The Great Indie Discography

The Great Indie Discography

Second Edition

M.C. Strong

Zweitausendeins

Lizenzausgabe von Zweitausendeins,
Postfach, D-60381 Frankfurt am Main,
mit freundlicher Genehmigung von Canongate Books Ltd,
14 High Street, Edinburgh EH1 1TE

Copyright © 1999 and 2003, M. C. Strong
The moral rights of the author have been asserted

Alle Rechte vorbehalten, insbesondere das Recht der
mechanischen, elektronischen oder fotografischen Vervielfältigung,
der Einspeicherung und Verarbeitung in elektronischen Systemen,
des Nachdrucks in Zeitschriften oder Zeitungen, des öffentlichen Vortrags,
der Verfilmung oder Dramatisierung, der Übertragung durch Rundfunk,
Fernsehen oder Video, auch einzelner Text- und Bildteile.

Der gewerbliche Weiterverkauf und der gewerbliche Verleih
von Büchern, CDs, CD-ROMs, DVDs, Videos, Downloads oder anderen
Sachen aus der Zweitausendeins-Produktion bedürfen in jedem Fall der
schriftlichen Genehmigung durch die Geschäftsleitung vom
Zweitausendeins Versand in Frankfurt am Main.

Dieses Buch gibt es nur bei Zweitausendeins im Versand,
Postfach, D-60348 Frankfurt am Main, Telefon 069-420 8000,
Fax 069-415 003. Internet www.Zweitausendeins.de,
E-Mail Info@Zweitausendeins.de. Oder in den Zweitausendeins-Läden
in Berlin, Düsseldorf, Essen, Frankfurt am Main, Freiburg,
2 x in Hamburg, in Hannover, Köln, Mannheim, München, Nürnberg, Stuttgart.

In der Schweiz über buch 2000, Postfach 89, CH-8910 Affoltern a. A.

ISBN 3-86150-615-7

The Great Indie Discography

The Great Indie Discography

Second Edition

M.C. Strong

Zweitausendeins

Lizenzausgabe von Zweitausendeins,
Postfach, D-60381 Frankfurt am Main,
mit freundlicher Genehmigung von Canongate Books Ltd,
14 High Street, Edinburgh EH1 1TE

Copyright © 1999 and 2003, M. C. Strong
The moral rights of the author have been asserted

Alle Rechte vorbehalten, insbesondere das Recht der
mechanischen, elektronischen oder fotografischen Vervielfältigung,
der Einspeicherung und Verarbeitung in elektronischen Systemen,
des Nachdrucks in Zeitschriften oder Zeitungen, des öffentlichen Vortrags,
der Verfilmung oder Dramatisierung, der Übertragung durch Rundfunk,
Fernsehen oder Video, auch einzelner Text- und Bildteile.

Der gewerbliche Weiterverkauf und der gewerbliche Verleih
von Büchern, CDs, CD-ROMs, DVDs, Videos, Downloads oder anderen
Sachen aus der Zweitausendeins-Produktion bedürfen in jedem Fall der
schriftlichen Genehmigung durch die Geschäftsleitung vom
Zweitausendeins Versand in Frankfurt am Main.

Dieses Buch gibt es nur bei Zweitausendeins im Versand,
Postfach, D-60348 Frankfurt am Main, Telefon 069-420 8000,
Fax 069-415 003. Internet www.Zweitausendeins.de,
E-Mail Info@Zweitausendeins.de. Oder in den Zweitausendeins-Läden
in Berlin, Düsseldorf, Essen, Frankfurt am Main, Freiburg,
2 x in Hamburg, in Hannover, Köln, Mannheim, München, Nürnberg, Stuttgart.

In der Schweiz über buch 2000, Postfach 89, CH-8910 Affoltern a. A.

ISBN 3-86150-615-7

Contents

Acknowledgements vi
Introduction vii
A Very Brief History of Indie Music ix
How to Read the Book xii
Formats and Abbreviations xiii

The 1970s (A — Z) 1
The 1980s (A — Z) 189
The 1990s + (A — Z) 583

Index 1077
Out-takes 1088

Acknowledgements

I'd like to thank the following "GREAT" people who've helped me with this book, namely co-biographers/friends ADAM STAFFORD, BRENDON GRIFFIN, BARNEY MIERS, STUART McDONALD, BEN ROSS and a sabotaging Grim Reaper who wishes to remain anonymous (although he uses my name/book in job references!) – I couldn't have finished the book without 5/6th of them. They put in around 400 hours between them and took half of my advance, but it was worth every penny. Also typesetter and volunteer proof-reader ALAN LAWSON, UK chart 2002 researcher NEIL WARWICK (co-author of "British Charts") and TERRY HOUNSOME ("Singles/Albums File" author).

I'd also like to thank girlfriend DAWN FORD (+ all her family including daughter JENNA, son LUKE, sister DEBBIE, brother-in-law JOHN, mum JEAN, dad JIM, etc.), ALLAN and ELAINE BREWSTER, VIC ZDZIEBLO, DOUGIE NIVEN, MIKEY KINNAIRD, IAN 'HARRY' HARRISON, ANDY RISK, SANDY and CAROLINE McCRAE, PETER McGUCKIN, TONY HUGHES, EILEEN SCOTT-MONCRIEFF (+ family), PAUL HUGHES, ELAINE BROWN, JOHN HILL (deceased January 2003), BARRY DEVLIN, WATTIE MORRISON, DANNY DICKSON, TAM MORRISON, STEF + MARIE, MICHAEL FLETCHER, HAMISH BRUCE + everyone at Alex SMITH's bar in Falkirk (including manager ALLAN MANN + SIMON), PAUL KLEMM, BILL FISHER, BRIAN McLAUGHLIN, JOHN McARDLE, LAURIE DOOLAN, BILLY and ANN ROSS, BRIAN and MARGARET HUNTER, JIM + ANN CONNELL, CAROLINE and ARCHIE, BARRY MOORE, GRANT BAILEY, RAB BELL, JAMES BEATTIE (deceased July 2003), GERRY + SANDY, JOE SIMPSON, TONY WEIR, MARTIN McDERMOTT, PAUL BAAS, IAIN McLEAN, DAVIE GALLOWAY, CARRIE DRUMMOND, COLIN, MARTIN No.7, ALEC GRAY, ALAN LIDDEL, BILLY MYLES, C.O.C., RICHIE WELSH, JIMMY + BETTY McLEAN, wee GREG, JIMMY, MICK MICK, JOHN HANLON, TONY & ANDREANA BAIRD, GORDON MURRAY + NINA.

Also not forgetting everyone at Canongate, EDWARD 'KIP' HANNAN and the Olympic Gardens crew, RICHARD MIDNIGHT HATSIZE SNYDER (ex-Captain Beefheart & The Magic Band), HAMISH McLEOD-PRENTICE, BRIAN VAUSE, RUSSELL MAYES, ROY JACK, SHUG MACKIE, IAIN SUTHERLAND, GEORGE MAIN, RAY NOTLEY, DEREK IRVINE, DAVIE BLAIR, LES O'CONNOR (deceased), CHRIS REID (deceased), GEORDIE YOUNG (deceased), BUFF, TED MOCHAR, DAVIE SEATH, my accountant GRAHAM MINTO, SEAN, TOM + CATHERINE at Mercat Press, my Scots book agent DAVID FLETCHER, my solicitor RAY MORTON, DAVID BLUE, HUNTER WATT, DEREK CLARKIN, GYLLA-FIONA SIMPSON, KIRSTIN ROSE, BOB PARR, ANDY MILNER, VIC GALLOWAY, JAMIE WATSON, GRANT McNAMARA, STEWART CRUICKSHANK, COLIN (and staff at Rialto Bar, Falkirk), ALISTAIR McGHEE (BBC Wales), LINDSAY HUTTON, JOEL McIVOR (@ Record Collector; they finally reviewed The Great Rock Discography in its 6th edition!), ED PYBUS, JOHN RYAN, GEORGE SHAW, ALAN DUNCAN, BRUCE FINDLAY, STEVE + KATY (@ Gilded Cage), MALCOLM STEWART (of Jimpress fanzine), the Hebrides pub guys DAVIE BISSETT, MALCOLM YORK, ANDY SUTHERLAND and JOHN BISSETT, EWAN (of Europa Records, Friar Street, Stirling; a brilliant shop for every type of music buff). Music journos I read and thank are the NME, LASERLOG/R.E.D., RECORD COLLECTOR, BILLBOARD, KERRANG! and MOJO; hope that AMG can give me that job, now.

A very special mention to my daughters SUZANNE and SHIRLEY, my grandson IVOR, my granny ZENA MACKAY (who sadly passed away on the 15th of April 2000), my auntie JOYCE (+ uncle MICHAEL, now deceased), my cousins PAUL, STEPHEN (+ NINA), BRIAN + LORRAINE, KEVIN (+ KAREN) and MAUREEN McELROY (died tragically on 26th May 2003), AVRIL and JACKIE, uncle FRANK in Australia, RONNIE (now deceased) and MAISIE, ISOBEL and DANNY BUCHANNAN, JENNIFER and DANIEL.

* * * * *

Introduction

It's been four busy years since the first publication of the original, "big cousin", 726-page 'THE GREAT ALTERNATIVE & INDIE DISCOGRAPHY', a subsequent 'ARSC 2000 Certificate of Merit' winner (in the field of Recorded Rock, Rhythm & Blues, or Soul). Since the date of its, er, launch in autumn 1999, four other tomes have hit the shops, namely 'THE GREAT ROCK DISCOGRAPHY – 5th Edition' (autumn 2000), 'THE GREAT METAL DISCOGRAPHY – 2nd Edition' (autumn 2001), 'THE GREAT ROCK DISCOGRAPHY – 6th Edition' (autumn 2002) and last but certainly not least 'THE GREAT SCOTS MUSICOGRAPHY' (winter 2002). The latter had been rejected by a handful of top Scottish-based publishers (as named in the book itself) as a non-viable commodity, but since its publication by Edinburgh-based Mercat Press just over seven months ago, it has surpassed the 2,000 sales mark – a second print-run is in the pipeline. I'm very proud of its achievements and more than proud a lot of music-loving Scots have not been denied the right to read their musical heritage.

So, here it is, 'THE GREAT INDIE DISCOGRAPHY', No.13 in the "Discography" series and hopefully not "unlucky for some", well for me anyway – a dozen of them issued by Canongate Books, an expanding and enterprising business (and 'Publisher Of The Year' 2002) who have sold over 250,000 copies of my books since the first edition of THE GREAT ROCK DISCOGRAPHY, way back nearly nine years ago in December, 1994.

"THE GREAT INDIE DISCOGRAPHY", 2nd Edition, has kept me busy over the last 9 months or so – over 2000 hours (plus the acknowledged additional work from co-biographers). When I took on this project I had no idea how long I would be sat at my computers and what shape the book (or indeed, myself) would take on. I'm putting on the weight as I write.

Firstly I had to dismiss the "ALTERNATIVE" part of the book as my publisher was requesting me to include psychedelic/jazz icon SUN RA and reggae/dub giant LEE PERRY. I thought they understood the 1st Edition was for post-Punk/New Wave acts. So I removed all "ALTERNATIVE" and non-Indie groups (i.e. The PRODIGY, ORBITAL, MOBY, SOUNDGARDEN and bands that have been catered for in "ROCK" + "METAL" editions). This left me with around under 500 pages from the original 726. I wanted to name it "THE GREAT NEW WAVE & INDIE DISCOGRAPHY", but it was decided to simply call it what you see now. I complaineth not. When I got my head around "INDIE"-only, the vision of the 2nd Edition began to shape up. Little did I know that in the last half a decade or so, there have been thousands of indie-type outfits sprouting out from all corners of the Earth, but mainly in America where a plethora of independent labels from the ever-evolving scene have emerged.

Number one priority was to track down by hook or by crook or by the internet, all the missing B-sides, track listings, etc, that I omitted to do – for one reason or another – first time around. I achieved around 99% of my target – and, incidentally, if you the reader can fill in whatever's missing (through having the actual recording or whatever), feel free to write to me with details. Thanks. This took around four solid months of constant telephone line-clogging and e-mailing of bands, labels or any connections. Thanks again to all them. This brought the tally of pages up somewhat, as did updating every biography. Incidentally, around 75% of the bands in the book are still on the go in some way or another – through re-forming, changing their moniker, joining another band, or going solo.

As previously mentioned, there were new bands/artists (over 1,000) to research for discographies, biographies, etc. This took up the remainder of my time. But I'm still surprised at hitting the 1100-page mark and I could have listed 2 outtakes sections to bring it even higher! If I've missed any band out, I do apologise but time, money and energy was drained. I think I've picked the best "indie" bands around.

At the start of the summer this year, I had a brainwave to divide the book into three sections (i.e. The 70's – for pioneers of Punk & New Wave; The 80's – for Alternative/Indie, grunge-pop, twee/C-86, etc; and The 90's+ for Lo-Fi, Riot Grrrl, retro, etc.). In my opinion, this has made the book a lot easier for all generations (I'd say between age 12 and whatever JOHN PEEL is) to get to grips with their faves of the last 27/28 years or so. Anyway, the book has an index (for the first time) to help you locate any particular band.

To add to this, instead of fitting in my 6 Innovators at the start of the book, I've added another 50 or so of the most influential "Icons of Indie" and incorporated them into the appropriate section. You might be surprised at some of the 50 – eg, The BEATLES, BURT BACHARACH and TOM WAITS, but do think OASIS/Brit-pop, SAINT ETIENNE/Twee-pop and WILL OLDHAM/Lo-fi respectively. (I had to be secretive enough not to tell my publishers in case they thought this idea too adventurous or even crazy.)

So, DO NOT tell me this is the same award-winning "Indie" book you bought in the last 4 years, or I will explain to you (in no uncertain terms!) your complete disregard for my efforts. This book has nearly 2000 entries, plus over 1000 sub-entries, and my blood, sweat and joyous tears are splattered all over it.

The book would have been a lot easier to concentrate on if the taxman hadn't kept hounding me every other day for backtaxes that I was paying off when I could. It didn't help also that they mislaid £3,000 for around a couple of months (although it was removed from my bank account) and still kept threatening me with sequestration (ouch!)

after I gave them another £5,000. I thank Jamie Byng (boss of Canongate) for lending me enough to sort out the initial payment. Pity it had to come to this.

What now then, a holiday? No! unless I win the lottery as I'm skint again. I'm looking forward to taking time off discographies (probably over a year!) to concentrate on renovating my property, getting a properly paid job and finishing off that novel I've promised everyone over the last half decade; the title is hidden somewhere in this Introduction. A few have said I'm court-ing disaster but I'm confident that just around the corner I'll get all the things I've worked for.

Signing off before I sign on – MC's (not) in the house!

From me to all of you,
M.C. STRONG
Falkirk, July 2003

A Very Brief History of Indie Music

Basically, what follows is a selfishly opinionated attempt to summarise the evolution of "indie" music which has (initially) positioned itself outside the mainstream of conventional "pop" music or has attempted to redefine musical boundaries. As for "indie", well it certainly doesn't refer to classical sitar music from New Delhi – although Brit Asian bands such as CORNERSHOP do actually draw on this tradition – an illusion that more than a few well-oiled pub dwellers seem to have been labouring under. Of course, most readers will recognise the term as the slang abbreviation for Independently released alternative records (i.e. not issued on a major label).

Let's go back, way back in time, well before Punk Rock first gobbed on a stagnant music scene around 1976/77. We're talking mid to late 60's here, a time when flower power 'n' peace was the order of the day; not everyone was sold on the hippy trip, though, and, like the proverbial mad scientist beavering away in his lab, a few disparate US-based mavericks were cooking up something dangerously different. In New York, The VELVET UNDERGROUND (LOU REED, JOHN CALE, STERLING MORRISON, MO TUCKER and NICO) were doing strange things with dark psychedelia and twisted pop while over in sunny L.A., DON VAN VLIET aka CAPTAIN BEEFHEART & HIS MAGIC BAND were alchemising a bizarre but effective avant-garde Rhythm & Blues cocktail (the rhythm of course, being mangled beyond recognition). More importantly though, the former soul stronghold of Detroit (home of 'Tamla Motown') had given birth to both The STOOGES and MC5, primal sonic riffmeisters with a penchant for white-noise nihilism and rock'n'roll revolution respectively. IGGY POP (from the aforementioned STOOGES) needs no introduction, a man who has generally come to be regarded as "The Godfather Of Punk", while MC5's WAYNE KRAMER is still motoring 30-odd years on. Last but not least, early 70's cross-dressing 'STONES wannabes, The NEW YORK DOLLS, fashioned a make-up-smeared blueprint for many a shambolic DIY punk band. For the purposes of this book, the aforementioned innovators slide into the book through "Icons of Indie" slots, the logic being that these artists preceded the Punk/New Wave explosion without being an intrinsic part of it; they were all going on or past thirty by the mid-70's, virtual dinosaurs in the eyes of the angry new youth brigade.

Always touted as an English/British phenomenon, the first rumblings of the Punk revolution were actually felt in and around New York where acts like poetess PATTI SMITH, TELEVISION, RICHARD HELL, The HEARTBREAKERS (with ex-NY DOLLS), RAMONES, TALKING HEADS and BLONDIE were all using the guitar-rock format in exciting new ways and providing an eclectic alternative to the mainstream domination of hard/AOR-rock and watered down disco-pop. Most of these bands were associated with the CBGB's and Max's Kansas City venues which formed the hub (along with Seymour Stein's 'Sire' records) of what was dubbed the "New Wave" scene; even more leftfield confrontational artists like SUICIDE, TEENAGE JESUS & THE JERKS (i.e. LYDIA LUNCH), etc, were getting decent crowds, forming the basis of the short-lived nihilistic "No-Wave" scene that BRIAN ENO documented with his subsequent compilation of the same name. Elsewhere in the USA, there were isolated pockets of punk-related activity; in Boston, The MODERN LOVERS (with JONATHAN RICHMAN) had attracted a cult following while the state of Ohio was home to both PERE UBU and DEVO, the former one of the first avant-garde New Wave outfits and the latter a proto-electro quasi-pop band.

If Britain was slower off the mark, it certainly made up for lost time as the full filth and fury of the punk time-bomb hit the musical establishment square on. While the thriving pub-rock scene had created a sympathetic environment with its back-to-basics R&B ethos, it took maverick fashion guru turned musical opportunist Malcolm McLaren to light the touchpaper by dreaming up the concept of the SEX PISTOLS after seeing out the last days of The NEW YORK DOLLS as manager. Rounding up prospective members (STEVE JONES, PAUL COOK, GLEN MATLOCK and carrot-topped frontman, JOHNNY ROTTEN) from regular customers in his Kings Road 'Sex' boutique, he set out to shock the music industry into submission with a sound and image so confrontational that the media couldn't resist demonising them. After a string of riotous gigs including an infamous date at Oxford Street's 100 Club, the punk figureheads transformed the genre into a nationwide phenomenon by signing to 'E.M.I.' and releasing the inflammatory 'ANARCHY IN THE UK' towards the end of 1976. Fed up with a bloodless music scene and a stagnant political climate, the nation's restless youth adopted the record as an anthem and made sure the SEX PISTOLS made the Top 40.

All across the country, safety-pinned, spiky-topped kids were arming themselves with guitars, a couple of chords and an enterprising DIY attitude. The DAMNED had already established themselves as one of the first leading lights of the punk-rock generation with the single, 'NEW ROSE'; released on pioneering indie imprint, 'Stiff' (who also boasted "New Wave" acts, ELVIS COSTELLO, IAN DURY, etc, artists who combined the newfound creative freedom and attitude of punk with traditional songwriting); the track was the first bonafide punk song to make it onto vinyl. While Radio One DJ John Peel provided a platform for punk on his night-time show, ALTERNATIVE TV frontman MARK PERRY gave the movement a voice through his influential 'Sniffin Glue' fanzine; the NME had already championed the new breed with many a cover story.

1977 also proved a pivotal year with The CLASH, The STRANGLERS, The JAM, (Australia's) The SAINTS and the BUZZCOCKS amongst others all releasing seminal 7" singles (with picture covers!) before finally putting together enough material for an LP. After having "celebrated" the Silver Jubilee year by releasing 'GOD SAVE THE QUEEN' (originally released on 'A&M' before the ROTTEN and Co were politely asked to leave), The SEX PISTOLS ended the year by delivering the definite punk album, appropriately titled 'NEVER MIND THE BOLLOCKS . . . HERE'S . . .'. The record was a massive-selling No.1 success, and the face of the music industry changed irreversibly.

The bulk of the charts had now become the domain of New Wave/Punk acts, bands like SIOUXSIE & THE BANSHEES, X-RAY SPEX (a band that were first brought to attention via gigs at the infamous 'Roxy' venue) and MAGAZINE making their name over the course of 1978. Although rumours of punk's death were greatly exaggerated (especially after the following year's messy demise of the 'PISTOLS and the controversial death of their iconic bassman, SID VICIOUS), the initial flash of angry energy had dimmed slightly as the music branched out into more experimental, individualistic and claustrophobic territory.

While second generation punk bands like SHAM 69, UK SUBS, STIFF LITTLE FINGERS and The ANGELIC UPSTARTS (from which was formed the genesis of the much-derided "Oi" movement) followed the tried and tested formula, outfits like The FALL, WIRE, the SLITS, The CURE and PUBLIC IMAGE LTD (Johnny Rotten's post-'PISTOLS band) were heading into the dark uncharted waters of post-punk. And they didn't come much darker than Manchester's JOY DIVISION, a bleak, coldly minimalistic pre-goth band led by the enigmatic IAN CURTIS. After two classic albums ('UNKNOWN PLEASURES' and 'CLOSER') and a hit single 'LOVE WILL TEAR US APART' in 1980, their career was cut short as the troubled epileptic singer took his own life; the remaining members chose to carry on as NEW ORDER, an equally influential group that laid the foundations for Manchester's alternative dance scene. 'Factory', the label that spawned these two outfits, was arguably one of the most creative imprints of the 1980's, being instrumental in the careers of A CERTAIN RATIO, DURUTTI COLUMN, etc, as well as the development of the 'Madchester' indie/dance phenomenon. Liverpool also made itself heard as The TEARDROP EXPLODES (with arch eccentric JULIAN COPE) and ECHO & THE BUNNYMEN (with the moody IAN McCULLOCH) took a post-punk ferry across the Mersey, while the "Sound Of Young Scotland" was aired via 'Postcard' acts, ORANGE JUICE, JOSEF K and AZTEC CAMERA alongside future 'Virgin'-signed stadium rockers, SIMPLE MINDS. Meanwhile, Northern Ireland had been getting its 'TEENAGE KICKS' with Power-Pop punks, The UNDERTONES.

The independent ethos engendered by the "New Wave" had also given rise to such key labels as 'Rough Trade' (home to electronic experimentalists CABARET VOLTAIRE), 'Mute' and '4 a.d.'. The latter served as a launching pad for proto-Goth act, BAUHAUS and Aussie avant-noise terrorists, The BIRTHDAY PARTY; while 'Mute' helped inspire a whole brood of black-clad "gothic" bands led by Leeds' SISTERS OF MERCY, the latter were beloved of the "psychobilly" crew, bequiffed afficionados of a punk/rockabilly hybrid that had its roots back in America with The CRAMPS. Led by the inimitable LUX INTERIOR (an IGGY POP clone if ever there was one!), the latter outfit had actually been loosely associated with the original CBGB's scene. This venue was now the focus for a new breed of US hardcore/avant-punk acts including the hugely influential feedback merchants, SONIC YOUTH. The West Coast mirrored the developments in the Big Apple with a brace of ear-bleeding new talent including the establishment-baiting DEAD KENNEDYS whose JELLO BIAFRA had instigated his own 'Alternative Tentacles' label (later home to Canadians, D.O.A.) after the independent success of two politico-punk classics, 'CALIFORNIA UBER ALLES' and 'HOLIDAY IN CAMBODIA'. California was also the base for 'S.S.T.', a label that spawned a slew of hardcore/alternative bands such as BLACK FLAG, HUSKER DU and The MEAT PUPPETS. The latter band were partly influenced by the desert rock twang of NEIL YOUNG (an "Icon of Indie"), also a touchstone for the Paisley underground psychedelic/jangle-pop scene that numbered R.E.M., The RAIN PARADE, The DREAM SYNDICATE, GREEN ON RED and The LONG RYDERS (all influenced by DYLAN, The BYRDS, The BEATLES, LOVE, The DOORS, VELVET UNDERGROUND, etc, in no particular order)

Back in Britain, The SMITHS were rescuing the term "alternative" from electro-popsters/New Romantics with a highly original sound hinged on JOHNNY MARR's legendary jangling guitar and MORRISSEY's equally legendary miserabilist lyrics/vocals. From the summer of '83 onwards (after the 'HAND IN GLOVE' single), the MORRISSEY-MARR partnership inspired hitherto unseen obsessive fan worship and dominated the Top 20 until it all ended in tears at the end of 1987. The SMITHS aside, the mid-80's indie scene was dominated by Glaswegian Alan McGee's 'Creation', a label that first made its name with the surf-pop/noise feedback kings, The JESUS & MARY CHAIN, before going on to help define the archetypal "indie" band by signing a long list of shambling, jangling guitar outfits such as The PASTELS and PRIMAL SCREAM (also both hailing from north of the border!). The NME-created C-86 scene (named after that year's similarly-titled cassette) also centred on these types of bands, providing a platform for John Peel Festive 50 favourite, The WEDDING PRESENT.

As the 80's neared their conclusion, more and more indie bands were cross-fertilizing their music with dance rhythms after experiencing the euphoric high of the insurgent acid-house culture and the "first summer of love". The scene coalesced around Manchester where working-class heroes The HAPPY MONDAYS were gettin' it on with a sleazy combination of groovy 'Stones rhythms, scratchy funk-guitar and of course SHAUN RYDER's glassy-eyed, fookin' tuneless vocals and x-rated cartoon lyrics. Scottish stalwarts, PRIMAL SCREAM, also saw the strobelight after becoming hooked on London's club scene, BOBBY GILLESPIE and Co finally coming of age in 1991 with the genre-defining 'SCREAMADELICA'. Most legendary of all though were The STONE ROSES, the classic psychedelic guitar-pop of their 1989 eponymous debut album setting them up as one of the most revered bands in Rock history. In the right place at the right time, the 'ROSES were adopted by the indie dance crowd as homecoming Messiahs, while their rock/funk crossover classic, 'FOOL'S GOLD', still stands as a benchmark for any aspiring group. Running parallel to "Madchester" was the more exclusively alternative "Shoegazing" scene, so-called because those involved had a tendency to er . . . study their feet while "tripping" the night away to swathes of swirling feedback melodica. Armed with a collection of albums and EP's by SPACEMEN 3, MY BLOODY VALENTINE and the COCTEAU TWINS (all hugely influential sound pioneers in their own right), outfits such as RIDE, SLOWDIVE and LUSH enjoyed a brief period of music press acclaim before the genre died a swift death along with the painful last remnants of the "baggy"/Madchester scene.

Neither of these scenes cut much ice in America where "Grunge" was beginning to ferment in deepest, darkest Seattle via the reborn 'Sub Pop' label. Influenced equally by mid-80's alternative/hardcore punk (i.e. The PIXIES, DINOSAUR JR, etc), 70's heavy-metal and 60's garage, NIRVANA, MELVINS and MUDHONEY redefined the whole American music scene, breaking the stranglehold of the cucumber'n'spandex hard-rock brigade and uniting alternative music fans. With precision perfect timing, NIRVANA stormed onto the international stage with the incendiary 'SMELLS LIKE TEEN SPIRIT' single and the 'NEVERMIND' album in Autumn '91, paving the way for a plethora of often second-rate imitators. Although the likes of The SMASHING PUMPKINS and their ilk continued to sell million of records, in reality the scene died with the controversial April '94 suicide of KURT COBAIN (whose wife, COURTNEY LOVE and her band, HOLE, were the most famous in a long list of femme-punks). Yet still the shockwaves continued to be felt in America where an insatiable appetite for everything punk saw the re-issue of obscure 70's/80's UK material and the success of workaday bands like GREEN DAY and anything from the 'Lookout!' imprint. The success of Grunge also opened up the market for all kinds of previously marginalised sub-genres – eg, Industrial, a noisy electronic percussion-driven punk-metal style which is catered for in THE GREAT METAL DISCOGRAPHY.

Of course, Britain could only stomach so many hairy, check-shirted noise merchants and finally re-invented its Rock history with the advent of Brit-Pop in the mid-90's. Chief protagonists, BLUR (who had already been once around the "baggy" block) and new lads on the block, OASIS, battled it out in a media-fuelled race to the top spot reminiscent of the BEATLES/ROLLING STONES heyday. By this point the bands had already released their landmark albums, 'PARKLIFE' and 'DEFINITELY MAYBE' respectively, while SUEDE, PULP (JARVIS COCKER's long-standing outfit) and SUPERGRASS all topped the charts with their own brand of alt/indie pop. When the GALLAGHER brothers weren't at each other's throats, they were embroiled in a war of words with DAMON ALBARN, the gossip-column overload helping to breathe life into an ailing music industry.

"Lo-Fi" was another buzz word of the era, originally coined for US post-grunge slacker outfits like PAVEMENT, MERCURY REV and SEBADOH, although it has since been used to cover the massive spectrum of experimental knob-twiddling music made by artists as creatively and geographically wide-ranging as TORTOISE and STEREOLAB. In fact, this scene could be taken as a microcosm of the melting pot that constitutes the current alternative landscape, a free-for-all no man's land where diversity is the key word. In the wake of Brit-pop, hardened campaigners, RADIOHEAD, THE VERVE and SPIRITUALIZED (a SPACEMEN 3 offshoot!) all released navel-gazing but groundbreaking career peak albums while Wales finally put itself on the map with a clutch of eclectic talent (i.e. SUPER FURRY ANIMALS, GORKY'S ZYGOTIC MYNCI, STEREOPHONICS and CATATONIA) to back up the long-running success of The MANIC STREET PREACHERS. Scotland, of course, was where arguably the most innovative music was being made by the likes of the mighty MOGWAI (my personal favourite of the 90's), Falkirk "bairns" ARAB STRAP, and cross-border marauders, The BETA BAND.

Post-millennium, nearly everyone has waited for another scene to take over, and while the classy COLDPLAY and TRAVIS have kept the home fires burning, America has set the world alight once again (and we're not just talking Iraq here!) with their biggest exports, The STROKES and The WHITE STRIPES. While the former instigated a mini retro-New Wave movement in NY, the latter has, and have been for some time, generating a musical revolution for the city of Detroit, alongside other bands which mainly featured 'STRIPES main guy JACK WHITE and the multifarious MICK COLLINS (ex-GORIES, etc). What's next? Who knows?

M.C. STRONG

How To Read The Book

The book is divided into 3 main sections – the 1970s, the 1980s, and the 1990s+ (ie, including the years of the new millennium). Within each of these sections, the bands/artistes are organised in alphabetical order.

There are over 60 bands/artistes which are presented as "Icons of Indie": these having grey shading and jagged lines around them.

If you're struggling in any way how to comprehend some of the more complex parts of each discography, here are some examples to make it easier. Read below for around 10 minutes, taking a step at a time. The final lines/examples you see will give you a good guide before you proceed with the actual chronological discographies. However, I think that once you've read your own favourites you'll have a good idea.

GROUP / ARTIST

Formed/Born: Where/When ... biography including style/analysis, songwriters, cover versions, trivia, etc.

Album rating: i.e. rating between 1-10 amalgamated between music press reviews, your letters and my own personal opinion.

SINGER (born; b. day/month/year, town/city, country) – vocals, whatever (ex-GROUP; if any) / **MUSICIAN** (b. BIRTH NAME, 8 Sep'60, Musselburgh, Scotland) – instruments / **OTHER MUSICIANS** – other instruments, vocals, etc.

UK Label US Label

UKdate. (single, ep or album) *(UK cat.no.)* <*US cat.no.*> **THE TITLE** ☐ ☐ US date
- note:- UK label – might be another country's label if not released in UK.
- also:- Labels only appear when the group signs to a new one.
- note:- UK date – might be foreign, <even American at times>, if not initially issued in Britain.
- note:- (UK catalogue number; in curved brackets) <US catalogue no.; in angle brackets>
- note:- chart positions, UK + US, are in the boxes below labels.
- also:- the boxes in the above example have been left blank, thus they did not hit either UK or US charts.
- note:- US date after the boxes indicates a variation from its UK counterpart.
- also:- Any other info on the right of the boxes (e.g. German) indicates it was not issued in the US.

UKdate. (7") *(UK cat.no.)* **A-SIDE. / B-SIDE** ☐ -
US date. (7") <*US cat.no.*> **A-SIDE. / DIFFERENT B-SIDE** - ☐
- note:- The two examples above show that the UK + US release did not have an identical A-side & B-side, thus the chart boxes are marked with a – to indicate it was not released in either the UK or the US.

UKdate. (7"/c-s) *(CATNO 1/+C)* **A-SIDE. / B-SIDE** ☐ -
- note:- above had two formats with the same tracks (i.e. 7"/c-s). However, catalogue numbers will always vary among different formats – often only slightly (e.g. CATNO 1/+C). Each cat.no. would read thus:- (7")=*(CATNO 1)* and (c-s)=*(CATNO 1C)*. To save space the (/) slash comes into effect. The (/) means "or" and in this case it is prefixed with a + sign for the equivalent cassette (c-s).

UKdate. (7"/c-s) *(example same as above)* **SEE ABOVE** ☐ -
(12"+=/cd-s+=) *(CATNO 1-12/1-CD)* – Extra tracks.
- note:- If there are more formats with extra or different tracks, a new line would be used. Obviously there would also be alternative catalogue numbers utilising the "(/)" as before. Extra tracks would therefore mean the addition of the sign "(+=)" to each format.

UKdate. (lp/c/cd) *(CATNO 200/+MC/CD)* <*US catno 4509*> **ALBUM TITLE** ☐ ☐
- Track listing / Track 2 / And so on. *(re-issued = re-iss. A later date, and other 'Label' mentioned, if different from original; new cat.no.) (could be re-iss. many times and if "(+=)" sign occurs there will be extra tracks from the original)* <*could also apply to the US release if in pointed brackets*>
- note:- Album above released in 3 formats, thus 3 catalogue numbers are neccessary. The "long-player" lp *(CATNO 200)* is obvious. The "cassette" c = +MC *(CATNO 200MC)* or "compact disc" CD *(CATNO 200CD)*. The US <*cat.no.*> will normally be just one set of numbers (or see further below for other details).

UKdate. (cd/c/lp) *(CD/TC+/CATNO+200)* <*UScatno 4509*> **ALBUM TITLE** ☐ ☐ US date
- note:- This time a prefix is used instead of a suffix, hence the difference before the standard lp catalogue number. For instance, the cd would read as *(CDCATNO 200)*.

Jun 97. (cd/c/lp) <*5557 49860-2/-4/-1*> **ALBUM TITLE** 1 1 May97
- note:- Some catalogue numbers don't include any letters, but instead consist of a number sequence followed by one digit which universally corresponds with the format (i.e. 2 = cd / 4 = c / 1 = lp).
- also:- If the US numbers are identical, there would be no need to list them separately, i.e. <*(the numbers)*>
- note:- I've also marked down an actual date of release and its variant in the US (you'll find this fictitious album also hit No.1 in both charts "and ah've no even heard it yet, man!")

—— **NEW MUSICIAN/SINGER** (b.whenever, etc.) – instruments (ex-GROUP(s) replaced = repl. DEPARTING MUSICIAN/SINGER, who joined whatever
- note:- Above denotes a line-up change.

GROUP or ARTIST with major change of name

note:- above would always be in grey.

UK Label US Label

Jun 97. (cd/c/lp; GROUP or ARTIST with minor change of name) <*(5557 49860)*> **ALBUM TITLE** 1 1 May97

– compilations, etc. –

UKdate. (cd) *compilation Label only; (cat.no.)* **ALBUM TITLE** 100 -
- Track listing would be selective, only included if the release was deemed essential.

Formats & Abbreviations

VINYL (black coloured unless stated)

(lp) = The (LONG PLAYER) record ... circular 12" plays at $33^{1/3}$ r.p.m., and has photo or artwork sleeve. Approximate playing time ... 30–50 minutes with average 10 tracks. Introduced in the mid-50's on mono until stereo took over in the mid-60's. Quadrophonic had a spell in the 70's, but only on mainly best-selling lp's, that had been previously released. Because of higher costs to the manufacturer and buyer, the quad sunk around 1978. Also note that around the mid-50's, some albums were released on 10 inch. Note:– average cost to the customer as of now = £9.00 (new). Collectors can pay anything from £1 to over £500, depending on the quality of the recording. Very scratched records can be worthless, but unplayed-mint deletions are worth a small fortune to the right person. Auctions and record fairs can be the place to find that long lost recording that's eluded you. This applies to all other vinyl below.

(d-lp) = The (DOUBLE-LONG PLAYER) record ... as before. Playing time 50–90 minutes on 4 sides, with average 17 tracks. Introduced to rock/pop world in the late 60's, to complement compilations, concept & concert (aka live) albums.[1]
Compilations:– are a selection of greatest hits or rare tracks, demos, etc.
Concepts:– are near-uninterrupted pieces of music, based around a theme.
Note that normal lp's could also be compilations, live or concept. Some record companies through the wishes of their artists, released double lp's at the price of one lp. If not, price new would be around £15.

(t-lp) = The (TRIPLE-LONG PLAYER) record ... as before. Playing time over 100 minutes with normally over 20 tracks. Because of the cost to the consumer, most artists steered clear of this format. Depending on the artwork on the sleeve, these cost over £17.50. (See its replacement, the CD.)

(4-lp-box) = The (BOXED-LONG PLAYER) record (could be between 4 and 10 in each boxed-set). As the triple album would deal with live, concept or compilation side, the boxed-set would be mostly re-issues of all the artist's album material, with probably a bonus lp thrown in, to make it collectable. Could be very pricey, due to lavish outlay in packaging. They cost over £25 new.

(m-lp) = The (MINI-LONG PLAYER) record ... playing time between 20 and 30 minutes and containing on average 7 tracks. Introduced for early 80's independent market, and cost around £5.
= Note:– This could be confused at times with the extended-play 12" single.

(pic-lp) = The (PICTURE DISC-LONG PLAYER) record... as before but with album artwork/ design on the vinyl-grooves. Mainly for the collector because of the slightly inferior sound quality. If unplayed, these can fetch between £10 and £250.

(coloured lp) = The (COLOURED-LONG PLAYER) record; can be in a variety of colours including ... white / blue / red / clear / purple / green / pink / gold / silver.

(red-lp) = The (RED VINYL-LONG PLAYER) record would be an example of this.

(7") = The (7 INCH SINGLE). Arrived in the late 50's, and plays at 45 r.p.m. Before this its equivalent was the 10" on 78 r.p.m. Playing time now averages 4 minutes per side, but during the late 50's up to mid-60's, each side averaged $2^{1/2}$ minutes. Punk rock/new wave in 1977/78 resurrected this idea. In the 80's, some disco releases increased playing time. Another idea that was resurrected in 1977 was the picture sleeve. This had been introduced in the 60's, but mostly only in the States.
Note:– cost in mid-98 was just under £2.50; second-hand rarities can cost between 25p and £200, depending again on their condition. These might also contain limited freebies/gifts (i.e. posters, patches, stickers, badges, etc). Due to the confusion this would cause, I have omitted this information, and kept to the vinyl aspect in this book. Another omission has been DJ promos, demos, acetates, magazine freebies, various artists' compilations, etc. Only official shop releases get a mention.

(7" m) = The (7 INCH MAXI-SINGLE). Named so because of the extra track, mostly on the B-side. Introduced widely during the early 70's; one being ROCKET MAN by ELTON JOHN.

(7" ep) = The (7 INCH EXTENDED PLAY SINGLE). Plays mostly at $33^{1/3}$ r.p.m., with average playing time 10–15 minutes and 4 tracks. Introduced in the late 50's as compilations for people to sample their albums. These had a *title* and were also re-introduced from 1977 onwards, but this time for punk groups' new songs.

(d7") = The (DOUBLE 7 INCH SINGLE). Basically just two singles combined ... 4 tracks. Introduced in the late 70's for the "new wave/romantics", and would cost slightly more than normal equivalent.

(7" pic-d) = The (7 INCH PICTURE-DISC SINGLE). This was vinyl that had a picture on the grooves, which could be viewed through a see-through plastic cover.

(7" sha-pic-d) = The (7 INCH SHAPED-PICTURE-DISC SINGLE). Vinyl as above but with shape (i.e. gun, mask, group) around the edge of the groove. Awkward because it would not fit into the collector's singles box. Initially limited, and this can still be obtained at record fairs for over £3. Note:– However, in the book the type of shape has not been mentioned, to save space.

(7" coloured) = The (7 INCH COLOURED SINGLE). Vinyl that is not black (i.e. any other colour; red, yellow, etc). Note:– (7" multi) would be a combination of two or more colours (i.e. pink/purple).

1: **Note**:– Interview long players mainly released on 'Babatak' label, have not been included due to the fact this book only gives artists' music discography.

(7" flexi)	=	The (7 INCH FLEXIBLE SINGLE). One-sided freebies, mostly given away by magazines, at concerts or as mentioned here; free with single or lp. Worth keeping in mint condition and well protected.
(12")	=	The (12 INCH SINGLE). Plays at 45 r.p.m., and can have extended or extra tracks to its 7" counterpart (+=) or (++=). B-side's playing speed could be at 33 r.p.m. Playing time could be between 8 and 15 minutes. Introduced in 1977 with the advent of new wave and punk. They were again a must for collectors, for the new wave of British heavy metal scene.
(12"ep)	=	The (12 INCH EXTENDED PLAY SINGLE). Virtually same as above but *titled* like the 7" ep. Playing time over 12 minutes, and could have between 3 and 5 tracks.
(d12")	=	The (DOUBLE 12 INCH SINGLE). See double 7". Can become very collectable and would cost new as normal 12", £4.50.
(12" pic-d)	=	The (12 INCH PICTURE-DISC SINGLE). As with 7" equivalent ... see above.
(12" sha-pic-d)	=	The (12 INCH SHAPED-PICTURE-DISC SINGLE). See above 7" equivalent.
(12" colrd)	=	The (12 INCH COLOURED SINGLE). Not black vinyl ... see above 7" equivalent.
(10")	=	The (10 INCH SINGLE). Plays at 45 r.p.m. and, like the 12", can have extra tracks (+=). Very collectable, it surfaced in its newer form around the early 80's, and can be obtained in shops at £4.50. Note:– also (10" ep) / (d10") / (10" coloured) / (10" pic-d) / (10" sha-pic-d).

CASSETTES

(c)	=	The (CASSETTE) album ... size in case $4^{1/2}$ inches high. Playing-time same as lp album, although after the mid-80's cd revolution, some were released with extra tracks. Introduced in the late 60's, to compete with the much bulkier lp. Until the 80's, most cassettes were lacking in group info, lyric sheets, and freebies. Note:– cost to the consumer as of now = £8 new. But for a few exceptions, most do not increase in price, and can be bought second-hand or budget-priced for around £5.
(d-c)	=	The (DOUBLE-CASSETTE) album ... as above, and would hold same tracks as d-lp or even t-1p. Price between £12 and £16.
(c-s)	=	The (CASSETTE-SINGLE). Now released mostly with same two tracks as 7" equivalent. The other side played the same 2 or 3 tracks. Introduced unsuccessfully in the US around the late 60's. Re-introduced there and in Britain in the mid-80's. In the States, it and its cd counterpart have replaced the charting 7" single for the 90's. Cost new is around £1.50–£2.50, and might well become quite collectable.
(c-ep)	=	The (CASSETTE-EXTENDED PLAY SINGLE). Same as above but *titled* as 12".

COMPACT DISCS

(cd)	=	The (COMPACT DISC) album. All 5" circular and mostly silver on its playing side. Perspex casing also includes lyrics & info, etc. Introduced late in 1982, and widely the following year (even earlier for classical music). Initially for top recording artists, but now in 2002 nearly every release is in cd format. Playing time normally over 50 minutes with some containing extra tracks or mixes. Possible playing time is just over 75 minutes. Marketed as unscratchable, although if they go uncleaned, they will stick just as vinyl. Average price now is £15, and will become collectable if, like most gloomy predictions, they do not deteriorate with time.
(d-cd)	=	The (DOUBLE-COMPACT DISC) album ... same as above although very pricey, between £20 and £25.
(cd-s)	=	The (COMPACT DISC-SINGLE). Mainly all 5" (but some 3" cd-s could only be played with a compatible gadget inside the normal cd player). Playing time over 15 minutes to average 25 minutes, containing 4 or 5 tracks. Introduced in 1986 to compete with the 12" ep or cassette. 99% contained extra tracks to normal formats. Cost new: over £4.50.
(pic-cd-s)	=	The (PICTURE-COMPACT DISC-SINGLE). Has picture on disc, which gives it its collectability. Also on (pic-cd-ep).
(vid-pic-s)	=	The (VIDEO-COMPACT DISC-SINGLE). A video cd, which can be played through stereo onto normal compatible TV screen. Very costly procedure, but still might be the format of the future. Promo videos can be seen on pub jukeboxes, which has made redundant the returning Wurlitzer style.

DIGITAL AUDIO TAPE

(dat)	=	The (DIGITAL AUDIO TAPE) album. Introduced in the mid-80's and, except for Japan and the rich yuppie, are not widely issued. It is a smaller version of the cassette, with the quality of the cd.

Another format (which I have not included) is the CARTRIDGE, which was available at the same time as the cassette. When the cassette finally won the battle in the early 80's, the cartridge became redundant. All car-owners of the world were happy when thieves made them replace the stolen cartridge player with the resurrected cassette. You can still buy these second-hand, but remember you'll have to obtain a second-hand 20-year-old player, with parts possibly not available.

Other abbreviations: repl. = replaced / comp. = compilation / re-iss. = re-issued / re-dist. = re-distributed

The 1970s

✻ ✻ ✻

THE GREAT INDIE DISCOGRAPHY — The 1970s

ADAM & THE ANTS

Formed: London, England ... April '77 by STUART GODDARD (aka ADAM ANT) along with LESTER SQUARE, ANDY WARREN and PAUL FLANAGAN. Initially a fairly rote punk act with attitude, what got the band noticed was their lurid stage show and penchant for S&M trappings. Derek Jarman was sufficiently enamoured to offer ADAM a part in his controversial punk flick, 'Jubilee' (released Feb '78), a revised ANTS line-up (featuring new members DAVE BARBE and MARK GAUMONT) recording two songs for the soundtrack, 'Plastic Surgery' and 'Deutcher Girls'. Later that year, the group released a one-off debut single for 'Decca', 'YOUNG PARISIANS', before releasing their rated debut album, 'DIRK WEARS WHITE SOX' in late '79. A morose slab of post-punk doom-mongering, the record stood in stark contrast to their later albums by a remodelled ADAM & THE ANTS. The shake-up came courtesy of none other than ex-SEX PISTOLS svengali, MALCOLM McLAREN, who, after dreaming up the flamboyant new image (a surprisingly effective if retrospectively ridiculous Native Indian cum swashbuckling pirates concept), whisked ADAM's band off to become BOW WOW WOW. Virtually written off by his critics, ADAM came swaggering back with a new line-up (MARCO PIRRONI, CHRIS HUGHES aka MERRICK, KEVIN MOONEY and TERRY LEE MIALL), a new sound and a new album (his first for 'C.B.S.'), 'KINGS OF THE WILD FRONTIER' (1980). Taking their cue from the Burundi drummers of Africa, the band had stumbled on a unique musical mutant which combined retro rock'n'roll with pseudo-tribal, dayglo pouting pop; teenyboppers loved it and a string of anthemic singles, 'DOG EAT DOG', 'ANT MUSIC' and the thundering title track all made the UK Top 5. The album itself rode to the top of the charts (even scaping into the US Top 50) and for a brief but warpainted period, Britain was gripped with "Antmania". The sight of the ever photogenic ADAM striding boldly through his video adventures like some dandy Indiana Jones was the stuff of girly fantasy and if you didn't have a white stripe across your nose, well, you could forget about getting lucky at the school disco. ANT was clever enough to slightly tweak his image on the follow-up set, 'PRINCE CHARMING' (1981), this time going for a dashing highwayman cum 18th century courtier get-up. It was even more effective, the group scoring two No.1 singles in quick succession with 'STAND AND DELIVER' and the title track, while 'ANT RAP' made the Top 3. To be fair to the man, he had the good sense to disband ADAM & THE ANTS at the height of their fame, although by carrying on as ADAM ANT in a vaguely similar vein, he was bound to suffer a backlash sooner or later. Retaining sidekick, PIRRONI, ANT's solo career nevertheless got off to an auspicious start with No.1 single, 'GOODY TWO SHOES', while the accompanying album, 'FRIEND OR FOE' (1982) made the Top 5 (and bizarrely the US Top 20). The following three years brought only one major hit in 'PUSS 'N' BOOTS' and after the 'VIVE LE ROCK' (1985) set, ANT took four years off to develop his acting career while PIRRONI joined SPEAR OF DESTINY. By the turn of the decade, the pair were back with an underwhelming new single, 'ROOM AT THE TOP', and album, 'MANNERS & PHYSIQUE', both enjoying a brief stint in the charts but largely ignored as the nation's pop kids raved to acid house. Of late, the ageing ADAM/STUART has run into a bit of trouble due to him brandishing a WWII gun in a pub when he was refused entry. Early in 2002, he was arrested by police and taken to a mental unit of the Royal Free Hospital in Hampstead, North London. • **Trivia:** He acted in stage production of 'Entertaining Mr. Sloane'. After retiring to the States in 1986 he took parts in 'Slam Dance' film, and 'Equalizer' TV serial.

Album rating: DIRK WEARS WHITE SOX (*7) / KINGS OF THE WILD FRONTIER (*7) / PRINCE CHARMING (*5) / FRIEND OR FOE (*5) / STRIP (*4) / VIVE LE ROCK (*4) / MANNERS AND PHYSIQUE (*4) / WONDERFUL (*5) / HITS (1980-1985) compilation (*7)

ADAM ANT (b. STUART GODDARD, 3 Nov'54) – vocals, guitar / **MATTHEW ASHMAN** (b.'62) – guitar, vocals (ex-KAMERAS) / **ANDY WARREN** (b.'61) – bass, vocals / **DAVE BARBE** (b.'61) – drums (ex-DESOLATION ANGELS)

			Decca	not iss.
Oct 78.	(7")	(F 13803) **YOUNG PARISIANS. / LADY**	-	-
		(re-act.Dec80; hit No.9)		

			Do-It	not iss.
Jun 79.	(7")	(DUN 8) **ZEROX. / WHIP IN MY VALISE**	-	-
—	(some copies had B-side playing 'PHYSICAL (YOU'RE SO)') (re-act.Jan81; hit No.45)			
Nov 79.	(lp/c)	(RIDE 3/+M) **DIRK WEARS WHITE SOX**	-	-

– Cartrouble (part 1 & 2) / Digital tenderness / Nine plan failed / Day I met God * / Tabletalk / Cleopatra / Catholic day / Never trust a man (with egg on his face) / Animals and men / Family of noise / The idea. (re-act.Jan81; hit No.16) (remixed & re-iss. Apr83 on 'C.B.S.' lp/c; CBS/40 25361) (track * replaced by) – Zerox / Kick! / Whip in my valise. (cd-iss. Jul95 on 'Columbia'; 480521-2)

— **LEIGH GORMAN** – bass (on B-side) repl. WARREN who joined MONOCHROME SET

Feb 80.	(7")	(DUN 10) **CARTROUBLE. / KICK!**	-	-
		(re-act.Jan81; hit No.33)		

— (Jan80) until (Mar'80 when ADAM brought in entire new group) **MARCO PIRRONI** (b.27 Apr'59) – guitar, vocals (ex-MODELS) repl. ASHMAN / **MERRICK** (b.CHRIS HUGHES, 3 Mar'54) – drums repl. BARBE / **KEVIN MOONEY** – bass, vocals repl. GORMAN (who with above 2 formed BOW WOW WOW) / added **TERRY LEE MIALL** (b. 8 Nov'58) – 2nd drummer (ex-MODELS)

			C.B.S.	Columbia
Jul 80.	(7")	(CBS 8877) **KINGS OF THE WILD FRONTIER. / PRESS DARLINGS**	48	-
		(re-act.Feb81; hit No.2)		
Sep 80.	(7")	(CBS 9039) **DOG EAT DOG. / PHYSICAL (YOU'RE SO)**	4	-
Nov 80.	(lp/c)	(CBS/40 84549) <37033> **KINGS OF THE WILD FRONTIER**	1	44 Feb81

– Dog eat dog / Ant music / Feed me to the lions / Los Rancheros / Ants invasion / Killer in the home / Kings of the wild frontier / The magnificent five / Don't be square (be there) / Jolly Roger / Making history / The human beings. (cd-iss. Oct93 & Dec98 on 'Sony Europe'; 477902-2)

Nov 80.	(7")	(CBS 9352) **ANT MUSIC. / FALL IN**	2	-
Jan 81.	(7")(12")	<02042><01061> **ANT MUSIC. / DON'T BE SQUARE (BE THERE)**	-	-

— **GARY TIBBS** (b.25 Jan'58)- bass (ex-ROXY MUSIC, ex-VIBRATORS) repl. MOONEY

May 81.	(7")<US-12">	(A-1065) <02193> **STAND AND DELIVER. / BEAT MY GUEST**	1	-
Sep 81.	(7")	(A-1408) **PRINCE CHARMING. / CHRISTIAN D'OR**	1	-
Nov 81.	(lp/c)	(CBS/40 85268) <37615> **PRINCE CHARMING**	2	94

– Prince charming / The Scorpios / Picasso visita el Planeta de los Simios / 5 guns west / That voodoo / Stand and deliver / Mile high club / Ant rap / Mowhok / S.E.X. (re-iss. cd Mar96 on 'Columbia'; 474606-2)

Dec 81.	(7"/7"pic-d)	(A/+11 1738) **ANT RAP. / FRIENDS**	3	-
—	they broke up early '82			

ADAM ANT

continued solo augmented by **PIRRONI** and sessioners

			C.B.S.	Epic
May 82.	(7"/7"pic-d)	(A/+11 2367) **GOODY TWO SHOES. / RED SCAB**	1	-
Sep 82.	(7"/7"pic-d)	(A/+11 2736) **FRIEND OR FOE. / JUANITO THE BANDITO**	9	-
Oct 82.	(lp/c)	(CBS/40 25040) <38370> **FRIEND OR FOE**	5	16

– Friend or foe / Something girls / Place in the country / Desperate but not serious / Here comes the grump / Hello I love you / Goody two shoes / Crackpot history and the right to lie / Made of money / Cajun twisters / Try this for sighs / A man called Marco. (cd-iss. Jul96 on 'Columbia'; 484436-2)

Oct 82.	(7")	<03367> **GOODY TWO SHOES. / CRACKPOT HISTORY**	-	12
Nov 82.	(7"/7"pic-d)	(A/+11 2892) **DESPERATE BUT NOT SERIOUS. / WHY DO GIRLS LOVE HORSES?**	33	-
Feb 83.	(7")	<03688> **DESPERATE BUT NOT SERIOUS. / PLACE IN THE COUNTRY**	-	66
Oct 83.	(7"/7"pic-d/ext.12")	(A/WA/TA 3614) <04461> **PUSS 'N' BOOTS. / KISS THE DRUMMER**	5	May84
Nov 83.	(lp/c)	(CBS/40 25705) <39108> **STRIP**	20	65

– Baby let me scream at you / Libertine / Spanish games / Puss'n'boots / Playboy / Strip / Montreal / Navel to neck / Amazon. (cd-iss. Jul84; CD 25705)

Dec 83.	(7"/7"pic-d/ext.12")	(A/WA/TA 3589) <04337> **STRIP. / YOURS, YOURS, YOURS**	41	42
Sep 84.	(7"/'A'-Orbit mix-12")	(A/TA 4719) **APOLLO 9. / B SIDE BABY**	13	
		(12") (QTA 4719) – ('A'-Splashdown remix & acappella instrumental).		
Jul 85.	(7")	(A 6367) <05574> **VIVE LE ROCK. / GRETA X**	50	
		(12"+=) (TA 6367) – ('A'instrumental dub mix).		
Sep 85.	(lp/c)	(CBS/40 26583) <40159> **VIVE LE ROCK**	42	

– Vive le rock / Miss Thing / Razor keen / Rip down / Scorpio rising / Apollo 9 / Hell's eight acres / Mohair lockeroom pin-up boys / No zap / P.O.E. (c+=) – Human bondage den. (cd-iss. 1988+=; CD 26583) – Apollo 9 (acappella). (re-iss. cd Mar95 on 'Rewind'; 478504-2)

— ADAM retired for 4 years. MARCO joined SPEAR OF DESTINY

ADAM ANT

brought back MARCO to resurrect career.

			M.C.A.	M.C.A.
Feb 90.	(7"/7"s/c-s)	(MCA/+R/C 1387) <53679> **ROOM AT THE TOP. / BRUCE LEE**	13	17
		(cd-s+=/12"+=) (D+/MCAT 1387) – ('A'house vocals).		
		(cd-s+=) (DMCAX 1387) – ('A'mixes).		
Mar 90.	(cd/lp)(c)	(D+/MCG 6068)(MCGC 6068) <6315> **MANNERS & PHYSICIQUE**	19	57

– Room at the top / If you keep on / Can't set rules about love / Bright lights black leather / Young dumb and full of it / Rough stuff / Manners & physicique / U.S.S.A. / Piccadilly / Anger Inc.

Apr 90.	(7"/c-s)	(MCA/+C 1404) **CAN'T SET RULES ABOUT LOVE. / HOW TO STEAL THE WORLD**	47	
		(cd-s+=/12"+=) (D+/MCAT 1404) – Brand new torso.		
		(cd-s++=) (DMCAP 1404) – ('A'-lp version).		
Jun 90.	(7")	<79042> **BRIGHT LIGHTS BLACK LEATHER. / ROUGH STUFF**	-	-

ADAM & THE ANTS (cont) — THE GREAT INDIE DISCOGRAPHY — The 1970s

				E.M.I.	Capitol
Jan 95.	(c-s/7")	(TC+/EM 366) <58239>	**WONDERFUL. / GOES AROUND**	32	39 Mar95
	(cd-s+=)	(CDEMS 366)	– Norman / Woman love run through me.		
	(cd-s)	(CDEM 366)	– ('A'side) / If / Phoenix.		
Mar 95.	(c-s/7"; withdrawn)		**BEAUTIFUL DREAM. / LET'S HAVE A FIGHT**		
	(cd-s+=; w-drawn)	– Billy boy / Wonderful (acoustic).			
	(cd-s; w-drawn)	– ('A'side) / Shake your hips / Ant music (acoustic) / ('A'-Lucas master mix).			
Apr 95.	(c-s/7")	(TC+/EMC 3687) <30335>	**WONDERFUL**	24	39
	– Won't take that talk / Beautiful dream / Wonderful / 1969 again / Yin & Yang / Image of yourself / Alien / Gotta be a sin / Vampires / Angel / Very long ride. (cd re-iss. Sep97; same)				
May 95.	(c-s)	(TCEM 379)	**GOTTA BE A SIN / DOG EAT DOG** (live)	48	
	(cd-s)	(CDEM 379)	– ('A'side) / Cleopatra (live) / Beat my guest (live) / Red scab (live).		
	(cd-s)	(CDEMS 379)	– ('A'side) / Desperate but not serious (live) / Car trouble (live) / Physical (you're so) (live).		

– compilations, others, etc. –

Feb 82.	(7")	E.G.; (EGO 5)	**DEUTCHER GIRLS. / PLASTIC SURGERY**	13	-
Mar 82.	(7"ep/7"pic-ep)	Do-It; (DUN/+X 20)	**THE B-SIDES**	46	-
	– Friends / Kick! / Physical (you're so).				
	(12"ep+=)	**ANTMUSIC** (DUNIT 20) – Cartrouble (pts. 1 & 2).			
1982.	(7"; as MANEATERS)	E.G.; (EGO 8)	**NINE TO FIVE. / (SUZI PINNS**: Jerusalem)		-
	(above another from the film 'Jubilee' & featuring TOYAH)				
Sep 86.	(lp/c)	C.B.S.; (CBS/40 450074-1/-4)	**HITS**		
	– Kings of the wild frontier / Dog eat dog / Ant music / Stand and deliver / Prince Charming / Ant rap / Goody two shoes / Friend or foe / Desperate but not serious / Puss 'n' boots / Strip / Apollo 9 / Vive le rock. (re-iss. Jul90 & Jul98 on 'Columbia' cd/c; R 450074-2/-4)				
Jan 88.	(7")	Old Gold; (OG 9739)	**ANT MUSIC. / STAND AND DELIVER**		-
Oct 89.	(12"white/12"pic-d)	Damaged Goods; (FNARR/+P 7)	**YOUNG PARISIANS / LADY. / (interview)**		-
Nov 90.	(7")	Old Gold; (OG 9953)	**PRINCE CHARMING. / GOODY TWO SHOES**		-
Feb 91.	(cd/c/lp)	Strange Fruit; (SFR CD/MC/LP 115)	**THE PEEL SESSIONS** (early 1979 material)		
Jun 91.	(cd/c)	Columbia; (468762-2/-4)	**ANTICS IN THE FORBIDDEN ZONE**		
Aug 93.	(cd/c)	Arcade; (ARC 31000 5-2/6-4)	**ANTMUSIC – THE VERY BEST OF ADAM ANT**	6	-
	(re-iss. Mar94 d-cd+ 'LIVE'; ARC 310000-2); hit No.30)				
Oct 94.	(cd)	Columbia; (477513-2)	**THE BEST (ADAM ANT)**		
May 95.	(cd)	Columbia; (480362-2)	**B SIDES BABIES**		-
Mar 99.	(cd)	Columbia; (494229-2)	**THE VERY BEST OF . . .**	56	

ADVERTS

Formed: London, England . . . late 1976 by singer TV SMITH (aka TIM) and one of punk's first female icons, the sultry GAYE ADVERT (his future wife). Enlisting HOWARD PICKUP and LAURIE DRIVER, the group gigged constantly at the infamous Covent Garden punk club, The Roxy, appearing on the 1977 compilation, 'Live At The Roxy' with their first recording, 'BORED TEENAGERS'. Subsequently signed for a one-off single deal with 'Stiff' through the help of The DAMNED, the band released the self explanatory 'ONE CHORD WONDERS' in Spring '77. While the track generated some interest, it was the amphetamine rush of 'GARY GILMORE'S EYES' which launched them into the UK Top 20. Based on the request of the notorious death row inmate to have his eyes donated to science, the single predictably caused a minor furore in the tabloid press. Yet despite this publicity and major label muscle courtesy of CBS subsidiary 'Bright', both a third single, 'NO TIME TO BE 21' and debut album, 'CROSSING THE RED SEA WITH THE ADVERTS' (1978) barely scraped into the Top 40. The general concensus was that the band had failed to capture the energy of their live shows in the studio and an increasingly mainstream sound and attitude ensured that 'CAST OF THOUSANDS' (1979) and its attendant singles would sink without trace. Line-up changes dogged the band as they went through a succession of drummers Spinal Tap-style, even recruiting a former MIKE OLDFIELD synth player (TIM CROSS) and blowing the remnants of their fast dissipating street cred. Following the tragic electrocution of manager, Michael Dempsey, TV and GAYE finally threw in the towel in late '79 and embarked on solo projects. SMITH formed TV SMITH'S EXPLORERS before ploughing a singer/songwriter vein, releasing a debut solo effort, 'CHANNEL 5', in 1983. Absent from the mainstream music scene for most of the 80's, SMITH re-emerged in 1992 on 'Cooking Vinyl' with 'MARCH OF THE GIANTS'. Follow-ups 'IMMORTAL RICH' (1995) and 'GENERATION Y' (1999), kept the singer in the retro-punk spotlight, although clearly fans were still counting the days of an ADVERTS re-union.

Album rating: CROSSING THE RED SEA WITH THE ADVERTS (*7) / CAST OF THOUSANDS (*4) / TV Smith: THE LAST WORDS OF THE GREAT EXPLORER (*5) / CHANNEL FIVE (*5) / MARCH OF THE GIANTS (*5) / R.I.P. . . . EVERYTHING MUST GO! (*5) / IMMORTAL RICH (*6) / GENERATION Y (*6) / USELESS compilation (*7)

TV SMITH (b. TIM, 1956, Devon, Cornwall) – vocals / **GAYE ADVERT** – bass (b. GAYE BLACK, 29 Aug'56) / **HOWARD PICKUP** – guitar / **LAURIE DRIVER** – drums

				Stiff	not iss.
Apr 77.	(7")	(BUY 13)	**ONE CHORD WONDERS. / QUICKSTEP**		-
				Anchor	not iss.
Aug 77.	(7")	(ANC 1043)	**GARY GILMORE'S EYES. / BORED TEENAGERS**	18	-
Oct 77.	(7")	(ANC 1047)	**SAFETY IN NUMBERS. / WE WHO WAIT**		-
				Bright-CBS	not iss.
Jan 78.	(7")	(BR 1)	**NO TIME TO BE 21. / NEW DAY DAWNING**	38	-
Feb 78.	(lp,red-lp)	(BRL 2001)	**CROSSING THE RED SEA WITH THE ADVERTS**	38	-
	– One chord wonders / Bored teenagers / New church / On the roof / New boys / Gary Gilmore's eyes / Bombsite boy / Mo time to be 21 / Safety in numbers / New day dawning / Drowning men / On wheels / Great British mistake. (re-iss. Oct81 & Sep83 [red-lp] on 'Butt'; ALSO 2) (re-iss. Dec88 on 'Bright' cd/lp; CD+/BUL 2) (cd-iss. Mar97 on 'Essential'; ESMCD 451) – Gary Gilmore's eyes / We who wait / New day dawning. (cd re-iss. Apr02 on 'Snapper'+=; SFIRE 004CD) – One chord wonders / Quickstep / Gary Gilmore's eyes / Bored teenagers / Safety in numbers / We who wait / On wheels (live) / Newboys (live) / New church (live) / Gary Gilmore's eyes (live) / Drowning men (live) / No time to be 21 (live).				
—	**JOHN TOWE** – drums (ex-ALTERNATIVE TV, ex-GENERATION X) repl. DRIVER (Spring'78) **ROD LATTER** – drums (ex-MANIACS, ex-RINGS) repl. TOWE				
				R.C.A.	not iss.
Nov 78.	(7")	(PB 5128)	**TELEVISION'S OVER. / BACK FROM THE DEAD**		-
Jun 79.	(7")	(PB 5160)	**MY PLACE. / NEW CHURCH** (live)		-
Sep 79.	(7")	(PB 5191)	**CAST OF THOUSANDS. / I WILL WALK YOU HOME**		-
—	added **TIM CROSS** – keyboards, synthesizers (of MIKE OLDFIELD)				
Oct 79.	(lp/c)	(PL/PK 25246)	**CAST OF THOUSANDS**		-
	– Cast of thousands / The adverts / My place / Male assault / Television's over / Fate of criminals / I looked at the Sun / Love songs / I surrender / I will walk you home. (<cd-iss. Feb98 on 'Anagram'+=; CDPUNK 102>) – Television's over / Back from the dead / New church / Cast of thousands.				
—	**PAUL MARTINEZ** repl. HOWARD (he died in 1997) / his brother **RICK** repl. ROD. After manager MICHAEL DEMPSEY was electrocuted to death, TV, GAYE and TIM decided to split late 1979.				

– compilations, others, etc. –

May 83.	(7"m)	Bright-CBS; (BULB 1)	**GARY GILMORE'S EYES / WE WHO WAIT / NEW DAY DAWNING**		-
Oct 87.	(12"ep)	Strange Fruit; (SFPS 034)	**THE PEEL SESSIONS (25.4.77)**		-
	– Quickstep / Gary Gilmore's eyes / Bored teenagers / New boys / One chord wonders.				
Nov 90.	(cd/c/lp)	Receiver; (<RR CD/LC/LP 136>)	**LIVE AT THE ROXY** (live)		
May 97.	(cd)	Anagram; (CDPUNK 95)	**THE PUNK SINGLES COLLECTION**		-
Oct 97.	(lp)	Get Back; (GET 24)	**THE WONDERS DON'T CARE** (the radio sessions)		-
	(<cd-iss. Feb01 on 'Burning Airlines'; PILOT 003>)				
Jun 98.	(lp)	Get Back; (<GET 30>)	**THE ADVERTS SINGLES COLLECTION**		
Oct 98.	(cd)	Anagram; (<CDPUNK 107>)	**THE BEST OF THE ADVERTS**		Jun00 Sep99
Sep 02.	(cd; shared w/ the RUTS)	Step 1; <STEP 44>	**LIVE AND LOUD** (live)		

TV SMITH'S EXPLORERS

were formed late 79 by **TV** and **TIM CROSS**, **JOHN TOWE**, plus **ERIC RUSSELL** – guitar / **COLIN STONER** – bass (ex-DOCTORS OF MADNESS)

— (Mar'80) **MEL WESSON** repl. CROSS who rejoined MIKE OLDFIELD / **DAVE SINCLAIR** (of LONDON ZOO) repl. TOWE, who later joined UK SUBS

				Big Beat	not iss.
Nov 80.	(7")	(NS 64)	**TOMAHAWK CRUISE. / SEE EUROPE**		-
	(re-iss. Jan81 on 'Chiswick'; CHIS 140)				
				Kaleidoscope	Epic
Apr 81.	(7")	(KRLA 1162)	**THE SERVANT. / LOOKING DOWN ON LONDON**		-
	(ltd.c-s+=)	(KRLA40 1162)	– Walk in a straight line.		
Jun 81.	(7")	(KRLA 1359)	**HAVE FUN. / IMAGINATION**		-
Jul 81.	(lp/c)	(KRL/40 85087)	**THE LAST WORDS OF THE GREAT EXPLORER**		
	– The perfect life / The servant / Have fun / Walk away / The last words of the great explorer / I live for everything / Imagination / The easy way / The unwelcome guest. (w/ free 7"; SXPS 119) (c+=) – WALK IN A STRAIGHT LINE / WORLD OF MY OWN (cd-iss. Nov98 on 'Ozit'+=; OZITCD 0043) – Tomahawk cruise / See Europe / Looking down on London / Walk of my own / Walk in a straight line / The servant (live) / The last of the great explorer (live) / Walk away (live) / Looking down on London (live).				
Oct 81.	(7")	(KRLA 1590)	**THE PERFECT LIFE. / IMAGINATION**		-
—	(Oct'81) disbanded				

TV SMITH

went solo, recruiting yet again **TIM CROSS** plus **TIM RENWICK** – guitar (ex-MIKE OLDFIELD, ex-SUTHERLAND BROTHERS)

				Expulsion	not iss.
Jan 83.	(lp)	(EXIT 4)	**CHANNEL FIVE**		-
	– A token of my love / On your video / Dominator / London beach / War fever / Burning rain / Fire in the darkness / Cracking up / Your haunted heart / The suit / Beautiful bomb. (<cd-iss. Jul99 on 'Ozit'+=; OZITCD 0044>) – Coming round / Woodpecker / Lies / Treasure / New ways are best / On your video (alt.take) / The suit (alt.take).				
May 83.	(7")	(OUT 2)	**WAR FEVER. / LIES**		-

ADVERTS (cont) — THE GREAT INDIE DISCOGRAPHY — The 1970s

		Production House	not iss.
May 85.	(7"; as PRODUCTION HOUSE) *(PH 1)* **COMING ROUND. / WOODPECKER**		-

CHEAP

— were formed late '86 by T.V. plus **SIMON BUDD** – drums / **ANDY BENNY** – bass (ex-SLEAZE) / **MIK HESLIN** – guitar (ex-CHAOTIC DISCHORD) they donated a few songs to V/A albums before recording 7" in '89 **MARTIN DENTZ** – drums; repl. BUDD (in 1988)

		Deltic	not iss.
May 90.	(7") *(DELT 4)* **THIRD TERM. / BURIED BY THE MACHINE**		-

TV SMITH

		Cooking Vinyl	not iss.
Jul 92.	(cd/c/lp) *(COOK CD/C/LP 047)* **MARCH OF THE GIANTS**		-

– Lion and the lamb / March of the giants / Can't pay won't pay / Atlantic tunnel / Haves and have-nots / Straight and narrow / Free world / Ship in a bottle / Empty wallet / Useless / Runaway train driver / Borderline. *(cd re-iss. Mar94; same)*

		Humbug	Thirsty Ear
Feb 95.	(cd) *(BAH 21)* <21306> **IMMORTAL RICH**		1996

– Immortal rich / Living world / Walk the plank / We want the road / High society / Head on! dear! / The day we caught the big fish / Thin green line / Let 'em go / In there / Earth 2.

| May 96. | (cd-s) *(HUM 8)* **THIN GREEN LINE /** | | - |

		Cherry Red	not iss.
Feb 99.	(cd) *(CDMRED 151)* **GENERATION Y**		-

– Expensive being poor / Generation Y / What if? / Roll like a river / Strong horse / This year, next year / Momentous changes / I know what you want / Last true thing / Happy homeland / Statue of liberty.

– compilations, etc. –

Jun 93. (cd; by T.V. SMITH'S CHEAP) *Humbug; (BAH 5) / Griffin; <380>* **RIP... EVERYTHING MUST GO!** (rec. late 80's)
– Leisure time / My string will snap / New ways are best / Free world / Silicon Valley holiday / Luxury in exile / Buried by the machine / Ghosts / Ready for the axe to drop / The newshound / Beauty treatment / The Lord's Prayer.
1999. (cd-ep; as T.V. SMITH & PUNK LUREX O.K.) *Hiljaiset Levyt;* **THE FUTURE USED TO BE BETTER**
– The future used to be better / Gary Gilmore's eyes / My punk rock poem / One chord wonder / World just got smaller.
Apr 01. (cd) *J.K.P.; (JKP 43)* **USELESS – THE VERY BEST OF TV SMITH**

ALBERTO Y LOST TRIOS PARANOIAS

Formed: Manchester, England... 1976 by actors/musicians, C.P. LEE and BRUCE MITCHELL along with a BONZO DOG BAND-like entourage of LES PRIOR, BOB HARDING, JIMMY HIBBERT, TONY BOWERS and SIMON WHITE. Although serious musicians in their own right, The ALBERTO's dealt in scathing parodies of 60's/70's icons; among those unlucky enough to be singled out for treatment on their first two albums, 'ALBERTO Y...' (1976) and 'ITALIANS FROM OUTER SPACE' (1977), included LOU REED/V.U. (substituting 'ANADIN' for 'Heroin'; surprisingly effective!) and that portly Greek tent-wearer ('HAPPY TO BE ON – AN ISLAND AWAY FROM DEMIS ROUSSOS'). Moving from 'Transatlantic' records to "new wave" bastion, 'Stiff', for a one-off EP, 'SNUFF ROCK', the band decided to set their satirical sights on the thriving punk and reggae movement. The record fooled many afficionados who believed its A-side (featuring the tracks, 'KILL' and 'GOBBIN' ON LIFE') to be the work of an authentic punk band, its release tied to a London Royal Court Theatre stage play, Sleak', in which ALBERTO and Co. presented the concept of "snuff rock" i.e. faked onstage suicide. Subsequently signing to 'Logo' (home of The TOURISTS), they hit the Top 50 with a STATUS QUO pastiche, 'HEADS DOWN NO NONSENSE MINDLESS BOOGIE', a track taken from their third and final album, 'SKITE' (1978). The aforementioned 'Sleak' subsequently enjoyed another run in the early 80's alongside a further production, 'Never Mind The Bullocks', although The ALBERTOS were all but finished (bar a one-off reunion 45 in 1982) after the untimely death (from leukaemia) of LES PRIOR on the 31st January, 1980. HIBBERT released a metal-ish solo album, 'HEAVY DUTY', before going on to become the man behind TV cartoon, 'Count Duckula'. C.P. LEE enjoyed live appearances under the guise of LORD BUCKLEY, a spoof show, 'RADIO SWEAT', was released on cassette in '81. The remaining members, BOWERS, HARDING and MITCHELL, made more successful attempts at breaking back into the pop limelight via The MOTHMEN, DURUTTI COLUMN and SIMPLY RED (just BOWERS that is).

Album rating: SNUFF ROCK – THE BEST OF THE ALBERTOS compilation (*7)

C.P. 'Chris' LEE – vocals, guitar / **BOB HARDING** – vocals, guitar, bass / **TONY BOWERS** – guitar, bass / **JIMMY HIBBERT** – vocals / **LES PRYOR** – vocals / **SIMON WHITE** – guitar, steel guitar / **BRUCE MITCHELL** – drums, percussion

		Transatla.	not iss.
Apr 76.	(7") *(BIG 541)* **DREAD JAWS. / DE VERSION**		-
May 76.	(lp) *(TRA 316)* **ALBERTO Y LOST TRIOS PARANOIAS**		-

– Torture you / Pavlov / I like gurls / Dread jaws / Follow the guru / Dead meat / Anadin / 6:45 / Jesus wept / Mandrax sunset variations pt.1, pt.2, pt.3.

| Jul 77. | (lp) *(TRA 349)* **ITALIANS FROM OUTER SPACE** | | - |

– Old Trust / Brrrr / I'll come if you let me / Invocation of the fundamental orrifice of St. Agnes / No change / Peon in the neck / Happy to be on (an island away from Demis Roussos) / Teenager in schtuck / Italians from Outer Space: (a) The ballad of Colonel Callan, (b) A fistfull of spaghetti / Mandrax sunset variations pt.IV / Neville / Breakfast / Wholefood love / Holiday frog / Teenage Paradise / Willie Baxter's blues / It never rains in El Paso / Whispering grass / Death of rock'n'roll.

		Stiff	not iss.
Sep 77.	(7"ep) *(LAST 2)* **SNUFF ROCK E.P.**		-

– Kill / Gobbin' on life / Snuffin' / Snuffin' in a Babylon.

		Logo	not iss.
Nov 77.	(7"m) *(GO 106)* **OLD TRUST. / NEVILLE / TEENAGER IN SCHTUCK**		-
Sep 78.	(7") *(GO 323)* **HEADS DOWN NO NONSENSE MINDLESS BOOGIE. / THANK YOU**	47	-
Sep 78.	(lp) *(1009)* **SKITE**		-

– Juan Lopez / Mother Superior / Heads down no nonsense mindless boogie / Where have all the flowers gone / 23 / Peter Parker / Rockin' sav'yer / **** you / Where have all the flowers gone (dub) / Anarchy in the U.K. / God is mad.

Nov 78.	(7") *(GO 335)* ****** YOU. / DEAD MEAT (pt.2)**		-
Dec 78.	(d7") *(GOD 340)* **JUAN LOPEZ. / TEENAGE PARADISE // DEAD MEAT (pt.3)**		-
Jul 80.	(lp) *(MOGO 4008)* **THE WORST OF THE BERTS** (compilation)		-

— Disbanded 1979, PRYOR died of cancer in 1980. HIBBERT made a solo album, 'HEAVY DUTY'. LEE became a music journalist and as LORD BUCKLEY, recorded a live album, 'M'LORDS & LADIES'. BOWERS and HARDING formed indie outfit, The MOTHMEN, who released two sets, 'PAY ATTENTION' and 'ONE BLACK DOT'. MITCHELL, with the aforementioned MOTHMEN, were also part of DURUTTI COLUMN. The ALBERTOS re-formed in 1982 for one-off 45.

		New Hormones	not iss.
Dec 82.	(7") *(ORG 30)* **CRUISIN' WITH SANTA. /**		-

– compilations, etc. –

		Mau Mau	
Apr 91.	(cd) *Mau Mau; (MAUCD 604)* **SNUFF ROCK – THE BEST OF THE ALBERTOS**		-

– Old Trust / Brrrr / I'll come if you let me / Invocation of the fundamental orrifice of St.Agnes / No change / Peon in the neck / Happy to be on (an island away from Demis Roussos) / Teenager in schtuck / Italians from Outer Space: (a) The battle of Colonel Callan, (b) A fistfull of spaghetti / Mandrax variations part IV / Naville breakfast / Whole food love / Holiday frog / Teenage paradise / Willie Baxter's blues / It never rains in El Paso / Whispering grass / Death of rock and roll / Heads down, no nonsense, mindless boogie / Jesus wept / Kill / Gobbin' on life / Snuffin' like that / Snuffin' in a Babylon / 23 / Dead meat / Juan Lopez / Anadin / Pavlov / Anarchy in the UK.

| Feb 97. | (cd) *Overground; (OVER 56CD)* **RADIO SWEAT** | | - |
| Jan 01. | (d-cd) *Castle; (CMDDD 115)* **MANDRAX SUNSET VARIATIONS** | | - |

ALTERNATIVE TV

Formed: London, England... 1976 by "Sniffin Glue" fanzine editor, MARK PERRY. Completing the initial line-up with ALEX FERGUSSON, TYRONE THOMAS and JOHN TOWE, the band's first recording was given away with an issue of the aforesaid pamphlet in the form of a flexi-disc (the track in question, 'LOVE LIES LIMP' – a subsequent B-side). A debut ATV single proper, 'HOW MUCH LONGER' / 'YOU BASTARD', arrived on the punk scene in late '77 via the local 'Deptford Fun City' indie imprint. A humourously cynical cockney rant against everything and everyone, the track was one of the genre's rawest missives to date and set the tone for what was to come. In the Spring of '78, PERRY and Co. surprised many commentators by taking a diversion into reggae/dub with the less offensive 'LIFE AFTER LIFE/DUB'. PERRY sought out new personnel in the shape of DENNIS BURNS and CHRIS BENNETT, after his previous backing bailed out for pastures new. This line-up recorded the seminal 'IMAGE HAS CRACKED' (1978) album, a commercially overlooked masterpiece containing such powerhouse gems as 'ACTION TIME VISION', 'VIVA LA ROCK'N'ROLL' and 'SPLITTING IN TWO', while even tackling a Frank Zappa number, 'WHY DON'T YOU DO ME RIGHT' with characteristic sarcasm. Contrary to the last, PERRY ended the year with a defiantly experimental and commercially suicidal follow-up, 'VIBING UP THE SENILE MAN (PART 1)', a difficult, intense and paranoid record which nevertheless yielded up a minimalist treat, 'FACING UP TO THE FACTS'. Its release coincided with a split live set, 'WHAT YOU SEE IS WHAT YOU ARE' with commune-dwelling hippies HERE & NOW, PERRY moving even further left of centre as he attempted to distance himself from the increasingly homogenised punk/new wave industry. ATV delivered a final single before PERRY and BURNS formed The GOOD MISSIONARIES (named after an ATV track) with the former's wife GILLIAN HANNA, releasing one 1979 set, 'FIRE FROM HEAVEN'. Ever industrious, PERRY subsequently juggled a solo venture (one album, 'SNAPPY TURNS') with yet more avant-garde knob-twiddling in the form of The DOOR AND THE WINDOW. However, early in 1981, PERRY, BURNS and the returning ALEX FERGUSSON decided to switch their ATV back on, signing to Miles Copeland's burgeoning 'I.R.S.' label and releasing a one-off album, 'STRANGE KICKS'. Splitting in two once more when FERGUSSON went off to join PSYCHIC TV, PERRY floundered for a spell until he inevitably re-formed his beloved project and continued to sporadically release the odd experimental set.

Album rating: THE IMAGE HAS CRACKED (*9) / VIBING UP THE SENILE MAN (PART ONE) (*4) / STRANGE KICKS (*4) / SPLITTING IN 2 compilation (*8) / PEEP

ALTERNATIVE TV (cont)

SHOW (*4) / DRAGON LOVE (*4) / MY LIFE AS A CHILD STAR (*4) / PUNK LIFE (*4) / APOLLO (*4) / ACTION TIME VISION: THE BEST OF . . . compilation (*8)

MARK PERRY – vocals, guitar / **ALEX FERGUSSON** (b.16 Dec'52, Glasgow) – guitar / **TYRONE THOMAS** – bass / **CHRIS BENNETT** – drums

Deptford Fun City / not iss.

Dec 77. (7") (DFC 02) **HOW MUCH LONGER. / YOU BASTARD**
May 78. (7") (DFC 04) **LIFE AFTER LIFE. / LIFE AFTER DUB**

— FERGUSSON formed CASH PUSSIES. PERRY brought in **JOHN TOWE** – drums; repl. BENNETT / **DENNIS BURNS** – bass; repl. THOMAS
Added guests **KIM TURNER** – rhythm guitar / **JOOLS HOLLAND** – piano (on 2)

May 78. (lp) (DLP 01) **THE IMAGE HAS CRACKED**
 – Alternatives / Action time vision / Why don't you do me right / Good times / Still life / Viva la rock'n'roll / Nasty little lonely / Red / Splitting in 2.
Jun 78. (7") (DFC 07) **ACTION TIME VISION. / ANOTHER COKE**
Nov 78. (7") (DFC 06) **LIFE. / LOVE LIES LIMP**

— Trim to duo of PERRY & BURNS with **GENESIS P.ORRIDGE** / **MARK LINEHAN** (TOWE joined The ADVERTS)

Dec 78. (lp) (DLP 03) **VIBING UP THE SENILE MAN (PART 1)**
 – Release the natives / Serpentine gallery / Poor association / The radio story / Facing up to the facts / The good missionary / Graves of deluxe green / Smile in the day. *(re-iss. Feb02 on 'Get Back'; GET 88)*
Dec 78. (lp; shared with HERE & NOW) (DLP 02) **WHAT YOU SEE IS WHAT YOU ARE** (live)
 – Action time lemon / Circles / Fellow sufferer / Splitting in 2.
May 79. (7") (DFC 10) **THE FORCE IS BLIND. / LOST IN ROOM**

— PERRY went on an experimental mission via The GOOD MISSIONARIES, some solo material, The DOOR & THE WINDOW plus the REFLECTIONS before ATV were resurrected

GOOD MISSIONARIES

— PERRY and BURNS. MARK's girlfriend **GILLIAN HANNA** – recorder / plus **DAVE GEORGE** – guitar / **HENRY BADOWSKI** – drums

Aug 79. (lp) (DLP 04) **FIRE FROM HEAVEN**
 – Another coke / The body / The force is blind / Thief of fire / The radio story / Strange loons / Fire from Heaven / Release the natives / Fellow sufferer in dub / Bugger the cat.

— without PERRY, released more singles in 1980/81 on 'Unnormality' UK indie label.
VIBING UP THE SENILE WORLD (NORM 001) **DERANGED IN HASTINGS** (NORM 002)

MARK PERRY

Mar 80. (7") (DFC 12) **WHOLE WORLD'S DOWN ON ME. / I LIVE – HE DIES**
Jun 80. (lp) (DLP 06) **SNAPPY TURNS**
 – Snappy turns / The object is to love / You know / Inside / At war / Death looks down / The game is over / Quagga's last stand.

DOOR AND THE WINDOW

off-shoot band featuring **PERRY, BENDLE** and **NAG**

N.B. / not iss.

1979. (7"ep) (NB 3) **PERMANENT TRANSCIENCE**
 – He feels like a Doris / I like sound / Innocent / Dig / Production line.
1980. (lp) (NB 5) **DETAILED TWANG**
 – Dads / Habits / We do scare each other / Order and obey / He feels like a Doris / Part time punks / In the car / Subculture fashion slaves / Sticks and stones / Positive / Why must you build walls around us / Detailed twang.
1980. (c) (NB 9) **MUSIC AND MOVEMENT** (live)

— they made other recordings without PERRY; **FIRST & SECOND ep's**

MARK PERRY & DENNIS BURNS (one-off)

N.B. / not iss.

Mar 80. (7") (NB 7) **YOU CRY YOUR TEARS. / MUSIC DEATH?**

REFLECTIONS

PERRY, BURNS / + **NAG** (b. LEE) – bass, vocals / **KARL BLAKE** – drums (of-LEMON KITTENS) / **GRANT SHOWBIZ** – bass / others

Cherry Red / not iss.

Nov 81. (lp) (BRED 22) **SLUGS AND TOADS**
 – Tightrope walker / Zigzagging / Keep it easy / Toy dog ripped by cat / Demon of my desires / The human touch / The interpreter / Oh baby, look out / I had love in my hands / Clamming up / Nag takes a ride / The parting.
Jan 82. (7") (CHERRY 33) **4 COUNTRIES. / THE CORONER AND THE INQUEST**
Jan 84. (7") (CHERRY 75) **SEARCHING. / ('A'remix)**

ALTERNATIVE TV

— ATV reformed with **PERRY, BURNS** and **FERGUSSON** plus (ex-CASH PUSSIES) / **ALAN GRUNER** – keyboards / **RAY WESTON** – drums

I.R.S. / I.R.S.

Jun 81. (7") (PFP 1006) **THE ANCIENT REBELS. / SLEEP IN DUB**
Jul 81. (lp) (SP 70023) **STRANGE KICKS**
 – The ancient rebels / Strange kicks / Communicate / Mirror boy / Anye is back / My hand is still wet / Fun city / TV operator / There goes my date with Doug / Cold rain / Who are they / Sleep in dub.
Oct 81. (7") (PFP 1009) **COMMUNICATE. / OBSESSION**

— PERRY went into production, and FERGUSSON joined PSYCHIC TV. ATV reformed in 1984 with **PERRY, DAVE GEORGE, PROTAG + NAG**

— by 1985 **MARK** and **DAVE** were joined by **STEVEN CANDEL** – bass / **ALISON PHILIPS** – drums

Noiseville / not iss.

Feb 86. (12"ep) (VOO 1T) **WELCOME TO THE END OF FUN. / ANTI / DEATH TIME**
Jul 86. (12"ep) (VOO 2T) **LOVE / SEX EP**
 – Victory / Repulsion / You never know.

Anagram / not iss.

Aug 87. (12"m) (ANA 36) **MY BABY'S LAUGHING (EMPTY SUMMER'S DREAM). / LOOK AT HER EYES / I HAD LOVE IN MY HANDS**
Nov 87. (lp) (GRAM 32) **PEEP SHOW**
 – Chrissie's moom / Let's sleep now / Tumble time / The river / Boy eats girl / My baby's laughing (empty summer dream) / Scandal / White walls / Animal. *(cd-iss. Oct96 on 'Overground'; OVER 54CD)*

— were now **PERRY + JAMES KYLIO**

Chapter 22 / not iss.

Apr 90. (12"ep) (12CHAP 46) **THE SOL EP**
 – Everyday / The word / Affecting people / Pain barrier.
Nov 90. (lp) (CHAPLP 51) **DRAGON LOVE**
 – Coming of age / Something happened / Last rites / You pushed it a little too far / Captured fantasy / Never gonna give it up / Dragon love / Few feathers fall / (Do you believe) The time / We're through / Don't you leave me.

Overground Feel Good All Over

Nov 94. (7") <FGAO 6> **BEST WISHES. / WESTERN WORLD**
Nov 94. (cd) (OVER 39CD) <FGAO 16> **MY LIFE AS A CHILD STAR** — 1995
 – Child star / Magic / Reflections on a strange existence / Melting pot / Parasite / Don't you lie to me / Reunion / Breakdown / I'll put aside my feelings for awhile / It's over / Give me love / Emotional inner world / Decline and fall / Best wishes (new mix) / Magic (alternative mix). *(re-iss. May02; same)*
Oct 95. (7") <FGAO 22> **PURPOSE IN MY LIFE. / COMPANY OF LIES**

— MARK re-formed the band with **TYRONE THOMAS, ALEX FERGUSSON**, the latter subsequently being replaced by a guy called **CLIVE** (1996) / in '97:- **PERRY + MIKE COOK, IAN McKAY, STEVE CONNELL + STEPHEN O'NEIL**

Jan 98. (cd) (OVER 70CD) **PUNK LIFE**
 – Unlikely star / Punk life / Guntai wa Moumoku / Give me love / I had my love in my hands / Jane's not at home / Alternative TG / Jesus on the mainline / You never know / God saves! / Purpose in my life / A bold chance / Alternative television.
Jan 99. (cd) (OVER 82CD) **APOLLO**
 – Introducing / Apollo / Communication failure / I loked at your face / Hello, I'm Mika . . . / Where? / Propaganda / Return of the crack / Politics in every sausage / A long song / Oh shit, we fell from grace / Slap and tickle / The green hair / Jane's bath / Just a memory / Do you know what time it is? *(re-iss. Apr02; same)*

Sorted / not iss.

Apr 99. (7") (SRS 017) **UNLIKELY STAR. /**

– compilations, others, etc. –

Dec 79. (lp) Crystal; (CLP 1) **LIVE AT THE RAT CLUB** (live '77)
Mar 80. (lp) Deptford Fun City; (DLP 05) **ACTION TIME VISION**
1980. (c; shared with The GOOD MISSIONARIES) Weird Noise; (WEIRD 001) **SCARS ON SUNDAY**
Aug 80. (c; shared with The GOOD MISSIONARIES) Conventional; (CON 14) **AN YE AS WELL**
Feb 89. (lp) Anagram; (GRAM 40) **SPLITTING IN 2 – SELECTED VIEWING**
 – Action time vision / Love lies limp / Life / How much longer / Another coke / Still life / You bastard / Nasty little lonely / Why don't you do me right / Facing up to the facts / Lost in room / Force in blind / Splitting in two.
Jul 93. (cd) Overground; (OVER 29) **LIVE 1978** (live)
Feb 94. (cd) Anagram; (CDPUNK 24) **THE IMAGE HAS CRACKED – THE ALTERNATIVE TV COLLECTION**
 (lp-iss.Apr98 on 'Get Back'; GET 26LP)
Oct 95. (cd) Overground; (OVER 44CD) **THE RADIO SESSIONS**
 (re-iss. May02; same)
Mar 96. (cd) Anagram; (<CDMGRAM 102>) **VIBING UP THE SENILE MAN / WHAT YOU SEE IS WHAT YOU ARE**
Apr 96. (cd) Overground; (OVER 49CD) **THE INDUSTRIAL SESSIONS 1977**
 (re-iss. Jun02; same)
Oct 99. (cd) (CDMRED 163) **ACTION TIME VISION (THE BEST OF ATV)**
Aug 01. (cd) Public Domain; (DOMCD 009) **REVOLUTION**

Laurie ANDERSON

Born: LAURA PHILLIPS ANDERSON, 5 Jun'47, Chicago, Illinois, USA. Graduating from Columbia University in the early 70's, she soon became the Mother Superior of the New York art-rock cognescenti, after moving there to sculpture in the mid 70's. In 1977, a debut 45 'IT'S NOT THE BULLET THAT KILLS YOU', saw her turn her talents to music although the single did nothing. Gave up history tuition to concentrate more on performance art and fashion, utilising her weird violin playing to great effect. It wasn't until 1981 that her recording career took off, when a surprise 8-minute nauseating UK hit, 'O SUPERMAN', paved the way for debut 'Warners' album 'BIG SCIENCE'. This highlighted her speech-based, hypnotic minimalism, rounding on such topics as technology, culture and alienation with a wry, unsightful ease. The follow-up, 'MR HEARTBREAK', was a slightly more mainstream effort, due in part to BILL LASWELL's production on a couple of tracks. Two live albums were released during the mid-80's, one of them the latter 'HOME OF THE BRAVE', with its accompanying concert film, was a flop despite garnering critical plaudits at Cannes. 'STRANGE ANGELS' (1989) saw

ANDERSON move towards "real" singing and a more melodious approach while 1994's 'BRIGHT RED', co-produced by BRIAN ENO was characterised by a more claustrophobic feel. Another live album and tour cemented her reputation as a witty and succinct cultural commentator, although her recorded output, while often being innovative, sometimes veered too close to theatre to warrant repeated listening. Another hiatus for LAURIE ended in 2001 when she released 'LIFE ON A STRING', a musical theatre work based on the novel 'Moby Dick'. The violinist (complete with numerous other string-ed instrumentation) developed her experimental side to the fore on the majority on the set while a song, 'SLIP AWAY', saw her depicting the recent death of her father. A month later, and to mark the horrific terrorist act that befell her native city on the 11th of September 2001, she performed 'LIVE AT THE TOWN HALL, NEW YORK CITY, SEPTEMBER 19-20, 2001' (the title of her next set in 2002), her lyrics "here comes the planes . . ." from 'O SUPERMAN' poignant to these fearful days as when they were written by her over 20 years ago. • **Trivia:** Her audio-visual concerts, complete with orchestra lasted for around 7 hours. Guests on her 1984 set were PETER GABRIEL, NILE RODGERS and WILLIAM S. BURROUGHS. She was romantically involved with LOU REED in the early 90's. • **Bibliography:** THE PACKAGE: A MYSTERY (1971) / TRANSPORTATION (1974) / NOTEBOOK (1977) / WORDS IN REVERSE (1979) / HOME OF THE BRAVE (1979) / EMPTY PLACES (1991) / STORIES FROM THE NERVE BIBLE (1994).

Album rating: BIG SCIENCE (*6) / UNITED STATES LIVE (*5) / MISTER HEARTBREAK (*7) / HOME OF THE BRAVE (*6) / STRANGE ANGELS (*7) / BRIGHT RED (*6) / THE UGLY ONE WITH THE JEWELS AND OTHER STORIES (*7) / TALK NORMAL – THE LAURIE ANDERSON ANTHOLOGY compilation (*7) / LIFE ON A STRING (*4) / LIVE AT TOWN HALL . . . (*5)

LAURIE ANDERSON – vocals, multi-instrumentalist (violin / synthesizers)

—— with many on session incl. **DAVID VAN TIEGHEM** – percussion, drums / **ROMA BARAN** – accordian / **BILL OBRECHE** – sax, flute / **CHICK FISHER** – sax, clarinet / **PETER GORDON** – clarinet, sax / etc

not iss. | Holly Solomon Gallery

1977. (7"ltd) *<004>* **IT'S NOT THE BULLET THAT KILLS YOU – IT'S THE HOLE** | – |

not iss. | One-Ten

Sep 81. (7") *<OT 005>* **O SUPERMAN. / WALK THE DOG** | – |

Warners | Warners

Oct 81. (7") *(K 17870) <49876>* **O SUPERMAN. / WALK THE DOG** | 2 |

Jan 82. (7") *(K 17941)* **BIG SCIENCE. / EXAMPLE 22** | | –

Apr 82. (lp/c) *(K/K4 57002) <3674>* **BIG SCIENCE** | 29 |
– From the air / Big science / Sweaters / Walking and falling / Born, never asked / O Superman (for Massenet) / Example #22 / Let x = x / It tango. *(cd-iss. Apr84; K2 57002)*

Jul 82. (7") *(K 17956)* **LET X = X. / IT TANGO** | | –
(12"+=) *(K 17956)* – Sweaters.

Feb 84. (lp/c) *(925077-1/-4) <25077>* **MISTER HEARTBREAK** | 93 | 60
– Sharkey's day / Language d'amour / Gravity's angel / Kokoku / Excellent birds / Blue lagoon / Sharkey's night. *(cd-iss. Jul84; 925077-2)*

Jan 85. (5-lp-box) *(925192-1) <25192>* **UNITED STATES LIVE (live)** | |
– Say hello / Walk the dog / Violin solo / Closed circuits / For a large and changing rooms / Pictures of it / The language of the future / Cartoon song / Small voice / Three walking songs / The healing horn / New Jersey turnpike / So happy birthday / English / Dance of electricity / Three songs for paper, film and video / Sax solo / Sax duet / Born, never asked / From the air / Beginning French / O Superman (for Massenet) / Talkshow / Frames for the pictures / Democratic why / Looking for you walking and falling / Private property / Neon duet / Let x = x / The Mailman's nightmare / Difficult listening hour / Language is a virus from Outer Space – (William S. Burroughs) / Reverb / If you can't talk about it, point to it / Violin walk / City song / Finnish farmers / Red map / Hey ah / Bagpipe solo / Steven Weed / Time and a half / Voices on paper / Example #22 / Strike / False documents / New York social life / A curious phenomenon / Yankee see / I dreamed I had to take a test . . . / Running dogs / Four, three, two, one / The big top / It was up in the mountains / Odd objects / Dr. Miller / Big science / Big science (reprise) / Cello solo / It tango / Blue lagoon / Hothead (la langue d'amour) / Stiff neck / Telephone song / Sweaters / We've got four big clocks (and they're all ticking) / Song for two Jims / Over the river / Mach 20 / Rising sun / The visitors / The stranger / Classified / Going somewhere / Fireworks / Dog show / Lighting out for the territories.

Apr 86. (lp/c/cd) *(925400-1/-4/-2) <25400>* **HOME OF THE BRAVE** | |
– Smoke rings / White lily / Late show / Talk normal / Radar / Language is a virus from outer space / Sharkey's night / Credit racket.

May 86. (7"/12") *(W 8701/+T)* **LANGUAGE IS A VIRUS FROM OUTER SPACE (edit). / WHITE LILY** | | –

Nov 89. (lp/c)(cd) *(WX 258/+C)(K 925900-2) <25900>* **STRANGE ANGELS** | |
– Strange angels / Monkey's paw / Coolsville / Ramon / Babydoll / Beautiful red dress / The day the Devil / The dream before / My eyes / Hiawatha.

Oct 94. (cd/c) *<(9362 45534-2/-4)>* **BRIGHT RED** | |
– Speechless / Bright red / The puppet motel / Speak my language / World without end / Freefall / Muddy river / Beautiful pea green boat / Love among the sailors / Poison / In our sleep / Night in Baghdad / Tightrope / Same time tomorrow.

Mar 95. (cd/c) *<(9362 45347-2/-4)>* **THE UGLY ONE WITH THE JEWELS & OTHER STORIES FROM THE NERVE BIBLE** | |
– The end of the world / The salesman / The night flight from Houston / Word of mouth / The soul is a bird / The ouija board / The ugly one with the jewels / The geographic North Pole / John Lilly / The rotowhirl / On the way to Jerusalem / The Hollywood strangler / Maria Teresa Teresa Maria / Someone else's dream / White lily / The mysterious "J" / The cultural ambassador / Same time tomorrow. *(re-iss. Jul00; same)*

Apr 95. (cd-ep) *<43515>* **IN OUR SLEEP** | – |
– In our sleep / Poison / The ouija board / In our sleep (trance mix) / Poison (trance mix) / The ugly one with jewels / Poison (instrumental) / In our sleep (instrumental).

Nonesuch – Atlantic | Nonesuch – Atlantic

Aug 01. (cd) *<(7559 75939-2)>* **LIFE ON A STRING** | |
– One white whale / The island where I come from / Pieces and parts / Here with you / Slip away / My compensation / Dark angel / Broken / Washington Street / Statue of liberty / One beautiful evening / Life on a string.

Jun 02. (d-cd) *<(7559 79681-2)>* **LIVE AT TOWN HALL, NEW YORK CITY, SEPTEMBER 19-20, 2001 (live)** | | May02
– Here with you / Statue of liberty / Let x=x / Sweaters / My compensation / Washington Street / Pieces and parts / Strange angels / Dark angel / Wildebeests / One beautiful evening / Poison / Broken / Progress / Animals / Life on a string / Beginning French / O Superman / Slip away / White lily / Puppet motel / Love among the sailors / Coolsville.

– compilations, etc. –

Nov 00. (d-cd) *Rhino; <(8122 76648-2)>* **TALK NORMAL – THE LAURIE ANDERSON ANTHOLOGY** | |
– o Superman (for Massenet) / From the air / Big science / Born, never asked / It tango / Gravity's angel / Excellent birds / Langue d'amour / Sharkey's day / Walk the dog / Cartoon song / So happy birthday / City song / The big top / Dr. Miller / Lighting out for the territories / Smoke rings / Talk normal / Language is a virus / Credit racket / Strange angels / Babydoll / Coolsville / My eyes / The dream before / The day the Devil / Speak my language / Love among the sailors / Poison / In our sleep / Night in Baghdad / The night flight from Houston / The rotowhirl / The ouija board / The end of the world.

ANGELIC UPSTARTS

Formed: Brockley Whim, South Shields, England . . . 1977 by MENSI along with MOND, RONNIE WOODEN and DECCA. Perhaps unsurprisingly for a northern punk band, The ANGELIC UPSTARTS cited the injustice of the class divide as one of their driving motivations and there was certainly no love lost between them and their more intellectual London-centric cousins. The boys in blue were another sitting target for their righteous anger, an independently released 1978 debut single, 'MURDER OF LIDDLE TOWERS', condemning police brutality and winning them both the patronage of SHAM 69 mainman, JIMMY PURSEY and a deal with 'Warners'. The PURSEY-produced 'TEENAGE WARNING' (1979) was a straightahead three-chord assault on all things right wing, including the creeping plague of racism and the menace of the new Thatcher government. Like fellow working class heroes, SHAM 69, The ANGELIC UPSTARTS were beleaguered by fascist skinheads disrupting their gigs and misinterpreting their political stance. Still, it didn't take a genius to work out which side of the fence MENSI was on from the lyrical content of follow-up set, 'WE GOTTA GET OUT OF THIS PLACE' (1980), another tirade aimed at Britain's would-be oppressors. A switch to 'E.M.I.' at the dawn of the 80's was shortlived as the punk revolution filtered out into the mainstream, the band defiantly carrying on with their collectivist crusade over a series of independently released albums inlcuding 'REASON WHY' (1983) and 'POWER OF THE PRESS' (1986). While their musical palate had broadened to include the use of keyboards etc., the message remained the same, if even more vitriolic than ever. The contentious 'BRIGHTON BOMB' single paid tribute to the IRA's failed attempt at killing the whole Conservative cabinet; after almost a decade of Tory rule, MENSI (who found himself taken up on obscenity charges!) was obviously reaching the end of his tether. Most of the band's fans were also giving up the ghost and in 1986, The ANGELIC UPSTARTS finally called it a day. An ill-advised reformation in 1992 saw the group sign to metal/hardcore specialist, 'Roadrunner', hardly a natural home. The resulting album, 'BOMBED OUT' (1992) was met with little enthusiasm, by either old fans or new. • **Songwriters:** MENSI and MOND, except WE GOTTA GET OUT OF THIS PLACE (Animals) / GREEN FIELDS OF FRANCE (Eric Bogle) / WHITE RIOT (Clash).

Album rating: TEENAGE WARNING (*5) / WE GOTTA GET OUT OF THIS PLACE (*5) / 2,000,000 VOICES (*4) / LIVE (*4) / STILL FROM THE HEART (*4) / REASON WHY? (*5) / LAST TANGO IN MOSCOW (*3) / LIVE IN YUGOSLAVIA (*3) / THE POWER OF THE PRESS (*4) / BOMBED OUT (*3) / ANGEL DUST (THE COLLECTED HIGHS) compilation (*6)

MENSI (b. THOMAS MENSFORTH) – vocals / **MOND** (b. COWIE) – guitar / **RONNIE WOODEN** (b. WARRINGTON) – bass; repl. STEVE due to drug problems / **DECCA** (b. TAYLOR) – drums

Dead | not iss.

Jun 78. (7") *(IS-AU 1024)* **THE MURDER OF LIDDLE TOWERS. / POLICE OPPRESSION** | | –
(re-iss. Sep78 on 'Rough Trade/Small Wonder'; RT-SW 001)

Warners | not iss.

Apr 79. (7",7"green/12") *(K 17354/+T)* **I'M AN UPSTART. / LEAVE ME ALONE** | 31 | –

Jul 79. (7"/7"red) *(K 17426/+C)* **TEENAGE WARNING. / THE YOUNG ONES** | 29 | –

Aug 79. (lp/c) *(K/K4 56717)* **TEENAGE WARNING** | 29 | –
– Teenage warning / Student power / The yong ones / Never again / We are the people / Liddle Towers / I'm an upstart / Small town, small mind / Youth leader / Do anything / Let's speed / Leave me alone.

Oct 79. (7") *(K 17476)* **NEVER 'AD NOTHING. / NOWHERE LEFT TO HIDE** | 52 | –

Jan 80. (7") *(K 17558)* **OUT OF CONTROL. / SHOTGUN SOLUTION** | 58 | –

Mar 80. (7") *(K 17586)* **WE GOTTA GET OUT OF THIS PLACE. / UNSUNG HEROES PART 2** | 65 | –

Apr 80. (lp/c) *(K/K4 56906)* **WE GOTTA GET OUT OF THIS PLACE** | 54 | –
– Never 'ad nothing / Police oppression / Lonely man of Spandau / Their destiny is coming / Shotgun solution / King Coal / Out of control / Ronnie is a rocker / Listen to the steps / Can't kill a legend / Capital city / We gotta get out of this place.

Zonophone | not iss.

Jul 80. (7") *(Z 7)* **LAST NIGHT ANOTHER SOLDIER. / THE MAN WHO CAME IN FROM THE BEANO** | 51 | –

Nov 80. (7") *(Z 12)* **ENGLAND. / STICK'S DIARY** | | –

ANGELIC UPSTARTS (cont)

Jan 81.	(7") (Z 16) **KIDS ON THE STREET. / THE SUN NEVER SHINES**		57	-
May 81.	(7") (Z 22) **I UNDERSTAND. / NEVER COME BACK** (12"+=) (12Z 22) – Heath's lament.			-
Jun 81.	(lp) (ZONO 104) **2,000,000 VOICES**		32	-

– 2,000,000 voices / Ghost town / You're nicked / England / Heath's lament / Guns for the Afghan rebels / I understand / Mensi's marauders / Mr. Politician / Kids on the street / We're gonna take the world / Last night another soldier / I wish. *(re-iss. May93 on 'Dojo'; DOJOLP 081) (cd-iss. Jan98; DOJOCD 081) (<cd re-iss. Feb01 on 'Captain Oi'; AHOYCD 158)>*

Sep 81.	(lp) (ZEM 102) **ANGELIC UPSTARTS LIVE (live)**		27	-

– Teenage warning / Never 'ad nothing / Four words / Last night another soldier / Guns for the Afghan rebels / I understand / Mr. Politician / Shotgun solution / Pride without prejudice / England / Police oppression / Kids on the street / I understand / You're nicked / 2,000,000 voices / I'm an upstart. *(c+=) –* (free live flexi 7"with above) – THE YOUNG ONES / WHITE RIOT. / WE'RE GONNA TAKE THE WORLD / LEAVE ME ALONE *(cd-iss. Feb94 on 'Dojo'; DOJOCD 169)*

Oct 81.	(7") (Z 25) **DIFFERENT STROKES. / DIFFERENT DUB**			-

—— **TONY FEEDBACK** – bass repl. DECCA who went solo

Mar 82.	(7") (Z 28) **NEVER SAY DIE. / WE DEFY YOU**			-
Apr 82.	(lp) (ZONO 106) **STILL FROM THE HEART**			-

– Never say die / Flames of Brixton / Action man / Wasted (loved by none) / Here comes trouble / Theme for lost souls / I stand accused / Black knights of the 80's / Cry wolf / Soldier. *(cd-iss. Nov93 on 'Dojo'; DOJOCD 144)*

—— (MENSI, MOND and FEEDBACK) were joined by **BRYAN HAYES** – rhythm guitar / **PAUL THOMPSON** – drums

Anagram   not iss.

Nov 82.	(7"/12") (ANA/12ANA 3) **WOMAN IN DISGUISE. / LUST FOR GLORY**			-
Mar 83.	(7"/12") (ANA/12ANA 7) **SOLIDARITY. / FIVE FLEW OVER**			-
Jul 83.	(7"; w-drawn) (ANA 12) **THE BURGLAR.**			-

—— next 45 with guest vocalist MAX SPLODGE (ex-SPLODGENESSABOUNDS)

Sep 83.	(7") (ANA 13) **NOT JUST A NAME. / THE LEECH** (12"+=) (12ANA 13) – Leave me alone / Liddle Towers.			-
Dec 83.	(lp) (GRAM 04) **REASON WHY?**			-

– Woman in disguise / Never give up / Waiting, hating / Reason why? / Nobody was saved / Geordie's wife / Loneliness of the long distance runner / 42nd Street / The burglar / Solidarity / As the passion / A young punk / Where we started. *(cd-iss. Nov92; CDGRAM 04) (cd re-iss. Jan97 on 'Summit'; SUMCD 4086) (cd re-iss. Mar01 on 'Anagram'; CDPUNK 17)*

Picasso   not iss.

Oct 84.	(7") (PIK 001) **MACHINE GUN KELLY. / PAINT IT IN RED** (12"+=) (PIKT 001) – There's a drink in it.			-
Aug 85.	(lp) (PIK 004) **LAST TANGO IN MOSCOW (live)**			-

– One more day / Machine gun Kelly / Progress / Blackleg miner / Who's got the money / Last tango in Moscow / I think it should be free / Never return / Rude boy / No news / Jarrow woman / Nowhere to run / Paint it in red. *(re-iss. Feb88 on 'Razor'; RAZ 004) (cd-iss. Nov93 on 'Great Expectations'; PIPCD 047) (cd re-iss. May98 on 'Captain Oi'+=; AHOYCD 087)* – There's a drink in it / Listen to the silence / She don't cry anymore / I won't pray for liberty / Never return to Hell / When will they learn / No nukes.

Sep 85.	(lp) (HCLP 002M) **LIVE IN YUGOSLAVIA (live)**			-

– Never ad nothing / Leave me alone / Teenage warning / Solidarity / Last night another soldier / Guns for the Afghan rebels / Machine gun Kelly / Police oppression / Kids on the street / Women in disguise / 2,000,000 voices / One more day / Upstart / Who killed Liddle Towers / White riot. *(re-iss. Feb88 on 'Razor'; RAZM 32) (cd-iss. Aug93 on 'Great Expectations'; PIPCD 048) (cd re-iss. Oct95 on 'Punx'; PUNXCD 2)*

Gas   Chameleon

Jun 85.	(7") (GM 1010) **BRIGHTON BOMB. / SOLDIER** (12"+=) (GM 3010) – Thin red line.			-
Jan 86.	(m-lp) (GAS 4012) **THE POWER OF THE PRESS**			-

– I stand accused / Nottingham slag / Joe where are you now? / Empty street / Soldier / Brighton bomb / The power of the press / Stab in the back / Here I come / Thin red line / I'd kill her for six pence / Green fields of France. *(re-iss. Jun90 on 'Streetlink'; CLINK 006) (<cd-iss. Nov00 on 'Step 1'; STEPCD 039>)*

1987.	(c) <CHC 8603> **BRIGHTON BOMB**	-		-

—— disbanded 1986 and little or nothing heard of until 1992

Roadrunner   not iss.

May 92.	(cd/lp) **BOMBED OUT**			-

– Red till dead / Albert's gotta gun / Victim of deceit / Open your eyes / Still fighting / The writing on the wall / A real rain / Let's build a bomb / Proud and loud / Stone faced killer. *(re-iss. Aug94 on 'Dojo'; DOJOCD 198)*

– compilations, others, etc. –

Apr 81.	(c-s) Warners; (SPZ 2) **I'M AN UPSTART / NEVER 'AD NOTHING**			-
Sep 83.	(lp/c) Anagram; (GRAM/CGRAM 07) **ANGEL DUST (THE COLLECTED HIGHS)**			-

– The murder of Liddel Towers / Police oppression / I'm an upstart / Teenage warning / Never 'ad nothing / Shotgun solution / England / Last night another soldier / 2,000,000 voices / Kids on the street / Never say die / Heath's lament / I understand / Woman's disguise / Solidarity. *(cd-iss. Oct88; CDMGRAM 7)* – REASON WHY. *(<cd re-iss. Sep93 & Oct99; same>)*

Mar 86.	(lp) Dojo; (DOJOLP 7) **BOOTLEGS AND RARITIES** *(cd-iss. Nov93 on 'Great Expectations'; PIPCD 049)*			-
Dec 87.	(lp) Link; (LINKLP 019) **BLOOD ON THE TERRACES** *(<cd-iss. Jun99 on 'Harry May'; AHOYCD 116>)*			-
Jul 88.	(12"ep) Skunx; (MENSIX 1) **ENGLAND'S ALIVE (live)**			-

– England / We're gonna take the world / Liddle Towers / The young ones.

Jan 92.	(cd) Streetlink; (AOK 102) **ALTERNATIVE CHARTBUSTERS**			-
Jul 92.	(cd) Streetlink; (STRCD 027) **GREATEST HITS LIVE (live)** *(re-iss. Mar93 on 'Dojo'; DOJOCD 127)*			-
Aug 92.	(cd) Soundtrack Music; (SLOGCD 1) **BLOOD ON THE TERRACES / LOST AND FOUND** *(re-iss. Feb94 on 'Loma'; LOMACD 11)*			-
Jun 95.	(cd) Anagram; (<CDPUNK 59>) **THE INDEPENDENT PUNK SINGLES COLLECTION**			1999
Dec 97.	(cd) Captain Oi; (<AHOYCD 80>) **RARITIES**			Oct00
Jun 99.	(cd) Harry May; (MAYOCD 116) **NEVER 'AD NOTHING**			Apr00
Sep 99.	(cd) Captain Oi; (<AHOYCD 121>) **THE E.M.I. PUNK YEARS**			Jan00
May 00.	(cd) Captain Oi; (<AHOYCD 138>) **THE BBC PUNK SESSIONS**			
Nov 00.	(cd) Harry May; (MAYOCD 505) **LOST AND FOUND**			-

Adam ANT (see under ⇒ ADAM & THE ANTS)

ART & LANGUAGE
(see under ⇒ RED CRAYOLA; in 90's section)

ART ATTACKS

Formed: London, England ... 1977 by 'Sounds' cartoonist extrordinaire, SAVAGE PENCIL (aka EDWIN POUNCEY), who turned his talents to "singing" against a 3-chord punk-rock backdrop provided by STEVE SPEAR, MARION FUDGER and JD HANEY (who replaced WIRE bound, ROBERT GOTOBED). Although they only gigged sporadically, they definitely had their moments, two of which ('Frankenstein's Heartbeat' & 'Animal Bondage') were the only classic punk tracks on that year's otherwise dull Various Artists lp, 'Live At The Vortex'. The ART ATTACKS contributed to yet another V/A compilation, 'Streets', the track in question being 'ARABS IN 'ARRADS', another slice of Dalek-voxed DIY. Appropriately titled, 'I AM A DALEK', became their debut 45 in Spring '78, although the scene had moved on leaps and bounds in such a short time span that their amateurism seemed outdated. They were still flogging a dead horse at the turn of the decade when they issued their wannabe final effort, 'PUNK ROCK STARS'. POUNCEY continued to record occasionally under various pseudonyms while keeping an illustrious career as a cartoonist. As SAVAGE PENCIL, he penned an obscure one-off solo album, 'ANGEL DUST' (1988), the soundtrack to the 'Bikers' movie which did nothing.

Album rating: never released one!

EDWIN POUNCEY – vocals / **STEVE SPEAR** – guitar / **M.S.** (MARION FUDGER) – bass (ex-DERELICTS) / **J.D. HANEY** – drums; repl. ROBERT GOTOBED who joined WIRE

Albatross   not iss.

Apr 78.	(7") (TIT 1) **I AM A DALEK. / NEUTRON BOMB**			-

—— had already split. ? replaced HANEY who joined MONOCHROME SET

Fresh   not iss.

Dec 79.	(7"m) (FRESH 3) **PUNK ROCK STARS. / RAT CITY / FIRST AND LAST**			-

TAGMEMICS

were formed by EDWIN or an ex-member.

Index   not iss.

1980.	(7"m) (INDEX 003) **CHIMNEYS. / (DO THE) BIG BABY / TAKE YOUR BRAIN OUT FOR A WALK**			-

SAVAGE PENCIL

Furthur   not iss.

Apr 88.	(lp) (FU 3) **ANGEL DUST** (music from the movie, Bikers')			-

KRAY CHERUBS

formed by EDWIN? or other.

Fierce   not iss.

1988.	(7"-1 sided) (FRIGHT 014) **NO**			-

Snakeskin   not iss.

1989.	(7"ltd.) (SS 002) **RIOT IN HELL MOM. / "SAUCERMAN":- Motor Drag**			-

—— split for final time; SAVAGE PENCIL guested for ETHER HOGG

AVANT GARDENERS

Formed: London, England ... 1977 by RUSSELL MURCH, MARTIN SAUNDERS, NIGEL RAE and MIKE KELLY. One of the many "New Wave" acts to hitch a ride on the 'Punk' bandwagon via Richard Branson's 'Virgin' records, The AVANT GARDENER (as they were called then) debuted with an eponymous EP later that summer. The green-fingered ones then disappeared from the scene for a few years, returning in 1980 with MURCH as the sole remaining original alongside a new line-up of MIKE ROBERTS, ROB HILL and guest drummers. More popular on the continent, The AVANT GARDENERS found a deal with Italy's 'Appaloosa' imprint and issued their long-awaited debut set, 'DIG IT' (1980), basically re-hashed versions of their early material alongside a Roky Erickson cover, 'TWO HEADED DOG'. The band further pursued their interest in warped 60's psychedelia with their final lp, 'THE CHURCH OF THE INNER COSMOS' (1983/84) their final rake through retro muck before they paved their proverbial way out of the music business.

Album rating: DIG IT (*6) / THE CHURCH OF THE INNER COSMOS (*6)

RUSSELL MURCH – vocals, guitar / **MARTIN SAUNDERS** – guitar / **NIGEL RAE** – bass / **MIKE KELLY** – drums

AVANT GARDENERS (cont)

		Virgin	not iss.
Aug 77.	(7"ep; as The AVANT GARDENER) (VEP 1003) **THE AVANT GARDENER EP**		-

– Gotta turn back / Back door / Bloodclad boogie / Strange gurl in clothes.

—— split for a time, while **MURCH** recruited entirely new musicians **MIKE ROBERTS** – guitar / **ROB HILL** – bass / plus guest drummers **STEVE HARTLEY, ED LEWIS + SID SLATER** (RAE played keyboards)

		Appaloosa	not iss.
1980.	(lp) (AP 013) **DIG IT**	-	- Italy

– Strange gurl in clothes / Where are my hormones / Gotta turn back / Johnny Cash / Dateless night / Two-headed dog / Bloodclad boogie baby / Never turn your back on a silicon chip.

—— the trio also increased guest list including drummers **HARTLEY, STEVE SATURN + MARTIN HUGHES**

| Jan 84. | (lp) (AP 027) **THE CHURCH OF THE INNER COSMOS** | | - |

– Looking for a sun / C.D.C. / Loose in the sky / $30 / Pe 13th son of Rameses / Looking for another sun / Jennifer Jones / The lecture / The force is with you / The kitchen of oblivion.

		Speed	not iss.
Dec 83.	(7"m) (SPEED 11) **DEADWOOD STAGE. / JOHN PRIEST / WHERE ARE MY HORMONES**		-

—— nothing was heard from them after above

AVENGERS

Formed: San Francisco, California, USA ... 1977 by PENELOPE HOUSTON, DANNY FURIOUS, JONATHAN POSTAL and GREG WESTERMARK (the latter two were subsequently replaced by JIMMY WILSEY, BRAD KENT and GREG INGRAHAM before any recordings). Their debut release was a maxi-single featuring the lead track, 'CAR CRASH', a head-on collision of raw punk and primitive hardcore for the 'Dangerhouse' imprint that made its mark on the fertile San Fran underground scene. Garnering a minor degree of fame by supporting the SEX PISTOLS at their final gig in December '78 at the city's Winterland Ballroom, The AVENGERS subsequently worked with ex-PISTOL, STEVE JONES on a follow-up release, 'THE AMERICAN IN ME' EP. However, the file was closed on the group shortly after, PENELOPE HOUSTON going on to become a singer/songwriter.
• **Covered:** JOKER'S WILD (Ventures; Batman hit) / MONEY (Barrett Strong).

Album rating: THE AVENGERS 1977-1979 compilation (*6) / DIED FOR YOUR SINS compilation (*7)

PENELOPE HOUSTON – vocals / **GREG INGRAHAM** – guitar; repl. GREG WESTERMARK / **JIMMY WILSEY** – bass; repl. JONATHAN POSTAL / **DANNY FURIOUS** – drums / added **BRAD KENT** – second guitar

		not iss.	Dangerhouse
Dec 77.	(7"m) <SFD 400> **CAR CRASH. / WE ARE THE ONE / I BELIEVE IN ME**	-	
		not iss.	White Noise
Jan 79.	(7"ep) <WNR 002> **THE AMERICAN IN ME / UH-OH. / CORPUS CHRISTI / WHITE NIGGER**	-	

<re-iss. 1981 with diff.sleeve; same>

—— split in 1979, PENELOPE HOUSTON later became a singer/songwriter, releasing one album, 'BIRDBOYS' for 'Subterranean'.

– compilations, etc. –

| Aug 86. | (cd) CD Presents; (CD 007) **THE AVENGERS 1977-1979** | | - |

– We are the one / Car crash / I believe in me / Open your eyes / No martyr / Desperation / Thin white line / Paint it black / The American in me / White nigger / Uh-oh / Second to none / Corpus Christi / Fuck you (live). (re-iss. Apr90 as 'CADILLACS AND LINCOLNS' on 'Rockhouse'; ROCK 8901)

| Mar 99. | (cd/lp) Lookout; <(LK 217 CD/LP)> **DIED FOR YOUR SINS** | | Feb99 |

– Teenage rebel / Friends of mine / White nigger / The good, the bad and the Kowalskis / I want in / Crazy homocide / The end of the world / Fools or hippies / The American in me / Get up / Open your eyes / Car crash / Tiny pink noise / Fuck you / Joker's wild / Something's wrong / Wrong town / Desperation / I believe in me / Money (that's what I want) / We are the one.

| Sep 02. | (d-cd) Castle; (CMDDD 571) <72287> **TOO WILD TO TAME: ANTHOLOGY** | | Nov02 |

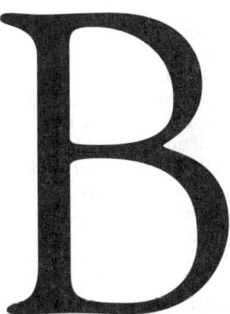

Henry BADOWSKI

Born: London, England. Having played for a variety of "Conference League" punk outfits in '77, the following year saw BADOWSKI sign for "1st Division/Premier League" punk contenders, CHELSEA. Switching from bass to drums (an unusual occurrence during these DIY times!), the man served time with singer, WRECKLESS ERIC before taking up keyboards and vocal duties for KING (no relation to PAUL's 80's outfit!). A one-off project exploring the unlikely link between punk and psychedelia, the band also featured KIM BRADSHAW, DAVE BERK (from JOHNNY MOPED) and CAPTAIN SENSIBLE, the latter soon inviting HENRY to play bass with the new short-lived incarnation of the DAMNED; The DOOMED. The following year BADOWSKI hooked up with another influential punk, MARK PERRY (ex-ALTERNATIVE TV), requesting his drumming talents in The GOOD MISSIONARIES while he procured some solo studio time and recorded a debut single, 'MAKING LOVE WITH MY WIFE', for 'Deptford Fun City'. Inspired by late 60's idol, SYD BARRETT, the single included BERK, ALEKSANDER KOLKOWSKI (another JOHNNY MOPED sidekick) and CHELSEA's JAMES STEPHENSON. The multi-instrumentalist almost immediately signed to 'A&M' (SQUEEZE had made a similar move a few years previous!), a series of solo flops being succeeded by a full-blown long-player, 'LIFE IS A GRAND' (1981). However, despite some favourable press reaction, HENRY disappeared from view for the rest of the 80's (and the 90's!) . . .. where are you now?

Album rating: LIFE IS A GRAND (*6)

HENRY BADOWSKI – vocals, saxophone, bass, keyboards, percussion / with **JAMES STEPHENSON** – guitar, bass (of CHELSEA) / **ALEKSANDER KOLKOWSKI** – violin (of JOHNNY MOPED) **DAVE BERK** – drums (of JOHNNY MOPED)

		Deptford Fun City	not iss.
Jul 79.	(7") (DFC 11) **MAKING LOVE WITH MY WIFE. / BABY, SIGN HERE WITH ME**		-
		A&M	not iss.
Sep 79.	(7") (AMS 7478) **BABY, SIGN HERE WITH ME. / MAKING LOVE WITH MY WIFE**		-
Feb 80.	(7") (AMS 7503) **MY FACE. / FOUR MORE SEASONS**		-

—— now without BERK

| Jun 81. | (7") (AMS 8135) **HENRY'S IN LOVE. / LAMB TO THE SLAUGHTER** | | - |
| Jul 81. | (lp) (AMLH 68527) **LIFE IS A GRAND** | | - |

– My face / Henry's in love / Swimming with the fish in the sea / The inside out / Life is a grand / Silver trees / This was meant to be / Anywhere else / Baby, sign here with me / Rampant.

—— HENRY retired from the music scene

Chris BAILEY (see under ⇒ SAINTS)

Edward BALL

Born: 23 Nov'59, Chelsea, London, England. After leaving school, ED and DAN TREACY put together "DIY" punk outfit, TV PERSONALITIES. Late in 1977, they gained national airplay on the John Peel show with a self-financed debut 45, '14TH FLOOR'. Meanwhile, ED initiated his own outfit, O-LEVEL, who, after a number of gigs, released 'EAST SHEEN'. An EP, 'MALCOLM', surfaced later in '78, although it was overshadowed by another TELEVISION PERSONALITIES gem, 'WHERE'S BILL GRUNDY NOW?'. Enjoying a sales boost courtesy of its B-side, 'PART-TIME PUNKS', it sold its limited run of copies in a matter of weeks and the band became overnight underground cult legends dabbling in SYD BARRETT-type psychedelia. In 1979, The O-LEVEL became The TEENAGE FILMSTARS. This outfit released three 45's before ED (still with TVP's) formed retro-mod combo, The TIMES. ED and DAN subsequently initiated the 'Whaam!' label as an outlet for both groups' material while also functioning as a starting point for fellow indie acts, SMALL WORLD, The PASTELS, DOCTOR & THE MEDICS, DIRECT HITS, etc. The TIMES created some fine tunes, including a TEENAGE FILMSTARS re-make of 'I HELPED PATRICK McGOOHAN ESCAPE' (the main actor in cult 60's TV series 'The Prisoner'; "I am not a number!"). ED re-released the debut album, 'POP GOES ART!', for his new 'Art Pop' label in 1983, enjoying something of a mini-cult TVP following. He finally left the TVP's in 1985 and concentrated wholly on The TIMES, the latter outfit signing to Alan McGee's 'Creation' in 1988 and issuing the album, 'BEAT TORTURE'. Although sales were nothing spectacular, Alan McGee kept faith with ED as he ventured into yet more side projects, i.e. LOVE CORPORATION, TEENAGE FILMSTARS (again!), CONSPIRACY OF NOISE. At the same time, EDWARD (as he was now calling himself), attempted to carve out a solo career, a move which brought minor success in 1996 with the single, 'THE MILL HILL SELF HATE CLUB'. In the 90's, he was also involved in The BOO RADLEYS with fellow baldy, SICE, while his solo albums, 'IF A MAN EVER LOVED A WOMAN' (1996) and 'CATHOLIC GUILT' (1997), performed well enough for BALL to retain his informal position on the slimmed-down 'Creation' roster. A fashion-conscious near-genius with a taste for melancholy eccentricity, the man could yet become a smaller version of the Millennium Dome if he continues to elicit regular hype from McGee and the music press. • **Songwriters:** Self-penned except covers; YOU CAN GET IT IF YOU REALLY WANT (Jimmy Cliff) / YOUR GENERATION (Generation X) / NOWHERE TO RUN (hit; Martha & The Vandellas) / MAN FROM UNCLE (Jerry Goldsmith) / BLUE MONDAY (as 'LINDI BLEU') (New Order).

Album rating: IF A MAN EVER LOVED A WOMAN (*6) / CATHOLIC GUILT (*7) / Times: PURE (*7) / Times: PINK BALL, BROWN BALL, RED BALL (*8) / Teenage Filmstars: A DAY IN THE LIFE OF GILBERT & GEORGE (*7)

O-LEVEL

ED BALL – vocals, organ / **JOHN BENNETT** – bass / **GERARD BENNETT** – drums (both also of TELEVISION PERSONALITIES) / **DICK SCULLY** – guitar

Psycho   not iss.

Jul 78. (7") *(PSYCH 2)* **EAST SHEEN. / PSEUDO PUNK**

Kings Road   not iss.

Dec 78. (7"ep) *(KR 002)* **THE MALCOLM EP**
– We love Malcolm / Leave me / Everybody's on Revolver / Stairway to boredom.

— In 1979, ED financed a DRY RIB ep 'THE DRY SEASON' on 'Clockwork'.

TEENAGE FILMSTARS

ED BALL – vocals, organ / **DAN TREACY** – bass (of TELEVISION PERSONALITIES) / **JOE FOSTER** – guitar (of TELEVISION PERSONALITIES) / **PAUL DAMIEN** – drums

Clockwork   not iss.

Sep 79. (7") *(COR 002)* **(THERE'S A) CLOUD OVER LIVERPOOL. / SOMETIMES GOOD GUYS DON'T FOLLOW TRENDS**

Wessex   not iss.

Mar 80. (7") *(WEX 275)* **ODD MAN OUT. / I APOLOGISE**
(re-iss. Jun80 on 'Blueprint'; BLU 2013)

Fab Listen   not iss.

Nov 80. (7") *(FL 1)* **I HELPED PATRICK McGOOGHAN ESCAPE. / WE'RE NOT SORRY**

TIMES

EDWARD BALL – vocals, guitar / **JOHN EAST** – bass, vocals / **PAUL DAMIEN** – drums, vocals

Whaam!   not iss.

May 81. (7") *(WHAAM 002)* **RED WITH PURPLE FLASHES. / BIFF! BANG! POW!**
Jul 82. (lp) *(LP 01)* **POP GOES ART!**
– Picture gallery / Biff! bang! / It's time / If now is the answer / A New arrangement / Looking through the world through dark glasses / I helped Patrick McGastan escape / Pop goes art! / Miss London / The Sun never sets / This is tomorrow. (re-iss. Jul83 on 'Art Pop' pic-lp Jul90; ART 20)

Art Pop   not iss.

Jun 82. (7"; as JONI DEE & THE TIMES) *(POP 50)* **HERE COMES THE HOLIDAYS. / THREE CHEERS FOR THE SUN**
Jul 83. (lp) *(ART 19)* **THIS IS LONDON**
– This is London / Goodbye Piccadilly / Whatever happened to Thamesboat / Big painting / If only / Goodnight children everywhere / The party / Stranger than fiction / (There's a) Cloud over Liverpool / Will success spoil Frank Summit? / The chimes of Big Ben.
Sep 83. (7") *(POP 49)* **I HELPED PATRICK McGOOGHAN ESCAPE. / THE THEME FROM 'DANGER MAN'**
Nov 83. (m-lp) *(ARTPOP 1)* **I HELPED PATRICK McGOOGHAN ESCAPE**
– Big painting / Stranger than fiction / Danger Man theme / I helped Patrick McGooghan escape / All systems go / Up against it.
Jul 84. (7") *(POP 46)* **BOYS BRIGADE. / POWER IS FOREVER**
Oct 84. (7") *(POP 45)* **BLUE FIRE. / WHERE THE BLUE REIGNS**
Nov 84. (lp) *(ART 17)* **HELLO EUROPE**
– Dada Europe (I'm so cut up about you) / Boys brigade / The things we've learnt / Ra diate / Blue fire / Everything turns to black and white / Where the blue begins / Public reaction killed this cat / Kultureshock.

— Early in 1985 he made another for 'Art Pop!' under EDWARD BALL'S L'ORANGE MECHANIK name; 'SYMPHONY. / INTERMEZZO (SPRECHSTIMME) / SCHERZO'. Four years later an lp was given away free with ED's Edgar Allen Poe poems for 'Creation'.

Mar 85. (m-lp) *(ARTPOP 2)* **BLUE PERIOD**
Sep 85. (12"ep) *(POP 43DOZ)* **BOYS ABOUT TOWN EP**
– David Jones (is on his way) / Victim 1960 / Up against it / Song for Joe Walton.
Apr 86. (lp) *(ART 16)* **UP AGAINST IT (soundtrack)**
– Up against it / Last tango for one / Boy's about town / Gordon into moonlight / W.P.C. Boon / Most modern woman in the world / Jade's revolution / Ladies of the cause / Mutiny in the British Empire / Escape / She's a professional / It's a cabaret time / The way / The wedding song.

Unicorn   not iss.

Apr 86. (7") *(PHZ 1)* **LONDON BOYS. / (WHERE TO GO) WHEN THE SUN GOES DOWN**

Fire   not iss.

Oct 86. (7") *(BLAZE 16S)* **TIMES TV. / TRAILER FROM 'ENJOY'**
(12"+=) *(BLAZE 16T)* – The policeforce / El Aragma / Pick it up.

Creation   not iss.

Oct 88. (lp/cd) *(CRELP/+CD 038)* **BEAT TORTURE**
– God evil / Heaven sent me an angel / I'll be your volunteer / Department store / Love like haze or rain / It had to happen / Chelsea green / How to start your own country // On the peace line / Scarlet and Sapphire / Angel / Volunteer / Country / Love. *(re-iss. May94)*
Oct 89. (lp/cd) *(CRELP/+CD 053)* **E FOR EDWARD**
– Manchester / Valvaline / Snow / Catherine Wheel / Crashed on you / Count to five / All your life / French film bleurred / No love on Haight street / Acid Angel of Ecstasy / Gold / Sold / Life.
Feb 90. (7") *(CRE 71)* **MANCHESTER. / LOVE AND TRUTH**
(12") *(CRE 71T)* – ('A'side) / Dada won't buy me a Bauhaus / ('A'extended).
(cd-s) *(CRESCD 71)* – ('A'side) / ('A'extended) / Ulysses / Shoom!.
Oct 90. (7") *(CAFF 13)* **EXTASE. / SLEEP (by "BIFF! BANG! POW!")**
(above single on 'Caff' label)
Oct 90. (lp/cd) *(CRELP/CD 070)* **ET DIEU CREA LA FEMME**
– Septieme ciel / Aurore boreale / Confiance / Chagrin d'amour / Volupte / Baisers voles / Pour Kylie / Sucette / 1990 Annee erotique / Extase.
Mar 91. (lp/cd) *(CRELP/+CD 091)* **PURE**
– From Chelsea Green to Brighton Beach / A girl called Mersey / Lindi bleu / From L.A. to Edgbaston / Ours is wonderlove world / Another star in Heaven. *(re-iss Sep 92)*
Apr 92. (lp/cd) *(CRELP/+CD 123)* **AT THE ASTRADOME LUNAVILLE (GOLDEN OLDIES OF THE 1990's)**
Jul 92. (7"/c-s) *(CRE/+CS 114)* **LINDI BLEU (version Francais de Blue Monday). / ('A'instrumental)**
(12") *(CRE 114T)* – 'A'- Grid & Bandulu mixes; Praise the Lord / Grid World communications / Bandulu smiling mixes).
(cd-s+=) *(CRESCD 114)* – (above 3) / (Brazilian, Japanese, German & Spanish versions).
Apr 93. (lp/cd) *(CRELP/+CD 137)* **ALTERNATIVE COMMERCIAL CROSSOVER**
– Obligatory grunge song / Finnegan's break / How honest are Pearl Jam / Sweetest girl / Ballad of Georgie Best / Lindi bleu (praise the lord mix by the GRID) / Palace in the sun / Sorry, I've written a melody / Finnegan's break (corporate rock mix) / Whole world's turning seaface / All I want is you to care.
May 93. (7"; TIMES featuring TIPPA IRIE) *(CRE 158)* **FINNEGAN'S BREAK. / HEARTBROKEN LOST IN BLUE**
(12"+=)(cd-s+=) *(CRE 158T)(CRESCD 158)* – Soultight / Come alive.
Jun 93. (12"ep/cd-ep) **BABY GIRL. / THE COLOUR OF MY LOVE / MASH IT UP / PRIMROSE 0822**

– (TIMES) compilations, etc. –

May 85. (lp) *Pastell; (POW 3)* **GO! WITH THE TIMES** (rec.1980)   *German*
– You can get it / I'm with you / Your generation / Pinstripes / Dressing up for the cameras / Red with purple flashes / The joke's on Zandra / Nowhere to run / No hard feelings / My Andy Warhol poster / Man from Uncle Reflections in an imperfect mirror.
Nov 86. (lp) *Art Pop; (ART 15)* **ENJOY**
Jul 91. (lp/cd) *Creation; (CRELP/+CD 073)* **PINK BALL, BROWN BALL, ED BALL**
Nov 92. (cd) *Rev-Ola; (CREV 005CD)* **A DAY IN THE LIFE OF GILBERT & GEORGE** (O-LEVEL & TEENAGE FILMSTARS)
Nov 93. (cd) *Rev-Ola; (CREV 028CD)* **THIS IS LONDON / HELLO EUROPE**
Dec 93. (cd) *Rev-Ola; (CREV 029CD)* **ENJOY / UP AGAINST IT**
Apr 94. (cd) *Rev-Ola; (CREV 030CD)* **GO! WITH THE TIMES / POP GOES ART!**

— ED BALL was also part of BIFF BANG POW, another 'Creation' outfit and in the 90's joined The BOO RADLEYS

LOVE CORPORATION

aka **ED BALL** solo

Creation   not iss.

Feb 90. (lp/cd) *(CRELP/+CD 056)* **TONES**
– Fleshtones / Monumental / Tones of incorporation / World / Palatial.
Apr 90. (7") *(CRE 076)* **PALATIAL. / PALATIAL II**
(cd-s+=) *(CRESCD 076)* – Palatial III / (b-side extended).
(12") *(CRE 176T)* – ('A'-Danny Rampling extended remix) / ('A'-II extended).
Feb 91. (lp/cd) *(CRELP/+CD 068)* **LOVERS**
– L-O-V-E / Warm / Crystal / Sun / Happy days and lonely nights / Nice / Lovers / Smile.
Mar 91. (12") *(CRE 086T)* **GIME ME SOME LOVE. / ('A'version)**
(12") *(CRE 086X)* – ('A'-Andrew Weatherall remix) / Lovers.
Nov 94. (lp/cd) *(CRELP/+CD 116)* **INTELLIGENTSIA**
– Translucent / Don't fight it, flaunt it / Twilight in Babylon / Cathedrals of glitter / And then we'll have world peace / Unconditional love's going out of fashion / The majesty of melancholia / Beware the tranquil trap / Mind gangsters / Your mama don't dance and your daddy don't acid house / What price art? / Translucence.
Jun 97. (cd/d-lp) *(CRE CD/LP 199)* **DANCE STANCE**
– Cathedrals of glitter (Monkey Mafia mix) / Don't fight it flaunt it (Kris Needs mix) / Palatial (Danny Rampling mix) / Give me some love (Andy Weatherall mix) / And then we have world peace (Tim Brown mix) / Beware the tranquil trap (Midfield General mix) / You mamma don't dance and your daddy don't acid house (Ultra Living mix) / Twilight of Babylon (Mekon mix) / Palatial (Scuba mix).

TEENAGE FILMSTARS

— re-united in 1992 for below.

Creation   not iss.

Mar 92. (lp/cd) *(CRELP/+CD 111)* **STAR**
– Kiss me / Loving / Inner space / Apple / Flashes / Kaleidoscope / Vibrations / Soulful / Hallucinations / Moon.
Mar 93. (lp/cd) *(CRELP/+CD 141)* **ROCKET CHARMS – SPLASHDOWN AVEC LES TEENAGE FILMSTARS**
– Pressure / Tension / Frantic / Bad thoughts / Lapse / Alone / Lost / Broken / Dark / Nothing.

Edward BALL (cont) — THE GREAT INDIE DISCOGRAPHY — The 1970s

CONSPIRACY OF NOISE

ED BALL with PHIL KANE or DEAN JONES – vocals (of EXTREME NOISE TERROR)

		Creation	not iss.
Oct 93.	(lp/cd) (CRELP/+CD 161) **CHICKS WITH DICKS AND SPLATTER FLICKS**		-

– Losing my grip / Business is business / Content and contempt / Jerkoff / Hurt / Henry / I'd love to plug in / F.L.D. / Young, dumb and full of cum / E:Meriker.

EDWARD BALL

with ANDY BELL, MARTIN CARR, NICK HEYWARD, SICE IDHAR, TIM BROWN, ALAN McGEE, NOEL JOYCE & THE IAN SHOW ORCHESTRA featuring NAOMI ZOOB

		Creation	not iss.
Feb 95.	(d-lp/cd) (CRELP/+CD 183) **WELCOME TO THE WONDERFUL WORLD OF ED BALL** (compilation)		-
Apr 95.	(7") (CRE 197) **IF A MAN EVER LOVED A WOMAN. / FIREHORSE BLUES / 12 NOON 28.8.93**		-
	(cd-s+=) (CRESCD 197) – United States of loneliness.		
Jun 95.	(cd/lp) (CRELP/+CD 195) **IF A MAN EVER LOVED A WOMAN**		-

– It's kinda lonely where I am (acoustic) / Fire horse / If a man ever loved a woman / She's just high maintenance, baby / The Arizona loner / You only miss me when I'm bleeding / The ballad of a lonely man / A ton of blues / You're an idiot babe / It's kinda lonely where I am.

Jun 95.	(7") (CRE 208) **IT'S KIND OF LONELY WHERE I AM / DOCKLANDS BLUES**		-
	(cd-s+=) (CRESCD 208) – Bled a river over you / Another member of the Mill Hill Self Hate Club.		
Jun 96.	(7") (CRE 233) **THE MILL HILL SELF HATE CLUB. / WRAPPED UP IN LONESOME BLUES**	57	-
	(cd-s+=) (CRESCD 233) – I'm going out of your mind / An act of faith.		
Sep 96.	(7"/c-s) (CRE/+CS 239) **TRAILBLAZE. / THE OTHER SIDE OF LOVE IS GUILT**		
	(cd-s+=) (CRESCD 239) – Blues for Brian Wilson.		
Feb 97.	(7"/c-s) (CRE/+CS 244) **LOVE IS BLUE / WHEN YOU LOSE YOUR LOVER, LEARN TO LOSE**	59	
	(cd-s+=) (CRESCD 244) – The Mill Hill Self Hate Club (acoustic) / Love is blue (acoustic).		
Apr 97.	(7") (CRE 260) **THE MILL HILL SELF HATE CLUB. / FOR THE SOULS OF DEAD HORSES**		-
	(cd-s+=) (CRESCD 260) – Ma blues / Never live to love again.		
May 97.	(cd/lp) (CRE CD/LP 200) **CATHOLIC GUILT**		

– The Mill Hill Self Hate Club / Love is blue / Docklands blues / Controversial girlfriend / Hampstead therapist / Tilt / Trailblaze / Never live to love again / This is the story of my love / This is real.

Honey BANE (see under ⇒ FATAL MICROBES)

Ed BANGER (see under ⇒ NOSEBLEEDS)

BANNED

Formed: Croydon, nr. London, England ... in the summer of '77 by drummer/vocalist PAUL SORDID, PETE FRESH, BEN DOVER and TOMMY STEAL (obviously not their real names!). One of the many pub-rock acts (i.e. The MOTORS, etc) to turn punk-rock/new wave, the BANNED self-financed the release of their version of The Syndicate's 1966 US hit, 'LITTLE GIRL'. Two months later in November, 'Harvest' records signed the group to their roster (the label had also recently signed WIRE) and with radio airplay it became a surprise UK Top 40 hit. Their early '78 follow-up, 'HIM OR ME' (another cover; PAUL REVERE & THE RAIDERS the source this time), failed to capture the same fanbase, however and the BANNED er... dis-banded-ed.

Album rating: none released!

PAUL SORDID – vocals, drums / PETE FRESH – guitar / BEN DOVER (b. RICK MANSWORTH) – guitar / TOMMY STEAL (b. JOHN THOMAS) – bass

		Can't Eat	not iss.
Sep 77.	(7") (EATUP 1) **LITTLE GIRL. / C.P.G.J.'s**		-
		Harvest	Harvest
Nov 77.	(7") (HAR 5145) **LITTLE GIRL. / C.P.G.J.'s**	36	-
Mar 78.	(7") (HAR 5149) **HIM OR ME. / YOU DIRTY RAT**		-

— split sometime in 1978, although they'll no doubt be featuring on an upcoming edition of Mark Lamaar's BBC2 pop quiz show, 'Never Mind The Buzzcocks'.

Stiv BATORS (see under ⇒ DEAD BOYS)

B-52's

Formed: Athens, Georgia, USA ... late '76, by KATE PIERSON, FRED SCHNEIDER, KEITH STRICKLAND, RICKY WILSON and his sister CINDY. After one self-financed 45 sold out its limited 2,000 copies, they drew the attention of Island's Chris Blackwell, who signed them after they played residency at Max's Kansas City late in 1978. They subsequently re-issued their 'ROCK LOBSTER' debut, the single making UK Top 40 lists the following year. Combining a kitsch image and sound which took in everything from rock'n'roll and 60's beat to new wave REZILLOS-style dual harmonies, The B-52's brightened up the increasingly dour late 70's/early 80's punk/pop scene. The marine madness of the classic 'ROCK LOBSTER' eventually made its way into the US charts in early 1980, by which time the eponymous '79 debut album had made UK Top 30. Even JOHN LENNON was a fan, the former BEATLES man surprisingly admitting that The B-52's were one of the groups who inspired him to start writing again. A strong follow-up set, 'WILD PLANET' (1980), made the Top 20 in both Britain and America, although critics weren't quite so enamoured with the more mannered 'MESOPOTAMIA' set (1982), produced by DAVID BYRNE of TALKING HEADS. The mid-80's were a bleak time for the band as RICKY finally died from AIDS on the 12th October, 1985, and the group struggled to capture the inspired creativity of their earlier period (fans were content in making 'ROCK LOBSTER' an even bigger UK hit than before). Signing a new deal with 'Reprise', The B-52's reunited with their roots on the 'BOUNCING OFF SATELLITES', an album which should have spawned a hit single, 'WIG'. DON WAS / NILE RODGERS-produced 'COSMIC THING' (1989), a remarkable comeback that showcased their alternative dancefloor smash, 'LOVE SHACK', the album becoming their most successful release to date, making the US Top 5. Trimmed to a trio of PIERSON, SCHNEIDER and STRICKLAND following the departure of CINDY in 1992, the group recorded another album in the classic B-52's style, 'GOOD STUFF', before setting to work on the soundtrack for the revamped 'Flintstones' movie. Something of a canny pairing, SCHNEIDER's nasal-voiced nonsense was a perfect backdrop for Fred and family's stone age adventures. • **Songwriters:** All mainly STRICKLAND or group compositions. PLANET CLAIRE (w/ Henry Mancini) • **Trivia:** In 1981, during lay-off, STRICKLAND, PIERSON and CINDY WILSON did one-off Japan venture as "MELON" with group The PLASTICS and ADRIAN BELEW. Late 1990, PIERSON contributed on singles by IGGY POP (Candy) and R.E.M. (Shiny Happy People).

Album rating: THE B-52's (*8) / WILD PLANET (*6) / PARTY MIX! remixes (*3) / MESOPOTAMIA mini (*4) / WHAMMY! (*5) / BOUNCING OFF THE SATELLITES (*4) / COSMIC THING (*7) / DANCE THIS MESS AROUND – THE BEST OF THE B-52's compilation (*9) / GOOD STUFF (*5) / Fred Schneider: FRED SCHNEIDER AND THE SNAKE SOCIETY (*5) / JUST . . . FRED (*5)

KATE PIERSON (b.27 Apr'48, Weehawken, N.J.) – vocals, organ, bass / **CINDY WILSON** (b.28 Feb'57) – vocals, percussion, guitar / **RICKY WILSON** (b.19 Mar'53) – guitar / **FRED SCHNEIDER** (III) (b. 1 Jul'56, Newark, N.J.) – vocals, keyboards / **KEITH 'Julian' STRICKLAND** (b.26 Oct'53) – drums

		not iss.	Boo-Fant
Nov 78.	(7") <DB-52> **ROCK LOBSTER. / 52 GIRLS**	-	
		Island	Warners
Jul 79.	(7") (WIP 6506) **ROCK LOBSTER. / RUNNING AROUND**	37	-
Jul 79.	(lp/c) (WIP/ICT 9580) <3355> **THE B-52's**	22	59

– Planet Claire / 52 girls / Dance this mess around / Rock lobster / Lava / There's a Moon in the sky (called the Moon) / Hero worship / 6060-842 / Downtown. (lp w/ free 7") (PSR 438) – ROCK LOBSTER. / 52 GIRLS (re-iss. May86; same) (cd-iss. Jan87; CID 9580) (re-iss. Jan94 + May94)

Sep 79.	(7") (WIP 6527) **6060-842. / HERO WORSHIP**		
Nov 79.	(7"pic-d/7") (P+/WIP 6551) <WBS 49212> **PLANET CLAIRE. / THERE'S A MOON IN THE SKY (CALLED THE MOON)**		May80
Jan 80.	(7") <WBS 49173> **ROCK LOBSTER. / 6060-842**	-	56
Jul 80.	(7") (WIP 6579) **GIVE ME BACK MY MAN. / STROBE LIGHT**	61	-
Sep 80.	(lp/c) (ILPS/ICT 9622) <BSK 3471> **WILD PLANET**	18	18

– Party out of bounds / Dirty back road / Runnin' around / Give me back my man / Private Idaho / Devil in my car / Quiche Lorraine / Strobe light / 53 miles west of Venus. (cd-iss. May90; 842436-2)

Oct 80.	(7") <WBS 49537> **PRIVATE IDAHO. / PARTY OUT OF BOUNDS**	-	74
Nov 80.	(7") (WIP 6685) **DIRTY BACK ROAD. / STROBE LIGHT**	-	-
Jan 81.	(7") <WBS 49717> **QUICHE LORRAINE. / LAVA**	-	-
Jul 81.	(m-lp/c) (IPM/ICT 1001) <MINI 3596> **THE PARTY MIX ALBUM** (remixes)	36	55

– Party out of bounds / Private Idaho / Give me back my man / Lava / Dance this mess around / 52 girls. (cd-iss. May90; 846044-2)

Aug 81.	(7") (WIP 6727) **GIVE ME BACK MY MAN (Party mix). / PARTY OUT OF BOUNDS (version)**		-
Feb 82.	(m-lp/c) (ISSP/ICT 4006) <3641> **MESOPOTAMIA**	18	35

– Loveland / Deep sleep / Mesopotamia / Cake / Throw that beat in the garbage can / Nip it in the bud. (cd-iss. May90; 846239-2) (cd re-iss. Aug01; IMCD 107)

Mar 82.	(7") <50064> **DEEP SLEEP. / NIP IT IN THE BUD**	-	
Jun 82.	(7") <29971> **MESOPOTAMIA. / THROW THAT BEAT IN THE GARBAGE CAN**	-	
Apr 83.	(7") (IS 107) **SONG FOR A FUTURE GENERATION. / ('A'instrumental)**	63	-
	(12"+=) (12IS 107) – Planet Claire.		
	(d7"+=) (ISD 107) – There's a moon in the sky (called the moon).		
May 83.	(lp/c) (ILPS 9759) <23819> **WHAMMY!**	33	29

– Legal tender / Whammy kiss / Song for a future generation / Butterbean / Trism / Queen of Las Vegas / Don't worry / Big bird / Work that skirt. (cd-iss. May90; 842445-2) (cd re-iss. Aug01; IMCD 109)

Jul 83.	(7") <29579> **LEGAL TENDER. / MOON 83**	-	81
Oct 83.	(7") <29561> **SONG FOR A FUTURE GENERATION. / TREASON**	-	

— RICKY suffering from full blown AIDS, died 12 Oct'85.

May 86.	(7"/7"sha-pic-d; rock/planet/lobster) (BFT+/G/P/L 1) **ROCK LOBSTER (new version). / PLANET CLAIRE**	12	-
	(d7"+=) (BFTD 1) – Song for a future generation / 52 girls.		
	(12"+=) (12BFT 1) – Song for a future generation / Give me back my man.		

— They carry on, augmented by session man **RALPH CARNEY** – guitar

Jun 87.	(7"/7"pic-d) (BFT+/P 2) **WIG. / SUMMER OF LOVE**		
	(c-s+=/12+=) (BFTD/12BFT 2) – Song for a future generation.		
Jul 87.	(lp/c/cd) (ILPS/ICT/CID 9871) <25504> **BOUNCING OFF THE SATELLITES**	74	85 Sep86

– Summer of love / Girl from Ipanema goes to Greenland / Housework /

B-52's (cont)

Detour thru your mind / Wig / Theme for a nude beach / Ain't it a shame / Juicy jungle / Communicate / She brakes for rainbows. *(cd-iss. May90; 842480-2)*

Sep 87. (7") **SUMMER OF LOVE. / HOUSEWORK** | - | |

—— added on tour **PAT IRWIN** – keyboards / **ZACH ALFORD** – drums / **PHILIPPE SASSE** – (studio keyboards) / **SARA LEE** – bass (ex-GANG OF FOUR) (also studio)

	Reprise	Reprise
Jul 89. (lp/c)(cd) *(WX 283/+C)(925854-2) <25854>* **COSMIC THING**	8	4

– Cosmic thing / Dry country / Deadbeat club / Love shack / Junebug / Roam / Bushfire / Planet Z / Topaz / Follow your blues.

| Aug 89. (7") *<22817>* **LOVE SHACK. / CHANNEL Z** | - | 3 |
| Sep 89. (7") *(W 2831)* **CHANNEL Z (remix). / JUNEBUG** | 61 | - |

(12")(cd-s) *(W 2831 T/CD)* – ('A'-Rock mix) / ('A'side) / ('A'dub mix). *(re-iss. Aug90;)*

| Dec 89. (7") *<22667>* **ROAM. / BUSHFIRE** | - | 3 |
| Feb 90. (7"/7"g-f/7"pic-d/c-s/cd-s) *(W 9917/+X/P/CD)* **LOVE SHACK. / PLANET CLAIRE (live) / ROCK LOBSTER (live)** | 2 | - |

(12") *(W 9917T)* – ('A'-Dany Rampling remix) / ('A'-Ben Grosse mix) / ('A'side).

| Apr 90. (7") *<19938>* **DEADBEAT CLUB. / PLANET CLAIRE** | - | 30 |
| May 90. (7"/c-s/cd-s) *(W 9827/+C/CD)* **ROAM. / WHAMMY KISS (live) / DANCE THIS MESS AROUND (live)** | 17 | - |

(12"/12"w-poster) *(W 9827T/+W)* – ('A'-Radio mix) / ('A'remix) / ('A'extended remix).

| Sep 90. (7"/c-s) **DEADBEAT CLUB. / LOVE SHACK** | | |

(12"+=/cd-s+=) – B-52's megamix.

—— now trimmed to basic trio of **PIERSON, SCHNEIDER** – vox / + **STRICKLAND** – guitar with guest musicians **IRWIN / ALFORD / LEE** / plus **JEFF PORCARO + STERLING CAMPBELL** – drums / **DAVID McMURRAY** – sax / **JAMIE MULHOBERAC + RICHARD HILTON** – keyboards / **LENNY CASTRO** – percussion / **TRACY WORMWORTH** – bass

| Jun 92. (7"/c-s) *(W 0109/+C) <18895>* **GOOD STUFF. / BAD INFLUENCE** | 21 | 28 |

(12"+=/cd-s+=) *(W 0109 T/CD)* – Return to Dreamland.
(12") *(W 0109TX)* – (4-'A'mixes).

| Jul 92. (cd/c/lp) *(7599 26943-2/-4/-1)* **GOOD STUFF** | 8 | 16 |

– Tell it like it t-i-is / Hot pants explosion / Good stuff / Revolution Earth / Dreamland / Is that you Mo-Dean? / The world's green laughter / Vision of a kiss / Breezin' / Bad influence. *(re-iss. Feb95 cd/c;)*

| Sep 92. (7"/c-s) *(W 0130/+C)* **TELL IT LIKE IT T-I-IS. / THE WORLD'S GREEN LAUGHTER** | 61 | |

(12"/cd-s) *(W 0130 T/CD)* – ('A'-4 other mixes).

| Nov 92. (7"/c-s) **IS THAT YOU MO-DEAN?. / ('A'-Moby mix)** | | |

(12"+=/cd-s+=) – ('A'-2 other mixes) / Tell it like it t-i-is.

| Feb 93. (7"/c-s) **HOT PANTS EXPLOSION. / LOVE SHACK** | | |

(cd-s+=) – Channel Z / Roam.

—— **SCHNEIDER, PIERSON + STRICKLAND**

	M.C.A.	M.C.A.
Jun 94. (7"/c-s; BC-52's) *(MCS/+CS 1986) <54839>* **(MEET) THE FLINTSTONES. / ('A'-Barney's mix)**	3	33 May94

(cd-s+=) *(MCSTD 1986)* – (2-'A'mixes).
(above from that year's movie, 'The Flintstones')

— **compilations, others, etc.** —

| Jun 90. (cd/c/lp) *Island; (ILPS/ICT/CID 9959)* **DANCE THIS MESS AROUND THE BEST OF THE B-52's** | 36 | - |

– Party out of bounds / Devil in my car / Dirty back road / 6060-842 / Wig / Dance this mess around / Private Idaho / Rock lobster / Strobe light / Give me back my man / Song for a future generation / Planet Claire / 52 girls. *(cd+=)* – (2 extra mixes).

Feb 91. (cd) *Reprise; <26401>* **PARTY MIX! / MESOPOTAMIA**	-	
Nov 92. (d-cd) *Island; (ITSCD 1)* **THE B-52'S / WILD PLANET**		-
Sep 95. (cd) *Spectrum; (551210-2)* **PLANET CLAIRE**		-
Jul 98. (cd/c) *Reprise; (9362 46995-2/-4) <46920>* **TIME CAPSULE – SONGS FOR A FUTURE GENERATION**		93 Jun98

– Planet Claire / 52 girls *[US-only]* / Rock lobster / Party out of bounds *[US-only]* / Strobelight *[US-only]* / Private Idaho / Quiche Lorraine (live) / Mesopotamia / Songs for a future generation *[US-only]* / Summer of love (original unreleased mix) / Channel Z / Deadbeat club / Love shack / Roam / Good stuff / Is that you Mo-Dean? / (Meet) The Flintstones *[UK-only]* / Debbie / Hallucinating Pluto.

| Jan 99. (c-s) *Reprise; (W 0461C)* **LOVE SHACK '99 (mix)** | 66 | |

(cd-s+=) *(W 0461CD)* –

FRED SCHNEIDER

solo, recorded 1984 and written with COTE

—— with various session people

	Reprise	Reprise
May 91. (cd/c/lp) *<(7559 26592-2/-4/-1)>* **FRED SCHNEIDER & THE SHAKE SOCIETY**		

– Monster / Out the concrete / Summer in Hell / Orbit / I'm gonna haunt you / It's time to kiss / This planet's a mess / Wave / Boonga (the New Jersey caveman).

| Jun 91. (cd-s) *<19262>* **MONSTER /** | - | 85 |

—— next with **STEVE ALBINI** – producing backing from **DEADLY CUPCAKE, SHADOWY MEN ON A SHADOWY PLANET + SIX FINGER SATELLITE**

	WEA	WEA
Jun 96. (cd) *<(9362 46215-2)>* **JUST . . . FRED**		

– Whip / Helicopter / Sugar in my hog / Bulldozer / Coconut / Center of the universe / Radioactive lady eyeball / Lick / Bad dream / Secret sharer / Stroke of genius.

Jello BIAFRA (see under ⇒ DEAD KENNEDYS)

BID (see under ⇒ MONOCHROME SET)

BIG IN JAPAN

Formed: Liverpool, England . . . 1977 by BILL DRUMMOND, KEVIN WARD and PHIL ALLEN. They completed the line-up with singer JAYNE CASEY, IAN BROUDIE and CLIVE LANGER, who issued a self-titled debut 45 for the 'Eric's' label, run by the local club of the same name; it's b-side was actually recorded by local mates, The YACHTS, under the guise of the CHUDDY NUDDIES. 1978 was a year when they found AMBROSE REYNOLDS, although he was subsequently replaced by HOLLY JOHNSON – yes, another who would make the grade in the 80's! – in time for their second single and final single/EP, 'FROM A TO Z AND NEVER AGAIN'. Released on DRUMMOND's own label, 'Zoo', the record didn't fully prepare listeners for the full-on live show wherein the shaven-headed CASEY would often appear with false electrodes attached to her skull. With all the personnel comings and goings, it was inevitable that the band would split, nearly all of them finding major fame in one form or another (i.e. DRUMMOND with the KLF, BROUDIE with the LIGHTNING SEEDS and JOHNSON with FRANKIE GOES TO HOLLYWOOD).

Album rating: FROM A TO Z AND NEVER AGAIN EP (*6)

JAYNE CASEY – vocals / **BILL DRUMMOND** – guitar, vocals / **KEVIN WARD** – bass, vocals / **PHIL ALLEN** – drums / **IAN BROUDIE** – guitar / **CLIVE LANGER** – guitar (ex-DEAF SCHOOL)

	Eric's	not iss.
Nov 77. (7") *(ERIC'S 0001)* **BIG IN JAPAN. / (CHUDDIE NUDDIES: Do The Chud)**		-

—— **HOLLY (JOHNSON)** – bass; repl. AMBROSE REYNOLDS who joined WALKIE TALKIES, after repl. CLIVE LANGER (to The BOXES)

—— **BUDGIE** – drums; repl. PHIL ALLEN

	Zoo	not iss.
Nov 78. (7"ep) *(CAGE 001)* **FROM A TO Z AND NEVER AGAIN**		-

– Nothing special / Cindy & the Barbi dolls / Suicide a gogo / Taxi.

—— **DAVE BALFE** – bass; repl. STEVE LINDSAY (ex-DEAF SCHOOL) who had repl. HOLLY, who formed HOLLYCAUST and later FRANKIE GOES TO HOLLYWOOD (LINDSAY was later part of The SECRETS, The PLANETS, etc). When BIG IN JAPAN split in 1979, most went onto greater things. JAYNE formed PINK MILITARY / INDUSTRY. After being main part of LORI & THE CHAMELEONS, DRUMMOND and BALFE, went into production. The former managed The TEARDROP EXPLODES and ECHO & THE BUNNYMEN, went solo and formed duo KLF, while the latter joined TEARDROP EXPLODES and later formed 'Food' records; home of EMI subsidised BLUR). BROUDIE formed The ORIGINAL MIRRORS, The CARE, went into production for nearly everybody! and made The LIGHTNING SEEDS a household name. The last member BUDGIE, joined The SLITS and later SIOUXSIE & THE BANSHEES (also The CREATURES). BROUDIE and BUDGIE were also in The SECRETS during late 70's. Phew!

BIRTHDAY PARTY (see under ⇒ CAVE, Nick)

BISHOPS (see under ⇒ COUNT BISHOPS)

BLACK FLAG

Formed: Hermosa Beach, California, USA . . . 1976 by GREG GINN and CHUCK DUKOWSKI. In 1977, their demo reached local indie label 'Bomp', who, after over half a year decided not to release BLACK FLAG's debut 45, 'NERVOUS BREAKDOWN'. Instead, GREG and CHUCK, with sound men MUGGER and SPOT, formed their own label, 'S.S.T.' (Solid State Tuners), issuing the aforesaid single in 1978. By the time BLACK FLAG's debut lp, 'DAMAGED', was released in 1981, the group had suffered label difficulties with 'MCA-Unicorn', who didn't like the outrageous content of the tracks. Numerous personnel changes had also occurred, mainly the substitution of KEITH MORRIS, with the harder looking and now legendary HENRY ROLLINS. SST took the major label to court and although the pivotal hardcore group won, they had to pay out a 6-figure sum. The influential label went on to help kickstart the careers of many hardcore/alternative acts such as HUSKER DU, MINUTEMEN, DINOSAUR JR, MEAT PUPPETS, etc. Meanwhile, BLACK FLAG (with GINN and ROLLINS at the helm), completed a series of near brilliant albums, ROLLINS even contributing a spoken word side on the half instrumental album, 'FAMILY MAN' (1984), a thing that he would do more when he took off on a successful solo venture that year. GINN and some new cohorts completed two more mid 80's sets, 'IN MY HEAD' and 'WHO'S GOT THE 10 1/2', before he too pursued a solo sojourn, although at first with instrumental punk-jazz fusion, GONE. BLACK FLAG were one of the first US acts to take DIY punk into hardcore, a hybrid sound that would later be revered by metal fans who had picked up on 90's US hardcore/punk groups like BAD RELIGION and OFFSPRING.

Album rating: DAMAGED (*8) / EVERYTHING WENT BLACK (*5) / THE FIRST FOUR YEARS (*7) compilation / MY WAR (*6) / FAMILY MAN (*4) / SLIP IT IN (*5) / LOOSE NUT (*5) / IN MY HEAD (*6) / WHO'S GOT THE 10 1/2 (*6) / WASTED . . . AGAIN (*7)

KEITH MORRIS – vocals / **GREG GINN** (b. 8 Jun'54) – guitar / **CHUCK DUKOWSKI** – bass / **BRIAN MIGDOL** – drums

	not iss.	S.S.T.
Oct 78. (7"ep) *<SST 001>* **NERVOUS BREAKDOWN. / FIX ME / I'VE HAD IT / WASTED**	-	

<US 10"colrd-ep/12"ep/cd-ep iss.1990; same>

BLACK FLAG (cont)

— CHAVO PEDERAST (aka RON REYES) – vocals (ex-RED CROSS) repl. KEITH who formed CIRCLE JERKS. ROBO – drums repl. MIGDOL
Mar 80. (12"ep) <SST 003> JEALOUS AGAIN / REVENGE. / WHITE MINORITY / NO VALUES / YOU BET WE'VE GOT SOMETHING PERSONAL AGAINST YOU!
(UK-iss.Mar83; same) <US 10"colrd-ep/12"ep/cd-ep iss.1990; same>

— DEZ CADENA – vocals, guitar (ex-RED CROSS) repl. REYES
Jan 81. (7"ep) <SST 005> SIX PACK. / I'VE HEARD IT ALL BEFORE / AMERICAN WASTE
(UK-iss.Dec81 on 'Alternative Tentacles'; VIRUS 9) <US 10"colrd-ep/12"/cd-ep iss.1990; same>

— HENRY ROLLINS (b. HENRY GARFIELD, 13 Feb '61, Washington, D.C.) – vocals (ex-SOA) repl. CHUCK who formed WURM (with ED DANKY and SIMON SMALLWOOD (vocalist of DEAD HIPPIE) – one lp surfaced in '85, 'FEAST' <SST 041>. CHUCK later formed SWA and was part of OCTOBERFACTION
— group now ROLLINS, GINN, CADENA (now rhythm guitar only) + ROBO
Nov 81. (lp) <(SST 007)> DAMAGED
 – Rise above / Spray paint / Six pack / What I see / TV party / Thirsty and miserable / Police story / Gimmie gimmie gimmie / Depression / Room 13 / Damaged II / No more / Padded cell / Life of pain / Damaged I.
— In the US, 'Posh Boy' issued '79 recording LOUIE LOUIE. / DAMAGED 1 (PBS 13) (This was finally issued 10"coloured 1988 on 'SST' US) (re-iss. cd/c/lp Oct95; same) LOUIE LOUIE was a KINGSMEN original.
— BILL STEVENSON + guest EMIL – drums repl. ROBO
1982. (7"ep) <SST 012> TV PARTY. / I'VE GOT TO RUN / MY RULES
<US 12"+cd-ep iss.1990; same>
— guest on half DALE NIXON – bass (actually GREG under pseudonym) repl. CADENA who formed DC3
Mar 84. (lp) <(SST 023)> MY WAR
 – My war / Can't decide / Beat my head agaist the wall / I love you / The swinging man / Forever time / Nothing left inside / Three nights / Scream. (cd-iss. 1990; SST 023CD) (re-iss. cd/c/lp Oct95; same)
— added KIRA ROESSLER – bass
Sep 84. (lp) <(SST 026)> FAMILY MAN
 – Family man / Salt on a slug / The pups are doggin' it / Let your fingers do the walking / Long lost dog of it / I won't stick any of you unless and until I can stick all of you / Hollywood diary / Armageddon man / Account for what? / Shred reading (rattus norvegicus) / No deposit, no return. (cd-iss. 1990; SST 026CD) (re-iss. cd/c/lp Oct95; same)
Oct 84. (12") <(SST1 2001)> FAMILY MAN. / I WON'T STICK ANY OF YOU UNLESS AND UNTIL I CAN STICK ALL OF YOU
Dec 84. (lp) <(SST 029)> SLIP IT IN
 – Slip it in / Black coffee / Wound up / Rat's eyes / Obliteration / The bars / My ghetto / You're not evil. (cd-iss. 1990; SST 029CD) (re-iss. cd/c/lp Oct95; same)
Jan 85. (c) <(SST 030)> LIVE '84 (live)
 – The process of weeding out / My ghetto / Jealous again / I love you / Swinging man / Three nights / Nothing left inside / Black coffee. (cd-iss. 1990; SST 030CD) (re-iss. cd/c/lp Oct95; same)
Jun 85. (lp) <(SST 035)> LOOSE NUT
 – Loose nut / Bastard in love / Annihilate this week / Best one yet / Modern man / This is good / I'm the one / Sinking / Now she's black. (cd-iss. 1990; SST 035CD) (re-iss. cd/c/lp Oct95; same)
— trimmed to GINN, KIRA + STEVENSON when ROLLINS went solo
Sep 85. (m-lp) <(SST 037)> THE PROCESS OF WEEDING OUT
 – Your last affront / Screw the law / The process of weeding out / Southern rise. (US 10"colrd/m-cd iss.1990)
Nov 85. (lp) <(SST 045)> IN MY HEAD
 – Paralyzed / The crazy girl / Black love / Retired at 21 / Drinking and driving / White hot / In my head / Society's tease / It's all up to you / You let me down. (cd-iss. 1990 +=; SST 045CD) – Out of this world / I can see you. (cd re-iss. Oct95; same)
— ANTHONY MARTINEZ – drums; repl. STEVENSON who had already joined OCTOBERFACTION
May 86. (lp) <(SST 060)> WHO'S GOT THE 10 1/2 (live in Portland 23/8/85)
 – I'm the one / Loose nut / Bastard in love / Slip it in / This is good / Gimmie gimmie gimmie / Drinking and driving / Modern man / My war. (cd-iss. 1990) (re-iss. cd/c/lp Oct95; same) (cd+=) – Annihilate / Wasted / Sinking / Jam / Louie Louie / Best one yet.
— had already split earlier in '86. KIRA continued with DOS, alongside MIKE WATT of The MINUTEMEN. After playing bass on a one-off trio project/eponymous album in 1985 with TOM TROCCOLI'S DOG <SST 047> – solo artist GINN had also been part of TOM's own quintet, OCTOBERFACTION – he also teamed up with ANDREW WEISS to form instrumental group, GONE.

– compilations, others, etc. –

on 'S.S.T.' unless mentioned otherwise
Mar 83. (d-lp) <(SST 015)> EVERYTHING WENT BLACK (rare 78-81)
(re-iss. Oct95 lp/c/cd; SST 015/+C/CD)
1984. (lp) <SST 021> THE FIRST FOUR YEARS
(UK-iss.Oct95 & Oct99 lp/c/cd; SST 021/+C/CD)
Dec 87. (lp/c/cd) <(SST 166/+C/CD)> WASTED . . . AGAIN
 – Wasted / TV party / Six pack / I don't care / I've had it / Jealous again / Slip it in / Annihilate this week / Loose nut / Gimme gimme / Louie Louie / Drinking and driving. (re-iss. Oct95; same)
Jun 93. (12"/c-s/cd-s) (SST 226/+C/CD) I CAN SEE YOU

GONE

— GREG GINN – guitar / ANDREW WEISS – bass

Jul 86. (lp) <(SST 061)> LET'S GET REAL, REAL GONE FOR A CHANGE
 – Insideous detraction / Get gone / Peter gone / Rosanne / Climbing Rat's wall / Watch the tractor / Last days of being stepped on / CH 69 / Lawndale Rock City / Hypercharge – the wait (the fifth force suite). (re-iss. May93 cd/c; SST 061 CD/C)
Jan 87. (lp) <(SST 086)> GONE II – BUT NEVER TOO GONE!
 – Jungle law / New vengeance / Unglued / Turned over stone / Drop the bat / Adams / Time of entry / Left holding the bag / GTV / Daisy strut / Cut off / Put it there / Utility hole / Yesterday is teacher / How soon they forget / Cobra XVIII. (re-iss. May93 cd/c; SST 086 CD/C)
— In 1993, GREG released 'COLLEGE ROCK' EP as POINDEXTER STEWART
— GINN re-formed GONE with STEVE SHARP – bass / GREGORY MOORE – drums
Jan 94. (lp/cd) <(SST 300/+CD)> THE CRIMINAL MIND
 – Poor losers / Punch drunk / Pull it out / Pump room / Snagglepuss / PS was wrong / Off the chains / Smoking gun in Waco / Spankin' plank / Piled one higher / Row nine / Toggle / Big check / Ankle strap / Hand out / Freeny / Unknown calibar.
Apr 94. (12"/cd-s) <(SST 303)> SMOKING GUN IN WACO. /
(re-iss. Feb96; same)
Aug 94. (lp/c/cd) <(SST 306/+C/CD)> ALL THE DIRT THAT'S FIT TO PRINT
 – Picket fence asylum / Upward spiral / Mutilated fade / Damage control / Kattiwompus / 39051 / White tail / Crawdad / Meet me in the van / Bosco pit / Huntin w/ a rich man / 4 a.m.
Sep 95. (12") <(SST 303)> DAMAGE CONTROL. / SMOKING GUN (IN WACO)
Apr 96. (cd) <(SST 313)> BEST LEFT UNSAID
 – Bicycle riding assassin / My name is on the masthead but . . . / Hotheaded butchers / Closet courtaholic / Stray bullet / We have pigs / Closeted publishers / Second gunman / Bomb plot case / Mother called Ill / Hostile witness.
Jul 98. (cd) <(SST 344)> COUNTRY DUMB
 – Dinky cat / (Lost in) Filegate / Big government, small mind / Pentagon expands / Cut your hair, drink Coors / "Punks" in government / Rage against intelligence / Another existential excuse / Paula Jones Clinton / Hip Castro conservative / Woozy news hound / "Punk" and the cash narcotic / Country dumb or city stupid? / Sugar bear.

GREG GINN

— with GREGORY MOORE – tom-tom / DAVID RAVEN – drums / later added STEVE SHARP – bass
Jun 93. (12"/c-s/cd-s) <(CRZ 028/+C/CD)> PAYDAY. / PAYDAY / PIG MF
Jun 93. (lp/c/cd) <(CRZ 029/+C/CD)> GETTING EVEN
 – I've changed / Kill burn fluff / You drive me crazy / Pig MF / Hard thing / Payday / Nightmares / Torn / PF flyer / I can't wait / Short fuse / Not that simple / Yes officer / Crawling inside.
Sep 93. (lp/c/cd) <(CRZ 032/+C/CD)> DICK
 – Never change baby / I want to believe / You wanted it / I won't give in / Creeps / Strong violent type / Don't tell me / You dirty rat / Disgusting reference / Walking away / Ignorant order / Slow fuse / You're gonna get it.
Mar 94. (12"/cd-s) (CRZ 033/+CD) DON'T TELL ME / DON'T TELL ME (instrumental). / YES OFFICER (remix) / YOU'RE GOING TO GET IT (remix)
Aug 94. (lp/c/cd) <(CRZ 036/+C/CD)> LET IT BURN (BECAUSE I DON'T LIVE THERE ANYMORE)
 – On a roll / Taking the other side / Lame Hollywood cop / Lame excuses / In your face motherfucker / Hey, stupid face / Venting / Let it burn / Drifting away / Military destroys mind/body / I don't want it / Destroy my mind / Exiled from Lame Dome.

KILLER TWEEKER BEES

GREG GINN + ANDY BATWINAS

Sep 97. (cd) <(SST 345CD)> TWEEKER BLUES
 – Buyer's club / Grounds to indict / Big phoney / Tweeker blues / Erotic edge / Rat zombie / The government protects me / Pure police for now people / Rage against your mother / Now that I've solved society's problem / Junk cool.

BLACK RANDY & THE METRO SQUAD

Formed: Los Angeles, California, USA . . . 1977 by caucasian punk rocker, BLACK RANDY. With a free'n'easy attitude to recruitment, The METRO SQUAD were probably the genuine definition of the punk DIY philosophy and the line-up varied accordingly. Tagged after the punk club of the same name, the 'Dangerhouse' label was home to the band's debut single, 'TROUBLE AT THE CUP', featuring such classic B-side material as 'LONER WITH A BONER' and 'SPERM BANK BABY'. Clearly untroubled by the American work ethic, RANDY and co. released a single a year through '78 and '79 – 'IDI AMIN' and 'I SLEPT IN AN ARCADE' respectively – before bowing out with a solitary album, 'PASS THE DUST, I THINK I'M BOWIE' (1980). No prizes for guessing what the dust in the title referred to, RANDY's alleged fondness for PCP no doubt contributing to the chaos surrounding the band. The 'SQUAD's subsequent demise was followed by RANDY's mysterious death while GARRETT went on to play with The DILS. • **Covered:** GIVE IT UP OR TURNIT A LOOSE + I'M BLACK AND PROUD (James Brown).

Album rating: PASS THE DUST, I THINK I'M BOWIE (*4)

BLACK RANDY – vocals / **DAVID BROWN** – keyboards, vocals / **BOB DEADWYLER** – guitar, vocals / **PAT GARRETT** – bass, guitar, vocals / **KK BARRETT** – guitar / **JOE RAMIREZ** – bass / **TOM HUGHES** – guitar, bass / **JOE NANINI** – drums, percussion

	not iss.	Dangerhouse
Dec 77. (7"m) <MO 721> **TROUBLE AT THE CUP. / LONER WITH A BONER / SPERM BANK BABY**	-	□
1978. (7"ep) <IDI 722> **IDI AMIN / I'M BLACK AND PROUD PART 3. / I'M BLACK AND PROUD PART 14 / I WANNA BE A NARK**	-	□
Jul 79. (7") <KY 724> **I SLEPT IN AN ARCADE. / GIVE IT UP**	-	□
Jan 80. (lp) <PCP 725> **PASS THE DUST, I THINK I'M BOWIE**	-	□

– I slept in an arcade / Marlon Brando / Down at the laundromat / I tell lies every day / San Francisco / Give it up or turn it a loose / Idi Amin / Barefootin' on the wicked picket / Shaft / I wanna be a nark / Sperm bank baby / Tellin' lies / I'm black and proud.

—— split early 1980 when RANDY died of drug related causes. PAT GARRETT later joined The DILS. RAMIREZ, BROWN, NANINI + bassist JIMMY LEACH were also part of The EYES, who had a few releases in the late 70's.

Andy BLADE (see under ⇒ EATER)

BLONDIE

Formed: New York City, New York, USA ... August 1974 by former Playboy bunny girl, DEBBIE HARRY and boyfriend CHRIS STEIN. Other original members excluding female backing singers were sticksman, BILLY O'CONNOR (soon replaced by CLEM BURKE), bassist FRED SMITH (later of TELEVISION) and guitarist IVAN KRAL (later of PATTI SMITH GROUP). After line-up changes which saw the latter two replaced by GARY VALENTINE and JIMMY DESTRI respectively, the group soon found themselves supporting the likes of punk legend, IGGY POP. Subsequently hooking up with veteran producer, Richard Gottehrer, the group released their debut single, 'X-OFFENDER', on his 'Private Stock' label in late '76. This was followed up with a second track, 'IN THE FLESH', while the eponymous debut hit the shelves later that Spring. Trawling tacky 60's girly pop and sprucing it up with a healthy dose of punk muscle and attitude, BLONDIE laid the foundations for their swoonsomely infectious late 70's/early 80's hits. With HARRY as the peroxide Marilyn Monroe of new wave, BLONDIE almost immediately caught the eye of the UK scene, where a follow-up album, 'PLASTIC LETTERS', made the Top 10 in Spring '78. By this point BLONDIE had signed to 'Chrysalis' (who had reputedly bought the contract out for $500,000 in August of the previous year) and had replaced VALENTINE with FRANK INFANTE. A cover of Randy & The Rainbows 60's nugget, 'DENISE' (aka 'DENIS') almost topped the British charts, while another single pulled from the album, '(I'M ALWAYS TOUCHED BY YOUR) PRESENCE DEAR', made the Top 10. With the subsequent recruitment of bassist NIGEL HARRISON, INFANTE switched to rhythm guitar, the music taking on a whole new dimension with the seminal 'PARALLEL LINES' (1978). Produced by legendary pop picker, MIKE CHAPMAN, the album spawned a UK Top 5 in 'HANGING ON THE TELEPHONE', plus two No.1's with 'SUNDAY GIRL' and 'HEART OF GLASS'. The latter track's throbbing disco feel was further developed on fourth album, 'EAT TO THE BEAT', a set which featured yet another UK chart topper in the moody dancefloor classic, 'ATOMIC' (later famous for providing the aural backdrop to the disco scene in 'Trainspotting'). BLONDIE even teamed up with electro disco guru, GEORGIO MORODER, for 'CALL ME' (recorded for the soundtrack to 'American Gigolo'), the band's second transatlantic No.1. They repeated this feat with 'THE TIDE IS HIGH', a wonderfully dreamy cover of a track originally cut by reggae outfit, The PARAGONS, while also having a bash at hip hop with 'RAPTURE', their fourth US No.1. Both tracks were included on 1980's 'AUTOAMERICAN', an album which suggested BLONDIE were beginning to lose their musical curls. Although 'THE HUNTER' (1982) spawned a further British No.1 in 'ISLAND OF LOST SOULS', the album met with a less than rapturous reception, likewise their final tour. The band finally split in summer '82, STEIN forming his own 'Chrysalis'-backed label, 'Animal', before falling ill the following year. This put HARRY's solo career (begun rather noneventfully with 1981's BERNARD EDWARDS / NILE RODGERS collaborative set, 'KOO KOO') temporarily on the back burner, the singer re-emerging in late '86 with the UK Top 10, 'FRENCH KISSIN' IN THE U.S.A.'. The accompanying album, 'ROCKBIRD' made the Top 40 although 1989's 'DEF, DUMB AND BLONDE' was more successful, its shiny, poppy single 'I WANT THAT MAN' making the UK Top 20. If nothing else, she proved herself an adaptable stylist although much more interesting was the tongue in cheek duet with IGGY POP in 1990, 'WELL, DID YOU EVAH!'. Throughout her career, HARRY had also made the occasional venture into celluloid (see below). At the tender age of 53, but still looking every inch (or two) the ideal peroxide sex symbol, DEBBIE and her slightly younger crew of CHRIS, JIMMY and CLEM, re-formed BLONDIE for round the world tours. By early 1999, the band were topping the UK charts with the catchy 'MARIA', a song lifted from their aptly-titled Top 5 (US Top 40) parent album, 'NO EXIT'. A year later, BLONDIE opted for a quick follow-up, the 'greatest hits live' package 'LIVID' (2000) – I know I was. • **Songwriters:** Most written by STEIN-HARRY except; HANGING ON THE TELEPHONE (Jack Lee; Nerves) / RING OF FIRE (Johnny Cash) / HEROES (David Bowie). • **Trivia:** DEBBIE HARRY filmography:- UNION CITY (1979) / ROADIE (1980) / VIDEODROME (1982) / HAIRSPRAY (1982) / Broadway play 'TEANECK TANZI: THE VENUS FLYTRAP' (1983), which bombed after one night. She also appeared on 'The Muppet Show' circa 1980.

Album rating: BLONDIE (*6) / PLASTIC LETTERS (*7) / PARALLEL LINES (*8) / EAT TO THE BEAT (*6) / AUTOAMERICAN (*5) / THE BEST OF BLONDIE compilation (*9) / THE HUNTER (*4) / THE COMPLETE PICTURE – THE VERY BEST OF DEBORAH HARRY & BLONDIE compilation (*9) / BLONDE AND BEYOND compilation (*5) / NO EXIT (*6) / LIVID (*3) / Debbie Harry: KOOKOO (*5) / ROCKBIRD (*6) / DEF, DUMB & BLONDE (*5) / DEBRAVATION (*4)

DEBBIE HARRY (b. 1 Jul'45, Miami, Florida) – vocals (ex-WIND IN THE WILLOWS) / **CHRIS STEIN** (b. 5 Jan'50, Brooklyn, New York) – guitar / **JIMMY DESTRI** (b.13 Apr'54) – keyboards (ex-KNICKERS) / **GARY VALENTINE** – bass / **CLEM BURKE** (b.CLEMENT, 24 Nov'55) – drums (ex-SWEET REVENGE)

	Private Stock	Private Stock
Dec 76. (7") <PVT 90> **X OFFENDER. / IN THE SUN**	-	□
Dec 76. (lp) <PS 2023> **BLONDIE**	-	□

– X offender / Little girl lies / In the flesh / Look good in blue / In the sun / A shark in jet's clothing / Man overboard / Rip her to shreds / Rifle range / Kung Fu girls / The attack of the giant ants. <re-iss. Feb77; PVLP 1017> (UK-iss.Dec77 on 'Chrysalis'; CHR 1165) – (hit UK No.75 in Mar79) (re-iss. Oct82 on 'Hallmark' lp/c; SHM/HSC 3119) (re-iss. Apr85 on 'M.F.P.' lp/c; MFP 41-5696-1/-4) (cd-iss. Sep94 on 'Chrysalis'; CDCHR 6081)

Feb 77. (7") <PVT 105> **IN THE FLESH. / MAN OVERBOARD**	-	□
May 77. (7") (PVT 105) **IN THE FLESH. / X OFFENDER**	□	-

	Chrysalis	Chrysalis
Nov 77. (7"m/12"m) <CHS 2180/+12> **RIP HER TO SHREDS. / IN THE FLESH / X OFFENDER**	□	-

(re-iss. 12"m Dec81; same)

—— (Oct'77) **FRANK INFANTE** – bass (ex-WORLD WAR III) repl. VALENTINE

Feb 78. (7"m/12"m) <CHS 2180/+12> **DENIS. / CONTACT IN RED SQUARE / KUNG FU GIRLS**	2	□

(re-iss. 12"white Dec81; same)

| Feb 78. (lp/c) <(CHR/ZCHR 1166)> **PLASTIC LETTERS** | 10 | 72 Feb78 |

– Fan mail / Denis / Bermuda Triangle blues (Flight 45) / Youth nabbed as sniper / Contact in Red Square / (I'm always touched by your) Presence, dear / I'm on E / I didn't have the nerve to say no / Love at the pier / No imagination / Kidnapper / Detroit 442 / Cautious lip. (cd-iss. Sep94; CDCHR 6085)

| Apr 78. (7"m/12"m) <(CHS/+12 2217)> **(I'M ALWAYS TOUCHED BY YOUR) PRESENCE, DEAR. / POET'S PROBLEM / DETROIT 442** | 10 | □ |

(re-iss. Dec81; same)

—— (Nov77 on recording of 2nd lp) added **NIGEL HARRISON** – bass (b.24 Apr'51, Stockport, England) now sextet with **INFANTE** – now on rhythm guitar

Aug 78. (7"yellow) <(CHS 2204)> **PICTURE THIS. / FADE AWAY (AND RADIATE)**	12	□
Sep 78. (7") <2251> **I'M GONNA LOVE YOU TOO. / JUST GO AWAY**	-	□
Sep 78. (lp/c) <(CHR/ZCHR 1192)> **PARALLEL LINES**	1	6

– Fade away (and radiate) / Hanging on the telephone / One way or another / Picture this / Pretty baby / I know but I don't know / 11:59 / Will anything happen / Sunday girl / Heart of glass / I'm gonna love you too / Just go away. (re-iss. Nov83 on 'Fame' lp/c; FA/TCFA 3089-1/-4) (re-iss. Jul88 lp/cd/cd; CDL/ZCDL/CCD 1192) (re-iss. Dec92 on 'Fame' cd/c; CD/TC FA 3282) (re-iss. Jul94 cd/c; CCD/ZCDL 1192)

Nov 78. (7") <CHS 2266> **HANGING ON THE TELEPHONE. / WILL ANYTHING HAPPEN**	5	-
Nov 78. (7") <CHS 2266> **HANGING ON THE TELEPHONE / FADE AWAY AND RADIATE**	-	□
Jan 79. (7") (CHS 2275) **HEART OF GLASS. / RIFLE RANGE**	1	-
(12"+=) – ('A'instrumental). (re-iss. 12" Dec81; same)		
Feb 79. (7") <CHS 2275> **HEART OF GLASS. / 11:59**	-	1
May 79. (7") (CHS 2320) **SUNDAY GIRL. / I KNOW BUT I DON'T KNOW**	1	-
(12"+=) (CHS/+12 2320) – ('A' French version).		
(re-iss. 12"clear Dec81; same)		
May 79. (7") <CHS 2336> **ONE WAY OR ANOTHER. / JUST GO AWAY**	-	24
Sep 79. (7") <CHS 2350> **DREAMING. / SOUND ASLEEP**	2	-
Sep 79. (7") <CHS 2379> **DREAMING. / LIVING IN THE REAL WORLD**	-	27
Oct 79. (lp/c) <(CHR/ZCHR 1225)> **EAT TO THE BEAT**	1	17

– Dreaming / The hardest part / Union city blue / Shayla / Eat to the beat / Accidents never happen / Die young stay pretty Slow motion / / Atomic / Sound-a-sleep / Victor / Living in the real world. (cd-iss. Jun87; CPCD 1225) (cd-iss. Nov92; CDCHR 1225)

Nov 79. (7") (CHS 2400) **UNION CITY BLUE. / LIVING IN THE REAL WORLD**	13	-
Jan 80. (7") <CHS 2408> **THE HARDEST PART. / SOUND-A-SLEEP**	-	84
Feb 80. (7") <(CHS 2410)> **ATOMIC. / DIE YOUNG STAY PRETTY**	1	39 May80
(12"+=) (CHS12 2410) – Heroes. (re-iss. 12" Dec81; same)		
Apr 80. (7") <(CHS 2414)> **CALL ME. / ('A'instrumental)**	1	1 Feb80
(12"+=) (CHS12 2414) – ('A'-Spanish version).		
Oct 80. (7") <(CHS 2465)> **THE TIDE IS HIGH. / SUZIE AND JEFFREY**	1	1 Nov80
Nov 80. (lp/c) <(CDL/ZCDL 1290)> **AUTOAMERICAN**	3	7

– Europa / Live it up / Here's looking at you / The tide is high / Angels on the balcony / Go through it / The hardest part / Rapture / Faces / Do the dark / T-Birds / Walk like me / Follow me. (cd-iss. Sep94; CDCHR 6084)

Jan 81. (7") <(CHS 2485)> **RAPTURE. / WALK LIKE ME**	5	1
(12") (CHS12 2485) – ('A'side) / Live it up.		
Oct 81. (lp/c) <(CDLTV/ZCLTV 1) <1371> **THE BEST OF BLONDIE** (compilation)	4	30

– Denis / The tide is high / In the flesh / Sunday girl / (I'm always touched by your) Presence dear / Hanging on the telephone / Rapture / Picture this / Union city blue / Call me / Atomic / Rip her to shreds / Heart of glass. (cd-iss. Jan88; CCD 1371)

Apr 82. (7"/7"pic-d) <(CHS/+P 2608)> **ISLAND OF LOST SOULS. / DRAGONFLY**	1	37 May82
May 82. (lp/c/pic-lp) <(CDL/ZCDL/PCDL 1384)> **THE HUNTER**	9	33

– Orchid club / Island of lost souls / Dragonfly / For your eyes only / The beast / War child / Little Caesar / Danceaway / (Can I) Find the right words (to say) / English boys / The hunter gets captured by the game. (cd-iss. Sep94; CDCHR 6083)

| Jul 82. (7"/7"pic-d/12") <(CHS/+P/12 2624)> **WAR CHILD. / LITTLE CAESAR** | 39 | □ |

BLONDIE (cont)   THE GREAT INDIE DISCOGRAPHY   The 1970s

— (Aug'82) STEIN formed own 'Animal' label through 'Chrysalis'. CLEM BURKE joins EURYTHMICS and later RAMONES. He also teams up with HARRISON to form CHEQUERED PAST. A solo album, 'HEART ON THE WALL', was released by JIMMY DESTRI in 1982 and featured most of BLONDIE.

DEBBIE HARRY

solo, with **NILE RODGERS** and **BERNARD EDWARDS** on production, etc.

		Chrysalis	Chrysalis
Jul 81. (7"/12") <(CHS/+12 2526)> **BACKFIRED. / MILITARY RAP**		32	43
Aug 81. (lp/c) <(CHR/ZCCHR 1347)> **KOO KOO**		6	23

– Jump jump / The jam was moving / Chrome / Under arrest / Inner city spillover / Surrender / Backfired / Now I know you / Military rap / Oasis. (cd-iss. Sep94; CDCHR 6082)

Sep 81. (7") <(CHS 2554)> **THE JAM WAS MOVING. / CHROME**	82
(12"+=) (CHS12 2554) – Inner city spillover.	

— now worked with various session musicians.

	Chrysalis	Geffen
Jan 84. (7") **RUSH RUSH. / DANCE DANCE DANCE**	–	
Jan 84. (7"/12") (CHS/12CHS 2752) **RUSH RUSH. / RUSH RUSH (dub)**		–
Nov 86. (7") (CHS 3066) **FRENCH KISSIN' IN THE U.S.A. / ROCKBIRD**	8	–

('A'dance; 12"+=/12"pic-d+=) (CHS12 3066/+B) – ('A'dub version).

Nov 86. (7") <28546> **FRENCH KISSIN' IN THE U.S.A. / BUCKLE UP**	–	57
Nov 86. (lp/c/cd) (CHR/ZCHR/CCD 1540) <24123> **ROCKBIRD**	31	97

– I want you / French kissin' in the U.S.A. / Buckle up / In love with love / You got me in trouble / Free to fall / Rockbird / Secret life / Beyond the limit. (cd re-iss. Sep94; CCD 1540)

Feb 87. (7") <(CHS 3093)> **FREE TO FALL. / FEEL THE SPIN**	46	
(12"+=/12"pic-d+=) (CHS12 3093/+B) – Secret life.		
(d7"+=) (CHSD 3093) – French kissin' in the U.S.A. / Rockbird.		
Apr 87. (7") (CHS 3128) **IN LOVE WITH LOVE. / FEEL THE SPIN**	45	–

(12"+=/12"pic-d+=) (CHS/P 12-3128) – French kissin' in the U.S.A. (French version).

| Jun 87. (7") <28476> **IN LOVE WITH LOVE. / SECRET LIFE** | – | 70 |

DEBORAH HARRY

— with **CHRIS STEIN** – guitar / **LEIGH FOXX** – bass / **TERRY BOZZIO** – drums / **TOMMY PRICE** – drums / **PHIL ASHLEY** – synthesizers / **STEVE GOLDSTEIN** – keyboards, etc.

	Chrysalis	Sire
Sep 89. (7"/c-s) (CHS/+MC 3369) **I WANT THAT MAN. / BIKE BOY**		
(12"pic-d+=/cd-s+=) (CHS 12P/CD 3369) – ('A'remix) / ('A'instrumental).		
Oct 89. (lp/c/cd) (CHR/ZCHR/CCD 1650) <25938> **DEF, DUMB AND BLONDE**	12	

– I want that man / Lovelight / Kiss it better / Bike boy * / Get your way / Maybe for sure / I'll never fall in love / Calmarie / Sweet and low / He is so / Bugeye / Comic books / Brite side / End of the run *. (cd+=*) (cd re-iss. Sep94; CCD 1650)

Nov 89. (7"/7"s) (CHS/+PB 3452) **BRITE SIDE. / BUGEYE**	59	
(12"+=/cd-s+=) (CHS 12/CD 3452) – In love with love.		
('A'remix-cd-s++=) (CHSCCD 3452) – French kissin' in the U.S.A.		

— Her touring group at time included STEIN and FOXX plus **SUZY DAVIS** – keyboards / **CARLA OLLA** – rhythm guitar / **JIMMY CLARK** – drums

Mar 90. (7"/7"s) (CHS/+PB 3491) **SWEET AND LOW. / LOVELIGHT**	57	
(12"/12"pic-d/cd-s) (CHS 12/P12/CD 3491) – (3-'A'mixes).		
May 90. (7") (CHS 3537) **MAYBE FOR SURE. / GET YOUR WAY**		
(12"+=/cd-s+=) (CHS 12/CD 3537) – ('A'extended).		

below featured on a Cole Porter tribute album, 'Red Hot & Blue'.

Dec 90. (7"/12"; by DEBORAH HARRY & IGGY POP) (CHS/+12 3646) **WELL DID YOU EVAH! / (b-side by The Thompson Twins)**	42	
(cd-s+=) (CHSCD 3646) – (track by 'Aztec Camera').		
Jun 93. (c-s/7") (TC+/CHS 4900) **I CAN SEE CLEARLY. / STANDING IN MY WAY**	23	
(12"+=/cd-s+=) (12/CD CHS 4900) – Atomic / Heart of glass.		
(cd-s+=) (CDCHSS 4900) – Call me / In love with love.		
Jul 93. (cd/c/lp) (CD/TC+/CHR 6033) **DEBRAVATION**	24	

– I can see clearly / Stability / Strike me pink / Rain / Communion / Lip service / Mood ring / Dancing down the moon / Standing in my way / The fugitive / Dog star girl.

Sep 93. (c-s) (TCCHS 5000) **STRIKE ME PINK / 8 AND A HALF RHUMBA**	46	
(cd-s) (CDCHS 5000) – Dreaming.		
(12"pic-d/cd-s) (12CHSPD/CDCHSS 5000) – ('A'side) / Sweet and low / On a breath.		

BLONDIE

— re-formed in 1998 with **DEBBIE, CHRIS, CLEM + JIMMY**

	Beyond-RCA	Logic
Feb 99. (c-s) (74321 64563-4) <78040> **MARIA / MARIA (Soul Soultion mix)**	1	82 Mar99
(cd-s+=) (74321 64563-2) – Maria (Talvin Singh remix).		
(cd-s) (74321 63737-2) – ('A'side) / In the flesh (live) / Screaming skin (live).		
Feb 99. (cd/c) (74321 64114-2/-4) <78003> **NO EXIT**	3	18

– Screaming skin / Forgive & forget / Maria / No exit / Double take / Nothing is real but the girl / Boom boom in the zoom zoom room / Night wind sent / Under the gun / Out in the streets / Happy dog (for Caggy) / The dream's lost on me / Divine / Dig up the Congo. (cd re-iss. Aug02 on 'Epic'+=; 501408-2) – Hot shot / Rapture (live) / Heart of glass (live).

Jun 99. (c-s) (74321 66948-4) **NOTHING IS REAL BUT THE GIRL (Boilerhouse mix) / RIP HER TO SHREDS (live)**	26	
(cd-s) (74321 66380-2) – ('A'side) / 'A'-Danny Tenaglia mix) / 'A'-Danny Tenaglia instradub).		
(cd-s) (74321 66947-2) – ('A'-US radio mix) / Hanging on the telephone (live) / Shayla (live).		

Nov 99. (cd-ep) (74321 71653-2) **NO EXIT / MARIA (J&B mix) / MARIA (Talvin Singh rhythmic mix) / NOTHING IS REAL BUT THE GIRL (Danny Tenaglia mix & his trance version)**		
Feb 00. (cd/c) (501409-2) **LIVID – THE GREATEST HITS LIVE (live)**	–	–

– Dreaming / Hanging on the telephone / Screaming skin / Atomic / Forgive and forget / The tide is high / Shayla / Sunday girl / Maria / Call me / Under the gun / Rapture / Rip her to shreds / X-offender / No exit / Heart of glass / One way or another.

– compilations, others, etc. –

on 'Chrysalis' unless mentioned otherwise

Dec 82. (d-c) (2CDP 101) **EAT TO THE BEAT / AUTOAMERICAN**	–	–
Feb 87. (7") Old Gold; (OG 9672) **DENIS. / PICTURE THIS**	–	–
Feb 87. (7") Old Gold; (OG 9674) **SUNDAY GIRL. / HANGING ON THE TELEPHONE**	–	–
Feb 87. (7") Old Gold; (OG 9676) **CALL ME. / UNION CITY BLUE**	–	–
Feb 87. (7") Old Gold; (OG 9678) **HEART OF GLASS. / THE TIDE IS HIGH**	–	–
Feb 87. (7") Old Gold; (OG 9680) **DREAMING. / ATOMIC**	–	–
Nov 88. (7") (CHS 3328) **DENIS (remix). / RAPTURE (Teddy Riley remix)**	50	–
(12"+=/12"pic-d+=/cd-s+=) (CHS/+12/12P/CD 3328) – Heart of glass (remix) / Atomic (remix).		
Dec 88. (lp/c/cd) (CJB/ZCJB/CDJB 2) **ONCE MORE INTO THE BLEACH (GREATEST HITS)**	50	–

– Denis / Heart of glass / Call me / Rapture / Rapture (bonus beats) / The tide is high / The jam was moving (DEBBIE HARRY) / In love with love (DEBBIE HARRY) / Rush rush (DEBBIE HARRY) / French kissin' in the U.S.A. (DEBBIE HARRY) / Feel the spin (DEBBIE HARRY) / Backfired (DEBBIE HARRY) / Sunday girl (French version).

Dec 88. (lp/c) Star; (84026-1/-4) **BLONDIE HIT COLLECTION**	–	–
Feb 89. (7") (CHS 3342) **CALL ME. / CALL ME (version)**	61	–
(12"+=/cd-s+=) (CHS 12/CD 3342) – Backfired (DEBBIE HARRY).		
Mar 91. (cd/c/d-lp) (CCD/ZCHR/CHR 1817) **THE COMPLETE PICTURE – THE VERY BEST OF DEBORAH HARRY & BLONDIE**	3	–

– Heart of glass / I want that man / Call me / Sunday girl / French kissin' in the USA / Denis / Rapture / Brite side / (I'm always touched by your) Presence dear / Well, did you evah! / The tide is high / In love with love / Hanging on the telephone / Island of lost souls / Picture this / Dreaming / Sweet and low / Atomic / Rip her to shreds.

Jan 94. (cd/c) (CD/TC CHR 6063) **BLONDIE AND BEYOND – RARITIES AND ODDITIES**	–	–
Aug 94. (c-s/12"/cd-s) (12/ZC/CD CHS 5013) **ATOMIC (re-mix). / ('A'mixes by Diddy & Alan Thompson)**	19	–
(cd-s) (CDCHSS 5013) – ('A'side) / Sunday girl (re-mix) / Union City blues (re-mix).		
Nov 94. (d-cd) (CDCHR 6089) **THE PLATINUM COLLECTION**	–	–
Jun 95. (12") (12CHS 5023) **HEART OF GLASS (re-mix). / CALL ME (re-mix)**	15	–
(c-s) (CDCHSS 5023) – ('A'side) / Rapture (re-mix) / Atomic (re-mix).		
(cd-s+=) (CDCHSS 5023) – ('A'mixes).		
Jul 95. (cd/c/d-lp) (CD/TC+/CHR 6105) **BEAUTIFUL – THE REMIX ALBUM**	25	–
Oct 95. (12"blue/cd-s) (12/CD CHS 5027) **UNION CITY BLUE (re-mix) / I FEEL LOVE (live)**	31	–
(cd-s) (CDCHSS 5027) – (other mixes by:- Diddy / The Burger Queens / OPM / Vinny Vero & Jammin' Hot).		
Jul 98. (cd/c) E.M.I.; (494996-2/-4) **ATOMIC – THE VERY BEST OF…**	12	–
(d-cd-iss. Feb99 +=; 499288-2) – ATOMIX		
Jul 98. (c-s) E.M.I.; (TCATOM 150) **ATOMIC (1998 remix)**	–	–
(12"+=/cd-s+=) (12/CD ATOM 150) – ('A'mixes).		
Mar 99. (cd) EMI Gold; (499421-2) **THE ESSENTIAL COLLECTION**	–	–
Jun 99. (cd) E.M.I.; (521233-2) **LIVE (live Philadelphia 1978 / Dallas 1980)**	–	–
Oct 02. (cd) E.M.I.; (543105-2) **GREATEST HITS**	38	–

– Dreaming / Call me / One way or another / Heart of glass / The tide is high / X-offender / Hanging on the telephone / Rip her to shreds / Rapture / Atomic / Picture this / In the flesh / Denis / I'm always touched by your presence dear / Union city blue / The hardest part / Island of lost souls / Sunday girl / Maria.

BOOMTOWN RATS

Formed: Dun Laoghaire (near Dublin), Ireland … 1975 by former NME journalist BOB GELDOF, JOHNNIE FINGERS, GERRY COTT, PETE BRIQUETTE, GERRY ROBERTS and SIMON CROWE. Moving to London in late 1976, they signed to the newly formed 'Ensign' records. Though their music was rooted in R&B and they were more of a New Wave outfit than anything, The BOOMTOWN RATS were loosely affiliated with the burgeoning punk scene, at least initially. In the long, hot summer of '77, their debut single, 'LOOKIN' AFTER No.1' made the UK Top 20. This was closely followed by a similarly successful eponymous debut album and a second Top 20 hit, 'MARY OF THE 4th FORM'. With a lean sound lying somewhere between EDDIE & THE HOT RODS and The ROLLING STONES, The BOOMTOWN RATS were also a compelling live proposition, GELDOF's moody charisma helping to give the band a distinct identity. Major success came with 'A TONIC FOR THE TROOPS' (1978), this album spawning a number of hits including their first No.1 in the insistent 'RAT TRAP'. They scored a second number one and a massive worldwide hit with 'I DON'T LIKE MONDAYS', a stunningly effective, piano-driven belter inspired (if that's the appropriate word) by schoolgirl Brenda Spencer, who snipered/shot dead several of her school colleagues. The accompanying album, 'THE ART OF SURFACING' (1979) showed the 'RATS at the peak of their power, although subsequent albums increasingly followed a more mundane pop/rock direction and the band slowly faded from view, finally splitting in 1984. GELDOF's profile remained high, however, the Irishman helping to mastermind the mammoth undertaking that was LIVE AID. He and ULTRAVOX's MIDGE URE, assembled together all the major stars of the time to sing 'DO THEY KNOW IT'S CHRISTMAS', the resulting 45 making millions of pounds/dollars/etc for famine relief in Ethiopia. Not content with this, BOB and MIDGE reunited most of them again for the LIVE AID concert at Wembley Stadium on the 13th of July '85 (this was simultaneously broadcast over the Atlantic at JFK Stadium, Philadelphia). At the time, it amassed well over £10m, the money also being spread around other needy charities as well as Ethiopia (the total at the end of 1991 was over £100m). In June 1986, BOB was now Sir BOB GELDOF, after being knighted by the Queen and two months later he married long-time fiancee, PAULA YATES (TV presenter/writer/etc). She gave birth to FIFI TRIXIBELLE and in 1989, their second daughter, PEACHES, was born. During the latter half of a very busy decade for GELDOF, he managed to maintain a solo career, a hit single, 'THIS IS THE WORLD CALLING', was appropriate enough to become a Top 30 hit in 1986, while 1990's 'THE GREAT SONG OF INDIFFERENCE' went one step better. His backing band at the time, The VEGETARIANS OF LOVE, provided the title of the single's folky/cajun parent album, which also sold reasonably well. His last solo album, 'THE HAPPY CLUB' (1992), was something of a disappointment and Sir BOB virtually retired from the studio side of things to run his own Planet 24 company and The Big Breakfast on Channel 4. PAULA was also part of the latter, although by 1995, she had opted to bed MICHAEL HUTCHENCE of INXS, citing BOB as the adulterer. BOB and PAULA were subsequently divorced as the new couple became the media focal point (tragically, this was cut short when MICHAEL took his own life on the 22nd November, 1997 – see INXS). • **Songwriters:** Most written by GELDOF except; BAREFOOTIN' (Robert Parker). GELDOF solo covered SUNNY AFTERNOON (Kinks). • **Trivia:** GELDOF starred in the feature films, 'The Wall' (1982) and 'Number One' (1984).

Album rating: THE BOOMTOWN RATS (*6) / A TONIC FOR THE TROOPS (*5) / THE FINE ART OF SURFACING (*5) / MONDO BONGO (*4) / V DEEP (*4) / IN THE LONG GRASS (*5) / Bob Geldof: DEEP IN THE HEART OF NOWHERE (*5) / THE VEGETARIANS OF LOVE (*5) / THE HAPPY CLUB (*4) / LOUDMOUTH – THE BEST OF THE BOOMTOWN RATS AND BOB GELDOF compilation (*8)

BOB GELDOF (b. 5 Oct'54, Dublin, Ireland) – vocals / **JOHNNIE FINGERS** (b. JOHNNY MOYLETT) – keyboards, vocals / **GERRY COTT** – guitar / **PETE BRIQUETTE** (b. PATRICK CUSACK) – bass / **GERRY ROBERTS** – guitar, vocals / **SIMON CROWE** – drums, vocals

		Ensign	Mercury
Aug 77.	(12"m) (ENY 4) **LOOKIN' AFTER No.1. / BORN TO BURN** (live) / **BAREFOOTIN'** (live)	11	-
Sep 77.	(lp/c) (ENVY/ENCAS 1) <SRM 1188> **THE BOOMTOWN RATS**	18	
	– Lookin' after No.1 / Neon heart / Joey's on the street again / Never bite the hand that feeds / Mary of the 4th form / (She gonna) Do you in / Close as you'll ever be / I can make it if you can / Kicks. (re-iss. Dec83 on 'Mercury' lp/c; PRICE/PRIMC 57)		
Nov 77.	(7") (ENY 9) **MARY OF THE 4th FORM. / DO THE RAT**	15	-
		Ensign	Columbia
Mar 78.	(7") (ENY 13) **SHE'S SO MODERN. / LYING AGAIN**	12	
Jun 78.	(7") (ENY 14) **LIKE CLOCKWORK. / HOW DO YOU DO?**	6	
Jul 78.	(lp/c) (ENVY/ENCAS 3) <35750> **A TONIC FOR THE TROOPS**	8	
	– Like clockwork / Blind date / (I never loved) Eva Braun / Living in an island / Don't believe what you read / She's so modern / Me and Howard Hughes / Can't stop * / (Watch out for) The normal people / Rat trap. <US version repl.* with – Joey> (re-iss. Dec83 on 'Mercury' lp/c; PRICE/PRIMC 58)		
Oct 78.	(7") (ENY 16) **RAT TRAP. / SO STRANGE**	1	-
Nov 78.	(7") (ENY 17) **RAT TRAP. / DO THE RAT**		
Jul 79.	(7") (ENY 30) <11117> **I DON'T LIKE MONDAYS. / IT'S ALL THE RAGE**	1	73 Jan80
Oct 79.	(lp/c) (ENROX/ENCAS 11) <36248> **THE FINE ART OF SURFACING**	7	
	– Someone's looking at you / Diamond smiles / Wind chill factor (minus zero) / Having my picture taken / Sleep (Fingers' lullaby) / I don't like Mondays / Nothing happened today / Keep it up / Nice 'n' neat / When the night comes. (re-iss. Nov84 on 'Mercury' lp/c; PRICE/PRIMC 73)		
Nov 79.	(7") (ENY 33) **DIAMOND SMILES. / LATE LAST NIGHT**	13	-
Jan 80.	(7",12") (ENY 34) **SOMEONE'S LOOKING AT YOU. / WHEN THE NIGHT COMES**	4	-
May 80.	(7") <11248> **SOMEONE'S LOOKING AT YOU. / I DON'T LIKE MONDAYS** (live)	-	
		Mercury	Columbia
Nov 80.	(7") (BONGO 1) **BANANA REPUBLIC. / MAN AT THE TOP**	3	-
Dec 80.	(lp/c) (6359/7150 042) <37062> **MONDO BONGO**	6	
	– Please don't go / The elephant's graveyard (guilty) / Banana republic / Fall down / Hurt hurts / Whitehall 1212 * / Mood mambo / Straight up / This is my room / Another piece of red / Under my thumb . . . is under my thumb / Go man go. <US version repl.* with – Don't talk to me>		
Jan 81.	(7") (BONGO 2) **THE ELEPHANT'S GRAVEYARD (GUILTY). / REAL DIFFERENT**	26	-

— (Mar'81) trimmed to a quintet when GERRY COTT left to go solo

Nov 81.	(7") <60512> **UP ALL NIGHT. / ANOTHER PIECE OF RED**	-	
Nov 81.	(7") (MER 87) **NEVER IN A MILLION YEARS. / DON'T TALK TO ME**	62	-
Mar 82.	(7"/12") (MER/+X 91) **HOUSE ON FIRE. / EUROPE LOOKED UGLY**	24	-
Mar 82.	(lp/c) (6359/7150 082) **V DEEP**	64	
	– Never in a million years / The bitter end / Talking in code / He watches it all / Storm breaks / Charmed lives / House on fire / Up all night / Skin on skin / Little death.		
Jun 82.	(7") (MER 106) **CHARMED LIVES. / NO HIDING PLACE**		-
	(d7"+=) (MER 106-2) – Nothing happened (live) / Storm breaks (instrumental).		
	(12") (MERX 106) – ('A'side) / A storm breaks.		
Aug 82.	(7") <03386> **CHARMED LIVES. / NEVER IN A MILLION YEARS**	-	
Jan 84.	(7") (MER 154) **TONIGHT. / PRECIOUS TIME**	73	-
	(12"+=) (MERX 154) – Walking downtown.		
May 84.	(7") (MER 163) **DRAG ME DOWN. / AN ICICLE IN THE SUN**	50	-
	(12"+=) (MERX 163) – Rat trap / She's so modern.		
Nov 84.	(7"pic-d) (MER 179) **DAVE. / HARD TIMES**		-
	(d7"+=) (MER 179-2) – I don't like Mondays / It's all the rage.		
	(12"+=) (MERX 179) – Banana republic (live) / Close as you'll ever be (live).		
Dec 84.	(lp/c) (MERL/+C 38) <39335> **IN THE LONG GRASS**		
	– A hold of me / Drag me down / Dave / Over again / Another sad story / Tonight / Hard times / Lucky / Icicle in the Sun / Up or down.		
Feb 85.	(7") (MER 184) **A HOLD OF ME. / NEVER IN A MILLION YEARS**		-
	(12"+=) (MERX 184) – Say hi to Mick.		
Mar 85.	(7") <04892> **ICICLE IN THE SUN. / RAIN**	-	
Jun 85.	(7") <05590> **DRAG ME DOWN. / HARD TIMES**	-	

— had already split late '84. FINGERS and CROWE formed GUNG HO. BOB GELDOF pieced together BAND/LIVE AID before going solo.

– compilations, others, etc. –

Dec 83.	(6x7"box) Mercury; (none) **RAT PACK** (6 best of singles pack)		-
Jan 88.	(7") Old Gold; (OG 9790) **I DON'T LIKE MONDAYS. / RAT TRAP**		-
	Note; below single by BOOMTOWN RATS (also compilation tracks *)		
Jun 94.	(7"colrd/c-s) (VER/+MC 87) **I DON'T LIKE MONDAYS. / BORN TO BURN / DO THE RAT**	38	
	(cd-s) (MERCD 87) – ('A'side) / Looking after No.1 / Mary of the 4th form / She's so modern.		
	(cd-s) (MERCX 87) – ('A'side) / Rat trap / Someone's looking at you / Banana republic.		
Jul 94.	(cd/c) (522 283-2/-4) **LOUDMOUTH – THE BEST OF THE BOOMTOWN RATS & BOB GELDOF** (compilation)	10	
	– I don't like Mondays * / This is the world calling / Rat trap * / The great song of indifference / Love or something / Banana republic * / Crazy / The elephant's graveyard (guilty) * / Someone's looking at you * / She's so modern * / House on fire * / The beat of the night / Diamond smiles * / Like clockwork * / Room 19 (sha la la la lee) / Mary of the 4th form * / Looking after No.1 *. (* tracks by The BOOMTOWN RATS)		

Adrian BORLAND
(see under ⇒ SOUND; see 80's section)

BOYS

Formed: London, England ... summer 1976 by JOHN PLAIN, KID REID, JACK BLACK and two slightly more experienced musicians MATT DANGERFIELD and Norwegian CASINO STEEL, the latter fresh from The HOLLYWOOD BRATS. After supporting JOHN CALE on his Spring '77 tour, the lads signed to the 'NEMS' label, debuting almost immediately with the single, 'I DON'T CARE'. Power-pop punk sounding like a less abrasive hybrid of BUZZCOCKS and RAMONES, the track didn't chart but seemingly sold well in Scandinavia and Europe. Their second 45, 'FIRST TIME', deserved a better fate, although its inclusion as a highlight of their UK Top 50 eponymous debut album no doubt boosted sales. They couldn't repeat the formula however, and it didn't help when they inaugurated their annual Christmas appearance as The YOBS. After a second long-player, 'ALTERNATIVE CHARTBUSTERS' (1978) failed to make the grade, The BOYS signed to 'Safari', also home of TOYAH whom DANGERFIELD was asked to produce. At the turn of the decade, the improbably named crew released the poorly received 'TO HELL WITH THE BOYS' (1979); presumably this was also what their fans thought as their support dwindled and they faded from view after swansong set, 'BOYS ONLY' (1981). • **Songwriters:** STEEL / DANGERFIELD, except YOU BETTER MOVE ON (Arthur Alexander) / SABRE DANCE (Love Sculpture). • **Question:** What was The BOYS' connection with other late 70's outfits. The ROWDIES and COCKNEY & WESTERNS. Was MATT on production?

Album rating: THE BOYS (*6) / ALTERNATIVE CHARTBUSTERS (*5) / TO HELL WITH THE BOYS (*6) / BOYS ONLY (*4) / THE VERY BEST OF THE BOYS compilation (*6)

MATT DANGERFIELD – vocals, guitar (ex-LONDON SS) / **CASINO STEEL** (b. Norway) – keyboards (ex-LONDON SS, ex-HOLLYWOOD BRATS) / **KID REID** (b. DUNCAN) – vocals, bass / **JOHN PLAIN** (b. Leeds, England) – guitar / **JACK BLACK** – drums

		NEMS	not iss.
Apr 77.	(7") (NES 102) **I DON'T CARE. / SODA PRESSING**		-
Jul 77.	(7"m) (NES 111) **FIRST TIME. / WHATCHA GONNA DO / TURNING GREY**		-
Sep 77.	(lp) (NEL 6001) **THE BOYS**	50	-
	– Sick on you / I call your name / Tumble with me / Tonight / I don't care / Soda pressing / No money / First time / Box number / Kiss like a nun / Cop cars / Kep running / Tenement kids / Living in the city. (<cd-iss. Mar99 on 'Captain Oi'+=; AHOYCD 101>) – Watcha gonna do / Turning grey / The first time / Lonely school days (demo) / I don't care / Take a heart (demo) / Run Rudolph run / The worm song.		
Dec 77.	(7"; as The YOBS) (NES 114) **RUN RUDOLPH RUN. / THE WORM SONG**		-
Feb 78.	(7") (NES 116) **BRICKFIELD NIGHTS. / TEACHER'S PET**		-
Mar 78.	(lp) (NEL 6015) **ALTERNATIVE CHARTBUSTERS**		-
	– Brickfield nights / Usi / Taking on the world / Sway / Do the contract / Heroine / Not ready / Classified Susie / T.C.P. / Neighbourhood brat / Stop stop stop /		

BOYS (cont) THE GREAT INDIE DISCOGRAPHY The 1970s

Backstage pass / Talking / Cast of thousands. (cd-iss. Mar99 on 'Captain Oi'+=; AHOYCD 104) – Teacher's pet / School days / Lies / She's no angel / You're the other man / Silent night. (lp re-iss. Jun99 on 'Get Back'; GET 53)

		Yob	not iss.
Dec 78.	(7"; as The YOBS) (YOB 79) **SILENT NIGHT. / STILLE NACHT**		-

		Safari	not iss.
Nov 79.	(7") (SAFE 21) **KAMIKAZE. / BAD DAYS**		-
Nov 79.	(lp) (1-2 BOYS) **TO HELL WITH BOYS**		-

– Kamikaze / Lonely cowboy / Waiting for the lady / Bad day / Independent girl / You better move on / Sabre dance / Rue Morgue / Terminal love / See ya later / You can't hurt a memory. (cd-iss. Jun99 on 'Captain Oi'+=; AHOYCD 113) – Schoolgirls / Rub a dum dum (YOBS) / Another Christmas (YOBS). (lp re-iss. May00 on 'Get Back'; GET 51)

Dec 79.	(7"; as the YOBS) (YULE 1) **RUB-A-DUM-DUM. / ANOTHER CHRISTMAS**		-
Jan 80.	(7") (SAFE 23) **TERMINAL LOVE. / I LOVE ME**		-
May 80.	(7") (SAFE 27) **YOU BETTER MOVE ON. / SCHOOLGIRLS**		-

— now without STEEL. (JOHN PLAIN joined LURKERS man PETE STRIDE for an album and single, before returning to the fold)

Sep 80.	(7") (SAFE 31) **WEEKEND. / COOL**		-
Dec 80.	(lp; as the YOBS) (RUDE 1) **CHRISTMAS ALBUM** (compilation)		-
Feb 81.	(lp) (4) **BOYS ONLY**		-

– Weekend / Wrong arm of the law / Poor little rich girl / Monotony / Nothing ventured / Wonderful world / Scrubber / Satisfaction guarenteed / Gabrielle / Miss you / Little white lifeline / Let it rain. (cd-iss. Jun99 on 'Captain Oi'+=; AHOYCD 117) – Cool / Lucy / Terminal love. (lp re-iss. May00 on 'Get Back'; GET 52)

Mar 81.	(7") (SAFE 33) **LET IT RAIN. / LUCY**		-

		Fresh	not iss.
Jan 82.	(7"; as the YOBS) (FRESH 1) **YOBS ON 45. / THE BALLAD OF WARRINGTON**		-

— disbanded after above

– compilations, etc. –

Nov 90.	(cd/lp) Receiver; (RRCD/RRLP 135) **LIVE AT THE ROXY** (live)		-
Feb 94.	(cd) Loma; (LOMACD 12) **THE BOYS / ALTERNATIVE CHARTBUSTERS**		-
Mar 95.	(cd) Dojo; (DOJOCD 137) **THE BEST OF THE BOYS**		-
Nov 96.	(cd) Anagram; (<CDPUNK 85>) **THE COMPLETE PUNK SINGLES COLLECTION**		
Feb 99.	(cd) Anagram; (CDMGRAM 119) **POWER CUT**		Jun00
Jun 99.	(cd) Harry May; (<MAYOCD 113>) **SICK ON YOU** (lp-iss.May00 on 'Get Back'; GET 51)		Apr99
Jun 99.	(cd) Captain Oi; (<AHOYCD 144>) **TO ORIGINAL HELL / ODDS 'N' SODS**		Apr00
Jun 99.	(cd) Anagram; (<CDPUNK 112>) **THE VERY BEST OF THE BOYS**		Jul00
Aug 99.	(cd/lp) Vinyl Japan; (ASK CD/LP 089/088) **THE BBC SESSIONS**		Jul02
Aug 99.	(lp) Vinyl Japan; (ASKLP 090) **IN CONCERT** (live)		-
Sep 99.	(cd) Captain Oi; (<AHOYCD 120>) **PUNK ROCK RARITIES**		Jan00

BOYS NEXT DOOR (see under ⇒ CAVE, Nick)

BRINSLEY SCHWARZ

Formed: Tunbridge Wells, England ... 1965 as the beat/psychedelic combo KIPPINGTON LODGE by SCHWARZ and NICK LOWE. After 5 flop singles between '67 & '69 (the first 'SHY BOY', should have been a hit), they renamed themselves in Autumn '69. They came under the wing of DAVID ROBINSON, former tour manager for JIMI HENDRIX, who now headed the Famepushers Agency. On 3rd April '70, he chartered a plane to fly 150 music journalists to New York to see them support VAN MORRISON at East Fillmore. This proved to be a six-figure sum disaster, due to an admittedly dodgy performance. Predictably, the press ignored their debut album for 'United Artists' and not surprisingly it bombed. Unbowed, they went off to take stock and write new material, resurfacing late in the year with follow-up 'DESPITE IT ALL'. The preceding single 'COUNTRY GIRL' was reminiscent of 'SWEETHEART OF THE RODEO'-era BYRDS and was as fine an example of country-rock as anything coming out of America at the time. Pioneers of the genre in the UK, the band went on to experiment with many other areas of American roots music, evidenced on their 1972 album, 'NERVOUS ON THE ROAD'. Their interest in the "down home" sound had deepened upon seeing American bar band EGGS OVER EASY playing at the Tally Ho club in London. The venue had become a focus for the burgeoning "pub rock" scene of which The BRINSLEY's would soon be such an integral part, along with acts such as BEES MAKE HONEY and DUCKS DELUXE. As well as digging the band's R&B boogie, BRINSLEY SCHWARZ were heavily influenced by EGGS OVER EASY's freewheeling attitude which didn't give a fig for the banks of Marshall stacks and sprawling concept albums which were de rigeur in the early 70's. The same back to basics spirit that inspired the BRINSLEY's to scale down the length of their songs and cut their hair, laid the foundations for the punk explosion later in the decade as well as breaking such important figures as ELVIS COSTELLO and JOE STRUMMER (101'ERS). For the moment though, the band had found a comfortable niche and the track 'HAPPY DOING WHAT WE'RE DOING', from the 'NERVOUS ON THE ROAD' set seemed to confirm this. Another two excellent albums followed, showcasing LOWE's comprehensive songwriting talent on such classic tracks as '(WHAT'S SO FUNNY 'BOUT) PEACE, LOVE AND UNDERSTANDING'. Ironically, no commercial breakthrough came and the band split amicably in 1975, with NICK LOWE going on to a successful solo career, while BRINSLEY and keyboard player BOB ANDREWS helped to form The RUMOUR (GRAHAM PARKER's backing band). • **Covered:** (The Beatles') I SHOULD HAVE KNOWN BETTER. / TELL ME WHY as 'The LIMELIGHT' in '75. • **Trivia:** In 1974, they were featured as The ELECTRICIANS (with DAVE EDMUNDS; their sometimes producer) in the film 'Stardust'.

Album rating: BRINSLEY SCHWARZ (*5) / DESPITE IT ALL (*5) / SILVER PISTOL (*7) / NERVOUS ON THE ROAD (*6) / PLEASE DON'T EVER CHANGE (*6) / THE NEW FAVOURITES OF BRINSLEY SCHWARZ (*7) / SURRENDER TO THE RHYTHM (THE BEST OF BRINSLEY SCHWARZ) compilation (*7)

KIPPINGTON LODGE

BRINSLEY SCHWARZ – guitar, sax / **NICK LOWE** (b.25 Mar'49, Woodbridge, England) – vocals, bass / **BARRY LANDERMAN** – organ / **PETE WHALE** – drums

		Parlophone	Capitol
Oct 67.	(7") (R 5645) **SHY BOY. / LADY ON A BICYCLE**		-
Mar 68.	(7") (R 5677) <2236> **RUMOURS. / AND SHE CRIED** (above 4 tracks re-iss. Nov78.7"ep on 'EMI')		

— BOB ANDREWS (b.20 Jun'49) – organ, vox repl. BARRY to VANITY FARE

Aug 68.	(7") (R 5717) **TELL ME A STORY. / UNDERSTAND A WOMAN**		-
Dec 68.	(7") (R 5750) **TOMORROW TODAY. / TURN OUT THE LIGHT**		-
May 69.	(7") (R 5776) **IN MY LIFE. / I CAN SEE HER FACE**		-

BRINSLEY SCHWARZ

— (BRINSLEY, NICK + BOB) recruited **BILLY RANKIN** – drums; to repl. PETE

		U.A.	Capitol
Apr 70.	(lp) (UAS 29111) <SWBC 11869> **BRINSLEY SCHWARZ**		

– Hymn to me / Shining brightly / Rock & roll women / Lady constant / What do you suggest / Mayfly / Ballad of a has-been beauty queen. (cd-iss. Feb94 on 'Repertoire'; REP 4421WY)

May 70.	(7") (UP 35118) **SHINING BRIGHTLY. / WHAT DO YOU SUGGEST**		-
Jun 70.	(7") <3004> **HYMN TO ME. / ROCK & ROLL WOMAN**	-	

		Liberty	not iss.
Nov 70.	(7") (LBY 15419) **COUNTRY GIRL. / FUNK ANGEL** (re-iss. 1972 on 'United Artists'; UP 35312)		-
Dec 70.	(lp) (LBG 83427) **DESPITE IT ALL**		-

– Country girl / The slow one / Funk angel / Piece of home / Love song / Starship / Ebury down / Old Jarrow.

— added **IAN GOMM** (b.17 Mar'47) – guitar, vocals

		U.A.	U.A.
Oct 71.	(lp) (UAS 29217) <5566> **SILVER PISTOL**		

– Dry land / Merry go round / One more day / Nightingale / Silver pistol / The last time I was fooled / Unknown number / Range war / Egypt / Niki Hoeke speedway / Ju ju man / Rockin' chair. (re-iss. Apr86 on 'Edsel'; ED 190) (cd-iss. Sep90; EDCD 190)

Jan 72.	(7") <50915> **SILVER PISTOL. / NIGHTINGALE**	-	

— Contributed 5 tracks to 'GREASY TRUCKERS' live lp, Apr72.

Sep 72.	(lp) (UAS 29374) <5647> **NERVOUS ON THE ROAD**		

– It's been so long / Happy doing what we're doing / Surrender to the rhythm / Don't lose your grip on love / Nervous on the road (but can't stay at home) / Feel a little funky / I like it like that / Brand new you, brand new me / Home in my hand / Why, why, why, why, why. (re-iss. Dec80 on 'Liberty'; LBR 1040) (cd-iss. Oct95 on 'Beat Goes On'; BGOCD 289)

Oct 72.	(7") <50976> **NERVOUS ON THE ROAD. / HARRY DOING WHAT WE'RE DOING**		
May 73.	(7"; as The HITTERS) (UP 35530) **THE HYPOCRITE. / THE VERSION**		-
Aug 73.	(7") (UP 35588) **SPEEDO. / I WORRY**		-
Oct 73.	(lp) (UAS 29489) **PLEASE DON'T EVER CHANGE**		-

– Hooked on love / Why do we hurt the one we love? / I worry ('bout you baby) / Don't ever change / Home in my hand / Play that fast thing (one more time) / I won't make it without you / Down in Mexico / Speedo / Hypocrite (the version). (re-iss. Jan88 on 'Edsel'; ED 237) (cd-iss. Sep90; EDCD 237)

Mar 74.	(7") (UP 35642) **I'VE CRIED MY LAST TEAR. / (IT'S GONNA BE A) BRINGDOWN**		-
May 74.	(7") (UP 35700) **(WHAT'S SO FUNNY 'BOUT) PEACE, LOVE AND UNDERSTANDING. / EVER SINCE YOU'RE GONE**		-
Jul 74.	(lp) (UAS 29641) **THE NEW FAVOURITES OF BRINSLEY SCHWARZ**		-

– Peace, love and understanding / Ever since you're gone / Ugly things / I got the real thing / Look what's in your eye tonight / Now's the time / Small town, big city / Trying to live my life without you / I like you I don't love you / Down in the dive. (re-iss. Aug80 on 'Liberty'; LBR 1033)

Jan 75.	(7") (UP 35768) **I LIKE YOU, I DON'T LOVE YOU. / EVERYBODY**		-
Jan 75.	(7"; as LIMELIGHT) (UP 35779) **I SHOULD HAVE KNOWN BETTER. / TELL ME WHY**		-
Mar 75.	(7") (UP 35812) **THERE'S A CLOUD IN MY HEART. / I GOT THE REAL THING**		-

— Disbanded Mar75. SCHWARZ and RANKIN joined DUCKS DELUXE, The former latter joining with ANDREWS in GRAHAM PARKER & THE RUMOUR. IAN GOMM later went solo, as did NICK LOWE.

– compilations, others, etc. –

on 'United Artists' unless mentioned otherwise

Mar 74.	(lp) (USP 101) **ORIGINAL GOLDEN GREATS**		-
Jun 76.	(7"m) (UP 36409) **COUNTRY GIRL. / HOOKED ON LOVE / SURRENDER TO THE RHYTHM**		-
Jul 78.	(lp) (UAK 30177) **FIFTEEN THOUGHTS OF BRINSLEY SCHWARZ**		-

BRINSLEY SCHWARZ (cont)

Sep 78.	(7")	(UP 36466)	**PEACE, LOVE AND UNDERSTANDING. / I'VE CRIED MY LAST TEAR**
1978.	(7"ep; by KIPPINGTON LODGE)	E.M.I.; (NUT 2894)	**KIPPINGTON LODGE**
May 88.	(lp/c)(cd on 'Charly')	Decal; (LIK/TCLIK 22)(CDCHARLY 22)	**IT'S ALL OVER NOW**
Jul 91.	(cd/c/lp)	E.M.I.; (CD/TC+/EMS 1407)	**SURRENDER TO THE RHYTHM (THE BEST OF BRINSLEY SCHWARZ)**

– Country girl / Surrender to the rhythm / Ugly things / Happy what we're doing / The look what's in your eyes / Last time I was fooled / Silver pistol / Nightingale / Hypocrite / Trying to live my life without you / I like it like that / Nervous on the road / Down in Mexico / I worry ('bout you baby) / Play that fast thing (one more time) / Don't lose your grip on love / Ju Ju man / Down in the dive / Home in my hand. *(cd re-iss. Jun00 on 'Liberty'; 796746-2)*

Jul 94.	(cd)	Beat Goes On; (BGOCD 239)	**BRINSLEY SCHWARZ / DESPITE IT ALL**
Dec 95.	(cd)	Beat Goes On; (BGOCD 289)	**NERVOUS ON THE ROAD / THE NEW FAVOURITES OF . . .**
Apr 98.	(cd)	Edsel; (EDCD 546)	**HEN'S TEETH**
Mar 00.	(cd)	Beat Goes On; (BGOCD 476)	**ORIGINAL GOLDEN GREATS / FIFTEEN THOUGHTS OF BRINSLEY SCHWARZ**
Oct 01.	(cd)	Hux; (HUX 023)	**WHAT'S SO FUNNY 'BOUT PEACE, LOVE AND UNDERSTANDING**

Steven BROWN (see under ⇒ TUXEDOMOON)

J.J. BURNEL (see under ⇒ STRANGLERS)

JAKE BURNS & THE WHEEL (see under ⇒ STIFF LITTLE FINGERS)

BUZZCOCKS

Formed: Manchester, England . . . April 1976 by HOWARD DEVOTO and PETE SHELLEY who met at Bolton Institute Of Higher Education. Having recruited STEVE DIGGLE and JOHN MAHER, they played their first gig on the 20th of July '76 supporting the SEX PISTOLS. Early the following year, they released the first ever DIY punk "indie" 45 on 'New Hormones' in the form of the 'SPIRAL SCRATCH' EP. They then suffered a major bust up when frontman DEVOTO departed (to form MAGAZINE), although the rest carried on having signed to 'United Artists' on the strength of featuring on the now famous 'LIVE AT THE ROXY' Various artists compilation (with tracks 'Breakdown' and 'Love Battery'). By this time, SHELLEY had taken over vocal duties, while DIGGLE switched to guitar, having found a new bassist, GARTH SMITH. Early in 1978, they stormed the charts with the brooding love gem, 'WHAT DO I GET', a two-minute rush of bittersweet pop/punk angst which saw SHELLEY emerging as a strong frontman in his own right. The previous year's masturbating classic, 'ORGASM ADDICT', was too frenetic to allow SHELLEY's effeminate romance'n'roll stylings a look-in, although he blossomed on subsequent releases. A debut album, 'ANOTHER MUSIC IN A DIFFERENT KITCHEN' (1978), made the UK Top 20, while another SHELLEY-penned classic, 'EVER FALLEN IN LOVE (WITH SOMEONE YOU SHOULDN'T'VE?)', almost made the Top 10 later that year. With fervent support from Radio One DJ, John Peel, the band had squarely cornered the more accessible end of the punk market, although the 'LOVE BITES' album marked a move away from the short, sharp melodic shock which had become their trademark as songwriting duties were more democratically distributed. A final clutch of Top 30 hits, 'PROMISES' (their fifth hit in 1978), 'EVERYBODY'S HAPPY NOWADAYS' and 'HARMONY IN MY HEAD', saw the increasing influence of DIGGLE. 1979's 'A DIFFERENT KIND OF TENSION' saw SHELLEY's influence begin to dissipate and the album's mixed reviews signalled the band were running out of creative steam. After 'Liberty' took over their contract in 1980 and a further three 45's flopped, the BUZZCOCKS split, DIGGLE forming FLAG OF CONVENIENCE with MAHER. SHELLEY, meanwhile, went solo, making his debut in 1981 with the 'HOMOSAPIEN' album. Although the album made little commercial headway in Britain, the title track, bizarrely enough, topped the Australian charts. He released another two sets, 'XL-1' (1983) and 'HEAVEN AND THE SEA' (1986) to mild interest; far more newsworthy was the band's reformation in 1990 with a line-up of SHELLEY, DIGGLE, STEVE GARVEY and ex-SMITHS drummer, MIKE JOYCE. A comeback album, 'TRADE TEST TRANSMISSION' (1993) was lapped up by old punks and new converts alike, while a slightly modified line-up undertook a heartily received tour. A live set culled from the dates, 'FRENCH', was released in 1995, while a follow-up album, 'ALL SET' appeared a year later. The band's classic late 70's output remains one of the most influential bodies of work from the punk era, second only to perhaps the SEX PISTOLS. • **Covered:** HERE COMES THE NICE (Small Faces). • **Trivia:** In 1978, SHELLEY produced fun group, ALBERTO Y LOST TRIOS PARANOIAS.

Album rating: ANOTHER MUSIC IN A DIFFERENT KITCHEN (*9) / LOVE BITES (*7) / DIFFERENT KIND OF TENSION (*6) / SINGLES – GOING STEADY compilation (*9) / TRADE TEST TRANSMISSION (*5) / FRENCH (*4) / ALL SET (*5) / Pete Shelley: SKY YEN (*4) / HOMOSAPIEN (*7) / XL-1 (*5) / HEAVEN AND THE SEA (*6)

HOWARD DEVOTO (b.HOWARD TRAFFORD) – vocals / **PETE SHELLEY** (b.PETER McNEISH, 17 Apr'55) – guitar, vocals / **STEVE DIGGLE** – bass, vocals / **JOHN MAHER** – drums

New Hormones / not iss.

| Jan 77. | (7"ep) (ORG 1) | **SPIRAL SCRATCH** |

– Breakdown / Times up / Boredom / Friends of mine. *(re-iss. Aug79 credited as "BUZZCOCKS with HOWARD DEVOTO"; same); hit No.31) (re-iss. 1994 on 'Document' 12"ep/cd-ep)*

— (Mar'77) **GARTH SMITH** – bass; repl. DEVOTO who formed MAGAZINE
SHELLEY now lead vocals, guitar / DIGGLE switched to guitar, vocals

U.A. / not iss.

| Oct 77. | (7") (UP 36316) | **ORGASM ADDICT. / WHATEVER HAPPENED TO . . . ?** |

— **STEVE GARVEY** – bass repl. GARTH (on tour at first)

| Jan 78. | (7") (UP 36348) | **WHAT DO I GET?. / OH SHIT** | 37 | — |

U.A. / I.R.S.

| Mar 78. | (lp/c) (UAG/TCK 30159) | **ANOTHER MUSIC IN A DIFFERENT KITCHEN** | 15 | — |

– Fast cars / No reply / You tear me up / Get on our own / Love battery / 16 / I don't mind / Fiction romance / Autonomy / I need / Moving away from the pulsebeat. *(re-iss. Aug85 on 'Liberty' lp/c; ATAK/TC-ATAK 51) (re-iss. Jun87 on 'Fan Club' blue-lp; FC 021) (re-iss. May88 on 'Fame' lp/c/cd; FA/TC-FA/CD-FA 3199) (re-iss. cd Jul88 on 'E.M.I.'; CDP 790299-2) (cd re-iss. Jul96; PRDFCD 3) (cd re-iss. Aug01 on 'E.M.I.'+=; 534405-2)* – Orgasm addict / Whatever happened to? / What do I get / Oh shit.

Apr 78.	(7") (UP 36386)	**I DON'T MIND. / AUTONOMY**	55	—
Jul 78.	(7") (UP 36433)	**LOVE YOU MORE. / NOISE ANNOYS**	34	—
Sep 78.	(7") (UP 36455)	**EVER FALLEN IN LOVE (WITH SOMEONE YOU SHOULDN'T'VE?). / JUST LUST**	12	—
Sep 78.	(lp/c) (UAG/TCK 30197)	**LOVE BITES**	13	—

– Real world / Ever fallen in love with someone you shouldn't've / Operator's manuel / Nostalgia / Just lust / Sixteen again / Walking distance / Love is lies / Nothing left / E.S.P. / Late for the train. *(re-iss. Mar87 on 'Fame' lp/c; FA/TC-FA 3174) (re-iss. Jun87 on 'Fan Club' blue-lp; FC 022) (cd-iss. Jul88 on 'Fame'; CD-FA 3174) (cd re-iss. Jul96; PRDFCD 4) (cd re-iss. Aug01 on 'E.M.I.'+=)* – Love you more / Noise annoys / Promises / Lipstick.

Nov 78.	(7") (UP 36471)	**PROMISES. / LIPSTICK**	20	—
Mar 79.	(7") (UP 36499)	**EVERYBODY'S HAPPY NOWADAYS. / WHY CAN'T I TOUCH IT?**	29	—
Jul 79.	(7") (UP 36541)	**HARMONY IN MY HEAD. / SOMETHING'S GONE WRONG AGAIN**	32	—
Sep 79.	(7") (BP 316)	**YOU SAY YOU DON'T LOVE ME. / RAISON D'ETRE**		—
Sep 79.	(lp/c) (UAG/TCK 30260) <SP 009>	**A DIFFERENT KIND OF TENSION**	26	

– Paradise / Sitting round at home / You say you don't love me / You know you can't help it / Mad mad Judy / Raison d'etre / I don't know what to do with my life / Money / Hollow inside / A different kind of tension / I believe / Radio Nine. *(initial copies cont. previous 45) (re-iss. Jun87 on 'Fan Club' blue-lp; FC 023) (cd-iss. Jul88 on 'E.M.I.'; CZ 93)*

| Nov 79. | (lp/c) <010> | **SINGLES – GOING STEADY** (compilation) | — | |

– Orgasm addict / What do I get / I don't mind / Love you more / Ever fallen in love with someone you shouldn't've / Promises / Everybody's happy nowadays / Harmony in my head / Whatever happened to . . . ? / Oh shit! / Autonomy / Noise annoys / Just luck / Lipstick / Why can't I touch it / Something's gone wrong again. *(UK-iss.Nov81 on 'Liberty' lp/c; LBR/TC-LBR 1043) (re-iss. Aug85 lp/c; ATAK/TC-ATAK 52) (cd-iss. Jun87 + Jun88 on 'E.M.I.'; CDP 746449-2) (re-iss. Sep90 cd/c/lp; CD/TC+/FA 3241) (cd re-iss. Aug01 on 'E.M.I.'+=; 534442-2)* – (extra tracks).

Liberty / I.R.S.

Feb 80.	(7") <IR 9010>	**I BELIEVE. / SOMETHING'S GONE WRONG AGAIN**	—	
Aug 80.	(7") (BP 365)	**WHY SHE'S A GIRL FROM THE CHAINSTORE. / ARE EVERYTHING**	61	—
Oct 80.	(7") (BP 371)	**STRANGE THING. / AIRWAVES DREAM**		—
Nov 80.	(7") (BP 392)	**RUNNING FREE. / WHAT DO YOU KNOW**		—

— (split Feb'81) DIGGLE went solo and formed FLAG OF CONVENIENCE, with MAHER

PETE SHELLEY

— augmented by **STEVE GARVEY** – bass / **JIM RUSSELL** – drums

Genetic-Island / Arista

| Aug 81. | (7"/12") (WIP/12WIP 6720) | **HOMOSAPIEN. / KEAT'S SONG** | | — |
| Sep 81. | (lp/c) (ILPS/ICT 9676) | **HOMOSAPIEN** | | Jun82 |

– Homosapien / Yesterday's here / I generate a feeling / Keat's song / Qu'est-ce que c'est que ca / I don't know what it is / Guess I must have been in love with myself / Pusher man / Just one of those affairs / It's hard enough knowing. *(re-iss. cd Sep94 on 'Grapevine'; GRACD 201) (cd re-iss. May98 on 'Razor & Tie'; RE 2126)*

| Nov 81. | (d7"/12") (U/12 WIP 6740) | **I DON'T KNOW WHAT IT IS. / WITNESS THE CHANGE/ / IN LOVE WITH SOMEBODY ELSE. / MAXINE** | | — |
| Apr 82. | (7"/12") (WIP/12WIP 6720) | **HOMOSAPIEN. / LOVE IN VAIN** | | — |

— **BARRY ADAMSON** – bass (ex-MAGAZINE, ex-BIRTHDAY PARTY) repl. GARVEY / added **MARTIN RUSHENT** – keyboards, producer

Island / Arista

| Feb 83. | (7"/12") (XX/+T 1) | **TELEPHONE OPERATOR. / MANY A TIME** | 66 | — |
| Apr 83. | (lp) (XL 1) | **XL-1** | 42 | Jul83 |

– Telephone operator / If you ask me (I won't say no) / What was Heaven? / You better than I know / Twilight / (Millions of people) No one like you / Many a time / I just wanna touch / You and I / XL-1 *. (c+= dub tracks) (track* = only playable on ZX Spectrum computer) *(re-iss. cd Sep94 on 'Grapevine'; GRACD 202)*

Immaculate / not iss.

| Nov 84. | (7") (IMMAC 1) | **NEVER AGAIN. / ONE ONE ONE** | | — |

(12"+=) (12IMMAC 1) – Give it to me.

— SHELLEY brought in new **JOHN DOYLE** – drums / **MARK SANDERSON** – bass /

BUZZCOCKS (cont)

NORMAN FISCHER-JONES – guitar / GERARD COOKSON – keyboards / JIM GARDNER – synth.

Mercury | Mercury

Mar 86. (7"/12") (MER/+X 215) **WAITING FOR LOVE. / DESIGNER LAMPS**
May 86. (7"/12") (MER/+X 221) **ON YOUR OWN. / PLEASE FORGIVE ME . . . BUT I CANNOT ENDURE IT ANY LONGER**
Jun 86. (lp/c)(cd) (MERH/+C 90)(830004-2) **HEAVEN AND THE SEA**
– Never again / My dreams / Blue eyes / You can't take that away / No Moon . . . / Waiting for love / On your own / They're coming for you / I surrender / Life without reason / Need a minit.
Aug 86. (7"/12") (MER/+X 225) **BLUE EYES. / NELSON'S RIDDLE**
Nov 86. (7"/12") (MER/+X 234) **I SURRENDER. / I NEED A MINUTE**

—— In 1988, SHELLEY formed ZIP with COOKSON and SANDERSON.

– his compilations, others, etc. –

Apr 80. (m-lp) Groovy; (STP 2) **SKY YEN** (rec.1974)
Apr 89. (7"/12") Immaculate; (IMMAC/12IMMAC 11) **HOMOSAPIEN. PETE SHELLEY VS. POWER, WONDER AND LOVE / ('A'mix)**
(3"cd-s+=) (IMMACD 11) – ('A'-Icon mix) / ('A'-shower mix).

STEVE DIGGLE

Liberty | not iss.

Feb 81. (7"m) (BP 389) **SHUT OUT THE LIGHTS. / 50 YEARS OF COMPARATIVE WEALTH / HERE COMES THE FIRE BRIGADE**

FLAG OF CONVENIENCE

were formed by DIGGLE, MAHER + DAVE FARROW – bass / D.P. – keyboards

Sire | not iss.

Sep 82. (7") (SIR 4057) **LIFE ON THE TELEPHONE. / THE OTHER MAN'S SIN**

—— DIGGLE, MAHER + GARY HAMER – bass / MARK – keyboards

Weird Systems | not iss.

Dec 84. (7") **CHANGE. / LONGEST LIFE**

—— JOHN CAINE – drums repl. MAHER and MARK

M.C.M. | not iss.

Apr 86. (7") (MCM 186) **NEW HOUSE. / KEEP ON PUSHING**

Flag of Convenience | not iss.

Apr 87. (12") (FOC 1) **LAST TRAIN TO SAFETY. / ?**

M.C.M. | not iss.

Oct 87. (12"ep; as F.O.C.) (MCM 001) **SHOULD I EVER GO DEAF / PICTURES IN MY MIND. / THE GREATEST SIN / DROWNED IN YOUR HEARTACHES**
Aug 88. (12"ep; as F.O.C.) (MCM 002) **EXILES / I CAN'T STOP THE WORLD. / SHOT DOWN WITH YOUR GUN / TRAGEDY IN MARKET SQUARE**

BUZZCOCKS F.O.C.

—— DIGGLE, HAMMER + ANDY COUZENS – guitar / CHRIS GOODWIN – drums

Thin Line | not iss.

Jul 89. (12"/cd-s) (THIN 003/+CD) **TOMORROW'S SUNSET. / LIFE WITH THE LIONS / ('A'version)**

BUZZCOCKS

—— re-formed in 1990 SHELLEY, DIGGLE, GARVEY and MIKE JOYCE – drums (ex-SMITHS) repl. ANDY and CHRIS who formed The HIGH

Planet Pacific | not iss.

Apr 91. (7"ep/12"ep/c-ep/cd-ep) **ALIVE TONIGHT**
– Alive tonight / Successful street / Serious crime / Last to know.

—— JOHN MAHER – drums returned to repl. MIKE who joined PIL.
—— TONY BARBER – bass / PHIL BARKER – drums repl.GARVEY and MAHER

Essential | Caroline

May 93. (7") (ESS 2025) **INNOCENT. / WHO'LL HELP ME TO FORGET**
(12"+=/cd-s+=) (ESS T/X 2025) – Inside.
Jun 93. (cd/c/lp) (ESM CD/MC/LP 389) <1747> **TRADE TEST TRANSMISSION**
– Innocent / Smile / Palm of your hand / Last to know / Do it/ Who will help me to forget / Energy / Alive tonight / Inside / Isolation / Never gonna give it up / Crystal night / 369 / Chegga / It's unthinkable / Somewhere. (reiss.cd Jul96; same)
Aug 93. (12"/cd-s) (ESS T/X 2031) **DO IT. / TRASH AWAY / ALL OVER YOU**
Apr 94. (12"/cd-s) **LIBERTINE ANGEL. / ROLL IT OVER / EXCERPT FROM PRISON RIOT HOSTAGE**

Dojo | I.R.S.

Nov 95. (cd) (DOJOCD 237) <36761> **FRENCH (live in Paris 12th April 1995)** Jan96
– I don't mind / Who'll help me to forget / Get on our own / Unthinkable / Strange thing / Energy / Breakdown / Innocent / Roll it over / Why she's a girl from the chainstore / Last to know? / Running free / Libertine angel / Why can't I touch it / Noise annoys / Isolation / Boredom / Do it / Harmony in my head / I believe.

I.R.S. | I.R.S.

Apr 96. (cd) (EIRSCD 1078) <36962> **ALL SET**
– Totally from the heart / Without you / Give it to me / Your love / Point of no return / Hold me close / Kiss & tell / What am I supposed to do? / Some kind of wonderful / (What you) Mean to me / Playing for time / Pariah / Back with you.

– compilations, others, etc. –

Apr 87. (lp/c) Weird Systems; (WS 021/+X1) **TOTAL POP**
Jan 88. (12"ep) Strange Fruit; (SFPS 044) **THE PEEL SESSIONS (7.9.77)**
– Fast cars / What do I get / Moving away from the pulsebeat.
Oct 88. (c) R.O.I.R.; (A 158) **LEST WE FORGET (live)**
(cd-iss. Nov94; RE 158CD)
Sep 89. (lp/cd) Absolutely Free; (FREE LP/CD 002) **LIVE AT THE ROXY CLUB, 2 APRIL 1977 (live)**
(cd+=) – (1 extra track). (re-iss. Jul90 & Jul93 on 'Receiver'; RR CD/LC/LP 131)
Oct 89. (7"ep/12"ep/cd-ep) E.M.I.; (EM/12EM/CDEM 104) **THE FAB FOUR**
– Ever fallen in love with someone you shouldn't've / Promises / Everybody's happy nowadays / Harmony in my head.
Nov 89. (4xlp/2xd-c/2xd-cd) E.M.I.; (LP/TC/CD PROD 1) **PRODUCT**
– (cont. first 3 albums + 1 live and rare) (re-iss. May95 cd; PRODUCT 1)
Feb 90. (cd/lp) Strange Fruit; (SFR CD/LP 104) **THE PEEL SESSIONS ALBUM**
Sep 91. (cd/c/d-lp) E.M.I.; (CD/TC+/EM 1421) **OPERATOR'S MANUAL (BUZZCOCKS BEST)**
May 92. (cd) EMI Gold; (CDGOLD 1029) **ENTERTAINING FRIENDS LIVE AT THE HAMMERSMITH ODEON – MARCH 1979 (live)**
Oct 92. (cd-s) Old Gold; (OG 6182) **EVER FALLEN IN LOVE WITH SOMEONE . . . / WHAT DO I GET / PROMISES**
Apr 94. (cd) E.M.I.; (CDPRDT 12) **ANOTHER MUSIC IN A DIFFERENT KITCHEN / LOVE BITES**
1995. (7") One Stop Music; (ONE 7001) **NOISE ANNOYS. / ISOLATION (live)**
Jul 95. (cd) Dojo; (DLP 2) **TIME'S UP**
(re-iss. Mar00 on 'The Grey Area'; SCRATCH 2/+CD)
Nov 95. (cd-s) Old Gold; (12623 6332-2) **EVER FALLEN IN LOVE WITH SOMEONE YOU SHOULDN'T HAVE FALLEN IN LOVE WITH / PROMISES**
Jun 97. (cd) EMI Gold; (CDGOLD 2073) **CHRONOLOGY**
Sep 97. (cd) EMI Gold; (CDGOLD 1093) **I DON'T MIND**
Oct 98. (cd) E.M.I.; (497771-2) **THE BBC SESSIONS**
Jun 99. (cd) Almafame; (YEAAH 1) **PARIS ENCORE DU PAIN**
Sep 99. (d-cd) E.M.I.; (521767-2) **MODERN / A DIFFERENT KIND**
Mar 00. (lp/cd) Go Kart; (GK 058/+CD) **MODERN**
Jul 00. (d-cd) Burning Airlines; (PILOT 078) **BEATING HEARTS (LIVE IN MANCHESTER 1978)**
(d-lp-iss.Feb01 on 'Get Back'; GET 74)
Jul 01. (cd) Castle Pie; (PIESD 259) **LIVE IN PARIS (live)**
Sep 01. (d-lp) Get Back; (GET 80) **SMALL SONGS WITH BIG HEARTS**
Nov 01. (cd) Dressed To Kill; (MIDRO 805) **ORGASM ADDICTS**
Apr 02. (cd) EMI Gold; (538464-2) **FINEST (EVER FALLEN IN LOVE)**
Jun 02. (cd) N.M.C.; (SJLTD 01) **NOISE ANNOYS – MANCHESTER APOLLO 1978 (live)**
Jun 02. (cd) N.M.C.; (SJLTD 02) **LIVE TENSION – RAINBOW THEATRE, LONDON, 09/11/79)**
Jul 02. (lp) Get Back; (GET 92) **FAST CARS**

STEVE DIGGLE & THE FLAG OF CONVENIENCE

3:30 | not iss.

Nov 93. (cd-ep) (330001) **HEATED AND RISING / OVER AND OUT / TERMINAL / WEDNESDAYS FLOWERS**

Ax-s | not iss.

Oct 95. (cd) (AXSO 2CD) **HERE'S ONE I MADE EARLIER**

3.30 | not iss.

Apr 01. (cd) (DIGGLECD 001) **SOME REALITY**

– compilations, etc. –

Feb 94. (cd) Anagram; (CDMGRAM 74) **THE BEST OF . . . THE SECRET PUBLIC YEARS 1981-1989**
(re-iss. Aug00; same)

THE GREAT INDIE DISCOGRAPHY — The 1970s

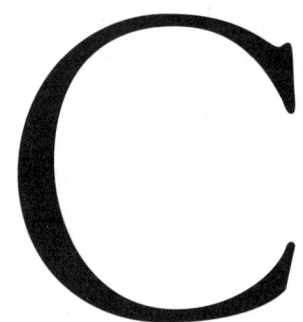

CABARET VOLTAIRE

Formed: Sheffield, England ... 1973 by STEPHEN MALLINDER, RICHARD H. KIRK and CHRIS WATSON, naming themselves after the experimental Parisian Dadaist performances of pre-20's France. A farcical 1975 debut gig saw them using a backing tape of a steamhammer while KIRK played clarinet; his jacket was also covered in fairy lights (!), the whole set up not going down with a rioting audience who proceeded to beat him up! Inspired by the likes of CAN and BRIAN ENO, the CABS contributed two songs (one of them, 'BAADER MEINHOF', was nearly chosen as a debut 45!) to a 1978 various artists double EP, 'A FACTORY SAMPLER', before they signed to Geoff Travis's new independent operation, 'Rough Trade'. Later that year, the trio issued their debut release, 'EXTENDED PLAY', a four track EP that included their industrial mangling of The Velvet Underground's 'HERE SHE COMES NOW'. A classic follow-up, 'NAG NAG NAG', fused electronic sound with the yobbish rush of adrenaline-fuelled punk to devastating effect. 1979 also saw the release of their debut long-player, 'MIX-UP', a pivotal experimental affair which, although marking out new territory, was a challenging listen end to end. The early years of the following decade found CABARET VOLTAIRE ploughing their own idiosyncratic furrow over the course of three studio albums (two live events were also issued), namely 'THE VOICE OF AMERICA' (1980), 'RED MECCA' (1981) and '2 X 45' (1982), before WATSON's departure left MALLINDER and KIRK as a duo. In 1983, they were sought out by Virgin off-shoot, 'Some Bizzare', their avant-garde inaccessibility now taking on a more commercial hue with 'THE CRACKDOWN', an album which nearly took them into the UK Top 30. Incorporating elements of Eastern exotica, the record was also more dancefloor friendly than anything they had recorded to date; tracks such as 'JUST FASCINATION', '24-24', 'ANIMATION' and 'WHY KILL TIME (WHEN YOU CAN KILL YOURSELF)', were lent the rhythmic expertise of SOFT CELL's DAVE BALL (later of The GRID). Ironically, the more overtly pop approach of SOFT CELL and their ilk (DEPECHE MODE, HUMAN LEAGUE and OMD) led to the more adventurous CABS being squeezed out of the market. They did, however, maintain a loyal if not massive following who stuck by them through a series of lesser mid-80's albums, 'MICRO-PHONIES' (1984), 'THE COVENANT, THE SWORD AND THE ARM OF THE LORD' (1985) and 'CODE' (1987), the latter set their first for 'Parlophone'. Since 1983, both MALLINDER and KIRK had moonlighted in various side projects, the former releasing a solo album, 'POW-WOW', the latter far more prolific in his output with 'BLACK JESUS VOICE' (1986) the pick of the bunch. The late 80's house scene, meanwhile, saw CABARET VOLTAIRE cited as a prominent influence on many of the genre's prime movers; the result was a creative renaissance of sorts which led to a remix by PETE WATERMAN (!) for the 'KEEP ON' single, while house producer, MARSHALL JEFFERSON, took controls on the comeback set, 'GROOVY, LAID BACK AND NASTY' (1990). Despite this uncharacteristic dalliance with the mainstream, the CABS slipped back into semi-obscurity with their former Belgian label, 'Les Disques Du Crepescule' releasing a handful of low profile sets, 'BODY AND SOUL' (1991), 'PERCUSSION FORCE' (1991), 'INTERNATIONAL LANGUAGE' (1993) and 'THE CONVERSATION' (1994).

Album rating: MIX-UP (*5) / THE VOICE OF AMERICA (*4) / RED MECCA (*7) / 2x45 (*7) / JOHNNY YES NO soundtrack (*3) / THE CRACKDOWN (*8) / MICRO-PHONIES (*6) / DRINKING GASOLINE (*6) / THE COVENANT, THE SWORD & THE ARM (*6) / CODE (*7) / GROOVY, LAIDBACK & NASTY (*6) / THE LIVING LEGENDS compilation (*9) / THE GOLDEN MOMENTS OF CABARET VOLTAIRE compilation (*7) / LISTEN UP WITH CABARET VOLTAIRE compilation (*7) / COLOURS (*5) / PLASTICITY (*5) / Stephen Mallinder: POW WOW (*6) / Richard H. Kirk: BLACK JESUS VOICE (*6)

STEPHEN MALLINDER – vocals, bass, electronics, percussion, trumpet, piano / **RICHARD H. KIRK** – guitar, vocals, synthesizer, bongos, piano / **CHRISTOPHER R. WATSON** – electronics, tapes
 (issued cassette 25 copies LIMITED EDITION in 1976 on own label)

Rough Trade   not iss.

- Nov 78. (7"ep) (RT 003) **EXTENDED PLAY**
  – Talkover / Here she comes now / Do the Mussolini – headkick / The set up.
- Jun 79. (7") (RT 018) **"NAG NAG NAG." / IS THAT ME (FINDING SOMEONE AT THE DOOR AGAIN)?**
- Oct 79. (lp) (ROUGH 4) **MIX-UP**
  – Kurlian photograph / No escape / 4th shot / Heaven and Hell / Eyeless sight (live) / Photophobia / On every other street / Expect nothing / Capsules. (re-iss. Sep90 on 'Mute' lp/cd; CABS 8/+CD)
- Dec 79. (7") (RT 035) **SILENT COMMAND. / The Soundtrack 'CHANCE VERSUS CAUSALITY'**
- — added guest **MARK TATTERSALL** – drums
- Jan 80. (lp) (ROUGH 7) **LIVE AT THE Y.M.C.A. 27.10.79 (live)**
  – Untitled / On every other street / Nag nag nag / The set up / Havoc / Expect nothing / Here she comes now / No escape / Baader Meinhof. (re-iss. Jun90 on 'Mute' lp/cd; CABS 4/+CD)
- — now with guests **JOHN CLAYTON** – percussion / **JANE** – tapes
- Mar 80. (12"ep) (RT 038) **THREE MANTRAS**
  – Eastern mantra / Western mantra. (re-iss. Jun90 on 'Mute' m-lp/cd; CABS 7/+CD)
- — with guest **HAYDN BOYES-WESTON** – drums (ex-2.3) (also on debut lp)
- Jul 80. (lp) (ROUGH 11) **THE VOICE OF AMERICA**
  – The voice of America / Damage is done / Partially submerged / Kneel to the boss / Premonition / Black mask / This is entertainment / If the shadows could march? / Stay out of it / Obsession / News from nowhere / Messages received. (re-iss. Jun90 on 'Mute' lp/cd; CABS 2/+CD)
- Nov 80. (7") (RT 060) **SECONDS TOO LATE. / CONTROL ADDICT**
- Jul 81. (12"ep) (TWI 018) **3 CREPUSCULE TRACKS**   – Belg.
  – Sluggin' fer Jesus (Pt.1) / Your agent man / Sluggin' fer Jesus (Pt.2). (above released on 'Crepuscule')
- — **NICK ALLDAY** – drums (ex-GRAPH) repl. HAYDN
- Aug 81. (lp) (ROUGH 27) **RED MECCA**
  – Touch of evil / Sly doubt / Landslide / A thousand ways / Red mask / Split second feling / Black mask / Spread the virus / A touch of evil (reprise). (re-iss. Jun90 on 'Mute' lp/cd; CABS 3/+CD)
- Sep 81. (lp) (COPY 002) **LIVE AT THE LYCEUM (live)**
  – Taxi music / Seconds too late / Your agent man / Split second feeling / Sluggin' fer Jesus (Pt.1) / Kneel to the bass / Obsession / A thousand ways. (re-iss. Sep90 on 'Mute' lp/cd; CABS 13/+CD)
- Nov 81. (7") (RT 095) **JAZZ THE GLASS. / BURNT TO THE GROUND**
- Dec 81. (12") (RT 096) **EDDIE'S OUT. / WALLS OF JERICHO**
  (limited copies contained last 7" free) (below on 'Solidarity')
- Mar 82. (12"ep; by PRESSURE COMPANY) (SOLID 1) **LIVE IN SHEFFIELD 19th JANUARY 1982 (live)**
  – War of nerves / Wait & shuffle / Get out of my face / Vitrions China (paradox).
- — **ALAN FISH** – drums, percussion (of HULA) repl. ALLDAY / guest **ERIC RANDOM** – guitar (also a solo artist)
- Jun 82. (2x12"lp) (ROUGH 42) **2 x 45**   98
  – Breathe deep / Yashar / Protection / War of nerves (T.E.S.) / Wait and shuffle / Get out of my face. (re-iss. Sep90 on 'Mute' lp/cd; CABS 9/+CD)
- Nov 82. (lp) (RTD 7) **HAI! (live)**   – German
  – Walls of Kyoto / 3 days monk / Yashar (version) / Over and over / Diskono / Taxi music (version). (re-iss. Sep90 on 'Mute' lp/cd; CABS 11/+CD)
- — trimmed to a duo (**MALLINDER + KIRK**) when WATSON departed. Retained **ALAN FISH** and brought in **DAVE BALL** – keyboards (of SOFT CELL)
- Feb 83. (12") (TWI 020) **FOOLS GAME (SLUGGIN' FER JESUS Pt.3). / GUT LEVEL**   – Belg.
  (above released on 'Crepuscule')

Some Bizzare – Virgin   not iss.

- Jul 83. (7") (CVS 1) **JUST FASCINATION. / EMPTY WALLS**
  (12") (CVS 1-12) – ('A'side) / The crackdown.
- Aug 83. (lp/c) (CV/TCV 1) **THE CRACKDOWN**   31
  – 24-24 / In the shadows / Talking time / Animation / Over and over / Just fascination / Why kill time (when you can kill yourself) / Haiti / Crackdown. (free 12"w/ above + on c+cd) – MOSCOW / BADGE OF EVIL / DISKONO / DOUBLE VISION (cd-iss. 1984; CDCV 1) (re-iss. Aug86 lp/c; OVED/+C 156)
- Nov 83. (lp) (DVR 1) **JOHNNY YESNO** (1982 video)
  – Taxi music / Hallucination sequence / DT's / Cold turkey / The quarry (in the wilderness) / Title sequence / Taxi music dub. (re-iss. Sep90 on 'Mute' lp/cd; CABS 10/+CD)
  (above released on 'DoubleVision')
- Dec 83. (7"/ext.12") (CVS 2/+12) **THE DREAM TICKET. / SAFETY ZONE**
- Sep 84. (7"/ext.12") (CVS 3/+12) **SENSORIA. / CUT THE DAMN CAMERA**
- Nov 84. (lp/c/cd) (CV/TCV/CVCD 2) **MICRO-PHONIES**   69
  – Do right / The operative / Digital rasta / Spies in the wires / Theme from Earthshaker / James Brown / Slammer / Blue heat / Sensoria. (cd+=) – Blue heat (extended) / Sensoria (extended). (re-iss. Sep91 on 'Virgin'; cd/c; same)
- Jan 85. (7"/12") (CVS 4/+12) **JAMES BROWN. / BAD SELF (part 1)**
- Jun 85. (2x12"/c) (CVM/TCVM 1) **DRINKING GASOLINE**   71
  – Kino / Sleepwalking / Big funk / Ghost talk. (re-iss. Sep91 on 'Virgin'; same)
- Sep 85. (7") (CVS 5) **I WANT YOU. / DRINK YOUR POISON**
  (12") (CVS 5-12) – ('A'side) / Drink your poison, C.O.M.A.
- Oct 85. (lp/c/cd) (CV/TCV/CDCV 3) **THE COVENANT, THE SWORD AND THE ARM OF THE LORD**   57
  – L21st / I want you / Hell's home / Kickback / The arm of the Lord / Warm / Golden halos / Motion rotation / Whip blow / The web. (cd+=) – Sleepwalking / Big funk (re-iss. Sep91 on 'Virgin'; same)
- — guest **DEE BOYLE** – drums (of CHAAK) repl. FISH

DoubleVision   not iss.

- Jun 86. (12"ep) (DVR-DVRP 21) **THE DRAIN TRAIN**
  – Shakedown (the whole thing) / Menace / Electro-motive.
  (w/ free-12") – SHAKEDOWN (The Whole Thing). / SHAKEDOWN (dub).

Parlophone   Manhattan

- Jul 87. (7") (R 6157) **DON'T ARGUE. / DON'T ARGUE (WHO'S ARGUING)**   69
  (12") (12R 6157) – ('A'extended) / ('A'-Hate & Destroy mix).
  (12") (12RX 6157) – ('A'dance mix) / ('A'dub).
- Sep 87. (7") (R 6166) **HERE TO GO. / HERE TO GO (dub)**
  (12") (12R 6166) – ('A'extended mix) / ('A'-Space dub mix).
  (12") (12RX 6166) – ('A'-Linn drum mix) / ('A'-Eleven Eleven mix).
- Oct 87. (lp/c/cd) (PCS/TCPCS/CDPCS 7312) <46999> **CODE**
  – Don't argue / Sex, money, freaks / Thank you America / Here to go / Trouble (won't stop) / White car / No one here / Life slips by / Code. (cd+=) – Here to go (little dub) / Hey hey.

CABARET VOLTAIRE (cont)

Oct 89. (7") *(RS 6227)* **HYPNOTISED (Daniel Miller mix). / ('A'-Gerald's vocal mix)** `66` `-`
(12") *(12RS 6227)* – ('A'-Fon Force mix) / ('A'-Fon Force dub) / ('A'-Daniel Miller dub mix) / ('A'-Robert Gordon mix).
(cd-s) *(CDCDR 6227)* – ('A'-Fon Force mix) / ('A'-Gerald's vocal mix).
(12") *(12RX 6227)* – (cd tracks) / ('A'-A Guy Called Gerald's music mix) / ('A'-Western Works mix).

Mar 90. (7") *(R 6250)* **KEEP ON. / KEEP ON (Les dub)** `55` `-`
(12") *(12R 6250)* – ('A'-Sweet Exorcist mix) / ('A'-Sleazy Dog mix) / ('A'-Mayday mix).
(cd-s) – ('A'-western works mix) / ('A'club mix).

Jun 90. (cd/c/lp) *(CD/TC+/PCS 7338)* <92249> **GROOVY, LAIDBACK AND NASTY**
– Searchin' / Hypnotised / Minute by minute / Runaway / Keep on (I got this feeling) / Magic / Time beats / Easy life. *(free 12"ep w/above)* **GROOVY, LAIDBACK AND NASTY** (remixes) – Runaway / Magic / Searchin' / Rescue me (city lights) * / Easy life. *(cd+= *)*

Jul 90. (7") *(R 6261)* **EASY LIFE. / ('A'-Robert Gordon mix)** `61` `-`
(12") *(12R 6261)* – ('A'side) / Fluid / Positive I.D.
(cd-s) *(CDR 6261)* – ('A'side) / ('A'-Jive Turkey mix) / Fluid.
(12") *(12RX 6261)* – ('A'vocal) / ('A'-Strange mix) / ('A'-Very strange mixes by Robert Gordon and Fon Force).

Crepescule   not iss.
Feb 91. (12") *(TWI 948)* **WHAT IS REAL. / ('A'-Virtual reality mix)**
(cd-s+=) *(TWI 948-2)* – Legacy of a computer.

Mar 91. (lp/cd) *(TWI 944/+2)* **BODY AND SOUL**
– No resistance / Shout / Happy / Decoy / Bad chemistry / Vibration / What is real / Western land. *(cd+=)* – What is real (dreamtime mix).

Jul 91. (m-lp/cd) *(TWI 951/+2)* **PERCUSSION FORCE**
– Don't walk away / Keep on pushin' / Don't walk away (Robert Gordon mix) / Dynamic zone / Jazz the computer (part 1) / Keep on pushin' (version). *(cd+=)* – T.Phunk / Don't walk away (version) / Jazz the computer part 2.

Plastex   Instinct
Oct 91. (m-lp) *(EXL 001)* <93> **COLOURS**
– Colours (original style mix) / Alright / Smooth / Colours (thunder mix) / Wildlife / Colours (club mix) / Ex.

Oct 92. (lp/c/cd) *(EXL/+C/CD 003)* <255> **PLASTICITY**
– Low cool / Soul vine (70 billion people) / Resonator / Inside the electronic revolution / From another source / Deep time / Back to Brazilia / Neuron factory / Delmas 19 / Cooled out / Invisible generation / Soulenoid (scream at the right time). *(cd re-iss. Mar96 on 'Crepescule'; TWI 975-2)*

Jun 93. (cd) *(EXLCD 004)* <264> **INTERNATIONAL LANGUAGE**
– Everything is true / Radical chic / Taxi mutant / Let it come down / Afterglow / The rest / Millenium / Belly of the beast (back in Babylon) / Other world.

Apollo-R&S   Instinct
Jul 94. (q-lp/d-cd) *(AMB 4934/+CD)* <273> **THE CONVERSATION**
– Exterminating angel (intro) / Brutal but clean / The message / Let's start / Night rider / Night rider / I think / The heat / Harmonic parallel / Project 80 (parts 1-4) / Exterminating angel (outro).

—— disbanded soon after above

– compilations, others, etc. –

1981. (c) *Industrial; (IRC 35)* **74-76**
(cd-iss. Jun92 on 'Grey Area-Mute'; CABS 15CD)

Feb 88. (lp/cd) *Crepescule; (TWI 749/+2)* **8 CREPESCULE TRACKS** `-` `-` Belgium
(cd re-iss. Mar96; same)

Jul 83. (12") *Factory Benelux; (FBN 25)* **YASHAR (5.00). / YASHAR (7.20)** `-` `-` Belgium

Nov 87. (cd) *Rough Trade; (RUFCD 6001)* **THE GOLDEN MOMENTS OF CABARET VOLTAIRE**
– Do the Mussolini (Head Kick) / Nag nag nag / Photophobia / Expect nothing / Seconds Too late / This is entertainment / Obsession / Sluggin for Jesus / Landslide / Red mask / Get out of my face.
(below releases on 'Mute' unless otherwise mentioned)

May 90. (cd-ep) *(CABS 1CD)* **"NAG NAG NAG." / YASHAR / YASHAR (John Robie remixes)**

Jun 90. (lp/c/cd) *(CABS 5/+C/CD)* **LISTEN UP WITH CABARET VOLTAIRE** (rare demos)

Jun 90. (d-lp/c/cd) *(CABS 6/+C/CD)* **THE LIVING LEGENDS... CABARET VOLTAIRE** (the singles)
– Do the Mussolini (head kick) / Talk over / Here she comes now / The set up / Nag, nag, nag / Silent command / Jazz the glass / Walls of Jericho / Seconds too late / Eddie's out / Burnt to the ground / Extract from : Chance Verses Casuality / Control addict / Is that me (finding someone at the door again).

Jun 90. (c) *(CABS 2C)* **LIVE AT THE LYCEUM / THE VOICE OF AMERICA**
Jun 90. (c) *(CABS 7C)* **THE DRAIN TRAIN / THREE MANTRAS**
Jun 90. (c) *(CABS 8C)* **MIX-UP / LIVE AT THE Y.M.C.A.**
Jun 90. (c) *(CABS 10C)* **2 x 45 / JOHNNY YESNO**
Jun 90. (c) *(CABS 11C)* **HAI! / RED MECCA**

Apr 92. (12"ep/cd-ep) *Virgin; (CVT 5)* **I WANT YOU hardcore hell) / KINO 4. / I WANT YOU (808 heaven mix) / KINO 5**
– (Altern 8 remixes / Western re-works '92)

May 92. (d-lp/c)(cd) *Virgin; (CV/+D 7)(TCV 4)* **TECHNOLOGY** (remixes late 70's & early 80's)

Oct 00. (cd) *Burning Airlines; (PILOT 039)* **RADIATION (BBC SESSIONS)**
(lp-iss.Sep01 on 'Get Back'; GET 82)

Apr 01. (cd) *E.M.I.; (532573-2)* **REMIXED**
Nov 01. (3xcd-box) *Virgin; (CVBOX 1)* **CONFORM TO DEFORM – THE VIRGIN YEARS**
Dec 01. (cd) *Virgin; (CVCD 5)* **THE ORIGINAL SOUND OF SHEFFIELD – THE BEST OF THE VIRGIN/EMI YEARS**

Oct 02. (12") *Nova Mute; (12NOMU 103)* **NAG NAG NAG. / NAG NAG NAG (R.H. Kirk 4 remix)**
(12") *(L12NOMU 103)* – ('A'-Tiga & Zyntherius radio version) / ('A'-Akufen's karaoke slam mix).
(cd-s) *CDNOMU 103)* – (all of the above).

Oct 02. (cd) *The Grey Area; (CABS 16CD)* **THE ORIGINAL SOUND OF SHEFFIELD – THE BEST OF CABARET VOLTAIRE 1978-1982**
– Do the Mussolini (headkick) / Set up / Baader Meinhof / Nag nag nag / Silent command / No escape / This is entertainment /Obsession / Seconds too late / Split second feeling / Spread the virus / Yashar / Wait and shuffle / Loosen the clamp.

STEPHEN MALLINDER

Fetish   not iss.
Nov 81. (12") *(FE 12)* **TEMPERATURE DROP. / COOL DOWN**
(above with DAVE BALL and ROBERT GORDON)

Jan 83. (m-lp) *(FM 2010)* **POW-WOW**
– Temperature Drop / The Devil In Me / 0.58 / Pow Wow / Three Piece Swing / Cool Down / 1.37 / In Smoke / 1.59 / Length Of Time / Going Out / Del Sol / *(re-iss. Oct85 as 'POW-WOW PLUS' on 'DoubleVision'; DVR 16) (cd-iss. Jun92 on 'Grey Area-Mute'; MAL 1CD)*

Parlophone   not iss.
Jun 88. (7"/12"; as LOVE STREET) *(R/12R 6183)* **GALAXY. / COME ON DOWN TO LOVE STREET**

—— LOVE STREET also included DAVE BALL + RUTH JOY (of SOFT CELL)

RICHARD H. KIRK

Industrial   not iss.
1981. (c) *(IRC 34)* **DISPOSABLE HALF-TRUTHS**
– Synesthesia / Outburst / Information therapy / Magic words command / Thermal damage / Plate glass replicas / Insect friends of Allah / Scatalist / False erotic love / L.D. 50 / L.D. 60 / Amnesic disassociation. *(cd-iss. Jun92 on 'Grey Area-Mute'; KIRK 1CD)*

DoubleVision   not iss.
Dec 83. (d-lp) *(DVR 2)* **TIME HIGH FICTION**
– Shaking down the tower of Babel / Force of habit / Day of waiting / Black honeymoon / Nocturnal children / Wiretrap / The power of autosuggestion / Dead relatives (part one) / Dead relatives (part two) / The greedy eye. *(d-cd-iss. Oct94 on 'Grey Area-Mute'; KIRK 2CD)*

Oct 85. (12"; by PETER HOPE & RICHARD H. KIRK) *(DVR 15)* **LEATHER HANDS (master mix). / ('A'radio mix) / ('A'crash mix)**
(above featured PETER HOPE of The BOX)

Rough Trade   not iss.
Aug 86. (12") *(RTT 199)* **HIPNOTIC. / MARTYRS OF PALESTINE**
Sep 86. (lp) *(ROUGH 99)* **BLACK JESUS VOICE**
– Street gang / Hipnotic / Shala / Black Jesus voice / Martyrs of Palestine / This is the H-bomb sound / Short wave. *(cd-iss. Mar95 on 'Grey Area-Mute'; KIRK 3CD)*

Oct 86. (m-lp) *(RTM 189)* **UGLY SPIRIT**
– The emperor / Confession / Infantile / Frantic machine (part 1 & 2) / Hollywood Babylon / Thai voodoo. *(cassette re-iss. Nov86 of all Sep86 releases) (cd-iss. Mar95 on 'Grey Area-Mute'; KIRK 4CD)*

Native   not iss.
Nov 87. (lp/cd; by RICHARD H. KIRK & PETER HOPE) *(NTV LP/CD 28)* **HOODOO TALK**
– Intro / Numb skull / N.O. / Cop out / Surgeons / 50 tears / Leather hands / 50 tears (reprise). *(cd re-iss. Aug00 on 'Grey Area'+=; KIRK 5CD)* – Sugar can you feel the drums / Upbeat / Leather hands (12"mix) / Leather hands (crash mix).

Nov 88. (12"ep; by PETER HOPE & RICHARD H. KIRK) *(NTV 36)* **SURGEONS / BEATS. / RESURGENCY / N.O.**

—— SWEET EXORCIST were RICHARD H. KIRK & DJ BARRETT

Warp   not iss.
Feb 90. (12"ep; as SWEET EXORCIST) *(WAP 3)* **TEST ONE**
– Test 1 / Test 2 / Test 3.
(12"ep+=) *(WAP 3R)* **TEST FOUR** – Test 4 / Test 5 / Test 6.

Dec 90. (12"ep; as SWEET EXORCIST) *(WAP 9)* **CLONK**
– Clonk / Clonk (Hombase mix) / Clonk (Freebase mix).
(12"ep+=) *(WAP 9R)* **CLONK REMIX** – Per Clonk / Samba / Bonus Samba.

Jan 91. (cd/lp; as SWEET EXORCIST) *(WARP CD/LP 1)* **CLONK'S COMING**
– Mad Jack / Track Jack / Jack Jack / Trick Jack / Kick Jack / Psych Jack / Clonk's coming. *(cd re-iss. Apr96; same)*

Plastex   not iss.
1991. (12"ep; as SWEET EXORCIST) *(EXL 002)* **POPCONE**

Network   not iss.
Jan 91. (7"ep; as XON) *(NWKT 17)* **THE MOOD SET**

—— (XON = RICHARD H. KIRK with ROBERT GORDON)

Warp   not iss.
Jan 94. (cd/c/lp) *(WARP CD/MC/LP 19)* **VIRTUAL STATE**
– November x-ray Mexico / Frequency band / Come / Freezone / Clandestine transmission / The feeling (of warmth and beauty) / Velodrome / Soul catcher / World War Three / Lagoon west.

Sub-Level-Touch   not iss.
Jul 94. (cd/d-lp; as SWEET EXORCIST) *(STO 33.13 CD/LP)* **SPIRIT GUIDE TO LOW TECH**
– Part of the scene / African / Feel your hands / Nice / We are about to funk / Acid / wing / Jazz / What it is / Scat / Ghettos of the mind.

Beyond   not iss.
Sep 94. (d-cd/q-lp-box) *(RBAD CD/LP 8)* **ELECTRONIC EYE**

Warp   not iss.
Jul 95. (cd/c/lp) *(WARP CD/MC/LP 32)* **THE NUMBER OF MAGIC**
– Lost souls on funk / Love is deep / So digital / Indole ring / East of Nina / Atomic / Poets saints revolutionaries / Monochrome dream / The number of magic.

Alphaphone   not iss.
Jun 98. (cd; as TRAFFICANTE) *(ALPHACD 4)* **IS THIS NOW?**
– Energy / This is channel one / Bump the 45 / Vaporetti / Soul and salvation / Art of darkness / El Cid inna dub / How you know.

—— in Jul'98, KIRK was credited on IT's cd, 'CONCUBIA NOCTE'

CABARET VOLTAIRE (cont)

Date	Format	Cat#	Title	Label
Oct 99.	(cd-ep)	(TO 41)	**DARKNESS AT NOON**	Touch / not iss.
May 00.	(12"ep)	(TONE 12 12)	**LOOPSTATIC**	

– Devil in your name / All in vain / With false identity / Crimes against humanity.

May 00. (cd) (TONE 12) **LOOPSTATIC**
– Devil in your name / All in vain / With false identity / Chemicals and Easter bunnies / Do you transmit? / One zero / Get our heads straight / Monday morning.

John CALE

Born: 9 Mar'42, Garnant, Carmarthen, Wales. He studied classical piano and later viola at London's Guildhall School Of Music. As an 8 year old schoolboy prodigy, he'd already composed music for the BBC. In 1963, he moved to New York on a scholarship, and under JOHN CAGE and LaMONTE YOUNG's tuition, he experimented with avant-garde music. In 1965, he met LOU REED, and formed the legendary VELVET UNDERGROUND, CALE's wailing viola and white noise experimentation meshing with REED's pop sensibilities and dark lyrics to create their distinctive sound. After being fired by the band in 1968, he went solo, releasing a couple of albums for 'Columbia'. His debut in 1970 'VINTAGE VIOLENCE', saw him exhibiting a more traditional side to his enigmatic persona, with gentle folky songs. A collaboration entitled 'CHURCH OF ANTHRAX', with minimalist composer TERRY RILEY, followed in 1971. CALE continued the trend towards his roots with 'ACADEMY OF PERIL', before returning once more to the songwriter format of his first album. With LITTLE FEAT members LOWELL GEORGE and RICHIE HAYWARD among his backing band, he cut the classic 'PARIS 1919', which infused his melancholic songwriting with a disturbing unease. This was the template for much of CALE's 70's output with 1974's 'FEAR' also introducing a more aggressive element. 'HELEN OF TROY' (1975), featured a version of 'HEARTBREAK HOTEL' guaranteed to send a shiver up anyone's spine, although the album was generally disappointing overall. In 1976, he cemented his reputation by producing the legendary PATTI SMITH album, 'HORSES', having previously worked on the classic blast of primal noise that was THE STOOGES first album. His career went into a bit of a slump in the latter half of the 70's, and after an infamous incident in which he allegedly beheaded a chicken onstage (!), he had a brief dalliance with the New York punk scene. He regained his footing with 1982's 'MUSIC FOR A NEW SOCIETY', an intelligent, minimalistic affair. The mid-80's saw him sign to British label 'Beggars Banquet', and release the more mainstream 'ARTIFICIAL INTELLIGENCE'. 'WORDS FOR THE DYING', released in 1989, was a return to the classical field which included a collaboration with BRIAN ENO. They also teamed up on the sparse 'WRONG WAY UP' from 1990. 'SONGS FOR DRELLA' (a tribute to mentor ANDY WARHOL), saw CALE hook up once more with his old sparring partner LOU REED, together producing an album that outshone CALE's more recent solo outings. He and REED re-united with the others in VELVET UNDERGROUND for live work which resulted in the comeback album 'LIVE MCMXCIII'. A year later, another collaboration, this time with BOB NEUWIRTH, was largely ignored by the public. Throughout his career, he also sessioned for others, including ENO, and produced MODERN LOVERS (JONATHAN RICHMAN), SQUEEZE, etc. • **Style:** Described initially as 'Baroque'n'roll', he drifted back into avant-garde. As an 'Island' artist, he shifted into more accessible rock forms, becoming one of the genre's most gifted and influential artists. His vocal monotone drew comparisons with stablemates like NICK DRAKE or even KEVIN AYERS.

Album rating: VINTAGE VIOLENCE (*5) / CHURCH OF ANTHRAX with Terry Riley (*5) / THE ACADEMY IN PERIL (*5) / PARIS 1919 (*8) / FEAR (*7) / SLOW DAZZLE (*6) / HELEN OF TROY (*5) / GUTS compilation (*7) / SABOTAGE – LIVE (*4) / HONI SOIT (*4) / MUSIC FOR A NEW SOCIETY (*6) / CARIBBEAN SUNSET (*4) / COMES ALIVE (*4) / ARTIFICIAL INTELLIGENCE (*5) / WORDS FOR THE DYING (*6) / SONGS FOR DRELLA with Lou Reed (*7) / WRONG WAY UP with Eno (*7) / EVEN COWGIRLS GET THE BLUES live collection (*5) / FRAGMENTS OF A RAINY SEASON (*7) / LAST DAYS ON EARTH with Bob Neuwirth (*5) / SEDUCING DOWN THE DOOR a collection (*7) / PARIS S'EVEILLE... (*5) / 23 SOLO PIECES FOR LA NAISSANCE DE L'AMOUR (*5) / THE ISLAND YEARS compilation (*7) / WALKING ON LOCUSTS (*4) / EAT/KISS: MUSIC FOR THE FILMS OF ANDY WARHOL (*5)

JOHN CALE – vocals, viola, keyboards, bass, guitar (with session people)

C.B.S. / Columbia

Nov 70. (7") *<45154>* **FAIRWEATHER FRIEND. / CLEO**
Dec 70. (lp) *(64256) <CS 1037>* **VINTAGE VIOLENCE**
– Hello there / Gideon's bible / Adelaide / Big white cloud / Cleo / Please / Charlemagne / Bring it on up / Amsterdam / Ghost story / Fairweather friend. *(re-iss. May87 on 'Edsel' lp/cd; ED/+CD 230) (cd-iss. Sep94 on 'Columbia'; 477356-2)*
Jan 71. (7") *<45266>* **GIDEON'S BIBLE. / BIG WHITE CLOUD**
Apr 71. (lp; JOHN CALE & TERRY RILEY) *(64259) <CS 30131>* **CHURCH OF ANTHRAX**
– Church of anthrax / The hall of mirrors in the palace at Versailles / The soul of Patrick Lee / Ides of March / The protege. *(cd-iss. Oct93 on 'Sony Europe';) (cd re-iss. Mar96 on 'Columbia'; 476640-2)*

Reprise / Reprise

Apr 72. (lp) *(K 44212) <MS 2079>* **ACADEMY IN PERIL**
– The philosopher / Brahms / Legs Larry at Television Centre / Academy in peril / Intro: days of steam: (a) Faust, (b) The balance, (c) Capt. Morgan's lament / King Harry / John Milton. *(re-iss. Apr86 on 'Edsel'; XED 182) (cd-iss. Apr89; EDCD 182) (cd-iss. Oct93 on 'Warners'; 7599 26930-2)*

May 72. (7") *<1108>* **DAYS OF STEAM. / LEGS LARRY AT TELEVISION CENTER**
Mar 73. (lp) *(K 44239) <MS 2131>* **PARIS 1919**
– Child's Christmas in Wales / Hanky panky nohow / The endless plain of fortune / Andalucia / Macbeth / Paris 1919 / Graham Greene / Half past France / Antartica starts here. *(cd-iss. Oct93 on 'Warners'; 7599 25926-2)*

— Around this time he contributed to album 'JUNE 1st, 1974' on 'Island' with others ENO, NICO, KEVIN AYERS. *(ILPS 9291)*

— now with **ENO** – synth / **PHIL MANZANERA** – guitar / **ARCHIE LEGGAT** – bass / **FRED SMITH** – drums guest on below 'A'side **JUDY NYLON** – vocals

Island / A&M

Jul 74. (7") *(WIP 6202)* **THE MAN WHO COULDN'T AFFORD TO ORGY. / SYLVIA SAID**
Sep 74. (lp) *(ILPS 9301)* **FEAR**
– Fear is a man's best friend / Buffalo ballet / Barracuda / Emily / Ship of fools / Gun / The man who couldn't afford to orgy / You know more than I know / Momamma scuba. *(re-iss. Aug91 cd)(c; IMCD 140)(ICM 9301)*

— with **CHRIS SPEDDING + PHIL MANZANERA** – guitar / **PAT DONALDSON** – bass / **TIMI DONALD + GERRY CONWAY** – drums / **ENO** – synthesizer / **CHRIS THOMAS** – violin, electric piano

Apr 75. (lp) *(ILPS 9317)* **SLOW DAZZLE**
– Mr. Wilson / Taking it all away / Dirty ass rock'n'roll / Darling I need you / Rollaroll / Heartbreak hotel / Ski patrol / I'm not the loving kind / Guts / The jeweller. *(cd-iss. Jun88; CID 9317) (re-iss. cd Aug94; IMCD 202)*

— **PHIL COLLINS** – drums repl. CONWAY, MANZANERA + THOMAS.

Nov 75. (lp) *(ILPS 9350)* **HELEN OF TROY**
– My Maria / Helen of Troy / China sea / Engine / Save us / Cable Hogue / I keep a close watch / Pablo Picasso / Leaving it up to you * / Baby what you want me to do? / Sudden death. *(some copies repl.* by)* – Coral Moon. *(cd-iss. Apr94; IMCD 177)*
Feb 77. (lp) *(ILPS 9459)* **GUTS** (compilation)
– Guts / Mary Lou / Helen of Troy / Pablo Picasso / Leaving it up to you / Fear is a man's best friend / Gun / Dirty ass rock 'n' roll / Heartbreak hotel. *(cd-iss. Aug94; IMCD 203)*

— with **RITCHIE FLIEGLER** – lead guitar / **BRUCE BRODY** – mogg synthesizer / **JIMMY BAIN** – bass / **KEVIN CURRIE** – drums

Illegal / not iss.

Sep 77. (7"ep) *(ILL 003)* **ANIMAL JUSTICE**
– Chicken shit / Memphis / Hedda Gabbler.

— with **MARK AARON** – guitar / **JOE BIDWELL** – keyboards / **GEORGE SCOTT** – bass / **DOUG BROWN** – drums / **DEERFRANCE** – vocals

not iss. / Spy

Dec 79. (lp) *<SP 004>* **SABOTAGE (live)**
– Mercenaries (ready for war) / Baby you know / Evidence / Dr.Mudd / Walkin' the dog / Captain Hook / Only time will tell / Sabotage / Chorale.

not iss. / I.R.S.

1980. (7") *<9008>* **MERCENARIES (READY FOR WAR). / ROSEGARDEN FUNERAL OF SORES**

— with **STURGIS NIKIDES** – guitar, vocals / **JIM GOODWIN** – keyboards, synth. / **PETER MUNY** – bass / **ROBERT MEDECI** – drums

A&M / A&M

Mar 81. (lp) *(AMLH 64849)* **HONI SOIT**
– Dead or alive / Strange times in Casablanca / Fighter pilot / Wilson Joliet / Streets of Laredo / Honi soit (la premiere Lecon de Francaise) / Riverbank / Russian roulette / Magic & lies. *(cd-iss. Jul94; CDMID 1936)*
Apr 81. (7") *(AMS 8130)* **DEAD OR ALIVE. / HONI SOIT**

— now w/ **ALAN LANIER** – keyboards / **D. J. YOUNG** – guitar / **DAVID LICHTENSTEIN** – drums / **JOHN WONDERLING** / **MIKE McCLINTOCK** / **ROBERT ELK**

Ze-Island / Passport

Aug 82. (lp/c) *(ILPS/ICT 7019) <PB 6019>* **MUSIC FOR A NEW SOCIETY**
– Taking your life in your hands / Thoughtless kind / Sanities / If you were still around / Close watch / Mama's song / Broken bird / Chinese envoy / Changes made / Damn life / Rise, Sam and Rimsky Korsakov. *(cd-iss. Mar94 on 'Yellow Moon'; YMCD 019)*
Apr 83. (7") *(IS 113)* **I KEEP A CLOSE WATCH. / CLOSE WATCH (instrumental)**

— **ANDY HEERMANS** – bass, vocals repl. LANIER

Ze-Island / Ze-Island

Jun 83. (lp/c) *(<ILPS/ICT 7024>)* **CARIBBEAN SUNSET**
– Hungry for love / Experiment number 1 / Model Beirut recital / Caribbean sunset / Praetorian underground / Magazines / Where there's a will / The hunt / Villa Albani.
Aug 84. (7") *(IS 197)* **OOH LA LA. / MAGAZINES**
Sep 84. (lp/c) *(ILPS/ICT 7026) <8402>* **JOHN CALE COMES ALIVE (live)**
– Ooh la la / Evidence / Dead or alive / Chinese envoy / Leaving it up to you / Dr. Mudd / Waiting for the man / Heartbreak hotel / Fear / Never give up on you.

— with **DAVID YOUNG** – guitar / **JAMES YOUNG** – keyboards / **GRAHAM DOWDALL** – percussion

Beggars Banquet / P.V.C.

Jul 85. (7"/12") *(BEG 145/+T)* **DYING ON THE VINE. / EVERYTIME THE DOGS BARK**
Nov 85. (lp/c) *(BEG A/C 68) <PVC 8947>* **ARTIFICIAL INTELLIGENCE**
– Everytime the dogs bark / Dying on the vine / The sleeper / Vigilante lover / Chinese takeaway (Hong Kong 1997) (medley) / Song of the valley / Fade away tomorrow / Black rose / Satellite walk. *(re-iss. Jan89 on 'Lowdown-Beggars Banquet' lp/c; BBL/+C 68) (cd-iss. Mar96; BBL 68CD)*
Nov 85. (12"m) *(BEG 153T)* **SATELLITE WALK. / DYING ON THE VINE / CRASH COURSE IN HARMONICS**

— now w/ **BRIAN ENO** – synthesizers, keyboards / **NEIL CATCHPOLE** – viola, violin, choir

Land / Warners

Oct 89. (lp/c/cd) *(LAND/+C/CD 009) <26024>* **WORDS FOR THE DYING**

– The Falkland suite:- Introduction-There was a saviour – Interlude 1 / On a wedding anniversary – Interlude II – Lie still, sleep becalmed – Do not go gentle into that good night / Songs without words 1 & 2 / The soul of Carmen Miranda. *(re-iss. cd Oct95 & Aug99 on 'All Saints'; ASCD 009)*

— Apr'90, CALE & Lou REED⇒, collaborated on Andy Warhol tribute album SONGS FOR DRELLA. On 'Warners' records lp/c/cd*WX 345/+C //7599 26140-2*. It was CALE's first excursion into the Top 30.

— Oct'90, he teamed up with ENO on the album 'WRONG WAY UP' on 'Land'

		Delabel	not iss.
Nov 91.	(cd) **PARIS S'EVEILLE, SUIVI D'AUTRES COMPOSITIONS**	–	France

– Paris S'eveille, suivi d'autres / Sanctus (four etudes for electronic orchestra) / Animals at night / The cowboy laughs at round-up / Primary motive 1) Factory speech, 2) Strategy session, 3) Closing titles / Antartica starts here / Booker T. (by VELVET UNDERGROUND) *(UK-iss.Mar93 on 'Crepuscule'; TWI 952-2) (re-iss. Nov95 on 'Yellow Moon'; YMCD 007)*

		Crepuscule	not iss.
Nov 93.	(cd) *(TWI 9542)* **23 SOLO PIECES FOR LA NAISSANCE DE L'AMOUR**		–

– La naissance de l'amour / If you love me no more / And if I love you still / Judith / Converging themes / Opposites attract / I will do it, I will keep it / Keep it to yourself / Walk towards the sea / Unquiet heart / Waking up to love / Mysterious relief / Never been so happy / Beyond expectations / Conversations in the garden / La naissance de l'amour II / Secret dialogue / Roma / On the dark side / La naissance de l'amour III / Eye to eye / Maria's car crash and hotel rooms / La naissance de l'amour IV. *(re-iss. Nov95 on 'Yellow Moon'; YMCD 007)*

		M.C.A.	M.C.A.
May 94.	(cd; JOHN CALE / BOB NEUWIRTH) *(11037)* **LAST DAY ON EARTH** (soundtrack)		

– Overture- a) A tourist, b) A contract, c) A prisoner / Cafe Shabu / Pastoral angst / Who's in charge? / Short of time / Angel of death / Paradise Nevada / Old China / Ocean life / Instrumental / Modern world / Streets come alive / Secrets / Maps of the world / Broken hearts / The high and the mighty road.

		Hannibal	Hannibal
Sep 96.	(cd) *(<HNCD 1395>)* **WALKING ON LOCUSTS**		

– Dancing undercover / Set me free / So what / Crazy Egypt / So much for love / Tell me why / Indistinct notion of cool / Secret corrida / Circus / Gatorville and points east / Some friends / Entre nous.

| Jun 97. | (cd) *(<HNCD 1407>)* **EAT / KISS – MUSIC FOR THE FILMS OF ANDY WARHOL** | | |

– KISS:- Infinite guitar, quartet / Frozen warning, Jimmy, metal-violin solo – Daid Tiye (backing vocal) / B.J., quartet, Moe / Violin solo – Todd, Tiye, quartet / Harpsichord, infinite guitar / Quartet, cello solo – Dawn, harpsichord / B.J., quartet, electric piano / Quartet solo / Solo Tiye, strings // EAT:- B.J., 12-string guitar intro – David / Reading from 'Melanethon' (Swedenborg) / Todd solo, 12-string, Moe / Piano, B.J.

		Erato	Erato
Nov 98.	(cd) *(<3984 22122-2>)* **NICO**		

– intro / New York underground / Night club theme / Modelling / Out of China / Death camp / Ari sleepy / Iceberg / Jim / Iceberg / Espana / Nibelungen.

– compilations, etc. –

Jul 91.	(c) *Danceteria;* (*DANCD 113*) **EVEN COWBOYS GET THE BLUES** (live 1978-79 at CBGB's)		
	(cd-iss. Jun97; same)		
Oct 92.	(cd) *Hannibal;* (*HNCD 1372*) **FRAGMENTS OF A RAINY SEASON** (live)		–
Oct 92.	(cd) *Traditional Line;* (*TL 001326*) **BROKEN HEARTS LIVE 1984-1992** (live)		–
Jul 94.	(d-cd) *Rhino;* <*R2 71685*> **SEDUCING DOWN THE DOOR: A JOHN CALE COLLECTION**	–	–
Sep 96.	(d-cd) *Island;* (*524235-2*) **THE ISLAND YEARS ANTHOLOGY**		–
Feb 99.	(cd) *Island;* (*IMCD 259*) **CLOSE WATCH (AN INTRODUCTION TO JOHN CALE)**		

– Paris 1919 / Mr. Wilson / Leaving it up to you / Dying on the vine / Guts / Heartbreak hotel / Ship of fools / Cable hogue / Gun / Riverbank / Child's Christmas in Wales / Fear is a man's best friend / If you were still around / Wilson Joilet / I keep a close watch.

CAPTAIN SENSIBLE

Born: RAYMOND BURNS, 23 Apr'55, Balham, South London, England. A founding member of legendary punk band, The DAMNED (along with DAVE VANIAN, BRIAN JAMES and RAT SCABIES), BURNS played bass in the band's initial incarnation (1976-78) before switching to guitar as the outfit re-emerged minus JAMES following a temporary hiatus. One-half of The DAMNED's in-house loony duo alongside SCABIES, BURNS' reputation for high jinks preceded him. Always the most colourful, animated member of The DAMNED, it was perhaps inevitable that sooner or later he'd find an alternative outlet for his manic energy and humour; during the aforementioned lull in DAMNED activities, The CAPTAIN made his first foray into solo waters with the 'JET BOY, JET GIRL' single. By the time he got round to recording a follow-up EP, 'THIS IS YOUR CAPTAIN SPEAKING' (issued on the 'Crass' label) in '81, The DAMNED had released two of the best albums of their career, 'MACHINE GUN ETIQUETTE' (1979) and 'THE BLACK ALBUM' (1980); SENSIBLE played a pivotal role in both and would continue as a full-time member even after his solo career took off big time in '82 as he signed to 'A&M'. With backing from The DOLLY MIXTURES (who'd first worked with him on the 'Crass' EP) and the added talents of ROBYN HITCHCOCK, CAPTAIN SENSIBLE sailed to No.1 in the summer of '82 with a chirpy cockney reading of the Rodgers/Hammerstein 'South Pacific' standard, 'HAPPY TALK'. From punk upstart to dayglo pop star overnight, The CAPTAIN became the acceptable face of rock'n'roll and a favourite fixture of Saturday morning TV. A follow-up single, 'WOT', made the Top 30 although the subsequent debut album, 'WOMEN AND CAPTAINS FIRST' (1982) barely scraped into the Top 75. The following year's 'POWER OF LOVE' album also failed to make much chart headway although it did put SENSIBLE back in the Top 10 with the anti-Falklands War song, 'GLAD IT'S ALL OVER'. 1984's compilation album, 'SENSIBLE SINGLES' smacked of desperation, SENSIBLE's days of pop fame numbered as he followed his own eccentric path throughout the remainder of the 80's. 1984 was also the year SENSIBLE finally left The DAMNED, although he continued to help them out on an occasional basis. As well as being a staunch peace campaigner, the CAPTAIN was also a committed vegetarian, releasing the 'WOT, NO MEAT' single in '85 as CAPTAIN SENSIBLE & THE MISSUS (the spouse in question was actually girlfriend and DOLLY MIXTURE, RACHEL BOR). Parting company with 'A&M' in the late 80's, SENSIBLE formed his own label, 'Deltic', for the release of the 1989 double set, 'REVOLUTION NOW'. If his star had faded somewhat, there were still a hardcore of SENSIBLE admirers and ageing DAMNED fans willing to shell out their hard earned cash and the man's career extended into the 90's via albums such as 'UNIVERSE OF GEOFFREY BROWN' (1993) and 'MEATHEAD' (1995).

Album rating: WOMEN AND CAPTAINS FIRST (*5) / THE POWER OF LOVE (*4) / SENSIBLE SINGLES compilation (*5) / REVOLUTION NOW (*4) / THE UNIVERSE OF GEOFFREY BROWN (*4) / LIVE AT THE MILKY WAY (*6) / MEATHEAD (*6) / MAD COWS & ENGLISHMEN (*4) / SENSIBLE LIFESTYLES compilation (*6)

CAPTAIN SENSIBLE – vocals, guitar, bass, etc

		Dutch Poker	not iss.
Jul 78.	(7") *(POS 15077)* **JET BOY, JET GIRL.** / the Softies: **CHILDREN OF THE DAMNED**		–
	(re-iss. May82 on 'Big Beat' 7"/7"pic-d; NS/+P 77)		

— with **DOLLY MIXTURES** – vocals

		Crass	not iss.
Nov 81.	(7"ep) *(321984-5)* **THIS IS YOUR CAPTAIN SPEAKING**		–

– The Russians are coming / Oursoles to you / (What d'ya give) The man who's gotten everything.

— retained The DOLLY MIXTURES + enlisted **ROBYN HITCHCOCK** – guitar / **TONY MANSFIELD** – synthesizer, producer / **ROD BOWKETT** – noises

		A&M	not iss.
Jun 82.	(7"/7"pic-d) *(CAP/+P 1)* **HAPPY TALK. / I CAN'T STAND IT**	1	–
Aug 82.	(7"/7"pic-d) *(CAP/+P 2)* **WOT. / STRAWBERRY DROSS**	26	–
Sep 82.	(lp/c) *(AMLH/CAM 68548)* **WOMEN AND CAPTAINS FIRST**	64	–

– Wot / A nice cup of tea / Brenda (part 1) / Brenda (part 2) / Yanks with guns / Happy talk / Martha the mouth / Nobody's sweetheart / What d'ya give a man who's gotten everything / Who is Melody Lee, Sid? / Gimme a uniform / Croydon.

| Oct 82. | (7"pic-d) *(CAPP 3)* **CROYDON. / JIMI HENDRIX'S STRAT** | | – |

— next added various session people incl. **DAVE RUFFY** – drums

Jul 83.	(7"/7"pic-d) *(CAP/+P 4)* **STOP THE WORLD. / BACK TO SCHOOL**		–
Nov 83.	(7") *(CAP 5)* **I'M A SPIDER. / WOMEN SAGA**		–
Nov 83.	(lp/c) *(AMLX/CXM 68561)* **THE POWER OF LOVE**		–

– I'm a spider / I love her / Stop the world / Sir Donald's song / It's hard to believe I'm not / Thanks for the night / Glad it's all over / Royal rave up / Secrets / It would be so nice / The power of love / I love you.

Mar 84.	(7"/7"pic-d) *(CAP/+P 6)* **GLAD IT'S ALL OVER. / DAMNED ON 45**	6	
	(12"+=) *(CAPX 6)* – Happy talk.		
Jul 84.	(7") *(CAP 7)* **THERE ARE MORE SNAKES THAN LADDERS. / THE FOUR MARY'S GO-GO DANCE ALL NIGHT AT THE GROOVY CELLAR**	57	–
	(12"+=) *(CAPX 7)* – ('A'remix).		
Nov 84.	(7") *(CAP 8)* **ONE CHRISTMAS CATALOGUE. / RELAX**		–
	(12"+=) *(CAPY 8)* – Pocketful of dosh / Wendy, where's my snaps?		
Dec 84.	(lp/c) *(AMA/AMC 5026)* **SENSIBLE SINGLES** (compilation)		–

– Happy talk / Wot / It would be so nice / Martha the mouth / Stop the world / Relax / I love her / Glad it's all over / It's hard to believe I'm not / There are more snakes than ladders / I'm a spider / One Christmas catalogue / I love you.

| Jul 85. | (7"; as CAPTAIN SENSIBLE + THE MISSUS) *(TOUCH 3)* **WOT, NO MEAT? / A MEAT SANDWICH** | | – |

(above was with girlfriend, RACHEL BOR (of DOLLY MIXTURES) / released on 'Animus' imprint) *(re-iss. Nov86; FEEL 3)*

— his backing band now **DAVE BERK** – drums / **CLIVE GATES** – keyboards / **BRIAN KERR** – guitar / **ROBBIE ROMP** – bass

Nov 85.	(7") *(AM 290)* **COME ON DOWN. / SHE TAKES ME**		–
	(12"+=) *(AMY 290)* – ('A'side) / Beggar's can be choosers / Like margarine / The ballad of Sheila and Mark.		
Jun 87.	(7") *(AM 395)* **REVOLUTION NOW. / COWARD OF TREASON COVE**		–
	(12"+=) *(AMY395)* – The groove.		

		Trax	not iss.
Apr 88.	(7") *(HS 1)* **THE SNOOKER SONG. / MIDNIGHT SMOKE**		–

		Deltic	not iss.
Jun 88.	(7") *(DELT 1)* **THE TOYS TAKE OVER. / A SPORTING LIFE**		–
	(12"+=) *(DELT 1T)* – V.O.A.		
Nov 88.	(7") *(DELT 2)* **I GET SO EXCITED. / THE DELTIC SUITE (parts 3-6)**		–
Aug 89.	(d-lp/c/cd) *(DELT LP/MC/CD 4)* **REVOLUTION NOW**		–

– Missing the boat / Smash it up (part 4) / The toys take over / A riot on Eastbourne pier / Wake up (you're only dreaming) / Green light / Lib 2-3 / Revolution now / Phone-in / I get so excited / Vosene. *cd+=)* – The kamikaze millionaire / Exploding heads and teapots / The coward of Treason Cove. *(cd re-iss. 1991 & Jul96 on 'Humbug'; BAH 3) (cd re-iss. Sep98 on 'Blueprint'; BP 293CD)*

CAPTAIN SENSIBLE (cont)

Aug 90.	(7"; as CAPTAIN SENSIBLE & The BROTHERHOOD OF LIZARDS) *(DELT 5)* **SMASH IT UP (PART 4). / MARKET PLACE**	XYZ	not iss.
1993.	(cd-s) *(7086-8)* **WOT '93 / WOT '93 (extended) / LIFE UP IN THE STARS**	Humbug	not iss.
Apr 93.	(cd/c) *(BAH/+MC 4)* **THE UNIVERSE OF GEOFFREY BROWN**		
	– Holiday in my head / Come on Geoffrey Brown / Getting to me / Street of shame / Geoff loosens his tie / Home / Govt. Dirty Tricks Dept. WC1 / Life up in the stars / The message / A trip to Cornwall / The universe of Geoffrey Brown. *(cd re-iss. Sep98 on 'Blueprint'; BP 294CD)*		
Aug 94.	(cd) *(BAH 12)* **LIVE AT THE MILKY WAY (live)**		
	– Interstellar overcoat / Jet boy, jet girl / Smash it up / Back to school / Come on Geoffrey Brown / Happy talk / The kamikaze millionaire / Exploding heads & teapots (past their prime) / Love song / Neat neat neat / New rose / Wot / Lookin' at you / Hey Joe / Glad it's all over. *(re-iss. Apr99 on 'Cherry Red'; CDMRED 159)*		
Dec 94.	(c-s/7") *(CA+/HOKEY 1)* **THE HOKEY COKEY. / (version)**	71	-
	(cd-s+=) – *(CDHOKEY 1)* – ('A' version). (above issued on 'Have A Nice Day' records)		
Sep 95.	(cd-s) *(HUM 7)* **FLIP TOP WORLD**		
Sep 95.	(d-cd) *(BAH 14)* **MEATHEAD**		
	– Sally blue shoes / Rough justice / Bare arm situations / The love policeman / Crazy fish / Elephant dung / Hammond solo / Zarbo Nebula (parts 1-4) / Freedom / Eric Clapton's wallet / Pasties / Love thing / Bruce Forsythe / Flip top world / Pompous overture / Aliens of the lord / Space shuttle / A brief hiccup / Meathead / Honeymoon in Acapulco / Can you hear me / The snow queen / Business trip to Saturn / Inventing the wheel / The last train / Festival radio jingles / Aliens? we are the aliens / Stabilizer jam / Plastic arcade. *(re-iss. Nov99 on 'Cherry Red'+=; CDMRED 160)* – (4 extra tracks).		
		Scratch	not iss.
1996.	(cd) *(SCRCD 017)* **MAD COWS & ENGLISHMEN**		
	– While wrecking the car / Bob's brown nose / Neverland / The stately homes of England / Smashing the chains / Mr. Brown's exploding wallet / Monty's revenge / Mr. Farmer / The lottery love rat / One hit wonder / The world of Matilda Free.		
		Empty	not iss.
1997.	(cd-s) *(MT 378)* **WHILE WRECKING THE CAR**		
		Jarmusic	not iss.
1998.	(cd-ep) *(JAR 025)* **THE UNIVERSE OF CAPTAIN SENSIBLE EP**		
1999.	(7") *(JAR 028)* **MISSING THE BOAT**		
—	THE CAPTAIN returned to The DAMNED		

– compilations, etc. –

Oct 88.	(7") *Old Gold; (OG 9811)* **HAPPY TALK. / GLAD IT'S ALL OVER**		
Jun 97.	(cd) *Humbug; (BAH 30)* **A SLICE OF GEOFFREY BROWN**		
Jun 97.	(d-cd) *Humbug; (BAH 32)* **THE CAPTAIN'S BOX**		
Aug 97.	(cd) *Cleopatra; (CLP 0041-2)* **SENSIBLE LIFESTYLES: THE BEST OF CAPTAIN SENSIBLE**		
Mar 98.	(cd) *Eagle; (EABCD 101)* **THE MASTERS**		

CARPETTES

Formed: Newcastle, England . . . 1977 by GEORGE MADDISON, NEIL THOMPSON and KEVIN HEARD, the latter being replaced by TIM WILDER prior to the release of a debut EP, 'RADIO WUNDERBAR'. Released on Walthamstow (London) label, 'Small Wonder' (also home to the CRAVATS), the single did relatively well on the punk/indie circuit, prompting the Geordie youngsters to name their follow-up track, 'SMALL WONDER', in the label's honour. Following in the footsteps of fellow punks The LURKERS, the trio signed to 'Beggars Banquet', although it would be Autumn '79 before their third single, 'I DON'T MEAN IT', hit the shelves. With punk-rock well past its honeymoon period, The CARPETTES didn't fit in with the more experimental musical upholstery of the 'New Wave' scene and the accompanying album, 'FRUSTRATION PARADISE', didn't exactly cut a rug with the critics. A follow-up set, 'FIGHT AMONG YOURSELVES' (1980), followed a similar tack and with the emerging "oi" scene just around the corner, The CARPETTES were rolled up for good.

Album rating: FRUSTRATION PARADISE (*5) / FIGHT AMONGST YOURSELVES (*4) / THE BEST OF THE CARPETTES compilation (*5)

NEIL THOMPSON – vocals, guitar / **GEORGE MADDISON** – bass / **TIM WILDER** – drums; repl. KEVIN HEARD

		Small Wonder	not iss.
Dec 77.	(7"ep) *(SMALL 3)* **RADIO WUNDERBAR EP**		
	– How about me and you / Help I'm trapped / Radio wunderbar / Cream of youth.		
Jul 78.	(7") *(SMALL 9)* **SMALL WONDER. / 2 NE 1**		
		Beggars Banquet	not iss.
Oct 79.	(7") *(BEG 27)* **I DON'T MEAN IT. / EASY WAY OUT**		
Nov 79.	(lp) *(BEGA 14)* **FRUSTRATION PARADISE**		
	– Frustration Paradise / Reach the bottom / I don't mean it / 3 a.m. / Away from it all / Johnny won't hurt you / Lost love / It don't make sense / A.B.C. / Cruel honesty / How to handle a woman / Indo-China. *(re-iss. 1988;)*		
Mar 80.	(7") *(BEG 32)* **JOHNNY WON'T HURT YOU. / FRUSTRATION PARADISE**		
	(w/ free 7") *(SAM 119)* – TOTAL INSECURITY. / KEYS TO YOUR HEART		
Aug 80.	(7"m) *(BEG 47)* **NOTHING EVER CHANGES. / YOU NEVER REALISE / FRUSTRATION PARADISE**		
Oct 80.	(lp) *(BEGA 21)* **FIGHT AMONGST YOURSELVES**		
	– Nothing ever changes / Since you went away / False foundations / Fight amongst yourselves / Dead or alive / If your heart stopped now / Friday night, Saturday morning / The last lone ranger / Youth rebellion / The reason I'm lonely / Total insecurity / Silly games.		
Dec 80.	(7"m) *(BEG 49)* **THE LAST LONE RANGER. / LOVE SO STRONG / FAN CLUB**		
—	disbanded soon after above		

– compilations, etc. –

Sep 97.	(cd) *Overground; (OVER 68CD)* **THE EARLY YEARS**		
Jul 00.	(cd) *Anagram; (CDPUNK 80)* **THE BEST OF THE CARPETTES**		
	– How about me and you / Radio Wunderbar / Small wonder / 2 No.1 / I don't mean it / Johnny won't hurt you / Frustration paradise / Reach the bottom / 3 a.m. / Away from it all / Lost love / Cruel honesty / Nothing ever changes / You never realise / Since you went away / Fight amongst yourselves / Dead or alive / Friday night . . . Saturday morning / The last lone ranger / Silly game / Fan club. *(re-iss. Mar02; same)*		
Nov 00.	(cd) *Captain Oi; (AHOYCD 065)* **FRUSTRATION / FIGHT AMONGST YOURSELVES**		

Nick CAVE

Born: NICHOLAS EDWARD CAVE, 22 Sep'57, Warracknabeal, Australia. He was the main man behind punk/power-pop outfit, The BOYS NEXT DOOR, completing the band with neighbours MICK HARVEY, TRACY PEW and PHIL CALVERT. Formed in Caulfield, Melbourne in late '77, they issued a one-off version of Nancy Sinatra's 'THESE BOOTS WERE MADE FOR WALKING', before they added a fifth member, ROWLAND S. HOWARD. After an album, 'DOOR, DOOR', was released on 'Mushroom' records in 1979, they came to England as The BIRTHDAY PARTY, taking their name from a Harold Pinter play. The band were subsequently snapped up by IVO on the (then) new indie label '4 a.d.', after a recent 'HEE-HAW' EP was given some night time airing by John Peel. About as extreme as any music ever released by the label, The BIRTHDAY PARTY were more a wake than a celebration, albeit one with more than its fair share of black humour. Their first UK album, 'PRAYERS ON FIRE' (1981), featured such enduringly sharp material as 'ZOO MUSIC GIRL', 'CRY', 'CAPERS' and 'NICK THE STRIPPER', although for many obsessive fans and critics alike, 'RELEASE THE BATS' remains the definitive track. Issued in summer '81, the single was a gothic slice of avant-garde that took over the territory once belonging to the likes of PERE UBU and The POP GROUP. Later that year, TRACY PEW was jailed for drunk driving, a revolving cast of BARRY ADAMSON, CHRIS WALSH and HARRY HOWARD deputising for him on tour. Live, The BIRTHDAY PARTY were even more unhinged than on vinyl, their demented stage show setting them apart from the masses of up and coming goth-rock acts around at the time. While TRACY was behind bars, NICK, ROWLAND and MICK teamed up as The TUFF MONKS with fellow Australians, The GO-BETWEENS on a one-off 45, 'AFTER THE FIREWORKS'. A further album, 'JUNKYARD' (which hit UK Top 75 in 1982), assured The BIRTHDAY PARTY's position as cult favourites among those who favoured black as a fashion statement. Later that year, ROWLAND hooked up with mistress of soft-porn new wave, LYDIA LUNCH, for a cover of Lee Hazlewood & Nancy Sinatra's 'SOME VELVET MORNING', while The BIRTHDAY PARTY were trimmed to a quartet for 'THE BAD SEED' EP. Released in early '83, the set included the incendiary 'SONNY'S BURNING', arguably the group's finest track. Having moved to Berlin to escape the pressures of critical adulation, the party was finally over after the appropriately titled 'MUTINY' EP. CAVE, who at the time also lived in London, played a few low-key gigs in '83 backed by The CAVEMEN who subsequently became The BAD SEEDS. Including a couple of his cronies from the BIRTHDAY PARTY days, MICK HARVEY and BLIXA BARGELD (also a member of cheery industrial types, EINSTURZENDE NEUBAUTEN), the initial line-up also boasted ex-MAGAZINE man, BARRY ADAMSON, who stayed with the band for the first four albums. Released on 'Mute' (whom CAVE was still contracted to), the debut long player, 'FROM HER TO ETERNITY' (1984), introduced CAVE's preoccupation with the ELVIS myth on a cover of 'IN THE GHETTO', an obsession indulged in greater depth on 'THE FIRSTBORN IS DEAD' (1985). The spit and thrash of the BIRTHDAY PARTY had now been replaced with a skeletal, funereal musical backing to accompany CAVE's ominous crooning. Part hellfire preacher, part damned sinner, CAVE's tales of murder most foul and general debauchery were almost always set in a context (real or implied) of Old Testament morality. Yep, this crazy cat's got that old-time religion, his songs steeped in the shadowy blues of the Mississippi Delta and the lure of his namesake, Old Nick himself. While 'KICKING AGAINST THE PRICKS' (1986), an album of covers, saw the likes of 'BLACK BETTY' and 'BY THE TIME I GET TO PHOENIX', falling under CAVE's dark spell like lambs to the slaughter, the singer came into his own on 'YOUR FUNERAL . . . MY TRIAL' later that year. Rich in dark, dense imagery, the compelling narratives of crime and punishment were further developed on 'TENDER PREY' (1988). In the couple of years preceding the next BAD SEEDS release, CAVE published his first novel, 'AND THE ASS SAW THE ANGEL', and appeared in the film, 'GHOSTS OF THE CIVIL DEAD', as well as scoring the soundtrack (along with HARVEY and BARGELD). Largely acoustic, 'THE GOOD SON' (1990) saw CAVE and his BAD SEEDS return in moodily intense style, grandiose string arrangements complementing CAVE's sombre intonations. 'HENRY'S DREAM' (1992) was somewhat more menacing with the chilling 'JACK THE RIPPER', although 'STRAIGHT TO YOU' found CAVE applying his vocal intensity in lovelorn ballad mode with impressive results. Further musings on the nature of love pervaded 'LET LOVE IN' (1994), although the apocalyptic antipode was back on familiar blood-stained ground with 'MURDER BALLADS' a couple of years later. Against a minimal musical backdrop, CAVE recounted tales of a lyrical savagery that made his earlier work read like nursery rhymes. As well as a duet with POLLY HARVEY, the record saw an unlikely, but interesting pairing with KYLIE MINOGUE (!) on

'WHERE THE WILD ROSES GROW'. In comparison, 'THE BOATMAN'S CALL' (1997) was almost evangelical, an opus that seemed to find NICK as at peace with himself and the world as he's ever been. That's not to say this was a happy record, far from it, as CAVE reflected on the redemptive power of love, and the pain of love lost. Mooted by many critics as his best work to date, it was certainly his most accessible and possessed an atmosphere of meditative grace that set it apart from much of his previous output. In a music world of MTV mediocrity, CAVE's dark, defiantly individual stance is somehow comforting, though you wouldn't necessarily want to meet the man down a dark alley late at night. Later in 1997, CAVE was rumoured to be working on a blues covers album with TIM ROSE, while he was also set to star alongside Ewan Bremner in the film, 'Rhinoceros Hunting In Budapest'. A second volume of 'King Ink' hit the book shops in March '98 although more publicity was generated via the release of a long-overdue NICK CAVE & THE BAD SEEDS best of compilation. • **Covered:** RUNNING SCARED (Roy Orbison) / BLACK BETTY (Ram Jam) / BY THE TIME I GET TO PHOENIX (Jim Webb) / MUDDY WATER (Johnny Rivers) / HEY JOE (Jimi Hendrix) / ALL TOMORROW'S PARTIES (Velvet Underground) / THE CARNIVAL IS OVER (Seekers) / SOMETHING'S GOTTEN HOLD OF MY HEART (Gene Pitney) / HELPLESS (Neil Young) / WHAT A WONDERFUL WORLD (Ray Charles) / etc. mainly from his covers album KICKING AGAINST THE PRICKS.

Album rating: Boys Next Door: DOOR DOOR (*6) / Birthday Party: PRAYERS ON FIRE (*8) / DRUNK ON THE POPE'S BLOOD (*6) / JUNKYARD (*6) / HITS compilation (*8) / LIVE 1981-1982 collection (*7) / Nick Cave & The Bad Seeds: FROM HER TO ETERNITY (*7) / THE FIRSTBORN IS DEAD (*8) / KICKING AGAINST THE PRICKS (*6) / YOUR FUNERAL... MY TRIAL (*6) / TENDER PREY (*6) / THE GHOST OF THE CIVIL DEAD soundtrack (*5) / THE GOOD SON (*8) / HENRY'S DREAM (*8) / LIVE SEEDS (*6) / LET LOVE IN (*8) / MURDER BALLADS (*7) / THE BOATMAN'S CALL (*9) / THE BEST OF NICK CAVE & THE BAD SEEDS compilation (*9) / NO MORE SHALL WE PART (*7)

BOYS NEXT DOOR

NICK CAVE – vocals / **MICK HARVEY** (b.29 Sep'58, Rochester, Australia) – guitar / **TRACY PEW** – bass / **PHIL CALVERT** – drums

Suicide / not iss.

May 78. (7") *(103140)* **THESE BOOTS ARE MADE FOR WALKING. / BOY HERO** – / – Austra

— (Dec'78) added **ROWLAND S. HOWARD** (b.24 Oct'59, Melbourne) – guitar (ex-YOUNG CHARLATANS)

Mushroom / not iss.

May 79. (7") *(K 7492)* **SHIVERS. / DIVE POSITION** – / – Austra
May 79. (lp) *(L 36931)* **DOOR, DOOR** – / – Austra
 – The nightwatchman / Brave exhibitions / Friends of my world / The voice / Roman Roman / Somebody's watching / After a fashion / Dive position / I mistake myself / Shivers. *(Australian cd-iss. 1987; D 19227) (cd-iss. Mar93 on 'Grey Area-Mute';)*

Missing Link / not iss.

Dec 79. (12"ep) *(MLEP-3)* **HEE-HAW** – / – Austra
 – Catholic skin / The red clock / Faint heart / The hair shirt / Death by drowning. *(Australia re-iss. Dec83; credited as BIRTHDAY PARTY; ING 008)*
Feb 80. (7"gig freebie) *(MLS 16)* **HAPPY BIRTHDAY. / THE RIDDLE HOUSE** – / – Austra

BIRTHDAY PARTY

— (same line-up & label)

Jul 80. (7") *(MLS 18)* **MR. CLARINET. / HAPPY BIRTHDAY** – / – Austra
Nov 80. (lp) *(LINK 7)* **THE FIRST ALBUM** (originally credited to BOYS NEXT DOOR) – / – Austra
 – Mr. clarinet / Hats on wrong / The hair shirt / Guilt parade / Riddle house / The friend catcher / Waving my arms / The red clock / Cat man / Happy birthday.
 (below Australian releases only are with different label mentioned)

4.a.d. / not iss.

Oct 80. (7"m) *(AD 12)* **THE FRIEND CATCHER. / WAVING MY ARMS / CATMAN** – / –
Apr 81. (lp) *(CAD 104)* **PRAYERS ON FIRE** – / –
 – Zoo music girl / Cry / Capers / Nick the stripper / Ho-ho / Figure of fun / King Ink / A dead song / Yard / Dull day / Just you and me. *(cd-iss. Apr88+=; CAD 104CD)* – Blundertown / Kathy's kisses.
Jun 81. Missing Link; (12"m) *(MSD 479)* **NICK THE STRIPPER. / BLUNDER TOWN / KATHY'S KISSES** – / – Austra
Aug 81. (7") *(AD 111)* **RELEASE THE BATS. / BLAST OFF** – / –
Oct 81. (7") *(AD 114)* **MR. CLARINET. / HAPPY BIRTHDAY** – / –
Feb 82. (m-lp) *(JAD 202)* **DRUNK ON THE POPE'S BLOOD** (live) – / –
 – (Sometimes) Pleasure heads must burn / King Ink / Zoo music girl / Loose / LYDIA LUNCH:- The Agony Is The Ecstasy.

— (Dec81) while **TRACY PEW** was in jail for drunk driving he was replaced on tour only by either BARRY ADAMSON, CHRIS WALSH or **HARRY HOWARD**

May 82. (lp) *(CAD 207)* **JUNKYARD** 73 / –
 – She's hit / Dead Joe / Dim locator / Hamlet (pow-pow-pow) / Several sins / Big-Jesus-trash-can / Kiss me suck / 6" gold blade / Kewpie doll / Junkyard. *(cd-iss. Apr84+=; CAD 207CD)* – Dead Joe (version) / Release the bats / Blast off.

— In Sep'82, ROWLAND S. HOWARD did duet with LYDIA LUNCH on 12" 'Some Velvet Morning. / I Fell In Love With A Ghost'; *BAD 210)*

Nov 82. Missing Link; (7") *(MLS 32)* **NICK THE STRIPPER. / BLUNDERTOWN** – / – Austra

— Now quartet when **CALVERT** joined **PSYCHEDELIC FURS**. (HARVEY now drums)

Feb 83. (12"ep) *(BAD 301)* **THE BAD SEED** – / –
 – Sonny's burning / Wild world / Fears of gun / Deep in the woods.

— **JEFFREY WEGENER** – drums (ex-LAUGHING CLOWNS) repl. HARVEY Also **BLIXA BARGELD** – guitar (of EINSTURZENDE NEUBAUTEN) repl. absent HOWARD

Mute / not iss.

Nov 83. (12"ep) *(12MUTE 29)* **MUTINY!** – / –
 – Jennifer's veil / Mutiny in Heaven / Swampland / Say a spell.

— Disbanded Autumn 1983. TRACY joined The SAINTS. (He was later to die late '86 of epileptic fit aged 28). ROWLAND HOWARD formed CRIME & THE CITY SOLUTION. NICK CAVE went solo, forming his BAD SEEDS taking with him MICK HARVEY.

– compilations, etc. – (mostly UK)

on '4 a.d.' unless otherwise stated

Jun 83. (12"ep) *(BAD 307)* **THE BIRTHDAY PARTY EP** – / –
 – Release the bats / Blast off / The friend catcher / Mr. Clarinet / Happy birthday.
Apr 85. (d-lp) *Missing Link; (ING 009)* **IT'S STILL LIVING** (live) – / – Austra
Dec 85. (lp) *Missing Link; (LINK 22)* **A COLLECTION – BEST AND RAREST** – / – Austra
Feb 87. (12"ep) *Strange Fruit; (SFPS 020)* **THE PEEL SESSION** (21.4.81) – / –
 – Release the bats / Rowland around in that stuff / (Sometimes) Pleasure heads must burn / Loose. *(re-iss. Aug88 cd-ep; SFPSCD 020)*
Oct 88. (12"ep/cd-ep) *Strange Fruit; (SFPS/+CD 058)* **THE PEEL SESSIONS** (2.12.81) – / –
 – Big-Jesus-trash-can / She's hit / Bully bones / 6" gold blade.
Aug 89. (cd) *(CAD 301CD)* **MUTINY / THE BAD SEED** – / –
Aug 89. (cd) *(CAD 307CD)* **HEE-HAW** – / –
 – (contains tracks from THE BIRTHDAY PARTY lp)
Oct 92. (d-lp/cd)(c) *(DAD 2016/+CD) (DADC 2016)* **HITS** – / – 1998
 – The friend catcher / Happy birthday / Mr. Clarinet / Nick the stripper / Zoo music girl / King Ink / Release the bats / Blast off / She's hit / 6" gold blade / Hamlet (pow, pow, pow) / Dead Joe / Junkyard / Big-Jesus-Trash-Can / Wild world / Sonny's burning / Deep in the woods / Swampland / Jennifer's veil / Mutiny in Heaven.
Jul 99. (cd) *(CAD 9005CD)* **LIVE 1981-1982** (live) – / –

NICK CAVE & THE BAD SEEDS

— **NICK CAVE** – vocals / **MICK HARVEY** – guitar, keyboards / **BLIXA BARGELD** (b.12 Jan'59, Berlin, Germany) – guitar (of EINSTURZENDE NEUBAUTEN) / **BARRY ADAMSON** (b. 1 Jun'58, Manchester, England) – bass, guitar (ex-MAGAZINE, ex-PETE SHELLEY) / **HUGO RACE** – drums

Mute / Restless

Jun 84. (7") *(MUTE 32)* **IN THE GHETTO. / THE MOON IS IN THE GUTTER** – / –

— added **ANITA LANE** – synthesizers (ex-solo artist)

Jun 84. (lp) *(STUMM 17) <71435>* **FROM HER TO ETERNITY** 40 / –
 – Avalanche / Cabin fever / Well of misery / From her to eternity / Wings of flies / Saint Huck / A box for black Paul. *(cd-iss. 1987+=; CDSTUMM 17)* – In the ghetto / The Moon is in the gutter / From her to eternity (1987).

— **THOMAS WYDLER** (b. 9 Oct'59, Zurich, Switzerland) – drums (ex-DIE HAUT) repl. HUGO + ANITA

Mute / Homestead

Jun 85. (lp/c) *(STUMM/CSTUMM 21) <HMS 026>* **THE FIRSTBORN IS DEAD** 53 / –
 – Tupelo / Say goodbye to the little girl tree / Train long suffering / Black crow king / Knockin' on Joe / Wanted man / Blind Lemon Jefferson. *(cd-iss. Apr88+=; CDSTUMM 21)*
Jul 85. (7") *(7MUTE 38)* **TUPELO. / THE SIX STRINGS THAT DREW BLOOD** – / –
Jun 86. (7") *(7MUTE 47)* **THE SINGER. / RUNNING SCARED** – / –
 (12"+=) *(12MUTE 47)* – Black Betty.
Aug 86. (cd/c/lp) *(CD/C+/STUMM 28) <HMS 065>* **KICKING AGAINST THE PRICKS** 89 / –
 – Muddy water / I'm gonna kill that woman / Sleeping Annaleah / Long black veil / Hey Joe / Jesus met the woman at the well / Black Betty * / Running scared * / All tomorrow's parties / By the time I get to Phoenix / The hammer song / Something's gotten hold of my heart / Jesus met the woman at the well / The carnival is over. *(cd+= *)*
Nov 86. (cd/c/lp) *(CD/C+/STUMM 34) <HMS 073>* **YOUR FUNERAL . . . MY TRIAL** – / –
 – Sad waters / The Carny / Your funeral . . . my trial / Stranger than kindness / Jack's shadow / Hard on for love / She fell away / Long time man. *(cd+=) – Scum.*

— CAVE retained HARVEY, BARGELD and WYDLER, bringing in **ROLAND WOLF** – bass / **KID CONGO POWERS** (b. BRIAN TRISTAN, 27 Mar'61, La Puente, Calif.) – guitar (ex-CRAMPS, ex-GUN CLUB)

Mute / Mute-Elektra

May 88. (7") *(MUTE 52)* **THE MERCY SEAT. / NEW DAY** – / –
 (12"+=) *(12MUTE 52)* – ('A' video mix).
 (cd-s+=) *(CDMUTE 52)* – From her to eternity (film version) / Tupelo (version).
Sep 88. (cd/c/lp) *(CD/C+STUMM 52) <75401>* **TENDER PREY** 67 / –
 – The mercy seat / Up jumped the Devil / Deanna / Watching Alice / Mercy / City of refuge / Slowly goes the night / Sunday's slave / Sugar, sugar, sugar / New morning. *(cd+=)* – The mercy seat (video mix). *(free-12"ep.w/above)* **AND THE ASS SAW THE ANGEL** (narration/book) – One Autumn / Animal static / Mah sanctum / Lamentation.
Sep 88. (12") *(12MUTE 86)* **DEANNA. / THE GIRL AT THE BOTTOM OF MY GLASS** – / –
Mar 89. (cd/c/lp; NICK CAVE – MICK HARVEY – BLIXA BARGELD) *(<CD/C+/IONIC 3>)* **GHOSTS . . . OF THE CIVIL DEAD** (Soundtrack w/ dialogue) – / –
 – The news / Introduction – A prison in the desert / David Hale – I've been a prison guard since I was 18 years old / Glover – I was 16 when they put me in prison / David Hale – you're danglin' us like a bunch of meat on a hook / Pop mix / Glover – we were united once / David Hale – the day of the murders / Lilly's theme ("A touch of warmth") / Maynard mix / David Hale – what I'm tellin' is the truth / Outro – The free world / Glover – one man released so they can imprison the rest of the world.

— (now a 5-piece, without WOLF)

Mar 90. (12"/cd-s/7") *(12CD+/MUTE 108)* **THE SHIP SONG. / THE TRAIN SONG** – / –
Apr 90. (cd/c/lp) *(CD/C+/STUMM 76) <60988>* **THE GOOD SON** 47 / – Oct90
 – Foi na cruz / The good son / Sorrow's child / The weeping song / The ship song /

	The hammer song / Lament / The witness song / Lucy. *(w/-7"/cd-s)* **THE MERCY SEAT / CITY OF REFUGE / DEANNA (all acoustic)**
Sep 90.	(12"/7") *(12+/MUTE 118)* **THE WEEPING SONG. / COCKS 'N' ASSES**
	(cd-s+=) *(12/CD MUTE 118)* – Helpless *(some with hidden track).*
—	**CONWAY SAVAGE** (b.27 Jul'60, Foster, Australia) – keyboards + **MARTYN P. CASEY** – 10 Jul'60, Chesterfield, England) – bass (ex-TRIFFIDS) repl. KID CONGO
Mar 92.	(7") *(MUTE 140)* **STRAIGHT TO YOU. / JACK THE RIPPER (acoustic)** — 68
	(12"+=/cd-s+=) *(12/CD MUTE 140)* – Blue bird.
Apr 92.	(cd/c/lp) *(CD/C+/STUMM 92) <61323>* **HENRY'S DREAM** — 29 May92
	– Papa won't leave you Henry / I had a dream, Joe / Straight to you / Brother, my cup is empty / Christina the astonishing / When I first came to town / John Finn's wife / Loom of the land / Jack the ripper.
Aug 92.	(7") *(LMUTE 147)* **I HAD A DREAM, JOE. / THE GOOD SON (live)**
	(12"/cd-s) *(12/CD MUTE 147)* – ('A'side) / The Carny (live) / The mercy seat (live) / The ship song (live).
Nov 92.	(c-s/7"; by NICK CAVE & SHANE MacGOWAN) *(C+/MUTE 151)* **WHAT A WONDERFUL WORLD. / A RAINY NIGHT IN SOHO** — 72
	(7") *(MUTE 151D)* – ('A'side / Lucy (by SHANE MacGOWAN).
	(12"/cd-s) *(12/CD MUTE 151)* – (all 3 tracks).
Sep 93.	(cd) *(CDMUTE 122) <61554>* **LIVE SEEDS (live)** — 67
	– Mercy seat / Deanna / The ship song / Papa won't leave you Henry / Plain gold ring / John Finn's wife / Tupelo / Brother my cup is empty / The weeping song / Jack the ripper / The good son / From her to eternity. *(re-iss. Sep96; LCDSTUMM 122)*
Mar 94.	(12/cd-s/7"silver) *(12/CD+/MUTE 160)* **DO YOU LOVE ME? / CASSIEL'S SONG / SAIL AWAY** — 68
Apr 94.	(cd/c/lp) *(CD/C+/STUMM 123) <61645>* **LET LOVE IN** — 12
	– Do you love me? / Nobody's baby now / Loverman / Jangling Jack / Red right hand / I let love in / Thirsty dog / Ain't gonna rain anymore / Lay me low / Do you love me? (part 2).
—	**JAMES JOHNSON** – guitar (of GALLON DRUNK) repl. on tour only BLIXA
Jul 94.	(7"pic-d) *(MUTE 169)* **LOVERMAN. / (I'LL LOVE YOU) TILL THE END OF THE WORLD**
	(12"/cd-s) *(12/CD MUTE 169)* – ('A'side) / B side.
Oct 94.	(7"red) *(MUTE 172)* **RED RIGHT HAND. / THAT'S WHAT JAZZ IS TO ME**
	(cd-s+=) *(CDMUTE 172)* – Where the action is.
Oct 95.	(c-s/7"; NICK CAVE & THE BAD SEEDS featuring KYLIE MINOGUE) *(C+/MUTE 185)* **WHERE THE WILD ROSES GROW. / THE BALLAD OF ROBERT MOORE & BETTY COLTRANE** — 11
	(cd-s+=) *(CDMUTE 185)* – The willow garden.
Feb 96.	(cd/c/lp) *(CD/C+/STUMM 138) <46195>* **MURDER BALLADS** — 8
	– Song of joy / Stagger Lee / Henry Lee / Lovely creature / Where the wild roses grow (featuring KYLIE MINOGUE) / The curse of Millhaven / The kindness of strangers / Crow Jane / O'Malley's bar / Death is not the end.
Feb 96.	(7"; by NICK CAVE & PJ HARVEY) *(MUTE 189)* **HENRY LEE. / KING KONG KITCHEE KITCHEE KI-MI-O** — 36
	(c-s+=/cd-s+=) *(C/CD MUTE 189)* – Knoxville girl.
—	<most UK singles were given a US release in 1996>
—	JOHNSON was repl. by **JIM SCLAVUNOS + WARREN ELLIS**
Feb 97.	(7") *(MUTE 192)* **INTO MY ARMS. / LITTLE EMPTY BOAT** — 53
	(cd-s+=) *(CDMUTE 192)* – Right now I'm a-roaming.
Mar 97.	(cd/c) *(CD/C+/STUMM 142) <46530>* **THE BOATMAN'S CALL** — 22
	– Into my arms / Lime tree harbour / People ain't no good / Brompton oratory / There is a kingdom / (Are you) The one that I've been waiting for? / Where do we go now but nowhere? / West country girl / Black hair / Idiot prayer / Far from me / Green eyes.
May 97.	(7") *(MUTE 206)* **(ARE YOU) THE ONE THAT I'VE BEEN WAITING FOR? / COME INTO MY SLEEP** — 67
	(cd-s+=) *(CDMUTE 206)* – Black hair (band version) / Babe, I got you bad.
May 98.	(cd/c/d-lp) *(CD/C+/MUTEL 004) <46960>* **THE BEST OF NICK CAVE & THE BAD SEEDS** (compilation) — 11
	– Deanna / Red right hand / Straight to you / Tupelo / Nobody's baby now / Stranger than kindness / Into my arms / (Are you) The one that I've been waiting for? / The Carny / Do you love me? / The mercy seat / Henry Lee (feat. PJ HARVEY) / The weeping song / The ship song / Where the wild roses grow (feat. KYLIE MINOGUE) / For her to eternity. *(special d-cd; LCDMUTEL 004)* **LIVE AT THE ROYAL ALBERT HALL** – Stranger than kindness / The ship song / Let love in / Brompton oratory / Red right hand / Lime tree arbour / The weeping song / Henry Lee / Where the wild roses grow / Deanna / Straight to you / Tupelo / Nobody's baby now / Into my arms / (Are you) The one that I've been waiting for? / The Carny / Do you love me? / The mercy seat / From her to eternity.
Mar 01.	(10"/cd) *(10/CD MUTE 249)* **AS I SAT SADLY BY HER SIDE. / LITTLE JANEY'S GONE / GOOD GOOD DAY** — 42
Apr 01.	(cd/c/d-lp) *(CD/C+/STUMM 164) <48039>* **NO MORE SHALL WE PART** — 15
	– As I sat sadly by her side / And no more shall we part / Hallelujah / Love letter / Fifteen feet of pure white snow / God is in the house / Oh my Lord / Sweetheart come / The sorrowful wife / We came along this road / Gates to the garden / Darker with the day. *(special cd+=; LCDSTUMM 164)* – Bless his ever loving heart / Grief came riding.
May 01.	(10") *(10MUTE 262)* **FIFTEEN FEET OF PURE WHITE SNOW. / GOD IS IN THE HOUSE (westside session) / AND NO MORE SHALL WE PART (westside session)** — 52
	(cd-s) *(CDMUTE 262)* – (first 2 tracks) / We came along this road (westside session).

Exene CERVENKA (see under ⇒ X)

Eugene CHADBOURNE

Born: 4 Jan'54, Mount Vernon, New York, USA. Raised in Boulder, Colorado, the guitarist initially took up journalism before fleeing to Canada to avoid the Vietnam draft. EUGENE returned to New York after the government relaxed their hardline policy, hooking up with avant-garde saxophonist, JOHN ZORN and releasing rare recordings, 'SCHOOL' and '2000 STATUES: THE ENGLISH CHANNEL'. Having been inspired by folk protest icon, PHIL OCHS at an early age, CHADBOURNE developed more wayward tastes as he grew older, getting into classic psychedelia and free-form jazz. He subsequently found a sympathetic musical ally in the form of bassist, MARK KRAMER, the pair instigating SHOCKABILLY in 1982 along with drummer, DAVID LICHT. Signing to UK indie outlet, 'Rough Trade', the madcap trio delivered a series of weird and wonderful releases including their inaugural recording, 'THE DAWN OF SHOCKABILLY EP' and 1983's covers jamboree (see below) 'EARTH VS. SHOCKABILLY'. Three more sets followed over the course of the next two years, namely 'COLOSSEUM' (1984), 'VIETNAM' (1985) and 'HEAVEN' (1985), the latter two issued on 'Fundamental' shortly before their demise. With KRAMER going on to join The BUTTHOLE SURFERS and start up his own 'Shimmy-Disc' label, CHADBOURNE had already prepared for a solo career by releasing a late 1985 set of warped C&W, 'COUNTRY PROTEST', re-activating the radical sentiments previously aired by his hero, OCHS. A series of largely collaborative albums appeared over the latter half of the 80's, notably 'THERE'LL BE NO TEARS TONIGHT' (1987; a 1980 recording with JOHN ZORN), 'VERMIN OF THE BLUES' (1987) with EVAN JOHNS & THE H BOMBS, 'THE LSD C&W' (1987; a turn of the decade recording as The CHADBOURNES) and 'CAMPER VAN CHADBOURNE' (1988), obviously a joint effort with alt-country bumpkins, CAMPER VAN BEETHOVEN. The 90's saw the maverick New Yorker setting up home at JELLO BIAFRA's 'Alternative Tentacles' label and releasing another dual opus with EVAN JOHNS, 'TERROR HAS SOME STRANGE KINFOLK' (1993); fan(s) of BILLY RAY CYRUS should listen out for the pastiche, 'ACHEY RAKEY HEART'. In 1996, the ubiquitous CHADBOURNE collaborated with ex-MOTHERS OF INVENTION drummer, JIMMY CARL BLACK, on an album of ZAPPA and BEEFHEART covers, 'THE JACK AND JIM SHOW – PACHUCO CADAVAR'. • **Covered:** 19th NERVOUS BREAKDOWN (Rolling Stones) / DAY TRIPPER (Beatles) / EIGHT MILES HIGH (Byrds) / I MUST HAVE BEEN BLIND (Tim Buckley) / PEOPLE ARE STRANGE (Doors) / INSTANT KARMA + OH YOKO (John Lennon) / ARE YOU EXPERIENCED + PURPLE HAZE (Jimi Hendrix) / LUCIFER SAM + CAREFUL WITH THAT AXE, EUGENE (Pink Floyd) / etc.

Album rating: Shockabilly: EARTH VS. SHOCKABILLY (*6) / COLOSSEUM (*5) / VIETNAM (*5) / HEAVEN (*5) / Eugene Chadbourne: COUNTRY PROTEST (*5) / CORPSES OF FOREIGN WAR (*5) / THERE'LL BE NO TEARS TONIGHT (*7) / VERMIN OF THE BLUES with Evan Johns & The H-Bombs (*5) / THE LSD C&W (*5) / CAMPER VAN CHADBOURNE (*6) / I'VE BEEN EVERYWHERE (*5) / THE EDDIE CHATTERBOX DOUBLE TRIO LOVE ALBUM (*5) / COUNTRY MUSIC IN THE WORLD OF ISLAM (*5) / EUROPE VAN BEETHOVEN – SINFUNNY (*5) / TERROR HAS SOME STRANGE KINFOLK (*5) / PACHUCO CADAVAR (*6)

EUGENE CHADBOURNE

		not iss.	Parachute
1975.	(ltd-lp) *<POO-1>* **SOLO ACOUSTIC GUITAR VOL.1**	—	
1976.	(ltd-lp) *<POO-2>* **SOLO ACOUSTIC GUITAR VOL.2**	—	
	<cd-iss. Aug98 on 'Rastacan'; 32>		
1977.	(ltd-lp) *<POO 3>* **GUITAR TRIOS: VOLUME THREE**	— not iss.	Merge
1977.	(lp) *<MGE 9>* **IMPROVISED MUSIC FOR ACOUSTIC PIANO AND GUITAR MUSIC GALLERY EDITIONS**		
		not iss.	Parachute
Sep 79.	(d-lp; with JOHN ZORN) *<POO 4&6>* **SCHOOL**	—	
Dec 79.	(lp) *<POO 7>* **THE ENGLISH CHANNEL**	—	
1980.	(lp) *<PO 13>* **THERE'LL BE NO TEARS TONIGHT**	—	
	<(UK+re-iss. Jan87 on 'Fundamental'; SAVE 016)> <(cd-iss. Jul90; SAVE 016CD)>		
1981.	(lp; w/ POLLY BRADFIELD) *<POO 10>* **TORTURE TIME**	—	
1983.	(c) **CHICKEN ON THE WAY**	—	

SHOCKABILLY

EUGENE CHADBOURNE – vocals, guitar / **MARK KRAMER** – bass / **DAVID LICHT** – drums

		Rough Trade	Fundam.
Nov 82.	(12"ep) *(RTT 120)* **THE DAWN OF SHOCKABILLY**		—
Mar 83.	(7") *(RT 127)* **19th NERVOUS BREAKDOWN. / CITY OF CORRUPTION**		—
1983.	(lp) *(ROUGH 48) <SAVE 17>* **EARTH VS. SHOCKABILLY**		1988
	– 19th nervous breakdown / Are you experienced? / Psychedelic basement / Big money broad / Tennessee flat top box / City of corruption / People are strange / Day tripper / Purple haze / Wrestling woman / Oh Yoko. *(re-iss. 1988 on 'Shimmy Disc'; SHIMMY 017)*		
1983.	(12"ep) *(RED 006)* **GREATEST HITS** (compilation)		—
	– Blue grass breakdown / Burma shave / Voodoo vengeance / People are strange / Wrestling woman / Train.		
	(above issued on 'Red Music')		
Apr 84.	(lp) *(ROUGH 68)* **COLOSSEUM**		—
	– Our daily lead / BYOB club / Roman man / Too big for it's cage / Eight miles high / Dang me / Secret of the cooler / Hattiesburg, Miss. / You dungeon my brain / Homeward bound / National bummer.		
		Fundam.	Fundam.
Aug 85.	(lp) *<(SAVE 001)>* **VIETNAM**		
	– Pile up all architecture / Born on the bayou / Your U.S.A. and my face / Vietnam /		

Eugene CHADBOURNE (cont)

Flying / Nicaragua / Paris / Iran into Tulsa / Georgia in a jug / Lucifer Sam / Signed D.C.

Nov 85. (lp) *(SAVE 008)* **HEAVEN**
– Instant karma / She was a living breathing piece of dirt / Red headed stranger / When you dream about bleeding / Tau and the soldier / Life's a gas / Tray-panning the man / Hendrix buried in Tacoma / How can you kill me, I'm already dead / Vampire tiger girl strikes again / Pity me Sheena / Happy new year / Our metempsychosis.

— they split in 1985, KRAMER joined BUTTHOLE SURFERS before forming BONGWATER and B.A.L.L.

– compilations, etc. –

1989. (cd) *Shimmy Disc;* **THE GHOST OF SHOCKABILLY**
– (EARTH VS. SHOCKABILLY + COLOSSEUM)
Jan 90. (cd) *Shimmy Disc;* <SHIMMY 026> **VIETNAM + HEAVEN**
(UK-iss.Aug01; SHM 5026)
Feb 90. (cd) *Shimmy Disc;* <SHIMMY 027> **LIVE JUST BEAUTIFUL**
– Intro / Georgia in a Ju / 8 miles high / Plunger routine / Are you experienced / Burma shave / Rake (birdcage routine) / Outro / Oh Yoko! / Dang me / Lucifer Sam / Nobody's place (dawn of Shockabilly) / Heart full of soul / Good girl's gonna go bad / Psychotic reaction / A hard day's night / Train kept a rollin' / Our daily lead / Byob club / Roman man / Too big for its cage / 8 miles high / Dang me / Secret of the cooler / Hattiesburg, Miss. / You dungeon my brain / Homeward bound / National bummer. *(cd re-iss. 1993; 8914)*

EUGENE CHADBOURNE

not iss. Iridescent
1984. (lp) <none> **THE PRESIDENT: HE IS INSANE**

not iss. Hot
1985. (lp) <Hot 1017> **THE RELATIVE BAND '85**

— next with RED CLAY RAMBLERS, DAVID LICHT, LENNY KAYE, etc
Fundam. Fundam.
Nov 85. (lp) <(SAVE 007)> **COUNTRY PROTEST**
– Convention of melodies / Melody in C / Always on my mind / I started a joke / The shah sleeps in / Lee Harvey's gone / Waltz across Texas. *(cd-iss. Jul90; SAVE 007CD)*

below with BRIAN RITCHIE – (of VIOLENT FEMMES)

Jul 86. (lp/c) (SAVE/CAVE 010) <SF 27> **CORPSES OF FOREIGN WARS**
– Universal soldier / When I'm gone / Fightin' side of me / etc
(cd-iss. Jul90; SAVE 010CD)
Jun 87. (lp; as EUGENE CHADBOURNE, EVAN JOHNS & THE H BOMBS) <(SAVE 018)> **VERMIN OF THE BLUES**
(cd-iss. Jul90; SAVE 018CD)
Jun 87. (d-lp) <(SAVE 019-020)> **THE LSD C&W** (recorded 1979-81 as The CHADBOURNES)
Feb 88. (lp; EUGENE CHADBOURNE & CAMPER VAN BEETHOVEN) <(SAVE 046)> **CAMPER VAN CHADBOURNE**
– Reason to believe / I talk to the wind / Fayettenam / Evil filthy preacher / Games people play / Zappa medley / Ba-lue bolivar ba-lues are / Boy with the coins / Psychedelic basement / Hum-allah hum-allah / Careful with that axe, Eugene / They can't make it rain bombs. *(cd-iss. Jul90; SAVE 046CD) (cd re-iss. Aug97; HYMN 7)*
Feb 89. (lp/c/cd) <(SAVE 068/+MC/CD)> **I'VE BEEN EVERYWHERE**
Feb 89. (lp/c/cd) <(SAVE 069/+MC/CD)> **THE EDDIE CHATTERBOX DOUBLE TRIO LOVE ALBUM**
– Sword & shield / Someday / Life x 2 minus 1 / Used record pile / Voodoo vengeance / I must have been blind / Chase the blues away / The river / Blue melody / Strange melody.
May 90. (lp/cd) <(SAVE 080/+CD)> **COUNTRY MUSIC IN THE WORLD OF ISLAM**
Sep 90. (d-lp/cd) **EUROPE VAN BEETHOVEN – SINFUNNY** (live)

EUGENE CHADBOURNE & EVAN JOHNS

Alternative Alternative
Tentacles Tentacles
Jun 93. (lp/cd) <(VIRUS 19/+CD)> **TERROR HAS SOME STRANGE KINFOLK**
– Achey rakey heart / Redneck jazz / Sail my ship alone / I gotta pee / I cut the wrong man / George Bush's bones jig / Desert storm chewing gum / Let 'em drink while they're young / Mister Jones / Missing engineer / Killbillies / Got the blues and can't be satisfied / Checkers of blood / There was gloom / Land of used to be / Living in the country.
Jul 93. (7") <(VIRUS 125)> **ACHEY RAKEY HEART. /**

EUGENE CHADBOURNE

— next feat. JIMMY CARL BLACK – drums, vocals (ex-FRANK ZAPPA)
not iss. Fundam.
1994. (cd; as The JACK AND JIM SHOW) <HYMN 2> **LOCKED IN A DUTCH COFFEE SHOP**
– Dropped another needle / Big boss man / B.Y.O.B. club / Captain Beefheart medley: Neon meate dream of an octafish – Sheriff of Hong Kong – The blimp / The umbrella / Expense account meeting / Call to Opal / Hey baby, que paso? / Dawn of the living dread / Colorado kool-aid / Fresh garbage / Prelude to chili in Navajo taco / Le hippie dogg / Ethnic cleansing / Crybaby umbrella. *(UK-iss.Aug97 by EUGENE CHADBOURNE; same)*
Fireant Fireant
Dec 95. (cd; EUGENE CHADBOURNE & JIMMY CARL BLACK) *(facd 1007)* **THE JACK AND JIM SHOW – PACHUCO CADAVER**
– That buggie boogie woogie / Willie the pimp / Drop out boogie / Sure 'nuff n' yes ah do / Clear spot / Steal softly through snow / The past is tense / Veteran's day puppy / I'm gonna booglarize you baby / Pachuco Cadaver / The dust blows forward and the dust blows back.
Jul 96. (cd) **JESSE HELMS BUSTED WITH PORNOGRAPHY**
not iss. Victo
Feb 97. (cd) <46> **PATRIZIO**

not iss. Intakt
Mar 97. (cd; by EUGENE CHADBOURNE & HELLINGTON COUNTY) <052> **HELLINGTUNES**

– compilations, others, etc. –

1986. (cd) *RR Records;* **COUNTRY MUSIC OF SOUTH EASTERN AUSTRALIA**
1986. (cd) *Parachute;* **CALGARY EXILE**
1987. (cd) *Placebo; (PLCD 5)* **DEAR EUGENE**
– Ollie's playhouse / How can you kill me / Eight miles high / Women against porno / Purple haze / The plunger / Oh Yoko / Ramblin' man / I must have been blind / Big boys will be little boys / Lucifer Sam / Price of Paradise / In the cemetary / Monk medley / Permanent lonely / Secret of the cooler.
1987. (c) *Parachute;* **MEGADEATH**
1987. (c) *Parachute;* **THIRD WORLD SUMMIT MEETING**
1987. (c) *Parachute;* **TUCSON, ARIZONA**
1988. (c) *Parachute;* **FUCK CHUCK**
1988. (c) *Parachute;* **WICHITA, KANSAS**
1993. (cd) *Leo;* **WORMS WITH STRINGS**
May 95. (cd) *Overtone;* <001> **ELECTRIC RAKE CAKE**
1997. (cd) *Leo;* <256> **INSECT AND WESTERN ATTRACTER**

James CHANCE

Born: JAMES SIEGFRIED, 20 Apr'53, Milwaukee, Wisconsin, USA. Having dropped out of Wisconsin Conservatory music school, JAMES took his saxophone to New York in 1976 and after a short-lived period studying under DAVID MURRAY, he formed The CONTORTIONS (i.e. ADELE BEREI, JODY HARRIS, PAT PLACE, GEORGE SCOTT III and DON CHRISTENSEN). With the city in the grip of punk fever, CHANCE took the opportunity to fuse aggressive nihilism with wildly improvised sax scree and twisted funk rhythms; reputed to be as obsessively meticulous as BEEFHEART during his "Trout Mask Replica" period, CHANCE and his CONTORTIONS' unhinged live shows often degenerated into improvised violence as the man confronted punters indiscriminately. Although they gained infamy in the Big Apple, it wasn't until 1978 that CHANCE and Co reached a wider audience when Avant Garde curator, BRIAN ENO, collected the sounds of various "No Wave" artists (including TEENAGE JESUS & THE JERKS, DNA and MARS) together on the album, 'No New York'; four tracks were featured, namely 'I CAN'T STAND MYSELF', 'JADED', 'DISH IT OUT' and 'FLIP YOUR FACE'. Finally, after nearly three years of aural terrorism, The CONTORTIONS unleashed their one and only studio set, hopefully titled 'BUY' (late '79). By this time, CHANCE had decided to re-invent himself and the band as JAMES WHITE AND THE BLACKS, two albums 'OFF-WHITE' (1980) and 'SAX MANIAC' (1982) offering up a less crazed but still off-beat take on funk and jazz drawing heavily from MACEO PARKER's heyday with JAMES BROWN. In 1980, he also found time to collaborate with ARTO LINDSAY, BRADLEY FIELD and band member, GEORGE SCOTT, on a soundtrack of Diego Cortez's film, 'Grutzi Elvis' (SCOTT was to die of a heroin overdose soon after its release). While The CORTORTIONS were still the subject of a posthumous release schedule, JAMES (WHITE) had already moved to Paris, returning periodically to New York City, mainly to record albums, most notably 1983's solo effort, 'JAMES WHITE PRESENTS THE FLAMING DELMONICS'. In 1987, after spells with trombonist JOSEPH BOWIE (later leader of DEFUNKT) and HENRY THREADGILL (of jazz outfit, AIR), he took on work with The FALSE PROPHETS, his alto sax clearly making the grade on their 'Implosion' set. Of late, CHANCE re-formed his CONTORTIONS, although recordings have been sparse thus far.

Album rating: Contortions: BUY (*7) LIVE IN NEW YORK (*6) / James Chance & The Blacks: OFF-WHITE (*6) / SAX MANIAC (*5) / JAMES WHITE PRESENTS THE FLAMING DELMONICS (*5)

CONTORTIONS

JAMES CHANCE – vocals, saxophone / ADELE BERTEI – organ / JODY HARRIS – guitar / PAT PLACE – slide guitar / GEORGE SCOTT II – bass / DON CHRISTENSEN – drums
Ze-Island Ze
Oct 79. (12") <ZEA12 001> **DESIGNED TO KILL. / THROW ME AWAY**
Mar 80. (lp) (ILPS 7002) <ZEA-33 002> **BUY** Nov79
– Designed to kill / My infatuation / I don't want to be happy / Anesthetic / Contort yourself / Throw me away / Roving eye / Twice removed / Bedroom athlete. *(cd-iss. Mar96 on 'Infinite Zero-BMG'; 74321 32757-2)*

JAMES WHITE & THE BLACKS

— virtually the same group members except BERTEI who was retained as guest although she had joined the BLOODS
Ze-Island Ze
May 80. (lp) (ILPS 7008) <ZEA33 003> **OFF-WHITE**
– Contort yourself / Stained sheets / Almost black / Heat wave / Almost black / White savages / Off black / White devil / Bleached black. *<(cd-iss. Oct95 on 'Infinite Zero-BMG'+=; 74321 31879-2)>* – Christmas with Satan.
Aug 80. (12") <ZE12 006> **CONTORT YOURSELF. / (TROPICAL) HEATWAVE**

— PAT joined BUSH TETRAS, while SCOTT joined LYDIA LUNCH in 8-EYED SPY, before re-grouping with HARRIS and CHRISTENSEN in The RAYBEATS. Meanwhile, JAMES recruited new band; JERRY ANTONIUS + CHRIS CUNNINGHAM – guitar / COLIN WADE – bass / RALPH ROLLE – drums / CHERIE MARILYN + ROBIN MARLOWE – vocals / ROBERT AARON – tenor sax / LUTHER THOMAS – saxes

Sep 82. (lp) <(CHR 1401)> **SAX MANIAC**   Chrysalis Chrysalis
- Irresistable impulse / That old black magic / Disco jaded / Money to burn / Sax maniac / Sax machine / The twitch. (cd-iss. 1996 on 'Infinite Zero'; 43066-2>

JAMES WHITE

— **RODNEY FORSTALL** – bass; repl. WADE

                                                              Ze-Island   not iss.
1983.   (lp) (ILPS 7023) **JAMES WHITE PRESENTS THE FLAMING DEMONICS**
- The Devil made me do it / Boulevard of broken dreams / Rantin' & ravin' / The natives are restless / Caravan / It don't mean a thing / Melt yourself down / I danced with a zombie.

– compilations, etc. –

May 80. (lp) *Invisible;* (SCOPA 1008) **LIVE AUX BAINS DOUCHES PARIS** (live with new CONTORTIONS)   –   –   French
- Don't stop till you get enough / I danced with a zombie / My infatuation / I got you (I feel good) / Almost black / King Heroin / Put me back in my cage / Contort yourself.
   above with **GINGER LEE** – vocals / **PATRICK GEOFFROIS + FRED WELLS** – guitar / **AL MacDOWELL** – bass / **RICHARD HARRISON** – drums / **LORENZO WYCHE** – trumpet
1981.   (c) *R.O.I.R.;* <A 100> **LIVE IN NEW YORK** (live with The CONTORTIONS)   –
- I got you (I feel good) / That old black magic / Sophisticated cancer / King heroin / White cannibal / Money to burn / Contort yourself. (UK cd-iss. Nov94 on 'Danceteria'; DANCD 082)
Apr 91. (lp/c) *R.O.I.R.;* <(A 191/+C)> **SOUL EXORCISM** (live Amsterdam June 1980 with The CONTORTIONS)
- Intro / Don't stop 'til you get enough / I danced with a zombie / Exorcise the funk / Disposable you / The twitch / The Devil made me do it / Melt yourself down / King heroin / Put me back in my cage / Contort yourself. <(cd-iss. Nov94; RE 191CD)>
Oct 95. (cd) *ROIR USA;* <(RUSCD 8214)> **LOST CHANCE** (live Chicago September 1981 with The Contortions)
- Super bad / Sax maniac / Almost black / White cannibal / I got you (I feel good) / Melt yourself down / Hell on earth / King heroin / My infatuation. (re-iss. Oct00; same)
Sep 97. (cd) *Enemy;* (EMY 157-2) **MOLOTOV COCKTAIL LOUNGE**
Oct 00. (cd) *ROIR USA;* <(RUSCD 8267)> **WHITE CANNIBAL** (live)

CHELSEA

Formed: London, England ... October '76 initially as LSD by GENE OCTOBER. He was soon left to take up the reins when other members, BILLY IDOL, TONY JAMES and JOHN TOWE went off to form the more successful GENERATION X. Early the following year, GENE founded CHELSEA along with JAMES STEVENSON, CAREY FORTUNE and SIMON VITESSE, the latter a replacement for short-lived member, HENRY BADOWSKI. Signed to Miles Copeland's new independent imprint, 'Step Forward', CHELSEA released the political protest, 'RIGHT TO WORK' as their debut single in the summer of '77. The people's punks followed up with another anthemic dig at government complacency in the shape of 'HIGH RISE LIVING', a heavy touring schedule taking in the country's more deprived areas as well as the normal city dates. Around this period (Autumn '77), GENE had a bit part in Derek Jarman's controversial punk film, 'Jubilee', alongside the likes of ADAM ANT, TOYAH and WAYNE COUNTY; a couple of CHELSEA songs were to feature on its soundtrack. A new line-up of OCTOBER, STEVENSON, GEOFF MYLES and CHRIS BASHFORD re-emerged in late summer '78 (with 'URBAN KIDS') after a lengthy absence and it was to be a further year before the belated release of their eponymous first album. By this point in time, GENE and Co had been overtaken by the musical experimentation of their now post-punk peers, the band relegated to the Vauxhall Conference Division of straggling punk diehards. Through varying line-ups, CHELSEA continued to fight the punk wars over the course of the 80's and some of the 90's, GENE's last effort to date being 1995's appropriately titled solo set, 'LIFE AND STRUGGLE'. • **Songwriters:** OCTOBER penned, except STREET FIGHTING MAN (Rolling Stones), and his solo SUFFERING IN THE LAND (Jimmy Cliff). • **Trivia:** In 1985, OCTOBER made an appearance on LWT's rock programme alongside JOOLS HOLLAND and MEAT LOAF!

Album rating: CHELSEA (*4) / ALTERNATIVE HITS compilation (*5) / EVACUATE (*3) / LIVE AND WELL (*4) / JUST FOR THE RECORD compilation (*5) / ROCKS OFF (*3) / UNDERWRAPS (*3) / THE ALTERNATIVE (*3) / TRAITOR'S GATE (*3) / Gene October: LIFE AND STRUGGLE (*3)

GENE OCTOBER – vocals / **JAMES STEVENSON** – lead guitar / **CAREY FORTUNE** – drums / **SIMON VITESSE** – bass; repl. HENRY BADOWSKI who joined WRECKLESS ERIC, The DAMNED, and later HELLIONS, before UK SUBS.

                                                        Step Forward   I.R.S.
Jun 77. (7") (SF 2) **RIGHT TO WORK. / THE LONER**
Oct 77. (7") (SF 5) **HIGH RISE LIVING. / NO ADMISSION**

— **OCTOBER + STEVENSON** were joined by **DAVE MARTIN** – guitar / **GEOFF MYLES** – bass / **CHRIS BASHFORD** – drums (CAREY later guested on JJ BURNEL's solo album)

Aug 78. (7") (SF 8) **URBAN KIDS. / NO FLOWERS**
Jul 79. (lp) (SFLP 2) **CHELSEA**
- I'm on fire / Decide / Free the fighters / Your toy / Fools and soldiers / All the downs / Government / Twelve men / Many rivers / Trouble is the day. (cd-iss. Oct98 on 'Captain Oi'; AHOYCD 91) (lp re-iss. Sep99 on 'Get Back'; GET 38)
Feb 80. (7") (SF 14) **NO ONE'S COMING OUTSIDE. / WHAT WOULD YOU DO?**
Apr 80. (7") (SF 15) **LOOK AT THE OUTSIDE. / DON'T GET ME WRONG**
Jul 80. (7") (SF 16) **NO ESCAPE. / DECIDE**
Nov 80. (lp) (SFLP 5) <SP 70010> **ALTERNATIVE HITS** <US-title 'NO ESCAPE'> (compilation)
- No escape / Urban kids / No flowers / All the downs / Right to work / Look at the outside / What would you do / No one's coming outside / The loner / Don't get me wrong / Decide / Come on. (<cd-iss. Oct98 on 'Captain Oi'+=; AYOYCD 92>) – High rise living / No admission.

— disbanded again when DAVE MARTIN joined PINK MILITARY, and STEVENSON was poached by GENE's favourite group GENERATION X

— **OCTOBER** recruited **NIC AUSTIN** – guitar / **TIM GRIFFIN** – bass / **SOL MINTZ** – drums

May 81. (7") (SF 17) **ROCKIN' HORSE. / YEARS AWAY**
Sep 81. (7"m) (SF 18) **FREEMANS. / I.D. PARADE / HOW DO YOU KNOW?**
Nov 81. (7") (SF 20) **EVACUATE. / NEW ERA**

— **SOL MINTZ** – drums; repl. JONES

Mar 82. (7") (SF 21) **WAR ACROSS THE NATION. / HIGH RISE LIVING** (remix)
Apr 82. (lp) (SFLP 7) <SP 70603> **EVACUATE**
- Evacuate / How do you know? / Cover up / Looks right / Tribal song / War across the nation / Forty people / Running free / Last drink / Only thinking. (cd-iss. Nov98 on 'Captain Oi'+=; AHOYCD 94) – Years away / Freemans / I.D. parade / How do you know? / New era / War across the nation / Stand out.
Oct 82. (7",7"pic-d) (SF 22) **STAND OUT. / LAST DRINK**

— disbanded again early in 1983. AUSTIN joined BANDITS AT 4 O'CLOCK, and LINC joined LIGOTAGE.

GENE OCTOBER

                                                        Illegal   not iss.
Jan 83. (7") (ILS 034) **SUFFERING IN THE LAND. / SUFFERING DUB**
                                                        Slipped Discs   not iss.
Jan 84. (7") (SPLAT 001) **DON'T QUIT. / BURNING SOUNDS**

CHELSEA

— were back for mid-83, with **GENE** plus **PETER DIMMOCK** – bass (ex-CHRON GEN) / **DAVEY JONES** (b. Scotland) – guitar / **GEOFF SEWELL** (or) **COLVILLE** – drums

                                                        Picasso   not iss.
May 84. (lp) (PIK 003) **LIVE AND WELL** (live)
- Tribal song / Evacuate / No admission / How do you know / No flowers / Only thinking / Running wild / Urban kids / The last time / Right to work. (cd re-iss. Oct95 on 'Razor'; PUNXCD 1) (cd re-iss. Sep01 on 'Rhythm Vicar'; PREACH 033CD)

— **PHOENIX + TIM BRIFFA** – guitar; repl. DAVEY

                                                        Communique not iss.
Jun 85. (7") (LITTLE 1) **VALIUM MOTHER. / MONICA, MONICA** (12"+=) – (12LITTLE 1) – Break this town.
Aug 85. (lp) (LARGE 1) **ORIGINAL SINNERS**
Mar 86. (7") **SHINE THE LIGHT. / BELIEVE ME**
                                                        Jungle   not iss.
Nov 86. (lp) (FREUD 14) **ROCKS OFF**
- Fool's Paradise / Revolution No.9 / Hard-up baby / Memory fades / Give me more / Inside out / You and me / Street fighting man / Little princess / Sidewinder.
                                                        Chelsea   not iss.
May 88. (7") (CH 001) **GIVE ME MORE. / SYMPATHY FOR THE DEVIL**

— next featured **TOPPER HEADON** – drums (ex-CLASH); on 2 tracks / plus **STEVE TANNETT** – guitar (ex-MENACE) / **NIC AUSTIN**

                                                        I.R.S.   not iss.
Jun 89. (lp/c/cd) (EIRSA/+C/CD 1011) **UNDERWRAPS**
- Somebody got murdered / Cheat / Give me mercy / Nice girls / No respect / Life of crime / Switchblade / Fool / Time after time / Come on.
                                                        Alter-Ego   not iss.
Apr 93. (cd) (ALTGOCD 002) **THE ALTERNATIVE**
- The alternative / Weirdos in wonderland / More than a giro / Wasting time / Ever wonder / Where is everything / You can be there too / What's wrong with you / Oh no / Too late / Dreams of dreams / Ode to the travellers. (re-iss. Oct94 on 'Weser'; WL 2466-2)
                                                        Weser   not iss.
Aug 94. (cd) (WL 2480-2) **TRAITORS GATE**
- Streets of anarchy / Be what you want to be / Traitors gate / Power for a day / Fireworks / S.A.D. / My hotel room / Guns in paradise / We dare / Floating in the dark / This is now / Nightmares.
May 95. (7") (WL 2482-7) **WE DARE. / WHAT'S WRONG WITH YOU** (live) / **RIGHT TO WORK** (live)

— CHELSEA finally split in 1995

– compilations, etc. –

May 85. (lp) *Step Forward;* (SFLP 10) **JUST FOR THE RECORD**
Sep 88. (lp) *Illegal;* (ILP 024) **BACKTRAX**
Aug 89. (lp) *Clay;* (CLAYLP 101) **UNRELEASED STUFF**
- I'm on fire / Come on / No flowers / Urban kids / 12 men / Trouble is the day / Young toy / Decide / Curfew / Look at the outside / Don't get me wrong / Fools and soldiers. (<cd-iss. May93 & Jul94 lp/cd; CLAY/+CD 101>)
Mar 92. (cd) *Released Emotions;* (REM 016CD) **LIVE AT THE MUSIC MACHINE 1978** (live)
Jul 97. (cd) *Receiver;* (<RRCD 242>) **FOOLS AND SOLDIERS**   Aug97
Dec 98. (cd) *Captain Oi;* (<AHOYCD 98>) **THE PUNK SINGLES COLLECTION 1977-1982**
Apr 99. (cd) *Captain Oi;* (<AHOYCD 106>) **PUNK ROCK RARITIES**
Feb 01. (cd) *Captain Oi;* (<AHOYCD 159>) **THE BBC PUNK SESSIONS**

Feb 02. (cd) *Red Steel; (RMCCD 9224)* **METALLIC F.O.** (live at CBGB's)

GENE OCTOBER

— with **JAMES STEVENSON** – guitar / **EMILE LOBO** – guitar / **JAMES HALLAWELL** – organ / **GLEN MATLOCK** – bass /

Receiver / Receiver

Mar 95. (cd) *(<RRCD 196>)* **LIFE AND STRUGGLE**
– Born to keep on running / Count to ten / Watch out / Welcome home / Butterfly / Life and struggle / It hurts / I owe you nothing / Big tears / Curfew / Everytime I see you I know I just gotta go.

Phil CHEVRON (see under ⇒ RADIATORS FROM SPACE)

Wild Billy CHILDISH

Born: STEPHEN JOHN HAMPER, 1958, Chatham, Kent, England. Having formed the POP RIVETS in 1977 – they only lasted a few years and a couple of albums – he went on to form The MILKSHAKES (subsequently known as THEE MILKSHAKES) with original guitarist, BRUCE BRAND (who was relegated to the drum stool when CHILDISH became 6-string proficient). This psychobilly/garage outfit toured alongside fellow Medway bands, The PRISONERS and The DENTISTS, while BILLY also turned his hand to poetry (his published works are now in double figures, something of an achievement in itself bearing in mind the man's chronic dyslexia!). In the early 80's, the MILKSHAKES released numerous albums, combining a plethora of R&B cover versions somewhat akin to what the COUNT BISHOPS had been doing several years earlier. In 1985, the hard-drinking WILD BILLY formed another outlet for his irrepressible creativity, THEE MIGHTY CAESARS, while also combining a solo career (!). Towards the end of the 80's, he virtually re-formed THEE MILKSHAKES, although this time around they were known as THEE HEADCOATS. In 1990, the group (featuring MICKEY HAMPSHIRE, RUSS WILKINS and BRUCE BRAND) were back on form with the rockin' brilliant third set, 'BEACH BUMS MUST DIE', followed almost immediately by 'HEAVENS TO MURGATROYD...' (1991), a set that would find its way on to US grunge bastion 'Sub Pop'. Around the same time, THEE HEADCOATS had the wonderfully amateurish promo for 'MATCHSTICK GIRL' featured on a V/A 'Sub Pop' video collection. While CHILDISH also undertook solo work, he worked with yet another associated project, THEE HEADCOATEES, who initially released the 'SECT' EP on his own 'Hangman's Daughter' imprint. In 1995, CHILDISH celebrated by inviting all his previous musical incarnations to farewell gigs at London's 'Wild West Rooms'. With a neolithic plethora of recordings behind him and his cohorts (a bloody discographical nightmare, to be blunt!), BILLY formed the post-millennial trio, The BUFF MEDWAYS, a harder-edged garage-rock act who've so far released a couple of albums. It's no wonder, the man has been cited as the inspiration to a string of Detroit outfits, top of them being The WHITE STRIPES. • **Covered:** Too numerous to mention although The Buff Medways did:- FIRE + MANIC DEPRESSION + HIGHWAY CHILE (Jimi Hendrix) / HOUND DOG (Leiber-Stoller) / IVOR (Pete Townshend) / LEAVE MY KITTEN ALONE (Little Willie John) / etc. • **Trivia:** 'A MIGHTY CHILDISH' various artists tribute album was issued late '95 under the title of 'No Hit'; *VEND 007*)

Album rating (a beginner's guide): 25 YEARS OF BEING CHILDISH double compilation (*8) / Thee Headcoats: ELEMENTARY HEADCOATS double compilation (*7)

POP RIVETS

WILD BILLY CHILDISH – vocals / **WILL POWER** – guitar, vocals / **BIG RUSS** – bass, vocals / **LI'L RUSS** – drums

Hypocrite / not iss.

1979. (7") *(HEP 1)* **POP RIVITS**
– When I came back / Souvenirs / Glanced the look.
1979. (7") *(HEP 002)* **POP RIVITS. / SULPHATE**
1979. (d7"ep) *(JIM 1)* **FUN IN THE U.K.**
– (above tracks)
1979. (lp) *(HIP-O)* **EMPTY SOUNDS FROM ANARCHY RANCH**
– Hang loose, mongoose / Skip off school / 2 is 2 / The spoken voice / I looked twice / The Pop Rivets mak show / Anarchy ranch / I'm just a satellite for your love / Empty sounds / Return to anarchy ranch...
May 80. (lp) *(HIP 007)* **THE POP RIVETS GREATEST HIS** (compilation)

MILKSHAKES

WILD BILLY CHILDISH – vocals, guitar / **MICK HAMPSHIRE** – guitar, vocals / **MARK GILBERT** – bass / **BRUCE BRAND** – drums

Milkshakes / not iss.

1981. (lp) *(MILK-O)* **TALKING 'BOUT MILKSHAKES**
– She'll be mine / Pretty baby / For she / I wantcha / Rugurge beat / After midnight / Bull's nose / Shed country / Don't love another / Tell me where's that girl / Can'tcha see / Love you the whole night through / There's nothing you can say or do / I say you lie. *(re-iss. Feb86)*

— **LI'L RUSS** – bass (ex-POP RIVETS) repl. MARK

Bilko / not iss.

May 82. (7") *(BILK-O)* **PLEASE DON'T TELL MY BABY. / IT'S YOU**

Big Beat / not iss.

Feb 83. (lp) *(NED 4)* **14 RHYTHM AND BEAT GREATS**
– Seven days / Black sails / Exactly like you / A girl called Mine / Sad girl mambo / I want you / Cadalina / No-one else / I need no-one / You did her wrong / Can you tell me / Red monkey / Take you home tonight / Wo' now.

Upright / not iss.

Mar 83. (7") *(UP 6)* **SOLDIERS OF LOVE. / SHIMMY SHIMMY**
May 83. (lp) *(UPLP 1)* **AFTER SCHOOL SESSION**
– Shimmy shimmy / I can tell / Tell me child / Goodbye girl / More honey / Soldiers of love / El Salvador / Let's stomp / Hide and scatter / Jaguar / That girl of mine / You can only lose / Little Minnie / Cadillac. *(re-iss. Jan89 on 'Hangman'; HANG 24LP)*

Wall City / not iss.

Mar 84. (lp) *(EFA 065403)* **THE MILKSHAKES IN GERMANY**

THEE MILKSHAKES

JOHN AGNEW – bass; repl. WILKINS

Milkshakes / not iss.

Mar 84. (lp) *(HARP-O)* **NOTHING CAN STOP THESE MEN**
– You got me girl / Little Bettina / Ida honey (let me tell you you'll be mine) / She's no good to me / Chatham train / Dull knife / She's just fifteen years / The grim reaper / Everywhere I look / I'm the one for you / That's my revenge / You've been lyin'.
Dec 84. (lp) *(GARB-0)* **THEE KNIGHTS OF TRASHE**
(re-iss. Oct95 on 'Hangman'; SCRAG 5LP)

Big Beat / not iss.

Feb 84. (lp) *(WIKM 20)* **20 ROCK & ROLL HITS OF THE 50'S & 60's**
– Hippy hippy shake / Rip it up / I'm gonna sit right down and cry over you / Say mama / Peggy Sue / Jaguar and the thunderbirds / Commanche / I'm talking 'bout you / Sweet little sixteen / Money (that's what I want) / Carol / Boys / Something else / Some other guy / Who do you love / Jezebel / Hidden charms / Little Queenie / Ya ya (twist) / I wanna be your man. *(re-iss. Mar91 cd/lp; CD+/WIKM 20)*
Mar 84. (7"ep) *(NS 94)* **BRAND NEW CADILLAC / COMMANCHE. / JEZEBEL / JAGUAR AND THUNDERBIRD**
Dec 84. (7"ep) *(SW 105)* **THE AMBASSADORS OF LOVE / NO MORE. / GRINGLES AND GROYLES AGAIN / REMARKABLE**
Mar 85. (lp) *(WIK 30)* **THEY CAME, THEY SAW, THEY CONQUERED**
– Bo Diddlius / Did I tell you / Little girl / I'm needing you / Quiet lives / The best things in life / This feeling inside / Wounded Knee / Just like you / Shed country / Thinking 'bout that girl / Gringles and groyles / Mother I want your daughter / How can I love you / Don't destroy me.

Empire / not iss.

Jan 86. (lp) *(MIC 001)* **LAST NIGHT AT THE MIC CLUB** (live w/ PRISONERS)

— WILKINS + BRAND had already joined LEN BRIGHT COMBO, which was fronted by WRECKLESS ERIC.

Aug 86. (7") *(UXF 228)* **LET ME LOVE YOU. / SHE TELLS ME SHE LOVES ME**

Media Burn / not iss.

Nov 86. (d-lp) *(MB 9)* **107 TAPES**
(cd-iss. Feb92 on 'Vinyl Japan'; ASKCD 8)

Hangman / not iss.

Jun 87. (lp) *(HANG 1UP)* **THE MILKSHAKES REVENGE... LEGENDARY MISSING LP**
(cd-iss. Sep93 on 'Hand Of Glory'; HOG 001)
Mar 88. (lp) *(HANG 11UP)* **LIVE FROM CHATHAM** (live)

– others, etc. –

Jul 90. (d-cd) *Big Beat; (CDWIKD 939)* **19th NERVOUS SHAKEDOWN**
Sep 92. (lp/cd) *Vinyl Japan; (ASK 10/+CD)* **STILL TALKIN' BOUT**
May 95. (7"ep) *Wonderlamp; (OIL 01)* **BITTE NICHT SPICKEN EP**
Jul 95. (cd/lp) *Hangman's Daughter; (SCRAG 4 CD/LP)* **TALKIN' ABOUT THE MILKSHAKES**

THEE MIGHTY CAESARS

WILD BILLY CHILDISH – vocals, guitar / **GRAHAM DAY** – guitar, vocals (ex-PRISONERS) / +2

Milkshakes / not iss.

Aug 85. (lp) *(NER-O)* **THEE MIGHTY CAESARS**

Big Beat / not iss.

Jan 86. (lp) *(WIK 45)* **BEWARE THE IDES OF MARCH**
– It ain't no sin / You'll be sorry now / Young man afraid of his horses / All of your love / Cyclonic / Little by little / Give it to me / This man's determined / You can't judge a book by the cover / Baby please / Rumble / Roadrunner.

Empire / not iss.

Feb 86. (7") *(LWC 604Q)* **TEN BEARS OF THE COMMANCHES. / BABY WHAT'S WRONG**

Media Burn / not iss.

Feb 86. (12"ep) *(MB 5)* **LITTLE BY LITTLE / THE SWAG. / I WANT WHAT YOU GOT / CYCLONIC**

Ambassador / not iss.

Feb 87. (lp) *(AMBAS 2)* **WISEBLOOD**
– I can't find pleasure / Come into my life / Signals of love / I self destroy / The wiseblood / The Bay of Pigs / The double axe / Tushunka witko / Stay the same / Kinds of women / Signals of love / Slight return / Action time vision. *(re-iss. Jun89 on 'Hangman')*

Big Beat / not iss.

Apr 87. (lp) *(WIK 60)* **LIVE IN ROME** (live)
– Wily coyote / Give it to me / When the night comes / I've got everything indeed / Commanche / Devious means / Little by little / Neat neat neat / The Bay of Pigs / Don't say it's a lie / Too much monkey business / Submission / All of my love / Baby what's wrong.

Hangman / not iss.

Aug 87. (lp) *(HANG 3UP)* **DON'T GIVE ANY DINNER TO HENRY CHINASKI**
Dec 87. (lp) *(HANG 7UP)* **THE PUNK ROCK SHOWCASE**

Milkshakes / not iss.

Feb 89. (lp) *(PLAT-O)* **ACROPOLIS NOW**
– I've got everything indeed / When the night comes / (Miss America) Got to get you outside / Ask the dust / I don't need no baby / Dictator of love / Now I know /

I can judge a daughter / Lil' red riding hood / Loathsome n' wild / Despite all this / I feel like giving in / I was led to believe.

Mar 89. (lp/c/cd; as APOLLO 440) (APOLL-O) **THE CAESARS OF TRASH**
— It's you I hate to lose / Don't say it's a lie / Devious means / Not fade away / I've been waiting / Don't break my laws / Man taken from guts / Oh yeah / All night worker / Jack the ripper / True to you / Psycho.

— GRAHAM DAY formed PRIME MOVERS

– compilation, etc. –

Feb 94. (d-cd) *Big Beat; (CDWIKD 124)* **CAESAR'S PLEASURE**

WILD BILLY CHILDISH

Empire   not iss.

Apr 87. (lp; by BILLY CHILDISH & RUSS WILKINS) (LPO 195) **LAUGHING GRAVY**
— Baby what you want me to do / We are what we own / 2 x 7 / Black girl / Little Bettina / Laughing gravy / I need lovin' / Quartet after nine / Gotta get you out of my little head . . . / Bring it on home.

Hangman   not iss.

Jul 87. (lp) (HANG 2-UP) **I'VE GOT EVERYTHING I NEED**
Oct 87. (lp; by BILLY CHILDISH & SEXTON MING) (HANG 5-UP) **WHICH DEAD DONKEY DADDY?**
— Muscle horse / Smousgiss / I ain't gonna see Kansas no more / Mi mi and Mi / The cable sausage girls / Major dog be kind to cats / O'Riley / The woods are dangerous / Here on my knee / Sweat and grit with Arnie / Yummy yellow girls / Sons of the desert / Fry-up / The firework man / The caribou of intelligence / Bizzer oxen / The wild breed is here / Dearest.

Jan 88. (lp) (HANG 9-UP) **THE 1982 CASSETTES**
— Oh Maude / Col' col' chillen / When I got no one / I hate my little baby / Dog end of a dog end / Tennessee blues / Ammonia '81 / Monkey bissness / Let's make it / Guillotine device / Today's menu / A matter of timing / Evil snake catcher / I'm home grown / Little Queenie.

Feb 88. (lp; by BILLY CHILDISH & SEXTON MING) (HANG 10-UP) **PLUMP PRIZES AND LITTLE GEMS**

Mar 88. (lp; by BILLY CHILDISH & SEXTON MING) (HANG 12-UP) **YPRES 1917 OVERTURE**

Mar 88. (lp) (HANG 13-UP) **I REMEMBER . . .**

Jun 88. (lp) (HANG 16-UP) **POEMS OF LAUGHTER AND VIOLENCE**
— People don't need oetry / Warts grown like flys / The talking lites / Me 'n' my father / Hawk and spitfire / Heaven she said / In here we believe / The terrible bull / Catastropy / Mercy.

(below with The BLACKHANDS)

Jul 88. (lp; as WILD BILLY CHILDISH & THE BLACKHANDS) (HANG 21-UP) **PLAY CAPTAIN CALYPSO'S HOODOO PARTY**
— Rum and coca cola / Under the mango tree / I love Paris / Long tall Shorty / Capt'n Jack is boss / 'Sen' me to the 'lectric chair / Anarchy in the UK / Three blind mice / Tequila / Yella skinned babies / Dread luck.

Nov 89. (lp; as WILD BILLY CHILDISH & THE NATURAL BORN LOVERS) (HANG 30-UP) **LONG LEGGED BABY**

– spoken word LP's on 'Hangman's Daughter' –

Jun 88. (lp) (WORDUP 001) **COMPANIONS IN A DEATH BOAT**
Jun 88. (lp) (WORDUP 003) **POEMS FROM THE BARRIER BLOCK**
Jun 88. (lp) (WORDUP 004) **POEMS WITHOUT RHYME**
Jun 88. (lp) (WORDUP 005) **MONKS WITHOUT GOD**
Jun 88. (lp) (WORDUP 006) **CONVERSATIONS WITH DOCTOR X**
Jun 88. (lp) (WORDUP 007) **TO THE QUICK**

THEE HEADCOATS

WILD BILLY CHILDISH – vocals, guitar / **MICKEY HAMPSHIRE** – guitar / **RUSS WILKINS** – bass (ex-LEN BRIGHT COMBO) / **BRUCE BRAND** – drums (ex-LEN BRIGHT COMBO)

Hangman's Daughter   not iss.

Jul 89. (lp) (HANG 29-UP) **HEADCOATS DOWN!**
— Smile now / Please little baby / You're looking fine / In your hand / Child's death letter / I'll make you mine / Headcoat and the mortar-board / Wily coyote / Let me touch / I'm the doctor / John the revelator / Young blood. (<cd-iss. Jul01 on 'Damaged Goods'; DAMGOOD 201CD>)

May 90. (lp) (HANG 32-UP) **THE KIDS ARE ALL SQUARE**
— I'm a gamekeeper / Davey Crockett (gabba hey) / Monkey's paw / Meet Jacqueline / Ballad of the fog-bound pinhead / All my feelings denied / Cowboys are square / I can destroy all your love / Poccahontas was her name / Nanook of the north / A town named Squaresville / Karasai.

Crypt   Crypt

1990. (lp) (<CR 020>) **THE EARLS OF SUAVEDOM**
— No escape / I'm a Headcoat, baby / Alone / Our little rendezvous / Everyday / She's got a strange attractor / Branded / Round every corner / Poka Hontas / My 7th girl Eve / The killing hold / Jaguar and Thunderbird / We can only lose / Going outside my head.

not iss.   Dog Meat

1990. (7") <DOG 010> **EARL OF SUAVE. / TROUBLED TIMES**

Hangman   not iss.

1990. (7"ep; as THEE HEADCOAT SECT) (LYNCH 1EP) **THEE HEADCOAT SECT**
— Headcoats on / Be a sect maniac / (I don't like) The man I am / She's got a strange attractor.

not iss.   K

1990. (m-lp) <KLP 09> **CAVERN BY THE SEA**
— Mama keep your big mouth shut / She's just fifteen years old / All my feelings denied / Young blood / Cavern by the sea.

not iss.   Sub Pop

1990. (7") <IPU 21> **SHOULDN'T HAPPEN TO A DOG. / MASK OF THE SQUAXIN**

Dec 90. (7") <SP 71> **TIME WILL TELL. / DAVEY CROCKETT (GABBA-HAY!)**

Feb 91. (cd/c/lp) <SP 82/A/B> **HEAVENS TO MURGATROYD, EVEN IT'S THEE HEADCOATS ALREADY**
— Mantrap / No way out / Reindeer are wild / Hand to hand / Headcoat man / Girl of matches / I don't like the man I am / Pokerhuntus was her name / We'er gone / Stewball / I ain't about to give you my name / Rusty hook. *(UK-iss.May93 on 'Sub Pop' cd/lp; SP CD6-119/6-117)*

Shakin' Street   not iss.

May 91. (lp) (YEAHHUP 018) **HEADCOATITUDE**
— My dear Watson / Everybody lies / Troubled times / Hog's jaw / By hook or by crook / It's gonna hurt you (more than it hurts me) / Neither fish nor fowl / I wonder why people don't like me / Snitch baby / Gonna get inside that girl's mind / Headcoatitude / I don't like you.

not iss.   Sympathy..

1991. (7") <SFTRI 138> **HATED, RIDICULE & CONTEMPT. / NEITHER FISH NOR FOUL**

not iss.   Regal Select

1991. (7") <RS 013> **GIRL FROM '62. / SOMEONE LIKE ME**

not iss.   Dionysus

1991. (7") <IDO 74535> **SOMETHING WENT WRONG. / IT'S YOUR OWN FAULT**

Damaged Goods   not iss.

1992. (7") (DAMGOOD 1) **LAKOTA WOMAN. / (other by Thee Headcoatees)**

not iss.   Estrus

1992. (7") <ES 726> **MY DEAR WATSON. / HOG'S JAW**

Crypt   Crypt

1992. (lp) (<CR 024>) **BEACH BUMS MUST DIE** (rec.1990)
— Youngblood / You broke my very mind / Strangler of Boston town / Beach bums must die / A town names Squaresville / Slide / That special kind of clay / Headcoat on backwards / Murder on the moors / All my feelings denied / Pow wow / I ain't never found / No such animal / In your hand / The case of the thundering dunderhead / Give me that apple, Eve. *(UK cd re-iss. Apr93 as 'BEACHED EARLS'+=; EFA 11563D)* – THE EARLS OF SUAVEDOM

Munster   not iss.

Sep 92. (7") (MR 7037) **I CAN DESTROY ALL YOUR LOVE. / FATBACK**

Clawfist   not iss.

1992. (7") (Claw 17) **PAEDOPHILE. / NO SUCH NUMBER**

Damaged Goods   not iss.

1992. (7") (DAMGOOD 7) **HEADCOAT LANE. / COMANCHE**
1992. (cd; split w/ THEE HEADCOATEES) (DAMGOOD 9) **GIRLSVILLE**

not iss.   Cleopatra

1992. (7") <CLEO 6> **LOUIS RIEL. / NARDWUAR V. PIERRE BERTON / DON'T TRY AND TELL ME**

not iss.   Sympathy..

1992. (7") <SFTRI 178> **HAVE LOVE WILL TRAVEL. / GIVE IT TO ME**

Twist   not iss.

1992. (7") <SFTRI 221> **TUB'S TWIST. / SAD SACK**

Apr 93. (7") (TWIST 5) **BRANDED. / Thee Headcoatees: STRYCHNINE**

Damaged Goods   not iss.

May 93. (7") (DAMGOOD 17) **EVERY BIT OF ME. / NEVER TO LOVE AGAIN**

Jul 93. (7") (DAMGOOD 19) **(WE HATE THE FUCKIN') NME. / HELP**

not iss.   Royal

1993. (7"m) <ROY 701> **THOUGHTS OF A HANGMAN**
— Thoughts of a hangman / Reasons for hating you / Now is not the best time / Please won't you tell me.

not iss.   Y.M.A.H.

1993. (7"flexi) <001> **TEAR IT TO PIECES. / GIRLSVILLE**

Hangman   not iss.

1993. (7") (Gibbet 3) **EVERY LITTLE THING. / SITTING IN MY CORNER**

Damaged Goods   not iss.

1993. (lp; w/ THEE HEADCOATEES) (DAMGOOD 30) **LIVE AT THE WESTERN WORLD**

not iss.   Sympathy..

1993. (7") <SFTRI 267> **I'M A CONFUSED MAN. / NOW YOUR HUNGER'S GONNA BE COMIN'**

Vinyl Japan   not iss.

Nov 93. (cd/lp) (ASK CD/LP 28) **THE GOOD TIMES ARE KILLING ME**
— Got to get what's been forbidden / I wasn't made for this world / It was too late / Double face / I'll be out of here / Picket fence / The good times are killing me / House on the water / Paedophile / At the bridge / Strychnine / Every little thing / Walk of the lost / She'll keep you on standby.

not iss.   Sub Pop

Jan 94. (7") (PAD 009) **ACTION TIME VISION. / I WASN'T MADE FOR THIS WORLD**

not iss.   Get Hip

1994. (7") <SP 239> **WHEN YOU STOP LOVIN' ME. / PAPA DOC**

1994. (cd) <GH 1022> **W.O.A.H. BO IN THE GARAGE**
— Roadrunner intro / Crackin' up / Can't judge a book / Who do you love / Greatest lover in the world / Diddy wah diddy / One ugly child / Keep your big mouth shut / I can tell / She's fine, she's mine / Dearest darlin' / Before you accuse me / Roadrunner.

Damaged Goods   not iss.

Mar 94. (7"ep; as THEE HEADCOATS featuring SEXTON MING) (DAMGOOD 32) **NO ONE**
— No one / Goldfish murder / Your little fight / Kyras vowels.

Hangman's Daughter   Super Electro

Sep 94. (cd/lp) (SCRAG 2 CD/LP) <super 04> **CONUNDRUM: INFLUENCING THE STARS OF TOMORROW, RIPPING OFF THE NON-ENTITIES OF YESTERDAY**
— Every bit of me / Bitten off more than you can chew / I wish I'd never been / We ain't gonna go / What smashed me / Crazy horse / Again & again / Girl from 62 / Thief / Watch me fall / He's so popular with the girls / I'm an idiot / Hoping. <US+=> – I wish I knew what I was living for.

Wild Billy CHILDISH (cont)

			not iss.	Sympathy..
Jan 95.	(7")	<SFTRI 335> **LOUIE LOUIE. / LOUIE LOUIE (WHERE DID SHE ROAM)**	-	

			Twist	not iss.
Feb 95.	(7")	(TWIST 17) **GUN IN MY FATHER'S HAND. / THE DAY I BEAT MY FATHER UP**		-

			Damaged Goods	Damaged Goods
May 95.	(7")	(DAMGOOD 62) **A-Z OF YOUR HEART. / (other by BILLY CHILDISH)**		-
May 95.	(7")	(DAMGOOD 63) **SUFFERENCE WHARF. /** Thee Headcoatees: **JOHNNY JACK**		-
Jun 96.	(lp/cd)	(<DAMGOOD 96/+CD>) **IN TWEED WE TRUST**		

– Everybody's wiser now / Too afraid / Want me, win me / I'm good enough / Fingers in the sun / This day to bust / It don't come easy / I'm hurtin' / Going down / The man with eyes like fishes / I was weak / Sex and flies.

			not iss.	Wild Wild
1996.	(7")	<WILD 7> **THEE WILD WILD HEADCOATS** – Shadow / No escape.	-	

			Karls Grammofon	not iss.
1996.	(7")	(carls 745-003) **THIS HEART. / IT'S BAD**		-

			not iss.	German Birdman
1996.	(7")	<BMR 014> **SHE'S IN DISGUISE. / COWBOYS ARE SQUARE**	-	

			not iss.	360 Twist!
1996.	(7")	<36T-011> **THIEF. / AUTOMATIC LOVE**	-	

—— next added The DOWNLINER'S SECT

			Hangman's Daughter	not iss.
Sep 96.	(cd/lp; by THEE HEADCOAT SECT)	(SCRAG 8 CD/LP) **DEERSTALKING MEN**		-

– Strychnine / My dear Watson / Fog-bound pinhead / Troubled times / Cowboys are square / Baby what's wrong / Why don't you smile now / The witch / Squaresville / Lie detector / Deerstalking men / I'm a gamekeeper.

			SmartGuy	not iss.
1997.	(7")	(smart 001) **THE MESSERSCHMITT PILOT'S SEVERED HAND. / I'VE BEEN FUCKING YOUR DAUGHTERS AND PISSING ON YOUR LAWN**		-

			Get Hip	Get Hip
Jun 97.	(10"m-lp)	(<GH 1029>) **JIMMY REED EXPERIENCE**		

– Baby what's wrong / High and lonesome / Ain'y that lovin' you baby / Bright lights, big city / Upside your head / Honest I do / I remember / I got everything indeed.

			Hangman's Daughter	not iss.
1997.	(7")	(KETCH 18) **ORGANIC FOOTPRINTS. / CLARABELLA**		-

			Damaged Goods	Damaged Goods
Apr 98.	(lp/cd)	(<DAMGOOD 140/+CD>) **THE MESSERSCHMITT PILOT'S SEVERED HAND**		

– The Messerschmitt pilot's severed hand / A beauty of love that splits the body in two / We hate the fucking NME / Organic footprints / I suppose I'm a poseur / Blood, piss and sperm / Where are the children that Hitler kissed? / I wouldn't want to be you / Good morning little snob / I've been fucking your daughters and pissing on your lawn / I wanna stop this world / Punk rock ist nicht tot.

			Vinyl Japan	Vinyl Japan
Sep 98.	(7")	(DAMGOOD 155) **THE RISE AND FALL OF A DOUBLE. /** Thee Headcoatees: **JACKIE CHAN DOES KUNG FU**		-
Apr 98.	(cd/lp)	(<ASK CD/LP 070>) **BROTHER IS DEAD . . . BUT FLY IS GONE**		

– Louie Louie / Boredom / Diddy wah diddy / What's my name / Whatcha gonna do about it / Love comes in spurts / Don't gimme no lip / 1077 / Loathsome and wild / Punk rock ist nicht tot! / You gotta lose / Viva la rock'n'roll / Darling, let's have another baby / Agitated.

Mar 00.	(cd/lp)	(ASK CD/LP 099) **READY SECT GO**		-

– Ain't that just like me / Down in the bottom / I'm a king bee / Take out some insurance on me / Knight of the Baskervilles / I'm a lover not a fighter / Mean red spider / A certain girl / She's fine, she's mine / I got love if you want it / Ready sect go / I'm ready.

– other HEADCOATS / HEADCOATEES releases

Jul 93.	(lp)	Tom Tom; (TOM 15) **THE WURST IS YET TO COME (live in Schaffhausen, 18 September 1990)**		-

– Smile now / Pretty baby / Comanche / Yo lookin' fine / In yur hand / Cowboys are square / Keep you big mouf shut / Troubled times / Oh yea / I can destroy all yu love / Jack the ripper / Mony / Davy Crockett / Lil Red Riding Hood.

Sep 93.	(cd)	Damaged Goods; (DAM 9CD) **THE KIDS ARE ALL SQUARE / GIRLSVILLE**		-
Mar 94.	(lp/cd)	Damaged Goods (DAMGOOD 30/+CD) **LIVE IN LONDON (live)**		-
Dec 95.	(lp/cd; with THEE HEADCOATEES)	Overground; (OVER 42/+CD) / Birdman; <BMR 013> **KNIGHTS OF THE BASKERVILLES**		

– She's in disguise / You can choose / Meet me / I'm unkind / Knights of the Baskervilles / By the hairs of my chinny chin chin / What you see is what you are / She's fine, she's mine / What's wrong with me / This wondrous day / Like a flag / It ain't mine.

| Aug 00. | (cd/d-t-lp) | Damaged Goods; (DAMGOOD 178 CD/LP) **ELEMENTARY HEADCOATS** | | Sep00 |

– Troubled times / The earl of suave / Headcoats on / Be a sect maniac / I don't like the man I am / She's got a strange attractor / Shouldn't happen to a dog / Neither fish nor fowl / Girl from '62 / Someone like me / Something went wrong again / My dear WAtson / Hog's jaw / I can destroy all your love / Fat back / Louie Riel / Don't try & tell me / Paedophile / Headcoat lane / Comanche / Every bit of me / Never to love again / (We hate the fuckin') NME / Help / Thoughts of a hangman / Now is not the best time / Every little thing / Tub's twist / Sad sack / Action time vision / I'm a confused man / Now your hunger's gonna be a-comin' / Louie Louie / Louie Louie (where did she roam) / When you stop loving me / Papa Doc / No one / The gun in my father's hand / The day I beat my father up / A-Z of your heart / Shadow / No escape / Thief / She's in disguise / The Messerschmitt pilot's severed hand / I've been fucking your daughters and pissing on your lawn / Organic footprints / Clarabella / I'm hurting / Art or arse (you be the judge).

WILD BILLY CHILDISH

			Sub Pop	Sub Pop
1991.	(7")	<SP 151> **THE BALLAD OF HOLLIS BROWN. / GRIZZERLY BEAR**		-
Oct 92.	(cd/lp; by BILLY CHILDISH & THE BLACKHANDS)	(SP 209CD/47-209) **THE ORIGINAL CHATHAM JACK**		-

– This is the Blackhands / Chatham Jack / I love my woman / Bottle up and go / For the deceived / Millionaire / The axeman cometh / Evil thing / Crying blvd. / Broken stone / Louis Riel / Politics of greed and pain / Rumble / John Hardy.

			Damaged Goods	not iss.
Apr 93.	(7")	(DAMGOOD 15) **CHATHAM JACK. / FINE AND MELLOW**		-

			Twist	not iss.
Sep 93.	(7")	(TWIST 8) **WHO DO YOU THINK YOU'RE KIDDING MR. HITLER. /**		-

BILLY CHILDISH & THE BLACKHANDS

			Hangman's Daughter	not iss.
Sep 93.	(lp)	(HANG 053UP) **LIVE IN THE NETHERLANDS (live May 1993)**		-

– Mr. Hitler / Chatham Jack / Fine and mellow / Bottle up and go / Evil thing / Yellow skinned babys / Black girl / She's fine, she's mine / Louis Riel / I love my woman / John Hardy / It's a long way to Tipperary / The Lambeth Walk.

BILLY CHILDISH & THE SINGING LOINS

—— with **CHRIS BRODERICK** + **CHRIS ALLEN**

			Damaged Goods	not iss.
Oct 93.	(cd)	(DAM 22CD) **AT THE BRIDGE**		-

– The bitter cup / Pocahontas was her name / The hanged man's dance / You make me die / I don't like the man I am / The double axe / At the bridge / Every bit of me / Somebody else / The ferry man (Zeebrugge) / One way you die / Brimfull of hate / Dragging through this / One more bottle to drink. (re-iss. lp Apr94; SCRAG 1UP)

			Lissy's	not iss.
Dec 95.	(7")	(LISS 10) **THE MAN WITH EYES LIKE LITTLE FISHES. / STUPID SONG**		-

BILLY CHILDISH & SEXTON MING

with **SEXTON MING** – guitar

			Hangman's Daughter	not iss.
Mar 95.	(7")	(KETCH 5UP) **GAUD BLESS OLD MITCHELL. / MUSCLE HORSE**		-

BILLY CHILDISH / DAN MELCHIOR

—— with **MELCHIOR** – guitars, vocals

			not iss.	Sympathy F
Jan 98.	(lp/cd)	<SFTRI 529/+CD> **DEVIL IN THE FLESH**	-	

– Trouble no more / Length of pipe / Bottom of the sea / Deep down in my heart / Two mewn / Heart in hand / I feel so bad / I'm hurtin' / Just to be with you / Honey bee / Gave myself away / Devil in the flesh.

BILLY CHILDISH & SEXTON MING

with **SEXTON MING** – guitar

			Damaged Goods	Damaged Goods
Mar 99.	(cd/lp)	(<DAMGOOD 159 CD/LP>) **THE CHEEKY CHEESE**		

– Intro / Sing shed sing / The glug glug car / Insects in your stars / Oma-laka-wee / In the land of the lusty bees / Don't be a misery guts / Buds and shoots / The cheeky cheese / Mussel horse in Holland / God bless old Mitchell / Arnie the scaffolder / The curious old woman / Daddy was a charger / The goldfish murder / Hide in the cellar / Outro.

| Oct 02. | (cd/lp) | (<DAMGOOD 208 CD/LP>) **HERE COME THE FLEECE GEESE** | | |

– Muscle horse was in the war / Here come the fleece geese / Days and numbers / Old horse of the nations tea party / Tractor of the cosmos / Torment of the insects / Goose of the Moon / Annie – Ice cream sargeant / Honk honk gray geese / They call me Mister Tibbs / Monkeys in space / The old barn yard / Smile / Here come the fleece geese (reprise).

BILLY CHILDISH & HOLLY GOLIGHTLY

			Wabana	Wabana
Nov 99.	(cd/lp)	(<ORE 22 CD/LP>) **IN BLOOD**		

– Step out / In blood / Let me know you / You got that thing / Demolition girl / Upside mine / You move me / I believe / It's a natural fact / I'm the robber / Move on up / Hold me.

WILD BILLY CHILDISH & THE FAMOUS HEADCOATS

—— with **JIMMY JOHNSON** – bass + **BRUCE BRAND** – drums

			not iss.	Cock1up
2000.	(cd)	<7623> **I AM THE OBJECT OF YOUR DESIRE**	-	

– I am the object of your desire / Hurt me (slight return) / An image of you / In a dead man's suit / Chatham Town welcomes desperate men / In blood / Come into my mind / Great grandfather / I'm a desperate man / Strange looking woman / Your crying means nothing to me / The same tree.

THEE HEADCOATS

				Friends Of..	not iss.
2000.	(7")	(FOBMFA 1)	**PUNK ROCK IST NICHT TOT. / WHEN THE NIGHT COMES**		-

BUFF MEDWAYS

BILLY CHILDISH – vocals, guitar / **JOHNNY BARKER** – bass (of DAGGERMEN) / **WOLF HOWARD** – drums (of DAGGERMEN)

				Friends Of..	not iss.
2000.	(7")	(FOBMFA 2)	**FIRE. / MANIC DEPRESSION**		-
				Damaged Goods	not iss.
Mar 01.	(7")	(DAMGOOD 188)	**DON'T HOLD ME BACK. / DEMOLITION GIRL** (re-iss. Aug02; same)		-
				SmartGuy	not iss.
2001.	(7"ep)	(smart 010)	**'TIL IT IS OVER** – 'Til it is over / Archive from 1959 / Medway sadness / Just explain.		-
				Vinyl Japan	Vinyl Japan
Oct 01.	(7")	(PAD 074)	**INTO YOUR DREAMS. / HIGHWAY CHILE**		
Oct 01.	(cd/lp)	<ASK CD/LP 132>	**THIS IS THIS** – No mercy / Don't hold me back / Teach me what you know / Till the end of time / This won't change / Into your dreams / Til it is over / Don't give up on love / Cross lines / This is this.		
				Transcopic	not iss.
Oct 01.	(7")	(TRAN 012)	**A STRANGE KIND OF HAPPINESS. / HOUND DOG**		-
Dec 01.	(7")	<gibbet 4>	**SALLY SENSATION. / DAWN SAID "WHAT HAVE I DONE?"** (above iss. on 'Hangman' below on 'Sympathy For The Record Industry')	-	
Feb 02.	(7"ep)	<SFTRI 664>	**TRIBUTE TO THE DAGGERMEN** – One more letter / Every moment / Ivor.		
Apr 02.	(7")	(TRAN 015)	**TROUBLED MIND. / LEAVE MY KITTEN ALONE**		-
May 02.	(cd/lp)	(TRAN CD/LP 016)	**STEADY THE BUFFS** – Troubled mind / Dawn said / A strange kind of happiness / Archive from 1959 / Times up / Sally sensation / Vanessa does favours / Strood lights / Misty water / Well well / You piss me off / Ivor.		-
Sep 02.	(7")	(TRAN 017)	**STROOD LIGHTS. / YOU MAKE ME DIE**		-

– BILLY CHILDISH compilations, etc. –

Feb 91.	(d-cd)	Hangman's Daughter; (HANG 037UP) / Sub Pop; <SP 116B>	**I AM THE BILLY CHILDISH: 50 SONGS FROM 50 RECORDS** – Fun in the UK / Kray twins / Laughing at you / Skip off school / Pretty baby / For she / I hate my little baby / Red monkey / Black sales / Dog watch / We can only lose / A girl called mine / One day you die / Chatham train / Comanche / I want you / Can't seem to make you mine / Mumble the peg / I'm needing you / Why don't you try me love? / I love that girl Ammonia / Verdun osserry / Baby please / Man take from guts / I feel givin' in / Living in a grave / Got to get you outside my head / Temptress of love / I was led to believe / Don't die it's a lie / I've got everything indeed / You got me restless / Double axe / You make me die / Cosmetic women / Give it to me / True to you / Prostitutes on Chatham hi street / Come into my life / Somebody else / Just is / Yellow skinned babys / Brimfull of hate / Can't you see? / In your hand / Everyday / Squaresville / All my feelings denied / Rusty hook / Child's death letter.
Mar 94.	(cd)	Sub Pop; <SP 206B>	**NATIVE AMERICAN SAMPLER – A HISTORY** (Jun93) – Tushunka Wittko' / Crazy horse / Comanche / Pocahontas was her name / Youngman afraid of his horses / Thunderbird / Dull knife / Reindeer are wild / Wounded Knee / Playing pool with a Salish Indian drug dealer in the Dodson bar down town Vancouver / Cowboys are square / Man taken from guts / Black elk speaks / Pocahontas / Louis Riel / Ten bears of the Comanches / Lakota woman / We'er gone.
Apr 94.	(lp)	Tom Tom; (TOM 17)	**KITCHEN RECORDINGS**
Sep 94.	(cd)	Hangman's Daughter; (SCRAG 3UP)	**CAPTAIN CALYPSO'S HOODOO PARTY / LIVE IN THE NETHERLANDS**
Sep 96.	(cd)	Sympathy For The Record Industry; <SFTRI 449>	**MADE WITH A PASSION: KITCHEN DEMO'S** – A-to-Z of your heart / Automatic love (part of) / Fingers in the sun / I'm good enough / This is unacceptable / Made we fall / Judging them all to hell / Names / The naked poet / The bitter cup / Your rite I'm rong / Art or arse (you be the judge) / Billy B. Childish / This wonderous day / Every little thing / Anchor me / Easy peasy / Laughter and violence.
Sep 98.	(cd; by BILLY CHILDISH & HIS FAMOUS HEADCOATS)	Slab-o-Concrete; (SLAB 018) / Sympathy For The Record Industry; <SFTRI 552>	**17% HENDRIX WAS NOT THE ONLY MUSICIAN** – Art or arse (you be the judge) / My girl does kung fu / Salty dog / The rise and fall of a double / Do things right / The bitter cup / Pinhead / Speak to me / I see shining / This wondrous day / That was then, this is now / I want a punk girl / You make me die / Teenage kicks.
Sep 99.	(d-lp/cd)	Sympathy For The Record Industry; <(SFTRI 582/+CD)>	**CRIMES OF THE FUTURE (BLUES MUSIC 1986-1999)** – I've got everything indeed / Strange words / I love that girl Ammonia / Get out of here pretty girl / The greatest lover in the world / Coming upside your head / Mister Elisabeth / I remember / Why don't you try my love? / Burn and blind me / Not many of my kind / This whole wide world / Grinning in your face / Yellow skin baby / Bourgeois blues / Cosmetic woman / Troubled times / I love my woman / Bottle up and go / John Hardy / The ballad of Hollis Brown / Cowboys and square / I feel so bad / I'm hurting / Iodine in my coffee / Cold chills / Crimes of the future.
Nov 02.	(t-lp/d-cd)	Damaged Goods; (<DAMGOOD 210/+CD>)	**25 YEARS OF BEING CHILDISH** – POP RIVETS: Whatcha gonna do about it / Fun in the UK (demo) / Beatle boots / MILKSHAKES: Pretty baby (demo) / Please don't tell my baby / For she / I need loving / THEE MIGHTY CAESARS: Wily coyote / True to you / You make me die / THEE MIGHTY CAESARS: Lie detector / with SEXTON MING:

Muscle horse / as JACK KETCH & CROWMEN: Somebody else / Who could be proud / solo: I remember / The noble beast (poetry) / THEE HEADCOATS: Earl of suave / Smile now // THEE HEADCOATS: Wild man / THEE HEADCOATEES: Girl from '62 / THEE HEADCOATS: Davey Crockett / with ARMITAGE SHANKS: Shirts off / THEE HEADCOATS: We'er gone / BLACKHANDS: Anarchy in the UK / with SINGING LOINS: One more bottle to drink / THEE HEADCOATS: All my feelings denied / BLACKHANDS: I love my woman / THEE HEADCOATS SECT: Deer stalking man / solo: The bitter cup / Ballad of Hollis Brown / KYRA: This wondrous day / THEE HEADCOATS: Punk rock ist nict tot / I'm hurtin / THEE HEADCOATEES: Hurt me / THEE HEADCOATS: The same tree / with HOLLY GOLIGHTLY: I believe / Buff Medways: Archive from 1959 / Troubled mind / Fire.

DELMONAS

SARAH – vocals / **HILARY** – vocals / **LOUISE** – vocals

				Big Beat	not iss.
Dec'84.	(7"m)	(SW 101)	**COMIN' HOME BABY. / WOA NOW / HE TELLS ME HE LOVES ME**		-
Dec'84.	(7"m)	(SW 102)	**HELLO WE LOVE YOU. / I'M THE ONE FOR YOU / PETER GUNN LOCOMOTION**		-
Jun'85.	(lp)	(WIK 35)	**DANGEROUS CHARMS** – Peter Gunn locomotion / You did him wrong / Hello we love you / Comin' home baby / Lies / C.C. rider / He tells me he loves me / Hidden charms / Twist and shout / I'm the one for you / Fever / Chains / Please don't tell my baby / I want you / Take me home tonight / Woa now.		
				Empire	not iss.
Aug'85.	(7")	(JLM 14C)	**SALLY-SHE-BROWN. /**		-

— added **MISS IDA RED** – vocals / **LUDELLA BLACK** – vocals
— backed by THEE MIGHTY CAESARS

				Hangman	Skyclad
Aug'86. (lp)	(UXF 228)	**DELMONA 5!** – Dr. Goldfoot / Heard about him / Why don't you smile now / Black elk speaks / Hound dog / Delmona / I feel like giving in / Keep your big mouth shut / When I want you / Black Ludella / Your love / Don't fall in love (every single time) / Jealousy. (re-iss. 1987; SYF 095) (re-iss. Jul88 on 'Hangman'; HANG 20UP)				
Jul'89.	(lp)	(HANG 28UP) <57>	**THE DELMONAS** <US-title 'DO THE UNCLE WILLY'> – Jealousy (French version) / That boy of mine / Can't sit down / Kiss me honey / I've got everything I need / Uncle Willy / Farmer John / You did him wrong / Dangerous charms / Long drop / I feel alright.		

— split later in 1989

– compilations, etc. –

Oct'93.	(cd)	Vinyl Japan; (ASKCD 032)	**DELMONA 5! / THE DELMONAS**		-

CHOU PAHROT

Formed: Glasgow, Scotland . . . 1978 by M. ZARB, EGGY BEARD, MAMA VOOT and THE AMPHIBIAN, the North's answer to The POP GROUP (CAPTAIN BEEFHEART also springs to mind!). Taking a wide berth from conventional punk/New Wave (unusual as the group's of a Caledonian group), CHOU PAHROT became something of a catch around the West Coast of Scotland, their 'Oor Wullie'-type sense of fun and frolics going down a proverbial storm for anyone lucky enough to witness them live. However, only a few releases surfaced – the single, 'BUZGO TRAM CHORUS' and the privately pressed album, 'LIVE' (1979) – before they were free soles once more.

Album rating: LIVE (*5)

MAMA VOOT – guitar, vocals, saxophones / **M. ZARB** – bass, guitar, vocals / **EGGY BEARD** – violin / **THE AMPHIBIAN** – drums

				Klub	not iss.
Feb 79.	(7"ep)	(KEP 101)	**BUZGO TRAM CHORUS. / GWIZGWEELA GWAMPHNOO / LEMONS**		-
Nov 79.	(lp)	(KLP 19)	**LIVE** – Pantomine schrub / Syphionic diplivits / The wee thing / The random shoggy / Itchy face / Lemons / Mary submarine / Day o' the mug / The yaw yaw song.		

— continued to make do with some sporadic (quite literally) gigs

CHROME

Formed: San Francisco, California, USA . . . 1975 by DAMON EDGE, JOHN LAMBDIN and GARY SPAIN. CHROME interpreted the wigged-out psychedelic heritage of their hometown in bizarre sequences of sci-fi obsessed mechanical noise and their two late 70's albums, 'ALIEN SOUNDTRACKS' and 'HALF MACHINE LIP MOVES' were a significant influence on the industrial and grunge scenes of the 80's and 90's. The wonderfully named HELIOS CREED (having joined their ranks by the release of the former) steered the band towards their experimental techno-goth sound. Signing to British indie, 'Beggars Banquet', the group were reduced to the duo of EDGE and CREED and subsequently moved to a more technology-based style. HELIOS departed in 1983, going on to record a string of suitably nasty grunge albums for the American 'Amphetamine Reptile' label. Meanwhile, DAMON EDGE, along with various collaborators maintained a highly prolific recording schedule under the CHROME moniker, releasing more than 20 albums. Sadly, DAMON was to die in 1995. HELIOS CREED, therefore, took up the opportunity to reunite past and new CHROME members for a new mini-set, 'THIRD SEED FROM THE BUD' (1996). • **Songwriters:** EDGE mainly, with others contributing.

Album rating: THE VISITATION (*5) / ALIEN SOUNDTRACKS (*6) / HALF MACHINE LIP MOVES (*7) / RED EXPOSURE (*6) / BLOOD ON THE MOON (*6) / 3RD FROM THE SUN (*6) / RAINING MILK (*5) / INTO THE EYES OF THE ZOMBIE KING (*4) / CHRONICLES (*4) / ANOTHER WORLD (*4) / ALIEN SOUNDTRACKS II (*4) / NO HUMANS ALLOWED compilation (*7) / CHROME BOX boxed set (*7) / RETRO TRANSMISSION (*6) / TIDAL FORCES (*6) / Helios Creed: X-RATED FAIRY TALES (*4) / SUPERIOR CATHOLIC FINGER (*5) / THE LAST LAUGH (*5) / BOXING THE CLOWN (*5) / Damon Edge: ALLIANCE (*4) / THE WIND IS TALKING (*3) / GRAND VISIONS (*4) / THE SURREAL ROCK (*3)

DAMON EDGE – vocals, guitar, keyboards, drums, Moog / **JOHN LAMBDIN** – guitar / **GARY SPAIN** – bass, violin

not iss.   Siren

Feb 77. (lp) <DE 1000> **THE VISITATION**
 – How many years too soon / Raider / Return to Zanzibar / Caroline / Riding you / Kinky lover / Sun control / My time to live / Memory chords over the body.

—— **HELIOS CREED** – guitar, vocals repl. LAMBDIN

Feb 78. (lp) <DE 2200> **ALIEN SOUNDTRACKS**
 – Chromosome damage / The monitors / All data lost / S.S. Lygni / Nova feedback / Pygmies in Zee Park / Slip it to the android / Pharoah chromium / St. 31 / Re pt.II.

Beggars Banquet   Siren

Mar 80. (lp) (BEGA 15) **RED EXPOSURE**   1979
 – New age / Rm 10 / Eyes on Mars / Jonestown / Animal / Static gravity / Eyes in the center / Electric chair / Night of the Earth / Isolation.
Apr 80. (7") (BEG 36) **NEW AGE. / INFORMATION**   1979

—— now down to duo **DAMON EDGE + HELIOS CREED**

Aug 80. (lp) (BEGA 18) <DE 333> **HALF MACHINE LIP MOVES**   1979
 – TV as eyes / Zombie warfare (can't let you down) / March of the Chrome police (a cold clamey bombing) / You've been duplicated / Mondo anthem / Half machine lip moves / Abstract nympho / Turned around / Zero time / Creature eternal / Critical mass. <cd-iss. 1990's on 'Dossier'; 2607496>

Red-Siren   Siren

May 80. (12"ep) (RS 12007) **READ ONLY MEMORY**   1979
 – You can't see them – They can't touch you / Inacontract / Read only memory / In front of the crowd / I am the jaw.

—— added **JOHN STENCH** – drums + **HILARY STENCH** – bass

Don't Fall   Don't Fall

Jan 81. (12"ep) (Y 3) **INWORLDS. / DANGER ZONE / IN A DREAM**
Jun 81. (lp) (X 6) **BLOOD ON THE MOON**
 – The need / Inner vacuum / Perfumed metal / Planet strike / The strangers / Insect human / Out of reach / Brain on scan / Blood on the Moon. (re-iss. Apr87 on 'Dossier'; DOSSIER 001)

—— added guest **FABIENNE SHINE** – vocals

Apr 82. (7") (Z 17) **FIREBOMB. / SHADOW OF A THOUSAND YEARS**
Apr 82. (lp) (X 18) **3RD FROM THE SUN**
 – Firebomb / Future ghosts / Armageddon / Heartbeat / Off the line / 3rd from the Sun / Shadows of a thousand years.

not iss.   Expanded

1983. (lp) <EX 40> **NO HUMANS ALLOWED**
 – Danger zone / The manifestation (of the idea) / In a dream / Information / Read only memory.

—— added guest **BETSY HILL** – vocals

Mosquito   not iss.

1983. (lp) (MOS 001) **RAINING MILK**   France
 – Wings born in the night / Tribes (ultra) / Gehenna to Canaan / La legende des sentences du futur / Beacons to the eye / Raining milk / Anorexic sacrifice / Gehenna lion.

—— HELIOS CREED went on to sign for 'Subterranean', releasing two albums, 'X-RATED FAIRY TALES' and 'SUPERIOR CATHOLIC FINGER' in 1985 and 1986 respectively. 'Amphetamine Reptile' also issued three sets, 'THE LAST LAUGH' (1989), 'BOXING THE CLOWN' (1990) and 'KISS TO THE BRAIN' (1992). Later albums included 'NUGG THE TRANSPORT' and 'CHROMAGNUM MAN' for 'Dossier' and 'ACTIVATED CONDITION' for 'Man's Ruin' (1998).

DAMON EDGE / CHROME

—— with **FABIENNE SHINE** – vocals / **REMY DeVILLA** – guitar / **RENAUD THOREZ** – bass / **PATRICK IMBERT** – drums

1984. (lp) (MOS 003) <260 5318> **INTO THE EYES OF THE ZOMBIE KING**   France
 – And then the red sun / You can't do anything / Walking and looking for you / Into the eyes of the Zombie King / Trip the switch / It wasn't real / Humans in the rain / Don't move like that. (UK-iss.Apr87 on 'Dossier'; ST 7513) <US-iss.Aug88 on 'Dossier'; DCD 9004>

DAMON EDGE

with **FABIENNE SHINE** – vocals / **REMY DEVILLIARD** – guitar / **RENAUD THOREZ** – bass

New Rose   not iss.

Mar 85. (7") (NEW 51) **I'M A GENTLEMAN. /**
Mar 85. (lp) (ROSE 51) **ALLIANCE**   France
 – Blue nights / I'm a gentleman / When I'm not alone / Why not give me your next trance / Alliance of the hearts / Angel fire / Coming at la Mer to a world left behind / Rhapsody in maroon.
Jun 85. (lp) (ROSE 64) **THE WIND IS TALKING**   France
 – I don't know why / Moror at my head / I'm exploring you – Shake / Don't ask me / Circles of time / Prelude – The wind is talking / The wind is talking.
Jun 86. (lp) (ROSE 90) **GRAND VISIONS**   France

Dossier   not iss.

1987. (lp) <ST 7537> **THE SURREAL ROCK**

CHROME

DAMON EDGE + FABIENNE SHINE, CLIFF MARTIN etc.

Dossier   Dossier

Apr 86. (lp) (ST 7503) **ANOTHER WORLD**
 – If you come around / I found out today / Our good dreams / Stranger from another world / Moon glow / The sky said / Loving lovely lover.
Feb 87. (lp) (ST 7527) **DREAMING IN SEQUENCE**
 – Everyone's the same / Sanity / Seeing everything / Touching you / Windows in the wind / The Venusian dance / White magic / Love to my rock (cause of me) / She is here.
Apr 87. (lp) (ST 3004) **THE LYON CONCERT (live)**
 – We are connected / Moror at my head / We stand here in time / March of the rubber people / Ghosts of the long forgotten future / Version 2 (Raining milk) / The service improves / Frankenstein's party.
Oct 87. (lp) (DOSSIER 002) **THE CHRONICLES**
 – The chronicles of the sacrifice / The chronicles of the tribes / The chronicles of the open door / The chronicles of born in the night.
Jul 88. (lp) (ST 003) **THE CHRONICLES II**
 – The chronicles of the beacons / The chronicles of Gehenna / The chronicles of Canaan. (cd-iss. Jun89 'CHRONICLES I & II'; 260 7499)
Feb 89. (lp) (ST 7553) **ALIEN SOUNDTRACKS II**
Sep 89. (clear-lp) (ST 7559) **LIVE IN GERMANY (live)**
Sep 90. (cd)(lp) (DCD 9026)(DLP 10) **LIQUID FOREST**
 – You remain / Down the river / Hey hey / Look away / Tibetian nights / Let me have it / As rabbits run / We can be together.
Feb 91. (cd)(lp) (DCD 9020)(DLP 7556) **MISSION OF THE ENTRANCED**
 – We are not haunted pt.1 / We are not haunted pt.2 / Mission of the entranced pt.1 / Mission of the entranced pt.2.
Jul 94. (cd) (EFA 06456-2) **THE CLAIRAUDIENT SYNDROME**
 – Hercules cave / Monkey zoo / One day in springtime / Glowing going away / The clairaudient syndrome.

—— after DAMON's death, **HELIOS** re-formed CHROME with **HILARY STENCH** – bass / **JOHNNY STENCH** – drums, backwards percussion / **TOMMY L. SIBOURG** – synths / **VOVA CAIN** – guitar / **PAUL DELLA PELLA** – drums

Consolidated   not iss.

May 95. (12") (CSD 22003) **BUMPER /**
Sep 95. (12") (CSD 22006) **I WANT YOU. /**

Man's Ruin   Man's Ruin

Sep 96. (10"clear-ep) <(MR 035)> **CHROME EP**
 – Third seed from the bud / Old time fuck n roll / Monkey shines / See ya.

—— In Apr'97, they split a single 'TORQUE POUND' for 'Gearhead' mag

Cleopatra   Cleopatra

Jan 98. (cd) <(CLP 0080-2)> **RETRO TRANSMISSION**   Sep97
 – Intro – Chili con carnage / Artificial human / Sirius system / More space / Retro transmission / Aratus / Phoebeus / Saint Jimmy's birthday / Mithras.

Man's Ruin   Man's Ruin

Feb 98. (cd) <(MR 061CD)> **TIDAL FORCES**
 – No humans allowed pt.II (the night) / A partial washing (air & water) / The ring of fire (fire and earth) / Descent into the lower worlds (lvel 1,2 & 3) / Dragon slayer / The ring of fire – reprise (a higher flame) / Bring 'em back / Mountain in the middle / Fudge bunny (the day) / The fate. (re-iss. Aug00; same)

Dossier   Dossier

May 02. (cd) <(DCD 9082)> **ANGEL OF THE CLOUDS**   Jul02
 – Death's door / Help / The spider / Torque pound / The viewer / Distance / The crimson sea / Lost in space / Down the road / Take it for me one time / Angel of the clouds.
 (above featured the taped work of DAMON)
Nov 02. (cd) <(DCD 9100)> **GHOST MACHINE**
 – Requiem / The wind / Roots / The farm / Ghost machine / Parameters / The magic bong / Santa will I die / Inner space / Black plastic bag / Drown.

– compilations, others, etc. –

Jun 89. (cd) *Dossier; (260 7490CD)* **BLOOD ON THE MOON / ETERNITY**
Jun 89. (cd) *Dossier; (260 7709CD)* **THE LYON CONCERT / ANOTHER WORLD**
Feb 95. (cd) *Dossier; (EFA 08461-2)* **CHROME SAMPLER VOLUME I: HAVING A WONDERFUL TIME WITH THE TRIPODS**
Mar 95. (cd) *Dossier; (EFA 08462-2)* **CHROME SAMPLER VOLUME II: HAVING A WONDERFUL TIME IN THE JUICE DROME**
Aug 95. (cd) *Cleopatra; (CLEO 9533-2)* **3RD FROM THE SUN / INTO THE EYES OF THE ZOMBIE KING**
Jan 98. (c-cd-box) *Cleopatra; <(CLP 97702)>* **CHROME BOX 1978-1983**
Feb 99. (cd) *Cleopatra; <472>* **CHROME FLASHBACK: THE BEST OF CHROME LIVE**
Sep 00. (d-cd) *Cleopatra; <919>* **CHROME AND FRIENDS**

John Cooper CLARKE

Born: 25 Jan'49, Salford, Manchester, England. After beginning his career in the city's folk clubs, where he met and subsequently hooked up with RICK GOLDSTRAW and his band The FERRETS, self-styled "punk poet" CLARKE signed to the independent 'Rabid' label, releasing his debut EP, 'INNOCENTS', in 1977. Recited in a heavy Manc accent, CLARKE's pulverising but witty and often hilarious verbal assaults saw him adopted by the embryonic punk scene, his uncompromising attitude and disregard for standard poetry mores drawing comparisons with the 50's Beats and influencing such early 80's wordsmiths as ATILLA THE STOCKBROKER and SEETHING WELLS. After touring with BE-BOP DELUXE in 1978, CLARKE secured a deal with 'Epic' and released a debut album, 'DISGUISE IN LOVE' (1978). Produced by BILL NELSON and with musical backing from The INVISIBLE GIRLS, the record kicked off with 'I DON'T WANT TO BE NICE', a tongue-in-cheek rant for the teenager in all of us. It also featured '(I MARRIED A) MONSTER FROM OUTER SPACE', a comment on racial prejudice via a highly amusing tale of intergalactic love as well as masturbation ode, 'READERS WIVES', set of course, to a mellow piano groove. He scored his first and only Top 40 single with 'GIMMIX!' early the following year, yet CLARKE wasn't so popular with music critics who saw him as an extension of the emerging alternative comedy scene. Live work was certainly his forte, CLARKE releasing his first live set, 'WALKING BACK TO HAPPINESS' later that summer, the record boasting one of his most vicious broadsides, 'TWAT', apparently dedicated to leading Tarzan Tory, Michael Heseltine. In 1980, the quick-fire Bard Of Broadsides toured with reggae poet LINTON KWESI JOHNSON and appeared in The Poetry Olympics at Westminster Abbey. That year's, 'SNAP, CRACKLE & BOP', was an altogether more accomplished collection, drawing praise for such gritty pieces as 'BEASLEY STREET'. While the album made the UK Top 30, CLARKE's career subsequently went into decline with third and final studio set, 'ZIP STYLE METHOD' (1982) issued to a muted response. The poet succumbed to drug abuse as the decade wore on, co-habiting with fellow addict NICO. Overcoming his problems, the 90's found CLARKE once again venturing onto the stage although new material has yet to surface. • **Trivia:** Late in 1982, his docu-film, 'TEN YEARS IN AN OPEN NECKED SHIRT' (based on his book of the same name), was seen on UK-TV Channel 4.

Album rating: DISGUISE IN LOVE (*6) / WALKING BACK TO HAPPINESS mini (*5) / OU EST LA MAISON DE FROMAGE compilation (*7) / SNAP, CRACKLE & POP (*6) / ME AND MY BIG MOUTH compilation (*7) / ZIP STYLE METHOD (*5) / WORD OF MOUTH – THE VERY BEST OF compilation (*7)

JOHN COOPER CLARKE – words, vocals / with The INVISIBLE GIRLS: **MARTIN HANNETT** – bass, producer / **PAUL BURGESS** – drums / **JOHN SCOTT** – guitar / **LYN OAKLEY** – guitar / guest **PETE SHELLEY** – guitar (of BUZZCOCKS) / **STEVE HOPKINS** – keyboards

		Rabid	not iss.
Oct 77.	(7"ep) *(TOSH 103)* **INNOCENTS**		-

– Psycle sluts (part 1 & 2) / Innocents / Suspended sentence. *(re-Sep82; same)*

—— solo with backing musicians, (INVISIBLE GIRLS)

		Epic	not iss.
Aug 78.	(7") *(EPC 6541)* **POST-WAR GLAMOUR GIRLS. / KUNG FU INTERNATIONAL (live)**		-
Oct 78.	(lp) *(EPC 83132)* **DISGUISE IN LOVE**		-

– I don't want to be nice / Psycle sluts 1 & 2 / (I've got a brand new) Tracksuit / Teenage werewolf / Readers wives / Post war glamour girl / (I married a) Monster from Outer Space / Salome Maloney / Health fanatic / Strange bed fellows / Valley of the lost women. *(cd-iss. Jun95; 480530-2)*

| Feb 79. | (7"/7"sha-orange-d) *(EPC/+12 7009)* **GIMMIX! (PLAY LOUD). / I MARRIED A MONSTER FROM OUTER SPACE (third version)** | 39 | - |
| Jun 79. | (10"clear-lp) *(JCC 1)* **WALKING BACK TO HAPPINESS** | | - |

– Gaberdine Angus / Majorca / Bronze adonis / Twat / The pest / Who stole the marble index / Gimmix! (play loud) / Nothing / Spilt beans.

| Oct 79. | (7") *(EPC 7982)* **SPLAT. / TWAT. / SLEEPWALK** | | - |

(above 'A'side was double grooved to play 2 tracks)

| Apr 80. | (lp) *(EPC 84083)* **SNAP, CRACKLE & BOP** | 26 | - |

– Evidently Chickentown / Conditional discharge / Sleepwalk / 23rd / Beasley Street / 36 hours / Belladonna / The it man / Limbo / A distant relation. *(cd-iss. Sep94; 477380-2)*

| May 80. | (7") *(EPC 8655)* **THE IT MAN. / 36 HOURS** | | - |
| May 81. | (lp) *(EPC 84979)* **ME AND MY BIG MOUTH** (compilation) | | - |

– I married a monster from Outer Space / I don't want to be nice / Valley of the lost women / 36 hours / The it man / Kung Fu international / Twat / Majorca / Bronze Adonis / Gimmix! (play loud) / Beasley Street.

| Apr 82. | (7") *(EPC 2077)* **THE DAY MY PAD WENT MAD. / A DISTANT RELATION** | | - |
| May 82. | (lp) *(EPC 85667)* **ZIP STYLE METHOD** | 97 | - |

– Midnight shift / The new assassin / Face behind the scream / I travel in biscuits / The day the world stood still / A heart disease called love / The ghost of Al Capone / Ninety degrees in the shade / The day my pad went mad / I wanna be yours / Drive she said / Night people.

| Jun 82. | (7") *(EPC 2521)* **NIGHT PEOPLE. / FACE BEHIND THE SCREAM** | | - |

—— He retired from recording, but still recited occasionally. He lived with American girlfriend/singer NICO until her death on 18th July 1988. He went into TV-advertisements for Sugar Puffs, etc.

– compilations, others, etc –

| Jul 80. | (lp) *Rabid; (NOZE 1)* **OU EST LA MAISON DE FROMAGE?** | | - |

– The serial (part 1) / Letter to Fiesta / Film extra's extra / Majorca / Action man / Kung Fu international / Sperm test / Missing persons / Spilt beans / Dumb row laughs / Bunch of twigs / Trains / The cycle accident / Gimmix / Reader's wives / Ten years in an open neck shirt (part 1) / Nothing / I married a monster from outer space / Ten years in an open neck shirt (part 2) / Daily express (you never see a nipple in) / Ten years in an open neck shirt (part 3) / Salome Malone / Psycle sluts (part 1). *(re-iss. Mar89 on 'Receiver'; RRLP 110) (cd-iss. Nov96; RRCD 110)*

| Aug 02. | (cd) *Sony; (<506343-2>)* **WORD OF MOUTH: THE VERY BEST OF** | | Sep02 |

– (I married a) Monster from outer space / I don't want to be nice / Valley of the lost women / Postwar glamour girls / Kung Fu international / Psycle sluts / Twat / Majorca / Gimmix! play loud / Beasley Street / Evidently chickentown / Conditional discharge / Limbo (baby limbo) / The it man / Thirty six hours / Midnight shift / I wanna be yours / The day my pad went mad / A heart disease called love / Night people.

CLASH

Formed: London, England ... early '76, by MICK JONES, PAUL SIMONON, JOE STRUMMER (ex-101'ers) and TERRY CHIMES (future PIL member, KEITH LEVENE, also had a brief spell). After a riotous tour supporting the SEX PISTOLS, their manager, BERNIE RHODES, attained a deal with major label big boys 'C.B.S.' in early '77 and subsequently unleashed the two minute classic, 'WHITE RIOT'. A driving chantalong stomp, the record smashed into the UK Top 40 and announced the arrival of a band whose influence and impact was second only to the 'PISTOLS. In contrast to LYDON and Co., The CLASH manipulated the energy of punk as a means of political protest and musical experimentation. 'THE CLASH' (1977) was a blinding statement of intent, a finely balanced masterwork of infectious hooklines and raging conviction. 'I'M SO BORED WITH THE U.S.A.' and 'CAREER OPPORTUNITIES' railed against inertia, while a cover of Junior Murvin's 'POLICE AND THIEVES' was the first of many sporadic forays into dub reggae. The album went Top 20, lauded by many critics as the definitive punk set, while a further two classic singles (not on the album), 'CLASH CITY ROCKERS' and 'WHITE MAN IN HAMMERSMITH PALAIS' made the Top 40 (the latter addressing the issue of racism, a subject never far from the band's agenda). CBS (and no doubt the band themselves) were keen to break America, subsequently enlisting the production services of BLUE OYSTER CULT guru, SANDY PERLMAN for follow-up set, 'GIVE 'EM ENOUGH ROPE' (1978). The album's more rock-based, less frenetic approach met with some criticism and despite the label's best efforts, the record just failed to crack the American Top 100. It had, however, made No.2 in Britain and spawned the band's first Top 20 hit in 'TOMMY GUN'. The CLASH subsequently set out to tour the States, while British fans lapped up 'THE COST OF LIVING' EP and its incendiary cover of Sonny Curtis's 'I FOUGHT THE LAW'. Finally, in late '79, The CLASH delivered their marathon masterwork, 'LONDON CALLING'. Overseen by seasoned producer, Guy Stevens, the double set showed The CLASH at an assured creative peak, from the anthemic echo of the title track to the brooding 'GUNS OF BRIXTON'. A UK Top 10'er, it finally cracked the States (Top 30), its universal acclaim spurred them on to ever more ambitious endeavours. After the plangent dub of the 'BANKROBBER' and 'THE CALL-UP' singles, the band unleashed the sprawling, triple vinyl set, 'SANDINISTA!' in December 1980. The record's wildly experimental material met with critical pasting, the bulk of the album's tracks failing to withstand repeated listening. Its relatively poor sales (still at single vinyl price!) forced a back to basics rethink for 'COMBAT ROCK' (1982). Although the record was a healthy seller, it sounded laboured; ironically, it became The CLASH's biggest selling album in America, where the 'ROCK THE CASBAH' single made the Top 10. Drummer TOPPER HEADON was already long gone by this point and was replaced by CHIMES, who had left after the 1977 debut; JONES too, was kicked out the following year. The band stumbled on for a further album, 'CUT THE CRAP' in 1985, before finally disbanding the following month. While JONES enjoyed mid-80's success with BIG AUDIO DYNAMITE, STRUMMER embarked on a low key solo career before working with his pal SHANE MacGOWAN in The POGUES. The CLASH fever gripped the nation again in 1991 when 'SHOULD I STAY OR SHOULD I GO' (a Top 20 hit in 1983), hit the top of the charts after being used in a Levi jeans advert (what else!?). A best of double set, 'THE STORY OF THE CLASH VOL.1', flew off the shelves and rumours were rife of a CLASH reunion (unceremoniously quashed by STRUMMER). Come the late 90's, STRUMMER was back from music biz oblivion fronting his own band, The MESCALEROS. Debut set, 'ROCK ART & THE X-RAY STYLE' (1999) ran a gamut of genres without really asserting STRUMMER's personality on any of them. 'GLOBAL A GO-GO' (2001) was significantly more focused and cohesive, the former CLASH man casting his witty, worldly wise perspective over a series of ventures into off-kilter world-beat. Tragically, JOE was to die of heart failure at his home in Somerset on the 22nd of December, 2002. • **Songwriters:** Either STRUMMER / – JONES until 1980 group penned, except PRESSURE DROP (Maytals) / POLICE ON MY BACK (Equals) / ARMAGIDEON TIME (Willie Williams) / JUNCO PARTNER + ENGLISH CIVIL WAR (unknown trad) / EVERY LITTLE BIT HURTS (Ed Cobb) / BRAND NEW CADILLAC (Vince Taylor). • **Trivia:** Early in 1980, the band featured live in the docu-film 'Rude Boy' about a fictionalised CLASH roadie. JOE STRUMMER went into acting 1986 (Straight To Hell) / 1989 (Lost In Space).

Album rating: THE CLASH (*10) / GIVE 'EM ENOUGH ROPE (*8) / LONDON CALLING (*9) / SANDINISTA! (*7) / COMBAT ROCK (*6) / CUT THE CRAP (*4) / THE STORY OF THE CLASH, VOL.1 compilation (*9) / CLASH ON BROADWAY (*7) / SUPER BLACK MARKET CLASH (*7) / FROM HERE TO ETERNITY live collection (*8) / Joe Strummer: EARTHQUAKE WEATHER (*5) / ROCK ART AND THE X-RAY STYLE (*5) / GLOBAL A GO-GO (*6)

JOE STRUMMER (b. JOHN GRAHAM MELLOR, 21 Aug'52, Ankara, Turkey / raised London) – vocals, guitar (ex-101'ers) / **PAUL SIMONON** (b.15 Dec'55, Brixton, England) – bass, vocals / **MICK JONES** (b. MICHAEL JONES, 26 Jun'55) – guitar, vocals / **TORY CRIMES** (b. TERRY CHIMES, 25 Jan'55) – drums

		C.B.S.	Epic
Mar 77.	(7") *(S-CBS 5058)* **WHITE RIOT. / 1977**	38	-
Apr 77.	(lp/c) *(CBS/40 82000)* **THE CLASH**	12	-

– Janie Jones / Remote control / I'm so bored with the U.S.A. / White riot / Hate and war / What's my name / Deny / London's burning / Career opportunities / Cheat / Protex blue / Police and thieves / 48 hours / Garage land. *<US-iss.Aug79 on 'Epic'; 36060>* (tracks differed & contained free 7") – GROOVY TIMES. / GATES OF THE WEST *(this lp version UK-iss.Jan91 on cd)* *(re-iss. Nov82*

CLASH (cont) THE GREAT INDIE DISCOGRAPHY The 1970s

lp/c; CBS/40 32232) (cd-iss. Apr89 on 'Columbia'; CD 32232) (cd re-iss. Aug91 on 'Columbia'; 468783-2) (cd re-iss. Oct99 on 'Columbia' cd/lp; 495344-2/-1; US version; 495345-2/-1) (lp re-iss. Oct99 on 'Simply Vinyl'; SVLP 131)

— (Jan'77) (NICKY) **TOPPER HEADON** (b.30 May'55, Bromley, Kent, England) – drums; repl. CHIMES who later joined COWBOYS INTERNATIONAL and GENERATION X

May 77. (7") *(S-CBS 5293)* **REMOTE CONTROL. / LONDON'S BURNING (live)** [ ] [-]
Sep 77. (7") *(S-CBS 5664)* **COMPLETE CONTROL. / THE CITY OF THE DEAD** [28] [-]
Feb 78. (7") *(S-CBS 5834)* **CLASH CITY ROCKERS. / JAIL GUITAR DOORS** [35] [-]
Jun 78. (7") *(S-CBS 6383)* **(WHITE MAN) IN HAMMERSMITH PALAIS. / THE PRISONER** [32] [-]
Nov 78. (lp/c) *(CBS/40 82431) <35543>* **GIVE 'EM ENOUGH ROPE** [2] [ ] Feb79
– Safe European home / English civil war / Tommy gun / Julie's been working for the drug squad / Guns on the roof / Drug-stabbing time / Stay free / Cheapstakes / All the young punks (new boots and contracts). *(re-iss. 1984 lp/c; CBS/40 32444) (cd-iss. Jan91; CD 32444) (re-iss. Oct99 on 'Columbia' cd/lp; 495346-2/-1)*
Nov 78. (7") *(S-CBS 6788)* **TOMMY GUN. / 1, 2, CRUSH ON YOU** [19] [-]
Feb 79. (7") *(S-CBS 7082)* **ENGLISH CIVIL WAR. / PRESSURE DROP** [25] [-]
May 79. (7"ep) *(S-CBS 7324)* **THE COST OF LIVING** [22] [-]
– I fought the law / Groovy times / Gates of the west / Capital radio.
Jul 79. (7") *<50738>* **I FOUGHT THE LAW. / (WHITE MAN) IN HAMMERSMITH PALAIS** [-] [ ]

— added on tour MICKEY GALLAGHER – keyboards (ex-IAN DURY)

Dec 79. (7") *(S-CBS 8087)* **LONDON CALLING. / ARMAGIDEON TIME** [11] [-]
(12"+=) *(CBS12 8087)* – Justice tonight (version) / Kick it over (version).
Dec 79. (d-lp/c) *(CLASH/+C 3) <36328>* **LONDON CALLING** [9] [27] Jan80
– London calling / Brand new Cadillac / Jimmy Jazz / Hateful / Rudie can't fail / Wrong 'em boyo / Death or glory / Koka Kola / The card cheat / Spanish bombs / The right profile / Lost in the supermarket / The guns of Brixton / Lover's rock / Four horsemen / I'm not down / Revolution rock / Train in vain. *(re-iss. Feb88 on 'Columbia' d-lp/c; 460114-1/-4) (cd-iss. Apr89 on 'Columbia'; 460114-2) (re-iss. Oct99 on 'Columbia' cd/d-lp; 495347-2/-1) (d-lp re-iss. Oct99 on 'Simply Vinyl'; SVLP 133)*
Mar 80. (7") *<50851>* **TRAIN IN VAIN (STAND BY ME). / LONDON CALLING** [-] [27]
Aug 80. (7") *(S-CBS 8323)* **BANKROBBER. / Mickey Dread: ROCKERS GALORE . . . UK TOUR** [12] [-]
Nov 80. (7") *(S-CBS 9339)* **THE CALL-UP. / STOP THE WORLD** [40] [-]
Nov 80. (10"m-lp) *<36846>* **BLACK MARKET CLASH** [-] [74]
– Time is tight / Capital radio / Bankrobber / Pressure drop / The prisoner / City of the dead / Justice tonight – kick it over (version). *(UK-iss.Sep91 on 'Columbia' cd/c; 468763-2/-4)*
Dec 80. (t-lp/d-c) *(CBS/40 FSLN 1) <37037>* **SANDINISTA!** [19] [24]
– The magnificent seven / Hitsville U.K. / Junco partner / Ivan meets G.I. Joe / The leader / Something about England / Rebel waltz / Look here / The crooked beat / Somebody got murdered / One more time / One more dub / Lightning strikes (not once but twice) / Up in Heaven (not only here) / Corner soul / Let's go crazy / If music could talk / The sound of the sinners / Police on my back / Midnight log / The equaliser / The call up / Washington bullets / Broadway / Lose this skin / Charlie don't surf / Mensforth Hill / Junkie slip / Kingston advice / The street parade / Version city / Living in fame / Silicone on sapphire / Version pardner / Career opportunites (version) / Shepherds delight. *(d-cd-iss. Apr89 on 'Columbia'; 463364-2) (re-iss. Oct99 on 'Columbia' d-cd/d-lp; 495348-2/-1)*
Jan 81. (7") *(S-CBS 9480)* **HITSVILLE U.K. / RADIO ONE** [56] [-]
Feb 81. (7") *<51013>* **HITSVILLE U.K. / POLICE ON MY BACK** [-] [ ]
Apr 81. (12"ep) *<02036>* **THE CALL-UP / THE COOL-OUT. / THE MAGNIFICENT SEVEN / THE MAGNIFICENT DANCE** [-] [ ]
Apr 81. (7"/12") *(A/+12 1133)* **THE MAGNIFICENT SEVEN. / THE MAGNIFICENT DANCE** [34] [-]
Nov 81. (7") *(A 1797)* **THIS IS RADIO CLASH. / RADIO CLASH** [47] [-]
(12"+=) *(A12 1797)* – Outside broadcast / Radio 5.

— **TERRY CHIMES** returned to repl. HEADON who later went solo (signed to 'Mercury', released a couple of singles – 'DRUMMIN' MAN', LEAVE IT TO LUCK' and 'I'LL GIVE YOU EVERYTHING' – all from the 1986 album, 'WAKING UP', which featured 60's soul singer, JIMMY HELMS)

Apr 82. (7") *(A 2309)* **KNOW YOUR RIGHTS. / FIRST NIGHT BACK IN LONDON** [43] [-]
May 82. (lp/c) *(CBS/40 FMLN 2) <37689>* **COMBAT ROCK** [2] [7]
– Know your rights / Car jamming / Should I stay or should I go / Rock the Casbah / Red angel dragnet / Straight to Hell / Overpowered by funk / Atom tan / Sean Flynn / Ghetto defendant / Inoculated city / Death is a star. *(re-iss. Nov86 lp/c; CBS/40 32787) (cd-iss. Jan91 on 'Columbia'; CD 32787) (re-iss. Oct99 on 'Columbia' cd/lp; 495349-2/-1) (lp re-iss. Oct99 on 'Simply Vinyl'; SVLP 132)*
May 82. (7") *<03006>* **SHOULD I STAY OR SHOULD I GO. / INNOCULATED CITY** [-] [ ]
Jun 82. (7"/7"pic-d) *(A/+11 2479) <03245>* **ROCK THE CASBAH. / LONG TIME JERK** [30] [8] Sep82
(12") *(A12 2479)* – ('A'side) / Mustapha dance.
Jul 82. (7") *<03061>* **SHOULD I STAY OR SHOULD I GO. / FIRST NIGHT BACK IN LONDON** [-] [45]
Sep 82. (7"/7"pic-d/12") *(A/+11/12 2646)* **SHOULD I STAY OR SHOULD I GO. / STRAIGHT TO HELL** [17] [-]
Feb 83. (7") *<03547>* **SHOULD I STAY OR SHOULD I GO? / COOL CONFUSION** [-] [50]

— (Feb83-Jan84) **STRUMMER & SIMONON** brought in new musicians **PETE HOWARD** – drums (ex-COLD FISH),repl. CHIMES who later joined HANOI ROCKS / **NICK SHEPHERD** – guitar (ex-CORTINAS) + **VINCE WHITE** – guitar; repl. JONES who formed BIG AUDIO DYNAMITE

Sep 85. (7") *(A 6122)* **THIS IS ENGLAND. / DO IT NOW** [24] [-]
(12"+=) *(A12 6122)* – Sex mad roar.
Nov 85. (lp/c) *(CBS/40 26601) <40017>* **CUT THE CRAP** [16] [88]
– Dictator / Dirty punk / We are The Clash / Are you red.. Y / Cool under heat / Movers and shakers / This is England / Three card trick / Play to win / Fingerpoppin' / North and south / Life is wild. *(cd-iss. Apr89 on 'Columbia'; CD 465110-2) (cd-iss. Dec92 on 'Columbia';)*

— disbanded Dec'85 and STRUMMER went solo (see below). SHEPHERD formed HEAD. In the early 90's, SIMONON formed HAVANA 3 A.M. who comprised NIGEL DIXON (ex-WHIRLWIND), GARY MYRICK and TRAVIS WILLIAMS. Signing to 'I.R.S.', they released only one 50's style eponymous rock album in 1991 before splitting their quiffs.

– compilations, others, etc. –

on 'C.B.S.' unless mentioned otherwise

Nov 82. (c-ep) *(A40 2907)* **COMPLETE CONTROL / LONDON CALLING / BANKROBBER / CLASH CITY ROCKERS** [ ] [-]
Sep 86. (c-ep) *(450 123-4)* **THE 12" TAPE** [ ] [-]
– London calling / The magnificent dance / This is Radio Clash / Rock the Casbah / This is England. *(cd-iss. Nov92 on 'Columbia'; 450123-2)*
Mar 88. (7") *(CLASH 1)* **I FOUGHT THE LAW. / THE CITY OF THE DEAD / 1977** [29] [-]
(12"+=/cd-s+=) *(CLASH T/C 1)* – Police on my back / 48 hours.
Mar 88. (d-lp/c/cd) *(460244-1/-4/-2) <44035>* **THE STORY OF THE CLASH** [7] [ ]
– The magnificent seven / Rock the Casbah / This is Radio Clash / Should I stay or should I go / Straight to Hell / Armagideon time / Clampdown / Train in vain / Guns of Brixton / I fought the law / Somebody got murdered / Lost in the supermarket / Bank robber / White man in Hammersmith Palais / London's burning / Janie Jones / Tommy gun / Complete control / Capital radio / White riot / Career opportinities / Clash city rockers / Safe European home / Stay free / London calling / Spanish bombs / English civil war / Police and thieves. *(re-iss. Mar91 as THE STORY OF THE CLASH VOL.1, on 'Columbia'; same)* – (hit UK 13) *(re-iss. Oct95 on 'Columbia'; same) (re-iss. Oct99 on 'Columbia' cd/d-lp; 495351-2/-4)*
Apr 88. (7"/7"box) *(CLASH/+B 2)* **LONDON CALLING. / BRAND NEW CADILLAC** [46] [-]
(12"+=) *(CLASHT 2)* – Rudie can't fail.
(cd-s+=) *(CLASHC 2)* – The street parade.
Jul 90. (7"/c-s) *(656072-7/-4)* **RETURN TO BRIXTON (remix). / ('A'-SW2 mix)** [57] [-]
(12"+=/cd-s+=) *(656072-6/-2)* – The guns of Brixton.
Feb 91. (7"/c-s) *Columbia; (656667-7/-4)* **SHOULD I STAY OR SHOULD I GO. / B.A.D. II: Rush** [1] [-]
(12"+=/cd-s+=) *(656667-6/-2)* – ('B'dance mix) / Protex blue.
(cd-s) *(656667-5)* – ('A'side) / London calling / Train in vain / I fought the law.
Apr 91. (7"/c-s) *Columbia; (656814-7/-4)* **ROCK THE CASBAH. / MUSTAPHA DANCE** [15] [-]
(12"+=/cd-s+=) *(656814-6/-2)* – The magnificent dance / This is Radio Clash.
(cd-s) *(656814-5)* – ('A'side) / Tommy gun / (White man) In Hammersmith Palais / Straight to Hell.
Jun 91. (7"/c-s) *Columbia; (656946-7/-4)* **LONDON CALLING. / BRAND NEW CADILLAC** [64] [ ]
(12"+=) *(656946-6)* – Return to Brixton (remix).
(cd-s++=) *(656946-2)* – The call-up.
Oct 91. (7"/c-s) *Columbia; (656-7/-4)* **TRAIN IN VAIN (STAND BY ME). / THE RIGHT PROFILE** [ ] [-]
(cd-s+=) *(656-2)* – Groovy times / Gates to the west.
(pic-cd-s+=) *(656-5)* – ('A'remix) / Death or glory.
Nov 91. (cd/c) *Columbia; (468946-2/-4)* **THE SINGLES COLLECTION** [68] [ ]
Nov 93. (cd/d-lp) *Columbia; (474546-2) <63895>* **SUPER BLACK MARKET CLASH** [ ] [ ]
(re-iss. Oct99 cd/d-lp; 495352-2/-1)
May 94. (3xcd-box/3xc-box) *Columbia; (469308-2/-4)* **THE CLASH ON BROADWAY** [ ] [ ]
(re-iss. Feb00 on 'Legacy'; 497453-2)
Oct 99. (cd/c/d-lp) *Columbia; (496183-2/-4/-1) <65747>* **FROM HERE TO ETERNITY (live)** [13] [ ]
– Complete control / London's burning / What's my name / Clash city rockers / Career opportunities / White man in Hammersmith Palais / Capitol radio / City of the dead / I fought the law / London calling / Armagideon time / Train in vain / Guns of Brixton / The magnificent seven / Know your rights / Should I stay or should I go / Straight to Hell. *(cd re-iss. Dec01; same)*
Oct 02. (3xcd-box) *Epic; (509662-2)* **THE CLASH (US version) / LONDON CALLING / COMBAT ROCK** [ ] [ ]
Oct 02. (12") *Columbia; (VJAY 26)* **ROCK THE CASBAH. / THE MAGNIFICENT SEVEN** [ ] [-]

— The CLASH also appeared under different guises for singles below

May 83. (12"; FUTURA 2000 with The Clash) *Celluloid; (CYZ 104)* **ESCAPADES OF FUTURA 2000** [ ] [-]
Dec 83. (7"; JANIE JONES & THE LASH) *Big Beat; (NS 91)* **HOUSE OF THE JU-JU QUEEN. / SEX MACHINE** [ ] [-]

— They can also be heard on TYMON DOGG's 45; 'Lose This Skin' (May80)

JOE STRUMMER

C.B.S. Epic

Oct 86. (7"/12") *(A/TA 7244)* **LOVE KILLS. / DUM DUM CLUB** [69] [-]

Virgin Virgin

Feb 88. (cd/c/lp) *(CD/TC+/V 2497) <90686>* **WALKER (Soundtrack)** [ ] [ ]
– Filibustero / Omotepe / Sandstorm / Machete / Viperland / Nica libre / Latin romance / The brooding side of madness / Tennessee rain / Smash everything / Tropic of no return / The unknown immortal / Musket waltz.

Epic Epic

Jun 88. (7"/7"s) *(TRASH/+P 1)* **TRASH CITY. / THEME FROM A PERMANENT RECORD** [ ] [-]
(12"+=/pic-cd-s+=) *(TRASH T/C 1)* – Nerfititi rock.

— STRUMMER was augmented by new band **JACK IRONS** – drums (of RED HOT CHILI PEPPERS) **ZANDON SCHLOSS** – guitar (ex-CIRCLE JERKS) / **RONNIE MARSHALL** – bass (of TONE LOC)

Aug 89. (7"/c-s) *(STRUM/+M 1)* **GANGSTERVILLE. / JEWELLERS AND BUMS** [ ] [-]
(7"ep+=) *(STRUME 1)* – Passport to Detroit / Punk rock blues.
(12"+=/cd-s+=) *(STRUM T/C 1)* – Don't tango with my django.
Sep 89. (lp/c/cd) *(465347-1/-4/-2) <45372>* **EARTHQUAKE WEATHER** [58] [ ]
– Gangsterville / King of the bayou / Island hopping / Slant six / Dizzy's goatee /

Shouting street / Boogie with your children / Leopardskin limousines / Sikorsky parts / Jewellers and bums / Highway on zero street / Ride your donkey / Passport to Detroit / Sleepwalk.

Oct 89. (7") *(STRUM 2)* **ISLAND HOPPING. / CHOLO VEST**
(12"+=/cd-s+=/7"ep+=) *(STRUM T/C/E 2)* – Mango street / Baby o' boogie.

— STRUMMER joined The POGUES on tour, deputising when SHANE McGOWAN was under the bottle. At the start of 1992, he had begun writing with them, so who knows? At least it will quell the dogged persistent rumours of a CLASH reformation.

JOE STRUMMER & THE MESCALEROS

— STRUMMER with **RICHARD NORRIS** – keyboards / **GED DYSON** – drums / **SCOTT SHIELDS** – bass / **ANTHONY GENN** – strings

Mercury   Epitaph

Aug 99. (12"/cd-s) *(MER/+CD 523)* **YALLA YALLA. / X-RAY STYLE / TIME AND THE TIDE**
Oct 99. (cd/c/lp) *(546654-2/-4/-1)* <80424> **ROCK ART & THE X-RAY STYLE**   71
– Tony Adams / Sandpaper blues / X-ray style / Techno D-day / The road to rock'n'roll / Nitcomb / Diggin' the new / Forbidden city / Yalla yalla / Willesden to Cricklewood.

— STRUMMER, SHIELDS + GENN recruited **MARTIN SLATTERY** – bass, flute, synthesizers, etc + **TYMON DOGG** – guitars, etc.

Hellcat   Hellcat

Jul 01. (7") *(1057-7)* **JOHNNY APPLESEED. /**
Jul 01. (cd/lp) *(<8 0440-2/-1>)* **GLOBAL A GO-GO**   68
– Johnny Appleseed / Cool 'n' out / Global a go-go / Bhindi bhagee / Gamma ray / Mega bottle ride / Shaktar Donetsk / Mondo bongo / Bummed out city / At the border, guy / Minstrel boy.

CONTORTIONS (see under ⇒ CHANCE, James)

Hugh CORNWALL (see under ⇒ STRANGLERS)

CORTINAS

Formed: London, England... early 1977 by fresh-faced R&B fans, JEREMY VALENTINE, NICK SHEPHERD, MIKE FEWINGS, DEXTER DALWOOD and DANIEL SWAN. Inspired by the onset of punk, the lads were the first act to release a single on 'Step Forward', 'FASCIST DICTATOR' drawing an imaginary line between The JAM, DR. FEELGOOD and SLAUGHTER & THE DOGS. A late '77 follow-up, 'DEFIANT POSE', packed a harder punch although in retrospect both the "sick" cover art and naive lyrics seem faintly ridiculous. Riotous gigs and a healthy major label deal with 'C.B.S.' saw the band dilute the punk influence on the disappointing debut album, 'TRUE ROMANCES' (1978), although cheeky tracks such as 'ASK MR. WAVERLY' (a subsequent B-side which should have been an A-side) and 'I TRUST VALERIE SINGLETON' (a clean living 'Blue Peter' children's TV presenter!) rescued it from bland oblivion. Not surprisingly, The CORTINAS consigned themselves to the scrapheap soon after, their career skidding to a halt after the belated 7" release of album opener, 'HEARTACHE'. The only member to enjoy his 15 minutes worth of fame was guitarist NICK SHEPHERD who became part of The CLASH prior to their mid-80's demise.

Album rating: TRUE ROMANCES (*4)

JEREMY VALENTINE – vocals / **MIKE FEWINGS** – lead guitar / **NICK SHEPPARD** – guitar / **DEXTER DALWOOD** – bass / **DANIEL SWAN** – drums

Step Forward   not iss.

Jun 77. (7") *(SF 1)* **FASCIST DICTATOR. / TELEVISION FAMILIES**
Dec 77. (7",12") *(SF 6)* **DEFIANT POSE. / INDEPENDENCE**

C.B.S.   not iss.

Apr 78. (lp) *(CBS 82831)* **TRUE ROMANCES**
– Heartache / Ask Mr. Waverly / Radio rape / Broken not twisted / I don't really want to get involved / Have it with you / Tribe of the city / I trust Valerie Singleton / Further education / Youth club dance / First I look at the purse / I'll keep my distance / Take that light away.

Nov 78. (7") *(CBS 6759)* **HEARTACHE. / ASK MR. WAVERLY**

— disbanded late '78, FEWINGS joined ESSENTIAL BOP, SHEPPARD later joined The CLASH after a two-year spell with the SPICS.

Elvis COSTELLO

Born: DECLAN McMANUS, 25 Aug'55, Liverpool, England. The son of a jazz bandleader, he grew up listening to the sounds of the day. The BEATLES (he was a member of his fanclub), the KINKS, the WHO and the sounds of Motown were all to instil in him a love of rock'n'roll and help shape his own musical style. Dividing his time between playing clubs at night and working as a computer operator during working hours (the strain on his eyes leading to the wearing of his now trademark glasses), he subsequently moved to London in 1974 to become frontman and songwriter for a country-rock group called Flip City. Flogging his demos far and wide, the newly formed 'Stiff' label duly took on his talent, McMANUS changing his name to ELVIS COSTELLO; 'Elvis', a challenge to the rock establishment, and 'Costello', his mother's maiden name. While at Stiff he met his long time collaborators NICK LOWE and Jake Rivera, who would in turn become producer and manager to COSTELLO. His first album was recorded in 24 hours, backed by CLOVER, a country and western bar band with a certain HUEY LEWIS at the helm (although he did not participate in the sessions). After little success with the first two singles, 'ALISON' and 'LESS THAN ZERO', the man resorted to playing outside a CBS Records international convention taking place at the Hilton in London. Although arrested, the stunt worked, and in '77 his first album, 'MY AIM IS TRUE' was released by 'Columbia' (US), stand out tracks including the aforementioned singles and 'WATCHING THE DETECTIVES'. Produced by LOWE, the record was hailed as one of the finest debuts in rock history, blending the Stiff sound of punk and new wave with COSTELLO's cynical observations on life. Voted Album of the Year in Rolling Stone's annual poll, COSTELLO toured the States with his newly assembled backing band, The ATTRACTIONS. America got its first taste of COSTELLO's independent stance when his appearance on Saturday Night Live turned into a scathing attack on the media. His next two albums, 'THIS YEARS MODEL' and 'ARMED FORCES' (originally titled Emotional Fascism) were to prove an artistic peak, as well as being commercially successful, the latter charting in the Top 10. Released in 1980, 'GET HAPPY' abandoned the new wave sound for a more 60's Motown approach. With 20 songs on the original LP (and 10 more on the CD reissue), it proved COSTELLO was in prime songwriting mode, the record swiftly followed by his fifth set, 'TRUST' (1981), sounding as captivating and twisted as its predecessor was fast and loose. In between these two sets was the Nashville covers album, 'ALMOST BLUE', more a curiosity than a stand out success. 'IMPERIAL BEDROOM', released in '82, is often cited as COSTELLO's best album, and was produced by the Beatles engineer, Geoff Emerick (who would later go on to produce the '96 effort 'ALL THIS USELESS BEAUTY'). Not surprisingly then, it was compared to the masterpieces of the BEATLES and the BEACH BOYS, and included such fan favourites as 'MAN OUT OF TIME' and 'THE LONG HONEYMOON'. 'PUNCH THE CLOCK', released in '83, and featuring CHET BAKER on the track 'SHIPBUILDING', was less ambitious than the previous album, while 'GOODBYE CRUEL WORLD', released the following year, was his worst record by some margin, starting out as an attempt at folk-rock, but ending up as an example of the '80s sound gone wrong. By this time, a split had developed between COSTELLO and the ATTRACTIONS, and 'KING OF AMERICA' was the penultimate album recorded with this combination until 'BRUTAL YOUTH' in '94. With backing from The CONFEDERATES and co-production by T-BONE BURNETT, it featured a mixture of country and folk with a fair splattering of rockabilly with varied success. 'BLOOD & CHOCOLATE' (1986) was notable both for the return of NICK LOWE as producer and the man's split from the ATTRACTIONS. With LOWE at the helm, the record was far removed from his '84 effort, featuring a nastier, meatier version of 'THIS YEARS MODEL' plus 'POISONED ROSE', the latter track boasting the bass playing of the legendary jazz bassist RAY BROWN. Subsequently signing to 'Warner Brothers', his first release was the darkly comic and commercially successful 'SPIKE' (1989), its considerable sales due largely to the hit single, 'VERONICA', although it also featured songs of genuine outrage such as 'TRAMP THE DIRT DOWN' and 'LET HIM DANGLE'. The next few years saw COSTELLO become more adventurous in an attempt to break away from the past, symbolised by a change of image. 'MIGHTY LIKE A ROSE' remains arguably his most underrated album, while the follow up, 'THE JULIET LETTERS' (featuring The Brodsky Quartet), mixed pop with chamber music to commercial failure but critical praise. 'BRUTAL YOUTH' in '94 saw the reunion of COSTELLO and the ATTRACTIONS (dubbed the Distractions) and included one of the most beautiful recordings of his career in 'ROCKING HORSE ROAD', while the follow up, 'ALL THIS USELESS BEAUTY', was the ATTRACTIONS' swansong and inexplicably a commercial failure. Collaborations outside of his albums for 'Columbia' and 'Warners' are numerous, COSTELLO winning a BAFTA with RICHARD HARVEY for the soundtrack to 'G.B.H.' and also contributing the track, 'MY MOOD SWINGS' to the Cohen Brothers film, 'The Big Lebowski'. Perhaps the most intriguing partnership never to see the light of day, save for three releases as obscure B-Sides, was his collaboration with country legend, GEORGE JONES, singing 'non-country' songs such as Hoagy Carmichael's 'MY RESISTANCE IS LOW' and Bruce Springsteen's 'BRILLIANT SURPRISE'. A collaboration was released at the back end of '98 featuring an album's worth of COSTELLO and BURT BACHARACH material, 'PAINTED FROM MEMORY', together again after the magnificent 'God Give Me Strength' (which was originally recorded on the 'Grace Of My Heart' soundtrack). A subsequent tribute album of COSTELLO's songs by the likes of JOHNNY CASH, JUNE TABOR, NICK LOWE and ROBERT WYATT demonstrated both the man's musical versatility and the songwriting skills which have made him such an integral part of the last 25 years of popular music. Solo once again, ELVIS COSTELLO was back in chart land courtesy of stripped-down, bare-bones set, 'WHEN I WAS CRUEL' (2002). Possibly short of production techniques, once provided by Mitchell Froom or Marc Ribot, the record still managed to encompass all of ELVIS's songwriting craft. • **Songwriters:** All penned by COSTELLO, bar NEAT NEAT NEAT (Damned) / I CAN'T STAND UP FOR FALLING DOWN (Sam & Dave) / SWEET DREAMS (Patsy Cline) / A GOOD YEAR FOR THE ROSES (Jerry Chestnut) / DON'T LET ME BE MISUNDERSTOOD (Nina Simone) / I WANNA BE LOVED (Farnell Jenkins) / THE UGLY THINGS (Nick Lowe) / YOU'RE NO GOOD (Swinging Blue Jeans) / FULL FORCE GALE (Van Morrison) / YOU'VE GOT TO HIDE YOUR LOVE AWAY (Beatles) / STEP INSIDE LOVE (Cilla Black) / STICKS & STONES (Ray Charles) / FROM HEAD TO TOE (Smokey Robinson) / CONGRATULATIONS (Paul Simon) / STRANGE (Screaming Jay Hawkins) / HIDDEN CHARMS (Willie Dixon) /

REMOVE THIS DOUBT (Supremes) / I THREW IT ALL AWAY (Bob Dylan) / LEAVE MY KITTEN ALONE (Little Willie John) / EVERYBODY'S CRYIN' MERCY (Mose Allison) / I'VE BEEN WRONG BEFORE (Randy Newman) / BAMA LAMA BAMA LOO (Little Richard) / MUST YOU THROW DIRT IN MY FACE (Louvin Bros.) / POURING WATER ON A DROWNING MAN (James Carr) / THE VERY THOUGHT OF YOU (Ray Noble) / PAYDAY (Jesse Winchester) / PLEASE STAY (Bacharach-David) / RUNNING OUT OF FOOLS (Jerry Ragavoy) / DAYS (Kinks) / SHE (hit; Charles Aznavour) / etc. • **Trivia:** He has also produced The SPECIALS (1979) / SQUEEZE (1981) / POGUES (1985) retaining a latter acquaintance in CAIT O'RIORDON, whom he married on 16 May'86.

Album rating: MY AIM IS TRUE (*9) / THIS YEAR'S MODEL (*9) / ARMED FORCES (*9) / GET HAPPY!! (*8) / TRUST (*8) / ALMOST BLUE (*5) / IMPERIAL BEDROOM (*8) / PUNCH THE CLOCK (*7) / GOODBYE CRUEL WORLD (*5) / KING OF AMERICA (*7) / BLOOD & CHOCOLATE (*7) / OUT OF OUR IDIOT collection (*5) / SPIKE (*5) / MIGHTY LIKE A ROSE (*5) / THE JULIET LETTERS with Brodsky Quartet (*5) / BRUTAL YOUTH (*6) / KOJAK VARIETY (*4) / ALL THIS USELESS BEAUTY (*5) / EXTREME HONEY compilation (*6) / PAINTED FROM MEMORY with Burt Bacharach (*5) / THE SWEETEST PUNCH re-working (*4) / THE VERY BEST OF ELVIS COSTELLO & THE ATTRACTIONS compilation (*8) / WHEN I WAS CRUEL (*5)

ELVIS COSTELLO

(solo) – vocals, guitar with backing band The **SHAMROCKS,** (alias CLOVER) / **JOHN McFEE** – guitar / **ALEX CALL** – guitar, vocals / **SEAN HOPPER** – keyboards / **JOHN CIAMBOTTI** – bass / **MICHAEL SHINE** – drums

Stiff Columbia

Mar 77. (7") *(BUY 11)* **LESS THAN ZERO. / RADIO SWEETHEART** -
May 77. (7") *(BUY 14)* **ALISON. / WELCOME TO THE WORKING WEEK**
Jun 77. (7") *<3-10641>* **ALISON. / MIRACLE MAN** -
Jul 77. (7") *(BUY 15)* **(THE ANGELS WANNA WEAR MY) RED SHOES. / MYSTERY DANCE** -
Jul 77. (lp/c) *(SEEZ/ZSEEZ 3) <JC 35037>* **MY AIM IS TRUE** 14 32 Nov77
– Welcome to the working week / Miracle man / No dancing / Blame it on Cain / Alison / Sneaky feelings / (The angels wanna wear my) Red shoes / Less than zero / Mystery dance / Pay it back / I'm not angry / Waiting for the end of the world. *<re-iss. US Mar78 +=> (AL 35037>* – Watching the detectives. *(re-iss. Jul86 on 'Imp' lp/c/cd; FIEND/+CASS/CD 13) (re-mast.Mar93 & Aug99 on 'Demon'++=; DPAM 1)* – Radio sweetheart / Stranger in the house / Imagination (is a powerful deceiver) / Mystery dance / Cheap reward / Jump up / Wave a white flag / Blame it on Cain / Poison moon. *(d-cd iss.Sep01 on 'Demon' MANUS 101)*

ELVIS COSTELLO & THE ATTRACTIONS

— **STEVE NIEVE** (b.NASON)– keyboards repl. HOPPER to HUEY LEWIS & THE NEWS **BRUCE THOMAS** – bass, vocals (ex-QUIVER)repl. CIAMBOTTI, CALL + McFEE / **PETE THOMAS** (b.9 Aug'54, Sheffield, England)– drums (ex-CILLI WILLI, ex-WILKO JOHNSON)repl. SHINE

Oct 77. (7"m) *(BUY 20)* **WATCHING THE DETECTIVES. / BLAME IT ON CAIN (live) / MYSTERY DANCE (live)** 15 -
Nov 77. (7" *<3-10705>* **WATCHING THE DETECTIVES. / ALISON** -

Radar Columbia

Mar 78. (7") *(ADA 3)* **(I DON'T WANT TO GO TO) CHELSEA. / YOU BELONG TO ME** 16 -
Mar 78. (lp/c) *(XX LP/C 11) <35331>* **THIS YEAR'S MODEL** 4 30
– No action / This year's girl / The beat / Pump it up / Little Triggers / You belong to me / Hand in hand / (I don't want to go to) Chelsea * / Lip service / Living in Paradise / Lipstick vogue / Night rally *. *(free-7"w/ above) (SAM 83)* – STRANGER IN THE HOUSE. / NEAT NEAT NEAT *<tracks * repl. by* 'Radio Radio' *on US version> (re-iss. May80 on 'F-Beat'; XXLP 4) (re-iss. Apr84 on 'Imp'; FIEND/+CASS 18) (cd-iss. Jan86; FIENDCD 18) (re-mast.Mar93 & Aug99 on 'Demon'++=; DPAM 2)* – Big tears / Crawling to the USA / Running out of angels / Green shirt / Big boys.
May 78. (7") *(ADA 10)* **PUMP IT UP. / BIG TEARS** 24 -
Jul 78. (7") *<3-10762>* **THIS YEAR'S GIRL. / BIG TEARS** -
Oct 78. (7") *(ADA 24)* **RADIO RADIO. / TINY STEPS** 29
Jan 79. (lp/c) *(RAD/RAC 14) <35709>* **ARMED FORCES** 2 10
– Accidents will happen / Senior service / Oliver's army / Big boys / Green shirt / Party girl / Goon squad / Busy bodies / Sunday's best * / Moods for moderns / Chemistry class / Two little Hitlers. *(free 7"w/ above) (SAM 90) <AE 71171>* LIVE AT HOLLYWOOD HIGH EP:- Accidents Will Happen / Alison / Watching The Detectives. *<track * repl. by* '(What's So Funny 'Bout) Peace, Love And Understanding' *on US version + re-issue> (re-iss. May80 on 'F-Beat'; XXLP 5) (re-iss. Apr84 on 'Imp' lp/c; FIEND/+CASS 21) (cd-iss. Jan86; FIENDCD 21) (re-mast.Mar93 & Aug99 on 'Demon'+=; DPAM 3)* – My funny valentine / Tiny steps / Clean money / Talking in the dark / Wednesday week / (above EP). *(d-cd re-iss. Oct02 on 'Demon'+=; MANUS 103)* – (live tracks).
Feb 79. (7") *(ADA 31)* **OLIVER'S ARMY. / MY FUNNY VALENTINE** 2
May 79. (7"m) *(ADA 35)* **ACCIDENTS WILL HAPPEN. / TALKING IN THE DARK / WEDNESDAY WEEK** 28

ELVIS COSTELLO

solo, but still used ATTRACTIONS

F-Beat Columbia

Feb 80. (7") *(XX 1)* **I CAN'T STAND UP FOR FALLING DOWN. / GIRLS TALK** 4
Feb 80. (lp/c) *(XX LP/C 1) <36347>* **GET HAPPY!!** 2 11
– Love for tender / Opportunity / The imposter / Secondary modern / King Horse / Possession / Man called Uncle / Clowntime is over / New Amsterdam / High fidelity / I can't stand up for falling down / Black and white world / Five years in reverse / B movie / Motel matches / Human touch / Beaten to the punch / Temptation / I stand accused / Riot act. *(re-iss. Apr84 on 'Imp' lp/c; FIEND/+CASS 24) (cd-iss. Jan86; FIENDCD 24) (re-mast.May94 & Aug99 on 'Demon'+=; DPAM 5)* – Girls talk / Clowntime is over No.2 / Getting mighty crowded So young / Just a memory / Hoover factory / Ghost train / Dr. Luther's assistant / Black & white world / Riot act.

Apr 80. (7") *(XX 3)* **HIGH FIDELITY. / GETTING MIGHTY CROWDED** 30
(12"+=) *(XX 3T)* – Clowntime is over (version 2).
Jun 80. (7") *(XX5)* **NEW AMSTERDAM. / DR. LUTHER'S ASSISTANT** 36
(7"ep+=) *(XX 5E)* – Ghost train / Just a memory.

ELVIS COSTELLO & THE ATTRACTIONS

(same line-up)
Dec 80. (7"m) *(XX 12)* **CLUBLAND. / CLEAN MONEY / HOOVER FACTORY** 60
Jan 81. (lp/c) *(XX LP/C 11) <37051>* **TRUST** 9 28
– Clubland / Lovers walk / You'll never be a man / Pretty words / Strict time / Luxembourg / Watch your step / New lace sleeves / From a whisper to a scream / Different finger / White knuckles / Shot with his own gun / Fish 'n' chip paper / Big sister's clothes. *(re-iss. Apr84 on 'Imp'; lp/c; FIEND/+CASS 30) (cd-iss. Jan86; FIENDCD 30) (re-mast.May94 & Aug99 on 'Demon'+=; DPAM 6)* – Black sails in the sunset / Big sister / Sad about girls / Twenty-five to twelve / Love for sale / Weeper's dream / Gloomy Sunday / Boy with a problem / Seconds of pleasure.
Feb 81. (7") *(XX 14)* **FROM A WHISPER TO A SCREAM. / LUXEMBOURG**
Sep 81. (7") *(XX 17)* **GOOD YEAR FOR THE ROSES. / YOUR ANGEL STEPS OUT OF HEAVEN** 6
Oct 81. (lp/c) *(XX LP/C 13) <37562>* **ALMOST BLUE** 7 50
– Why don't you love me (like you used to do) / Sweet dreams / Sucess / I'm your toy / Tonight the bottle let me down / Brown to blue / Good year for the roses / Sittin' and thinkin' / Colour of the blues / Too far gone / Honey hush / How much I lied. *(re-iss. Apr84 on 'Imp' lp/c; FIEND/+CASS 33) (cd-iss. Jan86; FIENDCD 33) (re-mast.Oct94 & Aug99 on 'Demon'+=; DPAM 7)* – He's got you (live) / Cry cry (live) / There won't be me anymore (live) / Sittin' and thinkin' (live) / Honey hush (live) / Psycho (live) / Your angel steps out of Heaven / Darling, you know I wouldn't lie / My shoes keep walking back to you / Tears before bedtime / I'm your toy (live).
Dec 81. (7") *(XX 19)* **SWEET DREAMS. / PSYCHO (live)** 42
Apr 82. (7"m) *(XX 21)* **I'M YOUR TOY (live). / CRY CRY CRY / WONDERING** 51
(12"ep) *(XX 21T)* – ('A'side) / My shoes keep walking back to you / Blues keep calling / Honky tonk girl. (w/ The ROYAL PHILHARMONIC)
Jun 82. (7"m) *(XX 26)* **YOU LITTLE FOOL. / BIG SISTER / THE STAMPING GROUND (The Emotional Toothpaste)** 52
Jul 82. (lp/c) *(XX LP/C 17) <38157>* **IMPERIAL BEDROOM** 6 30
– Beyond belief / Tears before bedtime / Shabby doll / The long honeymoon / Man out of time / Almost blue / . . .And in every home / The loved ones / Human hands / Kid about it / Little savage / Boy with a problem / Pidgin English / You little fool / Town cryer. *(re-iss. Apr84 on 'Imp' lp/c; FIEND/+CASS 36) (cd-iss. Jan86; FIENDCD 36) (re-mast.Oct94 & Aug99 on 'Demon'+=; DPAM 8)* – From head to toe / The world of broken hearts / Night time / Really mystified / I turn around / Seconds of pleasure / The stamping ground / Shabby doll / Imperial bedroom. *(d-cd iss.Oct02 on 'Demon'+=; MANUS 108)* – (alt. & live tracks).
Jul 82. (7") *(XX 28)* **MAN OUT OF TIME. / TOWN CRYER (alt.take)** 58 -
Jul 82. (7") *<CNR 03269>* **MAN OUT OF TIME. / (one-side)** -
(12"+=) *(XX 28T)* – Imperial bedroom.
Sep 82. (7") *(XX 30)* **FROM HEAD TO TOE. / THE WORLD OF BROKEN HEARTS** 43
(below from the film 'Party Party' and released on 'A&M')
Nov 82. (7") *(AMS 8267)* **PARTY PARTY. / IMPERIAL BEDROOM** 48
(below ELVIS as "The IMPOSTER" and issued on 'Imp-Demon')
May 83. (7") *(IMP 001)* **PILLS AND SOAP. / ('A'extended)** 16
Jul 83. (7") *(XX 32) <04045>* **EVERYDAY I WRITE THE BOOK. / HEATHEN TOWN** 28 36
(12"+=) *(XX 32T) <44-04115>* – Night time.
Jul 83. (lp/c) *(XX LP/C 19) <38897>* **PUNCH THE CLOCK** 3 24
– Let them all talk / Everyday I write the book / The greatest thing / The element within her / Love went mad / Shipbuilding / T.K.O. (boxing day) / Charm school / The invisible man / Mouth almighty / King of thieves / Pills and soap / The world and his wife. *(re-iss. Sep84 lp/c/cd; ZL/ZK/ZD 70026) (re-iss. Jan88 on 'Demon' lp/c/cd; FIEND/+CASS/CD 72) (re-mast.Feb95 & Aug99 on 'Demon'+=; DPAM 9)* – Heathen town / The flirting kind / Walking on thin ice / Town where time stood still / Shatterproof / The world and his wife (live) / Everyday I write the book (live).
Sep 83. (7"/ext.12") *(XX 33/+T) <04266>* **LET THEM ALL TALK. / KEEP IT CONFIDENTIAL** 59
(below also as "The IMPOSTER" and issued on 'Imp')
Apr 84. (7") *(TRUCE 1)* **PEACE IN OUR TIME. / WITHERED AND DEAD** 48
Jun 84. (7") *(XX 35) <05625>* **I WANNA BE LOVED. / TURNING THE TOWN RED** 25
(12"+=) *(XX 35T)* – ('A'extended smoochy'n'runny mix).
(12"+=) *(XX 35Z)* – ('A'discotheque version).
Jun 84. (lp/c) *(ZL/ZK 70317) <39429>* **GOODBYE CRUEL WORLD** 10 35
– The only flame in town / Home truth / Room with no number / Inch by inch / Worthless thing / Love field / I wanna be loved / The comedians / Joe Porterhouse / Sour milk cow blues / The great unknown / The deportees club / Peace in our time. *(cd-iss. Mar86; ZD 70317) (re-iss. Jan88 on 'Demon' lp/c/cd; FIEND/+CASS/CD 75) (cd re-mast.Feb95 & Aug99 on 'Demon'+=; DPAM 10)* – Turning the town red / Baby it's you / Get yourself another fool / I hope you're happy now / The only flame in town (live) / Worthless thing (live) / Motel matches (live) / Sleepless nights (live) / Deportee.
Aug 84. (7"/'A'disco-12") *(XX 37/+T) <04502>* **THE ONLY FLAME IN TOWN. / THE COMEDIANS** 71 56 Jul84
('A'disco-12"+=) *(XX 37Z) <44-05081>* – Pump it up (1984 dance mix).

— (In May'85, guested on JOHN HIATT single 'Living A Little')
(below as The COWARD BROTHERS (w/ T-BONE BURNETT) + issued on 'Imp')
Jul 85. (7") *(IMP 006)* **THE PEOPLE'S LIMOUSINE. / THEY'LL NEVER TAKE THEIR LOVE FROM ME**

Elvis COSTELLO (cont) — THE GREAT INDIE DISCOGRAPHY — The 1970s

The COSTELLO SHOW

featuring The ATTRACTIONS and The CONFEDERATES

— added **JAMES BURTON** – guitar / **MITCHELL FROOM** – keyboards / **JERRY SCHEFF** – bass / **JIM KELTNER** – drums / **RON TUTT** – drums (i.e. The CONFEDERATES)

F-Beat / Columbia

Jan 86. (7") (ZB 40555) <05809> **DON'T LET ME BE MISUNDERSTOOD. / BABY'S GOT A BRAND NEW HAIRDO** — 33
 (12"+=) (ZT 40556) – Get yourself another fool.

Feb 86. (lp/c/cd) (ZL/ZK/ZD 70946) <40173> **KING OF AMERICA** — 11 / 39
 – Brilliant mistake / Lovable / Our little angel / Don't let me be misunderstood / Glitter gulch / Indoor fireworks / Little palaces / I'll wear it proudly / American without tears / Eisenhower blues / Poisoned rose / The big light / Jack of all parades / Suit of lights / Sleep of the just. (re-iss. Jan88 on 'Demon' lp/c/cd; FIEND/+CASS/CD 78) (re-mast.Jul95 & Aug99 on 'Demon' cd+=/d-lp+=; DPAM/+LP 11) – LIVE ON BROADWAY – Coward Brothers:- The people's limousine / They'll never take her love from me / Suffering face / Shoes without heels / King of confidence.

ELVIS COSTELLO & THE ATTRACTIONS

ELVIS, BRUCE, STEVE & PETE plus guest **NICK LOWE** – guitar

Imp-Demon / Columbia

Aug 86. (7") (IMP 007) <06326> **TOKYO STORM WARNING. / (part 2)** — 73
 (12"+=) (IMP 007T) – Black sails in the sunset.

Sep 86. (lp/c/cd) (FIEND/+CASS/CD 80) <40518> **BLOOD & CHOCOLATE** — 16 / 84
 – Uncomplicated / I hope you're happy now / Tokyo storm warning / Home is anywhere you hang your head / I want you / Honey are you straight or are you blind? / Blue chair / Battered old bird / Crimes of Paris / Poor Napoleon / Next time around. (cd re-mast.Sep95 & Aug99 on 'Demon'+=; DPAM 12) – Seven day weekend / Forgive her anything / Blue chair / Baby's got a brand new hairdo / American without tears No.2 / A town called big nothing (really big nothing). (cd w/ bonus interview disc) (d-cd iss.Feb02 on 'Demon' +=; MANUS 112) <US-iss on 'Rhino'; 78355> – Leave my kitten alone / New rhythm method / Forgive her anything / Crimes of Paris / Uncomplicated / Battered old bird / Seven day weekend / Blue chair / Baby's got a brand new hairdo (live) / American without tears No.2 / A town called big nothing / Pouring water on a drowning man / Running out of fools / Tell me right now / Lonely blue boy.

Nov 86. (7") (IMP 008) **I WANT YOU. / (part 2)**
 (12"+=) (IMP 008T) – I hope you say you're happy.

Demon / Columbia

Jan 87. (7") (D 1047) **BLUE CHAIR. / AMERICA WITHOUT TEARS NO.2 (Twilight version)**
 (12"+=) (D 1047T) – Shoes without heels.

May 87. (7"/12") (D 1052/+T) **A TOWN CALLED BIG NOTHING. / RETURN TO BIG NOTHING** — — / -
 (above as "McMANUS GANG" featuring SY RICHARDSON)

ELVIS COSTELLO

solo, with mostly **FROOM, KELTNER, PETE THOMAS** (2), **MICHAEL BLAIR** – percussion / **MARC RIBOT** – guitar / **JERRY MAROTTA** – drums / **PAUL McCARTNEY, ROGER McGUINN, CAIT O'RIORDAN, T-BONE BURNETT, CHRISSIE HYNDE** on 1 or 2, plus The DIRTY DOZEN BRASS BAND (GREGORY DAVIS, EFREM TOWNS, ROGER LEWIS, KEVIN HARRIS, KIRK JOSEPH, C. JOSEPH, plus loads more)

Warners / Warners

Feb 89. (lp/c)(cd) (WX 238/+C)(925848-2) <25848> **SPIKE** — 5 / 32
 – ...This town... / Let him dangle / Deep dark truthful mirror / Veronica / God's comic / Chewing gum / Tramp the dirt down / Stalin Malone / Satellite / Pads, paws and claws / Baby plays around / Miss Macbeth / Any king's shilling / Coal train robberies * / Last boat leaving. (cd+= *) (<d-cd iss.Sep01 on 'Rhino'+=; 8122 74286-2>) – demos:- Miss Macbeth / This town / Deep dark truthful mirror / Coal train robberies / Satellite / Pads, paws and claws / Let him dangle / Veronica / Tramp the dirt down / Baby plays around / Put your big toe in the milk of human kindness / Last boat leaving / Ugly things / You're no good / Point of no return / Room nobody lives in / Stalin Malone (vocal version).

Feb 89. (7") (W 7558) <22981> **VERONICA. / YOU'RE NO GOOD** — 31 / 19
 (12"+=/12"poster+=/cd-s+=/pic-cd-s) (W 7558 T/TW/CD/CDX) – The room nobody lives in / Coal train robberies.

May 89. (7"ep/10"ep) (W 2949/+TE) **BABY PLAYS AROUND / POISONED ROSE. / ALMOST BLUE / MY FUNNY VALENTINE** — 65
 (c-ep/12"ep/cd-ep) (W 2949 C/T/CD) – (2nd track repl. by) Point of no return.

Apr 91. (7"/c-s) (W 0025/+C) **THE OTHER SIDE OF SUMMER. / COULDN'T CALL IT UNEXPECTED #4** — 43
 (12"+=/cd-s+=) (W 0025 T/CD) – The ugly things.

May 91. (lp/c/cd) (WX 419/+C/CD) <26575> **MIGHTY LIKE A ROSE** — 5 / 55
 – The other side of summer / How to be dumb / All grown up / Invasion hit parade / Harpers bizarre / Hurry down doomsday (the bugs are taking over) / After the fall / Georgie and her rival / So like Candy / Interlude: Couldn't call it unexpected #2 / Playboy to a man / Sweet pear / Broken / Couldn't call it unexpected #4. (re-iss. cd Feb95; 7599 26675-2) (<d-cd-iss. Nov02 on 'Rhino'+=;8122 78189-2>) – Mischievous ghost / St. Stephen's day murders / The other side of summer / Deep dark truthful mirror / Hurry down doomsday / All growing up / Georgia and her rival / Forgive her anything / It started to come to me / I still miss someone / The last town I painted / Put your big toe in the milk of human kindness / Invasion hit parade / Just another mystery train / Broken.

— in Jul'91, ELVIS COSTELLO & RICHARD HARVEY issued the TV soundtrack for 'G.B.H.'; they later teamed up for 'JAKE'S PROGRESS'

Oct 91. (7") (W 0068) **SO LIKE CANDY. / VERONICA (demo)**
 (12"+=/cd-s+=) (W 0068 T/CD) – Couldn't call it unexpected (live) / Hurry down doomsday (the blues are taking over).

— In 1992, he wrote material for WENDY JAMES (Transvision Vamp)

ELVIS COSTELLO / THE BRODSKY QUARTET

with **MICHAEL THOMAS + IAN BELTON** – violins / **PAUL CASSIDY** – viola / **JACQUELINE THOMAS** – violincello (all co-wrote music with him)

Jan 93. (cd/c) (<9362 45180-2/-4>) **THE JULIET LETTERS** — 18
 – Deliver us / For other eyes / Swine / Expert rites / Dead letter / I almost had a weakness / Why? / Who do you think you are? / Taking my life in your hands / This offer is unrepeatable / Dear sweet filthy world / The letter home / Jacksons, Monk and Rowe / This sad burlesque / Romeo's seance / I thought I'd write to Juliet / Last post / The first to leave / Damnation's cellar / The birds will still be singing. (cd re-iss. Dec96; same)

Feb 93. (c-s) (W 0159) **JACKSONS, MONK AND ROWE / THIS SAD BURLESQUE** — — / -
 (cd-s+=) (W 0159CDX) – (interviews).

Elvis COSTELLO

Mar 94. (7"/c-s) (W 0234/+C) **SULKY GIRL. / A DRUNKEN MAN'S PRAISE OF SOBRIETY** — 22
 (cd-s+=) (W 0234CD) – Idiophone / ('A'album version).

Mar 94. (cd/c) (<9362 45535-2/-4>) **BRUTAL YOUTH** — 2 / 34
 – Pony St. / Kinder murder / 13 steps lead down / This is Hell / Clown strike / You tripped at every step / Still too soon to know / 20% amnesia / Sulky girl / London's brilliant parade / My science fiction twin / Rocking horse road / Just about glad / All the rage / Favourite hour. (<d-cd iss.Feb02 on 'Rhino' +=; 8122 78390-2>) – This is Hell (alt.) / Idiophone / Abandon words / Poisoned letter / A drunken man's praise of sobriety / Pony St. / Just about glad / Clown strike / Rocking horse road (demo) / 13 steps lead down (demo) / All the rage (demo) / Sulky girl (demo) / You tripped at every step (alt.)

Apr 94. (7"/c-s) (W 0245/+C) **13 STEPS LEAD DOWN. / DO YOU KNOW WHAT I'M SAYING?** — 59
 (cd-s) (W 0245CD) – ('A'side) / Puppet girl / Basement kiss / We despise you.

Jul 94. (7"/c-s) (W 0251/+C) **YOU TRIPPED AT EVERY STEP. / YOU'VE GOT TO HIDE YOUR LOVE AWAY**
 (cd-s+=) (W 0251CD) – Step inside love / Sticks & stones.

Nov 94. (c-s) (W 0270C) **LONDON'S BRILLIANT PARADE / LONDON'S BRILLIANT** — 48
 (12"+=) (W 0270T) – My resistance is low / Congratulations.
 (cd-s+=) (W 270CD1) – ('A'side) / Sweet dreams / The loved ones / From head to toe.
 (cd-s+=) (W 270CD2) – ('A'side) / New Amsterdam / Beyond belief / Shipbuilding.

May 95. (cd/c) (<9362 45903-2/-4>) **KOJAK VARIETY** — 21
 – Strange / Hidden charms / Remove this doubt / I threw it all way / Leave my kitten alone / Everybody's cryin' mercy / I've been wrong before / Bama lama bama loo / Must you throw dirt in my face / Pouring water on a drowning man / The very thought of you / Payday / Please stay / Running out of fools / Days. (cd re-iss. Dec96; same)

Aug 95. (cd; by ELVIS COSTELLO & BILL FRISELL) (<9362 46073-2>) **DEEP DEAD BLUE** — — / Nov95
 – Weird nightmare / Love field / Shamed into love / Gigi / Poor Napoleon / Baby plays around / Deep dead blue.

ELVIS COSTELLO & THE ATTRACTIONS

Apr 96. (c-s) (W 0348C) **IT'S TIME / LIFE SHRINKS** — 58
 (cd-s+=) (W 0348CD) – Brilliant disguise.

May 96. (cd/c) (<9362 46198-2/-4>) **ALL THIS USELESS BEAUTY** — 28 / 53
 – The other end of the telescope / Little atoms / All this useless beauty / Complicated shadows / Why can't a man stand alone / Distorted angel / Shallow grave / Poor fractured atlas. (cd re-iss. Jul00; same) (<d-cd iss.Sep01 on 'Rhino'+=; 8122 74284-2>)Starting to come with me / You bowed down / It's time / I want to vanish / Almost ideal eyes / My dark life (with BRIAN ENO) / The day is done (with FAIRFIELD FOUR) / What do I do now / The bridge I burned / demos:- It's time / Complicated shadows / You bowed down / Mistress and maid / Distorted angel / The world's greatest optimist / The only flame in town / The comedians (demo) / Days take care of everything / Hidden shame / Why can't a man stand alone.

Jul 96. (cd-s) (W 0364CD) **LITTLE ATOMS / WHY CAN'T A MAN STAND ALONE / ALMOST IDEAL EYES / JUST ABOUT GLAD**

Jul 96. (cd-s) (W 0365CD) **THE OTHER END OF THE TELESCOPE / ALMOST IDEAL EYES / BASEMENT KISS (live) / COMPLICATED SHADOWS (demo)**

Jul 96. (cd-s) (W 0366CD) **DISTORTED ANGEL / ALMOST IDEAL EYES / LITTLE ATOMS (DJ Food mix) / Lush: ALL THIS USELESS BEAUTY**

Jul 96. (cd-s) (W 0367CD) **ALL THIS USELESS BEAUTY / ALMOST IDEAL EYES / Sleeper: THE OTHER END OF THE TELESCOPE / DISTORTED ANGEL (Tricky mix)**

ELVIS COSTELLO with BURT BACHARACH

Mercury / Mercury

Sep 98. (cd/c) (<538002-2/-4>) **PAINTED FROM MEMORY** — 32 / 78
 – In the darkest place / Toledo / I still have that other girl / This house is empty now / Tears at the birthday party / Such unlikely lovers / My thief / Long division / Painted from memory / The sweetest punch / What's her name today? / God give me strength. (special iss.Apr99; 546165-2)

Apr 99. (cd-s) (870965-2) **TOLEDO / TEARS AT THE BIRTHDAY PARTY (live) / INCH BY INCH (live)** — 72
 (cd-s) (870967-2) – ('A'side) / Such unlikely lovers (live) / Baby plays around (live).

Jul 99. (c-s) (MERMC 521) **SHE / THE HOUSE IS EMPTY NOW** — 19
 (cd-s+=) (MERDD 521) – What's her name today.
 (cd-s) (MERCD 521) – ('A'side) / Painted from memory / Sweetest punch.

Sep 99. (cd; ELVIS COSTELLO / BURT BACHARACH / BILL FRISELL) (<559865-2>) **THE SWEETEST PUNCH** (re-workings of above)

ELVIS COSTELLO

Mercury Mercury

Apr 02. (7") *(582887-7)* **TEAR OFF YOUR OWN HEAD (IT'S A DOLL'S REVOLUTION). / WHEN I WAS CRUEL** 58 -
(cd-s) *(582887-2)* – ('A'side) / The Imposter vs. the floodtide (dust and petals) / Revolution doll.

Apr 02. (cd)(d-lp) *(<586 829-2>)(586 775-1)* **WHEN I WAS CRUEL** 17 20
– 45 / Spooky girlfriend / Tear off your own head (it's a doll's revolution) / When I was cruel No.2 / Soul for hire / 15 petals / Tart / Dust 2 . . . / Dissolve / Alibi / . . .Dust / Daddy can I turn this? / My little blue window / Episode of blonde / Radio silence. *(d-cd iss.Sep02 +=; 63894-2)* – Smile (New York sudio version) / When I was cruel (studio) / 15 petals (live) / Spooky girlfriend (live) / Honeyhouse (Imposter mix) / Watching the detectives / My funny valentine (live) / Dust (live) / Uncomplicated (live) / Smile (live).

Sep 02. (7") *(063915-7)* **45. / MY MOOD SWINGS** -
(cd-s+=) *(063915-2)* – Peroxide side (blunt cut).

- compilations, others, etc. -

Mar 80. (c) *F-Beat; (XXC 6)* **TEN BLOODY MARYS & TEN HOW'S YOUR FATHERS** -
– Clean money / Girls talk / Talking in the dark / Radio sweetheart / Big tears / Crawling to the USA / Just a memory / Watching the detectives / Stranger in the house / Clowntime is over (N.2) / Getting mighty crowded / Hoover factory / Tiny steps / (What's so funny 'bout) Peace, love and understanding / Dr. Luther's assistant / Radio radio / Black and white world (No.2) / Wednesday week / My funny valentine / Ghost train. *(re-iss. Apr84 on 'Imp' lp/c; FIEND/+CASS 27) (cd-iss. Jan86; FIENDCD 27) (re-iss. cd Mar93; FIENDCD 27X)*

Oct 80. (lp) *Columbia; <JC 36839>* **TAKING LIBERTIES** (virtually 'TEN BLOODY MARYS') - 28

Apr 85. (lp/c/cd) *Telstar; (STAR/STAC/TCD 2247)* **THE BEST OF ELVIS COSTELLO – THE MAN** 8 -
– Watching the detectives / Oliver's army / Alison / Accidents will happen / Pump it up / High fidelity / Pills and soap (THE IMPOSTER) / (I don't want to go to) Chelsea / New lace sleeves / A good year for the roses / I can't stand up for falling down / Clubland / Beyond belief / New Amsterdam / Green shirt / Everyday I write the book / I wanna be loved / Shipbuilding (THE IMPOSTER). *(re-iss. May86 on 'Imp' lp/c/cd; FIEND/+CASS/CD 52) (re-iss. cd Mar93 on 'Demon'; FIENDCD 52X)*

Apr 85. (7",7"green) *F-Beat; (ZB 40086)* **GREEN SHIRT. / BEYOND BELIEF** 68 -
(12"+=,12"green+=) *(ZT 40086)* – ('A'extended).
(d7"+=) *(ZB 40085-7)* – Oliver's army / A good year for the roses.
(Nov85; d7"+=) *(same)* – The people's limousine / They'll never take her love away from me.

Nov 85. (12"ep) *Stiff; (BUYIT 239)* **WATCHING THE DETECTIVES / RADIO SWEETHEART. / LESS THAN ZERO / ALISON** -

Oct 87. (lp/c/cd; under various pseudonyms) *Demon; (<FIEND/+CASS/CD 67>)* **OUT OF OUR IDIOT**
– Seven day weekend / Turning the town red / Heathen town / The people's limousine / So young / American without tears No.2 / Get yourself another fool / Walking on thin ice / Blue chair / Baby it's you / From head to toe / Shoes without heels / Baby's got a brand new hairdo / The flirting kind / Black sails in the sunset / Imperial bedroom / The stamping ground / Little goody two shoes / Withered and died / A town called big nothing / Big sister. *(re-iss. cd Mar93; FIENDCD 67X)*

Oct 89. (d-lp/c/d-cd/dat) *Demon; (D-)FIEND CASS/CD/DAT 160)* **GIRLS, GIRLS, GIRLS** 67 -
– Watching the detectives / I hope you're happy now / This year's girl / Lover's walk / Pump it up / Strict time / Temptation / (I don't want to go to) Chelsea / High fidelity / Lovable / Mystery dance / Big tears / Uncomplicated / Lipstick vogue / Man out of time / Brilliant mistake / New lace sleeves / Accidents will happen / Beyond belief / Black and white world / Green shirt / The loved ones / New Amsterdam / Red shoes / King horse / Big sister's clothes // Alison / Men called uncle / Party girl / Shabby doll / Motel matches / Tiny steps / Almost blue / Riot act / Loved filed / Possession / Poisoned rose / Indoor fireworks / I want you / Oliver's army / Pills and soap / Sunday's best / Watch your step / Less than zero / Clubland / Tokyo storm warning / Shipbuilding. *(d-cd iss.Sep96 & Oct99; same)*

Nov 89. (c) *Demon; (FIENDCASS 161)* **GIRLS, GIRLS, GIRLS, VOL.2** (see above) -

Nov 93. (4xcd-box) *Demon; (DPAM BOX1)* **THE FIRST 2 1/2 YEARS** -
– (MY AIM IS TRUE / THIS YEAR'S MODEL / ARMED FORCES / LIVE AT EL MOCAMBO).

Nov 94. (cd/c/lp) *Demon; (DPAM CD/MC/LP 13) / Rykodisc; <40203>* **THE VERY BEST OF ELVIS COSTELLO** 57 Oct94
– Alison / Watching the detectives / (I don't want to go to) Chelsea / Pump it up / Radio, radio / (What's so funny 'bout) Peace, love and understanding / Oliver's army / Accidents will happen / I can't stand up for falling down / New Amsterdam / High fidelity / Clubland / Watch your step / Good year for the roses / Beyond belief / Man out of time / Everyday I write the book / Shipbuilding / Love field / Brilliant mistake / Indoor fireworks / I want you. *(cd re-iss. Oct99; same)*

Oct 97. (cd) *Warners; (9362 46801-2)* **EXTREME HONEY: THE VERY BEST OF THE WARNER BROS. YEARS**
– The bridge I burned / Veronica / Sulky girl / So like candy / 13 steps lead down / All this useless beauty / My dark life / Other side of summer / Kinder murder / Deep dark truthful mirror / Hurry down doomsday (the bugs are taking over) / Poor fractured atlas / Birds will still be singing / London's brilliant parade / Tramp the dirt down / Couldn't call it unexpected, No.4 / I want to vanish / All the rage.

Aug 99. (d-cd/d-c) *Universal TV; (546490-2/-4)* **THE VERY BEST OF ELVIS COSTELLO** 4 -
– (What's so funny 'bout) Peace, love and understanding / Oliver's army / Watching the detectives / Alison / (I don't want to go to) Chelsea / Accidents will happen / Pump it up / I can't stand up for falling down / Radio, radio / Clubland / Good year for the roses / Man out of time / I wanna be loved / Everyday I write the book / Brilliant mistake / The other side of summer / Tokyo storm warning / Sulky girl / So like candy / Veronica / She / Big tears / Beyond belief / Lipstick vogue / Green shirt / Pills and soap / Tramp the dirt down / Shipbuilding / High fidelity / New lace sleeves / (The angels wanna wear my) Red shoes / Talking in the dark / New Amsterdam / I hope you're happy now / Riot act / My funny valentine / Indoor fireworks / Almost blue / I want you / God give me strength / That day is done / I want to vanish.

— his first 4 singles were also re-issued together around 1980 and could be found on 'Stiff' 10-pack Nos.11-20).

— The ATTRACTIONS released two singles and an album (Aug80) 'MAD ABOUT THE WRONG BOY' on 'F-Beat'.

COUNT BISHOPS

Formed: London, England . . . mid 70's by MIKE SPENCER, JOHNNY GUITAR, ZENON DE FLEUR HEROWSKI, STEVE LEWINS and PAUL BALBI. One of the bigger attractions on the pub-rock scene just as punk was waiting in the wings, the COUNT BISHOPS specialised in a similar vein of revved-up R&B to the likes of DR. FEELGOOD and the 101'ERS. Signed to the influential rock'n'roll revival label, 'Chiswick', the band made their vinyl debut in late '75 with the 'SPEEDBALL' EP and although this featured SPENCER's vocals, the singer was quickly deposed by the sandpaper-throated DAVE TICE. Despite their promising start, 1976 was a quiet year on the recording front with a sole single release, 'TRAIN TRAIN', The COUNT BISHOPS' eponymous debut album finally unveiled in 1977. While paling next to the white-hot nihilism of that summer's punk crop, the record was an invigorating listen nonetheless, footstomping its way through a set of trad 60's influenced R&B that included covers of The Kinks' 'I NEED YOU', The Standells' 'GOOD GUYS DON'T WEAR WHITE' and Chuck Berry's 'DOWN THE ROAD APIECE'. Following the release of a Dutch-only live set, 'GOOD GEAR' (1977), the band re-emerged the following year as The BISHOPS, new bassist PAT McMULLEN having replaced LEWINS. A single, 'I TAKE WHAT I WANT', was withdrawn although a live set recorded at London's Roundhouse surfaced in April. Later that summer, a further single, 'MR. JONES' was withdrawn, replaced on the 'Chiswick' release schedule by 'I WANT CANDY'. These minor niggles were put in perspective the following year as ZENON suffered a fatal heart attack after a car crash, effectively bringing a premature end to the band's career; the poorly received 'CROSS CUT' (1979) proved a less than thrilling swansong, JOHNNY GUITAR going on to better things in DR. FEELGOOD. • **Covered:** SOMEBODY'S GONNA GET THEIR HEAD KICKED IN TONIGHT (Fleetwood Mac).

Album rating: THE COUNT BISHOPS (*7) / THE BISHOPS LIVE AT THE ROUNDHOUSE (*5) / THE BEST OF THE COUNT BISHOPS compilation (*7)

MIKE SPENCER (b. Brooklyn, New York, USA) – vocals / **JOHNNY GUITAR** – guitar / **ZENON DE FLEUR HEROWSKI** – guitar, vocals / **STEVE LEWINS** – bass / **PAUL BALBI** – drums

Chiswick not iss.

Nov 75. (7"ep) *(SW 1)* **SPEEDBALL** -
– Route 66 / I ain't got you / Beautiful Delilah / Teenage letter.

— **DAVID TICE** – vocals, harmonica; repl. SPENCER

Aug 76. (7") *(NS 5)* **TRAIN TRAIN. / TAKING IT EASY** -

Apr 77. (7") *(NS 12)* **BABY YOU'RE WRONG. / STAY FREE** -

Apr 77. (lp) *(WIK 1)* **THE COUNT BISHIPS** -
– I need you / Stay free / Down in the bottom / Talk to you / Shake your money maker / Down the road apiece / Baby you're wrong / Don't start crying now / Someone's got my number / Sometimes, good guys don't wear white / You're in the way / Taste and try. *(re-iss. 1979; CWK 3006)*

Dynamo not iss.

1977. (lp) *(DYR33 001)* **GOOD GEAR** - - Dutch
– Don't start cryin' now / Shake / Walkin' the dog / Somebody / Candy / Wang dang doodle / Dear dad / Confessin' the blues / Little by little / Carol / Johnny B. Goode / Dust my blues / Shake your money maker. *(French-rel.May84 on 'Lolita'; LOLITA 5014)*

BISHOPS

— **PAT McMULLEN** – bass; repl. LEWINS

Chiswick not iss.

Mar 78. (7"; w-drawn) *(NS 33)* **I TAKE WHAT I WANT. / NO LIES** - -

Apr 78. (10"m-lp) *(CH 7)* **THE BISHOPS LIVE AT THE ROUNDHOUSE (live)** -
– Too much too soon / Till the end of the day / Taking it easy / Somebody's gonna get their head kicked in tonight / Sometimes, good guys don't wear white / Don't start me talking / Baby you're wrong / I don't like it / I want Candy. *(re-iss. 1979; CWM 2001)*

Jun 78. (7"; w-drawn) *(NS 35)* **MR. JONES / HUMAN BEAN. / ROUTE 66 / TOO MUCH TOO SOON** - -
(re-iss. Mar79; CHIS 111)

Jun 78. (7") *(NS 37)* **I WANT CANDY. / SEE THAT WOMAN** -
(re-iss. 1979, 6"/10"; NS 37-6/-10) (re-iss. 1979 as 6"; CHIS 101-6)

— after a car crash, DE FLEUR died of heart attack on 17th March 1979

Jun 79. (lp) *(CWK 3009)* **CROSS CUT** -
– I take what I want / Could you would you / What's your number / Your daddy don't mind / Good times / Too much too soon / Rolling man / I want Candy / Somebody's gonna get their head kicked in tonight / Hands on the wheel / Don't start me talkin' / These arms of mine / No lies / Mr. Jones.

— **CHARLIE MORGAN** – drums; repl. BALBI, although they split due to DE FLEUR's death. JOHNNY GUITAR subsequently joined DR. FEELGOOD

- compilations, etc. -

Aug 95. (cd; as The BISHOPS) *Chiswick; (CDWIKD 150)* **THE BEST OF THE BISHOPS** -
– Train train / Baby you're wrong / Stay free / I want Candy / I take what I want / Mr. Jones / I need you / Down in the bottom / You're in my way / Talk to you / Taste and try / Someone's got my number / Good times / Your daddy won't mind / What's your number / Till the end of the day / These arms of mine / Rolling man / Paul's blues / No lies / Too much, too soon / Sometimes good guys don't wear white / Don't start me talkin' / Somebody's gonna get their head kicked in tonight / I don't like it / Route 66 / Train train.

Nov 95. (cd) *Chiswick; (CDWIKM 161)* **SPEEDBALL + 11** -
– Route 66 / I ain't got you / Beautiful Delilah / Teenage letter / Cry to me / Buzz me babe / Sweet little sixteen / Honey I need / Carol / Don't start crying now / Mercy mercy mercy / Reelin' and rockin' / Down the road apiece / I'm a man / I want candy.

Wayne/Jayne COUNTY

Born: WAYNE COUNTY, c.1950, Georgia, Atlanta, USA. WAYNE left for New York in 1968 where he appeared in a female role alongside PATTI SMITH in an off-Broadway production of 'Femme Fatale' before tackling the role of Florence Nightingale in 'World'. In 1970, the actor/singer encountered ANDY WARHOL, who cast him in his stage show, 'Pork'; the review subsequently arrived in England, impressing DAVID BOWIE and inspiring him to sign COUNTY to his 'Mainman' publishing company. By this point he was already a fully fledged transvestite and began singing in New York band, QUEEN ELIZABETH; their drummer, JERRY NOLAN, was soon to join other cross-dressers, The NEW YORK DOLLS. In 1973, WAYNE found new sidemen, The BACKSTREET BOYS, although BOWIE's manager, Tony DeFries dropped him from Mainman's bulging roster (ooer!). A further setback came a few years later when 'E.S.P.' (former stable of The FUGS) delayed issue of his new group's proposed album, citing it as unsuitable for release, probably due to the fact that it included future singles, 'FUCK OFF' and 'STUCK ON YOU'; it was said the master tapes were lost in an accidental fire. In 1976, the group appeared at Max's Kansas City where three tracks (including one named after the venue itself) were cut for a V/A compilation, John Peel subsequently airing the songs on his night time Radio One show. With punk rock and new wave now dominating the music scene, COUNTY was becoming more accepted and after an infamous gig at another great club, CBGB's (in 1977), Miles Copeland of 'Illegal' records (who had already snapped up brother, STEWART COPELAND and his band The POLICE), signed up the gender-bending punk and his backing band, The ELECTRIC CHAIRS. Based in the less conservative land of Britain, they released their eponymous debut EP which included the tracks 'STUCK ON YOU', 'PARANOIA PARADISE' and The Rolling Stones' 'THE LAST TIME'. Later that year, WAYNE and Co flitted to 'Safari' records (run by DEEP PURPLE's management team), although their controversial second 45, 'FUCK OFF', saw the label issuing it under the pseudonymous guise of the 'Sweet F.A.' imprint. Around the same time, The ELECTRIC CHAIRS re-hashed 'PARANOIA PARADISE' on the punk movie, 'Jubilee', WAYNE kitted out in his trademark blonde wig, pink mini and fish-net stockings. If they were ever to have had a chance to have a hit single, it was surely with 'EDDIE & SHEENA', although its commercial sheen alienated many harder core punks. Hot on the record's heels was the group's eponymous debut album, full of second and occasionally first division sleazy punk rock. WAYNE COUNTY was subsequently given priority billing on their second set that year, 'STORM THE GATES OF HEAVEN' (featuring The Electric Prunes' 'I HAD TOO MUCH TO DREAM LAST NIGHT'), yet The ELECTRIC CHAIRS found it hard to make the big time. Released on either side of the decade, albums 'THINGS YOUR MOTHER NEVER TOLD YOU' (1979) and the live 'ROCK'N'ROLL RESURRECTION' (1980) represented The 'CHAIRS' final sitting as the band had already split. WAYNE was now taking hormone treatment to become his alter-ego, JAYNE, full-time although she never went through with the final operation. After spells in Berlin, JAYNE relocated to London where she released a comeback album, 'PRIVATE OYSTER' (1986); US title 'AMERIKAN CLEOPATRA'. She continues to release the "odd" single and album, although her solo career has been sporadic. WAYNE/JAYNE was the shock formula transvestite turned transexual whose no-holds barred NEW YORK DOLLS meets DUSTY SPRINGFIELD punk'n'roll never survived the "so-called" death of punk rock when the 'PISTOLS split. Her autobiography, 'Man Enough To Be A Woman: The Trials And Tribulations Of An Underground Cult Figure, Wayne County', was published in 1995 and obviously paints a fuller portrait of a bizarre life.

Album rating: THE ELECTRIC CHAIRS (*6) / STORM THE GATES OF HEAVEN (*6) / THINGS YOUR MOTHER NEVER TOLD YOU (*4) / ROCK'N'ROLL RESURRECTION (*5) / THE BEST OF THE ELECTRIC CHAIRS compilation (*7) / ROCK'N'ROLL CLEOPATRA compilation (*7) / PRIVATE OYSTER (*4) / GODDESS OF WET DREAMS (*4) / DEVIATION (*4)

WAYNE COUNTY & THE BACKSTREET BOYS

WAYNE – vocals with **GREG VAN COOK** – guitar / + 3

                                                    not iss.   Max's Kan.

1976. (7"m) <*MAX 1213*> **MAX'S KANSAS CITY 1976. / FLIP YOUR WIG / CREAM IN MY JEANS**

— all above tracks also on US various artists lp 'MAX'S KANSAS CITY', released 1976 on 'Ram'; *1213* (re-iss. Mar78 as 'NEW YORK NEW WAVE, MAX'S KANSAS CITY' on 'C.B.S.'; CBS 82670)

ELECTRIC CHAIRS

WAYNE + GREG added **VAL HALLER** – bass / **J.J. JOHNSON** – drums

                       Illegal   not iss.

Jul 77. (7"ep) *(IL 002)* **THE ELECTRIC CHAIRS EP**
 – Stuck on you / Paranoia Paradise / The last time.

                      Sweet F.A. not iss.

Nov 77. (7") *(WC 1)* **FUCK OFF. / ON THE CREST**

— guest on below **JOOLS HOLLAND** – piano (of SQUEEZE)

                      Safari   not iss.

Feb 78. (7") *(SAFE 1)* **EDDIE & SHEENA. / ROCK'N'ROLL CLEOPATRA**

Feb 78. (lp) *(LONG 1)* **THE ELECTRIC CHAIRS**
 – Eddie & Sheena / Bad in bed / Hot blood / Worry wart / Twenty eight Model 'T' / Out of control / On the crest / Nazca / Big black window / Max's / Toilet love / Rock & roll resurrection.

May 78. (7";w-drawn) *(SAFE 6)* **I HAD TOO MUCH TO DREAM LAST NIGHT. / FUCK OFF**

WAYNE COUNTY AND THE ELECTRIC CHAIRS

— added **HENRY PADOVANI** – guitar (ex-POLICE)

Jun 78. (7"gold+grey-ep) *(WC 2)* **BLATANTLY OFFENZIVE EP**
 – Fuck off / Night time / Toilet love / Mean muthafuckin' man.

— **ELIOT MICHAELS** – guitar repl. COOK who joined The VIBRATORS

Aug 78. (7") *(SAFE 9)* **TRYING TO GET ON THE RADIO. / EVIL MINDED MOMMA**

Aug 78. (lp-grey+multi) *(GOOD 1)* **STORM THE GATES OF HEAVEN**
 – Storm the gates of Heaven / Cry of angels / Speed demon / Mr. Normal / Man enough to be a woman / Trying to get on the radio / I had too much to dream last night / Tomorrow is another day.
 above album featured MORGAN FISHER keyboards and DARRYL WAY violin

May 79. (lp) *(GOOD 2)* **THINGS YOUR MOTHER NEVER TOLD YOU**
 – Wonder woman / Wall city girl / Boy with the stolen face / Un-con-troll-able / Things / Berlin / C3 / Midnight pal / Waiting for the marines / Think straight.

— producer & synth-man on above; DAVID CUNNINGHAM (FLYING LIZARDS)

Jun 79. (7") *(SAFE 13)* **BERLIN. / WAITING FOR THE MARINES**
 (ext.12"pink+=) *(SAFELS 13)* – Midnight pal.

Nov 79. (7") *(SAFE 18)* **SO MANY WAYS. / J'ATTENDS LES MARINES**

— **WAYNE + ELIOT** went back to the States and found new members; **PETER JORDAN** – bass / **SAMMY MINELLI** – drums (they replaced HALLER and JOHNSON who joined FLYING LIZARDS after above ELECTRIC CHAIRS credited recording without WAYNE!)

May 80. (lp; as JAYNE COUNTY) *(LIVE 1)* **ROCK'N'ROLL RESURRECTION (live final gig)**
 – Night time / Rock'n'roll Cleopatra / Are you a boy / Bad in bed / Hanky panky / Rock'n'roll resurrection / Fucked by the Devil / Cream in my jeans / Stuck on you / Fuck off.

— had already disbanded his/her group at the end of '79. He/she went to Berlin, before relocating to London, England and going solo

JAYNE COUNTY

w/ 1985 band JC5; **MICK ROBINSON** – guitar / STUART 'Dick' CLARKE – lead guitar / **SNIDE** – bass / **BASIL CREECE** – drums

                      Heighway R   not iss.

May 86. (7") *(SAD 002)* **SAN FRANCISCO. / WHEN QUEENS COLLIDE (part 1)**

                      Revolver not iss.

Oct 86. (lp) *(REVLP 86)* **PRIVATE OYSTER**
 – Private oyster / Man enough to be a woman / Fun in America / I feel in love with a Russian soldier / Bad in bed / Are you a boy or are you a girl? / When queens collide (part 1) / Double shot / Xerox that man / That Lady Dye twist / Love lives on lies. (re-iss. Feb87 as 'AMERIKAN CLEOPATRA' for 'Konnexion'; KOMA 788016)

                      Jungle   not iss.

Jul 89. (7"ep) *(FREUD 27)* **BETTY GRABLE'S LEGS**

Jul 89. (7") *(JUNG 49)* **TIME MACHINE. / TAKE A DETOUR**

                      not iss.   E.S.P.

Oct 93. (cd) <*ESP 2002-2*> **GODDESS OF WET DREAMS**
 – Night time / Cream in my jeans / Paranoia paradise / Looking for a kiss / If you don't want to fuck – fuck off / Johnny gone to Heaven / Private world / Brainwashed / Take a detour / Party till armageddon. (lp-iss.Oct98 on 'Get Back'; GET 32LP)

                      Thunderbird not iss.

Jun 95. (cd) *(CSA 105)* **DEVIATION**
 – Transgender rock'n'roll / That's what the new breed say / Cherry bomb / Deviation / I'm in love with Dusty Springfield / Everyone's an asshole but me / Texas chainsaw manicurist / Little star / Come on down to my boat / Nuclear age vampires / That's what the new breed say (psychedelic mix).

– compilations, etc. –

Feb 79. (7") *Illegal; (IL 005)* **THUNDER WHEN SHE WALKS. / WHAT YOU GOT**

1981. (lp) *Safari; (NEN 1)* **THE BEST OF THE ELECTRIC CHAIRS**

Jun 83. (7"pic-d) *Safari; (WCP 3)* **FUCK OFF. / TOILET LOVE**

Dec 93. (cd) *R.P.M.; (RPM 119)* **ROCK'N'ROLL CLEOPATRA: FROM SNEAKERS TO STILETTOS – THE ESSENTIAL ... VOLUME 1**

Jul 95. (cd) *R.P.M.; (RPM 145)* **LET YOUR BACKBONE SLIP! – THE ESSENTIAL ... VOLUME 2**

CRAMPS

Formed: New York City, New York, USA ... 1975 by LUX INTERIOR and POISON IVY, who recruited fellow weirdos BRYAN GREGORY and PAM 'BALAM' GREGORY (the latter was replaced by MIRIAM LINNA, who in turn was superseded by NICK KNOX). The trashiest, sleaziest 50's throwbacks to ever besmirch the good name of rock'n'roll, The CRAMPS took the genre's inherit debauchery to its thrilling (and often hilarious) conclusion. Crawling from the mire of CBGB's punk scene like the proverbial Swamp Thing in one of their beloved B-movies, The CRAMPS started as they meant to go on, initiating their vinyl career in 1978 with an obscure cover, 'THE WAY I WALK'. The single was backed with a riotous mangling of The Trashmen's 'SURFIN' BIRD', as close to a theme tune as the band came. A follow-up, 'HUMAN FLY', introduced LUX's impressive capacity for disturbingly accurate animal (and insect!) noises, its voodoo surf twang and creeping tempo scarier than the frontman's skintight leotard. Subsequently signed to Miles Copeland's 'I.R.S.' label, The CRAMPS set up shop in Sun Studios, Memphis (where else?!) with producer ALEX CHILTON at the production helm, working on the material for their acclaimed debut set, 'SONGS THE LORD TAUGHT US' (1980).

Featuring such bad taste gems as 'GARBAGEMAN' (more animal noises!), 'I WAS A TEENAGE WEREWOLF' and 'STRYCHNINE', the record further boosted the band's cult following. The departure of GREGORY after the 'DRUG TRAIN' single was the first in a long series of line-up changes through which IVY (the sexiest thing in stockings!) and INTERIOR were the only constants. With KID CONGO POWERS as a replacement, the band cut the less convincing 'PSYCHEDELIC JUNGLE' (1981), their final release for Copeland whom they later sued. A short spell with the French 'New Rose' label and then 'Big Beat' saw the release of the live mini 'SMELL OF FEMALE' (1983). This went at least some way to capturing the cheap thrills of a CRAMPS gig, though readers are advised to experience the real thing; if the primeval spirit of raw rock'n'roll doesn't move you, then the sight of a grown man in a leather thong and high heels just might! INTERIOR had always modelled himself on a kind of ELVIS-from-the-crypt and in 1986, The CRAMPS met their maker, so to speak, on the classic 'A DATE WITH ELVIS'. The likes of 'THE HOT PEARL SNATCH', 'CAN YOUR PUSSY DO THE DOG?' and 'WHAT'S INSIDE A GIRL?', need no further explanation save that THE KING was no doubt turning in his grave. Though this marked a creative and commercial peak of sorts, The CRAMPS continued to think up the best song titles in the Western World over a string of late 80's/90's albums, including 'STAY SICK' (1990), 'LOOK MOM, NO HEAD' (1991; essential if only for the IGGY POP collaboration, 'MINISKIRT BLUES'), 'FLAME JOB' (1994) and 'BIG BEAT FROM BADSVILLE' (1997). Though they've hardly pushed back the boundaries of music, The CRAMPS are arguably even more essential now than in their heyday, if only to remind the current crop of indie dullards what it REALLY means to play "The Devil's Music". • **Songwriters:** Most written by LUX and IVY except SURFIN' BIRD (Trashmen) / FEVER (Little Willie John) / THE WAY I WALK (Robert Gordon) / GREEN DOOR (Jim Lowe) / JAILHOUSE ROCK (Elvis Presley) / MULESKINNER BLUES (Fendermen) / PSYCHOTIC REACTION (Count Five) / LONESOME TOWN (Ricky Nelson) / HARD WORKIN' MAN (Jack Nitzche) / HITSVILLE 29 B.C. (Turnbow) / WHEN I GET THE BLUES (Larry Mize) / HOW COME YOU DO ME? (…Joiner) / STRANGE LOVE (…West) / BLUES BLUES BLUES (…Thompson) / TRAPPED LOVE (Kohler-Fana) / SINNERS (…Aldrich) / ROUTE 66 (Bobby Troup) / etc. • **Trivia:** Their fan club was surprisingly based in Grangemouth, Scotland (wee Marty fi the Nash ran it!)

Album rating: SONGS THE LORD TAUGHT US (*7) / PSYCHEDELIC JUNGLE (*7) / OFF THE BONE compilation (*8) / SMELL OF FEMALE (*6) / A DATE WITH ELVIS (*7) / STAY SICK (*6) / LOOK MOM, NO HEAD! (*5) / FLAMEJOB (*6) / BIG BEAT FROM BADSVILLE (*5)

LUX INTERIOR (b. ERICK LEE PURKHISER, 1948, Akron, Ohio) – vocals / **POISON IVY RORSCHACH** (b. KIRSTY MARLANA WALLACE, 1954, Sacramento, Calif.) – guitar / **BRYAN GREGORY** (b. Detroit, Mich.) – guitar / **NICK KNOX** (b. NICHOLAS STEPHANOFF) – drums repl. MIRIAM LINNA (later to The ZANTEES & The A-BONES) who had repl. PAM 'BALAM' GREGORY

not iss. *Vengeance*
Apr 78. (7") <666> **THE WAY I WALK. / SURFIN' BIRD**
Illegal *I.R.S.*
Nov 78. (7") <668> **HUMAN FLY. / DOMINO**
Jun 79. (12"ep) (ILS 12-013) **GRAVEST HITS**
– Human fly / The way I walk / Domino / Surfin' bird / Lonesome town. *(re-iss. Sep82 – 7"blue-ep / re-iss. Mar83- 7"red-ep; same)*
Mar 80. (7") (ILS 0017) **FEVER. / GARBAGEMAN**
Apr 80. (lp) (ILP 005) <SP 007> **SONGS THE LORD TAUGHT US**
– TV set / Rock on the Moon / Garbageman / I was a teenage werewolf / Sunglasses after dark / The mad daddy / Mystery plane / Zombie dance / What's behind the mask / Strychnine / I'm cramped / Tear it up / Fever. *(cd-iss. Jul98 on 'E.M.I.'; 493836-2)*
May 80. (7") <IR 9014> **DRUG TRAIN. / GARAGEMAN**
Jul 80. (7"m) (ILS 021) **DRUG TRAIN. / LOVE ME / I CAN HARDLY STAND IT**

— KID CONGO POWERS (b. BRIAN TRISTAN, 27 Mar'61, La Puente, Calif.) – guitar; repl. JULIEN BOND, who had repl. GREGORY for two months mid 1980.
I.R.S. *I.R.S.*
May 81. (7"yellow) (PFS 1003) <IR 9021> **GOO GOO MUCK. / SHE SAID** Aug81
May 81. (lp) <(SP 70016)> **PSYCHEDELIC JUNGLE** Jul81
– Green fuzz / Goo goo muck / Rockin' bones / Voodoo idol / Primitive / Caveman / The crusher / Don't eat stuff off the sidewalk / Can't find my mind / Jungle hop / The natives are restless / Under the wires / Beautiful gardens / Green door. *(cd-iss. Sep98 on 'E.M.I.'; 496504-2)*
Oct 81. (12"m) (PFSX 1008) **THE CRUSHER. / SAVE IT / NEW KIND OF KICK**

— (LUX, IVY & NICK were joined by **IKE KNOX** (Nick's cousin) – guitar; repl. KID CONGO who returned to GUN CLUB (appeared on live tracks 83-84)
Big Beat *not iss.*
Nov 83. (red-m-lp) (NED 6) **SMELL OF FEMALE (live)** 74
– Faster pussycat / I ain't nuthin' but a gorehound / Psychotic reaction / The most exhalted potentate of love / You got good taste / Call of the wig hat. *(pic-lp Jun84; NEDP 6) (re-iss. Feb91 cd+=/c+=; CDWIKM/WIKMC 95) – Beautiful gardens / She said / Surfin' dead. (lp re-mast.Nov01 on 'Vengeance'; VENG 670)*

— (signed to below label in France)
New Rose *New Rose*
Mar 84. (7"/7"pic-d) (NEW 28/+P) **FASTER PUSSYCAT. / YOU GOT GOOD TASTE** — French
Mar 84. (7"cold;various) (NEW 33) **I AIN'T NUTHIN' BUT A GOREHOUND. / WEEKEND ON MARS** — French

— **CANDY FUR** (DEL-MAR) – guitar; repl. IKE

Big Beat *not iss.*
Nov 85. (7"orange) (NS 110) **CAN YOUR PUSSY DO THE DOG? / BLUE MOON BABY** 68
(12"blue+=) (NST 110) – Georgia Lee Brown.
Feb 86. (blue-lp/c/cd) (WIKA/WIKC/CDWIK 46) **A DATE WITH ELVIS** 34
– How far can too far go / The hot pearl snatch / People ain't too good / What's inside a girl? / Can your pussy do the dog? / Kizmiaz / Cornfed dames / Chicken (Hot pool of) Woman need / Aloha from Hell / It's just that song. *<US-iss.1994 on 'Capitol'; 73579> (lp re-mast.Nov01 on 'Vengeance'; VENG 671)*
May 86. (7") (NS 115) **WHAT'S INSIDE A GIRL? / GET OFF THE ROAD**
(12"+=) (NST 115) – Give me a woman.
(Mar87; cd-s++=) (CRAMP 1) – Scene / Heart of darkness.

Enigma *Enigma*
Jan 90. (7"/7"sha-pic-d/c-s) (ENV/+PD/TC 17) **BIKINI GIRLS WITH MACHINE GUNS. / JACKYARD BACKOFF** 35
(12"+=/cd-s+=) (12ENV/ENVCD 17) – Her love rubbed off.
Feb 90. (cd/c/lp) (CDENV/TCENV/ENVLP 1001) <73543> **STAY SICK** 62
– Bop pills / Goddam rock'n'roll / Bikini girls with machine guns / All women are bad / Creature from the black leather lagoon / Shortenini' bread / Daisy's up your butterfly / Everything goes / Journey to the centre of a girl / Mama oo pow pow / Saddle up a buzz buzz / Muleskinner blues. *(cd+=) – Her love rubbed off. (pic-lp Nov90; ENVLPPD 1001) (re-iss. Feb94 cd/lp; CD+/WIKD 126) (lp re-mast.Nov01 on 'Vengeance'; VENG 672)*
Apr 90. (7"/c-s) (ENV/+TC 19) **ALL WOMEN ARE BAD. / TEENAGE RAGE**
(12"+=/12"pic-d+=/cd-s+=) (12ENV/12ENVPD/ENVCD 19) – King of the drapes (live) / High school hellcats (live).
Aug 90. (7") (ENV 22) **CREATURE FROM THE BLACK LEATHER LAGOON. / JAILHOUSE ROCK**
(12"+=/12"pic-d+=/cd-s+=) (12ENV/12ENVPD/CDENV 22) – Beat out my love.
Sep 90. (cd-ep) <773617-2> **CREATURE FROM THE BLACK LEATHER LAGOON / JAILHOUSE ROCK / JACKYARD BACKOFF / BEAT OUT MY LOVE / HER LOVE RUBBED OFF**

— **LUX & IVY** were joined by **SLIM CHANCE** – guitar (ex-PANTHER BURNS) / **JIM SCLAVUNOS** – drums
Big Beat *Restless*
Sep 91. (7") (NST 135) **EYEBALL IN MY MARTINI. / WILDER WILDER FASTER FASTER**
(12"+=/cd-s+=) (12/CD NST 135) – Wilder wilder faster faster.
Sep 91. (cd/c/lp) (CDWIK/WIKDC/WIKAD 101) <72586> **LOOK MOM, NO HEAD!**
– Dames, booze, chains and boots / Two headed sex change / Blow up your mind / Hard workin' man / Miniskirt blues / Alligator stomp / I wanna get in your pants Bend over, I'll drive / Don't get funny with me / Eyeball in my martini / Hipsville 29 B.C. / When I get the blues (the strangeness in me). *(also pic-lp/pic-cd; WIKDP/CDWIKD 101) (lp re-mast.Nov01 on 'Vengeance'; VENG 673)*

— **NICKY ALEXANDER** – drums (ex-WEIRDOS); repl. JIM
Sep 92. (cd-ep) (CDNST 136) **BLUES FIX EP**
– Hard workin' man / It's mighty crazy / Jelly roll rock / Shomblalor.

— **HARRY DRUMDINI** – drums; repl. NICKY
Creation *Medicine – Warners*
Oct 94. (7") (CRE 180) **ULTRA TWIST! / CONFESSIONS OF A PSYCHO CAT**
(12"+=)(cd-s+=) (CRE 180T)(CRESCD 180) – No club love wolf.
Oct 94. (cd/c/lp) (CRECD/C-CRE/CRELP 170) <24592> **FLAMEJOB**
– Mean machine / Ultra twist / Let's get f*cked up / Nest of the cuckoo bird / I'm customized / Sado country auto show / Naked girl falling down the stairs / How come you do me? / Inside out and upside down (with you) / Trapped love / Swing the big eyed rabbit / Strange love / Blues blues blues / Sinners / Route 66 (get your kicks on). *(cd re-iss. Jan01; same)*
Feb 95. (7") (CRE 196) **NAKED GIRL FALLING DOWN THE STAIRS. / LET'S GET F*CKED UP**
(cd-s+=) (CRESCD 196) – Surfin' bird.
Epitaph *Epitaph*
Oct 97. (cd/c/lp) <(6516-2/-4/-1)> **BIG BEAT FROM BADSVILLE**
– Cramp stomp / God monster / It thing hard on / Like a bad girl should / Sheena's in a goth gang / Queen of pain / Monkey with your tail / Devil behind that bush / Super goo / Hypno sex ray / Other world, burn / Wet nightmare / Badass bug / Haulass hyena. *(lp re-mast.Nov01 on 'Vengeance'; VENG 674)*
Dec 97. (7") (6527-7) **LIKE A BAD GIRL SHOULD. / WET NIGHTMARE**
(cd-s+=) (6527-2) – I walked all night.

– compilations, others, etc. –

May 83. (lp) *Illegal;* (ILP 012) */ I.R.S.;* <SP 70042> **OFF THE BONE** 44 Feb84
<US-title 'BAD MUSIC FOR BAD PEOPLE'>
– Human fly / The way I walk / Domino / Surfin' bird / Lonesome town / Garbageman / Fever / Drug train / Love me / I can't hardly stand it / Goo goo muck / She said / The crusher / Save it / New kinda of kick. *(cd-iss. Jan87; ILPCD 012) (cd re-iss. 1992 on 'Castle'+=;) – Uranium Rock / Good taste (live). (cd re-iss. Apr98 on 'E.M.I.'; 493837-2) (lp re-iss. May01 on 'Simply Vinyl'; SVLP 327)*
1984. (4x7"box) *New Rose;* **I AIN'T NUTHIN' BUT A GOREHOUND. / WEEKEND ON MARS // FASTER PUSSYCAT. / YOU GOT GOOD TASTE // CALL OF THE WIG HAT. / THE MOST EXHALTED POTENTATE OF LOVE // PSYCHOTIC REACTION.** (one sided) — French
(all 4 either blue/white/black/green)
May 86. (7") *New Rose;* (NEW 71) **KIZMIAZ. / GET OFF THE ROAD** — —
(12"+=) (NEW 70) – Give me a woman.
Nov 87. (lp) *Vengeance;* **ROCKIN' AND REELIN' IN AUCKLAND, NEW ZEALAND (live)**
(UK cd-iss. Sep94 on 'Big Beat'; CDWIKD 132) (lp re-mast.Nov01 on 'Vengeance'; VENG 669)
Sep 00. (3xcd-box) *EMI;* (528203-2) **SONGS THE LORD TAUGHT US / OFF THE BONE / PSYCHEDELIC JUNGLE**

CRASS

Formed: North Weald, Essex, England ... 1978 by commune dwellers STEVE IGNORANT and PENNY RIMBAUD. With a line-up completed by PHIL FREE, JOY DE VIVRE, N.A. PALMER, PETE WRIGHT and MICK G., the pseudonymous crew unleashed the first instalment of their anarchist manifesto in late '78 on indie label, 'Small Wonder'. 'THE FEEDING OF THE FIVE THOUSAND' EP introduced the raging punk blitzkrieg of CRASS in full flow, an "Oi!-Guv" cockney vocal raging over military-style drumming and shouting down religion and "the system" in all its multifarious guises. Forming their own label (an operation which subsequently released material by a range of protest bands including POISON GIRLS, CONFLICT and RUDIMENTARY PENI) was the logical next step for such an avowedly anti-establishment operation and Autumn '79 saw the release of 'STATIONS OF THE CRASS', a (part-live) double album's worth of bile directed at all the usual subjects and some surprising ones (i.e. The CLASH in 'WHITE PUNKS ON HOPE'), even taking a pot shot at media outrage over Myra Hindley on 'MOTHER EARTH'. Two politically incendiary 45's appeared in the early 80's, the first, 'BLOODY REVOLUTIONS' was a shared affair with The POISON GIRLS, while the peerless epic, 'NAGASAKI NIGHTMARE', represented the pinnacle of punk outrage. The CRASS line-up fluctuated according to whoever was living with them at the time, the band's democratic approach seeing EVE and PENNY take on the vocal chores for feminist tract, 'PENIS ENVY' (1981). Not a band to do things by halves, CRASS released their second double set with 'CHRIST THE ALBUM' (1983), a record that saw them widen their musical horizons and intersperse songs with spoken word poetry. If the band were straying too far into neo-hippy territory for some fans comfort, there was no doubting the strength of feeling behind 'HOW DOES IT FEEL (TO BE THE MOTHER OF 1000 DEAD)?', directed squarely at Margaret Thatcher and taking her to task over the Falklands conflict. As the war raged, CRASS had tapes confiscated by the government and found themselves charged under The Obscene Publications Act. Not surprisingly, no records were ever given a release outside the UK! The album that had spawned such apparently dangerous fare ('SHEEP FARMING IN THE FALKLANDS' being another sarcastic classic) was 'YES SIR, I WILL' (1983), an even more experimental set that divided opinion. It also proved to be the band's swansong, and, staying true to their original vow of breaking up in early '84 (which was the meltdown year predicted by George Orwell in 1948) following a final single, 'YOU'RE ALREADY DEAD'. While EVE and PENNY worked together on a set of poetry, 'ACTS OF LOVE' (1986), IGNORANT subsequently joined fellow anarchists CONFLICT, for whom he'd deputised in the past.

Album rating: THE FEEDING OF THE FIVE THOUSAND (*8) / STATIONS OF THE CRASS (*6) / PENIS ENVY (*6) / CHRIST THE ALBUM (*5) / YES SIR, I WILL (*4) / BEST BEFORE 1984 compilation (*7)

EVE LIBERTINE – vocals / **JOY DE VIVRE** – vocals / **STEVE IGNORANT** – vocals / **PHIL FREE** – lead guitar / **N.A. PALMER** – guitar, vocals / **PENNY RIMBAUD** – drums / **PETE WRIGHT** – bass / **MICK G.** (DUFFIELD) – flute, film-maker /

Small Wonder / not iss.

Dec 78. (12"ep) *(WEENY 2)* **THE FEEDING OF THE FIVE THOUSAND**
– Asylum / Do they owe us a living? / End result / They've got a bomb / Punk is dead / Reject of society / General Bacardi / Banned from The Roxy's / G's song / Fight war, not wars / Women / Securicor / Sucks / You pay / Angels / What a shame / So what / Well? ... do they. (re-iss. Nov80 & Oct81 / Dec87 as 'FEEDING OF THE 5,000 EP (2nd SITTING)' on 'Crass'; 621984) (cd-iss. Oct90 +=; 621984CD)
– Reality asylum. (lp re-iss. Sep02 on 'Crass'; same)

Crass / not iss.

May 79. (7") *(521984-1)* **REALITY ASYLUM. / SHAVED WOMAN**
(re-iss. Dec80; CRASS 19454U)

Sep 79. (d-lp) *(CRASS 521984)* **STATIONS OF THE CRASS**
– Mother Earth / White punks on hope / You've got big hands / Darling / System / Big man, big M.A.N. / Hurry up Garry / Fun going on / Crutch of society / Heard too much about / Chairman of the bored / Tired / Walls / Uptight citizen / Time out / The gasman cometh / Democrats / Contaminational power / I ain't thick it's just a trick. // live:- System / Big man, big M.A.N. / Banned from the Roxy / Hurry up Garry / Time out / They've got a bomb / Fight war, not wars / Women / Shaved women / You pay / Heard too much about / Angels / What a shame / So what / G's song / Do they owe us a living? / Punk is dead. (re-iss. Oct81 & Dec87; same) (cd-iss. Oct90; 521984CD)

May 80. (7") *(421984-1)* **BLOODY REVOLUTIONS. / Poison Girls: PERSONS UNKNOWN**
(re-iss. Dec80 as above on 'Crass/Xntrix' joint label outing)

Feb 81. (7") *(421984-5)* **NAGASAKI NIGHTMARE. / BIG A LITTLE A**

Oct 81. (lp) *(CRASS 321984-1)* **PENIS ENVY**
– Bat a motel / Systematic death / Poison in a pretty pill / What the fuck / Where next Columbus / Berkertex bribe / Smother love / Health surface / Dry weather. (re-iss. Dec87 lp/c; CRASS 321984-1/-4) (cd-iss. Oct90; 321984CD) (lp re-iss. Sep02; same)

Dec 81. (7") *(COLD TURKEY 1)* **MERRY CRASSMAS. / MERRY CRASSMAS – HAVE FUN**

Aug 82. (7"promo+flexi) *(421984-6)* **RIVAL TRIBAL REBEL REVEL / BULLY BOYS GO OUT FIGHTING**

Aug 82. (d-lp) *(BOLLOX 2U2)* **CHRIST THE ALBUM** (some live)   26
– Have a nice day / Mother love / Nineteen eighty bore / I know there is love / Beg your pardon / Birth control 'n' rock'n'roll / Reality white-wash / It's the greatest working class rip-off / Deadhead / You can be who / Buy no pay as you go / Rival tribal revel rebel part 2 / Bumhooler / Sentiment / Major General despair / Banned from the Roxy / The sound of one hand / Punk is dead / Nagasaki nightmare / Bat a motel blues / Berkertex bribe / Fold it in half / Big hands / Heart-throb of the mortuary / Bumhooler / Big A little A / First woman / Arlington 73 / Bomb plus bomb bomb / Contaminational power / I ain't thick / G's song / Securicor / I can't stand it / Shaved women / A part of life / Do they owe us a living? / So what / Salt'n'pepper. (cd-iss. Oct90; BOLLOX 2U2CD) (d-lp re-iss. Sep02; same)

Oct 82. (7") *(221984-6)* **HOW DOES IT FEEL (TO BE THE MOTHER OF 1000 DEAD?). / THE IMMORTAL DEATH / DON'T TELL ME YOU CARE**

May 83. (lp) *(121984-2)* **YES SIR, I WILL**
– Yes sir, I will / The pig's head controversy – the aesthetics of anarchy. (cd-iss. Oct90; 121984-2CD) (lp re-iss. Sep02; same)

May 83. (7") *(121984-3)* **SHEEP FARMING IN THE FALKLANDS. / GOTCHA!** (live)
(free-7"brown+=) *(121984-4)* **WHO DUNNIT? / WHO DUNNIT** (part 2)

Jan 84. (7") *(CATNO 4)* **YOU'RE ALREADY DEAD. / DON'T GET CAUGHT / NAGASAKI IS YESTERDAY'S DOG END**

— broke up 1984. STEVE joined CONFLICT
— note: all albums were issued by CRASS in the States around mid-90's

– compilations, others, etc. –

Jul 86. (d-lp) *Crass; (CATNO 5)* **BEST BEFORE 1984**
– Intro / Do they owe us a living? / Major general despair / Angela Rippon / Reality asylum / Shaved women / Bloody revolutions / Nagasaki nightmare / Big a little a / Rival tribal rebel revel – Sheep farming in the Falklands (Flexidisc version) / How does it feel / The immortal death / Don't tell me that you care / Sheep farming in the Falklands / Gotcha / Nagasaki is yesterdays dogend / Don't get caught / Smash the mac / Do they owe us a living? (live) (cd-iss. Oct90; CRASS 5CD) (d-lp re-iss. Sep02; same)

Nov 86. (12") *Crass; (CATNO 6)* **TEN NOTES ON A SUMMER'S DAY. / (instrumental mix)**
(re-iss. Aug98, 12"/cd-s; CATNO 6/+CD)

Dec 93. (cd) *Pomona; (ONA 002CD)* **YOU'LL RUIN IT FOR EVERYONE** (live '81)
(re-iss. Aug01; same)

Nov 96. (cd) *Allied; (ALLIED 76CD)* **CHRIST THE BOOTLEG**
(re-iss. Jun99 on 'No Idea'; NIR 082)

– others, solo, etc. –

on 'Crass' unless mentioned otherwise

May 81. (7"white-flexi; by JOY DE VIVRE) *(CRASS ENVY 1)* **OUR WEDDING**

Nov 92. (cd; by EVE LIBERTINE) *Red Herring; (RH 2CD)* **SKATING**

PENNY RIMBAUD

Crass / not iss.

Jun 85. (lp; by PENNY RIMBAUD & EVE LIBERTINE) *(1984-4)* **ACT OF LOVE**
– (short poems written 1968-73 by Joy's deceased friend, WALLY HOPE) (re-iss. Oct95; same) <US cd-iss. 2000 on 'Orchard'; 5647>

Jul 92. (cd/lp) **CHRIST'S REALITY ASYLUM** (spoken word)

Red Herring / Red Herring

Mar 01. (cd) *(<RH 3>)* **THE DEATH OF IMAGINATION**   Jul01
– A cross to bear / Another me? / Dreams they be / Flesh, fleshness / The seed of words / Falling / Savage flesh / Yes, my body / Savage utopia / Together in the silence.

CRAVATS

Formed: Redditch, Worcestershire, England ... late 70's by CHRIS SHEND (aka THE SHEND), RICK LONDON, ETHOS YAPP and NIBBS (aka SIR ROBIN RAYMOND). Signed to indie label, 'Small Wonder', the quartet released the sad tale of 'GORDON' as their debut single towards the end of '78. A demented musical cocktail of choppy post-punk guitar, strange bleating sax and Vivien (of 'Young Ones' fame)-style vocal exhortations, The CRAVATS were one of the era's more obscure but interesting propositions. A string of singles ensued including 1979's 'BURNING BRIDGES' EP and 'PRECINCT' single, while a bonafide indie long player, 'THE CRAVATS IN TOYTOWN', emerged in 1980. Although a further handful of singles appeared on various labels over the course of the next few years – including an indie chart hit on the 'Crass' label with 'RUB ME OUT' – The CRAVATS were subsumed under the wider banner of the mysterious 'Dada Cravats Laboratory' organisation. Operating under a Dadaist (influential 1920's French art movement) criterion via various musical endeavours – including The CRAVATS, D.C.L. LOCOMOTIVE (who covered the Hollies' 'KING MIDAS IN REVERSE') and The BABYMEN – the project's most successful venture was The VERY THINGS. Including THE SHEND and SIR ROBIN amongst their number, this outfit debuted with a single, 'THE GONG MAN', on the 'Crass' label before recording a John Peel session and signing to the 'Reflex' label. A suitably bizarre debut album, 'THE BUSHES SCREAM WHILE MY DADDY PRUNES', appeared in 1984 and the band even secured a slot on legendary Channel 4 music show, 'The Tube'. Very reminiscent of BOBBY PICKETT's 'Monster Mash', with a side serving of NICK CAVE/LUX INTERIOR gardening with actor Boris Karloff, the album's comical title track is surely a classic waiting to be unearthed by a new generation. The VERY THINGS re-emerged sporadically over the next few years, a cover of R. Dean Taylor's 'THERE'S A GHOST IN MY HOUSE', withdrawn in May '87 due to The FALL's version being released simultaneously. It was to be a further year, however, before the release of follow-up set, 'MOTORTOWN' (on 'One Little Indian'), by which time the band had folded.

Album rating: IN TOYTOWN (*7) / Very Things: THE BUSHES SCREAM WHILE MY DADDY PRUNES (*7) / MOTORTOWN (*5)

NIBBS (aka SIR ROBIN RAYMOND) – vocals, guitar / **CHRIS SHENDO** (aka THE SHEND) – bass, vocals / **RICK LONDON** (b. SVOR MANN) – saxophone / **ETHOS YAPP** (b. DAVE BENNETT) – drums

Cravats / not iss.

Sep 78. (7") *(CH 004)* **GORDON. / SITUATIONS VACANT**

Small Wonder / not iss.

Jun 79. (7") *(SMALL 15)* **THE END. / BURNING BRIDGES / I HATE THE UNIVERSE**

CRAVATS (cont)

Oct 80.	(7")	(SMALL 24)	**PRECINCT. / WHO'S IN HERE WITH ME?** (w/ free-7"flexi) – Fireman / A FLUX IN 3D: Divide.		–
Oct 80.	(lp)	(CRAVAT 1)	**IN TOYTOWN** – All around the corner / All on standby / Pressure sellers / Welcome / One in a thousand / X.M.P. / Tears on my machine / Gordon / In your eyes / Still / The hole / Ceasing to be / Live for now / Triplex zone.		–
Mar 81.	(7")	(SMALL 25)	**YOU'RE DRIVING ME. / I AM THE DREG**		–
Nov 81.	(7")	(SMALL 26)	**OFF THE BEACH. / AND THE SUN SHONE**	Glass	not iss.
Feb 82.	(7")	(GLASS 021)	**TERMINUS. / LITTLE YELLOW FROGGY**		–
Aug 82.	(12"ep)	(GLASS 021/12)	**CRAVATS SING TERMINUS AND OTHER HITS**	Crass	not iss.
Jul 82.	(7")	(221984/4)	**RUB ME OUT. / WHEN WILL WE FALL**	Corpus Christi	not iss.
1983.	(12"ep; abandoned)	(none)	**THE COLOSSAL TUNE'S OUT**		–

— had already disbanded late in '82. SVOR formed The PIG BROS

VERY THINGS

— were formed by **THE SHEND** – lead vocals / **SIR ROBIN** – guitar; plus **GORDON DISNEYTIME** – drums / Horn section – **VINCENT JOHNSON, JOHN GRAHAM, ROBERT HOLARD + PAUL GREEN**

				Corpus Christi	not iss.
Nov 83.	(7")	(CHRIST ITS 2)	**THE GONG MAN. / THE COLOURS (ARE SPEAKING TO ME)**	Reflex	not iss.
Jun 84.	(12"; as D.C.L. LOCOMOTIVE)	(12RE 4)	**KING MIDAS IN REVERSE. / LAST BLACK TIE**		–
Jun 84.	(7")	(RE 5)	**THE BUSHES SCREAM WHILE MY DADDY PRUNES. / SHEARING MACHINE**		–
Aug 84.	(lp)	(LEX 3)	**THE BUSHES SCREAM WHILE MY DADDY PRUNES** – The conqueror / The bushes scream while my daddy prunes / Information / Down the final flight / Message from Disney time / Philip's world service / Wall of fir / Shearing machine / World of difference. (re-iss. Mar94 on 'Fire' cd/lp; REFIRE CD/LP 12)		–

— back to the basic trio.

Jul 85.	(12"ep)	(12RE 9)	**MUMMY YOU'RE A WRECK. / WHEN FATHER PAPERED THE PARLOUR / THE LIGHT POURS OUT OF MUMMY'S HOUSE**		–
Feb 86.	(12"ep; as The CRAVATS)	(12RE 10)	**IN THE LAND OF THE GIANTS**	DCL Electric	not iss.
Sep 86.	(7"/12")	(DCL 1/+T)	**THIS IS MOTORTOWN. / MOTORTOWN EPILOGUE (version A)**	One Little Indian	not iss.
Aug 87.	(12"; as The BABYMEN)	(12TP 3)	**FOR KING WILLY. /**		–
Sep 88.	(7")	(7TP 8)	**LET'S GO OUT. / THE MOTORTOWN TRAILER** (12"+=) (12TP 8) – ('A'version).		–
Sep 88.	(lp)	(TPLP 6)	**MOTORTOWN** – Let's go out / This is Motortown / There's a ghost in my house / She's standing still / Walking in the sand / Robin Holland is God / Motortown epilogue. (re-iss. Mar94 on 'Fire' cd/lp; REFIRE CD/LP 14)		–

— Had already disbanded. THE SHEND became an actor and appeared in some episodes of 'Eastenders' and 'The Bill'.

– compilations, etc. –

Mar 87.	(lp)	B.P.;	**LIVE AT THE ZAP CLUB, BRIGHTON (live)**	–	– mail-o
Jan 88.	(12"ep)	Strange Fruit; (SFPS 046)	**THE PEEL SESSION (17.12.83)** – Message from Disney Time / Down the final flight / Philip's world service / Wall of fir.		–
Mar 94.	(cd/lp)	Fire; (REFIRE CD/LP 13)	**IT'S A DRUG, IT'S A DRUG** – Mummy you're a wreck / When father papered the parlour / The gong man / Where's the rest of me? (link) / Transfusion / The hole / The colours are speaking to me / Motorlogue / (+ other versions).	–	–

CRIME

Formed: San Francisco, California, USA . . . 1976 . . . by FRANKIE FIX, JOHNNY STRIKE, RON THE RIPPER GRECO and RICKY JAMES. Possibly holding the crown of being the first US punk act to release a single, the self-financed double A-side, 'HOT WIRE MY HEART' and 'BABY YOU'RE SO REPULSIVE', appeared as CRIME's debut at the tail end of '76. By the following year's 'MURDER BY GUITAR' the STOOGES influenced crew were minus RICKY who joined FLIPPER and was superseded by BRITTLEY BLACK. He in turn was replaced by the brilliantly named HANK RANK, who stayed around between early '78 and mid '79, studio takes subsequently released as a bootleg, 'SAN FRANCISCO'S DOOMED'. Featuring two raw sessions (the first of which was produced by Elliott Mazer, who'd previously worked on Neil Young's 'Harvest'!), the album included such choice cuts as 'PISS ON YOUR DOG' (not advice that Great British dog trainer, Mrs. Woodhouse would have given readily!). After a brief stint with The FLAMIN' GROOVIES, BLACK was back on the drum stool for one last 7" effort in 1980, 'MASERATI'.
Album rating: SAN FRANCISCO'S DOOMED posthumous bootleg (*4)

JOHNNY STRIKE – vocals, guitar / **FRANKIE FIX** – guitar / **RON THE RIPPER GRECO** – bass (ex-CHOSEN FEW, aka FLAMIN' GROOVIES) / **RICKY JAMES** – drums

			not iss.	Crime
Dec 76.	(7")	**HOT WIRE MY HEART. / BABY YOU'RE SO REPULSIVE**	–	–
—		**BRITTLEY BLACK** – drums; repl. RICKY who joined FLIPPER		
Dec 77.	(7")	**MURDER BY GUITAR. / FRUSTRATION**	–	–
—		**HANK RANK** – drums; repl. BLACK who briefly joined FLAMIN' GROOVIES before moving to DEATH (he rejoined for below)		
			not iss.	B Square
1980.	(7")	**MASERATI. / GANGSTER FUNK**	–	–

— split in 1980, STRIKE formed REV, while RANK formed OTHER MUSIC. A bootleg, 'SAN FRANCISCO'S DOOMED' appeared in 1983 on US 'Solar Lodge'.

– compilations, etc. –

Feb 94.	(cd)	Overground; (OVER 33CD)	**SAN FRANCISCO'S DOOMED** – Frustration / Crime wave / I knew this nurse / San Francisco's doomed / Rock'n'roll enemy No.1 / Piss on your dog / Feel the beat / I stupid anyway / Twisted / Murder by guitar / Instrumental instrumental / Flyeater / Rockabilly drugstore / Dillinger's brain / Flipout / Emergency music ward / Monkey on your back / Yakuza / Rockin' weird / Samurai.		

CUBAN HEELS

Formed: Glasgow, Scotland . . . late 1977 by ex-JOHNNY & THE SELF-ABUSERS (the embryonic SIMPLE MINDS) singer, JOHN MILARKY. While JIM KERR & Co. went on to explore experimental post-punk territory, The CUBAN HEELS kicked up a more straightforward blend of new-wave power-pop and 60's retro sounds. After debuting with a charged-up cover of Petula Clark's 'DOWNTOWN' in Spring '78 on the tiny 'Housewife's Choice' label, the group underwent a shift in personnel as NICK CLARKE replaced ARMOUR and ALI McKENZIE replaced DUNCAN. A further two singles, 'LITTLE GIRL' and 'WALK ON WATER', appeared on their own 'Greville' and 'Cuba Libre' labels respectively, ushering in a major label deal with 'Virgin'. Released in Spring '81, the CUBAN HEELS' first single for the label, 'SWEET CHARITY', sounded like The B-52's FRED SCHNEIDER fronting a poppier SKIDS, a band with whom The 'HEELS were comparable in image terms as well as musical. Frantic follow-up single, 'MY COLOURS FLY', previewed the band's long awaited debut album, 'WORK OUR WAY TO HEAVEN' (1981). With a muted response from both press and punters alike, the band released a last gasp remake of 'WALK ON WATER' before calling it a day the following year. • **Covered:** MATTHEW AND SON (Cat Stevens).
Album rating: WORK OUR WAY TO HEAVEN (*4)

JOHN MILARKY – vocals / **LAURIE CUFFE** – guitar / **PAUL ARMOUR** – bass / **DAVIE DUNCAN** – drums

				Housewife's Choice	not iss.
Apr 78.	(7")	(JW 1-2)	**DOWNTOWN. / DO THE SMOKE WALK**		–
—			**NICK CLARK** – bass; repl. ARMOUR		
—			**ALI MacKENZIE** – drums; repl. DUNCAN	Greville	not iss.
Aug 80.	(7")	(GR 1)	**LITTLE GIRL. / FAST LIVING FRIEND**	Cuba Libre	not iss.
Jan 81.	(7")	(DRINK 1)	**WALK ON WATER. / TAKE A LOOK**	Virgin	not iss.
May 81.	(7")	(VS 413)	**SWEET CHARITY. / PAY AS YOU GO**		–
Aug 81.	(7")	(VS 439)	**MY COLOURS FLY. / CUBA LIBRE**		–
Oct 81.	(lp)	(V 2210)	**WORK OUR WAY TO HEAVEN** – Liberty hall / Move up a grade / A matter of time / Homes for heroes / The old school song / Walk on water / Hard times / Coming up for air / Work our way to Heaven / My colours fly.		–
Nov 81.	(7")	(VS 440)	**WALK ON WATER. / HARD TIMES** (with free 7"flexi) – Matthew and son.		–

— split some time in 1982

CUDDLY TOYS

Formed: Ireland-based . . . 1977 out of the ill-advisedly monikered RAPED, by SEAN PURCELL, TONY BAGGETT, FAEBHEAN KWEST, PADDY PHIELD and BILLY SURGEONER. This bunch of peroxide blonde BOWIE-cloning glam-punks released a couple of singles in 1978, 'PRETTY PAEDOPHILES' and 'CHEAP NIGHT OUT', although none were taken seriously by the press. 1980 saw a much needed change of group name to CUDDLY TOYS, their cheap electro-pop never making any inroads commercially. By this point, SURGEONER was replaced by ALIG FODDER and NICKY BROCKWAY, their debut album, 'GUILLOTINE THEATRE', duly issued by RAPED's old label, 'Parole', in 1980. After a few singles ('MADMEN' and 'ASTRAL JOE') found few buyers, TERRY NOAKES and ROBERT BARKER were subsequently drafted in to supersede FAEBHEAN and PADDY, the new line-up completing only one single, 'SOMEONE'S CRYING', before further personnel troubles ensued; S. PAUL WILSON and DAVID KOVACEVIC would come in for BAGGETT, FODDER and BROCKWAY. The second album, 'TRIALS AND CROSSES' (1982), was given short shrift by most critics resulting in the disbandment of the group shortly afterwards.
Album rating: GUILLOTINE THEATRE (*5) / TRIALS AND CROSSES (*5) / THE BEST OF THE CUDDLY TOYS compilation (*5) / Raped: PHILES AND SMILES (*3) / THE COMPLETE RAPED COLLECTION (*4)

RAPED

SEAN PURCELL – vocals / **FAEBHEAN KWEST** – guitar / **BILLY SURGEONER** – keyboards / **TONY BAGGETT** – bass / **PADDY PHIELD** – drums

				Parole	not iss.
Jan 78.	(7"ep)	(KNIT 1)	**PRETTY PAEDOPHILES** – Moving target / Raped / Escalator hater / Normal.		–
Nov 78.	(7")	(PURL 1)	**CHEAP NIGHT OUT. / FOREPLAY PLAYGROUND**		–

CUDDLY TOYS

ALIG FODDER (b. LEVILLIAN) + **NICKY BROCKWAY** – keyboards; repl. BILLY

		Fresh	not iss.
Apr 80.	(lp) *(FRESHLP 1)* **GUILLOTINE THEATRE**	☐	-

– Introvenus / Brain saviour / Join the girls / Wolf / Madman / Universe / Astral Joe / My commando / Full circle / Alien / Guillotine theatre / Time warp.

| Jul 80. | (7") *(FRESH 10 – PURL 7)* **MADMAN. / JOIN THE GIRLS** | ☐ | - |
| Nov 80. | (7") *(FRESH 20)* **ASTRAL JOE. / SLOW DOWN** | ☐ | - |

TERRY NOAKES – guitar; repl. FAEBHEAN. **ROBERT BARKER** – drums; repl. PADDY

| Feb 81. | (7") *(FRESH 25)* **SOMEONE'S CRYING. / BRING ON THE RAVERS** | ☐ | - |

(12") *(FRESH 25-12)* – ('A'side) / Dancing glass (instrumental) / Slide / Broken mirrors.

S. PAUL WILSON – bass; repl. BAGGETT

DAVID KOVACEVIC – keyboards; repl. FODDER (who formed FAMILY FODDER) + BROCKWAY

| Feb 82. | (7") *(FRESH 39)* **IT'S A SHAME. / FALL DOWN** | ☐ | - |
| Feb 82. | (lp) *(FRESHLP 6)* **TRIALS AND CROSSES** | ☐ | - |

– It's a shame / Trials and crosses / Action / Colombine's song / Fall down / One close step / Normandy nightfall / Lo and behold / Malice thru the looking glass . . . Pierrot Lunaire.

disbanded some time in '82

– compilations, etc. –

1984.	(lp; as RAPED) *Iguana; (PILLAGED 1)* **PHILES AND SMILES**	☐	-
Jul 94.	(cd; as RAPED) *Anagram; (CDPUNK 35)* **THE COMPLETE RAPED COLLECTION**	☐	-
Jul 01.	(cd) *Cherry Red; (CDMRED 191)* **THE BEST OF THE CUDDLY TOYS**	☐	-

– It's a shame / Trials and crosses / Madman / Slide / One close step / Join the girls / Someone's crying / Universe / Fall down / Full circle / Broken mirrors / Action / Astral Joe / Bring on the ravers / Guillotine theatre / Malice thru the looking glass / Pierrot lunaire / Slow down / Madman (video).

David CUNNINGHAM (see under ⇒ FLYING LIZARDS)

CURE

Formed: Crawley, Sussex, England . . . 1976 initially as The EASY CURE by ROBERT SMITH, LAWRENCE TOLHURST and MICHAEL DEMPSEY. In 1978, following a brief liaison with the small 'Hansa' label the previous year, the band recorded a one-off '45, 'KILLING AN ARAB', for indie operation, 'Small Wonder'. Although actually inspired by classic Albert Camus novel, 'The Outsider', the track was met with its fair share of controversy upon its early '79 re-release by Chris Parry's new 'Fiction' imprint. A subsequent debut album, 'THREE IMAGINARY BOYS' (1979) remains among The CURE's finest work, their strangely accessible post-punk snippets lent an air of suppressed melancholy to SMITH's plangent whine. The record almost scraped into the Top 40, while the pop brilliance of accompanying single, 'BOYS DON'T CRY', saw The CURE lauded as one of the UK's most promising young bands. With SIMON GALLUP replacing DEMPSEY (who joined The ASSOCIATES), the group again drew critical plaudits for the insidious 'JUMPING SOMEONE ELSE'S TRAIN'. A track railing against fashion victims, The CURE carved out their own solitary path over the course of the next three albums. Claustrophobic is normally the favoured critical bon mot in getting to grips with The CURE's sound and few would argue that the spiralling disorientation of 'A FOREST' was easy listening. SMITH and CO.'s first Top 40 hit, the track previewed follow-up set, 'SEVENTEEN SECONDS' (1980), an album which took them into the UK Top 20 despite its gloomy sound. Revered by the more pasty faced among the group's fanbase, 'FAITH' (1981) and 'PORNOGRAPHY' (1982) ploughed a similarly grim furrow, although the latter set went Top 10. Internal feuding subsequently led to the departure of GALLUP, SMITH and TOLHURST taking charge and effecting a bit of a stylistic departure on the more flippantly pop-friendly 'LET'S GO TO BED' (not before you take that eyeliner off, BOB) single. Finally, in summer of the following year, The CURE scored a long awaited breakthrough hit with 'THE WALK', the track narrowly missing the Top 10. Nevertheless, SMITH was simultaneously busying himself with SIOUXSIE AND THE BANSHEES, contributing guitar to their Top 5 cover of The Beatles' 'Dear Prudence' and playing on the 'Hyaena' album as well as hooking up with BANSHEES man, STEVE SEVERIN, for side project, The GLOVE. Meanwhile, the flouncing 'LOVECATS' single introduced the group to a whole new audience, a song with an alarmingly high irritability factor that still gets played to death by radio. With SMITH back on board in a full-time capacity by Spring '84, The CURE again managed to take their skewered pop vision into the pop charts with 'THE CATERPILLAR', a track lifted from bizarre new album, 'THE TOP' (1984). More line-up changes occurred prior to the recording of the band's breakthrough set, 'HEAD ON THE DOOR' (1985), including the return of SIMON GALLUP. Trailed by the classic 'IN BETWEEN DAYS', the record spawned a further major hit in the glockenspiel weirdness of 'CLOSE TO ME', its breathy claustrophobia segueing into a sassy, brassy finale. The track was also accompanied by a celebrated video (directed by long standing associate Tim Pope), featuring the whole band, erm, playing inside a wardrobe (honestly!). A subsequent two year lull was punctuated by an impressive singles retrospective, 'STANDING ON A BEACH' (1986), before the band returned with the sprawling 'KISS ME, KISS ME KISS ME' (1987) double set. Hardly an easy ride, the record showcased the many strange faces of The CURE and more, incredibly making the US Top 40 where they'd slowly been building up a cult following. This time around there was no stellar pop to liven up the Stock, Aitken & Waterman-clogged Top 10 although the record did spawn a trio of minor hits in 'WHY CAN'T I BE YOU', 'CATCH' and 'JUST LIKE HEAVEN'. The latter track was later privy to a genius fuzz-pop mangling courtesy of DINOSAUR JR., an interpretation that reportedly impressed SMITH no end. The CURE were now a formidable commercial proposition on both sides of the Atlantic, which probably explains why the ponderous 'DISINTEGRATION' (1989) album made the UK Top 3 and the 'LOVESONG' single almost topped the American Hot 100. The turn of the decade saw major upheaval as TOLHURST finally bailed out after clashing with SMITH, a pared down line up of SMITH, GALLUP, PORL THOMPSON, BORIS WILLIAMS and PERRY BAMONTE seeing the group through most of the following decade. A remix album, 'MIXED UP', appeared in 1990, its sensual dancefloor appeal illustrating just how adaptable the band's music was, bearing in mind that SMITH and Co. were sometimes dismissed as whimsical, goth-pop throwbacks. New material finally arrived in Spring '92 with the 'WISH' album, the huge hit 'FRIDAY I'M IN LOVE' following in their occasional tradition of jangling dreaminess. The album itself became The CURE's first UK No.1, missing the top of the American charts by a whisker; the band were now sufficiently world dominating that they could almost get away with two double live albums, 'SHOW' and 'PARIS', released simultaneously in late '93. The remainder of the decade saw the band's profile at its lowest since their shadowy beginnings, a low-key 1996 set, 'WILD MOOD SWINGS' their sole studio output in almost five years. While that album flirted with pop stylings, The CURE resorted to navel-gazing type with 'BLOODFLOWERS' (2000), presented as the third and final part of a trilogy that already featured 'PORNOGRAPHY' and 'DISINTEGRATION'. While the record undoubtedly qualified as classic CURE, there were few glimpses of the maverick streak which made their mid-period work so interesting. • **Songwriters:** Group compositions, except covers of FOXY LADY + PURPLE HAZE (Jimi Hendrix), HELLO I LOVE YOU (Doors). • **Trivia:** SMITH married childhood sweetheart Mary Poole on the 13th of August '88.

Album rating: THREE IMAGINARY BOYS (*8) / BOYS DON'T CRY exploitation (*7) / SEVENTEEN SECONDS (*6) / FAITH (*6) / PORNOGRAPHY (*6) / JAPANESE WHISPERS mini (*6) / THE TOP (*7) / CONCERT: LIVE (*5) / THE HEAD ON THE DOOR (*7) / STANDING ON THE BEACH / STARING AT THE SEA: THE SINGLES compilation (*9) / KISS ME, KISS ME, KISS ME (*7) / DISINTEGRATION (*8) / MIXED UP (*4) / WISH (*6) / PARIS (*4) / SHOW (*4) / WILD MOOD SWINGS (*5) / GALORE – THE SINGLES 1987-1997 compilation (*6) / BLOODFLOWERS (*6) / GREATEST HITS compilation (*8)

ROBERT SMITH (b.21 Apr'59, Blackpool, England) – vocals, lead guitar / **LAWRENCE TOLHURST** (b. 3 Feb'59) – drums, keyboards / **MICHAEL DEMPSEY** – bass

		Small Wonder	not iss.
Aug 78.	(7") *(SMALL 11)* **KILLING AN ARAB. / 10.15 SATURDAY NIGHT**	☐	-

		Fiction	not iss.
Jan 79.	(7") *(FICS 001)* **KILLING AN ARAB. / 10.15 SATURDAY NIGHT**	☐	-
May 79.	(lp/c) *(FIX/+C 1)* **THREE IMAGINARY BOYS**	44	-

– 10.15 Saturday night / Accuracy / Grinding halt / Another day / Object / Subway song / Foxy lady / Meat hook / So what / Fire in Cairo / It's not you / Three imaginary boys. *(cd-iss. Apr90; 827 686-2)*

| May 79. | (7") *(FICS 002)* **BOYS DON'T CRY. / PLASTIC PASSION** | ☐ | - |

SIMON GALLUP (b. 1 Jun'60, Surrey, England) – bass, keyboards (ex-MAG-SPYS, ex-LOCKJAW) repl. DEMPSEY who joined The ASSOCIATES

| Oct 79. | (7") *(FICS 005)* **JUMPING SOMEONE ELSE'S TRAIN. / I'M COLD** | ☐ | - |

added **MATHIEU HARTLEY** – keyboards, synthesizers

| Nov 79. | (7") *(FICS 006)* **I'M A CULT HERO (as "CULT HERO"). / I DIG YOU** | ☐ | - |

(on above they backed FRANK BELL)

| Mar 80. | (7"/ext.12") *(FICS/+X 10)* **A FOREST. / ANOTHER JOURNEY BY TRAIN** | 31 | - |
| Apr 80. | (lp/c) *(FIX/+C 004)* **SEVENTEEN SECONDS** | 20 | - |

– A reflection / Play for today / Secrets / In your house / Three . . . / The final sound / A forest / M / At night / Seventen seconds. *(cd-iss. Jan86; 825 354-2)*

reverted to trio of **SMITH, TOLHURST & GALLUP** when HARTLEY left to form CRY.

		Fiction	P.V.C.
Mar 81.	(7"/ext.12") *(FICS/+X 12)* **PRIMARY. / DESCENT**	43	
Apr 81.	(lp/c) *(FIX/+C 6)* <2383 605> **FAITH**	14	

– The holy hour / Primary / Other voices / All cats are grey / The funeral party / Doubt / The drowning man / Faith. *(cd-iss. Jan86; 827 687-2) (c+=)* **CARNAGE VISORS** (film soundtrack)

| Oct 81. | (7") *(FICS 14)* **CHARLOTTE SOMETIMES. / SPLINTERED IN HER HEAD** | 44 | - |

(12"+=) *(FICSX 14)* – Faith (live).

		Fiction	A&M
Apr 82.	(lp/c) *(FIX D/C 7)* <4902> **PORNOGRAPHY**	8	

– One hundred years / A short term effect / The hanging garden / Siamese twins / The figurehead / A strange day / Cold / Pornography. *(cd-iss. Jan86; 827 688-2)*

| Jul 82. | (7") *(FICS 15)* **THE HANGING GARDEN. / KILLING AN ARAB (live)** | 34 | - |

(d7"+=) *(FICG 15)* – One hundred years (live) / A forest (live).

STEVE GOULDING – bass repl. GALLUP who later joined FOOLS DANCE. (LOL now keyboards)

| Nov 82. | (7"/ext.12") *(FICS/+X 17)* **LET'S GO TO BED. / JUST ONE KISS** | 44 | - |

trimmed to duo of **SMITH + TOLHURST**

| Jul 83. | (7"/7"pic-d) *(FICS/+P 18)* **THE WALK. / THE DREAM** | 12 | - |

(12"+=) *(FICXT 18) <23928>* – The upstairs room / Lament.
(free 12"w/ free 12") *(FICSX 17)* – Let's go to bed / Just one kiss.

added **PHIL THORNALLEY** – bass / **ANDY ANDERSON**-drums (ex-BRILLIANT)

| Oct 83. | (7"/7"pic-d) *(FICS/+P 19)* **THE LOVECATS. / SPEAK MY LANGUAGE** | 7 | - |

(ext.12"+=) *(FICSX 19)* – Mr. Pink eyes.

Date	Release info	Chart (Fiction)	Chart (Elektra)
Dec 83.	(m-lp/c) (FIXM/+C 8) <25076> **JAPANESE WHISPERS** – Let's go to bed / The dream / Just one kiss / The upstair's room / The walk / Speak my language / Lament / The lovecats. *(cd-iss. Apr87; 817 470-2)*	26	
Mar 84.	(7"/7"pic-d) (FICS/+P 20) **THE CATERPILLAR. / HAPPY THE MAN** (12"+=) (FICSX 20) – Throw your foot.	14	-
Apr 84.	(lp/c)(cd) (FIXS/+C 9)(821 136-2) <25086> **THE TOP** – Shake dog shake / Birdmad girl / Wailing wall / Give me it / Dressing up / The caterpillar / Piggy in the mirror / The empty world / Bananafishbones / The top.	10	
	added **PORL THOMPSON** (b.8 Nov'57, London, England) – guitar, saxophone, keyboards (a member in '77)		
Oct 84.	(lp/d-c)(cd) (FIXH/+C 10)(823 682-2) **CONCERT – THE CURE LIVE** (live) – Shake dog shake / Primary / Charlotte sometimes / The hanging garden / Give me it / The walk / One hundred years / A forest / 10.15 Saturday night / Killing an Arab. *(d-c+=)* **CURIOSITY: CURE ANOMALIES 1977-1984** – Heroin face / Boys don't cry / Subway song / At night / In your house / The drowning man / Other voices / The funeral party / All mine / Forever.	26	-
	SIMON GALLUP returned to repl. PORL. **BORIS WILLIAMS** (b.24 Apr'57, Versailles, France) – drums (ex-THOMPSON TWINS) repl. ANDERSON who joined JEFFREY LEE PIERCE (of The GUN CLUB)		
Jul 85.	(7") (FICS 22) **IN BETWEEN DAYS. / EXPLODING BODY** (12"+=) (FICSX 22) – A few hours after this.	15	-
Aug 85.	(lp/c)(cd) (FIXH/+C 11)(827 231-2) <60435> **THE HEAD ON THE DOOR** – In between days / Kyoto song / The blood / Six different ways / Push / The baby screams / Close to me / A night like this / Screw / Sinking.	7	59
Sep 85.	(7"/7"poster) (FICS/+G 23) **CLOSE TO ME** (remix). / **A MAN INSIDE MY MOUTH** (12"+=) (FICST 23) – Stop dead. (10"++=) (FICST 23) – New day.	24	-
Jan 86.	(7") <69604> **IN BETWEEN DAYS. / STOP DEAD**	-	99
Mar 86.	(7") <69551> **CLOSE TO ME. / SINKING**	-	
Apr 86.	(7") (FICS 24) **BOYS DON'T CRY** (new mix). / **PILLBOX BLUES** (club-12"+=) (FICSX 24) – Do the Hansa.	22	-
May 86.	(lp/d-c)(cd) (FIXH/+C 12)(829 239-2) <60477> **STANDING ON THE BEACH / STARING AT THE SEA** (compilation of A's & B's) – Killing an Arab / Boys don't cry / Jumping someone else's train / A forest / Primary / Charlotte sometimes / The hanging garden / Let's go to bed / The walk / The lovecats / The caterpillar / In between days / Close to me. *(cd+=)* – 10.15 Saturday night / Play for today / Other voices / A night like this. *(re-iss. Feb91; same)*	4	48
Apr 87.	(7"/ext.12") (FICS/+X 25) <69474> **WHY CAN'T I BE YOU? / A JAPANESE DREAM** (d7"+=) (FIGSG 25) – Six different ways (live) / Push (live).	21	54 Jun87
May 87.	(d-lp/c)(cd) (FIXH/+C 13)(832 130-2) <60737> **KISS ME KISS ME KISS ME** – The kiss / Catch / Torture / If only tonight we could sleep / Why can't I be you? / How beautiful you are / Snakepit / Hey you / Just like heaven / All I want / Hot hot hot!!! / One more time / Like cockatoos / Icing sugar / The perfect girl / A thousand hours / Shiver and shake / Fight. *(pic-lp.Dec87; FIXP 13)* (free-ltd.12"orange / or green,w/cd) – A Japanese dream / Breathe / Chain of flowers / Sugar girl / Snow in summer / Icing sugar (remix).	6	35
	added on tour **ROBERT O'CONNELL** – keyboards (ex-PSYCHEDELIC FURS)		
Jul 87.	(7"/7"clear) (FICS/+P 26) **CATCH. / BREATHE** (c-s+=/12"+=) (FICS C/X 26) – A chain of flowers. (7"ep+=) (FICSE 26) – Kyoto song (live) / A night like this (live).	27	
Oct 87.	(7",7"white/7"pic-d) (FICS/+P 27) **JUST LIKE HEAVEN. / SNOW IN SUMMER** (12"+=/cd-s+=) (FICSX/FIXCD 27) – Sugar girl.	29	-
Oct 87.	(7") <69443> **JUST LIKE HEAVEN. / BREATHE**	-	40
Feb 88.	(12"/cd-s) (FICSX/FIXCD 28) <69424> **HOT HOT HOT!!! (extended remix). / HOT HOT HOT!!! (remix) / HEY YOU!!! (extended remix)**	45	65
Apr 89.	(7"/7"gf/7"clear) (FICS/+G/P 29) **LULLABY** (remix). / **BABBLE** (ext.12"+=/ext.12"pink+=) (FIC SX/VX 29) – Out of mind. (3"cd-s++=) (FICCD 29) – ('A'extended).	5	74
May 89.	(lp/c)(cd) (FIXH/+C 14)(839 353-2) <60855> **DISINTEGRATION** – Plainsong / Pictures of you / Closedown / Lovesong / Lullaby / Fascination street / Prayers for rain / The same deep water as you / Disintegration / Untitled. *(cd+=)* – Last dance *(pic-lp Apr90; FIXHP 14)*	3	12
May 89.	(7") <69300> **FASCINATION STREET. / BABBLE**	-	46
Aug 89.	(7"/7"box/c-s) (FIC S/SG/CD 30) <69280> **LOVESONG. / 2 LATE** (ext.12"+=) (FICSX 30) – Fear of ghosts. (cd-s++=)(cd-vid++=) (FICCD 30)(081398-2) – ('A'-12"mix).	18	2
Nov 89.	(c-s) <69249> **LULLABY / HOMESICK**	-	74
	(Mar'89) reverted to a quintet when TOLHURST left **SMITH, GALLUP, THOMPSON, WILLIAMS + PERRY BAMONTE** (b. 6 Sep'60, London, England) – keyboards		
Mar 90.	(7"/7"green/c-s) (FIC A/PA/CA 34) **PICTURES OF YOU** (remix). / (ext.12"+=/ext.12"green+=/cd-s+=) (FICXA/FIXPA/FICDA 34) – Fascination Street (live). (7"/7"purple/c-s) (FIC B/PB/CB 34) <64974> – PICTURES OF YOU (remix). / PRAYERS FOR RAIN (12"+=/12"purple+=/cd-s+=) (FICXB/FIXPB/FICDB 34) – Disintegration (live).	24	71
	(W.H. Smith's released ENTREAT (May90) a live EP, which featured the 5 tracks +=) – Closedown / Homesick / Untitled.		
Sep 90.	(7")/c-s) (FIC S/CS 35) **NEVER ENOUGH. / HAROLD AND JOE** (12"+=/cd-s+=/pic-cd-s+=) (FICSX/FICCD/FICDP 35) – Let's go to bed (milk mix).	13	72 Oct90
Oct 90.	(7")/c-s) (FIC S/CS 36) <64911> **CLOSE TO ME (closet remix). / JUST LIKE HEAVEN (dizzy mix)** (12"+=/cd-s+=) (FICSX/FICCD 36) – Primary (red mix). (cd-s+=) (FICDR 36) – Why can't I be you? (extended).	13	97 Jan91
Nov 90.	(cd)(d-lp/c) (847 009-2)(FIXH/+C 18) <60978> **MIXED UP** (remix album) – Lullaby (extended mix) / Close to me (closer mix) / Fascination Street (extended mix) / The walk (everything mix) / Lovesong (extended mix) / A forest (tree mix) / Pictures of you (extended dub mix) / Hot hot hot!!! (extended mix) / The caterpillar (flicker mix) / Inbetween days (shiver mix) / Never enough (big mix).	8	14
Apr 91.	(cd)(lp/c) (843 359-2)(FIXH/+C 17) **ENTREAT** (live) – (finally nationally released; see above)	10	
Mar 92.	(7"/c-s) (FIC S/CS 39) <64766> **HIGH. / THIS TWILIGHT GARDEN** ('A'-Higher mix-12"+=) (FICSX 39) – Play. (cd-s+=) (FICCD 39) – (all above).	8	42
Apr 92.	(12"clear) (FICSX 41) **HIGH (trip mix). / OPEN (fix mix)** (cd-s+=) (FICCD 41) – (see last cd-s for 4 tracks).	44	43
Apr 92.	(cd)(d-lp/c) (513 261-2)(FIXH/+C 20) <61309> **WISH** – Open / High / Apart / From the edge of the deep green sea / Wendy time / Doing the unstuck / Friday I'm in love / Trust / A letter to Elise / Cut / To wish impossible things / End.	1	2
May 92.	(7"/c-s) (FIC S/CS 42) <64742> **FRIDAY I'M IN LOVE. / HALO** ('A'-Strangelove mix-12"colrd+=) (FICSX 42) – Scared as you. (cd-s+=) (FICCD 42) – (all above).	6	18
Oct 92.	(7"/c-s) (FIC S/CS 46) **A LETTER TO ELISE. / THE BIG HAND** (Blue mix-12"+=) (FICSX 46) – A foolish arrangement. (cd-s+) (FICCD 46) – (all above).	28	
Sep 93.	(d-cd/d-c/d-lp) (FIX CD/MC/LP 25) <61551> **SHOW** (live) – Tape / Open / High / Pictures of you / Lullaby / Just like Heaven / Fascination Street / A night like this / Trust / Doing the unstuck / The walk / Let's go to bed / Friday I'm in love / In between days / From the edge of the deep green sea / Never enough / Cut / End.	29	42
	PORL departed after the above.		
Oct 93.	(cd/c/d-lp) (FIX CD/MC/LP 26) <61552> **PARIS** (live) – The figurehead / One hundred years / At night / Play for today / Apart / In your house / Lovesong / Catch / A letter to Elise / Dressing up / Charlotte sometimes / Close to me.	56	
Apr 96.	(c-s) (576468-4) **THE 13TH (swing radio mix) / IT USED TO BE ME** (cd-s+=) (576469-2) – ('A'-Killer bee mix). (cd-s) (576493-2) – ('A'-Two chord cool mix) / Ocean / Adonais.	15	-
Apr 96.	(c-s) <64292> **THE 13TH / ADONAIS**	-	44
May 96.	(cd/c/lp) (FIX CD/MC/LP 28) <61744> **WILD MOOD SWINGS** – Want / Club America / This is a lie / The 13th / Strange attraction / Mint car / Jupiter crash / Round & round & round / Gone! / Numb / Trap / Treasure / Bare.	9	12
Jun 96.	(c-s) (FICCS 52) <64275> **MINT CAR / HOME** (cd-s+=) (FICCD 52) – ('A'-buskers mix). (cd-s) (FISCD 52) – ('A'-electric mix) / Waiting / A pink dream.	31	58
Nov 96.	(c-s) (FICCS 53) **GONE! / THIS IS A LIE (ambient mix)** (cd-s+=) (FICD 53) – Strange attraction (strange mix) / The 13th (feels good mix).	60	
Nov 97.	(cd/c/lp) (FIX CD/MC/LP 30) <62117> **GALORE – THE SINGLES 1987-1997** (compilation) – Why can't I be you / Catch / Just like Heaven / Hot, hot, hot / Lullaby / Fascination Street / Love song / Pictures of you / Never enough / Close to me / High / Friday I'm in love / Letter to Elise / The 13th / Mint car / Strange attraction / Gone / Wrong number.	37	32
Nov 97.	(c-s) (FICMC 54) **WRONG NUMBER / ('A'-radio mix mix)** (12"/cd-s+=) (FIC SX/D 54) – ('A'mixes).	62	
Feb 00.	(d-lp/cd) (FIX/+CD 31) <62236> **BLOODFLOWERS** – Out of this world / Watching me fall / Where the birds always sing / Maybe someday / The last day of summer / There is no if . . . / The loudest sound / 39 / Bloodflowers.	14	16
Oct 01.	(cd-s) (587389-2) **CUT HERE / SIGNAL TO NOISE / CUT HERE (missing mix) / CUT HERE (video)**	54	-
Nov 01.	(cd) (589435-2) <62726> **GREATEST HITS** (compilation) – Boys don't cry / A forest / Let's go to bed / The walk *[US-only]* / The lovecats / Caterpillar *[UK-only]* / Inbetween days / Close to me / Why can't I be you? / Just like Heaven / Lullaby / Lovesong / Pictures of you *[UK-only]* / Never enough / High / Friday I'm in love / Mint car / Wrong number / Cut here / Just say yes. *(d-cd-iss. +=; 589434-2)* – (acoustic versions).	33	58

– compilations, etc. –

Aug 83.	(lp/c) Fiction; (SPE LP/MC 26) / P.V.C.; <7916> **BOYS DON'T CRY** – Boys don't cry / Plastic passion / 10.15 Saturday night / Accuracy / Object * / Jumping someone else's train / Subway song / Killing an Arab / Fire in Cairo / Another day / Grinding halt / World war * / Three imaginary boys. *(cd-iss. Nov86; 815 011-2)* (w/ out tracks * +=) – So what.	71	Aug80
May 86.	(c) Fiction; **BOYS DON'T CRY. / LET'S GO TO BED**	-	-
May 88.	(12"ep/cd-ep) *Strange Fruit*; (SFPS/+CD 050) **PEEL SESSIONS** – Killing an Arab / Boys don't cry / 10:15 Saturday night / Fire in Cairo.	-	-
Oct 88.	(vid-cd) Fiction; (080184-2) **WHY CAN'T I BE YOU (video) / JAPANESE DREAM / HEY YOU / WHY CAN'T I BE YOU**		-
Oct 88.	(vid-cd) Fiction; (080182-2) **IN BETWEEN DAYS (video) / SIX DIFFERENT WAYS (live) / PUSH (live)**		-
Oct 88.	(vid-cd) Fiction; (080186-2) **CATCH (video) / CATCH / BREATHE / A CHAIN OF FLOWERS / ICING SUGAR (new mix)**		-

THE GREAT INDIE DISCOGRAPHY — The 1970s

DAMNED

Formed: London, England ... May 1976 by BRIAN JAMES and RAT SCABIES who soon found The CAPTAIN and former undertaker, DAVE VANIAN. Signed to new UK indie label, 'Stiff', by JAKE RIVERA, they released the classic track, 'NEW ROSE', produced by stablemate, NICK LOWE. The DAMNED became the first "New Wave Punks" to release and chart with an album, namely the enduring 'DAMNED DAMNED DAMNED' (1977). One of the classic punk debuts, the album pogo'd and thrashed its way through a frenetic set of three-chord wonders, LOWE's garden shed production underlining the riotous pandemonium. The band had also broken into the Top 40, although ironically enough, prolonged chart success would come later in the 80's when The DAMNED had changed almost beyond recognition. Live, the band were also one of the major attractions on the London scene; with VANIAN's proto-goth affectations, SENSIBLE's beret-topped antics and SCABIES' demented-drummer persona all competing against each other, The DAMNED were indeed a motley crew. Their musical assault was bolstered later that year by a second guitarist, LU EDMONDS, who debuted on the flaccid 'MUSIC FOR PLEASURE' (1977). The album was universally derided and SCABIES soon left for pastures new. Although future CULTURE CLUB man, JOHN MOSS was drafted in briefly as a replacement, the band splintered early the following year. After a period of solo work, VANIAN, SENSIBLE and SCABIES regrouped as The DAMNED early in '79 and emerged rejuvenated into the UK Top 20 via the impressive 'LOVE SONG'. With ALGY WARD completing the line-up, the band scored a second chart hit with 'SMASH IT UP', releasing their lauded 'MACHINE GUN ETIQUETTE' album later that year. Sure, they were still as swift and deadly as the title might suggest, but somehow they'd acquired a mastery of pop dynamics; a third single, 'I JUST CAN'T BE HAPPY TODAY', was the closest they'd yet come to a rock-solid tune. PAUL GRAY replaced WARD for 1980's 'UNTITLED (THE BLACK ALBUM)', an even more surprising, ambitious double set which flew in the face of punk convention with its rampant experimentalism. The poppy 'STRAWBERRIES' (1982) marked the last stand of CAPTAIN SENSIBLE, who'd scored with the annoying 'HAPPY TALK' earlier that summer, the first fruits of his solo deal with 'A&M'. VANIAN and SCABIES lumbered on with new members ROMAN JUGG and BRYN MERRICK, suprisingly enough enjoying major chart success with a string of overtly commercial, pseudo-goth rockers, the biggest of which, a cover of BARRY RYAN's 'ELOISE', made the Top 3. 'PHANTASMAGORIA' (1985) became their biggest selling album to date, catering to a whole new generation of fans. Most critics were agreed, however, that it paled in comparison to their earlier work, the DAMNED finally fading in the late 80's. For any interested parties, the band periodically get together with an amorphous line-up for all-dayers and one-off gigs; old punks never die, they just tour with The DAMNED. With the horsemen of the apocalypse holding fire just yet, The DAMNED made an unlikely return from the recording grave with 'GRAVE DISORDER' (2001). Boasting a line-up of VANIAN and SENSIBLE alongside newcomers PATRICIA MORRISON, MONTY OXY MORON and PINCH, the interminably resurrected rockers trawled familiar, if never exactly predictable, musical and lyrical territory with customary disregard for current trends. • **Songwriters:** Most written by JAMES, until he left, when group took over. Covered:- HELP! (Beatles) / I FEEL ALRIGHT (Stooges / Iggy Pop) / JET BOY JET GIRL (New York Dolls) / CITADEL (Rolling Stones) / ELOISE (Paul & Barry Ryan) / WHITE RABBIT (Jefferson Airplane) / ALONE AGAIN OR (Love) / WILD THING (Troggs) / LET THERE BE RATS (aka DRUMS) (Sandy Nelson). • **Trivia:** NICK MASON (Pink Floyd drummer) produced disappointing 2nd album MUSIC FOR PLEASURE. CAPTAIN SENSIBLE had UK-No.1 in 1982 with (Rogers-Hammerstein's) HAPPY TALK, and although briefly, became a top disco/pop act abroad.

Album rating: DAMNED DAMNED DAMNED (*8) / MUSIC FOR PLEASURE (*5) / MACHINE GUN ETIQUETTE (*7) / BLACK ALBUM (*6) / BEST OF THE DAMNED compilation (*8) / STRAWBERRIES (*5) / PHANTASMAGORIA (*5) / ANYTHING (*3) THE LIGHT AT THE END OF THE TUNNEL compilation (*7) / FINAL DAMNATION exploitation (*4)

DAVE VANIAN (b. DAVE LETTS) – vocals / **BRIAN JAMES** (b. BRIAN ROBERTSON) – guitar (ex-LONDON S.S.) / **CAPTAIN SENSIBLE** (b. RAY BURNS, 23 Apr'55) – bass, vocals / **RAT SCABIES** (b. CHRIS MILLER, 30 Jul'57) – drums (ex-LONDON S.S.)

		Stiff	Frontier
Nov 76.	(7") (BUY 6) **NEW ROSE. / HELP!**	□	-
Feb 77.	(7") (BUY 10) **NEAT NEAT NEAT. / STAB YOR BACK / SINGALONGASCABIES**	□	-
Feb 77.	(lp) (SEEZ 1) **DAMNED DAMNED DAMNED**	36	Apr77

– Neat neat neat / Fan club / I fall / Stab yor back / Feel the pain / New rose / Fish / See her tonite / 1 of the 2 / So messed up / I feel alright. (re-iss. Apr87 on 'Demon' lp/c/cd; FIEND/+CASS/CD 91) (pic-lp 1988; PFIEND 91) (<cd re-iss. Nov97 on 'Frontier'; 31033-2>) (cd re-iss. Aug00 on 'Edsel'; EDCD 677)

—— added (ROBERT) **LU EDMUNDS** – guitar

| Sep 77. | (7") (BUY 18) **PROBLEM CHILD. / YOU TAKE MY MONEY** | □ | - |
| Nov 77. | (lp) (SEEZ 5) **MUSIC FOR PLEASURE** | □ | - |

– Problem child / Don't cry wolf / One way love / Politics / Stretcher case / Idiot box / You take my money / Alone / Your eyes / Creep (you can't fool me) / You know. (re-iss. Apr88 on 'Demon' lp/c/cd; FIEND/+CASS/CD 108)

| Dec 77. | (7",7"purple) (BUY 24) **DON'T CRY WOLF. / ONE WAY LOVE** | □ | - |

—— **DAVE BERK** – drums (ex-JOHNNY MOPED) repl. SCABIES who formed various bands

—— **JOHN MOSS** – drums replaced BERK. They split Feb 78. VANIAN joined DOCTORS OF MADNESS. SENSIBLE formed SOFTIES then KING. EDMUNDS & MOSS formed THE EDGE. MOSS later joined ADAM & THE ANTS then CULTURE CLUB. EDMUNDS became part of ATHLETICO SPIZZ 80, The MEKONS, SHRIEKBACK, PIL. etc. BRIAN JAMES formed TANZ DER YOUTH, who released one single, 'I'M SORRY I'M SORRY' for 'Radar', before going solo the following year (1979) to issue his version of 'AIN'T THAT A SHAME'. He subsequently formed another punk supergroup, The HELLIONS, issuing one 1981 single for 'Illegal', 'WHY WHY WHY', before he jointly formed The LORDS OF THE NEW CHURCH. The DAMNED re-formed in Autumn '78 as The **DOOMED** with LEMMY of MOTORHEAD on bass. (1 gig) **HENRY BADOWSKI** – bass (ex-CHELSEA) replaced LEMMY. The group reverted to name The **DAMNED** with originals VANIAN, SENSIBLE (now guitar & keyboards) and **SCABIES**

—— **ALGY WARD** – bass (ex-SAINTS) replaced BADOWSKI who went solo

		Chiswick	Roadrunner
Apr 79.	(7",7"red) (CHIS 112) **LOVE SONG. / NOISE NOISE NOISE / SUICIDE**	20	-

(re-iss. 7"blue Feb82 on 'Big Beat'; NS 75)

| Oct 79. | (7") (CHIS 116) **SMASH IT UP. / BURGLAR** | 35 | - |

(re-iss. 7"red Mar82 on 'Big Beat'; NS 76)

| Nov 79. | (lp) (CWK 3011) **MACHINE GUN ETIQUETTE** | 31 | Dec79 |

– Love song / Machine gun etiquette / I just can't be happy today / Melody Lee / Anti-Pope / These hands / Plan 9 channel 7 / Noise noise noise / Looking at you / Smash it up (parts 1 & 2). (re-iss. Jun85 on 'Ace' lp/c; DAM/+MC 3) (cd-iss. 1986 +=; CDWIK 905) – Ballroom blitz / Suicide / Rabid (over you) / White rabbit.

| Nov 79. | (7") (CHIS 120) **I JUST CAN'T BE HAPPY TODAY. / BALLROOM BLITZ / TURKEY SONG** | 46 | - |

—— **PAUL GRAY** – bass, vocals (ex-EDDIE AND THE HOT RODS) repl. WARD who formed TANK

Jun 80.	(7";w-drawn) (CHIS 130) **WHITE RABBIT. / RABID (OVER YOU) / SEAGULLS**	□	-
Sep 80.	(7"m/12"m) (CHIS/+12 135) **THE HISTORY OF THE WORLD (part 1). / I BELIEVE THE IMPOSSIBLE / SUGAR AND SPITE**	□	-
Nov 80.	(d-lp) (CWK 3015) **UNTITLED** (THE BLACK ALBUM) (1/2 studio, 1/4 live, 1/4 concept)	29	-

– Wait for the blackout / Lively arts / Silly kids games / Drinking about my baby / Hit and miss / Doctor Jekyll and Mr. Hyde / 13th floor vendetta / Twisted nerve / Sick of this and that / History of the world (part 1) / Therapy // Curtain call / live side:- Looking at you / Second time around / Smash it up (parts 1 & 2) / Plan 9 / I just can't be happy today / Plan 9 Channel 7. (re-iss. Aug82 on 'Ace' as one-lp/d-c; DAM/+MC 3) (c-iss.Jun85; TCWIK 3015) (cd-iss. Mar90; CDWIK 906) – (omits live tracks)

| Nov 80. | (7"m) (CHIS 139) **THERE AINT NO SANITY CLAUS. / HIT OR MISS / LOOKING AT YOU (live)** | □ | - |

		N.E.M.S.	not iss.
Nov 81.	(d7"ep) (TRY 1) **FRIDAY THE 13th**	50	-

– Disco man / The limit club / Citadel / Billy bad breaks.

		Bronze	not iss.
Jul 82.	(7"m/7"pic-d) (BRO/+P 149) **LOVELY MONEY. / LOVELY MONEY (disco) / I THINK I'M WONDERFUL**	42	-
Sep 82.	(7"ep) (BRO 156) **DOZEN GIRLS. / TAKE THAT / MINE'S A LARGE ONE, LANDLORD / TORTURE ME**	□	-
Oct 82.	(lp/c) (BRON 542) **STRAWBERRIES**	15	-

– Ignite / Generals / Stranger on the town / Dozen girls / The dog / Gun fury / Pleasure and the pain / Life goes on / Bad time for Bonzo / Under the floor again / Don't bother me. (re-iss. Mar86 on 'Legacy' red-lp/c; LLM/+K 3000) (re-iss. Dec86 on 'Dojo' lp/cd; DOJO LP/CD 46) (cd re-iss. Nov92 on 'Dojo'; DOJOCD 46) (cd-iss. Apr94 on 'Cleopatra'; CLEO 1029-2) (cd re-iss. Mar97 on 'Essential'; ESMCD 473) (cd re-iss. JUn01 on 'Castle'; CMRCD 246)

| Nov 82. | (7"m) (BRO 159) **GENERALS. / DISGUISE / CITADEL ZOMBIES** | □ | - |

		Damned	not iss.
Nov 83.	(pic-lp/lp) (P+/DAMU 2) **LIVE IN NEWCASTLE (live)**	-	- mail-o

(cd-iss. Jan94 on 'Receiver'; RRCD 181)

		Plus One	not iss.
May 84.	(7"colrd/7"pic-d) (DAMNED 1/+P) **THANKS FOR THE NIGHT. / NASTY**	□	-

(re-iss. 12"-ltd.1985 +=; DAMNED 1T) – Do the blitz.

—— **VANIAN** and **SCABIES** recruited new guys **ROMAN JUGG** (b. Barry, Wales) – guitar, keyboards / who replaced the CAPTAIN who carried on with solo career. **BRYN MERRICK** (b. Barry, Wales) – bass; repl. GRAY

		M.C.A.	Off Beat
Mar 85.	(7"/7"pic-d/ A'-Spic'n'Spec mix-12") (GRIM/+P/T 1) **GRIMLY FIENDISH. / EDWARD THE BEAR**	21	-

(12"white+=) (GRIMX 1) – ('A'-Bad Trip mix).

| Jun 85. | (7") (GRIM 2) **SHADOW OF LOVE. / NIGHTSHIFT** | 25 | □ |

('A'-Ten Inches Of Hell mix-10"+=) (GRIMX 2) – Would you.
(12"+=) (GRIMT 2) – Would you.
(d7"+=) (GRIMY 2) – Let there be Rats / Wiped out.

Jul 85. (lp/c/pic-lp/white-lp/blue-lp) (MCF/+C/P/W/B 3275)
PHANTASMAGORIA — 11
– Street of dreams / Shadow of love / There'll come a day / Sanctum sanctorum / Is it a dream / Grimly fiendish / Edward the bear / The eighth day / Trojans. (free 7"w.a.) I JUST CAN'T BE HAPPY TODAY (re-iss. 1986; same) – (contains free 12"blue ELOISE) (cd-iss. Aug89; DMCL 1887)

Sep 85. (7") (GRIM 3) **IS IT A DREAM (Wild West End mix) / STREET OF DREAMS (live)** — 34
(12"+=) (GRIMT 3) – Curtain call (live) / Pretty vacant (live) / Wild thing (live).

Jan 86. (7") (GRIM 4) **ELOISE. / TEMPTATION** — 3
(12"blue+=/'A'-No Sleep Until Wednesday mix-12") (GRIM T/X 4) – Beat girl.

Nov 86. (7") (GRIM 5) **ANYTHING. / THE YEAR OF THE JACKAL** — 32
(10"blue+=,10"yellow+=) (GRIMX 5) – ('A'mixes).
(12"+=) (GRIMT 5) – Thanks for the night.

Nov 86. (lp/c/cd) (MCG/MCGC/DMCG 6015) <5966> **ANYTHING** — 40
– Anything / Alone again or / The portrait / Restless / In dulce decorum / Gigolo / The girl goes down / Tightrope walk / Psychomania.

Feb 87. (7"colrd/12"clear) (GRIM/+T 6) **GIGOLO. / THE PORTRAIT** — 29

Apr 87. (7") (GRIM 7) **ALONE AGAIN OR. / IN DULCE DECORUM** — 27
(12"+=) (GRIMT 7) – Psychomania.
(d7"++=) (DGRIM 7) – Eloise.

Nov 87. (7") (GRIM 8) **IN DULCE DECORUM. / PSYCHOMANIA** — 72
(12"+=) (GRIMT 8) – ('A'dub).

— disbanded in the late 80's (ROMAN + BRYN formed The MISSING MEN) although re-union gigs were forthcoming

                                                           Essential Restless
Aug 89. (green-lp) (ESCLP 008) <72385> **FINAL DAMNATION** (live '88 reunion)
– See her tonite / Neat neat neat / Born to kill / I fall / Fan club / Fish / Help / New rose / I feel alright / I just can't be happy today / Wait for the blackout / Melody Lee / Noise noise noise / Love song / Smash it up (parts 1 & 2) / Looking at you / The last time. (cd-iss. Apr94 on 'Castle'; CLACD 338) (cd re-iss. Jun01 on 'Castle'; CMRCD 247)

— the DAMNED re-formed in 2001 with **VANIAN**, **SENSIBLE**, plus **PATRICIA MORRISON** – bass (ex-SISTERS OF MERCY) / **MONTY OXY MORON** – keyboards / **PINCH** – drums (ex-ENGLISH DOGS)

                                                           Nitro Nitro
Aug 01. (cd/lp) (<15844-2/-1>) **GRAVE DISORDER**
– Democracy / Song.com / Thrill kill / She / Looking for action / Would you be so hot (if you weren't dead?) / Absinthe / Amen / Neverland / 'Til the end of time / Obscene. <US+=> – W / Beauty of the beast.

– compilations, etc. –

1981. (4x7"box) Stiff; (GRAB 2) **FOUR PACK**
– (NEW ROSE / NEAT NEAT NEAT / PROBLEM CHILD / DON'T CRY WOLF)

Nov 81. (lp/c) Ace; (DAM/+C 1) **THE BEST OF THE DAMNED** — 43
– New rose / Neat neat neat / I just can't be happy today / Jet boy jet girl / Hit or miss / There ain't no sanity claus / Smash it up (parts 1 & 2) / Plan 9 channel 7 / Rabid (over you) / Wait for the blackout / History of the world (part 1). (cd-iss. Oct87; CDDAM 1)

May 82. (7"/7"pic-d) Big Beat; (NS/+P 77) **WAIT FOR THE BLACKOUT. / Captain Sensible & The Softies: JET BOY, JET GIRL**

Oct 82. (7"green) Big Beat; (NS 80) **LIVELY ARTS. / TEENAGE DREAM**
(10"+=) (NST 80) – I'm so bored.

Nov 82. (lp) Ace; (NED 1) **LIVE SHEPPERTON 1980 (live)**
– Love song / Second time around / I just can't be happy today / Melody Lee / Help / Neat neat neat / Looking at you / Smash it up (parts 1 & 2) / New rose / Plan 9 channel 7. (also iss.Nov82 on 'Big Beat'; WIKM 27) (c-iss.Jun85; WIKC 27) (cd-iss. Jun88; CDWIKM 27)

Nov 85. (12"ep) Stiff; (BUYIT 238) **NEW ROSE / NEAT NEAT NEAT. / STRETCHER CASE / SICK OF BEING SICK**

Jan 86. (lp/c/cd) Dojo; (DOJO LP/TC/CD 21) **DAMNED BUT NOT FORGOTTEN**
(cd re-iss. Nov92; same) (cd re-iss. Feb97 on 'Essential'; ESMCD 472) (cd re-iss. Jun01 on 'Castle'; CMRCD 245)

Jun 86. (12"ep) Strange Fruit; (SFPS 002) **THE PEEL SESSIONS (10.5.77)**
– Sick of being sick / Stretcher case / Feel the pain / Fan club. (c-ep.1987; SFPSC 002) (cd-ep.May88; SFPSCD 002)

Jul 86. (blue-m-lp) Stiff; (GET 4) **THE CAPTAIN'S BIRTHDAY PARTY – LIVE AT THE ROUNDHOUSE**
(cd-iss. Nov91 on 'Demon'; VEXCD 7)

Jul 87. (12"ep) Strange Fruit; (SFPS 040) **THE PEEL SESSIONS (30.11.76)**
– Stab yor back / Neat neat neat / New rose / So messed up / I fall.

Oct 87. (cd/lp) I.D.; (C+/NOSE 18) **MINDLESS, DIRECTIONLESS, ENEMY (live)**
(re-iss. Jun89 cd/c/lp; CDOSE/KOSE/NOSE 18X)

Dec 87. (d-lp) M.C.A.; (MCSP 312) **THE LIGHT AT THE END OF THE TUNNEL** — 87
(d-cd-iss. Apr92; MCLDD 19007)

Jun 88. (lp/c) Big Beat; (WIK/+C 80) **THE LONG LOST WEEKEND: BEST OF VOL.1/2**

1990. (cd) Marble Arch; (cd) **THE DAMNED LIVE (live)**

Dec 90. (cd/c/d-lp) Castle; (CCS CD/MC/LP 278) **THE COLLECTION**

Jan 91. (12"blue-ep) Deltic; (DELT 7T) **FUN FACTORY ('82). / Captain Sensible: FREEDOM / PASTIES / A RIOT ON EASTBOURNE PIER**

Jun 91. (cd/colrd-lp) Receiver; (RR CD/LP 159) **BALLROOM BLITZ – LIVE AT THE LYCEUM (live)**

Dec 91. (cd) Dojo; (DOJOCD 65) **TOTALLY DAMNED (live + rare)**

Jan 92. (cd) Street Link; (AOK 101) **ALTERNATIVE CHARTBUSTERS**

Feb 92. (clear-lp) Receiver; (RRLP 159) **LIVE AT THE LYCEUM (live)**

Aug 92. (cd) Connoisseur; (VSOPCD 174) **THE MCA SINGLES A'S & B'S**

Sep 92. (cd) Demon; (VEXCD 12) **SKIP OFF SCHOOL TO SEE THE DAMNED (THE STIFF SINGLES A'S & B'S)**

May 93. (cd) Receiver; (RRCD 179) **SCHOOL BULLIES**

Jul 93. (cd) Success; (550 747-2) **THE DAMNED: FROM THE BEGINNING**

Nov 93. (cd) Strange Fruit; (SFRSCD 070) **SESSIONS OF THE DAMNED**

Jun 94. (cd/c) M.C.I.; (MUS CD/MC 017) **ETERNALLY DAMNED – THE VERY BEST OF THE DAMNED**

Dec 94. (cd) Cleopatra; (CLEO 7139-2) **TALES FROM THE DAMNED**

May 95. (cd) Spectrum; (550 747-2) **FROM THE BEGINNING**

Sep 95. (cd/c) Emporio; (EMPR CD/MC 592) **NOISE – THE BEST OF: LIVE**

Jun 96. (cd) Nighttracks; (CDNT 011) **THE BBC RADIO 1 SESSIONS**

Oct 96. (cd) Cleopatra; (CLP 9804) **FIENDISH SHADOWS**

Feb 97. (3xcd-box) Demon; (FBOOK 14) **NEAT NEAT NEAT**

Mar 97. (cd) Cleopatra; (CLP 9960) **THE CHAOS YEARS**

Apr 97. (cd/c) The Record Label; (MOCDR/MOMC 1) **I'M ALRIGHT JACK AND THE BEANSTALK**

May 97. (d-cd) Snapper; (SMDCD 143) **BORN TO KILL**

Jun 97. (lp) Cleopatra; (CLP 9782) **SHUT IT**

Nov 97. (7") Skinnies Cut; (AVL 1077) **PROKOFIEV. /**

Nov 97. (7") Marble Orchard; (MOS 7) **TOUR SINGLE. /**

Jul 98. (cd) Strange Fruit; (SFRSCD 070) **THE SESSIONS OF THE DAMNED**

Oct 98. (7") Musical Tragedy; (MT 418) **PRETTY VACANT. / DISCO MAN**

Jun 99. (t-cd) Cleopatra; (CLP 542) **THE DAMNED BOX SET**

Dec 99. (cd) Chiswick; (CDWIKK 198) **MARVELLOUS: THE BEST OF THE DAMNED**

Dec 99. (cd) Musical Tragedies; (efa 12354-2) / Sudden Death; <5> **MOLTEN LAGER (live)** — — Sep00

Jun 00. (d-cd) Essential; (ESACD 901) **ANTHOLOGY**

DAVE VANIAN & THE PHANTOM CHORDS

                                                  Camden Town not iss.
Dec 92. (7") **TOWN WITHOUT PITY. /**

                                                  Big Beat   not iss.
Mar 95. (cd) (CDWIKD 140) **BIG BEAT PRESENTS . . .**
– Voodoo doll / Screamin' kid / Big town / This house is haunted / You and I / Whiskey and me / Fever in my blood / Frenzy / Shooting Jones / Jezebel / Tonight we ride / Johnny Guitar / Chase the wild wind / Swamp thing.

DANGEROUS GIRLS

Formed: Worcester, nr. Birmingham, England . . . 1978 by lads MIKOCUPA (alias MICHAEL COOPER), ROB RAMPTON, CHRIS AMES and ROB PETERS. A year into their musical account, The DANGEROUS GIRLS released their debut single, the eponymous 'DANGEROUS GIRLS' on their own 'Happy Face' records. After their 'TAAGA' EP hit the shops a few months later, the er 'GIRLS signed to 'Human' records (home to fellow Brummies, The AU PAIRS), where they delivered two more, 'MAN IN THE GLASS' and 'STEP OUT'. Squeezed in between the aforementioned 7 inchers, the quirky rock quartet completed a session for the BBC's Mike Read; the tracks being 'INSTINCT', 'SUMMERTIME BLUES', 'DOMESTIC BLISTERS' and a polished version of their debut A side.

Album rating: never released any

MYKOCUPA (b. MICHAEL ROBERT COOPER) – vocals, guitar / **BEETMOLL** (b. CHRIS AMES) – guitar, bongos / **ROB RAMPTON** – bass, vocals / **ROB PETERS** – drums, vocals

                                                  Happy Face not iss.
Aug 79. (7") (MM 115) **DANGEROUS GIRLS. / I DON"T WANT TO EAT (WITH THE FAMILY)**

Nov 79. (7"ep) (MM 116) **TAAGA EP**
– Safety in numbers / Sex / Jump up and down / Down on the file.

                                                  Human   not iss.
Nov 80. (7") (HUM 1) **MAN IN THE GLASS. / MO7's**

Apr 81. (7"m) (HUM 6) **STEP OUT. / PSYCHIC PHENOMENA / MEN IN SUITS**

— (an album was shelved with the cat.no; HUMAN 2)

— a few years after their split, ROB PETERS joined EVERYTHING BUT THE GIRL

dB's

Formed: Winston-Salem, North Carolina, USA . . . early 1978 by CHRIS STAMEY (ex-RITTENHOUSE SQUARE) and fellow ex-SNEAKERS, WILL RIGBY and GENE HOLDER. Under this moniker, they released two singles between 1976-77 for STAMEY's 'Car' label while the band also featured MITCH EASTER (later a producer and leader of LET'S ACTIVE). A posthumous SNEAKERS ep, 'IN THE RED', surfaced a year later, while a compilation, 'RACKET', was finally put together in the early 90's. In 1977, meanwhile, STAMEY issued a solo 45, 'SUMMER SUN' for the legendary US 'Ork' label, before returning to 'Car' as leader of the dB's. STAMEY had already moved to New York City by this point, playing with ALEX CHILTON (ex-BOX TOPS, ex-BIG STAR) and undertaking a one-off stint with RICHARD LLOYD (of TELEVISION). A debut single, 'IF

AND WHEN' (as CHRIS STAMEY & THE dB's) backed with 'I THOUGHT (YOU WANTED TO KNOW)' arrived in mid-'78 and although shunned by every major record company in the States, they found a UK home with 'Albion', who released a string of singles and two BEATLES-esque albums, 'STANDS FOR DECIBELS' (1981) and 'REPERCUSSION' (1982). Like the considerably more successful LENNON and McCARTNEY songwriting partnership before them, STAMEY and PETER HOLSAPPLE acted as foils for each others respective styles; while the former concerned himself with highly melodic but often off-beat pop and psychedelia, the latter's rootsy approach helped to anchor the sound. However, the pairing was severed when STAMEY upped sticks for a solo career in 1983, HOLSAPPLE recruiting bass player, RICK WAGNER, while the band signed for 'Bearsville'. Unfortunately, the band were dogged by legal problems following the death of label boss, Albert Grossman, the subsequent album, 'LIKE THIS' (1984), was bogged down in the ensuing confusion despite being a spirited set of earthier country-orientated sounds. Following an absence of three years, HOLSAPPLE and Co, emerged with their long-awaited comeback album, 'THE SOUND OF MUSIC' (1987), after inking a new deal with 'I.R.S.' and supporting new labelmates, R.E.M.; HOLSAPPLE would subsequently guest for STIPE and Co, guesting on their 'Out Of Time' classic in 1991. The dB's continued to work together well into the 90's, although it would only be HOLSAPPLE and RIGBY who would feature on 1994's umpteenth comeback set, 'PARIS AVENUE'.

Album rating: STANDS FOR DECIBELS (*8) / REPERCUSSION (*7) / LIKE THIS (*5) / THE SOUND OF MUSIC (*5) / RIDE THE WILD TOM (*4) / PARIS AVENUE (*5)

CHRIS STAMEY (b. 6 Dec'54, Chapel Hill, N. Carolina) – vocals, guitar / after debut 45; **PETER HOLSAPPLE** (b.19 Feb'56, Greenwich, Connecticut) – guitar, organ, vocals / **GENE HOLDER** (b.10 Jul'54, Pennsylvania) – bass / **WILL RIGBY** (b.17 Mar'56) – drums

Jul 78. (7") **I THOUGHT (YOU WANTED TO KNOW). / IF AND WHEN** — not iss. / Car

1980. (7") <SHK 100> **BLACK AND WHITE. / SOUL KISS (part one & two)** — not iss. / Shake

Dec 80. (7") (ION 1005) **DYNAMITE. / FIGHT** — Albion / not iss.
Mar 81. (7") (ION 1010) **BIG BROWN EYES. / BABY TALK**
Apr 81. (lp/c) (ALB/+C 105) **STANDS FOR DECIBELS**
— Black and white / Dynamite / She's not worried / The fight / Espionage / Tearjerkin' / Cycles per second / Bad reputation / Big brown eyes / I'm in love / Moving in your slee / Judy. (re-iss. Oct87 on 'Line'; ALLP 400009)
May 81. (7") (ION 1013) **JUDY. / CYCLES PER SECOND**
Nov 81. (7") (ION 1024) **AMPLIFIER. / ASK FOR JILL**
(w/ free 7") **UPS AND DOWNS. / WE WERE HAPPY THERE**
Feb 82. (7") (ION 1030) **NEVERLAND. / Ph FACTOR**
Jun 82. (lp/c) (ALB/+C 109) **REPERCUSSIONS**
— Happenstance / We were happy there / Living a lie / From a window to a screen / Ask for Jill / Amplifier / Neverland / Storm warning / Ups and downs / Nothing is wrong / In Spain / I feel good. (re-iss. Oct87 on 'Line'; ALLP 400032)
Jun 82. (7") (ION 1034) **LIVING A LIE. / IN SPAIN**

— **RICK WAGNER** – bass (HOLDER now guitar) repl. STAMEY (to solo)

1984. (lp) <24516> **LIKE THIS** — not iss. / Bearsville
— Love is for lovers / She got soul / Spitting in the wind / Lonely is not cool / Amplifier / A spy in the house of love / Rendezvous / New gun in town / On the battlefront / White train / Darby Hall. (re-iss. Jun88 on 'Rhino' lp/cd; RN LP/CD 70891)

— split for a while in 1984. WILL RIGBY released solo album 'SIDEKICK PHENOMENON' for US 'Egon'.

— **JEFF BENINATO** – bass; repl. WAGNER

Nov 87. (lp/c) (MIRF/+C 1031) <42055> **THE SOUND OF MUSIC** — IRS-MCA / I.R.S.
— Never say when / Change with the changing times / Molly says / Bonneville / Any old thing / Think too hard / Working for somebody else / Never before and never again / A better place / Looked at the sun too long / Today could be the day.

— In 1991 for below label, PETER HOLSAPPLE and CHRIS STAMEY released album 'MAVERICKS'. It featured HOLDER, MICHAEL BLAIR and JANE SCARPENTONI.

— new dB's; **ERIC PETERSON** – guitar + **HAROLD KELT** – keyboards repl. HOLDER who became a producer for WYGALS and his own band The INDIVIDUALS

Nov 94. (cd) <(RSACD 805)> **RIDE THE WILD TOM TOM** — Special Delivery / Rhino Aug93
— We should be in bed / Everytime anytime / Let's live for today / Little hands / You got it wrong / Tell me two times / Nothing is wrong / Purple hose / Ash I read New York rocker / Walking the ceiling (it's good to be alive) / Baby talk / Dynamite (original) / Soul kiss (part one) / Bad reputation / Modern boys and girls / What about the cat / What's the matter with me? / The fight / She's green, I'm blue / If and when / Soul kiss (part two) / The death of rock / Purple hose (light return) / Hardcore Judy / A spy in the house of love.

Apr 95. (cd) <(MON 6122)> **PARIS AVENUE** — Monkey Hill / Monkey Hill Oct94
— Morning bugle / Ride the roller coaster / Lines and dots / Huey, Dewey, and "Louie, Louie" / Girlfriend / Baldhead baby / Window on the world / I can't look her in the eye / Barometers, thermometers / Running over / This is where I belong / We gold / Visible man.

— disbanded and PETER featured with The CONTINENTAL DRIFTERS on self-titled album (& same label) with new wife SUSAN COWSILL (ex-COWSILLS)

– compilations, etc. –

Aug 86. (lp) Dojo; (DOJOLP 33) **AMPLIFIER**
— Nothing is wrong / Neverland / In Spain / Happenstance / Living a lie / From a window to a scream / Ask for Jill / Amplifier / Bad reputation / Big brown eyes / Moving in your sleep / Black and white / I feel good Toady / Ups and downs.

Apr 92. (d-cd) Line; <(LICD 921191)> **STANDS FOR DECIBELS / REPERCUSSION** Dec96
<(US/UK re-iss. Nov01 on 'Collector's Choice'; CCM 0250-2)>

DEAD BOYS

Formed: Cleveland, Ohio, USA . . . mid '76 by CHEETAH CHROME and JOHNNY BLITZ, both ex-ROCKET FROM THE TOMBS (same band as DAVID THOMAS and PETER LAUGHNER of PERE UBU), who relocated to New York with frontman STIV BATORS (also a short-lived RFTT member), JIMMY ZERO and JEFF MAGNUM. Under The DEAD BOYS moniker, they played the infamous CBGB's, a nightclub owned at the time by their manager, Hilly Kristal. America's answer to The DAMNED, they signed to 'Sire' in 1977, finally unleashing their brash HEARTBREAKERS meets STOOGES debut set, 'YOUNG, LOUD & SNOTTY'. Featuring at least two seminal punk classics in 'SONIC REDUCER' and 'ALL THIS AND MORE' (also available on the V/A album, 'New Wave'), it sold moderately enough to make the US Top 200 for a month. The FELIX PAPPALARDI-produced follow-up, 'WE HAVE COME FOR YOUR CHILDREN' (1978), was everything that punk's critics railed against (i.e. brutally nihilistic, musically limited and sheer bloody-minded), although it did feature 'AIN'T IT FUN' (later covered by GUNS 'N ROSES) and was also graced by the presence of two RAMONES, JOEY and DEE DEE. The DEAD BOYS were finally laid to rest when STIV went solo in 1979, recording a handful of singles (including a version of The Choirs' 'IT'S COLD OUTSIDE') and an album for Greg Shaw's 'Bomp', 'DISCONNECTED' (1980). After putting in a brief stint as an actor in John Waters' 'Polyester', BATORS teamed up with ex-SHAM 69 Brits, DAVE TREGANNA, DAVE PARSONS and MARK GOLDSTEIN to form the short-lived WANDERERS. A solitary album, 'THE ONLY LOVERS LEFT ALIVE' (1981), appeared on UK 'Polydor', before he and TREGANNA hooked up with old DAMNED friend, BRIAN JAMES as The LORDS OF THE NEW CHURCH. With ex-BARRACUDAS' drummer NICKY TURNER in tow, the punk supergroup were inaugurated via a low key gig in Paris towards the end of 1981. Signed to Miles Copeland's 'Illegal/I.R.S.' imprint, the LORDS delivered their first vinyl sermon in the shape of an eponymous 1982 debut album, a lacklustre sub-metal affair dabbling in pseudo gothic imagery and religious doom-mongering. This set the tone for the remainder of the band's career, two further studio albums, 'IS NOTHING SACRED?' (1983) and 'METHOD TO OUR MADNESS' (1984) hardly adding to their legacy; bizarrely enough, ex-MANFRED MANN'S EARTH BAND keyboard player/bassist, MATT IRVING joined for the latter. As the band's studio output dwindled to almost nothing, BATORS finally sacked his whole band in 1989 and took flight to London where he gathered together a bunch of old punk friends (DEE DEE RAMONE, NEIL X and JOHNNY THUNDERS) for a one-off gig billed as 'Return Of The Living Boys'. Although this loose aggregation actually laid down around half a dozen studio tracks, BATORS was to die in his sleep on the 4th of June, 1990, after he was run over by an automobile in Paris the previous day.

Album rating: YOUNG, LOUD & SNOTTY (*7) / WE HAVE COME FOR YOUR CHILDREN (*5) / Stiv Bators: DISCONNECTED (*5) / Lords Of The New Church: LORDS OF THE NEW CHURCH (*5) / IS NOTHING SACRED? (*4) / THE METHODS TO OUR MADNESS (*4) / KILLER LORDS compilation (*5) / LIVE AT THE SPIT (*3)

STIV BATORS (b. STEVEN BATOR, 22 Oct'56, Cleveland) – vocals / **CHEETAH CROME** (b. GENE CONNOR) – guitar, vocals / **JIMMY ZERO** – guitar / **JEFF MAGNUM** – bass / **JOHNNY BLITZ** – drums

Oct 77. (lp) (9103 329) <SR 6038> **YOUNG, LOUD & SNOTTY** — Sire / Sire
— Ain't nothin' to do / All this and more / Caught with the meat in your mouth / Down in flames / Hey little girl / High tension wire / I need lunch / Not anymore / Sonic reducer / What love is. <cd-iss. Feb00; 7599 26038-2)>
Dec 77. (7"m)(12"m) (SRE 1004)(6078 609) **SONIC REDUCER. / LITTLE GIRL / DOWN IN FLAMES**
Aug 78. (7"m) (SRE 1029) **TELL ME. / NOT ANYMORE / AIN'T NOTHIN' TO DO**
Aug 78. (lp) <(SRK 6054)> **WE HAVE COME FOR YOUR CHILDREN** Jun78
— Third generation nation / I won't look back / Catholic boy / Flame thrower love / Son of Sam / Tell me / Big city / Calling on you / Dead and alive / Ain't it fun. <(cd-iss. Feb00; 7599 26054-2)>

— now without MAGNUM, they disbanded in 1979. BATORS went solo

– compilations, etc. –

May 81. (lp) Bomp; (BLP 4017) **NIGHT OF THE LIVING DEAD BOYS (live)**
— Detention home / Caught with the meat in your mouth / All this and more / 3rd generation nation / Tell me / Catholic boy / Won't look back / Ain't it fun / What love is / Ain't nothin' to do / Need lunch / Sonic reducer / Route 66 / Hang on Sloopy / It's all over now / Ain't it fun / Sonic reducer. (cd-iss. Apr94 & Mar99; BCD 4017) (lp re-iss. Jul97; same)
1989. (lp/cd) Bomp; <BLP/BCD 4064> **YOUNGER, LOUDER AND SNOTTIER**
(UK-iss.Jul97; same)
Nov 97. (cd/lp) Bacchus Archives; (BA 1121 CD/LP) **TWISTIN' ON THE DEVIL'S FORK**
Aug 98. (d-cd) Bomp; <(BCD 4066)> **ALL THIS AND MORE**
May 99. (cd/lp) Bad Boy; (RUDE CD/LP 00010) **3rd GENERATION NATION**
Mar 01. (7") Cold Front; (CF 035) **BURIED GEMS**
Apr 02. (cd) Burning Airlines; <(PILOT 112)> **LIVER THAN YOU'LL EVER BE**

STIV BATORS

with band; **GEORGE HARRISON** – guitar (no not that one!) / **FRANK SELICH** – bass / **DAVID QUINTON** – drums

	London	Bomp
Sep 79. (7") (HLZ 10575) <BMP 124> **IT'S COLD OUTSIDE. / THE LAST YEAR**		
	Bomp	Bomp
May 80. (7") <BMP 128> **NOT THAT WAY ANYMORE. / CIRCUMSTANTIAL EVIDENCE**		
May 80. (lp) <BLP 4015> **DISCONNECTED**	–	

– Evil boy / Bad luck charm / A million miles away / Make up your mind / Swingin' a go-go / Too much to dream / Ready anytime / The last year / I wanna forget you (just the way you are). (re-iss. Oct87 on 'Line' lp/cd; LILP4/LICD9 00174) (cd re-iss. Feb94; BCD 4043)

| 1980. (12"ep) <BEP 1202> **TOO MUCH TO DREAM. / MAKE UP YOUR MIND** | – | |

In Aug'87, BATORS released mini-lp, 'HAVE LOVE WILL TRAVEL' *BMP 12-136*

BATORS joined The WANDERERS (with ex-SHAM 69 members). They released a few singles and an album in 1981; 'THE ONLY LOVERS LEFT ALIVE'. He then was part of punk supergroup . . .

LORDS OF THE NEW CHURCH

STIV BATOR plus **BRIAN JAMES** – guitar, vocals (ex-DAMNED, ex-TANZ DER YOUTH, ex-HELLIONS) / **DAVE TREGANNA** – bass, vocals (ex-WANDERERS, ex-SHAM 69) / **NICKY TURNER** – drums (ex-BARRACUDAS)

	Illegal	I.R.S.
Apr 82. (7") (ILS 0028) **NEW CHURCH. / LIVIN' ON LIVIN'**		
Jul 82. (7") (ILS 0030) **OPEN YOUR EYES. / GIRLS GIRLS GIRLS**		
Jul 82. (lp) (ILP 009) **LORDS OF THE NEW CHURCH**		

– New church / Russian roulette / Question of temperature / Eat your heart out / Portobello / Open your eyes / Livin' on livin' / Li'l boys play with dolls / Apocalypso / Holy war. (cd-iss. Apr87; ILPCD 009)

Nov 82. (7"/7"pic-d) (ILS/+P 0033) **RUSSIAN ROULETTE. / YOUNG DON'T CRY**		
	I.R.S.	I.R.S.
Jun 83. (7") (PFP 1015) **LIVE FOR TODAY. / OPENING**		
Aug 83. (lp/c) (SP/CS 70039) **IS NOTHING SACRED?**		

– Dance with me / Bad timing / Johnny too bad / Don't worry children / The night is calling / Black – white girl / Goin' downtown / Tales of two cities / World without end / Partners in crime / Live for today.

Sep 83. (7"/12"colrd-pic-d) (PFP/PFSX 1022) **DANCE WITH ME. / I'M NOT RUNNING HARD ENUFF**

added guest **MATT IRVING** – bass, keyboards (ex-MANFRED MANN'S EARTH BAND)

Oct 84. (7") (IRS 113) **M STYLE. / SORRY FOR THE MAN**		
(d7"+=) (IRSY 113) – Dance with me / I'm not running hard enuff.		
Nov 84. (lp) (IRSA 7049) **THE METHOD TO OUR MADNESS**		

– Method to my madness / I never believed / Pretty baby scream / Fresh flesh / When blood runs cold / M style / The seducer / Kiss of death / Do what thou wilt / My kingdom come.

	Illegal	not iss.
Apr 85. (7"pic-d) (LORDSP 1) **LIKE A VIRGIN. / METHOD TO MY MADNESS**		–
(12"+=) (LORDS 1) – Gun called Justice.		
Nov 85. (lp/c) (ILP 016) **KILLER LORDS** (compilation)		

– Dance with me / Hey tonight / Russian roulette / M style / Lord's prayer / Live for today / Method to my madness / Open your eyes / I never believed / Black girl – white girl / New church / Like a virgin. (re-iss. Aug90 cd/lp; ILP 016) (cd re-iss. Feb99 on 'E.M.I.'; 713178-2)

trimmed to quartet again, when IRVING joined PAUL YOUNG BAND

	BondageInt	not iss.
Aug 87. (7") (B 11) **REAL BAD TIME. / THINGS GO BAD**		–
	Illegal	not iss.
May 88. (lp/c) (ILP/+C 021) **LIVE AT THE SPIT** (live)		–

– Method to my madness / Partners in crime / Kiss of death / Bad timing / Dance with me / M style / Livin' on livin' / The seducer / Open your eyes / Holy war / Gun called Justice / When blood runs cold / Pretty baby scream / Live for today / Holy war / Black girl – white girl / New church. (w/ free 45) – Gun called Justice / Johnny too bad / Light and shade / All or nothing. (re-iss. Aug90 cd; ILPCD 021)

	Perfect B.	not iss.
May 89. (d-lp; as STIV BATORS & HIS EVIL BOYS) (PB 003) **SCENE OF THE CRIME** (live at the Limelight 1985)	–	– German

– Introduction / Evil boy / It's cold outside / Have love, will travel / Not that way anymore / The last year / Story in your eyes / It's trash / Ready to snap / Do you believe in magic / Dreams & desires / Sonic reducer / 3rd generation nation.

split, when BATORS sacked the rest, because they were going to sack him. He started to work with ex-members of SIGUE SIGUE SPUTNIK and HANOI ROCKS, but he died in his sleep in 1990 after being knocked down by a car in Paris.

– compilations, etc. –

| Mar 00. (cd) Wargasm; (30551CD) **ANTHOLOGY** | | – |

– STIV BATORS compilations, others, etc. –

| May 94. (cd) New Rose; (64200-2) **THE DEAD BOYS** | | – |
| Apr 98. (cd) Bond Age; (BRCD 96129) **THE LAST RACE** | | – |

DEAD KENNEDYS

Formed: San Francisco, California, USA . . . early 1978 by JELLO BIAFRA and EAST BAY RAY, who recruited KLAUS FLOURIDE, TED and briefly, the mysterious 6025. Inspired by British punk rock, BIAFRA formed The DEAD KENNEDYS primarily as a vehicle for his raging, razor-sharp satire of America and everything it stood for. Public enemy #1 from the off, major labels steered well clear of the band, BIAFRA and Co. subsequently forming their own label, the legendary 'Alternative Tentacles', releasing 'CALIFORNIA UBER ALLES' as their debut 45 in late '79. A scathing critique of California governor, Jerry Brown, the record introduced the singer's near-hysterical vocal undulations set against a pulverising punk/hardcore musical backdrop. Released on the independent 'Fast' imprint in Britain, the record's initial batch of copies sold like proverbial hotcakes. The 1980 follow-up, 'HOLIDAY IN CAMBODIA' (released on Miles Copeland's 'Faulty' label; 'Cherry Red' in the UK), remains The DEAD KENNEDYS' most viciously realised moment, a dark, twisting diatribe on American middle-class liberal trendies. Later in the year, the group kept up their aural assault with a debut album, 'FRESH FRUIT FOR ROTTING VEGETABLES', an unexpected Top 40 entry in the seemingly "Punk Is Dead" Britain, which contained the aforesaid 45's plus perennial favourites, 'LET'S LYNCH THE LANDLORD', 'DRUG ME' and the forthcoming UK hit, 'KILL THE POOR'. The record also offered a glimpse of BIAFRA's reassuringly twisted sense of humour in such surreal cuts as 'STEALING PEOPLE'S MAIL' and 'VIVA LAS VEGAS' (the latter was a hit for Elvis!). In 1981, drummer D.H. PELIGRO replaced TED, making his debut on the bluntly-titled 'TOO DRUNK TO FUCK', the only UK Top 40 charting single in musical history (up to that point!) to utilise the "f***" word. Once again mocking the inherent hypocrisy of corporate America, The DEAD KENNEDYS released a frenetic 10" mini-set, 'IN GOD WE TRUST INC.' (1981), highlights being the self-explanatory 'NAZI PUNKS FUCK OFF' (a US-only single) and a deadpan version of 'RAWHIDE'. The band then took a brief hiatus, busying themselves with an 'Alternative Tentacles' compilation of promising unsigned American bands, entitled 'Let Them Eat Jellybeans'. That same year (1982), the group released their second album proper, 'PLASTIC SURGERY DISASTERS'; issued on 'Statik' in the UK, it featured the singles 'BLEED FOR ME' and 'HALLOWEEN'. Spending the ensuing few years touring, the band resurfaced in 1985 with 'FRANKENCHRIST', an album that finally saw BIAFRA's upstanding enemies closing in (ie. the PMRC, the US government, etc) due to the album's free "penis landscape" poster by Swiss artist H.R. Giger. Although BIAFRA and Co. (including some senior label staff) were tried in court for distributing harmful material to minors (a revised obscenity law), the case was subsequently thrown out after a hung jury. Nevertheless, the cost of the trial effectively put the band out of business, The DEAD KENNEDYS poignantly-titled finale, 'BEDTIME FOR DEMOCRACY' being issued late in 1986. Although KLAUS and RAY followed low-key solo careers, the ever-prolific BIAFRA vociferously protested against his treatment on spoken-word sets, 'NO MORE COCOONS' (1987) and 'THE HIGH PRIEST OF HARMFUL MATTER' (1989). He subsequently collaborated with a wide range of hardcore/industrial acts such as D.O.A., NO MEANS NO and TUMOR CIRCUS, although it was with LARD (a project with MINISTRY mainmen, AL JOURGENSEN and PAUL BARKER) that BIAFRA really came into his own. A late 80's mini-set, 'THE POWER OF LARD' preceded a full-length album, 'THE LAST TEMPTATION OF LARD', a minor UK hit early in 1990. This demented set included such hilarious BIAFRA monologues as 'CAN GOD FILL TEETH?' and even a rendition of Napolean XIV's 'THEY'RE COMING TO TAKE ME AWAY'. In 1994, he hooked up with another likeminded soul in hillbilly punk, MOJO NIXON, releasing one album, 'PRAIRIE HOME INVASION' (the title possibly a parody of an ICE-T album). BIAFRA continues to work at 'Alternative Tentacles', supplying the country with suitably deranged hardcore and occasionally taking time out for other projects, most recently a second LARD set, 'PURE CHEWING SATISFACTION' (1997). • **Trivia:** In 1979, BIAFRA stood in the elections for Mayor of San Francisco (he came 4th!).

Album rating: FRESH FRUIT FOR ROTTING VEGETABLES (*9) / IN GOD WE TRUST INC. mini (*5) / PLASTIC SURGERY DISASTERS (*6) / FRANKENCHRIST (*6) / BEDTIME FOR DEMOCRACY (*5) / GIVE ME CONVENIENCE OR GIVE ME DEATH compilation (*8) / Jello Biafra: NO MORE COCOONS spoken (*5) / HIGH PRIEST OF HARMFUL MATTER spoken (*5) / THE LAST TEMPTATION OF LARD with Lard (*6) / THE LAST SCREAM OF THE MISSING NEIGHBORS with D.O.A. (*6) / THE SKY IS FALLING AND I WANT MY MOMMY with No Means No (*5) / I BLOW MINDS FOR A LIVING (*6) / HIGH VOLTAGE CONSPIRACY FOR RADICAL FREEDOM with Tumor Circus (*5) / PRAIRIE HOME INVASION with Mojo Nixon (*6) / BEYOND THE VALLEY OF THE GIFT POLICE (*5) / PURE CHEWING SATISFACTION with Lard (*5)

JELLO BIAFRA (b. ERIC BOUCHER, 17 Jun'58, Boulder, Colorado) – vocals / **EAST BAY RAY** (b. RAY GLASSER, Castro Valley, California) – guitar, (synthesisers-later 80's) / **KLAUS FLUORIDE** (b. Detroit, Michigan) – bass, vocals / **BRUCE SLESINGER** (aka TED) – drums

	Fast	Alternative Tentacles
Oct 79. (7") (FAST 12) <AT 95-41> **CALIFORNIA UBER ALLES. / MAN WITH THE DOGS**		
	Cherry Red	Faulty-IRS
Jun 80. (7")12" (CHERRY/12CHERRY 13) <IR 9016> **HOLIDAY IN CAMBODIA. / POLICE TRUCK**		
(re-iss. 7"/cd-s Jun88 & Mar95; same)		
Sep 80. (lp) (B-RED 10) <SP 70014> **FRESH FRUIT FOR ROTTING VEGETABLES**	33	Nov80

– Kill the poor / Forward to death / When ya get drafted / Let's lynch the landlord / Drug me / Your emotions / Chemical warfare / California uber alles / I kill children / Stealing people's mail / Funland at the beach / Ill in my head / Holiday in Cambodia / Viva Las Vegas. (cd-iss. Nov87 & Mar95 & Sep01; CDBRED 10) (d-cd-iss. Sep01 +=; CDSBRED 155) – (bonus tracks).

| Oct 80. (7") (CHERRY 16) **KILL THE POOR. / IN SIGHT** | 49 | – |
| (re-iss. Nov87 & Mar95; CDCHERRY 16) | | |

D.H. PELIGRO (b. DARREN, East St.Louis, Illinois) – drums; repl. BRUCE/TED

DEAD KENNEDYS (cont)

				Cherry Red	Alternative Tentacles
May 81.	(7"/12") (CHERRY/12CHERRY 24) <VIRUS 2> **TOO DRUNK TO FUCK. / THE PREY** (re-iss. May88 & Mar95 cd-s; CDCHERRY 24)			36	

		Statik	Alternative Tentacles
Nov 81.	(10"ep) (STATEP 2) <VIRUS 5> **IN GOD WE TRUST INC.** – Religious vomit / Moral majority / Kepone factory / Dog bite / Nazi punks fuck off / We've got a bigger problem now / Rawhide. <US c-ep+=; VIRUS 5C> – Too drunk to fuck / The prey / Holiday in Cambodia. (re-iss. Jun92 cd-ep; STATEP 2CD)		
Dec 81.	(7") <VIRUS 6> **NAZI PUNKS FUCK OFF. / MORAL MAJORITY**	-	
Jul 82.	(7"/12") (STAT/+12 22) <VIRUS 23> **BLEED FOR ME. / LIFE SENTENCE** (cd-s Jun92; STAT 22CD)		
Nov 82.	(lp) (STATLP 11) **PLASTIC SURGERY DISASTERS** – Government flu / Terminal preppie / Trust your mechanic / Well paid scientist / Buzzbomb / Forest fire / Halloween / Winnebago warrior / Riot / Bleed for me / I am the owl / Dead end / Moon over Marin. (re-iss. Oct85; same) (cd-iss. Nov86 & Jun92 & Jun98 +=; same) – IN GOD WE TRUST INC. (cd re-iss. Feb01 on 'Decay'+=; DKS 6/9CD) – IN GOD WE TRUST INC.		-
Nov 82.	(7"/12") (STAT/+12 27) <VIRUS 28> **HALLOWEEN. / SATURDAY NIGHT HOLOCAUST** (cd-s Jun92; STAT 27CD)		

— meanwhile KLAUS and EAST BAY released solo singles (see below)

		Alternative Tentacles	Alternative Tentacles
May 82.	(12"; KLAUS FLUORIDE) <(VIRUS 12)> **SHORTNING BREAD. / DROWNING COWBOY**		
Jun 84.	(7"; EAST BAY RAY) <(VIRUS 34)> **TROUBLE IN TOWN. / POISON HEART** (12 re-iss. Apr89 on 'New Rose' France; GMO 40)		
Aug 84.	(12"ep; KLAUS FLUORIDE) **CHA CHA CHA WITH MR. FLUORIDE** – Ghost riders / etc.		-
Dec 85.	(lp) <(VIRUS 45)> **FRANKENCHRIST** – Soup is good food / Hellnation / This could be anywhere (this could be everywhere) / A growing boy needs his lunch / Chicken farm / Macho-rama (invasion of the beef-patrol) / Goons of Hazzard / At my job / M.T.V. / Get off the air / Stars and stripes of corruption. (cd-iss. 1986 & Jun98; VIRUS 45CD) (cd re-iss. Feb01 on 'Decay'; DKS 11CD)		
Dec 86.	(lp/c/cd) <(VIRUS 50/+C/CD)> **BEDTIME FOR DEMOCRACY** – Take this job and shove it / Hop with the jet set / Dear Abby / Rambozo the clown / Fleshdunce / The great wall / Shrink / Triumph of the swill / I spy / Macho insecurity / Cesspools in Eden / One-way ticket to Pluto / Do the slag / Gone with the wind / A commercial / Anarchy for sale / Chickenshit conformist / Where do ya draw the line / Potshot heard round the world / D.M.S.O. / Lie detector. (cd re-iss. Jun98; same) (cd re-iss. Feb01 on 'Decay'; DKS 12CD)		

— split December '86 when RAY departed (he subsequently turned up in SKRAPYARD). KLAUS FLUORIDE went solo, releasing albums 'BECAUSE I SAY SO' (1988) and 'THE LIGHT IS FLICKERING' (1991) and forming acoustic outfit FIVE YEAR PLAN

– compilations, etc. –

on 'Alternative Tentacles' unless mentioned otherwise

Jun 87.	(lp/cd) <(VIRUS 57/+CD)> **GIVE ME CONVENIENCE OR GIVE ME DEATH** – Police truck / Too drunk to f*** / California uber alles / Man with the dogs / In sight / Life sentence / A child and his lawnmower / Holiday in Cambodia / Night of the living rednecks / I fought the law / Saturday night holocaust / Pull my strings / Short songs / Straight A's / Kinky sex makes the world go round / The prey. (cd+=/free flexi-disc) – BUZZBOMB FROM PASADENA (cd re-iss. Feb01 on 'Decay'; DKS 13CD)	84	
Jun 93.	(7"ep) Subterranean; (SUB 24) **NAZI PUNKS **** OFF / ARYANISMS. / ('A'live) / CONTEMPTUOUS** (re-iss. Dec97 & Jul00; same)		-
Feb 01.	(cd) Decay; (DKS 14CD) / Manifesto; <42905> **MUTINY ON THE BAY** (live)		Apr01

JELLO BIAFRA

Nov 87.	(lp) <(VIRUS 59)> **NO MORE COCOONS** (spoken word) (cd-iss. Mar93; VIRUS 59CD)		
Jul 89.	(d-lp) <(VIRUS 66)> **HIGH PRIEST OF HARMFUL MATTER (TALES OF THE TRIALS, LIVE)** (spoken word) (cd-iss. Mar93; VIRUS 66CD)		

LARD

BIAFRA, AL JOURGENSEN + PAUL BARKER (Ministry) / JEFF WARD – drums

Nov 89.	(12"ep/c-ep/cd-ep) <(VIRUS 72 T/C/CD)> **THE POWER OF LARD / HELL FUDGE. / TIME TO MELT (31 mins.)**		
Jul 90.	(lp/cd) <(VIRUS 84/+CD)> **THE LAST TEMPTATION OF LARD** – Forkboy / Pineapple face / Hate, spawn and die / Drug raid at 4a.m. / Can God fill teeth? / Bozo skeleton / Sylvestre Matuschka / They're coming to take me away / I am your clock.	69	

JELLO BIAFRA & D.O.A.

w/ JOE KEITHLEY + CHRIS PROHOM – guitar, vocals / BRIAN GOBLE – bass, vocals / JON CARD – drums

May 90.	(lp/cd) <(VIRUS 78/+CD)> **THE LAST SCREAM OF THE MISSING NEIGHBORS** – That's progress / Attack of the peacekeepers / Wish I was in El Salvador / Power is boring / We gotta get out of this place / Full metal jackoff.		

JELLO BIAFRA & NO MEANS NO

with TIPPER GORE BOB WRIGHT – guitar / JOHN WRIGHT – drums / JON CARD – percussion

Mar 91.	(lp/c/cd) <(VIRUS 85/+C/CD)> **THE SKY IS FALLING AND I WANT MY MOMMY** – The sky is falling and I want my mommy (falling space junk) / Jesus was a terrorist / Bruce's diary / Sad / Ride the flume / Chew / Sparks in the Gene pool / The myth is real – let's eat.		

JELLO BIAFRA

Jun 91.	(d-lp/c/cd) <(VIRUS 94/+C/CD)> **I BLOW MINDS FOR A LIVING** – Pledge of allegience / Talk on censorship – let us prey / Die for oil, sucker – higher octane version / I was a teenage pacifist / If voting changed anything . . . / Running for mayor / Grow more pot / Lost orgasm / Talk on censorship-Better living through new world orders + Fear of a free planet.		

TUMOR CIRCUS

— DARREN MOR-X / DALE FLAT-UM + MIKE MDRASKOID (of STEEL POLE BATH TUB) / KING GRONG CHARLIE (TOLNAY) (of LUBRICATED GOAT) + J. BIAFRA

Nov 91.	(lp/c/cd) <(VIRUS 087/+C/CD)> **TUMOR CIRCUS – HIGH VOLTAGE CONSPIRACY FOR RADICAL FREEDOM** – Hazing for success / Human cyst / The man with the corkscrew eyes / Fireball / Calcutta a-go-go / Turn off the respirator. (cd+=) Swine flu / Take me back or I'll drown our dog / Meathook up my rectum.		
Feb 92.	(7") <(VIRUS 102)> **MEATHOOK UP MY RECTUM. / (etched side)** (12"+=/cd-s+=) <(VIRUS 102 T/CD)> – Take me back or I'll drown the dog / Swine flu / Fireball.		

JELLO BIAFRA & MOJO NIXON

Nov 93.	(7") (VIRUS 136) **WILL THE FETUS BE ABORTED? / THE LOST WORLD** (cd-s+=) (VIRUS 136CD) – Drinkin' with Jesus / Achey raky heart.		-
Feb 94.	(lp/cd) <(VIRUS 137/+CD)> **PRAIRIE HOME INVASION** – Buy my snake oil / Where are we gonna work (when the trees are gone) / Convoy in the sky / Atomic power / Are you drinkin' with me Jesus / Love me, I'm a liberal / Burgers of wrath / Nostalgia for an angel that never existed / Hammer chicken plant disaster / Mascot mania / Let's go burn de Nashville down / Will the fetus be aborted? / Plastic Jesus. (cd re-iss. Apr00; same)		

JELLO BIAFRA

Oct 94.	(d-lp) <(VIRUS 150)> **BEYOND THE VALLEY OF THE GIFT POLICE** (spoken word) – Message to our sponsor / Experts / Ban everything / I have a dream / Talk on censorship / What we are not being told / President McMuffin tightens the belt / Talk on censorship / What we are not being told / In the belly of the wrong beast / Talk on censorship / Eric meets the moose diarrhea / Virturcrats unreality.		-

LARD

— see last line-up + add BILL RIEFLIN – drums

May 97.	(lp/c/cd) <(VIRUS 199/+MC/CD)> **PURE CHEWING SATISFACTION** – War pimp renaissance / I wanna be a drug sniffing dog / Moths / Generation execute / Faith hope and treachery / Peeling back the foreskin of liberty / Mangoat / Sidewinder.		
Jan 00.	(12"ep/cd-ep) <(VIRUS 235/+CD)> **70'S ROCK MUST DIE. / VOLCANUS 2000 (WE WIPE THE WORLD) / BALLAD OF MARSHALL LEDBETTER**		

JELLO BIAFRA

— (spoken word)

Oct 98.	(t-lp/d-cd) <(VIRUS 201/+CD)> **IF EVOLUTION IS OUTLAWED ONLY OUTLAWS WILL EVOLVE** – Depends on the drug / Wake up and smell the coffee / The murder of Mumia Abu Jemal / Clinton comes to Long Beach / Half time / Hex flies space shuttle sequel / New Soviet Union / Talk on censorship.		
Dec 01.	(3xcd-box) <(VIRUS)> **BECOME THE MEDIA**		Oct00
Apr 02.	(cd) <VIRUS 276> **THE BIG KA-BOOM – part one**	-	
Oct 02.	(3xcd-box) <VIRUS 290> **MACHINE GUN IN THE CLOWN'S HAND**	-	

– others, etc. –

Jul 00.	(12"; by JELLO BIAFRA, EAST BAY RAY & CHRISTIAN LUNCH) Subterranean; <(SUB 017)> **THE WITCH TRIALS**		

DEAF SCHOOL

Formed: Liverpool, England …early 1974 by large ensemble; BETTE BRIGHT, CLIFF HANGER, MR.AVERAGE, Rev. MAX RIPPLE, TIM WHITTAKER, ERIC SHARK, ENRICO CADILAC, IAN RITCHIE, MIKE EVANS, ROY HOLDER, ANN BRIGHT and HAZEL BARTRAM. The latter 4 departed before they were joined by PAUL PILNICK and this bunch won the prestigious at the time Melody Maker Rock Contest award, which led to a contract from 'Warners'. Their "New Wave" sound of Vaudevillian rock was highly popular for a time when punk rock and diversified fashions were the rage. Three albums were released, before all took off for greater pastures. BETTE BRIGHT cameod in the SEX PISTOLS film 'The Great Rock'n'roll Swindle' and 3 years later in 1981 married MADNESS singer

DEAF SCHOOL (cont) — THE GREAT INDIE DISCOGRAPHY — The 1970s

SUGGS. In 1988, BRIGHT, LANGER, LINDSAY, CADILLAC, SHARK and RIPPLE re-united for 5 sell-out concerts, to celebrate 10 years of separation. • **Songwriters:** LANGER / BRIGHT / ALLEN etc. • **Trivia:** Some members played for PORTSMOUTH SINFONIA ORCHESTRA on various intentional out-of-tune performances.

Album rating: SECOND HONEYMOON (*6) / DON'T STOP THE WORLD (*5) / ENGLISH BOYS, WORKING GIRLS (*4) / SECOND COMING compilation (*6)

ENRICO CADILLAC (b. STEVE ALLEN) – vocals / **BETTE BRIGHT** (b. ANN MARTIN, Whitstable, Kent) – vocals / **ERIC SHARK** (b. THOMAS DAVIS) – vocals / **CLIFF HANGER** (b. CLIVE LANGER) – guitar, piano, vocals / **The Rev. MAX RIPPLE** (b. JOHN WOOD) – keyboards, accordion / **MR. AVERAGE** (b. STEVE LINDSAY) – bass, piano, vocals / **IAN RITCHIE** – sax / **TIM WHITTAKER** – drums / **PAUL PILNICK** – guitar (ex-STEALER'S WHEEL)

		Warners	Warners
Aug 76.	(lp) (K 56280) **SECOND HONEYMOON**		-
	– What a way to end it all / Where's the weekend / Cocktails at 8 / Bigger splash / Knock knock knocking / 2nd honeymoon / Get set ready go / Nearly moonlit night motel / Room service / Hi Jo hi / Snapshots / Final act.		
Sep 76.	(7") (K 16812) **WHAT A WAY TO END IT ALL. / NEARLY MOONLIT NIGHT MOTEL**		-
—	now without PILNICK who had already left mid-76.		
Feb 77.	(7") (K 16870) **TAXI. / LAST NIGHT**		-
Mar 77.	(lp) (K 56364) **DON'T STOP THE WORLD**		-
	– Don't stop the world / What a jerk / Darling / Everything for the dancer / Capaldi's cafe / Hypertension / It's a boy's world / End / Operator.		
1977.	(d-lp) <2LS 3011> **DON'T STOP THE WORLD / SECOND HONEYMOON**	-	
Jan 78.	(7") (K 17087) **ALL QUEUED UP. / GOLDEN SHOWERS**		-
Feb 78.	(lp) (K 56450) <3169> **ENGLISH BOYS, WORKING GIRLS**		
	– Working girls / Golden showers / Thunder and lightning / What a week / Refugee / Ronny Zamora / English boys (with guns) / All queued up / I wanna be your boy / Morning after / Fire / O blow.		
Feb 78.	(7") (K 17100) **THUNDER AND LIGHTNING. / WORKING GIRLS**		-
—	Disbanded in Apr'78. STEVE ALLEN formed The ORIGINAL MIRRORS. WHITTAKER joined LORI & THE CHAMELEONS, before BIG IN JAPAN then PINK MILITARY. LINDSAY also joined BIG IN JAPAN and later The SECRETS then The PLANETS. RITCHIE went to JANE AIRE & THE BELVEDERES. BETTE BRIGHT went solo as did renowned producer to be CLIVE LANGER.		

– compilations, others, etc. –

Dec 88.	(lp) Demon; (FIEND 135) **SECOND COMING**		-
	– What a way to end it all / Shake some action / Hi Jo hi / Nearly moonlit night motel / Taxi / Ronny Zamora / Thunder and lightning / Blue velvet / Princess princess / I wanna be your boy / Lines / Capaldi's cafe / 2nd honeymoon / Final act. (cd-iss. Jan91; FIENDCD 135)		

DESPERATE BICYCLES

Formed: New Cross, London, England... March 1977 by DANNY WIGLEY (a man who later bravely attempted to rehabilitate the Rolf Harris-endorsed stylophone!), along with NICKY STEPHENS, ROGER STEPHENS and DAVE PAPWORTH. In a similar makeshift DIY-punk mould to the SWELL MAPS or SPIZZ, The DESPERATE BICYCLES released a handful of 45's throughout '77 and '78 on their own 'Refill' imprint. All limited edition affairs, the likes of 'SMOKESCREEN', 'THE MEDIUM WAS TEDIUM', the 'NEW CROSS NEW CROSS' EP and 'OCCUPIED TERRITORY' were successful without ever raising them above cult status. By the release of their debut album, 'REMORSE CODE' (1980), DANNY and NICKY were the only remaining members from the original line-up, DAN ELECTRO and JEFF TITLEY having replaced the rhythm section; after one final single, 'GRIEF IS VERY PERSONAL', WIGLEY and Co got on their bikes for good.

Album rating: REMORSE CODE (*6)

DANNY WIGLEY – vocals (later added stylophone!) / **NICKY STEPHENS** – organ / **ROGER STEPHENS** – bass / **DAVE PAPWORTH** – drums

		Refill	not iss.
Aug 77.	(7") (RR 1) **SMOKESCREEN. / HANDLEBARS**		-
Feb 78.	(7") (RR 2) **THE MEDIUM WAS TEDIUM. / DON'T BACK THE FRONT**		-
May 78.	(7"ep) (RR 3) **NEW CROSS NEW CROSS**		-
	– Holidays / The housewife song / Cars / (I make the) Product / Paradise lost / Advice on arrest.		
Jul 78.	(7") (RR 4) **OCCUPIED TERRITORY. / SKILL**		-
—	**DANNY + NICKY** (now on bass) recruited **DAN ELECTRO** – guitar / **JEFF TITLEY** – drums		
Feb 80.	(lp) (RR 6) **REMORSE CODE**		-
	– I am nine / Walking the talking channel / A can of lemonade / Pretty little analyse / Acting / It's somebody's birthday today / Sarcasm / Trendy feelings / Natural history / Blasting radio.		
Mar 80.	(7") (RR 7) **GRIEF IS VERY PERSONAL. / OBSTRUCTION CONUNDRUM**		-
—	disbanded after above		

DESTROY ALL MONSTERS

Formed: Detroit, Michigan, USA... 1973 by former model and visual artist NIAGARA, who was to be joined by veterans of the garage-punk era MIKE DAVIS (ex-MC5) and RON ASHETON (ex-STOOGES). In 1977, they played a handful of experimental gigs by which time the line-up had expanded to include LARRY and BEN MILLER. The following year, DESTROY ALL MONSTERS released a debut single, 'BORED', a record licensed to UK indie label, 'Cherry Red'. Punk-ish rock'n'roll characterised by NIAGARA's sexual monotone, the band's sound was developed over a further couple of singles, namely 'MEET THE CREEPER' and 'NOBODY KNOWS'. A disappointing tour of Britain led to them disbanding a year later, although two further US-only EP's did surface around the turn of the decade.

Album rating: BORED compilation (*7)

NIAGARA (b. LYNN ROVNER) – vocals, violin / **RON ASHETON** – guitar (ex-STOOGES) repl. CARY LOREN / **LARRY MILLER** – guitar repl. MIKE KELLY / **MIKE DAVIS** – bass (ex-MC5) / **RON KING** – drums repl. JIM SHAW / **BEN MILLER** – saxophone

		Cherry Red	Idibi
Jan 79.	(7"red) (CHERRY 3) **BORED. / YOU'RE GONNA DIE**		1978
Jun 79.	(7") (CHERRY 7) **MEET THE CREEPER. / NOVEMBER 22nd, 1963**		1978
Sep 79.	(7") (CHERRY 9) **NOBODY KNOWS. / WHAT DO I GET**		
		not iss.	Black Hole
1979.	(7"ep) <18551> **LIVE** (live)	-	
	– Assassination photograph / Dream snug / Destroy all monsters / There is no end.		
1980.	(7"ep) **BLACK OUT IN THE CITY**	-	
	– No change / Switch the topic / Time bomb 1977.		
—	disbanded; ASHETON formed NEW RACE		

– compilations, etc. –

1989.	(lp) Fan Club; (FC 050) **LIVE** (live)		-
	– Anyone can fuck her / Bored / Party girl / Fast city / Go away / Having it all / Boots / Little boyfriend / November 22nd, 1963 / Right stuff / Ground zero.		
1989.	(cd) Revenge; (MIG 11) **NOVEMBER 22nd, 1963 – SINGLES AND RARITIES**		-
	– Bored / You're gonna die / Meet the creeper / November 22nd, 1963 / Jesus is a shotgun / Nobody knows / What do I get / These boots are made for walking / Anybody can / Party girl / A/D (angel in the daytime, Devil at night).		
Oct 91.	(cd) Cherry Red; (CDMRED 94) **BORED**		-
	– Bored / You're gonna die / November 22nd 1963 / Meet the creeper / Nobody knows / What do I get? / Goin' to lose. (re-iss. Apr97 & Aug00; same)		
Oct 96.	(cd) Sympathy For The Record Industry; (SFTRI 444) **SILVER WEDDING**		-
Apr 98.	(lp) Get Back; (GET 31LP) **AMAZING...**		-

DEVIANTS (see under ⇒ PINK FAIRIES)

Willy DeVILLE (see under ⇒ MINK DeVILLE)

DEVO

Formed: Akron, Ohio, USA... 1972 by two sets of brothers, MARK and BOB MOTHERSBAUGH together with GERALD and BOB CASALE (drummer, ALAN MYERS completed the line-up. From the early 70's, they had been known as The DE-EVOLUTION BAND, before sensibly abbreviating the name to DEVO. This bunch of lab-coated weirdos (taking up The RESIDENTS terminally skewed vision) issued two obscure 45's on their own indie label, 'Booji Boy', which was heavily imported into Britain through leading indie outlet, 'Stiff', late in 1977. Early the following year, both the double A-sided 'MONGOLOID' / 'JOCKO HOMO' and a hilarious electro-fied rendition of The Rolling Stones' '(I CAN'T GET NO) SATISFACTION', were repressed due to popular demand, the singles subsequently becoming minor chart entries. After a third classic, 'BE STIFF' also hit UK Top 75, the flowerpot-headed, potato-faced futurists secured a deal with 'Virgin' ('Warners' in the US) and continued to inject a quirky humour into the po-faced New Wave movement with a fourth hit, 'COME BACK JONEE'. A debut album, inspiringly titled 'Q: ARE WE NOT MEN? A: WE ARE DEVO!' (produced by BRIAN ENO, who else!?), was released a month later to a confused but appreciative audience who helped propel the record into the Top 20 (Top 100 US). However, their follow-up set, 'DUTY NOW FOR THE FUTURE' (1979), suffered a slight backlash, the novelty wearing thin without the impact of a hit single. 1980's 'FREEDOM OF CHOICE' would have suffered a similar fate, but for a freak US Top 20 single, 'WHIP IT'. The rest of their 80's output lacked their early wit, although America embraced such albums as 'DEV-O LIVE' (1981), 'NEW TRADITIONALISTS' (1981), 'OH NO, IT'S DEVO' (1982) and 'SHOUT' (1984). Having disbanded in the middle of the decade, DEVO (with new drummer, DAVID KENDRICK) reformed in 1988, signing to 'Enigma' and releasing one non-event of an album after another. Their days of inspired innovation now behind them, the legacy of DEVO was nevertheless plundered to unusual effect when SOUNDGARDEN, SUPERCHUNK and even ROBERT PALMER!!! covered their 1980 classic, 'GIRL U WANT'. • **Songwriters:** GERALD and MARK wrote most of material, SECRET AGENT MAN (Johnny Rivers) / ARE U EXPERIENCED (Jimi Hendrix) / WORKING IN A COALMINE (Lee Dorsey). • **Trivia:** In 1982, DEVO had contributed services to choreographer TONI BASIL on her debut solo album 'WORD OF MOUTH'. In the late 70's, MARK had appeared on HUGH CORNWALL (of The STRANGLERS) and ROBERT WILLIAMS collaboration 'Nosferatu'.

DEVO (cont)

Album rating: Q: ARE WE NOT MEN? A: WE ARE DEVO! (*8) / DUTY NOW FOR THE FUTURE (*7) / FREEDOM OF CHOICE (*7) / DEV-O LIVE mini (*2) / NEW TRADITIONALISTS (*6) / OH NO! IT'S DEVO (*6) / SHOUT (*4) / E-Z LISTENING DISC collection (*4) / TOTAL DEVO (*4) / NOW IT CAN BE TOLD (DEVO AT THE PALACE 12/9/88) live (*5) / SMOOTH NOODLE MAPS (*4) / HARDCORE DEVO, VOL.1 compilation (*6) / THE GREATEST HITS compilation (*7) / HARDCORE DEVO, VOL.2 compilation (*5) / DEVO LIVE: THE MONGOLOID YEARS compilation (*4) / HOT POTATOES: THE BEST OF DEVO compilation (*8)

BOB MOTHERSBAUGH – vocals, guitar / **MARK MOTHERSBAUGH** – keyboards, synthesizers / **BOB CASALE** – guitar / **JERRY CASALE** – bass, vocals / **ALAN MYERS** – drums repl. JIM MOTHERSBAUGH

			Stiff	Booji Boy
Feb 78.	(7")	*(DEV 1)* <7033-14> **MONGOLOID. / JOCKO HOMO**	62	1977
Apr 78.	(7")(12")	*(DEV 2)(BOY 1)* **(I CAN'T GET ME NO) SATISFACTION. / SLOPPY (I SAW MY BABY GETTING)** <re-iss. 1978 on 'Bomp'; 72843>	41	1977

			Stiff	not iss.
Jul 78.	(7"clear,7"lemon)	*(BOY 2)* **BE STIFF. / SOCIAL FOOLS**	71	–

			Virgin	Warners
Aug 78.	(7"grey)	*(VS 223)* **COME BACK JONEE. / SOCIAL FOOLS**	60	–
Sep 78.	(lp/c)	*(V/TCV 2106)* <3239> **Q: ARE WE NOT MEN? A: WE ARE DEVO!**	12	78

– Uncontrollable urge / (I can't get no) Satisfaction / Praying hands / Space junk / Mongoloid / Jocko homo / Too much paranoias / Gut feeling – (slap your mammy) / Come back Jonee / Sloppy (I saw my baby getting) / Shrivel-up. (w/free flexi-7"; VDJ 27) (pic-lp; VP 2106)

Jan 79.	(7")	<WB 8745> **COME BACK JONEE. / PRAYING HANDS**	–	
Jun 79.	(7")	*(VS 265)* **THE DAY MY BABY GAVE ME A SURPRIZE. / PENETRATION IN THE CENTREFOLD**	–	
Jun 79.	(lp/c)	*(V/TCV 2125)* <3337> **DUTY NOW FOR THE FUTURE**	49	73

– Devo corporate anthem / Clockout / Timing X / Wiggly world / Blockhead / Strange pursuit / S.I.B. (Swelling Itching Brain) / Triumph of the will / The day my baby gave me a surprize / Pink pussycat / Secret agent man / Smart patrol – Mr. DNA / Red eye. (re-iss. Mar84 lp/c; OVED/+C 38)

Jul 79.	(7")	<WBS 49028> **SECRET AGENT MAN. / RED EYE EXPRESS**	–	–
Aug 79.	(7")	*(VS 280)* **SECRET AGENT MAN. / SOO BAWLS**	–	–
May 80.	(7")	*(VS 350)* **GIRL U WANT. / TURN AROUND**	–	–
May 80.	(lp/c)	*(V/TCV 2162)* <3435> **FREEDOM OF CHOICE**	47	22

– Girl u want / It's not right / Whip it / Snowball / Ton o' luv / Freedom of choice / Gates of steel / Cold war / Don't you know / That's Pep! / Mr. B's ballroom / Planet Earth. (re-iss. Mar84 lp/c; OVED/+C 39)

Jul 80.	(7")	<WBS 49524> **GIRL U WANT. / MR. B'S BALLROOM**	–	–
Aug 80.	(7")	<WBS 49550> **WHIP IT. / TURN AROUND**	–	14
Nov 80.	(7")	*(VS 383)* **WHIP IT. / SNOWBALL**	51	–
	(12"+=)	*(VS 383-12)* – Gates of steel.		
Nov 80.	(7")	<WBS 49621> **FREEDOM OF CHOICE. / SNOWBALL**	–	–
Mar 81.	(7")	<WBS 49711> **GATES OF STEEL. / BE STIFF (live)**	–	–
May 81.	(m-lp/m-c)	*(OVED 1)* <3548> **DEV-O LIVE (live)**	49	Apr81

– Freedom of choice (theme song) / Whip it / Girl u want / Gates of steel / Be stiff / Planet Earth.

Jun 81.	(7")	<WBS > **THROUGH BEING COOL. / GOING UNDER**	–	–
Aug 81.	(7")	*(VS 450)* **THROUGH BEING COOL. / RACE OF DOOM**	–	–
Aug 81.	(lp/c)	*(V/TCV 2191)* <3595> **NEW TRADITIONALISTS**	50	24

– Through being cool / Jerkin' back 'n' forth / Pity you / Soft things / Going under / Race of doom / Love without anger / The super thing / Beautiful world / Enough said. (re-iss. Aug87 lp/c; OVED/+C 73)

| Aug 81. | (7") | <WBS 47204> **WORKING IN A COALMINE. / PLANET EARTH** | – | – |

<above issued on 'Full Moon' US>

Oct 81.	(7")	*(VS 457)* **WORKING IN A COALMINE. / ENOUGH SAID**	–	–
Oct 81.	(7")	<WBS 49834> **BEAUTIFUL WORLD. / ENOUGH SAID**	–	–
Jan 82.	(7")	*(VS 470)* **BEAUTIFUL WORLD. / THE SUPER THING**	–	–
Mar 82.	(7")	<WBS 50010> **JERKIN' BACK 'N' FORTH. / MECHA MANIA BOY**	–	–
Oct 82.	(7")<US-7"/12">	*(VS 536)* <WBS 29931/29906> **PEEK-A-BOO. / FIND OUT**	–	–
Oct 82.	(lp/c)	*(V/TCV 2241)* <23741> **OH NO! IT'S DEVO**	–	47

– Time out for fun / Peek-a-boo / Out of synch / Explosions / That's good / Patterns / Big mess / Speed racer / What I must do / I desire / Deep sleep. (re-iss. Aug88 lp/c; OVED/+C 122)

| Jan 83. | (7") | <WBS 29811> **THAT'S GOOD. / WHAT MUST I DO** | – | – |
| Jun 83. | (7"/12") | *(MCA/+T 822)* <52215> **THEME FROM DOCTOR DETROIT. / (track by James Brown)** | | 59 May83 |

(above issued on 'M.C.A.' UK / 'Backstreet' US)

			Warners	Warners
Oct 84.	(7")	<29133> **ARE YOU EXPERIENCED?. / GROWING PAINS**	–	–
Oct 84.	(lp/c)	*(925 097-1/-4)* <25097> **SHOUT!**	–	83

– Shout / The satisfied mind / Don't rescue me / The 4th dimension / C'mon / Here to go / Jurisdiction of love / Puppet boy / Please please / Are you experienced?

| Mar 85. | (7") | *(W 9119)* **SHOUT. / C'MON** | – | – |
| | (d7"+=) | *(W 9119F)* – Mongoloid / Jocko homo. | | |

— **DAVID KENDRICK** – drums; repl. MYERS

			Enigma	Enigma
Jul 88.	(lp/c/cd)	*(ENVLP/TCENV/CDENV 503)* <73303> **TOTAL DEVO**	–	Jun88

– Baby doll / Disco dancer / Some things never change / Plain truth / Happy guy / Don't be cruel / I'd cry if you died / Agitated / Man turned inside out / Blow up. (cd re-iss. Mar95 on 'Restless'; 72756-2)

| Jul 89. | (3 sided-lp/cd) | *(ENVLP/CDENV 532)* **NOW IT CAN BE TOLD (DEVO AT THE PALACE 12/9/88) (live)** | – | – |

(cd re-iss. Mar95 on 'Restless';)

Oct 90.	(7")	**POST-POST MODERN MAN. / WHIP IT (live)**	–	–
	(12"+=)	– ('A'-Ultra post mix).		
	(cd-s++=)	– Baby doll (mix).		

| Oct 90. | (cd/c/lp) | *(CDENV/TVENV/ENVLP 1006)* <73526> **SMOOTH NOODLE MAPS** | – | Jun90 |

– Stuck in a loop / Post-post modern man / When we do it / Spin the wheel / Morning dew / A chance is gonna cum / The big picture / Pink jazz trancers / Devo has feelings too / Jimmy / Danghaus. (re-iss. cd Mar95 on 'Restless'; 72757-2)

– compilations, etc. –

Jan 79.	(m-lp)	*Stiff; (ODD 1)* **BE STIFF** (first 3 singles)	–	–
May 83.	(12"ep)	*Virgin; (VS 594-12)* **COME BACK JONEE. / WHIP IT / + 2**	–	–
Aug 87.	(cd)	*Rykodisc; <RCD2 0031>* **E-Z LISTENING DISC** (UK-iss.Nov91; same as US)	–	–
Oct 90.	(cd)	*Fan Club; (FC 065) / Rykodisc; <RCD/RLP 10188>* **HARDCORE DEVO, VOL.1** (demos 74-77) (re-iss. c Mar94 on 'New Rose'; 422105)		Aug90
Dec 90.	(cd)	*Warners;* <26449> **THE GREATEST HITS**	–	–
Dec 90.	(cd)	*Warners;* <26450> **THE REST: GREATEST MISSES**	–	–
Dec 91.	(cd)	*Rykodisc;* <(RCD 20208)> **HARDCORE DEVO, VOL.2: 1974-1977** (re-iss. c Mar94; RACS 0208)		Aug91
Oct 92.	(cd)	*Rykodisc;* <(RCD 20209)> **DEVO LIVE: THE MONGOLOID YEARS (live)**		
Jun 93.	(cd)	*Virgin; (CDV 2106)* **Q: ARE WE NOT MEN? A: WE ARE DEVO / DEV-O LIVE**		
Jun 93.	(cd)	*Virgin; (CDV 2125)* **DUTY NOW FOR THE FUTURE / NEW TRADITIONALISTS**		
Jun 93.	(cd)	*Virgin; (CDV 2241)* **OH NO! IT'S DEVO / FREEDOM OF CHOICE**		
Sep 93.	(cd/c)	*Virgin; (CDVM/TCVM 9016)* **HOT POTATOES: THE BEST OF DEVO**		–

– Jocko homo / Mongoloid / Satisfaction (I can't get me no) / Whip it / Girl u want / Freedom of choice / Peek-a-boo / Thru being cool / That's good / Working in a coalmine / Devo corporate anthem / Be stiff / Gates of steel / Come back Jonee / Secret agent man / The day my baby gave me a surprise / Beautiful world / Big mess / Whip it (HMS & M remix). (lp-iss.Apr01 on 'Simply Vinyl'; SVLP 320)

| Oct 94. | (3xcd-box) | *Virgin; (TPAK 38)* **THE COMPACT COLLECTION** | | |

– (Q: ARE WE NOT MEN / DUTY NOW FOR THE FUTURE / OH NO IT'S DEVO!)

Aug 96.	(cd-rom)	*Discovery; <none>* **ADVENTURES OF SMART PATROL**	–	–
May 00.	(d-cd)	*Rhino;* <(8122 75967-2)> **PIONEERS WHO GOT SCALPED: THE ANTHOLOGY**		
Apr 02.	(cd)	*Rhino;* <76037> **THE ESSENTIALS**	–	–

Howard DEVOTO (see under ⇒ MAGAZINE)

DICKIES

Formed: San Fernando Valley, California, USA ... 1977 by CHUCK WAGON, STAN LEE, BILLY CLUB, LEONARD PHILLIPS and KARLOS KABALLERO. Forebears to the likes of GREEN DAY and a poppier prototype of English cover fiends, SNUFF, the DICKIES initially made a name for themselves on the L.A. punk scene through their rabid, tongue-in-cheek versions of rock's sacred cows. Signed to 'A&M', the band's eponymous debut three-tracker surfaced in Spring '78, leading with a frantic reading of Black Sabbath's 'PARANOID'. This was subsequently released as a single in its own right, followed up by a trashing of the Barry McGuire protest classic, 'EVE OF DESTRUCTION'. Christmas '78, meanwhile, saw what else but a rendition of 'SILENT NIGHT', DICKIES style (backed with a none too quiet cover of Simon & Garfunkel's 'SOUNDS OF SILENCE'), a track that gave them an early Top 50 hit. While not featured on debut album, 'THE INCREDIBLE SHRINKING DICKIES' (1979), early '79's version of The Moody Blues' 'NIGHTS IN WHITE SATIN' was a stage favourite and a hit second time around later that year. The DICKIES' defining moment, however, came with their punked-up pilgrimage to classic 70's kids TV, a cover of the theme tune to 'Banana Splits'. A Top 10 UK hit, it cemented the band's reputation as a punk novelty act although the DICKIES' self-penned good-time three-chord anthems won them respect among the safety-pin crew on both sides of the Atlantic. A prolific year came to a close with the release of a follow-up album, 'DAWN OF THE DICKIES', again drawing inspiration from B-movies and assorted American cultural debris. Sadly, CHUCK committed suicide in summer '81, effectively halting the band's career. Although 1983's 'STUKAS OVERT DISNEYLAND' comprised recordings made before CHUCK's death, the band didn't re-emerge with new material until the late 80's. With a line-up of PHILLIPS, LEE, LORENZO BUNHE, JEROME ANGEL, ENOCH HAIN and CLIFF MARTINEZ, the DICKIES inked a deal with 'Enigma' and released the 'KILLER KLOWNS FROM OUTER SPACE' EP in late '88. An album, 'SECOND COMING', followed in '89, replete with the usual helping of cover versions including Gene Pitney's 'TOWN WITHOUT PITY'. The early 90's saw future SMASHING PUMPKINS keyboard player, JONATHON MELVOIN, come on board while a new deal with L.A.'s 'Triple X' label was inaugurated with 'ROADKILL' (1993). Come 1998, the DICKIES were still chasing their proverbial tail with 'DOGS FROM THE HARE THAT BIT US', basically a covers set ripping into Iron Butterfly's 'UNCONSCIOUS POWER', Uriah Heep's 'EASY LIVIN', the Beatles' 'THERE'S A PLACE', etc. Just when we thought The DICKIES had popped their proverbial clogs, they were back once again with a ... er, fresh batch of songs, 'ALL THIS AND PUPPET STEW' (2001), featuring the Human Beinz' 'NOBODY BUT ME'. When will groups move on from cartoon punk-pop? Don't hurry back lads.

DICKIES (cont)

Album rating: THE INCREDIBLE SHRINKING DICKIES (*7) / DAWN OF THE DICKIES (*7) / STUKAS OVER DISNEYLAND (*6) / WE AREN'T THE WORLD (*5) / SECOND COMING (*4) / GREAT DICTATIONS (THE DEFINITIVE DICKIES COLLECTION) compilation (*6) / IDJIT SAVANT (*5) / DOGS FROM THE HARE THAT BIT US (*5) / ALL THIS AND PUPPET STEW (*4)

LEONARD GRAVES PHILLIPS – vocals, keyboards / **STAN LEE** (b.24 Sep'56) – guitar, vocals / **CHUCK WAGON** (b. BOB DAVIS) – keyboards, guitar / **BILLY CLUB** – bass, vocals / **KARLOS KABALLERO** – drums

A&M / A&M

- May 78. (12"m) <12-008> **THE DICKIES**
  – Paranoid / Hideous / You drive me ape (you big gorilla).
- Jun 78. (7",7"clear) *(AMS 7368)* **PARANOID. / I'M OK, YOU'RE OK**
  (re-iss. Jul79; same) – hit UK No.45
- Aug 78. (7",7"pink) *(AMS 7373)* **EVE OF DESTRUCTION. / DOGGIE DO**
- Oct 78. (7",7"white) *(AMS 7391)* **GIVE IT BACK. / YOU DRIVE ME APE (YOU BIG GORILLA)**
- Dec 78. (7",7"white) *(AMS 7403)* **SILENT NIGHT. / THE SOUNDS OF SILENCE** — 47
- Jan 79. (7") <2225> **NIGHTS IN WHITE SATIN. / MANNY, MOE & JACK**
- Feb 79. (lp,yellow-lp,blue-lp,orange-lp) *(AMLE 64742)* **THE INCREDIBLE SHRINKING DICKIES**
  – Give it back / Poodle party / Paranoid / She / Shadow man / Mental ward / Eve of destruction / You drive me ape (you big gorilla) / Waterslide / Walk like an egg / Curb job / Shake and bake / Rondo. *<cd-iss. Sep00 on 'Captain Oi' cd/lp; AHOY CD/LP 149)> (pic-lp iss.Mar01; AHOYPD 149)*
- Apr 79. (7",7"clear) *(AMS 7431)* **BANANA SPLITS (TRA LA LA SONG). / HIDEOUS / GOT IT AT THE STORE** — 7
- May 79. (7") <2241> **BANANA SPLITS (TRA LA LA SONG). / THE SOUNDS OF SILENCE**
- Jun 79. (7",7"purple; by CHUCK WAGON) *(AMS 7450)* **ROCK'N'ROLL WON'T GO AWAY. / THE SPY IN MY FACE**
- Aug 79. (7"white) *(AMS 7469)* **NIGHTS IN WHITE SATIN. / WATERSLIDE** — 39
- Oct 79. (lp,blue-lp) *(AMLH 68510)* **DAWN OF THE DICKIES**
  – Where did his eye go / Fan mail / Manny, Moe & Jack / Infedil zombie / I'm a chollo / Nights in white satin / (I'm stuck in a pagoda) With Tricia Toyota / I've got a splitting headache / Attack of the mole men / She loves me not. *<cd-iss. Sep00 on 'Captain Oi' cd/lp; AHOY CD/LP 150)>*
- Nov 79. (7") *(AMS 7491)* **MANNY, MOE & JACK. / SHE LOVES ME NOT**
- Jan 80. (7"red) *(AMS 7504)* **FAN MAIL. / (I'M STUCK IN A PAGODA) WITH TRICIA TOYOTA**
- Jul 80. (7"yellow) *(AMS 7544)* **GIGANTOR. / BOWLING WITH BEDROCK BARNEY**

— CHUCK WAGON committed suicide in June '81 as the band continued in a lower profile (below recordings between 1980-83 with CHUCK)

— other people used incl. **SCOTT SINDON + STEVE HUFSTETER** – guitar / **LORENZO BUHNE** – bass / **JEROME ANGEL** – drums, percussion

not iss. / P.V.C.

- 1983. (lp) <6903> **STUKAS OVER DISNEYLAND**
  – Rosemary / She's a hunch back / Out of sight, out of mind / Communication breakdown / Pretty please me / Wagon train / If Stuart could talk / Stukas over Disneyland. *(UK cd-iss. Jul95 on 'Restless'; 772247-2) (re-iss. Jul98 on 'Overground' 10"lp/cd; OVER 76/+CD) <cd re-iss. May00 on 'Triple X'; TX 51265CD)>*

— **PHILLIPS, LEE, ANGEL + BUHNE** plus newcomers **ENOCH HAIN** – guitar / **CLIFF MARTINEZ** – drums

Enigma-Virgin / Enigma

- Nov 88. (12"ep) <D2 73322> **KILLER KLOWNS FROM OUTER SPACE**
  – Killer klowns / Booby trap / Jim Bowie / Magoomba / Eep oop ork (uh uh). *(UK cd-iss. Jul95 on 'Restless'; 772554-2)*
- May 89. (lp/c/cd) *(ENVLP/TCENV/CDENV 526)* <73289> **SECOND COMING** — Feb89
  – Hair / Monster island / Town without pity / Cross-eyed Tammy / Going homo / Dummy up / Booby trap / Magoomba / Caligula / I'm Stan / Monkey see, monkey do. *(cd re-iss. Jul95 on 'Restless'; 772553-2)*

Overground / not iss.

- Jul 90. (7"white,7"mauve,7"blue) *(OVER 12)* **JUST SAY YES. / AYATOLLAH YOU SO**
- Oct 90. (7"flexi-tour) *(OVER 17)* **ROADKILL**

Receiver / not iss.

- Apr 91. (cd/c/lp) *(RR CD/LC/LP 137)* **LIVE IN LONDON – LOCKED 'N' LOADED 1990 (live)**
  – Attack of the killer clowns from Outer Space / Eve of destruction / Nights in white satin / Pretty please me / You drive me ape (you big gorilla) / Give it back / Just say yes / (Stuck in a pagoda) With Tricia Toyota / Curb job / Cross-eyed Tammy / Going homo / She's a hunch back / If Stuart could talk / Manny, Moe & Jack / Paranoid / Gigantor / Communication breakdown / Banana splits / Fan mail. *<US-iss.Sep02 on 'Sanctuary'; 81164>*

— now with **JONATHAN MELVOIN** – keyboards (of SMASHING PUMPKINS)

Triple X / Relativity

- May 93. (cd-ep) <(TX 51149CD)> **ROADKILL**
  – Roadkill / Just say yes / Dead heat.
- Sep 94. (cd/c) <(51168-2/-4)> **IDJIT SAVANT** — Jan95
  – Welcome to the diamond mine / Golden boys / Pretty ballerina / Elevator / Oh baby / Make it so / I'm on crack / I'm stuck in a condo (with Marlon Brando) / Zeppelina / Roadkill / House of Raoul / Song of the dawn. *(cd re-iss. Mar95 & Aug99 on 'Golf'; CDHOLE 002)*
- 1995. (7") *(HOLE 008)* **MAKE IT SO. / OH BABY**
  (above issued on 'Golf' records)
- Jun 98. (10"lp/cd) <TX 51232/+CD> **DOGS FROM THE HARE THAT BIT US**
  – Intro / Solitary confinement / Easy livin' / Unconscious power / There's a place / Nobody but me / Can't let go / Let me out / Epistle to Dippy.

Fat Wreck Chords / Fat Wreck Chords

- Apr 01. (7"blue) <(FAT 629)> **FREE WILLY. / SHORT MUSIC FOR SHORT PEOPLE**
- May 01. (lp/cd) <(FAT 608/+CD)> **ALL THIS AND PUPPET STEW**
  – See my way / Keep watchin' the skies / Free Willy / Donut man / Howdy doody in the woodshed II / Marry me, Ann / Sobriety / I did it / Whack the Dalai Lama / He's courtin' Courtney / Nobody but me / My pop the cop / It's huge.

– compilations, etc. –

- Apr 86. (c) *R.O.I.R.; <A 140>* **WE AREN'T THE WORLD (live '78-'85)**
  (cd-iss. Nov94; RE 140CD)
- Mar 89. (lp/c/cd) *A&M; (AMA/AMC/CDA 5236)* **GREAT DICTATIONS (THE DEFINITIVE DICKIES COLLECTION)**
  – Hideous / You drive me ape (you big gorilla) / Give it back / Paranoid / I'm ok, you're ok / Got it at the store / The sounds of silence / Banana splits (tra la la song) / Nights in white satin / (Stuck in a pagoda) With Tricia Toyota / Manny, Moe & Jack / Fan mail / Attack of the mole men / Gigantor / Eve of destruction / Silent night.
- Jun 99. (cd) *R.O.I.R.; <(RUSCD 8252)>* **STILL LIVE EVEN IF YOU DON'T WANT IT**

DICTATORS

Formed: The Bronx, New York, USA ... 1974 by ROSS THE BOSS FUNICELLO, MARK "The Animal" MENDOZA, main songwriter ADNY (ANDY) SHERNOFF, SCOTT KEMPNER and STU BOY KING, who were soon joined by "Handsome" DICK MANITOBA. Exploding onto the embryonic NY punk scene at the same time as bands like The RAMONES and The HEARTBREAKERS, the group harnessed the energy of garage-rock to a raucous pre-MOTORHEAD metallic bludgeon. Signed to the 'Epic' label, they nevertheless delivered a rather poorly-received debut album in 1975, 'GO GIRL CRAZY!', which included a few covers including Sonny & Cher's 'I GOT YOU BABE'. 'Asylum' subsequently took up the reins, releasing the much-improved 'MANIFEST DESTINY' (1977), a hard-rocking set that featured their version of Iggy (Pop) & The Stooges' 'SEARCH & DESTROY' (one of the first ever tracks to be released on the 12" format). The single, which also featured new drummer RITCHIE TEETER, surprisingly hit the UK Top 50, although a third album, 'BLOOD BROTHERS' failed to garner any wider support from the evolving punk scene, The DICTATORS were also misunderstood by purist metal fans. ROSS THE BOSS and MENDOZA finally found some degree of recognition with MANOWAR and TWISTED SISTER respectively. Missing from the 80's and 90's, ROSS, SCOTT, ANDY, DICK and J.P. THUDERBOLT PATTERSON combined their resources for another stab at the rock world. The album 'D.F.F.D.' (2001) – meaning Dictators Forever Forever Dictators – was a barrage of heavy-meets-punk sounds, from the opener 'WHO WILL SAVE ROCK AND ROLL?' to the savage finale 'BURN, BABY, BURN!!', the bloodthirsty masters of rock were back.

Album rating: GO GIRL CRAZY (*7) / MANIFEST DESTINY (*6) / BLOODBROTHERS (*6) / FUCK 'EM IF THEY CAN'T TAKE A JOKE (*6) / D.F.F.D. (*7)

'HANDSOME' DICK MANITOBA (b. RICHARD BLUM, 29 Jan'54) – vocals / **ROSS THE BOSS FUNICELLO** (b. 3 Jan'54) – guitar, vocals / **ADNY SHERNOFF** (b. ANDY, 19 Apr'52) – vocals, bass / **SCOTT KEMPNER** (b. 6 Feb'54) – guitar, vocals / **STU BOY KING** – drums, percussion

Epic / Epic

- Dec 75. (lp) *(EPC 80767)* <33348> **GO GIRL CRAZY!**
  – The next big thing / I got you babe / Back to Africa / Master race rock / Teengenerate / California sun / Two tub man / Weekend / (I live for) Cars and girls. *(cd-iss. Jul93 on 'Sony Europe';)*

— **RITCHIE TEETER** (b.16 Mar'51, Long Island, N.Y.) – drums; repl. STU

— added **MARK MENDOZA** (b.13 Jul'56, Long Island) – bass

Asylum / Asylum

- Jun 77. (7") <45420> **DISEASE. / HEY BOYS**
- Jun 77. (lp) *(K 53061)* <7E 1109> **MANIFEST DESTINY**
  – Exposed / Heartache / Sleepin' with the T.V. on / Disease / Hey boys / Steppin' out / Science gone too far! / Young, fast, scientific / Search & destroy.
- Aug 77. (7") <45470> **SLEEPIN' WITH THE T.V. ON. / SCIENCE GONE TOO FAR**
- Sep 77. (7"/12") *(K 13091/+T)* **SEARCH & DESTROY. / SLEEPIN' WITH THE T.V. ON** — 49

— now without MENDOZA who later joined TWISTED SISTER

- Aug 78. (lp) *(K 53083)* <147> **BLOODBROTHERS**
  – Faster & louder / Baby let's twist / No tomorrow / The Minnesota strip / Stay with me / I stand tall / Borneo Jimmy / What is it / Slow death.
- Aug 78. (7") <45523> **I STAND TALL. / TOO MUCH FUN**

not iss. / Hampore

- 1980. (lp) <10017> **DICTATORS**
  – The next big thing / Disease / Hey boys / Two tub man / The moon upstairs / Weekend / New York, New York / I stand tall / Slow death.

— disbanded 1980. ROSS formed SHAKIN' STREET and later MANOWAR. DICK and SHERNOFF later formed MANITOBA'S WILD KINGDOM. In 1990, they were joined by FUNICELLO, MANITOBA, KEMPNER and FRANK FUNARO – drums (ex-DEL-LORDS), SHERNOFF and FRANK FUNARO – drums reformed The DICTATORS. In 2001, the same line-up were back again

Dictators / Dictators

- Oct 01. (cd) <(DFFD 2)> **D.F.F.D.**
  – Who will save rock and roll / I am right! / Pussy and money / The moronic inferno / It's alright / What's up with that? / The savage beat / In the presence of a new god / Avenue A / Channel surfing / Jim Gordon blues / Burn, baby, burn!!

DICTATORS (cont)

		Norton	Norton
Oct 01.	(7") <(45052)> **I AM RIGHT! / LOYOLA**	☐	☐
Oct 01.	(7") <(45103)> **AVENUE A. / NEW YORK NEW YORK** (live)	☐	☐

– compilations, others, etc. –

1981.	(c) *R.O.I.R.;* <A 102> **FUCK 'EM IF THEY CAN'T TAKE A JOKE** (cd-iss. Nov94 on 'Danceteria'; DANCD 052)	-	☐
Jan 97.	(cd-s) *White Jazz;* (JAZZ 003CD) **I AM RIGHT**	☐	-
Nov 97.	(7"; split with The NOMADS) *Next Big Thing;* (NBT 4527)	☐	-
Dec 98.	(cd) *ROIR;* <(RUSCD 8247)> **NEW YORK NEW YORK – THE DICTATORS LIVE** (live)	☐	☐

— (there is also two tribute albums out there on 'Roto' RTI 205/206)

DIFFORD & TILBROOK (see under ⇒ SQUEEZE)

Steve DIGGLE / FLAG OF CONVENIENCE (see under ⇒ BUZZCOCKS)

DILS

Formed: San Diego, California, USA ... early 1977, by brothers CHIP and TONY KINMAN, who recruited drummer ENDRE ALQUOVER. This seminal punk act released two much sought after 45's, 'I HATE THE RICH' and 'CLASS WAR', before a succession of drummers passed through their ranks. In 1980, The DILS issued their finale in the shape of the 'MADE IN CANADA' EP, the KINMAN siblings changing direction and moniker completely for the 80's. Enlisting the help of ALEJANDRO ESCOVEDO and subsequently SLIM EVANS, the new RANK & FILE set up home in New York. The KINMAN brothers were well versed in the application of razor sharp attitude; combining this with a rootsy, gritty country sound, they almost singlehandedly initiated the ubiquitous cowpunk genre of the early-mid 80's. Signed to 'Slash', a label which became synonymous with the scene, the group released their debut album, 'SUNDOWN', in 1982 to widespread critical acclaim; The EVERLY BROTHERS later covered one of the stand-out tracks, 'AMANDA RUTH'. Lacing poppy melodies and clear-eyed harmonies with darker lyrical and musical hues, the band were unfortunately never fully accepted by either the punk or the country fraternity. A subsequent split led to the departure of both EVANS and ESCOVEDO, the KINMANS heading to Austin, Texas, where they cut a further couple of albums, 'LONG GONE DEAD' (1984) and 'RANK AND FILE' (1987) to minimal interest. ESCOVEDO meanwhile, formed the TRUE BELIEVERS with his brother JAVIER before going on to a solo career in the 90's. Eventually dissolving RANK AND FILE, the KINMANS formed BLACKBIRD, an experimental project combining elements from the burgeoning industrial scene with their trademark alt-country sound. • **Covered:** WHAT GOES ON (Velvet Underground) / WRECK OF THE OLD 97 (Lewey-Noell-Work).

Album rating: LIVE: DILS (*6) / Rank & File: SUNDOWN (*5) / LONG GONE DEAD (*5) / RANK AND FILE (*4)

DILS

CHIP KINMAN (b. 4 Oct'57, Edenton, North Carolina) – vocals, guitar / **TONY KINMAN** (b. 3 Apr'56, Quantico, Virginia) – bass, vocals / **ENDRE ALQUOVER** – drums

		not iss.	What
Sep 77.	(7") <WHAT 02> **I HATE THE RICH. / YOU'RE NOT BLANK**	-	☐
		not iss.	Dangerhouse
Dec 77.	(7") <SLA 268> **198 SECONDS OF THE DILS** – Class war / Mr. Big.	-	☐

— **RAND McNALLY** (aka ZIPPY PINHEAD) – drums (ex-DOA) repl. JOHN SILVERS, who repl. ALQUOVER

		not iss.	Rogelletti
Apr 80.	(d7"ep) <RR 001> **MADE IN CANADA** – Sound of the rain / Not worth it / Red rockers.	-	☐

— split when the brothers formed RANK & FILE. McNALLY formed LOS POPULAROS

– compilations, etc. –

Aug 87.	(lp) *Triple XXX;* <(51003-1)> **LIVE: DILS** (live 1980) – I hate the rich / You're not blank / Tell her you love her / Tell me what I want to hear / It's not worth it / You're not blank / Red rockers rule / Mr. Big / Sound of the rain / Gimme a break / Modern Don Juan / Class war. <(re-iss. Jan00 as 'CLASS WAR' on 'Bacchus Archives' lp/cd; BA 1132/+CD)>	☐	☐
1990.	(lp) *Lost;* **THE DILS** (live) (UK cd-iss. Jul92 on 'Damaged Goods'; DAMGOOD 008)	-	☐
Dec 01.	(lp/cd) *Bacchus Archives;* <(BA 1166/+CD)> **DILS DILS DILS** – Blow up / Class war / Mr. Big / Sound of the rain / It's not worth it / Red rockers / Citizen / National Guard / What goes on / Wimp / LOve house / Wreck of the Old 97 / New kicks / C.A.R. / Before the law / Some things never change.	☐	Nov01

RANK & FILE

CHIP KINMAN – guitar, vocals / **TONY KINMAN** – bass, vocals / **ALEJANDRO ESCOVEDO** (b.10 Jan'51, San Antonio, Texas) – vocals, guitar (ex-NUNS, ex-JUDY NYLON)

		not iss.	Jackalope
1981.	(7") **LUCKY DAY. / AMANDA RUTH**	-	☐

— added **SLIM EVANS** (b. JIM) – drums

		Rough Trade	Slash
Jan 84.	(lp) (ROUGH 67) <23833> **SUNDOWN** – Amanda Ruth / (Glad I'm) Not in love / Rank and file / The conductor wore black / Sundown / I went walking / Lucky day / I don't go out much anymore / Coyote. (re-iss. Jan87 on 'Slash' lp/c; SLMP/SLMC 18)	☐	Apr83

— **KINMAN's** recruited session people **STAN LYNCH** – drums, percussion (of TOM PETTY & THE HEARTBREAKERS) / **RICHARD GREENE** – fiddle / **JEFF ROSS** – guitar / **PETER GRANT** – guitar, steel guitar, banjo / **BILL MEYERS** – woodwind

— ESCOVEDO joined The TRUE BELIEVERS before going solo

		Slash	Slash
Jun 84.	(7") (LASH 2) **RANK & FILE. / AMANDA RUTH** (12"+=) (LASHX 2) – I'm an old man.	☐	☐
Jul 84.	(lp) (SLAP 2) **LONG GONE DEAD** – Long gone dead / I'm an old man / Sound of the rain / Hot wind / Tell her I love her / Saddest girl in the world / Timeless love / John Brown / Last night I dreamed / It don't matter.	☐	☐
		not iss.	Rhino
1987.	(cd) <RNCD 70830> **RANK AND FILE** – Black book / One big thing / Golden age / Rbt / Pistol dawn / Sweet life / Good times / Oh! that girl / Unlucky in love / Love house.	-	☐

— split after above and the KINMAN's formed BLACKBIRD who released three self-titled sets.

DIODES

Formed: Toronto, Canada ... early 1977 by PAUL ROBINSON, JOHN CATTO, IAN MacKAY and JONATHAN HAMILTON. Certainly one of the purveyors from the New Wave Power Pop nucleus north of the American border, The DIODES (meaning:- a two-way electrode semi-conductor evolving from crystal rectifiers) issued a split single with The CURSE before signing to major 'Epic' records. Bouncy follow-up 45, 'RED RUBBER BALL' (a PAUL SIMON number and a No.2 US hit for the CYRKLE in 1966), was also featured on their classic BIG STAR-meets-RAMONES-esque eponymous set, as was the electifying 'TIRED OF WAKIN' UP TIRED'. MIKE LENGYELL took up the drumstool thereafter (replacing HAMILTON), although their sound waned when their contemporaries moved into other territories; The DIODES soon moved too, but only across the water to England. With LP's, 'RELEASED' (1979) and 'ACTION / REACTION' (1980), failing to generate interest outside of Canada, The DIODES tried to crack the lucrative British market, however covers package 'SURVIVORS' (1982) shook up no one.

Album rating: THE DIODES (*7) / RELEASED (*6) / ACTION – REACTION (*3) / SURVIVORS (*4) / TIRED OF WAKING UP TIRED compilation (*7)

PAUL ROBINSON – vocals / **JOHN CATTO** – guitar / **IAN MacKAY** – bass, piano, vocals / **JONATHAN HAMILTON** – drums, vocals

		not iss.	Crash'n'burn
Aug 77.	(7") <CAEC> **RAW. / (other track by The CURSE)**	-	Canada
		Epic	Epic
Oct 77.	(7") <CH 4168> **RED RUBBER BALL. / WE'RE RIPPED**	-	☐
Aug 78.	(lp) (EPC 6531) <E4 4186> **TIRED OF WAKIN' UP TIRED. / CHILD STARS**	☐	Jun78
		C.B.S.	Columbia
Dec 78.	(lp) (CBS 82681) <PES 90441> **THE DIODES** – Red rubber ball / Child star / Tennis (again) / Blonde fever / Plastic girls / Death in the suburbs / Behind those eyes / Midnight movie star / We're ripped / China doll / Shapes of things to come / Time damage.	☐	Nov77

— **MIKE LENGYELL** – drums; repl. HAMILTON (he later joined TRUE CONFESSIONS)

		not iss.	Epic
Dec 79.	(lp) <PEC 80002> **RELEASED** – Red rubber ball / Teenage nation / Photographs from Mars / Madhouse / Mercenary flight / Tired of waking up tired / Jewnny's in a sleep world / Weekend / No right to make me bleed / Terminal rock.	-	Canada
		not iss.	Orient-RCA
1980.	(7") <045-001> **STRANGE TIME. / ROCKET OVER & UNDER**	-	☐
1980.	(lp) <OLP 001> **ACTION – REACTION**	-	Canada
1980.	(7") <045-003> **CAT WALKER. / ACTION – REACTION**	-	Canada

— split in 1981; most now all work in the computer business

– compilations, etc. –

1982.	(lp) *Fringe;* **SURVIVORS** (rare odds'n'ends) – Survivors / When I was young / Hot sands / Heat or the beat / Lost in the dark / Burn down your daddy's house / Curiosity girl / Roses and thorns / Coma / Play with fire (live at the Horseshoe).	-	Canada
Nov 98.	(cd) *Epic;* <80320> **TIRED OF WAKING UP TIRED: THE ORIGINAL RECORDINGS – 1977-1979** – Noise / Red rubber ball / Child star / Tennis (again) / Blonde fever / Plastic girls / Death in the suburbs / Behind those eyes / Midnight movie star / We're ripped / China doll / Shapes of things to come / Time damage / Headache / Burn down your daddy's house / Teenage nation / Photographs from Mars / Madhouse / Mercenary flight / Tired of waking up tired / Jenny's in a sleep world / Weekend / No right to make me bleed / Terminal rock / Dead on arrival.	-	Canada

DISTRACTIONS

Formed: Manchester, England ... late 1977 by students MIKE FINNEY and STEVE PERRIN-BROWN, who had played several live gigs in the previous two years with the rhythm section of LAWRENCE TICKLE and TONY TRAP. These originals were replaced by ADRIAN WRIGHT, PIP NICHOLLS and ALEC SIDEBOTTOM (former drummer with 60's combo, The PURPLE

GANG), after their jubilee year resurrection. During a hectic touring schedule supporting the likes of MAGAZINE, The BUZZCOCKS and just about every Mancunian New Wave act around at the time, The DISTRACTIONS signed a one-off deal with 'T.J.M.' and unveiled their debut EP, 'YOU'RE NOT GOING OUT DRESSED LIKE THAT', early in '79. That year also saw the lads sign another one-off contract, this time to Tony Wilson's 'Factory', the results coming in the shape of the strongly melodic double-header, 'TIME GOES BY SO SLOW' / 'PILLOW TALK'. At the turn of the decade, The DISTRACTIONS' critical stock had risen to the extent that 'Island' offered them an album deal. Preceded by a re-recorded 'IT DOESN'T BOTHER ME' (originally from the debut EP) and a re-vamped version of (Eden Kane's 1964 Top 10 hit) 'BOYS CRY', 'NOBODY'S PERFECT' (1980) was surprisingly disappointing. One further single for the independent 'That' outlet, 'AND THEN THERE'S', surfaced the following year, singer JULIE FINNEY replacing PERRIN-BROWN before their attention was diverted to other activities.

Album rating: NOBODY'S PERFECT (*4)

MIKE FINNEY – vocals / **STEVE PERRIN-BROWN** – guitar / **ADRIAN WRIGHT** – guitar / **PIP NICHOLLS** – bass / **ALEC SIDEBOTTOM** – drums (ex-PURPLE GANG)

	T.J.M.	not iss.
Mar 79. (7"ep) (TJM 2) **YOU'RE NOT GOING OUT DRESSED LIKE THAT EP** – It doesn't bother me / Waiting for the rain / Do the.		-

	Factory	not iss.
Sep 79. (7") (FAC 12) **TIME GOES BY SO SLOW. / PILLOW FIGHT**		-

	Island	not iss.
Jan 80. (7") (WIP 6533) **IT DOESN'T BOTHER ME. / ONE WAY LOVE**		-
Apr 80. (7") (WIP 6568) **BOYS CRY. / PARACETAMOL PARALYSIS**		-
May 80. (lp) (ILPS 9604) **NOBODY'S PERFECT** – Waiting for Lorraine / Something for the weekend / Boys cry / Sick and tired / Leave you to dream / Louise / Paracetamol paralysis / Fantasy / Nothing / Wonder girl / Untitled / Still it doesn't ring / Looking for a ghost / Valerie.		-
Sep 80. (7") (WIP 6650) **SOMETHING FOR THE WEEKEND. / WHAT'S THE USE**		-

	That	not iss.
Apr 81. (7"ep) (THAT 1) **AND THEN THERE'S / 24 HOURS. / GHOST OF A CHANCE / LOVE IS NOT FOR ME**		-

— **JULIE FINNEY** – vocals; repl. PERRIN-BROWN

— changed their moniker to FIRST CIRCLE, although there were no records

DMZ

Formed: Boston, Massachusetts, USA ... early 1977 by MONOMAN (aka JEFF CONOLLY), PETER GREENBERG, JAY RASSLER, RICK CORACCIO and PAUL MURPHY. Purveyors of rousing garage rock, once the territory of The SEEDS, ? & THE MYSTERIANS and the early TROGGS, DMZ unleashed their debut self-titled EP for seminal indie 'Bomp!' records. Without mainman MONOMAN (who formed the legendary LYRES), the band signed to 'Sire', where they delivered the poorly-produced – courtesy of FLO & EDDIE – long-player, 'DMZ' (1978). Further recordings subsequently surfaced, but this was after MURPHY trailed in JEFF's footsteps and into The LYRES. • **Covered:** YOU'RE GONNA MISS ME (13th Floor Elevators) / TEENAGE HEAD (Flamin' Groovies) / SINDERELLA (Sonics) / etc. • **Note:** Not to be confused with US punks DMZ who issued the double-CD, 'Fight The Power'!.

Album rating: DMZ (*5) / RELICS or WHEN I GET OFF or THE FIRST TIME collection (*5/*6/*6)

MONOMAN (JEFF CONOLLY) – vocals, organ, percussion / **PETER GREENBERG** – guitar / **JAY RASSLER** – guitar / **RICK CORACCIO** – bass / **PAUL MURPHY** – drums

	not iss.	Bomp!
Sep 77. (7"ep) <BEP 111> **DMZ** – Busy man / Can't stand the pain / You're gonna miss me / When I get off.	-	

— now without CONOLLY who formed The LYRES

	Sire	Sire
1978. (lp) <(SRK 6051)> **DMZ** – Mighty Idy / Bad attitude / Watch for me girl / Cinderella / Don't jump me mother / Destroyer / Baby boom / Out of our tree / Border line / Do not enter / From home.		

— decided to split after above, MURPHY followed CONOLLY into The LYRES

– compilations, etc. –

1981. (m-lp) Voxx; (VOXX 200.004) **RELICS** – Busy man / Can't stand the pain / You're gonna miss me / When I get off / Do not enter / Guilty child / Shirt loop / Lift up your hood / Barracuda. (UK-iss.Jan91; same as US) (cd-iss. Jul93 as 'WHEN I GET OFF' +=; VOXXCD 2004) – Comin' after me / Bloody Englishmen / First time / Oedipus show / Rosalyn / Mighty have I.D. / From home / Are you gonna be there / Pretty girl. <US lp/cd-iss. Sep95 as 'THE FIRST TIME'; same as German/UK>	-	- German
1983. (lp) Crypt; <CR 009> **LIVE AT ST. BARNABY'S** (live)	-	
1985. (lp) Crypt; <CR 025> **1976-77 DEMOS / LIVE**	-	
1986. (m-lp) Crypt; <CR-45 2> **LIVE AT ST. BARNABY'S 1978!!** (live) – You're gonna miss me / Can't do that / Baby boom / Are you gonna be there?	-	
Nov 01. (lp/cd) Bomp; <(BLP/BCD 4081)> **LIVE AT THE RAT**		Aug01

DNA

Formed: New York City, New York, USA ... 1977 by ARTO LINDSAY, who had been brought up in a Brazilian village by his missionary father. In 1975, he arrived in the Big Apple where he initially worked for the 'Village Voice' newspaper. Having nearly joined the band, MARS (for whom he'd later write lyrics) as a drummer, ARTO chose to form his own trio together with ROBIN CRUTCHFIELD and Japanese drummer, IKUE ILE MORI. In 1978, DNA released their debut 45, 'LITTLE ANTS', before contributing four tracks to the BRIAN ENO-produced V/A album, 'No New York' (along with the aforementioned MARS, James Chance's CONTORTIONS and Lydia Lunch's TEENAGE JESUS & THE JERKS). TIM WRIGHT subsequently replaced CRUTCHFIELD and in 1981 a 10-minute EP of six songs, 'A TASTE OF DNA', showcased the man's experimental "No Wave", highlighting his untuned staccato guitar. ARTO had already moonlighted with JOHN LURIE's "fake-jazz" group, The LOUNGE LIZARDS, his unique style an integral part of their eponymous debut set in '81. That year too, MORI surprisingly surfaced as a cellist, violist and violinist on MARS' 'John Gavanti', while WRIGHT played bass on BRIAN ENO & DAVID BYRNE's 'My Life In The Bush Of Ghosts'. Inevitably, DNA had already reached the end of its natural lifespan, ARTO going on to work with the likes of JAMES CHANCE, The GOLDEN PALOMINOS and poet, JOHN GIORNO, on his 1984 album, 'Better An Old Demon Than A New God'. With PETER SCHERER on keyboards, ARTO LINDSAY & The AMBITIOUS LOVERS were formed the following year, the ever adventurous guitarist striving to incorporate the complex rhythms of his beloved Brazil into 1985's 'ENVY'. The AMBITIOUS LOVERS returned in 1988 with an all-star cast of hip New Yorkers including VERNON REID (of LIVING COLOR), JOHN ZORN, BILL FRISELL and the aforementioned LURIE, these multi-talented musicians playing on their only album for 'Virgin', 'GREED' (1988). After becoming the curator of 'The Kitchen' (New York's foremost meeting place for the experimentally inclined) 'LUST' continued LINDSAY's search for an immaculate marriage of sonic chaos and exotic South American funk. In 1992, he formed ARTO with likeminded veterans, BERNIE WORRELL, MARC RIBOT and MELVIN GIBBS, although it would be in a solo capacity that LINDSAY would release his next album, an eponymous set for 'Knitting Factory'. The following year, the enigmatic guitarist delivered two albums for 'Bar None', 'O CORPO SUTIL (THE SUBTLE BODY)' and 'MUNDO CIVILIZADO', the latter covered work by AL GREEN, PRINCE and SANTANA. Bypassing, but obviously not forgetting some excellent musicianship on 1998's 'NOON CHILL', LINDSAY was back with another piece of textured experimentation, 'PRIZE' (1999). If fitting the sounds of Latin America into New York might've been extremely formidable (DAVID BYRNE was also trying the same thing), ARTO proved to be worthy of leading the cause. Three years on, LINDSAY returned with 'INVOKE' (2002), a slide into smoochy late-night mood music that was miles away from his No Wave days and more in keeping with groovy SANTANA-ish style (CARLOS SANTANA co-wrote the track, 'UMA').

Album rating: A TASTE OF DNA mini (*7) / Ambitious Lovers: ENVY (*6) / GREED (*6) / LUST (*6) / Arto Lindsay: ARTO LINDSAY (*6) / AGGREGATES 1-26 (*5) / MUNDO CIVILIZADO (*5) / O CORPO SUTIL (THE SUBTLE BODY) (*6) / NOON CHILL (*7) / PRIZE (*6) / INVOKE (*5)

ARTO LINDSAY (b.28 May'53, Richmond, Virginia) – vocals, guitar / **IKUE ILE MORI** (b.17 Dec'53, Tokyo, Japan) – drums / **ROBIN CRUTCHFIELD** – keyboards

	not iss.	Lust/Unlust
Dec 78. (7") <11-CAN 234> **LITTLE ANTS. / YOU AND YOU**	- not iss.	DNA
1980. (7") <DNA 1> **DO THE SHOPPING. / ZOO TANGO**	-	

— **TIM WRIGHT** – bass, guitar (ex-PERE UBU) repl. CRUTCHFIELD who formed DARK DAY

	Rough Trade	American Clave
Aug 81. (12"ep) (RT 086) <AMCL 1003EP> **A TASTE OF DNA** – New fast / 5:30 / Blondie red head / 32123 / New life / Lying on the sofa of life.		May81

— TIM formed HOME & GARDEN

– compilations, etc. –

Aug 93. (cd) Avant; (AVANT 006) **DNA** (live at CBGB's June '82)		-

ARTO LINDSAY and The AMBITIOUS LOVERS

ARTO LINDSAY with **PETER SCHERER** – keyboards / **TONI NOGUEIRA** / **CLAUDIO SILVA** / **REINALDO FERNANDES** / **M.E. MILLER**

	EditionsEG	EG
Feb 85. (lp) (EGED 39) **ENVY** – Cross your legs / Trouble maker / Pagode Americano / Nothings monstered / Crowning roar / Too many mansions / Let's be adult / Venus lost her shirt / Badu / Dora / Beberibe / Locus coruleus. (cd-iss. Jan87; CDEGED 39) (re-iss. cd Jul96 on 'Virgin'; CDOVD 469)		

AMBITIOUS LOVERS

LINDSAY + SCHERER plus others **VERNON REID** – guitar, vocals / **JOHN ZORN + JOHN LURIE** – saxophone / **BILL FRISELL** – guitar / **NANA VASCONCELOS** – percussion / **MELVIN GIBBS** – bass / **JOEY BARON** – drums / **JILL JAFFE** – violin / **D.K. DYSON + GAIL LOU** – vocals

	Virgin	Virgin
Oct 88. (7") (VS 1128) **LOVE OVERLAP. / IT ONLY HAS TO HAPPEN ONCE** (12"+=) (VST 1128) – ('A'-Stretched out long mix) / ('A'-Stuck in love mix).		

Nov 88. (lp/c/cd) (V/TCV/CDV 2545) <90903> **GREED**
– Copy me / Privacy / Caso / King / Omotesando / Too far / Love overlap / Admit it / Steel wool / Para nao contrariar voce / Quasi you / It only has to happen once / Hot stuff. (re-iss. cd Jul96; same)

— duo with **GIBBS, RIBOT, VASCONCELOS** plus **TONY LEWIS** – drums / **LORELEI McBROOM** – vocals

                                                    Elektra Elektra

Jan 91. (12"ep) (66583) **PONTA DE LANCA AFRICANO EP**
Apr 91. (cd/c) <(7559 60981-2/-4)> **LUST**
– Lust / It's gonna rain / Tuck it in / Ponta de lanca Africano umbabarauma / Monster / Villain / Half out of it / Slippery / Make it easy / More light / E preciso perdoar.

ARTO LINDSAY

— with **MELVIN GIBBS** – bass (of ROLLINS BAND) / **DOUGIE BOWNE** – drumsb(ex-LOUNGE LIZARDS)

                                      Knitting Knitting
                                      Factory Factory

Apr 95. (cd) <(KFWCD 164)> **ARTO LINDSAY: AGGREGATES 1-26**
– Be great / Recognize / In love / GTR drums #2 / Stitches / Imbue / Tap GTR / Tap / Absurd children / Noise / Flag of friendship / Venus / Looks like you / Flourish / Awfully short / Voice & lips / GTR bass / Founder / Two / 3 / Four / Bag pipes / Drug finger / GTR drums #1 / Head in a paper bag / Very good.

— now with a plethora of session people incl. RYUICHI SAKAMOTO

                                    Rykodisc Bar None

Aug 96. (cd) (RCD 10369) <078> **O CORPO SUTIL (THE SUBTLE BODY)**
– Four skies / Child prodigy / Anima animale / Este seu olhar / My mind is going / Enxugar / No meu sotaque / Unbearable / Nobody in bed / Astronauts / Sovereign.
Jun 97. (cd) (RCD 10410) <082> **MUNDO CIVILIZADO**   Dec96
– Complicity / Q samba / Simply beautiful / Mundo civilizado / Titled / Horizontal / Mar de Gavea / Ibassai / Pleasure / Erotic city / Clown.
Jun 97. (cd) <(GLP 79519)> **HYPER CIVILIZADO** (DJ remixes)
(above issued on 'GramaVision')
Mar 98. (d-cd) (RCD 10436) <102> **NOON CHILL**
– Noon chill / Whirlwind / Simply are / Blue eye shadow / Mulata fuzarqueira / Ridiculously deep / Anything / Gods are weak / Take my place / Daily life / Light moves away / Why compare / Auguri // Re-entry / Ambassador Jr. / 3348 / Size / Channel 17.

                                    Rykodisc Righeous Babe

Oct 99. (cd) (RCD 10498) <RBRCD 16> **PRIZE**
– Ondina / The prize / Pode ficar / Prefeelings / Modos / Ex-preguica / Unsure / Resemblances / O nome dela / Tone / Interior life / E ai esqueco.

                                      Righteous Righteous
                                      Babe Babe

Jun 02. (cd) <(RBRCD 27)> **INVOKE**
– Illuminated / Predigo / Ultra privileged / Over – Run / Invoke / You decide / In the city that reads / Delegada / Uma / Clemency / Unseen / Beija-me.

D.O.A.

Formed: Vancouver, Canada … early 1978 with an initial line-up of JOEY 'SHITHEAD' KEITHLEY, RANDY RAMPAGE and CHUCK BISCUITS, their moniker an acronym for DEAD ON ARRIVAL. The name reflected their no-messing approach, D.O.A.'s unceasingly radical stance and uncompromising musical approach doing much to shape the early 80's American hardcore scene. Following a clutch of early 7"/12" EP's and an album 'HARDCORE '81', the group signed to JELLO BIAFRA's 'Alternative Tentacles' and released the influential 'POSITIVELY D.O.A.' EP, such raging political barbs as 'FUCKED UP RONNIE' underlining the band's agit-punk approach. The lean three-chord attack which formed the basis of much of their material was much in evidence on 1984's top compilation 'BLOODIED BUT UNBOWED'. This included the 'WAR ON 45' EP, which introduced new members DAVE GREGG (actually around since 1980), GREGG JAMES and BRIAN GOBLE, recruited as replacements for RAMPAGE and BISCUITS, the latter moving on to CIRCLE JERKS, then BLACK FLAG and later DANZIG. These punk lumberjacks of the North American scene finally released an album's worth of new material, 'LET'S WRECK THE PARTY' in 1985, a set that saw the band's deceptively simple approach reach fruition. JAMES subsequently departed, JON CARD taking up the post prior to the release of their next hardcore delivery, 'TRUE (NORTH) STRONG AND FREE' (1987). More personnel changes were to follow, when DAVE GREGG split to form GROOVAHOLICS, CHRIS PROHOM coming in for the 1990 album, 'MURDER'. This was released around the same time as a collaboration set with JELLO BIAFRA (ex-DEAD KENNEDYS) entitled 'LAST SCREAM OF THE MISSING NEIGHBORS'. The band stuck by their hardcore principles into the 90's with albums like 'TALK – ACTION = 0' (1991), '13 FLAVOURS OF DOOM' (1992) and 'LOGGERHEADS' (1993), the latter two finding D.O.A. back with 'Alternative Tentacles'. • **Covers:** WE GOTTA GET OUT OF THIS PLACE (Animals) / FOLSOM PRISON BLUES (Johnny Cash) / COMMUNICATION BREAKDOWN (Led Zeppelin). • **Note:** To the Canadian guy who wrote to me a few years ago and pointed out a certain error, I've intentionally retained this original uncorrected biography – I think I threw out your "nice" letter.

Album rating: SOMETHING BETTER CHANGE mini (*6) / BLOODED BUT UNBOWED compilation (*8) / LET'S WRECK THE PARTY (*7) / TRUE (NORTH) STRONG AND FREE (*5) / MURDER (*6) / TALK – ACTION = 0 (*6) / 13 FLAVOURS OF DOOM (*6) / LOGGERHEADS (*5)

JOEY "SHITHEAD" KEITHLEY – vocals, guitar / **RANDY RAMPAGE** – bass / **CHUCK BISCUITS** – drums

                                      not iss. Sudden Death

May 78. (7"ep) <SD 001> **DISCO SUCKS EP**
– Royal police / Woke up screaming / Disco sucks / Nazi training camp. (re-iss. Apr79 on 'Quintessence'; QEP 002) <(re-iss. Jan94 on 'Alternative Tentacles'; VIRUS 133)>

                                      not iss. Quintessence

1978. (7") <QS 102> **THE PRISONER. / 13**
Dec 79. (7") <QD 206> **WHATCHA GONNA DO? / WORLD WAR 3**

                                      not iss. Friends

1979. (12"ep) <FR 001> **TRIUMPH OF THE IGNOROIDS EP**
– Nazi training camp / Want some bondage / Woke up screaming / Rich bitch / Let's fuck.
Sep 80. (m-lp) <FR 003> **SOMETHING BETTER CHANGE EP**
– New age / The enemy / 2 + 2 / Get out of my life / Woke up screaming / Last night / 13 / Great white hope / The prisoner / Rich bitch / Take a chance / Whatcha gonna do? / World War 3.
Jun 81. (12"ep) <FR 010> **HARDCORE '81**
– D.O.A. / Unknown / Unknown / Waiting for you.

                                      not iss. Sudden Death

1983. (7") <SD 003> **BURN IT DOWN. / FUCK YOU**
1983. (7") <SD 004> **GENERAL STRIKE. / THAT'S LIFE**

                                    Alternative Alternative
                                    Tentacles Tentacles

Jan 82. (7"ep) <(VIRUS 7)> **POSITIVELY D.O.A.**
– Fucked up Ronnie / World War Three / The enemy / My old man's a bum / New wave sucks. (re-iss. Jul93; same)

— **KEITHLEY** was now joined by **DAVE GREGG** – guitar, vocals / **GREGG JAMES** – drums / **BRIAN "SUNNY BOY ROY" GOBLE** – bass, vocals (they repl. RAMPAGE + BISCUITS; latter to CIRCLE JERKS, BLACK FLAG then DANZIG)

Nov 82. (7"ep) <(VIRUS 24)> **WAR ON 45**
– America the beautiful / Unknown / Rich bitch / Let's fuck war / I hate you / War in the east / Class war.
Feb 84. (lp) <(VIRUS 31)> **BLOODED BUT UNBOWED** (compilation 1978-83)
– Liar for hire / Fuck you / The prisoner / I'm right, you're wrong / Smash the state / Slumlord / New age / I don't give a shit / Waiting for you / Whatcha gonna do / World War 3 / 2 + 2 / The enemy / Fucked up Ronnie / Woke up screaming / 001 Loser's club / 13 / Get out of my life / D.O.A. (cd-iss. Mar92 w/ 'WAR ON 45' on 'Restless'; LS 91852)
Dec 84. (12"ep) <(VIRUS 42)> **DON'T TURN YER BACK (ON DESPERATE TIMES)** (The John Peel session)
– General strike / Race riot / A season in Hell / Burn it down.
Sep 85. (lp) <(VIRUS 44)> **LET'S WRECK THE PARTY**
– Our world / Dangerman / Race riot / Singin' in the rain / Dance o'death / General strike / Let's wreck the party / Shout out / Murder in Hollywood / The warrior ain't no more / No way out / Trial by media.

— split for a while, reformed in '87

— **JON CARD** – drums (ex-PERSONALITY CRISIS, ex-SNFU) repl. JAMES

                                      not iss. Profile

Mar 87. (cd) <1228> **TRUE (NORTH) STRONG AND FREE**

— **CHRIS PROHOM** – guitar (ex-RED TIDE) repl. GREGG

                                      Restless Restless

Mar 90. (cd/lp) <(72376-2/-4)> **MURDER**
– We know what you you want / Guns, booze & sex / Boomtown / Afrikana security / Waiting for you / No productivity / The agony and the ecstasy / The midnight special / Bananaland / The warrior lives again / Concrete beach / Suicidal. (re-iss. cd Jul95; same)

— In May'90, teamed up w/ JELLO BIAFRA (ex-DEAD KENNEDYS) to release 'Alternative Tentacles' album 'LAST SCREAM OF THE MISSING NEIGHBORS' (Soundtrack to 'Terminal City Ricochet')

Dec 91. (cd/lp) <(72506-2/-1)> **TALK – ACTION = 0**
– America the beautiful / 13 / Burn it down / Murder in Hollywood / Lumberjack city / Waiting for you (part 2) / F*** you / Woke up screaming / Liar for hire / 2 + 2 / Let's wreck the party / The prisoner / Do or die / F*** that shit / General strike / Race riot. (re-iss. cd Jul95; same)

                                    Alternative Alternative
                                  Tentacles Tentacles

Feb 92. (cd) <(VIRUS 106CD)> **THE DAWNING OF A NEW ERROR** (compilation of EP's, etc.)
Oct 92. (lp/c/cd) <(VIRUS 117/+MC/CD)> **13 FLAVOURS OF DOOM**
– Already dead / Death machine / Bombs away / The living dead / I played the fool / Too f***in' heavy / Hole in the sky / Hey sister / Use your raincoat / Legalized theft / Rosemary's baby / Beatin' rock'n'roll to death / Time of illusion. (c+=/cd+=) – Phantom zone.
Mar 93. (7") <(VIRUS 120)> **IT'S NOT UNUSUAL . . . BUT IT'S UGLY!. / DEAD MEN TELL NO TALES**
(cd-s) <(VIRUS 120CD)> – ('A'side) / Blue to brown / Help me get out of here / Runaway world.
Oct 93. (lp/c/cd) <(VIRUS 130/+MC/CD)> **LOGGERHEADS**
– Logjam / I see you cross / You little weiner / Overpowering urges / That turbulent uneasy feeling / The only green thing / Overtime / Cocktail time in Hell / Cut and dried / Burning in anger / Liberation and execution / Witch hunt / Knots / I can't take much more. (c+=/cd+=) – Fulsom prison dirge.
Oct 93. (7") <(VIRUS 131)> **THE ONLY THING GREEN. / FOLSOM PRISON BLUES**
(above a benefit single for the "Friends Of Clayoquot Sound" to save the region of Tofino, British Columbia, Canada from commercial logging)

                                    Essential Essential
                                  Noise Noise

Dec 96. (cd) <(35299-2)> **THE BLACK SPOT**   Oct95
– Blind men / Kill ya later / Order / Marijuana motherfuckers / You're playing for your body now / Worries / Rock hill / Get away / More / Je declare / Big guys like D.O.A. / I know who you are / 1 bound for glory / Unchained melody / Cut time / Running out of time.

                                    Earache not iss.

Jan 97. (cd; various artists) (MOSH 164CD) **NEW YORK CITY SPEEDCORE**
– Total annihilation / Ya mutha / Brooklyn mob / NYC speedcore / Wanna be a gangsta / Zu leiten / Uncle Bill's message / Pound down on your brain / Kill / Uncle Bill's message / Minute madness / Extreme gangsta / Our father / Our father / Ya mutha III / Noize core / I'll give you hard / Ya mutha II / You're dead / This is D.O.A.

D.O.A. (cont)   THE GREAT INDIE DISCOGRAPHY   The 1970s

– compilations, etc. –

Mar 98.	(cd) *Golf; (CDHOLE 015)* **THE LOST TAPES**		
May 98.	(cd) *Golf; (CDHOLE 014)* **A FESTIVAL OF ATHEISTS**		

DOCTORS OF MADNESS

Formed: London, England ... mid-70's by RICHARD 'KID' STRANGE, COLIN 'STONER' BROWN, PETER DILEMMA and URBAN BLITZ. Signed to 'Polydor', this oddball group made their debut in 1976 with the album, 'LATE NIGHT MOVIES, ALL NIGHT BRAINSTORMS', an amalgam of spaced-out ballads and full throttle fiddle-enhanced avant-rock. Vaguely associated with the emerging punk scene (vocalist STRANGE could snarl with the best of them when he felt like it), The DOCTORS released a follow-up set, 'FIGMENTS OF EMANCIPATION' later the same year. A new wave QUEEN might be the best way to describe this lot, favouring as they did overblown violin flourishes (similar to ULTRAVOX!) and ambitious arrangements. The initial burst of creativity dissipated and 1977's recorded output amounted to a solitary single, 'BULLETIN', predictably their most punk-like recording to date. A third album, 'SONS OF SURVIVAL', finally arrived the following year to general public apathy, the band unable to compete in the musically fertile wake of punk and its aftershocks. The record proved to be their epitaph although STRANGE pursued a solo career, recording for both 'Cherry Red' and 'Virgin'.

Album rating: LATE NIGHT MOVIES ALL NIGHT BRAINSTORMS (*7) / FIGMENTS OF EMANCIPATION (*5) / SONS OF SURVIVAL (*5) / 1975-1978 REVISIONISM compilation (*6)

RICHARD 'KID' STRANGE – vocals, guitar, keyboards, percussion / **URBAN BLITZ** – guitar, violin / **COLIN 'STONER' BROWN** – bass, vocals, percussion / **PETER DILEMMA** – drums, percussion, vocals

		Polydor	U.A.
Mar 76.	(lp) *(2383 378)* **LATE NIGHT MOVIES ALL NIGHT BRAINSTORMS**		-
	– Waiting / Afterglow / Mitzi's cure / I think we're alone / The noises of the evening / Billy watch out / B-movie bedtime / Mainlines. (<cd-iss. Jan99 on 'Ozit'+=; OZITCD 0042>) – Mitzi's cure (acoustic) / I think we're alone (acoustic) / B-movie bedtime (acoustic) / Marie and Joe (live) / Who cries for me (live).		
Sep 76.	(lp) *(2383 403)* **FIGMENTS OF EMANCIPATION**		
	– Brothers / Suicide city / Perfect pest / Marie and Joe / In camera / Doctors of madness / Out. (cd-iss. Jul02 on 'Ozit'+=; OZITCD 0045) – (extra tracks).		
Aug 77.	(7") *(2058 921)* **BULLETIN. / WAITING**		-
Mar 78.	(7") *(2059 009)* **SONS OF SURVIVAL. / OUT**		-
Apr 78.	(lp) *(2383 472)* **SONS OF SURVIVAL**		
	– 50's kids / Into the strange / No limits / Bulletin / Network / Sons of survival / Back from the dead / Triple vision / Kiss goodbye tomorrow / Cool. (cd-iss. Jul02 on 'Ozit'+=; OZITCD 0046) – Don't panic England / Last human being in the world / Triple vision.		
May 78.	(lp) *<871>* **DOCTORS OF MADNESS**	-	

— disbanded after ex-DAMNED vocalist DAVE VANIAN repl. STRANGE on brief tour. STONER later joined The ADVERTS.

– compilations, etc. –

Jul 81.	(lp) *Polydor; (2478 146)* **1975-1978 REVISIONISM**		-
	– Mainlines / Prologue / Waiting / B-movie bedtime / Triple vision / In camera / Network / Sons of survival / Marie and Joe / Mitzi's cure / Afterglow / Bullitin / Mainlines.		

RICHARD STRANGE

— solo with **STEVE BOLTON + ANGUS McLEAN** – guitar / **PETE O'SULLIVAN** – bass / **MARTIN GRIFFIN** – drums / **DAVE WINTHROP** – saxophone (on lp)

		Cherry Red	P.V.C.
Jan 80.	(7") *(CHERRY 10)* **INTERNATIONAL LANGUAGE. / KISS GOODBYE TOMORROW**		-
Nov 80.	(lp) *<7917>* **THE LIVE RISE OF RICHARD STRANGE** (live 24/6/80)	-	
	– The phenomenal rise of Richard Strange / On top of the world / I make plans / The hero runs away / International language / Replay / Gutter press / I won't run away.		
		Virgin	not iss.
Apr 81.	(7"/12") *(VS 419/+12)* **INTERNATIONAL LANGUAGE. / GOD IS SCIENCE**		-
May 81.	(lp) *(V 2203)* **THE PHENOMENAL RISE OF RICHARD STRANGE**		-
	– The phenomenal rise of Richard Strange / On top of the world / Hearts and minds / Magic man / Gutter press / International language / Who cries for me / Premonition / The road to the room / I won't run away.		
Jun 81.	(7") *(VS 431)* **THE PHENOMENAL RISE OF RICHARD STRANGE. / ON TOP OF THE WORLD**		-
		Albion	not iss.
May 83.	(12") *(SLAM 1)* **NEXT! /**		-

RICHARD STRANGE & The ENGINE ROOM

— with **JULIE HEPBURN + RENE EYRE**

		Arista	Arista
Sep 84.	(7"/12"; as The ENGINE ROOM) *(ARIST/+12 587)* **WILD TIMES. / I LOVE HER (SHE'S POISON)**		
Mar 85.	(7"/7"pic-d; as The ENGINE ROOM) *(ARIST/+P 593)* **YOUR KISS IS A WEAPON. / FALL OF THE HOUSE OF USHER**		
	(12"+=) *(ARIST 12593)* – ('A'extended).		

		Nightshift	not iss.
Jul 88.	(lp) *(NISHI 205)* **GOING-GONE**		-
	– Damascus / The lion's den / Banco celestial / Dominoes / The fall of the House Of Usher / Fear is the engine / Wounded / Love scare / Pride, time & inspiration / Pioneering surgery.		
Dec 88.	(12"ep) *(NISHI 206T)* **DAMASCUS**		-
	– Damascus / Haj caravan / Damascus (alt.version) / Pioneering surgery.		
		Ausfahrt	not iss.
1990.	(lp) *(2606.143)* **THE REST IS SILENCE**	German	-
	– Low life / God help the wealthy man / Endless winter / Waterlillies / Wake up, America / Inch' Allah / Down comes the hammer / The ghost of Brian Jones.		

— RICHARD retired from the music business in the 90's having already cut two albums with German act, The INTERNATIONAL NOISE ORCHESTRA

John DOE (see under ⇒ X)

DOLL

Formed: London, England ... October '77 by MARION VALENTINE, ADONIS YIANNI, his brother CHRISTOPHER YIANNI and MARIO WATTS. Bandwagoneers with a catchy line in disposable New Wave punk, The DOLL almost immediately signed to 'Beggars Banquet' (home of The LURKERS and TUBEWAY ARMY), through whom they released their pop-friendly debut 45, 'DON'T TANGO ON MY HEART'. A fusion of The REZILLOS and BLONDIE, the track failed to ignite public interest, although follow-up single, 'DESIRE ME', cracked the Top 30 and saw the leopard-skin clad MARION and Co pout their stuff on Top Of The Pops. With MARION receiving all the press attention, internal tensions came to a head and caused a sizeable split in the ranks; with only CHRISTOS and VALENTINE remaining, new members DENNIS HAINES, JAMIE WEST-ORAM and PAUL TURNER were recruited. After nearly a year's lay off, the band returned to find themselves shunned by fans and critics alike as they attempted to hit the singles chart again via 'CINDERELLA WITH A HUSKY VOICE'. The accompanying debut album, 'LISTEN TO THE SILENCE' (1979) suffered a similar fate as the record buying public took their advice all too literally; The DOLL wound up proceedings shortly after.

Album rating: LISTEN TO THE SILENCE (*3)

MARION VALENTINE (b.1952, Brighton, England) – vocals, rhythm guitar / **ADONIS YANNI** (b.10 Oct'57) – keyboards / **CHRISTOPHER YIANNI** (b. CHRISTOS, 6 Sep'54) – bass / **MARIO WATTS** (b.1958) – drums

		Beggars Banquet	not iss.
Jan 78.	(7") *(BEG 4)* **DON'T TANGO ON MY HEART. / TRASH**		-
Dec 78.	(7"/ext.12") *(BEG 11/+T)* **DESIRE ME. / T.V. ADDICT**	28	-
	(with free 7") *(SAM 93)* **BURNING UP LIKE A FIRE. / DESIRE ME**		

— **MARION + CHRISTOS** enlisted **DENNIS HAINES** – keyboards / **JAMIE WEST-ORAM** – lead guitar / **PAUL TURNER** – drums

Oct 79.	(7") *(BEG 26)* **CINDERELLA WITH A HUSKY VOICE. / BECAUSE NOW**		-
Oct 79.	(lp) *(BEGA 12)* **LISTEN TO THE SILENCE**		-
	– The one kiss / Zero heroes / Ce soir, Cheri / Cinderella with a husky voice / Memories / You used to be my hero / True love / Frozen fire / Carmina / Listen to the silence / Something rare, something beautiful.		
Jan 80.	(7") *(BEG 31)* **YOU USED TO BE MY HERO. / ZERO HEROES**		-
Apr 80.	(7") *(BEG 38)* **BURNING UP LIKE A FIRE. / FROZEN FIRE**		-

— split in the Spring of 1980, MARION retired after songwriting failed

— JAMIE WEST-ORAM went on to be successful with The FIXX

DOLL BY DOLL

Formed: London, England ... 1977 by Fife-born JACKIE LEVEN, although it would be a few years later that the band – which also comprised JO SHAW, ROBIN SPREAFICO and DAVID McINTOSH – would make their mark. LEVEN had previously cut his teeth as a singer/songwriter performing under the assumed name of JOHN ST. FIELD, gigging with the likes of MAN until the onset of punk rock captured his imagination and inspired him to form a band. DOLL BY DOLL emerged in punk's wake after signing to Warner Brothers off-shoot, 'Automatic', releasing a debut album, 'REMEMBER', early in 1979. Having replaced SPEARFICO with TONY WAITE, DBD issued a second album that year, 'GYPSY BLOOD', LEVEN's Celtic fringe lyrics and stirring vocals sitting rather uneasily beside the band's elaborate rock arrangements. An unusual signing to pop label, 'Magnet', the quartet delivered two further sets, 'DOLL BY DOLL' (1981) and 'GRAND PASSION' (1982), the latter seeing LEVEN employ a new band including co-vocalist, HELEN TURNER and an array of rock establishment veterans, i.e. DAVE GILMOUR and MEL COLLINS. The following year, LEVEN disbanded the group for a solo deal with 'Charisma', although only two flop singles were forthcoming. Things went horribly wrong as the singer found himself the victim of a street attack in London, amongst other injuries suffering damage to his larynx; it went from bad to worse as LEVEN fell into a spiral of heroin abuse. He nevertheless managed to turn things around, curing himself (with help from his wife, Carol) and setting up a support network, C.O.R.E., for fellow drug addicts. During this period in the musical wilderness, he did actually manage a few gigs with ex-SEX PISTOLS and RICH KIDS bass player, GLEN MATLOCK, as the short-lived C.B.I (CONCRETE BULLETPROOF INVISIBLE). In 1994, LEVEN finally emerged as a fully-fledged solo artist, signed to roots label 'Cooking Vinyl'. Recorded in Scotland and released only north of the border, the mini-set, 'SONGS FROM THE ARGYLL CYCLE', re-introduced LEVEN as a folk-rock artist leaving behind all traces of his punk days amid lyrical images of windswept Highland scenes. LEVEN has since released several more sets in a similar vein while working with American poet, ROBERT BLY and fellow ex-punk Fifer, RICHARD JOBSON.

Album rating: REMEMBER (*6) / GYPSY BLOOD (*7) / DOLL BY DOLL (*5) / GRAND PASSION (*4) / Jackie Leven: SONGS FROM THE ARGYLL CYCLE (*6) / THE MYSTERY OF LOVE IS GREATER THAN THE MYSTERY OF DEATH (*7) / THE FORBIDDEN SONGS OF THE DYING WEST (*7) / FAIRY TALES FOR HARD MEN (*6) / CONTROL (*5)

JACKIE LEVEN (b. 1950, Fife, Scotland) – vocals (later added guitar) / **JO SHAW** – guitar, vocals / **ROBIN SPREAFICO** – bass, vocals / **DAVID McINTOSH** – drums, vocals

Automatic-Warners / not iss.

Mar 79. (7") (K 17330) **THE PALACE OF LOVE. / FOUNTAIN IS RED, FOUNTAIN IS WHITE**
Mar 79. (lp/c) (K/K4 56618) **REMEMBER**
 – Butcher boy / Chances / Sleeping partners / More than human / Lose myself / Janice / The palace of love.

— **TONY WAITE** – bass, vocals; repl. ROBIN

Oct 79. (lp) (K 56755) **GYPSY BLOOD**
 – Teenage lightning / Gypsy blood / Strip show / The human face / Hey sweetheart / Binary fiction / Hell games / Forbidden worlds / Highland rain / Endgame / When a man dies.
Nov 79. (7") (K 17496) **TEENAGE LIGHTNING. / ONE TWO BLUES**
Jan 80. (7") (K 17559) **GYPSY BLOOD. / LOVE MYSELF**

Magnet / Magnet

May 81. (7") (MAG 188) **MAIN TRAVELLED ROADS. / BE MY FRIEND**
May 81. (lp/c) (MAGL/ZCMAG 5039) **DOLL BY DOLL**
 – Figure it out / Carita / Soon new life / Main travelled roads / Those in peril / I never saw the movie / The perfect romance / Fantastic sensation / The street I love / Be my friend / Up / A bright green field.
Aug 81. (7") (MAG 195) **CARITA. / MURDER ON THE HIGHWAY**
 (12"+=) (12MAG 195) – An honest woman.

— LEVEN recruited an entire new line-up with **HELEN TURNER** – vocals, keyboards / **TOM NORDON** – vocals, guitar, bass / plus a plethora of famous people in session incl. DAVE GILMOUR, MEL COLLINS, JON FIELD, GRAHAM BROAD, TIM CROSS + MAGGIE RILEY

Aug 82. (7") (MAG 229) **UNDER MY THUMB. / ETERNAL**
Sep 82. (lp/c) (MAGL/ZCMAG 5057) **GRAND PASSION**
 – Strong hands / Under my thumb / Dancing shoes / Cool skies / Eternal / onely kind of show / Natural / Grand passion / City of light / Dawn of the rain girls / Boxers hit harder when women are around / So long kid.

— subsequently split when LEVEN went solo

JACKIE LEVEN

Charisma / not iss.

Aug 83. (7") (JACK 1) **LOVE IS SHINING DOWN ON ME. / GREAT SPIRIT CALLS**
Jul 84. (7") (JACK 2) **UPTOWN. / TROPIC OF COOL**
 (12"+=) (JACK 2-12) – Beautiful train.

— JACKIE was attacked in a London street and suffered severe larynx problems which stopped him singing for a long spell. In March '88, he and GLEN MATLOCK surfaced as CONCRETE BULLETPROOF INVISIBLE, releasing the single, 'BIG TEARS', for 'Radioactive'. JACKIE was again a solo artist in the mid 90's

Cooking Vinyl / not iss.

Mar 94. (m-cd) (COOKCD 065) **SONGS FROM THE ARGYLL CYCLE** — Scot
 – Stranger on the square / Walking in Argyll / Honeymoon hill / Looking for love / Grievin' at the mish nish / Ballad of a simple heart / As we sailed into Skibbereen / Some ancient misty morning / History of rain / Gylen Gylen / Fly / Crazy song. (full UK-iss.Apr96; COOKCD 101)
Jul 94. (d-lp/c/cd) (COOK/+C/CD 064) **THE MYSTERY OF LOVE IS GREATER THAN THE MYSTERY OF DEATH**
 – Clay jugg / Shadow in my eyes / Call mother a lonely field / The crazy song / Farm boy / The garden / Snow in Central Park / Looking for love / Heartsick land / Gylen Gylen / I say a little prayer / Bars of Dundee. (d-lp+=) – Donna Karan / Ballad of a simple heart / Stranger on the square / Horseshoe and jug / Mary Jone's dog / So my soul can sing. (also iss.Sep94 cd+=; COOKCDS 064) **THE RIGHT TO REMAIN SILENT** (with ROBERT BLY & JAMES HALLAWELL)
Jan 95. (cd-ep) (FRY 036) **I SAY A LITTLE PRAYER / HONEYMOON HILL / AS WE SAILED INTO SKIBBEREEN / THE BONNIE EARL O' MORAY**
Sep 95. (d-lp/c/cd) (COOK/+C/CD 090) **THE FORBIDDEN SONGS OF THE DYING WEST**
 – Young male suicide blessed by invisible woman / Some ancient misty morning / Working alone – A blessing / Leven's lament / Marble city bar / The wanderer / Exultation / Men in prison / Birds leave shadows / Stornoway girl / Silver roof / Lammermuir hills / Come back early or never of come / By the sign of the sheltered star / The scene that haunts my memory / My Lord, what a morning. (d-lp+=) – Exultation.
Apr 97. (d-lp/cd) (COOK/+CD 115) **FAIRY TALES FOR HARD MEN**
 – Boy trapped in a man / Desolation blues / Extremely violent man / Old West African song / aint Judas / Poortoun / Fear of woman / Walled covers of Ravenscraig / Sad Polish song / Sexual danger / Jim o' Windygates / Mad as the mist and snow / Kirkconnell flow / Listening to crows pray / Sir Patrick Spens . . . / Sunflower / Torture blues / Story which could be true / Scotland the brave.
Sep 97. (cd; by JOHN ST. FIELD & JACKIE LEVEN) (COOKCD 131) **CONTROL** (rec.1973-5)
 – Soft lowland tongue / Raerona / Mansion tension / Dog star / Ruins / I'm always a Prinlaws boy / Problem / Dune voices / Sleeping in bracken. (LP was iss.1975 by JOHN ST. FIELD on a Spanish label)
Mar 01. (4xcd-box) (COOKCD 212) **GREAT SONGS FROM ETERNAL BARS**
 – (CONTROL / FAIRYTALES FOR HARDMEN / FORBIDDEN SONGS OF THE DYING WEST / THE WANDERER).
Aug 01. (cd; as JACKIE LEVEN & DAVID THOMAS) (COOKCD 213) **CREATURES OF LIGHT AND DARKNESS**
 – My Spanish dad / Exit wound / The sexual loneliness of Jesus Christ / Hidden world of she / Billy ate my pocket / Rainy day Bergen women / Friendship between men and women / Stopped by woods on a snowy evening / Washing by hand / Wrapped up in blue.
Jun 02. (cd) **BAREFOOT DAYS** (official bootleg)

DR. MIX & THE REMIX (see under ⇒ METAL URBAIN)

DRONES

Formed: Manchester, England . . . late 1976 by M.J. DRONE, GUS GANGRENE, STEVE 'WHISPER' CUNDALL and PETE PURFECT. Bonafide DIY three-chord wonders, The DRONES were there at punk's inception; while their fuzzy guitar anthems mightn't have been in the same league as The SEX PISTOLS or even The DAMNED, the pogo-tastic likes of 'BONE IDOL' and 'LOOKALIKES' were loud, dumb and a hell of a lot more fun than the latest REO SPEEDWAGON offering. Making their vinyl debut on the 'Ohm' label in 1977 with the 'TEMPTATIONS OF A WHITE COLLAR WORKER' EP, the band followed up with the aforementioned 'BONE IDOL' (a double A-side with 'I JUST WANNA BE MYSELF') on their self-financed 'Valer' imprint later that year. The DRONES' one and only album, 'FURTHER TEMPTATIONS', also surfaced late in 1977, their two-minute formula not exactly suited to a long playing format (probably in the same way as The SUBURBAN STUDS and The LURKERS). Prior to their inevitable demise in the early 80's, they did manage to have material included on two various artists compilations – the 'Beggars Banquet' compilation, 'Streets' and live punk effort, 'Short Circuit: Live At The Electric Circus' – as well as releasing a final single, 'CAN'T SEE' on the 'Fabulous' label.

Album rating: FURTHER TEMPTATIONS (*5)

M.J. DRONE (b. HOWELLS) – vocals, rhythm guitar / **GUS GANGRENE** (b. CALLENDAR) – lead guitar, vocals / **WHISPER** (b. STEVE CUNDELL) – bass / **PETE PURFECT** (b. LAMBERT) – drums

O.H.M.S. / not iss.

May 77. (7"ep) (GOOD MIX 1) **TEMPTATIONS OF A WHITE COLLAR WORKER**
 – Lookalikes / Corgi crap / Hard on me / You'll lose.

Valer / not iss.

Oct 77. (7") (VRS 1) **BONE IDOL. / I JUST WANNA BE MYSELF**
Dec 77. (lp) (VRLP 1) **FURTHER TEMPTATIONS**
 – Persecution complex / Bone idol / Movement / Be my baby / Corgi crap / Lookalikes / The underdog / No more time / City drones / I just wanna be myself / Lift off the bans. (<cd-iss. Oct93 & Sep01 on 'Anagram'+=; CDPUNK 20>) – TEMPTATIONS OF A WHITE COLLAR WORKER (tracks) / I just wanna be myself / Bone idol / Can't see / Fooled today. (lp re-iss. Oct96 on 'Get Back'; GET 6)
Jan 78. (12"; w-drawn) (VRSP 1) **BE MY BABY. / LIFT OFF THE BANS**

— continued to work sporadically until final single below

Fabulous / not iss.

Mar 80. (7") (JC 4) **CAN'T SEE. / FOOLED TODAY**

– compilations, etc. –

Apr 97. (cd) Overground; (OVER 60CD) **EXPECTATIONS: TAPES FROM THE ATTIC 1975-1982**
 (lp-iss.Oct97 on 'Get Back'; GET 25)
May 99. (cd) Captain Oi; (<AHOYCD 111>) **SORTED** — May00
 – Sorted / Johnny go home (remix) / Dirty bastards / Nightman / Psychotic woman / American pie / The phone / Good girl / I'll get back to you / I don't care / Jon the postman / I heard it through the grapevine.

DROOGS

Formed: Los Angeles, California, USA . . . 1972 by vocalist RIC ALBIN, guitarist ROGER CLAY, bassist PAUL MOTTER and drummer KYLE RAVEN. The latter two were replaced during the next decade by a long list of rhythm players, finally stabilising with DAVID PROVOST and JON GERLACH respectively. Produced by EARLE MANKEY (ex-SPARKS), their first albums, 'STONE COLD WORLD' (1984) and 'KINGDOM DAY' (1987), established the band on the fringe of the Paisley underground scene alongside the likes of The DREAM SYNDICATE and GREEN ON RED, who occasionally augmented their studio efforts. They subsequently signed to German outlet, 'Music Maniac', the albums 'MAD DOG DREAMS' (1990), 'LIVE IN EUROPE' and 'GUERILLA LOVE-IN' (1991) surfacing at the turn of the decade. • **Covered:** HE'S WAITIN' (Sonics) / LIGHT BULB BLUES (Shadows Of Knight) / I'M NOT LIKE EVERYBODY ELSE (Kinks) / OFF THE HOOK (Rolling Stones) / GARDEN ON MY MIND (Mickey Finn) / I'M WAITING FOR THE MAN (Velvet Underground) / YOU MUST BE A WITCH (Lollipop Shoppe) / BORN TO BE WILD (Steppenwolf) / ZERO HOUSE (John Hiatt) / I WANT SOMETHING (Bad Religion) / WINGS OF MERCURY + MARIA + WEATHERED AND TORN (Dream Syndicate) / WE ALL FALL DOWN (dB's) / PAPER DOLLS (. . . Lee) / MORNING DEW (Tim Rose) / I GOT A RIGHT (Stooges) / etc.

Album rating: STONE COLD WORLD (*6) / KINGDOM DAY (*5) / ANTHOLOGY compilation (*6) / MAD DOG DREAMS (*6) / WANT SOMETHING (*5) / LIVE IN EUROPE mini (*4) / GUERILLA LOVE-IN (*5) / ATOMIC GARAGE (*4)

RIC ALBIN – vocals, harmonica, acoustic guitar / **ROGER CLAY** – guitar, vocals / **PAUL MOTTER** – bass / **KYLE RAVEN** – drums

		not iss.	Plug n Socket
1973.	(7") <PNS 001> **HE'S WAITIN'. / LIGHT BULB BLUES**	–	

— **KEVIN McMANUS** – bass; repl. MOTTER

| 1974. | (7") <PNS 002> **SET MY LOVE ON YOU. / I'M NOT LIKE EVERYBODY ELSE** | – | |

— **JOEY HOEY** – bass; repl. McMANUS (on A-side)

| 1974. | (7") <PNS 003> **AHEAD OF MY TIME. / GET AWAY** | – | |

— **BOB KASEY** – bass; repl. HOEY

| 1975. | (7") <PNS 004> **OVERNIGHT SUCCESS. / LAST LAUGH** | – | |

— **J R KRUGER** – bass; repl. KASEY
— **ADRIAN FOLTZ** – drums; repl. RAVEN

| 1979. | (7") <PNS 005> **AS MUCH AS I WANT. / OFF THE HOOK** (live) | – | |
| 1980. | (c-30) **MEMORIAL** | – | |

<above issued on 'Stapled Chin Music'>

— **TOM MUSICK** – bass; repl. KRUGER

| 1981. | (7") <PNS 006> **ONLY GAME IN TOWN. / GARDEN OF MY MIND** | – | |

— **CLAY + ALBIN** recruited **DAVID PROVOST** – bass / **TOM MORGAN** – keyboards / **PHIL COHEN** – drums

| 1983. | (12"ep) <PNSEP 101> **HEADS EXAMINED EP** | – | |

– 98 steps / You must be a witch / Train she's on / Born to be wild.

— **JON GERLACH** – drums; repl. COHEN + MORGAN

| 1984. | (7") <PNS 007> **CHANGE IS GONNA COME. / I'M WAITING FOR THE MAN** (live) | – | |
| 1984 | (lp) <6919> **STONE COLD WORLD** | – | |

– Change is gonna come / Set my love on you / For these remaining days / Stone cold world / Mr. Right / From another side / He's waitin' (live NYC) / Only game in town (soundtrack version). *(UK-iss.May86 on 'Spindrift'+=; SPIN 117)* – I'm waiting for the man (live). *(German-iss.Feb92 on 'Music Maniac' cd+=/lp+=; MM CD/LP 034)* – KINGDOM DAY

<above issued for 'Passport' US>

1986.	(7") <PNS 008> **COLLECTOR'S ITEM. / WEBSTER FIELD**	–	P.V.C.
		not iss.	
1987.	(lp/cd) <PVC/+CD 8956> **KINGDOM DAY**	–	

– Stranger in the rain / Quarry street / Call off your dogs / Jack of all trades / Kingdom day / Webster field / Collector's item / When angels fall / Countdown to zero. *(German-iss.1989 on 'Music Maniac'; MMLP 011)*

— in 1988, 'WEATHERED AND TORN' featured on the 7" for Bucketful Of Brains fanzine (BOB 22)

— **BRIAN HUDSON** – drums; repl. GERLACH

		Music Maniac	not iss.
Aug 89.	(lp) (MMLP 026) **MAD DOG DREAMS**	–	– German

– Zero house / Paper dolls / Echo of an empty heart / I want something / Reach the dawn / Devil left to pay / Wings of mercury / Mad dog dreams / We all fall down.

| May 90. | (lp) <75> **WANT SOMETHING** | | |

– Other end of town / Zero house / Maria / Long dark night / Paper dolls / Echo of an empty heart / I want something / Reach the dawn / Devil left to pay / Wings of Mercury / County line / Mad dog dreams / She's got everything / We all fall down. <issued in the States on 'Skyclad'>

— **HOT ROD STEVE** – drums; repl. HUDSON

| Dec 90. | (m-lp) (MMLP 037) **LIVE IN EUROPE 1990** (live) | – | – German |

– Contdown to zero / Long dark night / Paper dolls / Jack of trades / 98 steps / Zero house.

— **TY RIO** – drums; repl. HUDSON (on 1/2 of below)

| Nov 91. | (cd/lp) (MMCD/MMLP 041) **GUERILLA LOVE-IN** | – | – German |

– Maria / Cruel highway / Other end of town / Smoke and mirrors / Saints of Mexico / Tempt me / Morning dew / Long dark night / Close to the sun / County line (instrumental). *(cd+=)* – I got a right.

		not iss.	Plug n Socket
1993.	(7") <PNS 009> **TV MAN. / LETTER TO THE TIMES**	–	
		Hitch-Hyke	not Iss.
1993.	(7") (LIFT7-002) **COME HEAVEN OR HELL. / I GOT A RIGHT**	–	– Greece

— disbanded in 1993 but re-formed '96/'97

		not iss.	Lakota
1997.	(cd) <003> **ATOMIC GARAGE**	–	

– Puzzled mynds / Guerilla love-in / TV man / Letter to the times / For the roses / Gold inside a shrine / Come Heaven or Hell / Two headed snake / Tell the world / That dangerous year / Talk thru the night.

– compilations, etc. –

| Dec 87. | (lp/cd) *Music Maniac*; (MM LP/CD 005) **ANTHOLOGY** (compilation of all their 'Plug n Socket' 45's) | – | – German |

Ian DURY

Born: 12 May '42, Upminster, Essex, England. At age seven he became partially crippled from contracting polio. In 1970, he was employed as a teacher / lecturer at Canterbury College. The following year, he formed KILBURN & THE HIGH ROADS, who embarked on pub/college circuit in London. After 1 album in the mid-70's and many line-up changes, they disbanded, leaving DURY and manager DAVE ROBINSON to create solo deal for the singer. Signing to Jake Riviera's new indie label, 'Stiff', he soon raced up album charts in 1977 with the new wave favourite 'NEW BOOTS AND PANTIES!!!'. DURY's articulate patter and intelligent lyrics fused well with funky/jerky group backing which alternated between rock'n'roll and disco. He also developed many areas of Cockney rhyme-slang into rude but clever lyrics. The album made the UK Top 5, preceded by the brilliant 'SEX AND DRUGS AND ROCK AND ROLL', DURY's typically wry comment on the excesses of the music business. The following year, the singer's cast of sidemen became The BLOCKHEADS, the line-up of CHAZ JANKEL, NORMAN WATT-ROY, CHARLEY CHARLES, MICKEY GALLAGHER, JOHN TURNBULL and DAVY PAYNE playing on DURY's first hit single, 'WHAT A WASTE'. However, it was the follow-up, 'HIT ME WITH YOUR RHYTHM STICK' which really earned DURY a smutty place in the annals of pop history, its half-spoken narrative style breaking into a gloriously demented chorus. The track sat astride the UK singles chart for a few weeks, while the attendant album, 'DO IT YOURSELF' (1979) made No.2. The DURY/JANKEL writing partnership was to end soon after, however, the latter embarking on solo work and freeing up a position for ex-DR. FEELGOOD guitarist, WILKO JOHNSON. The resulting album, 'LAUGHTER' (1980), met with limited success, prompting a musical Spring clean from DURY; signing to 'Polydor', securing the esteemed services of SLY & ROBBIE and reuniting with JANKEL, the cheeky cockney released the acclaimed 'LORD UPMINSTER'. Commercial success continued to elude him, however, and DURY semi-retired in the mid-80's following the '4,000 WEEKS HOLIDAY' (1984) opus. He eventually resurfaced in 1989 with the 'APPLES' soundtrack, although he proved his inimitable sense of humour hadn't deserted him on 1992's 'THE BUS DRIVERS PRAYER & OTHER STORIES'. Having been diagnosed with cancer of the colon in 1995 (it was soon to spread into his liver), IAN DURY wanted to bow out with a bang not a whimper. In the summer of '98, the man did just that (with the help from his ever faithful BLOCKHEADS). His comeback album, 'Mr LOVE PANTS', even returned him back into the charts, but sadly, this was IAN's last lyrical message – he died on the 27th March, 2000; they said he died with a smile on his face. A posthumous final recording, the LP 'TEN MORE TURNIPS FROM THE TIP' (2002), kept the man on a high note. • **Songwriters:** DURY – words / JANKEL – music, until his departure from The BLOCKHEADS. • **Trivia:** After he semi-retired in the mid-80's, he started an acting career in films:- NUMBER ONE (1985) / PIRATES (1986) / HEARTS OF FIRE (1987), and TV plays:- KING OF THE GHETTOS (1986) / TALK OF THE DEVIL (1986) / NIGHT MOVES (1987). His other work on TV was mainly for commercials, etc.

Album rating: NEW BOOTS AND PANTIES!! (*8) / DO IT YOURSELF (*7) / LAUGHTER (*6) / JUKEBOX DURY compilation (*6) / LORD UPMINSTER (*6) / 400 WEEKS HOLIDAY (*5) / SEX AND DRUGS AND ROCK AND ROLL compilation (*7) / APPLES (*5) / THE BUS DRIVER'S PRAYER AND OTHER STORIES / Mr LOVE PANTS (*6) / TEN MORE TURNIPS FROM THE TIP (*6)

KILBURN & THE HIGH ROADS

IAN DURY – vocals / **KEITH LUCAS** – guitar / **DAVEY PAYNE** – sax / **CHARLIE SINCLAIR** – bass repl. HUMPHREY OCEAN who had repl. CHARLIE HART / **LOUIS LAROSE** then **GEORGE BUTLER** – drums

— Early 1974, recorded lp for 'Raft', which was shelved after 'Warners' took over label. It was later issued by them in Oct'78 as 'WOTABUNCH', after DURY was top of the charts.

— (mid-74) **DAVID ROHOMAN** – drums repl. BUTLER / **ROD MELVIN** – piano repl. HARDY

		Dawn	not iss.
Nov 74.	(7") (DNS 1090) **ROUGH KIDS. / BILLY BENTLEY**		–
Feb 75.	(7") (DNS 1102) **CRIPPLED WITH NERVES. / HUFFETY PUFF**		–
Jun 75.	(lp) (DNLS 3065) **HANDSOME**		–

– The roadette song / Pam's mood / Crippled with nerves / Broken skin / Upminster kid / Patience / Father / Thank you mum / Rough kids / The badger and the rabbit / The mumble rumble and the cocktail rock / The call up. *(re-iss. Nov85 on 'Flashback' lp/c; FBLP/ZCFBL 8094)*

— Disbanded mid-75, although IAN gigged at times with a new line-up as IAN DURY & THE KILBURNS. KEITH LUCAS was later to become NICK CASH and form 999. There were also other KILBURN material re-released after DURY's success.

1977.	(lp) *Warners*; (K 56513) **WOTABUNCH**		–
Sep 78.	(7") *Warners*; (K 17225) **BENTLEY. / PAM'S MOODS**		–
Jul 83.	(lp/c) *P.R.T.*; (DOW/ZCDOW 17) **UPMINSTER KIDS**		–

IAN DURY

— - vocals solo with **CHAZ JANKEL** – guitar, keyboards (ex-BYZANTIUM) plus session men that became The BLOCKHEADS (see below)

		Stiff	Stiff
Aug 77.	(7",7"orange) (BUY 17) **SEX AND DRUGS AND ROCK AND ROLL. / RAZZLE MY POCKET**		
Sep 77.	(lp/gold-lp/c) (SEEZ/SEEZG/ZSEEZ 4) <0002> **NEW BOOTS AND PANTIES!!!**	5	Apr78

– Sweet Gene Vincent / ake up and make love with me / I'm partial to your abracadabra / My old man / Billericay Dickie / Clevor Trever / If I was with a woman / Plainstow Patricia / Blockheads / Blackmail man. *(re-iss. Sep86 on 'Demon' lp/c/cd+=; FIEND/+CASS/CD 63)* – (interview). *(re-iss. cd Aug98 & Apr00 on 'A Hit Label'; AHLCD 57)* *(cd re-iss. Jun00 on 'REpertoire'; REP 4546)*

| Nov 77. | (7") (BUY 23) **SWEET GENE VINCENT. / YOU'RE MORE THAN FAIR** | | – |

Ian DURY (cont) — THE GREAT INDIE DISCOGRAPHY — The 1970s

IAN DURY AND THE BLOCKHEADS

— with **JANKEL** plus **NORMAN WATT-ROY** – bass (ex-LOVING AWARENESS, ex-GLENCOE) / **CHARLEY CHARLES** – drums (ex-LOVING AWARENESS, ex-GLENCOE) / **MICKEY GALLAGHER** – keyboards (ex-LOVING AWARENESS, ex-FRAMPTON'S CAMEL) / **JOHN TURNBULL** – guitar (ex-LOVING AWARENESS) / **DAVEY PAYNE** – saxophone (ex-WRECKLESS ERIC)

Apr 78. (7"/12") (BUY 27/+12) **WHAT A WASTE. / WAKE UP AND MAKE LOVE WITH ME** — 11

Nov 78. (7"; as IAN & THE BLOCKHEADS) (BUY 38) **HIT ME WITH YOUR RHYTHM STICK. / THERE AIN'T HALF BEEN SOME CLEVER BASTARDS** — 1

May 79. (lp/c) (SEEZ/ZSEEZ 14) <36104> **DO IT YOURSELF** — 2 — Jul79
– Inbetweenies / Quiet / Don't ask me / Sink my boats / Waiting for your taxi / This is what we find / Uneasy sunny hotsy totsy / Mischief / Dance of the screamers / Lullaby for Francies. (re-iss. Feb90 on 'Demon' lp/c/cd; FIEND/+CASS/CD 133) (re-iss. cd May95 on 'Disky'; Sep98 on 'Repertoire'; REP 4547) (cd re-iss. Apr00 on 'A Hit Label'; AHLCD 58)

Jul 79. (7") (BUY 50) **REASONS TO CHEERFUL (pt.3). / COMMON AS MUCK** — 3

Aug 80. (7") (BUY 90) **I WANT TO BE STRAIGHT. / THAT'S NOT ALL HE WANTS** — 22

— **WILKO JOHNSON** – guitar (ex-DR. FEELGOOD, solo artist) repl. JANKEL who went solo

Oct 80. (7") (BUY 100) **SUEPERMAN'S BIG SISTER. / F***ING ADA** — 51
(12"+=) (BUYIT 100) – You'll see glimpses.

Nov 80. (lp/c) (SEEZ/ZSEEZ 30) <36998> **LAUGHTER** — 48 — Jan81
– Sueperman's big sister / Pardon / Delusions of grandeur / Yes and no (Paula) / Dance of the crackpots / Over the points / (Take your elbow out of the soup you're sitting on the chicken) / Uncoolohol / Hey, hey, take me away / Manic depression / Oh, Mr. Peanut / F***ing Ada. (cd re-iss. May95 on 'Disky'; (cd re-iss. Aug98 & Apr00 on 'A Hit Label'; AHLCD 59)

— IAN DURY now brought in the services of rhythm boys **SLY & ROBBIE** plus **JANKEL** + **TYRONE DOWNIE** – keyboards

Polydor   Polydor

Aug 81. (7"/12") (POSP/+X 285) **SPASTICUS AUSTICIOUS. / ('A'instrumental)**

Sep 81. (lp/c) (POLD/+C 5042) <16337> **LORD UPMINSTER** — 53
– Funky disco pops / Red letter / Girls watching / Wait for me / The body song / Lonely town / Trust is a must / Spasticus austicious. (re-iss. Dec89 on 'Great Expectations' lp/cd; PIP LP/CD 005)

IAN DURY & THE MUSIC STUDENTS

— with many musicians including **JANKEL, PAYNE + RAY COOPER**

Nov 83. (7"/12") (POSP/+C 646) **REALLY GLAD YOU CAME. / INSPIRATION**

Jan 84. (lp/c) (POLD/+C 5112) **4,000 WEEKS HOLIDAY** — 54 —
– (You're my) Inspiration / Friends / Tell your daddy / Peter the painter / Ban the bomb / Percy the poet / Very personal / Take me to the cleaners / The man with no face / Really glad you came. (re-iss. Dec89 on 'Great Expectations' lp/cd; PIP LP/CD 004)

Feb 84. (7") (POSP 673) **VERY PERSONAL. / BAN THE BOMB**
(12"+=) (POSPX 673) – The sky's the limit.

IAN DURY

— solo, with **PAYNE, GALLAGHER, COOPER** plus **STEVE WHITE** – drums / **MICHAEL McEVOY** – bass, synth / **MERLIN RHYS-JONES** – guitar / **FRANCES RUFELLE** – vocals / etc.

E.M.I.   not iss.

Oct 89. (7"/7"pic-d) (EMI/+P 5534) **PROFOUNDLY IN LOVE WITH PANDORA. / EUGENIUS (YOU'RE A GENIUS)** — 45 —
(above from the TV series, 'Adrian Mole')

WEA   not iss.

Oct 89. (7") (YZ 437) **APPLES. / BYLINE BROWN**

Oct 89. (lp/c/cd) (WX 326/+C)(246355-2) **APPLES** (soundtrack)
– Apples / Love is all / Byline Browne / Bit of kit / Game on / Looking for Harry / England's glory / Bus driver's prayer / P.C. Honey / The right people / All those who say okay / Riding the outskirts of fantasy.

— In Sep'90 he reformed IAN DURY & THE BLOCKHEADS for two reunion gigs

IAN DURY

Demon   not iss.

Apr 91. (lp/cd) (FIEND/+CD 777) **WARTS 'N' AUDIENCE (live 22 December 1990)**
– Wake up / Clever Trevor / If I was with a woman [cd-only] Billericay Dickie / Quiet / My old man / Spasticus autisticus / Plaistow Patricia / Clever bastards / Sweet Gene Vincent / What a waste / Hit me with your rhythm stick / Blockheads. (cd re-iss. Sep00 on 'Diablo'+=; DIAB 8037) – Inbetweenies / Reasons to be cheerful (part 3).

Nov 92. (cd/c) (FIEND CD/CASS 702) **THE BUS DRIVERS PRAYER & OTHER STORIES**
– That's enough of that / Bill Haley's last words / Poor Joey / Quick quick slow / Fly in the ointment / O'Donegal / Poo-poo in the prawn / Ave a word / London talking / D'orine the cow / Your horoscope / No such thing as love / Two old dogs without a name / Bus driver's prayer.

IAN DURY & THE BLOCKHEADS

— with **CHAZ JANKEL, MICKEY GALLAGHER, DAVEY PAYNE, JOHN TURNBULL, NORMAN WATT-ROY, STEVEN MONTI** (drums) / **The BREEZEBLOCKS** – backing vocals

Ronnie Harris   Ronnie Harris

Jun 98. (cd) (DUR 1) <61863> **Mr LOVE PANTS** — 57
– Jack shit George / The passing show / You're my baby / Honeysuckle highway / Itinerant / Geraldine / Cacka boom / Bed 'o' roses No.9 / Heavy living / Mash it up Harry.

— sadly, IAN was to die on the 27th of March, 2000; his last recording was left for a few years . . .

Mar 02. (cd) (DUR 002) <63145> **TEN MORE TURNIPS FROM THE TIP** — 60 — Apr02
– Dance little rude boy / I believe / It ain't cool / Cowboys / Ballad of the sulphate strangler / I could lie / One love / Happy hippy / Books and water / You're the why (with ROBBIE WILLIAMS).

May 02. (cd-s) (DUR 004) **ONE LOVE / JOCK'S POEM / BALLAD OF THE SULPHATE STRANGLER**

— compilations etc. —

Nov 81. (lp/c) Stiff; (SEEZ/ZSEEZ 41) **JUKE BOX DURY**
(re-iss. Sep82 as 'GREATEST HITS' on 'Fame' lp/c; FA/TC-FA 3031)

May 85. (7") Stiff; (BUY 214) **HIT ME WITH YOUR RHYTHM STICK (Paul Hardcastle mix). / SEX AND DRUGS AND ROCK AND ROLL** — 55 —
(12"+=) (BUYIT 214) – Reasons to be cheerful / Wake up and make love to me (Paul Hardcastle mix).

Apr 87. (lp/c/cd) Demon; (FIEND/+CASS/CD 69) **SEX AND DRUGS AND ROCK AND ROLL**
– Hit me with your rhythm stick / I want to be straight / There ain't half been some clever bastards / What a waste! / Common as muck / Reasons to be cheerful (pt.3) / Sex and drugs and rock and roll / Sueperman's big sister / Razzle in my pocket / You're more than fair / Inbetweenies / You'll see glimpses.

Jul 91. (7"/c-s) Flying; (FLYR 1/+C) **HIT ME WITH YOUR RHYTHM STICK '91 (The Flying Remix Version) / HIT ME WITH YOUR RHYTHM STICK** — 73 —
(12"+=/cd-s+=) (FLYR 1 T/CD) – ('A'mix).

Aug 91. (3xcd-box) Demon; (IAN 1) **IAN DURY & THE BLOCKHEADS**
– (NEW BOOTS AND PANTIES / DO IT YOURSELF / SEX AND DRUGS AND ROCK AND ROLL)

Aug 96. (cd) Disky; (DC 88975-2) **THE BEST OF IAN DURY**

Sep 99. (cd) E.M.I.; (522888-2) **REASONS TO BE CHEERFUL – THE VERY BEST OF IAN DURY & THE BLOCKHEADS** — 40 —
– Reasons to be cheerful / Wake up and make love with me / Hit me with your rhythm stick / Clevor Trever / What a waste / Sex and drugs and rock and roll / This is what we find / Itinerant child / Sweet Gene Vincent / I want to be straight / Blockheads / Mash it up Harry / There ain't half been some clever bastards / Billericay Dickie / Inbetweenies / Sparticus (autisticus) / My old man / Lullaby for Francis.

Apr 00. (d-cd) Repertoire; (REP 4592) **REASONS TO BE CHEERFUL**

May 00. (cd) Repertoire; (REP 4507) **THE BEST OF IAN DURY**

— The BLOCKHEADS also released their own singles and lp early 80's

THE GREAT INDIE DISCOGRAPHY — The 1970s

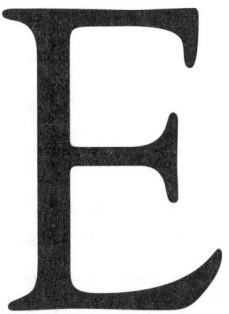

EATER

Formed: London, England ... late 1976 by ANDY BLADE, BRIAN CHEVETTE, IAN WOODGATE and 15 year-old DEE GENERATE. Signed to DIY label, er ... 'The Label', they released their debut 45, 'OUTSIDE VIEW', in March '77. Around this time their songs '15' and 'DON'T NEED IT' were used on the live seminal various artists album 'LIVE AT THE ROXY'. Their debut album finally saw light at the end of that punk year, encompassing EATER's basic boy-ish punk rock – showing not every Punk band had talent.
• **Songwriters:** BLADE except; JEEPSTER (T.Rex).

Album rating: THE ALBUM (*4) / THE HISTORY OF EATER VOL.1 compilation (*5)

ANDY BLADE – vocals / **BRIAN CHEVETTE** – guitar / **IAN WOODGATE** – bass / **DEE GENERATE** (b. PHIL ROWLANDS) – drums

			The Label	not iss.
Mar 77.	(7")	*(TLR 001)* **OUTSIDE VIEW. / YOU**	☐	-
Jun 77.	(7")	*(TLR 003)* **THINKIN' OF THE USA. / SPACE DREAMIN' / MICHAEL'S MONETARY SYSTEM**	☐	-
Oct 77.	(7"/12")	*(TLR 004/+12)* **LOCK IT UP. / JEEPSTER**	☐	-
Jan 78.	(lp)	*(TLRLP 001)* **THE ALBUM**	☐	-

– You / Public toys / Room for one / Lock it up / Sweet Jane / 15 / I don't need it / Ann / Get raped / Space dreaming / Queen bitch / My business / Waiting for the man / No more / No brains / Peace and luv (H-bomb). *(re-iss. Apr98 on 'Get Back'; GET 27LP)*

| Sep 78. | (7"white-ep/12"white-ep) | *(TLR 007/+12)* **GET YOUR YO-YO'S OUT (live)** | ☐ | - |

– Debutantes ball / No more / Thinkin' of the USA / Holland.

| Nov 78. | (7") | *(TLR 009)* **WHAT SHE WANTS SHE NEEDS. / REACHING FOR THE SKY** | ☐ | - |

—— they split early next year. ANDY BLADE owned the group name and recruited BILLY DUFFY, BOB GURNEY and DAVID JOHNSON. In 1980, BLADE released a solo single 'BREAK THE NEWS' for 'SMS'; *SMS 001)*. He later formed The ROYTERS, while ROWLAND joined SLAUGHTER & THE DOGS, after a spell in RADIO SWEETHEARTS.

– compilations, etc. –

| Feb 85. | (colrd-lp) | *De Lorean; (EAT 1)* **THE HISTORY OF EATER** (above w/ free 7"; *EAT FREEBIE 1*) | ☐ | - |
| Apr 93. | (cd/lp) | *Anagram; (CD+/PUNK 10)* **THE COMPLEAT EATER** | ☐ | - |

– (THE ALBUM tracks) / (cd+=) – Outside view / Thinking of the U.S.A. / Michaels monetary system / She's wearing green / Notebook / Jeepster / Debutantes ball / Holland / What she wants she needs / Reach for the sky / Point of view / Typewriter babies.

| Mar 98. | (cd) | *Creative Man; (<CMCD 024>)* **ALL OF EATER** | ☐ | ☐ |

ANDY BLADE

			Creative Man	Creative Man
May 95.	(cd)	*(<CMCD 007>)* **FROM THE PLANET POP TO THE MENTAL SHOP**	☐	☐

– Big bad world / The church bell / Three weeks / Playtime / Creature / The big plan / Beautiful failure / Speed of life / Sad / All I want from you / All of the girls / Horsefly / Heart / The girl who forgets everything / The amazing adventures / Without using hands / Wednesday Jones / The effervescing elephant / Face the window / Speed of life jazz.

| Apr 96. | (cd-ep) | *(CMCDS 24)* **JUNKIE SHOOTING STAR** | ☐ | - |

– Heart / The girl who forgets everything / Horsefly / Church bell / The amazing adventures.

EDDIE & THE HOT RODS

Formed: Canvey Island, Essex, England ... 1975 by DAVE HIGGS, alongside former amateur boxer turned singer, BARRIE MASTERS, STEVE NICOLS, PETE WALL and ROB STEEL (the latter pair soon to be replaced by schoolboy, PAUL GRAY and harmonica player, LEW LEWIS). After ripping up the tarmac on the thriving London pub-rock circuit, manager/producer/lyricist, ED HOLLIS, secured them a deal with 'Island'. With precision timing, EDDIE & Co emerged as a catalyst for the nascent punk scene, just edging out ahead of R&B contemporaries (e.g. DR. FEELGOOD and The COUNT BISHOPS) with a raw, rasping three-chord blast more attuned to the intensity of early WHO. Sandwiched between the release of their first two singles, 'WRITING ON THE WALL' and 'WOOLY BULLY' (a Sam The Sham & The Pharaohs cover), was an infamous gig at the Marquee where unknown support act, SEX PISTOLS, made their mark in more ways than one. In fact the 'HOT RODS' subsequent EP was recorded at the same venue, featuring garage/R&B standards, 'GET OUT OF DENVER' (Bob Seger) and '96 TEARS' (? & The Mysterians) together with a medley of 'GLORIA'-'SATISFACTION' (Them – Rolling Stones). The first punk-affiliated record to make the Top 50, the EP's success was improved upon in October that year when the 'TEENAGE DEPRESSION' single made the Top 40. A debut album of the same name also charted, an R&R (i.e. Rough'n'Ready rather than Rock'n'Roll) powerhouse that nevertheless didn't entirely succeed in capturing the spark of their live set. Having already sacked LEW LEWIS prior to the aforementioned 'PISTOLS gig, the group's sound was fuel-injected by the addition of second guitarist, GRAEME DOUGLAS (ex-KURSAAL FLYERS), his introduction coinciding with the release of another Top 50 hit, 'I MIGHT BE LYING'. The latter actually co-wrote what would become the band's biggest hit and signature tune, 'DO ANYTHING YOU WANNA DO'; suspiciously reminiscent of Springsteen's 'Born To Run', this tough-talking power-pop belter became a massive summer '77 hit, giving The RODS (a one-off pseudonym) their only Top 10 hit. That year's album, 'LIFE ON THE LINE', also made it into the UK Top 30, although the band's increasingly sanitised sound and image alienated the spiky-top, safety-pin punk brigade who'd previously lent them their support. While the album spawned a last-ditch Top 40 hit, 'QUIT THIS TOWN', 1979's subsequent 'THRILLER' set was a let down and their last effort for 'Island'. Surprisingly, it would be 'E.M.I.' who'd come to their rescue, although they no doubt regretted their investment as three singles crashed along with a 1981 album, 'FISH 'N' CHIPS', unhealthy listening at its greasiest. The group disbanded shortly after, MASTERS going on to front The INMATES, although he would sporadically re-group EDDIE & THE HOT RODS to minimal interest throughout the 80's and 90's.
• **Songwriters:** Group with HOLLIS lyrics, except covers of THE KIDS ARE ALRIGHT (Who) / YOU BETTER RUN (Rascals) / etc. • **Miscellaneous:** One-time member LEW LEWIS was jailed for 7 years in 1987, due to his part in a P.O. robbery.

Album rating: TEENAGE DEPRESSION (*6) / LIFE ON THE LINE (*7) / THRILLER (*4) / FISH 'N' CHIPS (*3) / ONE STORY TOWN mini (*3) / GASOLINE DAYS (*3) / LIVE AT THE PARADISO (*4) / DO ANYTHING YOU WANNA DO compilation (*6)

BARRIE MASTERS – vocals / **DAVE HIGGS** – guitar / **PAUL GRAY** – bass / **STEVE NICOL** – drums / plus **LEW LEWIS** – mouth harp

			Island	not iss.
Jan 76.	(7")	*(WIP 6270)* **WRITING ON THE WALL. / CRUISIN' (IN THE LINCOLN)**	☐	-

—— now without LEW LEWIS who was sacked due to unruly behavior

| Jun 76. | (7") | *(WIP 6306)* **WOOLY BULLY. / HORSEPLAY (WEARY OF THE SCHMALTZ)** | ☐ | - |
| Aug 76. | (7"ep) | *(IEP 2)* **LIVE AT THE MARQUEE (live)** | 43 | - |

– 96 tears / Get out of Denver / Medley: Gloria – Satisfaction.

| Oct 76. | (7") | *(WIP 6354)* **TEENAGE DEPRESSION. / SHAKE** | 35 | - |
| Dec 76. | (lp) | *(WIP 6354)* **TEENAGE DEPRESSION** | 43 | - |

– Get across to you / Why can't it be? / Show me / All I need is money / Double checkin' woman / The kids are alright / Teenage depression / Horseplay (weary of the schmaltz) / Been so long / Shake / On the run. *(cd-iss. May98 on 'Edsel'; EDCD 563) (<cd re-iss. Mar00 on 'Captain Oi'; AHOYCD 132>)*

—— added **GRAEME DOUGLAS** – guitar (ex-KURSAAL FLYERS)

| Apr 77. | (7") | *(WIP 6388)* **I MIGHT BE LYING. / IGNORE THEM** | 44 | - |
| Jun 77. | (7"ep,12"ep) | *(IEP 5)* **AT THE SPEED OF SOUND** | ☐ | - |

– Hard driving man / Horseplay / Double checkin' woman / All I need is money.

| Aug 77. | (7"/12"; as The RODS) | *(WIP/12WIP 6401)* <IS 091> **DO ANYTHING YOU WANNA DO. / SCHOOLGIRL LOVE** | 9 | - |
| Nov 77. | (lp) | *(ILPS 9509)* **LIFE ON THE LINE** | 27 | - |

– Do anything you wanna do / Quit this town / Telephone girl / What's really going on / Ignore them (still life) / Life on the line / (And) Don't believe your eyes / We sing ... the cross / Beginning of the end. *(<cd-iss. Mar00 on 'Captain Oi'+=; AHOYCD 133>)* – I might be lying / Ignore them (always crashing in the same car) / Schoolgirl love / 'Til the night is gone (let's rock) / Flipside rock / Do anything you wanna do (live) / What's really going on (live) / Why can't it be? (live) / Distortion may be expected.

| Dec 77. | (7"; as ROB TYNER & THE HOT RODS) | *(WIP 6418)* **'TIL THE NIGHT IS GONE (LET'S ROCK). / FLIPSIDE ROCK** | ☐ | - |

(above was with the former MC5 on vocals & guitar)

| Jan 78. | (7") | *(WIP 6411)* **QUIT THIS TOWN. / DISTORTION MAY BE EXPECTED** | 36 | - |
| Mar 78. | (7") | *(WIP 6438)* **LIFE ON THE LINE. / DO ANYTHING YOU WANNA DO (live)** | ☐ | - |

(12"+=) – *(12WIP 6438)* – (I don't know) What's really going on (live) / Why can't it be (live).

Oct 78.	(7")	*(WIP 6464)* **MEDIA MESSIAHS. / HORROR THROUGH THE STRAIGHTNESS**	☐	-
Mar 79.	(7")	*(WIP 6474)* **POWER AND THE GLORY. / HIGHLANDS ONE, HOPEFULS TWO**	☐	-
Mar 79.	(lp)	*(ILPS 9563)* **THRILLER**	50	-

– Power and the glory / Echoes / Media messiahs / Circles / He does it with mirrors / Strangers on the payphone / Out to lunch / Breathless / Take it or leave it / Living dangerously. *(<cd-iss. Mar02 on 'Captain Oi'+=; AHOYCD 192>)* – Horror through straightness / Highlands one Hopefuls two.

			E.M.I.	not iss.
Mar 80.	(7")	*(EMI 5052)* **AT NIGHT. / YOU BETTER RUN / LOOKING AROUND**	☐	-

—— now quartet of **MASTERS, HIGGS, DOUGLAS** / + **T.C.** – bass, (GRAY joined DAMNED)

| Nov 80. | (7") | *(EMI 5110)* **WIDE EYED KIDS. / LEAVE US ALONE** | ☐ | - |

—— guests **RUFUS JENKINS** – accordion / **AL KOOPER** – keyboards, guitar, vocals

EDDIE & THE HOT RODS (cont) — THE GREAT INDIE DISCOGRAPHY — The 1970s

Apr 81. (7") *(EMI 5160)* **FARTHER ON DOWN THE ROAD. / FISH 'N' CHIPS**

Apr 81. (lp) *(EMC 3344)* **FISH 'N' CHIPS**
– Fish 'n' chips / Wide eyed kids / You better run / Time won't let me / Unfinished business / Another party / This is today / Farther on down the road / Call it quits / We want more. *(cd-iss. Oct00; 529472-2)*

―― split '81, BARRIE MASTERS joined The INMATES until he and *NICOL* re-formed **EDDIE & THE HOT RODS** '84 with **WARREN KENNEDY** – guitar / **TONY CRANNEY** – bass

Waterfront not iss.

Feb 85. (7") *(WFS 9)* **FOUGHT FOR YOU. / HEY TONIGHT**

Sep 85. (m-lp) *(WF 023)* **ONE STORY TOWN (live)**
– Teenage depression / Quit this town / Telephone girl / Move town / You better run / Do anything you wanna do.

―― split finally '85; recent recruit, TEX AXILE, later joined TRANSVISION VAMP. **MASTERS, NICOL, HIGGS + GRAY** re-formed EDDIE & THE HOT RODS in the mid 90's / **MICK RODGERS** (ex-MANFRED MANN'S EARTH BAND) repl. GORDON RUSSELL who repl. STEVE WALWYN

Creative Man not iss.

Apr 96. (cd) *(CMCD 008)* **GASOLINE DAYS**
– Human touch / Emergency / Just do it / Love runaway / Love lies bleeding / It's killing me / (Oh no) What you gonna do / Crazy / Gasoline days / Love love love / Alive. *(<re+US-iss.Feb01 on 'Anagram'; CDMGRAM 137>)*

Pub not iss.

Oct 98. (cd) *(PUB 003CD)* **LIVE AT THE PARADISO (live October 1997)** – Dutch
– LOve love love / The kids are all right / Quit this town / Telephone girl / The hunter / Emergency / Alive / Hard driving man / Once bitten twice shy / Killing me / Do anything you wanna do / Human touch / Ignore them.

– compilations, others, etc. –

Aug 92. (cd) *Street Link; (LINKCD 157)* **THE CURSE OF THE HOT RODS**
(re-iss. Jun93 on 'Dojo'; DOJOCD 142)

Sep 93. (cd) *Receiver; (<RRCD 177>)* **LIVE & RARE (live)**

Feb 94. (cd) *Dojo; (DOJOCD 173)* **TIES THAT BIND**

Jul 94. (cd) *Windsong; (WINCD 062)* **BBC RADIO 1 LIVE IN CONCERT (live)**

Aug 94. (cd) *Island; (IMCD 156) <61292>* **THE END OF THE BEGINNING – THE BEST OF EDDIE & THE HOT RODS**
– Do anything you wanna do / Quit this town / Telephone girl / Teenage depression / The kids are alright (live) / Get out of Denver (live) / 'Til the night is gone (let's rock) / Schoolgirl love / Hard drivin' man (live) / On the run (live) / The power and the glory / Ignore them / Still life / Life on the line / Circles / Take it or leave it / Echoes / We sing the cross / The beginning of the end / Gloria (live) / (I can't get no) Satisfaction.

Jan 95. (cd) *Loma; (LOMACD 44)* **THE CURSE OF THE HOT RODS / TIES THAT BIND**

Mar 96. (cd) *Skydog; (622412)* **GET YOUR BALLS OFF**

Aug 96. (cd) *Anagram; (CDMGRAM 108)* **DOING ANYTHING THEY WANNA DO . . .**

Sep 00. (cd) *Spectrum; (544332-2)* **DO ANYTHING YOU WANNA DO**

Jul 02. (cd) *Jungle; (<FREUDCD 079>)* **GET YOUR ROCKS OFF**

Damon EDGE (see under ⇒ CHROME)

ELECTRIC CHAIRS (see under ⇒ COUNTY, Wayne/Jayne)

ELECTRIC EELS

Formed: Cleveland, Ohio, USA . . . 1973 by JOHN MORTON, DAVID E (McMANUS), BRIAN McMAHON and PAUL MAROTTA. They played regularly at a pub owned by JAMIE LYONS (ex-MUSIC EXPLOSION), until, that is, their experimentations went too far after adding industrial and garden equipment. This, together with MORTON's GBH-attitude to the rest of the band led to MAROTTA moving on despite this line-up supporting ROCKET FROM THE TOMBS and the MIRRORS late in '74. The 'EELS soon found a drummer (their first!), NICK KNOX, although this new incarnation was also short-lived as the group split in May '75 after a bust-up on stage. KNOX subsequently joined The CRAMPS, while the remaining quartet (MAROTTA was back in the fold) added ANTON FIER and two former MIRRORS members, JIM JONES and JAIME KLIMEK. By the following year, this group (briefly called MEN FROM U.N.C.L.E.) had evolved into The STYRENES, although only KLIMEK, MAROTTA and FIER were mainstays (MORTON and JONES guested on the odd show). With punk/new wave and avant-garde (fellow Clevelanders, PERE UBU, the prime example) getting a fair crack of the whip in 1978, UK indie imprint 'Rough Trade' decided to issue a posthumous ELECTRIC EELS single, 'AGITATED', as The STYRENES carried on in similarly uncompromising fashion. • **Note:** There was an unconnected English band called The ELECTRIC EELS, who released a few singles on 'Slippery Discs & Rocket'.

Album rating: HAVING A PHILOSOPHICAL INVESTIGATION posthumous (*6)

JOHN MORTON – guitar, vocals / **DAVID E (McMANUS)** – vocals, clarinet (ex-EX-BLANK-EX) / **BRIAN McMAHON** – guitar / **PAUL MAROTTA** – guitar / added **NICK KNOX** – drums

Rough Trade not iss.

Jan 79. (7"; as DIE ELECTRIC EELS) *(RT 008)* **AGITATED. / CYCLOTRON**
(above actually recorded early 1975 with stated line-up)

―― McMANUS subsequently formed the COOL MARRIAGE COUNSELORS, while KNOX joined The CRAMPS. The ELECTRIC EELS briefly reformed adding **ANTON FIER**, who soon joined The FEELIES, The LOUNGE LIZARDS and then PERE UBU (**JIM JONES** also connected to both). Another to be added was **JAIME 'George' KLIMEK** – guitar (he and MAROTTA evolved into the STYRENES)

– compilations, etc. –

Oct 81. (7") *Mustard; <MUST-107>* **SPIN AGE BLASTERS. / BUNNIES (live)**

1989. (lp) *Tinnitus; <191304>* **HAVING A PHILOSOPHICAL INVESTIGATION WITH THE ELECTRIC EELS** (final session in '75)
– Agitated / Cyclotron / Refrigerator / Tidal wave / Anxiety / Natural situation / Cold meat / Cyclotron (giganto) / Sewercide / Jaguar ride / You're full of shit / No nonsense / Accident / Bunnies / Cards and fleurs / Spin age blasters. *<cd-iss. 1991 as 'GOD SAYS FUCK YOU' on 'Homestead'+=; HMS 174-2>* – (see above).

Mar 98. (cd) *Overground; <(OVER 71CD)>* **THE BEAST 999 PRESENTS THE ELECTRIC EELS IN THEIR ORGANIC MAJESTY'S REQUEST**
– Agitated / Cyclotron / Refrigerator / Spin age blasters / Tidal wave / Bunnies / No no / Jazz is / No nonsense / Anxiety / Natural situation / Cold meat / No nonsense / Cyclotron / Sewercide / Jaguar ride / You're full of shit / No nonsense / Accident / Cards and fleurs / As if I cared / Almost beautiful you. *(re-iss. Apr02; same)*

Nov 01. (d-lp/cd) *Scat; <(SCAT 62/+CD)>* **THE EYEBALL OF HELL** (the 1975 recordings) Oct01

ESSENTIAL LOGIC (see under ⇒ LOGIC, Lora)

THE GREAT INDIE DISCOGRAPHY — The 1970s

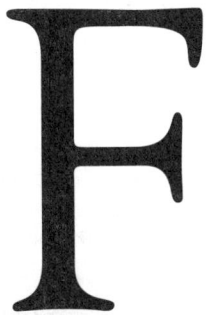

Jad FAIR (see under ⇒ HALF JAPANESE)

FALL

Formed: Salford, Manchester, England . . . late '76 by vocalist MARK E. SMITH, guitarist MARTIN BRAMAH and bassist TONY FRIEL. Completing the line-up with UNA BAINES (electric piano) and KARL BURNS (drums), the unusual punk band completed a 1977 session for Radio One's John Peel show, before signing to indie outlet, 'Step Forward'. In summer of the following year, The FALL released their debut, the 'BINGO-MASTERS BREAK-OUT! EP'. Sharp-witted right from the outset, the shrieking MARK E traversed the minefield of punk sterotypes, the last track, 'REPETITION' a slow teaser to the other quickfire numbers, 'PSYCHO MAFIA' and 'BINGO-MASTER'. The first of many personnel changes was to occur soon after, MARC RILEY and YVONNE PAWLETT coming in for the departing FRIEL (to The PASSAGE) and BAINES (to The BLUE ORCHIDS) respectively. A weird, disappointing follow-up, 'IT'S THE NEW THING' was thankfully not on their glorious Bob Sergeant-produced debut album, 'LIVE AT THE WITCH TRIALS'. Unleashed to an ever-changing alternative rock audience (who were probably now holding down office jobs while daydreaming of their pogoing dancefloor days of yore!?), the studio set (recorded in two days) packed a lyrical angst not heard since the days of The VELVET UNDERGROUND (one of MARK E's inspirators). Quirky punk tracks such as 'FUTURES AND PASTS' and 'REBELLIOUS JUKEBOX' fitted in nicely with longer excursions into experimentation, 'FRIGHTENED' and 'MUSIC SCENE', making this a classic debut worthy of more listeners. MARK E was now in full control after the remaining founding members, BRAMAH and BURNS bailed out (also joining BLUE ORCHIDS and The PASSAGE) to be subsequently replaced by STEVE HANLEY and MIKE LEIGH respectively. What came next was a piece of punk rock genius, the single 'ROWCHE RUMBLE' ditching conventional rhythms in mindblowing style. PAWLETT left the band soon after and was replaced by guitarist, CRAIG SCANLON, just in time for yet another masterful set that year, 'DRAGNET' (1979). A darker, even more experimental affair, MARK E's twisted tales of life's stranger characters were summed up best on tracks such as 'MUZOREWI'S DAUGHTER', 'A FIGURE WALKS', 'SPECTRE VS. RECTOR' and the "rockabilly" 'PSYKICK DANCEHALL'. The FALL kickstarted the 80's in fine fashion with another punkabilly classic, 'FIERY JACK', an ever better version appearing on 'THE FALL LIVE – TOTALE'S TURNS', their first for 'Rough Trade' a couple of months later. With PAUL HANLEY taking over the vacant drum stool, Mark and Co. delivered two more classic 45's, 'HOW I WROTE ELASTIC MAN' and 'TOTALLY WIRED', their third studio set, 'GROTESQUE (AFTER THE GRAMME)', being released later in 1980. An impressive if not brilliant album, it featured acidic, "Manc-abilly" screechers, 'THE CONTAINER DRIVERS', 'PAY YOUR RATES' and 'NEW FACE IN HELL', the kazoo backing provided by the group's manager and MARK E's girlfriend, KAY CARROLL. Next up was another unusual concept, the 10" mini-set that was 'SLATES' (1981), a patchy affair that nevertheless contained another gem, 'AN OLDER LOVER ETC'. With founder member KARL BURNS (the second drummer! and extra keyboard player) now back in tow, The FALL signed to 'Kamera', releasing another diamond of a single, 'LIE DREAM OF A CASINO SOUL' (backed by 'FANTASTIC LIFE' on the B-side; like all 45's at this time, not from the accompanying album). They finally found some degree of commercial success when 1982's 'HEX ENDUCTION HOUR' broke silently into the Top 75. Recorded in Iceland, it was sixty minutes of lyrical abandon, excellent songs, however confusing, came in the shape of 'THE CLASSICAL', 'WHO MAKES THE NAZIS?', 'HIP PRIEST' and their most commercial tune to date, 'JAW-BONE AND THE AIR-RIFLE'. Later that year, the most prolific band on earth issued yet another long-player, 'ROOM TO LIVE', a more self-indulgent delivery that disappointed their growing college/uni fanbase. In 1983, they lost the talents of MARC RILEY, who formed his own outfit, The CREEPERS (another great band!), KAY also leaving after she split (not for the first time!) with the grumpy one. Returning to 'Rough Trade', The FALL excelled once more with two splendid singles, 'THE MAN WHOSE HEAD EXPANDED' and 'KICKER CONSPIRACY', before MARK E's new Californian girlfriend, BRIX, came into the fold. She immediately made her mark, augmenting on vocals, playing guitar and co-writing a few numbers on The FALL's late 1983 album, 'PERVERTED BY LANGUAGE'. This set was another to whet the appetite of the faithful (and another illustrious indie chart topper), MARK's mental execution of tracks like 'EAT Y'SELF FITTER' and 'TEMPO HOUSE' the pick of a bizarre bunch. Advancing to 'Beggars Banquet', MARK E, BRIX E and Co. delivered a couple of odd pop singles in the shape of 'OH BROTHER' and 'C.R.E.E.P.', the records not featuring on their forthcoming eighth set, 'THE WONDERFUL AND FRIGHTENING WORLD OF . . .' (1984). Their buoyant rockabilly was back in full flow on two numbers, 'LAY OF THE LAND' and '2 x 4', while GAVIN FRIDAY of The VIRGIN PRUNES guested on a couple of tracks. A month later, a 12"ep, 'CALL FOR ESCAPE ROUTE', saw The FALL experimenting once more, although this was their last with PAUL HANLEY, who was superseded by the numerous talents of SIMON ROGERS (he had been a member of panpipes afficionados, INCANTATION!). With STEVE HANLEY on summer vacation in 1985, the band released the disappointing 'COULDN'T GET AHEAD' single, its flipside containing their first cover, Gene Vincent's 'ROLLIN DANY'. STEVE was back in time to record their most accessible recording to date, 'THIS NATION'S SAVING GRACE' (1985). Regarded as their best work since their debut, the UK Top 60 album housed the excellent 'PAINTWORK', 'MY NEW HOUSE' and 'I AM DAMO SUZUKI', the latter track MARK E's tribute (sort of!) to the CAN singer. BURNS jumped ship after the obligatory set of singles, SIMON WOOLSTENCROFT taking his place for The FALL's first hit (well, No.75), a cover version of The Other Half's 'MR. PHARMACIST'. This seemed to pay off commercially, especially when the accompanying (for once) 'BEND SINISTER' album reached the dizzy heights of the Top 40 in 1986. Another minor hit 45, 'HEY! LUCIANI' (Top 60 this time), preceded the following year's Top 30 embarrassment coming in the shape of R. Dean Taylor's 'THERE'S A GHOST IN MY HOUSE'. Some time later in 1987, BRIX brought in her old friend, MARSHA SCHOFIELD (both were in BANDA DRATSING together), the keyboard player and vocalist arriving in time for two more hits, 'HIT THE NORTH' and 'VICTORIA' (the latter from the pen of Ray Davies). Now without SIMON, who stayed on as their producer, MARK E and Co. hit the charts (Top 20!) with 'THE FRENZ EXPERIMENT' (1988), a confused set that nevertheless contained one standout song, 'CARRY BAG MAN'. Having also been a friend of ballet dancer, MICHAEL CLARK (who used FALL tapes as his backing soundtrack), MARK E and The FALL collaborated with the bare-arsed performer on the band's next ambitious concept, 'I AM KURIOUS ORANJ' (1988). It was indeed, curious, although the Top 40 album did have its moments, especially in 'CAB IT UP!' and a tongue-in-cheek rendition of William Blake's 'JERUSALEM' (segued with the 'DOG IS LIFE' poem). A concert set, 'SEMINAL LIVE' (1989) filled in time during which MARK and BRIX split up, the blonde (who had initiated her own band, ADULT NET, some time ago) eventually becoming the girlfriend of posh/cockney (you choose) classical violinist, NIGEL KENNEDY; he had previously guested on an earlier FALL album (she stunned many after appearing on 'This Is Your Life', which looked back over NIGEL's short career). BRAMAH was now back in the fold, enrolling in time for their umpteenth long-player, 'EXTRICATE' (1990), their first album jointly controlled by the group's new imprint, 'Cog Sinister' and major 'Fontana' label. Premiered by a hit version of Cold Cut's 'TELEPHONE THING', the cynical but accessible set featured other acidic attacks, 'SING! HARPY', 'THE LITTLEST REBEL' and two more obscure covers, 'POPCORN DOUBLE FEATURE' (Searchers) and 'BLACK MONK THEME' (Monks). MARK then trimmed the band down to a quartet, retaining only CRAIG, STEVE and JOHN to record an excellent SID VICIOUS-esque version of Big Bopper's 'WHITE LIGHTNING'. This minor hit was followed by an uncharacteristic flop, 'HIGH TENSION LINE', although both tracks appeared on the follow-up album, 'SHIFT-WORK' (1991), which added a fifth member, violinist KENNY BRADY. Split into two, titled sides, the UK Top 20 record was highlighted by two more excellent pieces of wordplay, 'EDINBURGH MAN' (still makes me sad) and their umpteenth rockabilly delivery, 'A LOT OF WIND' (as in, you talk . . .). BRADY was let go soon after, DAVID BUSH coming in as a more permanent fixture on their next set, 'CODE: SELFISH' (1992). The album disappointed many of the faithful, although some FALL diehards regard it as one of the best (I'm in the former I'm afraid), its re-working of Hank Williams' 'JUST WAITING' not the MARK E of old, although the hit single, 'FREE RANGE' gets back to grips. Moving to 'Permanent' records (not the most appropriate label title for them), MARK and the lads released their biggest seller to date, 'THE INFOTAINMENT SCAN', which went Top 10 in 1993. Short of a classic MARK E song, it collected together another bunch of covers, this time in the shape of Sister Sledge's 'LOST IN MUSIC', S. Bent's (who?!) 'I'M GOING TO SPAIN' and Lee Perry's 'WHY ARE PEOPLE GRUDGEFUL?' (a Top 50 hit). For many, The FALL "lost it" from then on, their formula of sticking several good (not brilliant) songs together with a few obscure covers saw their fanbase dwindle dramatically. Early in '94, a collaboration between MARK and The INSPIRAL CARPETS on the brilliant 'I WANT YOU' single gave him another hit, the mainman subsequently being invited to do similar things for other acts (notably, COLD CUT and DOSE). The return of KARL BURNS for the disappointing 'MIDDLE CLASS REVOLT' (Top 50, 1994) and BRIX for the bittersweet 'CEREBRAL CAUSTIC' (Top 75, 1995), did little to rectify this change in commercial climate. Now signed to 'Jet' records (once home to ELO!), they added JULIA NAGLE and a few guest members to the fold for their next effort, 'THE LIGHT USER SYNDROME' (1996), gaining some critical respect once again, as well as brief chart action. Returning early '98 on 'Artful' records with 'LEVITATE', MARK E and his crew seemed a tad "lost in music", the album being under par for once. Evidently, there had been friction between him and his "employees", three of them (STEVE HANLEY, KARL BURNS and guitarist TOMMY CROOKS) subsequently bailing out after the frontman became "impossible" to work with. Unperturbed, MARK E talked about a spoken-word album, 'THE POST NEARLY MAN', while the DOSE track, 'INCH' (a No.7 in John Peel's 1997 Festive 50), finally hit the shops early in '99. The FALL (Mk.1998/99) were back soon after, NAGLE standing by her man while newcomers NEVILLE WILDING, TOM HEAD and ADAM HALAL (the former two both session men on the last set – ADAM replaced KAREN LATHAM) were beginning to "fall" into place. That spring, album number thirty odd, 'THE MARSHALL SUITE', was dispatched to the shops and although it was a slight improvement the record found no new fans in the way of sales. Never far from the music biz tabloids, MARK E appeared (as a janitor!) in the low-budget movie, 'Glow Boys', while he collaborated with the CLINT BOON EXPERIENCE (ex-INSPIRAL CARPETS man) on the track, 'I Wanna Be Your Dog'. The millennium finally kicked off for The FALL in November 2000 via studio set, 'THE UNUTTERABLE'. Synth-riddled, sharp-lyrically and positively beaming with chaotic rhythms, the set shone out in all the right places, the obscure cover this time being 'HANDS UP BILLY'. A year on and returning to their own 'Cog Sinister' imprint (having escaped for the previous shot on elephant's graveyard label 'Eagle' – once home to STATUS QUO and GARY NUMAN), MARK E and his "classmates" drove out album #f---knows, 'ARE YOU ARE MISSING WINNER' (2001). A winner it was certainly not, from the obscure nine and a half minutes of 'IBIS-AFRO MAN' trailing after a decent cover of R Dean Taylor's 'GOTTA SEE JANE', it failed to register among even the loyal fanbase. Get back to basics was the call. • **Other covers:** A DAY IN THE LIFE (Beatles) / LEGEND OF XANADU (Dave Dee, Beaky, Mick and Tich) / SHUT UP! (Monks) / JUNK MAN (McFree) / WAR (Slapp Happy) / I'M NOT SATISFIED (Frank Zappa) / JUST WAITING (Hank Williams) / ROADHOUSE (John Barry) / STAY AWAY (OLD WHITE TRAIN) (Johnny Paycheck) / LAST CHANCE TO TURN AROUND (hit; Gene Pitney) / JUNGLE ROCK (Hank Mizell) / THIS PERFECT DAY (Saints) / F-'OLDIN' MONEY (Tommy Blake). • **Trivia:** MARK E. featured on TACKHEAD b-side of 'Dangerous Sex' in mid 1990, alongside ADRIAN SHERWOOD and GARY CLAIL. Just previous to this, he had a solo track 'ERROR-ORROR I' for the Various Artists compilation 'HOME'.

Album rating: LIVE AT THE WITCH TRIALS (*9) / DRAGNET (*8) / THE FALL LIVE – TOTALE'S TURNS (IT'S NOW OR NEVER) (*6) / GROTESQUE (AFTER THE GRAMME) (*7) / SLATES (*6) / EARLY YEARS 77-79 compilation (*7) / HEX ENDUCTION HOUR (*8) / ROOM TO LIVE (*6) / PERVERTED BY LANGUAGE (*7) / THE WONDERFUL AND FRIGHTENING WORLD OF… (*7) / HIP PRIESTS & KAMERADS compilation (*6) / THIS NATION'S SAVING GRACE (*8) / BEND SINISTER (*7) / IN PALACE OF SWORDS REVERSED collection (*6) / THE FRENZ EXPERIMENT (*6) / I AM KURIOUS, ORANJ (*7) / SEMINAL LIVE (*4) / 458489 A-SIDES compilation (*8) / 458489 B-SIDES compilation (*7) / EXTRICATE (*8) / SHIFT-WORK (*8) / CODE: SELFISH (*7) / THE INFOTAINMENT SCAN (*7) / MIDDLE CLASS REVOLT (*6) / CELEBRAL CAUSTIC (*6) / THE TWENTY-SEVEN POINTS (*5) / THE LIGHT USER SYNDROME (*7) / LEVITATE (*6) / THE MARSHALL SUITE (*7) / THE UNUTTERABLE (*7) / ARE YOU ARE MISSING WINNER (*5)

MARK E. SMITH (b. MARK EDWARD SMITH, 5 Mar'57) – vocals / **TONY FRIEL** – bass / **MARTIN BRAMAH** – guitar / **UNA BAINES** – electric piano / **KARL BURNS** – drums

Step Forward / I.R.S.

Jun 78. (7"ep) (SF 7) **BINGO-MASTERS BREAK-OUT!**
– Psycho Mafia / Bingo-Master / Repitition.

— **MARC RILEY** – bass; repl. ERIC and JOHNNIE BROWN who had repl. FRIEL (he formed The PASSAGE) / **YVONNE PAWLETT** – keyboards; repl. BAINES who formed BLUE ORCHIDS

Nov 78. (7") (SF 9) **IT'S THE NEW THING. / VARIOUS TIMES**
Jan 79. (lp) (SFLP 1) <SP 003> **LIVE AT THE WITCH TRIALS**
– Frightened / Crap rap 2 / Like to blow / Rebellious jukebox / No Xmas for John Quays / Mother-sister! / Industrial estate / Underground medecin / Two steps back / Live at the witch trials / Futures and pasts / Music scene. (cd-iss. Jun97 & Nov01 on 'Cog Sinister'; COGVP 103CD) <US cd-iss. 1997 on 'Resurgent'; 4107> (lp re-iss. Aug02 on 'Turning Point'; TPM 2208) (cd re-iss. Nov01 on 'Cog Sinister'; COGVP 103CD) <US+cd re-iss. Nov02 on 'Cog Sinister'+=; COGVP 138CD>) – Bingo master / Psycho mafia / Repetition.

— MARK E. (now sole founder), RILEY (now guitar) and PAWLETT recruited **STEVE HANLEY** (b.20 May'59, Dublin, Ireland) – bass repl. BRAMAH who also joined BLUE ORCHIDS / **MIKE LEIGH** – drums repl. BURNS who also joined The PASSAGE and P.I.L.

Jul 79. (7") (SF 11) **ROWCHE RUMBLE. / IN MY AREA**

— **CRAIG SCANLON** (b. 7 Dec'60) – guitar (RILEY now guitar, keyboards) repl. PAWLETT

Oct 79. (lp) (SFLP 4) **DRAGNET**
– Psykick dancehall / A figure walks / Printhead / Dice man / Before the Moon falls / Your heart out / Muzorewi's daughter / Flat of angles / Choc-stock / Spectre vs. rector / Put away. (re-iss. Dec90 lp/cd; SFAL/SPLPCD 4) (cd re-iss. Nov01 on 'Cog Sinister'; COGVP 113CD) (lp re-iss. Aug02 on 'Turning Point'; TPM 02209) (<US+cd re-iss. Nov02 on 'Cog Sinister'+=; COGVP 140>) – Rowche rumble / In my area / Fiery Jack / 2nd dark age / Psykick dancehall No.2.

Jan 80. (7") (SF 13) **FIERY JACK. / SECOND DARK AGE / PSYKICK DANCEHALL II**

Rough Trade / not iss.

May 80. (lp) (ROUGH 10) **THE FALL LIVE – TOTALE'S TURNS (IT'S NOW OR NEVER)** (live)
– (intro) / Fiery Jack / Rowche rumble / Muzorewi's daughter / In my area / Choc-stock / Spectre vs. rector 2 / Cary Grant's wedding / That man / New puritan / No Xmas for John Quays. (cd-iss. Nov92 on 'Dojo'; DOJOCD 83)

— **PAUL HANLEY** – drums repl. LEIGH

Jun 80. (7") (RT 048) **HOW I WROTE ELASTIC MAN. / CITY HOBGOBLINS**
Sep 80. (7") (RT 056) **TOTALLY WIRED. / PUTTA BLOCK**

— **KAY CARROLL** their manager augmented lp/cd on backing vocals, kazoo

Nov 80. (lp) (ROUGH 18) **GROTESQUE (AFTER THE GRAMME)**
– Pay your rates / English scheme / New face in Hell / C'n'c Smithering / The container drivers / Impression of J. Temperance / In the park / W.M.C. – Blob 59 / Gramme Friday / The N.W.R.A. (<cd-iss. Sep93 on 'Castle'; CLACD 391>) (cd re-iss. Jun98 on 'Essential'; ESMCD 640) (lp re-iss. Oct02 on 'Turning Point'; TPM 02210)

Apr 81. (10"m-lp) (RT 071) **SLATES**
– Middle mass / An older lover etc. / Prole art threat / Fit and working again / Slates, slags, etc. / Leave the capitol.

— **KARL BURNS** – drums returned now alongside SMITH, RILEY, SCANLON, S and P HANLEY

Kamera / not iss.

Nov 81. (7") (ERA 001) **LIE DREAM OF A CASINO SOUL. / FANTASTIC LIFE**
Mar 82. (lp) (KAM 005) **HEX ENDUCTION HOUR** — 71
– The classical / Jaw-bone and the air-rifle / Hip priest / Fortress – Deer park / Mere psued mag. ed / Winter / Winter 2 / Just step s'ways / Who makes the Nazis? / Iceland / And this day. (re-iss. 1987 on 'Line'; LILP 400126) (<cd-iss. Sep89 & Mar98; LICD 900126>) <US cd-iss. 1999 on 'Resurgent'; 4486> (<cd re-iss. Nov02 on 'Cog Sinister'; COGVP 141CD>)
Apr 82. (7") (ERA 004) **LOOK KNOW. / I'M INTO C.B.**
Nov 82. (lp) (KAM 011) **ROOM TO LIVE**
– Joker hysterical face / Marquee cha-cha / Hard life in the country / Room to live / Detective instinct / Solicitor in studio / Papal visit. (re-iss. Oct87 on 'Line'; LILP 400109) (cd-iss. Apr98 & Nov01 on 'Cog Sinister'; COGVP 105CD) <US cd-iss. 1998 on 'Resurgent'; 4257> (cd re-iss. Apr02 on 'Cog Sinister'; COGVP 119CD) (<US+cd re-iss. Nov02 on 'Cog Sinister'; COGVP 139CD>)

— reverted to quintet when RILEY left to form MARC RILEY & THE CREEPERS (note that their manager and p/t member KAY CARROLL also departed)

Rough Trade / not iss.

Jun 83. (7") (RT 133) **THE MAN WHOSE HEAD EXPANDED. / LUDD GANG**
Oct 83. (d7") (RT 143) **KICKER CONSPIRACY. // WINGS / CONTAINER DRIVERS (live) / NEW PURITANS (live)**

— added **LAURA-ELISE** (now BRIX E. SMITH) (b. California, USA) – guitar, vocals (ex-BANDA DRATSING) P. HANLEY added keyboards and BURNS added lead bass to their repertoire

Dec 83. (lp/c) (ROUGH/+C 62) **PERVERTED BY LANGUAGE**
– Eat y'self fitter / Neighbourhood of infinity / Garden / Hotel Bloedel / I feel voxish / Tempo house / Hexen definitive / Strife knot. (re-iss. Oct87 on 'Line'; LILP 400116) (cd-iss. Sep89+=; LICD 900116) – Oh! brother / Good-box / C.R.E.E.P. / Pat-trip dispenser. (<cd re-iss. Sep93 on 'Castle'; CLACD 392>) (cd re-iss. Feb98 on 'Cog Sinister – Voiceprint'; COGVP 104CD) (cd re-iss. Jun98 on 'Essential'; ESMCD 639)

Beggars Banquet / Beggars Banquet

Jun 84. (7") (BEG 110) **OH BROTHER. / GOD-BOX**
(12"+=) (BEG 110T) – ('A'instrumental).
Aug 84. (7") (BEG 116) **C.R.E.E.P. / PAT-TRIP DISPENSER**
(12"green+=/12"s) (BEG 116T/+P) – ('A'extended).

— added **GAVIN FRIDAY** – some vocals (of VIRGIN PRUNES) (on next 2 releases)

Sep 84. (lp/c) (<BEGA/+C 58>) **THE WONDERFUL AND FRIGHTENING WORLD OF…** — 62
– Lay of the land / 2 x 4 / Copped it / Elves / Slang king / Bug day / Stephen song / Craigness / Disney's dream debased. (re-iss. Jul88 on 'Beggars Banquet' lp/c(cd+=; BBL/+C 58)(BBL 58CD) – Oh! brother / Draygo's guilt / God-box / Clear off! / C.R.E.E.P. / Pat-trip dispenser / No bulbs.
Oct 84. (12"ep) (BEG 120E) **CALL FOR ESCAPE ROUTE**
– Draygo's Guilt / No bulbs / Clear Off!.
(with free-7") **NO BULBS 3. / SLANG KING**

— **SIMON ROGERS** – bass, keyboards repl. P. HANLEY (he cont. with KISS THE BLADE) (GAVIN returned to VIRGIN PRUNES and S. HANLEY took a holiday)

Jul 85. (7") (BEG 134) **COULDN'T GET AHEAD. / ROLLIN' DANY**
(12"+=) (BEG 134T) – Petty (thief) lout.

— **STEVE HANLEY** returned to join MARK E., BRIX, CRAIG, KARL and SIMON

Sep 85. (lp/c)(cd) (<BEGA/BEGC 47)(BEGA 67CD>) **THIS NATION'S SAVING GRACE** — 54
– Mansion / Bombast / Barmy / What you need / Spoilt Victorian child / L.A. / Out of the quantifier / My new house / Paintwork / I am Damo Suzuki / To nkroachment: yarbles. (re-iss. Feb90 lp/c)(cd+=; BBL/+C 67)(BBL 67CD) – Vixen / Couldn't get ahead / Pretty (thief) lout / Rollin' Dany / Cruiser's creek.
Oct 85. (7") (BEG 150) **CRUISER'S CREEK. / L.A.**
(12"+=) (BEG 150T) – Vixen.
Jul 86. (7") (BEG 165) **LIVING TOO LATE. / HOT AFTER-SHAVE BOP**
(12"+=) (BEG 165T) – Living too long.

— **JOHN SIMON WOOLSTENCROFT** (b.19 Jan'63, Altringham, England) – drums (ex-WEEDS) repl. BURNS who formed THIRST

Sep 86. (7") (BEG 168) **MR. PHARMICIST. / LUCIFER OVER LANCASHIRE** — 75
(12"+=) (BEG 168T) – Auto-tech pilot.
Oct 86. (lp/c) (BEGA/BEGC 75) **BEND SINISTER** — 36
– R.O.D. / Dktr. Faustus / Shoulder pads #1 / Mr. Pharmicist / Gross chapel – British grenadiers / U.S. 80's-90's / Terry Waite sez / Bournemouth runner / Riddler / Shoulder pads #2. (cd-iss. Jan88+=; BEGA 75CD) – Living too late / Auto-tech pilot.
Nov 86. (7") (BEGA 176) **HEY! LUCIANI. / ENTITLED** — 59
(12"+=) (BEG 176T) – Shoulder pads.
Apr 87. (7") (BEG 187) **THERE'S A GHOST IN MY HOUSE. / HAF FOUND, BORMAN** — 30
(12"+=/c-s+=) (BEG 187 T/C) – Sleepdebt / Snatches / Mark'll sink us.

— added **MARSHA SCHOFIELD** (b.1963, Brooklyn, N.Y.) – keyboards, vocals of ADULT NET, (ex-BANDA DRATSING)

Oct 87. (7"/7"pic-d) (BEG 200/+P) **HIT THE NORTH. / (part 2)** — 57
(12"+=) (BEG 200T) – Australians in Europe.
(cd-s+=) (BEG 200C) – Northerns in Europe / (Hit the north versions).

FALL (cont) — THE GREAT INDIE DISCOGRAPHY — The 1970s

— reverted back to sextet of **MARK E., BRIX, CRAIG, JOHN S., STEVE** and **MARSHA** when **SIMON** became their producer & studio guitarist only

Jan 88. (7") (BEG 206) **VICTORIA. / TUFF LIFE BOOGIE** — 35
(12"+=) (BEG 206T) — Guest informant / Twister.

Mar 88. (lp/c)(cd) (BEGA/BEGC 91)(BEGA 91CD) <6987> **THE FRENZ EXPERIMENT** — 19
— Frenz / Carry bag man / Get a hotel / Victoria / Athlete cured / In these times / The steak place / Bremen nacht / Guest informant (excerpt) / Oswald defence lawyer. (c/c+=) — Tuff life boogie / Guest informant / Twister / There's a ghost in my house / Hit the north (part 1).

Oct 88. (lp/c)(cd) (BEGA/BEGC 96)(BEGA 96CD) <9582> **I AM KURIOUS, ORANJ** — 54
— New big prinz / Overture from 'I Am Curious, Orange' / Dog is life / Jerusalem / Wrong place, right time / Guide me soft * / C.D. win fall 2088 ad / Yes, o yes / Van plague? / Bad news girl / Cab it up! / Last nacht * / Big new priest *. (c+=/cd+= *)

Nov 88. (d7"ep/d3"cd-ep) (FALL 2 B/CD) **JERUSALEM / ACID PRIEST 2088. / BIG NEW PRINZ / WRONG PLACE, RIGHT TIME** — 59

Jun 89. (7") (BEG 226) **CAB IT UP. / DEAD BEAT DESCENDENT** (out take from ballet)
(12"+=) (BEG 226T) — Kurious oranj (live) / Hit the north (live).

Beggars Banquet – Lowdown / not iss.

Jun 89. (lp/c)(cd) (BBL/+C 102)(BBL 102CD) <9807> **SEMINAL LIVE** (some studio) — 40
— Dead beat descendent / Pinball machine / H.O.W. / Squid law / Mollusc in Tyrol / 2 x 4 / Elf prefix – L.A. / Victoria / Pay your rates / Cruiser's creek. (c+=/cd+=) — Kurious oranj / Hit the north / In these times / Frenz.

— **MARTIN BRAMAH** – guitar returned to repl. BRIX E. who continued with ADULT NET.

Cog Sinister-Fontana / Fontana

Jan 90. (7"/c-s) (SIN/+MC 4) **TELEPHONE THING. / BRITISH PEOPLE IN HOT WEATHER** — 58
(12"+=)(cd-s+=) (SIN 4-12)(SINCD 4) — Telephone (dub).

Feb 90. (cd/c/lp) (<842204-2/-4/-1>) **EXTRICATE** — 31
— Sing! Harpy / I'm Frank / Bill is dead / Black monk theme part 1 / Popcorn double feature / Telephone thing / Hilary / Chicago, now! / The littlest rebel / British people in hot weather / And therein. (c+cd+=) — Arms control poseur / Black monk theme part II / Extricate. (cd re-iss. Nov01 on 'Cog Sinister'; COGVP 122CD)

Mar 90. (7"/c-s) (SIN/+MC 5) **POPCORN DOUBLE FEATURE. / BUTTERFLIES 4 BRAINS**
(12"+=) (SIN 5-12) — Arms control poseur.
(cd-s+=) (SINCD 5) — Zandra / Black monk theme part II.

— trimmed to basic quartet of **MARK E, CRAIG, STEVE** and **JOHN.**

Aug 90. (7") (SIN 6) **WHITE LIGHTNING. / BLOOD OUTTA STONE** — 56
(12"+=) (SINR 6-12) — Zagreb.
(12"ep+=)(cd-ep+=) (SIN 6-12)(SINCD 6) — Life just bounces.

Dec 90. (7") (SIN 7) **HIGH TENSION LINE. / XMAS WITH SIMON**
(12"+=)(cd-s+=) (SIN 7-12)(SINCD 7) — Don't take the pizza.

— added guest **KENNY BRADY** – violin

Apr 91. (cd/c/lp) (<848594-2/-4/-1>) **SHIFT-WORK** — 17
— EARTH'S IMPOSSIBLE DAY :-So what about it? / Idiot joy showland / Edinburgh man / Pittsville direkt / The book of lies / High tension line / The war against intelligence! / NOTEBOOKS OUT PLAGIARISTS :-Shift-work / You haven't found it yet / The mixer / White lightning / A lot of wind / Rose / Sinister waltz. (<US+cd re-iss. Sep02 on 'Cog Sinister'+=; COGVP 134CD>) — Blood outta stone / Xmas with Simon.

— **DAVID BUSH** (b. 4 Jun'59, Taplow, England) – keyboards, machines repl. BRADY

Mar 92. (7") (SINS 8) **FREE RANGE. / EVERYTHING HURTZ** — 40
(12"+=)(pic-cd-s+=) (SIN 8-12)(SINCD 8) — Dangerous / Return.

Mar 92. (cd/c/lp) (<512162-2/-4/-1>) **CODE: SELFISH** — 21
— The Birmingham school of business school / Free range / Return / Time enough at last / Everything hurtz / Immorality / Two-face! / Just waiting / So-called dangerous / Gentlemen's agreement / Two kids / Crew filth. (cd re-iss. Aug93; same) (<US+cd re-iss. Sep02 on 'Cog Sinister'+=; COGVP 133CD>) — Ed's babe / Free ranger.

Jun 92. (12"ep)(cd-ep) (SIN 9-12)(SINCD 9) **ED'S BABE / PUMPKIN HEAD XSCAPES / THE KNIGHT, THE DEVIL AND DEATH / ARID'S AL'S DREAM / FREE RANGER**

Permanent / Matador

Apr 93. (7") (SPERM 9) <OLE 053> **WHY ARE PEOPLE GRUDGEFUL? / GLAM-RACKET** — 43
(12"+=)(cd-s+=) (12/CD SPERM 9) <OLE 054> — The re-mixer / Lost in music.

Apr 93. (cd/c/lp) (PERM CD/MC/LP 12) <OLE 055> **THE INFOTAINMENT SCAN** — 9 — May93
— Ladybird (green grass) / Lost in music / Glam-racket / I'm going to Spain / It's a curse / Paranoia man in cheap sh*t room / Service / The league of bald-headed men / A past gone mad / Light fireworks / League Moon monkey mix. (cd+=) — Why are people grudgeful? (cd re-iss. Jul99 on 'Artful'; ARTFULCD 22)

— added the returning **KARL BURNS** – percussion(now 6-piece yet again)

Dec 93. (d-cd-ep/d12"ep) (CD/12 SPERM 13) **BEHIND THE COUNTER EP** — 75
— Behind the counter / War / M5 / Happy holiday / Cab driver / (1).

— Feb 94; MARK guested for INSPIRAL CARPETS on their single 'I Want You'.

Apr 94. (10"clear-ep/12"ep/cd-ep) (10/12/CD SPERM 14) <OLE 094> **15 WAYS. / HEY! STUDENT / THE $500 BOTTLE OF WINE** — 65 — May94

May 94. (cd/c/lp) (PERM CD/MC/LP 18) <OLE 095> **MIDDLE CLASS REVOLT (aka THE VAPOURISATION OF REALITY** — 48 — Jul94
— 15 ways / The reckoning / Behind the counter / M5#1 / Surmount all obstacles / Middle class revolt! / You're not up to much / Symbol of Mordgan / Hey! student / Junk man / The $500 bottle of wine / City dweller / War / Shut up!. (cd re-iss. Jul99 on 'Artful'; ARTFULCD 23)

— added on tour the returning **BRIX SMITH** – guitar, vocals

Permanent / Permanent

Feb 95. (cd/c/lp) (<PERM CD/MC/LP 30>) **CEREBRAL CAUSTIC** — 67 — May95
— The joke / Don't call me darling / Rainmaster / Feeling numb / Pearl city / Life just bounces / I'm not satisfied / The aphid / Bonkers in Phoenix / One day / North west fashion show / Pine leaves. (cd re-iss. Jul99 on 'Artful'; ARTFULCD 24)

Aug 95. (d-cd/d-c/d-lp) (<PERM CD/MC/LP 36>) **THE TWENTY-SEVEN POINTS (live)** — — Sep95
— Mollusc in Tyrol / Return / Lady bird (green grass) / Idiot – Walk-out / Ten points Idiot – Walk-out / Big new prinz / Intro: Roadhouse / The joke / ME's jokes – The British people in hot weather / Free range / Hi-tension line / The league of the bald headed men / Glam racket: Star / Lost in music / Mr. Pharmacist / Cloud of black / Paranoia man in cheap shit room / Bounces / Outro / Passable / Glasgow advice / Middle class revolt: Simon, Dave and John / Bill is dead / Strychnine / War! / Noel's chemical effluence / Three points – Up too much.

— added **JULIA NAGLE** – keyboards, guitar / + 7th & 8th members **LUCY RIMMER** – vocals / **MIKE BENNETT** – vocals, co-producer (to MARK E., BRIX, SIMON, STEPHEN + KARL)

Jet / Jet

Feb 96. (12"ep/c-ep/cd-ep) (JET/+MC/SCD 500) **THE CHISELERS / CHILINIST. / INTERLUDE / CHILINISM** — 60

— MARK E. worked with DOSE on their single 'PLUG MYSELF IN', released on Pete Waterman's new label 'Coliseum'!

Jun 96. (cd/c/lp) (<JET CD/MC/LP 1012>) **THE LIGHT USER SYNDROME** — 54
— D.I.Y. meat / Das vulture ans ein nutter-wain / He Pep! / Hostile / Stay away (old white train) / Spinetrak / Interlude – Chilinism / Powder keg / Oleano / Cheetham Hill / The Coliseum / Last chance to turn around / The ballard of J. Drummer / Oxymoron / Secession man. (cd re-iss. Feb99 on 'Receiver'; RRCD 264) (cd re-iss. Sep02 on 'Castle'; CMRCD 570)

Artful / Artful

Feb 98. (10"ep/cd-ep) (10/CD ARTFUL 1) **MASQUERADE / CALENDAR. / SCAREBALL / OL' GANG (live)** — 69
(cd-ep) (CXARTFUL 001) — ('A'side) / Ivanhoes two pence / Spencer must die / Ten houses of Eve.

Feb 98. (cd/c/lp) (<ARTFUL CD/MC/LP 9>) **LEVITATE**
— Ten houses of Eve / Masquerade / Hurricane Edward / I'm a mummy / Quartet of Doc Shanley / Jap kid / 4 1/2 inch / Spencer must die / Jungle rock / Ol' gang / Tragic days / I come and stand at your door / Levitate / Everybody but myself. (cd re-iss. May99; ARTFULCDX 9)

— **SMITH** retained **NAGLE** and recruited **NEVILLE WILDING** – guitar + **TOM HEAD** – drums

— **ADAM HALAL** – bass; repl. temp. KAREN LATHAM

Mar 99. (12"/cd-s) (12/CD ARTFUL 2) **TOUCH SENSITIVE. / ANTIDOTE / TOUCH SENSITIVE (dance mix)**

Apr 99. (cd/c/lp) (<ARTFUL CD/MC/LP 17>) **THE MARSHALL SUITE** — — Oct99
— Touch sensitive / F-'oldin' money / Snake-off / Bound / This perfect day / (Jung Nev's) Antidotes / Inevitable / Anecdotes + anecdotes in B# / Early life of crying Marshal / Birthday song / Mad. men-eng, dog / On my own.

Aug 99. (cd-s) (CDARTFUL 3) **F-'OLDIN' MONEY / THIS PERFECT DAY (remix) / BIRTHDAY SONG (remix)**
(cd-s) (CDXARTFUL 3) — ('A'side) / The early life of the crying marshall (remix) / Tom Raggazzi (remix).

Eagle / not iss.

Nov 00. (cd) (EAGCD 164) **THE UNUTTERABLE**
— Cyber insekt / Two Librans / W.B. / Sons of temperance / Dr. Buck's letter / Hot runes Way round / Octo realm – Ketamine sun / Serum / The unutterable / Pumpkin soup and mashed potatoes / Hands up Billy / Midwatch 1953 / Devolute / Das katerer.

Cog Sinister / not iss.

Nov 01. (cd) (COGVP 131CD) **ARE YOU ARE MISSING WINNER**
— Jim's the fall / Bourgeois town / Crop dust / My ex-classmate's kids / Kick the can / Gotta see Jane / Ibis afro man / Acute / Hollow mind / Reprise (Jane – Prof Mick – Ey bastardo). (pic-lp iss.Feb02; COGVP 131LP)

Action / not iss.

Nov 02. (7"ep/cd-ep) (TAKE 020/+CD) **FALL VS. 2003** — 64
— Susan vs. nightclub / Janet vs. Johnny.

– compilations, etc. –

Sep 81. (lp) Step Forward; (ROUGH 18) **77-EARLY YEARS-79**
— Repetition / Bingo-masters breakout / Psycho mafia / Various times / It's the new thing / Rowche rumble / In my area / Dice man / Psykick dancehall / Second dark age / Fiery Jack / Stepping out / Last orders. <US cd-iss. 2000 on 'Resurgent'; 4540> (re-iss. Nov01 on 'Cog Sinister'; COGVP 123CD) (cd re-iss. Dec02 on 'Cog Sinister'; COGVP 136CD)

Mar 82. (c) Chaos; (LIVE 006) **LIVE AT ACKLAM HALL, LONDON 1980**
(cd-iss. Jan96 as 'THE LEGENDARY CHAOS TAPES'; SAR 1005) (re-iss. Jul97 & Nov01 on 'Cog Sinister – Voiceprint'; COGVP 101CD)

Nov 82. (lp) Cottage; <none> **A PART OF AMERICA THEREIN**

Nov 83. (7") (KAM 014) **MARQUEE CHA-CHA. / ROOM TO LIVE // (PAPAL VISIT original b-side)**

Mar 85. (lp/c) Situation 2; (SIT U/C 13) **HIP PRIESTS AND KAMERADS** (81-82 material)
(c+=) — (has 4 extra tracks) (cd-iss. Mar88+= same 4; SITU 13CD) (re-iss. 1988 on 'Situation 2-Lowdown' lp/c+=; SITL/+C 13)(SITU 13CD) (re-iss. Sep95 on 'Beggars Banquet')

May 87. (12"ep/c-ep) Strange Fruit; (<SFPF/SFPSC 028>) **THE PEEL SESSIONS** (28.11.78) — — 1991
— Put away / No Xmas for John Quay / Like to blow / Mess of my.

Nov 87. (cd/c/lp) Cog Sinister; (CD/C+/COG 1) **IN PALACE OF SWORDS REVERSED (80-83)**
(cd re-iss. Nov01; COGVP 107CD)

Sep 90. (cd)(lp/c) Beggars Banquet; (BEGA 111CD)(BEGA/+C 111) <2430> **458489** ('A'sides; 1984-89) — 47
— Oh! brother / C.R.E.E.P. / No bulbs 3 / Rollin' Dany / Couldn't get ahead / Cruiser's creek / L.A. / Living too late / Hit the north (part 1) / Mr. Pharmacist / Hey! student / There's a ghost in my house / Victoria / Big new prinz / Wrong place, right time No.2 / Jerusalem / Dead beat descendent. // God-box / Pat-trip dispenser / Slang king / Draygo's guilt / Clear off! / No bulbs / Petty thief lout / Vixen / Hot aftershave bop / Living too long / Lucifer over Lancashire / Auto tech pilot / Entitled / Shoulder pads #1 / Sleep debt snatches / Mark'll sink us / Haf found Bormann / Australians in Europe / Northerns in Europe / Hit the north (part 2) / Guest informant / Tuff life boogie / Twister / Acid priest 2088 / Cab it up. <US cd re-iss. 1994 on 'Atlantic'; 92380>

Date	Format/Label/Catalogue	Title		
Dec 90.	(cd)(d-lp/c) *Beggars Banquet*; (BEGA 116CD)(BEGA/+C 116) <2430> **458489** (B'sides; 1984-89) – God-box / Pat-trip dispenser / Slang king 2 / Draygo's guilt / Clear off! / No bulbs / Petty thief lout / Vixen / Hot aftershave bop / Living too long / Lucifer over Lancashire / Auto tech pilot / Entitled / Shoulder pads £1 / Sleep debt snatches / Mark'll sink us / Haf found Bormann / Australians in Europe / Northerns in Europe / Hit the north (part 2) / Guest informant / Tuff life boogie / Twister / Acid priest 2088 / Cab it up. *(cd+=)* – Bremen nache run out / Mark'll sink us (live) / Kurious oranj. <US cd re-iss. 1994 on 'Atlantic'; 92474>			
Mar 93.	(7"ep/cd-ep) *Strange Fruit*; (SFPS/SFPCD 087) / Dutch East India; <8355> **KIMBLE** – Kimble / C'n'c hassle schmuk / Spoilt Victorian child / Words of expectation.			
Apr 93.	(cd) *Castle*; (CCSCD 365) **THE COLLECTION**			-
Aug 93.	(m-cd) *Windsong*; (WINCD 038) / Griffin; <404> **BBC RADIO 1 LIVE IN CONCERT**			
Feb 94.	(cd) *Loma*; (LOMACD 10) **SLATES / PART OF AMERICA IN THERIN 1981**			-
Aug 94.	(cd) *Matador*; <OLE 62> **THE LEAGUE OF BALD HEADED MEN**		-	
Feb 96.	(cd) *Receiver*; (<RRCD 209>) **SINISTER WALTZ**			
Apr 96.	(cd) *Receiver*; (<RRCD 211>) **FIEND WITH A VIOLIN**			
Apr 96.	(cd/lp) *Receiver*; (<RRCD/RRLP 213>) **OSWALD DEFENCE LAWYER**			
Oct 96.	(3xcd-box) *Receiver*; (<RRXCD 506>) **THE OTHER SIDE OF THE FALL** (above 3 albums)			
Apr 97.	(d-cd) *Cog Sinister – Voiceprint*; (COGVP 102CD) **FALL IN A HOLE** (was originally a New Zealand release on 'Flying Nun') (re-iss. Nov97 on 'Resurgence'; RSG 4016) (re-iss. Nov01 on 'Cog Sinister'; COGVP 102CD) (re-iss. Dec02 on 'Cog Sinister'; COGVP 137CD)			-
Jun 97.	(d-cd) *Snapper*; (<SMDCD 132>) **THE LESS YOU LOOK THE MORE YOU FIND**			
Aug 97.	(cd) *Receiver*; (RRCD 239) **15 WAYS TO LEAVE YOUR MAN (live)**			
Nov 97.	(cd) *Receiver*; (RRCD 246>) **OXYMORON**			-
Nov 97.	(cd) *Rialto*; (<RMCD 214>) **THE FALL ARCHIVES**			
Dec 97.	(cd) *Receiver*; (<RRCD 247>) **CHEETHAM HILL**			
Mar 98.	(cd) *Strange Fruit*; (SFRSCD 048) **THE PEEL SESSIONS**			-
Mar 98.	(cd) *Castle*; (CCSCD 823) **SMILE . . . IT'S THE BEST OF THE FALL**			
Apr 98.	(cd) *Cog Sinister – Voiceprint*; (COGVP 108CD) **LIVE ON AIR IN MELBOURNE 1982 (live)** (re-iss. Nov01; same)			
Jun 98.	(cd) *M.C.I.*; (MCCD 350) **NORTHERN ATTITUDE**			
Jun 98.	(cd) *Artful*; (ARTFULCD 3) **IN THE CITY (live in Manchester 1995)**			
Aug 98.	(cd) *Cog Sinister – Voiceprint*; (COGVP 111CD) **LIVE VARIOUS YEARS (live)** (re-iss. Nov01; same)			
Jan 99.	(3xcd-box) *Receiver*; (RRXCD 508) **THE FALL BOX SET**			
Jan 99.	(cd) *Strange Fruit*; (SFRSCD 048) **THE PEEL SESSIONS**			-
Feb 00.	(cd/d-lp) *Artful*; (ARTFUL CD/LP 30) **A PAST GONE MAD (THE BEST OF 1990-2000)**			
Aug 00.	(3xcd-box) *Eagle*; (EEECD 010) **PSYKICK DANCEHALL – THE MASTERS**			
Feb 01.	(d-cd) *Artful*; (ARTFULCD 35) **A WORLD BEWITCHED – THE BEST OF THE FALL 1990-2000**			
Feb 01.	(cd) *Cog Sinister*; (COGVP 115CD) **LIVE IN CAMBRIDGE 1988 (live)**			
Jun 01.	(cd) *Cog Sinister*; (COGVP 109CD) **LIVE IN ZAGREB (live)**			
Nov 01.	(cd) *Cog Sinister*; (COGVP 125CD) **LIVE IN REYKJAVIK (May 6th 1983)**			
Nov 01.	(cd) *Cog Sinister*; (COGVP 127CD) **BACKDROP**			
Nov 01.	(cd) *Cog Sinister*; (COGVP 110CD) **LIVE IN NOTTINGHAM (live)**			
Dec 01.	(cd) *Cog Sinister*; (COGVP 118CD) **LIVERPOOL '78 – LIVE AT MR. PICKWICK'S LIVERPOOL 1978**			
Apr 02.	(cd) *Cog Sinister*; (COGVP 114CD) **LIVE 1977**			
Jun 02.	(cd) *Cog Sinister*; (COGVP 112CD) **LIVE AT THE DERBY HALL, BURY 1982 (live)**			
Jul 02.	(d-cd) *Castle*; (CMDDD 461) / *Sanctuary*; 81205> **TOTALLY WIRED: THE ROUGH TRADE ANTHOLOGY**			Aug02
Jul 02.	(4xcd-box) *Castle*; (CMEBX 526) **THE ROUGH TRADE SINGLES BOX**			
Sep 02.	(d-cd) *Snapper*; (SMDCD 443) **HIGH TENSION LINE**			
Nov 02.	(cd) *Cog Sinister*; (COGVP 132CD) **LISTENING IN SINGLES 1990-2001**			-

Mick FARREN (see under ⇒ PINK FAIRIES)

FASHION

Formed: Birmingham, England . . . 1977 by LUKE (JAMES), (JOHN) MULLIGAN and DIK DAVIS. A bizarre hybrid of arty post-punk/neo new romantic synth experimentation and Brummie reggae influences, FASHION kickstarted their career via their own label, 'Fashion Music' (distributed by Miles Copeland's 'Faulty' products). Influenced by the likes of ROXY MUSIC, BOWIE and BE-BOP DELUXE, the band were actually more palatable than the aforementioned description might suggest, their debut album, 'PRODUCT PERFECT', possessing a certain mutoid attraction and period fascination (especially for LUKE's brilliantly affected vocals). Prior to 1980's 'SILVER BLADE' single, however, the tonsil-distorting frontman was replaced with DEE HARRIS, the band subsequently adding MARTIN RECCI, MARTIN STOKER and TONY before securing a major label deal with 'Arista'. Following a hiatus of more than a year, FASHION broke the silence with 'MOVE ON', sporting a radically different sound closer to a discofied SIMPLE MINDS with CHIC-slapping bass. Aiming straight at the heart of the electro/dance-pop crossover market, the new-look FASHION were certainly willing to change with the times, earning themselves a major label hit with the funky 'STREETPLAYER – MECHANIK' in early '82. Both tracks – along with third single, 'SOMETHING IN YOUR PICTURE' – were featured on the long awaited second album, 'FABRIQUE', later that summer. Despite making the UK Top 10, the album surprisingly failed to provide FASHION with that all important breakthrough single and following a final minor hit, 'LOVE SHADOW', their fortunes faded. Former TEARDROP EXPLODES man, TROY TATE, was briefly installed as frontman before making way for Fife lad, ALAN DARBY, the latter spearheading the band's comeback attempt in 1984. Armed with a new deal courtesy of 'Epic', an increasingly threadbare FASHION scored a minor Top 75 hit with both the single, 'EYE TALK' and album, 'TWILIGHT OF IDOLS' (1984), before finally stepping off the music business catwalk for good later that year. • **Songwriters:** MULLIGAN-DAVIS wrote most of the songs. • **Trivia:** MULLIGAN also made videos for The STRANGLERS.

Album rating: PRODUCT PERFECT (*6) / FABRIQUE (*5) / TWILIGHT OF IDOLS (*4) / THE HEIGHT OF FASHION compilation (*5)

LUKE (JAMES) – vocals, guitar, effects / **(JOHN) MULLIGAN** – bass, synthesizers, vocals / **DIK** (b. DICK DAVIS) – percussion, vocals, harp

			Fashion Music	I.R.S.
Nov 78.	(7") (FM 001) **STEADY EDDIE STEADY. / KILLING TIME**			-
Jan 79.	(lp) (FML 1) <SP 002> **PRODUCT PERFECT** – Product perfect / Die in the west / Red, green and gold / Burning down / a) Big John, b) Hanoi annoys me, c) The innocent / Citinite / Don't touch me, touch me / Bike boys / Fashion / Technofascist.			Sep79
Jun 79.	(7") (FM 002) **CITINITE. / WASTELIFE**			-
Sep 79.	(7") <IR 9502> **THE INNOCENT. / RED, GREEN AND GOLD / SODIUM PENTHATOL NEGATIVE**		-	

—— **DEE HARRIS** (b.DAVE) – vocals, guitar; repl. LUKE to France

Mar 80.	(7") (FM 003) **SILVER BLADES. / SILVER BLADES (A DEEPER CUT)**			-

—— added **MARTIN RECCI** – bass, vocals 1980 had also saw them extended to sextet with **MARTIN STOKER** – drums / **TONY** – vox (ex-NEON HEARTS) before reverting to quartet

			Arista	Arista
Nov 81.	(7") (ARIST 440) **MOVE ON. / MUTANT DANCE MOVE** (12") (ARIST 440) – ('A'-audio extra).			-
Feb 82.	(7"/12") (ARIST/+12 456) **STREETPLAYER – MECHANIK. / ('A' version)**		46	-
May 82.	(7") (ARIST 472) **SOMETING IN YOUR PICTURE. / ('A'-alt.version)** (12"+=) (ARIST12 472) – Motor drive / Smokey dialogue.			
Jun 82.	(lp/c) (SPART/TCART 1185) <6604> **FABRIQUE** – Move on / Streetplayer – mechanik / Dressed to kill / Do you wanna make love / It's alright / Slow blue / Whitestuff / You only left your picture / Something in your picture / Love shadow.		10	
Aug 82.	(7") (ARIST 483) **LOVE SHADOW. / LET'S PLAY DIRTY** (12"+=) (ARIST12 483) – Let's play dirty (centrefold).		51	-

—— (Oct'82) **TROY TATE** – vocals, guitar (ex-TEARDROP EXPLODES) repl. DEE HARRIS who formed ZEE with RICHARD WRIGHT (of Pink Floyd)

—— (1983) **ALAN DARBY** (b.1952, Dunfermline, Scotland) – vocals, guitar (ex-CADO BELLE) repl. TATE who continued solo. (others still in band:- **MULLIGAN, DAVIES + RECCI**).

			Epic	Epic
Jan 84.	(7"/12") (A/TA 4106) **EYE TALK. / SLOW DOWN**		69	-
Apr 84.	(7"/12") (A/TA 4327) **DREAMING. / WHITE LINE FEVER**			
May 84.	(lp/c) (EPC/+40 25909) <39427> **TWILIGHT OF IDOLS** – Eye talk / Dreaming / Ice girl / Trader / Too much too soon / Slow down / Hurricane / You in the night / Twilight of idols / Delirious. *(c+=)* – (alternate mixes).		69	
Jun 84.	(7") (A 4502) **YOU IN THE NIGHT. / YAMASHATA THEME** *(c-s+=)* (CA 4502) – Hurricane *(d7"++=)* (DA 4502) – White stuff.			

—— split 1984, DARBY went on to session for BONNIE TYLER, PAUL YOUNG and ROBERT PALMER

– compilations, others, etc. –

Apr 90.	(cd/c) *Arista*; (260/410 626) **THE HEIGHT OF FASHION** – (virtually 'FABRIQUE' re-issued with extra tracks). (cd re-iss. Aug01 on 'Cherry Red'; CDMRED 193)			-

FATAL MICROBES

Formed: London, England . . . 1978 by 14 year-old singing schoolgirl, DONNA 'HONEY' BANE, DEREK HADLEY and KEITH HUDSON. Augmented by relative veteran, PETE FENDER (of The POISON GIRLS), the young band were invited to share an EP with the latter's outfit. HONEY, however, had been AWOL from a detention centre at the time of the recording. Released via 'Small Wonder' early in '79, the two tracks, 'VIOLENCE GROWS' and 'BEAUTIFUL PICTURES', were also issued in 7" format later that year. The English answer to LYDIA LUNCH (Teenage Jesus) or JUDY NYLON (Snatch), the peroxide-pink HONEY and her glass-shattering shriek was best sampled on the couch-punk plea for public transport peace of mind,

'VIOLENCE GROWS'. However, the band took a backseat when HONEY opted for a solo career, releasing a self-financed single, 'GUILTY', in late 1980. Early the following year, she signed to EMI subsidiary, 'Zonophone' (COCKNEY REJECTS were among her labelmates!), attempts to transform her into a pouting teen-pop starlet initially paying off as 'TURN ME ON TURN ME OFF' hit the UK Top 40. With her DIY/punk beginnings now just a vague memory, BANE had one more feeble stab at the charts with a cover of the Supremes' 'BABY LOVE'. Three further singles flopped unceremoniously, although she did revisit her radical past one more time on a late 1981 EP, 'YOU CAN BE YOU', mates CRASS (whose label the single also appeared on) backing her as the pseudonymous KEBABS. Prior to the final demise of her short-lived career, HONEY turned her talents to acting and starred in the controversial Mai Zettering film, 'Scrubbers'.

Album rating: still awaiting a comprehensive retrospective

HONEY BANE (b. DONNA BANE) – vocals / **PETE FENDER** – guitar (of POISON GIRLS) / **KEITH HUDSON** – bass / **DEREK HADLEY** – drums

	Small Wonder	not iss.
Mar 79. (12"ep) *(WEENY 3)* **FATAL MICROBES MEET THE POISON GIRLS** – Violence grows / Beautiful pictures / (POISON GIRLS:- Close shop / Piano lessons).	☐	-
Nov 79. (7"m) *(SMALL 20)* **VIOLENCE GROWS. / BEAUTIFUL PICTURES / CRY BABY**	☐	-

— DANNY TRICKETT + DAVE MALTBEY – guitar; repl. PETE
— disbanded in 1980

HONEY BANE

	Honey Bane	not iss.
Dec 80. (7") *(HB 946)* **GUILTY. / GUILTY (dub)**	☐	-

	Zonophone	not iss.
Jan 81. (d7") *(Z 15)* **TURN ME ON TURN ME OFF. / IN DREAMS // T'AIN'T NOBODYS BUSINESS / NEGATIVE EXPOSURE**	37	-
Mar 81. (7") *(Z 19)* **BABY LOVE. / MASS PRODUCTION**	58	-
Jun 81. (7") *(Z 23)* **JIMMY (LISTEN TO ME). / NEGATIVE EXPOSURE**	☐	-
Oct 81. (7"m; DONNA & KEBABS) *(Crass; 521984-1)* **YOU CAN BE YOU** – Girl on the run / Porno grows / Boring conversations.	☐	-
Jun 82. (7") *(Z 32)* **I WISH IT COULD BE ME. / CHILDHOOD PRINCE**	☐	-
Feb 83. (7") *(Z 36)* **DIZZY DREAMERS. / ONGOING SITUATION**	☐	-

— her last 45 was credited to "HONEY BANE & JONATHAN MOORE"

John FELICE & THE LOWDOWNS
(see under ⇒ REAL KIDS)

FINGERPRINTZ

Formed: London, England … 1978 by Scots-born JIMMIE O'NEILL alongside CHA BURNZ, KENNY ALTON and BOB SHILLING. One of the earliest bands to translate the energy and anger of punk into a more accessible New Wave style, The FINGERPRINTZ were an obvious choice for 'Virgin' who released their debut single, 'DANCING WITH MYSELF', in early '79. A further two singles, 'WHO'S YOUR FRIEND' and 'TOUGH LUCK', preceded their first long player, 'THE VERY DAB', at the tail end of the year, a musically upbeat album that nevertheless concentrated on the lyrical preoccupations that would come to dominate the post-punk era, i.e. alienation, paranoia, urban decay etc. Produced by ex-DUCKS DELUXE man, NICK GARVEY, 'DISTINGUISHING MARKS' (1980) carried on in a similar, if more streamlined vein while 1981's 'BEAT NOIR' was an ambitious attempt to combine the rhythmic drive of funk with new wave pop sensibilities. Yet like their predecessors, none of the album's three singles made any commercial impact, FINGERPRINTZ finally marking their books after the last of these, 'THE BEAT ESCAPE'. After another aborted project, INTRO (with JACQUI BROOKS), O'NEILL went on to greater recognition if not acclaim with The SILENCERS.

Album rating: THE VERY DAB (*6) / DISTINGUISHING MARKS (*5) / BEAT NOIR (*5)

JIMMIE O'NEIL – vocals, guitar / **CHA BURNZ** – guitar, vocals / **KENNY ALTON** – bass, vocals / **BOB SHILLING** – drums

	Virgin	not iss.
Jan 79. (7") *(VS 235)* **DANCING WITH MYSELF. / SEAN'S NEW SHOES** (12"+=) *(VS 235-12)* – Sync unit.	☐	-
Mar 79. (d7"blue) *(VS 252)* **WHO'S YOUR FRIEND. / DO YOU WANT TO KNOW A SECRET // NERVZ. / NIGHT NURSE**	☐	-
Aug 79. (7") *(VS 278)* **TOUGH LUCK. / DETONATOR**	☐	-
Oct 79. (lp) *(V 2119)* **THE VERY DAB** – Tough luck / Temperamental / Close circuit connection / Beam me up Scotty / Punchy Judy / On the hop / Fingerprintz / Hey Mr.Smith / Wet job / Invisible seams.	☐	-
Jul 80. (7") *(VS 358)* **BULLET PROOF HEART. / HIDE AND SEEK**	☐	-
Aug 80. (lp) *(V 2170)* **DISTINGUISHING MARKS** – Yes eyes / Houdini love / Criminal mind / Bullet proof heart / Remorse code / Amnesia / Ringing tone / Radiation / Jabs / Hide and seek.	☐	-
Oct 80. (7") *(VS 375)* **HOUDINI LOVE. / ALL ABOUT YOU**	☐	-

— BOGDAN WIEZLING – drums, percussion; repl. SHILLING

May 81. (7") *(VS 420)* **SHADOWED. / MADAME X**	☐	-
Jun 81. (lp) *(V 2201)* **BEAT NOIR** – The beat escape / The chase / Cat walk / Changing / Get civilised / Shadowed / Touch sense / Echo head / Going going gone / Famous last words.	☐	-
Jul 81. (7") *(VS 432)* **BOHEMIAN DANCE. / COFFEE & SCREAMS**	☐	-
Oct 81. (7") *(VS 452)* **THE BEAT ESCAPE. / DISORIENT EXPRESS** (12") *(VS 452-12)* – ('A'side) / Catwalk.	☐	-

— disbanded after above single. JIMMIE O'NEIL + JACQUI BROOKS formed INTRO who recorded one 'M.C.A.' single in '83, 'LOST WITHOUT YOUR LOVE'. JIMMIE subsequently formed The SILENCERS

FISCHER-Z

Formed: London, England … early 1978 by JOHN WATTS, along with STEVE SKOLNIK, DAVID GRAHAM and STEVE LIDDLE. Signed to 'United Artists', this frantic, edgy, guitar/keyboards-dominated New Wave outfit made their vinyl debut in September '78 with the 'WAX DOLLS' single, following it up early in 1979 with 'REMEMBER RUSSIA'. The quartet finally dented the lower regions of the chart later that Spring with 'THE WORKER', all three singles featuring on the attendant debut album, 'WORD SALAD' (1979). As the 70's turned into the 80's, FISCHER-Z scored a further (very) minor hit with 'SO LONG' although that would be the sum total of their success and a follow-up album, 'GOING DEAF FOR A LIVING' (1980) failed to chart. Moving to 'Liberty', the group released one more single, 'LIMBO', before being reduced to a trio following the departure of SKOLNIK. 1981 saw the release of their third and final album, 'RED SKIES OVER PARADISE', the band finally calling it a day after a final, charmingly titled single, 'WRISTCUTTER'S LULLABY'. WATTS (whose yelping prog-rock vocals were something of an acquired taste) subsequently embarked on a similarly commericially fruitless solo career, inking a deal with 'E.M.I.' and releasing two albums in two years, 'ONE MORE TWIST' (1982) and 'THE ICEBERG MODEL' (1983). Incredibly, perhaps, 'Arista' decided to sign up a reformed 'FISCHER-Z' in the late 80's, obviously hoping to succeed where their rivals had earlier failed. Having recruited a new line-up of IAN PORTER, DENIS HAINES, ALAN MORRISON, JENNIE CRUSE and STEVE KELLNER, WATTS proceeded to record a comeback album, 'REVEAL' (1988), before going on to record a German-only follow-up, 'FISH'S HEAD' for the affiliated 'Ariola' label. Mainstream recognition remained as far off as ever and although WATTS carried on with the band into the 90's, nothing more was heard from them after a proposed 1995 set, 'STREAM', was cancelled.

Album rating: WORD SALAD (*5) / GOING DEAF FOR A LIVING (*4) / RED SKIES OVER PARADISE (*4) / REVEAL (*4) / FISH'S HEAD (*4) / DESTINATION PARADISE (*4) / KAMIKAZE SHIRT (*4) / John Watts: ONE MORE TWIST (*5) / THE ICEBERG MODEL (*5)

JOHN WATTS – vocals, guitar, keyboards / **STEVE SKOLNIK** – keyboards / **DAVID GRAHAM** – bass / **STEVE LIDDLE** – drums, percussion

	U.A.	U.A.
Sep 78. (7") *(UP 36478)* **WAX DOLLS. / THE ANGRY BRIGADE**	☐	-
Feb 79. (7") *(UP 36486)* **REMEMBER RUSSIA. / BIGGER SLICE NOW**	☐	-
May 79. (7",7"pic-d) *(UP 36509)* **THE WORKER. / KITTEN CURRY**	53	-
Jun 79. (lp) *(UAG 30232)* **WORD SALAD** – Pretty paracetamol / Acrobats / The worker / Spiders / Remember Russia / The French let her / Lies / Wax dolls / Headlines / Nice to know / Billy and the motorway police / Lemmings. (cd-iss. Nov87; CDP 746684-2)	66	-
Aug 79. (7") *(BP 305)* **FIRST IMPRESSIONS. / HIGH WIRE WORKER**	☐	-
Apr 80. (7") *(BP 342)* **SO LONG. / HIDING**	72	-
May 80. (lp) *(UAG 30295)* **GOING DEAF FOR A LIVING** – Room service / So long / Crazy girl / No right / Going deaf for a living / Pick up, slip up / The crank / Haters / Four minutes in Durham (with you) / Limbo. (cd-iss. Nov87; CDP 746685-2)	☐	-

	Liberty	Liberty
Sep 80. (7") *(BP 360)* **LIMBO. / THE RAT MAN**	☐	-

— now a trio when SKOLNIK departed

Mar 81. (7") *(BP 387)* **MARLIESE. / RIGHT HAND MEN**	☐	-
Apr 81. (lp) *(LBG 30326)* **RED SKIES OVER PARADISE** – Berlin / Marliese / Red skies over paradise / In England / You'll never find Brian here / Battalions of strangers / Song and dance brigade / The writer / Bathroom scenario / Wristcutter's lullaby / Cruise missiles / Luton to Lisbon / Multinationals bite. (cd-iss. Nov87; CDP 746683-2)	☐	-
May 81. (7") *(BP 398)* **WRISTCUTTER'S LULLABY. / YOU'LL NEVER FIND BRIAN HERE**	☐	-

— disbanded after above; JOHN WATTS went solo

JOHN WATTS

now solo / with **DAVE PURDYE** – bass / **DEREK BALLARD** – drums

	E.M.I.	not iss.
Oct 81. (7") *(EMI 5239)* **SPEAKING IN A DIFFERENT LANGUAGE. / HOLIDAY IN FRANCE**	☐	-
Mar 82. (7") *(EMI 5266)* **ONE VOICE. / HOLIDAY IN FRANCE**	☐	-
Apr 82. (lp) *(EMC 3402)* **ONE MORE TWIST** – One voice / Lagonda lifestyle / Watching you / Carousel / That's not enough for me / I know it now / Victims of fashion / Speaking in a different language / Involuntary movement / Relax.	☐	-
Jun 82. (7") *(EMI 5298)* **YOUR FAULT. / SARAWEGO**	☐	-

— now without BALLARD who was repl. by session people **DICK ADLAND** – drums / **ROSA B.** – violin, vocals / **DENIS HAINES** – keyboards / **BRIAN BRUMMIT + MICK DONNELY + JIM PATERSON + PAUL SPEARE** – wind instruments

| Jan 83. (7") *(EMI 5361)* **I SMELT THE ROSRES (IN THE UNDERGROUND). / I NEED ACTION** | ☐ | - |

FISCHER-Z (cont)

Mar 83. (lp) (EMC 3427) **THE ICEBERG MODEL**
- Interference / Man in someone else's skin / I smelt roses (in the underground) / I was in love with you / Money and power / The prisoner's dilemma / Mayday mayday / Menargerie makers / A face to remember / The iceberg model.

May 83. (7") (EMI 5387) **MAYDAY MAYDAY. / TURN THE LIGHT ON**

FISCHER-Z

— WATTS + IAN PORTER – bass, keyboards, electric drums / DENIS HAINES – keyboards / ALAN MORRISON – guitar / JENNIE CRUSE – vocals / STEVE KELLNER – drums

Arista / Arista

Feb 88. (7") (109 396) **THE PERFECT DAY. / MARGUERITE**
(12"+=) (609 396) – ('A'extended).

Mar 88. (lp/c/cd) (208/408/258 620) **REVEAL**
- The perfect day / Leave it to the businessmen to die young / I can't wait that long / Tallulah tomorrow / Realistic man / Fighting back the tears / Big drum / Heartbeat / It takes love / So far.

Apr 88. (7") (109 704) **BIG DRUM. / THE CAMERA LIES**
(12"+=) (609 704) – ('A'extended).

— now without MORRISON + HAINES

Jun 89. (7") (112 301) **SAY NO. / PSYCHOJAZZ SHUFFLE**
(12"+=/cd-s+=) (612/662 301) – ('A'extended).

Ariola – not iss. – German

Jul 89. (lp/cd) (209/259 772) **FISH'S HEAD**
- Say no / Masquerade / It could be you / Sticky business / Huba / Oh mother / Just words / It's only a hurricane / She said / Ho ho ho.

Marquee not iss.

Oct 90. (12") (MARQX 002) **SAUSAGES AND TEARS. / SAUSAGES AND TEARS (instrumental) / DANGEROUS TALK**

Welfare not iss.

1992. (cd-s) **DESTINATION PARADISE / DESTINATION PARADISE / VENILLION LIPS**

Nov 92. (cd) (WELFD 3) **DESTINATION PARADISE**
- Destination paradise / Will you be there / Tightrope / Say when / Caruso / Marguerite Yourcenar / Saturday night / Mockingbird again / Still in flames / Time for Rita / Of all the / Count to ten / So hard / Further from love.

Apr 94. (cd) (WELFD 6) **KAMIKAZE SHIRT**
- The peaches and cream / Killing time / Marlon / And this we call crime / Kamikaze shirt / Polythene / Human beings / Stripper in the mirror / Stars / Blue anemone / Radio K.I.L.L.

— an album, 'STREAM' (WELFD 8), was cancelled in 1995

– compilations, etc. –

May 90. (cd/c/lp) E.M.I.; (CDP 794132-2/-4/-1) **GOING RED FOR A SALAD (THE UA YEARS 1979-1982)**
- So long / Acrobats / The worker / Wax dolls / Remember Russia / Going deaf for a living / Room service / Pretty paracetamol / Marliese / You'll never find Brian here / Berlin / Battalions of strangers / Bathroom scenario / Wristcutter's lullaby / Crazy girl. (cd+=) – One voice / Involuntary movement / Mayday mayday / I smelt roses (in the underground).

Jun 95. (cd) Welfare; (WELFD 7) **STILL IN FLAMES (THE BEST OF FISCHER-Z)**

Feb 98. (cd) Disky; (DC 882812) **THE WORKER**

Patrik FITZGERALD

Born: 19 Mar'56, Bow, East London, England. Inspired by the energy and anti-establishment stance of punk, FITZGERALD attempted to carve out a niche as the genre's acoustic troubadour and often found himself on the receiving end of skinhead intolerance as a result. Signed to the independent 'Small Wonder' label, the singer-songwriter made his debut with the acclaimed 'SAFETY-PIN STUCK IN MY HEART' EP, following it up with another four-tracker, 'BACKSTREET BOYS', the latter's title track a comment on mob violence. Following cult acclaim for these early releases, FITZGERALD recorded a 17-track debut album, GRUBBY STORIES (1979), wherein his alternately affecting and ironic, cockney-intoned tales (highlights being 'LITTLE FISHES' and 'NO FUN FOOTBALL') were augmented by BUZZCOCKS sticksman JOHN MAHER and PENETRATION bass player ROBERT BLAMIRE. Subsequent efforts such as 'GIFTS AND TELEGRAMS' (1982) – now on 'Red Flame' – and 'DRIFTING TOWARDS VIOLENCE' (1984) met with little interest, however, and by the mid-80's, the man had left the music business completely. The following decade saw PATRIK the bard return for some sporadic performances, although no studio material was forthcoming.

Album rating: GRUBBY STORIES (*5) / GIFTS AND TELEGRAMS (*5) / DRIFTING TOWARDS SILENCE (*5) / TUNISIAN TWIST (*4) / THE VERY BEST OF... compilation (*6)

PATRIK FITZGERALD – vocals, acoustic guitar

Small Wonder not iss.

Dec 77. (7"ep) (SMALL 4) **SAFETY-PIN STUCK IN MY HEART**
- Banging and shouting / Safety-pin stuck in my heart / Work, rest, play, reggae / Set we free / Optimism Reject.

Jul 78. (7"ep) (SMALL 6) **THE BACKSTREET BOYS**
- Buy me, sell me . . . / The little dippers / Trendy / The backstreet boys.

Oct 78. (12"ep) (WEENY ONE) **THE PARANOID WARD / THE BEDROOM TAPES**
- Babysitter / Irrelevant battles / Cruelist crime / The paranoid ward / The bingo crowd / Ragged generation for real / Live out my stars / George / Live at the top. (re-iss. Dec78 as 7"ep 'THE PARANOID WARD'; first 5 tracks only)

— added band; ROBERT BLAMIRE – bass (of PENETRATION) / JOHN MAHER – drums (of BUZZCOCKS) / PETER WILSON – guitar, keyboards, producer

Polydor not iss.

Mar 79. (7") (2059 091) **ALL SEWN UP. / HAMMERSMITH ODEONS**

Apr 79. (lp) (2383 533) **GRUBBY STORIES**
- As ugly as you / Nothing to do / All my friends are dead now / Adopted girl / Don't tell me because I'm young / When I get famous / Little fishes / Lover's pact / All the years of trying / But not anymore / Suicidal wreck / My secret life / Conventions of life / Parent games / No fun football / Make it safe / Your hero.

Jun 79. (7"m) (2059 135) **IMPROVE MYSELF. / THE BINGO CROWD / MY NEW FAMILY**

— toured with COLIN PEACOCK – guitar / CHARLIE FRANCIS – bass / RAB FAE BEITH – drums

— completely solo again. RAB joined The WALL and CHARLIE joined TOYAH

Red Flame not iss.

Sep 82. (7") (RF 708) **PERSONAL LOSS. / STRAIGHT BOY**

Nov 82. (lp) (RF 8) **GIFTS AND TELEGRAMS**
- One little soldier / Exist / Personal loss / Travel through a dark though scented county / Grey echoes / World is getting better / Solve / My death / Work / Gifts and telegrams / Punch / Island of lost souls.

Himalaya not iss.

Feb 84. (lp) (HIM 009) **DRIFTING TOWARDS SILENCE**
- Smile / In this world / Family outing / Domestication / Working hu-mans casino / We seemed so suited / My perfect world / Scattered villages / A life sentence / Down / Drifting towards silence / Mystery / My perfect world (part 2).

Final Solution not iss.

Apr 84. (7"ep) (FSEP 001) **TONIGHT EP** (rec.1981)
- Mrs & Mrs / Animal mentality / Tonight / A superbeing / Waiting for the final clue.

— now with PETER McDONNELL – keyboards / ALISDAIR ROBERTS – bass / GILLY JARMAN – drums

Red Flame not iss.

Jun 86. (lp) (RF 48) **TUNISIAN TWIST**
- Factory of wines / The finger of Lesotho / Putting wings on aeroplanes / 10,000 years of weeping / Pilot of a private yacht / Down Mexico way / Poor John / Tunisian twist.

— retired from music scene and went to work as a waiter in the House Of Commons. He went to live in Normandy, France, until his return in the early 90's to try his hand at acting.

— new tracks, 'Volcano', 'One by one', 'The early warning' and 'Thee serving classes' were available on 'Red Flame' V/A comp 'Treasures From The Wax Museum' in 1993

– compilations, etc. –

Apr 94. (cd) Anagram; (CDPUNK 31) **SAFETY PIN STUCK IN MY HEART – THE VERY BEST OF PATRIK FITZGERALD**
- Banging and shouting / Safety pin stuck in my heart / Work rest play reggae / Set we free / Optimism reject / Buy me sell me / The little dippers / Trendy / Backstreet boys / Babysitter / Irrelevant battles / Cruelist crime / The paranoid ward / The bingo crowd (instrumental) / Life at the top / Ragged generation for real / Live out my stars / George / All sewn up (demo) / Improve myself (new version) / Tonight / Mr. & Mrs. / Animal mentality / A superbeing / Waiting for the final cue / Without sex / Pop star pop star. (re-iss. Mar00; same)

FLAMIN' GROOVIES

Formed: Bay Area, San Francisco, California, USA . . . 1965 originally as The CHOSEN FEW and then The LOST AND FOUND, by CYRIL JORDAN, ROY LONEY, GEORGE ALEXANDER and TIM LYNCH. In 1967, they issued a self-financed debut lp, the 10" 'SNEAKERS', which resulted in a deal with 'Epic'. After one poorly promoted lp, 'SUPERSNAZZ', they left to join the roster of the 'Kama Sutra' label, aided by producer Richard Robinson in 1970. There, they issued two well-received albums, 'FLAMINGO' and 'TEENAGE HEAD', before again moving stables to 'United Artists' in '72. Critically acclaimed, the albums highlighted The 'GROOVIES' characteristic high-energy rock'n'roll, updating 50's material into 60's-style garage punk. The following years resulted in many personnel changes, and after touring Europe in 1976, they finally released the DAVE EDMUNDS-produced 'Sire' comeback, 'SHAKE SOME ACTION' (he had previously worked on their 1972 album, 'SLOW DEATH'). Although the band were associated with the embryonic new wave/punk movement, the album's power-pop harmonies found little credibility with this scene. The band released a further two albums in the same vein before splitting then re-forming for the live comeback lp, 'ONE NIGHT STAND' (1987). • **Songwriters:** JORDAN-LONEY, until the latter's departure in '71. Recorded many covers including; SOMETHIN' ELSE (Eddie Cochran) / PISTOL PACKIN' MAMA (Gene Vincent) / SHAKIN' ALL OVER (Johnny Kidd) / THAT'LL BE THE DAY (Buddy Holly) / KEEP A KNOCKIN' (Little Richard) / MOVE IT (Cliff Richard) / FEEL A WHOLE LOT BETTER (Byrds) / PAINT IT BLACK + JUMPIN' JACK FLASH + 19th NERVOUS BREAKDOWN (Rolling Stones) / MARRIED WOMAN (Frankie Lee Sims) / TEENAGE CONFIDENTIAL (Jerry Lee Lewis) / WEREWOLVES OF LONDON (Warren Zevon) / ABSOLUTELY SWEET MARIE (Bob Dylan) / TALLAHASSEE LASSIE (Freddy Cannon) / KICKS (Mann-Weill) / CALL ME LIGHTNING (Who) / MONEY (Barrett Strong) / PLEASE PLEASE ME + MISERY + THERE'S A PLACE (Beatles) / etc. • **Trivia:** Long-time fan GREG SHAW, issued 1975 single 'YOU TORE ME DOWN', for his own 'Bomp' magazine label.

Album rating: SNEAKERS (*5) / SUPERSNAZZ (*6) / FLAMINGO (*7) / TEENAGE

FLAMIN' GROOVIES (cont)

HEAD (*8) / SHAKE SOME ACTION (*8) / FLAMIN' GROOVIES NOW! (*7) / JUMPIN' IN THE NIGHT (*6) / ONE NIGHT STAND (*4) / GROOVIES GREATEST GROOVES compilation (*8)

ROB LONEY (b.13 Apr'46) – vocals / **CYRIL JORDAN** (b. 1948) – lead guitar / **TIM LYNCH** (b.18 Jul'46) – rhythm guitar / **GEORGE ALEXANDER** (b.18 May'46, San Mateo, Calif.) – bass / **DANNY MIHM** – drums (ex-WHISTLING SHRIMP) repl. RON GRECO

		not iss.	Snazz
1967.	(10"m-lp) <2371> **SNEAKERS**	–	–

– The slide / I'm drowning / Babes in the sky / Love time / My yada / Golden clouds / Prelude in A flat to afternoon of a plad. <US re-iss. 1975 on 'Skydog'; FGG 803>

		not iss.	Epic
1968.	(7") <10501> **ROCKIN' PNEUMONIA AND THE BOOGIE WOOGIE FLU. / THE FIRST ONE'S FREE**	–	–
1968.	(7") <10564> **SOMETHIN' ELSE. / LAURIE DID IT**	–	–
1970.	(lp) <26487> **SUPERSNAZZ**	–	–

– Love have mercy / The girl can't help it / Laurie did it / Apart from that / Rockin' pneumonia and the boogie woogie flu / The first one's free / Pagan Rachel / a) Somethin' else, b) Pistol packin' mama / Brushfire / Bam balam / Around the corner. (UK-rel.Feb86 on 'Edsel'; ED 173) (cd-iss. Aug93 on 'Columbia'; 467073-2)

		Kama Sutra	Kama Sutra
1971.	(lp) <KSBS 2021> **FLAMINGO**		

– Roadhouse / Headin' for the Texas border / Gonna rock tonite / Comin' after you / Sweet roll me on down / Keep a knockin' / Second cousin / Childhood's end / Jailbait. (UK cd-iss. Jan90 on 'Big Beat'+=; CDWIK 925) – Walkin' the dog / Somethin' else / My girl Josephine / Louie Louie / Rockin' pneumonia and the boogie woogie flu / Going out theme (version 2).

| 1971. | (d-lp) <KSBS 2031> **TEENAGE HEAD** | – | – |

– Teenage head / Whiskey women / Yesterday's numbers 32:20 / High flyin' baby / City lights / Have you seen my baby / Evil-hearted Ada / Doctor Boogie / Rumble / Shakin' all over / That'll be the day / Round and round / Going out theme. ('FLAMINGO' + 'TEENAGE HEAD' iss.UK as 'FLAMIN' GROOVIES' on 'Kama Sutra' d-lp; 2683 003) (UK re-iss. 1989 on 'Dojo' lp/cd; DOJO LP/CD 58) (cd re-iss. Jan90 on 'Big Beat'; CDWIK 926)

| Aug 71. | (7") (2013 031) **TEENAGE HEAD. / EVIL-HEARTED ADA** | | |
| Mar 72. | (7"ep) (2013 042) **GONNA ROCK TONITE / KEEP A-KNOCKIN'. / (3 others by 'Sha Na Na')** | | |

— **CHRIS WILSON** (b.10 Sep'52, Waltham, Massachusetts, USA) – vocals (ex-LOOSE GRAVEL) repl. LONEY / **JAMES FARRELL** – guitar (ex-LOOSE GRAVEL) repl. LYNCH who formed HOT KNIVES

— changed to The DOGS for a short while, before returning to same

		U.A.	U.A.
Jun 72.	(7") (UP 35392) **SLOW DEATH. / TALAHASSIE LASSIE**		–
Jun 72.	(lp) <7521> **SLOW DEATH**	–	

– Sweet little rock'n'roller / Doctor Boogie / Walking the dog / Roadhouse / Teenage head / Slow death / Shakin' all over / Louie Louie / Have you seen my baby / Can't explain.

| Jan 73. | (7") (UP 35464) **MARRIED WOMAN. / GET A SHOT OF RHYTHM & BLUES** | | |

— JORDAN, WILSON, FARRELL and ALEXANDER recruited new member **DAVID WRIGHT** – drums; repl. TERRY RAE who had repl. MIHM (to HOT KNIVES)

		Skydog	not iss.
1974.	(7") **JUMPIN' JACK FLASH. / BLUES FROM PHILLYS** (re-iss. '77 on 12";)	–	– France
1974.	(7"ep) <66001> **GREASE**	–	– France

– Let me rock / Dog meat / Sweet little rock'n'roller.

		Philips	not iss.
1975.	(7") **LET THE BOY ROCK'N'ROLL. / YES IT'S TRUE**	–	– France
		not iss.	Bomp
1975.	(7") <101> **YOU TORE ME DOWN. / HIM OR ME**	–	–
		Sire	Sire
Jun 76.	(lp) (9103 251) **SHAKE SOME ACTION**		

– Shake some action / Sometimes / Yes it's true / St. Louis blues / You tore me down / Please please girl / Let the boy rock'n'roll / Don't you lie to me / She said yeah / I'll cry alone / Misery / I saw her / Teenage confidential / I can't hide. (re-iss. Sep78; SRK 6021) (cd-iss. Sep93 on 'Aim'; AIMCD 1017)

Jul 76.	(7"m) (6198 086) **DON'T YOU LIE TO ME. / SHE SAID YEAH / SHAKE SOME ACTION**		
Nov 76.	(7") (6078 602) **SHAKE SOME ACTION. / TEENAGE CONFIDENTIAL**		
Nov 76.	(7") <731> **TEENAGE CONFIDENTIAL. / I CAN'T HIDE**	–	

— MIKE WILHELM – guitar; repl. FARRELL who joined PHANTOM MOVERS

| Apr 78. | (lp) (9103 333) **THE FLAMIN' GROOVIES NOW!** | | |

– Feel a whole lot better / Bewteen the lines / Ups and downs / There's a place / Take me back / Reminiscing / Good laugh man / Yeah my baby / House of blue lights / All I wanted / Blue turns to grey / When I heard your name / Move it / Don't put me on. (re-iss. Sep78; SRK 7059)

Apr 78.	(7"m,12"m) (6078 619) **FEEL A WHOLE LOT BETTER. / PAINT IT BLACK / SHAKE SOME ACTION**		
Aug 78.	(7") (SIR 4002) **MOVE IT. / WHEN I HEARD YOUR NAME**		
Jun 79.	(lp) (SRK 6067) **JUMPING IN THE NIGHT**		

– Please please girl / Next one crying / Down down down / Tell me again / Absolutely sweet Marie / (You're my) Wonderful one / Jumpin' in the night / 19th nervous breakdown / Boys / 5D / First plane home / Lady friend / In the U.S.A. <US-different tracks>

| 1979. | (7") (SIR 4018) **ABSOLUTELY SWEET MARIE. / WEREWOLVES OF LONDON / NEXT ONE CRYING** | | |

— **DANNY MIHM** – drums (ex-PHANTOM MOVERS) re-repl. WRIGHT before split CHRIS WILSON joined BARRACUDAS in '82, **CYRIL JORDAN** re-formed FLAMIN' GROOVIES in 1986

— JACK JOHNSON – guitar + PAUL ZAHL – drums; repl. WILSON, WRIGHT + WILHELM

		A.B.C.	not iss.
Jul 87.	(7") (ABCS 015) **SHAKE SOME ACTION (live). / ?**		–
Jul 87.	(lp) (ABCLP 10) **ONE NIGHT STAND (live)**		–

– Kicks / Bittersweet / I can't hide / Money / Call me Lightning / Shake some action / Slow death / Teenage head / Slow down / Tallahassie lassie. (cd-iss. Apr89; ABCD 10) (re-iss. Sep93 on 'Aim' cd/c; AIM CD/C 1008)

– compilations etc. –

| Jun 76. | (7") Kama Sutra; (KSS 707) **TEENAGE HEAD. / HEADIN' FOR TEXAS BORDER** | – | – |
| Nov 76. | (7"ep) United Artists; (REM 406) **SLOW DEATH EP** | – | – |

– Slow death / Talahassie lassie / Married woman / Get a shot of rhythm & blues.

May 84.	(lp) Skydog; (SK 12226) **SUPERGREASE**	–	– France
1980's.	(7") Skydog; **I CAN'T EXPLAIN. / LITTLE QUEENIE**	–	– France
Nov 84.	(lp) Eva; (12044) **'68 (live)**	–	– France
Nov 84.	(lp) Eva; (12045) **'70 (live)**	–	– France
Jul 85.	(lp/c) Buddah; (252262-1/-4) **STILL SHAKIN'**		
May 86.	(lp/c) Edsel; (ED/CED 183) **ROADHOUSE**		

– (compilation of 'FLAMINGO' + 'TEENAGE HEAD').

| Aug 88. | (lp) Voxx; (200009) **BUCKET OF BRAINS** | – | |

(UK cd-iss. Apr95 on 'E.M.I.'; CZ 542)

| Aug 89. | (lp/c/cd) Sire; (K 925948-1/-4/-2) **GROOVIES GREATEST GROOVES** | | |

– Shake some action / Teenage head / Slow death / Tallahassie lassie / Yeah my baby / Yes it's true / First plane home / In the U.S.A. / Between the lines / Don't you lie to me / Down down down / I'll cry alone / You tore me down / Please please girl / Yes I am / Teenage confidential / I can't hide / Absolutely sweet Marie / Don't put me on / I saw her / All I wanted / Jumpin' in the night / There's a place / River deep, mountain high. (cd re-iss. Jan96 on 'Warners'; 7599 25948-2)

Nov 89.	(lp) Aim; (COLLECT 2) **ROCKFIELD SESSIONS**		–
Apr 93.	(cd/lp) Marilyn; **RARE DEMOS & LIVE RECORDINGS**		
Sep 93.	(cd/c) Aim; (AIM CD/C 1030) **STEP UP**		
Oct 93.	(cd) Aim; (COLLECT 1-2) **SNEAKERS / ROCKFIELD SESSIONS**		–
Nov 93.	(cd) Mystery; **ROCKIN' AT THE ROUNDHOUSE – LIVE IN LONDON 1976/78 (live)**		
May 94.	(cd) Eva; (842070) **LIVE 68/70 (live)**		
Nov 94.	(10"lp) Bomp; **EP**		
Apr 95.	(cd) Aim; (AIM 1051CD) **LIVE AT THE FESTIVAL OF THE SUN BARCELONA (live)**		
Apr 97.	(cd) Aim; (AIM 2001CD) **OLDIES BUT GOLDIES: BEST OF**		

FLESH EATERS

Formed: Los Angeles, California, USA ... 1977 by CHRIS 'D' DESJARDINS, who has been the only constant fixture in the band's line-up over its decade and a half lifespan. A cast of DAVE ALVIN, JOHN DOE, BILL BATEMAN, DON BONEBRAKE and STEVE BERLIN were present on their debut album, 'NO QUESTIONS ASKED', at the turn of the decade, although the revolving door personnel policy led them on to better things. CHRIS D and Co delivered a series of average post-punk albums that verged on alternative heavy-metal, although lack of interest led the singer to change direction in the mid 80's via the rootsier DIVINE HORSEMEN. While their music might have less intensity, a sinister lyrical edge was never far from the surface, 'S.S.T.' albums such as 'DEVIL'S RIVER' (1986) and 'SNAKE HANDLER' (1987) finding DESJARDINS splitting the vocals with his partner, JULIE C (CHRISTENSEN). Towards the end of the decade, CHRIS D founded yet another vehicle for his dark talent, issuing 'I PASS FOR HUMAN' as STONE BY STONE in 1989. The 90's, meanwhile, saw The FLESH EATERS return with a convincing comeback album, 'DRAGSTRIP RIOT' (1991), although the following year's 'SEX DIARY OF MR VAMPIRE' would be their final offering. • **Covered:** Divine Horsemen: GIMME SHELTER (Rolling Stones) / VOODOO IDOL (Cramps).

Album rating: NO QUESTIONS ASKED (*6) / A MINUTE TO PRAY, A SECOND TO DIE (*6) / FOREVER CAME TODAY (*6) / DRAGSTRIP RIOT (*5) / SEX DIARY OF MR VAMPIRE (*5) / GREATEST HITS – DESTROYED BY FIRE compilation (*6) / PREHISTORIC FITS compilation (*6) / ASHES OF TIME (*5) / Divine Horsemen: TIME STANDS STILL (*5) / DEVIL'S RIVER (*5) / MIDDLE OF THE NIGHT (*5) / SNAKE HANDLER (*5) / Stone By Stone: I PASS FOR HUMAN (*5)

CHRIS 'D' DESJARDINS – vocals / **DAVE ALVIN** – guitar / **JOHN DOE** – bass / **BILL BATEMAN** – drums / **DON BONEBRAKE** – marimbas, percussion / **STEVE BERLIN** – saxophone

		not iss.	Upsetter
1978.	(7"ep) **THE FLESH EATERS**	–	

– Disintegration nation / Agony shorthand / Radio dies screaming / Twisted road.

		Initial	Ruby
1980.	(lp) <UPCD 34> **NO QUESTIONS ASKED**		
Sep 81.	(lp) (IRC 007) <JRR 101> **A MINUTE TO PRAY, A SECOND TO DIE**		

– Digging my grave / Pray til you sweat / River of fever / Satan's stomp / See you in the boneyard / So long / Cyrano de Berger's back / Divine horsemen.

— **DON KIRK** – guitar; repl. ALVIN who was already part of The BASTERS / **ROBYN JAMESON** – bass; repl. DOE / BONEBRAKE who were part of X / **CHRIS WAHL** – drums; repl. BATEMAN (also of BLASTERS)

| 1982. | (lp) **FOREVER CAME TODAY** | – | – |

– My life to live / A minute to pray, a second to die / Secret life / Shallow water / The rosy hours / The wedding dice / Hand of glory / Drag my name in the mud / Because of you / Tightrope of fire.

| 1983. | (lp) **A HARD ROAD TO FOLLOW** | – | |

— split after above

DIVINE HORSEMEN

CHRIS D – vocals / with **DAVE ALVIN** – lead guitar / **JULIE C** (b. CHRISTENSEN) – vocals / **ROBYN JAMESON** – bass / **JEFFREY LEE PIERCE** – guitar / **CHRIS CACAVAS** – piano / **JOHN DOE** – acoustic guitar / **ANN DEJARNETT** – violin, percussion / **DAN STUART** – guitars / + others

FLESH EATERS (cont)

1984. (lp/c; as CHRIS D. / DIVINE HORSEMEN) *(ROSE 46)* <E 1130/+C> **TIME STANDS STILL** — New Rose / Enigma / – / French
– When the rain comes down / Lilly white hands / Post all dishonor / Frankie Silver / Sanctuary / Heat from the sun / Little sister / Hell's belle / Time stands still.

— now a basic 6-piece **CHRIS D., JULIE C. + ROBYN, WAYNE JAMES + CAM KING** (guitars) + **REX ROBERTS** (drums, vocals)

Dec 86. (lp/cd) *(ROSE 102/+CD)* <SST 091/+CD> **DEVIL'S RIVER** — New Rose / S.S.T.
– My sin / Sapphire / Devil's river / He rode right out / Come into this night / Tenderest kiss / Love call / Too young to die / It doesn't matter / Middle of the night. (cd+=) – Field of stone / Little sister / Mother's worry / Gimme shelter / If I only could. (re-iss. May93 on 'S.S.T.' lp/cd; same as US)

Jan 87. (lp) *(NEW 87)* <SST 090> **MIDDLE OF THE NIGHT**
– Middle of the night / Field of stone / If I only could / Little sister / Mother's worry / It doesn't matter / Gimme shelter / Voodoo idol.

— **PETE ANDRUS** – guitar; repl. CAM + WAYNE

Oct 87. (lp/cd) *(ROSE 134/+CD)* <SST 140/+CD> **SNAKE HANDLER**
– Snake handler / Kiss tomorrow goodbye / Stone by stone (fire is my home) / Curse of the crying woman / Someone like you / Fire kiss / What is red / The blind leading the blind / That's no way to live. (cd+=) – Superlungs / Frankie Silver / Past all dishonour / Sanctuary. (re-iss. May93 on 'S.S.T.' lp/cd; same as US)

Mar 88. (m-lp) *(NEW 110)* <SST 176> **HANDFUL OF SAND**
– Handful of sand / Curse of the crying woman / Tenderest kiss / Frankie Silver (live) / Past all dishonor (live) / Sanctuary (live).

— broke up the partnership, although CHRIS D formed below solo project with **JOHN NAPIER, ERIC MARTIN + CHRIS HASKETT**

Jul 89. (lp/c/cd; as STONE BY STONE with CHRIS D) <(SST 247/+C/CD)> **I PASS FOR HUMAN**

— **MATT LEE** – guitar; repl. ANDRUS

1990. (7") *SX 010)* **MY SIN. / DEVIL'S RIVER** — Shock / not iss.

FLESH EATERS

— re-formed with of course **CHRIS D** at the helm / + **WAYNE JAMES** – guitar / **GLENN HAYS** – bass / **RAY TORRES** – drums, percussion / **TERRI LAIRD** – backing vocals

Nov 90. (lp/c/cd) <(SST 264/+C/CD)> **PREHISTORIC FITS VOL.2** — S.S.T. / S.S.T.
(compilation)
– My life to live / Pray til you sweat / Satan's stomp / Kiss on my cheek – Suicide saddle / No questions asked / So long / Buried treasure / Because of you / Tightrope on fire / I take what I want / Fistful of vodka / Poison arrow. (re-iss. May93; same)

Mar 91. (d-lp/c/cd) <(SST 273/+C/CD)> **DRAGSTRIP RIOT**
– Tomorrow never comes / Youngest profession / Soul kiss / Dragstrip riot / Bedful of knives / My baby's done her best / Sugarhead and panther breath / Out of nowhere / Dove's blood ink / Take my hand / Agony shorthand / Agony sorehead / The moon upstairs / Slipped, tripped, fell in love / Fur magnet. (re-iss. May93; same)

— **CHRISTIAN FREE** – drums, percussion; repl. TORRES

May 93. (cd/c) <(SST 292 CD/C)> **THE SEX DIARY OF MR. VAMPIRE** — / Nov92
– Death installment plan / Cemetery without crosses / Better tomorrow / Soft knife and a brick pillow / Covert counter-insurgency man / Five dolls for an August moon / I love you so / Car named Ego / Diary of a psycho / Diamond in my eye / Eyes of lightning / Kill, baby, kill.

Dec 92. (12"ep/cd-ep) <SST/+CD 297> **CRUCIFIED LOVERS IN WOMAN HELL** — -

— disbanded after above; CHRIS D subsequently released a solo album, 'LOVE CANNOT DIE' for 'Sympathy For The Record Industry'

— the FLESH EATERS re-formed for one more stab in '99

Jan 01. (cd) <UPCD 001> **ASHES OF TIME** — not iss. / Upsetter
– Salty black water / Crosseyed butterfly / Kisses draw blood / Red spell spells red / Mourning becomes you / Blood wedding / House amid the thickets / Double snake bourbon / Gate of flesh / Evil flower / Cut down the setting sun / Nobody lives forever / Black-and-blue bird / My love has been burning / Crucified lovers.

– compilations, etc. –

May 87. (lp) *Fan Club; (FC 025)* / S.S.T.; <SST 094> **DESTROYED BY FIRE – GREATEST HITS** — / 1986
– See you in the boneyard / Cyrano / Dominoes / Impossible crime / Secret life / Hard road to follow / The wedding dice / Pony dress / We'll never die / Digging my grave / Lake of burning fire. (re-iss. May93 on 'S.S.T.'; same as US)

Mar 89. (lp) *Homestead; <(HMS 124-1)>* **LIVE (live 1979-83)**
– Version nation / Digging my grave / So long / Divine horsemen / Cinderella / A minute to pray, a second to die / Because of you / My destiny / Poison arrow / My life to live / I take what I want / Shallow water / Buried treasure / Digging my grave.

FLESHTONES

Formed: Queens, New York, USA . . . 1976 by KEITH STRENG, PETER ZAREMBA and JAN MAREK PAKULSKI; BILL MILHIZER subsequently coming in for the departing LENNY CALDERONE. Like most bands of the era, they started out by playing at both the legendary CBGB's and Max's Kansas City venues. A debut single, 'AMERICAN BEAT', was issued in 1979, leading to a contract with Miles Copeland's 'I.R.S.' the following year. Meanwhile, a UK package tour alongside the dB'S and the BUSH TETRAS introduced British audiences to the band's punk/garage revivalist sound complete with melodic fuzz guitar and Farfisa organ. After a few singles were issued, The FLESHTONES finally released their debut album, 'ROMAN GODS' (1982), translating at least some of their live chemistry to vinyl. Adding GORDON SPAETH, they unleashed a second collection of bad-assed rock'n'roll in the shape of the slightly superior 'HEXBREAKER!' (1983).

A further personnel change was effected when PAKULSKI was replaced by ROBERT BURKE WARREN, the latter sticking around for two more albums, 'LIVE IN PARIS' (1985) and 'THE FLESHTONES VS REALITY' (1987). The new bassist on the Spanish-only 'SOUL MADRID' was FRED SMITH, although he in turn made way for ANDY SHERNOFF then KEN FOX. Throughout the 90's they have continued to unearth the occasional long-player, 'MORE THAN SKIN DEEP' (1998), their first for their new label, 'Epitaph'.
• **Covered:** ROCKET USA (Suicide) / medleys by Kingsmen, etc. • **Trivia:** The guest on the 'BLAST OFF!' album was ALAN VEGA (of Suicide).

Album rating: ROMAN GODS (*7) / HEXBREAKER! (*8) / BLAST OFF! collection (*6) / FLESHTONES VS REALITY (*6) / SOUL MADRID (*5) / POWERSTANCE! (*5) / BEAUTIFUL LIGHT (*5) / LABORATORY OF SOUND (*5) / MORE THAN SKIN DEEP (*5) / HITSBURG REVISITED (*5)

PETER ZAREMBA (b.16 Sep'54) – vocals, keyboards, harmonica / **KEITH STRENG** (b.18 Sep'55) – guitar, vocals / **JAN MAREK PAKULSKI** (b.22 Aug'56, Lewiston, Maine) – bass, vocals / **BILL MILHIZER** (b.21 Sep'49, Troy, N.Y.) – drums (ex-HARRY TOLEDO, ex-ACTION COMBO) repl. LENNY CALDERONE in 1979

1979. (7") *<RSS 1>* **AMERICAN BEAT. / CRITICAL LIST** — not iss. / Red Star

Aug 80. (12"ep) *<SP 70402>* **UP-FRONT** — I.R.S. / I.R.S.
– The girl from Baltimore / Cold cold shoes / Feel the heat / Play with fire / Theme from 'The Vindicators'.

May 81. (7") *(PFP 1004)* **GIRL FROM BALTIMORE. / FEEL THE HEAT** — / -

Jun 81. (7") *(IR 9024)* **THE WORLD HAS CHANGED. / ALL AROUND THE WORLD**

Feb 82. (lp) *<SP 70018>* **ROMAN GODS**
– The dreg / I've gotta change my life / Stop fooling around / Hope come back / The world has changed / R-I-G-H-T-S / Let's see the sun / Shadow line / Chinese kitchen / Ride your pony / Roman gods.

Mar 82. (7") *<(PFP 1012)>* **SHADOW LINE. / ALL AROUND THE WORLD**

— added **GORDON SPAETH** (b.21 Sep'50, New York City) – organ, saxophone, harmonica

Jul 83. (7") *(PFP 1018)* **RIGHT SIDE OF A GOOD THING. / (LEGEND OF A) WHEELMAN**

Aug 83. (lp) *<SP 70605>* **HEXBREAKER!**
– Deep in my heart / What's so new (about you) / Screaming skull / (Legend of a) Wheelman / New scene / Hexbreaker / Right side of a good thing / Brainstorm / This house is empty / Want / Burning hell.

Nov 83. (7") *<PFP 1024>* **SCREAMING SKULL. / BURNING HELL**

1985. (lp) *<IRS 5627>* **SPEED CONNECTION: THE FINAL CHAPTER**
– Hide and seek / Watch this / Kingsmen like medley: Trouble – Haunted / Return to the haunted house / Hope come back / B.Y.O.B. / One more time / Dreg / Extended super rock medley: Stop . . . / When the night falls / Wind out / La reprise.

— **ROBERT BURKE WARREN** (b.29 Mar'65, Quantico, Virginia) – bass repl. PAKULSKI

1985. (lp) *(D 26412)* **LIVE IN PARIS** (live) — - / - German
– Hide and seek / Watch this / Kingsmen like medley: Trouble – Haunted castle – Twelve month later / Return to the haunted house / Let's see the sun / Hope come back / B.Y.O.B. / This house is empty / Last chance / Super rock medley: Theme from "The Vindicators" – Hexbreaker – Roman gods / I'm back / La la la la.

Mar 87. (cd/lp) *(EM 34/+9634)* **THE FLESHTONES VS REALITY** — Emergo / Emergo
– Another direction / Way up here / Way down south / Treat her like a lady / Too late to run / The return of the leather kings / Jump back / Our own time / Whatever makes you happy / Mirror, mirror / The end of the track / Nothing's gonna bring me.

— Mar 88, 'New Rose' released various artists lp 'FLESHTONES PRESENT TIME BOMB'; *(ROSE 137)*

— **FRED SMITH** – bass repl. WARREN

1989. (lp) **SOUL MADRID** — Impossible / not iss. / - Spain

— **ANDY SHERNOFF** (b.19 Apr'52, Bronx, N.Y.) – bass repl. SMITH

— (1990) **KEN FOX** (b.19 Feb'65, Toronto, Canada) – bass repl. SHERNOFF

May 91. (cd/c) *(CDWIK/WIKC 99)* <NAK 6101CD> **POWERSTANCE!** — Big Beat / Naked Language
– Armed and dangerous (remix) / I'm still thirsty / Waiting for a message / Let it rip / 3 fevers / Living legends / I can breathe / Mod teepee / House of rock / Irresistible / Candy ass.

Feb 94. (cd/c) *(NAK 6116 CD/MC)* **BEAUTIFUL LIGHT** — Naked Language / Naked Language
– Mushroom cloud / Take a walk with the Fleshtones / Beautiful light / Big heart / Not everybody's Jesus / Whistling past the grave / Outcast / D.T. shadows / Pickin' pickin' / Pocketful of change / Push on thru / Worried boy blues.

Oct 95. (cd/c) *(11854-2/-4)* <24861-2/-4> **LABORATORY OF SOUND** — Musidisc / Ichiban
– Let's go / High on drugs / Sands of our lives / Nostradamus Jr. / The sweetest thing / Hold on / Accelerated emotion / Train of thought / One step less / A motor needs gas / Psychedelic swamp / Fading away / We'll never forget.

Jan 98. (m-cd/m-lp) *(6529-2/-1)* <24940> **MORE THAN SKIN DEEP** — Epitaph / Ichiban
– I'm not a sissy / Laugh it off / My love machine / I wanna feel something now / Gentlemen's twist / Smash crash / Dig in / Blow job / God damn it / Dance with the ghoulman / Anywhere you go / Medley: My kinda lovin' – The . . . / Better days.

May 99. (cd) *(TR 035CD)* <6558-2> **HITSBURG REVISITED** — Telstar / Epitaph
– Rock and roll baby / Comin' home baby / Don't stop now / Take my love (I want to give it all to you) / Little Lou / Going down to Tia Juana / Find somebody / Tribute to Hank Ballard / Voodoo voodoo / Tearing me apart / Soul city / Keelee's twist / I'm over twenty-five (but you can trust me) / Hitsburg USA.

FLESHTONES (cont)   THE GREAT INDIE DISCOGRAPHY   **The 1970s**

– compilations, etc. –

Feb 82. (c) *R.O.I.R.*; <(A 107)> **BLAST OFF!** (rec.1978)
— Soul struttin' / American beat / Cara-Lin / Shadow line / Comin' in-dead stick / Rocket U.S.A. / Atom spies / B.Y.O.B. / The way I feel / Watch Junior go! / Judy / Critical list / Rockin' this joint. *(cd-iss. May90 on 'Danceteria'; DANCD 039) (cd re-iss. Jul97; RE 107CD) <(lp re-iss. Apr01 on 'Munster'; MR 202LP)>*
1989. (cd/c) *I.R.S.*; <44797-0057-2/-4> **LIVING LEGENDS SERIES**
1994. (cd) *Impossible*; **THE ANGRY YEARS** — Spain
(UK-iss.Mar99 on 'Amsterdamned'; 2)
Jul 97. (cd) *Essential*; (ESMCD 573) **FLESHTONES**
— BYOB / Critical list / Shadowline / American beat / Cara Lin / Watch Junior go / Atom spies / The way I feel / comin' in dead stick / Judy / Soul struttin' / Rockin' this joint / Rocket USA.
Jul 01. (cd) *Wagram*; (306835CD) **SOLID GOLD GROUND**

— ZAREMBA was also part of The LOVE DELEGATION in 1982 (one lp, 'SPREAD THE WORD') and STRENG was in the FULL-TIME MEN who also issued records

FLYING LIZARDS

Formed: based – Kent, England ... 1978 by Irish-born DAVID CUNNINGHAM, a former art college graduate and conceptual artist who had issued a solo album, 'GREY SCALE'. Subsequently discovering monotone chanteuse, DEBORAH EVANS and pianist/keyboardist, JULIAN MARSHALL, CUNNINGHAM signed to 'Virgin' and recorded a DIY cover of Eddie Cochran's 'SUMMERTIME BLUES' on a basic tape recorder for a sum total of £6 (!). Barrett Strong's 'MONEY' was next up for the minimalist, monochromatic treatment, the bizarre but catchy results hooking a UK Top 5 placing in late summer '79 before going on to storm the US Top 50 later that year! Early 1980's self-penned follow-up, 'T.V.', stalled outside the Top 40 and although an eponymous debut album made the Top 60, a cover of Curtis Mayfield's 'MOVE ON UP' (featuring the debut of new vocalist, PATTI PALLADIN) failed to chart. A further couple of original singles followed before CUNNINGHAM added sticksman, JJ JOHNSON and recorded 'THE FOURTH WALL' (1981) with the help of such alternative luminaries as ROBERT FRIPP and GARETH SAGER. After taking a few years out to concentrate on production work, CUNNINGHAM returned in summer '84 with a savage reading of James Brown's 'SEX MACHINE'. Too much to take for some fans, the single sold poorly, as did a follow-up version of Larry Williams' 'DIZZY MISS LIZZY' and a wholesale covers set, 'TOP TEN' (1984). CUNNINGHAM made a belated comeback in the mid-90's with a series of solo and collaborative albums, the last of which, 'ARTIFICIAL HOMELAND' (1988), saw him working with ANGELA JAEGAR. • **TOP TEN covers:** TUTTI FRUTTI (Little Richard) / PURPLE HAZE (Jimi Hendrix Experience) / GREAT BALLS OF FIRE + WHOLE LOTTA SHAKIN' GOIN' ON (Jerry Lee Lewis) / WHAT'S NEW PUSSYCAT? (hit; Tom Jones) / THEN HE KISSED ME (Crystals) / SUZANNE (Leonard Cohen) / DIZZY MISS LIZZY (Larry Williams) / TEARS (Bobby Vinton).

Album rating: THE FLYING LIZARDS (*5) / THE FOURTH WALL (*4) / TOP TEN (*2)

DAVID CUNNINGHAM – synthesizer, electronics, keyboards, guitar / **DEBORAH EVANS** – vocals / **JULIAN MARSHALL** – piano, keyboards

			Virgin	Virgin
Oct 78.	(7")	(VS 230) **SUMMERTIME BLUES. / ALL GUITARS**		–
Aug 79.	(7")	(VS 276) <67003> **MONEY. / MONEY** (instrumental)	5	50 Nov79

— added **STEVE BERESFORD** – keyboards, bass, guitar

| Jan 80. | (7") | (VS 325) **T.V. / TUBE** | 43 | |
| Feb 80. | (lp) | (V 2150) <13137> **THE FLYING LIZARDS** | 60 | 99 |

— Der song Von Mandelay / Her story / T.V. / Russia / Summertime blues / Money / The flood / Trouble / Events during flood / The window.

— **PATTI PALLADIN** – vocals (ex-SNATCH) repl. DEBORAH

Oct 80.	(7")	(VS 381) **MOVE ON UP. / PORTUGAL**		–
Jan 81.	(7")	(VS 392) **HANDS 2 TAKE. / CONTINUITY**		–
May 81.	(7")	(VS 421) **LOVERS AND OTHER STRANGERS. / WIND**		–

— added **JJ JOHNSON** – drums (ex-ELECTRIC CHAIRS)
— guests incl. ROBERT FRIPP, GARETH SAGER + PETER GORDON

| Jun 81. | (lp) | (V 2190) **THE FOURTH WALL** | | – |

— Lovers and other strangers / Glide spin / In my lifetime / Cirrus / A-train / New voice / Hands 2 take / On age / Steam away / Move on up / Another story / Lost and found.

— CUNNINGHAM returned after a few years on the production front

— others:- **BERESFORD, MARSHALL, GORDON** + / **SALLY** – vocals / **JOHN GREAVES** – bass / **ELIZABETH PERRY** + **ALEX BALANESCH** – strings

			Statik	not iss.
Jul 84.	(7")	(TAK 19) **SEX MACHINE. / FLESH AND STEEL**		–
	(12"+=)	(TAK 19-12) – Machine sex.		
Oct 84.	(7")	(TAK 25) **DIZZY MISS LIZZY. / DIZZY**		–
	(12"+=)	(TAK 25-12) – ('A'extended).		
Nov 84.	(lp/c)	(STAT LP/C 20) **TOP TEN**		–

— Tutti frutti / Sex machine / What's new pussycat? / Whole lotta shakin' goin' on / Purple haze / Great balls of fire / Dizzy Miss Lizzy / Suzanne / Then he kissed me / Tears. *(cd-iss. Dec86; CDST 20)*

— folded after the above dive bombed

– compilations, etc. –

| Nov 88. | (7") | *Old Gold*; (OG 9828) **MONEY. / T.V.** | | – |

DAVID CUNNINGHAM

— with **STEPHEN REYNOLDS** – glockenspiel, keyboards / **ALAN HUDSON** – bass / **DEREK ROBERTS** – piano, percussion / **MICHAEL DOHERTY** – percussion

			Piano	not iss.
1979.	(lp)	(PIANO 001) **GREY SCALE**		–

— Error system (Bagfgab) / Error system (C pulse solo recording) / Error system (C pulse group recording) / Error system (E based group recording) / Error system (Efga) / Ecuador / Water systemised / Venezuela I / Guitar systemised / Venezuela II / Bolivia.

			Made To Measure	Made To Measure
Apr 95.	(cd)	(<MTM 31>) **WATER**		

— Stars / Next day / Once removed / Fourth sea / White, blue and grey / Shade creek / Short winter's day / Blue river / Beneath the vines / Yellow river / Low sun / Only shadows / Liquid hand / Dark ocean / Same day. *(re-iss. Jun96; same)*

— next with **JAH LLOYD**

			Piano	Resurgent
Jan 96.	(cd)	(PIANO 501) **THE SECRET DUB LIFE OF THE FLYING LIZARDS**		–

— Preface / Shake / Lime and salt / Mute / Skin and stone / Crab claw / Outside / Inside / Ash and diamond / Flicker / Postscript / (untitled).

| Jul 96. | (cd; PETER GORDON & DAVID CUNNINGHAM) (PIANO 504) **THE YELLOW BOX** | | |
| Jul 96. | (cd) (PIANO 505) <4003> **VOICEWORKS** | | Nov97 |

— Siren sign / Engine window / Magic words / At one remove / Engine definite / Not speech / Masks and voices / Mass / Canta / Collective / Resolution / Black air tower / Belgrano / True air / Idiolect / Invisible.
(above was originally a 1992 Japanese-only set, 'VOICES')

| Aug 98. | (cd; DAVID CUNNINGHAM & ANGELA JAEGAR) (PIANO 509) <4293> **ARTIFICIAL HOMELAND** | | |

— Silver thread / Artificial homeland / Beyond that star / Wood and glass / Fortuna / Turning left / Made of sand / Unlock the hills / Blue gold seven / Forsythia / Hot day / Time can make a difference / Radioloop / River west.

FLYS

Formed: Coventry, England ... 1976 out of MIDNIGHT CIRCUS by NEIL O'CONNOR, DAVID FREEMAN, JOE HUGHES and relative newcomer PETE KING. Inspired by punk's DIY ethic, the band issued 'BUNCH OF FIVE' as a debut EP on their own 'Zama' label in 1977. The ominous mob-chorus strains of 'LOVE AND A MOLOTOV COCKTAIL' attracted the attentions of 'E.M.I.', who subsequently signed the band and issued the track as a single in its own right in early '78. Despite the ensuing buzz, The FLYS failed to land a chart placing, another couple of singles and a debut album, 'WAKIKI BEACH REFUGEES' (1978) making little commercial headway despite strong critical support. Nevertheless, 'E.M.I.' stayed behind them for a further string of singles and a follow-up album, 'OWN' (1979) before the band moved along the corridor to 'Parlophone' for early 1980's 'FOUR FROM THE SQUARE' EP and a swansong single, 'WHAT WILL MOTHER SAY?'. Their continuing chart drought combined with internal pressures to hasten the FLYS' inevitable demise, NEIL going on to work with his more famous sister, HAZEL. DAVID FREEMAN and JOE HUGHES, meanwhile, formed The LOVER SPEAKS, a mid-late 80's act discovered by DAVE STEWART of The EURYTHMICS and signed to 'A&M'. Despite an initial Top 60 hit in summer '86 with 'NO MORE "I LOVE YOU"S' (later covered by ANNIE LENNOX) the group's eponymous album failed to chart.

Album rating: WAKIKI BEACH REFUGEES (*5) / OWN (*5) / THE FLYS compilation (*6)

NEIL O'CONNOR – vocals, guitar, keyboards / **DAVID FREEMAN** – guitar, vocals / **JOE HUGHES** – bass / **PETE KING** – drums / **LYN DOBSON** – saxophone

			Zama	not iss.
1977.	(7"ep)	(ZA 10EP) **BUNCH OF FIVE**		–

— Can I crash here? / Civilization / Love and a molotov cocktail / E.C.4.

— **GRAHAM DEACON** – drums (ex-SNIPS, ex-FRANKIE MILLER, ex-JOHN ENTWISTLE'S OX) repl. KING who joined AFTER THE FIRE (later died)

			E.M.I.	not iss.
Jan 78.	(7"m)	(EMI 2747) **LOVE AND A MOLOTOV COCKTAIL. / CAN I CRASH HERE? / CIVILIZATION**		–
May 78.	(7")	(EMI 2795) **FUN CITY. / E.C.4**		–
Oct 78.	(7"/7"yellow)	(EMI/+Y 2867) **WAKIKI BEACH REFUGEES. / WE DON'T MIND THE RAVE**		–
Nov 78.	(lp)	(EMC 3249) **WAKIKI BEACH REFUGEES**		–

— We don't mind the rave / Oh Beverley / She's the one / Some kind of girl / Looking for new hearts / Monsoon sky / Wakiki beach refugees / I don't know / Dark nights / Fun city / Don't moonlight on me / Saturday sunrise.

Jan 79.	(7")	(EMI 2907) **OH BEVERLEY. / DON'T MOONLIGHT ON ME**		–
Apr 79.	(7")	(EMI 2936) **NAME DROPPING. / FLY V FLY**		–
Jul 79.	(7")	(EMI 2976) **WE ARE THE LUCKY ONES. / LIVING IN THE STICKS**		–
Oct 79.	(lp)	(EMC 3316) **OWN**		–

— Energy boy / Let's drive / Fascinate me / Taking to the world / 16 down / Fortunes / Night creatures / When 2 & 5 make 9 / Undercover agent zero / Cheap days / Walking the streets / Through the windscreen / Freezing / Frenzy is 23.

			Parlophone	not iss.
Feb 80.	(7"ep)	(R 6030) **FOUR FROM THE SQUARE EP**		–

— 16 down / Night creatures / Lois Lane / Today belongs to me.

| Apr 80. | (7") | (R 6036) **WHAT WILL MOTHER SAY? / UNDERCOVER AGENT ZERO** | | – |

— disbanded 1980 when NEIL joined his sister HAZEL O'CONNOR's group.

FREEMAN, meanwhile briefly went solo while reuniting with HUGHES in The LOVER SPEAKS

– compilations, etc. –

Jan 91. (lp/cd) *See For Miles; (SEE/+CD 304)* **THE FLYS BUZZ BACK**
(re-iss. Apr93; same)

FRESHIES

Formed: Manchester, England ... mid-70's by sole conspirator, CHRIS SIEVEY. The man had previously reputedly barged his way into London's Abbey Road studios, demanding the listening attention of the engineers, secretaries or indeed anyone who happened to be there at the time. Having literally suffered a catalogue of record company rejection notices, SIEVEY finally formed his own label ('Razz') and proceeded to release a plethora of DIY cassettes over the period 1975 to 1985. However, SIEVEY and his FRESHIES would make their mark via the 7" market, the man's eccentric humour landing him a belated radio hit with 'I'M IN LOVE WITH THE GIRL ON THE MANCHESTER VIRGIN MEGASTORE CHECKOUT DESK', 'M.C.A.' picking it up in early '81 and making it a minor hit. A further series of chart attempts failed to make the grade, although 'I CAN'T GET BOUNCING BABIES BY THE TEARDROP EXPLODES' was just as bizarrely memorable. The mid-80's found SIEVEY re-inventing himself as FRANK SIDEBOTTOM, a decidedly childish alter-ego that recalled the freaky anonymity of The RESIDENTS minus the surreal humour. His tongue-in-cheek tributes to KYLIE MINOGUE, QUEEN, etc, consigned him to children's TV land, adult programmers (save some mad Manchester shows with 'Factory boss', Tony Wilson!) giving him a body swerve.

Album rating: THE VERY VERY BEST OF THE FRESHIES compilation (*6)

CHRIS SIEVEY – vocals / with various musicians including **MARTIN JACKSON + BILLY DUFFY** (before they made their name)

Razz — not iss.

Feb 78. (7"ep) *(RAZZXEP 1)* **WASHED UP / MOON MIDSUMMER. / Chris Sievey: BAISER / TWO OF THE SAME GIRL**

— now with **BARRY SPENCER** – guitar, vocals / **EDDIE CARTER** – guitar, vocals / **BOB DIXON** – drums

Nov 78. (7"ep) *(RAZZXEP 2)* **STRAIGHT IN AT NO.2**
– Johnny Radar / U-boat / Skid room / Last.

— now with **BARRY SPENCER** – guitar / **RICK SARKO** – bass (ex-ED BANGER & THE NOSEBLEEDS) / **MIKE DOHERTY** – drums (ex-SMIRKS)

Jul 79. (7"; as CHRIS SIEVEY) *(TOSH 109)* **BAISER. / LAST**
(above issued on 'Rabid') (re-iss. Sep80 as 'SKIP THE FIGHT'. / 'JIM BAISER' on 'Razz'; RAZZ 9)

Nov 79. (7"ep) *(RAZZ 3)* **THE MEN FROM BANANA ISLAND WHOSE STUPID IDEAS NEVER CAUGHT ON IN THE WESTERN WORLD AS WE KNOW IT**
– Amoco Cadiz / Children of the world / Octopus.

Mar 80. (mag+7") *(RAZZ 4)* **MY TAPE'S GONE. / MOON MIDSUMMER**

May 80. (7") *(RAZZ 5)* **WE'RE LIKE YOU. / Chris Sievey: HEY**
Aug 80. (7") *(RAZZ 6)* **YELLOW SPOT. / IF IT'S NEWS**
Sep 80. (7") *(RAZZ 7)* **NO MONEY. / OH GIRL**
Sep 80. (7"ep; as FRESHIES with CHRIS SIEVEY) *(RAZZ 8)* **RED INDIAN MUSIC**
– Sue of the Sioux / Riding out to Devil's Ridge / Return of Sue of the Sioux.

Oct 80. (7") *(RAZZ 11)* **I'M IN LOVE WITH THE GIRL ON THE MANCHESTER VIRGIN MEGASTORE CHECKOUT DESK. / SINGALONG VERSION**
(also radio bleeped out "Virgin" version; RAZZ 12) (re-iss. Jan81 on 'M.C.A.'; MCA 670) – hit No.54 in UK charts.

— early in 1981, CHRIS + BARRY augmented JILTED JOHN in his new band, GOING RED?; one single 'SOME BOYS'.

M.C.A. not iss.

Mar 81. (7") *(MCA 693)* **WRAP UP THE ROCKETS. / IT'S GONNA GET BETTER**
(remixed; c-s+=/12"+=) *(MCA S/T 693)* – Tell her I'm ill.

Jun 81. (7") *(MCA 725)* **I CAN'T GET BOUNCING BABIES BY THE TEARDROP EXPLODES. / TELL HER I'M ILL**

CV not iss.

1981. (7") *(CVS 1)* **IF YOU REALLY LOVE ME, BUY ME A SHIRT. / I AM A WALRUS**

Razz – Pinnacle not iss.

Oct 81. (7") *(RP 8)* **DANCIN' DOCTORS. / ONE TO ONE**

Stiff not iss.

Aug 82. (7") *(BUY 158)* **FASTEN YOUR SEAT BELYS. / BEST WE CAN DO**

— had already decided to abandon The FRESHIES

E.M.I. not iss.

Jun 83. (c-s/7") *(TC+/EMI 5398)* **CAMOUFLAGE. / (ZX 81 programme "CAMOUFLAGE"). / FLYING TRAIN / F.T.**

— (also issued on 'Random; RND 1)

– others, unofficial specials, etc. –

1975. (c; CHRIS SIEVEY) *Hey Boss; (none)* **GIRL IN MY BLUE JEANS**
1976. (c; CHRIS SIEVEY) *Razz; (RAZZCS-1)* **ALL SLEEPS SECRETS**
1979. (c) *Razz; (RAZZCS-2)* **MANCHESTER PLAYS**
1979. (c) *Razz; (RAZZCS-3)* **SING THE GIRLS FROM BANANA ISLAND ...**
1980. (c) *Razz; (RAZZCS-4)* **ROUGH AND READY**
1981. (c) *Razz; (RAZZCS-5)* **LONDON PLAYS**
1981. (12"white label) *(HANNA 1)* **VIRGIN MEGASTORE / WRAP UP THE ROCKETS. / BUY ME A SHIRT / TELL HER I'M ILL / FRANK TALKS TO CHRIS (conversation)**
1985. (c,lp) *E.T.S.; (1)* **JOHNNY RADAR STORY**
1985. (c) *E.T.S.; (3)* **EARLY RAZZ**
1985. (c) *E.T.S.; (4)* **STUDIO OUT-TAKES**
1986. (lp) *Cordelia; (ERICAT 015)* **CHRIS SIEVEY'S BIG RECORD**
(w/ free 7"; TOSH 109) – BAISER. / LAST
Apr 96. (cd) *Cherry Red; (CDMRED 129)* **THE VERY VERY BEST OF THE FRESHIES**
(re-iss. Jun99; same)

FRANK SIDEBOTTOM

Regal Zonophone not iss.

Aug 85. (7") *(Z 39)* **POPULAR MEDLEY**
– Bohemian rhapsody / Anarchy in the UK / Every breath you take / Material boy / God save the queen.

Nov 85. (7"ep) *(Z 40)* **OH BLIMEY IT'S CHRISTMAS:- OLIVER'S ARMY – CHRISTMAS IN AUSTRALIA – IN THE SUMMERTIME – OLD LANG ZINE – LIFE IN A NORTHERN TOWN**
(12"+=) *(12Z 40)* – Greengrocer on the corner.

Jul 86. (7"/7"pic-d) *(Z/+P 41)* **I'M THE URBAN SPACEMAN. / OH SUPERMUM**
(12"+=) *(12Z 41)* – Sci-fi medley: Space is ace – Robot Frank – Fireball ZL5 – Life on Mars – Close encounters of the third kind.

In Tape not iss.

Dec 86. (7") *(IT 041)* **CHRISTMAS IS REALLY FANTASTIC. / O COME ALL YE FAITHFUL (ADESTE FIDELIS) / I WISH IT COULD BE CHRISTMAS EVERDAY**
(12"+=) *(ITT 041)* – Xmas medley: Twist 'n' shout – The benefit of Mr. Kyte – Flying – It was nearly 20 years ago today – Mull of Timperley.

Jul 87. (12"ep) *(ITT 045)* **SALUTES THE MAGIC OF FREDDIE MERCURY & K MINOGUE**
– I should be so lucky – Love poem for Kylie – Radio Ga Ga – Save me – We will rock you – Frank Gordon – Queen (hip hop disco mix) – Everybody sings Queen – I am the champion.

Nov 87. (7"ep/12"ep) *(IT/+T 048)* **TIMPERLEY SUNSET**
– Born in Timperley / Anarchy in Timperley / Timperley sunset / Wild thing in Timperley / Next train to Timperley / Oh Timperley / Surfin' Timperley.

Sep 88. (lp) *(IT 058)* **5.9.88**
Sep 88. (c) *(IT 060)* **13.9.88**
Oct 88. (cd) *(ITCD 063)* **11.10.88**
Jul 90. (10"m-lp) *(IT 069-10)* **MEDIUM PLAY**

— continued to work on mainly children's TV

– compilations, etc. –

Apr 97. (cd) *Cherry Red; (CDMRED 143)* **FRANK SIDEBOTTOM'S ABC AND D** (all his singles)

GANG OF FOUR

Formed: Leeds, England ... 1977 by journalist ANDY GILL, JON KING, DAVE ALLEN and HUGO BURNHAM. After releasing a debut EP, 'DAMAGED GOODS' for Bob Last's 'Fast' label, they signed to 'E.M.I.' in late '78. Their debut 45 for the label, 'AT HOME HE'S A TOURIST', hit the Top 60 and should have reached a lot higher but for a BBC ban due to the use of the word 'Rubbers' (i.e. contraceptives) in the lyrics. In Autumn '79, their debut album 'ENTERTAINMENT' hit the Top 50, a startling showcase for the band's adrenaline fuelled post-punk sound, GILL's rifling staccato guitar slicing through the twisted funk rhythms. Lyrically, they were also pretty incendiary, although their radical political agenda rarely descended into heavy handed preaching or took precedence over the music. It would be another couple of years before they released a follow-up, 'SOLID GOLD' (1981) mixing down GILL's patented feedback assault and coming in for some critical stick. Although he played on the landmark 'TO HELL WITH POVERTY' single (released in summer '81), ALLEN subsequently left the band to form his own outfit, SHRIEKBACK, his replacement being SARA LEE. Thereafter, the band favoured a more conventional approach, 'SONGS OF THE FREE' (1982) notable for its barbed comments on the Falklands war, 'CALL ME UP' and 'I LOVE A MAN IN UNIFORM' (another single blacklisted by Radio 1). Following the departure of BURNHAM, they moved further towards a slick funk/Philly sound with 'HARD' (1983), employing a cast of studio professionals and female backing singers. With diminishing artistic and commercial returns, the band finally split in mid-'84 following the release of live set, 'AT THE PALACE' (1984). While GILL subsequently relocated to America and concentrated on production work, renewed interest in the band towards the end of the decade saw a GANG OF FOUR reformation, although GILL and KING were the only original members involved in the project. The result was a one-off album for 'Polydor', 'MALL' (1991), the label soon losing interest after it failed to sell; there was more grief for them the following year when, despite their best efforts in supplying the soundtrack for the Labour Party's 1992 campaign, the Tories romped home yet again. The duo initiated yet another reincarnation of the band in 1995 for the 'SHRINKWRAPPED' set, although sales were again disappointing. • **Songwriters:** Penned by KING / ALLEN / GILL, until ALLEN departed. Covered SOUL REBEL (Bob Marley).

Album rating: ENTERTAINMENT (*7) / SOLID GOLD (*6) / SONGS OF THE FREE (*6) / HARD (*5) / AT THE PALACE (*3) / A BRIEF HISTORY OF THE 20TH CENTURY compilation (*8) / MALL (*4) / SHRINKWRAPPED (*5)

JON KING (b. 8 Jun'55, London) – vocals, melodica / **ANDY GILL** (b. 1 Jan'56, Manchester) – guitar / **DAVE ALLEN** (b.23 Dec'55, Cumbria) – bass / **HUGO BURNHAM** (b.25 Mar'56, London) – drums

		Fast	not iss.
Oct 78.	(7"m) (*FAST 5*) **DAMAGED GOODS. / LOVE LIKE ANTHRAX / ARMALITE RIFLE**		–
		E.M.I.	Warners
Mar 79.	(7") (*EMI 2956*) **AT HOME HE'S A TOURIST. / IT'S HER FACTORY**	58	–
Sep 79.	(lp/c) (*EMC/TC-EMC 3313*) <*BSK 3446*> **ENTERTAINMENT**	45	
	– Ether / Natural's not in it / Not great men / Damaged goods / Return the gift / Guns before butter / I found that essence rare / Glass / Contract / At home he's a tourist / 5-45 / Anthrax. (*re-iss. 1985 lp/c; ATAK/TC-ATAK 41*) (*cd-iss. Feb95; CZ 541*) <*cd-iss. 1995 on 'Infinite Zero'+=; 14502-2*> – YELLOW EP		
		Regal Zonophone	not iss.
Apr 80.	(7") (*Z 1*) **OUTSIDE THE TRAINS DON'T RUN ON TIME. / HE'D SEND IN THE ARMY**		–
		Regal Zonophone	Warners
Oct 80.	(12"ep) <*MINI 3494*> **OUTSIDE THE TRAINS DON'T RUN ON TIME / HE'D SEND IN THE ARMY. / IT'S HER FACTORY / ARMALITE RIFLE**	–	
Mar 81.	(7"/12") (*EMI/12EMI 5146*) **WHAT WE ALL WANT. / HISTORY'S BUNK**		
Mar 81.	(lp/c) (*EMC/TC-EMC 3364*) <*BSK 3565*> **SOLID GOLD**	52	
	– Paralysed / What we all want / If I could keep it for myself / Outside the trains don't run on time / Why theory? / Cheeseburger / The republic / In the ditch / A hole in the wallet / He'd send in the army.		
May 81.	(7") (*EMI 5177*) **CHEESEBURGER. / PARALYSED**		–
—	(tour) **BUSTA CHERRY JONES** – bass (ex-SHARKS) repl. ALLEN (to SHRIEKBACK)		
Jul 81.	(7"/12") (*EMI/12EMI 5193*) **TO HELL WITH POVERTY. / CAPITAL (IT FAILS US NOW)**		
Feb 82.	(m-lp) <*MINI 3646*> **ANOTHER DAY / ANOTHER DOLLAR**	–	
	– To hell with poverty / What we all want / Cheeseburger / Capital (it fails us now) / History's bunk!		
—	**SARA LEE** – bass, vocals (ex-JANE AIRE, ex-ROBERT FRIPP) repl. BUSTA		
Apr 82.	(7"/12") (*EMI/12EMI 5299*) **I LOVE A MAN IN A UNIFORM. / WORLD AT FAULT**	65	–
May 82.	(lp/c) (*EMC/TCEMC 3412*) <*23683*> **SONGS OF THE FREE**	61	
	– Call me up / I love a man in a uniform / Muscle for brains / It is not enough / Life, it's a shame / I will be a good boy / History of the world / We live as we dream, alone / Of the instant.		
Jun 82.	(7") <*29921*> **I LOVE A MAN IN A UNIFORM. / I WILL BE A GOOD BOY**	–	
	(12"+=) <*29907*> – ('A'extended).		
Jul 82.	(7") (*EMI 5320*) **CALL ME UP. / I WILL BE A GOOD BOY**		–
—	(KING, GILL + BURNHAM were joined by) **JON ASTROP / CHUCK KIRKPATRICK + JOHN SOMBATERO** – bass repl. SARA / added backing singers **ALFA ANDERSON** and **BRENDA WHITE**		
Aug 83.	(7"/12") (*EMI/12EMI 5418*) **IS IT LOVE. / MAN WITH A GOOD CAR**		
Sep 83.	(lp/c) (*EMC 165219-1/-4*) <*23936*> **HARD**		
	– Is it love / I fled / Silver lining / Woman town / A man with a good car / It don't matter / Arabic / A piece of my heart / Independence.		
Sep 83.	(7") <*29449*> **IS IT LOVE. / ARABIC**	–	
Nov 83.	(7") (*EMI 5440*) **SILVER LINING. / INDEPENDENCE**		–
—	**STEVE GOULDING** – drums (ex-RUMOUR) repl. BURNHAM who joined ILLUSTRATED MAN		
		Mercury	not iss.
Oct 84.	(12"m) (*GANG 12*) **I WILL BE A GOOD BOY (live). / IS IT LOVE (live) / CALL ME UP (live)**		–
Nov 84.	(lp/c) (*MERL/+C 51*) **AT THE PALACE (live)**		–
	– We live as we dream, alone / History is not made by great men / Silver lining / The history of the world / I love a man in uniform / Paralysed / Is it love / Damaged goods / At home he's a tourist / To hell with poverty. (*c+=*) – I will be a good boy / Call me up.		
—	(split mid-84) **JON** later formed KING BUTCHER		

ANDY GILL

—	finally went solo		
		Survival	not iss.
Aug 87.	(12") (*SUR12 039*) **DISPOSSESSION. / GENUINE**		–

GANG OF FOUR

—	re-formed 1990 w/ **JON KING + ALAN GILL** added **HIROMI + STAN LOUBIERES**		
		Scarlett	not iss.
Jun 90.	(7") (*SCART 4*) **MONEY TALKS (The Money mix). / USE THE COLOUR FROM THE TUBE**		–
	(12") (*SCART 4T*) – ('A'side) / ('A'dub version).		
	(cd-s) (*SCART 4CD*) – ('A'extended) / (above 3 tracks).		
		Polydor	Polydor
May 91.	(cd/c/lp) (*849 124-2/-4/-1*) **MALL**		
	– Cadillac / Motel / Satellite / F.M.U.S.A. / Don't fix what ain't broke / Impossible / Money talks / Soul rebel / Hiromi & Stan talk / Colour from the tube / Hey yeah / Everybody wants to come / World falls apart.		
Aug 91.	(12") (*P2 152DJ*) **CADILLAC. / MOTEL / FAVOURITES**		–
—	disbanded again when their record label dropped them. GILL then supplied the soundtrack in 1992 for the Labour Party's unsuccessful general election campaign. Re-formed again in 1994.		
—	**GILL + KING + STEVE MONTI** (ex-CURVE) + **PHIL BUTCHER** (ex-IGGY POP)		
		When!	not iss.
Aug 95.	(7"/c-s) (*WEN 7/M 1002*) **TATTOO. / BANNED WORDS / COP GOES HOME**		–
	(cd-s+=) (*WENX 1002*) – ('A' Quiet guy mix).		
Sep 95.	(cd/c) (*WEN CD/MC 003*) **SHRINKWRAPPED**		–
	– Tattoo / Sleepwalker / I parade myself / Unburden / Better him than me / Something 99 / Showtime, valentine / Unburden, unbound / The dark side / I absolve you / Shrinkwrapped. (*cd re-iss. Apr01 on 'Castle'; CMRCD 197*)		

– compilations etc. –

Oct 86.	(12"ep) *Strange Fruit; (SFPS 008)* **THE PEEL SESSIONS** (16.1.89)		–
	– I found that essence rare / Return the gift / 5-45 / At home he's a tourist. (*c-ep.iss.Jun87; SFPSC 008*)		
May 90.	(lp/c/cd) *Strange Fruit; (SFR LP/C/CD 107)* / *Dutch East India; <8101>* **THE PEEL SESSIONS (COMPLETE SESSIONS 1979-81)**		
Mar 90.	(cd) *Greenlight - Capitol; (CDP 795051-2)(TC+/GO 2028)* **YOU CATCH UP WITH HISTORY (1978-1983)**		–
Nov 90.	(cd/c/lp) *E.M.I.; (CD/TC+/EMC 3583)* / *Warners: <26448>* **A BRIEF HISTORY OF THE 20th CENTURY**		Dec90
	– At home he's a tourist / Damaged goods / Natural's not in it / Not great men / Anthrax / Return the gift / It's her factory / What we all want (live) / Paralysed / A hole in the wallet / Cheeseburger / To hell with poverty / Capital (it fails us now) / Call me up / I will be a good boy / History of the world / I love a man in uniform / Is it love / Woman town / We live as we dream, alone. (*c+cd.+=*) – (4 tracks)		
Jan 91.	(7"ep/c-ep/12"ep/cd-ep). *E.M.I.; (EMS/TCEM/12EM/CDEM 172)* **TO HELL WITH POVERTY (the loaded edit) / ('A'-original version). / CHEESEBURGER (live) / CALL ME UP**		
Oct 95.	(cd) *Warners; <43035>* **SOLID GOLD / ANOTHER DAY – ANOTHER DOLLAR**	–	
Nov 98.	(d-cd) *Rhino; <RCD 75479>* **100 FLOWERS BLOOM** (rare tracks)	–	

GENERATION X

Formed: London, England ... 1976 by aspiring young punk, BILLY IDOL, alongside BOB ANDREWS and ex-CHELSEA members, TONY JAMES and JOHN TOWE (the latter was soon replaced by former SUBWAY SECT man, MARK LAFF). Though they attracted a loyal fanbase, GENERATION X were never considered a dyed-in-the-wool punk band per se, their more commercial, hook-filled power pop at odds with the genre's inherent nihilism. Signed to 'Chrysalis', the band hit the Top 40 with their first single, 'YOUR GENERATION', following it up with 'WILD YOUTH' and 'READY STEADY GO', the latter track a decidedly un-punk 60's tribute. An eponymous debut album hit the Top 30 in Spring '78, while the band's sound grew increasingly commercial on successive albums, 'VALLEY OF THE DOLLS' (1979; produced by IAN HUNTER) and 'KISS ME DEADLY' (1981; released under the slightly clipped moniker of GEN X). Following their split in '81, JAMES later formed SIGUE SIGUE SPUTNIK, while the bleached-blond IDOL was free to pursue his barely concealed desire for pop stardom. Relocating to New York, he met manager, Bill Aucoin and producer, Keith Forsey, recruiting guitarist STEVE STEVENS and cutting a cover of Tommy James & The Shondells' 'MONY MONY' (along with a few other tracks – including the GENERATION X song, 'DANCING WITH MYSELF' – it formed part of a US-only mini-set, 'DON'T STOP'). • **Covers:** GIMME SOME TRUTH (John Lennon) / SHAKIN' ALL OVER (Johnny Kidd).

Album rating: GENERATION X (*6) / VALLEY OF THE DOLLS (*5) / KISS ME DEADLY (*5) / PERFECT HITS compilation (*7)

BILLY IDOL (b. WILLIAM BROAD, 30 Nov'55, Stanmore, Middlesex, England) – vocals (ex-CHELSEA, ex-INFANTS) / **BOB 'Derwood' ANDREWS** – guitar / **TONY JAMES** – bass, vocals (ex-CHELSEA, ex-INFANTS) / **MARK LAFF** – drums (ex-SUBWAY SECT) repl. JOHN TOWE (ex-CHELSEA, ex-INFANTS) who joined ALTERNATIVE TV then ADVERTS, etc

			Chrysalis	Chrysalis
Sep 77.	(7") *(CHS 2165)*	**YOUR GENERATION. / DAY BY DAY**	36	
Dec 77.	(7") *(CHS 2189)*	**WILD YOUTH. / WILD DUB**		

(some copies were mispressed with b-side 'NO NO NO')

Mar 78.	(7") *(CHS 2207)*	**READY STEADY GO. / NO NO NO**	47	
Mar 78.	(lp/c) *(CHR/ZCHR 1169)*	**GENERATION X**	29	

– From the heart / One hundred punks / Listen / Ready steady go / Kleenex / Promises promises / Day by day / The invisible man / Kiss me deadly / Too personal / Youth, youth, youth. *(cd-iss. Jan86; CCD 1169) (re-iss. cd Mar94; CD25CR 14) (cd re-iss. Jul96 on 'EMI Gold'; CDGOLD 1039) (cd re-iss. Apr02 on 'EMI Gold'+=; 538936-2)* – Your generation / Wild youth / Wild dub / No no no / Trying for kicks / This heat.

Jan 79.	(7",7"red,7"pink,7"orange,7"yellow) *(CHS 2261)* **KING ROCKER. / GIMME SOME TRUTH**			11	
Jan 79.	(lp/c) *(CHR/ZCHR 1193)* **VALLEY OF THE DOLLS**			51	

– Running with the boss sound / Night of the Cadillacs / Paradise west / Friday's angels / King rocker / Valley of the dolls / Love like fire / Paradise west / The prime of Kenny Silvers. *(cd-iss. Jan86; CCD 1193) (cd re-iss. Apr02 on 'EMI Gold'+=; 538935-2)* – The prime of Kenny Silvers (part 2) / Gimme some truth / Shakin' all over.

Mar 79.	(7",7"brown) *(CHS 2310)* **VALLEY OF THE DOLLS. / SHAKIN' ALL OVER**			23	
Jun 79.	(7",7"pink) *(CHS 2330)* **FRIDAY'S ANGELS. / TRYING FOR KICKS / THIS HEAT**			62	

— **TERRY CHIMES** – drums (ex-CLASH, ex-COWBOYS INTERNATIONAL) repl. LAFF / **JAMES STEPHENSON** – guitar (ex-CHELSEA) repl. 'DERWOOD' (later to WESTWORLD)

GEN X

Sep 80.	(7") *(CHS 2444)* **DANCING WITH MYSELF. / UGLY RASH**			62	
	(12"+=) *CHS12 2444)* – Loopy dub / What do you want				
Jan 81.	(lp/c) *(CHR/ZCHR 1327)* **KISS ME DEADLY**				

– Dancing with myself / Untouchables / Happy people / Heaven's inside / Triumph / Revenge / Stars look down / What do you want / Oh mother. *(cd-iss. Jan86; CCD 1327)*

Jan 81.	(7"ep,7"clear-ep/12"ep) *(CHS/+12 2488)* **DANCING WITH MYSELF / UNTOUCHABLES. / KING ROCKER / ROCK ON**			60	

— split early '81, when BILLY went solo. CHIMES rejoined The CLASH, TONY JAMES later formed SIGUE SIGUE SPUTNIK. STEPHENSON later joined GENE LOVES JEZEBEL, then The CULT.

– compilations, etc. –

on 'Chrysalis' unless otherwise mentioned

Nov 85.	(lp/c) *(CHM/ZCHM 1521)* **THE BEST OF GENERATION X**				
Feb 87.	(7") *Old Gold; (OG 9693)* **KING ROCKER. / VALLEY OF THE DOLLS**				
Jun 87.	(lp) *M.B.C.; (JOCKLP 9)* **THE ORIGINAL GENERATION X**				–
Jun 88.	(lp) *M.B.C.; (JOCKLP 11)* **GENERATION X LIVE (live)**				–
Oct 91.	(cd/c/lp) *(CCD/ZCHR/CHR 1854)* **PERFECT HITS (1975-81)**				

– Dancing with myself / Your generation / Ready steady go / The untouchables / Day by day / Wild youth / Wild dub / One hundred punks / King rocker / Kiss me deadly / Gimme some truth / New order / English dream / Triumph / Youth, youth, youth. *(cd re-iss. May99; same)*

May 98.	(cd) *Mutiny; (MUTINY 14)* **SWEET REVENGE**				–

GERMS

Formed: Los Angeles, California, USA ... April '77 by DARBY CRASH, PAT SMEAR, LORNA DOOM and BELINDA CARLISLE. The latter soon departed before groundbreaking debut 45, 'FORMING' (she later helped to form The GO-GO'S). The GERMS signed to the (then) indie, 'Slash', finally issuing a debut album proper, '(GI)', in '79, this highly influential (KURT COBAIN was a massive fan!) outfit doing more than their fair share to define the boundaries of American punk/hardcore. In keeping with their incendiary nature, the band burned out in early 1980, only to reform approximately a year later. This incarnation was even more short-lived, CRASH dying of a suicide heroin overdose on the 7th of December 1980, aged only 22. Pioneers of hardcore punk, The GERMS made way for The DEAD KENNEDYS, BLACK FLAG and a host of grunge devotees including NIRVANA, HOLE, etc. • **Covered:** ROUND AND ROUND (Chuck Berry) / DEATHFOLK covered AUTOMATIC (Go-Go's). • **Trivia:** They were given tribute from many of the aforementioned bands on 1996 album, 'GERMS (TRIBUTE) – A SMALL CIRCLE OF FRIENDS' on 'Grass Grow' label; (10042). In March '95, PAT SMEAR, now a member of DAVE GROHL's post-Nirvana outfit, FOO FIGHTERS, was part of HOLEZ (aka COURTNEY LOVE, PATTY & ERIC) on their 7" tribute to The GERMS, 'CIRCLE 1' (released by 'Dutch East India'; (9037-7); The B-side was by MONKEYWRENCH)

Album rating: GERMICIDE (*4) / (GI) (*8) / GERMICIDE: LIVE AT THE WHISKY live (*4) / ROCK'N'RULE rare (*4) / THE COMPLETE ANTHOLOGY compilation (*7) / Pat RuthenSmear: RUTHENSMEAR (*4) / Deathfolk: DEATHFOLK (*6) / DEATHFOLK II (*5) / Pat Smear: SO YOU FELL IN LOVE WITH A MUSICIAN (*4)

DARBY CRASH (b. JAN PAUL BEAHM, 26 Sep'58) – vocals / **PAT SMEAR** (b. GEORGE RUTHENBERG, 5 Aug'59) – guitar / **LORNA DOOM** – bass / **D.J. BONEBRAKE** (b. DON BOLES) – drums; repl. BELINDA CARLISLE who later joined GO-GO'S and is currently top solo chanteuse

			not iss.	Mohawk
Sep 77.	(lp) *<SCALP 001>* **GERMICIDE** (recorded live at the Whisky in their first ever performance – June 1977)		–	

– Forming / Sex boy / Victim / Street dreams / Let's pretend / Get a grip / Suicide machine / Sugar sugar / Teenage clone (wild baby) / Grand old flag. *<re-iss. Apr81; same> <c-iss.Nov81 on 'R.O.I.R.'; A 108> (cd-iss. Nov94; RE 108CD)*

			not iss.	What?
Nov 77.	(ltd-7") *<WHAT 01>* **FORMING. / SEXBOY (live)**		–	

<re-iss. 1982; same> <re-iss. Jun89 on 'Iloki'; IR 23> <re-iss. 1990 on 'Gift Of Life'; GIFT 008> <re-iss. 1995 on 'Alive'; 0036>

			not iss.	Slash Scam
May 78.	(7"m) *<SLASH 101>* **LEXICON DEVIL. / CIRCLE ONE / NO GOD**		–	

<re-iss. Nov78; SLASH 002>

— **DON BOLLES** – drums (of 45 GRAVE) repl. BONEBRAKE who joined X

Dec 79.	(lp) *<SR 103>* **GI**		–	

(UK-iss.Nov80 +=; same) – Flower child. *<c-iss.1989 +=; same>* – Caught in my eye. *<US re-iss. 1990's on 'Warners'+=; 23932>* – (7" singles).

— split early in 1980, but featured on various artists lp 'The Decline' for 'Slash'; *<SR 105>*. Had to split once more, when on the 7th December '80, CRASH died of heroin overdose.

— PAT SMEAR later went solo, initially as PAT RUTHENSMEAR

– compilations, etc. –

Feb 81.	(12"ep) *Slash; <SREP 108>* **WHAT WE DO IS SECRET**		–	

– Round and round / Lexicon devil / Circle one / Caught in my eye / No god / The other newest one / My love.

Aug 85.	(lp) *Gasatanka; <G 12>* **LET THE CIRCLE BE UNBROKEN (live)**		–	– German
Nov 85.	(lp) *Ghost o' Darb; <WDG>* **LION'S SHARE** (live at the Starwood Dec 3, 1980, their reunion-farewell gig)		–	
Mar 86.	(lp) *X.E.S.; <XT 3>* **ROCK N' RULE (live at the Masque reunion Christmas 1979)**		–	
Nov 92.	(ltd-7"ep) *Crash!; <CRASH 001>* **(GI)**		–	

– Manimal / Dragon lady / Strange notes.

Apr 93.	(7"ep) *Gasatanka-Rockville; <(ROCK 6094-7)>* **(DCC)**			Nov92

– Communist eyes / Forming / What we do is secret.

Jun 93.	(cd-ep) *Munster; <MR 25>* **CAT'S CLAUSE (live, rare rehearsals)**		–	
Aug 93.	(cd) *Slash; <45239-2>* **(MIA)** (the complete anthology)		–	

– Forming / Sexboy / Lexicon devil / Circle one / No God / What we do is secret / Communist eyes / Land of treason / Richie Dagger's crime / Strange notes / American leather / Lexicon devil / Manimal / Our way / We must bleed / Media blitz / Other newest one / Let's pretend / Dragon lady / Slave / Shut down (annihilation man) / Caught in my eye / Round and round / My tunnel / Throw it away / Not all right / No I hear the laughter / Going down / Lion's share / Forming 2.

Jan 94.	(cd) *Cleopatra; <(CLEO 3731-2)>* **MEDIA BLITZ**			Jun93

– Forming / Round 'n' round / Sex boy / Strange notes / Caught in my eye / Let's pretend / Lexicon devil / Manimal / Our way / Shut down / What we do is secret / Art / Communist eyes / Lion's share / Media blitz / What we do is secret 2 / Lion's share / Throw it away.

PAT RUTHENSMEAR

— with **PAUL ROESSLER** – keyboards (of DC3)

			S.S.T.	S.S.T.
Jan 88.	(lp/c) *<(SST 154/+C)>* **RUTHENSMEAR**			

– Sahara hotel / Golden boys / Odenora / Princes / Magic candle tragic canary / The area of the circle / Xmas song / I heart / A gentle axe. *<re-iss. May93; same>*

DEATHFOLK

PAT SMEAR + GARY JACOBY (also of CELEBRITY SKINS)

		not iss.	New Alliance

1990. (lp/c/cd) <NAR 047/+C/CD> **DEATHFOLK**
 – Hobos / Yellow 1 / Smiley Jack / Jack frost / Monkey brains / Rad man / Frostina / Typical girl / '39 / Jack / Amsterdam / Work! *(UK-iss.May93; same as US)*
Apr 92. (lp/c/cd) <NAR 076/+C/CD> **DEATHFOLK II**
 – Freedom / Scary girl / Romeo Bob / Regina boxing party / Jojo luv / Azreal / Adream / Motherfucker / Medley / Baby Hugh / Lulu bell / Automatic. *(UK-iss.May93; same as US)*

PAT SMEAR

— with **WALTER SPENCER** – bass / **GARY JACOBY** – drums / **MICHELE GREGG** – voices

May 93. (cd/c) <(SST 294 CD/C)> **SO YOU FELL IN LOVE WITH A MUSICIAN** — Nov92
 – I'll find you / Lulu Belle / Creep street / Holy Bulsara / Ever alone with thee / All my cheating / Innocent X / Cold towne / Yummy yuck / Love your friends / Lazy.

— he joined NIRVANA in '93 and helped form FOO FIGHTERS with DAVE GROHL

GILBERT & LEWIS (see under ⇒ WIRE)

Andy GILL (see under ⇒ GANG OF FOUR)

Greg GINN / GONE (see under ⇒ BLACK FLAG)

Vic GODARD (& SUBWAY SECT)

Born: VIC KNAPPER, c.1959, Mortlake, London, England, although raised in nearby Barnes. Heavily inspired by the 1976 punk revolution and the SEX PISTOLS in particular, VIC formed SUBWAY SECT along with schoolfriends, ROB SIMMONS, PAUL MYERS and PAUL PACKHAM, the band's shortlived original singer (who was later replaced by MARK LAFF). The lads made their live debut on the 20th of September that year, kicking off a punk festival at the 100 Club, a night that featured SIOUXSIE & THE BANSHEES, BUZZCOCKS, STINKY TOYS, VIBRATORS, CLASH and the 'PISTOLS. Their performance (free of the safety-pin chic favoured by their peers) prompted CLASH manager, Bernie Rhodes, to take them under his wing and release an early '78 single, 'NOBODY'S SCARED', for his own 'Braik' label. The track was a punk era classic although by this time, LAFF had been snatched up by GENERATION X and substituted with ROB WARD; Rhodes subsequently sacked both MYERS and SIMMONS, replacing them with three newcomers, STEVE ATKINSON, JOHNNY BRITTON and, fresh from school, COLIN SCOTT. This was the line-up to back VIC on SUBWAY SECT's more professional but sedate late 1978 follow-up, 'AMBITION', a one-off for 'Rough Trade'. A mooted album never appeared, VIC being groomed by his manager to try his hand at other vocal styles. In the Spring of 1980, having signed to an offshoot of 'M.C.A.', VIC GODARD & SUBWAY SECT re-emerged with a completely overhauled sound and style on the album, 'WHAT'S THE MATTER BOY?', leaving behind all traces of punk in the process. The record was nevertheless loved by the critics, although the follow-up, 'SONGS FOR SALE' (still co-crediting SUBWAY SECT), did not impress 'Island' who sold the rights to 'London' records for release in '82. VIC's Bristol-based backing band at the time (ROB MARCHE, DAVE COLLARD, CHRIS BOSTOCK and SEAN McLUSKY) soon pursued their own career as hitmakers, JoBOXERS, GODARD going into semi-retirement until the mid-80's. The former punk turned jazzy crooner was tempted back into the biz when Geoff Travis and Mike Always signed him to their newly formed 'Blanco Y Negro' imprint. However, the cost of numerous backing musicians led to them shelving a proposed album ('T.R.O.U.B.L.E.') and subsequently seeing VIC back on the dole and washing-up in a cafe to make ends meet. The aforementioned tapes were given another lease of life in Spring '86 when Travis' 'Rough Trade' label gave it a belated release; Always, meanwhile, had already issued a single, 'HOLIDAY HYMN', for his own 'El' label. Amid all the business wrangling etc, VIC retired from the music scene to become a postman in Kew (London), although he did return again in 1992 to pay tribute to the recently deceased 'JOHNNY THUNDERS' on a one-off single for 'Rough Trade Singles Club'. Perhaps inspired by some renewed interest from EDWYN COLLINS, GODARD, with help of both the former ORANGE JUICE frontman and dub producer, DENNIS BOVELL, recorded a 1993 comeback album, 'END OF THE SURREY PEOPLE', for the newly resurrected Scottish 'Postcard' label. EDWYN (and guest RODDY FRAME) were featured on yet another "comeback" set, 'LONG TERM SIDE-EFFECT' (1998), a blend of loose soul and lounge rock complemented by his distinguished crooning vox. • **Covered:** LANDSLIDE (Tony Clarke) / LOVE FOR SALE (Cole Porter) / etc.

Album rating: WHAT'S THE MATTER BOY? (*5) / SONGS FOR SALE (*6) / A RETROSPECTIVE compilation (*7) / Vic Godard: T.R.O.U.B.L.E. (*5) / END OF THE SURREY PEOPLE (*5) / LONG TERM SIDE-EFFECT (*5)

SUBWAY SECT

VIC GODARD – vocals / **ROB SIMMONS** – guitar / **PAUL MYERS** – bass / **BOB WARD** – drums; repl. MARK LAFF (to GENERATION X) who repl. PAUL PACKHAM

		Braik	not iss.

Mar 78. (7") (BRS 01) **NOBODY'S SCARED. / DON'T SPLIT IT**

— **JOHNNY BRITTON** – guitar + **STEVE ATKINSON** – keyboards repl. SIMMONS / **COLIN SCOTT** (b.1962) – bass; repl. MYERS who later joined The PROFESSIONALS (former SEX PISTOLS)

		Rough Trade	not iss.

Dec 78. (7") (RT 007) **AMBITION. / DIFFERENT STORY**

VIC GODARD & SUBWAY SECT

VIC plus **BRITTON** / the returning **MYERS** + **TERRY CHIMES** – drums (ex-CLASH)

		Oddball-MCA	not iss.

Apr 80. (7") (MCA 585) **SPLIT UP THE MONEY. / OUT OF TOUCH**
Apr 80. (lp/c) (MCF/+C 3070) **WHAT'S THE MATTER BOY?**
 – Birth and death / Stand back / Watching the Devil / Enclave / Out of touch – View / Vertical integration / Split up the money / Making him sad. (re-iss. Jul82 lp/c; MCL/+C 1687) (<cd-iss. Apr96 on 'Mau Mau'; MAUCD 645>) (cd re-iss. Aug00 on 'Universal'+=; 844973-2) – Watching the Devil (BBC Peel session) / Stool pigeon (BBC Peel session) / Double negative (BBC Peel session) / Head held high (BBC Peel session).

— now backed by singers The BLACK ARABS

		Rough Trade	not iss.

Jan 81. (7") (RT 068) **STOP THAT GIRL. / INSTRUMENTALLY SCARED / VERTICAL INTEGRATION**

		Club Left	not iss.

Nov 81. (7") (CLUB 1) **STAMP OF A VAMP. / HEY NOW (I'M IN LOVE)**
(above was VIC GODARD solo)

VIC GODARD & THE SUBWAY SECT

— now with Bristol lads and future JO BOXERS; **ROB MARCHE** – guitar / **DAVE COLLARD** – keyboards / **CHRIS BOSTOCK** – bass / **SEAN McLUSKY** – drums

		London	not iss.

May 82. (7") (LON 005) **HEY NOW (I'M IN LOVE). / JUST IN TIME**
(10"+=/12"+=) (LON X/T 005) – Mr. Bennett.
Jun 82. (lp/c) (SH/KSAC 8549) **SONGS FOR SALE**
 – Hey now (I'm in love) / Crazy, crazy / Mr. Bennett / What's your name / Nola's salon / Be your age / Moving bed / Swing gently / Stamp of a vamp / Love for sale / Dilletante / Just in time / No style.

— VIC retired for a few years, although 'Rough Trade' were to have released single 'T.R.O.U.B.L.E.' mid-83 RT 126)

		Rough Trade	not iss.

Feb 85. (lp) (ROUGH 56) **A RETROSPECTIVE (1977-81)**
(compilation)

VIC GODARD

with **SIMON BOOTH** + others from WORKING WEEK

		El	not iss.

Jul 85. (7") (EL 4) **HOLIDAY HYMN. / NICE ON THE ICE**
(12"+=) (EL 4T) – Stop that girl / Ice on the volcano / T.R.O.U.B.L.E.

		Rough Trade	not iss.

Apr 86. (lp) (ROUGH 86) **T.R.O.U.B.L.E.**
 – Up on icing sugar mountain / T.R.O.U.B.L.E. / 20th century blues / Tidal wave / The Devil's in league with you / Caribb-blu / I'm gonna write a musical / Chain smoking / (Stayin' outta) View / Stop that girl / Nice on the ice / Holiday hymn / Ice on a volcano / Miss Sadie / The wave. *(cd-iss. May98 as 'IN TROUBLE AGAIN' on 'Tugboat'; TUG 001CD) <US cd-iss. Oct99 on 'Triple X'; 70027>*

— retired for a long spell but returned on the same label

Sep 92. (7") (45rev12) **JOHNNY THUNDERS. / IMBALANCE**

— now with **EDWYN COLLINS** – guitar (ex-ORANGE JUICE) / **CLAIRE KENNY** – bass (ex-AMAZULU) / **PAUL COOK** – drums (ex-SEX PISTOLS)

		Postcard	not iss.

May 93. (7") (DUBH 937) **WON'T TURN BACK. / ('A'version)**
(cd-s+=) (DUBH 937CD) – ('A'side) / The water was bad / Conscience be your guide / Same mistakes.
Jun 93. (lp/cd) (DUBH 936/+CD) **END OF THE SURREY PEOPLE**
 – Imbalance / Johnny Thunders / The water was bad / Malicious love / On the shore / Nullify my reputation (I'm gonna) / Won't turn back / Talent to follow / Same mistakes / The pain barrier / I can't stop you / The end of the Surrey people.

		Garcia	not iss.

Sep 96. (7") (POUM 002) **NO LOVE NOW. / SHE'S MY BEST FRIEND**

— Around this time, VIC was working with MARK PERRY (Alternative TV) in a band called The LONG DECLINE.

		Tugboat	Triple X

Nov 98. (cd) (TUG 003CD) <70028> **LONG TERM SIDE-EFFECT** — Oct99
 – We'll keep our chains / Outrageous things / One step from the gutter, baby / Common thief / No love (now) / Cold London blues / S-T-R-E-S-S / Don't do me down / The three bells / I barely exist / Zero tolerance / I wish . . . / I the shadow of your ego / One step / George Blake – masterspy.

		Creeping Bent	not iss.

Nov 99. (ltd-7") (BENT 048) **PLACE WE USED TO LIVE. / (other track by SECRET GOLDFISH)**

– compilations, etc. –

Apr 96. (7"ep/cd-ep) Overground; (OVER 45/+CD) **AMBITION / DIFFERENT STORY. / CHAIN SMOKING / AMBITION**
Dec 96. (cd; by SUBWAY SECT) Overground; (OVER 53CD) **WE OPPOSE ALL ROCK'N'ROLL**
 – Nobody's scared / Don't split it / Parallel lines / Chain smoking / Rock'n'roll even / Ambition / Double negative / Head held high / Stool pigeon / Watching the Devil / Spring is grey / Stop that girl / Exit no return / Staying out of view / Parallel lines.

Vic GODARD (& SUBWAY SECT) (cont) THE GREAT INDIE DISCOGRAPHY The 1970s

Oct 99. (d-cd) Motion; (PACECD 10) **20 ODD YEARS (THE BEST OF VIC GODARD & SUBWAY SECT)**

GORILLAS

Formed: Hammersmith, London, England ... 1974 by JESSE HECTOR (formerly of mid-60's outfit, The CLIQUE) and his cohorts ALAN BUTLER and GARY ANDERSON. Around well before the punk explosion of '76, this dynamic R&B trio nevertheless became an integral part of the London scene, HECTOR's "You Beauty" mutton chops distinguishing them from the spiky-topped pack. Way back in '74, The HAMMERSMITH GORILLAS (as they were known then) debuted with a cover of the Kinks' 'YOU REALLY GOT ME' before signing to local label, 'Chiswick' (home of the COUNT BISHOPS and the 101'ERS). Wearing their influences proudly on their sleeves, The GORILLAS recalled the ghosts of everyone from ELVIS PRESLEY to JIMI HENDRIX (they subsequently covered 'FOXY LADY') with their hard-gigging escapades around the capital. In 1976, HECTOR and Co recorded two singles, 'SHE'S MY GAL' and 'GATECRASHER' for 'Chiswick', before moving on to the 'Raw' label (home of punk-rockers, The UNWANTED and The USERS) for a further couple of tracks, 'IT'S MY LIFE' and 'MESSAGE TO THE WORLD' (the latter the title track of their one and only album, released in '78).

Album rating: MESSAGE TO THE WORLD (*4)

JESSE HECTOR – vocals, guitar / **ALAN BUTLER** – bass / **GARY ANDERSON** – drums, percussion

Penny Farthing / not iss.

Sep 74. (7"; as HAMMERSMITH GORILLAS) (PEN 849) **YOU REALLY GOT ME. / LEAVING 'OME**
(re-iss. Aug77 on 'Raw'; RAW 2)

Chiswick / not iss.

Jul 76. (7") (S 4) **SHE'S MY GAL. / WHY WAIT TILL TOMORROW**
Jan 77. (7") (S 8) **GATECRASHER. / GORILLA GOT ME**

Raw / not iss.

Jan 78. (7") (RAW 14) **IT'S MY LIFE. / MY SON'S ALIVE**
Nov 78. (7") (RAW 26) **MESSAGE TO THE WORLD. / OUTTA MY BRAIN**
Dec 78. (lp) (RWLP 103) **MESSAGE TO THE WORLD**
– Foxy lady / I'm a liar / I need her / Going fishing / New York groover / Outta my brain / Waitin' for you / No way in / Last train / Message to the world. (cd-iss. Nov94 on 'Damaged Goods'; DAMGOOD 49)

Chiswick / not iss.

Aug 81. (7") (CHIS 151) **MOVE IT. / SONG FOR RITA**

— split in the early 80's, although a decade later HECTOR was still on the London live circuit

Dave GREENFIELD & J.J. BURNEL
(see under ⇒ STRANGLERS)

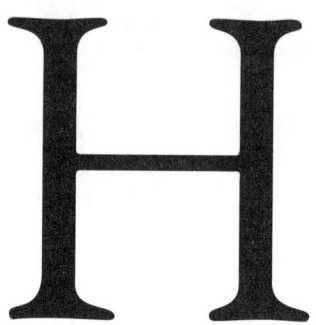

Nina HAGEN

Born: KATHERINA HAGEN, 11 Mar'55, East Berlin, Germany. Raised in the Eastern Bloc by her mother and dissident poet/songwriter stepfather, Walter Biermann, HAGEN excelled in her musical studies while moonlighting in dance groups such as AUTOMOBIL and FRITZENS DAMPFERBAND. In 1976, she followed her stepfather into exile in West Germany where she found it easy to secure a record deal with 'C.B.S.'. Inspired by her subsequent experience of the burgeoning London punk scene (where she met the SLITS), NINA formed her own posse of German musicians and proceeded to record an eponymous debut album, 'THE NINA HAGEN BAND' (1978). Despite the record's sizeable success on the continent, HAGEN chose to temporarily neglect her budding musical career and instead moved to the Netherlands where she struck up a friendship with HERMAN BROOD and LENE LOVICH, both of whom appeared with her in the late 70's cult movie, 'Cha Cha'. The LOVICH connection ultimately proved fairly profitable as HAGEN recycled her UK smash, 'LUCKY NUMBER' (having already tackled The Tubes' 'WHITE PUNKS ON DOPE' – aka 'TV GLOTZER' – on her debut) for German then American fans. A contract filling second album, 'UNBEHAGEN' (1980), was all the rage in her German homeland, while Austrians also developed a taste for her after allegedly witnessing the singer's simulated masturbation on TV. Having relocated to Los Angeles, she released her esoteric third set, 'NUNSEXMONKROCK' (1982), a US Top 200 record inspired by an apparent sighting of a UFO; HAGEN's newfound mysticism coincided with her decision to "sing" in English, the result being a banshee howl compared by many to a more extreme YOKO ONO. For her next project, the 1984 GIORGIO MORODER/KEITH FORSEY-produced set, 'FEARLESS', HAGEN moved into electro-dance territory, even roping in the fledgling RED HOT CHILI PEPPERS on the track, 'WHAT IT IS'. HAGEN subsequently fused her newfound dance leanings with metal-punk, although the choice of cover material on 'IN EKSTASY' (1985), suggested NINA was running out of ideas. She reunited with her old friend, LENE LOVICH on a one-off single in '87, 'DON'T KILL THE ANIMALS', while the same year saw her controversially marry one of her teenage fans! It would be 1989 before the release of another HAGEN long-player, the virtually ignored eponymous 'Mercury' set being followed a few years later by 'STREET' (1991). Her final album to date, 'REVOLUTION BALLROOM' (1995), failed to renew any interest in her flagging career, HAGEN's heyday long gone. • **Covered:** MY WAY (Paul Anka) / SPIRIT IN THE SKY (Norman Greenbaum) / MOVE OVER (Janis Joplin) / VIVA LAS VEGAS (hit; Elvis) / AVE MARIA + THE LORD'S PRAYER (trad.) / etc.

Album rating: THE NINA HAGEN BAND (*5) / UNBEHAGEN (*4) / NUNSEXMONKROCK (*4) / FEARLESS (*5) / IN EKSTASY (*3) / NINA HAGEN (*3) / STREET (*3) / REVOLUTION BALLROOM (*4) / 14 FRIENDLY ABDUCTIONS: BEST OF compilation (*5)

NINA HAGEN BAND

NINA HAGEN – vocals / with **BERNHARD POTSCHKA** – guitar (ex-LOK KREUZBERG) / **MANFRED PRAEKER** – bass (ex-LOK KREUZBERG) / **HERWIG MITTEREGGER** – drums / **REINHOLD HEIL** – keyboards

C.B.S. / Columbia

Dec 78. (lp) (CBS 83136) **THE NINA HAGEN BAND**
– TV glotzer / Rangehn / Unbeschreiblich weiblich / Auf'm bahnhof / Naturtrane / Superboy / Heiss / Fisch im wasser / Auf'm Friedhof / Der spinner Pank. (cd-iss. 1988; CD 83136)
Aug 79. (7") (CBS 7804) **TV GLOTZER (WHITE PUNKS ON DOPE). / NATURTRANE**
Feb 80. (7") (CBS 8304) **AFRICAN REGGAE. / WAU WAU**
Apr 80. (lp) (CBS 84159) **UNBEHAGEN**
– African reggae / Alptraum / Wir leben immer noch / Wenn oich ein junge war / Hermann heiss er / Auf'n rummel / Wau wau / Fall in love mit mir / No way.

NINA HAGEN

— now with **ALLAN SCHWARTZBERG** – drums / **KARL RUCKER** – bass / **CHRIS SPEDDING** – guitar / **PAUL SCHAFFER + PAUL ROSTLER** – piano + synthesizer / **AXEL GOTHE** – clarinet, wind

Jul 82. (lp) (CBS 85774) <38008> **NUNSEXMONKROCK**
– Antiworld / Smack Jack / Taitschi – Tarot / Dread love / Future is now / Born in Xixax / Iki maska / Dr. Art / Cosma shiva / U.F.O.

— her main band:- **KARL RUCKER** – bass, keyboards / **STEVE SCHIFF** – guitar, keyboards / **RICHIE ZITO** – guitar

Nina HAGEN (cont)

Jan 84. (lp) (CBS 25667) <39214> **ANGSTIOS** <US-title 'FEARLESS'>
– New York New York / What it is / Flying saucers / Zarah / Springtime in Paris / I love Paul / My sensation / T.V. snooze / The change.
Feb 84. (7") (A 4216) **ZARAH.** / (version)

—— **PETER KRAUSE + ALEX LAROQUE** – drums; repl. SCHIFF + ZITO

—— she used a plethora of musicians from now on

May 85. (7"/12") (ATX 6278) **UNIVERSAL RADIO. / PRIMA NINA IN EKSTASY**
May 85. (lp) (CBS 26421) **IN EKSTASY**
– Universal radio / Gods of Aquarius / Russian reggae / My way / 1983 Ekstasy Drive / Prima Nina in Ecstasy / Spirit in the sky / Atomic flash deluxe / The Lord's prayer / Gott im Himmel.

Arista   not iss.

Jan 87. (7"/12"; NINA HAGEN & LENE LOVICH) (RIS/+T 3) **DON'T KILL THE ANIMALS.** /

Mercury   Mercury

Sep 89. (lp/c/cd) (838505-1/-4/-2) **NINA HAGEN**
– Move over / Super freak family / Love heart attack / Hold me / Viva Las Vegas / Live on Mars / Dope sucks / Only seventeen / Where's the party / Michail, Michail (Gorbachev rap) / Ave Maria. (cd re-iss. Feb96 on 'Activ'; ACTIVCD 6)
Aug 91. (cd/c/lp) (848716-2/-4/-1) **STREET**
– Blumen fur die damen / Divine, love, sex and romance / Ruler of my heart / Nine 4 president / Keep it live / Berlin / In my world / Gretchen / Erfurt and Gera / All 4 Frankie. (cd re-iss. Feb96 on 'Activ'; ACTIVCD 4)

Activ   not iss.

Jun 95. (cd/c/lp) (ACTIV CD/MC/LP 3) **REVOLUTION BALLROOM**
– So bad / Revolution ballroom / Right on time / Pollution pirates / King of hearts / L'amore / Pillow talk / Berlin / I'm going to live the life / Gypsy love / Dmhadahandi.
Sep 95. (c-s/12"/cd-s) (C/12/CD TV 4) **SO BAD (Utah Saints mixes)**

– compilations, etc. –

1987. (lp) Polygram; (460454) **LOVE**
Oct 93. (cd) Sony Europe; (471675-2) **THE GOLD COLLECTION**
Mar 96. (cd) Legacy; <64790> **14 FRIENDLY ABDUCTIONS: THE BEST OF**

HALF JAPANESE

Formed: Uniontown, Maryland, USA … 1977 by San Franciscan-born brothers JAD and DAVID FAIR; a few years previously, together with friend, DAVID STANSKY, the pair had practised daily in the basement of their parents' Michigan home. A debut EP, 'CALLING ALL GIRLS … ' was released that year, its deliberate amateurism and wilful experimentation heralding a long and chequered career for the FAIR siblings. After they issued a further EP in 1979, 'NO DIRECT LINE FROM MY BRAIN TO MY HEART', the pair decided to recruit two other brothers, RUCKY and JOHN DREYFUSS, their inaugural appearance coming in the shape of 1980's UK-only single, 'THE ZOMBIES OF MORA-TAU'. By 1981, they had amassed enough material to fill a triple album, 'HALF GENTLEMEN, NOT BEASTS', a schizoid trip through the brothers' warped muse featuring numerous crazed cover versions (see below) alongside defiantly DIY creations which set the tone for homemade US underground music throughout the 80's. From then on they assembled various musicians to augment them on each album project, JAD simultaneously juggling a prolific solo career with HALF JAPANESE albums such as 'LOUD' (1981), the KRAMER-produced 'MUSIC TO STRIP BY' (1987), 'CHARMED LIFE' (1988) and 'THE BAND THAT WOULD BE KING' (1989); DAVID would now be just part-time in '88. JAD subsequently worked with the likes of DON FLEMING (of VELVET MONKEYS, etc), JOHN ZORN and FRED FRITH (ex-HENRY COW), to mention but a few. At the turn of the decade, JAD collaborated with fellow maverick, DANIEL JOHNSTON on their demon-exorcising 1989 album and went on to work with Scottish spiritual cousins, The PASTELS. In 1993, a feature-length film, 'HALF JAPANESE: THE BAND THAT WOULD BE KING' was being screened in art-house cinemas, while the band came perilously close to fame as fans, NIRVANA, asked them to support them on tour. Back to the obscure, HALF JAPANESE were back in 1997 via 'HEAVEN SENT', which opened with the 60-minute + title track followed by nine lo-fi ditties! Squeezed in between a HJ follow-up, 'HELLO' (2001), JAD FAIR collaborated twice again, the first with YO LA TENGO ('STRANGE BUT TRUE'), the second with JASON WILLETT ('ENJOYABLE SONGS'); a further joint effort 'LUCKY SPERMS' (2001) with DANIEL JOHNSTON compounded the theory that JAD was indeed a bit of an all-round oddball.
• **Songwriters:** JAD FAIR except; 10th AVENUE FREEZE OUT (Bruce Springsteen) / TANGLED UP IN BLUE (Bob Dylan) / RAVE ON (Buddy Holly) / AIN'T TOO PROUD TO BEG (Temptations) / SHE CRACKED (Modern Lovers) / I CAN'T STAND IT ANYMORE + I HEARD HER CALL MY NAME (Velvet Underground) / THE SPY (Doors) / BLUE MONDAY (Fats Domino) / GLORIA (Them) / HIDDEN CHARMS (Willie Dixon) / LA BAMBA (Richie Valens) / TOMORROW NEVER KNOWS (Beatles) / BLUE MONDAY (Fats Domino) / SHANTY TOWN (Desmond Dekker) / GOING HOME (Love) / ELEVATOR BOY Orthotonics) / EVERY HOUR (Little Richard) / ALL OF ME (Marks-Simons) / TEARS STUPID TEARS (Daniel Johnston) / IT'S NO WONDER (Roky Erickson) / EAR (… Brookings) / MEMPHIS TENNESSEE + CHARMED LIFE (Chuck Berry) / I'LL CHANGE MY STYLE (Jerry Reed) / CHERRY PIE (… Josea) / FUTURISTIC LOVERS (Laureate-Mitchell) / SILVER AND KATHERINE (trad) / CASPER (c/o cartoon; Carmichael). Jad Fair also covered numerous songs etc. • **Trivia:** In 1991, they were produced by MO TUCKER (former VELVET UNDERGROUND drummer).

Album rating: HALF GENTLEMEN, NOT BEASTS compilation (*7) / LOUD (*5) / OUR SOLAR SYSTEM (*4) / SING NO EVIL (*4) / MUSIC TO STRIP BY (*6) / CHARMED LIFE (*7) / THE BAND THAT WOULD BE KING (*7) / WE ARE THEY WHO ACHE WITH AMOROUS LOVE (*6) / FIRE IN THE SKY (*6) / HOT (*6) / GREATEST HITS compilation (*8) / BONE HEAD (*6) / HEAVEN SENT (*6) / HELLO (*5) / Jad Fair: EVERYBODY KNEW. BUT ME (*6) / MONARCHS (*4) / BEST WISHES (*5) / GREAT EXPECTATIONS (*6) / ROLL OUT THE BARREL (*4) / IT'S SPOOKY with Daniel Johnston (*7) / I LIKE IT WHEN YOU SMILE (*6) / HONEY BEE (*5) / STRANGE BUT TRUE (*4) / ENJOYABLE SONGS (*6) / SOMEWHAT HUMOROUS by the Lucky Charms (*5)

JAD FAIR – vocals, guitar, drums / **DAVID FAIR** – guitar, vocals, drums

Armageddon   50..Watts

1977. (7"ep) <7094-18> **CALLING ALL GIRLS EP**
– Dream date / Calling all girls / School of love / Battle of the bands / Bogue millionaires / Cool millionaires / Ann Arbor MI / Shy around girls / Her parents came home / Worst I'd ever do.
1978. (7"m) <no No> **NO DIRECT LINE FROM MY BRAIN TO MY HEART. / (I DON'T WANT TO HAVE) MONO (NO MORE) / RIP MY SHIRT TO SHREDS**

—— added **RICKY DREYFUSS** – drums / **JOHN DREYFUSS** – saxophone

May 81. (7"/12") (AS 009) **SPY. / I KNOW HOW IT FEELS … BAD / MY KNOWLEDGE WAS WRONG**
Oct 81. (t-lp-box)<d-c> (ABOX 1)<519-60> **1/2 GENTLEMEN, NOT BEASTS** (compilation 77-79)   1979
– No direct line from my brain to my heart / 10th Ave. freezeout / Ta Sheri ta ta / My girlfriend lives like a beatnik / Her parents came home / Shhh-shhh-shhh / Girls like that / Rrrrrr / No more Beatlemania / Tangled up in blue / Patti Smith / School of love / Jodi Foster / Shy around girls / Grrrrrrrrrrr / Bogue millionaires / Cool millionaires / Tn tn tn tn ki / I can't stand it anymore / I love Oriental girls / Dream date / Du du du du du du / Ain't too proud to beg / Ann Arbor MI / I'm going to the zoo / Shi Yi Yi / Rave on / I ta na si na mi eee / Till victory / Rip my shirt to shreds / I don't want to have mono no more / She cracked / Bbbbbb-bbbbbb-bbbbbb / Funky Broadway medley / I'm sorry / TT-T-T-T-T-T / The worst I'd ever do / Live. <US d-cd-iss. 1993 on 'T.E.C. Tones'; 9256-2>

—— added **MARK JICKLING** – guitar / **LANA ZABKO** – saxophone

May 82. (lp) (ARM 7) **LOUD**
– My concentration, oh no / 2 hearts = 1 / If my father answers, don't say nothing / Scientific devices / Gift / Dumb animals / Popular / I know how it feels … bad / Perfume / New brides of Frankenstein / Forget you / Loud, louder, loudest / Spy / No danger / Love lasts forever / Nurse / Only dancing / Bad to your best friend / Baby wants music / High school tonight.

not iss.   Press

1983. (12"ep) <P 2005> **HORRIBLE**
– Think with a hook / Don't go to bed / Rosemary's baby / Vampire / Walk through walls. (UK-iss.Jul86; same)

—— added **RICHIE LaBRIE** – drums

not iss.   Iridescence

Dec 84. (lp) <K-6> **OUR SOLAR SYSTEM**
– Dance when I say dance / Girl athletes / Because I love you / Danger danger Rachel Lang / E.S.P. / Classical music / You're gonna miss me / Little girls have to be home early / Too much adrenalin / Fire to burn / Rhonda / Electricity request / Knocked down on the dancefloor / European son / There's a girl / Hall of the mountain king / Louie Louie / Young hearts break / Did you miss me / The thing with the hook. <(cd-iss. May00 on 'Drag City'; DC 174)>
Dec 85. (lp) <I-10> **SING NO EVIL**
– Firecracker firecracker / On the one hand / Too bad about Elizabeth / Dearest darling / Sing no evil / Double trouble / Rub every muscle / Nicole told me / Tell me I'm wrong / Acupuncture / I have a secret / House of voodoo. <(cd-iss. May00 on 'Drag City'; DC 173)>

Shadowline   50 Skidillion Watts

1987. (lp) <WAT 2> **MUSIC TO STRIP BY**
– Stripping for cash / Thick and thin / Diary / Big mistake / Hot dog and hot damn / Price was right / Blue Monday / U.S. teens are spoiled bums / Point – Counterpoint / Sex at your parents house / The 1st straw / Gator bait / La bamba / Colleen / Ouija board summoning Satan / You must obey me / Salt and pepper / Ancient life / Silver and Katherine / Money to burn / Hidden charms / How / My sordid past. (cd-iss. Jul93 on 'Paperhouse'+=; PAPCD 017) – Silver and Katherine / Dusk to dawn / Everybody knows / Go go go go go / Scratch / Colleen / Salt and pepper / 'T' for Texas / Terminator / Shiek of Araby. <cd-iss. 1994; 80002>
Feb 88. (7"m) (SR 0188) <no No> **U.S. TEENS ARE SPOILED BUMS**
– Silver and Katherine / Patty Hearst / Patti Smith. (re-iss. Jun93; HJ 4)

No Man's   50 Land   Skidillion Watts

Nov 88. (lp) (NML 8815) <WATT 5> **CHARMED LIFE** (rec.1985)
– Said and done / Penny in the fountain / Evidence / Vietnam / Roman candles / Love at first sight / Snake line / Bright lights, big city / Face rake / Later in a magazine / Red dress / Charmed life / Day and night / 1,000,000,000 kisses / Terminator / I'll change my style / Fortunate / Poetic license / Day and night / 1,000,000,000 kisses / Madonna nude / I'll change my style / George Steele / Real cool time / How many moe years / King Kong Bundy / Something new in the ring / Terminator. (cd-iss. Jul93 on 'Paperhouse'; PAPCD 016) <cd-iss. 1994; 80005>
1988. (c) <none> **BIG BIG SUN (live)** (tracks * by Velvet Monkeys)
– * Little doll / Later in a magazine / T for Texas / * We call it rock / I know how it feels … bad / * She's not a girl / Fortunate / King Kong Bundy / * Hey Joe / Nicole told me / * Nervous communication breakdown / What I say / * Rock party.
(above issued on 'K')

—— now **JAD** with **DON FLEMING, KRAMER, SCOTT JARVIS, Mr. J. RICE, ROB KENNEDY, FRED FRITH, GEORGE CARTWRIGHT + JOHN ZORN**

Apr 89. (lp) <HALF 8> **THE BAND WHO WOULD BE KING**
– Open your eyes – Close your eyes / Daytona beach / Lucky star / Some things last a long time / My most embarrassing moment / Buried treasure / Open book / Little records / Deadly alien spawn / Postcard from faraway / Ventriloquism made easy / Something in the wind / Bingo's not his name / Put some sugar on it / What more can I do. (re-iss. cd Jul93 on 'Paperhouse'+=; PAPCD 018) – Brand new moon / Another world / Every word is true / I live for love / Werewolf / Ride ride ride / Sugar cane / I wish I may / Ashes on the ground / Curse of the doll people / Horse

shoes / Bluebirds / Frankenstein meets Billy The KId / My bucket's got a hole in it / Africans built the pyramids / Better than before / Daytona / Back home / Mule skinner blues / Sugar cane / Jump up / Postcard from far away / Big wheels / Ordeal / Jump down / Cowboys / Man without a head. *<cd-iss. 1994; 80008>*

not iss. TEC Tones

Jan 91. (cd/d-lp) *<9060-2/-1>* **WE ARE THEY WHO ACHE WITH AMOROUS LOVE**
– Every hour / Elevator boy / Gloria / Ear / Titanic / Our eyes / Spin / Up and down / Run / All of me / Hand without a body / Going home / Three rings / How did you know? Then we walk / Secret / Best / The house I live in / Shanty town *[cd-only]* / Everything is right?

—— **JAD, DON FLEMING, JOHN SLUGGET + HANK BECKMEYER**

Seminal Twang not iss.

Jun 91. (7") *(TWANG 1CD)* **EVERYBODY KNOWS / TURN YOUR LIFE AROUND / ALWAYS**

Paperhouse Safe House

Mar 92. (cd) *(PAPCD 010) <SH 2113-2>* **FIRE IN THE SKY**
– UFO expert / Tears stupid tears / This could be the night / Possum head / Frosty head / Turn your life around / I love a mystery / 12 houses / Hangar 18 / Magic kingdom / It's no wonder / Fire in the sky / Good luck / Gates of glory. *<US+=>* – Everyone knows / I heard her call my name / Eye of the hurricane.

Apr 92. (7") *(PAPER 017)* **EYE OF THE HURRICANE**

not iss. TEC Tones

May 94. (cd) *<94602>* **BOO! LIVE IN EUROPE 1992 (live)**
– Open your eyes / Big mistake / One million kisses / Fire to burn / Mule in the corn / If he says he did / King Kong / Postcard / I'll change my style / Cherry pie / Rrrrrsssssstttttt / Sex at your parent's house / Secret / Said and done / Charmed life / Casper / Around around / Rocking chair / Turn your life around / Firecracker / Silver and Katherine / Frankenstein must fie! / By and by / Fire in the sky.

—— with **MICK HOBBS** – bass, guitar / **JOHN SLUGGETT** – guitar / **JASON WILLETT** – bass, guitar

Fire Safe House

Jun 95. (cd) *(FIRECD 47) <SH 2125>* **HOT** Aug95
– Drum straight / True believers / Well / Dark night / Part of my plan / Vampire / Lucky ones / Vast continent / Guess again / Black fruit / Sleep talk / Smile / Lucky town.

Mar 96. (m-cd) *<SH 2132>* **TBD**

—— retained only **SLUGGETT** + enlisted other co-writers **TIM FOLJAHN** – guitar / **GILLES V. RIEDER** – percussion, drums, etc

Alternative Tentacles Alternative Tentacles

Mar 97. (cd/lp) *<(VIRUS 197 CD/LP)>* **BONE HEAD**
– Monkey head / A night like this / Sometimes / Zombie eyes / Song of joy / Oww / Do it / He walks among us / Diamonds and . . . / Kiss me like a frog / Rhumba / Intergalactic aliens / Celebration / C'mon baby / Somehow I knew / Now I know / Brand new sky / Should I? / Song of joy / Futuristic lovers / Movin' on up.

Nov 97. (cd) *<(EJ 12CD)>* **HEAVEN SENT**
– Heaven sent / Good & true & fine / A fine line / Outer Space / Well worth while / Better than no / Dynasty / Goldfish & the trout / This is our night / The day we met. (above issued on 'Emperor Jones')

Feb 01. (cd/lp) *<(VIRUS 245 CD/LP)>* **HELLO**
– All the angels said go to her / Patty / Temptation / The legend of hillbilly John / Mississippi / No doubt / 10:00 a.m. / Jump into the mess / Red sun / Whatever the outcome / Best of the best / Summer nights / Our turn / Starlight / The good side / Super-size it / Happyland.

– compilations, etc. –

Nov 96. (d-cd) *Safe House; <(SH 2118-2)>* **GREATEST HITS** Mar95
– Firecracker / Daytona beach / Said and done / Dance when I say dance / Postcard from far away / Worst I'd ever do / Horseshoes / Open/close your eyes / This could be the night / Put some sugar on it / Caling all girls / Bamba / Love at first sight / Rub every muscle / Silver and Katherine / My sordid past / Ride, ride, ride / Day and night / Last straw / Nicole / Miracles happen every day / U.S. teens / School of love / T for Texas / Colleen / Red dress / Charmed life / Rosemary's baby / I know how it feels . . . bad / Roman candles / Dream date / Moving on up / No more Beatlemania / How did you know? / Penny in the fountain / King Kong / Secret / B./C. millionaires / Amazing clock / Thick and thin / 1,000,000 kisses / Big mistake / Little records / No direct line / The house I live in / UFO expert / Identical twins / Double trouble / Evidence / Stripping for cash / On the one hand / Snake line / Too much adrenalin / Trouble in the water / Ball and chain / Her parents came home / Deadly alien spawn / Ancient life / Poetic license / Uncertain feelings / Something new / Fire to burn / Acupuncture / Salt and pepper / Guitar solo / A little bit more / Mono / Better than before / Everything is right?

JAD FAIR

Armageddon Press

Jun 80. (7"ep) *(AEP 003)* **THE ZOMBIES OF MORA-TAU** 1982
– Frankenstein must die / Dead men talk / The thing with the atomic brain / Angela / It walks at night / The zombies of Mora-Tau / The invisible ray.

1982. (7") *<P 1002>* **XXOO**
– How will I know / That's what they say / Tracks of my tears.

1983. (lp) *<P 4005>* **EVERYBODY KNEW . . . BUT ME**
– Love research / Girl trouble / I'm going to go out / Jumbalaya / I'm going to come back to you / Amy / Walking with Candy / Everyone knew . . . but me / Fish can talk / All my love / I got you / Another silent night / Things with eyes / Oh / Amy you went away / Mil mascaras / I want to be loved / Monster island / Sex machine / I / Will you go with me? / Snake on my head / Want / Roses for Karen / You / It saw ME / Lonely week-ends / Back / Again.

not iss. Iridescence

1985. (lp) *<G 2>* **MONARCHS**
– Starry eyes / Thank you / Amnesia / She went downtown / Hang seven / Folsom prison blues / I changed my mind twice / Stephanie / Early in the morning / I told lies / Ring / Rambi shimba / Lucille / . . .To reveal yet another face – This one even more frightening than the one before – Immediately I jumped from my chair and ran toward the door – I now know what I needed to – Unfortunately . . . So did he / Guess who / Toad / All shook up / From where I stood I could see the shape that once was formless take on the characteristics of a human being – Who are you? I gasped – Do you not know me?, he replied – I was once a very powerful man / No no no no / We are good / Say it again / The end. *<(cd-iss. Jul97 on 'Dr.Jim'; DRJIM 20)>*

1985. (12"ep) *<O-9>* **BETWEEN MEALS**
– Don't you know / Do you have a friend? / John Lennon and the Beatles / Matchbox / Sink or swim? / What'd I say / How will I know? / Route 66.

1986. (lp) *<I 16>* **BEST WISHES**
– OK / AOK / OK / AOK / . . ..

Bad Alchemy TEC Tones

1988. (d-lp) *(BAAL 22)* **GREAT EXPECTATIONS** German
– And / Now I see / Snakes / Snake on my head / Everyone knew but me / Outlaw blues / Space sound / Want / Roses for Karen / Rocket ship / Moon / Tiger / Robot / Love research / Baseball / Lion / All my love / Hogwild / Like a bird / Shakespear / Parade / Angela / The tracks of my tears / Frankenstein must die / Weee / All / Amy / You / Frankenstein monster / Checkers / It saw me / Jambalaya / Horses / Dog / Whale / I got you / Deadmen walk / Fish / Zombies of Mora-Tau / Another silent night / This / New Orleans / Vampire / Amy you went away / Owl / Radio / Romeo and Juliet / Girl-trouble / Shoestrings / Mule / I want to be loved / Thing with the atomic brain / Lonely weekends / Again / Invisible ray / Duck / I'm gonna go out / XXOO / Went / Hotdog / I'm gonna come back to you / Eifel Tower / Cherry pie / Linda Lou / Bear / Will you go out with me? / Hillbillies / It walks at night / Monster is land / Elephant / Things with eyes / Pajamas / Wild West / Me and the boys / Fish can talk / I heard his footsteps beat against the attic floor / I knew my time had come / Don't you want to live forever? / Face your lord and master / There is no escape / The time has come / Nosferatu is among us.

1989. (cd) *<91062>* **GREATER EXPECTATIONS**
– Elephant / Hillbillies / Pajamas / Wild West / Me & the boys / Vampire / Wise old owl / Radio / Romeo & Juliet / Shoe strings / Mule / The tracks of my tears / Weeeeeeeeee / All / Frankenstein monster / Checkers / Horses / Dog / Whale / Speed of sound / Rocket ship / Moon / A great big tiger / Robot / Baseball / Lion / And / And now I can see / Snakes / Outlaw blues / Hog wild / Like a bird / Shakespeare / And then I went / Hot dog / Eiffel Tower / Cherry pie / Linda Lou / A big bear / Water / Salt & pepper / Cheese / Chairs / Cha-cha / Thank you, bye.

—— next with also **SONIC YOUTH, JOHN ZORN, DAVID LICHT**, etc

Black Lion ShimmyDisc

Jan 89. (lp; by JAD FAIR & KRAMER) *(BLP 60904) <SDE 8912>* **ROLL OUT THE BARREL**
– Cheerleaders wild weekend / Double for me / Bird of prey / Subterranean homesick blues / If it's OK / Better safe than sorry / DEn of angels / Blind hope / California / When is she coming / Second thought / Best left unsaid / By and by / Help / Around and around / What I've been waiting for / Load and mount / Nosferatu / Twist and shout / King Kong / Rockin' chair / It's easy to see / On the sunny side of the street / Paths of glory. *<(cd-iss. Apr99 on 'Shimmy Disc'+=; SHM 5012)>* – Eye of the hurricane / No one knows / Flower of the north.

50 Skidillion Watts 50 Skidillion Watts

Apr 89. (lp/c/cd; by JAD FAIR AND DANIEL JOHNSTON) *<(JAD 9-1/-4/-2)>* **IT'S SPOOKY**
– It's spooky / Summertime / I met Roky Erickson / Happy talk / McDonalds on the brain / I did acid with Caroline / If I'd only known / Tongues wag in this town / Tomorrow never knows / Oh honey / A vow of love / When love calls / Frankenstein conquers the world / Hands of love / Kicking the dog / What I've seen / Something's got a hold on me / Villain / Chords of fame / Ostrich / Casper the friendly ghost / First day at work / Nothing left / Memphis, Tennessee / Come back. *(cd+=)* – Tears stupid tears / The making of the album / Get yourself together / What the world needs now / Sweet loafed. *(cd-iss. Jul93 on 'Paperhouse'; PAPCD 019) <US cd-iss. Jun01 on 'Jagjaguwar'; JAG 33>*

Seminal Twang Shimmy Disc

1990. (cd; by JAD FAIR & KRAMER) *<SHIMMY 035>* **THE SOUND OF MUSIC**
– Beverly / Candace / Elenor / Faceless man / Our cause to worry / Here comes Roxanne / Zorro's black whip / Sleeping beauty / Pretty angel eyes / Something to sing about / Annie Oakley / The sound of music.

1991. (cd-ep) **THE MAKING OF THE ALBUM**
– The making of the album / Get yourself together / Day / Night / When.

—— now with **TERRY ADAMS** – harmonica, percussion, keyboards / plus guests **DON FLEMING + MICK HOBBS + STEVE SHELLEY + J MASCIS**etc

Paperhouse TEC Tones

Feb 92. (cd/lp) *(PAP CD/LP 009) <9260-2>* **I LIKE IT WHEN YOU SMILE**
– A little bit more / The only one left / Sunny side of the street / Something inside of me / Surprise party / Secret life / Dot / Roadrunner / If he says he did / You'll never know / Big as the sun / Crown / Take a chance / I like candy / Mule in the corn / Big top / I had a dream last night / Angel / The eyes of the world / Brand new moon / Texas / Better than before.

—— next with the Scottish band, The PASTELS

Feb 92. (12"ep/cd-ep; as JAD FAIR & THE PASTELS) *(PAPER 013 T/CD)* **THIS COULD BE THE NIGHT. / WHEN WE TOUCH / A LONELY SONG**

Jun 92. (12"ep/cd-ep; as JAD FAIR & THE PASTELS) *(PAPER 018 T/CD)* **HE CHOSE HIS COLOURS WELL**

—— next with NAO = NAOFUMI ISHIMARU

Jan 94. (cd; by JAD FAIR & NAO) *(PAPCD 015)* **HALF ROBOT**
– Population is only 2 / Walk right in / Art? ha! / Hope-Bogart / ETC's / Happy together / Smile pretender / Our love has come / Neat beings / I like it / Gone with window / Pu-14 is is 4 of GB 10 / Brigham's coffee shop / Distorted moon / Kukaimanimani / Navel cake / Intuition / Broom of love / Zui zui zukkorobash / Amy's smile / Coffee me / Water / I don't know / April / Egg'n'ham / Haircuts / Do hachamecha / Nihon no Otoko / 999 years loan / Fresh meat / Pepper and salt / Forever / Hana o meshimasho / Junkful junk / Made in Paradise / The band / Do you like America? / Debt for debt / Beast wishes / Charlie Chaplin / As seen on T.V. / Oh! my buddha / $1.99, $2.99, $3.99 / Time / Protecting / Simon, not Simon / Nynyusa / Bride with cowboy boots / Candy / Pornographies in the safe / Happy birthday / Can't buy my money / Typewriter / Curious crowd's faces / My name is Jad Fair / Morale booster / Bob Hope / Industrial refuse / Freaks / Miserable shit / Yes, I'm not tired / Too much car / Tattoo of hello Kitty / Cold summer / Vegetarian puts leather / Kiss tribe / Sleep / Newborn babies / Tokolo de Kowela Nani / Cato and Dogu / 40 monsters / Watch T.V. 'til you die / Taking a bath / Rocky mountain oyster / Blue suede shoes / Homosexual teacher.

HALF JAPANESE (cont) — THE GREAT INDIE DISCOGRAPHY — The 1970s

		not iss.	Smells Like
1993.	(7"ep) <5> **SHORT SONGS ep**	-	

– Shoes / Birds / Breakfast / Oh my word / Movies / Jack / Morning / Books / July / Cape Fear / Sandwich / I felt O.K.

―― in 1994, JAD (alongside GOD IS MY CO-PILOT) released 7"ep 'Gunfighter Ballads' on 'The Making Of Americans'

		Derivative	not iss.
Oct 95.	(7"; as JAD FAIR & PHONO COMB) (DVH 020) **IN A HAUNTED HOUSE. /**		-

		not iss.	Shake
Jun 96.	(cd; as PHONO-COMB & JAD FAIR) <226> **MONSTERS, LULLABIES . . . AND THE OCCASIONAL FLYING SAUCER**	-	

– Close my eyes / Too sweet to be forgotten / The beast within / Object: to serve man / My astonished heart / Just across the street / Life of the party / Evil eye / You will have it all / That's where I went right / Lucinda / I feel good / Dreamy eyes / UFO – IFO / All for you / TV guide / Nightclub / Null.

		Vesuvius	not iss.
Nov 95.	(7"; as JAD & DAVID FAIR) (pomp 003) **JAD AND DAVID FAIR**		-

– What do you want / Idiot wind / Strange life / Voodoo master.

| Nov 96. | (cd; as JAD & DAVID FAIR) (pomp 006) **BEST FRIENDS** | | - |

– Blessed by angels / Love train wreck / Voodoo master says / Nancy is an angel-o / Howlin Wolf / What do you want? / Face on the ceiling / Everybody loves the tinklers / Strange life / Everynight I have the dream / Godzilla vs. mecha Godzilla / Incredible journey 2000 / It really doesn't matter / They were shocked / Rage and fire / That love / Pergatory, atleast / Best friend / A club about loving you / Someone fell in love / Perry Mason in the way / King Kong / Band like me / Andy Griffith show 2000 / Hell enough alone / Rock and roll r.o.p. / The tinklers rule my world / Jupiter, Saturn, Pluto, Sue / 2, 2, 3 / Well, I'll be John Brown.

―― now with **KIM M. RANCOURT** – sax, vocals, etc / + others

		not iss.	Avant
Apr 97.	(cd; as JAD FAIR & THE SHAPIR-O-RAMA) <AVANT 52> **WE ARE THE RAGE**	-	

– Meet me by the prison wall / I comb my hair with my hand / The book of love / Love in stores / Jamboree / I love honey / I saw Chris Economaki / Caterpillar / We are the rage / Shnella / Call me / Electric / I knew I know (just one look) / Convert / Lots of room for love / Party / Olives / Evelyn day / Don't change a thing / Summer – Winter / Rice a roni / Be it again / And I love her.

		Dr. Jim	not iss.
Jul 97.	(cd; by JAD FAIR and JASON WILLETT) (DRJIM 19) **HONEY BEE**		-

– Honey bee / We will never stop / Now is why / Sweet as honey / I can't wait / Kiss my ass / Come along for the ride / We are pure / Your pretty smile / Batman on the double / First comes love / My dream og genie / I got a promise / Jenny Wood / Let's all sing / Punk rovk 1996 (part 2) / Crazy cubist / I have made you a promise / Brand new red / We did try / I love the high test / Tally ho / Mad about you / Advice column / Sound of the sea. (lp-iss.Apr98 on 'Lissys'; LISS 26)

		Kill Rock Stars	Kill Rock Stars
May 98.	(cd; by JAD & DAVID FAIR) <(KRS 292)> **26 MONSTER SONGS FOR CHILDREN**		

– Abominable snowman / Big foot / Creature / Dracula / E.T. / Frankenstein / Godzilla / Headless horseman / Invisible man / Jabberwocky / King Kong / Loch Ness monster / Mummy / Nosferatu / Ogre / Phantom / Queen Kong / Rodan / Sasquatch / Troll / Urchin / Vampire / Werewolf / The man with the x-ray eyes / Yeti / Zombie.

		Matador	Matador
Oct 98.	(cd; by JAD FAIR & YO LA TENGO) <(OLE 309)> **STRANGE BUT TRUE**		

– Helpful monkey wallpapers entire room / Texas man abducted by aliens for outer space joy ride / National sports association hires retired English professor to name new wrestling holds / Dedicated thespian has teeth pulled to play newborn baby in high school play / Three-year-old genius graduates high school at top of her class / Embarrassed teen accidentally uses valuable rare postage stamp / Principal punishes students with bad impressions and tired jokes / Retired grocer constructs tiny Mount Rushmore entirely of cheese / X-ray reveals doctor left wristwatch inside patient / Clumsy grandmother serves delicious dessert by mistake #2 / Retired woman starts new career in monkey fashions / Circus strongman runs for PTA president / High school shop class constructs bicycle built for 26 / Clumsy grandmother serves delicious dessert my mistake #1 / Ohio town saved from killer bees by hungry vampire bats / Nevada man invents piano on 21 extra keys / Clever chemist makes chewing gum from soap / Minnesota man claims monkey bowled perfect game / Ingenius scientist invents car of the future / Car gears stick in reverse, daring driver crosses town backwards / Shocking fashion statement terrorizes town / Feisty millionaire fills potholes with hundred-dollar bills.

		Marginal Talent	not iss.
Dec 98.	(cd; as JAD FAIR and JASON WILLETT) (efa 06981-2) **THE MIGHTY SUPER HEROES**		

		Alternative Tentacles	Alternative Tentacles
Apr 99.	(lp/cd; as JAD FAIR and JASON WILLETT) <(VIRUS 228/+CD)> **ENJOYABLE SONGS**		

– Sticky cotton candy dress / Roll Johnny roll / Olive / Valerie / Tabatha / Damage done / Enjoy the morning / The mummy / You can do it if you try / Big boots / Robot vs. the Aztec mummy / Insatiable / Lemondrops and gumdrops / Students of the take / The beast with a million miles / Sweet honey / I dig this mess / Wild Andrea / Eat that cake / Natalie / They could be vampires / Stand up / Bernadette / Invisible ray / Sally / Ask me about vampires / Hand me the lotion / Sweet valentine / Welcome to the night / Lovely Linda / Amelia / You name this song / Tony to Shirley / Animal orchestra / On the town.

		Ubik	not iss.
Sep 99.	(cd; by JAD & DAVID FAIR) (UBIK 3) **SING YOUR LITTLE BABIES TO SLEEP**		-

		Wire Monkey	not iss.
Oct 99.	(cd; by JAD FAIR & THE SHAPIR-O-RAMA) (WRMM 001CD) **I LIKE YOUR FACE**		-

– A certain smile / Starpower / Frankenstein / Lucky / Naoko / Apple pie / Winnie lake / Cupid shot me / A day like any other / Lift me up / The helmet maker's wife / Grand champion / I'll do Mary's wash / Radiation pill / Better than better than before / Bzzzzzz / The death of Clayton Peacock / Kiss of the vampire / It doesn't take a lot / Yellow lemon / Open book / Norman / Goya's head.

―― next was a collaboration with **R. STEVIE MOORE**

		not iss.	Old Gold
Jul 02.	(cd) <002> **FAIR MOORE**	-	

LUCKY SPERMS

are **JAD FAIR + DANIEL JOHNSTON** (also **CHRIS BULTMAN**)

		Jagjaguwar	Jagjaguwar
Nov 01.	(cd) <(JAG 34CD)> **SOMEWHAT HUMOROUS**		Oct01

– Movie / Yes, we can / She starts fire / Cow at the sacrifice / Yellow buttons / Michelle / Ruby Tuesday / Loony take me home / Stale spaghetti / Lost / Grey / All the while / Screw / Pancakes flop / Undying love / Easter bunny / Death / Coffee cup / Melody / Beserk.

Charlie HARPER (see under ⇒ UK SUBS)

Deborah / Debbie HARRY (see under ⇒ BLONDIE)

Charles HAYWARD (see under ⇒ THIS HEAT)

Jowe HEAD (see under ⇒ SWELL MAPS)

HEARTBREAKERS (see under ⇒ THUNDERS, Johnny)

Richard HELL

Born: RICHARD MYERS, 2 Oct'49, Lexington, Kentucky, USA. Raised in Wilmington, Delaware, he later moved to New York in his late teens, where he wrote poetry and experimented with drugs. Along with his sidekick, TOM MILLER and BILLY FICCA, he formed The NEON BOYS in 1971. By '73, they'd metamorphosed into TELEVISION, MYERS adopting his RICHARD HELL moniker (while MILLER became TOM VERLAINE) and helping to initiate the city's new wave/punk scene. As legend has it, a sharp eyed MALCOLM McLAREN was rather taken by HELL's dragged-through-a-hedge-backwards attire and mop of spiked hair, initially attempting to secure his services for his new baby, The SEX PISTOLS; when this failed, well, at least he could go back to England with a few ideas . . . HELL subsequently split with VERLAINE and co., briefly joining JOHNNY THUNDERS in The HEARTBREAKERS, where he co-penned (along with a RAMONE!) the seminal 'CHINESE ROCKS'; like THUNDERS, HELL was well acquainted with the pleasures of heroin, which no doubt accounted for his haphazard career. HELL subsequently formed his own outfit, RICHARD HELL & THE VOIDOIDS along with future LOU REED guitarist ROBERT QUINE, IVAN JULIAN and MARC BELL. They hastily recorded an independently released debut EP before signing to 'Sire'; with the resulting 'BLANK GENERATION' (1977) album, HELL had finally succeeded in capturing his brutally nihilistic poetical/musical vision, if only fleetingly. With his drug problems reaching critical levels, HELL's only release over the next five years was 'THE KID WITH THE REPLACEABLE HEAD', a 1978 NICK LOWE-produced single. A belated follow-up album, 'DESTINY STREET' (1982), eventually appeared in Spring '82, although the momentum had long since dissipated. HELL was absent from the music scene for the next ten years (although he did star in the film, 'Smithereens' as well as scoring a cameo role as MADONNA's boyfriend in 'Desperately Seeking Susan'), finally re-emerging with art-noise veterans, THURSTON MOORE and DON FLEMING for a solo EP, before adding STEVE SHELLEY and recording an album under the DIM STARS moniker. • **Songwriters:** HELL penned all, co-writing 'LOVE COMES IN SPURTS' with VERLAINE. He also covered CRUEL WAY TO GO DOWN (Allen Toussaint) / I'M FREE + VENTILATOR BLUES (Rolling Stones) / CROSSTOWN TRAFFIC (Jimi Hendrix) / WALKING ON THE WATER (Creedence Clearwater Revival) / I WANNA BE YOUR DOG (Stooges); DIM STARS covered RIP OFF (Marc Bolan) / NATCHEZ BURNING (Johnny Burnette). • **Trivia:** He also wrote a column for East Village Eye in the 80's. His biography 'Artifact: Notebooks from Hell' was issued by Hanuman in 1990.

Album rating: BLANK GENERATION (*8) / DESTINY STREET (*5) / R.I.P. – THE ROIR SESSIONS collection (*5) / FUNHUNT live collection (*5) / ANOTHER WORLD collection (*4) / TIME double compilation (*7) / Dim Stars: DIM STARS (*6)

RICHARD HELL & THE VOID-OIDS

RICHARD HELL – vocals, bass / **ROBERT QUINE** (b.30 Dec'42, Akron, Ohio) – guitar, vocals / **IVAN JULIAN** (b.26 Jun'55, Washington, D.C.) – guitar, vocals / **MARC BELL** (b.15 Jul'56, New York City) – drums (ex-WAYNE COUNTY & THE ELECTRIC CHAIRS)

		Stiff	Ork
Nov 76.	(7"ep) (BUY 7) <81976> **(I COULD LIVE WITH YOU IN) ANOTHER WORLD. / YOU GOTTA LOSE / (I BELONG TO THE) BLANK GENERATION**		

(re-iss. Jun94 on 'Overground' 7"ep/cd-ep; OVER 36/+CD)

		Sire	Sire
Sep 77.	(7") (6078 608) <SRE 1003> **BLANK GENERATION. / LOVE COMES IN SPURTS**		

(12") (6078 608) – ('A'side) / Liars beware / Who says.

| Sep 77. | (lp) (SR 6037) <6037> **BLANK GENERATION** | | |

– Love comes in spurts / Liars beware / New pleasure / Betrayal takes two / Down at the rock and roll club / Who says / Blank generation / Walking on the water / The plan / Another world. (cd-iss. Jun90; 7599 26137-2)

―― **FRED MAURO** – drums repl. BELL who joined RAMONES

Richard HELL (cont)

    added **JERRY ANTONIUS** – keyboards, vocals

                                                                Radar not iss.

Nov 78. (7") *(ADA 30)* **THE KID WITH THE REPLACEABLE HEAD. / I'M YOUR MAN**

— **HELL** and **JULIAN** recruited **FRED MAHER** – drums repl. MAURO / **NAUX** (b.29 Jul'51, San Jose, Calif.) – guitar repl. QUINE to LYDIA LUNCH

                                                       I.D. Red Star

May 82. (lp) *(NOSE 2)* **DESTINY STREET**
– The kid with the replaceable head / You gotta move / Going going gone / Lowest common dominator / Downtown at dawn / Time / I can only give you everything / Ignore that door / Staring in her eyes / Destiny street. *<US cd-iss. 1991 on 'Relativity'; 5036> (cd-iss. Sep93 & Mar95 on 'Danceteria'; DAN 9306CD) (cd re-iss. Jul97 on 'Essential'; ESMCD 574) (lp re-iss. Dec00 on 'Munster'; MR 192)*

— Split 1982, RICHARD HELL starred in the film 'Smithereens'. MAHER joined SCRITTI POLITTI. In 1986, he made brief cameo in the film 'Desperately Seeking Susan' as Madonna's boyfriend.

RICHARD HELL

— (solo) with **THURSTON MOORE** + **DON FLEMING** – guitar (of GUMBALL)

                                               Overground not iss.

Feb 92. (7"ep/cd-ep) *(OVER 24/+CD)* **3 NEW SONGS EP**
– The night is coming on / Baby Huey (Baby do you wanna dance?) / Frank Sinatra.

                                                Codex Tim Kerr

Apr 95. (cd-ep/10"ep) *(CODE 3/+X)* <TK 9410 080 CD> **GO NOW** (spoken word)   Oct96

– compilations etc. –

Feb 80. (7"ep; The NEON BOYS) *Shake*; <SHK 101> **DON'T DIE / TIME. / LOVE COMES IN SPURTS ('73) / THAT'S ALL I KNOW (RIGHT NOW)**
(UK-iss.Feb90 as 'TIME EP' on 'Overground' 7"purple; OVER 11)

Dec 84. (c) R.O.I.R.; <A-134> **R.I.P. (live)**
– Love comes in spurts / Can't keep my eyes on you / Hurt me / I'm your man / Betrayal takes two / Crack of dawn / Ignore that door / I live my life / Going, going, gone / I can only give you everything (live) / I been sleepin' on it / Cruel way to go down / The hunter was drowned / Hey sweetheart. *(UK cd-iss. Jun90 on 'Danceteria'; DANCD 040) (lp-iss.Sep92; DANLP 040)*

Apr 90. (c) R.O.I.R.; <A-172> **FUNHUNT (live at the CBGB's & Max's 1978 & 1979)**
– Love comes in spurts / I'm free / Funhunt / Lowest common dominator / Staring in her eyes / You gotta lose / Crosstown traffic / Liars beware / Don't die / Ignore that door / Walking on the water / Ventilator blues / Blank generation / I wanna be your dog / Hell has left the building – All the way. *(cd/lp-iss.Jul92 on 'Danceteria'; DAN CD/LP 088)*

Apr 91. (12"clear/cd-ep; A-side as The NEON BOYS) *Overground; (OVER 19/+CD)* **THAT'S ALL I KNOW (RIGHT NOW) / LOVE COMES IN SPURTS / HIGH HEELED WHEELS. / DON'T DIE / TIME**

Jan 98. (cd) *Overground; <(OVER 36)>* **ANOTHER WORLD**

Mar 02. (d-cd) *Matador; <(OLE 530-2)>* **TIME**
– (R.I.P. + other sessions/live).

DIM STARS

RICHARD HELL + **DON FLEMING** with **THURSTON MOORE** + **STEVE SHELLEY** (both of SONIC YOUTH)

                                       Paperhouse Caroline

Apr 92. (12"ep/cd-ep) *(PAPER 015 T/CD)* <CAROL 1468> **THE PLUG / DIM STAR THEME. / CHRISTIAN RAP ATTACK / YOU GOTTA LOSE**

Jun 92. (cd/lp) *(PAP CD/LP 014)* <CAROL 1724> **DIM STARS**
– She wants to die / All my witches come true / Memo to Marty / Monkey / Natchez burning / Stop breakin' down / Baby Huey (do you wanna dance?) / The night is coming on / Downtown at dawn / Try this / Stray cat generation / Rip off.

Robyn HITCHCOCK

Born: 3 Mar'53, East Grinstead, London, England. Aged 21, he set out for Cambridge to locate the home of his idol, SYD BARRETT but ended up busking instead. 1976 found him forming a string of bands including The WORST FEARS, The BEETLES, MAUREEN & THE MEATPACKERS and, finally by the end of the year, DENNIS AND THE EXPERTS, who were the embryonic SOFT BOYS; alongside ROBYN were ALAN DAVIES, ANDY METCALFE and MORRIS WINDSOR. In March '77, they were offered a deal with indie label, 'Raw', who soon issued their debut release, 'GIVE IT TO THE SOFT BOYS EP'. The record included three trash-punk songs, notably 'WADING THROUGH A VENTILATOR'. KIMBERLEY REW replaced DAVIES before the band embarked on a UK tour supporting ELVIS COSTELLO and The DAMNED. This, in turn, led to a contract with 'Radar', although after only one 45 and many disagreements, they parted company. Taking matters into their own hands, the SOFT BOYS set up their own label, 'Two Crabs', and issued a debut album, 'A CAN OF BEES' (1979). The record was a resounding failure although it has since been the subject of many re-issues in different versions. In 1980 – by which time MATTHEW SELIGMAN had replaced METCALFE – they eventually established themselves, critically at least, with the much heralded follow-up, 'UNDERWATER MOONLIGHT'. HITCHCOCK and Co. had finally managed to translate their quirky post-punk psychedelia to vinyl, pointing the way towards the direction of the frontman's erratic solo career. By the following year The SOFT BOYS had split, playing their final shows to more appreciative US audiences. HITCHCOCK subsequently completed a solo album, 'BLACK SNAKE DIAMOND ROLE' (1981), featuring the cult classics, 'BRENDA'S IRON SLEDGE' and the single, 'THE MAN WHO INVENTED HIMSELF'. Clearly the man had lost none of his BARRETT-esque lyrical daftness in the interim, his tongue-in-cheek, surreal humour occasionally even outstripping CAPTAIN BEEFHEART. After the disastrous STEVE HILLAGE-produced 'GROOVY DECAY' (1982), however, ROBYN decided enough was enough. Until 1984, that is, when he returned with an affecting acoustic album, 'I OFTEN DREAM OF TRAINS', the record seeing him reinstate the SOFT BOYS rhythm section (MORRIS WINDSOR and ANDY METCALFE) under the guise of ROBYN HITCHCOCK & THE EGYPTIANS. In 1985, their first product, 'FEGMANIA!', hit the shops, songs like 'THE MAN WITH THE LIGHTBULB HEAD' and 'EGYPTIAN CREAM', resurrecting the man's public profile. After a few more albums in the mid-80's, he and his band were signed to 'A&M', the resulting album, 'GLOBE OF FROGS' (1988), worthy of anything he'd previously recorded. It brought recommendations from R.E.M., who were longtime fans of HITCHCOCK. His band became firm faves on the US college circuit, especially when indie idols, MICHAEL STIPE and PETER BUCK guested on the two mediocre either-side-of-the-decade albums, 'QUEEN ELVIS' and 'PERSPEX ISLAND'. In 1993, he returned to the eccentric brilliance of old with the highly regarded, John Leckie-produced 'RESPECT', a creative renaissance of sorts which even inspired him to re-unite The SOFT BOYS early in 1994 for some Bosnia benefit concerts. A further couple of solo sets appeared in the mid-90's, 'YOU AND OBLIVION' (1995) and 'MOSS ELIXIR' (1996), the latter with a quintessentially HITCHCOCK, engagingly fantastical life-after-death yarn printed on the inner sleeve. Back to the zaniness of his old self, the man was to bow out of the 90's with a low-key effort, 'JEWELS FOR SOPHIA' (1999). Towards the end of 2002, ROBYN delivered a whole set of Dylan tunes under the guise of 'ROBYN SINGS', while he also found time to re-form The SOFT BOYS for a one-off album 'NEXTDOORLAND' (2002); HITCHCOCK, REW, SELIGMAN and WINDSOR had performed live the previous year. Had it really been over 21 years since their last?

Album rating: A CAN OF BEES (*7) / UNDERWATER MOONLIGHT (*8) / INVISIBLE HITS compilation (*7) / THE SOFT BOYS 1976-81 compilation (*8) / Robyn Hitchcock: BLACK SNAKE DIAMOND ROLE (*6) / GROOVY DECAY (*4) / I OFTEN DREAM OF TRAINS (*7) / FEGMANIA! (*8) / GOTTA LET THIS HEN OUT (*8) / ELEMENT OF LIGHT (*7) / INVISIBLE HITCHCOCK collection (*5) / GLOBE OF FROGS (*7) / QUEEN ELVIS (*7) / EYE (*7) / PERSPEX ISLAND (*4) / RESPECT (*5) / YOU & OBLIVION (*4) / MOSS ELIXIR (*6) / GREATEST HITS compilation (*8) / JEWELS FOR SOPHIA (*5) / Soft Boys: NEXTDOORLAND (*7)

SOFT BOYS

ROBYN HITCHCOCK – vocals, guitar, bass / **ALAN DAVIS** – guitar / **ANDY METCALFE** – bass / **MORRIS WINDSOR** (aka OTIS FAGG) – drums

                                             Raw not iss.

Jul 77. (7"ep) *(RAW 5)* **GIVE IT TO THE SOFT BOYS**
– Wading through a ventilator / The face of death / Hear my brane. *(re-iss. Oct79; RAW 37)*

— **KIMBERLEY REW** – guitar, harmonica, vocals repl. DAVIS

                                             Radar not iss.

May 78. (7") *(ADA 8)* **(I WANT TO BE AN) ANGELPOISE LAMP. / FAT MAN'S SON**

                                           Two Crabs not iss.

Feb 79. (lp) *(CLAW 1001)* **A CAN OF BEES**
– Give it to the soft boys / The pigworker / Human music / Leppo and the jooves / The rat's prayer / Do the chisel / Sandra's having her brain out / The return of the sacred crab / Cold turkey / Skool dinner blues / Wading through a ventilator. *(re-iss. Feb80 on 'Aura'; AUL 709) (re-iss. Jun84 on 'Two Crabs'; same) (cd-iss. Feb95 on 'Rhino'+=; RCD 20231) – Sandra's having her brain out / Skool dinner blues / Fatman's son / (I want to be an) Angelpoise lamp / Ugly Nora. <cd re-iss. Nov92 & May96 on 'Rykodisc'; RCD 20231>*

— In Oct'79, 'Raw' quickly withdrew release of 45 'WHERE ARE THE PRAWNS'; *RAW 41*

— **MATTHEW SELIGMAN** – bass, keyboards (ex-SW9) repl. ANDY to FISH TURNED HUMAN

                                    Armageddon Armageddon

Jun 80. (7"ep) *(AEP 002)* **NEAR THE SOFT BOYS**
– Kingdom of love / Vegetable man / Strange.

Jul 80. (lp) *(ARM 1)* **UNDERWATER MOONLIGHT**
– I wanna destroy you / Kingdom of love / Positive vibrations / I got the job / Insanely jealous / Tonight / You'll have to go sideways / Old pervert / The queen of eyes / Underwater moonlight. *(cd-iss. Feb95 on 'Rhino'+=; – Vegetable man / Strange / Only the stones remain / Where are the prawns / Dreams / Black snake diamond role / There's nobody like you / Song No.4. (<cd re-iss. Nov92 & May96 on 'Rykodisc'; RCD 20232>) (<re-iss. Mar01 on 'Matador' as t-lp+7"/d-cd+=; OLE 500-1/-2>) – (extra tracks).*

Aug 80. (7") *(AS 005)* **I WANNA DESTROY YOU. / (I'M AN) OLD PERVERT (DISCO)**

Oct 81. (7") *(AS 029)* **ONLY THE STONES REMAIN. / THE ASKING TREE**

Mar 82. (lp) *(BYE 1)* **TWO HALVES FOR THE PRICE OF ONE** (half live)   Oct81
– Only the stones remain / Where are the prawns / The bells of Rhymney / There's nobody like you / Innocent box / Black snake diamond role / Underwater moonlight / Astronomy domine / Outlaw blues / Mystery train. *<US-title; ONLY THE STONES REMAIN>*

— disbanded in 1982, SELIGMAN who joined The THOMPSON TWINS

ROBYN HITCHCOCK

was already solo, using session people, including most ex-SOFT BOYS

Armageddon not iss.

Apr 81. (7") *(AS 008)* **THE MAN WHO INVENTED HIMSELF. / DANCING ON GOD'S THUMB**
 (free 7"flexi w-above) (4SPURT 1) IT'S A MYSTIC TRIP. / GROOVING ON AN INNER PLANE
May 81. (lp) *(ARM 4)* **BLACK SNAKE DIAMOND ROLE**
 – The man who invented himself / Brenda's iron sledge / Do policemen sing? / The lizard / Meat / Acid bird / I watch the cars / Out of the picture / City of shame / Love. *(re-iss. May86 on 'Aftermath'; AFT 1) (cd-iss. 1988; AFTCD 1) (cd re-iss. Feb95 on 'Rhino-Sequel'+=; RSACD 819)* – Dancing on God's thumb / Happy the golden prince / I watch the cars / It was the night / Grooving on an inner plane.

— now w/ **SARA LEE** – bass / **ANTHONY THISTLETHWAITE** – sax / **ROD JOHNSON** – drums repl. SELIGMAN to THOMAS DOLBY (and REW who re-joined The WAVES, who added Czech KATRINA; now KATRINA & THE WAVES)

Albion not iss.

Mar 82. (7") *(ION 103)* **AMERICA. / IT WAS THE NIGHT / HOW DO YOU WORK THIS THING?**
Mar 82. (lp) *(ALB 110)* **GROOVY DECAY**
 – Night ride to Trinidad / Fifty-two stations / Young people scream / The rain / America / The cars she used to drive / Grooving on an inner plane / St. Petersburg / When I was a kid / Midnight fish. *(some with free various 'Albion' artists; RH track '52 STATIONS') (re-iss. Dec85 on 'Midnight Music'; CHIME 00.15) (cd-iss. Nov89 & Oct94 on 'Line'; ALCD 9.000008) (cd-iss. Feb95 as 'GRAVY DECO (THE COMPLETE GROOVY DECAY / DECOY SESSIONS)' on 'Rhino-Sequel'+=; RSACD 820)* – (extra mixes)

Midnight Music   Slash

Nov 82. (7"m) *(DING 2)* **EATEN BY HER OWN DINNER. / LISTENING TO THE HIGSONS / DR. STICKY**
 (12"ep; Oct86) (DONG 2) – ('A'side) / Grooving on an inner plane / Messages of the dark / The abandoned brain / Happy the golden prince.

— now w/ **WINDSOR + METCALFE** / + **ROGER JACKSON** – keyboards

Aug 84. (lp) *(CHIME 00.05S)* **I OFTEN DREAM OF TRAINS**
 – Nocturne / Uncorrected personality traits / Sounds great when you're dead / Flavour of night / This could be the day / Trams of old London / Furry green atom bowl / Heart full of leaves / Autumn is your last chance / I often dream of trains. *(cd-iss. Oct86; CHIME 00.05CD) (cd re-iss. Feb95 on 'Rhino-Sequel'+=; RSACD 821)* – Ye sleeping knights of Jesus / Sometimes I wish I was a pretty girl / Cathedral / Mellow together / Winter love / The bones in the ground / My favourite buildings / I used to say I love you.

Nov 84. (12"m) *(DONG 8)* **THE BELLS OF RHYMNEY / FALLING LEAVES. / WINTER LOVE / THE BONES IN THE GROUND**

ROBIN HITCHCOCK & THE EGYPTIANS

— same as solo line-up

Mar 85. (lp) *(CHIME 00.08)* <25316> **FEGMANIA!**
 – Egyptian cream / Another bubble / I'm only you / My wife and my dead wife / Goodnight I say / The man with the lightbulb head / Insect mother / Strawberry mind / Glass / The fly / Heaven. *(cd-iss. 1986 +=; CHIME 00.08CD)* – The bells of rhymney / Dwarfbeat / Some body. *(re-iss. Mar95 on 'Rhino-Sequel'+=; RSACD 822)* – Egyptian cream (demo) / Heaven (live) / Insect mother (demo) / Egyptian cream (live) / The pit of souls: I) The plateau – II) The descent – III) The spinal dance – IV) Flight of the iron lung.

May 85. (12"m) *(DONG 12)* **HEAVEN. / DWARFBEAT / SOME BODY**

Midnight   Relativity

Oct 85. (lp/c) *(CHIME 00.15 S/C)* **GOTTA LET THIS HEN OUT (live)**
 – Sometimes I wish I was a pretty girl / Kingdom of love / Acid bird / The cars she used to drive / My wife and my dead wife / Brenda's iron sledge / The fly * / Only the stones remain * / Egyptian cream * / Leppo & the Jooves / America / Heaven / Listening to The Higsons / Face of death. *(cd-iss. Oct86 += *; CHIME 00.15CD) (re-iss. cd Mar95 on 'Rhino-Sequel'; RSACD 823)*
Feb 86. (12"ep) *(DONG 17)* **BRENDA'S IRON SLEDGE (live). / ONLY THE STONES REMAIN (live) / THE PIT OF SOULS (part I-IV)**
Mar 86. (pic-lp)(c) *(BM 80)(BMC 80-4) <EMC 8074>* **EXPLODING IN SILENCE**

Glass Fish   Combat

Jun 86. (lp) *(MOIST 2)* **INVISIBLE HITCHCOCK** (compilation)
 – All I wanna do is fall in love / Give me a spanner, Ralph / A skull, a suitcase, and a long red bottle of wine / It's a mystic trip / My favourite buildings / Falling leaves / Eaten by her own dinner / Pits of souls / Trash / Mr. Deadly / Star of hairs / Messages of dark / Vegetable friend / I got a message for you / Abandoned brain / Point it at gran / Let there be more darkness / Blues in A. *(re-iss. cd Mar95 on 'Rhino-Sequel'+=; RSACD 825)* – Listening to the higsons / Dr. Sticky.
Sep 86. (lp/c/cd) *(MOIST 3/+CD) <885618130>* **ELEMENT OF LIGHT**
 – If you were a priest / Winchester / Somewhere apart / Ted, Woody and Junior / The president / Raymond Chandler evening / Bass / Airscape / Never stop bleeding / Lady Waters & the hooded one / The black crow knows / The crawling / The leopard / Tell me about your drugs. *(re-iss. cd Mar95 on 'Rhino-Sequel'+=; RSACD 824)* – The can opener / Raymond Chandler evening (demo) / President (demo) / If you were a priest (demo) / Airscape (live) / The leopard (demo).
Jan 87. (7") *(OOZE 1)* **IF YOU WERE A PRIEST / THE CRAWLING**
 (12"+=) (OOZE 1T) – Tell me about your drugs / The can opener.

A&M   A&M

Feb 88. (lp/c/cd) *<(AMA/AMC/CDA 5182)>* **GLOBE OF FROGS**
 – Trapped flesh Mandela / Vibrating / Balloon man / Luminous rose / Sleeping with your devil mask on / Unsettled / Flesh number one / Chinese bones / A globe of frogs / Beatle Dennis / The shapes between us / Turn to animals.
Apr 88. (7") **GLOBE OF FROGS. / BALLOON MAN**

— still with **METCALFE + WINDSOR** + guest **PETER BUCK** – guitar (of R.E.M.)

Mar 89. (lp/c/cd) *<395241-1/-4/-2>* **QUEEN ELVIS**
 – Madonna of the wasps / The Devils coachman / Wax doll / Knife / Swirling / One long pair of eyes / Veins of the Queen / Freeze / Autumn sea / Superman. *(cd+=)* – Veins of the Queen (royal mix) / Freeze (shatter mix).
Jul 89. (7") **MADONNA OF THE WASPS. / RULING CLASS**
 (12"+=/cd-s+=) – Veins of the queen (royal mix) / Freeze (shatter mix).

ROBIN HITCHCOCK

Glass Fish   Twin/Tone

Nov 90. (lp/cd) *(MOIST 8/CD) <89175>* **EYE**
 – Cynthia mask / Certainly clickot / Queen Elvis / Flesh cartoons / Chinese water python / Executioner / Linctus House / Sweet ghosts of light / College of ice / Transparent lover / Beautiful girl / Raining twilight coast / Clean Steve / Agony of pleasure / Glass hotel / Satellite / Aquarium / Queen Elvis II. *(UK cd-iss. Mar95 on 'Rhino-Sequel'+=; RSACD 826)* – Raining twilight coast (demo) / Agony of pleasure (demo) / Queen Elvis III (demo).

Go! Discs   A&M

Oct 91. (cd/c) *(828 292-2/-4) <75021 5368-2>* **PERSPEX ISLAND**   Aug91
 – Oceanside / So you think you're in love / Birds in perspex / Ultra unbelievable love / Vegetations and dines / Lysander / Child of the universe / She doesn't exist / Ride / If you go away / Earthly Paradise.
Jan 92. (7") *(GOD 65)* **SO YOU THINK YOU'RE IN LOVE. / WATCH YOUR INTELLIGENCE**
 (12"+=/cd-s+=) (GOD X/CD 65) – Dark green energy.
 (above featured STIPE + BUCK of R.E.M.)
Jun 93. (cd/c; with ARCHIE ROACH) *(RHE CD/MC 1) <540064>* **RESPECT**   Feb93
 – The yip song / The arms of love / The moon inside / Railway shoes / When I was dead / The wreck of Arthur Lee / Driving aloud (radio storm) / erpnt at the gates of wisdom / Then you're dust / Wafflehead. *(cd re-iss. Oct96; same)*

Rhino-Sequel   Rhino-Sequel

Mar 95. (cd) *(<RSACD 827>)* **YOU & OBLIVION**
 – You've got / Don't you / Birdshead / She reached for a light / Victorian squid / Captain Dry / Mr. Rock I / August hair / Take your knife out of my back / Surgery / The dust / Polly on the shore / Aether / Fiend before the shrine / Nothing / Into it / Stranded in the future / Keeping still / September clones / Ghost ship / You & me / If I could look.
Feb 95. (cd-ep) *(CDSEQ 2)* **MY WIFE AND MY DEAD WIFE / I SOMETHING YOU / ZIPPER IN MY SPINE / MAN WITH A WOMAN'S SHADOW**

— now with **DENI BONET** – violin / **NITSHUKS BONGA** – sax / **TIM KEEGAN** – guitar / **JAKE KYLE** – bass / **PATCH HANNAN** – drums / **MORRIS WINDSOR** – vocals, percussion / etc

Warners   Warners

Aug 96. (cd/c) *<9362 46302-2/-4>* **MOSS ELIXIR**
 – Sinister but she was happy / The Devil's radio / Heliotrope / Alright, yeah / Filthy bird / The speed of things / Beautiful queen / Man with a woman's shadow / I am not me / De Chirico Street / You and oblivion / This is how it feels.
Sep 99. (cd) *<9362 47433-2>* **JEWELS FOR SOPHIA**   Jul99
 – Mexican God / Cheese alarm / Viva! sea-tac / I feel beautiful / You've got a sweet mouth on you, baby / NASA clapping / Sally was a legend / Antwoman / Elizabeth Jade / No, I don't remember Guildford / Dark princess / Jewels for Sophia.

– compilations, etc. –

May 83. (12"ep) *Albion; (12ION 1036)* **NIGHT RIDE TO TRINIDAD (long version). / KINGDOM OF LOVE / MIDNIGHT FISH**
1984. (7"flexi; w-mag) *Bucketful Of Brains; (BOB 8)* **HAPPY THE GOLDEN PRINCE**
Jun 94. (cd) *Strange Roots; (ROOTCD 001)* **KERSHAW SESSIONS**
 (re-iss. Jul98 on 'Strange Fruit'; SFRSCD 075)
Sep 96. (cd) *A&M; (540 570-2)* **GREATEST HITS**
Jan 98. (cd) *Rhino-Sequel; (<RSACD 957>)* **THE COLLECTION: UNCORRECTED PERSONALITY TRAITS**
Oct 98. (cd) *Strange Fruit; (CAFECD 004)* **LIVE AT THE CAMBRIDGE FOLK FESTIVAL (live)**
 (re-iss. Jul00 on 'Varese Sarabande'; 0302061070-2)
Nov 98. (cd) *Warners; (<9362 46846-2>)* **STOREFRONT HITCHCOCK: MUSIC FROM DEMME PICTURE (live)**   Oct97
 – 1974 / Let's go thundering / I'm only you / Glass hotel / I something you / Yip! song / Freeze / Alright, yeah / Where do you go when you die? / The wind cries Mary / No, I don't remember Guildford / Beautiful queen.
2000. (cd) *Editions PAF; <PAF 001CD>* **A SONG FOR BRAM**
Jul 02. (d-cd) *Editions PAF; (<PAF 002CD>)* **ROBYN SINGS: A TRIBUTE TO BOB DYLAN**   Nov02
 – Visions of Johanna / Tangled up in blue / Not dark yet / 4th time around / Desolation row / It's all over now, baby blue / Dignity / Visions of Johanna // live:- Tell me mama / I don't believe you / Baby let me follow you down / Just like Tom Thumb's blues / Leopard-skin pillbox hat / One too many mornings / Ballad of a thin man / Like a rolling stone.

SOFT BOYS

ROBYN HITCHCOCK with **KIMBERLEY REW, MATTHEW SELIGMAN + MORRIS WINDSOR**

Matador   Matador

Sep 02. (cd/lp) *(<OLE 553-2/-1>)* **NEXTDOORLAND**
 – I love Lucy / Pulse of my heart / Mr. Kennedy / Unprotected love / My mind is connected to your dreams / Sudden town / Strings / Japanese captain / La cherite / Lions and tigers.

– compilations, others, etc –

1982. (7"w/mag) *Bucketful Of Brains; (BOB 1)* **LOVE POISONING. / WHEN I WAS A KID**
Nov 83. (7") *Midnight Music; (DING 4)* **HE'S A REPTILE. / SONG NO.4**
Nov 83. (7") *Midnight Music; (CHIME 0002)* **INVISIBLE HITS**
 – Wey-wey-hep-uh-hole * / Have a heart Betty (I'm not fireproof) * / The asking tree / Muriel's hoof / The rout of the clones / Let me put it next to you / When I was a kid * / Rock & roll toilet * / Love poisoning * / Empty girl / Blues in the dark / He's a reptile. *(cd-iss. Feb96 on 'Rhino' +=;)* – (alt.takes of *). *(cd re-iss. May96 on 'Rykodisc'; RCD 20233)*
Aug 85. (lp/pic-lp) *De Laurean; (SOFT 1/+P)* **WADING THROUGH A VENTILATOR**

1987.	(7"flexi; w-mag) *Bucketful Of Brains; (BOB 17)* **DECK OF CARDS. /** Robyn Hitchcock & Peter Buck: **FLESH NO.1**	-	-
Dec 87.	(lp) *Midnight Music; (MOIST 4)* **LIVE AT THE PORTLAND ARMS (live)**		
1989.	(7"yellow,7"white; ltd) *Overground; (OVER 4)* **THE FACE OF DEATH. / THE YODELLING HOOVER**		-
Sep 93.	(d-cd) *Rykodisc; (RCD 10234-35)* **THE SOFT BOYS 1976-1981**		-
	– (mostly all of their material).		

Kristian HOFFMAN (see under ⇒ MUMPS)

HOLLYWOOD BRATS

Formed: London, England ... 1973 by Canadian frontman ANDREW MATHESON, Norwegian keyboard man CASINO STEEL, along with EUNON BRADY, WAYNE MANOR and LOUIS SPARKS. Despite their failure to secure a UK deal, the 'BRATS did actually record an album, 'GROWN UP WRONG', for a Scandinavian label although it was subsequently withdrawn. Definitely ahead of their time, the band were belatedly acknowledged as progenitors of underground sleaze/glam-punk upon the release of the album (now re-titled simply, 'HOLLYWOOD BRATS') by 'Cherry Red' at the turn of the decade. By this point, however, they had been defunct for nearly five years, STEEL having had minor success with power-pop punks, The BOYS.

Album rating: HOLLYWOOD BRATS (*6)

ANDREW MATHESON – vocals / **CASINO STEEL** – keyboards / **EUNON BRADY** – guitar / **WAYNE MANOR** – bass / **LOUIS SPARKS** – drums

— split in 1975 with an impending album, 'GROWN UP WRONG', withdrawn from release in Scandinavia and America; the 1973 recordings surfaced below. MATHESON and BRADY went into sessions with WRECKLESS ERIC's LAST ORDERS, while STEEL found a little fame with The BOYS.

– posthumous, etc. –

		Cherry Red	not iss.
May 79.	(7") *(CHERRY 6)* **THEN HE KISSED ME. / SICK ON YOU**		-
Feb 80.	(lp) *(ARED 6)* **HOLLYWOOD BRATS**		-
	– Chez maximes / Another schoolday / Nightmare / Empty bottles / Courtesan / Then he kissed me / Tumble with me / Zurich 17 / Southern belles / Drowning sorrows / Sick on you. *(cd-iss. Dec93 & Apr00; CDMRED 106) (lp re-iss. May99 on 'Get Back'; GET 047)*		

HUMAN LEAGUE

Formed: Sheffield, England ... Autumn 1977 by computer operators MARTYN WARE and IAN CRAIG-MARSH. As The FUTURE, with vocalist ADI NEWTON, they recruited former hospital porter PHIL OAKEY, who soon replaced ADI (later to CLOCKDVA). Now as HUMAN LEAGUE, the trio recorded demo, which was accepted by Edinburgh-based indie 'Fast', run by Bob Last. Their debut 45 'BEING BOILED', became NME single of the week in mid-78. They added ADRIAN WRIGHT on visuals and synths, and after a dire instrumental EP 'THE DIGNITY OF LABOUR', they signed to 'Virgin' in Apr'79. Their first 45 for the label, 'I DON'T DEPEND ON YOU', was credited to The MEN, but their credibility was restored later that year when 'EMPIRE STATE HUMAN', nearly gave them a hit. This was duly followed by a debut album, 'REPRODUCTION', which failed to build on their early promise. In Spring 1980, they went into UK Top 60 with double-7" EP, 'HOLIDAY '80', and Top 20 with album, 'TRAVELOGUE'. In October '80, OAKEY and WRIGHT brought in teenage girls JOANNE and SUZANNE to replace WARE and CRAIG-MARSH who left to form HEAVEN 17. Twelve months later, with new additions IAN BURDEN and JO CALLIS, they were at No.1 with the 'DARE' album, and 'DON'T YOU WANT ME' single, which also peaked at the top in the States. By now, the experimental industrial leanings of their early work had given way to a chart dominating new romantic/pop synth sound which made 'DARE' one of the definitive albums of the era. They were also responsible, or at least OAKEY was, for perhaps the worst 80's haircut of them all (yes, even worse than the mullet), the accident-with-a-pair-of-garden-shears number that featured one side long and erm . . . one side short! Barnet's aside, the hits were consistent ('KEEP FEELING FASCINATION', 'MIRROR MAN', 'THE LEBANON'), if not exactly prolific and, like many similar 80's acts, by the time they got around to releasing a follow-up set, the fuss had died down. Nevertheless, 'HYSTERIA' (1984) made the UK Top 3, while OAKEY teamed up with disco veteran, GIORGIO MORODER, for the soppy but brilliant 'TOGETHER IN ELECTRIC DREAMS', another massive Top 5 hit in Autumn '84 (the pair subsequently recorded a full length album together, 'CHROME'). Produced by the soul/R&B team of Jimmy Jam and Terry Lewis, 'CRASH' (1986) didn't do the band any favours, although it did spawn the melancholy 'HUMAN', a surprise US No.1 and their biggest hit single since the early 80's heyday. Though a 1988 greatest hits album kept the band's profile high, poor sales of 'ROMANTIC' (1990) saw the end of their tenure with 'Virgin', and it looked like permanent relegation was imminent. A new deal with 'East West' and a 1994 Top 10 album, 'OCTOPUS', suggested otherwise, things coming full circle when a remixed version of 'DON'T YOU WANT ME' made the Top 20 in late '95. Conspicuous only by his absence, PHIL OAKEY has since provided some vocals (alongside 60's crooner, TONY CHRISTIE) on the ALL SEEING I album in '99. With 'SECRETS' (2001), The HUMAN LEAGUE entered their fourth decade of recording although you wouldn't have guessed it by OAKEY's ever youthful looks. A fair attempt at reconciling current trends in electronic music with their classic sound, this largely instrumental effort scraped into the UK Top 50. • **Songwriters:** WARE and CRAIG-MARSH before their departure, and OAKEY and WRIGHT on all since early 80's. The 90's, featured OAKEY composing alongside new member NEIL SUTTON. Covered:- YOU'VE LOST THAT LOVIN' FEELIN' (Righteous Brothers) / ROCK'N'ROLL (Gary Glitter) / NIGHTCLUBBIN' (Iggy Pop) / ONLY AFTER DARK (Mick Ronson).

Album rating: REPRODUCTION (*5) / TRAVELOGUE (*5) / DARE (*8) / LOVE AND DANCING mixes set (*4) / HYSTERIA (*5) / CRASH (*5) / GREATEST HITS compilation (*8) / ROMANTIC? (*4) / OCTOPUS (*6) / SECRETS (*4) / Phil Oakey & Giorgio Moroder: CHROME (*4)

PHIL OAKEY (b. 2 Oct'55) – vocals / **IAN CRAIG-MARSH** (b.19 Nov'56) – synthesizers / **MARTYN WARE** (b.19 May'56) – synthesizers

		Fast	not iss.
Jun 78.	(7") *(FAST 4)* **BEING BOILED. / CIRCUS OF DEATH**		-
	(re-iss. Jan82 reached No.6 UK; same)		

— added **ADRIAN WRIGHT** (b.30 Dec'56) – synthesizers, visuals

| Apr 79. | (12"ep) *(FAST 10)* **THE DIGNITY OF LABOUR** | | - |
| | – (part 1 / part 2 / part 3 / part 4) *(contains free spoken word flexi; VF 1)* | | |

		Virgin	A&M
Jul 79.	(7"/12"; as The MEN) *(VS 269/+12)* **I DON'T DEPEND ON YOU. / CRUEL (instrumental)**		-
Sep 79.	(7") *(VS 294)* **EMPIRE STATE HUMAN. / INTRODUCING**		-
Oct 79.	(lp/c) *(V/TCV 2133)* **REPRODUCTION**		-
	– Almost medieval / Circus of death / The path of least resistance / Blind youth / The word before last / Empire state human / Morale / You've lost that lovin' feelin' / Austerity / Girl one / Zero as a limit. *(re-pro.Aug81, hit UK No.49) (re-iss. Jun88 lp/c; OVED/+C 114) (cd-iss. Dec88; CDV 2133)*		
Apr 80.	(d7"ep) *(SV 105)* **HOLIDAY '80**	56	-
	– Rock'n'roll / Being boiled / Nightclubbing / Dancevision. *(re-iss. Nov81 as 12"ep+=)* – Marianne. *(hit UK No.46)*		
May 80.	(lp/c) *(T/TCV 2160)* **TRAVELOGUE**	16	-
	– The black hit of space / Only after dark / Life kills / Dreams of leaving / Toyota city / Crow and a baby / The touchables / Gordon's Gin / Being boiled / WXJL tonight. *(re-iss. Jun88 lp/c; OVED/+C 115)*		
Jun 80.	(7") *(VS 351)* **ONLY AFTER DARK. / TOYOTA CITY**	62	-
	(free 7" w/) – EMPIRE STATE HUMAN. / INTRODUCING		

— **JO CATHERALL** (b.18 Sep'62) & **SUSANNE SULLEY** (b.22 Mar'63) – b.vocals repl. WARE and MARSH who formed HEAVEN 17. also added **IAN BURDEN** (b.24 Dec'57) – bass, synthesizers

| Feb 81. | (7") *(VS 395)* **BOYS AND GIRLS. / TOM BAKER** | 48 | - |
| Apr 81. | (7"/ext.12"; as HUMAN LEAGUE RED) *(VS 416/+12)* **THE SOUND OF THE CROWD. / ('A'instrumental)** | 12 | - |

— added **JO CALLIS** (b. 2 May'55, Glasgow, Scotland) – guitar (ex-REZILLOS, ex-BOOTS FOR DANCING, ex-SHAKE)

Jul 81.	(7"; as HUMAN LEAGUE RED) *(VS 435)* **LOVE ACTION (I BELIEVE IN LOVE). / HARD TIMES**	3	Apr82
	(12"+=) *(VS 435-12)* – ('A'&'B'instrumental). *(cd-ep.iss.Jun88; – the four 12"tracks)*		
Oct 81.	(7"; as HUMAN LEAGUE BLUE) *(VS 453)* **OPEN YOUR HEART. / NON-STOP**	6	-
	(12"+=) *(VS 453-12)* – ('A'instrumental) / ('B'instrumental).		
Oct 81.	(lp/pic-lp/c) *(T/TP/TCV 2192)* <4892> **DARE**	1	3 Feb82
	– Things that dreams are made of / Open your heart / The sound of the crowd / Darkness / Do or die / Get Carter / I am the law / Seconds / Love action (I believe in love) / Don't you want me. *(re-iss. 1983; OVED 177) (re-iss. Sep90 lp/c; OVED/+C 333) (cd-iss. Nov01; SACDV 2192)*		
Nov 81.	(7"; as HUMAN LEAGUE 100) *(VS 466)* <2397> **DON'T YOU WANT ME. / SECONDS**	1	1 Feb82
	(2"+=) *(VS 466-12)* – ('A'extended).		
Jul 82.	(lp/c; as LEAGUE UNLIMITED ORCHESTRA) *(OVED/OVEC 6)* <3209> **LOVE AND DANCING**	6	Sep92
	– (instrumental versions of "DARE" except;) / Get Carter / Darkness. *(cd-iss. Jan86; CDOVED 6)*		
Aug 82.	(7") **THINGS THAT DREAMS ARE MADE OF. / ('A' instrumental)**		-
Oct 82.	(7"; as LEAGUE UNLIMITED ORCHESTRA) **DON'T YOU WANT ME. / (part 2)**		-
Nov 82.	(7"/7"pic-d) *(VS/+Y 522)* **MIRROR MAN. / (YOU REMIND ME OF) GOLD**	2	-
	(ext.12"+=) *(VS 522-12)* – Gold (instrumental).		
Apr 83.	(7"; as HUMAN LEAGUE RED) *(VS 569)* <2547> **KEEP FEELING) FASCINATION. / TOTAL PANIC**	2	8 May83
	(ext.12"+=) *(VS 569-12)* – ('A'improvisation).		
Jul 83.	(m-lp) <12501> **FASCINATION** (import, recent hits)	-	22
Sep 83.	(7") <2587> **MIRROR MAN. / NON-STOP**	-	30
Apr 84.	(7") *(VS 672)* <2641> **THE LEBANON. / THIRTEEN**	11	64 Jul84
	(ext.12"+=) *(VS 672-12)* – ('A'instrumental).		
May 84.	(lp/c/cd) *(T/TCV/CDV 2315)* <4923> **HYSTERIA**	3	62
	– I'm coming back / I love you too much / Rock me again and again and again and again and again and again / Louise / The Lebanon / Betrayed / The sign / So hurt / Life on your own / Don't you know I want you. *(re-iss. Feb88 lp/c; OVED/+C 177)*		
Jun 84.	(7") *(VS 688)* **LIFE ON YOUR OWN. / THE WORLD TONIGHT**	16	-
	(12"+=) *(VS 688-12)* – ('A'extended).		
Aug 84.	(7") **DON'T YOU KNOW I WANT TO. / THIRTEEN**	-	-
Oct 84.	(7"/7"pic-d)(12") *(VS/+Y 723)(VS 723-12)* **LOUISE. / THE SIGN**	13	-
Oct 84.	(7") **LOUISE. / THE WORLD TONIGHT**	-	-

HUMAN LEAGUE (cont)

— Trimmed down to main trio of **PHIL, SUSANNE, JOANNE** plus **ADRIAN / JIM RUSSELL** – synthesizer repl. BURDEN and CALLIS

				UK	US
Aug 86.	(7") *(VS 880)* <2861>	**HUMAN.** / ('A'instrumental)		8	1
	(ext.12"+=) *(VS 880-12)* – ('A'acappella).				
Sep 86.	(lp/c/cd) *(V/TCV/CDV 2391)* <5129>	**CRASH**		7	24

– Money / Swang / Human / Jam / Are you ever coming back? / I need your loving / Party / Love on the run / The real thing / Love is all that matters.

Nov 86.	(7") *(VS 900)* **I NEED YOUR LOVING.** / ('A'instrumental)	72	-
	(ext.12"+=) *(VS 900-12)* – ('A'dub).		
Nov 86.	(7") <2893> **I NEED YOUR LOVING.** / **ARE YOU EVER COMING BACK**	-	44
Jan 87.	(7") **LOVE IS ALL THAT MATTERS.** / ('A'instrumental)	-	-
Apr 87.	(7") **ARE YOU EVER COMING BACK.** / **JAM**	-	-
Oct 88.	(7") *(VS 1025)* **LOVE IS ALL THAT MATTERS.** / **I LOVE YOU TOO MUCH**	41	
	('B'dub.12"+=/'B'dub.cd-s+=) *(VS T/CD 1025)* – ('A'extended).		
Nov 88.	(lp/c/cd/pic-cd) *(HL TV/MC/CD/CDP 1)* <75021 5227-1/-4/-2> **GREATEST HITS** (compilation)	3	

– Mirror man / (Keep feeling) Fascination / The sound of the crowd / The Lebanon / Human / Together in electric dreams (PHIL OAKEY & GIORGIO MORODER) / Don't you want me? / Being boiled (re-boiled) / Love action (I believe in love) / Louise / Open your heart / Love is all that matters / Life on your own. *(re-iss. Nov95 cd/c;)*

— The basic trio, added **RUSSELL BENNETT** – guitar / **NEIL SUTTON** – keyboards

Aug 90.	(7"/c-s) *(VS/+C 1262)* <1520> **HEART LIKE A WHEEL.** / **REBOUND**	29	32 Sep90
	(12"+=) *(VST 1262)* – ('A'extended).		
	(cd-s++=) *(VSCDT 1262)* – ('A'remix).		
	(cd-s++=) *(VSCDX 1262)* – A doorway (dub mix).		
Sep 90.	(cd/c/lp) *(V/TCV/CDV 2624)* <75021 5316-2/-4/-1> **ROMANTIC?**	24	

– Kiss the future / A doorway / Heart like a wheel / Men are dreamers / Mister Moon and Mister Sun / Soundtrack to a generation / Rebound / The stars are going out / Let's get together again / Get it right this time.

Nov 90.	(7"/c-s) *(VS/+C 1303)* **SOUNDTRACK TO A GENERATION.** / ('A'instrumental)	-	-
	(12"+=) *(VST 1303)* – ('A'-Orbit mix).		
	(cd-s+=) *(VSCDT 1303)* – ('A'-Pan Belgian mix).		
	(cd-s) *(VSCDX 1303)* – ('A'-Pan Belgian dub) / ('A'-808 instrumental mix) / ('A'-Dave Dodd's mix) / ('A'-acappalla).		

East West   East West

Dec 94.	(c-s) *(YZ 882C)* <64443> **TELL ME WHEN.** / ('A'mix 1)	6	31 Mar95
	(cd-s+=) *(YZ 882CD1)* – Kimi ni mune kyun / The bus to Crookes.		
	(12"/cd-s) *(YZ 882 T/CD2)* – ('A'side) / ('A'-Overworld mix) / ('A'-Red Jerry mix) / ('A'-Strictly blind dub mix).		
Jan 95.	(cd/c/lp) *(4509 98750-2/-4/-1)* <61788> **OCTOPUS**	6	

– Tell me when / These are the days / One man in my heart / Words / Filling up with Heaven / House full of nothing / John Cleese; is he funny? / Never again / Cruel young lover.

Mar 95.	(c-s/cd-s) *(YZ 904 C/CD1)* **ONE MAN IN MY HEART** / **THESE ARE THE DAYS** (Ba ba mix)	13	-
	(cd-s+=) *(YZ 904CD2)* – These are the days (sonic radiation) / ('A'version).		
	(12") *(YZ 904T)* – ('B'side) / ('B'-Symphone Ba Ba mix) / ('B'instrumental) / ('A'-T.O.E.C. unplugged).		
Jun 95.	(c-s/cd-s) *(YZ 944 C/CD1)* **FILLING UP WITH HEAVEN** / **JOHN CLEESE, IS HE FUNNY?**	36	-
	(cd-s) *(YZ 944CD2)* – ('A'side) / ('A'-Hardfloor mix) / ('A'-Neil McLellen mix).		
Jan 96.	(c-s) *(EW 020C)* **STAY WITH ME TONIGHT** / ('A'mix)	40	-
	(cd-s) *(EW 020CD)* – ('A'mixes).		

Papillion   Ark 21

Jul 01.	(cd-s) *(BTFLYS 0012)* <1220> **ALL I EVER WANTED** / **TRANQUILITY** / **ALL I EVER WANTED** (vanity case mix)	47	
	(cd-s) *(BTFLYX 0012)* – ('A'-original) / ('A'-Oliver Lieb mix).		
Aug 01.	(cd) *(BTFLYCD 0019)* <810075> **SECRETS**	44	

– All I ever wanted / Nervous / Love me madly? / Shameless / 122.3 bpm / Never give your heart / Ran / The snake / Ringinglow / Liar / Lament / Reflections / Brute / Sin city / Release / You'll be sorry.

– compilations, etc. –

Oct 90.	(3xcd-box) *Virgin; (TPAK 3)* **DARE** / **HYSTERIA** / **CRASH**	-	-
Oct 95.	(c-s) *Virgin; (VSC 1557)* **DON'T YOU WANT ME** (remix) / ('A'-Snap remix) / (2-'A'-Red Jerry mix)	16	
	(12") *(VST 1557)* – ('A'-Snap remix extended) / ('A'-Red Jerry remix extended).		
	(cd-s) *(VSCDT 1557)* – (all 6-'A'versions).		
Oct 96.	(cd) *Disky; (VI 87530-2)* **SOUNDTRACK TO A GENERATION**	-	-
Apr 02.	(12") *Klang; (KLANG 62)* **ALL I EVER WANTED** (mixes)	-	-

JAM

Formed: Woking, Surrey, England ... late '73 by PAUL WELLER, BRUCE FOXTON, RICK BUCKLER and 4th member STEVE BROOKS – guitar. This quartet first gigged mid-74, progressing to the likes of London's Marquee, 101 Club & Red Cow in late '76, by which time BROOKS had departed. Peddling amphetamine charged retro R&B, the band rode in on the first wave of punk's brave new musical world. Incendiary live performances had generated a loyal following and considerable record company interest, the band signing with 'Polydor' early the following year via A&R man Chris Parry. In Spring '77, their debut, 'IN THE CITY', cracked the UK Top 40, an album of the same name following a month later. Image wise, the band were kitted out in unashamed allegiance to the mod masterplan of yore; sharp suits, parkas, scooters etc., another factor that set the band apart from the anti-fashion of punk. Something WELLER did share with his glue-sniffing peers was anger; yep, before WELLER the 'red-wedge' soul smoothie and WELLER the patron of 'Dad Rock' came WELLER the angry young man, so angry in fact, that he professed to voting conservative. Politics aside, 'IN THE CITY' was a cut above the average three chord punk thrash, bristling with adolescent fury yet possessed of an irresistible melodic verve. 'THIS IS THE MODERN WORLD' (1977) was a hastily recorded follow-up, and it showed. Only the pounding title track (the single backed with a cover of Arthur Conley's 'SWEET SOUL MUSIC') really hit the target, the rest of the album pointlessly recycling WHO riffs ad nauseum. With 'ALL MOD CONS' (1978), however, The JAM were onto something big, WELLER's cutting social reportage and songwriting genius translating into such gems as 'DOWN IN THE TUBE-STATION AT MIDNIGHT', a cover of The Kinks' 'DAVID WATTS' indicating the heights he was aiming for. Come 'SETTING SONS' (1979), and with the bile-spewing 'ETON RIFLES', in particular, WELLER came pretty damn close to updating RAY DAVIES' class-conscious agenda for a harsh new age. The single gave the band their first Top 5 success and the album achieved a similar feat upon its release a month later. In February of the following year, the band went straight in at No.1 with 'GOING UNDERGROUND', a snarling critique of the establishment. The band followed this up with 'START!', a virtual remake (well, intro definitely) of George Harrison/Beatles' 'TAXMAN', quite why there's never been a court case over the matter remains a mystery. Still, the single marked a move into more ambitious musical territory, WELLER penning his most accomplished tune to date in the lilting, understated ennui of 'THAT'S ENTERTAINMENT'. The album, 'SOUND AFFECTS' (1980), confirmed the shift away from powerchord aggression with the use of horns and more obviously black music-derived rhythms. By this point, THE JAM were one of, if not the, biggest band in Britain although, despite repeated attempts, the American market was apparently impossible for the band to crack. Then again, it's not hard to see that their defiantly British sound just didn't translate in the States, in much the same way as, more recently, BLUR's idiosyncratic Englishness has precluded US recognition. Back home though, the band were No.1 again in early 1982 with the heavily Motown-influenced 'TOWN CALLED MALICE', 'THE GIFT' album being released the following month. It was to be the band's swansong as WELLER, at the peak of the band's fame later that summer, announced he was to break the group up to explore his soul fixation with The STYLE COUNCIL. After a final kiss-off with 'THE BITTEREST PILL' and the brilliant 'BEAT SURRENDER', the band were no more. While WELLER went on to a undergo many musical rebirths, there was no such joy for FOXTON, who later joined aging punks STIFF LITTLE FINGERS. BUCKLER, meanwhile, forsook the evils of the music business for furniture restoration. Thankfully, with no reunion so far, and the possibility of one rather slim, the legend of The JAM remains intact. • **Songwriters:** WELLER penned except; BACK IN MY ARMS AGAIN (Holland-Dozier-Holland) / DAVID WATTS (Kinks) / MOVE ON UP (Curtis Mayfield). • **Trivia:** In Oct'81, WELLER started own record company 'Respond', and signed acts The QUESTIONS and TRACIE.

Album rating: IN THE CITY (*6) / THIS IS THE MODERN WORLD (*5) / ALL MOD CONS (*8) / SETTING SONS (*8) / SOUND EFFECTS (*8) / THE GIFT (*6) / DIG THE NEW BREED live collection (*6) / SNAP! compilation (*10) / GREATEST HITS compilation (*8) / DIRECTION REACTION CREATION boxed compilation (*9) / THE

JAM (cont)

VERY BEST OF THE JAM compilation (*8) / THE SOUND OF THE JAM compilation (*8)

PAUL WELLER (b. JOHN WELLER, 25 May'58) – vocals, guitar / **BRUCE FOXTON** (b. 1 Sep'55) – bass, vocals / **RICK BUCKLER** (b. PAUL RICHARD BUCKLER, 6 Dec'55) – drums

			Polydor	Polydor
Apr 77.	(7") (2058 866)	**IN THE CITY. / TAKIN' MY LOVE**	40	-
	(re-iss. Apr80) – hit No.40 (re-iss. Jan83) – hit No.47 (re-iss. Apr02; 587611-7) – hit No.36			
May 77.	(lp) (2383 447) <6110>	**IN THE CITY**	20	
	– Art school / I've changed my address / Slow down / I got by in time / Away from the numbers / Batman / In the city / Sounds from the street / Non stop dancing / Time for truth / Takin' my love / Bricks and mortar. (re-iss. Aug83 lp/c; SPE LP/MC 27) (re-iss. Jul90 cd/c/lp; 817124-2/-4/-1) (cd re-iss. Jul97; 537417-2)			
Jul 77.	(7") (2058 903)	**ALL AROUND THE WORLD. / CARNABY STREET**	13	-
	(re-iss. Apr80) – hit No.43 (re-iss. Jan83) – hit No.38			
Oct 77.	(7"m) (2058 945)	**THE MODERN WORLD. / SWEET SOUL MUSIC (live) / BACK IN MY ARMS AGAIN (live) / BRICKS AND MORTAR (live)**	36	-
	(re-iss. Apr80) – hit No.52 (re-iss. Jan83) – hit No.51			
Nov 77.	(lp) (2383 475) <6129>	**THIS IS THE MODERN WORLD**	22	
	– The modern world / London traffic / Standards / Life from the window / The combine / Don't tell them you're sane / In the street today / London girl / I need you / Here comes the weekend / Tonight at noon / In the midnight hour. (re-iss. Aug83 lp/c; SPE LP/MC 66) (re-iss. Jul90 cd/c/lp; 823281-2/-4/-1) (cd re-iss. Jul97; 537418-2)			
Feb 78.	(7") <14462>	**I NEED YOU. / IN THE CITY**	-	
Mar 78.	(7"m) (2058 995)	**NEWS OF THE WORLD. / AUNTIES AND UNCLES / INNOCENT MAN**	27	-
	(re-iss. Apr80) – hit No.53 (re-iss. Jan83) – hit No.39			
Aug 78.	(7") (2059 054)	**DAVID WATTS. / 'A' BOMB IN WARDOUR STREET**	25	-
	(re-iss. Apr80) – hit No.54 (re-iss. Jan83) – hit No.50			
Oct 78.	(7"m) (POSP 8)	**DOWN IN THE TUBE STATION AT MIDNIGHT. / SO BAD ABOUT US / THE NIGHT**	15	-
	(re-iss. Apr80) – hit No.30			
Nov 78.	(lp/c) (POLD/+C 5008) <6218>	**ALL MOD CONS**	6	
	– All mod cons / To be someone (didn't we have a nice time) / Mr. Clean / David Watts / English rose / In the crowd / Billy Hunt / It's too bad / Fly 3.18 / The place I love / 'A' bomb in Wardour Street / Down in the tube station at midnight. (cd-iss. 1989; 823282-2) (cd re-iss. Jul97; 537419-2) (lp re-iss. Aug99 on 'Simply Vinyl'; SVLP 108)			
Mar 79.	(7") (POSP 34) <14553>	**STRANGE TOWN. / THE BUTTERFLY COLLECTOR**	15	-
	(re-iss. Apr80) – hit No.44 (re-iss. Jan83) – hit No.42			
Jun 79.	(7") <14566>	**DOWN IN THE TUBE STATION AT MIDNIGHT. / MR. CLEAN**	-	
Aug 79.	(7") (POSP 69)	**WHEN YOU'RE YOUNG. / SMITHERS-JONES**	17	-
	(re-iss. Jan83) – hit No.53			
Oct 79.	(7") (POSP 83)	**THE ETON RIFLES. / SEE-SAW**	3	-
	(re-iss. Jan83) – hit No.54			
Nov 79.	(lp/c) (POLD/+C 5028) <6249>	**SETTING SONS**	4	
	– Girl on the phone / Thick as thieves / Private hell / Little boy soldiers / Waste land / Burning sky / Smithers-Jones / Saturday's kids / The Eton rifles / Heat wave. (cd-iss. May88; 831314-2) (cd re-iss. Jul97; 537420-2) (lp re-iss. May00 on 'Simply Vinyl'; SVLP 209) (cd re-iss. Nov01 on 'Collectors Choice'+=; CCM 0247-2) – Strange town / When you're young / Smithers-Jones / See saw / Going underground / Dreams of children / So sad about us / Hey mister / Start.			
Dec 79.	(7") <2051>	**THE ETON RIFLES. / SMITHERS-JONES**	-	
Feb 80.	(7") (POSP 113)	**GOING UNDERGROUND. / DREAMS OF CHILDREN**	1	-
	(d7"+=) (POSPJ 113 – 2616 024) – The modern world (live) / Away from the numbers (live) / Down in the tube station at midnight (live). (re-iss. Jan83) – hit No.21			
Apr 80.	(7") (2074)	**SATURDAY'S KIDS. / (LOVE IS LIKE A) HEATWAVE**	-	
Aug 80.	(7") (2059 266)	**START! / LIZA RADLEY**	1	-
	(re-iss. Jan83) – hit No.60			
Sep 80.	(7") <2155>	**START! / WHEN YOU'RE YOUNG**	-	
Nov 80.	(lp/c) (POLD/+C 5035) <6315>	**SOUND AFFECTS**	2	72
	– Pretty green / Monday / But I'm different now / Set the house ablaze / Start! / That's entertainment / Dreamtime / Man in the cornershop / Music for the last couple / Boy about town / Scrape away. (re-iss. Apr90 cd/c/lp; 823284-2/-4/-1) (cd re-iss. Jul97; 537421-2)			
Jan 81.	(7") (0030 364)	**THAT'S ENTERTAINMENT. / DOWN THE TUBE STATION AT MIDNIGHT (live)**	21	-
	(above 45, was actually imported into Britain by German 'Metrognome') (re-iss. Jan83 on 'Polydor'; 2059 482) – hit No.60			
May 81.	(7") (POSP 257)	**FUNERAL PYRE. / DISGUISES**	4	
	(re-iss. Jan83)			
Oct 81.	(7") (POSP 350)	**ABSOLUTE BEGINNERS. / TALES FROM THE RIVERBANK**	4	
	(re-iss. Jan83)			
Dec 81.	(m-lp) <503>	**THE JAM**	-	
	– Absolute beginners / Funeral pyre / Liza Radley / Tales from the riverbank / Disguises.			
Feb 82.	(7"/12") (POSP/+X 400)	**TOWN CALLED MALICE. / PRECIOUS**	1	
	(re-iss. Jan83) – hit No.73			
Mar 82.	(lp/c) (POLD/+C 5055) <6349>	**THE GIFT**	1	82
	– Happy together / Ghosts / Precious / Just who is the 5 o'clock hero? / Trans-global express / Running on the spot / Circus / The planner's dream goes wrong / Carnation / Town called Malice / The gift. (re-iss. Apr90 cd/c/lp; 823285-2/-4/-1) (cd re-iss. Jul97; 537422-2)			
Jun 82.	(7") (2059 504)	**JUST WHO IS THE 5 O'CLOCK HERO?. / THE GREAT DEPRESSION**	6	
	(12"+=) (2141 558) – War.			
Sep 82.	(7") (POSP 505)	**THE BITTEREST PILL (I EVER HAD TO SWALLOW). / PITY POOR ALFIE / FEVER – PITY POOR ALFIE**	2	
	<US-iss.Nov82 as 12"m-lp> – Great depression.			
Nov 82.	(7") (POSP 540)	**BEAT SURRENDER. / SHOPPING**	1	Mar83
	(d7"+=)<m-lp> (POSPJ 540 – JAM 1) <810751> – Move on up / War / Stoned out of my mind.			
Dec 82.	(lp/c) (POLD/+C 5075) <6365>	**DIG THE NEW BREED (live 77-82)**	2	
	– In the city / All mod cons / To be someone / It's too bad / Start! / Big bird / Set the house ablaze / Ghosts / Standards / In the crowd / Going underground / Dreams of children / That's entertainment / Private hell. (re-iss. Jun87 lp/c; SPE LP/MC 107) (re-iss. Jun90 cd/c/lp; 810041-2/-4/-1) (cd re-iss. Sep95)			

— They split late '82. WELLER formed The STYLE COUNCIL, before making it huge as a solo star. FOXTON, meanwhile, went solo, delivering a solitary solo album, 'TOUCH SENSITIVE' (May 1984) for 'Arista'; the Top 75 breaker contained his only Top 30 hit, 'FREAK', released a year earlier. BUCKLER formed TIME UK who had one minor hit, 'THE CABARET' (Sep'83), before he and FOXTON teamed up with TIME UK singer, JIMMY EDWARDS, to become mid-late 80's outfit, SHARP.

– compilations, etc. –

on 'Polydor' unless mentioned otherwise

Sep 80.	(d-lp) (2683 074)	**IN THE CITY / THIS IS THE MODERN WORLD**		-
	(re-iss. Jan91 cd/c; 847730-2/-4)			
Jan 83.	(d-c) (TWOMC 1)	**SOUND AFFECTS / THE GIFT**		-
Feb 83.	(d-c) (1574 098)	**ALL MOD CONS / SETTING SONS**		-
Oct 83.	(d-lp/d-c) (SNAP/+C 1)	**SNAP!**	2	
	– In the city / Away from the numbers / All around the world / The modern world / News of the world / Billy Hunt / English Rose / Mr. Clean / David Watts / 'A' bomb in Wardour Street / Down in the tube station at midnight / Strange town / The butterfly collector / When you're young / Smithers-Jones / Thick as thieves / The Eton rifles / Going underground / Dreams of children / That's entertainment / Start! / Man in the cornershop / Funeral pyre / Absolute beginners / Tales from the riverbank / Town called Malice / Precious / The bitterest pill (I ever had to swallow) / Beat surrender. (d-lp.with free 7"ep) **LIVE AT WEMBLEY** (live) – The great depression / But I'm different now / Move on up / Get yourself together. (cd-iss. Sep84 as 'COMPACT SNAP'; 821712-2) – omits 8 tracks. (re-iss. Jun90 cd/c/lp; 815537-2/-4/-1)			
Mar 90.	(7") Old Gold; (OG 9894)	**TOWN CALLED MALICE. / ABSOLUTE BEGINNERS**		-
Mar 90.	(7") Old Gold; (OG 9895)	**BEAT SURRENDER. / THE BITTEREST PILL (I EVER HAD TO SWALLOW)**		-
Mar 90.	(7") Old Gold; (OG 9896)	**THE ETON RIFLES. / DOWN IN THE TUBE STATION AT MIDNIGHT**		-
Mar 90.	(7") Old Gold; (OG 9897)	**GOING UNDERGROUND. / START!**		-
Sep 90.	(12"ep/cd-ep) Strange Fruit; (SFPS/+CD 080)	**THE PEEL SESSIONS** (26.4.77)		-
	– In the city / Art school / I've changed my address / The modern world. (cd-ep re-iss. Sep96; same)			
Jun 91.	(7")/c-s) (PO/+CS 155)	**THAT'S ENTERTAINMENT. / DOWN IN THE TUBE-STATION AT MIDNIGHT (live)**	57	
	(12"+=/cd-s+=) (PZ/+CD 155) – Town called Malice (live).			
Jul 91.	(cd/c/lp) (849554-2/-4/-1)	**GREATEST HITS**	2	
	– In the city / All around the world / Modern world / News of the world / David Watts / A bomb in Wardour Street / Down in the tube-station at midnight / Strange town / When you're young / Eton rifles / Going underground / Dreams of children / Start / That's entertainment / Funeral pyre / Absolute beginners / A town called Malice / Precious / Just who is the 5 o'clock hero / The bitterest pill (I ever had to swallow) / Beat surrender.			
Mar 92.	(7"/c-s) (PO/+CS 199)	**THE DREAMS OF CHILDREN. / AWAY FROM THE NUMBERS (live)**		-
	(12"+=/cd-s+=) (PZ/+CD 199) – This is the modern world (live).			
Apr 92.	(cd/c/lp) (513177-2/-4/-1)	**EXTRAS: A COLLECTION OF RARITIES**		-
Oct 92.	(cd/c) Pickwick; (PWK S/MC 4129P)	**WASTELAND**		-
Oct 93.	(cd/c/d-lp) (519667-2/-4/-1)	**LIVE JAM (live)**	28	
	– The modern world / Billy Hunt / Thick as thieves / Burning sky / Mr. Clean / Smithers-Jones / Little boy soldiers / The Eton Rifles / Away from the numbers / Down in the tube station at midnight / Strange town / When you're young / 'A' Bomb In Wardour Street / Pretty green / Boy about town / Man in the cornershop / David Watts / Funeral pyre / Move on up / Carnation / The butterfly collector / Precious / Town called Malice / Heatwave. (cd re-iss. Apr02; same)			
Jul 96.	(d-cd/d-c/d-lp) (531493-2/-4/-1)	**THE JAM COLLECTION**	58	-
May 97.	(5xcd-box) (537143-2)	**DIRECTION REACTION CREATION**	8	-
Sep 97.	(7"/c-s) (571598-7/-4)	**THE BITTEREST PILL (I EVER HAD TO SWALLOW). / THE BUTTERFLY COLLECTOR**	30	-
	(cd-s+=) (571598-2) – That's entertainment / ('A' version).			
Oct 97.	(cd/c) (537423-2/-4)	**THE VERY BEST OF THE JAM** (all the singles 1977-1982)	9	-
	– (see 'GREATEST HITS' for track details).			
Nov 98.	(cd/c) Spectrum; (550006-2/-4)	**BEAT SURRENDER**		-
Apr 01.	(9xcd-s-box) (587610-2)	**THE SINGLES 1977-1979**		-
Apr 01.	(9xcd-s-box) (587620-2)	**THE SINGLES 1980-1982**		-
May 02.	(cd/d-lp) (589781-2/-1)	**THE SOUND OF THE JAM**	3	-
Jun 02.	(3xcd-box) (589690-2)	**THE JAM AT THE BBC**	33	-

JANSEN / BARBIERI (see under ⇒ JAPAN)

JAPAN

Formed: Catford / Lewisham, London, England ... mid-70's by DAVID SYLVIAN, his brother STEVE JANSEN, MICK KARN and RICHARD BARBIERI. In 1977, they added a second guitarist, ROB DEAN, subsequently signing to 'Ariola-Hansa' after winning a talent competition run by the label. They released a debut album, 'ADOLESCENT SEX', in the Spring of '78, followed six months later by 'OBSCURE ALTERNATIVES'. Basically pop music at the more accessible end of the avant-garde spectrum, JAPAN's proto-New Romantic image contrasted with SYLVIAN's (FERRY-esque) monotone croon. The following year, JAPAN scored a major hit in (of all places) Japan, with the GIORGIO MORODER-produced single, 'LIFE IN TOKYO'; a year on they finally gained a UK chart placing with 'QUIET LIFE'. By the turn of the decade, they'd secured a deal with 'Virgin', releasing the John Porter-produced Top 50 album, 'GENTLEMEN TAKE POLAROIDS'. The next year, after three minor hits in Britain, they went overground with a top selling classic album, 'TIN DRUM'. The record subsequently spawned the spectral 'GHOSTS' single in early '82, which hit the UK Top 5 after their former label had initiated a string of re-issues with 'EUROPEAN SON'; these exploitation releases graced the charts over the course of the next eighteen months while JAPAN officially folded. All band members went on to other projects, DAVID SYLVIAN enjoying most success. After a 1982 collaboration with RYUICHI SAKAMOTO ('BAMBOO HOUSES' and 'FORBIDDEN COLOURS' from the movie, 'Merry Xmas Mr. Lawrence'), the immaculately fringed frontman released his debut solo album, 'BRILLIANT TREES' (1984). The Top 5 album utilised the talents of world trumpeter, JON HASSELL, while JAPAN cohorts JANSEN and BARBIERI also helped to sculpt its sophisticated ambience. On future albums such as 'GONE TO EARTH' (1986), 'SECRETS OF THE BEEHIVE' (1987), 'PLIGHT AND PREMONITION' (1988) and 'FLUX AND MUTATION' (1989) – the latter two were collaborations with HOLGER CZUKAY (ex-CAN) – he worked with left-field luminaries like BILL NELSON and ROBERT FRIPP. In 1991, JAPAN re-formed as RAIN TREE CROW, although it became clear this set-up was only temporary, as all members (especially SYLVIAN), continued to pursue solo careers. SYLVIAN briefly returned to the charts in 1993 with the ROBERT FRIPP collaboration, 'THE FIRST DAY', a more accessible yet still inventive set. Although MICK KARN began a solo career at the same time as SYLVIAN (the bassist's work reminiscent of ENO or BILL NELSON), he went on to work as a sculptor; his track, 'TRIBAL DAWN' (from the album, 'TITLES' – 1982), was used on Channel 4's arty TV programme, 'Altered States'. SYLVIAN was still gaining respect in some quarters of the music world when he turned up courtesy of a fresh set of scrumptious solo songs entitled 'DEAD BEES ON A CAKE' (1999), his aura and presence still on show when this returned him to the Top 40 (as did single, 'I SURRENDER'). • **Songwriters:** SYLVIAN lyrics / group compositions except; DON'T RAIN ON MY PARADE (Rogers-Hammerstein) / AIN'T THAT PECULIAR (Marvin Gaye) / I SECOND THAT EMOTION (Smokey Robinson) / ALL TOMORROW'S PARTIES (Velvet Underground).

Album rating: ADOLESCENT SEX (*6) / OBSCURE ALTERNATIVES (*6) / QUIET LIFE (*6) / GENTLEMEN TAKE POLAROIDS (*7) / TIN DRUM (*9) / ASSEMBLAGE compilation (*7) / OIL ON CANVAS live (*6) / EXORCISING GHOSTS compilation (*9) / Rain Tree Crow: RAIN TREE CROW (*4) / David Sylvian: BRILLIANT TREES (*8) / GONE TO EARTH (*6) / SECRETS OF THE BEEHIVE (*7) / PLIGHT AND PREMONITION with Holger Czukay (*7) / FLUX AND MUTABILITY with Holger Czukay (*6) / THE FIRST DAY with Robert Fripp (*6) / DEAD BEES ON A CAKE (*8) / APPROACHING SILENCE (*5) / EVERYTHING AND NOTHING compilation (*8) / Mick Karn: TITLES (*7) / DREAMS OF REASON PRODUCE (*6) / BESTIAL CLUSTER (*5) / POLLYTOWN (*5) / THE TOOTH MOTHER (*5) / Jansen & Barbieri: CATCH THE FALL (*5) / STORIES ACROSS THE BORDER (*5) / BEGINNING TO MELT with Karn (*5) / SEED with Karn (*5) / STONE TO FLESH (*5) / OTHER WORLDS IN A SMALL ROOM (*4)

DAVID SYLVIAN (b. DAVID BATT, 23 Feb'58) – vocals, guitar, keyboards / **RICHARD BARBIERI** (b.30 Nov'57) – keyboards, synthesizers / **ROB DEAN** – guitar, mandolin / **MICK KARN** (b. ANTHONY MICHAELIDES, 24 Jul'58) – bass, saxophone / **STEVE JANSEN** (b. STEVE BATT, 1 Dec'59) – drums, percussion

		Ariola Hansa	Ariola
Mar 78.	(7") (AHA 510) **DON'T RAIN ON MY PARADE. / STATELINE**		–
Apr 78.	(lp) (AHAL 8004) <50037> **ADOLESCENT SEX**		–
	– Transmission / The unconventional / State line / Wish you were black / Performance / Lovers on Main Street / Don't rain on my parade / Suburban love / Adolescent sex / Communist China / Television. (re-iss. Sep82; same) (re-iss. Sep84 on 'Fame' lp/c; FA41 3108-1/-4) (cd-iss. 1989 on 'Hansa Germany'; VDP 1153)		
Aug 78.	(7") (AHA 525) **THE UNCONVENTIONAL. / ADOLESCENT SEX**		–
Nov 78.	(lp) (AHAL 8007) <50047> **OBSCURE ALTERNATIVES**		
	– Automatic gun / Rhodesia / Love is infectious / Sometimes I feel so low / Obscure alternatives / Deviation / Suburban Berlin / The tenant. (re-iss. Sep82; same) (re-iss. Apr84 on 'Fame' lp/c; FA41 3098-1/-4) (cd-iss. 1989 on 'Hansa Germany'; CDP 1154)		
Nov 78.	(7",7"blue) (AHA 529) <7727> **SOMETIMES I FEEL SO LOW. / LOVE IS INFECTIOUS**		
May 79.	(7"red/ext.12"red) (AHA/+D 540) **LIFE IN TOKYO. / LIFE IN TOKYO (part 2)**		–
Jul 79.	(12") <7756> **LIFE IN TOKYO. / LOVE IS INFECTIOUS**	–	
Jan 80.	(lp) (AHAL 8011) **QUIET LIFE**	53	–
	– Quiet life / Fall in love with me / Despair / In-vogue / Halloween / All tomorrow's parties / Alien / The other side of life. (re-iss. Sep82 on 'Fame'; FA/TCFA 3037) (cd-iss. 1989 on 'Hansa Germany'; VDP 1155)		
Feb 80.	(7",7"maroon) (AHA 559) **I SECOND THAT EMOTION. / QUIET LIFE**		–

		Virgin	not iss.
Oct 80.	(7") (VS 379) **GENTLEMEN TAKE POLAROIDS. / THE EXPERIENCE OF SWIMMING**	60	–
	(d7"+=) (VS 379) – The width of a room / Burning bridges.		
Oct 80.	(lp/c) (V/TCV 2180) **GENTLEMEN TAKE POLAROIDS**	45	–
	– Gentlemen take polaroids / Swing / Some kind of fool / My new career / Methods of dance / Ain't that peculiar / Night porter / Taking islands in Africa. (re-iss. Aug88 lp/c; OVED/+C 138) (cd-iss. Jun88; CDV 2180) <US cd-iss. 1991 on 'Caroline'; CAROL 1829-2>		

— Trimmed to quartet when ROB DEAN left, to later form ILLUSTRATED MAN

Apr 81.	(7"/12") (VS 409/+12) **THE ART OF PARTIES. / LIFE WITHOUT BUILDINGS**	48	–
Oct 81.	(7") (VS 436) **VISIONS OF CHINA. / TAKING ISLANDS IN AFRICA**	32	–
	(12"+=) (VS 436-12) – Swing. (re-iss. Dec84; same)		
Nov 81.	(lp/c) (V/TCV 2209) **TIN DRUM**	12	–
	– The art of parties / Talking drum / Ghosts / Canton / Still life in mobile homes / Visions of China / Sons of pioneers / Cantonese boy. (re-iss. Apr86 lp/c; OVED/+C 158) (cd-iss. Jun88; CDV 2209) <US cd-iss. 1991 on 'Caroline'; CAROL 1830-2>		
Jan 82.	(7"/7"pic-d/12") (VS/+Y 472)(VS 472-12) **GHOSTS. / THE ART OF PARTIES (version)**	5	–
Feb 82.	(7") **VISIONS OF CHINA. / CANTON**	–	
May 82.	(d7") (VS 502) **CANTONESE BOY. / BURNING BRIDGES // GENTLEMEN TAKE POLAROIDS / THE EXPERIENCE OF SWIMMING**	24	–

— They had earlier in the year quietly branched out into new projects. DAVID SYLVIAN went solo after a brief collaboration with RYUICHI SAKAMOTO. MICK KARN went solo, had a one-off single with MIDGE URE, then went into sessions before forming DALI'S CAR with PETE MURPHY in '84. BARBERI and JANSEN produced Swedes LUSTAN LAKEJER. The pair formed their own duo (The DOLPHIN BROTHERS) before joining DAVID SYLVIAN again.

– compilations, exploitation releases etc. –

— on 'Hansa-Ariola' unless otherwise mentioned

Apr 81.	(7"/12") (HANSA/+12 4) **LIFE IN TOKYO. / EUROPEAN SON**		–
Aug 81.	(7"/12") (HANSA/+12 6) **QUIET LIFE. / A FOREIGN PLACE / FALL IN LOVE WITH ME**	19	–
Sep 81.	(lp)(c) (HANLP 1)(ZCHAN 003) **ASSEMBLAGE**	26	–
	– Adolescent sex / State line / Communist China / Rhodesia / Suburban Berlin / Life in Tokyo / European son / All tomorrow's parties / Quiet life / I second that emotion. (c+=) – (12"extended versions). (re-iss. Sep85 on 'Fame' lp/c; FA41 3136-1/-4)		
Jan 82.	(7"/12") (HANSA/+12 10) **EUROPEAN SON. / ALIEN**	31	–
Jun 82.	(7"/12") (HANSA/+12 12) **I SECOND THAT EMOTION. / HALLOWEEN**	9	–
Sep 82.	(7"/12") (HANSA/+12 17) **LIFE IN TOKYO. / THEME**	28	–

— now on 'Virgin' unless mentioned otherwise

Nov 82.	(7") (VS 554) **NIGHT PORTER. / AIN'T THAT PECULIAR**	29	–
	(12"+=) (VS 554-12) – Methods of dance.		
Feb 83.	(7"/12") Hansa; (HANSA/+12 18) **ALL TOMORROW'S PARTIES. / IN VOGUE**	38	–
May 83.	(7") (VS 581) **CANTON (live). / VISIONS OF CHINA (live)**	42	–
Jun 83.	(d-lp/c) (VD/TCVD 2513) **OIL ON CANVAS (live)**	5	–
	– Oil on canvas / Sons of pioneers / Gentlemen take polaroids / Swing / Cantonese boy / Visions of china / Ghosts / Voices raised in welcome, hands held in prayer / Night porter / Still life in mobile homes / Methods of dance / Quiet life / The art of parties / Canton / Temple of dawn. (cd-iss. Apr85; CDVD 2513)		
Aug 83.	(d-c) (XTWO 24) **ADOLESCENT SEX / OBSCURE ALTERNATIVES**		
Nov 84.	(d-lp/c/cd) (VGD/+C/CD 3510) **EXORCISING GHOSTS**	45	–
	– Methods of dance / Swing / Gentlemen take polaroids / Quiet life / A foreign place * / Night porter / My new career / The other side of life / Visions of China / Sons of pioneers * / Talking drum / The art of parties / Taking islands in Africa / Voices raised in welcome, hands held in prayer / Life without buildings / Ghosts. (cd-omits *)		
Jun 88.	(3"cd-ep) (CDT 11) **GHOSTS / THE ART OF PARTIES / VISIONS OF CHINA**		
Nov 88.	(3"cd-ep) (CDT 32) **GENTLEMEN TAKE POLAROIDS / CANTONESE BOY / METHODS OF DANCE**		
Sep 87.	(7") Old Gold; (OG 9666) **I SECOND THAT EMOTION. / ALL TOMORROW'S PARTIES**		
	(12"+=) (OG 4020) – Life in Tokyo.		
Nov 87.	(7") Old Gold; (OG 4031) **QUIET LIFE. / LIFE IN TOKYO**		
Nov 88.	(7") Old Gold; (OG 9817) **GHOSTS. / CANTONESE BOY**		
Dec 89.	(c/cd) R.C.A.; (410/260 360) **A SOUVENIR FROM JAPAN**		
Nov 90.	(3xcd-box) (TPAK 6) **COLLECTOR'S EDITION**		
	– (GENTLEMEN TAKE POLAROIDS / TIN DRUM / OIL ON CANVAS)		
Nov 92.	(cd-ep) Old Gold; (OG 6187) **I SECOND THAT EMOTION / QUIET LIFE / LIFE IN TOKYO**		
Oct 91.	(cd/c) Receiver; (RR CD/MC 150) **THE OTHER SIDE OF JAPAN**		
Aug 96.	(cd) B.M.G.; (74321 39338-2) **IN VOGUE**		

DAVID SYLVIAN

— vocals, instruments (ex-JAPAN) / **RYUICHI SAKAMOTO** – synthesizers (ex-YELLOW MAGIC ORCHESTRA)

		Virgin	Caroline
Jul 82.	(7"/ext.12") by SYLVIAN / SAKAMOTO (VS 510) **BAMBOO HOUSES. / BAMBOO MUSIC**	30	–
	(below from the the film soundtrack 'Merry Christmas Mr.Lawrence')		
Jun 83.	(7") by DAVID SYLVIAN & RYUICHI SAKAMOTO (VS 601) **FORBIDDEN COLOURS. / THE SEED AND THE SOWER (by RYUICHI SAKAMOTO)**	16	
	(12"+=) (VS 601-12) – Last regrets.		
	(3"/5"cd-ep of SYLVIAN tracks was iss.Aug88; CDT 18)		

— now solo – vocals, keyboards, guitar, percussion, with **RICHARD BARBIERI** and

JAPAN (cont) — THE GREAT INDIE DISCOGRAPHY — The 1970s

STEVE JANSEN (ex-JAPAN) / **RYUICHI SAKAMOTO** – synthesizers / **HOLGER CZUKAY** – tapes / **DANNY THOMPSON** – upright bass / **KENNY WHEELER** – horns

May 84. (7"/7"pic-d)(12") (VS/+Y 633)(VS 633-12) **RED GUITAR. / FORBIDDEN COLOURS** (version) — 17 / -

Jun 84. (lp/c/cd) (V/TCV/CDV 2290) <CAROL 1812> **BRILLIANT TREES** — 4 / -
– Pulling punches / The ink in the well / Nostalgia / Red guitar / Weathered wall / Backwaters / Brilliant trees. (re-iss. Apr90 lp/c; OVED/+C 239)

Aug 84. (7"/12") (VS 700/+12) **THE INK IN THE WELL** (remix). / **WEATHERED WALL** (instrumental) — 36 / -

Oct 84. (7"/ext.12") (VS 717/+12) **PULLING PUNCHES. / BACKWATERS** (remix) — 56 / -

— now with **JOHN HASSELL** and **ROBERT FRIPP** – guitar / **HOLGER CZUKAY** – tapes / **KENNY WHEELER** – horns

Nov 85. (12"ep) (VS 835-12) **WORDS WITH THE SHAMEN** — 72 / -
– Part 1: Ancient evening / Part 2: Incantation / Part 3: Awakening.

Dec 85. (c) (SLY 1) **ALCHEMY (AN INDEX OF POSSIBILITIES)** — / -
– WORDS WITH THE SHAMEN / Preparations for a journey / Steel cathedrals.

— now with **ROBERT FRIPP** and **BILL NELSON** – guitar / **PHIL PALMER** – accoustic guitar / **MEL COLLINS** – soprano sax. / **KENNY WHEELER** – flugel horn

Jul 86. (7"/7"sha-pic-d) (VS/+Y 815) **TAKING THE VEIL. / ANSWERED PRAYERS** — 53 / - (Virgin / Virgin)
(remix-12"+=) – (VS 815-12) – Bird of prey vanishes into a bright blue sky.

Aug 86. (d-lp)(c)(cd) (VDL/TCVDL/CDVDL 1) <96003> **GONE TO EARTH** — 24 / -
– Taking the veil / Laughter and forgetting / Before the bullfront / Gone to earth / Wave / River man / Silver moon / The healing place / Answered prayers * / Where the railroad meets the sea / The wooden cross * / Silver moon over sleeping steeples * / Campfire: Coyote country * / A bird of prey vanishes into a blue cloudless sky * / Sunlight seen through the towering trees * / Upon this Earth. (cd-omits tracks *)

Sep 86. (7"/s7") (VS/+P 895) **SILVER MOON. / GONE TO EARTH** — / -
(12"+=) – (VS 895-12) – Silver moon over sleeping steeples.

— DAVID was also credited on VIRGINIA ASTLEY's Feb87 'Some Small Hope'.

— now with **SAKAMOTO, PALMER, JANSEN** plus **DANNY CUMMINGS** – percussion / **DAVID TORN** – guitar / **DANNY THOMPSON** – d. bass / **MARK ISHAM** – trumpet

Oct 87. (lp)(c)(cd) (V/TCV/CDV 2471) <86028> **SECRETS OF THE BEEHIVE** — 37 /
– September / The boy with the gun / Maria / Orpheus / The Devil's own / When poets dreamed of angels / Mother and child / Let the happiness in / Waterfront.

Oct 87. (7") (VS 1001) **LET THE HAPPINESS IN. / BLUE OF MOON** — 66 / -
(12"+=) – (VS 1001-12) – Buoy (remix).

Apr 88. (7") (VS 1043) **ORPHEUS. / THE DEVIL'S OWN** — / -
(12"+=) – (VS 1043-12) – Mother and child.

— His touring band JANSEN, BARBIERI, TORN, ISHAM plus IAN MAIDMAN – bass, percussion / ROBBY ALEDO – guitar

DAVID SYLVIAN & HOLGER CZUKAY

with **JAKI LIEBEZEIT** – drums (ex-CAN)

Mar 88. (lp/c/cd) (VE/TCVE/CDVE 11) <86053> **PLIGHT AND PREMONITION** — 71 / - (Venture / Virgin)
– Plight (the spiralling of winter ghosts) / Premonition (giant empty iron vessel).

— with LIEBEZEIT, MICHAEL KAROLI – guitar / MARKUS STOCKHAUSEN – flugel horn / MICHI – vocals

Sep 89. (lp/c/cd) (VE/TCVE/CDVE 43) <CAROLCD 1602> **FLUX AND MUTABILITY** — / - (Venture / Caroline)
– Flux (a big, bright, colourful world) / Mutability ("a new beginning is in the offing").

DAVID SYLVIAN

Nov 89. (7") (VS 1221) **POP SONG. / A BRIEF CONVERSATION ENDING IN DIVORCE** — / - (Virgin / not iss.)
(12"+=/cd-s+=) (VST/VSCDX 1221) – ('A'remix).
(cd-s+=) (VSCD 1221) – Stigmas of childhood.

Nov 89. (5-cd-box) (DXCD 1) **WEATHERBOX** — / -
– (BRILLIANT TREES / GONE TO EARTH / GONE TO EARTH (instrumental) / SECRETS OF THE BEEHIVE / ALCHEMY – AN INDEX OF POSSIBILITIES)

Nov 91. (cd) (DSRM 1) **EMBRE GLANCE (THE PERMANENCE OF MEMORY)** — / -
– The beekeeper's apprentice / Epiphany.

— JAPAN had reformed quartet in 1990, but as . . .

RAIN TREE CROW

Mar 91. (7"/c-s) (VS/+C 1340) **BLACK WATER. / RAIN TREE CROW / I DRINK TO FORGET** — 62 / - (Virgin / Virgin)
(12") (VST 1340) – (1st + 3rd track) / Red Earth (as summertime ends).
(cd-s) (VSCD 1340) – (all above 4).

Apr 91. (cd/c/lp) (CD/TC/+V 2659) <91774> **RAIN TREE CROW** — 24 / -
– Big wheels in Shanty town / Every colour you are / Rain tree crow / Red Earth (as summertime ends) / Rocket full of charge / Boat's for burning / New Moon Red Deer wallow / Black water / A reassuringly dull Sunday / Blackcrow hats shoe shine city.

SLYVIAN – SAKAMOTO

— next with **INGRID CHAVEZ**

Jun 92. (7"/c-s) (VUS/+C 57) **HEARTBEAT (TAINAI KAIKI II) RETURNING TO THE WOMB. / NUAGES** — 58 / - (Virgin America / Virgin Am.)
(cd-s+=) (VUSCD 57) – The lost emperor.
(cd-s) (VUSCDG 57) – ('A'side) / Forbidden colours / Heartbeat.

DAVID SYLVIAN & ROBERT FRIPP

with **FRIPP** – guitar (of-KING CRIMSON & solo artist) / **TREY GUNN** – synthesizers, vocals, co-writer plus band **DAVID BOTTRILL** – synthesizers / **JERRY MAROTTA** – drums, percussion / **MARC ANDERSON** – percussion / **INGRID CHAVEZ** – backing vocals

Jul 93. (cd/c/lp) (CD/TC+/V 2712) <88208> **THE FIRST DAY** — 21 / (Virgin / Virgin)
– God's monkey / Jean the birdman / Firepower / Brightness falls / 20th century dreaming (a shaman's song) / Darshan (the road to Graceland).

Aug 93. (c-ep/cd-ep) (VSC/DG 1462) **JEAN THE BIRDMAN / EARTHBOUND – STARBLIND / ENDGAME** — 68 / -
(cd-ep) (VSCDT 1462) – ('A'side) / Tallow moon / Dark water / Gone to Earth.

Dec 93. (cd/c/lp) (SYL CD/MC/LP 1) **DARSHAN** (mixes) — / -
– Darshan (the road to Graceland) (remixed by The GRID & others).

Sep 94. (cd) (DAMAGE 1) <39905> **DAMAGE** (live) — / -
– Damage / God's monkey / Brightness falls / Every colour you are / Firepower / Gone to Earth / 20th century dreaming (a shaman's song) / Wave / Riverman / Darshan (the road to Graceland) / Blinding light of Heaven / The first day. (re-iss. Nov01 on 'Venture'; CDVE 958)

— In 1996, SYLVIAN was credited on soundtrack of 'Marco Polo' film alongside NICOLA ALESINI & PIER LUIGI ANDREONI. It was released on 'Materiali Sonori'; MASOCD 90069)

DAVID SYLVIAN

Mar 99. (cd-s) (VSCDT 1722) **I SURRENDER / LES FLEURS DU MAL / STARRED AND DREAMING** — 40 / -
(cd-s) (VSCDX 1722) – ('A'side) / Whose trip is this / Remembering Julia.

Mar 99. (cd/c) (CDV/TCV 2876) <47071> **DEAD BEES ON A CAKE** — 31 / -
– I surrender / Dobro #1 / Midnight sun / Thalhelm / Godman / Alphabet angel / Krishna blue / Shining of things / Cafe Europe / Pollen path / All of my mother's name / Wanderlust / Praise / Darkest dreaming.

Sep 99. (cd-s) (VEND 8) **GODMAN (mixes) / SHADOWLAND** (mixes) — / - (Venture / Virgin)

Sep 99. (m-cd) (CDVE 943) <848177> **APPROACHING SILENCE** — / Oct99
– The beekeeper's apprentice / Epiphany / Approaching silence.

– compilations, etc. –

Oct 00. (d-cd/d-c) Virgin; (CDVD/TCVD 2897) <50017> **EVERYTHING AND NOTHING** — 57 /
– The scent of magnolia / Heartbeat (Tainai kaiki II) / Blackwater / Albuquerque (dobro No.6) / Ride / The golden way / Ghosts / Pop song / Every colour you are / Wanderlust / God's monkey / Let the happiness in / I surrender / Thoroughly lost to logic / Jean the birdman / Cover me with flowers / The boy with the gun / Riverman / Aparna and Nimisha (dobro No.5) / Midnight sun / Orpheus / Some kind of fool / Cries and whispers / Godman / Laughter and forgetting / Buoy / Weathered wall / Bamboo houses / Come morning. (3xcd-box+=; CDVDX 2897) – Scent of magnolia (edit) / Blinding light of Heaven / Scent of magnolia (Portobello mix) / Brilliant trees (version 2000).

May 02. (cd/d-cd) Venture; (CDVE/+X 962) / E.M.I.; <812201> **CAMPHOR** (out-takes) — / -

MICK KARN

- vocals, bass, keyboards, synthesizers (ex-JAPAN) with session

Jun 82. (7"/12") (VS 508/+12) **SENSITIVE. / THE SOUND OF WAVES** — / - (Virgin / Caroline)

Nov 82. (lp/c) (V/TCV 2249) <CAROL 1675> **TITLES** — 74 / -
– Tribal dawn / Lost affections in a room / Passion in moisture / Weather the windmill / Saviour, are you with me / Trust me / Sensitive / Piper blue. (re-iss. Aug88 lp/c; OVED/+C 91) (cd-iss. Oct90/ CDV 2249)

— In Jun83, he teamed up with ULTRAVOX's MIDGE URE, on the single AFTER A FASHION which reached UK No.39. In 1984 KARN formed DALI'S CAR with PETE MURPHY (ex-BAUHAUS) and PAUL VINCENT LAWFORD.

— MICK KARN returned to solo '86

Jan 87. (lp/c/cd) (V/TCV/CDV 2389) <CAROL 1864> **DREAMS OF REASON PRODUCE MONSTERS** — 89 / -
– First impression / Language of ritual / Buoy / Land / The three fates / When love walks in / Dreams of reason / Answer.

Jan 87. (7"; by MICK KARN featuring DAVID SYLVIAN) (VS 910) **BUOY. / DREAMS OF REASON** — 63 / -
(12"+=) (VST 910) – Language of ritual.

Oct 93. (cd) (CMPCD 1002) **BESTIAL CLUSTER** — / - (C.M.P. / not iss.)
– Bestial cluster / Back in the beginning / Beard in the letterbox / The drowning dream / The sad velvet breath of Summer & Winter / Saday, Maday / Liver and lungs / Bones of mud.

May 94. (cd; by DAVID TORN, MICK KARN + TERRY BOZZIO) (CMPCD 1006) **POLYTOWN** — / -
– Honey sweating / Palms for Lester / Open letter to the heart of diaphora / Bandaged by dreams / Warrior horsemen of the spirit thundering / Snail hair dune / This is the abduction scene / Red sleep / Res majuko.

— with RICHARD BARBIERI – keyboards / STEVE JANSEN – drums / DAVID TORN – guitar / DAVID LIEBMAN – soprano sax

May 95. (cd) (CMPCD 1008) **THE TOOTH MOTHER** — / -
– Thundergirl mutation / Plaster the magic tongue / Lodge of skins / Gossip's cup / Feat funk / The tooth mother / Little less hope / There was not anything but nothing.

– compilations, etc. –

Apr 98. (cd) C.M.P.; (CMPCD 1014) **THE MICK KARN COLLECTORS EDITION** — / -

JANSEN / BARBIERI

JANSEN – vocals, etc / **BARBIERI** – keyboards, etc

		Pan-East	not iss.
Oct 86.	(lp/c/cd) *(NEW LP/MC/CD 105)* **WORLDS IN A SMALL ROOM**	☐	-

– Breaking the silence / Toys / Blue lines / Mission / The way the light falls / Balance / Moving circles / Distant fire.

—— (at same time JANSEN w/ YUKIHURO TAKAHASHI released 7"; STAY CLOSE. / BETSU-NI on 'Rime'; *RIM 1*)

—— The JAPAN duo now

The DOLPHIN BROTHERS

—— with **DAVID RHODES** – guitar / **DANNY THOMPSON** – ac. bass / **MATTHEW SELIGMAN + ROBERT BELL** – bass / **PHIL PALMER** – acoustic guitar / **MARTIN DITCHAM** – percussion

		Virgin	Caroline
Jun 87.	(7") *(VS 969)* **SHINING. / MY WINTER** (12"+=) – *(VS 969-12)* – ('A'-Am-ex mix).	☐	-
Jul 87.	(lp/c/cd) *(V/TCV/CDV 2434)* <*CAROL 1828*> **CATCH THE FALL**	☐	

– Catch the fall / Shining / Second sight / Love that you need / Real life, real answers / Host to the holy / My winter / Pushing the river. *(cd re-iss. Mar91; same)*

| Aug 87. | (7"/12") *(VS 997/+12)* **SECOND SIGHT. / HOST TO THE HOLY** | ☐ | - |

STEVE JANSEN & RICHARD BARBIERI

		Venture	Virgin
Sep 91.	(cd) *(CDVE 908)* **STORIES ACROSS BORDERS**	☐	

– Long tales, tall shadows / When things dream / Luman / The insomniac's bed / The night gives birth / Celebration 1988 remix (saw) / Nocturnal sightseeing / One more zombie.

		Medium	not iss.
Mar 94.	(cd; by STEVE JANSEN, RICHARD BARBIERI & MICK KARN) *(MPCD 1)* **BEGINNING TO MELT**	☐	-

– Beginning to melt / The wilderness / March of the innocents / Human agie / Shipwrecks / Ego dance / The orange asylum. *(re-iss. Oct96; same)*

| Oct 94. | (cd; by STEVE JANSEN, RICHARD BARBIERI & MICK KARN) *(MPCD 2)* **SEED** | ☐ | - |

– Beginning to melt / In the black of desire / The insect tribe / Prey.

| Oct 95. | (cd) *(MPCD 3)* **STONE TO FLESH** | ☐ | - |

– Mother London / Sleepers awake / Ringing the bell backwards: Siren – Drift / Swim there / Closer than "I" / Everything ends in darkness. *(re-iss. Oct96 & Apr97; same)*

| Oct 96. | (cd) *(MPCD 4)* **OTHER WORLDS IN A SMALL ROOM** | ☐ | - |

– Remains of a fragile illusion / Light years / Disturbed sense of distance / Breaking the silence / Blue lines / Way the lights falls / Distant fire.

JILTED JOHN

Born: GRAHAM FELLOWS, Manchester, England. Having been an actor from the mid 70's, GRAHAM turned his attention to er . . . "singing" after being slightly influenced by the New Wave/Punk scene. His eponymous debut single, 'JILTED JOHN', was unleashed in the summer of '78 by local independent label, Rabid'. Its woeful tales of two-timing teen-angst were backed up by a pogo-punk beat, the record's potential leading to major 'EMI International' taking up its cause. Helped by daytime radioplay and an appearance on the prestigious (at the time!) Top Of The Pops TV show, the record shot up to No.4 in the charts and gave him not fifteen, but three minutes of fame. Subsequent follow-ups, including a MARTIN HANNETT-produced pseudo-concept long-player, 'TRUE LOVE STORIES' (1978) and two 45's by his winning rival/alter-ego, GORDON THE MORON, failed to shake off the one hit wonder/novelty tag and GRAHAM returned to acting; amongst other things, he went on to work in TV soap, 'Coronation Street'. After virtually disappearing throughout the 80's, the following decade saw GRAHAM resurface as Northern entertainer, JOHN SHUTTLEWORTH. Introduced through Jonathan Ross' Channel 4 TV show, the "old man" SHUTTLEWORTH character embarrassingly sang while programming his Bontempi organ, gaining cult status in the process. He went on to star in his own TV series, '500 Bus Stops' and did a mock Eurovision entry in 1997, singing the gloriously catchy 'Pigeons In Flight' (would have been a winner for me anyway!?).

Album rating: TRUE LOVE STORIES (*5)

JILTED JOHN – vocals / with session people

		Rabid	not iss.
Jul 78.	(7") *(TOSH 105)* **JILTED JOHN. / GOING STEADY**	☐	-
Sep 78.	(7"; as GORDON THE MORON) *(TOSH 107)* **DE DO DOUGH DON'T BE DOUGH. /**	☐	-
Dec 78.	(7"; as GORDON THE MORON) *(TOSH 111)* **FIT FOR NOTHING. / SOLD ON YOU**	☐	-

		EMI Internat.	not iss.
Aug 78.	(7") *(INT 567)* **JILTED JOHN. / GOING STEADY**	4	-
Nov 78.	(lp) *(INS 3024)* **TRUE LOVE STORIES**	☐	-

– Going steady / Baz's party / I know I'll never / I was a pre-pubescent / Fancy mile / Jilted John / The birthday kiss / The paperboy song / True love / In the bus shelter / Karen's letter / Shirley / Goodbye, Karen. *(cd-iss. Sep99 on 'Essential'+=; ESMCD 771)* – Jilted John (single version) / Fit for nothing / Sold on you.

| Jan 79. | (7") *(INT 577)* **TRUE LOVE. / I WAS A PRE-PUBESCENT** | ☐ | - |
| Apr 79. | (7") *(INT 587)* **BIRTHDAY KISS. / BAZ'S PARTY** | ☐ | - |

—— made one last effort, 'SOME BOYS', under the moniker, GOING RED (with fellow nutters, FAMILY FODDER), before retiring from the business. He subsequently re-appeared in the early 90's as tongue-in-cheek comedian/singer, JOHN SHUTTLEWORTH.

Richard JOBSON (see under ⇒ SKIDS)

JOHNNY & THE SELF-ABUSERS (see under ⇒ SIMPLE MINDS)

JOY DIVISION

Formed: Salford, Manchester, England . . . mid '77 initially as The STIFF KITTENS by IAN CURTIS, BERNARD ALBRECHT, PETER HOOK and STEPHEN MORRIS. By the time they were ready to take the stage for the first time, the group were going under the WARSAW moniker, finally settling on JOY DIVISION later that year. A term used by the Nazis for Jewish prostitutes, the band had taken the name from the book, 'House Of Dolls'; unsurprisingly, they ran into a little media trouble, the press subsequently speculating about their supposedly fascistic tendencies and unfairly branding them little Adolfs. Particularly controversial was the track, 'AT A LATER DATE', included on the 'Virgin' various artists punk sampler, 'Short Circuit: Live At The Electric Circus'. A vinyl debut proper came with the limited EP, 'AN IDEAL FOR LIVING', although it was through manager Rob Gretton and a subsequent deal with the emerging 'Factory' records that JOY DIVISION's career really got off the ground. Their first recordings for the label were a couple of tracks, 'GLASS' and 'DIGITAL', featured on a 'Factory' sampler (in mid-'79, a further two tracks, 'AUTO-SUGGESTION' and 'FROM SAFETY TO WHERE', surfaced on the 'Fast' records compilation EP, 'Earcom 2'), while their legendary Martin Hannett-produced debut album, 'UNKNOWN PLEASURES' was finally released later that summer. Groundbreaking in its bass-heavy, skeletal sound and evocation of urban alienation, isolation and despair, the record ensured CURTIS's position as a latter day messiah of existential angst; while his lyrics trawled the underbelly of the human psyche with disturbing clarity, his sub-JIM MORRISON ruminations were a blueprint for every pasty-faced goth pretender of the next decade. Tony Wilson's faith in the band was such that he contributed his life savings of over £8,000 towards the album's cost, the 'Factory' supremo's investment rewarded as the record topped the indie charts and JOY DIVISION became the foremost post-punk cult act. Yet even as the hypnotic rhythms of sublime new single, 'TRANSMISSION', hinted at an equally compelling new direction, CURTIS's robotic contortions and trance-like stage presence were giving way to epileptic fits as the singer struggled to cope with the increasing demands of live work. Tragically, on the 18th May, 1980, depressed with the break-up of his marriage and his worsening illness, CURTIS hanged himself. Ironically, JOY DIVISION scored their first chart hit a month later with the seminal 'LOVE WILL TEAR US APART'; the loss of such a fiercely individual talent was underlined as the track suggested a singer (and indeed, band) at the very apex of their creative potential. CURTIS had actually recorded a full album's worth of material before his death, released that summer as 'CLOSER'; even more lyrically unsettling, the record's bleak vision nevertheless pre-empted rock's dancefloor embrace on the synth-laced likes of 'ISOLATION', as well as forming the basis for NEW ORDER's experiments in cross-genre innovation. The latter act were formed later that year from JOY DIVISION's ashes, while further CURTIS-era material was posthumously released in late '81 as 'STILL'. The band remain one of the most revered and certainly one of the most influential outfits to emerge from the punk 'revolution', the best of NEW ORDER's work an indication as to what musical heights JOY DIVISION might have scaled had CURTIS prolonged the battle with his personal demons.

Album rating: UNKNOWN PLEASURES (*10) / CLOSER (*10) / STILL part compilation/live (*8) / SUBSTANCE compilation (*9) / PERMANENT: JOY DIVISION 1995 remixes (*6)

IAN CURTIS (b.15 Jul'56, Macclesfield, England) – vocals / **BERNARD ALBRECHT** (b. BERNARD DICKEN, 4 Jan'56) – guitar, vocals / **PETER HOOK** (b.13 Feb'56, Salford, Manchester) – bass / **STEPHEN MORRIS** (b.28 Oct'57, Macclesfield) – drums

		Enigma	not iss.
Jun 78.	(7"ep) *(PSS 139)* **AN IDEAL FOR LIVING**	☐	-

– An ideal for living / Warsaw / Leaders of men / No love lost / Failures. *(re-iss. Jul78 on 'Anonymous' 12"ep; ANON 1)*

		Factory	not iss.
Aug 79.	(lp) *(FACT 10)* **UNKNOWN PLEASURES**	☐	-

– Disorder / Day of the lords / Candidate / Insight / New dawn fades / She's lost control / Shadowplay / Wilderness / Interzone / I remember nothing. *(re-dist.Jul80, hit No.71) (re-iss. Jul82; same) (c-iss.Nov84; FACT 10C) (cd-iss. Apr86; FACD 10) (re-iss. Jul93 on 'Centredate-London' cd/c; 520016-2) <US-iss.1989 on 'Qwest' lp/c/cd; 1-/4-/2-25840> (cd re-iss. Jan00; 3984 28223-2)*

| Oct 79. | (7") *(FAC 13)* **TRANSMISSION. / NOVELTY** | | |

(re-iss. Oct80 as 12"; FAC 13-12)

| Mar 80. | (7") *(SS 33-002)* **ATMOSPHERE. / DEAD SOULS** | - | - France |

(above single released on 'Sordide Sentimentale' & now worth lots)

| Jun 80. | (7") *(FAC 23)* **LOVE WILL TEAR US APART. / THESE DAYS** | 13 | - |

(re-iss. Oct80 as 12"+=; FAC 23-12) – ('A'version). *(re-iss. Oct83; same; hit UK No.19)*

| Jul 80. | (lp) *(FACT 25)* **CLOSER** | 6 | - |

– Heart and soul / 24 hours / The eternal / Decades / Atrocity exhibition / Isolation / Passover / Colony / Means to an end. *(c-iss.Jul82; FACT 25C) (cd-iss. Apr86; FACD 25) (re-iss. Jul93 on 'Centredate-London' cd/c; 520015-2) <US-iss.1989 on 'Qwest' lp/c/cd; 1-/4-/2-25841> (cd re-iss. Sep99 on 'Factory Too'; 3984 28219-2)*

JOY DIVISION (cont)   THE GREAT INDIE DISCOGRAPHY   The 1970s

— After another fit of depression, IAN CURTIS hanged himself 18th May 1980. The others became NEW ORDER

– compilations, others, etc. –

Sep 80. (12") *Factory Benelux; (FACTUS 2)* **ATMOSPHERE. / SHE'S LOST CONTROL**
Apr 81. (free 7"flexi) *Factory; (FAC 28)* **KOMAKINO. / INCUBATION**
May 81. (7"ep/12"ep; as WARSAW) *Enigma; (PSS 138)* **THE IDEAL BEGINNING**
– Inside the line / Gutz / At a later date.
Oct 81. (d-lp) *Factory; (FACT 40)* **STILL (live & rare)**   5
– Exercise one / Ice age / The sound of music / Glass / The only mistake / Walked in line / The kill / Something must break / Dead souls / Sister Ray / Ceremony / Shadowplay / Means to an end / Passover / New dawn fades / Transmission / Disorder / Isolation / Decades / Digital. (c-iss.Dec86; FACT 40C) (cd-iss. Mar90; FACD 40) (re-iss. Jul93 on 'Centredate-London' cd/c; 520014-2/-4) <US-iss.1989 on 'Qwest' lp/c/cd; 26495> (cd re-iss. Jan00 on 'Factory Too'; 3984 28222-2)
Nov 86. (12"ep) *Strange Fruit; (SFPS 013)* **THE PEEL SESSIONS (31.1.79)**
– Exercise one / Insight / She's lost control / Transmission. (re-iss. Jul88 cd-ep; SFPSCD 013)
Sep 87. (12"ep) *Strange Fruit; (SFPS 033)* **THE PEEL SESSIONS 2 (26.11.79)**
– Love will tear us apart / 24 hours / Colony / The sound of music. (re-iss. Jul88 cd-ep; SFPSCD 033)
1987. (7"ep+book) *Stampa; (SCONIC 001)* **YOU'RE NO GOOD FOR ME / KOMAKINO / INCUBATION / INCUBATION (version)**   –   – Italy
Jun 88. (7") *Factory; (FAC 213-7)* **ATMOSPHERE. / THE ONLY MISTAKE**   34
(12"+=) *(FAC 213)* – The sound of music.
(cd-s) *(FACD 213)* – ('A'side) / Love will tear us apart / Transmission.
Jul 88. (lp/c/dat)(cd) *Factory; (FACT 250/+C/D)(FACD 250) / Qwest; <1-/4-/2-25747>* **SUBSTANCE** (The best of..)   7
– She's lost control / Dead souls / Atmosphere / Love will tear us apart / Warsaw / Leaders of men / Digital / Transmission / Auto-suggestion. (cd+=) – (7 extra tracks). (re-iss. Jul93 on 'Centredate-London' cd/c; 520 014-2/-4) (cd re-iss. Sep99 on 'Factory Too'; 3984 28224-2)
Sep 90. (cd/c) *Strange Fruit; (SFR CD/MC 111)* **COMPLETE PEEL SESSIONS**
Jun 95. (c-s) *London; (YOJC 1)* **LOVE WILL TEAR US APART (radio version) / ('A'-original version)**   19
(12"+=/cd-s+=) *(YOJ T/CD 1)* – These days / Transmission.
Jun 95. (cd/c/d-lp) *London; (828 624-2/-4/-1) / Warners; <45979>* **PERMANENT: JOY DIVISION 1995** (remixes)   16   Aug95
– Love will tear us apart / Transmission / She's lost control / Shadow play / Day of the lords / Isolation / Passover / Heart and soul / 24 hours / These days / Novelty / Dead souls / The only mistake / Something must break / Atmosphere / Love will tear us apart (Permanent mix). (cd re-iss. Sep99; 3984 28221-2)
Jan 98. (4xcd-box) *London; (<828 968-2>)* **HEART AND SOUL** (all material)   70
(re-iss. Sep99; 3984 29040-2)
Feb 98. (cd+book) *Sonic Book; (SB 10)* **ALL THE LYRICS**
Jul 00. (cd) *Fractured; (FACD 260)* **PRESTON – THE WAREHOUSE 28/2/80 (live)**
(lp-iss.Oct00 on 'Get Back'; GET 69)
Aug 00. (cd) *Strange Fruit; (SFRSCD 094)* **THE COMPLETE RADIO ONE RECORDINGS**
(lp-iss.Apr01; SFRSCD 084)
Apr 01. (cd) *Fractured; (FACD 261)* **LES BAINS DOUCHES**
(d-lp-iss.Jun01 on 'Get Back'; GET 79)

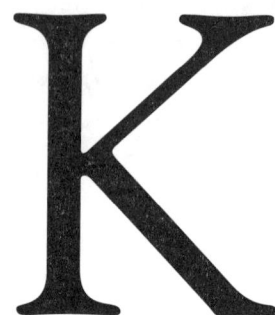

Mick KARN (see under ⇒ JAPAN)

Klark KENT (see under ⇒ POLICE)

KILBURN & THE HIGH ROADS (see under ⇒ DURY, Ian)

KILLJOYS

Formed: Stoke, England . . . 1977 by main writer, KEVIN ROLAND (aka ROWLAND, i.e. future lead singer for DEXY'S MIDNIGHT RUNNERS), alongside HEATHER TONGE, MARK PHILLIPS, GEM STONE (later bass player of GIRLSCHOOL) and JOE 45 (apparently, only half the man of puppet, JOE 90!). The KILLJOYS managed only one blasting raw punk anthem, 'JOHNNY WON'T GET TO HEAVEN' (a prophetic tale for JOHNNY ROTTEN!), before all but KEVIN disappeared from punk's underground limelight. However, an "oi" crew formed another KILLJOYS (not this lot!) for a one-off single, 'THIS IS NOT LOVE', late in 1982. • **Note:** Not to be confused with the Canadian power-pop outfit of the 90's.

Album rating: NAIVE mini compilation (*4)

KEVIN ROLAND – vocals / **GEM (STONE)** – bass / **HEATHER TONGE** – vocals / **MARK PHILLIPS** – guitar / **JOE 45** – drums

                                                                   Raw   not iss.

Nov 77. (7") *(RAW 3)* **JOHNNY WON'T GET TO HEAVEN. / NAIVE**
— they split for a long period while KEVIN advanced his DEXY's career
— GEM joined RUBELLA BALLET and later GIRLSCHOOL

– compilations, etc. –

May 92. (m-lp) *Damaged Goods; (FNARRLP 10)* **NAIVE**
— note: another KILLJOYS (not this one!) issued an album for 'Mushroom'.

KIPPINGTON LODGE
(see under ⇒ BRINSLEY SCHWARZ)

Richard H. KIRK
(see under ⇒ CABARET VOLTAIRE)

KLEENEX

Formed: Geneva, Switzerland . . . 1978 by RAMONA CARLER, MARLENE MARDER, KLAUDI SCHIFF and LISLOT HA. One of the first bands to sign with 'Rough Trade', this highly regarded Euro punk outfit released only two singles, 'AIN'T YOU' and 'HEIDI'S HEAD' before the threat of legal action from the tissue giant of the same name convinced them to adopt the LILIPUT moniker. With the addition of sax, the band's jerky, stop-start chants assumed a new depth and a vaguely X-RAY SPEX/SLITS-like sound, especially on the moody 'DIE MATROSSEN' (the B-side of debut single, 'SPLIT'). A second single, 'EISERGWIND', preceded an eponymous debut set in 1983, yet by the time of the album's release the band had already ceased to exist. A further album, 'SOME SONGS', surfaced as a German-only release later the same year, MARDER subsequently formed DANGER MICE before going on to work in record retail.

Album rating: LILIPUT (*7) / SOME SONGS (*5) / COMPLETE RECORDINGS compilation (*8)

REGULA SING (b. RAMONA CARLIER) – vocals / **MARLENE MARDER** – guitar / **KLAUDI SCHIFF** – bass, vocals / **LISLOT HA** – drums

                                                                   Rough Trade   not iss.

Nov 78. (7") *(RT 009)* **AIN'T YOU. / HEIDI'S HEAD**
— **CRIGELE FREUND** – vocals repl. REGULA who joined MO-DETTES
May 79. (7") *(RT 014)* **YOU. / U**

LILIPUT

— added **ANGIE BARRACK** – saxophone

		Rough Trade	not iss.
Jun 80.	(7") *(RT 047)* **SPLIT. / DIE MATROSEN**	□	-
Feb 81.	(7") *(RT 062)* **ELSIGER WIND. / WHEN THE CAT'S AWAY, THE MICE WILL PLAY**	□	-

— **ASTRID SPIRIT** – vocals, violin, bass, percussion repl. CRIGELE and LISLOT

| 1982. | (lp) *(ROUGH 43)* **LILIPUT** | □ | - |

– Do you mind my dream / In a mess / Birdy / Feel like snakes, twisting / Through the fog / Tschik-Mo / Outburst / Umamm / Might is right / Like it or lump it / Ichor / Tong-tong. *(re-iss. Aug84)*

| Jul 83. | (7") *(RTD 01)* **YOU DID IT. / THE JAZZ** | - | - German |

— added guest drummer **BEAT SCHLATTER**

| Dec 83. | (lp) *(RTD 15)* **SOME SONGS** | - | - German |

– Ring-a-ding-dong / A silver key can open an iron lock, somewhere / Yours is mine / Blue is all in rush / Terrified / Etoile / On streets without names / Boat-song / His head all red.

— disbanded after above; MARDER went onto form DANGER MICE who released two singles, 'I HAVE GOT YOU' & 'BROKEN NEW HEART'. She returned to Zurich to run a record shop, while SCHIFF became one of her countries best known modern painters.

– compilations, etc. –

| Feb 01. | (d-cd) For Us; *(FU 014CD)* / Kill Rock Stars; *<KRS 373>* **THE COMPLETE RECORDINGS** | □ | □ |

(above was actually issued in Switzerland in 1993 as 'LILIPUT')

Wayne KRAMER (see under ⇒ MC5)

Ed KUEPPER
(see under ⇒ LAUGHING CLOWNS; in 80's section)

Jon LANGFORD (see under ⇒ MEKONS)

LAST

Formed: Los Angeles, California, USA . . . 1976 by brothers JOE, MIKE and DAVID NOLTE, along with VITUS MATARE and JACK REYNOLDS. Inspired by 60's garage, psychedelia and bubblegum, this seminal New Wave/Power Pop outfit hit out with three self-financed 45's, 'SHE DON'T KNOW WHY I'M HERE', 'EVERY SUMMER DAY' and 'L.A. EXPLOSION', in 1978. The latter was also used as their major label debut LP for 'London' the following year. Back on the roster of their own 'Backlash' imprint, The LAST delivered sophomore set, 'LOOK AGAIN' (1980), which was followed by a few low-key EP's. With DAVID departing to his own WEDNESDAY WEEK project, the remaining brothers took a sabbatical until 1988; MIKE and JOE recruited ROBBIE RIST (drums), LUK LOHNES (guitar) and MISSY BUETTNER (bass) for a stint with established hardcore/punk label, 'S.S.T.'. Following further line-up changes, The LAST cut two more LP's, 'AWAKENING' (1989) and the long-awaited 'GIN & INNUENDO' (1996). • **Covered:** BE-BOP-A-LULA (Gene Vincent) / SHE LOVES YOU (Beatles) / BABY IT'S YOU (Bacharach-David).

Album rating: L.A. EXPLOSION (*7) / LOOK AGAIN (*5) / PAINTING SMILES ON A DEAD MAN (*5) / CONFESSION (*5) / AWAKENING (*7) / GIN AND INNUENDO (*4)

MIKE NOLTE – vocals / **JOE NOLTE** – lead guitar, vocals / **VITUS MATARE** – keyboards, flute / **DAVID NOLTE** – bass / **JACK REYNOLDS** – drums

		not iss.	Backlash
Feb 78.	(7") *<BLS 001>* **SHE DON'T KNOW WHY I'M HERE. / BOMBING OF LONDON**	-	□

<re-iss. 1979 on 'Bomp'; BMP 119>

| Jun 78. | (7") *<BLS 002>* **EVERY SUMMER DAY. / HITLER'S BROTHER** | - | □ |
| Nov 78. | (7") *<BLS 003>* **L.A. EXPLOSION. / HITLER'S BROTHER** | - | □ |

		London	Bomp!
Nov 79.	(7") *<BMP 126>* **EVERY SUMMER DAY. / SLAVEDRIVER**	-	□
Dec 79.	(lp) *(SH-Z 8540) <BLP 4004>* **L.A. EXPLOSION**	□	□

– She don't know why I'm here / This kind of feeling / Bombing of London / Century city rag / Walk like me / Slavedriver / Every summer day / Rack / Objections / Fool like you / Someone's laughing / I don't wanna be in love / Be-bop-a-lula / Looking at you.

| 1980. | (lp) *<private>* **LOOK AGAIN** | - | - |

— *<above issued on 'Backlash'>*

| 1982. | (12"ep) *<BMP12 132>* **FADE TO BLACK** | - | - |
| 1982. | (7") **BE-BOP-A-LULA. / OBJECTIVES** | - | - |

		not iss.	Warfrat
1982.	(12") **UP IN THE AIR. / WRONG TURN**	-	□

— **JOHN ROSEWALL** – bass; repl. DAVID (on most) who joined WEDNESDAY WEEK and later LUCKY / **JOHN FRANK** – drums; repl. JACK / added **STEVE ANDREWS** – guitar

		Lolita	not iss.
1985.	(lp) *(5005)* **PAINTING SMILES ON A DEAD MAN**	-	- French

– Wrong turn / It had to be you / Isn't anybody there / Lightning strikes / Louie Louie / December song / Everybody's had it with you / Weekend girl / Failing heart / Leper colony / What is in there / Up in the air.

— **JOE + MIKE** re-formed adding **LUK LOHNES** – guitar, vocals / **MISSY BUETTNER** – bass / **ROBBIE RIST** – drums

		S.S.T.	S.S.T.
Jul 88.	(lp/c/cd) *<(SST 189/+C/CD)>* **CONFESSION**	□	□

– So quick to say / Another side / Going gone / And they laugh / I saw your eyes / It isn't really you / Don't care / Soldiers of love / Book / Dancing / Everywhere you turn / Confession.

— **DAVE NAZWORTHY** – drums; repl. RIST

— **LARRY P. MANKE** – bass; repl. BUETTNER

| Jul 89. | (lp/c/cd) *<(SST 230/+C/CD)>* **AWAKENING** | □ | □ |

– No love / Assembly line / You / Somebody new / Garden grow / Your wings / Book of life / Dreaming / Tired / Awakening / She loves you / Baby it's you.

| May 96. | (cd) *<SST 323CD>* **GIN & INNUENDO** | - | □ |

– Drywood town / Sleep / It's not that way / Sirens / Don't make no sound / Song - Unordinary substance / Guls / 7-21 / You won't win / Let there be Naz / Withdrawal / Blessed / Time is gone / Look for me / Slug / Time is gone.

above was finally their last album

Thomas LEER

Born: THOMAS WISHART, 1960, Port Glasgow, Scotland. As a young teenager at school, the young THOMAS played and sang in a variety of local experimental pop groups, although with the advent of punk rock he moved down south to London, forming the group, PRESSURE, in the process. By late 1978, again returning to his love of electro-pop and CAN, LEER self-financed his debut single, 'PRIVATE PLANE', a machine-friendly minor classic. The following year, together with ROBERT RENTAL (former musical associate of The NORMAL), he issued a collaboration set, 'THE BRIDGE', although only one track, 'ATTACK DECAY', stood out. In the summer of '81, THOMAS resurfaced as a solo artist with the EP, '4 MOVEMENTS', his first of three promising releases for the stalwart indie imprint, 'Cherry Red'. The last of these, 'ALL ABOUT YOU' (a single and his most commercial so far), paved the way for 'Arista' to snap him up (partly reviving his 'Oblique' set-up), although their idea to release his debut's B-side, 'INTERNATIONAL', was certainly questionable. However, the mid-80's was definitely his most creative period, the long-awaited debut album proper, 'THE SCALE OF TEN', finally delivered towards the end of '85. Two years later, LEER abandoned his ineffectual solo career to help initiate the 'Z.T.T.' duo, ACT, with former PROPAGANDA chanteuse, CLAUDIA BRUCKEN. This partnership began reasonably well with a minor hit single, 'SNOBBERY AND DECAY', although their short-lived professional affair was over after their one and only long-player, 'LAUGHTER, TEARS AND RAGE' (1988), was panned by the press.
• ACT covered: WHITE RABBIT (Jefferson Airplane) / HEAVEN KNOWS I'M MISERABLE NOW (Smiths).

Album rating: THE SCALE OF TEN (*5) / CONTRADICTIONS – THE CHERRY RED COLLECTION compilation (*7*) / Act: LAUGHTER, TEARS & RAGE (*4)

THOMAS LEER – vocals, keyboards, synthesizer

		Oblique	not iss.
Nov 78.	(7") *(ER 101)* **PRIVATE PLANE. / INTERNATIONAL**		–
		Industrial	not iss.
1979.	(lp; by THOMAS LEER & ROBERT RENTAL) *(IR 0007)* **THE BRIDGE** – Attack decay / Monochrome days / Day breaks, night heals / Connotations / Fade away / Interferon / 6 a.m. / The hard way & the easy way out / Perpetual. *(cd-iss. Jun92 on 'Grey Area'; BRIDGE 1CD)*		–
		Cherry Red	not iss.
Jul 81.	(12"ep) *(12CHERRY 28)* **4 MOVEMENTS** – Don't / Letter from America / Light as a drum / West End.		–
Jan 82.	(2x12"m-lp) *(ERED 26)* **CONTRADICTIONS** – Hear what I say / Mr. Nobody / Contradictions / Looks that kill / Soul gypsy / Choices / Gulf stream.		–
Nov 82.	(7"/12") *(CHERRY/12CHERRY 52)* **ALL ABOUT YOU. / SAVING GRACE**		–
		Arista	Arista
Jul 84.	(7"/12") *(LEER/+12 1)* **INTERNATIONAL. / EASY WAY**		–
Feb 85.	(7"/12") *(LEER/+12 2)* **HEARTBEAT. / CONTROL YOURSELF**		–
May 85.	(7") *(LEER 3)* **NO.1. / CHASING THE DRAGON** (12"+=) *(LEER 3T)* – Trust me.		–
Nov 85.	(lp/c) *(207/407 208)* **THE SCALE OF TEN**		

ACT

THOMAS LEER + CLAUDIA BRUCKEN – vocals (ex-PROPAGANDA)

		Z.T.T.	Island
May 87.	(7") *(ZTAS 28)* **SNOBBERY AND DECAY. / POISON** ('A'-That's Entertainment mix-12"+=) *(12ZTAS 28)* – I'd be surprisingly good for you. (12") *(12ZACT 28)* – ('A'-Naked Civil remix) / Strong poison / ('A'-...Theme from). (cd-s) *(CID 28)* – ('A'extended) / I'd be surprisingly good for you / Poison / ('A'-...Theme from). (c-s) *(CTIS 28)* – Snobbery and Decay Cabaret Cassette.	60	
Aug 87.	(7") *(IMM 1)* **ABSOLUTELY IMMUNE. / BLOODRUSH** (12"+=) *(TIMM 1)* – White rabbit. (12"+=) *(VIMM 1)* – States of logic.		–
Feb 88.	(7") *(IMM 2)* **I CAN'T ESCAPE FROM YOU. / DEAR LIFE** (12"+=/cd-s+=) *(T/CD IMM 2)* – ('A'-Love And Hate) / Heaven knows I'm miserable now.		–
Jun 88.	(7"; w-drawn) *(BET 1)* **CHANCE. / WINNER '88** (12"+=/cd-s+=) *(BET T/CD 1)* – Chance (we give you another chance).	–	–
Jul 88.	(lp/c/cd) *(ZQ CD/MC/LP 1)* **LAUGHTER, TEARS & RAGE** – Absolutely immune / Chance / Laughter / I can't escape from you / Poison / Under the nights of Germany / Gestures / A friendly warning / Certified / Where love lies bleeding / Snobbery and decay. *(c+=)* – Bloodrush / Poison. *(cd++=)* – Heaven knows I'm miserable now / The 3rd planet.		

— when CLAUDIA went solo the duo split and LEER retired

– (THOMAS LEER) compilation –

| Jan 94. | (cd) *Cherry Red; (CDBRED 105)* **CONTRADICTIONS – THE CHERRY RED COLLECTION** – CONTRADICTIONS (tracks) / Private plane / International / Kings of sham / Dry land / Don't / Letter from America / Tight as a drum / West end / All about you / Love and flowers / Togetherness and unity. *(re-iss. Oct00; CDMRED 105)* | | – |

Jackie LEVEN (see under ⇒ DOLL BY DOLL)

LEYTON BUZZARDS

Formed: Leyton, East London, England... late '77 by GEOFFREY DEANE (aka NICK NAYME) and DAVID JAYMES (DAVE DEPRAVE), who almost immediately recruited VERNON AUSTIN (CHIP MONK) and KEVIN STEPTOE (GRAY MARE). Leaving behind their pub rock beginnings, The LEYTON BUZZARDS got in on the punk/New Wave act and signed a one-off deal with the indie imprint, 'Small Wonder', releasing their debut, '19 AND MAD', the following year. Subsequently scooping first prize in a high profile Battle Of The Bands competition (jointly run by BBC Radio One and The Sun), the group were rewarded with a major label deal courtesy of 'Chrysalis'. Early in '79, they swooped into the lower regions of the UK charts with the easier-going 'SATURDAY NIGHT (BENEATH THE PLASTIC PALM TREES)', their claim to fame being a Top Of The Pops appearance. However, their follow-up single, 'I'M HANGING AROUND', failed to take them any higher up the proverbial pecking order, even an abbreviation of their moniker to The BUZZARDS not helping to stave off the encircling critical vultures. A debut album, 'JELLIED EELS TO RECORD DEALS' (1979), was savaged by the critics, leaving the band with only a bucketful of the former as their contract flew out the window, so to speak. Once bitten, twice shy(te), should have been the guiding motto of DEANE and JAYMES as they returned to terrorise the pop charts with the frankly embarrassing MODERN ROMANCE ("The Best Years Of Our Lives", "Ay Ay Ay Ay...." right!).

Album rating: Buzzards: JELLIED EELS TO RECORD DEALS (*4)

GEOFF DEANE (b.10 Dec'54) – vocals / **VERNON AUSTIN** – guitar / **DAVID JAYMES** (b.28 Dec'54, Woodford, Essex, England) – bass / **KEVIN STEPTOE** – drums

		Small Wonder	not iss.
Jul 78.	(7") *(SMALL 7)* **19 AND MAD. / VILLAIN / YOUTHANASIA**		–
		Chrysalis	not iss.
Feb 79.	(7") *(CHS 2288)* **SATURDAY NIGHT (BENEATH THE PLASTIC PALM TREES). / THROUGH WITH YOU**	53	–
May 79.	(7") *(CHS 2328)* **I'M HANGING AROUND. / I DON'T WANT TO GO TO ART SCHOOL / NO DRY ICE OR FLYING PIGS**		–
Aug 79.	(7"; as the BUZZARDS) *(CHS 2360)* **WE MAKE A NOISE. / DISCO ROMEO**		–
Oct 79.	(lp; as the BUZZARDS) *(CHR 1213)* **JELLIED EELS TO RECORD DEALS** – Sharp young men / Saturday night (beneath the plastic palm trees) / I don't want to go to art school / British justice / The greatest story ever told / Land of the free / I'm hanging around / Can't get used to losing you / Sweet dreams little one / Mixed marriages / We make a noise / 19 and mad / People on the street / Disco Romeo / Through with you / No dry ice or flying pigs / Baby if you love me say yes if you don't say no.		–
		WEA	not iss.
Jul 80.	(7"; as LEYTON BUZZARDS) *(K 18284)* **CAN'T GET USED TO LOSING YOU. / WEIRD FRENZ**		–

— DEANE and JAYMES evolved the group into salsa popsters, MODERN ROMANCE, enjoying a string of hits in the first half of the 80's.

Arto LINDSAY (see under ⇒ DNA)

Richard LLOYD (see under ⇒ TELEVISION)

Lora LOGIC

Born: SUSAN WHITBY, c.1961, London, England. Alongside POLY STYRENE, she came to prominence in 1977 as the saxophonist with punk group, X-RAY SPEX. LORA departed however, immediately after the release of their debut 45, 'Oh Bondage Up Yours'; the classic punk track was originally a highlight on the infamous 'Live At The Roxy' V/A album. The following year, LORA re-emerged with a new outfit, ESSENTIAL LOGIC, a frenetic avant-New Wave project who debuted with the single, 'AEROSOL BURNS'. After signing a one-off deal with 'Virgin' in 1979 for a follow-up single, 'WAKE UP', they secured a longer-term contract with 'Rough Trade'. By this time, ESSENTIAL LOGIC were comprised of LORA, PHILIP LEGG, MARK TURNER, WARBLING DAVID WRIGHT and RICH TEA, this line-up featuring on a debut album, 'BEAT RHYTHM NEWS' (1979). During this period, LORA guested for the likes of the SWELL MAPS, RED CRAYOLA, the STRANGLERS and the RAINCOATS, prior to initiating her own short-lived solo career. However, after only one solitary lp in 1982, 'PEDIGREE CHARM', LORA chose the same spiritual path as her former X-RAY SPEX bandmate, giving up the music business to join the Hare Krishna movement.

Album rating: Essential Logic: BEAT RHYTHM NEWS (*6) / PEDIGREE CHARM (*6)

ESSENTIAL LOGIC

LORA LOGIC – vocals, saxophone (ex-X-RAY SPEX) / **STUART ACTION** – guitar / **TIM WRIGHT** – bass / **RICH TEA** – drums

		Cells	not iss.
Jun 78.	(7") *(CELLS ONE)* **AEROSOL BURNS. / WORLD FRICTION**		–

— STUART + TIM were repl. **PHILIP LEGG** – guitar / **WILLIAM BENNETT** – guitar / **MARK TURNER** – bass / **WARBLING DAVID WRIGHT** – tenor sax

		Virgin	not iss.
May 79.	(12"ep) *(VS 261-12)* **ESSENTIAL LOGIC EP** – Wake up / Eagle bird / Quality crayon wax O.K. / Bod's message.		–

— now without BENNETT

				Rough Trade	not iss.
Oct 79.	(7")	(RT 029)	**POPCORN BOY. / FLORA FORCE**		-
Oct 79.	(lp)	(ROUGH 5)	**BEAT RHYTHM NEWS**		-

– Quality crayon wax o.k. / The order form / Shabby Abbott / World friction / Wake up / Albert / Alkaline loaf in the area / Collecting dust / Popcorn boy.

Nov 80.	(7")	(RT 050)	**EUGENE. / TAME THE NEIGHBOURS**		-
Jan 81.	(7")	(RT 053)	**MUSIC IS A BETTER NOISE. / MOONTOWN**		-
Jun 81.	(7")	(RT 074)	**FANFARE IN THE GARDEN. / THE CAPTAIN**		-

— split soon after above, some members joined RIP, RIG & PANIC

LORA LOGIC

— with **PHIL LEGG** + **BEN ANNESLEY** – bass / **RICH TEA** + **CHARLES HAYWARD** (ex-THIS HEAT) – drums

				Rough Trade	not iss.
Oct 81.	(7")	(RT 087)	**WONDERFUL OFFER. / STEREO**		-
Feb 82.	(lp)	(ROUGH 28)	**PEDIGREE CHARM**		-

– Brute fury / Horrible party / Stop halt / Wonderful offer / Martian man / Hiss and shake / Pedigree charm / Rat alley / Crystal gazing.

— split when she converted to Hare Krishna. LEGG joined The GIST.

Lene LOVICH

Born: LILI MARLENE PREMILOVICH, 30 Mar'49, Detroit, Michigan, USA, the daughter of a Yugoslavian father and English mother. In the early 60's, LENE and her mother took up residence in London, although she ran away from home a few years later. The budding singer/songwriter subsequently received a place at London's Central School of Art where she studied sculpture and met future husband and writing partner, LES CHAPPELL. Together they formed a band, The DIVERSIONS, signing to 'Polydor' in the mid-70's. Their one and only album was rejected however, although a solo LENE did release an embarrassing Xmas novelty (1976) single, 'I SAW MOMMY KISSING SANTA CLAUS'. Influenced by the onset of Punk Rock/New Wave and having also put her distinctive shriek to good use in the horror-film industry, LENE moved to the forefront of the musical revolution via a deal with 'Stiff'. Although the label's magic touch didn't work first time around with the flop cover of Tommy James & The Shondells' 'I THINK WE'RE ALONE NOW', her breakthrough came early in '79 with UK Top 3 smash, 'LUCKY NUMBER'. An infectious, quirky pop tune, its robotic simplicity focused around LOVICH's banshee-on-speed vocal style while a Top Of The Pops appearance found her cast as a more extravagant, intense punk cousin to KATE BUSH. Over the course of the following year, LENE and her shaven-headed sidekick, LES, completed two moderately successful albums, 'STATELESS' (1979) and 'FLEX' (1980), both of which contained further hits including the Top 20 third single, 'SAY WHEN'. However, the limited appeal of this singer/sax-player was all too obvious as subsequent releases – including third set, 'NO MAN'S LAND' (1982) – failed miserably both critically and commercially. As well as scoring bit parts in the movies, 'Cha Cha' and 'Mati Hari', LENE also hooked up with German punkstress, NINA HAGEN, for a one-off pro-Animal Rights single, 'DON'T KILL THE ANIMALS'. The latter track represented her only musical excursion during a 7-year itch, finally broken when she made a belated comeback album, 'MARCH', in '89.

Album rating: THE VERY BEST OF LENE LOVICH compilation (*6)

LENE LOVICH – vocals, saxophone; with session people

				Polydor	not iss.
Nov 76.	(7")	(2058 812)	**I SAW MOMMY KISSING SANTA CLAUS. / CHRISTMAS SONG (MERRY CHRISTMAS TO YOU) / HAPPY CHRISTMAS**		-

				Stiff	Stiff
Aug 78.	(7")	(BUY 32)	**I THINK WE'RE ALONE NOW. / LUCKY NUMBER**		-
Feb 79.	(7"/12")	(BUY/12BUY 42)	**LUCKY NUMBER. / HOME**	3	
Mar 79.	(lp,pic-lp,red-lp)	(SEEZ 7) <36102>	**STATELESS**	35	

– Home / Sleeping beauty / Lucky number / Too tender (to touch) / Say when / Writing on the wall / Telepathy / Momentary breakdown / I think we're alone now / One in a million / Tonight. (cd-iss. May94 on 'Disky'; STIFFCD 20) (cd re-iss. Oct94 on 'Line'; LICD 901066)

Apr 79.	(7")	(BUY 46)	**SAY WHEN. / ONE LONELY HEART**	19	
	(12"+=)	(12BUY 46)	– ('A' version).		
Sep 79.	(7")	(BUY 53)	**BIRD SONG. / TRIXI**	39	
	(12"+=)	(12BUY 53)	– Too tender to touch.		
Jan 80.	(7")	(BUY 63)	**ANGELS. / THE FLY**		
	(12"+=)	(12BUY 63)	– The fall.		
Jan 80.	(lp)	(SEEZ 19) <36308>	**FLEX**	19	94

– Bird song / What will I do without you / Angels / The night / You can't kill me / Egg head / Wonderful one / Monkey talk / Joan / The freeze. (cd-iss. May94 on 'Disky'; STIFFCD 21) (cd re-iss. Oct94 on 'Line'; LICD 901071)

Mar 80.	(d7")	(BUY 69)	**WHAT WILL I DO WITHOUT YOU. / JOAN // MONKEY TALK (live) / THE NIGHT (live). / TOO TENDER (live) / YOU CAN'T KILL ME (live)**	58	
Feb 81.	(7"/12")	(BUY/+IT 97)	**NEW TOY. / CATS AWAY**	53	
	(c-s+=)	(ZBUY 97)	– ('A' extended).		
Oct 82.	(lp/c)	(SEEZ/ZSEEZ 44) <38399>	**NO-MAN'S-LAND**		

– It's you, only you (mein schmerz) / Blue hotel / Rocky road / Sister video / Faces / Special star / Maria / Savages / Walking low. (cd-iss. May94 on 'Disky'; STIFFCD 22)

Nov 82.	(7"/7"pic-d)	(BUY/+P 164)	**IT'S YOU, ONLY YOU (MEIN SCHMERZ). / BLUE**	68	

— She retired for a while until a recording with German solo star, NINA HAGEN, appeared in 1986. The one-off single, 'DON'T KILL THE ANIMALS', was released in 7"/12" on 'Arista'; RIS/+T 3)

				not iss.	Pathfinder
1989.	(cd/c)	<PAT 8909>	**MARCH**	-	

– Life / Wonderland / Nightshift / Hold on to love / Rage / Natural beauty / Make believe / Shadow walk / Vertigo / Sharman. (Uk-iss.Oct95 on 'Evidence'; ECD 28001-2)

– compilations, etc. –

Sep 90.	(cd)	Great Expectations; (PIPCD 007)	**THE STIFF YEARS VOL.1**		-
Sep 90.	(cd)	Great Expectations; (PIPCD 008)	**THE STIFF YEARS VOL.2**		-

(above 2 re-iss. cd Feb94 on 'Disky'; HRCD 8035)

May 97.	(cd)	Disky; (DC 87858-2)	**THE VERY BEST OF LENE LOVICH**		-

– Lucky number / Tonight / Say when / Be stiff / What will I do without you / Angels / Too tender (to touch) / New toy / Momentary breakdown / It's you, only you (mein schmerz) / Once in a million / Home / Bird song / Writing on the wall / Telepathy / I think we're alone now / Special star / Big bird / Sleeping beauty.

Nick LOWE

Born: 24 Mar'49, Woodchurch, Suffolk, England. In 1963, LOWE formed his first semi-serious musical enterprise, SOUND 4 PLUS 1, with schoolfriend, BRINSLEY SCHWARZ. This subsequently evolved into KIPPINGTON LODGE, a pseudo-psychedelic outfit which released a series of flop singles before re-launching in 1969 under the BRINSLEY SCHWARZ banner. Despite a disastrous beginning (see separate entry), the band became one of the leading lights of the 70's pub-rock scene and released a clutch of fine, rootsy albums before their eventual demise in 1975. As well as handling bass and vocal duties, LOWE had penned the bulk of the band's material, finally embarking on a solo career the following year. Although his first releases were a couple of pseudonymous, tongue-in-cheek singles (TARTAN HORDE – 'Bay City Rollers We Love You' / 'Rollers Theme' and DISCO BROTHERS – 'Let's Go To The Disco' / 'Everybody Dance'), LOWE was also making a name for himself as a producer (GRAHAM PARKER & THE RUMOUR, DR. FEELGOOD etc.) and in 1976 had a hand in setting up Jake Rivera's seminal 'Stiff' label. His debut single, 'SO IT GOES', was also Stiff's very first release, LOWE helping to shape both the operation's identity and the careers of its artists i.e. The DAMNED, IAN DURY, ELVIS COSTELLO amongst others. LOWE joined the latter in late '77 at Rivera's new venture, 'Radar', where he recorded the UK Top 10 single, 'I LOVE THE SOUND OF BREAKING GLASS', and Top 30 album, 'THE JESUS OF COOL' (1978). Released in America under the title, 'PURE POP FOR NOW PEOPLE', the album saw LOWE's writing take a distinctly more sardonic turn although his lyrical barbs were rarely as razor sharp as those of labelmate COSTELLO. He nevertheless proved himself to be witty, articulate and intelligent as well as a consummate musical chameleon capable of traversing rock'n'roll boundaries while injecting his songs with a rootsy authenticity. 1979's 'LABOUR OF LUST' spawned a second major hit single in 'CRUEL TO BE KIND', the song also making the American Top 20. From the summer of '77 onwards, LOWE had also been a member of DAVE EDMUND's band, ROCKPILE (EDMUNDS and other band members played on LOWE's solo material), the outfit graduating from live work to releasing an album, 'Seconds Of Pleasure', in 1980. Although the record was a minor success, the group folded shortly after and LOWE divided his time between production (working with The PRETENDERS, PAUL CARRACK, FABULOUS THUNDERBIRDS and JOHN HIATT amongst others) and solo work. The turn of the decade also saw him marrying CARLENE CARTER (daughter of JOHNNY CASH), a successful country singer in her own right who numbered among LOWE's production clients. Recorded with new backing band, The CHAPS (subsequently NOISE TO GO), 'NICK THE KNIFE' (1980) was his first album for 'Columbia' and his last to enjoy any kind of chart success. The 80's were a difficult period for LOWE; increasingly countrified sets such as 'THE ABOMINABLE SHOWMAN' (1983) and 'NICK LOWE & HIS COWBOY OUTFIT' (1984) were enjoyable enough if never threatening to break him into the mainstream. Towards the end of the decade, he sunk into depression and considered retiring from the music business before making a convincing return to form with 1990's 'PARTY OF ONE', an infectious, invigorating album which saw him reunited with EDMUNDS and featured the likes of JIM KELTNER and RY COODER. The latter two hooked up with LOWE and JOHN HIATT in a kind of critics' supergroup, LITTLE VILLAGE (the same formation that played on HIATT's 1987 album, 'Bring The Family'), releasing an eponymous, one-off album in 1992. A fairly average affair, the album nevertheless saw LOWE back in the UK Top 30 for the first time in more than a decade. Yet this success failed to have a knock-on effect in terms of his solo career, 'THE IMPOSSIBLE BIRD' (1994) failing to cross over to a wider audience despite widespread critical acclaim. It's typical of LOWE's career, the man remaining something of an unsung, backroom hero when at the very least, he deserves some kind of recognition for his contributions to popular music over a career spanning more than thirty years. While 1998's 'DIG MY MOOD' found LOWE in balladeering mode, the equally laid back musings of 'CONVINCER' (2001) proved that, if his muse flows as easily as it does on this record, then he doesn't actually need to convince anybody at all, least of all his fans.

• **Songwriters:** Self-penned except; PEACE, LOVE & UNDERSTANDING (Brinsley Schwarz) / HALFWAY TO PARADISE (Billy Fury) / ENDLESS SLEEP (Joey Reynolds) / I KNEW THE BRIDE (Dave Edmunds) / etc.

Album rating: JESUS OF COOL (aka PURE POP FOR NOW PEOPLE) (*8) / LABOUR OF LUST (*7) / NICK THE KNIFE (*6) / THE ABOMINABLE SHOWMAN (*4) / NICK LOWE AND HIS COWBOY OUTFIT (*6) / THE ROSE OF ENGLAND (*6) / PINKER AND PROUDER THAN PREVIOUS (*5) / BASHER: THE BEST OF

NICK LOWE compilation (*7) / PARTY OF ONE (*4) / THE WILDERNESS YEARS early stuff (*5) / THE IMPOSSIBLE BIRD (*6) / DIG MY MOOD (*6) / THE CONVINCER (*5) / Little Village: LITTLE VILLAGE (*5)

NICK LOWE – vocals, bass, guitar (ex-BRINSLEY SCHWARZ) He was also a member of DAVE EDMUNDS' ROCKPILE group between Jul77-Feb81. His solo band included **EDMUNDS** – guitar and other ROCKPILE members **BILLY BREMNER** – guitar and **TERRY WILLIAMS** – drums (ex-MAN, etc.) used mainly on 2 albums below.

		Stiff	not iss.
Aug 76.	(7") *(BUY 1)* **SO IT GOES. / HEART OF THE CITY**		–
May 77.	(7"ep) *(LAST 1)* **BOWI**		–
	– Born a woman / Shake that rat / Marie Provost / Endless sleep.		
Oct 77.	(7") *(BUY 21)* **HALFWAY TO PARADISE. / I DON'T WANT THE NIGHT TO END**		–

		Radar	Columbia
Feb 78.	(7") *(ADA 1)* **I LOVE THE SOUND OF BREAKING GLASS. / THEY CALLED IT ROCK**	7	–
Feb 78.	(lp/c) *(RAD/RAC 1)* <35329> **THE JESUS OF COOL** <US-title 'PURE POP FOR NOW PEOPLE'>	22	
	– Music for money / I love the sound of breaking glass / Little Hitler / Shake & pop / Tonight / So it goes / No reason / 36 inches high / Marie Provost / Nutted by reality / Heart of the city. *(re-iss. Oct88 & Aug00 on 'Demon' lp/c/cd; FIEND/+CASS/CD 131)*		
May 78.	(7") *(ADA 12)* **LITTLE HITLER. / CRUEL TO BE KIND**	–	–
Jul 78.	(7") <10734> **HEART OF THE CITY. / SO IT GOES**	–	–
Sep 78.	(7") <10844> **I LOVE THE SOUND OF BREAKING GLASS. / ENDLESS SLEEP**	–	
Nov 78.	(7") *(ADA 26)* **AMERICAN SQUIRM. /** Nick Lowe & His Sound: **(WHAT'S SO FUNNY 'BOUT) PEACE, LOVE AND UNDERSTANDING**		–
May 79.	(7") *(ADA 34)* **CRACKING UP. / BASING STREET**	34	–
Jun 79.	(lp/c) *(RAD/RAC 21)* <36087> **LABOUR OF LUST**	43	31
	– Cruel to be kind / Cracking up / Big kick, plain scrap / Born fighter / You make me / Skin deep / Switchboard Susan / Grey ribbon / Without love / Dose of you / Love so fine. <US cd-iss. Jun88; CK 36087> *(cd-iss. Apr90 & Aug00 on 'Demon'; FIENDCD 182)*		
Aug 79.	(7") *(ADA 43)* <11018> **CRUEL TO BE KIND. / ENDLESS GREY RIBBON**	12	12 Jul79
Dec 79.	(7") <11131> **SWITCHBOARD SUSAN. / BASING STREET**	–	

After he split from ROCKPILE in Feb'81, LOWE formed his own band, **NICK LOWE & THE CHAPS** (They became NOISE TO GO early '82) **MARTIN BELMONT** – guitar / **PAUL CARRACK** – keyboards / **BOBBY IRWIN** – drums

		F-Beat	Columbia
Feb 82.	(7") *(XX 20)* **BURNING. / ZULU KISS**		–
Feb 82.	(lp/c) *(XX LP/MC 14)* <37932> **NICK THE KNIFE**	99	50
	– Burning / Heart / Stick it where the sun don't shine / Queen of Sheba / My heart hurts / Couldn't love you (any more than I do) / Let me kiss ya / Too many teardrops / Ba doom / Raining raining / One's too many / Zulu kiss. *(cd-iss. Apr90 & Aug00 on 'Demon'; FIENDCD 183)*		
Apr 82.	(7") *(XX 23)* **MY HEART HURTS. / PET YOU AND HOLD YOU**		–
	(d7"+=) *(XX 23F – SAM 147)* – Cracking up / (What's so funny 'bout) Peace, love and understanding.		
Apr 82.	(7") <02813> **MY HEART HURTS. / STICK IT WHERE THE SUN DON'T SHINE**	–	

added **JAMES ELLER** – bass

Apr 83.	(7") *(XX 31)* **RAGIN' EYES. / TANGUE-RAE**		–
	(12"+=) *(XX 31T)* – Cool reaction.		
Jun 83.	(lp/c) *(XX LP/MC 18)* **THE ABOMINABLE SHOWMAN**		–
	– We want action / Ragin' eyes / Cool reaction / Time wounds all heels / Man of a fool / Tanque-Rae / Wish you were here / Chicken and feathers / Paid the price / Mess around with love / Saint beneath the paint / How do you talk to an angel. *(cd-iss. Apr90 & Aug00 on 'Demon'; FIENDCD 184)*		
Jun 83.	(7") <03837> **HOW DO YOU TALK TO AN ANGEL / I WISH YOU WERE HERE**	–	

NICK LOWE AND HIS COWBOY OUTFIT

with **PAUL CARRACK**, etc

		F-Beat/RCA	Columbia
May 84.	(7") *(XX 340)* **HALF A BOY AND HALF A MAN. / AWESOME**	53	–
	(12"+=) *(XX 34T)* – Cruel to be kind.		
May 84.	(lp/c) *(ZL/ZK 79250)* <39371> **NICK LOWE & HIS COWBOY OUTFIT**		
	– Half a boy and half a man / You'll never get me up / (in one of those) / Maureen / God's gift to women / The Gee and the Rick and the three card trick / (Hey big mouth) Stand up and say that / Awesome / Breakaway / Love like a glove / Live fast, love hard, die young / L.A.F.S. *(cd-iss. Aug00 on 'Demon'; FIENDCD 185)*		
Aug 84.	(7") *(XX 36)* **L.A.F.S. / (HEY BIG MOUTH) STAND UP AND SAY THAT**		
	(12"+=) *(XX 36T)* – Baby it's you.		
Jul 85.	(7") *(ZB 40303)* **I KNEW THE BRIDE (WHEN SHE USE TO ROCK AND ROLL). / DARLIN' ANGEL EYES**		
	(12"+=) *(ZT 40303)* – Seven nights to rock.		
Aug 85.	(lp/c) *(ZL/ZK 70765)* <39958> **THE ROSE OF ENGLAND**		
	– Darlin' angel eyes / She don't love nobody / 7 nights to rock / Long walk back / The rose of England / Lucky dog * / I knew the bride (when she use to rock and roll) / Indoor fireworks / (Hope to God) I'm right / I can be the one you love / Everyone * / Bobo ska diddle daddle. *(re-iss. Dec88 & Aug00 on 'Demon' lp/c/cd; FIEND/+CASS/CD 73)* – omits tracks *		
Nov 85.	(7") <05570> **I KNEW THE BRIDE (WHEN SHE USE TO ROCK AND ROLL). / LONG WALK BACK**	–	77

NICK LOWE

		Demon	Columbia
Jan 88.	(7") **CRYING IN MY SLEEP. / LOVER'S JAMBOREE**	–	
Feb 88.	(lp/c/cd) *(FIEND/+CASS/CD 99)* **PINKER AND PROUDER THAN PREVIOUS**		

– (You're my) Wildest dream / Crying in my sleep / Big hair / Love gets strange / I got the love / Black Lincoln Continental / Cry it out / Lover's jambouree / Geisha girl / Wishing well / Big big love.

now with **DAVE EDMUNDS, PAUL CARRACK, JIM KELTNER** / plus **BILL KIRCHEN** – electric guitar / **AUSTIN DE LONE** – piano, guitar / **RY COODER** – steel guitar

		Warners	Reprise
Apr 90.	(7") *(W 9821)* **ALL MEN ARE LIARS. / GAI-GIN MAN**		–
	(12"+=/cd-s+=) *(W 9821 T/CD)* – I love the sound of breaking glass / Cruel to be kind.		
Apr 90.	(cd)(lp/c) (<7599 26132-2>)*(WX 337/+C)* **PARTY OF ONE**		
	– You got the look I like / (I want to build a) Jumbo ark / Gai-gin man / Who was that man? / What's shakin' on the hill / Shting-shtang / All men are liars / Rocky road / Refrigerator white / I don't know why you keep me on / Honeygun. *(cd re-iss. Nov95 on 'Demon'; FIENDCD 767)* – (extra tracks)		

LITTLE VILLAGE

were another amalgamation of near superstars; **NICK LOWE** – vocals, bass / **RY COODER** – vocals, guitar / **JOHN HIATT** – vocals, guitar / **JIM KELTNER** – drums, percussion, guitar, composer

		Reprise	Reprise
Feb 92.	(cd)(lp/c) (<7599 26713-2>)*(WX 462/+C)* **LITTLE VILLAGE**	23	66
	– Solar sex panel / The action / Inside job / Big love / Take another look / Do you want my job / Don't go away mad / Fool who knows / She runs hot / Don't think about her when you're trying to drive / Don't bug me when I'm working.		
Mar 92.	(7"/c-s) **SOLAR SEX PANEL. / DO WITH ME WHAT YOU WANT TO DO**		
	(12"+=/cd-s+=) – Haunted house.		
May 92.	(7"/c-s) **DON'T GO AWAY MAD. / BIG LOVE**		
	(12"+=/cd-s+=) – Do with me what you want to do.		

NICK LOWE

		Demon	Upstart
Nov 94.	(cd-s) *(NICKA 315)* **TRUE LOVE TRAVELS ON A GRAVEL ROAD EP**		
	– I am the cancer / Two seater / Rag doll / Laying blame.		
Nov 94.	(cd) *(FIENDCD 757)* <13> **THE IMPOSSIBLE BIRD**		
	– Soulful wind / The beast in me / True love travels on a gravel road / Trail of tears / Shelly my love / Where's my everything / 12-step program / Lover don't go / Drive-thru man / Withered on the vine / I live on a battlefield / 14 days / I'll be there.		
Jul 95.	(cd-ep) <21> **LiVe! ON THE BATTLEFIELD (live)**	–	
	– I live on a battlefield / 36 inches high / Without love / Dream girl / In the middle of it all.		
Jan 98.	(cd) *(FIENDCD 939)* <38> **DIG MY MOOD**		
	– Faithless lover / Lonesome reverie / You inspire me / What lack of love has done / Time I took a holiday / Failed Christian / The man that I've become / Freezing / High on a hilltop / Lead me not / I must be getting over you / Cold grey light of dawn.		
Jun 98.	(cd-ep) *(VEXCD 17)* **YOU INSPIRE ME EP**		
	– You inspire me / Soulful win (live) / She don't love nobody (live) / Cruel to be kind (live) / Half a boy and half a man (live).		

		Proper	Yep Roc
Sep 01.	(cd) *(PRPCD 12)* <2027> **THE CONVINCER**		Oct01
	– Homewrecker / Only a fool breaks his own heart / Lately I've let things slide / She's got soul / Cupid must be angry / Indian queens / Poor side of town / I'm a mess / Between dark and dawn / Bygones (won't go) / Has she got a friend? / Let's stay in and make love.		
Nov 01.	(cd-s) *(DDTB 1)* **LATELY I'VE LET THINGS SLIDE / SHE'S GOT SOUL / THERE WILL NEVER BE ANY PEACE**		–

– compilations etc. –

on 'Demon' unless mentioned otherwise

Sep 84.	(lp/c) *(FIEND/+CASS 20)* **16 ALL-TIME LOWES**		–
	– Born fighter / Marie Provost / American squirm / Skin deep / When I write the book / Little Hitler / Cruel to be kind / Heart of the city / Switchboard Susan / (I love the sound of) Breaking glass / Big kick plain scrap / Cracking up / Without love / Nutted by reality / So it goes / They called it rock. *(cd-iss. 1986 as '20 ALL-TIME LOWES'; FIENDCD 20)* – (4 extra tracks). *(cd re-iss. Oct93 on 'Diablo'; DIAB 801)*		
Mar 86.	(lp/c/cd) *(FIEND/+CASS/CD 59)* **NICK'S KNACK**		–
Aug 89.	(d-lp/c/cd) *(FIEND/+CASS/CD 142)* **BASHER: THE BEST OF NICK LOWE**		–
Jun 91.	(cd) *(FIENDCD 203)* **THE WILDERNESS YEARS**		–
	– (rare material 1974-1977)		
Jan 94.	(4xcd-box) *(NICK 1)* **BOXED SET**		–
	– (JESUS OF COOL / ROSE OF ENGLAND / NICK LOWE AND HIS COWBOY OUTFIT / PINKER AND PROUDER THAN PREVIOUS)		
Jul 99.	(4xcd-box) *Demon; (LOWE 50)* **THE DOINGS**		–

Lydia LUNCH

Born: LYDIA KOCH, 2 Jun'59, Rochester, New York, USA. She became part of New York's 'No Wave' scene in 1976-78 when her punk band, TEENAGE JESUS & THE JERKS exploded onto the scene with their discordant, tortured classic, 'ORPHANS'. Towards the end of the decade, the stunning (in more ways than one!) punk banshee disbanded the 'JERKS, forming the short-lived BEIRUT SLUMP. After a solitary US-only single, 'TRY ME', LYDIA embarked on a solo career with the more vocally subdued debut album, 'QUEEN OF SIAM' (1980), a schizoid record that found LUNCH entertaining a gamut of styles including avant-swing-jazz in the shape of the TOM WAITS-esque 'LADY SCARFACE' (!). Ever the experimentalist, LYDIA tried out R&B and funk in her next project, 8-EYED SPY, although this too was just as brief as only a single and a mini eponymous set appeared in '81. The following year, LYDIA unleashed her second solo album, '13:13', an intense, heavy-duty precursor to the girl-grunge likes of

HOLE and BABES IN TOYLAND, it featured three of her most effective numbers, 'AFRAID OF YOUR COMPANY', 'THIS SIDE OF NOWHERE' and 'STARES TO . . .'. Subsequent collaborations with The BIRTHDAY PARTY, ROWLAND S. HOWARD, EINSTURZENDE NEUBAUTEN, DIE HAUT and Danish band, SORT SOL, took her overseas to Berlin, although she returned in her own right in 1984 with 'IN LIMBO' (released on CABARET VOLTAIRE's indie imprint, 'DoubleVision'). The following year, LYDIA founded her own 'Widowspeak' label, issuing her 'UNCENSORED' cassette which unearthed her girlhood traumas in the shape of 'DADDY DEAREST'. This mid-80's period also found the provocative punk queen featuring in a series of NY "artistic" films, including 'Fingered', in which she gets to grips, so to speak, with long-time beau, JIM THIRLWELL (of FOETUS). Musically, LUNCH kept up her profile via a collaborative effort with mates SONIC YOUTH, 'DEATH VALLEY '69', a spiralling maelstrom of disturbing guitar-noise (inspired by the MANSON killings) over which she stamped her uncompromising authority. In between further solo work, LYDIA spent time in the studio with MICHAEL GIRA (Swans) and JIM FOETUS (as STINKFIST), while also lending her talents to the all-female project, HARRY CREWS, alongside KIM GORDON (of SONIC YOUTH) in late 80's splinter group HARRY CREWS. In the 90's, LUNCH continued to swim against the musical mainstream, her solo albums interspersed with further collaborative work featuring the likes of former X singer, EXENE CERVENKA. • **Songwriters:** LYDIA, except SPOOKY (Association) / DON'T FEAR THE REAPER (Blue Oyster Cult) / WHY DON'T WE DO IT IN THE ROAD (Beatles) / IN MY TIME OF DYING (trad/ Led Zeppelin).

Album rating: QUEEN OF SIAM (*6) / 8-EYED SPY mini (*5) / 13:13 (*7) / IN LIMBO (*5) / THE UNCENSORED (*5) / THE DROWNING OF LUCY HAMILTON mini (*5) / HYSTERIE compilation (*7) / HONEYMOON IN RED (*6) / ORAL FIXATION (*5) / NAKED IN GARDEN HILLS with Harry Crews (*6) / CONSPIRACY OF WOMEN (*6) / SHOTGUN WEDDING with Rowland S. Howard (*5) / RUDE HIEROGLYPHICS with Exene Cervenka (*5) / CRIMES AGAINST NATURE compilation (*7) / WIDOWSPEAK – THE BEST OF LYDIA LUNCH compilation (*8)

TEENAGE JESUS & THE JERKS

LYDIA LUNCH – vocals, guitar / **GORDON STEVENSON** – bass; repl. JIM SCLAVUNOS who repl. JAMES CHANCE / **BRADLY FIELD** – drums; repl. RECK who joined FRICTION

			not iss.	Migraine
Apr 78.	(7") <CC-333>	**ORPHANS. / LESS OF ME**	-	
Mar 79.	(7") <CC-334>	**BABY DOLL. / FREUD IN FLOP / RACE MIXING**	-	
Aug 79.	(12"ep,12"pink-ep) <CC-336>	**PINK**	-	
	– Freud in flop / Race mixing / Baby doll / Burning rubber / Red alert / Orphans / Less of me.			
			not iss.	Ze
Nov 79.	(12"ep) <12011>	**PRE-TEENAGE JESUS**	-	
	– The closet / Less of me / My eyes.			
	disbanded when she formed . . .			

BEIRUT SLUMP

LYDIA LUNCH – vocals, guitar / **ROBERT QUINE** – guitar / **PAT IRWIN** – sax / **GEORGE SCOTT** – bass

			not iss.	Migraine
Apr 79.	(7") <CC-335>	**TRY ME. / STAIRCASE**	-	

LYDIA LUNCH

went solo added piano & was backed by **ROBERT QUINE** – guitar / **PAT IRWIN** – guitar, keyboards / **JACK RUBY** – bass / **DOUGLAS BROWNE** – drums

			Celluloid	Ze
Nov 80.	(lp) (CEL 2-6561) <33006>	**QUEEN OF SIAM**		
	– Mechanical flattery / Gloomy Sunday / Tied and twisted / Spooky / Los banditos / Atomic bongos / Lady Scarface / A cruise to the Moon / Carnival fat man / Knives in the drain / Blood of tin. (cd-iss. Jul91 on 'UFO'; WSP 001) (re-iss. cd Aug95 on 'Triple X')			

8 EYED SPY

were formed by **LUNCH / IRWIN + SCOTT** plus **JIM SCLAVUNOS** – sax / **MICHAEL PAUMGARDEN** – drums

			Fetish	not iss.
Oct 81.	(m-lp) (FR 2003)	**8 EYED SPY**		-
	– Diddy wah diddy / Lazy in love / Love split / Dead you me B side / Swamp / Run through the jungle / Motor oil shanty / You twist I shout / Looking for someone / Lightning's girl / Innocence / Boy meets girl / 2 square / I want candy / Ran away dark. <cd-iss. Sep97 on 'Atavistic'; ALP 75CD>			
Feb 82.	(7") FE 19)	**DIDDY WAH DIDDY. / DEAD YOU ME B SIDE**		-
	Had already disbanded, after SCOTT died late in 1981.			

LYDIA LUNCH

went solo, but she first half shared an album with The BIRTHDAY PARTY, then a single with their guitarist ROWLAND S. HOWARD

			4 a.d.	not iss.
Feb 82.	(lp) (JAD 202)	**THE AGONY & THE ECSTASY** (other side 'Drunk On The Pope's Blood' by BIRTHDAY PARTY)		-
	– Afraid of your company / (2).			
Sep 82.	(12") (BAD 210)	**SOME VELVET MORNING. ("ROWLAND S.HOWARD & LYDIA LUNCH") / I FELL IN LOVE WITH A GHOST**		-

now w/ **DIX DENNEY** – guitar / **GREG WILLIAMS** – bass / **CLIFF MARTINEZ** – drums;

			Situation2	Ruby
Jun 82.	(lp) (SITU 6) <JRR 806>	**13:13**		
	– Stares to . . . / 3*3 / This side of nowhere / Snakepit breakdown / Dance of the dead children / Suicide ocean / Lock your door / Afraid of your company. (cd-iss. Oct89 + Oct94 on 'Line'; LICD 9.00096)			

Between 1982 + Aug83, she guested on 2 German 12"ep's on labels 'Ripoff' & 'Zensor' respectively. These were; **EINSTURZENDE NEUBAUTEN** – 'DURSTIGES TIER' the B-side of 'THIRSTY ANIMAL' + **DIE HAUT** – 'DER KARIBISCHE WESTERN'.

Next with musicians **PAT PLACE** – guitar / **THURSTON MOORE** – bass + RICHARD EDSON – drums (of SONIC YOUTH) / **KRISTIAN HOFFMAN** – piano / **JIM SCLAVUNOS** – sax

			DoubleVision	not iss.
Sep 84.	(m-lp; some red) (DVR 5)	**IN LIMBO**		-
	– I wish . . . I wish / Friday afternoon / 1000 lies / Some boys / Still burning / What did you do. (re-iss. 1986 on 'Widowspeak'; WSP 6)			

Early in 1985, she was again credited on a 12", this time **SONIC YOUTH's** 'DEATH VALLEY '69', which was released on 'Blast First' UK 'Irredescence' US.

			Widowspeak	Widowspeak
Mar 85.	(c) (WSP 1)	**THE UNCENSORED**	-	
	– Dear whores / Shotgun / Black Romeo / Daddy dearest. (cd-see ORAL . . .)			
Jun 85.	(lp) (WSP 2)	**THE DROWNING OF LUCY HAMILTON**		-
	– Emerald pale has disappeared / The drowning / How men die in their sleep / Lucy's lost her head again / 3:20 Thursday morning / A quiet night of murder in . . .			
Oct 85.	(10"ep) (WSP 3)	**HEART OF DARKNESS (with NO TREND)**		-
Mar 87.	(d-lp) (WSP 8)	**HYSTERIE** (compilation of all material 1976-1986)		-
	– Red alert / Orphans / The closet / Burning rubber / I woke up dreaming / Reud in flop / Baby doll / Race mixing / Crown of thorns / Red alert / Try me / Staircase / I am the Lord Jesus / Case #14 / See pretty / C-I blue / Tornado warnings / Sidewalk / Swamp / Run through the jungle / Motor oil shanty / Love split with blood / Ran away dark / Diddy wah diddy / Lazy in love / Dead me you B side / I fell in love with a ghost / As she weeps / Caribbean western. (cd-iss. 1989; WSP 008CD)			
Mar 88.	(12"m) (WSP 013T)	**THE CRUMB. (with THURSTON MOORE) / DONE DUN / DEAD RIVER**		-
	next featured backing from **BIRTHDAY PARTY** + recorded 1983-84			
Apr 88.	(lp) (WSP 12)	**HONEYMOON IN RED**		-
	– Done dun / Still burning / Fields of fire / Dead in the head / Some velvet morning / Come fall / So your heart / Dead river / Three kings. (cd-iss. May90; WSP 12CD)			
Nov 88.	(m-lp) (WSP 14)	**STINKFIST (with CLINT RUIN)**		-
	– Stinkfist / Meltdown oratorio (part 1,2,3) / Son of Stink.			
Sep 89.	(lp) (WSP 16)	**ORAL FIXATION** (spoken word live in Detroit)		-
	– Dear whores / Shotgun / Black Romeo / Daddy dearest / Oral fixation.			

HARRY CREWS

LYDIA LUNCH – vocals, guitar / **KIM GORDON** – bass (of SONIC YOUTH) / **SADIE MAE** – drums

			Big Cat	Widowspeak
Apr 90.	(lp/cd) (ABB 21/+CD) <24>	**NAKED IN GARDEN HILLS (live in Vienna; late 1988)**		Nov89
	– About the author / Distopia / Gospel singer / (She's in a) Bad mood / Bring me down / S.O.S. / Man hates a man / You're it / Knockout artist / Way out / Car / Orphans.			

LYDIA LUNCH

			Big Cat	not iss.
Oct 91.	(12"ep)(cd-ep) (ABB 26T)(ABBSCD 26)	**(with CLINT RUIN): DON'T FEAR THE REAPER / CLINCH. / SERPENTINE / WHY DON'T WE DO IT IN THE ROAD**		-
			Pathological	not iss.
May 91.	(cd) (PATH 6CD)	**C.O.W. (CONSPIRACY OF WOMEN)**		-
	– The right to revolt / The conspiracy of women.			
			UFO	not iss.
Oct 91.	(cd)(lp) (UFO-WSP 2CD)(WSP 002)	**SHOTGUN WEDDING** (with ROWLAND S. HOWARD)		-
	– Burning skulls / In my time of dying / Solar hex / Endless fall / What is memory / Pigeon town / Cisco sunset / Incubator / Black juju. <(re-iss. cd Aug95 on 'Triple X'+; 51111)> – Gospel singer. (d-cd Sep94 w/ 'TRANCE MUTATION' cd on 'Trident') (d-cd re-iss. Feb01 on 'Burning Airlines'; PILOT 047)			
			Clawfist	not iss.
Feb 93.	(7") (X-PIG 19)	**UNEARTHLY DELIGHTS. / BUSTED**		-
			Rykodisc	Rykodisc
Nov 95.	(cd; LYDIA LUNCH & EXENE CERVENKA) <(RCD 10326)>	**RUDE HIEROGLYPHICS**		
	– Rude hieroglyphics.			

– compilations, etc. –

on 'Widowspeak' unless mentioned otherwise

May 81.	(c) R.O.I.R.) <A 101>	**LIVE (8 EYED SPY)**	-	
	(UK-iss.1992 on 'Danceteria' cd/lp; DAN CD/LP 087)			
Feb 90.	(cd) (WSP 19CD)	**DROWNING IN LIMBO**		-
	– (THE DROWNING OF LUCY HAMILTON / IN LIMBO) <US cd-iss. 1995 on 'Atavistic'; 52>			
May 90.	(cd) (WSP 20CD)	**STINKFIST / THE CRUMB**		-
Jul 90.	(cd) (WSP 23CD)	**THE UNCENSORED / ORAL FIXATION**		-
Jul 93.	(3xcd-box) Triple X; <51157-2>	**CRIMES AGAINST NATURE**	-	
	– Crimes against nature / The beast / Unearthly delights / Cruel story of youth / Daddy dearest / Terminal distraction / Shock corridor / Oral fixation / The right to revolt / Conspiracy of women. (re-iss. Aug98; same) (re-iss. Nov99 on 'Atavistic'; APL 114CD)			
Apr 98.	(d-cd) CDH Wax; (efa 043992)	**MATRIKAMANTRA**		-
Jun 99.	(d-cd) Burning Airlines; (6501131045-2) <PILOT 009>	**WIDOWSPEAK – THE BEST OF LYDIA LUNCH**		
	– Death valley '69 / Endless fall / Why don't we do it in the road? / Some velvet morning / Four cornered room / Suicide ocean / No excuse / A short history of decay			

(parts 1 & 2) / Escape / A quiet night of murder in Greenwich Connecticut / The need to feed / Der karibische western / Twisted / Past glas / Done dun / Lock your door / Diddy wah diddy / Run through the jungle / Orphans / Son of stink / Still burning / Tornado warnings / Lady scarface. *(re-iss. Feb01; same as US)*

Nov 00. (cd) *Almafame; (ALMACD 18)* **THE DEVIL'S RACETRACK**

LURKERS

Formed: Uxbridge, London, England ... late 1976 by HOWARD WALL, ARTURO BASSICK, PETE STRIDE and MANIC ESSO. The first act to be signed to fledgling DIY independent, 'Beggars Banquet', The LURKERS' debut single, 'SHADOW' / 'LOVE STORY', was initially handed out free at gigs in the summer of '77. The flipside, rather than the lead track, stood out for its relentless, uncompromising barrage of 100 mph raw punk rock, taking its lead from the RAMONES but replacing the bubblegum factor with an aggressive edge more akin to MOTORHEAD. ARTURO was soon to be replaced by KYM BRADSHAW in time for their next single, 'FREAK SHOW', another brutally simplistic two and a half minutes which came packaged in artwork courtesy of SAVAGE PENCIL (an illustrator for Sounds and the frontman of fellow punk conspirators, The ART ATTACKS). Another personnel change ensued when brief member, KYM, was substituted by the more experienced NIGEL MOORE, the revised line-up hitting the Top 50 with the more chorus-friendly 'AIN'T GOT A CLUE'. A taster from their Top 60 debut set, 'FULHAM FALLOUT' (1978), its moderate success consolidated by their second Top 50 entry, 'I DON'T NEED TO TELL HER'. 1979 started off promisingly enough when the single, 'JUST THIRTEEN', dented the charts, although the accompanying album, 'GOD'S LONELY MEN', failed to generate much interest either critically or commercially. After two further 45's only just managed to scrape into the charts, The LURKERS began a long slide into oblivion when after losing their frontman. Although replacement, MARK FINCHAM took up the reins from 1982's 'THIS DIRTY TOWN', the band joined the bulging ranks of the redundant punk has-beens and continued to churn out albums of limited appeal throughout the 80's and even the 90's. • **Songwriters:** WALL lyrics / STRIDE music. In 1982 STRIDE and EAGLE were the main writers with BASSICK returning in '88 replacing EAGLE. Covered; LITTLE OL' WINE DRINKER ME (Dean Martin) / etc? • **Trivia:** Their early sleeve artwork was created by Sounds journalist and ART ATTACKS frontman SAVAGE PENCIL.

Album rating: FULHAM FALLOUT (*6) / GOD'S LONELY MEN (*5) / LAST WILL AND TESTAMENT – GREATEST HITS compilation (*7) / THIS DIRTY TOWN (*4)

HOWARD WALL – vocals / **PETE STRIDE** – guitar / **ARTURO BASSICK** (b. ARTHUR BILLINGSLEY) – bass / **MANIC ESSO** (b. PETE HAYNES) – drums

		Beggars Banquet	not iss.
Jul 77.	(7") *(BEG 1)* **SHADOW. / LOVE STORY**		-
	(re-iss. Aug78 red, blue or white; same)		

— KYM BRADSHAW – bass; repl. ARTURO

Oct 77.	(7") *(BEG 2)* **FREAK SHOW. / MASS MEDIA BELIEVER**		-

— NIGEL MOORE – bass repl. KYM

May 78.	(7") *(BEG 6)* **AIN'T GOT A CLUE. / OOH OOH I LOVE YOU**	45	-
	(with free gold 7"flexi) **CHAOS BROTHERS FULHAM FALLOUT FIRTY FREE!'**) *(BEG 6 1/2)*		
Jun 78.	(lp) *(BEGA 2)* **FULHAM FALLOUT**	57	-
	– Ain't got a clue / I don't need to tell her / Total war / Hey you / Shadow / Then I kicked her / Go go go / Jenny / Time of year / Self destruct / It's quiet here / Gerald / I'm on heat / Be my prisoner. *(<cd-iss. Nov97 on 'Captain Oi'+=; AHOYCD 073>)* – Shadow / Love story / Freak show / Mass media believer / Ohh ohh I love you / Pills / We are the Chaos brothers / Be my prisoner / Total war / Then I kissed her / I love the dark / Freak show.		
Jul 78.	(7") *(BEG 9)* **I DON'T NEED TO TELL HER. / PILLS**	49	-
Jan 79.	(7") *(BEG 14)* **JUST THIRTEEN. / COUNTDOWN**	66	-
Apr 79.	(lp/c) *(BEGA/BEGC 8)* **GOD'S LONELY MEN**		-
	– She knows / God's lonely men / Out in the dark / Cyandide / Whatever happened to Mary / Take me back to Babylon / Room 309 / I'll be with you / Non contender / Seven o'clock someday / Sleep on diamonds / Bad times. *(<cd-iss. Nov97 on 'Captain Oi'+=; AHOYCD 074>)* – Just thirteen / Countdown / Suzie is a floozie / Cyanide / New guitar in town / Little old wine drinker / Cold old night / Pick me up / Mary's coming home / New guitar in town / Little old wine drinker.		
May 79.	(7") *(BEG 19)* **OUT IN THE DARK. / CYANIDE**	72	-
	(d7"+=) *(BEG 19)* – Suzie is a floozie / Cyanide (pub version).		
Nov 79.	(7") *(BEG 28)* **NEW GUITAR IN TOWN. / PICK ME UP / LITTLE OL' WINE DRINKER ME**	72	-

— STRIDE teamed up with BOYS member JOHN PLAIN (see below).

— Split for a while. STRIDE, HAYNES and MOORE brought in new members **MARK FINCHAM** – vocals repl. WALL

		Clay	not iss.
Jun 82.	(7") *(CLAY 12)* **THIS DIRTY TOWN (I CAN'T FIND WAY OUT). / WOLF AT THE DOOR**		-
Jul 82.	(lp) *(CLAY 104)* **THIS DIRTY TOWN**		-
	– This dirty town / Drag you out / Frankenstein again / Heroin it's all over / One man's meat / Wolf at the door / Shut out the light / Let's dance now / Midnight hour / By the hat. *(re-iss. Dec89; same)* <*cd-iss. Apr93; CLAYCD 104*>		
Nov 82.	(7"/7"pic-d) *(CLAY 17/+P)* **DRAG YOU OUT. / HEROIN (IT'S ALL OVER)**		-
Feb 83.	(7") *(CLAY 21)* **FRANKENSTEIN AGAIN. / ONE MAN'S MEAT...**		-
Mar 84.	(12"ep) *(PLATE 7)* **FINAL VINYL**		-
	– Let's dance now (no time to be strangers) / Midnight hour / By the heart / Frankenstein again.		
May 84.	(7") *(CLAY 32)* **LET'S DANCE NOW. / MIDNIGHT HOUR**		-

— split '84. Re-formed late '88, **STRIDE & BASSICK** plus **ESSO + MOORE**

		Weser	not iss.
Feb 89.	(lp) *(efa 2433)* **WILD TIMES AGAIN**		-
	– Sidewinder / In Soho / Wolverine / Don't fall down / Miss World / Love commando / Rubber room / I can be good / Don't ask me / She go solo / Wild games / Someone out there / In my own world / Fanatical heart / Uptown or downtown. *(cd-iss. Nov94; WL 024332CD)*		

		Link	not iss.
Jun 89.	(m-lp) *(LINKLP 087)* **KING OF THE MOUNTAIN**		-
	– Brou blue / Never had a beech head / Unfinished business / Going monkee again / King of the mountain (part 1) / Lucky John / King of the mountain (pt.2).		
Nov 89.	(lp) **LIVE AND LOUD (live early '89)**		-
	– Ain't got a clue / I don't need to tell her / Unfinished business / Pills / Barbara blue / Rubber room / Just thirteen / Uptown or downtown / Going Monkee again (hey hey hey) / Shadow / New guitar in town / Miss World / I'm on heat / Freak show / Take me back to Babylon / Then I kissed her / Drag you out / Cyanide / Jenny.		

		Released Emotions	not iss.
Oct 90.	(cd)(lp) **POWERJIVE**		-
	– Powerjive / Lipstick and shampoo / Solitaire / Waiting for you / Things will never be the same / The world of Jenny Brown / Walk like a superstar (talk like a zombie) / Go go girl / Strange desire (burn, burn, burn) / Raven's wings / I close my eyes / Lullaby.		

— **DAN TOZER** – drums joined STRIDE, PLAIN + BASSICK

		Weser	Weser
Nov 94.	(cd) *(<WL 02460CD>)* **NON-STOP NITROPOP**		Jul96
	– Don't need a reason / Melt away / Can't stand my room / Hand in the fire / She's another man / Unknown / The show goes on / Frozen out / Jungle creature / Storm in my mind / Rags to riches / Feel it coming / In a dark room.		

— they've since split

– compilations, etc. –

on 'Beggars Banquet' unless mentioned otherwise

1979.	(d7"ep) *(BACK 1)* **SHADOW / LOVE STORY. / FREAK SHOW / MASS MEDIA BELIEVER**		-
1979.	(d7"ep) *(BACK 3)* **I DON'T NEED YO TELL HER. / PILLS / JUST THIRTEEN / COUNTDOWN**		-
Nov 80.	(lp) *(BOPA 2)* **LAST WILL AND TESTAMENT – GREATEST HITS**		-
	– I'm on heat / Cyanide / Shadow / Little ol' wine drinker me / Out in the dark / Freak show / Jenny / Self destruct / Ain't got a clue / Take me back to Babylon / Total war / Love story / Then I kissed her / Just thirteen / New guitar in town / She knows. *(re-iss. Jul88 on 'Beggars Banquet-Lowdown' lp/c)(cd; BBL/+C 2)(BBL 2CD)*		
Dec 92.	(cd) *Dojo; (DOJOCD 74)* **TOTALLY LURKERED**		-
Nov 95.	(cd) *Anagram; (CDPUNK 69)* **POWERJIVE / KING OF THE MOUNTAIN**		-
May 97.	(cd) *Anagram; (<CDPUNK 94>)* **THE BEGGARS BANQUET PUNK SINGLES**		-
Dec 97.	(cd) *Receiver; (<RRCD 243>)* **TAKE ME BACK TO BABYLON**		-
Jun 99.	(cd) *Harry May; (<MAYOCD 114>)* **AIN'T GOT A CLUE**		Apr00
May 00.	(cd) *Captain Oi; (<AHOYCD 137>)* **THE BBC PUNK SESSIONS**		
Nov 01.	(cd) *Captain Oi; (<AHOYCD 178>)* **WILD TIMES AGAIN / NON STOP NITRO POP**		
Mar 02.	(cd) *Captain Oi; (<AHOYCD 188>)* **THE PUNK SINGLES COLLECTION**		

PETE STRIDE and JOHN PLAIN

(PLAIN was from The BOYS) + **TONY BATEMAN** – bass / **JACK BLACK** – drums

		Beggars Banquet	not iss.
Jan 80.	(lp) *(BEGA 17)* **NEW GUITAR IN TOWN**		-
	– Laugh at me / School girls / Cold cold night / He'll have to go / Just like a clown / Half the time / New guitar in town / Cure for love / Restless kind / You better move on / Pick me up.		
May 80.	(7") *(BEG 41)* **LAUGH AT ME. / JIMMY BROWN**		-

John LYDON (see under ⇒ PUBLIC IMAGE LTD.)

THE GREAT INDIE DISCOGRAPHY — The 1970s

MAGAZINE

Formed: Manchester, England ... spring 1977 by former BUZZCOCKS frontman HOWARD DEVOTO and guitarist JOHN McGEOGH, who recruited the rhythm section of BARRY ADAMSON and MARTIN JACKSON along with keyboard player, BOB DICKINSON. After six months of rehearsals, they played their debut gig on the final night of legendary Manchester punk club, The Electric Circus, subsequently signing to 'Virgin' on the strength of a demo. A classic debut single, 'SHOT BY BOTH SIDES' established MAGAZINE's post-punk credentials, its stark, uncompromising approach and lyrical despair paving the way for countless gaggles of miserable young men in trenchcoats. Although DICKINSON had left prior to recording the single, the band had recruited a replacement, DAVE FORMULA, in time for the debut album, 'REAL LIFE' (1978). Its icy keyboard textures and spiky sonic artistry announced the arrival of a unique talent although DEVOTO's hyper-intelligent wayward genius was nothing new for fans who'd admired the punk maverick since his BUZZCOCKS days. With major radio support from John Peel and a growing cult fanbase, the album made the UK Top 30, while JACKSON was replaced with JOHN DOYLE following the obligatory tour. A follow-up set, 'SECONDHAND DAYLIGHT' (1979), was even more liberal in its use of keyboards although MAGAZINE's leftfield approach could hardly be accused of straying into New Romantic territory (some of MAGAZINE did dip a toe into these waters when they guested for VISAGE). Although a further three singles (including the unsettling 'A SONG FROM UNDER THE FLOORBOARDS' and an unlikely cover of Sly Stone's 'THANK YOU') failed to chart, a third album, 'THE CORRECT USE OF SOAP' (1980), became their most successful to date. DEVOTO wasn't happy with the direction the band were headed, however, and the defection of McGEOGH to SIOUXSIE & THE BANSHEES led to a slow decline and a patchy final effort in 'MAGIC, MURDER AND THE WEATHER' (1981). By the time of the album's release, DEVOTO had already announced his departure, effectively ending MAGAZINE's limited shelf life. The singer went on to release a solo set, 'JERKY VERSIONS OF THE DREAM' before forming LUXURIA with NOKO. He subsequently quit the music business; BARRY ADAMSON has enjoyed greater recognition, initially with NICK CAVE & The Bad Seeds and latterly with his acclaimed solo career. • **Songwriters:** DEVOTO penned all except; I LOVE YOU BIG DUMMY (Captain Beefheart). LUXURIA covered JEZEBEL (Marty Wilde).

Album rating: REAL LIFE (*9) / SECONDHAND DAYLIGHT (*6) / THE CORRECT USE OF SOAP (*8) / MAGIC, MURDER AND THE WEATHER (*6) / AFTER THE FACT compilation (*8) / RAYS AND HAIL compilation (*8) / Howard Devoto: JERKY VERSIONS OF THE DREAM (*5) / Luxuria: THE UNANSWERABLE LUST (*5) / BEAST BOX (*4)

HOWARD DEVOTO – vocals (ex-BUZZCOCKS) / **JOHN McGEOGH** – guitar / **BARRY ADAMSON** – bass / **MARTIN JACKSON** – drums / **BOB DICKINSON** – keyboards (latter left before debut recording)

		Virgin	Int
Jan 78.	(7") (VS 200) **SHOT BY BOTH SIDES. / MY MIND AIN'T SO OPEN**	41	-
Apr 78.	(7") (VS 207) **TOUCH AND GO. / GOLDFINGER**		-

— added **DAVE FORMULA** – keyboards

Jun 78.	(lp/c) (V/TCV 2100) **REAL LIFE**	29	

– Definitive gaze / My tulpa / Shot by both sides / Recoil / Burst / Motorcade / The great beautician in the sky / The light pours out of me / Parade. (re-iss. Mar84; OVED 62) (cd-iss. Oct88; CDV 2100)

— **JOHN DOYLE** – drums repl. JACKSON (to CHAMELEONS, then SWING OUT SISTER)

Nov 78.	(7") (VS 237) **GIVE ME EVERYTHING. / I LOVE YOU, YOU BIG DUMMY**		-
Feb 79.	(7") (VS 251) **RHYTHM OF CRUELTY. / T.V. BABY**		-
Mar 79.	(lp/c) (V/TCV 2121) **SECONDHAND DAYLIGHT**	38	

– Feed the enemy / Rhythm of cruelty / Cut-out shapes / Talk to the body / I wanted your heart / The thin air / Back to nature / Believe that I understand / Permafrost. (re-iss. 1987 lp/c; OVED/+C 84) (cd-iss. Oct88; CDV 2121)

Feb 80.	(7") (VS 321) **A SONG FROM UNDER THE FLOORBOARDS. / TWENTY YEARS AGO**		-
Mar 80.	(7") (VS 328) **THANK YOU (FALETTINME BE MICE ELF AGIN). / THE BOOK**		-
Apr 80.	(7") (VS 334) **UPSIDE DOWN. / THE LIGHT POURS OUT OF ME** (live)		-
May 80.	(lp/c) (V/TCV 2156) <13144> **THE CORRECT USE OF SOAP**	28	

– Because you're frightened / Model worker / I'm a party / You never knew me / Philadelphia / I want to burn again / Thank you (falettinme be mice elf agin) / Sweetheart contract / Stuck / A song from under the floorboards. (re-iss. 1988 lp/c; OVED/+C 116) (cd-iss. Oct88; CDV 2156)

Jul 80.	(d7"/12"ep) (VS 368/+12) **SWEETHEART CONTRACT. / FEED THE ENEMY** (live) // **TWENTY YEARS AGO. / SHOT BY BOTH SIDES** (live)	54	-

— **ROBIN SIMON** – guitar (ex-ULTRAVOX) repl. McGEOGH who joined SIOUXSIE ... (above now alongside DEVOTO, ADAMSON, FORMULA and DOYLE)

		Virgin	I.R.S.
Nov 80.	(lp/c) (V/TCV 2184) <70015> **PLAY** (live at Melbourne Festival Hall)	69	

– Give me everything / A song from under the floorboards / Permafrost / The light pours out of me / Model worker / Parade / Thank you (falettinme be mice elf agin) / Because you're frightened / Twenty years ago / Definitive gaze. (re-iss. 1988 lp/c; OVED/+C 117) (cd-iss. Oct88; CDV 2184)

— **BEN MANDELSON** – guitar (ex-AMAZORBLADES) repl. ROBIN.

May 81.	(7") (VS 412) **ABOUT THE WEATHER. / IN THE DARK**		-
	(12"+=) (VS 412-12) – The operative.		
Jun 81.	(lp/c) (V/TCV 2200) <70020> **MAGIC, MURDER AND THE WEATHER**	39	

– About the weather / So lucky / The honeymoon killers / Vigilante / Come alive / The great man's secrets / This poison / Naked eye / Suburban Rhonda / The garden. (re-iss. 1988 lp/c; OVED/+ 141) (cd-iss. Oct88; CDV 2200)

— They split mid '81. DEVOTO went solo with help from FORMULA (see below). BEN MANDELSON joined The MEKONS, JOHN DOYLE later joined ARMOURY SHOW. BARRY ADAMSON joined PETE SHELLEY then later NICK CAVE & THE BAD SEEDS. FORMULA had also joined the group DESIGN FOR LIVING.

– compilations, etc. –

on 'Virgin' unless mentioned otherwise

May 82.	(lp/c) (VM/+C 1) **AFTER THE FACT** (best of)		-
May 83.	(12"ep) (VS 592-12) **SHOT BY BOTH SIDES**		-

– Shot by both sides / Goldfinger / Give me everything / A song from under the floorboards.

May 87.	(cd) (COMCD 5) **RAYS AND HAIL 1978-81** (best of)		-

– Shot by both sides / Definitive gaze / Motorcade / The light pours out of me / Feed the enemy / Rhythm of cruelty / Back to nature / Permafrost / Because you're frightened / You never knew me / A song from under the floorboards / I want to burn again / About the weather / Parade. (re-iss. Jul93; CDVM 9020)

Jul 90.	(cd) (CDOVD 312) **SCREE** (rarities 76-81)		-
Aug 93.	(cd) Windsong; (WINCD 040) **BBC RADIO 1 LIVE IN CONCERT**		-
Oct 00.	(cd) (CDV 2924) **MAGAZINE: WHERE THE POWER IS**		-
Oct 00.	(3xcd-box) (MAGBOX 1) **MAGAZINE: MAYBE IT'S RIGHT TO BE NERVOUS NOW**		-

(above two releases were B-sides, out-takes, Peel sessions)

HOWARD DEVOTO

— went solo, with **DAVE FORMULA** – keyboards / **PAT AHORN** – drums / **ALAN ST. CLAIR** – guitar / **NEIL PYZER** – keyboards, synth / **MARTIN HEATH** – bass

		Virgin	I.R.S.
Jun 83.	(7"/12") (VS 598/+12) **RAINY SEASON. / RAIN FOREST**		-
Aug 83.	(lp/c) (V/TCV 2272) <SP 70036> **JERKY VERSIONS OF THE DREAM**	57	

– Cold imagination / Topless / Rainy season / I admire you / Way out of shape / Some will pay (for what others pay to avoid) / Waiting for a train / Out of shape with me / Taking over Heaven / Seeing is believing. (re-iss. Aug88; OVED 129) (cd-iss. Apr90; CDV 2272)

Aug 83.	(7"/12") (VS 642/+12) **COLD IMAGINATION. / OUT OF SHAPE WITH ME**		-

— PYZER and ST.CLAIR joined SPEAR OF DESTINY. HEATH and AHORN joined DAVE HOWARD SINGERS, DEVOTO guested for B.SZAJNER a French electronic wizard. He then took 4 years off before his new venture ...

LUXURIA

DEVOTO with **NOKO** (b. Liverpool) – guitar, co-composer

		Beggars Banquet	Beggars Banquet
Jan 88.	(7") (BEG 204) **REDNECK. / SHE'S YOUR LOVER NOW (pt.1)**		-
	(12"+=) (BEG 204T) – She's your lover now (pt.2).		
Feb 88.	(lp/c)(cd) (BEGA/BEGC 90)(BEGA 90CD) <6990> **THE UNANSWERABLE LUST**		

– Redneck / Flesh / Public highway / Pound / Lady 21 / Celebrity / Rubbish / Mile / Luxuria.

May 88.	(7") (BEG 211) **PUBLIC HIGHWAY (Short cut) / SICKLY THUG AND I**		-
	(12"+=) (BEG 211T) – Luxuria (The wilderness mix).		
Mar 90.	(7"ep/12"ep/cd-ep) (BEG 233/+T/CD) **THE BEAST BOX IS DREAMING / BEAST BOX / USELESS LOVE**		-
Apr 90.	(cd)(c/lp) (BEGA 106CD)(BEGC/BEGA 106) <2233-2/-4/-1> **BEAST BOX**		

– The beast box is dreaming / Stupid blood / Against the past / Our curious leader / We keep on getting there / Ticket / Animal in the mirror / Dirty beating heart / Smoking mirror / I've been expecting you / Karezza / Beast box / Jezebel.

May 90.	(7") (BEG 242) **JEZEBEL. / SMOKING MIRROR (instrumental)**		-
	(12"+=) (BEG 242T) – Sickly thug and I (live).		
	(cd-s++=) (BEG 242CD) – Luxuria (live).		

— after their split, NOKO went to ground for a while, re-emerging later in the 90's with hard techno act, APOLLO 440

Stephen MALLINDER
(see under ⇒ CABARET VOLTAIRE)

MARS

Formed: New York, USA ... 1977 by DON BURG, SUMNER CRANE, NANCY ARLEN and MARK CUNNINGHAM. The following year, the quartet made it onto vinyl with a four track contribution ('PUERTO RICAN GHOST', 'HELEN FORDSDALE', 'TUNNEL' and 'HAIRWAVES') to the BRIAN ENO-produced V/A set, 'No New York' alongside fellow No Wavers, TEENAGE JESUS & THE JERKS, The CONTORTIONS and DNA. 1978 also saw the band record a debut single in their own right, '3E', released on the 'Ze' label (then home of SUICIDE) as well as an eponymous EP. By the time of the latter's belated release in 1980, MARS had already entered the black hole of music business oblivion, the various space cadets engaging in their own solar missions; BURG and CUNNINGHAM resurfaced in the band, DON KING, alongside DUNCAN LINDSAY. The latter and his brother, ARTO, together with three MARS originals (NANCY wasn't involved) and DNA's IKUE MORI released a critically savaged reworking of the famous opera, 'Don Giovanni', released in 1981 as 'JOHN GAVANTI'.

Album rating: 78 compilation (*6) / JOHN GAVANTI (*2)

DON BURG – vocals, guitar / **SUMNER CRANE** – vocals, guitar / **MARK CUNNINGHAM** – vocals, bass / **NANCY ARLEN** – drums

			not iss.	Ze
1978.	(12") <ZE12 010>	**3E. / 11,000 VOLTS**	-	
			not iss.	Lust-Unlust
Jun 80.	(12"ep) <JMB 232>	**MARS** (rec.1978)	-	

– N.N. end / Scorn / Outside Africa / Monopoly / The immediate stages of the erotic.

—— had already split; BURG and CUNNINGHAM forming DON KING with DUNCAN LINDSAY (brother of ARTO). All three (and ARTO) with CRANE and IKUE MORI (of DNA) re-worked DON GIOVANNI below

			not iss.	Hyrax
Jan 81.	(lp) <HY 101>	**JOHN GAVANTI**	-	

– compilation, etc. –

Dec 86.	(lp) Widowspeak; <(WSP 10)> **78**

– 3-E / 11,000 volts / Tunnel / Helen Forsdale / Puero Rican ghost / Immediate stages of the erotic / Monopoly / Cats / Cairo / Hairwaves / Outside Africa. (cd-iss. 1996 on 'Atavistic'; 48)

| Apr 90. | (lp) Danceteria; <(DANLP 360)> **VENUS FLY TRAP** |
| Mar 94. | (cd) Semantic; (CDSA 54025) **MARS LIVE** (live) |

MARTHA & THE MUFFINS

Formed: Toronto, Canada ... late '77 by ex-CADS organist, MARTHA JOHNSON (one single, 'DO THE CRABWALK'), alongside CARL FINKLE, MARK GANE, TIM GANE and ANDY HAAS; MARTHA LADLY was soon added. A Canadian-only debut single, 'INSECT LOVE', appeared in 1978, the track introduced to the British market a year later via a deal with Virgin subsidiary, 'Dindisc'. Its follow-up, the infectious 'ECHO BEACH', struck a chord in the collective post-New Wave consciousness and heralded a new era of futuristic 80's style pop, the MARK GANE-penned classic climbing into the UK Top 10. Unfortunately, their accompanying album, 'METRO MUSIC' (1980), received mixed reviews and was unable to sustain its Top 40 chart run as a further single, 'SAIGON', failed miserably. Seemingly not concerned with saturating the market for want of another hit, MARTHA & THE MUFFINS tried to shake off the one-hit wonder tag with another two flop singles and an equally unsuccessful second album, 'TRANCE AND DANCE', all in the same year. By the time they returned to the studio, only one MARTHA remained as LADLY first opted for a one-off solo career then went on to join The ASSOCIATES. FINKLE had also bailed out, the remaining members bringing in then unknown producer, DANIEL LANOIS, in a dual capacity on their third set, 'THIS IS THE ICE AGE' (1981). With LANOIS' sister, JOCELYN, now in tow, the group moved in an increasingly Euro-pop direction, the result being a German-only release for their 1983 set, 'DANSEPARC'. The following year, MARK GANE and MARTHA JOHNSON sweetened their moniker by slimming it down to M + M, the revamp initially paying off with a transatlantic Top 75 dancefloor hit, 'BLACK STATIONS – WHITE STATIONS'. However, the failure of two albums, 'MYSTERY WALK' (1984) and 'THE WORLD IS A BALL' (1985), led to the outfit taking several years out during which they dabbled in soundtrack work.

Album rating: FARAWAY IN TIME compilation (*5)

MARTHA JOHNSON – vocals, keyboards / **MARK GANE** – guitar / **ANDY HAAS** – saxophone / **CARL FINKLE** – bass / **TIM GANE** – drums / **MARTHA LADLY** – keyboards, trombone, vocals

			not iss.	M+M
Jun 78.	(7") <MM 001>	**INSECT LOVE. / SUBURBAN DREAM**	-	- Canada
			Dindisc	Virgin
Oct 79.	(7") (DIN 4)	**INSECT LOVE. / CHEESIES AND GUM**		-
Feb 80.	(7") (DIN 9)	**ECHO BEACH. / TEDDY THE DINK**	10	
Mar 80.	(lp) (DID 1) <13145>	**METRO MUSIC**	34	Aug80

– Echo beach / Paint by number heart / Saigon / Indecision / Terminal twilight / Hide and seek / Monotone / Sinking land / Revenge (against the world) / Cheesie and gum. (re-iss. Mar84 lp/c; OVED/+C 54)

Apr 80.	(7") (DIN 17) **SAIGON. / COPACABANA**

Jun 80.	(7"green) (DIN 19) **ABOUT INSOMNIA. / 1 4 6**
Aug 80.	(7") (DIN 21) **SUBURBAN DREAM. / GIRL FAT**
Sep 80.	(lp/c) (DID/+C 5) **TRANCE AND DANCE**

– Luna park / Suburban dream / Was ezo / Teddy the dink / Symptomatic love / Primal weekend / Halfway through the week / Am I on / Motorbikin' / About insomnia / Be blase / Trance and dance. (re-iss. Aug88; OVED 78)

| Nov 80. | (7") (DIN 27) **WAS EZO. / TRANCE AND DANCE** |

—— now without FINKLE + LADLY (the latter joined the ASSOCIATES after one solo single in May'81, 'FINLANDIA' / 'TASMANIA'; DIN 32)

—— added **DANIEL LANOIS** – producer, etc

| Aug 81. | (7") (DIN 34) **WOMEN AROUND THE WORLD AT WORK. / TWENTY-TWO IN CINCINNATI** |
| Sep 81. | (lp) (DID 10) **THIS IS THE ICE AGE** |

– Swimming / Women around the world at work / Casualties of glass / Body without filters / Jets seem slower in London skies / This is the ice age / One day in Paris / You sold the cottage / Three hundred years / Chemistry. (re-iss. 1988; OVED 79)

—— (Mar'82) JOHNSON + MARK GANE recruited **JOCELYN LANOIS** – bass, vocals / **NICK KENT** – drums, percussion (also many guests)

		R.C.A.	R.C.A.
May 83.	(7"/12") (RCA/+T 331) **DANSEPARC (EVERY DAY IT'S TOMORROW). / WHATEVER HAPPENED TO RADIO VALVE ROAD?**		
May 83.	(lp) (PL 14664) <4664> **DANSEPARC**	-	German

– Obediance / World without borders / Walking into walls / Danseparc / Sins of children / Several styles of blonde girls dancing / Boys in the bushes / What people do for fun / Whatever happened to radio valve road?

M + M

—— was adopted by the duo (**MARK + MARTHA**) plus a plethora of session people incl. **DANIEL LANOIS** / **TINKER BARFIELD + DAVID PILTCH** – bass / **YOGI HORTON + FRED MAHER** – drums / etc

		R.C.A.	Current
Jul 84.	(7"/12") (RCA/+T 426) <13824> **BLACK STATIONS – WHITE STATIONS. / XOA OHO**	46	63 Jun84
Aug 84.	(lp/c) (PL/PK 70246) <3> **MYSTERY WALK**		Jul84

– Black stations – white stations / Cooling the medium / Come out and dance / I start to stop / Big trees / In between sleep and reason / Garden in the sky / Nation of followers / Alibi room / Rhythm of life.

| Sep 84. | (7"/12") (RCA/+T 452) **COOLING THE MEDIUM. / COME OUT AND DANCE** |
| Nov 85. | (lp) (PL 70841) **THE WORLD IS A BALL** |

– The world is a ball / I watch, I wait / Watching the boys fall down / Only you / By the waters of Babylon / Song in my heart / Don't jump the gun / Stuck on the grid / Someone else's shoes / As a matter of fact.

| Oct 86. | (7"/12") (PB/PT 40835) **SONG IN MY HEART. / RIVERINE** |

—— split up some time in the mid-80's; re-formed some time later

MARTHA + THE MUFFINS

MARK GANE + MARTHA JOHNSON

		not iss.	Intrepid
1992.	(cd) <N21S 0014> **MODERN LULLABY**	-	- Canada

– To dream about you / Fighting the monster / Rainbow sign / Modern lullaby / Paradise / The looking time / Birdcage walk / Everybody has a place / Show me your magic / Million dollars / Where blue meets green.

– compilations, etc. –

May 88.	(cd) Virgin; (COMCD 12) **FARAWAY IN TIME**

– Echo beach / Paint by number heart / Saigon / Indecision / Terminal twilight / Hide and seek / Monotone / Sinking land / Revenge (against the world) / Cheesies and gum / Insect love / About insomnia / Motorbikin' / Suburban dream / Was ezo / Women around the world at work / This is the ice age.

Nov 88.	(7") Old Gold; (OG 9824) **ECHO BEACH. / WOMEN AROUND THE WORLD AT WORK**
Jun 98.	(cd) EMI Music; <7243 4 96001-2> **THEN AGAIN: A RETROSPECTIVE** – – Canada
Sep 00.	(cd) One Way; <(466371003-2)> **DANSEPARC / MYSTERY WALK**

MC5

Formed: Detroit, Michigan, USA ... 1965 by ROB TYNER, FED 'SONIC' SMITH and WAYNE KRAMER. After two limited single releases, MC5 (MOTOR CITY FIVE) signed a contract with 'Elektra' in mid '68, helped by counter-cultural activist and DJ, John Sinclair. In addition to becoming the band's manager, he heavily influenced both their political extremism and warped takes on free jazz improvisation. Reflecting the harsher geographical and economic climate of Detroit, the band espoused revolution and struggle as opposed to the love and peace ethos of the sun-kissed Californian flower children. The riotous proto-punk of their legendary, acid-fuelled live show was captured on the controversial debut, 'KICK OUT THE JAMS'. Recorded in late October '68, it eventually hit the shops in May '69 and while the original uncensored pressings contained the line "Kick Out The Jams, Motherfuckers!", the offending word was later supplanted with the milder "Brothers And Sisters". Unfortunately, this wasn't enough to prevent some record stores from refusing to stock the lp, and after the band explicitly aired their views on one of the aforementioned dealers in a local newspaper, they were duly given the boot by Elektra. Nevertheless, the album reached No.30 in America and although it sounds a bit dated to modern ears, it was way radical for the time, remaining an inspiration to each new generation of noiseniks. After a split with Sinclair, the band signed with Atlantic and began to move away from the overtly subversive nature of their earlier material to a more straightahead rock approach, evidenced on their Jon Landau-produced follow-up album, 'BACK IN THE U.S.A.'. Wired rock'n'roll of an impeccable degree, the record didn't fare well in the laid-back, doped-up climate of the early 70's. An ambitious third album in 1971, 'HIGH TIME', featuring horns and even Salvation Army musicians, still failed to cut any commercial ice and the band split in 1972. KRAMER subsequently spent five years in jail for cocaine dealing before embarking on a low key solo career while former manager, Sinclair, was sentenced to ten years in the early 70's for a minor dope charge, serving only two after appeal. Tragically, ROB TYNER died from a heart attack in 1991 aged only 46. Pioneers in the true sense of the word, the MC5 together with the STOOGES were the first real punk bands, the originators who were never bettered. Although KRAMER released the odd obscure 7" throughout the late 70's/80's – during which time he teamed up with JOHNNY THUNDERS as GANG WAR and even worked with the mad, bad and dangerous to know G.G. ALLIN – his solo career only really got back on track via a mid-90's deal with hardcore/punk label 'Epitaph'. The first fruits of this partnership were unleashed in the shape of 'THE HARD STUFF' (1995), an abrasively unsentimental trawl through life's piss-stinking back alleys with guest support from the likes of HENRY ROLLINS and BAD RELIGION. The 'DANGEROUS MADNESS' album followed in 1996, KRAMER once again taking bitter lyrical inspiration from his school-of-hard-knocks background while kicking out the jams 90's style with more ferocity and bile than many of the young pretenders. The same year saw a collaborative effort with fellow Detroit veterans SCOTT MORGAN and DENIZ TEK entitled 'DODGE MAIN', while his rejuvenated solo career continued apace in 1997 with 'CITIZEN WAYNE'. 'LLMF (LIVE LIKE A MOTHERFUCKER)' (1998) found KRAMER in his element while a further studio set, 'BEYOND CYBERPUNK', appeared in 2002. • **Songwriters:** Group compositions, except; I CAN ONLY GIVE YOU EVERYTHING (Them) / TUTTI FRUTTI (Little Richard).

Album rating: KICK OUT THE JAMS (*9) / BACK IN THE USA (*7) / HIGH TIME (*5) / BABES IN ARMS collection (*5) / LOOKING AT YOU collection (*4) / POWER TRIP collection (*5) / THE BEST OF MC5 compilation (*9) / Wayne Kramer: DEATHTONGUE (*4) / THE HARD STUFF (*7) / DANGEROUS MADNESS (*5) / CITIZEN WAYNE (*5) / LLMF (*5)

ROB TYNER (b. ROBERT DERMINER, 12 Dec'44) – vocals, harmonica / **WAYNE KRAMER** (b.30 Apr'48) – guitar, vocals, keyboards / **FRED 'SONIC' SMITH** (b. West Virginia) – guitar / **MICHAEL DAVIS** – bass / **DENNIS THOMPSON** – drums

not iss.   A.M.G.
1966. (7") <AMG 1001> **I CAN ONLY GIVE YOU EVERYTHING. / I JUST DON'T KNOW**
(above credited to MOTOR CITY FIVE)

not iss.   A2.
Mar 68. (7") <A2 333> **LOOKING AT YOU. / BORDERLINE**

— added 6th member **Brother J.C.CRAWFORD** – rapper / narrative

Elektra   Elektra
May 69. (7") (EKSN 45056) <EK 45648> **KICK OUT THE JAMS. / MOTOR CITY IS BURNING**   82 Mar 69
May 69. (lp) (mono/stereo; EKL/EKS 74042) **KICK OUT THE JAMS**   30 Mar 69
– Ramblin' rose / Kick out the jams / Come together / Rocket reducer No.62 (rama lama fa fa) / Borderline / Motor city is burning / I want you right now / Starship. (re-iss. May77.) (re-iss. +cd.Nov91) (re-iss. cd+c Mar93 on 'Pickwick') (re-iss. cd/c Sep95 on 'Warners')
Aug 69. (7") (EKSN 45067) **RAMBLIN' ROSE. / BORDERLINE**

Atlantic   Atlantic
Oct 70. (7") <2678> **TONIGHT. / LOOKING AT YOU**
Nov 70. (lp) (2400 016) <SD 8247> **BACK IN THE U.S.A.**   Feb 70
– Tutti frutti / Tonight / Teenage list / Looking at you / Let me try / High school / Call me animal / The American ruse / Shakin' Street / The human being lawnmower / Back in the U.S.A. (re-iss. Feb77.) (cd-iss. May93 on 'Rhino-Atlantic')
1970. (7") <2724> **SHAKIN' STREET. / THE AMERICAN RUSE**
Oct 71. (lp) (2400 123) <SD 8285> **HIGH TIME**
– Sister Anne / Baby won't ya / Miss X / Gotta keep movin' / Future – Now / Poison / Over nnd over / Skunk (sonically speaking). (cd-iss. May93 on 'Rhino-Atlantic')

— (split early '72 when DAVIS departed) THOMPSON, SMITH and DAVIS formed short-lived ASCENSION. FRED SMITH married PATTI SMITH and later formed SONIC'S RENDEZVOUS BAND. TYNER was credited on HOT RODS single, late'77. (see ⇒ EDDIE & THE HOT RODS.

– compilations, etc. –

1969. (7") A.M.G.; <AMG 1001> **I CAN ONLY GIVE YOU EVERYTHING. / ONE OF THE GUYS**
Jul 83. (c) R.O.I.R.; <A 122> **BABES IN ARMS**
(re-iss. Apr90 & Dec92 on 'Danceteria' lp/cd; DAN LP/CD 031)
May 94. (cd) Receiver; (RRCD 185) **BLACK TO COMM**
Oct 94. (10"lp/cd) Alive; (ALIVE 005/+CD) **POWER TRIP**
Nov 94. (cd) Receiver; (RRCD 193) **LOOKING AT YOU**
Feb 95. (10"lp/cd) Alive; (NER/+CD 2001) **THE AMERICAN RUSE**
Mar 95. (10"lp) Alive; (ALIVE 008) **ICE PICK SLIM**
(cd-iss. Feb97; ALIVECD 8)
Sep 95. (10"ep/cd) Alive; (ALIVE 0010/+CD) **FRIDAY, THE 13TH**
Dec 96. (cd) Dressed To Kill; (DTKLP 002) **THUNDER EXPRESS – ONE DAY IN THE STUDIO**
Mar 97. (lp) Alive; (NER 3008) **TEENAGE LUST**
Feb 00. (cd) Rhino; (8122 79783-2) **BIG BANG – THE BEST OF MC5**

WAYNE KRAMER

— went solo after spending 5 years in prison for cocaine dealing.

Stiff-Chiswick   not iss.
Oct 77. (7") (DEA-SUK 1) **RAMBLIN' ROSE. / GET SOME**

Radar   not iss.
Jul 79. (7") (ADA 41) **THE HARDER THEY COME. / EAST SIDE GIRL**

not iss.   Pure&Easy
1983. (7") <PE 017> **NEGATIVE GIRLS. / STREET WARFARE**

— GANG WAR formed in 1980 with **JOHNNY THUNDERS** – vocals

Zodiac   not iss.
1987. (7"ep; WAYNE KRAMER'S GANG WAR) (800) **GANG WAR (live at Max's May 1980)**
May 90. (lp) (LP 1001) **GANG WAR (live/studio)**

— WAYNE had joined the DEVIANTS in 1984 for their album HUMAN GARBAGE.

Curio   Progressive
1987. (7"; as WAYNE KRAMER'S DEATH TONGUE) **SPIKE HEELS EP**

— (WAYNE played late 80's with DAS DAMEN and G.G. ALLIN)
Nov 91. (d-cd/d-lp) (ITEM 2 CD/LP) <PRO 023> **DEATH TONGUE**
– Take your clothes off / Sike heels / Spend the rent / Negative girls / Death tongue / Leather skull / The scars never show / McArthur Park / Fun in the final days / Who shot you Dutch.

— In Sep'91, ROB TYNER was found dead after suffering heart attack. He was 46.

— with on first **KEITH MORRIS, BRETT REED, MATT FREEMAN, DALE CROVER, JOSH FREESE, BRETT GUREWITZ, CHRIS BAGAROZZI**, etc

Epitaph   Epitaph
Jan 95. (cd/c/lp) <(E 86447-2/-4/-1)> **THE HARD STUFF**
– Crack in the universe / Junkie romance / Bad seed / Poison / Realm of the pirate kings / Incident on Stock Island / Pillar of fire / Hope for sale / Edge of the switchblade / Sharkskin suit.
Feb 96. (cd/lp) <(86458-2/-1)> **DANGEROUS MADNESS**
– Dangerous madness / Back to DEtroit / Wild America / Something broken in the promised land / Take exit '97 / God's worst nightmare / The boy's got that look in their eyes / Dead man's vest / It's never enough / Rats of illusion / Dead movie stars.
May 97. (cd) <(6488-2)> **CITIZEN WAYNE**
– Stranger in the house / Back when dogs could talk / Revolution in apt.29 / Down on the ground / Shining Mr. Lincoln's shoes / Dope for democracy / No easy way out / You don't know my name / Count time / Snatched defeat / Doing the work / Farewell to whiskey.

— MC5 were about to reform with KRAMER, DAVIS + THOMSON

— next with rhythm **DOUGLAS LUNN + RIC PARNELL**
Nov 98. (cd/lp) <(86539)> **LLMF (Live Like A Motherfucker)**
– Bad seed / Stranger in the house / It's never enough / Something broken in the promised land / Take your clothes off / Down on the ground / Junkie romance / Poison / Count time / No easy way out / Crack in the universe / So long, Hank / Kick out the jams / Bomb day in Paris.

– others, etc. –

Nov 96. (cd; by WAYNE KRAMER – DENIZ TEK – SCOTT MORGAN) Alive; <(ALIVE 25)> **DODGE MAIN**
– City slang / 1.94 / Citizen of time / Future – Now / Fire comin' / 100 fools / The harder they come / Over and over / Better than that / I got a right.
Oct 00. (cd; by WAYNE KRAMER & PINK FAIRIES) Table Of Elements; <(TOE 3028)> **COCAINE BLUES 1974-1978**
(re-iss. Nov00 on 'Alive'; NER 3028 CD/LP)

MEDIUM MEDIUM
(see under ⇒ C-CAT TRANCE; in 80's section)

MEKONS

Formed: Leeds, England ... 1977 by art students TOM GREENHALGH and JON LANGFORD. The pair signed to Edinburgh's 'Fast' records, soon surfacing on vinyl in early '78 with the two-chord wonder, 'NEVER BEEN IN A RIOT', reputedly a reply to the macho overtones of the CLASH's 'White Riot'. This three song ultra-DIY assault was played to death by late night DJ, John Peel, a fervent supporter through thick and thin over the ensuing two decades. To end the year, The MEKONS delivered the classic lovesick punk anthem, 'WHERE WERE YOU', a track which perhaps encapsulated the genre's yellow-haired heyday more vividly than many of their peers (i.e. the BUZZCOCKS and WIRE). Limited by the extent of their musical talent and subject to the pressures of a major label deal ('Virgin'), LANGFORD and GREENHALGH enlisted the help of ANDY CARRIGAN, MARK WHITE, KEVIN LYCETT and ROS ALLEN, the latter borrowed from fellow Leeds cohorts, DELTA 5. At the turn of the decade, The MEKONS finally delivered their debut album, 'THE QUALITY OF MERCY IS NOT STRNEN' (1980), an overly ambitious collection which marked a premature departure from their early ramshackle charm in favour of GANG OF FOUR-style politico experimentation. They were dropped by their record label the following year amid poor sales, a string of low-key independent releases via various labels, namely 'Red Rhino' and the more political 'C.N.T.'. The core trio of GREENHALGH, LANGFORD and LYCETT (although the latter was soon to leave) recruited various musicians (SALLY TIMMS and SUSIE HONEYMAN being the more stable) over the years, their style of music constantly evolving in line with the personnel comings and goings; LANGFORD moonlighted with the THREE JOHNS. Although maintaining their uncompromising punk ideals and politics (especially with regards to the plight of the miners), 1985's 'FEAR AND WHISKEY' saw The MEKONS baptised by country/roots/folk fire. 'THE MEKONS HONKY TONKIN' (1987) and 'SO GOOD IT HURTS' (1988), continued in a rootsy, if more eclectic vein, the latter encompassing elements of various world music folk styles. Moving from their own 'Sin' records to UK's 'Blast First' ('A&M' in America), the band were once more critically reborn with the blisteringly defiant 'MEKONS ROCK'N'ROLL' (1989), proving they weren't yet ready to sink into worthy middle age. In the early 90's, they (GREENHALGH, LANGFORD, TIMMS and HONEYMAN) continued to release the odd album, although geographical problems (half the band had taken flight to the States!) precluded an overly prolific release schedule. Having signed to 'Quarter Stick' in 1993, they issued a number of albums including the 1996 collaborative set, 'PUSSY, KING OF THE PIRATES', featuring narration by American writer, KATHY ACKER. Of late, the ever-industrious LANGFORD has completed his first solo set, 'SKULL ORCHARD' (1998), a disappointing album which seemed to be retreading the heady radical politics of the mid 80's. Meanwhile, back at the ranch, The MEKONS were still getting it down musically. 1998's 'ME', 2000's 'JOURNEY TO THE END OF THE NIGHT' and 2002's 'OOOH! (OUT OF OUR HEADS)' maintained that bit of eclectic rootsy rock'n'roll that has seen them survive a quarter of a century. • **Covered:** MAKES NO DIFFERENCE (Robbie Robertson) / FANCY (Kinks) / FOLSOM PRISON BLUES (Johnny Cash) / CRAP RAP (Ex) / YOU WEAR IT WELL (Rod Stewart) / HAVING A PARTY (Kevin Coyne) / etc. • **Trivia:** Named themselves after the green-headed alien in the 50's US comic-strip 'Dan Dare'.

Album rating: THE QUALITY OF MERCY IS NOT STRNEN (*6) / UNTITLED (*4) / THE MEKONS STORY compilation (*7) / FEAR AND WHISKEY (*6) / THE EDGE OF THE WORLD (*6) / THE MEKONS HONKY TONKIN' (*5) / SO GOOD IT HURTS (*5) / MEKONS ROCK'N'ROLL (*6) / THE CURSE OF THE MEKONS (*6) / I LOVE MEKONS (*5) / RETREAT FROM MEMPHIS (*6) / PUSSY, KING OF THE PIRATES with Kathy Acker (*6) / ME (*5) / I HAVE BEEN TO HEAVEN AND BACK . . . compilation (*5) / WHERE WERE YOU? HENS TEETH . . . compilation (*6) / JOURNEY TO THE END OF THE NIGHT (*6) / OOOH! (OUT OF OUR HEADS) (*6) / Jon Langford: SKULL ORCHARD (*5)

TOM GREENHALGH (b. 4 Nov'56, Stockholm, Sweden) – vocals, guitar / **JON LANGFORD** (b.11 Oct'57, Newport, Wales) – drums, vocals

Fast Prod. / not iss.

Feb 78. (7"m) *(FAST 1)* **NEVER BEEN IN A RIOT. / 32 WEEKS / HEART AND SOUL**
Dec 78. (7") *(FAST 7)* **WHERE WERE YOU? / I'LL HAVE TO DANCE THEN (ON MY OWN)**

— added **ANDY CARRIGAN** – vocals / **MARK WHITE** – lyrics / **KEVIN LYCETT** – guitar / **ROSS ALLEN** – bass (of DELTA 5)

Virgin / not iss.

Sep 79. (7") *(VS 300)* **WORK ALL WEEK. / UNKNOWN WRECKS**
Feb 80. (lp) *(V 2143)* **THE QUALITY OF MERCY IS NOT STRNEN**
 – Like spoons no more / Join us in the countryside / Rosanne / Trevira trousers / After 6 / What are we going to do tonight? / What / / Watch the film / Beetroot / I saw you dance / Lonely and wet / Dan Dare. *(cd-iss. Apr90 +=; VCD 2143)* – Teeth / Guardian / Kill / Stay cool / Work all week / Unknown wrecks. *<US cd-iss. 1990 on 'Caroline'; 1621>*
Mar 80. (d7") *(VS 101)* **TEETH. / GUARDIAN // KILL. / STAY COOL**

Red Rhino

Dec 80. (lp) *(RR 001)* **UNTITLED** (aka 'DEVILS RATS AND PIGGIES A SPECIAL MESSAGE FROM GODZILLA')
 – Snow / St. Patrick's day / D.P. Miller / Institution / I'm so happy / Chopper squad / Business tango / Trimden Grange explosion / Karen / Corporal Chalkie / John Barry / Another one / Killer Ken / Another set of teeth. *(re-iss. Jun85; same)* *<US cd-iss. 1997 on '1/4 Stick'; QS 66>*
Sep 81. (7") *(RED 7)* **SNOW. / ANOTHER ONE TIME**

C.N.T. / not iss.

Oct 81. (12"m) *(CNT 1)* **THIS SPORTING LIFE. / FRUSTRATION / (mystery live track; NEVER BEEN IN A RIOT)**
Nov 82. (7"ltd.) *(CNT 008)* **THIS SPORTING LIFE. / FIGHT THE CUTS**
Nov 82. (lp) *(CNT 009)* **THE MEKONS STORY – IT FALLETH LIKE GENTLE RAIN FROM HEAVEN** (compilation)
 – The letter's in the post / Not a dancing master / Dance and drink the Mekons / Bomb train / Trouble down south / Car-men / Eden / Frustrations / Fight the cuts / Byron / This sporting life / Rosanne / Garden fence of sound / Miriam always / The walking song / Building / I'm so happy / I bought you these / He beat up his boyfriend / 1st guitarist. *<US cd-iss. 1993 on 'Feel Good All Over'>*

— **GREENHALGH, LANGFORD + LYCETT** recruited new members **BEN MANDELSON** – guitar (ex-MAGAZINE) / **DICK TAYLOR** – guitar (ex-PRETTY THINGS) / **ROB WAREY** – bass (all these 3 left after 1985 recordings)

Sep 83. (12"ep) *(CNT 014)* **THE ENGLISH DANCING MASTER**
 – The last dance / No confess / No country dance / Parsons farewell.

— **LU KNEE** (aka **LU EDMUNDS**) – bass, guitar (ex-DAMNED, ex-EDGE) repl. LYCETT / added **SALLY TIMMS** – vocals (ex-guest & solo artist) / **SUSIE HONEYMAN** – violin / **STEVE GOULDING** – drums (ex-RUMOUR)

Sin / not iss.

Jul 85. (lp) *(SIN 001)* **FEAR AND WHISKEY**
 – Chivalry / Trouble down south / Hard to be human again / Darkness and doubt / Psycho cupid (danceband on the edge of town) / Flitcraft / Country / Abernant 1984-1985 / The last dance / Lost highway. *(cd-iss. Mar89 as 'ORIGINAL SIN' on 'R.T.D.'+=; RTCD 105)* *<US cd-iss. Mar89 as 'ORIGINAL SIN' on 'Twin/Tone'+=; 89164>* – (A dancing master such as) Mr Confess / Beaten and broken / Chop that child in half / Hey! Susan / Garage d'or / Slightly south of the border / Coal hole / $1000 wedding / Rescue mission. *(cd re-mast.Jan02 on 'Quarter Stick'; QS 80CD)*
Feb 86. (12"ep) *(SIN 002R)* **CRIME AND PUNISHMENT** (Peel session)
 – Beaten and broken / Chop that child in half / Hey! Susan / Deep end.
Jun 86. (lp) *(SIN 003)* **THE EDGE OF THE WORLD**
 – Hello cruel world / Bastard / Oblivion / King Arthur / Ugly band / Shanty / Garage d'or / Big zombie / Sweet dreams / Dream dream dream / Slightly south of the border / Alone and forsaken / The letter. *(<cd-iss. 1996 on '1/4 Stick'; 42)>*
Jun 86. (7") *(SIN 004)* **HELLO CRUEL WORLD. / ALONE AND FORSAKEN**
Oct 86. (10"ep) *(SIN 005)* **SLIGHTLY SOUTH OF THE BORDER / $1,000 WEDDING. / COOL HOLE / RESCUE MISSION**

— trimmed slightly when LU (already a brief PUBLIC IMAGE LTD member) joined SHRIEKBACK

— over the next few years, they (**GREENHALGH, LANGFORD, TIMMS, HONEYMAN + GOULDING**) used others:- **RICO BELL** – accordion / **BRENDAN CROKER** – guitar / **JOHN GILL** – mellotron / **SARAH CORINA** – bass / etc.

Sin / Twin/Tone

Mar 87. (lp/c) *(SIN/+C 006)* *<TTR 87113/+C>* **THE MEKONS HONKY TONKIN'**
 – I can't find my money / Hole in the ground / Sleepless nights / Keep hoppin' / Charlie cake park / If they hang you / Prince of darkness / Kidnapped / Sympathy for The Mekons / Spit / The Trimdon Grange explosion / Please don't let me love you / Gin palace. *(c+=)* – Sin city / Derion.
Aug 87. (12"m) *(SIN 007T)* **HOLE IN THE GROUND. / SIN CITY / PRINCE OF DARKNESS**
Mar 88. (lp/c/cd) *(SIN/+C/CD 008)* *<TTR 88114/+C/CD>* **SO GOOD IT HURTS**
 – I'm not here (1967) / Ghosts of American astronauts / Road to Florida / Johnny miner / Dora / Poxy lips / (Sometimes I feel like) Fletcher Christian / Fantastic voyage / Robin Hood / Heart of stone / Maverick / Vengeance. *(cd+=)* – Revenge.
Apr 88. (7") *(SIN 009)* **GHOSTS OF AMERICAN ASTRONAUTS. / ROBIN HOOD**
 (12") *(SIN 009T)* – ('A'side) / 1967 (revisited) / Revenge.

Blast First / A&M

Aug 89. (10"ep/cd-ep) *(BFFP 53/+CD)* **DREAM AND LIE OF THE MEKONS**
 – Amnesia / Heaven and back / Club Mekon / Blow your tuneless trumpet.
Sep 89. (lp/c/cd) *(BFFP 40/+C/CD)* *<75021 5277-1/-4/-2>* **MEKONS ROCK'N'ROLL**
 – Memphis, Egypt / Club Mekon / Only darkness has the power / Ring o'roses / Learning to live on your own / Cocaine Lil / Empire of the senseless / Someone / Amnesia / I am crazy / Heaven and back / Blow your own tuneless trumpet / Echo / When darkness falls. *(cd re-iss. Jul01 on 'Collector's Choice'; CCM 0201-2)*
Oct 90. (m-lp/c/cd) *(BFFP 62/+C/CD)* **F.U.N. '90**
 – Makes no difference / Having a party / Sheffield park / One town / Hashis in Marseilles / One horse dub.
Feb 91. (7") *(BFFP 80/+C/CD)* **MAKES NO DIFFERENCE. / HAVING A PARTY**
Jun 91. (lp/c/cd) *(BFFP 80/+C/CD)* **THE CURSE OF THE MEKONS**
 – The curse / Blue arse / Wild and blue / Authority / Secrets / Nocturne / Sorcerer / Brutal / Funeral / Lyric / Waltz / 100% song.

— now 2 boy/ 2 girl (**GREENHALGH, LANGFORD, TIMMS + HONEYMAN**) with others on call at various times

not iss. / Loud-WEA

Dec 92. (12"ep) *<89014>* **WICKED MIDNITE / ALL I WANT. / THE CURSE (live) / WALTZ (live) / AMNESIA (live)**

1/4 Stick / 1/4 Stick

Oct 93. (lp/c/cd) *(<QS 19/+C/CD>)* **I LOVE MEKONS**
 – Millionaire / Wicked midnite / I don't know / Dear sausage / All I want / Special / St. Valentine's day / I love apple / Love letter / Honeymoon in Hell / Too personal / Point of no return.
Nov 93. (cd-s) *(<QS 823CD>)* **MILLIONAIRE EP**
 – Millionaire / He beat up his boyfriend / All I want (live) / Blow your tuneless trumpet (live) / Fletcher Christian, (sometime I feel like) (live).
May 94. (cd/lp) *(<QS 26 CD/LP>)* **RETREAT FROM MEMPHIS**
 – Eve future / Lucky devil / Insignificance (conversation with . . .) / His bad dream / Our bad dream / The flame that killed John Wayne / Ice rink in Berlin / Spinning round in flames / Machine / Hostile mascot / Chemical wedding / Spirals of paranoia / Missing you all / Submerged / Soldier / Never work.
May 95. (7") *(<QS 31>)* **UNTITLED 1. / UNTITLED 1 (continued) / UNTITLED 2**
Jan 96. (cd/lp; as The MEKONS & KATHY ACKER) *(<QS 36 CD/LP>)* **PUSSY, KING OF THE PIRATES**
 – Ange's song as she crawled through London / Song of the dogs / Ostracism's song to pussycat / Antigone speaks about herself / My song at night / Into the strange / Captured by pirates / A prayer for all sailors / My name is O / I want to tell you about myself / We're just outside London / Antigone, you see her / Now let me tell you / Since Ange and me are innocent.
May 98. (cd) *(<QS 53CD>)* **ME**
 – Enter the lists / Down / Narrative / Tourettes / Flip flop / Gin & it / Back to back / Come and have a go if you think you're hard enough / Men united / Mirror / Far sub dominant / Whiskey sex shack / Thunder / Belly to belly.
Mar 00. (cd) *(<QS 60CD>)* **JOURNEY TO THE END OF THE NIGHT**
 – Myth / Out in the night / Last weeks of the war / City of London / Tina / The flood / Cast no shadows / Ordinary night / Powers & horror / Neglect / Something to be scared of / Last night on Earth.

— next virtually a reunion of all present/past MEKONS

Aug 02. (cd) *(<QS 77CD>)* **OOOH! (OUT OF OUR HEADS)**
 – Thee olde trip to Jerusalem / Dancing in the head / This way through the fire / Hate is the new love / Take his name in vain / Only you and your ghost will know / Lobe pilgrim / Winter / One x one / Bob Hope and charity / Stonehead.

– compilations, etc. –

Jan 88. (c)<cd> *R.O.I.R.; (A 154) / Combat; <5026>* **MEKONS N.Y. 1986-1987 (live)**
 – (Chicago introduction) Big zombie / Trouble down south / Slightly south of the border / The story of nothing / Flitcraft at the Iron Horse / Abernant 84-87 / I can't find my money / The shape I'm in / Hard to be human / Beaten and broken / Not long ago / Shanty / Revenge / Sophie / Chivalry. *(cd re-iss. Dec00; RUSCD 8269)*
1988. (12") *Materiali Sonori; (MASO 70008)* **GREETINGS EIGHT** — Italy
Mar 94. (cd) *Anagram; (CDMGRAM 76)* **THE MEKONS**
Apr 99. (cd) *Quarter Stick; <QS 57CD>* **I HAVE BEEN TO HEAVEN AND BACK, VOLUME 1**

MEKONS (cont)

– I have been to heaven and back / The ballad of Sally / This funeral is for the wrong corpse (full version) / (untitled) / Orange and lemons / Ring o' roses / Gill & Vicky / (untitled) / Now we have the bomb / (untitled) / You wear it well / Betrayal / Orpheus / Roger Troutman / (untitled) / Circle city (Mekons vs. peace love hooligans) / (untitled) / Cowboy boots / Lucky star / Axcerpt / (untitled) / Born to choose / Unknown song.

Sep 99. (cd) *Quarter Stick; (<QS 59CD>)* **WHERE WERE YOU?: HENS TEETH AND OTHER LOST FRAGMENTS OF POPULAR CULTURE, VOL.2**
– Fancy / One horse dub / Mekons rock'n'roll / Dick's van 1 / Nice Julie (waltz) / East is red / 1967 revisited / Darkness / Dick's van 2 / Hashish in Marseilles / Folsom Prison blues / My song at night / Polaroid (I don't own I only date) / Brixton-Leeds phone tune / Where were you? / Untitled 1 / Dick's van 3 / Noisy Gertie / Crap crap woof talk / Crap rap / Angel dog / Dick's van 4 / Untitled 2 / Dick's van end.

Jul 01. (cd) *Collector's Choice; (<CCM 0202-2>)* **CURSE OF THE MEKONS / F.U.N. 90**

JON LANGFORD

— next with **STEVE GOULDING + TOM RAY** + others

                                                          not iss.   Scout

1995. (cd; as JONBOY LANGFORD & THE PINE VALLEY COSMONAUTS) *<sr 1001>* **MISERY LOVES COMPANY**
– Cocaine blues / Tennessee flat-top box / Guess things happen that way / What is truth? / I got stripes / Busted / Big river / Sunday morning coming down / There you go / I still miss someone / Thing called love / Give my love to Rose / Next in line / Home of the blues.

— now with **ALAN DOUGHTY** – bass, vocals / **MARC DURANTE** – guitars / **STEVE GOULDING** – drums

                                    Sugar Free Sugar Free

Jul 98. (cd) *(<sf 006>)* **SKULL ORCHARD**   Feb98
– Tubby brothers / Penny arcades / Butter song / Sentimental marching song / Youghal / Trapdoor / Inside the whale / I am the law / Pill sailor / The last count / My own worst enemy / I'm stopping this train / Deep sea diver / Tom Jones levitation.

— The PINE VALLEY COSMONAUTS released their own set, 'SALUTE THE MAJESTY OF BOB WILLS' in October '98 for 'Bloodshot'

MEMBERS

Formed: Camberley, Surrey, England ... 1977 by NICKY TESCO and French-born JEAN-MARIE CARROLL along with GARY BAKER and ADRIAN LILLYWHITE. Following the subsequent replacement of BAKER with NIGEL BENNETT and the addition of CHRIS PAYNE the band made their first foray into DIY punk with the raw 'FEAR ON THE STREETS' single. Released on the tiny (self-financed) 'X.S.' label, the track alerted the recently formed 'Stiff' who signed them to a one-single deal. The result was 'SOLITARY CONFINEMENT', a paean to the delights of living in the bedsit-land of London's lovely Earls Court. Amateurish but addictive, it landed them a major label deal with 'Virgin', Richard Branson's operation releasing punk classic, 'THE SOUND OF THE SUBURBS', in 1979. A singalong mob anthem for semi-detached youth up and down the country, the track was the finest example of The MEMBERS' knack for three-chord chaos baited on the sharpest of hooklines; the band were memorably described as the intelligent bloke's SHAM 69. The fact that both a TV series (charting the history of the genre) and a best selling compilation album – both part of the ever enduring nostalgia for punk's heyday – were named in the track's honour is testament to its importance. Yet like many of their peers, the band made the tragic mistake of recording a cod-reggae follow-up; it may have been amusing but 'OFFSHORE BANKING BUSINESS' fell flat. A Steve Lillywhite (brother of ADRIAN)-produced debut album, 'AT THE CHELSEA NIGHTCLUB' (1979), met with some positive critical noises but the lack of a worthy successor to 'SOUND ...' eventually sounded the death knell on The MEMBERS' career. A second 'Virgin' album, 'THE CHOICE IS YOURS' (1980), met with little enthusiasm and signalled the end of their contract. The independently released 'GOING WEST' (1983) was a last-ditch effort, TESCO already having long since abandoned ship.

Album rating: AT THE CHELSEA NIGHTCLUB (*5) / THE CHOICE IS YOURS (*4) / GOING WEST (*4)

NICKY TESCO – vocals / **GARY BAKER** – lead guitar / **J.C. MAINMAN** (b. JEAN-MARIE CARROLL) – guitar, vocals / **CHRIS BAYNE** – bass, vocals / **ADRIAN LILLYWHITE** – drums

                                     X.S.   not iss.

Jul 77. (7"; w-drawn) *(XS 1)* **FEAR ON THE STREETS**

                                    One Off-Stiff not iss.

May 78. (7") *(OFF 3)* **SOLITARY CONFINMENT. / RAT UP A DRAINPIPE**

— **NIGEL BENNETT** – lead guitar; repl. BAKER

                                  Virgin   not iss.

Jan 79. (7"clear) *(VS 242)* **THE SOUND OF THE SUBURBS. / HANDLING THE BIG JETS**   12
Mar 79. (7"/12") *(VS 248/+12)* **OFFSHORE BANKING BUSINESS. / SOLITARY CONFINEMENT**   31
Apr 79. (lp) *(V 2120)* **AT THE CHELSEA NIGHTCLUB**   46
– Love in a lift / Electricity / Don't push / Offshore banking business / Soho a go-go / Frustrated bagshot / The sound of the suburbs / Solitary confinment / Sally / Stand up and spit / Phone-in show / Chelsea nightclub. *(re-iss. Mar84; OVED 44)*
Sep 79. (7") *(VS 292)* **KILLING TIME. / G.L.C.**
Mar 80. (7") *(VS 333)* **ROMANCE. / THE BALLAD OF JOHN MARTIN**
Apr 80. (lp) *(V 2153)* **THE CHOICE IS YOURS**
– Brian was / Killing time / Clean men / Romance / Flying again / Solitary confinement / Chelsea nightclub / Gang war / Police car.
May 80. (d7") *(VS 352)* **FLYING AGAIN. / DISCO OUI OUI // LOVE IN A LIFT. / RAT UP A DRAINPIPE**

— now a quartet when TESCO went solo (J.C. & C.B. took over vocals)

                                     Albion   not iss.

May 81. (7") *(ION 1012)* **WORKING GIRL. / HOLIDAY IN TANGANIKA**
(12"+=) *(12ION 1012)* – Everybody's a holiday.

                                     Island   Arista

Apr 82. (7") *(WIP 6773)* **RADIO. / IF YOU CAN'T STAND UP**
Jan 83. (7") **BOYS LIKE US. / AT THE ARCADE**

                                     Albion   not iss.

Jul 83. (7") *(ION 1050)* **WORKING GIRL (re-recorded). / THE FAMILY**
(12"+=) *(12ION 1050)* – The arcade.
Aug 83. (lp) *(ALB 115)* **GOING WEST**
– Working girl / The family / You and me against the world / Chairman of the board / Boys like us / Going west / Radio / Fire (in my heart) / The model / We, the people.
Aug 83. (7"/12") *(ION/12ION 153)* **GOING WEST. / MEMBERSHIP**

— split 1983

– compilations, others, etc. –

on 'Virgin' unless mentioned otherwise

Apr 83. (7"/12") *(VS 584/+12)* **THE SOUND OF THE SUBURBS. / OFFSHORE BANKING BUSINESS**
Feb 91. (cd) *(CDOVD 310)* **THE CHOIVE IS YOURS / AT THE CHELSEA NIGHTCLUB**
Mar 95. (cd) *(CDOVD 455)* **THE SOUND OF THE SUBURBS ...THE FINEST MOMENTS**
– Handling the big jets / Sally / G.L.C. / Offshore banking business / Pennies in the pound / Soho a go-go / Muzak machine / Rat up a drainpipe / Sound of the suburbs / Phone-in show / Brian was / Killing time / Clean men / Romance / Flying again / Solitary confinement / Chelsea nightclub / Gang war / Police car.

METAL URBAIN

Formed: Paris, France ... 1977 as possibly the first Gallic punk-rock act. The band also took the honour of being the first act to release a record on British independent, 'Rough Trade', the track in question being early '78's 'PARIS MAQUIS'. However, CLAUDE PANIK, ERIC DEBRIS, HERMAN SCHWARTZ and NANCY LUGER (a male!) had already issued a French-only debut 7", 'PANIK', two months previously. Pitting growling, politically motivated lyrics against a background/foreground blast of cheap fuzz noise-guitar and a bizarre syncopated drumbeat, METAL URBAIN were musically distinct from most of their UK cousins. Over the course of the next year or so, the Frenchmen released two more singles, 'HYSTERIE CONNECTIVE' and 'SWEET MARILYN', the latter the first to appear under the moniker of the METAL BOYS. DEBRIS also fronted another 'Rough Trade' act, DR. MIX & THE REMIX, releasing a cover of The Stooges' 'NO FUN'. Towards the end of the decade, DEBRIS and Co tackled another cover, 'I CAN'T CONTROL MYSELF', once a hit for the Troggs. The two acts continued to release material simultaneously although both had disappeared in the space of a year.

Album rating: L'AGE D'OR compilation (*6)

CLAUDE PANIK – vocals / **ERIC DEBRIS** – synthesizer, electric drums / **HERMAN SCHWARTZ** – guitar / male **NANCY LUGER** – guitar

                                  Cobra   not iss.

Oct 77. (7") *(COB 7004)* **PANIK. / LADY COCA COLA**   French

                                   Rough Trade not iss.

Jan 78. (7") *(RT 001)* **PARIS MAQUIS. / CLE DE CONTACT**

                                   Radar   not iss.

Sep 78. (7") *(ADA 20)* **HYSTERIE CONNECTIVE. / PAS POUBELLE**

— now without DEBRIS who joined METAL BOYS and DR. MIX & THE REMIX

— METAL URBAIN issued two further albums, 'LES HOMMES MORT SONT DANGEREUX' (1980 – Byzz; BLPS 8101) and 'DEAD MEN' (1981 – Byzz; BLPS 8107). The former had a free 7" below on 'Celluloid'

Sep 80. (7") *(CEL 16216)* **HYSTERIE CONNECTIVE (mix 2). / ATLANTIS**   French

DR. MIX & THE REMIX

— **ERIC DEBRIS** – vocals / **PAT VINCENT** – guitar / **MARK TURNER** – bass, synthesizers / **JEAN-PIERRE** – bass, synthesizers / **NICK TURNER** – drums / **LUCY** – saxophone

                                   Rough Trade not iss.

Jun 79. (7"; as METAL BOYS) *(RT 016)* **SWEET MARILYN. / FUGUE FOR A DARKENED ISLAND**
Jun 79. (7") *(RT 017)* **NO FUN. / NO FUN (Dr.Mix alone version)**
Dec 79. (7") *(RT 032)* **I CAN'T CONTROL MYSELF. / ('A'version)**
Dec 79. (m-lp) *(ROUGH 6)* **WALL OF NOISE**
– Out of the question / Grey lagoons / No fun / Six dreams / I can't control myself / Supermen / Sister Ray. *(cd-iss. Aug92 on 'Creation – Rev-Ola';)*

                                   Celluloid   not iss.

Oct 80. (12"ep) *(CEL 6585)* **PSYCHEDELIC DESERT EP**
Dec 80. (lp; as METAL BOYS) *(CEL 2.6560)* **TOKIO AIRPORT** (John Peel session)
Oct 81. (lp) *(CEL 6589)* **DR. MIX & THE REMIX**

— disappeared after above

– (METAL URBAIN) compilations –

1989. (lp/cd) *Fan Club; (FC 011/+CD)* **L'AGE D'OR**
– Hysterie connective / Ghetto / Cle de contact / Lady Coca Cola / Panik / Futurama / Paris maquis / Pop poubelle / 50-50 / Anarchie au palace / E 202 / Numero / Colt 45 / Lady Coke / No fun / Metal urbain / Atlantis / Creve salope / Snuff movie / Ultra violence / Tango sudiste.

Aug 90. (cd/lp; by DR. MIX & THE REMIX) *A.B.C.; (ABCD/BR 041)* **1979-1982**

MINK DeVILLE

Formed: San Francisco, California, USA ... 1974 by WILLY DeVILLE (he had lived in London for the past few years), the singer relocating his new outfit – who included RUBEN SIGUENZA, THOMAS 'MANFRED' ALLEN and LOUIS X. ERLANGER – to his native New York where they became favourites on the New York new wave underground scene. Snapped up by 'Capitol' on the strength of a few tracks on the celebrated V/A collection, 'Live At CBGB'S', the group broke through with their 1977 debut 45, 'SPANISH STROLL'. A surprise UK chart hit in light of its characteristic Hispanic singing crossed between LOU REED and the more soulful R&B American singers, the track was one of the few highlights from their patchy eponymous debut set. Produced by Jack Nitzsche, the album failed to generate anticipated interest, although it was notable for the inclusion of Patti & The Emblems cover, 'MIXED UP, SHOOK UP GIRL'. Follow-up set, 'RETURN TO MAGENTA' (1978), fared little better, DeVILLE turning his interpretive skills this time around to a cover of Moon Martin's 'ROLENE'. Ever the ladies man, WILLY relocated his musical endevours to Paris for the recording of third album, 'LE CHAT BLEU' (1980), he and ERLANGER joined by a clutch of seasoned former session men enlisted to make the most of the part-DOC POMUS penned songs. With each subsequent release, MINK DeVILLE (or just basically WILLY solo) became an increasingly mainstream/AOR operation, culminating in a collaborative effort with MARK KNOPFLER, 'Storybook Love', in 1988.

Album rating: SAVOIR FAYRE compilation (*5)

WILLY DeVILLE (b. WILLIAM BORAY, 27 Aug'53, New York City) – vocals, guitar, mouth harp / **RUBEN SIGUENZA** – bass / **THOMAS 'MANFRED' ALLEN** – drums / **LOUIS X. ERLANGER** – guitar, vocals / **BOBBY LEONARDS** – keyboards

		Capitol	Capitol
Jun 77.	(7") **SPANISH STROLL. / MIXED UP, SHOOK UP**	–	–
Jun 77.	(7"/12") (CL/12CLX 103) **SPANISH STROLL. / GUNSLINGER**	20	–
Jun 77.	(lp/c) <(EST/TC-EST 11631)> **MINK DeVILLE**		

– Venus of Avenue D / Little girl / One way street / Mixed up, shook up girl / Gunslinger / Can't do without it / Cadillac walk / Spanish stroll / She's so tough / Party girls. (re-iss. Feb87 on 'Razor'; as 'CABRETTA'; RAZ 24) (cd-iss. Mar93 as 'SPANISH STROLL' on 'Raven'; RVCD 32)

Sep 77.	(7") (CL 15942) **LITTLE GIRL. / SHE'S SO TOUGH**		–
Nov 77.	(7") (CL 15952) **CADILLAC WALK. / CAN'T DO WITHOUT IT**		–
Dec 77.	(7") **CADILLAC GIRL. / LITTLE GIRL**		
May 78.	(7") (CL 15989) **JUST YOUR FRIEND. / ONE WAY STREET**	–	
Jun 78.	(7") **GUARDIAN ANGEL. / EASY SLIDER**	–	
Jul 78.	(lp/c) <(EST/TC-EST 11780)> **RETURN TO MAGENTA**		Jun78

– Guardian angel / Soul twist / "A" train lady / Rolene / Desperate days / Just your friends / Steady drivin' man / Easy slider / I broke that promise / Confidence to kill. (cd-iss. May93 on 'Wotre Music'; WM 339003)

| Aug 78. | (7") (CL 16005) **SOUL TWIST. / ROLENE** | | – |

— WILLY retained ERLANGER and brought in new men **RICK BORGIA** – guitar / **KENNY MARGOLIS** – keyboards / **JERRY SCHEFF** – bass / **RON TUTT** – drums

| Apr 80. | (7") (CL 16134) **THIS MUST BE THE NIGHT. / MIXED UP, SHOOK UP GIRL** | | – |

(12"+=) (CLX 16134) – Lipstick traces.

| Apr 80. | (lp/c) (EST/TC-EST 25390) <11955> **LE CHAT BLEU** | | Sep80 |

– This must be the night / Savoir faire / That world outside / Slow drain / You just keep holding on / Lipstick traces / Bad boy / Mazurka / Just to walk that little girl home / Heaven stood still. (cd-iss. May93 on 'Wotre Music'; WM 339002)

| Jun 80. | (7") **LIPSTICK TRACES. / JUST TO WALK THAT LITTLE GIRL HOME** | – | – |

— disbanded in Spring 1980

		C.B.S.	Columbia
Sep 80.	(7"; by WILLY DeVILLE) (CBS 8526) **HEAT OF THE MOMENT. / PULLIN' MY STRING**		

— MINK DEVILLE re-grouped in 1981. WILLY, RICK + KENNY recruited **JOEY VASTA** – bass / **TOMMY PRICE** – drums

		Atlantic	Atlantic
Oct 81.	(7") (K 11688) **YOU BETTER MOVE ON. / SHE WAS MINE**		
Oct 81.	(lp/c) (K/K4 50833) <19311> **COUP DE GRACE**		

– Just give me one good reason / Help me to make it / Maybe tomorrow / Teardrops must fall / You better move on / Love & emotion / So in love are we / Love me like you did before / She was made in Heaven / End of the line.

| Jan 82. | (7") (K 11703) **MAYBE TOMORROW. / SO IN LOVE ARE WE** | | |
| Dec 83. | (lp/c) (780115-1/-4) **WHERE THE ANGELS FEAR TO TREAD** | | |

– Each word's a beat of my heart / River of tears / Demasiado / corazon (Too much heart) / Lilly's daddy's Cadillac / Around the corner / Pick up the pieces / Love's got a hold on me / Keep your monkey away from my door / Are you lonely tonight / The moonlight let me down.

| Apr 84. | (7") (A 9750) <89750> **EACH WORD'S A BEAT OF MY HEART. / RIVER OF TEARS** | | 89 Jan84 |

(12"+=) (AT 9750) – Harlem nocturne / Maybe tomorrow.

| Apr 84. | (7") **PICK UP THE PIECES. /** | – | – |

— now with complete new personnel of session people

| Jun 85. | (7") (POSP 745) **IN THE HEART OF THE CITY. / PRIDE AND JOY** | | – |

(12"+=) (POSPX 745) – Italian shoes (New York mix).

| Jun 85. | (lp/c/cd) (825776-1/-4/-2) **SPORTIN' LIFE** | | |

– In the heart of the city / I must be dreaming / Italian shoes / Slip away / When you walk my way / A woman's touch / Easy street / Little by little / There's no living (without your loving) / Something beautiful is dying.

| Oct 85. | (7") (POSP 773) **I MUST BE DREAMING. / IN THE HEART OF THE CITY** | | |

(12"+=) (POSPX 773) – ('A'mix).

— split late '85

WILLY DE VILLE

— continued a solo career

		Polydor	A&M
Nov 87.	(7") **ASSASSIN OF LOVE. / I CALL YOUR NAME**	–	–
Nov 87.	(7") (POSP 887) **MIRACLE. / I CALL YOUR NAME**		–

(12"+=) (POSPX 887) – Stand by me.
(c-s+=/cd-s+=) (PO C/CD 887) – Could you would you.

| Jan 88. | (lp/c)(cd) (POLH/+C 39)(833669-2) **MIRACLE** | | |

– (Due to) Gun control / Could you would you / Heart & soul / Assassin of love / Spanish Jack / Miracle / Angel eyes / Nightfalls / Southern politician / Storybook love. (cd-iss. Dec94 on 'Raven'; RVCD 41)

| Feb 88. | (7") (POSP 904) **ASSASSIN OF LOVE. / SPANISH JACK** | | – |

(12"+=) (POSPX 904) – ('A'extended remix) / Spanish stroll (live).
(cd-s++=) (POCD 904) Desperate ways (live).

— WILLY was credited with MARK KNOPFLER (Dire Straits) on 'Storybook Love', (circa Mar88).

		Skyranch	Skyranch
Mar 92.	(cd) <(SR 652304)> **VICTORY MIXTURE**		

– Hello my lover / It do me good / Key to my heart / Beating like a tom-tom / Every dog has its day / Big blue diamonds / Teasin' you / Ruler of my heart / Who shot the la-la / Junker's blues. (re-iss. Mar95; same)

		F.N.A.C.	not iss.
Apr 94.	(cd) (592254) **WILLY DeVILLE LIVE** (live)		

		not iss.	Forward-Rhino
May 94.	(cd-s) **HEY! JOE /**	–	
May 94.	(cd) <71686> **BACKSTREETS OF DESIRE**	–	

– Empty heart / All in the name of love / Lonely hunter / Even while I sleep / Voodoo charm / Come to poppa / Chemical warfare / Hey! Joe / I call your name / I can only give you everything / Jump city / Bamboo road / All in the name of love (reprise).

		East West	WEA
Nov 95.	(c-s) (EW 019C) **STILL / WHEN YOU'RE AWAY FROM ME**		

(cd-s+=) (EW 019CD) – Still (I love you still).

| Jan 96. | (cd/c) <(0630 12456-2/-4)> **LOUP GAROU** | | |

– (MINK DeVILLE) compilations, etc. –

| Nov 81. | (lp/c) Capitol; (EST/TC-EST 26716) **SAVOIR FAIRE** | | |

– This must be the night / "A" train lady / Spanish stroll / Cadillac walk / Soul twist / Just your friends / Mixed up, shook up girl / Gunslinger / One way street / Mazurka / I broke that promise / Just to walk that little girl home.

Jul 84.	(7") EMI Gold; (G45 27) **SPANISH STROLL. / CADILLAC WALK**		–
Nov 95.	(3xcd-box) E.M.I.; (CDOMB 013) **CABRETTA / RETURN TO MAGENTA / LE CHAT BLEU**		
Jan 96.	(cd; by WILLY DeVILLE) Wotre Music; (122151) **BIG EASY FANTASY**		
Oct 96.	(cd) Raven; (RVCD 59) **CABRETTA / RETURN TO MAGENTA**		
Sep 97.	(cd) E.M.I.; (CTMCD 333) **THE CENTENARY COLLECTION (THE BEST OF MINK DeVILLE)**		–

MIRRORS (see under ⇒ STYRENES)

MISFITS

Formed: Lodi, New Jersey, USA ... 1977 by GLENN DANZIG and JERRY ONLY. B-movie punks dominated by the brooding presence and sneering croon of DANZIG, the group (BOBBY STEELE and JOEY IMAGE completing the line-up) gigged at the usual NY haunts such as CBGB's before releasing their debut single, 'COUGH COOL', on the self-financed 'Plan 9' label. This was closely followed by such endearingly amateurish slices of low-rent melodic splatter-punk as 'HORROR BUSINESS' and 'NIGHT OF THE LIVING DEAD EP', as well as a special 'HALLOWEEN' single released in, you guessed it, October (1980). Around the same time, GLENN and Co. supported The DAMNED on a European tour, during which DANZIG wound up in jail after fisticuffs with their roadies. By this point, STEELE had been replaced with JERRY's brother DOYLE, this line-up playing on the belated debut album, 'WALK AMONG US' (1982; one of their only releases issued in the UK). Taking DANZIG's horror/sci-fi obsession to its comic-book conclusion, tracks like 'ASTRO ZOMBIES' and 'I TURNED INTO A MARTIAN' would've done ROKY ERICKSON proud. The painful 'LIVE/EVIL' (1983) featured a guest spot from HENRY ROLLINS on 'We Are 138', while the final album, 'EARTH A.D. / WOLFSBLOOD' (1984) saw the group opting for a decidedly more brutal sonic assault. Although their career spanned only six short years during which time they struggled to achieve even the most passing interest, The MISFITS have since come to be regarded as eminent cult heroes, GUNS N' ROSES, METALLICA and more recently MARILYN MANSON admitting their fondness for the band. A Various Artists tribute compilation, 'VIOLENT WORLD', was released early in 1997 featuring PRONG, NOFX, THERAPY?, while the original band, well at least JERRY and DOYLE, along with new members DR. CHUD and MICHAEL GRAVES, reformed for an album on 'Geffen', 'AMERICAN PSYCHO' (1997) thankfully without heavy-metal frontman DANZIG; another set, 'FAMOUS MONSTERS' was issued in '99.

Album rating: WALK AMONG US (*7) / EVIL – LIVE (*5) / EARTH A.D. (*5) / THE MISFITS compilation (*7) / AMERICAN PSYCHO (*6) / STATIC AGE (*6) / THE MISFITS boxed-set (*7) / FAMOUS MONSTERS (*6)

GLENN DANZIG (b.23 Jun'55, Lodi, New Jersey) – vocals / **BOBBY STEELE** – guitar / **JERRY ONLY** – bass / **JOEY IMAGE** – drums

MISFITS (cont)

				not iss.	Plan 9
1977.	(7") <PL 1001> **COUGH – COOL. / SHE**			-	
1977.	(7") <PL 1009> **BULLET EP**			-	
	– Horror business / Teenagers from Mars / Children in heat.				
1979.	(7"ep) <PL 1011> **NIGHT OF THE LIVING DEAD EP**			-	
	– Night of the living dead / Where eagles dare / Rat fink.				

— **DOYLE ONLY** – guitar; repl. STEELE who joined The UNDEAD
— **(ARTHUR) GOOGY** (aka EERIE VON) repl. JOEY

Apr 81. (7"ep) <PL 1013> **THREE HITS FROM HELL EP** — -
– London dungeon / Horror hotel / Ghoul's night out.
(below release licensed to 'Cherry Red' in the UK)

Jul 81. (m-lp) (PLP 9) **BEWARE EP** — -
– Cough – Cool / She / Bullet / We are 138 / Attitude / Hollywood Babylon / Horror business / Teenagers from Mars / Children in heat / Night of the living dead / Where eagles dare / Rat fink / London dungeon / Horror hotel / Ghouls night out. (cd-iss. 1990's;) – Halloween / Halloween 2 / 20 eyes (live) / Night of the living dead (live) / Astrozombies (live) / Horror business (live) / London dungeon (live) / All hell breaks loose (live) / We are 138 (live w/ HENRY ROLLINS) / Return of the fly / Last caress.

Oct 81. (7") <PL 1017> **HALLOWEEN. / HALLOWEEN II** — -

not iss. Ruby-WEA

1982. (lp) <925756-1> **WALK AMONG US** —
– 20 eyes / I turned into a Martian / All Hell breaks loose / Vampira / Nike a go-go / Hate breeders / Mommy, can I go out & kill tonight / Night of the living dead / Skulls / Violent world / Devils whorehouse / Astro zombies / Brain eaters. (re-iss. +cd Sep88 on 'Ruby-WEA')

not iss. Aggressive Rock

1983. (lp) <AG 023> **EVIL – LIVE (live)** — -
– 20 eyes / Night of the living dead / Astro zombies / Horror business / London dungeon / All Hell breaks loose / We are 138. (re-iss. Sep87 on 'Plan 9'; PL 908) (UK-iss.Mar97 on 'Plan 9' lp/cd; PL9/+CD 08)

— **ROBO** – drums; repl. GOOGY

Feb 84. (lp) <AG 024> **EARTH A.D. / WOLF'S BLOOD** — -
– Earth a.d. / Queen wasp / Devilrock / Death comes ripping / Green Hell / Wolf's blood / Demonomania / Bloodfeast / Hellhound / Die die my darling / We bite. (cd-iss. Jul91; AGO 572) (cd re-iss. Jan97 on 'Plan 9' lp/cd+=; PL9 02) – DIE DIE MY DARLING ep

had already split the previous year. DANZIG released a solo single and formed SAMHAIN with EERIE VON. JERRY and DOYLE formed KRYST THE CONQUEROR, releasing five track EP augmented by future SKID ROW frontman DAVID SABO.

— The MISFITS re-formed in 1996 with **JERRY ONLY** – bass / **DOYLE** – guitar / **MICHAEL GRAVES** – vocals / **DR. CHUD** – drums

Geffen Geffen

May 97. (cd) <(GED 24939)> **AMERICAN PSYCHO**
– Abominable Dr. Phibes / American psycho / Speak of the Devil / Walk among us / The hunger / From Hell they came / Dig up your bones / Blacklight / Resurrection / This island Earth / Crimson ghost / The day of the dead / The haunting / Mars attacks / Hate the living, love the dead / The shining / Don't open til doomsday.

— **MYKE HIDEOUS** – vocals; repl. GRAVES

Roadrunner Roadrunner

Oct 99. (cd/lp) <(RR 8658-2/-1)> **FAMOUS MONSTERS**
– King at the gates / Forbidden zone / Lost in space / Dust to dust / Crawling eye / Scream / Witch hunt / Saturday night / Pumpkinhead / Scarecrow man / Di monster die / Living hell / Descending angel / Them / Fiend club / Hunting humans / Helena / Kong unleashed. (ltd-cd; RR 8658-5) – Devil doll / 1000 b.c. / Helena.

— **compilations, etc.** —

1986. (lp/cd) Plan 9; <PL9/+CD 06> **LEGACY OF BRUTALITY** — -
– Angelfuck / Who killed Marilyn? / Where eagles dare / She / Halloween / American nightmare / Static age / T.V. casualty / Hybrid moments / Spinal remains / Come back / Some kinda hate / Theme for a jackal. (UK-iss.Jul97; same)

Jul 86. (lp) Revolver; (REVLP 74) **BEST OF THE MISFITS** — -
Nov 87. (12"ep) Plan 9; **DIE DIE MY DARLING** — -
May 88. (cd) Plan 9; <PL9CD 1> **THE MISFITS COLLECTION** — -
(UK-iss.Jul97 cd/lp; same)
Oct 95. (cd/lp) Caroline; <(CAROL 7515-2/-1)> **THE MISFITS COLLECTION VOL.2**
Feb 97. (4xcd-box) Caroline; <(CDCAR 7529-2)> **THE MISFITS BOX SET**
Jul 97. (cd/lp) Caroline; (CAROL 7520-2/-1) **STATIC AGE**
– (debut album GLENN DANZIG, JERRY ONLY, FRANCHE COME, MR. JIM) – 14 tracks +; 'She', 'Spinal Remains' and 'In The Doorway')
Mar 00. (cd) <(PL9CD 02-3)> **EARTH A.D. / WOLFSBLOOD**

MODELS

Formed: London, England ... 1977 by CLIFF HARRIS, MICK ALLEN, MARCO PIRRONI and TERRY LEE MIALL, the short-lived punk-rock group were a launching pad for ADAM & THE ANTS members (the latter two actually) and subsequently The WOLFGANG PRESS, through the line of REMA REMA and MASS member, MICK ALLEN. Although they only ever released one single, 'FREEZE', for 'Step Forward' (home of CHELSEA and The CORTINAS), the track was raw and hard-hitting enough to ensure The MODELS a minor footnote in punk history. Worth tracking down for its 'PISTOLS-style attitude and radical political stance, the single still sounds as fresh today as it ever did, only serving to underline the lack of any discernible charisma or drive in the current crop of Kerrang's pseudo heavy/punk brigade.

Album rating: never released any

CLIFF HARRIS – vocals, guitar / **MARCO PIRRONI** (b.27 Apr'59) – guitar (ex-INFANTS, ex-SIOUXSIE & THE BANSHEES) / **MICK ALLEN** – bass / **TERRY LEE MIALL** (b. 8 Nov'58) – drums

Step Forward not iss.

Aug 77. (7") (SF 003) **FREEZE. / MAN OF THE YEAR** — -

just prior to their split, **MARK ROBERTSON** – drums; repl. MIALL + HARRIS (both formed MUSIC CLUB); the former later joined ADAM & THE ANTS. MARCO + MICK formed REMA REMA, the latter evolving the group into the WOLFGANG PRESS. ROBERTSON later joined The TALL BOYS.

MODERN LOVERS (see under ⇒ RICHMAN, Jonathan)

MONOCHROME SET

Formed: London, England ... early 1978 by BID and LESTER SQUARE, who had comprised one half of punk outfit The B-SIDES. While the other half formed ADAM & THE ANTS, BID and SQUARE recruited a rhythm section in JEREMY HARRINGTON and J.D. HANEY, signing to 'Rough Trade' and releasing a string of quirky but compelling singles, 'HE'S FRANK (SLIGHT RETURN)', 'EINE SYMPHONIE DES GRAUENS' and subtropical signature tune, 'THE MONOCHROME SET (I PRESUME)', SET-ting the tone for an eclectic and generally low-key career. Characterised by the lugubrious, sardonic vocals of BID – the alternative JAKE THACKARY! – The MONOCHROME SET's offbeat guitar-based musings won them a cult following and a modicum of critical acclaim but precious little in the way of commercial rewards. Hardly surprising then, that they were shunted around from label to label, the band moving on to 'Dindisc' for 1980's debut album, 'STRANGE BOUTIQUE'. As well as marking the arrival of ANDY WARREN (another ex-B-SIDE who had initially played with ADAM & THE ANTS), the album stands as the band's one and only flirtation with the charts, skirting the UK Top 60. A further two singles followed in '405 LINES' and 'APOCALYPSO', previewing another full length album, 'LOVE ZOMBIES' (1980) in the space of only six months. Yet the band were dogged by personnel changes, LEXINGTON CRANE replacing HANEY for 'ELIGIBLE BACHELORS' (1982). The first fruits of a new deal with 'Cherry Red', the record featured such memorable MONOCHROME SET moments as ironic Latin America commentary, 'JET SET JUNTA' and the wry 'MATING GAME', the latter set to a hilarious 'Young Ones'-era CLIFF RICHARD style tune. Despite indie chart success and an obvious influence on upcoming bands like The SMITHS, BID & co. couldn't quite manage a significant breakthrough, the line-up changes continuing apace as CARRIE BOOTH joined on keyboards and (ex-SOFT BOYS) MORRIS WINDSOR took up the vacant drum seat. The latter pair were subsequently replaced by FOZ and NICK WESOLOWSKI as the band moved to 'Blanco Y Negro' and came close to wider recognition with their most accessible singles – 'JACOB'S LADDER', 'WALLFLOWER' – and album, 'THE LOST WEEKEND' (1985) to date. It wasn't to be though and disillusioned, the band split soon after with BID subsequently becoming involved in the short-lived RAJ QUARTET. Come 1989, BID, SQUARE and WARREN regrouped to give it another go, recruiting new member, ORSON PRESENCE, and releasing an album, 'DANTE'S CASINO' on 'Vinyl Japan'. The revamped MONOCHROME SET subsequently renewed their acquaintance with 'Cherry Red' in the early 90's, delivering material such as 'MISERIE' and 'TRINITY ROAD' at their usual prolific pace to a generally disinterested music scene.

Album rating: STRANGE BOUTIQUE (*5) / LOVE ZOMBIES (*4) / ELIGIBLE BACHELORS (*6) / VOLUME, BRILLIANCE, CONTRAST compilation (*7) / THE LOST WEEKEND (*5) / DANTE'S CASINO (*5) / JACK (*5) / CHARADE (*5) / MISERIE (*5) / TRINITY ROAD (*4) / THE BEST OF THE MONOCHROME SET compilation (*8)

BID (b. J.BIVOUAC, Calcutta, India) – vocals, guitar / **LESTER SQUARE** – lead guitar, vocals (ex-ADAM & THE ANTS, ex-B-SIDES) / **JEREMY HARRINGTON** – bass, percussion (ex-GLORIA MUNDI and MEAN STREET) repl. SIMON CROFT who had replaced CHARLIE / **J.D. HANEY** – drums (ex-ART ATTACKS) / plus 5th member **TONY POTTS** – visuals

Rough Trade I.R.S.

Dec 78. (7") (RT 005) <IR 9002> **ALPHAVILLE. / HE'S FRANK** — Oct79
Apr 79. (7") (RT 019) **EINE SYMPHONIE DES GRAUENS. / LESTER LEAPS IN** — -
Sep 79. (7") (RT 028) **THE MONOCHROME SET (I PRESSUME). / MR. BIZARRO** — -

Disques Bleu not iss.

Dec 79. (7") (BL 1) **HE'S FRANK (SLIGHT RETURN). / SILICON CARNE / FALLOUT (all live)** — -

— **ANDY WARREN** – bass (ex-ADAM & THE ANTS, ex-B SIDES) repl. JEREMY

Dindisc not iss.

Apr 80. (7") (DIN 18) **STRANGE BOUTIQUE. / SURFING S.W.12** — -
Apr 80. (lp) (DID 4) **STRANGE BOUTIQUE** 62 -
– The Monochrome Set (I pressume) / Expresso / The Puerto Rican fence climber / Martians go home / Love goes down the drain / Ici les enfants / The ecetera stroll / Goodbye Joe / Strange boutique / The lighter side of dating / Tomorrow will be too long. (re-iss. Mar84 on 'Virgin'; OVED 55)
Jun 80. (7") (DIN 23) **405 LINES. / GOODBYE JOE** — -
Oct 80. (7") (DIN 26) **APOCALYPSO. / FIASCO BONGO** — -
Oct 80. (lp) (DID 8) **LOVE ZOMBIES** — -
– Apocalypso / Adesta fiedes / Love zombies / 405 lines / Kama Sutra / B.I.D. spells Bid / R.S.V.P. / The man with the black moustache / In love, cancer? / The weird, wild and wonderful world of Tony Potts. (re-iss Mar84 on 'Virgin'; OVED 56)

Pre not iss.

Jul 81. (7") (PRE 018) **TEN DON'TS FOR HONEYMOONERS. / STRAITS OF MALACCA** — -

— **LEXINGTON CRANE** – drums; repl. HANEY

MONOCHROME SET (cont)

		Cherry Red	not iss.
Jul 82.	(7") *(CHERRY 42)* **THE MATING GAME. / J.D.H.A.N.E.Y.**	□	-
Aug 82.	(lp) *(BRED 34)* **ELIGIBLE BACHELORS**		-

– The jet-set junta / The mating game / Cloud 10 / The ruling class / The great barrier reef / I'll cry instead / Fun for all the family / The Devil rides out / On the 13th day / March of the eligible bachelors. (<US+cd-iss. May91 & Jun00; CDBRED 34>)

— **CARRIE BOOTH** – keyboards (ex-THOMPSON TWINS) repl. LESTER who went solo

— **MORRIS WINDSOR** – drums (ex-SOFT BOYS) repl. LEXINGTON

Oct 82.	(7") *(CHERRY 51)* **CAST A LONG SHADOW. / THE BRIDGE**	□	-
May 83.	(7"m) *(CHERRY 60)* **THE JET-SET JUNTA. / LOVE GOES DOWN THE DRAIN / NOISE**	□	-
May 83.	(lp) *(MRED 47)* **VOLUME! BRILLIANCE! CONTRAST!** (compilation)		-

– Eine symphonie des grauens / The jet-set junta / Love zombies / Silicon Carne / The ruling class / Viva death row / The man with the black moustache / He's Frank (slight return) / Fun for all the family / Lester leaps in / Ici les enfants / Fat fun / Alphaville / Avanti. (cd-iss. May91 & Jul93 & Jun00; CDBRED 47)

— **BID + WARREN** recruited **NICK WESOLOWSKI** – drums; who repl. WINDSOR

— **FOZ** (b. JAMES FOSTER) – guitar; repl. CARRIE (to The SING MARKET)

		Blanco Y Negro	not iss.
Jan 85.	(7") *(NEG 4)* **JACOB'S LADDER. / ANDIANO**	□	-
	(12"+=) *(NEG 4T)* – La boom boom / Sailor beware / Starry nowhere.		
May 85.	(7"/12") *(NEG 12/+T)* **WALLFLOWER / BIG BEN BONGO**	□	-
Jun 85.	(lp/c) *(BYN/+C 5)* **THE LOST WEEKEND**		-

– Wallflower / Sugar plum / Take Foz / Starry nowhere / Jacob's ladder / Cargo / Don't touch / Letter from Viola / The twitch / Cowboy country / La boom boom.

— disbanded after above album

BID

		El	not iss.
Jun 86.	(7") *(GPO 10)* **REACH FOR YOUR GUN. / SWEET CHARIOTS**	□	-
	(12"+=) *(GPO 10T)* – Love.		

RAJ QUARTET

were formed by **BID**

		El	not iss.
Mar 87.	(12"ep) *(GPO 26T)* **WHOOPS: WHAT A PALAVER / INVOCATION OF TOTH. / RAZBOYNIKA / THE MANEATER OF SURREY GREEN**	□	-

Split, and BID went onto join KING OF LUXEMBOURG in '86-87

MONOCHROME SET

re-formed 4-piece late 1989 with **BID, LESTER, WARREN** plus **ORSON PRESENCE** – guitar, keyboards

		Vinyl Japan	not iss.
Sep 90.	(lp/cd) *(ASK 4/+CD)* **DANTE'S CASINO**		-

– Bella morte / Walking with the beast / Hate male / Wilderness / Golden waters / House of God / Up / Mindfield / White lightning / Reverie. (<US+cd re-iss. Mar01 on 'Cherry Red'; CDMRED 180>)

		Honeymoon	not iss.
Nov 91.	(12"/cd-s) *(JAKK 1T)* **KILLING DAVE. / HOUSE OF GOD (live) / SWEET DEATH**	□	-
Nov 91.	(cd/c/lp) *(MONO CD/MC/LP 1)* **JACK**	□	-

– Big wheel / Jack / Blood act / Sweet death / Cerebella / Killing Dave / Jane / Black are the flowers / Yo Mo fo / Ground zero. (re-iss. Nov93; same)

		Cherry Red	not iss.
Mar 93.	(cd/lp) *(CD+/BRED 102)* **CHARADE**	□	-

– Prelude / Forever young / Clover / Snowgirl / White garden / Her pain / Little noises / Crystal chamber / Girl / Oh Angie / Talking about you / No time for girls / Christine / Tilt.

| Mar 93. | (cd-ep) *(CDCHERRY 126)* **FOREVER YOUNG / HURTING YOU / LITTLE NOISES** | □ | - |
| May 94. | (cd) *(<CDBRED 114>)* **MISERIE** | □ | 1995 |

– Milk and honey / Pauper / Dr. Robinson / Achilees / Leather jacket / Bed / Handsome / The ethereal one / UFO / Intergrate me / Twang 'em high.

| Sep 95. | (cd-ep) *(CDCHERRY 138)* **I LOVE LAMBETH / KISSY KISSY / ALL OVER / CLOSING TIME** | □ | - |
| Sep 95. | (cd) *(CDBRED 122)* **TRINITY ROAD** | □ | - |

– Flamen dialis / All over / I love Lambeth / Kissy kissy / The mousetrap / Snakefingers / Hula honey / Albert Bridge / Two fists / The wurst is yet to come / The golden apples of the sun / Hobb's end / Bar Madiera / Bliss / The April dance affair. <US-iss.Sep99; same as UK>

— they split after above

– compilations, etc. –

| Jun 86. | (lp) *El; (ACME 1)* **FIN! (live)** | □ | - |

– He's Frank / Martians go home / Straits of Malacca / Sugar plum / B-I-D spells BID / Alphaville / Heaven can wait / Goodbye Joe / The strange boutique / Jacob's ladder / Wallflower / Apocalypso / Mr. Bizarro / I'll cry instead / Expresso / 405 lines / Ein symphonie des grauens / The Monochrome Set.

| Jun 87. | (cd) *Virgin; (COMCD 9)* **COLOUR TRANSMISSION** | □ | - |

– The Monochrome Set (I pressume) / The lighter side of dating / Expresso / The Puerto Rican fence climber / Tomorrow will too long / Martians go home / Love goes down the drain / Ici les enfants / Adeste fideles / 405 lines / B-I-D spells BID / R.S.V.P> / Apocalypso / Karma sutre / The man with the black moustache / The weird, wild and wonderful world of Tony Potts / In love cancer?

| Aug 88. | (lp/c/cd) *El; (ACME 17/+CD)* **WESTMINSTER AFFAIR – BANDE ORIGINALE DU FILM** | □ | - |

– The jet-set junta / Cast a long shadow / The ruling class / Lester leaps in / The mating game / On the 13th day / March of the eligible bachelors / Devil rides out / Fun for all the family / Andiamo / Cowboy country / J.D.H.A.N.E.Y. / Noise / Eine symphonie des grauens / Apocalypso / Avanti. (cd+=) – Viva death row / Jacob's ladder / Ici les enfants. (cd re-iss. Nov93; same)

Apr 92.	(lp/cd) *Richmond; (MONDE 2/+CD)* **WHAT A WHOPPER!** <US cd-iss. Nov99; same>	□	-
Oct 92.	(cd) *Richmond; (MONDE 8CD)* **THE GOOD LIFE**	□	-
May 93.	(cd) *Code 90; (<NINETY 4>)* **LIVE (live)**	□	Nov95
Mar 95.	(cd) *Virgin; (CDOVD 458) / Caroline; <CAROL 1252>* **TOMORROW WILL BE TOO LONG – THE BEST OF THE MONOCHROME SET**	□	Apr95

– The Monochrome Set (I presume) / The lighter side of dating / Expresso / Puert Rican fence climber / Tomorrow will too long / Martians go home / Love goes down the drain / Ici les enfants / Etcetera stroll / Goodbye Joe / Strange boutique / Love zombies / O come all ye faithful (adeste fidelis) / 405 lines / B.I.D. spells Bid / R.S.V.P. / Apocalypso / Karma suture / The man with the black moustache / The weird wild world of Tony Potts / In love, cancer?

Mar 95.	(cd) *Cherry Red; (CDMRED 118)* **BLACK & WHITE MINSTRELS – 1975-1979**	□	-
May 96.	(cd) *Cherry Red; (<CDBRED 128>)* **COMPENDIUM: A HISTORY: 1979-95**	□	Sep99
Sep 97.	(d-cd) *Snapper; (SMDCD 134) / Recall; <134>* **CHAPS**	□	-
Sep 00.	(cd) *Cherry Red; (<CDMRED 174>)* **THE BEST OF THE MONOCHROME SET**	□	-

– He's Frank (slight return) / Eine symphonie des grauens / The Monochrome Set (I presume) / Strange boutique / 405 lines / Jet set junta / The ruling class / Mating game / Cast a long shadow / Jacob's ladder / Up / Jack / Killing Dave / Her pain / Forever young / Christine / Milk and honey / Leather jacket / I love Lambeth / Mousetrap / Bliss / Kissy kissy.

Johnny MOPED

Born: PAUL HALFORD, Croydon, London, England. PAUL/JOHNNY initially started out in the early 70's playing under various guises: BLACK WITCH CLIMAX BLUES BAND, The GENETIC BREAKDOWN, The ARROGANT SUPERSTARS and JOHNNY MOPED'S ASSAULT AND BUGGERY. The latter numbered RAY BURNS (aka CAPTAIN SENSIBLE) among their rank, The CAPTAIN asking MOPED to support his band The DAMNED after they became more famous. The JOHNNY MOPED outfit also featured more permanent members, the BERK brothers (aka DAVE and FRED), although SENSIBLE's brother PHIL and astonishingly, CHRISSIE HYNDE (later of The PRETENDERS), also passed through briefly. Early in 1977, SLIMEY TOAD became the band's resident guitarist, playing on the original (very rough!) version of 'HARD LOVIN' MAN' from the infamous V/A live album, 'Live At The Roxy'. Moronic punk'n'roll fusing future 'Chiswick' labelmates, MOTORHEAD with the manic humour of JOHN OTWAY, the latter track a pogo-floor favourite at many a punk disco. The aforementioned London independent were either brave or stupid enough to give the man a break, releasing his/their debut single, 'NO ONE', in the summer of '77. Romantically inclined, or at least in his own mind, MOPED delivered his somewhat mellower follow-up, 'DARLING, LET'S HAVE ANOTHER BABY', a taster from his retrospectively feted debut long-player, 'CYCLEDELIC' (1978). The collection featured his inimitable interpretation of Chuck Berry's R&R classic, 'LITTLE QUEENIE', a laugh a minute for those with a sense of humour, sacrilege for anyone over forty (at the time!). However, HALFORD dismounted his JOHNNY MOPED and subsequently quit the music scene altogether; that is, until 1991, when the outfit played live again and released a comeback LP, 'THE SEARCH FOR XERXES' (the name referring to a mysterious early member). • Covered: SOMETHIN' ELSE + CUT ACROSS SHORTY! (Eddie Cochran).

Album rating: CYCLEDELIC (*8) / THE SEARCH FOR XERXES (*5)

JOHNNY MOPED – vocals, organ / **SMILEY TOAD** – guitar, piano / **FRED BERK** – bass, piano, guitar / **DAVE BERK** – drums, percussion / **CAPTAIN SENSIBLE + PHIL BURNS** also contributed

		Chiswick	not iss.
Aug 77.	(7") *(NS 15)* **NO ONE. / INCENDIARY DEVICE**	□	-
Jan 78.	(7") *(NS 27)* **DARLING, LET'S HAVE ANOTHER BABY. / SOMETHING ELSE / IT REALLY DIGS**	□	-
Apr 78.	(lp) *(WIK 8)* **CYCLEDELIC**	□	-

– Mystery track / V.D. boiler / Panic button / Little Queenie / Maniac / Darling, let's have another baby / Groovy Ruby / 3D time / Wee wee / Make trouble / Wild breed / Hell razor / Incendiary device. (some w/ free 7") – BASICALLY, THE ORIGINAL JOHNNY MOPED TAPE

| Jun 78. | (7") *(NS 41)* **LITTLE QUEENIE. / HARD LOVIN' MAN** | □ | - |

— split after above and DAVE joined The DAMNED to replace RAT SCABIES on tour. SLIMEY TOAD as SLIME issued a single in 1978; 'CONTROVERSIAL'.

— **CAPTAIN SENSIBLE, KIRSTY MacCOLL** and revived group featured on return album.

		Deltic	not iss.
May 91.	(lp) *(DELT-LP6)* **THE SEARCH FOR XERXES**	□	-

– I believed her lies / Edwina / Every dream came true / Corpse boogie / Cut across Shorty! / I wanna die / Zogaloogajergabrox / Sad sack / Soldiers / SAve the baby seals / Moped crash / I'm a spasm / Hiawatha.

— JOHNNY MOPED retired after above although his big band re-unite from time to time

– compilations, etc. –

| Sep 95. | (cd) *Chiswick; (CDWIKD 144)* **BASICALLY (THE BEST OF JOHNNY MOPED)** | □ | - |

– No one / V.D. boiler / Panic button / Little Queenie / Maniac / Darling, let's have another baby / Groovy Ruby / 3D time / Wee wee / Make trouble / Wild breed / Hell

Elton MOTELLO

Born: ALAN WARD, London, England. A one-time member of BASTARD (which included noneother than soon-to-be DAMNED guitarist, BRIAN JAMES), WARD changed his stage name to ELTON MOTELLO and released a one-off Belgian-only single, 'JET BOY JET GIRL', at the tail end of '77. While MOTELLO's version sank without trace, PLASTIC BERTRAND would subsequently take the track into the UK Top 10 early the following year as 'Ca Plane Pour Moi'. Roping in a cast of backing musicians who included ex-PINK FAIRIES and PRETTY THINGS drummer, TWINK, ELTON continued to record in Belgium, putting together the album 'VICTIM OF TIME' (1979). With a fresh bunch of sidemen, the singer worked on a follow-up set, 'POP ART', released this time around in North America and Britain. In the event, it proved to be MOTELLO's final effort despite never having had a proper UK release to his name.

Album rating: VICTIM OF TIME (*5) / POP ART (*5)

ELTON MOTELLO – vocals (ex-BASTARDS) / with session people

		Pinball	not iss.
Dec 77.	(7") (6.12186) **JET BOY JET GIRL. / POGO POGO** (UK-iss.Feb78 on 'Lightning'; LIG 508)	-	- Belgian

— now with **PETER GOFF** – guitar / **WILLIE CHANGE** – bass / **NOBBY GOFF** – drums / + guests **JET STAXX** – guitar / **TONY BOAST** – guitar / **TWINK** – drums (ex-PINK FAIRIES, ex-PRETTY THINGS)

Mar 79.	(lp) (623650) **VICTIM OF TIME**	-	- Belgian

– Victim of time / I am the marshall / Jet boy jet girl / He's a rebel / He's crying / Pipe line / Get the guy / Tuttie fruttie Teen pimp / Sha la la la lee / Artificial incemination / Pogo pogo / Apocalipstic.

— with **MIKE BUTCHER** – guitar / **ANDREW GOLDBERG** – keyboards / **J.P. MARTINS** – bass, guitar / **WALTER METER** – drums

		Edge	Passport
Jan 80.	(lp) (HOB 1) <PB 9846> **POP ART**		Jan81

– Pop art / In the heart of the city / Queen / Pocket calculator / When all the boys are English / Out of limit / Night sister / Falling like a domino / Can't explain / Pay the radio / Out cast / 20th century fox.

Oct 80.	(7") (EDGE 4) **20th CENTURY FOX. / FALLING LIKE A DOMINO**		
Nov 80.	(7") <PS 7920> **POP ART. / 20th CENTURY**	-	-

— ELTON/ALAN retired from the music business

MUMPS

Formed: New York City, New York, USA ... 1977 by LANCE LOUD, alongside songwriter KRISTIAN HOFFMAN, TOBY DUPREY, KEVIN KIELEY and PAUL RUTNER. The toast of the NY punk/New Wave elite, The MUMPS were more infamous for their unhinged stage show than their studio output, although they did manage to release two one-off singles in 1977/78. The first of these, 'CROCODILE TEARS', was jointly issued by Greg Shaw's 'Bomp' label and 'Exhibit', while 'ROCK & ROLL THIS, ROCK & ROLL THAT', appeared on 'Perfect'. A precursor to the likes of The B-52's or REDD KROSS, The MUMPS' infectious update of 70's kitsch was more fully showcased on 1994's 'Eggbert' outtakes/rare/demos compilation, 'FATAL CHARM'. An early 80's singer with The SWINGING MADISONS (and later a member of BLEAKER ST. INCIDENT), HOFFMAN finally returned on the solo circuit with two rather retro-fied power-pop albums, 'I DON'T LOVE MY GURU ANYMORE' (1994) and 'EARTHQUAKE WEATHER' (1997).

Album rating: FATAL CHARM compilation (*7) / Kristian Hoffmann: I DON'T LOVE MY GURU ANYMORE (*5) / EARTHQUAKE WEATHER (*6)

LANCE LOUD – vocals / **KRISTIAN HOFFMAN** – keyboards (vocalist with JAMES CHANCE / CONTORTIONS) / **TOBY DUPREY** – guitar / **KEVIN KIELEY** – bass / **PAUL RUTNER** – drums

		not iss.	Bomp-Exhibit
1977.	(7") <BES 1> **CROCODILE TEARS. / I LIKE TO BE CLEAN**	-	
		not iss.	Perfect
1978.	(7") <PR 1> **ROCK & ROLL THIS, ROCK & ROLL THAT. / MUSCLEBOYS / THAT FATAL CHARM**	-	

— split in the late 70's after KIELEY + RUTNER departed, HOFFMAN founded The SWINGING MADISONS (one 1981 US-only EP, 'APPEARIMNG NITELY') before fronting anti-folk act, BEAKER ST. INCIDENT

– compilations, etc. –

Dec 97.	(cd) Eggbert; <(ER 80011CD)> **FATAL CHARM**		1994

– I like to be clean / Crocodile tears / Crocodile tears / Rock and roll this, rock and roll that / Muscleboys / Fatal charm / Brain massage / Scream and scream again / Just look, don't touch / Did you get the girl? / Anyone but you / Not again / Awkward age / Before the accident / Forget me not / Teach me / S.O.S. / We ended up / Dutch boy / Stupid / Dance tunes for underdogs / Photogenia / Gimme gimme / Crocodile tears.

KRISTIAN HOFFMAN

— with on session **EARLE MANKEY, WILLIAM COOPER, ROBERT MACHE, JIM SCLAVUNOS, RONNIE GOMEZ, CHUCK MANCILLAS + SALLY NORVELL**

		not iss.	Eggbert
1994.	(cd) <ER 80009CD> **I DON'T LOVE MY GURU ANYMORE**	-	

– Odd man out / Garbage turns to gold / I don't love my guru anymore / I fell from grace / Science fiction / Don't believe your eyes / Bridget who / Cold but not over / New old flame / Shanty town / Always / My generation / What I meant to say.

Dec 97.	(cd) <ER 80023> **EARTHQUAKE WEATHER**	-	

– He means well / Life of the world / Earthquake weather / Morose colored glasses / Man in a hurry / Gaper's club / That beautiful word / I had my chance / That's our secret / Rehearsal / But I didn't / Reasonable man / Fool is back upon the hill / Now I understand.

Pauline MURRAY (& THE INVISIBLE GIRLS)
(see under ⇒ PENETRATION)

MX-80 SOUND

Formed: Bloomington, Indiana, USA ... 1975 by BRUCE ANDERSON, DAVE SOPHIEA and JEFF ARMOUR. Relocating to San Francisco, they were joined by RICH STIM and DAVE MAHONEY, releasing a few low-key singles for a local independent imprint. Signed to a UK deal with 'Island', they issued their debut album, 'HARD ATTACK' in 1977, an experimental New Wave affair that, being American, lay closer in spirit to BEEFHEART or ZAPPA. They resurfaced a further twice in the early 80's on The RESIDENTS, 'Ralph' records with 'OUT OF THE TUNNEL' (1980) and 'CROWD CONTROL' (1981), although little was heard of them since; ANDERSON and SOPHIEA were said to be behind The GIZZARDS, HALF-LIFE and O-TYPE on their 'Quadroped' label. Save for MAHONEY (who was replaced by MARC WEINSTEIN), the original members re-formed MX-80 SOUND in the early 90's and recorded one final album, 'DAS LOVE BOAT'.

Album rating: HARD ATTACK (*7) / OUT OF THE TUNNEL (*6) / CROWD CONTROL (*6) / DAS LOVE BOAT (*4)

RICH STIM – vocals, guitar, keyboards, sax / **BRUCE ANDERSON** – guitar / **DAVE SOPHIEA** – bass / **DAVE MAHONEY** – drums / **JEFF ARMOUR** – drums

		not iss.	6r6q
1976.	(7"ep) **BIG HITS – HARD POP FROM THE HOSSIERS**	-	

– Train to loveland / You turn me on / SCP / Till death us do part / Myonga von Bontee / Boy trouble girl trouble / Tidal wave. <re-iss. 1977 on 'Gulcher'; GULCH 003>

		Island	not iss.
Oct 77.	(lp) (ILPS 9520) **HARD ATTACK**		

– Man on the move / Kid stuff / Fascination / Summer 77 / P.C.B.'s / Crushed ice / Tidal wave / Checkmate / Facts – facts / You're not alone / Civilised – Demeyes / Afterbirth – Aftermath. (UK cd-iss. Apr97 on Atavistic'+=; ALP 30CD) – BIG HITS EP

— **KEVIN TEARE** – drums repl. ARMOUR (although he left in 1979)

		not iss.	Ralph
Mar 80.	(7") <MX 8001S> **SOMEDAY YOU'LL BE KING. / WHITE KNIGHT**	-	
Mar 80.	(lp) <MX 8002L> **OUT OF THE TUNNEL**	-	

– It's not my fault / Follow that car / Fender bender / I walk among them / Someday you'll be king / Frankie I'm sorry / Gary and Priscilla / Man in a box / Metro-teens.

Dec 80.	(7") <MX 8055-2> **O TYPE (part 1). / O TYPE (part 2)**	-	
Mar 81.	(lp) <8102> **CROWD CONTROL**	-	

– Face of the Earth / Crowd control / Why are we here / Obsessive devotion / More than good / Night rider / City of fools / Theme from Sisters / Cover to cover / Pharoah's sneakers / Promise of love.

— split after above. STIM entered law school and ANDERSON joined The HENRY KAISER BAND. MX-80 SOUND re-formed, although drummer MAHONEY was replaced by **MARC WEINSTEIN**

		not iss.	A&R Enter.
Oct 90.	(lp) **DAS LOVE BOAT**	-	

– Clown sex / Das love boat / Mystery meat / Pink carnations / Rock rock rock / Halloween theme / Crowd control / Theme from sisters / Pharoah's sneakers / O-type / Fender bender / I left my heart in San Francisco / Theme from Checkmate / SCP / Theme from Batman / Hey art / Life insurance / Theme from Route 66 / Hard. (UK-iss.Apr97 on 'Atavistic'; ALP 56CD)

– compilations, etc. –

Apr 97.	(cd) Atavistic; (ALP 32CD) **OUT OF CONTROL**		
Apr 97.	(cd) Atavistic; (ALP 67CD) **I'VE SEEN ENOUGH**		

NERVES

Formed: San Francisco, California, USA . . . 1976 by JACK LEE, PETER CASE and PAUL COLLINS, although it would be in L.A. that they would establish their Stateside power-pop base. Towards the end of the year, the band self-financed the release of their debut EP, a record that contained the original LEE-penned version of 'HANGIN' ON THE TELEPHONE'. By the time it became a massive hit for BLONDIE in 1978, The NERVES had broken down as COLLINS formed The BREAKAWAYS and CASE formed the more fruitful PLIMSOULS. LEE, meanwhile, put together a solo set which featured another future BLONDIE track, 'WILL ANYTHING HAPPEN?'. In the late 70's, COLLINS was reunited with CASE when the former founded The BEAT (the trio also included HARLAN HOLLANDER), although the latter was already occupied with own group. Under the wing of veteran manager, Bill Graham, The BEAT (no relation to the UK 2-Tone act of the same name who were forced to prefix the moniker with ENGLISH for American releases) inked a deal with 'Columbia'. COLLINS and his new cohorts (i.e. LARRY WHITMAN, STEVEN HUFF and MICHAEL RUIZ) released a couple of strident, college-friendly pop singles before delivering their eponymous debut set (issued as 'PAUL COLLINS' BEAT' for the UK market) in the Spring of 1980. After a poor performance on the sales front, The BEAT downshifted slightly to 'Passport' records, emerging with what proved to be their final releases, 'THE KIDS ARE THE SAME' (1982) album and 'TO BEAT OR NOT TO BEAT' (1983) EP.

Album rating: THE NERVES compilation (*6)

JACK LEE – vocals, guitar / **PETER CASE** (b. 5 Apr'54, Buffalo, New York, USA) – bass, vocals / **PAUL COLLINS** (b. New York) – drums

		not iss.	Nerves
Dec 76.	(7"ep) <N45-01> **THE NERVES EP**	–	

– Hangin' on the telephone / When you find out / Give me some time / Working too hard. *(rel.1985 on French 'Fence' as lp +=;)* – (6 demos).

— disbanded early in '78 when COLLINS formed The BREAKAWAYS, CASE formed The PLIMSOULS and JACK LEE went solo in 1981, 'JACK LEE'S GREATEST HITS VOL.1' lp was released by 'Maiden America'.

BEAT

PAUL COLLINS – vocals, drums / **PETER CASE** – bass, vocals / **HARLAN HOLLANDER** – guitar

— actually named PAUL COLLINS' BEAT (in the UK only), after CASE formed The PLIMSOULS and HOLLANDER departed

COLLINS – (now) vocals, guitar / **LARRY WHITMAN** – guitar, vocals / **STEVEN HUFF** – bass, vocals / **MICHAEL RUIZ** – drums

		C.B.S.	Columbia
Jan 80.	(7") <1-11161> **WALKING OUT ON LOVE. / LET ME INTO YOUR LIFE**	–	
Feb 80.	(7") (CBS 8135) **DON'T WAIT UP FOR ME. / WALK OUT ON LOVE**		–
Apr 80.	(7") <1-11211> **DON'T WAIT UP FOR ME. / WORKING TOO HARD**	–	
May 80.	(7") (CBS 8575) **ROCK'N'ROLL BEAT. / LOOK BUT DON'T TOUCH**		–
May 80.	(lp) (CBS 83895) <36195> **PAUL COLLINS' BEAT**		Nov79

– Rock'n'roll girl / I don't fit in / Different kind of girl / Don't wait up for me / You won't be happy / Walking out on love / Work a day world / USA / Let me into your life / Working too hard / You and I / Look but don't touch.

		not iss.	Passport
Mar 82.	(lp) <ARC 36794> **THE KIDS ARE THE SAME**	–	

– That's what life is all about / Dreaming / On the highway / Will you listen / Crying won't help / The kids are the same / Trapped / It's just a matter of time / Met her yesterday / I will say no / Down. <cd-iss. 1995 on 'Wagon Wheel'; 3>

— **JIMMY RIPP** – guitar; repl. WHITMAN

— **JAY DEE DAUGHERTY** – drums (ex-PATTI SMITH) repl. RUIZ

| 1983. | (12"ep) <5002> **TO BEAT OR NOT TO BEAT** | – | |

— split after above failed to sell

NERVOUS EATERS

Formed: Boston, Massachusetts, USA . . . 1974 out of The PSYCHO PUNKS by mainman/songwriter STEVE CATALDO, SCOTT BAERENWALD and JEFF WILKINSON (the latter's mother had intervened with the group's risky moniker!). Inspired by local legend WILLIE ALEXANDER, the band played their inaugural gig at Jim Harold's 'Rat Club' in 1976; the said boss also released their first 45, 'LORETTA', on his own 'Rat' label. Enthusiastic and energetic, the trio launched themselves onto many memorable stage shows, and after another 'Rat'-invested 45, 'JUST HEAD' (in 1979), they were attracting the attention of RIC OCASEK (his CARS and The 'EATERS shared the same manager, Fred Lewis). Having deposited a demo to many record companies including 'Columbia', the quartet – they had added JONATHAN PALEY while ROBB SKEEN replaced SCOTT – subsequently settled for 'Elektra'. With production by Harry Maslin and a guest list that included STEVE CROPPER, NICKY HOPKINS and ANDY PALEY, their eponymous debut (with toned-down lyrics!) should have had all the ingredients to make it a success. Wrong. Maslin's confusion with where to take this raunchy New Wave act were somewhat bewildering: "the Rolling Stones of Boston were sounding like Mother Teresa of Massachusetts" came from the mouth of one journo objector. CATALDO had even openly knocked back a place in LOU REED's band around this time because the VU man didn't want the rest of the group. Rock'n'roll ain't fair and The NERVOUS EATERS were out to lunch for over half a decade. Their comeback mini-set, 'HOT STEEL AND ACID' (1986) was a low-key release on the French-based 'New Rose' records, but even a cover of Dylan's 'THE TIMES THEY ARE A-CHANGIN', couldn't set them free this time. Pity.

Album rating: NERVOUS EATERS (*5) / HOT STEEL AND ACID mini (*4)

STEVE CATALDO – vocals, guitar / **SCOTT BAERENWALK** – bass / **JEFF WILKINSON** – drums

		not iss.	Rat
1976.	(7") <RR 5282> **LORETTA. / ROCK WITH ME**	–	
1979.	(7") <RR 5286> **JUST HEAD. / GET STUFFED**	–	

— **ROBB SKEEN** – bass; repl. SCOTT

— added **JONATHAN PALEY** – guitar

		not iss.	Elektra
Jan 80.	(7") <E 47025> **NO SLEEP TONITE (mono). / NO SLEEP TONITE (stereo)**	–	
Jun 80.	(7") <E 47072> **LORETTA. / GET STUFFED**	–	
Jul 80.	(lp) <6E 282> **NERVOUS EATERS**	–	

– Loretta / By yourself / No sleep tonight / Walkout / No time / All except you / Get stuffed / Girl next door / Last chance / Hooked / Out on a date (she said no) / She's got the kind of love.

— split in 1981; but re-formed later; **STEVE, JEFF + JONATHAN** plus **ALAN HEBDITCH** – lead guitar

		New Rose	Ace Of Hearts
Nov 86.	(m-lp) (ROSE 104) <AHS 1007> **HOT STEEL AND ACID**		1987

– Nazi concentration camp blues / Shit for brains / Got a hold on it born to die / On the avenue / The times they are a-changin' / She's gonna be my baby.

Colin NEWMAN (see under ⇒ WIRE)

NEW YORK DOLLS

Formed: New York City, New York, USA . . . late '71 by JOHNNY THUNDERS, DAVID JOHANSEN, BILLY MURCIA, ARTHUR KANE and RICK RIVETS. In March the following year, RIVETS left to form The BRATS, being swiftly replaced by SYLVAIN SYLVAIN. After a promising start as support act on a FACES British tour, the 'DOLLS' first casualty was MURCIA who died on the 6th of November '72 after drowning in his own bath (not, as widely believed, from a drug overdose). With JERRY NOLAN as a replacement, they signed to 'Mercury' in March '73 and promptly began work on an eponymous debut album with TODD RUNDGREN producing. Released in the summer of that year, 'THE NEW YORK DOLLS' was a proto-punk revelation, a way cool schlock of visceral rock'n'roll which combined the more essential moments of MC5, The PRETTY THINGS, PINK FAIRIES and The SHANGRI-LAS. The ROLLING STONES were another obvious reference point, JOHANSEN a dead-ringer for MICK JAGGER in terms of both vocal style and mascara'd looks. Inevitably, then, THUNDERS was the glam-punk KEITH RICHARDS, Glitter Twins to the JAGGERS/RICHARDS Glimmer coupling. The 'DOLLS' trashy transvestite attire also borrowed heavily from the 'STONES (circa '66 'Have You Seen Your Mother . . .'), although being American they'd obviously taken it to almost cartoon-esque proportions. The likes of 'PERSONALITY CRISIS', 'TRASH' and 'JET BOY' were seminal squalls of guitar abuse, making up in attitude what they lacked in musical ability. Although the record had the critics salivating, commercial success wasn't forthcoming and, unhappy with the record's production, the band opted for SHANGRI-LA's producer, GEORGE MORTON to work on 'TOO MUCH TOO SOON' (1974). Though the album had its moments, again the band had been paired with the wrong producer and the music press were emphatically unimpressed. The lukewarm reviews heightened inter-

NEW YORK DOLLS (cont) — THE GREAT INDIE DISCOGRAPHY — The 1970s

band tension and the 'DOLLS demise was swift and inevitable. Early the following year, Londoner MALCOLM McLAREN made a last-ditch attempt to save the band, revamping their image to no avail. THUNDERS was the first to leave, departing in 1975 to form The HEARTBREAKERS, while JOHANSEN and SYLVAIN subsequently sacked KANE before finally calling it a day the following Christmas. While THUNDERS went on to most acclaim with his HEARTBREAKERS (dying from an overdose on 23rd April '91), JOHANSEN recorded a number of solo albums, 'DAVID JOHANSEN' (1978), 'IN STYLE' (1979) and 'HERE COMES THE NIGHT' (1981) as well as releasing a 1988 set under the pseudonym of BUSTER POINDEXTER. NOLAN also met an untimely death, almost a year on from THUNDERS (14th January, 1992), suffering a fatal stroke while undergoing treatment for meningitis and pneumonia. A pivotal reference point for not only punk, but the US sleaze/glam metal movement of the mid-80's (FASTER PUSSYCAT, L.A. GUNS, GUNS N' ROSES, et al), The NEW YORK DOLLS influence remains hugely disproportionate to their relatively slim recorded legacy. • **Songwriters:** JOHANSEN with THUNDERS or SYLVAIN. Covered PILLS (Bo Diddley) / DON'T START ME TALKIN' (Sonny Boy Williamson) / SHOWDOWN (Archie Bell) / SOMETHIN' ELSE (Eddie Cochran) / etc. • **Trivia:** Two songs 'PERSONALITY CRISIS' & 'WHO ARE THE MYSTERY GIRLS', appeared on the 1977 Various Artists compilation 'NEW WAVE'. **JOHANSEN's filmography:** 'Married To The Mob', 'Scrooged' and 'The Fisher King'.

Album rating: NEW YORK DOLLS (*8) / TOO MUCH TOO SOON (*7) / LIPSTICK KILLERS exploitation (*5) / ROCK & ROLL compilation (*7).

DAVID JOHANSEN (b. 9 Jan'50, Staten Island, N.Y.) – vocals / **JOHNNY THUNDERS** (b. JOHN GENZALE, 15 Jul'52) – guitar, vocals / **SYLVAIN SYLVAIN** (b. SIL MIZRAHI) – guitar, vocals repl. RICK RIVETS / **ARTHUR KANE** (b. 3 Feb'51) – bass / **JERRY NOLAN** (b. 7 May'51) – drums repl. BILLY MURCIA who died.

			Mercury	Mercury
Jul 73.	(7")	<73414> **TRASH. / PERSONALITY CRISIS**	–	
Aug 73.	(lp)	(6338 270) <SRM 675> **NEW YORK DOLLS**		Jul73

– Personality crisis / Looking for a kiss / Vietnamese baby / Lonely planet boy / Frankenstein / Trash / Bad girl / Subway train / Pills / Private world / Jet boy. <US re-iss. 1984; same>

| Nov 73. | (7") | (6052 402) **JET BOY. / VIETNAMESE BABY** | | |
| Jul 74. | (lp) | (6338 498) <SRM 1001> **TOO MUCH TOO SOON** | | May74 |

– Babylon / Stranded in the jungle / Who are the mystery girls? / (There's gonna be a) Showdown / It's too late / Puss 'n' boots / Chatterbox / Bad detective / Don't start me talkin' / Human being. <US re-iss. 1984; same>

Jul 74.	(7")	(6052 615) <73478> **STRANDED IN THE JUNGLE. / WHO ARE THE MYSTERY GIRLS?**		
Sep 74.	(7")	<73615> **(THERE'S GONNA BE A) SHOWDOWN. / PUSS 'N' BOOTS**	not iss.	Trash
1974.	(fan club-7"ep)	<TR 001> **LOOKING FOR A KISS (live). / WHO ARE THE MYSTERY GIRLS? (live) / SOMETHIN' ELSE (live)**	–	

—— **PETER JORDAN** – bass (the roadie filled in on stage when KANE was drunk)

—— Disbanded mid-1975, after **BOBBY BLAIN** – keyboards repl. CHRIS ROBINSON who had repl. THUNDERS (he formed The HEARTBREAKERS with NOLAN). **TOMMY MACHINE** (was last drummer). The NEW YORK DOLLS reformed again with JOHANSEN and SYLVIAN but only toured until late '76. SYLVIAN later formed The CRIMINALS. DAVID JOHANSEN went solo in 1978.

– compilations, others, etc. –

| Jun 77. | (7"m) | Mercury; (6160 008) **JET BOY. / BABYLON / WHO ARE THE MYSTERY GIRLS?** | | – |
| Jul 77. | (d-lp) | Mercury; (6641 631) **NEW YORK DOLLS / TOO MUCH TOO SOON** | | – |

(re-iss. Apr86; PRID 12)

| Nov 81. | (c) | R.O.I.R.; <A 104> **LIPSTICK KILLERS – MERCER ST. SESSIONS** | – | |

(re-iss. May90 on 'Danceteria' cd/lp; DAN CD/LP 038) (re-iss. cd Feb95 & Jun97 on 'ROIR Europe'; 885615027-2) (cd re-iss. Aug00 on 'R.O.I.R.'; RUSCD 8266)

| Sep 82. | (12"ep) | Kamera; (ERA 13-12) **PERSONALITY CRISIS / LOOKING FOR A KISS. / SUBWAY TRAIN / BAD GIRL** | | – |

(re-iss. Jul90 on 'See For Miles' cd-ep; SEACD 3)

| Sep 84. | (red-m-lp) | Fan Club; (FC 007) **RED PATENT LEATHER (rec. 75)** | – | – France |

– Girls / Downtown / Private love / Personality crisis / Pills / Something else / Daddy rollin' stone / Dizzy Miss Lizzy. (cd-iss. Feb93 on 'Receiver'+=; RRCD 173) (cd re-iss. Apr97 on 'Last Call'; 42241-2)

Oct 84.	(7"white)	Fan Club; (NYD 1) **PILLS (live). / DOWN, DOWN, DOWN TOWN (live)**	–	– France
1985.	(lp)	Mercury; <8260 941> **NIGHT OF THE LIVING DOLLS**	–	
Feb 86.	(7",12"pic-d,12"red)	Antler; (DOLLS 1) **PERSONALITY CRISIS. / SUBWAY TRAIN**		–
Feb 86.	(7",12"pic-d,12"blue)	Antler; (DOLLS 2) **LOOKING FOR A KISS. / BAD GIRL**		–
1986.	(lp; one-side by SEX PISTOLS)	Receiver; (RRLP 102) **AFTER THE STORM**		–

(cd-iss. Jul93; RRCD 102)

Jul 93.	(cd)	Receiver; <(RRCD 163)> **SEVEN DAY WEEKEND**		
Jul 93.	(cd)	Receiver; <(RRCD 173)> **IN NYC 1975**		
Oct 94.	(cd)	Mercury; (522 176-2) **ROCK'N'ROLL**		
Mar 96.	(cd)	Skydog; <(62256-2)> **PARIS BURNING**		
Mar 96.	(cd)	Skydog; <(62257-2)> **NEW YORK TAPES 1972-1973**		

<(re-iss. Feb00 on 'Munster'; MR 167/+CD)>

Oct 97.	(cd)	Red Star; <(RS 7006)> **TEENAGE NEWS**		
Nov 98.	(cd; shared w/ JOHNNY THUNDERS)	Recall; <(SMDCD 207)> **STREET TRASH**		
Nov 98.	(cd)	Receiver; <(RRCD 260)> **I'M A HUMAN BEING (live)**		
Sep 98.	(cd)	Red Star; <(RSR 7006)> **LIVE IN CONCERT PARIS 1974**		

<(re-iss. Jun99 on 'Essential'; ESMCD 734)>

| Jul 99. | (cd) | Big Ear; (109634022-2) **GLAMOROUS LIFE – LIVE** | | |
| Apr 00. | (lp/cd) | Get Back; (GET 60/+CD) **THE BIRTH OF THE NEW YORK DOLLS** | | |

999

Formed: London, England ... 1977 as 48 HOURS by former KILBURN & THE HIGH ROADS man, NICK CASH along with GUY DAYS, PABLO LABRITAIN and JON WATSON. Building on CASH's pub-rock CV, the band amassed a healthy live following in the capital and snagged a deal with 'United Artists' on the strength of a self-financed debut single, 'I'M ALIVE'. A headlong rush of anti 9-5 rebellion complete with a bruising power-pop punk guitar attack and rent-a-yob pitched-in vocals, the track was quickly followed with 'NASTY NASTY' and 'EMERGENCY' while an eponymous debut album confirmed their position in punk's vanguard. Things began to go awry, however, with follow-up set, 'SEPARATES' (1978), an album which embraced a more straightahead but colourful rock sound and thus appealed more to the US market. Subsequently taking off for a prolonged bout of transatlantic touring, the band were criticised for losing direction and neglecting British fans who had to make do with a live set, 'BIGGEST PRIZE IN SPORT' (1980). The latter represented the first fruits of a new deal with 'Polydor' while a long awaited studio set, 'CONCRETE' (1981), failed to cement their fading profile at home. The same year, 999 almost broke into the Top 50 with their version of John D. Loudermilk's 'INDIAN RESERVATION'. 1983's '13TH FLOOR MADNESS' saw many fans give up the ghost and the band looked all but washed up; as it was, they redeemed themselves with a more accomplished final effort, 'FACE TO FACE' (1985). Almost a decade later, they answered the call of duty once more, touring the punk nostalgia circuit and releasing an album's worth of new material, 'YOU, US, IT' (1993). Still pounding the beat, 999 rarely instigate a real emergency these days but still command a fair sized audience, issuing their sixth proper album, 'TAKEOVER', in '98.

Album rating: 999 (*5) / SEPARATES (*5) / THE BIGGEST PRIZE IN SPORT (*5) / CONCRETE (*5) / THIRTEENTH FLOOR MADNESS (*4) / FACE TO FACE (*5) / YOU, US, IT (*3) / THE SINGLES ALBUM compilation (*6) / TAKEOVER (*6)

NICK CASH (b. KEITH LUCAS, 6 May'50, Gosport, England) – vocals, guitar / **GUY DAYS** – guitar, vocals / **JON WATSON** – bass / **PABLO LABRITAIN** – drums

			LaBritain	not iss.
Jul 77.	(7")	(LAB 999) **I'M ALIVE. / QUITE DISAPPOINTING**		–

(re-iss. 1979 on 'United Artists'; UP 36519)

			U.A.	S.P.V.
Oct 77.	(7",7"green)	(UAG 36299) **NASTY NASTY. / NO PITY**		
Mar 78.	(lp)	(UAG 30199) **999**	53	–

– Crazy / Hit me / Emergency / No pity / Pick it up / I'm alive / Your number is my number / Direct action briefing / Me and my desire / Chicane destination / Titanic (my over) reaction / Nobody knows. (re-iss. Jun87 on 'Fan Club'; FC 026) (cd-iss. 1990 +=; FC 026C) – (3 extra). (cd re-iss. Sep93 on 'Dojo'; DOJOCD 145) (<cd re-iss. Sep00 on 'Captain Oi'; AHOYCD 147>)

Apr 78.	(7")	(UP 36376) **ME AND MY DESIRE. / CRAZY**		–
Jun 78.	(7")	(UP 36399) **EMERGENCY. / MY STREET STINKS**		–
Aug 78.	(7")	(UP 36435) **FEELING ALRIGHT WITH THE CREW. / TITANIC (MY OVER) REACTION**		–
Sep 78.	(lp)	(UAG 30209) **SEPARATES**		

– Let's face it / Homocide / Feeling alright with the crew / Tulse Hill night / Real man / Out of reach / High energy plan / Wolf / Crime (part 1 & 2) / Subterfuge / Brightest view. (re-iss. Jun87 on 'Fan Club'; FC 027) (cd-iss. 1990 +=; FC 027CD) – (4 extra). (cd re-iss. Sep93 on 'Dojo'; DOJOCD 150) (cd re-iss. Sep00 on 'Captain Oi'; AHOYCD 148)

			LaBritain	not iss.
Oct 78.	(7",7"green)	(UP 36467) **HOMOCIDE. / SOLDIER**	40	
			Radar	not iss.
Dec 78.	(12"freebie)	(12FREE 10) **WAITING. / ACTION**	–	– mail-o
Sep 79.	(7")	(ADA 46) **FOUND OUT TOO LATE. / LIE LIE LIE**	69	

—— **ED CASE** – drums; repl. LABRITAIN

			Polydor	not iss.
Jan 80.	(7")	(POSP 99) **TROUBLE. / MAKE A FOOL OF YOU**		–
Jan 80.	(lp)	(POLS 1013) **THE BIGGEST PRIZE IN SPORT**		–

– Boys in the gang / Inside out / Trouble / So long / Fun thing / The biggest prize in sport / Hollywood / Stranger / Stop stop / English wipeout / Shake / Boiler. (cd-iss. Nov95 & Aug99 on 'Anagram'; CDPUNK 67)

| Apr 80. | (7") | **HOLLYWOOD. / BOILER** | | – |

—— **PABLO LABRITAIN** – drums; returned to repl. CASE

			Albion	Polydor
Apr 81.	(7"m)	(ION 1011) **OBSESSED. / CHANGE / LIE LIE LIE (live)**	71	–
Apr 81.	(lp)	(ITS 999) **CONCRETE**		

– So greedy / Li'l red riding hood / Break it up / Taboo / Mercy mercy / Fortune teller / Obsessed / Silent anger / That's the way it goes / Bongos on the Nile / Don't you know I need you / Public enemy No.1. (re-iss. Oct87 on 'Link'; NALLP 400017) (cd-iss. May91; ALCD 9.00017)

May 81.	(7")	**OBSESSED. / FORTUNE TELLER**		–
Jun 81.	(7"m)	(ION 1017) **LI'L RED RIDING HOOD. / WAITING FOR YOUR NUMBER TO BE CALLED / I AIN'T GONNA TELL YA (live)**	59	–
Nov 81.	(7",7"clear)	(ION 1023) **INDIAN RESERVATION. / SO GREEDY (remix) / TABOO (remix)**	51	–
Jun 82.	(7"red-or-yellow)	(ION 1033) **WILD SUN. / SCANDAL IN THE CITY / BONGOS ON THE NILE**		–

(12"red-or-yellow+=) (12ION 1033) – Don't you know I need you.

999 (cont)

Oct 83. (7") *(ION 155)* **13th FLOOR MADNESS. / NIGHTSHIFT**
(12"+=) *(12ION 155)* – Arabesque.
Nov 83. (lp/c) *(AS/CAS 8502)* **13th FLOOR MADNESS**
– Use your imagination / Lookin' like you do / Book of love / It's what you've got / Don't want you back / 13th floor madness / Good to see you / Arabesque / Custer's last stand / Hang it all / Night shift. *(c+=)* – (4 extra). *(cd-iss. May91; ALCD 9.00073)*
—— **DANNY PALMER** – bass repl. WATSON on tour

LaBritain not iss.

Mar 85. (lp) *(LABLP 1000)* **FACE TO FACE**
– Hallelujah / Black sunshine / 20 years / Walk in the meadow / Dancing on me / Spiritual independence / Vicious circle / Lucy dead / I can't face it / Maybe someday / This is just a lie / Dancing in the wrong shoes. *(cd-iss. Jun93 on 'Obsession'; OBSESSCD 003)*

A.B.C. Rough Trade

May 87. (lp/c/cd) *(ABC LP/K/D 11)* **LUST POWER AND MONEY (live)**
– Inside out / Hit me / Don't you know I need you / White trash / Feelin' alright with the crew / Obsessed / On the line / Let's face it / Emergency / English wipe out / Nasty nasty / Homocide / Lust power and money / My street stinks / Titanic reaction / I'm alive. *(cd-iss. Jun93 on 'Dojo'+=; DOJOCD 129)* – (2 extra). *(cd re-iss. Oct92 as 'GREATEST HITS LIVE' on 'Streetlink'; STRCD 026)*

—— split but re-formed in 1993

Anagram not iss.

Nov 93. (cd) *(CDGRAM 71)* **YOU, US, IT!**
– Black flowers for the bride / There is no glory in Mary's story / Signed dangerous from Hollywood / Bye bye bones / Everybody needs it / It's over now / Bye bye England / All of the days / Big fast car / Absolution / Deep in the shadow / Run for your life / Don't tell me / Crazy crazy crazy / White light. *(re-iss. Apr97; CDPUNK 92)*

—— **ARTURO BASSICK** – bass (ex-LURKERS) repl. DANNY

Get Back Get Back

Mar 98. (cd) *(<GBR 010CD>)* **TAKEOVER** Apr98
– Takeover / Didn't mean to / No prisoners / Headcase / Salvage mission / Fit up / Out of our heads / I can't wait / Split personality / Damp with tears / Edge of the world / Falling / Really like you / Jam me up (with something nice) / Pile up.

– compilations, etc. –

Jun 80. (lp/c) *United Artists; (SOS 999)* **THE SINGLES ALBUM**
– Nasty nasty / No pity / Me and my desire / Crazy / Emergency / My street stinks / Feelin' alright with the crew / Titanic (my over) reaction / You can't buy me / Homocide / Soldier / I'm alive / Quite disappointing / Waiting / Action.
Mar 84. (lp/c) *Albion; (ALB/CALB 118)* **IDENTITY PARADE**
(c+=) – (4 extra).
Nov 86. (lp) *Dojo; (DOJOLP 31)* **IN CASE OF EMERGENCY**
Nov 89. (lp/c) *Link; (LINK LP 107)* **LIVE AND LOUD (live)**
(cd-iss. Jan91; LINKCD 107)
May 92. (cd) *E.M.I.; (CDGO 2032)* **THE EARLY STUFF (THE UNITED ARTISTS YEARS)**
Dec 92. (lp) *Link; (LINKLP 125)* **THE CELLBLOCK TAPES**
Dec 94. (d-cd; shared with SLAUGHTER & THE DOGS)
Step 1; (STEPCD 045) **THE CELLBLOCK TAPES / The Slaughterhouse Tapes**
Dec 95. (d-cd; shared with SHAM 69) *Step 1; (STEPCD053)* **LOVE AND LOUD / Live And Loud**
Jun 96. (cd) *Anagram; (<CDPUNK 78>)* **THE ALBION PUNK YEARS (THE INDEPENDENT PUNK SINGLES COLLECTION)** Sep99
Apr 97. (cd) *Anagram; (CDPUNK 93)* **LIVE AT THE NASHVILLE 1979 (live)**
Aug 97. (cd) *Receiver; (RRCD 245)* **EMERGENCY**
– Don't know I love you / Crazy / Feeling alright with the crew / Emergency / Pick it up / Indian reservation / Quite disappointing / My street stinks / Rael raen / Subterfuge / Hollywood / Inside out / The biggest prize in sport / Chicane destination / Obsessed / Hit me / Nasty nasty / Tulse Hill nights / Mercy mercy / English wipeout / Fun thing / Titanic reaction / Boys in the gang / Lil' red riding hood / Me and my desire / Homocide / Let's face it / I'm alive / Found out too late.
May 99. (cd) *Rhythm Vicar; (PREACH 012CD)* **THE SINGLES**
Jun 99. (cd) *Receiver; (<RRCD 266>)* **DANCING IN THE WRONG SHOES**
Oct 01. (cd) *Captain Oi; (<AHOYCD 176>)* **THE PUNK SINGLES COLLECTION: 1977-1980**
Oct 01. (cd) *Overground; (OVER 84CD)* **SLAM**
Apr 02. (cd) *Overground; (<OVER 90VPCD>)* **ENGLISH WIPEOUT (live)**
Sep 02. (cd) *Captain Oi; (<AHOYCD 207>)* **THE BIGGEST TOUR IN SPORT / THE BIGGEST PRIZE IN SPORT**

NORMAL

Formed: London, England … 1977/78 as the brainchild of futuristic electronic entrepreneur-to-be, DANIEL MILLER. He created and self-financed The NORMAL's one and only single (the first on his 'Mute' imprint), the classic double-header, 'T.V.O.D.' & 'WARM LEATHERETTE'. Almost immediately, both sides were compared to KRAFTWERK / THROBBING GRISTLE on punk pills, the latter track being subsequently covered in impressively monotonic fashion by GRACE JONES. However, with MILLER's indie label now in full swing, he abandoned The NORMAL (after his/their last live appearance was on the 6th March 1979 with ROBERT RENTAL), choosing instead to sign his first act, FAD GADGET; he would soon snap up DEUTSCH AMERIKANISCHE FREUNDSCHAFT, SILICON TEENS and DEPECHE MODE. The rise of such prestigious loyal acts like the aforementioned DEPECHE MODE, YAZOO and later ERASURE and NICK CAVE, ensured MILLER and his 'Mute' crew would be shopping at Harrod's (so-to-speak) for years to come.

Album rating: never released any

DANIEL MILLER – electronics, vox

Mute not iss.

Feb 78. (7") *(MUTE 001)* **T.V.O.D. / WARM LEATHERETTE**
(re-iss. Jun95 on cd-s; 771400-2)

—— The NORMAL with ROBERT RENTAL issued a live one-sided lp, 'LIVE – AT WEST RUNTON PAVILLION' on 'Rough Trade' *(ROUGH 17)<ROUGHUS 2>*

NOSEBLEEDS

Formed: Manchester, England … 1977 by ED BANGER, VINI REILLY, PETE CROOKS and TOBY. Although this raw punk outfit only managed to bring out one single, the brilliant 'AIN'T BIN TO NO MUSIC SCHOOL' (complete with orchestra intro, chunky guitars and griping chorus line!), each member went on to better things: ED to fellow 'Rabid' combo, SLAUGHTER & THE DOGS and VINI (with later PETE and TOBY) to the more subdued DURUTTI COLUMN. Billed at times as ED BANGER & THE NOSEBLEEDS, it was no surprise when the loud frontman went solo leaving the rest to audition the likes of STEPHEN MORRISSEY (yes, that one!); future CULT guitarist, BILLY DUFFY, also made an appearance before their final demise.

Album rating: never released any

ED BANGER – vocals / **VINI REILLY** – guitar / **PETE CROOKS** – bass / **TOBY** – drums

Rabid not iss.

Sep 77. (7") *(TOSH 102)* **AIN'T BIN TO NO MUSIC SCHOOL. / FASCIST PIGS**

—— ED joined SLAUGHTER & THE DOGS after a solo single, VINI joined V2 (prior to any releases) and later recalled PETE and TOBY to his DURUTTI COLUMN, the latter also becoming part of The BLUE ORCHIDS.

ED BANGER

Jul 78. (7") *(TOSH 106)* **KINNEL TOMMY. / BABY WAS A BABY**
(re-iss. Aug78 on 'EMI International'; INT 570)

Spiv not iss.

Nov 81. (7") *(DIV 1)* **I'VE JUST HAD ME CAR NICKED. / P.C. PLOD / SPONGE**

Cloud Nine not iss.

Jan 83. (7") *(CNS 01)* **POOR PEOPLE. / VICARS IN THE PARK**

—— ED retired from solo work

NOTSENSIBLES

Formed: Burnley, Lancashire, England … 1978 by frontman HAGGIS, and his motley crew of SAGE, KEV, ROG and GARY. "Celebrating" the election of a new Conservative government, these northern lads made their memorable debut with a frantic, fun-packed JILTED JOHN-esque ode to the Iron Lady, '(I'M IN LOVE WITH) MARGARET THATCHER'. Tongue-in-cheek shoutalong punk at its vintage best, the track was a turn of the decade favourite and even laid into Sun pundit, Gary Bushell on the B-side. A possible precursor to the TOY DOLLS, they never quite managed to send-up any target as entertainingly as their debut, although they made a fair attempt with their one and only LP, 'INSTANT CLASSIC' (1980).

Album rating: INSTANT CLASSIC (*4)

HAGGIS – vocals / **SAGE** – guitar / **ROG SENSIBLE** – keyboards, bass / **GARY BROWN** – bass / **KEV HEMMINGWAY** – drums

Bent not iss.

Apr 79. (7"m) *(SMALL BENT 5)* **DEATH TO DISCO. / CORONATION STREET HUSTLE / LYING ON THE SOFA**

Redball not iss.

Nov 79. (7"m) *(RR 02)* **(I'M IN LOVE WITH) MARGARET THATCHER. / LITTLE BOXES / GARY BUSHELL'S BAND OF THE WEEK**
(re-iss. Jan80 on 'Snotty Snail'; NELCOL 1)

Snotty Snail not iss.

Mar 80. (lp) *(SSLP 1)* **INSTANT CLASSIC**
– Instant classic / Girl with scruffy hair / Freedom / King Arthur / Death to disco / Ploppy / I am a clone / Little boxes / Sick of being normal / (Love is like) Banging my head against a brick wall / Because I'm mine / Wrong love / Blackpool rock / Daddy won't let me love you song / Don't wanna work anymore.
1980. (7"m) *(NELCOL 3)* **I THOUGHT YOU WERE DEAD. / I MAKE A BALLS OF EVERYTHING I DO / TEENAGE REVOLUTION**
Sep 81. (7") *(NELCOL 6)* **I AM THE BISHOP. / THE TELEPHONE RINGS AGAIN**

—— sensibly split up after above

– compilations, etc. –

Sep 94. (cd) *Anagram; (CDPUNK 38)* **INSTANT PUNK CLASSICS** (all material)

Gary NUMAN

Born: GARY WEBB, 8 Mar '58, Hammersmith, London, England. Inspired by 70's glam icons such as BOLAN and BOWIE as well as synthmeisters like KRAFTWERK, NUMAN formed punk outfit, MEAN STREET in 1977, subsequently appearing on the Various Artists compilation, 'Live At The Vortex'. To end the year, he set up TUBEWAY ARMY, basically his solo project although he was accompanied on live work by PAUL GARDINER and his uncle, GERALD LIDYARD. The debut vinyl outing, 'THAT'S TOO BAD', was issued by indie punk label, 'Beggars Banquet' in early '78. An eponymous debut album passed virtually unnoticed, although things changed dramatically in June '79, when they/he had a first No.1 with the monotonic synth-noir of 'ARE FRIENDS ELECTRIC', spurred on by a compelling appearance on UK's 'Top Of The Pops'. Its parent album, 'REPLICAS', also shot to the top the same month. A busy year for NUMAN, in addition to collaborating with ROBERT PALMER, of all people (he was initially part of offshoot outfit, DRAMATIS), he found time to record a second No.1 album, 'THE PLEASURE PRINCIPLE'. This collection was previewed with the hypnotic, sweeping electronica of the 'CARS' single, by far his most well known track and one that enjoyed a rejuvenation in 1996 after it was used in a British TV advert. NUMAN scored yet another No.1 album with 'TELEKON' (1980) the following year, his futuristic synth-based pop/rock gracing the upper reaches of the singles chart in the form of 'WE ARE GLASS' and 'I DIE: YOU DIE'. By this point, however, NUMAN was well on his way to becoming perhaps one of most visible targets of critical derision in the whole of the music industry, his neo-futurist posturing, dalek vocals, pretentious lyrics and worst of all, his vocal support of Margaret Thatcher raising the not inconsiderable ire of the music press. Nevertheless, NUMAN had a fiercely loyal grassroots following of clone-like fans (second only to NUMAN himself as figures of fun among rock circles) who ensured most of his subsequent output made the Top 50 at least. Despite the presence of such luminaries as MICK KARN (JAPAN), ROGER TAYLOR (QUEEN) and erm, NASH THE SLASH (solo artist from Canada, apparently), 'DANCE' (1981) was a decidedly ungroovy set of steely electronica and his last to achieve mainstream success. NUMAN released two further, increasingly pompous albums, 'I, ASSASSIN' (1982) and 'WARRIORS' (1983) before forming his own label, 'Numa', in 1984 to issue his own product along with material by his brother JOHN's outfit, HOHOKAM. 80's albums like 'THE FURY' (1985), 'STRANGE CHARM' (1986), 'METAL RHYTHM' (1988) and 'AUTOMATIC' (1989) continued to appeal mainly to hardcore fans although 'OUTLAND' (1991) managed to nudge into the Top 40. However, since the awful 'MACHINE AND SOUL' (1992), NUMAN has fallen further into cult status, his releases failing to even break the Top 100. Come the new millennium, NUMAN was still churning out the albums, the harsh industrialised textures of 'PURE' (2000) suggesting that he could easily give the young pretenders to goth electronica a run for their money. It also suggested that after years in the musical wilderness, NUMAN may have found a creatively profitable niche for himself. • **Songwriters:** Wrote own material, with inspiration from psi-fi writers (i.e. WILLIAM S. BURROUGHS). Covered 1999 + U GOT THE LOOK (Prince). • **Trivia:** In the early 80's, he took up flying planes and bought his own aircraft (mainly warplanes).

Album rating: Tubeway Army: TUBEWAY ARMY (*4) / REPLICAS (*7) / Gary Numan: THE PLEASURE PRINCIPLE (*7) / TELEKON (*6) / LIVING ORNAMENTS 1979 (*4) / LIVING ORNAMENTS 1980 (*4) / DANCE (*4) / I, ASSASSIN (*5) / WARRIORS (*4) / BERSERKER (*4) / WHITE NOISE (*4) / THE FURY (*4) / STRANGE CHARM (*3) / EXHIBITION compilation (*7) / METAL RHYTHM (*4) / AUTOMATIC (*3; as Sharpe & Numan) / THE SKIN MECHANIC (*4) / OUTLAND (*4) / MACHINE AND SOUL (*4) / THE BEST OF ... compilation (*7) / DREAM CORROSION (*4) / DARL LIGHT (*4) / DARK LIGHT (*4) / HUMAN (*4) / EXILE (*3) / PURE (*6)

TUBEWAY ARMY

GARY NUMAN – vocals, guitar, synthesizer, keyboards (ex-MEAN STREET) / **PAUL 'Scarlett' GARDINER** – bass / **GERALD 'Rael' LIDYARD** – drums

		Beggars Banquet	Atco
Feb 78.	(7") (BEG 5) **THAT'S TOO BAD. / OH! DIDN'T I SAY**		–

— BARRY BENN – drums repl. BOB SIMMONDS who had repl. LIDYARD / added SEAN BURKE – guitar

| Jul 78. | (7"m) (BEG 8) **BOMBERS. / O.D. RECEIVER. / BLUE EYES** | | – |
| Aug 78. | (lp,blue-lp) (BEGA 4) **TUBEWAY ARMY** | | – |

– Listen to the sirens / My shadow in vain / The life machine / Friends / Something's in the house / Every day I die / Steal and you / My love is a liquid / Are you real / The dream police / Jo the waiter / Zero bass. (re-iss. Aug79 lp/c; BEGA/BEGC 4); hit No.14) (re-iss. May83 on 'Fame' lp/c; FA/TC-FA 3060) (re-iss. Jul88 lp/c; BBL/+C 4)

— JESS LIDYARD – drums returned to replace BARRY and SEAN

| Mar 79. | (7") (BEG 17) **DOWN IN THE PARK. / DO YOU NEED THE SERVICE?** | | – |

(12"+=) (BEG 17T) – I nearly married a human 2.

| May 79. | (7"/7"pic-d) <US-7"/c-s> (BEG 18/+P) **ARE 'FRIENDS' ELECTRIC?. / WE ARE SO FRAGILE?** | 1 | |
| Jun 79. | (lp/c) <credited as GARY NUMAN & TUBEWAY ARMY> (BEGA/BEGC 7) <117> **REPLICAS** | 1 | |

– Me I disconnect from you / Are 'friends' electric / The machman / Praying to the aliens / Down in the park / You are in my vision / Replicas / It must have been years / When the machines rock / I nearly married a human. (re-iss. +cd.Sep88) (re-iss. cd/c Apr95 on 'Music Club')

GARY NUMAN

— solo retaining **PAUL GARDINER** – bass / **CEDRIC SHARPLEY** – drums / **CHRIS PAYNE** – synth, viola / **BILLY CURRIE** – keyboards

| Aug 79. | (7") (BEG 23) **CARS. / ASYLUM** | 1 | – |
| Sep 79. | (lp/c) (BEGA/BEGC 10) <38120> **THE PLEASURE PRINCIPLE** | 1 | 16 Jan80 |

– Airplane / Metal / Complex / Films / M.E. / Tracks / Observer / Conversation / Cars / Engineers. (re-iss. Sep88 lp/c; BBL/+C 10)

| Nov 79. | (7") (BEG 29) **COMPLEX. / BOMBERS (live)** | 6 | |

(12"+=) (BEG 29T) – Me I disconnect from you (live).

| Jan 80. | (7") <7211> **CARS. / METAL** | – | 9 |

— **DENNIS HAINES** – keyboards repl. CURRIE who returned to ULTRAVOX and VISAGE; added **RUSSELL BELL** – guitar (on tour).

May 80.	(7") (BEG 35) **WE ARE GLASS. / TROIS GYMNPEDIES (1st MOVEMENT)**	5	
Aug 80.	(7") (BEG 46) **I DIE: YOU DIE. / DOWN IN THE PARK (piano version)**	6	–
Sep 80.	(lp/c) (BEGA/BEGC 19) <32103> **TELEKON**	1	64

– This wreckage / The aircrash bureau / Telekon / Remind me to smile / Sleep by windows / I'm an agent / I dream of wires / Remember I was a vapour / Please push no more / The joy circuit. (free-7"w/ lp) – REMEMBER I WAS A VAPOUR. / ON BROADWAY (re-iss. Jul88 lp/c; BBL/+C 19)

Sep 80.	(7") **I DIE: YOU DIE. / SLEEP BY WINDOWS**	–	–
Dec 80.	(7") **REMIND ME TO SMILE. /**		
Dec 80.	(7") (BEG 50) **THIS WRECKAGE. / PHOTOGRAPH**	20	
Apr 81.	(d-lp/c) (BOX/C 1) **LIVING ORNAMENTS 1979-1980 (live)**	2	–
Apr 81.	(lp) (BEGA 24) **LIVING ORNAMENTS 1979 (live)**	47	–

– Airplane / Cars / We are so fragile? / Films / Something's in the house / My shadow in vain / Conversation / We are glass / Metal.

| Apr 81. | (lp) (BEGA 25) **LIVING ORNAMENTS 1980 (live)** | 39 | – |

– This wreckage / I die: you die / M.E. / Everyday I die / Down in the park / Remind me to smile / The joy circuit / Tracks / Are 'friends' electric? / We are glass.

— GARY now recruited famous stars to replace BELL, SHARPLEY, HAINES and PAYNE. They became DRAMATIS. Jul'81 he guested on PAUL GARDINER single 'STORMTROOPER IN DRAG' (BEG 61/+T), which hit UK No.49. Next with stars **MICK KARN** – bass (of JAPAN) / **ROGER TAYLOR** – drums (of QUEEN) + **NASH THE SLASH** – violin (Canadian solo artist)

| Aug 81. | (7") (BEG 62) **SHE'S GOT CLAWS. / I SING RAIN** | 6 | – |

(12"+=) (BEG 62T) – Exhibition.

| Sep 81. | (lp/c) (BEGA/BEGC 28) <38-143> **DANCE** | 3 | |

– Slowcar to China / Night talk / A subway called you / Cry the clock said / She's got claws / Crash / Boys like me / Stories / My brother's time / You are you are / Moral. (re-iss. Jan89 lp/c; BBL/+C 28)

| Nov 81. | (7"; by GARY NUMAN and DRAMATIS) (BEG 68) **LOVE NEEDS NO DISGUISE. / TAKE ME HOME** | 33 | |

(12"+=) (BEG 68T) – Face to face.

— GARY NUMAN now used session people.

| Feb 82. | (7") (BEG 70) **MUSIC FOR CHAMELEONS. / NOISE NOISE** | 19 | |

(ext.12"+=) (BEG 70T) – Bridge? what bridge.

| Jun 82. | (7") (BEG 77) **WE TAKE MYSTERY (TO BED). / THE IMAGE IS** | 9 | |

(ext.12"+=) (BEG 77T) – ('A'early version).

| Aug 82. | (7") (BEG 81) **WHITE BOYS AND HEROES. / WAR GAMES** | 20 | |

(ext.12"+=) (BEG 81T) – Glitter and ash.

| Sep 82. | (lp/c) (BEGA/BEGC 40) <900141> **I, ASSASSIN** | 8 | |

– White boys and heroes / War songs / A dream of Siam / Music for chameleons / This is my house / I, assassin / The 1930's rust / We take mystery (to bed). (re-iss. Jan89 lp/c; BBL/+C 40)

| Aug 83. | (7"/7"sha-pic-d) (BEG 95/+P) **WARRIORS. / MY CAR SLIDES (1)** | 20 | – |

(ext.12"+=) (BEG 95T) – My car slides (2).

| Sep 83. | (lp/c) (BEGA/BEGC 47) **WARRIORS** | 12 | |

– Warriors / I am render / The iceman comes / This prison moon / My centurion / Sister surprise / The tick tock man / Love is like clock law / The rhythm of the evening. (re-iss. Jan89 lp/c; BBL/+C 47)

| Oct 83. | (7") (BEG 101) **SISTER SUPRISE. / POETRY AND POWER** | 32 | |

(ext.12"+=) (BEG 101T) – Letters.

Numa   not iss.

| Oct 84. | (7"/7"sha-pic-d) (NU/+P 4) **BERSERKER. / EMPTY BED, EMPTY HEART** | 32 | – |

(12"+=) (NUM 4) – ('A'extended).

| Nov 84. | (lp/c) (NUMA/+C 1001) **BERSERKER** | 45 | – |

– Berserker / This is new love / The secret / My dying machine / Cold warning / Pump it up / The God film / A child with the ghost / The hunter. (c+=) – (6 extra tracks). (cd-iss. Dec95; NUMACD 1001)

| Dec 84. | (7") (NU 6) **MY DYING MACHINE. / HERE I AM** | 66 | – |

(ext.12"+=) (NUM 6) – She cries.

— next 45 with BILL SHARPE of SHAKATAK; and on 'Polydor' album 'Famous People'.

| Feb 85. | (7"/7"pic-d; by SHARPE & NUMAN) (POSP/+P 722) **CHANGE YOUR MIND. / REMIX, REMAKE, REMODEL** | 17 | |

(ext.12"pic-d+=) (POSPX 722) – Fools in a world of fire.

| Apr 85. | (d-lp/c) (NUMA D/C 1002) **WHITE NOISE (live)** | 29 | – |

– (intro) / Berserker / Metal / Me, I disconnect from you / Remind me to smile / Sister surprise / Music for chameleons / The iceman comes / Cold warning / Down in the park / This prison moon / I die; you die / My dying machine / Cars / We take mystery (to bed) / We are glass / This is new love / My shadow in vain / Are 'friends' electric?. (d-cd-iss. May93; NUMACD 1002)

| May 85. | (7"ep/12"ep,12"blue-ep,12"white-ep) (NU/+M 7) **THE LIVE EP (live)** | 27 | – |

– Are 'friends' electric? / Berserker / Cars / We are glass.

| Jul 85. | (7"/7"pic-d) (NU/+P 9) **YOUR FASCINATION. / WE NEED IT** | 46 | – |

(ext.12"+=/ext.12"pic-d+=) (NUM/+P 9) – Anthem.

| Sep 85. | (7") (NU 11) **CALL OUT THE DOGS. / THIS SHIP COMES APART** | 49 | – |

(ext.12"+=) (NUM 11) – No shelter.

| Sep 85. | (lp/pic-lp/c) (NUMA/+P/K 1003) **THE FURY** | 24 | – |

– Call out the dogs / This disease / Your fascination / Miracles / The pleasure skin / Creatures / Tricks / God only knows / Creatures / I still remember. (c+) – (all tracks extended). (cd-iss. 1986; CDNUMA 1003) (re-iss. cd Nov96; NUMACDX 1003)

| Nov 85. | (7",7"red,7"white/ext-12",ext-12"red,ext-12"white) (NU/+M 13) **MIRACLES. / THE FEAR** | 49 | – |
| Apr 86. | (7"/7"pic-d/ext-12"/ext-12"pic-d) (NU/+P/M/MP 16) **THIS IS LOVE. / SURVIVAL** | 28 | – |

(all w/ free 7"flexi)

(d12"+=) (NUMX 16) – Call out the dogs (extended) / No shelter / This ship comes apart.

Gary NUMAN (cont)

Jun 86. (7"/7"sha-pic-d/ext-12"/picture-12"pic-d/club-10") (NU/+P/M/MP/DJ 17) **I CAN'T STOP. / FACES** (all w/ free 7"flexi) — 27 / -

Sep 86. (7"/7"pic-d/ext-12"/ext-12"pic-d; as SHARPE & NUMAN) (NU/+P/M/MP 19) **NEW THING FROM LONDON TOWN. / TIME TO DIE** — 52 / -

Oct 86. (lp/c)(cd) (NUMA/+C 1005)(CDNUMA 1005) **STRANGE CHARM** — 59 / -
 – My breathing / Unknown and hostile / The sleep room / New thing from London Town / I can't stop / Strange charm / The need / This is love. (re-iss. cd Nov96; NUMACDX 1005)

Nov 86. (7"/7"pic-d/ext-12"pic-d) (NU/+P/M/MP 21) **I STILL REMEMBER. / PUPPETS** — 74 / -

— Early in 1987, he teamed up with RADIO HEART (see further below)

Polydor / not iss.

Jan 88. (7",7"white,7"blue,7"clear/7"pic-d/ext-12"/ext-12"pic-d; as SHARPE & NUMAN) (POSP/+P/X/PX 894) **NO MORE LIES. / VOICES** — 34 / -
 (cd-s+=) (POCD 894) – ('A'extended) / Change your mind.

Illegal / I.R.S.

Sep 88. (7"/7"w-poster) (ILS/+P 1003) **NEW ANGER. / I DON'T BELIEVE** — 46 / -
 (12"+=/12"g-f+=) (ILST/ILSG 1003) – Children.
 (cd-s+=) (ILSCD 1003) – Creatures (live) / I can't stop (live).

Oct 88. (lp/c/cd) (ILP/+C/CD 035) <IRS/+D 82005> **METAL RHYTHM** — 48 / -
 – Respect / Don't call my name / New anger / America / Hunger / Voix / Young heart / Cold metal rhythm / This is emotion. (pic-lp iss.Mar89; ILPX 035)

Nov 88. (7"/7"pic-d) (ILS/+PD 1004) **AMERICA (remix). / RESPECT (live)** — 49 / -
 (12"+=) (ILST 1004) – New anger (live).
 (cd-s++=) (ILSCD 1004) – Call out the dogs (live).

— again with ROGER ODELL – drums / TESSA MILES + LINDA TAYLOR – backing vocals

SHARPE & NUMAN

Polydor / not iss.

May 89. (7"/7"pic-d) (PO/+PD 43) **I'M ON AUTOMATIC. / LOVE LIKE A GHOST** — 44 / -
 (ext.12"+=/ext.12"pic-d+=) (PZ/+PD 43) – Voices ('89 remix).
 (7"w-poster) (POPB 43) – ('A'side) / No more lies (new version).
 (cd-s+=) (POCD 43) – (all 4 above).

Jun 89. (lp/c/cd) (839520-1/-4/-2) **AUTOMATIC** — 59 / -
 – Change your mind / Turn off the world / No more lies / Breathe in emotion / Some new game / I'm on automatic / Rip it up / Welcome to love / Voices / Nightlife.
 (cd+=) – No more lies (12"version) / I'm on automatic (12"version).

GARY NUMAN

— solo with RUSSELL BELL – guitar / CHRIS PAYNE – keyboards, violin / ADE ORANGE – keyboards / CEDRIC SHARPLY – drums / JOHN WEBB – saxophone / ANDY COUGHLAN – bass / VAL CHALMERS + EMMA CHALMER – backing vocals

I.R.S. / Capitol

Oct 89. (lp/cd) (EIRSA/+CD 1019) **THE SKIN MECHANIC (live Sep88)** — 55 / -
 – Survival / Respect / Call out the dogs / Cars / Hunger / Down in the park / New anger / Creatures / Are 'friends' electric / Young heart / We are glass / I die: you die.

Mar 91. (7",7"red/c-s) (NUMAN 1/+C) **HEART. / SHAME** — 43 / -
 (12") – ('A'side) / Icehouse.
 (cd-s) – ('A'side) / Tread careful.
 (12") – ('A'side) / Are 'friends' electric?.

Mar 91. (lp/c/cd) (EIRSA/+MC/CD 1039) <13077> **OUTLAND** — 39 / -
 – Confession / My world storm / Interval 1 / From Russia infected / Interval 2 / They whisper you / Dark Sunday / Heart / Devotion / Outland / Interval 3 / 1999 / Dream killer.

Numa / not iss.

Sep 91. (7"/c-s) (NUD/NUC 22) **EMOTION. / IN A GLASSHOUSE** — — / -
 (12"+=) (NUM 22) – Hanoi.
 (cd-s++=) (NUCD 22) – ('A'-different mix).

Mar 92. (7"/c-s) (NU/+C 23) **THE SKIN GAME. / DARK MOUNTAIN** — 68 / -
 (12"+=/cd-s+=) (NUM/NUCD 23) – U got the look / ('A'-digi mix).

Jul 92. (7") (NU 24) **MACHINE + SOUL. / ('A'-promo mix)** — 72 / -
 (cd-s+=) (NUCD1 24) – Cry baby / Wonder eye.
 (cd-s+=) (NUCD2 24) – 1999 / The hauntings.
 (12"+=) (NUM1 24) – Your fascination (live) / Outland (live) / Respect (live).
 (12") (NUM2 24) – ('A'side) / Soul protection (live) / Confession (live) / From Russia infected (live).

Jul 92. (lp/c/cd) (NUMA/+C/CD 1009) **MACHINE + SOUL** — 42 / -
 – Machine + soul / Generator / The skin game / Poison / I wonder / Emotion / Cry / U got the look / Love isolation. (ext.cd re-iss. Sep93)

— Apr 94; He guested for GENERATOR on their version of 'ARE FRIENDS' ELECTRIC'.

— NUMAN & DADAGANG; Apr 94 12"/cd-s LIKE A REFUGEE (I WON'T CRY) on 'Record Label', re-iss. Aug 94 as GARY NUMAN & FRIENDS

Aug 94. (12"ep/cd-ep) (NU M/CD 25) **DREAM CORROSION (THE LIVE EP)** — — / -
 – Noise, noise / It must have been years / I'm an agent / Jo the waiter.

Aug 94. (t-lp/d-c/d-cd) (NUMA/+C/CD 1010) **DREAM CORROSION (live)** — — / -
 – Mission / Machine and soul / Outland / Me, I disconnect from you / We are so fragile / Respect / Shame / Films / Dream killer / Heart / My world storm / Machman / Generator / Noise, noise / Cars / Voix / You are in my vision / It must have been years / That's too bad / Remind me to smile / I'm an agent / Are 'friends' electric / My breathing / I don't believe / Bombers / Jo the waiter / We are glass.

Oct 94. (12"ep/cd-ep) (NU M/CD 26) **A QUESTION OF FAITH** — — / -
 – A question of faith (agnostic edit) / Play like God / Whisper of truth / A question of faith (devout edit).

Mar 95. (cd/c/lp) (NUMA/+C/CD 1011) **SACRIFICE** — — / -
 – Pray / Deadliner / A question of faith / Desire / Scar / Love and napalm / You walk in my soul / Magic / Bleed / The seed of life.

Mar 95. (12"/12"pic-d/cd-s/pic-cd-s) (NU/+MP/CD/CDP 27) **ABSOLUTION. / MAGIC (trick mix) / MAGIC (extended)** — — / -

Jun 95. (12"ep/cd-ep) (NUM/+CD 28) **DARK LIGHT LIVE E.P. (live)** — — / -
 – Bleed / Everyday I die / The dream police / Listen to the sirens.

Jul 95. (d-cd/d-c) (NUMA CD/C 1012) **DARK LIGHT (live)** — — / -
 – Pray / A question of faith / I dream of wires / Noise noise / Listen to the sirens / Everyday I die / Desire / Friens / Scar / Magic / Praying to the aliens / Replicas / Mean street / Stormtrooper in drag / Dead liner / Bleed / The dream police / I die, you die / The hunter / Remind me to smile / Are friends "electric"? / Do you need the service? / Love and napalm / Jo the waiter / I'm an agent.

Nov 95. (d-c/d-cd; with MICHAEL R. SMITH) (NUMA C/CD 1013) **HUMAN** — — / -
 – Navigators / Bombay / We fold space / Cry in the dark / Manic / Empire / Little lost soul / Visitor / Magician / Undercover / Halloween / Embryo / Elm Street / Harmonos / Big alten / Blind faith / New life / Fairy tales / Disease / Tidal wave / Alone and afraid / Sahara / Cold / Do you wonder / Betrayal / Suspicion / Unborn / Lethal injection / Frantic / Mother / Black heart / Thunder road / Law and order / Needles / Climax / Inferno.

Eagle / Spitfire

Oct 97. (cd/c) (EAG CD/MC 008) **EXILE** — 48 / -
 – Dominion day / Prophecy / Dead heaven / Dark / Innocence bleeding / The angel wars / Absolution / An alien cure / Exile.

Apr 98. (c-s) (EAGCS 008) **DOMINION DAY / ANGEL WARS (extended)** — — / -
 (cd-s+=) (EAGXS 008) – ('A'side) / Voix (20th anniversary) / Dead heaven (extended) / Cars (live).
 (cd-s) (EAGXA 008) – ('A'side) / Metal (20th anniversary) / Down in the park (20th anniversary) / Dominion day (live).

— now with STEVE HARRIS – guitar / ROB HOLIDAY – guitar, keyboards / MONTI – drums, prog / RICHARD BEASLEY – drums

Oct 00. (cd) (EAGCD 078) <15088> **PURE** — 58 / Nov00
 – Pure / Walking with shadows / Rip / One perfect lie / My Jesus / Fallen / Listen to my voice / A prayer for the union / Torn / Little Invitro / I can't breathe. (d-cd+=; EAGTE 078) – (live):- Pure / My Jesus / R.I.P. / Cars / Replicas / A prayer for the unborn (Greyed up remix) / Listen to my voice (Greyed up remix).

Jagged Halo / not iss.

May 02. (d-cd) (JHCD 001) **EXPOSURE – THE BEST OF GARY NUMAN 1977-2002** (compilation) — — / -

Jul 02. (cd-s) (JHCDS 1) **RIP** — 29 / -
 (cd-s) (JHCDSX 1) –

– compilations, etc. –

on 'Beggars Banquet' unless otherwise mentioned / * = TUBEWAY ARMY

Aug 79. (d7"*) (BACK 2) **THAT'S TOO BAD. / OH! I DIDN'T SAY/ / BOMBERS. / O.D. RECEIVER / BLUE EYES** — — / -

Apr 81. (c-s*) WEA; (SPC 4) **ARE 'FRIENDS' ELECTRIC? / WE ARE SO FRAGILE? / DOWN IN THE PARK** — — / -

Nov 82. (lp/c) TV-Virgin; (TVA/TVC 7) **NEW MAN NUMAN – THE BEST OF GARY NUMAN** — 45 / -

Apr 83. (12"ep,12"yellow-ep*) (BEG 92E) **TUBEWAY ARMY '78 VOL.1** — — / -
 – That's too bad (alternate mix) / Oh! didn't I say / Bombers / O.D. receiver / Blue eyes / Do you need the service.

Sep 84. (lp/pic-lp*) (BEGA 55/+P) **THE PLAN** — 29 / -
 (re-iss. Jul88 lp/c; BBL/+C 55)

Dec 84. (12"ep,12"red-ep*) (BEG 123E) **TUBEWAY ARMY '78-'79 VOL.2** — — / -
 – Fade out / 1930 / The crazies / Only a downstate / We have a technical.

Dec 84. (12"ep,12"blue-ep*) (BEG 124E) **TUBEWAY ARMY '78-'79 VOL.3** — — / -
 – The Monday troup / Crime of assikon / The life machine / A game called Echo / Random / Oceans.

Aug 87. (12"ep/c-ep;*) Strange Fruit; (SFPS/+C 032) **THE PEEL SESSIONS** — — / -
 – Me I disconnect from you / Down in the park / I nearly married a human.

Aug 87. (7"/7"pic-d) (BEG 199/+P) **CARS (E-REG MODEL). / ARE FRIENDS ELECTRIC?** — 16 / -
 (c-s+=/ext-12"+=) (BEG 199 C/T) – We are glass / I die: you die.
 (ext-12"+=) (BEG 199TR) – ('A'-Motorway mix).

Sep 87. (d-lp/d-cd) (BEGA 88/+CD)(BEGC 88) **EXHIBITION** — 43 / -
 – Me, I disconnect from you / That's too bad / My love is a liquid / Music for chameleons / We are glass / Bombers / Sister Surprise / Are 'friends' electric / I dream of wires / Complex / Noise noise / Warriors / Everyday I die / Cars / We take mystery to bed / I'm an agent / My centurion / Metal / You are in my vision / I die: you die / She's got claws / This wreckage / My shadow in vain / Down in the park / The iceman comes. (d-cd+=) – (11 tracks)

Dec 87. (cd) (BEGA 4CD) **REPLICAS / THE PLAN** — — / -
 (re-iss. d-cd Dec93; BEGA 152CD)

Dec 87. (cd) (BEGA 7CD) **TUBEWAY ARMY / DANCE** — — / -
 (re-iss. d-cd Dec93; BEGA 152CD)

Dec 87. (cd) (BEGA 10CD) **THE PLEASURE PRINCIPLE / WARRIORS** — — / -
 (re-iss. d-cd Dec93; BEGA 153CD)

Dec 87. (cd) (BEGA 19CD) **TELEKON / I, ASSASSIN** — — / -
 (re-iss. d-cd Dec93; BEGA 154CD)
 (above series of cd's, omitted some tracks on each)

Oct 89. (d-lp/cd) Castle; (CCS LP/CD 229) **THE GARY NUMAN COLLECTION** — — / -

Dec 89. (m-lp/cd) Strange Fruit; (SFPMA/+CD 202) **DOUBLE PEEL SESSIONS** — — / -

1990. (pic-cd-ep) **THE SELECTION** — — / -
 – Cars ('E' reg.model) / Down in the park / I die: you die / Are 'friends' electric? / We are glass / Music for chameleons.

1990. (7") Old Gold; (OG 9917) **ARE FRIENDS ELECTRIC?. / I DID YOU** — — / -

1990. (7") Old Gold; (OG 9919) **CARS. / WE ARE GLASS** — — / -

Mar 92. (lp/c/cd) Numa; (NUMA/+C/CD 1008) **ISOLATE** — — / -

Oct 92. (d-cd) Numa; (NUMACD 1007) **GHOST** — — / -

Gary NUMAN (cont)

Date	Format	Details	Chart	
Oct 92.	(cd/lp)	*Receiver; (RR CD/LP 170)* **THE OTHER SIDE OF GARY NUMAN**		-
Dec 92.	(cd)	*Connoisseur; (CSAPCD 113)* **DOCUMENT SERIES PRESENTS . . .**		-
Aug 93.	(7"/c-s)	*(BEG 264/+C)* **CARS.** / ('A'mix) (12"sha-pic-d+=/cd-s+=) *(BEG 264 L/CD)* – Cars ('93 sprint mix) / Cars (Top Gear mix).	53	-
Sep 93.	(d-cd)(c)	*(BEGA 150CD)(BEGC 150)* **THE BEST OF GARY NUMAN 1978-1983**	70	-
Jul 94.	(cd)	*Receiver; (RRCD 186)* **HERE I AM**		-
Mar 95.	(cd/c)	*Polygram TV; (531 149-2/-4)* **GREATEST HITS**		-
Feb 96.	(cd)	*When!; (WHENCD 006)* **TECHNO ARMY**		-
Mar 96.	(7"/c-s/cd-s)	*Premier; (PRM/+MC/CD 1)* **CARS (premier mix)** / **ARE FRIENDS ELECTRIC (live)** / **DOWN IN THE PARK (live)**	17	-
Mar 96.	(cd/c)	*Premier;* **THE PREMIER HITS** (compilation)	21	-
Jul 96.	(3xcd)	*Receiver; (RRXCD 505)* **THE STORY SO FAR**		-
Sep 96.	(cd/c)	*Emporio; (EMPR CD/MC 666)* **THE BEST OF GARY NUMAN**		-
Oct 97.	(12")	*Random; (RANDOM 2.1)* **METAL** (remixes). / **DANS LE PARC**		-
Nov 97.	(12"green)	*Random; (RANDOM 2.2)* **I DIE YOU DIE** (Greenhaus mix) / **CARS** (Mike Dearborn mix) / **CARS** (Dave Clarke mix)		-
Jan 98.	(12"blue)	*Random; (RANDOM 2.3)* **WARRIORS** (Dave Angel mix). / **ARE 'FRIENDS' ELECTRIC** (Liberator DJ's mix) / **REMEMBER I WAS VAPOUR** (Steve Stoll mix)		-
Feb 98.	(12")	*Random; (RANDOM 2.4)* **WE ARE GLASS** (Claude Young mix) / **FILMS** (Alex Hazzard remix) / **THE ICEMAN COMES** (Peter Lazonby mix)		-
Feb 02.	(d-cd)	*Snapper; (SMDCD 372)* **DARK WONDERS**		-
Apr 02.	(3xcd-box)	*Castle; (CNETD 466)* / *Sanctuary; <81214>* **DISCONNECTION**		Oct02

—— GARY has also contributed to other DRAMATIS recordings as well as joining RADIO HEART for one eponymous set

NUNS

Formed: San Francisco, California, USA . . . 1977 by RITCHIE DETRICK, ALEJANDRO ESCOVEDO, JENNIFER MIRO, PAT RYAN and JEFF RAPHAEL. One of many bands said to have pioneered the US New Wave scene (which paved the way for fellow Californians The DEAD KENNEDYS and The GERMS), The NUNS made their vinyl debut late in 1978 with the blistering single, 'SAVAGE'. The following few years saw the lads release a couple of 45's for the 'Rosco' imprint, before signing to the influential 'Posh Boy' (home of BLACK FLAG, etc). However, immediately prior to this they disbanded for a while, only to re-form again early 1980 with slightly new personnel on their eponymous debut album. A few more line-up changes ensued, leading to another break-up soon after, although a new look NUNS completed a comeback pop-orientated album, 'RUMANIA', in the mid 80's. In the interim, ESCOVEDO had helped form RANK & FILE with former DILS members.

Album rating: NUNS (*7) / RUMANIA (*5) / 4 DAYS IN A MOTEL ROOM: THEIR GREATEST SINS collection (*6)

RITCHIE DETRICK – vocals / **ALEJANDRO ESCOVEDO** – guitar / **JENNIFER MIRO** – keyboards / **PAT RYAN** – bass / **JEFF RAPHAEL** – drums

			not iss.	415
Nov 78.	(7"m)	*<S 0001>* **SAVAGE.** / **DECADENT JEW** / **SUICIDE CHILD**	-	

			not iss.	Rosco
1979.	(7")	**THE BEAT.** / **MEDIA CONTROL**	-	
1980.	(7")	*<4166>* **WW III.** / **COCK IN MY POCKET**	-	

—— split after recording of above. **KEVIN FOLEY** – drums; repl. RAPHAEL / **JOEY TERRANOVA** – bass; repl. PAT

			not iss.	Posh Boy
Nov 80.	(lp)	*<PBS 105>* **THE NUNS**	-	

			Butt	Watteau
Jan 82.	(7")	*(FUN 2) <002>* **WILD.** / **SUICIDE CHILD**		Nov81
Mar 82.	(lp)	*(ALSO 001)* **1ST** (UK-issue of US debut)		
1982.	(lp)	*<PBS 106>* **WILD**	-	

—— ESCOVEDO helped form RANK AND FILE in 1981. The NUNS re-formed later

MIKE VARNEY – bass; repl. JOEY TERRANOVA

JEFF OLENER – vocals repl. DETTRICK

			Hive	P.V.C.
1986.	(lp)	**RUMANIA**	-	
May 87.	(7")	*(HIVE 8)* **THE SUN IS GONNA GET TO ME.** /		

			not iss.	Posh Boy
1993.	(7")	*<PBS 23>* **IN THE SHADOWS.** / **INVISIBLE PEOPLE**	-	
1993.	(cd)	*<PBCD 88158>* **DESPERATE CHILDREN**	-	

– Don't let it go / It's a dream / My religion / The night is calling / Fire in the night / Walkin' the beat / In the shadows / Invisible people / World without you / Falling apart / Suicide child II.

—— no more heard of them after above

– compilations, etc. –

Feb 94.	(cd)	*Musical Tragedies; (EFA 122012)* / *Posh Boy; <PBCD 88159-2>* **4 DAYS IN A MOTEL ROOM: THEIR GREATEST SINS**		

– Elvis said / Rodney's English disco / Do you want me on my knees? / 4 days in a motel room / Suicide child / The underground / Just do it! / The more I want you / Platinum princess / My religion / In the shadows / Are you the enemy! / To your soul / Savage / Media control / World War III / You think you're the best / Walkin' the beat / Wild / Getting straight / Confused / Child molester / Lazy / Sex dream.

Judy NYLON (see under ⇒ SNATCH)

Gene OCTOBER (see under ⇒ CHELSEA)

O-LEVEL (see under ⇒ BALL, Edward)

101'ERS

Formed: Brixton, London, England . . . summer '74 by JOE STRUMMER, CLIVE TIMPERLEY, DAN KELLEHER and RICHARD DUDANSKI, their first gig being on the 7th of September, 1974, at the local Telegraph venue. However, eighteen months later the quartet had broken-up, only a posthumous issue – in June '76 – of their modern R&B gem, 'KEYS TO YOUR HEART', hitting the small record shops. All four group members went on to greater things, frontman, STRUMMER, becoming a punk icon when he joined The CLASH (KELLEHER subsequently formed MARTIAN SCHOOLGIRLS, while TIMPERLEY joined The PASSIONS and DUDANSKI initially played with PUBLIC IMAGE LTD and The RAINCOATS).

Album rating: ELGIN AVENUE BREAKDOWN posthumous (*4)

JOE STRUMMER (b. JOHN MELLOR, 21 Aug'52, Ankara, Turkey) – vocals, guitar / **CLIVE TIMPERLEY** – guitar, vocals (ex-DERELICTS) / **DAN KELLEHER** – bass, vocals / **RICHARD DUDANSKI** – drums

			Chiswick	not iss.
Jun 76.	(7")	*(NS 3)* **KEYS TO YOUR HEART.** / **5 STAR ROCK'N'ROLL PETROL**		-

—— had already split (see biog for details).

– posthumous collections, etc.

Feb 81.	(7")	*Chiswick; (NS 63)* **SWEET REVENGE.** / **RABIES (FROM THE DOGS OF LOVE)**		-
Sep 81.	(lp)	*Andalucia; (AND 101)* **ELGIN AVENUE BREAKDOWN** (live recordings & rare items)		-

ONLY ONES

Formed: South London, England . . . 1976 by singer/guitarist PETER PERRETT out of the recently defunct ENGLAND'S GLORY (which also comprised HARRY KAKOULLI – bass and JON NEWEY – drums). They were initially managed by HARRY's sister, ZENA, who also provided some backing vocals alongside fourth member, MICHAEL KEMP – keyboards. When HARRY quit to join SQUEEZE in 1974, PERRETT found seasoned musicians, JOHN PERRY, MIKE KELLIE and ALAN MAIR, subsequently adopting The ONLY ONES tag. Their vinyl debut, 'LOVERS OF TODAY', was released in Summer '77 on Zena & Peter's own 'Vengeance' label, selling sufficiently to attract the attentions of major label, 'C.B.S.'. April '78 saw the release of their exhilarating 'ANOTHER GIRL, ANOTHER PLANET', a legendary track that remains to this day in the "One That Got Away" bracket. An eponymous debut album followed a few months later, its low-rent, faded glamour tales of life's seedier side drawled out by the charismatic PERRETT against an authentic but professional new wave backdrop. The record's humble Top 60 position was a poor reflection of its quality bearing in mind the number of two-bit amateurs clogging up the charts at the time. With bountiful critical acclaim on their side, The ONLY ONES ploughed on, releasing a second instalment of PERRETT's doomed romanticism in 1979's 'EVEN SERPENTS SHINE'. Another impressive self-produced effort, the album's success was hindered by the snowballing tensions, both internally within the group itself and with their record company. Perhaps as a result, a third set, 'BABY'S GOT A GUN' (1980) sounded flaccid and tired in comparison, although it did provide PERRETT and Co. with a belated Top 40 placing. Sales weren't sufficient to please CBS, however, and, minus a deal, the group called it a day. While PERRY formed DECLINE AND FALL, PERRETT faded into drug-fuzzed obscurity, only re-emerging more than a decade later as PETER PERRETT IN THE ONE. An album, 'WOKE UP STICKY' (1996), appeared on 'Demon' in summer '96 to encouraging reviews, although whether he can last the course this time around remains to be seen.
• **Songwriters:** PERRETT compositions except; FOOLS (Johnny Duncan) / MY WAY OF GIVING (Small Faces) / SILENT NIGHT (trad.carol) / I'M NOT LIKE EVERYBODY ELSE (Kinks). • **Trivia:** PERRETT is known to have made recordings with SQUEEZE man GLENN TILBROOK in the mid-70's.

Album rating: THE ONLY ONES (*8) / EVEN SERPENTS SHINE (*7) / SPECIAL VIEW compilation (*6) / BABY'S GOT A GUN (*5) / REMAINS (*4) / THE IMMORTAL STORY – THE BEST OF ... compilation (*8) / DARKNESS AND LIGHT – THE COMPLETE BBC RECORDINGS collection (*7) / Peter Perrett In The One: WOKE UP STICKY (*5)

PETER PERRETT – vocals, guitar (ex-ENGLAND'S GLORY) / **JOHN PERRY** – lead guitar, keyboards (ex-RATBITES FROM HELL) / **MIKE KELLIE** (b.24 Mar'47, Birmingham, England) – drums (ex-SPOOKY TOOTH, ex-FRAMPTON'S CAMEL) / **ALAN MAIR** – bass (ex-BEATSTALKERS)

Vengeance / not iss.

Jun 77. (7",12") *(VEN 001)* **LOVERS OF TODAY. / PETER AND THE PETS**

C.B.S. / Epic

Apr 78. (7") *(S-CBS 6228)* **ANOTHER GIRL, ANOTHER PLANET. / SPECIAL VIEW**
May 78. (lp/c) *(CBS/40 82830)* **THE ONLY ONES** — 56
 – The whole of the law / Another girl, another planet / Breaking down / City of fun / The beast / Creature of doom / It's the truth / Language problem / No peace for the wicked / Immortal story. *(re-iss. 1984; CBS 32077)* *(re-iss. cd Sep94 on 'Columbia'; 477379-2)*
Aug 78. (12") *(S-CBS12 6576)* **ANOTHER GIRL, ANOTHER PLANET. / AS MY WIFE SAYS**
Feb 79. (7") *(S-CBS 7086)* **YOU'VE GOT TO PAY. / THIS AIN'T ALL (IT'S MADE OUT TO BE)**
Mar 79. (lp/c) *(CBS/40 83451)* **EVEN SERPENTS SHINE** — 42
 – From here to eternity / Flaming touch / You've got to pay / No solution / In betweens / Out there in the night / Curtains for you / Programme / Someone who cares / Miles from nowhere / Instrumental. *(re-iss. 1985; same)* *(cd-iss. Feb95 on 'Columbia'; 478503-2)*
Apr 79. (7") *(S-CBS 7285)* **OUT THERE IN THE NIGHT. / LOVERS OF TODAY**
 (12"blue+=) *(SCBS12-7285)* – Peter and the pets.
Jun 79. (lp) *<36199>* **SPECIAL VIEW** (compilation 77-79)
 – Another girl, another planet / Lovers of today / Peter and the pets / The beast / City of fun / The whole of the law / Out there in the night / Someone who cares / You've got to pay / Flaming torch / Curtains for you / From here to eternity.
Nov 79. (7") *(S-CBS 7963)* **TROUBLE IN THE WORLD. / YOUR CHOSEN LIFE**
Apr 80. (lp/c) *(CBS/40 84089)* *<36584>* **BABY'S GOT A GUN** — 37
 – The happy pilgrim / Why don't you kill yourself / Me and my shadow / Deadly nightshade / Strange mouth / The big sleep / Oh Lucinda (love becomes a habit) / Reunion / Trouble in the world / Castle built on sand / Fools / My way out of here. *(re-iss. 1985; same)* *(cd-iss. Mar96 on 'Columbia'; 483662-2)*
May 80. (7"; ONLY ONES with PAULINE MURRAY) *(S-CBS 8535)* **FOOLS. / CASTLE BUILT ON SAND**

— Disbanded March '81, PERRY formed DECLINE AND FALL but soon disappeared. In Autumn 91, PERRETT augmented the HEARTTHROBS live in Canada.

– compilations, others, etc. –

Jan 83. (7") *Vengeance; (VEN 002)* **BABY'S GOT A GUN. / Peter Perrett: SILENT NIGHT**
 (re-press.Aug85; same)
— (next lp featured on session **GLENN TILBROOK + GORDON EDWARDS** to repl. KELLIE + MAIR.
Jun 84. (lp) *Closer; (CL 012)* **REMAINS** (out-takes from their last album) — France
 – Prisoners / Watch you drown / Flowers die / Devon song / My rejection / Baby's got a gun / Hope valley blues / Counterfeit woman / River of no return / I only wanna be your friend / Oh no / Don't hold your breath / Silent night / Don't feel too good. *(cd-iss. Dec88; CLCD 012)* *(UK-iss.Sep93 on 'Anagram'; CDMGRAM 67)* *(lp re-iss. Dec00 on 'Munster'; MR 191)*
Oct 86. (lp) *Dojo; (DOJOLP 43)* **ALONE IN THE NIGHT**
 (cd-iss. Oct91; DOJOCD 43)
May 87. (lp; by ENGLAND'S GLORY) *5 Hours Back; (TOCK 004)* **ENGLAND'S GLORY – THE LEGENDARY LOST RECORDINGS**
 – Devotion / The wide waterway / City of fun / First time I saw you / Broken arrows / Bright lights / It's been a long time / The guest / Peter and the pets / Showdown / Predictably blonde / Weekend / Trouble in the world. *(this was originally privately released in 1973 for 'Vengeance'; VEN 105)* *(cd-iss. Apr94 & Sep96 on 'Anagram'; CDMGRAM 73)*
Aug 89. (lp/cd) *Mau Mau; (MAU/+CD 603)* **THE ONLY ONES LIVE (live)**
 (cd has extra tracks)
Dec 89. (lp/c/cd) *Strange Fruit; (SFR/+MC/CD 102) / Dutch East India; <DEI 8109>* **DOUBLE PEEL SESSIONS**
 (re-iss. Jul94; same)
Jan 92. (7") *Columbia; (657750-7)* **ANOTHER GIRL, ANOTHER PLANET. / ('B' by 'Psychedelic Furs')** — 57
 (12"+=/12"red+=/cd-s+=) *(657750-0/-2)* – Lovers of today.
May 92. (cd/c/d-lp) *Columbia; (471267-2/-4/-1)* **THE IMMORTAL STORY: THE BEST OF THE ONLY ONES**
 – Lovers of today / Peter and the pets / The whole of the law / Another girl, another planet / Special view (aka Telescopic love) / The beast / It's the truth / No peace for the wicked / The immortal story / From here to eternity / In betweens / No solution / Curtains for you / Someone who cares / Miles from nowhere / Instrumental / Your chosen life / Baby's got a gun / Why don't you kill yourself / Oh Lucinda (love becomes a habit) / The big sleep. (
Nov 93. (lp/cd) *Jungle; (<FREUD/+CD 045>)* **THE BIG SLEEP (live)** — 1997
Dec 95. (cd) *Windsong; (WINCD 080)* **IN CONCERT**
Sep 02. (d-cd) *Hux; (<HUX 030>)* **DARKNESS AND LIGHT: THE COMPLETE BBC RECORDINGS**

PETER PERRETT IN THE ONE

Dwarf / not iss.

Nov 94. (12"ep/cd-ep) *(VEN 003)* **CULTURED PALATE**
 – Baby don't talk / Twilight world / Made to fall apart / A company of strangers.

Demon / Demon

Apr 96. (7"one-sided) *(VEX 14)* **WOKE UP STICKY**
 (cd-s+=) *(VEXCD 14)* – Transfixed / Wildlife / Dead love syndrome.
Jun 96. (lp/c/cd) *(<FIEND/+CASS/CD 773>)* **WOKE UP STICKY**
 – Deep freeze / Woke up sticky / Nothing worth doing / Falling / The shame of being you / I'm not like everybody else / Sirens / Law of the jungle / Land of the free / Shivers / My sweet angel.

– (PETER PERRETT) compilations, etc. –

Feb 99. (cd) *Dwarf; (VEN 004)* **LIVE WITH THE ONE (live)**
 – Lovers of today / The shame of being you / Hearts on fire / The big sleep / Shivers / Falling / You gave birth / Skin like armour / The company of strangers / Another girl another planet / Baby don't talk / Daughter / The beast / Made to fall apart / Flaming torch / Land of the free / Law of the jungle. *(<re-iss.Jul00 as 'HEARTS ON FIRE' on 'Burning Airlines'+=; PILOT 065>)* – Another girl another planet (CD-Rom) / No peace for the wicked (CD-rom).

OUTCASTS

Formed: Belfast, N.Ireland ... 1977 by the COWAN brothers, MARTIN (the main songwriter), COLIN and GREG, the trio invited GETTY to join a little later. Early the following year, the quartet issued their debut 7", 'FRUSTRATION', before signing to up and coming local imprint, 'Good Vibrations' (who'd just had a hit with The UNDERTONES' 'Teenage Kicks'). Towards the end of '78, The OUTCASTS delivered their take on the classic punk-pop anthem with 'JUST ANOTHER TEENAGE REBEL', glammin' it up for unsavoury murder "ballad", 'THE COPS ARE COMIN', which subsequently featured on a V/A EP, 'Battle Of The Bands'. Their final single for the label, 'SELF CONSCIOUS OVER YOU', was also the title track of the accompanying debut album, released at the turn of the decade as punk's initial spark was dying out. Rejecting the majors and adamantly refusing to budge from the independent sector, The OUTCASTS delivered a further handful of 45's (including two on their own imprint), although tragedy struck when COLIN was killed in a car crash in '82. While the band struggled on with new drummer, RAYMOND FALLS, they failed to recapture the bite of their early work.

Album rating: SELF CONSCIOUS OVER YOU (*5) / BLOOD AND THUNDER (*5) / SEVEN DEADLY SINS (*5) / THE PUNK SINGLES COLLECTION (*6)

GREG COWAN (b.1961) – vocals, bass / **MARTIN COWAN** (b.1955) – guitar, vocals / **GETTY** (b. COLIN GETGOOD, 1960) – lead guitar / **COLIN COWAN** (b.1957) – drums

It / not iss.

Mar 78. (7"m) *(IT 4)* **FRUSTRATION. / DON'T WANT TO BE NO ADULT / YOU'RE A DISEASE**

Good Vibrations / not iss.

Nov 78. (7") *(GOT 3)* **JUST ANOTHER TEENAGE REBEL. / LOVE IS FOR SOPS**
Feb 79. (d7"; with Various Artists) *(GOT 7)* **THE COPS ARE COMIN' (from 'Battle Of The Bands')**
Nov 79. (7") *(GOT 17)* **SELF CONSCIOUS OVER YOU. / LOVE YOU FOR NEVER**
Dec 79. (lp) *(BIG 1)* **SELF CONSCIOUS OVER YOU**
 – Self conscious over you / Clinical love / One day / Love is for sops / Love you for never / The princess grew up a frog / Cyborg / School teacher / Spiteful Sue / The cops are comin'. *(cd-iss. Feb94 on 'Dojo'+=; DOJOCD 182)* – Just another teenage rebel.

G.B.H. / not iss.

Aug 81. (7") *(GBH 001)* **MAGNUM FORCE. / GANGLAND WARFARE**

Outcasts Only / not iss.

Nov 81. (7") *(OO 001)* **PROGRAMME LOVE. / BEATING AND SCREAMING (pt.1 & 2) / MANIA**
Jun 82. (7") *(OO 200)* **ANGEL FACE. / GANGLAND WARFARE**

— **RAYMOND FALLS** – drums; repl. COLIN (on some of below album) when he died in a car crash in '82

Abstract / not iss.

Jan 83. (lp) *(ABT 004)* **BLOOD AND THUNDER**
 – Winter / Machine gun / Sex and glory / Gangland warfare / Programme love / Frustration / Magnum force / Beating and screaming (parts 1 & 2) / Mania. *(cd-iss. 1984 on 'New Rose'; ROSE 16CD)*
Jun 83. (7") *(ABS 017)* **NOWHERE LEFT TO RUN. / THE RUNNING'S OVER TIME TO PRAY**
 (12"+=) *(12ABS 017)* – ('A'instrumental) / Ruby.

New Rose / not iss.

Aug 84. (7") *(NEW 38)* **SEVEN DEADLY SINS. / SWAMP FEVER**
Aug 84. (lp) *(NEW 40)* **SEVEN DEADLY SINS**
Jul 85. (12"m) *(NEW 52)* **1969 (extended). / PSYCHOTIC SHAKEDOWN / BLUE MURDER**
— disbanded after above

– compilations, etc. –

Sep 95. (cd) *Anagram; (CDPUNK 62)* **THE PUNK SINGLES COLLECTION**
Nov 00. (cd) *Captain Oi; (AHOYCD 68)* **BLOOD AND THUNDER / SEVEN DEADLY SINS**

OUTSIDERS (see under ⇒ SOUND; in 80's section)

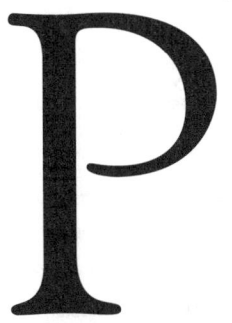

PAGANS

Formed: Cleveland, Ohio, USA . . . 1977 by MIKE HUDSON and TOMMY GUNN METOFF along with TIM ALLEE and BRIAN MORGAN. Hailing from the same American city that spawned PERE UBU, DEAD BOYS, etc, The PAGANS certainly kicked up an ungodly racket while their brutally defiant lyrics took no prisoners, thriving on alienation and offence. Despite being overlooked during punk's first wave, the greasoid garage crew were subsequently namechecked by a host of latter day hardcore/punk bands. Only four (independently-released) singles appeared during their short career span, the first three on 'Drome': 'THE STREET WHERE NOBODY LIVES', 'NOT NOW, NO WAY' and 'DEAD END AMERICA'. A final 7", 'SIX AND CHANGE', surfaced on 'Neck' records at the turn of the decade, rounding up their short sharp legacy. They re-formed for the odd gig or two throughout the 80's, sparking interest in a handful of retrospective releases for Mark Trehus' 'Treehouse' imprint. • **Covered:** HEART OF STONE (Rolling Stones) / CAN'T EXPLAIN (Who) / SEVENTH SON WIPED OUT (Willie Dixon / Surfaris) / BOY I CAN DANCE GOOD (. . . Carlton) / FEVER (Cooley – Davenport) / LITTLE BLACK EGG (. . . Conlon) / THERE SHE GOES AGAIN (Velvet Underground) / I'M MOVING ON (Hank Snow) / EIGHTEEN (Alice Cooper) / FINAL SOLUTION (Pere Ubu) / SEARCH AND DESTROY (Stooges) / IT'S ALL OVER NOW (Bobby Womack) / SECRET AGENT MAN (Johnny Rivers) / FORTUNE TELLER (Aaron Neville).

Album rating: THE PINK ALBUM (*6) / BURIED ALIVE compilation (*7) / THE GODLIKE POWER OF THE PAGANS compilation (*7) / EVERYBODY HATES YOU compilation (*7) / SHIT STREET collection (*6)

MIKE HUDSON – vocals / **TOMMY GUNN METOFF** – guitar (ex-CHRONIC) / **TIM ALLEE** – bass / **BRIAN MORGAN** – drums

not iss. Drome

1978. (7") <DR 1> **STREET WHERE NOBODY LIVES. / WHAT'S THIS SHIT CALLED LOVE?**
1978. (7") <DR 5> **NOT NOW NO WAY. / I JUVENILE**
1978. (7") <DR 7> **DEAD END AMERICA. / LITTLE BLACK EGG**

not iss. Neck

1979. (7") <1143> **SIX AND CHANGE. / SIX AND CHANGE**

—— disbanded Sep'79, METOFF went on to work with DAVE DELUCA, MORGAN with The FRENCHMEN – The PAGANS (aka HUDSON + METOFF) re-formed

Treehouse Treehouse

1986. (lp,red-lp) <TR 002> **BURIED ALIVE**
 – Streey where nobody lives / Haven't got the time / I juvenile / Dead end America / I don't understand / Not now no way / Heart of stone / Boy can I dance good / What's this shit called love? / Eyes of Satan / Little black egg / Yeah yeah / Real world / Can't explain / Give up / Dream lover / Six and change.
Aug 87. (7") <TR 003> **DEAD END AMERICA '87. / SECRET AGENT MAN**
Sep 87. (lp) <(TR 004)> **THE GODLIKE POWER OF THE PAGANS**
 – I'm moving on / There she goes again / Fever / Not now no way / Mixed emotions / Street where nobody lives / What's this shit called love? / Dead end America (live) / Little black egg (live) / What's this shit called love (live) / I don't understand (live) / Six and change (live) / Eighteen / Final solution.
1988. (lp) <TR 006> **THE PINK ALBUM**
 – Nowhere to run / Give till it hurts / Multiple personalities / When I die / Slow street / Cry 815 / Angela / Seventh son wiped out / Multiple personalities / When I die / Cleveland confidential / Dead end America / Wall of shame / Six and change. <(re-iss. Jun01 as 'THE PINK ALBUM . . . PLUS' on 'Crypt' cd+=/lp; CRYPT 91/+LP)>
 – THE GODLIKE POWER OF THE PAGANS
1989. (7") <TR 021> **HER NAME WAS JANE. / I DO**

– compilations, etc. –

May 89. (lp)(cd) *Resonance; (R33 8921)(08908-2)* **STREET WHERE NOBODY LIVES (live)**
May 95. (cd) *Crypt; <CR-036>* **EVERYBODY HATES YOU**
 – What's this shit called love / Dead end America / Eyes of Satan / The street where nobody lives / Boy I can dance good / Give up / Real world / Six and change / Haven't got the time / Little black egg / Yeah yeah / Heart of stone / Not now no way / I juvenile / Can't explain / Have / Give till it hurts / Slow street / Cry 815 / Angela / Seventh son wiped out / Multiple personalities / When I die / Cleveland confidential (real world) / Dead end America / Wall of shame / She's a cadaver (and I gotta have her) / I stand alone / I don't understand / Her name was Jane.
Apr 98. (cd) *Sonic Swirl; (SWIRL 024)* **LIVE ROAD KILL 1978-1979 (live)**
Jun 01. (cd/lp) *Crypt; <(CRYPT 90/+LP)>* **SHIT STREET** May01
 – What's this shit called love / Street where nobody lives / Haven't got the time / I juvenile / Eyes of Satan / I don't understand / Not now no way / Don't leave me alone / Boy can I dance good / Six and change / Dead end America / She's a cadaver / Little black egg / Yeah yeah / Heart of stone / Real world / Fortune teller / Give up / I can't explain / Say no (live) / Fortune teller (live) / I don't understand (live) / Yeah yeah (live) / Street where nobody lives (live) / Heart of stone (live) / Eyes of Satan (live) / Real world (live) / I juvenile (live) / Secret agent man (live) / She's a cadaver (live) / Not now no way (live) / It's all over now (live) / Search and destroy (live).

Andy PARTRIDGE (see under ⇒ XTC)

PASSAGE

Formed: Manchester, England . . . 1978 by mult-instrumentalist, DICK WITTS who recruited LORRAINE HILTON and ex-FALL bassist TONY FRIEL. WITTS' eccentricity was extended to both the musical and lyrical vision of his band, as heard on their first two EP's, 'NEW LOVE SONGS' and 'ABOUT TIME', in the late 70's. Their debut album, 'PINDROP', was issued late in 1980, although many were put off by WITTS' self-indulgent and often directionless musical experimentation and cryptic narratives. He was left in the dark following the departure of his bandmates, although there was light at the end of the tunnel when ANDREW WILSON, JOEY McKECHNIE and TERESA SHAW entered the fray. Another, slightly improved effort, 'FOR ALL AND NONE', hit the shops in summer '81, 'Cherry Red' subsequently signed The PASSAGE after they'd trimmed down to a duo of WITTS and WILSON. The third album, 'DEGENERATES', appeared a year later, its way-out, schizophrenic avant-indie occasionally reminiscent of a bizarre rock musical in which the campy WITTS played the lead role. One further set, 'ENFLAME' (1983), rounded off the 'Cherry Red' era and surprisingly the band signed to 'Arista'. Their major label tenure was short-lived however, only a solitary revamped version of 'SHARP TONGUE' being released before The PASSAGE finally reached a dead end. WITTS had already made his mark on television by presenting the music programme, The Oxford Road Show.

Album rating: PINDROP (*4) / FOR ALL AND NONE (*5) / DEGENERATES (*5) / ENFLAME (*5) / THROUGH THE PASSAGE compilation (*6) / SEEDY (THE BEST THE PASSAGE) compilation (*7)

DICK WITTS – vocals, drums, cello / **LORRAINE HILTON** – keyboards / **TONY FRIEL** – bass, guitar (ex-FALL)

Object not iss.

Dec 78. (7"ep) *(OM 02)* **NEW LOVE SONGS**
 – Love song / Competition / Slit machine / New kind of love.
Oct 79. (7"ep) *(OM 08)* **ABOUT TIME**
 – Taking my time / Clock paradox / Sixteen hours / Time.
Nov 80. (lp) *(OBJ 11)* **PINDROP**
 – PIN: Fear / Troops out / Carnal / Watching you dance / Hunt / Anderton's hall / From the heart / DROP: Locust / 2711 / 16 hours / Carmen / A certain way to go / Prelude.

—— added **IZZY JOHNSON**

Night & Day   not iss.

Feb 81. (7") *(AM:PM 24.00)* **DEVILS AND ANGELS. / WATCHING YOU DANCE**

—— **JOEY McKECHNIE** – drums (ex-MODERN EON); repl. HILTON
—— **ANDREW WILSON** – guitar + **TERESA SHAW** – vocals; repl. FRIEL (to CONTACT)

May 81. (7") *(AM:PM 22.00)* **TROOPS OUT. / HIP REBELS**
Jun 81. (lp) *(PM:AM 23.00)* **FOR ALL AND NONE**
 – Dark times / Lon Don / The shadows / Do the Bastinado / One to one / A good and useful life begun / A good and useful life revisited / Flag night / Shave your head / Tangled / Photo romance / The great refusal.

—— now a duo of **WITTS + WILSON**

Cherry Red   not iss.

Nov 81. (12") *(12CHERRY 30)* **TABOOS. / TABOO DUB**

—— added **PAUL MAHONEY** – drums

May 82. (7") *(CHERRY 35)* **XOYO. / ANIMAL IN ME**
 (12"+=) *(12CHERRY 35)* – Born every minute.
Jun 82. (lp) *(BRED 29)* **DEGENERATES**
 – Revelation / Love is as / Flock / Time will tell / Ourselves / Xoyo / Go to seed / Armour / Empty words.
Oct 82. (7") *(CHERRY 50)* **WAVE. / ANGLELAND**
 (12"=) *(12CHERRY 50)* – Drugface.

—— **JOEY McKECHNIE** – drums; returned to repl. PAUL

Mar 83. (lp/c) *(BRED/CBRED 45)* **ENFLAME**
 – Sharp tongue / The half of it: Twats / Clear as crystal / Drugface / Man of war / Dogstar – ?th day / Horseplay / Sunburn / The half of it: Sissies / BRD USA GDR JFK.
Mar 83. (7") *(CHERRY 58)* **SHARP TONGUE. / BRD USA GDR JFK**
Nov 83. (lp) *(BRED 56)* **THROUGH THE PASSAGE** (compilation)
 – Xoyo / Sharp tongue / Devils and angels / Good and useful life / Taboos / Born every minute / Sixteen houses / Watching you dance / Love is as / Carnal / Wave.

—— disbanded in 1984 (FRIEL was also part of CONTACT)

– compilations, others, etc. –

Apr 85. (7"/12"; w-drawn) *Arista; (ARIST/+12 525)* **SHARP TONGUE**
Sep 97. (cd) *Cherry Red; (<CDMRED 146>)* **SEEDY (THE BEST OF THE PASSAGE)**
 – Xoyo / Carnal / Horseplay / Devils and angels / Sharp tongue / Man of war / Armour / Fear / A good and useful life / Drugface / Love is as / Angleland / A certain way to go / Time will tell / 2711 / Wave / Taboos.

PENETRATION

Formed: Newcastle / Middlesborough, England ... 1976 by PAULINE MURRAY and ROBERT BLAMIRE alongside GARY CHAPMAN and GARY SMALLMAN, all four hailing from the small mining village of Ferrybridge. Following a valuable support slot to GENERATION X at London's punk nerve centre, The Roxy, PENETRATION began to make a name for themselves in the capital and duly secured a deal with 'Virgin'. Late 77's debut single, 'DON'T DICTATE', revealed a decidedly more "rawk" proposition than many of the three-chord trainee anarchists on the scene, MURRAY drawing inevitable comparisons with both PATTI SMITH and SIOUXSIE SIOUX for her force of personality and the strength/style of her voice. Replacing CHAPLIN with NEALE FLOYD and adding keyboard player FRED PURSER, the band released a fine follow-up in 1978's 'FIRING SQUAD', the track, like its predecessor, generating only limited interest amid charges that the band were "going heavy". Certainly, the debut album, 'MOVING TARGETS' (1978) had a few nifty guitar solos but MURRAY's songs were firmly rooted in punk's guiding light of social awareness and integrity. Also featuring a sterling choice of cover material in the Buzzcocks' 'NOSTALGIA', the album met with a generally positive press reaction and narrowly missed the UK Top 20. Yet things went inexorably awry from here on in as the band struggled, both with live commitments and new material, 'Virgin' pressing them for a new album which arrived in the shape of 1979's 'COMING UP FOR AIR'. The response was less than enthusiastic and amid increasing frustration, the band split soon after its release. While PURSER confirmed the suspicions of the band's detractors and went on to play with NWOBHM (New Wave Of British Heavy Metal) band, TYGERS OF PAN TANG, MURRAY launched her solo career with 'PAULINE MURRAY & THE INVISIBLE GIRLS' (1980). Backed by BLAMIRE, STEVE HOPKINS, JOHN MAHER and MARTIN HANNETT, MURRAY had recorded a set of much poppier, more experimental/electronic material which cracked the Top 30. The project was short-lived, however, MURRAY only surfacing occasionally with the odd single over the coming decade before releasing an album, 'STORM CLOUDS', in 1989. Over a decade later and into the new millennium, PAULINE was back with a new release, 'HALLOWEEN 2000', an EP featuring three ROKY ERICKSON-penned nuggets. • **Songwriters:** MURRAY lyrics / group music. PAULINE solo: – CLOSE WATER (John Cale). • **Trivia:** In 1979, Pauline guested for THE ONLY ONES on their final album, 'Baby's Got A Gun', and duetted with their leader, PETER PERRETT, on a single/track, 'Fools'.

Album rating: MOVING TARGETS (*7) / COMING UP FOR AIR (*5) / DON'T DICTATE – THE BEST OF PENETRATION compilation (*8) / PAULINE MURRAY & THE INVISIBLE GIRLS (*7)

PAULINE MURRAY (b. 8 Mar'58, Durham, England) – vocals / **GARY CHAPLIN** – guitar / **ROBERT BLAMIRE** – bass / **GARY SMALLMAN** – drums

		Virgin	not iss.
Nov 77.	(7") (VS 192) **DON'T DICTATE. / MONEY TALKS**		-

— NEALE FLOYD – guitar repl. CHAPLIN. / added FRED PURSER – keyboards

May 78.	(7") (VS 213) **FIRING SQUAD. / NEVER**		-
Sep 78.	(7") (VS 226) **LIFE'S A GAMBLE. / V.I.P.**		-
Oct 78.	(lp,luminous-lp/c) (V/TCV 2109) **MOVING TARGETS**	22	-

– Future daze / Life's a gamble / Lovers of outrage / Vision / Silent community / Stone heroes / Movement / Too many friends / Reunion / Nostalgia / Free money. (re-iss. Mar84; OVED 40) (cd-iss. Dec89; CDV 2109)

Apr 79.	(7") (VS 257) **DANGER SIGNS. / STONE HEROES**		-
	(12"+=) (VS 257-12) – Vision (live).		
Aug 79.	(7") (VS 268) **COME INTO THE OPEN. / LIFELINE**		-
Sep 79.	(lp/c) (V/TCV 2131) **COMING UP FOR AIR**	36	-

– Shout about the noise / She is the slave / Last saving grace / Killed in the rush / Challenge / Come into the open / What's going on / The party's over / On reflection / Lifeline / New recruit. (re-iss. 1988; OVED 203) (<cd-iss. Jun01 on 'Captain Oi'+=; AHOYCD 174)> – Danger signs / Stone heroes (live) / Vision (live).

— (split late 1979) CHAPLIN later formed SOUL ON ICE; PURSER subsequently joined the TYGERS OF PAN TANG.

– compilations, etc. –

Oct 79.	(lp) Cliffdayn; (PEN 1) **RACE AGAINST TIME** (official bootleg)		-
May 83.	(12"ep) Virgin; (VS 593-12) **DON'T DICTATE / FREE MONEY. / LIFE'S A GAMBLE / DANGER SIGNS**		-
Jan 92.	(cd; shared with The RUTS) Windsong; (WINCD 009) **BBC RADIO 1 LIVE IN CONCERT (live)**		-
Nov 93.	(cd) Burning Airlines; (PILOT 001) / Griffin; <381> **PENETRATION**		May95
	– (live, demos, Peel sessions, solo PAULINE MURRAY, etc)		
Mar 95.	(cd) Virgin; (CDOVD 450) **DON'T DICTATE ... THE BEST OF PENETRATION**		-
	– Come into the open / Lifeline / Firing squad / Never / Life's a gamble / V.I.P. / Danger signs / Stone heroes / Don't dictate / Free money / Shout above the noise / She is the slave / Party's over / Future daze.		
Apr 97.	(lp) Get Back; (GET 13) **THE EARLY YEARS**		-

PAULINE MURRAY & THE INVISIBLE GIRLS

— with **ROBERT BLAMIRE** – bass / **STEVE HOPKINS** – keyboards / **JOHN MAHER** – drums (ex-BUZZCOCKS) / **MARTIN HANNETT** – keyboards

		Illusive	not iss.
Jul 80.	(7"/10") (IVE/+X 1) **DREAM SEQUENCE 1. / DREAM SEQUENCE 2**	67	-
Sep 80.	(lp) (2934 277) **PAULINE MURRAY & THE INVISIBLE GIRLS**	25	-

– Screaming in the darkness / Dream sequence 1 / European eyes / Shoot you down / Sympathy / Time slipping / Drummer boy / Thunder tunes / When will we learn / Mr. X / Judgement day. (cd-iss. Jun93 on 'Trident'; PSTRCD 01) (cd re-iss. Mar97 on 'Burning Airlines'+=; PILOT 002) – The visitor / Animal crazy / Searching for Heaven. (cd re-iss. Nov00 on 'N.M.C.'+=; PSTRCD 01)

Oct 80.	(7") (IVE 2) **MR. X. / TWO SHOTS**		-
Apr 81.	(7") (IVE 3) **SEARCHING FOR HEAVEN. / ANIMAL CRAZY** (10"+=) (IVEX 3) – The Visitor.		-

— split in 1981

PAULINE MURRAY

— with **ROBERT BLAMIRE** – bass / **PAUL HARVEY** – guitar / **TIM JOHNSON** – drums

		Polestar	not iss.
Oct 84.	(7") (PSTR 001) **HOLOCAUST. / DON'T GIVE UP** (12"+=) (PSTR 12-001) – Aversion.		-
Oct 86.	(7") (PSTR 003) **NEW AGE. / BODY MUSIC** (12"+=) (PSTR 12-003) – Archangel.		-

— (from 1984-86 by PAULINE MURRAY & THE STORM, below with The SAINT)

Mar 87.	(12"ep) (PSTR 002) **HONG KONG EP**		-

– Close watch / All I want / Body music / Holocaust.

		Cat&Mouse	not iss.
Apr 89.	(12"m) (ABBO 9T) **THIS THING CALLED LOVE. / MR. MONEY / PRESSURE ZONE**		-
Jul 89.	(lp) (ABB 10) **STORM CLOUDS**		-

– This thing called love / Holocaust / Soul power / No one like you / Another world / Don't give up / Pressure zone / Close watch / Everybody's talkin' / New age / Time. (re-iss. Jun91 on 'Polestar'; 834445-1)

		Polestar	not iss.
Oct 00.	(cd-ep) (PSTRCD 002) **HALLOWEEN 2000**		-

– Stand for the fire demon / Night of the vampire / Creature with the atom brain.

PERE UBU

Formed: Cleveland, Ohio, USA ... September '75 out of ROCKET FROM THE TOMBS, by DAVID THOMAS (aka CROCUS BEHEMOTH; his alter-ego) and PETER LAUGHNER. Along with CHARLIE WEINER (guitar), GLEN 'THUNDERHAND' HACH (guitar) and TOM 'FOOLERY' CLEMENTS (drums), they became residents at THOMAS's workplace, the Viking Saloon; he was apparently a bouncer! A revamped RFTT saw THOMAS and LAUGHNER being joined by CRAIG BELL (bass), GENE 'CHEETAH CHROME' O'CONNOR (guitar) and 'JOHNNY BLIZ' MADANSKY (drums), and it was this line-up who recorded sessions for WMMS radio stations, later to surface as a posthumous 1990 cd, 'LIFE STINKS'. A few embryonic UBU tracks, 'FINAL SOLUTION' and '30 SECONDS OVER TOKYO', plus covers of 'SATISFACTION' (Rolling Stones) and 'SEARCH AND DESTROY' (Stooges), featured on these rare master tapes. Even 'SONIC REDUCER' was hijacked by The DEAD BOYS bound, CHEETAH and BLITZ, the pair being united with STIV BATORS, who replaced THOMAS before the ROCKETS split. Meanwhile, PERE UBU (THOMAS and LAUGHNER) recruited other musicians; TIM WRIGHT, ALLEN RAVENSTINE, TOM HERMAN plus SCOTT KRAUSS, and took their name from a play by French writer, Alfred Jarry. The large-framed THOMAS formed his own 'Hearthan' label, issuing a classic debut, '30 SECONDS OVER TOKYO', which led to gigs at (New York's) Max's Kansas City in early '76. Another gem, 'FINAL SOLUTION', was unleashed soon after, although LAUGHNER departed (at this stage the line-up numbered THOMAS, RAVENSTINE, HERMAN, KRAUSE and newcomer, TONY MAIMONE) prior to the release of their third and fourth rare 45's, 'STREET WAVES' and 'THE MODERN DANCE'. The latter subsequently became the name of their debut album which gained a release early in 1978 on the obscure US 'Blank' label (a few months later it surfaced in the UK on 'Mercury'). The sound was clearly a break from the "New Wave", echoing as it did a revival of the avant-garde (CAPTAIN BEEFHEART and ENO-era ROXY MUSIC). On the strength of this masterwork, they signed to the major 'Chrysalis' label and, six months later, wowed the music world with another abstract beauty, 'DUB HOUSING' (1978). After the disappointing 'NEW PICNIC TIME' (1979), however, they were unceremoniously dropped by their label, the band's wayward eccentricity floating right over the average pop picker's head. PERE UBU (who had replaced HERMAN with veteran, MAYO THOMPSON – formerly of RED CRAYOLA) subsequently found a home with UK indie, 'Rough Trade', although they split after two poorly-received studio sets, 'THE ART OF WALKING' (1980) and 'SONG OF THE BAILING MAN' (1982), the latter boasting the drumming talents of ANTON FIER. Over the course of the next five years, having released a debut album, 'THE SOUND OF THE SAND' early in '82, THOMAS embarked on an equally weird and anti-commercial solo career with albums, the live 'WINTER COMES HOME' (1983), 'VARIATIONS ON A THEME' (1983), 'MORE PLACES FOREVER; (1985), 'MONSTER WALKS THE WINTER LAKE' (1986) and 'BLAME THE MESSENGER' (1987). PERE UBU released a belated comeback album, 'THE TENEMENT YEARS', in 1988, a record which gathered together old UBU men, THOMAS, RAVENSTINE, MAIMONE and KRAUSE, while retaining CHRIS CUTLER and JIM JONES (previously part of THOMAS' solo band). For the 1989 set, 'CLOUDLAND', the group sought out former CAPTAIN BEEFHEART employee, ERIC DREW FELDMAN, who remained for a further two albums, 'WORLDS IN COLLISION' (1991) and 'STORY OF MY LIFE' (1993). Subsequently signing to 'Cooking Vinyl' (also now the rest home of BILLY BRAGG and The WEDDING PRESENT), PERE UBU cut one final effort, 'RAY GUN SUITCASE' (1995), before THOMAS once again opted for solo pastures with 'EREWHON' (1996). Sidestepping between solo and PERE UBU releases, THOMAS continued to create his own creative pop. UBU's 'PENNSYLVANIA' (1998) found him in a reflective mood – he had been living in England for some time now – while the solo DAVID THOMAS AND TWO PALE BOYS release 'MIRROR MAN' (1999) was pure rock-opera mixed with readings. To start the millennium, DAVID THOMAS AND FOREIGNERS (mainly Danish musicians!) got together for improv live set, 'BAY CITY' (2000); THOMAS AND TWO PALE BOYS (aka ANDY DIAGRAM and KEITH MOLINE) delivered a second batch of songs, 'SURF'S UP!', the following year. PERE UBU returned in the summer of 2002 via 'ST. ARKANSAS', their body of sound now over a quarter of a century old but still viable and conscious of today's discerning and fickle market. • **Songwriters:** All group compositions. THOMAS collaborated with others on solo work and covered SLOOP JOHN B. (Beach Boys).

Album rating: THE MODERN DANCE (*9) / DUB HOUSING (*7) / NEW PICNIC TIME (*7) / THE ART OF WALKING (*6) / 390 DEGREES OF SIMULATED STEREO (*4) / SONG OF THE BAILING MAN (*5) / TERMINAL TOWER: AN ARCHIVAL COLLECTION compilation (*9) / THE TENEMENT YEAR (*6) / ONE MAN DRIVES WHILE THE OTHER MAN SCREAMS early live (*5) / CLOUDLAND (*6) / WORLDS IN COLLISION (*6) / STORY OF MY LIFE (*6) / RAYGUN SUITCASE (*7) / DATAPANIK IN THE YEAR ZERO boxed collection (*8) / PENNSYLVANIA (*6) / APOCALYPSE NOW live (*6) / ST. ARKANSAS (*6) / David Thomas: THE SOUND OF THE SAND... (*6) / WINTER COMES HOME (*5) / VARIATIONS ON A THEME (*6) / MORE PLACES FOREVER (*5) / MONSTER WALKS THE WINTER LAKE (*4) / BLAME THE MESSENGER (*5) / MIRROR MAN (*7) / BAY CITY (*5) / SURF'S UP! (*6) / Rocket From The Tombs: THE DAY THE EARTH MET THE... (*6)

DAVID THOMAS (b.14 Jun'53) – vocals / **PETER LAUGHNER** (b.1953) – guitar / **TIM WRIGHT** – bass, guitar / **TOM HERMAN** (b.19 Apr'49) – guitar, bass / **SCOTT KRAUSE** (b.19 Nov'50) – drums / **ALLEN RAVENSTINE** (b. 9 May'50) – synthesizer

not iss. Hearthan

Dec 75. (7"ltd) <HR 101> **30 SECONDS OVER TOKYO. / HEART OF DARKNESS**

— **DAVE TAYLOR** – synthesizer repl. RAVENSTINE

Mar 76. (7"ltd) <HR 102> **FINAL SOLUTION. / CLOUD 149**

— **ALLEN RAVENSTINE** – synthesizer returned to repl. TAYLOR / **ALAN GREENBLATT** – guitar; repl. LAUGHNER who formed FRICTION (he died of drug & alcohol abuse 22nd June '77)

— **TONY MAIMONE** (b.27 Sep'52) – bass, piano repl. WRIGHT who joined DNA. (GREENBLATT left also) (were now a quintet with **THOMAS, HERMAN, KRAUSE, MAIMONE + RAVENSTINE**)

Nov 76. (7"ltd) <HR 103> **STREET WAVES. / MY DARK AGES**
Aug 77. (7"ltd) <HR 104> **THE MODERN DANCE. / HEAVEN**

Mercury Blank

Apr 78. (lp) (9100 052) <001> **THE MODERN DANCE** *Jan78*
 – Non-alignment pact / The modern dance / Laughing / Street waves / Chinese radiation / Life stinks / Real world / Over my head / Sentimental journey / Humor me. (re-iss. Jan81 on 'Rough Trade'; ROUGH 22) (re-iss. Feb88 on 'Fontana' lp/cd; SF LP/CD 3) (cd re-iss. Jun98 on 'Cooking Vinyl'; COOKCD 141) <US cd-iss. Jun98 on 'Geffen'; 25206> (lp re-iss. May99 on 'Get Back'; GET 054)

Radar not iss.

Apr 78. (12"ep) (RDAR 1) **DATAPANIK IN THE YEAR ZERO (remixes compilation)**
 – Heart of darkness / 30 seconds over Tokyo / Cloud 149 / Untitled / Heaven.

Chrysalis Rough Trade

Nov 78. (lp) (CHR 1207) <ROUGH-US 14> **DUB HOUSING**
 – Navy / On the surface / Dub housing / Cagliari's mirror / Thriller / I will wait / Drinking wine Spodyody / Ubu dance party / Blow daddy-o / Codex. (cd-iss. Mar89 on 'Rough Trade'; ROUGHCD 6002) (cd re-iss. Mar99 on 'Cooking Vinyl'; COOKCD 170) (lp re-iss. Feb00 on 'Get Back'; GET 58)

Sep 79. (lp) (CHR 1248) <ROUGH-US 20> **NEW PICNIC TIME**
 – One less worry / Make hay / Goodbye / The voice of the sand / Jehovah's kingdom comes / Have shoes will walk / 49 guitars and 1 girl / A small dark cloud / Small was fast / All the dogs are barking. (cd-iss. Mar89 on 'Rough Trade'; ROUGHCD 6003) (cd re-iss. Mar99 on 'Cooking Vinyl'; COOKCD 171) (lp re-iss. Feb00 on 'Get Back'; GET 59)

Oct 79. (7"m) (CHS 2372) **THE FABULOUS SEQUEL (HAVE SHOES WILL WALK). / HUMOR ME (live). / THE BOOK IS ON THE TABLE**

— **MAYO THOMPSON** (b.26 Feb'44) – guitar, vocals (ex-RED CRAYOLA) repl. HERMAN who went solo

Rough Trade not iss.

Jun 80. (7") (RT 049) **FINAL SOLUTION. / MY DARK AGES**
Sep 80. (lp) (ROUGH 14) **THE ART OF WALKING**
 – Go / Rhapsody in pink / Arabia * / Miles * / Misery goats / Loop / Rounder / Birdies / Lost in art / Horses / Crush this horn. (re-iss. 1981; same) / Arabian nights / Tribute to Miles; repl. *) (cd-iss. as re-issue; ROUGHCD 14)<US = ROUGH-US-4CD> (cd re-iss. Nov99 on 'Cooking Vinyl'; COOKCD 157) <US cd re-iss. Nov99 on 'Thirsty Ear'; 57079> (lp re-iss. Sep01 on 'Get Back'; GET 81)

Feb 81. (7") (RT 066) **NOT HAPPY. / LONESOME COWBOY DAVE**
May 81. (lp) (ROUGH 23) **390° OF SIMULATED STEREO – UBU LIVE: VOLUME 1 (live 76-79)**
 – Can't believe it / Over my head / Sentimental journey / 30 seconds over Tokyo / Humor me / Real world / My dark ages / Street waves / Laughing / Non-alignment pact / Heart of darkness / The modern dance. (cd-iss. Apr89; ROUGHCD 23)

— added **ANTON FIER** (b.20 Jun'56) – drums, percussion (ex-FEELIES) / guest **EDDIE THORNTON** – trumpet

Jun 82. (lp) (ROUGH 33) **SONG OF THE BAILING MAN**
 – The long walk home / Use of a dog / Petrified / Stormy weather / West Side story / Thoughts that go by steam / Big Ed's used farms / A day such as this / The vulgar boatman bird / My hat / Horns are a dilemma. (cd-iss. Apr89; ROUGHCD 33) (cd re-iss. Nov99 on 'Cooking Vinyl'; COOKCD 158) <US cd-iss. Nov99 on 'Thirsty Ear'; 57080> (lp re-iss. Jun02 on 'Get Back'; GET 90)

— split mid 1982. MAYO returned to RED CRAYOLA (which also incl. most UBU's). KRAUSE + WRIGHT formed HOME & GARDEN, who released one album for 'Dead Man's Curve', 'HISTORY & GEOGRAPHY' (1986)

DAVID THOMAS & THE PEDESTRIANS

Rough Trade Recommended

Dec 81. (12"ep; by DAVID THOMAS) (TRADE 5-12) **VOCAL PERFORMANCES**

— included **THOMPSON, KRAUSE, FIER & RAVENSTINE** plus **CHRIS CUTLER** (b. 4 Jan'47) – drums / **JOHN GREAVES** – bass (both ex-HENRY COW) / **PHILIP MOXHAM** – multi (ex-YOUNG MARBLE GIANTS) / **RICHARD THOMPSON** – guitar

Jan 82. (lp) (ROUGH 30) **THE SOUND OF THE SAND AND OTHER SONGS OF THE PEDESTRIANS**
 – The birds are good ideas / Yiki Tiki / The crickets in the flats / Sound of the sand / The new atom mine / Big dreams / Happy to see you / Crush this horn – part 2 / Confuse did / Sloop John B. / Man's best friend.

Oct 82. (7") **PETRIFIED. /**

— w/ **CHRIS CUTLER & LINDSAY COOPER** – bassoon (ex-MIKE OLDFIELD)

Feb 83. (lp; DAVID THOMAS & HIS LEGS) (DTLP) **WINTER COMES HOME (live Munich, 1982)**
 – A day such as this / Winter comes home / West side story / Sunset / Stormy weather / Poetic license / Rhapsody in pink / Dinosaurs like me / Petrified / Bones in action / Contrasted views of the archaeopterix.

— added **RICHARD THOMPSON** etc. (CUTLER, COOPER)

Dec 83. (lp) (ROUGH 60) **VARIATIONS ON A THEME**
 – A day at the Botanical Gardens / Pedestrians walk / Bird town / The egg and I / Who is it / Song of hoe / Hurry back / The ram / Semaphore.

— **TONY MAIMONE** – bass repl. GREAVES who joined The FLYING LIZARDS

Rough Trade Twin/Tone

May 85. (lp) (ROUGH 80) <TTR 8551> **MORE PLACES FOREVER**
 – Through the magnifying glass / Enthusiastic / Big breezy day / About true friends / Whale head king / Song of the bailing man / The farmer's wife / New broom.

DAVID THOMAS & THE WOODEN BIRDS

(**DAVID** retained **MAIMONE** and **CUTLER**) brought in **RAVENSTINE** again. (**DAVID HILD** – accordion of LOS LOBOS guested)

Apr 86. (lp/cd) (ROUGH 90) <TTR/+CD 8667> **MONSTER WALKS THE WINTER LAKE**
 – My theory of simultanious similtude – Red tin bus / What happened to me / Monster walks the winter lake / Bicycle / Coffee train / My town / Monster Magge king of the seas / Monster thinks about the good days / What happened to us.

— **JIM JONES** (b.12 Mar'50) – guitar was added

Mar 87. (lp) (ROUGH 120) <TTR 87105> **BLAME THE MESSENGER**
 – The long rain / My town / King Knut / A fact about trains / When love is uneven / Storm breaks / Having time / Velikovsky / The two-step.

PERE UBU

(**THOMAS, RAVENSTINE, MAIMONE, CUTLER, JONES** and **KRAUSE**)

Fontana Enigma

Mar 88. (lp/c)(cd) (SF LP/MC 5)(834 537-2) <73343> **THE TENEMENT YEAR**
 – Something's gotta give / George had a hat / Talk to me / Busman's honeymoon / Say goodbye / Universal vibration / Miss you / Dream the Moon / Rhythm kind / The hollow Earth / We have the technology.

Jul 88. (7") (UBU 1) **WE HAVE THE TECHNOLOGY. / THE B-SIDE**
 (12"+=/cd-s+=) (UBU 1-12/CD1) – The postman drove a caddy / ('A'-different mix).

— **ERIC DREW FELDMAN** (b.16 Apr'55) – drums (ex-CAPTAIN BEEFHEART) repl. RAVENSTINE + CUTLER

Fontana not iss.

Mar 89. (7") (UBU 2) **WAITING FOR MARY (WHAT ARE WE DOING HERE?). / WINE DARK SPARKS**
 (12"+=/cd-s+=) (UBU 2-12/CD2) – Flat.

May 89. (lp/c/cd) (838 237-1/-4/-2) **CLOUDLAND**
 – Breath / Bus called happiness / Race the sun / Waiting for Mary / Cry / Flat * / Ice cream truck / Lost nation road / Monday night / Pushin' / The wire * / The waltz. (cd+= *)

Jun 89. (7") (UBU 3) **LOVE LOVE LOVE. / FEDORA SATELLITE**
 (cd-s+=) (UBUCD 3) – Say goodbye.
 (12") (UBU 3-12) – ('A' cajun house mix) / ('A' 132 bpm mix) / ('A' side).

Oct 89. (7") (UBU 4) **BREATH. / BANG THE DRUM**
 (12"+=) (UBU 4-12) – Over my head (live) / Universal initiation (live).
 (cd-s+=) (UBUCD 4) – Humor me (live).

Mar 91. (7") (UBU 5) **I HEAR THEY SMOKE THE BARBEQUE. / INVISIBLE MAN**
 (12"+=/cd-s+=) (UBU 5-12/CD5) – Around the fire.

May 91. (cd/c/lp) (848 564-2/-4/-1) **WORLDS IN COLLISION**
 – Oh Catherine / I hear they smoke the barbeque / Turpentine / Goodnight Irene / Mirror man / Cry cry / World's in collision / Life of Riley / Over the Moon / Don't look back / Playback / Nobody knows / Winter in the Netherlands.

May 91. (7") (UBU 6) **OH CATHERINE / LIKE A ROLLING STONE**
 (12"+=/cd-s+=) (UBU 6-12/CD6) – Down by the river.

Fontana Imago

Jan 93. (cd/c) (514159-2/-4) <21024> **STORY OF MY LIFE**
 – Wasted / Come home / Louisiana train wreck / Fedora satellite II / Heartbreak garage / Postcard / Kathleen / Honey Moon / Sleep walk / The story of my life / Last will and testament.

— **THOMAS / KRAUSS / JONES / TEMPLE / YELLIN**

Cooking Vinyl Tim/Kerr

Aug 95. (cd) (COOKCD 089) <TK 100> **RAY GUN SUITCASE**
 – Folly of youth / Electricity / Beach Boys / Turquoise fins / Vacuum in my head / Memphis / Three things / Horse / Don't worry / Ray gun suitcase / Surfer girl / Red sky / Montana / My friend is a stooge for the media priests / Down by the river II.

PERE UBU (cont)

THE GREAT INDIE DISCOGRAPHY — The 1970s

Oct 95. (cd-ep) *(FRYCD 043)* <*TK 111-2*> **FOLLY OF YOUTH / BALL 'N' CHAIN (jam) / DOWN BY THE RIVER II (demo) / MEMPHIS (demo)**
Mar 96. (cd-ep) <*TK 830121*> **B EACH B OYS SEE DEE +** — Feb96
 – Beach Boys / Down by the river / Louisiana train wreck / Montana.

DAVID THOMAS

— with **ANDY DIAGRAM** – trumpet (ex-PALE FOUNTAINS) / **PAUL HAMANN** – upright bass / **JIM JONES** – backing vocals

 Cooking Vinyl / Tim/Kerr

Sep 96. (cd; DAVID THOMAS & TWO PALE BOYS) *(COOKCD 105)* <*TK 145*> **EREWHON**
 – Obsession / Planet of fools / Nowheresville / Fire / Lantern / Morbid sky / Weird cornfields / Kathlen / Highway 61 revisited.

PERE UBU

— **THOMAS** with **TOM HERMAN + JIM JONES** newcomer + **ROBERT WHEELER** – synthesizer / **MICHELE TEMPLE** – bass

Mar 98. (cd) *(COOKCD 139)* <*TK 155*> **PENNSYLVANIA**
 – Woolie bullie / Highwaterville / Sad. TXT / Urban lifestyle / Drive / Indiangiver / Monday morning / Perfume / Silent spring / Mr. Wheeler / Muddy waters / Slow / Fly's eye / The duke's Saharan ambitions / Wheelhouse.

DAVID THOMAS

— with **ANDY DIAGRAM, LINDA THOMPSON, JACKIE LEVEN**, etc

 Cooking Vinyl / Thirsty Ear

Mar 99. (cd; by The PALE ORCHESTRA conducted by DAVID THOMAS) *(COOKCD 175)* <*57068*> **MIRROR MAN**
 – Mirror man sees / Mirror man speaks – Lost nation road / The flying Dutchman of the interstate / Ballad of Florida – Montana / Ribbons on the road / Morbid sky / Nowheresville / Shadows on the face – Memphis / Over the moon – If the deer blinks / Bus called happiness / Weird cornfields.
 next with **JORGEN TELLER** – guitar, organ / **PER BUHL ACS** – clarinet, bass / **P.O. JORGENS** – percussion

 Hearpen / Thirsty Ear

Aug 00. (cd; as DAVID THOMAS AND FOREIGNERS) *(HR 111)* <*57085*> **BAY CITY**
 – Clouds of you / White room / Black coffee dawn / Salt / Nobody lives on the moon / Charlotte / The doorbell / 15 seconds / The radio talks to me / Shaky hands / Black rain / Turpentine / Untitled track.

— back with **DIAGRAM + KEITH MOLINE** – guitar

 Glitterhouse / Thirsty Ear

Mar 01. (cd; as DAVID THOMAS AND TWO PALE BOYS) *(GRCD 519)* <*57096*> **SURF'S UP!** — Feb01
 – Runaway / Man in the dark / Night driving / Surf's up / River / Ghosts / Spider in my stew / Come home – Green river.

 – compilations, etc. –

Jun 97. (5xcd-box) *Hearpen; (HR 110)* **MONSTER** (compilation of all his solo work)
 (re-iss. Oct02; same)

PERE UBU

 Glitterhouse / SpinArt

May 02. (cd) *(GRCD 554)* <*SPART 108*> **ST. ARKANSAS** — Jun02
 – The fevered dream of Hernando DeSoto / Slow walking daddy / Michele / 333 / Hell / Lisbon / Steve / Phone home Jonah / Where's the truth / Dark.

 – compilations, others, etc. –

Nov 85. (lp/cd) *Rough Trade; (ROUGH 83) / Twin/Tone;* <*TTR/+CD 8561*> **TERMINAL TOWER: AN ARCHIVAL COLLECTION** (early work)
 – Heart of darkness / 30 seconds over Tokyo / Final solution / Cloud 149 / Untitled / My dark ages / Heaven / Humor me / The book is on the table / Not happy / Lonesome cowboy Dave. *(cd re-iss. Jun98 on 'Cooking Vinyl'; COOKCD 142)* <*US cd re-iss. Jun98 on 'Geffen'; 25207*> *(lp re-iss. Feb01 on 'Get Back'; GET 73)*
Mar 89. (cd) *Rough Trade; (ROUGHCD 93)* **ONE MAN DRIVES WHILE THE OTHER MAN SCREAMS – LIVE VOL.2: PERE UBU ON TOUR**
Nov 95. (4x7"box) *Cooking Vinyl; (FRY 045) / Tim/Kerr;* <*TK 107*> **THE HEARTHAN SINGLES**
Nov 95. (d-cd) *Movieplay Gold; (MPG 74178)* **THE MODERN DANCE / TERMINAL TOWER**
Sep 96. (5xcd-box) *Cooking Vinyl; (COOKCD 098) / Geffen;* <*24969*> **DATAPANIK IN THE YEAR ZERO**
 – (first 5 albums + 1 free rarities album)
Aug 99. (cd) *Cooking Vinyl; (COOKCD 185) / Thirsty Ear;* <*57074*> **APOCALYPSE NOW (live in Chicago 1991)**
Oct 00. (cd) *Hearpen;* <*113*> **THE SHAPE OF THINGS** (live, April 7, 1976)

ROCKET FROM THE TOMBS

CROCUS BEHEMOTH (aka DAVID THOMAS) – vocals, guitar / **PETER LAUGHNER** – guitar, vocals / **CHEETAH CHROME** (b. GENE O'CONNOR) – guitar, organ / **CRAIG "C.W." BELL** – bass / **JOHNNY BLITZ** (b. JOHNNY MADANSKY) – drums

— released no singles during their lifespan (Jan-Aug 1975); CHEETAH + BLITZ helped to form The DEAD BOYS

 – compilations, etc. –

Mar 02. (cd) *Glitterhouse; (GRCD 549)* **THE DAY THE EARTH MET THE ... ROCKET FROM THE TOMBS**
 – Raw power / So cold / What love is / Ain't it fun / Transfusion / Life stinks / Muckraker / 30 seconds over Tokyo / Satisfaction / Sonic reducer / Never gonna kill myself again / Final solution / Foggy notion / Amphetamine / Read it and weep / Seventeen / Frustration / Down in flames / Search and destroy.

— (some tracks were initially from 1990 bootleg, 'LIFE STINKS')

Peter PERRETT (see under ⇒ ONLY ONES)

Mark PERRY (see under ⇒ ALTERNATIVE TV)

PiL (see under ⇒ PUBLIC IMAGE LTD.)

PINK FAIRIES

Formed: London, England ... 1966 as The SOCIAL DEVIANTS, by RUSSELL HUNTER, MICK FARREN – vocals, SID BISHOP – guitar, CORD REES – bass and two others. In 1967, they shortened their name to The DEVIANTS, luckily finding a millionaire who put up the cash for an album, 'PTOOF', which sold reasonably well on mail order. With DUNCAN SANDERSON replacing CORD, and the recruitment of a new manager (Canadian, Jamie Mandelkau), they issued a second lp, 'DISPOSABLE', another effort showcasing their heavily percussive prog-rock set. Early in '69, PAUL RUDOLPH replaced BISHOP, their third lp, 'DEVIANTS', being issued by 'Transatlantic'. When FARREN left to go solo in October '69, the new line-up (HUNTER, SANDERSON and RUDOLPH) augmented SHAGRAT member TWINK on his debut 'Polydor' album, 'THINK PINK'. The latter had already initiated the idea of The PINK FAIRIES in Colchester, subsequently teaming up with the aforesaid trio under that name. TWINK had also drummed at various stages with The IN-CROWD (who evolved into TOMORROW), and The PRETTY THINGS. Early in 1971, The PINK FAIRIES unleashed their first official 'Polydor' single, 'THE SNAKE', preceding the hippie celebration of the 'NEVER NEVER LAND' album. Their 1972 follow-up, 'WHAT A BUNCH OF SWEETIES', (recorded without TWINK, who had briefly formed The STARS together with another acid casualty, SYD BARRETT) scraped into the UK Top 50. With numerous personnel changes, they decided to disband in March '74, although many re-incarnations lay ahead (for touring purposes only, mainly with friends HAWKWIND).

Album rating: Deviants: Ptoof! (*5) / DISPOSABLE (*5) / DEVIANTS (*5) / Pink Fairies: NEVER NEVER LAND (*6) / WHAT A BUNCH OF SWEETIES (*6) / KINGS OF OBLIVION (*7) / FLASHBACK: PINK FAIRIES compilation (*7) / KILL 'EM & EAT 'EM (*5) / Deviants: HUMAN GARBAGE (*5)

DEVIANTS

DUNCAN SANDERSON – bass / **SID BISHOP** – guitar, sitar / **MICK FARREN** – vocals, piano / **CORD REES** – bass, guitar / **RUSS HUNTER** – drums

 Underground / not iss.

1967. (lp) *(IMP 1)* **PTOOFF!**
 – Opening / I'm coming home / Child of the sky / Charlie / Nothing man / Garbage / Bun / Deviation street. *(re-iss. May69 on 'Decca' mono/stereo; LK-R/SKL-R 4993) (re-iss. Dec83 on 'Psycho'; PSYCHO 16) (cd-iss. Nov92 on 'Drop Out'; DOCD 1988) (cd re-iss. Sep95 on 'Alive';)*

— **PAUL RUDOLPH** – guitar repl. CORD

 Stable / not iss.

Oct 68. (lp) *(SLE 7001)* **DISPOSABLE**
 – Somewhere to go / Sparrows and wires / Jamie's song / You've got to hold on / Fire in the city / Let's loot the supermarket / Papa-oo-Mao-Mao / Slum lord / Blind Joe McTurk's last session / Normality jam / Guaranteed too dead / Sidney B. Goode / Last man.
Nov 68. (7") *(STA 5601)* **YOU'VE GOT TO HOLD ON. / LET'S LOOT THE SUPERMARKET**

— now a trio of SANDERSON, RUDOLPH + HUNTER when BISHOP left, FARREN went solo and released lp in 1970 'MONA (THE CARNIVEROUS CIRCUS).'

 Transatla. / not iss.

Jan 70. (lp) *(TRA 204)* **THE DEVIANTS**
 – Billy the monster / Broken biscuits / First line / The people suite / Rambling 'B' ask transit blues / Death of dream machine / Play time / Black George does it weith his mouth / Junior narco raiders / People of the city / Metamorphosis exploration. *(re-iss. 1978 on 'Logo'; MOGO 4001) (re-iss. Oct88 on 'Demon'; DEMON 8)*

TWINK

TWINK (b. JOHN ADLER) – drums, vocals (ex-SHAGRAT) (solo, with DEVIANTS)

 Polydor / not iss.

Jan 71. (lp) *(2343 032)* **THINK PINK**
 – Coming of the other side / Ten thousand words in a cardboard box / Dawn of magic / Tiptoe on the highest hill / Fluid / Mexican grass war / Rock an' roll the joint / Suicide / Three little piggies / Sparrow is a sign. *(re-prom.Apr71; same) (re-iss. Nov97 on 'Twink' cd/lp; TWK CD/LP 7) (re-iss. Jul99 on 'Akarma' cd/lp; AK 64 CD/LP)*

PINK FAIRIES

PAUL RUDOLPH – guitar, vocals / **DUNCAN SANDERSON** – bass, vocals / **RUSSELL HUNTER** – drums now with **TWINK**

			Polydor	Polydor
Jan 71.	(7")	*(2058 059)* **THE SNAKE. / DO IT**		-
May 71.	(lp,pink-lp)	*(2383 045)* **NEVER NEVER LAND**		

– Do it / Heavenly man / Say you love me / Wargirl / Never never land / Track one side two / Thor / Teenage rebel / Uncle Harry's last freak-out / The dream is just beginning.

— Trimmed to a trio when TWINK joined STARS, before flitting to Morocco. His spot filled by guest **TREVOR BURTON** – guitar (ex-MOVE)

| Jul 72. | (lp) | *(2383 132)* **WHAT A BUNCH OF SWEETIES** | 48 | |

– Right on, fight on / Portobello shuffle / Marilyn / The pigs of Uranus / a) Walk, don't run, b) Middle run / I went up, I went down / X-ray / I saw her standing there.

— **MICK WAYNE** – guitar, vox (ex-JUNIOR'S EYES) repl. RUDOLPH (to UNCLE DOG)

| Nov 72. | (7") | *(2059 302)* **WELL WELL WELL. / HOLD ON** | | - |

— **LARRY WALLIS** – guitar, vocals (ex-UFO, ex-SHAGRAT, ex-BLODWYN PIG) repl. MICK. (trio now consisted of LARRY, DUNCAN + RUSSELL)

| Jun 73. | (lp) | *(2383 212)* <5537> **KINGS OF OBLIVION** | | |

– City kids / I wish I was a girl / When's the fun begin? / Chromium plating / Raceway / Chambermaid / Street urchin. *(cd-iss. Apr98 on 'Raceway'; RWY 001CD)*

— broke-up Mar74, although DUNCAN, RUSSELL, PAUL, TWINK & LARRY re-formed for one-off reunion gig at The Roundhouse 13th Jul'75. Autumn 1975, they officially re-united w / DUNCAN, RUSSELL & LARRY. When they added (mid'76) **MARTIN STONE** – guitar (ex-CHILI WILLI, ex-MIGHTY BABY, ex-ACTION, etc.) they returned to studio.

			Stiff	not iss.
Sep 76.	(7")	*(BUY 2)* **BETWEEN THE LINES. / SPOILING FOR A FIGHT**		-

— Break-up again, and LARRY went solo in 1977.

TWINK & THE FAIRIES

— solo with ex-PINK FAIRIES (**PAUL RUDOLPH**; who had been recently seen in HAWKWIND, etc. / **DUNCAN + RUSSELL**)

			Chiswick	not iss.
Feb 78.	(12"ep)	*(SWT 26)* **DO IT '77. / PSYCHEDELIC PUNKAROO / ENTER THE DIAMONDS**		-

— Disbanded once again when TWINK moved to Belgium. DUNCAN joined The LIGHTNING RAIDERS.

MICK FARREN

with **TWINK** – drums, percussion, vocals / **SHAGRAT THE VAGRANT** – vocals, percussion / **STEVE HAMMOND** – guitar / **JOHNNY GUSTAFSON** – bass / **PETE ROBINSON** – keyboards

			Transatla.	not iss.
Apr 70.	(lp)	*(TRA 212)* **MONA (THE CARNIVEROUS CIRCUS)**		-

– Mona (a fragrant) / Carniverous circus part 1: The whole thing starts – But Charlie it's still moving – Observe the ravens – Society 4 the horsemen – Summertime blues / Carniverous circus part 2: Don't talk to Mary – You can't move me – In my window box – An epitaph can point the way – Mona (the whole trip). *(re-iss. Mar84 on 'Psycho'; PSYCHO 20)*

			Stiff	not iss.
Nov 77.	(7"ep; MICK FARREN & DEVIANTS)	*(LAST 4)* **SCREWED UP**		-

– Outrageous contagious / Let's loot the supermarket / Screwed up / Shock horror

— now with **WILKO JOHNSON** – guitar / **ALAN POWER** – drums / **ANDY COLQUHOUN** – bass / **WILL STALL** – brass / **CHRISSIE JANE + SONJA KRISTINA** – backing vox.

			Logo	not iss.
1978.	(lp)	*(LOGO 2010)* **VAMPIRES STOLE MY LUNCH MONEY**		-

– Trouble coming every day / Half price drinks / I don't want to go this way / I want a drink / Son of a millionaire / Zombie (live) / Bela Lugosi / People call you crazy / Fast Eddie / Let me in damn you / Self destruction / Drunk in the morning.

| 1978. | (7") | *(GO 321)* **HALF PRICE DRINKS. / I DON'T WANT TO GO THIS WAY** | | - |
| May 79. | (7") | *(GO 345)* **BROKEN STATUE. / IT'S ALL IN THE PICTURE** | | - |

DEVIANTS

— re-formed with **MICK FARREN** – vocals / **LARRY WALLIS + WAYNE KRAMER** – guitar / **DUNCAN SANDERSON** – bass / **GEORGE BUTLER** – drums

			Psycho	not iss.
May 84.	(lp)	*(PSYCHO 25)* **HUMAN GARBAGE** (live at Dingwalls '84)		-

– Outrageous contagious / Broken statue / Ramblin' Rose / Hey thanks / Screwed up / I wanna drink / Takin' LSD / Police car / Trouble coming every day.

– compilations, etc. –

| Sep 92. | (cd) | *Drop Out; (DOCD 1989)* **PARTIAL RECALL** | | - |

– (from DEVIANTS 3 / VAMPIRES / all 'MONA; THE CARNIVOROUS CIRCUS')

| Jun 97. | (cd; MICK FARREN & THE DEVIANTS) | *Captain Trip; (CTCD 046)* **FRAGMENTS OF BROKEN DREAMS** | | - |

MICK FARREN'S TIJUANA BIBLE

			Big Beat	not iss.
Feb 93.	(cd)	*(CDWIK 117)* **GRINGO MADNESS**		-

– Leader hotel / Mark of Zorro / Lone sungularity / Solitaire devil / Spider kissed /

Jezebel / Long walk with the devil / Jumping Jack Flash / Movement of the whores on Revolution Plaza / Hippie death cult / Last night the Alhambra burned down / Eternity is a very long time / Memphis psychosis / Riot in Cell Block #9.

PINK FAIRIES

— re-formed 1987 with **TWINK, LARRY, RUSSELL, ANDY + SANDY** (aka DUNCAN)

			Demon	not iss.
Oct 87.	(lp/cd)	*(FIEND/+CD 105)* **KILL 'EM AND EAT 'EM**		-

– Broken statue / Fear of love / Undercover of confusion / Waiting for the ice cream to melt / Taking LSD / White girls on amphetamine / Seeing double / Fool about you / Bad attitude / I might be lying. *(cd re-iss. May97; VEXCD 16)*

— Once again, they bit the dust, and TWINK joined MAGIC MUSCLE who made live lp in 1989 'ONE HUNDRED MILES BELOW'. TWINK released another solo lp 'MR. RAINBOW' and then 'MAGIC EYE' both in 1990 for 'Woronzow' label. Reformed in the mid-90's, **TWINK** – drums / **PAUL RUDOLPH** – guitar / **MATTHEW BAILEY** – bass / **CHRIS PINKERTON** – drums

			H.T.D.	not iss.
Jan 96.	(cd)	*(HTDCD 46)* **OUT OF THE BLUE AND INTO THE PINK**		-

– Out of the pink / Red house / Going home / Find yourself another fool / Talk to me babe / Oye come va / Youngblood / Steppin' out / Tulsa time / Kansas city / Rambling / Out go the lights: (a) A midnight rambler (excerpt from Stone The Dragon solo), (b) Midnight rambler return.

– compilations, others, etc. –

| Jul 75. | (lp) | *Flashback-Polydor; (2384 071)* **PINK FAIRIES** | | - |

– The snake / City kids / Wargirl / Portobello shuffle / Heavenly man / Do it / pigs of Uranus / Well well well / Chromium plating / I went up, I went down / Say you love me / Street urchin.

| Jun 82. | (m-lp) | *Big Beat; (WIK 14)* **AT THE ROUNDHOUSE** (live July '75) | | - |

– City kids / Waiting for the man / Lucille / Uncle Harry's last freakout / Going down.

| Oct 84. | (m-lp) | *Big Beat; (NED 9)* **PREVIOUSLY UNRELEASED** | | - |

– As long as the price is right / Waiting for the lightning to strike / Can't find a lady / No second chance / Talk of the Devil / I think it's coming back again.

Oct 90.	(cd/c)	*Polydor; (843894-2/-4)* **THE BEST OF THE PINK FAIRIES**		-
Jul 91.	(cd)	*Big Beat; (CDWIK 965)* **LIVE AT THE ROUNDHOUSE / PREVIOUSLY UNRELEASED / TWINK & THE FAIRIES (ep)**		-
Jan 98.	(cd)	*Twink; (TWKCD 8)* **NO PICTURE**		-
Mar 98.	(cd)	*Cleopatra; (<CLP 01882>)* **THE GOLDEN YEARS 1969-1971**		-
Jul 98.	(d-lp)	*Get Back; (GET 514)* **UNCLE HARRY**		-
Nov 98.	(lp/cd)	*Total Energy; (NER 3017/+CD)* **DO IT (live)**		-
May 99.	(lp)	*Get Back; (GET 527)* **LIVE AT THE WEELY FESTIVAL**		-

TWINK

			Twink	not iss.
Mar 86.	(7")	*(TWK 1)* **APOCALIPSTIC. / HE'S CRYING**		-
Jul 86.	(12"ep)	*(TWK 2)* **SPACE LOVER** (Rock'n'roll mix 1 & 2). / ('A'-percussion mix) / ('A'-psychedelic mix) / ('A'instrumental)		-
Jun 87.	(7")	*(TWK 3)* **DRIVING MY CAR. / WAR GIRL**		-
Mar 90.	(lp/cd)	*(TWK LP/CD 1)* **MR. RAINBOW**		-

– Psychedelic punkaroo / Baron Saturday / Teenage rebel / Mr. Rainbow / Seize the time / The snake / Three jolly little dwarfs / Waygirl / Balloon burning / Do it.

| Jun 90. | (7") | *(7TWK 5)* **PSYCHEDELIC PUNKAROO.** | | - |

(12"+=) – (12TWK 5) –

— in 1991, TWINK collaborated with BEVIS FROND on the album 'Magic Eye'

– compilations, etc. –

Jan 98.	(cd/lp)	*Twink; (TWK CD/LP 3)* **ODDS AND BEGINNINGS**		-
Dec 99.	(lp)	*Get Back; (GET 526)* **FROM THE VAULTS**		-
Mar 00.	(d-lp/cd)	*Get Back; (GET 0572 CD/LP)* **THE LOST EXPERIMENTAL RECORDINGS 1970**		-

PLASMATICS

Formed: New York, USA ... 1978 by porn magnate ROD SWENSON, the brains behind this outrageous, shock-hungry post-punk outfit. To front the band he recruited ex-stripper and porn-star WENDY O'WILLIAMS, backing her up with the colourful RITCHIE STOTTS, WES BEECH, STU DEUTSCH and CHOSEI FUNAHARA, the latter subsequently being replaced by JEAN BEAUVOIR. With a string of US-only indie 45's behind them, The PLASMATICS arrived in Britain under a storm of protest, especially from London's GLC who vehemently objected to their much publicised high-octane stage show (blowing up cars and chainsawing the odd instrument a speciality, while WENDY's topless, sometimes bottomless attire further provoked police heavy-handedness!). Appropriately signing to 'Stiff' records, the spiky-nippled O'WILLIAMS and her crew finally unleashed their debut set, 'NEW HOPE FOR THE WRETCHED' amid a sea of hype in 1980. Although lambasted by the critics it nevertheless hit the UK charts, as did the controversial 'BUTCHER BABY' single. WENDY and the band released two further forgettable albums the following year and it was quite surprising 'Capitol' records took up the option to sign them. Now without BEAUVOIR and DEUTSCH (who were replaced by JUNIOR ROMANELLI and T.C. TOLLIVER), they released the heavier 'COUP D'ETAT' (1982), a change in music and image which left them with few fans. This proved to be The PLASMATICS' epitaph, the bondage-loving WENDY going solo, taking her cue from wildman sidekick, LEMMY and releasing three albums in as many years. The last of these, 'MAGGOTS: THE RECORD', came in 1987, both its concept and cover art reaching a nadir in bad taste. She made her final stand for rock'n'roll excess with the aforementioned LEMMY on a version of Tammy Wynette's country standard, 'STAND BY YOUR MAN'. Spookily enough, both WENDY and TAMMY were to die on the same day (6th April '98), O'WILLIAMS taking her own life by shooting herself. • **Songwriters:** BEECH-BEAUVOIR penned most, until the latter's departure; also covered DREAM LOVER (Bobby Darin) / JAILBAIT (Motorhead).

Album rating: NEW HOPE FOR THE WRETCHED (*6) / BEYOND THE VALLEY OF 1984 (*4) / COUP D'ETAT (*5) / Wendy O'Williams: W.O.W. (*5) / KOMMANDER OF CHAOS (*4) / MAGGOTS: THE RECORD (*3) / DEFFEST! AND BADDEST! (*1)

WENDY O'WILLIAMS – vocals, saxophone, electric chain saw / **RITCHIE STOTTS** – lead guitar / **WES BEECH** – rhythm guitar / **JEAN BEAUVOIR** – bass; repl. CHOSEI FUNAHARA / **STU DEUTSCH** – drums

		Vice Squad	P.V.C.
Nov 78.	(7";7"red) <VS 101/102> **BUTCHER BABY. / FAST FOOD SERVICE / CONCRETE SHOES**	-	
Oct 79.	(7"/7"lavender) <VS 103/104> **DREAM LOVER. / CORRUPTION / WANT YOU BABY**	-	
Dec 79.	(12"ep/12"ep;yellow) <VS 105/106> **MEET THE PLASMATICS** – Sometimes I / Won't you? / Want you baby.	-	

		Stiff	Stiff
Jun 80.	(7",7"multi-colrd) <BUY 76> **BUTCHER BABY. / TIGHT BLACK PANTS**	55	-
Jul 80.	(12"ep) (BUYIT 76) **BUTCHER BABY (re-recorded). / LIVING DEAD (live) / SOMETIMES I (FEEL IT WHEN YOU'RE DOWN ON YOUR KNEES)**		
Sep 80.	(7"multi-colrd) (BUY 91) **MONKEY SUIT. / SQUIRM (live)**	-	-
Sep 80.	(lp,multi-colrd-lp) (SEEZ 24) <USE 9> **NEW HOPE FOR THE WRETCHED** – Concrete shoes / Butcher baby / Squirm (live) / Corruption / Want you baby / Dream lover / Won't you / Sometimes I / Tight black pants / Monkey suit / Living dead / Test-tube babies. (cd-iss. Dec92 on 'Dojo'; DOJOCD 79) (re-iss. cd Feb94 on 'Disky'; STIFFCD 16) (cd re-iss. Mar02 on 'Cherry Red'; CDMRED 204)	55	

—— **JOEY REESE** – drums; repl. DEUTSCH

| Nov 81. | (m-lp) <WOW 666> **METAL PRIESTESS** (The 2nd Album) – Lunacy / Doom song / Sex junkie / Black leather monster / 12 noon / Masterplan. | - | |

—— **'JUNIOR' CHRIS ROMANELLI** – bass repl. BEAUVOIR who went solo, after joining LITTLE STEVEN & THE DISCIPLES OF SOUL

| Jun 81. | (lp) (WOW 2) **BEYOND THE VALLEY OF 1984** – Incantation / Masterplan / Headbanger / Sumer nite / Nothing / Fast food service / Hit man / Living dead / Sex junkie / Plasma jam / Pig is a pig. | | |

—— **T.C. TOLLIVER** – drums, percussion; repl. REESE

		Capitol	Capitol
Nov 82.	(lp/c) <(EST/TC-EST 12237)> **COUP D'ETAT** – Put your love in me / Stop / Rock and roll / Counting fairs / No class / Just like on TV / Lightning breaks / Mistress of taboo / Path of glory. (re-iss. 1986 on 'Revolver' lp/c; REV LP/MC 78) (cd-iss. Mar96 on 'Dojo'; DOJOCD 239) (cd re-iss. Oct00 on 'Razor & Tie'; RE 82215-2)		

—— split 1983; WENDY O'WILLIAMS went into heavy metal

PLASTIC BERTRAND

Born: ROGER JORRET, 1958, Belgium. A former musical child prodigy, ROGER went on to drum with New Wave ironists, HUBBLE BUBBLE, who issued a couple of singles and two French lp's for 'Barclay', 'HUBBLE BUBBLE' (1977) and 'FAKING' (1978). Subsequently plucked from Euro obscurity by 'Sire' records, the hyperactive BERTRAND thrilled UK audiences with his Top 10 teen-friendly pogo-punk classic, 'CA PLANE POUR MOI'. Bafflingly, his label declined to grant a UK release for a debut album of the same name, 'Vertigo' taking over his Brit business for a follow-up Top 40 version of The Small Faces' 'SHA LA LA LEE'. By the turn of the decade this colourful character had been sidelined to the more sympathetic markets of Belgium and French-speaking Canada. A more mature BERTRAND recently turned up as a guest on that naughtee leetle TV show, 'Eurotrash', talking about his failed bid for Eurovision glory!

Album rating: CA PLANE POUR MOI (*5)

PLASTIC BERTRAND – vocals / with session people incl. **ELTON MOTELLO**

		Sire	Sire
May 78.	(7") (6078 616) <1020> **CA PLANE POUR MOI. / POGO POGO** (above was released in France 1977 on 'Vogue'; 140.316) (below was released same name as 'AN 1' on 'Vogue'; VO 15008)	8	Apr78
Jun 78.	(lp) <SRK 6061> **CA PLANE POUR MOI** – Le petit toptillard / Bambino / Naif song / Ca plane pour moi / Sha la la lee / Pognon pognon / Dance dance / 5-4-3-2-1 / Pogo pogo / Wha wha (je suis un chien, nous sommes des chiens, vous des chiens) / Solo naif song.	-	

		Vertigo	not iss.
Jul 78.	(7") (6059 209) **SHA LA LA LEE. / NAIF SONG**	39	-
Dec 78.	(7") (6059 215) **C'EST LE ROCK'N'ROLL. / AFFECTION**	-	-

		Sire	Sire
Mar 79.	(7") (SIR 4012) **TOUT PETITE LA PLANETE. / JE FAIT UN PLAN / HIT 78**	-	-

		Vogue	R.K.M.
1979.	(7") (VG 108) **SENTIMENTALE MOI. / OUAIS, OUAIS, OUAIS, OUAIS**	-	- French
1979.	(7") <101.251> **LE MONDE EST MERVEILLEUX. / J'TE FAIS UN PLAN**	-	- French
1979.	(pink-lp) (9250 8508) **J'TE FAIS UN PLAN** – J'te fais un plan / Affection / Telephone, telephone / Super cool / Hit 78 / C'est le rock'n'roll (walk like a man) / Cliche / Tout petit la planete.	-	French
1980.	(7") (101.394) **SANS AMOUR. / PLASTIC BOY**	- not iss.	- French Attic
1980.	(7") <ATF 506> **TELEPHONE A TELEPHONE MON BIJOU. / STOP OU ENCORE**	-	- Canada
1980.	(lp) <LATF 5004> **L'ALBUM** – Telephone a telephone mon bijou (mon rock'n'roll attrappe des cheveaux blancs) / Stop ou encore / Rock'n'roll je te hais / Je t'aime trop danger / Kangourou / Une fille moche / Express ca presse / Chacun son truc / Jeaune et insouciant.	-	- Canada
1981.	(lp) <LATF 5006> **GREATEST HITS** (compilation) – Telephone a telephone mon bijou / Sans amour / Super cool / Les monde est merveilleux / Tout petit la planete / Stop ou encore / Ouais, ouais, ouais, ouais / Intro / Je t'aime trop danger / Telephone a telephone / Ca plane pour moi / Hula hoop / Sentimentale moi / Au bout / Stop or go.	-	- Canada
1982.	(lp) <LATF 5007> **PLASTIQUEZ VON BAFFLES** – Jacques Cousteau / Coeur d'acier / Victime de l'amour / Si ma tete fait ding dong, . . . mon coeur est dingue donc / Le pantin / Shoe bi dou bi . . . baby / Baby doll / Boum dans le coeur / Kili watch / Chewing-gum / Paradis / Hula hoop.	-	- Canada

—— BERTRAND/ROGER retired from recording

– compilations, etc. –

| Apr 02. | (cd) EMI France; (537364-2) **L'ESSENTIEL PLASTIC BERTRAND** | - | - French |

POISON GIRLS

Formed: Brighton, England . . . 1977 by VI SUBVERSA, LANCE D'BOYLE and RICHARD FAMOUS. In her mid-40's by the time of the group's shared debut EP, 'FATAL MICROBES MEET THE POISON GIRLS' – the FATAL MICROBES being a punk band featuring VI's kids! – SUBVERSA was an unlikely but highly articulate and committed hippy-turned-punk frontwoman, guiding the band through more than a decade of anti-establishment, pro-feminist musical activity. The subsequent 'HEX' EP was released on Crass' own label, while the 'GIRLS collaborated with the staunchly anarchist punks themselves on 1980's bludgeoning 'PERSONS UNKNOWN'. The POISON GIRLS also shared their beliefs and lifestyle, choosing to live in a London commune and spending their spare time campaigning against racism and fascism. A full length debut set, 'CHAPPAQUIDDICK BRIDGE' (1980) followed on the band's own 'Xentrix' label and by the release of 'WHERE'S THE PLEASURE' (1982), the group had begun to widen their musical scope and had moved on from their affiliation with CRASS. Following a brief dalliance with the 'Illuminated' label for 1983's 'SEVEN YEAR SCRATCH', the group reactivated 'Xentrix' with their swansong album, 'SONGS OF PRAISE' (1985), the material, at least lyrically, as uncompromising as ever. Although they kept on keeping on until the end of the 80's, The POISON GIRLS last vinyl release was 1986's EP, 'THE PRICE OF GRAIN AND THE PRICE OF BLOOD', railing against injustice to the last. While VI's occasionally cackling vocal style may be something of an acquired taste and the slightly GONG-hippy feel to some tracks may be off-putting, 1995's 4CD box set, 'STATEMENT', provides an interesting overview of the band's career.

Album rating: CHAPPAQUIDDICK BRIDGE (*5) / TOTAL EXPOSURE (*4) / WHERE'S THE PLEASURE (*6) / 7 YEAR SCRATCH compilation (*6) / SONGS OF PRAISE (*4) / STATEMENT – THE COMPLETE RECORDINGS boxed set (*6)

VI SUBVERSA – vocals, guitar / **RICHARD FAMOUS** – guitar, vocals / **LANCE D'BOYLE** – drums / **PETE FENDER** – bass

		Small Wonder	not iss.
Mar 79.	(12"ep) (WEENY 3) **FATAL MICROBES MEET THE POISON GIRLS** – Piano lessons / Closed shop / (2 by FATAL MICROBES).		-

—— **BERNHARDT REBOURS** – bass; repl. FENDER (of FATAL MICROBES)

—— additional vocals **EVE LIBERTINE** – vocals (guest)

| Jul 79. | (12"ep) (WEENY 4) **HEX** – Old tarts song / Crisis / Ideologically unsound / Bremen song / Political love / Jump mama jump / Under the doctor / Reality attack. (re-iss. Apr81 on 'Crass'; 421984-1) | | - |

		Crass	not iss.
May 80.	(7") (421984-1) **PERSONS UNKNOWN. / (other track by CRASS)**		-

—— added guests **GEM STONE** – vocals (ex-KILLJOYS) / **NIL** – violin

Oct 80.	(lp) (421984-2) **CHAPPAQUIDDICK BRIDGE** – Another hero / Hole in the wall (Thisbe's song) / Underbitch / Alienation / Pretty Polly / Good time (I didn't know Sartre played piano) / Other / Daughters and sons.		-
Apr 81.	(7"m) (421984-8) **ALL SYSTEMS GO. / PROMENADE IMMORTELLE / DIRTY WORK**		-
Jun 81.	(7"flexi-free) (421984-10) **PRETTY POLLY. / BULLY BOYS (live)**		-

		Xntrix	not iss.
Oct 81.	(lp) (XN 2003) **TOTAL EXPOSURE (live)** – Persons unknown / Old tart's song / State control / Tension / Bully boys / Another hero bites / Don't go home tonight / S.S. snoopers / Other / Daughters and sons / Alienation / Fucking mother / Dirty work.		-

—— **CHRIS GRACE** + guest **PETE FENDER** – bass repl. REBOURS

| Nov 82. | (lp) (XN 2006) **WHERE'S THE PLEASURE** – Where's the pleasure / Lovers are they worth it / I've done it all before / Whisky voice / Menage abattoir / Take the toys / Soft touch / Take the toys – reprise / Velvet launderette / Rio disco stink / Cry no more / Mandy is having a baby / Fear of freedom. | | - |

—— added **CYNTH ETHICS** – keyboards

		Illuminated	not iss.
Jul 83.	(7") (ILL 23) **ONE GOOD REASON. / CINNAMON GARDEN**		-
Oct 83.	(7") (ILL 25) **ARE YOU HAPPY NOW?. / CREAM DREAM**		-

---- **MARTIN HEATH** – bass; repl. CHRIS

		Xntrix	not iss.
Nov 84.	(7") (XN 2009) **(I'M NOT A) REAL WOMAN. / TAKE THE TOYS FROM THE BOYS**		-
	(12"+=) (12XN 2009) – Perfect crime / Tension.		
Jun 85.	(lp) (XN 2008) **SONGS OF PRAISE**		-

---- **AGENT ORANGE** – drums; repl. D'BOYLE

		Upright	not iss.
Nov 85.	(12"ep) (UPT 12) **THE PRICE OF GRAIN AND THE PRICE OF BLOOD**		-

---- **MAX VOLUME** – bass; repl. HEATH + ETHICS

---- still until split in 1989 after Zagreb concert, but nothing new was released after '86; however, they did a one-off gig in June '95

– compilations, etc. –

Mar 84.	(d-lp) Xntrix; (RM 101) **7 YEAR SCRATCH**		-
Mar 85.	(12"ep) Illuminated; (ILL 33-12) **ARE YOU HAPPY NOW? (remix) / CREAM DREAM. / MENAGE ABATTOIR / WHISKY VOICE**		-
May 95.	(cd) Cooking Vinyl; (<COOKCD 086>) **REAL WOMAN**		Feb97
May 95.	(4xcd-box) Cooking Vinyl; (<COOKCD 087>) **STATEMENT – THE COMPLETE RECORDINGS 1977-1989** (re-iss. Jun00; same)		
Jun 98.	(d-cd) Snapper; (<SMDCD 137>) **POISONOUS**		Sep98
	– Piano lessons / Old tarts song / Idealogically unsound / Jump mama jump / Reality attack / Persons unknown / State control / Promenade immortelle / Underbitch / Pretty Polly / Daughters and sons / Statement / Fuckin' mother / Tender love / Dirty work / Where's the pleasure / Lovers are they worth it / Take the toys / Rio disco stink / Fear of freedom / Cream dream / Offending article / Real women / Rockface / No more lies / The price of grain / Jenny / Girls over there / Cupid / All the way.		

POLICE

Formed: London, England ...early 1977 by drummer STEWART COPELAND, vocalist/bassist STING (b. GORDON SUMNER) and guitarist HENRY PADOVANI. In May '77, this line-up released a debut punk single, 'FALL OUT', for Miles Copeland's (brother of STEWART) indie label, 'Illegal'. Immediately after the record's release, they were invited by GONG member MIKE HOWLETT to join veteran guitarist ANDY SUMMERS in live band, STRONTIUM 90. Following PADOVANI's departure in August of the same year (to form the brilliantly monikered FLYING PADOVANI BROTHERS), SUMMERS took his place in The POLICE, this modified line-up initially sessioning on EBERHARD SCHOENER's 'Video Flashback' album. Like all the best 'punk' bands of the time, The POLICE weren't actually punk at all, the members all coming from some kind of 'muso' background, SUMMERS having noodled for the likes of KEVIN AYERS and KEVIN COYNE while COPELAND had drummed for prog-rock merchants, CURVED AIR and STING had plucked his bass for the jazzy LAST EXIT. Not exactly the best credentials for the 'anyone can play' ethos of punk but The POLICE succeeded by infusing their complex reggae-tinged pop/rock with insidiously catchy hooks and radio friendly melodies while keeping most of their songs down to an acceptable post-hippy playing time. They also cultivated a trendy bleached haired image, sporting their new blonde barnets on a Wrigley's Spearmint Gum TV ad. After supporting SPIRIT of all people, the group signed to 'A&M', releasing their debut single, 'ROXANNE', soon after. Initially, this paean to a lady of the night failed to score a chart position, although it was subsequently released a year later, reaching No.12 in the UK charts. The follow-up, 'CAN'T STAND LOSING YOU', was a minor chart hit as was the debut album, 'OUTLANDOS D'AMOUR' (1978). An impressive collection with a strong rhythmic thrust and a few token nods to punk, the album was finally given its due when it was resurrected the following year, reaching the Top 10 in the Spring of '79. Later that summer The POLICE captured their first No.1 single with the power pop of the 'MESSAGE IN A BOTTLE' single, swiftly followed by a No.1 album in 'REGATTA DE BLANC' (aka WHITE REGGAE; 1979). Again the record illustrated the band's masterful grasp of dynamics, using time changes to enhance rather than detract from the pop appeal of their songs. From the space reggae of 'WALKING ON THE MOON' to the melodic lament of 'THE BED'S TOO BIG WITHOUT YOU', The POLICE were continually charting new musical territory. It was only a matter of time before the group broke through worldwide, including the lucrative American market. That break came with the 'ZENYATTA MONDATTA' (1980) album and its attendant hits, 'DON'T STAND SO CLOSE TO ME' and the lyrically rhythmic genius of 'DE DO DO DO, DE DA DA DA'. By the release of 'GHOSTS IN THE MACHINE' (1981), The POLICE were now a world beating act, once more delivering the goods with a more instrumentally diverse opus best sampled on the exotically effervescent 'EVERY LITTLE THING SHE DOES IS MAGIC'. STING's lyrics were also taking on a new depth, notably on 'INVISIBLE SUN', wherein the singer commented on the strife-torn Northern Ireland. Bearing in mind that STING's songs formed the bulk of the band's output – leading to simmering discontentment in the ranks – it's surprising how well the trio gel on their final release and undisputed masterpiece, 'SYNCHRONICITY' (1983). The brooding atmospherics of 'EVERY BREATH YOU TAKE' (a massive worldwide No.1) formed the album's centrepiece while the melancholy 'WRAPPED AROUND YOUR FINGER' and the pummelling 'SYNCHRONICITY 2' illustrated the band's ability to craft a consistently satisfying but varied musical palate. The aforementioned tensions ultimately led to the band's demise, although an official announcement wasn't made until 1986, the trio working on solo projects in the meantime. Predictably, STING was the only member who went on to any commercial success – massive success in the event – while COPELAND and SUMMERS lingered in relative obscurity. The former had already released a string of 7"s under the KLARK KENT moniker at the turn of the decade as well as scoring the soundtrack for cult film 'Rumblefish' (featuring vocals of ex-WALL OF VOODOO man, STAN RIDGWAY). During the mid-80's, he went on to make an album of African music, 'THE RHYTHMATIST' (1985) for 'A&M' and a one-off 7" with ADAM ANT, 'OUT OF BOUNDS'. More recently, COPELAND has scored various films including 'Talk Radio', 'Wall Street' and 'First Power', going on to form ANIMAL LOGIC with bassist STANLEY CLARKE and vocalist DEBORAH HOLLAND. SUMMERS, meanwhile, continued his collaboration with ROBERT FRIPP (they'd released the 'I ADVANCE MASKED' album in 1982) on 'BEWITCHED' (1984) before going on to release a series of eclectic solo albums.

Album rating: OUTLANDOS D'AMOUR (*8) / REGATTA DE BLANC (*7) / ZENYATTA MONDATTA (*7) / GHOST IN THE MACHINE (*7) / SYNCHRONICITY (*8) / EVERY BREATH YOU TAKE – THE SINGLES compilation (*9) / GREATEST HITS compilation (*9) / LIVE! collection (*4)

STING (b. GORDON SUMNER, 2 Oct'51, Wallsend, England) – vocals, bass (ex-LAST EXIT) / **HENRY PADOVANI** (b. Corsica) – guitar, vocals / **STEWART COPELAND** (b.19 Jul'52, Alexandria, Egypt) – drums, vocals (ex-CURVED AIR)

		Illegal	not iss.
May 77.	(7") (IL 1) **FALL OUT. / NOTHING ACHIEVING** (re-act.Dec79 reached UK No.47)		-

---- **ANDY SUMMERS** (b. ANDREW SOMERS, 31 Dec'42, Blackpool, England) – guitar (ex-KEVIN AYERS, ex-KEVIN COYNE, ex-ERIC BURDON, ex-SOFT MACHINE) soon repl. HENRY (after brief spell as 4-piece) left to form his FLYING PADOVANI BROTHERS

		A&M	A&M
Apr 78.	(7",12") (AMS 7348) **ROXANNE. / PEANUTS** (re-iss. Apr79; same) – hit UK No.12		-
Aug 78.	(7",7"sha-pic-d,7"in most colours) (AMS 7381) **CAN'T STAND LOSING YOU. / DEAD END JOB** (re-iss. Jun79; same) – hit UK No.2	42	-
Oct 78.	(lp/blue-lp/c) (AMLH/AMLN/CAM 68502) <4753> **OUTLANDOS D'AMOUR** – Next to you / So lonely / Roxanne / Hole in my life / Peanuts / Can't stand losing you / Truth hits everybody / Born in the 50's / Be my girl / Sally / Masoko tanga. (resurrected Apr79 made No.6) (cd-iss. Mar89; CDA 68502) (re-iss. Oct92 cd/c; CD/C MID 126)		23 Feb79
Oct 78.	(7") (AMS 7402) **SO LONELY. / NO TIME THIS TIME** (re-dist.Feb80; same) – hit UK No.6		-
Jan 79.	(7") <2096> **ROXANNE. / DEAD END JOB**	-	32
Apr 79.	(7") <2147> **CAN'T STAND LOSING YOU. / NO TIME THIS TIME**	-	
Sep 79.	(7",7"green,7"sha-pic-d) (AMS 7474) <2190> **MESSAGE IN A BOTTLE. / LANDLORD**	1	74 Nov79
Oct 79.	(lp/c) (AMLH/CAM 64792) <4792> **REGATTA DE BLANC** – Message in a bottle / Reggatta de blanc / It's alright for you / Bring on the night / Deathwish / Walking on the Moon / On any other day / The bed's too big without you / Contact / Does everyone stare / No time this time. (cd-iss. Mar89; CDA 64792) (re-iss. Oct92 cd/c; CD/C MID 127)	1	25
Nov 79.	(7"/12") (AMS/+P 7494) **WALKING ON THE MOON. / VISIONS OF THE NIGHT**	1	-
Jan 80.	(7") **BRING ON THE NIGHT. / VISIONS OF THE NIGHT**	-	-
Sep 80.	(7"/7"sha-pic-d) (AMS/+P 7564) **DON'T STAND SO CLOSE TO ME. / FRIENDS**	1	-
Oct 80.	(lp/c) (AMLH/CAM 64831) <4831> **ZENYATTA MONDATTA** – Don't stand so close to me / Driven to tears / When the world is running down, you make the best of what's still around / Canary in a coalmine / Voices in my head / Bombs away / De do do do, de da da da / Behind my camel / Man in a suitcase / Shadows in the rain / The other way of stopping. (cd-iss. Sep86; CDA 64831)	1	5
Oct 80.	(7") <2275> **DE DO DO DO, DE DA DA DA. / FRIENDS**	-	10
Dec 80.	(7"/7"pic-d) (AMS/+P 7578) **DE DO DO DO, DE DA DA. / A SERMON**	5	-
Feb 81.	(7") <2301> **DON'T STAND SO CLOSE TO ME. / A SERMON**	-	10
Sep 81.	(7") (AMS 8164) **INVISIBLE SUN. / SHAMELLE**	2	-
Sep 81.	(7") (AMS 2371) **EVERY LITTLE THING SHE DOES IS MAGIC. / SHAMBELLE**	-	3
Oct 81.	(lp/c) (AMLK/CKM 63730) <3730> **GHOST IN THE MACHINE** – Spirits in the material world / Every little thing she does is magic / Invisible sun / Hungry for love / emolition man / Too much information / Rehumanize yourself / One world (not three) / Omega man / Darkness / Omega man / Secret journey / Darkness. (cd-iss. 1983; CDA 63730)	1	2
Oct 81.	(7"/7"pic-d) (AMS/+P 8174) **EVERY LITTLE THING SHE DOES IS MAGIC. / FLEXIBLE STRATEGIES**	1	-
Dec 81.	(7") (AMS 8194) **SPIRITS IN THE MATERIAL WORLD. / LOW LIFE**	12	-
Jan 82.	(7") <2390> **SPIRITS IN THE MATERIAL WORLD. / FLEXIBLE STRATEGIES**	-	11
Apr 82.	(7") <2408> **SECRET JOURNEY. / DARKNESS**	-	46
May 83.	(7"/7"pic-d) (AM/+SP 117) <2542> **EVERY BREATH YOU TAKE. / MURDER BY NUMBERS** (d7"+=) (AM 117) – Truth hits everybody / Man in a suitcase.	1	1
Jun 83.	(lp/c/cd) (AMLX/CXM/CDA 63735) <3735> **SYNCHRONICITY** – Synchronicity / alking in your footsteps / O my God / Mother / Miss Gradenko / Synchronicity II / Every breath you take / King of pain / Wrapped around your	1	1

	finger / Tea in the sahara. (c+=/cd+=) – Murder by numbers. (re-iss. Mar93 cd/c; CD/C MID 186)		
Jul 83.	(7"/7"pic-d-x3) (AM/+P 127) **WRAPPED AROUND YOUR FINGER. / SOMEONE TO TALK TO** (12"+=/12"pic-d+=) (AMX/+P 127) – Message in a bottle (live) / I burn for you.	7	–
Aug 83.	(7") <2569> **KING OF PAIN. / SOMEONE TO TALK TO**	–	3
Oct 83.	(7") (AM 153) <2571> **SYNCHRONICITY II. / ONCE UPON A DAYDREAM**	17	16
Jan 84.	(7"/12") (AM/+P 176) **KING OF PAIN. / TEA IN THE SAHARA (live)**	17	–
Jan 84.	(7") <2614> **WRAPPED AROUND YOUR FINGER. / TEA IN THE SAHARA (live)**	–	8

Split up although not officially, until 1986. STING, ANDY SUMMERS and STEWART COPELAND

– compilations, etc. –

on 'A&M' unless otherwise mentioned

Jun 80.	(6x7"box) (AMPP 6001) **SIX PACK** – (first 5 – A&M singles re-issued in blue vinyl, plus added 45 below) THE BED'S TOO BIG WITHOUT YOU. / TRUTH HITS EVERYBODY	17	
Sep 86.	(7"/12") (AM/+Y 354) <2879> **DON'T STAND SO CLOSE TO ME '86. / (live version)**	24	46
Nov 86.	(lp/c/cd) (EVERY/EVERC/EVECD 1) <3902> **EVERY BREATH YOU TAKE – THE SINGLES** – Roxanne / Can't stand losing you / Message in a bottle / Walking on the Moon / Don't stand so close to me '86 / De do do do, de da da da / Every little thing she does is magic / Invisible Sun / Spirits in the material world / Every breath you take / King of pain / Wrapped around your finger. (c+=/cd+=) – So lonely. (re-iss. UK Mar92 hit No.31)	1	7
Nov 86.	(7"/12") (AM/+Y 363) **ROXANNE '86. / SYNCHRONICITY II**		
Jan 87.	(7") **WALKING ON THE MOON. / MESSAGE IN A BOTTLE**	–	–
Apr 88.	(3"cd-ep) (AMCD 905) **COMPACT HITS** – Roxanne / Can't stand losing you / Canary in a coalmine / Bed's too big without you.	–	–
Jun 89.	(d-c) (AMC 24103) **REGATTA DE BLANC / SYNCHRONICITY**	–	–
Oct 92.	(cd/c/lp) (540030-2/-4/-1) **THE POLICE: GREATEST HITS** (like above)	10	
Oct 93.	(4xcd-box) <0150> **MESSAGE IN A BOX: THE COMPLETE RECORDINGS**	–	79
May 95.	(7"sha-pic-d/12") (581037-7/-1) **CAN'T STAND LOSING YOU (live). / VOICES IN MY HEAD (mix)** (cd-s+=) (581037-2) – Roxanne live). (d12") (581061-1) – Voices in my head (8 remixes).	27	
May 95.	(d-cd/d-c) (540222-2/-4) <0222> **THE POLICE LIVE!** (live) – Next to you / So lonely / Truth hits everybody / Walking on the Moon / Hole in my life / Fall out / Bring on the night / Message in a bottle / The bed's too big without you / Peanuts / Roxanne / Can't stand losing you / Landlord / Born in the 50's / Be my girl – Sally / Synchronicity I / Synchronicity II / Walking in your footsteps / Message in a bottle / O my God / De do do do, de da da da / Wrapped around your finger / Tea in the Sahara / Spirits in the material world / King of pain / Don't stand so close to me / Every breathe you take / Roxanne / Can't stand losing you / So lonely.	25	86

see also STING (GRD-only) for combined STING & THE POLICE releases

KLARK KENT

pseudonym used by **STEWART COPELAND**

		Kryptone	not iss.
May 78.	(7"green) (KK 1) **DON'T CARE. / THRILLS / OFFICE GIRLS** (re-iss. Jul78 on 'A&M' 7"green; AMS 7376) – hit No.48		–
Nov 78.	(7"green) (KMS 7390) **TOO KOOL TO KALYPSO. / THEME FROM KINETIC RITUAL**		–
		A&M	A&M
May 80.	(7"green) (AMS 7532) **AWAY FROM HOME. / OFFICE TALK**		–
Jul 80.	(10"green-lp) (AMLE 68511) **KLARK KENT** (compilation)		–
Aug 80.	(7"green) (AMS 7554) **RICH IN A DITCH. / GRANDELINQUENT**		

Iggy POP

Born: JAMES JEWEL OSTERBERG, 21 Apr'47, Ypsilanti, Michigan, USA. The son of an English father and American mother, he joined The IGUANAS as a drummer in 1964. They issued a cover of Bo Diddley's 'MONA', which was limited to 1,000 copies sold at gigs. The following year, he became IGGY POP and joined The PRIME MOVERS with bassist RON ASHETON, although they folded, IGGY subsequently moving to Chicago. In 1967, he returned to Michigan and formed The (PSYCHEDELIC) STOOGES with RON and his drummer brother SCOTT. They were soon joined by DAVE ALEXANDER, IGGY making his celluloid debut in the avant-garde film, 'Francois De Moniere' with girlfriend NICO. In 1968, the band gigged constantly, on one occasion IGGY being charged with indecent exposure. The following year, A&R man Danny Fields, while looking to sign MC5, instead signed The STOOGES to 'Elektra', furnishing them with a $25,000 advance. Their eponymous debut (produced by JOHN CALE – another VELVET UNDERGROUND connection), later proved to be way ahead of its time. Tracks such as 'NO FUN', '1969' and 'I WANNA BE YOUR DOG', were howling proto-punk, garage classics, later covered by The SEX PISTOLS, SISTERS OF MERCY and SID VICIOUS! respectively. The album just failed to secure a Top 100 placing, the second album faring even worse commercially, although it was hailed by the more discerning critics of the day as a seminal work. From the primal nihilism of 'DIRT', to the psychedelic kiss-off, 'I FEEL ALRIGHT (1970)', it seemed, to The STOOGES at least, as if flower-power had never happened. They were subsequently dropped by their label, following drug-related problems and dissension in the ranks. IGGY moved to Florida, becoming a greenkeeper while taking up golf more seriously, a healthier pastime than his penchant for self-mutilation. In 1972, he had a chance meeting with DAVID BOWIE and manager TONY DeFRIES, who persuaded IGGY to reform his STOOGES and sign a MainMan management deal, this in turn leading to a 'C.B.S.' contract. After his/their flawed classic, 'RAW POWER' (not one of BOWIE's best productions), they folded again, citing drugs as the cause. It was, however, even more of an embryonic punk record, the amphetamine rush of 'SEARCH AND DESTROY' highly influential on the "blank generation" that would trade-in their STEELY DAN albums for anything with two chords and a sneering vocal. In 1975, IGGY checked in to a psychiatric institute, weaning himself off heroin. His only true friend, BOWIE, who regularly visited him in hospital, invited him to appear on his 'LOW' album. He signed to 'R.C.A.' (home of BOWIE) in 1977, issuing the BOWIE-produced debut solo album, 'THE IDIOT', which, due to the recent "new wave" explosion, broke him into the UK Top 30 and US Top 75. It contained the first BOWIE/POP collaboration, 'CHINA GIRL', later a smash hit for BOWIE. His second solo release, 'LUST FOR LIFE' (also produced by BOWIE in '77), was another gem, again deservedly reaching the UK Top 30 (the title track was later resurrected in 1996 after appearing on the soundtrack to the cult Scottish movie, 'Trainspotting'). In 1979, IGGY moved to 'Arista' records, shifting through various infamous personnel, although his commercial appeal was on the wane. The first half of the 80's saw IGGY desperately trying to carve out a successful solo career while combating his continuing drug problems. Albums such as, 'SOLDIER' (1980), 'PARTY' (1981) and 'ZOMBIE BIRDHOUSE' (1982) marking the nadir of POP's chequered career. Finally teaming up again with BOWIE for 1986's 'BLAH BLAH BLAH', the proclaimed "Godfather Of Punk" at last gained some belated recognition, his revival of a 1957 Johnny O'Keefe hit, 'REAL WILD CHILD', giving IGGY his first Top 10 hit (UK). Still with 'A&M' records and adding ex-SEX PISTOLS guitarist STEVE JONES, he consolidated his recovery with 'INSTINCT' (1988). His new lease of life prompted 'Virgin America' to give IGGY (who had recently taking up acting) a new contract, the 1990 set, 'BRICK BY BRICK' featuring the GN'R talents of SLASH and DUFF McKAGAN. To end the year, IGGY showed his caring side by duetting with former punkette, DEBORAH HARRY, on AIDS benefit single, 'WELL DID YOU EVAH!' (a bigger hit for NANCY Sinatra & LEE Hazlewood in 1971). He resurfaced once again in 1993 with 'AMERICAN CAESAR', a full-length set which contained some of his raunchiest tracks for some time, including 'WILD AMERICA', 'F***** ALONE' and Richard Berry's 'LOUIE LOUIE'. Busying himself with more film work, he eventually broke his recording silence with an umpteenth album, 'NAUGHTY LITTLE DOGGIE' (1996). Mr. POP was back on song in the Autumn of '99, the album 'AVENUE B' delivering his usual raw power with all the finesse of a man taking a motorcycle ride to Hell. 'NAZI GIRLFRIEND', 'LONG DISTANCE' and even a cover of Johnny Kidd's 'SHAKIN' ALL OVER', all testament to a guy not yet ready to get out his pipe and slippers. Seeing as he's only ever enjoyed fleeting run-ins with the pop charts, it probably didn't bother the IG one iota that 'BEAT 'EM UP' (2001) didn't come within sniffing distance of the Top 40. Still, he's always got plenty of other subjects to rail against and his latest record is no exception. Apart from anything else, 'BEAT 'EM UP' should surely scoop the most gratuitously tasteless sleeve of the year award. • **IGGY covered;** SOMETHING WILD (John Hiatt) / LIVIN' ON THE EDGE OF THE NIGHT (Rifkin / Rackin) / SEX MACHINE (James Brown). • **Trivia:** In 1987, IGGY made a cameo appearance in the film, 'The Color Of Money'. In 1990, his film & TV work included, 'Cry Baby', 'Shannon's Deal', Tales From The Crypt' & 'Miami Vice'. In 1991, he starred in the opera! 'The Manson Family' and five years later, 'The Crow'.

Album rating: Stooges: THE STOOGES (*8) / FUN HOUSE (*10) / RAW POWER as Iggy & the Stooges (*7) / METALLIC K.O. (*5) / Iggy Pop: THE IDIOT (*9) / LUST FOR LIFE (*9) / TV EYE (*3) / NEW VALUES (*5) / SOLDIER (*5) / PARTY (*4) / ZOMBIE BIRDHOUSE (*4) / BLAH-BLAH-BLAH (*6) / INSTINCT (*5) / BRICK BY BRICK (*7) / AMERICAN CAESAR (*6) / NAUGHTY LITTLE DOGGIE (*5) / NUDE & RUDE: THE BEST OF IGGY POP compilation (*8) / AVENUE B (*7) / BEAT 'EM UP (*5)

STOOGES

IGGY POP – vocals / **RON ASHETON** (b. RONALD RANKLIN ASHETON JR., 17 Jul'48, Washington, D.C.) – guitar / **DAVE ALEXANDER** (b. DAVID MICHAEL ALEXANDER, 3 Jun'47, Ann Arbor) – bass / **SCOTT ASHETON** (b. SCOTT RANDOLPH ASHETON, 16 Aug'49, Washington) – drums

		Elektra	Elektra
Sep 69.	(lp) <(EKS 74051)> **THE STOOGES** – 1969 / I wanna be your dog / We will fall / No fun / Real cool time / Ann / Not right / Little doll. (re-iss. Mar77; K 42032) <US cd-iss. 1988; 74051-2> (cd-iss. Nov93; 7559 60667-2).		Aug69
Oct 69.	(7") <EK 45664> **I WANNA BE YOUR DOG. / 1969**	–	

added guests **STEVE MACKAY** – saxophone / **BILL CHEATHAM** – 2nd guitar

Dec 70.	(lp) <(EKS 74071)> **FUN HOUSE** – Down on the street / Loose / T.V. eye / Dirt / I feel alright (1970) / Fun house / L.A. blues. (re-iss. Mar77; K 42051) <US cd-iss. 1988; 74071-2> (cd-iss. Nov93; 7559 60669-2).		
Dec 70.	(7") <EKM 45695> **I FEEL ALRIGHT (1970). / DOWN ON THE STREET**	–	

broke-up in 1972. **IGGY** re-formed the group with **SCOTT** and **RON** (now bass)

Iggy POP (cont)   THE GREAT INDIE DISCOGRAPHY   The 1970s

IGGY AND THE STOOGES

JAMES WILLIAMSON – guitar repl. DAVE (died 10 Feb'75)

		C.B.S.	Columbia
Jun 73.	(lp) (CBS 65586) <KC 32111> **RAW POWER**		May73

– Search and destroy / Gimme danger / Hard to beat * / Penetration / Raw power / I need somebody / Shake appeal / Death trip. (re-iss. May77 on 'CBS-Embassy'; 31464), hit UK No.44, *track repl. by – Your pretty face is going to Hell. (re-iss. Nov81; CBS 32081) <US cd-iss. 1988 on 'Columbia'; > (UK re-iss. May89 on 'Essential' cd/c/lp; ESS CD/MC/LP 005) (cd-iss. all tracks) (re-iss. May94 & Apr97 on 'Columbia' cd/c; 485176-2/-4) (lp re-iss. Jul98 on 'Simply Vinyl'; SVLP 33)

Jun 73. (7") <45877> **SEARCH AND DESTROY. / PENETRATION**

— added **SCOTT THURSTON** – keyboards (on last 1974 tour, before disbanding) The ASHETONS formed The NEW ORDER (US version), with RON moving on to DESTROY ALL MONSTERS who had three 45's for UK label 'Cherry Red' in the late 70's.

– compilations, others, etc. –

1977. (white-d-lp) Visa; <IMP 1015> **METALLIC K.O.**
– Raw power / Head on / Gimme danger / Rich bitch / Cock in my pocket / Louie Louie. (originally issued 1976 on French 'Skydog'; SGIS 008) (re-iss. May88 as 'METALLIC KO x 2' on 'Skydog' lp/cd; 62232-1/2) (cd-iss. Sep94; same) (re-iss. Sep96 & May98 on 'Dressed To Kill'; DTKLP 001)

1977. (7"ep) Bomp; <EP 113> **I'M SICK OF YOU**
– I'm sick of you / Tight pants / Scene of the crime.

1977. (7"ep; by IGGY POP & JAMES WILLIAMSON) Bomp; <EP 114> **JESUS LOVES THE STOOGES**
– Jesus loves the Stooges / Consolation prizes / Johanna. (re-iss. 10"ep.Nov94;)

1977. (7") Siamese; <PM 001> **I GOT A RIGHT. / GIMME SOME SKIN**
(UK-iss.Dec95 on 'Bomp'; REVENGE 2)

Feb 78. (lp,green-lp; as IGGY POP with JAMES WILLIAMSON) Radar; (RAD 2) / Bomp; <BLP 4001> **KILL CITY**   Nov77
– Sell your love / Kill city / I got nothin' / Beyond the law / Johanna / Night theme / Night theme reprise / Master charge / No sense of crime / Lucky monkeys / Consolation prizes. (re-iss. ! on 'Elektra';) (cd-iss. Feb89 on 'Line'; LICD 9.00131) (cd-iss. Jan93;) (re-iss. 10"lp Feb95 on 'Bomp'; BLP 4042-10) (cd-iss. ; BCD 4042)

Apr 78. (7") Radar; (ADA 4) **KILL CITY / I GOT NOTHIN'**
1978. (7"ep) Skydog; (SGIS 12) **(I GOT) NOTHING**   France
– I got nothing / Gimme danger / Heavy liquid.

Aug 80. (lp/c) Elektra; (K/K4 52234) <EF 7095> **NO FUN** (1969-70 best of THE STOOGES)

1983. (lp) Invasion; <E 1019> **I GOT A RIGHT**
1987. (lp) Revenge; (MIG 2) **I GOT A RIGHT**   France
1987. (7") Revenge; (SS 1) **I GOT A RIGHT. / NO SENSE OF CRIME**   France
1987. (7") Revenge; (BF 50) **KILL CITY. / I'M SICK OF YOU**   France
Dec 87. (lp) Fan Club; (FC 037) **RUBBER LEGS**   France
– Rubber legs / Open up and bleed / Johanna / Cock in my pocket / Head on the curb / Cry for me. (free 7") – GIMME DANGER (live). / I NEED SOMEBODY (live) (cd-iss. Apr97 on 'Last Call'; 422248)

1988. (cd-ep) Revenge; (CAX 1) **PURE LUST**   France
– I got a right / Johanna / Gimme some skin / I got nothing.
1988. (cd-ep) Revenge; (CAX 2) **RAW POWER**   France
– Raw power / Head on the curb / Purple haze / Waiting for the man.
1988. (12"pink-ep,cd-ep) Revenge; (CAX 3) **GIMME DANGER**   France
– Gimme danger / Open up and bleed / Heavy liquid / I got nothing / Dynamite boogie.
1988. (7") Revenge; (SS 6) **JOHANNA. / PURPLE HAZE**   France
Sep 88. (pic-lp; as IGGY & THE STOOGES) Revenge; (LPMIG 6) **DEATH TRIP**   France
May 88. (cd; as IGGY & THE STOOGES) Revenge; (HTM 16) **OPEN UP AND BLEED**   France
(re-iss. Feb96 on 'Bomp' cd/lp; BCD/BLP 4051) (cd re-iss. Jul96; 890016)
Dec 88. (lp; as IGGY & THE STOOGES) Revenge; (MIG 7) **LIVE AT THE WHISKEY A GO-GO**
(cd-iss. Nov94 & Feb97; 895104F)
Dec 88. (lp; as IGGY & THE STOOGES) Electric; (190069) **RAW STOOGES VOL.1**   German
Dec 88. (lp; as IGGY & THE STOOGES) Electric; (190070) **RAW STOOGES VOL.2**   German
May 92. (cd) Line; (LICD 921175) **I'M SICK OF YOU / KILL CITY**
Jun 94. (cd; IGGY & THE STOOGES) New Rose; (890028) **MY GIRL HATES MY HEROIN**
(re-iss. Feb97 on 'Wrote Music'; 7890028) (re-iss. Sep97 on 'Revenge'; MIG 28)
Jul 94. (cd; IGGY & THE STOOGES) New Rose; (642100) **NIGHT OF DESTRUCTION**
(re-iss. as 6xcd-s-box on 'Wind'; WM 375)
Jul 94. (cd; IGGY & THE STOOGES) New Rose; (642042) **TILL THE END OF THE NIGHT**
(re-iss. Apr97; same) (re-iss. Sep97 on 'Revenge'; MIG 42)
Sep 94. (cd; IGGY & THE STOOGES) New Rose; (642011) **LIVE 1971 & EARLY LIVE RARITIES** (live)
(re-iss. Apr97; same)
Sep 94. (cd; IGGY & THE STOOGES) New Rose; (895002) **RAW MIXES VOL.1**
Sep 94. (cd; IGGY & THE STOOGES) New Rose; (895003) **RAW MIXES VOL.2**
Sep 94. (cd; IGGY & THE STOOGES) New Rose; (895004) **RAW MIXES VOL.3**
Feb 95. (10"lp/cd) Bomp; (BLP/BCD 4049) **ROUGH POWER**
— Also in France; THE STOOGES(12"ep) / **SHE CREATURES OF HOLLYWOOD HILLS**
Jul 96. (cd) Revenge; (642050) **WILD ANIMAL** (live 1977)
Jul 96. (cd) Revenge; (893334) **PARIS HIPPODROME 1977** (live)
Jul 96. (cd; as IGGY & THE STOOGES) Trident; (PILOT 008) **YOUR PRETTY FACE IS GOING TO HELL**
Mar 97. (cd; IGGY & THE STOOGES) Bomp; (BCD 4063) **YEAR OF THE IGUANA**

Apr 97. (cd; STOOGES) Arcade; (301563-2) **THE COMPLETE RAW MIXES**
Sep 97. (cd/lp; IGGY & THE STOOGES) Bomp; (BCD/BLP 4069) **CALIFORNIA BLEEDING**
Nov 97. (cd) King Biscuit; (88203) **KING BISCUIT FLOWER HOUR**
Mar 98. (cd) Snapper; (SMMCD 528) **LIVE IN L.A. 1973** (live)
Apr 98. (cd) King Biscuit; (KBFHCD 001) **KING BISCUIT PRESENTS . . .**
May 88. (12"ep; IGGY & THE STOOGES) Revenge; (CAX 8MAXI) **I GOT NOTHING. / SEARCH AND DESTROY / COCK IN MY POCKET**
Jun 98. (lp; IGGY & THE STOOGES) Get Back; (GET 33LP) **RUBBER**
Nov 99. (7"pic-d; as IGGY & THE STOOGES) Munster; (MR 7125) **I GOT NOTHING. /**

IGGY POP

— had already gone solo, augmented by **DAVID BOWIE** – producer, keyboards / **RICKY GARDINER** – guitar / **TONY SALES** – bass / **HUNT SALES** – drums (latter 2; ex-TODD RUNDGREN) / guest **CARLOS ALOMAR** – guitar

		R.C.A.	R.C.A.
Feb 77.	(7") <10989> **SISTER MIDNIGHT. / BABY**	-	72
Mar 77.	(lp/c) (PL/PK 12275) <2275> **THE IDIOT**	30	

– Sister midnight / Nightclubbing / Fun time / Baby / China girl / Dum dum boys / Tiny girls / Mass production. (re-iss. Apr90 on 'Virgin' lp/c/cd; OVED/OVEDC/CDOVD 277)

May 77. (7") (PB 9093) **CHINA GIRL. / BABY**

— **STACEY HEYDON** – guitar / **SCOTT THURSTON** – keyboards repl. BOWIE + ALOMAR

Sep 77. (lp/c) (PL/PK 12488) <2488> **LUST FOR LIFE**   28
– Lust for life / Sixteen / Some weird sin / The passenger / Tonight / Success / Turn blue / Neighbourhood threat / Fall in love with me. (re-iss. 1984 lp/c; NL/NK 82488) (re-iss. Apr90 on 'Virgin' lp/c/cd; OVED/OVEDC/CDOVD 278) (lp re-iss. Nov97 on 'Virgin'; LPCENT 40)

Oct 77. (7") (PB 9160) **SUCCESS. / THE PASSENGER**

— **IGGY** retained **THURSTON**, and recruited **SCOTT ASHETON** – drums / **FRED 'SONIC' SMITH** – guitar (ex-MC5) / **GARY RAMUSSEN** – bass (The SALES brothers later to BOWIE's TIN MACHINE)

Apr 78. (7") (PB 9213) **I GOT A RIGHT** (live). / **SIXTEEN** (live)
May 78. (lp/c) (PL/PK 12796) **TV EYE** (live 1977)
– T.V. eye / Funtime / Sixteen / I got a right / Lust for life / Dirt / Nightclubbing / I wanna be your dog. (cd-iss. Jul94 on 'Virgin'; CDOVD 448)

— **IGGY / THURSTON** now with **JAMES WILLIAMSON** – guitar, producer / **JACKIE CLARKE** – bass (ex-IKE & TINA TURNER) / **KLAUS KREUGER** – drums (ex-TANGERINE DREAM) / **JOHN HORDEN** – saxophone

		Arista	Arista
Apr 79.	(lp/c) (SPART/TC-SPART 1092) <4237> **NEW VALUES**	60	

– Tell me a story / New values / Girls / I'm bored / Don't look down / The endless sea / Five foot one / How do ya fix a broken part / Angel / Curiosity / African man / Billy is a runaway. (re-iss. Mar87; 1201144) (cd-iss. Oct90 cd/lp; 260/210 997)

May 79. (7") (ARIST 255) <0438> **I'M BORED. / AFRICAN MAN**
Jul 79. (7"/7"pic-d) (ARIP/+D 274) **FIVE FOOT ONE. / PRETTY FLAMINGO**

— **IGGY / KREUGER** recruited **IVAN KRAL** – guitar (ex-PATTI SMITH) / **PAT MORAN** – guitar / **GLEN MATLOCK** – bass (ex-SEX PISTOLS, ex-RICH KIDS) / **BARRY ANDREWS** – keyboards (ex-XTC, ex-LEAGUE OF GENTLEMEN) (THURSTON formed The MOTELS)

Jan 80. (lp/c) (SPART/TC-SPART 1117) <4259> **SOLDIER**   62
– Knockin' 'em down (in the city) / I'm a conservative / I snub you / Get up and get out / Ambition / Take care of me / I need more / Loco mosquito / Mr. Dynamite / Play it safe / Dog food. <US cd-iss. Oct87; 201160> (re-iss. Apr91; 251 160)

Jan 80. (7") (ARIST 327) **LOCO MOSQUITO. / TAKE CARE OF ME**

— **IGGY / KRAL** now with **ROB DuPREY** – guitar / **MICHAEL PAGE** – bass / **DOUGLAS BROWNE** – drums (BARRY ANDREWS formed SHRIEKBACK)

May 81. (7") (ARIST 407) **BANG BANG. / SEA OF LOVE**
Jun 81. (lp/c) (SPART/TC-SPART 1158) <9572> **PARTY**
– Pleasure / Rock and roll party / Eggs on plate / Sincerity / Houston is hot tonight / Pumpin' for Jill / Happy man / Bang bang / Sea of love / Time won't let me. (re-iss. Jan87 lp/c; 203/403 806) (cd-iss. Sep89 on 'R.C.A.'; 253 806)

— **IGGY / DuPREY** found new people **CHRIS STEIN** – guitar, producer (ex-BLONDIE) / **CLEM BURKE** – drums (ex-BLONDIE)

		Animal-Chrysalis	Animal
Aug 82.	(7") (CHFLY 2634) **RUN LIKE A VILLAIN. / PLATONIC**		
Sep 82.	(lp/c) (CHR/ZCHR 1399) <APE 6000> **ZOMBIE BIRDHOUSE**		

– Run like a villain / The villagers / Angry hills / Life of work / The ballad of Cookie McBride / Ordinary bummer / Eat to be eaten / Bulldozer / Platonic / The horse song / Watching the news / Street crazies.

— In 1984, he sang the title song on Alex Cox's movie 'REPO MAN'. For the same director, he appeared in the 1985 film 'SID & NANCY' about SID VICIOUS.

— **IGGY** now with **ERDAL KIZILCAY** – drums, bass, synthesizers / **KEVIN ARMSTRONG** – guitar / **BOWIE + STEVE JONES** (guest writers)

		A&M	A&M
Sep 86.	(7"/12") (AM/+Y 358) <2874> **CRY FOR LOVE. / WINNERS & LOSERS**		
Oct 86.	(lp/c/cd) <(AMA/AMC/CDA 5145)> **BLAH-BLAH-BLAH**	43	75

– Real wild child (wild one) / Baby, it can't fail / Shades / Fire girl / Isolation / Cry for love / Blah-blah-blah / Hideaway / Winners and losers / Little Miss Emperor. (cd re-iss. 1989; 395 145-2) (re-iss. Jun91 cd/c; CD/C+/MID 159)

Nov 86. (7"/12") (AM/+Y 368) <2909> **REAL WILD CHILD (WILD ONE). / LITTLE MISS EMPEROR**   10
Feb 87. (7") (AM 374) **SHADES. / BABY IT CAN'T FAIL**
(12"+=) (AMY 374) – Cry for love.
Apr 87. (7"/12") (AM/+Y 392) **FIRE GIRL. / BLAH-BLAH-BLAH** (live)

119

Iggy POP (cont) — THE GREAT INDIE DISCOGRAPHY — The 1970s

Jun 87. (7") (AM 397) **ISOLATION. / HIDEAWAY**
(12"+=) (AMY 397) – Fire girl (remix).

—— IGGY now with **STEVE JONES** – guitar / **PAUL GARRISTO** – drums (ex-PSYCHEDELIC FURS) / **SEAMUS BEAGHEN** – keyboards / **LEIGH FOXX** – bass

Jul 88. (lp/c/cd) <(AMA/AMC/ADA 5198)> **INSTINCT** — 61
– Cold metal / High on you / Strong girl / Tom tom / Easy rider / Power & freedom / Lowdown / Tuff baby / Squarehead.

Aug 88. (7") (AM 452) **COLD METAL. / INSTINCT**
(12"+=/12"pic-d+=) (AM Y/P 452) – Tuff baby.

Nov 88. (7") (AM 475) **HIGH ON YOU. / SQUAREHEAD**
(12"+=) (AMY 475) – Tuff baby (remix).

—— **ALVIN GIBBS** – guitar (ex-UK SUBS) repl. STEVE JONES (continued solo) / **ANDY McCOY** – bass (ex-HANOI ROCKS) repl. FOXX (to DEBORAH HARRY)

Nov 88. (lp/c/cd) **LIVE AT THE CHANNEL** (live 17.9.88)
– Instinct / Kill city / 1969 / Penetration / Power & freedom / Your pretty face / High on you / 5 foot 1 / Johanna / Easy rider / Tuff baby / 1970 / Search & destroy / Squarehead / No fun / I wanna be your dog. (UK-iss.May94 on 'New Rose'; 642005) (re-iss. cd Sep97 on 'Revenge'; MIG 40-41)

—— now with **SLASH** – guitar / **DUFF McKAGAN** – bass (both of GUNS N' ROSES) / **KENNY ARONOFF** – drums

                        Virgin   Virgin America

Jan 90. (7"/c-s) (VUS/+C 18) <VSC 1228> **LIVIN' ON THE EDGE OF THE NIGHT. / THE PASSENGER** — 51
(12"+=/12"pic-d+=/cd-s+=) (VUS T/TE/CD 18) – Nightclubbing / China girl.

Jun 90. (7"/c-s) (VUS/+C 22) **HOME. / LUST FOR LIFE**
(12"+=/cd-s+=) (VUS T/CD 22) – Pussy power / Funtime.

Jul 90. (cd/c/lp) (CDVUS/VUSMC/VUSLP 19) <91381> **BRICK BY BRICK** — 50   90
– Home / Main street eyes / I won't crap out / Candy / Butt town / The undefeated / Moonlight lady / Something wild / Neon forest / Stormy night / Pussy power / My baby wants to rock & roll / Brick by brick / Livin' on the edge of the night. (c re-iss. Apr92; OVEDC 426)
(below 'A'side featured **KATE PIERSON** – vox of B-52's)

Oct 90. (7"/c-s) (VUS/+C 29) <98900> **CANDY. / PUSSY POWER** (acoustic demo) — 67   28
(10"+=/cd-s+=) (VUS 29) – My baby wants to rock'n'roll (acoustic demos).
(12"/cd-s) (VUS T/CD 29) – ('A'side) / The undefeated / Butt town (acoustic demo).

—— Oct 90, IGGY duetted with DEBORAH HARRY on UK Top 50 single 'DID YOU EVAH'; Chrysalis; CHS 3646)

—— with **LARRY MULLEN** (U2) – drums, percussion / **HAL CRAGIN** – bass / **ERIC SCHERMERHORN** – guitar plus guests **MALCOLM BURN** – guitars, etc

Aug 93. (7"ep/c-ep/12"ep/cd-ep) (VUS/+C/T/CD 74) **THE WILD AMERICA EP** — 63
– Wild America / Credit card / Come back tomorrow / My angel.

Sep 93. (cd/c/d-lp) (CDVUS/VUSMC/VUSLP 64) <39002> **AMERICAN CAESAR** — 43
– Character / Wild America / Mixin' the colors / Jealousy / Hate / It's our love / Plastic & concrete / F***in' alone / Highway song / Beside you / Sickness / Boogie boy / Perforation / Problems / Social life / Louie Louie / Caesar / Girls of N.Y

May 94. (10"ep) (VUS A/C 77) **BESIDE YOU / EVIL CALIFORNIA. / HOME** (live) **/ FUCKIN' ALONE** — 47
(cd-ep) (VUSCD 77) – ('A'side) / Les amants / Louie Louie (live) / ('A'acoustic).

Feb 96. (cd/c/lp) (CDVUS/VUSMC/VUSLP 102) <41327> **NAUGHTY LITTLE DOGGIE**
– I wanna live / Pussy walk / Innocent world / Knucklehead / To belong / Keep on believing / Outta my head / Shoeshine girl / Heart is saved / Look away.

Sep 99. (cd) (CDVUS 163) <48216> **AVENUE B**
– No shit / Nazi girlfriend / Avenue B / Miss Argentina / Afraid to get close / Shakin' all over / Long distance / Corruption / She called me daddy / I felt the luxury / Espanol / Motorcycle / Facade.

Oct 99. (7") (VUS 155) **CORRUPTION. / ROCK STAR GRAVE**
(cd-s+=) (VUSCD 155) – Hollywood affair.

Jun 01. (cd) (CDVUS 200) <10574> **BEAT 'EM UP**   Jul01
– Mask / L.O.S.T. / Howl / Football / Saviour / Beat 'em up / Talking snake / The jerk / Death is certain / Go for the throat / Weasels / Drink new blood / It's all shit / Ugliness / V.I.P.

– compilations, etc. –

May 82. (7") RCA Gold; (GOLD 549) **THE PASSENGER. / NIGHTCLUBBING**

Sep 84. (lp/c) R.C.A.; (PL/PK 84597) **CHOICE CUTS**

Apr 88. (cd-ep) A&M; (AMCD 909) **COMPACT HITS**
– Real wild child (the wild one) / Isolation / Cry for love / Shades.

Jan 92. (cd) Arista; (262 178) **POP SONGS**

Jan 93. (3xcd-box) Virgin; (TPAK 21) **LUST FOR LIFE / THE IDIOT / BRICK BY BRICK**

Jun 93. (cd) Revenge; (642044) **LIVE NYC RITZ '86** (live)

Aug 93. (cd/c) Revenge; (642/644 050) **SUCK ON THIS!**

Aug 95. (cd) Skydog; **WE ARE NOT TALKING ABOUT COMMERCIAL SHIT**

Aug 95. (cd) Skydog; **WAKE UP SUCKERS**

Aug 96. (cd) M.C.A.; (MCD 84021) **THE BEST OF IGGY POP LIVE** (live)

Sep 96. (cd) Camden RCA; (74321 41503-2) **POP MUSIC**

Oct 96. (cd/c/d-lp) Virgin; (CDVUS/VUSMC/VUSLP 115) <42351> **NUDE & RUDE: THE BEST OF IGGY POP**
– I wanna be your dog / No fun / Search & destroy / Gimme danger / I'm sick of you / Funtime / Nightclubbing / China girl / Lust for life / The passenger / Kill city / Real wild child / Cry for love / Cold metal / Candy / Home / Wild America.

Nov 96. (7"colrd/c-s) Virgin; (VUS/+C 116) **LUST FOR LIFE / (GET UP I FEEL LIKE BEING A) SEX MACHINE** — 26
(cd-s+=) (VUSCD 116) – ('A'live) / I wanna be your dog (live).

Dec 96. (cd) The Network; (3D 013) **IGGY POP**

Apr 97. (cd) Wotre; (642007) **LIVE IN BERLIN '91**

Sep 97. (d-cd) Snapper; (SMDCD 142) **HEAD ON**

Nov 97. (cd) Other People's Music; (OPM 2116CD) **HEROIN HATES YOU**

Nov 97. (cd) Eagle; (EABCD 011) **THE MASTERS**

Feb 98. (c-s) Virgin; (VSC 1689) **THE PASSENGER / LUST FOR LIFE** — 22
(12"+=/cd-s+=) (VS T/CDT 1689) – Nightclubbing.

Aug 98. (cd) A&M; (540943-2) **BLAH BLAH BLAH / INSTINCT**

POP GROUP

Formed: Bristol, England ... 1978 by MARK STEWART, JON WADDINGTON, DAVID WRIGHT, SEAN OLIVER and BRUCE SMITH. Inspired by punk's nihilistic energy and influenced by everyone from ROLAND KIRK to CAN and LEE PERRY, The POP GROUP harnessed their competing forces into a funky but defiant howl of rage at newly elected Prime Minister, Margaret Thatcher, with 1979's debut single, 'SHE IS BEYOND GOOD AND EVIL'. Issued on Jake Riviera's newly established 'Radar' label, the track was hailed as one of the most innovative releases of the post-punk era. With OLIVER and WRIGHT subsequently replaced by SIMON UNDERWOOD and GARETH SAGER – the latter introducing screeching free-jazz sax into the equation – The POP GROUP recorded a landmark debut album, 'Y' (1979). Produced by reggae veteran DENNIS BOVELL, the record presaged the primal intensity of The BIRTHDAY PARTY with spontaneous layers of visceral noise, militant lyrics and tortured vocals underpinned by CHIC-style basslines and dub dynamics. NICK CAVE, for one, was irrevocably changed after witnessing The POP GROUP in full flight, confessing (early 1999) on Channel 4 that the seminal 'WE ARE ALL PROSTITUTES' was among the most "violent, paranoid" music he'd ever heard. Essential ingredients for decent rock'n'roll of course, the band's first single for 'Rough Trade' offering it up in spades. A second album, 'FOR HOW MUCH LONGER DO WE TOLERATE MASS MURDER' (1980), was, if anything, even more intense but hardly helped widen the band's limited appeal. Something had to give and inevitably it all ended in tears, the band subsequently embroiled in legal wrangles with their label and signing off after a split single with The SLITS. STEWART went on to work with The ON-U SOUND posse, issuing records as MARK STEWART & THE MAFFIA (and later solo in his own right), while SAGER went on to form RIP, RIG + PANIC. UNDERWOOD achieved brief but enduring acclaim as founder of PIGBAG while WADDINGTON formed MAXIMUM JOY. OLIVER, sadly, was to die of heart failure in 1990, having recently co-written TERENCE TRENT D'ARBY's massive 'Wishing Well'. As cult as they come, The POP GROUP are widely acknowledged as laying the foundations for a fertile Bristol music scene which would subsequently spawn such revered artists as MASSIVE ATTACK, NENEH CHERRY, NELLEE HOOPER, PORTISHEAD, TRICKY etc. • **Songwriters:** STEWART lyricist / group compositions.

Album rating: Y (*7) / FOR HOW MUCH LONGER ... (*8) / WE ARE TIME (*5) / WE ARE ALL PROSTITUTES compilation (*7) / Mark Stewart: LEARNING TO COPE WITH COWARDICE (*6) / AS THE VENEER OF DEMOCRACY BEGINS TO FADE (*6) / MARK STEWART (*5) / METATRON (*5) / CONTROL DATA (*5)

MARK STEWART – vocals / **JOHN WADDINGTON** – guitar / **DAVID WRIGHT** – saxophone / **SEAN OLIVER** – bass / **BRUCE SMITH** – drums, percussion

                        Radar   not iss.

Mar 79. (7"/12") (ADA 29/1229) **SHE IS BEYOND GOOD AND EVIL. / 3:38**

—— **SIMON UNDERWOOD** – bass; repl. OLIVER who joined ESSENTIAL LOGIC / **GARETH SAGER** – guitar, saxophone; repl. WRIGHT who joined ESSENTIAL LOGIC

Apr 79. (lp) (RAD 20) **Y**
– Thief of fire / Snowgirl / Blood money / Savage sea / We are time / Words disobey me / Don't call me Pain / The boys from Brazil / Don't sell your dreams. (re-iss. May96 on 'Radarscope' cd+=/lp; SCAN CD/LP 14) – She is beyond good and evil.

—— **DAN KATSIS** – bass (also of GLAXO BABIES) repl. SIMON who joined PIGBAG / added **TRISTAN HONSINGER** – cello

                        Rough Trade   not iss.

Oct 79. (7") (RT 023) **WE ARE ALL PROSTITUTES. / OUR CHILDREN SHALL RISE UP AGAINST**

—— **PAUL STUART** – drums; repl. SMITH who joined SLITS

Mar 80. (7") (RT 039 – Y1) **(In The Beginning – by SLITS). / WHERE THERE'S A WILL THERE'S A WAY**

Mar 80. (lp) (ROUGH 9 – Y2) **FOR HOW MUCH LONGER DO WE TOLERATE MASS MURDER?**
– Forces of oppression / Feed the hungry / One out of many / Blind faith / How much longer . . . / Justice / There are no spectators / Communicate / Rob a bank.

Dec 80. (lp) (ROUGH 12 – Y5) **WE ARE TIME** (live)
– Kiss the book / Amnesty report / Springer / Sense of purpose / We are time / Trap / Thief of fire / Genius or lunatic / Colour blind / Spanish inquisition. (re-iss. Aug84; same)

—— split 1980, when GARETH formed RIP, RIG & PANIC with other ex-POP GROUP members, SEAN and BRUCE. WADDINGTON and CATSIS formed MAXIMUM JOY

– compilations, etc. –

Jun 98. (cd/lp) Radarscope; (SCAN CD/LP 31) **WE ARE ALL PROSTITUTES**
– We are all prostitutes / Blind faith / Justice / Amnesty report / Feed the hungry / Where there's a will / Forces of oppression / Spanish inquisition / No spectators / Amnesty report II.

POP GROUP (cont)

MARK STEWART

May 82. (10"/7"; as MOUTH 2) *(10+/Y 20)* **WHO'S HOT. / CATCH A CAB**
— with **CHARLES 'ESKIMO' FOX** – drums / **EVAR** – bass / **NOAH** – keyboards

Oct 82. (10"ep; as MARK STEWART & THE MAFFIA) *(ONUDP 5)* **JERUSALEM. / HIGH IDEALS AND CRAZY DREAMS / LIBERTY CITY**
— **FATFINGERS** – keyboards; repl. NOAH
Jun 83. (lp; as MARK STEWART & THE MAFFIA) *(ONULP 24)* **LEARNING TO COPE WITH COWARDICE**
– Learning to cope with cowardice / Liberty city / Blessed are those / Who struggle / None dare / Call it conspiracy / Don't you ever lay down / Your arms / The paranoia of power / To have the vision / Jerusalem.
— he again worked with **ADRIAN SHERWOOD** – producer / **KEITH LA BLANCA** – drums (ex-MALCOLM X) / **DOUG WIMBUSH** – bass / **SKIP McDONALD** – keyboards, guitar

May 85. (7") *(7MUTE 37)* **HYPNOTISED. / DREAMERS**
(12"+=) *(12MUTE 37)* – The veneer of democracy starts to fade.
Nov 85. (lp) *(<STUMM 24>)* **AS THE VENEER OF DEMOCRACY BEGINS TO FADE**
– Passcreation programme / Bastards / The resistance of the cell / As the veneer of democracy starts to fade / Hypnotised / Slave of love / The waiting room. *(cd-iss. Apr88 +=; CDSTUMM 24)* – Dreamers.
Sep 87. (7") *(MUTE 59)* **THIS IS STRANGER THAN LOVE. / ANGER IS HOLY**
(12"+=) *(12MUTE 59)* – Survival / ('A'dub).
Oct 87. (cd/lp) *(<CD+/STUMM 43>)* **MARK STEWART**
– Survival / Survivalist / Anger is holy / Hell is empty / Stranger / Forbidden colour – Forbidden dub / Fatal attraction / This is stranger than love.
Mar 90. (12"/cd-s) *(12/CD MUTE 92)* **HYSTERIA. / MY POSSESSION / HYSTERIA (dub)**
Apr 90. (cd/c/lp) *(<CD/C+/STUMM 62>)* **METATRON**
– Hysteria / Shame / Collision / Faith healer / These things happen / My possession / Possession dub / Mammon.
Mar 96. (12"/cd-s) *(12/CD MUTE 130)* **DREAM KITCHEN. / CRAWL SPACE / FORBIDDEN LOVE (dub)**
Apr 96. (cd/d-lp) *(CD+/STUMM 93) <69013>* **CONTROL DATA** Jun96
– Dream kitchen / Forbidden love / Red zone / Scorpio / Consumed / Data blast / Digital justice / Simulacra / Half / Blood money 2.
Aug 98. (cd-s/12") *(CD+/MUTE 213)* **CONSUMED – THE REMIX WARS**
– Consumed:- mixes Ultraviolence Voiceprint / Alec Empire's Digital Hardcore / The program (no U-turn) / Ultraviolence / original Mark Stewart & Adrian Sherwood.

POP RIVETS (see under ⇒ CHILDISH, Wild Billy)

PORK DUKES

Formed: London, England … mid 1977 by brothers VILOS STYLES and RON DODGE, together with er … SCABS and NIKON BONK. Ah, the days when politically correct was just a figment of a Utopian future and punk rock sexist crudity was all the rage. If only. The PORK DUKES via their debut double A-side, 'BEND AND FLUSH' and 'THROBBING GRISTLE' (on 'Wood' records) was under par rock music with a comic twist … it wasn't funny. Subsequent titles such as 'MAKING BACON', 'TIGHT PUSSY' and 'TELEPHONE MASTURBATOR', barely raised a chuckle far less anything else. Twenty years on (the late 90's to be exact!), The PORK DUKES were touring with The CLAP. Yes, I'm tempted, but no.

Album rating: THE PORK DUKES (*3) / PIG OUT OF HELL (*3) / PIG IN A POKE (*4) / ALL THE FILTH compilation (*4)

VILOS STYLES – vocals, guitar / **RON DODGE** – guitar / **SCABS** – bass / **NIKON BONK** – drums

Aug 77. (7") *(WOOD 9)* **BEND AND FLUSH. / THROBBING GRISTLE**
Mar 78. (12"yellow) *(BRANCH 9)* **MAKING BACON. / TIGHT PUSSY**
Jun 78. (7") *(WOOD 56)* **TELEPHONE MASTURBATOR. / MELODY MAKERS**
— **MARK E. VALLEY** – keyboards; repl. SCABS
— **GERMUM LE PIG** – drums; repl. NIKON who became ROCKY RHYTHM and joined The REVILLOS
Nov 78. (pink-lp) *(PORK 001)* **THE PORK DUKES**
– Dirty boys / Stuck up / Bend and flush / Melody makers / Telephone masturbator / Sick of sex / Down down down / Soho girls / Tight pussy / Big tits / Penicillan princess / Loser. *(re-iss. Mar82 as 'PIG IN A POKE' on 'Butt'; PORK 1)*
— added **THE GUARDIAN ANGEL** – keyboards
1980. (lp) *(PORK 2)* **PIG OUT OF HELL**
– Devil driver / House of the rising sun / Three men in an army truck / My mother / Gin sin / Let's spend the night together / I'm a guitar / Day tripper / Do you love me / Marxist Leninist feminist / Stop / Around and around. *(re-iss. May83 & Aug86; same)*
— decided enough was enough after above

– compilations, others, etc. –

Oct 89. (7") *Damaged Goods; (FNARR 8)* **THE FILTHY AND THE NASTY. /**
1990's. (lp) *Vinyl Japan; (ASK 66)* **TELEPHONE MASTURBATOR**

Nov 99. (cd/lp) *Vinyl Japan; (<ASK CD/LP 98>)* **ALL THE FILTH**
– Bend and flush / Throbbing gristle / Making bacon / Melody maker / Telephone masturbator / Cocksucker blues / I like your big tits / Dirty boys / Penicillin princess / My mother gave me a gun for Xmas / Stuck up you / Soho girls / Sick for sex / Tight pussy / Around and around / Lady Diana. *(cd+=)* – Powers / Devil driver / Banana man / Chat line / Marxist Leninist feminist / Bend and flush (organ mix) / I wanna fuck.

PRAG VEC

Formed: London, England … 1978 by ex-DERELICTS members SUSAN GOGAN and JOHN STUDHOLME, plus DAVID BOYD and NICHOLAS CASH. Not one of the better female-fronted punk rock outfits, PRAG VEC delivered only two singles, 'CIGARETTES' and 'THE FOLLOWER' before New Wave fizzled out at the turn of the decade. While GOGAN's hard-nosed vocal chords were uncannily similar to those of PENETRATION's PAULINE MURRAY, the overall PRAG VEC effect was akin to a less entertaining hybrid of BLONDIE and the SLITS. In fact, the band were more famous for the inclusion of JIM THIRLWELL (soon-to-be FOETUS), who contributed synth-noise on their one and only LP, 'NO COWBOYS' (1981).

Album rating: NO-COWBOYS (*4)

SUSAN GOGAN – vocals / **JOHN STUDHOLME** – guitar / **DAVID BOYD** – bass / **NICHOLAS CASH** – drums

Dec 78. (7"ep) *(SP 001)* **WOLF / CIGARETTES. / EXISTENTIAL / BITS**
Jun 79. (7") *(SP 002)* **EXPERT. / THE FOLLOWER**
(all tracks re-iss. Feb80 on French 'Celluloid'; LTD 1040)
— they disbanded for around a year, returning in 1981 with additional musicians, **JIM THIRLWELL** – synthesizer, vocals / **SURESH SINGH** – vocals, marimba / + guest **ART MORAN** – alto sax
Oct 81. (lp) *(reSPECt 1)* **"NO-COWBOYS"**
– Laugh / Nervous / Happy valley / By the sea / Uh oh erotic / Welcome home / You're the gun / Third person / Breaking point / Cigarettes.
— split again after above; CASH joined FAD GADGET and THIRLWELL formed his own outfit, FOETUS

Peter PRINCIPLE (see under ⇒ TUXEDOMOON)

PUBLIC IMAGE LTD.

Formed: London, England … July '78 by ex-SEX PISTOLS frontman, JOHNNY ROTTEN, who reverted to his real name, JOHN LYDON. He recruited local friends, guitarist KEITH LEVENE (ex-CLASH), bassist JAH WOBBLE and Canadian drummmer JIM WALKER, re-signing to 'Virgin' in the process. 'PUBLIC IMAGE', both the debut single and the title track of the debut album, was a raucous slice of post-PISTOLS sonic energy, the record coming wrapped in a mock-newspaper sleeve and reaching the UK Top 10 late in 1978. The album followed it into the Top 30 at the end of the year, hardly a departure from punk but a convincing statement of intent nevertheless; tracks such as 'RELIGION', 'ANNA LISA' and 'ATTACK' formed the basis for LYDON's subsequent experiments. Preceded by the bizarre 'DEATH DISCO' single, 'METAL BOX 1' (1979) was a strikingly differeent beast, its pristine packaging (three 12" 45's inside a metal film can, something much copied by record company marketing departments in the years to come) rather deceptively encasing a dark, often disturbing set of experimental, Eastern-influenced material. As far from punk as LYDON has ever ventured, the record utilised monotonic repetition, LEVENE's shards of splintered guitar dissecting the vague structures of WOBBLE's rubbery basslines while LYDON wailed and ranted like a damned soul. John Peel was a particular champion of the record, playlisting virtually all its disturbing but accessible tracks, 'CAREERING', 'POPTONES' and 'GRAVEYARD' highlighting what came to be regarded as one of the last classic "punk/alternative" albums of the 70's. Surely one of the most avant-garde releases to ever grace the Top 20, the album even hit the charts a second time (Top 50) when it was re-issued in double-album format as 'SECOND EDITION' two months later. Following a patchy live album, 'PARIS AU PRINTEMPS' (1980), WOBBLE departed on a sour note, leaving LYDON and LEVENE to mastermind 'FLOWERS OF ROMANCE' (1981). A comparatively weaker effort, the record nevertheless almost made the Top 10 and the more contrived moments were interspersed with a few gems, notably the Burundi-esque title track, a Top 30 hit single. LEVENE was also soon to leave in less than pleasant circumstances following the success of 'P.I.L.'s biggest hit single to date, the compelling 'THIS IS NOT A LOVE SONG'. LYDON subsequently completed the lacklustre 'THIS IS WHAT YOU WANT … THIS IS WHAT YOU GET' opus with the help of session musicians, disbanding the group around the time of the album's release in the summer of '84. By this point, LYDON had moved to Los Angeles and his career slowed up somewhat, although he subsequently reformed 'P.I.L.' in late '85. Using such respected (and glaringly un-punk) musos as STEVE VAI, RYUICHI SAKAMOTO, GINGER BAKER and RAVI SHANKAR, LYDON recorded the minimally titled 'ALBUM' (also released as 'CASSETTE' and 'COMPACT DISC', of course). The BILL LASWELL-produced effort remains his last consistent collection, the 'SINGLE', 'RISE', almost making the Top

PUBLIC IMAGE LTD. (cont)

10, a driving, resonating, infectiously commercial example of LYDON doing what he does best (although I could be wrong . . .). For the remainder of the 80's, LYDON was content to churn out formula 'JOHNNY ROTTEN'-to-order type material that often incorporated bland Americanised rock backing. This only served to further entrench him in the mire of self-parody. Albums like 'HAPPY?' (1987) and '9' (1989) achieved only minimal commercial success although LYDON was back in the Top 20 in 1990 with 'DON'T ASK ME', the punk veteran's comment on the topical subject of the environment. The single was cannily included by 'Virgin' on a best of set, the hopefully titled 'GREATEST HITS – SO FAR' (1990). Then again, LYDON proved he could still cut the mustard with his late '93 LEFTFIELD collaboration, 'OPEN UP'. When LYDON lets rip, as he does here (a blood curdling wail of 'Burn, Hollywood, burn'), he is still the most frightening man in rock, no contest. Just to prove it, he hooked up once more with the original SEX PISTOLS line-up for the aptly titled 'Filthy Lucre' tour, appearing on 'Top Of The Pops' and scaring young children all over again with his gravity-defying hairdo.

Album rating: PUBLIC IMAGE (*9) / METAL BOX 1 (*10) / FLOWERS OF ROMANCE (*5) / LIVE IN TOKYO (*5) / THIS IS WHAT YOU WANT . . . THIS IS WHAT YOU GET (*4) / ALBUM (*7) / HAPPY? (*6) / 9 (*5) / GREATEST HITS – SO FAR compilation (*8) / THAT WHAT IS NOT (*4) / PLASTIC BOX boxed set (*8) / John Lydon: PSYCHO'S PATH (*4)

JOHN LYDON (b.31 Jan'56, Finsbury Park, London, England) – vocals (ex-SEX PISTOLS) / **KEITH LEVENE** (b. London, England) – guitar (ex-CLASH) / **JAH WOBBLE** (b. JOHN WORDLE) – bass / **JIM WALKER** (b. Canada) – drums (ex-FURIES)

—— (most singles just credit "PiL")

			Virgin	Warners
Oct 78.	(7") (VS 228)	**PUBLIC IMAGE. / THE COWBOY SONG**	9	-
Dec 78.	(lp/c) (V/TCV 2114) <3288>	**PUBLIC IMAGE**	22	-

– Theme / Religion I / Religion II / Annalisa / Public image / Low life / Attack / Fodderstompf. (re-iss. Apr86 lp/c; OVED/+C 160) (cd-iss. Jun88; CDV 2114)

—— **DAVE CROWE** – drums repl. WALKER who joined The PACK (with KIRK BRANDON) added **JEANNETTE LEE** – keyboards, synthesizer

Jun 79.	(7") (VS 274) **DEATH DISCO. / NO BIRDS DO SING**	20	-

(12"+=) (VS 274-12) – Death disco megamix.

| Sep 79. | (7"/ext.12") (VS 299/+12) **MEMORIES. / ANOTHER** | 60 | - |
| Dec 79. | (3x12"box)<lp> (METAL 1) <3288> **METAL BOX 1** <US-title 'SECOND EDITION'> | 18 | Jul80 |

– Albatross / Memories / Swan lake// Poptones / Careering / No birds / Graveyard / / The suit / Bad baby / Socialist – Chant – Radio 4. (re-iss. Feb80 as 'SECOND EDITION' d-lp/c; VD/TCVD 2512); hit UK No.46) (cd-iss. Jun86; CDVD 2512) (original; cd-iss. Jun90; MTLLCD 1)

—— **RICHARD DUDANSKI** – drums (ex-101'ERS, ex-BASEMENT 5) repl. CROWE

—— (he had joined during Apr-Sep'79) (below French titles of above songs)

| Nov 80. | (lp/c) (V/TCV 2183) **PARIS AU PRINTEMPS** (live 'PARIS IN THE SPRING') | 61 | - |

– Theme / Psalmodie (Chant) / Precipitamment (Careering) / Sale bebe (Bad baby) / La vie ignoble (Low life) / Attaque (Attack) / Timbres de pop (Poptones). (re-iss. Mar84 lp/c; OVED/+C 50)

—— (Jul80) Trimmed to a quartet when JAH WOBBLE went solo. / **MARTIN ATKINS** (b. 3 Aug'59, Coventry, England) (aka BRIAN BRAIN) – drums repl. DUDANSKI who joined RAINCOATS. (ATKINS was sacked Jul80, most of drums by LYDON and LEVENE)

| Mar 81. | (7") (VS 397) **FLOWERS OF ROMANCE. / HOME IS WHERE THE HEART IS** | 24 | - |

(12"+=) (VS 397-12) – ('A'instrumental).

| Apr 81. | (lp/c) (V/TCV 2189) <3536> **FLOWERS OF ROMANCE** | 11 | - |

– Four enclosed walls / Track 8 / Phenagen / Flowers of romance / Under the house / Hymie's him / Banging the door / Go back / Francis massacre. (re-iss. Mar84 lp/c; OVED/+C 51) (cd-iss. Apr90 & Mar94; CDV 2189)

—— **KEN LOCKIE** – keyboards (ex-COWBOYS INTERNATIONAL, ex-Solo) repl. LEE / added (May82) **MARTIN ATKINS** – drums / **PETE JONES** – bass

| Aug 83. | (7") (VS 529) **THIS IS NOT A LOVE SONG. / PUBLIC IMAGE** | 5 | - |

(12"+=) (VS 529-12) – Blue water / ('A'remix).
(re-iss. Jun88 cd-ep; CDT 14)

—— LYDON + ATKINS were joined by US session people from New Jersey; **JOSEPH GUIDA** – guitar / **TOM ZVONCHECK** – keyboards / **LOUIE BERNARDI** – bass

		Virgin	Elektra
Sep 83.	(2x12"/c) (VGD/+C 3508) **LIVE IN TOKYO** (live)	28	-

– Annalisa / Religion / Low life / Solitaire / Flowers of romance / This is not a love song / Death disco / Bad life / Banging the door / Under the house. (cd-iss. 1986; VGDCD 3508)

| May 84. | (7"/ext.12") (VS 675/+12) **BAD LIFE. / QUESTION MARK** | 71 | - |
| Jul 84. | (lp/c) (V/TCV 2309) <60365> **THIS IS WHAT YOU WANT . . . THIS IS WHAT YOU GET** | 56 | |

– Bad life / This is not a love song / Solitaire / Tie me to the length of that / The pardon / Where are you? / 1981 / The order of death. (re-iss. 1986 lp/c; OVED/+C 176) (cd-iss. Apr90; CDV 2309)

| Aug 84. | (lp; as KEITH LEVENE & PiL) <XYZ 007> **THE COMMERCIAL ZONE** | - | |

– (as last album, with LEVENE's guitar parts more obvious)

—— Disbanded mid'84, but reformed by LYDON late '85 with on session **STEVE VAI** – guitar (ex-ALCATRAZZ) / **RYUICHI SAKAMOTO** – keys (ex-YELLOW MAGIC ORCHESTRA) / **GINGER BAKER** (ex-CREAM, etc) / **TONY WILLIAMS** (ex-MILES DAVIES, etc) / **RAVI SHANKER** – violin

| Jan 86. | (7"/12") (VS 841/+12) **RISE.** / ('A'instrumental) | 11 | - |
| Feb 86. | (cd/c/lp) (CD/TC/V 2366) <60438> **ALBUM** | 14 | |

– FFF / Rise / Fishing / Round / Bags / Home / Ease. (re-iss. 1989 lp/c; OVED/+C 245)

| Apr 86. | (7") (VS 855) **HOME. / ROUND** | 75 | - |

(12"+=) (VS 855-12) – ('A'-lp version).
(d7"+=) (VSD 855) – Rise / ('A'instrumental).

—— (Feb86) LYDON recruited **LU EDMUNDS** – guitar, keys (ex-DAMNED, ex-MEKONS) / **JOHN McGEOGH** – guitar (of ARMOURY SHOW, ex-SIOUXSIE & THE BANSHEES) / **ALAN DIAS** – bass / **BRUCE SMITH** – drums (ex-RIP, RIG & PANIC, ex-SLITS, ex-POP GROUP)

		Virgin	Virgin
Aug 87.	(7") (VS 988) **SEATTLE. / SELFISH RUBBISH**	47	-

(12"+=/c-s+=) (VS/+C 988-12) – The suit.

| Sep 87. | (cd/c/lp) (CD/TC+/V 2455) <90642> **HAPPY?** | 40 | |

– Seattle / Rules and regulations / The body / Save me / Hard times / Open and revolving / Angry / Fat chance hotel. (re-iss. Apr90 lp/c; OVED/+C 299)

| Oct 87. | (7") (VS 1010) **THE BODY. / RELIGION** (new version) | 100 | - |

(12"+=) (VST 1010) – Angry.
(12") (VSR 1010) – ('A' extended remix) / ('A'-U.S. remix) / Angry.

—— trimmed to a quartet when EDMUNDS dispersed.

| Apr 89. | (7") (VS 1181) **DISAPPOINTED. / SAME OLD STORY** | 38 | - |

(ext.12"+=/12"pic-d+=/3"cd-s+=) (VS T/TY/CD 181) – ('A'version).

| Jun 89. | (cd/c/lp) (CD/TC+/V 2588) <91062> **9** | 36 | |

– Happy / Disappointed / Warrior / U.S.L.S. 1 / Sand castles in the snow / Worry / Brave new world / Like that / Same old story / Armada.

| Jul 89. | (7"/7"g-f) (VS 1195) **WARRIOR. / U.S.L.S. 1** | | |

(ext.12"+=) (VST 1195) – ('A'instrumental).
(3"cd-s+=) (VSCD 1195) – ('A'extended).
(12") (VSTX 1195) – ('A'-Dave Dorrell remix) / ('A'instrumental).

| Oct 90. | (7"/c-s) (VS/+C 1231) **DON'T ASK ME. / RULES AND REGULATIONS** | 22 | - |

(cd-s+=) (VSCD 1231) – Warrior (original).
(12") (VST 1231) – ('A'extended) / Warrior (remix).

| Oct 90. | (cd/c/lp) (CD/TC+/V 2644) <86196> **GREATEST HITS – SO FAR** (compilation) | 20 | |

– Public image / Death disco / Memories / Careering / Flowers of romance / This is not a love song / Rise / Home / The body / Rules and regulations / Disappointed / Warrior / Don't ask me / Seattle.

—— **MIKE JOYCE** – drums (ex-SMITHS, ex-BUZZCOCKS) repl. BRUCE

| Feb 92. | (7") (VS 1390) **CRUEL. / LOVE HOPE** | 49 | - |

(cd-s+=) (VSCD 1390) – Rise (live) / Home (live).
(10"+=) (VST 1390) – Happy (live).

| Feb 92. | (cd/c/lp) (CD/TC+/V 2681) <86263> **THAT WHAT IS NOT** | 46 | |

– Acid drops / Lucks up / Cruel / God / Covered / Love hope / Unfairground / Think tank / Emperor / Good things.

—— In Nov'93, LYDON was credited on acclaimed dance hit & UK No.19 'Open Up' by LEFTFIELD / LYDON on 'Hard Hands' records.

—— Early '96, JOHN LYDON (ROTTEN) re-grouped with The SEX PISTOLS for summer tours in Britain, Europe and America.

– compilations, etc. –

| Mar 99. | (4xcd-box) Virgin; PILBOX 1) **PLASTIC BOX** | | - |

JOHN LYDON

		Virgin America	Virgin America
Jun 97.	(cd/c) (CDVUS/VUSMC 130) <44209> **PSYCHO'S PATH**		

– Grave ride / Dog / Psychopath / Sun / Another way / Dis-ho / Take me / No and a yes / Stump / Armies / Open up.

| Jul 97. | (12"/cd-s) (VUS T/CD 122) **SUN. / GRAVE RIDE / PSYCHOPATH** | 42 | - |

PUNISHMENT OF LUXURY

Formed: Newcastle, England . . . 1976 by NEVILLUXURY and his co-writer BRIAN BOND alongside RED HELMET, JIMI GIRO and LIQUID LES DENHAM. With their origins in radical theatre, this punk-era oddity was driven by an attempt to combine three-chord aggression with quirky prog-rock. Initially signed to the 'Small Wonder' label, the group released a debut single, 'PUPPET LIFE', in summer '78. A couple of John Peel sessions also added to their credibility, the band subsequently signing to 'United Artists' for whom they cut a further two singles, 'ENGINE OF EXCESS' and 'SECRETS', prior to their one and only album, 'LAUGHING ACADEMY' (1979). Retrospectively bestowed with the honour of appearing in a 'Mojo' magazine poll of 100 all-time worst albums, the record's political sermonising and woefully self-indulgent guitar work was certainly not your average New Wave fare. A subsequent deal with 'Liberty' saw the release of the album's title track prior to a lengthy break. NEVILLE, BOND and JIMI eventually resurfaced as PUNILUX (alongside new recruits STEVE SEKRIT and TIM MAGENTA) with a one-off single, 'HOLD ME (NEVER MOULD ME)' on 'Red Rhino' in 1983. The following year saw the outfit's swansong release, mini-set, '7', NEVILLE going on to release a solo album, 'FEELS LIKE DANCING WARTIME'.

Album rating: LAUGHING ACADEMY (*5) / Punilux: 7 (*4)

BRIAN BOND – vocals / **NEVILLUXURY** – guitars, vocals / **RED HELMET** – guitar, vocals / **JIMI GIRO** – bass, vocals / **LIQUID LES (DENHAM)** – drums

		Small Wonder	not iss.
Jul 78.	(7") (SMALL 8) **PUPPET LIFE. / THE DEMON**		
		U.A.	not iss.
Apr 79.	(7") (UP 36507) **ENGINE OF EXCESS. / JELLYFISH**		-
Jul 79.	(7") (UP 36537) **SECRETS. / BRAINBOMB**		-
Sep 79.	(lp) (UAG 30258) **LAUGHING ACADEMY**		-

– Puppet life / Funk me / The message / All white Jack / Obsession / Radar bug / Metropolis / British baboon / Babalon / Excess bleeding heart / Laughing academy. (cd-iss. Sep93 on 'Dojo'+=; DOJOCD 147) – Secrets / Brainbomb / Baby don't jump / Engine of excess / Jellyfish.

			Liberty	not iss.
Feb 80. (7") *(BP 317)* **LAUGHING ACADEMY. / BABY DON'T JUMP**

—— (early in 1982) NEVILLE + BOND + JIMI recruited new members **STEVE SEKRIT** – guitar + **TIM MAGENTA** – guitar

			Red Rhino	not iss.
Mar 83. (7"; as PUNILUX) *(RED 33)* **HOLD ME (NEVER MOULD ME). / GOLDEN CORSETS**

—— **RAB AITCH** – guitar, vocals; repl. MAGENTA

Sep 84. (m-lp; as PUNILUX) *(REDLP 34)* **7**
– Funghi / The bird and the elephant / Gasman / Revelations / Golden corsets / Tria-dance.

—— disbanded; BRIAN BOND was later in MADAM X as guitarist

NEVILLE LUXURY

with **SEKRIT** plus **MARK DUNCAN** – bass / **DAVE EXCESS** – guitar (on live gigs)

Jun 85. (m-lp) *(REDLP 46)* **FEELS LIKE DANCING WARTIME**
– The dragon / Feels like dancing wartime / Eyes / Motivator / Welcome / The prisoner / Rock out of the box.

PUNISHMENT OF LUXURY

—— **NEVILLUXURY** re-formed the group with **EDDIE HALL** – bass, vocals / **TONY WRIGHT** – drums, vocals

			P.U.K.	not iss.
1989. (7") *(PUK 1)* **ALIEN CONTACT. / PARTY GOBLINS**

– compilations, etc. –

Aug 97. (lp/cd) *Overground; (OVER 66/+CD)* **REVOLUTION BY NUMBERS**
– Blood money / Damaging man / Why don't you / Snowqueen / You eat too much / Revolution by numbers / My wife's in love with a polar bear / Double agent / Funghi / The bird and the elephant / Revelations / Golden corsets / Tria dance / Alien contact / Party goblins.

Sep 98. (cd) *Overground; (OVER 75CD)* **GIGANTIC DAYS** (the shelved LP)
– Plants and insects / Fasciculi Barbaraclique / Empire of idiots / No admittance / Destiny / Death and boogie / Auschwitz / Love decayed / All change / The dragon / Feels like dancing wartime / Eyes / Motivator / Welcome / The prisoner / Rock out the box.

Jimmy PURSEY (see under ⇒ SHAM 69)

R

RADIATORS FROM SPACE

Formed: Dublin, Ireland ... 1976 initially as GRETA GARBAGE & THE TRASHCANS by STEVE RAPID and PETER HOLIDAI, the pair recruiting PHILIP CHEVRON, MARK MEGARAY and JAMES CRASH as they became The RADIATORS FROM SPACE. The first Irish band of the punk era to get a single out in the UK (having already signed to 'C.B.S.' in Eire), Spring '77's 'TELEVISION SCREEN' was a heady slice of R&B-influenced punk-pop. Having subsequently relocated to London (home of 'Chiswick' records), they issued a second single, 'ENEMIES' and an accompanying album, 'TV TUBE HEART', later that year. While rivals The BOOMTOWN RATS invaded their space, so to speak, the band trimmed down their moniker and their personnel after losing vocalist STEVE RAPID. The RADIATORS, as they were now known, returned in 1979 with a series of singles (including near hit, 'MILLION DOLLAR HERO'), all featuring on their belated and difficult second set, 'GHOSTOWN'. After another batch of 45's the wanna-be-stars finally burned out, HOLIDAI striking out to join LIGHT A BIG FIRE while CHEVRON issued a few solo singles. The RADIATORS were turned on again – but only briefly this time – releasing a one-off set for 'Warners' (Ireland), 'BUYING GOLD IN HEAVEN' (1987), after which CHEVRON was invited to join The POGUES.

Album rating: THE RADIATORS FROM SPACE (*6) / GHOSTOWN (*5) / COCKLES AND MUSCLES compilation (*7) / ALIVE-ALIVE-O! (*5)

STEVE RAPID – vocals / **PHILIP CHEVRON** (b.17 Jun'57) – guitar, vocals / **PETER HOLIDAI** – guitar, vocals / **MARK MEGARAY** – bass, vocals / **JAMES CRASH** – drums

			Chiswick	not iss.
Apr 77. (7") *(NS 10)* **TELEVISION SCREEN. / LOVE DETECTIVE**
Oct 77. (7") *(NS 19)* **ENEMIES. / PSYCHOTIC REACTION**
Oct 77. (lp) *(WIK 4)* **TV TUBE HEART**
– Television screen / Prison bars / Great expectations / Roxy girl / Press gang / Contact / Sunday world / Electric shares / Enemies / Ripped and torn / Not too late / Blitzin' at the Ritz / Party line.
Sep 78. (7"w/drawn) *(NS 24)* **PRISON BARS. / (WHY CAN'T I BE A) TEENAGER IN LOVE**

RADIATORS

—— now without STEVE RAPID

Jan 79. (7") *(NS 29)* **MILLION DOLLAR HERO (IN A FIVE AND TEN CENTS STORE). / BLITZIN' AT THE RITZ**
May 79. (7"w/drawn) *(NS 45)* **WALKIN' HOME ALONE AGAIN. / TRY AND STOP ME / THE HUCKLEBUCK**
Jun 79. (7") *(CHIS 113)* **LET'S TALK ABOUT THE WEATHER. / THE HUCKLEBUCK / TRY AND STOP ME**
Jun 79. (lp) *(CWK 3003)* **GHOSTOWN**
– Million dollar hero / Let's talk about the weather / Johnny jukebox / Confidential / They're looting in the town / Who are the strangers? / Ballad of Kitty Rickets / Song of the faithful departed / Walkin' home alone again / Dead the beast, dead the poison.
Aug 79. (7") *(CHIS 115)* **KITTY RICKETS. / SONG OF THE FAITHFUL DEPARTED**
Jul 80. (7") *(CHIS 126)* **STRANGER THAN FICTION. / PRISON BARS / WHO ARE THE STRANGERS?**
Sep 80. (7") *(CHIS 133)* **THE DANCING YEARS. / (part 2 – instrumental)**
Dec 80. (7") *(CHIS 144)* **SONG OF THE FAITHFUL DEPARTED. / THEY'RE LOOTING IN THE TOWN** — — Irish

—— split and HOLIDAI later joined LIGHT A BIG FIRE

PHILIP CHEVRON

			Mosa	not iss.
Nov 81. (12"ep) *(MOEP 412)* **SONGS FROM BILL'S DANCE HALL**

			Imp-Demon	not iss.
Oct 83. (7") *(IMP 002)* **THE CAPTAIN AND THE KINGS. / FAITHFUL DEPARTED**

—— The RADIATORS returned and signed to 'WEA' in Ireland

			Hotwire	not iss.
Jun 87. (lp; w-drawn) *(HWLP 8503)* **BUYING GOLD IN HEAVEN**

—— PHIL CHEVRON went on to join The POGUES

– compilations, etc. –

Jul 79. (7"ep) *Big Beat; (NS 57)* **FOUR ON THE FLOOR**
– Enemies / Teenager in love / Television screen / Psychotic reaction.

RADIATORS FROM SPACE (cont) — THE GREAT INDIE DISCOGRAPHY — The 1970s

Feb 89. (7") *Ace-Chiswick*; (NS 128) **UNDER CLEARY'S CLOCK. / TAKE MY HEART AND RUN**
(12"+=) (NST 128) – Strangers in fiction.
Oct 95. (cd) *Chiswick*; (CDWIKD 156) **COCKLES & MUSSELS (THE BEST OF THE RADIATORS)**
– Television screen / Love detective / Sunday world / Prison bars / Party line / Roxy girl / Enemies / Try and stop me / Million dollar hero (in a five and ten cents store) / Let's talk about the weather / Johnny Jukebox / Confidential / They're looting in the town / Who are the strangers / Kitty Ricketts / Ballad of the faithful departed / Walking home alone again / Dead the beast, dead the poison / Stranger than fiction / The dancing years / Under Cleary's clock / Plura bell / Television screen.
Jun 96. (cd) *Chiswick*; (CDWIKD 164) **ALIVE-ALIVE-O! (live)**
– Contact / Sunday world / Roxy girl / Electric shares / Press gang / Prison bars / Million dollar hero / Television screen / Walking home alone again / Psychotic reaction / Blitzin' at the Ritz / Enemies / Teenager in love / Hucklebuck / Teenage head / Shake some action / 1970 (I feel alright) / Private world / Strangers in fiction / Take my heart and run / Buying gold in Heaven / Gold diggers of 1981 (hits for the blitz) / Ballad of the faithful departed.

RADIO BIRDMAN

Formed: Sydney, Australia . . . September 1974 by American medical students DENIZ TEK and PHILIP 'PIP' HOYLE, alongside ROB YOUNGER, WARWICK GILBERT, RON KEELY and CARL ROURKE. Being a part-time project, RADIO BIRDMAN weren't exactly the most prolific of New Wave acts, releasing only two domestic singles prior to their first UK visit early in '78. By this time, new guitarist CHRIS MUSUAK had replaced bassist CARL ROURKE and with their Australian singles selling well on import, 'Sire', signed them up to re-issue their debut LP, 'RADIOS APPEAR' (1977/78) – albeit with a change of track listing. Very much in the balls-out MC5/STOOGES mould, 'BIRDMAN couldn't quite break the already congested UK/US market and subsequently flew back to their homeland. After a further Australian-only album, 'LIVING EYES' (1981), YOUNGER, TEK and GILBERT hooked up with their long-time heroes, RON ASHETON (ex-STOOGES) and DENNIS THOMPSON (ex-MC5) to form The NEW RACE; the appropriately-title concert set, 'THE FIRST AND THE LAST', was the sole recorded output of this short-lived project. YOUNGER subsequently concentrated on a production career as well as playing in his own band, The NEW CHRISTS. Some belated RADIO BIRDMAN reunions saw the band briefly plucked from obscurity and even seminal grunge label 'Sub Pop' got in on the act by releasing a great 'ESSENTIAL' collection in 2001.

Album rating: RADIOS APPEAR (*7) / LIVING EYES (*8) / THE ESSENTIAL RADIO BIRDMAN 1974-1978 compilation (*7)

ROB YOUNGER – vocals / **DENIZ TEK** (b. Detroit, Michigan, USA) – guitar / **PIP HOYLE** (b. USA) – organ, guitar / **CHRIS MUSUAK** – guitar, piano; repl. CARL ROURKE / **WARWICK GILBERT** – bass / **RON KEELY** – drums

Trafalgar / not iss.
Jan 77. (7"ep) (ME 109) **BURN MY EYE EP** – Austra
– Smith Wesson blues / Snake / I-94 / Burned my eye.
Jun 77. (7") (TRS 11) **NEW RACE. / TV EYE** – Austra
Jul 77. (lp) (TRL 1001) **RADIOS APPEAR** – Austra
– TV eye / Murder city nights / Anglo girl desire / Man with the golden helmet / Descent into maelstrom / Monday morning gunk / Do the pop / Love kills / Hand of law / New race.
May 78. (7") (TRS 12) **ALOHA STEVE AND DANNO. / ANGLO GIRL DESIRE** – Austra

Sire / Sire
Mar 78. (7") (6078 617) **WHAT GIVES? / ANGLO GIRL DESIRE**
Apr 78. (lp) (9103 332) <SRK 6050> **RADIO APPEAR**
– What gives? / Non-stop girls / Do the pop / Man with the golden helmet / Descent into the maelstrom / New race / Aloha Steve and Danno / Anglo girl desire / Murder city nights / You're gonna miss me / Hand of law / Hit them again. (cd-iss. +re-mast.Jan98 on 'Red Eye'; REDCD 49) (cd w/cd-iss. Jun02 on 'Citadel'; CITCD 550SP)

WEA / not iss.
Mar 81. (lp) (600085) **LIVING EYES** – Austra
– More fun / TPBR combo / 455 SD / Do the movin' change / I-94 / Iskender time / Burn my eye '78 / Time to fall / Smith and Wesson blues / Breaks my heart / Alone in the endzone / Hanging on. (cd-iss. +re-mast.Jan98 on 'Red Eye'; REDCD 53) (cd w/cd-iss. Jun02 on 'Citadel'; CITCD 551SP)
Apr 81. (7") (100160) **ALONE IN THE ENDZONE. / BREAKS MY HEART** – Austra

— disbanded after above and YOUNGER became top-notch producer. In 1982, WARWICK and MUSUAK formed The HITMEN with ex-SAINTS drummer IVOR HAY and future HOODOO GURUS members (not to be confused with UK band of same name 1980-82).

– compilations, etc. –

1992. (d-cd) *WEA*; (255991-2) **UNDER THE ASHES** – Austra
Jan 97. (cd+book) *Crying Sun*; (CSREC 001) **RITUALISM**
Mar 99. (cd) *Murder One*; (ARK 003) **MURDER CITY NIGHTS**
(re-iss. Aug02 on 'Bite My Tongue'; BITE 852)
Apr 99. (lp) *Mission*; (RB 001) **ROCK'N'ROLL WAR 1976-1978**
Aug 01. (d-lp/cd) *Sub Pop*; <(SP/+CD 553)> **THE ESSENTIAL RADIO BIRDMAN 1974-1978**
– Aloha Steve and Danno / Murder cirt nights / New race / Love kills / Descent into the maelstrom / Burn my eye '78 / I-94 / Anglo girl desire / Hand of law / Snake / Do the pop / Non-stop girls / What gives? / Man with the golden helmet / Hanging on / Crying sun / Smith and Wesson blues / Time to fall / Alone in the endzone / Breaks my heart (live) / More fun (live) / Dark surprise (live).

NEW RACE

ROB YOUNGER – vocals / **DENIZ TEK** – guitar / **WARWICK GILBERT** – bass / **RON ASHETON** – guitar (ex-STOOGES) / **DENNIS THOMPSON** – drums (ex-MC5)

Statik / not iss.
Jun 83. (lp) (STATLP 16) **THE FIRST AND THE LAST (live 1981)**
– Crying sun / Haunted road / Sad T.V. / Breaks my heart / Looking at you / November 22, 1963 / Alone in the endzone / Love kills / Gotta keep movin' / Columbia. (cd-iss. Oct97 on 'Total Energy'; NER 3013)

— YOUNGER went on to form NEW CHRISTS, who made two turn of the decade albums for 'Citadel'; 'DISTEMPER' & 'DIVINE RITES'. On the latter, they (others being :- CHARLIE OWEN, JIM DICKSON + NICK FISHER) were joined by MUSUAK.

RADIO STARS

Formed: London, England . . . early 1977 by former JOHN'S CHILDREN and JET frontman, ANDY ELLISON, alongside IAN McLEOD and MARTIN GORDON (also ex-JET). Almost immediately joined by NEO drummer, PAUL SIMON (no, not that one!), they signed a deal with 'Chiswick' records and wasted no time in getting debut single, 'DIRTY PICTURES', on the shelves (but not the top ones). Shifting to a different frequency from their past musical endeavours, The RADIO STARS presented a more refined blend of power-pop/new wave bandwagoneering. Finding a more permanent drummer in STEVE PARRY, the colourful quartet released an EP, 'STOP IT', prior to achieving short-lived chart glory with the Top 40, 'NERVOUS WRECK'. Towards the end of the year, the seasoned 'STARS delivered their first album, the sarcastically-titled 'SONGS FOR SWINGING LOVERS' (actually the name of a classic FRANK SINATRA lp). With new wave moving on to a more experimental channel, The RADIO STARS were left behind, the result being poor sales of their subsequent 45's and follow-up set, 'HOLIDAY ALBUM' (1978). Nevertheless, the band's off-kilter sense of humour shone through on the likes of '(I'VE GOT DEM OLD) SEX IN CHAINS BLUES (AGAIN MAMA)', alongside a cover of The Beatles' 'NORWEGIAN WOOD'. By this time, MARTIN had been replaced by JAMIE CROMPTON, although the latter was in turn succeeded by JOHN MACKIE and former SPARKS guitarist TREVOR WHITE. However, further personnel changes left the band effectively dead, although ELLISON briefly resurrected the name in 1982.

Album rating: SONGS FOR SWINGING LOVERS (*5) / HOLIDAY ALBUM (*4) / SOMEWHERE THERE'S A PLACE FOR US compilation (*6)

ANDY ELLISON – vocals, guitar (ex-JOHN'S CHILDREN, ex-JET) / **IAN McLEOD** – guitar (ex-JET) / **MARTIN GORDON** – bass (ex-JET) / **PAUL SIMON** – drums (also of NEO)

Chiswick / not iss.
Apr 77. (7") (NS 9) **DIRTY PICTURES. / SAIL AWAY**

— (Jul'77) **STEVE PARRY** – drums; repl. PAUL who joined COWBOYS INTERNATIONAL
Aug 77. (7"ep) (SW 17) **STOP IT**
– No Russians in Russia / Box 29 / Johnny Mekon / Sorry I'm tied up.
Oct 77. (7"/12") (NS/+T 23) **NERVOUS WRECK. / HORRIBLE BREATH** — 39
Dec 77. (lp) (WIK 5) **SONGS FOR SWINGING LOVERS**
– Good personality / Is it really necessary / Eric / The beast of Barnsley / Nervous wreck / Nothing happened today / Buy Chiswick records / Don't waste my time / Arthur is dead boring / Macaroni and mice / Nice girls / Talkin' 'bout you. (free-7"w.a.) – NO RUSSIANS IN RUSSIA. / DIRTY PICTURES
Apr 78. (7",6") (NS 36) **FROM A RABBIT. / TO A BEAST**

— **JAMIE CROMPTON** – drums (ex-NEW HEARTS) repl. MARTIN to BLUE MEANIES
Sep 78. (7") (CHIS 102) **RADIO STARS. / ACCOUNTANCY BLUES**
Sep 78. (lp) (CWK 3001) **THE RADIO STARS HOLIDAY ALBUM**
– Radio stars / Boy meets girl / Baffin Island / (I've got dem old) Sex in chains blues (again mama) / Sitting in the rain / The real me / Rock and roll for the time being / Norwegian wood / Get on a plane / I'm down / No Russians in Russia / It's all over / Goodnight.

— (tour after lp) **JOHN MACKIE** – drums (ex-STUKAS) repl. CROMPTON / added **TREVOR WHITE** – guitar (ex-SPARKS)
Jan 79. (7") (CHIS 109) **THE REAL ME. / GOOD PERSONALITY**

— (Feb'79) **STEVE PARRY** – drums; returned to repl. MACKIE + WHITE

— disbanded but re-formed in 1982 by **ELLISON**, etc

Moonlight / not iss.
May 82. (7") (MNS 001) **GOOD PERSONALITY. / TALKING 'BOUT YOU**

Snat / not iss.
Sep 82. (7") (ECG 1) **MY MOTHER SAID. / TWO MINUTES MR SMITH**

– compilations, etc. –

May 82. (lp) *Moonlight*; (MNA 001) **TWO MINUTES MR. SMITH**
Oct 92. (cd) *Chiswick*; (CDWIKD 107) **SOMEWHERE THERE'S A PLACE FOR US**
– Radio stars / Dirty pictures / The beast of Barnsley / Nervous wreck / Boy meets girl / My mother said / Is it really necessary? / Arthur is dead boring (let's rot) / Johnny Mekon / Good personality / Dear Prudence / Nothing happened today / Eric / Macaroni & mice / (I got dem old) Sex in chains blues (again mama) part 1 / From a rabbit / SAil away / It's all over / Talking about you / Accountancy blues / Baffin island / This is your next life / Sitting in the rain / Rock'n'roll for the time being / No Russians in Russia / The real me / Somewhere there's a place for us / Goodnight.

RAINCOATS

Formed: Ladbroke Grove, London, England . . . 1977 by ANA DA SILVA and GINA BIRCH (other early members included NICK TURNER, ROSS CRIGHTON, KATE KORUS (ex-SLITS), JEREMIE F and SHIRLEY O'LOUGHLIN). Featuring a line-up subsequently completed by VICKY ASPINAL and future SLITS member, PALMOLIVE, this all-female outfit are held up as having redefined the musical possibilities for women in what was still – even with the supposed liberation of punk – a male dominated bastion. Signed to fledgling indie label, 'Rough Trade', the band debuted in 1979 with the groundbreaking guitar scree and distinctive drumroll chorus of the 'FAIRYTALE IN A SUPERMARKET' single, promptly notching up an NME Single Of The Week award. Later that year, they released their much acclaimed debut album, 'THE RAINCOATS', commentators falling over themselves to praise its emotionally stark noise collages. Somewhere in deepest Seattle, a young KURT COBAIN was similarly entranced, the future grunge architect at least partly responsible for resurrecting interest in the 90's. In the meantime, The RAINCOATS began writing material for a follow-up set, minus PALMOLIVE, who had departed for foreign shores in pursuit of spiritual enlightenment. The resulting album, 'ODYSHAPE' (1981) was more abstract than anything they'd recorded to date, eschewing conventional song structures for a near-improvisational approach and off-kilter time signatures. It was also largely recorded with the absence of a solid drum beat, deep, dubby bass and minimalist percussion the only instruments providing any kind of rhythmic anchor among the ethereal vocals, violin shards and angular guitar. The third and final RAINCOATS studio album, 'MOVING' (1984) was radically different again, far more accessible in a kind of knotty, avant-disco/funk stylee, lead track and single, 'ANIMAL RHAPSODY' carrying on where their cover of Sly Stone's 'RUNNING AWAY' left off and rendering the band virtually unrecognisable from their previous incarnation. ASPINALL's scraping violin was ever present of course, even if it did jar against the hotch-potch of competing musical strands. The disparate sound suggested a band coming apart at the seams, the girls subsequently going their separate ways for the remainder of the 80's. While the 90's was characterised by reformation mania, few could've predicted The RAINCOATS reunion. As mentioned above, NIRVANA mainman, KURT COBAIN made sure their legacy lived on, instrumental as he was in the CD re-issue of their albums. The interest from COBAIN and many of his peers encouraged the girls to give it another go and in 1993, DA SILVA and BIRCH teamed up with violinist ANNE WOOD and SONIC YOUTH's STEVE SHELLEY to record an EP, 'EXTENDED PLAY' (1994) and an album, 'LOOKING IN THE SHADOWS' (1995). BIRCH would subsequently turn out for indie-pop supergroup, The HANGOVERS.
• **Songwriters:** BIRCH and ASPINALL, except LOLA (Kinks) / STILL WAITING (Prince). • **Trivia:** GINA was also part of RED CRAYOLA, and VICKY played violin for the NEW AGE STEPPERS.

Album rating: THE RAINCOATS (*7) / ODYSHAPE (*8) / MOVING (*8)

ANA DA SILVA (b.1949, Portugal) – vocals, guitar / **VICKY ASPINALL** – guitar, violin / **GINA BIRCH** (b.1956) – bass / **PALMOLIVE** (b.Spain) – drums (ex-SLITS)

Rough Trade Rough Trade

Apr 79. (7"m) *(RT 013)* **FAIRYTALE IN A SUPERMARKET. / IN LOVE / ADVENTURES CLOSE TO HOME**
Nov 79. (lp) *(ROUGH 3)* **THE RAINCOATS**
– Fairytale in a supermarket / No side to fall in / Adventures close to home / Off duty trip / Black and white / Lola / The void / Life on the line / You're a million / In love / No looking. *(cd-iss. Sep93; R 302-2) <US-iss.Sep93 on 'DGC'; 24622>*

—— **INGRID WEISS** (b.1961) drums repl. PALMOLIVE who returned to Spain.
—— guests on next **ROBERT WYATT + CHARLES HAYWARD** (of THIS HEAT)

Jun 81. (lp/c) *(ROUGH 13/+C)* **ODYSHAPE**
– The Raincoats / Shouting out loud / Family treat / Only loved at night / Dancing in my head / And then it's o.k. / Baby song / Red shoes / Go away. *(cd-iss. Jan94; R 304-2) <US-iss.Jan94 on 'DGC'; 24623>*

—— **RICHARD DUDANSKI** – drums repl. INGRID

Jul 82. (7") *(RT 093)* **RUNNING AWAY. / NO-ONE'S LITTLE GIRL**

—— basic trio **BIRCH, DA SILVA, ASPINALL + DUDANSKI** plus guests **PADDY O'CONNELL** – saxophone / **DEREK GODDARD** – percussion

Nov 83. (12"m) *(RT 153)* **ANIMAL RHAPSODY. / NO-ONE'S LITTLE GIRL / HONEY MAD WOMAN**
Feb 84. (lp) *(ROUGH 66)* **MOVING**
– Ooh ooh la la la / Dreaming in the past / Mouth of a story / Hoey mad woman / Rainstorm / The dance of the hopping mad / Balloon / I saw a hill / Overheard / The body / Avidoso / Animal rhapsody. *(cd-iss. Feb94; R 306-2) <US-iss.Feb94 on 'DGC'; 24624>*

—— disbanded after above album

DOROTHY

were a duo formed by **GINA + VICKY**

BlueGuitar not iss.

Jul 88. (7"/12") *(AZUR 8/+T)* **STILL WAITING. / THE FROG PRINCE**
Jan 89. (7"/12"/cd-s) *(AZUR 11/+T/CD)* **LOVING FEELING. / SEXUAL OBSESSION**

Cooltempo not iss.

Jul 89. (7"/12") *(COOL 187/+T)* **REFLECTIONS. / ('A'version)**

—— They split after above dance flop.

RAINCOATS (cont.)

—— re-formed w / **BIRCH, DA SILVA, + ANNE WOOD** – violin / **STEVE SHELLEY** (b.23 Jun'62, Midland, Michigan) – drums (of SONIC YOUTH)

Blast First Smells Like

Jun 94. (10"ep/cd-ep) *(BFFP 99/+CD) <12>* **EXTENDED PLAY**   Apr95
– Don't be mean / We smile / No-one's little girl / Shouting out loud.

Rough Trade Geffen

May 96. (7"ep/cd-ep) *(R 404-7/-3)* **DON'T BE MEAN**   -
Jun 96. (cd/lp) *(R 403-2/-1) <24957>* **LOOKING IN THE SHADOWS**   May96
– Only tonight / Don't be mean / Forgotten words / Pretty / Truth is hard / Babydog / You ask why / 57 ways to end it all / So damn early / You kill me / Love a loser / Looking in the shadows.

—— BIRCH subsequently formed The HANGOVERS

– compilations, etc. –

1983. (c) *R.O.I.R.; <A 120>* **THE KITCHEN TAPES (live)**   -
(cd-iss. Feb95 & Mar98 on 'ROIR Europe'; RUSCD 8238)

RAMONES

Formed: Forest Hills, New York, USA . . . August '74 as a trio by JOHNNY, JOEY and DEE DEE, who all took the working surname RAMONE (although they were brothers only in the loosest sense of the term). One of the prime movers (many would subsequently cite them as the first) in the emergent US punk scene, the band began a residency at the legendary NY club, CBGB's, TOMMY coming in on the drum stool in order to free JOEY up for suitably deranged vocal duties. In June '75, the band were dealt a slight setback when they failed an audition for RICK DERRINGER's 'Blue Sky' label in front of 20,000 fans at a JOHNNY WINTER concert, although later that year manager, Danny Fields, found up and coming new wave label, 'Sire' (run by Seymour Stein) considerably more receptive. Released around the same time as their pivotal (and highly influential) London Roundhouse gig, the band's eponymous summer '76 debut album presented a sound every bit as exhilaratingly juvenile and humorously warped as their leering, mop-topped scruffiness might suggest. Ripping out gloriusly dumb, two-minute buzz-saw classics on such perennial punk subjects as solvent abuse ('I WANNA SNIFF SOME GLUE'), girls (most of the album) and erm, chainsaws ('CHAIN SAW'), The RAMONES had invented themselves as larger than life, cartoon yob no-wavers well ahead of their time, their attitude alone copied by countless two-bit punk bands (and a few great ones) the length and breadth of the British Isles. Barely pausing for breath (or whatever it was these guys inhaled), the new yoik brudders followed up with 'LEAVE HOME' (1977), another strychnine-fuelled session of primitive but tuneful terrace chant anthems, RAMONES style; from this point onwards, the words 'Gabba Gabba Hey' would be forever carved in the stone of the punk lexicon. The album even managed a minor dent in the UK charts, a full scale assault led later that year with the brilliantly throwaway 'SHEENA IS A PUNK ROCKER'. The climax of the early RAMONES blitzkrieg came with 'ROCKET TO RUSSIA' (1977), the lads easing ever so slightly off the gas pedal and taking the credo of mangled, two minute surf-pop to its dayglo conclusion; the hilarious 'CRETIN HOP', 'ROCKAWAY BEACH' and 'TEENAGE LOBOTOMY' remain among the most definitive moments in the RAMONES' dog-eared catalogue. A rather disappointing Top 60 placing failed to do the record justice, although by this stage the band were beginning to make some inroads into the home market. Further evidence, if any was needed, that The RAMONES' chief writer was at the peak of his powers came with the blistering 'Chinese Rocks', a HEARTBREAKERS track co-penned by DEE DEE. With the departure of TOMMY (into production work) the following year, ex-VOID-OID MARC BELL was recruited in his place, rechristened, of course, MARKY RAMONE. Incredibly, the tried and tested formula (with a few notable exceptions, a guitar solo (!) on 'GO MENTAL' and a ballad, 'QUESTIONINGLY') continued to excite with 'ROAD TO RUIN' (1978), their first album to break into the UK Top 40 and the resting place of the legendary 'I WANNA BE SEDATED'. The riotous 'IT'S ALIVE' (1979) captured the RAMONES concert experience head-on, neatly wrapping up the first stage of the boys' career and providing a handy overview of their career to date. Every punk band coped with the scene's fragmentation in their own way, The RAMONES not so wisely choosing to indulge their love of classic 60's pop via the genre's guru, Phil Spector. The results were predictably confused, many longtime RAMONES headbangers balking at their UK Top 10 cover of The Ronettes' 'BABY I LOVE YOU'. Subsequent 80's efforts such as 'PLEASANT DREAMS' (1981) and 'SUBTERRANEAN JUNGLE' (1983) lacked the ragged glory of their earlier work although with the replacement of MARKY with RICHIE (aka RICHARD REINHARDT) in 1984, 'TOO TOUGH TO DIE' (1985) found the band sharpening their attack and presenting a united front against the hardcore pretenders of the day. They couldn't keep it up though, and the limitations of their art really began to bite deep on the bedraggled 'ANIMAL BOY' (1986) and 'HALFWAY TO SANITY' (1987). DEE DEE bailed out after 'BRAIN DRAIN' (1989), replacement C.J. effecting something of a rejuvenation on 'MONDO BIZARRO' (1992). The following year's 'ACID EATERS' saw the band pay tribute to the 60's sounds which had inspired them, while in turn, many of the younger bands who had actually been inspired by The RAMONES would soon be calling the shots at America's major labels. Yet despite this punk revival and the success of such acts as GREEN DAY and OFFSPRING, The RAMONES finally decided to call it a day in early 1996 following the release of the 'ADIOS AMIGOS' set and the accompanying tour. Fans of all ages were shocked to hear the news of JOEY's death (of lymphoma) in NY on the 15th of April, 2001. Barely a year later (5th June 2002), DEE DEE also passed away. • **Songwriters:** DEE DEE and group, except; DO YOU WANNA DANCE (Bobby Freeman) / SURFIN' BIRD (Trashmen) / BABY I LOVE YOU (Ronettes; Phil Spector) / NEEDLES AND PINS (Searchers) / STREET FIGHTIN' MAN (Rolling Stones) / TAKE IT AS IT COMES (Doors) / R.A.M.O.N.E.S. (Motorhead) / ANY WAY YOU WANT IT (Dave Clark) / SPIDER-MAN (Harris-Webster) / etc. In '77, DEE DEE co-wrote 'CHINESE ROCKS' for The HEARTBREAKERS. • **Trivia:** The RAMONES featured in the films 'Blank Generation' (1976) & 'Rock'n'roll High School' (Roger Corman 1979).

Album rating: RAMONES (*9) / LEAVE HOME (*8) / ROCKET TO RUSSIA (*8) / ROAD TO RUIN (*7) / IT'S ALIVE (*6) / END OF THE CENTURY (*7) / PLEASANT DREAMS (*6) / SUBTERRANEAN JUNGLE (*6) / TOO TOUGH TO DIE (*7) / ANIMAL BOY (*6) / HALFWAY TO SANITY (*4) / RAMONES MANIA compilation (*9) / BRAIN DRAIN (*4) / LOCO LIVE (*3) / MONDO BIZARRO (*3) / ACID EATERS (*3) / ADIOS AMIGOS (*5) / WE'RE OUTTA HERE (*5)

JOEY RAMONE (b. JEFFREY HYMAN, 19 May'51) – vocals (was drummer) / **JOHNNY RAMONE** (b. JOHN CUMMINGS, 8 Oct'51, Long Island, N.Y.) – guitar, vocals / **DEE DEE RAMONE** (b. DOUGLAS COLVIN, 18 Sep'52, Fort Lee, Virginia) – bass, vocals / **TOMMY RAMONE** (b. TOM ERDELYI, 29 Jan'49, Budapest, Hungary) – drums

Sire Sire

Jul 76. (lp) *(9103 253)* *<7520>* **RAMONES** [ ] [ ] May76
– Blitzkrieg bop / Beat on the brat / Judy is a punk / I wanna be your boyfriend / Chain saw / Now I wanna sniff some glue / I don't wanna go down to the basement / Loudmouth / Havana affair / Listen to my heart / 53rd & 3rd / Let's dance / I don't wanna walk around with you / Today your love, tomorrow the world. *(re-iss. Sep78; SRK 6020) <cd-iss. Oct99 on 'Rhino'; 7559 27421-2> <cd re-mast.Jun01 on 'Rhino'+=; 8122 74306-2>* – (extra tracks).

Jul 76. (7") *(6078 601)* *<725>* **BLITZKRIEG BOP. / HAVANA AFFAIR** [ ] [ ] May76

Oct 76. (7"m) *<734>* **I WANNA BE YOUR BOYFRIEND. / CALIFORNIA SUN (live) / I DON'T WANNA WALK AROUND WITH YOU (live)** [-] [ ]

Feb 77. (7"m) *(6078 603)* **I REMEMBER YOU. / CALIFORNIA SUN (live) / I DON'T WANNA WALK AROUND WITH YOU (live)** [ ] [-]

Mar 77. (lp) *(9103 254)* *<7528>* **LEAVE HOME** [45] [ ] Feb77
– Glad to see you go / Gimme gimme shock treatment / I remember you / Oh oh I love her so / Babysitter * / Suzy is a headbanger / Pinhead / Now I wanna be a good boy / Swallow my pride / What's your game / California sun / Commando / You're gonna kill that girl / You should never have opened that door / California sun. *(re-iss. Jun77 'Carbona Not Glue' replaced *; other re-iss's same) (re-iss. Sep78; SRK 6031) (re-iss. Nov87 on 'Mau Mau'; MAU 602) <cd re-iss. Oct99 on 'Rhino'; 7599 27422-2> <cd re-mast.Jun01 on 'Rhino'+=; 8122 74307-2>* – (extra tracks).

May 77. (7"m,12"m) *(6078 606)* *<746>* **SHEENA IS A PUNK ROCKER. / COMMANDO / I DON'T CARE** [22] [81]

Jul 77. (7"m) *(6078 607)* *<738>* **SWALLOW MY PRIDE. / PINHEAD / LET'S DANCE (live)** [36] [ ] Mar77

Nov 77. (7"m,12"m) *(6078 611)* **ROCKAWAY BEACH. / TEENAGE LOBOTOMY / BEAT ON THE BRAT** [ ] [-]

Nov 77. (7") *<1008>* **ROCKAWAY BEACH. / LOCKET LOVE** [-] [66]

Dec 77. (lp) *(9103 255)* *<6042>* **ROCKET TO RUSSIA** [60] [49] Nov77
– Cretin hop / Rockaway beach / Here today, gone tomorrow / Locket love / I don't care / Sheena is a punk rocker / We're a happy family / Teenage lobotomy / Do you wanna dance? / I wanna be well / I can't give you anything / Ramona / Surfin' bird / Why is it always this way. *(re-iss. Sep78; SRK 6042) <cd-iss. Oct99 on 'Rhino'; 7559 27424-2> <cd re-mast.Jun01 on 'Rhino'+=; 8122 74309-2>* – (extra tracks).

Feb 78. (7") *<1017>* **DO YOU WANNA DANCE?. / BABYSITTER** [-] [86]

Mar 78. (7"m) *(6078 615)* **DO YOU WANNA DANCE? / IT'S A LONG WAY BACK TO GERMANY / CRETIN HOP** [ ] [-]

— **MARKY RAMONE** (b. MARC BELL, 15 Jul'56) – drums (ex-RICHARD HELL & THE VOID-OIDS, ex-DUST) repl. TOMMY who continued producing others.

Sep 78. (7",7"yellow,12"yellow,12"red) *(SRE 1031)* *<1025>* **DON'T COME CLOSE. / I DON'T WANT YOU** [38] [ ]

Oct 78. (yellow-lp) *<(SRK 6063)>* **ROAD TO RUIN** [32] [ ]
– I just want to have something to do / I wanted everything / Don't come close / I don't want you / Needles and pins / I'm against it / I wanna be sedated / Go mental / Questioningly / She's the one / Bad brain / It's a long way back. *(cd-iss. Oct99; 7559 27426-2) <(cd re-mast.Jun01 on 'Rhino'+=; 8122 74308-2)>* – (extra tracks).

Nov 78. (7") *<1045>* **NEEDLES AND PINS. / I WANTED EVERYTHING** [-] [ ]

Jan 79. (7") *(SIR 4009)* **SHE'S THE ONE. / I WANNA BE SEDATED** [ ] [-]

May 79. (d-lp/c) *(SRK/SRC 26074)* **IT'S ALIVE (live)** [27] [-]
– Rockaway beach / Teenage lobotomy / Blitzkrieg bop / I wanna be well / Glad to see you go / Gimme gimme shock treatment / You're gonna kill that girl / I don't care / Sheena is a punk rocker / Havana affair / Commando / Here today, gone tomorrow / Surfin' bird / Cretin hop / Listen to my heart / California sun / I don't wanna walk around with you / Pinhead / Do you wanna dance? / Chain saw / Today your love, tomorrow the world / Now I wanna be a good boy / Judy is a punk / Suzy is a headbanger / Let's dance / Oh oh I love her so / Now I wanna sniff some glue / We're a happy family. *(cd-iss. Nov93 on 'Warners'; 7599 26069-2) (cd re-iss. Jan96; 9362 46045-2)*
(above album features TOMMY on drums)

Sep 79. (7") *<1051>* **DO YOU WANNA DANCE? / ROCK'N'ROLL HIGH SCHOOL** [-] [ ]

Sep 79. (7") *(SIR 4021)* **ROCK'N'ROLL HIGH SCHOOL. / SHEENA IS A PUNK ROCKER (live) / ROCKAWAY BEACH (live)** [67] [-]

Jan 80. (lp/c) *<(SRK/SRC 6077)>* **END OF THE CENTURY** [14] [44]
– Do you remember rock'n'roll radio? / I'm affected / Danny says / Chinese rock / The return of Jackie and Judy / Let's go / Baby I love you / I can't make it on time / This ain't Havana / Rock'n'roll high school / All the way / High risk insurance. *(re-iss. cd Mar94; 7599 27429-2) <(cd re-mast.Aug02 on 'Rhino'+=; 8122 78155-2)>* – (bonus tracks).

Jan 80. (7") *(SIR 4031)* *<49182>* **BABY, I LOVE YOU. / HIGH RISK INSURANCE** [8] [ ]

Apr 80. (7") *<49261>* **DO YOU REMEMBER ROCK'N'ROLL RADIO?. / LET'S GO** [-] [ ]

Apr 80. (7") *(SIR 4037)* **DO YOU REMEMBER ROCK'N'ROLL RADIO?. / I WANT YOU AROUND** [54] [-]

Jul 81. (7") *(SIR 4051)* *<49812>* **WE WANT THE AIRWAVES. / ALL'S QUIET ON THE EASTERN FRONT** [ ] [ ]

Jul 81. (lp/c) *<(SRK/SRC 3571)>* **PLEASANT DREAMS** [ ] [58]
– We want the airwaves / All's quiet on the Eastern front / The KKK took my baby away / Don't go / You sound like you're sick / It's not my place / She's a sensation / 7-11 / You didn't mean anything to me / Come on now / This business is killing me / Sitting in my room. *(re-iss. cd Mar94 & Jun00; 7599 23571-2) <(cd re-mast.Aug02 on 'Rhino'+=; 8122 78156-2)>* – (bonus tracks).

Oct 81. (7") *(SIR 4052)* **SHE'S A SENSATION. / ALL'S QUIET ON THE EASTERN FRONT** [ ] [-]

May 83. (lp/c) *(WX/+C 3800)* *<23800>* **SUBTERRANEAN JUNGLE** [ ] [83]
– Little bit o' soul / I need your love / Outsider / What'd ya do / Highest trails above / Somebody like me / Psycho therapy / Time has come today / My-my kind of girl / In the park / Time bomb / Everytime I eat vegetables It makes me think of you. *(re-iss. cd Mar94 & Jun00; 7599 23800-2) <(cd re-mast.Aug02 on 'Rhino'+=; 8122 78157-2)>* – (bonus tracks).

Jun 83. (7") *(W 9606)* **TIME HAS COME TODAY. / PSYCHO THERAPY** [ ] [-]
(12"+=) *(W 9606T)* – Baby I love you / Don't come close.

— **RICHIE RAMONE** (b. RICHARD REINHARDT, aka BEAU) – drums (ex-VELVETEENS) repl. MARC

Beggars Banquet Sire

Nov 84. (7") *<29107>* **HOWLING AT THE MOON (SHA LA LA). / WART HOG** [-] [ ]

Jan 85. (lp/c) *(BEGA/BEGC 59)* *<25187>* **TOO TOUGH TO DIE** [63] [ ] Oct84
– Mama's boy / I'm not afraid of life / Too young to die / Durango 95 / Wart hog / Danger zone / Chasing the night / Howling at the Moon (sha-la-la) / Daytime dilemma (dangers of love) / Planet Earth 1988 / Human kind / Endless vacation / No go. *<cd re-mast.Aug02 on 'Rhino'+=; 8122 78158-2>* – (bonus tracks).

Jan 85. (7") *(BEG 128)* **HOWLING AT THE MOON (SHA-LA-LA). / CHASING THE NIGHT** [ ] [-]
(d7"+=)(12"pic-d+=) *(BEG 128D)(BEGTP 128)* – Smash you / Street fighting man.

Jun 85. (7") *(BEG 140)* **BONZO GOES TO BITBURG. / DAYTIME DILEMMA (DANGERS OF LOVE)** [ ] [-]
(12"+=) *(BEG 140T)* – Go home Annie.

Apr 86. (7") *(BEG 157)* **SOMETHING TO BELIEVE IN. / SOMEBODY PUT SOMETHING IN MY DRINK** [69] [-]
(12"+=) *(BEG 157T)* – (You) Can't say anything nice.

May 86. (lp/c) *(BEGA/BEGC 70)* *<25433>* **ANIMAL BOY** [38] [ ]
– Somebody put something in my drink / Animal boy / Love kills / Apeman hop / She belongs to me / Crummy stuff / My brain is hanging upside down (Bonzo goes to Bitburg) / She belongs to me / Mental hell / Eat that rat / Freak of nature / Hair of the dog / Something to believe in.

Jun 86. (7") *<28599>* **SOMETHING TO BELIEVE IN. / ANIMAL BOY** [-] [ ]

Jul 86. (7") *(BEG 167)* **CRUMMY STUFF. / SHE BELONGS TO ME** [ ] [-]
(12"+=,12"red+=) *(BEG 167 T)* – I don't want to live this life.

— **MARKY RAMONE** – drums returned to repl. CLEM BURKE (ex-BLONDIE) who had repl. RICKY (above now with originals JOEY, DEE DEE and JOHNNY)

Sep 87. (7") *(BEG 198)* **A REAL COOL TIME. / INDIAN GIVER** [ ] [-]
(12"+=) *(BEG 198T)* – Life goes on.

Sep 87. (lp/c) *(BEGA/BEGC 89)* *<25641>* **HALFWAY TO SANITY** [78] [ ]
– I wanna live / Bop 'til you drop / Garden of serenity / Weasel face / Go lil' Camaro go / I know better now / Death of me / I lost my mind / A real cool time / I'm not Jesus / Bye bye baby / Worm man. *(cd-iss. Dec87 +=; BEGA 89CD)* – Indian giver / Life goes on.

Nov 87. (7"/12") *(BEG 201/+T)* **I WANNA LIVE. / MERRY CHRISTMAS (I DON'T WANT TO FIGHT TONIGHT)** [ ] [ ]

Chrysalis Sire

Aug 89. (lp/c/cd) *(CHR/ZCHR/CCD 1725)* *<25905>* **BRAIN DRAIN** [75] [ ] Jun89
– I believe in miracles / Zero zero UFO / Don't bust my chops / Punishment fits the crime / All screwed up / Palisades Park / Pet sematary / Learn to listen / Can't get you outta my mind / Ignorance is bliss / Come back, baby / Merry Christmas (I don't want to fight tonight).

Sep 89. (7") *(CHS 3423)* **PET SEMATARY. / ALL SCREWED UP** [ ] [-]
(12"+=) *(CHS12 3423)* – Zero zero UFO.

Sep 89. (7") *<22911>* **PET SEMATARY. / SHEENA IS A PUNK ROCKER** [-] [ ]

— **C.J. RAMONE** (b. CHRISTOPHER JOSEPH WARD, 8 Oct'65, Long Island, N.Y.) – bass repl. DEE DEE who became rap artist DEE DEE KING

Oct 91. (cd/c/d-lp) *(CCD/ZCHR/CHR 1901)* **LIVE LOCO (live)** [ ] [-]
– The good, the bad and the ugly / Django 95 / Teenage lobotomy / Psycho therapy / Blitzkrieg bop / Rock'n'roll radio / I believe in miracles / Gimme gimme shock treatment / Rock'n'roll high school / I wanna be sedated / The KKK took my baby away / I wanna live / Bonzo goes to Bitzburg / Too tough to die / Sheena is a punk rocker / Rockaway beach / Pet semetary / Don't bust my shape / Palisades park / Mama's boy / Animal boy / Wart hog / Surfin' bird / Cretin hop / I don't wanna walk around with you / Today your love, tomorrow the world / Pinhead / Somebody put something in my drink / Beat on the brat / Judy is a punk / Chinese rocks / Love kills / Ignorance is bliss.

Radioactive Radioactive

Sep 92. (cd/c/lp) *<(RAR D/C 10615)>* **MONDO BIZARRO** [ ] [ ]
– Censorshit / The job that ate my brain / Poison heart / Anxiety / Strength to endure / It's gonna be alright / Take it as it comes / Main man / Tomorrow she goes away / I won't let it happen again / Cabbies on crack / Heidi is a heartache / Touring.

Chrysalis Radioactive

Nov 92. (c-s/7"yellow) *(TC+/CHS 3917)* **POISON HEART. / CENSORSHIT (live)** [69] [-]
(12"+=) *(12CHS 3917)* – Chinese rocks (live) / Sheena is a punk rocker (live).
(cd-s+=) *(CDCHS 3917)* – Rock and roll radio (live).

Dec 93. (cd/c/lp) *(CD/TC+/CHR 6052)* *<10913>* **ACID EATERS** [ ] [ ]
– Journey to the center of the mind / Substitute / Out of time / The shape of things to come / Somebody to love / When I was young / 7 and 7 is / My back pages / Can't seem to make you mine / Have you ever seen the rain / I can't control myself / Surf city.

RAMONES (cont) — THE GREAT INDIE DISCOGRAPHY — **The 1970s**

— Album of covers; SUBSTITUTE (Who) / I CAN'T CONTROL MYSELF (Troggs) / SURF CITY (Jan & Dean) / OUT OF TIME (Rolling Stones) / THE SHAPE OF THINGS TO COME (Headboys) / etc.

Jun 95. (cd/c/lp) (CD/TC+/CHR 6104) <11273> **ADIOS AMIGOS** [62]
 – I don't want to grow up / I'm makin' monsters for my friends / It's not for me to know / The crusher / Life's a gas / Take the pain away / I love you / Cretin family / Have a nice day / Scattergun / Got a lot to say / She talks to rainbows / Born to die in Berlin.

— split after tour early the following year, although they had a brief reunion on the 6th August, 1996 at The Palace, Los Angeles

                                                                                        Eagle   Radioactive
Nov 97. (cd) (EAGCD 010) <11555> **WE'RE OUTTA HERE!** (their last show)
 – Durango 95 / Teenage lobotomy / Psycho therapy / Blitzkrieg bop / Do you remember rock and roll radio / I believe in miracles / Gimme gimme shock treatment / Rock'n'roll high school / I wanna be sedated / Spider-man / The K.K.K. took my baby away / I just want to have something to do / Commando / Sheena is a punk rocker / Rockaway beach / Pet sematary / The crusher / Love kills / Do you wanna dance / Someone put something in my drink / I don't want you / Wart hog / Cretin hop / R.A.M.O.N.E.S. / Today your love, tomorrow the world / Pinhead / 53rd & 3rd / Listen to your heart / We're a happy family / Chinese rock / Beat on the brat / Any way you want it.

— after what we think is their final release, MARKY RAMONE went solo

– compilations, etc. –

Aug 80. (7") R.S.O.; (RSO 70) / Sire; <2090 512> **I WANNA BE SEDATED. / THE RETURN OF JACKIE AND JUDY**
— (above from Various Artists Film Soundtrack 'Rock'n'roll High School' also incl. 'Medley: Blitzkrieg bop – Teenage lobotomy – California sun – Pinhead – She's the one')
Nov 80. (7"ep) Sire; (SREP 1) **MELTDOWN WITH THE RAMONES**
 – I just wanna have something to do / Questioningly / I wanna be your boyfriend / Here today, gone tomorrow.
Jun 88. (7") Sire; <27663> **I WANNA BE SEDATED. / (part 2)**
Jun 88. (d-lp/c/cd) (925709-1/-4/-2) <25709> **RAMONES MANIA**
 – I wanna be sedated / Teenage lobotomy / Do you remember rock'n'roll radio? / Gimme gimme shock treatment / Beat on the brat / Sheena is a punk rocker / I wanna live / Pinhead / Blitzkrieg bop / Cretin hop / Rockaway beach / Commando / I wanna be your boyfriend / Mama's boy / Bop 'til you drop / We're a happy family / Bonzo goes to Bitburg / The outsider / Psycho therapy / Wart hog / Animal boy / Needles and pins / Howlin' at the Moon / Somebody put something in my drink / We want the airwaves / Chinese rocks / I just want to have something to do / The KKK took my baby away / Indian giver / Rock'n'roll high school.
Sep 90. (cd/c/d-lp) Sire; (7599 26220-2/-4/-1) **ALL THE STUFF (AND MORE)** (demos 1976-77, etc)
May 99. (d-cd+book) Megaworld; (MEGBK 02) **BLITZKREIG BOP**
Aug 99. (d-cd) Sire; (8122 7581-2) **HEY HO LET'S GO – THE RAMONES ANTHOLOGY**
Aug 00. (cd) Burning Airlines; <(PILOT 79)> **YOU DON'T COME CLOSE**
May 01. (cd) Sire; <8122 73557-2> **HEY HO LET'S GO! (THE RAMONES ANTHOLOGY)** [74]
Aug 01. (cd) E.M.I.; (534609-2) **MASTERS OF ROCK – THE VERY BEST OF THE RAMONES**
Sep 01. (7"/cd-s) Musical Tragedies; (EFA 12615-7/-2) **JUDY IS A PUNK. / (other track by New York Dolls)**
Apr 02. (cd) EMI Gold; (538472-2) **THE BEST OF THE CHRYSALIS YEARS**
Aug 02. (3xcd-box) E.M.I.; (541080-2) **THE CHRYSALIS YEARS**
Nov 02. (cd) W.S.M.; (8122 76101-2) **LOUD FAST RAMONES – THEIR TOUGHEST HITS**

— JOEY also on "HOLLY & JOEY" 7" – 1982 'I Got You Babe' on 'Virgin'.
— In August '88, JOHNNY teamed up with DEBBIE HARRY for 7" – 'Go Lil Camara Go'. In 1994, JOEY RAMONE featured (+ on cover sleeve) of SIBLING RIVALRY's 'In A Family Way' EP for 'Alternative Tentacles'.

JOEY RAMONE

with a plethora of session players
                                                                    Sanctuary Sanctuary
Dec 01. (cd-s) <84541> **MERRY CHRISTMAS (I DON'T WANT TO FIGHT TONIGHT)**
Feb 02. (cd) (SANC 108CD) <84542> **DON'T WORRY ABOUT ME**
 – What a wonderful world / Stop thinking about it / Mr. Punchy / Maria Bartiromo / Spirit in my house / Venting (it's a different world today) / Like a drug I never did before / Searching for something / I got knocked down (but I'll get up) / 1969 / Don't worry about me.
Dec 02. (cd-ep) <84589> **CHRISTMAS SPIRIT … IN MY HOUSE**
 – Christmas (baby please come home) / Merry Christmas (I don't want to fight tonight) / Spirit in my house / Don't worry about me / What a wonderful world.

DEE DEE RAMONE

writes with REY
                                                                    World Dom. World Dom.
Jun 94. (cd/lp) <(1571757-2/-1)> **I HATE FREAKS LIKE YOU**
 – I'm making monsters for my friends / Don't look in my window / Chinese bitch / It's not for me to know / Runaway / All's quiet on the Eastern Front / I hate it / Life is like a little smart Alleck / I hate creeps like you / Trust me / Curse on me / I'm seeing strawberry's again / Lass mich in Fuhe / I'm making monsters for my friends.
                                                                    Other People's Music Other People's Music
Sep 97. (cd) <(OPM 2118CD)> **ZONKED**
 – I'm zonked, los hombres / Fix yourself up / I am seeing UFO's / Get off the scene / Never never again / Bad horoscope / It's so bizarre / Get out of my room / Someone who don't fit in / Victim of society / My Chico / Disguises / Why is everybody always against Germany.

                                                                    Blackout Blackout
Oct 97. (7") (BLK 5008E7) **I AM SEEING UFO'S. / BAD HOROSCOPE**
Nov 97. (cd) (BLK 5008ECD) **AIN'T IT FUN**
 – I'm zonked los hombres / Fix yourself up / I am seeing UFO's / Get off the scene / Never never again / Bad horoscope / Get out of the room / Someone who doesn't fit in / Victim of society / My Chico / Disguises / Why is everyone always against Germany / Please kill me.
                                                                    Corazong not iss.
Mar 00. (cd) (2000 006) **HOP AROUND**
 – I don't wanna die in the basement / Mental patient / Now I wanna be sedated / Rock & roll vacation in L.A. / Get out of this house / 38th & 8th / Nothin' / Hop around / What about me? / I saw a skull instead of my head / I wanna you / Master plan / Born to lose / Hurtin' kind / I'm horrible. (re-iss. Jul02; same)
                                                                    Eagle Conspiracy
Sep 00. (cd) (EAGCD 156) <10> **GREATEST AND LATEST**
 – Blitzkrieg bop / Timebomb / Sheena is a punk rocker / Shaking all over / I wanna be sedated / Cretin hop / Teenage lobotomy / Gimme gimme shock treatment / Motorbikin' / Come on now / Cathy's clown / Pinhead / Rockaway beach / Fix yourself up / Sidewalk surfin' / Beat on the brat. (re-iss. Mar02; same)

RAPED (see under ⇒ CUDDLY TOYS)

REAL KIDS

Formed: Boston, Massachusetts, USA … 1975 out of The KIDS by songwriter JOHN FELICE (also a sometime J.RICHMAN/MODERN LOVERS sidekick), who enlisted ALLEN 'ALPO' PAULINO, BILLY BORGIOLI and HOWARD FERGUSON. With the Punk/New Wave explosion providing a perfect platform for FELICE's brand of slap-dash high-octane rock'n'roll, the RAMONES-alike (definitely image wise at least) REAL KIDS were a regular draw at New York's CBGB's club. Bizarrely enough, the band became a leading light of the Paris punk scene after issuing their debut single, 'ALL KINDSA GIRLS', as a French-only release in '77. American and British fans had to wait for 1978's eponymous LP which featured the song as its opening track, the record subsequently achieving underground cult status for its combination of raw beer-drenched originals and spirited covers of material by BUDDY HOLLY and EDDIE COCHRAN. The band was put on hold however, as FELICE became part of the RAMONES' road crew, the man (along with a new cast of musicians) later releasing an EP as the TAXI BOYS, taking the moniker from an old REAL KIDS track. A near original line-up of the latter combo regrouped in '82, signing to French label 'New Rose' for a trio of albums, 'OUTTA PLACE' (1982), the live 'ALL KINDSA JERKS' (1983) and 'HIT YOU HARD' (1983). With the band again put on ice, JOHN FELICE & HIS LOWDOWNS returned in '88 with a collection of songs entitled 'NOTHING PRETTY'; The REAL KIDS were back on the block one last time in 1999 with a new EP, 'DOWN TO YOU'.

Album rating: THE REAL KIDS (*7) / OUTTA PLACE mini (*5) / ALL KINDSA JERKS (*4) / HIT YOU HARD (*4) / BETTER BE GOOD compilation (*7) / John Felice & The Lowdowns: NOTHING PRETTY (*5)

JOHN FELICE – vocals, guitar / **BILLY BORGIOLI** – guitar / **ALLEN 'ALPO' PAULINO** – bass / **HOWARD FERGUSON** – drums
                                                                    Sponge not iss.
1977. (7") (SPSP 10) **ALL KINDSA GIRLS. / COMMON AT NOON** – French
 <US re-iss. 1999 on 'Norton'; 45-081>
                                                                    Bronze Red Star
Jun 78. (lp) (BRON 509) <RS 2> **THE REAL KIDS**
 – All kindsa girls / Better be good / She's alright / Solid gold (thru and thru) / Just like darts / Do the boob / My baby's book / Reggae reggae / My ways / Taxi boys / Roberta / Rave on. (re-iss. Jul85 on 'Fan Club'; FC 010)
Jun 78. (7") (BRO 54) **ALL KINDSA GIRLS. / TAXI BOYS**

— **SCOTT PARMENTAR** – guitar; repl. BORGIOLI
— **BILLY COLE** – bass; repl. PAULINO
— **BOBBY McNABB** – drums; repl. FERGUSON
                                                                    not iss. Bomp
Jul 81. (12"ep; as the TAXI BOYS) <EC 4019> **TAXI BOYS EP**
 – She / Bad to worse / Happens all the time / What she don't know / What's it to you / Everybody's girl.

— **ROBBY 'MOROCCO' MORIN** – drums; repl. McNABB
— **PAULINO + BORGIOLI** would return to repl. SCOTT + BILLY
                                                                    New Rose Star-Rhythm
Jul 82. (m-lp) (ROSE 14) <103> **OUTTA PLACE**
 – Can't talk to that girl / No place fast / Senseless / It's been real / I'd rather go to jail (live at Jacks) [not US] / Every day is a Saturday / Small town / Problems / Outta place.
Mar 83. (lp/c) (ROSE/ROSK 21) **ALL KINDSA JERKS (live)**
 – Outta place / No place fast / She don't know / Common at noon / Boob / Baby's book / Can't talk to that girl / Bad to worse / She got everything / My way / All kindsa girls.

— added **ANDY PALEY** – keyboards, slide guitar, harmonica
Jun 83. (7") (NEW 17) **SHE. / SHE'S A MESS (live)**
Jul 83. (lp) (ROSE 24) **HIT YOU HARD**
 – She / Hit you hard / Now you know / Where I wanna be / Take it slow / Right when it's right / She's a mess / Face to face / Some love / On the blink.
                                                                    Lolita not iss.
1983. (m-lp; split w/ TAXI BOYS) (5002) **GIRLS! GIRLS! GIRLS!** – French
 – Now you know / Up is up / She comes alive / Who needs ya / TAXI BOYS:- Whats it to you / Bad to worse / What she don't know / Everybody's girl / Happens all the time / She.

REAL KIDS (cont)

— disbanded in 1984, but originals re-formed in the mid 90's

			T.K.O.	T.K.O.
Nov 99.	(7") <(ROUND 31)> **DOWN TO YOU. / MAKE IT GO AWAY**			
	(cd-s+=) <(ROUND 32)> – I'll say it / Something bad.			
			not iss.	D.U.I.
2000.	(7") <DUI 002> **LIVE IN DETROIT** (live)		-	
	– I can't kick it / Who needs you.			

— FELICE continued to tour with a REAL KIDS outfit featuring **BILLY COLE** – guitar / **CHRIS BARNARD** – bass (ex-QUEERS) / **JUDD WILLIAMS** – drums

– compilations, etc. –

on 'Norton' unless mentioned otherwise

Jun 97. (cd/lp) <(C+/ED 231)> **GROWN UP WRONG** (live) [ ] [Nov93]
– Bad to worse / No fun no more / Do the boob / Jeannie, Jeannie, Jeannie / Common at noon / Shake outta control / I'd rather go to jail / All night boppin' / Hit you hard / Some love like yours / She don't take it / Don't talk to strangers / Grown up wrong / Can't shake that girl. (cd+=) – She come alive / Up is up / Down to you / Got it made / She's alright / Solid gold / Hot dog / Who needs you / Better be good / All kindsa girls.

1993. (7") <45-018> **HOT DOG. / JUST LIKE DARTS** [-] [ ]
(above both live 1976 + 1978) (UK-iss.Feb98; same as US)

Sep 99. (cd/lp) <(CED/NRT 266)> **BETTER BE GOOD** [ ] [ ]
– All kindsa girls / Common at noon / Solid gold / Better be good / Just like darts / Roberta / Reggae, reggae / Taxi boys / She / Up is up / Now you know / She comes alive / My way / She's alright / Do the boob / My baby's back / Rave on / All kindsa girls.

Sep 99. (cd/lp) <(CED/NRT 267)> **NO PLACE FAST** [ ] [ ]
– (OUTTA PLACE + TAXI BOYS + She).

Jun 01. (m-cd/m-lp) <CED/NRT 286> **SENSELESS (Live at Cantone's '82)** [-] [ ]
– Senseless / Outta place / Now you know / Problems / What she don't know / Common at noon / She's got everything / Happens all the time / My way [cd-only] / I'd rather go to jail [cd-only] / All kindsa girls.

Nov 01. (7"ep) <EP 102> **SHE'S GOT EVERYTHING (live 1982)** [ ] [ ]
– She's got everything / My way / I'd rather go to jail.

JOHN FELICE & THE LOWDOWNS

		New Rose	not iss.
Feb 88.	(lp/cd) (ROSE 141/+CD) **NOTHING PRETTY**		-

– Don't be telling me / Ain't we having fun / I'll never sing that song again / Not the one / Perfect love / Nowadaze kids / Nothing pretty / Dreams / Don't make me wait / Can't play it safe.

RECORDS

Formed: Southend, England ... early 1978 by ex-KURSAAL FLYERS, WILL BIRCH and JOHN WICKS, the pair creating a songwriting partnership in the process. The former was a veteran of the local music scene, having played drums in various bands beginning with mid-60's combo, The GEEZENSTACKS through to the aforementioned mid-70's pub-rock act. The RECORDS' line-up was completed by PHIL BROWN, HUW GOWER and IAN GIBBONS, the latter in place in time for their debut lp, 'SHADES IN BED' (1979); he subsequently became a full-time member thereafter. One track from the album, a revamped 'STARRY EYES' (the song had originally appeared in 1978 as RECORDS' independently released debut single prior to their deal with 'Virgin'), nudged into the Top 60 later that year, the band's one and only hit. Fine in small doses, their trademark power-pop was a mite too sickly to stomach over a whole album, the underwhelming 'CRASHES' (1980) being a case in point. Endless variations on the same squeaky clean harmonies and earnest, often cringeworthy lyrics (see 'MAN WITH A GIRLPROOF HEART' and 'WORRIERS') were the order of the day. By the time of the record's release, GOWER had decamped to play with former NEW YORK DOLL, DAVID JOHANSEN, his place filled initially by BILLY MARTIN and more permanently JUDE COLE. More line-up changes then ensued with the replacement of COLE and GIBBONS (who remained on a part-time basis) with CHRIS GENT and DAVE WHELAN prior to swansong album, 'MUSIC ON BOTH SIDES' (1982). Splitting after BIRCH embarked on a fruitful career in production, the band later reformed for a one-off album, 'A SUNNY AFTERNOON IN WATERLOO' (1988). • **Covers:** HAVE YOU SEEN HER MOTHER BABY . . . (Rolling Stonnes).

Album rating: SHADES IN BED (*5) / CRASHES (*4) / MUSIC ON BOTH SIDES (*4) / SMASHES, CRASHES & NEAR MISSES compilation (*5)

JOHN WICKS – vocals, rhythm guitar (ex-KURSAAL FLYERS) / **WILL BIRCH** (b.1950) – drums, vocals (ex-KURSAAL FLYERS) / **HUW GOWER** – lead guitar, vocals (ex-RATBITES FROM HELL) / **PHIL BROWN** – bass, vocals

		N.B.	not iss.
Nov 78.	(7") (NB 2) **STARRY EYES. / PAINT HER FACE**		-
		Virgin	Virgin
Mar 79.	(7") (VS 247) **ROCK'N'ROLL LOVE LETTER. / WIVES AND MOTHERS OF TOMORROW**		-
	(12"+=) (VS 247-12) – Starry eyes.		

— added as a guest at first, **IAN GIBBONS** – keyboards

May 79.	(7") (VS 250) **TEENARAMA. / HELD UP HIGH**		
Jun 79.	(lp) (V 2122) <VA 13130> **SHADES IN BED** <US-title 'THE RECORDS'>		41 Aug79

– All messed up and ready to go / Teenarama / Girls that don't exist / Starry eyes / Up all night / Girl / Insomnia / Affection rejected / The phone / Another star. (w/ free 7"ep) **HIGH HEELS** – Abracadabra (have you seen her) / See my friends / 1984 / Have you seen her mother baby (standing in the shadows).

Aug 79.	(7") <VA 67000> **STARRY EYES. / PAINT HER FACE**	-	56

— **JUDE COLE** – guitar, vocals (ex-MOON MARTIN); repl. BILLY MARTIN, who repl. GOWER (latter to DAVID JOHANSEN group)

May 80.	(7") (VS 330) **HEARTS IN HER EYES. / SO SORRY**		-
Jun 80.	(lp) (V 2155) <VA 13140> **CRASHES**		-

– Rumour sets the woods alight / Hearts in her eyes / I don't remember your name / Man with a girlproof heart / The same mistakes / Girl in golden disc / Spent a week with you last night / Hearts will be broken / Worriers / Guitars in the sky.

— **DAVE WHELAN** – guitar; repl. JUDE + IAN

— **CHRIS GENT** – vocals, saxophone; repl. GIBBONS (was p/t again)

Aug 81.	(7") (VS 442) **IMMITATION JEWELLERY. / YOUR OWN SOUNDTRACK**		-
Mar 82.	(lp) (V 2206) **MUSIC ON BOTH SIDES**		-

– Immitation jewellery / Heather and Hell / Selfish love / Clown around town / Not so much time / Keeping up with Joneses / Third hand information / Real life / King of kings / Cheap detective music / Everyday nightmare.

— split when BIRCH went into production work (re-formed late 80's for a one last recording session (**WICKS, BIRCH, GOWER + BROWN**)

		Waterfront	not iss.
Apr 88.	(lp) (WF 042) **ON A SUNNY AFTERNOON IN WATERLOO**		-

– Night driving / Lovin' in the back row / Level in the bottle / You changed the lock / In the eyes of a blindman / Third degree burns / 36-24-36 / Living out of a suitcase.

– compilations, etc. –

Oct 88. (cd) Virgin; (COMCD 13) **SMASHES, CRASHES AND NEAR MISSES** [ ] [-]
– Starry eyes / Girl in golden disc / Teenarama / Up all night / I don't remember your name / Girls that don't exist / Hearts will be broken / All messed up and ready to go / Hearts in her eyes / Girl / Spent a week with you last night / Held up high / Rumour set the woods alight / The same mistakes / Selfish love / Not so much the time / Affection rejected / Paint her face / Imitation jewellery / Rock and roll love letter. (re-iss. Feb95; CDOVD 456)

May 01. (cd) Angel Air; (<SJPCD 78>) **PAYING FOR THE SUMMER OF LOVE** (demos) [ ] [ ]
– Teenarama / Up all night / Wives and mothers of tomorrow / Girls don't exist / Held up high / Coin machine / Starry eyes / All messed up and ready to go / Insomnia / Affection rejected / The phone / Hearts in eyes / Coca-Cola jingle / If I write your name in my book.

Blaine L. REININGER (see under ⇒ TUXEDOMOON)

RESIDENTS

Formed: Shreveport, North Louisiana, USA ... 1966 by mysterious line-up. Soon relocating to San Mateo, California in the early 70's, they made a few untitled homemade recordings. They subsequently sent these to Hal Haverstadt of 'Warners' who promptly returned them, the address marked; 'for the attention of the residents'. Adopting the latter as their moniker, they later issued the two newly named tapes in the early 70's, 'RUSTY COAT HANGER FOR THE DOCTOR' and 'THE BALLAD OF STUFFED TRIGGER' respectively. In 1972, they shifted base to San Francisco, founding the independently distributed 'Ralph' records. Their "real" debut lp, 'MEET THE RESIDENTS' was issued in 1974, its title and cover art a tongue-in cheek take-off of The BEATLES. They then released a series of very limited edition lp's, 'THIRD REICH AND ROLL' in 1976, a collection of mangled 50's and 60's covers, carrying on where FRANK ZAPPA left off (albeit in a much weirder fashion). Later in the year, The RESIDENTS and DEVO competed for the best re-constructed version of The STONES' 'SATISFACTION', however, the latter won out in the end. After more comical parodying of The BEATLES and others, they unleashed the 'ESKIMO' set in 1979. This seminal meisterwork was recorded over a lengthy period of time, weird in the extreme, it featured tribal rhythms behind sub-lingual voices (VIC REEVES in "club style" must have taken inspiration). In 1980, the 'COMMERCIAL ALBUM' was released, containing forty tracks of exactly one minute in length, it was another to explore the barren frontiers of possibilities in music. They continued throughout the 80's with even more obscurity than their earlier 70's work. This included highlights 'MARK OF THE MOLE' (1981), 'THE TUNE OF TWO CITIES' (1982) and the biblical opera 'GOD IN THREE PERSONS' (1988). The following decade, 'FREAK SHOW' (1991), was first to emerge from the pack, its fake-theatrical doodlings too much for new fans to take on. With the advent of the CD-ROM, The RESIDENTS produced the interactive 'GINGERBREAD MAN' (1995), its play-at-will approach making it never the same twice. The safer 'HAVE A BAD DAY' soundtrack in 1996 was accompanied by yet another interactive CD, 'BAD DAY ON THE MIDWAY'; it was getting beyond a joke, so to speak. In October, 1998, the one-eyeball'd legends set out their religious stall via, 'WORMWOOD: CURIOUS STORIES FROM THE BIBLE', a post-modernist look into the teaching and doctrine of the great book, although with their usual bizarre rhythms. 'ROADWORMS: THE BERLIN SESSIONS' (2000) and the 30th anniversary 'DEMONS DANCE ALONE' (2002) – post-9/11-penned – showed The RESIDENTS were no-one's fools when it comes to uncompromising individualism. • **Songwriters:** Group penned, except tribute/covers lp's of ELVIS PRESLEY, HANK WILLIAMS, GEORGE GERSHWIN and JAMES BROWN material.

Album rating: MEET THE RESIDENTS (*7) / THE THIRD REICH AND ROLL (*6) / FINGERPRINCE (*6) / NOT AVAILABLE (*6) / DUCK STAB – BUSTER AND GLEN (*7) / ESKIMO (*8) / NIBBLES compilation (*6) / THE COMMERCIAL

RESIDENTS (cont) THE GREAT INDIE DISCOGRAPHY The 1970s

ALBUM (*8) / MARK OF THE MOLE (*6) / THE TUNES OF TWO CITIES (*4) / INTERMISSION mini (*4) / RESIDUE OF THE RESIDENTS (*4) / TITLE IN LIMBO with Renaldo & The Loaf (*4) / GEORGE AND JAMES (*4) / RALPH BEFORE '84 – VOLUME 1 compilation (*6) / WHATEVER HAPPENED TO VILENESS FATS (*4) / RALPH BEFORE '84 – VOLUME 2 compilation (*6) / THE BIG BUBBLE – PART 4 OF THE MOLE TRILOGY (*4) / THE PAL TV LP (*4) / HEAVEN? collection (*6) / HELL? collection (*6) / 13th ANNIVERSARY SHOW (*5) / STARS AND HANK FOREVER – THE AMERICAN COMPOSERS SERIES VOL.2 (*4) / GOD IN THREE PERSONS (*4) / THE MOLE SHOW earlier recording (*4) / THE KING AND EYE (*4) / FREAKSHOW (*4) / PRESENT OUR FINEST FLOWERS (*4) / GINGERBREAD MAN (*4) / RESIDUE DEUX (*4) / HAVE A BAD DAY (*7) / WORMWOOD: CURIOUS STORIES FROM THE BIBLE (*7) / ROADWORMS: THE BERLIN SESSIONS (*) / DEMONS DANCE ALONE (*6)

The RESIDENTS (4) – instruments, vocals, noises / assisted by **SNAKEFINGER** (b. PHILIP LITHMAN) (ex-CHILLI WILLI & THE RED HOT PEPPERS)

not iss. Ralph

Dec 72. (d-7"ltd) <RR 1272> **SANTA DOG** (under false psedonyms) –
– Fire (IVORY & THE BRAINEATERS) / Lightning (DELTA NUDES) / Explosion (COLLEGE WALKERS) / Aircraft damage (credited to ARF + OMEGA).

Feb 74. (lp-ltd) <RR 0274> **MEET THE RESIDENTS** –
– Boots / Numb erone / Guylum Bardot / Breath and length / Consuelo's departure / Smelly tongues / Rest aria / Skratz / Spotted pinto bean / Infant tango / Seasoned greetings / N-ER-GEE (crisis blues). *(re-iss. re-mixed Aug77; RR 0677)* – (lost 7 minutes). *(re-iss. Dec88 on 'Torso' cd/lp; CD/40 416) (cd re-iss. Mar98 on 'Euro Ralph'; CD 018)*

— In Oct'75, they issued 500 copies US of lp 'BLORP ESETTE' for 'LAFMS'; *005*>

Feb 76. (lp-ltd) <RR 1075> **THE THIRD REICH AND ROLL** –
– Swastikas on parade / Hitler was a vegetarian. *<re-iss. 1978; same>*

Sep 76. (7"ltd) <RR 0776> **SATISFACTION. / LOSER = WEED** –
<re-iss. Aug78 as 7"yellow; RR 7803>

Jan 77. (7"ep-ltd) <RR 0377> **BABYFINGERS** –
– Monstrous intro / Death in Barstow / Melon collie lassie / Flight of the bumble roach / Walter Westinghouse. *<re-iss. 1979 on 'W.E.I.R.D.' 7"pink; 1>*

Feb 77. (lp-ltd) <RR 1276> **FINGERPRINCE** –
– You yesyesyes / Home age conversation / Godsong / March de la winni / Bos sy / Boo who / Tourniquet of roses / You yesyesyes again / Six things to a cycle. *(re-iss. twice 1978; same) (cd-iss. Dec87 on 'Torso'; TORSOCD 047)*

Aug 77. (7") <RR 0577> **(THE BEATLES PLAY THE RESIDENTS AND THE RESIDENTS PLAY THE BEATLES)** –
– Beyond the valley of a day in the life / Flying.

Feb 78. (7"ep) <RR 1177> **DUCK STAB EP** –
– Constantinople / Sinister exaggerator / The Booker tease / Blue rosebuds / Laughing song / Bach is dead / Elvis and his boss.

Oct 78. (lp) <RR 1174> **NOT AVAILABLE** –
– Edweena / The making of a soul / Ships a going down / Never known questions epilogue. *(UK-iss.cd Sep94 on 'Indigo'; 7539-2)*

Nov 78. (lp) <RR 0278> **DUCK STAB / BUSTER AND GLEN** –
– DUCK STAB + / Lizard lady / Semolina / Birthday boy / Weight-lifting Lulu / Krafty cheese / Hello skinny / The electrocutioner. *(cd-iss. Jul87 on 'Torso'; TORSOCD 406>*

Dec 78. (7") <RR 7812> **SANTA DOG 78. / SANTA DOG** –

Aug 79. (lp) <SM 7908> **SUBTERRANEAN MODERN** –

— more guests **CHRIS CUTLER** – percussion / **DON PRESTON** – synth

Sep 79. (lp,white-lp) <ESK 7906> **ESKIMO** –
– The walrus hunt / Birth / Arctic hysteria / The angry Angakok / A spirit steals a child / The festival of death. *(cd-iss. Jul87 on 'Torso'; TORSOCD 404) (cd re-iss. 1996 on 'Ralph Euro'; CD 016)*

Virgin Ralph

Sep 79. (lp; with SNAKEFINGER) *(VR 3)* <DJ 7901> **NIBBLES** <US title 'PLEASE DO NOT STEAL IT' – DJ compilation> Mar79
– Yesyesyesyes / Santa dog '78 / Gloria / Rest aria / Semolina / The spot / Never known questions / Constantinople / Laughing song / The mocking of a soul / Skratz / Good lovin' / Blue rosebuds / Six things to a cycle / The electrocutioner.

Pre Ralph

Oct 80. (lp) *(PREX 2)* <6559> **THE RESIDENTS COMMERCIAL ALBUM**
– Easter woman / Perfect love / Picnic boy / End of home / Amber / Japanes watercolour / Red rider / My second wife / Suburban bathers / Floyd / Dimples and toes / The nameless souls / Die in terror / Love leaks out / Act of being polite / Medicine man / Tragic bells / Loss of innocence / The simple song / Ups and downs / Possessions / Give it someone else / Phantom / Less not more / My work is so behind / Birds in the trees / Handful of desire / Moisture / Love is . . . / Troubled man / La la loneliness / Nice old man / The talk of creatures / Fingertips / In between dreams / Margaret Freeman / The coming of the crow / When we were young.

Oct 80. (7"ep) *(PRE 009)* **THE RESIDENTS COMMERCIAL SINGLE**
– Amber / Red rider / Picnic boy / When we were young / Phantom / Moisture.

1980. (12"ep) <RZ 8006-D> **DISKOMO** –
– Diskomo / Goosebump: Disasterplants – Farmers – Twinkle.

1981. (lp) <8152> **MARK OF THE MOLE** –
– Hole-worker at the mercies of nature / Voices of the air / The ultimate disaster / Won't you keep us working / First warning / Back to normality / The sky falls / Why are we crying / The tunnels are filling / It never stops / Migration / March to the sea / The observer / Hole-worker's new hymn / Hole-worker's vs Man and machine / Another land / Rumors / Arrival / Deployment / Saturation / The new machine / Idea / Construction / Failure / Reconstruction / Success / Final confrontation / Success / Final confrontation / Driving the moles away / Don't tread on me / The short war / Resolution. *(UK cd-iss. Sep94 on 'Indigo'; 7540-2)*

Ralph Recommended

May 82. (lp) *(RZ 8202)* **THE TUNES OF TWO CITIES** Mar82
– Serenade for Missy / Mousetrap / Smack your lips clap your teeth / A maze of jigsaws / God of darkness / Smokebams / Mourning the undead / Song of the wild / Happy home / The secret seed / The evil disposer.

Jul 83. (12"ep) *(RALPH 1)* <RZ 8252> **INTERMISSION**
– Lights out / Shorty's lament / Moles are coming / Would we be alive / New hymn. *(lp-iss.1989 on 'Torso'; TORSO 33-055)*

1983. (lp) <RZ 8302> **RESIDUE OF THE RESIDENTS** –
– The sleeper / Whoopy snorp / Kamakazi lady / Boy in love / Shut up! shut up! / Anvil forest / Diskomo / Jailhouse rock / Up & down / Walter Westinghouse / Saint Nix / Open up.

New Ralph New Ralph

Jan 84. (lp; with RENALDO & THE LOAF) *(RR 8351)* **TITLE IN LIMBO**

Korova Recommended

Jul 84. (7") *(KOW 36)* **IT'S A MAN'S MAN'S MAN'S WORLD. / I'LL GO CRAZY**

Aug 84. (lp/c) *(KODE/CODE 9)* <RZ 8402> **GEORGE & JAMES** (some live)
– Rhapsody in blue / I got rhythm / Summertime / Live at the Apollo: I'll go crazy / Try me / Think / I don't mind / Lost someone / Please please please / Night train. *(c+=)* – (extra track). *(cd-iss. Sep94 & Oct00 on 'Indigo'; 2122-2)*

DoubleVision Ralph

Dec 84. (lp) *(DV 9)* <RZ 8452> **WHATEVER HAPPENED TO VILENESS FATS**
– Whatever happened to Vileness Fats / Atomic shopping carts / Adventures of a troubled heart / Search for the short man / The importance of evergreen / Broccoli and saxophone / Disguised as meat / Thoughts busily betraying / Lord, it's lonely / The knife fight. *(UK cd-iss. Sep94 on 'Indigo'; 7537-2)*

1985. (lp) <RZ 8552> **THE BIG BUBBLE – PART 4 OF THE MOLE TRILOGY** –
– Sorry / Hop a little / Go where ya wanna go / Gotta gotta get / Cry for the fire / Die stay-go / Vinegar / Fire fly / The big bubble / Fear for the future / Kula bocca says so. *(cd-iss. Sep94 on 'Indigo'; 7541-2)*

Sep 85. (red-lp) *(DVR 17)* **THE PAL TV LP** –

Torso Torso

Oct 86. (d-lp) *(TORSO 33-018)* <2614220> **13TH ANNIVERSARY SHOW (live in Japan & Holland)**
– Jailhouse rock / Where is she? / Picnic in the jungle / I got rhythm / Passing in the bottle / Monkey and Bunny / This is a man's man's man's world / Walter Westinghouse / Easter woman guitar solo / Diskomo / Hello skinny / Constantinople / Hop a little / Cry for the fire / Kamikaze. *(cd-iss. Sep94 on 'Indigo'; 7534-2)*

Nov 86. (lp) *(TORSO33 022)* <2614202> **STARS & HANK FOREVER! – THE AMERICAN COMPOSER'S SERIES VOL.II (THE MUSIC OF HANK WILLIAMS AND JOHN PHILIP SOUSA)**
– Hank Williams:- Hey good lookin' / Six more miles (to the graveyard) / Kaw-liga / Ramblin' man / Jambalaya / John Philip Sousa:- Sousaside: a) Nobles of the mystic shrine, b) The stars & stripes forever, c) El capitan, d) The liberty bell, e) Semper fidelis, f) The Washington post. *(re-iss. Sep94 on 'Indigo'; 7530-1)*

Dec 86. (7"pic-d) *(TORSO7 022)* **KAW-LIGA. / THE STARS AND STRIPES FOREVER**
(12"pic-d) *(TORSO12 022)* – (mixes; prairie / single / original / horror).

Jun 87. (7") *(TORSO7 032)* **HIT THE ROAD JACK. / ELSIE**
(12") *(TORSO12 032)* – ('A'side) / Jambalaya / Firefly (live) / The big bubble (live) / Cry for the fire (live).

Aug 88. (d-lp/cd/dat) *(TORSO 33/CD/DAT 055)* <2614226> **GOD IN THREE PERSONS**
– Hard and tenderly / Devotion / The thing about them / Their early yearsx / Loss of a loved one / The touch / The service / Confused / Fine fat flies / Time / Silver sharp / Kiss of flesh / Pain and pleasure. *(re-iss. lp Sep94 & Oct00 on 'Indigo'; 7531-1)*

Mar 89. (cd-s) *(TORSOCD 322)* **KAW-LIGA (the housey mix / the stripped mix / Nightmare mix II)**

1989. (lp/cd) <2614262> **THE MOLE SHOW LIVE (live)** –
– Voices of the air / The secret seed / Narration / The ultimate disaster / God of darkness / Migration / Smack your lips clap your feet / Another land / The new machine / Call of the wild / Final confrontation / Satisfaction / Happy home. *(UK cd-iss. Sep94 on 'Indigo'; 7542-2)*

1989. (3"pic-cd-ep) *(TORSOCD 355)* **DOUBLE SHOT / LOSS OF LOVED ONE (extended) / KISS OF FLESH (instrumental)** –

1989. (lp/cd) <14263-26> **THE KING AND EYE** –
– Blue suede shoes / Don't be cruel / Heartbreak hotel / All shook up / Return to sender / Teddy bear / Devil in disguise / Stuck on you / Big hunk o' love / A fool such as I / Little sister / His latest flame / Burning love / Viva Las Vegas / Love me tender / Hound dog. *(UK cd-iss. Sep94 on 'Indigo'; 7535-2)*

1989. (cd-ep) *(TORSOCD 421)* **DISKOMO / WHOOPY SNORP / SAINT NIX / DISKOMO LIVE** –

May 90. (7") *(70166)* **DON'T BE CRUEL. / DON'T / SUPPOSING**
(cd-s+=) *(CD166)* – The toy factory / Ghost music.

Indigo East Side Digital

1991. (cd/lp) <8060-2/-1> **FREAKSHOW** –
– Everyone comes to the freak show / Harry the head / Herman the human mole / Wanda the worm woman / Jack the boneless boy / Benny the bouncing bum / Mickey the mumbling midget / Lillie / Nobody laughs when they leave. *(re-iss. Sep94 on 'Indigo' cd)(lp; 2125-2)(7532-1)*

1992. (7") <SP 02> **BLOWOFF** –
(above issued on 'Cryptic')

1995. (cd) *(INDIGO 2129-2)* <8107-2> **GINGERBREAD MAN**
– The weaver / The dying oilman / The confused transsexual The sold-out artist / The ascetic / The old soldier / The aging musician / The butcher / The old woman / Ginger's lament.

Aug 96. (cd) *(INDIGO 2133-2)* <8120-2> **HAVE A BAD DAY**
– Bad day on the midway / Dagmar, the dog woman / I ain't seen no rats / Tears of the taxman / God's teardrops / The seven tattoos / The marvels of mayhem / Lottie the human log / Ugly liberation / Daddy's poems / The red head of death / Timmy.

— returned in 1998

Sep 98. (cd) *(8535-2)* <81332> **WORMWOOD: CURIOUS STORIES FROM THE BIBLE** Oct98
– In the beginning / Fire fall / They are the meat / Melncholy clumps / How to get a head / Cain and Abel / Mr. Misery / Tent peg in the temple / God's magic finger / Spilling the seed / Dinah and the unclean skin / Bathsheba bathes / Bridegroom of blood / Hanging by his hair / Seven ugly cows / Burn baby burn / Kill him / I hate Heaven / Judas slaves / Revelation.

Jul 00. (cd/d-lp) *(9431-2/-1)* <8153> **ROADWORMS: THE BERLIN SESSIONS** (on the road)
– Un-American band / How to get a head / Hanging by his hair / God's magic finger / Tent pig in the temple / Fire fall / Cain and Abel / Dinah and the unclean skin / Abraham / Burn baby burn / Judas saves.

Ralph Euro East Side Digital

Nov 02. (cd) *(2048-2)* <8167-2> **DEMONS DANCE ALONE** Sep02
– Tongue / Loss: Life would be wonderful – The weatherman – Ghost child –

RESIDENTS (cont)   THE GREAT INDIE DISCOGRAPHY   The 1970s

Caring – Honey bear – The car thief – Neediness / Denial:- Thundering skies – Mickey Macaroni – Betty's body – My brother Paul – Baja / Three metaphors:- Beekeeper's daughter – Wolverines – Make me moo / Demons dance alone. (d-cd-iss. ; 2079-2)

– others, etc. –

Sep 94. (lp)(cd) Torso; (TORSO 33-199)(7536-2) **CUBE E**
Sep 94. (cd) Indigo; (2124-2) **POOR KAW LIGA'S PAIN**
Sep 94. (cd/lp) Indigo; (7543-2/-6) **POOR KAW LIGA (housey mix)**
Oct 94. (cd) Cargo; (2129-2) **THE RESIDENTS**

– compilations, etc. –

Oct 84. (lp/c) Korova; (KODE/CODE 10) **RALPH BEFORE '84 – VOLUME 1**
– It's a man's man's man's world / Diskomo / Hello skinny / (I left my heart in) San Francisco / Happy home / Smack your lips / Yesyesyesyes / Jailhouse rock / Monkey and Bunny / Festival of death.
Jan 85. (lp) Korova; (KODE 12) **RALPH BEFORE '84 – VOLUME 2**
– Eva's warning / Halloween / Evolution / What use / Mahogany wood / Same ole me / Tritone / Melvyn's repose / Yeti: what are you / Nelda danced at day break / Norrgarden nyvia.
Jan 86. (cd) Rykodisc; <RCD 20012> **HEAVEN?**
– The importance of evergreen / It's a man's man's man's world / H.E.L.L. no! / Japanese watercolours / I got rhythm / Ups and downs / Serenade for Missy / Eastern woman / Amber / The census taker / Happy home / Crashing / Redrider / Floyd / The moles are coming / Resolution / Mahogany wood / Simple song / Kula bocca says no / Love leaks out / New hymn / Whater happened to Vileness Fats / Twinkle / Festival of death (excerpt).
Jan 86. (cd) Rykodisc; <RCD 20013> **HELL?**
– The ultimate disaster (excerpt) / Lights out / Where is she? / The coming of the crow / Lizard lady / Die interior / Shut up! shut up! / Shorty's lament / Hello skinny / Kamikaze lady / Secret seed / Sonny / Smelly tongues / Monkey and Bunny / Farmers / Satisfaction / Sinister exaggerator / Loss of innocence / The sleeper / Final confrontation (excerpt).
Nov 92. (cd/c/lp) Euro Ralph; (80782) **PRESENT OUR FINEST FLOWERS**
– Gone again / Sour song / Six amber things / Mr. Lonely / Perfect goat / Blue tongues / Jungle bunny / I'm dreaming of a white sailor / Or maybe a marine / Kick a picnic / Dead wood / Baby sister / Forty-four no more / He also serves / Ship of fools / Be kind to U-web footed friends. (re-iss. cd Sep94 & Oct00 on 'Indigo'; 2121-2)
May 97. (4xcd-box) Cargo; (RESBOX 1) **25th ANNIVERSARY BOX SET**
Jul 97. (4xcd-box) Euro Ralph; (INDIGO 2137-2) **OUR TIRED, OUR POOR, OUR HUDDLED MASSES**
Apr 98. (cd) East Side Digital; <8132-2> **RESIDUE DEUX**
– Sleeper / Whoopy snorp / Kamikazi lady / A boy in love / Shut up! shut up! / Anvil forest / Diskomo / Jailhouse rock / Ups and downs / Scent of mint / Saint Nix / Open up / From the plains of Mexico / In San Francisco / Dumbo the clown / Is he really bringing roses? / Time's up / Daydream believer / Prelude for a toddler / Toddler's lullaby / Sagety is cootie wootie / Daydream in space.
Mar 01. (cd) Euro Ralph; (9846-2) <8157-2> **ICKY FLIX**
Apr 02. (cd) East Side Digital; <8166-2> **PETTING ZOO**

Martin REV (see under ⇒ SUICIDE)

REVILLOS (see under ⇒ REZILLOS)

REZILLOS

Formed: Edinburgh, Scotland . . . March '76 by EUGENE REYNOLDS and JO CALLIS (aka LUKE WARM), alongside art school colleagues MARK 'HI-FI' HARRIS, DR. D.K. SMYTHE, ANGEL PATERSON, GAYLE WARNING and inimitable frontwoman, FAY FIFE. Early in 1977, the band signed a one-off deal with Lawrie Love's 'Sensible' records and released the semi-legendary 'CAN'T STAND MY BABY'. Three-chord dumbness in the vein of The RAMONES with the added advantage of FIFE's Scots twang, the track was followed by '(MY BABY DOES) GOOD SCULPTURES' towards the end of the year. As well as being the first fruits of their deal with 'Sire', the record marked the debut of new man, WILLIAM MYSTERIOUS, recruited as a replacement for early departees, SMYTHE, HARRIS and WARNING. By the summer of '78, The REZILLOS were performing the tongue-in-cheek 'TOP OF THE POPS' on that self same programme as their multi-coloured freakshow crashed into the UK Top 20. A debut album, 'CAN'T STAND THE REZILLOS' also hit the Top 20 that summer, offering up for closer inspection the band's obsession with American beat/girl groups and general trash culture competing with British influences like DR. FEELGOOD. MYSTERIOUS didn't hang around long, replaced by SIMON TEMPLAR (yeah, right) as the 'DESTINATION VENUS' single carried on the sci-fi malarky but failed to crack the Top 40. Splitting before the year was out, The REZILLOS splintered in two, with CALLIS, TEMPLAR and PATERSON forming SHAKE – CALLIS would subsequently join the more successful HUMAN LEAGUE – while FIFE and REYNOLDS remained on much the same track with The REVILLOS. Featuring a line-up completed by ROCKY RHYTHM, a returning HARRIS and a trio of female backing singers, the new-look band immersed themselves even further in retro Americana with a string of singles, 'WHERE'S THE BOY FOR ME?', 'MOTORBIKE BEAT' and 'SCUBA SCUBA'. Despite encouraging press, neither these nor an album, 'REV UP' (1980) notched up sufficient sales as the group underwent constant personnel upheaval with MYSTERIOUS and new man KID KRUPA coming and going. Over the course of the next three years, the band hopped from label to label as they continued to crank out inimitably titled material like '(SHE'S FALLEN IN LOVE WITH A) MONSTER MAN' and 'BONGO BRAIN'. Following a final couple of singles for 'E.M.I.', the band called it a day in 1985, FIFE moving into TV acting and subsequently appearing in the likes of 'Taggart' and 'The Bill'. Like spiritual descendants BIS, the band were big in Japan, choosing the Far East as their destination for a mid-90's reunion tour. • **Songwriters:** EUGENE and JO penned most, except; I WANNA BE YOUR MAN (Beatles) / I LIKE IT (Gerry & The Pacemakers) / GLAD ALL OVER (Dave Clark Five) / TWIST AND SHOUT (Isley Brothers) / BALLROOM BLITZ (Sweet) / TELL HIM (Exciters) / LAND OF A 1,000 DANCES (Cannibal & The Headhunters) / ON THE BEACH (hit; Cliff Richard) / THUNDERBIRDS ARE GO (Barry Gray).
Album rating: CAN'T STAND THE REZILLOS (*7*) / MISSION ACCOMPLISHED ... BUT THE BEAT GOES ON (*5*) / REV UP (*5*) / LIVE AND ON FIRE IN JAPAN (*4*)

FAY FIFE (b. SHEILAGH HYNDE) – vocals / **EUGENE REYNOLDS** (b. ALAN FORBES, USA) – vocals / **LUKE WARM** (b. JO CALLIS, England) – guitar, vocals (both ex-KNUTSFORD DOMINATORS) / **MARK 'HI-FI' HARRIS** – guitar / **Dr. D.K. SMYTHE** – bass / **ANGEL PATERSON** – drums / **GAYLE WARNING** – backing vocals

	Sensible	not iss.
Aug 77. (7") (FAB 1) **CAN'T STAND MY BABY. / I WANNA BE YOUR MAN** (re-iss. Aug79; SAB 1) – hit No.71	□	-

—— **WILLIAM MYSTERIOUS** (b.DONALDSON) – bass finally repl. SMYTHE, HARRIS & WARNING

	Sire	Sire
Nov 77. (7") (6078.612) **(MY BABY DOES) GOOD SCULPTURES. / FLYING SAUCER ATTACK**	□	-
May 78. (7";w-drawn) (6198.215) **COLD WARS. / WILLIAM MYSTERIOUS OVERTURE**	□	-
Jul 78. (7") (SIR 4001) **TOP OF THE POPS. / 20,000 REZILLOS UNDER THE SEA** (c-s) (SPC 3) – ('A'side) / Destination Venus.	17	-
Jul 78. (lp/c) (K/K4 56530) <SRK 6057> **CAN'T STAND THE REZILLOS** – Flying saucer attack / No / Someone's gonna get their heads kicked in tonight / Top Of The Pops / 2000 AD / It gets me / Can't stand my baby / Glad all over / My baby does good sculptures / I like it / Gettin' me down / Cold wars / Bad guy reaction. (cd-iss. Jan96; 7599 26942-2)	16	□

—— **SIMON TEMPLAR** (b. BLOOMFIELD) – bass, vocals repl. WILLIAM

| Nov 78. (7") (SIR 4008) **DESTINATION VENUS. / MYSTERY ACTION** | 43 | - |

—— disbanded late '78; JO, SIMON + ANGEL formed SHAKE, who released a couple of singles, 'CULTURE SHOCK' and 'INVASION OF THE GAMMA MEN'. JO CALLIS released an EP for 'Pop Aural', 'WOAH YEAH!', in 1981. They subsequently became part of BOOTS FOR DANCING.

—— The REZILLOS gave us a few more exploitation releases

| Apr 79. (7"m) (SIR 4014) **COLD WARS. / FLYING SAUCER ATTACK (live) / TWIST AND SHOUT (live)** | □ | - |
| Apr 79. (lp/c) (SRK/SRC 6069) **MISSION ACCOMPLISHED ... BUT THE BEAT GOES ON (live)** – Top of the pops / Mystery action / Somebody's gonna get their head kicked in tonight / Thunderbirds are go / Cold wars / Teenbeat / Land of 10,000 dances / I need you / Gettin' me down / Culture shock / Ballroom blitz / Destination Venus / (My baby does) Good sculptures. | 30 | - |

REVILLOS

—— (a slight change in name) brought together again **FAY & EUGENE** (also now on bass) / **HI-FI HARRIS** – guitar / **ROCKY RHYTHM** (b. NICKY FORBES) – drums (ex-PORK DUKES) / **JANE WHITE, JANE BROWN, TRICIA BRYCE** – backing vocals

	Dindisc	not iss.
Sep 79. (7") (DIN 1) **WHERE'S THE BOY FOR ME?. / THE FIEND**	□	-

—— (Aug'79) added **KID KRUPA** – guitar (on tour) / **FELIX** – bass / **CHERIE & BABS REVETTE** – backing vocals repl. last backing trio

| Jan 80. (7") (DIN 5) **MOTORBIKE BEAT. / NO SUCH LUCK** | 45 | - |

—— **WILLIAM MYSTERIOUS** – bass returned to repl. FELIX (to HEY ELASTICA)

Apr 80. (7") (DINZ 16) **SCUBA SCUBA. / BOY BOP**	□	-
Sep 80. (lp) (DIDX 3) **REV UP** – Secret of the shadow / Rev up / Rock-a-boom / Voodoo / Bobby come back to me / Scuba scuba / Boy bop / Yeah yeah / Hungry for love / Jukebox sound / On the beach / Cool jerk / Hippy hippy sheik / Motorbike beat. (re-iss. Mar84 on 'Virgin'; OVED 53) (cd-iss. Jun01 on 'Captain Oi'+=; AHOYCD 173) – Where's the boy for me / The fiend / No such luck / Scuba scuba / Voodoo (part 2).	□	-
Sep 80. (7") (DINZ 20) **HUNGRY FOR LOVE. / VOODOO 2**	□	-

—— **KID KRUPA** (b. JON McLOUGHLIN) – guitar now totally repl. HARRIS / **DRAX** – b.vox repl. **BABS** / **VINCE SANTINI** – bass repl. MYSTERIOUS

	Superville	not iss.
Sep 81. (7") (SV 1001) **(SHE'S FALLEN IN LOVE WITH A) MONSTER MAN. / MIND BENDING CUTIE DOLL**	□	-
Jan 82. (lp;w-drawn) (SV 4001) **ATTACK**	-	-
Feb 82. (7"m) (SV 2001) **BONGO BRAIN. / HIP CITY / YOU WERE MEANT FOR ME**	□	-

—— **MAX ATOM** – guitar repl. KRUPA / **TERRI REVETTE** – b.vox repl. DRAX

	Aura	not iss.
Nov 82. (7") (AUS 135) **TELL HIM. / GRAVEYARD GROOVE**	□	-

—— **FABIAN WONDERFUL** – guitar repl. ATOM

	E.M.I.	not iss.
Oct 83. (7") (RVL 1) **BITTEN BY A LOVE BUG. / TRIGGER HAPPY JACK** (12"+=) (12RVL 1) – Cat call.	□	-

REZILLOS (cont)

Mar 84. (7") *(RVL 2)* **MIDNIGHT. / Z-X-7**
(12"+=) *(12RVL 2)* – ('A'extended).
— **BUDDY MOON** – bass; repl. SANTINI
— disbanded early 1985, FAY went into acting and later featured in 'Taggart' and 'The Bill'.
— REVILLOS re-formed with main originals (see above)

Vinyl Japan not iss.

Dec 94. (12"ep/cd-ep) *(TASK/+CD 033)* **YEAH YEAH / CRUSH. / SCUBA SCUBA / SCUBA SCUBA** (Japanese version)
May 95. (cd/lp) *(ASK CD/LP 046)* **LIVE AND ON FIRE IN JAPAN (live)**
– Secret of the shadow / Bongo brain / Rockaboom / She's fallen in love with a monster man / Where's the boy for me / Rev up! / Bitten by a lovebug / Mad from birth to death / Bobby come back to me / The fiend / Scuba scuba / My baby does good sculptures / Do the mutilation / Somebody's gonna get their head kicked in tonight / A-yeah-yeah.

Damaged Goods not iss.

Sep 96. (7"m) *(DAMGOOD 93)* **JACK THE RIPPER. / A-YEAH-YEAH / MEET THE REVILLOS**
Sep 96. (cd) *(DAMGOOD 97CD)* **FROM THE FREEZER** (demos & live tracks from 1979, 1982 & 1994)
– Sputnik kiss / Superville / Jack the ripper / Motorbike beat (demo) / The last one to know / You were meant for me / Voodoo / Jukebox soul / Call me the cat / No such luck (demo) / Where's the boy for me (demo) / Snatzmobile (live) / Motorbike beat (live) / Mind bending cutie doll (live) / 1982 – make a wish / Manhunt (rehearsal) / The vampire strikes / Boys (live) / Wipeout (live) / Tango (rehearsal). *(re-iss. Jul02; same)*

– compilations, etc. (REZILLOS or REVILLOS) –

Jul 95. (cd) *Mau Mau; (MAUCD 643)* **MOTORBIKE BEAT**
Aug 95. (cd) *Receiver; <RRCD 204>* **ATTACK OF THE GIANT REVILLOS**
Sep 98. (cd) *Vinyl Japan; (ASKCD 80)* **THE BBC RADIO SESSIONS**
Nov 01. (cd) *Captain Oi; (AHOYCD 179)* **TOTALLY ALIVE (live)**

RICH KIDS

Formed: London, England . . . Autumn 1977 by sacked SEX PISTOLS bass player, GLEN MATLOCK, who founded the band along with Scots-born MIDGE URE (a one-time chart-topping star with SLIK). Spoiled by press expectation, the RICH KIDS' wealth of talent (which also included STEVE NEW and RUSTY EGAN) promised much but delivered relatively little. Although MATLOCK and his fellow 'PISTOLS had been unceremoniously ousted from the 'E.M.I.' roster a year previously, the bass player was cynically welcomed back with open arms. A watered-down "Power-pop" version of what E.M.I. would probably have wanted the 'PISTOLS to sound like, the RICH KIDS' eponymous debut single confounded the label's expectations by stalling at No.24 in early 1978. Later that summer, The RICH KIDS dynasty went bankrupt, metaphorically speaking, as two further singles, 'MARCHING MEN' and 'GHOSTS OF PRINCES IN TOWERS', failed to chart. The accompanying MICK RONSON-produced album, 'GHOSTS OF PRINCES IN TOWERS', just missed the Top 50, the 'KIDS finally falling out with each other as the strained relationship between MATLOCK and URE came to a head. While the latter found fame and fortune with ULTRAVOX, a solo career and BAND AID, the former scraped a living on the fringes of the rock scene until 1996 when re-united with JOHNNY ROTTEN and Co for the self-explanatory 'Filthy Lucre' tour. At the same time, GLEN signed to 'Creation' for a one-off solo album, 'WHO'S HE THINK HE IS WHEN HE'S AT HOME'.
• **Songwriters:** MATLOCK-URE penned most, except HERE COMES THE NICE (Small Faces).

Album rating: GHOSTS OF PRINCES IN TOWERS (*5)

MIDGE URE (b. JAMES URE, 10 Oct'53, Cambuslang, Scotland) – vocals, guitar (ex-SLIK, ex-PVC 2) / **STEVE NEW** – guitar (ex-SEX PISTOLS briefly '75) / **GLEN MATLOCK** (b. 21 Aug'56) – bass, vocals (ex-SEX PISTOLS) / **RUSTY EGAN** (b. 19 Sep'57) – drums

E.M.I. not iss.

Jan 78. (7"red) *(EMI 2738)* **RICH KIDS. / EMPTY WORDS** 24
May 78. (7") *(EMI 2804)* **MARCHING MEN. / HERE COMES THE NICE**
Aug 78. (7") *(EMI 2848)* **GHOSTS OF PRINCES IN TOWERS. / ONLY ARSENIC**
Aug 78. (lp) *(EMI 3263)* **GHOSTS OF PRINCES IN TOWERS** 51
– Strange one / Hung on you / Ghosts of princes in towers / Cheap emotion / Marching men / Put you in the picture / Young girls / Bullet proff lover / Rich kids / Lovers and fools / Burning sounds. *(re-iss. Nov83 on 'Fame' lp/c; FA/TC-FA 4130771) (cd-iss. Sep93 on 'Dojo'; DOJOCD 154) (cd re-iss. Mar99 on 'Cherry Red'+=; CDMRED 157)* – Empty words / Here comes the nice (live) / Only arsenic.
— disbanded early 1979. MIDGE joined ULTRAVOX after a brief spell with THIN LIZZY!. He also was part of the initial guest list of VISAGE who had recruited RUSTY EGAN, who was later to join SKIDS. GLEN joined IGGY POP's band and later formed the SPECTRES in '81, followed by The LONDON COWBOYS. In the mid 90's, he was back with a re-united SEX PISTOLS (for live gigs) and released his first solo set, 'WHO'S HE THINK HE IS WHEN HE'S AT HOME?' for 'Creation. STEVE NEW formed UK act, PEARL HARBOUR.

Jonathan RICHMAN

Born: 16 May'51, Boston, Massachusetts, USA. After a period in the late 60's working as a contributor for local music papers, 'Vibrations' & 'Fusion', he formed his first real band, MODERN LOVERS, in 1971. With the help of producer KIM FOWLEY, they recorded a successful demo for 'Warners' in 1972, although the label subsequently shelved their JOHN CALE-produced debut album and soon dropped the group. RICHMAN & Co. finally split in late '74, only to re-form again six months later and record a debut single, 'ROADRUNNER', for 'United Artists'. They then moved to West Coast label 'Beserkley', who bought the unreleased Warners tapes and finally packaged the songs as an eponymous album in 1976. Featuring the classic MODERN LOVERS line-up of JERRY HARRISON, ERNIE BROOKS and DAVID ROBINSON, the album was one of the more genuine efforts to lay claim to the vastly oversubscribed 'first punk album' tag. Carrying on where his heroes The VELVET UNDERGROUND left off, RICHMAN fashioned an idiosyncratic update of late 60's garage-rock, his REED-y vocals carrying epistles of adolescent angst over a simplistic but effective musical backing. While UK Top 20 hit, 'ROADRUNNER', may have whetted fans appetites for more of the same, a belated follow-up album, 'JONATHAN RICHMAN & THE MODERN LOVERS' (1977) was a different beast altogether. While HARRISON and BROOKS were now tending greener new wave pastures with The TALKING HEADS and The CARS respectively, the revamped MODERN LOVERS line-up of ROBINSON, LEROY RADCLIFFE and GREG KERANEN were following RICHMAN's more whimsically eccentric path, cutting retro pop, acoustic-based tracks about aliens, insects and erm, abominable snowmen. A second album that year, 'ROCK'N'ROLL WITH THE MODERN LOVERS', confirmed RICHMAN's new strategy, hitting the British Top 50 despite itself and spawning a second hit (Top 5) in the bizarre instrumental, 'EGYPTIAN REGGAE'. Critics were divided, some hailing the man as a wayward genius, some confounded at what they perceived as a waste of good talent. Whatever, after a late 70's lay-off, RICHMAN continued to plow his singular furrow throughout the following decade with an ever changing cast of musicians and different labels. Amid the grating childishness, the man was still capable of a wistful charm and the occasional sting of biting poignancy, fans and critics alike generally agreed that 'JONATHAN SINGS!' (1984) remains his finest release from this period. Towards the end of the decade, he recruited BRENDAN TOTTEN and JOHNNY AVILA for the leaner 'MODERN LOVERS '88' before abandoning the backup for good and going it alone. His 1989 eponymous solo debut was followed up with a misguided attempt at C&W, 'JONATHAN GOES COUNTRY' (1990), while a Spanish-language set, '!JONATHAN, TE VAS A EMOCIONAR!' (1994) surely tested the patience of even his most loyal fans. Much more promising were 1995's 'YOU MUST ASK THE HEART' and the following year's 'SURRENDER TO JONATHAN', the latter his first for a major label ('WEA') after years in the commercial wilderness. During the latter half of the 90's, RICHMAN stuck to his task of coming up with the odd album, 1999's 'I'M SO CONFUSED', a slight return to the old fun JONNO of yore. Fans however were disappointed with RICHMAN's US-only issued 'HER MYSTERY NOT OF HIGH HEELS AND EYE SHADOW' (2001), which showcased two instrumentals and four songs sung in Spanish. However, live, the old Modern Lover still packed a retro punch. • **Trivia:** JOHN CALE (ex-Velvet Underground), went on to record his brilliant 'PABLO PICASSO'.

Album rating: THE MODERN LOVERS (*8) / JONATHAN RICHMAN & THE MODERN LOVERS (*7) / ROCK'N'ROLL WITH THE MODERN LOVERS (*6) / THE MODERN LOVERS LIVE (*5) / BACK IN YOUR LIFE (*6) / THE JONATHAN RICHMAN SONGBOOK compilation (*7) / JONATHAN SINGS! (*6) / ROCKIN' AND ROMANCE (*5) / IT'S TIME FOR JONATHAN RICHMAN & THE MODERN LOVERS (*5) / MODERN LOVERS '88 (*5) / JONATHAN RICHMAN (*4) / JOHNATHAN GOES COUNTRY (*4) / 23 GREAT RECORDINGS BY JONATHAN RICHMAN & THE MODERN LOVERS compilation (*8) / HAVING A PARTY WITH JONATHAN RICHMAN collection (*4) / I, JONATHAN (*6) / JONATHAN, TE VAS A EMOCIONAR! (*5) / YOU MUST ASK THE HEART (*5) / SURRENDER TO JONATHAN (*6) / I MUST BE KING: THE BEST OF JONATHAN RICHMAN compilation (*6) / I'M SO CONFUSED (*6) / HER MYSTERY NOT OF HIGH HEELS AND EYE SHADOW (*5)

MODERN LOVERS

were formed by **RICHMAN** – vocals, guitar / with **JERRY HARRISON** – keyboards, vocals / **ERNIE BROOKS** – bass, vocals / **DAVID ROBINSON** – drums (left Nov73 to DMZ, after recording debut)

U.A. U.A.

Jun 75. (7") *(UP 36006)* **ROADRUNNER. / IT WILL STAND**

Beserkley Beserkley

Oct 76. (7") *<5701>* **ROADRUNNER. / Friday On My Mind (by Earthquake)**
Oct 77. (lp/c) *(BSERK/BSERC 1) <BZ/+CA 0050>* **THE MODERN LOVERS** (1972 demos) Oct76
– Roadrunner / Astral plane / Old world / Pablo Picasso / I'm straight / She cracked / Hospital / Someone I care about / Girlfriend / Modern world. *(re-iss. Nov87; same) <re-iss. Nov89 on 'Rhino'; RNLP 70091> (cd-iss. Feb93 on 'Rev-Ola'+=; CREV 007CD)* – (3 extra tracks). *(lp re-iss. Jun00 on 'Get Back'; GET 66)*
— HARRISON (also to TALKING HEADS) and BROOKS joined ELLIOTT MURPHY

JONATHAN RICHMAN & THE MODERN LOVERS

with also **LEROY RADCLIFFE** – guitar, vox / **GREG KERANEN** – bass, vox / **DAVID ROBINSON** – drums

Feb 77. (7") *<5743>* **NEW ENGLAND. / HERE COME THE MARTIAN MARTIANS**
Jun 77. (7") *(BZZ 1)* **ROADRUNNER (once). / ROADRUNNER (twice)** 11
(re-iss. Jul82 on 'Old Gold'; OG 9113)
Oct 77. (lp/c) *(BSERK/BSERC 2) <BZ/+CA 0048>* **JONATHAN RICHMAN & THE MODERN LOVERS** Jan77
– Rockin' shopping center / Back in the U.S.A. / Important in your life / New

England / Lonely financial zone / Hi dear / Abominable snowman in the market / Hey there little insect / Here comes the Martian Martians / Springtime / Amazing Grace. <re-iss.Nov87; same> (cd-iss. Feb93 on 'Rev-Ola'; CREV 008CD)

Aug 77. (lp/c) (BSERK 9) <BZ/+CA 0053> **ROCK'N'ROLL WITH THE MODERN LOVERS** — 50 — Feb77
— The sweeping wind (kwa ti feng) / Ice cream man / Rockin' rockin' leprechauns / Summer morning / Afternoon / Fly into the mystery / South American folk song / Roller coaster by the sea / Dodge veg-o-matic / Egyptian reggae / Coomyah / The wheels on the bus / Angels watching over you. <re-iss. Nov87; same> (cd-iss. Feb93 on 'Rev-Ola'; CREV 009CD)

Sep 77. (7") (BZZ 2) **EGYPTIAN REGGAE. / ROLLER COASTER BY THE SEA** — 5

— D.SHARPE – drums repl. ROBINSON / ASA BREMNER – bass repl. KERANEN

Dec 77. (lp/c) (BSERK/BSERC 12) <BZ/+CA 055> **THE MODERN LOVERS LIVE** (live)
— I'm a little airplane / Hey there little insect / Egyptian reggae / Ice cream man / I'm a little dinosaur / My little kookenhaken / South American folk song / New England / Morning of our lives. <re-iss. Nov87; same> (cd-iss. Feb93 on 'Rev-Ola'; CREV 010CD) (cd re-iss. Apr97 on 'Wooded Hill'; HILLCD 15)

Jan 78. (7"; as MODERN LOVERS) (BZZ 7) **MORNING OF OUR LIVES** (live). / **ROADRUNNER** (thrice) (live) — 28

Apr 78. (7"; as MODERN LOVERS) (BZZ 14) **NEW ENGLAND. / ASTRAL PLANE** (live) — —

Jul 78. (7") (BZZ 19) **ABDUL & CLEOPATRA. / OH CAROL**

Dec 78. (7") (BZZ 25) **BUZZ BUZZ BUZZ. / HOSPITAL** (live)

Feb 79. (lp/c) (BSERK/BSERC 17) <BZ/+CA 0060> **BACK IN YOUR LIFE**
— Abdul and Cleopatra / (She's gonna) Respect me / Lover please / Affection / Buzz buzz buzz / Back in your life / Party in the woods tonight / My love is a flower (just beginning to bloom) / I'm nature's mosquito / Emaline / Lydia / I hear you calling me. <re-iss. Nov86; same> (cd-iss. Feb93 on 'Rev-Ola'; CREV 011CD) (cd re-iss. Apr97 on 'Wooded Hill'; HILLCD 14)

Mar 79. (7") (BZZ 28) **LYDIA. / IMPORTANT IN YOUR LIFE**

JONATHAN RICHMAN

Jan 80. (lp) (DSERK 19) **JONATHAN RICHMAN SONGBOOK – THE BEST OF . . .** (compilation)

JONATHAN retired in the late 70's, until 1982. Joining him were KEN FORFIA – keyboards / BETH HARRINGTON – guitar / GREG KERANEN – bass, vocals / MICHAEL GUARDABASCIO – drums, vocals / ELLIE MARSHALL – backing vocals

Rough Trade   Sire

Aug 84. (lp/c) (ROUGH/+C 52) **JONATHAN SINGS!**
— That summer feeling / This kind of music / The neighbors / Somebody to hold me / These conga drums / Stop this car / Not yet three / Give Paris one more chance / You're the one for me / When I'm walking.

May 85. (7") (RT 152) **THAT SUMMER FEELING. / THIS KIND OF MUSIC**
(12"+=) (RTT 152) – The tag game.

— re-formed again with JONATHAN, ELLIE, MICHAEL and newcomer ANDY PALEY – toy piano

Jun 85. (lp/c) (ROUGH/+C 72) **ROCKIN' AND ROMANCE**
— The beach / My jeans / Bermuda / The U.F.O. man / Down in Bermuda / V. Van Gogh / Walter Johnson / I'm just beginning to live / The fenway / Chewing gum wrapper / The Baltimores / Up in the sky sometime / Now is better than before.

Aug 85. (7") (RT 154) **I'M JUST BEGINNING TO LIVE. / CIRCLE I**
(12"+=) (RTT 154) – Shirin & Fahrad.

JONATHAN RICHMAN & THE MODERN LOVERS

Feb 86. (lp/c) (ROUGH/+C 92) **IT'S TIME FOR JONATHAN RICHMAN & THE MODERN LOVERS**
— It's you / Let's take a trip / This love of mine / Neon sign / Double chocolate malted / Just about seventeen / Corner store / The desert / Yo Jo Jo / When I dance / Shirin & Fahrad / Ancient and long ago.

— JONATHAN recruited complete new line-up BRENDAN TOTTEN – guitar / JOHNNY AVILA – drums

Demon   Rounder

Feb 88. (lp/cd) (FIEND/+CD 106) <ROUNDER/+CD 9014> **MODERN LOVERS '88**
— Dancin' late at night / When Harpo played his harp / Gail loves me / New kind of neighborhood / African lady / I love hot nights / California desert party / Everything's gotta be right / Circle 1 / I have come out to play / The theme from 'Moulin Rouge'!.

JONATHAN RICHMAN

Special Delivery   Rounder

Aug 89. (lp/c/cd) <(SPD/+C/CD 1024)> **JONATHAN RICHMAN**
— Malagueno de Jojo / Action packed / Everyday clothes / Fender Stratocaster / Blue Moon / Closer / I eat with Gusto / Damn!! you bet / Miracles will start to happen / Sleepwalk / Que reste t'll de nos amours / A mistake today for me / Cerca.

— now with TOM BRUMLEY – guitar

Aug 90. (lp/c/cd) <(SPD/+C/CD 1037)> **JONATHAN GOES COUNTRY**
— Since she started to ride / Reno / You're the one for me / Your good girl's gonna go bad / I must be king / You're crazy for takin' the blues / Rodeo wind / Corner store / The neighbours / Men walks among us / I can't stay mad at you / Satisfied mind.

Rounder   Rounder

Dec 92. (cd/c) <(ROU CD/C 9036)> **I, JONATHAN**
— Parties in the U.S.A. / Tandem jump / You can't talk to the dude / Velvet underground / I was dancing in the lesbian bar / Rooming house on Venice beach / That summer feeling / Grunion run / A higher power / Twilight in Boston.

May 94. (cd) <(ROUCD 9040)> **JONATHAN, TE VAS A EMOCIONAR!**
— Pantomima del amor Brujo / Harpo en su Harpa / No te oye / No mas por fun / Papel de chicle / Los vecinos / Compadrito corazon / Melodia tradicional Ecuadoriana / Shirin y Farad / Reno / Cerca / El U.F.O. man / Ahora es Mejor / Sabor A.Mi / Una Fuerza alla.

May 95. (cd/c) <(ROU CD/C 9047)> **YOU MUST ASK THE HEART**
— To hide a little thought / The heart of Saturday night / Vampire girl / Just because I'm Irish / That's how I feel / Let her go into darkness / The rose / You must ask the heart / Nothing can change this love / Amorcito corazon / City vs. country / Walter Johnson / Nishi.

Vapor – Vapor – Warners Warners

Sep 96. (cd/c) <(9362 46296-2/-4)> **SURRENDER TO JONATHAN**
— Just look at me / That little sleeper car / Not just a plus list on the guest list anymore / My little girl's got a full time daddy now / Rock'n'roll drummer straight from the hospy-tel / atisfy / When she kisses me / Egyptian reggae / To hide a little thought / I was dancing in the lesbian bar / Surrender / Floatin' / French style.

— next with DARRYL JENIFER – bass / TOMMY LARKINS – drums

Feb 99. (cd) <(9362 47086-2/-4)> **I'M SO CONFUSED**
— When I dance / Nineteen in Naples / I'm so confused / True love is not nice / Love me like I love / Hello from Cupid / If she don't love me / The lonely little thrift store / Affection / I can hear her fighting with herself / The night is still young / I can't find my best friend.

not iss.   Vapor

Oct 01. (cd) <48216> **HER MYSTERY NOT OF HIGH HEELS AND EYE SHADOW** — —
— Her mystery not of high heels and eye shadow / Springtime in New York / Me and her got a good thing goin' baby / Couples must fight / I took a chance on her / Maybe a walk home from Natick High School / Give Paris one more chance / My love for her ain't sad / Leaves on the sidewalk after the rain / Tonight / Yo tengo una novia / El joven se estremece / Con el merengue / Vampiresa mujer (Vampire girl).

– compilations, etc. –

Oct 81. (lp) Bomp; <LBOM 1> **THE ORIGINAL MODERN LOVERS** — —
(UK-iss.Jun87 on 'Link'; 400.310) <re-iss. 1991 on 'Ubik'; BAKTUN 004> <(UK-iss.Feb97 & Nov00 on 'Bomp'; BLP 4021)>

Jul 82. (7") Old Gold; (OG 9112) **EGYPTIAN REGGAE. / MORNING OF OUR LIVES** (live) — —

1987. (cd) Rhino; <RNCD 75889> **THE BEST OF JONATHAN RICHMAN AND THE MODERN LOVERS** — —

1988. (cd) Rounder; (CDS1) **JONATHAN RICHMAN & BARRENCE WHITFIELD** — —

Feb 91. (cd/c/lp) Essential; (ESS CD/MC/LP 128) **23 GREAT RECORDINGS BY JONATHAN RICHMAN AND THE MODERN LOVERS** — —
— Roadrunner / Dignified & old / Pablo Picasso / I'm straight / Astral plane / Girl friend / Government centre / New teller / It will stand / Morning of our lives / Abominable snowman in the market / Important in your life / My little kookenhaken / Dodge veg-o-matic / Lonely financial zone / Roller coaster by the sea / New England / Egyptian reggae / Ice cream man / Buzz buzz buzz / Abdul & Cleopatra / Roadrunner (twice). (c+=) – She cracked / Hospital. (re-iss. cd Sep93 on 'Castle'; CSCD 397)

Nov 91. (cd) Cheree; (CHEREE 22) **HAVING A PARTY WITH JONATHAN RICHMAN** (live US tour in '83) — —
— The girl stands up to me now / Cappuccino bar / my career as a homewrecker / She doesn't laugh at my jokes / When she kisses me / They're not tryin' on the dance floor / At night / When I say wife / 1963 / Monologue about bermuda / Our swingin' pad / Just for fun.

Apr 94. (cd) Castle; (CCSCD 397) **THE COLLECTION**

May 94. (cd) New Rose; (422439) **LIVE AT THE LONGBRANCH SALOON** (live)
<(US+re-iss. Aug98 on 'Last Call'; 303821)>

Apr 95. (cd; by MODERN LOVERS) Rounder; (ROUCD 9042) **PRECISE MODERN LOVERS ORDER**
(originally issued in 1992 on French 'Fan Club'; 422439)

Jun 95. (cd) Nectar; (NPMCD 506) **A PLEA FOR TENDERNESS**

Jul 97. (cd) Snapper; (SMDCD 115) **RADIO ON / STOP AND SHOP**

Aug 98. (cd) Castle; (SELCD 521) **ROADRUNNER**

Nov 98. (cd) Cooking Vinyl; (COOKCD 166) **I MUST BE KING: THE BEST OF JONATHAN RICHMAN**
— That summer feeling / Fender stratocaster / Foggy notion / No mas po fun (Just for fun) / You're the one for me / Girls stand up to me now / Satisfied mind / Velvet underground / Pablo Picasso / A plea for tenderness / Corner stone / Neighbours / Dignified and old / Parties in the USA / I must be king / El UFO man / Action packed / Roadrunner.

Sep 00. (cd) Target; (47038) **BUZZ BUZZ BUZZ: AN INTROSPECTIVE**

Feb 02. (cd) Rounder; <(ROUCD 11596)> **ACTION PACKED: THE BEST OF JONATHAN RICHMAN**

Penny RIMBAUD (see under ⇒ CRASS)

Tom ROBINSON

Born: 1 Jun'50, Cambridge, England. Sent to reform school as a lad, the young ROBINSON met guitarist DANNY KUSTOW and subsequently formed DAVANQ in the early 70's. Duly relocating to London, ROBINSON put together cabaret-folk outfit, CAFE SOCIETY, releasing an eponymous solo album on RAY DAVIES' (KINKS) 'Konk' label in 1974. Relations between the band and DAVIES soon soured, the project falling by the wayside as ROBINSON formed his own outfit, The TOM ROBINSON BAND. With a stable line-up cementing around KUSTOW, MARK AMBLER and DOLPHIN TAYLOR, the group were signed up by 'E.M.I.', immediately hitching a ride on the emerging punk juggernaut with stompalong classic, '2-4-6-8 MOTORWAY'. The track's UK Top 5 success was followed with the live EP, 'RISING FREE', ROBINSON's radical political manifesto introduced with the celebratory 'SING IF YOU'RE GLAD TO BE GAY' and the defiant 'DON'T TAKE NO FOR AN ANSWER'. Adopted by the music press as something of a new wave cause celebre, TRB, along with the likes of The CLASH, espoused a more positive strand of protest than the bleak nihilism of many punk acts, their anti-racist, pro-individual freedom stance represented by the clenched fist logo on debut album, 'POWER IN THE DARKNESS' (1978). Brimming with anthemic rallying cries for the disaffected yet rarely lapsing into laboured preaching, the album confirmed ROBINSON's credentials as an articulate spokesman for the punk generation. And it wasn't just empty rhetoric, ROBINSON putting his politics where his mouth was and playing a host of benefit gigs (chiefly anti-racism and gay/lesbian rights events) both at home and in the States where he was something of a minor hero on the college circuit. Following the departure of AMBLER and TAYLOR, however, ROBINSON struggled through a TODD RUNDGREN-produced follow-up set, 'TRB 2' (1979). Preceded by the flop PETER GABRIEL collaboration, 'BULLY FOR YOU', the album's bland sloganeering was met with a frosty critical reception and relatively poor sales (despite a UK Top 20 placing); the TOM ROBINSON BAND fell apart, its mainman subsequently suffering a nervous breakdown. Upon his recovery, the singer formed a new outfit, SECTOR 27, initiating his own label, 'Panic' and releasing an eponymous album in 1980. A more experimental post-punk affair, the album was well received but failed to sell and again, ROBINSON changed his plans. Moving to Hamburg, Germany in early '82, he cut his first solo album proper, 'NORTH BY NORTHWEST', another strong effort which found him developing a more conventional singer/songwriter style. This paid dividends the following year when 'WAR BABY' made the UK Top 10, its laidback, swinging sophistication contrasting with the three-chord assault of old. An equally classy follow-up, 'LISTEN TO THE RADIO: ATMOSPHERICS', just nudged into the Top 40 later that year, another collaboration with PETER GABRIEL. Together with a further minor hit in Steely Dan's 'RIKKI DON'T LOSE THAT NUMBER', the singles were included on the fine 1984 set, 'HOPE AND GLORY', ROBINSON's most successful album since the late 70's. 'STILL LOVING YOU' (1986) saw the man's muse become increasingly mellow as he entered fatherhood (it emerged that he was actually bi-sexual, not homosexual) although the album failed to match even its predecessor's limited success. Throughout the remainder of the 80's and on into the 90's, ROBINSON regularly performed with original members of TRB as well as touring, writing and recording as a solo artist. Featuring such disparate guests as CHRIS REA and T.V. SMITH, 1994's 'LOVE OVER RAGE' album boasted ROBINSON's most confident set of songs in almost a decade, proving that he didn't have to rely on mere nostalgia to make a living.

Album rating: POWER IN THE DARKNESS (*8) / TRB TWO (*5) / SECTOR 27 (*4; by SECTOR 27) / TOM ROBINSON BAND compilation (*7) / NORTH BY NORTHWEST (*7) / HOPE AND GLORY (*6) / STILL LOVING YOU (*5) / WE NEVER HAD IT SO GOOD with Jakko M. Jakszuk (*4) / LIVING IN A BOOM TIME (*5) / LOVE OVER RAGE (*5) / HAVING IT BOTH WAYS (*5) / RISING FREE – THE BEST OF TOM ROBINSON compilation (*7)

TOM ROBINSON BAND

TOM ROBINSON – vocals, bass (ex-CAFE SOCIETY, ex-DAVANQ) / **DANNY KUSTOW** – guitar (ex-DAVANQ) / **MARK AMBLER** – keyboards repl. ANTON MAUVE, BRET SINCLAIR & MARK GRIFFITHS / **DOLPHIN TAYLOR** – drums, vocals repl. NICK TREVISICK (ex-CAFE SOCIETY)

			E.M.I.	Harvest
Oct 77.	(7")	(EMI 2715) <4533> **2-4-6-8 MOTORWAY. / I SHALL BE RELEASED**	5	
Feb 78.	(7"ep)	(EMI 2749) **RISING FREE (live)** – Don't take no for an answer / Right on sister / Sing if you're glad to be gay / Martin.	18	–
May 78.	(7")	(EMI EMI 2787) **UP AGAINST THE WALL. / I'M ALRIGHT JACK**	33	–
May 78.	(lp/c)	(EMC/TC-EMC 3226) <11778> **POWER IN THE DARKNESS** – Up against the wall / Grey Cortina / Too good to be true / Ain't gonna take it / Long hot summer / Winter of 79 / Man you never saw / Better decide which side you're on / You gotta survive / Power in the darkness / 2-4-6-8 Motorway. (re-iss. Aug83 lp/c; EMS/TC-EMS 106668-1/-4) (re-iss. Oct94 on 'Cooking Vinyl' cd/c; COOK C/CD 076) (cd re-iss. Aug96 on 'Razor & Tie'; RE 2018)	4	
Aug 78.	(7")	(EMI 2847) **TOO GOOD TO BE TRUE. / POWER IN THE DARKNESS**		
Sep 78.	(7")	(<4568>) **RIGHT ON SISTER. / GLAD TO BE GAY**	–	

— (mid'78) **IAN PARKER** – keyboards repl. NICK PLYTAS (ex-ROOGALATOR) who had repl. AMBLER (Apr'78).

— (Dec78) **PRESTON HEYMAN** – drums (ex-BRAND X) repl. DOLPHIN who joined STIFF LITTLE FINGERS.

Mar 79.	(7")	(EMI 2916) <4726> **BULLY FOR YOU. / OUR PEOPLE**	68	
Mar 79.	(lp/c)	(EMC/TC-EMC 3296) <11930> **TRB TWO** – All right all night / Why should I mind / Black angel / Let my people be / Blue murder / Bully for you / Crossing over the road / Sorry Mr. Harris / Law and order / Days of rage / Hold out. (re-iss. Aug83 lp/c; EMS/TC-EMS 165215-1/-4) (re-iss. Oct94 on 'Cooking Vinyl' cd/c; COOK CD/C 077) (cd re-iss. Aug96 on 'Razor & Tie'; RE 2019)	18	
May 79.	(7"; w-drawn)	(EMI 2946) **ALRIGHT ALL NIGHT. / BLACK ANGEL**		–

— **CHARLIE MORGAN** – drums repl. the returning TREVISICK who had repl. HEYMAN. The latter joined KATE BUSH. **GEOFF SHARKEY** – guitar repl. KUSTOW / added **GRAHAM COLLIER** – double bass / **GEOFF DALY** – saxophone

| Aug 79. | (7"; TOM ROBINSON & THE VOICE SQUAD) | (EMI 2967) **NEVER GONNA FALL IN LOVE (AGAIN). / GETTING TIGHTER** | | – |

— Disbanded late summer '79. **TOM ROBINSON** now vocals, guitar went solo with back-up from SECTOR 27. **STEVE BLANCHARD** – guitar / **DEREK QUINTON** – drums / **JO BURT** – bass (recorded one withdrawn lp, 'SECTOR 27', on 'Regal Zonophone')

SECTOR 27

— were now given full billing.

			Panic	not iss.
Jul 80.	(7")	(SEC 27) **NOT READY. / CAN'T KEEP AWAY**		–
Oct 80.	(7")	(SEC 28) **INVITATION, WHAT HAVE WE GOT TO LOSE? / DUNGANNON**		–

			Fontana	I.R.S.
Nov 80.	(lp)	(6359 039) <70013> **SECTOR 27** – Invitation / Not ready / Mary Lynne / Looking at you / 523 / Total recall / Where can we go tonight / Take it or leave it / Bitterly disappointed / One fine day. (cd-iss. Jun96 +=; 532642-2) – (extra tracks).		

			Panic	not iss.
Jan 81.	(7")	(SEC 29) **TOTAL RECALL. / STORNOWAY**		–
May 81.	(7")	(SEC 30) **MARTIN'S GONE. / CHRISTOPHER CALLING**		–

TOM ROBINSON

— went solo again. (SECTOR 27 as a trio branched out on own). **TOM** added **STEVE LAURIE** – drums / **RICHARD MAZDA** – guitar, producer / etc

			Panic	Geffen
Jun 82.	(lp)	(ROBBO 1) **NORTH BY NORTHWEST** – Now Martin's gone / Atmospherics / Can't keep away (part 2) / Looking for a bonfire / Merrily up on high / Those days / In the cold / The night tide / Dungannon / Love comes. (re-iss. 1986 on 'Castle' lp/c/cd; CLA LP/MC/CD 128) (cd-iss. Jun97 & Apr02 on 'Castaway Northwest'+=; CNWVP 003CD) – Tango an der wand / Now Richard's gone / Airtraum tango dob / Any favours / Out to lunch.		–
Jul 82.	(7")	(NIC 1) **NOW MARTIN'S GONE. / ATMOSPHERICS** (re-iss. Feb83 as 5-track-12"ep; NIC 1-12) – ATMOSPHERICS		–
Jun 83.	(7")	(NIC 2) **WAR BABY. / HELL YES** (12"+=) (NIC 2-12) – Martin's gone (original).	6	Sep84
Nov 83.	(7")	(NIC 3) **LISTEN TO THE RADIO: ATMOSPHERICS. / DON'T DO ME ANY FAVOURS** (12"+=) (NIC 3-12) – Out to lunch.	39	–

			Castaway-RCA	Geffen
Jun 84.	(7")	(TR 1) **BACK IN THE OLD COUNTRY. / BEGGIN'** (12"+=) (TRT 1) – ('A'live version).		
Sep 84.	(7"/12")	(ZL/ZK+T 2) **RIKKI DON'T LOSE THAT NUMBER. / CABIN BOY (live)**	58	–
Sep 84.	(lp/c)	(ZL/ZK 70484) **HOPE AND GLORY** – War baby / Atmospherics: Listen to the radio / Cabin boy / Blond and blue / Hope and glory / Murder at the end of the day / Prison / Rikki don't lose that number / Old friend / Looking for a bonfire.	21	
May 85.	(7"/12")	(ZB/ZT 400 19/20) **PRISON. / MORE LIVES THAN ONE**		–

— TOM brought back **BLANCHARD + BURT** plus **RED** – drums

Jul 86.	(7")	(TR 3) **(IT AIN'T NOTHIN' LIKE) THE REAL THING. / THE WEDDING** (12"+=) (TRT 3) – ('A'extended).		–
Sep 86.	(lp/c/cd)	(ZL/ZK/ZD 71129) **STILL LOVING YOU** – Feels so good – Hurt so bad / (It ain't nothin' like) The real thing / Still loving you / Take me home again / You tattooed me / Drive all night / Living in a love town / Spain / This little romance / The wedding. (cd re-iss. Sep00 on 'Castaway Northwest'; CNWVP 006CD)		–
Sep 86.	(7"/12")	(TR/+T 4) **STILL LOVING YOU. / THE SATURDAY DISCO**		–
Jan 87.	(7"; TOM ROBINSON & KIKI DEE)	(TR 5) **FEELS SO GOOD. / NORTHERN RAIN** (12"+=) (TRT 5) – You tattooed me / Change.		–
Jun 87.	(7")	(ZB 41333) **SPAIN. / DRIVE ALL NIGHT** (12"+=) (ZT 41333) – (It ain't nothin' like) The real thing.		–

			Musidisc	not iss.
Oct 90.	(cd/c/lp; TOM ROBINSON & JAKKO M. JAKSZUK)	(10666-2/-4/-1) **WE NEVER HAD IT SO GOOD** – We never had it so good / Drinking through the desert / Blood brother / What have I ever done to you / The baby rages on / Tomboy / Kiss and roll over / Hard cases / Can't stop: Peter's theme / My own sweet way.		–
Nov 90.	(7"; as TOM ROBINSON & JAKKO M. JAKSZUK)	(10666-7) **BLOOD BROTHER. / ('A'version)** (12"+=) (10666-6) – What have I ever done to you / Rigging.		–

			Cooking Vinyl	Scarface
Sep 92.	(lp/c/cd)	(COOK/+C/CD 052) **LIVING IN A BOOM TIME** – Folk song (intro) / Living in a boom time / More lives than one / Yuppie scum / My own sweet way / Castle island / Digging it up / The Brits / War baby / Back in the old country. (re-iss. Mar94 cd/c; same)		
Jan 93.	(c-ep/cd-ep)	(FRY C/CD 022) **WAR BABY (live). / BLOOD BROTHER / WE DIDN'T KNOW (WHAT WAS GOING ON)**		–

— now w / **ROBIN MILLAR** – rhythm guitar / **CHRIS REA** – slide guitar / **MARK AMBLER** – keyboards / **WINSTON BLISSETT** – bass / **MARTIN DITCHAM** – drums / **MARK RAMSDEN** – saxophone / **T.V.SMITH + ANDY MITCHELL** – backing vocals

May 94.	(lp/c/cd)	(COOK/+C/CD 066) <53913> **LOVE OVER RAGE** – Roaring / Hard / Loved / Days / Driving / Green / DDR / Fifty / Silence / Chance.		
Jun 94.	(cd-ep)	(FRYCD 028) **HARD / GREEN / LIVING IN A BOOM TIME / PORTOBELLO TERRACE**		–
Jul 94.	(cd-ep)	(FRYCD 029) **LOVED / FIFTY / YUPPY SCUM / GLAD TO BE GAY '94**		–
Sep 94.	(cd-ep)	(FRYCD 031) **DAYS (THAT CHANGED THE WORLD) / ROARING / THE BRITS COME ROLLING BACK**		–
May 96.	(cd/c)	(COOK CD/C 097) **HAVING IT BOTH WAYS** – Disrepect / One / Rum thunderbird / Cold cold ground / Fool to myself / Hot dog / Sorry / Raining in Connecticut / Congo blue / Castaway / The last word.		
Jul 96.	(cd-ep)	(FRYCD 050) **RAINING IN CONNECTICUT / DISRESPECT / RUM THUNDERBIRD / RAINING IN CONNECTICUT (mix)**		–

Tom ROBINSON (cont)

– compilations, etc. –

Dec 81.	(lp)	E.M.I.; (EMS 1005)	**TOM ROBINSON BAND**
		(re-iss. May82 on 'Fame'; FA 3028)	
Nov 82.	(lp)	Panic; (ROBBO 2)	**CABARET '79 (live)**
Oct 83.	(7")	Old Gold; (OG 9379)	**2-4-6-8 MOTORWAY. / DON'T TAKE NO FOR AN ANSWER**
Apr 87.	(lp/c; TOM ROBINSON & THE CREW)	Dojo; (DOJO LP/CD 51)	**MIDNIGHT AT THE FRINGE (live)**
Sep 87.	(7")	E.M.I.; (EM 28)	**2-4-6-8 MOTORWAY (live). / ('A'original)**
	(12"+=) (12EM 28) – Sing if you're glad to be gay.		
Sep 87.	(cd/c/lp)	E.M.I.; (CD/TC+/EMC 3540)	**COLLECTION 77-87**
Mar 89.	(lp/cd)	Line; (MS LP4/CD9.00695)	**GLAD TO BE GAY CABARET**
Jun 89.	(cd)	Line; (LICD 9.005888)	**LAST TANGO**
Oct 89.	(d-lp/c/cd)	Connoisseur; (VSOP LP/MC/CD 138)	**BACK IN THE OLD COUNTRY**

– Listen to the radio: Atmospherics / Too good to be true / Up against the wall / Northern rain / I shall be released / 2-4-6-8 motorway / Don't take no for an answer / Where can we go tonight / Back in the old country / Alright all night / War baby / Power in the darkness / Crossing over the road / Rikki don't lose that number / Looking for a bonfire / Hard cases / Still loving you / Not ready / Bully for you / Long hot summer. (d-lp/c+=) – Mary Lynne / Bitterly disappointed.

Jun 92.	(d-cd)	Line; (LICD 921215)	**GLAD TO BE GAY / LAST TANGO**
	(re-iss. Aug95; same)		
Aug 92.	(cd)	Pop Almanac; (PACD 7005)	**WINTER OF '89**
Jun 93.	(cd/c)	Optima; (OPTM CD/C 012)	**TOM ROBINSON**
Jul 94.	(cd)	Music De-Luxe; (MSCD 6)	**MOTORWAY**
Mar 96.	(cd/c)	EMI Gold; (CD/TC GOLD 1015)	**THE GOLD COLLECTION**
Jun 96.	(cd)	Fontana; (532642-2)	**SECTOR 27 COMPLETE**
	(re-iss. Apr02 on 'Castaway Northwest'; CNWVP 012CD)		
Jun 97.	(cd)	EMi Gold; (CDGOLD 1098)	**RISING FREE – THE BEST OF TOM ROBINSON**
Jun 97.	(cd; with JAKKO M. JAKSZUK)	Castaway Northwest; (CNWVP 001CD)	**BLOOD BROTHER**
	(above was virtually 'WE NEVER HAD IT SO GOOD' & extra tracks)		
Jul 97.	(cd)	Castaway Northwest; (CNWVP 002CD)	**LAST TANGO / MIDNIGHT AT THE FRINGE**
Aug 97.	(cd)	Castaway Northwest; (CNWVP 003CD)	**GLAD TO BE GAY (CABARET '79)**
Apr 98.	(d-cd)	Snapper; (<SMDCD 118>)	**THE UNDISCOVERED: MODERN CLASSICS** Sep98
Sep 00.	(cd)	Castaway Northwest; (CNWVP 007CD)	**WAR BABY**
Nov 00.	(cd)	Secret; (SECRET 001CD)	**THE CAFE SOCIETY ARCHIVES**
Mar 01.	(cd)	Castaway Northwest; (CNWVP 011CD)	**RARE**
May 01.	(cd)	Castaway Northwest; (CNWVP 013CD)	**SMELLING DOGS**
	(some BBC archives)		

ROCKET FROM THE TOMBS
(see under ⇒ PERE UBU)

RUDI

Formed: Belfast, N. Ireland ... 1975 by RONNIE MATTHEWS, BRIAN YOUNG, GORDON BLAIR and GRAHAM MARSHALL. Alongside fellow Belfast acts STIFF LITTLE FINGERS, VICTIM, The OUTCASTS, The IDIOTS and FLYING SQUAD, RUDI were tipped for stardom after a classy punk-pop debut 45, 'BIG TIME', for 'Good Vibrations' in May '78. A Battle Of The Bands EP the following year secured a little exposure until their follow-up proper, 'I SPY', that August. Now without BLAIR, RUDI continued to release the odd record, although they could never match the highs of SLF.

Album rating: BIG TIME – THE BEST OF RUDI compilation (*5)

RONNIE MATTHEWS – vocals, guitar / **BRIAN YOUNG** – guitar, vocals / **GORDON BLAIR** – bass, vocals / **GRAHAM MARSHALL** – drums

Good Vibrations   not iss.

May 78.	(7")	(GOT 1)	**BIG TIME. / NUMBER 1**
Feb 79.	(d7"ep; various artists)	(GOT 7)	**Battle Of The Bands EP**
	– Overcome by fumes / (other artists).		
Aug 79.	(7"ep)	(GOT 12)	**I SPY. / GENUINE REPLY. / SOMETIMES / RIPPED IN TWO**

— now without BLAIR

Jamming 1   not iss.

| Aug 81. | (7"m) | (CREATE 1) | **WHEN I WAS DEAD. / BEWARE WOLF! / THE PRESSURE'S ON** |
| Mar 82. | (7") | (CREATE 3) | **CRIMSON. / 14 STEPS** |

— split after above

– compilations, etc. –

| Aug 96. | (cd) | Anagram; (CDPUNK 77) | **BIG TIME – THE BEST OF RUDI** |

– Big time / Number 1 / Overcome by fumes / I spy / Genuine reply / Sometimes / Ripped in two / Who you / Time to be proud / Without you / The pressure's on / Yummy, yummy, yummy / Tigerland / When I was dead / Beware wolf! / Prince of pleasure / Love goes on / Crimson / 14 steps / Cops. (re-iss. Apr00; same)

RUNAWAYS

Formed: Los Angeles, California, USA ... mid-1974 by the notorious solo star turned record producer KIM FOWLEY (along with teen lyricist, KARI KROME), who set out to create a female RAMONES. After successfully applying to his music paper ad, JOAN JETT became the first to join, followed soon after by SANDY WEST and MICKI STEELE. With a few gigs under their belt, STEELE was replaced by CHERIE CURRIE, while the line-up was finalised with the addition of LITA FORD and JACKIE FOX. This was the formation that played a rooftop session on a Los Angeles apartment block in early 1976, an event that helped secure a record deal with 'Mercury'. While their eponymous debut was hitting the shops, the girls (average age 16) made their New York debut at CBGB's in September '76 supporting TELEVISION and TALKING HEADS. Dragging glam-metal by the pubic hair and injecting it with punk energy, tracks such as 'CHERRY BOMB' and 'HOLLYWOOD' saw The RUNAWAYS lumped in with the fermenting US New Wave scene. Early in '77, they released a second album, 'QUEENS OF NOISE', and like its predecessor it too failed to capitalize on the hype. Internal tensions were coming to a head around the time of the Japanese-only (The RUNAWAYS were huge in the Far East) live set, VICKI BLUE standing in for the worn out JACKIE FOX, while the blonde CURRIE finally split for a solo career (JOAN JETT taking over vocal duties). Adopting a harder-edged approach, the new line-up released yet another album, 'WAITIN' FOR THE NIGHT' (1978), the last to feature LITA FORD (another RUNAWAY to go on to a semi-successful solo career) and VICKI BLUE (who had attempted suicide). Although LAURIE McCALLISTER was brought in as a brief replacement, she didn't play on a posthumous covers set, 'AND NOW ... THE RUNAWAYS', the band having already finally split. JOAN JETT was the third and most successful member to carve out a solo niche, however, FOWLEY subsequently resurrected the name (minus any original members!) for a less than impressive 1987 set, 'YOUNG AND FAST'. • **Trivia:** The JOAN JETT & THE RUNAWAYS album was entirely made up of covers; Slade's 'MAMA WEER ALL CRAZEE NOW' being one of them.

Album rating: THE RUNAWAYS (*7) / QUEENS OF NOISE (*6) / LIVE IN JAPAN (*5) / WAITIN' FOR THE NIGHT (*4) / AND NOW ... THE RUNAWAYS (*3) / THE BEST OF THE RUNAWAYS compilation (*6) / YOUNG AND FAST (*3)

CHERIE CURRIE (b.1960) – vocals who repl. MICKI STEELE (was part-time vox, bass) / **LITA FORD** (b.23 Sep'59, London, England) – lead guitar, vocals / **JOAN JETT** (b.22 Sep'60, Philadelphia, Pennsylvania) – rhythm guitar, vocals / **JACKIE FOX** – bass / **SANDY WEST** (b.1960) – drums

Mercury   Mercury

Sep 76.	(7")	(6167 392) <73819>	**CHERRY BOMB. / BLACKMAIL**
Nov 76.	(lp)	(9100 029) <SRM1 1090>	**THE RUNAWAYS** Jun 76
	– Cherry bomb / You drive me wild / Is it day or night? / Thunder / Rock and roll / Lovers / American nights / Blackmail / Secrets / Dead end justice.		
Feb 77.	(lp)	(9100 032) <SRM1 1126>	**QUEENS OF NOISE** Jan 77
	– Queens of noise / Take it or leave it / Midnight music / Born to be bad / Neon angels on the road to ruin / Midnight music / I love playin' with fire / California Paradise / Hollywood heartbeat / Johnny Guitar.		
Feb 77.	(7")	<73890>	**HEARTBEAT. / NEON ANGELS ON THE ROAD TO RUIN**
Feb 77.	(7")	(6167 493)	**QUEENS OF NOISE. / BORN TO BE BAD**
Oct 77.	(lp)	(9100 046)	**LIVE IN JAPAN (live)**
	– Queens of noise / California Paradise / All right you guys / Wild thing / Gettin' hot / Rock and roll / You drive me wild / Neon angels on the road to ruin / I wanna be where the boys are / Cherry bomb / American nights / C'mon.		

— (Jul'77) **VICKI BLUE** – bass repl. FOX who suffers from nervous exhaustion. JETT took over lead vocals, when CURRIE left to go solo.

Oct 77.	(7")	(6167 587)	**SCHOOL DAYS. / WASTED**
Dec 77.	(lp)	(9100 047) <SRM1 3075>	**WAITIN' FOR THE NIGHT**
	– Little sister / Wasted / Gotta get out tonight / Wait for me / Fantasies / School days / Trash can murders / Don't go away / Waitin' for the night / You're too possessive.		

— **LAURIE McCALLISTER** – bass repl. VICKI BLUE when she attempted suicide. Split late 1978, when LITA FORD went solo after the recording of final album below.

Cherry Red   not iss.

| Jul 79. | (lp,colrd-lp) | (ARED 3) | **AND NOW ... THE RUNAWAYS** |

– Saturday night special / Eight days a week / Mama weer all crazee now / I'm a million / Right now / Takeover / My buddy and me / Little lost girls / Black leather. <re-iss. US 1981 as 'LITTLE LOST GIRLS' on 'Rhino' lp><pic-lp; RNLP 70861><RNDF 250> <cd-iss. US 1987; R2 70861> (cd-iss. Jul93 & Mar97 on 'Anagram'; CDGRAM 63)

| Aug 79. | (7") | (CHERRY 8) | **RIGHT NOW. / BLACK LEATHER** |

— JOAN JETT went solo backed by her BLACKHEARTS

— re-formed for a one-off (with no originals)

not iss.   Allegience

| 1987. | (lp) | | **YOUNG AND FAST** |

– compilations, others, etc. –

Feb 80.	(lp)	Cherry Red; (BRED 9)	**FLAMING SCHOOLGIRLS** (live/studio)
Sep 82.	(lp/c)	Mercury; (MERB/+C 12)	**THE BEST OF THE RUNAWAYS**
1981.	(12"ep)	Rhino; <RNEP 602>	**MAMA WEER ALL CRAZEE NOW**
Apr 82.	(pic-lp/lp; JOAN JETT & THE RUNAWAYS)	Cherry Red; (P+/LAKER 1)	**I LOVE PLAYING WITH FIRE**
1992.	(cd)	Mercury; <838 583-2>	**NEON ANGELS**
Jun 94.	(10"lp)	Marilyn; (FM 1004)	**BORN TO BE BAD** France

RUTS

Formed: London, England ... 1978 by MALCOLM OWEN, PAUL FOX, SEGS and DAVE RUFFY. One of the most revered punk acts to emerge in the seismic wake of The SEX PISTOLS and The CLASH, The RUTS shared the latter outfit's love of reggae and dub as well as their Rock Against Racism politics. Released as a one-off by tiny reggae label, 'People Unite', the seething 'IN A RUT' served as the band's debut single in May '78, earning them a series of John Peel sessions and a major label contract courtesy of 'Virgin'. The tinderbox intensity of follow-up track, 'BABYLON'S BURNING' was enough to break The RUTS into the UK Top 10 later that summer while the equally anthemic 'SOMETHING THAT I SAID' scraped the Top 30 ahead of debut album, 'THE CRACK' (1979). Alternating scathing politico-punk with defiant dub excursions, the album cut to the fractured heart of late 70's youth culture with a precision lacking in some of their clumsier peers; third single, 'JAH WAR', recounted an anti-fascist riot to a hypnotic dub backing while 1980's classic 'STARING AT THE RUDE BOYS' displayed a spiritual solidarity with the emerging 2-tone movement. Sadly, it also proved to be the band's epitaph as OWEN succumbed to his heroin habit later that summer. While a compilation set of live and rare tracks, 'GRIN AND BEAR IT' (1980), served as a stop-gap release, the remainder of the band eventually resurfaced in early '81 as RUTS DC with FOX taking over lead vocals and GARY BARNACLE joining on sax. The subsequent two albums, 'ANIMAL NOW' (1981) and 'RHYTHM COLLISION' (1982) took a more commercial approach and met with little enthusiasm. Clearly struggling without OWEN's guiding influence, the band finally split in mid '83 with BARNACLE going on to work with VISAGE and RUFFY joining AZTEC CAMERA. • **Trivia:** In 1980, they were the backing band of KEVIN COYNE on his album, 'Sanity Stomp'.

Album rating: THE CRACK (*7) / SOMETHING THAT I SAID – THE BEST OF ... compilation (*8)

MALCOLM OWEN – vocals / **PAUL FOX** – guitar, vocals / **SEGS** (b. JOHN JENNINGS) – bass / **DAVE RUFFY** – drums

	People Unite	not iss.
May 78. (7") *(SJP 795)* **IN A RUT. / H-EYES** *(re-iss. Jun79; RUT 1)*	–	–

	Virgin	Virgin
Jun 79. (7"/12") *(VS 271/-12)* **BABYLON'S BURNING. / SOCIETY**	7	–
Aug 79. (7") *(VS 285)* **SOMETHING THAT I SAID. / GIVE YOUTH A CHANCE**	29	–
Sep 79. (lp/c) *(<V/TCV 2132>)* **THE CRACK**	16	

– Babylon's burning / Dope for guns / S.U.S. / Something that I said / You're just a . . . / It was cold / Savage circle / Jah war / Criminal mind / Backbiter / Out of order / Human punk. *(re-iss. Aug88; OVED 80) (cd-iss. Jul90; CDV 2132)(+=)* – Give youth a chance / I ain't so satisfied / The crack. *(re-iss. cd Mar94)*

Nov 79. (7") *(VS 298)* **JAH WAR. / I AIN'T SOFISTICATED**		–
Apr 80. (7") *(VS 327)* **STARING AT THE RUDE BOYS. / LOVE IN VAIN**	22	–

—— On 14th July '80, MALCOLM OWEN died of a drug overdose. Posthumous releases below.

Aug 80. (7") *(VS 370)* **WEST ONE (SHINE ON ME). / THE CRACK**	43	–
Oct 80. (lp/c) *(V/TCV 2188)* **GRIN AND BEAR IT** (new, live & rare)	28	–

– In a rut / Love in vain / S.U.S. / Babylon's burning / Society / West one (shine on me) / Staring at the rude boys / Demolition dancing / Secret soldier / H eyes. *(re-iss. Mar84; OVED 57)*

RUTS D.C.

remaining trio (with PAUL on lead vocals) / added **GARY BARNACLE** – saxophone, keyboards

Feb 81. (7") *(VS 396)* **DIFFERENT VIEW. / FORMULA BOYS**		–
May 81. (lp/c) *(V/TCV 2193)* **ANIMAL NOW**		–

– Mirror smashed / Dangerous minds / Slow down / Despondency / Different view / No time to kill / Fools / Walk or run / Parasites.

	Bohemian	not iss.
Jul 82. (7") *(BO 2)* **WHATEVER WE DO. / PUSH YOURSELF – MAKE IT WORK**		–
Jul 82. (lp) *(BOLP 4)* **RHYTHM COLLISION**		–

– Whatever we do / Militant / Push yourself (make it work) / Rhythm collision / Accusation / Pleasures of the dance / Weak heart (dub) / Love and fire.

Mar 83. (12"ep) *(12BO 3)* **WEAK HEART. / MILITANT / ACCUSATION**		–

RUTS

May 83. (7"m) *(BO 4)* **STEPPING BONDAGE. / LOBOTOMY / RICH BITCH**		–

—— Folded mid '83. BARNACLE joined VISAGE, etc, and RUFFY joined AZTEC CAMERA.

– compilations, etc. –

Apr 83. (12"ep) Virgin; *(VS 583-12)* **BABYLON'S BURNING / SOMETHING THAT I SAID. / STARING AT THE RUDE BOYS / WEST ONE (SHINE ON ME)**		–
Dec 86. (12"ep) Strange Fruit; *(SFPS 011)* **PEEL SESSIONS** (21.5.79)		–

– S.U.S. / Society / You're just a . . . / It was cold / Something that I said. *(re-iss. Jun87 c-ep; SFPSC 011)*

Mar 87. (lp) Dojo; *(DOJOLP 52)* **LIVE!** (live)		–
Aug 87. (c) R.O.I.R.; *<A 151>* **RHYTHM COLLISION DUB VOL.1** (with MAD PROFESSOR)	–	

(re-iss. Mar91 on French 'Danceteria' cd/lp; DANCD/DANLP 054) (cd re-iss. Nov94; RE 151CD) (cd re-iss. Jun98 on 'Echo Beach'; EB 002)

1987. (cd) Virgin; *(COMCD 7)* **YOU'VE GOTTA GET OUT OF IT**		–
Dec 87. (lp) Link; *(LINKLP 013)* **LIVE AND LOUD** (live)		–

(cd-iss. Aug92 on 'Street Link'; LINKCD 013)

Nov 88. (7") Old Gold; *(OG 9829)* **BABYLON'S BURNING. / STARING AT THE RUDE BOYS**		–
May 90. (cd/c/lp) Strange Fruit; *(SFR CD/MC/LP 109)* **PEEL SESSIONS – COMPLETE SESSIONS 1979-1981**		–
Jan 92. (cd; shared with PENETRATION) Windsong; *(WINCD 009)* **BBC RADIO 1 LIVE IN CONCERT** (live)		–
1992. (cd-ep; shared with SKIDS) Virgin; **THE SKIDS VS THE RUTS EP**		–
Mar 94. (cd) Receiver; *(<RRCD 182>)* **DEMOLITION DANCING**		Dec94
Jul 94. (cd) Vince Lombard; efa 12303-2) **RULES**		–
Mar 95. (cd) Virgin; *(CDOVD 454)* / Caroline; *<CAROL 1251>* **SOMETHING THAT I SAID . . . THE BEST OF THE RUTS**		

– In a rut / Babylon's burning / Dope for guns / Sus / Something that I said / You're just a . . . / It was cold / Savage circle / Jah war / Criminal mind / Backbiter / Out of order / Human punk / Staring at the rude boys / Love in vain / West one (shine on me).

Mar 95. (cd; shared with The ADVERTS) Step 1; **LIVE AND LOUD** (live)		–
Nov 99. (cd; vs ZION TRAIN) Echo Beach; *(<EB 021>)* **RHYTHM COLLISION REMIX**		–
Jun 00. (cd) Harry May; *(<CANCAN 009CD>)* **IN A CAN** *(re-iss. Sep02; MAYOCD 523)*		Jul00
Jan 01. (cd) Past & Present; *(AFUNCD 01)* **ARCHIVE LIVE**		–
May 01. (d-cd) Snapper; *(SMDCD 332)* **CRIMINAL MINDS**		–
Jun 01. (cd) E.M.I.; *(533590-2)* **BUSTIN' OUT – THE ESSENTIAL RUTS COLLECTION**		
May 02. (d-cd/d-lp; with MAD PROFESSOR & ZION TRAIN) Select Cuts; *(<efa 334004-2/-1>)* **RHYTHM COLLISION VOL.1 & REMIXES**		

THE GREAT INDIE DISCOGRAPHY — The 1970s

SAINTS

Formed: Brisbane, Australia... 1976 by ED KUEPPER and CHRIS BAILEY alongside KYM BRADSHAW and IVOR HAY. The quartet had barely begun an apprenticeship on the Sydney music scene when their debut effort, 'I'M STRANDED' (released on 'Fatal' in Australia), won a Single Of The Week award in punk-friendly music paper, 'Sounds'. Hi-octane rock'n'roll ignited by KUEPPER's scathing guitar playing and IGGY POP-style drawl, the domestically released track saw The SAINTS hailed as Australia's most vital contribution to the punk war effort and bagged them a major label deal with 'Harvest' into the bargain. Relocating to the UK, the band enjoyed widespread acclaim for their similarly titled debut album, released in the summer of '77 alongside their only Top 40 hit, 'THIS PERFECT DAY'. A subsequent EP, 'ONE TWO THREE FOUR', found them demolishing standards, 'LIPSTICK ON YOUR COLLAR' and 'RIVER DEEP MOUNTAIN HIGH', while 1978's 'KNOW YOUR PRODUCT' single and accompanying album, 'ETERNALLY YOURS', flirted with a brassier sound. Never a punk band in the conventional sense, The SAINTS refused to kow-tow to prevailing fashion and suffered the resulting damage to their credibilty. To make matters worse, KUEPPER left after the release of 1978's 'PREHISTORIC SOUNDS' with the remaining line-up having crumbled by the end of the year. While the former frontman went on to follow his own idiosyncratic path and enjoy cult acclaim with The LAUGHING CLOWNS and a subsequent solo career, CHRIS BAILEY later reformed The SAINTS at the turn of the decade with a line-up of CHRIS BARRINGTON, JANINE HALL, MARK BIRMINGHAM and IVOR HAY. Signed to French label, 'New Rose', the remodelled band released 'THE MONKEY PUZZLE' in 1981, the following year's 'CASABLANCA' and 1984's 'WHAT WE DID ON OUR HOLIDAYS' issued as BAILEY solo albums. Featuring former BIRTHDAY PARTY man, TRACY PEW, until his untimely death in 1986, The SAINTS continued to record sporadically throughout the 80's and on into the 90's with varying line-ups. • **Songwriters:** Penned by BAILEY and KUEPPER, until the latter's departure. Covered RIVER DEEP MOUNTAIN HIGH (Phil Spector) / LIPSTICK ON YOUR COLLAR (Connie Francis).

Album rating: I'M STRANDED (*7) / ETERNALLY YOURS (*6) / PREHISTORIC SOUNDS (*6) / THE MONKEY PUZZLE (*4) / OUT IN THE JUNGLE (*5) / A LITTLE MADNESS TO BE FREE (*5) / LIVE IN A MUD HUT (*5) / ALL FOOLS DAY (*6) / SONGS OF SALVATION compilation (*8) / HOWLING (*5) / EVERYBODY KNOWS THE MONKEY (*5) / SPIT THE BLUES OUT (*5) / Chris Bailey (selective): 54 DAYS AT SEA (*5) / ENCORE (*5)

CHRIS BAILEY – vocals / **ED KUEPPER** (b. EDMUND) – guitar / **KYM BRADSHAW** – bass / **IVOR HAY** – drums

	Fatal	Sire
Sep 76. (7") *(MA 7158)* <*1005*> **(I'M) STRANDED. / NO TIME**		
	Harvest	Sire
May 77. (7") *(HAR 5123)* **EROTIC NEUROTIC. / ONE WAY STREET**		-
May 77. (lp) *(SHSP 4065)* <*SRK 6039*> **(I'M) STRANDED**		Jun77

– (I'm) Stranded / One way street / Wild about you / Messin' with the kid / Erotic neurotic / No time / Kissin' cousins / Story of love / Demolition girl / Nights in Venice. *(<cd-iss. Nov97 on 'Triple X'; TX 51243CD>) (<cd re-iss. Nov00 on 'Captain Oi'+=; AHOYCD 129)* – Lipstick on your collar / River deep mountain high.

Jul 77. (7") *(HAR 5130)* **THIS PERFECT DAY. / LIES** — 34
(12") *(12HAR 5130)* – ('A'side) / Do the robot.

— **ALGY WARD** – bass repl. BRADSHAW who joined The LURKERS

Sep 77. (7"ep) *(SHSM 2028)* **ONE TWO THREE FOUR**
– Lipstick on your collar / One way street / Demolition girl / River deep mountain high.

Feb 78. (7") *(11673)* **KNOW YOUR PRODUCT. / RUN DOWN**
Mar 78. (lp) *(SHSP 4078)* <*SRK 6055*> **ETERNALLY YOURS**
– Know your product / Lost and found / Memories are made of this / Private affair / A minor aversion / No, your product / This perfect day / Run down / Ostralia / New center of the universe / Untitled / I'm misunderstood. *(re-iss. Nov87 on 'Fan Club'; FC 035) (cd-iss. May94 on 'New Rose'; 422309) (<cd re-iss. Nov00 on 'Captain Oi'+=; AHOYCD 127>)* – International robots / Lies / Do the robot.

Aug 78. (7") *(11795)* **SECURITY. / ALL TIMES THROUGH PARADISE**
Sep 78. (lp) *(SHSP 4094)* **PREHISTORIC SOUNDS**
– Swing for the crime / All times through Paradise / Everyday's a holiday, every night's a party / Brisbane / Church of indifference / Crazy Googenheimer blues / Everything's fine / The prisoner / Security / This time / This heart of mine / The chameleon / Save me. *(re-iss. Nov87 on 'Fan Club'; FC 036) (cd-iss. May94 on 'New Rose'; 422312)*

— Disbanded late 1978. KUEPPER formed The LAUGHING CLOWNS and WARD joined The DAMNED. In 1980, **CHRIS BAILEY** re-formed The SAINTS recruiting **CHRIS BARRINGTON** – guitar / **JANINE HALL** – bass / **MARK BIRMINGHAM** – drums / guest **IVOR HAY** – keyboards

	New Rose	not iss.
Apr 80. (12"ep) *(NEW 1)* **PARALYTIC TONIGHT DUBLIN TOMORROW EP**		-
Oct 80. (7") *(NEW 3)* **ALWAYS. / IN THE MIRROR**		-
Jan 81. (lp) *(ROSE 1)* **THE MONKEY PUZZLE**		-

– Simple love / Roses / On the waterfront / Call it mine.
– Miss wonderful / Always / Paradise / Let's pretend / Someday / Monkeys (let's go) / Mystery dream / Simple love / The ballad / Dizzy Miss Lizzy. *(free live 7"m w.a.)* – (I'M) STRANDED. / SECURITY / THIS PERFECT DAY *(cd-iss. 1980's+=; ROSE 1CD)* – (above 12"ep)

— **IAIN SHEDDEN** – drums; repl. BIRMINGHAM

Mar 82. (lp) *(ROSE 11)* **OUT IN THE JUNGLE**
– Follow the leader / Rescue / Senile dementia / Casablanca / Curtains / Come on / A 1000 faces / Animal / Out in the jungle / Beginning of the tomato party. *(cd-iss. 1988+=; ROSE 11CD)* – Out a sight / Simple love / Dizzy Miss Lizzy / Gypsy woman call it mine / Roses. *(re-iss. Oct90 on 'Flicknife'; SHARP 106)*

	Flicknife	not iss.
Feb 83. (7") *(FLS 215)* **FOLLOW THE LEADER. / ANIMAL**		-

CHRIS BAILEY

BAILEY – vocals, guitar

	New Rose	not iss.
Jan 83. (lp) *(ROSE 20)* **CASABLANCA**		-

– Home again / Rescue / It's only time / Insurance on me / Wait till tomorrow – Look at me / Junko partner / Always the same / Follow the leader / Why does it make me feel this way / Country boy.

Mar 84. (lp) *(ROSE 30)* **WHAT WE DID ON OUR HOLIDAYS (live)**
– Ghost ships / I'm drinking / Careless love / Amsterdam / Walk on / In the midnight hour – Cherokee dance / Bring it on home to me / I heard it through the grapevine / All night long / Another Saturday night. *(cd-iss. Aug90; ROSE 30CD)* – CASABLANCA

SAINTS

— **TRACY PEW** – bass (ex-BIRTHDAY PARTY) repl. JANINE HALL

	New Rose	not iss.
Dec 84. (7") *(NEW 43)* **IMAGINATION. / PRISONER (live)**		-
Dec 84. (lp/cd) *(ROSE 38/+CD)* **A LITTLE MADNESS TO BE FREE**		-

– Down the drain / Ghost ships / Someone to tell me / The hour / Imagination / It's only time / Wrapped up and blue / Walk away / Photograph / Heavy metal / Angels. *(cd+=)* – LIVE IN A MUD HUT

Mar 85. (7") *(NEW 37)* **GHOST SHIP. / WRAPPED UP AND BLUE**
Mar 85. (lp) *(ROSE 55)* **LIVE IN A MUD HUT (live)**
– Follow the leader / Let's pretend / Always / Walk away / Imagination roses / Ghost ships / Someone to tell me / On the waterfront / Angels / Know your product.

— TRACY PEW died of cancer in November '86

— **BAILEY + HAY** with **RICHARD BURGMANN** – bass + **ARCHIE LaRIZZA** – drums

	Polydor	TVT
Oct 86. (7") *(POSP 825)* **THE TEMPLE OF THE LORD. / CELTIC BALLAD**		-
(12"+=) *(POSPX 825)* – How to avoid disaster.		
Oct 86. (lp/c) *(POLD/+C 5203)* <*TVT 2111-1/-4/-2*> **ALL FOOLS DAY**		1987

– Just like fire would / First time / Hymn to Saint Jude / See you in Paradise / Love or imagination / Celtic ballad / Empty page / Big hits (on the underground) / How to avoid disaster / Blues on my mind / Temple of the Lord / All fools day.

Mar 87. (7") *(POSP 848)* **JUST LIKE FIRE WOULD. / EAST IS EAST** — -
(12"+=) *(POSPX 848)* – Casablanca.

— split but BAILEY re-formed 1989 with LaRIZZA / + **IAIN SHEDDEN** – drums / **BARRINGTON 'BAZ' FRANCIS** – guitar / **JOE CHIOFALO** – keyboards

	Mushroom	TVT
Jan 90. (7") *(MRI 01)* **GRAIN OF SAND. / MAD RACE**		-
(12"+=) *(MRI 01T)* – Minus a ride.		
Jan 90. (cd/c/lp) *(MRI CD/MC/LP 001)* <*TVT 2121-2/-4/-1*> **PRODIGAL SON**		Nov89

– Grain of sand / Fire and brimstone / Friend of the people / Before Hollywood / Sold out / Ghost ships / Massacre / Tomorrow / Stay / Shipwreck / The music goes round my head.

1992. (12"etched) **GRAIN OF SAND. / CARTOON** — -

— disbanded after above but re-formed in the mid-90's; **BAILEY** with **IAN WALSH** – guitar + **ANDREAS JORNVILL** – drums

	Blue Rose	Triple X
Oct 96. (cd) *(BLUCD 029)* <*TX 51245CD*> **HOWLING**		Jan98

– Howling / Shadows / Something, somewhere, sometime / Something wicked / Only stone / Good Friday / Blown away / Last and laughing mile / You know I know / Only dreaming / Second coming / All for nothing.

— **BAILEY** now with **MICHAEL BAYLISS** – bass, vocals / **MARTIN BJERREGAARD** – drums / **ANDY FAULKNER** – guitar

	Last Call	Amsterdamned
Apr 98. (cd) *(303777-2)* <*70019*> **EVERYBODY KNOWS THE MONKEY**		Oct98

– What do you want / Easy money / Working overtime / Fall of an empire / Mustard / Vaguely Jesus / What are you waiting for / Everything turns sour / Playboy of the western world / Come back and visit / S+M+M's / Glorious wonder.

— **PATRICK MATHE** – guitar, harmonica; repl. MARTIN + ANDY

	Axe Killer	not iss.
Nov 00. (cd) *(AXE 306372CD)* **SPIT THE BLUES OUT**		-

– A gentleman came walking / Who's been talking? / Waiting for God (OH!) / The beginning of a beautiful friendship Louis / Where did my mind go / I want to be with you tonight / Spit the blues out / Mojo erectus howls / Before you accuse me / You got a tale babe / It hurts me too. *(<re+US-iss.Nov01 as 'SPIT THE BLUES OUT... PLUS' on 'Raven'+=; RVCD 135>)* – Good Friday / I want to be with you tonight / Who's been talking? / Ghost ships / Howling.

SAINTS (cont)

– compilations, etc. –

Date	Format	Label	Cat#	Title	UK	US
Aug 77.	(7")	Power Exchange;	(PX 242)	**(I'M) STRANDED.** / (B-side by Chuck Stanley)	–	–
Nov 86.	(lp)	Razor;	(RAZ 21)	**THE BEST OF THE SAINTS (77-78)**	–	–
Dec 89.	(lp)	Raven;		**SCARCE SAINTS**	–	Austra
Jan 90.	(lp/c/cd)	Fan Club;	(FC 060/+C/CD)	**THE NEW ROSE YEARS (GREATEST HITS)**	–	–

(cd+=) – (5 extra tracks)

| Feb 91. | (cd) | Raven; (<RVCD 9>) | **SONGS OF SALVATION 1976-1988** | – | Austra |

(UK re-iss. Aug02; same)

| 1992. | (cd) <1053> | **PERMANENT REVOLUTION** (unofficial bootleg) | – | Austra |

– Grain of sand (Zydeco version) / One night with you / Wild and wicked world / Pick up the pieces / Running away / Revolution in my life / Friday the 13th / Love or imagination / Cartoon life / Idiot blues.

| Jul 95. | (lp/cd) | Hot; (HOT 1053/+CD) | **THE MOST PRIMITIVE BAND IN THE WORLD (live from The Twilight Zone, Brisbane 1974)** | – | – |

– Wild about you / Do the robot / One way street / Knock on wood / Erotic neurotic / River deep mountain high / Lies / Stranded / Messin' with the kid / Misunderstood.

| Oct 96. | (lp) | EMI Gold; (CDGO 2069) | **KNOW YOUR PRODUCT (THE BEST OF THE SAINTS)** | – | – |

– (I'm) Stranded / This perfect day / Lipstick on your collar / River deep mountain high / Demolition girl / One way street / Story of love / Kissin' cousins / No time / Wild about you / Messin' with the kid / Nights in Venice / Do the robot / Know your product / Run down / Lost and found / Memories are made of this / Private affaie / Minor aversion / No. your product / Swing for the crime / All times through paradise.

Aug 99.	(d-cd)	Last Call; (LC 305151CD)	7799	–	–
Oct 00.	(d-cd)	Raven; (RVCD 107)	**WILD ABOUT YOU 1976-1979: COMPLETE STUDIO RECORDINGS**	–	–
Aug 02.	(cd; SAINTS & CHRIS BAILEY) Fire Would; (1298) **RARITIES**	–	–

CHRIS BAILEY

Mushroom / not iss.

| Mar 91. | (cd/lp) | **DEMONS** |

– Demons / Marquis of Queensberry / Return to zero / Bridges / Edgar Allan Poe / Running away from home / Fade away / Marie Antoinette / Rusting in the moonlight / That's the way it goes / Up all night.

| Nov 92. | (cd) | **SAVAGE ENTERTAINMENT** | – | Austra |

– Road to oblivion / Key to Babylon / Do they come from you / Broken mirrors / World gone slightly mad / Hotel de la gare / Queen of the hour / Savage entertainment / Life's a comedy / Getting friendly with the Devil / What am I doing here.

—— next with **EDWARD NYSTROM** – guitar / **MAGNUS BORJESON** – bass, keyboards / **STELLAN COLE** – drums / etc.

| Mar 94. | (cd) | (D 31145) **54 DAYS AT SEA** | – | – |

– Fountain of life / Everything I need / On the avenue / Unfamiliar circles / Gone with the wind / Vampyres / Lazarus / Nothing's as it seems / Drowned by the sound / She says / In the desert.

– compilations, etc. –

| Oct 95. | (cd) | Last Call; (422009) **ENCORE** | – | – |

– Do they come from you / Road to oblivion / Queen of the hour / Just like firewould / Ain't nobody's business / Mists of time / Savage entertainment / Look at me / Photography / Casablanca / The prisoner / Swing for the crime / Can't help falling in love / I hear you knocking / In the midnight hour / All night long / I'm drinking / Careless love / Amsterdam / Suspicious minds.

SATAN'S RATS (see under ⇒ PHOTOS; in 80s section)

SAVAGE PENCIL (see under ⇒ ART ATTACKS)

SCRITTI POLITTI

Formed: London, England . . . late '77 by Leeds art student (and former Young Communist), 'GREEN' GARTSIDE, along with NIAL JINKS and TOM MORLEY. Politically motivated punks, their first release, 'SKANK BLOC BOLOGNA' (issued on their own 'St. Pancras' label) created enough interest for a John Peel session, the tracks subsequently released on 'Rough Trade' in 1979. By the release of the classic 'SWEETEST GIRL' single in summer '81, only MORLEY remained from the original line-up, GREEN now steering the band in an altogether more endearing new-wave art-pop/white reggae vein. The track (which featured the piano talents of ROBERT WYATT) was a minor chart hit, likewise the follow-up singles, 'FAITHLESS' and 'JERUSALEM'. All three were included on the much anticipated debut set, 'SONGS TO REMEMBER' (1982), GREEN's dreamy falsetto, musical eclecticism and unerring way with an insidious pop hook (not to mention clever-clever lyric) making him – by this juncture SCRITTI POLITTI were basically a studio vehicle for GREEN – a critical darling and one of 'Rough Trade's most unlikely success stories; the album almost made the UK Top 10, becoming the label's biggest selling release to date. Subsequently relocating to New York and moving up to 'Virgin', GREEN sought out such accomplished US musicians as MARCUS MILLER (former bassist for MILES DAVIS), who accompanied him on his first (UK) Top 10 hit, 'WOOD BEEZ (PLAY LIKE ARETHA FRANKLIN)' in 1984. A succession of different sessioners played on subsequent singles, 'ABSOLUTE', 'HYPNOTISE' and 'THE WORD GIRL', although FRED MAHER and DAVID GAMSON went on to augment GREEN on the follow-up album, 'CUPID AND PSYCHE '85' (1985). Again including all the singles, this slick set of Arif Mardin-produced dancefloor pop-soul also included 'PERFECT WAY', the track which broke SCRITTI POLITTI (albeit briefly) in the States and was later given the honour of a cover by aforementioned jazz legend, MILES DAVIS. The trumpeter also contributed to 'OH PATTI (DON'T FEEL SORRY FOR LOVERBOY)', GREEN's first single after three years of beavering away in the studio. The accompanying album, 'PROVISION' (1988), further refined the man's luxuriant pop vision with an altogether more straightforward approach, GAMSON again providing the lush synth textures. Despite the quality, further singles, 'FIRST BOY IN TOWN (LOVESICK)' and 'BOOM! THERE SHE WAS' lingered in the lower regions of the singles chart. After another interminable lay-off, GREEN returned in 1991 for a Top 20 collaborative cover of The Beatles' 'SHE'S A WOMAN' with ragga loveman, SHABBA RANKS, a further duet with SWEETIE IRIE (a version of Gladys Knight's hit, 'TAKE ME IN YOUR ARMS') not quite so successful. With no album forthcoming in the 90's so far, it does seem as if GREEN had finally abandoned SCRITTI POLITTI as a front for his musical activities although it's likely that this pop maverick will emerge at one point in one form or another. Ah, to see a prophecy come true. Re-inventing himself as a bearded rapper type (well his backing group were anyhow), GREEN and SCRITTI POLITTI came storming back from oblivion on the long-awaited fourth set, 'ANOMIE AND BONHOMIE' (1999). • **Trivia:** SCRITTI POLITTI is nearly Italian for political writing. MADNESS had a 1986 hit with 'THE SWEETEST GIRL'. That year also saw GREEN and GAMSON write the title track for AL JARREAU's album, 'L Is For Lover'.

Album rating: SONGS TO REMEMBER (*8) / CUPID & PSYCHE (*7) / PROVISION (*4) / ANOMIE AND BONHOMIE (*6)

GREEN (b. GREEN STROHMEYER-GARTSIDE, 22 Jun'56, Cardiff, Wales) – vocals, guitar / **TOM MORLEY** – linn drum / **MATTHEW 'K'** – programme organiser / **NIAL JINKS** – bass

St.Pancras / not iss.

| Nov 78. | (7") | (SCRIT 1) **SKANC BLOG BOLOGNA.** / **IS AND OUGHT OF THE WESTERN WORLD** | – | – |

Rough Trade / not iss.

| Sep 79. | (12"ep) | (RT 027T) **4 A SIDES** | – | – |

– Doubt beat / Confidences / Bibbly O'tek / P.A.'s.

| Nov 79. | (7"ep) | (SCRIT 2 – RT 034) **WORK IN PROGRESS (PEEL SESSIONS)** | – | – |

– Hegamony / Scritlocks door / Opec-Immac / Messthetics.

—— added **MIKE MacEVOY** – synthesizers, vocoder / **MGOTSE** – d.bass / guest **ROBERT WYATT** – piano

| Aug 81. | (7"/12") | (RT 091/+T) **THE SWEETEST GIRL.** / **LIONS AFTER SLUMBER** | 64 | – |

—— **JOE CANG** – bass repl. NIAL / **STEVE SIDWELL** – trumpet / **JAMIE TALBOT** – saxophone repl. MGOTSE

| Apr 82. | (7"/12") | (RT 107/+T) **FAITHLESS.** / **FAITHLESS PART II (instrumental)** | 56 | – |
| Jul 82. | (7"/7"pic-d) | (RT 111/+P) **ASYLUMS IN JERUSALEM.** / **JAQUES DERRIDA** | 43 | – |

(12"+=) (RT 111T) – ('A' extended).

| Aug 82. | (lp) | (ROUGH/+C 20) **SONGS TO REMEMBER** | 12 | – |

– Asylums in Jerusalem / A slow soul / Jacques Derrida / Lions after slumber / Faithless / Sex / Rock-a-boy blue / Gettin' havin' & holdin' / The sweetest girl. (cd-iss. May87; ROUGH/+CD 20) (cd re-iss. Oct01 on 'Virgin'; CDV 2944)

—— GREEN recruited US musicians **MARCUS MILLER** – bass (ex-MILES DAVIS) / **STEVE FERRONE** – drums (ex-BRIAN AUGER) / **PAUL JACKSON Jnr.** – guitar / (MORLEY went solo and released one 1985 single for 'Zarjazz', 'WHO BROKE THE LOVE?')

Virgin / Warners

| Mar 84. | (7"/7"pic-d) | (VS 657/+P) <28811> **WOOD BEEZ (PLAY LIKE ARETHA FRANKLIN).** / ('A'dub) | 10 | 91 Jan86 |

(12"+=) (VS 657T) – ('A' extended).

—— GREEN with **ROBBIE BUCHANAN** + **DAVID FRANK** – keyboards / **FRED MAHER** – drums

| Jun 84. | (7"/7"pic-d) | (VS 680/+P) **ABSOLUTE.** / ('A' version) | 17 | – |

(12"+=) (VS 680T) – ('A' extended).

—— GREEN now with **DAVID GAMSON** – keyboards / **ALLAN MURPHY** – guitar

| Nov 84. | (7"/7"pic-d) | (VS 725/+P) **HYPNOTISE.** / ('A' version) | 68 | – |

(12"+=) (VS 725T) – ('A' extended).

—— **NICK MOROCH** – guitar was added to above guests for album below.

| May 85. | (7"/7"sha-pic-d) | (VS 747/+P) **THE WORD GIRL.** / **FLESH AND BLOOD** | 6 | – |

(12"+=) (VS 747-12) – ('A' & 'B' versions).

| Jun 85. | (lp/c/cd) | (V/TCV/CDV 2350) <25302> **CUPID AND PSYCHE '85** | 5 | 50 |

– The word girl / Small talk / Absolute / A liitle knowledge / Don't work that way / Perfect way / Lover to fall / Wood beez (pray like Aretha Franklin) / Hypnotize. (cd+=)– (other versions). (re-iss. Apr90 lp/c; OVED/C 294)

| Aug 85. | (7") | (VS 780) <28949> **PERFECT WAY.** / ('A' version) | 48 | 11 |

(12"+=) (VS 780-12) – ('A' extended).

—— GREEN with numerous session people, + guest MILES DAVIS

| Apr 88. | (7") | (VS 1006) **OH PATTI (DON'T FEEL SORRY FOR LOVERBOY).** / ('A'instrumental) | 13 | – |

(12"+=/12"pic-d+=) (VST/+P 1006) – ('A' extended).
(cd-s+=) (VSCD 1006) – Best thing ever.
(c-s++=) (VSTC 1006) – ('A'-Drumless mix).

| Jun 88. | (lp/c/cd) | (V/TCV/CDV 2515) <25686> **PROVISION** | 8 | – |

– Boom! there she was / Overnite / First boy in this town / All that we are / Best thing ever / Oh Patti (don't feel sorry for loverboy) / Bam salute / Sugar and spice / Philosophy now. (cd+=) – Oh Patti (extended) / Boom! . . . (dub). (re-iss. Aug91 cd/c;)

137

SCRITTI POLITTI (cont)

Jul 88.	(7") (VS 1082) **FIRST BOY IN TOWN (LOVESICK). / WORLD COME BACK TO LIFE**	63	-
	(12"+=) (VST 1082) – ('A'instrumental).		
	(cd-s+=) (VSCD 1082) – ('A'extended remix).		
Oct 88.	(7") (VS 1143) <27973> **BOOM! THERE SHE WAS. / PHILOSOPHY NOW**	55	53 Jun88
	(12"+=/3"cd-s+=) (VS T/CD 1143) – ('A'mix) / ('A'dub version).		
Mar 91.	(7"/c-s; SCRITTI POLITTI & SHABBA RANKS) (VS/+C 1333) **SHE'S A WOMAN. / LITTLE WAY** (different)	20	-
	(12"+=) (VST 1333) – ('A'-Apollo 440 remix).		
	(cd-s+=) (VSCD 1333) – Wood beez (pray like Aretha Franklin).		
	(12") (VSTX 1333) – ('A'-William Orbit remix) / ('A'-Tutology business mix).		
Jul 91.	(7"/c-s) (VS/+C 1346) **TAKE ME IN YOUR ARMS. / ('A'instrumental) / ('A'mix)**	47	-
	(12"+=/cd-s+=) (VS T/CD 1346) – She's a woman.		
	above single credited SWEETIE IRIE on the sleeve. GREEN abandoned SCRITTI although he still writes for and with others until . . .		
Jul 99.	(cd-s) (VSCDT 1731) **TINSEL TOWN TO THE BOOGIEDOWN / DEAD CERTAINTY**	46	-
	(12"/cd-s) (VST/VSCDX 1731) – ('A'mixes).		
Jul 99.	(cd/c) (CDV/TCV 2884) <8 47488> **ANOMIE AND BONHOMIE**	33	
	– Umm / Tinsel town to the boogiedown / First goodbye / Die alone / Mystic handyman / Smith n' slappy / Born to be / World you understand is over and over / Here come July / Prince among men / Brushed with oil dusted with powder.		

– compilations, others, etc. –

on 'Virgin' unless mentioned otherwise

Jun 88.	(3"cd-ep) (CDT 13) **THE WORD GIRL / FLESH AND BLOOD** / ('A'-Turntable mix)		-
Nov 88.	(3"cd-ep) (CDT 34) **WOOD BEEZ (PRAY LIKE ARETHA FRANKLIN)** / ('A'dub) / **SMALL TALK**		-
Apr 90.	(3"cd-ep) (VVCS 1) **ABSOLUTE** / (3 tracks by other artists)		-

SEX PISTOLS

Formed: London, England . . . summer 1975 out of The SWANKERS by PAUL COOK, STEVE JONES and GLEN MATLOCK, the latter two regular faces at MALCOLM McLAREN's 'Sex' boutique on the capital's King's Road. With the NEW YORK DOLLS already on his CV, McLAREN was well qualified to mastermind the rise and fall of The SEX PISTOLS as he dubbed his new plaything, the entrepreneur/svengali installing another 'Sex' customer, the green-haired JOHN LYDON, as a suitably sneering frontman. JONES soon renamed the latter JOHNNY ROTTEN, informing his farting rear-end, "You're rotten, you are"; the tone of the SEX PISTOLS was set. After a few local gigs, the group supported JOE STRUMMER's 101'ers in April '76, their bedraggled, low-rent bondage chic troupe of followers including the likes of SIOUXSIE SIOUX (later of BANSHEES fame) and one SID VICIOUS, allegedly the perpetrator behind the infamous glass-throwing incident at the 100 Club punk all-dayer in which a girl was partially blinded. Controversy, intentional or otherwise, hung around the group like a bad smell and made The SEX PISTOLS into minor legends with barely one single under their belts. Signed to 'E.M.I.' for £40,000, their debut release, 'ANARCHY IN THE U.K.' (having already shocked those of a sensitive disposition after being aired on the 'So It Goes' TV pop show) was finally released in November '76. An inflammatory slice of primal nihilism which surpassed even The STOOGES' finest efforts, the track initially climbed into the Top 40 before being unceremoniously withdrawn following the band's riotous appearance on a local chat/news programme, 'Today'. With JONES swearing copiously at presenter Bill Grundy, the tabloids had a field day, stirring up the moral majority and prompting more "must we subject our pop kids to this filth" editorials than you could shake a snotty stick at. 'E.M.I.' of course, bailed out (writing off the advance as a particularly bad debt) early the following year, while MATLOCK was fired around the same time for being, well, er . . . too nice. His replacement was the aforementioned VICIOUS, a suitably violent and abusive character who duly became more of a punk anti-hero/caricature than McLAREN could ever have dreamed. After a short period in label limbo, The 'PISTOLS signed to 'A&M' in March '77 for another six figure sum; the honeymoon period was probably the shortest in recording history as the band's infamous antics at the post-signing party, together with protests from other artists on the label saw the UK's foremost punk band once again minus a recording contract. Once again, the band retained the loot from the advance and once again, a single, 'GOD SAVE THE QUEEN', was withdrawn (some copies did find their way into circulation and now fetch considerably more than the original 50p price tag). Arguably The SEX PISTOLS' defining moment, this jaw-clenching two-fingered salute to the monarchy and everything it represented was to truly make the band public enemy No.1, its release coinciding sweetly with her highness' silver jubilee year. Re-released by new label 'Virgin' (virtually the only company willing to take the band on for a meagre £15,000 advance), the single was predictably banned by the BBC, though that didn't prevent it from outselling the official No.1 at the time, Rod Stewart's 'I Don't Want To Talk About It'. That long, hot summer also saw the band hiring a boat and sailing up and down the Thames in a publicity stunt which ended in chaos; cue yet more controversy and howls of derision from the nation's moral guardians. Knuckle-headed English royalists decided to take matters into their own hands, both COOK and ROTTEN attacked in separate incidents as another blankly brilliant single, 'PRETTY VACANT', gatecrashed the Top 10. Previewed by the seething, squalling outrage of 'HOLIDAYS IN THE SUN', the legendary debut album, 'NEVER MIND THE BOLLOCKS, HERE'S THE SEX PISTOLS' was finally released at the end of the year. While the record undeniably contained some filler, it remains the classic punk statement, the blistering 'BODIES' and the gleeful kiss-off to their former employers, 'E.M.I.', almost standing up against the intensity of the singles (included in their entirety). As ever, controversy clouded its release, the album reaching No.1 in spite of the word 'Bollocks' – a near contravention of the 1889 Indecent Advertisements Act(!) – resulting in boycotts from many major outlets. Constantly on the verge of falling apart, the band subsequently flew to America for a string of chaotic dates, the final round of blanks in The SEX PISTOLS' depleted armoury. Amid sporadic showdowns with Deep South cowboys and SID's ever worsening heroin problem, ROTTEN (bowing out on stage in San Francisco with the immortal phrase "Ever get the feeling you've been cheated") effectively ended the whole sorry affair with his departure after the final gig. While LYDON (the name he now reverted back to) went on to form PUBLIC IMAGE LTD., McLAREN had other ideas for the splintered remains of the band, namely jetting off to Rio De Janeiro to record a single with exiled trainrobber, RONNIE BIGGS. The result, 'NO ONE IS INNOCENT (A PUNK PRAYER BY RONNIE BIGGS)', made the Top 10 in summer '78, although VICIOUS was absent from the recording, holed up in New York with his similarly addicted girlfriend, Nancy Spungeon. He did find time to record a peerless rendition of Paul Anka's 'MY WAY', the single taking on an added poignancy following his untimely but hardly surprising death early the following year; out on bail after being charged with the murder of Spungeon in October, VICIOUS succumbed to a fatal heroin overdose on the 2nd of February '79. The following month saw the belated release of McLAREN's pet project, an artistically licensed celluloid account of The SEX PISTOLS' history entitled 'THE GREAT ROCK'N'ROLL SWINDLE'. Widely criticised for its blatant exclusion of GLEN MATLOCK, the glaring absence of ROTTEN as an active participant and its paper-thin storyline, the movie was nevertheless an occasionally exhilarating, often hilarious trip through the misspent youth of Britain's best-loved punk band. While a perfunctory cover of Eddie Cochran's 'C'MON EVERYBODY' (a posthumous VICIOUS recording) made the Top 10 later that summer and 'Virgin' continued to flog The SEX PISTOLS' dead corpse with a variety of exploitation jobs, COOK and JONES formed the short-lived PROFESSIONALS. Although they didn't invent punk, The SEX PISTOLS certainly helped popularise it and while they were at least partly responsible for an avalanche of unlistenably amateurish shit, the band's uncompromising approach permanently altered the machinations of the music industry and took three-chord rock'n'roll to its ultimate conclusion. Despite the fact original fans had long since given up on the UK ever descending into anarchy, the original 'PISTOLS line-up of LYDON, MATLOCK, JONES and COOK reformed in summer '96 for a handful of outdoor gigs and an accompanying live album. Opinion was divided as to whether this blatantly commercial venture (billed as "The Filthy Lucre Tour") was in keeping with the original punk spirit; probably not, although few paying punters complained about what was subsequently hailed as one of the events of the summer and it was certainly a safer bet than the new GREEN DAY album . . . • **Songwriters:** Group compositions, until COOK & JONES took over in 1978. They also covered; NO FUN (Stooges) / ROCK AROUND THE CLOCK (Bill Haley) / JOHNNY B. GOODE (Chuck Berry) / STEPPING STONE (Boyce-Hart) / etc. • **Trivia:** In 1979, they took McLAREN to court for unpaid royalties. In 1986, the official receiver, through McLAREN paid a 7-figure out of court settlement to LYDON, JONES, COOK and SID's mother.

Album rating (selective): NEVER MIND THE BOLLOCKS, HERE'S THE SEX PISTOLS (*10) / THE GREAT ROCK'N'ROLL SWINDLE soundtrack (*8) / FLOGGING A DEAD HORSE compilation (*8) / KISS THIS compilation (*8) / FILTHY LUCRE LIVE (*6) / JUBILEE compilation (*8)

JOHNNY ROTTEN (b. JOHN LYDON, 31 Jan'56) – vocals / **STEVE JONES** (b. 3 Sep'55) – guitar / **GLEN MATLOCK** (b.27 Aug'56) – bass / **PAUL COOK** (b.20 Jul'56) – drums

		E.M.I.	not iss.
Nov 76.	(7") (EMI 2566) **ANARCHY IN THE U.K. / I WANNA BE ME**	38	-

— (Feb'77) **SID VICIOUS** (b.JOHN RITCHIE, 10 May'57) – bass, vocals (ex-SIOUXSIE & THE BANSHEES) repl. MATLOCK who soon formed RICH KIDS

		A&M	not iss.
Mar 77.	(7"w-drawn) (AMS 7284) **GOD SAVE THE QUEEN. / NO FEELINGS**	-	-

— Were soon paid off yet again. Above copies filtered through and soon became a collectors item).

		Virgin	Warners
May 77.	(7") (VS 181) **GOD SAVE THE QUEEN. / DID YOU NO WRONG**	2	-

— (above was banned by the BBC, and outsold the official No.1 at the time; Rod Stewart's 'I Don't Want To Talk About It'.

Jul 77.	(7") (VS 184) **PRETTY VACANT. / NO FUN**	6	-
Oct 77.	(7") (VS 191) **HOLIDAYS IN THE SUN. / SATELLITE**	8	-
Nov 77.	(7") **PRETTY VACANT. / SUBMISSION**	-	
Nov 77.	(lp/c) (V/TCV 2086) <3147> **NEVER MIND THE BOLLOCKS, HERE'S THE SEX PISTOLS**	1	106
	– Holidays in the sun / Bodies / No feelings / Liar / God save the Queen / Problems / Seventeen / Anarchy in the UK / Submission / Pretty vacant / New York / E.M.I. (7" free w/some copies of 'Submission'; SPOTS 001) – **SUBMISSION** (one-sided). (pic-lp Jan78; VP 2086) (re-iss. Oct86 lp/c; OVED/+C 136) (cd-iss. Oct86; CDV 2086) (re-iss. cd May93; CDVX 2086) (re-iss. 1996 on cd w/ free 'SPUNK' bootleg tracks) <cd-iss. Jul96 on 'Alex'; 5695>		

— ROTTEN left, reverted to JOHN LYDON and created new band PUBLIC IMAGE

SEX PISTOLS (cont)

LTD. His place was temporarily taken by **RONNIE BIGGS** (the Great Train Robber escapee now exiled in Brazil) 'A'-side vocals / **SID VICIOUS** – 'B'side vocals

Jun 78. (7") (VS 220) **NO ONE IS INNOCENT (A PUNK PRAYER BY RONNIE BIGGS). / MY WAY** — 7 / -
(12") (VS 220-12 A1/2) – The biggest blow (a punk prayer by Ronnie Biggs) / My way.
(12"+=) (VS 220-12 A3) – (above listing) / (interview).

— On 11 Oct'78, SID was charged with the murder of girlfriend NANCY SPUNGEON. MALCOLM McLAREN/'Virgin' bailed him out, but he died 2 Feb'79 of drug overdose. The 1979/80 singles were all taken from THE GREAT ROCK'N'ROLL SWINDLE film.

Feb 79. (7") (VS 240) **SOMETHING ELSE. / FRIGGIN' IN THE RIGGIN'** — 3 / -
Mar 79. (d-lp/d-c) (VD/TCV 2510) <45083> **THE GREAT ROCK'N'ROLL SWINDLE (Film Soundtrack)** — 7 / -
– God save the Queen symphony / Rock around the clock / Johnny B. Goode / Roadrunner / Black Arabs / Watcha gonna do about it (* on some) / Who killed Bambi? / Silly thing / Substitute / No lip / (I'm not your) Stepping stone / Lonely boy / Somethin' else / Anarchie pour le UK / Einmal war Belsen vortrefflich / No one is innocent / My way / C'mon everybody / E.M.I. / The great rock'n'roll swindle / You need hands / Friggin' in the riggin'. (re-iss. 1-lp May80; V 2168) (re-iss. Apr89 lp/c; OVED/+C 234) (d-cd iss.Jul93; CDVD 2510) (re-iss. cd May93; CDVDX 2510)

Apr 79. (7") (VS 256) **SILLY THING. / WHO KILLED BAMBI?** — 6 / -
— (above 'A'vocals – **STEVE JONES**, 'B' vocals – **EDDIE TENPOLE TUDOR**) (below 'A'vocals – **SID VICIOUS**)

Jun 79. (7") (VS 272) **C'MON EVERYBODY. / GOD SAVE THE QUEEN SYMPHONY / WATCHA GONNA DO ABOUT IT** — 3 / -
Aug 79. (lp/c) (VR/ 2) **SOME PRODUCT: CARRI ON SEX PISTOLS** — 6 / -
– The very name (the Sex Pistols) / From beyond the grave / Big tits across America / The complex world of Johnny Rotten / Sex Pistols will play / Is the Queen a moron / The fuckin' rotter. (cd-iss. May93; CDVR 2)

Oct 79. (7") (VS 290) **THE GREAT ROCK'N'ROLL SWINDLE. / ROCK AROUND THE CLOCK** — 21 / -
Dec 79. (lp/c; by SID VICIOUS) (V/TCV 2144) **SID SINGS** — 30 / -
– Born to lose / I wanna be your dog / Take a chance on me / (I'm not your) Stepping stone / My way / Belsen was a gas / Somethin' else / Chatterbox / Search and destroy / Chinese rocks / My way. (re-iss. Aug88 lp/c; OVED/+C 85) (cd-iss. Feb89; CDV 2144)

— There were other SID VICIOUS exploitation releases later.

Feb 80. (lp/c) (V/TCV 2142) **FLOGGING A DEAD HORSE** — 23 / -
– (singles compilation) (re-iss. Apr86 lp/c; OVED/+C 165) (cd-iss. Oct86; CDV 2142)

Jun 80. (7") (VS 339) **(I'M NOT YOUR) STEPPING STONE. / PISTOLS PROPAGANDA** — 21 / -

— COOK and JONES were now The PROFESSIONALS

– compilations, exploitation releases –

Note; on 'Virgin' until mentioned otherwise.

Jan 80. (lp) Flyover; (YX 7247) **THE BEST OF... AND WE DON'T CARE**
Dec 80. (6x7"box) (SEX 1) **PISTOLS PACK**
– GOD SAVE THE QUEEN. / PRETTY VACANT // HOLIDAYS IN THE SUN. / MY WAY // SOMETHING ELSE. / SILLY THING // C'MON EVERYBODY. / THE GREAT ROCK'N'ROLL SWINDLE // STEPPING STONE. / ANARCHY IN THE U.K. / BLACK LEATHER. / HERE WE GO AGAIN
(below 45 credited EDDIE TENPOLE TUDOR)

Sep 81. (7") (VS 443) **WHO KILLED BAMBI?. / ROCK AROUND THE CLOCK**
1983. (7") (VS 609) **ANARCHY IN THE UK. / NO FUN**
(12"+=) (VS 609-12) – E.M.I.
Jan 85. (7"/7"pic-d/12") Cherry Red; (PISTOL 76P)(12PISTOL 76) **LAND OF HOPE AND GLORY. ("EX-PISTOLS") / FLOWERS OF ROMANSK** — 69 / -
Jan 85. (m-lp) Chaos; (MINI 1) **THE MINI-ALBUM**
(pic-m-lp.Jan86; AMPL 37) (cd-iss. Mar89; APOCA 3)
Mar 87. (7"/7"yellow,7"pink) Chaos; (DICK 1) **SUBMISSION. / NO FEELINGS**
(12",12"colrd) (EXPORT 1) – ('A'side) / Anarchy in the U.K.
Feb 85. (lp) Receiver; (RRLP 101) **THE ORIGINAL PISTOLS LIVE (live)**
(pic-lp Jun86 on 'American Phono.'; APKPD 13) (re-iss. Jan89 on 'Dojo'; DOJOLP 45) (re-iss. May86 on 'Fame' lp/c; FA 41-3149-1/-4) (cd-iss. Jul89; CDFA 3149)
1985. (lp) Receiver; (RRLP 102) **AFTER THE STORM**
(above with tracks by NEW YORK DOLLS) (cd-iss. Jul91; RRCD 102)

Aug 85. (lp) Konnexion; **LIVE WORLDWIDE (live)**
Nov 85. (lp) Receiver; **WHERE WERE YOU IN '77**
Nov 85. (lp/pic-lp) Bondage; **BEST OF SEX PISTOLS LIVE (live)**
Nov 85. (lp) Hippy; **NEVER TRUST A HIPPY**
Nov 85. (lp) '77 Records; **POWER OF THE PISTOLS**
Feb 86. (lp) McDonald-Lydon; (JOCK 1) **THE LAST SHOW ON EARTH (live)**
Apr 86. (12") McDonald-Lydon; (JOCK 1201) **ANARCHY IN THE U.K. (live). / FLOGGING A DEAD HORSE**
Aug 86. (lp) McDonald-Lydon; (JOCKLP 3) **THE SEX PISTOLS 10th ANNIVERSARY ALBUM**
Aug 86. (12"ep) Archive 4; (TOF 104) **ANARCHY IN THE UK / I'M A LAZY SOD. / PRETTY VACANT / SUBSTITUTE**
Jan 87. (6xlp-box) McDonald-Lydon; (JOCK BOX1) **THE FILTH AND THE FURY**
– FILTH & THE FURY / LAST SHOW ON EARTH / 10th ANNIVERSARY ALBUM / ITALIAN DEMOS / NO FUTURE USA / THE REAL SID & NANCY
May 88. (lp/cd) Restless; <72255-1/-2> **BETTER LIVE THAN DEAD (live)**
Jun 88. (cd/lp) M.B.C.; (JOCK/+LP 12) **IT SEEMED TO BE THE END UNTIL THE NEXT BEGINNING**
Jun 88. (3"cd-s) (CDT 3) **ANARCHY IN THE U.K. / E.M.I. / NO FUN**
Oct 88. (m-lp) Specific; (SPAW 101) **ANARCHY WORLDWIDE**

Oct 88. (cd-ep) Specific; (SPCFC 102) **CASH FOR CHAOS**
– Submission (live) / God save the Queen / Liar.
Oct 88. (cd-ep) Classic Tracks; (CDEP 13C) **THE ORIGINAL PISTOLS (live)**
– Anarchy in the U.K. / Pretty vacant / No fun / Substitute.
Dec 88. (3"cd-s) (CDT 37) **GOD SAVE THE QUEEN / DID YOU NO WRONG / DON'T GIVE ME NO LIP CHILD**
Jun 89. (lp,pink-lp,green-lp/c) Link; (LINK LP/MC 063) **LIVE AND LOUD (live)**
(cd-iss. Oct92; LINKCD 063)
Dec 89. (lp/c/cd,pic-cd) Receiver; (RR LP/MC/CD 117) **NO FUTURE U.K.?**
Feb 90. (cd/c) Action Replay; (CDAR/ARLC 1008) **THE BEST OF AND THE REST OF THE SEX PISTOLS**
1990. (12"blue-ep) Receiver; (REPLAY 3012) **THE EARLY YEARS LIVE**
– Anarchy in the U.K. / Pretty vacant / Liar / Dolls (aka 'New York').
Jan 91. (d-lp) Receiver; (RRLD 004) **PRETTY VACANT**
(d-cd-iss. Jul93; RRDCD 004)
Sep 92. (7"/c-s) (VS/+C 1431) **ANARCHY IN THE U.K. / I WANNA BE ME** — 33 / -
(cd-s+=/s-cd-s+=) (VSCD T/X 1431) – ('A'demo).
Oct 92. (cd) Streetlink; (STRCD 019) **EARLY DAZE – THE STUDIO COLLECTION**
(re-iss. May93 on 'Dojo'; DOJOCD 119)
Oct 92. (cd/c/d-lp) (V/TC/CDV 2702) / Alex; <2931> **KISS THIS** — 10 / -
– Anarchy in the UK / God save the Queen / Pretty vacant / Holidays in their Sun / I wanna be me / Did you no wrong / No fun / Satellite / Don't give me no lip child / (I'm not your) Stepping stone / Bodies / No feelings / Liar / Problems / Seventeen / Submission / New York / E.M.I. / My way / Silly thing. // (cd w/bonus cd+=) **LIVE IN TRONDHEIM 21st JULY 1977** :- Anarchy in the UK / I wanna be me / Seventeen / New York / E.M.I. / No fun / No feelings / Problems / God save the Queen.
Nov 92. (7") (VS 1448) **PRETTY VACANT. / NO FEELINGS (demo)** — 56 / -
(12"+=) (VST 1448) – Satellite (demo) / Submission (demo).
(cd-s+=) (VSCDG 1448) – E.M.I. (demo) / Satellite (demo).
(cd-s) (VSCDT 1448) – ('A'side) / Seventeen (demo) / Submission (demo) / Watcha gonna do about it?
Mar 93. (cd) Dojo; (DOJOCD 66) **LIVE AT CHELMSFORD PRISON**
Nov 93. (cd) Dojo; (DOJOCD 73) **BETTER LIVE THAN DEAD**
Jul 95. (cd) Dojo; (DOJOCD 216) **WANTED – THE GOODMAN TAPES**
Oct 95. (d-cd) Essential; (ESDCD 321) **ALIVE**
Jan 96. (cd) Dojo; (DOJOCD 222) **PIRATES OF DESTINY**
Jan 97. (7") Man's Ruin; (MR 053) **split with the UGLYS**
Mar 97. (7") Man's Ruin; (MR 056) **split with the SOPHISTICATES**
Jun 97. (cd) Emporio; (EMPRCD 716) **RAW**
May 02. (7") (VS 1832) **GOD SAVE THE QUEEN. / GOD SAVE THE QUEEN** (Neil Barnes & Sex Pistols extended mix) — 15 / -
(12"+=/cd-s+=) (VST/VSCDT 1832) – ('A'-Neil Barnes dance mix).
Jun 02. (cd) (CDV 2961) **JUBILEE** — 29 / -
– God save the Queen / Anarchy in the UK / Pretty vacant / Holidays in the sun / No one is innocent / My way / Somethin' else / Friggin' in the riggin' / Silly thing / C'mon everybody / The great rock'n'roll swindle / I'm not your stepping stone / Pretty vacant (live) / E.M.I. (unlimited edition) / God save the Queen (video) / Anarchy in the UK (video) / Pretty vacant (video).

PROFESSIONALS

STEVE JONES – vocals, guitar / **PAUL COOK** – drums / **ANDY ALLEN** – guitar, vocals / **RAY McVEIGH** – guitar, vocals / **PAUL MYERS** – bass (ex-SUBWAY SECT)

Virgin / not iss.

Jul 80. (7") (VS 353) **JUST ANOTHER DREAM. / ACTION MAN**
Aug 80. (lp/c) (V/TCV 2167) **THE PROFESSIONALS**
– All the way / Are you? / Kick down the doors / Crescendo / Little boys in blue / Does anybody care / Kamikaze / 1-2-3 / Rockin' Mick.
Sep 80. (7"m) (VS 376) **1-2-3. / BABY I DON'T CARE / WHITE LIGHT, WHITE HEAT** — 43 / -
May 81. (7") (VS 426) **JOIN THE PROFESSIONALS. / HAS ANYBODY GOT AN ALIBI**
Oct 81. (7") (VS 456) **THE MAGNIFICENT. / JUST ANOTHER DREAM**
Nov 81. (lp/c) (V/TCV 2220) **I DIDN'T SEE IT COMING**
– The magnificent / Payola / Northern slide / Friday night square / Kick down the doors / Little boys all the way / Crescendo / Madhouse / Too far to fall.

— PROFESSIONALS split early in '82 and COOK subsequently joined CHIEFS OF RELIEF. STEVE JONES augmented IGGY POP and went solo in 1987. He released two albums, 'MERCY' (1987) and 'FIRE AND GASOLINE' (1989).

SEX PISTOLS

— The original SEX PISTOLS re-formed at the back end of '95. Messrs LYDON, JONES, COOK + MATLOCK finally returned live on 24th June 1996, with packed out Finsbury Park concert. Embarked on their 'Filthy Lucre' tour soon after.

Virgin America / Caroline

Jul 96. (7"silver) (VUS 113) **PRETTY VACANT – LIVE. /** — 18 / -
(cd-s+=) (VUSCD 113) –
Aug 96. (cd/c/lp) (41926) <7541> **FILTHY LUCRE LIVE (live)** — 26 / -
– Seventeen / New York / Did you no wrong / God save the Queen / Liar / Satellite / (I'm not your) Stepping stone / Holidays in the sun / Submission / No feelings / Pretty vacant / E.M.I. / Problems / Anarchy in the UK / No fun.

— JONES was also part-member of trans-Atlantic supergroup, NEUROTIC OUTSIDERS, alongside DUFF McKAGAN and MATT SORUM (Guns N' Roses) and JOHN TAYLOR (Duran Duran). They released an eponymous album for 'Maverick' in August '96 and from it they lifted the single, 'JERK'.

SHAKE (see under ⇒ REZILLOS)

SHAM 69

Formed: London, England . . . 1976 by JIMMY PURSEY, ALBIE SLIDER, MARK CAIN and DAVE PARSONS (the latter two replacing original members BILLY BOSTIK and NEIL HARRIS – who himself had replaced the curiously monikered JOHN GOODFORNOTHING – respectively). Inspired by The SEX PISTOLS, PURSEY set out making pogo-friendly, dumbly anthemic punk with a fiercely working class agenda, issuing a statement of intent with an independently released, JOHN CALE-produced single, 'I DON'T WANNA'. Subsequently signing with 'Polydor', the band made their major label debut with the inimitable 'BORSTAL BREAKOUT' in early '77, following it up with a partly live album, 'TELL US THE TRUTH'. What really took their terrace chant appeal to the masses, however, was the subsequent trio of hit singles led by 'ANGELS WITH DIRTY FACES'; 'HURRY UP HARRY' and 'IF THE KIDS ARE UNITED' followed into the Top 10 shortly after, the latter track (complete with hilarious chirpy cockney intro) a well meant but naive call for youthful brotherhood. Which kind of summed up SHAM 69's fate; PURSEY's idealistic working class warrior philosophy backfired as the air-punching punk-by-numbers began attracting more and more face-punching neo-Nazi skinheads. Despite a considered attempt to brush up on the lads-on-the-loose formula with their third set, 'THE ADVENTURES OF THE HERSHAM BOYS' (1979), Top 10 success only seemed to make the situation worse. PURSEY finally disbanded SHAM 69 in the summer of '79 only to reform a couple of months later for a final album, 'THE GAME' (1980). This failed to chart and PURSEY subsequently pursued a low key solo career, initially with 'Polydor' (who released his 1980 debut set, 'IMAGINATION CAMOUFLAGE') then with 'Epic', before going on to record a series of one-off singles for various indie labels. With this going nowhere fast, PURSEY and PARSONS resurrected SHAM 69 in 1987, releasing a largely ignored album, 'VOLUNTEER' the following year. Retreating from view for a further four years, they were back yet again in the 90's, releasing a string of albums for the diehards and playing regular gigs on the punk nostalgia circuit. • **Songwriters:** Penned by PURSEY-PARSONS except; YOU'RE A BETTER MAN THAN I (Yardbirds) / WITH A LITTLE HELP FROM MY FRIENDS (Beatles). The WANDERERS covered THE TIMES THEY ARE A-CHANGIN' (Bob Dylan). • **Trivia:** PURSEY appeared on Various Artists lp, 'The Whip', in '83.

Album rating: TELL US THE TRUTH (*6) / THAT'S LIFE (*5) / ADVENTURES OF THE HERSHAM BOYS (*5) / THE GAME (*4) / THE FIRST, THE BEST AND THE LAST compilation (*7) / VOLUNTEER (*2) / INFORMATION LIBRE (*2) / KINGS AND QUEENS (*3) / SOAPY WATER & MR MARMALADE (*1)

JIMMY PURSEY (b. Hersham, Surrey, England) – vocals / **DAVE PARSONS** – guitar repl. NEIL HARRIS who had repl. JOHNNY GOODFORNOTHING / **ALBIE SLIDER** (b. ALBERT MASKAIL) – bass, vocals / **MARK CAIN** – drums repl. BILLY BOSTIK

Step Forward / not iss.

Oct 77. (7"m/12"m) *(SF 4/+12)* **I DON'T WANNA. / RED LONDON / ULSTER**
(re-iss. 1979; same)

—— **DAVE TREGANNA** – bass, vocals repl. ALBIE

Polydor / Sire

Jan 78. (7") *(2058 966)* **BORSTAL BREAKOUT. / HEY LITTLE RICH BOY**
Feb 78. (lp) *(2383 491)* <6060> **TELL US THE TRUTH** (some live) 25
 – We gotta fight / Rip off / Ulster / George Davis is innocent / They don't understand / Borstal breakout / Family life / Hey little rich boy / I'm a man, I'm a boy / What about the lonely / Tell us the truth / It's never too late / Whose generation. *(re-iss. Mar89 on 'Receiver'; RRD 001) (cd-iss. Mar96 on 'Dojo'; DOJOCD 256)*
Apr 78. (7") *(2059 023)* **ANGELS WITH DIRTY FACES. / COCKNEY KIDS ARE INNOCENT** 19
Jul 78. (7") *(2059 050)* **IF THE KIDS ARE UNITED. / SUNDAY MORNING NIGHTMARE** 9
Oct 78. (7") *(POSP 7)* **HURRY UP HARRY. / NO ENTRY** 10
Nov 78. (lp) *(2442 158)* **THAT'S LIFE** 27
 – Leave me alone / Who gives a damn / Everybody's right, everybody's wrong / That's life / Win or lose / Hurry up Harry / Evil way (live) / Reggae pick up (part 1) / Sunday morning nightmare / Hurry up Harry (part 2) / Angels with dirty faces / Is this me or is this you. *(re-iss. Jul88 on 'Skunx'; SHAMX 1) (cd-iss. Mar96 on 'Dojo'; DOJOCD 257)*
Mar 79. (7"m) *(POSP 27)* **QUESTIONS AND ANSWERS. / I GOTTA SURVIVE (live) / WITH A LITTLE HELP FROM MY FRIENDS** 18
Jul 79. (7"m) *(POSP 64)* **HERSHAM BOYS. / I DON'T WANNA (live) / TELL US THE TRUTH (live)** 6
(12"m+=) *(POSPX 64)* – I'm a man, I'm a boy (live).
Sep 79. (lp) *(POLD/+C 5025)* **THE ADVENTURES OF THE HERSHAM BOYS** 8
 – Money / Fly dark angel / Joey's on the street / Cold blue in the night / You're a better man than I / Hersham boys / Lost on Highway 46 / Voices / Questions and answers / What have we got. *(free 12")* (2812 045) – IF THE KIDS ARE UNITED. / BORSTAL BREAKOUT. *(cd-iss. Mar96 on 'Dojo'; DOJOCD 258)*
Oct 79. (7") *(POSP 82)* **YOU'RE A BETTER MAN THAN I. / GIVE A DOG A BONE** 49

—— Disbanded for two months Jul'79. **MARK GOLDSTEIN** – drums repl. CAIN

Mar 80. (7") *(POSP 136)* **TELL THE CHILDREN. / JACK** 45
May 80. (lp) *(2442 173)* **THE GAME**
 – The game / Human zoo / Lord of the flies / Give a dog a bone / In and out / Tell the children / Spray it on the wall / Dead or alive / Simon / Deja vu / Poor cow / Run wild run free / Unite and win. *(re-iss. Mar89 on 'Receiver'; RRLD 002) (cd-iss. Mar96 on 'Dojo'; DOJOCD 259)*
Jun 80. (7") *(2059 259)* **UNITE AND WIN. / I'M A MAN**

Nov 80. (lp) *(2383 596)* **THE FIRST, THE BEST AND THE LAST** (compilation)
 – Borstal breakout / Hey little rich boy / Angels with dirty faces / Cockney kids are innocent / If the kids are united / Sunday morning nightmare / Hurry up Harry / Questions and answers / Give the dog a bone / Hersham boys / Tell the children / Unite & win. *(free 7"ep live)(RIOT 1 – 2816 028) (cd-iss. Apr94; 513429-2).*

—— Had already splintered, with PURSEY going solo

WANDERERS

(TREGANNA, PARSONS + GOLDSTEIN) added **STIV BATORS** – vocals (ex-DEAD BOYS)

Polydor / not iss.

Mar 81. (7") *(POSP 237)* **READY TO SNAP. / BEYOND THE LAW**
May 81. (lp) *(POLS 1028)* **THE ONLY LOVERS LEFT ALIVE**
 – Fanfare for 1984 / No dreams / Dr.Baker / Take them and break them / Little bit frightening / It's all the same / The times they are a-changin' / Ready to snap / Can't take you anymore / Sold your soul for fame / Circles of time / There'll be no end fanfare.
Jun 81. (7") *(POSP 284)* **THE TIMES THEY ARE A-CHANGIN'. / (IT'S A) LITTLE BIT FRIGHTENING**

—— Split Aug'81, TREGANNA followed BATORS into LORDS OF THE NEW CHURCH. PARSONS formed FRAMED later in 1982.

JIMMY PURSEY

Polydor / not iss.

Sep 80. (7") *(POSP 154)* **LUCKY MAN. / BLACK AND WHITE ROCK REGGAE**
Oct 80. (lp) *(2442 180)* **IMAGINATION CAMOUFLAGE**
 – Moon morning funday / Have a nice day / Lucky man / You never can tell / Situation's vacant / Playground soldier / White trash / Fifty-fifty / Freak show / Your mother should have told you / Just another memory.

Epic / not iss.

Jun 81. (7") *(EPCA 1336)* **ANIMALS HAVE MORE FUN. / SUS**
Nov 81. (7") *(EPCA 1830)* **NAUGHTY BOYS LIKE NAUGHTY GIRLS. / WHO'S MAKING YOU HAPPY**
Feb 82. (lp) *(EPC 85235)* **ALIEN ORPHAN**
 – Alien orphan / The first deadly kiss / I'm a human being / One invite only / Why (he shouldn't be here) / Who's making you happy / Spies / Jungle west one / Oh isn't it a weird weird world / One night in Paris / Technical / Naughty boys like naughty girls.
Feb 82. (7") *(EPCA 2118)* **ALIEN ORPHAN. / CONVERSATIONS**

Code Black / not iss.

Jan 83. (lp) **REVENGE IS NOT THE PASSWORD**
Feb 83. (7") **MAN WORRIES MAN. / ?**

An Eskimo / not iss.

May 84. (12"/7"; as JAMES T. PURSEY) *(CODE 02/+7)* **IF ONLY BEFORE. / ABOVE AND BEYOND**

Videocat / not iss.

Sep 86. (7"/12") *(JIMMY/+T 1)* **ZAP POW. / ('A'-Bass camp mix)**

SHAM 69

—— re-formed in '87. (PURSEY, PARSONS, +2)

Legacy / Legacy

Jul 87. (7") *(LGY 69)* **RIP AND TEAR. / THE GREAT AMERICAN SLOWDOWN**
Feb 88. (7") *(LGY 71)* **OUTSIDE THE WAREHOUSE. / ('A'version)**
(12"+=) *(LGY+T 71)* – How the west was won.
Jun 88. (lp/c) *(<LLP/LLK 117>)* **VOLUNTEER**
 – Outside the warehouse / Wicked tease / Wallpaper / Mr.Know it all / As black as sheep / How the west was won / That was the day / Rip and tear / Bastard club / Volunteer. *(cd-iss. Dec89; LLCD 117) (cd re-iss. Mar92 on Castle'; CLACD 274)*

Rotate / not iss.

Nov 92. (cd/lp) *(ROT CD/LP 006)* **INFORMATION LIBRE**
 – Break on through / Uptown / Planet trash / Information libertaire / Caroline's suitcase / Feel it / King Kong drinks Coca-Cola / Saturdays and Strangeways / Breeding dinosaurs / Wild and wonderful. *(cd re-iss. Nov95 on 'Dojo'; DOJOCD 236)*
Nov 92. (12") *(ROTST 03)* **M25. / CAROLINE'S SUITCASE / INFORMATION LIBERTAIRE**

C.M.P. / not iss.

Mar 93. (7") *(CMP 1)* **UPTOWN. / BORSTAL BREAKOUT**
(12"+=) *(CMP 1T)* – Flowers / Wild and wonderful.
Nov 93. (cd) *(CMCCD 69)* **KINGS & QUEENS**
 – Action time vision / I don't wanna / Ulster boy / They don't understand / Tell us the truth / Borstal breakout / Family life / The kids are united / Hurry up Harry / Hey little rich boy / Bosnia / Reggae giro. *(re-iss. Jul95 on 'Dojo'; DOJO 235)*
Oct 93. (cd-ep) *(CMCCD 002)* **ACTION TIME VISION / BOSNIA / HEY LITTLE RICH BOY / REGGAE GIRO**

Plus 1 / not iss.

Jul 95. (cd) *(A1CD 001)* **SOAPY WATER & MR. MARMALADE**
 – Listen up / Girlfriend / Little bit of this / Otis Redding / Junkie / The doctor's song / Alice / Stevie / Chasing the moon / Spunky candy. *(re-iss. May98 on 'Rhino'; 301279-2)*
Aug 95. (cd-s) *(AISCD 001)* **GIRLFRIEND / 25 YEARS / RAINBOW WARRIOR**
1997. (cd-ep) *(AISCD 005)* **PUNK FICTION**
 – Swampy / Geoffrey Thomas / Studenthead / Windowstare.

– compilations, others, etc. –

Oct 82. (12"ep) *Polydor; (POSPX 602)* **ANGELS WITH DIRTY FACES. / BORSTAL BREAKOUT. / HURRY UP HARRY / IF THE KIDS ARE UNITED**
Nov 86. (lp/c) *Receiver; (RRLP/RRLC 104)* **ANGELS WITH DIRTY FACES – THE BEST OF SHAM 69**
Dec 87. (lp) *Link; (LINKLP 004)* **LIVE AND LOUD (live)**
Apr 88. (lp) *Link; (LINKLP 025)* **LIVE AND LOUD VOL.2**
May 89. (lp/cd) *Receiver; (RRLP/CD 112)* **THE BEST OF THE REST OF SHAM 69**

				Castle	
Oct 89.	(cd/c/lp)	*Castle;* (CLA CD/MC/LP 153)	**COMPLETE LIVE** (live)		-
Apr 90.	(cd/c)	*Action Replay;* (CDAR/ARLC 1011)	**SHAM 69 LIVE** (live)		-
Aug 90.	(cd/lp)	*Receiver;*	**LIVE AT THE ROXY** (live tapes '77)		-
Jul 91.	(cd)	*Dojo;* (DOJOCD 62)	**LIVE AT THE CBGB'S**		-
Apr 93.	(cd)	*Dojo;* (DOJOCD 95)	**SHAM'S LAST STAND**		-
		(re-iss. Jun99 on 'Snapper'; SMMCD 540)			
Oct 93.	(cd)	*Dojo;* (DOJOCD 105)	**LIVE IN JAPAN** (live)		-
Nov 93.	(cd)	*Windsong;* (WINCD 049)	**BBC RADIO 1 LIVE IN CONCERT** (Live)		-
Mar 95.	(cd; shared with 999)	*Step-1;*	**LIVE AND LOUD**		-
Sep 95.	(cd)	*Emporio;* (EMPRCD 582)	**SHAM 69 LIVE**		-
Dec 95.	(cd)	*Essential;* (ESDCD 350)	**LIVE / THE BEST OF SHAM 69**		-
Jun 96.	(cd/c)	*Hallmark;* (30446-2/-4)	**UNITED**		-
Jun 97.	(cd)	*Essential;* (<ESMCD 512>)	**THE BEST OF SHAM 69**		-
Jul 97.	(cd)	*Empty;* (efaCD 12359)	**THE A FILES**		-
Mar 98.	(d-cd)	*Eagle;* (EDMCD 030)	**THE MASTERS**		-
Mar 98.	(cd/c)	*Castle Select;* (SEL CD/MC 504)	**THE VERY BEST OF THE HERSHAM BOYS**		-
Oct 98.	(7"; shared with DIE TOTEN HOSEN)	*M Tradegy;* (MT 385)	**SAWBLADE SERIES #19**		-
Jun 99.	(cd)	*Essential;* (ESMCD 733)	**LIVE IN ITALY**		-
Oct 99.	(d-cd)	*Essential;* (<ESDCD 780>)	**ANGELS WITH DIRTY FACES – THE BEST OF SHAM 69**		-
May 00.	(cd)	*Captain Oi;* (<AHOYCD 139>)	**RARITIES 1977-1980**		-

JIMMY PURSEY

				Store For Music	not iss.
Apr 02.	(cd)	(SFMMCD 001)	**CODE FOR BLACK**		-

– Die in Disneyland / Menu / Starring with the animals tonight / Sex worm / Death Dr. war / Movement interior / Speechless / Weybridge hotel / Code black (independence day).

SHAPES

Formed: Leamington Spa, Midlands, England ... 1976 by weird and wonderful frontman SEYMOUR BYBUSS, and his motley crue of musicians TIM JEE, STEVE RICHARDS, BRIAN HELICOPTER and DAVE GEE. Inspired by the BUZZCOCKS, The REZILLOS and SPIZZ (the latter they supported on their first gig), The SHAPES eventually surfaced record-wise in March 1979 via the self-financed 'PART OF THE FURNITURE' EP. Heralded by John Peel (who else!?), the 7" featured such oddities as 'WOT'S FOR LUNCH MUM? (NOT BEANS AGAIN!)' and '(I SAW) BATMAN (IN THE LAUNDERETTE)', both given airwave time of the DJ's Radio One night-time show. Subsequent support slots to The CURE and The FALL, led to them being snapped up by Northern Ireland's 'Good Vibrations' imprint, who rushed-released their sophomore 45, the double-A side 'BLAST OFF' / 'AIRLINE DISASTER' (both singles are now worth around £16 each). With 2-Tone and ska bands virtually breaking through on their doorstep, The SHAPES were sent, not to, but out of Coventry. A third single, 'JENNIFER THE CONIFER' in 1980, failed to get by the printing stage and the band disappeared. However, it was revealed just recently, that BYBUSS was the weirdo transvestite nun, Sister Bendy, from the Eurotrash late-night shows for Channel 4. It's true!

Album rating: SONGS FOR SENSIBLE PEOPLE compilation (*7)

SEYMOUR BYBUSS – vocals / **STEVE RICHARDS** – lead guitar / **TIM JEE** – rhythm guitar / **BRIAN HELICOPTER** – bass / **DAVE GEE** – drums

				Sofa	not iss.
Mar 79.	(7"ep)	(SEAT 1)	**THE SHAPES – PART OF THE FURNITURE**		-

– Wot's for lunch mum? (not beans again!) / College girls / (I saw) Batman (in the lauderette) / Chatterbox.

				Good Vibrations	not iss.
Aug 79.	(7")	(GOT 13)	**BLAST OFF. / AIRLINE DISASTER**		-
—	now without STEVE RICHARDS				
1980.	(7"m; w-drawn)		**JENNIFER THE CONIFER. / LET'S GO TO PLANET SKARO / MY HOUSE IS A SATELLITE**	-	-

— after a disastrous tour, The SHAPES split up; JEE briefly joined The CAPTAIN BLACK SOLUTION (he now sells cravats); GEE went on to be an all-nude wrestler in Scandinavia, HELICOPTER became a Californian and top skydiver, while, most bizarrely, BYBUSS is now Sister Bendy, the transvestite nun in Eurotrash!

– compilations, etc. –

Nov 98.	(cd)	*Overground;* (<OVER 81CD>)	**SONGS FOR SENSIBLE PEOPLE**		

– (interview) / Kids' stuff / Wot's for lunch mum? (not beans again!) / Leamington / College girls / Wot's for lunch mum? (not beans again!) (EP version) / College girls (1979 version with deluxe guitar bits) / (I saw) Batman (in the lauderette) / Chatterbox (disco mix) / Bedtime stories / Alien love / Airline disaster / Business calls / Leamington / Let's go to Planet Skaro / My house is a satellite / Jennifer the conifer / Blast off! / (interview).

Pete SHELLEY (see under ⇒ BUZZCOCKS)

SHIRTS

Formed: Brooklyn, New York, USA ... early 1975 out of The LACKEYS and The SCHEMERS by ANNIE GOLDEN, ARTIE LaMONICA, RONNIE ARDITO, JOHN PICCOLO, ROBERT RACIOPPO and JOHN CRISCIONE. Originally conceived as a pop covers outfit, The SHIRTS fitted right in to the burgeoning New Wave scene after building up a loyal following at clubs such as CBGB's. A major signing to 'Capitol' ('Harvest' in Britain), the sartorial Noo Yoikers found favour on the continent with their summer '78 debut single, 'TELL ME YOUR PLANS'. This was accompanied by a slightly disappointing eponymous debut album that failed to break America, although GOLDEN's voice did shine on standout track, 'TEENAGE CRUTCH' and the aforementioned single. Even a subsequent support slot to the more mainstream PETER GABRIEL failed to raise their profile and despite a further two albums, 'STREET LIGHT SHINE' (1979) and 'INNER SLEEVE' (1980), GOLDEN became more famous for her role in the 1979 movie adaptation of 'Hair' and her work on Broadway.

Album rating: THE SHIRTS (*5) / STREET LIGHT (*4) / INNER SLEEVE (*4) / TELL ME YOUR PLANS compilation (*5)

ANNIE GOLDEN (b.1953) – vocals / **ARTIE LaMONICA** – lead guitar, vocals / **RONNIE ARDITO** – rhythm guitar, vocals / **JOHN PICCOLO** – keyboards / **ROBERT RACIOPPO** – bass / **JOHN CRISCIONI** – drums, percussion

				Harvest	Capitol
Jul 78.	(7")	(HAR 5165)	**TELL ME YOUR PLANS. / CYRINDA**		-
Jul 78.	(lp)	(SHSP 4089) <SW 11791>	**THE SHIRTS**		

– Reduced to a whisper / Tell me your plans / Empty never after / Teenage crutch / Tenth floor clown / The story goes / Lonely android / Running through the night / They say the sun shines / Poe.

Oct 78.	(7")	(HAR 5170)	**RUNNING THROUGH THE NIGHT. / LONELY ANDROID**		-
Aug 79.	(7")	(HAR 5190)	**OUT ON THE ROPES. / MAYBE, MAYBE NOT**		-
Oct 79.	(lp)	(SHSP 4104) <ST 11986>	**STREET LIGHT SHINE**		

– Laugh and walk away / Love is a fiction / Don't you hesitate / Milton at the Savoy / Ground zero / Triangulum / Out on the ropes / Starts with a handshake / Can't cry anymore / I feel so nervous / Outside the cathedral door / Kensington gardens.

Oct 79.	(7")	<4750>	**CAN'T CRY ANYMORE. / I'M IN LOVE AGAIN**	-	
Dec 79.	(7")	<4783>	**DON'T YOU HESITATE (HOLD ME). / GROUND ZERO**	-	
Feb 80.	(7")	(HAR 5195)	**LAUGH AND WALK AWAY. / TRIANGULUM**		-

				Capitol	Capitol
Aug 80.	(7")	(CL 16161)	**ONE LAST CHANCE. / TOO MUCH TROUBLE**		
Oct 80.	(lp)	(EST 12085)	**INNER SLEEVE**		

– I'm not one of those / One last chance / Can't get it through my head / I've had it / I don't wanna know / Pleasure is the pain / As long as the laughter lasts / Too much trouble / Hanging around / Small talk.

— disbanded the following year, with GOLDEN having a short-lived solo career in '84

– compilations, etc. –

Feb 98.	(cd)	*Disky;* (DC 88608-2)	**TELL ME YOUR PLANS**		-

– Tell me your plans / Laugh and walk away / Too much trouble / Out on the ropes / Running through the night / Triangulum / Can't cry anymore / Lonely android / Reduced to a whisper / Empty never after / Teenage crutch / Tenth floor clown / The story goes / They say the sun shines / Poe.

SHOES

Formed: Zion, Illinois, USA ... 1974 by GARY KLEBE, JEFF MURPHY, his brother JOHN and SKIP MEYER. Wearing their classic BEATLES influences proudly, The SHOES made their first tentative steps into the music business with a couple of self-financed cassettes before spreading the net wider via debut album proper, 'BLACK VINYL SHOES' (1977). Strangely enough, it was released in Britain by 'Sire' while the band moved on to Greg Shaw's 'Bomp' for a one-off double-A 45, 'OKAY' / 'TOMORROW NIGHT'. With power-pop increasingly in vogue (in the States at least) on the back of the New Wave explosion, The SHOES kicked off their deal with 'Elektra' via the 'PRESENT TENSE' (1979) album. Containing the minor hit, 'TOO LATE', the record scraped into the US Top 50, although the 1981 follow-up, 'TONGUE TWISTER', failed to make the grade. Subsequent releases, 'SILHOUETTE' (1984), 'BOOMERANG' (1987) and 'STOLEN WISHES' (1990), extended their polished legacy and rounded off the first chapter in their career. A mid-90's reformation resulted in the two quickfire sets, 'PROPELLER' and 'FRET BUZZ', proving that these veterans weren't ready to hang up their boots just yet.

Album rating: BLACK VINYL SHOES (*7) / PRESENT TENSE (*6) / TONGUE TWISTER (*6) / SILHOUETTE (*6) / STOLEN WISHES (*5) / BOOMERANG (*6)

GARY KLEBE – vocals, guitar / **JEFF MURPHY** – vocals, bass, guitar / **JOHN MURPHY** – vocals, guitar / **SKIP MEYER** – drums

				Sire	Black Vinyl
Dec 77.	(lp)	(SRK 6075) <51477>	**BLACK VINYL SHOES**		

– Boys don't lie / Do you wanna get lucky / She'll disappear / Tragedy / Writing a postcard / Not me / Someone finer / Capital gain / Fatal running start / Okay it really hurts / Fire for a while / If you'd stay / Nowhere so fast. <re-iss. 1978 on 'P.V.C.'; 7904> (cd-iss. Sep93 on 'Creation Rev-Ola'; CREV 016CD) (cd re-iss. Nov96 on 'Black Vinyl'; BV 10092-2)

				not iss.	Bomp
Jun 78.	(7")	<BMP 116>	**OKAY. / TOMORROW NIGHT**	-	

				Elektra	Elektra
Oct 79.	(lp)	(K 52187) <GE 244>	**PRESENT TENSE**		50

– Tomorrow night / Too late / Hangin' around with you / Your very eyes / In my arms again / Somebody has what I had / Now and then / Every girl / I don't miss you / Cruel you / Three times: See me – say it – Listen / I don't wanna hear it.

Feb 80.	(7")	(K 12404) <46557>	**TOO LATE. / NOW AND THEN**		75 Oct79
Feb 80.	(7")	<46598>	**I DON'T MISS YOU. /**	-	

SHOES (cont)

Apr 81.	(7") (K 12520) **YOUR IMAGINATION. / THE THINGS YOU DO**
Jun 81.	(lp) (K 52201) <303> **TONGUE TWISTER** — Jan81

– Your imagination / Burned out love / The things you do / Only in my sleep / Karen / She satisfies / Girls of today / Hopin' she's the one / When it hits / Yes or no / Found a girl / Hate to run.

Demon   not iss.

Sep 84. (lp) (FIEND 19) **SILHOUETTE**
– Get my message / Will you spin for me / When push comes to shove / Shining / It's only you / Twist and bend it / I wanna give it to you / Turn around / Running wild / Oh, Angeline / Bound to fade / Suspicion. (re-iss. 1985 on 'New Rose' lp/c; ROSE 44/+C) (cd-iss. Nov96 on 'Black Vinyl'; BV 15191-2)

Jan 85. (7") (D 1029) **WHEN PUSH COMES TO SHOVE. / DORMANT LOVE**

New Rose   not iss.

1985. (7") (NEW 49) **WILL YOU SPIN FOR ME. / DORMANT LOVE**

— SKIP MEYER had now departed

Fan Club   not iss.

Jul 87. (lp) (FC 028) **BOOMERANG**
– In her shadow / Curiosity / Mayday / Too soon / Double talk / Summer rain / Under the gun / The tube / What love means / Bound to be a reason / Shake it away / Tested charms.

New Rose   Black Vinyl

May 90. (lp/cd) (ROSE 202/+CD) <SPV 54012> **STOLEN WISHES** — Dec89
– Feel the way that I do / I'll follow you / Love does / Let it go / Your devotion / I know you'd be mine / Want you bad / Torn in two / She's not the same / Untangled / I don't know why / Inside of you / I can't go wrong / Love is like a bullet / Never had it better. (cd re-iss. Nov96 on 'Black Vinyl'; BV 10189-2)

— disbanded in the early 90's but re-formed again later with **GARY KLEBE, JEFF + JOHN MURPHY** plus **RIC MENCK + MIKE ZELENKO** – drums

Black Vinyl   Black Vinyl

Nov 96. (cd) <(BV 10294-2)> **PROPELLER** — Apr94
– Animal attraction / Treading water / Don't do this to me / Last of you / Slipping through your fingers / Tore a hole / Bittersweet / If all I had was you / In my mind / Silence is deadly / Thing of the past / Never ending.

— **JOHN RICHARDSON** – drums; repl. drummers

Nov 96. (cd) <(BV 10495-2)> **FRET BUZZ** — May95
– Animal attraction / Mayday / When push comes to shove / Want you bad / I don't wanna hear it / Turnaround / Love is like a bullet / Your devotion / Feel the way I do / Silence is deadly / Tore a hole / In harm's way.

– compilations, etc. –

on 'Black Vinyl' unless mentioned otherwise

Aug 88. (cd) <(BV 19787-2)> **SHOES BEST** — 1987
– Burned out love / Tomorrow night / Turnaround / Get my message / Love is like a bullet / Karen / Mayday / She satisfies / When push comes to shove / Too late / Your imagination / Now and then / Summer rain / Curiosity / Piece of glass / Will you spin for me? / Too soon / Double talk / Boys don't lie / Will I / I don't miss you / Hate to run. (re-iss. Nov96; same)

Nov 96. (cd) (BV 18190-2) **BOOMERANG / SHOES ON ICE**
Nov 96. (cd) (BV 19888-2) **PRESENT TENSE / TONGUE TWISTER**
Jan 97. (d-cd) (BV 10596-2) **AS IS**
May 02. (d-cd) Hunter; (HM 1389-2) **SINGLES A'S AND B'S**

**Chris SIEVEY / Frank SIDEBOTTOM
(see under ⇒ FRESHIES)**

SIMPLE MINDS

Formed: Gorbals, Glasgow, Scotland ... early 1978 after four members (frontman JIM KERR, guitarists CHARLIE BURCHILL and DUNCAN BARNWELL and drummer BRIAN McGEE) had left punk band, JOHNNY & THE SELF ABUSERS. Taking the group name from a line in a BOWIE song, the band gigged constantly at Glasgow's Mars Bar, finally being signed on the strength of a demo tape by local Edinburgh music guru and record store owner, Bruce Findlay. Also becoming the band's manager, Findlay released their debut album, 'LIFE IN A DAY' (1979) on his own 'Zoom' label, the record scoring a Top 30 placing. Its minor success led to a deal with 'Arista' who released the follow-up, 'REEL TO REEL CACOPHONY' (1979), a set of post-punk, electronic experimentation best sampled on the evocative synth spirals of 'FILM THEME'. SIMPLE MINDS took another about turn with 'EMPIRES AND DANCE' (1980), an album heavily influenced by the harder end of the Euro-disco movement, the abrasive electro pulse of the 'I TRAVEL' single becoming a cult dancefloor hit. Initially released as a double set, 'SONS AND FASCINATION' / 'SISTER FEELINGS CALL' (1981), marked the first fruits of a new deal with 'Virgin' and gave the group their first major success, peaking at No.11 in the UK chart on the back of the Top 50 single, 'LOVE SONG'. SIMPLE MINDS were beginning to find their niche, incorporating their artier tendencies into more conventional and melodic song structures. This was fully realised with 'NEW GOLD DREAM (81-82-83-84)' (1982), a record which marked the pinnacle of their early career and one which arguably, they've since failed to better. Constructed with multiple layers of synth, the band crafted a wonderfully evocative and atmospheric series of undulating electronic soundscapes, often married to pop hooks, as with 'GLITTERING PRIZE' and 'PROMISED YOU A MIRACLE' (the group's first Top 20 hits), but more effectively allowed to veer off into dreamier territory on the likes of 'SOMEONE SOMEWHERE IN SUMMERTIME'. While SIMPLE MINDS and U2 were often compared in terms of their anthemic tendencies, a closer comparison could be made, in spirit at least, between 'NEW GOLD..'

and U2's mid-80's experimental classic, 'The Unforgettable Fire'. The album reached No.3 in the UK charts, a catalyst for SIMPLE MINDS' gradual transformation from an obscure cult act to stadium candidates, this process helped along nicely by the success of 'SPARKLE IN THE RAIN' (1984), the band's first No.1 album. Though it lacked the compelling mystery of its predecessor, the record featured such quintessential SIMPLE MINDS' moments as 'UP ON THE CATWALK', 'SPEED YOUR LOVE TO ME' and an inventive cover of Lou Reed's 'STREET HASSLE'. For better or worse, the album also boasted SIMPLE MINDS' first truly BIG anthem, the sonic bombast of 'WATERFRONT'. But the track that no doubt finally alienated the old faithful was 'DON'T YOU (FORGET ABOUT ME)', the theme tune for quintessentially 80's movie, 'The Breakfast Club' and surely one of the most overplayed records of that decade. The song had stadium-friendly written all over it, subsequently scaling the US charts and paving the way for the transatlantic success of 'ONCE UPON A TIME' (1985). Unashamedly going for the commmercial pop/rock jugular, the album was heady, radio orientated stuff, the likes of 'ALIVE AND KICKING', 'SANCTIFY YOURSELF' and 'OH JUNGLELAND' among the most definitive anthems of the stadium rock genre. Predictably, the critics were unimpressed, although they didn't really stick the knife in until the release of the overblown 'BELFAST CHILD', a UK No.1 despite its snoozeworthy meandering and vague political agenda. The accompanying album, 'STREET FIGHTING YEARS' (1989) brought more of the same, although it cemented SIMPLE MINDS' position among the coffee table elite. Down to a trio of KERR, BURCHILL and and drummer, MEL GAYNOR, the group hired a team of session players for their next album, 'REAL LIFE' (1991), the record almost spawning a Top 5 hit in the celebratory 'LET THERE BE LOVE'. Although the album narrowly missed the UK top spot, it held nothing new, nor did their next release, 'GOOD NEWS FROM THE NEXT WORLD' (1995). Although KERR and BURCHILL brought back DEREK FORBES and signed a new deal with 'Chrysalis' for 1998's 'NEAPOLIS' set, the band only managed to scrape into the UK Top 20. You couldn't help feeling a little sorry for JIM KERR (one-time spouse of CHRISSIE HYNDE), not only does a young pretender like LIAM GALLAGHER hook up with his then wife (PATSY KENSIT), but his band became something of an anachronism in the ever changing world of 90's music. This was realized come their 2002 release 'CRY', a leap backwards into the world of old SIMPLE MINDS. Granted, the group had started using loops and adding a little guitar playing here and there, but what remained was a keyboard-driven album that gave us little in the way of musical vision. While U2 have at least made an attempt to move with the times, SIMPLE MINDS' sound is so deeply rooted in the 80's that it seems inconceivable they could ever make any kind of relevant departure. • **Songwriters:** All group compositions or KERR-BURCHILL. Covered BIKO (Peter Gabriel) / SIGN O' THE TIMES (Prince) / DON'T YOU FORGET ABOUT ME (Keith Forsey-Steve Chiff) / GLORIA (Them) / THE MAN WHO SOLD THE WORLD (David Bowie) / HOMOSAPIEN (Pete Shelley) / DANCING BAREFOOT (Patti Smith) / NEON LIGHTS (Kraftwerk) / HELLO I LOVE YOU (Doors) / BRING ON THE DANCING HORSES (Echo & The Bunnymen) / THE NEEDLE & THE DAMAGE DONE (Neil Young) / FOR YOUR PLEASURE (Roxy Music) / ALL TOMORROW'S PARTIES (Velvet Underground). • **Trivia:** SIMPLE MINDS played LIVE AID and MANDELA DAY concerts in 1985 and 1988 respectively.

Album rating: LIFE IN A DAY (*7) / REAL TO REAL CACOPHONY (*5) / EMPIRES AND DANCE (*8) / SONS AND FASCINATION – SISTER FEELING CALL (*8) / CELEBRATION compilation (*7) / NEW GOLD DREAM (81-82-83-84) (*8) / SPARKLE IN THE RAIN (*8) / ONCE UPON A TIME (*8) / LIVE IN THE CITY OF LIGHT (*6) / STREET FIGHTING YEARS (*5) / REAL LIFE (*5) / GLITTERING PRIZE – SIMPLE MINDS 81-92 compilation (*9) / GOOD NEWS FROM THE NEXT WORLD (*4) / NEAPOLIS (*3) / NEON LIGHTS (*4) / THE BEST OF SIMPLE MINDS compilation (*8) / CRY (*4)

JOHNNY & THE SELF ABUSERS

JIM KERR (b. 9 Jul'59) – vocals / **CHARLIE BURCHILL** (b.27 Nov'59) – guitar / **BRIAN McGEE** – drums / **TONY DONALD** – bass / **JOHN MILARKY** – guitar / **ALAN McNEIL** also

Chiswick   not iss.

Nov 77. (7") (NS 22) **SAINTS AND SINNERS. / DEAD VANDALS**

SIMPLE MINDS

— (KERR, BURCHILL + McGEE) recruited **MICK McNEILL** (b.20 Jul'58) – keyboards / **DEREK FORBES** (b.22 Jun'56) – bass (ex-SUBS) + **DUNCAN BARNWELL** – guitar (left before recording)

Zoom   not iss.

Apr 79.	(7") (ZUM 10) **LIFE IN A DAY. / SPECIAL VIEW**	62	-
Apr 79.	(lp) (ZULP 1) **LIFE IN A DAY**	30	-

– Someone / Life in a day / Sad affair / All for you / Pleasantly disturbed / No cure / Chelsea girl / Wasteland / Destiny / Murder story. (re-iss. Oct82 on 'Virgin' lp/c; VM/+C 6) (re-iss. 1985 on 'Virgin' lp/c; OVED/+C 95) (cd-iss. Jul86; VMCD 6)

Jun 79. (7") (ZUM 11) **CHELSEA GIRL. / GARDEN OF HATE**

Arista   Arista

Nov 79. (lp/c) (SPART/TC-SPART 1109) **REAL TO REAL CACOPHONY**
– Real to real / Naked eye / Citizen (dance of youth) / Carnival (shelter in a suitcase) / Factory / Cacophony / Veldt / Premonition / Changeling / Film theme / Calling your name / Scar. (re-iss. Oct82 on 'Virgin' lp/c; V/TCV 2246) (re-iss. 1985 on 'Virgin' lp/c; OVED/+C 124) (cd-iss. May88; CDV 2246)

Jan 80. (7") (ARIST 325) **CHANGELING. / PREMONITION (live)**

Sep 80. (lp/c) (SPART/TC-SPART 1140) **EMPIRES AND DANCE** | 41 |
– I travel / Today I died again / Celebrate / This fear of gods / Capital city / Constantinople line / Twist-run-repulsion / Thirty frames a seconds / Kant-kino / Room. (re-iss. Oct82 on 'Virgin' lp/c; V/TCV 2247) (cd-iss. May88; CDV 2247)

SIMPLE MINDS (cont)

Oct 80. (7") *(ARIST 372)* **I TRAVEL. / NEW WARM SKIN**
(w/ free 7"blue flexi) – KALEIDOSCOPE. / FILM DUB THEME
(12") *(ARIST 12-372)* – ('A'side) / Film dub theme.
Feb 81. (7") *(ARIST 394)* **CELEBRATE. / CHANGELING (live)**
(12"+=) *(ARIST 12-394)* – I travel (live).

                                                                Virgin   A&M

May 81. (7"/remix.12") *(VS 410/+12)* **THE AMERICAN. / LEAGUE OF NATIONS**   [59] [ ]

──── **KENNY HYSLOP** (b.14 Feb'51, Helensburgh, Scotland) – drums (ex-SKIDS, ex-ZONES, ex-SLIK) repl. McGEE who joined ENDGAMES; in 1994 he became a songwriter for LES McKEOWN (ex-BAY CITY ROLLERS)

Aug 81. (7"/12") *(VS 434/+12)* **LOVE SONG. / THE EARTH THAT YOU WALK UPON (instrumental)** [47] [–]
Sep 81. (2xlp/d-c) *(V/TCV 2207)* **SONS AND FASCINATION / SISTER FEELINGS CALL** [11] [ ]
 – SONS AND FASCINATION – In trance as mission / Sweat in bullet / 70 cities as love brings the fall / Boys from Brazil / Love song / This Earth that you walk upon / Sons and fascination / Seeing out the angels. SISTER FEELINGS CALL – Theme for great cities * / The American / 20th Century promised land / Wonderful in young life / League of nations / Careful in career / Sound in 70 cities. *(issued separately Oct81; V 2207 / OVED 2) (cd-iss. Apr86 + Apr90; CDV 2207)* – (omits tracks *)
Oct 81. (7") *(VS 451)* **SWEAT IN BULLET. / 20th CENTURY PROMISED LAND** [52] [–]
(d7"+=) *(VSD 451)* – League of nations (live) / Premonition (live).
(12"+=) *(VS 451-12)* – League of nations (live) / In trance as mission (live).
Apr 82. (7") *(VS 488)* **PROMISED YOU A MIRACLE. / THEME FOR GREAT CITIES** [13] [–]
(12"+=) *(VS 488-12)* – Seeing out the angel (instrumental mix).

──── **MIKE OGLETREE** – drums (ex-CAFE JAQUES) repl. HYSLOP who formed SET THE TONE

Aug 82. (7"/12") *(VS 511/+12)* **GLITTERING PRIZE. / GLITTERING THEME** [16] [ ]

──── **MEL GAYNOR** (b.29 May'59) – drums (ex-sessions) repl. MIKE who joined FICTION FACTORY

Sep 82. (lp/c)<gold-lp> *(V/TCV 2230)* <4928> **NEW GOLD DREAM (81-82-83-84)** [3] [69] Jan83
 – Someone, somewhere in summertime / Colours fly and the Catherine wheel / Promised you a miracle / Big sleep / Somebody up there likes you / New gold dream (81-82-83-84) / Hunter and the hunted / King is white and in the crowd. *(cd-iss. Jul83 & Apr92; CDV 2230) (re-iss. Apr92 lp/c; OVED/+C 393)*
Nov 82. (7"/7"pic-d) *(VS/+Y 538)* **SOMEONE, SOMEWHERE IN SUMMERTIME. / KING IS WHITE AND IN THE CROWD (live)** [36] [ ]
(12"+=) *(VS 538-12)* – Soundtrack for every Heaven.
Nov 82. (7") **PROMISED YOU A MIRACLE. / THE AMERICAN** [–] [ ]
Nov 83. (7"/12") *(VS/+ 636/+12)* **WATERFRONT. / HUNTER AND THE HUNTED (live)** [13] [ ]
Jan 84. (7"/7"pic-d) *(VS/+Y 649)* **SPEED YOUR LOVE TO ME. / BASS LINE** [20] [ ]
(12"+=) *(VS 649-12)* – ('A'extended.)
Feb 84. (cd/c/lp,white-lp) *(CD/TC/+V 2300)* <4981> **SPARKLE IN THE RAIN** [1] [64]
 – Up on the catwalk / Book of brilliant things / Speed your love to me / Waterfront / East at Easter / White hot day / Street hassle / "C" Moon cry like a baby / The kick inside of me / Shake off the ghosts. *(re-iss. cd Mar91; same)*
Mar 84. (7"/7"pic-d)(12") *(VS/+Y 661)(VS 661-12)* **UP ON THE CATWALK. / A BRASS BAND IN AFRICA** [27] [ ]
Apr 85. (7"/7"sha-pic-d)(12") *(VS/+S 749)(VS 749-12)* <2703> **DON'T YOU (FORGET ABOUT ME). / A BRASS BAND IN AFRICA** [7] [1] Feb85
(re-iss. Jun88 cd-s; CDT 2)

──── **KERR, BURCHILL, McNEILL + GAYNOR** brought in new member **JOHN GIBLING** – bass (ex-PETER GABRIEL sessions) to repl. FORBES

Oct 85. (7"/12") *(VS 817/+12)* **ALIVE AND KICKING. / ('A'instrumental)** [7] [ ]
(12"+=) *(VS 817-13)* – Up on the catwalk (live).
Oct 85. (cd/c/lp,pic-lp) *(CD/TC/+V 2364)* <5092> **ONCE UPON A TIME** [1] [10]
 – Once upon a time / All the things she said / Ghost dancing / Alive and kicking / Oh jungleland / I wish you were here / Sanctify yourself / Come a long way. *(lp re-iss. Mar01 on 'Simple Vinyl'; SVLP 312)*
Oct 85. (7") <2783> **ALIVE AND KICKING. / UP ON THE CATWALK (live)** [–] [3]
Jan 86. (7") *(SM 1)* <2810> **SANCTIFY YOURSELF. / ('A'instrumental)** [10] [14]
(d7"+=) *(SMP 1)* – Love song (live) / Street hassle (live).
(12") *(SM 1-12)* – ('A'mix). / ('A'dub instrumental).
Apr 86. (7") *(VS 860)* <2828> **ALL THE THINGS SHE SAID. / DON'T YOU (FORGET ABOUT ME)** [9] [28]
(12"+=) *(VS 860-12)* – Promised you a miracle (US mix).
Nov 86. (7") *(VS 907)* **GHOSTDANCING. / JUNGLELAND (instrumental)** [13] [ ]
(12"+=/cd-s+=) *(VS/MIKE 907-12)* – ('A'instrumental) / ('B'instrumental).
May 87. (d-cd/d-c/d-lp) *(CDVSM/SMDCX/SMDLX 1)* <6850> **LIVE IN THE CITY OF LIGHT (live)** [1] [96] Jul87
 – Ghostdancing / Big sleep / Waterfront / Promised you a miracle / Someone somewhere in summertime / Oh jungleland / Alive and kicking / Don't you (forget about me) / Once upon a time / Book of brilliant things / East at Easter / Sanctify yourself / Love song / Sun City – Dance to the music / New gold dream (81-82-83-84).
Jun 87. (7"/10") *(SM 2/+10)* **PROMISED YOU A MIRACLE (live). / BOOK OF BRILLIANT THINGS (live)** [19] [ ]
(12"+=/c-s+=) *(SM/+C 2-12)* – Glittering prize (live) / Celebrate (live).

──── **KERR, BURCHILL + McNEILL** were basic trio, w/other 2 still sessioning.

Feb 89. (7") *(SMX 3)* **BELFAST CHILD. / MANDELA DAY** [1] [ ]
(c-s+=/12"ep+=/12"box-ep+=/cd-ep+=) **BALLAD OF THE STREETS** *(SMX C/T/C/CD 3)* – Biko.
Apr 89. (7") *(SMX 4)* **THIS IS YOUR LAND. / SATURDAY GIRL** [13] [ ]
(c-s+=/12"+=/12"g-f+=/3"cd-s+=) *(SMX C/T/TG/CD 4)* – Year of the dragon.

May 89. (cd/c/lp) *(MIND D/C/S 1)* <3927> **STREET FIGHTING YEARS** [1] [70]
 – Soul crying out / Wall of love / This is your land / Take a step back / Kick it in / Let it all come down / Biko / Mandela day / Belfast child / Street fighting years. *(re-iss. Dec89 box-cd/c +=; SMBX D/C 1)* – (interview cassettes).
Jul 89. (7"/c-s) *(SMX/+C 5)* **KICK IT IN. / WATERFRONT ('89 mix)** [15] [ ]
(12"+=/cd-s+=) *(SMX T/CD 5)* – Big sleep (live).
(12"g-f+=) *(SMXTG 5)* – ('A'mix).
Dec 89. (7"ep/c-ep/12"ep/cd-ep) *(SMX/+C/TCD 6)* **THE AMSTERDAM EP** [18] [ ]
 – Let it all come down / Sign o' the times / Jerusalem.
(12"ep+=/cd-ep+=) *(SMX TR/X 6)* – Sign o' the times (mix).

──── **KERR, BURCHILL + GAYNOR** brought in sessioners **MALCOLM FOSTER** – bass / **PETER JOHN VITESSE** – keyboards / **STEPHEN LIPSON** – bass, keyboards / **ANDY DUNCAN** – percussion / **GAVIN WRIGHT** – string leader / **LISA GERMANO** – violin

Mar 91. (7"/c-s) *(VS/+C 1332)* **LET THERE BE LOVE. / GOODNIGHT** [6] [ ]
(12"+=) *(VST 1332)* – Alive and kicking (live).
(cd-s++=) *(VSCD 1332)* – East at Easter (live).
Apr 91. (cd/c/lp) *(CD/TC/+V 2660)* <5352> **REAL LIFE** [2] [74]
 – Real life / See the lights / Let there be love / Woman / Stand by love / African skies / Let the children speak / Ghostrider / Banging on the door / Travelling man / Rivers of ice / When two worlds collide.
May 91. (7"/c-s) *(VS/+C 1343)* **SEE THE LIGHTS. / THEME FOR GREAT CITIES ('91 edit)** [20] [ ]
(12"+=/cd-s+=) *(VS T/CD 1343)* – Soul crying out (live).
May 91. (c-s,cd-s) <1553> **SEE THE LIGHTS / GOODNIGHT** [–] [40]
Aug 91. (7"/c-s) *(VS/+C 1358)* **STAND BY LOVE. / KING IS WHITE AND IN THE CROWD (live)** [13] [ ]
(12"+=/cd-s+=) *(VS T/CD 1358)* – Let there be love (live).
Oct 91. (7"/c-s) *(VS/+C 1382)* **REAL LIFE. / SEE THE LIGHTS** [34] [ ]
(ext.12"+=) *(VST 1382)* – Belfast child (extended).
(cd-s++=) *(VSCD 1382)* – Ghostrider.
Oct 92. (7"/c-s) *(VS/+C 1440)* **LOVE SONG. / ALIVE AND KICKING** [6] [ ]
(ext.cd-s+=) *(VSCDG 1440)* – ('B'instrumental.)
(cd-s++=) *(VSCDX 1440)* – Travelling man / Oh jungleland.
Oct 92. (cd/c/lp) *(SMTV D/C/S 1)* **GLITTERING PRIZE – SIMPLE MINDS 81-92** (compilation) [1] [–]
 – Waterfront / Don't you (forget about me) / Alive and kicking / Sanctify yourself / Love song / Someone somewhere / See the lights / Belfast child / The American / All the things she said / Promised you a miracle / Ghostdancing / Speed your love to me / Glittering prize / Let there be love / Mandela Day. *(lp re-iss. Oct00 on 'Simply Vinyl'; SVLP 258)*

──── **KERR + BURCHILL** with guests **MARK BROWNE, MALCOLM FOSTER, MARCUS MILLER + LANCE MORRISON** – bass / **MARK SCHULMAN, TAL BERGMAN + VINNIE COLAIUTA** – drums

                                               Virgin   Virgin

Jan 95. (7"/c-s/cd-s) *(VS/+C/DG 1509)* <38467> **SHE'S A RIVER. / E55 / ('A'mix)** [9] [52]
(cd-s) *(VSCDX 1509)* – ('A'side) / Celtic strings / ('A'mix).
Jan 95. (cd/c/lp) *(CD/TC/+V 2760)* <39922> **GOOD NEWS FROM THE NEXT WORLD** [2] [87]
 – She's a river / Night music / Hypnotised / Great leap forward / 7 deadly sins / And the band played on / My life / Criminal world / This time.
Mar 95. (7"/c-s) *(VS/+C 1534)* **HYPNOTISED. / #4** [18] [–]
(cd-s+=) *(VSCDX 1534)* – ('A'-Tim Simenon extended remixes) / ('A'-Malfunction mix).
(cd-s) *(VSCDT 1534)* – ('A'side) / Up on the catwalk (live) / And the band played on (live) / She's a river (live).

──── **KERR + BURCHILL** brought back **DEREK FORBES** – bass / **MEL GAYNOR** – drums / also **HAMI LEE** – additional programming

                                            Chrysalis not iss.

Mar 98. (c-s) *(TCCHS 5078)* **GLITTERBALL / WATERFRONT (Union Jack mix)** [18] [–]
(cd-s+=) *(CDCHSS 5078)* – Love song (Philadelphia Bluntz mix).
(cd-s) *(CDCHS 5078)* – ('A'side) / Don't you (forget about me) (Jam & Spoon mix) / Theme for great cities (Fila Brazillia mix).
Mar 98. (cd/c) *(493712-2/-4)* **NEAPOLIS** [19] [–]
 – Song for the tribes / Glitterball / War babies / Tears of a guy / Superman v supersoul / Lightning / If I had wings / Killing Andy Warhol / Androgyny.
May 98. (ext;c-s/7") *(TC/+/CHS 5088)* **WAR BABIES. / I TRAVEL (Utah Saints mix)** [43] [–]
('A'-Bascombe mix;cd-s+=) *(CDCHS 5088)* – Theme for great cities '98 (Fluke's Atlantis mix) / ('A'-Johnson Somerset extended mix).

                                           Eagle Red Ink

Sep 01. (cd-ep) *(EAGEP 198)* **DANCING BAREFOOT EP** [ ] [ ]
 – Dancing barefoot / Gloria / Being boiled / Love will tear us apart.
Sep 01. (cd) *(EAGCD 194)* <55944> **NEON LIGHTS** [ ] [ ] Oct01
 – Gloria / The man who sold the world / Homosapien / Dancing barefoot / Neon lights / Hello I love you / Bring on the dancing horses / The needle & the damage done / For your pleasure / All tomorrow's parties.
Dec 01. (12") *(REMOTE 016)* **HOMOSAPIEN (Malcolm Duffy mix). / HOMOSAPIEN (Malcolm Duffy dub mix)** [–] [–]
(cd-s+=) *(REMOTE 016CD)* – ('A'-Malcolm Duffy edit).
(above issued on 'Remote')
Mar 02. (cd-s) *(EAGXA 218)* **CRY / LEAD THE BLIND / HOMOSAPIEN (Vince Clarke remix)** [47] [–]
(cd-s) *(EAGXS 218)* – ('A'side) / For what it's worth / The garden.
Apr 02. (cd) *(EAGCD 196)* <59145> **CRY**
 – Cry / Spaceface / New sunshine morning / One step closer / Face in the sun / Disconnected / Lazy lately / Sugar / Sleeping girl / Cry again / Slave nation / The floating world.
Jun 02. (cd-s) *(EAGXS 232)* **SPACEFACE / NEW SUNRISE** [ ] [–]

──── in Jun'02, LIQUID PEOPLE vs. SIMPLE MINDS had a hit with 'Monster' which sampled 'CHANGELING'

                                           Absolute not iss.

Sep 02. (12") *(ABR 014)* **CRY (phunk investigation club mix). / CRY (dub mix) / CRY (radio)** [ ] [–]
(cd-s) *(ABR 015)* – ('A'-Tazz Glasgoal vocal + tech-house dub).

– compilations, others, etc. –

on 'Virgin' unless otherwise mentioned

Jan 82. (7") *Arista; (ARIST 448)* **I TRAVEL. / THIRTY FRAMES A SECOND (live)** [ ] [-]
(12"+=) *(ARIST12 448)* – ('A'live).

Feb 82. (lp/c) *Arista; (SPART/TCSPART 1183)* **CELEBRATION** [45] [ ]
(re-iss. Oct82 on 'Virgin' lp/c; V/TCV 2248) (re-iss. Apr89 on 'Virgin' lp/c; OVED/+C 275) (cd-iss. Aug89; CDV 2248)

Apr 83. (12") *(VS 578-12)* **I TRAVEL (mix). / FILM THEME** [ ] [-]

Aug 90. (5xcd-box-ep) *(SMTCD 1)* **THEMES – VOLUME ONE** [ ] [-]
– (Apr79 – LIFE IN A DAY – Apr82 – PROMISED YOU A MIRACLE singles)

Sep 90. (5xcd-box-ep) *(SMTCD 2)* **THEMES – VOLUME TWO** [ ] [-]
– (Aug82 – GLITTERING PRIZE – Apr85 – DON'T YOU (FORGET ABOUT ME) singles)

Oct 90. (5xcd-box-ep) *(SMTCD 3)* **THEMES – VOLUME THREE** [ ] [-]
– (Oct85 – ALIVE AND KICKING – Jun87 – PROMISED YOU A MIRACLE (live) singles)

Nov 90. (5xcd-box-ep) *(SMTCD 4)* **THEMES – VOLUME FOUR** [ ] [-]
– (Feb89 – BELFAST CHILD, Dec89 – THE AMSTERDAM EP)

Nov 90. (3xcd-box) *(TPAK 2)* **COLLECTOR'S EDITION** [ ] [-]
– (LIFE IN A DAY / REEL TO REAL CACOPHONY / EMPIRES AND DANCE)

Nov 01. (d-cd) *(CDVD 2953)* **THE BEST OF SIMPLE MINDS** [34] [-]

SIOUXSIE & THE BANSHEES

Formed: London, England . . . September '76 by SIOUXSIE SIOUX and STEVE SEVERIN, both members of the infamous 'Bromley Contingent' punk troupe who religiously followed The SEX PISTOLS during the turbulent early years of their career; an early incarnation of The BANSHEES even featured future PISTOL, SID VICIOUS on drums, the outfit mangling the Lord's Prayer at the legendary 100 Club punk all-dayer in summer '76. SIOUX gained further notoriety following her appearance (as a fan) on the fateful edition of Bill Grundy's 'Today' programme wherein his tete-a-tete with the 'PISTOLS outraged the country's more upstanding citizens. Cutting a striking dash through the punk scene with her Nazi chic and proto-goth garb, SIOUXSIE and her BANSHEES (who, after much to-ing and fro-ing, were eventually completed by JOHN McKAY amd KENNY MORRIS) toured constantly throughout 1977, eventually signing to 'Polydor' the following year after their original label, 'Track', went bust. A debut single, 'HONG KONG GARDEN' was a sprightly slice of oriental flavoured post-punk which hit the Top 10 with ease and introduced the band outwith the confines of the London scene. 'THE SCREAM' (1978) was instantly hailed as a classic upon its release a few months later, the record's queasy, churning goth-psychedelia breaking new ground and spearheading a new direction for many bands inspired by a movement already dying on its feet. For many recent converts, then, 'JOIN HANDS' (1979) was a disappointment, a turgid affair which lacked the bite of its predecessor and presaged a band breakdown; McKAY and MORRIS upped sticks and left mid-tour, ROBERT SMITH (The CURE) briefly deputising before a new guitarist was eventually found in erstwhile MAGAZINE man, JOHN McGEOGH. The drum seat, meanwhile, was taken by ex-SLITS man, BUDGIE, who would subsequently become SIOUXSIE's beau and eventual husband. The revamped line-up bounced back in 1980 with the enchanting 'HAPPY HOUSE' (a Top 20 hit that Spring) and an accompanying Top 5 album, 'KALEIDOSCOPE', investing their sound with a newly acquired accessibility and ensuring a degree of crossover success for SIOUXSIE's icy sensuality. 'JU JU' (1981) further refined the group's subtle gothic tapestries, again taking the band into the UK Top 10 and spawning a clutch of minor hits while 'ONCE UPON A TIME – THE SINGLES' neatly rounded up the first instalment in The BANSHEES' career. More overtly experimental was the following year's 'A KISS IN THE DREAMHOUSE', utilising strings and flirting with club sounds. 1983 saw a flurry of side project activity as SIOUXSIE and BUDGIE formed The CREATURES, releasing 'FEAST', the first of two albums together (they also had a major hit with Mel Torme's 'RIGHT NOW'). SEVERIN, meanwhile, formed The GLOVE with SMITH (who had also rejoined the BANSHEES ranks as a part-time, temporary replacement for the departing McGEOGH), releasing the 'BLUE SUNSHINE' album the same year. No new BANSHEES material surfaced, although an atmospheric cover of The Beatles' 'DEAR PRUDENCE' hit No.3 and gave them their biggest selling single to date. The track featured on 1983's live set, 'NOCTURNE', while the following year's 'HYAENA', saw SMITH making his presence felt over the course of a haunting set that was unfairly panned by the critics. With SMITH subsequently finding the demands of a dual lifestyle too tiring, ex-CLOCKDVA man, JOHN CARRUTHERS was drafted in for 'TINDERBOX' (1986), an album which carried on in much the same vein, spawning a sizeable hit with the infectious 'CITIES IN DUST'. Perhaps the band really were running out of ideas as their detractors suggested, a suitably gothic Top 20 rendition of Bob Dylan's 'THIS WHEEL'S ON FIRE' trailing a whole album's worth of competent but hardly inspiring cover versions. Featuring yet another guitarist, JON KLEIN, 1988's 'PEEPSHOW' was a much more compelling proposition, a perversely eclectic selection best sampled on the mutant dancefloor hit, 'PEEK-A-BOO'. Now something of an alternative institution, SIOUXSIE & THE BANSHEES cruised into the 90's with their most chart-friendly original material to date, the swooning 'KISS THEM FOR ME' (the band's first – and to date only – major US hit) single and attendant 'SUPERSTITION' (1991) album. Despite the latter set's commercial and critical success, the group reached the end of its natural lifespan in the mid-90's, bowing out on a high with the majestic 'THE RAPTURE'. Officially splitting in April '96, SIOUXSIE was working on new CREATURES material with spouse BUDGIE, while SEVERIN scored the soundtrack for the movie, 'Visions Of Ecstasy'. The aforementioned CREATURES finally resurfaced via 'ANIMA ANIMUS' (1999), an album that boasted a few minor hits; SIOUXSIE was now looking rather Elizabeth Taylor-ish although when she wailed and her BUDGIE drummed it was safe there was no lasting comparison. • **Songwriters:** All written by SIOUXSIE / SEVERIN except; HELTER SKELTER (Beatles) / 20th CENTURY BOY (T.Rex) / IL EST NE LE DIVIN ENFANT (French festive song) / ALL TOMORROW'S PARTIES (Velvet Underground). THROUGH THE LOOKING GLASS was a covers album containing THE PASSENGER (Iggy Pop) / YOU'RE LOST LITTLE GIRL (Doors) / GUN (John Cale) / THIS TOWN AIN'T BIG ENOUGH FOR THE BOTH OF US (Sparks) / SEA BREEZES (Roxy Music) / STRANGE FRUIT (Billie Holiday) / WALL OF MIRRORS (Kraftwerk) / LITTLE JOHNNY JEWEL (Television) / TRUST IN ME ('Jungle Book' animated film). • **Trivia:** SEVERIN produced ALTERED IMAGES debut 45 'Dead Pop Stars'.

Album rating: THE SCREAM (*9) / JOIN HANDS (*7) / KALEIDOSCOPE (*7) / JU JU (*7) / ONCE UPON A TIME – THE SINGLES compilation (*9) / A KISS IN THE DREAMHOUSE (*7) / NOCTURNE (*5) / HYAENA (*7) / TINDERBOX (*7) / THROUGH THE LOOKING GLASS (*5) / PEEP SHOW (*5) / SUPERSTITION (*5) / TWICE UPON A TIME compilation (*7) / THE RAPTURE (*5) / THE BEST OF SIOUXSIE & THE BANSHEES compilation (*6) / Creatures: FEAST (*5) / BOOMERANG (*4) / ANIMA ANIMUS (*6) / Glove: BLUE SUNSHINE (*5)

SIOUXSIE SIOUX (b. SUSAN DALLION, 27 May'57) – vocals / **STEVEN SEVERIN** (b. STEVEN BAILEY, 25 Sep'55) – bass / **JOHN McKAY** – guitar; repl. PT FENTON; who had repl. MARCO PIRRONI (he joined The MODELS and later ADAM & THE ANTS) / **KENNY MORRIS** – drums repl. SID VICIOUS who later became bassman for SEX PISTOLS

Polydor Polydor

Aug 78. (7") *(2059 052)* **HONG KONG GARDEN. / VOICES** [7] [-]

Oct 78. (7") **HONG KONG GARDEN. / OVERGROUND** [-] [ ]

Nov 78. (lp/c) *(POLD/+C 5009) <6207>* **THE SCREAM** [12] [ ]
– Pure / Jigsaw feeling / Overground / Carcass / Helter skelter / Mirage / Metal postcard / Nicotine stain / Suburban relapse / Switch. *(cd-iss. Mar89 & Mar95 on 'Wonderland'; 839 008-2) (cd re-iss. Mar95)*

Mar 79. (7") *(POSP 9)* **THE STAIRCASE (MYSTERY). / 20th CENTURY BOY** [24] [-]

Jun 79. (7") *(POSP 59)* **PLAYGROUND TWIST. / PULLED TO BITS** [28] [-]

Sep 79. (lp/c) *(POLD/+C 5024)* **JOIN HANDS** [13] [-]
– Poppy day / Regal zone / Placebo effect / Icon / Premature burial / Playground twist / Mother / Oh mein papa / The Lord's prayer. *(cd-iss. Mar89 & Mar95 on 'Wonderland'; 839004-2)*

Sep 79. (7") *(2059 151)* **MITTAGEISEN (METAL POSTCARD). / LOVE IN A VOID** [47] [-]

— **BUDGIE** (b.PETER CLARK, 21 Aug'57, St.Helens, England) – drums (ex-SLITS, ex-PLANETS, ex-BIG IN JAPAN, etc.) repl. MORRIS who bailed out (he subsequently released a solo 12", 'LA MAIN MORTE', for 'Temple' records in '86) / **JOHN McGEOGH** (b. 1955, Greenock, Scotland) – guitar (of MAGAZINE) finally repl. ROBERT SMITH (of The CURE) + JOHN CARRUTHERS who repl. McKAY (he finally formed ZOR GABOR in 1986 – with vocalist LINDA CLARK – and released one single, 'TIGHTROPE', for 'In-Tape' early '87)

Mar 80. (7") *(POSP 117)* **HAPPY HOUSE. / DROP DEAD** [17] [-]

May 80. (7") *(2059 249)* **CHRISTINE. / EVE WHITE EVE BLACK** [24] [-]

Aug 80. (lp)(c) *(2442 177)(3184 146)* **KALEIDOSCOPE** [5] [-]
– Happy house / Tenant / Trophy / Hybrid / Lunar camel / Christine / Desert kisses / Red light / Paradise place / Skin. *(cd-iss. Mar89 & Mar95 on 'Wonderland'; 839006-2)*

Nov 80. (7"/dance-12") *(POSP/+X 205)* **ISRAEL. / RED OVER WHITE** [41] [-]

May 81. (7") *(POSP 273)* **SPELLBOUND. / FOLLOW THE SUN** [22] [-]
(12"+=) *(POSPX 273)* – Slap dash snap.

Jun 81. (lp/c) *(POLS/+C 1034)* **JU JU** [7] [-]
– Spellbound / Into the light / Arabian knights / Halloween / Monitor / Night shift / Sin in my heart / Head cut / Voodoo dolly. *(cd-iss. Mar89 & Mar95 on 'Wonderland'; 839005-2)*

Jul 81. (7") *(POSP 309)* **ARABIAN KNIGHTS. / SUPERNATURAL THING** [32] [-]
(12"+=) *(POSPX 309)* – Congo conga.

— SIOUXSIE & BUDGIE as The CREATURES hit Top 30 with WILD THINGS EP.

Dec 81. (lp/c) *(POLS/+C 1056)* **ONCE UPON A TIME – THE SINGLES** [21] [-]
– Hong Kong garden / Mirage / The staircase (mystery) / Playground twist / Happy house / Christine / Israel / Spellbound / Arabian knights / Fireworks. *(cd-iss. Mar89 on 'Wonderland'; 831542-2)*

May 82. (7") *(POSPG 450)* **FIREWORKS. / COAL MIND** [22] [-]
(12"+=) *(POSPX 450)* – We fall.

Sep 82. (7") *(POSP 510)* **SLOWDIVE. / CANNIBAL ROSES** [41] [-]
(12"+=) *(POSPX 510)* – Obsession II.

Nov 82. (lp/c) *(POLD/+C 5064)* **A KISS IN THE DREAMHOUSE** [11] [-]
– Cascade / Green fingers / Obsession / She's a carnival / Circle / Melt! / Painted bird / Cocoon / Slowdive. *(cd-iss. Apr89 & Mar 95 on 'Wonderland'; 839007-2)*

Nov 82. (7") *(POSP 539)* **MELT! / IL EST NE LE DIVIN ENFANT** [49] [ ]
(12"+=) *(POSPX 539)* – A sleeping rain.

— **ROBERT SMITH** – guitar (of The CURE) returned part-time to repl. McGEOGH who later joined The ARMOURY SHOW.

— In 1983, SMITH and SEVERIN had also splintered into The GLOVE, with SIOUXSIE and BUDGIE re-uniting as The CREATURES (see further on).

Wonderland – Polydor Geffen

Sep 83. (7") *(SHEG 4)* **DEAR PRUDENCE. / TATTOO** [3] [-]
(12"+=) *(SHEX 4)* – There's a planet in my kitchen.

Nov 83. (d-lp/c) *(SHAH/+C 1)* **NOCTURNE (live)** [29] [-]
– Intro – The rite of Spring / Israel / Dear Prudence / Paradise place / Melt! / Cascade / Pulled to bits / Night shift / Sin in my heart / Slowdive / Painted bird / Happy house / Switch / Spellbound / Helter skelter / Eve white eve black / Voodoo dolly. *(cd-iss. Apr89 & Mar95; 839009-2)*

Mar 84. (7") *(SHE 6)* **SWIMMING HORSES. / LET GO** [28] [-]
(12"+=) *(SHEX 6)* – The humming wires.

SIOUXSIE & THE BANSHEES (cont) *THE GREAT INDIE DISCOGRAPHY* **The 1970s**

May 84. (7") *(SHE 7)* **DAZZLE. / I PROMISE** — 33 / -
(12"+=) *(SHEX 7)* – Throw them to the lions / ('A'mix).
Jun 84. (lp/c)(cd) *(SHEH P/C 1)(821510-2) <24030>* **HYAENA** — 15 / □
– Dazzle / We hunger / Take me back / Belladonna / Swimming horses / Bring me the head of the preacher man / Running town / Pointing bone / Blow the house down. *(re-iss. cd Mar95; same)*

——— **JOHN CARRUTHERS** – guitar (ex-CLOCKDVA, ex-JEFFREY LEE PIERCE) returned to repl. SMITH who had CURE commitments.

Oct 84. (12"ep) *(SHEEP 8)* **THE THORN** (live) — 47 / -
– Voices / Placebo effect / Red over white / Overground.
Oct 85. (7") *(SHE 9)* **CITIES IN DUST. / AN EXECUTION** — 21 / -
(12"+=) *(SHEX 9)* – Quarter drawing of the dog.
Feb 86. (7") *(SHE 10)* **CANDYMAN. / LULLABY** — 34 / -
(12"+=) *(SHEX 10)* – Umbrella.
Apr 86. (lp/c)(cd) *(SHE LP/MC 3)(829145-2) <24092>* **TINDERBOX** — 13 / 88
– Candyman / The sweetest chill / Cities in dust / Cannons / Partys fall / 92° / Lands End. *(cd+=)* – An execution / Quarter drawing of the dog / Lullaby / Umbrella / Candyman (extended). *(re-iss. cd Mar95; same)*
Jan 87. (7") *(SHE 11)* **THIS WHEEL'S ON FIRE. / SHOOTING SUN** — 14 / -
(12"+=) *(SHEX 11)* – Sleepwalking (on the high wire).
Feb 87. (lp/c)(cd) *(SHE LP/MC 3)(831474-2) <24134>* **THROUGH THE LOOKING GLASS** — 15 / □
– Hall of mirrors / Trust in me / This wheel's on fire / Strange fruit / This town ain't big enough for the both of us / You're lost little girl / The passenger / Gun / Sea breezes / Little Johnny Jewel. *(re-iss. cd Mar95; same)*
Mar 87. (7") *(SHE 12)* **THE PASSENGER. / SHE'S CUCKOO** — 41 / -
(12"+=) *(SHEX 12)* – Something blue.

——— **JON KLEIN** (b. 9 May'??, Bristol, England) – guitar (ex-SPECIMEN) repl. CARRUTHERS / added **MARTIN McCARRICK** (b.29 Jul'??) – cello, keyboards (ex-MARC ALMOND, ex-The GLOVE) (to SIOUXSIE, SEVERIN, BUDGIE + KLEIN)

Jul 87. (7"/7"pic-d/c-s) *(SHE/+P/PC 13)* **SONG FROM THE EDGE OF THE WORLD. / THE WHOLE PRICE OF BLOOD** — 59 / -
(12"+=) *(SHEX 13)* – Mechanical eyes.
Jul 88. (7"/7"g-f) *(SHE/+G 14) <27760>* **PEEK-A-BOO. / FALSE FACE** — 16 / 53
(c-s+=/cd-s+=) *(SHE CS/CD 14)* – Catwalk / ('A'-Big suspender mix).
(12"+=) *(SHEXR 14)* – ('A'-2 other mixes).
Sep 88. (lp/c)(cd) *(SHE LP/MC 5)(837240-2) <24205>* **PEEPSHOW** — 20 / 68
– Peek-a-boo / Killing jar / Scarecrow / Carousel / Burn-up / Ornaments of gold / Turn to stone / Rawhead and bloodybones / The last beat of my heart / Rhapsody. *(re-iss. cd Mar95; same)*
Sep 88. (7"/7"g-f/7"pic-d) *(SHE/+G/P 15)* **KILLING JAR. / SOMETHING WICKED (THIS WAY COMES)** — 41 / -
(12"+=/cd-s+=) *(SHE X/CD 15)* – Are you still dying, darling.
Nov 88. (7"/7"g-f) *(SHE/+G 16)* **THE LAST BEAT OF MY HEART. / EL DIABLO LOS MUERTOS** — 44 / -
(12"+=) *(SHEX 16)* – Sunless.
(cd-s+=) *(SHECD 16)* – ('B'mix).

——— In Autumn'89, The CREATURES issued singles and 'BOOMERANG' album.

May 91. (7"/c-s) *(SHE/+CS 19) <19031>* **KISS THEM FOR ME. / RETURN** — 32 / 23
(ext-12"+=/12"pic-d+=) *(SHE X/XD 19)* – Staring back.
(cd-s++=) *(SHECD 19)* – ('A'side).
Jun 91. (cd/c/lp) *(847731-2/-4/-1) <24387>* **SUPERSTITION** — 25 / 65
– Kiss them for me / Fear (of the unknown) / Cry / Drifter / Little sister / Shadowtime / Silly thing / Got to get up / Silver waterfalls / Softly / The ghost in you. *(re-iss. cd Mar95; same)*
Jul 91. (7"/c-s) *(SHE/+CS 20)* **SHADOWTIME. / SPIRAL TWIST** — 57 / -
(12"+=/cd-s+=) *(SHE X/CD 20)* – Sea of light. / ('A'-Eclipse mix).

——— Below single from the film 'Batman Returns'.

Jul 92. (7"/c-s) *(SHE/+CS 21)* **FACE TO FACE. / I COULD BE AGAIN** — 21 / -
(cd-s+=) *(SHECD 21)* – Hothead.
(12") *(SHEX 21)* – ('A'side) / ('A'-catatonic mix) / Hothead.
Oct 92. (cd/c/lp) *(517160-2/-4/-1)* **TWICE UPON A TIME – THE THING** — 26 / -
– Fireworks / Slowdive / Melt / Dear Prudence / Swimming horses / Dazzle / Overground (from The Thorn) / Cities in dust / Candyman / This wheel's on fire / The passenger / Peek-a-boo / The killing jar / The last beat of my heart / Kiss them for me / Shadowtime / Fear (of the unknown) / Face to face. *(re-iss. cd Mar95; same)*

——— In Aug 94, SIOUXSIE partnered MORRISSEY on his single, 'INTERLUDE'.

Dec 94. (c-s) *(SHECS 22)* **O BABY. / OURSELVES** — 34 / -
(cd-s+=) *(SHECD 22)* – ('A'-Manhattan mix).
(cd-s) *(SHECDX 22)* – ('A'side) / Swimming horses (live) / All tomorrow's parties (live).
Jan 95. (cd/c/lp) *(523725-2/-4/-1) <24630>* **THE RAPTURE** — 33 / □
– O baby / Tearing apart / Stargazer / Fall from grace / Not forgotten / Sick child / The lonely one / Falling down / Forever / The rapture / The double life / Love out me.
Feb 95. (7"/c-s) *(SHE/+CS 23)* **STARGAZER. / HANG ME HIGH** — 64 / □
(cd-s+=) *(SHECD 23)* – Black Sun.
(cd-s) *(SHECDX 23)* – ('A'-Mambo sun) / ('A'-Planet queen mix) / ('A'-Mark Saunders mix).

——— Split Apr'96 although SIOUXSIE and BUDGIE recorded a third album as The CREATURES. SEVERIN has written for the film 'Visions Of Ecstacy'.

– compilations, etc. –

Feb 87. (12"ep) *Strange Fruit; (SFPS 012)* **THE PEEL SESSIONS (29.11.77)** — □ / □
– Love in a void / Mirage / Suburban relapse / Metal postcard. *(c-ep-iss.Jun87; SFPSC 012) (cd-ep-iss.Mar88; SFPSCD 012)*
Feb 89. (12"ep/cd-ep) *Strange Fruit; (SPPS/+CD 066)* **THE PEEL SESSIONS** (Feb'78) — □ / □
– Hong Kong garden / Carcass / Helter skelter / Overground.
Sep 02. (cd) *Universal; (<065152-2>)* **THE BEST OF SIOUXSIE & THE BANSHEES** — □ / Nov02
– Dear Prudence / Hong Kong garden / Cities in dust / Happy house / KIss them for me / Face to face / Dizzy / Israel / Christine / Spellbound / Stargazer /

Arabian knights / The killing jar / This wheel's on fire. *(<d-cd+=; 065150-2>)* – (bonus mixes).

CREATURES

(SIOUXSIE & BUDGIE)

Polydor / not iss.

Sep 81. (d7"ep/d7"gf-ep) *(POSP D/G 354)* **WILD THINGS** — 24 / -
– Mad-eyed screamer / So unreal / But not them / Wild thing / Thumb.

Wonderland / Geffen

May 83. (7") *(SHE 1)* **MISS THE GIRL. / HOT SPRING IN THE SNOW** — 21 / -
May 83. (lp/c) *(SHE LP/MC 1)* **FEAST** — 17 / -
– Morning dawning / Inoa 'ole / Ice house / Dancing on glass / Gecko / Sky train / Festival of colours / Miss the girl / Dancing / A strutting rooster / Flesh.
Jul 83. (7") *(SHE 2)* **RIGHT NOW. / WEATHERCADE** — 14 / -
(12"+=) *(SHEX 2)* – Festival of colours.
Oct 89. (7") *(SHEP 17)* **STANDING THERE. / DIVIDED** — 53 / -
(12"+=/cd-s+=) *(SH X/CD 17)* – Solar choir / ('A'-Andalucian mix).
('A'-La Frontera mix-10"+=) *(SHET 17)* – Solar choir.
Nov 89. (lp/c/cd) *(841463-1/-4/-2) <24275>* **BOOMERANG** — □ / □
– Standing there / Manchild / You! / Pity / Killing time / Willow / Pluto drive / Solar choir * / Speeding * / Fury eyes / Fruitman / Untiedundone * / Simoom * / Strolling wolf / Venus sands / Morriha. *(extra tracks on cd= *)*
Feb 90. (7"/7"box) *(SHE/+B 18)* **FURY EYES. / ABSTINENCE** — □ / -
(12"/cd-s) *(SHE P/CD 18)* – ('A'-20/20 mix) / ('A'dub) / ('A'-Fever mix).

Sioux / Record Of Substance

Jun 98. (7") *(SIOUX 1)* **SAD CUNT. / SAD CUNT** (chix'n'dix mix) — □ / □
Aug 98. (10"ep/cd-ep) *(SIOUX 2 V/CD) <1>* **ERASER CUTS** — □ / □
– Pinned down / Guillotine / Thank you / Slipping away.
Oct 98. (7"green) *(SIOUX 3V)* **2ND FLOOR. / TURN IT ON** — □ / □
(12"on 'Hydrogen Jukebox'+=)(cd-s+=) *(DUKE 044DJV)(SIOUX 3CD)* – ('A'-Girl eats boy mix) / ('A'-Emperor Sly mix).
Dec 98. (cd-ep) *(SIOUX 5CD)* **EXTERMINATING ANGEL** — - / - mail-o
– Exordium (one night in France) / Interim (NYC & Paris) / Remake (the James Hardway) / Remodel (album mix).

Sioux / Instinct

Feb 99. (cd/c/2x10"lp) *(SIOUX 4 CD/C/V) <413>* **ANIMA ANIMUS** — □ / □
– 2nd floor / Disconnected / Turn it on / Take mine / Say / I was me / Prettiest thing / Exterminating angel / Another planet / Don't go to sleep without me.
Mar 99. (7"clear) *(SIOUX 6V)* **SAY. / ALL SHE COULD ASK FOR** — 72 / -
(cd-s) *(SIOUX 6CD)* – ('A'side) / Broken.
(cd-s) *(SIOUX 6CDX)* – ('A'-Witchman remix) / ('A'-Justice & Endemic void remix).
Mar 99. (12"ltd) *(DUKE 055DJV)* **SAY (Witchman 4x4 mix). / THANK YOU (Dub Pistols brings you joy mix)** — □ / -
Jul 99. (12"ltd) *(DUKE 064DJV)* **DISCONNECTING (Beloved's mix). / PRETTIEST THING (Super Chumbo's mix)** — □ / -
(above singles on 'Hydrogen Dukebox')
Sep 99. (10"blue/cd-s) *(SIOUX 9 V/CD)* **PRETTIEST THING (Super Chumbo's waking dream mix) / TURN IT ON (Emperor Sly's elemental mix) / GUILLOTINE (bitten by the black dog)** — □ / -
(cd-s) *(SIOUX 9CDX)* – ('A'-mixes; Howie B hormonal / album / subsonic legacy).
Nov 99. (cd/d-lp) *(DUKE 066 CD/DJV) <433>* **HYBRIDS** (remixes) — □ / □
(re-iss. Aug01; same)
Dec 00. (m-cd) *<516>* **U.S. RETRACE** (compilation) — - / □
– Pinned down / Guillotine / Turn it on (bound 'n' gagged mix) / All she could ask for / Broken / Turn it on (Emperor Sly's elemental mix) / Thank you / Slipping away.

not iss. / Sioux

Jun 01. (cd) *<79611>* **SEQUINS IN THE SUN** (compilation) — - / □
– All she could ask for / Disconnected / Turn it on / Take mine / Pinned down / Guillotine / 2nd floor / Pluto drive – Nightclubbing / Prettiest thing / Exterminating angel.

The GLOVE

(SEVERIN & ROBERT SMITH) also incl. **MARTIN McCARRICK** – cello / **ANNE STEPHENSON + GINNY HEWES** – strings / **ANDY ANDERSON** – drums / (JEANETTE) LANDRAY – dual vocals w/SMITH

Wonderland / Rough Trade

Aug 83. (7") *(SHE 3)* **LIKE AN ANIMAL. / MOUTH TO MOUTH** — 52 / -
(12"+=) *(SHEX 3)* – Animal (club mix).
Aug 83. (lp/c) *(SHE LP/MC 2) <ROUGHUS 85>* **BLUE SUNSHINE** — 35 / □
– Like an animal / Looking glass girl / Sex-eye-make-up / Mr. Alphabet says / A blues in drag / Punish me with kisses / This green city / Orgy / Perfect murder / Relax. *(re-iss. Sep90 lp/c/cd+=; 815019-1/-4/-2)* – Mouth to mouth / The tightrope / Like an animal (club mix).
Nov 83. (7") *(SHE 5)* **PUNISH ME WITH KISSES. / THE TIGHTROPE** — □ / -

SKIDS

Formed: Dunfermline, Scotland ... spring 1977 by RICHARD JOBSON and STUART ADAMSON together with BILL SIMPSON and TOM KELLICHAN. Careering into the wreckage of the post-punk music scene with the self-financed 'CHARLES' single, the band soon found themselves with a deal courtesy of the ever eclectic 'Virgin' label. After a couple of minor hit singles, the group hit the UK Top 10 with 'INTO THE VALLEY', a shining example of The SKIDS' anthemic, new wave warriors style. In addition to JOBSON's highly distinctive, affected vocals and ADAMSON's strident axework (which he'd later perfect in BIG COUNTRY), The SKIDS were notable for their clever visual image (i.e. JOBSON's kick-dance and ultra-slick wavey hairdo). A debut album, 'SCARED TO DANCE' (1979), made the UK Top 20 and established the group as a more tasteful Caledonian alternative to The BAY CITY ROLLERS. Later that Spring, The SKIDS scored another Top 20 hit single with 'MASQUERADE', a highlight of the BILL NELSON-produced follow-up album, 'DAYS IN EUROPA' (1979), alongside the almost militaristic clarion call of 'WORKING FOR THE YANKEE DOLLAR'. All wasn't well within The SKIDS camp, however, personnel upheaval (leading to an all-new rhythm section of RUSSELL WEBB and MIKE BAILLIE) adding to criticisms of JOBSON's increasing lyrical complexities and the group's more schitzo pop/experimental sound. Despite all this, a third album, 'THE ABSOLUTE GAME' (1980) saw a return to form of sorts, furnishing the group with their one and only Top 10 set. ADAMSON became increasingly disillusioned, however, and finally departed the following summer. Left to his own devices, JOBSON dominated The SKIDS' final album, 'JOY' (1981), an at times trad/folk concept effort which met with a frosty critical reception and signalled the subsequent demise of the group early in '82. While ADAMSON went on to massive success with "bagpipe"-guitar rockers, BIG COUNTRY, JOBSON concentrated on a solo career which extended to writing (and recording) poetry. He then went on to form the short-lived and critically derided ARMOURY SHOW along with ex-MAGAZINE men, JOHN McGEOGH and JOHN DOYLE, releasing a sole album, 'WAITING FOR THE FLOODS' (1985). More recently, JOBSON's recording career has taken a backseat to his more successful forays into modelling and TV journalism. • **Songwriters:** JOBSON lyrics/group compositions, except ALL THE YOUNG DUDES (hit; Mott The Hoople) / BAND PLAYED WALTZING MATILDA (Australian trad.). • **Trivia:** In 1981, JOBSON published book of poetry, 'A MAN FOR ALL SEASONS'.

Album rating: SCARED TO DANCE (*8*) / DAYS IN EUROPA (*6*) / THE ABSOLUTE GAME (*6*) / JOY (*4*) / DUNFERMLINE compilation (*7*) / SWEET SUBURBIA – THE BEST OF THE SKIDS compilation (*8*)

RICHARD JOBSON (b. 6 Apr'60) – vocals, guitar / **STUART ADAMSON** (b. WILLIAM STUART ADAMSON, 11 Apr'58, Manchester, England) – lead guitar, vocals / **BILL SIMPSON** – bass / **TOM KELLICHAN** – drums

		No-Bad	not iss.
Mar 78.	(7"m) (NB 1) **CHARLES. / REASONS / TEST-TUBE BABIES**		-
		Virgin	not iss.
Sep 78.	(7",7"white) (VS 227) **SWEET SUBURBIA. / OPEN SOUND**	70	-
Oct 78.	(7"red-ep/12"red-ep) (VS 232/+12) **WIDE OPEN**	48	-
	– The saints are coming / Of one skin / Confusion / Night and day.		
Feb 79.	(7",7"white) (VS241) **INTO THE VALLEY. / T.V. STARS**	10	-
Feb 79.	(lp/c) (V/TCV 2116) **SCARED TO DANCE**	19	-
	– Into the valley / Scared to dance / Of one skin / Dossier (of fallibility) / Melancholy soldiers / Hope and glory / The saints are coming / Six times / Calling the tune / Integral plot / Charles / The Scale. *(re-iss. Apr84 lp/c; OVED/+C 41) (cd-iss. Jun90+=; CDV 2116)* – Sweet suburbia / Open sound / TV stars / Night and day / Contusion / Reasons / Test tube babies. <US cd-iss. 1991 on 'Caroline'; CAROL 1817-2>		
May 79.	(7") (VS 262) **MASQUERADE. / OUT OF TOWN**	14	-
	(d7"+=) (VS 262-12) – Another emotion / Aftermath dub.		

— **RUSTY EGAN** – drums (ex-RICH KIDS) repl. KELLICHAN

Sep 79.	(7") (VS 288) **CHARADE. / GREY PARADE**	31	-
Oct 79.	(lp/c) (V/TCV 2138) **DAYS IN EUROPA**	32	-
	– Animation * / Charade / Dulce et decorum (pro patria mor) / Pros and cons / Home of the saved / Working for the Yankee dollar / The olympian / Thanatos / Masquerade / A day in Europa / Peaceful times. *(re-dist.Mar80 += *) (re-iss. Mar84 lp/c; OVED/+C 42) (cd-iss. Jun01 on 'Captain Oi'+=; AHOYCD 172)* – Out of town / Another emotion / Aftermath dub / Grey parade / Working for the yankee dollar / Vanguard's crusade.		
Nov 79.	(7") (VS 306) **WORKING FOR THE YANKEE DOLLAR. / VANGUARD'S CRUSADE**	20	-
	(d7"+=) (VS 306) – All the young dudes / Hymns from a haunted ballroom.		

— **RUSSELL WEBB** – bass, vocals (ex-ZONES, ex-SLIK) repl. SIMPSON / **MIKE BAILLIE** – drums (ex-INSECT BITES) repl. EGAN who joined VISAGE

Feb 80.	(7") (VS 323) **ANIMATION. / PROS AND CONS**	56	-
Jul 80.	(7") (VS 359) **CIRCUS GAMES. / ONE DECREE**	32	-
Sep 80.	(lp/c) (V/TCV 2174) **THE ABSOLUTE GAME**	9	-
	– Circus games / Out of town / Goodbye civilian / The children saw the shame / A woman in winter / Hurry on boys / Happy to be with you / The Devil's decade / One decree / Arena. *(free-lp w.a.) (VDJ 333)* **STRENGTH THROUGH JOY** *(re-iss. Mar84 lp/c; OVED/+C 43) (cd-iss. Oct01 on 'Track'; TRK 0006CD)*		
Oct 80.	(7"/7"pic-d) (VS/+P 373) **GOODBYE CIVILIAN. / MONKEY McGUIRE MEETS SPECKY POTTER BEHIND THE LOCHORE INSTITUTE**	52	-
Nov 80.	(7") (VSK 101) **A WOMAN IN WINTER. / WORKING FOR THE YANKEE DOLLAR (live)**	49	-

— **KENNY HYSLOP** (b.14 Feb'51, Helensburgh, Scotland) – drums (ex-ZONES, ex-SLIK) repl. BAILLIE who joined EPSILON.

| Aug 81. | (7"/12") (VS 401/+12) **FIELDS. / BRAVE MAN** | | - |

— **JOBSON + WEBB** recruited **PAUL WISHART** – saxophone, flute to repl. ADAMSON who formed BIG COUNTRY and HYSLOP who joined SIMPLE MINDS. Session people on album incl. **J.J. JOHNSON** – drums / The ASSOCIATES / **VIRGINIA ASTLEY** / **MIKE OLDFIELD** – guitar / **KEN LOCKIE** / **TIM CROSS** – piano / **ALAN DARBY** – guitar

Oct 81.	(7") (VS 449) **IONA. / BLOOD AND SPOIL**		-
Nov 81.	(lp/c) (V/TCV 2217) **JOY**		-
	– Blood and soil / A challenge, the wanderer / Men of mercy / A memory / Iona / In fear of fire / Brothers / And the band played Waltzing Matilda / The men of the fall / The sound of retreat (instrumental) / Fields. *(re-iss. 1988 lp/c; OVED/+C 200)*		

— folded early '82 with JOBSON already concentrating on poetry & solo work

– compilations, etc. –

on 'Virgin' unless mentioned otherwise

May 82.	(lp/c) (VM/+C 2) **FANFARE**		-
May 83.	(12"ep) (VS 591-12) **INTO THE VALLEY / MASQUERADE. / SCARED TO DANCE / WORKING FOR THE YANKEE DOLLAR**		-
Jul 87.	(cd) (CDVM 9022) **DUNFERMLINE (THE SKIDS' FINEST MOMENTS)**		-
Feb 92.	(m-cd) Windsong; (<WINCD 008>) **BBC RADIO 1 LIVE IN CONCERT (live)**		-
Jan 95.	(cd) (CDOVD 457) **SWEET SUBURBIA – THE BEST OF THE SKIDS**		-
	– Into the valley / Charles / The saints are coming / Scared to dance / Sweet suburbia / Of one skin / Night and day / Animation / Working for the Yankee dollar / Charade / Masquerade / Circus games / Out of town / Goodbye civilian / A woman in winter / Hurry on boys / Iona / Fields.		

— in May'02 – through STUART ADAMSON's death – 'Universal TV' records delivered a BIG COUNTRY 'GREATEST HITS' collection with SKIDS tracks

RICHARD JOBSON

solo with **JOHN McGEOGH** – guitar / **VIRGINIA ASTLEY** – piano, flute / **JOSEPHINE** – wind, piano

		Cocteau	not iss.
Oct 81.	(lp) (JC 1) **THE BALLAD OF ETIQUETTE** (some poetry)		-
	– India song / Don't ever tell anybody anything / Pavillion pole / Etiquette / Joy / Thomas / Anonymous / The night of crystal / Orphee / Stormy weather. *(re-iss. Jul85)*		
		Crepescule	not iss.
Feb 83.	(lp) **10:30 ON A SUMMER NIGHT**		-

— with **VINI REILLY** – guitar (of DURUTTI COLUMN) / **WIM MERTENS** (of SOFT VERDICT) / **BLAINE L. REININGER** (of TUXEDO MOON) / **PAUL HAIG** – synthesizers (ex-JOSEF K) / **STEVEN BROWN** – sax

Jul 84.	(lp; as THOMAS THE IMPOSTER) **AN AFTERNOON IN COMPANY**		-
	– Autumn / The return to England / Auden / The Pyrenees / Verbier / The Rhur Valley / Hollow men / Savannah / Jericho 1 / Meditation / Oran / Aragon / Jericho 2 / Dignity / Mount Fuji / The end of the era.		
Feb 86.	(d-lp) (TWI 615) **THE OTHER MAN**		-
Jan 87.	(lp) (TWI 807) **16 YEARS OF ALCOHOL**		-

ARMOURY SHOW

was formed by **RICHARD JOBSON** – vocals + **RUSSELL WEBB** – bass / plus **JOHN McGEOGH** – guitar (ex-SIOUXSIE & THE BANSHEES, ex-MAGAZINE) / **JOHN DOYLE** – drums (ex-MAGAZINE) / **EVAN CHARLES** – keyboards (ex-COWBOYS INTERNATIONAL)

		Parlophone	Capitol
Aug 84.	(7") (R 6109) **CASTLES IN SPAIN. / INNOCENTS ABROAD**	69	-
	(12"+=) (12R 6109) – Is it a wonder.		
Jan 85.	(7") (R 6087) **WE CAN BE BRAVE AGAIN. / A FEELING**	66	-
	(12"+=) (12R 6087) – Catherine.		
Jul 85.	(7") (R 6098) **GLORY OF LOVE. / HIGHER THAN THE WORLD (instrumental)**		-
	(12"+=) (12R 6098) – ('A'part 2) / ('A')instrumental).		
Sep 85.	(lp/c) (ARM/TC-ARM 1) **WAITING FOR THE FLOODS**	57	-
	– Castles in Spain / Kyria / A feeling / Jungle of cities / We can be brave again / Higher than the world / Glory of love / Waiting for the floods / Sense of freedom / Sleep city sleep / Avalanche.		
Oct 85.	(7") (R 6079) **CASTLES IN SPAIN. / A GATHERING**		-
	(12"+=) (12R 6079) – Ring those bells.		
Jan 87.	(7"/12") (R/12R 6149) **LOVE IN ANGER. / TENDER IS THE NIGHT**	63	-
Apr 87.	(7") (R 6153) **NEW YORK CITY. / WHIRLWIND**		-
	(12"+=) (12R 6153) – ('A')versions).		

— Crumbled around mid'87, with . . .

RICHARD JOBSON

again tried solo career augmented by co-writer RUSSELL WEBB

		Parlophone	not iss.
Aug 88.	(7"/12") (R/12R 6181) **BADMAN. / THE HEAT IS ON**		-
	(cd-s+=) (CDR 6181) – Big fat city.		
Nov 88.	(cd/c/lp) (CD/TC+/PCS 7321) **BADMAN**		-
	– Badman / This thing caled love / Monkey's cry / The heat is on / Uptown – downtown / A boat called Pride / Angel / Fire. (cd+=) – Big fat city.		

— JOBSON, who was now a successful male model while also taking up TV work mainly interviews. Most people now know of him winning his battle against alcohol and epilepsy. In the late 80's, his marriage to TV presenter, Mariella Frostrup failed, although they remained very good friends. He subsequently went on to present late night TV shows including 'Hollywood Report'.

SLAUGHTER & THE DOGS

Formed: Manchester, England . . . 1976 by WAYNE BARRETT, MIKE ROSSI, HOWARD BATES and MAD MUFFET. Emerging from a fertile Manchester punk scene concentrated around the city's Electric Circus venue, SLAUGHTER AND THE DOGS were initially signed to local independent label, 'Rabid', through which they issued a debut single, 'CRANKED UP REALLY HIGH'. Signed to 'Decca' in the wake of the punk explosion, the band issued their one and only album, the provocatively titled 'DO IT DOG STYLE', in 1978. Featuring such enduring aggro anthems as 'WHERE HAVE ALL THE BOOT BOYS GONE' (their major label debut single), the record was a first-wave mini-classic played out with more than a passing nod to the proto-punk glam of The NEW YORK DOLLS (especially with regards to BARRETT's THUNDERS-like vocals!). One famous admirer, of course, was a young STEVEN MORRISSEY, auditioned but not taken on for the vacant role of lead singer after BARRETT's subsequent departure. With ROSSI eventually

taking over the post and future CULT man BILLY DUFFY added on guitar, the group re-emerged as SLAUGHTER (nothing to do with the American metal-boys!). When that name didn't work, they rather unadvisedly adopted the STUDIO SWEETHEARTS moniker before finally splitting after a brief period with BARRETT back in the fold. More often mentioned for the big name connections rather than their actual music, SLAUGHTER AND THE DOGS nevertheless remain one of the key players in the early punk scene.
• **Songwriters:** BARRETT-ROSSI except; QUICK JOEY SMALL (Kasenetz-Katz Singing Orchestral Circus) / I'M WAITING FOR THE MAN (Velvet Underground) / A HARD DAY'S NIGHT (Beatles). .
Album rating: DO IT DOG STYLE (*5) / BITE BACK (*4) / WHERE HAVE ALL THE BOOT BOYS GONE compilation (*6) / BEWARE OF . . . (*3) / ANTHOLOGY double compilation (*6)

WAYNE BARRETT – vocals / **MIKE ROSSI** – guitar / **HOWARD BATES** – bass / **MAD MUFFET** (b. BRIAN CRANFORD) – drums

Rabid   not iss.

Jun 77. (7") (TOSH 101) **CRANKED UP REALLY HIGH. / THE BITCH**

Decca   not iss.

Sep 77. (7") (FR/LF 13723) **WHERE HAVE ALL THE BOOT BOYS GONE. / YOU'RE A BORE**
Nov 77. (7") (FR 13743) **DAME TO BLAME. / JOHNNY T**
Feb 78. (7") (FR 13758) **QUICK JOEY SMALL. / COME ON BACK**
 – above featured MICK RONSON – guitar (ex-DAVID BOWIE)
May 78. (lp) (SKL 5292) **DO IT DOG STYLE**
 – Where have all the boot boys gone / Victims of the vampire / Boston babies / I'm waiting for the man / I'm mad / You're a bore / Quick Joey Small / Keep on trying / We don't care / Since you went away / Who are the mystery girls / Dame to blame. *(re-iss. 1989 colrd-lp on 'Damaged Goods'; FNARR 2) (<cd-iss. Mar00 on 'Captain Oi'; AHOYCD 131>)*

Rabid   not iss.

Dec 78. (lp) (HAT 23) **LIVE SLAUGHTER RABID DOGS (live)**
 (re-iss. Mar 89 on 'Receiver'; RRLP 109)

 —— **ED BANGER** (EDDIE GARRITY) – guitar (ex-NOSEBLEEDS) repl. WAYNE

T.J.M.   not iss.

Mar 79. (12"ep) (TJM 3) **IT'S ALRIGHT / EDGAR ALLEN POE. / TWIST & TURN / UFO**

D.J.M.   not iss.

Jun 79. (7") (DJS 10915) **I BELIEVE. (as "STUDIO SWEETHEARTS") / IT ISN'T ME**
Nov 79. (7") (DJS 10927) **YOU'RE READY NOW. / RUNAWAY**

SLAUGHTER

 —— **PHIL ROWLAND** – drums (ex-EATER) repl. MUFFET
 —— WAYNE BARRETT also returned to repl. BILLY DUFFY who joined THEATRE OF HATE
Feb 80. (7") (DJS 10936) **EAST SIDE OF TOWN. / ONE BY ONE**
Mar 80. (lp) (DJF 20566) **BITE BACK**
 – Now I know / What's wrong boy / Won't let go / All over now / She ain't gonna show / Heel in New York / Crashing out with Lucy / Chasing me / It's in the mind / East side of town / Don't wanna die. *(<cd-iss. Jun00 on 'Captain Oi'+=; AHOYCD 142>)* – I'm the one / One by one / What's wrong boy (live).
Jun 80. (7") (DJS 10945) **I'M THE ONE. / WHAT'S WRONG BOY? (live) / HELL IN NEW YORK**

SLAUGHTER & THE DOGS

 —— now without ED BANGER

Thrush   not iss.

Feb 83. (12"ep) (THRUSH 1) **HALF ALIVE**
 – Twist and turn / Cranked up really high (live) / Where have all the boot boys gone (live).

 —— split after above; BARRETT + ROSSI re-formed in the late 90's

Captain Oi   Knock Out

Oct 01. (cd) (AHOYCD 175) <KOCD 73> **BEWARE OF . . .**
 – Saturday night 'til Sunday morning / Welcome to our town / Blow / I got your number / Message from a ghost / A hard day's night / Hell in New York / Car thief / The rope around your neck / Schizophrenic / (Come on) Let's do it / Anthem for the kids. *(lp-iss.Apr02 on 'Knock Out'; KOLP 143-6)*

– compilations, etc. –

Jun 83. (lp) Thrush; (THRUSHLP 1) **THE WAY WE WERE**
Nov 88. (7",7"red or green) Damaged Goods; (FNARR 1) **WHERE HAVE ALL THE BOOT BOYS GONE. / YOU'RE A BORE / JOHNNY T**
May 89. (lp) Receiver; (RRLP 14) **LIVE AT THE FACTORY (live 1981)**
 – Now I know / Hell in New York / Runaway / Mystery girls / What's wrong boy? / You're ready now / Johnny T / Boston babies / All over now.
Jun 89. (lp) Link; (LINKLP 092) **SLAUGHTERHOUSE TAPES**
Feb 92. (cd/lp) Receiver; (RR CD/LP 151) **SHOCKING**
Mar 94. (cd) Receiver; (RRCD 183) **WHERE HAVE ALL THE BOOT BOYS GONE**
Sep 98. (cd) Captain Oi; (<AHOYCD 050>) **CRANKED UP REALLY HIGH**
Nov 00. (cd) Captain Oi; (<AHOYCD 154>) **THE PUNK SINGLES COLLECTION**
Oct 01. (d-cd) Castle; (<CMDDD 356>) **ANTHOLOGY**
Mar 02. (cd; split w/ 999) Step 1; (STEPCD 045) **THE SLAUGHTERHOUSE TAPES / THE CELLBLOCK TAPES**

SLITS

Formed: London, England . . . early 1977 as the foremost all-girl outfit on the punk scene (until BUDGIE joined that is) and initially comprising ARI UP (aka ARIANNA FOSTER), KATE KORUS, SUZI GUTSY and PALMOLIVE. By the time the group had secured a support slot on The CLASH's Spring 1977 tour, KORUS and GUTSY had been replaced by VIV ALBERTINE and TESSA POLLITT respectively, the band's infamously amateurish approach compensated by their bolshy hardline feminist attitude. Although they had two John Peel sessions under their belts, The SLITS didn't actually sign a deal until 1979, having turned down the 'Real' label (home to The HEARTBREAKERS and PRETENDERS) the previous year. In the event the not-so "TYPICAL GIRLS" signed with 'Island' and set to work on a debut album with reggae producer, Dennis Bovell, the aforementioned BUDGIE (PETER CLARK) coming in as a replacement for PALMOLIVE who departed midway through the recording sessions. A Top 30 hit upon its release in late '79, the seminal 'CUT' showcased ARI's distinctive vocal phrasing against a compelling backdrop of unorthodox tribal rhythms and raw guitar abrasion, the sleeve's cover shot of the lasses getting butt naked and muddy generating almost as much interest as the music. With BUDGIE decamping to SIOUXSIE & THE BANSHEES, BRUCE SMITH was recruited in his place and despite the presence of respected jazz trumpeter, DON CHERRY (father of NENEH), a dreadful untitled bootleg/jam affair did the band no favours. Much more enjoyable was the subsequent cover of John Holt's 'MAN NEXT DOOR', released as a single a couple of months later in the summer of 1980. A further single followed on the 'Human' label before The SLITS signed to 'C.B.S.' for a final disappointing patchy album, 'RETURN OF THE GIANT SLITS' (1981), the group disbanding in early '82. While SMITH joined Bristolian avant-funk collective RIP, RIG & PANIC, the remaining members (minus POLLITT) went on to be part of colossus ensemble, The NEW AGE STEPPERS. • **Songwriters:** Group compositions, except I HEARD IT THROUGH THE GRAPEVINE (Marvin Gaye). • **Trivia:** Early in 1978, they were sighted in the punk film, 'Jubilee'.
Album rating: CUT (*9) / UNTITLED (*1) / RETURN OF THE GIANT SLITS (*6) / IN THE BEGINNING collection (*4) / THE PEEL SESSIONS collection (*7)

ARI UP (b. ARIANNA FOSTER) – vocals / **VIVIEN ALBERTINE** – guitar (ex-FLOWERS OF ROMANCE) repl. KATE KORUS to KLEENEX (Feb77) / **TESSA POLLITT** – bass repl. SUZI GUTSY who formed The FLICKS. / **PALMOLIVE** – drums (ex-FLOWERS OF ROMANCE) was repl. (Oct78) by **BUDGIE** (b. PETER CLARK, 21 Aug'??, St.Helens, England) – percussion, drums (ex-BIG IN JAPAN, ex-SECRETS, etc)

Island   Antilles

Sep 79. (lp/c) (ILPS/ZC1 9573) <7072> **CUT**
 – Instant hit / So tough / Spend spend spend / Shoplifting / FM / Newtown / Ping pong affair / Love and romance / Typical girls / Adventures close to home. *(cd-iss. Apr90; IMCD 89) (cd re-mast.Oct00 +=; IMCD 275)* – I heard it through the grapevine / Liebe and romanza (slow version).
Sep 79. (7") (WIP 6505) **TYPICAL GIRLS. / I HEARD IT THROUGH THE GRAPEVINE**   60
 (12"+=) (12WIP 6505) – Typical girls (brink style) / Liebe and romanze.

 —— **BRUCE SMITH** – drums (of POP GROUP) repl. BUDGIE to SIOUXSIE & BANSHEES jazz-trumpeter **DON CHERRY** guested

Y – Rough Trade   not iss.

Mar 80. (7") (Y1 – RT 039) **IN THE BEGINNING THERE WAS RHYTHM. / (B-side by the Pop Group)**
May 80. (lp) (Y3LP) **UNTITLED (Y3LP)** (bootleg demo jam)
 – A boring life / Slime / Or what it is / No.1 enemy / Once upon a time in a living room / Bongos on the lawn / Face place / Let's do the split / Mosquitos / Vaseline / No more rock and roll for you.
Jun 80. (7") (Y4 – RT 044) **MAN NEXT DOOR. / MAN NEXT DOOR (dub version)**

 —— added guest **STEVE BERESFORD** – keyboards, guitar (of FLYING LIZARDS)

Human   not iss.

Nov 80. (7") (HUM 4) **ANIMAL SPACE. / ANIMAL SPACIER**

C.B.S.   Epic

1981. (12"m) **ANIMAL SPACE. / ANIMAL SPACIER / IN THE BEGINNING THERE WAS RHYTHM**
Aug 81. (7") (A 1498) **EARTHBEAT. / BEGIN AGAIN RHYTHM**
 (12"+=) (A13 1498) – Earthdub.
Oct 81. (lp/c) (CBS/40 85269) **RETURN OF THE GIANT SLITS**
 – Earthbeat / Or what it is? / Face place / Walkabout / Difficult fun / Animal space – Spacier / Improperly dressed / Life on Earth. *(free-7"w/ lp) (XPS 125)* – AMERICAN RADIO INTERVIEW (Winter 1980). / FACE DUB
Dec 81. (7") (49-02567> **EARTHBEAT. / OR WHAT IT IS?**

 —— Parted ways early 1982. BRUCE joined RIP, RIG & PANIC. All except TESSA were part of colossus band NEW AGE STEPPERS.

– compilations, others, etc. –

on 'Strange Fruit' unless otherwise mentioned
Feb 87. (12"ep) (SFPS 021) **THE PEEL SESSION** (27.9.77)
 – Love and romance / Vindictive / Newtown / Shoplifting.
Nov 88. (m-lp/m-cd) (SFPMA/+CD 207) **THE DOUBLE PEEL SESSIONS** (27.9.77 + 22.5.78)
 – (THE PEEL SESSION) + So tough / Instant hit / FM.
Aug 97. (cd) Jungle; (FREUDCD 057) / Cleopatra; <65> **IN THE BEGINNING (live)**
 – Vindictive / A boring life / Slime / New town / Love and romance / Shoplifting / Number one enemy / Number one enemy (acoustic) / In the beginning / New town / Man next door / I heard it through the grapevine / Typical girls / Fade away / In the beginning.

Pat SMEAR/RUTHENSMEAR (see under ⇒ GERMS)

Patti SMITH

Born: 31 Dec'46, Chicago, Illinois, USA. She started to write for New York magazine 'Rock' in 1969, having earlier being shipped around by her family between Paris and London. In the early 70's, PATTI began writing poetry full-time and met fellow rock-scribe, LENNY KAYE, who provided guitar accompaniment for her beat-poet monologues at readings/gigs. By 1971 she was writing for 'Creem' magazine and soon developed a professional musical partnership with playwright, SAM SHEPHERD. A prolific time for SMITH, come Christmas '72 she had two books of poetry, 'Witt' and '7th Heaven' in the stores and, after contributing to TODD RUNDGREN's 'A WIZARD, A TRUE STAR' album, he credited her for nicknaming him 'Runt'. RICHARD SOHL was recruited alongside SMITH and KAYE for a one-off single in 1974, 'HEY JOE / PISS FACTORY' on the small 'MER' label. A suitably caustic slice of proto-punk, it later gained airplay after being picked up by 'Sire' records. Meanwhile, SMITH completed the line-up of what would become The PATTI SMITH GROUP with IVAN KRAAL and JAY DEE DAUGHERTY, signing to 'Arista' and starting work on the 'HORSES' (1975) album with JOHN CALE producing. From the monochrome androgyny of the cover shot to the DIY three chord thrash which formed the bulk of the musical backing, the album was a blueprint for a generation of both American and British punk/new wave artists. Although SMITH's vocals were something of an acquired taste, her distinctive intonation was a perfect vehicle for the image rich symbolism of her free flowing lyrics. 'GLORIA' and 'LAND OF 1,000 DANCES' were transformed into wired, beat-inspired flashes of nervous energy, while quieter moments like the intro to 'REDONDO BEACH' and 'FREE MONEY' possessed a stark beauty. After this alternative tour de force, the follow-up, 'RADIO ETHIOPIA' (1976), came as something of a departure. Possessing a more straightforward hard-rock approach save for the chaotic feedback-drenched exploration of the title track, the album received mixed reviews. After SMITH survived breaking her neck after falling from the stage at a gig, it was to be another two years before the release of her next album. 'EASTER' (1978) was a confident comeback which moved even further into commercial rock territory without extinguishing the livewire spark that had made 'HORSES' so compelling. The record contained an unlikely collaboration with BRUCE SPRINGSTEEN, 'BECAUSE THE NIGHT', which saw SMITH breach the upper reaches of the singles charts on both sides of the Atlantic and propelled the album to similar success. 'WAVE' (1979) sounded slightly unfocused although it attained a higher chart placing Stateside than its predecessor. After a final tour in 1979, SMITH bowed out of the music business for domestic bliss with her new husband FRED 'SONIC' SMITH (ex-MC5). Together with her spouse, SOHL and DOUGHERTY, she recorded a low-key comeback album in 1988, 'DREAM OF LIFE', although tragedy struck in the 90's when both SOHL and her husband died from heart failure. With many artists namechecking her as an influence, SMITH recorded 'GONE AGAIN' (1996) amid a mini-renaissance. A tribute to FRED, it was filled with a sense of loss and yearning, echoing the intensity of her earlier work. 'PEACE AND NOISE' (1997), was surprisingly released only a year later than its predecessor and showed signs she could easily get back to her poetic past. Three years later, 'GUNG HO' (2000), delivered all sorts of emotions, from its opener, 'ONE VOICE' (a tribute to the work of Mother Teresa) to the heartbreaking 'LO AND BEHOLDEN', all marked a fine return to form for the former goddess of punk. • **Songwriters:** Lyrics PATTI, some music KAYE. Covered HEY JOE (Jimi Hendrix) / LAND OF A THOUSAND DANCES (Cannibal & The Headhunters) / MY GENERATION (The Who) / GLORIA (Them) / SO YOU WANNA BE A ROCK'N'ROLL STAR (Byrds) / 5-4-3-2-1 (Manfred Mann) / DOWNTOWN TRAIN (Tom Waits) / WICKED MESSENGER (Bob Dylan) / WHEN DOVES CRY (Prince). • **Trivia:** In 1974, she co-wrote with ex-boyfriend ALLEN LANIER, his groups' (BLUE OYSTER CULT) 'Career Of Evil'. Her albums were produced by JOHN CALE (1st) / JACK DOUGLAS (2nd) / JIMMY IOVINE (3rd) / TODD RUNDGREN (4th) / FRED SMITH and JIMMY IOVINE (1988).

Album rating: HORSES (*9) / RADIO ETHIOPIA (*7) / EASTER (*7) / WAVE (*6) / DREAM OF LIFE (*5) / GONE AGAIN (*6) / PEACE AND NOISE (*6) / GUNG HO (*6) / LAND (1975-2002) compilation (*8)

PATTI SMITH – vocals, poetry / with **LENNY KAYE** – guitar / **RICHARD SOHL** – piano

		not iss.	M.E.R.
Aug 74.	(7") <601> **HEY JOE. / PISS FACTORY** (UK-iss.Mar78 on 'Sire'; SRE 1009)	–	

— added **IVAN KRAL** – bass, guitar, piano / **JAY DEE DAUGHERTY** – drums

		Arista	Arista
Dec 75.	(lp) (ARTY 122) <4066> **HORSES** – Gloria / Redondo Beach / Birdland / Free money / Kimberly / Break it up / Land: Horses – Land of a thousand dances – La mer (de) / Elegie. (re-iss. Aug88 lp/c; 201/401/252-112) (cd re-iss. Jul96+=; 18827-2) – My generation (live).		47
Apr 76.	(7") (ARIST 47)<AS 0171> **GLORIA. / MY GENERATION (live)** (re-iss. 12"-Sep77; ARIST 12135)		
Oct 76.	(lp/c) (SPARTY/TCSPARTY 1001) <4097> **RADIO ETHIOPIA** – Ask the angels / Ain't it strange / Poppies / Pissing in the river / Pumping (my heart) / Distant fingers / Radio Ethiopia / Abyssinia. (re-iss. Aug88 lp/c/cd; 201/401/251-117) (re-iss. cd Jul96; 18825-2)		

— Her tour featured **LEIGH FOXX** – bass repl. SOHL. Others augmenting at the time **ANDY PALEY** (ex-ELLIOT MURPHY) + **BRUCE BRODY** – keyboards (ex-JOHN CALE)

PATTI SMITH GROUP

with KAYE, KRAAL, DAUGHERTY, BRODY + SOHL

Mar 78.	(7") (ARIST 181) <AS 0318> **BECAUSE THE NIGHT. / GOD SPEED**	5	13
Mar 78.	(lp/c) (SPARTY/TCSPARTY 1043) <4171> **EASTER** – Till victory / Space monkey / Because the night / Ghost dance / Babelogue / Rock'n'roll nigger / Privilege (set me free) / We three / 25th floor / High on rebellion / Easter. (re-iss. Jan83 on 'Fame' lp/c; FA/TCFA 3058) (re-iss. Aug88 lp/c/cd; 201/401/251-128) (re-iss. cd Jul96; 18826-2)	16	20
Jun 78.	(7") (ARIST 191) **PRIVILEGE (SET ME FREE). / ASK THE ANGELS** (12"+=) (ARIST 12191) – 25th floor (live) / Bablefield (live).	72	–

— **FRED 'Sonic' SMITH** – drums (ex-MC5) repl. DAUGHERTY to TOM VERLAINE

May 79.	(7") (ARIST 264) **FREDERICK. / FIRE OF UNKNOWN ORIGIN**	63	–
May 79.	(lp/c) (SPART/TCART 1086) <4221> **WAVE** – Frederick / Dancing barefoot / Citizen ship / Hymn / Revenge / So you want to be a rock'n'roll star / Seven ways of going / Broken flag / Wave. (re-iss. Aug88 lp/c/cd; 201/401/251-139) (re-iss. cd Jul96; 18829-2)	41	18
Jun 79.	(7") <AS 0427> **FREDERICK (live)**	–	90
Jul 79.	(7") (ARIST 281) **DANCING BAREFOOT. / 5-4-3-2-1 (live)**	–	–
Aug 79.	(7"m) <AS 0453> **SO YOU WANT TO BE A ROCK'N'ROLL STAR. / 5-4-3-2-1 / FIRE OF UNKNOWN ORIGIN**	–	–
Sep 79.	(7") (ARIST 291) **SO YOU WANT TO BE A ROCK'N'ROLL STAR. / FREDERICK (live)**		–

— PATTI retired Mar'80 with her new husband FRED SMITH to bring up children. BRUCE BRODY was another to join ex-TELEVISION singer TOM VERLAINE's band.

PATTI SMITH

re-appeared in 1988 with still **SOHL, DAUGHERTY & SONIC**

		Fierce	Fierce
Feb 88.	(7"m) (white label) **BRIAN JONES. / STOCKINGED FEET / JESUS CHRIST**		–
		Arista	Arista
Jul 88.	(7")<US-c-s> (109877) <AS1/CAS 9689> **PEOPLE HAVE THE POWER. / WILD LEAVES** (12"+=) (609877) <AD1 9688> – Where duty calls. (cd-s++=) (659877) – ('A'-album version).		
Jul 88.	(lp/c/cd) (209/409/259-172) <8453> **DREAM OF LIFE** – People have the power / Going under / Up there, down there / Paths that cross / Dream of life / Where duty calls / (I was) Looking for you / The Jackson song. (re-iss. cd.Apr92;) (cd re-iss. Jul96; 18828-2)	70	65

— RICHARD SOHL was to die from a cardiac arrest on 3 Jun'90. PATTI returned to reciting and recording her poetry in 1995. Now with some of her original group (**DAUGHERTY + KAYE**), **TONY SHANAHAN** – bass / **LUIS RESTO** – keyboards and on some **TOM VERLAINE** – guitar (ex-TELEVISION) / **OLIVER RAY** – guitars. Album featured guest spots from JOHN CALE, JEFF BUCKLEY and JANE SCARPANTONI – cello

Jul 96.	(cd/c) (74321 38474-2/-4) <18747> **GONE AGAIN** – Gone again / Beneath the Southern Cross / About a boy / My madrigal / Summer cannibals / Dead to the world / Wing / Ravens / Wicked messenger / Fireflies / Farewell reel.	44	55
Aug 96.	(cd-ep) (74321 40168-2) **SUMMER CANNIBALS / COME BACK LITTLE SHEEBA / GONE AGAIN (live) / PEOPLE HAVE THE POWER** (cd-ep) (74321 40299-2) – ('A'side) / People have the power (live) / Beneath the Southern cross / Come in my kitchen.		–

— **OLIVER RAY** ; repl. RESTO

Nov 97.	(cd/c) <(07822 18986-2/-4)> **PEACE AND NOISE** – Waiting underground / Whirl away / 1959 / Spell / Don't say nothing / Dead city / Blue poles / Death singing / Memento Mori / Last call.		Sep97
Mar 00.	(cd) <(07822 14618-2)> **GUNG HO** – One voice / Lo and beholden / Boy cried wolf / Persuasion / Gone pie / China bird / Glitter in their eyes / Strange messengers / Grateful / Upright come / New party / Libbie's song / Gung ho.		

– compilations, others, etc. –

Apr 83.	(7") Arista; (ARIST 513) **BECAUSE THE NIGHT. / GLORIA** (12") (ARIST 12513) – ('A'side) / Redondo beach / Dancing barefoot / Free money.		–
Jul 84.	(7") Old Gold; (OG 9458) **BECAUSE THE NIGHT. / GLORIA**		–
Sep 91.	(3xcd-box) R.C.A.; (354.226) **BOX SET** – (RADIO ETHIOPIA / HORSES / WAVE albums)		
Apr 02.	(cd) Arista; <(07822 14708-2)> **LAND (1975-2002)** – Dancing barefoot / Babelogue / Rock'n'roll nigger / Gloria / Pissing in a river / Free money / People have the power / Because the night / Frederick / Summer cannibals / Ghost dance / Ain't it strange / 1959 / Beneath the southern cross / Glitter in their eyes / Paths that cross / When doves cry. (free cd+=) – Piss factory (version) / Redondo beach (demo) / Distant fingers (demo) / 25th floor (live) / Come back little Sheba (live) / Wander I go (version) / Dead city (live) / Spell (live) / Wing (live) / Boy cried wolf (live) / Birdland (live) / Higher learning (live) / Notes to the future (live).		Mar02

t.v. SMITH (see under ⇒ ADVERTS)

SNATCH

Formed: Lower East Side, New York, USA ... 1976 by JUDY NYLON and PATTI PALLADIN, a pair of Noo Yoik proto-punks influenced by the pioneering work of PATTI SMITH. Having cut a number of demos, SNATCH were finally taken on by Bomp's GREG SHAW, who released the double-A sided 7", 'STANLEY' / 'I.R.T.' early the following year. Featuring an intro of which even LYDIA LUNCH would be proud, the former track was typical of the band's barebones, razor-wire R&B-punk with obligatory snotty vocals. UK distributor, 'Lightning', would later re-issue the record and go on to release a follow-up, 'ALL I WANT' / 'WHEN I'M BORED', while English ambient boffin, ENO, invited them to collaborate with him on the B-side ('R.A.F.') of his own 'King's Lead Hat'. British label, 'Fetish', would subsequently issue some unearthed recordings in the summer of 1980 as the 'SHOPPING FOR CLOTHES' EP, PALLADIN having already joined the FLYING LIZARDS. She would go on to work with JOHNNY THUNDERS, while her partner in crime, NYLON delivered her ADRIAN SHERWOOD-produced solo set, 'PAL JUDY', in '82. A belated retrospective of all SNATCH's material surfaced around a year later, an essential listen for anyone interested in the deepest roots of US DIY "No Wave", especially the femme-friendly variation.

Album rating: SNATCH compilation (*6) / Judy Nylon: PAL JUDY (*5)

JUDY NYLON – vocals / **PATTI PALLADIN** – vocals / with **KEITH PAUL** – guitar / **NICK PLYTAS** – piano / **BRUCE DOUGLAS** – bass / **JERRY NOLAN** – drums

		Lightning	Bomp
Feb 77.	(7") <BP 108> **STANLEY. / I.R.T.** (UK-iss.Jul78 on 'Lightning'; LIG 502)	-	
Jan 78.	(7") (LIG 006) **ALL I WANT. / WHEN I'M BORED**		-

—— Jan'78, were credited on ENO b-side of 'KINGS LEAD HAT' 45 with 'R.A.F.' on 'Polydor'; 2001 762).

—— PATTI PALLADIN moved to England and joined The FLYING LIZARDS. She later teamed up with JOHNNY THUNDERS (ex-Heartbreakers).

		Fetish	Fetish
Jul 80.	(12"ep) (FET 004) **SHOPPING FOR CLOTHES. / JOEY / RED ARMY**		-

—— finally split after above. DOUGLAS joined DECLINE AND FALL.

– compilations, etc. –

| Nov 83. | (lp) *Pandemonium;* (WITCH 1) **SNATCH** (demos & singles, etc) |

JUDY NYLON

with session people incl. GEORGE OBAN, CHRIS JOYCE and SEAN OLIVER

		Demon	not iss.
Feb 82.	(7") (D 1011) **CARLOTTA. / SLEEPLESS NIGHTS**		-

		On-U-Sound	R.O.I.R.
May 82.	(lp) (ONULP 16) <A-179> **PAL JUDY** – Information rain / Dateline Miami / Live in a lift / Jailhouse rock / Triai by fire / Slepless nights / Others / The dice / Room without a view. (cd-iss. Aug91 on 'R.O.I.R.'; same as US)		

—— virtually retired from music biz. An album 'BITE YOUR TONGUE' by a different indie SNATCH on Jul'93.

SNIVELLING SHITS

Formed: London, England ... summer 1977 by Zig Zag journalist GIOVANNI DADAMO. With the sound of 'Never Mind The Bollocks' LP probably ringing in his ears, GIO and various musicians (mainly from EDDIE & THE HOT RODS) set about recording the novelty-punk record, 'I CAN'T COME'. Released late in '77 by 'Ghetto Rockers' records, it sold reasonably well for a pure indie/punk record; it's now worth over £20. DADAMO was also the main man behind ARTHUR COMIX who surfaced early 1978 with the religious-ripping 'ISGODAMAN?' via the V/A punk band set, 'Streets'. The vocalist subsequently helped out The DAMNED, co-writing two of their best known turn-of-the-decade numbers, 'I Just Can't Be Happy Today' and 'There Ain't No Sanity Clause'. Towards the end of the 80's (and when the man was working at Notting Hill's Records & Tape Exchange), further cuts/demos were found and cleaned up (by DAVE GOODMAN) and released as a mini-set, 'I CAN'T COME'. Sadly, GIOVANNI was to die around the start of the millennium, leaving behind a brief legacy and a CD re-issue of the said collection.

Album rating: I CAN'T COME mini compilation (*6)

GIOVANNI DADAMO – vocals / **PETE MAKOWSKI** – guitar / **DAVE FUDGER** – guitar / **BARRY MYERS** – bass / **STEVE NICOL** – drums (of EDDIE & THE HOT RODS) / other members on recordings:- **STEVE LILLYWHITE** – bass / **ADE LILLYWHITE + LOU SALVONI + NICK RATBITE** – drums

		Ghetto Rockers	not iss.
Oct 77.	(7") (PRE 2) **TERMINAL STUPID. / I CAN'T COME**		-

—— DADAMO had another guise under the banner of ARTHUR COMIX and the hard-to-get 'ISGODAMAN?' 45, a record that found its way on to the 'Streets' V/A compilation for 'Beggars Banquet' in 1978

– compilations, etc. –

on 'Damaged Goods' unless mentioned otherwise

| Jan 89. | (brown m-lp) (FNARR 3) **I CAN'T COME** – I can't come / Terminal stupid / Isgodaman? / Crossroads / I wanna be your biro / Et moi moi et moi / Bring me the head of Yukio Mishima / Only 13. (re-iss. 1990 on red or blue vinyl) (<cd-iss. Oct02 +=; DAMGOOD 205CD>) – There ain't no sanity claus / Isgodaman? (demo) / Terminal stupid (demo) / I can't come (demo). |
| Jul 89. | (7"m/7"brown-box) (FNARR 4/+B) **ISGODAMAN? / TERMINAL STUPID / I CAN'T COME** (above tracks were actually the original demos) |

SOFT BOYS (see under ⇒ HITCHCOCK, Robyn)

SONICS

Formed: Tacoma, Washington, USA ... 1964 by brothers LARRY and ANDY PARYPA, ROB LIND, GERRY ROSLIE and BOB BENNETT. Signing to the local 'Etiquette' label, they released their debut single, 'KEEP A KNOCKIN'. The record's B-side, 'THE WITCH', was a pioneering garage-punk classic which gained the band some degree of notoriety and a cult following in the Pacific Northwest. A further string of 45's, mostly covers, failed to break the band nationally, only 'PSYCHO' achieving a modicum of success locally. Their third album, 'INTRODUCING THE SONICS' (1967) was their first release for a major label, although the band subsequently split, only to reform a few times in the 70's. At the turn of the decade, with new wave still very much in vogue, The SONICS re-formed for a one-off album, 'SINDERELLA'.

Album rating: HERE ARE THE SONICS (*8) / THE SONICS BOOM (*6) / INTRODUCING THE SONICS (*5) / EXPLOSIVES (*4) / SINDERELLA (*5) / PSYCHO-SONIC compilation (*6)

GERRY ROSLIE – vocals, organ, piano / **ROB LIND** – sax, harmonica / **LARRY PARYPA** – lead guitar, vocals / **ANDY PARYPA** – bass, vocals / **BOB BENNETT** – drums

		not iss.	Etiquette
1964.	(7") <11> **THE WITCH. / KEEP A KNOCKIN'**	-	
1964.	(7") <16> **BOSS HOSS. / THE HUSTLER**	-	
1964.	(7") <18> **SHOT DOWN. / DON'T BE AFRAID OF THE DARK**	-	
Nov 64.	(7") <22> **DON'T BELIEVE IN CHRISTMAS. / (b-side by The WAILERS)**	-	
Feb 65.	(7") <23> **LOUIE LOUIE. / CINDERELLA**	-	
Mar 65.	(lp) <024> **HERE ARE THE SONICS** – The witch / Do you love me / Roll over Beethoven / Boss hog / Dirty robber / Have love will travel / Psycho / Money / Walkin' the dog / Night time is the right time / Strychnine / Good golly Miss Molly. (UK-iss.Aug86 on 'Fan Club'; FC 017) (cd-iss. Feb88 +=; FC 017CD) – (below singles). (cd re-iss. Jun99 on 'Norton'+=; CNW 903) – Keep a knockin' / Don't believe in Christmas / Santa Claus / The village idiot.	-	
1966.	(lp) <027> **THE SONICS BOOM** – Cinderella / Don't be afraid of the dark / Skinny Minny / Let the good times roll / Don't you just know it / Jenny Jenny / He's waiting / Louie Louie / Since I feel for you / Hitch hike / It's alright / Shot down / Psycho (live) / The witch (live). (UK-iss.Jan87 on 'Fan Club'; FC 020) (re-iss. Jan99 on 'Norton'; NW 905) (cd-iss. Jun99; CNW 905)	-	

		not iss.	Jerden
1966.	(7") <809> **LOVE LIGHTS. / YOU GOT YOUR HEAD ON BACKWARDS**	-	
1966.	(7") <810> **THE WITCH. / LIKE NO OTHER MAN**	-	
1966.	(7") <811> **PSYCHO. / MAINTAINING MY COOL**	-	
1967.	(lp) <JR 7007> **INTRODUCING THE SONICS** (re-iss. Aug00 on 'Beatrocket'; BR 114)	-	

—— **JIM BRADY** – vocals, repl. LIND

		not iss.	Piccadilly
1967.	(7") <244> **LOST LOVE. / ANY WAY THE WIND BLOWS**	-	

		not iss.	Uni
1967.	(7") <55039> **ANY WAY THE WIND BLOWS. / LOST LOVE**	-	

		not iss.	Buckshot
1973.	(lp) <001> **EXPLOSIVES**	-	

		not iss.	Burdette
1975.	(7") <106> **DIRTY OLD MAN. / BAMA LAMA BAMA LOO**	-	

—— disbanded after above. Re-formed in the 80's with **GARY ROSLIE + GEORGE WALLACE** – guitar, vocals / **GEORGE CROWE** – bass / **MICHAEL GONE** – guitar / **BILL SHAW** or **JAMES N. BUTSCH** – drums / **LES KINGBEARD** – sax

		not iss.	Bomp
1980.	(lp) <4011> **SINDERELLA** (UK cd-iss. Jan97; BCD 4011)	-	

– compilations, etc. –

1977.	(lp) *S.R.T.;* <77079> **SONICS**	-	
1979.	(7") *Great Northwest;* <702> **THE WITCH. / BAMA LAMA BAMA LOO**		
1979.	(lp) *First;* <7715> **ORIGINAL NORTHWEST PUNK**		
1980.	(lp) *First;* <7719> **UNRELEASED**		
Nov 87.	(lp) *Fan Club;* (FC 033) **LIVE FANZ ONLY**		-
Mar 88.	(lp) *Line;* (LILP 400387) **FULL FORCE (THE BEST OF THE SONICS)**		-
Jun 88.	(lp) *Bam Caruso;* (KIRI 104) **PSYCHO**		-
Mar 93.	(cd) *Big Beat;* (CDWIKD 115) **PSYCHO-SONIC** – The witch / Do you love me / Roll over Beethoven / Boss Hoss / Dirty robber / Have love will travel / Psycho / Money (that's what I want) / Walking the dog / Night time is the right time / Strychnine / Good golly Miss Molly / The hustler / Psycho (live) / Sinderella / Don't be afraid of the dark / Skinny Minnie / Let the good times roll / Don't you just know it / Jenny Jenny / He's waitin' / Louie Louie / Since I fell for you / Hitch hike / It's all right / Shot down / Keep a knockin' / The witch (live) / The witch (version 2).		-

Oct 96.	(cd) *Jerden;* <(JRCD 7007)> **MAINTAINING MY COOL**		
Oct 96.	(cd) *Jerden;* <(JRCD 7009)> **FIRE AND ICE – THE LOST TAPES**		
Oct 99.	(7") *Norton;* (813) **PSYCHO. / HAVE LOVE WILL TRAVEL**		-
Oct 99.	(7") *Norton;* (816) **BOSS HOG. / THE HUSTLER**		-
Oct 99.	(7") *Norton;* (819) **LOUIE LOUIE. /**		-

SPIZZ

Formed: London, England ... August '77 by one-man DIY punk act, SPIZZ (surname, SPIERS), who first entertained an audience at that summer's Barbarellas Punk Festival. A few months later, SPIZZ 77 (his new group name at the time), hired the services of guitarist PETE PETROL and subsequently became the first act to sign for Geoff Travis' 'Rough Trade' label having been playlisted on the John Peel show. In the first of many name changes, the outfit released their first two maxi-singles, '6,000 CRAZY' and 'COLD CITY', towards the end of '78 under the SPIZZ OIL moniker. Both were 2-minute gems, proving that punk-rock was best sampled stripped down to its bare bones, the futuristic lyrics marking SPIZZ out from the bulk of his "New Wave" contemporaries. The following year saw the project expand into a full band set-up (going under the name SPIZZENERGI) with the addition of MARK COALFIELD, JIM SOLAR and BRIAN B. BENZINE. Boasting a beefed-up sound built around bass and plink-plonk keyboards, SPIZZ's third single, 'SOLDIER, SOLDIER' was backed up by a spikey version of Roxy Music's 'VIRGINIA PLAIN'. The space theme continued as the man went "Warp Factor 2" on the classic punk anthem, 'WHERE'S CAPTAIN KIRK?', even putting in his best BUDDY HOLLY on speed impression to fill out the chorus line. The new decade saw the birth of ATHLETICO SPIZZ '80, the band's most successful incarnation to date. A goodbye 45 for 'Rough Trade', the double-A sided 'NO ROOM' / 'SPOCK'S MISSING', suggested that SPIZZ had finally located his vocal chords. Almost immediately, the punk startroopers appeared on 'A&M' with the single, 'HOT DESSERTS' and debut album, 'DO A RUNNER', the latter surprisingly denting the UK Top 30. However, the album fell short of expectations and for many fans the SPIZZ spark had fizzled out. Obviously running out of ideas, the man (alongside SOLAR and SNARE) returned in 1981 as The SPIZZLES, the new moniker displaying almost as much of a lack of imagination as the accompanying album, 'SPIKEY DREAM FLOWERS'. Looking to regain his indie credibility, he resurrected the SPIZZENERGI moniker (Mk.2, that is) and returned to 'Rough Trade', although two singles, 'WORK' and 'JUNGLE FEVER', were woefully short of requirements. SPIZZ sensibly retired from the scene for almost five years, eventually staging another comeback attempt when he revamped his most famous three minutes, 'WHERE'S CAPTAIN KIRK?', as a solo artist in '87.

Album rating: DO A RUNNER (*6) / SPIKEY DREAM FLOWERS (*4) / SPIZZ HISTORY compilation (*7)

SPIZZ OIL

SPIZZ (b. SPIERS) – vocals, keyboards, guitar, etc / **PETE PETROL** (b. HYDE) – guitar

		Rough Trade	not iss.
Oct 78.	(7"m) *(RTS 01)* **6,000 CRAZY. / 1989 / FIBRE**		-
Dec 78.	(7"m) *(RTS 02)* **COLD CITY / RED AND BLACK. / SOLARISATION (SHUN) / PLATFORM 3**		-

SPIZZENERGI

added **MARK COALFIELD** – keyboards / **JIM SOLAR** – bass / **BRIAN B. BENZINE** – drums

Sep 79.	(7") *(RTS 03)* **SOLDIER, SOLDIER. / VIRGINIA PLAIN**		-
Dec 79.	(7") *(RTS 04)* **WHERE'S CAPTAIN KIRK? / AMNESIA**		-

ATHLETICO SPIZZ '80

DAVE SCOTT – guitar (ex-BANK OF DRESDEN) repl. PETROL who joined REPETITION

Jun 80.	(7") *(RTS 05)* **NO ROOM. / SPOCK'S MISSING**		-

C.P. SNARE (b. CLIVE PARKER) – drums; repl. BENZINE

		A&M	A&M
Jul 80.	(7") *(AMS 7550)* **HOT DESSERTS. / LEGAL PROCEEDINGS**		-
Jul 80.	(lp) *(AMLE 68514)* **DO A RUNNER**	27	-
	– Touched / New species / Intimate / Effortless / European heroes / Energy / Red and black / Rhythm inside / Person impersonator / Clocks are big / Airships.		

LU EDMUNDS – drums (ex-DAMNED, etc) repl. SCOTT

Oct 80.	(7") *(AMS 7566)* **CENTRAL PARK. / CENTRAL PARK (Dr. & Nurses dub version)**		-

SPIZZLES

SPIZZ, SOLAR + SNARE

Feb 81.	(7") *(AMS 8107)* **RISK. / MELANCHOLY**		-
Apr 81.	(lp) *(AMLE 68253)* **SPIKEY DREAM FLOWERS**		-
	– Brainwashing time / Five year mission / Dangers of living / Robots holiday / Soldier soldier / Risk / Central Park / Scared / Melancholy.		
Apr 81.	(7") *(AMS 8124)* **DANGERS OF LIVING. / SCARED**		-

CLIVE (C.P.) joined BIG COUNTRY on a temp. basis

SPIZZENERGI 2

		Rough Trade	not iss.
Feb 82.	(7") *(RT 096)* **WORK. / MEGACITY III**		-
Jun 82.	(7") *(RT 108)* **JUNGLE FEVER. / MEANING**		-

retired for half a decade

SPIZZ

returned in solo form 1987 with a re-working of his old classic

added **MARK FERDA** – guitar

		Hobo Railway	not iss.
Sep 87.	(7") *(HOBO 001)* **WHERE'S CAPTAIN KIRK? / LIVING IS BETTER WITH FREEDOM**		-
	(12"+=) *(HOBO12 001)* – ('A'extended).		

		Plastic Head	not iss.
Nov 88.	(12") *(PLASPOP 2)* **LOVE ME LIKE A ROCKET. /**		-

SPIZZ's career again fizzled out

– compilations, etc. –

Nov 83.	(lp) *Rough Trade;* (ROUGHSO 1) **SPIZZ HISTORY** (compilation of singles, etc)		-
	(above was scheduled for release in March '82)		
Feb 87.	(12"ep) *Strange Fruit;* (SFPS 022) **THE PEEL SESSIONS** (7.8.78) (early material)		-
	– Cold city / 6,000 crazy / Pure noise / Alien language / Protect from heat / Platform 3 / Switched off.		
Mar 94.	(cd; as SPIZZ ENERGI) *Damaged Goods;* (DAMGOOD 36) **UNHINGED**		-
	– Soldier soldier / Where's Captain Kirk? / Spock's missing / We want the world / Central park / Mega city 3 / Energy crisis / Brainwashing time / Hot desserts / Media messiah / Angel baby / 6000 crazy / Platform: 3 / Fibre / Love me like a rocket / Scared.		
May 96.	(cd) *Cherry Red;* (CDMRED 130) **SPIZZ NOT DEAD SHOCK: A DECADE OF SPIZZ HISTORY 1978-1988**		-
	– No room / Red & black / Where's Captain Kirk? / Spock's missing / Soldier soldier / Mega city 3 / Jungle fever / Central park / Work / Amnesia / The meaning / Virginia plain / 6000 crazy / Cold city / 1989 / Platform: 3 / Solarisation (shun) / Pure noise – Alien language – P.F.H. / On my own / Where's Captain Kirk? / Living is better with freedom / Three lions in the sky. (re-iss. Sep99; same)		
May 02.	(cd; as SPIZZ ENERGI) *Cherry Red;* <(CDMRED 212)> **WHERE'S CAPTAIN KIRK? – THE VERY BEST OF SPIZZ ENERGI**		

SQUEEZE

Formed: Deptford, South London, England ... March '74 by CHRIS DIFFORD and GLENN TILBROOK, the pair initially forming a writing partnership whereby the former penned the lyrics with the latter writing the music. Their genius was subsequently incorporated into a group format as the pair recruited ace pianist, JOOLS HOLLAND, bassist HARRY KAKOULLI and drummer PAUL GUNN, forming SQUEEZE in the process. Early 1977 saw the group's vinyl debut on the independent 'B.T.M.' label with the mock-Egyptian new wave pop/rock of 'TAKE ME I'M YOURS'. Despite the single being subsequently withdrawn, the group replaced GUNN with GILSON LAVIS and proceeded to release the JOHN CALE-produced 'PACKET OF THREE' EP on the 'Deptford Fun City' label. This duly attracted the attentions of 'A&M', keen to get in on the new wave act after their abortive signing of the SEX PISTOLS earlier that year. Immediate Top 20 chart success came with the re-release of 'TAKE ME..', an eponymous debut surfacing soon after. With the addition of JOHN BENTLEY on bass as a replacement for the departing KAKOULLI, the group narrowly missed No.1 in Spring '79 with the cockney wide-boy rap of 'COOL FOR CATS', a similarly titled follow-up album almost breaking the Top 40. The record consolidated the growing reputation of the DIFFORD/TILBROOK songwriting axis; their sagely observed, often darkly amusing social commentary drew inevitable comparisons with prime RAY DAVIES, definitely more accurate than the fanciful LENNON & McCARTNEY references. 'UP THE JUNCTION' was a perfect example, a compelling, hard-bitten tale of love on the breadline leading to broken-hearted disillusionment, a swooning, deceptively melancholy keyboard refrain holding the whole thing together. The song clearly struck a chord in the populace at large, SQUEEZE once again coming within a whisker of No.1. 'ARGYBARGY' (1980) gave the group their first Top 40 album, although the comparatively lowly placings afforded SQUEEZE's long players never really reflected the enduring quality of the songs contained within. Tracks like 'PULLING MUSSELS (FROM THE SHELL)', a brilliant slice of pop genius featuring a rollicking piano break courtesy of the illustrious HOLLAND. The latter left soon after to follow his boogie-woogie muse with JOOLS HOLLAND AND THE MILLIONAIRES and more famously, to present Channel 4's legendary music show, 'The Tube', alongside a young Paula Yates. Finding a replacement in respected vocalist/pianist, PAUL CARRACK (ex-ACE, ex-FRANKIE MILLER etc.), SQUEEZE cut their most successful album to date, 'EAST SIDE STORY' (1981). Co-produced by ELVIS COSTELLO, the album had a rootsier feel, CARRACK's COCKER-esque vocals gracing the grittily soulful 'TEMPTED', while the poignant 'LABELLED WITH LOVE' proved SQUEEZE could 'do' country better than most country artists. The latter song (Top 5) marked the end of their reign as a singles band, however, with the evocative 'BLACK COFFEE IN BED'

SQUEEZE (cont)

not even breaching the Top 40. By this point CARRACK had left for a solo career, DON SNOW brought in for a final, patchy album, 'SWEETS FROM A STRANGER' (1982). Though the group were at the height of their popularity, creatively they were beginning to stall and wisely decided to quit while they were still on top. Later that year, the compilation, 'THE SINGLES – 45 AND UNDER', brought the era neatly to a close, a seminal record (no household is complete without a copy!) illustrating why SQUEEZE have aged better than many "new wave" bands of the era. This wasn't the end, though, and after a solo 'DIFFORD & TILBROOK' (1984) album, the pair reunited with HOLLAND, recruiting KEITH WILKINSON on bass. A new album, 'COSI FAN TUTTI FRUTTI' appeared in summer '85, although they didn't really recapture anything resembling the old magic until 'BABYLON AND ON' (1987). That album gave SQUEEZE their first UK Top 20 hit in years with 'HOURGLASS', as well as some belated US chart action, the single reaching No.15 in the States while the album made the Top 40. 'FRANK' (1989) failed to capitalise on the momentum and SQUEEZE were subsequently dealt a double blow when HOLLAND left once again to concentrate on TV work and A&M finally let the band go. The band soldiered on, releasing a sole album, the acclaimed 'PLAY' (1991), for 'Reprise' before eventually regrouping with CARRACK and re-signing with 'A&M' for a further couple of 90's albums, 'SOME FANTASTIC PLACE' (1993) and 'RIDICULOUS' (1995). While the latter set featured at least a handful of bonafide DIFFORD/TILBROOK gems, 'DOMINO' (1998) was something of a career low. If the staleness of the record suggested the writing partnership was past its sell-by date, then 'THE INCOMPLETE GLENN TILBROOK' (2001) offered an opportunity to see what one half of it could achieve on their own. Despite having decided to record alone due to a disagreement over touring rather than writing, TILBROOK grabbed the bull by the proverbial horns nevertheless, turning out a consummately crafted, often charming effort that proved he could go it alone and then some. Although there were contributions from the likes of RON SEXSMITH and AIMEE MANN, the record had TILBROOK's trademarks stamped all over it. Although lyrics were traditionally DIFFORD's bag, TILBROOK proved he was no slouch when it came to wordsmithery. • **Songwriters:** Mostly DIFFORD & TILBROOK compositions, and some by CARRACK who joined late 1980. Covered END OF THE CENTURY (Blur).

Album rating: SQUEEZE (*6) / COOL FOR CATS (*7) / ARGYBARGY (*8) / EAST SIDE STORY (*7) / SWEETS FROM A STRANGER (*4) / THE SINGLES – 45 AND UNDER compilation (*8) / DIFFORD & TILBROOK (*5; as Difford & Tilbrook) / COSI FAN TUTTI FRUTTI (*6) / BABYLON AND ON (*5) / FRANK (*4) / A ROUND AND A BOUT early live (*3) / PLAY (*5) / GREATEST HITS compilation (*8) / SOME FANTASTIC PLACE (*6) / RIDICULOUS (*5) / DOMINO (*5) / THE BIG SQUEEZE – THE VERY BEST OF SQUEEZE compilation (*8)

CHRIS DIFFORD (b. 4 Nov'54) – vocals, guitar / **GLENN TILBROOK** (b.31 Aug'57) – vocals, guitar / **JOOLS HOLLAND** (b.JULIAN, 24 Jan'58) – keyboards / **HARRY KAKOULLI** – bass / **PAUL GUNN** – drums (below 45 withdrawn from release)

	B.T.M.	not iss.
Jan 77. (7"; w-drawn) *(SBT 107)* **TAKE ME I'M YOURS. / NO DISCO KID, NO**	-	-

— **GILSON LAVIS** (b.27 Jun'51) – drums (ex-MUSTARD) repl. GUNN

	Deptford Fun City	not iss.
Aug 77. (7"ep,12"ep) *(DFC 01)* **PACKET OF THREE** – Cat on a wall / Back track / Night ride. *(re-iss. Nov79 12"ep; same)*		-

	A&M	A&M
Feb 78. (7"/12") *(AMS/+P 7335)* **TAKE ME, I'M YOURS. / NIGHT NURSE**	19	
Mar 78. (lp/c) *(AMLH/CAM 68465) <4687>* **SQUEEZE** – Sex master / Bang bang / Strong in reason / Wild sewerage tickles Brazil / Out of control / Take me, I'm yours / The call / Model / Remember what / First thing wrong / Hesitation (rool Britania) / Get smart. *(re-iss. Mar82 lp/c; AMID/CMID 122)*		
May 78. (7",7"green) *(AMS 7360)* **BANG BANG. / ALL FED UP**	49	-

— **JOHN BENTLEY** (b.16 Apr'51) – bass; repl. KAKOULLI who went solo (he released an album, 'EVEN WHEN I'M NOT', in 1980 and subsequently released a handful of singles in the first half on the 80's)

Nov 78. (7") *(AMS 7398)* **GOODBYE GIRL. / SAINTS ALIVE**	63	-
Mar 79. (7",7"pale pink,7"pink,7"red/12"pink) *(AMS/+P 7426)* **COOL FOR CATS. / MODEL**	2	-
Apr 79. (lp/c) *(AMLH/CAM 68503) <4759>* **COOL FOR CATS** – Slap and tickle / Revue / Touching me, touching you / It's not cricket / It's so dirty / The knack / Hop, skip and jump / Up the junction / Hard to find / Slightly drunk / Goodbye girl / Cool for cats. *(cd-iss. Mar91; CDMID 131)*	45	
May 79. (7",7"lilac) *(AMS 7444)* **UP THE JUNCTION. / IT'S SO DIRTY**	2	-
Jun 79. (7") *<2168>* **SLIGHTLY DRUNK. / GOODBYE GIRL**	-	
Aug 79. (7",7"red) *(AMS 7466)* **SLAP AND TICKLE. / ALL'S WELL**	24	-
Nov 79. (7",7"white) *(AMS 7495)* **CHRISTMAS DAY. / GOING CRAZY**		
Jan 80. (7",7"clear) *(AMS 7507)* **ANOTHER NAIL IN MY HEART. / PRETTY THING**	17	-
Feb 80. (7") *<2229>* **IF I DIDN'T LOVE YOU. / PRETTY ONE**	-	
Feb 80. (lp/c) *(AMLH/CAM 64802) <4802>* **ARGYBARGY** – Pulling mussels (from the shell) / Another nail in my heart / Separate beds / Misadventure / I think I'm go go / Farfisa beat / Here comes that feeling / Vicky Verky / If I didn't love you / Wrong side of the Moon / There at the top.	32	71
Apr 80. (7",7"red) *(AMS 7523)* **PULLING MUSSELS (FROM THE SHELL). / WHAT THE BUTLER SAW**	44	-
Jun 80. (7") *<2247>* **PULLING MUSSELS (FROM THE SHELL). / PRETTY ONE**	-	
Sep 80. (7"m) *<2263>* **ANOTHER NAIL IN MY HEART. / GOING CRAZY / WHAT THE BUTLER SAW** *<re-iss. Sep82>*	-	

— **PAUL CARRACK** (b. Apr'51, Sheffield, England) – keyboards (ex-ACE, ex-FRANKIE MILLER, ex-ROXY MUSIC) repl. JOOLS who formed his own MILLIONAIRES

Apr 81. (7") *(AMS 8129)* **IS THAT LOVE. / TRUST**	35	-
May 81. (lp/c) *(AMLH/CAM 64854) <4854>* **EAST SIDE STORY** – In quintessence / Someone else's heart / Tempted / Piccadilly / There's no tomorrow / A woman's world / Is that love / F-hole / Labelled with love / Someone else's bell / Mumbo jumbo / Vanity fair / Messed around. *(cd-iss. Jan87; CDA 3253)*	19	44
Jul 81. (7") *(AMS 8147)* **TEMPTED. / YAP YAP YAP** (free 5"w.a.) **ANOTHER NAIL IN MY HEART. / IF I DIDN'T LOVE YOU**	40	-
Jul 81. (7") *<2345>* **TEMPTED. / TRUST**	-	49
Sep 81. (7") *(AMS 8166)* **LABELLED WITH LOVE. / SQUABS ON FORTY FAB**	4	
Oct 81. (7") *<2377>* **MESSED AROUND. / YAP YAP YAP**	-	

— **DON SNOW** (b.13 Jan'57, Kenya) – keyboards (ex-VIBRATORS, ex-SINCEROS) repl. CARRACK (now solo)

Apr 82. (7",7"pic-d) *(AMS 8219) <2424>* **BLACK COFFEE IN BED. / THE HUNT**	51	Jul82
Apr 82. (12") *<2413>* **WHEN THE HANGOVER STRIKES. / I'VE RETURNED**	-	
May 82. (lp/c) *(AMLH/CAM 64899) <4899>* **SWEETS FROM A STRANGER** – Out of touch / I can't hold on / Points of view / Stranger than the stranger on the shore / Onto the dance floor / When the hangover strikes / Black coffee in bed / I've returned / Tongue like a knife / His house her home / The very last dance / The elephant ride.	37	32
Jul 82. (7",7"pic-d) *(AMS 8237)* **WHEN THE HANGOVER STRIKES. / THE ELEPHANT RIDE**		-
Oct 82. (7") *(AMS 8259) <2518>* **ANNIE GET YOUR GUN. / SPANISH GUITAR**	43	Feb83
Nov 82. (lp/c) *(AMLH/CAM 68552) <4922>* **SINGLES – 45 AND UNDER** (compilation) – Take me I'm yours / Goodbye girl / Cool for cats / Up the junction / Slap and tickle / Another nail in my heart / Pulling mussels (from the shell) / Tempted / Is that love / Labelled with love / Black coffee in bed / Annie get your gun. *(cd-iss. Dec84; CDA 64922)*	3	47
Dec 82. (7") *<2534>* **ANOTHER NAIL IN MY HEART. / GOING CRAZY – WHAT THE BUTLER SAW**	-	

— Split at same time of compilation.

DIFFORD & TILBROOK

— carried on as duo, augmented by **KEITH WILKINSON** (b.24 Sep'54, Southfield, England) – bass / + other musicians

Jun 84. (7"/ext.12") *(AM/+X 193)* **LOVE'S CRASHING WAVES. / WITHIN THESE WALLS OF WITHOUT YOU**	57	-
Jun 84. (lp/c) *(AMLX/CXM 64985) <4985>* **DIFFORD & TILBROOK** – Action speaks faster / Love's crashing waves / Picking up the pieces / On my mind tonight / Man for all seasons / Hope fell down / Wagon train / You can't hurt the girl / Tears for attention / The apple tree.	47	55
Jun 84. (7") *<2648>* **PICKING UP THE PIECES. / WITHIN THESE WALLS OF WITHOUT YOU**	-	
Oct 84. (7"/12") *(AM/+X 219)* **HOPE FELL DOWN. / ACTION SPEAKS FASTER**		-

SQUEEZE

— re-formed '78 line-up except **KEITH WILKINSON** – bass (- HARRY)

Jun 85. (7"/12") *(AM/+Y 255)* **LAST TIME FOREVER. / SUITE FROM FIVE STRANGERS**	45	
Aug 85. (lp/c/cd) *(AMLH/AMC/CDA 5085) <5085>* **COSI FAN TUTTI FRUTTI** – Bang bang / By your side / King George Street / I learnt how to pray / Last time forever / No place like home / Heartbreakin' world / Hits of the year / Break my heart / I won't ever go drinking again.	31	57
Sep 85. (7") *<2776>* **HITS OF THE YEAR. / THE FORTNIGHT SAGA**	-	
Sep 85. (7") *(AM 277)* **NO PLACE LIKE HOME. / THE FORTNIGHT SAGA** (12"+=) *(AMY 277)* – Last time forever.		
Nov 85. (7") *(AM 291)* **HEARTBREAKING WORLD. / BIG BANG** (10"+=) *(AMY 291)* – Tempted (live) / By your side (live).		
Apr 86. (7") *(AM 306)* **KING GEORGE STREET. / LOVE'S CRASHING WAVES (live)** (12"+=) *(AMY 306)* – Up the junction (live).		

— added **ANDY METCALFE** – keyboards (ex-SOFT BOYS)

Aug 87. (7") *(AM 400) <2967>* **HOURGLASS. / WEDDING BELLS** (12"+=) *(AMY 400)* – Splitting into three.	16	15
Sep 87. (lp/c/cd) *(<AMA/AMC/CDA 5161>)* **BABYLON AND ON** – Hourglass / Footprints / Tough love / The prisoner / 853-5937 / In today's room / Trust me to open my mouth / Striking matches / Cigarette of a single man / Who are you? / The waiting game / Some Americans.	14	36
Sep 87. (7") *(AM 412)* **TRUST ME TO OPEN MY MOUTH. / TAKE ME, I'M YOURS (live)** (12"+=) *(AMY 412)* – Black coffee in bed (live).	72	
Nov 87. (7") *(AM 420)* **THE WAITING GAME. / LAST TIME FOREVER** (12"+=) *(AMY 420)* – The prisoner.		
Dec 87. (7") *<2994>* **853-5937. / TAKE ME I'M YOURS (live)**	-	32
Jan 88. (7"/ext.12") *(AM/+Y 426)* **853-5937. / TOUGH LOVE**		-
Apr 88. (7") *<3021>* **FOOTPRINTS. / BLACK COFFEE IN BED (live)**	-	
Jun 88. (7") *(AM 450)* **FOOTPRINTS. / STRIKING MATCHES (INSTANT BUFF)** (ext.12"+=) *(AMY 450)* – In today's room.		

— Reverted back to 5-piece when METCALFE departed.

| Sep 89. (7") *(AM 350) <1457>* **IF IT'S LOVE. / FRANK'S BAG** (12"+=/cd-s+=) *(AMY/CDEE 350)* – Vanity fair (piano version). | | |
| Sep 89. (lp/c/cd) *(<AMA/AMC/CDA 5278>)* **FRANK** | 58 | |

– Frank / If it's love / Peyton Place / Rose I said / Slaughtered, gutted and heartbroken / (This could be) The last time / She doesn't have to shave / Love circles / Melody hotel / Can of worms / Dr. Jazz / Is it too late.

Jan 90. (7") *(AM 535)* **LOVE CIRCLES. / RED LIGHT**
(12"+=/cd-s+=) *(AMY/CDEE 535)* – Who's that?

Deptford Fun City / I.R.S.

Mar 90. (cd/c/lp) *(DFC CD/MC/LP 1) <82040>* **A ROUND AND A BOUT (live 1974-1989)** | 50 |
– Footprints / Pulling mussels (from the shell) / Black coffee in bed / She doesn't have to shave / Is that love / Dr. Jazz / Up the junction / Slaughtered, gutted and heartbroken / Is it too late / Cool for cats / Take me, I'm yours / If it's love / Hourglass / Labelled with love / Annie get your gun / Boogie woogie country girl / Tempted. *(free 7"ep 'PACKET OF THREE')*

___ JOOLS left again to go solo and take up more TV work. In 1991 he was repl. by **MATT IRVING + STEVE NIEVE** – keyboards / **TONY BERG** – guitar, keyboards / **BRUCE HORNSBY** – accordion

Reprise / Reprise

Jul 91. (7"/c-s) *(W 0054/+C)* **SUNDAY STREET. / MAIDSTONE**
(12"+=/cd-s+=) *(W 0054 T/CD)* – Mood swings.

Aug 91. (lp/c)(cd) *(WX 428/+C)(<7599 26644-2>)* **PLAY** | 41 |
– Satisfied / Crying in my sleep / Letting go / The day I get home / The truck / House of love / Cupid's toy / Gone to the dogs / Walk a straight line / Sunday street / Wicked and cruel / There is a voice. *(re-iss. cd Feb95; same)*

Nov 91. (7"/c-s) *(W 0071/+C)* **SATISFIED. / HAPPINESS IS KING**
(12"+=/cd-s+=) *(W 0071 T/CD)* – Laughing in my sleep.

___ **DIFFORD + TILBROOK + WILKINSON** plus returning **PAUL CARRACK** – keyboards / **PETE THOMAS** – drums

A&M / A&M

Jul 93. (7"/c-s) **THIRD RAIL. / COOL FOR CATS - STRONG IN REASON (live medley)** *(580334-7/-4)* | 39 |
(cd-s+=) *(580335-2)* – Take me I'm yours (Paul Dakeyne remix).
(cd-s) *(580337-2)* – ('A'side) / The truth (live) / Melody hotel (live) / Walk a straight line (live).

Aug 93. (7"/c-s) *(580376-7/-4)* **SOME FANTASTIC PLACE. / JUMPING** | 73 |
(cd-s+=) *(580377-2)* – Dark saloons / Discipline.
(cd-s) *(580379-2)* – ('A'side) / Is that the time? / Don't be a stranger / Stark naked.

Sep 93. (cd/c/lp) *(<540140-2/-4/-1>)* **SOME FANTASTIC PLACE** | 26 |
– Everything in the world / Some fantastic place / Third rail / Loving you tonight / It's over / Cold shoulder / Talk to him / Jolly comes home / Images of loving / True colours (the storm) / Pinocchio.

Oct 93. (7"/c-s/12") *(580412-7/-4/-1)* **LOVING YOU TONIGHT. / ('A'edit)**
(cd-s+=) *(580413-2)* – Tempted (session) / Third rail (session).

Feb 94. (7"/c-s) *(580506-7/-4)* **IT'S OVER. / IS THAT LOVE (live)**
(cd-s+=) *(580507-2)* – Pulling mussels (from the shell) (live) / Goodbye girl (live).

___ they were joined by drummer **KEVIN WILKINSON** (b.1957, Swindon)

A&M / IRS-Capitol

Aug 95. (c-s) *(581189-4)* **THIS SUMMER / GOODBYE GIRL (live)** | 47 |
(cd-s+=) *(581191-2)* – All the king's horses.
(cd-s) *(581189-2)* – ('A'side) / End of a century (live acoustic) / Periscope.

Nov 95. (c-ep/cd-ep) *(581271-4/-2)* **ELECTRIC TRAINS / CRACKER JACK / FIGHTING FOR PEACE / COLD SHOULDER (live)** | 44 |
(cd-ep) *(581269-2)* – ('A'side) / Some fantastic place / It's over / Hour glass.

Nov 95. (cd/c) *(540440-2/-4) <38304>* **RIDICULOUS** | 50 |
– Electric trains / Heaven knows / Grouch of the day / Walk away / This summer / Got to me / Long face / I want you / Daphne / Lost for words / Great escape / Temptation for love / Sound asleep / Fingertips. *(re-iss. Sep97 cd/c; same)*

Jun 96. (cd-s) *(581605-2)* **HEAVEN KNOWS / GOODBYE GIRL (live) / LABELLED WITH LOVE (live) / IS THAT LOVE? (live)** | 27 |
(cd-s) *(581607-2)* – ('A'side) / Tempted (live) / Walk away (live) / Some fantastic place (live).
(cd-s) *(581609-2)* – ('A'side) / Take me I'm yours (live) / Annie get your gun (live) / Slap and tickle (live).

Aug 96. (cd-s) *(581837-2)* **THIS SUMMER (remix) / ELECTRIC TRAINS / HEAVEN KNOWS / THIS SUMMER** | 32 |
(cd-s) *(581839-2)* – ('A'side) / Cool for cats / Up the junction / Black coffee in bed.
(cd-s) *(581841-2)* – ('A'side) / Sweet as a nut / In another lifetime / Never there.

___ **DIFFORD, TILBROOK** with **CHRIS HOLLAND** – keyboards, vocals / **HILAIRE PENDA** – bass / **ASHLEY SOAN** – drums, vocals

Quixotic / Valley

May 98. (cd-s) *(QRCSQ 098)* **DOWN IN THE VALLEY / DOWN IN THE VALLEY (mixes; crowd / jug band / instrumental)**

Nov 98. (cd) *(QRSQD 098) <15046>* **DOMINO** Sep99
– Play on / Bonkers / What's wrong with this picture? / Domino / To be a dad / Donkey talk / Sleeping with a friend / Without you here / In the morning / A moving story / Little king / Short break.

___ tragedy struck, when former member KEVIN committed suicide 17 Jul'99

– compilations, etc. –

1981. (10"m-lp) *A&M; <SP 3413>* **SIX SQUEEZE SONGS CRAMMED ONTO ONE TEN INCH RECORD**

Oct 83. (7") *Old Gold; (OG 9364)* **TAKE ME, I'M YOURS. / UP THE JUNCTION**

Sep 85. (7") *Old Gold; (OG 9546)* **COOL FOR CATS. / LABELLED WITH LOVE**

Apr 92. (7"/c-s) *A&M; (AM/+MC 860)* **COOL FOR CATS. / TRUST ME TO OPEN MY MOUTH** | 62 |
(cd-s+=) *(AMCD 860)* – Squabs on forty fab (medley hits).

May 92. (cd/c/d-lp) *A&M; (397181-2/-4/-1)* **GREATEST HITS** | 6 |
– (as THE SINGLES 45 AND UNDER +) Take me, I'm yours / Goodbye girl / Cool for cats / Up the junction / Slap and tickle / Another nail in my heart / Pulling mussels (from the shell) / Tempted / Is that love / Labelled with love / Black coffee in bed / Annie get your gun / King George Street / Last time forever / No place like home / Hourglass / Trust me to open my mouth / Footprints / If it's love / Love circles.

Oct 93. (cd) *A&M; (CDA 24120)* **BABYLON AND ON / EAST SIDE STORY**
Aug 96. (cd) *A&M; <540425-2>* **PICCADILLY COLLECTION**
Nov 96. (d-cd) *A&M; (540651-2)* **EXCESS MODERATION**
Oct 97. (6xcd-box) *(540801-2)* **SIX OF ONE**
Aug 00. (cd) *Spectrum; (544229-2)* **UP THE JUNCTION**
Jun 02. (cd) *Universal TV; (493253-2)* **THE BIG SQUEEZE – THE VERY BEST OF SQUEEZE** | 8 |
– Take me I'm yours / Goodbye girl / Cool for cats / Up the junction / Slap and tickle / Another nail in my heart / Pulling mussels from a shell / Is that love / Tempted / Black coffee in bed / Annie get your gun / Labelled with love / Last time forever / Hourglass / Some fantastic place / Third rail / This summer / Electric trains / Heaven knows / Domino / Suites from five strangers / Squabs on forty five / Model / Spanish guitar / Elephant girl / Trust / Yap yap yap / Fortnight saga / Wedding bells / What the butler saw / Going crazy / Introvert / Who's that / Vanity fair / Christmas day / Maidstone / Discipline / Periscope / All's well that ends well.

Chris STAMEY

Born: 6 Dec'54, Chapel Hill, North Carolina, USA. Formerly a member of the RITTENHOUSE SQUARE in 1972 along with with future dB, PETER HOLSAPPLE, STAMEY subsequently founded The SNEAKERS with WILL RIGBY and GENE HOLDER. Following a move to New York in early '77, the singer released a solo single, 'SUMMER FUN' for Alex Chilton's 'Ork' imprint (STAMEY was also helping the former BIG STAR man with his current album project), before HOLSAPPLE, RIGBY, HOLDER and STAMEY adopted the dB's moniker (mid-'78). CHRIS was an integral part of The dB's prior to his departure in 1984, having already begun the process of carving out a respectable solo career for himself. A single, 'IN THE WINTER OF LOVE', preceded a full-length debut album, 'IT'S A WONDERFUL LIFE' (1983), proving that STAMEY's songwriting talent was valid in its own right. He continued to record sporadically throughout the 80's, most notably 1987's 'IT'S ALRIGHT', boasting a star-studded cast of friends including CHILTON, ANTON FIER, BERNIE WORRELL, MITCH EASTER, RICHARD LLOYD and JANE SCARPANTONI. The 90's got off to a relatively prolific start with a STAMEY solo set, 'FIREWORKS' (1991) and a collaborative reunion effort with HOLSAPPLE, 'MAVERICKS' (1991). Another combined effort, this time with KIRK RUSS, was released in 1995 as the snappily-titled, 'THE ROBUST BEAUTY OF IMPROPER LINEAR MODELS IN DECISION MAKING: COMPOSITIONS AND IMPROVISATIONS FOR GUITAR'.

Album rating: CHRISTMAS TIME (*5) / IT'S A WONDERFUL LIFE (*5) / IT'S ALRIGHT (*5) / FIREWORKS (*5) / THE ROBUST BEAUTY... (*4)

CHRIS STAMEY – vocals, guitar (ex-SNEAKERS)

not iss. / Ork

1977. (7") *<81982>* **SUMMER FUN. / WHERE THE FUN IS**

___ subsequently formed The dB's and kicked off with the single 'I THOUGHT YOU WANTED TO KNOW'

Albion / Palo Alto

Jun 83. (12") *(12ION 1045)* **IN THE WINTER OF LOVE. / IT'S A WONDERFUL LIFE**

Jan 84. (lp) *(ALB 114) <PA 8022>* **IT'S A WONDERFUL LIFE** Nov83
– Winter of love / Never enters my mind / Get a job / Oh yeah / Brushfire in Hoboken / It's a wonderful life / Still life #3 / Depth of field / Face of the crowd. *<cd-iss. Nov92 as 'WONDERFUL LIFE' on 'East Side Digital'+=; ESD 80682>* – Excitement / Instant karma! / When we're alone / Ghost story / Something came over me (demo) / Winter of love (power station version) / It's a wonderful life (violin version).

___ with **ALEX CHILTON, PETER HOLSAPPLE, WILL RIGBY, TED LYONS, WES LACHOT, GENE HOLDER, JODY STEPHENS, ALAN BEZOZI + JOHN HOWIE**

not iss. / Twin/Tone-Coyote

1984. (7"ep) *<TTC 8554>* **INSTANT EXCITEMENT EP**
– Excitement / Instant karma! / When we're alone / Ghost story.

1986. (lp) *<TTC 8564>* **CHRISTMAS TIME**
– Christmas time / Christmas is the only time (I think...) / Sha la la / O holy night / The only law that Santa Claus understood / Jesus Christ / Silent nocturne / Holiday spirit / (I'm always touched by you) Presence dear / The snow is falling / Occasional shivers / You're what I want (for Christmas) / Santa's moonlight sleighride / Silver bells / I's a wonderful life / Feliz Vavidad.

___ next also with a host of session men including; MITCH EASTER, ANTON FIER, RICHARD LLOYD, BERNIE WORRELL, ALEX CHILTON and JANE SCARPANTONI

not iss. / A&M

Oct 87. (lp) *<SP 65180>* **IT'S ALRIGHT**
– From the word go / When we're alone / The seduct / It'a alright / Of time and all she to mind / Big time / In the dark / If you hear my voice / 27 years in a single day / Incredible happiness.

Rhino / Rhino

Oct 91. (cd) *(<98695-2>)* **FIREWORKS**
– The company of light / Something came over me / Glorious delusion / Time is running out / Two places at once / Perfect time / The newlyweds / On the radio / All the heart's desire – Black orchids / Fireworks / The brakeman's consolation / I want you / You don't miss your water.

___ In 1991, he collaborated with old mate PETER HOLSAPPLE on the album 'MAVERICKS' for 'Rhino'.

S.O.L. / not iss.

Apr 93. (7") *(SOL 250)* **ALIVE. / STOP**

not iss. / East Side Digital

Apr 95. (cd; as CHRIS STAMEY with KIRK ROSS) *<ESD 81052>* **THE ROBUST BEAUTY OF IMPROPER LINEAR MODELS IN DECISION MAKING: COMPOSITIONS AND IMPROVISATIONS FOR GUITAR**

– Love / Dahlia gradual / (I'm in with) The out crowd / The Indianapolis two thousand / Rail spike melody / Fog harbor, 1943 / Dog worrying a bone / Meditation on a theme / The arsonist and the fire engine / Puzzle / Ping pong / Bukowski attends his funeral march (suite) / Puzzle: reprise and twang / Shimmerish / The Kurdish shepherd / Staircase descending a nude / The big clock: a fanfare for appliances / Sargasso a la carte / While watching the Led Zeppelin reunion.

STATIC
(see under ⇒ BRANCA, Glenn; in 80's section)

Mark STEWART (see under ⇒ POP GROUP)

STIFF LITTLE FINGERS

Formed: Belfast, N.Ireland ... 1977 by teenagers JAKE BURNS, HENRY CLUNEY, ALI McMORDIE and GORDON BLAIR, the latter soon being replaced by BRIAN FALOON. Famously taking their name from a line in a VIBRATORS b-side, the group began life as a CLASH covers band. Taken under the wing of journalist, GORDON OGILVIE (who subsequently became both band manager and BURNS' writing partner), the group began to rely on original material, releasing their incendiary 1978 debut single, 'SUSPECT DEVICE'. / 'WASTED LIFE' on the self-financed 'Rigid Digits' label. Wound tight, both lyrically and musically, with the frustration and anger of living in war-torn Belfast, the record introduced SLF as one of the most visceral and compelling punk bands since The SEX PISTOLS. Championed by the ever vigilant John Peel, the single led to a deal with 'Rough Trade' who jointly released a follow-up single, 'ALTERNATIVE ULSTER', the track rapidly assuming legendary status, although it was originally penned for release as a magazine flexi-disc. A debut album, 'INFLAMMABLE MATERIAL', followed in early '79, a raging, politically barbed howl of punk protest which lined up all the aforementioned tracks alongside such definitive SLF material as 'STATE OF EMERGENCY' and 'JOHNNY WAS'. Storming into the Top 20, the album expanded their already voracious fanbase, the group undertaking their first major headlining tour to promote it. The insistent, bass-heavy pop-punk dynamics of 'GOTTA GETAWAY' marked the debut of JIM REILLY (replacing the departing FALOON on the drum stool) and no doubt fuelled a thousand teenage runaway fantasies while the vicious 'STRAW DOGS' marked the group's major label debut for 'Chrysalis'. Early the following year, SLF scored their sole Top 20 hit with 'AT THE EDGE', another seething account of BURNS' troubled youth in Northern Ireland and arguably one of the group's finest moments. 'NOBODY'S HEROES' (1980) saw a move towards a more varied musical palette and a distinctly melodic feel, notably on the title track although 'TIN SOLDIERS' was as brutal as ever. The seminal live album, 'HANX!' (1980) gave the band their only Top 10 success later that year, surprising given the band's increasingly commercial approach as witnessed on the infectious 'JUST FADE AWAY' (possibly the only song ever written about a woman harassing a man!). A centerpiece of the 'GO FOR IT' (1981) set, the single stood in stark contrast to the insipid cod-reggae that so many punk bands, SLF unfortunately included, were now falling back on. 'NOW THEN' (1982) was an uncomfortable attempt to branch out even further into uncharted pop/rock territory, BURNS leaving soon after to form JAKE BURNS & THE BIG WHEEL. This effectively spelled the end for the band, and after a farewell tour, they called it a day. The live demand for SLF was so strong, however, that they were able to regroup in 1987, new material eventually surfacing in 1991 following the replacement of the disillusioned McMORDIE with ex-JAM bassist BRUCE FOXTON. The album in question, 'FLAGS AND EMBLEMS', hardly set the rock world alight, gigs predictably characterised by diehard fans shouting for old favourites. 'GET A LIFE' (1994) was similarly formulaic and, without being precious, one can't help but wonder how such a vital, influential band are now reduced to basically retreading past glories for a greying audience. • **Songwriters:** BURNS penned, some with OGILVIE. They also covered JOHNNY WAS (Bob Marley) / RUNNING BEAR (Johnny Preston) / WHITE CHRISTMAS (Bing Crosby) / LOVE OF THE COMMON PEOPLE (Nicky Thomas) / THE MESSAGE (Grandmaster Flash). • **Trivia:** JAKE once applied for a job as a Radio 1 producer.

Album rating: INFLAMMABLE MATERIAL (*8) / NOBODY'S HEROES (*7) / HANX! (*6) / GO FOR IT (*5) / NOW THEN (*5) / ALL THE BEST compilation (*8) / NO SLEEP TILL BELFAST (*5) / SEE YOU UP THERE! (*5) / FLAGS AND EMBLEMS (*5) / GET A LIFE (*4) / TINDERBOX (*4)

JAKE BURNS – vocals, lead guitar / **HENRY CLUNEY** – guitar / **ALI McMORDIE** – bass / **BRIAN FALOON** – drums; repl. GORDON BLAIR who later joined RUDI

		Rigid Digits	not iss.
Mar 78.	(7") (SRD-1) **SUSPECT DEVICE. / WASTED LIFE**	☐	-
	(re-iss. Jun78) (re-iss. Mar79 on 'Rough Trade'; RT 006)		

		Rough Trade	not iss.
Oct 78.	(7") (RT 004) **ALTERNATIVE ULSTER. / '78 R.P.M.**	☐	-
Feb 79.	(lp) (ROUGH 1) **INFLAMMABLE MATERIAL**	14	-

– Suspect device / State of emergency / Here we are nowhere / Wasted life / No more of that / Barbed wire love / White noise / Breakout / Law and order / Rough trade / Johnny was / Alternative Ulster / Closed groove. (re-iss. Mar89 on 'E.M.I.' lp/c(cd); EMC/TC-EMC 3554)(CDP 792105-2) <US cd-iss. 1992 on 'Restless'; 72363> (cd re-iss. Oct01 on 'E.M.I.'+=; 535886-2) – Suspect device (single version) / 78 rpm / (Jake Burns interview).

— **JIM REILLY** – drums; repl. FALOON

| May 79. | (7") (RT 015) **GOTTA GETAWAY. / BLOODY SUNDAY** | ☐ | - |

		Chrysalis	Chrysalis
Sep 79.	(7") (CHS 2368) **STRAW DOGS. / YOU CAN'T SAY CRAP ON THE RADIO**	44	-
Feb 80.	(7") (CHS 2406) **AT THE EDGE. / SILLY ENCORES: RUNNING BEAR – WHITE CHRISTMAS**	15	-
Mar 80.	(lp/c) (CHR/ZCHR 1270) **NOBODY'S HEROES**	8	-

– Gotta getaway / Wait and see / Fly the flag / At the edge / Nobody's hero / Bloody dub / Doesn't make it alright / I don't like you / No change / Tin soldiers. (re-iss. Mar89 on 'E.M.I.' lp/c(cd); EMC/TC-EMC 3555)(CDP 792106-2) <US cd-iss. 1992 on 'Restless'; 72364> (cd re-iss. Oct01 on 'E.M.I.'+=; 535887-2) – Bloody Sunday / Straw dogs / You can't say crap on the radio / (Jake Burns interview).

May 80.	(7") (CHS 2424) **TIN SOLDIERS.**	36	-
Jul 80.	(7") (CHS 2447) **BACK TO FRONT. / MR FIRE COAL-MAN**	49	-
Sep 80.	(lp/c) (CHR/ZCHR 1300) **HANX!** (live)	9	-

– Nobody's hero / Gotta getaway / Wait and see / Barbed wire love / Fly the flag / Alternative Ulster / Johnny was / At the edge / Wasted life / Suspect device. (re-iss. Feb89 on 'Fame-EMI' lp/c/cd; FA/TC-FA/CD-FA 3215) <US cd-iss. 1992 on 'Restless'; 72365> (cd re-iss. Oct01 on 'E.M.I.'+=; 535884-2) – Running bear / White Christmas / (Jake Burns interview).

| Mar 81. | (7"m) (CHS 2510) **JUST FADE AWAY. / GO FOR IT / DOESN'T MAKE IT ALRIGHT** (live) | 47 | - |
| Apr 81. | (lp/c) (CHR/ZCHR 1339) **GO FOR IT** | 14 | - |

– Roots, radicals, rockers and reggae / Just fade away / Go for it / The only one / Hits and misses / Kicking up a racket / Safe as houses / Gate 49 / Silver lining / Piccadilly Circus. (re-iss. Feb89 on 'Fame-EMI' lp/c/cd+=; FA/TC-FA/CD-FA 3216) <US cd-iss. 1992 on 'Restless'; 72366> (cd re-iss. Sep93 on 'Dojo'+=; DOJOCD 148) (<cd re-iss. Oct00 on 'Captain Oi'++=; AHOYCD 151>) – Mr Fire coal man / Doesn't make it alright (live).

| May 81. | (7") (CHS 2517) **SILVER LINING. / SAFE AS HOUSES** | 68 | - |

— **BRIAN 'DOLPHIN' TAYLOR** – drums (ex-TOM ROBINSON BAND) repl. REILLY

| Jan 82. | (7"ep) (CHS 2580) **R.E.P. PAY 1.10 OR LESS EP** | 33 | - |

– Listen / Sad-eyed people / That's when your blood bumps / Two guitars clash.

Apr 82.	(7") (CHS 2601) **TALK BACK. / GOOD FOR NOTHING**	☐	-
Aug 82.	(7"/12") (CHS/+12 2637) **BITS OF KIDS. / STANDS TO REASON**	73	-
Sep 82.	(lp/c) (CHR/ZCHR 1400) **NOW THEN**	24	-

– Falling down / Won't be told / Love of the common people / The price of admission / Touch and go / Stands to reason / Bits of kids / Welcome to the whole week / Big city night / Talkback / This must have been what fought the war for. (cd-iss. Dec94 on 'Fame'; CDFA 3306) (cd re-iss. Apr97 on 'EMI Gold'; CDGOLD 1090) (<cd re-iss. Oct00 on 'Captain Oi'+=; AHOYCD 152>) – Listen Sad eyed people / That's when your blood bumps / Two guitars clash / Good for nothing.

| Jan 83. | (d-lp/d-c) (CTY/ZCTY 1414) **ALL THE BEST** (compilation) | 19 | - |

– Suspect device / Wasted life / Alternative Ulster / '78 R.P.M. / Gotta getaway / Bloody Sunday / Straw dogs / You can't say crap on the radio / At the edge / Running bear / White Christmas / Nobody's hero / Tin soldiers / Back to front / Mr. Fire coal-man / Just fade away / Go for it / Doesn't make it alright / Silver lining / Safe as houses / Sad eyed people / Two guitars clash / Listen / That's when your blood bumps / Good for nothing / Talkback / Stand to reason / Bits of kids / Touch and go / The price of admission / Silly encores [not on cass]. (d-cd-iss. Jun88; CCD 1414) (re-iss. Sep91 on 'E.M.I.' d-cd-d/c; CD/TC EM 1428) <US d-cd-iss. 1995 on 'One Way'; 18429>

| Feb 83. | (7") (CHS 2671) **THE PRICE OF ADMISSION. / TOUCH AND GO** | ☐ | - |

— Had already disbanded late 1982. McMORDIE joined FICTION GROOVE and DOLPHIN joined SPEAR OF DESTINY after stint with GO WEST.

JAKE BURNS & THE BIG WHEEL

— were formed by **JAKE** plus **NICK MUIR** – keyboards / **SEAN MARTIN** – bass / **STEVE GRANTLEY** – drums

		Survival	not iss.
Jul 85.	(7"/12") (SRD/+T 2) **ON FORTUNE STREET. / HERE COMES THAT SONG AGAIN**	☐	-
Mar 86.	(7"/12") (SRD/+T 3) **SHE GREW UP. / RACE YOU TO THE GRAVE**	☐	-

		Jive	not iss.
Feb 87.	(7"/ext.12") (JIVE/+T 139) **BREATHLESS. / VALENTINE'S DAY**	☐	-

STIFF LITTLE FINGERS

— re-formed in 1987 by **BURNS, TAYLOR, CLUNEY & McMORDIE**

		Link	not iss.
Apr 88.	(d-lp,green-d-lp) (LP 026) **LIVE AND LOUD** (live)	☐	-

– Alternative Ulster / Roots radicals rockers and reggae / Silver lining / Wait and see / Gotta getaway / Just fade away / Wasted life / The only one / Nobody's hero / At the edge / Listen / Barbed wire love / Fly the flag / Tin soldiers / No sleep till Belfast / Suspect device / Johnny was. (re-iss. May88 as 'NO SLEEP TILL BELFAST' on 'Kaz' c/cd; KAZ MC/CD 6) (cd-iss. Sep89; CD 026) ('NO SLEEP...' re-iss. Jun99 on 'Camden'; 74321 67786-2)

		Skunx	not iss.
Jun 88.	(12"ep) (SLFX 1) **NO SLEEP TILL BELFAST** (live)	☐	-

– Suspect device / Alternative Ulster / Nobody's hero.

		Virgin	Caroline
Mar 89.	(12"ep/cd-ep) (SLF/+CD 1) **ST. PATRIX** (the covers live)	☐	-

– The wild rover / Love of the common people / Johnny Was.

| Apr 89. | (d-lp/d-c/d-cd) (VGD/+C/CD 3515) <CAROL 1377-1/-4/-2> **SEE YOU UP THERE!** (live) | ☐ | |

– (intro: Go for it) / Alternative Ulster / Silver lining / Love of the common people / Gotta getaway / Just fade away / Piccadilly Circus / Gate 49 / Wasted life / At the edge / Listen / Barbed wire love / Fly the flag / Tin soldiers / The wild rover / Suspect device / Johnny was.

— (Mar'91) **BRUCE FOXTON** – bass (ex-JAM, ex-solo) repl. McMORDIE

		Essential	Taang!
Oct 91.	(cd/c/lp)(pic-lp) (ESS CD/MC/LP 171)(EPDLP 171) **FLAGS & EMBLEMS**	☐	-

– (It's a) Long way to Paradise (from here) / Stand up and shout / Each dollar a

STIFF LITTLE FINGERS (cont)

bullet / The cosh / Beirut Moon / The game of life / Human shield / Johnny 7 / Dread burn / No surrender. *(cd re-iss. Jul95 on 'Dojo'; DOJOCD 243)*

Oct 91. (cd-ep) *(ESSX 2007)* **BEIRUT MOON / STAND UP AND SHOUT / (JAKE interview)**

Jan 94. (12"ep) *(ESS 2035)* **CAN'T BELIEVE IN YOU. / SILVER LINING (unplugged) / LISTEN (unplugged) / WASTED LIFE (unplugged)**
(cd-ep) *(ESSX 2035)* – ('A'side) / ('A'extended) / Alternative Ulster (featuring RICKY WARWICK of The ALMIGHTY) / Smithers-Jones (live with BRUCE FOXTON vocals).

Feb 94. (cd/c) *(ESS CD/MC 210) <TAANG 100>* **GET A LIFE** Oct94
– Get a life / Can't believe in you / The road to kingdom come / Walk away / No laughing matter / Harp / Forensic evidence / Baby blue ((what have they been telling you?) / I want you / The night that the wall came down / Cold / When the stars fall from the sky / What if I want more? i(re-iss. Apr97; ESMCD 488)

Jun 94. (12"cd-s) *(ESS T/X 2040)* **HARP. / SHAKE IT OFF / NOW WHAT WE WERE (PRO PATRIA MORI)**

—— **STEVE GRANTLEY** – drums (ex-JAKE BURNS . . .) repl. TAYLOR

Spitfire   Taang!

Jun 97. (cd/lp) *(SLF 100 CD/LP) <T 137>* **TINDERBOX** Jul97
– You never hear the one that hits you / (I could) Be happy yesterday / Tinderbox / Dead of night / The message / My ever changing moral stance / Hurricane / You can move mountains / River flowing / You don't believe in me / In your hand / Dust in my eye / Roaring boys (part 1) / Roaring boys (part 2). *(cd re-iss. Mar99; ABT 104CD) (cd re-iss. Oct02 on 'E.M.I.'+=; 543134-2)* – Wasted life / Hope Street / You can get it if you really want it / Fly the flag / Tin soldiers.

– compilations, etc. –

Sep 86. (12"ep) *Strange Fruit; (SFPS 004)* **THE PEEL SESSIONS (12.9.78)**
– Johnny was / Law and order / Barbed wire love / Suspect device. *(c-ep-iss.May87; SFPSC 004) (cd-ep-iss.Jul88; SFPCD 004)*

Nov 89. (lp/c/cd) *Strange Fruit; (SFR LP/MC/CD 106) / Dutch East India; <8103>* **THE PEEL SESSIONS**

Oct 89. (12"ep) *Link; (LINK 1203)* **THE LAST TIME. / MR.FIRE-COAL MAN / TWO GUITARS CLASH**

Apr 91. (cd) *Streetlink; (STRCD 010)* **GREATEST HITS LIVE (live)**
(re-iss. May93 on 'Dojo'; DOJOCD 110) (re-iss. Feb99 on 'Recall'; SMMCD 538)

Oct 91. (cd) *Link; (AOK 103)* **ALTERNATIVE CHARTBUSTERS**

Oct 89. (cd/green-lp) *Limited Edition; (LTD EDT 2 CD/LP)* **LIVE IN SWEDEN (live)**

Dec 92. (cd) *Dojo; (<DOJOCD 75>)* **FLY THE FLAGS – LIVE AT BRIXTON ACADEMY (27/9/91)** Oct94

Aug 93. (cd) *Windsong; (<WINCD 037>)* **BBC RADIO 1 LIVE IN CONCERT (live)**

Mar 95. (cd) *Dojo; (DOJOCD 224)* **PURE FINGERS LIVE – ST.PATRIX 1993**

Sep 98. (cd) *PinHead; (PINCD 105)* **STAND UP AND SHOUT**

Feb 99. (d-cd) *E.M.I.; (498816-2)* **AND BEST OF ALL . . . HOPE STREET**

Mar 99. (cd) *Harry May; (<MAYOCD 105>)* **TIN SOLDIERS (live)**

Jun 99. (cd) *Snapper; (SMMCD 516)* **PURE FINGERS LIVE**

Mar 00. (d-cd) *Recall; (<SMMCD 276>)* **LIVE INSPIRATION**

Apr 01. (cd) *E.M.I.; (532469-2)* **BACK AGAINST THE WALL**

Mar 02. (3xcd-box) *E.M.I.; (537756-2)* **ANTHOLOGY**

Apr 02. (cd) *EMI Gold; (538560-2)* **LIVE IN ABERDEEN (live)**

Aug 02. (cd) *Strange Fruit; (SFRSCD 110)* **THE COMPLETE JOHN PEEL SESSIONS**

Nov 02. (cd) *Strange Fruit; (SFRSCD 113)* **THE RADIO ONE SESSIONS**

STINKY TOYS

Formed: Paris, France . . . mid 1976 by songwriter ELLI MEDEIROS and cohorts BRUNO CARONE, JAN COLRTH, ALBIN DERIAT and HERVE ZENOUDA. After opening at the second night of the 100 Club Punk Festival on the 21st of September, 1976 (The DAMNED, The VIBRATORS and the BUZZCOCKS also featured), STINKY TOYS set about trying to woo audiences in other parts of London. With their brash, STONES-meets-DOLLS type of punk rock, the quintet subsequently signed to 'Polydor' records (a label who also signed SIOUXSIE & THE BANSHEES). In June 1977, their debut 45, 'BOOZY CREED', was finally unleashed to mixed reviews which resulted in Polydor pulling the plug (although not in France) of their eponymous debut set. The sexy ELLI went on to have a solo pop career in France and had a few hits including 'BOM BOM'.

Album rating: STINKY TOYS (*4)

ELLI MEDEIROS – vocals / **BRUNO CARONE** – lead guitar / **JAN COLRTH** – rhythm guitar / **ALBIN DERIAT** – bass / **HERVE ZENOUDA** – drums

Polydor   not iss.

Jun 77. (7") *(2056 630)* **BOOZY CREED. / DRIVER BLUES**

Jun 77. (lp) *(2393 174)* **STINKY TOYS** French
– Plastic faces / You close your eyes / City life / Jack the ripper / Driver blues / Boozy creed / More than me / Lonely lovers / Sun sick / Pepe Gestapo.

—— went back into their box; MEDEIROS went solo

STOOGES (see under ⇒ POP, Iggy)

Richard STRANGE
(see under ⇒ DOCTORS OF MADNESS)

STRANGLERS

Formed: Chiddington, Surrey, England ... Autumn 1974 as The GUILDFORD STRANGLERS by ex-science teacher, HUGH CORNWELL, history graduate JEAN-JACQUES BURNEL and jazz drummer JET BLACK. Augmented by organist DAVE GREENFIELD in the Spring of '75, they commenced gigging around the pub-rock circuit, developing their boorish, black-clad brand of DOORS/ELECTRIC PRUNES/Dr.FEELGOOD retro rock with scant encouragement from the press. Late in '76, after supporting the likes of The FLAMIN' GROOVIES and The RAMONES, The STRANGLERS were signed to 'United Artists' and initially lumped in with the fermenting punk/new wave scene. Released early the following year, '(GET A) GRIP (ON YOURSELF)' found the band at their sneering, leering best, GREENFIELD's churning organ characterising a sound with which they'd stick fairly closely over the early part of their career. The single stalled outside the UK Top 40 – reportedly due to a chart mistake – although its controversial follow-up, 'PEACHES', made the Top 10 and immediately brought the band into conflict with feminists and the more liberal contingent of the music press. It was also banned by the BBC (a slightly modified version was later deemed acceptable), the surrounding controversy the first of many throughout the band's career and one which certainly didn't harm sales of the classic debut album, 'STRANGLERS IV – RATTUS NORVEGICUS' (1977). A Top 5 success comprising both singles and the enduring STRANGLERS favourite, 'HANGING AROUND', the record met with enthusiastic reviews as the group enjoyed the briefest of honeymoon periods with the press. A not entirely convincing attempt at political comment, 'SOMETHING BETTER CHANGE', gave the band a second Top 10 hit later that summer, closely followed by the vicious momentum of 'NO MORE HEROES'. Also released in '77, the album of the same name narrowly missed No.1, another solid set which armed their detractors with more ammunition in the form of 'BRING ON THE NUBILES'; a notorious, stripper-enhanced gig at Battersea Park didn't help matters and The STRANGLERS' were firmly tarred as sexist yobs. Not that their fans cared, helping put a further two singles, 'FIVE MINUTES' and 'NICE 'N' SLEAZY', into the Top 20, both tracks featuring on the album, 'BLACK AND WHITE' (1978). The latter set came free with a limited edition 7" featuring the lads' interesting cover of the BACHARACH/DAVID standard, 'WALK ON BY' tastefully placed side by side with the inimitable 'TITS'. More promising and certainly more memorable was the surprisingly melodic 'DUCHESS', a Top 20 hit lifted from accompanying album, 'THE RAVEN' (1979). That year also saw the release of solo albums from both J.J. BURNEL and HUGH CORNWELL (with ROBERT WILLIAMS), the former's 'EUROMAN COMETH' barely making the Top 40 while the latter's 'NOSFERATU' failed to make any impression on the charts. Worse was to come for CORNWELL when, on the 7th of January 1980, the singer was found guilty of drug possession and sentenced to three months in prison. Later that year, the whole band fell foul of the law, this time in the South of France where they were accused of inciting a riot; although threatened with serious jail terms, they were susbsequently let off with fines, later claiming it was 'NICE IN NICE' on 1986's 'DREAMTIME' album. The STRANGLERS' commercial fortunes didn't fare much better with 'THE MEN IN BLACK' (1981), a tongue-in-cheek (but critically derided nonetheless) pseudo-concept affair about alien undercover agents. Boasting the exquisite harpsichord stylings of 'GOLDEN BROWN', 'LA FOLIE' (1981) was a considerably more successful album, if somewhat pretentious. In line with the prevailing trend, The STRANGLERS moved perilously closer to synth-pop as the 80's wore on, 'Epic' albums such as 'FELINE' (1983) and 'AURAL SCULPTURE' (1984) seeing the band's hardcore fanbase dwindle. Even a return to their former stamping ground (and the UK Top 10) with a musclebound run-through of The Kinks' 'ALL DAY AND ALL OF THE NIGHT' couldn't rejuvenate them and the subsequent studio album, '10' (1990) was the last to feature CORNWELL. Deciding to carry on with new frontman, JOHN ELLIS, the band recorded for various indie labels in the 90's and although the likes of 'STRANGLERS IN THE NIGHT' (1992) and 'ABOUT TIME' (1995) made the Top 40, most commentators (and many fans) were agreed that the band's glory days were definitely behind them. • **Songwriters:** Mostly CORNWALL-penned except some by BURNEL. They also covered; 96 TEARS (? & The Mysterians).

Album rating: STRANGLERS IV – RATTUS NORVEGICUS (*8) / NO MORE HEROES (*7) / BLACK AND WHITE (*7) / LIVE (X CERT) (*5) / THE RAVEN (*6) THE MEN-IN-BLACK (*5) / LA FOLIE (*7) / THE COLLECTION 1977-1982 compilation (*7) / AURAL SCULPTURE (*6) / DREAMTIME (*6) / ALL LIVE AND ALL OF THE NIGHT (*4) / 10 (*5) / THE STRANGLERS' GREATEST HITS compilation (*9) / STRANGLERS IN THE NIGHT (*4) / SATURDAY NIGHT SUNDAY MORNING (*3) / ABOUT TIME (*4) / WRITTEN IN RED (*4) / THE HIT MEN – THE COMPLETE SINGLES 1977-1990 compilation (*8) / COUP DE GRACE (*4) / PEACHES – THE VERY BEST OF THE STRANGLERS compilation (*8) / JJ Burnel: EUROMAN COMETH (*3) / Dave Greenfield & Jean-Jacques Burnel: FIRE AND WATER (*4) / Hugh Cornwall & Robert Williams: NOSFERATU (*2)

HUGH CORNWALL (b.28 Aug'48, London, England) – vocals, guitar / **JEAN-JAQUES BURNEL** (b.21 Feb'52, London; French parents) – bass / **DAVE GREENFIELD** (b.29 Mar'49, Brighton, England) – keyboards / **JET BLACK** (b. BRIAN DUFFY, 26 Aug'43, Ilford, England) – drums

U.A.   A&M

Jan 77. (7") *(UP 36211)* **(GET A) GRIP (ON YOURSELF). / LONDON LADY**   44

Apr 77. (lp/c) *(UAG/UAC 30045) <4648>* **STRANGLERS IV – RATTUS NORVEGICUS**   4
– Sometimes / Goodbye Toulouse / London lady / Princess of the streets / Hanging

around / Peaches / (Get a) Grip (on yourself) / Ugly / Down in the sewer: (a) Falling – (b) Down in the sewer – (c) Trying to get out again – (d) Rats rally. *(free ltd.7"w.a.)* **CHOOSEY SUSIE. / IN THE BIG SHITTY (live)** *(re-iss. May82 on 'Fame' lp/c; FA/TC-FA 3001) (cd-iss. Apr88; CDFA 3001) (cd-iss. Feb88 on 'Liberty'; CZ 85) (lp re-iss. Jan01 on 'Simply Vinyl'; SVLP 291) (cd re-iss. Aug01 on 'EMI Gold'+=; 534406-2)* – Choosey Susie / Go buddy go / Peasant in the big shitty (live).

May 77. (7") *(UP 36248)* **PEACHES. / GO BUDDY GO** 8 -

— Jun77; They backed CELIA & THE MUTATIONS on cover single 'MONY MONY'.

Jul 77. (7") *(UP 36277)* **SOMETHING BETTER CHANGE. / STRAIGHTEN OUT** 9 -

Sep 77. (7") *(UP 36300)* **NO MORE HEROES. / IN THE SHADOWS** 8 -

Oct 77. (lp/c) *(UAG/UAC 30200) <4659>* **NO MORE HEROES** 2
– I feel like a wog / Bitching / Dead ringer / Dagenham Dave / Bring on the nubiles / Something better change / No more heroes / Peasant in the big shitty / Burning up time / English towns / School mam / In the shadows. *(re-iss. 1985 lp/c; ATAK/TC-ATAK 32) (cd-iss. Feb88 on 'E.M.I.'; CDP 746613-2) (re-iss. Sep87 on 'Fame' lp/c; FA/TC-FA 3190) (cd-iss. Aug88; CDFA 3190) (cd re-iss. Aug01 on 'EMI Gold'+=; 534407-2)* – Straighten out / Five minutes / Rok it to the Moon.

Nov 77. (7"pink-ep) **SOMETHING BETTER CHANGE / STRAIGHTEN OUT. / GRIP / HANGIN' AROUND** -

Jan 78. (7") *(UP 36350)* **FIVE MINUTES. / ROK IT TO THE MOON** 11 -

Apr 78. (7") *(UP 36379)* **NICE 'N' SLEAZY. / SHUT UP** 18 Aug78

May 78. (lp/c)<US-grey-lp> *(UAK/TCK 30222) <4706>* **BLACK AND WHITE** 2
– Tank / Nice 'n' sleazy / Outside Tokyo / Mean to me / Hey! (rise of the robots) / Sweden (all quiet on the Eastern Front) / Toiler on the sea / Curfew / Threatened / Do you wanna? / Death and night and blood (Yukio) / Enough time. *(free ltd.7"w.a.) (FREE 9)* **WALK ON BY. / TITS / MEAN TO ME** *(re-iss. Jan86 on 'Epic' lp/c; EPC/40 26439) (cd-iss. Jul88 on 'E.M.I.'+=; CZ 109)* – (free 7" tracks). *(cd re-iss. Aug01 on 'E.M.I.'+=; 534691-2)* – Mean to me / Shut up / Walk on by / Sveridge / Old codger / Tits.

Jul 78. (7"m) *(UP 36429)* **WALK ON BY. / OLD CODGER / TANK** 21 -

U.A. I.R.S.

Mar 79. (lp/c) *(UAG/TCK 30224) <70011>* **X-CERT (live)** 7
– (Get a) Grip (on yourself) / Dagenham Dave / Burning up time / Dead ringer / Hanging around / I feel like a wog / Straighten out / Do you wanna – Death and night and blood (Yukio) / Five minutes / Go buddy go. *(re-iss. 1985 lp/c; ATAK/TC-ATACK 33) (cd-iss. Jul88 +=; CZ 110)* – In the shadows / Peasant in the big shitty. *(cd re-iss. Aug01 on 'E.M.I.'++=; 534687-2)* – In the shadows / Sometimes / Mean to me / London lady / Goodbye Toulouse / Hangin' around.

Aug 79. (7") *(BP 308)* **DUCHESS. / FOOLS RUSH OUT** 14

Sep 79. (lp/c) *(UAG/TCK 30262)* **THE RAVEN** 4 -
– Longships / The raven / Dead Loss Angeles / Ice / Baroque bordello / Nuclear device / Shah shah a go go / Don't bring Harry / Duchess / Meninblack / Genetix. *(re-iss. Sep85 on 'Fame' lp/c; FA/TC-FA 3131) (cd-iss. Aug88; CDFA 3131) (cd-iss. Oct87 on 'E.M.I.'+=; CZ 20)* – Bear cage. *(cd re-iss. Aug01 on 'E.M.I.'++=; 534689-2)* – Fools rush out / N'emmenes pas Harry / Yellowcake UFO.

Oct 79. (7") *(BP 318)* **NUCLEAR DEVICE (THE WIZARD OF AUS). / YELLOWCAKE UF6** 36 -

Nov 79. (7"ep) *(STR 1)* **DON'T BRING HARRY** 41 -
– Don't bring Harry / Wired / Crabs (live) / In the shadows (live).

Liberty I.R.S.

Jan 80. (7") **DUCHESS. / THE RAVEN** -

Jan 80. (lp) *<SP 70011>* **STRANGLERS IV** -
– (5 tracks from 'THE RAVEN', plus recent singles)
(above w/ free 7"ep) – Do The European / Choosie Suzie / Wired / Straighten out.

Mar 80. (7"/12") *(BP/12BP 344)* **BEAR CAGE. / SHAH SHAH A GO GO** 36 -

May 80. (7") *(BP 355)* **WHO WANTS THE WORLD. / MENINBLACK** 39 -

Jan 81. (7") *(BP 383)* **THROWN AWAY. / TOP SECRET** 42 -

Feb 81. (lp/c) *(LBG/TC-LBG 30313)* **THE MEN• IN• BLACK** 8 -
– Waltzinblack / Just like nothing on Earth / Second coming / Waiting for the meninblack / Turn the centuries, turn / Two sunspots / Four horsemen / Thrown away / Manna machine / Hallo to our men. *(re-iss. 1985 lp/c; ATAK/TC-ATAK 34) (re-iss. Sep88 on 'Fame' lp/c/cd; FA/TCFA/CDFA 3208)* – Top secret / Maninwhite. *(cd re-iss. Aug01 on 'E.M.I.'++=; 534690-2)* – Tomorrow was hereafter.

Mar 81. (7") *(BP 393)* **JUST LIKE NOTHING ON EARTH. / MANINWHITE** -

Nov 81. (7") *(BP 405)* **LET ME INTRODUCE YOU TO THE FAMILY. / VIETNAMERICA** 42 -

Nov 81. (lp/c) *(LBG/TC-LBG 30342)* **LA FOLIE** 11 -
– Non stop / Everybody loves you when you're dead / Tramp / Let me introduce you to the family / The man they love to hate / Pin up / It only takes two to tango / Golden brown / How to find true love and happiness in the present day / La folie. *(re-iss. Nov83 on 'Fame' lp/c; FA/TC-FA 3083) (cd-iss. Aug88; CDFA 3083) (cd-iss. Feb88 +=; CZ 86)* – Cruel garden. *(cd re-iss. Aug01 on 'E.M.I.'++=; 534688-2)* – Cocktail nubiles / Vietnamerica / Love 30 / You hold the key to my love in your hands / Strange little girl.

Jan 82. (7") *(BP 407)* **GOLDEN BROWN. / LOVE 30** 2 -

Apr 82. (7") *(BP 410)* **LA FOLIE. / WALTZINBLACK** 47 -

Jul 82. (7") *(BP 412)* **STRANGE LITTLE GIRL. / CRUEL GARDEN** 7 -

Sep 82. (lp/c) *(LBG/TC-LBG 304353)* **THE COLLECTION 1977-1982** (compilation) 12 -
– (Get a) Grip (on yourself) / Peaches / Hanging around / No more heroes / Duchess / Walk on by / Waltzinblack / Something better change / Nice'n'sleazy / Bear cage / Who wants the world / Golden brown / Strange little girl / La folie. *(cd-iss. 1985; CDP 746066-2) (re-iss. Aug89 on 'Fame' cd/c/lp; CD/TC+/FA 3230)*

Epic Epic

Nov 82. (7"/7"pic-d) *(EPCA/+11 2893)* **THE EUROPEAN FEMALE. / SAVAGE BEAST** 9 -

Jan 83. (lp/c) *(EPC/40 25237) <38542>* **FELINE** 4
– Midnight summer dream / It's a small world / Ships that pass in the night / The European female / Let's tango in Paris / Paradise / All roads lead to Rome / Blue sister / Never say goodbye. *(free ltd.one-sided-7"w.a.)* **AURAL SCULPTURE** *(re-iss. Apr86 lp/c; EPC/40 32711) <US lp+=>* – Golden brown. *(cd-iss. Jul97; 484469-2) (cd re-iss. Oct01 +=; 504592-2)* – SAvage breast / Pawsher / Permission / Midnight summer dream / European female (live) / Vladimir and Olga / Aural sculpture manifesto.

Feb 83. (7"/12") *(A/+13 3167)* **MIDNIGHT SUMMER DREAM. / VLADIMIR AND OLGA** 35 -

Jul 83. (7") *(A 3387)* **PARADISE. / PAWSHER** 48 -
(12"+=) *(A13 3387)* – Permission.

Jul 83. (12") **MIDNIGHT SUMMER DREAM. / PARADISE** -

Sep 84. (7") *(A 4738)* **SKIN DEEP. / HERE AND NOW** 15 -
(12"+=) *(TA 4738)* – Vladimir and the beast.

Nov 84. (lp/c) *(EPC/40 26220) <39959>* **AURAL SCULPTURE** 14
– Ice queen / Skin deep / Let me down easy / No mercy / North winds / Uptown / Punch & Judy / Spain / Laughing / Souls / Mad Hatter. *(re-iss. May87 lp/c; 450488-1/-4) (cd-iss. 1987; 450488-2) (re-iss. cd Sep93 on 'Sony Collectors'; 983285-2) (cd re-iss. Feb97; 474676-2)*

Nov 84. (7"/7"sha-pic-d) *(A/WA 4921)* **NO MERCY. / IN ONE DOOR** 37 -
(12"+=) *(TA 4921)* – Hot club (riot mix).
(d7"++=) *(GA 4921)* – Head on the line.

Feb 85. (7") *(A 6045)* **LET ME DOWN EASY. / ACHILLES HEEL** 48 -
(12"+=) *(TA 6045)* – Place des victories.
(12"++=) *(QTA 6045)* – Vladimir goes to Havana / The aural sculpture manifesto.

Aug 86. (7"/12"/7"sha-pic-d) *(650055-7/-6/-0)* **NICE IN NICE. / SINCE YOU WENT AWAY** 30 -

Oct 86. (7"/7"sha-pic-d) *(SOLAR/+P 1)* **ALWAYS THE SUN. / NORMAN NORMAL** 30 -
(12"+=) *(SOLART 1)* – Soul.
(d7"+=) *(SOLARD 1)* – Nice in Nice / Since you went away.

Oct 86. (lp/c/cd/pic-lp) *(EPC/40/CD/11 26648) <40607>* **DREAMTIME** 16
– Always the sun / Dreamtime / Was it you? / You'll always reap what you sow / Ghost train / Nice in Nice / Big in America / Shakin' like a leaf / Mayan skies / Too precious. *(re-iss. Feb89 lp/c/cd; 463366-1/-4/-2) (cd re-iss. Oct01 +=; 504593-2)* – Since you went away / Norman normal / Dry day / Hitman / Was it you / Burnham beaches.

Dec 86. (7"/7"sha-pic-d) *(HUGE/+P 1)* **BIG IN AMERICA. / DRY DAY** 48 -
(12"+=) *(HUGET 1)* – Uptown.
(d7"+=) *(HUGED 1)* – Always the sun / Norman normal.

Feb 87. (7"/7"sha-pic-d) *(SHEIK/+P 1)* **SHAKIN' LIKE A LEAF. / HIT MAN** 58 -
('A'-Jelly mix-12"+=) *(SHEIKQ 1)* – Was it you?
('A'live-12") *(SHEIKB 1)* – (an evening with Hugh Cornwall).

Dec 87. (7"/7"sha-pic-d) *(VICE/+P 1)* **ALL DAY AND ALL OF THE NIGHT (live). / VIVA VLAD** 7
(12"+=) *(VICET 1)* – Who wants the world (live).
(cd-s+=) *(CDVICE 1)* – Strange little girl.

Feb 88. (lp/c/cd) *(460259-1/-4/-2) <44209>* **ALL LIVE AND ALL OF THE NIGHT (live)** 12
– No more heroes / Was it you? / Down in the sewer / Always the sun / Golden brown / North winds / The European female / Strange little girl / Nice 'n' sleazy / Toiler on the sea / Spain / London lady / All day and all of the night. *(cd re-iss. Oct01 +=; 504594-2)* – Souls / Uptown / Shakin' like a leaf / Who wants the world / Peaches / Straighten out / Nuclear device / Punch and Judy.

Feb 90. (7"/c-s) *(TEARS/+M 1)* **96 TEARS. / INSTEAD OF THIS** 17 -
(12"+=/cd-s+=/pic-cd-s+=) *(TEARS T/C/P 1)* – Poisonality.

Mar 90. (cd/c/lp/pic-lp) *(466483-2/-4/-1/-0)* **10** 15 -
– The sweet smell of success / Someone like you / 96 tears / In this place / Let's celebrate / Man of the Earth / Too many teardrops / Where I live / Out of my mind / Never to look back. *(cd re-iss. Oct01 ++; 504595-2)* – Instead of this / Personality / Motorbike / Something / You / Viva Vlad / All day and all of the night (studio) / Always the sun (sunny side up mix).

Apr 90. (7"/c-s/7"pic-d) *(TEARS/+M/P 2)* **THE SWEET SMELL OF SUCCESS. / MOTORBIKE** 65 -
(12"+=/cd-s+=) *(TEARS T/C 2)* – Something.

Nov 90. (cd/c/lp/pic-cd) *(467541-2/-4/-1/-9) <47081>* **THE STRANGLERS' GREATEST HITS 1977-1990** (compilation) 4
– Peaches / Something better change / No more heroes / Walk on by / Duchess / Golden brown / Strange little girl / The European female / Skin deep / Nice in Nice / Always the sun / Big in America / All day and all of the night / 96 tears / No mercy.

Dec 90. (7"/c-s) *(656 430-7/-4)* **ALWAYS THE SUN. / BURNHAM BEECHES** 29 -
(12"+=) *(656 430-6)* – Straighten out.
(cd-s) *(656 430-2)* – ('A'side) / Nuclear device (live) / All day and all of the night (live) / Punch and Judy (live).

Mar 91. (7"/c-s) *(656 761-7/-4)* **GOLDEN BROWN (re-mix). / YOU** 68 -
(cd-s+=) *(656 761-2)* – Skin deep (extended) / Peaches.

— (late 1990) **JOHN ELLIS** (b. 1 Jun'52, London) – guitar, vocals (once p/t member) (ex-VIBRATORS, etc.) repl. CORNWALL who has already ventured solo.

— (Jan'91) also added **PAUL ROBERTS** (b.31 Dec'59, London) – vocals (ex-SNIFF 'N' THE TEARS)

China Viceroy

Aug 92. (7") *(WOK 2025)* **HEAVEN OR HELL. / DISAPPEAR** 46 -
(12"+=/c-s+=/cd-s+=) *(WOK T/C/CD 2025)* – Brainbox / Hanging around.

Sep 92. (lp/c/cd) *(WOL/+MC/CD 1030) <8007>* **STRANGLERS IN THE NIGHT** 33 Feb93
– Time to die / Sugar bullets / Heaven or Hell / Laughing at the rain / This town / Brainbox / Southern mouintains / Gain entry to your soul / Grand canyon / Wet afternoon / Never see / Leave it to the dogs.

Psycho not iss.

Oct 92. (7"/c-s) *(PSY/+MC 002)* **SUGAR BULLETS. / SO UNCOOL** -
(cd-s+=) *(PSYCD 002)* – ('A'version).

— **TIKAKE TOBE** – drums repl. JET BLACK

Essential Viceroy

Jun 93. (cd/c/lp) *(ESS CD/MC/LP 194) <ESM 388>* **SATURDAY NIGHT SUNDAY MORNING (live)** Mar96
– Toiler on the sea / 96 Tears / Always the sun / No more heroes / Golden brown / Tank / Strange little girl / Something better change / Hanging around / All day and all of the night / Duchess / *Medley / Was it you? / Down in the sewer.

— In Jun'93, old Strangler HUGH CORNWALL released album 'WIRED' on 'Transmission' label. Nearly a year earlier as CCW, he, ROGER COOK & AND WEST issued cd 'CCW FEATURING HUGH CORNWALL • ROGER COOK • ANDY WEST' on 'UFO'.

STRANGLERS (cont)

— JET BLACK returned

				When!	Beacon
May 95.	(cd/c/lp) *(WEN CD/MC/LP 001)* <51568> **ABOUT TIME**			31	Jan96

– Golden boy / Money / Sinister / Little blue lies / Still life / Paradise row / She gave it all / Lies and deception / Lucky finger / And the boat sails by.

Jun 95. (12"/cd-s) *(WEN T/X 1007)* **LIES AND DECEPTION. / SWIM / DANNY COOL**
(cd-s) *(WENX 1008)* – ('A'side) / Kiss the world goodbye / Bed of nails.

Jan 97. (pic-cd/cd/c) *(WEN PD/CD/MC 009)* **WRITTEN IN RED** — 52 / –
– Valley of the birds / In heaven she walks / In a while / Silver into blue / Blue sky / Here / Joy de viva / Miss you / Daddy's riding the range / Summer in the city / Wonderful land. *(cd re-iss. Mar98 on 'Eagle'; EAMCD 001)*

Feb 97. (c-s/cd-s) *(WEN N/X 1018)* **IN HEAVEN SHE WALKS / GOLDEN BROWN** (live)
(cd-s) *(WENX 1020)* – ('A'side) / Grip (live) / Something better change (live).

		Eagle	Festival
Oct 98.	(cd) *(EAGCD 042)* <31965> **COUP DE GRACE**		Mar99

– God is good / You don't know what you've done is wrong / Tonight / Jump over my shadow / Miss you / Coup de grace (S-O-S) / In the end / No reason / Known only unto God / The light.

– compilations, etc. –

Mar 84. (7") *EMI Gold; (G45 6)* **GOLDEN BROWN. / STRANGE LITTLE GIRL**
Sep 86. (lp/c) *Liberty; (LBG/TCLBG 5001)* **OFF THE BEATEN TRACK** — 80 / –
Nov 88. (lp/c) *Liberty; (EMS/TCEMS 1306)* **THE RARITIES**
  (cd-iss. Oct02 on 'E.M.I.'; 541079-2)
Jan 89. (7"/7"red) *E.M.I.; (EM/+R 84)* **GRIP '89. / WALTZINBLACK** — 33 / –
  (12"+=) *(12EM 84)* – Tomorrow was thereafter.
  (cd-s++=) *(CDEM 84)* – ('A'mix).
Feb 89. (cd/c/lp) *E.M.I.; (CD/TC+/EM 1314)* **THE SINGLES** — 57 / –
Jun 89. (12"ep) *Nighttracks; (SFNT/+CD 020)* **RADIO 1 SESSION (1982)**
  – The man they love to hate / Nuclear device / Genetix / Down in the sewer.
Dec 90. (3xcd-box) *Epic; (467395-2)* **FELINE / AURAL SCULPTURE / DREAMTIME**
  (re-iss. Oct02 on; 509722-2)
Feb 92. (cd/c/d-lp) *Newspeak; (SPEAK CD/MC/LP 101)* **THE EARLY YEARS 74-75-76, RARE LIVE & UNRELEASED**
Mar 92. (cd/c) *Epic; (471416-2/-4)* **ALL TWELVE INCHES**
May 92. (cd/c) *(CDGO/TCGO 2033)* **LIVE AT THE HOPE AND ANCHOR** (live)
  (cd re-iss. Feb95 on 'Fame'; CDFA 3316)
Jul 92. (d-cd) *Epic; (466835-2)* **FELINE / DREAMTIME**
Dec 92. (4xcd-box) *E.M.I.; CDS 799924-2)* **THE OLD TESTAMENT – THE U.A. STUDIO RECORDINGS** (demos)
May 94. (cd) *Receiver; (<RRCD 187>)* **DEATH AND NIGHT AND BLOOD**
Jun 94. (cd) *Castle; (CLACD 401)* **THE EARLY YEARS 1974-76**
Feb 95. (cd) *Receiver; (RRCD 195)* **LIVE IN CONCERT** (live w/ FRIENDS)
Nov 95. (cd) *Essential; <ESM 283>* **RADIO ONE**
Nov 95. (cd-s) *Old Gold; (12623 6339-2)* **GOLDEN BROWN / NO MORE HEROES**
Feb 97. (cd/c) *E.M.I.; (CD/TC EMC 3759)* **THE HIT MEN (The Complete Singles 1977-1990)**
Apr 97. (cd) *EMI Gold; (CDGOLD 171)* **THE COLLECTION**
Dec 97. (cd) *Rialto; (<RMCD 220>)* **STRANGLERS ARCHIVE LIVE IN LONDON** (live)
Feb 98. (cd) *Disky; (DC 88187-2)* **THE COLLECTION**
Feb 98. (cd) *Cleopatra; <206>* **FRIDAY THE THIRTEENTH**
Mar 98. (cd) *Eagle; (EABCD 111)* **THE MASTERS**
Apr 98. (cd) *Stranglers; (SOF 001CD) / Voiceprint; <1>* **ACCESS ALL AREAS** (live) — / Jul98
May 98. (cd) *Stranglers; (SOF 002CD)* **FROM BIRTH TO BEYOND**
Oct 98. (cd) *E.M.I.; (497773-2)* **THE BBC SESSIONS / LIVE AT THE HAMMERSMITH ODEON 1981**
Jan 00. (cd) *Eagle; (EAGCD 006)* **FRIDAY 13TH** (live at the Royal Albert Hall)
Feb 01. (cd) *S.P.V.; (SPV 0857105-2)* **5 LIVE VOL.1**
Jun 01. (10xcd-s; box) *E.M.I.; (889172-2)* **THE U.A. SINGLES 1977-1979**
Aug 01. (cd) *Armoury; (ARMCD 053)* **THE STRANGLERS**
Oct 01. (5xcd-box) *Epic; (504596-2)* **THE EPIC YEARS**
Jan 02. (cd) *Castle; (CMRCD 455)* **DEATH AND NIGHT AND BLOOD – THE STRANGLERS LIVE** (live)
Jan 02. (cd) *Castle; (CMRCD 459)* **LIVE IN CONCERT** (live)
Jan 02. (d-cd) *Snapper; (<SMDCD 373>)* **LIES AND DECEPTION** (live)
Mar 02. (cd) *Stable; (STABLE 1)* **CLUBBED TO DEATH – THE GREATEST HITS REMIXED**
Jun 02. (cd) *Liberty; (540202-2)* **PEACHES – THE VERY BEST OF THE STRANGLERS** — 21 / –
  – Peaches / Golden brown / Walk on by / No more heroes / Skin deep / Hanging around / All day and all of the night / Straighten out / Nice 'n' sleazy / Strange little girl / Who wants the world? / Something better change / Always the sun (sunny side up mix) / European female / Grip (1989 mix) / Five minutes / Don't bring Harry / La folie / 96 tears.
Jul 02. (12") *Tried & Twisted; (TT 2001)* **GOLDEN BROWN (earth loop remix). / GOLDEN BROWN (slipped disco remix)**
Aug 02. (cd) *Zenith; (ZEN 0031-2)* **LAID BACK**
Oct 02. (cd) *Epic; (487997-2)* **THE BEST OF THE EPIC YEARS**
Oct 02. (cd) *Delta; (CD 47103)* **OUT OF THE BLACK**

J.J. BURNEL

— solo with **BRIAN JAMES** – guitar / **CAREY FORTUNE** – drums / **LEW LEWIS** – harmonica

		U.A.	not iss.
Mar 79.	(7") *(UP 36500)* **FREDDIE LAKER (CONCORDE AND EUROBUS). / OZYMANDIAS**	–	–
Apr 79.	(lp/c) *(UAG/TCK 30214)* **EUROMAN COMETH**	40	–

– Euroman / Jellyfish / Freddie Laker (Concorde and Eurobus) / Euroness / Deutschland nicht uber alles / Do the European / Tout comprendre / Triumph (of the good city) / Pretty face / Crabs / Eurospeed (your own speed). *(re-iss. Feb88 on 'Mau Mau' pic-lp/lp; P+/MAU 601) (cd-iss. Jan92 on 'EMI' +=; CDP7 98535-2)* – (9 tracks). *(cd re-iss. May98 on 'Eastworld'; EW 002CD)*

— toured with **ELLIS, PETER HOWELLS & PENNY TOBIN**.

		Epic	Epic
Jul 80.	(7"w-drawn) *(BP 361)* **GIRL FROM SNOW COUNTRY. / ODE TO JOY** (live) **/ DO THE EUROPEAN** (live)	–	–
1988.	(7") *(652836-7)* **LE WHISKEY. / EL WHISKEY**	–	– French
	(12"+=/cd-s+=) *(652836-6/-3)* – Garden of Eden.		
1988.	(lp/cd) *(462424-1/-4)* **UN JOUR PARFAIT**	–	– French

– Un jour parfait / Si j'etais / Weekend / Tristeville ce soir / Via dolorose / La whiskey / Crazy / Garden of Eden / Reves / Waltz. *(cd-iss. Sep98 on 'Eastworld'+=; EW 003CD)* – (bonus versions).

| 1988. | (7") *(654576-7)* **REVES. / (SHE DRIVES ME) CRAZY** | – | – French |

(12"+=/cd-s+=) *(654576-6/-3)* – ('A'extended).

DAVE GREENFIELD & JEAN-JAQUES BURNEL

		Epic	Epic
Dec 83.	(lp/c) *(EPC/40 25707)* **FIRE AND WATER**	–	–

– Liberation / Rain, dole & tea / Vladimir and Sergei / Le soir / Trois pedophiles pour Eric Sabyr ino rap / Nuclear power (yes please) / Detective privee / Consequences.

Feb 84. (7") *(A 4076)* **RAIN, DOLE & TEA. / CONSEQUENCES**

— In 1989, they with **ALEX GIFFORD, MANNY ELIAS** and **JOHN ELLIS** splintered as The **PURPLE HELMUTS**. They made an album RIDE AGAIN for 'New Rose' Jan89.

HUGH CORNWALL & ROBERT WILLIAMS

with **ROBERT WILLIAMS** – drums, bass, guitar, vocals, synthesizer / **MARK + BOB MOTHERSBAUGH** – synth + guitar (of DEVO) / **DAVID WALLDROOP** – guitar / **IAN UNDERWOOD** – synth, saxes

		U.A.	not iss.
Oct 79.	(lp) *(UAG 30251)* **NOSFERATU**		–

– Nosferatu / Losers in a lost land / White room / Irate caterpillar / Rhythmic itch / Wired / Big bug / Mothra / Wrong way round / Puppets. *(cd-iss. May92 on 'E.M.I.'; CDP 799104-2)*

Nov 79. (7") *(BP 320)* **WHITE ROOM. / LOSERS IN A LOST LAND** — / –

HUGH CORNWALL

— (solo with session people)

		Portrait	Portrait
Sep 85.	(7"/12") *(A/TX 6509)* **ONE IN A MILLION. / SIREN SONG**		
Sep 85.	(lp) **BLEEDING STAR** (various Soundtrack)		
		Virgin	not iss.
Jan 87.	(7"/12") *(VS 922)* **FACTS AND FIGURES. / ('A'version)**		
Apr 88.	(7") *(VS 945)* **ANOTHER KIND OF LOVE. / REAL PEOPLE**		

(12"+=)(cd-s+=) *(VS 945-12)(VSCD 945)* – Nothing but the groove / Where is this place . . .

Jun 88. (cd/c/lp) *(CD/TC+/V 2420)* **WOLF** — 98 / –
– Another kind of love / Cherry rare / Never never / Real slow / Break of dawn / Clubland / Dreaming away / Decadence / All the tea in China / Getting involved.
Jul 88. (7") *(VS 1093)* **DREAMING AWAY. / BLUE NOTE**
  (12"+=) *(VST 1093)* – Getting involved.
  (cd-s++=) *(VSCD 1093)* The English walk.

In May92, ex-member **HUGH CORNWALL** teamed up with **COOK & WEST** (ex-BLUE MINK) to release single 'Sweet Sister'.

Pete STRIDE & John PLAIN (see under ⇒ LURKERS)

Joe STRUMMER (see under ⇒ CLASH)

Poly STYRENE (see under ⇒ X-RAY SPEX)

STYRENES

Formed: Cleveland, Ohio, USA . . . 1971 as The MIRRORS by high school musicians JAMIE KLIMEK, CRAIG BELL and MIKE WELDON; they added JIM CROOK soon afterwards. With a plethora of punk/new wave acts stemming from the Cleveland area (i.e. ROCKET FROM THE TOMBS, PERE UBU, The ELECTRIC EELS, The DEAD BOYS, etc.), this noisy pop act found it difficult to get live work. However, a solitary single, 'SHE SMILED WILD' (recorded in '75), was unearthed by 'Hearthan' (home of PERE UBU) after their first demise; JIM JONES had already replaced BELL. KLIMEK almost immediately found a new crew of backers – including keyboard man, PAUL MAROTTA – and formed the arty, experimental STYRENES. A series of limited edition 45's surfaced from time to time, 'DRANO IN YOUR VEINS', their debut from '75 even snatching a melody from Syd Barrett's 'BABY LEMONADE'. To ignite the 80's, a new STYRENES line-up formulated in New York City based around KLIMEK and MAROTTA, and they even managed to release an album, 'GIRL CRAZY' (1981). With the addition of former PAGANS singer, MIKE HUDSON, The STYRENES (i.e. "HUDSON/STYRENE") re-surfaced in 1989 courtesy of LP, 'A MONSTER AND A DEVIL'. A few years later, KLIMEK, MAROTTA, CROOK and BELL were back as The MIRRORS, although subsequent recordings in 1991 only brought about one further long-player, 'ANOTHER NAIL IN THE COFFIN' (released belatedly in '94). With interest at a high and a handful of STYRENES/MIRRORS compilations in the shops (or in the can), The STYRENES – aka MAROTTA and HUDSON – signed to 'Drag City', where they issued the patchy 'WE CARE, SO YOU DON'T HAVE TO' (1998); it featured a cover of The Velvet Underground's 'VENUS IN FURS'.

Album rating: GIRL CRAZY (*5) / IT'S ARTASTIC! compilation (*6) / WE CARE, SO YOU DON'T HAVE TO (*5) / ALL THE WRONG PEOPLE ARE DYING compilation (*5) / IT'S STILL ARTASTIC collection (*5) / Mirrors: ANOTHER NAIL IN THE COFFIN (*5) / HANDS IN MY POCKETS compilation (*6)

MIRRORS

JAMIE KLIMEK – vocals, guitar / CRAIG BELL – bass, vocals / MIKE WELDON – drums / added JIM CROOK – guitar, theremin

                                                                          not iss.   Hearthan
1977.   (7") <HR-105> **SHE SMILED WILD. / SHIRLEY**
         (above was recorded in 1975 before they broke-up)

—   JIM JONES – bass, vocals; had already repl. BELL

STYRENES

KLIMEK + PAUL MAROTTA – keyboards / plus ANTON FIER plus part-timers, MIKE ANTLE – bass / TOMMY AMATO – drums / PETE HASKINS – sax / DAVE FRANDUTO – guitar / DAVE KLAMUT – drums / PETE HASKINS + PHIL CAPONE – sax / TOM KIRCHMER + ALBERT DENNIS + JOHN ZIMMERMAN – bass / also with vocalist/collaboration BOBBY MYERS

                                                                          not iss.   Mustard
Sep 75. (7"; as POLYSTYRENE JASS BAND) <MM-101> **DRANO IN YOUR VEINS. / CIRCUS HIGHLIGHTS**
Feb 77. (7"; as STYRENE MONEY) <MM-102> **RADIAL ARM SAWS. / JUST WALKING**
Sep 77. (7"m; as STYRENE MONEY) <MM-103> **I SAW YOU. / JAGUAR RIDE / EVERYTHING NEAR ME**
1979.   (7"; as STYRENE MONEY) <MM-104> **LEAVE THE GIRLS. / INSIDE OF HERE**   w-drawn
Apr 81. (lp) <MRDS-4001> **GIRL CRAZY**
         – Leave the girls / Inside of here / Girl crazy / Cheap and vulgar / Where the girls are / Brian's song / Social whirlpool / Just walking / Outer limits / Electricity / My problem / Drano in your veins / Opus 12 / It's artastic.
Oct 81. (7"m) <MUST-108> **JENNIFER GYMSHORTS. / EXASPERATION / NO DEPOSIT NO RETURN**

—   KLIMEK + MAROTTA added MIKE HUDSON – vocals (ex-PAGANS) / also in band TOM KIRCHMER – bass / PAUL LAWRENCE – drums

                                                                          not iss.   Tinnitus
1989.   (lp; as HUDSON/STYRENE) **A MONSTER AND THE DEVIL**

—   others members had been DAVID LICHT (drums, ex-SHOCKABILLY), FRED LONBERG-HOLM (cello), MARTY EHRLICH

MIRRORS

KLIMEK + MAROTTA + CROOK + BELL re-formed

                                                                          not iss.   Resonance
1994.   (cd/lp) <33-9135> **ANOTHER NAIL IN THE COFFIN**
         (rec.1991)

– compilations, etc. –

Nov 01. (cd) Overground-Voiceprint; <(OVER 93VPCD)> **HANDS IN MY POCKETS**
         – Hands in my pockets / Shirley / Beaver girls / We'll see / She smiled wild / Everything near me / Frustration / Cheap and vulgar / Cindy and Kathy / Penthouse legend / All my life / How could I / Inside of here / I've been down / Jaguar ride / Muckraker / Living without you / Fog-shrouded mist / Violent shadows – House on the hill.

STYRENES

—   HUDSON + MAROTTA re-formed with various sidekicks AL MARGOLIS – drums

                                                                          Drag City Drag City
Dec 96. (12") <(DC 108)> **ONE FANZINE READER WRITES. / ALL THE WRONG PEOPLE ARE DYING**   Feb99
                                                                          Scat   Scat
Apr 98. (cd) <(SCAT 63CD)> **WE CARE, SO YOU DON'T HAVE TO**   Mar98
         – Green lamp / Silver daggers / Half of nothin' / Heavy streets / Anything / Westies / He was a loser / Variations on three blind mice / Hour of the gun / Venus in furs / Thanks for coming home.

– compilations, etc. –

1991.   (cd) Homestead; <HMS 173> **IT'S ARTASTIC!: CLEVELAND '75 TO '79** (compilation)
         – Drano in your veins / Circus highlights / Radial arms saws / Just walking / Jaguar ride / Everything near me / I saw you / Social whirlpool / As if I cared / Leave the girls / Inside of here / Outer limits / Electricity / Cheap and vulgar / Brian's song / Where the girls are / Tom's problem / Drano in your veins / Opus XII / It's artastic.
Sep 98. (cd) Overground; <(OVER 74CD)> **ALL THE WRONG PEOPLE ARE DYING** (1982-1993; incl. 'A MONSTER AND THE DEVIL')

– One fanzine reader writes / East side story / Memory of you / Two up two down / Last hot day / Opus 12 / All the wrong people are dying / True confessions / Back in Hell / Jetsam. (re-iss. Apr02; same)

Aug 02. (cd) ROIR; <RUSCD 8276> **IT'S STILL ARTASTIC**   Jul02

SUBHUMANS

Formed: Vancouver, Canada . . . 1978 by WIMPY BOY, MIKE GRAHAM, GERRY USELESS and GREG DIMWIT. Pioneering the Canadian hardcore/punk scene, they released a series of singles beginning with 'DEATH TO THE SICKOIDS', in late '78. Two further 45's for 'Quintessence', 'DEATH WAS TOO KIND' and 'FIRING SQUAD', displayed the uncompromisingly politically correct stance which would eventually see GERRY end up in jail. Following their debut album, 'INCORRECT THOUGHTS' later in 1980, the bass player was sentenced to ten years for his part in a bombing campaign which took in such targets as a nuclear components factory, a hydro-power station and several sex shops. He was subsequently replaced by bass player, RON, while the band had already found a new drummer, JIM IWAGAMA to fill in for GREG JAMES. The upheaval undoubtedly put a brake on their career and only one further album ('NO WISHES, NO PRAYERS') appeared before WIMPY BOY (BRIAN GOBLE) and GREG joined D.O.A.

Album rating: INCORRECT THOUGHTS (*7) / NO WISHES, NO PRAYERS (*6)

WIMPY BOY (b. BRIAN GOBLE) – vocals (ex-SKULLS) / **MIKE GRAHAM** – guitar / **GERRY USELESS** (b. GERRY HANNAH) – bass / **GREG DIMWIT** (b. GREG JAMES) – drums

                                                                   not iss.   SI
Dec 78. (7") <A00> **DEATH TO THE SICKOIDS. / OH CANADUH**
                                                                   not iss.   Quintessence
Feb 80. (12"ep) <QEP12 02> **DEATH WAS TOO KIND / FUCK YOU. / INQUISITION DAY / SLAVE TO MY DICK**
Jun 80. (7") <QS 105> **FIRING SQUAD. / NO PRODUCTIVITY**
                                                                   not iss.   Friends
Nov 80. (lp) <FR 008> **INCORRECT THOUGHTS**
         – The scheme / New order / Behind my smile / Out of line / Big picture / Dead at birth / Urban gorillas / War in my head / Firing squad / Slave to my dick / Death to the sickoids / Greaser boy / Model of stupidity / We're alive / Refugee / Let's go down to Hollywood and shoot people. (UK-iss.Apr88 on 'CD Presents'; CD 036)

—   JIM IWAGAMA – drums; repl. GREG JAMES who joined POINTED STICKS, although he returned and was joined by RON – bass; who had repl. the jail-bound GERRY (see above)

                                                                   not iss.   S.S.T.
1983.   (lp) **NO WISHES, NO PRAYERS**

—   they split when GOBLE and JAMES joined D.O.A. (the latter was the elder brother of their CHUCK BISCUITS)

SUBWAY SECT (see under ⇒ GODARD, Vic)

Nikki SUDDEN (see under ⇒ SWELL MAPS)

SUICIDE

Formed: New York, USA . . . 1971 by ALAN VEGA and ex-jazz band organist MARTIN REV. After a series of sporadic, performance art-style gigs in the early 70's, the duo laid low until the emergence of the CBGB's punk/new wave scene a few years later. Signed to US independent, 'Red Star' (run by Marty Thau, former manager of The NEW YORK DOLLS), the duo released one of the most influential records of the era in 1977's eponymous 'SUICIDE'. Delivering shock screams and whispered goth-rockabilly vocals over brooding, churning Farfisa organ, the duo laid the foundations for the industrial/electro experimentation of the following decade and in 'ROCKET U.S.A.' and 'FRANKIE TEARDROPS', penned two of the most compelling compositions in the NY avant-garde pantheon. Now almost universally heralded as being ahead of their time, punters of the day weren't always so appreciative; SUICIDE performances were infamous for audience stand-off's, a tour with the CLASH running into trouble while a gig in Belgium ended in a full-on riot (the same gig documented on the 1978 "official bootleg", '24 MINUTES OVER BRUSSELS'). Unperturbed, the pair moved to 'Ze' records ('Island' in the UK) and recorded a follow-up, 'ALAN VEGA / MARTIN REV – SUICIDE' (1980). Produced by CARS mainman, RIC OCASEK, the record presented a slightly more palatable version of SUICIDE's patented synth apocalypse, although sales remained minimal. Subsequently embarking on solo careers, the pair met with little more than cult success, although VEGA's eponymous 1980 solo debut spawned a Top 5 hit in France, 'JUKEBOX BABE'. Following his eponymous 1980 solo debut, REV devoted his time to sculpture with his work exhibited in 1982-83. VEGA continued working with OCASEK, also bringing in a young AL JOURGENSEN (later of MINISTRY fame) for 1983's 'SATURN STRIP' (featuring an unlikely but entertaining cover of Hot Chocolate's 'EVERYONE'S A WINNER') and guesting for SISTERS OF MERCY re-incarnation, The SISTERHOOD in 1986. VEGA and REV eventually reformed SUICIDE in 1988 and recorded 'A WAY OF LIFE' (1989) for 'Wax Trax!' (licensed to 'Chapter 22' in the UK), a label heavily indebted to the duo's pioneering electronics. With the album afforded little interest, VEGA resumed his solo activities on through the 90's, collaborating with STEPHEN LIRONI on his REVOLUTIONARY CORPS OF TEENAGE JESUS project and also ALEX CHILTON on their 1997 set, 'Cubist Blues'. Ironically, there's been something of an upsurge of interest

SUICIDE (cont)   THE GREAT INDIE DISCOGRAPHY   The 1970s

in SUICIDE of late, the duo receiving renewed press attention after their performances with critical darlings SPIRITUALIZED. It was no surprise then, that the inevitable comeback album would appear. The thought-provoking 'AMERICAN SUPREME' (2002), sarcastically waved the stars'n'stripes aloft through the confrontational, snidey words of VEGA and REV. Tracks such as opener 'TELEVISED EXECUTIONS', plus 'SWEARING TO THE FLAG' and 'DACHAU, DISNEY, DISCO', pounded their caustic messages from stark funky beats. Nothing's changed on both fronts then.

Album rating: SUICIDE (*8) / ALAN VEGA – MARTIN REV (*5) / HALF ALIVE exploitation (*6) / GHOST RIDERS exploitation (*5) / A WAY OF LIFE (*7) / Y.B. BLUE (*4) / AMERICAN SUPREME (*4) / Alan Vega: ALAN VEGA (*4) / COLLISION DRIVE (*5) / SATURN STRIP (*7) / JUST A MILLION DREAMS (*4) / DEUCE AVENUE (*5) / POWER ON TO ZERO HOUR (*4) / NEW RACEION (*4) / DUJANG PRANG (*3) / CUBIST BLUES with Alex Chilton & Ben Vaughn (*5) / Martin Rev: MARTIN REV (*4) / CLOUDS OF GLORY (*6) / CHEYENNE (*5) / SEE ME RIDIN' (*7) / STRANGEWORLD (*4)

ALAN VEGA (b. 1948) – vocals / **MARTIN REV** – keyboards, percussion

                                                                    Bronze   Red Star
Nov 77. (lp) *(BRON 508)* <RS 1> **SUICIDE**
 – Ghost rider / Rocket U.S.A. / Cheree / Frankie Teardrops / Johnny / Girl / Che. (re-iss. Sep86 on 'Demon'; FIEND 74) (cd-iss. Jun88; FIENDCD 74)
Jul 78. (7",12") *(BRO 57)* **CHEREE. / I REMEMBER**
 (re-iss.Nov86 on 'Demon' 12"; D 1046T)
1978. (lp-ltd; official bootleg) *(FRANKIE 1)* **24 MINUTES OVER BRUSSELS (live)**
                                                                    Island   –Ze
Nov 79. (ext.12"/7") *(12+/WIP 6543)* **DREAM BABY DREAM. / RADIATION**
                                                                    Island   –
May 80. (lp) *(ILPS 7007)* <7080> **ALAN VEGA / MARTIN REV – SUICIDE**
 – Diamonds, furcoats, champagne / Mr. Ray / Sweetheart / Fast money music / Touch me / Harlem / Be bop kid / Las Vegas man / Shadazz / Dance. (re-iss. Jun99 on 'Blast First' d-lp/d-cd+=; BFFP 162/+CD) – Super subway comedian / Dream baby dream / Radiation / Speed queen / Creature feature / Tough guy / Man / Sneakin' around / Too fine for you / See you around / Be my dream / Space blue mambo / Spaceship / Into my eyes / C'mon babe / New city / Do it nice.

— split partnership in the early 80's and both went solo

ALAN VEGA

with **PHIL HAWK** – guitar
                                                                    not iss. P.V.C.
1980. (lp) <PVC 7915> **ALAN VEGA**   –
 – Jukebox babe / Fireball / Kung Foo cowboy / Love cry / Speedway / Ice drummer / Bye bye bayou / Lonely.

— w/band 81-83 **MARK KUGH** – guitar / **LARRY CHAPLAN** – bass / **SESU COLEMAN** – drums
                                                                    Island   Island
Nov 81. (lp) <(ILPS 9692)> **COLLISION DRIVE**
 – Magdalena 82 / Be bop a lula / Outlaw / Raver / Ghost rider / I believe / Magdalena 83 / Rebel / Viet vet.
Nov 81. (ext.12"/7") *(12+/WIP 6744)* **JUKEBOX BABE. / LONELY**   –

— added **AL JOURGENSEN** – keyboards (of MINISTRY) / **STEPHEN GEORGE** – drums / **GREG HAWKES** – synth, sax (of CARS) / **RIC OCASEK** – guitar, producer (of CARS)
                                                                    Elektra Elektra
Sep 83. (lp) *(K 960259-1)* <60259-1> **SATURN STRIP**
 – Saturn drive / Video babe / American dreamer / Wipeout beat / Je t'adore / Angel / Kid Congo / Goodbye darling / Every 1's a winner.

— retained **OCASEK** + added **KENNAN KEATING** – guitar / **CHRIS LORD** – synth
Oct 85. (7") *(EKR 24)* **ON THE RUN. / CRY FIRE**   –
 (12"+=) *(EKR 24T)* – Rah rah baby.
Dec 85. (lp/c) *(EKT 15/+C)* <60434-1/-4> **JUST A MILLION DREAMS**
 – On the run / Shooting for you / Hot fox / Too late / Wild heart / Creation / Cry fire / Ra ra baby.

— In 1986, VEGA guested for SISTERS OF MERCY re-incarnation, SISTERHOOD

MARTIN REV

                                                                    not iss. Infidelity
Feb 80. (lp) <228> **MARTIN REV**   –
 – Mari / Baby o baby / Nineteen 86 / Temptation / Jomo / Asia. <(cd-iss. Nov02 on 'R.O.I.R.'; RUSCD 8279)> – Coal train / Marvel / 5 to 5 / Wes / Daydreams.
                                                                    New Rose Red Star
Mar 85. (lp) *(ROSE 52)* <RS 700> **CLOUDS OF GLORY**
 – Rodeo / Clouds of glory / Metatron / Whisper / Rocking horse / Parade / Island. (cd-iss. May98 on 'Mau Mau'; MAUCD 648) (cd re-iss. Jun00; RS 700-2>

SUICIDE

re-formed in 1988
                                                                    Chapter 22 Wax Trax!
Jan 89. (lp/cd) *(CHAP LP/CD 35)* <WAX/+CS/CD 7072> **A WAY OF LIFE**
 – Wild in blue / Surrender / Jukebox baby 96 / Rain of ruin / Sufferin' in vain / Dominic Christ / Love so lonely / Devastation.
Feb 89. (12") *(12CHAP 36)* **RAIN OF RUIN. / SURRENDER**   –
                                                                    Brake Out Brake Out
Jun 92. (cd) <(OUT 108-2)> **Y B BLUE**
 – Why be blue / Cheat-cheat / Hot ticket / Universe / The last time / Play the dream / Pump it / Flashy love / Chewy-chewy / Mujo.

ALAN VEGA

returned to solo work for the 90's. **LIZ LAMERA** – drums
                                                                    Chapter 22 Infinite Zero
Feb 90. (cd/lp) *(CHAP CD/LP 45)* <43032> **DEUCE AVENUE**
 – Body bop jive / Sneaker gun fire / Jab Gee / Bad scene / La la bola / Deuce avenue / Faster blaster / Sugee / Sweet sweet money / Love on / No tomorrow / Future sex. (re-iss. Jun90 on 'Musicdisc' cd/c/lp; 10812-2/-4/-1)
                                                                    Musidisc Warners
Jul 91. (cd/c/lp) *(10812-2/-4/-1)* <43027> **POWER ON TO ZERO HOUR**
 – Bring in the year 2000 / Sucker / Fear / Doomo dance / Automatic terror / Jungle justice / Full force of them nuclear shoes / Believe it / Cry a sea of tears / Quasi.
May 93. (cd/c) *(11012-2/-4)* <43051> **NEW RACEION**
 – The pleaser / Christ dice / Gamma pop / Viva the legs / Do the job / Junior's little sister's dropped to cheap / How many lifetimes / Holy skips / Keep it alive / Go Trane go / Just say.

— next with **LIZ LAMERE** – keyboards, vocals
                                                                    Thirsty Ear Thirsty Ear
Dec 96. (cd) <(21308)> **DUJANG PRANG**   Jul96
 – Dujang prang / Hammered / Chennaroka / Saturn drive 2 (subtalk) / Jaxson gnome / Life ain't life / Flowers, candles, crucifixes / Big daddy stat's livin' on Tron / Sacrifice / Kiss.
                                                                    Last Call Thirsty Ear
May 97. (cd; ALAN VEGA, ALEX CHILTON, BEN VAUGHN) *(422466)* <21314> **CUBIST BLUES**   Oct96
 – Fat city / Fly away / Freedom / Candyman / Come on Lord / Promised land / Lover of love / Sister / Too late / Do not do not / Werewolf / Dream baby revisited.

MARTIN REV

                                                                    Marilyn Alive
Jul 92. (cd) *(FM 1006CD)* <ALIVE 2> **CHEYENNE**   Jan95
 – Wings of the wind / Red Sierra / Dakota / Cheyenne / River of tears / Buckeye / Little Rock / Prairie star / Mustang.
                                                                    R.O.I.R. R.O.I.R.
Jan 96. (cd) <(RUSCD 8220)> **SEE ME RIDIN'**
 – See me ridin' / Pillars / I heard your name / No one knows / Be mine / Mari go round / Small talk / Secret teardrops / I made you cry / Here we go / Ten two / Hop and scotch / Told the moon / Yours tonight / Tell me why / Post card.
                                                                    Sahko   Sahko
Mar 00. (cd/lp) <(efa 50167-2/-1)> **STRANGEWORLD**
 – My strange world / Sparks / Solitude / Funny / Ramplin' / Trouble / Splinters / Cartoons / One track mind / Chalky / Reading my mind / Jacks and aces / Day and night.

SUICIDE

REV + VEGA re-united
                                                                    Blast First Mute
Oct 02. (lp/cd) *(BFFP 168/+CD)* <9196> **AMERICAN SUPREME**
 – Televised executions / Misery train / Swearin' to the flag / Beggin' for miracles / American mean / Wrong decisions / Death machine / Power au go-go / Dachau, Disney, disco / Child, it's a new world / I don't know.

– compilations, etc. –

Dec 81. (c) *R.O.I.R.*; <(A 103)> **HALF-ALIVE (half studio)**
Oct 86. (c) *R.O.I.R.*; <(A 145)> **GHOST RIDERS (live)**
 (cd-iss. Apr90 on 'Danceteria'; DANCD 029) (cd-iss. Feb95 on 'ROIR Europe'; RE 145CD)
Mar 96. (cd; by ALAN VEGA) *Infinite Zero*; <43069> **JUKEBOX BABE / COLLISION DRIVE**   –
Jan 98. (12"ep) *Blast First; (BFFP 115)* **CHEREE. / HARLEM / I REMEMBER**   –

— Their classic 'FRANKIE TEARDROP' was used by STEPHEN LIRONI (producer and ex- ALTERED IMAGES guy) on project REVOLUTIONARY CORPS, etc

SUICIDE COMMANDOS
(see under ⇒ BEAT RODEO; see 80's section)

SWELL MAPS

Formed: Solihull, Midlands, England... 1972 by brothers NIKKI SUDDEN and EPIC SOUNDTRACKS, who, in 1976, were joined by PHONES SPORTSMAN, RICHARD EARL and JOWE HEAD. This loose aggregate of D-I-Y punks (who also included early contributor, JOHN COCKRILL at this time) finally issued their semi-legendary debut 45, 'READ ABOUT SEYMOUR', on their own 'Rather' label early in 1978. Favoured by John Peel for their pared down noise assaults, the band secured many sessions for the man's Radio One show, the cream of these released (jointly by 'Rather' and 'Rough Trade') as singles, 'DRESDEN STYLE' and 'REAL SHOCKS'. These clattering FALL-esque tracks didn't even feature on their 1979 debut set, 'A TRIP TO MARINEVILLE', a love-it-or-hate-it affair which found a vocal supporter in journalist, Paul Morley. Completed on a 4-track in under a week and characterised by SUDDEN's scuzzy guitar freak-outs and his flat larynx, the album placed the energetic nihilism of punk in the context of Kraut-rock experimentalism and, in the sporadic piano interludes of EPIC SOUNDTRACKS, recalled the likes of FAUST and CAN. The 80's got off to a productive start with what has retrospectively come to be regarded as their finest three minutes, 'LET'S BUILD A CAR', a speaker-busting example of the 'MAPS at their off-kilter piano-abusing best. Later in the year, after an ill-starred tour of Italy (where they had found a sizeable fanbase!), they finally fell apart having already completed the bulk of the work for a new album. 'JANE FROM OCCUPIED EUROPE', hit the shelves that summer, a more confident piece of work that threw in everything but the kitchen sink. Despite the split, fans were kept busy with a slew of archive releases including 1981's home-recorded outtakes set, 'WHATEVER HAPPENS NEXT . . .' and the following years' singles collection, 'COLLISION TIME'. PHONES SPORTSMAN had already begun a solo career, having released an EP, 'I REALLY LOVE YOU', in summer 1980, prior to playing alongside solo bound JOWE HEAD in 1982. JOWE released the first of several albums that year, 'PINCER MOVEMENT', while in the mid 80's he fronted another recording outfit, The PALOOKAS. Meanwhile, EPIC SOUNDTRACKS issued two singles in '81/'82, the solo 'POPULAR, CLASSICAL' and a JOWE HEAD collaboration, 'RAIN RAIN RAIN'. EPIC subsequently joined former BIRTHDAY PARTY members in CRIME & THE CITY SOLUTION, while simultaneously moonlighting with NIKKI SUDDEN's outfit, The JACOBITES. SUDDEN himself had kickstarted his solo career in 1981 with 'BACK TO THE START' trailing it with an album, 'WAITING ON EGYPT' (1982). Following another solo album and two JACOBITES (a trio featuring NIKKI, EPIC and DAVE KUSWORTH) sets, the former SWELL MAPS leader signed to 'Creation', releasing several albums starting with 1986's mini-set, 'TEXAS' (which featured an obscure Neil Young cover, 'CAPTAIN KENNEDY'). In 1998, the JACOBITES (SUDDEN and KUSWORTH) dedicated a fresh batch of songs, 'GOD SAVE US POOR SINNERS', to the former's brother who died (suicide?) in his flat on 22nd November 1997. • **Trivia:** SONIC YOUTH are known to be admirers of their early attitude and sound.

Album rating: A TRIP TO MARINEVILLE (*6) / JANE FROM OCCUPIED EUROPE (*6) / WHATEVER HAPPENS NEXT . . . (*5) / COLLISION TIME compilation (*8) / TRAIN OUT OF IT (*4) / Nikki Sudden: WAITING ON EGYPT (*6) / THE BIBLE BELT (*6) / JACOBITES (*6) / ROBESPIERRE'S VELVET BASEMENT with the Jacobites (*6) / DEAD MEN TELL NO TAILS mini (*5) / KISS YOU KIDNAPPED CHARABANC with Roland S. Howard (*6) / FORTUNE OF FAME with Dave Kusworth (*5) / GROOVE (*5) / BACK TO THE COAST (*5) / THE JEWEL THIEF (*5) / OLD SCARLETT (*5) / GOD SAVE US POOR SINNERS (*6) / Nikki Sudden: SEVEN LIVES LATER (*4) / RED BROCADE (*5) / Jowe Head: PINCER MOVEMENT (*5) / STRAWBERRY DEUTSCHMARK (*5) / THE JOWE HEAD PERSONAL ORGANIZER (*5) / UNHINGED (*5)

NIKKI SUDDEN (b.19 Jul'56) – guitar, vocals / **EPIC SOUNDTRACKS** (b. KEVIN PAUL GODFREY, 1960) – drums, vocals, some keyboards / **PHONES SPORTSMAN** (b.DAVID BARRINGTON) – vocals / **JOWE HEAD** (JOE HENDON) – bass, vocals / **RICHARD EARL** – vocals / guest on a couple **JOHN (GOLDEN) COCKRILL** – vocals

Rather   not iss.

Feb 78. (7"m) *(GEAR ONE)* **READ ABOUT SEYMOUR. / RIPPED AND TORN / BLACK VELVET**
– *(re-iss. Oct79 on 'Rough Trade-Rather'; RT 10-GEAR ONE MK.2)*

— (next releases were jointly issued on own 'Rather')

Rough Trade   not iss.

Feb 79. (7"m) *(RT 012 – GEAR 3)* **DRESDEN STYLE / MYSTERY TRACK. / AMMUNITION TRAIN / FULL MOON (dub)**
– *(re-iss. Sep80; same) – (new vocal 'A';- mystery track).*

Jun 79. (7"m) *(RT 021 – GEAR 6)* **REAL SHOCKS. / AN ENGLISH VERSE / MONOLOGUES**

Jul 79. (lp) *(ROUGH 2 – TROY 1)* **A TRIP TO MARINEVILLE**
– H.S. art / Another song / Vertical slum / Spitfire parade / Harmony in your bathroom / Don't throw ashtrays at me / Midget submarines / Bridge head / Full moon in my pocket / Blam!! / Full Moon (reprise) / Gunboats / Adventuring into basketry / My little shops / Ripped and torn / International rescue / Loin of the surf / Shoot the angels. *(free-7"ep) (GEAR FIVE)* **LOIN OF THE SURF / DOCTOR AT CAKE. / STEVEN DOES / BRONZE & BABY SHOES** *(re-iss. Feb90 on 'Mute' cd/lp; CD+/MAPS 1)* (+=) – (8 extra tracks).

Jan 80. (7"m) *(RT 036 – GEAR 7)* **LET'S BUILD A CAR. / BIG MAZ IN THE COUNTRY / . . . THEN POLAND**

Jul 80. (lp) *(ROUGH 15)* **JANE FROM OCCUPIED EUROPE**
– Robot factory / Let's buy a border / Border country / Cake shop / The helicopter spies / Big Maz in the desert / Big empty field / Mining villages / Collision with a frogman vs. the Mangrove Delta Plan / Secret island / Whatever happens next / Blenheim shots / Raining in my room. *(re-iss. Feb90 on 'Mute' cd/lp; CD+/MAPS 2)* (cd+=) – Let's build a car / Epic's trip / Uh / Secret island (instrumental) / Amphitheatres / Big empty field (No.2) / The stairs are like an avalanche / . . . Then Poland.

— Disbanded later in 1980, with all going off to solo careers, etc.

– compilations, others, etc. –

on 'Rough Trade' unless otherwise mentioned

May 81. (d-lp) *(ROUGH 21)* **WHATEVER HAPPENS NEXT . . .**
– Read about Seymour / Fashion cult / Armadillo / (I am) The greatest plumming! – Radio ten / Here's the cupboard (thrash) / Terribly insect / Midget submarines / Whatever happens next / Clearasil record (stuck) / Blam / Down with tractors / Amphibious landing craft / Paul's dead / Sheep dip / avoc all ended / The Himalayas / The stairs are like an avalanche / Vertical slum / Forest fire / Midget submarines (II) / Armadillo (II) / Bandits one five. *(cd-iss. Aug91 on 'Mute'; CDMAPS 4)*

May 82. (lp) *(ROUGH 41)* **COLLISION TIME**
– Read about Seymour / Ammunition train / Full Moon in my pocket / Blam / Real shocks / Midget submarines / Let's build a car / . . .Then Poland / Secret Island / Whatever happens next / Big Maz in the desert from the trolley / Big empty field / Blenheim shots / A raincoat's room. *<US-iss.Jul89 as 'COLLISION TIME REVISITED' d-lp/cd; 7 71421-1/-2>*

May 87. Antar; (lp) *(ANTAR 4)* **TRAIN OUT OF IT**
(cd-iss. Oct91 on 'Mute'; CDMAPS 3) – (8 extra tracks).

May 99. (cd/lp) *Alive; (<ALIVE CD/LP 35>)* **THE INTERNATIONAL RESCUE**

Feb 01. (cd/lp) *Alive; (<ALIVE CD/LP 41>)* **SWEEP THE DESERT**

— SWELL MAPS associated releases ('Rather' or 'Rough Trade')

Aug 78. (7"ep; by STEVE TREATMENT) *(GEAR 2)* **5-A-SIDED 45**
– The hippy posed engrosement / Hooked on a trend / Negative nights / Taste your own medicine / Danger zone.

Jul 79. (7"m; as CULT FIGURES) *(RT 020)(GEAR 4)* **ZIP NOLAN (HIGHWAY PATROLMAN). / PLAYING WITH TOYS / ZIP DUB**

May 80. (7"ep; as CULT FIGURES) *(GEAR 8)* **IN LOVE EP**
– I remember / Almost a love song / Laura Kate.

Jun 80. (7"ep; by PHONES SPORTSMAN BAND) *(GEAR 9)* **I REALLY LOVE YOU EP**
– I realy love you / Get down & get with it / I woke up this morning / Wah wah track / The Olton.

Aug 81. (7"ep; by EPIC SOUNDTRACKS) *(RT 084)* **POPULAR, CLASSICAL**
– Jelly babies / A 3-acre floor / Pop in packets.

Jun 82. (12") *(RTT 104)* by EPIC SOUNDTRACKS & JOWE HEAD **RAIN RAIN RAIN. / GHOST TRAIN**

— EPIC went on to join CRIME & THE CITY SOLUTION, who later evolved into THESE IMMORTAL SOULS. Returned to solo work in 1992, augmented by LEE RANALDO, KIM GORDON (both SONIC YOUTH), J. MASCIS (DINOSAUR JR), ROWLAND S. HOWARD. In Nov'92 he released album 'RISE ABOVE' and in Sep'95 'SLEEPING STAR' on 'Normal'.

— SWELL MAPS also guested on singles by METROPHASE; 'IN BLACK'. / 'NEO BEAUTY' / 'COLD REBELLION' (Jul79 on 'Neo London', re-iss. 1980 on 'Fresh') & 'NEW AGE'. / 'FRAMES OF LIFE' (Mar89 on 'Neo London').

NIKKI SUDDEN

— now with **PHONES** – bass / **HUGO BURNHAM** – drums (of GANG OF FOUR) / **STEVE TAYTON** – saxophone / **JOHN RIVERS** – keyboards

Rather   not iss.

Mar 81. (7") *(GEAR 11)* **BACK TO THE START. / RUNNING ON MY TRAIN**

1983. (c) *(RATHER 10)* **BEAU GESTE** (rec.1981)

— now with **EMPIRE** – drums (of TELEVISION PERSONALITIES) / **PHONES** – bass / **RICHARD EARL** – guitar / **PAUL PAPYRUS** – bass / **ANTHONY THISTLETWAITE** – saxophone

Abstract   not iss.

Apr 82. (7") *(ABS 009)* **CHANNEL STEAMER. / CHELSEA EMBANKMENT**

May 82. (lp) *(ABT 003)* **WAITING ON EGYPT**
– Channel steamer / Still full of shreds / Back to the coast / Stuck on China / Knife my next / Fashion cult / Forest fire.

Flicknife   not iss.

May 83. (lp) *(SHARP 110)* **THE BIBLE BELT**
– Gold painted fingernails / English girls / Cathy / Chelsea embankment / Bethlehem castle / The road of broken dreams / Six hip princes / Out of Egypt / The angels are calling / Missionary boy / The only boy in heaven.

JACOBITES

— NIKKI with the ex-RAG DOLLS member & **EPIC SOUNDTRACKS** – drums

Glass   not iss.

Apr 84. (lp; as NIKKI SUDDEN & DAVE KUSWORTH) *(GLALP 008)* **JACOBITES**
– Big store / Kissed you twice / Hurt me more / Jacobites grave / Kings and queens / Silver street / Hanging out the banners / Need a friend / Little bird / Angels in my arms / For the roses. *(cd-iss. Aug88; GLACD 008) (cd re-iss. Jun93 on 'Carlton'; JANIDA 001) <US cd-iss. 1994 on 'Mammoth'; MR 84>*

Sep 84. (12"ep; as NIKKI SUDDEN & DAVE KUSWORTH) *(Pawnhearts; 1747-01)* **THE SHAME OF THE ANGELS EP**

— added **MARK LEMON** – bass, vocals / **ANDY WICKETT** – organ / **TYLA** – guitar / etc

Aug 85. (lp) *(GLALP 012)* **ROBESPIERRE'S VELVET BASEMENT**
– I'm just a broken heart / Only children sleeping / Fortune of fame / It'll end up in tears / Ambulance station / Where the rivers end. *(cd-iss. Aug88; GLACD 012) (cd re-iss. Sep93 on 'Carlton'; JANIDA 002)*

Sep 85. (7"ep) *(GLAEP 102)* **PIN YOUR HEART TO ME NIKKI, DAVE + EPIC**

Feb 86. (7"/12") *(GLASS/+12 045)* **WHEN THE RAIN COMES. / COUNTRY GIRL**

not iss.   What's So Funny About

1985. (lp) **LOST IN A SEA OF SCARVES**

— In Aug'86, NIKKI teamed up with SIMON CARMODY (of GOLDEN HORDE) & JOHNNY FEAN (ex-HORSLIPS) for album 'THE LAST BANDITS IN THE WORLD' on 'Hotwire'; *(HWLP 8504)*.

NIKKI SUDDEN

— (solo) with **ROWLAND S. HOWARD** – guitar (ex-BIRTHDAY PARTY) / **EPIC SOUNDTRACKS** – drums (the new JACOBITES, who repl. KUSWORTH)

Creation   not iss.

Oct 86. (7") *(CRE 033)* **JUNGLE TOWN. / THE LAST BANDIT**
(12"+=) (CRE 033T) – When you're alone / Captain Kennedy.

Oct 86. (m-lp; NIKKI SUDDEN & THE JACOBITES) *(CRELP 012)* **TEXAS**
– Jungle town / Death is hanging over me / In your room / Glass-such a little girl / Broken tooth / Stuka / Basement tapes / Wedding dress / When I left you / Captain Kennedy / Captain Kennedy (instrumental).

— In Mar'87, he featured on JEREMY GLUCK's lp 'I Knew Buffalo Bill'.

Apr 87. (m-lp) *(CRELP 016)* **DEAD MEN TELL NO TAILS**
– When I cross the line / Before I leave you / Dog latin / Wooden leg / Dog rose / How many lies / Cupful of change / Kiss at dawn. *(cd-iss. Feb91 +=; CRECD 016)* – TEXAS

SWELL MAPS (cont)

— In Jun'87, he was augmented by The TIMES & The NECESSARITARIANS on 12"ep 'LUNACY IS DEAD' on 'Barracuda'; *12UTA 9)*

Aug 87. (12"ep; by NIKKI SUDDEN & ROLAND S. HOWARD) *(CRE 040T)* **WEDDING HOTEL. / GIRL WITHOUT A NAME / HELLO WOLF (LITTLE BABY)**

Nov 87. (lp; NIKKI SUDDEN & ROLAND S. HOWARD) *(CRELP 022)* **KISS YOU KIDNAPPED CHARABANC**
– Wedding hotel / Rebel grave / Sob story / Snow plough / Quick thing / Feather beds / French revolution blues / Crossroads / Don't explain / Hello wolf (little baby) / Better blood / Debutante blues / Girl without a name / Wedding hotel (the moose) *(cd-iss. Mar90; CRECD 022)*

Jul 88. (lp/cd; JACOBITES) *(GLA LP/CD 029)* **FORTUNE OF FAME** (compilation)
– When the rain comes / Country girl / Pin your heart to me / Slave for the angels / Road of broken dreams / Into my arms / The old church steps / Heart of hearts / Ratcliffe highway / Romance / Every girl / Fortune of fame. *(cd+=)* – (7 tracks).

Apr 89. (d-lp/cd; by NIKKI SUDDEN & THE FRENCH REVOLUTION) *(CRELP 041 D/CD)* **GROOVE**
– See my rider / Murder valley / French revolution blues / Breaking lines / Groove / Sea dog blues / Great pharoah / Poor relation / Wild cathedral / Beethoven's ring / Back to the coast / Too bad for you / Village Green.

Dec 90. (cd/lp) *(CRE CD/LP 083)* **BACK TO THE COAST**
– Back to the coast / Death is hanging over me / In your life / Jangle town / Feather beds / Flower bed romance / The last bandit / Great pharoah / Crossroads / Broken tooth.

— (solo) with R.E.M. backing (except STIPE)

Oct 91. (lp/c/cd) *(UFO 004/+MC/CD)* **THE JEWEL THIEF**
– I belong to you / The bagman and the twangman / Mountains of New York / Spend a little gold with me / Paying the way / Hotel blues / Failing / Liquor, guns and ammo / Don't let them mess with you / Grievous angel.

Nov 91. (12"/cd-s) **I BELONG TO YOU. / ALLEY OF THE STREET / JIGSAW BLUES**

JACOBITES

— NIKKI SUDDEN + DAVE KUSWORTH (also a solo artist in his own right) + GLENN TRANTER (b. 7 Jul'62, Dudley, England) – acoustic guitar / CARL EUGENE PICOT (b.11 May'64, Weymouth, England) / MARK WILLIAMS (b.30 Oct'65, Birmingham, England) – drums

Jun 94. (cd/lp) *(JANIDA/+LP 004)* **HOWLING GOOD TIMES**
– Don't you ever leave me / Can't you see / 100 miles from here / Howling good times / Some people / Ambulance / Chelsea springtime / Older women / Margarita / Flying / Don't ever leave me (reprise).

Oct 95. (cd) *(PCP 012CD)* **HEART OF HEARTS (THE SPANISH ALBUM)**

Dec 95. (cd) *(GRCD 382)* **OLD SCARLETT**
– Over & over / When angels die / Falling apart / Down on my own / Boutique / What am I living for? / Puppeteer's son / Liquor, guns and ammo / Love's cascade / Penicillin / Tire rolling of the hearse / Wasted.

Jan 99. (cd) *(<BCD 4072>)* **GOD SAVE US POOR SINNERS**
– God save us / I miss you / Heartbreaks / The wishing well / Second time around / I'll care for you / So unkind / Never apart / Blonde angel / She sleeps alone / Teenage Christmas / Cramping my own style / Elizabethan balladeer. *(re-iss. Mar00 on 'Glitterhouse'; GRCD 434)*

NIKKI SUDDEN

with various back-up

Oct 97. (cd) *(ISAM 1004)* **SEVEN LIVES LATER**
– Cellar door / Whiskey priest / Golden dawn / Love nest / Evangeline / French lipstick / All my sinking ships / Quand les rivieres finissent / Behind the lines / Valley of hearts / Flowerbox / Venetian rags / Thorns of gold / Butterfly. *(re-iss. Nov98 on 'Glitterhouse'; GRCD 403)*

Mar 00. (cd) *(GHCD 448) <8004>* **RED BROCADE**
– Scent / Broken door / Countess / Farewell, my darling / Stained sheets / Tie you up / Miss you so / Silver blanket / Undressed / Scarred again / Take me back home. *(re-iss. Mar01 on 'Wagging Dog'; WAGG 005)*

– compilations, etc. –

May 95. (cd) *Carlton; (JANIDA 003)* **HAWKS GET RELIGION**
Mar 01. (d-cd) *Alive; (ALIVECD 42)* **THE LAST BANDIT**
(re-iss. Mar02 on 'Wagging Dog'; WAGG 004)
Nov 01. (d-cd) *Secretly Canadian; (<SC 51CD>)* **WAITING ON EGYPT / THE BIBLE BELT**
Nov 01. (d-cd) *Secretly Canadian; (<SC 52CD>)* **TEXAS / DEAD MEN TELL NO TALES**
Feb 02. (d-cd) *Secretly Canadian; (<SC 53CD>)* **GROOVE / CROWN OF THORNS**
Feb 02. (d-cd) *Secretly Canadian; (<SC 54CD>)* **JACOBITES**
Feb 02. (d-cd) *Secretly Canadian; (<SC 55CD>)* **JACOBITES / ROBESPIERRE'S VELVET BASEMENT**
Oct 02. (d-cd) *Secretly Canadian; (<SC 56CD>)* **NIKKI SUDDEN'S AND DAVE KUSWORTH'S JACOBITES**
Oct 02. (d-cd) *Secretly Canadian; (<SC 57CD>)* **KISS YOU KIDNAPPED CHARABANC / LIVE IN AUSBERG**

JOWE HEAD

solo with BARRY – organ / PRINCE EMPIRE – drums / PHONES – bass, etc / JOSEPH – bass, organ

Mar 82. (lp) *(HEDON 5)* **PINCER MOVEMENT**
– Vatican chime / Cake shop girl / Blood bank / Glistening pincers / Curt replies / Leeches / Mermaid / Quartermass & the pulpit / Son of crawfish / Wimoweh / Radio Vatican / Crawfish / Swissair / Diesel loco / Feeding time / Glass animal colony / Cake shop chime / Locotrain / Beergarten / Uncle Mac's revenge / Vatican chime.

— JOWE went off to join The TELEVISION PERSONALITIES for a few years

— now w/ EMPIRE / SPORTSMAN / JOHN RIVERS – keyboards / CARMEL – vocals / EPIC SOUNDTRACKS + guest CARMEL

Feb 86. (lp) *(CON 00001)* **STRAWBERRY DEUTSCHMARK** — German
– Cakeshop girl / Crawfish / The lion sleeps tonight / Cold finger / Son of a crawfish / Insect flavour valentine / Shiney black shirt / February / Swissair / Sliding down / Nearest faraway place / Coding fires / Chad valley / Tar babies / Slow babies.

HOUSEHUNTERS

JOWE HEAD and others (see below)

Jul 86. (12") *(AGARR 002)* **CUTICLES. / SHOPPING CITY**
Jan 88. (12") *(AGARR 011)* **COOLER THAN THOU. / I AM A MOLE**
Oct 88. (7") *(HOP 003)* **WARP FACTOR 13. / DORSEL FIN**
Nov 88. (lp) *(HOLP 001)* **FEEDING FRENZY**

JOWE HEAD

— w/ TRUDI HOLT + MARTIN GILES – keyboards / LUCY THE HOLY GHOST – sax / MERCEDES MOLE – vox

Oct 88. (lp) *(HOLP 002)* **THE JOWE HEAD PERSONAL ORGANIZER**
– Sudden shower / For who the bell tolls / Lolita / Shy town / Mosquito / Exhibition / Shoe horn / Nebel werger / Town shy / Crabson land. *(re-iss. Sep89 on 'Constrictor'; CON 00042)*

Oct 88. (7") *(HOP 004)* **SUDDEN SHOWER. /**

1991. (7"ep) *(Grey 4)* **THE LEGENDARY EP**
– Constantinople / Frenzy / Marzipan / Exhibition (coda).

– compilations, etc. –

Nov 94. (cd) *Overground; (<OVER 35CD>)* **UNHINGED**

PALOOKAS

— JOWE with PAUL HOLT – guitar / TRUDI HOLT – keyboards / JAMES ROWBOTTAM – bass / RITCHIE PRALINE – drums

Jul 85. (7"m/12"m) *(PROFIT 11)* **CLEAR DAY. / VIRGINIA'S WOLF / PHANTOM OF THE GAUMONT**

Apr 86. (lp) *(CON 00002)* **GIFT** — German
– Clear day / Hot tin roof / Cut the rug / Hobby hoss / Saddle in the ground / Raise the Titanic / Anaesthesia / Wooden hills / Hedge hog / Red letter day.

1987. (7") *(CON 00012)* **I WANT TO BE FREE. /** — German
1987. (lp) *(CON 00012)* **DUMP**
– I want to be free / Fondest regards / Only get to heaven / Phantom of the Gaumont / All the will in the world.

Nov 87. (7") *(HOP 001.2)* **RUN RABBIT. / A HAPPY SONG**
(12"+=) *(HOP 001)* – Hit the bottle.
(above single on 'Hollow Planet'; shared with SPIT LIKE PAINT)

Aug 88. (lp) *(CON 00032)* **HIT THE BOTTLE**
– Hit the bottle / Quality street / The girl with everything / Leggo land / Chicken in a basket / Dr. No / Run rabbit / Black Peter / Rubber Johnny.

1989. (lp) *(CON 00039)* **CLASSICAL MUSIC** (compilation) — German
– Hit the bottle / Clear day / Virginia's wolf / Leggo land / Girl with every thing / Fondest regards / Phantom of the Gaumont / Swim head / Take me back / Quality street / Run rabbit / I want to be free / Only get to Heaven / Dr. No / Cufflinks / Black Peter.

— now w/out ROWBOTTAM

1991. (7") *(STAR 9101)* **SCHMALOOKAS** — German
– Monopoly / Babysham / Hippy song / Hygiene high / Paint the town / Wandering / Nest egg / Mummy / Piss me off / Country builders.

David SYLVIAN (see under ⇒ JAPAN)

THE GREAT INDIE DISCOGRAPHY — The 1970s

TABLE

Formed: Cardiff, Wales ... late '76 by TONY BARNES and RUSSELL YOUNG, the latter a singer and player of the "space-age" guitar. The pair had performed earlier in the 70's as JOHN STABBER (debut gig at Windsor Festival, 1974) and DO YOU WANT A TABLE before being picked up by 'Virgin' records. Recruiting LEN LEWIS and MICKY O'CONNOR, The TABLE – who didn't have touring equipment and were virtually a studio band – delivered their debut 45, 'DO THE STANDING STILL'. In spring '77, the single was awarded the NME "Single Of The Week", its classy WIRE-meets-ENO-like ("Baby's On Fire"-period), was undeservedly overlooked by many New Wave pundits. Unfortunately, by the time it took 'Chiswick' records to issue a disappointing follow-up, 'SEX CELLS', The TABLE were last year's dish.

Album rating: awaiting someone to issue a collection?

RUSSELL YOUNG – vocals, guitar, keyboards, bass / **TONY BARNES** – guitar, bass / **MICKY O'CONNOR** – guitar / **LEN LEWIS** – drums, percussion

		Virgin	not iss.
Apr 77.	(7") (VS 176) **DO THE STANDING STILL (CLASSICS ILLUSTRATED). / MAGICAL MELON OF THE TROPICS**	☐	–
		Chiswick	not iss.
Mar 78.	(7") (NS 31) **SEX CELLS. / THE ROAD OF LYFE**	☐	–

— went out to lunch after above

TALKING HEADS

Formed: Manhattan, New York, USA ... May '75 by former art & design students DAVID BYRNE, TINA WEYMOUTH and CHRIS FRANTZ. Their first gig was supporting The RAMONES at the CBGB's club in New York, circa mid '75. The band were soon spotted by Seymour Stein, who duly signed them to his new US label, 'Sire' and in late 1976 they released their debut 45, 'LOVE GOES TO A BUILDING ON FIRE'. Although this flopped, the following year's '77' album sold well enough to reach the lower regions of the album chart. The record's centerpiece was the spastic, new wave-funk of 'PSYCHO KILLER', BYRNE's compelling eccentricity making the number a live favourite. By this point the band were well established as one of the leading lights in the New York art-punk scene, firing subversively intelligent broadsides at the overblown rock establishment. The follow-up album, 'MORE SONGS ABOUT BUILDINGS AND FOOD' (1978) was produced by BRIAN ENO whom the band had met on a British tour the previous year. Sharing ENO's disregard for the workmanlike, the band were spurred on to new heights, FRANTZ and WEYMOUTH fashioning intricate but gloriously funky rhythms, BYRNE turning around Al Green's 'TAKE ME TO THE RIVER' with his wonderfully idiosyncratic vocal style. ENO stuck around for 'FEAR OF MUSIC' (1979), an album which saw them experimenting with complex ethnic rythms and instrumentation, an area that was further explored on the BYRNE/ENO collaboration, 'MY LIFE IN THE BUSH OF GHOSTS' (1981). Bolstered by a crew of esteemed session musicians, the band cut 'REMAIN IN LIGHT' (1980). Swathed in giddy funk and rooted by African polyrhythms, the album spawned the wondrous 'ONCE IN A LIFETIME' single. The band had now established themselves as a top live draw and were notching up increasing record sales, although it was to be three years before the next TALKING HEADS studio album as the band divided their time between solo projects and live work. Worth the wait, 'SPEAKING IN TONGUES' (1983) was another classy outing, spawning the trance-rock of the 'SLIPPERY PEOPLE' (1984) single and the jittery 'BURNING DOWN THE HOUSE' (1983) which went top 10 in the UK. The Jonathon Demme-directed concert movie 'STOP MAKING SENSE' contained some of the most innovative live footage ever commited to celluloid and further increased The TALKING HEADS' burgeoning reputation. Another groundbreaking piece of film came with the video for 'ROAD TO NOWHERE' (1985), the band's biggest chart hit to date. Its parent album, 'LITTLE CREATURES' (1985), marked a return to a more basic sound. From this point on, the band began to spend an increasing amount of time on solo projects. 'TRUE STORIES' (1986) was a patchy TALKING HEADS version of the soundtrack to the DAVID BYRNE film of the same name while 'NAKED' (1986) came on like an over-produced version of 'REMAIN IN LIGHT'. Following this album, the various 'HEADS went on to do their own thing, BYRNE concentrating on his solo career. The band officially split in 1991, although The HEADS (as WEYMOUTH, FRANTZ and HARRISON were now known) made a comeback album of sorts in '96 entitled 'NO TALKING, JUST HEAD', a record that utilised an array of vocal talent including SHAUN RYDER on the minor hit single, 'DON'T TAKE MY KINDNESS FOR WEAKNESS'. • **Songwriters:** Group compositions except; TAKE ME TO THE RIVER (Al Green) / SLIPPERY PEOPLE (Staple Singers). TOM TOM CLUB:- UNDER THE BOARDWALK (Drifters) / FEMME FATALE (Velvet Underground) / YOU SEXY THING (Hot Chocolate). DAVID BYRNE: – GREENBACK DOLLAR (Hoyt Axton) / GIRLS ON MY MIND (Toquinnho Vinicius) / DON'T FENCE ME IN (Cole Porter). • **Trivia:** FRANTZ and WEYMOUTH (later TOM TOM CLUB) married on the 18th of June '77. BYRNE produced The B-52's on their 1982 album, 'Mesopotamia' and FUN BOY THREE on their 1983, 'Waiting' album. HARRISON produced The VIOLENT FEMMES on 1986 album, 'The Blind Leading The Naked'. TOM TOM CLUB started out producing in 1988 with ZIGGY MARLEY, later working with HAPPY MONDAYS.

Album rating: TALKING HEADS '77 (*9) / MORE SONGS ABOUT BUILDINGS AND FOOD (*8) / FEAR OF MUSIC (*8) / REMAIN IN LIGHT (*8) / THE NAME OF THIS BAND IS TALKING HEADS (*6) / SPEAKING IN TONGUES (*7) / STOP MAKING SENSE (*7) / LITTLE CREATURES (*7) / TRUE STORIES soundtrack (*5) / NAKED (*5) / ONCE IN A LIFETIME – THE BEST OF TALKING HEADS compilation (*9) / Tom Tom Club: TOM TOM CLUB (*5) / CLOSE TO THE BONE (*4) / BOOM BOOM CHI BOOM BOOM (*3) / DARK SNEAK LOVE ACTION (*3) / Jerry Harrison: THE RED AND THE BLACK (*4) / CASUAL GODS (*4) / WALK ON WATER (*4) / Heads: NO TALKING, JUST HEADS (*4) / David Byrne: SONGS FROM 'THE CATHERINE WHEEL' (*6) / MUSIC FOR THE KNEE PLAYS (*6) / REI MOMO (*7) / THE FOREST soundtrack (*4) / UH-OH (*5) / DAVID BYRNE (*4) / FEELINGS (*5)

DAVID BYRNE (b.14 May'52, Dumbarton, Scotland) – vocals, guitar / **TINA WEYMOUTH** (b.22 Nov'50, Coronado, Calif.) – bass, vocals / **CHRIS FRANTZ** (b. CHARLTON CHRISTOPHER FRANTZ, 8 May'51, Fort Campbell, Kentucky) – drums

		Sire	Sire
Feb 77.	(7") (6078 604) <737> **LOVE GOES TO A BUILDING ON FIRE. / NEW FEELING**	☐	☐
—	added **JERRY HARRISON** (b.21 Feb'49, Milwaukee, Wisconsin) – guitar, keyboards (ex-JONATHAN RICHMAN & THE MODERN LOVERS)		
Sep 77.	(lp) (9103 328) <SR 6306> **TALKING HEADS '77**	60	97
	– Uh-oh, love comes to town / New feeling / Tentative decisions / Happy day / Who is it? / No compassion / The book I read / Don't worry about the government / First week – last week ... carefree / Psycho killer / Pulled up. (re-iss. Sep78; SR 6036) (cd-iss. Feb87; K2 56647)		
Oct 77.	(7") <1002> **UH-OH, LOVE COMES TO TOWN. / I WISH YOU WOULDN'T SAY THAT**	–	☐
Dec 77.	(7") (6078 610) **PSYCHO KILLER. / I WISH YOU WOULDN'T SAY THAT**	☐	–
	(12"+=) (same) – Psycho killer (acoustic).		
Jan 78.	(7") <1013> **PSYCHO KILLER. / PSYCHO KILLER (acoustic)**	–	92
May 78.	(7") (6078 620) **PULLED UP. / DON'T WORRY ABOUT THE GOVERNMENT**	☐	–
Jul 78.	(lp/c) (K/K4 56531) <SR 6058> **MORE SONGS ABOUT BUILDINGS AND FOOD**	21	29
	– Thank you for sending me an angel / With our love / The good thing / Warning sign / Girls want to be with the girls / Found a job / Artists only / I'm not in love / Stay hungry / Take me to the river / The big country. (double-play cass. includes debut album) (cd-iss. Jan87; K2 56531)		
Oct 78.	(7") <1032> **TAKE ME TO THE RIVER. / THANK YOU FOR SENDING ME AN ANGEL**	–	26
Jun 79.	(7") (SIR 4004) **TAKE ME TO THE RIVER. / FOUND A JOB**	☐	–
	(d7"+=) (SAM 87) – Love goes to a building on fire / Psycho killer.		
Aug 79.	(lp/c) (K/K4 56707) <SRK 6076> **FEAR OF MUSIC**	33	21
	– Air / Animals / Cities / Drugs / Electric guitar / Heaven / I Zimbra / Life during wartime / Memories can't wait / Mind / Paper. (re-iss. Sep79 lp/c; SRK/SRC 6076) (w/ free 7") – PSYCHO KILLER (live). / NEW FEELING (live) (cd-iss. Jul84; K2 56707)		
Oct 79.	(7") (SIR 4027) <49075> **LIFE DURING WARTIME. / ELECTRIC GUITAR**	☐	80
Feb 80.	(7") (SIR 4033) **I ZIMBRA. / PAPER**	☐	–
Jun 80.	(7") (SIR 4040) **CITIES. / CITIES (live)**	☐	–
	(12"+=) (SIR 4040T) – Artists only.		
—	basic 4 added **BUSTA CHERRY JONES** – bass / **ADRIAN BELEW** – guitar / **BERNIE WORRELL** – keyboards / **STEVEN SCALES** – percussion / **DONETTE McDONALD** – backing vox		
Oct 80.	(lp/c) <(SRK/SRC 6095)> **REMAIN IN LIGHT**	21	19
	– The great curve / Crosseyed and painless / Born under punches / Houses in motion / Once in a lifetime / Listening wind / Seen and not seen / The overlord. (cd-iss. Mar84; K2 56867)		
Feb 81.	(7"/ext.12") (SIR 4048/+T) <40649> **ONCE IN A LIFETIME. / SEEN AND NOT SEEN**	14	☐
May 81.	(7") <49734> **HOUSES IN MOTION (remix). / THE OVERLORD**	–	☐
May 81.	(7") (SIR 4050) **HOUSES IN MOTION (remix). / AIR**	50	–
	(ext.12"+=) (SIR 4050T) – ('A'live).		
—	In 1981, all 4 diversed into own projects		
Mar 82.	(7") (SIR 4055) **LIFE DURING WARTIME (live). / LIFE DURING WARTIME**	☐	–
	(12"+=) (SIR 4055T) – Don't worry about the government (live).		
Apr 82.	(d-lp/d-c) <(SRK/SRC 23590)> **THE NAME OF THIS BAND IS TALKING HEADS (live)**	22	31
	– I Zimbra / Drugs / Houses in motion / Life during wartime / Take me to the river / The great curve / Cross-eyed and painless / New feeling / A clean break / Don't worry about the government / Pulled up / Psycho killer / Artists only / Stay hungry / Air / Building on fire / Memories can't wait. (cd-iss. May87; K2 66112)		
Jun 83.	(lp,clear-lp/c/cd) (923883-1/-4/-2) <23883> **SPEAKING IN TONGUES**	21	15
	– Burning down the house / Making flippy floppy / Girlfriend is better / Slippery people / I get wild – Wild gravity / Swamp / Moon rocks / Pull up the roots / This must be the place (naive melody). (c+=/cd+=) – (6 extra mixes).		

161

TALKING HEADS (cont)

Date	Details	UK	US
Jul 83.	(7") (W 9565) <29565> **BURNING DOWN THE HOUSE. / I GET WILD – WILD GRAVITY** (12"+=) (W 9565T) – Moon rocks.		9
Jan 84.	(7") (W 9451) <29451> **THIS MUST BE THE PLACE (NAIVE MELODY). / MOON ROCKS** (ext.d12"+=) (W 9451T / SAM 176) – Slippery people (remix) / Making flippy floppy (remix).	51	62 Oct83
Feb 84.	(7") <29163> **ONCE IN A LIFETIME (live). / THIS MUST BE THE PLACE (live)**	– E.M.I.	– Sire
Oct 84.	(7"/ext.12") (EMI/12EMI 5504) **SLIPPERY PEOPLE (live). / THIS MUST BE THE PLACE (NAIVE MELODY) (live)**	68	–
Oct 84.	(lp/c) (TAH/+TC 1) <25121> **STOP MAKING SENSE (live)** – Psycho killer / Swamp / Slippery people / Burning down the house / Girlfriend is better / Once in a lifetime / What a day that was / Life during wartime / Take me to the river. (cd-iss. Feb85; CDP 746064-2) (c+=/cd+=) – (extra tracks) (re-iss. Mar90 cd)(c/lp; CZ 289)(TC+/ATAK 147) (re-iss. Nov93 on 'Fame' cd/c; CD/TC FA 3302) (lp-iss.Apr99 on 'E.M.I.'; 499471-1)	37	41
Nov 84.	(7"/ext.12") (EMI/12EMI 5509) **GIRLFRIEND IS BETTER (live). / ONCE IN A LIFETIME (live)**		–
Dec 84.	(7") <29080> **STOP MAKING SENSE (GIRLFRIEND IS BETTER) (live). / HEAVEN**	–	
May 85.	(7"/ext.12") (EMI/12EMI 5520) **THE LADY DON'T MIND. / GIVE ME BACK MY NAME** (d12"+=) (12EMID 5520) – Slippery people (live) / This must be the place (naive melody) (live).		–
Jun 85.	(lp/c)(cd) (TAH/+TC 2)(CDP 746158-2) <25035> **LITTLE CREATURES** – And she was / Give me back my name / Creatures of love / The lady don't mind / Perfect world / Stay up late / Walk it down / Television man / Road to nowhere. (c+=) – The lady don't mind (extended). (re-iss. Mar90 cd)(c/lp; CZ 287)(TC+/ATAK 146) (re-iss. Nov93 on 'Fame' cd/c; CD/TC FA 3301) (lp-iss.Dec99 on 'Simply Vinyl'; SVLP 152)	10	20
Jun 85.	(7") <28987> **ROAD TO NOWHERE. / GIVE ME BACK MY NAME**	–	
Sep 85.	(7") <28917> **AND SHE WAS. / ('A')dub**	–	54
Sep 85.	(7"/7"pic-d) (EMI/+P 5530) **ROAD TO NOWHERE. / TELEVISION MAN** (d12"+=) (12EMID 5530) – Slippery people (extended live) / This must be the place (naive melody) (live).	6	–
Feb 86.	(7") (EMI 5543) **AND SHE WAS. / PERFECT WORLD** (12"pic-d+=) (12EMIP 5543) – ('A'extended).	17	–
Apr 86.	(7") <29163> **ONCE IN A LIFETIME (live). / THIS MUST BE THE PLACE (live)** (above re-generated from 1984 album & taken from 'Down And Out In Beverly Hills')	–	91
Aug 86.	(7") (EMI 5567) <28629> **WILD WILD LIFE. / PEOPLE LIKE US** (movie version) (12"+=/12"pic-d+=) (12EMI/+P 5567) – ('A'extended).	43	25
Sep 86.	(lp/c)(cd) (EU/TCEU 3511)(CDP 746345-2) <25512> **TRUE STORIES** – Love for sale / Puzzlin' evidence / Hey now / Radio head / Papa Legba / Wild wild life / Radio head / Dream operator / People like us / City of dreams. (cd+=) – Wild (ET mix). (re-iss. Sep89 on 'Fame' cd/lp; CD/TC+/FA 3231)	7	17
Nov 86.	(7") <28497> **LOVE FOR SALE. / HEY NOW**	–	
Nov 86.	(lp/c) (ENC/TCENC 3520) <25515> **SONGS FROM 'TRUE STORIES'** (Original DAVID BYRNE Film Soundtrack; w/ other artists) – Cocktail desperado / Road song / Freeway son / Brownie's theme / Mall muzak: Building a highway – Puppy polka / Party girls / Dinner music / Disco hits / City of steel / Love theme from 'True Stories' / Festa para um Rei Negro / Buster's theme / Soy de Tejas / I love metal buildings / Glass operator.		
Apr 87.	(7") (EM 1) **RADIO HEAD. / HEY NOW (movie version)** (d7"+=)(12"+=/cd-s+=) (EMD 1)(12/CD EM 1) – ('A'remix) / ('B'-Milwaukee remix).	52	–
Mar 88.	(cd/c/lp) (CD/TC+/EMD 1005) <26654> **NAKED** – Blind / Mr. Jones / Totally nude / Ruby dear / (Nothing but) Flowers / The Democratic circus / The facts of life / Mommy daddy you and I / Big daddy / Cool water. (other cd+=; CDP 790156-2) – Bill. (re-iss. Nov93 on 'Fame' cd/c; CD/TC FA 3300)	3	19
Aug 88.	(c-s/7") (TC+/EM 68) <27948> **BLIND. / BILL** (ext.d12"+=/cd+=) (12/CD EM 68) – ('A'-Def, dub & blind mix).	59	
Oct 88.	(c-s/7") (TC+/EM 53) <27992> **(NOTHING BUT) FLOWERS. / RUBY DEAR** (10"+=) (10EM 53) – Facts of life / Mommy, daddy, you and I. (12") (12EM 53) – ('A'extended) / ('B'-Lillywhite mix). (cd-s) (CDEM 53) – ('A'side) / ('B'-bush mix) / Mommy, daddy, you and I ('A'-Lillywhite mix).		– Apr88

—— cease to function as a group, after last recording. Officially split 1991.

– compilations, others, etc. –

on 'E.M.I.' UK / 'Sire' US unless mentioned otherwise

Date	Details	UK	US
Apr 81.	(c-s) WEA; (SPC 9) **TAKE ME TO THE RIVER / PSYCHO KILLER**		–
1989.	(3"cd-ep) Sire; (921 135-2) **LOVE GOES TO A BUILDING ON FIRE / PSYCHO KILLER / ONCE IN A LIFETIME / BURNING DOWN THE HOUSE**		–
Oct 92.	(c-s/7") (TC+/EM 250) **LIFETIME PILING UP. / ROAD TO NOWHERE** (cd-s+=) (CDEM 250) – Love for sale / The lady don't mind (extended). (cd-s) (CDEMS 250) – ('A'side) / Stay up late / Radio head / Take me to the river.	50	
Oct 92.	(d-cd/d-c/d-lp) (CD/TC+/EQ 5010) <26760> **POPULAR FAVOURITES 1976-1992** – ONCE IN A LIFETIME:- Psycho killer / Take me to the river / Once in a lifetime / Burning down the house / This must be the place (naive melody) / Slippery people (live) / Life during wartime (live) / And she was / Road to nowhere / Wild wild life / Blind / (Nothing but) Flowers / Sax and violins / Lifetime piling up. // SAND IN MY VASELINE:- Sugar on my tongue / I want to live / Love goes to a building on fire / I wish you wouldn't say that / Don't worry about the government / The big country / No compassion / Warning sign / Heaven / Memories can't wait / I Zimbra / Crosseyed and painless / Swamp / Girlfriend is better (live) / Stay up late / Love for sale / City of dreams / Mr. Jones / Gangster of love / Popsicle.	7	
Nov 95.	(3xcd-box) (CDOMB 003) **THE ORIGINALS** – (STOP MAKING SENSE / LITTLE CREATURES / TRUE STORIES). (re-iss. Mar97; same)	–	–
Sep 99.	(cd) E.M.I.; (522453-2) **STOP MAKING SENSE: 15th ANNIVERSARY EDITION**		
Sep 00.	(3xcd-box) E.M.I.; (5283722-2) **LITTLE CREATURES / TRUE STORIES / NAKED**		
Apr 01.	(cd) E.M.I.; (532569-2) **REMIXED**	–	–
Sep 01.	(c-s/12"/cd-s) (W 571 C/T/CD) **ONCE IN A LIFETIME**		

TEENAGE JESUS & THE JERKS
(see under ⇒ LUNCH, Lydia)

TELEVISION

Formed: New York City, New York, USA based ... late '73 by TOM VERLAINE, RICHARD HELL and BILLY FICCA who had all been members of The NEON BOYS. In 1975, William Terry Ork gave them a deal on his own self-named indie label, for whom they issued a one-off flop single, 'LITTLE JOHNNY JEWEL'. By this point, HELL (who went on to form the equally seminal RICHARD HELL & THE VOID-OIDS) had been replaced by ex-MC5 man, FRED 'SONIC' SMITH, TELEVISION subsequently signing with 'Elektra' and unleashing their classic debut album, 'MARQUEE MOON'. Although virtually ignored in America (more astute British punk/new wave fans placed it in the UK Top 30) upon its 1977 release, the album has since been acknowledged as a landmark release. The hypnotic near-10 minute title track (also a UK Top 30 hit) breathtakingly showcased the driving/free-form cool guitar interplay between LLOYD and virtuoso VERLAINE (the track first debuted at their early CBGB's shows and perfected/modified over the next couple of years), while the album as a whole testified to VERLAINE's barely disguised passion for The ROLLING STONES, PINK FLOYD and the darker moments of The VELVET UNDERGROUND. While VERLAINE's tortured vocals were reminiscent of LOU REED/PATTI SMITH, his molten-spark histrionics resolutely distinguished the band from the more wilfully amateurish new wave pack and TELEVISION remain the most musically adept band of the era. Unsurprisingly, however, they found it difficult following up such a milestone and although 'ADVENTURE' (1978) contained sporadic moments of genius, TELEVISON were beginning to lose clarity. Ironically, as the New York scene was at its height, LLOYD effectively pulled the plug on the group after walking out mid-tour later that year. VERLAINE tried unsuccessfully to translate his distinctive sound into a more mainstream rock setting with his solo career, retaining his characteristic vocals and of course, his trademark guitar alchemy. TELEVISION eventually re-formed in the 90's with the classic line-up of VERLAINE, LLOYD, SMITH and FICCA, recording the acclaimed 'TELEVISION' (1992) for 'Capitol' and suggesting that what VERLAINE's solo career was lacking was the anchor and foil of LLOYD's rhythm playing. The latter kept himself busy during the 90's with guest spots for the likes of MATTHEW SWEET although parental considerations also took up much of his time. He eventually returned to solo work with 'THE COVER DOESN'T MATTER' (2001), a belated – 15 years (!) – set of pared-back alt-rock recorded with PETER STUART and CHRIS BUTLER. Meanwhile, news of another TELEVISION comeback for summer 2002 were proved true ... • **Songwriters:** VERLAINE lyrics / group compositions, except early live material; FIRE ENGINE (13th Floor Elevators) / KNOCKIN' ON HEAVEN'S DOOR (Bob Dylan) / SATISFACTION (Rolling Stones). • **Trivia:** VERLAINE played guitar on PATTI SMITH's 1974 single 'Hey Joe'.

Album rating: MARQUEE MOON (*10) / ADVENTURE (*6) / THE BLOW UP exploitation (*4) / TELEVISION (*5) / Tom Verlaine: TOM VERLAINE (*7) / DREAMTIME (*6) / WORDS FROM THE FRONT (*6) / COVER (*7) / FLASH LIGHT (*7) / THE WONDER (*7) / WARM AND COOL (*5) / THE MILLER'S TALE: A TOM VERLAINE ANTHOLOGY compilation (*8) / Richard Lloyd: ALCHEMY (*6) / FIELD OF FIRE (*5) / REAL TIME (*5) / THE COVER DOESN'T MATTER (*4)

TOM VERLAINE (b. THOMAS MILLER, 13 Dec'49, Mt.Morris, New Jersey) – vocals, lead guitar / **RICHARD LLOYD** – guitar, vocals / **RICHARD HELL** (b. RICHARD MYERS, 2 Oct'49, Lexington, Kentucky) – bass, vocals / **BILLY FICCA** – drums

Date	Details	not iss.	Ork
Oct 75.	(7") <81975> **LITTLE JOHNNY JEWEL. / (part 2)**	–	

—— **FRED SMITH** (b.10 Apr'48) – bass, vocals (ex-BLONDIE) repl. RICHARD HELL who went solo

Date	Details	Elektra	Elektra
Feb 77.	(lp/c) (K/K4 52046) <7E 1098> **MARQUEE MOON** – See no evil / Venus / Friction / Marquee moon / Elevation / Guiding light / Prove it / Torn curtain. (cd-iss. 1989; 960616-2)	28	
Mar 77.	(12",2-part-7") (K 12252) **MARQUEE MOON (stereo). / MARQUEE MOON (mono)**		
Jul 77.	(7"/12",12"green) (K 12262/+T) **PROVE IT. / VENUS**	25	–
Apr 78.	(lp,red-lp/c) (K/K4 52072) <6E 133> **ADVENTURE** – Glory / Days / Foxhole / Careful / Carried away / The fire / Ain't that nothin' / The dream's a dream. (cd-iss. Nov93 on 'WEA'; 7559 60523-2)	7	
Apr 78.	(7"/12"red) (K 12287/+T) **FOXHOLE. / CAREFUL**	36	–
Jul 78.	(7") (K 12306) **GLORY. / CARRIED AWAY**	–	–
Jul 78.	(7") <45516> **GLORY. / AIN'T THAT NOTHIN'**	–	

—— Broke ranks in Aug'78. FICCA joined The WAITRESSES, FRED joined The PATTI SMITH GROUP and RICHARD LLOYD went solo.

TELEVISION (cont) — THE GREAT INDIE DISCOGRAPHY — The 1970s

TOM VERLAINE

— went solo augmented mainly by **FRED SMITH** – bass / **JAY DEE DAUGHERTY** – drums / **BRUCE BRODY** – keyboards / **ALLAN SCHWARTZBERG** – drums, percussion

Elektra Elektra

Sep 79. (lp/c) *(K/K4 52156)* <2156> **TOM VERLAINE**
 – The grip of love / Souvenir from a dream / Kingdom come / Mr. Bingo / Yonki time / Flash lightning / Red leaves / Last night / Breakin' in my heart.

Warners Warners

Sep 81. (lp/c) *(K/K4 56919)* <BSK 3559> **DREAMTIME**
 – There's a reason / Penetration / Always / The blue robe / Without a word / Mr. Blur / Fragile / A future in noise / Down on the farm / Mary Marie.
Sep 81. (7"/12") *(K 17855/+T)* **ALWAYS. / THE BLUE ROBE**

— **JIMMY RIPP** – guitar; repl. BRODY

Virgin Warners

May 82. (lp/c) *(V/TCV 2227)* <BSK 3685> **WORDS FROM THE FRONT**
 – Present arrived / Postcard from Waterloo / True story / Clear it away / Words from the front / Coming apart / Days on the mountain. *(cd-iss. Aug88; OVED 87) (re-iss. cd Jun89; CDV 2227)*
May 82. (7"/12") *(VS 501/+12)* **POSTCARD FROM WATERLOO. / DAYS ON THE MOUNTAIN**
Jun 84. (7") *(VS 696)* **LET'S GO TO THE MANSION. / ('A'version)**
 (12"+=) *(VS 696/+12)* – Lindi Lu.
Aug 84. (7") *(VS 704)* **FIVE MILES OF YOU. / YOUR FINEST HOUR**
 (12"+=) *(VS 704/+12)* – Dissolve reveal.
Sep 84. (lp/c) *(V/TCV 2314)* <25144> **COVER**
 – Five miles of you / Let's go to the mansion / Travelling / O foolish heart / Dissolve – Reveal / Miss Emily / Rotation / Swim. *(re-iss. Apr86 lp/c; OVED/+C 168) (cd-iss. Jun89; CDV 2314)*

— **ANDY NEWMARK** – drums; repl. JAY DEE

Fontana Mercury-IRS

Feb 87. (7") *(FTANA 1)* **A TOWN CALLED WALKER. / SMOOTHER THAN JONES**
 (12"+=) *(FTANA 1-12)* – ('A'version) / Caveman flashlight.
Feb 87. (lp/c/cd) *(SF LP/MC 1)(830861-2)* <42050> **FLASH LIGHT** 99
 – Cry mercy, judge / Say a prayer / A town called Walker / Song / The scientist writes a letter / Bomb / 4 a.m. / The funniest thing / Annie's tellin' me / One time at sundown.
Mar 87. (7") *(FTANA 2)* **CRY MERCY JUDGE. / CALL ME THE CIRCLING**
 (12"+=) *(FTANA 2-12)* – At this moment (live) / Lover of the night (live) / Strange things happening.
Jun 87. (7") *(VLANE 3)* **THE FUNNIEST THING. / ONE TIME AT SUNDOWN**
 (12"+=) *(VLANE 3-12)* – Marquee Moon ('87 version).
Aug 87. (7") *(VLANE 4)* **THE SCIENTIST WRITES A LETTER. / ('A'-Paris version)**
Oct 89. (7") *(VLANE 5)* **SHIMMER. / BOMB**
 (cd-s+=) *(VLANE 5-12)(VLACD 5)* – The scientist writes a letter.
Mar 90. (7") *(VLANE 6)* **KALEIDOSCOPIN'. / SIXTEEN TULIPS**
 (12"+=)(cd-s+=) *(VLANE 6-12)(VLACD 6)* – Vanity fair.
Apr 90. (cd/c/lp) *(842420-2/-4/-1)* **THE WONDER**
 – Kaleidoscopin' / August / Ancient Egypt / Shimmer / Stalingrad / Pillow / Storm / 5 hours from Calais / Cooleridge / Prayer.

Rough Trade Rykodisc

Apr 92. (cd/lp) *(R 288-2/-1)* <10216> **WARM AND COOL**
 – Those harbour lights / Sleepwalkin' / The deep dark clouds / Saucer crash / Depot (1951) / Boulevard / Harley Quinn / Sor Juanna / Depot (1957) / Spiritual / Little dance / Ore.

– compilation –

Apr 96. (cd) *Virgin; (CDVDM 9034)* **A MILLER'S TALE (The Tom Verlaine Story)**
 – Kingdom come / Souvenir from a dream / Clear it away / Always / Postcard from Waterloo / Penetration / Breakin' in my heart / Marquee moon / Days on the mountain / Prove it / Venus / Glory / The grip of love / Without a word / Words from the front / Let's go to the mansion / Lindi-Lu / O foolish heart / Five miles of you / Your finest hour / Anna / Sixteen tulips / Call me the / At 4 a.m. / Stalingrad / Call Mr. Lee / No glamour for Willi / The revolution.

RICHARD LLOYD

— solo augmented by **JIM MAESTRO** – guitar (ex-BONGOS) / **MATTHEW MacKENZIE** – guitar, piano / **MICHAEL YOUNG** – guitar, synthesizer / **FRED SMITH** – bass / **VINNY DeNUNZIO** – drums

Elektra Elektra

Jan 80. (lp) *<(K 52196)>* **ALCHEMY**
 – Misty eyes / In the night / Alchemy / Womans ways / Number nine / Should've known better / Blue and grey / Summer rain / Pretend / Dying words.
Apr 80. (7") **BLUE AND GREY. / PRETEND**

— enlisted new line-up

Mistlur Moving Target

Jan 86. (lp/c) *(MLR 046)* <MT/+C 005> **FIELD OF FIRE**
 – Watch yourself / Losin Anna / Soldier blue / Back / Keep on dancin / Pleading / Lovin man / Black to white / Field of fire.

Celluloid GrandSlamm

Oct 87. (lp/c/cd) *(CELL 6135/+C/CD)* <32> **REAL TIME (live)**
 – Fire engine / Misty eyes / Alchemy / Spider talk / Lost child / No.9 / The only feeling / Soldier blue / Field of fire / Pleading / Watch yourself / Louisianna Anna / Black to white. (cd+=) – Watch yourself / Losin' Anne / Black to white. *(cd re-iss. Nov97 on 'Charly'; CDGR 194)*

— LLOYD went onto join JOHN DOE (ex-X)

Evangeline Upsetter

Apr 01. (cd) *(GEL 4023)* <4001> **THE COVER DOESN'T MATTER**
 – The knock down / Ain't it time / She loves to fly / I thought / Dtrangestrange / Torn shirt / Downline / Raising the serpent / Submarine / Cortege.

TELEVISION

— re-formed for one-off with **VERLAINE, LLOYD, FICCA + SMITH**

Capitol Capitol

Sep 92. (cd/c/lp) *<(CD/TC+/EST 2181)>* **TELEVISION**
 – 1880 or so / Shane, she wrote this / In world / Call Mr. Lee / Rhyme / No glamour for Willi / Beauty trip / The rocket / This fire / Mars. *(cd re-iss. Feb99; CDESTV 2181)*

– compilations, others, etc. –

Jan 83. (c) *R.O.I.R.; <A-114>* **THE BLOW UP (live)**
 – The blow up / See no evil / Prove it / Elevation / I don't care / Venus de Milo / Foxhole / Ain't that nothin' / Knockin' on Heaven's door / Little Johnny Jewel / Friction / Marquee moon / Satisfaction. *(UK cd-iss. Feb90 on 'Danceteria'; DANCD 030) (cd re-iss. Nov94 on 'R.O.I.R.'; RE 114CD) <cd-iss. Apr99; RUSCD 8249)> <(d-lp iss.May01; RUSLP 8249)>*
1979. (12"m) *Ork-WEA; (NYC 1T)* **LITTLE JOHNNY JEWEL (parts 1 & 2). / ('A'live version)**

TELEVISION PERSONALITIES

Formed: Chelsea, London, England . . . 1976 by schoolmates DAN TREACY and EDWARD BALL, who found JOE FOSTER and later added brothers JOHN and GERARD BENNETT. After originally going under the moniker of TEEN 78, they came up with the name TV PERSONALITIES, parading themselves as HUGHIE GREEN, BRUCE FORSYTHE, BOB MONKHOUSE, RUSSELL HARTY and NICHOLAS PARSONS. Their first 45, '14th FLOOR', was released in the early summer of 1978, and with the help of airplay from John Peel, sold out of its 867 print run. The TVP's soon formed their own 'King's Road' label, (distributed initially by 'Rough Trade') and released an EP, 'WHERE'S BILL GRUNDY NOW?', which included the superb title track, alongside another sarcastic gem, 'PART-TIME PUNKS'. Around this time ED and GERARD were also part of The O-LEVEL, who, after one 45, became The TEENAGE FILMSTARS (with DAN and JOE). In 1980, after a short retirement, they gigged for the first time and issued the 'SMASHING TIME' single, a more retro-themed affair as the band moved increasingly towards punk-influenced psychedelic whimsy. Their recordings over the course of the previous year were issued on the album, 'AND DON'T THE KIDS JUST LOVE IT' (1981), a record that paid homage (of sorts!) to one of the band's mentors in the shape of the classic 'I KNOW WHERE SYD BARRETT LIVES' alongside naively charming cockney tales, 'GEOFFREY INGRAM' and 'JACKANORY STORIES'. A year later, DAN and ED set up their own label, 'Whaam!', although they were subsequently forced to fold it after a only few releases (including two TVP albums, 'MUMMY YOU'RE NOT WATCHING ME' and 'THEY COULD HAVE BEEN BIGGER THAN THE BEATLES') due to pressure from pop duo, WHAM. As a result, the proposed 1983 release of 'THE PAINTED WORD' was shelved and the album later released by 'Illuminated', early in '85. Later that year, they chose another name for their recording venture, 'Dreamworld', although this too became defunct, even after signing The MIGHTY LEMON DROPS. The TVP's (now minus BALL who had been replaced with former SWELL MAPS man, JOWE HEAD) broke their long silence in 1989 when 'Fire' records finally issued their remarkable comeback 45, 'SALVADOR DALI'S GARDEN PARTY', soon to be included on the following year's 'PRIVILEGE' set. By 1992's 'CLOSER TO GOD' they had lost their initial impact and TREACY became more heavily into drugs, leading to bouts of depression and little creative output. In the Autumn of '95, he was back to his near best with the sarcastic 'I WAS A MOD BEFORE YOU WERE A MOD'. • **Songwriters:** DAN and ED penned most, until latters' departure. Covered BIKE (Pink Floyd) / NO ONE'S LITTLE GIRL (Raincoats) / SEASONS IN THE SUN (Jacques Brel). • **Trivia:** While in the studio, DAN once tried to decapitate another member at the time, MARK SHEPPARD, although producer, DALE GRIFFIN, reportedly locked him in the cupboard!

Album rating: AND DON'T THE KIDS JUST LOVE IT (*8) / MUMMY YOU'RE NOT WATCHING ME (*6) / THEY COULD HAVE BEEN BIGGER THAN THE BEATLES (*6) / THE PAINTED WORD (*7) / PRIVILEGE (*8) / CLOSER TO GOD (*6) / I WAS A MOD BEFORE YOU WERE A MOD (*6) / YES DARLING, BUT IS IT ART? compilation (*7)

DAN TREACY – vocals / **EDWARD BALL** – organ, vocals / **JOE FOSTER** – guitar / **JOHN BENNETT** – bass / **GERARD BENNETT** – drums

W1 Teen not iss.

May 78. (7"; as TV PERSONALITIES) *(SRTS-CUS 77089)* **14th FLOOR. / OXFORD STREET**
 (re-iss. Aug89 on 'Overground', 7" + yellow or white; OVER 03)

— now as trio (ED, DAN & JOE)

Kings Road not iss.

Nov 78. (7"ep) *(LYN 5976-7)* **WHERE'S BILL GRUNDY NOW?**
 – Part-time punks / Where's Bill Grundy now? / Happy families / Posing at the Roundhouse. *(re-iss. Nov79 on 'Rough Trade'; RT 033)*

— disbanded for a year. **MARK 'EMPIRE' SHEPPARD** – drums (of SWELL MAPS)

Rough Trade not iss.

Jul 80. (7") *(RT 051)* **SMASHING TIME. / KING AND COUNTRY**

— JOE FOSTER left and soon became The MISSING SCIENTISTS who released a 45 in Sep80 'BIG CITY BRIGHT LIGHTS'. / 'DISCOTEQUE X', which featured DAN TREACY and DANIEL MILLER of Mute label.

TELEVISION PERSONALITIES (cont)

Jan 81. (lp; as TV PERSONALITIES) *(ROUGH 24)* **AND DON'T THE KIDS JUST LOVE IT**
– This angry silence / The glittering prizes / World of Pauline Lewis / A family affair / Silly girl / Diary of a young man / Geoffrey Ingram / I know where Syd Barrett lives / Jackanory stories / Parties in Chelsea / La grande illusion / A picture of Dorian Gray / The crying room / Look back in anger. *(cd-iss. Aug91 on 'Fire'; REFIRECD 7) (cd re-iss. Mar02 on 'Fire'; SFIRE 002CD)*

Feb 81. (7") *(RT 063)* **I KNOW WHERE SYD BARRETT LIVES. / ARTHUR THE GARDENER**

— were now just **DAN + EMPIRE** + new bassman **BERNARD COOPER** (ED BALL had formed The TIMES.)

Whaam! not iss.

May 81. (7"; as GIFTED CHILDREN) *(WHAAM 001)* **PAINTING BY NUMBERS. / LICHTENSTEIN GIRL**

— **ED** returned on guitar & bass. **SLAUGHTER JOE FOSTER** also returned.

Jan 82. (lp) *(WHAAM 3)* **MUMMY YOU'RE NOT WATCHING ME**
– Adventure playground / A day in heaven / Scream quietly / Mummy you're not watching me / Brians magic ear / Where the rainbow ends / David Hockney's diaries / Painting by numbers / Lichtenstein painting / Magnificent dreams If I could write poetry. *(re-iss. Jun86 on 'Dreamworld'; BIG DREAM 4) (re-iss. Sep91 on 'Fire' cd/lp; REFIRE CD/LP 8) (cd re-iss. Apr02 on 'Fire'; SFIRE 007CD)*

Aug 82. (lp) *(BIG 5)* **THEY COULD HAVE BEEN BIGGER THAN THE BEATLES**
– Three wishes / David Hockney's diary / In a perfumed garden / Flowers for Abigail / King and country / The boy in the Paisley shirt / Games for boys / Painter man / Psychedelic holiday / 14th floor / Sooty's disco party / Makin time / When Emily cries / The glittering prizes / Anxiety block / Mysterious ways.. *(re-iss. Jun86 on 'Dreamworld'; BIG DREAM 2) (re-iss. Sep91 on 'Fire' cd/lp; REFIRE CD/LP 9) (cd re-iss. Jul02 on 'Fire'; SFIRE 014CD)*

Sep 82. (7"m) *(WHAAM 4)* **THREE WISHES. / GEOFFREY INGRAM / AND DON'T THE KIDS JUST LOVE IT**

— **DAN + ED** added **DAVE MUSKER** – organ / **JOE FOSTER** – guitar / **MARK FLUNDER** – bass / (JOWE HEAD repl. MARK who joined ROBYN HITCHCOCK)

Rough Trade not iss.

Dec 83. (7") *(RT 109)* **A SENSE OF BELONGING. / PARADISE ESTATE**
(below lp should have been issued by 'Whaam!' in Nov83)

Illuminated not iss.

Jan 85. (lp) *(JAMS 37)* **THE PAINTED WORD**
– Stop and smell the roses / The painted word / A life of her own / Bright sunny smiles / Mentioned in dispatches / A sense of belonging / Say you won't cry / Someone to share my life with / You'll have to scream louder / Happy all the time / The girl who had everything / Paradise estates / Back to Vietnam. *(re-iss. Sep91 on 'Fire' cd/lp; REFIRE CD/LP 10) (cd re-iss. May02 on 'Fire'; SFIRE 029CD)*

— now with **JOWE HEAD** – bass / **JEFF BLOOM** – drums (FOSTER became SLAUGHTER JOE and MUSKER formed JASMINE MINKS. ED continued with The TIMES and later went solo

Dreamworld not iss.

Feb 86. (12"m) *(DREAM 4)* **HOW I LEARNED TO LOVE THE ...BOMB! / THEN GOD SNAPS HIS FINGERS. / NO YOU'RE JUST BEING RIDICULOUS**

Nov 86. (7"m) *(DREAM 10)* **HOW I LEARNED TO LOVE THE BOMB. / GROCER'S DAUGHTER / GIRL CALLED CHARITY**

— (next album was to have been issued a year earlier on 'Dreamworld')

Fire not iss.

Oct 89. (7") *(BLAZE 37S)* **SALVADOR DALI'S GARDEN PARTY. / ROOM AT THE TOP OF THE STAIRS**
(12"+=) *(BLAZE 37T)* – This time there is no happy ending / Part one: Fulfilling the contractual obligations.

Dec 89. (ltd.7") *(CAFF 5)* **I STILL BELIEVE IN MAGIC. / RESPECTABLE**
(above single on 'Caff' label)

Feb 90. (cd/c/lp) *(FIRE CD/MC/LP 21)* **PRIVILEGE**
– Paradise is for the blessed / Conscience tells me no / All my dreams are dead / The man who paints the rainbows / Sad Mona Lisa / Sometimes I think you know me / Good and faithful servant / My hedonistic tendencies / Salvador Dali's garden party / What if it's raining? / The engine driver song / Better than I know myself / Privilege. *(c+=/cd+=)* – The room at the top of the stairs / This time there's no happy ending / Fulfilling the contractual obligations (part one). *(cd re-iss. Jul02; SFIRE 014CD)*

Sep 91. (12"ep/cd-ep) *(BLAZE 48 T/CD)* **STRANGELY BEAUTIFUL / REACHING FOR THE STARS. / NOT EVEN A MAYBE / ('A'-Chill out mix)**

Feb 92. (12"ep/cd-ep) *(BLAZE 440/550 49)* **SHE NEVER READ MY POEMS / THE DAY THE DOPLINS LEAVE THE SEA. / CHRIST KNOWS I HAVE TRIED / ('A'extended)**

Sep 92. (7"/cd-s) *(TWANG 15/+CD)* **WE WILL BE OUR GURUS. / AN EXHIBITION BY JOAN MIRO / LOVE IS BETTER THAN WAR**
(above on 'Seminal Twang')

Oct 92. (cd/c/d-lp) *(FIRE CD/MC/DLP 032)* **CLOSER TO GOD**
– You don't know how lucky you are / Hard luck story No. 30 / Little works of art / Razorblades and lemonade / Coming home soon / Me and big ideas / Honey for the bears / Let me myself in you / Goodnight Mr. Spaceman / My very nervous breakdown / We will be your gurus / You are special and you always will be / Not for the likes of us / You're younger than you know / Very dark today / I hope you have a nice day / Baby you're only as good as you should be / Closer to God.

May 93. (7"/cd-s) *(BLAZE 65)* **GOODNIGHT MR. SPACEMAN. / IF I WAS YOUR GIRLDRIEND**
(cd-s+=) *(BLAZE 65CD)* – She loves it when he sings like Elvis / ('A'-Lost in space mix).

Vinyl Japan not iss.

May 94. (12"ep/cd-ep) *(TASK 28)* **FAR AWAY AND LOST IN JOY / I DON'T WANT TO LIVE THIS LIFE. / DO YOU KNOW WHAT THEY'RE SAYING ABOUT ME NOW? / I GET FRIGHTENED**

Oct 95. (12"ep/cd-ep) *(TASK/+CD 048)* **DO YOU THINK IF YOU WERE BEAUTIFUL YOU'D BE HAPPY / HE USED TO PAINT IN COLOURS / WHO WILL BE YOUR PRINCE / I SUPPOSE YOU THINK IT'S FUNNY**

Overground not iss.

Sep 95. (lp/cd; as TV PERSONALITIES) *(OVER 41/+CD)* **I WAS A MOD BEFORE YOU WAS A MOD**
– As John Belushi said I was a mod before you were a mod / A stranger to myself / Little Woody Allen / A long time gone / Evan doesn't ring me anymore / Things have changed since I was girl / Haunted / I can see my whole world crashing down / Something flew over my head / Everything she touches turns to gold. *(re-iss. Jun97 & May02; same)*

Twist not iss.

Jan 96. (7"m) *(TWIST 20)* **SEASONS IN THE SUN. / BIKE / NO ONE'S LITTLE GIRL**

– compilations, etc. –

1985. (lp) *Pastell; (POW 2)* **CHOCOLAT-ART (A TRIBUTE TO JAMES LAST) (live Germany 1984)** — German
(re-iss. Jul93 cd/lp; POW 2)

Aug 91. (lp/cd; as TV PERSONALITIES) *Overground; (OVER 21/+CD)* **CAMPING IN FRANCE (live '85)**

1994. (lp/cd; as TV PERSONALITIES) *Overground; (OVER 30/+CD)* **HOW I LEARNED TO LOVE THE BOMB**
(re-iss. Jun97; same)

Feb 95. (cd) *Fire; (FLIPCD 001)* **YES DARLING BUT IS IT ART?**

Mar 96. (cd; as TV PERSONALITIES) *Overground; (OVER 48CD)* **TOP GEAR**

1996. (7"/cd-s) *Overground; (OVER 50/+CD)* **I WAS A MOD BEFORE YOU WERE A MOD**

Oct 96. (cd; as TV PERSONALITIES) *Overground; (OVER 52/+CD)* **PAISLEY SHIRTS & MINI SKIRTS**

Sep 97. (cd) *Nectar; (NTMCD 529)* **PRIME TIME 1981-1992**
(re-iss. Jun98 on 'Reactive'; REMCD 529)

Oct 98. (cd/lp) *Damaged Goods; (<DAMGOOD 64 CD/LP>)* **DON'T CRY BABY ... IT'S ONLY A MOVIE**

Jun 99. (lp) *Little Teddy; (BITE 017)* **MADE IN JAPAN (live)**

May 00. (cd) *Vinyl Japan; (<ASKCD 112>)* **THE BOY WHO COULDN'T STOP DREAMING** — Jun00

Apr 01. (cd) *Cherry Red; (<CDMRED 152>)* **PART TIME PUNKS: THE VERY BEST OF TELEVISION PERSONALITIES**

May 02. (cd) *Little Teddy; (<BITE 026CD>)* **FASHION CONSCIOUS: THE LITTLE TEDDY YEARS** — Jun02

THEORETICAL GIRLS
(see under ⇒ BRANCA, Glenn; in 80's section)

THIS HEAT

Formed: Brixton, London, England ... late 1975 by CHARLES BULLEN, CHARLES HAYWARD and GARETH WILLIAMS. They were originally called RADAR FAVOURITES, later changing to DOLPHIN LOGIC. Setting up their own studio in a local disused meat factory, their line-up was augmented by tape editor CHRIS BLAKE, the band subsequently sending a demo to John Peel, who gave them airtime on his night time Radio One show in early '77. Going back into the studio with ANTHONY MOORE (Slapp Happy) and DAVID CUNNINGHAM (Flying Lizards), they recorded a self-titled debut album for CUNNINGHAM's label, 'Piano'. Experimental improvisers lying between THROBBING GRISTLE and CAN, THIS HEAT swapped instruments and multi-layered tracks on tape loops. During this period and after the album's release in 1979, they worked with "world music" musicians from India, Ghana (MARIO BOYER DIEKVUROH) and Senegal, branching out on tour the following year. After a further 12" single, the band signed to 'Rough Trade' and in '81, hooked up with reggae mixer, MARTIN FREDERICK on a follow-up album, 'DECEIT', this time around fusing industrial ethnic-folk with dub. However, THIS HEAT later split when WILLIAMS went to study Indian dance, drama and music theory, HAYWARD later surfacing in another trio, The CAMBERWELL NOW.

Album rating: THIS HEAT (*8) / DECEIT (*7)

CHARLES BULLEN (b. Liverpool) – guitar, clarinet, viola, vocals, tapes (also of PEOPLE IN CONTROL) / **CHARLES HAYWARD** (b. 1951) – percussion, keyboards, vocals, tapes (ex-QUIET SUN) / **GARETH WILLIAMS** – keyboards, guitar, bass, vocals, tapes

Piano not iss.

Aug 79. (lp) *(THIS 1)* **THIS HEAT**
– Testcard / Horizontal hold / Not waving / Water / Twilight furniture / 24 track loop / Diet of worms / Music like escaping gas / Rainforest / The fall of Saigon / Testcard. *(re-iss. Aug84 on 'These'; HEAT 1) (cd-iss. Nov91; HEAT 1CD)*

Sep 80. (12"ep) *(THIS 12-01)* **HEALTH AND EFFICIENCY. / GRAPHIC / VARISPEED**
(3"cd-ep iss.Sep98 on 'These'; THESE 12)

Rough Trade not iss.

Sep 81. (lp) *(ROUGH 26)* **DECEIT**
– Sleep / Paper hats / Triumph / S.P.Q.R. / Cenotaph / Shrink wrap / Radio Prague / Makeshift Swahili / Independence / A new kind of water. *(re-iss. Aug84 on 'These'; HEAT 2) (cd-iss. Nov91; HEAT 2CD)*

— split in 1982 when WILLIAMS' place was filled by tour temps **IAN HILL** – keyboards, vocals / **TREVOR GORONWY** – bass, vocals / **STEVE RICKARD** – engineer. BULLEN became a sound engineer and released one rare 'LIFETONES' lp in 1983

— HAYWARD went onto work with Rough Trade outfits LAURA LOGIC (Pedigree Charm) and RAINCOATS (Odyshape)

THIS HEAT (cont)   THE GREAT INDIE DISCOGRAPHY   The 1970s

– compilations, etc. –

1993. (cd) *These;* (THESE 6CD) **REPEAT**
– Repeat / Metal / Graphic – Varispeed. *(re-mast.Sep98; same)*
Jun 97. (cd) *These;* (THESE 010CD) **MADE AVAILABLE – PEEL SESSIONS**
(lp-iss.Sep98; THESE 10)
Jul 98. (2x12") *These;* (THESE 12-6) **REPEAT / HEALTH AND EFFICIENCY**

CAMBERWELL NOW

HAYWARD, GORONWY + RICKARD + guest BULLEN

Duplicate   not iss.

1983. (12"ep) *(0011)* **MERIDIANS**
– Cutty Sark / Trade winds / Pearl divers / Spirit of Dunkirk / Splash.

Ink   not iss.

May 86. (lp) *(INK 19)* **THE GHOST TRADE**
– Working nights / Sitcom / Wheat futures / Speculative fiction / Green lantern / The ghost trade.
—— added guest **MARIA LANBURN** – saxophone
Feb 87. (12") *(INK 12-24)* **GREENFINGERS. /**
—— HAYWARD's drum trio then recorded 'NOISY CHAMPS' as LES BATTERIES (on 'Ayaa Disques'; *AYAADT 0486*), alongside drummers GUIGOU CHENEBIER and RICK BROWN.

– compilations, etc. –

1992. (cd) *RecDec;* (CD 1015) **ALL'S WELL**

CHARLES HAYWARD

Ink   not iss.

Nov 87. (lp) *(INK 31)* **SURVIVE THE GESTURE**
– Make believe / Let's pretend / North Southwark / Pretend to believe / Crystal Palace / This misunderstanding / You and me / Time and motion / That distant light / Australia. *(cd-iss. Nov88; INKCD 004)*

Sub Rosa   Sub Rosa

1990. (cd) *(<SUBCD 01033>)* **SKEW WHIFF – A TRIBUTE TO MARK ROTHKO**
– The actor merges with the crowd / Cold blue sun / Smell of metal / Lopside / Thames water authority (parts 1 & 2).
1992. (cd) *(<SUBCD 01740>)* **SWITCH ON WAR – MUSIC FOR THE ARMCHAIR THEATRE OF WAR**
– Crying shame / Strong-arm deadline / Pinpoint / Sweetheart / Never before.
—— HAYWARD also drummed in outfits KEEP THE DOG and CAROL, SINGING, which included FRED FRITH (ex-HENRY COW) and NICK DOYNE-DITMUS (ex-PINSKI ZOO) respectively. He also sessioned for EVERYTHING BUT THE GIRL. With NICK DOYNE-IT, he issued cd/lp 'MY SECRET ALPHABET' *(SR 59)*

Marina   not iss.

Mar 97. (cd; CHARLES HAYWARD, DAVID SHEA & NUS)
(MAR 21) **SUB ROSA SESSIONS: BARI OCTOBER 1996**

David THOMAS (see under ⇒ **PERE UBU**)

THOSE NAUGHTY LUMPS

Formed: Liverpool, England ... 1977 by PETER HART, GERRY MULLIGAN, KEVIN WILKINSON, BILL DRUMMOND (from BIG IN JAPAN) and DAVID BALFE, the latter subsequently moving on to The TEARDROP EXPLODES. His replacement, PETE YOUNGER, was in place for the group's long-awaited debut 45, 'IGGY POP'S JACKET', a brilliant indie-pop tribute to the Godfather Of Punk. By the time of their 1980 follow-up, 'DOWN AT THE ZOO', a major upheaval in the ranks left only HART and WILKINSON at the core, the other three including 'Zoo' label boss, DRUMMOND, all went on to better things.

Album rating: never released any

PETER HART – vocals / **BILL DRUMMOND** – lead guitar (ex-BIG IN JAPAN) / **GERRY MULLIGAN** – saxophone / **KEVIN WILKINSON** – drums / **PETE YOUNGER** – bass; repl. DAVID BALFE (to TEARDROP EXPLODES)

Zoo   not iss.

Jan 79. (7") *(CAGE 002)* **IGGY POP'S JACKET. / PURE AND INNOCENT**
—— **BOBBY CARL** – guitar; repl. DRUMMOND who later formed KLF
—— **MARTIN COOPER** – saxophone (ex-DALEK I LOVE YOU) repl. MULLIGAN
—— **BREAM** – bass; repl. YOUNGER who joined WAH! HEAT

Open Eye   not iss.

1980. (7"ep) *(OEEP 1002)* **DOWN AT THE ZOO EP**
– Ice cream / Down at the zoo / I'm gonna die / Love is a reflex.
—— basically split when WILKINSON joined HOLLY & THE ITALIANS (and later CHINA CRISIS). COOPER went on to ORCHESTRAL MANOEUVRES IN THE DARK.

THROBBING GRISTLE

Formed: Manchester, England ... Autumn '75 by GENESIS P-ORRIDGE and girlfriend COSEY FANNI TUTTI, a nude model, the couple having previously met at an art exhibition in Hull. Defiantly unconventional from day one, their early live shows boasted some dubious attractions such as COSEY going topless, P-ORRIDGE and other member CHRIS CARTER slashing themselves and a backdrop of stomach-churning slides. In 1977, along with PETER CHRISTOPHERSON, the act set up their own independent label, 'Industrial', as a means of issuing limited edition material. A debut album, '2ND ANNUAL REPORT', was given a low-key release at the height of punk in '77. Although revelling in the genre's subversiveness, P-ORRIDGE & Co. were more interested in monotony electronic textures than three-chord rock. Beloved of the more arty avant-garde post-punk set, THROBBING GRISTLE were largely a vehicle for the bizarre P-ORRIDGE's psycho-sexual narratives, usually set to pioneering synth-musak (CABARET VOLTAIRE and SUICIDE were mining a similar seam). A doubled-header single, 'UNITED' / 'ZYKLON B ZOMBIE' emerged the following summer, pursued by a second set, 'D.O.A.', at the end of '78. The following year, THROBBING GRISTLE made a vague stab at commerciality with the cynically titled '20 JAZZ FUNK GREATS', unearthing the wild 'PERSUASION' and the tortuously ponderous 'CONVINCING PEOPLE'. The record unsurprisingly failed to win the band any new admirers, especially in the music press, a swansong album, 'HEATHEN EARTH' (1980), paving the way for new ground; the group split two ways, P-ORRIDGE forming PSYCHIC TV, while CHRIS AND COSEY formed their own duo. • **Songwriters:** GENESIS P-ORRIDGE or mainly group compositions. • **Trivia:** Many or all performance / art gigs were recorded on tape and video.

Album rating: GREATEST HITS: ENTERTAINMENT THROUGH PAIN compilation (*7) / 20 JAZZ FUNK GREATS (*7) / D.O.A. (*8)

GENESIS P-ORRIDGE (b. NEIL ANDREW MEGSON, 22 Feb'50) – vox, electric violin, bass (ex-PORK DUKES) / **COSEY FANNI TUTTI** – guitar, cornet, effects / **CHRIS CARTER** – synthesizers, keyboards / **PETER 'Sleazy' CHRISTOPHERSON** – tapes, synthesizers, trumpet

Industrial   not iss.

Dec 76. (ltd-c) *(IR 0001)* **BEST OF VOLUME II**
– Slug bait / Very friendly / We hate you / Seers of E / etc. *(cd-iss. Jun91 on 'Grey Area-Mute'; TGCD 1)*
Nov 77. (ltd-lp) *(IR 0002)* **SECOND ANNUAL REPORT** (some live)
– Industrial introduction / Slug bait (ICA) / Slug bait (live at Southampton) / Slug bait (live at Brighton) / Maggot death (live at the Rat Club) / Maggot death (live at Southampton) / Maggot death (live at Brighton) / After cease to exist – The original soundtrack of the Coum transmission film. *(re-iss. Nov78 + Apr79; same) (re-iss. Jun81 on 'Fetish'; FET 2001) (re-iss. Nov83 on 'Mute'; MIR 1) (re-iss. Jul91 on 'Grey Area-Mute'+=; TGCD2)* – Zyklon B Zombie / United. *<US cd-iss. 1993 on 'Mute-Warners'; 61093>*
Jun 78. (7"/7"white) *(IR 0003/+U)* **UNITED. / ZYKLON B ZOMBIE**
(re-iss. Jan80; same) – B-side longer.
Dec 78. (lp) *(IR 0004)* **D.O.A. – THE THIRD AND FINAL REPORT**
– I.B.M. / Hit by a rock / United / The valley of the shadow of death / Dead on arrival / Weeping / Hamburger lady / Hometime / Ab-7a / E-Coli / Death threats / Walls of sound / Blood on the floor. *(re-iss. Nov83 on 'Mute'; MIR 002) (cd-iss. Jul91 on 'Grey Area-Mute'; TGCD 3) <US cd-iss. 1993 on 'Mute-Warners'+=; 61094>* – Five knuckle shuffle / We hate you (little girls).
Jul 79. (7") *<SS45 001>* **WE HATE YOU (LITTLE GIRLS). / FIVE KNUCKLE SHUFFLE**   French
(above on 'Sordid Sentimentale') *<US-iss.Sep81 on 'Adolescent'; ARTI 010>*
Oct 79. (lp) *(IR 0008)* **20 JAZZ FUNK GREATS**
– 20 jazz funk greats / Beach Head / Still walking / Tanith / Convincing people / Exotica / Hot on the heels of love / Persuasion / Walkabout / What a day / Six six sixties. *(re-iss. Nov83 on 'Mute'; MIR 3) (cd-iss. Jul91 on 'Grey Area-Mute'+=; TGCD 4)* – Discipline (Berlin) / Discipline (Manchester). *<US cd-iss. 1993 on 'Mute-Warners'; 61095>*
Jun 80. (lp,blue-lp) *(IR 0009)* **HEATHEN EARTH**
– Heathen Earth (pts 1-8) / Adrenalin / Subhuman *(re-iss. Nov83 on 'Mute'; MIR 004) (cd-iss. Jul91 on 'Grey Area-Mute'; TGCD 5)* – (also on video). *<US cd-iss. 1993 on 'Mute-Warners'; 61696>*
Sep 80. (7") *(IR 0013)* **SUBHUMAN. / SOMETHING CAME OVER ME**
Sep 80. (7") *(IR 0015)* **ADRENALIN. / DISTANT DREAMS (Part Two)**

Fetish   Fetish

May 81. (12") *(FET 006)* **DISCIPLINE (live in Manchester). / DISCIPLINE (live in Berlin)**

—— dissolved in 1981 when P-ORRIDGE and CHRISTOPHERSON formed PSYCHIC TV; the other two formed duo CHRIS & COSEY

– compilations, others, etc. –

Oct 81. (lp) *Mute;* (*<61001-2>*) **GREATEST HITS: ENTERTAINMENT THROUGH PAIN**
– Hamburger lady / Hot on the heels of love / Subhuman / Ab 7a / Six six sixties / Blood on the floor / 20 jazz funk greats / Tiab guls / United / What a day / Adrenalin. *(UK-iss.Dec84 on 'Rough Trade'; ROUGHUS 23) (cd-iss. Oct90 & Jul91 on 'Grey Area-Mute'; TGCD 7) (<re-iss. Feb93 on 'Grey Area-Mute' c; 961001-4>)*
Nov 81. (lp) *Zensor;* (ZENSOR 1D) **FUNERAL IN BERLIN**   Germ'y
– Stained by dead horses / Trained condition of obedience zero's death / Nomon / Raudive bunker experiment / Denial of death / Funeral in Berlin / Trade deficit.
Feb 82. (5xlp-box) *Fetish;* (FX 1) **A BOXED SET**
– (5 original albums) *(cd's 1988 on 'Mute')*
1982. (ltd-lp) *Death;* (01) **MUSIC FROM THE DEATH FACTORY, MAY '79 (live)**
1982. (ltd-lp) *Walter Ulbricht;* (001) **JOURNEY THROUGH THE BODY**
(cd-iss. Oct93 on 'Grey Area-Mute'; TGCD 8)
1982. (ltd-lp) *Power Focus;* (001) **ASSUMING POWER FOCUS**   fanclub
(most rec.1975)
– Debris of murder / Freedom is a sickness / His arm was her leg / What a day! / Dead'd / Last exit / Propaganda vogananga / Sunstroke militia / Heathen earth / Urge to kill / Epping forest / Persuasion / Leeds ripper. *(<cd-iss. Oct95 on 'Paragoric'; PA 016CD>) (<cd re-iss. Apr98 on 'Triple X'; TX 6001CD>)*
Nov 82. (d-lp) *Karnage;* (KILL 1) **THEE PSYKICK SACRIFICE**
(re-iss. Aug86 as 'SACRIFICE' on 'Dojo'; DOJOLP 29)

THROBBING GRISTLE (cont)

1983. (lp) *Expanded;* **MISSION IS TERMINATED: NICE TRACKS** (free-12"w.a.) **DAMURA SUNRISE. / YOU DON'T KNOW**
1983. (10"lp) *Phonograph;* **FUHRER DER MEIN SHEAT**
1983. (lp) *Illuminated; (SJAMS 31S)* **EDITIONS FRANKFURT – BERLIN**
Nov 83. (lp) *Mute; (MIR 5)* **MISSION OF DEAD SOULS (THE LAST LIVE PERFORMANCE OF THROBBING GRISTLE) (live San Francisco)**
– Dead souls / Guts on the floor / Circle of animals / Looking for the Oto / Vision and voice / Funeral rites / Spirits flying / Persuasion U.S.A. / Process / Discipline / Distant dreams / Something came over me. *(cd-iss. Jul91 on 'Grey Area-Mute'; TGCD 6) <US cd-iss. Feb93 on 'Mute-Warners'; 61097>*
Feb 84. (lp) *Illuminated; (JAMS 35)* **IN THE SHADOW OF THE SUN (Soundtrack)**
(cd-iss. Oct93 on 'Grey Area-Mute'; TGCD 9)
Apr 84. (lp) *Casual Abandon; (CAS 1J)* **ONCE UPON A TIME**
May 84. (c) *Cause For Concern; (CFC 001)* **NOTHING SHORT OF TOTAL WAR**
(lp-iss.Oct87; CFC 016)
1984. (lp) *Mental Decay; (MD 01-1)* **SPECIAL TREATMENT**
(re-iss. May88; same)
1980's. (lp) *Sprut; (001)* **VERY FRIENDLY – THE FIRST ANNUAL REPORT OF T.G.**
(cd-iss. Oct96 on 'New Millennium'; CDTG 23) (cd re-iss. Apr01 on 'Yeaah'; YEAAH 50) (lp re-iss. Dec01 on 'Get Back'; GET 83)
1980's. (4xc-box) *Industrial; (IRC 1-IRC 24)* **24 HOURS**
Apr 93. (cd) *Grey Area-Mute; (TGCD 10)* **LIVE – VOLUME 1 (live 1976-1978)**
Apr 93. (cd) *Grey Area-Mute; (TGCD 11)* **LIVE – VOLUME 2 (live 1977-1978)**
Apr 93. (cd) *Grey Area-Mute; (TGCD 12)* **LIVE – VOLUME 3 (live 1978-1979)**
Apr 93. (cd) *Grey Area-Mute; (TGCD 13)* **LIVE – VOLUME 4 (live 1979-1980)**
Dec 93. (cd) *Dossier; (EFA 08450CD)* **FUNK BEYOND JAZZ**
Oct 94. (cd) *Dossier; (EFA 08458-2)* **GIFTGAS**
Dec 95. (cd) *Dossier; (EFA 08448-2)* **BLOOD PRESSURE**
Oct 96. (cd) *New Millennium; (CDTG 24)* **GRIEF**
(re-iss. Jul01 on 'Yeaah'; YEAAH 51)
Oct 97. (cd) *Dossier; (<EFA 08490-2>)* **KREEME HORN**
– Careless idle chatter / Merely nodding / Raw mode of life / Rumour and dishonour / Ugliness is a form of genius.
Dec 98. (cd) *Dossier; (<EFA 08493-2>)* **DIMENTIA IN EXCELSIS (live first US gig)** — Sep98
Nov 99. (cd) *Tin Toy; (TTCD 010)* **RAFTERS**
Jan 02. (cd) *Dressed To Kill; (MIDRO 849)* **FINAL MUSAK**

Johnny THUNDERS

Born: JOHN ANTHONY GENZALE, 15 Jul'52, Leesburg, Florida, USA. Having been an integral part of The NEW YORK DOLLS in the first half of the 70's, vocalist/guitarist THUNDERS formed new wave/punk act, The HEARTBREAKERS alongside ex-'DOLLS drummer, JERRY NOLAN and ex-TELEVISION bassist, RICHARD HELL. After an initial gig as a trio, they picked up extra guitarist, WALTER LURE, although this incarnation was short-lived as RICHARD promptly departed to form his own RICHARD HELL & THE VOID-OIDS. Filling the void with BILLY RATH, they were invited to London by ex-'DOLLS manager, MALCOLM McLAREN, who offered them a support slot with his punk proteges, The SEX PISTOLS (on their 'Anarchy' tour of late '76). The HEARTBREAKERS subsequently signed to UK label, 'Track', issuing their debut 45, 'CHINESE ROCKS' (a tribute to oriental narcotics co-written with DEE DEE RAMONE), in early '77; both the lead track and the B-side, 'BORN TO LOSE', drawled out with inimitably wasted NY cool. In September of that "Jubilee" year, the group released their much-anticipated debut album, 'L.A.M.F.' (New York street slang for 'Like A Mother F***** '), and although it suffered from terrible production provided by SPEEDY KEEN (ex-THUNDERCLAP NEWMAN), the set still managed a Top 60 placing in Britain. So bad was the record's sound that NOLAN left in protest, further calamity befalling the band as they found themselves on the wrong side of the immigration authorities having abandoned their label. Deported back to NY, the band inevitably splintered despite having recruited a replacement drummer, TY STYX. THUNDERS subsequently returned to London where he recorded a solo album, 'SO ALONE' (1978) aided and abetted by the cream of the UK new wave scene including PETER PERRETT (The Only Ones), CHRISSIE HYNDE (Pretenders), PAUL COOK and STEVE JONES (Sex Pistols) and even PHIL LYNOTT (Thin Lizzy)! In the interim, THUNDERS teamed up with SID VICIOUS in the ill-fated, unfortunately named, The LIVING DEAD (SID was to die shortly afterwards). Just prior to the turn of the decade, The HEARTBREAKERS regrouped in New York with THUNDERS masterminding the affair and prefixing the band name with his own; the resulting stage set, 'LIVE AT MAX'S KANSAS CITY' stands as testament to what might have been. In the 80's, THUNDERS released a series of sporadic albums/singles mostly for UK indie label, 'Jungle', although he never managed to shake off the cult legend tag. Sadly, THUNDERS died in New Orleans on the 23rd of April 1991, the circumstances remaining shrouded in mystery until a subsequent autopsy revealed what most people suspected, that he'd overdosed on heroin. • **Covered:** CAN'T KEEP MY EYES OFF YOU (Andy Williams) / DO YOU LOVE ME (Brian Poole & The Tremeloes) / DOWNTOWN (Petula Clark) / LIKE A ROLLING STONE (Bob Dylan) / CRAWFISH (Elvis Presley) / QUE SERA, SERA (hit; Doris Day). 'COPY CATS' was a complete covers album.

Album rating: Heartbreakers: L.A.M.F. (*7) / Johnny Thunders: SO ALONE (*7) / Johnny Thunders & The Heartbreakers: LIVE AT MAX'S KANSAS CITY (*7) / D.T.K. (*6) / Johnny Thunders: IN COLD BLOOD (*5) / TOO MUCH JUNKIE BUSINESS collection (*5) / HURT ME (*6) / QUE SERA, SERA (*5) / STATIONS OF THE CROSS collection (*4) / COPY CATS with Patti Palladin (*5) / GANG WAR (*4) / BOOTLEGGING THE BOOTLEGGERS (*4)

HEARTBREAKERS

JOHNNY THUNDERS – vocals, guitar / **JERRY NOLAN** (b. 7 May'46) – drums / **WALTER LURE** (b.22 Apr'49) – guitar, vocals / **BILLY RATH** – bass, vocals repl. RICHARD HELL who formed his own group

Track | not iss.

May 77. (7"/12") *(2094 135/+T)* **CHINESE ROCKS. / BORN TO LOSE**
Sep 77. (lp) *(2409 218)* **L.A.M.F.** — 55
– Born to lose / Baby talk / All by myself / I wanna be loved / It's not enough / Get off the phone / Chinese rocks / Pirate love / One track mind / I love you / Goin' steady / Let go. *(re-iss. May85 as 'L.A.M.F. – REVISITED' on 'Jungle' lp,pink-lp/pic-lp; FREUD 4/+P) <(re-iss. Sep96 as 'THE LOST '77 MIXES' cd/c/lp; FREUD CD/C/LP 044)> (cd re-iss. Oct00; FREUDCD 044E)*
Nov 77. (7") *(2094 137)* **ONE TRACK MIND. / CAN'T KEEP MY EYES OFF YOU (live) / DO YOU LOVE ME (live)**
Mar 78. (7"w-drawn) *(2094 142)* **IT'S NOT ENOUGH. / LET GO**

—— split early '78 after being deported back to New York, NOLAN joined SNATCH, while RATH and LURE disappeared

JOHNNY THUNDERS

—— returned to London and went solo using session people

Real-W.E.A. | not iss.

May 78. (7") *(ARE 1)* **DEAD OR ALIVE. / DOWNTOWN**
Sep 78. (7"/12"pink,12"blue) *(ARE 3/+T)* **YOU CAN'T PUT YOUR ARMS AROUND A MEMORY. / HURTIN'**
Oct 78. (lp) *(RAL 1)* **SO ALONE**
– Pipeline / You can't put your arms around a memory / Great big kiss / Ask me no questions / Leave me alone / Daddy rolling stone / London boys / Untouchable / Subway train / Downtown. *<(re-iss. Jul92 & Feb95 on 'Warners' lp/cd; 7599 26982-2)>*

JOHNNY THUNDERS & THE HEARTBREAKERS

—— re-formed '79, with **WALTER, BILLY** / + **STYX** – drums

Beggars Banquet | Max's Kansas

Jul 79. (7") *(BEG 21)* **GET OFF THE PHONE (live). / I WANNA BE LOVED (live)**
Sep 79. (lp) *(BEGA 9) <DTK 213>* **LIVE AT MAX'S KANSAS CITY (live)**
– (intro) / Milk me / Chinese rocks / Get off the phone / London / Take a chance / One track mind / All by myself / Let go / I love you / Can't keep my eyes on you / I wanna be loved / Do you love me?. *(cd-iss. Jul91; BBL 9CD) <(cd-iss. Dec95 on 'ROIR USA'; RUSCD 8219)>*

—— Split again '79. In 1980, THUNDERS joined WAYNE KRAMER'S GANG WAR.

JOHNNY THUNDERS

solo again with **WALTER LURE** – guitar / **BILLY ROGERS** – drums

New Rose | not iss.

Dec 82. (7") *(NEW 14)* **IN COLD BLOOD / ('A'live)** — — France
Jan 83. (d-lp) *(NR 18)* **IN COLD BLOOD (some live)** — — France
– In cold blood / Just another girl / Green onions / Diary of a lover / Look at my eyes / Live: (intro) / Just another girl / Too much junkie business / Sad vacation / Louie Louie / Gloria / Treat me like a nigger / Do you love me / Green onions / 10 commandments. *(re-iss. Apr94 lp/cd; 422367) (re-iss. cd Jun95 on 'Dojo'; DOJOCD 221) <(cd re-iss. Aug97 on 'Essential'; ESMCD 589)> (lp re-iss. Mar98 on 'Munster'; MR 142)*
Jan 84. (7"m) *(NEW 27)* **HURT ME. / IT'S NOT ENOUGH / LIKE A ROLLING STONE**
Jan 84. (lp) *(ROSE 26)* **HURT ME**
– So alone / It ain't me babe / Eve of destruction / You can't put your arms round a memory / You're so strange / I'm a boy in a girl / Lonely planet boy / Sad vacation / Hurt me / Diary of a lover / Ask me no questions. *(cd-iss. May94; 422366) (re-iss. cd Jul95 on 'Dojo'; DOJOCD 217) <(cd re-iss. Aug97 on 'Essential'; ESMCD 588)> (lp re-iss. Mar98 on 'Munster'; MR 142)*

Jungle | not iss.

Oct 85. (7"/7"pic-d; by JOHNNY THUNDERS with PATTI PALLADIN) *(JUNG 23/+P)* **CRAWFISH. / TIE ME UP (LOVE KNOT)**
(ext.12"+=) *(JUNG 23T)* – ('A'-Bayou mix).

—— with **PATTI PALLADIN** – vocals (ex-SNATCH, FLYING LIZARDS)

Dec 85. (lp) *(FREUD 9)* **QUE SERA, SERA**
– Que sera, sera / Short lives / M.I.A. / I only wrote this song for you / Little bit of whore / Cool operator / Blame it on mom / Tie me up / Alone in a crowd / Billy boy / Endless party. *(pic-lp iss.Jun87; FREUDP 09) <(cd-iss. Dec94; FREUDCD 49)> (cd re-iss. Apr01; FREUDCD 49E)*
Jun 87. (7") *(JUNG 33)* **QUE SERA SERA. / SHORT LIVES**
(12"+=) *(JUNG 33T)* – I only wrote this song.

JOHNNY THUNDERS & PATTI PALLADIN

May 88. (7") *(JUNG 38)* **SHE WANTS TO MAMBO. / UPTOWN**
(12"+=) *(JUNG 38T)* – Love is strange.
Jun 88. (lp/c/cd) *(FREUD/+C/CD 20)* **YEAH, YEAH, I'M A COPY CAT**
– Can't seem to make you mine / Baby it's you / She wants to mambo / Treat her right / Uptown to Harlem / Crawfish / Alligator wine / Two time loser / Love is

Johnny THUNDERS (cont)

Jan 89.	(7") *(JUNG 43)* **(I WAS) BORN TO CRY. / TREAT HER RIGHT**	
	(12"+=) *(JUNG 43T)* – Can't seem to make her mine.	

— THUNDERS died on the 23rd April '91, aged 38. He left three children from his first marriage plus another 3 year-old daughter, Jamie, conceived while he'd lived in Sweden with his girlfriend, Suzanne. JERRY NOLAN died on the 14th January '92 of a stroke (aged 45) after a bout of pneumonia and meningitis. Original drummer, BILLY MURCIA, also died in the 90's.

– compilations, etc. –

on 'Jungle' unless otherwise mentioned

Nov 82.	(lp,pink-lp,white-lp/pic-lp) *(FREUD/+P 1)* **D.T.K. – LIVE AT THE SPEAKEASY (live)**	
	<(cd-iss. Aug94 on 'Receiver'; R 191)>	
May 83.	(7"ep) *(JUNG 1)* **VINTAGE '77**	
	– Let go / Chinese rocks / Born to lose.	
1983.	(c) *R.O.I.R.; <A 118>* **TOO MUCH JUNKIE BUSINESS**	
	(cd-iss. Feb95 on 'ROIR Europe'; same) <US 'Combat'; 5029>	
Mar 84.	(7"/7"pic-d) *(JUNG 14/+P)* **GET OFF THE PHONE. / ALL BY MYSELF**	
	(12"+=) *(JUNG 14X)* – Pirate love.	
Jun 84.	(lp) *A.B.C.; (ABCLP 2)* **LIVE AT THE LYCEUM BALLROOM 1984 (live)**	
	<(re-iss. Jun91 on 'Receiver' lp/c/cd; RR LP/LC/CD 134)>	
Feb 85.	(7") *Twins; (T 1702)* **BORN TO LOSE.**	
May 85.	(7"ep/12"ep) *(JUNG 18/+X)* **CHINESE ROCKS / BORN TO LOSE / ONE TRACK MIND / I WANNA BE LOVED**	
Feb 87.	(c) *R.O.I.R.; (A 146) / Combat; <5028>* **STATIONS OF THE CROSS**	
	(re-iss. cd Jul94 on 'Receiver'; RRCD 188) (re-iss. cd Feb95 on 'ROIR Europe'; same)	
May 88.	(box-lp) *(JTBOX 1)* **THE JOHNNY THUNDERS ALBUM COLLECTION**	
Feb 90.	(lp/cd) *(FREUD/+CD 30)* **BOOTLEGGIN' THE BOOTLEGGERS**	
Jan 92.	(cd) *Fan Club;* **LIVE AT MOTHERS (live)**	
	(re-iss. Mar98 on 'Munster'; MR 140)	
Feb 92.	(cd) *Bomp; <(BCD 4039)>* **WHAT GOES AROUND (live)**	
Oct 92.	(cd) *Fan Club; (422365)* **HAVE FAITH (live solo)**	
	<(re-iss. Aug96 on 'Mutiny'; MUT 8005CD)>	
Dec 93.	(cd) *Anagram; (CDGRAM 70)* **CHINESE ROCKS – THE ULTIMATE LIVE COLLECTION (live)**	
	(lp-iss.Sep99 on 'Get Back'; GET 49) (re-iss. Nov02; same)	
Sep 94.	(cd) *Skydog; (62251)* **VIVE LE REVOLUTION – LIVE PARIS, 1977 (live JOHNNY THUNDERS & THE HEARTBREAKERS)**	
Nov 94.	(cd) *Essential; (ESDCD 226)* **ADD WATER AND STIR – LIVE IN JAPAN 1991 (live)**	
Apr 96.	(cd) *Dojo; (DOJOCD 231)* **THE STUDIO BOOTLEGS**	
Oct 97.	(cd) *Anagram; (CDMGRAM 117)* **BELFAST ROCKS**	
	(re-iss. Jul00 on 'Triple X'; TX 0031CD)	
Feb 99.	(cd) *Mogul; (MNR 003)* **LIVE CRISIS**	
Apr 99.	(d-cd) *Receiver; <(RRDCD 009)>* **SAD VACATION**	
May 99.	(cd) *Sonic; (SRCD 0020)* **INTERNAL POSSESSION**	
Sep 99.	(7"pink) *(JUNG 62)* **CHINESE ROCKS. /**	
Sep 99.	(7") *(JUNG 63)* **ONE TRACK MIND. /**	
Oct 99.	(d-cd) *Jungle; (FREUDCD 60)* **BORN TO LOSE**	
May 00.	(cd) *Amsterdamned; (TX 70030CD)* **IN THE FLESH**	
May 00.	(cd) *Receiver; <(RRCD 288)>* **PLAY WITH FIRE – JOHNNY THUNDERS LIVE**	
Nov 00.	(cd) *Receiver; (RRCD 297)* **LIVE AND WASTED – UNPLUGGED 1990 (live)**	
Apr 01.	(cd) *Triple X; <(TX 70032CD)>* **ENDLESS PARTY**	
Apr 02.	(cd) *Captain Trip; (CTCD 359)* **THUNDERSTORM IN DETROIT – LIVE AT THE SILVERBIRD 21/12/80 (live)**	
Jun 02.	(3xcd-box) *Castle; <(CMETD 468)>* **YOU CAN'T PUT YOUR ARMS AROUND A MEMORY**	
	– L.A.M.F. REVISITED / LIVE AT THE LYCEUM / LIVE & WASTED).	

TIGER LILY (see under ⇒ ULTRAVOX)

TIN HUEY

Formed: Akron, Ohio, USA ... 1977 by CHRIS BUTLER and RALPH CARNEY, who completed the line-up with HARVEY GOLD, STUART AUSTIN, MICHAEL AYLWARD and MARK PRICE. Following the release of a couple of singles on the indie label, 'Clone', namely 'PUPPETS WIVES' and 'BREAKFAST WITH ...', TIN HUEY's experimental blend of jazzy ZAPPA-rooted "New Wave" pop/rock was enough to convince 'Warners' of their potential. First up was an avant-pop version of The Monkees' 'I'M A BELIEVER', probably released too soon after ROBERT WYATT's UK Top 30 cover from '74. The resulting album, 'CONTENTS DISLODGED DURING SHIPMENT', proved too challenging for mainstream public consumption even in 1979 and the band split after a final Labor Day gig the following year. While BUTLER initiated The WAITRESSES, CARNEY formed The SWOLLEN MONKEYS (with DAVID BUCK, DAN KLAYMAN, MARS WILLIAMS, DON DAVIS, TED ORR, BILL YLITANO and CHRIS MORGAN), releasing one solitary lp, 'AFTERBIRTH OF THE COOL', for 'Cachelot' <CA 128> early in 1982. CARNEY subsequently teamed up with DAVID HILD and MARK KRAMER, the trio of CARNEY-HILD-KRAMER issuing a 1987 set, 'HAPPINESS FINALLY CAME TO THEM'.

Album rating: CONTENTS DISLODGED DURING SHIPMENT (*6)

CHRIS BUTLER – guitar, percussion, vocals / **RALPH CARNEY** – saxophones, clarinets / **HARVEY GOLD** – synthesizer, keyboards, vocals / **MICHAEL AYLWARD** – guitar + slide, vocals / **MARK PRICE** – bass, vocals / **STUART AUSTIN** – drums, percussion, synthesizer

not iss.   Clone

1977.	(7"ep) *<CL 002>* **PUPPET WIVES / CUYAHOGA CREEPING BENT. / POOR ALPHONSO (live) / THE TIN HUEY STORY**	
1978.	(7") *<CL 004>* **BREAKFAST WITH THE HUEYS**	
	– Robert takes the road to Liebernawash / Squirm you worm.	

not iss.   Warners

Jun 79.	(7") *<WBS 49001>* **I'M A BELIEVER. / NEW YORK'S FINEST DINING EXPERIENCE**	
Jul 79.	(lp) *<BSK 3297>* **CONTENTS DISLODGED DURING SHIPMENT**	
	– I'm a believer / Revelations of Dr. Modesto / I could rule the world if only I / Coronation / Slide / Hump day / Pink berets / Squirm, you worm / Chinese circus / Puppet wives / New York's finest dining experience.	

not iss.   Clone

1980.	(7") *<CL 011>* **ENGLISH KIDS. / SISTER ROSE**	

— CARNEY split the band in 1980

TOYAH

Born: TOYAH ANN WILLCOX, 18 May'58, King's Heath, Birmingham. Following a stint in drama school and a bit part in a BBC play, TOYAH's big break came when the late Derek Jarman offered her a prestigious role in his influential punk flick, 'Jubilee' (she later starred in his version of 'The Tempest'). Through this, the budding singer met ADAM ANT with whom she played in a short-lived outfit named The MAN EATERS. Soon after, TOYAH formed her own group with the help of JOEL BOGEN, PETE BUSH, MARK HENRY and STEVE BRAY. Securing a deal with burgeoning indie label, 'Safari', they released their debut single, 'VICTIMS OF THE RIDDLE', in the summer of '79. Unsurprisingly for a cringe-inducingly titled track, it failed to break the chart, with an accompanying album, ahem ... 'SHEEP FARMING IN BARNET' (1979) meeting a similar fate. Wisely perhaps, TOYAH continued to juggle an acting career simultaneously, scoring roles in TV and film including a part in 'The Corn Is Green' and in PETE TOWNSHEND's seminal mod-revisionist movie, 'Quadrophenia'. Though a follow-up album, 'THE BLUE MEANING', and a live effort, 'TOYAH! TOYAH! TOYAH!' (1981) gave the singer her first Top 40 action, it was only with the release of the 'FOUR FROM TOYAH' EP (1981) that the kids really took to her new wave/goth histrionics. The lead track, 'IT'S A MYSTERY', was infect-t-tious enough to take her into the Top 5, though it was largely her aggressively hyped image (dauntingly flame-haired, quintessentially 80's ice-queen) which turned her into an unlikely pop star. Next up was 'I WANT TO BE FREE', a rebel song up there with Cliff Richard's 'SUMMER HOLIDAY' in terms of anti-establishment ire but naively charming and annoyingly hummable nonetheless. TOYAH's third and final Top 10 single was 'THUNDER IN THE MOUNTAINS', a song as majestically bombastic as the title suggests. The latter two tracks both featured on the 'ANTHEM' (1981) set, TOYAH's most successful album by far, narrowly missing the No.1 spot. The singer continued her mythical/futuristic lyrical musings with 'THE CHANGELING' (1982) the following year, the set spawning two further Top 30 hits, 'BRAVE NEW WORLD' and 'BE LOUD BE PROUD (BE HEARD)'. Though she suffered constant music press jibes about her slight lisp, TOYAH retained a loyal following who put later albums like 'LOVE IS THE LAW' (1983) and 'MINX' (1985) into the Top 30 despite not having any major hits. Taking a sabbatical in the mid-80's during which she married ex-KING CRIMSON guitar maestro ROBERT FRIPP, TOYAH eventually returned in the summer of '87 with 'DESIRE', an album that followed a co-credited set, 'THE LADY OR THE TIGER' to both her and her new spouse. Though she never sees any chart action these days, TOYAH continues to collaborate with FRIPP, most recently on the 1994 set, 'DREAMCHILD'. The singer has also sidelined into TV presenting of late, living it up on far-flung exotic beaches for BBC 1's 'Holiday' programme, while also presenting videos on Sky channel show, 'VH1'. • **Songwriters:** She and band wrote music, except ECHO BEACH (Martha + The Muffins) / SCHOOL'S OUT (Alice Cooper). • **Trivia:** Her other acting attributions were in 1983's 'TRAFFORD TANZI' and in 1987, she acted in the West End play, 'CABARET'. Amongst other roles, she subsequently appeared in the TV detective series, 'Shoestring'.

Album rating: SHEEP FARMING IN BARNET (*6) / THE BLUE MEANING (*7) / TOYAH! TOYAH! TOYAH! (*5) / ANTHEM (*5) / THE CHANGELING (*5) / WARRIOR ROCK – TOYAH ON TOUR (*4) / LOVE IS THE LAW (*3) / TOYAH TOYAH compilation (*6) / MINX (*4) / THE LADY OR THE TIGER with Fripp (*4) / DESIRE (*3) / PROSTITUTE (*2) / OPHELIA'S SHADOW (*3) / DREAMCHILD (*3) / THE VERY BEST OF TOYAH compilation (*6)

TOYAH – vocals / with band **JOEL BOGEN** – guitar / **PETE BUSH** – keyboards / **MARK HENRY** – bass / **STEVE BRAY** – drums

Safari   not iss.

Jun 79.	(7") *(SAFE 15)* **VICTIMS OF THE RIDDLE. / VICTIMS OF THE RIDDLE (VIVESECTION)**	
Jul 79.	(7"ep) *(SAP 1)* **SHEEP FARMING IN BARNET**	
	– Neon womb / Indecision / Waiting / Our movie / Vivisection / Danced.	
Dec 79.	(lp/c) *(IC 064/264)* **SHEEP FARMING IN BARNET**	
	– Neon womb / Indecision / Waiting / Computer / Victims of the riddle / Elusive stranger / Our movie / Danced / Last goodbye / Victims of the riddle (vivisection) /	

TOYAH (cont)

Race through space. *(re-iss. Aug90 on 'Great Expectations' cd/c/lp; PIP MC/CD/LP 014)*

Jan 80. (7") *(SAFE 22)* **BIRD IN FLIGHT. / TRIBAL LOOK** | □ | - |

—— **CHARLIE FRANCIS** – bass; repl. MARK HENRY

May 80. (7"/ext.12"white) *(SAFE/+LS 28)* **IEYA. / SPACE WALKING (HELIUM SONG)** | □ | - |
(re-iss. Jul82 + 7"pic-d; SAFEX 28) – hit UK No.48.

May 80. (lp/c) *(IEYA/CIEYA 666)* **THE BLUE MEANING** | 40 | - |
– Ieya / Space walking (helium song) / Ghosts / Mummys / Blue meanings / She / Tiger tiger / Vision / Insects / Love me. *(re-iss. Jul90 on 'Great Expectations' cd/c/lp; PIP CD/MC/LP 015)*

Nov 80. (7"m) *(SAFE 32)* **DANCED (live). / GHOSTS (live) / NEON WOMB (live)** | □ | - |

Jan 81. (lp/c) *(LIVE/CLIVE 2)* **TOYAH! TOYAH! TOYAH! (live)** | 22 | - |
– Victims of the riddle / Indecision / Love me / Vision / Tribal look / Bird in flight / Danced / Insects / Race through space / Ieya. *(re-iss. Aug90 on 'Great Expectations' cd/c/lp; PIP CD/MC/LP 016)*

—— TOYAH retained only BOGEN, and recruited **ADRIAN LEE** – keys / **PHIL SPALDING** – bass (ex-ORIGINAL MIRRORS) / **NIGEL GLOCKER** – drums (ex-ASSOCIATES)

Feb 81. (7"ep) *(TOY 1)* **FOUR FROM TOYAH** | 4 | - |
– It's a mystery / War boys / Angels and demons / Revelations.

May 81. (7"m) *(SAFE 34)* **I WANT TO BE FREE. / WALKIE TALKIE / ALIEN** | 8 | - |

May 81. (pic-lp/c) *(VOOR/+C 1)* **ANTHEM** | 2 | - |
– I want to be free / Obsolete pop star / Elocution lesson (the door is a whore) / Jungles of Jupiter / I am / It's a mystery / Masai boy / Marionette / Demolition man / We are. *(cd-iss. Nov85 +=; VOORD 1)* – Thunder in the mountains / War boys / Angels and demons / Revelations. *(cd re-iss. Jan99 on 'Connoisseur'; EVSOPCD 263)*

—— **SIMON PHILIPS** – drums, percussion; repl GLOCKER who left to join SAXON. **ANDY CLARKE + SIMON DARLOW** – keyboards; repl LEE.

Sep 81. (7"pic-d) *(SAFE 38)* **THUNDER IN THE MOUNTAINS. / STREET ADDICT** | 4 | - |
(w/ free 7"flexi) *(SAFELS 38)* – STAND PROUD

Nov 81. (7"ep) *(TOY 2)* **FOUR MORE FROM TOYAH** | 14 | - |
– Good morning universe / Urban tribesman / In the fairground / The furious futures.

May 82. (7"pic-d) *(SAFE 45)* **BRAVE NEW WORLD. / WARRIOR ROCK** | 21 | - |

Jun 82. (lp/c) *(VOOR/+C 9)* **THE CHANGELING** | 6 | - |
– Creepy room / Street creature / Castaways / The druids / Angel and me / The pact / Life in the trees / Dawn chorus / Run wild run free / Brave new world. *(cd-iss. Jan99 on 'Connoisseur'; EVSOPCD 264)*

—— **KEITH HALE** – keyboards, vocals; repl. CLARKE

Sep 82. (7"pic-d) *(SAFE 52)* **BE LOUD BE PROUD (BE HEARD). / LAUGHING WITH THE FOOLS** | 30 | - |

Nov 82. (d-lp/d-c) *(TNT/CTNT 1)* **WARRIOR ROCK - TOYAH ON TOUR (live)** | 20 | - |
– Good morning universe / Warrior rock / Danced / Jungles of Jupiter / Castaways / Angel and me / Brave new world / The pact / Thunder in the mountains / We are / I want to be free / Dawn chorus / War boy / Ieya / Be loud be proud (be heard).

—— **ANDY DUNCAN** – drums; repl. PHILIPS

	Safari	not iss.
Sep 83. (7") *(SAFE 56)* **REBEL RUN. / MOUNTAINS HIGH**	24	-
Oct 83. (lp/c) *(VOOR/+C 10)* **LOVE IS THE LAW**	28	-

– Broken diamonds / I explode / Rebel of love / Rebel run / Martian cowboy / Dream scape / Tone is ours / Love is the law / Remember / The vow.

Nov 83. (7") *(SAFE 58)* **THE VOW. / I EXPLODE** | 50 | - |
(12"+=) *(SAFELS 58)* – Haunted.

—— now w / DARLOW / LEE / PETER VAN HOOKE – drums / AL HODGE + PHIL PALMER – guitar / IAN WHERRY + ANDY BROWN – bass

	Portrait	Portrait
Apr 85. (7"/12") *(A/TX 6160)* **DON'T FALL IN LOVE (I SAID). / SNOW COVERS THE KISS**	22	-
Jun 85. (7"pic-d) *(A 6359)* **SOUL PASSING THROUGH SOUL. / ALL IN A RAGE**	57	-

(12"+=) *(TA 6359)* – ('A'extended).

Jul 85. (lp/c/cd) *(PRT/40/CD 26415)* **MINX** | 24 | - |
– Soldier of fortune, terrorist of love / Don't fall in love (I said) / Soul passing through soul / Sympathy / I'll serve you well / All in a rage / Space between the sounds / School's out / World in action / America for beginners. *(c+=/cd+=)* – Over twenty-one / Vigilante.

Sep 85. (7"/12") *(A/TA 6545)* **WORLD IN ACTION. / SOLDIERS OF FORTUNE** | □ | - |

—— in Sep'85, she guested on TONY BANKS (of Genesis) EP track, 'You Call This Victory'.

below was credited with her new hubby, ROBERT FRIPP (ex-KING CRIMSON)

	E.G.	not iss.
Jan 87. (lp/c; TOYAH & FRIPP) *(EGED/+C 44)* **THE LADY OR THE TIGER**	□	-

– The lady or the tiger / Discourager of hesitancy.

Apr 87. (7"/12") *(EGO/+X 31)* **ECHO BEACH. / PLENTY** | 54 | - |

Jun 87. (lp/c/cd) *(EG LP/MC/CD 71)* **DESIRE** | □ | - |
– Echo beach / Moonlight dancing / Revive the world / The view / Moon migration / Love's unkind / Dear diary / Deadly as a woman / Goodbye baby / When a woman cries / Desire.

Jun 87. (7") *(EGO 35)* **MOONLIGHT DANCING. / SUN UP** | □ | - |
(12"+=) *(EGOX 35)* – R.E-N.T.R.Y. / Into dance.

—— now w / backing from **STEVE SIDEH** – drums, percussion, keyboards

Nov 88. (lp/c/cd; as TOYAH WILLCOX) *(EGED/EGEDC/EEGCD 59)* **PROSTITUTE** | □ | - |
– Hello / Prostitute / Wife / The show / Dream house / Homecraft / Obsession / Let the power bleed / Restless / Falling to Earth / Jazz singers in the trees / Vale of Evesham / Ghosts in the universe.

—— FRIPP appeared on above (their tour was billed as FRIPP & FRIPP)

new band:- GUNN, GEBALLE + BEAVIS and guest ROBERT FRIPP

Feb 91. (cd/c/lp) *(EGCD/EGMC/EGLP 78)* **OPHELIA'S SHADOW** | □ | - |
– Ophelia's shadow / The shaman says / Brilliant day / Prospect / Turning tide / Take what you will / Ghost light / The woman who had an affair with herself / Homeward / Lords of the never known.

—— now with **MIKE BENNETT** – guitar, producer, main writer / **PAUL MORAN** – keyboards, producer / **JAY STAPLEY** – guitar / **BOB SKEAT** – bass / **SASHA ADAMS** – tape operator

	Cryptic	not iss.
Nov 93. (12"/cd-s) *(12/CD TOY 1)* **OUT OF THE BLUE (Trancentral mix). / OUT OF THE BLUE (deep ocean mix)**	□	-

(12+=) – Out of The Blue (Transcentral radio mix).

Apr 94. (c-s/12"/cd-s) *(12/MC/CD TOY 2)* **NOW AND THEN. / ('A'mixes)** | □ | - |

May 94. (cd/c) *(TOY CD/MC 1001)* **DREAMCHILD** | □ | - |
– Now and then / Let me go / Unkind / Out of the blue / Dreamchild / World of tension / Lost and found / Over you / I don't know / Disappear / Tone poem.

—— TOYAH now concentrates on her television work

– compilations, etc. –

Feb 84. (lp/c) *K-Tel; (NE/C1 1268)* **TOYAH TOYAH** | 43 | - |
Nov 85. (lp/c) *Safari; (VOOR/+C 77)* **MAYHEM** | □ | - |
Mar 94. (cd) *Connoisseur; (CSAPCD 115)* **THE BEST OF TOYAH** | □ | - |
Nov 96. (cd) *Tring; (ANT 012)* **THE ACOUSTIC ALBUM** | □ | - |
Nov 96. (cd) *Tring; (QED 065)* **LOOKING BACK** | □ | - |
Apr 97. (cd) *Receiver; (<RRCD 235>)* **PHOENIX** | □ | May97 |
Feb 98. (cd) *Reactive; (REMCD 501)* **THE VERY BEST OF TOYAH** | □ | - |
– It's a mystery / Good morning universe / I want to be free / Be proud be loud be heard / Bird in flight / Rebel run / Brave new world / Thunder in the mountains / Ieya / Street creature / Elusive stranger / Martian cowboy / Love me / Broken diamonds / Castaways / She / Jungles of Jupiter / We are.

Jun 98. (cd) *Connoisseur; (CSAPCD 125)* **LIVE AND MORE (live)** | □ | - |
Sep 98. (cd) *Music Club; (MCCD 359)* **LOUD PROUD AND HEARD – THE BEST OF TOYAH** | □ | - |
Apr 02. (d-cd) *Safari; (VOORCD 4002)* **SHEEP FARMING IN BARNET / THE BLUE MEANING** | □ | - |

—— In Jun'82, a single as "The ANTEATERS", 'NINE TO FIVE', was lifted from the 1977 film, 'Jubilee', in which she appeared with ADAM ANT.

TUBES

Formed: Phoenix, Arizona, USA ... 1972 by BILL SPOONER, VINCE WELNICK and ex-drama student FEE WAYBILL, who moved the outfit to the Bay Area, San Francisco, the line-up completed by RICK ANDERSON, MICHAEL COTTEN, ROGER STEEN, PRAIRIE PRINCE and REG STYLES. Coming on like a perverted, pseudo-punk precursor to MEAT LOAF's theatrical overload, the group became infamous for their garish shows which placed scantily clad ladies against such unsavoury stage characters as Dr. Strangekiss and Quay Lude. Signed to 'A&M', their debut single was the legendary 'WHITE PUNKS ON DOPE', a UK Top 30 hit some three years later when Britain was in the grip of three-chord fever. The accompanying AL KOOPER-produced, eponymous debut album narrowly missed the US Top 100, while follow-up, 'YOUNG AND RICH' (produced by KEN SCOTT), broke them into the US Top 50 in 1976. But the music often took second place to the theatrics and in 1979, obviously bored with the limitations of the genre, swapped anthemic punk/new wave for easier going pop/rock on that year's TODD RUNDGREN-produced 'REMOTE CONTROL' album. A proposed 1980 set, 'SUFFER FOR SOUND', was shelved by 'A&M' prior to the band being dropped. Inking a new deal with 'Capitol', the group moved even further towards the mainstream with 'THE COMPLETION BACKWARD PRINCIPLE' (1981), an album which spawed a one-off Top 10 hit in 'SHE'S A BEAUTY'. After a final couple of albums, 'OUTSIDE INSIDE' (1983) and 'LOVE BOMB' (1986), The TUBES realised the joke had run its course and packed it in. Having already released a solo set, 'READ MY LIPS' (1984), WAYBILL went on to write material for RICHARD MARX (!), while SPOONER and WELNICK subsequently went on to work with Bay Area veterans, The GRATEFUL DEAD. Just when you thought WAYBILL and Co had fully retired from their musical extravaganzas, The TUBES were back on tour for a series of American and European dates c.1993. An album, 'GENIUS OF AMERICA' (1996), found little friends among the critics and their die-hard, loyal fanbase; 2000's 'TUBES WORLD TOUR 2001' album (yes, 2001) was worth the price of a ticket at least. • **Songwriters:** WAYBILL penned except I SAW HER STANDING THERE (Beatles) / etc. • **Trivia:** In 1980, they undertook a cameo performance in the film, 'Xanadu', soundtrack courtesy of ELECTRIC LIGHT ORCHESTRA and OLIVIA NEWTON-JOHN.

Album rating: THE TUBES (*5) / YOUNG AND RICH (*6) / NOW (5) / WHAT DO YOU WANT FROM LIVE (*5) / REMOTE CONTROL (*4) / THE COMPLETION BACKWARD PRINCIPLE (*6) / T.R.A.S.H. (TUBES RARITIES AND SMASH HITS) compilation (*7) / OUTSIDE INSIDE (*5) / LOVE BOMB (*4) / THE BEST OF THE TUBES compilation (*7) / GENIUS OF AMERICA (*3) / THE TUBES WORLD TOUR 2001 (*5) / Fee Waybill: READ MY LIPS (*3)

FEE WAYBILL (b. JOHN WALDO, 17 Sep'50, Omaha, Nebraska) – vocals / **BILL 'Sputnik' SPOONER** (b.16 Apr'49) – guitar / **VINCE WELNICK** (b.21 Feb'51) – keyboards / **RICK ANDERSON** (b. 1 Aug'47, St. Paul, Minnesota) – bass / **MICHAEL COTTEN** (b.25 Jan'50, Kansas City, Missouri) – synthesizer / **ROGER STEEN** (b.13 Nov'49, Pipestone, Minnesota) – guitar / **PRAIRIE PRINCE** (b. 7 May'50, Charlotte, New Connecticut) – drums / **REG STYLES** (b. 3 Mar'50) – vocals, guitar

TUBES (cont)

	A&M	A&M
Jul 75. (7") <1733> **WHITE PUNKS ON DOPE. / (part 2)**	–	–
Jul 75. (lp/c) (AMLH/CAM 64534) <4534> **THE TUBES**	–	–

– Up from the deep / Haloes / Space baby / Malaguena Saleroza / Mondo bondage / What do you want from life / Boy crazy / White punks on dope. (re-iss. May83 on 'Fame') (d-cd-iss. Dec85 on 'Mobile Fidelity', incl.next album)

Nov 75. (7") **WHAT DO YOU WANT FROM LIFE. / SPACE BABY** – –
Jan 76. (7") (AMS 7209) **WHAT DO YOU WANT FROM LIFE. / WHITE PUNKS ON DOPE** – 46
May 76. (lp/c) (AMLH/CAM 64580) <4580> **YOUNG AND RICH**
– Tubes world tour / Brighter day / Pimp / Stand up and shout / Don't touch me there / Slipped my disco / Proud to be an American / Poland whole / Madam I'm Adam / Young and rich.
Jun 76. (7") (AMS 7239) <1826> **DON'T TOUCH ME THERE. / PROUD TO BE AMERICAN** – 61
Jan 77. (7") **YOUNG AND RICH. / LOVE WILL KEEP US TOGETHER** – –

—— added MINGO LEWIS – percussion

May 77. (lp/c) (AMLH/CAM 64632) <4632> **THE TUBES NOW**
– Smoke (la vie en fumer) / Hit parade / Strung out on strings / Golden boy / My head is my house (unless it rains) / God-bird-change / I'm just a mess / Cathy's clone / This town / Pound of flesh / You're no fun.
Aug 77. (7") <1956> **I'M JUST A MESS. / THIS TOWN** – –
Nov 77. (7"m/12"m) (AMS 7323) **WHITE PUNKS ON DOPE. / DON'T TOUCH ME THERE / WHAT DO YOU WANT FROM LIFE** 28 –
Feb 78. (d-lp/d-c) (AMLM/CLM 68460) <6003> **WHAT DO YOU WANT FROM LIVE (live)** 38 82
– (overture) / Got yourself a deal / Show me a reason / What do you want from life / God-bird-change / Special ballet / Don't touch me there / Mondo bondage / Smoke (la vie en fumer) / Crime medley: (themes from 'Dragnet' – 'Peter Gunn' – 'Perry Mason' – 'The Untouchables') / I was a punk before you were a punk / I saw her standing there / (drum solo) / Boy crazy / You're no fun / Stand up and shout / White punks on dope. (cd-iss. Apr97; 396003-2)
Apr 78. (7") (AMS 7349) **SHOW ME A REASON (live). / MONDO BONDAGE (live)** – –
Jul 78. (7") <2037> **SHOW ME A REASON (live). / I SAW HER STANDING THERE (live)** – –
Feb 79. (7")(7"cold-7 diff.) (AMS 7423,) <2120> **PRIME TIME. / NO WAY OUT** – 34
May 79. (lp/c) (AMLH/CAM 64751) <4751> **REMOTE CONTROL** 40 46 Mar 79
– Turn me on / TV is king / Prime time / I want it all / No way out / Getoverture / No mercy / Only the strong survive / Be mine tonight / Love's a mystery (I don't understand) / Telecide.
May 79. (7") <2149> **LOVE'S A MYSTERY (I DON'T UNDERSTAND). / TELECIDE** – –
Jul 79. (7")(7"yellow) (AMS 7462,) **TV IS KING. / TELECIDE** – –

—— trimmed slightly when LEWIS + STYLES left.

	Capitol	Capitol
May 81. (7") <5016> **TALK TO YA LATER. / POWER TOOLS**	–	–
May 81. (7") (CL 201) **TALK TO YA LATER. / WHAT'S WRONG WITH ME**		–
May 81. (lp/c) (EST/TCEST 26285) <12151> **THE COMPLETION BACKWARD PRINCIPLE**		36

– Talk to ya later / Let's make some noise / Matter of pride / Mr. Hate / Attack of the fifty foot woman / Think about me / Sushi girl / Don't want to wait anymore / Power tools / Amnesia. (re-iss. Mar91 on 'Beat Goes On' cd/lp; BGO CD/LP 100)
Jul 81. (7") (CL 208) <5007> **DON'T WANT TO WAIT ANYMORE. / THINK ABOUT ME** 60 35 Jun81
Oct 81. (7") (CL 219) **SUSHI GIRL. / MR. HATE** – –
Apr 83. (7") (CL 288) <5217> **SHE'S A BEAUTY. / WHEN YOU'RE READY TO COME** 10
(12"+=) (12CL 288) – Fantastic delusion.
May 83. (lp/c) <(EST/TCEST 12260)> **OUTSIDE INSIDE** 77 18 Apr83
– She's a beauty / No not again / Out of the business / The monkey time / Glass house / Wild women of Wongo / Tip of my tongue / Fantastic delusion / Drums / Theme park / Outside lookin' inside. (cd-iss. Jul92 on 'Beat Goes On'; BGOCD 133)
above feat. guests MAURICE WHITE (of EARTH, WIND & FIRE) + MARTHA DAVIS – vocals (of MOTELS)
Jul 83. (7") <5258> **TIP OF MY TONGUE. / KEYBOARD KIDS** – 52
Sep 83. (7") <5254> **THE MONKEY TIME. / SPORTS FAN** – 68

—— In 1984, WAYBILL released a solo album, 'READ MY LIPS'

Mar 85. (7") <5443> **PIECE BY PIECE. / NIGHT PEOPLE** – 87
May 85. (lp) <12381> **LOVE BOMB** 87
– Piece by piece / Stella / Come as you are / One good reason / Bora Bora 2000 – Love bomb / Night people / Say hey / Eyes / Muscle girls / Theme from a wooly place – Wooly bully / Theme from a summer place / For a song / Say hey (part 2) / Feel it / Night people (reprise). (cd-iss. Aug93 on 'Beat Goes On'; BGOCD 188)

—— group disbanded after above album. WAYBILL continued to write and guest on albums by RICHARD MARX (1988). WELNICK joined GRATEFUL DEAD. The TUBES re-formed in 1993; WAYBILL, STEEN, PRINCE, ANDERSON / + GARY CAMBRA – vocals, keyboards / JENNIFER McFEE + AMY FRENCH – vocals

	Brilliant	Popular Critique
Oct 96. (cd) <12007> **GENIUS OF AMERICA**	–	–

– Genius of America / Arms of the enemy / Say what you want / How can you live with yourself / Big brothers still watching you / After all you said / Fishhouse / The fastest gun alive / I never saw it comin' / Who names the hurricanes / It's too late / Around the world.
Nov 99. (cd) (BT 33028) **HOODS FROM OUTER SPACE** – –
– Hoods from Outer Space / I know you / Say what you want / Around the world / Genius of America / Who names the hurricanes / It's too late / How can you live with yourself / I never saw it comin' / Arms of the enemy / Fishhouse / Big Brother's still watching you / The fastest gun alive / After all you said. (re-iss. Mar02; same)

	Sanctuary	C.M.C.
Oct 00. (cd) (SANCD 007) <86300> **THE TUBES WORLD TOUR 2001 (live)**		

– Introduction / The Tubes World Tour / She's a beauty / Digi-doll / T.V. king / Don't touch me there / Tip of my tongue / Loveline / Wild women of Wongo / Mondo bondage / White punks on dope / Talk to ya later.

– compilations, etc. –

Nov 81. (lp/c) A&M; (AMLH/CAM 64870) <4870> **T.R.A.S.H. (TUBES RARITIES AND SMASH HITS)**
– Drivin' all night / What do you want from life / Turn me on / Slipped my disco / Mondo bondage / Love will keep us together / I'm just a mess / Only the strong survive / Don't touch me there / White punks on dope / Prime time.
Sep 85. (7") Old Gold; (OG 9545) **PRIME TIME. / (B-side by STYX)** – –
Jan 87. (7") Old Gold; (OG 9545) **(above tracks)**
(12"+=) (OG 4013) – White punks on dope / (other by 'Styx').
Nov 86. (lp) Plastic Head; (PLASLP 006) **PRIME TIME**
Apr 93. (cd) Capitol; (C 298359) **THE BEST OF THE TUBES**
Oct 96. (d-cd) A&M; (540564-2) **GOING DOWN . . . THE TUBES**
Feb 98. (cd) Disky; <(DC 88611-2)> **DON'T WANT TO WAIT ANYMORE**
Feb 00. (cd) Hux; (HUX 017) <91263> **INFOMERCIAL: HOW TO BECOME TUBULAR (live)**
Aug 00. (cd) Spectrum; (544352-2) **WHITE PUNKS ON DOPE**
Oct 00. (cd) Universal; (AA69 490766-2) **THE MILLENNIUM COLLECTION: THE BEST OF THE TUBES** –

FEE WAYBILL

	Capitol	Capitol
Oct 84. (7") WHO SAID LIFE WOULD BE PRETTY. / YOU'RE STILL LAUGHING	–	–
Nov 84. (lp/c) <12369> **READ MY LIPS**		

-You're still laughing / Nobody's perfect / Who loves you baby / I don't even know your name (passion play) / Who said life would be pretty / Thrill of the kill / Saved my life / Caribbean sunsets / Star of the show / I could've been somebody.
Dec 84. (7") **STAR OF THE SHOW. / I DON'T EVEN KNOW YOUR NAME** – –

TUBEWAY ARMY (see under ⇒ NUMAN, Gary)

TUXEDOMOON

Formed: San Francisco, California, USA ... mid '77 by BLAINE REININGER and WINSTON TONG (an early line-up also included VICTORIA LOWE, MIKEL BELFER and PAUL ZAHL). In 1978 they issued their debut single, 'PINHEADS ON THE MOVE', on the self-financed 'Tidal Wave' imprint before the band set up their own 'Time Release' label for 1979's 'NEW MACHINE' EP. Late addition, STEVE BROWN, augmented the already exotic brew of violin-led, avant-garde electro with his sax playing; this four tracker (as 'NO TEARS'), along with a whole batch of TUXEDOMOON material received a UK release in the mid-80's on the 'Cramboy' label). Following the 1979 addition on PETER PRINCIPLE, the band subsequently took up residence at 'Ralph' records ('Pre' in the UK), home of er.. The RESIDENTS. The 'SCREAM WITH A VIEW' EP and full-length debut, 'HALF-MUTE' (1980), the former was recorded in the absence of TONG, who put in some part-time effort on the latter. The man himself could be heard in full monged-out flight on Belgian label, 'Les Disques Du Crepuscule's various artists set, 'The Fruit Of The Original Sin', memorably crawling his way through spoken word effort, 'THE LAST THING TO DEATH'. TONG was back in a full-time capacity for 1981's 'DESIRE' album alongside guest RAINCOAT, VICKY ASPINALL, the group subsequently relocating to Brussels, Belgium after a spell in Rotterdam, Netherlands. From this new base, the free-from space jazz/electro cadets released a clutch of European-only affairs including an album, 'SUITE EN SOUS-SOL' on Italian label, 'Expanded', sung in French (!). Pretentious ? Non! Founding members TONG and REININGER both departed to concentrate on solo careers (the latter had already released two sets, 'BROKEN FINGERS' and 'NIGHT AIR' on the aforementioned 'Crepuscule . . .' label in the mid-80's, TONG taking his leave after 1985's 'HOLY WARS' set. TUXEDOMOON continued with a line-up of PRINCIPLE, BRUCE GEDULDIG, LUC VAN LIESHOUT, JAN D'HAESE and IVAN GEORGIEV for a couple more albums, 'SHIP OF FOOLS' (1986) and 'YOU' (1987) before disbanding. Bizarrely enough, a posthumous live set emerged on 'R.C.A.' at the turn of the decade while a final, mysterious TUXEDOMOON studio set, 'THE GHOST SONATA', appeared in 1991. REININGER continued to record in Belgium for the bulk of the 80's, although only two albums, '(SONGS FROM THE) RAIN PALACE' and 'EXPATRIATE' have appeared in the 90's. TONG's last vinyl appearance, meanwhile, was 1985's 'THEORETICALLY CHINESE'. • **Covered:** 19th NERVOUS BREAKDOWN (Rolling Stones).

Album rating: HALF MUTE (*7) / DESIRE (*5) / DIVINE (*4) / A THOUSAND LIVES BY PICTURE (*4) / HOLY WARS (*5) / SHIP OF FOOLS (*5) / YOU (*4) / PINHEADS ON THE MOVE (*4) / TEN YEARS IN ONE NIGHT (*5) / 13 + 1 OF THE BEST compilation (*6) / THE GHOST SONATA (*4) / JOEBOY IN MEXICO (*4)

BLAINE L. REININGER – violin, keyboards, guitars / **MIKEL BELFER** – guitar / **PAUL ZAHL** – drums, electronic percussion / **WINSTON TONG** – vocals / **VICTORIA LOWE** – vocals

	not iss.	Tidal Wave
1978. (7") <001> **PINHEADS ON THE MOVE. / JOEBOY**	–	

<re-iss. 1978 on 'Time Release'; TRR 101>

—— **STEVEN BROWN** – vocals, keyboards, saxophone, etc; repl. LOWE

TUXEDOMOON (cont) — THE GREAT INDIE DISCOGRAPHY — The 1970s

		not iss.	Time Release
1979.	(12"ep) <TREP 101> **NEW MACHINE / LITE BULB OVERKILL. / NITE & DAY / NO TEARS** (UK-iss.Mar86 as 'NO TEARS EP' on 'Cramboy'; CBOY 7070)	–	

— **PETER PRINCIPLE** (b. DACHERT) – bass, guitar, etc; repl. ZAHL

| 1979. | (7") <TR 102> **STRANGER. / LOVE – NO HOPE** | – | |

— now without TONG (he returned for the following album)

		Pre	Ralph
Dec 79.	(12"ep) (PRE 1-12) **SCREAM WITH A VIEW** – Nervous guy / Where interest lie / Special treatment for the family man / Midnite stroll. (re-iss. Oct85 on 'Cramboy'; CBOY 4040)		

— now without BELFER

May 80.	(7") <TX 80032> **WHAT USE? / CRASH**		
Sep 80.	(lp) <TX 8004> **HALF-MUTE** – Nazca / 59 to 1 / Fifth column / Tritone / Loneliness / James Whale / What use? / Volo vivace / 7 years / Km / Seeding the clouds. (UK-iss.Oct84 on 'Cramboy'; CBOY 1010) (cd-iss. 1988 +=; CBOY 1040) – SCREAM WITH A VIEW		
Oct 80.	(7") (PRE 010) <TX 8054> **DARK COMPANION. / 59 TO 1** (remix)		

— **WINSTON TONG** – vocals (now a full-time member again)

— w/ guests VICKY ASPINALL – vocals (of RAINCOATS) / AL ROBINSON – cello

| Mar 81. | (lp/c) <PREX/PRICS 4> <TX 8104> **DESIRE** – East – Jinx / Blue suit / Music 1 / Victims of the dance / Incubus / Desire again / In the name of talent / Holiday for plywood. (re-iss. Oct85 on 'Cramboy'; CBOY 3030) (re-iss. Aug88 on 'Charisma'; CHC 66) (cd-iss. 1989 on 'Cramboy'+=; CBOY 3070) – NO TEARS EP | | |

— group now moved base to Brussels, Belgium

— added part-timer **BRUCE GEDULDIG** – visuals, films, percussion

		Operation Twilight	not iss.
Apr 82.	(12") (TWI 055) **NINOTCHKA. / AGAIN**		–
May 82.	(lp) (6399348) **DIVINE** – Mata Hari / Anna Christie / Grand hotel / Ninotchka / Conquest / Queen Christina / Camille.	–	– German
Jul 82.	(m-lp) (TWI 084) **TIME TO LOSE** – Time to lose / Music #2 / Blind / Cage / This beast.(cd-ep iss.Oct88 on 'Cramboy'; CBOY 8081)		–
Apr 83.	(12") **THE CAGE. /**	–	– Belgian

		Expanded	not iss.
Dec 82.	(d-lp) (EX 38-Y2) **SUITE EN SOUS-SOL** – Prelude / Allemande bleue / Courante marocaine / Sarabande en bas de l'escalier / Polonaise mecanique / L'etranger.		– Italian

		New Ralph	New Ralph
Jan 84.	(lp) <(TX 8354)> **A THOUSAND LIVES BY PICTURE (live)** – What use? / Incubus (blue suit) / 7 years / Tritone (musica diablo) / Desire / Dark companion / Jinx / 59 to 1 / Crash.		

		Joeboy	not iss.
Jul 84.	(7") (SW 7007) **SOMA. / HUGGING THE EARTH**	–	– Belgian

— now without mainman REININGER was already releasing solo material

— TONG, PRINCIPLE + BROWN recruited **LUC VAN LIESHOUT** – trumpet, flugelhorn / **ALAIN LeFEBVRE** – congas, percussion / **JAN D'HAESE** – vocals

		Cramboy	not iss.
Apr 85.	(lp/cd) (CBOY 2020/+CD) **HOLY WARS** – The waltz / St. John / Bonjour tristesse / Hugging the earth / In a manner of speaking / Some guys / Holy wars / Watching the blood flow / Egypt.		–

— **BRUCE GEDULDIG** – vocals (returned) to repl. TONG who had already initiated his own solo career

— **IVAN GEORGIEV** – keyboards, synths, vocals; repl. LeFEVRE

— **MARCIA BARCELLOS** – vocals; repl. D'HAESE

| Jun 86. | (m-lp) (CBOY 6060) **SHIP OF FOOLS** – Atlantis / Reeding, righting, phythmatic / Break the rules / A piano solo / Lowlands tone poem / Music for piano & guitar / An afternoon with N / The train. | | |

— now without MARCIA

| Sep 87. | (lp) (CBOY 9090) **YOU** – Roman P. / The train / 2000 / Never ending story / Boxman (Mr. Niles) / Spirits & ghosts / Boxman (the city) / You / Boxman (home). | | |

— disbanded the following year

		R.C.A.	not iss.
Aug 90.	(lp/cd) (PB 5921/+CD) **TEN YEARS IN ONE NIGHT (live 1985-1988)** – Michael's theme / Burning trumpet / The waltz / In a manner of speaking / The cage / Everything you want / Courante marocaine / Lite bulb overkill / Desire / Nervous guy / Pinheads on the move / No tears / In Heaven / Nazca. (d-cd was issued 1989 on 'Materiali Sonoro'; MASO 90006) (cd-iss. Jun98; MASOCD 90006)		–

		Les Tempes Modernes	not iss.
May 91.	(cd) (LTMCD 203) **THE GHOST SONATA** – Funeral of a friend / The ghost sonata / Catalyst / Affair at the soiree / Music No.2 / Drowning / Cascade / Mystic death / Basso pomade / Licorice stick ostinado / Laboratory / Les odalisques / Unsigned postcard. (re-iss. Oct97 on 'Cramboy'; CBOY 1414)		–

— above was their final release for a while

		Opcion Sonica	Opcion Sonica
Jan 99.	(cd) <(OPCD 48)> **JOEBOY IN MEXICO** – The door – Viaje en la Sierra Madre / Brad's loop / Les six / Shipwreck / Zombie paradise I / Zombie paradise II / Bitter bark / El pop / Hindi loop / Ambient pop / Keredwin's reel.		May98

– compilations, etc. –

Jan 88.	(d-lp/cd) Cramboy; <(CBOY 5050/+CD)> **PINHEADS ON THE MOVE** – Pinheads on the move / Joeboy the electronic ghost / Stranger / Jungle 7 / Love – No hope / In Heaven / I heard it through the grapevine / Fifth column / Touched / Waterfront seat / Nuit au fond de la frayere / I left my heart in San Francisco / Everything you want / Next to nothing / Egypt / Over his head / Martial – This land / Straight line forward / Jingle 9 / Pinheads on the move.		
Jan 94.	(cd) Cramboy; <(CBOY 1313)> **13 + 1 OF THE BEST** – What use? / No tears / The cage / Some guys / Dark companion / In a manner of speaking / Atlantis / The waltz / L'etranger / Tritone (music diablo) / East – Jinx / Desire / 59 to 1 / You (Christmas mix).		
1997.	(cd) Cramboy; <(CBOY 8081)> **SUITE EN SOUS SOL – TIME TO LOSE** – Suite en sous sol / Time to loose / Short stories. (re-iss. May01; same)		
Feb 01.	(cd) Gigolo; (efa 29555-2) **NO TEARS** (remastered)		

STEVEN BROWN

— with **REININGER** – violin (on 1st)

		Another Side	not iss.
1984.	(lp) (SIDE 8405) **MUSIC FOR SOLO PIANO** – Piano No.1 / Waltz / The ball / Hold me while I'm naked / Close little sixes / Fanfare / Egypt / The fall / Fantasie for clarinet & violin / R.W.F. / Rotterdam lullabye. (UK-iss.Jul88 on 'Crepuscule'; TWI 110) (cd-iss. Mar90; TWI 110-2)		– Belgian

— now with **LEW** – synths, tapes / **MARC HOLLANDER** – clarinet

		Crammed Discs	not iss.
1984.	(lp; by BENJAMIN LEW & STEVEN BROWN) (CRAM 020) **DOUZIEME JOURNEE: LA VERBE, LA PARURE, L'AMOUR** – Bamako ou ailleurs / Passage / De l'autre cote fleuve / L'ile l'hotel / A veugle, depuis / Elle s'avanca / Dans les jardins / Les autres, tou / Il, les quitta a l'aube. (re-iss. Mar88 on 'Made To Measure'; MTM 15)		–

— added **ALAIN LeFEBVRE** – drums, percussion / + guests **VINI REILLY** – guitar, piano (of DURUTTI COLUMN) / **FORTIS** – vocals

| 1985. | (lp; by BENJAMIN LEW & STEVEN BROWN) (CRAM 038) **A PROPOS D'UN PAYSAGE** – Moments / Les enormes et pourtant l'invisibles / Profondeurs des eaux des laques / Une telle richesse / S'ignorer / Pareseuse aussi / Au sujet d'un paysage / Face a ce qui se derobe / Noubelles observations / La vie aussi / Etendue. | | – |

		Play It Again Sam	not iss.
Jun 87.	(7") (BIAS 066) **THE LAST RENDEZVOUS. /**		–
Jun 87.	(cd/lp) (CD+/BIAS 055) **SEARCHING FOR CONTACT** – Habit / Audiences & stages / Does day / In praise of money / Manner of means / This land, scene 1-3 / De hamburger veermaster / Voxcon.		–

		Sub Rosa	not iss.
Jul 87.	(12") (SUB12 002-4) **ME & YOU & THE LICORICE STICK. /**		–
Oct 88.	(lp/cd; by BENJAMIN LEW & STEVEN BROWN) (MTM 17/+CD) **NEBKA** (above on 'Made To Measure')		
1989.	(lp/cd) (SUB 33/CD 00921) **THE DAY IS GONE**	–	–
Jan 90.	(12") (SUB12 007-28) **LOVE, YES. /**		–

		Les Tempes Modernes	not iss.
Apr 90.	(lp/cd) (LTM/+CD 2304) **LA GRACE DU TOMBEUR** – The labyrinth / The flight / The fall.		–

– (his) compilations, others, etc. –

| Nov 88. | (lp/c) Materiali Sonoro; (MASO 33044/+C) **ZOO STORY** | | – Italian |
| May 89. | (lp/cd) Crepuscule; (TWI 872/+2) **COMPOSES POUR LE THEATRE ET LE CINEMA** | | – |

PETER PRINCIPLE

— with **SASHKIA LUPINI** – flute

		Made To Measure	not iss.
Mar 84.	(lp) (MTM 2) **REVAUX AU BONGO** (cd-iss. Nov88; MTM 2CD)		
Mar 85.	(lp) (MTM 4) **SEDIMENTAL JOURNEY** – The anvil chorus / Pandemonium / Spring / Friends of extinction / Tippi rider / The eleventh race / Noon / Ain't superstitious / Dnieper / Before the wind. (cd-iss. Sep88; MTM 4CD)		
Nov 88.	(lp/cd) (MTM 18/+CD) **TONE POEMS** – Le maka / Sphinx / Sub-lunar folly / The observatory / Independence day / Pillar of salt / Orfal / Orion's shadow / Dolphins / Riding the silver chord.		

BLAINE L. REININGER

— with **PETER PRINCIPLE, STEVEN BROWN, MIKEL BELFER, JJ LaRUE + ALAIN GAUTIER**

		Crepuscule	not iss.
Jul 82.	(lp) (TWI 068) **BROKEN FINGERS** – Broken fingers / Nurr al Hajj / Magic time / Petite piece Chinoise / Right mind / Gigolo grasiento / Spiny doughboys / Sons of the silent age / Uptown / Les nuages / Magnetic life / Playin' your game. (cd-iss. May88; TWICD 068)		–
Oct 83.	(12") **MAGNETIC LIFE. /**		– Belgian

— **WINSTON TONG** – vocals; repl. LaRUE

— **MARC HOLLANDER** – clarinet; repl. PRINCIPLE

| Dec 83. | (lp) (TWI 267) **NIGHT AIR** – Night air / Birthday song / Beak people / Mystery and confusion / Bizarre bizarre / Intermission / Ash and bone / L'entree de l'hierophante / Un cafe au lait for Mr. XYZPTLK / Miraculous absense / El mensajero divino. | | – Belgian |
| Oct 84. | (lp; by BLAINE L. REININGER & MIKEL ROUSE) (MTM 3) **COLORADO (suite)** – Side wind / Windy outside / West wind / Sun study / Friendship '84 / Big pine II / Airland 2000 / Hardfall / Winter in Wyoming / The eloquent dissenter / A walk in the woods. (above issued on 'Made To Measure') | | |

— only retained **GOUTIER** + enlisted **THIERRY PLAS** – guitar / **WERNER PENSAERT** – keyboards / **BOB DI MARCO** – saxophone / **MARC BONNE** – drums

| Jul 85. | (lp; by BLAINE REININGER & ALAIN GOUTIER) (TWI 380) **PARIS EN AUTOMNE** | | – |

TUXEDOMOON (cont)

— Paris en automne / Singular world / Raise your hands / Burn like Rome / The homecoming.

— **KLAUS WANG** – vocals, keyboards; repl. WERNER + THIERRY
— **DANIEL WANG** – drums, trumpet; repl. MARC

May 86. (lp) *(TWICD 637)* **LIVE IN BRUSSELS (live)**
— Volo / Night air / Birthday song / What use indeed? / Uptown (extremely long concert version) / Broken fingers.

— **BLAINE** with **LEON VAN DEN ACKER + ERIC SLEICHIM**

Apr 87. (lp/cd) *(TWI/+CD 767)* **BYZANTIUM**
— Rolf and Florian go Hawaiian / Blood of a poet / Teenage theatre / Some fine day / Japanese dream / Too cool to die / Bird on the wire / Rosebud.

1988. (cd; by STEVEN BROWN & BLAINE L. REININGER) *(TWI 916-2)* **LIVE IN PORTUGAL (live)**
— Iberia / Egypt / The fall / L'arrivee dans le jour / Music number two / Fanfare / The waltz / Piano No.1 / Salad variation / Licorice stick ostinato / Volo vivace / Lite bulb overkill.

Oct 88. (7") *(NORMAL 72)* **EL PASO. /**
(12"+=/3"cd-s+=) *(NORMAL 72 T/CD)* –
(above issued on German label, 'Normal')

1989. (lp/cd) *(TWI 845/+2)* **BOOK OF HOURS**
— Zombie bop / St. Therese / To the green door / Salad days / El Paso / Letter from home / Come the Spring / Software pancake house.

Sep 90. (cd) *(TWI 909-2)* **(SONGS FROM THE) RAIN PALACE**   Giant / not iss.

1990's. (cd/lp) *(GRI 6042-2/-1)* **EXPATRIATE**

– (his) compilations, etc. –

1988. (lp) *Interior Music; (IM 008)* **INSTRUMENTALS 1982-86**
— Contempt / Les chose de la vie / Le dernier amant romantique / Les nuages / Petite piece Chinoise / Travelling / Music Number two / Licorice stick ostinato / Basso pomade – Dogs licking my heart.

May 96. (cd) *Crepescule; (TWI 964-2)* **BRUSSELS / USA – THE BEST OF BLAINE L. REININGER, VOL.1**
— Night air / Gigolo grasiento / Mystery and confusion / Ash and bone / Teenage theatre / Tombee de la nuit / Zen and Lulu / Software pancake house / To the green door / Cafe au lait / Come the Spring / Ralf and Florian go Hawaiian / Right mind / Letter from home / Broken fingers / One-way man / El mensajero divino.

WINSTON TONG

Crepescule / not iss. – Japan

Jun 83. (lp) *(044)* **LIKE THE OTHERS**

— with guests SUSAN DEHIM – vocals / DAVE FORMULA – keyboards (ex-MAGAZINE) / STEVE MORRIS – drums (of NEW ORDER) / ALAN RANKINE – guitar, synthesizer, percussion (ex-ASSOCIATES) / JAH WOBBLE – bass (Solo Artist) / SIMON TOPPING – trumpet (ex-A CERTAIN RATIO) / ALAIN LeFEBVRE – drums / PIETRO LACRIGINOLA – sax / NIKKI MONO – vocals

Dec 84. (12") *(TWI 310)* **THEORETICAL CHINA. / HUNGER**
Aug 85. (lp) *(6911)* **REPORTS FROM THE HEART**   German
— Phadre slips on her silver girdle / In a white room / What makes the click in me / Now we were misunderstood / Orpheus: The last march of a poet / The other half lives / Thirteenth hour / Silence / China he said / Soulsearch / Lost everywhere.

Operation Afterglow / not iss.

Nov 85. (lp) *(LPOPA 004)* **THEORETICALLY CHINESE**
— Big brother / Yellow peril / Theoretical China / Endgame / The quotidan / The principles of movement / No regrets / Reports from the heart. *(cd-iss. May86 on 'Crepescule'; CDTWI 549)*

TV PERSONALITIES (see under ⇒ TELEVISION PERSONALITIES)

20/20

Formed: Tulsa, Oklahoma, USA ... 1976 by schoolfriends STEVE ALLEN and RON FLYNT. Flitting west to L.A. the following year, the pair enlisted MIKE GALLO before emerging on Greg Shaw's seminal New Wave label, 'Bomp!'. Debut 45, 'GIVING IT ALL', in 1978, saw this power-pop act come of age, and with the addition of keyboard-player CHRIS SILAGYI and the signing to 'Portrait' records, 20/20 unleashed their critically-acclaimed eponymous set in 1979. Sadly ignored (except in Oklahoma), the quartet found it difficult to break through commercially. Subsequent efforts, 'LOOK OUT!' (1981) and 'SEX TRAP' (1983), found little respect in the musically blinkered post-New Wave world of rock'n'roll and it was inevitable the band would split. However, with a renewed interest in everything from the punk years, 20/20 re-united for a few more sets, '4 DAY TORNADO' (1995) and 'INTERSTATE' (1998). • **Trivia:** They guested on the 'Tribute To Badfinger' album.

Album rating: 20/20 (*7) / LOOK OUT! (*6) / SEX TRAP (*3) / 4 DAY TORNADO (*5) / INTERSTATE (*5)

STEVE ALLEN – vocals, guitar / **RON FLYNT** – bass, vocals / **MIKE GALLO** – drums

not iss. / Bomp!

Jul 78. (7") <*BOMP 115*> **GIVING IT ALL. / UNDER THE FREEWAY**

— added **CHRIS SILAGYI** – keyboards, synthesizer, vocals

Portrait / Portrait

Apr 80. (7") *(PRT 8184)* **TELL ME WHY. / BACKYARD GUYS**
May 80. (lp) *(PRT 83898)* <*JR 36205*> **20/20**   Oct79
— Sky is falling / Yellow pills / Cheri / Out of this time / Tell me why (can't understand you) / Tonight we fly / Remember the lightning / She's an obsession / Leaving your world behind / Backyard guys / Jet lag / Action now. *<cd-iss. 1995 on 'Oglio'+=; 81581>* – LOOK OUT!

Aug 80. (7") *(PRT 8557)* **CHERI. / ACTION NOW**
Jun 81. (lp) *<JB 37050>* **LOOK OUT!**
— Nuclear boy / Out of my head / Strange side of love / Alien / Girl like you / Life in the U.S.A. / Night I heard a scream / Beat city / Mobile unit 245 / American dream.

— disbanded but returned in 1983, the line-up being **ALLEN, FLYNT** and new drummer **DEAN KORTH**

not iss. / Mainway

1983. (lp) *<5RD 101>* **SEX TRAP**
— Jack's got a problem / Fast car (remix) / Sex trap (remix) / We can fly / Howard / Overload / Walking downtown / Bad night / Haunted people go / Kick it up twice.

— disbanded for over a decade, **BILL BELKNAP** – drums, percussion

not iss. / Oglio

Sep 95. (cd) *<89100>* **4 DAY TORNADO**
— Song of the universe / Stone cold / Nothing at all / My Tuesday / State of grace / Watching the headlights burn / Solid ground / For all our time / It goes on / Well, frankly.

Aug 98. (cd) *<89101>* **INTERSTATE**
— Land of the free / Trip in Hollywood / Picasso's big blue heart / What do you feel / Cool white Laura / I never did no Hitler / Best thing in the world / Julie / Sex / New thing / So many reasons.

TWINK (see under ⇒ PINK FAIRIES)

TWINKEYZ

Formed: Sacramento, California, USA ... 1976 by DONNIE JUPITER, KEITH McKEE, TOM DARLING and vocalist HONEY. One of California's first punk-influenced acts, the TWINKEYZ made their debut in 1977 with a single, 'ALIENS IN OUR MIDST', on the tiny 'Grok' label. Bizarrely enough, the band gained a foothold on continental Europe, where Dutch label, 'Plurex', released their one and only album, 'ALPHA JERK'. While the latter was available in the UK, a final single, 'WATCH OUT FOR HER KISS' was released exclusively onto the Dutch market in 1980 prior to the band's final split. • **Covered:** YOU'RE GONNA MISS ME (13th Floor Elevators).

Album rating: ALPHA JERK (*5) / ALIENS IN OUR MIDST compilation (*6)

DONNIE JUPITER – vocals, rhythm guitar / **HONEY** – vocals, bass, guitar / **TOM DARLING** – lead guitar, bass, vocals / **KEITH McKEE** – drums, vocals

not iss. / Grok

1977. (7"white) <*1.00*> **ALIENS IN OUR MIDST. / ONE THOUSAND REASONS**
1978. (7"opalescent) <*2.00*> **E.S.P. / CARTOON LAND**

Plurex / not iss.

Aug 79. (lp) *(1000)* **ALPHA JERK**   Dutch
— Aliens in our midst / Tonight again / Sweet nothing / 1000 reasons / Cartton land / E.S.P. / Twinkeyz theme / That's the way it goes / Alpha jerk / Strange feeling / Wild love.

Oct 80. (7") *(0019)* **WATCH OUT FOR HER KISS. /**   Dutch

— after they split, DARLING joined The VEIL (and later GAME THEORY)

– compilations, etc. –

Jun 98. (cd) *Anopheles; (ANOPHELES 003)* **ALIENS IN OUR MIST**
— Aliens in our midst / Tonight again / Sweet nothing / 1,000 reasons / Cartoon land / E.S.P. / Twinkeyz theme / That's the way it goes / Alpha jerk / Strange feeling / Wild love / My plea / Watch out for her kiss / Moonbabies / Little Joey / Cartoon land (live) / Twinkeyz theme (live) / Aliens in our midst (live) / Space-age rock queen (live) / Radar burning (live) / You're gonna miss me (live).

U

UK SUBS

Formed: London, England ... Spring '76 by former R&B singer CHARLIE HARPER and guitarist NICKY GARRETT. This hardy punk outfit – completed by PAUL SLACK and PETE DAVIS – made their vinyl debut in early '78 on the various artists LP, 'Farewell To The Roxy' before issuing a debut single on the small 'City' label. Although the band arrived a bit late for the punk party, their subsequent signing to R.C.A. subsidiary, 'Gem', resulted in a string of minor hit singles beginning with the frantic three-chord stomp of 'STRANGLEHOLD' in summer '79. Along with the excellent 'TOMORROW'S GIRLS', the track was featured on debut album, 'ANOTHER KIND OF BLUES' (1979), an amphetamine-fuelled collection of simple but effective hooklines and RAMONES-style lyrics. The following month saw the release of an EP with an unlikely cover of The Zombies' 'SHE'S NOT THERE' as the lead track, the busy schedule continuing apace with the classic 'WARHEAD' single early in 1980. 'BRAND NEW AGE' hit the Top 20 later that year, although its success was outstripped by seminal live set, 'CRASH COURSE'; while the UK SUBS were perhaps a second division outfit in the shadow of The CLASH etc., there was no doubting their onstage power and formidable aura of HARPER in full flight. The record made the Top 10, an all-time best that the 'SUBS would struggle to emulate as their commercial fortunes began to wane in the early 80's. Personnel upheavals dogged the band, SLACK and DAVIS replaced by ALVIN GIBBS and STEVE ROBERTS prior to the band's last charting album, 'DIMINISHED RESPONSIBILITY' (1981). The subsequent departure of co-songwriter GARRETT dealt a blow that the UK SUBS never really recovered from, HARPER continuing to release workmanlike albums such as 'FLOOD OF LIES' (1983) and 'HUNTINGTON BEACH' (1985) to an ever diminishing core of fans. At the dawn of the 90's HARPER was still fronting the latest incarnation of the UK SUBS, 'MAD COW FEVER's hackneyed collection of pub-rock favourites a far cry from the band's late 70's heyday. • **Covered:** SHE'S NOT THERE (Zombies) / I'M WAITING FOR THE MAN (Velvet Underground) / I WALKED WITH A ZOMBIE (13th Floor Elevators) / ROUTE '66 (hit; Nelson Riddle) / BABY PLEASE DON'T GO (hit; Them). • **Trivia:** HARPER had also been part of garage-influenced URBAN DOGS between 1983-85.

Album rating: ANOTHER KIND OF BLUES (*5) / BRAND NEW AGE (*5) / CRASH COURSE (*6) / DIMINISHED RESPONSIBILTY (*5) / ENDANGERED SPECIES (*4) / FLOOD OF LIES (*3) / GROSS OUT U.S.A. (*2) / HUNTINGTON BEACH (*4) / KILLING TIME (*3) / JAPAN TODAY (*3) / IN ACTION: TENTH ANNIVERSARY (*3) / MAD COW FEVER (*3) / NORMAL SERVICE RESUMED (*3) / SCUM OF THE EARTH – THE BEST OF... compilation (*6) / OCCUPIED (*3) / QUINTESSENTIALS (*4) / Charlie Harper: STOLEN PROPERTY (*3)

CHARLIE HARPER (b. DAVID CHARLES PEREZ, 25 Apr'44) – vocals, rhythm guitar / **NICKY GARRETT** – lead guitar / **PAUL SLACK** – bass / **PETE DAVIS** – drums

	City	not iss.
Dec 78. (7"clear,7"blue,7"green,7"orange,7"red) (NIK 5) **C.I.D. / I LIVE IN A CAR / B.I.C.**		-
(re-iss. Oct79 on 'Pinnacle'; PIN 22)		

	Gem-RCA	R.C.A.
Jun 79. (7"red) (GEMS 5) **STRANGLEHOLD. / WORLD WAR / ROCKERS**	26	-
Aug 79. (7"blue) (GEMS 10) <PB 11766> **TOMORROW'S GIRLS. / SCUM OF THE HEART / TELEPHONE NUMBERS**	28	
Oct 79. (blue-lp) (GEMLP 100) **ANOTHER KIND OF BLUES**	21	

– C.I.D. / I couldn't be you / Tomorrow's girl / Killer / World war / Rockers / I.O.D. / T.V. blues / Lady Esquire / All I wanna know / Crash course / Young criminals / B.I.C. / Disease / Stranglehold. (re-iss. Sep91 on 'Abstract' cd/c; AAB CD/TC 801) (cd-iss. Jul95 on 'Dojo'; DOJOCD 226) (cd re-iss. + Jul98 on 'Diabolo'; DIAB 86-2) (<cd re-iss. Mar00 on 'Captain Oi'; AHOYCD 134>)

Nov 79. (7"green-ep) (GEMS 14) **SHE'S NOT THERE / KICKS. / VICTIM / THE SAME THING**	36	-
Feb 80. (7"brown) (GEMS 23) **WARHEAD. / I'M WAITING FOR THE MAN / THE HARPER**	30	-
Apr 80. (clear-lp) (GEMLP 106) **BRAND NEW AGE**	18	-

– You can't take it anymore / Public servant / Warhead / Barbie's dead / Organised crime / Rat race / Emotional blackmail / Kicks / Teenage / Dirty girls / 500 c.c. / Bomb factory. (re-iss. Sep91 on 'Abstract' cd/c; AAB CD/TC 802) (cd-iss. Jul95 on 'Dojo'; DOJOCD 228) (<cd re-iss. May00 on 'Captain Oi'; AHOYCD 143>)

May 80. (7"pink,7"orange) (GEMS 30) **TEENAGE. / LEFT FOR DEAD / NEW YORK STATE POLICE**	32	-
Sep 80. (purple-lp) (GEMLP 111) **CRASH COURSE** (live)	8	-

– C.I.D. / I couldn't be you / I live in a car / Tomorrow's girl / Left for dead / Kicks / Rat race / New York state police / Warhead / Public servant / Telephone numbers / Organised crime / Rockers / Brand new age / Dirty girls / The same thing / Crash course / Teenage / Killer / Emotional blackmail. (w/ free-12") (re-iss. Sep91 on 'Abstract' cd/c; AAB CD/TC 803) (cd-iss. Jul95 on 'Dojo'; DOJOCD 229) (<cd re-iss. Jun00 on 'Captain Oi'; AHOYCD 140>)

--- **ALVIN GIBBS** – bass (ex-USERS, ex-HELLIONS) repl. SLACK --- **STEVE ROBERTS** – drums; repl. DAVIS

Oct 80. (7"yellow) (GEMS 42) **PARTY IN PARIS. / FALL OF THE EMPIRE**	37	-
Feb 81. (red-lp) (GEMLP 112) **DIMINISHED RESPONSIBILITY**	18	-

– You don't belong / So what / Confrontation / Fatal / Time and matter / Too tired / Party in Paris / Gangster / Face the machine / New order / Just another jungle / Collision cult. (re-iss. Sep91 on 'Abstract' cd/c; AAB CD/TC 804) (cd-iss. Jul95 on 'Dojo'; DOJOCD 232) (<cd re-iss. Jul00 on 'Captain Oi'; AHOYCD 143>)

Apr 81. (7"blue) (GEMS 45) **KEEP ON RUNNIN' (TILL YOU BURN). / PERFECT GIRL**	41	-

(7"ep+=) **KEEP RUNNIN' EP** (GEMEP 45) – Ice age / Party in Paris (French version).

	NEMS	not iss.
Nov 81. (7") (NES 304) **COUNTDOWN. / PLAN OF ACTION**		-

--- **KIM WYLIE** – drums; repl. ROBERTS who joined CYANIDE then LIGOTAGE

	Abstract	not iss.
Oct 82. (7"red-ep) (ABS 012) **SHAKE UP THE CITY**		-
– Self destruct / Police state / War of the roses.		
Oct 82. (red-lp) **ENDANGERED SPECIES**		-

– Endangered species / Living dead / Countdown / Ambition / Fear of girls / Lay down and die / Down on the farm / Sensitive boys / Divide by 8, multiply by 5 / Ice age / I robot / Flesh wound. (re-iss. Jun90 on 'Link'; CLINK 4) (<cd-iss. Dec98 on 'Captain Oi'; AHOYCD 097>)

--- **CHARLIE HARPER** recruited entire new band **CAPTAIN SCARLET** – guitar repl. GARRETT who formed REBEKKA FRAME / **PAUL SLACK** – bass returned to repl. GIBBS who joined URBAN DOGS / **STEVE JONES** – drums repl. WYLIE

	Fall Out	not iss.
Aug 83. (7") (FALL 017) **ANOTHER TYPICAL CITY. / STILL LIFE**		-
(12"+=) (FALL12 017) – Veronique.		
Oct 83. (lp/c) (FALL LP/CLP 018) **FLOOD OF LIES**		-

– Flood of lies / Veronique / Soldiers of fortune / Db's / Tampa Bay / After the war / Vilent revolution / In the red / Dress code / Still life / Revenge of the yellow devils / Another typical city / In the wild / Seas. (cd-iss. 1995; FALLCD 018) (<cd re-iss. Apr01 on 'Captain Oi'+=; AHOYCD 166>) – Another typical city / Still life / Spell / Private army / Multiple minds / Primary strength / Another typical city (12" version).

Sep 84. (12") (FALL12 024) **MAGIC / PRIVATE ARMY. / THE SPELL / MULTIPLE MINDS / PRIMARY STRENGTH**		-

--- **HARPER** again + new members **JOHN FALLON** – guitar / **JEZZ MONCUR** – bass / **RAB FAE BEITH** – drums (ex-WALL, ex-PATRIK FITZGERALD)

Jan 85. (lp) (FALLLP 031) **GROSS OUT U.S.A.** (live)		-

– Intro / Emotional blackmail / New barbarians / In the wild / Veronique / Flood of lies / Warhead / Limo life / Disease / Violent revolution / Soldiers of fortune / Ice-age / Dress code / Telephone numbers / Stranglehold / You don't belong / Party in Paris. (cd-iss. 1995; FALLCD 031)

Jun 85. (7"red,7"blue) (FALL 036) **THIS GUN SAYS. / SPEAK FOR MYSELF / WANTED**		-

	Red Flame	not iss.
Dec 85. (lp/c) (RFB LP/CA 1) **HUNTINGTON BEACH**		-

– Rock'n'roll savage / Between the eyes / Suicide taxi / Party animal / The unknown / Miss Tennage USA / Huntington / All the king's horses / Juke box / Sk8 tough / Death row / Bullshitter / Dirty boy / All change for Hollywood / Blinding stories. (re-iss. Jun90 on 'FM-Revolver' cd/c/lp; REV XD/MC/LP 150) (<cd re-iss. Jun99 on 'Captain Oi'; AHOYCD 114>)

Apr 86. (7"ep) (RFBSIN 1) **LIVE IN HOLLAND – TENTH ANNIVERSARY** (live)		-

– Stranglehold / New barbarians / Tomorrow's girls / Between the eyes.

Apr 86. (lp/c) (RFB LP/CA 2) **IN ACTION: TENTH ANNIVERSARY** (compilation)		-

(re-iss. Mar90 on 'FM-Revolver' cd/c/lp; REV XD/MC/LP 142) (cd re-iss. Jul99 on 'Solid Inc.'; CDRNB 001)

	Fall Out	New Red Archives
Dec 87. (12") (FALL12 044) **HEY SANTA (LEAVE THESE KIDS ALONE). / THUNDERBIRD**		-
Dec 87. (lp) (FALLLP 045) **JAPAN TODAY** (live)		-

– Another Cuba / Funk rap / Streets on fire / Sex object / Warzone / Japan inc. / (interview) / Comin' back / Thunderbird / Hey! Santa / Street legal / Captain Scarlett / Skateboard Billy / Surf bastard / Angel. (cd-iss. Apr93; FALLCD 045) (<cd re-iss. Apr01 on 'Captain Oi'+=; AHOYCD 167>) – Motivator / Combat zone / Fascist regime / Auld lang syne / Cycle sluts from hell.

Mar 89. (lp/c/cd) (FALL LP/C/CD 047) <06> **KILLING TIME** (reunion album)		

– Yellowman / Motivator / Lower East Side / Drag me down / Never say you won't / Magalopolis / Planet I / Killing time / Holy land / American motors / Big Apple / Killing with kindness / Sabre dance / No heart / Fear to go / Nico. (cd has extra tracks)

--- latest UK SUBS alongside **HARPER** were **ALAN LEE** – guitar / **FLEA DAVE FARRELLY** – bass / **MATTHEW McCOY** – drums

--- **DARRELL BARTH** – guitar; repl. LEE

	Released Emotions	not iss.
Feb 89. (12"ep) (REM 004) **THE MOTIVATOR / COMBAT ZONE / FASCIST REGIME. / AULD LANG SYNE / CYCLE SLUTS FROM HELL**		-

	Fall Out	Amsterdamned
Feb 91. (cd/c/lp) (FALL CD/C/LP 048) **MAD COW FEVER**		-

– I walked with a zombie / Mandarins of change / Boneyard / Welfare mother / Saints and sinners / Pearl divers / Roadhouse blues / Talkin' 'bout you / Road runner / Route '66 / Pills / Baby please don't go / Last bus boogie / Ecology blues.

--- **DAVIS + CAMPBELL** repl. LEE + FARRELLY

Sep 93. (cd/lp) (FALL CD/LP 050) **NORMAL SERVICE RESUMED**		-

– Dumfux / Killer time / Jodie Foster / Here comes Alex / Ozone death / Strangeways / Joyride / Believe in yourself / Down on the farm / Mohawk radio / Brixton / Reaper / All the people / Squat the world / Lydia.

UK SUBS (cont)   THE GREAT INDIE DISCOGRAPHY   The 1970s

Nov 93. (7"ep/cd-ep) (FALL 051/+CD) **THE ROAD IS HARD, THE ROAD IS LONG EP**
– Jodie Foster / Here comes Alex / Killer time / Another Cuba / Lydia.
Apr 96. (cd/lp) (FALL CD/LP 052) <5> **OCCUPIED**   Mar97
– Let's get drunk / Shove it / DF 118 / Solutions / Public address / Revolving boys / One of the girls / Darkness / Not so secret wars / Infidel / MPRI.

	Fall Out	New Red Archives
Apr 97. (cd/lp) (FALL CD/LP 054) <69> **QUINTESSENTIALS**		May97

– Jump on it / Your ego / War on the Pentagon (parts 1 & 2) / Quintessentials / State of alert / The day of the dead / AK47 / Media man / Mouth on a stick / Outside society / Bitter and twisted / Accident prone / Killer cops / Psychosis.
Apr 98. (7"red) (FALL 056) **RIOT '98. /**   -

– compilations, etc. –

Jun 82. (c-ep) *Chaos;* (LIVE 009) **LIVE AT GOSSIPS** (live)   -
Oct 82. (blue-lp) *Abstract;* (AABT 300) **RECORDED '79–'81**   -
Apr 84. (lp/c) *Mausoleum;* (AMOK/KOMA 788005) **DEMONSTRATION TAPES** (rare demos) -
Apr 86. (lp) *Dojo;* (DOJOLP 28) **SUB STANDARDS**   -
Jun 86. (c) *R.O.I.R.;* (A 142) **LEFT FOR DEAD (ALIVE IN HOLLYWOOD)**   -
(cd-iss. Nov94; RE 412CD) (cd re-iss. Nov99; RUSCD 8256)
Jul 86. (lp) *Killerwatt;* (KILP 2001) **RAW MATERIAL**   -
Apr 90. (lp) *Released Emotions;* **GREATEST HITS (LIVE IN PARIS)**   -
(cd-iss. Jun93 on 'Dojo'; DOJOCD 130)
May 91. (blue-lp) *Abstract;* (AABT 800) **THE SINGLES 1978-1982**   -
(cd-iss. Apr93 on 'Get Back'; GBR 001)
Dec 91. (cd) *Streetlink;* (STRCD 017) **DOWN ON THE FARM (A COLLECTION OF THE LESS OBVIOUS)** -
(re-iss. Apr93 on 'Dojo'; DOJOCD 117)
Mar 92. (cd) *Released Emotions;* (REM 012CD) **EUROPE CALLING**   -
(re-iss. Jul98 on 'Pinhead'; PINCD 101)
May 93. (cd) *Get Back;* (BGR 002) **ANOTHER KIND OF BLUES / CRASH COURSE**   -
May 93. (cd) *Get Back;* (BGR 003) **BRAND NEW AGE / DIMINISHED RESPONSIBILITY** -
Jun 93. (cd/c) *Optima;* (OPTM CD/C 016) **PUNK AND DISORDERLY**   -
Jul 93. (cd/lp) *Receiver;* (RRCD/RRLP 146) **LIVE AT THE ROXY** (live)   -
(lp re-iss. Jul00 on 'Get Back'; GET 61)
Aug 93. (cd/c) *Music Club;* (MCCD/MCTC 120) **SCUM OF THE EARTH – THE BEST OF THE UK SUBS** -
Feb 94. (cd) *Loma;* (LOMACD 7) **ENDANGERED SPECIES / HUNTINGTON BEACH**   -
May 95. (cd) *C.A.S.;* (CD 43000-2) **THE PUNK IS BACK**   -
Sep 95. (cd) *Anagram;* (CDPUNK 66) **THE PUNK SINGLES COLLECTION**   -
Jul 96. (cd) *Cleopatra;* (<CLP 9703-2>) **THE PUNK CAN TAKE IT**   -
Oct 96. (cd) *Cleopatra;* (<CLP 9826-2>) **SELF DESTRUCT: PUNK CAN TAKE IT VOL.2** -
Nov 96. (4xcd-box) *Abstract;* (SUBBOX 1) **UK SUBS BOX SET**   -
Mar 97. (cd/lp) *Fallout;* (FALL CD/LP 53) **THE PEEL SESSIONS (1978-1979)**   -
Jun 97. (cd) *Anagram;* (CDMGRAM 113) / *Cleopatra;* <9929> **RIOT**   Mar97
(re-iss. Mar00; CDPUNK 115)
Jul 98. (cd) *PinHead;* (PINCD 101) **EUROPE CALLING**   -
Oct 98. (cd) *Captain Oi;* (<AHOYCD 093>) **PUNK ROCK RARITIES**   -
Nov 98. (3xcd-box) *Get Back;* (GBRBOX 100CD) **FASCIST REGIME**   -
– (ANOTHER KIND OF BLUES / CRASH COURSE / BRAND NEW AGE / DIMINISHED RESPONSIBILITY / SINGLES 1978-1982)
Mar 99. (cd) *Harry May;* (MAYOCD 107) **WARHEAD**
May 99. (d-cd) *Fallout;* (FALLCD 055) **SUBMISSION – THE BEST OF UK SUBS 1982-1998** -
Nov 99. (cd) *Rejected;* (REJ 1000024) **LIVE AT THE WARZONE**   -
Jan 00. (cd) *Metrodome;* (METRO 323) **STRANGLEHOLD**   -
Mar 01. (cd) *Anagram;* (<CDPUNK 120>) **TIM WARP – GREATEST HITS**   -
(re-iss. Jul01 on 'Cleopatra'; CLP 099CD)
May 01. (d-cd) *Snapper;* (<SMDCD 331>) **DOWN ON THE FARM**   -
Jun 02. (7") *Captain Oi;* (AHOY 701) **DRUNKEN SAILOR. / RECLAIM THE STREETS** -
Jun 02. (cd) *Captain Oi;* (<AHOYCD 204>) **UNIVERSAL**

CHARLIE HARPER

	Gem	not iss.
Jul 80. (7") (GEMS 35) **BARMY LONDON ARMY. / TALK IS CHEAP**	68	-

	Ramkup	not iss.
Jul 81. (7") (CAC 005) **FREAKED. / JO**		-

	Flicknife	not iss.
Feb 82. (lp) (SHARP 100) **STOLEN PROPERTY**		-

– Hoochie coochie man / Femme fatale / Hey Joe / Louie Louie / Pills / Light my fire / I'm waiting for the man / etc.

	Fall Out	not iss.
Nov 82. (7"; CHARLIE HARPER'S URBAN DOGS) (FALL 008) **NEW BARBARIANS. / SPEED KILLS / COCAINE**		-
Mar 83. (7"; CHARLIE HARPER'S URBAN DOGS) (FALL 011) **LIMO LIFE. / WARHEAD**		-

ULTRAVOX

Formed: London, England . . . mid '76 out of TIGER LILY (whose one and only single was a bizarre cover of Fats Waller's 'AIN'T MISBEHAVIN', subsequently withdrawn from release) comprising frontman JOHN FOXX, CHRIS CROSS, STEVE SHEARS, BILLY CURRIE and WARREN CANN. With the addition of violin (courtesy of CURRIE) and added synth power, the group became ULTRAVOX, initially with a ! at the end!. The fact that the band were picked up by 'Island' records and their eponymous 1977 debut album produced by BRIAN ENO says a lot about where ULTRAVOX! were coming from; artsy avant-pop combining elements of a punked-up ROXY MUSIC, the group were something of a cult live act. This didn't translate into sales, however, and despite an improved second effort, 'HA! HA! HA!' (1977), the group languished in relative obscurity. With ROBIN SIMON replacing SHEARS, they decamped to Germany to begin work on a third set under the auspices of electronic maestro, CONNY PLANK. The underwhelming result, 'SYSTEMS OF ROMANCE' (1978), failed to change the group's fortunes and by the Spring of '79, FOXX had abandoned ship for a solo career while SIMON went on to join MAGAZINE. The ubiquitous MIDGE URE was brought in as lead man, the singer having already cut his music business teeth in such diverse outfits as SLIK, The RICH KIDS and THIN LIZZY. He was also an integral part of moody synth-poppers, VISAGE, co-writing some of their material alongside mainman, STEVE STRANGE. Ironically, all this upheaval seemed to work wonders for all concerned, FOXX going his experimental electronic way and scoring a Top 40 hit almost immediately with the brilliant 'UNDERPASS' (early '80), while the newly revamped ULTRAVOX (now without a ! and signed to 'Chrysalis') broke the Top 30 that summer with 'SLEEPWALK'. 'VIENNA' (1980; again produced by CONNY PLANK) was released later that year, its Top 5 placing indicating that the new-look outfit had effectively cornered the burgeoning new romantic/electropop market. This was confirmed early in '81 when the album's title track narrowly missed the UK No.1 spot, its chilly, grandiose Euro feel and indelible melody managing to combine pretentiousness with mass public appeal. This was a talent which was to serve the group well over the ensuing five years, ULTRAVOX scoring an impressive run of seven Top 10 albums and a string of Top 30 hits. 'RAGE IN EDEN' (1981) was another Top 5 success, spawning three Top 20 singles including the po-faced 'ALL STOOD STILL'. The album also marked the end of the group's tenure with PLANK, GEORGE MARTIN overseeing production duties on 'QUARTET' (1982). The result was a markedly warmer sound and more commercial appeal, evident on the preceding single, 'REAP THE WILD WIND'. By the release of 'LAMENT' (1984), ULTRAVOX were a fully fledged pop band, the evocative heartbreak of 'DANCING WITH TEARS IN MY EYES' giving the group their biggest hit since 'VIENNA'. A bonus new track on the best selling compilation, 'THE COLLECTION' (1984), 'LOVE'S GREAT ADVENTURE', was another pop odyssey, its rolling synth crescendos a taster for the latest chapter in URE's solo career. Strangely enough, ULTRAVOX's last hit single was the sombre 'ALL FALL DOWN', its subject matter the war-torn Northern Ireland, an almost militaristic rhythm and uillean pipes utilised for greater effect. The track was lifted from the 'U-VOX' (1986) set, an album featuring the drumming talents of BIG COUNTRY's MARK BRZEZICKI. Realising they'd reached a creative impasse, ULTRAVOX disbanded the following year, URE taking up the solo career that had begun so successfully in 1982 with a Top 10 cover of Tom Rush's 'NO REGRETS' (made famous by the WALKER BROTHERS) and continued with the soaring pop of 'IF I WAS', a No.1 single in summer '85 (URE had also helped to mastermind the Band Aid single, 'Do They Know It's Christmas). He struggled, however, to resurrect his flagging solo career, the 1988 set, 'ANSWERS TO NOTHING' barely scraping into the Top 40 while a Spring '89 single, 'SISTERS AND BROTHERS' was withdrawn by 'Chrysalis'. Subsequently securing a new contract with 'Arista', URE returned in 1991 with the Top 20 hit, 'COLD COLD HEART' and a Top 40 album, 'PURE'. While ULTRAVOX made a low-key comeback in 1993 with a new singer, TONY FENELLE, and a new album, 'REVELATION', URE was conspicuous by his absence from the charts for most of the 90's. • **Songwriters:** FOXX and group until URE replaced FOXX. Covered only KING'S LEAD HAT (Brian Eno). MIDGE URE's solo career included THE MAN WHO SOLD THE WORLD (David Bowie) / STRANGE BREW (Cream).

Album rating: ULTRAVOX! (*5) / HA! HA! HA! (*5) / SYSTEMS OF ROMANCE (*5) / THREE INTO ONE compilation (*7) / VIENNA (*7) / RAGE IN EDEN (*6) / QUARTET (*5) / MONUMENT – THE SOUNDTRACK (*4) / LAMENT (*5) / THE COLLECTION compilation (*7) / U-VOX (*4) / REVELATION (*3) / INGENUITY (*2) / Midge Ure: THE GIFT (*6) / ANSWERS TO NOTHING (*5) / PURE (*4) / IF I WAS: THE VERY BEST OF MIDGE URE & ULTRAVOX compilation (*7) / BREATHE (*5)

TIGER LILY

DENNIS LEIGH (JOHN FOXX) – vocals / **STEVE SHEARS** – guitar / **BILLY CURRIE** (b. 1 Apr'52, Huddersfield, Yorkshire, England) – keyboards / **WARREN CANN** (b.20 May'52, Victoria, Canada) – drums / **CHRIS ST. JOHN** (b. CHRISTOPHER ALLEN, 14 Jul'52) – bass

	Gull	not iss.
Mar 75. (7") (GULS 12) **AIN'T MISBEHAVIN'. / MONKEY JIVE**	-	w-drawn

(re-iss. Oct77; GULS 54) (re-iss. Oct80 on 'Dead Good'; DEAD 11)

ULTRAVOX!

LEIGH became **JOHN FOXX** and ST.JOHN now **CHRIS CROSS**. (CURRIE now added violin, synthesizers.)

	Island	Antilles
Feb 77. (7") (WIP 6375) **DANGEROUS RHYTHM. / MY SEX**		-
Mar 77. (lp/c) (ILPS/ICT 9449) **ULTRAVOX!**		-

– Saturday night in the city of the dead / Life at Rainbow End (for all the tax exiles on Main Street) / Slip away / I want to be a machine / Wide boys / Dangerous rhythm / The lonely hunter / The wild the beautiful and the damned / My sex. (cd-iss. Jul92; IMCD 146)

May 77. (7") (WIP 6392) **YOUNG SAVAGE. / SLIPAWAY**   -

ULTRAVOX (cont)

Oct 77. (7") *(WIP 6404)* **ROCKWROK. / HIROSHIMA MON AMOUR**
 (all 3 ULTRAVOX! singles were re-iss. Jul81)
Oct 77. (lp/c) *(ILPS/ICT 9505)* **HA! HA! HA!**
 – Rockwrok / The frozen ones / Fear in the western world / Distant smile / The man who dies every day / Artificial life / While I'm still alive / Hiroshima mon amour. *(free-7"w.a.)*– **QUIRKS. / MODERN LOVE (live).** *(cd-iss. Jul92; IMCD 147)*
Feb 78. (7"ep) *(IEP 8)* **RETRO E.P. (live)**
 – The wild the beautiful and the damned / Young savage / My sex / The man who dies every day.

—— **ROBIN SIMON** – guitar (ex-NEO) repl. SHEARS to COWBOYS INTERNATIONAL
Aug 78. (7"/12"violet) *(WIP/12WIP 6454)* **SLOW MOTION. / DISLOCATION**
Sep 78. (lp/c) *(ILPS/ICT 9555) <7069>* **SYSTEMS OF ROMANCE**
 – Slow motion / I can't stay long / Someone else's clothes / Blue light / Some of them / Quiet men / Dislocation / Maximum acceleration / When you walk through me / Just for a moment. *(cd-iss. Aug92; IMCD 148)*
Oct 78. (7"/12"white) *(WIP/12WIP 6459)* **QUIET MEN. / CROSS FADE**

—— *(Apr79)* **MIDGE URE** (b.JAMES, 10 Oct'53, Cambuslang, Scotland) – vocals, guitar (ex-SLIK, ex-RICH KIDS, ex-THIN LIZZY, ex-VISAGE) repl. JOHN FOXX who went solo. ROBIN also departed to MAGAZINE. Now as ULTRAVOX, after dropping the exclamation mark!

	Chrysalis	Chrysalis
Jun 80. (7",7"clear) *(CHS 2441)* **SLEEPWALK. / WAITING**	29	
Sep 80. (7",7"clear/12") *(CHS 2457/122457)* **PASSING STRANGERS. / SOUND ON SOUND**	57	
Oct 80. (lp/c) *(CHR/ZCHR 1296) <1296>* **VIENNA**	3	

 – Astradyne / New Europeans / Private lives / Passing strangers / Sleepwalk / Mr. X / Western promise / Vienna / All stood still. *(cd-iss. 1985; CCD 1296) (re-iss. Dec92 on 'Fame' cd/c; CDFA/TCFA 3283) (re-iss. cd Mar94 + Jul94; same) (cd re-iss. Apr00 on 'EMI Gold'; 5255230)*

Jan 81. (7",7"clear) *(CHS 2481)* **VIENNA. / PASSIONATE REPLY** — 2
 (12"+=) *(CHS 122481)* - Herr X.
Apr 81. (7",7"clear) *(CHS 2457)* **PASSING STRANGERS. / FACE TO FACE**
 (12"+=) *(CHA 122457)* – King's lead hat.
May 81. (7",7"clear) *(CHS 2522)* **ALL STOOD STILL. / ALLES KLAR** — 8
 (12"+=) *(CHS 122522)* – Keep talking.
Aug 81. (7",7"clear/ext-12") *(CHS 2549/122549)* **THE THIN WALL. / I NEVER WANTED TO BEGIN** — 14
Sep 81. (lp/c) *(CHR/ZCHR 1338) <1338>* **RAGE IN EDEN** — 4
 – The voice / We stand alone / Rage in Eden / I remember (death in the afternoon) / The thin wall / Stranger within / Accent on youth / The ascent / Your name has slipped my mind again. *(cd-iss. Jun87; CPCD 1338) (cd re-iss. Sep97 on 'EMI Gold'; CDGOLD 1097)*
Nov 81. (7",7"clear) *(CHS 2559)* **THE VOICE. / PATHS AND ANGELS** — 16
 (12"+=,12"clear+=) *(CHS 122559)* – All stood still (live) / Private lives (live).
Sep 82. (7",7"clear/c-s/12") *(CHS 2639/122639) <42682>* **REAP THE WILD WIND. / HOSANNA (IN EXCELIS DEO)** — 12 — 71 Mar 83
Oct 82. (lp/c/pic-lp) *(CDL/ZCDL/PCDL 1394) <1394>* **QUARTET** — 6 — 61 Mar83
 – Reap the wild wind / Serenade / Mine for life / Hymn / Visions of blue / When the scream subsides / We came to dance / Cut and run / The song (we go). *(cd-iss. 1988; CCD 1394) (cd re-iss. Sep98 on 'EMI Gold'; 496823-2)*
Nov 82. (7",7"clear) *(CHS 2557)* **HYMN. / MONUMENT** — 11
 (12"+=,12"clear+=) *(CHS 122557)* – The thin wall.
Mar 83. (7",7"clear,7"pic-d) *(CHS 2676)* **VISIONS IN BLUE. / BREAK YOUR BACK** — 15
 (12"+=,12"clear+=) *(CHS 122676)* – Reap the wild wind.
May 83. (7",7"pic-d,7"clear/12",12"clear) *(VOX/+X 1)* **WE CAME TO DANCE. / OVERLOOK** — 18
Oct 83. (lp/c) *(CUX/ZCUX 1452)* **MONUMENT – THE SOUNDTRACK (live)** — 9
 – Monument / Reap the wild wind / The voice / Vienna / Mine for life / Hymn. *(cd-iss. 1986 +=; CCD 1452)* – Passing strangers / Visions in blue. *(cd re-iss. Jul96 on 'EMI Gold'; CDGOLD 1025)*
Feb 84. (7",7"clear/12") *(VOX/+X 2)* **ONE SMALL DAY. / EASTERLY** — 27
Apr 84. (lp/c/pic-lp/cd) *(CDL/ZCDL/PCDL/CCD 1459) <41459>* **LAMENT** — 8
 – White China / One small day * / Dancing with tears in my eyes / Lament * / Man of two worlds / Heart of the country / When the time comes / I have a friend I called Desire. *(c+=/cd+=)* – (tracks * remixed). *(cd re-iss. Sep99 on 'EMI Gold'; 521834-2)*
May 84. (7",7"clear/12") *(UV/+X 1)* **DANCING WITH TEARS IN MY EYES. / BUILDING** — 3
Jul 84. (7",7"clear) *(UV 2)* **LAMENT. / HEART OF THE COUNTRY** — 22
 (12"+=) *(UVX 2)* – ('A'instrumental).
Oct 84. (7",7"clear,7"pic-d/12") *(UV/+X 3)* **LOVE'S GREAT ADVENTURE. / WHITE CHINA** — 12
Nov 84. (lp/c/cd) *(UTV/ZUTV 1)(CCD 1490)* **THE COLLECTION (compilation)** — 2
 – Dancing with tears in my eyes / Hymn / The thin wall / The voice / Vienna / Passing strangers / Sleepwalk / Reap the wild wind / All stood still / Visions in blue / We came to dance / One small day / Love's great adventure / Lament. *(w/ free 12")*

—— guest **MARK BRZEZICKI** (b.21 Jun'57) – drums (of BIG COUNTRY) repl. CANN to HELDEN
Sep 86. (7",7"clear,7"pic-d) *(UV 4)* **SAME OLD STORY. / 3** — 31
 (12",12"clear) *(UVX 4)* – ('A'side) / All in one day.
Oct 86. (lp/c/cd) *(CDL/ZCDL/CCD 1545) <207934>* **U-VOX** — 9
 – Same old story / Sweet surrender / Dream on / All fall down / Time to kill / Moon madness / Follow your heart / All in one day. *(cd re-iss. Oct00 on 'EMI Gold'; 525611-2)*
Nov 86. (7",7"clear) *(UV 5)* **ALL FALL DOWN. / DREAM ON** — 30
 (12"+=) *(UVX 5)* – ('A'version).
May 87. (7",7"clear) *(UV 6)* **ALL IN ONE DAY. / THE PRIZE (live)**
 (12"+=) *(UVX 6)* – Stateless.

—— disbanded 1987, although U-VOX was formed by BILLY CURRIE, ROBIN SIMON and MARCUS O'HIGGINS – vocals; they toured 1989 playing ULTRAVOX songs

—— **TONY FENELLE** – vocals; repl. MIDGE URE who was by now continuing solo

	D.S.B.	not iss.
May 93. (cd/c/lp) *(DSB 3098-2/-4/-1)* **REVELATION**		

 – I am alive / Revelation / Systems of love / Perfecting the common ground / The great outdoors / The closer I get to you / No turning back / True believer / Unified / The new frontier. *(cd re-iss. Sep02 on 'Puzzle'; PZLCD 106)*

Jun 93. (7"/c-s/7"clear) *(DSB 3097-7/-3/-1)* **I AM ALIVE. / SYSTEMS OF LOVE**
 (cd-s+=) *(DSB 30975)* – ('A'extended).

—— line-up: **CURRIE / BLUE / BURNS**

	Resurgence	not iss.
Nov 95. (cd) *(RES 109CD)* **INGENUITY**		

 – Ingenuity / There goes a beautiful world / Give it all back / Future picture forever / The silent cries / Distance / Ideals / Who'll save you / A way out, a way through / Majestic. *(re-iss. Mar02 on 'Puzzle'; PZLCD 105)*

– compilations, others, etc. –

Jun 80. (lp/c) *Island/ US= Antilles; (ILPS/ICM 9614) <7079>* **THREE INTO ONE**
 – Young savage / Rockwrok / Dangerous rhythm / The man who dies every day / The wild the beautiful and the damned / Slow motion / Just for a moment / My sex / Quiet men / Hiroshima mon amour. *(re-iss. Nov86, cd-iss. 1989; IMCD 30)*
Mar 81. (12"ep,12"clear-ep) *Island; (DWIP 6691)* **SLOW MOTION / DISLOCATION. / QUIET MEN / HIROSHIMA MON AMOUR** — 33
Dec 82. (d-c) *Chrysalis; (ZCDP 109)* **VIENNA / RAGE IN EDEN**
Feb 87. (7") *Old Gold; (OG 9675)* **VIENNA. / THE VOICE**
Apr 87. (7") *Old Gold; (OG 9698)* **DANCING WITH TEARS IN MY EYES. / REAP THE WILD WIND** *(12"-iss.Jan88)*
Apr 88. (12"ep) *Strange Fruit; (SFPS 047)* **THE PEEL SESSIONS** (21.7.77)
 – My sex / Artificial life / Young savage.
Sep 93. (cd/c) *Spectrum; (550112-2/-4)* **SLOW MOTION**
Aug 94. (cd) *Chrysalis; (CDCHR 6053)* **RARE VOLUME 2**
Jun 95. (cd) *Receiver; (RRCD 199)* **FUTURE PICTURE**
Aug 95. (cd-s) *Old Gold;* **VIENNA / REAP THE WILD WIND**
Oct 95. (cd) *MFP; (CDMFP 6175)* **DANCING WITH TEARS IN MY EYES**
Nov 95. (3xcd-box) *Island; (5241522)* **ULTRAVOX! / HA! HA! HA! / SYSTEMS OF ROMANCE**
Feb 98. (cd) *EMI Gold; (493465-2)* **EXTENDED – A COLLECTION OF 12" REMIXES**
Nov 98. (d-cd) *Disky; (HR 85380-2)* **ORIGINAL GOLD**
Mar 99. (cd) *Spectrum; (554898-2)* **THE ISLAND YEARS**
Jul 00. (cd) *Disky; (SI 25080-2)* **THE BEST OF THE 80'S**
Aug 01. (cd) *Armoury; (ARMCD 043)* **GREATEST HITS LIVE (live)**

UNDERTONES

Formed: Londonderry, N. Ireland ... late '75 by the O'NEILL brothers, DAMIAN and JOHN, alongside FEARGAL SHARKEY, MIKE BRADLEY and BILLY DOHERTY. Taking up the offer of a one-off singles deal with Belfast label, 'Good Vibrations', they released a debut EP in September '78 with the seminal 'TEENAGE KICKS' as the lead track. Immediately championed by DJ John Peel, this compelling slice of adolescent angst reached the collective ear of 'Sire' records leading to a prestigious deal. Their major label debut, 'GET OVER YOU', scraped into the Top 60 although they eventually cracked the chart later that Spring with 'JIMMY JIMMY', a boisterous post-punk stomper reminiscent of a wittier, more laid-back SHAM 69. This was closely followed by an eponymous debut album, establishing The UNDERTONES as one of the most promising and intelligent new-wave punk/pop bands in the UK. Like a more hyperactive KINKS, the band chronicled the nitty gritty, highs and lows of everyday life in such unforgettable pop nuggets as 'HERE COMES THE SUMMER', 'TRUE CONFESSIONS' and 'FAMILY ENTERTAINMENT'. Arguably, 'YOU'VE GOT MY NUMBER (WHY DON'T YOU USE IT), remains The UNDERTONES' finest moment, a jarring, insistent riff marking it out from the group's standard pop rush. While the song barely made the UK Top 40, The UNDERTONES were back in the Top 10 the following year with the sneering 'MY PERFECT COUSIN', a humorous tale of a goody-two-shoes relative which obviously struck a chord with more than a few disaffected youngsters. The accompanying album, 'HYPNOTISED' (1980), consolidated the group's standing, critically and commercially, a more assured set which also spawned another classic single in 'WEDNESDAY WEEK'. Inevitably, however, along with many of their contemporaries, The UNDERTONES increasingly moved away from the roughshod charm of old to a more refined sound. This was evident in the group's third album, 'THE POSITIVE TOUCH' (1981), only one track making the Top 20 ('IT'S GOING TO HAPPEN') despite such enduring material as the lovely 'JULIE OCEAN'. By 1983's 'THE SIN OF PRIDE', FEARGAL's quavering vocals and the group's boy-next-door image had been shelved for a blend of "alternative soul". Predictably, this didn't sit well with the group's more traditional fans who were unsurprisingly becoming increasingly critical of The UNDERTONES newfound sophistication. The imminent split eventually came in mid '83 with SHARKEY initially hooking up with VINCE CLARKE in The ASSEMBLY before launching a solo career. Following a minor hit on MADNESS' 'Zarjazz' label, SHARKEY signed to 'Virgin' and scored a massive No.1 hit with Maria McKee's 'A Good Heart'. A fully fledged, if brief, pop star, SHARKEY's eponymous solo debut hit the Top 10 around the same time in late '85, while he scored a follow-up Top 5 hit with 'YOU LITTLE THIEF'. Successive albums failed to chart, however, and SHARKEY moved into A&R work for 'Virgin'. The O'NEILL brothers, meanwhile, formed the

UNDERTONES (cont)

critically acclaimed THAT PETROL EMOTION. • **Songwriters:** O'NEILL brothers except UNDER THE BOARDWALK (Drifters). In the mid-80's, FEARGAL, solo, collaborated with DAVE STEWART of The EURYTHMICS. In 1991, he teamed up with writers SHERRILL and DiPIERO. Covered; TAKE ME TO THE RIVER (Al Green). • **More Info:** While spending time in Londonderry in February '86, FEARGAL's mother and sister were abducted by terrorists, although they were thankfully released after a number of hours.

Album rating: THE UNDERTONES (*9) / HYPNOTISED (*7) / POSITIVE TOUCH (*6) / THE SIN OF PRIDE (*5) / ALL WRAPPED UP compilation (*7) / CHER O'BOWLES – THE PICK OF THE UNDERTONES compilation (*8) / Feargal Sharkey: FEARGAL SHARKEY (*6) / WISH (*4) / SONGS FROM THE MARDI GRAS (*5)

FEARGAL SHARKEY (b.13 Aug'58) – vocals / **DAMIAN O'NEILL** (b.15 Jan'61, Belfast, N.Ireland) – guitar, bass / **JOHN O'NEILL** (b.26 Aug'57) – guitar / **MIKE BRADLEY** (b.13 Aug'59) – bass / **BILLY DOHERTY** (b.10 Jul'58, Larne, N.Ireland) – drums

		Good Vibrations	not iss.
Sep 78.	(7"ep) *(GOT 4)* **TEENAGE KICKS. / TRUE CONFESSIONS. / SMARTER THAN U / EMMERGENCY CASES**		-

– re-iss. Oct78 on 'Sire'; SIR 4007) – hit No.31 (re-iss. Jul83 on 'Ardeck'; ARDS 1) – hit 60 (re-iss. on 7"ep/cd-ep Apr94 on 'Dojo'; TONES/+CD 1)

		Sire	Sire
Jan 79.	(7"m) *(SIR 4010)* **GET OVER YOU. / REALLY REALLY / SHE CAN ONLY SAY NO**	57	
Apr 79.	(7",7"lime green) *(SIR 4015)* **JIMMY JIMMY. / MARS BARS**	16	
May 79.	(lp/c) *(SRK/+C 6071) <6081>* **THE UNDERTONES**	13	Jan 80

– Family entertainment / Girls don't like it / Male model / I gotta getta / Teenage kicks / Wrong way / Jump boys / Here comes the summer / Get over you / Billy's third / Jimmy Jimmy / True confessions / She's a runaround / I know a girl / Listening in. (re-iss. Jul83 on 'Ardeck'; ARDM 164739-1) (re-iss. Oct87 on 'Fame' lp/c/cd; FA/TCFA/CDFA 3188) (re-iss. May94 on 'Dojo' cd/c/lp; DOJO CD/MC/LP 191) – Smarter than u / Emergency cases / Top twenty / Really really / Mars Bars / She can only say no / One way love. (cd re-iss. Mar97 on 'Essential'; ESMCD 484) (re-iss. Feb00; ESMCD 831)

Jul 79.	(7") *(SIR 4022)* **HERE COMES THE SUMMER. / ONE WAY LOVE / TOP TWENTY**	34	
Sep 79.	(7") *(SIR 4024)* **YOU'VE GOT MY NUMBER (WHY DON'T YOU USE IT). / LET'S TALK ABOUT GIRLS**	32	
Mar 80.	(7"m) *(SIR 4038)* **MY PERFECT COUSIN. / HARD LUCK / I DON'T WANNA SEE YOU AGAIN**	9	

(d7"+=) (SIR 4038) – Here comes the summer.

| Apr 80. | (lp/c) *(SRK/+C 6088) <6088>* **HYPNOTISED** | 6 | |

– More songs about chocolate and girls / There goes Norman / Hypnotised / See that girl / Whizz kids / Under the boardwalk / The way girls talk / Hard luck / My perfect cousin / Boys will be boys / Tearproof / Wednesday week / Nine times out of ten / Girls that don't talk / What's with Terry?. (re-iss. Jul83 on 'Ardeck'; ARDM 164742-1) (re-iss. Mar86 on 'Fame' lp/c; FA/TCFA 3145) (re-iss. May94 on 'Dojo' cd+=/c/lp; DOJO CD/MC/LP 192) – You've got my number (why don't you use it?) / Hard luck (again) / Let's talk about girls / I told you so / I don't want to see you again. (cd re-iss. Mar97 on 'Essential'; ESMCD 486) (cd re-iss. Feb00; ESMCD 832)

| Jun 80. | (7") *(SIR 4042)* **WEDNESDAY WEEK. / I TOLD YOU SO** | 11 | |

		Ardeck-EMI	Rykodisc
Apr 81.	(7") *(ARDS 8)* **IT'S GOING TO HAPPEN. / FAIRLY IN THE MONEY NOW**	18	
May 81.	(lp/c) *(ARD/TCARD 103) <12159>* **THE POSITIVE TOUCH**	17	

– Fascination / Life's too easy / You're welcome / The positive touch / Julie Ocean / Crisis of mine / His good looking friend / When Saturday comes / It's going to happen / Sigh and explode / I don't know / Hannah Doot / Boy wonder / Forever Paradise. (re-iss. Apr84 on 'E.M.I.' lp/c; ATAK/TCATAK 46) (re-iss. May94 on 'Dojo' cd+=/c/lp; DOJO CD/MC/LP 193) – Kiss in the dark / Beautiful friend / Life's too easy / Fairly in the money now. (cd re-iss. Mar97 on 'Essential'; ESMCD 485) (cd re-mast.Apr00; ESMCD 853)

Jul 81.	(7") *(ARDS 9)* **JULIE OCEAN. / KISS IN THE DARK**	41	
Feb 82.	(7") *(ARDS 10)* **BEAUTIFUL FRIEND. / LIFE'S TOO EASY**		-
Jan 83.	(7") *(ARDS 11)* **THE LOVE PARADE. / LIKE THAT**		-
	(12"+=) *(12ARDS 11)* – You're welcome / Family entertainment / Crises of mine.		
Mar 83.	(7") *(ARDS 12)* **GOT TO HAVE YOU BACK. / TURNING BLUE**		-
	(12"+=) *(12ARDS 12)* – Bye bye baby blue.		
Mar 83.	(lp/c) *(ARD/TCARD 104)* **THE SIN OF PRIDE**	43	-

– Got to have you back / Valentine's treatment / Luxury / Love before romance / Untouchable / Bye bye baby blue / Conscious / Chain of love / Soul seven / The love parade / Save me / The sin of pride. (re-iss. Aug85 on 'E.M.I.' lp/c; ATAK/TCATAK 47) (re-iss. May94 on 'Dojo' cd+=/c/lp; DOJO CD/MC/LP 194) – Turning blue / Like that / Window shopping for new clothes / Bitter sweet / You stand so close (but you're never there) / I can only dream. (cd re-iss. Mar97 on 'Essential'; ESMCD 487) (cd re-mast.Apr00; ESMCD 854)

| Apr 83. | (7") *(ARDS 13)* **CHAIN OF LOVE. / WINDOW SHOPPING FOR NEW CLOTHES** | | - |

— split mid '83 with FEARGAL SHARKEY joining The ASSEMBLY; (see YAZOO) before going solo. The O'NEILL brothers formed THAT PETROL EMOTION.

– compilations, others, etc. –

| Nov 83. | (d-lp)(c) Ardeck-EMI; *(ARD 1654283)(1654289)* **ALL WRAPPED UP** | 67 | - |

– Teenage kicks / Get over you / Jimmy Jimmy / Here comes the summer / You've got my number (why don't you use it) / My perfect cousin / Wednesday week / It's going to happen / Julie Ocean / Beautiful friend / The love parade / Got to have you back / Chain of love.

— (note: all singles were re-iss. on 'Ardeck-EMI)

| May 86. | (lp/c) Ardeck-EMI; *(EMS/TCEMS 1172)* **CHER O'BOWLIES – THE PICK OF THE UNDERTONES** | 96 | - |

– Teenage kicks / True confessions / Get over you / Family entertainment / Jimmy Jimmy / Here comes the Summer / You got my number (why don't you use it) / My perfect cousin / See that girl / Tearproof / Wednesday week / It's going to happen / Julie Ocean / You're welcome / Forever Paradise / Beautiful friend / Save me / The love parade / Valentine's treatment / Love before romance. (re-iss. Oct89 on 'Fame' cd/c/lp; CD/TC+/FA 3226)

Jun 86.	(7") *Ardeck-EMI; (ARDS 14)* **SAVE ME. / TEARPROOF**		-
	(12"+=) *(12ARDS 14)* – I know a girl.		
Dec 86.	(12"ep) *Strange Fruit; (SFPS 016)* **THE PEEL SESSIONS** (21.1.79)		-
	– Listening in / Family entertainment / Here comes the summer / Billy's third. *(cd-ep iss.Mar88)*		
Dec 89.	(lp/c/cd) *Strange Fruit; (SFR LP/MC/CD 103)* **DOUBLE PEEL SESSIONS**		-
	(re-iss. cd Mar94 as 'THE PEEL SESSIONS ALBUM'; same)		
Sep 93.	(cd/c) *Castle / Rykodisc; (CTV CD/MC 121)* **THE BEST OF THE UNDERTONES – TEENAGE KICKS**	45	
	(cd re-iss. Jan97 on 'Renaissance'; CCSCD 808)		
Jul 95.	(cd-ep) *Dojo; (TONESCD 1)* **HERE COMES THE SUMMER / GET OVER YOU / JIMMY JIMMY / YOU'VE GOT MY NUMBER (WHY DON'T YOU USE IT)**		-
Sep 99.	(d-cd) *Essential; (ESDCD 788)* **TRUE CONFESSIONS: SINGLES A's & B's**		-
Jun 00.	(12xcd-s) *Essential; (ESFCD 893)* **THE SINGLES BOX SET**		-

UNWANTED

Formed: London, England . . . spring 1977 by OLLIE, VINCE ELY and PAUL GARDNER. Another DIY punk band to have at least one member (ELY) to subsequently find fame (i.e. the PSYCHEDELIC FURS). A regular feature at the infamous Roxy club, The UNWANTED appeared on the venue's seminal Various Artists LP, 'Live At The Roxy', with the track 'FREEDOM'. The UNWANTED. Now with postman DAVE LYNCH, the band signed to up and coming independent imprint, 'Raw'. Their first vinyl outing arrived in October 1977 via the 'WITHDRAWAL' / '1984' a double 'A' sided 45 the latter of which delivered the shouty topical lines "the ministry of punk is the one that bosses hate". Early the following year, they unleashed a second 7", 'SECRET POLICE', a quirky, cod-reggae punk piece with MEKONS-esque lyrics. However, The UNWANTED became somewhat, er . . . 'unwanted' when their label shelved a third outing, 'MEMORY MAN' – they split around the same time.

Album rating: SECRET PAST compilation (*5)

OLLIE – vocals / **DAVE LYNCH** – guitar; repl. PAUL GARDNER / **VINCE ELY** – drums

		Raw	not iss.
Oct 77.	(7"m) *(RAW 6)* **WITHDRAWAL / 1978. / BLEAK OUTLOOK**		-
	(re-iss. Jul78 as 12"m; RAWT 6) (re-iss. Dec00 on 'Damaged Goods'; DAMGOOD 183)		
Feb 78.	(7") *(RAW 15)* **SECRET POLICE. / THESE BOOTS WERE MADE FOR WALKING**		-
Dec 78.	(7"; w-drawn) *(RAW 30)* **MEMORY MAN. / GUNS OF LOVE**	-	-

— after their demise, VINCE ELY joined The PSYCHEDELIC FURS

– compilations, etc. –

| Jan 85. | (lp) *De Lorean; (NUMBER ONE)* **SECRET PAST** | | - |

URINALS

Formed: Orange County, California, USA . . . January '78 by L.A. film students, JOHN TALLEY-JONES, KEITH BARRETT and KJEHL JOHANSEN (originally as a parody 5-piece). Got serious in '79 and released three 7"er's, although their musical lifespan was mercifully brief. Clearly they became pissed off before their fans did and flushed away their musical ambitions in 1981; despite a second incarnation as 100 FLOWERS, success continued to elude them. Mid-80's releases (like an arty GANG OF FOUR such as '100 FLOWERS' and 'DRAWING FIRE', were better served as a posthumous compilation '100 YEARS OF PULCHRITUDE'. JOHANSEN and much later, TALLEY-JONES resurfaced with 'S.S.T.' outfit, TROTSKY ICEPICK. Initially cutting it as DANNY & THE DOORKNOBS, guitarist KJEHL JOHANSEN along with VITUS MATARE (from The LAST), the group delivered several records up to their split in the mid-90's; 'EL KABONG' (1991) featured Magazine's 'THE LIGHT POURS OUT OF ME' – the 1991 follow-up 'THE ULTRAVIOLET CATASTROPHE' contained two covers, The Monochrome Set's 'ALPHAVILLE' and Television's 'VENUS DE MILO'. • **Trivia:** An early D&tD cut, 'MELODY ARROW', featured on V/A compilation, 'The Happy Squid Sampler'. • **Songwriters:** JONES with JOHANSEN & BARRETT contributing to others except covers WHY ARE WE SLEEPING? (Soft Machine) / SHAPE OF THINGS TO COME (Mann-Weill) / YOU'RE GONNA MISS ME (13th Floor Elevators) / JETSON MAIN THEME (Barbera-Curtin-Hanna) / RETURN OF JAKE BODDLER (. . . Bludgeon) / GO AWAY GIRL (Last).

Album rating: NEGATIVE CAPABILITY compilation (*5) / 100 Flowers: 100 YEARS OF PULCHRITUDE collection (*5) / Trotsky Icepick: POISON SUMMER as DANNY & THE DOORKNOBS (*5) / POISON SUMMER (*5) / BABY (*7) / EL KABONG (*5) / THE ULTRAVIOLET CATASTROPHE (*4) / CARPETBOMB THE RIFF (*4) / HOT POP HELLO: A CHANCE MEDLEY (*4)

JOHN TALLEY-JONES – vocals, bass / **KJEHL JOHANSEN** – guitar, vocals / **KEITH BARRETT** – drums

		not iss.	Happy Squid
Jan 79.	(7"ep) *<HS-001>* **THE URINALS EP**	-	
	– Dead flowers / Hologram / The last days of man on Earth / Surfin' with the Shah.		
Jul 79.	(7"ep) *<HS-002>* **ANOTHER EP**	-	
	– Black holes / I'm white and middle class / I'm a bug / Ack ack ack ack.		

URINALS (cont)

Apr 80. (7") <HS-003> **SEX. / GO AWAY GIRL** — ☐

—— also the track, 'U', appeared on the label sampler 7"ep; HS-004

– compilations, etc. –

Nov 97. (cd) *Amphetamine Reptile;* <(AMREP 045-2)> **NEGATIVE CAPABILITY** ☐ Jan97
— Dead flowers / Hologram / The last days of man on Earth / Surfin' with the Shah / Black holes / I'm white and middle class / I'm a bug / Ack ack ack ack / Sex / Go away girl / U / Scholastic attitude / I hate / She's a drone / Male masterbation / Return of Jake Boddler / Presence of mind / Sex / I'm like you / Orange anal sin / Salmonella / I'm a bug / Ack ack ack ack / Mr. Encore / Why are we sleeping? / Shape of things to come / You're gonna miss me / Hologram / Jetsons main theme / Don't make me kill again / You piss me off.

100 FLOWERS

TALLEY-JONES + JOHANSEN

                                               not iss. Happy Squid

1983. (lp) <HS 010> **100 FLOWERS** – ☐
— Without limbs / All sexed up / Our fallout / Horizontal / Head, no heart / Presence of mind / I don't own my own heart / Motorboat to Hell / Strip club / Poltergeists at home / Pressing the point / Virtually nothing / Salad of speech / Funky Kjehl / Dizzy Ms. Lizzy / California's falling into the ocean.

1984. (12"ep) **DRAWING FIRE** – ☐
— Bunkers / Long arm of the social sciences / Triage / Contributions / Let's not.

– compilations, etc. –

1990. (cd) *Rhino;* <70751> **100 YEARS OF PULCHRITUDE** – ☐
— 100 FLOWERS lp tracks / Dyslexia / Mop dub / Reject yourself / I hate / I'm like you / From the fire / 100 flowers / DRAWING FIRE ep tracks.

TROTSKY ICEPICK

KJEHL JOHANSEN – vocals, guitars, bass / **VITUS MATARE** – guitar, keyboards, vocals (ex-LAST) / **JOHN FRANK** – drums / 4th member **JOHN ROSEWALL** – bass (of The LAST)

                       not iss. Old Scratch

1985. (lp; as DANNY & THE DOORKNOBS) **POISON SUMMER** – ☐
— Whispering glades / Poison summer / In exile / Northern lights / Harmonia / Little things you don't know / Full cone excursion / Love to hate / Wooden legs with real feet / Healing / Slow motion / Game / From a quiet heart / Wooden legs / Farewell. <(re-iss. Sep90 as 'TROTSKY ICEPICK presents DANNY & THE DOORKNOBS' on 'S.S.T.' lp/c/cd; SST 254/+C/CD)>

—— bassist now **JAMIE LENNON**

1986. (lp) **POISON SUMMER** – ☐
— The gaslight / The commissioner / Nightingale drive / Big dreams / Just the end of the world / Drawing fire / Set still the time / Clowns on fire / Clown on fire (version) / Hit parade / Ivory tour / You look like something Goya drew / Temporary faith rangers. <(re-iss. Dec89 on 'S.S.T.' lp/cd; SST 239/+CD)>

—— **JASON KAHN** – drums (ex-LEAVING TRAINS) repl. FRANK who joined The PEACE CORPS / bassist again **JOHN ROSEWALL**

                     S.S.T. S.S.T.

Sep 88. (lp/cd) <(SST 197/+CD)> **BABY**
— Incident / Dante's flame / Mar vista bus stop / A little push at the top of the stairs / Bury Manilow / Pillars of salt / Big daddy / Don't buy it / Windowpane / untitled / And it goes like this / Barricades / Robilussio rag. *(cd+=)* – (2 tracks).

—— **HUNTER CROWLEY** – drums (ex-LAST) repl. KAHN who joined UNIVERSAL CONGRESS OF / added **JOHN TALLEY-JONES** – vocals (ex-100 FLOWERS)

Jul 89. (lp/cd) <(SST 246/+CD)> **EL KABONG**
— Conveniences of life / The light pours out of me / Yolanda won't you give me a job / Cornfield / 106° / This car is not blue / About that boot of mine / Candidate / Unbuttoned / Astronomer / El Kabong / Long grey baggy soul / Hotel / Say goodnight.

—— **MIKE PATTON** – bass (repl. ROSEWALL during below)

Oct 91. (lp/c/cd) <(SST 279/+C/CD)> **THE ULTRAVIOLET CATASTROPHE**
— The ultraviolet catastrophe / Alphaville / Thing under the cosh / WDBS / Barbara Steele / Boy w/ book / God without a compass / Venus De Milo / Pstilence / August August / Martion manhunter / Q.E.D.

—— **JOHN GLOGOVAC** – drums; repl. CROWLEY

Sep 93. (cd/c) <(SST 295 CD/C)> **CARPETBOMB THE RIFF**
— Imagining Neptune / Invisible politicians / Bad girls go to Hell / Home surgery / Swallowing tongues / Local 63 / There goes salvation / Hate clown / Shaken / (Kinda like the) Berlin Wall / 1000 points of light / Mr. Caution's funeral.

—— nect album invited all past & present members to join in

May 94. (cd/c) <(SST 286 CD/C)> **HOT POP HELLO: A CHANCE MEDLEY**
— 20 nights with Godzilla / Father Murry's glass eye / Personal ad / Dark engine / Rubberband / Lord of the Medflies / David Charles / Natchez / Oh! general / Empty reel / Because love / Erase the sun / Scalpel city / Hot pop hello.

—— disbanded after above

USERS

Formed: London, England ... early '77 by JAMES HAIGHT, CHRIS 'PANIC' FREE, ALVIN GIBBS and ANDREW BOR. Much like The UNWANTED (whom they shared a label with 'Raw'), The USERS made their debut in spring 1977 with 'SICK OF YOU', an underrated punk classic in the mould of The STOOGES. However, after only one more effort, 'KICKS IN STYLE', the group changed their moniker to ACME SEWAGE CO. They made only a few recordings, including 'SMILE AND WAVE GOODBYE', which appeared on the 1978 compilation, 'Farewell To The Roxy'.

Album rating: never released any

JAMES HAIGHT – vocals / **CHRIS 'PANIC' FREE** – guitar / **ALVIN GIBB** – bass / **ANDREW BOR** – drums

                     Raw not iss.

May 77. (7"/12") *(RAW/+T 1)* **SICK OF YOU. / (I'M) IN LOVE WITH TODAY** ☐ –

—— **BOBBY KWOK** – bass; repl. GIBB who joined The HELLIONS before becoming part of UK SUBS

                     Warped not iss.

1978. (7") *(WARP 1)* **KICKS IN STYLE. / DEAD ON ARRIVAL** ☐ –

—— The USERS had already changed their moniker to The ACME SEWAGE CO.

THE GREAT INDIE DISCOGRAPHY | The 1970s

VALVES

Formed: Portobello, nr. Edinburgh ... 1977 by DEE ROBOT, G. DAIR, RONNIE MacKINNON and GORDON SCOTT. This quirky fun-punk/rock act were the first band to have a record – the double A-sided 'ROBOT LOVE' & 'FOR ADOLFS ONLY' – issued on Bruce Findlay's 'Zoom' label (he subsequently signed SIMPLE MINDS). The VALVES played a number of low-key hotel/venue gigs and managed to squeeze out another 45 before the year was out, namely 'TARZAN OF THE KING'S ROAD'. However, it took all of eighteen months to deliver a third, 'DON'T MEAN NOTHIN' AT ALL', although by this time the punk/new wave scene had gone down the tubes.

Album rating: never released any

DEE ROBOT (b. ROBERTSON) – vocals / **RONNIE MacKINNON** – lead guitar / **GORDON SCOTT** – bass / **G. DAIR** – drums

		Zoom	not iss.
Sep 77.	(7") (ZUM 1) **ROBOT LOVE. / FOR ADOLF'S ONLY**		-
Dec 77.	(7") (ZUM 3) **TARZAN OF THE KING'S ROAD. / AIN'T NO SURF IN PORTOBELLO**		-
		Albion	not iss.
Jul 79.	(7") (DEL 5) **DON'T MEAN NOTHIN' AT ALL. / LINDA VINDALCO**		-

— all retired from the music biz

Dave VANIAN & THE PHANTOM CHORDS
(see under ⇒ DAMNED)

Cherry VANILLA

Born: Staten Island, New York, USA. This obscure punky looking vocalist formed her first outfit, CHERRY VANILLA & HER STATEN ISLAND BAND in 1976, comprising GARY COHEN (piano), THOMAS MORRONGIELLO (guitar), BUZZY JOHN VIERNO (bass) and FRANK LA ROCCA (drums). They played the infamous Max's Kansas City in the heart of NY, the track 'SHAKE YOUR ASHES' appearing on that year's live Various Artists collection on 'Ram' <1213>; re-issued UK (CBS 82670). VANILLA's innuendo-laden anthemic new wave pop secured her a UK contract with 'R.C.A.' and led to the release of 'THE PUNK' single, a disastrous attempt to jump on the anarchy bandwagon. A debut album, 'BAD GIRL' (released early in '78) was even worse, titles like 'FOXY BITCH' and 'HARD AS A ROCK' left little to the imagination and showed she didn't have much herself. The album also featured (if that's the right word!) a version of Willie Dixon's 'LITTLE RED ROOSTER', conclusive proof of why the Americans shipped her overseas. A year later, VANILLA unleashed that "difficult" second album, 'VENUS DE VINYL', difficult that is, to get rid of once you've bought it.

Album rating: BAD GIRL (*3) / VENUS D'VINYL (*2)

CHERRY VANILLA – vocals / with **LOUIS LEPERE** – guitar / **ZECCA ESQUIBEL** – keyboards / **HOWIE FINKEL** – bass / **STUART ELLIOT** – drums

		R.C.A.	not iss.
Sep 77.	(7") (PB 5053) **THE PUNK. / FOXY BITCH**		-
Feb 78.	(lp) (PL 25217) **BAD GIRL**		-
	– I know how it took / So 1950's / Not so bad / The punk / No more canaries / Hard as a rock / Liverpool / Foxy bitch / Bad girl / Little red rooster.		

— session bassists **GEORGE FORD** + **DAVE QUINN** + **ROY BABBINGTON** repl. FINKEL + ESQUIBEL

Apr 79.	(7") (PB 5145) **MOONLIGHT. / MR. SPIDER**		-
Apr 79.	(lp) (PL 25217) **VENUS D'VINYL**		-
	– Amanda / The young boys / Lover like you / Wayni's sweet / Mr. Spider / You belong to me / California / Tear myself away / The round dance / Moonlight.		

— CHERRY retired from the music biz until the early 90's

		not iss.	Hot Prod.
Dec 91.	(12") <12283> **FONE**	-	
Jun 92.	(12") <12311> **TECHNO SEX**	-	
		not iss.	E.S.P.
May 93.	(cd) <2014> **BLUE ROSES**	-	

– compilations, etc. –

| Mar 00. | (cd) Renaissance; <179> **VENUS D'VINYL / BAD GIRL** | | - |

Alan VEGA (see under ⇒ SUICIDE)

Tom VERLAINE (see under ⇒ TELEVISION)

VIBRATORS

Formed: London, England ... 1976 by JOHN ELLIS and PAT COLLIER. Both veterans of pub rockers, BAZOOKA JOE, the pair teamed up with KNOX (aka IAN CARNOCHAN) and EDDIE (aka JOHN EDWARDS), turning their talents to the nascent punk scene. A meeting with session whizz, CHRIS SPEDDING, in Oxford Street's 100 Club, subsequently led to a SPEDDING-produced debut single, 'WE VIBRATE', on MICKIE MOST's 'Rak' label at the tail end of '76. Hardly the most auspicious of starts, it nevertheless led to a major label deal with 'Epic' and a debut album, 'PURE MANIA' (1977). More considered, mature and less snotty – the laid-back stomp of 'BABY BABY' would've sounded fine in the hands of TOM PETTY – than the bulk of the safety-pin brigade, the album featured such enduring VIBRATORS favourites as 'INTO THE FUTURE', S&M classic, 'WHIPS & FURS' and the track that inspired one of the era's most vital bands, 'STIFF LITTLE FINGERS'. The predicted success never materialised, however, and COLLIER promptly jumped ship to form new wave outfit, The BOYFRIENDS (later became a renowned producer). His replacement was GARY TIBBS, who played on the bulk of follow-up set, 'V2' (1978), a disappointing promo single, 'LONDON GIRLS' hardly boding well for the record's prospects. A second single, 'AUTOMATIC LOVER', scraped into the Top 40 but the band was already on its last legs; ELLIS left to play with PETER GABRIEL and later The STRANGLERS while the remainder limped on with replacement DAVE BIRCH and keyboard player DON SNOW. They managed a second and final VIBRATORS hit with 'JUDY SAYS (KNOCK YOU IN THE HEAD)' before finally falling apart as TIBBS and SNOW departed. A short-lived reformation featuring a line-up of EDDIE, KNOX, BEN BRIERLEY and GREG VAN COOK was doomed to failure, KNOX eventually going on to a solo career while EDDIE soldiered on as The NEW VIBRATORS. Incredibly, the original line-up re-formed in 1982 and went on to record a series of albums for heavy metal label, 'FM-Revolver', the most recent being 1994's 'HUNTING FOR YOU'. Needless to say, both COLLIER and ELLIS bailed out along the way with the line-up never staying the same for long. With the UK punk revival big in the States, The VIBRATORS were back with another stab at the music industry, KNOX and Co delivering the near-metal attack, 'ENERGIZE' (2002). • **Songwriters:** Most by KNOX-ELLIS-COLLIER, except covers GIMME SOME LOVIN' (Spencer Davis Group) / RIP IT UP (Little Richard) / JUMPIN' JACK FLASH (Rolling Stones) / HALFWAY TO PARADISE (Billy Fury) / SLOW DEATH (Flamin' Groovies) / etc. • **Trivia:** KNOX teamed up with UK SUBS man, CHARLIE HARPER, to form URBAN DOGS between 1983-85.

Album rating: PURE MANIA (*6) / V2 (*5) / BATTERIES NOT INCLUDED compilation (*6) / GUILTY (*5) / FIFTH AMENDMENT (*4) / RECHARGED (*4) / MELTDOWN (*4) / VICIOUS CIRCLE (*4) / VOLUME 10 (*5) / HUNTING FOR YOU (*4) / YEAH YEAH YEAH compilation (*6) / UNPUNKED (*4) / FRENCH LESSONS WITH CORRECTIONS (*4) / ENERGIZE (*5)

KNOX (b. IAN CARNOCHAN) – vocals, guitar / **JOHN ELLIS** – guitar, vocals / **PAT COLLIER** – bass, vocals / **EDDIE** (b.JOHN EDWARDS) – drums

		RAK	not iss.
Nov 76.	(7") (RAK 245) **WE VIBRATE. / WHIPS AND FURS**		-
Nov 76.	(7"; by The VIBRATORS with CHRIS SPEDDING) (RAK 246) **POGO DANCING. / THE POSE**		-
Mar 77.	(7") (RAK 253) **BAD TIMES. / NO HEART**		-
		Epic	Columbia
May 77.	(7") (EPC 5302) **BABY BABY. / INTO THE FUTURE**		-
Jun 77.	(lp) (EPC 82097) <35038> **PURE MANIA**	49	
	– Baby baby / London girls / You break my heart / Sweet sweet heart / Yeah yeah yeah / Bad times / Keep it clean / No heart / Into the future / Petrol / Whips and furs / She's bringing you down / Wrecked on you / I need a slave / Stiff little fingers. *(re-iss. Aug91 on 'Repertoire' lp/cd; REP 2001/+TO)*		

— **GARY TIBBS** – bass (ex-RED) repl. COLLIER who formed The BOYFRIENDS

Aug 77.	(7") (EPC 5565) **LONDON GIRLS – LIVE. / STIFF LITTLE FINGERS – LIVE**		-
Mar 78.	(7") (EPC 6137) **AUTOMATIC LOVER. / DESTROY**	35	-
Apr 78.	(lp) (EPC 82495) **V2**	33	
	– Automatic lover / 24 hour people / Feel alright / Pure mania / Troops of tomorrow / Wake up / War zone / Flying duck theory / Destroy / Nazi baby / Fall in love / Sulphate / Public enemy number one. *(re-iss. Aug91 on 'Repertoire' lp/cd; REP 2002/+TO) (cd-iss. Aug93; 471408-2) (cd re-iss. Feb99 on 'Columbia'; 493338-2)*		

— **DAVID BIRCH** – guitar; repl. ELLIS who joined PETER GABRIEL and went solo / added **DON SNOW** – keyboards (ex-RED)

| Jun 78. | (7") (EPC 6393) **JUDY SAYS (KNOCK YOU IN THE HEAD). / PURE MANIA** | | - |

— **GREG VAN COOK** – guitar (ex-ELECTRIC CHAIRS) repl. BIRCH to BRUCE WOOLLEY / **BEN BRIERLEY – bass** repl. TIBBS who joined ROXY MUSIC then ADAM & THE ANTS / SNOW also departed to SINCEROS then SQUEEZE. After a tour they disbanded with KNOX going solo (he released a few singles, 'GIGOLO AUNT' and 'SHE'S SO GOOD LOOKING' and an album in 1983, 'PLUTONIUM EXPRESS'). BRIERLEY joined NAZIS AGAINST RACISM.

— late 1979, The VIBRATORS re-formed with **EDDIE + KIP** – vocals, guitar / **PHIL ABLE** – guitar / + 1

		Rat Race	not iss.
Feb 80.	(7") (RAT 2) **GIMME SOME LOVIN'. / POWER CRY (live)**		-
May 80.	(7") (RAT 4) **DISCO IN MOSCOW. / TAKE A CHANCE**		-

VIBRATORS (cont) — THE GREAT INDIE DISCOGRAPHY — The 1970s

— folded again when KIP joins The CHORDS and PHIL forms ABLE RAM. Originals re-united The VIBRATORS. (see above)

Anagram / not iss.

Nov 82. (7") *(ANA 4)* **BABY BABY. / DRAGNET**
Jan 83. (lp) *(GRAM 02)* **GUILTY**
– Wolfman howl / Rocket to the moon / Sleeping / Parties / Jumpin' Jack Flash / Watch out baby / Do a runner / We name the guilty / Baby baby / Fighter pilot / The day they caught the killer / Kick it / A dot ain't a lot / Claws in my brain.
May 83. (7") *(ANA 8)* **GUILTY. / HANG TEN**

Ram / not iss.

Nov 83. (7") *(RAM 7005)* **MR AMERICA. / SHADOW LOVE**
Mar 84. (12"m) *(RAM 7007T)* **FLYING HOME. / FLASH FLASH FLASH / MX AMERICA**

Carrere / not iss.

May 84. (7") *(CAR 329)* **FLYING HOME. / PUNISH ME WITH KISSES**
(12"+=) *(CART 329)* – Mr America.
May 84. (lp) *(CAL 205)* **ALASKA 127**
– Amphetamine blues / Somnabulist / Baby blue eyes / Peepshow / 4875 / 3-D Jesus / Jesus always lets you down / Flying home / Shadow love / MX America / Flash flash flash / Punish me with kisses.
Jul 84. (7") *(CAR 338)* **BABY BLUE EYES. / AMPHETIMINE BLUES**
(12"+=) *(CART 338)* – Flying high.
Jun 85. (lp/c) *(CHIPL/ZCCH P002)* **FIFTH AMENDMENT**
– Blown away by love / Rip up the city / Tomorrow is today / Wipe away / Too late for love / The demolishers / Running right into your heart / Frankenstein stomp / Crazy dream / Criminal.

Revolver / not iss.

Oct 86. (lp) *(REVLP 85)* **VIBRATORS LIVE (live)**
–

— KNOX + EDDIE were joined by DUNCAN + OWEN
Jan 88. (lp/c) *(REV LP/MC 101)* **RECHARGED**
– String him along / Hey little doll / I don't trust you / Too dumb / Go go go / Hey nony no (instrumental) / Everyday I die a little / Picture of you / Rip it up / Someone stole my heart / Electricity / Tight black jeans / Reach for that star.
Mar 88. (7") *(REV 45)* **STRING HIM ALONG. / DISCO IN MOSCOW (live)**
Nov 88. (lp/c/cd) *(REV LP/MC/CD 121)* **MELTDOWN**
– Office girls / Don't cha lean on me / So young / Speedtrap / The other side of midnight / Cruel to you / (Na na na) U238 / Dynamite / Letting you go / Danger street / Let's go baby / Sally gardens. *(c+=)* – Wasted life. *(cd++=)* – Don't trust anyone.

— DONNELLY ; repl. OWEN
Nov 89. (lp/c/cd; The VIBRATORS & STEVE NUNN) *(REV LP/MC/XD 135)* **VICIOUS CIRCLE**
– No getting over you / Poll tax blues / I don't wanna fall / Rocket ride to Heaven / Count on me / Slow death / Fire / Halfway to Paradise / Ruby's got a heart / Don't trust anyone / No mercy / Work.
Dec 89. (7") *(REV 52)* **HALFWAY TO PARADISE. / DRIVE**
(cd-s+=) *(REVXD 52)* – Rocket ride to Heaven / Fire.
Oct 90. (cd/c/lp) *Revolver; (REV XD/MC/LP 159)* **VOLUME 10**
– Losing it / Hot for you / Rave on / Wonderful world / Outa my system / Cartel / Video girl / Hey America / Raintime / World in your hands / Don't know now / Can't have it all / Commanche.

— NIGEL BENNETT – guitar (ex-MEMBERS) repl. DONNELLY

Dojo / not iss.

Oct 94. (cd) *(DOJOCD 179)* **HUNTING FOR YOU**
– Hunting for you / The kid's a mess / Fever (you gimme) / Please please please / No no no / Modern world / Another day without you / Goodbye you stupid cow / Keep away from me / She's the one you need / Hey hey / Radium city.

Vibes / not iss.

1996. (cd) *(001)* **UNPUNKED** (acoustic best of)
– Hot for you / U238 (na na na) / She's the one you need / Juice on / Wrecked on you / Baby baby / Troops of tomorrow / Judy says (knock you in the head) / Automatic lover / Amphetamine blue / No getting over you / Dynamite / Don'tcha lean on me / She's bringing you down.

Anagram / Anagram

Sep 97. (cd) *(<CDGRAM 114>)* **FRENCH LESSONS WITH CORRECTION**
– Tired of living with you / The girl's screwed up / Shiver / Judy's killing herself / Cycle of violence / Cold cold cold / Party on / The rain must fall / A date with disaster / Juice on / The evil that men do / Don't you tell me / Johnny B. Bad / Money money / I hate 'Blind Date'.

Track / Track

Sep 02. (cd) *(<TRK 1016CD>)* **ENERGIZE**
– X-files / Your love is fading away / So far down / New brain / Rock the kids / 3/4 Angelina / Animals / 2night / Brand new / General purpose / Jukebox light / Tears are falling / Moonlight / I knew it must be love / Shine / No more.

– compilations, others, etc. –

Jun 80. (lp) *C.B.S.; (CBS 31840)* **BATTERIES INCLUDED**
Jan 88. (12"ep) ; **DISCO IN MOSCOW / RIP UP THE CITY. / AMPHETIMINE BLUES / YEAH YEAH**
Aug 91. (cd) *Repertoire; (REP 4001WZ)* **YEAH YEAH YEAH**
– Into the future / Yeah, yeah, yeah / Sweet, sweet heart / Baby, baby / No heart / She's bringing you down / Petrol / London girls / Stiff little fingers / Wrecked on you / I need a slave / Bad time / Pure mania / Automatic lover / Public enemy No.1 / Destroy / Nazi baby / Wake up / Feel alright / War zone / Troops of tomorrow / Wolfman howl / Jumpin' Jack Flash / Disco in Moscow.
Jun 92. (cd/c/lp) *Anagram; (CD/C+/GRAM 52)* **THE POWER OF MONEY (THE BEST OF THE VIBRATORS)**
Sep 92. (cd) *Released Emotions; (REM 018CD)* **LIVE AT THE MARQUEE 1977 (live)**
Jul 93. (cd; shared with The BOYS) *Windsong; (WINCD 036)* **BBC RADIO 1 LIVE IN CONCERT (live)**
Sep 93. (cd) *Anagram; (<CDPUNK 16>)* **GUILTY / ALASKA 127**
May 94. (cd) *Anagram; (<CDPUNK 34>)* **FIFTH AMENDMENT / RECHARGED**
Jan 95. (cd) *Anagram; (<CDPUNK 43>)* **THE BEST OF THE VIBRATORS**
Jun 95. (cd) *Anagram; (<CDPUNK 58>)* **MELTDOWN / VICIOUS CIRCLE**
May 96. (cd) *Anagram; (<CDPUNK 76>)* **THE INDEPENDENT PUNK SINGLES COLLECTION**
(lp-iss.Nov00 on 'Get Back'; GET 65)
Oct 97. (cd) *Cleopatra; (<CLP 0090>)* **WE VIBRATE (THE BEST OF THE VIBRATORS)**
– Automatic lover / 24 hour people / Baby baby / Stiff little fingers / Disco in Moscow / I need a slave / London girls / Judy says (knock you in the head) / We vibrate / Flying home / Dance to the music / Flying duck theory / She's bringing you down / He's a psycho / Whips and furs / Amphetamine blues.
Jan 98. (cd) *Dojo; (DOLECD 102)* **DEMOS 1976-1977**
Jun 98. (cd) *Overground; (OVER 73CD)* **VOLUME 10 / UNPUNKED**
Oct 98. (cd-s) *Raw Power; (UKPR 001)* **TROOPS OF TOMORROW /**
Jan 99. (cd) *Receiver; (<RRCD 263>)* **RIP UP THE CITY (live)**
Mar 99. (cd) *Harry May; (<MAYOCD 106>)* **PUBLIC ENEMY No.1**
May 99. (cd) *Gig; (GIG 1009-2)* **LIVE AT THE MARQUEE 1977**
May 99. (cd) *Gig; (GIG 1011-2)* **DEMOS AND RARITIES**
Sep 99. (cd) *Raw Power; (RP 008CD)* **BUZZIN'**
(<re-iss. Oct02 on 'Empty'; efa 12621-2>)
Mar 00. (cd) *Captain Oi; (<AHOYCD 135>)* **THE BBC PUNK SESSIONS 1977-1978**
Jul 00. (cd) *Receiver; (<RRCD 291>)* **NOISE BOYS**
Feb 01. (d-cd) *Epic; (500631-2)* **THE BEST OF THE VIBRATORS**
Sep 01. (cd) *Overground; (OVER 92VPCD)* **LIVE AT THE NASHVILLE AND 100 CLUB (live)**
Nov 01. (cd) *Captain Oi; (AHOYCD 181)* **PUNK ROCK RARITIES**
Jan 02. (cd) *Victory Works; (VICTORY 01)* **LIVE AT CBGB'S: PUNK'S SONIC GORMANDIZERS 5/5/2000 – 25th ANNIVERSARY**
May 02. (cd) *Track; (TRK 1013CD)* **V2 / PURE MANIA**

WAITRESSES

Formed: Akron & Cleveland, Ohio, USA ... late '77 by TIN HUEY guitarist, CHRIS BUTLER, alongside vocalist PATTY DONAHUE, TRACY WORMWORTH, session sax man extraordinaire MARS WILLIAMS, STUART AUSTIN and RICK DAILEY. The WAITRESSES first served USA's 'New Wave' clientele with an appearance on the 'Akron' compilation, 'Spirit Of America' and the release of a debut single, 'IN SHORT STACK'. However, it wasn't until 1980 and a deal with Island subsidiary 'Ze', that newly NY-based PATTY and her crew started turning heads with the tongue-in-cheek 'I KNOW WHAT BOYS LIKE'. Following some personnel changes (including former TELEVISION man BILLY FICCA coming in for AUSTIN), the band re-released the song in the States, PATTY's playful DEBBIE HARRY/GO-GO'S style nearly tipping them into the Top 60. This helped their debut set, 'WASN'T TOMORROW WONDERFUL?' (1982), gain a Top 50 booking, although chart success was off the menu for 1982's mini-set, 'I COULD RULE THE WORLD ...'. Nevertheless, this featured one of their most enduring tracks to date, 'CHRISTMAS WRAPPING', a surprise Yuletide novelty hit in Britain. The following year, the group released their second album proper, 'BRUISEOLOGY', their last effort as PATTY was briefly replaced by HOLLY BETH VINCENT. PATTY was to die of cancer late 1996.

Album rating: WASN'T TOMORROW WONDERFUL (*6) / BRUISEOLOGY (*4) / THE BEST OF THE WAITRESSES compilation (*6)

PATTY DONAHUE – vocals / **CHRIS BUTLER** – guitar (of/ex-TIN HUEY) / **MARS WILLIAMS** – saxophone (of SWOLLEN MONKEYS, of MASSACRE, of TERRORISTS) / **RICK DAILEY** – piano / **TRACY WORMWORTH** – bass / **STUART AUSTIN** – drums

		not iss.	Clone
1978.	(7") <CL 006> **IN SHORT STACK. / SLIDE**	–	
		Ze-Island	Ze-Antilles
Oct 80.	(7") <ANS 105> **I KNOW WHAT BOYS LIKE. / NO GUILT** <re-iss. 1982; ANS 4504>	–	

— **DAN KLAYMAN** – keyboards (of SWOLLEN MONKEYS) repl. DAILEY
— **BILLY FICCA** – drums (ex-TELEVISION, etc) repl. AUSTIN

| Nov 81. | (7") (WIP 6763) **CHRISTMAS WRAPPING. / CHRISTMAS FEVER (CHARLELIE COUTURE)** | | |

— **DAVID HOFSTRA** – bass; repl. TRACY

		Polydor	Polydor
Feb 82.	(7") (POSP 414) <PD 2196> **I KNOW WHAT BOYS LIKE. / IT'S MY CAR**		62
Apr 82.	(lp) (POLS 1063) <PD1 6346> **WASN'T TOMORROW WONDERFUL?** – No guilt / Wise up / Quit / It's my car / Wasn't tomorrow wonderful? / I know what boys like / Heat night / Redland / Pussy strut / Go on / Jimmy tomorrow.		41 Jan82

— now without KLAYMAN (still a SWOLLEN MONKEY)

Dec 82.	(m-lp) <507> **I COULD RULE THE WORLD IF I COULD ONLY GET THE PARTS** – I could rule the world if I could only get the parts / Make the weather / Bread and butter / Square pegs / The smartest person I know / Christmas wrapping.	–	
May 83.	(7") (POSP 582) **MAKE THE WEATHER. / BREAD AND BUTTER** (12"+=) (POSPX 582) – Square pegs / The smartest person I know.		–
May 83.	(lp/c) (POLD/+C 5080) <810980> **BRUISEOLOGY** – A girl's gotta do / Make the weather / Everything's wrong if my hair is wrong / Luxury / Open city / Thinking about sex again / Bruiseology / Pleasure / Spin / They're all out of liquor, let's find another party.		

— **HOLLY BETH VINCENT** – vocals (ex-HOLLY & THE ITALIANS) repl. PATTY (the latter died of cancer on the 9th December, 1996)
— served up their last platter on above album (MARS joined The PSYCHEDELIC FURS)

– compilations, etc. –

Dec 82.	(7"/12") Ze-Island; (WIP/12WIP 6821) **CHRISTMAS WRAPPING. / HANGOVER (FOR THE 1ST OF THE 1ST '83)**	45	–
Oct 90.	(cd) Polydor; <(847249-2)> **THE BEST OF THE WAITRESSES** – No guilt / I know what boys like / Wise up / Wasn't tomorrow wonderful? / Heat night / Jimmy tomorrow / Christmas wrapping / Bread & butter / Square pegs / The smartest person I know / A girl's gotta do / Make the weather / Thinking about sex again / Bruiseology / They're all about liquor, let's find another party.		
Mar 97.	(cd) King Biscuit; <88024> **KING BISCUIT FLOWER HOUR (live)**	–	

John WATTS (see under ⇒ FISCHER-Z)

Fee WAYBILL (see under ⇒ TUBES)

WEIRDOS

Formed: Los Angeles, California, USA ... 1976 initially as The BARBIES then The LUXURIOUS ADULTS by brothers JOHN and DIX DENNEY, with others CLIFF ROMAN, DAVID TROUT and NICKEY BEAT. In 1977, they unleashed the first of many cult-punk 45's, 'DESTROY ALL MUSIC', which somehow found its way by import to UK shores. A number of sporadic singles followed, although internal wrangles led to a split in 1981. They did however re-form in the early 90's, and even got round to an album going by the name of 'CONDOR'. Despite their lack of recognition during their short lifespan, this punk/new wave outfit are now regarded by many critics as US pioneers of the movement.

Album rating: CONDOR (*5) / WEIRD WORLD 1977-1981 TIME CAPSULE VOLUME ONE compilation (*8)

JOHN DENNEY – vocals / **DIX DENNEY** – guitar / **CLIFF ROMAN** – guitar / **DAVID TROUT** – bass / **NICKEY BEAT** – drums

		not iss.	Bomp
1977.	(7"m) <112> **DESTROY ALL MUSIC. / A LIFE OF CRIME / WHY DO YOU EXIST?**	–	
		not iss.	Dangerhouse
1978.	(7") <SP 1063> **WE GOT THE NEUTRON BOMB. / SOLITARY CONFINEMENT**	–	

— **BILLY PERSONS** – bass; repl. TROUT
— **DANNY BENAIR** – drums; repl. NICKEY

		not iss.	Bomp
1979.	(12"ep) <W 3> **WHO? WHAT? WHEN? WHERE? WHY?** – Jungle rock / Happy people / Big shot / Hitman / Idle life / Fort U.S.A.	–	
		not iss.	Numbskull
1979.	(7") <none> **SKATEBOARDS TO HELL. / ADULTHOOD**	–	

— **WILLY WILLIAMS** – bass; repl. PERSONS
— **ART FOX** – drums; repl. BENAIR

		not iss.	Rhino
1980.	(12"ep) <RNEP 508> **ACTION DESIGN** – The hideout / I feel / Break on through / Helium bar.	–	

— split but re-formed nearly a decade later. DENNEY's + ROMAN

		Frontier	Frontier
1990.	(cd/lp) <(4623-2L/1L)> **CONDOR** – Shining silver light / Cyclops helicopter / Tropical depression / W.W.Y.D.? (1981) / Terrain / Night after day / Her / Something's moving / Living thing / Condor.		
May 91.	(cd/lp) (4630-2L/-4L/-1L) **WEIRD WORLD 1977-1981 – TIME CAPSULE VOLUME ONE** (compilation) – Weird world / Arms race / Pagan / Helium bar / Rhythm syndrome / Fallout / Fort U.S.A. / Happy people / Message from the underworld / Teenage / I'm not like you / We got the neutron bomb / Solitary confinement / Life of crime. (lp re-iss. Aug00 on 'Munster'; MR 152)		

— THE WEIRDOS FEATURING MR. GASSER cd from '95 was from surf band

James WHITE (& THE BLACKS) (see under ⇒ CHANCE, James)

WIPERS

Formed: Portland, Oregon, USA ... 1977 by GREG SAGE, DAVE KOUPAL and SAM HENRY. The former two had begun their musical career in late 60's rock outfit, BEAUREGARDE, named after a professional wrestler (who actually featured on the sleeve of their one and only eponymous album!). The WIPERS debuted in '78 with the EP, 'BETTER OFF DEAD', a full album, 'IS THIS REAL?', emerging at the turn of the decade, the blitzkrieg 'D-7' later covered by NIRVANA (KURT COBAIN was only one of a number of alt-rock icons to cite The WIPERS as a seminal influence). After another EP, 'ALIEN BOY', some personnel changes took place, drummer HENRY making way for BRAD DAVIDSON and BRAD NAISH before the subsequent release of their second set, 'YOUTH OF AMERICA' (1982). Following the release of a Canadian-only LP, 'OVER THE EDGE' (1984), GREG signed to rising label 'Enigma' issuing a solo album, 'STRAIGHT AHEAD' (1986) in the process. The WIPERS returned to the fold (STEVE PLOUF replacing NAISH) with a fifth set, 'LAND OF THE LOST' (1986), a dirtier, metallic grunge sound which deserved a lot more success than it achieved. They continued ploughing a singular furrow to the end of the decade, remaining largely unsung until the advent of the Seattle grunge scene. SAGE subsequently went solo in the early '90's with the album 'SACRIFICE (FOR LOVE)', although the resulting surge in interest for all things WIPERS, led to a reformation in 1993. The 'SILVER SAIL' single (their first ever!) and an album of the same name appeared the following year, while 'Tim/Kerr' (the label) also issued another, 'THE HERD', in '96. Three years on, The WIPERS cast out another uncompromising set, 'THE POWER IN ONE' (1999), axegrinder SAGE and drummer PLOUF were never better. • **Trivia:** May '94 saw the release of a tribute album, 'SONGS FOR GREG SAGE & THE WIPERS', boasting contributions from the likes of NIRVANA, HOLE, POISON IDEA, etc.

WIPERS (cont)

Album rating: IS THIS REAL? (*7) / YOUTH OF AMERICA mini (*6) / OVER THE EDGE (*8) / LAND OF THE LOST (*6) / FOLLOW BLIND (*6) / THE CIRCLE (*6) / SILVER SAIL (*6) / THE HERD (*6) / POWER IN ONE (*6) / Greg Sage: STRAIGHT AHEAD (*6)

GREG SAGE – vocals, guitar / **DAVE KOUPAL** – bass / **SAM HENRY** – drums

not iss.   Trap

1978. (7"ep) <810X44> **BETTER OFF DEAD. / UP IN FLAMES / DOES IT HURT?**

not iss.   Park Avenue

Feb 80. (lp) **IS THIS REAL?**
– Return of the rat / Mystery / Up front / Let's go let's go away / Is this real? / Tragedy / Alien boy / D-7 / Potential suicide / Don't know what I am / Window shop for love / Wait a minute. <re-iss. Apr84 on 'Psycho'; PSYCHO 22> (UK-iss.Mar87 on 'Weird Systems'; WS 024) (cd-iss. Mar93 on 'Sub Pop'+=; SPCD 82-253) – ALIEN BOY EP

Aug 80. (7"ep) <PA 10EP> **ALIEN BOY**
– Image of man / Telepathic love / Voices in the rain.

—— **BRAD DAVIDSON** – bass + **BRAD NAISH** – drums repl. DAVE (on some) + SAM also departed

Feb 82. (m-lp) <82802> **YOUTH OF AMERICA**
– Taking too long / Can this be / Pushing the extreme / When it's over / No fair / Youth of America. <re-iss. Apr84 on 'Psycho'; PSYCHO 23> (cd-iss. Dec94 on 'Gift Of Life' lp/cd; GIFT 025/+CD)

not iss.   Brain Eater

Nov 84. (lp) <EATER 2> **OVER THE EDGE** — Canada
– Over the edge / Doom town / So young / Messenger / Romeo / Now is the time / What is / No one wants an alien / The lonely one / No generation gap / This time. (re-iss. Mar87 on 'Enigma'; 2187-1) (UK-iss.Aug94 on 'Gift Of Life' lp/cd; GIFT 020/+CD)

Enigma   Enigma

Jan 86. (lp; by GREG SAGE) <2007-1> **STRAIGHT AHEAD**
– Straight ahead / Soul's tongue / Blue cowboy / Your empathy / The illusion fades / Seems so clear / On the run / Astro clouds / Lost in space / Let it go / World without fear / Keep on keepin' on. (UK-iss.Aug94 on 'Gift Of Life' lp/cd; GIFT 022/+CD)

Mar 86. (lp) <(2026-1)> **LIVE: WIPERS (live)**
– Pushing the extreme / Messenger / Moon rider / Doom town / Think about it / Potential suicide / D-7 / Now is the time / Tell me / Window shop for love / Youth of America. (re-iss. Aug94 & Feb98 on 'Gift Of Life' lp/cd; GIFT 021/+CD)

—— **STEVE PLOUF** – drums; repl. NAISH

Nov 86. (lp/cd) <(2094-1/-2)> **LAND OF THE LOST**
– Just a dream away / Way of love / Let me know / Fair weather friends / Land of the lost / Nothing left to lose / The search / Different ways / Just say. (cd re-iss. Aug94 & Feb98 on 'Gift Of Life' lp/cd; GIFT 023CD)

Dec 87. (lp) <971194> **FOLLOW BLIND**
– Follow blind / Some place else / Any time you find / The chill remains / Let it slide / Against the wall / No doubt about it / Don't belong to you / Losers town / Coming down / Next time. (UK-iss.Aug94 & Feb98 on 'Gift Of Life' lp/cd; GIFT 024/+CD)

Enigma   Restless

Dec 88. (lp/c/cd) (ENVLP/TCENV/CDENV 516) <72339> **THE CIRCLE**
– I want a way / Time marches on / All the same / True believer / Good thing / Make or break / The circle / Goodbye again / Be there / Blue & red.

Feb 90. (cd/c) <72378-2/-4> **BEST OF WIPERS & GREG SAGE** (compilation)
– Nothing left to lose / The way of love / Some place else / The chill remains / Soul's tongue / Blue cowboy / Taking too long / The circle / Romeo / Messenger / Better off dead / No solution / My vengeance / Just a dream away / Different ways / Losers town.

Roadrunner   Restless

Oct 91. (cd; by GREG SAGE) (LS 9237-2) <772539-2> **SACRIFICE (FOR LOVE)**
– Stay by me / Sacrifice (for love) / Know by now / Forever (with BOBBY WOMACK) / The same guitar / No turning back / Ready or not / For your love / This planet Earth / Dreams. (cd re-iss. Jul95 on 'Restless'; same as US)

—— the WIPERS line-up still:- **SAGE / DAVIDSON / KOUPAL**

Tim/Kerr   Gift Of Life

Jun 94. (7"/cd-s) **SILVER SAIL**

Jun 94. (cd/lp) <(TK 92 CD/12 031)> **SILVER SAIL**
– Y I came / Back to the basics / Warning / Mars / Prisoner / Standing there / Sign of the times / Line / On a roll / Never win / Silver sail. (re-iss. Nov94 on 'Gift Of Life' lp/cd; GIFT 036/+CD)

Apr 96. (cd) <(TK 95CD 114)> **THE HERD** — Feb96
– Psychic vampire / No place safe / Last chance / Wind the clock slowly / The herd / Stormy / Green light region / Sinking as a stone / Sunrise / Defiant / Resist / Insane. (re-iss. Jul97; same)

Apr 96. (cd-s) <TK 116> **INSANE**

Zeno   Zeno

Dec 99. (cd) (ZE 8439) <3> **POWER IN ONE** — Oct99
– The fall / Power in one / Shaken / Misleading / Rockett / I'll be around / Still inside of me / Ship of dreams / Rest of my life / Loser's revenge / Take it now / Stay around / What's wrong? / Too many strangers.

—— split after above; SAGE will make an album 2002/3

– compilations, etc. –

Jun 02. (3xcd-box) Zeno; (0016249) **BOX SET**

WIRE

Formed: London, England ... October '76, by GRAHAM LEWIS, COLIN NEWMAN, BRUCE GILBERT and ROBERT GOTOBED. WIRE made their vinyl debut in April '77 when safety pin-pierced ears were subjected to their punk anthems, '12XU' and 'LOWDOWN' on the seminal Various Artists lp, 'Live At The Roxy'. The EMI backed label 'Harvest', desperate for some hip punk credibility, decided to give WIRE a contract and although unsuccessful with their first single attempt ('MANNEQUIN'), unleashed the Mike Thorne-produced 'PINK FLAG' at the end of '77. The record contained 21 short, sharp shocks of minimalist punk rock/new wave, possessed of a musical intelligence that dwarfed their more retro-fixated contemporaries. Early in 1978, they followed this with the classic 'I AM THE FLY', lyrically a simple piece of what can only be described as progressive punk. After another fruitless stab at the charts with 'DOT DASH', they returned with an even more engaging second set, the oblique, atmospheric 'CHAIRS MISSING'. This record surely deserved better than its Top 50 placing, featuring as it did the classy avant-punk tunes, 'PRACTICE MAKES PERFECT', 'I FEEL MYSTERIOUS TODAY' and the "minor" hit 45, 'OUTDOOR MINER'. In the Autumn of '79, WIRE's third set, '154' hit the Top 40, effectively displaying an even more experimental side to the one-time three-chord wonders. Sadly, however, it was their final outing for 'Harvest', the group moving on to the more appropriate indie label, 'Rough Trade', who released the 1981 single, 'OUR SWIMMER'. An anti-commercial, unproduced live set appeared around the same time, the band members having already taken off for solo projects. One of these, DOME (aka GILBERT & LEWIS), had been in the pipeline for some time, while NEWMAN went on to indie success with several albums. In 1986, the much-in-demand WIRE returned, completing a few EP's for top indie, 'Mute' before the following year's 'THE IDEAL COPY' album. They continued to enjoy cult success, which even spread across the Atlantic, the band signing to US label, 'Enigma'. In 1991, GOTOBED retired (to Bedfordshire, no doubt?!) and the band became WIR, releasing the disappointing 'THE FIRST LETTER' that year. For the remainder of the 90's, each took on individual projects, all fairly obscure of course. With the nasty 90's out of the way, WIRE were back with the internet-friendly series releases, 'READ & BURN 01' (2002), a record that opened with the basic and incise 'IN THE ART OF STOPPING'.
• **Songwriters:** Group compositions. • **Trivia:** COLIN NEWMAN produced The VIRGIN PRUNES in 1982 and FAD GADGET in 1984. He moved to India at this time, returning after a few years to live in Belgium, where he founded 'Crammed Discs' records.

Album rating: PINK FLAG (*8) / CHAIRS MISSING (*9) / 154 (*7) / DOCUMENT AND EYEWITNESS: ELECTRIC BALLROOM (*3) / THE IDEAL COPY (*7) / A BELL IS A CUP ... UNTIL IT IS STRUCK (*5) / ON RETURNING (1977-1979) compilation (*8) / IT'S BEGINNING TO & BACK AGAIN (*6) / MANSCAPE (*5) / THE FIRST LETTER (*4; as Wir)

COLIN NEWMAN (b.16 Sep'54, Salisbury, England) – vox, guitar, keyboards / **BRUCE GILBERT** (b.18 May'46, Watford, England) – guitar, vocals, synths. / **GRAHAM LEWIS** (b.22 Feb'53, Grantham, England) – bass, vocals, synthesizers / **ROBERT GOTOBED** (b. MARK FIELD, 1951, Leicester, England) – drums, percussion (ex-SNAKES, ex-ART ATTACKS) / **GEORGE GILL** – guitar (left before debut)

Harvest   Harvest

Nov 77. (7"m) (HAR 5144) **MANNEQUIN. / 12XU / FEELING CALLED LOVE**

Nov 77. (lp/c) (SHSP/TC-SHSP 4076) <11757> **PINK FLAG**
– Reuters / Field day for the Sundays / Three girl rhumba / Ex-lion tamer / Lowdown / Start to move / Brazil / It's so obvious / Surgeon's girl / Pink flag / The commercial / Straight line / 106 beats that / Mr. Suit / Strange / Fragile / Mannequin / Different to me / Champs / Feeling called love / 12XU. (cd-iss. 1990 on 'Restless'+=; 72360) – Options R. (re-iss. cd Aug94 on 'E.M.I.'; CDGO 2063) <cd-iss. 1995 on 'Capitol'; 29857-2>

Feb 78. (7") (HAR 5151) **I AM THE FLY. / EX-LION TAMER**

Jun 78. (7") (HAR 5161) **DOT DASH. / OPTIONS R**

Sep 78. (lp/c) (SHSP/TC-SHSP 4093>) **CHAIRS MISSING** — 48
– Practice makes perfect / French film blurred / Another the letter / Men 2nd / Marooned / Sand in my joints / Being sucked in again / Heartbeat / Mercy / Outdoor miner / I am the fly / I feel mysterious today / From the nursery / Used to / Too late. (cd-iss. 1990 on 'Restless'+=; 72361) – Go ahead / A question of degree / Former airline. (re-iss. cd Aug94 on 'E.M.I.'; CDGO 2065) <cd-iss. 1995 on 'Capitol'; 29858-2>

Jan 79. (7",7"white) (HAR 5172) **OUTDOOR MINER. / PRACTICE MAKES PERFECT** — 51
Harvest   Warners

Jun 79. (7") (HAR 5187) **A QUESTION OF DEGREE. / FORMER AIRLINE**

Sep 79. (lp/c) (SHSP/TC-SHSP 4105) <3398> **154** — 39
– I should have known better / Two people in a room / The 15th / The other window / Single k.o. / A touching display / On returning / A mutual friend / Blessed state / Once is enough / Map reference 41°N, 93°W / Indirect enquiries / 40 versions. (free-7"ep w.a) (Dome; PSR 444) – Song 2 / Get down (parts 1 & 2) / Let's panic / Later / Small electric piece. (cd-iss. 1990 on 'Restless'+= 72362) – (7"ep above). (re-iss. cd Aug94 on 'E.M.I.'; CDGO 2064) <cd-iss. 1995 on 'Capitol'; 39859> (cd re-iss. Jul99; CDGO 2064)

Oct 79. (7") (HAR 5192) **MAP REFERENCE 41°N 93°W. / GO AHEAD**

—— In 1980, WIRE also diverged into own activities; GILBERT & LEWIS became CUPOL and DOME, etc. The pair also joined THE THE. COLIN NEWMAN went solo taking ROBERT GOTOBED with him. The latter also became member of FAD GADGET. (see further on for these activities)

Rough Trade   not iss.

May 81. (7") (RT 079) **OUR SWIMMER. / MIDNIGHT BAHNHOF CAFE**

Jul 81. (lp) (ROUGH 29) **DOCUMENT AND EYEWITNESS: ELECTRIC BALLROOM (live)**
– 5 10 / 12XU (fragment) / Underwater experiences / Zegk hoqp / Everything's going to be nice / Instrumental (thrown bottle) / Piano tuner (keep strumming those guitars) / And then ... / We meet under tables / Revealing trade secrets / Eels sang lino / Eastern standard / Coda. (free 12"m-lp) **DOCUMENT AND EYEWITNESS: NOTRE DAME HALL (live)** – Underwater experiences / Go ahead / Ally in exile / Relationship / Our swimmer / Witness to the fact / 2 people in a room / Heartbeat. (re-iss. 1984 lp/c; same/ COPY 004) (cd-iss. Apr91 on 'Grey Area-Mute'; WIRE 80CD)

WIRE (cont)

Mar 83. (12"m) *(RTT 123)* **CRAZY ABOUT LOVE. / SECOND LENGTH (OUR SWIMMER) / CATAPULT 30**
— WIRE were now back to full-time membership.

Mute / Enigma

Nov 86. (12"ep) *(12MUTE 53)* <72245> **SNAKEDRILL**
— A serious of snakes / Advantage in height / Up to the sun / Drill.
Mar 87. (7") *(MUTE 57)* **AHEAD. / FEED ME (live)**
(12"+=) *(12MUTE 57)* – Ambulance chasers (live) / Vivid riot of red (live).
Apr 87. (cd/c/lp) *(CD/C+/STUMM 42)* <273270> **THE IDEAL COPY** 87
— Points of collapse / Ahead / Madman's honey / Feed me / Ambitious / Cheeking tongues / Still shows / Over theirs. *(cd+=)* – Ahead II / SNAKEDRILL EP tracks.
Mar 88. (7") *(MUTE 67)* **KIDNEY BONGOS. / PIETA**
(3"cd-s+=) *(CDMUTE 67)* – Drill (live).
(12"++) *(12MUTE 67)* – Over theirs (live).
May 88. (cd/c/lp) *(CD/C+/STUMM 54)* <73314-1> **A BELL IS A CUP... UNTIL IT IS STRUCK**
— Silk skin paws / The finest drops / The queen of Ur and the king of Um / Free falling divisions / It's a boy / Boiling boy / Kidney bongos / Come back in two halves / Follow the locust / A public place. *(cd+=)* – The queen of Ur and the king of Um (alternate take) / Pieta / Over theirs (live) / Drill (live).
Jun 88. (7") *(MUTE 84)* **SILK SKIN PAWS. / GERMAN SHEPHERDS**
(12"+=) *(12MUTE 84)* – Ambitious (remix).
(3"cd-s+=) *(CDMUTE 84)* – Come back in two halves.
Apr 89. (7"clear; withdrawn) *(MUTE 87)* **EARDRUM BUZZ. / THE OFFER** 68
(12"+=) *(12MUTE 87)* – It's a boy (instrumental).
(cd-s) *(CDMUTE 87)* – ('A'side) / Silk skin paws / A serious of snakes / Ahead (extended).
(live-12") *(LMUTE 87)* – BUZZ BUZZ BUZZ – Eardrum buzz / Ahead / Kidney bongos.

Mute / Mute

May 89. (cd/c/lp) *(CD/C+/STUMM 66)* <73516-2> **IT'S BEGINNING TO AND BACK AGAIN (live)**
— Finest drops / Eardrum buzz / German shepherds / Public place / It's a boy / Illuminated / Boiling boy / Over theirs / Eardrum buzz (12"version) / The offer / In vivo.
Jul 89. (7") *(MUTE 98)* **IN VIVO. / ILLUMINATED**
(12"+=/cd-s+=) *(12/CD MUTE 98)* – Finest drops (live).
May 90. (7"; w-drawn) *(MUTE 107)* **LIFE IN THE MANSCAPE. / GRAVITY WORSHIP**
(12"+=/cd-s+=) *(12/CD MUTE 107)* – Who has wine.
May 90. (cd/c/lp) *(CD/C+/STUMM 80)* <73559-2> **MANSCAPE**
— Patterns of behaviour / Goodbye ploy / Morning bell / Small black reptile / Torch it / Other moments / Sixth sense / What do you see? / Where's the deputation? / You hung your lights in the trees – A craftman's touch. <US cd+=> – Life in the manscape / Stampede / Children of groceries.
Apr 91. (cd/c/lp) *(CD/C+/STUMM 74)* **DRILL**
— (7 versions of out-takes from last album)

WIR

— slightly different name when GOTOBED left
Sep 91. (7") *(MUTE 107)* **SO AND SLOW IT GOES. / NICE FROM HERE**
(12") *(12MUTE 107)* – ('A'side) / ('A'-Orb mix) / Take it (LFO mix)
(cd-s+=) *(CDMUTE 107)* – (all 4 tracks).
Oct 91. (cd/c/lp) *(CD/C+/STUMM 87)* <61238> **THE FIRST LETTER**
— Take it (for greedy) / So and slow it goes (extended) / A bargain at 3 and 20 yeah! / Rootsi-rootsy / Ticking mouth / It continues / Looking at me (stop!) / Naked, whooping and such-like / Tailor made / No cows on the ice / A big glue canal.
— allo 4 members were back again

pinkflag.www / pinkflag.www

Nov 00. (7") *(VPF 3)* **TWELVE TIMES YOU. / X U (version)**
May 02. (m-cd) *<PF 4>* **READ & BURN 01**
— In the art of stopping / I don't understand / Comet / Germ ship / 1st fast / The Agfers of Kodack.

– compilations, others, etc. –

Mar 86. (m-lp) *Pink; (PINKY 7)* **PLAY POP**
Aug 86. (lp) *Dojo; (DOJOLP 36)* **IN THE PINK (live)**
Nov 87. (12"ep) *Strange Fruit; (SFPS 041)* **THE PEEL SESSIONS (18.1.78)**
— I am the fly / Culture vultures / Practice makes perfect / 106 beats that.
Jul 89. (cd)(c/lp) *Harvest; (CDP 792 535-2)(TC+/SHSP 4127) / Restless; <72358-1>* **ON RETURNING (1977-1979)**
— 12XU / It's so obvious / Mr. Suit / Three girl rhumba / Ex lion tamer / Lowdown / Strange / Reuters / Feeling called love / I am the fly / Practise makes perfect / French film blurred / I feel mysterious today / Marooned / Sand in my joints / Outdoor miner / A question of degree / I should have known better / The other window / 40 versions / A touching display / On returning. *(cd+=)* – Straight line / 106 beats that / Field day for the Sundays / Champs / Dot dash / Another the letter / Men 2nd / Two people in a room / Blessed state. *(cd re-iss. Feb00; same)*
Feb 90. (cd/c/lp) *Strange Fruit; (SFR CD/MC/LP 108)* **DOUBLE PEEL SESSIONS**
(cd re-iss. May96; same)
May 93. (cd/c/d-lp) *Mute; (CD/C+/STUMM 116)* **1985-1990 THE A LIST**
Sep 94. (cd; w/book) *Audioglobe; (SCONC 25)* **EXPLODING VIEWS**
May 95. (cd) *E.M.I. (CDGO 2066)* **BEHIND THE CURTAIN**
Dec 95. (12"; WIRE with HAFLER TRIO) *Touch; (TONE 5)* **THE FIRST LETTER / THE LAST LAST NUMBER**
May 96. (cd) *W.M.O.; (WMO 004CD)* **TURNS AND STROKES**
— Safe / Lorries / Panamanian craze / Remove for improvement / Spare one / Over my head / 12XU / Inventory / Ritual view / Part of our history / Second length (our swimmer) / Catapult 30.
(d-lp-iss.Apr97; same)
Oct 97. (cd) *W.M.O.; (WMO 014CD) / World Domination; <67>* **COATINGS**

Sep 00. (3xcd-box) *E.M.I.; (528357-2)* **PINK FLAG / CHAIRS MISSING / 154**
— Ambulance chasers / Series of snakes / Ambitious / Madman's honey / Kidney bongos / It's a boy / German shepherds / Boling boy / Drill / In vivo / Who has nine? / It can't be true can it? / Gravity worship. *(w/ free cd-s)* – AMBITIOUS

COLIN NEWMAN

(solo playing most instruments) **with ROBERT GOTOBED** – drums / **DESMOND SIMMONDS** – bass, guitar / **BRUCE GILBERT** – guitar / **MIKE THORNE** – keyboards

Beggars Banquet / not iss.

Oct 80. (lp) *(BEGA 20)* **A-Z**
— I waited for ages / And jury / Alone / Order for order / Image / Life on deck / Troisieme / S-S-S-Star eyes / Seconds to last / Inventory / But no / B. *(re-iss. Sep88 on 'Beggars Banquet-Lowdown' lp/c/cd; (BBL/+C 20/+CD)*
Nov 80. (7"m) *(BEG 48)* **B. / CLASSIC REMAINS / ALONE ON PIANO**
Mar 81. (7") *(BEG 52)* **INVENTORY. / THIS PICTURE**
— COLIN played everything.

4.a.d. / not iss.

Aug 81. (lp) *(CAD 108)* **PROVISIONALLY TITLED THE SINGING FISH**
— Fish 1 / Fish 2 / Fish 3 / Fish 4 / Fish 5 / Fish 6 / Fish 7 / Fish 8 / Fish 9 / Fish 10. *(d-cd-iss. Jan88 +=; CAD 108)* – NOT TO (lp tracks) / Not to (remix) / You and your dog / The grace you know / H.C.T.F.R. / No doubt.
— added **DES SIMMONDS + SIMON GILHAM** – bass, vocals
Jan 82. (lp) *(CAD 201)* **NOT TO**
— Lorries / Don't bring reminders / You me and happy / We meet under tables / Safe / Truculent yet / 5'10 / 1, 2, 3, beep beep / Not to / Indians / Remove for improvement / Blue Jay way.
May 82. (7") *(AD 209)* **WE MEANS WE STARTS. / NOT TO (remix)**

Crammed Discs / not iss.

Sep 86. (lp) *(CRAM 045)* **COMMERCIAL SUICIDE**
— Their terrain / 2-sixes / Metakest / But I . . . / Commercial suicide / I'm still here / Feigned hearing / Can I explain the delay / I can hear you . . .
Oct 86. (7") *(CRAM 1345-7)* **FEIGNED HEARING. / I CAN'T HEAR YOU . . .**
Aug 87. (12") *(CRAM 051)* **INTERVIEW. / INTERVIEW**
May 88. (7") *(CRAM 1745-7)* **BETTER LATE THAN NEVER. / AT LAST**
May 88. (lp/c/cd) *(CRAM 058/+C/CD)* **IT SEEMS**
— Quite unrehearsed / Can't help being / The rite of life / An impressive beginning / It seems / Better late than never / Not being in Warsaw / At rest / Convolutions / Round and round. *(w/ free label 'Various Artists' lp)*

Swim / not iss.

May 95. (12") **VOICE. /**

CUPOL

GILBERT & LEWIS under many guises (not initially chronological)

4.a.d. / not iss.

Jul 80. (12"ep) *(BAD 9)* **LIKE THIS FOR AGES. / KLUBA CUPOL**
(20min@'33rpm)

GILBERT & LEWIS

4 a.d. / not iss.

Nov 80. (m-lp) *(CAD 16)* **3R4**
— Barge calm / 3,4 / Barge calm / R.
Aug 81. (7") *(AD 106)* **ENDS WITH THE SEA. / HUNG UP TO DRY WHILE BUILDING AN ARCH**
— In May88, a cd-compilation '8 TIME' was issued by duo on '4 a.d.'; CAD 16CD

DOME

Dome / not iss.

Aug 80. (lp) *(DOME 1)* **DOME 1**
— Cancel your order / Cruel when complete / And then . . . / Here we go / Rolling upon my day / Say again / Lina sixup / Airmail / Ampnoise / Madmen. *(free-7")* – SO. / DROP
Feb 81. (lp) *(DOME 2)* **DOME 2**
— The red tent 1 + 2 / Long lost life / Breathless / Reading Prof. B / Ritual view / Twist up / Keep it.
Oct 81. (lp) *(DOME 3)* **DOME 3**
— Jasz / Ar-gu / An-an-an-d-d-d / Ba-dr / D-o-bo / Na-drm / Dasz / Ur-ur / Danse / Roor-an.
(above with also **RUSSELL MILLS** – percussion / **DANIEL MILLER** – saxophone / **E.C.RADCLIFFE** – guitar / **PETER PRINCE** – drums
— (1 & 2 and 3 & 4 were re-issued on 2 cd's for 'Grey Area-Mute' Aug92; *DOME 12CD & DOME 34CD*)

GILBERT, LEWIS & MILLS

Cherry Red / not iss.

May 82. (lp) *(BRED 27)* **MZUI (WATERLOO GALLERY)**
— Mzui (part 1) / Mzui (part 2).

W.M.O. / not iss.

Dec 95. (cd) **PACIFIC / SPECIFIC**

P'O

— aka **GILBERT + LEWIS** plus **ANGELA CONWAY** – bass, vocals / **DAVID TIDBALL** – vocals, clarinet / **PETER PRICE** – drums

Court / not iss.

Jan 83. (lp) *(COURT 1)* **WHILST CLIMBING THIEVES VIE FOR ATTENTION**

– Time and time / Back to back / Holy Joe / Earl / Vanite / Today's version / I will / Mhona / Blind Tim / Crystal streams. *(cd-iss. May00 on 'W.M.O.'+=; WMO 011CD)* – Only one I / Zinc lasso (noose) / Back to back / Vanite / Today's version / Mhona.

DUET EMMO

——— **GILBERT & LEWIS** augmented by **DANIEL MILLER** (label boss)

		Mute	not iss.
Aug 83. (7") *(MUTE 25)* **OR SO IT SEEMS. / HEART OF HEARTS (OR SO IT SEEMS)**			-
Aug 83. (lp) *(STUMM 11)* **OR SO IT SEEMS**			-

– Hill of men / Or so it seems / Friano / The first person / A.N.C. / Long sledge / Gatemmo / Last's card / Heart of hearts. *(cd-iss. Aug92 on 'Grey Area-Mute'; CDSTUMM 11)*

BRUCE GILBERT

	Dome	not iss.
Apr 83. (lp) **TO SPEAK**		-

– To speak / To walk, to run / To duck, to dive / This / Seven year / Atlas. *(iss.Sep84 as 'WILL YOU SPEAK THIS WORD?' on 'Uniton'; U 011)*

	Mute	Mute
Sep 84. (m-lp) *(STUMM 18)* **THIS WAY**		-

– Work for do you me / I did / Here visit. *(cd-iss. with next; CDSTUMM 18)*

Mar 87. (lp) *(STUMM 39)* **THE SHIVERING MAN**		-

– Angel food / The shivering man / Not in the feather / There are / Hommage / Eline Court li / Epitaph for Henran Brenlar.

1990. (cd/c) *<71432-2/-4>* **THIS WAY TO THE SHIVERING MAN**	-	
Jan 91. (cd/lp) *(CD+/STUMM 71) <61030>* **INSIDING (2 excerpts from 'SAVAGE WATER')**		

– Bloodlines (ballet) / Insiding.

Aug 91. (cd/lp) *(CD+/STUMM 91) <61197>* **MUSIC FOR FRUIT**		

– Music for fruit / Push / You might be called.

Oct 95. (7") **BI YO YO. /**		

(above single on 'Sub Pop')

Mar 96. (cd) *(<CDSTUMM 117>)* **AB OVO**		
May 96. (cd; by GILBERT – HAMPSON – KENDALL) *<1>* **ORR**	-	

(above issued on the 'Parallel' series)

Dec 97. (cd) *<69050>* **IN ESSE**		-

– Soli / Psycho / Eclectic / Extraction.

	Sahko	not iss.
Dec 98. (12"; by BRUCE GILBERT & RON WEST) *(efa 620966)* **FREQUENCY VARIATION. /**		-

HE SAID

(aka **GRAHAM LEWIS** solo) aug. by **JOHN FRYER** – drum prog

	Mute	Mute
Oct 85. (7"/12") *(7/12 MUTE 41)* **ONLY ONE I. / ONLY ONE I**		-
Apr 86. (7") *(7MUTE 43)* **PUMP. / PUMP** (instrumental)		-

(12"+=) *(12MUTE 43)* – To and fro.

Aug 86. (7") *(7MUTE 48)* **PULLING 3 G's. / PALE FEET**		-

(12"+=) *(12MUTE 48)* – ('A'&'B' extended versions).

——— added **BRUCE GILBERT** – guitar / **NIGEL H. KIND** – guitar / **E.C. RADCLIFFE** – prog. / **ANGELA CONWAY** – backing vocals / **ENO** (guested on 1)

Oct 86. (cd/c/lp) *(CD/C+/STUMM 29)* **HAIL**		-

– Kidnap yourself / Only one I / Pump / I fall in your arms / Do you mean that? / Flagwearing / Shades to escape / Pale feet.

Nov 88. (7"/12") *(MUTE/12MUTE 73)* **COULD YOU?. / HE SAID . . . SHE SAID**		
Feb 89. (cd/c/lp) *(CD/C+/STUMM 57) <75400>* **TAKE CARE**		

– Could you? / ABC Dicks love / Watch-take-care / Tongue ties / Not a soul / Halfway house / Get out of that rain / Hole in the sky.

WRECKLESS ERIC

Born: ERIC GOULDEN, 1950, Newhaven, England. Odd-job man turned pub-rock troubadour, GOULDEN took on the WRECKLESS ERIC mantle after netting a deal with 'Stiff' at the height of punk's first wave, causing a stir in 1977 with his anthemic debut single, 'WHOLE WIDE WORLD'. An eponymous debut album appeared the following year as ERIC trooped out alongside the likes of ELVIS COSTELLO and IAN DURY on the riotous 'Stiff' live shindigs. Despite living in the shadow of such talented labelmates, the man turned out a fine follow-up set of more retro-styled, punk-influenced pop/rock, 'THE WONDERFUL WORLD OF WRECKLESS ERIC' (1978). Amid mounting pressure to achieve some kind of breakthrough, he penned his most commercial singles to date in 'HIT AND MISS JUDY' and 'A POP SONG'; chart success remained tantalisingly out of reach, however and WRECKLESS ERIC effectively bowed out of the scene with 1980's sardonically titled 'BIG SMASH'. Reverting back to his real name, GOULDEN eventually resurfaced in 1985 with 'A ROOMFUL OF MONKEYS', musical support coming from members of IAN DURY's BLOCKHEADS. The shortlived LEN BRIGHT COMBO was ERIC's next project before he finally relocated to France and enjoyed a fairly fruitful career with LE BEAT GROUP ELECTRIQUE alongside CATFISH TRUTON and ANDRE BARREAU. Signed to the 'New Rose' label initially, the trio released an eponymous debut in 1989, going on to record a mini-set, 'AT THE SHOP' (1990) and releasing 'THE DONOVAN OF TRASH' in 1991 on the 'Sympathy For The Record Industry' label. • **Songwriters:** GOULDEN compositions except; CRYING, WAITING, HOPING (Buddy Holly) / I WISH IT WOULD RAIN (Temptations) / etc.
Album rating: WRECKLESS ERIC (*5) / THE WONDERFUL WORLD OF . . .

(*6) / BIG SMASH (*7) / GREATEST HITS compilation (*7) / AT THE SHOP (*6) / GREATEST STIFFS compilation (*7) / Captains Of Industry: A ROOMFUL OF MONKEYS (*5) / Len Bright Combo: PRESENT THE . . . (*6) / COMBO TIME! (*5)

ERIC – vocals, guitar with **COLIN FLETCHER** – lead guitar / **WALTER MACON** – guitar / **JOHN BROWN** – bass / **DAVE OTWAY** – drums

	Stiff	Stiff
Aug 77. (7") *(BUY 16)* **WHOLE WIDE WORLD. / SEMAPHORE SIGNALS**		-
Feb 78. (7") *(BUY 25)* **RECONNEZ CHERIE. / RAGS AND TATTERS**		-

——— now with **CHARLIE HART** – keyboards / **STEVE CURRIE** – bass / **JOHN GLYN** – sax / + **DAVE OTWAY, DAVID WHITTON + STEVE GOLDING** – drums

Mar 78. (lp/10"brown-lp) *(SEEZ/+B 6)* **WRECKLESS ERIC**	46	-

– Reconnez Cherie / Rags and tatters / Waxworks / Telephoning home / Grown ups / Whole wide world / Personal hygiene / Brain thieves / There isn't anything else. *(cd-iss. Aug91 on 'Repertoire'; REP 4217WY)*

——— his new band were **MALCOLM MORLEY + BRADY** – guitar / **PETE SOLLEY** – keyboards / **JOHN BROWN** – bass / **GIER WADE** – drums

Oct 78. (7") *(BUY 34)* **TAKE THE K.A.S.H. / GIRLFRIEND**		-
Oct 78. (lp,green-lp,pic-lp) *(SEEZ 9)* **THE WONDERFUL WORLD OF . . .**		-

– Walking on the surface of the moon / Take the K.A.S.H. / Dizzy / Veronica / Roll over rock-ola / I wish it would rain / Let's go to the pictures / The final taxi / Girlfriend / Crying, waiting, hoping.

Dec 78. (7") *(BUY 40)* **CRYING, WAITING, HOPING. / I WISH IT WOULD RAIN**		-
Oct 79. (7") *(BUY 49)* **HIT AND MISS JUDY. / LET'S GO TO THE PICTURES**		-

(12"orange+=) *(BUYIT 49)* – I need a situation.

Oct 79. (7") *<OWN 1>* **TAKE THE CASH (K.A.S.H.). / LET'S GO TO THE PICTURES**	-	
Dec 79. (lp) *<USE 1>* **WHOLE WIDE WORLD** (compilation)	-	
Jan 80. (7") *(BUY 64)* **A POPSONG. / RECONNEZ CHERIE**		-

	Stiff	Stiff-Epic
Feb 80. (lp/c) *(SEEZ/ZSEEZ 21) <36463>* **BIG SMASH**	30	Apr80

– A popsong / Tonight (is my night) / Too busy / Broken doll / Can I be your hero / Back in my hometown / It'll soon be the weekend / Strange towns / Excuse me / Break my mind / Out of the blue / Good conversation. *(re-iss. Nov80 w/ free GREATEST HITS lp 'WHOLE WIDE WORLD')* – Whole wide world / Take the cash / Let's go to the pictures / Walking on the surface of the Moon / Hit & Miss Judy / I wish it would rain / Reconnez Cherie / Veronica / Brain thieves / Semaphore signals / I need a situation / The final taxi / There isn't anything else. *(cd-iss. Feb94 on 'Disky'; STIFFCD 13)*

Mar 80. (7") *(BUY 75)* **BROKEN DOLL. / I NEED A SITUATION**		-

(12"+=) *(BUYIT 75)* – A little bit more.

Apr 80. (7") *<50870>* **BROKEN DOLL. / A LITTLE BIT MORE**	-	

——— retired from the music biz in the early 80's.

CAPTAINS OF INDUSTRY

were formed by **ERIC GOULDEN** in 1983 with **MICKEY GALLAGHER** – keyboards + **NORMAN WATT-ROY** – bass (both ex-IAN DURY . . .) / **BAZ MURPHY** – organ / **DAVID ADLAND** – drums (ex-PIRANHAS)

	Go! Discs	not iss.
Nov 84. (7") *(GOD 6)* **LIFELINE. / A GIRL IN A MILLION**		-

——— Reduced band to a quartet when BAZ departed

May 85. (lp) *(AGOLP 5)* **A ROOMFUL OF MONKEYS**		-

– Land of the faint at heart / Our neck of the woods / Julie / Home and away / Lucky ones / Reputation (a serious case of . . .) / Food factory / Lifeline / Lady of the manor / Playtime is over.

——— **DAVE CLARKE** – keyboards + **BILL HILL** – bass; repl. MICKEY + NORM who rejoined IAN DURY

LEN BRIGHT COMBO

——— were **ERIC** – vocals, guitar plus **RUSS WILKINS** – bass / **BRUCE BRAND** – drums (both ex-MILKSHAKES)

	Empire	not iss.
Feb 86. (lp) *(NICE 1)* **THE LEN BRIGHT COMBO PRESENTS THE LEN BRIGHT COMBO**		-

– You're gonna screw my head off / Shirt without a heart / Selina through the windshield / Lureland / Young, upwardly mobile . . . and stupid / The golden hour of Harry Secombe / Sophie (the dream of Edmund Hirondelle Barnes).

Apr 86. (7") *(LEN 1)* **SOMEONE MUST'VE NAILED US TOGETHER. / MONA**		-

	Ambassador	not iss.
Nov 86. (lp) **IT'S COMBO TIME**		-

– Pleasant valley Wednesday / (Swimming against) The tide of reason / Cut off my head / The house burned down / Phasers on stun / The awakening of Edmund Hirondelle Barnes / All charm / Club 18 to 30 / Ticking in my corner.

——— In 1988, **ERIC** returned to his old moniker

WRECKLESS ERIC

——— with **CATFISH TRUTON + ANDRE BARREAU**

	New Rose	not iss.
Sep 89. (lp) *(ROSE 179)* **LE BEAT ELECTRIQUE**		-

– Tell me I'm the only one / Wishing my life away / Depression / It's a sick sick world / Just for you / Sarah / I'm not going to cry / The Sun is pouring down / You sweet big thing / Fuck by fuck / Parallel bells / True happiness. *(cd-iss. Jun94; 422396)*

Oct 89. (7") *(NEW 100)* **IT'S A SICK SICK WORLD. / RECONNEZ CHERIE**		-
May 90. (7") *(NEW 136)* **HAUNTED HOUSE. / DEPRESSION (version Francaise)**		-

WRECKLESS ERIC (cont)

May 90. (m-lp) *(NR 312)* **AT THE SHOP** (recorded live in a record store 1 day)
– Big old world / If it makes you happy / (Waiting for the shit) To hit the fan / Semaphore signals / Our neck of the woods / You're the girl for me. *(cd-iss. Jun94; 422395)*

Hangman / Sympathy F

Feb 93. (7") *<SFTRI 226>* **JOE MEEK. / TELL ME I'M THE ONLY ONE**

Mar 93. (lp) *(HANG 050UP) <SFTRI 230>* **THE DONOVAN OF TRASH**
– Birthday blues / Duvet fever / Joe Meek / The consolation prize / Semi-porno statuette / Schoo / The nerd / Turkey song / Lureland / Harry's flat / Haunted house / If it makes you happy / Paris in June. *(<cd-iss. Jul98 on 'Sympathy For The Record Industry'; SFTRI 230>)*

—— the Wreckless one retired once more

– compilations, etc. –

Mar 01. (cd) *Metro; (<METROCD 44>)* **GREATEST STIFFS**
– Whole wide world / Reconnez Cherie / Semaphore signals / Take the cash (K.A.S.H.) / A pop song / Personal hygiene / Tonight (is my night) / Hit and miss Judy / Walking on the surface of the Moon / Veronica / Let's go to the pictures / Waxworks / Broken doll / Excuse me / It'll soon be the weekend / Strange towns / I wish it would rain / Out of the blue / Grown ups / The final taxi.

X

Formed: Los Angeles, California, USA ... 1977 by EXENE CERVENKA, BILLY ZOOM, JOHN DOE and original drummer MICK BASHER (the latter subsequently replaced by DJ BONEBRAKE). After a one-off debut in 1978, 'ADULT BOOKS' (for the US 'Dangerhouse' imprint), X marked their spot with the then newly formed indie label, 'Slash'. Pioneers of the cowpunk scene alongside WALL OF VOODOO, The GUN CLUB, etc, the quartet enlisted the help of RAY MANZAREK, the former DOORS organist producing their debut set, 'LOS ANGELES' (1980). A rock hybrid of country and raw punk, X were obviously influenced by 60's garage punks the FUGS and MC5 with a tone of 50's rockabilly, this combination of musical styles used most effectively on follow-up set, 'WILD GIFT' (also recorded with MANZAREK at the helm). The MANZAREK connection continued when X moved to 'Elektra', their third album, 'UNDER THE BIG BLACK SUN' (1982) breaking them into the US Top 100. A fourth set, 'MORE FUN IN THE NEW WORLD' (1983), fared just as well commercially, although the band were in turn accused of selling out. The previous year, EXENE and LYDIA LUNCH had a book of poetry, 'Adulterers Anonymous' (with that title, it's not surprising that EXENE and JOHN were divorced in '84) published in the States, the X frontwoman subsequently teaming up with DOE, DAVE ALVIN (Blasters), HENRY ROLLINS (Black Flag) and JONNY RAY BARTEL to form country-rock outfit, The KNITTERS. The latter project obviously had an effect on X themselves (ALVIN had now replaced ZOOM), who emerged with a more countrified sound on 1985's 'AIN'T LOVE GRAND'. The following year ALVIN was deposed by ex-LONE JUSTICE guitarist, TONY GILKYSON, a fuller heavy sound beginning to manifest itself on 1987's 'SEE HOW WE ARE'. A commercially disastrous double-live set was their last for some time, although the band returned after other solo projects with a disappointing comeback set, 'HEY ZEUS!' (1993). • **Covered:** WILD THING (Troggs) / ALL OR NOTHING (Small Faces) / IT'S IN HIS KISS (Betty Everett) / SOUL KITCHEN (Doors) / POSITIVELY 4th STREET (Bob Dylan) / U.S. MALE (hit; Elvis Presley) / HOME MOTEL (Willie Nelson).

Album rating: LOS ANGELES (*8) / WILD GIFT (*8) / UNDER THE BIG BLACK SUN (*6) / MORE FUN IN THE NEW WORLD (*5) / AIN'T LOVE GRAND (*6) / SEE HOW WE ARE (*5) / LIVE AT THE WHISKEY A GO-GO (*5) / HEY ZEUS! (*4) / UNCLOGGED (*4)

EXENE CERVENKA (b. CHRISTINE CERVENKA, 1 Feb'56, Chicago, Illinois) – vocals / **BILLY ZOOM** – guitar / **JOHN DOE** (b. JOHN NOMMENSEN, 25 Feb'53, Decatur, Illinois) – bass, vocals / **D.J. BONEBRAKE** (b. DON, 8 Dec'55, Hollywood, Calif.) – drums repl. MICK BASHER

not iss. / Dangerhouse

Jun 78. (7") *<D 88>* **ADULT BOOKS. / WE'RE DESPERATE**

not iss. / Slash

Jun 80. (lp) *<SR 104>* **LOS ANGELES**
– Your phone's off the hook, but you're not / Johnny hit and run Pauline / Soul kitchen / Nausea / Sugarlight / Los Angeles / Sex and dying in high society / The unheard music / The world's a mess / It's in my kiss. *(cd-iss. Sep01 on 'Rhino'+=; 8122 74370-2)>* – I'm coming over / Adult books (demo) / Delta 88 (demo) / Cyrano De Berger's back (rehearsal) / Los Angeles (dangerhouse version).

May 81. (lp) *<SR 107>* **WILD GIFT**
– The once over twice / We're desperate / Adult books / Universal corner / I'm coming over / It's who you know / In this house that I call home / Some other time / White girl / Beyond and back / Back 2 the base / When our love passed out on the coach / Year 1. *<(cd-iss. Sep01 on 'Rhino'+=; 8122 74371-2)>* – Beyond and back (live) / Blue spark (demo) / We're desperate (single) / Back 2 the base (live) / Heater (rehearsal) / White girl (single) / The once over twice (single).

Aug 81. (7") *<SRS 106>* **WHITE GIRL. / YOUR PHONE'S OFF THE HOOK**

Elektra / Elektra

Jul 82. (7") *<69885>* **BLUE SPARK. / DANCING WITH TEARS IN MY EYES**

Jul 82. (lp) *(K 52401) <60150>* **UNDER THE BIG BLACK SUN** — 76
– The hungry wolf / Motel room in my bed / Riding with Mary / Come back to me / Under the big black sun / Because I do / Blue spark / Dancing with tears in my eyes / Real child of Hell / How I (learned my lesson) / The have nots. *<(cd-iss. Sep01 on 'Rhino'; 8122 74372-2)>* – Riding with Mary (single) / X rewrites "El Paso" (rehearsal) / Because I do (instrumental) / Universal corner (live) / Breathless (single) / How I (learned my lesson) (live).

Jun 83. (7") *<69825>* **BREATHLESS. / RIDING WITH MARY**

Sep 83. (lp/c) *(K 960283-1/-4) <60283>* **MORE FUN IN THE NEW WORLD** — 86
– The new world / We're having much more fun / True love / Poor girl / Make the music go bang / Breathless / I must not think bad thoughts / Devil doll /

X (cont) THE GREAT INDIE DISCOGRAPHY The 1970s

Painting the town blue / Hot house / Drunk in my past / I see red / True love #2. <(cd-iss. May02 on 'Rhino'+=; 8122 78257-2)> – Poor girl (demo) / True love #2 (demo) / Devil doll (demo) / I must not think bad thoughts (demo).
Jan 84. (7") (E 9779) **THE NEW WORLD. / I MUST NOT THINK BAD THOUGHTS**
Jun 84. (12") <66966> **WILD THING. / TRUE LOVE (part 2)**
Jun 84. (7") <69709> **WILD THING. / DEVIL DOLL**

— In 1985, JOHN DOE splintered with country-western project The KNITTERS. They included HENRY ROLLINS (of BLACK FLAG), DAVE ALVIN (of BLASTERS) + JOHNNY RAY BARTEL and made one album POOR LITTLE CRITTER ON THE ROAD. In fact, X brought in **DAVE ALVIN** – guitar to repl. BILLY

Aug 85. (7") (EKR 18) **BURNING HOUSE OF LOVE. / LOVE SHACK**
(12"+=) (EKRT 18) – Wild thing.
Sep 85. (lp) (EKT 12) <60430> **AIN'T LOVE GRAND**   89 Aug85
– Burning house of love / Love shack / My soul cries your name / My goodness / Around my heart / What's wrong with me . . . / All or nothing / Watch the sun go down / I'll stand up for you / Little honey / Supercharged. <(cd-iss. May02 on 'Rhino'+=; 8122 78258-2)> – Wild thing (extended) / I will dare (demo) / My goodness (demo) / All or nothing.

— **TONY GILKYSON** (b. 6 Aug'52) – guitar (ex-LONE JUSTICE) repl. ALVIN who went solo

Jul 87. (lp/c) (K 960492-1/-4) <60492> **SEE HOW WE ARE**
– I'm lost / You / 4th of July / In the time it takes / Anyone can fill your shoes / See how we are / Left & right / When it rains . . . / Holiday story / Surprise surprise / Cyrano de Bergerac's back. <(cd-iss. May02 on 'Rhino'+=; 8122 78259-2)> – Holiday story (demo) / I'm lost (demo remix) / Highway 61 revisited (rough take) / In the time it takes (demo) / See how we are (alt. take).
Jul 87. (7") <69462> **4th OF JULY. / POSITIVELY 4th STREET**
May 88. (d-lp/c/cd) (K 960788-1/-4/-2) <60788> **LIVE AT THE WHISKEY A GO-GO ON THE FABULOUS SUNSET STRIP (live)**
– Los Angeles / House I call home / The new world / Around my heart / Surprise surprise / Because I do / Burning house of love / My goodness / Blue spark / The once over twice / In the time it takes / Devil doll / Hungry wolf / Just another perfect day / Unheard music / Riding with Mary / The world's a mess / True love / White girl / Skin deep town / So long / Call of the wreckin' ball / Year 1 / Johnny hit a run / Pauline.

Oct 89. (7") **WILD THING. / (part 2)**   R.C.A. D.G.C.
(ext;12"+=/cd-s+=) – Oh you angel / U.S. male.

— split after this final flop, although they re-formed in 1993

Jun 93. (cd/c) <519261-2/-4> **HEY ZEUS!**   Big Life Mercury
– Someone's watching / Big blue house / Clean like tomorrow / New life / Country at war / Arms for hostages / Into the light / Lettuce and vodka / Everybody / Baby you lied / Drawn in the dark.
Jul 93. (c-s) (BLRC 94) **COUNTRY AT WAR / YOU WOULDN'T TELL ME**
(12"+=/cd-s+=) (BLR T/D 94) – Drawn in the dark (acoustic).
Jun 95. (cd) <10812> **UNCLOGGLED** (acoustic live)   not iss. Infidelity
– White girl / Because I do / Lying in the road / Unheard music / I must not think bad thoughts / Burning house of love / Stage / See how we are / True love / Have nots / The world's a mess, it's in my kiss / I see red / What's wrong with me.

— when they finally split, EXENE fronted the band AUNTIE CHRIST who had signed to 'Lookout!'; included in their ranks, MATT FREEMAN (of RANCID).

– compilations, etc. –

Oct 97. (d-cd) Elektra; <62103> **BEYOND & BACK: THE X ANTHOLOGY**
– Los Angeles / The world's a mess, it's in his kiss / Yr ignition / Year one / Hungry wolf / We're desperate / Beyond and back / Back 2 the base / Blue spark / Some other time / Sex and dying in high society / Motel room in my bed / Heater / Once over twice / Because I do / In this house I call home / Soul kitchen / Universal corner / Delta 88 / Real child of hell / I'm coming over / White girl / Nausea / Johnny hit and run Paulene / My phone's off the hook but you're / Riding with Mary / New world / Breathless / Poor girl / What's wrong with me / How I (learned my lesson) / Have nots / Someone like you / Stage / See how we are / Surprise, surprise / 4th of July / Arms for hostages – Country at war / Wild thing / Burning house of love / Devil doll / True love / Call of the wreckin' ball / In the time it takes / I must not think bad thoughts.
Feb 00. (cd) Ascension; (XCD 1) **LIVE AT THE STAGEDOOR TAVERN (live)**
Jul 01. (lp/cd) Drop Kick; <(BEHIND 016/+CD)> **LIVE AT THE CIVIC 1979 (live)**

JOHN DOE

— with band; **JOHN DEE GRAHAM** – guitar / **RICHARD LLOYD** – guitar (ex-TELEVISION) / **TONY MARSICO** – bass / **JEFF DONAVAN** – drums
                                                                                D.G.C. D.G.C.
Jun 90. (cd/c/lp) <(7599 24291-2/-4/-1)> **MEET JOHN DOE**
– Let's be mad / A matter of degrees / Dyin' to get home / It's only love / The real one / Take #52 / Worldwide brotherhood / With someone like you / By the light / Knockin' around / Touch me, baby / My offering.

— next with various session people including EXENE + DJ BONEBRAKE (actress SANDRA BERNHARD also makes an appearance)

1995. (cd) <72134> **KISSINGSOHARD**   Forward Rhino
– Fallen tears / Safety / Love knows / Mo goodness / Tragedy by definition / Kissing / Hits the ground / Going down fast / TV set / Beer, gas, ride forever / Field of dirt / Williamette / Liar's market.
                                                                            not iss. Kill Rock Stars
Jan 98. (cd-ep; as JOHN THING DOE) <KRS 290> **FOR THE REST OF US**
– Step outside / Let's get lost / Unhappy song / Bad, bad feeling / This loving thing.

EXENE CERVENKA

                                                                            not iss. Freeway
Jan 86. (lp; EXENE CERVENKA WANDA COLEMAN) <FRWY 1057> **TWIN SISTERS: LIVE AT McCABE'S** (live poetry)

— with **TONY GILKYSON / STEVE NELSON / JIM CHRISTIE / KEN STRANGE / JULIE CHRISTENSEN / ELIZA GILKYSON** etc
                                                                            not iss. Rhino
1989. (lp/c/cd) <R2/R4/R1 70913> **OLD WIVES' TALES**
– She wanted / Biggest memory / Here come the crucifiers / Cocktail trees / Famous barmaid / Leave Heaven alone / Good luck / White trash wife / He's got a she / Gravel / Coyote on the town.
1990. (cd/c) <R2/R4 70757> **RUNNING SCARED**
– Slave labor / Clinic / Red dirt / Real estate / Curtains / The boy and his sister / Same denomination / Missing nature / It fell / The ballad of Roberta / Just another perfect day / Will Jesus wash the bloodstains from our souls.

— EXENE also released an album, 'RUDE HIEROGLYPHICS', with LYDIA LUNCH
                                                                            2.13.61 Thirsty Ear
Jun 96. (cd) <(213CD 04)> **SURFACE TO AIR SERPENTS**
– Big stain / Dream bodies / In the year of the ant / Unfortunate / Flies without borders / Living / Closing numbers / Truce / Magdalene / Deep end / Like morning / Three stories / Clay / I want questions / I want answers / I want / Good, then its unanimous/ Being and everythingness / Waiting / Hello / Debate / What is there to be at one with?

X-RAY SPEX

Formed: Brixton, London, England . . . 1977 by POLY STYRENE, JAK 'AIRPORT' STAFFORD, LORA LOGIC, PAUL DEAN and B.P. HURDING. Fronted by the inimitable STYRENE (a woman who turned metal-braced dentures and figure hugging black bin-liners into a punk fashion statement!), the group secured a residency at the infamous Roxy club, contributing live favourite, 'OH BONDAGE, UP YOURS!' to the club's celebrated v/a compilation. A considerably tamer studio version was released on 'Virgin' in late '77, after which STEVE 'RUDI' THOMPSON replaced LORA as the band's in-house sax player. Together with STYRENE's banshee wail, the demented sax honking (employed in a STOOGES kinda fashion) marked out X-RAY SPEX from the three-chord hordes and put a groovy spin on such memorable singles as 'THE DAY THE WORLD TURNED DAY-GLO' (the group's first single for 'E.M.I.' and the first of three chart hits), the seething 'IDENTITY' and 'GERMFREE ADOLESCENTS'. The latter track was also the title of the band's one and only album, STYRENE venting her spleen/wondering aloud at the absurdities of a production line society; listen to 'WARRIOR IN WOOLWORTHS' and weep, possibly. Released in late '78, the album made the Top 30 and spawned a further single in 'HIGHLY INFLAMMABLE' the following Spring. In true punk style, however, the band disbanded while their influence was being felt most acutely, only HURDING going on to anything resembling fame with CLASSIX NOUVEAUX. STYRENE, meanwhile, opted for Krishna consciousness, releasing a suitably blissed out solo set, 'TRANSLUCENCE' (1980), before taking an extended sabbatical. Finally, in 1995, STYRENE resurrected the original X-RAY SPEX line-up and released 'CONSCIOUS CONSUMER' on the independent 'Receiver' label.

Album rating: GERMFREE ADOLESCENTS (*8) / CONSCIOUS CONSUMER (*5) / ANTHOLOGY double compilation (*7) / Poly Strene: TRANSLUCENCE (*5)

POLY STYRENE (b. MARION ELLIOT, 1962) – vocals / **JAK 'AIRPORT' STAFFORD** – guitar / **LORA LOGIC** (b. SUSAN WHITBY, 1961) – saxophone / **PAUL DEAN** – bass / **B.P.HURDING** (b. CHRIS CHRYSLER) – drums
                                                                            Virgin not iss.
Oct 77. (7"/12") (VS 189/+12) **OH BONDAGE! UP YOURS!. / I AM A CLICHE**

— **STEVE 'RUDI' THOMPSON** – saxophone repl. LORA who formed ESSENTIAL LOGIC
                                                                            EMI Internat. E.M.I.
Mar 78. (7",7"orange) (INT 553) **THE DAY THE WORLD TURNED DAY-GLO. / IAMA POSEUR**   23
Jul 78. (7",7"pink) (INT 563) **IDENTITY. / LET'S SUBMERGE**   24
Oct 78. (7") (INT 573) **GERMFREE ADOLESCENTS. / AGE**   19
Nov 78. (lp/c) (INS/TCINS 3023) **GERMFREE ADOLESCENTS**   30
– The day the world turned day-glo / Obsessed with you / Genetic engineering / Identity / I live off you / Germfree adolescents / Art-i-ficial / Let's submerge / Warrior in Woolworths / Iama poseur / I can't do anything / Highly inflammable / Age / Plastic bag / I am a cliche / Oh bondage up yours!. (re-iss. Jun92 on 'Virgin' cd/c; CDTC/TC VM 9001) <US cd-iss. 1991 on 'Caroline'; CAROL 1813-2>
Apr 79. (7",7"red) (INT 583) **HIGHLY INFLAMMABLE. / WARRIOR IN WOOLWORTHS**   45

— **JOHN GLIN** – saxophone repl. THOMPSON. Disbanded soon after, GLIN formed The LIVING LEGEND. JAK and PAUL formed AIRPORT & DEAN, while HURDING joined CLASSIX NOUVEAUX.

POLY STYRENE

went solo augmented by **GT MOORE** – guitar / **RICHARD MOORE** – guitar / **KEVIN McALEA** – keyboards / **KUMA KARADA** – bass / **RICHARD BAILEY** – drums / **TED BUNTING** – horns / **DARYLL LEE QUE** – percussion
                                                                            U.A. not iss.
Sep 80. (7") (BP 370) **TALK IN TOYTOWN. / SUB-TROPICAL**
Nov 80. (lp) (UAG 30320) **TRANSLUCENCE**
– Dreaming / Talk in Toytown / Sky diver / The day that time forgot / Shades /

Essence / Hip city / Bicycle song / Sub-tropical / Translucent / Age / Goodbye. *(re-iss. Mar90 on 'Receiver' cd/c/lp; RRCD/RRLC/RRLP 128)*

— POLY (MARION) took a long sabbatical to bring up her family; she returned to the studio after five years.

Aug 86. (7"ep/12"ep) *(AOR 7/+T)* **GODS AND GODDESSES** [Awesome] [not iss.]
– Trick of the witch / Paramatma / Sacred temple / Big boys, big toys.

— In 1990, POLY was part of The DREAM ACADEMY

X-RAY SPEX

— re-formed with **POLY STYRENE / LAURA LOGIC / PAUL DEAN + HURDING**

Oct 95. (cd) *(<RRCD 205>)* **CONSCIOUS CONSUMER** [Receiver] [Receiver]
– Cigarettes / Junk food junkie / Crystal / India / Dog in Sweden / Hi chaperone / Good time girl / Melancholy / Sophia / Peace meal / Prayer for peace / Party.

– compilations, etc. –

Mar 91. (cd/c/lp) *Receiver; (<RR CD/MC/LP 140>)* **LIVE AT THE ROXY CLUB (live)**
Jul 91. (cd/lp) *Receiver; (<RR CD/LP 145>)* **OBSESSED WITH YOU**
Oct 01. (d-cd) *Castle; (<CMDDD 369>)* **ANTHOLOGY** — Mar02

XTC

Formed: Swindon, Wiltshire, England ... 1976 after 3 years of calling themselves The HELIUM KIDZ. Not an early version of acid house as the name might suggest, XTC traded in a quirky blend of pop that owed more to quintessential English psychedelia than the nihilistic three chord assault of their punk peers. Nevertheless, they were picked up by 'Virgin' in the signing scramble that followed The SEX PISTOLS early success in 1977. The debut album, 'WHITE MUSIC' (1978), introduced their tentative art-pop sound, PARTRIDGE's songwriting talent much in evidence even at this early stage. The JOHN LECKIE produced 'GO 2' (1978) was a more sonically adventurous follow-up, heavily influenced by BRIAN ENO and moulding their pop with quirky electronica. Soon after the record's release, ANDREWS left to join ROBERT FRIPP's 'LEAGUE OF GENTLEMEN' and was replaced by DAVE GREGORY. The new improved unit cut the successful 'DRUMS AND WIRES' (1979) album which spawned a top 20 hit single, the hypnotic, MOULDING-penned 'MAKING PLANS FOR NIGEL'. The rest of the tracks were just as catchy in their distinctive, left-of-centre way. This signalled the onset of a punishing touring/recording schedule during which time the band released a succession of impressive singles, some of which went top 20 and an album, 'BLACK SEA' (1980), that hinted at the psychedelic nostalgia which would characterise their later output. 'ENGLISH SETTLEMENT' (1982) is generally held to be band's finest hour. A double set, the record artfully blended rustic folk, ethnic rhythms and synthesizer pop, all shot through with the spectral hue of psychedelia. Although the stellar single, 'SENSES WORKING OVERTIME' was one of the band's biggest hits and XTC looked to be headed for the big time, PARTRIDGE, never comfortable with live performance, was dreading the inevitable round of touring. In the event, after a few disastrous shows he decided he could suffer it no longer and shortly after, announced that the band would never tour again. CHAMBERS promptly left, unhappy with such a prospect and although PARTRIDGE was now suffering from Agoraphobia, the band struggled on. With no full-time drummer and a string of producers, 'MUMMER' (1983) and 'THE BIG EXPRESS' (1983) were inconsistent and lacking in direction although 'EVERYDAY STORY OF SMALLTOWN' from the latter set was a charming piece of nostalgia-pop. It was clear the band needed some fresh inspiration and with the help of JOHN LECKIE they cut the '25 O'CLOCK' mini-album in 1985 under the pseudonym DUKES OF STRATOSPHERE. More overtly psychedelic than any previous XTC material, PARTRIDGE was given free range to indulge his obvious passions. Re-energised, the band were paired with TODD RUNDGREN for 'SKYLARKING' (1986) and although there were some well documented clashes between PARTRIDGE and the maverick American, the resultant album was a triumphant return to form. Embellishing the gentle hybrid of 'ENGLISH SETTLEMENT' with a 'PET SOUNDS'-like sonic richness, the album swayed the sultry single 'GRASS'. Its B-side, the semi-acoustic sweep of 'DEAR GOD' was picked up by American radio, with the end result that 'SKYLARKING' was a considerable stateside success. After a final DUKES OF STRATOSPHERE album, 'PSONIC PSUNSPOT', XTC began work on the 'ORANGES AND LEMONS' set. Released in 1989, the album was another resounding success, creatively at least, and spawned the charming 'MAYOR OF SIMPLETON' single. While the album was a relative success in America, it failed to make any lasting impact in the UK and after 'NONESUCH' (1992) stiffed completely, XTC faded into obscurity. Although sightings are rare, PARTRIDGE has surfaced occasionally, notably on the HAROLD BUDD collaboration, 'THROUGH THE HILL', in 1994. Without even an inkling that songwriters PARTRIDGE and MOULDING were about to unleash a new episode of quirky pop tunes, the public were happy to find out XTC were once again planning their comeback. Delivered early '99 for 'Cooking Vinyl', 'APPLE VENUS VOLUME 1' saw Swindon's finest regain the ground they had lost while securing a Top 30 entry in the process. The record's swelling, organic orchestrations delighted many longtime fans and whetted appetites for a follow-up. In the event, 'WASP STAR (APPLE VENUS, PT.2)' (2000) was a more straightforward XTC album rather than a continuation of its predecessor's grandiose pop, concentrating on the kind of nuts and bolts material that the band have long made their own. • **Covered:** ALL ALONG THE WATCHTOWER (Bob Dylan) / ELLA GURU (Captain Beefheart).

Album rating: WHITE MUSIC (*8) / GO 2 (*4) / DRUMS AND WIRES (*8) / BLACK SEA (*7) / ENGLISH SETTLEMENT (*8) / WAXWORKS (SOME SINGLES 1977-82) compilation (*8) / BEESWAX (SOME B-SIDES 1977-82) compilation (*5) / MUMMER (*7) / THE BIG EXPRESS (*7) / SKYLARKING (*8) / THE COMPACT XTC – THE SINGLES 1978-1985 (*8) / ORANGES AND LEMONS (*7) / EXPLODE TOGETHER (THE DUB EXPERIMENTS '78-'80) exploitation (*4) / RAG 'N' BONE BUFFET collection (*5) / NONESUCH (*8) / FOSSIL FUEL: THE XTC SINGLES 1977-1992 compilation (*8) / APPLE VENUS VOLUME 1 (*7) / WASP STAR – APPLE VENUS VOLUME 2 (*6) / Andy Partridge: TAKE AWAY (THE LURE OF SALVAGE) (*5) / Dukes Of Stratosfear: 25 O'CLOCK mini (*4) / PSONIC PSUNSPOT (*5)

ANDY PARTRIDGE (b.11 Dec'53) – vocals, guitar / **COLIN MOULDING** (b.17 Aug'55) – bass, vocals / **BARRY ANDREWS** (b.12 Sep'56, London) – keyboards repl. JONATHAN PERKINS / **TERRY CHAMBERS** (b.18 Jul'55) – drums

	Virgin	Virgin-Epic
Oct 77. (7") *(VS 188)* **SCIENCE FRICTION. / SHE'S SO SQUARE** (12"ep+=) *(VS 188-12)* **3-D** – Dance band.		-
Jan 78. (7") *(VS 201)* **STATUE OF LIBERTY. / HANG ON TO THE NIGHT**		-
Feb 78. (lp/c) *(<V/TCV 2095>)* **WHITE MUSIC**	38	

– Radios in motion / Cross wires / This is pop? / Do what you do / Statue of liberty / All along the watchtower / Into the atom age / I'll set myself on fire / I'm bugged / New town animal in a furnished cage / Neon shuffle. *(re-iss. Mar84 lp/c; OVED/+C 60) (cd-iss. Mar87 +=; CDV 2095)* – Science friction / She's so square / Dance band / Hang on to the night / Heatwave / Traffic light rock / Instant tunes. *(cd re-iss. Jun01 +=; CDVX 2095) <US cd-iss. May02 on 'Caroline'+=; 50691>*

Apr 78. (7") *(VS 209)* **THIS IS POP?. / HEATWAVE**		-
Oct 78. (7") *(VS 231)* **ARE YOU RECEIVING ME. / INSTANT TUNES**		-
Oct 78. (lp/c) *(<V/TCV 2108>)* **GO 2**	21	

– Mekanic dancing (oh we go!) / Battery brides / Buzzcity talking / Crowded room / The rhythm / Beatown / My weapon / Life is good in the greenhouse / Jumping in Gomorrah / My weapon / Super-tuff. *(free-12"ep w/ lp)* **GO +** – Dance with me Germany / Beat the bible / A dictionary of modern marriage / Clap, clap, clap / We kill the beast. *(re-iss. Mar84 lp/c; OVED/+C 61) (cd-iss. Jul87 +=; CDV 2108)* – Are you receiving me. *(cd re-iss. Jun01 +=; CDVX 2108) <US cd-iss. Jun02 on 'Caroline'+=; 50666>*

— **DAVE GREGORY** – synthesizers, guitar repl. ANDREWS who joined LEAGUE OF GENTLEMEN (w/ ROBERT FRIPP). He later went solo and formed SHRIEKBACK

May 79. (7",7"clear) *(VS 259)* **LIFE BEGINS AT THE HOP. / HOMO SAFARI**	54	-
	Virgin	Virgin Atlantic
Aug 79. (lp/c) *(V/TCV 2129) <VA 13134>* **DRUMS AND WIRES**	34	

– Making plans for Nigel / Helicopter / Life begins at the hop / When you're near me I have difficulty / Ten feet tall / Roads girdle the globe / Reel by reel / Millions / That is the way / Outside world / Scissor man / Complicated game. *(free-7"w/ lp)* – LIMELIGHT. / CHAIN OF COMMAND *(re-iss. 1986 lp/c; OVED/+C 113) (cd-iss. Jun88 +=; CDV 2129)* – Limelight / Chain of command. *(cd re-mast.Jun01 +=; CDVX 2129) <US cd-iss. Aug02 on 'Caroline'; 50653>*

Sep 79. (7"m) *(VS 282)* **MAKING PLANS FOR NIGEL. / BUSHMAN PRESIDENT (HSS 2) / PULSING, PULSING**	17	-
Nov 79. (7") **TEN FEET TALL. / HELICOPTER / THE SOMNAMBULIST**	-	
Feb 80. (7"m) *<VA 67009>* **MAKING PLANS FOR NIGEL. / THIS IS POP? / MEKANIC DANCING (OH WE GO!)**	-	
Mar 80. (7") *(VS 322)* **WAIT TILL YOUR BOAT GOES DOWN. / TEN FEET TALL (U.S. version)**		
Aug 80. (7") *(VS 365)* **GENERALS AND MAJORS. / DON'T LOSE YOUR TEMPER**	32	
(d7"+=) *(VS 365)* – Smokeless zone. / The somnambulist.		
Sep 80. (lp/c) *(V/TCV 2173) <VA 13147>* **BLACK SEA**	16	41

– Respectable Street / Generals and majors / Living through another Cuba / Love at first sight / Rocket from a bottle / No language in our lungs / Towers of London / Paper and iron (notes and coins) / Burning with optimism's flames / Sgt. Rock (is going to help me) / Travels in Nihilon. *(re-iss. 1986 lp/c; OVED/+C 83) (cd-iss. Mar87 +=; CDV 2172)* – Smokeless zone / Don't lose your temper / The somnambulist. *(cd re-mast.Jun01 +=; CDVX 2173) <US cd-iss. Jun02 on 'Caroline'+=; 50666>*

Oct 80. (7") *(VS 372)* **TOWERS OF LONDON. / SET MYSELF ON FIRE (live)**	31	
(d7"+=) *(VS 372)* – Battery brides (live) / Scissor man.		
Oct 80. (7"; as The COLONEL) *(VS 380)* **TOO MANY COOKS IN THE KITCHEN. / I NEED PROTECTION**		-
(above by The COLONEL; aka MOULDING + CHAMBERS)		
Nov 80. (7") *(RSO 71)* **TAKE THIS TOWN. / (b-side by The Ruts)**		
(above single was from 'Times Square' film soundtrack on 'R.S.O.')		
Dec 80. (7") **LOVE AT FIRST SIGHT. / ROCKET FROM A BOTTLE**	-	
Jan 81. (7"m) *(VS 384)* **SGT. ROCK (IS GOING TO HELP ME). / LIVING THROUGH ANOTHER CUBA (live) / GENERALS AND MAJORS (live)**	16	
Mar 81. (7"m) *(VS 407)* **RESPECTABLE STREET. / STRANGE TAILS, STRANGE TAILS / OFFICER BLUE**		
	Virgin	Epic
Jan 82. (7"m) *(VS 462)* **SENSES WORKING OVERTIME. / BLAME THE WEATHER / TISSUE TIGERS**	10	-
(12"+=) *(VS 462-12)* – Egyptian solution (HSS 3).		
Feb 82. (d-lp/c)<US-lp> *(V/TCV 2223) <37943>* **ENGLISH SETTLEMENT**	5	48 Mar82

– Runaways / Ball and chain / Senses working overtime / Jason and the Argonauts / No thugs in our house / Yacht dance / All of a sudden (it's too late) / Melt the guns / ** Leisure / It's nearly Africa * / Knuckle down * / Fly on the wall * / ** Down in the cockpit * / English roundabout / Snowman. *<US single-lp version omits *> (cd-iss. Jun88 +=; CDV 2223); omits tracks **) (cd re-iss. Jun01 +=; CDVX 2223)*

XTC (cont)

Mar 82. (7"m) *(VS 482)* **BALL AND CHAIN. / PUNCH AND JUDY / HEAVEN IS PAVED WITH BROKEN GLASS** 58
(12"+=) *(VS 482-12)* – Cockpit dance mixture.
May 82. (7"ep,9"ep) *(VS 490)* **NO THUGS IN OUR HOUSE / CHAIN OF COMMAND. / LIMELIGHT / OVER RUSTY WALLS** –
May 82. (7") **SENSES WORKING OVERTIME. / ENGLISH ROUNDABOUT** –
Nov 82. (lp/c) *(V/TCV 2251)* **WAXWORKS (SOME SINGLES 1977-82)** (compilation) 54 –
(free lp w/ above) **BEESWAX (SOME B-SIDES 1977-82)** (re-iss. Dec82 lp/c; OVED/+C 9)

—— trimmed to basic trio of **PARTRIDGE, MOULDING + GREGORY** plus on session **PETER PHIPPES** – drums (ex-GLITTER BAND) (CHAMBERS emigrated to Australia)

                          Virgin Geffen

Apr 83. (7") *(VS 553)* **GREAT FIRE. / GOLD** – –
(12"+=) *(VS 553-12)* – Frost circus (HSS 5) / Procession towards learning land (HSS 6).
Jul 83. (7"/7"pic-d) *(VS/+Y 606)* **WONDERLAND. / JUMP**
Aug 83. (lp/c) *(V/TCV 2264)* <4027> **MUMMER** 51
– Beating of hearts / Wonderland / Love on a farmboy's wages / Great fire / Deliver us from the elements / Human alchemy / Ladybird / In loving memory of a name / Me and the wind / Funk pop a roll. (re-iss. 1986 lp/c; OVED/+C 142) (cd-iss. Mar87 +=; CDV 2264) – Frost circus (HSS 5) / Jump / Toys / Gold / Procession towards learning land (HSS 6) / Desert island. (cd re-iss. Jun01 +=; CDVX 2264) <US cd-iss. Aug02 on 'Caroline' +=; 50672>
Sep 83. (7") *(VS 613)* **LOVE ON A FARMBOY'S WAGES. / IN LOVING MEMORY OF A NAME** 50
(d7"+=) *(VS 613)* – Desert island / Toys.
(12") *(VS 613-12)* – ('A'side) / Burning with optimism's flames (live / English roundabout (live) / Cut it out (live).
Nov 83. (7"; as THREE WISE MEN) *(VS 642)* **THANKS FOR CHRISTMAS. / COUNTDOWN TO CHRISTMAS PARTYTIME** –
Sep 84. (7") *(VS 709)* **ALL YOU PRETTY GIRLS. / WASHAWAY** 55 –
(12"+=) *(VS 709-12)* – Red brick dream.
Oct 84. (lp/c) *(V/TCV 2325)* <24054> **THE BIG EXPRESS** 38
– Wake up / All you pretty girls / Shake you donkey up / Seagulls screaming kiss her, kiss her / This world over / The everyday story of Smalltown / I bought myself a liarbird / Reign of blows / You're the wish you are I had / I remember the sun / Train running low on soul coal. (re-iss. 1987 +=; CDV 2325) – Red brick dreams / Washaway / Blue overall. (re-iss. 1988 lp/c; OVED/+C 142) (cd re-iss. Jun01 +=; CDVX 2325)
Oct 84. (7"/12") *(VS 721/+12)* **THIS WORLD OVER. / BLUE OVERALL**
Jan 85. (7"m) *(VS 746)* **WAKE UP. / TAKE THIS TOWN / MANTIS ON PAROLE (HSS 4)**
(12"+=) *(VS 746-12)* – Making plans for Nigel / Sgt. Rock (is going to help me) / Senses working overtime.

—— **IAN GREGORY** (DAVE's brother) – drums repl. PHIPPES

DUKES OF STRATOSPHEAR

Apr 85. (7") *(VS 763)* **THE MOLE FROM THE MINISTRY. / MY LOVE EXPLODES** –
Apr 85. (m-lp/c) *(WOW/+C 1)* **25 O'CLOCK**
– 25 o'clock / Bike ride to the Moon / My love explodes / What in the world . . . / Your gold dress / The mole from the ministry.

XTC

Aug 86. (7") *(VS 882)* **GRASS. / DEAR GOD**
(12"+=) *(VS 882-12)* – Extrovert.
Oct 86. (lp/c/cd) *(V/TCV/CDV 2399)* <24117> **SKYLARKING** 90 70
– Summer's cauldron / Grass / The meeting place / That's really super, Supergirl / Ballet for a rainy day / 1000 umbrellas / Season cycle / Earn enough for us / Big day / Another satellite / Mermaid smiled * / The man who sailed around his soul / Dying / Sacrificial bonfire. <re-iss. 1987; 'Dear God' repl. *> (cd re-iss. Jun01 +=; CDVX 2399)
Jan 87. (7"/7"clear) *(VS/+Y 912)* **THE MEETING PLACE. / THE MAN WHO SAILED AROUND HIS SOUL**
(12"+=) *(VS 912-12)* – Terrorism.
Jun 87. (7") *(VS 960)* **DEAR GOD. / BIG DAY** –
(12"+=) *(VS 960-12)* – Another satellite (live).
(cd-s) *(CDEP 3)* – ('A'side) / Homo safari series (HSS 1-6):- Homo safari / Bushman president / Egyptian solution / Mantis on parole / Frost circus / Procession towards learning land.
Jul 87. (7") **DEAR GOD. / MERMAID SMILED** –

DUKES OF STRATOSPHEAR

Jul 87. (7"/7"colrd) *(VS/+Y 982)* **YOU'RE A GOOD MAN ALBERT BROWN (CURSE YOU RED BARREL). / VANISHING GIRL** –
(12"+=) *(VS 982-12)* – The mole from the ministry / My love explodes.
Aug 87. (lp/colrd-lp/c) *(V/VP/TCV 2440)* **PSONIC PSUNSPOT**
– Vanishing girl / Have you seen Jackie? / Little lighthouse / You're a good man Albert Brown (curse you red barrel) / Collideascope / You're my drug / Shiny cage / Brainiac's daughter / The affiliated / Pale and precious.
1989. (cd) *(COMCD 11)* **CHIPS FROM THE CHOCOLATE FIREBALL**
– (25 O'CLOCK / PSONIC PSUNSPOT)

XTC

—— **PAT MASTELOTTO** – drums (of MR. MISTER) repl. IAN
Jan 89. (7") *(VS 1158)* **THE MAYOR OF SIMPLETON. / ONE OF THE MILLIONS** 46 72
(12"+=) *(VST 1158)* – Ella guru.
(3"cd-s) *(VSCD 1158)* – ('A'side) / Ella guru / Living in a haunted heart / The good thing.
(12") *(VSR 1158)* – ('A'side) / Dear God / Senses working overtime / Making plans for Nigel.

Feb 89. (d-lp/c/cd) *(V/TCV/CDV 2581)* <24218> **ORANGES AND LEMONS** 28 44
– Garden of earthly delights / The Mayor of Simpleton / King for a day / Here comes President Kill again / The loving / Poor skeleton steps out / One of the millions / Scarecrow people / Merely a man / Cynical days / Across this antheap / Hold me my daddy / Pink thing / Miniature sun / Chalkhills and children. (re-iss. Oct89, 3xcd-ep-box; CDVT 2581) (cd re-iss. Jun01; CDVX 2581)
Apr 89. (7") *(VS 1177)* **KING FOR A DAY. / HAPPY FAMILIES** –
(12"+=) *(VST 1177)* – ('A'extended).
(c-s+=) *(VSC 1177)* – Generals and majors / Towers of London.
(3"cd-s+=) *(VSCD 1177)* – ('A'extended) / ('A'side) / My paint heroes (home demo) / Skeletons (home demo).
Aug 89. (7") *(VS 1201)* **THE LOVING. / CYNICAL DAYS** –
(c-s) *(VSC 1201)* – ('A'side) / The world is full of angry young men.
(12"/cd-s) *(VS T/CD 1201)* – (all 3 tracks).
Sep 89. (cd-ep) <9-21236-2> **KING FOR A DAY (Czar mix) / ('A' Versailles mix) / TOYS / DESERT ISLAND** –
Mar 92. (7"/c-s) *(VS/+C 1404)* **THE DISAPPOINTED. / THE SMARTEST MONKEYS** 33 –
(10"+=) *(VST 1404)* – Humble Daisy.
(cd-s++=) *(VSCD 1404)* – ('B'demo).
May 92. (cd/c/d-lp) *(CD/TC/V 2699)* <24474> **NONESUCH** 28 97
– The ballad of Peter Pumpkinhead / My bird performs / Dear Madam Barnum / Humble Daisy / The smartest monkeys / The dismal / Holly up on poppy / Crocodile Rook / Omnibus / That wave / Then she appeared / War dance / Wrapped in grey / The ugly underneath / Bungalow / Books are burning. (cd re-iss. Jun01; CDVX 2699)
Jun 92. (7"/c-s) *(VS/+C 1415)* **THE BALLAD OF PETER PUMPKINHEAD. / WAR DANCE** 71 –
(cd-s+=) *(VSCD1 1415)* – Down a peg (demo) / ('A'demo).
(cd-s+=) *(VSCD2 1415)* – My bird performs (demo) / Always winter never Christmas (demo).

—— **PARTRIDGE + MOULDING** re-formed six years later

—— additional musicians **DAVE GREGORY, PRAIRIE PRINCE**, etc

                          Cooking Vinyl T.V.T.

Feb 99. (lp/c/cd) *(COOK/+C/CD 172)* <3250> **APPLE VENUS VOLUME 1** 42
– River of orchids / I'd like that / Easter theatre / Knights in shining karma / Frivolous tonight / Greenman / Your dictionary / Fruit nut / I can't own her / Harvest festival / Last balloon.
Apr 99. (cd-s) *(FRYCD 080)* **EASTER THEATRE / EASTER THEATRE (home demo) / HOW EASTER THEATRE CAME TO BE** –
Jun 99. (cd-s) *(FRYCD 083)* **I'D LIKE THAT / I'D LIKE THAT (home demo) / HOW I'D LIKE THAT CAME TO B** –
Sep 99. (lp/cd) *(COOK/+CD 188)* **HOMESPUN (APPLE VENUS VOLUME 1 HOME DEMOS)** –
May 00. (lp/c/cd) *(COOK/+C/CD 194)* <3260> **WASP STAR – APPLE VENUS VOLUME 2** 40
– Playground / Stupidly happy / In another life / My brown guitar / Boarded up / I'm the man who murdered love / We're all light / Standing in for Joe / Wounded horse / You and the clouds will still be beautiful / Church of women / The wheel and the maypole.
Jul 00. (cd-s) *(FRYCD 095)* **I'M THE MAN WHO MURDERED LOVE (mixes) / DIDN'T HURT A BIT** –

– compilations, others, etc. –

on 'Virgin' unless otherwise mentioned

Jan 87. (cd) *(CDV 2251)* **THE COMPACT XTC – THE SINGLES 1978-1985** –
– Science friction / Statue of liberty / This is pop? / Are you receiving me / Life begins at the hop / Making plans for Nigel / Wait till your boat goes down / Generals and majors / Towers of London / Sgt. Rock (is going to help me) / Senses working overtime / Ball and chain / Great fire / Wonderland / Love on a farmboy's wages / All you pretty girls / This world over / Wake up.
Jul 88. (3"cd-ep) *(VSCDT 9)* **SENSES WORKING OVERTIME / BLAME THE WEATHER / TISSUE TIGERS**
Nov 88. (7") *Old Gold; (OG 9819)* **MAKING PLANS FOR NIGEL. / SENSES WORKING OVERTIME**
Aug 90. (cd) *(CDOVD 308)* **EXPLODE TOGETHER (THE DUB EXPERIMENTS 78-80)**
– (included the ANDY PARTRIDGE album below)
Aug 90. (cd) *(CDOVD 311) / Geffen; <24417>* **RAG & BONE BUFFET (rare)**
Nov 94. (cd) *Night Tracks; (CDNT 008)* **DRUMS AND WIRELESS: BBC RADIO SESSIONS 77-89**
Jun 96. (d-cd) *Geffen; <25137>* **UPSY DAISY ASSORTMENT (A SELECTION OF SWEETEST HITS)** –
Sep 96. (cd/c) *(CD/TC VD 2811)* **FOSSIL FUEL: THE XTC SINGLES 1977-92** 33
– (nearly same tracks as 1987 collection + add more recent) *(d-cd; CDVDX 2811)*
Nov 98. (4xcd-box) *Cooking Vinyl; (COOKCD 152) / TVT; <3240>* **TRANSISTOR BLAST: BEST OF THE BBC SESSIONS**
Mar 02. (4xcd-box) *Virgin; (XTCBOX 1) / Caroline; <CAROL 11900>* **A COAT OF MANY CUPBOARDS**

MR. PARTRIDGE

Feb 80. (lp/c) *(V/TCV 2145)* **TAKE AWAY (THE LURE OF SALVAGE)** –
– Commerciality / The day the pulled the North Pole down / Cairo / Madhattan / The forgotten language of light / Steam fist futurist / The rotary / Shore leave ornithology (another 1950) / I sit in the snow / Work away Tokyo day / New broom. (re-iss. Aug88; OVED 130)

—— In Jun'94, **ANDY PARTRIDGE** co-released with **HAROLD BUDD** the cd 'THROUGH THE HILL' for 'All Saints' label.

—— Also in '94, **PARTRIDGE** with **MARTIN NEWELL**, issued album 'THE GREATEST LIVING ENGLISHMAN' for 'Pipeline'.

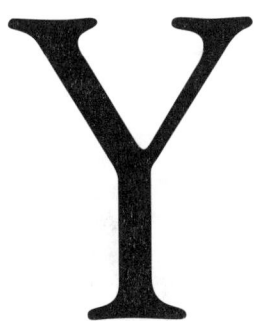

YACHTS

Formed: Liverpool, England ... 1977 as ALBERT AND THE COD FISH WARRIORS by HENRY PRIESTMAN, J.J. CAMPBELL, MARTIN WATSON, MARTIN DEMPSEY and BOB BELLIS. Adopting the YACHTS moniker, the band cruised onto the New Wave scene via a one-off single, 'SUFFICE TO SAY', launched from the scene's flagship operation, 'Stiff'. Later that year, they almost capsized, unadvisedly issuing a pseudonymous split single (with BIG IN JAPAN) as The CHUDDY NUDDIES, the subsequent departure of CAMPBELL (later to IT'S IMMATERIAL) leaving PRIESTMAN to take the helm (he was also a member of BETTE BRIGHT & THE ILLUMINATIONS). In 1978, The YACHTS charted a different course through a deal with 'Radar', also the home of ELVIS COSTELLO and NICK LOWE (they had supported the former at Eric's in '77). A stream of singles surfaced prior to their 1979 eponymous Richard Gottehrer-produced debut set, a record that revealed The YACHTS to be one of the many outfits jostling for recognition in the overcrowded pop/rock marketplace. With GLYN HAVARD substituting the PINK MILITARY-bound DEMPSEY, the crew turned their hand to an old R.Dean Taylor classic, 'THERE'S A GHOST IN MY HOUSE', although this floundered outside chart waters, as did the follow-up album, 'WITHOUT RADAR' (1980). After a final single on 'Demon', The YACHTS finally sailed off into the sunset, only PRIESTMAN finding mainstream pop fame with The CHRISTIANS.

Album rating: THE YACHTS (*5) / WITHOUT RADAR (*5)

HENRY PRIESTMAN – vocals, keyboards / **J.J. CAMPBELL** – vocals / **MARTIN J. WATSON** – guitar, vocals / **MARTIN DEMPSEY** – bass, vocals / **BOB BELLIS** – drums

	Stiff	not iss.
Sep 77. (7") *(BUY 19)* **SUFFICE TO SAY. / FREEDOM IS A HEADY WINE**	□	–

	Eric's	not iss.
Nov 77. (7"; as CHUDDY NUDDIES) *(0001)* **(A-side by Big In Japan). / DO THE CHUD**	□	–

— now without CAMPBELL who later formed IT'S IMMATERIAL

	Radar	Polydor
Sep 78. (7"blue) *(ADA 23)* **LOOK BACK IN LOVE (NOT IN ANGER). / I CAN'T STAY LONG ENOUGH**	□	–
Nov 78. (7") *(ADA 25)* **YACHTING TYPES. / HYPNOTISING LIES**	□	–
Feb 79. (7") *<PD 2027>* **YACHTING TYPES. / TANTAMOUNT TO BRIBERY**	–	□
May 79. (7") *(ADA 36)* **LOVE YOU, LOVE YOU. / HAZY PEOPLE**	□	–
Jun 79. (lp) *(RAD 19) <PD 6220>* **THE YACHTS** – Box 202 / In a second / Love you, love you / Tanytamount to bribery / Easy to please / Mantovani's hits / Then and now / Semaphore love / I can't stay long / Heads will turn / I'll be leaving you / Yachting types. *(w/ free 7"; SAM 98)* – SUFFICE TO SAY (live). / ON AND ON	□	□
Jul 79. (7") *(ADA 42)* **BOX 202. / PERMANENT DAMAGE (live)**	□	–
Nov 79. (7") *(ADA 49)* **NOW I'M SPOKEN FOR. / SECRET AGENTS**	□	–

— GLYN HAVARD – bass, vocals; repl. DEMPSEY who joined PINK MILITARY

Apr 80. (7") *(ADA 52)* **THERE'S A GHOST IN MY HOUSE. / REVERY / YACHTING TYPES**	□	–
May 80. (lp) *(RAD 27) <PD 16270>* **WITHOUT RADAR** – Consequences / On the bridge / Trust you / Out of luck / This thing, that thing / March of the moderates / There's a ghost in my house / Live saving's easy / Now I'm spoken for / The lush / Don't call us / Spimosa.	□	□
Aug 80. (7") *(ADA 57)* **I.O.U. / 24 HOURSE FROM TULSA**	□	–

	Demon	not iss.
Feb 81. (7") *(D 1005)* **A FOOL LIKE YOU. / DUBMARINE**	□	–

— after they split, PRIESTMAN joined IT'S IMMATERIAL; he subsequently joined The CHRISTIANS

The 1980s

✳ ✳ ✳

THE GREAT INDIE DISCOGRAPHY | **The 1980s**

ABLE TASMANS

Formed: Auckland, New Zealand . . . 1984 by GRAEME HUMPHREYS, DAVE BENISTON and CRAIG BAXTER; accordingly naming themselves after an early Dutch explorer of the region. Beginning life gigging around their local party circuit, the band soon recruited PETER KEEN, who relieved HUMPHREYS from vocal duties, resulting in the former singer being able to focus his attentions on guitar, a missing element from the original line-up. The year following their conception saw the release of their debut EP, 'THE TIRED SUN', a record which showcased an alternative pychedelic sound, helped by the musicianship of ANTHONY NEVISON (of HEADLESS CHICKEN fame) on a few of the tunes. With their initial release doing well on their native Kiwi-rock scene, the group subsequently delivered the single, 'BUFFALOES', and supplemented this with their inaugural LP, 'A CUPPA TEA AND A LIE DOWN' (1987). By the time of its recording the 'TASMANS had been joined by LESLIE JONKERS and JANE LEGGOTT; Aussie-born BAXTER stepping out with the strain of living and working between the two Antipodean countries. STUART GREENWAY ably stepped into his shoes and helped to make the album a competent listen, with a more folk-rock slant than its predecessor, although the few comedy sing-a-long tracks left critics divided. Over the next few years the band's ranks swelled again, with the introduction of ex-VERLAINES member JANE DODD and RON YOUNG. The revolving drum slot also took another spin with GREENWAY exiting and CRAIG MASON making his entrance. The beginning of the decade witnessed the release of their sophomore full-length outing, 'HEY SPINNER!', which again pushed into uncharted territories for the band, making use of a range of instrumentation, to create a fullsome indie pop sound, with such stand-out tracks as 'MICHAEL FAY' and 'GREY LYNN'. The teeming musical arrangements were extended on their third album, 'SOMEBODY ATE MY PLANET' (1992), where the range of instruments included cornet and bagpipes, while the subject-matter aligned itself in parts with a focus on environmental issues. The ensuing year saw the issue of EP, 'THE SHAPE OF DOLLS', which continued their forthright folk-pop mission and was superseded three years later by their fourth and final full set proper, 'STORE IN A COOL PLACE' (1996). Following its release the group parted company, KEEN keeping his ethics at the forefront with his next career as an environmental researcher at his hometown university.

Album rating: A CUPPA TEA AND A LIE DOWN (*5) / HEY SPINNER! (*5) / SOMEBODY ATE MY PLANET (*4) / THE SHAPE OF DOLLS mini (*4) / STORE IN A COOL PLACE (*5) / SONGS FROM THE DEPARTURE LOUNGE compilation (*7)

GRAEME HUMPHREYS – vocals, keyboards / **DAVE BENISTON** – bass / **CRAIG BAXTER** – drums / **PETER KEEN** – vocals, guitar / **ANTHONY NEVISON** – guitar

Flying Nun not iss.

1985. (12"ep) *(FN 043)* **THE TIRED SUN EP** – / – New Z.
– Patrick's mother / Rain in Tulsa / Tom song / Snow white chook / Nelson the cat?!! / Rhyme for orange.

— NEVISON departed (he later joined The HEADLESS CHICKENS)

1986. (7") *(FN 063)* **BUFFALOES. / Relapse: RAUCOUS LAUGHTER** – / – New Z.

— added **LESLIE JONKERS** – organ + guest **JANE LEGGOTT** – flute

— **STUART GREENWAY** – drums; repl. BAXTER

— (note:- KEEN now on vocals + HUMPHREYS on guitar, vocals)

1987. (lp/cd) *(FNE/+CD 18 – FN 075)* **A CUPPA TEA AND A LIE DOWN** – / –
– Inside the modern / What was that thing / Little hearts / And relax / Rainbow / I see now where / And we swam the magic bay / Fa fa fa fa / Sour queen / New sheriff / Virtues asunder / Evil barbeque. *(cd+=)* – Buffaloes (remix) / Caroline / Patrick's mother / Rhyme for orange / Snow white chook. *(cd re-iss. Jul96; FNCD 75)*

— **HUMPREYS, KEEN + JONKERS** (adding various instruments) recruited **JANE DODD** – bass (ex-VERLAINES, ex-CHILLS) / **RONALD YOUNG** – vocals, analogue synthesizer / **CRAIG MASON** – drums (of CHILLS)

1990. (lp/c) *(FN/+C 162)* **HEY SPINNER!** – / – New Z.
– Dileen / Angry martyr / Hold me I / Michael Fay / Hold me II / Wednesday (she's coming round) / Patience / The theory of continual disappointment / Grey Lynn / Hey, spinner! / Amelia.

Nov 92. (cd) *(FNCD 233)* **SOMEBODY ATE MY PLANET** – / –
– Circular / Fault on the frog / School is no good for you / Asian aphrodisiac solution / The cliff / Weight of love / Sweet state / Napoleons last letter to France / A conversation with Mark Byrami / Big fat / Not fat.

1993. (m-cd) *(FNCD 280)* **THE SHAPE OF DOLLS** – / – New Z
– Dog-whelk / The big bang theory / Coming up for air / Mayfly May / The shape of dolls.

— now without YOUNG

Mar 96. (lp/cd) *(FN/+CD 312)* **STORE IN A COOL PLACE** – / –
– That's why / Giant / Simple / The professional / My name is Peter Keen / GG 300 / The wind changed / Dog whelk 2 / Orenthal's face / Ladies & gentlemen / Mary Tyler Moore / Home on the range / The Klingon national anthem / Parallex.

— retired from the scene after above

– compilations, etc. –

Jan 00. (cd) *Flying Nun; (DFN 404)* **SONGS FROM THE DEPARTURE LOUNGE** – / –
– What was that thing? / Sour queen / Buffaloes / Michael's / Hold me / Grey Lynn / Dileen / Michael Fay / Angry martyr / The theory of continual disappointment / Hey, spinner! / Fault in the frog / The cliff / School is no good for you / Not fair / Coming up for air / The shape of dolls / That's why / Dog whelk / Mary Tyler Moore.

ABSOLUTE GREY

Formed: Rochester, New York, USA . . . Autumn 1983 by BETH BROWN, MITCH RASOR, PAT THOMAS and MATTHEW KITCHEN. After an initial gig early the following year, they surfaced on vinyl with mini-lp, 'GREEN HOUSE' (1984). Melancholy psychedelic/garage pop-rock, the album was heavily influenced by JEFFERSON AIRPLANE, The DREAM SYNDICATE or ECHO & The BUNNYMEN (although ABSOLUTE GREY featured haunting female vocals courtesy of BETH BROWN) and included a cracking rendition of the VELVET UNDERGROUND's 'Beginning To See The Light'. The band subsequently signed to 'Midnight' records for what might have been their last album, the deeper and emotional 'WHAT REMAINS' (1986) – produced by Tim Lee of The WINDBREAKERS – although they (BROWN and RASOR) re-formed in 1987 with the original line-up, releasing a fresh but low-key studio set, 'SAND DOWN THE MOON' at the turn of the decade. • **Covers:** HALLOWEEN (Dream Syndicate) / WANTED DEAD OR ALIVE (Bon Jovi) / ABIGAIL'S GHOST (Green On Red) / KNOCKIN' ON HEAVEN'S DOOR (Bob Dylan) / SEPTEMBER GURLS (Alex Chilton).

Album rating: GREEN HOUSE mini (*6) / WHAT REMAINS (*7) / SAND DOWN THE MOON (*5) / A JOURNEY THROUGH THE PAST re-issued collection (*6)

BETH BROWN – vocals (ex-HIT & RUN) / **MATTHEW KITCHEN** – guitar, viola / **MITCH RASOR** – bass / **PAT THOMAS** – drums

not iss. Earring

Dec 84. (m-lp) *<EAR 2>* **GREEN HOUSE** – –
– Beginning to see the light (live) / More walnuts / Memory of you (live) / Sidewalk / Remorse / Notes / Willow / +1. *<re-iss. 1986 on 'Midnight';>*

not iss. Midnight

Dec 86. (lp) *<MIRLP 125>* **WHAT REMAINS** – –
– My own / Untitled / Bad influence / Umbrella / Perfect life / No man's land / A joke / What remains / Little ditty / Grey farewell.

— now without PAT THOMAS who went on to release an eponymous solo album for the 'Heyday' imprint in 1988

— they were soon down to BROWN + RASOR when KITCHEN left

Jul 87. (12"ep) **PAINTED POST** – –
– Painted post / Closer apart / Sylvia / Abandon waltz.

Di-Di not iss.

1989. (cd) **A JOURNEY THROUGH THE PAST** (live in Rochester 1984) – – Greek
– Watching waiting / Song of / Elements / Out of the blue / We Autumn / Halloween / For some reason / Killing birds / Hug hug / Candy canes / Umbrella. *<US cd-iss. Sep01 on 'Paisley Pop'; POP-CDR 102361>* – Up to my shoulders in my love / Wanted dead or alive / Harvest / Sand down the moon / Abigails's ghost / Knockin' on Heaven's door / Memory of you / September gurls / (WCMF radio interview).

— the original quartet re-formed for last set below

1990. (lp) **SAND DOWN THE MOON** – – Greek

— nothing heard of BETH for the rest of the 90's; she could have been part of INNERSTATE

ACCELERATORS

Formed: North Carolina, USA . . . early 80's by mainman GERALD DUNCAN (not to be confused with the same named bands from Los Angeles, New Jersey or Liverpool). Recorded with the added expertise of DON DIXON and MITCH EASTER, The ACCELERATORS kickstarted their sporadic career with 'LEAVE MY HEART', an album that contained a power-pop cover of The Box Tops' 'THE LETTER'. Retaining only drummer DOUG WHELCHEL, GERALD enlisted guitarist BRAD RICE, although it would be around three to four years before the release of the eponymous follow-up set. Now signed for 'Profile', the band would take a further extended sabbatical before delivering a third offering, 'DREAM TRAIN' (1991). A comeback set in 2000, 'NEARER' (DUNCAN alongside drummer CHRIS 'CHUBBY' HENDERSON) featured a cover of Gershwin's 'SUMMERTIME'.

Album rating: LEAVE MY HEART (*5) / THE ACCELERATORS (*5) / DREAM TRAIN (*4) / NEARER (*5)

GERALD DUNCAN – vocals, guitar / **DOUG WHELCHEL** – drums

not iss. Dolphin

1983. (lp) **LEAVE MY HEART** – –

— added **BRAD RICE** – guitar / **MIKE JOHNS** – bass

ACCELERATORS (cont) THE GREAT INDIE DISCOGRAPHY The 1980s

			not iss.	Profile
1987.	(lp/c/cd) <PRO/PCT+/1246> **THE ACCELERATORS**		-	
	– Stayin' up in the city / (Why you) Hang up on me / Two girls in love / Black slacks / Under your wing / Radio / Ohh whee / You're a fool / What is real / Tears / Black and white / Letter.			
1991.	(cd,c) <1404> **DREAM TRAIN**		-	

—— disbanded after above; re-formed after several years with **GERALD DUNCAN** / + **CHRIS 'CHUBBY' HENDERSON** – drums

		not iss.	D.E.S.
May 00.	(cd) <1> **NEARER**	-	
	– Cry like a baby / House of love / That worries me / Waiting in line / All I want / Nearer / Serenade / Big machine / Summertime / One more one in a million / The killing kind / I had a dream last night / Daydreams.		

A CERTAIN RATIO

Formed: Manchester, England … 1977 by JEREMY KERR, PETER TERREL, SIMON TOPPING and MARTIN MOSCROP. One of the original 'Factory' bands, ACR came to shape and influence the nascent Manchester dance scene in much the same way as NEW ORDER, if never gaining even a fraction of the commercial success afforded that band. Signed to the label by head honcho Tony Wilson, the band's debut single, 'ALL NIGHT PARTY', appeared in late '79, closely followed by part-live, cassette only mini-set, 'THE GRAVEYARD AND THE BALLROOM'. By this point the drum machine had been replaced by a real live musician, BOB JOHNSON and ACR began expanding on their early bass-heavy, punk-funk/industrial sound towards an increasingly experimental, heavily rhythmic dance style. Released on 'Factory's Belgian sister label, 'Benelux', ACR's take on the BANBARRA funk classic, 'SHACK UP', suggested the direction the band were headed and following another one-off 12", they issued their first album proper, 'TO EACH', in 1981. With MARTHA TILSON taking over vocal duties and TOPPING moving to percussion, the sound was lent an even greater rhythmic dimension. 1982's 'SEXTET' was a benchmark of the band's early career and incredibly one of their few UK chart entries; an acclaimed collection taking in everything from funk and latin to avant-jazz, the album nevertheless struggled to make the Top 60. By the release of third album, 'I'D LIKE TO SEE YOU AGAIN' (1982), ACR had lost two of its founder members, TOPPING and TERREL, along with TILSON. A new vocalist, CAROL McKENZIE, was recruited for a series of 12" singles, with sax player, TONY QUIGLEY, further enhancing ACR's complex sonic textures. After a final album for 'Factory', 1986's 'FORCE', little was heard from the band – save an Italian 12" and live album on 'Dojo' – as they made the transition from cult indie band to a major label, 'A&M'. 1989's club hit, 'THE BIG E (I WON'T STOP LOVING YOU)', was released at the height of the house craze ACR had helped pioneer, yet both 'GOOD TOGETHER' (1989) and the live 'M.C.R.' failed to make any inroads into the mainstream chart. A subsequent move to dance label, 'Rob's' (set up by former NEW ORDER manager, Rob Gretton) saw future PRIMAL SCREAM collaborator, DENISE JOHNSON, guesting on the 'UP IN DOWNSVILLE' (1992) set, ACR now ploughing the most accessible furrow of their career. In recognition of their far reaching influence on both dance and independent music in general, 'Creation' released remix tribute set, 'LOOKING FOR A CERTAIN RATIO', in 1994, featuring such Manchester luminaries as ELECTRONIC. At various times throughout the 80's, MOSCROP and KERR were part of KALIMA with TONY and ANN QUIGLEY. Although a few albums hit the shops they were best remembered for covering Sarah Vaughan's 'SMILING HOUR' and featuring in the movie, 'Absolute Beginners'. • **Covered:** DON'T YOU WORRY 'BOUT A THING (Stevie Wonder). • **Trivia:** DONALD JOHNSON'S brother, BARRY, was a member of soul/pop outfit SWEET SENSATION. SHAUN RYDER of HAPPY MONDAYS and BARNEY SUMNER of NEW ORDER guested vocals on 1990 ep '4 FOR THE FLOOR'.

Album rating: THE GRAVEYARD AND THE BALLROOM (*6) / TO EACH … (*5) / SEXTET (*7) / I'D LIKE TO SEE YOU AGAIN (*4) / FORCE (*6) / THE OLD AND THE NEW compilation (*9) / LIVE IN AMERICA (*4) / GOOD TOGETHER (*5) / MCR (*5) / UP IN DOWNSVILLE (*5) / LOOKING FOR A CERTAIN RATIO remixes (*5) / CHANGE THE STATION (*5)

JEREMY KERR – bass, vocals / **SIMON TOPPING** – vocals, trumpet / **MARTIN MOSCROP** – guitar, vocals / **PETER TERREL** – guitar

		Factory	Factory
Sep 79.	(7"ltd.) (FAC 5) **ALL NIGHT PARTY. / THE THIN BOYS**		-

—— added **DONALD JOHNSON** – percussion, drums

Jan 80.	(c) (FACT 16C) **THE GRAVEYARD AND THE BALLROOM** (one-side live)		-
	– Flight / Faceless / Crippled child / Strain / Do the du (casse) / I feel / The choir / Flight / All night party / The fox / Genotype-phenotype / Oceans / The choir / Suspect. (re-iss. Nov85; same) (cd-iss. Nov94 on 'Creation Rev-Ola'; CREV 022CD)		
Jul 80.	(7") Factory Benelux; (FAC BN 1-004) **SHACK UP. / AND THEN AGAIN (live)**	-	- Belgian
Nov 80.	(12") (FAC 22) **BLOWN AWAY. / FLIGHT / AND THEN AGAIN**		-
Jan 81.	(12"ep) <FACUS 4> **SHACK UP / SON AND HEIR. / DO THE DU (casse) / THE FOX**	-	

—— added **MARTHA TILSON** – vocals (ex-OCCULT CHEMISTRY)

May 81.	(lp) (FACT 35) **TO EACH**		-
	– Felch / My spirit / Forced laugh / Choir / Back to the start / The fox / Loss / Oceans / Winter hill. (cd-iss. Nov94 on 'Creation Rev-Ola'; CREV 023CD)		
Sep 81.	(d12") (FACT 42) **THE DOUBLE 12"**		- Italian
	– (the EP's FAC 22 + FACUS 4)		

Dec 81.	(12") (FAC 52) **WATERLINE. / FUNAEZEKEA**		-
Jan 82.	(lp/c) (FACT 55/+C) **SEXTET**	53	-
	– Lucinda / Crystal / Gum / Knife slits water / Skipscada / Day one / Rub down / Rialto / Below the canal. (cd-iss. Nov94 on 'Creation Rev-Ola'; CREV 024CD)		
Jul 82.	(12") Factory Benelux; (FBN 17) **GUESS WHO?. / (part Two)**	-	- Belgian
Sep 82.	(7") (FAC 62-7) **KNIFE SLITS WATER. / TUMBA RUMBA**		-
	(12") (FAC 62T) – ('A'side) / Kether-Hot Knives mix-in special.		

—— reverted to quintet when MARTHA departed

Nov 82.	(lp/c) (FACT 65/+C) **I'D LIKE TO SEE YOU AGAIN**		-
	– I'd like to see you again / Axis / Saturn / Touch / Showcase / Guess who? / Hot knives / Sesano apriti-cordo vada. (cd-iss. Nov94 on 'Creation Rev-Ola'; CREV 025CD)		

—— **ANDY CONNELL** – keyboards, vocals repl. TERREL / **CAROL McKENZIE** – (guest) vocals; repl. TOPPING who went solo (one 1985 single, 'PROSPECT PARK') before forming T-COY with ex-QUANDO QUANGO member, MIKE PICKERING (later M-PEOPLE)

Sep 83.	(12") (FAC 72) **I NEED SOMEONE TONIGHT. / DON'T YOU WORRY BOUT A THING**		-

—— **TONY QUIGLEY** – sax (also of KALIMA) repl. McKENZIE

Nov 84.	(12") (FAC 112) **LIFE'S A SCREAM. / THERE'S ONLY THIS**		-
Feb 85.	(12") Factory Benelux; (FBN 32) **BRAZILIA. / BRAZILIA (extended)**	-	- Belgian
Jun 85.	(12") (FAC 128) **WILD PARTY. / SOUNDS LIKE SOMETHING DIRTY**		-
	(c-s+=) (FAC 128C) – Life's a scream (live) / Force (live) / Wild party (live).		
Dec 85.	(lp/c) (FACT 135/+C) **THE OLD AND THE NEW** (best of; remixed)		-
	– Flight / Do the du / And then again / The fox / Blown away / Sounds like something dirty / Life's a scream / There's only this / Wild party. (w/ free 7")(7FAC 135) – SHACK UP. / THE THIN BOYS (cd-iss. Nov94 on 'Creation Rev-Ola'; CREV 026CD)		

—— added guests **CORRINE DREWERY** – vocals / **TOM BARRISH** – trombone / **PAUL HARRISON** – bass programmer

		Factory	not iss.
Sep 86.	(12") (FAC 168) **MICKEY WAY (THE CANDY BAR). / INSIDE / SI FERMIR OGRIDO**		-
Nov 86.	(lp/c)(c) (FACT/FACD 166)(FACT 166C) **FORCE**		-
	– Only together / Bootsy / Fever / Naked and white / Mickey Way (the candy bar) / And then she smiles / Take me down / Anthem. (c+=) – Inside / Nostromo a go-go. (cd++=) – Si fermir Ogrido. (cd-iss. Nov94 on 'Creation Rev-Ola'; CREV 027CD)		

		Dojo	not iss.
Feb 87.	(lp/cd) (DOJO LP/CD 47) **LIVE IN AMERICA (live 1985)**		-
	– Sounds like something dirty / The fox / Shack up / Life's a scream / Wild party / Flight / And then again / Touch / Knife slits water / Si fermir Ogrido.		

		Materiali	not iss.
Jul 87.	(12"ep) (MASO 70004) **GREETINGS FOUR**	-	- Italy
	– The runner / Inside / Bootsy.		

—— now line-up KERR, MOSCROP, JOHNSON + QUIGLEY when CONNELL took guest DREWERY to form SWING OUT SISTER

		A&M	not iss.
Jun 89.	(7") (ACR 514) **THE BIG E (I WON'T STOP LOVING YOU). / LOVE IS THE WAY (instrumental)**		-
	(12"+=/cd-s+=) (ACR Y/CD 514) – Day 2.		
Aug 89.	(7") (ACR 517) **BACKS TO THE WALL. / BE WHAT YOU WANT TO BE**		-
	(12"+=/cd-s+=) (ACR Y/CD 517) – ('A' instrumental).		
Sep 89.	(lp/c/cd) (AMA/AMC/CDA 9008) **GOOD TOGETHER**		-
	– Your blue eyes / Your little world / The big E / God's own girl / Love is the way / Backs to the wall / River's edge / Every pleasure / Coldest days / Good together / Repercussions / 2000 a.d.		
Oct 89.	(7") (ACR 534) **YOUR BLUE EYES. / THIN GREY LINE**		-
	(12"+=/cd-s+=) (ACR Y/CD 534) – Coldest days.		
Feb 90.	(7") (ACR 550) **GOOD TOGETHER (live). / BE WHAT YOU WANNABE (live)**		-
	(12"ep+=/cd-ep+=) (ACR Y/CD 550) 4 FOR THE FLOOR EP – Spirit dance / Tribeca.		
Jun 90.	(7") (ACR 540) **WON'T STOP LOVING YOU. / THE BIG E**	55	-
	(7"/c-s) (ACR R/MC 540) – ('A'-Bernard Sumner mix) / ('A'-Norman Cook mix).		
	(12") (ACRY 540) – ('A'-Bernard Sumner mix) / Repercussions (live) / Love is the way (instrumental).		
	(cd-s) (ACRCD 540) – (3 tracks above) / ('A'extended).		
Jul 90.	(cd/c/lp; as ACR) (397057-2/-4/-1) **MCR (live)**		-
	– Spirit dance / Won't stop loving you / B.T.T.W.90 / Be what you wanna be / Good together / Funky Heaven / Tribeca / Repercussions.		

—— Promos of 'SHACK UP' were issued in Sep'90; ACR/+Y 590)

—— added on guest vocals **DENISE JOHNSON**

		Robs Records	not iss.
Jul 91.	(7"/ext.12") (7/12 ROB 2) **LOOSEN UP YOUR MIND. / THE PLANET**		-
	(cd-s+=) (CDROB 2) – ('A'+'B' versions).		
Nov 91.	(7") (7ROB 5) **27 FOREVER. / ('A'loose mix)**		-
	(12"+=) (12ROB 5) – ('A'instrumental dub).		
	(cd-s++=) (CDROB 5) – ('A'-Higher plane edit).		
	(12") (12ROB 5R) – ('A'-Da Silver mixes; Bubble bath + Soundstation).		
Oct 92.	(12"ep/cd-ep) (12/CD ROB 6) **MELLO (M-People mix) (part 1) / (part 2) / ('A'-Fon mix) / ('A'-Soundstation mix)**		-
	(12"ep) (12ROB 6) – Mello'd up / Mello dub / 27 forever (testimonial mix) / Mello (303 dub).		
Oct 92.	(cd/lp) (CD/L ROB 20) **UP IN DOWNSVILLE**		-
	– Manik / Turn me on / Mello / Wonder Y / Up in Downsville (pt.1) / 27 forever / Tekno 4 an answer / Salvador's (fish) / Up in Downsville (pt.2).		

ACR

				Creation	not iss.
Feb 93.	(12"ep/cd-ep)	*(12/CD ROB 11)*	**TURN ME ON** ("O" mix) / ('A'-Tackle mix) / ('A'-Primetime mix) / ('A'-M21 mix)	☐	-
Dec 93.	(12")	*(12ROB 18)*	**TEKNO** (Way out west mix). / **TEKNO** (Lip mix)	☐	-
May 94.	(12"ep)(cd-ep)	*(CRE 151T)(CRESCD 151)*	**SHACK UP** (3 mixes; Wipeout / Radio / Work) / **LIFE'S A SCREAM** (Shaven not stirred mix)	☐	-
Jul 94.	(cd/c/lp)(2x12")	*(CRE CD/MC/LP 159)(CRELP 159B)*	**LOOKING FOR A CERTAIN RATIO** (remixes)	☐	-

— still with **DENISE JOHNSON + LORNA BAILEY** – vocals

				Rob's	Rob's
Aug 96.	(12"ep/cd-ep)	*(<12/CD ROB 48>)*	**SOUNDSTATION VOLUME 1** (live) – Samba 123 / Yeah boy / Desire / Funk off.	☐	Mar97
Nov 96.	(cd)	*(<CDROB 50>)*	**CHANGE THE STATION** – Listen to the sound / Some day / You're on your own / Waiting for you / Yeah boy / Sister brother / Desire / Samba 123 / Pole / Do du beep / Golden balls / Funk off / Groov(e).	☐	Jan97
Mar 97.	(12"ep/cd-ep)	*(<12/CD ROB 52>)*	**SOUNDSTATION VOLUME 2** (live) – Samba 123 / Yeah boy / Yeah boy.	☐	Apr97

– compilations, others, etc. –

Dec 94.	(lp)	*Creation Rev-Ola; (CREV 013LP)*	**SAMPLER**	☐	-
Dec 01.	(12")	*Soul Jazz; (SJR 057)*	**SHACK UP. / Human League: BEING BOILED**	☐	-
Mar 02.	(7")	*Soul Jazz; (SJR 607)*	**DO THE DU. / SKIPSCADA**	☐	-
Apr 02.	(cd/d-lp)	*Soul Jazz; (SJR CD/LP 60)*	**EARLY** (cd w/ free cd)	☐	-
Jun 02.	(dx10"lp)	*Soul Jazz; (SJR 65-10)*	**B-SIDES, RARITIES AND SESSIONS**	☐	-

SIR HORATIO

— a reggae version and pseudonym for A CERTAIN RATIO

Jan 82.	(12")	*Rock Steady; (666 MIX 1T)*	**ABRACADUBRA. / SOMMADUB**	☐	-

SWAMP CHILDREN

MARTIN MOSCROP – percussion, drums / **ANN QUIGLEY** – vocals / **JOHN KIRKHAM** – guitar, percussion / **CLIFF SAFFER** – saxophone, clarinet / **ALAN** – bass

				Factory	not iss.
Oct 81.	(12"ep)	*(FAC 49)*	**HONEY** – Little voices / Call me honey / Boy.	☐	-

— now without ALAN; repl. by **TONY QUIGLEY** – bass, percussion / **CERI EVANS** – keyboards, bass, percussion, vocals

Nov 82.	(12")	*Factory Benelux; (FACBN 16)*	**TASTE WHAT'S RHYTHM. /**	☐	-
Jan 83.	(lp)	*(FACT 70)*	**SO HOT** – Samba zippy (part 1) / El Figaro / Tender game / Magic / Sunny weather / Samba zippy (part 2) / No sunshine / Spark the flame / Secret whispers.	☐	-

— they changed their moniker to . . .

KALIMA

Nov 83.	(7"/12")	*(FAC 87/+12)*	**SMILING HOUR. / FLYAWAY**	☐	-

— now a 4-piece **MARTIN, ANN, TONY + JOHN**

Jul 85.	(12"ep)	*(FAC 127-12)*	**4 SONGS** – Land of dreams / Sparkle / So sad / Trickery.	☐	-

— added **ANDY CONNELL** – keyboards / **JEREMY KERR** – bass / **CLIFF SAFFER** – saxophone

Apr 86.	(12"m)	*(FAC 147-12)*	**WHISPERED WORDS. / SUGAR 'N' SPICE / IN TIME**	☐	-
Jul 86.	(lp)	*(FACT 155)*	**NIGHT TIME SHADOWS** – Mystic rhymes / After hours / Green dolphin street / Backwater / In time / Father pants / Start the melody / Token freaky / Love suspended in time.	☐	-
May 87.	(7"/12")	*(FAC 187/+12)*	**WEIRD FEELINGS. / THE DANCE**	☐	-
Apr 88.	(lp/c)(cd)	*(FACT 206/+C/FACD 206)*	**KALIMA** – That twinkle / Casabel / Sad and blue / Over the waves / Now you're mine / The strangest thing / Special way / Autumn leaves (French version) / Julian.	☐	-
May 89.	(cd)	*(FACD 219)*	**FLYAWAY** (compilation) – Samba zippy / Tender games / Smiling hour / Flyaway / Trickery / Land of dreams / Sparkle / Whispered words / Sugar and spice / Mystic rhymes / After hours / Start the melody / Token freaky / Love suspended in time / Weird feelings / The dance.	☐	-
Jul 90.	(12")		**SHINE. /**	☐	-
Jul 90.	(cd/lp)	*(FACD/FACT 249)*	**FEELING FINE** – Shine / A thousand signs / Take it easy / Interstella / All the way through / Big fat city / The groovy one / Azure / Unreal.	☐	-

A.C. MARIAS

Formed: London, England . . . early 80's as a vehicle for chanteuse, ANGELA CONWAY. A one-off 45, 'DROP', for WIRE's "new music" showcase imprint, 'Dome' was issued in the summer of '81, before she became part of WIRE's (GILBERT & LEWIS) splinter outfit, DUET EMMO. This collaboration resulted in a sole album for 'Mute', 'OR SO IT SEEMS' (1983), the singer subsequently signing to the label in a solo capacity. Hardly prolific, A.C. MARIAS finally resurfaced in her/their own right towards the end of '86 (during this period she also provided backing vocals for GRAHAM LEWIS'S HE SAID project) with a comeback single, 'JUST TALK'. Sticking by musical mentor, BRUCE GILBERT and enlisting alternative stalwarts, ROWLAND S. HOWARD (ex-BIRTHDAY PARTY, now of CRIME & THE CITY SOLUTION) plus BARRY ADAMSON (ex-MAGAZINE and solo artist), she/they released a taster to her long awaited debut album, 'ONE OF OUR GIRLS (HAS GONE MISSING)' (1989). The record's title track was released early the following year, another slice of ethereal gothic weirdness which proved to be her music biz swansong.

Album rating: ONE OF OUR GIRLS (HAS GONE MISSING) (*4)

ANGELA CONWAY – vocals

				Dome	not iss.
Jul 81.	(7"; as A.C. MARIAS A.C.)	*(DOM45 1)*	**DROP. / SO**	☐	-

— guests included WIRE guys, GILBERT & LEWIS

				Mute	Enigma
Oct 86.	(7"/12")	*(MUTE/12MUTE 50)*	**JUST TALK. / JUST TALK (NO TALK)** (re-iss. Jun88)	☐	-

— now w/ **ROWLAND S. HOWARD / BRUCE GILBERT / BARRY ADAMSON**

Jan 88.	(7"/12")	*(MUTE/12MUTE 70)*	**TIME WAS. / SOMETHING**	☐	-
Aug 89.	(cd/c/lp)	*(CD/C+/STUMM 68) <71437>*	**ONE OF OUR GIRLS (HAS GONE MISSING)** – Trilby's couch / Just talk / There's a scent of rain in the air / Our dust / So soon / Give me / To sleep / Looks like / Sometime / One of our girls has gone missing / Time was.	☐	1990
Feb 90.	(12"/cd-s)	*(12/CD MUTE 105)*	**ONE OF OUR GIRL IS MISSING. / TIME WAS**	☐	-

— retired from the music biz

ACT (see under ⇒ LEER, Thomas; 70's section)

A.C. TEMPLE

Formed: Sheffield, England . . . 1985 by PAUL DORRINGTON and JANE BROMLEY; CHRIS TROUT being added in '86. Influenced by the harsh industrial environment of their native city, A.C. TEMPLE alchemised a disturbing percussive cacophony utilising crashing guitars and filtering them through an echo chamber. Similar in spirit to the BIRTHDAY PARTY, JESUS & MARY CHAIN or SONIC YOUTH, the band released their first two albums, 'SONGS OF PRAISE' (1987) and 'BLOWTORCH' (1988) on the independent 'Further' label before signing to influential experimental noise outlet, 'Blast First'. With the addition of TIM BECKHAM and MAT SILCOX, A.C. TEMPLE released a third set, 'SOURPUSS' (1989), although press reaction was lukewarm and the band struggled to scale the heights of labelmates like DINOSAUR JR, etc. Even with the production expertise of BONGWATER's KRAMER, a fourth set, 'BELINDA BACKWARDS' (1991), failed to bring the band any more recognition; DORRINGTON, in turn, defected to The WEDDING PRESENT as the TEMPLE finally crumbled.

Album rating: SOURPUSS (*4)

JANE BROMLEY – vocals / **PAUL DORRINGTON** – guitar / **CHRIS TROUT** – bass (of KILGORE TROUT) / + 1

				Further	not iss.
Jun 87.	(lp)	*(FU 001)*	**SONG OF PRAISE** – Ulterior / Make mine music / A motel in Kansas / Fear no more the heat of the sun / All hail discordia / 90 seconds.	☐	-
Jul 88.	(lp/cd)	*(FU 6 LP/CD)*	**BLOWTORCH** – Mincemeat / Yield / I dream of fraud / American / Weekend / Sheikh / Chinese burn / Shimmer queen / Hank / Armache / Ulterior.	☐	-

— new **TIM BECKHAM** – guitar / **MAT SILCOX** – drums

				Blast First	not iss.
Nov 89.	(lp/c/cd)	*(BFFP 45/+C/CD)*	**SOURPUSS** – Sundown pet corner / Miss Sky / Stymied / Mother tongue / Crayola / Devil you know / Horsetrading / A mouthful / Faith in a windsock / Ringpiece / (Dirty) Weekend.	☐	-
Apr 91.	(lp/cd)	*(BFFP 63/+CD)*	**BELINDA BACKWARDS** – Glitterball / Silver swimmer / Half-angel / Come sunrise / Girlseye / Lifesize / Spacebore / Skyhooks / Baby seals / P2.	☐	-

— disbanded when DORRINGTON joined The WEDDING PRESENT

Barry ADAMSON

Born: 1 Jun'58, Moss Side, Manchester, England. As the bassist of avant-punksters, MAGAZINE, ADAMSON played on such classic albums as 'Real Life' (1978) and 'The Correct Use Of Soap' (1980), before going on to work with ex-BUZZCOCKS man, PETE SHELLEY. This proved to be a short-lived collaboration as ADAMSON was subsequently recruited as one of NICK CAVE's BAD SEEDS. He remained with the ex-BIRTHDAY PARTY man until the late 80's, playing on four albums: 'From Her To Eternity' (1984), 'The Firstborn Is Dead' (1985), 'Kicking Against The Pricks' (1986) and 'Your Funeral . . . My Trial' (1986). An impressive musical CV by anyone's standard and one which ADAMSON put to good use in his first solo venture, 'MOSS SIDE STORY' (1989). With echoes of MAGAZINE's angular noise and The BAD SEEDS' black majesty, the record was conceived as a soundtrack to a would-be movie set in the seedy underbelly of Manchester's crime-ridden Moss Side area. By subverting the classic recipe of cheesy hammond

Barry ADAMSON (cont)

and setting it against both his feel for the avant-garde and the clever use of samples, ADAMSON created a noir collage which proved so effective he subsequently found himself writing and recording bonafide soundtracks to such cult films as 'Gas Food Lodging'. A similarly unsavoury follow-up album proper, 'SOUL MURDER', eventually appeared in 1992 while the following year's 'THE NEGRO INSIDE ME' mini explored more accessible and familiar musical territory duly examining ADAMSON's thoughts on cultural identity. 'OEDIPUS SCHMOEDIPUS' (1996) pleased his fans (it featured JARVIS COCKER and NICK CAVE) if not exactly breaking the established mould, ADAMSON remaining the kingpin of his self-created genre while his brooding shadow lurks in the recordings of trip hop artists like PORTISHEAD. The man – who was once labelled "the Ennio Morricone" of the 90's – issued his seventh album, 'AS ABOVE, SO BELOW' (1998), another delivery of class. Some four years later, the stylish ADAMSON resurfaced with his 7th set, 'KING OF NOTHING HILL' (2002), fusing smooth 60's-styled Gallic jazz/pop with funky FLOOD-produced soundscapes. • **Covered:** THESE BOOTS ARE MADE FOR WALKING (Nancy Sinatra).

Album rating: MOSS SIDE STORY (*7) / DELUSION soundtrack (*5) / SOUL MURDER (*6) / THE NEGRO INSIDE ME mini (*5) / OEDIPUS SCHMOEDIPUS (*7) / AS ABOVE, SO BELOW (*6) / THE MURKY WORLD OF BARRY ADAMSON compilation (*7) / THE KING OF NOTHING HILL (*6)

BARRY ADAMSON – bass, keyboards, vocals (ex-MAGAZINE, ex-NICK CAVE & THE BAD SEEDS, ex-IGGY POP)

Mute / Mute-Elektra

Nov 88. (7") *(MUTE 77)* **THE MAN WITH THE GOLDEN ARM. / BOMBASTO!**
(12"+=/cd-s+=) *(12/CD MUTE 77)* – Fifteen rounds / Suck on the honey of love.

Mar 89. (cd/c/lp) *(CD/C+/STUMM 53) <71420>* **MOSS SIDE STORY**
– (The ring's the thing): On the wrong side of relaxation / Under wraps / Central control / Round up the usual suspects / (Real deep cool): Sounds from the big house / Suck on the honey of love / Everything happens to me / The swinging detective / (Final irony): Auto destruction / Intensive care / The most beautiful girl in the world / Free at last / (For your ears only): Alfred Hitchcock presents / Chocolate milkshake / The man with the golden arm.

Oct 89. (12"ep/3"cd-ep) *(12/CD MUTE 97)* **TAMING OF THE SHREWD**
– (Samplers Against Apartheid): Diamonds / (Half-cast In The Movie Of Life): Boppin' out – Eternal morning / Splat goes the cat / From Rusholme with love.

Jul 91. (cd-s; as BARRY ADAMSON, ANITA LANE AND THE THOUGHT SYSTEMS OF LOVE) *(CDMUTE 119)* **THESE BOOTS ARE MADE FOR WALKING / THESE BOOTS ARE MADE FOR WALKING (Bonnie floats on air mix) / GO JOHNNY / THESE BOOTS ARE MADE FOR WALKING (sleepwalking mix)**

Ionic-Mute / Elektra

Aug 91. (cd/c/lp) *(CD/C+/IONIC 004) <61127-2/-4>* **DELUSION** (Original Soundtrack)
– Delusion / Crossin' the line / Il solitario / Patti's theme / A settlin' kinda scam / Fish face / Go Johnny / The life we leave behind / An amendment / La cucaracha / Diamonds / George's downfall / Got to bet to win / The track with no name / Patti's theme (Two stage variation) / Death valley junction / These boots are made for walking.

Mute / Mute

Apr 92. (cd/c/lp) *(<CD/C+/STUMM 105>)* **SOUL MURDER**
– Preface / Split / The violation of expectation / Suspicion / A gentle man of colour / Trance of hatred / Checkpoint Charlie / Reverie / Un petit miracle / 007, a fantasy Bond theme / The Adamson family / Cool green world / On the edge of atonement / Epilogue.

Sep 92. (cd-ep) *(CDMUTE 149)* **CINEMA IS KING EP**
– 007, a fantasy Bond theme / Autodestruction / Il solitario / From Rusholme with love.

Jun 93. (m-cd/m-lp) *(<CD+/STUMM 120>)* **THE NEGRO INSIDE ME** — Oct93
– The snowball effect / Dead heat / Busted (Michelangelo version) / Cold black preach / Je t'aime . . . moi non plus / A perfectly natural union.

Apr 95. (ltd-12"ep) *(12MUTE 183)* **MOVIEOLOGY EP**
– Busted (Michelangelo version) / 007, a fantasy Bond theme (dance version) / The snowball effect / The man with the golden arm / Dead heat.

Mute / Elektra

Jul 96. (12"ep/cd-ep) *(12/CD MUTE 186)* **THE BIG BAMBOOZLE EP**
– The big bamboozle / 007, a fantasy Bond theme (dance version) / Busted (Michelangelo version) / Dead heat.

Jul 96. (cd/lp) *(CD MUTE 134) <69019>* **OEDIPUS SCHMOEDIPUS** — Aug96
– Set the controls for the heart of the / Something wicked this way comes / Vibes ain't nothin' but the vibes / It's business as usual / Miles / Dirty Barry / In a moment of clarity / Achieved in the valley of the dolls / Vermillion kisses / Big bamboozle / State of contraction / Sweetest embrace / Se the controls again.

May 98. (12"ep/cd-ep) *(12/CD MUTE 188)* **CAN'T GET LOOSE / TROUBLE ASUNDER (ODEIPUS RETURNS). / HEAR THE ANGELS / NAMASTA MPC (END TITLE)**

Jun 98. (cd/lp) *(CD+/STUMM 161) <69035>* **AS ABOVE, SO BELOW**
– Can't get loose / What it means / Deja voodoo / Come hell or high water / Jazz devil / Still I rise / Girl / Monkey speaks his mind / Goddess of love / Jesus wept.

Jul 98. (12"ep) *(12MUTE 219)* **WHAT IT MEANS. / ('A'-Skylab plucked chicken mix) / ('A'-Subsonic legacy master mix)**
cd-s+= *(CDMUTE 219)* – Skylab a smokin' Japanese were – Chicken in Moss Side.

Mute / Mute

May 99. (cd) *(CDSTUMM 174) <9093-2>* **THE MURKY WORLD OF BARRY ADAMSON** (compilation)
– The man with the golden arm / Jazz devil / The big bamboozle / What it means / The vibes ain't nothin' but the vibes / Mitch and Andy / The snowball effect / Can't get loose / 007, a fantasy Bond theme / Something wicked this way comes / Walk the last mile / Saturn in the summertime.

1999. (7") *(SMALL 004)* **THE CRIME SCENE. / (other by Jon Spencer Blues Explosion)**
(above issued on 'Slut Smalls')

Nov 01. (cd; by BARRY ADAMSON & PAN SONIC) *(KM 4)* **MOTORLAB, VOL.3**
– The hymn of the 7th illusion / (untitled) / The illusion of the 7th hymn (Hafler Trio mix).
(above issued on 'Kitchen Motors')

Aug 02. (12") *(12MUTE 223)* **BLACK AMOUR. / BLACK AMOUR (Trojan extended pleasure mix) / AMOUR (FOR JOCELYN)**
(cd-s) *(CDMUTE 223)* – (first 2 tracks) / First light / ('A'video).

Sep 02. (cd/d-lp) *(CD+/STUMM 176)* **THE KING OF NOTHING HILL**
– Cinematic soul / Whispering streets / Black amour / When darkness calls / The second stain / Twisted smile / Le matin des noire / That fool was me / The crime scene / Cold comfort.

Nov 02. (12"/cd-s) *(12/CD MUTE 283)* **WHISPERING STREETS (mixes; edit / Aim / Funkstorung / original)**

ADULT NET

Formed: Manchester, England . . . late 1984 by native New Yorker, BRIX E. SMITH (aka LAURA ELISE), wife at the time of FALL mainman, MARK E. SMITH. She had joined the aforesaid Mancunian indie outfit as guitarist/co-singer in 1982, forming the ADULT NET as her extracurricular outfit. With help from fellow FALL musicians, MARSHA SCHOFIELD (also once a member of BRIX's former group, BANDA BRATSING) and SIMON ROGERS, the sultry retro-chick made her debut on 'Beggars Banquet' with a cover of the Strawberry Alarm Clock's late 60's US chart-topper, 'INCENSE AND PEPPERMINTS', in April '85. A follow-up single, 'EDIE', dealt with the life of the infamous VELVET UNDERGROUND sidekick/dancer, EDIE SEDGWICK. Two further commercially-orientated 45's appeared in quick succession, the latter of which, 'WAKING UP IN THE SUN', featured a cover of Shangri-la's '(REMEMBER) WALKING IN THE SAND' on its flip side. In a concerted attempt to break into the mainstream, she transformed her ADULT NET into an indie supergroup of sorts with the help of CRAIG GANNON (ex-AZTEC CAMERA), JAMES ELLER (ex-JULIAN COPE) and CLEM BURKE (ex-BLONDIE). Landing a major deal with 'Fontana' late in '88 (along with The FALL), BRIX and Co released a comeback single, 'TAKE ME', although it was to be yuppie violinist, NIGEL KENNEDY, who would accept her offer, not MARK E whom she would subsequently separate from. Having now also split from The FALL, she/ADULT NET had their first taste of chart success when 'WHERE WERE YOU' broke into the Top 75. The accompanying long awaited debut album, 'THE HONEY TANGLE' (1989), failed to give them the expected breakthrough despite being an enjoyable set of dreamy, psychedelic indie-pop. By this point divorced from MARK E. she was a surprise guest on long-running TV show, 'This Is Your Life', as the girlfriend of the aforementioned KENNEDY. The first half of the 90's were something of a musical wilderness, although she subsequently buried the proverbial hatchet with MARK E and rejoined The FALL.

Album rating: THE HONEY TANGLE (*5)

BRIX E. SMITH – vocals, guitar (of The FALL); with **MARSHA SCHOFIELD** – keyboards, vocals / **SIMON ROGERS** – bass (both of FALL)

Beggars Banquet / not iss.

Apr 85. (7"/12") *(BEG 137/+T)* **INCENSE AND PEPPERMINTS. / SEARCHING FOR THE NOW**

Nov 85. (7") *(BEG 148)* **EDIE. / GET AROUND**
(12"+=) *(BEG 148T)* – Phantom power.

Jun 86. (7"/12") *(BEG 164/+T)* **WHITE NIGHT (STARS SAY GO). / NAUGHTY OF ME**

Aug 86. (7"/12") *(BEG 171/+T)* **WAKING UP IN THE SUN. / (REMEMBER) WALKING IN THE SAND**

—— BRIX recruited new band; **CRAIG GANNON** – guitar (ex-SMITHS, ex-BLUEBELLS, ex-AZTEC CAMERA, etc.) / **JAMES ELLER** – bass (ex-JULIAN COPE, + of THE THE) / **CLEM BURKE** – drums (ex-BLONDIE, ex-RAMONES) / **CRAIG LEON** – keyboards, producer

Fontana / not iss.

Mar 89. (7") *(BRX 1)* **TAKE ME. / SEA OF RAIN**
(10"blue+=/12"+=/cd-s+=) *(BRX 1-10/12/CD)* – Going nowhere/ Incense and peppermints.

May 89. (7"/10"white) *(BRX 2/+10)* **WHERE WERE YOU. / OVER THE RIVER** — 66

Jul 89. (lp/c/cd) *(838125-1/-4/-2)* **THE HONEY TANGLE**
– Take me / August / Waking up in the Sun / Spin this web / Sad / Where were you / Honey tangle / Tiffany Tuesday / Tomorrow morning daydream / It's the way.

Jul 89. (7"/7"pic-d) *(BRX/+P 3)* **WAKING UP IN THE SUN. / AUGUST**
(12"+=/cd-s+=) *(BRX 3-12/CD)* – (Remember) Walking in the sand.

—— lost her recording contract not long after above, although she found a new beau in NIGEL KENNEDY. She subsequently rejoined The FALL later in the 90's.

AFRAID OF MICE

Formed: Liverpool, England . . . late 1978 out of BEANO, by PHILIP FRANZ JONES, the only mainstay of this initially unstable group. Original drummer CLIVE GEE moved over to keyboards with the arrival of TERRY STERLING, the line-up completed by SHAUN McLAUGHLIN who replaced JEFF KELLY. Part of the much lauded Merseyside new wave/alternative scene, AFRAID OF MICE signed to 'Charisma' (home of GENESIS!) and released a series of BOWIE-esque, spiky pop-punk singles between 1981 and '82. However, after the release of their eponymous debut set in early '83, the outfit receded back into obscurity as PHIL moved on to form TWO'S COMPANY (a duo that would subsequently evolve into UP AND RUNNING).

Album rating: AFRAID OF MICE (*5)

PHILIP FRANZ JONES – guitar, vocals (ex-NEXT) / **CLIVE GEE** – keyboards / **SAM BREW** – guitar / **SHAUN McLAUGHLIN** – bass; repl. JEFF KELLY / **TERRY STERLING** – drums

		Charisma	not iss.
Jul 81.	(7") *(CB 383)* **I'M ON FIRE. / DOWN IN THE DARK**	☐	-
Aug 81.	(12"m) *(CB 389)* **INTERCONTINENTAL. / HAVE A NICE DAY / WHAT SHALL WE DO?**	☐	-
Oct 81.	(7") *(CB 395)* **POPSTAR. / WHAT I WANT**	☐	-
Apr 82.	(7") *(CB 397)* **TRANSPARENTS. / THAT'S NOT TRUE**	☐	-
Aug 82.	(7") *(CB 398)* **AT THE CLUB. / I WILL WAIT**	☐	-
Jan 83.	(lp) *(CAS 1155)* **AFRAID OF MICE**	☐	-

— they continued to work under various guises but finally gave up when PHIL joined forces with ALEX McKECHNIE (ex-MODERN EON) and formed TWO'S A CROWD, aka UP AND RUNNING. In the late 80's two singles were issued, 'JOHNNY AND MARIE' and 'I CAN'T SAY NO', although a 'LIVE AT LIME STREET' album never saw light.

AGE OF CHANCE

Formed: Leeds, Yorkshire, England ... early 80's by STEVE ELVIDGE, NEIL HOWSON, GEOFF TAYLOR and JAN PERRY. Released on their own 'Riot Bible' label, the 'MOTOR CITY' single introduced their grating noise/dance fusion to a jingle-jangle indie scene, the band even securing a place on the infamous C86 compilation with the cacophonous 'FROM NOW ON, THIS WILL BE YOUR GOD'. While the 'BIBLE OF THE BEATS' single was even more dancefloor oriented, AGE OF CHANCE were at their most entertaining interpreting other artists' work; a cover of Prince's 'KISS' (before TOM JONES got hold of it!) set the scene while an alternative-dance trashing of The Trammps' 'DISCO INFERNO' almost cracked the Top 40. Securing a major label deal with 'Virgin', the band made their bid for the big time with the 'ONE THOUSAND YEARS OF TROUBLE' (1987) set. It went nowhere, as did a succession of singles, even vocalist ELVIDGE had bailed out as the more soulful sounding CHARLES HUTCHINSON was drafted in as a replacement. After the disappointing follow-up set, 'MECCA' (1990), AGE OF CHANCE again found themselves minus a frontman as HUTCHINSON departed. While PERRY stepped in temporarily, the band finally took fate into their own hands and killed off AGE OF CHANCE in 1991. ELVIDGE, meanwhile, formed MAD LOVE, before carving out a career as a DJ in his hometown of Leeds.

Album rating: THE TWILIGHT WORLD OF SONIC DISCO 12" (*6) / ONE THOUSAND YEARS OF TROUBLE (*5) / MECCA (*5)

STEVEN ELVIDGE – vocals / **NEIL HOWSON** – guitar / **GEOFF TAYLOR** – bass / **JAN PERRY** – drums

		Riot Bible	not iss.
Apr 85.	(7") *(RIOT 1)* **MOTOR CITY. / EVERLASTING YEAH!**	☐	-
Jan 86.	(7") *(RIOT 2)* **THE BIBLE OF THE BEATS. / THE LIQUID JUNGLE**	☐	-
May 86.	(12"ep; pink or yellow) *(BIBLE 001)* **THE TWILIGHT WORLD OF SONIC DISCO**	☐	-
	– Motor City / Everlasting yeah! / The bible of the beats / The liquid jungle.		

		Fon-MCA	not iss.
Nov 86.	(7"orange,7"green,12") *(AGE 5)* **KISS. / CRUSH COLLISION**	50	-
	(12"+=/d7"+=;-rel.Feb87) *(AGE 5M)* – Disco inferno / Kiss (remix).		

		Virgin	Charisma
May 87.	(7") *(VS 962)* **WHO'S AFRAID OF THE BIG BAD NOISE. / BIG BAD RAP**	☐	-
	(12"+=) *(VS 962-12)* – ('A'-symphony).		
Sep 87.	(7") *(VS 989)* **DON'T GET MAD GET EVEN. / GETTING MAD (instrumental)**	☐	-
	(12"+=) *(VS 989-12)* – ('A'mix) / Getting even / ('A'-bonus beats). *(re-iss. Jul88 with extra see below; same)*		
	(12"+=)(cd-s+=) *(VS 989-12)(CD-EP 7)* – New York's revenge / The beats of New York / NYC versus AOC.		
Oct 87.	(cd/c/lp) *(CD/TC/V 2473)* <90672> **ONE THOUSAND YEARS OF TROUBLE**	☐	-
	– Don't get mad get even / We've got trouble / Ready or not here we come / Shut up and listen / Big bad noise / Take it / This is crush collision / Learn to pay / Hold on.		
Jan 88.	(7") *(VS 1035)* **TAKE IT. / TAKING TOP DOLLARS**	☐	-
	(12"+=) *(VST 1035)* – ('A'mix)		

— CHARLES HUTCHISON – vocals; repl. ELVIDGE

Oct 89.	(7") *(VS 1133)* **TIMES UP. / FOUR MORE YEARS: MOTORCADE**	☐	-
	(12") *(VST 1133)* – Times up: Prove it / ('B'side) / Superpower.		
	(cd-s) *(VSCD 1133)* – ('A'side) / Times up: Prove it / Superpower / You can run.		
	(12") *(VSTX 1133)* – (3 versions of the 'A'side).		
Jan 90.	(7") *(VS 1228)* **HIGHER THAN HEAVEN. / ('A'-green mix)**	☐	-
	(12") *(VST 1228)* – (3 'A'versions).		
	(cd-s++=) *(VSCD 1228)* – Snowblind.		
Mar 90.	(cd/c/lp) *(CD/TC/V 2564)* <91366> **MECCA**	☐	-
	– Four more years / Higher than Heaven / Joyride / Refuse to lose / Snowblind / Mecca / Time's up / You can run but you can't hide / Playing with fire / What's happening.		
May 90.	(7") *(VS 1258)* **PLAYING WITH FIRE. / JOYRIDE**	☐	-
	(12") *(VST 1258)* – ('A'-playing with house mix) / Times up (pop mix).		
	(cd-s) *(VSCD 1258)* – (2 'A'versions) / Red alert / Higher than Heaven (mix).		
	(12") *(VSTX 1258)* – (3 versions of 'A'side).		

— disbanded soon after above

A HOUSE

Formed: Dublin, Ireland ... 1985 by DAVE COUSE, FEARGAL BUNBURY and MARTIN HEALY (along with additional part-time members, DAVE MORRISSEY, DAVE DAWSON and SUSAN KAVANAGH). Stamped with the characteristically broad-accented bile and wit of lyricist/vocalist COUSE, A HOUSE's highly individual take on Celtic rock was initially picked up on by 'Warners' alternative subsidiary, 'Blanco Y Negro'. The London-based label signed up the now Belfast-based band on the strength of three self-financed singles, issuing their first album, 'ON OUR BIG FAT MERRY GO ROUND', in 1988. Unfortunately, both the debut and its acclaimed follow-up, 'I WANT TOO MUCH' (1990) failed to meet major label sales targets and the band soon found themselves back at square one. All fuel for the fire of COUSE's barbed muse of course, the band trooping on against the odds and inking a subsequent deal with Keith Cullen's hip'n'happening new 'Setanta' label. An EP, 'DOODLE', was closely followed by arguably their most effective – and possibly most controversial – single, 'ENDLESS ART', a strangely hypnotic spoken-word 'list' of history's most famous painters, musicians, writers etc., spliced with a snippet of one of Mozart's symphonies. It certainly stood out from almost any other 'indie' release of the day, perhaps too much; its distinct lack of female achievers, perhaps understandably, riled many women. The band made up for it by cutting a revised version, made up entirely of the fairer sex, prior to the release of their third and most successful album, the EDWYN COLLINS-produced 'I AM THE GREATEST' (1991). Critics suggested that COUSE's edge seemed blunted on 1994's 'WILD EYED AND IGNORANT', a record that failed to build on the artistic and relative commercial feats of its predecessor. Nevertheless, A HOUSE haven't called in the removals people just yet, perhaps a little renovation is all that's needed. • **Covered:** CHILDREN OF THE REVOLUTION (T.Rex) / I FEEL LOVE (Donna Summer) / LOVE SONG (Damned).

Album rating: ON OUR BIG FAT MERRY GO ROUND (*5) / I WANT TOO MUCH (*6) / I AM THE GREATEST (*7) / WIDE EYED AND IGNORANT (*5) / NO MORE APOLOGIES (*6) / THE WAY WE WERE – THE BEST OF compilation (*7)

DAVE COUSE – vocals, acoustic guitar / **FEARGAL BUNBURY** – guitar / **MARTIN HEALY** – bass / **DERMOT WYLIE** – drums

		Rip	not iss.
Mar 87.	(7") *(ARIP 1)* **KICK ME AGAIN JESUS. / I WANT YOU**	☐	-
	(12"+=) *(ARIPT 1)* – When I change.		
Jun 87.	(7") *(ARIP 2)* **SNOWBALL DOWN. / Y.O.U.**	☐	-
Aug 87.	(12"ep) *(ARIPT 3)* **KISS ME AGAIN JESUS / I WANT YOU / WHEN I CHANGE. / SNOWBALL DOWN / Y.O.U.**	☐	-

		Blanco Y Negro	Sire
Nov 87.	(7") *(NEG 28)* **HEART HAPPY. / PRETTY SOMETHING**	☐	-
	(12"+=) *(NEGT 28)* – Oh God I hurt inside.		
Jun 88.	(7") *(NEG 35)* **CALL ME BLUE. / FREAK OUT**	☐	-
	(12"+=) *(NEGT 35)* – Michael / Plane or pearl.		
Sep 88.	(7") *(NEG 38)* **I'LL ALWAYS BE GRATEFUL. / FUNNYMAN**	☐	-
	(12"+=) *(NEGT 38)* – This child is yours not mine / There's only one thing wrong with the perfect.		
Oct 88.	(lp/c/cd) *(BYN/+C 18)(244079-2)* <25821> **ON OUR BIG FAT MERRY-GO-ROUND**	☐	-
	– Call me blue / I'll always be grateful / Don't ever think you're different / Love of the eighties / Love quarry / Stone the crows / I want to kill something / My little greenhouse / That's not the truth / Violent love / Clump of trees. *(cd+=)* – Make hay when the sun shines.		
Apr 90.	(7") *(NEG 43)* **I THINK I'M GOING MAD. / I WANT TOO MUCH**	☐	-
	(12"+=/cd-s+=) *(NEG 43 T/TCD)* – Why must we argue.		
May 90.	(cd)(lp/c) *(9031 71316-2)(BYN/+C 22)* <26204> **I WANT TOO MUCH**	☐	-
	– I want too much / Talking / The patron saint of mediocrity / Shivers up my spine / Marry me / I give you now / Now that I'm sick / I think I'm going mad / Bring down the beast / Manstrong / Keep the homefires burning / You'll cry when I die / Small talk.		

		Setanta	Radioactive
Nov 90.	(12"ep/cd-ep) **DOODLE EP**	☐	-
	– The last to know / Bugaboo / A minute of your time / Sometimes I feel.		
Sep 91.	(12"ep) **BINGO SPINSTER EP**	☐	-
	– Spinster / Easy way out / Senses / There is no time.		
	(c-ep/cd-ep) – (1st track) / Angeline / I want to be allowed to love you / I'll make it up to you.		
Oct 91.	(lp/c/cd) *(SET/+C/CD 3)* <RAR/+C/D 10600> **I AM THE GREATEST**	☐	Jan92
	– I don't care / You're too young / Endless art / Blind faith / Cotton pickers / How strong is love / When I first saw you / I am afraid / Victor / Take it easy on me / Creatures of craze / Slipping away / I wanted to die / I lied / Live life dead die / I am the greatest. *(cd re-iss. Aug92; same)*		
Jan 92.	(7") **YOU'RE TOO YOUNG. / TAKE IT EASY ON ME**	☐	-
	(12"ep+=) **ZOP EP** – Serious lovin' / When I first saw you (long).		
	(cd-ep+=) **ZOP EP** – Baby, you're too much / Our love is good enough.		
Jun 92.	(7") *(AHOU 1)* **ENDLESS ART. / MORE ENDLESS ART**	46	-
	(12"+=/cd-s+=) *(12/CD AHOU 1)* – Freak show / Charity.		
Aug 92.	(c-s/7") *(TC+/AHOU 2)* **TAKE IT EASY ON ME. / I LOVE YOU**	55	-
	(12"+=/cd-s+=) *(12/CD AHOU 2)* – Everything's wrong.		
	(w /free flexi) – Force fed.		
Sep 92.	(7"mail-order) *(AHOU 3)* **WHEN I FIRST SAW YOU (live). / I WANT TO KILL SOMETHING / SECOND WIND**	-	-
Jun 94.	(c-s/7") *(TC+/AHOU 4)* **WHY ME. / I HOPE I'M WRONG / MY HEART BLEEDS FOR YOU**	52	-
	(10") *(10AHOU 4)* – (first 2 tracks) / Angeline / You think you know.		
	(cd-s) *(CDAHOU 4)* – (first & third tracks) / I will never forget you / This hurts me.		

Jul 94. (cd/c/lp) *(AHOU CD/TC/LP 2)* **WIDE EYED AND IGNORANT**
– Intro / Here comes the good times / She keeps me humble / Why me / Make me proud / Everything I am / Curious / These things / The comedy is over / The strong & the silent / Big talk / Deadhead / I want to be allowed to love you.

Sep 94. (c-s/7") *(TC+/AHOU 5)* **HERE COME THE GOOD TIMES. / CHILDREN OF THE REVOLUTION / I FEEL LOVE** 37 -
(cd-s+=) *(CDAHOU 5)* – Love song.
(10"/cd-s) *(10/CD AHOUS 5)* – ('A'side) / Everybody needs something / Soon / All I need.

Sep 96. (cd/c) *(SET CD/MC 028)* **NO MORE APOLOGIES**
– The start / Into the light / Cry easily / No more apologies / My sweet life / Sister's song / Twist and squeeze / Love is . . . / Without dreams / Just because / I can't change / Clotheshorse / My mind / Broken / Happy ending.

Feb 97. (cd-ep) *(SETCD 029)* **WITHOUT DREAMS / DAYS LIKE THESE / MY SHELTERED LIFE / JEAN**

—— split after above

– compilations, etc. –

Aug 02. (cd) *Setanta; (SETCD 105)* **THE WAY WE WERE – THE BEST OF A HOUSE: 04.85 – 02.97**
– I'll always be grateful / Love is / Endless art / Why me? / The comedy is over / 13 wonderful love songs / I want too much / Here comes the good times / You're just too young / I can't change / Kick me again Jesus / Call me blue / Small talk / I am afraid / Just because / Spinster / Take it easy on me / Our love is good enough / No more apologies.

ALICE DONUT

Formed: New York, USA ... mid 80's by singer TOMAS ANTONA, MICHAEL JUNG, RICHARD MARSHALL, TED HOUGHTON, STEPHEN MOSES and DAVE GIFFIN. Described as nasty, horrible Americans, who like nothing better than to outrage people with their crazy lyrics and antics, ALICE DONUT found a natural home at JELLO BIAFRA's 'Alternative Tentacles' label. Fronted by a man who looks like GENESIS P. ORRIDGE (Psychic TV) leaving an Oxfam shop and characterised by a fondness for outlandishly juvenile song titles, ALICE DONUT accumulated a (very!) cult fanbase with releases such as 'DONUT COMES ALIVE' (1988) and 'BUCKETFULLS OF SICKNESS AND HORROR IN AN OTHERWISE MEANINGLESS LIFE' (1989). The lads began the 90's in much the same fashion, spinning their sub-JESUS LIZARD/DEAD KENNEDYS punk squall over a series of critically lambasted sets, their "unique" sense of humour one of their few saving graces. Having bulldozed through Black Sabbath's 'WAR PIGS' on the 'REVENGE FANTASIES OF THE IMPOTENT' album in '91, they virtually demolished The Beatles' 'HELTER SKELTER' on 1994's 'DRY HUMPING THE CASH COW'. The latter remains something of an oddity, featuring as it does a number of bonafide live tracks (at the CBGB's) alongside their best known songs dubbed over with a mock stadium crowd roar. A year later it seemed all over bar the shouting when they delivered their final set, 'PURE ACID PARK'. • **Covered:** SUNSHINE SUPERMAN (Donovan) / I WALKED WITH A ZOMBIE (Roky Erickson).

Album rating: DONUT COMES ALIVE (*4) / BUCKETFULLS OF SICKNESS AND HORROR IN AN OTHERWISE MEANINGLESS LIFE (*3) / MULE (*3) / REVENGE FANTASIES OF THE IMPOTENT (*2) / THE UNTIDY SUICIDES OF YOUR DEGENERATE CHILDREN (*2) / DRY HUMPING THE CASH COW part compilation (*5) / PURE ACID PARK (*4)

TOMAS ANTONA – vocals / **MICHAEL JUNG** – guitar, vocals / **RICHARD MARSHALL** – guitar, vocals / **TED HOUGHTON** – bass, vocals / **STEPHEN MOSES** – drums, trombone / **DAVE GIFFIN** – guitar

Alternative Tentacles / Alternative Tentacles

1988. (lp/cd) *<(VIRUS 61/+CD)>* **DONUT COMES ALIVE**
– Green pea soup / World profit / Mason Reece / Great great big big head / Diet cola syringe / New Jersey exit / American lips / Windshield of love / Mad dogs on a bone / Joan of arc / Bedpost / Sunshine superman / Love is a fickle thing / Tipper Gore / Death shield / I want your mother. *(cd re-iss. Apr00; same)*

Jul 89. (lp/cd) *<(VIRUS 73/+CD)>* **BUCKETFULLS OF SICKNESS AND HORROR IN AN OTHERWISE MEANINGLESS LIFE**
– Lydia's black lung / Testosterone gone wild / Sinead O'Connor on T.V. / Dorothy / Sky of bones / Egg / Consumer decency / My life is a mediocre piece of shit / Incinerator heart / Buckets, pock, fork / Demonologist / Lisa's father (waka baby) (live).

Aug 90. (7") *<(VIRUS 83)>* **MY BOYFRIEND'S BACK. / DEMONOLOGIST**

Sep 90. (lp/cd) *<(VIRUS 82/+CD)>* **MULE**
– Mother of Christ / Mrs. Hayes / Roaches in the sink / Crawlpappy / My severed heads / Bottom of the chain / Burlesque / Big ass / Roadkill / Tiny ugly world / J train downtown – A nest of murder / Cow's placenta to armageddon. *(cd+=)* – My boyfriend's back.

May 91. (lp/cd) *<(VIRUS 91/+CD)>* **REVENGE FANTASIES OF THE IMPOTENT**
– Rise to the skin / My best friend's wife / Telebloodprintmeadiadeathwhore / What / Dead river / Sleep / Naked, sharp and perfect / Come up with your hands out / War pigs / Good posture.

Oct 91. (12") *<(VIRUS 101)>* **BIGGEST ASS. / BIGGER ASS / BIG ASS** (live)
(cd-s+=) *<(VIRUS 101CD)>* – Mr Hayes' gimp leg.

—— SISSI SCHULMEISTER – bass, vocals; repl. HOUGHTON + GIFFIN

Jul 92. (7") *<(VIRUS 114)>* **MAGDALENE. / ONLY THE GOOD DIE YOUNG**
(cd-s+=) *<(VIRUS 114CD)>* –

Sep 92. (lp/cd) *<(VIRUS 115/+CD)>* **THE UNTIDY SUICIDES OF YOUR DEGENERATE CHILDREN**
– Magdalene / Untidy suicides / Loteria / The tingler / Every body is on sale / Hang the dog / Son of a disgruntled x-postal worker . . . / Annie's empty / Loteria / Medication / Things have never looked better / Wire mother / She loves you she wants you it's amazing / Loteria / In my head.

Mar 93. (7") *<(VIRUS 121)>* **MEDICATION. / LADY DI**
(cd-s+=) *<(VIRUS 121CD)>* – The yellow bridge.

Apr 94. (lp/cd) *<(VIRUS 143/+CD)>* **DRY-HUMPING THE CASH COW** (some live at CBGB's 1993)
– Green meat stew / Hose / The tingler / Dorothy / Every body is on sale / My best friend's wife / Mrs. Hayes / The son of a disgruntled x-postal worker reflects on his life while getting stoned in the parking lot of a Winn Dixie listening to Metallica / Dead river / Mother of Christ / Helter skelter / American lips / Egg / Demonologist / Buckets, pock, fork. *(cd re-iss. Nov97; same)*

—— In Oct'94, they teamed up with ICE PRINCESS for a single on 'Cargo'; *BEAT 013)*

Nov 94. (7") *<(VIRUS 154)>* **NADINE. / CHICKEN DOOR**
(cd-s+=) *<(VIRUS 154CD)>* – Empty streets.

Jul 95. (lp/cd) *<(VIRUS 163/+CD)>* **PURE ACID PARK**
– Millennium / Dreaming in Cuban / Freaks in love / Big cars and blow jobs / I walked with a zombie / The senator and the cabin boy / Mummenschantz Pachinko / Insane / Shining path / The unspeakable pleasure of being me / Lost in place / Cain. *(cd re-iss. Nov97; same)*

—— ALICE DONUT have since split up

ALIEN SEX FIEND

Formed: London, England ... 1982 by NIK WADE, a former DEMON PREACHERS member who enlisted the help of his wife, CHRISTINE (aka MRS. FIEND). The aforementioned band released a couple of 45's towards the end of the decade, recording for such established indie imprints as 'Illegal' and 'Small Wonder'. Adding DAVID JAMES (aka YAXI HIGHRIZER) and JOHNNY 'HA HA' FRESHWATER, the couple adopted the ALIEN SEX FIEND moniker and secured a residency at the infamous 'Batcave' club. Complete with thick ghoulish make-up, NIK led his band of ALICE COOPER devotees through a regular performance of cabaret goth, recording a live demo cassette 'THE LEWD, THE MAD, THE UGLY & OLD NIK' at their famous haunt. Carving out a deal with Cherry Red subsidiary, 'Anagram', the 'FIENDS released two singles, 'IGNORE THE MACHINE' and 'LIPS CAN'T GO', both highlights of their late 1983 debut set, 'WHO'S BEEN SLEEPING IN MY BRAIN?'. An almost permanent fixture in the indie charts from then on ('ACID BATH' – 1984, etc), the band also became massive in Japan, their third set, 'LIQUID HEAD IN TOKYO – LIVE' (1985) documenting this surprise phenomenon. Subsequently continuing as a trio without JOHNNY, they were finally offered the honour of supporting their schlock-rocker idol, ALICE COOPER, on his 1986 "Nightmare Returns" tour. Having contributed to three further mid-80's sets (' ... MAXIMUM SECURITY, 'IT – THE ALBUM' and 'HERE CUM GERMS'), YAXI was the next to depart, leaving the husband and wife team to record a one-off single, 'WHERE ARE BATMAN AND ROBIN', as The DYNAMIC DUO. ALIEN SEX FIEND returned to terrorize self-respecting indie fans with the likes of 'ANOTHER PLANET' (1988), 'TOO MUCH ACID?' (1989), although their shift to more electronically based territory ALIENated some of their more traditional fans. Later in the 90's, after a couple of patchy sets, including the 'INFERNO' CD-ROM game/album, they initiated their own '13th Moon Records' label. • **Songwriters:** NIK penned most except; SCHOOL'S OUT (Alice Cooper) / I WALK THE LINE (Johnny Cash) / HURRICANE FIGHTER PLANE (Red Crayola) / SILVER MACHINE (Hawkwind).

Album rating: WHO'S BEEN SLEEPING IN MY BRAIN (*4) / ACID BATH (*5) / LIQUID HEAD IN TOKYO – LIVE mini (*5) / (I'M DOIN' TIME IN A) MAXIMUM SECURITY TWILIGHT HOME (*6) / IT – THE ALBUM (*6) / HERE CUM GERMS (*4) / ANOTHER PLANET (*6) / TOO MUCH ACID? (*4) / CURSE (*4) / OPEN HEAD SURGERY (*6) / THE ALTERED STATES OF AMERICA (*5) / INFERNO (*6) / THE SINGLES 1983-1995 compilation (*6) / NOCTURNAL EMISSIONS (*5)

DEMON PREACHERS

NIK FIEND (b. Wales) – vocals, bass (ex-EARWIGS, ex-MR. & MRS. DEMEANOUR) / (+ 3 others)

Illegal / not iss.

1978. (7"m) *(SRTS-CUS 78110)* **ROYAL NORTHERN (N7) / LAUGHING AT ME. / STEAL YOUR LOVE / DEAD END KIDZ**

Small Wonder / not iss.

Aug 78. (7") *(SMALL TEN)* **LITTLE MISS PERFECT. / PERFECT DUB**

Crypt Music / not iss.

1980. (7"; as The DEMONS) *(DEM 1)* **ACTION BY EXAMPLE. / I WISH I WAS A DOG**

ALIEN SEX FIEND

NIK WADE – vocals, bass / **CHRISTINE WADE** – synthesizers / **DAVID JAMES** (aka YAXI HIGHRIZER) – guitar / **JOHNNY 'HA HA' FRESHWATER** – drums

Anagram / not iss.

Aug 83. (7") *(ANA 11)* **IGNORE THE MACHINE. / THE GIRL AT THE END OF MY GUN**
(12"+=) *(12ANA 11)* – I'm not mad.
(12"+=) *(12ANA 11X)* – Under the thunder.
(re-iss. Mar85 7"pic-d; (PANA 11) – ('A'mix) / ('A'dub version). *(pic-cd-s iss.Sep88; CDANA 11)*

ALIEN SEX FIEND (cont)   THE GREAT INDIE DISCOGRAPHY   **The 1980s**

Oct 83.	(7") (ANA 15) **LIPS CAN'T GO. / DRIVE MY ROCKET (UP URANUS)**
	(12"+=) (12ANA 15) – Toytown mix / 30 second coma.
Nov 83.	(lp) (GRAM 10) **WHO'S BEEN SLEEPING IN MY BRAIN?**
	– I wish I woz a dog / Wild women / I'm not mad / New Christian music / Wigwam wipeout / I'm her Frankenstein / I am a product / Ignore the machine / R.I.P. / Lips can't go / Black rabbit. (cd-iss. Sep98; CDGRAM 10) (cd re-iss. Feb01 +=; CDMGOTH 9) – New Christian music (live) / Crazee (live).
Feb 84.	(7"/7"red) (ANA 18) **R.I.P. / NEW CHRISTIAN MUSIC**
	(10"+=/12"+=) (10/12 ANA 18) – Crazee.
Aug 84.	(7"pic-d/7",7"red) (P+/ANA 23) **DEAD AND BURIED. / ATTACK**
	(12"+=) (12ANA 23) – Ignore the machine.
Oct 84.	(lp/c) (GRAM/CGRAM 18) **ACID BATH**
	– In God we trust / Dead and re-buried / Smoke my bones / She's a killer / E.S.T. (trip to the Moon) / Breakdown and cry (lay down and say goodbye) / Hee-haw (here come the bone people) / Attack / Boneshaker baby. (c+=) – WHO'S BEEN SLEEPING IN MY BRAIN? (cd-iss. Jun88 & Jun97 +=; CDMGRAM 18) – I am a product (live) / 30 second coma. <US-iss.1999; ASFLPC 2>
Oct 84.	(7") (ANA 25) **E.S.T. (TRIP TO THE MOON). / BONESHAKER BABY**
	(11"+=) (11ANA 25) – I am a product (live).
Jul 85.	(m-lp) (MGRAM 22) **LIQUID HEAD IN TOKYO (live)**
	– R.I.P. / E.S.T. / Dead and buried / In God we trust / Back to the egg / Attack / Lips can't go / Wild woman. (cd-iss. Jan97 on 'Summit'; SUMCD 4087)

— trimmed to a trio, when JOHNNY departed HA HA (it's not funny- ed)

Aug 85.	(12"m) (12ANA 30) **I'M DOIN' TIME IN A MAXIMUM SECURITY TWILIGHT HOME. / IN AND OUT OF MY MIND / BACKWARD BEAVER**
Sep 85.	(lp) (GRAM 24) **(I'M DOIN' TIME IN A) MAXIMUM SECURITY TWILIGHT HOME**
	– I'm doin' time in a maximum security twilight home / Spies / Depravity lane / Seconds to nowhere / The beaver destroys forest / Mine's full of maggots / In and out of my mind / Fly in the ointment / Do you sleep (not of one mind). (re-iss. Jun88 on 'Antler'; ANT037) (cd-iss. Nov88 & Apr94 as 'THE FIRST ALIEN SEX FIEND CD' =; CDGRAM 25) – E.S.T. (trip to the Moon) / Boneshaker baby / Ignore the machine / Attack!!!.

Flicknife   not iss.

May 86.	(7") (SFLEP 106) **I WALK THE LINE. / SCHOOL'S OUT**
	(d7"+=/12"+=) (DL/FL EP 106) – Here she comes/ Can't stop smoking. (d7"re-iss. Feb95; SFLEP 106)

Vat   not iss.

Aug 86.	(7") **GET INTO IT. / SOMEONE KEEPS ON BUGGIN' ME**

Anagram   not iss.

Oct 86.	(7"/12") (ANA/12ANA 32) **SMELLS LIKE SHIT. / SOMEOME KEEPS ON BUGGIN' ME**
Oct 86.	(lp/c) (GRAM/CGRAM 26) **IT - THE ALBUM**
	– Smells like shit / Manic depression / Believe it or not / Get into it / Wop bop / April showers / Lesson one / Do it right / To be continued . . . (re-iss. Jun88 on 'Antler' lp/c+=; ANT 048/+C) – TWILIGHT HOME (lp tracks) (cd-iss. Dec91 +=; CDGRAM 26) – Buggin' me / Hurricane fighter pilot / It lives again.
Feb 87.	(7") (ANA 33) **HURRICANE FIGHTER PLANE. / IT LIVES AGAIN**
	(12"+=) (12ANA 33) – ('A'mix).
Jun 87.	(7") (ANA 34) **THE IMPOSSIBLE MISSION. / MY BRAIN IS IN THE CUPBOARD ABOVE THE KITCHEN SINK**
	(12"+=) (12ANA 34) – Put A-Z.
Aug 87.	(7") (ANA 38) **HERE CUM GERMS. / ('A'-Ravi mix) / ('A'dub)**
	(12"+=) (12ANA 38) – Camel camel.
Oct 87.	(lp/c) (GRAM/CGRAM 31) **HERE CUM GERMS**
	– The mission impossible / Here cum germs (Ravi mix) / Isolation / My brain is in the cupboard above the kitchen / You are soul / Death / Boots on!. (cd-iss. Jun92 +=; CDGRAM 31) – Camel, camel / Stuff the turkey / They all call me crazee.
Nov 87.	(7",7"red,7"green) (ANA 40) **STUFF THE TURKEY. / THEY ALL CALL ME CRAZEE**

— now as duo when YAXI left

Oct 88.	(12"m) (12ANA 45) **BUN HO!. / SILVER MACHINE / SATISFACTION**
Oct 88.	(cd/c/lp) (CD/C+/GRAM 38) **ANOTHER PLANET**
	– Bun hol / Anybody's dream / Radiant city / Spot your lucky warts / Sample my sausage / Outer limits / Instant karma sutra / So much to do – So little time / Alien / Wild green fiendly liquid / Nightmare zone / Bun ho (time after time) / Another planet. (c+=) – Silver machine / Satisfaction. (cd re-iss. Jun97; same)
Mar 89.	(7") (ANA 46) **HAUNTED HOUSE. / ('A'dub version)**
	(12"+=/cd-s+=) (12/CD ANA 46) –
Sep 89.	(cd/c/d-lp) (CD/C+/GRAM 41) **TOO MUCH ACID? (live)**
	– It lives again / I walk the line / Nightmare zone / Get into it / E.S.T. (trip to the Moon) / So much to do, so little time / Bun ho! / Haunted house / Smells like shit / Hurricane fighter plane / Sample my sausage / Boneshaker baby. (cd re-iss. May93; same) (cd re-iss. Nov01; CDMGOTH 13)
Sep 90.	(7") **NOW I'M FEELING ZOMBIEFIED. /**
	(12"+=/cd-s+=) –
Oct 90.	(cd/c/lp) (CD/C+/GRAM 46) **CURSE**
	– Katch 22 / You – Along cums reality – Hubble bubble / Goodbye to space / Now I'm feeling zombiefied / Stress / Blessings of the state / Eat! eat! eat! (an eye for an eye) / Ain't got time to bleed. (cd+=/c+=) – Bleeding (reprise) / Dalsims / Burger bar baby / I think I . . . Mad daddy drives a UFO / Wuthering wind / Radio Jimi / Hands of the silken / Blessing in disguise. (cd re-iss. Mar02; CDMGOTH 15)
Mar 92.	(cd/c/lp) (CD/C+/GRAM 51) **OPEN HEAD SURGERY**
	– Clockwork banana banana – moon / Magic / Class of '69 / Aliensexfiend / Coma / Lickin' ma bone / Stressed out / B-B-Bone boogie.
Feb 93.	(cd/c/lp) (CD/C+/GRAM 60) **THE ALTERED STATES OF AMERICA**
	– Wild women / Now I'm feeling zombiefied / Class of '69 / Ignore the machine / Magic / Coma / Eat! eat! eat! / R.I.P. (blue crumb truck).
Jul 94.	(12") (MFF 007T) **INFERNO. /**
	(above issued on 'Cherry Red')
Oct 94.	(cd) (CDGRAM 80) <9529> **INFERNO**
	– Inferno / Human installation / Take off tune / Space 1 / Happy tune / Planet 1 / Human atmosphere / Happy finale / Alien installation / Aromatic tune / Moon toon / Planet 2 / Bad news / Space 2 / Alien atmosphere / Death tune / Sad finale / Moon ton (lunaphases mix) / Planet 2 (together dreamscape mix) / Inferno.
Mar 95.	(cd-ep) (CDGRAM 56) **INFERNO / INFERNO (Mix) / PLANET 2 / ECHOES**

13th Moon   13th Moon

Feb 96.	(12"/cd-s) (FULL T/CDS 001) **EVOLUTION. / ('A'mixes)**
Mar 97.	(cd/d-lp) (FULL CD/DLP 1301) **NOCTURNAL EMISSIONS** Nov98
	– Evolution / On a mission / Warp out / Big blue moon / Room 101 / Soaking wet, mate / Garbage / Tarot / Sticky. (re-iss. Jul00; FULLCD 1302) <US-iss.2001 on 'Resurgence'; 4642>
Aug 97.	(12") (FULLT 002R) **ON A MISSION (remix). /** Oct98
Nov 98.	(12") (FULLT 003R) **TAROT (7 mix). / ('A'-No.6 mix) / ('A'-POD dub mix)**

– compilations, etc. –

Mar 88.	(cd/c/lp) Anagram; (CD/C+GRAM 34) **ALL OUR YESTERDAZE (The Singles Collection 1983-87)**
	– Ignore the machine / Lips can't go / R.I.P. – Blue crumb truck / Dead & buried / E.S.T. – Trip to the Moon / I'm doing time in a maximum security twilight home / I walk the line / Smells like shit / Hurricane fighter pilot. (<cd re-iss. May93 & Dec99; same>)
Mar 88.	(12"; as DYNAMIC DUO) Anagram; (12ANA 42) **WHERE ARE BATMAN AND ROBIN? / BATMAN THEME**
Oct 93.	(cd/c) Anagram; (CD/C GRAM 69) **THE LEGENDARY BATCAVE TAPES (live)**
	(<re-iss. Jun98 as 'BAT CAVE MASTERS' on 'Cleopatra'; CLP 232)>
Aug 94.	(cd) Cleopatra; (<CLEO 9412-2>) **DRIVE MY ROCKET**
Jun 95.	(cd) Cleopatra; (<CLEO 9508CD>) **I'M HER FRANKENSTEIN**
Oct 95.	(d-cd) Anagram; (<CDGRAM 99>) **THE SINGLES 1983-1995** Feb96
Feb 98.	(d-cd) Snapper; (SMDCD 133) **WARDANCE OF THE ALIEN SEX FIEND**
May 99.	(d-cd) Anagram; (CDGRAM 120) Cleopatra; <694> **FIENDS AT THE CONTROLS VOL.1 & 2** Oct98
Feb 01.	(cd) Anagram; (CDMGOTH 1) **THE BEST OF ALIEN SEX FIEND**
Apr 02.	(cd) Yeaah; (YEAAH 52) **FLASHBACKS LIVE 1995-1998**

ALL ABOUT EVE

Formed: London, England . . . 1985 by music journalist JULIANNE REGAN and ex-AEMOTTI CRII member TIM BRICHENO. Named after a 1950 Bette Davis film, they released four indie hits on their own 'Eden' records, before landing a contract with 'Mercury' in mid-87. Their major label debut (a remix of their second 45, 'IN THE CLOUDS') hit the UK Top 50, and paved the way for late 80's chart status. Touting progressive "acid-folk" "hippygoth" influenced by early 70's acoustic LED ZEPPELIN or even CURVED AIR (imagery & mysticism), ALL ABOUT EVE were for a brief period in the late 80's something of an alluring alternative to the disposable pop clogging up the charts. A follow-up single, 'WILD HEARTED WOMAN', made the Top 40, although the band really broke through later that summer with the ethereal 'MARTHA'S HARBOUR', a single which crossed over to rock/pop fans and made the UK Top 10. Its success fuelled further sales of the eponymous debut album which achieved a similar chart position. The tricky momentum of simultaneously balancing a goth/indie and mainstream fanbase came undone with a more morose follow-up album, 'SCARLET AND OTHER STORIES' (1989). Though it made the Top 10, it failed to match the success of its predecessors, the record's downbeat sound possibly attributable to the internal ructions taking place. BRICHENO finally left for The SISTERS OF MERCY in 1990, his replacement being CHURCH-man, MARTY WILLSON-PIPER, initially on a temporary basis and subsequently full-time. Despite being touted as a return to form, 'TOUCHED BY JESUS' (1991) failed to meet commercial expectations and the band split from their label shortly after. Despite a comeback with a set for 'M.C.A.', 'ULTRAVIOLET', the band finally called it a day in early '93. REGAN subsequently formed HARMONY AMBULANCE (who released a one-off 45 for 'Rough Trade') before going on to work with BERNARD BUTLER and later form MICE. Towards the end of the decade, the acoustic ALL ABOUT EVE toured alongside The MISSION on their Resurrection tour, subsequent concert sets 'FAIRY LIGHT NIGHTS' (in two volumes) showcased their long-awaited return. • **Songwriters:** REGAN – lyrics / BRICHENO – music, until his departure, then group compositions. • **Trivia:** 1987 single 'OUR SUMMER' was produced by WAYNE HUSSEY and SIMON HINKLER (of The MISSION). JULIANNE returned the favour by guesting on their 'God's Own Medicine' album. BRICHENO also joined The MISSION for a time, after his relationship with REGAN floundered.

Album rating: ALL ABOUT EVE (*8) / SCARLET AND OTHER STORIES (*6) / TOUCHED BY JESUS (*5) / ULTRAVIOLET (*5) / WINTER WORDS – HITS AND RARITIES compilation (*6) / Mice: BECAUSE I CAN (*5) / All About Eve: FAIRY LIGHT NIGHTS (*6) / FAIRY LIGHT NIGHTS TWO (*5)

JULIANNE REGAN – vocals, (some) keyboards / **TIMOTHY BRICHENO** (b. 6 Jul'63, Huddersfield, England) – guitar / **ANDY COUSIN** – bass (group augmented by a drum machine)

Eden   not iss.

Jul 85.	(12") (1 EDEN) **D FOR DESIRE. / DON'T FOLLOW ME (MARCH HARE)**
Apr 86.	(12") (2 EDEN) **IN THE CLOUDS. / END OF THE DAY / LOVE LEADS NOWHERE**

ALL ABOUT EVE (cont) — THE GREAT INDIE DISCOGRAPHY — The 1980s

Apr 87.	(7") (EVEN 3) **OUR SUMMER. / LADY MIDNIGHT** (ext.12"+=) (EVENX 3) – Shelter from the rain.		–
Jul 87.	(7") (EVEN 4) **FLOWERS IN OUR HAIR. / PARADISE** (12"+=) (EVENX 4) – Devil woman.		–

— added **MARK PRICE** – drums

		Mercury	Mercury
Oct 87.	(7") (EVEN 5) **IN THE CLOUDS. / SHE MOVES THROUGH THE FAIR** (12"+=) (EVENX 5) – Calling your name.	47	–
Jan 88.	(7") (EVEN 6) **WILD HEARTED WOMAN. / APPLE TREE MAN** (c-s+=/12"+=) (EVEN M/X 6) – Like Emily. (12"box++=) (EVENX 6-22) – What kind of fool (live). (cd-s+=) (EVNCD 6) – Like Emily / In the clouds.	33	–
Feb 88.	(lp/c)(cd) (MERH/+C 119)(<834 260-2>) **ALL ABOUT EVE** – Flowers in our hair / Gypsy dance / In the clouds / Martha's harbour / Every angel / Like Emily / Shelter from the storm / She moves through the fair / Wild hearted woman / Never promise (anyone forever) / What kind of fool. (c+=/cd+=) – Apple tree man / In the meadow / Lady Midnight.	7	–
Mar 88.	(7"/7"g-f) (EVEN/+G 7) **EVERY ANGEL. / WILD FLOWERS** (12"+=) (EVENX 7) – Candy tree. (10"++=)(cd-s++=) (EVEN 710)(EVNCD 7) – More than this hour.	30	–
Jul 88.	(7") (EVEN 8) **MARTHA'S HARBOUR. / ANOTHER DOOR** (12"+=) (EVENX 8) – In the meadow (live). (c-s++=) (EVENM 8) – Never promise (anyone forever) (live). (cd-s+=) (EVNCD 8) – She moves through the fair (live) / Wild flowers (live). (12"+=) (EVENXB 8) – In the clouds (live) / Shelter from the rain (live).	10	–
Nov 88.	(7") (EVEN 9) **WHAT KIND OF FOOL. / GOLD AND SILVER** (12"+=) (EVENX 9) – The garden of Jane Delawney. (12"box++=/cd-s++=) (EVN XB 9/CD 99) – ('A'-Autumn rhapsody mix). (10"+=) (EVEN 9-10) – Every angel (live).	29	–
Sep 89.	(7"/c-s) (EVEN/EVNMC 10) **ROAD TO YOUR SOUL. / PIECES OF OUR HEART** (ext.12"+=)(pic-cd-s+=) (EVNXP/EVCDX 10) – Hard Spaniard.	37	–
Oct 89.	(lp/c/cd) (<838 965-1/-4/-2>) **SCARLET AND OTHER STORIES** – Road to your soul / Dream now / Gold and silver / Scarlet / December / Blind lemon Sam / More than the blues / Tuesday's child / Pieces of our heart ** / Hard Spaniard * / The empty dancehall / Only one reason / The pearl fisherman. (c+=*/cd++= **)	9	–
Dec 89.	(7"/c-s) (EVEN/+MC 11) **DECEMBER. / DROWNING** (7"pic-d+=/10"+=) (EVEN P/B 11) – Paradise ('89 remix). (c-s+=/12"+=/cd-s+=) (EVE MC/NX/NCD 11) – The witches' promise.	34	–
Apr 90.	(7"/c-s) (EVEN/+MC 12) **SCARLET. / OUR SUMMER (live)** (12"+=/cd-s+=) (EVENX/EVNCD 12) – Candy tree (live) / Tuesday's child (live).	34	–

— (Aug'90) – when BRICHENO went off to join SISTERS OF MERCY (also later TIN STAR), **MARTY WILLSON-PIPER** (of The CHURCH) came in temp. at first, then full-time

Jun 91.	(7") (EVEN 14) **FAREWELL MR. SORROW. / ELIZABETH OF GLASS** (12"+=/cd-s+=) (EVENX/EVNCD 14) – All the rings round Saturn.	36	–

		Vertigo	Mercury
Aug 91.	(7"/7"pic-d/c-s) (EVEN/+P/MC 15) **STRANGE WAY. / DRAWN TO EARTH** (pic-cd-s+=) (EVNCD 15) – Share it with me. (10"+=) (EVENB 15) – Share it with me / Nothing without you. (12"+=) (EVENX 15) – Nothing without you / Light as a feather.	50	–
Aug 91.	(cd/c/lp) (<51046-2/-4/-1>) **TOUCHED BY JESUS** – Strange way / Farewell Mr. Sorrow / Wishing the hours away / Touched by Jesus / The dreamer / Share it with me * / Rhythm of life / The mystery we are / Hide child / Ravens / Are you lonely. (c/cd+= *) (re-iss. Feb93; same)	17	–
Oct 91.	(7") (EVEN 16) **THE DREAMER (remix). / FRIDA OF BLOOD AND GOLD** (12"+=) (EVENX 16) – Road to Damascus / Strange way (demo). (cd-s+=) (EVNCD 16) – Road to Damascus / ('A'-nightmare mix).	41	–

		M.C.A.	M.C.A.
Sep 92.	(7"ep/c-ep/cd-ep/10"blue-ep) (MCS/+C/CD/T 1688) **PHASED EP** – Phased / Mine / Infrared / Ascent-descent.	38	–
Oct 92.	(cd/c/lp) (<MCD/MCC/MCA 10712>) **ULTRAVIOLET** – Phased / Yesterday goodbye / Mine / Freeze / Things he told her / Infrared / I don't know / Dream butcher / Some finer day / Blindfolded visionary / Outside the Sun.	46	–
Nov 92.	(7"/c-s) (MCS/+CS 1706) **SOME FINER DAY. / MOODSWING** (10"+=/cd-s+=) (MCS T/CD 1706) – Dive in.	57	–

— Disbanded early 1993, JULIANNE formed HARMONY AMBULANCE and released one-off 45 for 'Rough Trade'. In 1994, she began working with BERNARD BUTLER (ex-SUEDE), signing solo to 'Permanent' she soon formed her own band, MICE, with past AAE members. ALL ABOUT EVE (see final line-up trio) re-formed for gigs in 2000.

– compilations, others, etc. –

Feb 91.	(cd-ep) Mercury; (EVCDX 13) **THIRTEEN (live)** – In the clouds / Never promise (anyone forever) / Scarlet / More than the blues / Road to your soul.		–
Nov 92.	(cd/c/lp) Vertigo; (514 154-2/-4/-1) **WINTER WORDS – HITS AND RARITIES** (re-iss. Apr95 cd/c; same)		–
Nov 93.	(cd) Windsong; (WINCD 044) **BBC RADIO 1 LIVE IN CONCERT – GLASTONBURY FESTIVAL (live)**		–
Aug 99.	(cd) Spectrum; (544153-2) **THE BEST OF ALL ABOUT EVE**		–
Oct 01.	(cd) Castle; (CMRCD 332) **LIVE AND ELECTRIC AT THE UNION CHAPEL (live)** (re-iss. Nov01 on 'Jam Tart'; AAEVP 4)		–
Dec 01.	(cd) Almafame; (ALMACD 13) **B-SIDES AND C-SIDES**		–
Jan 02.	(cd) Dressed To Kill; (MIDRO 850) **MARTHA'S HARBOUR**		–
Jul 02.	(cd) Jam Tart; (AAEVP 5) **RETURN TO EDEN VOL.1 – THE EARLY RECORDINGS**		–

MICE

— **JULIANNE REGAN** – vocals / with **COUSIN + PRICE** and **BIC** – guitar (ex-CARDIACS)

		Permanent	Permanent
Nov 95.	(7"yellow/c-s) (7/CA SPERM 30) **MAT'S PROZAC. / BANG BANG** (cd-s+=) (CDSPERM 30) – Julie Christie.		–
Apr 96.	(7"/c-s/cd-s) (7/CA/CD SPERM 31) **THE MILKMAN (semi-skimmed version) / THE MILKMAN (full-cream version) / MARTIAN MAN / DIE UBERMAUS**		–
Jul 96.	(7"colrd/c-s) (7/CA SPERM 033) **DEAR SIR.** / ('A'mix) (cd-s+=) (CDSPERM 033) – Pyjamadrama / Tiny window.		– –
Aug 96.	(cd/c/lp) (<PERM CD/MC/LP 035>) **BECAUSE I CAN** – Mat's prozac / Star / Dear sir / Bang bang / The milkman / Trumpet song / Blue sonic boy / Julie Christie / Miss World / Battersea / Messed up.		–

ALL ABOUT EVE

— **REGAN + COUSINS + WILLSON-PIPER**

		Yeaah	Yeaah
Jun 00.	(cd) (<YEAAH 8>) **FAIRY LIGHT NIGHTS – LIVE ACOUSTIC (live)** – What kind of fool / In the clouds / Forever / Share it with me / Will I start to bleed / Miss World / Martha's harbour / Shelter from the rain / Are you lonely / Appletree man.		Aug00
Dec 01.	(cd) (YEAAH 24) **FAIRY LIGHT NIGHTS TWO – LIVE ACOUSTIC (live)** – Scarlet / The mystery we are / You bring your love to me / Freeze / Mine / More than the blues / Never promise (anyone forever) / Yesterday goodbye / Wild hearted woman / Every angel. (re-iss. Apr02 on 'Jam Tart'; AAEVP 1CD)		–

Marc ALMOND

Born: PETER MARC ALMOND, 9 Jul'59, Southport, England. Having met DAVE BALL at Leeds Polytechnic, the pair formed SOFT CELL and with the help of visual technician, STEVEN GRIFFITHS, they embarked on studio and live work in 1980 with the 'MUTANT MOMENTS' EP. After appearing on the infamous 'Some Bizzare Album', with cut, 'The Girl With The Patent Leather Face', they secured a bonafide deal with the 'Some Bizzare' label. The following year, after a debut single, 'MEMORABILIA' failed to make an impression, a darkly compelling, electro-fuelled cover of 'TAINTED LOVE' (once the dancefloor domain of disco diva, GLORIA JONES) slipped in the UK chart, peaking at No.1 for two weeks. To end the year, SOFT CELL cracked the Top 5 with both 'BEDSITTER' and their debut album, 'NON-STOP EROTIC CABARET', an early 80's classic which trawled the depths of ALMOND's black-leather, neon-lit fantasies to a sleazy musical backdrop of low-rent alternative disco. Apart from the aforementioned singles, tracks such as 'YOUTH', 'SEX DWARF', 'SEEDY FILMS', 'CHIPS ON MY SHOULDER' and the forthcoming hit, 'SAY HELLO, WAVE GOODBYE', even found a rampant audience in the gay disco community of New York. The extroverted ALMOND was a figurehead for young homosexuals, although the media were scathing in their criticism of what they saw as the singer's effeminate posturing. Nevertheless, SOFT CELL continued to chalk up the hits, 'TORCH' (an exquisite duet featuring CINDY ECSTACY) narrowly missing No.1, while a revamped dance model of the debut, 'NON-STOP ECSTATIC DANCING', marked time as BALL and ALMOND worked on a follow-up. Early in '83, their second set proper, 'THE ART OF FALLING APART', hit the shops and subsequently the Top 5, the record coming with a free 12" single that saw ALMOND bravely attempting a HENDRIX medley. As the pair increasingly concentrated on separate projects, MARC & THE MAMBAS and DAVE BALL solo, a split seemed imminent; by the release of 'THIS LAST NIGHT . . . IN SODOM' in January '84, SOFT CELL was no more. After many threats of impending retirement, ALMOND was back in his beloved spotlight with the 'VERMIN IN ERMINE' (1984) album, cut with new backing band, The WILLING SINNERS. Developing further as an interpretive balladeer/torch singer with each successive release, ALMOND's mid-late 80's output found him marginalised to cult appeal despite an impressive array of cover material from such luminaries as JACQUES BREL, SCOTT WALKER and JOHNNIE RAY. This approach finally resulted in a massive comeback hit duet with GENE PITNEY, the melodramatic 'SOMETHING'S GOTTEN HOLD OF MY HEART', originally a Top 5 hit in 1967 for the singing/songwriting heart-throb. In the early 90's, SOFT CELL enjoyed a bit of a renaissance, remixed versions of 'SAY HELLO WAVE GOODBYE' and 'TAINTED LOVE' making the charts, while ALMOND scored a surprise Top 20 hit with a dancefloor reworking of Jacques Brel's 'JACKY'. Taken from the album, 'TENEMENT SYMPHONY' (1991), this return to form also numbered future hits, 'MY HAND OVER MY HEART' and 'THE DAYS OF PEARLY SPENCER', the latter another blast from the 60's past and originally a hit for DAVID McWILLIAMS. ALMOND continued to work on various idiosyncratic projects, including a set of old French songs and poems, 'ABSINTHE' (1993). Having delivered what was to be a one-off album ('FANTASTIC STAR') for 'Mercury' in early '96, the long-suffering tainted soul that was MARC ALMOND made his re-appearance with the single 'BLACK KISS' in late '98. Having set up his own record label, 'Blue Star', the wee man unleashed his most advanced work since the early days in the shape of 'OPEN ALL NIGHT' (1999). With rave reviews (for once!), ALMOND set about publishing two works, the first a lyrics/poems collection entitled 'A Beautiful Twisted Night', the second an autobiography 'Tainted Life'. 'STRANGER THINGS' (2001) happened to ALMOND in the new millennium as he joined forces with Icelandic leftfield beats merchant JOHAN JOHANNSON. Well, not that strange, merely a trip into more widescreen territory courtesy of JOHANNSON's luxuriant string arrangements, the record even featuring the obligatory guest spot from SHIRLEY BASSEY to add that crucial 007 touch. Spurred on by a UK Top 40 "BEST OF..." compilation and with nearly every other post-New Wave outfit re-forming to rake in the spoils of money (or credibility!), it was no surprise that messrs ALMOND and BALL would resurrect SOFT CELL; it had been a full 18 years since their... er 'LAST NIGHT IN SODOM' came out. 'CRUELTY WITHOUT BEAUTY' (2002), stepped back to these heady days of yore. Opening with 'DARKER TIMES' and the minor hit single, 'MONOCULTURE', the set showed what might've been had ALMOND not ventured to croon land. • **Covered:** WHERE DID OUR LOVE GO (Supremes). MARC & THE MAMBAS covered IF YOU GO AWAY + THE BULLS (Jacques Brel) / CAROLINE SAYS (Lou Reed) / TERRAPIN (Syd Barrett) / CATCH A FALLEN STAR (Perry Como). MARC ALMOND solo:- A WOMAN'S STORY (Cher) / A SALTY DOG (Procol Harum) / THE LITTLE WHITE CLOUD THAT CRIED (Johnnie Ray) / THE PLAGUE (Scott Walker). • **Trivia:** In 1983, DAVE BALL scored the music for Tennessee Williams' play 'Suddenly Last Summer'. In mid 1987, ALMOND guested and wrote on SALLY TIMMS' single 'This House Is A House Of Tears'.

Album rating: Soft Cell: NON-STOP EROTIC CABARET (*8) / NON-STOP ECSTATIC DANCING remix collection (*4) / THE ART OF FALLING APART (*6) / THIS LAST NIGHT ... IN SODOM (*5) / MEMORABILIA – THE SINGLES compilation (*8) / Marc And The Mambas: UNTITLED (*8) / TORMENT AND TOREROS (*5) / Marc Almond: VERMIN IN ERMINE (*5) / STORIES OF JOHNNY (*5) / MOTHER FIST AND HER FIVE DAUGHTERS (*4) / THE STARS WE ARE (*5) / JACQUES (*5) / ENCHANTMENT (*5) / TENEMENT SYMPHONY (*4) / TWELVE YEARS OF TEARS (*5) / ABSINTHE (*5) / FANTASTIC STAR (*5) / THE SINGLES (1984-1987) compilation (*7) / THE BEST OF MARC ALMOND compilation (*6) / OPEN ALL NIGHT (*7) / STRANGER THINGS (*6)

SOFT CELL

MARC ALMOND – vocals / **DAVE BALL** – keyboards, synthesizer, drum programming

		Big Frock	not iss.
1980.	(7"ep) (ABF 1) **MUTANT MOMENTS**		–
	– Potential / L.O.V.E. feelings / Metro MRX / Frustration.		

		Some Bizzare	Sire
Mar 81.	(7") (HARD 1) **MEMORABILIA. / A MAN CAN GET LOST**		–
	(12") (HARD 12) – ('A'extended) / Persuasion (extended).		
Jul 81.	(7") (BZS 2) <49855> **TAINTED LOVE. / WHERE DID OUR LOVE GO**	1	8 Dec81
	(12"+=) (BZS 2-12) – Tainted dub / Memorabilia.		
	(re-iss. Jul82; hit 50, re-iss. Jan85; hit 43)		
Nov 81.	(7"/ext-12") (BZS 6/+12) **BEDSITTER. / FACILITY GIRLS**	4	
—	guests **CINDY ECSTACY** – dual vox / **DAVE TOFANI** – sax / **JOHN GATHELL** – trumpet		
Dec 81.	(lp/c) (BZ LP/MC 2) <3647> **NON-STOP EROTIC CABARET**	5	22 Jan82
	– Frustration / Tainted love / Seedy films / Youth / Sex dwarf / Entertain me / Chips on my shoulder / Bedsitter / Secret life / Say hello, wave goodbye. (re-iss. May90 on 'Vertigo' cd/c/lp; 800 061-2/-4/-1)		
Jan 82.	(7"/ext-12") (BZS 7/+12) **SAY HELLO, WAVE GOODBYE. / FUN CITY**	3	
May 82.	(7"/ext-12") (BZS 9/+12) **TORCH. / INSECURE ME**	2	
—	duo carried on without CINDY, who later formed SIX SEE RED		
Jun 82.	(m-lp/m-c) (BZ X/M 1012) <23694> **NON-STOP ECSTATIC DANCING** (remixes)	6	57 Jul82
	– Memorabilia / Where did our love go / What! / A man could get lost / Chips on my shoulder * / Sex dwarf. * (US version repl.* with –) – Insecure ... me? (re-iss. Mar92 on 'Mercury'; 510 295-2/-4) – (extra tracks).		
Aug 82.	(7"/ext-12") (BZS 11/+12) **WHAT! / ... SO** (remix)	3	
Nov 82.	(7"/ext-12") (BZS 16/+12) **WHERE THE HEART IS. / IT'S A MUG GAME**	21	
Feb 83.	(lp/c) (BIZL/+C 3) <23769> **THE ART OF FALLING APART**	5	84
	– Forever the same / Where the heart is / Numbers / Heat / Loving you, hating me / The art of falling apart. (12"ep with above +=) – MARTIN. / HENDRIX MEDLEY: HEY JOE – PURPLE HAZE – VOODOO CHILE (re-iss. Nov87; SOD 2) (re-iss. Mar92 on 'Mercury' cd/c; 510 296-2/-4) – (extra tracks).		
Feb 83.	(7"/ext-12") (BZS 16/+12) **NUMBERS. / BARRIERS**	25	–
Apr 83.	(7") **HEAT. / IT'S A MUGS GAME**	–	–
Sep 83.	(7") (BZS 20) **SOUL INSIDE. / YOU ONLY LIVE TWICE**	16	
	(12"+=) (BZS 20-12) – Loving you, hating me / 007 theme.		
	(d7"+=) (BZS 20-20) – Loving you, hating me / Her imagination.		
Feb 84.	(7") (BZS 22) **DOWN IN THE SUBWAY. / DISEASE AND DESIRE**	24	
	(ext-12"+=/12"remix+=) (BZS/+R 22-12) – Born to lose.		
Mar 84.	(lp/c) (BIZL/+C 6) **THIS LAST NIGHT ... IN SODOM**	12	
	– Mr. Self destruct / Slave to this / Little rough rhinestone / Meet murder my angel / The best way to kill / L'Esqualita / Down in the subway / Surrender (to a stranger) / Soul inside / Where was your heart (when you needed it most). (cd-iss. Aug84; 818 436-2)		
—	waved goodbye just prior to the above album		

– compilations, others, etc. –

1982.	(6x12"box) Some Bizzare; (CELBX 1) **THE 12" SINGLES**		–
Dec 86.	(lp/c/cd) Some Bizzare; (BZ LP/MC 3)(830 708-2) **SOFT CELL – THE SINGLES**	58	–
Mar 91.	(7"/c-s) Mercury; (SOF TMC 1) **SAY HELLO, WAVE GOODBYE '91. / MEMORABILIA (Grid remix)**	38	–
	(12"+=)(cd-s+=) (SOFT 1-12/SOFCD 1) – ('A'-Mendelsohn extended remix).		
	(cd-s) (SOFCP 1) – ('A'side) / Numbers / Torch (12"version).		
May 91.	(7"/c-s)(12") Mercury; (SOF T/MC 2)(SOFT 2-12) **TAINTED LOVE ('91 remix). / ('A'-Original)**	5	–
	(cd-s+=) (SOFCP 2) – Where did our love go?		
	(cd-s) (SOFCD 2) – Tainted love – Where the heart is / Loving you – hating me / Where the heart is.		
May 91.	(cd/c/lp) Mercury; (848 512-2/-4/-1) **MEMORABILIA – THE SINGLES**	8	
	– Memorabilia '91 / Tainted love / Bedsitter / Torch / What was the matter with Rachmaninov? / Say hello wave goodbye '91 / Where the heart is / I feel love / Tears run rings / A lover spurned / Something's gotten hold of my heart. (cd+=) – (Soul inside / Say hello wave goodbye (12"mix) / Waifs and strays (Grid twilight mix).		
Mar 96.	(cd/c) Spectrum; (550 189-2/-4) **DOWN IN THE SUBWAY**		
Mar 96.	(cd) Some Bizarre; (552 086-2) **SAY HELLO TO SOFT CELL**		
Feb 99.	(12"; as SOFT CELL vs CLUB 69) Twisted; (TWD 55530) **TAINTED LOVE**		
Apr 02.	(cd) Mercury; (586834-2) **THE VERY BEST OF SOFT CELL**	37	

MARC AND THE MAMBAS

with **ANNIE HOGAN** – piano / **TIM TAYLOR** – bass / **DAVE BALL** – multi instruments

Mar 82.	(12"; mail order) (BZS 5-12) **FUN CITY. / SLEAZE (TAKE IT, SHAKE IT) / TAKING IT SHAKING IT**	–	–
—	guests on next 2 albums were **GENESIS P. ORRIDGE + MATT JOHNSON**		
Oct 82.	(lp/c) (BZA/BZC 13) **UNTITLED**	42	–
	– Untitled / Empty eyes / Angels / Big Louise / Caroline says / Margaret / If you go away. (free-12"ep with above +=) – Terrapin / Twilights and lowlifes (street walking soundtrack) / Twilights and lowlifes. (re-iss. Mar92 on 'Mercury' cd/c; 510 298-2/-4)		
Nov 82.	(7";w-drawn) (BZS 15) **BIG LOUISE. / EMPTY EYES**	–	–
	(12";w-drawn) (BZS 15-12) – The dirt behind the neon.		
Jun 83.	(7") (BZS 19) **BLACK HEART. / YOUR AURA**	49	
	(12"+=) (BZS 19-12) – Mamba.		
Aug 83.	(d-lp/c) (BIZL/+C 4) **TORMENT AND TOREROS**	28	
	– The animal in you / Narcissus / Gloomy Sunday / Vision / Your love is a lesson / The untouchable one / My little book of sorrows / In my room / First time / The bulls / Boss cat / Intro / Catch a fallen star / Beat out dat rhythm on a drum / A million manias / Torment / Black heart. (re-iss. Mar92 on 'Mercury' cd/c; 812 872-2/-4) (cd re-iss. Oct97; SBZCD 028CD)		
Nov 83.	(12"ep) (BZS 21-12) **TORMENT / FIRST TIME. / YOU'LL NEVER SEE ME ON A SUNDAY / MAGAMILLIONMANIA-MULTIMANIAMIX**		–

MARC ALMOND

— went solo augmented by **The WILLING SINNERS: ANNIE HOGAN** – piano / **BILLY McGEE** – bass / **RICHARD RILEY** – guitar / **STEPHEN HUMPHRIES** – drums / **MARTIN McCARRICK** – cello

May 84.	(7") (BZS 23) **THE BOY WHO CAME BACK. / JOEY DEMENTO**	52	
	(10"/12") (BZS 23 10/12) – ('A'-Loud cut) / ('B'extended).		
Sep 84.	(7") (BZS 24) **YOU HAVE. / SPLIT UP**	57	
	(ext-10"+=) (BZS 24-10) – Black mountain blues.		
	(ext-12"+=) (BZS 24-12) – Joey Demento.		
Oct 84.	(lp/c)(cd) (BIZL/+C 8)(<822 832-2>) **VERMINE IN ERMINE**	36	
	– Shining sinners / Hell was a city / You have / Crime sublime / Gutter hearts / Ugly head / The boy who came back / Solo adultos / Tenderness is a weakness. (c+=/cd=) – Pink shack blues / Split lip / Joey Demento.		
Nov 84.	(7") (BZS 25) **TENDERNESS IS A WEAKNESS. / LOVE FOR SALE**		
	(10"+=) (BZS 25-10) – Pink shack blues (live) / The heel (live).		
—	In April '85, he teamed up with BRONSKI BEAT on Top 3 version of 'I FEEL LOVE'. Two months later, he featured anonymously on 12" 'SKIN' as The BURMOE BROTHERS		
Aug 85.	(7") (BONK 1) **STORIES OF JOHNNY. / STORIES OF JOHNNY (with The Westminster City School Choir)**	23	–
	(12"+=) (BONK 1-12) – Take my heart.		
	(d7"++=/10"++=) (BONK 1/+10) – Blond boy.		
Sep 85.	(lp/c/cd) (FAITH/TFTH/CDFTH 1) **STORIES OF JOHNNY**	22	
	– Traumas, traumas, traumas / Stories of Johnny / The house is haunted (by the echoes of your last goodbye) / Love letter / The flesh is willing / Always / Contempt / I who never / My candle burns / Love and little white lies. (c+=/cd+=) – Take my heart / Blond boy / Stories of Johnny (with The Westminster City School Choir).		
Oct 85.	(7") (BONKP 1) **LOVE LETTER. / LOVE LETTER (with The Westmonster City School Choir)**	68	–
	(10"/12") (BONK 2 10/12) – ('A'-Special mix) / ('B'side).		
Jan 86.	(d7") (GLOW D1) **THE HOUSE IS HAUNTED (BY THE ECHO OF YOUR LAST GOODBYE). / BROKEN BARRICADES // CARA A CARA (FACE TO FACE). / MEDLEY: (UNCHAIN MY HEART – BLACK HEART – TAKE MY HEART)**	55	–
	('A'-Ectoplasm mix-12"+=) (GLOW 1-12) – Burning boats.		
May 86.	(7") (GLOW 2) **A WOMAN'S STORY. / FOR ONE MOMENT**	41	
	(c-ep+=)(10"pic-d-ep+=)(12"ep+=) SOME SONGS TO TAKE TO THE TOMB EP (TGLOW 2-12)(GLOWY 2-12)(GLOW 2-12) – The heel / A salty dog / The plague / The little white cloud that cried / Just good friends.		
Oct 86.	(7") (GLOW 3) **RUBY RED. / I'M SICK OF YOU TASTING OF SOMEONE ELSE**	47	
	('A'-Arnacoma mix-12"+=) (GLOW 3-12) – Broken hearted and beautiful / Jackal jackal (Mustapha Tomb Stone Teeth).		
	('A'ext.dance mix-12") (GLOW 3-13) – ('A'instrumental).		
Jan 87.	(7") (GLOW 4) **MELANCHOLY ROSE. / GYP THE BLOOD**	71	–
	(12"+=) (GLOW 4-12) – A world full of people / Black lullaby.		
	(d7+=) (GLOWD 4) – Surabaya Johnny / Pirate Jenny.		
Mar 87.	(lp/c/cd) (FAITH/TFTH/CDFTH 2) **MOTHER FIST AND HER FIVE DAUGHTERS**	40	
	– Mother Fist / There is a bed / Saint Judy / The room below / Angel in her kiss / The hustler / Melancholy rose / Mr. Sad / The sea says / Champ / Ruby red / The river.		

Marc ALMOND (cont) — THE GREAT INDIE DISCOGRAPHY — The 1980s

Mar 87. (7") (GLOW 5) **MOTHER FIST. / TWO SAILORS ON THE BEACH**
(12"+=) (GLOW 5-12) – The hustler.
Nov 87. (lp/c/cd) (FAITH/TFTH/CDFTH 3) **THE SINGLES 1984-1987** (compilation)
– The boy who came back / You have / Tenderness is a weakness / Stories of Johnny / Love letters / The house is haunted / A woman's story / Ruby red / Melancholy rose / Mother Fist.

— He was now backed by LA MAGIA. (aka HOGAN, HUMPHRIES + McGEE)

Parlophone Capitol

Aug 88. (7"/7"box) (R/RX 6186) <44240> **TEARS RUN RINGS. / EVERYTHING I WANTED LOVE TO BE** 26 67 Jan89
(12"+=/cd-s+=) (12R/CDR 6186) – ('A'extended.
('A'-Justin Strauss mix-12"+=) (12RX 6186) – ('A'-La Magia dance mix).
Sep 88. (cd/c/lp) (CD/TC+/PCS 7324) <91042> **THE STARS WE ARE** 41 Jan89
– The stars we are / These my dreams are true / Bitter sweet / Only the moment / Your kisses burn / Tears run rings / Something's gotten hold of my heart / The sensualist / She took my soul in Instanbul. (c+=/cd+=) – The frost comes tomorrow / Kept boy. (cd re-iss. Apr02 on 'E.M.I.'+=; 539176-2) – Something's gotten hold of my heart (w/ GENE PITNEY).
Oct 88. (7"/7"g-f/7"clear) (R/RG/RC 6194) **BITTER SWEET. / KING OF THE FOOLS** 40 -
(12"+=/12"g-f+=/12"etched+=/'A'-Big Beat mix-12"+=/cd-s+=) (12R/12RG/12RS/12RX/CDR 6194) – Tears run rings (Justin Strauss remix).
Jan 89. (7"/7"box; by MARC ALMOND & GENE PITNEY) (R/RX 6201) **SOMETHING'S GOTTEN HOLD OF MY HEART. / ('A'-solo version)** 1
(12"+=/12"etched+=/cd-s+=) (12R/12RS/CDR 6201) – The frost comes tomorrow.
Mar 89. (7",7"clear) (R 6210) **ONLY THE MOMENT. / REAL EVIL** 47 -
(cd-s+=) (CDR 6210) – She took my soul in Instanbul (The Blue Mosque mix).
(12"/12"etched) (12R/+S 6210) – ('A'-All The Time In The World mix) / She took my soul in Instanbul (The Blue Mosque mix).
Feb 90. (7"/ext-7"square-pic-d/ext-c-s) (R/RPD/TCR 6229) **A LOVER SPURNED. / EXOTICA ROSE** 29 -
(12"+=/cd-s+=) (12R/CDR 6229) – ('A'version).
May 90. (c-s/7") (TC+/R 6252) **THE DESPERATE HOURS. / THE GAMBLER** 45 -
(12"+=/12"clear-pic-d+=/cd-s+=) (12R/12RPD/CDR 6252) – ('A'extended Flamenco mix).
Jun 90. (cd/c/lp) (CD/TC+/PCS 7344) <94404> **ENCHANTED** 52
– Madame de la luna / Waifs and strays / The desperate hours / Toreador in the rain / Widow weeds / A lover spurned / Death's diary / Sea still sings / Carnival of life / Orpheus in red velvet. (cd re-iss. Apr02 on 'E.M.I.'; 539177-2)
Oct 90. (c-s/7") (TC+/R 6263) **WAIFS AND STRAYS. / OLD JACK'S CHARM**
(12") (12R 6263) – (2 'A'-Grid mixes).
(cd-s+=) (CDR 6263) – City of nights.

— Wrote w/DAVE BALL + NORRIS (The GRID)

W.E.A. Sire

Sep 91. (7"/c-s) (YZ 610/+C) **JACKY. / DEEP NIGHT** 17 -
(12"+=) (YZ 610T) – ('A'-Alpine dub).
(cd-s+=) (YZ 610CD) – A love outgrown.
Oct 91. (cd/c/lp) (9031 75518-2/-4/-1) <26764> **TENEMENT SYMPHONY** 39
– Meet me in my dream / Beautiful brutal thing / I've never seen your face / Vaudeville and burlesque / Champagne / Tenement symphony (i) Prelude, (ii) Jacky, (iii) What is love?, (iv) Trois Chansons de Bilitis – extract, (v) The days of Pearly Spencer, (vi) My hand over my heart. (re-iss. cd Feb95; same)
Dec 91. (7"/c-s) (YZ 633/+C) **MY HAND OVER MY HEART. / DEADLY SERENADE** 33 -
(12"pic-d) (YZ 633TP) – ('A'-Grit & Glitter mix) / Money for love (2 versions).
(cd-s) (YZ 633CD) – (above 3 tracks) / Night and no morning.
Apr 92. (7"/c-s) (YZ 638/+C) **THE DAYS OF PEARLY SPENCER. / BRUISES** 4 -
(cd-s+=) (YZ 638CD) – Dancing in a golden cage / Extract from 'Trois Chanson De Bilitis'.

— with DAVE CLAYTON – keyboards, musical director / MARTIN WATKINS – piano / ANDY HAMILTON – saxophone / MICHELE DREES – drums, perc. / CRIS BONACCI – guitars / SHIRLEY LEWIS, ANNA ROSS & AILEEN McLAUGHLIN – b.vox / TENEMENT SYMPHONY ORCH.

Mar 93. (7"/c-s) (YZ 720/+C) **WHAT MAKES A MAN A MAN (live). / TORCH (live)** 60 -
(cd-s+=) (YZ 720CD) – The stars we are (live).
(cd-s) (YZ 720CDX) – ('A'side) / Tainted love (live) / Vision (live) / Only the moment (live).
Apr 93. (cd/c/lp) (4509 92033-2/-4/-1) <45247> **12 YEARS OF TEARS - LIVE AT THE ROYAL ALBERT HALL (live)** May93
– Tears run rings / Champagne / Bedsitter / Mr. Sad / There is a bed / Youth / If you go away / Jacky / Desperate hours / Waifs and strays / Something's gotten hold of my heart / What makes a man a man / Tainted love / Say hello wave goodbye.

Some Bizzarre not iss.

Sep 93. (cd/c/lp) (SBZ CD/MC/LP 10) **ABSINTHE: THE FRENCH ALBUM** -
– Undress me / Abel and Cain / Lost Paradise / Secret child / Rue Des Blancs Manteaux / The slave / Remorse of the dead / Incestuous love / A man / My little lovers / In your bed / Yesterday when I was young. <US cd-iss. 1996 on 'Thirsty Ear'; 57026>

Mercury Mercury

Apr 95. (c-s) (MERMC 431) **ADORED AND EXPLORED / ('A'-original)** 25 -
(cd-s) (MERCD 431) – ('A'side) / The user / Loveless world / ('A'-Andy Meecham's Slow Fat dub).
(cd-s) (MERDD 431) – ('A'side) / ('A'-Beatmasters 12 take 1) / ('A'-Andy Meecham club mix) / ('A'-X-Press 2 extre,me excess mix).
Jul 95. (c-s) (MERMC 437) **THE IDOL / ('A'-Tin Tin Out mix)** 44 -
(cd-s+=) (MERDD 437) – ('A'-Idolized mix) / ('A'-Teenage dream mix).
(cd-s) (MERCD 437) – ('A'-part 1) / Law of the night / Adored and explored (live) / Bedsitter (live).
Nov 95. (c-s) (MERMC 450) **CHILD STAR / EDGE OF HEARTBREAK** 41 -
(cd-ep+=) **CHILD STAR EP** (MERCD 450) – Christmas in Vegas / My guardian angel.
(cd-ep) **CHILD STAR EP** (MERDD 450) – ('A'side) / We need jealousy (live) / The idol (live) / Out there (live).
Feb 96. (c-s) (MERMC 444) **OUT THERE / BRILLIANT CREATURES**
(cd-s+=) (MERCD 444) – Lie (Beatmasters mix) / Lie.
(12") (MERX 444) – ('A'mixes:- Tony De Vite parts 1 & 2 / Non Eric / House Of Usher / Valerie Singleton).
Feb 96. (cd/c) (528 659-2/-4) **FANTASTIC STAR** 54
– Caged / Out there / We need jealousy / Idol (parts 1 & 2) / All gods fall / Baby night eyes / Adored and explored / Child star / Looking for love (in all the wrong places) / Addicted / Edge of heartbreak / Love to die for / Betrayed / On the prowl / Come in sweet assassin / Brilliant creatures / Shining brightly. (cd re-iss. Sep97; same)

— In Dec'96, MARC was credited on PJ PROBY minor hit single 'YESTERDAY HAS GONE' on 'EMI Premier' (PRESTC/CDPRES/CDPRESX 13).

Echo Instinct

Nov 98. (7"pic-d) (ECS 58) **BLACK KISS. / ('A'-DJ mix)**
(cd-s) (ECSCD 58) – ('A'side) / Satan's child / ('A'live).

Blue Star Incense

Mar 99. (cd-s) (BSRS 001) **TRAGEDY (TAKE A LOOK AND SEE) / BEAUTIFUL LOSERS / BLACK KISS (hard vocal mix)**
Apr 99. (cd) (BSRCD 01) <INS 435-2> **OPEN ALL NIGHT** Aug99
– Night & dark / Bedroom shine / Tragedy (take a look and see) / Black kiss / Almost diamonds / Scarlet bedroom / My love / Heart in velvet / Open all night / Threat of love / Bad people kiss / Sleepwalker / Midnight soul. <US+=> – Satan's child / Lonely go-go dancer / Beautiful losers.
Nov 99. (cd-s) (BRSCD 002) **MY LOVE / THREAT OF LOVE / ONE BIG SOUL**

— next with JOHANN JOHANNSON – keyboards, etc / JOHNNY GREEN – strings, keyboards, etc / PETUR HALLGRIMSSON – guitar

XIII Bis XIII Bis

Jun 00. (cd) (<533800-2>) **STRANGER THINGS** Jul00
– Glorious / Born to cry / Come out / Under your wing / Lights / Tantalise me / Moonbathe skin / Dancer / When it's your time / End in tears / Love in a time of science / Glorious (reprise).

– compilations, etc. –

Dec 89. (lp/c/cd) Some Bizzare; (BREL/+C/CD 001) **JACQUES** (most rec.1986)
– The Devil (okay) / If you need / The lockman / We must look / Alone / I'm coming / Litany for a return / If you go away / The town fell asleep / The bulls / (Never to be) Next / My death.
(above a tribute to Belgian singer, JACQUES BREL)
Sep 92. (cd/c) Virgin; (CD/TC VM 9010) **A VIRGIN'S TALE VOL.1 (1985-1988)**
Sep 92. (cd/c) Virgin; (CD/TC VM 9011) **A VIRGIN'S TALE VOL.2 (1988-1991)**
(re-iss. both above Nov92 as d-cd; DCDVM 901 0/1) (both re-iss. Nov97; SBZ 032/033 CD)
Aug 95. (d-cd) E.M.I.; (CDMATBOX 1) **TREASURE BOX**
(re-iss. Apr02 on 'E.M.I.'; 538915-2)
Sep 97. (cd; MARC ALMOND & FOETUS) Some Bizarre; (SBZ 022CD) **VIOLENT SILENCE**
Nov 97. (cd; MARC ALMOND & FOETUS) Some Bizarre; (SBZ 034CD) **FLESH VOLCANO / SLUT**
Nov 98. (cd-enhanced) Some Bizzare; (SBZ 037) **LIVE IN CONCERT AT THE ASTORIA (with LA MAGIA)**

SOFT CELL

— re-formed with ALMOND + BALL

Cooking Vinyl SpinArt

Sep 02. (12")(cd-s) (FRY 132T)(FRYCD 132) **MONOCULTURE / MONOCULTURE (extended). / ALL OUT OF LOVE / DANCING ALONE** 52
(cd-s) (FRYCD 132X) – ('A'-mixes; radio / Playgroup / Antoine 909 & Oggie-B).
Sep 02. (cd) (COOKCD 245) <SPIN 116> **CRUELTY WITHOUT BEAUTY** Oct02
– Darker times / Monoculture / Le grand guignol / The night / Last chance / Together alone / Desperate / Whatever it takes / All out of love / Sensation nation / Caligula syndrome / On an up.

ALTAMONT
(see under ⇒ PORCUPINE TREE; 90's section)

ALTERED IMAGES

Formed: Glasgow, Scotland … 1979 by JOHNNY McELHONE, TONY McDAID and MICHAEL 'TICH' ANDERSON, subsequently recruiting 'Gregory's Girl' bit actress, CLARE GROGAN, as a suitably kinetic frontwoman and second guitarist CAESAR. By mid 1980, they'd secured a support slot with SIOUXSIE & THE BANSHEES and following a promising John Peel session, were duly signed to 'Epic'. Following minor chart success in early '81 with cult classic, 'DEAD POP STARS', CAESAR was replaced with JIM McKINVEN and the band released a second single, 'A DAY'S WAIT', to minimal reaction. It was a case of third time lucky, however, and the celebrations began in earnest with the release of 'HAPPY BIRTHDAY', a song which narrowly missed the top of the UK charts and came to define the band's kaleidoscopic pop sound. Bouncing about like a demented rag doll, GROGAN made for a compelling stage presence, her little-girl-on-helium

ALTERED IMAGES (cont)

vocals among the most disinctive in the new wave pack. 'HAPPY BIRTHDAY' the album spawned a further two major hits, namely 'I COULD BE HAPPY' and 'SEE THOSE EYES', although the band's popularity began to dip after the release of a second album, 'PINKY BLUE' (1982). ANDERSON and McINVEN subsequently departed (the latter would later reappear with ambient popsters ONE DOVE), STEPHEN LIRONI brought in as a replacement. A change in direction (or at least an altered image) resulted in a one-off Top 10 hit, 'DON'T TALK TO ME ABOUT LOVE', lifted from the accompanying album, 'BITE' (1983), although with GROGAN increasingly concentrating her full-time efforts on an acting career, the band ground to a halt later that year. While LIRONI went on to form FLESH, McELHONE re-emerged initially with HIPSWAY, then TEXAS. Music wise, GROGAN released a lone 7" single, 'LOVE BOMB' in the mid-80's, later teaming up with LIRONI once more to form UNIVERSAL LOVE SCHOOL. Her cheeky grin was subsequently witnessed on cable music channel, VH1, for whom GROGAN works as a presenter. • **Songwriters:** McELHONE and group compositions / GROGAN lyrics. Also covered JEEPSTER (T.Rex) / SONG SUNG BLUE (Neil Diamond) / LITTLE TOWN FLIRT (Del Shannon). • **Trivia:** STEVE SEVERIN (Siouxsie & The Banshees) produced debut 45, and MARTIN RUSHENT the debut album.

Album rating: HAPPY BIRTHDAY (*6) / PINKY BLUE (*5) / BITE (*4) / COLLECTED IMAGES compilation (*7)

CLARE GROGAN (b. Mar'62) – vocals / **JOHNNY McELHONE** – guitar / **TONY McDAID** – bass / **MICHAEL 'Tich' ANDERSON** – drums / **CAESAR** – guitar

		Epic	Portrait
Feb 81.	(7") *(EPCA 1023)* **DEAD POP STARS. / SENTIMENTAL** (c-s+=) *(EPC40A 1023)* – Leave me alone.	67	

— JIM McKINVEN – guitar (ex-BERLIN BLONDES) repl. CAESAR who joined The WAKE

May 81.	(7") *(EPCA 1167)* **A DAY'S WAIT. / WHO CARES?**		
Aug 81.	(7") *(EPCA 1522)* **HAPPY BIRTHDAY. / SO WE GO WHISPERING** ('A' dance mix-12"+=) *(EPCA13 1522)* – Jeepster.	2	
Sep 81.	(lp/c) *(EPC/40 84893)* **HAPPY BIRTHDAY** – (intro – Happy birthday) / Love and insects / Real toys / Idols / Legionaire / Faithless / Beckoning strings / Happy birthday / Midnight / A day's wait / Leave me alone / Insects / (outro – Happy birthday). *(re-iss. Sep83 lp/c; EPC/40 32355) (cd-iss. Sep91 & Jun95 on 'Columbia'; 480528-2) (re-iss. May93 on 'Sony Collectors'; 932944-2)*	26	
Nov 81.	(7"/7"pic-d) *(EPCA/+11 1834)* **I COULD BE HAPPY. / INSECTS** ('A' dance mix-12"+=) *(EPCA13 1834)* – Disco pop stars.	7	
Mar 82.	(7"/7"pic-d) *(EPCA/+11 2198)* **SEE THOSE EYES. / HOW ABOUT THAT THEN (I MISSED MY TRAIN)** (12"+=) *(EPCA13 2198)* – ('A' extended).	11	
Apr 82.	(lp/c) *(EPC/40 85665)* **PINKY BLUE** – Pinky blue / See those eyes / Forgotten / Little brown head / See you later / Song sung blue / Funny funny me / Think that It might / I could be happy (version) / Jump jump / I could be happy (version) / Goodnight and I wish. *(cd-iss. Mar94 on 'Sony Collectors'; 983227-2)*	12	
May 82.	(7",7"pink) *(EPCA 2426)* **PINKY BLUE. / THINK THAT IT MIGHT (dance mix)** (12") *(EPCA13 2426)* – ('A' dance mix) / Jump jump – Think that it might (sequed dance mix).	35	

— STEPHEN LIRONI – guitar, drums (ex-RESTRICTED CODE) repl. ANDERSON and McKINVEN The latter reappeared in the early 90s in ONE DOVE. Also used session people including **ANDY HAMILTON** – saxophone

Mar 83.	(7"/7"pic-d/ext.12") *(EPCA/WA/EPCA13 3083)* **DON'T TALK TO ME ABOUT LOVE. / LAST GOODBYE**	7	
May 83.	(7"/ext.12"/7"pic-d/ext.12"pic-d) *(EPCA/TA 3398)(WA/WTA 3398)* **BRING ME CLOSER. / SURPRISE ME**	29	
Jun 83.	(lp/c) *(EPC/40 25413)* **BITE** – Bring me closer / Another lost look / Love to stay / Now that you're here / Don't talk to me about love / Stand so quiet / Change of heart / Thinking about you. *(c+=)* – Bring me closer (dance mix) / Don't talk to me about love (extended) / Surprise me / I don't want to know / Last goodbye.	16	
Jul 83.	(7"/ext.12") *(EPCA/TA 3582)* **LOVE TO STAY. / ANOTHER LOST LOOK (live)**	46	
Sep 83.	(7") *(EPCA 3735)* **CHANGE OF HEART. / ANOTHER LOST LOOK** (12"+=) *(TA 3735)* – Happy birthday / I could be happy.		

— added on summer tour **DAVID WILD** – drums / **JIM PRIME** – keyboards

— the inevitable split came late '83. LIRONI formed FLESH and in the mid-90's returned to cult status when he formed The REVOLUTIONARY CORPS OF TEENAGE JESUS (with augmentation from – of all people – SUICIDE's ALAN VEGA). GROGAN had a brief solo career while McELHONE formed HIPSWAY and, later in 1989, formed TEXAS.

– **compilations, others, etc.** –

on 'Epic' unless mentioned otherwise

Mar 83.	(7"ep/c-ep) *(EPCA/+40 2617)* **GREATEST ORIGINAL HITS** – Happy birthday / I could be happy / Dead pop stars / A day's wait.		-
May 84.	(lp/c) *(EPC/40 25973)* **COLLECTED IMAGES**		-
Jan 87.	(7") Old Gold; *(OG 9663)* **HAPPY BIRTHDAY. / I COULD BE HAPPY**		-
Jul 96.	(cd) *(484339-2)* **REFLECTED IMAGES (THE BEST OF ALTERED IMAGES)** – Happy birthday (intro) / Dead pop stars / Happy birthday / Love and kisses / Real toys / I could be happy / See those eyes / Pinky blue / Forgotten / See you later / Don't talk to me about love / Bring me closer / Love to stay / Change of heart / Thinking about you / Happy birthday (12" mix) / Don't talk to me about love (12" mix) / Love to stay (12" mix) / Bring me closer (12" mix) / Last goodbye (don't talk to me about love) / Happy birthday (outro). *(re-iss. Aug00; same)*		-

---

ALTERNATE LEARNING (see under ⇒ GAME THEORY)

ALWAYS

Formed: London, England . . . mid 80's as the brainchild of one KEVIN WRIGHT (aka MR. WRIGHT, to his friends?). ALWAYS kicked off the recording account via 'El' records (run by MIKE ALWAY), who released a handful of EP's before registering his/their debut long-player, 'THAMES VALLEY LEATHER CLUB' (1988). Defiantly arty and OTT, the record was a slow-burner for some time and surely influenced BELLE & SEBASTIAN and over a dozen twee-pop acts of the future. But for one solitary set in early 1990, the non-'El' release, 'LOOKING FOR MR. WRIGHT', little was heard from the man for some time – indeed, we were "looking for Mr. Wright" for some time to come! MR. WRIGHT (as he was now billed) did make his re-appearance in 1997 (through US-based 'Le Grand Magistery' imprint) on a low-key album, '. . .IS ALWAYS THE FANCY MAN' – a slight clue there then. With the poise of a modern-day crooner (draw a line through SCOTT WALKER to MOMUS), the debonair MR. WRIGHT touched the listener frequently with his romantic, lonely tales through the grooves of his sophomore release, 'STAR TIME' (1999). But was anybody listening? 'HELLO IS ANYONE OUT THERE', was the plea of his next title in summer 2001. Certainly not in Old Blighty who could only access his material through imports or the internet. Complete with chamber orchestral backing (once again), the missing MR. WRIGHT slightly disappointed on this venture.

Album rating: THAMES VALLEY LEATHER CLUB w/extra tracks (*6) / LOOKING FOR MR. WRIGHT (*5) / Mr. Wright: . . .IS ALWAYS THE FANCY MAN (*5) / STAR TIME (*6) / HELLO IS ANYONE OUT THERE (*4)

KEVIN WRIGHT – vocals, instruments

		El	not iss.
Oct 86.	(12"ep) *(GPO 16T)* **ARIEL ATLAS** – Dreams of leaving / Morning heights / Heavens / The flying display.		-
Mar 87.	(12"ep) *(GPO 27T)* **METROLAND** – Metroland / The arcade / W.C. Fields.		-
Mar 88.	(10") *(GPO 34)* **THAMES VALLEY LEATHER CLUB. / AMATEUR DEFECTION**		-
Mar 88.	(lp) *(ACME 12)* **THAMES VALLEY LEATHER CLUB** – The turf accountant's dream / My honeymoon hell / Thames Valley leather club / Amateur defection / Love and death in Metroland / Window without a view / London times / Mystery disappearance. *(cd-iss. Oct00 +=; ACME 12CD)* – Metroland / The arcade / W.C. Fields / Park now / Dreams of leaving / Morning heights / Heaven / The flying display.		-

		Suburbs Of Hell	not iss.
Mar 90.	(lp) *(SOH 005)* **LOOKING FOR MR. WRIGHT**		-

MR. WRIGHT

		not iss.	Le Grand Magistery
Nov 97.	(cd) *<HRH 002>* **. . .IS ALWAYS THE FANCY MAN** – Hanover Square / A dream / Bohemians / Death of love / Wonderful / Silent film / Blue cinema / Around the may pole / etc.	-	
May 99.	(cd) *<HRH 008>* **STAR TIME** – The man who was not / Lost in space / Lofe is everywhere / Don't walk in the dark (oh baby) / You're a queen / The moon and the stars / Star time / Paraphernalia / The balloon race / Strange feeling.	-	
Jul 01.	(cd) *<HRH 022>* **HELLO IS ANYONE OUT THERE** – Sailor on the sea / Darling honey / The nightwatchman / Coming home / Ocean boulevard / Missing you still / Winter on Harrow Road / I saw the light / New day / Voyage.	-	

AMBITIOUS LOVERS (see under ⇒ DNA; 70's section)

AMELIA (see under ⇒ TALULAH GOSH)

AMERICAN MUSIC CLUB

Formed: Burbank, California, USA . . . 1983 by MARK EITZEL, who had set up home in San Francisco after his Columbus, Ohio band The NAKED SKINNIES broke up in '82; they released one US-only single, 'ALL MY LIFE' / 'THIS IS THE BEAUTIFUL NIGHT' for 'Naked House'; (103457). With a line-up of MARK 'VUDI' PANKLER, DAN PEARSON, BRAD JOHNSON and MATT NORELLI, the AMERICAN MUSIC CLUB cut a debut album, 'RESTLESS STRANGER', for the small 'Grifter' label in 1985, before signing to 'Zippo' for the 'THE ENGINE' (1987). Regularly cited as one of the most criminally undervalued songwriters in the US, EITZEL has captured many a critic's ear with his neon-lit meditations on the tragic futility of human existence and the fleeting consolation of romantic love. Apart from a cult fanbase, however, AMC's appeal never translated to a wider audience, even after the band were picked up by 'Virgin' in the early 90's. By this point, the group had a clutch of austere, country-tinged classics under their belt, namely 'CALIFORNIA', 'UNITED KINGDOM' (1989) and 'EVERCLEAR' (1991), the latter set especially haunting in spite of its more accessible approach. EITZEL's wracked outpourings were often shot through with a kind of outraged desperation, the 'RISE' single, a poignant tribute to a friend who died of AIDS. Also featuring such bleakly beautiful material as 'SICK OF FOOD', the album saw EITZEL named as Rolling Stone magazine's songwriter of the year in 1991. The acclaim didn't sit particularly well with the AMC frontman; EITZEL, perhaps in response, accentuated the self-mocking tone of his work on the major label debut, 'MERCURY' (1993). Critically acclaimed once again, the album failed to sell, although it did almost scrape into the UK Top 40. It was the same story with 'SAN FRANCISCO' (1994). Parting company with 'Virgin', the band also saw fit to part company with each other, at least they'd given it their best shot. EITZEL remained with the label for a further solo album, '60 WATT SILVER LINING' (1996), another critical success seemingly doomed to obscurity. Switching labels for 'WEST' (1997 for 'Warners') and 'I CAN'T HOLD BACK . . .' (1998 for 'Matador'), EITZEL took a three-year hiatus before setting out his stall once more. 2001's 'THE INVISIBLE MAN' was a fine comeback encompassing all modern trites such as electronic sampling, etc. Indeed, his best song for some time, 'PROCLAIM YOUR JOY', closed the album and might've just given him a deserved hit single. The arch miserabilist was back in 2002 with 'MUSIC FOR COURAGE AND CONFIDENCE', presumably not a wholly ironic title for a record that, by its eclectic sweep alone, was worthy of close attention. Unsurprisingly perhaps, it was the countrified material which worked best, especially John Hartford's classic 'GENTLE ON MY MIND', although EITZEL reconstructed the likes of Bill Withers' 'AIN'T NO SUNSHINE' and even Culture Club's 'DO YOU REALLY WANT TO HURT ME' in his trademark skeletal style. • **Covered:** CALIFORNIA DREAMIN' (Mamas & The Papas). EITZEL covered THERE IS NO EASY WAY DOWN (Carole King) / SNOWBIRD (Anne Murray) / HELP ME MAKE IT THROUGH THE NIGHT (Kris Kristofferson) / I ONLY HAVE EYES FOR YOU (Flamingos) / MORE, MORE, MORE (Neil Diamond) / MOVE ON UP (Curtis Mayfield) / REHEARSALS FOR RETIREMENT (Phil Ochs) / I'LL BE SEEING YOU (Billie Holiday). • **Trivia:** EITZEL also moonlighted with The TOILING MIDGETS (a 5-piece also featuring early 90's AMC newcomer TIM MOONEY; he had always been part of the early 80's combo). They released an album, 'SON' (1993), before signing to 'Reprise' the same year.

Album rating: THE RESTLESS STRANGER (*5) / ENGINE (*6) / CALIFORNIA (*7) / UNITED KINGDOM (*7) / EVERCLEAR (*8) / MERCURY (*7) / SAN FRANCISCO (*6) / Mark Eitzel: SONGS OF LOVE: LIVE AT THE BORDERLINE – 1/19/91 (*6) / 60 WATT SILVER LINING (*6) / WEST (*7) / CAUGHT IN A TRAP AND I CAN'T BACK OUT (*5) / THE INVISIBLE MAN (*7) / MUSIC FOR COURAGE AND CONFIDENCE (*4)

MARK EITZEL (b.30 Jan'59, Walnut Creek, Calif.) – vocals, guitar, keyboards / **MARK "VUDI" PANKLER** (b.22 Sep'52, Chicago, Illinois) – guitar, accordion, bass / **DAN PEARSON** (b.31 May'59, Walnut Creek) – bass, guitar, dulcimer, vocals, etc. / **BRAD JOHNSON** – keyboards / **MATT NORELLI** – drums

not iss.   Grifter

Jan 86. (lp) <GR 001> **THE RESTLESS STRANGER**
 – $1,000,000 song / Away down my street / Yvonne gets dumped / Ms. Lucky / Point of desire / Goodbye reprise #54 / Tell yourself / When your love is gone / Heavenly smile / Broken glass / Hold on to your love. <US cd-iss. 1999 on 'Reprise'; 46675>

—— **TOM MALLON** – guitar, drums, vocals / **DAVE SCHEFF** – drums repl. JOHNSON + NORELLI

Zippo   Frontier

Oct 87. (lp/cd) (ZONG/+CD 020) <4612-1/-2> **ENGINE**
 – Big night / Outside this bar / At my mercy / Gary's song / Nightwatchman / Lloyd / Electric light / Mom's TV / Art of love / Asleep / This year.

—— now without SCHEFF

Demon   Frontier

Oct 88. (lp/cd) (FIEND/+CD 134) <4619-1/-2> **CALIFORNIA**
 – Firefly / Somewhere / Laughing stock / Lonely / Pale skinny girl / Blue and grey shirt / Bad liquor / Now you're defeated / Jenny / Western sky / Highway 5 / Last harbor. (cd re-iss. Apr93; FMCD 1)

—— **MIKE SIMMS** – drums; repl. MALLON

Oct 89. (lp/cd) (FIEND/+CD 151) **UNITED KINGDOM**
 – Here they roll down / Dreamers of the dream / Never mind / United kingdom / Dream is gone / Heaven of your hands / Kathleen / The hula maiden / Animal pen. (cd+=) – California (album). (cd re-iss. Apr93; FMCD 2)

—— added **BRUCE KAPHAN** (b. 7 Jan'55, San Francisco) – pedal steel guitar, keyboards, bass, producer (now full-time)

Alias   Alias

Oct 91. (lp/cd/cd) <(A 015/+C/D)> **EVERCLEAR**
 – Why won't you stay / Rise / Miracle on 8th Street / Ex-girlfriend / Crabwalk / The confidential agent / Sick of food / The dead part of you / Royal cafe / What the pillar of salt held up / Jesus' hands.

Nov 91. (cd-ep) <(A 014D)> **RISE / CHANNEL NUMBER / THE RIGHT THING / CRABWALK**

—— **TIM MOONEY** (b. 6 Oct'58, Las Vegas, Nevada) – drums (of TOILING MIDGETS) repl. SIMMS

Virgin   Reprise

Mar 93. (cd/c/lp) (CD/TC+/V 2708) <45226> **MERCURY** | 41 |
 – Gratitude walks / If I had a hammer / Challenger / I've been a mess / Hollywood 4-5-92 / What Godzilla said to God when his name wasn't found in the book of life / Keep me around / Dallas, airports, bodybags / Apology for an accident / Over and done / Johnny Mathis' feet / The hopes and dreams of Heaven's 10,000 whores / More hopes and dreams / Will you find me?

Apr 93. (c-s) (VSC 1445) **JOHNNY MATHIS' FEET / WILL YOU FIND ME / THE HOPES AND DREAMS OF HEAVEN'S 10,000** | 58 | - |
 (cd-s+=) (VSCDX 1445) – The amylnitrate dream of Pat Robertson.
 (cd-s) (VSCDT 1445) – ('A'side) / What Godzilla said to God when his name wasn't found in the book of life / Dallas, airports, bodybags (demo).

Jun 93. (c-ep) (VSC 1464) **KEEP ME AROUND / CHALLENGER / IN MY ROLE AS THE MOST HATED SINGER IN THE LOCAL UNDERGROUND MUSIC SCENE / MEMO FROM AQUATIC PARK**
 (cd-ep+=) (VSCDG 1464) – (no 2nd track) / Walking tune.

Aug 94. (7"/c-s) (VS/+C 1512) **WISH THE WORLD AWAY. / I JUST TOOK TWO SLEEPING PILLS AND NOW I'M LIKE A BRIDEGROOM** | 46 | - |
 (cd-s+=) (VSCDT 1512) – The revolving door (demo).
 (cd-s) (VSCDX 1512) – ('A'side) / The President's test for physical fitness / Cape Canaveral.

Sep 94. (cd/c/lp) (CD/TC+/V 2752) <45721> **SAN FRANCISCO** | 72 | |
 – Fearless / It's your birthday / Can you help me / Love doesn't belong to anyone * / Wish the world away / How many six packs to screw in a light? / Cape Canaverai * / Hello Amsterdam / The revolving door / In the shadow of the valley * / What holds the world together / I broke my promise / The thorn in my side is gone / I'll be gone / Fearless (reprise) * / I just took my two sleeping pills and now I'm like a bridegroom. (cd+=/c+= *)

Feb 95. (7"/c-s) (VS/+C 1523) **CAN YOU HELP ME. / THE THORN IN MY SIDE IS GONE**
 (cd-s+=) (VSCDT 1523) – California dreamin' (alt.version).

MARK EITZEL

not iss.   own label

1982. (c) <#1> **MEAN MARK EITZEL GETS FAT**
 – Swing low / You can be beautiful / Hold on to your love / I speak French / A tall black lady / Keep this dance for me / Shadow of my name.

Demon   Matador

Apr 91. (lp/cd) (FIEND/+CD 213) **SONGS OF LOVE: LIVE AT THE BORDERLINE 1/19/91 (live)**
 – Firefly / Chanel No.5 / Western sky / Blue and grey shirt / Gary's song / Outside this bar / Room above the club / Last harbour / Kathleen / Crabwalk / Jenny / Take courage / Nothing can bring me down. (cd re-iss. Nov97 on 'Diablo'; DIAB 838) (lp re-iss. Aug98 on 'Fruit Tree'; FRUITTREE 801)

Jul 92. (12") <OLE 016> **TAKE COURAGE**
 – On the emblematic use of jewelry as a metaphor for the disolution of our hopes and dreams / The ecstatic epiphany: A celebration of youth and beauty past, present, and future.

Virgin   Warners

Mar 96. (cd/c/lp) (CD/TC+/V 2798) <46152> **60 WATT SILVER LINING**
 – There is no way down / Sacred heart / Always turn away / Saved / Cleopatra Jones / When my plane finally goes down / Mission rock / Wild sea / Aspirin / Some bartenders have the gift of pardon / Southend on sea / Everything is beautiful.

Warners   Warners

Jun 97. (cd) <(9362 46602-2)> **WEST** | | May96 |
 – If you have to ask / Free of harm / Helium / Stunned and frozen / Then it really happens / In your life / Lower Eastside tourist / Three inches of wall / Move myself ahead / Old photographs / Fresh screwdriver / Live or die.

Matador   Matador

Feb 98. (cd/lp) <(OLE 179-2/-1)> **CAUGHT IN A TRAP AND I CAN'T BACK OUT** | | Jan98 |
 – Are you the trash / Xmas lights spin / Auctioneer's song / White rosary / If I had a gun / Goodbye / Queen of no one / Cold light of day / Go away / Atico 18 / Sun smog seahorse.

Apr 01. (7") (OLE 515-7) **IT IS IMPORTANT THROUGHOUT YOUR LIFE TO PROCLAIM YOUR JOY. / THE MAN WITH THE HOLE IN HIS FOOT**
 (cd-s) (OLE 515-2) – ('A'side) / Tell it to the lonely fairy in the forest (a rural gambol) / Proclaim your joy (swinging version).

May 01. (cd) <(OLE 505-2)> **THE INVISIBLE MAN**
 – The boy with the hammer in the paper bag / Can you see? / Christian science reading room / Sleep / To the sea / Shine / Steve I always knew / Bitterness / Anything / Without you / The global sweep of human history / Seeing eye to eye / Proclaim your joy.

New West   New West

Apr 02. (cd) <(NWCD 6038)> **MUSIC FOR COURAGE AND CONFIDENCE**
 – Snowbird / Ain't no sunshine / Do you really want to hurt me / Help me make it through the night / I only have eyes for you / Gentle on my mind / More, more, more / Move on up / Rehearsals for retirement / I'll be seeing you.

TOILING MIDGETS

TIM MOONEY – drums / **RICKY WILLIAMS** – vocals (ex-SLEEPERS) / **CRAIG GRAY** – guitar (ex-NEGATIVE TREND) / **PAUL HOOD** – guitar / with **JONATHAN HENDRICKSON** – bass

not iss.   Rough Trade

Apr 82. (lp) <ROUGHUS 11> **SEA OF UNREST**
 – Destiny / Trauma girl / Late show / Microage / Wishful thinking / All the girls cry / DJMC / Shooting gallery / Again / Big surprise / Sea of unrest. <cd-iss. Sep94 on 'Fist Puppet'; 16>

—— **KARL J GOLDRING** – bass; repl. HENDRICKSON

—— **MARK EITZEL** – guitar; repl. WILLIAMS

Hut   Matador

Oct 91. (7") <OLE 037> **MR. FOSTER. /**
Jan 93. (12"ep/cd-ep) (HUT 25 T/CD) **FAUX PONY. / GOLDEN FROG / MR. FOSTER'S SHOES**

—— **LISA DAVIS** – bass; repl. KARL

Jan 93. (cd/lp) (CDHUT/HUTLP 6) <OLE 030> **SON** | | Jul92 |
 – Faux pony / Fabric / Slaughter on Sumner St. / Mr. Foster's shoes / Process words / Clinging fire – Clams / Third chair / Listen / Chains.

—— signed to 'Reprise', although commitments elsewhere led to break-up

AND ALSO THE TREES

Formed: Inkberrow, Worcestershire, England ... 1979 by SIMON HUW-JONES, JO-JUSTIN JONES, STEVEN BURROWS and NICK HAVAS. Finally finding a home with the independent 'Reflex' imprint, the 'TREES released their debut single, 'SHANTELL', towards the end of '83. However, the song wasn't included on the following year's eponymous album, a record showcasing the quartet's alternative-rock. Firmly in the CURE-est tradition, tracks such as 'MIDNIGHT GARDEN', 'THE TEASE THE TEAR' and 'IMPULSE OF MAN', characterised by HUW-JONES' morbid monotone and delivered against a backdrop of spectral, downward spiralling guitars. Rapidly attracting a cult fanbase, AATT issued a further couple of 45's in the shape of 'THE SECRET SEA' and 'A ROOM LIVES IN LUCY', neither featured on the "difficult" second album, 'VIRUS MEADOW' (1986). The band carried on in much the same vein throughout the rest of the 80's without any mainstream success, even attempting a Cat Stevens number, 'LADY D'ARBANVILLE'. Finding more listeners on the continent, they secured a deal with Germany's 'Normal' label in the early 90's, who released 'GREEN IS THE SEA' (1992) and 'THE KLAXON' (1993), before re-issuing their entire back catalogue on CD.

Album rating: AND ALSO THE TREES (*7) / VIRUS MEADOW (*5) / A RETROSPECTIVE 1983-1986 compilation (*7) / THE EVENING OF THE 24th (*5) / THE MILLPOND YEARS (*5) / FAREWELL TO THE SHADE (*5) / GREEN IS THE SEA (*4) / FROM HORIZON TO HORIZON compilation (*6) / THE KLAXON (*5) / ANGELFISH (*5) / NAILED (*5) / SILVER SOUL (*5)

SIMON HUW-JONES – vocals / **JO-JUSTIN JONES** – guitar / **STEVEN BURROWS** – bass / **NICK HAVAS** – drums

Future / not iss.

Nov 83. (7") *(FS 9)* **SHANTELL. / WALLPAPER DYING**

Reflex / Troy

Feb 84. (lp) *(LEX 1)* **AND ALSO THE TREES**
– So this is silence / Talk without words / Midnight garden / The tease the tear / Impulse of man / Shrine / Twilights pool / Out of the moving life of circles. *(cd-iss. Nov88; LEX 1CD) (cd re-iss. Mar94 & Aug99 on 'Normal'; NORMAL 85CD)*

Apr 84. (7") *(RE 3)* **THE SECRET SEA. / SECRECY**
(12"+=) *(12RE 6)* – There were no bounds / The tease the tear / Midnight garden / Wallpaper dying.

Jan 85. (12"ep) *(12RE 8)* **A ROOM LIVES IN LUCY. / THERE WAS A MAN OF DOUBLE DEED / SCARLET ARCH**

Jun 86. (lp) *(LEX 6)* **VIRUS MEADOW**
– Slow pulse boy / Maps in her wrists and arms / The dwelling place / Vincent Crane / Jack / The headless clay woman / Gone... like the swallows / Virus meadow. *(cd-iss. Nov88; LEX 6CD) (cd re-iss. Mar94 & Aug99 on 'Normal'; NORMAL 90CD)*

May 87. (cd) *(LEX 7CD)* **A RETROSPECTIVE 1983-1986 (compilation)**
– Shantell / Talk without words / Shine / Midnight garden / Impulse of man / Twilights pool / A room lives in Lucy / Scarlet arch / Slow pulse boy / Maps in her wrists and arms / The dwelling place / Vincent Crane / Gone like the swallows / Virus meadow.

May 87. (lp) *(LEX 8)* **THE EVENING OF THE 24th**
– A room lives in Lucy / Twilights pool / Vincent Crane / Wallpaper dying / Shantell / Gone... like the swallows / The headless clay woman / Slow pulse boy / Virus meadow / So this is silence.

Jun 87. (12"m) *(12RE 12)* **THE CRITICAL DISTANCE. / SCYTHE AND SPADE / THE RENEGADE**

Nov 87. (7") *(RE 13)* **SHALETOWN. / L'UNICA STRADA**
(12"+=) *(12RE 13)* – Needle street.

May 88. (7") *(RE 014)* **THE HOUSE OF THE HEART. / THIS SHIP IN TROUBLE (instrumental)**
(12"+=)(cd-s+=) *(12RE 014)(RE 014CD)* – Anchor yard / Count Jefferey (the 1st).

May 88. (lp/cd) *(LEX 9/+CD)* **THE MILLPOND YEARS**
– The suffering of the stream / Simple Tom & the ghost of Jenny Bailey / The house of the heart / This ship in trouble / Count Jefferey / Shaletown / The sandstone man / From the silver frost / The millpond years. *(cd+=)* – Needle street / L'unica strada. *(cd re-iss. Mar94 & Aug99 on 'Normal'; NORMAL 100CD)*

Apr 89. (7") *(RE 15)* **LADY D'ARBANVILLE. / THE STREET ORGAN**
(12"+=)(cd-s+=) *(12RE 15)(RE 15CD)* – The harp.

Oct 89. (cd)(c/lp) *(LEX 10CD)(MC+/LEX 10)* <TROY 004 CD/CS/CD> **FAREWELL TO THE SHADE**   *Aug91*
– Prince Rupert / Macbeth's head / The Nobody Inn / Belief in the rose / The street organ / Lady D'Arbanville / Misfortunes / The pear tree / Ill omen / The horse fair. *(cd+=)* – The harp / Anchor yard. *(cd re-iss. Mar94 & Aug99 on 'Normal'; NORMAL 114CD)*

Dec 89. (7") *(RE 16)* **MISFORTUNES. / BELIEF IN THE ROSE (Instrumental)**

Apr 91. (12"ep) *<TROY 003S>* **THE PEAR TREE**   *French*
– The pear tree / Belief in the rose / Ill omen / Lady d'Arbanville.

Normal / not iss.

Jun 92. (cd) *(NORMAL 134CD)* **GREEN IS THE SEA**
– Red Valentino / The fruit room / Men of absolute / Tremendous risk for Mr. Ferdico / Blind opera / The dust sailor / The woodcutter / River of flame / Mermen of the Lea / Man who knew / Jacob fleet. *(re-iss. Aug99; same)*

Jun 93. (d-lp/cd) *(NORMAL 154/+CD)* **FROM HORIZON TO HORIZON (1983 TO 1992) (compilation)**
– Shantell / Wallpaper dying / The secret sea / There were no bounds / A room lives in Lucy / There was a man of double deed / Scarlet arch / Gone... like the swallows / The critical distance / The renegade / Scythe and spade / Shaletown / The house of the heart / Lady d'Arbanville / The street organ / Misfortunes / The pear tree (Robert Smith remix) / The fruit room.

Dec 93. (cd) *(NORMAL 164CD)* **THE KLAXON**
– Sickness divine / Red driver / Johnny Lexington / Sunrise / Dialogue / Wooden leg / The Dutchman / Bullet head / The flatlands. *(re-iss. Aug99; same)*

Jul 94. (cd) *(none)* **LE BATACLAN (live)**   *mail-o*
– Sickness divine / Red driver / The soul driver / Prince Rupert / The woodcutter / Dialogue / Slow pulse boy / Bullet head / Vincent Crane / The flatlands / Gone... like the swallows / There were no bounds / Shantell.

Mezentian / not iss.

Aug 96. (cd) *(MEXCD 1)* **ANGELFISH**
– Brother fear / Fighting in a lighthouse / The next flight to Rome / Paradiso / 6th floor elevator blues / Tremaine / Sea change / Roulette / The butcher's daughter / The lights of Phoenix / Missing. *(re-iss. Jun99 on 'Resurrection'; AATTCD 2)*

Resurrection / not iss.

Jun 99. (cd) *(AATTCD 1)* **NAILED**
– Nailed / III Omen III / The great alone / Highway 4287 (remix) / Paradiso (live) / The obvious (live) / Slow pulse boy (live).

May 00. (cd) *(AATTCD 3)* **SILVER SOUL**
– Nailed / Blue runner / Rose-Marie's leaving / The cyclone / Where the souls meet / Get critical / Before the power goes down / The obvious / Jewel park / Highway 4287.

—— a new album will be delayed until spring 2003

– compilations, etc. –

Oct 90. (12"box-set) *Reflex; (RE-BOX 1)* **AND ALSO THE TREES 12" BOX SET**

ANGEL CORPUS CHRISTI

Born: ANDREA ROSS, San Francisco, California, USA, the mysterious singer/songwriter and accomplished accordion player refusing to reveal much to the press. Two VERY low-key albums, 'I LOVE NEW YORK' and 'WAKE UP AND CRY', appeared in the mid-80's, although her self-described 'ACCORDION POP VOL.1' (containing covers of 'FEMME FATALE', 'IMAGINE' and 'YOU CAN'T ALWAYS GET WHAT YOU WANT'!!!) didn't surface until the turn of the decade. Despite being influenced by 60's icons such as LOU REED and LEONARD COHEN, both her music and her lyrics are firmly rooted in the present. Her talents were finally recognised by major (HERB ALPERT and JERRY MOSS) backed label, 'Almo Sounds', who issued the well-received 'WHITE COURTESY PHONE' in 1995 (incidentally co-written with her guitarist husband, RICH STIM (ex-MC5) – add a certain lady, CICCONE, for the 'THREW IT AWAY' track!). Of late, she has collaborated with alternative stalwarts, DEAN WAREHAM (ex-GALAXIE 500) and ALAN VEGA (of SUICIDE) on a cover of Serge Gainsbourg's naughty classic 'JE T'AIME'. • **Covered:** I'M 18 (Alice Cooper) / SLEEPING WITH THE TV ON (Dictators) / + a plethora of others.

Album rating: I LOVE NY (*5) / WAKE UP AND CRY mini (*5) / ACCORDION POP VOL.1 (*6) / WHITE COURTESY PHONE (*6)

ANDREA ROSS – vocals, accordion

Criminal Damage / Criminal Damage

Aug 85. (10"lp) *<CRIMLP 128>* **I LOVE NY**
– I love NY Cheree / Blank generation / Redondo beach / Dream, baby, dream / The day John Kennedy died / Femme fatale / Theme from Taxi Driver – New York, New York / Here today, gone tomorrow. *<(re-iss. Nov99 on 'Munster' lp/cd; MR 161/+CD)>*

Aug 86. (m-lp) *<CRIMLP 137>* **WAKE UP AND CRY**
– I can't make it / Never too late for Linda / Love in the shadows / Rock + roll heart / Wild Bill / Wake up and cry.

not iss. / a&r/ENT

1987. (c) **DIM THE LIGHTS**
– New red / Little surfer girl / California / Moon so bright / Dim the lights / Los Alamos / I wouldn't wanna be Bob Dylan / Way out west.

Stim / Stim

May 90. (c) *<STIM 001>* **ACCORDION POP VOL.1**
– Sleepwalk / Beast of burden / As tears go by / I love how you love me / To know him is to love him / Imagine / You can't always get what you want / Love me tender / Green fields / King of the road / Singin' the blues / Donna / Denise / Jennifer Juniper / I'm a believer / Downtown / Silhouettes / Femme fatale / Little surfer girl / Hey Jude.

Next Big Thing / Next Big Thing

Sep 90. (lp) *<NBT 007>* **THE 80's (compilation)**
– John Cassavettes / I'm 18 / Hell / Dream baby dream / Theme from Taxi Driver – New York, New York / Blank generation / The day John Kennedy died / Never too late for Linda / King of Los Alamos / Way out west.

1991. (7") *<NBT 025>* **LITTLE SURFER GIRL. / PULL GIRL**

not iss. / a&r/ENT

1992. (7") **PULL GIRL. / RUFF TUFF CREME PUFF**

1992. (7"blue) **BIG BLACK CLOUD. / DOWN**

—— now with **NANCY KRAVITZ** – bass / **WINDY WILD** – percussion, drums / **RICH STIM** – guitar / **JOEL 'POPEYE' JONES** – sax / + many guests incl. HERB ALPERT!, CASSELL WEBB, HAL BLAINE + producer CRAIG LEON

Almo Sounds / Almo Sounds

Nov 95. (cd) *(ALMOCD 004)* <80000> **WHITE COURTESY PHONE**
– Big black cloud / Threw it away / Homeboy / Candy / Nature girl / Dim the lights / Down / John Cassavetes / Lazy / Fall / Been there done that / Way out west. *(UK-only+=)* – Beretta.

Feb 96. (cd-ep) *(CDXALMOS 018)* **ME AND MY BERETTA / CANDY / I'M 18 / RUFF TUFF CREME PUFF (demo)**

Next Big Thing / not iss.

Nov 97. (7") *(NBT 452-7)* **SLEEPING WITH THE TV ON. / (other by MAGIC DIRT)**

Via Satellite / Munster

Feb 98. (7"; ANGEL CORPUS CHRISTI + DEAN WAREHAM) **JE T'AIME (I WANNA BOOGIE WITH YOU). / WILD BILL**

Mar 98. (7"pink) *(V-SAT 011)* **JE T'AIME – I WANNA BOOGIE WITH YOU. / CHEREE / SURFER GIRL**
(above A-side credited with DEAN WAREHAM, B-side with ALAN VEGA)

Emma's House / not iss.

Jul 01. (7"; by ANGEL CORPUS CHRISTI & DEAN WAREHAM) *<(EHR 004)>* **YOU. / I WANT EVERYTHING**

ANOTHER SUNNY DAY

Formed: Newlyn, nr. Penzance, Cornwall, England . . . 1987 as the brainchild of HARVEY WILLIAMS. This singer and multi-instrumentalist packed in a communications engineering course at Plymouth Polytechnic and devoted himself to his music. Having signed a singles deal with indie-pop label, 'Sarah', WILLIAMS' one-man band were initially heard via a flexi-single, 'ANORAK CITY', available free with the 'Are You Scared To Get Happy' fanzine. ANOTHER SUNNY DAY's debut single proper came in the shape of the long-winded 'I'M IN LOVE WITH A GIRL WHO DOESN'T KNOW I EXIST', WILLIAMS strumming along pleasantly enough although the saccharine-sweet vocals leave a bad taste in the ear. He continued in a similarly fey manner over a further clutch of singles, never quite managing to break the 2-minute barrier. WILLIAMS continued to feature in 'Sarah' acts The FIELD MICE and BLUEBOY; he also had a brief stint with The TREMBLING BLUE STARS (ex-FIELD MICE).

Album rating: LONDON WEEKEND compilation (*6) / Harvey Williams: REBELLION mini (*5) / CALIFORNIA mini (*4)

HARVEY WILLIAMS – vocals, guitar, bass, keyboards, drums, percussion

                                                                                                      Sarah not iss.

Apr 88. (6"flexi) *(SARAH 004)* **ANORAK CITY**
Jun 88. (7"m) *(SARAH 007)* **I'M IN LOVE WITH A GIRL WHO DOESN'T KNOW I EXIST. / THINGS WILL BE NICE / THE CENTRE OF MY LITTLE WORLD**
May 89. (7"m) *(SARAH 016)* **WHAT'S HAPPENED? / CAN'T TELL YOU IT'S TRUE. / IMPOSSIBLE**
Nov 89. (7"ltd) *(CAFF 7)* **GENETIC ENGINEERING. / KILLOWN TOWERS**
(above single on 'Caff')
Nov 89. (7"m) *(SARAH 022)* **YOU SHOULD ALL BE MURDERED. / HORSERIDING / GREEN**
Aug 90. (7"m) *(SARAH 035)* **RIO. / THE VERY BEGINNING**
Mar 92. (7") *(SARAH 060)* **NEW YEAR'S HONOURS. / I DON'T SUPPOSE I'LL GET A SECOND CHANCE**
Oct 92. (lp/cd) *(SARAH 613/+CD)* **LONDON WEEKEND** (compilation)
– Anorak city / I'm in love with a girl who doesn't know I exist / Things will be nice / The centre of my little world / What's happened to you, my dearest friend? / Can't you tell it's true? / Impossible / You should all be murdered / Horseriding / Green / Rio / The very beginning / I don't suppose I'll get a second chance / New Year's honours.

— HARVEY joined BLUEBOY

HARVEY WILLIAMS

Mar 94. (10"m-lp/m-cd) *(SARAH 406/+CD)* **REBELLION**
– Song for a weekend / The stunt-man / Song for close friends / The girl from East Tower / Don't shout at me / She sleeps around.

                                                                      Shinkansen not iss.

May 99. (m-cd) *(SHINKANSEN 16)* **CALIFORNIA**
– Cindy's been gone / The ballad of Katie and Amanda / Her boychart / Lost California love / On holiday / Everything's alright / Introducing . . . / Eurostar.

ANTIETAM

Formed: based New York, USA . . . 1983 out of Louisville, Kentucky arty power-pop outfit, the BABYLON DANCE BAND. Taking the rather non-descript moniker from a 19th century American civil war battle, this bizarre husband and wife team of TIM HARRIS and TARA KEY enlisted the first in a series of drummers, MICHAEL WEINERT. The influential 'Homestead' delivered their eponymous debut set, a self-indulgent collection which failed to make much of an impact. Borrowing violinist DANNA PENTES from FETCHIN BONES, they added a new dimension to their avant-indie rock, releasing a second album, 'MUSIC FROM ELBA', in '86. Four years elapsed before the group (with new sticksman, CHARLES SCHULTZ) resurfaced from the trenches of obscurity, releasing the IRA KAPLAN and GEORGE HUBLEY (YO LA TENGO)-produced 'BURGOO' (1990) on 'Triple X'. Half a decade later, ANTIETAM were still battling on, although TARA KEY enjoyed some belated recognition with a solo set, 'BOURBON COUNTY' (1993). Around the same time, interest was being shown in her other band, BABYLON DANCE BAND. • **Covered:** ASK THE ANGELS (Patti Smith).

Album rating: ANTIETAM (*4) / MUSIC FROM ELBA (*4) / BURGOO (*7) / EVERYWHERE OUTSIDE (*6) / COMES ALIVE (*4) / ROPE A DOPE (*4) / Tara Key: BOURBON COUNTY (*6) / EAR AND ECHO (*4) / Babylon Dance Band: FOUR ON ONE (*6)

TARA KEY – vocals, guitar, piano / **TIM HARRIS** – vocals, bass, guitar, piano / **WOLF KNAPP** – bass, vocals, guitar / **MICHAEL WEINERT** – drums, vocals, marimba, piano

                                                                      Homestead Homestead

Jul 85. (lp) <*(HMS 025)*> **ANTIETAM**
– Good kirk, bad kirk / Orange song / BMW / Red, black & blue / Shot in the dark / New crime! / Gospel according to John B. / Extra dry / Don't go back to Greenville / Shively spleen / The latest / Mikey / Ready, swing / Unhappiness diminishes intelligence.

— **SEAN MULHALL** – drums, mouth harp; repl. WEINERT
— added **DANNA PENTES** – violin (of FETCHIN BONES)

Sep 86. (7") <*(HMS 059)*> **UNTIL NOW. / RAIN**
Sep 86. (lp) <*(HMS 068)*> **MUSIC FROM ELBA**
– San Diego / Gordian / Love knot / Concord / Until now / Trouble net / M.V. Augusta / Fontaine ferry / In a glass house / Camp folk / War is (the health of the state) / Good life / The haunting of Rocky Face ridge.

— **CHARLES SCHULTZ** – drums; repl. MULHALL + KNAPP

                                                                      Triple X Triple X

Nov 89. (12"m) **EATEN UP BY HATE. / NAPLES / DAY BEFORE TOMORROW**
Feb 90. (lp/cd) <*(TX 51026/+CD)*> **BURGOO**
– After the tide / Hesitation / Really the blues / Naples / Eaten up by hate / Acid song / Imagining green / Something's happening / George / Pictures of you / Open letter. *(cd+=)* – Day before tomorrow.

— **JOSH MADELL** – drums; repl. SCHULTZ

May 91. (lp/cd) <*(TX 51083/+CD)*> **EVERYWHERE OUTSIDE**
– Monica / Stomp / Angels and strangers / Straight ahead / Sink or swim / World love / The boarder / Teleplay / Bought and sold / Tumbling down. *(cd+=)* – Some kinda Jones.
Jul 92. (cd) <*(TX 51112CD)*> **COMES ALIVE (live at CBGB's 7/10/91)**
– Track 13 / Monica / Open letter / George / Stomp / Glide / Angels & strangers / Sample for Sara / Ask the angels / Teleplay / Sink or swim / Eaten up by hate.

                                                      Homestead Homestead

Feb 95. (cd) <*(HMS 218-2)*> **ROPE-A-DOPE**   Nov94
– Hands down / What she will / Pine / Certain muse / Hardly believe / Graveyard / Rope-a-dope / Leave home / Betwixt / Silver solace.

                                                      not iss. Other Music

1996. (7") **ALIBI. / PEGASI**

TARA KEY

— with **TIM HARRIS, WOLF KNAPP + JOSH MADELL**, etc

                                                     Homestead Homestead

Mar 94. (cd) <*(HMS 210-2)*> **BOURBON COUNTY**   Nov93
– Northern star / Tranquility base / Jack of hearts / Long trail / Seraphim / Bender / V.O.B. / Kali / One spark / I found out / Turbo dog / Need to need / Gypsy village.
May 95. (cd) <*(HMS 222-2)*> **EAR AND ECHO**   Apr95
– All lit up / Burn / Breakin' in / In absinthe / Left-handed way / Rhythm jester / Lost and found / No reason now / Up and down / Get it straight / No tractor blues.

BABYLON DANCE BAND

TARA KEY + TIM HARRIS (had earlier released a US-only solo)

                                                      Matador Matador

Jun 94. (cd/lp) <*(OLE 033-2/-1)*> **FOUR ON ONE** (rec.early 80's)
– When I'm home / Bold beginnings / The reckoning / Shively spleen / My friend Roger / Leave / Resources / See that girl / Jacob's chain / ABC / Golden days / Someday / All radical / Shake!

ANTI-GROUP (see under ⇒ CLOCKDVA)

Annie ANXIETY

Born: New York, USA. A member of The ASEXUALS – a group of NY leather-clad types who frequented the seedier bars in town – the singer crossed the water to London in '81 and released a solo single, 'BARBED WIRE HALO', for the 'Crass' label. It would be a few years before the petite ANNIE (a pacifist boxing fan!) would finally unleash a full set of songs, 'SOUL POSSESSION' (1984), for 'Corpus Christi'. Produced by 'On-U-Sound' man, ADRIAN SHERWOOD, it also featured musicians from The POISON GIRLS and FLUX OF PINK INDIANS. In 1987, she formed ANNIE ANXIETY BANDEZ, although only a solitary set, 'JACKAMO', appeared on Derek Birkett's 'One Little Indian' operation. Another one-off vinyl appearance in 1990 (this time a single, 'SUGAR BOWL', for 'East West') was the only offering for some time. In 1993, LITTLE ANNIE (as she was now billed) was given a vital injection by SHERWOOD, who delivered her comeback set, 'SHORT AND SWEET'. Into funk/reggae dub'n'club sounds with help from the likes of ANDREW WEATHERALL, the melancholy chanteuse was back in town and looking to fight her corner (with words at least!).

Album rating: SOUL POSSESSION (*4) / JACKAMO (*4) / Little Annie: SHORT AND SWEET (*5)

ANNIE ANXIETY – vocals / with **MARTIN FREDERIX** – guitar / **DEREK BIRKETT** – bass / **PENNY RIMBAUD + PRISONER** – drums / **KISHI** – synthesizer, piano / **EVE LIBERTINE** – vocals / **BONJO** – percussion

                                                     Crass not iss.

Sep 81. (7"; as ANNIE ANXIETY BANDEZ / PENNY RIMBAUD) *(321984-3)* **BARBED WIRE HALO**
– Cyanide tears / Hello horror.

                                                 Corpus Christi not iss.

Feb 84. (lp) *(CHRIST ITS 10)* **SOUL POSSESSION**
– Closet love / Third gear / Turkey girl / Burnt offerings / To know evil / Sad shadows / Viet not mine, El Salvador yours / Waiting for the fun.

ANNIE ANXIETY BANDEZ

                                                 One Little Indian not iss.

Aug 87. (lp) *(TPLP 4)* **JACKAMO**
– As I lie in your arms / Bastinado / Chasing the dragon down Broadway / Jackamo / Jack yo mama / One mourning / Rise / Hier encore. *(cd-iss. 1989 +=; TPLP 4CD)* – Down by the station / Rise (dub). *(cd re-iss. 1996 ++=)* – Hier encore ('96 remix) / Rise dub ('96 remix) / As I lie in your arms ('96 remix).
Oct 87. (12"ep) *(12TP 6)* **AS I LIE IN YOUR ARMS. / DOWN BY THE STATION / RISE / RISE (dub)**
Mar 88. (12"; w-drawn) *(12TP 13)* **HIER ENCORE**

Annie ANXIETY (cont)

May 90. (7") *(B 8967)* **SUGAR BOWL. / DIAMONDS MADE OF GLASS** (East West / not iss.)
(12"+=) *(B 8967T)* – ('A'-Oedipus + bonus beats mixes).

— retired from her solo career until . . .

LITTLE ANNIE

(On-U-Sound / Restless)

Apr 92. (12") *(ONUDP 21)* **I THINK OF YOU (part 1). / I THINK OF YOU (part 2) / PRISONER OF PARADISE**
Apr 93. (10"ep) *(ONUDP 26)* **BLESS THOSE (part 1 & 2). / GOING FOR GOLD (part 1 & 2)**
Jun 93. (cd/lp) *(ONU CD/LP 60)* **SHORT AND SWEET**
– Watch the world go by / Bless those (Little Annie's prayer) / Going for gold / I think of you / I think of you (dub) / Give it to me / You the night and the music / Little man / Prisoner of paradise / Everything & more / If Cain were able.
Sep 94. (12"ep) *(ONUOP 30)* **IN DREAD WITH LITTLE ANNIE (FOUR PIECES OF HEART . . .)**
– 10 killer hurtz more / Miss the light / This town / Le mangers hereux.
Sep 94. (cd) <72797> **SHORT, SWEET AND DREAD** (compilation)
Oct 94. (12") <7 72911-0> **GOING FOR GOLD. / YOU, THE NIGHT AND THE MUSIC / THIS TOWN**

(not iss. / Streamline)

Aug 01. (12"/cd-s) <STREAM 1021/+CD> **DIAMONDS MADE OF GLASS. / LULLABY / DIAMONDS MADE OF GLASS (Christoph Heeman remix)**

APARTMENTS

Formed: Brisbane, Australia . . . 1978 by PETER MILTON WALSH, MICHAEL O'CONNOR, PETER WHITBY and PATER MARTIN. They released a one-off, 'HELP', for Australian indie, 'Able' (then also home of The GO-BETWEENS), before breaking up when WALSH moved to New York to form The COLORS; he subsequently joined The LAUGHING CLOWNS with ED KUEPPER (ex-SAINTS). WALSH later re-formed The APARTMENTS in 1984 after a stay in London, gaining support slots to EVERYTHING BUT THE GIRL in the process. With ex-TRIFFIDS steel guitar player GRAHAM LEE in tow, the outfit signed a contract with 'Rough Trade', releasing their long-awaited debut album, 'THE EVENING VISITS . . . AND STAYS FOR YEARS', in 1985. The critics gave it good reviews – especially the French ones – some remarking it was reminiscent of 60's hippie icons, LOVE and TIM BUCKLEY (SERGE GAINSBOURG also comes to mind). Early in 1987, WALSH and Co completed a part soundtrack to the John Hughes film, 'Some Kind Of Wonderful' and shifted stables to 'Glass'. After a lengthy hiatus (at least as far as UK releases were concerned), the group resurfaced in the early 90's, issuing a series of albums for Australian-based 'Hot' records; their aptly-titled 'DRIFT' set had found favour in France through 'New Rose' in '92. With varying line-ups, WALSH and his APARTMENTS subsequently toured their gallic foothold promoting works such as 'APART' (1997) and the acoustic mail order-only 'FETE FORAINE' (1998).

Album rating: THE EVENING VISITS . . . AND STAYS FOR YEARS (*7) / DRIFT (*5) / A LIFE FULL OF FAREWELLS (*6) / APART (*5) / FETE FORAINE (*4)

PETER MILTON WALSH – vocals, guitar / **MICHAEL O'CONNOR** – guitar, vocals / **PETER WHITBY** – bass, vocals / **PETER MARTIN** – drums

(Able / not iss.)

Oct 79. (7") *(AB 005)* **HELP. / NOBODY LIKE YOU** — Austra

— split when WALSH joined the LAUGHING CLOWNS; he also released a single on 'Prince Melon' with OUT OF NOWHERE, 'REMEMBER, REMEMBER' / 'NO RESISTANCE'.

— (1984) WALSH re-formed The APARTMENTS with **GRAEME BEAVIS** – guitar, vocals (ex-FUN THINGS) / **GARY WARNER** – piano / **JOE BORKOWSKI** – bass / **BRUCE CARRICK** – drums

(Hot / not iss.)

Nov 84. (7") **ALL YOU WANTED. / FEVER ELSEWHERE** — Austra

— **WALSH + CARRICK** added **GRAHAM LEE** – steel guitar (ex-TRIFFIDS) / plus guests **CLARE KENNY** – bass (ex-ORANGE JUICE) / **BEN WATT** – guitar (of EVERYTHING BUT THE GIRL)

(Rough Trade / not iss.)

Oct 85. (lp) *(ROUGH 88)* **THE EVENING VISITS . . . AND STAYS FOR YEARS**
– Sunset hotel / Mr. Somewhere / What's the morning for? / All the birthdays / Great fool / Speechless with Tuesday / Cannot tell the days apart / Lazarus, Lazarus / The black road shines. (cd-iss. Jul98 on 'Hot'; HOT 1059CD) <US cd-iss. 1997 on 'Twin/Tone'; 89331>
Mar 86. (7") *(RT 188)* **ALL I WANTED. / SUNSET HOTEL**
(12"+=) *(RTT 188)* – What's the morning for / The black road shines.

— WALSH added **MICHAEL COUVRET** – bass (ex-CELIBATE RIFLES) / **MARK DAWSON** – drums / **ASTRID MUNDAY** – backing vocals

(Glass / not iss.)

May 88. (7") *(GLASS 055)* **THE SHYEST TIME. /**
(12"+=) *(GLASS12 055)* –

— split once again, although they were by no means finished

— WALSH + DAWSON recruited **GREG ATKINSON** – guitar (ex-UPS AND DOWNS) / **JOHN WILLSTEED** – bass (ex-ZERO, ex-GO-BETWEENS)

(New Rose / Twin/Tone)

1992. (cd) *(422470)* <89330> **DRIFT** — French
– Goodbye train / On every corner / Mad cow / Nothing stops it / Over / Knowing you were loved / Places where the night is long / All his stupid friends / Could I hide here? / What's left of your nerve. (UK/Aust-iss.Jul98 on 'Hot'; HOT 1060CD)

(Hot / Restless)

Mar 95. (cd) *(HOT 1050CD)* <72955> **A LIFE FULL OF FAREWELLS**
– Things you'll keep / The failure of love is a brick wall / You became my big excuse / End of some fear / Not every clown can be in the circus / Thank you for making me beg / Paint the days white / She sings to forget you / All the time in the world.
Jun 95. (cd-ep) *(HIT 009)* **LIFE EP**
– Things you'll keep / All you wanted / The shyest time / Make it count.

— WALSH now with **KEN GORMLY** – bass (ex-CRUEL SEA) / **GENE MAYNARD** – drums

Jul 97. (cd) *(HOT 1063CD)* **APART**
– Doll hospital / No hurry / Breakdown in Vera Cruz / To live for / Welcome to Walsh world / Your ambulance rides / Friday rich – Saturday poor / World of liars / Place of bones / Cheerleader / Everything is given to be taken away.
Jul 98. (cd) *(HOT 1068CD)* **FETE FORAINE** (acoustic)
– What's the morning for / Knowing you were loved / Not every clown can be in the circus / On rvery corner / Sunset hotel / End of some fear / Thank you for making me beg / Things you'll keep / Paint the days white.

A PRIMARY INDUSTRY (see under ⇒ ULTRAMARINE)

A.R. KANE

Formed: East London, England . . . 1986 by ALEX AYULI and RUDI TAMBALA. They signed a one-off deal with 'One Little Indian', debuting in the indie charts with the 'WHEN YOU'RE SAD' EP in 1987. Described in the press as a unique fusion of COCTEAU TWINS meeting MILES DAVIS and ROBERT WYATT, their ROBIN GUTHRIE (Cocteau Twins)-produced follow-up, 'LOLITA', came out on '4 a.d.'. This led to a one-off collaboration with the label's COLOUR BOX; M/A/R/R/S. This project soon rose to No.1 simultaneously in the UK pop, dance and indie charts with the techno/dub classic 'PUMP UP THE VOLUME' (by the end of the year, it also hit No.13 in the States). During this fruitful period, they moved to 'Rough Trade', who issued their first long player '69'. This, together with their late 1989 follow-up, 'i', again topped the indie chart, although little was heard of them until they returned in 1994 with the album, 'NEW CLEAR CHILD'.

Album rating: 69 (*8) / i (*8) / AMERICANA compilation (*7) / NEW CLEAR CHILD (*6)

ALEX AYULI – guitars, etc / **RUDI TAMBALA** – guitars, etc

(One Little Indian / not iss.)

Feb 87. (12"ep) *(12TP 2)* **WHEN YOU'RE SAD. / WHEN YOU'RE SAD / THE HAUNTING**
(re-iss. Aug87; same)

(4 a.d. / Nesak)

Jul 87. (12"ep) *(BAD 704)* <704> **LOLITA. / SADO-MASOCHISM IS A MUST / BUTTERFLY COLLECTOR**
(above was to have been issued May87; 12TP 8)

(Rough Trade / Rough Trade)

Apr 88. (12"ep) *(RTT 201)* **UP HOME. / BABY MILK SNATCHER / W.O.G.S.**
Jun 88. (lp/c/cd) *(ROUGH/+C/CD 119)* **69**
– Crazy blue / Suicide kiss / Baby milk snatcher / Scab / Sulliday / Dizzy / Spermwhale trip over / The sun falls into the sea / The Madonna is with child / Spanish quay (3).
Nov 88. (7") *(RT 231)* **GREEN HAZED DAZE. / IS THIS IT?**
(12"ep+=) *(RTT 231)* **LOVESICK EP** – Sperm travels like a juggernaut / Is this dub?.
Jul 89. (7"/12"plays-@48rpm) *(RT/+T 239)* **POP. / WHAT'S ALL THIS THEN?**
(cd-s+=) *(RT 239CD)* – Snow joke.
Oct 89. (d-lp/c/cd) *(ROUGH/+C/CD 139)* **i**
– Snow joke / Off into space / Hello / Crack up / Yeti / What's all this then? / Honeysuckleswallow / In a circle / Insect love / Miles apart / Sugar wings / Down / And I say / Catch my drift / A love from outer space / Timewind / Conundrum / Long body / Fast kg / Pop / Mars / Spook / Back home / Super vixens / Sorry / Challenge.
May 90. (m-cd/m-lp) *(RT CD/CMC/D 171)* **REM'I'XES** (6 remixes)
– Miles apart / Crack up (space mix) / Sugarwings / Love from Outer Space / Catch my drift.

(not iss. / Luaka Bop-Sire)

Jan 92. (cd/c) <26669-2/-4> **AMERICANA** (compilation of first 2 albums)
– Love from Outer Space / Snow joke / Baby milk snatcher / Madonna is with child / In a circle / Miles apart / Green dazed haze / Water / Long body / Up / Supervixens / Spook / Crack up / And I Say / Sperm whale trip over.
Feb 92. (cd-s) <40373> **LOVE FROM OUTER SPACE**
– Love from outer space (2 mixes) / Sugarwings / A love from outer space (2 further mixes).

(3rd Stone / 3rd Stone)

Sep 94. (cd-s) <STONE 09CD> **SEA LIKE A CHILD / SEA LIKE A CHILD (IN THE SKY) / WATER / SEA LIKE A CHILD (UNDERWATER)**
Oct 94. (cd) (<STONE 11CD>) **NEW CLEAR CHILD**
– Deep blue breath / Grace / Tiny little drop of perfumed time / Surf motel / Gather / Honey be (for Stella) / Cool as moons / Snow White's world / Pearl / Sea like a child.

— split the following year

ARMOURY SHOW (see under ⇒ SKIDS; 70's section)

ARTERY

Formed: Sheffield, England . . . 1978, as an outlet for weird, extrovert singer, MARK GOLDTHORPE. Completing the line-up with TOYCE ASHLEY, NEIL MacKENZIE and GARRY WILSON, the band issued their self-financed debut 45, 'MOTHER MOON'. At the turn of the decade, ARTERY appeared at Leeds Futurama Festival, releasing a long awaited follow-up, 'UNBALANCED', later in 1980. After a further two indie 7"ers and the addition of MICK FIDLER and future MISSION-ary SIMON HINKLER (for the departing TOYCE), they were signed to the 'Red Flame' imprint through whom they delivered their first album, the DALE GRIFFIN (ex-Mott The Hoople) produced mini-set, 'OCEANS' (1982). With GOLDTHORPE contributing gothic, narrative-esque vocals against a backdrop of dense, mood-shattering post-punk textures, track highlights included the sinister carousel of 'THE CLOWN' and the repetitive bass-plucking of 'INTO THE GARDEN'. The first of many personnel upheavals occurred prior to the release of their first full-length effort, 'ONE AFTERNOON IN A HOT-AIR BALLOON' (1983), issued in conjunction with a non-album rendition of Jacques Brel's 'ALABAMA SONG'. In 1984, after relocating business to 'Golden Dawn', ARTERY attempted another moody classic, Leonard Cohen's 'DIAMONDS IN THE MINE', the single/track actually included on that year's lp, 'THE SECOND COMING'. Unfortunately their efforts were in vain, as the extremely shoddy 1986 live set proved that ARTERY's finger was no longer on the pulse. However, main songwriters GOLDTHORPE and HINKLER collaborated one last time on 'FLIGHT COMMMANDER SOLITUDE & THE SNAKE' (1986).

Album rating: OCEANS mini (*5) / ONE AFTERNOON IN A HOT-AIR BALLOON (*5) / THE SECOND COMING (*5)

MARK GOLDTHORPE – guitar / **TOYCE ASHLEY** – vocals, guitar / **NEIL MacKENZIE** – bass / **GARRY WILSON** – drums

		Take One	not iss.
Apr 79.	(7"m) *(TAKE 1)* **MOTHER MOON. / PRETENDS TO BE / HEINZ**	☐	-
		Aardvark	not iss.
Nov 80.	(7") *(STEAL 3)* **UNBALANCED. / THE SLIDE** (7"live-ep+=) – PERHAPS / TURTLE. / TOYTOWN / HEINZ	☐	-
—	added **MICHAEL FIDLER** – guitar, saxophone		
1981.	(7") *(AARD 15)* **CARS IN MOTION. / LIFE AND DEATH**	☐	-
		Armageddon	not iss.
Nov 81.	(7") *(AS 026)* **INTO THE GARDEN. / AFTERWARDS**	☐	-
—	**SIMON HINKLER** – keyboards, guitar (ex-TV PRODUCT) repl. ASHLEY		
—	(GOLDTHORPE took over vocals)		
		Red Flame	not iss.
Aug 82.	(7") *(RF 704)* **THE CLOWN 1. / THE CLOWN 2**	☐	-
Oct 82.	(m-lp) *(RFM 4)* **OCEANS** – The ghost of a small tour-boat captain / Into the garden / The clown 1 / Afterwards / The slide / The clown 2 / The sailor situation.	☐	-
—	**JOHN WHITE** – guitar; repl. FIDLER		
—	**CHRISTOPHER HENDRICK** – bass; repl. MacKENZIE		
—	added at gigs only **DAVID HINKLER** – keyboards		
—	now a trio of GOLDTHORPE, WILSON + multi-instrumentalist HENDRICK (JOHN WHITE formed UV POP himself & SIMON HINKLER produced PULP (not the same as the famous one!)		
Nov 83.	(lp) *(RF 18)* **ONE AFTERNOON IN A HOT-AIR BALLOON** – Perhaps / Being there / Unbalanced / Being there / One afternoon in a hot-air balloon / Song for Lena / Potential silence / Turtle / Butcher's wife / Louise / It's good to be alone.	☐	-
Nov 83.	(12"m) *(RFB 25-12)* **ALABAMA SONG. / SONG FOR LENA / THE DEATH OF PETER X**	☐	☐
—	**NEIL MacKENZIE** – bass; returned to repl. HENDRICK		
—	added **MURRAY FENTON** – guitar, organ		
		Golden Dawn	not iss.
May 84.	(12"m) *(GD 12-02)* **A BIG MACHINE. / BRINK OF EXTINCTION / I OPEN MY EYES & WALK**	☐	-
Oct 84.	(12"ep) *(GD 12-04)* **DIAMONDS IN THE MINE. / LOVE LIKE THE REST / ONEPENNY HORROR SHOW / BUTCHER'S SHOP**	☐	-
Nov 84.	(lp) *(GDLP 001)* **THE SECOND COMING** – The last song / My age, my beast / Diamonds in the mine / The father song / The mother song / Little boy blue / Ringing the bells.	☐	-
—	**TONY PERRIN** – bass, manager (1984 live 5th member) repl. MacKENZIE / added the returning **SIMON HINKLER** – now guitar		
Nov 85.	(lp) *(GDLP 002)* **NUMBER 4 (live in Amsterdam)**	☐	-
—	they disbanded in 1985, HINKLER was soon to join The MISSION		

– compilations, etc. –

		Pleasantly Surprised	not iss.
Apr 89.	(c) *(PS 011)* **AFTERWARDS** (demos, live & interviews) – Weak light / One afternoon in a hot air balloon / Louise / Afterwards / The sailor situation / So many people / A moment's thought / A mother's ruin / The Alabama song / One afternoon in a hot air balloon / It's good to be alone / Afterwards / Into the garden / The butcher's shop / Live like the rest / Diamonds in the mine.	☐	-

MARK GOLDTHORPE & SIMON HINKLER

		Golden Dawn	not iss.
Apr 86.	(lp) *(GDLP 003)* **FLIGHT COMMANDER SOLITUDE & THE SNAKE** – Monkey men / Message from a dead man / Another wild rose / Hold on tight / Dogs in leather / Serpent / Hidden for days / Shipwreck on the moon / Bad harvest / In late afternoon / Time & again / Wall of eyes.	☐	-

ART OBJECTS (see under ⇒ BLUE AEROPLANES)

Daniel ASH (see under ⇒ BAUHAUS)

ASSOCIATES

Formed: Dundee, Scotland . . . 1979 by BILLY MACKENZIE and ALAN RANKINE, who had worked as a duo in 1976 (the ABSORBIC ONES). After a debut single on their own 'Double-Hip' label, they signed to Chris Parry's 'Fiction', a subsidiary of 'Polydor' records. Their glorious debut set, 'THE AFFECTIONATE PUNCH', was followed by a series of highly rated 45's for the independent 'Situation 2' label. In 1982, they enjoyed their first taste of success when stylish 'PARTY FEARS TWO' and 'CLUB COUNTRY' both hit the UK Top 20. Energetic alternative dance rock, featuring high, passionate vocals of MACKENZIE, The ASSOCIATES inimitable, unclassifiable sound enjoyed only a very brief liaison with the pop charts. Now signed to 'Warners', the group's more accessible 'SULK' (1982) album made the UK Top 10, its lavish arrangements, white funk and stirring vocal histrionics going down well amid the craze for all things "New Romantic". Despite this belated recognition, the pair subsequently went their separate ways, losing their commercial momentum in the process. When they finally got back together in 1984 (with a line-up of STEVE GOULDING, IAN McINTOSH, ROBERT SUAVE and L. HOWARD JONES), MACKENZIE and RANKINE recorded only one further single together, 'THOSE FIRST IMPRESSIONS', before the latter finally bowed out. The remaining members recorded the 'PERHAPS' (1985) album, a relative flop which saw a further set, 'THE GLAMOUR CHASE' shelved and MACKENZIE returned in 1990 with an album on the 'Circa' label, 'WILD AND LONELY', to little reaction. The ASSOCIATES name had seemingly been laid to rest when, a couple of years later, the singer released a solo set, 'OUTERNATIONAL'. The next five years were quiet as MACKENZIE attended to his beloved greyhounds in his native Dundee. The music world was shocked, when, on the 22nd January '97, it was announced that he had taken his own life, reportedly depressed after the death of his mother a little earlier. Ironically, MACKENZIE had signed to the hip 'Nude' label (home of SUEDE), and had been working on new material at the time of his death. This material was posthumously released as 'BEYOND THE SUN', pundits and public alike mourning the death at 39 of one of music's forgotten geniuses. • **Songwriters:** Lyrics / music by duo (until RANKINE's departure), except BOYS KEEP SWINGING (David Bowie) / LOVE HANGOVER (Diana Ross) / GOD BLESS THE CHILD (Billie Holiday) / HEART OF GLASS (Blondie) / KITES (Simon Dupree & The Big Sound) / GROOVIN' WITH MR. BLOE (Mr. Bloe) / GREEN TAMBOURINE (Lemon Pipers) / I'M GONNA RUN AWAY FROM YOU (Tammi Lynn). • **Trivia:** MACKENZIE featured on B.E.F.'s (HEAVEN 17) single 'IT'S OVER' circa '82.

Album rating: THE AFFECTIONATE PUNCH (*6) / FOURTH DRAWER DOWN singles compilation (*9*) / SULK (*7) / PERHAPS (*5) / WILD AND LONELY (*4) / POPERA: THE SINGLES COLLECTION compilation (*8) / Billy MacKenzie: OUTERNATIONAL (*5) / BEYOND THE SUN (*8)

BILLY MACKENZIE (b.27 Mar'57) – vocals / **ALAN RANKINE** – keyboards, guitar, etc

		Double Hip	not iss.
Oct 79.	(7") *(DHR 1)* **BOYS KEEP SWINGING. / MONA PROPERTY GIRL** *(re-iss. Dec79 on 'M.C.A.'; MCA 537)*	☐	-
—	added **NIGEL GLOCKER** – drums / guest **ROBERT SMITH** – guitar (of-CURE) who replaced unknown guitarist		
		Fiction	not iss.
Aug 80.	(7") *(FICS 11)* **THE AFFECTIONATE PUNCH. / YOU WERE YOUNG**	☐	-
Aug 80.	(lp/c) *(FIX/+C 5)* **THE AFFECTIONATE PUNCH** – The affectionate punch / Amused as always / Logan time / Paper house / Transport to Central / A matter of gender / Even dogs in the wild / Would I . . . bounce back / Deeply concerned / A. *(remixed & re-iss. Nov82; FIXD 5) (re-iss. Aug83 on 'Polydor' lp/c; SPE LP/MC 33)*	☐	-
—	**JOHN MURPHY** (b. Australia) – drums repl. GLOCKER (to TOYAH)		
		Situation 2	not iss.
Apr 81.	(7"/12") *(SIT 1/+12)* **TELL ME EASTER'S ON FRIDAY. / STRAW TOWELS** *(re-iss. but w-drawn Nov82 on 'Beggars Banquet'; BEG 86)*	☐	-
Jun 81.	(7") *(SIT 4)* **Q: QUARTERS. / KISSED** (12"+=) – Q: Quarters (original).	☐	-
Aug 81.	(7"/12") *(SIT 7/+T)* **KITCHEN PERSON. / AN EVEN WHITER CAR**	☐	-
Oct 81.	(7"/12") *(SIT 10/+T)* **MESSAGE OBLIQUE SPEECH. / BLUE SOAP**	☐	-
Nov 81.	(7"/12") *(SIT 11/+T)* **WHITE CAR IN GERMANY. / THE ASSOCIATE**	☐	-
Jan 82.	(lp/c) *(SITU 2/+C)* **FOURTH DRAWER DOWN** – White car in Germany / A girl named Property / Kitchen person / Q; quarters / Tell me Easter's on Friday / The associate / Message oblique speech / An even whiter car. *(re-iss. Nov82 on 'Beggars Banquet' lp/c; BEGA/BEGC 43) (cd-iss. Apr02 on 'V2'; VVR 101202-2)*	☐	-
		R.S.O.	not iss.
1981.	(7"/12"; as 39, LYON STREET) *(RSO/+X 78)* **KITES. / A GIRL NAMED POVERTY**	☐	-
—	added **MICHAEL DEMPSEY** – bass (of CURE) / **MARTHA LADLY** – backing vocals (ex-MARTHA & THE MUFFINS)		

ASSOCIATES (cont)

		Associates	WEA
Mar 82.	(7"/12") (ASC 1/+T) **PARTY FEARS TWO. / IT'S BETTER THIS WAY**	9	
May 82.	(7") (ASC 2) **CLUB COUNTRY. / IT'S YOU AGAIN** (12"+=) (ASC 2T) – Ulcragyceptemol.	13	
Jun 82.	(lp/c) (ASCL/ASCC 1) **SULK**	10	–

– It's better this way / Party fears two / Club country / Love hangover / 18 carat love affair / Arrogance gave him up / No / Skipping / Nothing in something particular / Arrogance gave him up / White car in Germany / Gloomy Sunday / The associate. (re-iss. Oct82 on 'WEA' lp/c; 240 005-1/-4) (cd-iss. Jul88 on 'WEA'; K 240005-2) (cd re-iss. Apr02 on 'V2'; VVR 101201-2)

| Jul 82. | (7") (ASC 3) **18 CARAT LOVE AFFAIR. / LOVE HANGOVER** (12"+=) (ASC 3T) – Voluntary wishes, swapit production. | 21 | |

── split & re-formed 1984 by **MACKENZIE** + **RANKINE** recruiting **STEVE GOULDING** – drums / **IAN McINTOSH** – rhythm guitar / **ROBERT SUAVE** – bass / **L. HOWARD JONES** – keyboards

		WEA	WEA
May 84.	(7"/ext.12") (YZ 6/+T) **THOSE FIRST IMPRESSIONS. / THIRTEEN FEELINGS**		43

STEPHEN REID – guitar; repl. RANKINE who joined PAUL HAIG. He also had a solo career between 1986-87, releasing two albums, 'THE WORLD BEGINS TO LOOK HER AGE' for 'Crepescule' and 'SHE LOVES ME NOT' for 'Virgin'

Aug 84.	(7"/ext.12") (YZ 16/+T) **WAITING FOR THE LOVE BOAT. / SCHAMP OUT**		53
Jan 85.	(7"/7"pic-d) (YZ 28/+P) **BREAKFAST. / BREAKFAST ALONE** (12"+=) (YZ 28T) – Kites.		49
Feb 85.	(lp/c) (WX 9/+C) **PERHAPS**		23

– Those first impressions / Waiting for the love boat / Perhaps / Schampout / Helicopter helicopter / Breakfast / Thirteen feelings / The stranger in your voice / The best of you / Don't give me that I told you so look.

| Oct 85. | (7") (YZ 47) **TAKE ME TO THE GIRL. / PERHAPS** | | – |

(ext.12"+=) (YZ 47T) – The girl that took me / ('A'instrumental).
(10"+=) (YZ 47TE) – God bless the child (live) / Even dogs in the wild (live) / The boy that Santa Claus forgot (live).

── The above 'A'side was later (in Mar88) covered by group/artist JIH.

── (early 1986) HUGHES and SUAVE joined PETE MURPHY

── **MACKENZIE** now used session people under The ASSOCIATES

| Sep 88. | (7") (YZ 310) **HEART OF GLASS. / HER ONLY WISH** | 56 | |

(3"cd-s+=) (YZ 310CD) – Breakfast / Those first impressions.
('A'-Auchterhouse mix-12"+=) (YZ 310T) – ('A'-Auchterhouse instrumental).
(12"+=) (YZ 310TX) – ('A'-Temperamental mix) / Heavens blue.

| Nov 88. | (w-drawn lp/c)(cd) (WX 222/+C)(244619-2) **THE GLAMOUR CHASE** | – | – |
| Jan 89. | (w-drawn 7") (YZ 329) **COUNTRY BOY. / JUST CAN'T SAY GOODBYE** | – | – |

(w-drawn 12"+=) (YZ 329T) – Heart of glass (dub mix).
(w-drawn 3"cd-s++=) (YZ 329CD) – Take me to the girl.

		Circa	Charisma
Mar 90.	(c/cd/lp) (CIRC/+D/A 11) **WILD AND LONELY**	71	

– Fire to ice / Fever / People we meet / Just can't say goodbye / Calling all around the world / The glamour chase / Where there's love / Something's got to give / Strasbourg Square / Ever since that day / Wild and lonely / Fever in the shadows.

| Apr 90. | (7"/c-s) (YR/+C 46) **FEVER. / FEVER IN THE SHADOWS** | | |

(12"+=/s12"+=/3"cd-s+=/cd-s+=) (YR T/TB/CD/CDT 46) – Groovin' with Mr.Bloe.

| Aug 90. | (7"/c-s) (YR/+C 49) **FIRE TO ICE. / GREEN TAMBOURINE** | | |

(ext.12"+=) (YRT 49) – The glamour chase.
(10"++=/ext.cd-s++=) (YR TX/CD 49) – Groovin' with Mr.Bloe.

| Sep 90. | (12"ep) <096448> **FIRE TO ICE (mixes) / GREEN TAMBOURINE** | | |
| Jan 91. | (7"/c-s) (YR/+C 56) **JUST CAN'T SAY GOODBYE. / ONE TWO THREE** | | – |

(12") (YRT 56) – ('A'-Time Unlimited mix) / ('A'-Time Unlimited instrumental) / ('A'-US mix).
(12") (YRTX 56) – ('A'-Time Unlimited mix) / ('A'-Time Unlimited instrumental) / ('A'-Karma mix).
(cd-s) (YRCD 56) – ('A'side) / ('A'-Time Unlimited piano mix) / ('A'-US version) / I'm gonna run away from you.

BILLY MACKENZIE

| Jun 92. | (7") (YR 86) **BABY. / SACRIFICE AND BE SACRIFICED (CH 8032 mix)** | | – |

(cd-s+=) (YRCD 86) – Grooveature (D 1000 mix) / Colours will come (US 60659 mix).
(12") (YRT 86) – ('A'side) / Colours will come (Larry Heard remix) / Opal krush / Colours will come (Raw Stylus remix).

| Aug 92. | (7") (YR 91) **COLOURS WILL COME. / OPAL KRUSH** | | – |

(12"+=/cd-s+=) (YRT/YRCD 91) – Look what you've done / Feels like the richtergroove.

| Sep 92. | (c/cd) (CIRC/+D 22) **OUTERNATIONAL** | | – |

– Outernational / Feels like the richtergroove / Opal krusch / Colours wil come / Pastime paradise / Groovecture / Sacrifice and be sacrificed / Baby / What made me turn on the lights / Windows cell.

── In Jul'96, BILLY was featured on a single by LOOM, 'ANACOSTIA BAY'.

── Tragically on the 22nd January 1997, BILLY committed suicide in his father's garden shed; he had recently signed to 'Nude' records.

		Nude	not iss.
Oct 97.	(cd) (NUDE 8CD) **BEYOND THE SUN**	64	–

– Give me time / Winter academy / Blue it is / 14 mirrors / At the edge of the world / Beyond the sun / And this she knows / Sour jewel / 3 gypsies in a restaurant / Nocturne VII.

── early in 2000, a posthumous CD-album, 'MEMORY PALACE' (credited with PAUL HAIG) was released on 'Rhythm Of Life' (ROL 003)

		Rhythm Of Life	not iss.
Mar 01.	(cd; as BILLY MACKENZIE & STEVE AUNGLET) (ROL 005) **EUROCENTRIC**		–

– Falling out with the future / Homophobic / 14th Century nightlife / Liberty lounge / When the world was young / Sing that song again / Soul that sighs / Wild is the wind / Mother Earth / Return to love.

– (ASSOCIATES) compilations, others, etc. –

Sep 81.	(7"/12") Fiction; (FICS/+X 13) **A. / WOULD I . . . BOUNCE BACK**		–
Nov 82.	(7"/12") Fiction; (FIXS/+X 16) **A MATTER OF GENDER. / EVEN DOGS IN THE WILD**		–
Oct 89.	(12"ep/cd-ep) Strange Fruit; (SFPS/+CD 075) **THE PEEL SESSIONS** ('82)		–

– It's better this way / Nude spoons / Me myself and the tragic story / Natural gender / Ulcragyceptemol.

| Jan 91. | (cd)(lp/c) East West; (9031 72414-2)(WX 363/+C) **POPERA** | | – |

– Party fears two / Club country / 18 Carat love affair / Love hangover / Those first impressions / Waiting for the loveboat / Breakfast / Take me to the girl / Heart of glass / Country boy / The rhythm divine / Waiting for the loveboat (slight return) / Tell me Easter's on Friday / Q; quarters / Kitchen person / Message oblique speech / White car in Germany.

| Jan 91. | (7"/c-s) East West; (YZ 534/+C) **POPERETTA EP: WAITING FOR THE LOVEBOAT (Slight Return). / CLUB COUNTRY CLUB** | | – |

(12"+=/cd-s+=) (YZ 534 T/CD) – Waiting for the loveboat (extended voyage) / Club country club (Time Unlimited).

Sep 94.	(cd) Nighttracks; (CDNT 006) **THE RADIO ONE SESSION**		–
Apr 02.	(d-cd) V2; (VVR 101203-2) **DOUBLE HIPNESS**		–
May 02.	(d-cd) Warners; (8573 88496-2) **THE GLAMOUR CHASE / PERHAPS**		–

Virginia ASTLEY

Born: 26 Sep'59, Watford, England. After graduating from the Guildhall School Of Music, she co-founded The RAVISHING BEAUTIES along with NICKY HOLLAND and KATE ST. JOHN. At the turn of the decade they provided an unusual backdrop for many alternative-pop hitmakers including ECHO & THE BUNNYMEN, SIOUXSIE & THE BANSHEES and The SKIDS. After augmenting VICTIMS OF PLEASURE on a few rare singles, ASTLEY reconvened with her aforementioned 'BEAUTIES who backed her up on what would have been her debut album, 'SHE STOOD UP AND CRIED' (1981); initially shelved, the record finally appeared three years later as 'PROMISE NOTHING'. In the meantime she moved from 'Crespescule' records to 'Why-Fi', the label delivering two singles, the latter of which, 'LOVE'S A LONELY PLACE TO BE', hit high in the indie charts. 1983 proved to be a minor turning point for her, the angelic soprano signing to 'Rough Trade' for her first full release, 'FROM THE GARDENS WHERE WE FEEL SECURE', a delightfully dreamy collection of drifting neo-chamber music that was unique in the glitzy musical climate of the day. An English blueprint for the more commercial "new age" sounds created by the likes of ENYA later in the decade, VIRGINIA's style was marketed towards the mainstream charts as she signed to 'Elektra'/'WEA' in '85 and released the 'HOPE IN A DARKENED HEART' (1986) set. Augmented by kindred spirit, producer RYUICHI SAKAMOTO (ex-YMO), the album had its moments with the highlight being the single, 'SOME SMALL HOPE', a duet with ex-JAPAN mainman DAVID SYLVIAN. Although ASTLEY continued to maintain a low profile in Britain, she had more success in Japan where she secured a deal with 'Columbia'. To date, the "quiet-pop" queen has released two albums, 'ALL SHALL BE WELL' (1992) and 'HAD I THE HEAVENS' (1996), both finally given a belated British release via 'Rosebud' late '97.

Album rating: FROM GARDENS WHERE WE FEEL SECURE (*6) / PROMISE NOTHING (*5) / HOPE IN A DARKENED HEART (*6) / ALL SHALL BE WELL (*5) / HAD I THE HEAVENS (*5)

VICTIMS OF PLEASURE

VIRGINIA ASTLEY – synthesizer / **GEZ PRIOR** – guitar / **KENNY JONES** – bass / **CHRIS WYLES** – drums

		P.A.M.	not iss.
1980.	(7"m) (VOP 1) **WHEN YOU'RE YOUNG. / IF I WAS / SPORTING PASTIMES**		–
		Rialto	not iss.
Nov 81.	(7"/12") (RIA/12RIA 2) **SLAVE TO FASHION. / ON THE GAME**		–
Apr 82.	(7") (RIA 7) **JACK AND JILL. / RED MOON**		–
Oct 82.	(7"; w-drawn) (RIA 11) **WHEN YOU'RE YOUNG. /**		

VIRGINIA ASTLEY

── - vocals, piano / with **AUDREY RILEY** – cello / **ANNE STEPHENSON** – violin / **JOCELYN POOK** – viola (all ex-RAVISHING BEAUTIES)

		Crepsecule	not iss.
Nov 81.	(lp; w/drawn) (TWI 050) **SHE STOOD UP AND CRIED**		–
		Why-Fi	not iss.
Jan 82.	(10"ep) (WHYD 8) **4 BAO A QU**		–

– We will meet them again / Arctic death / Angels crying / Sanctus. (w/free 7"demos)

| Jan 83. | (7") (WFI 001) **LOVE'S A LONELY PLACE TO BE. / SOARING** | | – |

(12"+=) (WFIT 001) – A summer long since passed / It's too hot to sleep.

── now w/guest **JO WELLS** – clarinet (of KISSING THE PINK)

Virginia ASTLEY (cont)

| | | Rough Trade | not iss. |

Aug 83. (lp) *(ROUGH 58)* **FROM GARDENS WHERE WE FEEL SECURE**
– Morning: With my eyes wide open I'm dreaming / A summer long since passed / From gardens where we feel secure / Hiding in the ha-ha / Afternoon: Out in the lawn I lie in bed / Too bright for peacocks / Summer of their dreams / When the fields were on fire / It's too hot to sleep. *(cd-iss. 1993 on 'Happy Valley'+=; CY 4457)* – Sanctus / Melt the snow. *(cd re-iss. Nov97 on 'Rosebud'++=; RBXCD 1001)* – Melt the snow (instrumental 1 & 2). *(cd re-iss. May02; RETRADECD 001)*

Mar 85. (12"ep) *(RTT 158)* **MELT THE SNOW. / INSTRUMENTAL 1 / THE END OF TIME**
(also on 'Happy Valley'; HA 002)

──── added brothers **JON + TED**

| | | Elektra | Elektra |

Sep 85. (7") *(EKR 21)* **TENDER. / A LONG TIME AGO**
(ext-12"+=) *(EKR 21T)* – Mindless days / ('A'instrumental).

| | | W.E.A. | W.E.A. |

Dec 85. (7") *(YZ 53)* **DARKNESS HAS REACHED ITS END. / THE END OF TIME**
(12"+=) *(YZ 53T)* – Shadows will fall behind.

Nov 86. (lp)(cd) *(WX 78)(<242039-2>)* **HOPE IN A DARKENED HEART**
– Some small hope / A father / So like Dorian / Darkness has reached its end / I'm sorry / Tree top club / Charm / Love's a lonely place to be / A summer long since passed. *(cd re-iss. 1992 on 'WEA' Japan+=; WMC5 567)* – A day, a night. (below single credited with DAVID SYLVIAN. He and RYUICHI SAKAMOTO on above album)

Feb 87. (7") *(YZ 107)* **SOME SMALL HOPE. / A SUMMER LONG SINCE PASSED**
(12"+=) *(YZ 107T)* – So long Dorian (instrumental).

| | | Nippon Columbia | not iss. |

1992. (cd) *(COCY 9661)* **ALL SHALL BE WELL** — — Japan
– My smallest friend / All shall be well / You take me away / I live for the day / Love's eloquence / Although I know / Martin / Blue sky, white sky / How I miss you / My smallest friend (instrumental). *(UK-iss.Nov97 on 'Rosebud'; RBXCD 1002)*

1996. (cd) *(COCY 80070)* **HAD I THE HEAVENS** — — Japan
– It's over now / Over the edge of the world / Nothing is as it seems / Broken / Where I belong (a thousand nights) / I can't say goodbye / Had I the heavens / Another road / How can I do this to you / I know a tune we could sing / A long long year. *(UK-iss.Nov97 on 'Rosebud'; RBXCD 1003)*

– compilations, etc. –

Dec 84. (lp) *Crepescule; (TWI 194)* **PROMISE NOTHING**
– We will meet them again / Arctic death / Angels crying / Sanctus / Love's a lonely place to be / Soaring / Futility / A summer long since passed / It's too hot to sleep. *(cd-iss. 1993 on 'Nippon Columbia'; COCY 7533-2)*

Pete ASTOR (see under ⇒ WEATHER PROPHETS)

ATHLETICO SPIZZ '80
(see under ⇒ SPIZZ; 70's section)

ATTILA THE STOCKBROKER

Born: JOHN BAINE, 21 Oct'57, Southwick, West Sussex, England. After initially training to be a real stockbroker, the lure of the music biz proved too much and BAINE set himself up as performance poet, ATTILA THE STOCKBROKER. After brief stints in obscure Harlow-based punk bands, ENGLISH DISEASE and BRIGHTON RIOT SQUAD, he enjoyed another fleeting position with Belgian band, CONTINGENT (one single released in 1979, 'POLICE CONTROL'). Following a John Peel session, BAINE secured a deal with independent label, 'Cherry Red', who issued a belated debut album, 'RANTING AT THE NATION', in 1983. Described as the alternative LES DAWSON, his ranting was a light refreshment to the "oi" music around him and took up where JOHN COOPER CLARKE left off. Shot through with typically barbed humour, his state-of-the-nation commentaries were well observed if something of an acquired taste. Critical opinion wasn't exactly in his favour and perhaps as a result, ATTILA was increasingly developing the musical aspect of his work. Moving on from the sparse mandolin backing which had accompanied his earlier work, the release of 'SAWDUST AND EMPIRE' (1984) found the man moving in folkier circles alongside the likes of fellow erstwhile punk and general space cadet, JOHN OTWAY. With titles like 'LIBYAN STUDENTS FROM HELL' (1987) and 'SCORNFLAKES' (a book! in 1988), you know what to expect from this decidedly un-PC performer, you've been warned!

Album rating: RANTING AT THE NATION (*5) / SAWDUST & EMPIRE (*5) / LIBYAN STUDENTS FROM HELL (*4) / SCORNFLAKES (*4) / DONKEY'S YEARS (*4) / THE SIEGE OF SHOREHAM (*5) / JUST ONE LIFE . . . (*6)

ATTILA THE STOCKBROKER – vocals, fiddle, mandolin

| | | No Wonder | not iss. |

1981. (c-ep) *(E 1)* **PHAZING OUT CAPITALISM**

──── in 1982, he and SEETHING WELLS released the 'ROUGH, RAW AND RANTING' EP for 'Radical Wallpaper'.

| | | Cherry Red | not iss. |

Oct 82. (7"ep) *(CHERRY 46)* **COCKTAILS**
– Contributory negligence / The night I slept with Seething Wells / Fifth column / The oracle.

Apr 83. (lp) *(ARED 46)* **RANTING AT THE NATION**
– Away day / I slept with Seething Wells / Albanian football / A bang and a Wimpey / Burn it down / Flappin' in the wind / Contributory negligence / Nigel wants to go to C&A's / The perils of stealing half a bottle of wine / They must be Russians / Russians in the DHSS / Russians in MacDonalds / The oracle / Death in Bromley / Nigel wants to go and see Depeche Mode / Russians at the Henley regatta / Russians on the centre court / Fifth column / The fall of King Zog / Holiday in Albania / England are back (Luxembourg where are you?) / Where are you goin' with that flounder? / Hands off our halibuts / Gentlemen of the wrist / Eros products commercials / The Spencers croft cat (dead cat strat) / A very silly East European propaganda station / The fall of King Zog (reprise).

| | | Anagram | not iss. |

Mar 84. (lp) *(GRAM 13)* **SAWDUST & EMPIRE**
– Sawdust & empire / Boadicea uber alles / Factory gods / March of the levellers / Nigel's revenge / Recession / Diesirae (World War III) / Holiday in Albania / Alone in Sidco / Spare a thought / Midas the ground / Ghosts of the levellers.

| | | Cherry Red | not iss. |

Aug 84. (12"ep) *(12CHERRY 82)* **RADIO RAP! EP**
– Let the drain take the strain / Take a leak on a green / (Everytime) I eat vegetables / Vomit on a Viking / I don't talk to pop stars / Love and herpes / Albanian rifle poem / Nigel wants to join the S.A.S. / A letter from Nigel's mum / Russians versus the Tetley bitter man / Poetry requiem.

1984. (12"ep) **LIVINGSTONE RAP! EP**

| | | Plastic Head | not iss. |

Mar 87. (lp) *(PLASLP 009)* **LIBYAN STUDENTS FROM HELL**
– Libyan students from Hell / I'm so miserable / Airstrip one / The ballad of Comrade Enver / Pedi dies / The rapping mole / Another country / Glenzendes empire / The green fields of France.

| | | Probe Plus | not iss. |

Sep 88. (lp) *(PROBE 20)* **SCORNFLAKES**

──── in the early 90's, ATTILA & (JOHN) OTWAY released the joint 'CHERYL – A Rock Opera' CD.

| | | Musidisc | not iss. |

Apr 91. (cd/c/lp) *(10789-2/-4/-1)* **DONKEY'S YEARS**
– Jingo bells / Tyler smiles (22.11.90) / Roll up for the donkey derby / The iron men of rap / This is free Europe / Mountaineering in Belgium / Market sektor one / The ligger's song / Tammy's song / The bible according to Rupert Murdoch / Retrospective abortion / Dustbin poem / The pen and the sword (pre con-version) / Sawdust and empire / Libyan students from Hell! (mega city Paris mix).

| | | Larrikin | not iss. |

Jul 93. (cd/c) *(LRF CD/C 264)* **666: NEIGHBOUR OF THE BEAST** — — Austra

ATTILA THE STOCKBROKER'S BARNSTORMER

──── next with BARNSTORMER: **MARTIN FISH** – guitar / **DAN WOODS** – bass / **TIM O'TAY** – recorders / **M. M. McGHEE** – drums

| | | Demi-Monde | not iss. |

Aug 96. (cd/c) *(HELMET CD/CAS 1)* **THE SIEGE OF SHOREHAM**
– Bombarde (parts 1 & 2) / The one that got away / The Blanford forum / Cheering the plough / Sarajevo / Worms / March of the Levellers – The diggers song / Tyler smiles / Tirana / Old teenagers / The siege of Shoreham / Camelot by numbers / Horns / The torchbearer / And I won't run away / The Zen Stalinist manifesto / Joseph Porter's sleeping bag / Victoria road / (untitled).

| | | Townsend | not iss. |

Oct 00. (cd) *(none)* **JUST ONE LIFE . . .**
– Haider! / The ghost road / Game boy rude boy / Scumball pinochet (for Marc Bolan) / The worm & the archer / Cero / His master's voice / Another country / The comrade of Comrade Enver / 20 years / Just one life.

– compilations, others, etc. –

1990. (lp/c) *Festival;* **LIVE AT THE RIVOLI (live)** — — Canada
1999. (cd) *Roundhead-Mad Butcher;* **POEMS ANCIENT & MODERN: A LIVE ANTHOLOGY 1981-1999 (live)**
1999. (cd) *Roundhead-Mad Butcher;* **THE PEN & THE SWORD: SELECTED SONGS 1981-1995**

AU PAIRS

Formed: Birmingham, England . . . 1979 by lesbian feminist LESLEY WOODS, along with PAUL FOAD, JANE MUNRO and PETE HAMMOND. Pointedly political and musically eclectic, the AU PAIRS carried on where the likes of GANG OF FOUR and DELTA 5 left off, spiritually at least. Musically, the group were heavily influenced by the 2-tone scene and its mash-up of ska, reggae and pop (they had supported fellow Brummies, UB40), a healthy dose of quirky bass-led post-punk experimentalism keeping things interesting. In true DIY style, the band initiated their recording career with a self-financed EP, 'YOU', in 1980, following it up with a debut album, 'PLAYING WITH A DIFFERENT SEX' (1981) and a heavy touring schedule. While The AU PAIRS struggled to make any inroads into the mainstream, critics were generally supportive and WOODS' lyrics were often thought provoking in their presentation of a uniquely feminine perspective on gender and sexuality. Although a second album, 'SENSE AND SENSUALITY' (1982) appeared on 'Kamera' records (featuring members of The POP GROUP), it proved to be their epitaph as the band fell apart in 1983 after WOODS missed a gig in Belgium. She subsequently resurfaced fronting all-female band The DARLINGS while FOAD and HAMMOND formed END OF CHAT.
• **Songwriters:** Group compositions, except SEX MACHINE (James Brown).

Album rating: PLAYING WITH A DIFFERENT SEX (*8) / SENSE AND SENSUALITY (*5) / LIVE IN BERLIN (*5) / EQUAL BUT DIFFERENT: BBC SESSIONS 79-81 collection (*5) / SHOCK TO THE SYSTEM: THE VERY BEST OF . . . compilation (*7)

LESLEY WOODS (b.25 Jan'58, Hockley, Essex) – vocals, guitar / **JANE MUNRO** (b. 9 Dec'53) – bass, vocals / **PAUL FOAD** – guitar, vocals / **PETE HAMMOND** – drums

AU PAIRS (cont) — THE GREAT INDIE DISCOGRAPHY — The 1980s

	021	not iss.
1980. (7"m) (OTO 2) **YOU. / DOMESTIC DEPARTURE / KERB CRAWLER**		
Nov 80. (7") (OTO 4) **IT'S OBVIOUS. / DIET**	–	–

	Human	not iss.
Apr 81. (lp) (HUMAN 1) **PLAYING WITH A DIFFERENT SEX**	33	–

– We're so cool / Love song / Set-up / Repetition / Headache (for Michelle) / Come again / Armagh / Unfinished business / Dear John / It's obvious. (cd-iss. Nov92 & Apr00 on 'R.P.M.' +=; RPM 107) – You / Domestic departure / Kerb crawler / Diet / It's obvious (7"version) / Inconvenience (12"version) / Pretty boys / Headache (for Michelle) (remix).

Jul 81. (7") (HUM 8) **INCONVENIENCE. / PRETTY BOYS**
(12"+=) (HUM 8-12) – Heartache (remix).

	Kamera	not iss.
Aug 82. (lp) (KAM 010) **SENSE AND SENSUALITY**	79	–

– Don't lie back / (That's when) It's worth it / Instant touch / Sex without stress / Fiasco / In-tact / Tongue in cheek / Stepping out of line / Shakedown / America. (cd-iss. Sep93 & Apr00 on 'R.P.M.'; RPM 111) (cd re-mast.Mar02 on 'Castle'; CMRCD 470)

— disbanded early '83, FOAD and HAMMOND evolved the band into END OF CHAT with WOODS' replacement GRAHAM HAMILTON

– compilations, etc. –

Aug 83. (lp) a.k.a.; (AKA 6) **LIVE IN BERLIN (live 1981)** □ –
– Diet / Headache for Michelle / Dear John / Love song / Set up / Inconvenience / Armagh / Repetition / We're so cool / Cum again / Piece of my heart. (<cd-iss. Oct96 on 'Essential'; ESMCD 452>)

Jul 94. (cd) R.P.M.; (<RPM 139CD>) **EQUAL BUT DIFFERENT** □ –
– Monogamy / Pretty boys / Come again / Ideal woman / Dear John / The love song / It's obvious / Repetition / Unfinished business / Diet / We're so cool / Armagh / The set-up / Headache for Michelle / Intact / Shakedown / Instant touch / America / Sex without stress / Steppin' out of libne. (re-iss. Apr00; same)

Sep 99. (cd) Cherry Red; (<CDMRED 161>) **SHOCK TO THE SYSTEM: THE VERY BEST OF THE AU PAIRS** □ Oct99
– We're so cool / Repetition / Headache for Michelle / Come again / You / Diet / It's obvious / Inconvenience / Instant touch / America / Sex without stress / Steppin' out of line / Fiasco / Taking care of him / Love song.

A WITNESS

Formed: Stockport, near Manchester, England ... 1985 by RICK AITKEN, KEITH CURT and VINCE HUNT. Signed to C86 stalwart, 'Ron Johnson', A WITNESS became associated with the NME-created scene after having the track, 'SHARPENED STICKS', featured on the cassette of the same name. The band had already won praise from the same publication for their debut EP, 'LOUDHAILER SONGS'. Trading in the same jerky rhythms and crazed vocals as BEEFHEART, The FALL and The CRAVATS, the band had obviously cocked an ear at some point to new wave pioneers WIRE. A full length album, 'I AM JOHN'S PANCREAS', appeared in '86 and the group (soon to be with "real" drummer ALAN BROWN) enjoyed a brief period of cult acclaim until the collapse of both the scene which spawned them and the 'Ron Johnson' label itself. Another independent imprint, 'Communion', issued their belated follow-up set, 'SACRED COW HEART' (1988), before the band hooked up with The MEMBRANES' 'Vinyl Drip' label for a final single early in 1990, 'I LOVE YOU MR. DISPOSABLE RAZORS'. Inquisitive readers can sample an overview of A WITNESS's career (which was cut short by RICK's untimely death in a climbing accident 1989) via the 'DOUBLE PEEL SESSIONS' compilation of their recordings with the cult Radio One DJ and indie tastemaker. • **Covered:** BREAK ON THROUGH (Doors).

Album rating: I AM JOHN'S PANCREAS (*6) / SACRED COW HEART (*4) / THREAPHURST LANE compilation (*7)

KEITH CURTIS – vocals / **RICK AITKEN** (b.18 Aug'56) – guitar / **VINCE HUNT** – bass / + drum machine

	Ron Johnson	not iss.
Nov 85. (12"ep) (ZRON 5) **LOUDHAILER SONGS**	□	–

– Lucky in London / Kitchen sink drama / Regular round / Camera / Drill one.

Oct 86. (lp) (ZRON 12) **I AM JOHN'S PANCREAS** □ –
– Smelt like a pedestrain / O'Grady's dream / Car skidding / Red snake / Dipping bird / Sharpened sticks / The loudhailer song / Legs be sturdy / 4.49 stool / Hard days love.

May 87. (12"ep) (ZRON 26) **RED SNAKE EP** □ –
– red snake / Regular round / Hard days love.

— **ALAN BROWN** – drums; repl. drum machine

Feb 88. (12"ep) (ZRON 30) **RAW PATCH EP** □ –
– Raw patch / Faglane Morris wind / Zip up / Nodding dog moustache.

	not iss.	Communion
Oct 88. (lp/c) <COMM 003/+C> **SACRED COW HEART**	–	

	Vinyl Drip	not iss.
Feb 90. (12"ep) (SUK 010) **I LOVE YOU, MR. DISPOSABLE RAZORS**	□	–

— had already disbanded in 1989; RICK was to die the same year. CURTIS went on to The MEMBRANES and later GOLD BLADE; HUNT and BROWN (with PRAM's DAREN GARRATT) formed MARSHALL SMITH in 1997

– compilations, etc. –

Dec 89. (m-lp/m-cd) Strange Fruit; (SFPMA/+CD 206) **THE PEEL SESSIONS** □ –

Nov 00. (cd) Overground-Voiceprint; (OVER 88VPCD) **THREAPHURST LANE** □ □
– Sharpened sticks / I love you, Mr. Disposable razors / Tomorrow never knows / O'Grady's dream / The loudhailer song / Zip up / Dipping bird / Smelt like a pedestrian / Hard day's love / Car skidding / Lucky in London / 4.49 stool / Nodding dog moustache / Red snake / Faglane Morris wind / Threaphurst lane / Break on through / Dudefield.

AZTEC CAMERA

Formed: East Kilbride, Scotland ... early 1980 by 15 year-old, RODDY FRAME, who released two independent 45's on ALAN HORNE's now semi-famous 'Postcard' label, before moving on to 'Rough Trade' in 1982. The following year, RODDY and Co. hit the top of the indie charts (reached Top 30 nationally) with debut album, 'HIGH LAND, HARD RAIN', a largely acoustic-based affair combining folkish flights of fancy, Latin/jazz rhythms and an incisive lyrical flair with stunning results. The record's breezy lead track, 'OBLIVIOUS', was re-issued by new label 'Warners' later that year on the back of the album's success, one of the few AZTEC CAMERA singles to break the Top 20. FRAME brought in a new cast of musicians for 1984's MARK KNOPFLER-produced 'KNIFE' set, including seasoned Scots players CRAIG GANNON and MALCOLM ROSS. A more commercial offering, the record almost made the UK hit in 'ALL I NEED IS EVERYTHING'. After a world tour, FRAME laid low for more than two years, penning material for 'LOVE' (1987), the most successful album of his career. Initially something of a non-starter, this over-produced yet affecting album eventually made the Top 10 almost a year after its release following the massive Top 5 success of the plaintive 'SOMEWHERE IN MY HEART' single. Despite courting the pop mainstream, FRAME's subsequent effort, 'STRAY' (1990) veered off into more eclectic territory, the Top 20 hit, 'GOOD MORNING BRITAIN', featuring MICK JONES of BIG AUDIO DYNAMITE / CLASH fame. The 90's witnessed FRAME developing his earlier style, especially on the 1995 set, 'FRESTONIA'. Come 1998, the Scots veteran had signed to 'Independiente', releasing a minor hit, 'REASON FOR LIVING' which accompanied the relatively low-key pop-rock album, 'THE NORTH STAR'. • **Covered:** JUMP (Van Halen) / DO I LOVE YOU (Cole Porter) / I THREW IT ALL AWAY (Bob Dylan) / BAD EDUCATION (Blue Orchids) / IF PARADISE WAS HALF AS NICE (Amen Corner). • **Trivia:** In Autumn '83, while in the States supporting ELVIS COSTELLO, he lied about his age (19) to get into the country.

Album rating: HIGH LAND, HARD RAIN (*8) / KNIFE (*6) / LOVE (*5) / STRAY (*6) / DREAMLAND (*6) / FRESTONIA (*5) / THE BEST OF AZTEC CAMERA compilation (*8) / Roddy Frame: THE NORTH STAR (*5) / SURF (*6)

RODDY FRAME (b.29 Jan'64) – vocals, acoustic guitar / **DAVE MULHOLLAND** – drums / **CAMPBELL OWENS** – bass; who repl. ALAN WELSH late in 1980

	Postcard	not iss.
Mar 81. (7") (81-3) **JUST LIKE GOLD. / WE COULD SEND LETTERS**	□	–
Jul 81. (7") (81-8) **MATTRESS OF WIRE. / LOOK OUTSIDE THE TUNNEL**	□	–
Sep 81. (lp; w-drawn) (81-13) **GREEN JACKET GREY**	–	–

— (mid-'82) added temp. member **BERNIE CLARK** – keyboards / **DAVE RUFFY** – drums (ex-RUTS) repl. MULHOLLAND

	Rough Trade	Sire
Aug 82. (7"/7"pic-d) (RT 112/+P) **PILLAR TO POST. / QUEEN'S TATTOO**	□	–
Jan 83. (7") (RT 122) **OBLIVIOUS. / ORCHARD GIRL**	47	□

(12"+=) (RT 122T) – Haywire.

Apr 83. (lp) (ROUGH 47) <23899> **HIGH LAND, HARD RAIN** | 22 | Aug83
– Oblivious / The boy wonders / Walk out to winter / The bugle sounds again / We could send letters / Pillar to post / Release / Lost outside the tunnel / Back on board / Down the dip. (cd-iss. Feb87 +=; ROUGHCD 47) – Haywire / Queen's tattoo / Orchard girl. (re-iss. Sep93 on 'WEA' cd/c; 4509 92849-2/-4)

May 83. (7"/12") (RT/+T 132) **WALK OUT TO WINTER. / SET THE KILLING FREE** | 64 | □

	WEA	Sire
Oct 83. (d7") (AZTEC 1) **OBLIVIOUS. / ORCHARD GIRL // WE COULD SEND LETTERS (live). / BACK ON BOARD (live)**	18	□

— **RODDY FRAME** retained RUFFY and brought into line-up:- **CRAIG GANNON** – bass (ex-BLUEBELLS) repl. OWENS / added **MALCOLM ROSS** – guitar (ex-ORANGE JUICE, ex-JOSEF K) / guest / **GUY FLETCHER** – keyboards

Aug 84. (7") (AC 1) **ALL I NEED IS EVERYTHING. /** | 34 | □
(12") (AC 1T) – ('A'-Latin mix) / Jump (Loaded version).

Sep 84. (lp/c)(cd) (WX 8/+C)(240 483-2) <25183> **KNIFE** | 14 | □
– Still on fire / Just like the U.S.A. / Head is happy (heart's insane) / The back door to Heaven / All I need is everything / Backwards and forwards / Birth of the true / Knife. (cd-iss. Sep93; same) (cd re-iss. Jun02 on 'Wounded Bird'+=; WOU 5183) – AZTEC CAMERA mini-lp tracks.

Nov 84. (7"/7"sha-pic-d) (AC 2/+P) **STILL ON FIRE. / WALK OUT TO WINTER** □ □
(12"+=) (AC 2T) – Mattress of wire (live) / The boy wonders (live) / The bugle sounds again (live).

Apr 85. (10"m-lp) <25285> **AZTEC CAMERA (live)** – □
– Birth of the true / Mattress of wire / Jump / The bugle sounds again / Backwards and forwards.

— FRAME + RUFFY alongside other session musicians **MARCUS MILLER** – bass / **DAVID FRANK** – keyboards (ex-SYSTEM) / **STEVE JORDAN** – guitar

Sep 87. (7"/ext-12") (YZ 154/+T) **DEEP AND WIDE AND TALL. / BAD EDUCATION** □ □

Oct 87. (lp/c)(cd) (WX 128/+C)(242 202-2) <25646> **LOVE** | 10 | □
– Deep and wide and tall / How men are / Everybody is a number one / More than a law / Somewhere in my heart / Working in a goldmine / One and one / Paradise / Killermont Street. (cd-iss. Sep93; same)

Jan 88. (7") (YZ 168) **HOW MEN ARE. / THE RED FLAG** | 25 | □
(12"+=) (YZ 168T) – Killermont Street (live) / Pillar to post (live).
(cd-s+=) (248 028-2) – Oblivious / All I need is everything.

Apr 88. (7") (YZ 181) **SOMEWHERE IN MY HEART. / EVERYBODY IS A NUMBER ONE '86** | 3 | □
(12"+=) (YZ 181T) – Down the dip / Jump.
(cd-s+=) (YZ 181CD) – Walk out to winter / Still on fire.

209

AZTEC CAMERA (cont)

Jul 88. (7") *(YZ 199)* **WORKING IN A GOLDMINE. / I THREW IT ALL AWAY** — 31
(12"+=/12"s+=) *(YZ 199 T/W)* – ('A'version).
(cd-s++=) *(YZ 199CD)* – How men are.

Sep 88. (7") *(YZ 154)* **DEEP AND WIDE AND TALL. / BAD EDUCATION** — 55
(12"+=/cd-s+=) *(YZ 154 T/CD)* – More than a law.

— (live band '88: augmenting **FRAME + RUFFY**) **EDDIE KULAK** – keyboards / **GARY SANFORD** – guitar / **PAUL POWELL** – bass

— (by 1990, **FRAME** had lost **RUFFY** but retained **POWELL** / and new **GARY SANCTUARY** – keyboards / **FRANK TONTOH** – drums / guests **PAUL CARRACK, EDWYN COLLINS, MICKEY GALLAGHER & STEVE SI DELYNK.**

Jun 90. (cd)(lp/c) *(<9031 71694-2>)(WX 350/+C)* **STRAY** — 22
– Stray / The crying scene / Get outta London / Over my head / How it is / Good morning Britain (featuring MICK JONES) / The gentle kind / Notting Hill blues / Song for a friend. *(re-iss. cd+c Sep93)*

Jun 90. (7") *(YZ 492)* **THE CRYING SCENE. / TRUE COLOURS** — 70
(12"+=/cd-s+=) *(YZ 492 T/CD)* – Salvation.
(10"+=) *(YZ 492X)* – I threw it all away (live).

Sep 90. (7"/c-s; AZTEC CAMERA and MICK JONES) *(YZ 521/+C)* **GOOD MORNING BRITAIN. / ('A'live version)** — 19
(12"+=) *(YZ 521T)* – ('A'remix)
(cd-s+=) *(YZ 521CD)* – Consolation prize. (with EDWYN COLLINS).

Jul 92. (7"/c-s) *(YZ 688/+C)* **SPANISH HORSES. / JUST LIKE THE U.S.A. (live)** — 52
(cd-s) *(YZ 688CD1)* – ('A'side) / Killermont street (live) / The birth of the true (live) / Song for a friend (live).
(cd-s) *(YZ 688CD2)* – ('A'live version) / Stray (live) / The bugle sounds again (live) / Dolphins (live).

Apr 93. (7"/c-s) *(YZ 740/+C)* **DREAM SWEET DREAMS. / GOOD MORNING BRITAIN (live)** — 67
(cd-s+=) *(YZ 740CD1)* – Sister Anne (live) / How men are (live).
(cd-s) *(YZ 740CD2)* – ('A'side) / Mattress of wire (live) / Let your love decide (live) / Orchid girl (live).

May 93. (cd/c/lp) *(<4509 92492/-2/-4/-1>)* **DREAMLAND** — 21
– Birds / Safe in sorrow / Black Lucia / Let your love decide / Spanish horses / Dream sweet dreams / Piano's and clocks / Sister Ann / Vertigo / Valium Summer / Belle of the ball.

Jun 93. (7"/c-s) *(YZ 754/+C)* **BIRDS. / DEEP AND WIDE AND TALL** —
(cd-s) *(YZ 754CD1)* – ('A'side) / Working in a goldmine / Knife.
(cd-s) *(YZ 754CD2)* – ('A'side) / Somewhere in my heart / Oblivious / Good morning Britain.

WEA Reprise

Oct 95. (c-s) *(WEA 007C)* **SUN / SUNSET** —
(cd-s+=) *(WEA 007CD)* – The crying scene (live).
(cd-s) *(WEA 007CDX)* – ('A'side) / We could send letters (live) / Black Lucia (live) / The rainy season (live).

Nov 95. (cd/c) *(<0630 11929-2/-4>)* **FRESTONIA** —
– The rainy season / Sun / Crazy / On the avenue / Imperfectly / Debutante / Beautiful girl / Phenomenal world / Method of love / Sunset.

– compilations, etc. –

Sep 90. (7") *Old Gold; (OG 9945)* **SOMEWHERE IN MY HEART. / OBLIVIOUS** — -

— In Nov'90, 'DO I LOVE YOU?' appeared as the extra track on the 12" & cd-s of a Cole Porter tribute by The POGUES and KIRSTY MacCOLL

Oct 94. (cd) *Windsong; (WHISCD 006)* **LIVE ON THE TEST (live)** — -
Jul 99. (cd/c) *WEA; (3984 28984-2/-4)* **THE BEST OF AZTEC CAMERA** — 36 -
– Oblivious / Good morning Britain / Somewhere in my heart / Working in a goldmine / How men are / Birth of the true / Walk out winter / Jump / All I need is everything / Deep & wide & tall / The crying scene / Killermont street / Spanish horses / Reason for living.

RODDY FRAME

Independiente Sony

Sep 98. (c-s) *(ISOM 18CS)* **REASON FOR LIVING / WINTER HAVEN HIGH** — 45 Nov98
(cd-s) *(ISOM 18MS)* <66231A> – Rainy greys and blues.
(cd-s) *(ISOM 18SMS)* <66231B> – ('A'side) / Biba nova / The sea is wide.

Sep 98. (cd) *(ISOM 7CD)* <120123> **THE NORTH STAR** — 55 Nov98
– Back to the one / The north star / Here comes the ocean / River of brightness / Strings / Bigger brighter better / Autumn flower / Reason for living / Sister shadow / Hymn to grace.

Redemption not iss.

Aug 02. (cd) *(RRUK 2)* **SURF** —
– Over you / Surf / Small world / I can't start now / Abloom / Tough / Big Ben / High class music / Turning the world around / Mixed up love / For what it was.

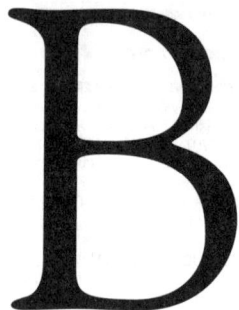

BABYLON DANCE BAND (see under ⇒ ANTIETAM)

BAD BRAINS

Formed: Washington DC, USA ... 1978 by Afro-Americans, H.R., his brother EARL, DR. KNOW and DARRYL JENNIFER. Prior to the advent of the punk rock movement in 1976/77, they had all played together in a jazz fusion outfit, carrying over the jazz dynamic to their frenetic, dub-wise hardcore. Subsequently relocating to New York, the late 70's saw the release of two classic 45's, 'PAY TO CUM' and 'BIG TAKEOVER'. These virtually went unnoticed, the band's UK profile remaining low after being refused work permits to support The DAMNED on a British tour. In 1983, they finally delivered their debut album, 'ROCK FOR LIGHT' (produced by RIC OCASEK of The CARS), a set that featured one side of hardcore and the other reggae. For three years, H.R. went solo, returning to the fold for 1986's 'I AGAINST I', a more metallic affair which anticipated the funk-rock explosion of the late 80's. H.R. (with EARL) subsequently departed to realise his more reggae orientated ambitions, releasing several albums for 'S.S.T.'. The remainder of BAD BRAINS parted company with this label, eventually reactivating the band for touring purposes with the addition of CHUCK MOSELEY (ex-FAITH NO MORE). H.R. and EARL returned to the fold for the 'QUICKNESS' album in 1989, remaining for the live set, 'THE YOUTH ARE GETTING RESTLESS'. Once again, H.R. and EARL decided to take off, their replacements being ISRAEL JOSEPH-I and the returning MACKIE. This line-up was in place for their major label debut for 'Epic', 'RISE' (1993), although incredibly yet again H.R. and EARL were invited back as BAD BRAINS were offered a place on MADONNA's 'Maverick' label. The resulting 1995 album, 'GOD OF LOVE' (again produced by OCASEK) focused more on dub reggae stylings, proving that the band were as open to experimentation as ever. However, during the accompanying tour, the athletic H.R. left the band for good in controversial circumstances, fighting with his fellow musicians and eventually being pulled up on a drugs charge (BAD BRAINS right enough!). • **Songwriters:** H.R. / DR. KNOW / group, except DAY TRIPPER (Beatles) / SHE'S A RAINBOW (Rolling Stones).

Album rating: BAD BRAINS (*7) / ROCK FOR LIGHT (*8) / I AGAINST I (*8) / LIVE (*5) / QUICKNESS (*4) / RISE (*4) / GOD OF LOVE (*6)

H.R. (b. PAUL HUDSON, 11 Feb'56, London, England) – vocals / **DR. KNOW** (b. GARY WAYNE MILLER, 15 Sep'58, Washington) – guitar, keyboards / **DARRYL AARON JENIFER** (b.22 Oct'60, Washington) – bass, vocals / **EARL HUDSON** (b.17 Dec'57, Alabama) – drums, percussion

not iss. Bad Brains

Jun 80. (7") <BB 001> **PAY TO CUM. / STAY CLOSE TO ME** —

Alternative Alternative Tentacles Tentacles

Jun 82. (12"ep) *(VIRUS 13)* **THE BAD BRAINS EP** —
– I luv jah / Sailin' on / Big takeover.

R.O.I.R. R.O.I.R.

Dec 82. (c) *(A 106)* **BAD BRAINS** —
– Sailin' on / Don't need it / Attitude / The regulator / Banned in D.C. / Jah calling / Supertouch / FVK / Big take over / Pay to cum / Right brigade / I love I jah / Intro / Leaving Babylon. *(cd-iss. Dec89 as 'ATTITUDE – THE ROIR SESSIONS' on 'We Bite' lp/cd; WB 056/+CD) <US re-iss. Nov89 on 'In-Effect'> (re-iss. cd/c/lp 1991 on 'Dutch East Wax' / re-iss. lp Mar93) (re-iss. cd Apr96; RUDCD 8223) (lp re-iss. Jul98 & Nov99; RUSLP 8223R)*

Food For Thought Important

Mar 83. (12"ep) *(YUMT 101)* **I AND I SURVIVE / DESTROY BABYLON EP** —

Abstract P.V.C.

Mar 83. (lp) *(ABT 007)* <PVC 8933> **ROCK FOR LIGHT** —
– Coptic times / Attitude / We will not / Sailin' on / Rally around jah throne / Right brigade / F.V.K. (Fearless Vampire Killers) / Riot squad / The meek shall inherit the Earth / Joshua's song / Banned in D.C. / How low can a punk get / Big takeover / I and I survive / Destroy Babylon / Rock for light / At the movies. *(re-mixed re-iss. Feb91 on 'Caroline' cd/c/lp; CAR CD/MC/LP 4) (re-iss. cd Sep91; same) (cd re-iss. Jun97; CAROLCD 1375)*

S.S.T. S.S.T.

Feb 87. (lp/c) <(SST 065/+C)> **I AGAINST I** — Nov86
– Intro / I against I / House of suffering / Re-ignition / Secret '77 / Let me help / She's calling you / Sacred love / Hired gun / Return to Heaven. *(cd-iss. Feb88 & May93; SST 065CD)*

— **CHUCK MOSELEY** – vocals (ex-FAITH NO MORE) repl. H.R.

— **MACKIE JAYSON** (b.27 May'63, New York City) – drums repl. EARL

BAD BRAINS (cont)

Nov 88. (lp/c/cd) <(SST 160 LP/C/CD)> **LIVE** (live)
– I cried / At the movies / The regulator / Right brigade / I against I / I and I survive / House of suffering / Re-ignition / Sacred love / She's calling you / Coptic times / F.V.K. (Fearless Vampire Killers) / Secret 77 / Day tripper. *(re-iss. May93; same)*

—— both **H.R.** + **EARL** returned

Caroline Caroline

Jul 89. (lp/c/cd) <(CAR LP/C/CD 4)> **QUICKNESS**
– Soul craft / Voyage into infinity / The messengers / With the quickness / Gene machine – Don't bother me / Don't blow bubbles / Sheba / Yout' juice / No conditions / Silent tears / The prophet's eye / Endtro. *(re-iss. cd Sep91; same)* *(cd re-iss. Jun97; CAROLCD 1375)*

S.S.T. S.S.T.

Oct 89. (10"m-lp/m-c/m-cd) <SST 228> **SPIRIT ELECTRICITY**
– Return to Heaven / Let me help / Day tripper / She's a rainbow / Banned in D.C. / Attitude / Youth are getting restless.

—— **ISRAEL JOSEPH-I** (b. DEXTER PINTO, 6 Feb'71, Trinidad) – vocals repl. H.R. / **MACKIE** returned EARL

Epic Epic

Sep 93. (cd/c/lp) <(474265-2/-4/-1)> **RISE**
– Rise / Miss Freedom / Unidentified / Love is the answer / Free / Hair / Coming in numbers / Yes jah / Take your time / Peace of mind / Without you / Outro.

—— **H.R.** + **EARL** returned to repl. JOSEPH-I + JAYSON

Maverick Maverick

May 95. (cd/c) <(9362 45882-2/-4)> **GOD OF LOVE**
– Cool mountaineer / Justic keepers / Long time / Rights of a child / God of love / Over the water / Tongue tee tie / Darling I need you / To the heavens / Thank jah / Big fun / How I love thee.

—— BAD BRAINS have since split

– compilations, etc. –

May 90. (cd/lp) *Caroline; (CARCD/LP 8)* <CAROL 1617> **THE YOUTH ARE GETTING RESTLESS** (live in Amsterdam 1987)
– I / Rock for light / Right brigade / House of suffering / Day tripper – She's a rainbow / Coptic times / Sacred love / Re-ignition / Let me help / The youth are getting restless / Banned in D.C. / Sailin' on / Fearless vampire killer / At the movies / Pay to cum / Big takeover. *(cd re-iss. Jun97; CAROLCD 1617)*

May 92. (d-cd) *Line; (LICD 921176)* **ROCK FOR LIGHT / I AGAINST I** — German

Oct 96. (cd/lp) *Caroline; (PCAROL 005CD/LP)* <7534> **BLACK DOTS** (rec.1979)
– Don't need it / At the Atlantis / Pay to cum / Supertouch – Shitfit / Regulator / You're a migraine / Don't bother me / Banned in D.C. / Why'd you have to go / Man won't annoy ya / Redbone in the city / Black dots / She does / How low can a punk get / Just another damn song / Attitude / Send you no flowers.

Nov 97. (10"ep/cd-ep) *Victory;* <(VR 064/+CD)> **THE OMEGA SESSIONS**
– I against you / Stay close to me / I love jah / At the movies / Attitude.

BAD DREAM FANCY DRESS
(see under ⇒ **KING OF LUXEMBOURG**)

BAILTER SPACE

Formed: Christchurch, New Zealand ... mid-80's, although mainman HAMISH KILGOUR had initiated the trio much earlier with ALISTER PARKER, the latter formerly of Kiwi FALL-like rock pioneers, The GORDONS. Tinted with a bit of WIRE, a bit of JOY DIVISION and a bit of this and bit of that, The GORDONS set out their stall as early as March 22, 1980 (their first gig). They secured a few mini-sets – the last without PARKER – before each member took their place (gradually) in BAILTER SPACE. Many readers will also recognise KILGOUR as being one of the founding members of another legendary NZ act, The CLEAN, alongside his brother DAVID. BAILTER SPACE originally began as a side project during a lull in The CLEAN activities, HAMISH and ALISTER teaming up with GLENDA BILLS and ROSS HUMPHRIES for what turned out to be an extended career, in NZ terms at least. Who else but that seminal Antipodean indie, 'Flying Nun', would release the first two domestic-only EP's, 1987's 'NELSH BAILTER SPACE' and the following year's 'GRADER SPADER' (former GORDONS bassist JOHN HALVORSEN replacing ROSS and GLENDA), both records well represented on the first European release, 'TANKER' (1988). Their first album proper, 'THERMOS' (1990), was the last to feature HAMISH, who erm, bailed out for a musical respite before concentrating on the re-formed CLEAN. His replacement, BRENT McLACHLIN (another ex-GORDONS member) made his inaugural appearance on 1992's comeback EP, 'THE AIM', also released in the US on 'Matador'. 1993's 'ROBOT WORLD' meanwhile, carried on the band's preoccupation with technology and alienation, although their driving fuzz-garage sound never strayed too far from rock's earthy roots. BAILTER SPACE continued their interstellar musical explorations into the mid-90's, reporting back to earth with two further sets, 'VORTURA' (1994) and 'WAMMO' (1995). Of late, the trio have concentrated on singles/EP's, future releases surfacing on the American-based 'Turnbuckle' imprint. 'CAPSUL' (1997) and 'SOLAR 3' (1999), saw the talented PARKER, HALVORSEN and McLACHLIN wig-out to a more conventional mode. Where 'WAMMO' was a little complex, these two sets recalled the stripped-down FALL comparisons, although these lads were only a trio.

Album rating: The Gordons: THE GORDONS mini (*6) / THE GORDONS VOLUME 2 mini (*5) / Bailter Space: TANKER (*6) / THERMOS (*5) / ROBOT WORLD (*7) / VORTURA (*6) / WAMMO (*5) / CAPSUL (*6) / SOLAR 3 (*6)

GORDONS

ALISTER PARKER – guitar, vocals / **JOHN HALVORSEN** – bass / **BRENT McLACHLAN** – drums

Harlequin not iss.

Jan 81. (ltd-12"ep) *(none)* **FUTURE SHOCK. / MACHINE SONG / ADULTS AND CHILDREN** — — New Z
(re-iss. 1987 on 'Flying Nun'; FN 093) (UK-iss.Sep88 on 'Flying Nun Europe'; FNE 17)

Dec 81. (m-lp) **THE GORDONS** — — New Z
– Spik and span / Right on time / Coalminer's song / Sometimes / I just can't stop / Growing up / Laughing now. *(UK-iss.Oct88 on 'Flying Nun Europe' m-lp/c+=; FNE/+CD 16)* – Future shock / Machine song / Adults and children.

—— **VINCE PINKER** – guitar, vocals; repl. ALISTER who formed BAILTER SPACE

Jul 84. (m-lp) **THE GORDONS VOLUME 2** — — New Z
– Quality control / Reactor / Lead room / Red line / Identity / Mono Flo / Gone machine / Joker / Mentus fugit.

—— after their split, HALVORSEN continued with The SKEPTICS and subsequently joined BAILTER SPACE (as did McLACHLIN)

BAILTER SPACE

ALISTER PARKER – vocals, guitar / **HAMISH KILGOUR** – drums, vocals (of The CLEAN) / **GLENDA BILLS** – keyboards / **ROSS HUMPHRIES** – bass (ex-PIN GROUP)

Flying Nun Matador

Dec 87. (12"ep/c-ep) *(FN/+MC 094)* **NELSH BAILTER SPACE EP** — — New Z
– New man / El whizzo / Our aim / I'm in love with these times / Separate circles / Now I will live.

Dec 87. (7") *(FN 096)* **NEW MAN. / INNER CITY WARDROBE** — — New Z

—— **JOHN HALVORSEN** – bass, vocals (ex-SKEPTICS, ex-GORDONS) repl. GLENDA + ROSS

1988. (12"ep) *(FN 106)* **GRADER SPADER EP** — — New Z
– Grader spader / The escalator song / N.B.S.

1988. (m-lp) *(FNE 31)* **TANKER** — —
– Glass / The "W" song / Grader spader / Titan / Your invisible life / Valve / The today song / Tanker / One more reason. *(re-iss. Aug94 lp/cd; FN/+CD 107)* <US cd-iss. Jan96 on 'Matador'+=; OLE 136> – NELSH BAILTER SPACE EP

1989. (cd/c/lp) *(FNCD/FNMC/FNLP 142)* **THERMOS** — —
– Fish eye / Zero return / Fused / The state / Earth fed / Hard wired / Ad man / Skin / Present. *(re-iss. Aug94; same)* <US cd-iss. Jan96 on 'Matador'+=; OLE 135> – The 'W' song / Your invisible life / Tanker / Titan.

—— **BRENT McLACHLIN** – drums (ex-GORDONS, + of-SKEPTICS) repl. HAMISH who eventually returned to The CLEAN

Aug 92. (cd-ep) *(FNCD 232)* <OLE 041> **THE AIM**
– The aim / We know / Shine / The unseen.

Jan 93. (7") *(HUNKA 014)* **THE AIM. / WE KNOW** — —

Apr 93. (7") *(HUNKA 016)* **SHINE. / THE UNSEEN** — —
(above 2 issued on 'Clawfist')

Apr 93. (cd/c/lp) *(FNCD 259)* <OLE 050> **ROBOT WORLD**
– Begin / Robot world / Morning / Be on time / Fascination / Ore / Get lost / EIP / Orbit / Make remain.

Mar 94. (cd-ep) *(FNCD 284)* <OLE 072> **BEIP** — Dec93
– X / Projects / Robot world / EIP.

Apr 94. (lp/cd) *(FN/+CD 295)* <OLE 093> **VORTURA** May94
– Projects / Process paid / X / Voices / No.2 / I.C.Y. / Dark blue / Shadow / Galaxy / Reactor / Control.

Jan 95. (c-ep) *(FNMC 328)* **SPLAT** — New Z
– Splat / Retro / At five we drive / Fascination.

Apr 95. (cd-ep) *(FNCD 345)* **RETRO / PROJECTS (live) / BEGIN (live)** — — New Z

Matador Matador

Jul 95. (7") <(OLE 147-7)> **SPLAT. / AT FIVE WE DRIVE** May95
(cd-s+=) <(OLE 147-2)> – Fascination.

Jul 95. (cd/lp) <(OLE 142-2/-1)> **WAMMO** May95
– Untied / Splat / At five we drive / Zapped / Colours / Retro / Glimmer / Voltage / D thing / Wammo. *(NZ-iss. on 'Flying Nun'; FNCD 325)*

Turnbuckle Orchard

Aug 97. (7") *(TB 003)* **THE CAPSUL. / AGRONAUT** —

Oct 97. (cd) *(TB 005CD)* <283> **CAPSUL**
– Shield / Pass it up / Velo / Sola / Picking up / Dome / Argonaut / The capsul / Tag / Collider / II / The sun / Shades / GA 9.

Aug 98. (cd-ep) *(TB 012)* <284> **PHOTON EP** May99
– Particle accelerator / Time machine / Torch / V 43 / U.H.F. / Nochen raum spatzel bitte / Flashback / Photon.

Turnbuckle Turnbuckle

Apr 99. (cd) (<TB 017>) **SOLAR 3** Mar99
– Two stars / Right now / So am I / Woke up / Live for you / Windows on the world / Big cat / Locher / Starand / Space X / Tide / Trekka.

BALANCING ACT

Formed: Los Angeles, California, USA ... 1984 by singer-songwriter JEFF DAVIS along with WILLIA ARON, STEVE WAGNER and ROBERT BLACKMON. Hardly typical for an 80's L.A. band, this lot attempted to balance the authenticity of traditional roots music with the spontaneity of rock's avant garde. After an obscure debut EP in '86, they laid down tracks with noted producer and former PLIMSOULS leader, PETER CASE, the results surfacing as 'NEW CAMPFIRE SONGS' on 'I.R.S.' subsidiary, 'Primitive Man'. Even featuring a cover of Captain Beefheart's 'ZIG ZAG WANDERER', the mini-set's quirky folk-rock sound was quite unlike anything else around at the time. Two further sets, 'THREE SQUARES AND A ROOF' (1987) and 'CURTAINS' (1988), developed their style without ever threatening the mainstream, the latter produced by ANDY GILL and featuring a cover of Funkadelic's 'CAN YOU GET TO THAT'.

BALANCING ACT (cont)

Album rating: NEW CAMPFIRE SONGS (*7) / THREE SQUARES AND A ROOF (*8) / CURTAINS (*7)

JEFF DAVIS – vocals, guitar / **WILLIE ARON** – guitar, vocals / **STEVE WAGNER** – bass, vocals / **ROBERT BLACKMON** – drums, vocals

                                                                                     Illegal   I.R.S.

May 86. (m-lp/m-c) *<IRS/+C 39097>* **NEW CAMPFIRE SONGS**
– Wonderful world tonight / Who got the pearls / A TV guide in the Olduvai gorge / A girl, her sister, and a train / The neighborhood phrenologist / Zig zag wanderer. *<originally issued on 'Type A'>*

Jul 88. (lp/c/cd) *(ILP 023) <IRS/+C/D 42082>* **THREE SQUARES AND A ROOF**   Nov87
– 3 cards / This is where it all begins / Kicking clouds across the sky / Whiskered wife / Adventure / Ballad of Art Snyder / Red umbrella / Governor of Pedro / Waiting for the mail / Searching for this thing / We're not lost. *<US cd+=>* – NEW CAMPFIRE SONGS

Nov 88. (lp/cd) *<IRS/+D 42237>* **CURTAINS**
– Generator / She doesn't work here / Lost in the mail / Red pants and romance / Dangerous roof / Can you get to that? / Understanding furniture / Sleep on the trusty floor / Fishing in your eye / Between two oceans / Learning how to cheat.

Jun 89. (7") *(EIRS 116)* **CAN YOU GET TO THAT? /**
(12"+=) *(EIRST 116)* –

— disbanded after above; 90's session man ARON teamed up with singer SIMON GLICKMAN (MILES LALLY on bass and PERRY OSTRIN on drums) to form power-pop outfit SPANISH KITCHEN (c. 1993). After one self-financed single they became MYSTERY POP and released an eponymous CD in 2002.

B.A.L.L.

Formed: New York, USA . . . 1987 by MARK KRAMER, DAVID LICHT, DON FLEMING and JAY SPIEGEL. All had indie rock pedigrees, the former two ex-members of SHOCKABILLY (KRAMER also of BONGWATER, and ex-BUTTHOLES), the latter both ex-HALF JAPANESE and VELVET MONKEYS. A twin-drum fuelled precursor to the late 80's grunge explosion, B.A.L.L.'s debut album, 'PERIOD' (ANOTHER AMERICAN LIE)', surfaced on KRAMER's own 'Shimmy Disc' label towards the end of that year. Next up was the following years' 'BIRD' album which parodied the sleeve design of The Beatles' "butcher-cover". The fab-four piss-take continued inside with a mock pastiche of George Harrison's 'CONCERT FOR BANGLA DESH', segueing Ringo Starr's 'IT DON'T COME EASY', Harrison's 'WAH WAH' and T.Rex's 'BUICK MACKANE'. Two further slices of slap-dash irreverence surfaced at the turn of the decade, 'TROUBLE DOLL' (1989) and 'BALL 4 – HARDBALL' (1990), before the culprits chose to take on other projects; KRAMER and LICHT carried on with BONGWATER. FLEMING and SPIEGEL, meanwhile, reunited in The VELVET MONKEYS (their album, 'RAKE' was released by 'Rough Trade' in 1990), at the same time joining DINOSAUR JR for a year before forming GUMBALL. This lot made a series of recordings for UK indie imprints 'Paperhouse' and 'Big Cat' (mainly the albums 'SPECIAL KISS' and 'SUPER TASTY'), before finally going corporate and signing a major deal with 'Columbia' in 1994 who issued third set, 'REVOLUTION ON ICE'. • **Covers:** Gumball: ALL I WANT (Troggs) / WHY DON'T WE DO IT IN THE ROAD (Beatles) / BACK OFF BOOGALOO (Ringo Starr). FLEMING + TOM SMITH; DIZZY (Tommy Roe). • **Trivia:** FLEMING took to production work for TEENAGE FANCLUB ('Bandwagonesque') and FREE KITTEN (the brainchild of KIM GORDON and JULIE CAFRITZ). Another SONIC YOUTH (90's) offshoot, DIM STARS, featured FLEMING alongside THURSTON MOORE, STEVE SHELLEY and Void-Oid legend, RICHARD HELL.

Album rating: BIRD (*7) / BALL 4 – HARDBALL (*6)

DON FLEMING – vocals, lead guitar (ex-HALF JAPANESE, ex-VELVET MONKEYS) / **JAY SPIEGEL** – drums (ex-HALF JAPANESE, ex-VELVET MONKEYS) / **MARK KRAMER** – bass, vocals, production (of-BONGWATER, ex-SHOCKABILLY, ex-BUTTHOLE SURFERS) / **DAVID LICHT** – drums (of-BONGWATER, ex-SHOCKABILLY)

                                                       Shadowline Shimmy Disc

Feb 88. (lp) *(SR 0388) <SHIMMY 006>* **PERIOD**   Nov87
– All I sought is progress / Ballad of Little Richard / King will never die / Favourite day / My TV is broke / Black spring / No song / Skull and cross / Treasure island / St. Vitus dance / In the woods / Theme B.A.L.L.

Jan 89. (lp) *(SD 8803) <SHIMMY 014>* **BIRD**
– When is a man / Bird / If I breakdown / Charm / Love was the end / Long ago / Burning wood / Buick Mackane / Another straight line / It don't come easy / Spit shine / Just like the last time / Wah-wah / Drink it on / Dylan side / Swim this way / Eye / Bangla-Desh / Scene's over // I could always be with you. *(cd-iss. Nov89 ++; SDE 8907)* – PERIOD

Oct 89. (lp/cd) *(SDE 8909 LP/CD)* **TROUBLE DOLL** (live + studio)
– Should brother kill / Never mant to say / Trouble world / This is war / Little Tex in trouble / Trash man / Trouble momma / I could always be with you / The cracked life of a cracked man / Floers grow on the wall / The French / When is a man / Bird / Charm / My T.V is broke / The king will never die / If I break down / It don't come easy / Love was the end / Just like the last time / Buick McKane. *(cd+=)* – Little Tex's prelude / Reagan's bush is on fire / Amazon / Trouble baby / TX-five / African sunset / Everywhere / Trouble finale.

Mar 90. (cd/lp) *(SDE 9018 CD/LP) <SHIMMY 030>* **BALL 4 – HARDBALL**
– Hard ball / She's always driving / Timmy the toad man / Mary Jane / The road to Heaven / Ball 4 prelude:- Ball 1 – Ball 2 – Ball 3 / Ball 4 R.I.P.

— split when FLEMING and SPIEGEL re-formed The VELVET MONKEYS and joined DINOSAUR JR for a year. Meanwhile KRAMER and LICHT carried on with BONGWATER.

VELVET MONKEYS

— early recordings included a 1982 US-only cassette collaboration with HALF JAPANESE, 'EVERYTHING IS RIGHT' (for 'Monkey Business') and in 1983, 'FUTURE' (for 'Fountain Of Youth'); both gathered together as 'ROTTING CORPSE AU GO-GO' in 1989 for 'Shimmy Disc' *<SHIMMY 018>*. Others included the cassette 'BIG BIG SUN' for 'K' in 1985

DON FLEMING (as "Rake") / **JAY SPIEGEL** (as "The Rummager") / **MALCOLM RIVIERA** (as "The Assassin") / **THURSTON MOORE** (as "The Action Pussy") / **J. MASCIS** (as "Sweet Dick") / **JULIA CAFRITZ** (as "Miss Sugar Bowl") / **JOHN HAMMILL** (as "Polack Johnny") / **DAISY VON FIRTH** (as "Chickley")

                                                   Rough Trade Rough Trade

Oct 90. (lp/c/cd) *(ROUGH/+C/CD 102)* **RAKE**
– We call it rock / She's not a girl / The ballad of 'Rake' / Something's in the air / Velvet monkey theme song / Rock the night / Harmonica hell house / Love to give / 7 angels / Rock party / Velvet monkey (Assassin mix) (theme). *(re-iss. cd Feb95 on 'Danceteria'; DANCD 061)*

GUMBALL

FLEMING + SPIEGEL plus **ERIC VERMILLION**

                                              Paperhouse Primo Scree

Nov 90. (12"ep/cd-ep) *(PAPER 006 T/CD) <SCREE-ONE>* **ALL THE TIME**

Jan 91. (12"ep/cd-ep) *<SCREE-TWO>* **THIS TOWN**

Jun 91. (lp/c/cd) *<SCREE-THREE>* **SPECIAL KISS** *<US-title 'GUMBALL'>*
– This town / All the time / Window pain / Wake up / Summer days / Yellow pants / Restless / Gone too far / Gettysburg / Alternate feed / You know / Pre / High or low / Gettysburg. *<re-iss. 1991 on 'Caroline'; 2703>*

Sep 91. (12"ep/cd-ep) *(PAPER 012 T/CD)* **LIGHT SHINES THROUGH**
– Light shines through / Restless / Talking 'bout / High or low / Damn! bam! / Alternate feed (alternate take) / Saint.

— In Nov'91, DON FLEMING & TOM SMITH (ex-Peach Of Immorality) collaborated on EP 'GIN BLOSSOMS' for 'Seminal Twang'.

— In Mar'92, DON teamed up with RICHARD HELL (---), THURSTON MOORE and STEVE SHELLEY to form DIM STARS, who released eponymous EP for 'Paperhouse'.

                                              not iss. Sony

Nov 92. (cd-ep) *<74754>* **NEW ROSE**

                                              Big Cat Columbia

Jan 93. (12"ep)(cd-ep) *(ABB 041T)(ABBSCD 041) <74754>* **WISCONSIN HAYRIDE**
– New rose / Tell me have you ever seen me / Butterfly potion / Depression / Awakening.

May 93. (lp/cd) *(ABB 46/+CD) <52023>* **SUPER TASTY**
– Accelerator / Hell of a message / Here it comes again / Tumbling / Marilyn / The damage done / Real gone deal / Thunder / Black payback / No more / Get the cure / Upsetters theme song.

May 93. (12"ep)(cd-ep) *(ABB 048T)(ABBSCD 048)* **ACCELERATOR. / STRAIGHT LINE / CHEW THE CHEW**

May 93. (cd-ep) *<44K 77138>* **THE DAMAGE DONE / THUNDER / CHEW THE CHEW / STRAIGHT LINE / UPSETTERS / ACCELERATOR**

                                              Columbia Columbia

Sep 94. (cd/c) *<(475927-2/-4)>* **REVOLUTION ON ICE**
– Revolution on the rocks / Free grazin' / With a little rain / Nights on fire / Whatcha gonna do? / Breath away / Gone to the moon / I ain't nothin' / Read the news / The boat race / Trudge / She's as beautiful as a foot.

                                              not iss. Gumball Ink

1995. (cd) **TOKYO ENCORE** (live)
– Hello there & depression / Gettysburg / Alternate feed / Caught in my eye / Upsetter's theme song / Why don't we do it in the road / Smoke on the water / Final upsetters.

BAND OF . . . BLACKY RANCHETTE
(see under ⇒ GIANT SAND)

BAND OF HOLY JOY

Formed: New Cross / Soho, London, England . . . summer 1983 by JOHNY BROWN and his sister MAXINE. They gathered up a host of friends including BRETT TURNBULL and proceeded to record two privately released cassettes. The following year, they signed to South London indie, 'Flim Flam', who issued their debut single, 'HAD A MOTHER WHO WAS PROUD'. POGUES-like in their make-up and approach, this extended musical family traded in a similar raucous folk sound, although based on European cabaret and influenced by the likes of JACQUES BREL or BERTOLD BRECHT. A mini debut lp, 'THE BIG SHIP SAILS', appeared the following year, while a more stabilised line-up (JOHNY recruiting a whole new cast including ADRIAN BAILEY, BILL LEWINGTON, BIG JOHN, KAREL VAN BERGEN, ALFIE THOMAS and JUB JENKINS) worked on 1987's debut album proper, 'MORE TALES FROM THE CITY'. 'Rough Trade' subsequently signed them and issued two acclaimed sets 'MANIC, MAGIC, MAJESTIC' (1989) and 'POSITIVELY SPOOKED' (1990), before the band clipped their moniker to HOLY JOY.

Album rating: MANIC, MAGIC, MAJESTIC (*8) / POSITIVELY SPOOKED (*8)

JOHNY BROWN – vocals / **BRETT TURNBULL** – organ, etc. / **MAXINE** – accordion, vocals

                                          Pleasantly Surprised not iss.

Jun 84. (c) *(PS 004)* **MORE FAVOURITE FAIRYTALES**
– First hour of the day / Today smashes down! / The only thing thats working in this

BAND OF HOLY JOY (cont)

town / Liquid lunch / I'd dream if I could sleep / Violence, adolescence, nightmare / Maybe one day? / Peters playground / Consumption / Mental / Snow white / Drug virgin / Anticipation / Bedtime again.

			own label	not iss.
1985.	(c)	**INTO THE CITY OF TALES**	Flim Flam	– not iss.
Oct 85.	(12"ep)	(HARP 1T) **HAD A MOTHER WHO WAS PROUD AND LOOK AT ME NOW. / CONSUMPTION / NYLON ROSE / DISGUST**	□	–
May 86.	(10"m-lp)	(HARP 1) **THE BIG SHIP SAILS**	□	–

– Prams, piers and bitter tears / Rosemary Smith / The boy sailor / Maybe one day.

Oct 86.	(7")	(HARP 4) **WHO SNATCHED MY BABY. / REAL BEAUTY PASSED ...**	□	–
	(12"+=)	(HARP 4T) –		

— **JOHNY** recruited new members **ADRIAN BAILEY** – trombone / **BILL LEWINGTON** – drums / **BIG JOHN** – keyboards, banjo / **KAREL VAN BERGEN** – violin / **ALFIE THOMAS** – accordion, keyboards / **JUB JENKINS** –

Apr 87.	(7")	(HARP 6) **ROSEMARY SMITH.** /	□	–
	(12"+=)	(HARP 6T) –		
May 87.	(lp)	(HARPLP 1) **MORE TALES FROM THE CITY**	□	–
Dec 87.	(lp)	(BYEBYE 1) **WHEN STARS COME OUT TO PLAY** (compilation)	□	–

– Don't stick knives in the babies' heads / Mad Dot / Janis – this one's for you / Nico – this is the way out / Tide of life / One child / Amsterdam / North Shields / Fishwives / Who snatched the baby / Yo!.

			Cause For Concern	not iss.
1988.	(lp)	(CFC 003) **THE DEVIL AND THE DEEP BLUE SEA**	□	–

— **MARK CAVENER** – double bass; repl. JUB JENKINS
— with guests **MISS ADELE WINTER** + **DAVID COULTER**

			Rough Trade	not iss.
Sep 88.	(7")	(RT 223) **TACTLESS.** /	□	–
	(12"+=)	(RTT 223) –		
Jan 89.	(lp/c/cd)	(ROUGH/+C/CD 125) **MANIC, MAGIC, MAJESTIC**	□	–

– Route to love / Baubles, bangles, emotional tangles / Nightjars / Tactless / You've grown so old in my dreams / Killy car thieves / Bride / Manic, magic, majestic / What the moon saw / Your not singing anymore / Blessed joy.

Nov 89.	(12")	(RTT 233) **EVENING WORLD HOLIDAY SHOW.** /	□	–
Apr 90.	(lp/c/cd)	(ROUGH/+C/CD 155) **POSITIVELY SPOOKED**	□	–

– Real beauty passed through / Evening world holiday show / Because it was never resolved / Unlikely girl / Shadows fall / Bitten lips / Here it comes / Hot little hopes / Freda Cunningham / Torch me / Positively spooked / Look who's changed with the times.

Jun 90.	(12"ep/cd-ep)	(RTT 243/+CD) **REAL BEAUTY PASSED THROUGH.** / **CHANTAL** / **LONELY COTTAGE** / **LONELY COTTAGE** (instr.)	□	–

HOLY JOY

JOHNY, BILL, ADRIAN, ALFIE, BIG JOHN + HOWARD, EMMET, CHESS + CHRIS

			Equador	not iss.
Jul 92.	(cd/lp)	(EQ CD/LP 004) **A TRACKSUIT VENDETTA**	□	–

– Ragman / Casual 983 / Well you've met this boy / Suit vendetta / 0898 intermission / Claudia dreams / By the light of a magical moon / Kitchen emigre / Marvin in Ostende / Soulstress / Trafalgar Square.

Jul 92.	(12"/cd-s)	**CLAUDIA DREAMS.** /		

			Rough Trade	not iss.
Aug 92.	(7")	**IT'S LOVEBITE CITY.** /	□	–

— split in 1993, although BROWN and LEWINGTON formed SUPERDRUG in '95

BAND OF SUSANS

Formed: Buffalo, New York, USA ... mid 80's by SUSAN STENGER, SUSAN TALLMAN, SUSAN LYALL and Susan.. no, er ... ROBERT POSS (the latter rejected a vacant position with PiL, formerly filled by KEITH LEVENE). Adding drummer RON SPITZER and signing to indie imprint, 'Further', the BAND OF SUSANS delivered an EP, 'BLESSING AND CURSE', prior to 1988's debut set, 'HOPE AGAINST HOPE'. Retaining their moniker despite losing two of their Susans (TALLMAN and LYALL), songwriters STENGER and POSS – plus SPITZER – recruited PAGE HAMILTON and KAREN HAGLOF, the latter also formerly a member of RHYS CHATHAM (with messrs., SUSAN and ROBERT). This configuration managed to secure a deal with 'Blast First' and complete another sonic guitar frenzy of an album, 'LOVE AGENDA', before the end of the decade. Yet more personnel upheaval dogged the band as they entered the 90's; PAGE exited to form HELMET while HAGLOF's dislike of touring led to her being temporarily substituted by WIRE's BRUCE GILBERT! – on a more permanent basis they were replaced by MARK LONERGAN and ANNE HUSICK. Inking a fresh deal with 'Restless', BOS unleashed two more sets, 'THE WORD AND THE FLESH' (1991) and 'VEIL' (1993), the second of which featured new drummer JOEY KAYE. Subsequently reuniting with 'Blast First', they issued a retrospective of their work to date entitled 'WIRED FOR SOUND', followed a few months later by new material in the shape of 'HERE COMES SUCCESS' (1995). Unfortunately, success is the one thing that has eluded the BAND OF SUSAN and Co. throughout their decade-plus lifespan. • **Covered:** PAINT IT BLACK (Rolling Stones).

Album rating: HOPE AGAINST HOPE (*7) / LOVE AGENDA (*7) / THE WORD AND THE FLESH (*6) / VEIL (*5) / HERE COMES SUCCESS (*7) / WIRED FOR SOUND: 1986-1993 compilation (*7)

ROBERT POSS (b.20 Nov'56) – vocals, guitar / **SUSAN STENGER** (b.11 May'55) – bass, vocals / **SUSAN TALLMAN** – guitar / **SUSAN LYALL** – guitar, vocals / **RON SPITZER** – drums / with also **ALVA ROGERS** – backing vocals (on debut)

			Further	Further
1987.	(12"ep)	(FU 2T) **BLESSING AND CURSE EP**	□	–

– Hope against hope / You were an optimist / Sometimes / Where have all the flowers gone.

Apr 88.	(lp/c/cd)	(FU 005/+C/CD) **HOPE AGAINST HOPE**	□	–

– Not even close / Learning to sin / Throne of blood / Elliott Abrahams in Hell / All the wrong reasons / I, the jury / No God / You were an optimist / Ready to bend / Hope against hope.

— **KAREN HAGLOF** – guitar, vocals (ex-RHYS CHATHAM ...) repl. LYALL
— **PAGE HAMILTON** – guitar, vocals; repl. TALLMAN

			Blast First	Blast First
Apr 89.	(lp/c/cd)	<(BFFP 043/+C/CD)> **LOVE AGENDA**	□	□

– The pursuits of happiness / It's locked away / Birthmark / Tourniquet / Thorn in my side / Sin embargo / Because of you / Hard light / Which dream came true / Child of the Moon / Take the express.

— **MARK LONERGAN** – guitar; repl. PAGE HAMILTON who formed HELMET
— **ANNE HUSICK** – guitar; repl. KAREN (she had been temp. repl. by BRUCE GILBERT of WIRE)

			World Service	Restless
Mar 91.	(cd/c)	(<72534-2/-4>) **THE WORD AND THE FLESH**	□	□

– Ice age / Now is now / Trouble follows / Plot twist / Estranged / Labor / Sermon on competition (part 2) / Bitter and twisted / Bad timing / Tilt / Silver lining / Guitar trio.

Apr 93.	(m-cd/m-cd)	(RTD 1591491-2) <72722-2/-4> **NOW**	□	□

– Pearls of wisdom / Following my heart / Trash train / Paint it black / Now is now (remix) / Paint it black (instrumental).

— **JOEY KAYE** – drums; repl. SPITZER

Jun 93.	(cd)	(RTD 1571561-2) <72733-2> **VEIL**	□	□

– Mood swing / Not in this life / The red and the black / Following my heart / Stained glass / The last temptation of Susan / Truce / Trouble spot / Out of the question / Pearls of wisdom / Troilbinders theme / Blind.

			Blast First	World Service
Apr 95.	(lp/cd)	(BFFP 114/+CD) <257> **HERE COMES SUCCESS**	□	□

– Elizabeth Stride (1843-1888) / Dirge / Hell bent / Pardon my French / As luck would have it / Two Jacks / Stone like a heart / In the eye of the beholder (for Rhys) / Sermon on competition, part 1 (nothing is recoupable).

— disbanded in 1996

– compilations, etc. –

Feb 94.	(cd)	*Strange Fruit;* (SFRCD 128) / *Dutch East India;* <8353> **THE PEEL SESSIONS**		

– I found that essence rare / Throne of blood / Child of the moon / Hope against hope / Which dream came true / Too late.

Jan 95.	(lp/cd)	*Blast First;* <(BFFP 111/+CD)> **WIRED FOR SOUND: 1986-1993**	□	□

– Hope against hope / Throne of blood / You were an optimist / All the wrong reasons / The pursuits of happiness / It's locked away / Birthmark / It's locked away / Now is now / Trouble follows (1994 remix) / Ice age (1994 remix) / Following my heart / Mood swing / The red and the black / Blind / Elliott Abrahms in Hell / Where have all the flowers gone / No God / Thorn in my side / Sin embargo / Bitter and twisted / Tilt / Paint it black / Trash train / Out of the question / Trollbinders theme / The last temptation of Susan / Guitar trio.

Lou BARLOW (see under ⇒ DINOSAUR JR.)

Richard BARONE (see under ⇒ BONGOS)

BARRACUDAS

Formed: London, England ... spring 1979 by a cosmopolitan crew of Canadian JEREMY GLUCK, American DAVID BUCKLEY, plus Brits ROBIN WILLS and NICKY TURNER. Like The RAMONES playing The BEACH BOYS garage-style, The BARRACUDAS splashed onto the scene via the independently released 'I WANT MY WOODY BACK'. After inking a major deal with EMI's 'Zonophone' imprint, their second single, 'SUMMER FUN', bit the arse-end of the UK Top 40 in 1980 and was followed by a wave of formulaic retro-surf singles prior to a debut album, 'DROP OUT WITH THE BARRACUDAS', early in '81. As the band progressed to more adventurous sounds, BUCKLEY and TURNER were replaced by JIM DICKSON and TERRY SMITH, while CHRIS WILSON (ex-FLAMIN' GROOVIES) added a new dimension. In 1982, 'Flicknife' (stable of HAWKWIND at the time) issued two limited edition 45's, although the band found it difficult to secure a UK album deal. However, they did find an outlet for their material through French label, 'Closer', who issued two albums, 'MEAN TIME' (1983) and 'ENDEVOUR TO PERSEVERE' (1984) prior to their untimely demise late in '84. While GLUCK ventured on a solo sojourn (one album in '87, 'I KNEW BUFFALO BILL'), WILLS formed the FORTUNATE SONS (named after a CREEDENCE CLEARWATER REVIVAL classic), filling in time before a belated BARRACUDAS reunion. The reformation was short-lived however, only a one-off single in 1990 and a solitary album, 'WAIT FOR EVERYTHING' (1992), seeing the light of day. • **Covered:** YOU'RE GONNA MISS ME (13th Floor Elevators) / FORTUNATE SON (Creedence Clearwater Revival) / SEVEN AND SEVEN IS (love) / etc.

Album rating: DROP OUT WITH THE BARRACUDAS (*6) / MEAN TIME (*6)

JEREMY GLUCK – vocals (ex-YOHAWKS) / **ROBIN WILLS** – guitar, vocals (ex-CHRYSLER ET LES NOUSTIQUAIRES, ex-R.A.F.) / **DAVID BUCKLEY** – bass, vocals (ex-SKYSCRAPERS, ex-R.A.F.) / **NICKY TURNER** – drums

BARRACUDAS (cont)

			Cells	not iss.
Aug 79.	(7")	(SELLOUT 1) **I WANT MY WOODY BACK. / SUBWAY SURFIN'**		

			Zonophone	Bomp
Jul 80.	(7")	(Z 5) **SUMMER FUN. / CHEVY BABY**	37	-
Sep 80.	(7"m)	(Z 8) **HIS LAST SUMMER. / BARRACUDA WAVER / SURFERS ARE BACK**		
Nov 80.	(7")	(Z 11) **(I WISH IT COULD BE) 1965 AGAIN. / RENDEZVOUS**		
Jan 81.	(7")	(Z 17) **I CAN'T PRETEND. / THE K.G.B. (MADE A MAN OUT OF ME)**		
Feb 81.	(lp/c)	(ZONO/ZC-ZONO 103) <BLP 4022> **DROP OUT WITH THE BARRACUDAS**		Jun82

– I can't pretend / We're living in violent times / Don't let go / Codeine / This ain't my time / I saw my death in a dream last night / Somewhere outside / Summer fun / His last summer / Somebody / Campus tramp / On the strip / California lament / (I wish it could be) 1965 again. <US cd-iss. Aug88 on 'Voxx'; 200009> (cd-iss. Jun94; VOXXCD 2009)

—— **JIM DICKSON** – bass; repl. BUCKLEY

—— **TERRY SMITH** – drums; repl. GRAEME POTTER who repl. TURNER who joined LORDS OF THE NEW CHURCH

—— added **CHRIS WILSON** – guitar, vocals (ex-FLAMIN' GROOVIES)

			Flicknife	not iss.
Feb 82.	(7")	(FLS 207) **INSIDE MIND. / HOUR OF DEGRADATION**		
May 83.	(12"ep)	(FLEP 103) **HOUSE OF KICKS**		

– House of kicks / Next time around / Dead skin / Takes what.

			Closer	not iss.
Mar 83.	(lp)	(CL 01) **MEAN TIME**		

– Grammar of misery / Bad news / I ain't no miracle worker / Be my friend again / Shades of today / Dead skin / Middle class blues / You've come a long way / Ballad of a liar / When I'm gone / Eleventh hour / Hear me calling. (cd-iss. May95 on 'Mau Mau'; MAUCD 641)

Feb 84.	(7")	(CL 06) **THEY SAY WE'VE CHANGED. / LAUGHING AT YOU**		
Apr 84.	(lp)	(CL 09) **ENDEAVOUR TO PERSEVERE**		

– Dealing with today / Leaving home again / Song for Lorraine / World turned upside down / See her eyes again / Black snake / The way we've changed / She knows / Man with money / Pieces broken / Losin' steak / Corrine / Barracuda. (cd-iss. May95 on 'Mau Mau'+=; MAUCD 642) – Stolen heart (single mix) / Laughing at you.

Aug 84.	(7")	(CL7 15) **STOLEN HEART. / I SEE HER EYES AGAIN**		

(12"+=) (CLI2 15) – Be my friend again (original demo).

—— split in December 1984, although all remained part of the scene. GLUCK and DICKSON became LIFE AHEAD CORPORATION, although they only issued a 12" EP, 'RICH MEN'S BURDEN' on 'Truth' (TRUET 02) in April '85.

JEREMY GLUCK

—— solo with various people including on the first NIKKI SUDDEN and ROWLAND S. HOWARD (ex-SWELL MAPS and BIRTHDAY PARTY respectively)

			Flicknife	not iss.
Apr 87.	(lp/c)	(SHARP/+C 037) **I KNEW BUFFALO BILL**		

– Looking for a place to fall / Too long / Gone free / Hymn / Time undone / Gallery wharf / Four seasons of trouble / All my secrets.

			Tuff Enuff	not iss.
Sep 87.	(12"ep)	(TUFFT 01) **THRILLING TALE OF BUFFALO BILL EP**		

– Thrilling tale of Buffalo Bill / Looking for a place to fall / Time goes faster / One more story.

FORTUNATE SONS

—— **ROBIN WILLS** – vocals, guitar / **STEVE LABINSO** – bass, vocals / **LEE ROBINSON** – drums, vocals

			Bam Caruso	not iss.
Jun 86.	(7")	(NRIC 043) **SOMETIMES YOU WIN . . . . / ME & MY UNCLE**		
Jun 86.	(lp)	(KIRI 050) **RISING**		

– Sometimes you win . . . / Under the light / Down down / Wastin' time / Just another day / Where we stand / Burning / Rock'n'roll time / All the time in the world / 20th century myth.

—— added **CHRIS WILSON** – guitar

Jul 87.	(12")	(PABL 087) **HAMMERHEAD. /**		
Nov 87.	(lp)	(KIRI 093) **KAREZZA**		

BARRACUDAS

—— reformed with **GLUCK + WILLS** plus **STEVE ROBINSON** – bass

			Brown Buffalo	Sympathy F
Apr 90.	(7"colrd; various) **NEXT TIME AROUND. / TAKE WHAT HE WANTS**			-	-
Feb 92.	(lp/c/cd)	(SAL/+C/CD 203) **WAIT FOR EVERYTHING**	-	-

– I thought you sounded that way yesterday / Throwin' it all away / Can't get away from you / Wait for everything / Outside my door / One from the heart / She's alive / It don't matter now / Burke & Willis / I'm the one / The best years.

—— split for the final time in 1993

– compilations, imports, etc.

Jun 82.	(7"ep)	Voxx-Bomp; **I CAN'T PRETEND**	-	

– I can't pretend / Surfers are back / You were on my mind / Surfer Joe.

Oct 83.	(lp)	Coyote; (COR 021) **LIVE 1983 (live)**	-	- French

– Inside mind / You've come a long way / Violent times / Codeine / Fortunate son / Middle class blues / Hour of degradation / Seven and seven is / Miracle worker / You're gonna miss me.

above featured **MARK SHEPPARD** (aka EMPIRE) – drums (not SMITH)

Jul 84.	(lp)	Coyote; (COR 022) **THE BIG GAP** (early demos 1978-81)	-	- French

Apr 85.	(m-lp)	Trust; (TRUST 001) **THE WORLD'S A BURN**		-

(re-iss. Dec88 on 'Flicknife'; BLUNT 044)

Jan 90.	(lp)	Shakin' Street; (YEAHHUP 006) **THE GARBAGE DUMP TAPES – THE COMPLETE HOUSE OF KICKS SESSIONS**		-

(remixes and re-recordings of early 80's material)

Nov 90.	(12"ep)	Shakin' Street; **GRAMMAR OF MISERY**		-

– Grammar of misery / Laughing at you / Slow death (live).

Jan 91.	(cd)	EMI Capitol; **THE COMPLETE EMI RECORDINGS**		

(UK-iss.May93 on 'Dojo'; DOJOCD 99)

Feb 93.	(cd)	Anagram; (CDGRAM 62) **TWO SIDES OF A COIN 1979-1984**		-

– I want my Woody back / Subway surfin' / Inside mind / Hour of degradation / Next time round / Take what he wants / DEad skin / Two sides of a coin / Kingdom of pain / 20th century myth / The very last day / Wastin' time / Daggers of justice / There's a world out there / Seven and seven is / Codeine / Song for Lorraine / Fortunate son.

May 94.	(cd)	New Rose; (899027) **SURF AND DESTROY**		-

Syd BARRETT

Born: ROGER KEITH BARRETT, 6 Jan'46, Cambridge, England. Earned the nickname SID (which he later changed to SYD), after regulars at the local Riverside Jazz Club found out his surname and christened him after an old drummer from the area, SID BARRET. SYD was talented enough to secure a place at the prestigious Camberwell Art School in 1963 and once in London, he teamed up with his old friend ROGER WATERS, who had asked him to join his band The SCREAMING ABDABS. At SYD's suggestion, the band renamed themselves PINK FLOYD after two Georgia bluesmen featured on an old record he owned. Turned onto LSD by a friend, he became fascinated by the mysteries of the Universe, even carrying around a Times Astronomical Atlas. This obsession would later inspire such FLOYD classics as 'ASTRONOMY DOMINE' and 'INTERSTELLAR OVERDRIVE'. The latter's main riff was famously derived from a chord pattern SYD worked out after hearing manager PETER JENNER attempting to hum LOVE's version of BURT BACHARACH's 'My Little Red Book'. The 1967 album 'THE PIPER AT THE GATES OF DAWN' on which these two tracks appeared, made the group and especially BARRETT, major league pop stars. This was something that did SYD's increasingly erratic mental health no good whatsoever. By the time of the album's release, he had moved into the infamous Cromwell Road flat in London, living on a daily diet of hallucinogenics and was beginning to develop a piercing stare, which would scare even the most hardened person in his company. At EMI's request, BARRETT recorded two further tracks, 'SCREAM THY LAST SCREAM' and 'VEGETABLE MAN', which were unsurprisingly rejected, EMI staff producer NORMAN SMITH dubbing them "lunatic ravings". His penultimate offering for FLOYD, 'APPLES AND ORANGES', flopped, and SYD's mental condition deteriorated further. After missing some shows and performances, WATERS eventually made it clear he was surplus to requirement. His last effort with PINK FLOYD, 'JUGBAND BLUES', appeared after his departure, on the second FLOYD album 'A SAUCERFUL OF SECRETS' (mid-68). It was his last poignant statement for FLOYD, a self-diagnosis of his encroaching schizophrenia. EMI (actually 'Harvest') still had enough confidence in SYD to offer him a solo deal, as he set about recording his debut, 'THE MADCAP LAUGHS'. Released early in 1970 after a laborious year in the studio, it featured drummer NICK MASON and other FLOYD-ians, thus its brief entry into the UK Top 40. Despite SYD being high on the tranquiliser Mandrax, the album had its moments, with the likes of 'OCTOPUS', 'DARK GLOBE', 'TERRAPIN', 'NO GOOD TRYIN' and 'LONG GONE', making up for the other lost-in-the-ether tracks. The hastily recorded 'BARRETT', released later the same year, used a band featuring DAVE GILMOUR (the friend who replaced him in PINK FLOYD), RICK WRIGHT and JERRY SHIRLEY, giving him some cohesion, and although it was more assured in depth, it lacked the fragility of its predecessor. The album was poorly received and SYD retreated to the cellar of his mother's home in Cambridge. He resurfaced in 1972 as part of the doomed STARS project (with TWINK & JACK MONK), before finally giving up music altogether. He never fully recovered from his debilitating mental illness and tragically, he's become almost blind due to diabetes related problems. Whether the drugs actually caused his decline or merely assisted it is something that will no doubt continue to be debated long into the future, although you can be sure SYD won't care to listen. A flawed genius whose legend and influence grows stronger with each passing year, SYD BARRETT was the whimsical child-like star, burning brightly in a kaleidoscope of technicolour sound, before dropping out into a haze of drug-induced psychosis. He has since been tributed and stylised by many, including TELEVISION PERSONALITIES, ROBYN HITCHCOCK and The LEGENDARY PINK DOTS. • **Trivia:** PINK FLOYD paid homage to SYD on their album SHINE ON YOU CRAZY DIAMOND track from album 'WISH YOU WERE HERE'. SYD attended these sessions but didn't contribute.

Album rating: THE MADCAP LAUGHS (*8) / BARRETT (*6) / OPEL collection (*6) / WOULDN'T YOU MISS ME – THE BEST OF SYD BARRETT compilation (*8)

SYD BARRETT – vocals, guitar; augmented by **DAVID GILMOUR + ROGER WATERS** with **MIKE RATLEDGE** – keyboards / **HUGH HOPPER** – bass / **ROBERT WYATT** – drums (all of SOFT MACHINE) plus **JOHN 'WILLIE' WATSON + JERRY SHIRLEY** – rhythm (latter of HUMBLE PIE)

Syd BARRETT (cont)

			Harvest	Harvest
Oct 69.	(7")	(HAR 5009) **OCTOPUS. / GOLDEN HAIR**		
Jan 70.	(lp)	(SHVL 765) <SABB 11314> **THE MADCAP LAUGHS**	40	

– Terrapin / No good trying / Love you / No man's land / Dark globe / Here I go / Octopus / Golden Hair / Long gone / She took a long cold look / Feel / If it's in you / Late night. (cd-iss. Oct87; CDP 746 607-2) (re-iss. cd Jun94; CDGO 2053) (re-iss. Feb97 on 'E.M.I.'; LPCENT 1) (lp re-iss. Jan01 on 'Simply Vinyl'; SVLP 289)

— SYD retained GILMOUR, SHIRLEY + WILSON adding **RICK WRIGHT** – keyboards (of PINK FLOYD) and guest on one **VIC SAYWELL** – tuba

| Nov 70. | (lp) | (SHSP 4007) **BARRETT** | | - |

– Baby lemonade / Love song / Dominoes / It is obvious / Rats / Maisie / Gigolo aunt / Waving my arms in the air / Wined and dined / Wolfpack / Effervescing elephant / I never lied to you. (cd-iss. May87; CDP 746 606-2) (re-iss. cd Jun94; CDGO 2054) (lp re-iss. Jan01 on 'Simply Vinyl'; SVLP 281)

— his solo career ended and he formed short-lived STARS early in '72, with **TWINK** – drums (ex-PINK FAIRIES) + **JACK MONK** – bass (they made no recordings)

— In 1982, he was living with his mother having hung up guitar.

– compilations, others, etc. –

Sep 74.	(d-lp) Harvest; (SHDW 404) **SYD BARRETT**		-

– (THE MADCAP LAUGHS & BARRETT).

| Jan 88. | (12"ep) Strange Fruit; (SFPS/+CD 043) **THE PEEL SESSIONS (24.2.70)** | | - |

– Terrapin / Gigolo aunt / Baby lemonade / Two of a kind / Effervescing elephant. (cd re-iss. Sep95; same)

| Oct 88. | (cd)(c/lp) Harvest; (CDP 791 206-2)(TC+/SHSP 4126) / Capitol; <91206> **OPEL** (recorded 68-70) | | Apr89 |

– Opel / Clowns and daggers (Octopus) / Rats / Golden hair (vocal) / Dollyrocker / Word song / Wined and dined / Swan Lee (Silas Lang) / Birdie hop / Let's split / Lanky (part 1) / Wouldn't you miss me / Golden hair (instrumental). (re-iss. cd Jun94; CDGO 2055) (lp re-iss. Dec99 on 'Simply Vinyl'; SVLP 153)

| Apr 93. | (3xcd-box) E.M.I.; (SYDBOX 1) **CRAZY DIAMOND – THE COMPLETE SYD BARRETT** | | |

– (all 3 albums above)

| Apr 94. | (cd) Cleopatra; (<CLEO 5771-2>) **OCTOPUS – THE BEST OF SYD BARRETT** | | May92 |

– Octopus / Swan Lee (Silas Lang) / Baby lemonade / Late night / Wined and dined / Golden hair / Gigolo aunt / Wolfpack / It is obvious / Lanky (pt.1) / No good trying / Clowns and jugglers (Octopus) / Waving my arms in the air / Opel. (re-iss. Jul01; CLP 2200CD)

| Apr 01. | (cd) Harvest; (532320-2) **WOULDN'T YOU MISS ME – THE BEST OF SYD BARRETT** | | |

– Octopus / Late night / Terrapin / Swan Lee / Wolfpack / Golden hair / Here I go / Long gone / No good trying / Opel / Baby lemonade / Gigolo aunt / Dominoes / Wouldn't you miss me / Wined and dined / Efferverscing elephant / Waving my arms in the air / I never lied to you / Love song / Two of a kind / Bob Dylan blues / Golden hair (instrumental).

BASTRO (see under ⇒ SQUIRREL BAIT)

Martyn BATES (see under ⇒ EYELESS IN GAZA)

BATHERS

Formed: Glasgow, Scotland . . . 1986 by former FRIENDS AGAIN frontman/songwriter, CHRIS THOMSON. After musical differences had put paid to FRIENDS AGAIN in the mid-80's, THOMSON was picked up by the ascendant 'Go! Discs' and together with DOUGLAS McINTYRE cut a debut BATHERS album, 'UNUSUAL PLACES TO DIE' (1987). Critics across the board hailed the album as a triumphant, modern interpretation of pop classicism yet its commercial potential was subsequently buried amid internal problems with the label. History repeated itself two years on as the similarly acclaimed 'SWEET DECEIT' (1990) fell victim to a period of instability at 'Island'. THOMSON then took time out in the form of a side project, BLOOMSDAY, with two members of LLOYD COLE & THE COMMOTIONS. The trio cut a one-off album, 'Fortuny', before CHRIS resumed BATHERS duty with 1994's 'LAGOON BLUES' set. The first of a series of albums for the German 'Marina' label, the record bore all the hallmarks of THOMSON's passionate muse: orchestral strings, heart-tinkling ivories, lovingly crafted arrangements and a Europhile's vision of doomed romance. Having attracted a cult following of frothing critics and discerning fans, he didn't disappoint them with 1995's 'SUNPOWDER', LIZ FRASER (COCTEAU TWINS) guesting on another set of elegantly lovelorn musings. 1997's 'KELVINGROVE BABY' was the final BATHERS set for 'Marina' before THOMSON inked a new deal with the London-based 'Wrasse' label (home to LADYSMITH BLACK MAMBAZO). Featuring an expanded, experienced line-up of CALLUM McNAIR, HAZEL MORRISON, KEN McHUGH, DAVID CRICHTON, IAIN WHITE, PAUL LEONARD and ROBERT HENDERSON as well as contributions from BELLE & SEBASTIAN's ISOBEL CAMPBELL and RICHARD COLBURN, 1999's 'PANDEMONIA' again had the critics in rapture. Early TOM WAITS, Astral Weeks-period VAN MORRISON and indigenous mood merchants The BLUE NILE were all consistent comparisons. To this list you could probably add TINDERSTICKS, PORTISHEAD ('THE BELLE SISTERS') and in THOMSON's wracked vocals, vague hints of DAVID BOWIE. All high praise indeed but praise which is, by and large, merited. Although THOMSON's vocal/lyrical ruminations occasionally veer too close to pretension for comfort, The BATHERS' languid, atmospheric tapestries of strings, piano, guitar and occasional brass surely rank them as one of Scotland's most sophisticated pop purveyors.

Album rating: UNUSUAL PLACES TO DIE (*5) / SWEET DECEIT (*5) / LAGOON BLUES (*5) / SUNPOWDER (*8) / KELVINGROVE BABY (*6) / PANDEMONIA (*5) / DESIRE REGAINED compilation (*8)

CHRIS THOMSON – vocals, guitar, piano (ex-FRIENDS AGAIN) / **DOUGLAS McINTYRE** – guitar / plus a few others

			Go! Discs	not iss.
Apr 87.	(7")	(GOD 17) **FANCY DRESS. / JU JU PEACH**		-

(12"+=) (GOD 18) – Yellow buckskin.

| Oct 87. | (lp/c) (A/Z GOLP 10) **UNUSUAL PLACES TO DIE** | | - |

– Perpetual adoration / Latta's dream / Fancy dress / Time regained / Take me back to the Brooklands / Candide / Ju ju peach / Unusual places to die / Isn't she shining? / Fortuny.

— THOMSON now with **JAMES LOCKE** – percussion / **SAM LOUP** – bass, organ / **GREER KITSON** – guitar, synths, etc / **FERMINA HAZE** – guitar, keyboards, percussion / **CAMPBELL OWENS** – bass

			C.G.T.-Island	not iss.
Apr 90.	(cd/c/lp) (CGTI 2/4/1) – (CID/ICT/ILPS 9953) **SWEET DECEIT**		-

– The pursuit of an orchid / Two cats on the piano / Memory fever / For the delicious C / Desire regained / Get out of life / Pistol crazed / The wreck in the bay / Reason to feel / Memory fever (2) / The idyll off Crown Circus / Perpetual adoration / Sweet deceit / The honeysuckle rose / On the steps at Park Circus.

— now down to THOMSON solo again

			Marina	not iss.
Apr 94.	(cd/c) (MA 2 – CD/MC 33962) **LAGOON BLUES**		-

– Lagoon blues pt.1 / Venice shoes / Gracefruit / Fermina fair / Sissoir / Never too late / The Ornella mutiny / Easter – for Edda Van Heemstra / Thru' the old Holmwood / Lolita / Via d'oro / Ave the leopards / Sweetheart sessions / Carnival / Easter Sorbonne / Lagoon blues pt.2

— with **KEN McHUGH** – bass / etc

| May 95. | (cd) (MA 12) **SUNPOWDER** | | - |

– Danger in love / The Dutch Venus / The angel of Ruskin / Delft / Weem rock muse / Faithless / She's gone forever / Send me your halo / For Saskia / The night is young / Sunpowder. (re-iss. Mar01 on 'Wraddle-Marina'; MAC 4460-2)

— now with **JAMES LOCKE** – co-producer, etc (ex-CHIMES, etc)

— also **KEN McHUGH, HAZEL MORRISON** (drums & percussion), **CARLO, COLIN, MARK + IAIN**

| Feb 97. | (cd) (MA 22 – MACD 44682) **KELVINGROVE BABY** | | - |

– Thrive / Girlfriend / If love could last forever / East of East Delier / No risk no glory / Once upon a time on the Rapenburg / Kelvingrove baby / Girl from the Polders / Lost certainties / Dial / The fragrance remains insane / Hellesporn in a storm / Twelve.

— CHRIS was now augmented mainly by **CALLUM McNAIR** – guitar, bass, vocals / **HAZEL + KEN** / plus others **IAIN WHITE + DAVY CRICHTON** – violin / **BARRY OVERSTREET** – sax / **ROBERT HENDERSON** – trumpet / NEIL CAMERON – double bass

			Wrasse	not iss.
Sep 99.	(cd) (WRASS 015) **PANDEMONIA**	-	- mail-o

– Twenty-two / Dreamless / Something precious has been destroyed (sleeper fragment I) / The Belle sisters / Tequila mockingbird / Sundown and longing / Trocadero girls / Huntly in love / The captives / Phantom sonata (sleeper fragment II) / Yellow crombie / Last night I loved you / Supernatural (sleeper fragment III) / Pandemonia.

— now with **PAUL LEONARD-MORGAN** – keyboards

– compilations, etc. –

| Oct 01. | (cd) Wrasse; (WRASS 034) **DESIRE REGAINED – THE BEST OF THE BATHERS** | | - |

– Unusual places to drive / Perpetual adoration / Two cats on the piano / Are the leopards / Pandemonia / Girlfriend / For Saskia / Thrive / Belle sisters / Sunpowder / Angel on Ruskin / Last night I loved you / Pandemonia (part 2) / The night is young / Danger in love / Kelvin grove baby / Desire regained / Once upon a time on the Rapenburg / Twenty two / If love could last forever.

BLOOMSDAY

CHRIS THOMSON + two members of the COMMOTIONS

			Island	not iss.
Oct 90.	(cd/c/lp) (CID/ICT/ILPS 9972) **FORTUNY**		-

– The day the colours died / Patience / Just the same / Song of five / Blue poetry / Vitamin / Pablo's diary / I remain yours / Soft / Weight.

— checking above + below for correct track listing

| 1990. | (cd-ep) **BLOOMSDAY EP** | | - |

– Blush / Television / Tuesday to Thursday / Girl with a black dress / Suddenly June.

Alec BATHGATE (see under ⇒ TALL DWARFS)

BATS

Formed: Christchurch, New Zealand . . . 1983 by former CLEAN member and main songwriter ROBERT SCOTT, along with PAUL KEAN, also from another Kiwi act, TOY LOVE. Adding KAYE WOODWARD and MALCOLM GRANT, The BATS signed to influential NZ label, 'Flying Nun', releasing a debut EP, 'BY NIGHT', the following year. In 1985, another 12" EP, 'MUSIC FOR THE FIRESIDE', continued in a similar roots pop-rock mould, no doubt confusing any goths who bought it on the strength of their moniker. The following year, The BATS became the first Kiwi act to appear on the UK branch of the aforementioned imprint with the 'MADE UP IN BLUE' EP (they also signed to 'Mammoth' in the States). In the Autumn of '88, The BATS finally released their first full-length set, 'DADDY'S HIGHWAY', a record fusing urban folk-rock, bluegrass and WIRE-esque garage. A two year sabbatical ensued during which time KAYE took maternity leave and KEAN regrouped The CLEAN. After a fine domestic release, 'THE LAW OF

THINGS' (1990), The BATS returned to the fray, this time for 'Rough Trade' with 'FEAR OF GOD' (1992). Homing in again on 'Flying Nun', the seasoned indie-pop campaigners issued two further sets, 'SILVERBEET' (1993) and 'COUCHMASTER' (1995), garnering the usual critical acclaim and steady sales. Setting aside The BATS for the time being, ROBERT SCOTT teamed up with singer JANE SINNOTT and initially DAVID MITCHELL (drummer of 3D's), to form new indie folk-pop outfit, the MAGICK HEADS. Sticksman JIM STRANG was in place for debut set, 'BEFORE WE GO UNDER' (1995), while 'Flying Nun' also released follow-up 'WOODY' (1997), which featured JIM's brother RICHARD on bass. In 2001, ROBERT released the BATS (so to speak) for good when he delivered his debut solo set, 'THE CREEPING UNKNOWN'.

Album rating: COMPILETELY BATS compilation (*7) / DADDY'S HIGHWAY (*7) / THE LAW OF THINGS (*8) / FEAR OF GOD (*6) / SILVERBEET (*6) / SPILL THE BEANS mini (*4) / COUCHMASTER (*6) / Magick Heads: BEFORE WE GO UNDER (*5) / WOODY (*5) / TRANSVECTION (*4) / Robert Scott: THE CREEPING UNKNOWN (*6)

ROBERT SCOTT – guitar, vocals (ex-CLEAN, of WEEDS) / **PAUL KEAN** – bass (ex-TOY LOVE) / **KAYE WOODWARD** – vocals, guitar, keyboards / **MALCOLM GRANT** – drums, percussion

			Flying Nun	Communion
1984.	(12"ep) *(FN 024)* **BY NIGHT**		-	- New Z

– I go wild / Jeweller's heart / By night / My way / Man in the moon / United airways.

| 1985. | (m-lp) *(FN 031)* **"AND HERE IS 'MUSIC FOR THE FIRESIDE'!"** | | - | - New Z |

– Earwig / Chicken bird run / Blindfold / Joe's again / Offside / Claudine / Neighbours.

| Oct 86. | (12"ep) *(FNUK 001 – FN 060)* **MADE UP IN BLUE** | | - | |

– Made up in blue / Trouble in this town / Mad on you.

| 1987. | (7"m) *(FN 084)* **BLOCK OF WOOD. / CALM BEFORE THE STORM / CANDIDATE** | | - | - New Z |

| Oct 88. | (12"ep) *(FNE 22 – FN 104)* **FOUR SONGS EP** | | - | - |

– North by north (remix) / Straight through my heart / Get fat / Best friend's brain.

| Oct 88. | (lp/cd) *(FNE 23/+CD – FN 079)* <5> **DADDY'S HIGHWAY** | | | |

– Treason / Sir Queen / Round and down / Take it / Tragedy / North by north / Block of wood / Miss these things / Mid city team / Some peace tonight / Had to be you / Daddy's highway / Calm before the storm / Candidate / Mad on you / Trouble in this town / Made up in blue. *<US cd re-iss. 1994 on 'Mammoth'; MR 0071-2>*

— in 1989, they took a sabbatical while KAYE had a baby and PAUL returned to The CLEAN

| 1989. | (cd) *(FNCD 121)* <15> **THE LAW OF THINGS** | | - | New Z |

– The other side of you / The law of things / Never said goodbye / Yawn vibes / Time to get ready / Ten to one / Mastery / I fall away / Cliff edge / Nine days / Bedlam / Smoking her wings. *<US re-iss. 1994 on 'Mammoth'; MR 0072-2>*

| 1989. | (7") *(FN 124)* **SMOKING HER WINGS. / MASTERY AND PASSED BY** | | - | - New Z |

| 1991. | (7"/cd-s) *(FN 168)* **THE BLACK AND THE BLUE. / WATCH THE WALLS** | | - | New Z |

| 1991. | (c-s/cd-s) *(FN 180)* **BOOGEY MAN / JETSAM / MAMA COME WATCH** | | - | - New Z |

| | | | Rough Trade | Mammoth |

| Mar 92. | (cd/c/lp) *(R 283-2/-4/-1)* <MR 0040-2/-4> **FEAR OF GOD** | | | |

– Boogey man / The black and the blue / Dancing as the boat goes down / Old ones / Hold all the butter / Fear of God / It's a lie / Straight image / Watch the walls / You know we shouldn't / Jetsam / Looming past. *(NZ-iss.on 'Flying Nun'; FNCD 217)*

| | | | Flying Nun | Mammoth |

| Sep 93. | (cd/c) *(FN CD/MC 260)* <MR 0051-2/-4> **SILVERBEET** | | | |

– Courage / Sighting the sound / Too much / Slow alight / Valley floor / Love floats two / Green / No time for your kind / Straight on home / Before the day / Stay away / Drive me some boars / Halfway to nowhere.

| Oct 93. | (cd-ep) *(FN 261)* <MR 0052> **COURAGE / MIND HOW YOU RUN / SLOW ALRIGHT / WIND IS SAD** | | | |

| 1994. | (7"ep) *(MRG 058)* **LIVE AT WFMU (live)** | | - | |

– North by north / Sir queen / Block of wood / Sighting the sound.

| 1994. | (7") **UNDER THE LAW. / SPILL THE BEANS / SIR QUEEN** | | | |

| Jul 94. | (cd-ep) *(FN 291)* <MR 0070-2> **SPILL THE BEANS EP** | | | |

– Spill the beans / Empty head / Make it clear / Give in to the sands / Under the law.

| Oct 95. | (lp/cd) *(FN/+CD 301)* <MR 0126> **COUCHMASTER** | | | |

– Outside / Afternoon in bed / Around you make snow / Work it out / Train / Lake o' keys / Chain home low / Supernova / Shoeshine / Crow song / Smorgasboard / Knowledge is power / It's happening to you / Lost weekend / For the ride / Out of bounds / Down to me.

| Dec 95. | (cd-s) *(FN 341)* **AFTERNOON IN BED** | | - | - NewZ |

— never got back together; SCOTT continued with The MAGICK HEADS

– compilations, etc. –

| Dec 92. | (cd) *Flying Nun; (FNCD 143) / Communion; <25>* **COMPILETELY BATS** (first 3 EP's) | | | |

MAGICK HEADS

ROBERT SCOTT – vocals, guitar, keyboards / with **JANE SINOTT** – vocals, tambourine, guitar / **DAVID MITCHELL** – guitar (of 3-D's) / **JIM STRANG** – drums

| | | | Flying Nun | Flying Nun |

| 1993. | (7") *(FN 224)* **MAGICK HEADS. /** | | - | - NewZ |

— JIM STRANG – drums; repl. MITCHELL

| Apr 95. | (cd) *(<FNCD 290>)* **BEFORE WE GO UNDER** | | | Jan96 |

– Standing at the side / Sweet angel / 42 degrees / Two different things / Seventh sense / Hear from you / Before we go under / New floor / Twilight / Light of the night / Gotta go home / The beast of Bodmin moor / Good books.

— added **RICHARD STRANG** – bass / **ALAN STARRETT** – violin, accordion (ex-3-D's, ex-BATS, ex-CLEAN)

| Oct 97. | (cd) *(FNCD 391)* **WOODY** | | - | - New Z |

– Better left unsaid / Some time to go / Who's watchin' out for you / Mystery train / Faith away / Take it on down / On the rocks / Walk on the wall / 12,000 miles / Nine minutes / Shadows / Lines of deception / Shivers / Particularly nasty weather.

| | | | Dark Beloved Cloud | not iss. |

| 1999. | (cd-ep) *(DBC 211)* **LAZY WAYS EP** | | - | - New Z |

– Save me from the sound / Domino / Just like the sun / This city.

— disbanded some time in '99

– compilations, etc. –

| Mar 00. | (cd) *Dark Beloved Cloud; (<DBC 222>)* **TRANSVECTION** | | | Feb00 |

– Truth / Pet / Roll on summer / Find a way home / Anemone / Give me a kiss / Two different things / Don't knock it down / Once apon a meeting / Use your charms / Who's watchin' out for you (live) / Better left unsaid / Part of it all / Love on the ground / One and the same / Floating.

ROBERT SCOTT

| | | | not iss. | Thirsty Ear |

| Feb 01. | (cd) <57097> **THE CREEPING UNKNOWN** | | - | |

– Harmonic deluxe / Shelf control / Details at play / Last outlaws / International loss adjuster / Fog and wind / Extinguisher / Footbridge / The creeping unknown / 2nd hand air / Somewhere on the coast / The wick effect / The slow room / When shade was made / Morepork makes it home / Greek country / Navigator / Upper lab / Near to a beautiful park.

BAUHAUS

Formed: Northampton, England ... late 1978, by PETE MURPHY, DANIEL ASH, DAVID J and KEVIN HASKINS, initially calling themselves BAUHAUS 1919. Obtaining a one-off deal with indie label 'Small Wonder', they released an 8-minute epic 'BELA LUGOSI'S DEAD', backed with the infamous 'DARK ENTRIES', the latter track subsequently issued as a follow-up 45. A gender-bending but hard-edged collage of glam and punk influences shrouded in gothic horror posturing, BAUHAUS carved out their own inimitable niche in the early 80's post-new wave wasteland. After an album, 'IN THE FLAT FIELD' (1981) and a couple of singles (one a cover of T.Rex's 'TELEGRAM SAM') on '4 a.d.', the band signed to 'Beggars Banquet', scoring a Top 30 hit with debut set, 'MASK' (1981). Featuring the minor hit singles, 'KICK IN THE EYE' and 'THE PASSION OF LOVERS', the album remains their most consistent set. Still, the underground cred was called into question after MURPHY appeared in a TV ad for Maxell tapes later that year. More appropriate, perhaps, was the band's performance of 'BELA LUGOSI'S DEAD' for 1982 vampire film, 'The Hunger' starring the band's boyhood hero, DAVID BOWIE. In fact, it was one of BOWIE's classics, 'ZIGGY STARDUST', that gave BAUHAUS their commercial breakthrough, the single's Top 20 success seeing the accompanying album, THE SKY'S GONE OUT' make the UK Top 5. The droning affectations of 'SHE'S IN PARTIES' remains one of the band's most recognisable tracks while the swan song album, 'BURNING FROM THE INSIDE' (1983), saw BAUHAUS signing off on an unsettling, if creatively high point. MURPHY soon reappeared with MICK KARN of JAPAN in a new outfit, DALI'S CAR, although only one album, 'THE WAKING HOUR', surfaced in '84. The singer went on to release a string of albums, surprising many in Britain when he had a US Top 50 placing with 'DEEP', which contained the 1990 hit, 'CUTS YOU UP'. Meanwhile, the rest were enjoying success as LOVE AND ROCKETS (from earlier incarnation of TONES ON TAILS and DAVID J solo) and this trio also took America by storm having had a Top 3 smash, 'SO ALIVE' in '89. With current offshoots failing to sparkle during the rest of the 90's, BAUHAUS decided to officially re-form in mid 1998 for two concerts, which enabled their record label to cash-in on an accompanying best-of collection, 'CRACKLE'. • **Covered:** THIRD UNCLE (Eno) / WAITING FOR THE MAN (Velvet Underground) / SEVERENCE (Dead Can Dance). PETER MURPHY solo, wrote with STREATHAM and covered; FINAL SOLUTION (Pere Ubu) / THE LIGHT POURS OUT OF ME (Magazine) / FUNTIME (Iggy Pop). LOVE AND ROCKETS covered BALL OF CONFUSION (Temptations) / BODY AND SOUL (trad). DAVID J covered 4 HOURS (ClockDva) / SHIP OF FOOLS (John Cale).

Album rating: IN THE FLAT FIELD (*5) / MASK (*6) / THE SKY'S GONE OUT (*6) / BURNING FROM THE INSIDE (*5) / BAUHAUS 1979-1983 compilation (*9) / CRACKLE collection (*6) / GOTHAM (*7)
Dali's Car: THE WAKING HOUR (*5) / Pete Murphy: SHOULD THE WORLD FAIL TO FALL APART (*5) / LOVE HYSTERIA (*5) / DEEP (*6) / CASCADE (*4) / Tones On Tails: NIGHT MUSIC compilation (*6) / Love And Rockets: LOVE AND ROCKETS (*5)

PETER MURPHY (b.11 Jul'57) – vocals / **DANIEL ASH** (b.31 Jul'57) – guitar, vocals / **DAVID J** (b. HASKINS, 24 Apr'57) – bass, vocals / **KEVIN HASKINS** (b.19 Jul'60) – drums, percussion

| | | | Small Wonder | not iss. |

| Aug 79. | (12",12"white) *(TEENY 2)* **BELA LUGOSI'S DEAD. / BOYS / DARK ENTRIES** | | | - |

(re-dist.Mar81 & Mar82; same) (re-iss. Sep86 in various colours; same) (12"pic-d.1987; TEENY 2P) (re-iss. May88 & Jun98, c-s/cd-s; TEENY 2 C/CD)

| | | | Axis | not iss. |

| Jan 80. | (7") *(AXIS 3)* **DARK ENTRIES. / UNTITLED** | | | - |

(re-iss. Feb80 on '4.a.d.'; AD 3) (some mispressed on 'Beggars Banquet'; BEG 37)

| | | | 4.a.d. | not iss. |

| Jun 80. | (7") *(AD 7)* **TERROR COUPLE KILL COLONEL. / SCOPES / TERROR COUPLE KILL COLONEL II** | | | - |

| Oct 80. | (lp) *(CAD 13)* **IN THE FLAT FIELD** | | 72 | - |

– Double dare / In the flat field / A god in an alcove / Dive / Spy in the cab / Small talk stinks / St. Vitus dance / Stigmata martyr / Nerves. *(cd-iss. Apr88 +=; CAD 13CD)* – Untitled. *(cd re-iss. Jul98; GAD 013CD)*

BAUHAUS (cont) — THE GREAT INDIE DISCOGRAPHY — The 1980s

			Beggars Banquet	A&M
Oct 80.	(7") *(AD 17)* **TELEGRAM SAM. / CROWDS**			–
	(12"+=) *(AD 17T)* – Rosegarden funeral of sores.			
Mar 81.	(7"/12") *(BEG 54/+T)* **KICK IN THE EYE. / SATORI**		59	–
Jun 81.	(7") *(BEG 59)* **THE PASSION OF LOVERS. / 1: 2: 3: 4:**		56	–
Oct 81.	(lp/c) *(BEGA/BEGC 29)* **MASK**		30	

– Hair of the dog / The passion of lovers / Of lillies and remains / Dancing / Hollow hills / Kick in the eye / Muscle in plastic / In fear of fear / Man with x-ray eyes / Mask. *(re-iss. Feb88 & Jul91 on 'Beggars Banquet-Lowdown' lp/c; BBL/+C 29) (cd-iss. Oct88 & Jul91 +=; BBL 29CD)* – Satori / Harry / Earwax / In fear of dub / Kick in the eye. *<US-iss.1995 on 'Atlantic'; 92576>*

Feb 82.	(7"ep) *(BEG 74)* **SEARCHING FOR SATORI**	45	–

– Kick in the eye / Harry / Earwax. (12"ep+=) *(BEG 74T)* – In fear of dub.

Jun 82.	(7"/7"pic-d) *(BEG 79/+P)* **SPIRIT. / TERROR COUPLE KILL COLONEL (live)**	42	–
Sep 82.	(7") *(BEG 83)* **ZIGGY STARDUST. / THIRD UNCLE (live)**	15	–

(12"+=) *(BEG 83T)* – Party of the first part / Waiting for the man.

Oct 82.	(d-lp/d-c) *(BEGA/BEGC 42) / (BEGA/BEGC 38)* *<SP 4918>* **THE SKY'S GONE OUT / PRESS THE EJECT BUTTON AND GIVE ME THE TAPE (live)**	4	

– Third uncle / Silent hedges / In the night / Swing the heartache / Spirit / The three shadows (parts 1, 2, 3) / Silent hedges / All we ever wanted was everything / Exquisite corpse. *(re-iss. Feb88 & Jul91 on 'Beggars Banquet-Lowdown' lp/c; BBL/+C 42) (cd-iss. Oct88 & Jul91 +=; BBL 42CD)* – Ziggy Stardust / Watch that grandad go / Party of the first part / Spirit (extended). **PRESS THE EJECT BUTTON AND GIVE ME THE TAPE** – In the flat field / Rosegarden funeral of sores / Dancing / Man with the x-ray eyes / Bela Lugosi's dead / Spy in the cab / Kick in the eye / In fear of fear / Hollow hills / Stigmata martyr / Dark entries. *(re-iss. Feb88 & Jul91 on 'Beggars Banquet-Lowdown'; BBL/+C 38) (cd-iss. Oct88 & Jul91 +=; BBL 38CD)* – Terror couple kill colonel / Double dare / Waiting for the man / Hair of the dog / Of lillies and remains. (free 7"ep with above; BH 1) – SATORI IN PARIS (live)

Jan 83.	(7") *(BEG 88)* **LAGARTIJA NICK. / PARANOIA! PARANOIA!**	44	–

(12"+=) *(BEG 88T)* – Watch that grandad go / In the flat field (live).

| Mar 83. | (7") *<2524>* **LAGARTIJA NICK. / ZIGGY STARDUST** | – | |
| Apr 83. | (7"/7"pic-d) *(BEG 91/+P)* **SHE'S IN PARTIES. / DEPARTURE** | 26 | |

(12"+=) *(BEG 91T)* – Here's the dub.

Jul 83.	(lp/c) *(BEGA/BEGC 45)* *<3325>* **BURNING FROM THE INSIDE**	13	

– She's in parties / Antonin Artaud / King Volcano / Who killed Mr. Moonlight? / Slice of life / Honeymoon croon / Kingdom's coming / Burning from the inside / Hope. *(re-iss. Feb88 & Jul91 on 'Beggars Banquet-Lowdown' lp/c; BBL/+C 45) (cd-iss. Oct88 & Jul91 +=; BBL 45CD)* – Lagartija Nick / Departure / Here's the dub / The sanity assassin.

—— disbanded mid 1983. DAVID J. continued splinter solo venture before forming LOVE AND ROCKETS with DANIEL and KEVIN who had come from own outfit, TONES ON TAIL. MURPHY went solo (see below).

– compilations, others, etc. –

on 'Beggars Banquet' unless mentioned otherwise

Sep 83.	(12"ep) *4 a.d.: (BAD 312)* **THE 4.A.D. SINGLES**		–

– Dark entries / Terror couple kill colonel / Telegram Sam / Rosegarden full of sores / Crowds.

| Oct 83. | (12"ep) *(BEG 100E)* **THE SINGLES 1981-83** | 52 | – |

– The passion of lovers / Kick in the eye / Spirit / Ziggy Stardust / Lagartija Nick / She's in parties. *(re-iss. Dec89 as 3"pic-cd; BBP 4CD)*

| Nov 85. | (d-lp/c) *(BEGA/BEGC 64)* **BAUHAUS 1979-1983** | 36 | |

(d-cd-iss. Feb88; BEG 64CD) (re-iss. d-cd Sep95)

| Jul 89. | (d-lp/c)(d-cd) *(BEGA/BEGC 103)(BEGA 103CD)* *<9804>* **SWING THE HEARTACHE** (the BBC sessions) | | |

(re-iss. 2xcd Sep95; BBL 64 CD1/CD2)

| Aug 98. | (cd) *(BEGL 2018CD)* **CRACKLE (live)** | | |

– Double dare / In the flat field / Passion of lovers / Bela Lugosi's dead / Sanity assassin / She's in parties / Hollow hills / Mask / Kick in the eye / Ziggy stardust / Dark entries / Terror couple kill colonel / Spirit / Burning from the inside / Crowds.

DALI'S CAR

were formed by **PETE MURPHY** – vocals / **MICK KARN** – bass, multi (ex-JAPAN) / **PAUL VINCENT LAWFORD** – rhythms

		Paradox	Beggars Banquet
Oct 84.	(7"/7"pic-d) *(DOX/+Y 1)* **THE JUDGEMENT IS THE MIRROR. / HIGH PLACES**	66	–
	(12"+=) *(DOX 1-12)* – Lifelong moment.		
Nov 84.	(lp/c/cd) *(DOX LP/C/CD 1)* **THE WAKING HOUR**	84	

– Dali's car / His box / Cornwall stone / Artemis / Create and melt / Moonlife / The judgement is the mirror. *(re-iss. Jan89 on 'Beggars Banquet-Lowdown'; lp/c)(cd; BBL/+C 52)(BBL 52CD)*

PETER MURPHY

went solo, augmented by **JOHN McGEOGH** – guitar / **HOWARD HUGHES** – keyboards / **ROBERT SUAVE** – bass / **STEVE YOUNG** – rhythm prog. / **PLUG** – harmonica

		Beggars Banquet	Beggars Banquet
Nov 85.	(7") *(BEG 143)* **THE FINAL SOLUTION. / THE ANSWER'S CLEAR**		–
	(12"+=) *(BEG 143T)* – ('A' full version).		
	(12"pic-d+=) *(BEG 143TP)* – ('A' club mix).		
Jun 86.	(7"/12") *(BEG 162/+T)* **BLUE HEART. / CANVAS BEAUTY**		
Jul 86.	(lp/c) *(BEGA/BEGC 69)* **SHOULD THE WORLD FAIL TO FALL APART**	82	

– Canvas beauty / The light pours out of me / Confessions / Should the world fail to fall apart / Never man / God . . . sends / Blue heart / The answer is clear / The final solution / Jemal. *(re-iss. Jul88 on 'Beggars Banquet-Lowdown' lp/c)(cd; BBL/+C 69)(BBL 69CD)*

Oct 86.	(7") *(BEG 174)* **TALE OF THE TONGUE. / SHOULD THE WORLD FAIL TO FALL APART**		

(12"+=) *(BEG 174T)* – ('A'-2nd version).

—— MURPHY brought in **PAUL STATHAM** – co-composer, keyboards (ex-B-MOVIE) / **EDDIE BRACH** – bass / **PETER BONAS** – guitar / **TERL BRYANT** – drums

Feb 88.	(7") *(BEG 207)* **ALL NIGHT LONG. / I'VE GOT A SECRET CAMERA**		–

(12"+=) *(BEG 207T)* – Funtime (in cabaret).

| Mar 88. | (lp/c/cd) *(BEGA/BEGC 92)(BEGA 92CD)* *<7634>* **LOVE HYSTERIA** | | |

– All night long / His circle and hers meet / Dragnet drag / Socrates the python / Indigo eyes / Time has got nothing to do with it / Blind sublime / My last two weeks / Funtime. *(cd+=)* – I've got a miniature secret camera / Funtime (cabaret mix).

| Mar 88. | (7") *<8670>* **ALL NIGHT LONG. / FUNTIME (Cabaret mix)** | – | |
| Apr 88. | (7"/7"box) *(BEG/+B 210)* **INDIGO EYES. / GOD SENDS (live)** | | |

(12"+=) *(BEG 210T)* – Confessions (live).

| Jun 88. | (7") *<8707>* **INDIGO EYES. / MY LAST TWO WEEKS** | – | |
| Mar 90. | (7") *(BEG 237)* *<9140>* **CUTS YOU UP. / STRANGE KIND OF LOVE** | 55 | |

(12"+=/cd-s+=) *(BEG 237 T/CD)* – Roll call (reprise).

| May 90. | (cd)(c/lp) *(BEGA 107CD)(BEGC/BEGA 107)* *<9877>* **DEEP** | | 44 |

– Deep ocean vast sea / Crystal waters / Marlene Dietrich's favourite poem / Seven veils / The line between the Devil's teeth (and that which cannot be repeated) / Cuts you up / A strange kind of love / Roll call. *(cd+=)* – Strange kind of love (alt.version).

| Apr 92. | (7") *(BEG 259)* **YOU'RE SO CLOSE. / THE SWEETEST DROP** | | – |

(12"+=/cd-s+=) *(BEG 259 T/CD)* – Cuts you up (live) / All night long (live).

| Apr 92. | (cd)(c/lp) *(BEGA 123CD)(BEGC/BEGA 123)* *<66007>* **HOLY SMOKE** | | |

– Keep me from harm / Kill the hate / You're so close / The sweetest drop / Low room / Let me love you / Our secret garden / Dream gone by / Hit song.

| Jul 92. | (7") *(BEG 261)* **HIT SONG. / SEVEN VEILS (live)** | | |

(12"+=/cd-s+=) *(BEG 261 T/CD)* – The line between the Devil's teeth (and that which cannot be repeated) (live).

| Apr 95. | (cd-ep) *(BBQ 52CD)* **THE SCARLET THING IN YOU / CRYSTAL WRISTS / WISH / DRAGNET DRAG (live)** | | |
| Apr 95. | (cd/c) *(BBQ CD/MC 175)* *<92541>* **CASCADE** | | |

– Mirror to my woman's mind / Subway / Gliding like a whale / Disappearing / Mercy rain / I'll fall with your knife / Scarlet thing in you / Sails wave goodbye / Wild birds flock to me / Huuvola / Cascade.

TONES ON TAILS

GLEN CAMPLING – vocals, bass, keyboards (roadie of BAUHAUS) / **DANIEL ASH** – guitar, vocals / **KEVIN HASKINS** – drums

		4.a.d.	not iss.
Apr 82.	(12"ep) *(BAD 203)* **A BIGGER SPLASH / COPPER. / MEANS OF ESCAPE / INSTRUMENTAL**		–
		Beggars Banquet	not iss.
Sep 82.	(12") *(BEG 85T)* **THERE'S ONLY ONE. / NOW WE LUSTRE**		–
		Situation 2	not iss.
May 83.	(7") *(SIT 21)* **BURNING SKIES. / OK, THIS IS THE POPS**		

(12"+=) *(SIT 21T)* – When you're smiling / You, the night and the music.

—— In 1983, they broke from BAUHAUS. ASH and HASKINS joined The JAZZ BUTCHER. TONES ON TAILS soon re-actified their line-up.

		Beggars Banquet	not iss.
Mar 84.	(7") *(BEG 106)* **PERFORMANCE. / SHAKES**		–
	(12"+=) *(BEG 106T)* – ('A' dub version).		
Apr 84.	(lp/c) *(BEGA/BEGC 51)* **POP**		

– Performance / War / Lions / Happiness / The never never / Real life / Slender fungus / Movement of fear / Rain. *(re-iss. Oct88 & Jul91 on 'Beggars Banquet-Lowdown' lp/c)(cd; BBL/+C 51)(BBL 51CD) (cd-iss. Oct88 as 'NIGHT MUSIC' +=; BEGA 51CD)* – (rest of material).

| May 84. | (7") *(BEG 109)* **LIONS. / GO! (LET'S GO TO YA YA'S NOW)** | | |

(12",12"red) *(BEG 109T)* – ('A'side) / Go! (club mix).

| Nov 84. | (7"/12"blue) *(BEG 121/+T)* **CHRISTIAN SAYS. / TWIST** | | |

—— split from this name

		Situation 2	not iss.
Feb 85.	(lp/c) *Situation 2; (SITU/SITC 12)* **TONES ON TAILS** (the singles compilation)		–

(re-iss. Oct88 on 'Situation 2-Lowdown' lp/c; SITL/+C 12)

LOVE AND ROCKETS

ASH + HASKINS were joined by **DAVID J.** – vocals, bass, keyboards (also ex-BAUHAUS + a solo artist)

		Beggars Banquet	Beggars Banquet
May 85.	(7"/12") *(BEG 132/+T)* **BALL OF CONFUSION. / INSIDE THE OUTSIDE**		
Sep 85.	(7"/12") *(BEG 146/+T)* **IF THERE'S A HEAVEN ABOVE. / GOD AND MR. SMITH**		
Oct 85.	(lp/c) *(BEGA/BEGC 66)* *<85071>* **7th DREAM OF TEENAGE HEAVEN**		

– If there's a Heaven above / A private future / 7th dream of teenage Heaven / Saudade / Haunted when the minutes drag / The dog-end of a day gone by / The game. *(cd-iss. May86; BEGA 66CD) (re-iss. Jan89 & Jul91 on 'Beggars Banquet-Lowdown' lp/c)(cd+=; BBL/+C 66)(BBL 66CD)* – Ball of confusion (USA mix) / God and Mr. Smith (Mars mix) / If there's a Heaven above (Canadian mix).

		Beggars Banquet	Big Time
Jun 86.	(12"m) *(BEG 163T)* **KUNDALINI EXPRESS. / LUCIFER SAM / HOLIDAY ON THE MOON**		

BAUHAUS (cont)

Sep 86. (7"/12") (BEG 166/+T) **YIN AND YANG (THE FLOWERPOT MEN). / ANGELS AND DEVILS**
Sep 86. (lp/c) (BEGA/BEGC 74) **EXPRESS** — 72
– Kundalini express / It could be sunshine / Love me / All in my mind / Life in Laralay / Yin and Yang (the flowerpot men) / An American dream / All in my mind (acoustic version). (cd-iss. Jan88; BEGA 74CD) (re-iss. Jan89 & Jul91 on 'Beggars Banquet-Lowdown' lp/c/cd; BBL/+C 74)(BEGA 74CD)
Sep 87. (lp/c)(cd) (BEGA/BEGC 84)(BEGA 84CD) <6011> **EARTH, SUN, MOON** — 64
– The light / Mirror people / Welcome tomorrow / Here on Earth / Lazy / Waiting for the flood / Rainbird / Telephone is empty / Everybody wants to go to Heaven / The sun / Youth. (re-iss. Jan89 & Jul91 on 'Beggars Banquet' lp/c/cd+=; BBL/+C 84)(BBL 84CD) – Mirror people (slow version).
Oct 87. (7"/12") (BEG 186/+T) **THE LIGHT. / MIRROR PEOPLE (slow version)**
Mar 88. (7") (BEG 209) **NO NEW TALE TO TELL. / EARTH, SUN, MOON**
(12"+=) (BEG 209T) – 7th dream of teenage Heaven.
May 88. (7") (BEG 213) **MIRROR PEOPLE. / DAVID LANFAIR**
(12"+=) (BEG 213T) – ('A'live version).
Aug 88. (7") (BEG 217) **LAZY. / THE DOG-END OF A DAY GONE BY**
(12"+=) (BEG 217T) – The purest blue.

Beggars Banquet / R.C.A.

Jan 89. (12"ep) (BEG 224T) **MOTORCYCLE / I FEEL SPEED. / BIKE / BIKEDANCE**
Jul 89. (7"/c-s/12") (BEG 229/+C/T) <8956> **SO ALIVE. / DREAMTIME** — 3 May89
(cd-s+=) (BEG 229CD) – Motorcycle / Bike. (re-dist.Jan90)
Sep 89. (lp/c)(cd) (BEGA/BEGC 99)(BEGA 99CD) <9715> **LOVE AND ROCKETS** — 14
– **** (Jungle law) / No big deal / The purest blue / Motorcycle / I feel speed / Bound for Hell / The teardrop collector / So alive / Rock and roll Babylon / No words no more.
Oct 89. (7") (BEG 234) <9045> **NO BIG DEAL. / NO WORDS NO MORE** — 82 Sep89
(12"+=) (BEG 234T) – 100 watts of your love.

Beggars Banquet / Beggars Banquet

Jul 94. (12"/cd-s) (BBQ 36 T/CD) **THIS HEAVEN / THIS HEAVEN (Secret Knowledge mix). / THIS HEAVEN (Lost In It) / THIS HEAVEN (Torched mix)**
Sep 94. (12"/cd-s) (BBQ 42 T/CD) **BODY AND SOUL. / BODY AND SOUL (Secret Knowledge out of body mix) / BODY AND SOUL (Delta Lady Rebel Trouser mix)**
above featured **NATACHA ATLAS** – vocals (of TRANS-GLOBAL UNDERGROUND)
Sep 94. (cd/c/d-lp) (BBQ CD/MC/LP 145) **HOT TRIP TO HEAVEN**
– Body and soul (parts 1 & 2) / Ugly / Trip and glide / This Heaven / No worries / Hot trip to Heaven / Eclipse / Voodoo baby / Be the revolution / Set me free. (re-iss. cd Sep95; BBL 145CD)
Mar 96. (cd-ep; unreleased) (BBQ 67CD) **SWEET F.A. / THE GLITTERING DARKNESS / TRIP AND GLIDE / RITUAL RADIO / BAD MONKEY**

DANIEL ASH

Beggars Banquet / Beggars Banquet

Jun 91. (cd)(c/lp) (BEGA 114CD)(BEGA/BEGC 114) <3014> **COMING DOWN**
– Blue moon / Coming down fast / Walk this way / Closer to you / Day tripper / This love / Blue angel / Me and my shadow / Candy darling / Sweet little liar / Not so fast / Coming down.
— Above features covers DAY TRIPPER (Beatles) / BLUE MOON (Rodgers / Hart) / ME AND MY SHADOW (Al Jolson) /
Jun 91. (7") **WALK THIS WAY. / HEAVEN IS WAITING**
(12") – ('A'side) / ('A'groovy vox) / ('A'groovy guitar).
(cd-s) – (all 4 tracks).
Apr 93. (12"ep/cd-ep) (BBQ 9 T/CD) **GET OUT OF CONTROL. / THE HEDONIST / GET OUT OF CONTROL (farewell mixes)**
May 93. (cd/c/lp) (BBQ CD/MC/LP 129) **FOOLISH THING DESIRE**
– Here she comes / Foolish thing desire / Bluebird / Dream machine / Get out of control / The void / Roll on / Here she comes again / The hedonist / Higher than this.

BAUHAUS

— re-formed for a live appearance

KK / Metropolis

Nov 99. (d-lp/d-cd) (KK 200/+CD) <150> **GOTHAM (live)**
– Double dare / In the flat field / A god in an alcove / In fear of fear / Hollow hills / Kick in the eye / Terror couple kill colonel / Silent hedges / Severence / Boys / She's in parties / The passion of lovers / Dark entries / Telegram Sam / Ziggy Stardust / Bela Lugosi's dead / All we ever wanted was everything / Spirit / Severence (studio version). (re-iss. Mar02; same)

DAVID J.

4 a.d. / not iss.

Sep 81. (7"; by DAVID JAY & RENE HACKETT) (AD 112) **NOTHING. / ARMOUR**

Situation 2 / not iss.

Aug 83. (7") (SIT 26) **JOE ORTON'S WEDDING. / THE GOSPEL ACCORDING TO FEAR**
(12"+=) (SIT 26T) – Requiem for Joe / Point of venture.
Oct 83. (lp) (SITU 8) **ETIQUETTE OF VIOLENCE**
– The gospel according to fear / I hear only silence now / No one's sending roses / The fugitive / Betrayal / Joe Orton's wedding / The promised land / With the Indians permanent / Say uncle / Disease / Roulette / Saint Jackie. (re-iss. Oct88 & Jul91 on 'Situation 2-Lowdown' lp/c/cd; SITL 8/+C/CD)

Glass / not iss.

Nov 83. (7"; as DAVID J. & J. WALKERS) (GLASS 031) **THE PROMISED LAND. / SAINT JACKIE**
(12"+=) (GLASS12 031) – A seducer, a doctor, a card you cannot trust.
Jun 84. (12"ep; by DAVID J. & ALAN MOORE) (GLASS12 032) **V FOR VENDETTA**
– This vicious cabaret / (AV.TV. broadcast) / V's theme (intro) / V's theme (outro).
Sep 84. (7"/12") (GLASS/+12 039) **I CAN'T SHAKE THIS SHADOW OF FEAR. / WAR GAME**
Mar 85. (lp) (GLALP 010) **CROCODILE TEARS & THE VELVET COSH**
– And the velvet cosh / Crocodile tears / Too clever by half / The first incision / Imitation pearls / Light & shade / Rene / Stop this city / Justine / The ballad of Cain / Vandal & the saint / Slip the rope / Greener. (cd-iss. Jun86; GLACD 010)
Apr 85. (7") (GLASS 042) **CROCODILE TEARS & THE VELVET COSH. / ELEGY**
(12"+=) (GLASS12 042) – Rene.
Jun 85. (12"ep) (GLAEP 101) **BLUE MOODS TURNING TAILS**
– 4 hours / The conjurors hand / Ship of fools.
Mar 86. (lp/c) (GLA LP/MC 017) **DAVID J. ON GLASS (singles compilation)**
(cd-iss. Jun88; GLACD 017)

— w/ **MAX KIDER** – guitar / **ANGUS WALLACE + OWEN JONES** – drums / **DAVE ANDERSON** – steel guitar / **ALEX GREEN** – sax / **BEN HEANEY** – violin / **BEN GREENAWAY** percussion / **JANIS ZAKIS** – accordian.

Beggars Banquet / Beggars Banquet

Jun 90. (7") (BEG 243) **I'LL BE YOUR CHAUFFEUR. / THE MOON IN THE MAN**
(12"+=) (BEG 243T) – ('A'original version).
Jul 90. (cd)(c/lp) (BEGA 112CD)(BEGA/BEGC 112) **SONGS FROM ANOTHER SEASON**
– Fingers in the grease / A longer look / Sad side to the sand boy / New woman is an attitude / Sweet ancenthexra / On the outskirts of a strange dream / I'll be your chauffeur (original) / The Moon in the man / Little star / Stranded Trans-Atlantic hotel nearly famous blues / The national anthem of nowhere / Nature boy.

not iss. / Arista

Apr 92. (12"ep) <54424> **CANDY ON A CROSS / ANTARTICA STARTS HERE. / MEMPHIS GHOST – ANTARTICA STARTS HERE (reprise)**

BEASTS OF BOURBON (see under ⇒ **SCIENTISTS**)

BEAT (see under ⇒ **NERVES; 70's section**)

BEAT HAPPENING

Formed: Olympia, Washington, USA . . . 1983 by CALVIN JOHNSON and his band of arty, JONATHAN RICHMAN-influenced alternative popsters. After two self-financed, mail-order cassettes, 'BEAT HAPPENING' (1983) and 'THREE TEA BREAKFAST' (1984), CALVIN and Co (HEATHER LEWIS and BRET LUNSFORD) brought BEAT HAPPENING to the wider indie public via their long-playing eponymous debut for UK's 'Rough Trade' in the mid 80's. Continuing the transatlantic connection, they signed to small Scottish-based label, '53rd & 3rd', unveiling their UK debut 45, 'CRASHING THROUGH EP', early in '88. A further EP, 'POLLY PEREGRIN' (shared with the SCREAMING TREES), was accompanied by a follow-up album, 'JAMBOREE' (1988). Later re-issued by American institution 'Sub Pop', the latter set remains one of their finest achievements featuring the classic 'INDIAN SUMMER' track. Side by side with BEAT HAPPENING, CALVIN was also running his own record label, 'K', releasing songs by the likes of TEENAGE FANCLUB and MELODY DOG, to mention two. This also included another JOHNSON offshoot, The GO TEAM, a trio of sorts who unleashed a series of rhythm-driven cassettes and 7" singles between 1989 and 1994; a certain KUR(D)T KOBAIN guested on one of the latter! Following a medicore set for 'Rough Trade', 'BLACK CANDY' (1989), the 'HAPPENING band (HEATHER was now co-writing a lot of the songs) wound down their career at 'Sub Pop' without pandering to the grunge craze over two final releases, 'DREAMY' (1991) and 'YOU TURN ME ON' (1992). CALVIN resurfaced with two other outfits, The HALO BENDERS (with BUILT TO SPILL's DOUG MARTSCH) and DUB NARCOTIC SOUND SYSTEM. The augmentation of LARRY BUTLER, BRIAN WEBBER and CHRIS SUTTON was much appreciated by the aforementioned mellifluous slacker when he recorded EP's 'INDUSTRIAL BREAKDOWN', 'RIDING SHOTGUN' and the brilliant 'SHIP TO SHORE' between '95 and '96 before the release of the debut DUB NARCOTIC album 'RHYTHM RECORD, VOL. 1: ECHOES FROM THE SCENE . . .'. The band (named after the studious recording cavity in 'K's headquarters) did their best to divert from any use of actual dub in their songs. The result was a groovy, swanky and, at times, melancholic mix of big drums, scratching, freeform jazz and guitars that were, literally, choked like chickens. It was like a field day for art students everywhere as they boarded the proverbial bus, transporting themselves into the perplexed and often muddled world of JOHNSON, which was painfully documented on a further four albums. • **Covered:** PLEASE PLEASE PLEASE LET ME GET WHAT I WANT (Smiths).

Album rating: BEAT HAPPENING (*6) / JAMBOREE (*7) / BLACK CANDY (*5) / DREAMY (*7) / YOU TURN ME ON (*8) / 1983-85 compilation (*6) / Halo Benders: GOD DON'T MAKE NO JUNK (*5) / DON'T TELL ME NOW (*7) / THE REBELS NOT IN (*6) / Dub Narcotic Sound System: INDUSTRIAL BREAKDOWN mini (*4) / RHYTHM RECORD VOL.1: ECHOES FROM THE SCENE CONTROL (*4) / RIDIN' SHOTGUN mini (*4) / BOOT PARTY (*5) / OUT OF YOUR MIND (*5) / SIDEWAYS SOUL (*4)

CALVIN JOHNSON – vocals, guitar / **HEATHER LEWIS + BRET LUNSFORD**

not iss. K

Jun 84. (c-ep) *<KLP 1C>* **THREE TEA BREAKFAST** mail-o
– Down at the sea / Primitives / I spy. *(UK-iss.Mar88; same)*

1984. (7") **OUR SECRET. / WHAT'S IMPORTANT**

Nov 85. (lp) *<KLP 1>* **BEAT HAPPENING**
– Our secret / What's important / Down at the sea / I love you / Fourteen / Run down the stairs / Primitives / I spy / Bad seeds (live) / Down at the sea / In my memory / Honey pot / Fall / Youth / Don't mix the colors / Foggy eyes / Bad seeds / I let him get to me / I spy / Run down the stairs / Christmas / Fourteen / Let's kiss / 1, 2, 3 / In love with you thing / Look around. *(UK-iss.Nov86 on 'Rough Trade'; ROUGH 105) <US cd-iss. 1992 as 'BEAT HAPPENING 1983-85' on 'Feel Good All Over'; 1> (re-iss. Apr96 cd+=/lp; KCD/KLP 1)* – THREE TEA BREAKFAST tracks

Jan 88. (7") *<L 26501>* **LOOK AROUND. / THAT GIRL**

53rd & 3rd K

Jan 88. (12"ep) *(AGARR 015T)* **CRASHING THROUGH EP**
– Crashing through / The this many boyfriends club / Look around / That girl.

Jul 88. (lp/pic-lp) *(AGAS 002/+F) <KLP 22>* **JAMBOREE**
– Bewitched / In between / Indian summer / Hangman / Jamboree / Ask me / Crashing through / Catwalk / Drive car girl / Midnight ago-go / The this many boyfriends club. *<US re-iss. Jun90 on 'Sub Pop' cd/c; SP 8/A> (UK cd-iss. Mar94 on 'Sub Pop'; SP 62B) (lp re-iss. Jan95 on 'K'; KLP 22)*

53rd & 3rd Homestead

Aug 88. (12"ep) *(AGARR 020) <HMS 110>* **POLLY PEREGUIN / TALES OF BRAVE APHRODITE. / (other tracks by SCREAMING TREES)**

1988. (7"flexi) *(ABENDI 001)* **HONEY POT. / DON'T MIX THE COLOURS**

Rough Trade K

Sep 89. (lp/cd) *(ROUGH/+CD 145) <KLP 23>* **BLACK CANDY**
– Other side / Black candy / Knick knack / Pajama party / In a haunted jive / Gravedigger blues / Cast a shadow / Bonfire / T.V. girl / Playhouse / Ponytail. *<US re-iss. Sep90 on 'Sub Pop; cd/c; SP 78 B/A>*

not iss. Chemical Imbalance

1989. (7") **FOGGY EYES. /**

Sub Pop Sub Pop

Sep 90. (7",7"red) *<SP 74>* **RED HEAD WALKING. / SECRET PICNIC SPOT**

Mar 91. (lp/c/cd) *<SP/+A/B 98>* **DREAMY**
– Me untamed (dreamy) / Left behind / Hot chocolate boy / I've lost you / Cry for a shadow / Collide / Nancy sin / Fortune cookie prize / Revolution come and gone / Red head walking.

1990. (7") *<IPU 15>* **NANCY SIN. / DREAMY**

1991. (7") *(Bijoop 025)* **SEA HUNT. / KNOCK ON ANY DOOR**
(above 2 issued on 'K' and 'Bi-Joopiter') (below on 'Tupelo')

1991. (12"ep) *(TUPEP 24)* **RED HEAD WALKING**
– Red head walking / Revolution come and gone / Secret picnic spot.

Sep 92. (7") **NOT A CARE IN THE WORLD. /**

Oct 92. (cd/lp) *<(SP 207CD/45-207)>* **YOU TURN ME ON**
– Tiger trap / Noise / Pinebox derby / Teenage caveman / Sleepy head / You turn me on / Godsend / Hey day / Bury the hammer.

— disbanded early in 1993, CALVIN having already formed The HALO BENDERS (with BUILT TO SPILL's DOUG MARTSCH) and DUB NARCOTIC SOUND SYSTEM. BEAT HAPPENING re-formed for a new 45.

K K

Nov 00. (7") *<(IPU 98)>* **ANGEL GONE. / ZOMBIE LIMBO THEME**

– compilations, etc. –

1991. (c; shared with VASELINES) *K;* **SPLIT**

May 02. (7xcd-box+book) *K; <(KLP 115CD)>* **CRASHING THROUGH**

GO TEAM

CALVIN JOHNSON with **TOBI VAIL** – guitar (of BIKINI KILL)

K K

Jan 88. (c) *<(KC 004)>* **YOUR PRETTY GUITAR**

Mar 88. (c) *<(KC 005)>* **DONNA PARKER POP**
– Brave aphrodite / Cherrydale / Lake Arrowhead / Loneliness march / Rexjohnnyhex / Wonderbirds.

— added **STEVE PETERS**

1988. (c) *<(KC 006)>* **LIVE IN WASHINGTON (live)**

Jan 89. (7") *<GTJA 89>* **SAND. / JIGSAW**

— added **BILLY KARREN** – guitar / **DAVID NICHOLS** – drums (of CANNANES) – STEVE PETERS had now left

Feb 89. (7") *<GTFE 89>* **OUTSIDE. / STAY READY**

— **THE LEGEND** – vocals; repl. BILLY + DAVID

Mar 89. (7") *<GTMA 89>* **BREAKFAST IN BED. / SAFE LITTLE CIRCLES**

— guest **JEFF KENNEDY** – vocals; repl. THE LEGEND

Apr 89. (7") *<GTAP 89>* **MILQUETOAST BRIGADE. / SHE WAS SAD**

May 89. (7") *<GTMY 89>* **RIBEYE. / 935 PATTERSON**

— added guests **QUANG H** – drums / **BRAD CLEMMONS + BILLY KARREN** – guitar

Jun 89. (7") *<GTJE 89>* **GO TEAM CALL. / THREE WAYS TO SUNDAY**

— guests now **TAMRA OHRMUND** – vocals / **CARLA OLSEN** – bass (of SOME VELVET SIDEWALK) / **DONNA BIDDLE + KURDT KOBAIN** – guitar (of NIRVANA)

Jul 89. (7") *<GTJL 89>* **SCRATCH IT OUT. / BIKINI TWILIGHT**

Aug 89. (7") *<GTAU 89>* **TUMMY HOP. / MAVERICK SUMMER**

— with guest **BRAD CLEMMONS** – guitar

Sep 89. (7"one-sided) *<GTSE 89>* **THE PINES OF ROME (excerpt)**

1989. (c) *<(KC 017)>* **ARCHER COME SPARROW**
– Acid autumn / Broken window / Crash cavern / Help me if you can / Intercept irradiate / Keep-a-way / My heart hurts / Open fire 3 guitars / Pledge of allegiance / Rainy day / Red headed ants / The golf pro / Treasure hunt.

HALO BENDERS

CALVIN JOHNSON – vocals, guitar / **DOUG MARTSCH** – guitar, vocals, bass, keyboards (of BUILT TO SPILL) / **WAYNE FLOWER** – bass / **RALF YOUTZ** – drums, guitar

not iss. Atlas

1994. (7"m) *(ATLAS 003)* **CANNED OXYGEN. / IT'S NOT ME / BIKINI (acoustic)**

— added **STEVE FISK** – producer

Fire K

Jan 95. (cd/lp) *(FIRE 43 CD/LP) <KLP 29 CD/LP>* **GOD DON'T MAKE NO JUNK** Nov94
– Snowfall / Don't touch my bikini / Will work for food / Freedom ride / Sit on it / Canned oxygen / Scarin' / On a tip / I can't believe it's true / Big rock candy mountain.

Apr 95. (7") *(7SM 5)* **DON'T TOUCH MY BIKINI. / PLEASE PLEASE PLEASE LET ME GET WHAT I WANT**
(cd-s+=) *(BLAZE 82CD)* –

K K

Jan 96. (cd/lp) *<(KLP 46 CD/LP)>* **DON'T TELL ME NOW**
– Phantom power / Halo bender / Mercury blues / Bombshelter / Volume mode / Inbread heart / Planned absolescence / Magic carpet rider / Blank equation / Crankenstein.

Jan 98. (cd/lp) *(KLP 81 CD/V)>* **THE REBELS NOT IN**
– Virginia reel around the fountain / Your asterisk / Lonesome sundown / Devil city destiny / Bury me / Surfers haze / Do that thing / Love travels faster / Turn it my way / Rebels got a hole in it / Foggy bottom.

DUB NARCOTIC SOUND SYSTEM

CALVIN JOHNSON with **LOIS MAFFEO** – vocals + DEAD PRESIDENTS: **LARRY BUTLER** – drums / **BRIAN WEBER** – organ, guitar / **TODD RANSLOW** – bass

K K

Oct 94. (7") *<DBN 101>* **DUB NARCOTIC. / (version)**

Oct 94. (7") *<DBN 102>* **FUCK SHIT UP. / (version)**

Oct 94. (7") *<DBN 103>* **BOOTY RUN. / (version)**

Oct 94. (7") *<DBN 104>* **BITE. / (mono version)**

Oct 94. (7") *<DBN 105>* **INDUSTRIAL BREAKDOWN. / (version)**

Jul 95. (lp/cd) *(SOUL 8/+CD) <KCD/KLP 39>* **INDUSTRIAL BREAKDOWN**
– Industrial breakdown / The beat from 20,000 fathoms / Typecast sanction / Run silent run deep / (Industrial) Revolution inclusion.
(above issued on 'Soul Static Sound' UK)

Nov 95. (lp) *<(KLP 45)>* **RHYTHM RECORD VOL.1: ECHOES FROM THE SCENE CONTROL ROOM** Jul95

Nov 95. (m-cd/m-lp) *<(KCD/KLP 50)>* **RIDIN' SHOTGUN** Oct95
– Ridin' shotgun / Int harvester / Harvester traveler / Half life / Isotopal Reg / Ridin shotgun.

May 95. (7") *<DB 106>* **R.U.A. BELIEVER. / (version by the MAKE-UP)**

May 95. (7") *<(DBN 107)>* **SHAKE-A-PUDDIN'. / (version)**

Jun 96. (lp/cd) *<(KLP 40/+CD)>* **BOOT PARTY**
– Test pattern / Monkey hips and rice / Ship to shore / Super dub narcotic / Afi-tione / Shake-a-puddin' / King Harvester / Robotica / Bunny echo / Boot party.

Oct 96. (m-lp/m-cd) *<(KLP 60/+CD)>* **SHIP TO SHORE** Sep96
– Ship to shore / DJ Dervishs ship shape / Rougher / Do that / Scat.

Feb 97. (12"ep/cd-ep) *<(KLP 68/+CD)>* **BONE DRY. / BASS HUMP / SUPERBALL / ROT GUT**

— **CHRIS SUTTON** – bass; repl. RANSLOW + MAFFEO

Jul 97. (7") *<(DBN 108)>* **WASTED. / GROOVE**

Aug 98. (lp/cd) *<(KLP 83/+CD)>* **OUT OF YOUR MIND**
– Wicked bad / Baseness / Teenage time bomb / Dub Narcotic's delight / Sawed off / Rebel makes rhymes / Out of your mind / Oslo calling / Belly warmer / Shock mount / Pappa's got a brand new burnbag.

Sep 98. (7") *<DBN 109>* **OLD TIME RELINJUN. / OFFICE BUILDING**

Dec 98. (7") *<DBN 110>* **K G SHOW ME. / K G (version)**

Sep 99. (cd; with JON SPENCER BLUES EXPLOSION) *<(KCD 103)>* **SIDEWAYS SOUL**
– Banana version / Love ain't on the run / Fudgy the whale / Banana meltdown / Frosty junction / Diamonds / Sideways soul / Chicken legs / Calvin's on a bummer.

BEAT RODEO

Formed: Minneapolis, Minnesota, USA . . . 1981/82 by former SUICIDE COMMANDOS and CRACKERS bassist, STEVE ALMAAS. The former revved-up punk outfit emerged out of the local new wave scene late '76, releasing their debut, 'MAKE A RECORD' (1978) for 'Blank'. After two US-only singles and a posthumous live set of the final outing in November '78, 'THE COMMANDOS COMMIT SUICIDE DANCE CONCERT', the group were no more. In 1981, ALMAAS cut a one-off EP alongside RICHARD BARONE (ex-BONGOS) and producer MITCH EASTER under the BEAT RODEO moniker, subsequently deciding to make the country-rock project a full-time concern albeit with new personnel. With the line-up of BILL SCHUNK, ALLAN GRELLER and PETER MOSER, ALMAAS initiated BEAT RODEO proper with a series of gigs before releasing their DON DIXON-produced debut set, 'STAYING OUT LATE', in 1984 on German imprint 'Zensor'. They subsequently signed a more lucrative deal with Miles Copeland's 'I.R.S.', the label re-issuing the debut in remixed form (courtesy of ALMAAS and DIXON), although by this time GRELLER and MOSER had been substituted by DAN PRATER and LOUIS KING respectively; the latter two made their debut on a couple of new bonus tracks. Produced by another future R.E.M. knob-twiddler (Scott Litt), the follow-up, 'HOME IN THE HEART OF THE BEAT' (1986) – their last – failed to achieve quite the same critical and commercial reaction as their Georgian contemporaries.

Album rating: Suicide Commandos: MAKE A RECORD (*6) / THE COMMANDOS COMMIT SUICIDE DANCE RECORD (*5) / Beat Rodeo: STAYING OUT LATE WITH . . . BEAT RODEO (*4) / HOME IN THE HEART OF THE BEAT (*5)

SUICIDE COMMANDOS

CHRIS OSGOOD – vocals, guitar / **STEVE ALMAAS** – bass, vocals / **DAVE AHL** – drums

		not iss.	P.S.
1976.	(7"m) <30254> **EMISSION CONTROL. / CLICHE OLE / MONSTER AU-GO-GO**	–	
1977.	(7") <30787> **MATCH – MISMATCH. / MARK HE'S A TERROR**	–	

		not iss.	Blank
1978.	(lp) <002> **MAKE A RECORD** – Shock appeal / Attacking the beat / Mosquito crucifixion / Mr. Dr. / Semi-smart / Call of the wild / You can't / I need a torch / Kidnapped / Premature / I don't get it / Real cool / She / Burn it down / Match – Mismatch. <cd-iss. 1996 on 'Polygram'; 532878>		

		not iss.	Twin Tone
Apr 79.	(lp) <TTR 7906> **THE COMMANDOS COMMIT SUICIDE** (dance concert – live)		–

— had already split late '78, although ALMAAS initiated another band

Jul 81. (12"ep; as The CRACKERS) <TTR 8122> **SIR CRACKERS** – Ultimato / I can't have faith / Light blue dress / Your heart.

— ALMAAS subsequently released an EP in 1981 under the name, BEAT RODEO, augmented by RICHARD BARONE (ex-BONGOS) and MITCH EASTER (of LET'S ACTIVE and the producer). BEAT RODEO were formed in 1982 . . .

BEAT RODEO

STEVE ALMAAS – vocals, guitar / **BILL SCHUNK** (b. Riverhead, New York, USA) – guitar / **ALLAN GRELLER** – bass / **PETER MOSER** – drums

		Zensor	Coyote	
1982.	(12"ep; by STEVE ALMAAS) **BEAT RODEO**	–		
1983.	(7") **WHAT'S THE MATTER. / MIMI**	–		
Jul 84.	(lp) <ZS 11> **STAYING OUT LATE WITH . . . BEAT RODEO** – She's more / Just friends / Heart attack / Who's gonna be around / Pet project / Mistake / Kind that says no / Without you / Not the girl loves me / Only for myself / You're the only reason / Take you home. (UK-iss.Dec84; ZSUK 01) <re-mixed & issued in US on 'I.R.S.' +=; > – (unknown 2 tracks).		–	German

— by this time, GRELLER + MOSER were repl. by **DAN PRATER** – bass, vocals / **LEWIS KING** – drums, percussion (guest on 1986 set, SYD STRAW)

		I.R.S.	I.R.S.
Nov 86.	(lp/c) (MIRF/+C 1019) <5774> **HOME IN THE HEART OF THE BEAT** – Twin hometowns / Everything I'm not / New love / It could happen here / (I have) Everything I need / I'm not afraid (doesn't matter to me) / In the summertime / Home in the heart of the beat / Song for an angry young man / It's been too long / While we're apart.		
Feb 87.	(12"ep) (IRMT 131) **EVERYTHING I'M NOT / NEW LOVE. / TRUE / STILL IN HOLLYWOOD**		–

— split in the late 80's after continuing to tour the States. STEVE ALMAAS subsequently released four LP's, 'EAST RIVER BLUES' (1993), 'BRIDGE SONGS' (1995), 'HUMAN, ALL TOO HUMAN' (1998) and 'KINGO A WILD ONE' (2000) – all on 'Lonesome Whippoorwill'.

Pete BECKER (see under ⇒ EYELESS IN GAZA)

BEEFEATER

Formed: Washington DC, USA . . . 1984, most members stemming from various local hardcore acts. The line-up consisted of TOMAS SQUIP JONES, DUG E. BIRD, BRUCE TAYLOR and FRED SMITH, breaking the 'Dischord' norm with an experimental hybrid of avant-jazz, dub, metal and of course hardcore. This soundclash was unleashed on two mid 80's albums, 'PLAYS FOR LOVERS' (1985) and 'HOUSE BURNING DOWN', although their lack of success led to a subsequent break-up (JONES and BIRD formed FIDELITY JONES).

Album rating: PLAYS FOR LOVERS (*6) / HOUSE BURNING DOWN (*6)

TOMAS SQUIP JONES – vocals (ex-RED C) / **FRED SMITH** – guitar / **DUG E. BIRD** (b. BIRDZELL) – bass (ex-UNDERGROUND SOLDIER) / **BRUCE TAYLOR** – drums (ex-CLEAR VISION, ex-HATE FROM IGNORANCE, ex-SUBTLE OPPRESION)

		Dischord	Dischord
1985.	(lp) <(DISCHORD 17)> **PLAYS FOR LOVERS** – Trash funk / Reaganomix / Song for lucky / 4 3 2 1 / Mr. Silverbird / Manic D / Mourning / Satyagraha / Dog day / Red carpet / Assholes / Beefeater / Fred's song / I miss you / Out of the woods.		
1987.	(lp) <(DISCHORD 23)> **HOUSE BURNING DOWN** – Just things / Bedlam rainforest / Move me strong / One soul down / Ain't got no time / Sinking me / Dover beach / Insurrection chant / 40 sonnets on plants / With you always / Freditude / Live the life.		

— disbanded when JONES and BIRD formed FIDELITY JONES

– compilations, etc. –

May 92. (cd) *Dischord; (DIS 64CD)* **PLAYS FOR LOVERS / HOUSE BURNING DOWN**
– (their 2 albums + Wars in space / Blind leads blind).

BEIRUT SLUMP
(see under ⇒ LUNCH, Lydia; 70's section)

Chris BELL

Born: 12 Jan'51, Memphis, Tennessee, USA. Influenced by classic British pop/rock, BELL began writing and performing while in high school. It was here that he met ALEX CHILTON, his future sparring partner in BIG STAR, one of America's great lost bands and a towering inspiration for countless indie hopefuls. Recorded while BELL was at university – he actually handed the album in for a class project! – '#1 RECORD' (1972) should've been massive but for the well documented disaster with its distribution; while critics reached for the collective thesaurus, 'Stax' subdivision, 'Ardent', proved themselves incapable of handling a white rock act. Devastated by the record's failure, BELL found himself at loggerheads with CHILTON on how best to proceed, finally departing in late '72 and falling into a deep depression which would dog him on and off for the next few years. During that time he briefly reunited with CHILTON and BIG STAR drummer, JODY STEPHENS, cutting a handful of tracks which turned up on BIG STAR's second album, 'RADIO CITY'. Yet such was the tension between the former writing partners that BELL subsequently refused to be credited. Instead, he cut three tracks, 'I GOT KINDA LOST', 'I DON'T KNOW' and the sublime 'I AM THE COSMOS' at 'Shoe' studios in Memphis before his brother, worried about his worsening emotional state, accompanied him to Chateau D'Herouville studios in France. The resulting sessions produced an impressive clutch of tracks which were subsequently mixed by BEATLES engineer, Geoff Emerick and which CHRIS and his brother duly attempted to hawk around the London record companies. Despite considerable interest, no concrete deal was forthcoming and CHRIS eventually resigned himself to working in his family's restaurant business. He nevertheless carried on with his music in his spare time, enthused by the mid-78 "2 on 1" re-issue of '#1 RECORD/RADIO CITY' and the belated release of his own 'I AM THE COSMOS / YOU AND YOUR SISTER' on New York indie label, 'Car'. Tragically, on the 27th of December 1978, BELL died instantly after the car he was driving struck a telegraph pole. Incredibly, BELL's unreleased masters gathered dust until the early 90's when a surge of interest in BIG STAR – due in no small part to the patronage of Scottish artists such as PRIMAL SCREAM and TEENAGE FANCLUB – saw 'Rykodisc' finally releasing the tracks as an album. From its meditative cover shot to the hypnotic beauty of the music contained within, 'I AM THE COSMOS' (1992) finally did the man justice. Worth the asking price alone for the opening salvo of 'I AM THE COSMOS', the LENNON-esque 'BETTER SAVE YOURSELF' and the lovely 'SPEED OF SOUND', the collection highlighted a criminally underrated talent whose inability to secure a recording contract in the 70's remains baffling.

Album rating: I AM THE COSMOS (*8)

CHRIS BELL – vocals, guitar (ex-BIG STAR) / with **ALEX CHILTON** + **BILL CUNNINGHAM**

		not iss.	Car
1977.	(7") <CRR 6> **I AM THE COSMOS. / YOU AND YOUR SISTER**	–	

— CHRIS had retired a few years previously before the release of the above single. He worked with a new band late in 1978, however tragedy struck (see above). Below was a posthumous release of his 1973 recordings, etc.

— with mainly **KEN WOODLEY** – bass, organ / **RICHARD ROSEBROUGH** – drums

		Rykodisc	Rykodisc
Mar 92.	(cd/c) <(RCD/RACS 10222)> **I AM THE COSMOS** – I am the cosmos / Better save yourself / Speed of sound / Get away / You and your sister / Make a scene / Look up / I got kinda lost / There was a light / Fight at the table / I don't know / Though I know she lies / I am the cosmos (slow version) / You and your sister (country version) / You and your sister (acoustic version).		

BELOVED

Formed: Camberwell, London, England . . . 1983/4 as JOURNEY THROUGH by JON MARSH, GUY GOUSDEN and TIM HARVARD. With the addition of Cambridge graduate STEVE WADDINGTON, the band assumed the BELOVED moniker and began releasing records through their own 'Flim Flam' label. Early efforts at indie psychedelia a la The SHAMEN had developed into a more bass-heavy pop-dance sound by the release of the 'WHERE IT IS' album in 1987 and the band were signed up by 'Warners'. A split in the ranks the following year led to GOUSDEN and HARVARD leaving MARSH and WADDINGTON to lead The BELOVED into the brave new world of the emerging 'house' culture by way of electronic bass and drums as evidenced on their early efforts for the label, 'LOVING FEELING' and 'YOUR LOVE TAKES ME HIGHER'. The blissed out vibe continued with 'THE SUN RISING', a second-summer-of-love-era classic placing a mesmerising female vocal over a near-ambient backing to stunning effect. Unsurprisingly, the track finally broke the band into the UK Top 30 as well as earning them a fair whack in licensing revenue after being used as a musical backdrop to many a TV ad. A kind of pop companion piece to A HOUSE's

'Endless Art', The BELOVED's follow-up single, 'HELLO', was another list of the great and the erm ... not so great (people, that is). Along with a third hit single, a revamped 'YOUR LOVE TAKES ME HIGHER', the track was one of the many highlights of the best selling 'HAPPINESS' (1990) album, an essential document of early 90's dance culture along with PRIMAL SCREAM's 'Screamadelica'. All good things come to an end, though, and with the departure of WADDINGTON to work with STEVE HILLAGE and his SYSTEM 7 project, MARSH recruited his other half, HELENA to work on new material. The resulting 'SWEET HARMONY' single in 1993 proved to be their most commercially successful effort to date, incredibly furnishing The BELOVED with its first UK Top 10 hit. The accompanying album, 'CONSCIENCE' (1993) narrowly missed the top of the charts despite being a less immediate collection. A further couple of minor hits followed before The BELOVED faded from view, their eventual return in 1996 with the 'X' album merely underlining the fact that the group had failed to keep pace with a dance scene continually in flux. • **Songwriters:** MARSH and WADDINGTON (until his departure), except a cover of GIVE IT TO ME (Bam Bam).

Album rating: HAPPINESS (*6) / BLISSED OUT (*5) / CONSCIENCE (*6) / X (*4) / SINGLE FILE: THE BEST OF THE BELOVED compilation (*7)

JON MARSH (b.1963) – vocals, guitar / **STEVE WADDINGTON** (b.1958) – guitar, keyboards / **TIM HARVARD** – bass / **GUY GAUSDEN** – drums

			Flim Flam	not iss.
Apr 86.	(12"m)	(HARP 2T) **A HUNDRED WORDS. / SLOW DANCING / IN TROUBLE AND SHAME**		-
Sep 86.	(7")	(HARP 3) **THIS MEANS WAR. / IF ONLY**		-
	(12")	(HARP 3T) – ('A'side) / Let it begin / Saints preserve us.		
Mar 87.	(12"ep)	(HARP 5T) **HAPPY NOW**		-
		– Righteous me / A kiss goodbye / If pennies came.		
Jul 87.	(7"/12")	(HARP 7/+T) **FOREVER DANCING. / SURPRISE ME**		-
	(12"+=)	(HARP 7E) – ('A'remix).		
Nov 87.	(lp)	(HARPLP 2) **WHERE IT IS**		-
		– A hundred words / Slow dancing / In trouble and shame / This means war / If only / Let it begin / Saints preserve us / If pennies came / Righteous me / A kiss goodbye / Surprise me / Forever dancing. (cd-iss. Jul90; HARPCD 2)		

— (trimmed to duo of MARSH and WADDINGTON & drum machine)

			W.E.A.	Atlantic
Oct 88.	(7"/12"/cd-s)	(YZ 311/+T/CD) **LOVING FEELING. / ACID LOVE**		-
Jan 89.	(7")	(YZ 357) **YOUR LOVE TAKES ME HIGHER. / PARADISE (MY DARLING, MY ANGEL)**		-
	(12"/cd-s)	(YZ 357 T/CD) – ('A'&'B'remix).		
Oct 89.	(7"/c-s/12"pic-d)	(YZ 414/+C/PD) <86126> **THE SUN RISING. / ('A'instrumental)**	26	Oct90
	(12"+=)	(YZ 414 T/CD) – (2 extra mixes).		
Jan 90.	(7"/c-s)	(YZ 426/+C) <86235> **HELLO. / ('A'-Dolly mix)**	19	Mar90
	(12"+=)	(YZ 426T) – ('A'mix).		
	(cd-s++=)	(YZ 426CD) – ('A'extra mix).		
Feb 90.	(cd/c/lp)	(2292 46253-2/-4/-1) <82047> **HAPPINESS**	14	Mar90
		– Hello / Your love takes me higher / Time after time / Don't you worry / Scarlet beautiful / The sun rising / I love you more / Wake up soon / Up, up and away / Found. (re-iss. cd/c Feb95; same)		
Mar 90.	(7"/c-s)	(YZ 463/+C) **YOUR LOVE TAKES ME HIGHER. / PABLO**	39	-
	(12")	(YZ 463T) – ('A'side) / ('A'version).		
	(cd-s++=)	(YZ 463CD) – (all above tracks).		
May 90.	(7"/c-s)	(YZ 482/+C) <86184> **TIME AFTER TIME. / ('A' through the round window mix)**	46	-
	(12"+=)	(YZ 482T) – ('A'-Muffin mix).		
	(cd-s+=)	(YZ 482CD) – ('A'extended mix).		
Oct 90.	(7"/c-s)	(YZ 541/+C) **IT'S ALRIGHT NOW. / ('A'instrumental)**	48	-
	(12"+=/cd-s+=)	(YZ 541 T/CD) – ('A'extra mix).		
Oct 90.	(cd)(lp/c)	(<9031 72907-2>)(WX 383/+C) **BLISSED OUT** (remixes of last album)	39	-
		– Up, up and away (happy sexy mix) / Wake up soon / Pablo (special K mix) / It's alright now (back to basics) / Hell (honky tonk) / Time after time (muffin mix) / The sun rising / Your love takes me higher. (re-iss. cd Feb95; same)		

— **HELENA MARSH** – producer, writer (wife of JON) repl. WADDINGTON

			East West	Atlantic
Jan 93.	(7"/c-s)	(YZ 709/+C) **SWEET HARMONY. / MOTIVATION (Empathised)**	8	-
	(12"+=/cd-s+=)	(YZ 709 T/CD) – (2 'A'mixes).		
Feb 93.	(cd/c/lp)	(4509 91483-2/-4/-1) <82457> **CONSCIENCE**	2	-
		– Spirit / Sweet harmony / Outer space girl / Lose yourself in me / Paradise found / You've got me thinking / Celebrate your life / Rock to the rhythm of love / Let the music take you / 1000 years from today / Dream on. (cd re-iss. Dec96; 4509 91483-2)		
Mar 93.	(7"/c-s)	(YZ 738/+C) **YOU'VE GOT ME THINKING. / CELEBRATE YOUR LIFE (Fit For Life Mix)**	23	-
	(12"+=/cd-s+=)	(YZ 738 T/CD) – ('B' dub mix) / Sweet harmony (club mix).		
Aug 93.	(7"/c-s)	(YZ 726/+C) **OUTER SPACE GIRL. / ('A'-Space Hopper mix)**	38	-
	(12")	(YZ 726T) – ('A'-Destination Moon + Organism mixes).		
	(cd-s+=)	(YZ 726CD) – ('A'-Space Cadet + Space Dust mixes).		
Jan 94.	(12")	<85716> **ROCK TO THE RHYTHM OF LOVE**	-	-
Mar 96.	(c-s)	(EW 034C) **SATELLITE / ('A'-Transformer vocal)**	19	-
	(cd-s+=)	(EW 034CD) – ('A'mixes; Hight 611's Kundalini Rising / freedom vocal / High lite dub).		
Apr 96.	(cd/c/lp)	(0630 13316-2/-4/-1) <82962> **X**	25	Oct96
		– Deliver me / Satellite / Ease the pressure / A dream within a dream / Crystal wave / For your love / Physical love / Missing you / Three steps to Heaven / Spacemen.		
May 96.	(c-s)	(EW 043C) **DELIVER ME / ('A'mix)**		-
	(cd-s+=)	(EW 043CD) – ('A'mixes; extended / Eau de Livami vocal / Salt City vocal / Coco dub / RoboDisco dub).		
	(12"+=)	(EW 043T) – ('A'mixes).		
Aug 96.	(c-s)	(EW 058C) **EASE THE PRESSURE / ('A'mix)**	43	-
	(cd-s+=)	(EW 058CD) – ('A'-guitarapella bonus freaks bass dub & backroom vocal) / Switchback.		
	(12")	(EW 058T) – ('A'mixes).		
Aug 97.	(12"/cd-s)	(EW 122 T/CD1) **THE SUN RISING / (mixes:- Back to the future / Tom's drum & bass / Zanzibar has risen / Deep breath vocal)**	31	-
	(cd-s+=)	(EW 122CD2) – ('A'side) / ('A'-mixes; Eurovisionary / Adam & Eve's house of the rising sun / Gentle night).		
Aug 97.	(cd/c)	(0630 19932-2/-4) **SINGLE FILE (THE BEST OF THE BELOVED)** (compilation)		-
		– The sun rising / Sweet harmony / Your love takes me higher / Satellite / Outerspace girl / Time after time / Hello / Ease the pressure / It's alright now / You've got me thinking / Deliver me / Mark's deep house.		

— The BELOVED had actually split well before above collection

BENNY PROFANE (see under ⇒ ROOM)

Heidi BERRY

Born: 1958, Boston, Massachusetts, USA, although she has resided in London since her remarried mother moved there in the early 70's. Having more than likely been inspired by the vocal dexterity of such female icons as SANDY DENNY, GRACE SLICK and JONI MITCHELL, HEIDI bizarrely enough got her first break on indie-guitar haven, 'Creation', in 1987. Alan McGee and Co. released her first work, the mini-set, 'FIREFLY', an atmospheric, string-cloaked piece of singer-songwriter melancholy which featured the keyboard talent of MARTIN DUFFY. In the Spring of '89 and now accompanied by her brother CHRISTOPHER BERRY and pianist ROCKY HOLMAN, HEIDI delivered her first full-length, 'BELOW THE WAVES', one of the highlights, the austere 'NORTH SHORE TRAIN' previously featured on her label's 99p album sampler 'Doin It For The Kids'. Invited by IVO's '4 a.d.' alternative ensemble, THIS MORTAL COIL, to interpret Rodney Crowell's 'Til I Gain Control Again', BERRY signed a full-time contract with the label around the same time. Augmented by the likes of MARTIN McCARRICK, LAURENCE O'KEEFE, TERRY BICKERS, LOL COXHILL and IAN KEARNEY, she delivered the 'LOVE' album in '91, a record that boasted her version of Bob Mould's 'UP IN THE AIR'. Throughout the 90's, HEIDI continued to plough her own idiosyncratic furrow to critical favour on the likes of 'HEIDI BERRY' (1993) and 'MIRACLE' (1996).

Album rating: FIREFLY (*5) / BELOW THE WAVES (*6) / LOVE (*5) / HEIDI BERRY (*7) / MIRACLE (*6) / POMEGRANATE: AN ANTHOLOGY compilation (*6)

HEIDI BERRY – vocals / with **MARTIN DUFFY** – piano (of FELT) / + others

			Creation	Positive
Sep 87.	(m-lp)	(CRELP 023) **FIREFLY**		-

— added **ROCKY HOLMAN** – piano, synthesizer / her brother **CHRISTOPHER BERRY** – acoustic guitar

May 89.	(lp/cd)	(CRE LP/CD 048) <6063> **BELOW THE WAVES**		
		– Ribbons / Below the waves / Little tragedy / Legacy / North shore train / Gather all the hours / River song / All for you / Living memory / ancer / Out of my hands / Firefly / Nobody tells you you / Will it all change / Houses made of wood / Hasten the buds to bloom.		

— added guests **MARTIN McCARRICK** (of SIOUXSIE & THE BANSHEES) / **TERRY BICKERS + LAURENCE O'KEEFE** (of LEVITATION) / **IAN KEARNEY** (of BLUE AEROPLANES) / **LOL COXHILL** (solo artist)

			4 a.d.	4 a.d.
Aug 91.	(cd)(lp/c)	<(CAD 1012CD)>(CAD/+C 1012) **LOVE**		
		– Washington Square / Up in the air / Gloria / Great big silver key / Wake / Cradle / Hand over head / Silver buttons / Lonely heart / Bright as day / Lily. (cd re-iss. Jul98; GAD 1012CD)		

			4 a.d.	4ad-Warners
Jun 93.	(12"ep/cd-ep)	(BAD 3010/+CD) **THE MOON AND THE SUN EP**		-
		– The moon and the sun / Unholy light / Zither song / You upset the grace of living when you lie.		
Jul 93.	(cd)(lp/c)	(CAD 3009CD)(CAD/+C 3009) <45301> **HEIDI BERRY**		Jan93
		– Mercury / Little fox / The moon and the sun / One-string violin / arling companion / Distant thunder / Heart like a wheel / For the rose / Follow / Ariel / Dawn. (cd re-iss. Jul98; GAD 3009CD)		
Jul 96.	(cd)(lp/c)	(CAD 6011CD)(CAD/+C 6011) <46020> **MIRACLE**		Sep96
		– Mountain / Time / The holy grail / Darkness, darkness / Miracle / Californian / Queen / Only human / Northern country. (cd re-iss. Jul98; GAD 6011CD)		

— In 1999, she and PATRICK FITZGERALD (ex-KITCHENS OF DISTINCTION) issued one single, 'NEEDLE'S EYE', under The LOST GIRLS moniker.

– compilations, etc. –

Mar 01.	(cd)	4 a.d.; (GAD 2KD010CD) **POMEGRANATE: AN ANTHOLOGY**		Jun01
		– Northern country / Time / The moon and the sun / Only human / Up in the air / Washington Square / Northshore train / The mountain (demo) / Mercury / One-string violin / Little fox / Follow / Cradle / Needle's eye / Up in the air (CD-Rom video).		

Cindy Lee BERRYHILL

Born: San Diego, California, USA. After pursuing theatre studies in L.A., CINDY LEE fell in with the local punk scene and formed her first band, The STOOPIDS (a few recordings do exist on cassette). Subsequently becoming disillusioned with her musical environment, BERRYHILL suffered a nervous breakdown and it was the second half of the decade before she fully recuperated. The stalwart singer-songwriter finally made it onto vinyl via a various artists compilation, 'The Radio Tokyo Tapes, Vol.3', the track in question being 'DAMN, WISH I WAS A MAN'. The latter song featured on her debut solo set, 'WHO'S GONNA SAVE THE WORLD' (1988), a record that gained a release through UK folkie imprint, 'New Routes'. Her LENNY KAYE-produced follow-up, 'NAKED MOVIE STAR' (1989) – on 'Awareness' UK – found her dabbling with jazz styles but failing to convince record buyers. At the turn of the decade, BERRYHILL suffered the loss of all her personal effects when they were stolen en route to her new home in San Diego. A few years later, her career was reactivated following interest from the 'Unique Gravity' stable, her long-awaited third set, 'GARAGE ORCHESTRA' (1994), named after her backing musicians. BERRYHILL suffered further misfortune as her boyfriend was injured in a serious motorbike crash. Although she nursed him through his ordeal, the resilient songstress found time to cut a fourth album, 'STRAIGHT OUTTA MARYSVILLE' (1996), issued via Britain's long-standing independent specialists, 'Demon'.
• **Covered:** SEASON OF THE WITCH (Donovan).

Album rating: WHO'S GONNA SAVE THE WORLD (*7) / NAKED MOVIE STAR (*7) / GARAGE ORCHESTRA (*6) / STRAIGHT OUTTA MARYSVILLE (*6) / LIVING ROOM 16 (*6)

CINDY LEE BERRYHILL – vocals, guitars, harmonica / with sessions from various personnel

New Routes / Rhino

Jun 88. (lp) *(RUE 001)* <70834> **WHO'S GONNA SAVE THE WORLD** – Nov87
– She had everything / Damn, I wish I was a man / Steve on H / Looking through portholes / Whatever works / Who's gonna save the world / Spe-c-i-al ingredient / Ceallaigh green / Ballad of a garage band / This administration / Heat.

Awareness / Rhino

Jul 89. (lp/c/cd) *(AWL/AWT/AWCD 1016)* <R1/R4/R2 70845> **NAKED MOVIE STAR**
– Me, Steve, Kirk and Keith / Old trombone routine / Supernatural fact / Indirectly yours / Trump / 12 dollar motel / Turn off the century / What's wrong with me / Yipee / Baby (should I have the baby?).

Sep 89. (7") *(AWP 001)* **ME, STEVE, KIRK AND KEITH. / BABY (SHOULD I HAVE THE BABY?)** – –
(12"+=) *(AWPX 001)* – 12 dollar motel.

—— In the early 90's, she encountered one ordeal after another (see above)

Unique Gravity / Earth Music – Cargo

Jul 95. (cd) *(UGCD 5502)* <008> **GARAGE ORCHESTRA** – Sep94
– Father of the seventh son / I wonder why / Radio astronomy / Gary Handeman / Song for Brian / UFO / Suite / I want stuff / Every someone tonight / The scariest thing in the world / Etude for ph. machine. *(re-iss. Apr98; same)*

Demon / Earth Music

Apr 96. (cd) *(FIENDCD 782)* <84503> **STRAIGHT OUTTA MARYSVILLE** – Mar96
– High jump / Unknown master painter / Diane / Season of the witch / Riddle riddle / Jane and John / The virtues of being apricot / Unwritten love song / Just like me / Talkin' with a mineral / I'm a tumbleweed / Caravan / Elvis of Marysville / California.

Griffith Park / Griffith Park

Mar 99. (cd) <*(GPR 001)*> **LIVING ROOM 16**
– Diane / She had everything / Family tree / Damn, I wish I was a man / This way up / UFO suite / Witness / I wonder why / Look at that grin / Gary Handeman / Every someone tonight.

BEVIS FROND

Formed: Walthamstow, London, England . . . 1987 by quintessential English eccentric, NICK SALOMAN, who had been part of the duo NICK & DICK, who became ODDSOCKS in 1975. They made one album, 'MEN OF THE MOMENT', for the 'Sweet Folk' label. In 1980, NICK formed the 5-piece, VON TRAPP FAMILY, which made an EP, 'BRAND NEW THRILL'. Two years later, the band became ROOM 13, releasing another single, 'MURDER MYSTERY'. Unfortunately, NICK was seriously injured in a motorcycle accident, using the compensation money to finance his next project, the solo BEVIS FROND. Early in 1987, he was back on vinyl with the 'MIASMA' album, a critically acclaimed, psychedelic guitar-rock feast – with influences ranging from JIMI HENDRIX and CREAM to folky punk – released on his own 'Woronzow' label. Another two albums, 'INNER MARSHLAND', and 'BEVIS THROUGH THE LOOKING GLASS', were issued during that year and several others followed, although he kept a low profile. In the late 80's, he also set up his own underground magazine 'Ptolemaic Terrascope'. In 1990, he recorded a collaboration album, 'MAGIC EYE', with the legendary PINK FAIRIES drummer TWINK. SALOMAN and The BEVIS FROND continued with his prolific release schedule, 'NORTH CIRCULAR' (1997), a double-CD that opened with 'STARS BURN OUT'; 'PSYCHEDELIC UNKNOWNS' was also a plus. Who was he lamenting about? The albums 'VAVONA BURR' (1999) – featuring 'Woodstock' icon COUNTRY JOE McDONALD on 'THE FROND CHEER' – 'VALEDICTORY SONGS' (2000) and 'WHAT DID FOR THE DINOSAURS' (2002) continued the trend, and he was now employing "dinosaur" musicians ADRIAN SHAW (of HAWKWIND) and ANDY WARD (CAMEL). • **Covered:** XPRESS MAN (Groundhogs) / POSSESSION (Iron Butterfly) / SUMMER HOLIDAY EP (Cliff & The Shadows) / etc.

Album rating: MIASMA (*8) / INNER MARSHLAND (*6) / BEVIS THROUGH THE LOOKING GLASS (*4) / TRIPTYCH (*7) / THE AUNTIE WINNIE ALBUM (*5) / ANY GAS FASTER (*6) / MAGIC EYE (*6) / NEW RIVER HEAD (*8) / A GATHERING OF FRONDS compilation (*7) / IT JUST IS (*6) / LONDON STONE (*6) / BEATROOTS as Fred Bison Five (*5) / SPRAWL (*5) / SUPERSEEDER (*6) / SON OF WALTER (*6) / NORTH CIRCULAR (*5) / VAVONA BURR (*6) / VALEDICTORY SONGS (*6) / WHAT DID FOR THE DINOSAURS (*6)

NICK SALOMAN – vocals, guitar / plus **BARI WATTS** – guitar / **MICK WILLS** – acoustic guitar / **GRAHAM CUMMING** – piano

Woronzow / not iss.

1980. (7"ep; as VON TRAPP FAMILY) *(WOO 1)* **BRAND NEW THRILL. / DREAMING / NO REFLEXES** – –

SALOMAN + 2 others

1982. (12"; as ROOM 13) *(WOO 2)* **MURDER MYSTERY. / NEED SOME DUB** – –

NICK SALOMAN – vocals, instruments

Mar 87. (lp) *(WOO 3)* **MIASMA** – –
– Garden party / She's in love with time / Wild mind / Wild afterthought / Splendid isolation / The Earl of Walthamstow / The Newgate wind / Release yourself / Maybe / Ride the train of thought / Confusion days. *(re-iss. Jul89 on 'Reckless'; RECK 13)* *(cd-iss. Mar89+=; CDRECK 13)* – Rat in a waistcoat / In another year / Mudman / Now you know / 1970 home improvements. *(cd re-mast.Oct01 on 'Rubric'+=; RUB 18)* – Find my way home / I eat the air / Song from room 13 / Need all your loving / High wind in the trees / South Hampstead rain / Looks like rain #1.

Aug 87. (lp) *(WOO 4)* **INNER MARSHLAND** – –
– Cries from the inner marshland / Termination station grey / Window eye / Once more / Defoliation part one / Reflections in a tall mirror / Hey Mr. Undecided / I've got eyes in the back of my head / Minsmere sphagnum Sienese acid blues / Defoliation part two. *(re-iss. Jul89 on 'Reckless'; RECK 14)* *(cd-iss. Mar89 +=; CDRECK 14)* – I can't get into your scene / Song for the sky / The shrine. *(cd re-mast.Oct01 on 'Rubric'+=; RUB 19)* – Walking in the lady's garden / Slave / Run at the sun / Parapsynquiry / The great mistake / Solid vimto.

Dec 87. (d-lp) *(WOO 5)* **BEVIS THROUGH THE LOOKING GLASS – THE GREAT MAGNET DISASTER** – –
– Rat in a waistcoat / In another year / Mudman / Now you know / 1970 home improvements / I can't get into your scene / Song for the sky / Shrine / Die is cast / Purtle sline / Die is cast. *(re-iss. Dec88 on 'Reckless'; RECKD 9)*

Jun 88. (lp) *(WOO 6)* **ACID JAM** – –
– Long journey into light / The miskatonic variations.

—— BEVIS featured on OUTSKIRTS OF INFINITY lp 'Lord Of The Dark Skies' *WOO 7)*

Aug 88. (lp) *(WOO 8)* **TRIPTYCH** – –
– Into the cryptic mist / Debbie's new song for drums / Lights are changing / Gemini machine / Phil exorcises the Daemons / Old man blank / The daily round / Hurt goes on / Corinthian / Nowhere fast / Tangerine infringement beak / Hey Joe. *(re-iss. Mar89 on 'Reckless' cd+=/lp; CD+/RECK 15)* – Purtle sline / Soot / Long journey into light.

used occasional musicians; **MARTIN CROWLEY** – drums / **SHAW + GOODWAY**

Reckless / Reckless

Jul 89. (cd/lp) *(<CD+/RECK 17>)* **THE AUNTIE WINNIE ALBUM**
– Malvolios dream – Journey to Pikes / Foreign laugh / Down again / Will to lose / Repressor / Winters blues / The mizmaze / Close / Without mind / City of the sun. *(cd+=)* – Die is cast / The miskatonic variations.

Feb 90. (cd/lp) *(<CD+/RECK 18>)* **ANY GAS FASTER**
– Lord Plentiful reflects / Rejection day (a.m.) / Ear song / This corner of England / Legendary / When you wanted me / Lost rivers / Somewhere else / These dark days / Head on a pole / Your mind's gone grey / Old sea dog / Rejection day (p.m.) / Olde world.

Oct 90. (12"ep) *(RECK 20)* **EAR SONG / OLDE WORLDE. / I'VE GOT EYES IN THE BACK OF MY HEAD (live) / MEDIAEVAL SIENESE ACID BLUES (live) / OLDE WORLDE (live) / RADIO BLOODBEAST (live)**

Woronzow / Reckless

Feb 91. (lp/cd; by BEVIS & TWINK) *(WOO 13)* **MAGIC EYE** – –
– Sorrow remembered / Flying igloos / The fairy / She darks the sun / Eclipse / Fractured sky / Black queen / Gryke / Bag drip.

SALOMAN with **BARRY DRANSFIELD** – violin + **MARTIN CROWLEY** – drums

Sep 91. (d-lp/cd) *(WOO 16/+CD)* <CDRECK 24> **NEW RIVER HEAD**
– White sun / Drowned / She's entitled to / Waving / New river head / Wild jack hammer / He'd be a diamond / Undertaker / Stain on the sun / Thankless task / Mistatonic variations II / It won't come again / Chinese burn / God speed you to earth. *(d-lp+=)* – Down in the well / Motherdust / Cuvie / Solar marmalade / Son of many mothers / Hillview.

Dec 91. (7"ep; with PTOLEMAIC TERRASCOPE 8) *(WOO 16 1/2)* **SNOW EP** (out-takes from 'NEW RIVER HEAD' album) – –

Mar 92. (lp/cd; as MAGIC MUSCLE) *(WOO 17/+CD)* **GULP** – –
– (spoken intro) / A hailer of taxis / Spaced and displaced / Pipe call / Umbrellamental / Psymonic / Leaders / Finally the voice of little Willy (now gross, hairy and monstrously reformed).
(above "supergroup" featured **SALOMAN, ADRIAN SHAW, ROD GOODWAY, SIMON HOUSE + STEVE BROUGHTON**)

Nov 92. (lp/cd) *(WOO 18/+CD)* **LONDON STONE** – –
– Stonedance / Coming round / That same morning / Living soul / Still trying / Well out of it / A most singular hole / Freedom falling / London stone / Lord of nothing / And now she's gone / On a liquid wheel.

SALOMAN now with **CANDICE HOSTETTLER** – drums, cello, vocals / **GRAHAM MILLS-WAINWRIGHT** – organ, guitar, vocals / **RAY DEAN** – bass, guitar, vocals (actually only a 4-piece)

Feb 93. (lp/cd; as the FRED BISON FIVE) *(WOO 19/+CD)* **BEATROOTS** – –
– Girl guitar / I'm on edge / Psychedelic garden pt.1 / Psychedelic garden pt. 2 / Tell me something / Quagmirehead pt. 1 / Here to cry / Be ready / Down time / Fried slice / Quagmirehead pt.2 / Confused / Theme from 'Action Inc.' / The prowler / Quagmirehead pt.3 / Blowin' smoke. *(cd+=)* – Fuse blews / Soul destruction / Can't seem to figure it out.

— In Feb'93, TODD DILLINGHAM & NICK SALOMAN collaborated on a 'Voiceprint' cd, 'ART INTO DUST' (VP 121CD).

Jul 93. (7"ep) (WOO 20) **SUMMER HOLIDAY EP**
– Summer holiday / Big news / Dancing shoes / Round and round.

Oct 93. (d-lp/cd) (WOO 21/+CD) **IT JUST IS** (live)
– Can't stop lying / Time-share heart / Idiot dance / Desperate / What's it all about / Day one / Let me live / Terrible day / Dreamboat sinking / A sorry tale / Human overload / I can't catch up with you / Hit the lights / Everyday sunshine / Not for now / All gone / Time piece / And then?

Jul 94. (7") (EFA 40304-7) **LET'S LIVE FOR TODAY. /**
(above issued on 'Helter Skelter')

                                                              Woronzow Imprint
Oct 94. (d-lp/cd) (WOO 22/+CD) <92422> **SPRAWL**   Feb99
– I know we're going / Awake! / Love you more / The puller / Oh Gideon / Right on (hippie dream) / I bought my love a lapdog / New Alexandria / Anodyne – See you.

— live band included; **ANDY WARD** – drums (ex-CAMEL) / **ADRIAN SHAW** – bass (ex-HAWKWIND) / with **RIC GUNTHER + MARTIN CROWLEY** – occasional drums

Oct 95. (d-lp/cd) (WOO 26/+CD) <92426> **SUPERSEEDER**   Feb99
(compilation)
– Superseded / Dolly bug / Stoned train driver / Animal tracks / Jaye / I can't cry / Could be / Flashy / Golden walks of London / House of mountains / The queen of May / Sue me / Loveland / Could you fly higher? / Stranger's mirror / Story ends.

Oct 95. (7") (DAMGOOD 81) **DOLLY BUG. / GREEN PARK SATURDAY**
(above issued on 'Damaged Goods')

                                                              Woronzow Flydaddy
Oct 96. (d-lp/cd) (WOO 28/+CD) <FLY 022CD> **SON OF WALTER**
– Plastic Elvis / Beautiful sister / Red hair / You saw me coming / Barking or false point blues / Forgiven / All hope is gone with you away / Dead man sitting on a train / It's not like you / Garden aeroplane trap / Driven away / Raining on TV / Requiem / Winner's way / Goodnight from the band.

Apr 97. (7") (SPAREME 004) **LITTLE TOWN PIER. /**
(above on 'Spare Me')

Nov 97. (t-lp/d-cd) (W 406/+CD) <FLY 029CD> **NORTH CIRCULAR**   Feb99
– Stars burn out / Hole song No.2 / Sun room / Eyeshine / He had you / That's why you need us / Where the old boys go / Pips / Blew me out / Love is / Heritage coast / Stay at home girl / Growing up / Mind blew all around me / There's always one / Book / Psychedelic unknowns / You make me feel / Revival / Gold and silver / Her father's daughter / Stoneground head / Timothy's powders / For want of you / Stranger's mirror / Story ends.

May 99. (d-lp/cd) (W 031/+CD) <FLY 035CD> **VAVONA BURR**
– The Frond cheer / Leave a light on / Virus / Caught in the headlights / National drag / To the lighthouse / Couldn't care less / Don Lang / You just don't feel that way about me / Let it ride / One leg sand dance / Bulldozer / Coming down on you / Temple falls / Almost like being alive / Looks like rain / In her eyes / Begging bowl.

                                                              Woronzow Rubric
Nov 00. (d-lp/cd) (W 042/+CD) <RUB 11> **VALEDICTORY SONGS**   Dec00
– Godsent / By the water's edge / Early riser / Let them beautify you / High on a downer / Artillery row / We are the dead / Portobello man / Can't feel it / Sugar voids / Back on my star / The speed of light / Old school rock / Child / Living in real time / China fry / Confession.

Mar 02. (cd) (W 050CD) <RUB 41> **WHAT DID FOR THE DINOSAURS**   Apr02
– What did for the dinosaurs / The wrong side / Return of the stylites / The real deal / Our number / Splitting clingfilm / Silver dart / Yo-de-lo / Hold me up / Breathe out / Lost soul's day / Candles / Courtrai / Nursery rhyme / Good enough for you / Down to earth / The inhibition twist / Dustbins in the rain.

– compilations, etc –

May 92. (cd) *Reckless; (CDRECK 25)* **A GATHERING OF FRONDS**
– Down in the well / Mother dust / Cuvie / Blurred vision / Solar marmalade / Son of many mothers / Hillview (PARTHENOGENTICK BROTHERHOOD) / Bad time / High in a flat / Snow / Express man / African violet / Possession / Visions (through dilated eyes) (VACANT PLOT) / Somewhere else / Alistair Jones.

1990's. (7") (HELPF 101) **AFRICAN VIOLET. / The Steppes: History Hates No Man**

Apr 98. (lp; by DOCTOR FROND) *Magic Gnome; (MG 429932-2)* **DOCTOR FROND**

BIBLE

Formed: Norwich, England . . . 1985 out of Cambridge outfit, The GREAT DIVIDE, by BOO HEWERDINE and KEVIN FLANAGAN. The latter combo released a handful of singles before the duo, along with newcomers TONY SHEPHERD and CLIVE LAWSON formed The BIBLE. A few classy 45's (including the definitive 'GRACELAND' and 'MAHALIA' – named after gospel singer, MAHALIA JACKSON) both from the mini-lp, 'WALKING THE GHOST BACK HOME', brought comparisons to The SMITHS. Released on local label, 'Backs', the record caused enough of a stir to see the band – now augmented by NEIL MacCOLL (brother of KIRSTY) and new drummer DAVE LARCOMBE – snapped up by 'Chrysalis'; the label duly re-issued the aforementioned 'GRACELANDS' early in 1987, confident of at least a decent sized hit. It flopped however, and the band retired to work on their first album proper, the STEVE EARLE-produced 'EUREKA' (1988). A collection of soft-ish romantic rock, lying somewhere between contemporaries CHINA CRISIS, DANNY WILSON or The BIG DISH, this UK Top 75 breakthrough surprisingly failed to spawn any hits, at least first time round; 'HONEY BE GOOD' became a belated minor success upon its re-release in summer '89. By this time, HEWERDINE had already found a new musical foil in the shape of Texas troubadour, DARDEN SMITH, the pair collaborating on a one-off album, 'EVIDENCE'. HEWERDINE's solo work – which also included 1992's 'IGNORANCE' – was similarly unsuccessful (although ironically EDDI READER took his 'Patience Of Angels' into the UK Top 40 in 1994) and together with SHEPHERD and LARCOMBE he re-formed The BIBLE. This proved to be short-lived, the band's guiding light taking his songs and releasing them (as 'BAPTIST HOSPITAL') under his own name. • **Songwriters:** HEWERDINE writes most w / SHEPHERD except; ABRAHAM, MARTIN & JOHN (Marvin Gaye) / ON BROADWAY (Drifters).

Album rating: WALKING THE GHOST BACK HOME mini (*6) / THE BIBLE (*8) / EUREKA (*7) / THE BEST OF THE BIBLE compilation (*7) / Boo Hewerdine: EVIDENCE with Darden Smith (*7) / IGNORANCE with Darden Smith (*6) / BAPTIST HOSPITAL (*6) / THANKSGIVING (*5) / ANON (*5)

GREAT DIVIDE

BOO HEWERDINE (b. MARCUS) – vocals, guitar / **KEVIN FLANAGAN** – saxophone / +?

                                                              Wimp   not iss.
Dec 82. (7") (WIMP 004) **WHO BROKE THE LOVE BANK. / BLESS MY SOUL**
                                                              Ensign   not iss.
Oct 83. (7"/12") (ENY/12ENY 504) **WHISPERED IN HEAVEN. / SWEAT**

Apr 84. (7"/12") (ENY/12ENY 512) **MONEY AND TIME. / ANIMATION TIME**
                                                              Blue
                                                              Murder   not iss.
Oct 84. (12"ep) (BLUE 701) **IT'S GOT TO BE LOVE / THE DYING ART OF CONVERSATION. / THE TALKING BLUES (LIE FOR YOU, DIE FOR YOU, DO ANYTHING FOR YOU) / I.O.U.T.L.C.**

BIBLE

BOO HEWERDINE + KEVIN FLANAGAN / plus **TONY SHEPHERD** – keyboards, drums / **CLIVE LAWSON** – bass

                                                              Backs   not iss.
Mar 86. (m-lp) (NCHLP 8) **WALKING THE GHOST BACK HOME**
– Red flag / Talk to me like Jackie Kennedy / Walking the ghost back home / She's my bible / Mahalia (Newport '58) / Kid Galahad and the chrome kinewa / King Chicago. *(cd-iss. Oct88; NCHCD 8) (cd re-iss. Nov95 on 'Haven'; HAVENCD 4)*

Apr 86. (7") (NCH 109) **GRACELAND. / SWEETNESS**

— **LEROY LENDOR** – bass; repl. LAWSON

Nov 86. (7") (NCH 111) **MAHALIA. / SPEND, SPEND, SPEND**
(12"+=) – (12NCH 111) – Sweetness.

— **DAVE LARCOMBE** – drums; repl. FLANAGAN (who was still a future guest)

— added **NEIL MacCOLL** – guitar, mandolin (ex-ROARING BOYS) / guest **CONSTANCE REDGRAVE** – bass

                                                              Chrysalis Chrysalis
Feb 87. (7") (BIB 1) **GRACELAND. / GLORYBOUND**
(12"+=) – (BIBX 2) – High, wide & handsome / The slow drag down (live) / Walking the ghost back home (live).
(d7"+=) – (BIBD 2) – Mahalia (Newport '58) / Spend, spend, spend.

— **GREG HAREWOOD** – bass; repl. CONSTANCE

Jan 88. (lp/c/cd) (CHR/ZCHR/CCD 1646) **EUREKA**   71
– Skywriting / Honey be good / Skeleton crew / November brides / Cigarette girls / Crystal Palace / The wishing game / Red Hollywood / Tiny lights / Blues shoes stepping. *(re-dist.May88; same) (cd re-iss. Nov95 on 'Haven'; HAVENCD 5)*

Apr 88. (7") (BIB 2) **CRYSTAL PALACE. / THE GOLDEN MILE**
(12"+=) – (BIBX 2) – Bubblehead / The slow drag down.
(cd-s+=) – (BIBCD 2) – Graceland / Mahalia (Newport '58).

Sep 88. (7") (BIB 3) **HONEY BE GOOD. / WHITE FEATHERS**
(12"+=) – (BIBX 3) – Coming of age / Up in smoke.
(cd-s+=) – (BIBCD 3) – Glorybound (live) / Abraham, Martin & John.

Nov 88. (7") <VS 443177> **SKYWRITING. / CRYSTAL PALACE**

Apr 89. (7") (BIB 4) **GRACELAND (new version). / EUREKA**   51
(c-s+=) – (BIBMC 4) – Graceland (original).
(12"+=/cd-s+=) – (BIB X/CD 4) – Hide, wide & handsome (parts 1 & 2).

Aug 89. (7"/c-s) (BIB/+MC 5) **HONEY BE GOOD. / KING CHICAGO (new version)**   54
(12"+=) – (BIBX 5) – Skywriting / Elastic money.
(cd-s+=) – (BIBCD 5) – Crystal Palace / On Broadway.

Sep 89. (lp/c/cd) (CHR/ZCHR/CCD 1732) **THE BEST OF THE BIBLE**   67
(compilation)
– Graceland / Crystal Palace / Honey be good / Skeleton crew / Red Hollywood / Abraham, Martin & John / Skywriting / Glory bound / Up in smoke / Blue shoes stepping / Cigarette girls / The golden mile.

BOO HEWERDINE

— with **DARDEN SMITH** who was a troubadour from Austin, Texas. Others on album; **MARTIN LASCELLES** – keyboards / **I.D. FOSTER** – bass / **PAUL PEARCY** – drums / **REESE WYNANS** – keyboards / **SONNY LANDREATH** – guitar / **CHRIS BIRKETT** – percussion / **SYD STRAW** – vocals

                                                              Ensign   Chrysalis
Jul 89. (7"; BOO HEWERDINE & DARDEN SMITH) (ENY 625) **ALL I WANT IS EVERYTHING. / SOUTH BY SOUTH WEST**
(12"+=/cd-s+=) – (ENY X/CD 625) – Tell me why.
                                                              Chrysalis Compas
Aug 89. (lp/c/cd; BOO HEWERDINE & DARDEN SMITH) (CHR/ZCHR/CCD 1726) <74232> **EVIDENCE**
– All I want is everything / Reminds me (a little of you) / These chains / Out of this world / Evidence / Who, what, where and why / Under the darkest Moon / South by south west / The first chill of winter / Love is a strange hotel / Oil on the water / A town called Blue. *(cd re-iss. Nov95 on 'Haven'; HAVENCD 6)*
                                                              Ensign   Compass
Feb 92. (cd)(c/lp) (CCD 1930)(Z+/CHEN 24) <7 4235-2> **IGNORANCE**
– I remember – The ship song / 59 yds / Sweet invisible / Swan silvertone / Touched / Little bits of zero / 16 miles / Gravity / Ignorance / A slow divorce / History. (cd+=) – Talk me down / The ghost of Johnny Ray / Liberty horses / The ghost of summer walking. *(re-iss. cd Nov95 on 'Haven')*

BIBLE (cont)

Mar 92. (12"ep/cd-ep) (ENY X/CD 653) **HISTORY / LITTLE BITS OF ZERO. / TALK ME DOWN / THE GHOST OF JOHNNY RAY**
May 92. (12"ep/cd-ep) (ENY X/CD 654) **59 YDS. / LIBERTY HORSES. / GHOST OF SUMMER WALKING / 16 MILES (version)**

BIBLE

— re-formed with **HEWERDINE, SHEPHERD + LARCOMBE**

Blanco Y Negro / Discovery

Dec 94. (c-ep/12"ep/cd-ep) (NEG 78 C/T/CD) **THE DREAMLIFE E.P.**
 – Mosquito / Firedogs / Explaining love to aliens.

— split just after the above's release. An album, RANDOM ACTS OF KINDNESS' was withdrawn by 'Haven'; HAVENCD 8) although HEWERDINE released the songs as his own solo material below …

BOO HEWERDINE

— with a plethora of musicians

Blanco Y Negro / Discovery

Nov 95. (c-s) (NEG 83 C/CD) **WORLD'S END / ONE SAD COWBOY**
 (cd-s+=) (NEG 83CDX) – A mess of blues.
Jan 96. (cd/c) (0630 12045-2/-4) <7704-2> **BAPTIST HOSPITAL**
 – World's end / The love thieves / Last cigarette / Dreamlife / Joke / Baptist hospital / A song for a friend / Candyfloss / Sycamore fall / Holy water / Junk / Greedy.
Feb 96. (c-s) (NEG 86C) **JOKE / AUCTIONEERS**
 (cd-s+=) (NEG 86CD) – Black cat / Firedog.
 (cd-s) (NEG 86CDX) – ('A'side) / First day in Hell / Buzz Aldrin / I miss you – Sha la la.

Black Burst / Compass

Apr 99. (cd) (BLACKCD 002) <7 4267-2> **THANKSGIVING**
 – The birds are leaving / Swansong / Hope is a name / Lazy heart / Water song / 'Our boy' / Bell, book and candle / Thanksgiving / Footsteps fall / Homesick son / Eve / A long winter / Murder in the dark / Please don't ask me to dance. (re-iss. Jan02; same)

Haven / not iss.

Oct 01. (cd-ep) (HAVENT 6CD) **EXTRAS**
 – Sweet on the vine / Extras / Dream baby / A cloud no bigger than your hand.
Jun 02. (cd) (HAVENCD 15) **ANON**
 – Kite / Anon / Dream baby / A cloud no bigger than your hand / Apple tree / The Devil takes care of his own / Extras / Peacetime / Roundabout / Hunger / Looking for a light on the rails / Mapping the human heart.

– compilations, etc. –

Mar 02. (cd) Madan; (LIVE 001) **A LIVE ONE** – / – gigs
 – Bell, book and candle / Sweet on the vine / Joke / Wings on my wheels / Murder in the dark / Graceland / Please don't ask me to dance / The border / Patience of angels / World's end / The birds are leaving / Lucky penny / Soul / Paper planes.

BIFF BANG POW! (see under ⇒ McGEE, Alan)

BIG BLACK

Formed: Evanston, Illinois, USA … 1982 by mainman STEVE ALBINI (vocals/guitar). The first official release, 'LUNGS' appeared later that year on local independent label, 'Ruthless', a six-track drum-machine driven EP that announced ALBINI's intent to take punk/hardcore into uncharted territory. Now with an expanded line-up numbering SANTIAGO DURANGO on guitar and JEFF PEZZATI on bass, the BIG BLACK trio unleashed two more 12"ep's/mini-lp's in the mid 80's, 'BULLDOZER' (1983) and 'RACER X' (1985), prior to the seminal 'IL DUCE' single in '86. Replacing PEZZATI with DAVE RILEY (aka LOVERING), they created a minor hardcore classic in 'ATOMIZER' (1986), its bleak examinations of small-town American despair a theme which would be echoed countless times by their grunge/industrial successors. With DURANGO off to study law, MERVIN BELLI came in for the inflammatory titled, 'SONGS ABOUT *!?KING', BIG BLACK giving their all on an album which they knew would be their last. However, they did bow out in uncharacteristic style with a double A-sided 45 covering Cheap Trick's 'HE'S A WHORE' and 'Kraftwerk's 'THE MODEL'. Taking his twisted vision to its warped conclusion, ALBINI formed the controversially named RAPEMAN with two former SCRATCH ACID players, DAVID WM. SIMS and REY WASHAM. It wasn't just the name that provoked outrage, tracks such as 'HATED CHINEE', 'SUPERPUSSY' and 'KIM GORDON'S PANTIES' causing a fuss which possibly contributed to ALBINI abandoning the operation early in '89. Having already turned in classic productions for the likes of The PIXIES ('Surfer Rosa'), ALBINI, along with BUTCH VIG became one of the highest profile and most respected/hard working figures of the grunge era (credits include NIRVANA, TAD, PJ HARVEY, etc). ALBINI's other side project, SHELLAC, was first conceived in 1992 along with drummer TODD TRAINER although it only took vinyl form after BOB WESTON began working for STEVE in his Chicago studio. A sporadic string of singles ('URANUS', 'THE ADMIRAL' and 'THE RUDE GESTURE: A PICTORIAL HISTORY') emerged on 'Touch & Go', suggesting a natural progression from BIG BLACK in terms of blackboard-scraping guitar, painfully sardonic lyrics and general sonic terrorism. A debut album, 'AT ACTION PARK', appeared in late '94 although given ALBINI's hectic schedule it'd be a further four years before the slightly disappointing 'TERRAFORM' (1998) hit the shelves. After further singles, haphazard live appearances and the obligatory Peel Session,

ALBINI & Co emerged blinking into the new millennium with '1000 HURTS' (2000). As raw, contrary and defiantly unconventional as ever, the record lurched along in the by now well established SHELLAC mould; unlikely to win over new fans but a rich source of perverse treats for diehards. • **Songwriters:** ALBINI and group compositions except; HEARTBEAT (Wire) / REMA REMA (Rema Rema) / Rapeman: JUST GOT PAID (ZZ Top).
Album rating: RACER-X mini (*5) / ATOMIZER (*7) / SONGS ABOUT *!?KING (*8) / PIGPILE live compilation (*7) / Rapeman: TWO NUNS AND A BLACK MULE (*7) / Shellac: AT ACTION PARK (*6) / TERRAFORM (*7) / 1000 HURTS (*8)

STEVE ALBINI – vocals, guitar

not iss. / Ruthless

Nov 82. (12"ep) <RRBB 02> **LUNGS**
 – Steelworker / Live in a hole / Dead Billy / I can be killed / Crack / R.I.P. (UK-iss.Nov92 on 'Touch & Go'; TG 89)

— added **SANTIAGO DURANGO** – guitar (ex-NAKED RAYGUN, ex-SILVER ABUSE) / **JEFF PEZZATI** – bass (ex-NAKED RAYGUN) / + on session 4th member **PAT BYRNE** – drums

Nov 83. (12"ep) <RRBB 07> **BULLDOZER**
 – Cables / Pigeon kill / I'm a mess / Texas / Seth / Jump the climb. (UK-iss.Nov92 on 'Touch & Go'; TG 90)

Homestead / Homestead

Apr 85. (m-lp) <(HMS 007)> **RACER-X** 1984
 – Racer-x / Shotgun / The ugly American / Deep six / Sleep! / Big payback. (re-iss. Nov92 on 'Touch & Go'; TG 91)
Sep 86. (7") (HMS 042) **IL DUCE. / BIG MONEY** 1985
 (re-iss. Nov92 on 'Touch & Go'; TG 96)

— **DAVE RILEY** (aka LOVERING) – bass (ex-SAVAGE BELIEFS) repl. PEZZATI / drum machine replaced BYRNE

Sep 86. (lp) <(HMS 43)> **ATOMIZER**
 – Jordan, Minnesota / Passing complexion / Big money / Kerosene / Bad houses / Kerosene / Fists of love / Stinking drunk / Bazooka Joe / Strange things. (re-iss. Nov86 on 'Blast First'; BFFP 11) (re-iss. Nov92 on 'Touch & Go' lp/cd; TG 93/+CD)

Blast First / Touch&Go

Jun 87. (12"ep/c-ep) (BFFP 14/+C) <TG 20> **HEADACHE** 1986
 – My disco / Grinder / Ready men / Pete, king of all detectives.
 (free 7"w.a./tracks on c-ep) (TG 21) – HEARTBEAT. / THINGS TO DO TODAY / I CAN'T BELIEVE (UK re-iss. Nov92 on 'Touch & Go'; TG 20)

— **MELVYN BELLI** – guitar; repl. DURANGO

Jul 87. (lp/c/cd) (BFFP 19/+C/CD) <TG 24/+C/CD> **SONGS ABOUT *!?KING**
 – The power of independent trucking / The model / Bad penny / El doper / Precious thing / Columbian neck-tie / Kitty empire / Ergot / Kashmir S. Pulasiday / Fish fry / Pavement saw / Tiny, the king of the Jews / Bombastic intro. (re-iss. Nov92 on 'Touch & Go' lp/cd +=; TG 24/+CD) – He's A Whore.
Aug 87. (7") (BFFP 24) <TG 23> **HE'S A WHORE. / THE MODEL**
 (re-iss. Nov92 on 'Touch & Go'; TG 23)

— Disbanded in 1988.

– compilations, etc. –

Mar 87. (lp) Homestead; (HMS 044) **THE HAMMER PARTY**
 – (LUNGS + BULLDOZER) (re-iss. Nov92 on 'Touch & Go' lp/cd +=; TG 92/+CD) – RACER-X
Jun 87. (lp) Not 2; (BUT 1) **SOUND OF IMPACT (live bootleg)**
 (re-iss. 1990)
Jan 88. (cd) Blast First; (BFFP 23) **THE RICH MAN'S EIGHT TRACK TAPE**
 – (ATOMIZER + HEADACHE + HEARTBEAT) (re-iss. Nov92 on 'Touch & Go'; TG 94CD)
Oct 89. (lp/c/cd) Blast First; (BFFP 49/+C/CD) **BIG BLACK LIVE** (live)
Oct 92. (lp/cd) Touch & Go; <(TG 81/+CD)> **PIGPILE** (live)

RAPEMAN

— were formed by **ALBINI** with **DAVID WM. SIMS** – bass / **REY WASHAM** – drums (both ex-SCRATCH ACID, latter ex-BIG BOYS)

not iss. / Fierce

1988. (7") <none> **HATED CHINEE. / MARMOSET**

Blast First / Touch & Go

Nov 88. (12"ep) (BFFP 27) <TG 34> **BUDD (live) / SUPERPUSSY (live). / LOG BASS (live) / DUTCH COURAGE**
Dec 88. (lp/c/cd) (BFFP 33/+C/CD) <TG 36/+C/CD> **TWO NUNS AND A BLACK MULE**
 – Steak and black onions / Monobrow / Up beat / Cotition ignition mission / Kim Gordon's panties / Hated Chinee / Radar love wizard / Marmoset / Just got paid / Trouser minnow. (cd+=) – Budd / Superpussy / Log brass / Dutch courage.

Sub Pop / Sub Pop

Aug 89. (7",7"clear) <SP 40)> **INKI'S BUTT CRACK. / SONG NUMBER ONE**

— Had to split in Feb'89 due to the backlash against group name. SIMS returned to Austin, where he re-united with ex-SCRATCH ACID members to form JESUS LIZARD. They were produced by ALBINI who continued as a producer, notably for others The PIXIES, The BREEDERS, NIRVANA, WEDDING PRESENT. ALBINI formed below in '93.

SHELLAC

STEVE ALBINI – guitar, vocals / **BOB WESTON** – bass (ex-VOLCANO SONS) / **TODD TRAINER** – drums (ex-RIFLE SPORT, etc)

Touch & Go / Touch & Go

1993. (7"ep) <TG 123> **THE RUDE GESTURE: A PICTORIAL HISTORY EP**
 – The guy who invented fire / Rambler song / Billiard player song.

BIG BLACK (cont)

1993.	(7"ep)	<TG 124>	**URANUS EP**	-	
			– Doris / Wingwalker.		
1994.	(7"ep)		**THE BIRD IS THE MOST POPULAR FINGER**	-	
			– XVI (aka Pull the cup) / The admiral.		
			(above issued on 'Drag City')		
Oct 94.	(lp/c/cd)	<(TG 141/+C/CD)>	**AT ACTION PARK**		Sep94
			– My black ass / Pull the cup / The admiral / Crow / Song of the minerals / A minute / The idea of north / Dog and pony show / Boche's dick / Il porno star.		
1997.	(cd)		**THE FUTURIST** (10 movements)	-	
May 98.	(lp/cd)	<(TG 200/+CD)>	**TERRAFORM**		Feb98
			– Didn't we deserve a look at you the way you really are / This is a picture / Disgrace / Mouthpiece / Canada / Rush job / House full of garbage / Copper.		
Jul 00.	(lp/cd)	<(TG 211/+CD)>	**1000 HURTS**		
			– Prayer to God / Squirrel song / Mama Gina / Q.R.L. / Ghosts / Song against itself / Canaveral / New number order / Shoe song / Watch song.		

BIG DIPPER (see under ⇒ EMBARRASSMENT)

BIG FLAME

Formed: Manchester, England . . . 1983 by ALAN BROWN, DAVID 'DIL' GREEN and GREG O'KEEFE. Taking up where The POP GROUP or PERE UBU left off, BIG FLAME unleashed their breakneck, psychotic BEEFHEART-like stutters on a number of 45's in the mid 80's for the cult 'Ron Johnson' imprint. A ten-inch compilation EP of the aforementioned tracks, 'TWO KAN GURU', was released in the summer of '86 immediately prior to their best and penultimate workfest, 'CUBIST POP MANIFESTO'. Having taken their chosen sound to its limits, the BIG FLAME finally extinguished itself as ALAN and DIL attempted to make a GREAT LEAP FORWARD. This revamped outfit issued a further couple of forgettable EP's in the latter half of the 80's, later disbanding at the turn of the decade.

Album rating: TWO KAN GURU (*6)

ALAN BROWN – vocals, guitar / **GREG O'KEEFE** – bass / **DAVID 'DIL' GREEN** – drums

				Laughing Gun	not iss.
Apr 84.	(7"m)	(PLAQUE 001)	**SINK. / THE ILLNESS / SOMETIMES**		-
				Ron Johnson	not iss.
Mar 85.	(7"ep)	(ZRON 3)	**RIGOUR**		-
			– Debra / Man of few syllables / Where's our Carol.		
Sep 85.	(7"ep)	(ZRON 4)	**TOUGH!**		-
			– All the Irish must go to Heaven / Sargasso / !Cuba!		
May 86.	(7"m)	(ZRON 7)	**WHY POPSTARS CAN'T DANCE. / !CHANEL SAMBA! / BREATH OF OF A NATION**		-
Jul 86.	(10"ep)	(RERON 8)	**TWO KAN GURU**		-
			– Sink / Sometimes / Man of few syllables / Sargasso / All the Irish (must go to Heaven) / Cuba!		
Dec 86.	(7"pink-ep)	(ZRON 13)	**CUBIST POP MANIFESTO**		-
			– Baffled island (the hard rock movement) / Cat with colic / Earsore.		
Feb 87.	(12"ep)	(ZRON 16)	**CUBIST POP MANIFESTO**		-
			– New way / Where's our Carol / Cat with colic / Baffled island / Let's rewrite the American constitution / XPQWRTZ / Earsore.		

— when GREG went off to become MEATMOUTH, **ALAN + DIL** changed their name (see further below)

– compilations, etc. –

| Dec 96. | (cd) | Drag City; (DC 19) | **RIGOUR** | | |

GREAT LEAP FORWARD

ALAN + DIL

Apr 87.	(12"ep)	(ZRON 20)	**CONTROLLING THE EDGES OF TONE**		-
			– Hope's not enough son, ask your parents / If the C.A.P.'s flat, waive it / Let's jive while we're still alive / My grandfather's cluck.		
Nov 87.	(12"ep)	(ZRON 27)	**A PECK ON THE CHEEK A LA POLITIQUE**		-
			– A peck on the cheek / The nose of the king / Propping up the nose of the king.		
Apr 88.	(12")	(ZRON 34)	**WHO WORKS THE WEATHER? / WHO WORKS THE WEATHER**		
				Communications Unique	not iss.
Apr 89.	(lp)	(CULP 1)	**DON'T BE AFRAID OF CHANGE** (compilation)		-
			– Bereavement of speech / Hope's not enough son / Let's jive while we're still alive / A peck on the cheek / Who works the weather? / Controlling the edges of tone / Ask your parents / My grandfathers clock / The noise of the king. (re-iss. Feb90 as 'THE GREAT LEAP FORWARD SEASON 87-88' lp/cd+=; CU 003/004) – (demos; see above).		
Nov 89.	(12"ep)	(12CU 002)	**HEART AND SOUL**		-

— split early in 1990

BIG STAR

Formed: when ALEX CHILTON headed back to Memphis, where he hooked up with his old schoolfriend CHRIS BELL to form the hugely influential but desperately unlucky BIG STAR. The first two albums sounded like a rougher take on the pop sensibilities of The BEATLES and The BEACH BOYS, with the 1972 debut 'NO.1 RECORD', especially, having great commercial potential. Guitarist BELL acted as a foil for CHILTON's inspired outpourings and the album contained such acoustic gems as 'BALLAD OF EL GOODOO'. Despite garnering rave reviews, the album failed to sell, due almost wholly to the distribution problems of their label 'Ardent' (a 'Stax' offshoot). BELL left at the end of '72, after a fallout with CHILTON over live work, the upshot being that BIG STAR became CHILTON's "power-pop" baby. Generally thought to be his artistic peak, early '74's 'RADIO CITY' had a gloriously raw spontaneity, with 'SEPTEMBER GURLS' proving the pained highlight. Distribution problems continued to dog Ardent and as the record stiffed, BIG STAR gradually broke up. Although released under the BIG STAR moniker, 'BIG STAR'S THE THIRD ALBUM', later re-released as 'SISTER LOVERS', was more or less the work of CHILTON. A difficult album, although none the less rewarding, it showcased a vulnerable man exorcising his demons in haunting and deeply introspective songs. CHRIS BELL's similarly downbeat 'I AM THE COSMOS', was recorded just before his death in a car accident in 1978, and was posthumously released by 'Rykodisc' in the early 90's. In 1979, CHILTON re-surfaced after a quiet period in New York, where his makeshift band toured with the likes of TELEVISION and The CRAMPS, whom he went on to produce. That same year saw him record the folk-punk 'BANGKOK' single and 'FLIES ON SHERBET', a cult classic which featured a hotch-potch of inspired covers and CHILTON originals. In the 80's, he worked with TAV FALCO under the name The PANTHER BURNS before releasing a solo album 'HIGH PRIEST' in 1987, a fairly enjoyable romp through a patchwork of ragged styles. The praise lavished upon BIG STAR by the likes of PRIMAL SCREAM and TEENAGE FANCLUB, brought about a renaissance of sorts, and CHILTON re-formed the band in 1993. He also released a further solo album in 1995, 'A MAN CALLED DESTRUCTION'.

Album ratings: Big Star: #1 RECORD (*7) / RADIO CITY (*7) / SISTER LOVERS – THIRD ALBUM (*8) / Alex Chilton: LIKE FLIES ON SHERBET (*7) / BLACK LIST (*4) / 19 YEARS: A COLLECTION compilation (*7) / COLUMBIA: LIVE AT MISSOURI UNIVERSITY (*4; Big Star) / CLICHES (*5) / A MAN CALLED DESTRUCTION (*3)

CHRIS BELL (b.12 Jan'51, Memphis) – vocals, guitar / plus **ALEX CHILTON** / **ANDY HUMMEL** (b.26 Jan'51) – bass / **JODY STEPHENS** (b. 4 Oct'52) – drums

				not iss.	Ardent
Apr 72.	(lp)	<ADS 1501>	**#1 RECORD**	-	
			– Feel / The ballad of El Goodo / In the street / Don't lie to me / Thirteen / The India song / When my baby's beside me / My life is right / Give me another chance / Try again / Watch the sunrise / St 100-6. (re-iss. Nov86 & Jan90 on 'Big Beat' lp/c; WIK/+C 53)		
Apr 72.	(7")	<2902>	**IN THE STREET. / WHEN MY BABY'S BESIDE ME**	-	
Jul 72.	(7")	<2904>	**DON'T LIE TO ME. / WATCH THE SUNRISE**	-	

— now trio when BELL left to go solo, He's killed in car crash 27th Dec'78.

Feb 74.	(lp)	<ADS 2803>	**RADIO CITY**	-	
			– O, my soul / Life is white / Way out west / What's going on / You got what you deserve / Mod Lang / Back of a car / Daisy glaze / She's a mover / September gurls / Morpha too – I'm in love with a girl. (re-iss. Nov86 & Mar95 on 'Big Beat' lp/c; WIK/+C 54)		
Feb 74.	(7")	<2909>	**O, MY SOUL. / MORPHATOO – I'M IN LOVE WITH A GIRL**	-	
May 74.	(7")	<2912>	**SEPTEMBER GURLS. / MOD LANG** (UK-iss.Sep78 on 'Stax'; STAX 504)	-	
1974.	(7"; as BOX TOPS)	<0199>	**WILLOBEE AND DALE. / I'M GONNA BE ALRIGHT**	-	

— ALEX CHILTON now sole BIG STAR with session people, incl. STEPHENS + STEVE CROPPER. In 1975, after recording below album, they disbanded. It was finally released.

				Aura	P.V.C.
Jul 78.	(lp)	(AUL 703) <7903>	**BIG STAR'S THE THIRD ALBUM**		
			– Stroke it Noel / For you / Kizza me / You can't have me / Nightime / Blue moon / Take care / Jesus Christ / Femme fatale / O Dana / Big black car / Holocaust / Kangaroo / Thank you friends. (re-iss. 1987 on 'Dojo' lp/cd; DOJO LP/CD 55) <US re-iss. Nov87 lp/c/cd; PVC/+C/CD 8917> (UK cd-iss. Mar92 & Apr97 on 'Rykodisc'; RCD 10220) (cd re-iss. Oct94 on 'Line'; LICD 900492)		
Jul 78.	(7")	(AUS 103)	**KIZZA ME. / DREAM LOVER**		-
Dec 78.	(7")	(AUS 107)	**JESUS CHRIST. / BIG BLACK CAR**		-

– (BIG STAR) compilations etc. –

Jul 78.	(d-lp)	Stax; (SXSP 302)	**#1 RECORD / RADIO CITY**		
			(cd-iss. Jun87 & Jan90 on 'Big Beat'; CDWIK 910) – (omits; In the street / St 100-6.		
1988.	(lp)	Line; (LILP 400509)	**BIG STAR'S BIGGEST**	-	- German
			– The ballad of El Goodo / In the street / Don't lie to me / When my baby's beside me / Try again / Watch the sunrise / Life is white / What's goin' ahn / Back of a car / She's a mover / Way out west / September gurls / Jesus Christ / O'Dana / Holocaust / Kangaroo / Big black car / Thank you friends. (UK cd-iss. Oct94; LICD 900509)		
Mar 92.	(cd)	Rykodisc; (RCD 10221)	**LIVE**		-
			(re-iss. Apr97; same)		
Dec 99.	(cd)	Big Beat; (CDWIKK 197)	**THE BEST OF BIG STAR**		-

ALEX CHILTON

went solo in 1977, with **RICHARD ROSEBROUGH** – drums / etc.

				not iss.	Ork
1977.	(lp)	<81978>	**ONE DAY IN NEW YORK**	-	
1977.	(12"ep)		**SINGER NOT THE SONG**	-	
				Aura	Peabody
Feb 80.	(lp)	(AUL 710)	**LIKE FLIES ON SHERBET**		
			– Boogie shoes / My rival / Hey! little child / Hook or crook / I've had it / Rock hard / Girl after girl / Waltz across Texas / Alligator man / Like flies on sherbet. (cd-iss. Sep92 on 'Great Expectations'+=; – No more the Moon shines on Lorena. (cd re-iss. Oct94 on 'Line'; LICD 900486) (cd re-iss. Jan96 on 'Cooking Vinyl'; COOKCD 095)		
Jun 80.	(7")	(AUS 117)	**HEY! LITTLE CHILD. / NO MORE THE MOON SHINES ON LORENA**		

— with **KNOX** – guitar / **MATTHEW SELIGMAN** – bass + **MORRIS WINDSOR** – drums

BIG STAR (cont)

				Line	not iss.
1981.	Line; (lp) <OLLP 5081> **BACH'S BOTTOM** (rec.1975)			-	- German

– Take me home / Make me like it / Everytime I close my eyes / All of the time / Oh baby I'm free / I'm so tired (parts 1 & 2) / Free again / Jesus Christ / The singer not the song / Summertime blues / Take me home again. *(cd-iss. Nov87; LICD 900091) (cd re-iss. Mar97 on 'Razor & Tie'; RE 2010)*

Jan 83. (lp) *(OLLP 5264)* **LIVE IN LONDON** (live)
– Bangkok / Tramp / In the street / Hey little child / Nightime / Rock hard / Alligator man / The letter / Train kept a rollin' / Kanga roo / My rival / Stranded on a dateless night / September gurls / No more the Moon shines on Lorena. *(cd-iss. May93 on 'Rev-Ola'; CREV 015CD)*

				New Rose	Big Time
Jul 85.	(m-lp) *(ROSE 68)* **FEUDALIST TARTS**			-	- France

– Tee ni nee ni noo – Tip on in / Stuff / B-A-B-Y / Thank you John / Lost my job / Paradise. *(cd-iss. 1986 as 'STUFF'; ROSE 68CD)* – (with 10 extra tracks).

May 86. (7") *(NEW 068)* **NO SEX. / UNDERCRASS** - - France
(12"+=) *(NEW12 068)* – Wild kingdom.
(d7"+=) *(NEW 69)* – September gurls / I'm gonna make you mine (live Paris'85).

Nov 87. (7") *(NEW 96)* **MAKE A LITTLE MOVE. / LONELY WEEKENDS** - - France
Nov 87. (lp/c/cd) *(ROSE 130/+C/CD)* **HIGH PRIEST** - - France
– Take it off / Let me get close to you / Dalai Lama * / Volare / Thing for you / Forbidden love / Make a little love / Trouble don't last / Don't be a drag / Nobody's fool / Come by here / Raunchy / Junkyard * / Lonely weekends / Margie * / Rubber room *. *(cd+= *)*

Feb 88. (d7"-ltd) *(NEW 102)* **DALAI LAMA. / MARGIE / / JUNKYARD. / RUBBER ROOM** - - France
Jan 90. (m-lp/cd) *(ROSE 194/+CD)* **BLACKLIST** - - France
– Little GTO / Guantanamerika / Jailbait / Baby baby baby / Nice and easy does it / I will turn your money green.
(above cont.some covers). In 1992 CHILTON resurrected BIG STAR (see below).

				New Rose	Ardent
Feb 94.	(cd) *(5481)* <71606> **CLICHES**				

– My baby just cares for me / Time after time / All of you / Gavotte / Save your love for me / Lets get lost / Funny (but I still love you) / Frame for the blues / The Christmas song / There will never be another you / Somewhere along the way / What was.

				Ruf	not iss.
Jun 95.	(cd) *(RRCD 90131-2)* **A MAN CALLED DESTRUCTION**			-	

– Sick and tired / Devil girl / Lies / It's your funeral / What's your sign girl / Il Ribelle / You don't have to go / Boplexity / New girl in school / You're lookin' good / Don't know anymore / Don't stop.

				Shoeshine	not iss.
Oct 96.	(7") *(SHOE 005)* **MARGIE. /**				-

– (ALEX CHILTON) compilations etc. –

Sep 85. (lp/cd) *Aura; (AURA 732)* **DOCUMENT**
– Kizza me / Downs / Holocaust / Big black car / Kangaroo / Dream lover / My rival / Hey little child / Hook or crook / Like flies on sherbet / Bangkok / September gurls / In the street.

Mar 86. (d-lp) *Fan Club; (FC 015)* **LOST DECADE (1969-77)** - - France
May 91. (cd/c) *Rhino; <R2/R4 70780>* **19 YEARS (1969-87)** - -
Feb 92. (cd) *New Rose;* **ALEX CHILTON** - - French
Mar 96. (cd) *Rev-ola; (CREV 044CD)* **1970** - -
Mar 97. (cd) *Razor & Tie; (RE 2032)* **FEUDALISTIC TARTS / NO SEX** - -
Mar 97. (cd) *Razor & Tie; (RE 2033)* **HIGH PRIEST / BLACKLIST** - -
May 97. (d-cd) *Arcade; (302108-2)* **TOP 30** - -

BIG STAR

re-formed with **CHILTON / JONATHAN BAUER** – guitar, vocals / **KEN STRINGFELLOW** – guitar, bass (ex-POSIES)

				Zoo	Zoo
Sep 93.	(cd/c) <(11060-2/-4)> **LIVE AT MISSOURI UNIVERSITY (4.25.93)** (live)				

– In the street / Don't lie to me / When my baby's beside me / I am the cosmos / The ballad of El Goodo / Back of a car / Way out west / Daisy glaze / Baby strange / For you / Fool / September gurls / Thank you friends / Slut / Jeepster.

—— CHILTON teamed up with VEGA (from SUICIDE) and BEN VAUGHN on album 'CUBIST BLUES' for 'Last Call'; (7422466)

BIRD NEST ROYS

Formed: Auckland, New Zealand . . . mid-80's by FATTY (aka DOMINIC STONES), LITTLE ROSS, er . . . BIG ROSS, WARRO WAKEFIELD, PETER MOERENHOUT and DEBERLY ROY. Launching their musical career on NZ's most famous of labels, 'Flying Nun' (where else!), The BIRD NEST ROYS – a silly moniker if ever there was one – flew back and forth between their homeland and Britain where interest in everything Antipodean was the rage. However, the 'ROYS were a different kettle of fish to their compatriots from Dunedin (i.e. The CHILLS, The CLEAN, The VERLAINES, etc). This lot were of the distorted guitar and crashing percussion variety expressed ever so genuinely on their debut 12" EP, 'WHACK IT ALL DOWN', in 1987. A splendid eponymous set the following year showed them creating more of the same grinding indie-rock, although this was to be their swansong LP. A cover of the Hollies' 'BUS STOP' featured on the flipside of single, 'JAFFA BOY', although by the time of its release, DOMINIC was performing with his new outfit, SNAPPER; he was later part of the 3D's. LITTLE ROSS and BIG ROSS were back in gear when they resurfaced in the mid 90's as The TUFNELS.

Album rating: BIRD NEST ROYS (*7) / Tufnels: LURID (*5)

FATTY (b. DOMINIC STONES) – guitar / **LITTLE ROSS (TUFNEL)** – vocals, guitar / **WARRO WAKEFIELD** – vocals, tambourine / **BIG ROSS (TUFNEL)** – vocals / **DEBERLY ROY** – bass / **PETER MOERENHOUT** – drums

				Flying Nun	not iss.
Jan 87.	(12"ep) *(FN 044)* **WHACK IT ALL DOWN**			-	- NewZ

– Ain't mutatin' / Batcave / Severed days / Cresta / Womcat stones.

Oct 88. (lp/cd) *(FNE/+CD 19 – FN 065)* **BIRD NEST ROYS** - -
– Five wheatabix and toast / Alien / Loving time / Jaffa boy / Bided / Joringel / Me want me get me need me have me love / Michael Jones / Who is the silliest Rossi? / Love / Wads of pork fat. *(cd+=)* – Ain't mutatin' / Severed days / I need your love.

Nov 88. (7") *(FN 067)* **JAFFA BOY. / BUS STOP** - - NewZ
Oct 89. (7"; w-drawn) *(FN 087)* **I NEED YOUR LOVE** - - NewZ

—— after their split, DOMINIC joined SNAPPER before he helped form 3D's

TUFNELS

BIG ROSS + LITTLE ROSS + guest **PETER**

				Globule	not iss.
1994.	(cd) *(GR-H 001)* **LURID**			-	- NewZ

– Fly away 1000's / Rather be alone / Husky vooms / Aiee! aiee! / Where's Bobby England / Hhrghhh / Pettibone / Don't call me blue / The hideous thing / Cack / Aiee! aiee! (rark mix) / Freak.

				Tristar	not iss.
1995.	(cd-ep) *(662296-2)* **BEAUTIFUL RIDE**			-	- NewZ

– Beautiful ride / Pettibone / Shady tree / Husky vooms.

—— they split after above

BIRDSONGS OF THE MESOZOIC

Formed: Boston, Massachusetts, USA . . . 1983 by ex-MISSION OF BURMA members, ROGER MILLER and MARTIN SWOPE, who recruited the aid of RICK SCOTT and ERIK LINDGREN, with guest percussion work provided by another MOB survivor, PETE PRESCOTT. BOTM took the experimentalism that the record-buying public had come to expect of MOB a stage further. Their output was in the truest sense of the word eclectic, helped by the classically trained, MILLER, it ranged from and blended classical innovation with rock, punk and more minimalist stylings, and used a variety of instrumentation and doubling up to create free-form and tight compositions. The group debuted in 1983 with an eponymously titled EP, and although they had been in existence in one form or another for the past three years, it was only with this release, and the definite break-up of MOB, that the band became a full-time venture. BOTM followed up this initial outing with the LPs, 'MAGNETIC FLIP' (1985), and 'SONIC GEOLOGY' (1986). Founding member, MILLER, subsequently departed the band and continued to please the critics with his ongoing solo career. He was replaced by saxophonist, KEN FIELD, an able and creative addition, whose introduction to the band added another string to their sonic investigations, as showcased on the succeeding sets, 'FAULTLINE', and 'PYROCLASTICS' (1991). Worthy of mention for its good humour, and connection with pop culture at large, is the latter LP's cover of 'The Simpsons' theme tune. Thereafter SWOPE also took his bow, his reins subsequently taken up by MICHAEL BIERYLO. BOTM did not release another LP until 1995's, 'DANCING ON A'A', although the fans were kept happy by the retrospective release, 'THE FOSSIL RECORD, 1980-1987'. Although the nineties saw few outings from the group, they were nonetheless kept busy with various projects including film scoring, and a joint theatre project in 1998 with David Greenberger, '1001 Real Apes'. Music from this piece found its way onto BOTM's long-awaited millennial release, 'PETROPHONICS'.
• **Covered:** SOMBRE REPTILES (Eno) / OUR PRAYER (Brian Wilson) / THE SIMPSONS (Danny Elfman) / PETER GUNN (Henry Mancini).

Album rating: MAGNETIC FLIP (*5) / SONIC GEOLOGY compilation (*6) / FAULTLINE (*7) / PYROCLASTICS (*5) / THE FOSSIL RECORD 1980-1987 compilation (*6) / DANCING ON A'A (*5) / PETROPHONICS (*6)

ROGER MILLER – piano, percussion (ex-MISSION OF BURMA) / **MARTIN SWOPE** – guitar, cymbals (ex-MISSION OF BURMA) / **RICK SCOTT** – organ, percussion / **ERIK LINDGREN** – synthesizers (of SPACE NEGROS, ex-FAMILY FUN)

			not iss.	Ace Of Hearts
1983.	(m-lp) <AHS 1008> **BIRDSONGS OF THE MESOZOIC EP**		-	

– Sound valentine / Transformation of Oz / Drift / The orange ocean / Triassic Jurassic, Cretaceous.

1984. (lp) <AHS 10018> **MAGNETIC FLIP** -
– Shiny golden snakes / Ptoccata / The rite of spring excerpts from) / International tours / Terry Riley's house / Theme from Rocky And Bulwinkle / The tyger / The fundamental / Bridge underwater / Chen – The arousing / Final motif.

1986. (12"ep) <AHS 1018> **BEAT OF THE MESOZOIC** -
– Lost in the B-zone / Waterwheel / Excavation No.32 / The beat of the Mesozoic (pt.1) / Scenes from a . . .

			not iss.	Rykodisc
1988.	(cd) <RCD 20073> **SONIC GEOLOGY** (compilation)			

– Shiny golden snakes / Ptoccata / Waterwheel / Pulse piece / The rite of spring / The orange ocean / The tyger / Scenes from a . . . / The beat of the Mesozoic (part 1) / International tours / Drift / Final motif / Theme from Rocky And Bullwinkle / The fundamental / Sound valentine / The common sparrow / Lost in the B-zone / Triassic, Jurassic, Cretaceous. *(UK-iss.Apr92; same)*

—— **KEN FIELD** – saxophone, keyboards, percussion; repl. MILLER

			not iss.	Cuniform
1989.	(cd) <RUNE 19> **FAULTLINE**		-	

– The true wheelbase / They walk among us / Coco Boudakian / I don't need no crystal ball / Chariots of fire / Magic fingers / Faultline / On the street where you live / Maybe I will / There is no one / Slo-boy / Pterobold / Just say yes.

BIRDSONGS OF THE MESOZOIC (cont)

Jun 91. (cd) <RUNE 35> **PYROCLASTICS**
– Shortwave longride / Pleasure island / I'm a pterodactyl / Why not circulate / Sled / The Simpsons / Tyronglaea II / Papercutsone / Sombre reptiles / Nothing but trouble / Tomorrow never came / Our prayer. *(UK-iss.Jun01; same)*

— **MICHAEL BIERYLO** – guitar; repl. SWOPE

1995. (cd) <CUNE 69> **DANCING ON A'A**
– A band of Deborahs (not Debbies) / Dancing on A'A / Ptinct / Readymen / Birdgam / Electric altamira / Swamp / Peter Gunn / Ray / Sirius the scorching / The pearly eyed march.

Mar 01. (cd) <(RUNE 137)> **PETROPHONICS** Sep00
– Petrophonics / Ptoccata II / One hundred cycles / Nevergreen / Study of unintended consequences / Birdhead / Allswell the endswell in Roswell / Time marches on theme / Dinosaurs theme / Gravity theme / Quincy sore throat theme:- part one – part two – part three.

– compilations, etc. –

1993. (cd) *Cuniform;* <RUNE 55> **THE FOSSIL RECORD 1980-1987**
– Sound valentine / Pulse piece / The transformation of Oz / Tyronglaea / Chen – The arousing / Sombre reptiles / Laramid revolution / Out of limits / Biff the brontosaurus / Carbon 14 / Modern warfare / March / Lqabblil insanya / Slo-boy / To a random / Studio talk.

BITCH MAGNET
(see under ⇒ SEAM; 90's section)

BITING TONGUES

Formed: Manchester, England ... 1980 by main composers GRAHAM MASSEY and HOWARD WALMSLEY. Commissioned to write film soundtracks, the latter duly recruited the aforesaid MASSEY together with KEN HOLLINGS, COLIN SEDDON and EDDIE SHERWOOD. BITING TONGUES' debut release came in the shape of 'DON'T HEAL', released on Beggars Banquet newly formed off-shoot label, 'Situation 2'. A fusion of jazzy punk and danceable soundscapes, the TONGUES oeuvre was developed over a further clutch of lp's including 'LIBREVILLE' (1984) and 'FEVERHOUSE', the latter for 'Factory' records. Having already lost SHERWOOD (to SIMPLY RED) and HOLLINGS, MASSEY and WALMSLEY recruited PHIL KIRBY and BASIL CLARKE, although both would in turn, go off to follow their own path with YARGO. 1988 saw the release of their pioneering video album, 'WALL OF SURF', although the following year, sessions for a new album, 'RECHARGE' (as yet unreleased), were abandoned when their label, 'Cut Deep', folded. It wasn't long before MASSEY was hitting the proverbial big time with 808 STATE, WALMSLEY working on film projects full-time.

Album rating: DON'T HEAL (*6) / LIBREVILLE (*6) / FEVERHOUSE (*7)

GRAHAM MASSEY (b. 4 Aug'60) – guitar / **HOWARD WALMSLEY** – saxophone / **KEN HOLLINGS** – vocals / **COLIN SEDDON** – bass / **EDDIE SHERWOOD** – drums

Situation 2 / not iss.

Apr 81. (lp) *(SITU 1)* **DON'T HEAL**
– Blue traces / Dog face / Heart disease / Or with eyes closed / Stabbing soft ice / You can choke like that / Walkway / Coil / R.R.O.R. / Give diamonds – You can't.

New Hormones / not iss.

Dec 81. (c) *(CAT 3)* **LIVE IT**
– Even state (the wave state) / (+ others).

Paragon / not iss.

Apr 84. (lp) *(VIRTUE 1)* **LIBREVILLE**
– First use all the G's / Forty four / Smash the strategie hamlets / Live it / The toucanostra / Doctor restore the sight / Dirt for 485 / Air care.

— **BASIL CLARKE** – vocals; repl. HOLLINGS

— **PHIL KIRBY** – drums; repl. SHERWOOD who joined SIMPLY RED

Factory / not iss.

Mar 85. (lp) *(FACT 105)* **FEVERHOUSE (soundtrack)**
– (parts 1-10).

Oct 85. (12"ep) *(FAC 134)* **TROUBLE HAND / PANORAMA. / MEAT MASK SEPARATIST / BOSS TOYOTA TROUBLE / PROBATE**

— were now a duo when BASIL and PHIL formed YARGO

May 87. (12"m) *(FAC 188)* **COMPRESSOR. / BLACK JESUS / BLACK AND WHITE JESUS**

Antler / not iss.

Jan 88. (12") *(AN 005)* **EVENING STATE. / EVENING STATE** – Belgian
Jan 88. (12"; shared with TANK OF DANZIG) *(AN 006)* **EVENING STATE / LOCK UP STATE** – Belgian

Cut Deep / not iss.

1989. (12"ep) *(CUT 12-004)* **LOVE OUT / LOVE OUT (brainwash mix instrumental). / SURRENDER (mellow mix) / SURRENDER**

— split in 1989, when MASSEY found 808 STATE. WALMSLEY however carried on with more film soundtracks.

BJORK

Born: BJORK GUDMUNDSDOTTIR, 21 Oct'65, Reykjavik, Iceland. Growing up in a creative communal family and something of a child prodigy, the strikingly unique BJORK enjoyed her first taste of the music business at the age of 11 when she impressed her teachers with her rendition of TINA CHARLES' No.1 'I LOVE TO LOVE', who in turn convinced a local radio station to play it. This led to her recording a self-titled album with many of Iceland's top musicians. It also included other covers; YOUR KISS IS SWEET (hit; Syreeta) / ALFUR UT UR HOL (FOOL ON THE HILL; Beatles) / CHRISTOPHER ROBIN (Melanie) / ALTA MIRA (Edgar Winter). BJORK graduated to her first band EXODUS, and in 1981 aged 14, she instigated another; TAPPI TIKARRASS, which meant 'Cork The Bitch's Arse'. In the next two years, the X-RAY SPEX-type outfit completed two albums 'BITID FAST I VITID' and 'MIRANDA'. She subsequently worked with KILLING JOKE theorists, JAZ COLEMAN and YOUTH, who had both fled to the frozen north in fear of a supposed impending apocalypse. In the interim, she guested for free-form jazz-rock duo STIFGRIM, who comprised of comedian/vocalist KRISTINN JON GUDMUNDSSON and guitarist STEINN SKAPTASON. They went down in the record books as one of over a hundred bands who took part in the longest ever continuous live performances (seven weeks!). She then spent two summer seasons playing synthesizer in a covers band named, CACTUS. In 1984, she teamed up with friends EINAR ORN BENEDIKTSSON (he of the legendary, erm, rapping "talent") and SIGTRYGGUR 'SIGGI' BALDERSSON to form KUKL ('Sorcery'), this FALL/BANSHEES influenced lot finding their way into Britain's earlobes (via the 'Crass' label) with two albums 'THE EYE' and 'HOLIDAYS IN EUROPE'. During this mid 80's period, she was also part of ROKHA ROKHA DRUM (as a drummer! and voice). They included lead vocalist JOHNNY TRIUMPH (b. SJON), who collaborated with BJORK's most famous and productive outfit The SUGARCUBES. Hooking up with BRAGI OLAFSSON, THOR ELDON (the father of BJORK's son, Sindri) and EINAR MELLAX, BJORK and Co. formed Iceland's first (and so far only) internationally renowned band. Signed to Derek Birkett's 'One Little Indian', the group had the critics frothing with their debut single, the sublime 'BIRTHDAY'. Like pop music from another planet, the song's reverberating bassline, celestial brass and ethereal production conspired to make this the aural equivalent of a particularly sensual massage. The track also introduced BJORK's inimitable vocals, a perversely melodic combination of wide-eyed child and Icelandic banshee. A further two slices of avant-garde strangeness, 'COLD SWEAT' and 'DEUS' followed into the UK Top 75 before a debut album, 'LIFE'S TOO GOOD', crashed into the Top 20 in Spring '88. An intoxicating blend of jazzy instrumentation, indie stylings and wilful weirdness, the album's success allowed the band to set up their own multi-media enterprise, 'Bad Taste Ltd.' back in Iceland. Though a follow-up, 'HERE TODAY, TOMORROW, NEXT WEEK' (1989) again made the UK Top 20, the critical reception was poor, particular vitriol reserved for EINER's (ORN) jarring vocal exhortations. After extensive touring the band headed back to Iceland to work on various outside jazz-styled projects, BJORK keeping her name in the music press via collaborative work with 808 STATE on their 'Ex:El' album. Then, in late '91, The SUGARCUBES bounced back with the celebratory avant-funk of 'HIT', the band putting in an unforgettable performance on Channel 4's 'The Word'. The accompanying album, 'STICK AROUND FOR JOY' (1992) saw the group back in critical favour, a brassy pot-pourri of spiked melody and faultless instrumental dexterity. To consolidate the new dancefloor-friendly direction, a set of remixes, 'IT'S-IT', was released in late '92, coinciding with the voluntary demise of The SUGARCUBES. It had been a short strange trip, but not as strange as BJORK's forthcoming rise to international pop superstardom. While she undoubtedly had a distinctive, beguiling charm, few would've predicted the massive critical and commercial achievements of her solo debut, entitled, er... 'DEBUT' actually. Released in summer '93, co-written with ex-SOUL II SOUL/MASSIVE ATTACK guru, NELLEE HOOPER and featuring such underrated talents as TALVIN SINGH and JHELISA ANDERSON, proceedings were dominated by pulsing, house-orientated material, although there was a fair smattering of off-the-wall BJORK oddities. Lauded by the indie and dance press alike, the album's kudos was further boosted by the success of the 'PLAY DEAD' single, a collaboration with soundtrack man, DAVID ARNOLD recorded for the movie, 'Young Americans'. A UK Top 3 success and a Mercury Music Prize nominee, 'DEBUT' turned BJORK into a household name, remixers clamouring to get to grips with her work. A true celebrity hobnobber, BJORK co-wrote the title track to MADONNA's 'Bedtime Stories' set, while 1995's follow-up album, 'POST', saw her working with everyone from TRICKY and SKUNK ANANSIE to The BRODSKY QUARTET and EVELYN GLENNIE! The latter two featured on the experimental/schizophrenic (delete according to taste) Top 5 hit, 'IT'S OH SO QUIET', an, ahem, 'adaptation' of Betty Hutton's 40's big band number which saw BJORK veer wildly from hushed reverence to shouting the rafters down in fine style. The song was characteristic of the album's more fragmented nature, a challenging listen but proof positive that the elfen firebrand wasn't content to rest on her laurels. The following year saw BJORK take up residence in the gossip columns rather than the charts, what with her highly publicised relationship with GOLDIE and her unfortunate fracas with a reporter at Bangkok airport (19th February '96). In September, an obsessed fan from Florida blew his brains out after sending a letter bomb to BJORK. Luckily neighbours contacted police after smelling his decomposed body and the bomb was averted, although unsurprisingly it caused her much distress. The stresses and strains of stardom formed the lyrical backbone for her acclaimed 1997 set, 'HOMOGENIC', a return to more electronic waters that was nevertheless more downbeat than dancefloor. One of the music world's more unpredictable stars, her maverick genius is sorely needed in a chart choked with indie loser clones. With a plethora of mixes behind her, BJORK looked set to be a film star, her part in the film, 'Dancer In The Dark' (alongside Catherine Deneuve) won her praise at Cannes 2000; she also wrote the score. With help from conductor/arranger Vincent

Mendoza, she composed the musical fantasies of her doomed character, Selma (as full-set 'SELMASONGS'). Deliciously different from her studio albums, the soundtrack presented a forum for BJORK's more esoteric ideas, poignantly capturing the light, shade and emotional extremes of Selma's life. In contrast, the celestial calm of 'VESPERTINE' (2001) was located squarely inside the meditative confines of the author's immediate environment. A reclusive rhapsody to private contentment, the record's spectral choir, angelic harp and head-nodding beats (courtesy of MATMOS) weaved a suitably spiritual spell to accommodate BJORK's uncharacteristically restrained and subdued vocals. Listen for instance to its heart-rending and emotive hit singles, 'THE HIDDEN PLACE' and 'PAGAN POETRY', to find out exactly how much this little lady had progressed. • **Songwriters:** SUGARCUBES – all written by BJORK and EINAR, except TOP OF THE WORLD (Carpenters) / MOTORCYCLE MAMA (Sailcat). • **Trivia:** BJORK was married to THOR, although after they had a child, he soon married new SUGARCUBE, MAGGI. SIGGI and BRAGI were former brother-in-laws who were married to twin sisters. In 1989, they divorced and moved to Denmark to get married to each other!. The first openly gay marriage in rock/pop history.

Album rating: Tappi Tikarrass: MIRANDA (*4) / Kukl: THE EYE mini (*4) / HOLIDAYS IN EUROPE mini (*4) / Sugarcubes: LIFE'S BEEN GOOD (*9) / STICK AROUND FOR JOY (*8) / HERE TODAY, TOMORROW, NEXT WEEK (*8) / IT'S-IT remixes (*6) / THE GREAT CROSSOVER POTENTIAL compilation (*7) / Bjork: DEBUT (*9) / POST (*8) / TELEGRAM remixes (*7) / HOMOGENIC (*7) / SELMASONGS soundtrack (*7) / VESPERTINE (*7) / GREATEST HITS compilation (*9) / FAMILY TREE boxed collection (*6)

BJORK GUDMUNDSDOTTIR

Falkinn / not iss.

Dec 77. (lp/c) *(FA 006/+C)* **BJORK** – – Icelan
– Arabadrengurinn / Bukolla / Alta mira / Johannes Kjarvalv / Fusi Hreindyr / Himnafor / Oliver / Alfur ut ur hol / Musastiginn / Baenin.

TAPPI TiKARRASS

BJORK – vocals, keyboards, etc / **JAKOB MAGNUSSON** – bass (ex-EXODUS) / etc.

Spor / not iss.

Sep 81. (m-lp) *(SPOR 4)* **BITID FAST I VITID** – – Icelan

Gramm / not iss.

Aug 83. (lp) *(GRAMM 16)* **MIRANDA** – – Icelan

KUKL

BJORK – vocals, keyboards / **EINAR ORN BENEDIKTSSON** (b.29 Oct'62, Copenhagen, Denmark) – trumpet, vocals / **SIGTRYGGUR 'Siggi' BALDURSSON** (b. 2 Oct'62, Stavanger, Norway) – drums, percussion / **EINAR MELLAX** – keyboards

Gramm / not iss.

Sep 83. (7") *(GRAMM 17)* **SONGULL. / POKN FYRIR BYRJENDUR** – – Icelan

Crass / not iss.

Nov 84. (m-lp) *(1984-1)* **THE EYE**
– Dismembered / Assassin / Anna. *(cd-iss. Mar97; 1984 2CD)*

Mar 86. (lp) *(Cat.No.4)* **HOLIDAYS IN EUROPE (THE NAUGHTY NOUGHT)**
– (8 untitled tracks).

SUGARCUBES

BJORK, EINAR, EINAR + SIGGI recruited **THOR ELDON JONSON** (b. 2 Jun'62, Reykjavik) – guitar / **BRAGI OLAFSSON** (b.11 Aug'62, Reykjavik) – bass

One Little Indian / Elektra

Sep 87. (7") *(7TP 7)* **BIRTHDAY. / BIRTHDAY (Icelandic)** 65 –
(12"+=) *(12TP 7)* – Cat (Icelandic).
(cd-s;Dec87;++=) *(7TP 7CD)* – Motorcrash.

Feb 88. (7") *(7TP 9)* **COLD SWEAT. / DRAGON (Icelandic)** 56 –
(12"+=) *(12TP 9)* – Traitor (Icelandic).
(12"++=) *(L12TP 9)* – Birthday (demo).
(cd-s+=) *(7TP 9CD)* – Traitor (Icelandic) / Revolution.

Apr 88. (7") *(7TP 10)* **DEUS. / LUFTGITAR (Icelandic) (with JOHNNY TRIUMPH)** 51 –
(10"+=/12"+=) *(10TP/12TP 10)* – Organic prankster.
(cd-s+=) *(7TP 10CD)* – Night of steel (Icelandic).

Apr 88. (lp/c/cd/dat) *(TPLP/TPC/TPCD/DTPLP 5)* **LIFE'S TOO GOOD** 14 54 Jun 88
– Mama / Delicious demon / Birthday / Traitor / Blue eyed pop / Petrol / F***ing in rhythm and sorrow / Cold sweat / Deus / Sick for toys. *(cd+=)* – I want.

May 88. (12"ep)(cd-ep) **COLD SWEAT / COLD SWEAT (meat mix). / BIRTHDAY (Icelandic) / DELICIOUS DEMON / COLD SWEAT (instrumental)**

— **MARGRET 'Magga' ORNOLFSDOTTIR** (b.21 Nov'67, Reykjavik) – keyboards repl. MELLAX

Sep 88. (7") *(7TP 11)* **BIRTHDAY. / CHRISTMAS (with Jesus & Mary Chain)** 65 –
(12")(cd-s) *(12TP 11)(7TP 11CD)* – ('A'side) / Fucking in rhythm and sorrow (live) / Cowboy (live) / Cold sweat (live).
(12"/cd-s) *(12TP 11L/7TP 11CDL)* – BIRTHDAY CHRISTMAS MIX: – Christmas eve / Christmas day / Christmas present / Petrol (live).
(US-green-ep title 'DELICIOUS DEMONS')

Dec 88. (c-s) **MOTORCRASH (live) / POLO** – –
(12"+=)(3"cd-s+=) – Blue eyed pop.

Aug 89. (7"/c-s) *(26 TP7/+C)* **REGINA / HOT MEAT** 55 –
(7"ep+=) *(26 TP7L)* – Hey / Propeller vs jet.
(12"+=) *(26 TP12)* – Regina (Icelandic).
(cd-s+=) *(26 TP7CD)* – Hey / Regina (Icelandic).
(12") *(26 TP12L)* – ('A'-Propeller mix) / ('A'-Jet mix).

Oct 89. (lp/silver-lp/c)(cd) *(TPLP 15/+SP/C)(TPCD 15)* **HERE TODAY, TOMORROW, NEXT WEEK** 15 70
– Tidal wave / Regina / Speed is the key / Dream T.V. / Nail / Pump / Eat the menu / Bee / Dear plastic / Shoot him / Water / Day called Zero / Planet. *(cd+=)* – Hey / Dark disco! / Hot meat.

Feb 90. (7") *(32 TP7)* **PLANET. / PLANET (somersault version)**
(12"+=/cd-s+=) *(32 TP 12/7CD)* – Planet (Icelandic) / Cindy.

Dec 91. (7") *(62 TP7)* **HIT. / HIT (instrumental)** 17
(12"+=) *(62 TP12)* – Theft.
(cd-s++=) *(62 TP7CD)* – Chihuahua (instrumental).
(12"+=) *(62 TP12L)* – Leash called love.

Feb 92. (lp/c/cd) *(TPLP 30/+C/CD)* **STICK AROUND FOR JOY** 16 95
– Gold / Hit / Leash called love / Lucky night / Happy nurse / I'm hungry / Walkabout / Hetero scum / Vitamin / Chihuahua.

Mar 92. (7"/c-s) *(72 TP7/+C)* **WALKABOUT (remix). / STONE DRILL (IN THE ROCK)**
(12"+=) *(72 TP12)* – Top of the world (live).
(cd-s+=) *(72 TP7CD)* – Bravo pop.

Aug 92. (12"ep) *(102 TP12)* **VITAMIN REMIXES** – –
– ('A'-Babylon's Burnin mix) / ('A'-Earth dub) / ('A'-Laser dub in Hell mix) / ('A'-Decline of Rome part II & III) / ('A'-Meditation mix).
(cd-ep+=) *(102 TP7CD)* – ('A'-E mix).

Sep 92. (c-ep/12"ep/cd-ep) *(104 TP7/12/7CD)* **BIRTHDAY REMIX EP** 64
– ('A'-Justin Robertson remix) / ('A'-Tommy D. dub mix) / ('A'-Jim & William Reid Christmas Eve mix) / ('A'original) / ('A'-Tommy D. 12" or dub mix) / ('A'-Justin Robertson dub) / ('A'-Jim & William Reid Christmas Day mix) / ('A'demo).
(cd-ep) *(104 TP7CD)* – Birthday (Justin Robertson mix) / Birthday (Tommy D. edit) / Hit (Tony Humphries mix) / Mama (Mark Saunders mix).

Oct 92. (lp/c/cd/d-cd) *(TPLP 40/+C/CD/CDL)* <61426> **IT'S-IT (remixes)** 47
– Birthday (Justin Robertson 12" mix) / Leash called love / Blue eyed pop / Motorcrash (Justin Robertson mix) / Planet / Gold (Todd Terry mix) / Water / Regina (Sugarcubes mix) / Mama (Mark Saunders mix) / Pump (Marius De Vries mix) / Hit (Tony Humphries sweet and low mix) / Birthday (Tommy D mix) / Coldsweat (DB/BP mix). *(cd w/ bonus cd)*

—— officially disbanded late 1992

– compilations, others, etc. –

all on 'One Little Indian' ('Elektra' US)

Apr 90. (11x12"box) *(TP BOX 1)* **12.11** (box set)
Apr 90. (8x7"box) *(TP BOX 2)* **7.8** (box set)
Apr 90. (6xcd-s-box) *(TP BOX 3)* **CD.6**
Jul 98. (cd/c/lp) *(TPLP 333 CD/MC/LP)* <62102> **THE GREAT CROSSOVER POTENTIAL**
– Birthday / Cold sweat / Mama / Motor crash / Deus / Regina / Pump / Planet / Water / Hit / Vitamin / Walkabout / Gold / Chihuahua.

BJORK GUDMUNDSDOTTIR & TRIO GUDMUNDAR INGOLFSSONAR

Smekkleysa / not iss.

Oct 90. (lp/c/cd) *(SM 27/+C/CD)* **GLING-GLO** – Icelan
– Gling-glo / Luktar-gvendur / Kata rokkar / Pabbi minn / Brestir og brak / Astartofrar / Bella simamaer / Litli tonlistarmadurinn / Pad sest ekki saetari mey / Bilavisur / Tondelevo / Eg veit ei hvad skal segja / I dansi med per / Bornin vid tjornina / Ruby baby / I can't help loving that man.

BJORK

—— solo, with **MARIUS DE VRIES, PAUL WALLER, MARTIN VIRGO + GARRY HUGHES** – keyboards / **NELLEE HOOPER** (co-writer of some), **LUIS JARDIM** (also bass) + **BRUCE SMITH** – drums, percussion / **JON MALLISON** – guitar / **TALVIN SINGH** – tabla / **CORKI HALE** – harp / **JHELISA ANDERSON** – backing vocals / **OLIVER LAKE, GARY BARNACLE, MIKE MOWER** – brass

One Little Indian / Elektra

Jun 93. (c-s) *(112 TP7C)* **HUMAN BEHAVIOUR / ATLANTIC** 36
(12") *(112 TP12)* – ('A'-Underworld mix) / ('A'-Close to human mix) / ('A'-Dom T. mix).
(cd-s) *(112 TP7CD)* – ('A'side) / (above extras) / ('A'-Bassheads edit).

Jul 93. (cd/c/lp) *(TPLP 31 CD/C/L)* <61468> **DEBUT** 3 61
– Human behaviour / Crying / Venus as a boy / There's more to life than this recorded live at the Milk Bar toilets / Like someone in love / Big time sensuality / One day / Aeroplane / Come to me / Violently happy / The anchor song. *(re-iss. Nov93 cd/c; TPLP 31 CDX/CX)(+=)* – Play dead.

Aug 93. (7"/c-s) *(122 TP7/+C)* **VENUS AS A BOY. / ('A'-Dream mix)** 29
(cd-s) *(122 TP7CD)* – ('A'side) / ('A'-Mykaell Riley mix) / There's more to life than this (non toilet mix) / Violently happy.
(cd-s) *(122 TP7CDL)* – ('A'side) / Stigdu mig / Anchor song (Black Dog mix) / I remember you.
(below single credited with DAVID ARNOLD and from the movie 'Young Americans', released on 'Island' records)

Oct 93. (7"/c-s) *(IS/CIS 573)* **PLAY DEAD. / ('A'-Tim Simenon remix)** 12
(12"+=/cd-s+=) *(12IS/CID 573)* – ('A'-Tim Simenon mixes; Orchestral / 12" / Instrumental) / ('A'-Original film mix).

Nov 93. (c-s) *(132 TP7C)* **BIG TIME SENSUALITY / SiDASTA EG** 17 –
(cd-s+=) *(132 TP7CD)* – Gloria / Come to me (Black Dog Productions).
(12"/cd-s) *(132 TP 12/7CDL)* – ('A'-Dave Morales def radio mix) / ('A'-Fluke mixes) / ('A'-Justin Robertson – Lionrock Wigout & Prankster's Joyride mix) / ('A'-Dom T. mix).

Jan 94. (c-s) <64561> **BIG TIME SENSUALITY / THERE'S MORE TO LIFE THAN THIS** – 88

—— In Mar'94, BJORK was accused by SIMON FISHER (LOVEJOY) of not crediting him on 4 of her songs on her 'DEBUT' album.

Mar 94. (c-s) *(142 TP7C)* **VIOLENTLY HAPPY. / ('A'-Fluke mix)** 13
(cd-s) *(142 TP7CD)* – ('A'side) / Anchor song (acoustic) / Come to me (acoustic) / Human behavior (acoustic).
(d-cd-s) *(142 TP7CDL)* – ('B'side) / ('A'-5 other mixes).

BJORK (cont)

Sep 94. (cd/c) *(MUM CD/SC 59)* **BEST MIXES FROM THE ALBUM DEBUT (For All The People Who Don't Buy White Labels)** ☐ -
(above rel. on 'Mother')
Apr 95. (c-s) *(162 TP7C)* **ARMY OF ME / ('A'-ABA All-Stars mix)** 10 ☐
(cd-s+=) *(162 TP7CD)* – You've been flirting again / Sweet intuition.
(cd-s+=) *(162 TP7CDL)* – ('A'-Massey mix) / ('A'-featuring SKUNK ANANSIE) / ('A'-ABA All-Stars instrumental).
(cd-s) *(162 TP7)* – ('A'side) / Cover me.
Jun 95. (cd/c/lp) *(TPLP 51 CD/C/L) <612740>* **POST** 2 32
– Army of me / Hyper-ballad / The modern things / It's oh so quiet / Enjoy / You've been flirting again / Isobel / Possibly maybe / I miss you / Cover me / Headphones. *(cd re-iss. Oct99; TPLP 51CD)*
Aug 95. (c-s/cd/s) *(172 TP7 C/CD)* **ISOBEL / CHARLENE (Black Dog mix) / I GO HUMBLE / VENUS AS A BOY (harpsicord version)** 23 ☐
(cd-s) *(172 TP7CDL)* – ('A'side) / ('A'-Goldie mix) / ('A'-Eumir Deodato mix) / ('A'-Siggi mix).
Nov 95. (c-s) *(182 TP7C)* **IT'S OH SO QUIET / YOU'VE BEEN FLIRTING AGAIN (flat is a promise mix)** 4 ☐
(cd-s+=) *(182 TP7CD)* – Hyper-ballad / Hyper-ballad (Over the edge mix) / Sweet sweet intuition.
(cd-s+=) *(182 TP7CDL)* – ('A'side) / Hyper-ballad (Girl's blouse mix) / Hyper-ballad (with The Brodsky Quartet) / My spine (featuring Evelyn Glennie).
Feb 96. (c-s) *(192 TP7C)* **HYPER-BALLAD / HYPER-BALLAD (Robin Hood riding through the glen mix)** 8 ☐
(cd-s+=) *(192 TP7CD)* – ('A'-The stomp remix) / ('A'-Fluke mix) / ('A'-Subtle abuse mix) / ('A'-Tee's freeze mix).
(cd-s) *(192 TP7CDT)* – ('A'side) / Isobel (the Carcass remix) / Cover me (Plaid mix) / ('A'-Towa Tei remix).
Oct 96. (cd-s) *(193 TP7CD)* **POSSIBLY MAYBE (mixes; Lucy / Calcutta Cyber Cafe / Dalas Austin)** 13 ☐
(cd-s) *(193 TP7CDT)* – ('A'-Calcutta Cyber Cafe dub) / Cover me (Dillinja mix) / One day (Trevor Morais mix) / I miss you (Photek mix).
(cd-s) *(193 TP7CDL)* – ('A'live mix) / Big time sensuality (Plaid remix) / Visur vatnsenda-rosu / Hyper-ballad (live).
Nov 96. (cd/c/lp) *(TPLP 51 CDT/CT/T) <61897>* **TELEGRAM** (remixes) ☐ 66 Jan97
(cd re-iss. Aug99; TPLP 51CDT)
Feb 97. (c-s) *(194 TP7C)* **I MISS YOU / I MISS YOU (Photek mix)** 36 ☐
(cd-s) *(194 TP7CD)* – ('A'side) / ('A'-Dobie part 2) / ('A'Darren Emerson mix) / Karvel (Graham Massey mix).
(cd-s) *(194 TP7CDL)* – ('A'-Dobie part 1) / Hyperballad (LFO) Violently happy (live) / Headphones (Miko Vainio remix).
Sep 97. (cd-s) *(202 TP7CD)* **JOGA (mixes; album / Alec Empire / Alec Empire Digital Hardcore 1 & 2)** ☐ ☐
(cd-s) *(202 TP7CDL)* – ('A'album mix) / Sod off / Immature (Bjork's version) / So broken.
(cd-s) *(202 TP7CDX)* – (mixes; Howie B. main / String & Vocal / Buzzwater) / All is full of love (original).
Sep 97. (lp/c/cd) *(TPLP 71/+C/CD) <62061>* **HOMOGENIC** 4 28
– Hunter / Joga / Unravel / Bachelorette / All neon like / 5 years / Immature / Alarm call / Pluto / All is full of love.
Dec 97. (c-s) *(212 TP7C)* **BACHELORETTE / ('A'-Howie "Spread" mix)** 21 ☐
(cd-s+=) *(212 TP7CD)* – My snare / Scary.
(12") *(212 TP12P1)* – ('A'-Alec Empire remix) / ('B'side).
(12") *(212 TP12P2)* – ('A'-Mark Bell "Optimism" remix) / ('A'-Mark Bell "Zip" remix).
(cd-s) *(212 TP7CDL)* – (mixes; above + RZA / Grooverider / etc).

—— In Aug'98. BJORK collaborated with FUNKSTORUNG on a single, 'ALL IS FULL OF LOVE', released on 'Fat Cat' cd-s; CDFAT 022)

Oct 98. (cd-s) *(222 TP7CD)* **HUNTER / ALL IS FULL OF LOVE (In Love With Funkstorung remix) / ('A'-U-Ziq remix)** 44 ☐
(cd-s) *(222 TP7CDL)* – ('A'side) / ('A'-State Of Bengal mix) / ('A'-Skothus mix).
(cd-s) *(222 TP7CDX)* – ('A'-Moodswing mix) / So broken (DK Krust remix) / ('A'live).
Nov 98. (cd-s) *(232TP7CD)* **ALARM CALL (mixes; radio / Rhythmic Phonetics / Bjeck)** 33 ☐
(cd-s) *(232 TP7CDL)* – (mixes; Potage du jour / French edit / French dub).
(cd-s) *(232 TP7CDX)* – (mixes; Phunk you / Gangsta / Locked).
(12") *(232 TP12P1)* – (mixes; Bjeck [Beck] / Rhythmic Phonetics [Matmos] / Speech therapy [Matmos]).
(12") *(232 TP12P2)* – (mixes; Enough is enough [Mark Bell] / Rise & shine [Mark Bell]) / All is full of love (Mark Bell mix).
(12") *(232 TP12P3)* – (mix; Repression [DJ Krust] / So broken (DJ Krush mix)).
(12") *(232 TP12P4)* – (mixes; A+E / Alan Braxe & Ben Diamond [Stardust] / Teesmade dub [Swag] / Alan Braxe & Ben Diamond).
(12") *(232 TP12P5)* – (mixes; Andy Bradford & Mark Bell / album / Snooze button [Dom T] / (Moodswing [Mark Bell]).
Jun 99. (cd-s) *(242 TP7CD)* **ALL IS FULL OF LOVE (mixes; original / Funkstorung exclusive / strings)** 24 ☐
(cd-s) *(242 TP7CDL)* – ('A'mixes; Howie B / Plaid / Guy Sigsworth).
(12") *(242 TP12)* – ('A'mixes; Mark Stent / Funkstorung exclusive / Mark Stent radio strings).
(12") *(242 TP12L)* – ('A'mixes; U-Ziq 7 minute / U-Ziq 1 minute / Funkstorung exclusive).
Sep 00. (lp/cd) *(TPLP 151/+CD) <62533>* **SELMASONGS** (Dancer In The Dark soundtrack) 34 41
– Overture / Cvalda / I've seen it all (with THOM YORKE) / Scatterheart / In the musicals / 107 steps / New world.
Aug 01. (cd-s) *(332 TP7CD)* **HIDDEN PLACE / GENEROUS PALMSTROKE / VERANDI** 21 -
(cd-s) *(332 TP7CDL)* – ('A'-acapella) / Mother heroic / Foot soldiers.
Aug 01. (d-lp/c/cd) *(TPLP 101/+C/CD) <62653>* **VESPERTINE** 8 19
– Hidden place / Cocoon / It's not up to you / Undo / Pagan poetry / Frosti / Aurora / An echo, a stain / Sun in my mouth / Heirloom / Harm of will / Unison.
Nov 01. (cd-s) *(352 TP7CD)* **PAGAN POETRY / DOMESTICA / BATABID** (DVD) 38 -
(cd-s) *(352 TP7CDL)* – ('A'side) / ('A'-Matthew Herbert mix) / Aurora (opiate mix).

Mar 02. (cd-s) *(332 TP7CD1)* **COCOON / PAGAN POETRY (new music box version) / SUN IN MY MOUTH (recomposed by ensemble)** 35 -
(cd-s) *(332 TP7CD2)* – ('A'-radio) / Aurora (new music box version) / Amphibian (DVD) / ('A'-video).
Nov 02. (d-lp/cd) *(TPLP 359/+CD) <62787>* **GREATEST HITS** 53 ☐
(compilation)
– All is full of love / Hyperballad / Human behaviour / Joga / Bachelorette / Army of me / Pagan poetry / Big time sensuality (the Fluke minimix) / Venus as a boy / Hunter / Hidden place / Isobel / Possibly maybe / Play dead / It's in our hands.
Nov 02. (6xcd-box) *(TPLP 365CD) <62815>* **FAMILY TREE** (collection) ☐ ☐
– Sidasta eg / Giora / Fuglar / Ammaeli / Mamma / Immature / Generous palmstroke / Joga / Mother heroic / The modern things / Karvel / I go humble / Nature is ancient / Unravel / Cover me / Possibly maybe / The anchor song / Hunter / All neon like / I've seen it all / Bachelorette / Play dead / Venus as a boy / Hyperballad / You've been flirting again / Isobel / Joga / Unravel / Bachelorette / All is full of love / Scatterheart / I've seen it all (with THOM YORKE) / Pagan poetry / It's not up to you.
Nov 02. (cd-s) *(366 TP7CD1)* **IT'S IN OUR HANDS / COCOON (rectangled by ensemble) / HUMAN BEHAVIOUR (live)** 37 -
(cd-s) *(366 TP7CD2)* – ('A'side) / Matmos (mix) / Arcade (mix).

– others, etc. –

Aug 96. (12"ltd) *(193 TP12TD)* **POSSIBLY MAYBE (Talvin Singh mix). / I MISS YOU (Dobie mix)** ☐ -
Sep 96. (12"ltd) *(193 TP12DM)* **POSSIBLY MAYBE (LFO mix). / ENJOY (Dom T mix)** ☐ -
Oct 96. (12"ltd) *(193 TP12PT)* **BIG TIME SENSUALITY (Plaid mix). / ONE DAY (Trevor Morais mix)** ☐ -
Jun 97. (12"ltd) *(193 TP12PT)* **BIG TIME SENSUALITY. / ONE DAY** ☐ -
Jun 97. (12"ltd) *(193 TP12PD)* **I MISS YOU (Photek mix). / COVER ME (Dillinja mix)** ☐ -
Jun 97. (12"ltd) *(193 TP12GH)* **ISOBEL'S LONELY HEART (Goldie remix). / HYPERBALLAD (Robin Hood Riding Through The Glen mix)** ☐ -
Jun 97. (12"ltd) *(193 TP12MO)* **POSSIBLY MAYBE (Lucy mix – Mark Bell). / ENJOY (Further Over The Edge mix – Outkast)** ☐ -
Jun 97. (12"ltd) *(193 TP12TT)* **HYPERBALLAD (Towa Tei remix). / ENJOY (The Beats mix – Dom T)** ☐ -
Aug 98. (12"/cd-s; BJORK & FUNKSTORUNG) Fat Cat; *(12/CD FAT 022)* **ALL IS FULL OF LOVE (mixes)** ☐ ☐
Mar 00. (4xcd-box) *(252TP 7BOX)* **A COLLECTION OF SINGLES** ☐ ☐

BLACK

Formed: Liverpool, England . . . 1980 by mainman, COLIN VEARNCOMBE. Following the recruitment of a couple of musical partners in crime, BLACK made their live debut as a trio on New Years' Day 1981. The group issued two independent 45's before getting a break in 1984 with 'WEA' subsidiary, 'Eternal', run by WAH! manager, Pete Fulwell. Despite major label backing, both the 'HEY PRESTO' and revamped 'MORE THAN THE SUN' singles failed to garner anything more than cult/critical acclaim and BLACK soon found themselves without a deal. Virtually running the show alone (mainstay DAVE 'DIX' DICKIE was only operating in a part-time capacity), VEARNCOMBE finally found an outlet for the 'WONDERFUL LIFE' single via the tiny 'Ugly Man' label. A brilliantly lugubrious pop ballad with more than a hint of BLACK humour, the track scraped into the UK Top 75 and prompted 'A&M' to sign the outfit for a second crack at mainstream success. Although the first single, 'EVERYTHING'S COMING UP ROSES' made little headway, 'A&M's investment was rewarded when BLACK finally hit the Top 10 in summer '87 with 'SWEETEST SMILE'. A re-issued 'WONDERFUL LIFE' followed into the Top 10 a couple of months later and a similarly titled debut album made the Top 3 as music lovers clamoured for VEARNCOMBE's soothing balm of intelligent, moodily romantic rock/pop (not unlike early ASSOCIATES or The CHAMELEONS). A follow-up set, 'COMEDY' (1988), made the Top 40 in late '88 although it was obvious BLACK's understated musings weren't quite to the taste of the average chart punter. Guest stars ROBERT PALMER and SAM BROWN were drafted in for cameos on 1991's 'BLACK', VEARNCOMBE's last effort for 'A&M' before heading back to semi-obscurity. No doubt resigned to such a fate anyhow, the BLACK stalwart set up his own label, 'Nero Schwarz', to release 'ARE WE HAVING FUN YET?' (1994), ironically released the same year as 'WONDERFUL LIFE' was trundled out for a third time after being used in a TV ad. • **Songwriters:** VEARNCOMBE with DICKIE on some, until latters departure. Covered SHADES (Iggy Pop – Bowie) / WHOLE WIDE WORLD (Wreckless Eric) / CONTROL (Janet Jackson).

Album rating: WONDERFUL LIFE (*6) / BLACK mini compilation (*6) / COMEDY (*5) / BLACK (*5) / ARE WE HAVING FUN YET? (*4)

COLIN VEARNCOMBE (b.26 May'61) – vocals, guitar, keyboards (ex-EPILEPTIC TITS) / **DAVE 'Dix' DICKIE** – keyboards, guitar (ex-LAST CHANT) / **JIMMIE SANGSTER** – bass

	Rox	not iss.
Jan 82. (7") *(ROX 17)* **HUMAN FEATURES. / ELECTRIC CHURCH**	☐	-

—— (Jun'82) trimmed to a duo of COLIN + DAVE

	W.W.O.	not iss.
Oct 82. (7") *(WW 3)* **MORE THAN THE SUN. / JUMP**	-	-
	Eternal	not iss.
Jan 84. (7") *(JF 3)* **HEY PRESTO. / STEPHEN**	☐	-
(12"+=) *(JF 3T)* – Liquid dream.		

BLACK (cont)

			WEA	not iss.
Jan 85.	(7") (BLACK 1) **MORE THAN THE SUN (remix). / BUTTERFLY MAN**		□	-
	(12"+=) (BLACKT 1) – I could kill you / Wide mouth / Stephen.			

— BLACK are virtually COLIN VEARNCOMBE, with DIX now just the engineer and on part-time keyboard sessions. Other contributions were from ROY CORKHILL – fretless bass / MARTIN GREEN – saxophone / JIMMY HUGHES – drums

			Ugly Man	not iss.
Aug 86.	(12") (JACK 001) **WONDERFUL LIFE. / BIRTHDAY NIGHT**		72	-
	(d7"+=) (JACK 071D) – Sometimes for the asking / Everything's coming up roses.			

			A&M	A&M
Apr 87.	(7"white) (AM 388) <2995> **EVERYTHING'S COMING UP ROSES. / RAVEL IN THE RAIN**		□	□ Nov87
	(12"+=) (AM 388) – It's not like you Lady Jane.			
Jun 87.	(7") (AM 394) <1205> **SWEETEST SMILE. / SIXTEENS**		8	□ Feb88
	(12"+=/cd-s+=) (AM Y/CD 394) – Leave yourself alone / Hardly star-crossed lovers.			
Aug 87.	(7"/c-s) (AM/+C 402) <2969> **WONDERFUL LIFE. / LIFE CALLS**		8	□
	(12"+=/cd-s+=) (AM Y/CD 402) – Had enough / All we need is money.			
Sep 87.	(lp/c/cd) (AMA/AMC/CDA 5165) **WONDERFUL LIFE**		3	□
	– Wonderful life / Everything's coming up roses / Something for the asking / Finder / Paradise / I'm not afraid / I just grew tired / Blue / Just making memories / Sweetest smile. (c+=) – Sixteens. (cd++=) – Hardly star-crossed lovers / Leave yourself alone / It's not like you Lady Jane / Ravel in the rain. (re-iss. Aug91 cd/c; CD/C MID 166)			
Oct 87.	(7") (AM 414) **I'M NOT AFRAID. / HAVE IT YOUR OWN WAY**		□	-
	(12"+=) (AMY 414) – My love.			
Dec 87.	(7") (AM 422) **PARADISE. / DAGGER REELS**		38	-
	(12"+=/cd-s+=) (AM Y/CD 422) – Sometimes for the asking (new version).			
Sep 88.	(7") (AM 468) **THE BIG ONE. / YOU ARE THE ONE**		54	-
	(12"+=/cd-s+=) (AM Y/CD 468) – Scrapbook.			
Oct 88.	(lp/c/cd) (AMA/AMC/CDA 5222) **COMEDY**		32	□
	– The big one / I can laugh about it now / Whatever people say you are / You're a big girl now / Let me watch you make love / Hey, I was right, you were wrong / All we need is money / You don't always do what's best for you / Now you're gone / No one done nothing. (cd+=) – It's not over yet / Paradise lost. (cd re-iss. Jul02 on 'Spectrum'; 839522-2)			
Nov 88.	(7") (AM 480) **YOU'RE A BIG GIRL NOW. / ENOUGH IS ENOUGH**		□	-
	(12"+=/12"pic-d/cd-s+=) (AMY/AMP/CDEE 480) – Reunion.			
Jan 89.	(7") (AM 491) **NOW YOU'RE GONE. / ('A'-Mardi Gras version)**		66	-
	(12"+=/cd-s+=) (AMY/CDEE 491) – Brother o' mine.			

— VEARNCOMBE retained GREEN – (sax, guitar, clarinet) plus ROY MARTIN – drums / BRAD LANG – bass / GORDON MORGAN – guitar / PETE DAVIS – keyboards / STEVE SIDWELL – trumpet / LUIS JARDIM – percussion / CAMILLA GRICHSEL-VEARNCOMBE – backing vocals

Apr 91.	(7"m) (AM 780) **FEEL LIKE CHANGE. / I NEVER WANTED TO WRITE THIS SONG / IT WON'T HELP WHAT'S GOING ON**	56	-
	(12"+=/cd-s+=) (AMY/CDEE 780) – Wonderful life.		
May 91.	(cd/c/lp) (387126-2/-4/-1) <75021 5365-2/-4> **BLACK**	42	□
	– Too many times / Feels like change / Here it comes again / Learning how to hate / Fly up to the Moon / Let's talk about me / Sweet breath of your rapture / Listen / She's my best friend / This is life.		
Jun 91.	(7"/c-s) (AM/+C 753) **HERE IT COMES AGAIN. / EVERY WAKING HOUR**	70	-
	(12"+=/cd-s+=) (AMY/CDEE 753) – Shades / Wonderful life (88 Christmas recording).		
Aug 91.	(7"/c-s) **FLY UP TO THE MOON. / YOU LIFT ME UP / WHAT YOU ARE**	□	-
	(cd-s+=) – Control.		
	(cd-s+=) – Whole wide world / Under wraps / What's right is right. (above featured SAM BROWN – vocals)		

		Nero Schwarz	not iss.
Mar 94.	(cd-s) (CDNERO 1) **(THAT'S) JUST LIKE LOVE / SURRENDER / PAPER CROWN**	□	-
Apr 94.	(cd/c/lp) (NERO CD/MC/LP 9401) **ARE WE HAVING FUN YET?**	□	-
	– Don't take the silence too hard / Swingtime / Wishing you were here / Leaving song / That's just like love / Ave Lolita / Wish the world awake / Paper crown / Change your mind / To take a piece.		

— COLIN disbanded BLACK soon after above

– compilations, others, etc. –

Nov 87.	(m-lp/m-c) WEA; (WX 137/+C) **BLACK** (84-85 material)	□	-
Nov 92.	(c-ep/cd-ep) A&M; **WONDERFUL LIFE / NOW YOU'RE GONE / YOU'RE A BIG GIRL NOW**	□	-
Feb 94.	(7"/c-s) Polygram TV; (580554-7/-4) **WONDERFUL LIFE. / SWEETEST SMILE**	42	-
	(cd-s+=) (580555-2) – The big one / Feel the change.		
Sep 01.	(cd) Polygram; <544257> **THE COLLECTION**	-	□

Frank BLACK (see under ⇒ PIXIES)

Karl BLAKE

Born: c.1958, Australia. Influenced by occult merchants like BLACK SABBATH and inspired by the experimental possibilities opened up by the punk explosion, BLAKE began making his own home spun recordings from 1977 onwards. During this period, the guitarist also initiated The LEMON KITTENS, who, after a solitary RESIDENTS-esque EP, 'SPOONFED AND WRITHING' (which featured a twisted cover of Johnny Kidd's 'SHAKIN' ALL OVER'), invited the equally bizarre multi-instrumentalist DANIELLE DAX into the fold. Based in Richmond, Surrey, the pair worked hard at flouting musical convention over three independently released sets, 'WE BUY A HAMMER FOR DADDY' (1980), 'CAKE FEAST' (1981) and 'THE BIG DENTIST', before DAX ventured solo. BLAKE was also the man behind the obscure GLAND SHROUDS, a series of cassette-only releases appearing on his own label during the early 80's. Slightly higher profile was the SHOCK HEADED PETERS project, a collaboration with DAVE KNIGHT which resulted in only one proper album, 'NOT BORN BEAUTIFUL' (1985). At times dark, rough and nightmarish, the 'PETERS, like most of BLAKE's repertoire, wasn't exactly easy listening. Incredibly, BLAKE would subsequently team up with hard-rock chick, KATERYNA BURBELA (a former guitarist with all-girl trio, ROCK GODDESS!), under the banner of the UNDERNEATH. After only a couple of EP outings, KARL formed the EVIL TWIN (apparently with a guy called DAVE MELLOR!) and augmented MARK PERRY's outfit, ALTERNATIVE TV. In 1988, while others still wanted his guitar/vocals, KARL joined SOL INVICTUS (with TONY WAKEFORD) and contributed bass to work such as 'In The Jaws Of The Serpent'. He subsequently formed BRITISH RACING GREEN, although a whole batch of songs have since been left in the can. Returning full circle, KARL augmented DANIELLE DAX on her early 90's work 'Blast The Human Flower'.

Album rating: Lemon Kittens: WE BUY A HAMMER FOR DADDY (*6) / CAKE FEAST (*5) / ... THE BIG DENTIST (*5) / Karl Blake: THE PREHENSILE TAPES collection (*5) / MANDIBLES (*4) / PAPER-THIN RELIGION collection (*5) / Shock Headed Peters: NOT BORN BEAUTIFUL (*4) / THE FEAR ENGINE (*4) / SEVERAL HEADED ENEMY (*4) / TENDERCIDE (*4)

KARL BLAKE – vocals, guitar, bass, etc.

			Daark Inc.	not iss.
1980.	(c) (D.I. 1) **TANK DEATH**		□	-
1981.	(c) (D.I. 2) **THE NEW POLLUTION**		□	-

LEMON KITTENS

KARK BLAKE – guitar, etc / **G. THATCHER** / **M. MERCER**

		Step Forward	not iss.
Oct 79.	(7"ep) (SF 10) **SPOONFED AND WRITHING**	□	-
	– Shakin' all over / This kind of dying / Morbotalk / Whom do I have to ask / Chalet d'amour / ...Nor a mirror. (re-iss. Apr96 as cd-ep on 'Biter Of Thorpe'; BOT 131-08CD)		

— basically BLAKE + DANIELLE DAX – vocals, keyboards, flute, multi / + live IAN STURGESS – bass / PETE FALLOWELL – drums / briefly joined in the studio MARK PERRY – drums (of ALTERNATIVE TV)

		United Dairies	not iss.
Aug 80.	(lp) (UD 02) **WE BUY A HAMMER FOR DADDY**	□	-
	– P.V.S. (Power Viewed Subjectively) / Small mercies (Evas song) / Coasters / Up in arms / The American cousin / Evidence / Rome burning / (Afraid of being) Bled by leeches / Pain topics / Reversal 2 / These men of old England / Wrist job – Once green and pleasant land / Lycanthrothene / Motet / Throat violence / False alarm (malicious). (cd-iss. Oct93 on 'Biter Of Thorpe'; BOT131 03CD)		
Feb 81.	(lp) (UD 07) **CAKE FEAST**	□	-
	– Kites / Only a rose / Popsykle.		

		Illuminated	not iss.
Dec 81.	(lp) (JAMS 131) **(THOSE THAT BITE THE HAND THAT FEEDS THEM, SOONER OR LATER MUST MEET...) THE BIG DENTIST**	□	-
	– They are both dirty / The hospital hurts the girl / Mylmus / No night not shared / Nudies. (cd-iss. Oct96 on 'Biter Of Thorpe'+=; BOT131 05CD) – Oath / An untimely end.		

— they split early in '82 when DANIELLE DAX went solo; BLAKE joined The REFLECTIONS (alongside MARK PERRY)

GLAND SHROUDS

KARL BLAKE

			Daark Inc.	not iss.
1981.	(c) (D.I. 3) **STAFF IN CONFIDENCE / TOYSHOP UNIVERSAL**		□	-
1982.	(c) (D.I. 4) **ANIMAL DANCE**		□	-
1982.	(c) (D.I. 5) **YOUR ANIMALS**		□	-
1983.	(c) (D.I. 6) **EVERYONE WANTS TO WIN**		□	-

			Detrimental History	not iss.
1980's.	(c) (DHSS 2) **FERTIVE CHEATS**		□	-
1980's.	(c) (DHSS 3) **A TELESCOPE IN THE SKY**		□	-
1980's.	(c) (DHSS 4) **MORGUE DREAMS** (as "HOMUNCULUS")		□	-

— KARL was also behind CHINESE FOUR ABREAST / ORANGE JELLYBABY & SIX WHITE CHOCOLATE MICE / PROBLEM 5.

SHOCK HEADED PETERS

KARL BLAKE + DAVE KNIGHT

		el	not iss.
Sep 84.	(7") (EL 1) **I, BLOOD BROTHER BE. / TRUTH HAS COME**	□	-
	(12"+=) (ONET) – Katabolism / Hate on sight.		
May 85.	(7") (EL3) **THE KISSING OF GODS. / ALWAYS BE WAITING**	□	-
	(12"+=) (ELT 3) – Heartbreak hotel / Mr. Very big.		
Jun 85.	(lp) (FIN 1) **NOT BORN BEAUTIFUL**	□	-
	(cd-iss. Oct96 on 'Cyclops'; CP131 03CD)		

— next with guest **DAVID CROSS** – violin (ex-KING CRIMSON)

Feb 86. (12"ep) (3BC) **LIFE EXTINGUISHER** — Beach Culture / not iss.
– Scorch / Life extinguisher / Son of thumbs of a murderer / Win on condition.

––– split 1986 …

UNDERNEATH

––– **KARL** with **KATERYNA BURBELA** – guitar (ex-ROCK GODDESS)

Oct 86. (7"ep) (GPO 17) **THE IMP OF THE PERSERSE** — el / not iss.
– Fire / Short term agreement.
(12"ep+=) (GPO 17T) – Have I the right? / Black roots: A tribute to Black Sabbath.

May 87. (12"ep) (ACME 9) **LUNATIC DAWN OF THE DISMANTLER**
– Positive force for good and evil / Thick black angular / Black England / White bomb / No / Tragedy boys and girls / Zophia / Bayonet / Smear / Another death in the family / Psranticide / Partyclens plus / This lady devoid / Hanging / Letter from an institution.

––– KARL with DAVE MELLOR formed The EVIL TWIN and worked with MARK PERRY in ALTERNATIVE TV and TONY WAKEFORD in SOL INVICTUS

KARL BLAKE

1992. (c) (TAK 07) **MANDIBLES: EN ROUTE TO TOOTHLESS** — Tak Tak Tak / not iss.
– Reversal 39: safe no happy / Below indigo / Sworn on oath (again) / Reversal 29: on route / Red fisherman / Bottomless, pitiless / Blindo chromo / Quality of love / Help now? I'm in love and no-one can / Page 5b: smalls / Toothy grin / Reversal 43: familiar hostile landscape / English culture for real / Blight on the bloody tower / New men of old England / Queens English / Bleu royale / Reversal 51: dark banner / More than an understanding / Reversal 7: who wins, ever? / Reversal 13: index of impossibility / I yearn and I burn / Hank scar / Reversal 27: victimiser / Reversal: Pistol-packing parson / Man stuff / Junior prig star / Reversal 16: breakfast only seen / Lord of the land / My little plots avail me not / Exit the harpy / Qs and As / Page 1b: The last green bottle / Reversal 19: she who must be obeyed / Reversal 49: Eightball CYA / Reversal 54: Want to tell me your future? / Fly cage rage / Archetypal archetype / Signifying nothing: of sound and fury full / One heaven in her? / Not a mirror to a blindman / The tray / Sandbag / Cabbage white / Again, whom do I have to ask? / Stationary waltz / Paul Pry, the san man / Reaching over / Reversal 22: a removal prayer / Reversal 21: night is a cloak for sinners / Full head start / Considering Pan / Never alone at night / Golden spires / Re-appropriated: not soon enough / Reversal 17: scissors a poem / "A katamaran is not just a boat …" / "Let's get wed and conceive in bed" / Riddle of the sounds: reversal 2 / Reversal 20: when lying is killing those who want only to love you. (cd-iss. Apr96 on 'Swordex Hieroglyph Proper'; SHP 616131-01CD)

– compilations, etc. –

1983. (lp) Glassl (GLASS 013) **THE PREHENSILE TAPES** (compilation 1977-81)
– Baby's in grey / Switchback / Whistle and weep / Blast the human flower / The waiting list / No limits / People with no shoulders / Dreams of Lichen Tester / A misogyny of song / Love so much like violent death.

Nov 87. (lp; by SHOCK HEADED PETERS) Produkt Korps; (PKLP 0020) **THE FEAR ENGINE**
(cd-iss. Oct96 on 'Cyclops'; CP131 05CD)

Nov 92. (cd; by SHOCK HEADED PETERS) Cyclops; (CP131 01CD) **SEVERAL HEADED ENEMY**

Oct 96. (cd; by SHOCK HEADED PETERS) Cyclops; (CP131 07CD) **TENDERCIDE**

Oct 96. (cd) Pro-Evil Pro-Devil; (USED 13102CD) **PAPER-THIN RELIGION: SOLO ARCHIVES 1977-1981**
– Me – in a single skull / Lullaby or knives / Weatherman / Sweeper of leaves / Lamentation blues / Fifty shilling gun / This intimacy / Church of latter-day taint / Dreams of sweet rain / Drogulus / The sky is false / Like flies to wanton boys / Rosette / Soul / The white worm / As electric poison / Slugabed / Characteristics of a rainy day / The malfunction house / Private preserved prohibited locked / Green fuse / Negative essay / Life in despair and afterwards.

BLAKE BABIES
(see under ⇒ HATFIELD, Juliana; 90's section)

BLOOD ON THE SADDLE

Formed: Los Angeles, California, USA … late 1981 by former DEAD HIPPIE, GREG DAVIS, who recruited likeminded RON BOTELHO and HERMANN SENAC. With the addition of ex-BANGLES bassist turned vocalist ANNETTE ZILINKAS, this critically revered cowpunk act completed their eponymous debut in 1984. It would be two years until their follow-up, 'POISON LOVE', although its lack of promotion was a contributing factor to the band's increasing disillusionment. Despite a third effort, 'FRESH BLOOD' (1987) on the influential American imprint 'S.S.T.', consistently poor sales led to these saddle-sore veterans calling it a day. DAVIS continued touring with others as BLOOD ON THE SADDLE and even moonlighted as a member of The VANDALS. In the early 90's, along with bassist CHRIS ENGEL and DANNY RICKARD on drums, the trio performed in and around L.A., although this was curtailed with the tragic death of ENGEL on the 13th of July, 1991. Eventually getting back on the road, GREG and various saddle tramps toured the West Coast and finally set about recording a comeback record for 'Kill Rock Stars' (also home to a legion of Riot Grrrl bands). A whole album's worth of fresh songs, 'NEW BLOOD', surfaced early in 1997 for 'Last Call'; it was indeed.

Album rating: BLOOD ON THE SADDLE (*6) / POISON LOVE (*5) / FRESH BLOOD (*5) / NEW BLOOD (*5)

GREG DAVIS – vocals, guitar, banjo / **ANNETTE ZILINSKAS** – vocals (ex-BANGLES) / **RON BOTELHO** – bass / **HERMANN SENAC** – drums

Apr 84. (lp) <NAR 15> **BLOOD ON THE SADDLE** — not iss. / New Alliance
– Blood on the saddle / I wish I was a single girl again / Car mechanic blues / Be my pretty baby / Ghost on my heart / Freight train / Banks of the Ohio / Do you wanna dance? / Landlord / It hurts me / I've never been married / Johnnies at the fair / Rumpelstiltskin. <cd-iss. 2000 +=; > – I wish I was a single girl again / Ghost on my heart.

Apr 86. (lp) (PETE 1) <CHLP 8601> **POISON LOVE** — Gates Of Heaven / Chameleon Jan86
– One step away / Police siren / Steal you away / Poison love / I thought I heard some thunder / Johnny's at the fair / A bed of roses / Colt 45 / Promise your heart to me / Down and out / In the pines / A mother's love / Abilene. (re-iss. Jun86 on 'New Rose'; ROSE 88)

Sep 87. (lp/cd) (ROSE 126/+CD) <SST 116> **FRESH BLOOD** — New Rose / S.S.T.
– Born with a hole in my pocket / Help wanted / Always there, never here / Rawhide / Endless highway / Burning sun / Black river / Baptist church blues (1 & 2) / Folsom prison / One step away / In the pines / Police siren / Steal you away / Poison love / A bed of roses / Mother's love / Abilene. (re-iss. May93 on 'S.S.T.'; same as US)

––– split later in the year but reformed a few years later

––– **GREG** with **CEASAR VISCARRA** – bass (ex-STAINS, ex-DC3) + **DAVE SHOLLENBARGER** (aka STEVE JONES) – drums

––– (1993/4) GREG with DAVE FRAPPIER – drums (ex-HATED PRINCIPLES) repl. CHRIS ENGEL who died 13/07/91 + JOHN STEPHENSON – bass (ex-NIP DRIVERS) repl. BILLY KOEPKE

Sep 94. (7"ep) <(KRS 235)> **4 SONG 7"** — Kill Rock Stars / Kill Rock Stars
– Please quit calling me from jail / I'm a poor lonesome cowboy / I wanna ramble and roam / Beer drinking man.

Feb 97. (cd) <(42206-2)> **NEW BLOOD** — Last Call / Last Call
– Julie / A little heroin song / Little house in the valley / Police siren / Be my pretty baby / Johnny Reb / Bonanza / Colt 45 (liquor store) / Born with a hole in my pocket / Lost highway / Hopeless / God save the south / Ramble & roam / Beer-drinking man / Poor lonesome cowboy / Quit calling me from jail / Ring of fire.

– compilations, etc. –

1995. (cd) Kill Rock Stars; <KRS 276> **SOME SONGS**

BLOW UP

Formed: Brighton, England … 1986 by NICK ROUGHLEY, who had just departed from 14 ICED BEARS. Completing the line-up with ALAN STIRNER, AZIZ HASHMIX (aye, right!) and CHRIS WINDOW, the jangly, melodic quartet entered the indie scene with two 1987 'Creation' singles, 'GOOD FOR ME' and 'POOL VALLEY'. Becoming more popular in the Netherlands, they released a compilation of these tracks, 'ROLLERCOASTER', having moved to 'Ediesta' then 'Cherry Red' in the process. Two singles, 'FOREVER HOLIDAY' and 'OWN WORLD WAITING', preceded their first album proper, 'IN WATERMELON SUGAR', a somewhat disappointing collection that was more sour than sweet.

Album rating: ROLLERCOASTER compilation (*5) / IN WATERMELON SUGAR (*4) / AMAZON EYEGASM (*4)

NICK ROUGHLEY – vocals (ex-14 ICED BEARS) / **ALAN STIRNER** – guitar / **AZIZ HASHMIX** – bass / **CHRIS WINDOW** – drums

Jun 87. (7") (CRE 045) **GOOD FOR ME. / TO YOU** — Creation / not iss.
(12") (CRE 045T) – ('A'side) / 125 / I won't hurt you.

Nov 87. (12") (CRE 049T) **POOL VALLEY. / WHEN YOU SMILE / WISH**

Jul 88. (lp) (MD 7918) **ROLLERCOASTER** (compilation) — Megadisc / not iss. / Ediesta / Dutch not iss.

Oct 88. (12") (CALC 066T) **FOREVER HOLIDAY. / GOOD FOR NOTHING / TAKE ME AS I WAS**

––– **WILL TAYLOR** (b.23 Aug'68) – bass (ex-14 ICED BEARS) repl. AZIZ

Oct 89. (7") (CHERRY 103) **FOREVER HOLIDAY. / HONKER'S CHA-CHA** — Cherry Red / not iss.
(12"+=) (12CHERRY 103) – Lovescene.

Feb 90. (7") (CHERRY 104) **OWN WORLD WAITING. / SLIP INTO SOMETHING**
(12"+=) (12CHERRY 104) – Little fool 52 / Gut rot.

Feb 90. (cd/c/lp) (CDBRED/BREDMC/BRED 85) **IN WATERMELON SUGAR**
– Own world waiting / Heaven tonight / Sweet skin / Beauty lies / Forever holiday / Baby superstar / What is in your mind? / I / Todd / Wish. (cd+=) – Honker's cha cha / Lovescene / Slip into something / Little fool 52.

Mar 91. (cd/lp) (CD+/BRED 91) **AMAZON EYEGASM**
– Somersault / Fly me across the ocean / World / Thorn of crowns / Caterpillar song / Just sin / She fades away / Different sounding sighs / Across me today.

––– disintegrated after above

BLUE AEROPLANES

Formed: Bristol, England ... 1984 out of The ART OBJECTS and EXPLODING SEAGULLS by GERARD LANGLEY, who has subsequently piloted The BLUE AEROPLANES with an extended, revolving cast of musicians over the course of the last decade. While NICK JACOBS, GERARD's brother, JOHN and dancer WOJTEK DMOCHOWSKI remained constants over the course of the band's career, others such as ANGELO BRUSCHINI came and went according to circumstance. In essence LANGLEY's concept, the BLUE AEROPLANES existed initially as a vehicle for combining GERARD's manic beat poetry with experimental, often psychedelic rock/folk. Following a debut album, 'BOP ART' (1984) on the 'Abstract' label, the band signed with 'Fire', where they developed their sound over further albums, 'TOLERANCE' (1986) and 'SPITTING OUT MIRACLES' (1897). With a serrated guitar sound embellished by backing tapes, banjos, mandolin etc., The BLUE AEROPLANES were nothing if not original although there were discernible BYRDS/FELT traces in their flight path. The late '88 compilation set, 'FRIENDLOVERPLANE', signalled the end of their tenure with 'Fire' and, following an incendiary Christmas gig at Camden's Electric Ballroom, the band were snapped up by 'Ensign'. As the band toured the UK as support to R.E.M. (MICHAEL STIPE guested on that year's album) and grazed the Top 75 with the near radio-friendly rumblings of 'JACKET HANGS', it seemed as if The BLUE AEROPLANES' moment had finally arrived. Their most accessible effort to date, 'SWAGGER' (1990), followed soon after and the band embarked on a hectic touring schedule taking them everywhere from Canada to the Far East. A second single, ' ...AND STONES', also scraped the charts later that summer, possibly one of their most effective marriages of ringing arpeggios and LANGLEY's slurred, half-spoken style. With an extended line-up including a returning BRUSCHINI, the ELVIS COSTELLO co-produced 'BEATSONGS' arrived in 1991 as the most fully formed and consistently listenable album of the band's chequered career, featuring such spiky, infectious pop gems as 'HUH!' and 'COLOUR ME'. Yet although it became their first and only Top 40 hit, the album surprisingly failed to produce a bonafide single and The BLUE AEROPLANES seemed to have missed the boat (or even the train) yet again. A period of instability ensued as the band transferred to 'Beggars Banquet' and underwent more line-up flux, the resulting 'LIFE MODEL' (1994) set failing to excite critics in quite the same fashion as its predecessor. The BLUE AEROPLANES nevertheless remained something of an institution until their split in late '95, content to release relentlessly experimental material to their adoring fans while being generally ignored by the rock, or even indie mainstream. This despite the promise shown by their final recordings for 'Beggars Banquet': 'ROUGH MUSIC' (album) and 'SUGARED ALMONDS' (EP). The BLUE AEROPLANES were flying high again in 2000, producing more of the same experimental and arty dirges on comeback set, 'CAVALIERS'. It was certainly one for the diehard fans, although the sets 15-minute highlight was 'ROUNDHEADS', repeat after me: "got to get to work" aarrgghh! LANGLEY, meanwhile was putting the finishing touches to what was to become his second solo outing, 'RECORD PLAYER', which hit the shops on his own 'Art Star' imprint in 2001. By the end of 2002, The BLUE AEROPLANES were still performing in and around their hometown. Weird shit, indeed, as the title of a compilation set – released in 2002 – suggested. • **Songwriters:** GERARD LANGLEY and JACOBS with other members until latters' departure. Covered; UNSQUARE DANCE (Dave Brubeck) / BAD MOON RISING (Creedence Clearwater Revival) / BREAKING IN MY HEART (Tom Verlaine) / THE BOY IN THE BUBBLE (Paul Simon) / I WANNA BE YOUR LOVER (Bob Dylan) / TOP OF THE POPS (Smithereens).

Album rating: Art Objects: BAGPIPE MUSIC (*5) / Blue Aeroplanes: BOP ART (*6) / TOLERANCE (*6) / SPITTING OUT MIRACLES (*6) / SWAGGER (*8) / BEATSONGS (*8) / LIFE MODEL (*5) / ROUGH MUSIC (*5) / FRIENDLOVERPLANE compilation (*7) / FRIENDLOVERPLANE 2 compilation (*6) / HUH! THE BEST OF THE BLUE AEROPLANES compilation (*8) / CAVALIERS (*6) / WEIRD SHIT collection (*4) / Gerard Langley: SIAMESE BOYFRIENDS mini with Ian Kearey (*4) / RECORD PLAYER (*5)

ART OBJECTS

GERARD LANGLEY – vocals / **JONATHAN KEY** – guitar, synthesizer, vocals / **WILLIAM STAIR** – bass, guitar / **JOHN LANGLEY** – drums, vocals / **ROBIN KEY** – guitar, bass, keyboards / **WOJTEK DMOCHOWSKI** – dance, percussion

	Heartbeat	not iss.
Oct 80. (7") (PULSE 10) **SHOWING OFF TO IMPRESS THE GIRLS. / OUR SILVER SISTER (live)**	☐	-
1981. (lp) (HB 5) **BAGPIPE MUSIC**	☐	-
– Dumbness / Showing off to impress / Conversation / Who switches off the light / Landscape workers / Batpoem / Miraculous birth / 20th century composites / Magog / Passengers of fortune / What am I supposed to do? / Underground market / The paperweight flood.		

	Fried Egg	not iss.
1981. (7"m) (EGG 007) **HARD OBJECTS. / BIBLIOTHEQUE / FIT OF PIQUE**	☐	-

BLUE AEROPLANES

GERARD LANGLEY – vocals / **NICK JACOBS** – rhythm guitar / **WOJTEK DMOCHOWSKI** – dancer / with **JOHN LANGLEY** – drums / **IAN KEAREY** – bass (of OYSTER BAND), + guests WILLIAM STAIR, J.KEY, R. KEY + MAXIMUM JOY members

	Abstract	not iss.
Apr 84. (lp) (ABT 009) **BOP ART**	☐	-
– Control of embassies / Pinkies hit the union / Gunning the works / Owls / Outback jazz / Chelsea wallpaper / Bagpipe music / Built in a day. (re-iss. Feb89 on 'Party'; PART 001RV)		

— added **ANGELO BRUSCHINI** – guitar, vocals (he was to leave and return soon) / **JOHN STAPLETON** – tapes / **RUTH COCHRANE** – bass, vocals / **DAVE CHAPMAN** – guitar, bass, vocals

	Fire	Restless
Mar 85. (12"ep) (FIRE 2) **ACTION PAINTING / LE PETIT CADEAU DE DON JUAN. / ASH TRAYS FROM MT. ETNA / POLICE (38 DIVINITY)**	☐	-
Mar 86. (12"ep) (FIRE 8) **LOVER AND CONFIDANTE PLUS OTHER STORIES**	☐	-
– Lover and confidante / Who built this station in the Midwest / Breaking in my heart / Weird heart.		
Jun 86. (lp) (FIRELP 3) **TOLERANCE**	☐	-
– Arriving / Journal of an airman / Rare flowers / Warhol's fifteen / 30 love / Lover and confidante / Tolerance / Ups / When the wave comes / Soul (seen and unseen). (cd-iss. Oct89 & Sep91; FIRECD 3)		
Oct 86. (7") (BLAZE 12) **TOLERANCE. / WHEN THE WAVE COMES**	☐	-
(12"+=) (BLAZE 12T) – Teaching English people through sex and death (remix) / And the couple in the next room / Complete blessing.		

— briefly added **CAROLINE HALCROW** – guitar (a member in '87) became CAROLINE TRETTINE and subsequently went solo, releasing one 1990 folk mini-set, 'BE A DEVIL', for 'Utility'; contained KEARNEY + JACOBS

Nov 87. (12"ep) (BLAZE 23T) **BURY YOUR LOVE LIKE TREASURE / KING OF THE SOAP BOX / VICE KING'S SON? / CONTINUALLY TORN APART**	☐	-
Nov 87. (lp) (FIRELP 10) <72254-1/4/-2> **SPITTING OUT MIRACLES**	☐	☐
– Goats / Cowardice and caprice / Julie / Spitting out miracles / Ceiling roses / In the mystery / Season ticket to a bad place / Bury your love like treasure / Days of 49 / Teaching English through sex and death / Winter sun / What do you mean (what I said) / Do the dead know what time it is? (free-7"flexi.w/a) – COWARDICE AND CAPRICE Instrumental) (cd-iss. Oct89; FIRECD 10) (re-iss. Oct91; FIRE 33/11 010)		
May 88. (12"ep) (BLAZE 24T) **VEILS OF COLOUR. / SPITTING OUT MIRACLES (remix) / ARRIVING / BUILT IN A DAY**	☐	-

— **RODNEY ALLEN** – vocals, rhythm guitar (ex-PRESS) repl. NICK / **ANDY McCREETH** – bass (ex-PRESS) repl. RUTH

— **GERARD + JOHN LANGLEY, RODNEY, ANDY, WOJTEK** and entourage, added **ALEX LEE** – guitar, keyboards, vocals (now a 7-piece)

	Ensign	Chrysalis
Jan 90. (7") (ENY 628) **JACKET HANGS. / RAZOR WALK**	72	-
(12"+=/cd-s+=) (ENY X/CD 628) – Different now / Big sky.		
Feb 90. (cd)(c/lp) (CCD 1752)(Z+/CHEN 13) **SWAGGER**	54	☐
– Jacket hangs / World view blues / Weightless / . . . and stones / Your ages / Love come around / The applicant / What it is / Anti-pretty / Careful boy / Picture framed / Cat-scan his'try.		
May 90. (7"/c-s) (ENY/+MC 632) **. . . AND STONES (remix). / ('A' lp version)**	63	-
(12"+=/cd-s+=) (ENY X/CD 632) – ('A'vocal) / ('A'-Lovers mix).		
Oct 90. (10"ep/12"ep/cd-ep) (ENY 10/X/CD 636) **THE LOVED EP**	☐	-
– You (are loved) / You're going to need somebody / Sweet Jane / World view blue (acoustic).		

— (Jan'91) **PAUL MULREANY** – drums (ex-JAZZ BUTCHER CONSPIRACY) repl. JOHN / **ANGELO BRUSCHINI** – guitar, accordion, vocals (returned from Saudi Arabia) guests on '91 album, **IAN KEAREY** – multi / **ALEX ACUNA** – percussion / **DANNY TIMMS** – keyboards / **DAVID MANSFIELD** – violins, bouzouki / **J.J. KEY** – guitar / **JERRY MAROTTA** – drums / guest JAZZ BUTCHER – b.vocals / **ELAINE SUMMERS** – vocals

Jul 91. (7") (ENY 647) **YR OWN WORLD. / PONY BOY**	☐	-
(12"+=/cd-s+=) (ENY X/CD 647) – Mis-firing / Autumn journal XXII.		
Aug 91. (cd)(c/lp) (CCD 1856)(Z+/CHEN 21) **BEATSONGS**	33	☐
– Huh! / Yr own world / Angel words / Fun / cardboard box / My hurricane / Jack leaves & back spring / Aeroplane blues / Colour me / Streamers / The boy in the bubble / sixth continent.		
Oct 91. (7") (ENY 649) **THE BOY IN THE BUBBLE. / TALKIN' ON THE OTHER PHONE / DISNEY HEAD**	☐	-
(12"+=) (ENYX 649) – Huh! (remix).		
(cd-s++=) (ENYCD 649) – Disneyhead.		

— added on tour August '91 **HAZEL KEY** – guitar; repl. injured ROBIN (JJ) and **MARCUS WILLIAMS** – bass (MIGHTY LEMON DROPS) repl. injured ANDY / **SUSIE HUGG** – vocals (of KATYDIDS) repl. HAZEL

— now a 5-piece after ANGELO left in July '92

	Beggars Banquet	Beggars Banquet
Jan 94. (12"ep/cd-ep) (BBQ 26 T/CD) **BROKEN AND MENDED / LOVE IS. / STAR CROSS'D / GET OUT!**	☐	-
Mar 94. (cd/c/lp) (BBQ CD/MC/LP 143) **LIFE MODEL**	59	☐
– Broken & mended / (I'm a) Smart drug / Ghost-nets / Frightened at night / Daughter movie / Open / Honey I / Vade mecum gunslinger / Mercury (Hold / Protect / Love) / Fragile.		
Nov 94. (7") (BBQ 39) **THE DETECTIVE SONG. / YOU'RE MINE AND ALWAYS WILL BE: JACK OF ALL HEARTS – JEALOUS TOWN – IT'S ALRIGHT**	☐	-
(cd-s+=) (BBQ 39CD) – A map below / Top of the pops.		
Jan 95. (cd/c/lp) (BBQ CD/MC/LP 167) **ROUGH MUSIC**	☐	-
– Detective song / Sugared almond / Scared / Worry beads / Contact high / A map below / James / Whatever hapened to our golden birds? / Wond'ring wild / Saint me and the Devil / Dark / Secret destination / Dear, though the night is gone.		
Mar 95. (cd-ep) (BBQ 53CD) **SUGARED ALMONDS EP**	☐	-
– Sugared almonds (remix) / Sacred (remix) / Bad moon rising / Broken and mended (live).		

— split later in '95; new guitarist **CALVIN TALBOT**

		Swarf Finger	not iss.
Feb 00.	(d-cd) (SF 038CD) **CAVALIERS**	☐	☐

– Cavaliers (parts 1-12) // Jazz baby / Get out! / Top of the pops / Star-cross'd . Ghosts / Here comes the queen / Smiler with the knyf / Roundheads.

– compilations, others, etc. –

Nov 88. (d-lp/cd) Fire; (FIRE LP/CD 15) / Restless; <72314>
FRIENDLOVERPLANE
– Veils of colour / Complete blessing / Weird heart / Le petit cadeau de Don Juan / Severn beach / Police (36 divinity) / Action painting / Who built this station in the mid west / Old men sleeping on the bowery / 88 out / Ashtrays from Mt.Etna / Gunning the works / King of the soap box / Tolerance / Etiquette! / Continually torn apart / Days of 49 / I wanna be your lover / For Tim Collins / Shame / The couple in the next room / Stripped. (cd+=) – (4 extra tracks). (re-iss. Oct91; FIRE 33/11 015) (cd re-iss. Apr02; SFIRE 008CD)

Nov 92. (cd/c/lp) Ensign; (CD/TC+/CHEN 28) **FRIENDLOVERPLANE 2 (UP IN A DOWNWORLD)**
– You (are loved) / Pony boy / Different now / World view blue (acoustic version) / . . .And stones (lovers all around mix) / Razor walk / Growing up, growing down / Autumn journal XV / Here it comes / For Tim Collins / Talkin' on the otherphone / You're going to need somebody / Missy Lane / Stranger / Trouble, tell me I'm alive / Big sky / Mis-firing / Disney head

Apr 88. (12"ep) Night Tracks; (SFNT 009) **THE EVENING SHOW SESSIONS** (15.2.87)
– Cowardice and Caprice / Coats / What do you mean / Shame.
Apr 96. (cd) Fire; (FIRECD 057) **FRUIT** (live compilation)
Aug 96. (12") Fantastic Plastic; (FP 002) **UP IN A DOWN WORLD.** /
Jun 98. (cd) Reactive; (REMCD 526) **THE BEST OF WARHOL'S 15**
Sep 98. (cd) Chrysalis; (CDCHRM 101) **HUH! (THE BEST OF THE BLUE AEROPLANES)**
– Jacket hangs / Huh! / Colour me / Razor walk / Growing up, growing down / Fun / Weightless / . . .And stones / You (are loved) / Jack leaves and back spring / Antipretty / Disney head / Yr. own world / What it is / Lovething – Higherthing / Sixth continent.
Feb 01. (cd) Swarf Finger; (SF 041CD) **WEIRD SHIT** (rec.1979- . . .)
– Showing off to impress the girls / Mau-Mau / Ticket taker / Popsicle Pete / On the trail of persephone's shoes / Through the smoke hole / Pre-fab buildings / Jacket hangs / Love come round / Vade mecum gunslinger No.1 / Mean time / Blood red roses / Streets of Laredo / Roundheads (on every corner) / Camus in the pocket.

GERARD LANGLEY & IAN KEAREY

(above with an OYSTER BAND member)

		Fire	not iss.
Feb 87.	(m-lp) (FIRELP 4) **SIAMESE BOYFRIENDS**	☐	☐

– Nicknames / Snow-walking / Joe Taylor's / La marisque / Good weather / Dear through the night has gone / The famous aren't.

GERARD LANGLEY

		Art Star	not iss.
Sep 01.	(cd) (AS 001) **RECORD PLAYER**	☐	☐

– Paper plane / Here comes the queen / Spiky young iconclast / 10000 miles / New caucasuan maps / Seymour's brother considered as a drug / Has it all, lost it . . . gone / Art star / Wishing up / Hush deep blue sea / X celebrity / I need.

BLUE NILE

Formed: Glasgow, Scotland . . . 1981 by songwriter PAUL BUCHANAN, PAUL JOSEPH MOORE and ROBERT BELL. After a debut 45 on 'R.S.O.' (just prior to the label going belly up!), they were offered an unusual record contract by East Lothian label, 'Linn', the hi-fi manufacturer using their tape as a demo and subsequently being sufficiently impressed to sign the band up for their recently formed music business venture. After an initial single, 'STAY', in spring '84, the label issued the languorous debut album, 'A WALK ACROSS THE ROOFTOPS'. Garnering gushing reviews, this classic set of understated pop elegance created enough of a buzz for 'Virgin' to take over distribution. Its relatively lowly final chart position of No.80 belied the record's influence and impact, although it would be another five years before a follow-up as the trio locked themselves in the studio and diligently attempted to create another masterpiece. After a few false starts, they finally emerged in 1989 with 'HATS', a record which arguably topped their debut in the late night sophistication stakes, its moody atmospherics delicately caressed by PAUL BUCHANAN's silky croon (a singer who undoubtedly has the potential of being the next SINATRA). A UK Top 20 hit, the record's success saw The BLUE NILE leave their studio cocoon in the early 90's for a tour of America where they ended up working with such luminaries as ROBBIE ROBERTSON and RICKIE LEE JONES amongst others. Now signed to 'Warners', it looked as if The BLUE NILE were finally destined to leave cultdom behind with a third set, 'PEACE AT LAST' (1996). Another classy effort, again the trio enjoyed critical plaudits and modest chart success while simultaneously failing to corner the wider pop market. Rumours are they are about to release their fourth set in not too distant future (another 7-year itch!).

Album rating: A WALK ACROSS THE ROOFTOPS (*8) / HATS (*8) / PEACE AT LAST (*6)

PAUL BUCHANAN – vocals, guitar, synthesizer / **PAUL JOSEPH MOORE** – keyboards, synthesizer, etc. / **ROBERT BELL** – bass, synthesizer, etc.

		R.S.O.	not iss.
Oct 81.	(7") (RSO 84) **I LOVE THIS LIFE. / SECOND ACT**	☐	☐

— added guests **CALUM MALCOLM** – keyboards, vocals (ex-BADGER, ex-HEADBOYS) / **NIGEL THOMAS** – drums

		Linn-Virgin	A&M
Apr 84.	(7"/12") (LKS 1/+12) **STAY. / SADDLE THE HORSES**	☐	☐ 1985

(re-iss. Jan89 remixed 7"/12"/d7"+=; same/same/LKSD 1) – Tinseltown in the rain / Heatwave (instrumental).

Apr 84.	(lp/c) (LKH/+C 1) **A WALK ACROSS THE ROOFTOPS**	80	☐ 1985

– A walk across the rooftops / Tinseltown in the rain / From rags to riches / Stay / Easter parade / Heatwave / Automobile noise. (cd-iss. Jan89; LKHCD 1)

Jul 84.	(7") (LKS 2) **TINSELTOWN IN THE RAIN. / HEATWAVE** (instrumental)	☐	–

('A'ext-12") (LKS 2-12) – Regret.

— now a basic trio plus session musicians.

Sep 89.	(7") (LKS 3) **THE DOWNTOWN LIGHTS. / THE WIRES ARE DOWN**	67	☐

(12"+=/3"cd-s+=) (LKS 3-12/CD3) – Halfway to Paradise (TV theme).

Oct 89.	(lp/c/cd) (LKH/+C/CD 2) <5284> **HATS**	12	☐

– Over the hillside / The downtown lights / Let's go out tonight / Headlights on the parade / From a late night train / Seven a.m. / Saturday night. (re-iss. Apr92 on 'Virgin' cd/c; OVED CD/C 391)

Sep 90.	(7"/c-s) (LKS/+C 4) **HEADLIGHTS ON THE PARADE (Bob Clearmount mix). / ('A'-lp version)**	72	☐

(12"+=/cd-s+=) (LKS 4-12/CD4) – Easter parade (with RICKIE LEE JONES).

Jan 91.	(7"/c-s) (LKS/+C 5) **SATURDAY NIGHT. / ('A'version)**	50	☐

(12"+=/cd-s+=) (LKS 5-12/CD5) – Seven a.m. (live in the U.S.) / or / Our lives.

		Warners	Warners
Jun 96.	(cd/c/lp) (<9362 45848-2/-4/-1>) **PEACE AT LAST**	13	☐

– Happiness / Tomorrow morning / Sentimental man / Love came down / Body and soul / Holy love / Family life / War is love / God bless you kid / Soon.

Sep 96.	(c-ep/cd-ep) (W 0373 C/CD2) **HAPPINESS / NEW YORK MAN / WISH ME WELL**	☐	☐

(cd-ep) (W 0373CD1) – ('A'side) / War is love / O Lolita.

BLUE ORCHIDS

Formed: Manchester, England . . . early 80's, by ex-FALL members MARTIN BRAMAH and UNA BAINES. Boasting a line-up completed by RICK GOLDSTRAW, STEVE TOYNE and JOE KIN, this fondly remembered alternative outfit bear inevitable comparison to The FALL, if only for BRAMAH's very MARK E.-esque vocals. Musically there was less resemblance, the emphasis placed on the harmonic discord of the organ pumping away behind the frontman's half-spoken/half-wailing efforts. The group signed to 'Rough Trade' and debuted with the 'DISNEY BOYS' single in late 1980, the first of many rhythm section replacements coming soon after as IAN ROGERS replaced KIN and TOYNE. Early '81 saw the release of a follow-up single, 'WORK', after which the drum stool was again vacated and subsequently filled by TOBY, a veteran of both The NOSEBLEEDS and DURUTTI COLUMN. The BLUE ORCHIDS' debut album, 'THE GREATEST HIT (MONEY MOUNTAIN)' (1982) made for interesting listening; 'SUN CONNECTION' could almost be described as a post-punk DOORS, the record's swirling hammond and angular guitar occasionally throwing up a treat like 'BAD EDUCATION'. After a further EP, 'AGENTS OF CHANGE', later that year, The BLUE ORCHIDS temporarily went to ground as BAINES joined The FATES and settled down to a life of married bliss with BRAMAH. The couple reactivated the band in 1985 for a one-off single, 'SLEEPY TOWN', BRAMAH subsequently forming THIRST with another ex-FALL man, KARL BURNS, along with his wife, CARRIE and the mysterious LEE. This was another one-off project, resulting in a sole EP, 'RIDING THE TIMES', in Autumn '87. BRAMAH later reformed The BLUE ORCHIDS for one last time in the early 90's, featuring a line-up of indie veteran, CRAIG GANNON alongside MARTIN HENNAN and DICK HARRISON. Signed to the established 'Playtime' label, they issued an EP, 'DIAMOND AGE', followed by an album, 'A VIEW FROM THE CITY' (1991). A final EP, 'SECRET CITY', appeared in late '92, the last chapter in The BLUE ORCHIDS' erratic career.

Album rating: THE GREATEST HIT – MONEY MOUNTAIN (*8) / A VIEW FROM THE CITY compilation (*6) / A DARKER BLOOM compilation (*8)

MARTIN BRAMAH – vocals, guitar (ex-FALL) / **UNA BAINES** – keyboards (ex-FALL) / **RICK GOLDSTRAW** – guitar / **STEVE TOYNE** – bass / **JOE 'KIN'** (b. IAN ROGERS – drums

		Rough Trade	not iss.
Nov 80.	(7") (RT 065) **DISNEY BOYS. / THE FLOOD**	☐	☐

— now without TOYNE

Feb 81.	(7") (RT 067) **WORK. / THE HOUSE THAT FADED OUT**	☐	☐

— **TOBY** – drums (ex-NOSEBLEEDS, ex-DURUTTI COLUMN) repl. ROGERS

1982.	(lp) (ROUGH 37) **THE GREATEST HIT (MONEY MOUNTAIN)**	☐	☐

– Sun connection / Dumb magician / Tighten my belt / A year with no head / Hanging man / Bad education / Wait / No looking back / Low profile / Money mountain.

— **MARK HELLYER** – bass; repl. GOLDSTRAW

Nov 82.	(12"ep) (RTT 117T) **AGENTS OF CHANGE**	☐	☐

– Agents of change / Release / Conscience / The long nights out.

— BAZ MURPHY replaced MARK for a time, before he joined CAPTAINS OF INDUSTRY. UNA took time out to join The FATES, and take up married life with BRAMAH. They both reformed BLUE ORCHIDS in 1985 with **NICK MARSHALL** – drums / **MICK** – bass

		Racket	not iss.
Jun 85.	(12") **SLEEPY TOWN. / THIRST**	☐	☐

— they disbanded again

BLUE ORCHIDS (cont) THE GREAT INDIE DISCOGRAPHY   The 1980s

THIRST

— were formed by **BRAMAH** and another (ex-FALL) drummer **KARL BURNS** / plus his wife **CARRIE BURNS** – guitar (ex-SEEDS) / **LEE** – bass

Rough Trade not iss.

Oct 87. (12"ep) *(RTT 206)* **RIDING THE TIMES**
– Riding the times / Let go / The unknown / Crystal kiss.

— they split and BRAHAM re-joined The FALL in 1989, but left 1990; another group of same name released the single 'Devious'

BLUE ORCHIDS

— re-formed with **BRAMAH** + **CRAIG GANNON** – guitar (ex-SMITHS, ex-AZTEC CAMERA, ex-BLUEBELLS) / **MARTIN HENNAN** – bass / **DICK HARRISON** – drums

Playtime not iss.

Mar 91. (12"ep) **DIAMOND AGE. / MOTH**

Authentic not iss.

Nov 92. (12"ep) **SECRET CITY**
– Dark matter kid / Out of sight / Love fiend / NY gargoyles.

— **BRAMAH** recruited **ALISTAIR 'BAZ' MURPHY** – keyboards / **STAURT KENNEDY** – bass / **ADRIAN WHITE** – drums

— split (1995) for the last time after 1993 album, 'THE SLEEPER' was shelved – until January 2003

– compilations, etc. –

Oct 91. (cd/lp) *Playtime; (AMUSE 011 CD/LP)* **A VIEW FROM THE CITY**
– The flood / Work / Agents of change / Sun connection / Bad education / Release / Low profile / Diamond age / Disney boys / Dumb magician / Wait / Sleepy town / A year with no head / Conscience / Moth / Tighten my belt / No looking back / The house that faded out / The long night out.

Jan 02. (cd) *Cherry Red; (CDMRED 203)* **A DARKER BLOOM – THE BLUE ORCHIDS COLLECTION**
– Disney boys / The flood / Work / The house that faded out / Sun connection / Wait / Dumb magician / Low profile / No looking back / Bad education / A year with no head / Tighten my belt / Agents of change / Conscience / Release / The long night out / Sleepy town / Diamond age / Out of sight.

BLURT

Formed: London, England . . . 1980 by poet TED MILTON and brother JAKE. Having previously toured his provocative one-man puppet theatre project, 'Mr. Pugh's Blue Show' around Britain and Europe, TED turned his eccentric talents to playing a mean sax and narrating/screaming his way through what could only loosely be described as songs. Along with guitarist PETE CREESE, the trio issued a debut single, 'MY MOTHER WAS A FRIEND OF AN ENEMY OF THE PEOPLE', in summer 1980, following it up with a live album, 'IN BERLIN' (1981), the latter featuring the classic 'PUPPETEERS OF THE WORLD UNITE'. MILTON had already released a solo EP, 'CONFESSIONS OF AN AEROPLANE FARTER'. A debut solo album proper, 'BLURT', appeared on 'Red Flame' in 1982, MILTON subsequently bringing in keyboard player HERMAN MARTIN and moving away from the initial guitar-orientated sound. The frontman's manic lyrical poetry remained the focal point of BLURT throughout the 80's, although the eventual replacement of MILTON's brother by sticksman/violinist, PAUL WIGENS (prior to 1986 album, 'POPPYCOCK'), added a further twist to BLURT's already twisted sound. A gap of three years ensued before 'KENNY ROGERS' GREATEST HIT: TAKE 2' (1989), a live set, 'THE BODY!..' released the same year. Sadly, MILTON hung up his instrument after 1992's 'PAGAN STRINGS', abandoning sax devotees to the mercy of KENNY G and his ilk.

Album rating: IN BERLIN (*7) / BLURT (*5) / POPPYCOCK (*5) / SMOKE TIME (*4) / KENNY ROGERS' GREATEST HIT (*4) / THE BODY LIVES (*4) / PAGAN STRINGS (*4)

TED MILTON – vocals, saxophone / **PETE CREESE** – guitar, trombone / **JAKE MILTON** – drums, vocals

Test Press not iss.

Aug 80. (7") *(TP 1)* **MY MOTHER WAS A FRIEND OF AN ENEMY OF THE PEOPLE. / GET**

Armageddon Ruby

Feb 81. (lp) *(ARM 6)* **IN BERLIN (live)**
– Cherry blossom polish / My mother was a friend of an enemy of the people / Puppeteers of the world unite / Dyslexia blues / Get / Tube plane / Paranoid blues / Ubu. *(re-iss. Apr84; same)*

Jun 81. (7") *(AS 013)* **THE FISH NEEDS A BIKE. / THIS IS MY ROYAL WEDDING SOUVENIR**

— added **HERMAN MARTIN** – keyboards

Red Flame not iss.

May 82. (m-lp) *(RF 1206)* **BLURT**
– Dog save my sole / Trees / Physical fitness / Empty vessels / Play the game / The ruminanth plinth / Arthur.

— **STEVE EAGLET** – guitar repl. CREESE

Devine not iss.

1984. (lp) **BULLETS FOR YOU** – French

Embryo not iss.

Jan 85. (7"; as MILTON) *(CELET 2)* **LOVE IS LIKE A VIOLENCE. / NOW THAT STARLINGS**

Another Side not iss.

Apr 85. (lp) *(SIDE 8418)* **WHITE LINE FEVER. / SHARKS OF PARADISE / NOMADS**

Apr 85. (lp) **FRIDAY THE 12th**
– Cherry blossom polish / Deepfrozen heart / Enemy ears / No go dada / Grave spit / Kill time / Dog save my soul / The fish needs a bike / Benighted.

— **PAUL WIGENS** – drums, violin; repl. JAKE

Toeblock not iss.

Nov 85. (12"; as TED MILTON) *(TBL 001)* **ODE: O TO BE SEEN THROUGH YOUR EYES**

Apr 86. (lp) *(TBL 002)* **POPPYCOCK**
– Domain of dreams / Down in the Argentine / Men to fly / etc.

Mar 87. (lp/cd) *(TB LP/CD 400307)* **SMOKE TIME**
– Smoke time / Nights before / Bulletproof vest / Aboule ton fric / Through by you / Congregate / The body that they built to fit the car / Schadenfreude / The tree is dead, long live the tree. *(re-iss. 1989 on 'Celluloid' lp/c/cd; MT/+C/CD 013)*

— **NICK MURCOTT** – drums; repl. WIGENS

Apr 89. (lp/cd) *(TB LP/CD 666)* **KENNY ROGERS' GREATEST HIT: TAKE 2**
– Shoot & shout / Kenny Rogers' greatest hit / Healthy shadows / Mirador / Am I lonesome tonight / Portage & Main / Sharks of Paradise / Forget about for whom the last bell / Chanson du sang / Nameless / Stroud the town of make-believe / Ubuture / The body that they built to fit the car / O to be seen through your eyes (ode).

Jul 89. (lp/cd) *(EFA 15081/+CD)* **THE BODY! LIVE! (live)**
– They bombed too soon / The body that they built to fit the car / Mickey / Enemy ears / Schadenfraude / Argentine / Nights before / Empty vessels / Poppycock / Jap zero / No there's a thing / Aboulton / Eric / Deep-frozen heart. (above issued on 'Heute')

1990. (cd) **THE BODY THAT THEY BUILT**
– The body that they built to fit the car / Mickey / Jap zero / Too bombed too soon / Now there's a thing.

Aug 92. (cd) *(TBCD 013)* **PAGAN STRINGS**
– Phone Monika / Alouette / Slow boat / Bright red white + blue / Authors / Violin sherbet / La clef des champs / Bird trigger / Machina machina / Universal love song / Planet you / Chouettes / Amour de ma vie / Mesopotamia / End of an era / People can fly / People can fly (2). *(re-iss. Feb97 on 'Spalax'; 14988)*

— split after above

TED MILTON

Embryo not iss.

1993. (lp) **LOVE IS LIKE A VIOLENCE**
(cd-iss. 2000 on ltd-'JohnJohn' records')

Bahia not iss.

1994. (cd; as TED MILTON & THE BLURT BIG BAND) **MAGIC MOMENTS** – German
– Burial mound / First World trombone / The A2 through thong / Click / The neutral territories / First dag issue / What's happening to you, Milton? / Columbus / A grace.

T.M. not iss.

1994. (7"; as TED MILTON & BOBONUS BEATS) **POSTCARD** – German
1994. (7"; as TED MILTON & GOZ OF KERMEUR) **THE INFLATABLE HEDGE** – German

1995. (cd; as TED MILTON & The BACK TO NORMAL ORCHESTRA) **NOGALES** – German
– Nogales / On ade & troop I swarm for free / Take your partners for the bullet that never left the gun in Denver, Colorado / Ver de verre / Wherever the unicorn mides / Say something sweet / I'm glad my photograph's come down / She spent a fortune on lipstick on me / My north face / Treise / Walk like a nubian / Cut / Listen to my South Sea bubble.

1997. (cd; by BLURT) **CELEBRATING THE BESPOKE: CELL OF LITTLE-EASE** – German

not iss. House Musik

1999. (12"; as TED MILTON & ANDREAS GERTH + PADDY STEER) **O PITY US**

— LOOPSPOOL is actually ANDREAS GERTH

Charhizma not iss.

Mar 00. (cd/lp; as TED MILTON & LOOPSPOOL) *(008)* **SUBLIME** – German
– Suck on the night / In your world / You've seen the light / L'Alpiniste / C'est ta faute / The room / Fragments / Don't let love pass you by / I've stolen all of your being.

BLYTH POWER

Formed: Camden Town, London, England . . . 1984 by Somerset lad, JOSEF PORTA, who had recently departed from Yeovil mob, er . . . called The MOB. This early 80's anarchist punk combo was completed by CURTESS and MARK WHO, a handful of singles (one for 'Crass', 'NO DOVES FLY HERE') and an album, 'LET THE TRIBE INCREASE' (1983), taking a similar line in defiant protest as the likes of CRASS. By 1984, PORTA had begun pursuing a rootsier direction with his new punk/folk outfit, BLYTH POWER (named after a Class 56 diesel engine), lyrically exploring the history of England's working classes from a largely rural perspective and taking in historical oppressors from Oliver Cromwell onwards. The missing link between NEW MODEL ARMY and The LEVELLERS, BLYTH POWER sparked their own mini-musical revolution, debut single 'CHEVY CHASE' sadly not evaluating the career of the latter day comic actor. Several albums later, PORTA and his merry band were commanding a small army of grass roots fans with their poetic evocations of past victories for the common man.

Album rating: The Mob: LET THE TRIBE INCREASE (5) / Blyth Power: A LITTLE TOUCH OF HARRY IN THE MIDDLE OF THE NIGHT cassette (*5) / WICKED WOMEN, WICKED MEN AND WICKET KEEPERS (*5) / THE BARMAN & OTHER STORIES (*5) / ALNWICK AND TYNE (*5) / THE GUNS OF CASTLE CARY (*4) / PASTOR SKULL (*4) / PARADISE RAZED (*4) / OUT FROM UNDER THE KING (*4) / PONT AU-DESSUS DE LA BRUE compilation (*5) / TEN YEARS INSIDE THE HORSE: THE BEST OF BLYTH POWER compilation (*6)

The MOB

JOSEF PORTA (b.21 Feb'62, Templecombe, Somerset, England) – drums / **MARK WHO** – vocals, guitar / **CURTESS YOUE** – bass

	All The Madmen	not iss.
Jan 80. (7") *(MAD 1)* **YOUTH. / CRYING AGAIN**	☐	–
Dec 80. (7"m) *(MAD 2)* **WITCH HUNT. / SHUFFLING SOUL / WHAT'S GOING ON**	☐	–
Apr 82. (7") *(321984-7)* **NO DOVES FLY HERE. / I HEAR YOU LAUGHING**	☐	–

(above issued on the 'Crass' label)

Feb 83. (lp) *(MAD 4)* **LET THE TRIBE INCREASE**
 – Another day, another death / Cry of the morning / Dance on (you fool) / Raised in a prison / Slayed / Our life, our world / Gates of Hell / I wish / Never understand / Roger / Witch hunt. (cd-iss. Oct95 on 'Rugger Bugger' lp/cd+=; SEEP 012/+CD) – Youth / Crying again / Shuffling souls / No doves fly here / I hear you laughing / The mirror breaks / Stay.

Oct 83. (7") *(MAD 6)* **THE MIRROR BREAKS. / STAY**

	Cause For Concern	not iss.
Nov 84. (lp/c; shared with APOSTLES) *(CFC 002/015)* **LIVE AT LMC** (live)	☐	–

– compilations, etc. –

Oct 86. (d7"ep) *All The Madmen; (MAD 13)* **CRYING AGAIN / YOUTH / NO DOVES FLY HERE. / GATES OF HELL / WHAT'S GOING ON**

BLYTH POWER

— **JOSEF PORTA** – vocals / **NEIL** – / **ANDY** – / **CURTESS** – bass / **SARAH LEWINGTON** – backing vocals / **GARY JAMES HATCHER** – drums

	96 Tapes	not iss.
Mar 85. (c) *(96 15)* **A LITTLE TOUCH OF HARRY IN THE MIDDLE OF THE NIGHT**	☐	–

	All The Madmen	not iss.
Sep 85. (7") *(MAD 9)* **CHEVY CHASE. / PFUCKE MASTICHE ROOM**	☐	–
May 86. (7") *(MAD 12)* **JUNCTION SIGNAL. / BIND THEIR KINGS IN CHAINS (& THE NOBLES WITH LINKS OF IRON)**	☐	–

(12"+=) *(MADT 12)* – Tribute to Admiral Byng / Pfucke mastiche room.

— JOSEF recruited **MARTIN 'PROTAG' NEISH** + **SIAN JEFFRIES** plus **LIBERTY KROPOTKIN** – drums

Apr 87. (lp) *(MADLP 006)* **WICKED WOMEN, WICKED MEN AND WICKET KEEPERS**
 – Goodbye General / Stand into danger / Bricklayers arms / Smoke from Cromwell's gun / John O'Grant / Hurling time / Probably going to rain / Caligula / Probably won't be easy / Marine's moves / Ixion / Some of Shelley's hang-ups.

	Midnight Music	not iss.
May 88. (lp) *(CHIME 0036S)* **THE BARMAN & OTHER STORIES**	☐	–

 – Up from the country / The barman / City of Morpeth / Boys in the bag / Me & Mr Absolutely / It's not going to happen again / The bishop at the gate / Chilterns / Hard summer long / He who would valient be / Bind their kings in chains / Goodbye to all that.

May 88. (12"ep) *(DONG 37)* **UP FROM THE COUNTRY. / A TALE OF A COCK AND A BULL / BLOW THE MAN DOWN**
Aug 88. (7") *(DONG 38)* **GOODBYE TO ALL THAT. /**
Jan 89. (lp) *(CHIME 0042S)* **PONT AU-DESSUS DE LA BRUE** (compilation)
 – Chevy Chase / My lady's games / God has gone wrong again / Song of the third cause / The ffucke masticke room / Junction signal / Emmanuel / Coriolanus / A tale of a cock and a bull / Blow the man down / The rookery / Father O'Brien / McArthur.
Jan 90. (7") *(DONG 58)* **BETTER TO BAT. /**
Apr 90. (lp) *(CHIME 0102)* **ALNWICK & TYNE**
 – Alnwick & Tyne / Lord of the isles / Shift / Under the sea wind / McArthur / When a knight won his spurs / Summer song / The thin red line / Song of the third cause / Right hand man / Better to bat / Execution song.
Apr 91. (lp/cd) *(CHIME 0116/+CD)* **THE GUNS OF CASTLE CARY**
 – Animal farm / The guns of Castle Cary / Trooper Shaw / Via quintana / The bugles of Company B / A little touch of Harry / A little touch of Harry II / Knights of Malta / Paradise sold / Inside the horse.

	Downward Spiral	not iss.
Nov 92. (cd) *(DR 001CD)* **KARPOV CROSSES THE BORDER**	☐	– German

 – Sunne in splendour / Westminster and Wandsworth / Stonehaven / Lambert simnel / House of cards / Breitenfeld / Pastor skull / Carlisle / Lines of graves / Stonehaven '92 / Man who came in third / Pandora's people.

Nov 93. (cd) *(DR 002CD)* **PASTOR SKULL**
 – Royal George / Pastor skull / The man who came in third / Gabriel the angel / In the lines of graves / Breitenfeld / General winter / The sunne in splendour / Stonehaven / Vane tempest / Pandora's people / Stitching in time. (re-iss. Dec98 as 'A REDEDICATION OF PASTOR SKULL – live in Harlow'; DR 006CD)
Feb 95. (cd) *(DR 003CD)* **PARADISE SOLD**
 – Bacchus on the wagon / Signalman white / Rowan's riding / Carlisle / Ghilbert de Haace / Milton's schemes / Letter from Reiffel / Burning Joan / Winter's tale / Cold war comforts / Cry Carlion / Stonehaven (version).
Sep 96. (cd) *(DR 004CD)* **OUT FROM UNDER THE KING**
 – God's orders / Lord Clay Cross / Westminster and Wandsworth / Emma / Katherine's will / Lambert simnel / Owen's tail / Father O'Brien / Swing / Battle of the nations / Holly band the ivy.
1998. (cd) *(DR 005CD)* **WHEN DEATH WENT TO BED WITH A LADY** – – German
1999. (cd) *(DR 007CD)* **GLADLY GIVE TO CAESAR** – – German
 – Westminster and Wandsworth / General winter / House of cards / Lambert and Simnel / Sunne in September / Burning Joan / Bomber Harris / Mary's mad army / Cold war comforts / On the Viking station / Alnwick and Tyne / Father O'Brien / Marius moves / Goodbye to all that / Animal farm / Ixion.
2000. (cd) *(DR 008CD)* **THE BRICKLAYER'S ARMS**
 – The bricklayer's arms / Blow the man down / It's probably going to rain / Coriolanus / Smoke from Cromwell's time / John O'Gaunt / Hurling time / Goodbye general to lose / God has it wrong again / Bind their kings in chains / Stand into danger / The junction signal.

Apr 01. (cd; as MAD DOGS AND ENGLISHMEN) *(WPTCD 19)* **GOING DOWN WITH ALICE**
 – Rich seam / House of war / Kater murr / Soldier on the mantelpiece / Canard's grace / Cynthia's revels / Seven hills / Land sea and sky / It's your time to leave / Full circle.
(above issued on 'Whippet')
Apr 02. (cd) *(DR 010CD)* **ON THE VIKING STATION**
 – McCullogh and guinea / Mary's mad army / Cider dreaming time / Armstrong goes to war / Rebels angels / Wintersfiend / House of cards / On the Viking station / To horse and away / Sometimes I wonder / To Wallis & sonnet / Edward lay bare.

– compilations, etc. –

Aug 94. (cd) *Anagram; (CDMGRAM 83)* **TEN YEARS INSIDE THE HORSE: THE BEST OF BLYTH POWER**
 – Stand into danger / Hurling time / Probably going to rain / Hard summer long / He who would valiant be / Me and Mr. Absolutely / Chilterns / Summer song / Song of the 3rd cause / Execution song / Inside the horse / Animal farm / Knights on Malta / Guns of Castle Cary / Vane tempest / Pastor skull / Royal George. (<re-US-iss.Sep00; same)>

B-MOVIE

Formed: Mansfield, Nottinghamshire, England ... 1979 by STEVE HOVINGTON and two former ABORTED members GRAHAM BOFFEY and PAUL STATHAM. Picked up by the local 'Dead Good' label, the band had a couple of tracks, 'REFUGE' and 'MAN ON A THRESHOLD', included on compilation set, 'East'. Adding a new dimension to their doomy guitar jangle with the addition of keyboard player, RICK HOLLIDAY, the band released the 'TAKE THREE' EP in 1980, earning themselves positive column inches in the process. Following a further 6-track EP 'NOWHERE GIRL', the band signed to Stevo's 'Some Bizzare' imprint – he also became their manager – and released the anthemic 'REMEMBRANCE DAY', the track's synth flourishes bizarrely reminiscent of ABBA's 'Gimme A Man After Midnight'(!). Yet it was B-MOVIE's association with the New Romantic scene rather than boy/girl Swedish pop that proved a thorn in their side as they attempted to break beyond the bounds of the indie chart. Major personnel changes resulted in an almost completely different line-up (HOVINGTON, STATHAM and newcomer MARTIN WINTER – RICK HOLLIDAY formed SIX SEE RED) by the release of the band's long awaited debut album, 'FOREVER RUNNING' (1985). Issued by major alternative player, 'Sire', and preceded by a single, 'A LETTER FROM AFAR', the record's release was marred by the band's collapse.

Album rating: FOREVER RUNNING (*5) / THE DEAD GOOD TAPES compilation (*6) / REMEMBRANCE DAY compilation (*6)

STEVE HOVINGTON – vocals, bass / **PAUL STATHAM** – guitar / **RICK HOLLIDAY** – keyboards, bass / **GRAHAM BOFFEY** – drums

	Dead Good	not iss.
Jul 80. (7"ep) *(DEAD 9)* **TAKE THREE EP**	☐	–

 – The soldier stood alone / Drowning man / Soundtrack.

Dec 80. (12"ep) *(BIG DEAD 12)* **NOWHERE GIRL EP**
 – Nowhere girl / This is still life / Institution walls / Aeroplanes and mountains / Left out in the cold / Remembrance day.

	Deram	not iss.
Mar 81. (12") *(DMX 437)* **REMEMBRANCE DAY. / INSTITUTION WALLS (remix)**	61	–
Jul 81. (7"/12") *(DM/+X 443)* **MARILYN DREAMS. / FILM MUSIC (Part 1)**	☐	–

— added (on tour only) **LUCIANO CODEMO** then **MIKE PEDHAM** – bass (ex-EVEREST THE HARD WAY)

	Some Bizzare	not iss.
Mar 82. (7") *(BZZ 8)* **NOWHERE GIRL. / SCARE SOME LIFE INTO ME**	67	–

(12"+=) *(BZZ 8-12)* – ('A' version).

— **AL CASH** – drums; repl. ANDY JOHNSON who temp'd for BOFFEY (he became a member of SLAUGHTERHOUSE 5)

— **MARTIN WINTER** – bass; repl. MARTIN SMEDLEY who repl. PEDHAM

— (1983) RICK HOLLIDAY left to form SIX SEE RED (and later MCX) with ex-SOFT CELL guest CINDY ECSTASY. One 12" single appeared in Feb'84, 'SHAKE IT RIGHT' / 'BANG 'EM RIGHT' on 'Sire' (SIR 4059T)

	Sire	Sire
Jan 84. (7"/ext.12") *(SIR 4058/+T)* **A LETTER FROM AFAR. / NO JOY IN HEAVEN**	☐	–

— trimmed to a trio of HOVINGTON, STATHAM + WINTER (CASH left)

— drumming was supplied by **GRAHAM BROAD** + **JAMIE LANE**

Sep 85. (7") *(W 8933)* **SWITCH ON SWITCH OFF. / JUST AN ECHO**
(12"+=) *(W 8933T)* – Forever running.
Oct 85. (lp/c) *(925272-1/-4)* **FOREVER RUNNING**
 – Forever running / Heart of gold / My ship of dreams / Just an echo / Remembrance day / Switch on switch off / Blind allegience / Arctic summer / Nowhere girl.

— split late in '85 when STATHAM joined PETE MURPHY's band. HOVINGTON formed ONE with SARA JANE (ex-BELLE STARS)

– compilations, etc. –

on 'Wax' records unless mentioned otherwise

May 87. (7") *(7WAX 2)* **REMEMBRANCE DAYS. / MARILYN DREAMS**
(12"+=) *(12WAX 2)* – Nowhere girl.
Mar 88. (lp/cd)(pic-lp) *(WAX LP/CD 1)(WAXLP 1P)* **THE DEAD GOOD TAPES**

Apr 88.	(12",12"pink,12"orange) *(12WAX 3)* **NOWHERE GIRL. / REMEMBRANCE DAY**
Aug 88.	(12"clear/cd-s) *(12/CD WAX 4)* **POLAR OPPOSITES. / TAXI DRIVER** *(re-iss. Jul89 as 12"pic-d; same)*
Nov 91.	(lp) *Dead Good; (GOOD 3)* **REMEMBRANCE DAYS** – Man on a threshold / Refugee / Drowning man / Soundtrack / Nowhere girl / Institution walls / This still life / Left out in the cold / Remembrance day / Aeroplanes and mountains / Remembrance day (version) / Remembrance day (version). *(with free 7")* – THE FOOL. / SWINGING LIGHTS *(cd-iss. Mar97 on 'Cherry Red'; CDMRED 137)*
Jun 01.	(cd) *Cherry Red: (CDMRED 186)* **BBC RADIO SESSIONS 1981-1984**

BMX BANDITS

Formed: Bellshill, Lanarkshire, Scotland ... summer 1985 by DUGLAS T. STEWART (ex-PRETTY FLOWERS) and future SOUP DRAGONS: SEAN DICKSON and JIM McCULLOCH. In 1986, they released a couple of 45's for Stephen Pastel's '53rd & 3rd' label, notably 'THE DAY BEFORE TOMORROW'. Later that year, DUGLAS was joined by drummer FRANCIS MACDONALD, although the pace slowed a little to let DUGLAS get out and support The SHOP ASSISTANTS (he was to mime Klaus Wunderlich on the organ and later host a night-time pop-TV show). In 1989, The BMX BANDITS' return was complete with the release of a debut long-player, 'C86' (1990!). A year later, having signed to Tokyo-based 'Vinyl Japan', DUGLAS and Co (this time around boasting a beefed up sound courtesy of MACDONALD, EUGENE KELLY, GORDON KEEN and JOE McALINDEN) issued a more up to date jangle-pop follow-up, 'STARWARS' (1991). Subsequently signing to 'Creation' (who else!?), the 'BANDITS enjoyed cult success with 'SERIOUS DRUGS' and 'KYLIE'S GOT A CRUSH ON US' (the latter boasting of Miss MINOGUE's surprising patronage!); the latter was also performed by local friends and cohorts, TEENAGE FANCLUB. During the mid-90's, this Bellshill pedal-(steel) powered supergroup delivered a further two sets of pleasant, harmony-fuelled retro-pop in 'GETTIN' DIRTY' (1995) and 'THEME PARK' (1996). In February '97, DUGLAS T. STEWART & COMPANY (i.e. NORMAN BLAKE) delivered what was to be a swansong set, 'FRANKENSTEIN'. • **Songwriters:** DUGLAS, until 1990 when he co-wrote with NORMAN BLAKE. Covered DON'T FIGHT IT, FEEL IT (Primal Scream) / C'EST LA VENT BETTY (Gabriel Yared) / GREEN GROW (Rabbie Burns; trad) / YO YO SONG (trad) / THINKIN' 'BOUT YOU BABY (Beach Boys) / GIRL AT THE BUS STOP (Television Personalities) / COME AND GET IT (Badfinger) / KYLIE'S GOT A CRUSH ON US (melody; Clydesmen) / LIKE A HURRICANE (Neil Young) / NAZI PUNKS FUCK OFF (Dead Kennedys) / CAST A SHADOW (Johnson-Lunsunda-Lewis) / I CAN'T STAY MAD AT YOU (Goffin-King) / THAT SUMMER FEELING (Jonathan Richman) / LITTLE RIVER OF SPRING (Okana-Takano). • **Trivia:** Took their name from children's bike film of the same name. 'KYLIE'S GOT A CRUSH ON US' was tongue-in-cheek humour about that lovely Australian singer!?

Album rating: C86 (*6) / A TOTALLY GROOVY LIVE EXPERIENCE (*5) / STARWARS (*6) / GORDON KEEN AND HIS BMX BANDITS mini (*5) / LIFE GOES ON (*7) / GETTIN' DIRTY (*5) / THEME PARK (*7)

DUGLAS STEWART – vocals / with **SEAN DICKSON** – bass / **JIM McCULLOCH** – guitar (both of SOUP DRAGONS) / **BILLY & WILLIE** (of SHOP ASSISTANTS?)

53rd & 3rd — *not iss.*

Jul 86.	(7") *(AGARR 003)* **SAD? / E102** (12"+=) *(AGARR 003-12)* – The cat from outer space (live) / Strawberry Sunday (live) / Groovy good luck friend (live).
—	now w /out SEAN (B-side only for JIM)
Jan 87.	(7") *(AGARR 006)* **WHAT A WONDERFUL WORLD. / THE DAY BEFORE TOMORROW** (12"+=) *(AGARR 006-12)* – Johnny Alucard / Sad? / Sandy's wallet.

DUGLAS w/ **FRANCIS MACDONALD** (b.11 Sep'70) – drums / + **GORDON KEEN** – guitar / + **NORMAN BLAKE** – guitar, vocals (of TEENAGE FANCLUB)

Jun 88.	(7") *(AGARR 018)* **FIGURE 4. / STARDATE 21.11.70.** (12"+=) *(AGARR 018T)* – In her hair / Bette Blue.

now w / **NORMAN BLAKE + GERRY** (from TEENAGE FANCLUB)

Click — *not iss.*

Mar 90.	(lp) *(LP 001)* **C86** – Right across the street / Top Shop girl / Rimbaud and me / Yo yo song (1969) / Medley: Disco girl – Disco daze and disco knights / Your class / Disco girl II / Whirlpool / C86 / On somedays / But tonight / Let Mother Nature be your guide / Heaven's daughter. *(cd-iss. Nov92 as 'C86 AND MORE' on 'Vinyl Japan'+=; ASKCD 19)* – Stardate / Figure 4 / Strawberry sundae / C'est la vent Betty / Thinkin' 'bout you baby / Let Mother Nature be your guide (karaoke mix) / Your class. *(cd re-iss. Jul97 on 'Elefant'; ER 1048)*

Avalanche — *not iss.*

Dec 90.	(cd/lp) *(ONLY CD/LP 007)* **TOTALLY GROOVY LIVE EXPERIENCE (live at Hattonrig Hotel)** – Whirl pool / Girl at the bus stop / Your class / In her hair / E102 / Bongo brains / Disco girl / The day before tomorrow / Like a hurricane / Nazi punks fuck off.

DUGLAS now w/ **EUGENE KELLY** (ex-VASELINES, of CAPTAIN AMERICA + EUGENIUS) + **GORDON KEEN | JOE McALINDEN** – guitar (of GROOVY LITTLE NUMBERS) / **FRANCIS MACDONALD** – drums

Vinyl Japan — *not iss.*

Oct 91.	(cd/lp) *(ASK CD/LP 007)* **STARWARS** – Come clean / Think tank / Smile for me / Green grow / Retitled / Life goes on / The sailor's song (pt.1) / Disguise / Studcats of life / Extraordinary / Do you really love me? / The sailor's song / Stars Wars.

Jan 92.	(12"ep/cd-ep) *(TASK 12005/+CD)* **COME CLEAN / LET MOTHER NATURE BE YOUR GUIDE. / RETITLED / ('A'-funky train mix)**

Sunflower — *not iss.*

Aug 92.	(red-lp) *(SUN 006)* **GORDON KEEN AND HIS BMX BANDITS** – Kylie's got a crush on us / Come and get it / Girl at the bus stop / etc.

Creation — *Tristar*

Nov 92.	(12"ep)(cd-ep) *(CRE 131T)(CRESCD 131)* **SERIOUS DRUGS / FUNNY FACE. / DON'T FIGHT IT FEEL IT (in concert) / SERIOUS DRUGS (demo)**
Jul 93.	(7"/c-s) *(CRE/+CS 154)* **KYLIE'S GOT A CRUSH ON US. / HOLE IN MY HEART** (12"+=)(cd-s+=) *(CRE 154T)(CRESCD 154)* – Thinkin' 'bout you baby / My generation.
Oct 93.	(cd/lp) *(CRE CD/LP 133)* <67207> **LIFE GOES ON** – Little hands / Serious drugs / Space girl / Scar / I'll keep on joking / Hole in my heart / Cast a shadow / Cats and dogs / Your dreams / My friend / It hasn't ended / Intermission (bathing beauties) / Kylie's got a crush on us.
Nov 93.	(12"ep)(cd-ep) *(CRE 168T)(CRESCD 168)* **LITTLE HANDS / THE NEXT GIRL. / WITCHI TAI TO (home recording) / BUT TONIGHT (acoustic session)**
Apr 94.	(7"ep/cd-ep) *(CRE/+SCD 181)* **SERIOUS DRUGS / LITTLE PONY. / I'LL KEEP ON JOKING / THE SAILOR'S SONG**

Creation — *Creation*

Mar 95.	(7") *(CRE 192)* **GETTIN' DIRTY. / I CAN'T STAY MAD AT YOU** (cd-s+=) *(CRESCD 192)* – Tiny fingers, tiny toes / This guy's in love with you.
May 95.	(cd/lp) *(CRE CD/LP 174)* **GETTIN' DIRTY** – Gettin' dirty / Hello again / Lost girl / Love, come to me / No future / Konnichiva #2 / On the road to Heaven / Little river of spring. *(below featured The MORLEY STRING QUARTET; b-side featured DAN PENN)*
Aug 95.	(7") *(CRE 207)* **LOVE, COME TO ME. / THAT SUMMER FEELING** (cd-s+=) *(CRESCD 207)* – Come summer / Sunshine day.
Sep 96.	(cd-ep) **WE'RE GONNA SHAKE YOU DOWN / LOVE AND MERCY (live) / LITTLE RIVER OF SPRING (live) / SERIOUS DRUGS (live)**
Oct 96.	(cd) *(CRECD 202)* **THEME PARK** – We're gonna shake you down / Girl nextdoor / Nuclear summertime / Teenage slaughtertime / This lonely guy / I wanna fall in love / One big heart / Opei mantra / Milky Way / Motorboat / Love makes the world go around / Before the blue moon / Lonely love / Evel Knievel / Ride the iron horse / In the afterglow / Sparkle finish / Our time has come.
—	FRANCIS also teamed up with (his) 'Shoeshine' band SPEEDBOAT

Shoeshine — *Elefant*

Oct 96.	(7") *(SHOE 002)* <ER 173> **HELP ME SOMEBODY. / GOLDEN TEARDROPS**		Jul97
—	Mar'97, they turned up with idol KIM FOWLEY on his CD, 'HIDDEN AGENDA' on 'Receiver'; *RRCD 231*)		

DUGLAS T. STEWART & COMPANY

with **NORMAN BLAKE** (of TEENAGE FANCLUB)

Vinyl Japan — *not iss.*

Feb 97.	(cd) *(MASKCD 60)* **FRANKENSTEIN** – Unbreakable heart / Hey little tomboy / Daddy daddy / Stupid / Tones / Airmail / Snow / Into the moon / Very / I'll be your baby tonight / Tones #2 / Gap (ten second of silence) / Frankenstein / And yes I'm still stupid.

BOB

Formed: North London, England ... 1986 by RICHARD BLACKBOROW, SIMON ARMSTRONG and JEM MORRIS. After using a drum machine for their debut EP, 'WHAT A PERFORMANCE', they subsequently required the services of a real drummer, GARY CONNORS, his first appearance being on the follow-up, 'KIRSTY'. Fortunate enough to have both records playlisted on John Peel's Radio One show, the lads took advantage of their rising profile by compiling the two EP's on one long-player, 'SWAG SACK' (1988). Soon afterwards, ex-JAMIE WEDNESDAY drummer, DEAN LEGGAT, substituted CONNORS just as the band were in the midst of delivering a further two 45's, 'PRUNE' and 'CONVENIENCE'. An indie pop outfit in the true sense of the word, BOB (whose idea was it to call them that?!) were never likely to stumble upon any great musical innovations although they were slightly influenced by the noisy, groovy psychedelia of the insurgent "baggy" scene. By the release of their fifth single, 'ESMERELDA BROOKLYN', MORRIS made way for STEPHEN HERSOM, the new bassist sticking around for a few more 12" singles and the belated release of their debut album proper, 'LEAVE THE STRAIGHT LIFE BEHIND' (1991). However, fate seemed to be against BOB as the financial collapse of the distribution arm of 'Rough Trade' affected sales, leading to their demise.

Album rating: SWAG SACK (*7) / LEAVE THE STRAIGHT LIFE BEHIND (*7)

RICHARD BLACKBOROW (b.21 Mar'66, Hackney, London) – vocals / **SIMON ARMSTRONG** (b.12 Feb'66, Hull, England) – guitar / **JEM MORRIS** (b. Aberdare, Wales) – bass / + drum machine

Sombrero — *not iss.*

Oct 87.	(12"ep) *(SOMBRERO ONE)* **WHAT A PERFORMANCE / DREARY ME. / PIGGERY / MEMORY OF A FREE FESTIVAL**
—	**GARY CONNORS** – drums; repl. drum machine
May 88.	(12"ep) *(SOMBRERO TWO)* **KIRSTY / THE HIPPY GOES FISHING. / BANWELL BLUES LIKE THESE (No.2) / TIMES LIKE THESE**

BOB (cont)

Dec 88. (lp) *(SOMBRERO FIVE)* **SWAG SACK**
– Kirsty / Piggery / Smelly summer / Prune / Deary me / The hippy goes fishing / What a performance / Times like these / Memory of a free lunch / Groove / Banwell blues No.2 / So far, so good.

— **DEAN LEGGETT** (b.30 Aug'63) – drums (ex-JAMIE WEDNESDAY) repl. CONNORS

	House Of Teeth	not iss.
Feb 89. (7"flexi) *(HOT 001)* **PRUNE (YOUR TRUE). / GROOVE / BRIAN WILSON'S BED**		-
May 89. (7"ep/12"ep) *(HOT 7/12-002)* **CONVENIENCE** – Convenience / Thinkful wishing / I fall upon the thorns of life! I bleed!! / So far, so good.		-

— **STEPHEN HERSOM** (b.28 Apr'63, Plaistow, London) – bass (ex-CARETAKER RACE) repl. MORRIS

Oct 89. (12") *(HOT 12-003)* **ESMERELDA BROOKLYN. / I DON'T KNOW**
May 90. (12"ep) *(HOT 12-004)* **STRIDE UP**
– Daymaker / Rain / My blood is drink / + 1.
May 91. (cd/lp) *(HOT CD/LP 013)* **LEAVE THE STRAIGHT LIFE BEHIND**
– Dynamite / Skylark III / Nothing for something / Who are you / Old Jean blues / Take take take / Skylark II / Trousercide / Saying goodbye / 95 tears / The belly / Leave the straight life behind.
Sep 91. (12") *(HOT 006)* **NOTHING FOR SOMETHING. /**

— they dissolved when the Rough Trade distribution collapsed

BODINES

Formed: Glossop, nr. Manchester, England . . . 1985 by MIKE RYAN, PAUL BROTHERTON, TIM BURTONWOOD and PAUL LILLEY. Heading out of the dole queue and onto the stage, the band (who took their moniker from Beverley Hillbillies character, Jethro Bodine) built up a healthy local following and signed to 'Creation' around the same time as the C86 phenomenon propelled The BODINES and their ilk (PRIMAL SCREAM, The WEDDING PRESENT, BOGSHED, The MIGHTY LEMON DROPS etc.) into the limelight via the infamous tape of the same name. Dreamt up by the NME (who else?), C86 gathered together a clutch of jangly indie hopefuls and created a short-lived and subsequently much derided scene in the process; while most of them aspired to be The BYRDS via The SMITHS, many never made it off the starting blocks, including The BODINES. A shame, as their three 'Creation' singles, 'GOD BLESS', the angst-ridden 'THERESE' (their most enduring, infectious track and their star turn on C86) and 'HEARD IT ALL' displayed definite potential – 'THERESE' introduced new drummer JOHN ROWLAND. While a further brace of singles including a remix of 'THERESE', 'SKANKING QUEENS' and 'SLIP SLIDE' were interspersed by a long overdue, IAN BROUDIE-produced album, 'PLAYED' (1987) on 'Magnet' records, none of their efforts met with much more than critical plaudits from the indie press. The final nail in the coffin was the collapse of their label, the group disappearing from view save a one-off reunion gig at Manchester's Hacienda in 1988. RYAN resurfaced in 1992 with MEDALARK 11 (something to do with basketball, no doubt), but even a return to 'Creation' for a couple of singles and an album, 'SHAPED UP, SHIPPED OUT', couldn't revive past glories.

Album rating: PLAYED (*5) / Medalark 11: SHAPED UP, SHIPPED OUT (*4)

MIKE RYAN – vocals / **PAUL BROTHERTON** – guitar / **TIM BURTONWOOD** – bass / **PAUL LILLEY** – drums

	Creation	not iss.
Sep 85. (7") *(CRE 016)* **GOD BLESS. / PARADISE**		-

— **JOHN ROWLAND** – drums; repl. LILLEY

Feb 86. (7") *(CRE 028)* **THERESE. / I FEEL**
(12"+=) *(CRE 028T)* – Scar tissue.
Aug 86. (7") *(CRE 030)* **HEARD IT ALL. / CLEAR**
(12"+=) *(CRE 030T)* – William Shatner.

	Magnet	not iss.
Feb 87. (7") *(BOD 1)* **THERESE (wear mix). / HEARD IT ALL** (ext.12"+=) *(BODT 1)* – ('A'original). (w/ free 7" CANADIAN BOOTLEG)		-
Jun 87. (7"m/12"m) *(BOD/+T 2)* **SKANKIN QUEENS. / 1000 TIMES / MY REMARKABLE MIND**		-
Aug 87. (lp/c) *(BODL/ZCBOD 2001)* **PLAYED** – Skankin queens / What you want / Scar tissue / Tall stories / Clear / Untitled / Therese / Slip slide / The back door / William Shatner. (cd-iss. Apr88; CDBOD 2001)		-
Sep 87. (7"/12") *(BOD/+T 3)* **SLIP SLIDE. / NAMING NAMES**		-

— split but re-formed late '88. **IAN** – bass; repl. BURTONWOOD
— **SPENCER** – drums; repl. ROWLAND who joined RAINKINGS

	Play Hard	not iss.
Mar 89. (12"m) *(DEC 18)* **DECIDE. / HARD ON / THE GROOVE**		-

— split again after above

MEDALARK 11

MIKE RYAN plus **GARETH THOMAS** – bass / **ADRIAN DONOHUE** – drums

	3 Bass	not iss.
May 92. (12"ep) *(3B 1)* **SNAKE. / DIVING / I CALL YOUR NAME**		-

	Creation	not iss.
Aug 92. (cd/lp) *(CRE CD/LP 145)* **SHAPED UP, SHIPPED OUT** (re-iss. Feb94; same)		-
Oct 92. (12"ep)(cd-ep) *(CRE 132T)(CRESCD 132)* **I CALL YOUR NAME. / MILES / MILES (Morocco mix)**		-
Aug 93. (12"ep)(cd-ep) *(CRE 144T)(CRESCD 144)* **SMOKE**		-

— split soon after above

BOGSHED

Formed: Hebden Bridge, Yorkshire, England . . . 1985 as THE AMAZING ROY NORTH PENIS BAND by PHIL HARTLEY, MARK McQUAID, MIKE BRYSON and TRISTAN KING. Sensibly adopting the marginally less offensive BOGSHED moniker, this absurdly humorous band were signed up by MEMBRANES man, JOHN ROBB, to his fledgling 'Vinyl Drip' label. A debut EP, 'LET THEM EAT BOGSHED', won them the patronage of John Peel who aired a couple of sessions, relaying the patented BOGSHED sound of herky-jerky, knotty rhythms and demented vocals provided by the madcap genius of HARTLEY. 1986 saw the release of the band's debut album, 'STEP ON IT', the group becoming inextricably linked to the much maligned C86 scene after having a track featured on the NME cassette of the same name. This association proved to be a thorn in the band's side as a fickle music press (in customary style) derided the scene they had helped create, BOGSHED's follow-up set, 'BRUTAL' receiving short shrift from critics. Undeterred, they ploughed their own idiosyncratic furrow until finances dictated otherwise. With the indie scene increasingly focusing on US alternative acts towards the end of the 80's, the 'EXCELLENT GIRL' single proved to be BOGSHED's epitaph, the lads finally discovering the luxuries of an inside loo. While KING went on to play with A WITNESS (not criminally though!), HARTLEY attempted a more sedate solo career. • **Trivia:** BRYSON did artwork on all the record sleeves and later went into animation.

Album rating: STEP ON IT (*8) / BRUTAL (*6)

PHIL HARTLEY – vocals / **MARK McQUAID** – guitar / **MIKE BRYSON** – bass / **TRISTAN KING** – drums

	Vinyl Drip	not iss.
Oct 85. (12"ep) *(DRIP 2)* **LET THEM EAT BOGSHED** – Panties please / Spencer Travis / Fat lad exam failure / Slave girls / City girls / Hand me down father.		-

	Shellfish	not iss.
May 86. (7") *(SHELF 1)* **MORNING SIR. / STORY OF BOGSHED**		-
Aug 86. (lp) *(SHELF 2)* **STEP ON IT** – Mechanical nun / Run to the temple / Adventure of dog / Tommy Steele record / Jobless youngsters / Tried to hide but forced to howl / Packed lunch to school / Summer in my lunchtime / The fastest legs / Oily stack / Hell bent on death / Thunderballs / Can't be beat / Little car.		-
Jan 87. (12"ep) *(SHELF 3)* **TRIED AND TESTED PUBLIC SPEAKER (The 1986 Peel Sessions)** – Tried and tested public speaker / Champion love shoes / Little grafter / Morning sir / Fastest legs / Adventure of dog.		-
Aug 87. (lp) *(SHELF 4)* **BRUTAL** – Raise the girl / Geoff's big problem / Old dog new dance / No to lemon mash / I'm the instrument / Opportunatist knocks / People equal greedy / Sing a little tune / C'mon everybody / Uncle death grip / Spring / Loaf.		-
Oct 87. (7"; shelved) *(SHELF 5)* **STOP REVOLVING**		-
Nov 87. (7") *(SHELF 6)* **EXCELLENT GIRL! / TRUE ROPE**		-

— disbanded in 1988 – KING joined JACKDAW WITH CROWBAR then A WITNESS, HARTLEY went solo although after a PEEL session he gave up

Marc BOLAN

Born: MARC FELD, 30 Sep'47, London, England. He began his performing career under the improbable moniker of TOBY TYLER, before ditching it and signing to 'Decca'. After 3 flop singles, he enjoyed a brief stint with JOHN'S CHILDREN ('Desdemona') before teaming up in 1968 with bongo player STEVE PEREGRINE TOOK to form TYRANNOSAURUS REX. Far from the hoary, chest-beating proto-metal that name might imply, the band's sound was a folky melange of acoustic guitar, manic bongos and pop melodies. Unfortunately the band were victims of their era and prone to lyrical flights of fancy that often broke down into hippy cliche, just check out the title of their debut mid-68 album 'MY PEOPLE WERE FAIR AND HAD SKY IN THEIR HAIR . . . BUT NOW THEY'RE CONTENT TO WEAR STARS ON THEIR BROWS'. A bit of a hippy himself at the time, Radio One DJ JOHN PEEL championed their first single 'DEBORA', as well as material from their next 3 albums. They became a big draw on the underground circuit, helping the albums gain minor placings in the UK charts. MARC's ex-model features and effeminate charisma did no harm in making him an object of hippy chick lust, and it was about time the band had a sexier name to match. Just before the group became T.REX, TOOK was replaced by MICKEY FINN, as they gradually adopted an all-electric sound. The spanking new single 'RIDE A WHITE SWAN', nearly nailed the No.1 spot in October 1970 and made BOLAN a fully fledged pop idol. A jaunty little number with a stabbing guitar-line, it heralded the band's strident new sound, although it retained the quasi-mystical lyrical schtick. STEVE CURRY and BILL LEGEND were drafted in and the band notched up 8 consecutive Top 3 hits, including 4 UK chart-toppers. The celebratory 'HOT LOVE' and the timeless 'GET IT ON' both hit the top spot as did the 'ELECTRIC WARRIOR' album, displaying a welcome move to raunchier (but often equally silly) lyrics. BOLAN then set up his own label through EMI after 'JEEPSTER' was re-issued without his consent. He almost single handedly invented the "glam-rock" phenomenon, achieving the rare feat of being a rock idol and pop star at the same time. 'TELEGRAM SAM', 'METAL GURU' and the evergreen '20th CENTURY BOY' are still guaranteed to get you dusting down your 6" platforms a quarter of a century on. After the single 'THE GROOVER' was released in 1973 and after splitting with his wife JUNE CHILD, BOLAN brought in his new girlfriend GLORIA JONES to record 'TRUCK ON (TYKE)'. This was the first single by T.REX not to make the Top 10. His creativity was ebbing and he moved to America to record some lacklustre formulaic material in a variety of styles. Like early fan JOHN PEEL, BOLAN embraced the subsequent punk takeover and had a new deal with 'R.C.A.' before he met his untimely end on 16th September 1977. In yet another bizarre rock'n'roll death, his girlfriend crashed their car into a tree near Barnes Common, which soon became a shrine. Since his death, obsessive fans and curious observers alike have lapped up a stream of documentaries, greatest hits packages, tributes and re-issues (mostly on fan club label 'Marc On Wax'), which show no sign of abating. • **Covers:** SUMMERTIME BLUES (Eddie Cochran) / DO YOU WANNA DANCE (Bobby Freeman) / DOCK OF THE BAY (Otis Redding) / TO KNOW HIM IS TO LOVE HIM (Teddy Bears) / RIP IT UP (Little Richard) / ENDLESS SLEEP (Joey Reynolds) / A TEENAGER IN LOVE (Dion).

Album rating: Tyrannosaurus Rex: MY PEOPLE WERE FAIR AND HAD SKY IN THE HAIR, BUT NOW THEY'RE CONTENT TO WEAR STARS ON THEIR BROWS (*6) / PROPHETS, SEERS AND SAGES, THE ANGEL OF THE AGES (*6) / UNICORN (*7) / A BEARD OF STARS (*6) / T.Rex: T.REX (*5) / ELECTRIC WARRIOR (*8) / THE SLIDER (*7) / TANX (*6)

MARC BOLAN

— solo using session men

Decca — not iss.

Nov 65. (7") *(F 12288)* **THE WIZARD. / BEYOND THE RISING SUN**
Jun 66. (7") *(F 12413)* **THE THIRD DEGREE. / SAN FRANCISCO POET**

Parlophone — not iss.

Dec 66. (7") *(R 5539)* **HIPPY GUMBO. / MISFIT**

— BOLAN then joined JOHN'S CHILDREN before forming own band

TYRANNOSAURUS REX

MARC – vocals, guitars / **STEVE PEREGRINE TOOK** (b.28 Jul'49, London) – bongos, vocals

Regal Zonophone — A&M

Apr 68. (7") *(RZ 3008)* **DEBORA. / CHILD STAR** — 34
Jun 68. (lp; stereo/mono) *(S+/LRZ 1003)* **MY PEOPLE WERE FAIR AND HAD SKY IN THEIR HAIR ... BUT NOW THEY'RE CONTENT TO WEAR STARS ON THEIR BROWS** — 15
– Red hot mama / Scenesof / Child star / Strange orchestras / Chateau in Virginia Waters / Dwarfish trumpet blues / Mustang Ford / Afghan woman / Knight / Graceful fat shake / Weilder of words / Frowning Atahuallpa. *(re-iss. May85 on 'Sierra' lp/c; FEDB/CFEDB 5013) (cd-iss. Oct98 on 'Polydor'; 541009-2)*

Regal Zonophone — Blue Thumb

Aug 68. (7") *(RZ 3011)* **ONE INCH ROCK. / SALAMANDA PALAGANDA** — 28
Oct 68. (lp; stereo/mono) *(S+/LRZ 1005)* **PROPHETS, SEERS AND SAGES, THE ANGELS OF THE AGES**
– Deboraarobed / Stacey grove / Wind quartets / Conesuala / Trelawny lawn / Aznagell the mage / The friends / Salamanda Palaganda / Our wonderful brownskin man / Oh Harley (the Saltimbanques) / Eastern spell / The travelling tragition / Juniper suction / Scenes of dynasty. *(re-iss. May85 on 'Sierra' lp/c; FEDB/CFEDB 5022) (cd-iss. Oct94 on 'Disky'; CUCD 10) (cd re-iss. Oct98 on 'Polydor'; 541010-2)*
Jan 69. (7") *(RZ 3016)* **PEWTER SUITOR. / WARLORD OF THE ROYAL CROCODILES**
May 69. (lp; stereo/mono) *(S+/LRZ 1007)* **UNICORN** — 12
– Chariots of silk / 'Pon a hill / The seal of seasons / The throat of winter / Cat black (the wizard's hat) / Stones of Avalon / She was born to be my unicorn / Like a white star, tangled and far, Tulip that's what you are / Warlord of the royal crocodiles / Evenings of Damask / The sea beasts / Iscariot / Nijinsky hind / The pilgrim's tale / The misty coast of Albany / Romany soup. *(re-iss. May85 on 'Sierra' lp/c; FEDB/CFEDB 5024) (cd-iss. Oct94 on 'Disky'; CUCD 11) (cd re-iss. Oct98 on 'Polydor'; 541012-2)*
Jul 69. (7") *(RZ 3022)* **KING OF THE RUMBLING SPIRES. / DO YOU REMEMBER?** — 44

— **MICKEY FINN** (b. 3 Jan'47) – bongos, vocals repl. TOOK who joined PINK FAIRIES (He died Nov80)

Jan 70. (7") *(RZ 3025)* **BY THE LIGHT OF THE MAGICAL MOON. / FIND A LITTLE WOOD**
Mar 70. (lp) *(SLRZ 1013)* **A BEARD OF STARS** — 21
– Prelude / A day laye / The woodland bop / First heart mighty dawn dart / Pavillions of sun / Organ blues / By the light of the magical Moon / Wind cheetah / A beard of stars / Great horse / Dragon's ear / Lofty skies / Dove / Elemental child. <*US-import had free 7"; BLUE THING*> *(re-iss. May85 on 'Sierra' lp/c; FEDB/CFEDB 5035) (cd-iss. Oct98 on 'Polydor'; 541003-2)*

T.REX

Fly — Blue Thumb

Oct 70. (7"m) *(BUG 1) <121>* **RIDE A WHITE SWAN. / IS IT LOVE / SUMMERTIME BLUES** — 2 — 76 Jan71

— added **STEVE CURRY** (b.21 May'47, Grimsby, England) – bass / **BILL LEGEND** (b. 8 May'44, Essex, England) – drums

Fly — Reprise

Dec 70. (lp/c) *(HIFLY/ZCFLY 2) <6440>* **T.REX** — 13 — Apr71
– The children of Rarn / Jewel / The visit / Childe / The time of love is now / Diamond meadows / Root of star / Beltane walk / Is it love / One inch rock / Summer deep / Seagull woman / Sun eye / The wizard / The children of Rarn (reprise). *(re-iss. Mar78 + Oct81; same) (re-iss. May85 on 'Sierra' lp/c; FEDB/CFEDB 5010) (cd-iss. May92 on 'Castle';) (cd re-iss. Oct98 on 'Polydor'; 541011-2)*
Feb 71. (7"m) *(BUG 6)* **HOT LOVE. / WOODLAND ROCK / KING OF THE MOUNTAIN COMETH** — 1 —
Apr 71. (7"m) *<1006>* **HOT LOVE. / ONE INCH ROCK / SEAGULL WOMAN** — — 72
Jul 71. (7"m) *(BUG 10)* **GET IT ON (BANG A GONG). / THERE WAS A TIME / RAW RAMP** — 1 —
Sep 71. (lp/c) *(HIFLY/ZCFLY 6) <6466>* **ELECTRIC WARRIOR** — 1 — 32 Oct71
– Mambo sun / Cosmic dancer / Jeepster / Monolith / Lean woman blues / Get it on (bang a gong) / Planet queen / Girl / The motivator / Life's a gas / Rip off. *(re-iss. Mar78 + Oct81; same) (cd-iss. May87 on 'Sierra'; CDTR 2) (re-iss. Apr90 on 'Castle' c/cd+=; CLA MC/CD 180)* – Hot love / Deborah. *(cd re-iss. Oct98 on 'Polydor'; 541007-2) (lp re-iss. Sep99 on 'Simply Vinyl'; SVLP 117)*
Nov 71. (7") *(BUG 16)* **JEEPSTER. / LIFE'S A GAS** — 2 —
Nov 71. (7") *<1056>* **JEEPSTER. / RIP OFF** — —

E.M.I. — Reprise

Dec 71. (7") *<1032>* **BANG A GONG (GET IT ON). /** — — 10
Jan 72. (7"m) *(T REX 1) <1078>* **TELEGRAM SAM. / CADILLAC / BABY STRANGE** — 1 — 67 Apr72
(re-iss. Mar82; same); hit No.69)
May 72. (lp/c) *(HIFLY/ZCFLY 8)* **BOLAN BOOGIE** (compilation) — 1
– Get it on (bang a gong) / The king of the mountain cometh / She was born to be my unicorn / Dove / Woodland bop / Ride a white swan / Raw ramp / Jeepster / First heart mighty dawn dart / By the light of the magical Moon / Summertime blues / Hot love. *(re-iss. Mar78 & Oct81; same) (re-iss. Apr89 on 'Castle' lp/c/cd; CLA LP/MC/CD 145) (cd re-iss. Oct98 on 'Polydor'; 541006-2)*
May 72. (7"m) *(MARC 1) <1095>* **METAL GURU. / LADY THUNDERWING** — 1
Jul 72. (lp/c) *(BLN/ 5001) <2095>* **THE SLIDER** — 4 — 17 Aug72
– Metal guru / Mystic lady / Rock on / The slider / Baby boomerang / Spaceball ricochet / Buick MacKane / Telegram Sam / Rabbit fighter / Baby strange / Ballrooms of Mars / Chariot choogle / Main man. *(re-iss. Nov89 on 'Marc On Wax' lp/c/cd; MARC L/K/D 503) (cd re-iss. Jul94 on 'Edsel'; EDCD 390)*
Jul 72. (7") *<1122>* **THE SLIDER. / ROCK ON** — —
Sep 72. (7"m) *(MARC 2)* **CHILDREN OF THE REVOLUTION. / JITTERBUG LOVE / SUNKEN RAGS** — 2
Dec 72. (7") *(MARC 3)* **SOLID GOLD EASY ACTION. / BORN TO BOOGIE** — 2
Mar 73. (7") *(MARC 4)* **20th CENTURY BOY. / FREE ANGEL** — 3
Mar 73. (lp/c) *(BLN/ 5002) <2132>* **TANX** — 4
– Tenement lady / Rapids / Mister mister / Broken hearted blues / Shock rock / Country honey / Electric Slim and the factory man / Mad Donna / Born to boogie / Life is strange / The street and the babe shadow / Highway knees / Left hand Luke and the beggar boys. *(re-iss. Oct87 on 'Marc On Wax' lp/pic-lp/c/cd; RAP/+D/CCD 504) (re-iss. Nov89 lp/c/cd; MARC L/K/D 504) (cd re-iss. Jul94 on 'Edsel'; EDCD 391)*

BOMB PARTY

Formed: Leicester, England ... early 80's initially as FARMLIFE, by SARAH CORINA, STEVE GERRARD, ANDY 'JESUS' MOSQUERA and MARK THOMPSON. Under this moniker they issued only one single, 'SUSIE'S PARTY', early in '82, although it might have been two but for the abandonment of a follow-up, 'BIG COUNTRY, a year later. BOMB PARTY were a different kind of proposition, taking an anti-American stance while treating us to a molotov cocktail of hardcore grebo gothabilly lying somewhere between The CRAMPS and BAUHAUS. Signing to the up and coming indie-punk label, 'Abstract' early in '85, the band blasted out with the 'RAY GUN' EP. Over the course of the next year, the BOMB PARTY unleashed two more, 'THE NEW MESSIAH' and 'LIFE'S A BITCH', before getting around to delivering their debut album, 'DRUGS' (1986). A slight shake up in the band's personnel resulted in the addition of LESZEK RATAJ and he was in place for their first album for 'Worker's Playtime', 'LIBERACE RISING' (1987). Around the same time, SARAH moonlighted with The JANITORS offshoot outfit, BIG ZAP. Augmented by the girls from VOICE OF THE BEEHIVE, the BOMB PARTY released what was to be their most commercial record to date, a cover of The Archies' 'SUGAR SUGAR'. Issued on Germany's 'Normal' label at the back end of '88, it was trailed by their third album, 'FISH' (1989); 'NATIVITY #3' followed a few years later.

Album rating: DRUGS (*5) / THE LAST SUPPER compilation (*5) / LIBERACE RISING (*5) / FISH (*4) / NATIVITY #3 (*4)

JESUS MOSQUERA (b. ANDY) – vocals / **STEVE GERRARD** – guitar / **SARAH CORINA** – bass / **MARK THOMPSON** – drums

Dining Out — not iss.

Feb 82. (7"; as FARMLIFE) *(TUX 19)* **SUSIE'S PARTY. / SIMPLE MEN**

Whaam! — not iss.

Sep 83. (7"; as FARMLIFE) *(WHAAM 13)* **BIG COUNTRY. / (part 2)** — — w/drawn

Abstract — not iss.

May 85. (12"ep) *(12ABS 032)* **RAY GUN EP**
– Harry the babysitter / Ray gun / Get lost my love / Knocking.
Aug 85. (12"ep) *(12ABS 035)* **THE NEW MESSIAH EP**
– Yeah yeah yeah / Great white hope / New messiah / Wasted.
Dec 85. (7"ep) *(ABS 038)* **LIFE'S A BITCH. / GET SO DOWN / THE NEW MESSIAH**
Jun 86. (lp) *(ABT 014)* **DRUGS**
– Kill your wife / Don't die Keith / Johnny took her breath away / Jesus was a pinko / Gas / Johnny Nero / Susie's party / Our love is pushing up daisies / Slide / Zombie head / Refugee.
May 87. (lp) *(ABT 016)* **THE LAST SUPPER** (compilation)

– Harry the babysitter / Ray gun / Get lost my love / Knocking / Fever / Life's a bitch / Hell sucks / New messiah / Wasted / Get so down / Yeah yeah yeah / Man hole / Life's a bitch (Spanish).

──── added **LESZEK RATAJ** – guitar

                                            Workers Playtime / not iss.

Oct 87. (m-lp) *(PLAYLP 2)* **LIBERACE RISING**
– Crawl / Don't talk just kiss / Come on and get closer / Evil eye / El savor del amor / Metropolis.

Dec 87. (7") *(WPCS 1)* **PRETTY FACE. / THESE ARE YOUR RIGHTS / I WANNA BE ABUSED**

                                            Normal / not iss.

Oct 88. (7") *(NORMAL 93)* **SUGAR SUGAR. / DO THE RIGHT THING**
(12"+=/cd-s+=) *(NORMAL 93 T/CD)* – Some people settle for less.

May 89. (lp/cd) *(NORMAL 103/+CD)* **FISH**
– Praise the Lord / L.S.D. / Some bodies / Venus in dirt / The last waltz / Do the right thing / Theme from "God Bless America" / Mephistopleles (a million worth of pillion) / Shakespeare / Why don't we talk / Love at any price / The only rule (there is no rule) / Car crash (on the highway of love) / Nobody's.

                                            Artlos / not iss.

Apr 91. (lp/cd) *(efa 01819/+CD)* **NATIVITY #3**
– The beginning and the end / Ship of fools / Hey Joe / 31st of September / Lucy gas / Unavoidably detained / Dreaming / Gimme summat to love / Use it / In this land / Touched / Tonight / The beginning and the end.

──── split soon after above

BONE ORCHARD

Formed: Brighton, England . . . 1983 by female singer CHRISSIE McGEE, MARK HORSE, TROY TYRO, MICK FINCH and PAUL HENDRICKSON. Led by CHRISSIE, a grunting banshee with gothic psychobilly overtones and described by music mags as "Nick Cave with tits", these post-punk crypt creepers signed to the 'Jungle' label following their fifteen minutes worth of fame on a John Peel session. Hot on the heels of their debut EP 'STUFFED TO THE GILLS', the band made an appearance at that year's Futurama festival, drummer RIM TIM CHEESE subsequently replacing MICK. 'SWALLOWING HAVOC' was the title of their follow-up EP, while BEN TISDALL became their new drummer on 1984's mini-set, 'JACK'. Given short shrift by the music press, BONE ORCHARD faded from view following the release of a low-key mini-album, 'PENTHOUSE POULTRY' (1985).

Album rating: JACK (*4) / PENTHOUSE POULTRY mini (*3)

CHRISSIE McGEE – vocals / **MARK HORSE** – guitar / **TROY TYRO** – guitar / **PAUL HENDRICKSON** – bass / **MICK FINCH** – drums

                                            Jungle / not iss.

Nov 83. (12"ep) *(JUNG 8)* **STUFFED TO THE GILLS**
– Fats terminal / Knuckle the butcher / Shall I carry the budgie woman / Picking appulheads / Kickin' up the sawdust.

──── **RIM TIM CHEESE** – drums; repl. MICK

Apr 84. (12"ep) *(JUNG 15)* **SWALLOWING HAVOC**
– Cold back stick! / Love has sin / I'm boned (boneabilly party)! / Slow red burn!

──── **BEN TISDALL** – drums; repl. TIM who joined SKELETAL FAMILY

Sep 84. (7") *(JUNG 18)* **JACK. / GIRL WITH A GUN**

Nov 84. (lp) *(FREUD 06)* **JACK**
– Jack / Lynched / Marianne / Touched / Five days in the neighboorhood / Girl with a gun / Tongue / Scarlet ropes.

──── had a new drummer; unknown to repl. BEN

                                            Vax / not iss.

Jun 85. (12"ep) *(JUNG 22T)* **PRINCESS EPILEPSY. / SAME OLD BALL AND CHAIN / YOU DON'T PRESS MY PANTS**

Nov 85. (m-lp) *(VAXLP 1)* **PENTHOUSE POULTRY**
– Eyesval / Scenic cruiser / Dead eighteen / The basement / Penthouse poultry / Dumb poet.

──── split some time in the mid 80's

BONGOS

Formed: Hoboken, New Jersey, USA . . . late '79 by RICHARD BARONE, FRANK GIANNINI and ROB NORRIS. Brought to London to feature in special gigs alongside other New York-based outfits BUSH TETRAS, dB's and The FLESHTONES, they signed to UK indie label, 'Fetish' (also home to a number of the more avant-garde new wave groups such as CLOCKDVA; CHARLIE COLLINS made an appearance for them early on). During the early 80's, the label issued a string of singles including debut 'TELEPHONE LENS' (after the release of which JAMES MASTRO joined as 4th member), along with two mini-sets, 'THE BONGOS' (1981) and 'TIME AND A RIVER' (1982). Guitar-based pop with a twist, The BONGOS were unashamedly retro yet managed to capture the imagination of the post New Wave cognoscenti. After a successful support slot to The B-52's, the quirky quartet signed an American deal with 'R.C.A.', releasing the Richard Gottehrer-produced 'NUMBERS WITH WINGS' EP in '83. A few years later, The BONGOS finally issued their first full-length album (barring compilation, 'DRUMS ALONG THE HUDSON'), 'BEAT HOTEL' (1985), ex-RICHARD HELL & The VOID-OIDS man, IVAN JULIAN coming in for MASTRO prior to their demise. BARONE later carved out a low-key solo career that took in albums such as 'COOL BLUE HALO' (1989), 'PRIMAL DREAM' (1990), 'CLOUDS OVER EDEN' (1993) and 'BETWEEN HEAVEN AND CELLO' (1994). • **BARONE covered:** THE VISIT + BALLROOMS OF MARS (T.Rex) / CRY BABY CRY (Beatles) / THE MAN WHO SOLD THE WORLD (David Bowie) / I'LL BE YOUR MIRROR (Velvet Underground) / GUINIVIERE (Donovan).

Album rating: TIME AND A RIVER mini (*6) / DRUMS ALONG THE HUDSON compilation (*5) / BEAT HOTEL (*4) / Richard Barone: COOL BLUE HALO (*7) / PRIMAL DREAM (*3) / CLOUDS OVER EDEN (*5) / BETWEEN HEAVEN AND CELLO (*6)

RICHARD BARONE (b. 1 Oct'60, Tampa, Florida) – vocals, guitar / **ROB NORRIS** (b. 1 Apr'55, New York City, N.Y.) – bass, vocals / **FRANK GIANNINI** (b. 6 Aug'59, Morristown, N.J.) – drums; augmented by **COSEY FANNI TUTTI** – concertina (of THROBBING GRISTLE) / **CHARLIE COLLINS** – saxophone (of CLOCKDVA)

                                            Fetish / not iss.

Apr 80. (12") *(FET 003)* **TELEPHONE LENS. / GLOW IN THE DARK**
Apr 81. (m-lp; w-drawn) *(FR 2004)* **THE BONGOS**
May 81. (12") *(FET 005)* **IN THE CONGO. / MAMBO SUN**
Dec 81. (7") *(FET 009)* **THE BULLRUSHES. / AUTOMATIC DOORS**
Feb 82. (m-lp) *(FR 2009)* **TIME AND A RIVER**
– Question ball / Clay midgets / Burning bush / Certain harbours / Speaking sand / Vieo eyes / Zebra club / Three wise men.
Feb 82. (7") *(FE 17)* **ZEBRA CLUB. / CERTAIN HARBOURS**
Apr 82. (7"/12") *(FE/+T 18)* **MAMBO SUN. / HUNTING**

──── added **JAMES MASTRO** (b. JAMES MASTRODIMUS, 9 Dec'60, Springfield, Ohio) – guitar, vocals

                                            not iss. / R.C.A.

1983. (12"ep) *<MFL1 8509>* **NUMBERS WITH WINGS**
– Numbers with wings / Tiger nights / Barbarella / Skydiving / Sweet blue cage.

1985. (lp) *<8043>* **BEAT HOTEL**
– Space jungle / Apache dancing / Brave new world / A story (written in the sky) / Beat hotel / Come back to me / Splinters / She starts shaking / Totem pole / Blow up / Barbarella (remix). *<cd-iss. Jul92 on 'Razor & Tie'+=; REC 1995>* – NUMBERS WITH WINGS

──── **IVAN JULIAN** – guitar (ex-RICHARD HELL) repl. MASTRO who released an album for 'Passport'; 'NUTS AND BOLTS' shared with RICHARD BARONE. MASTRO later released solo and with STRANGE CAVE plus The HEALTH AND HAPPINESS SHOW.

──── disbanded shortly after brief personnel change

– compilations, etc. –

1982. (lp) *P.V.C.; <8909>* **DRUMS ALONG THE HUDSON**
– In the Congo / The bullrushes / Clay midgets / Video eyes / Glow in the dark / Telephoto lens / Certain harbours / Speaking sands / Burning bush / Automatic doors hunting / Zebra club / Three wise men / Mambo sun / Question ball. *<cd-iss. 1992 on 'Razor & Tie'+=; REC 1999>* (UK-iss.Oct94 on 'Line'; LICD 900770) – Nuts and bolts.

RICHARD BARONE

──── with main musicians; **NICK CELESTE** – vocals, guitar / **JANE SCARPANTONI** – cello / **VALERIE NARANJO** – percussion

                                            Line / not iss.

1988. (cd-s) **CRY BABY CRY / I BELONG TO ME / TANGLED IN YOUR WEB**

                                            New Rose / Passport — German

Sep 89. (lp/cd) *(ROSE 171/+CD) <PB/+C/+CD 6058>* **COOL BLUE HALO (live at the Bottom Line)** — Nov87
– The bullrushes / I belong to me / The visit / Tangled in your web / Silent symphony / Flew a falcon / Cry baby cry / Sweet blue cage / The man who sold the world / Love is a wind that screams / Numbers with wings. *(also cd on 'Line'; LICD 9.00707)*

                                            M.C.A. / M.C.A.

1990. (lp/cd) *(MCA/+D 6370)* **PRIMAL DREAM**
– Where the truth lies / Before you were born / Something happens / River to river / Opposites attracting / I only took what I needed / Mr. Used-To-Be / Native tongue / To the pure . . . / I'll be your mirror / Roman circus.

1990. (cd-ep) **MR. USED-TO-BE (remix) / RIVER TO RIVER (live acoustic) / WHERE THE TRUTH LIES (live acoustic) / MR. USED-TO-BE (extended remix)**

                                            Line / not iss.

1990. (7") **RIVER TO RIVER. / I'LL BE YOUR MIRROR** — German
(cd-s+=) – Roman circus.

1991. (cd-ep) **PRIMAL CUTS EP** — German
1992. (cd-s) **NOBODY KNOWS ME / STANDING IN THE LINE / NATIVE TONGUE** — German
1992. (cd-s) **FORBIDDEN / FORBIDDEN (live Radio Berlin) / BEFORE YOU WERE BORN** — German

──── now with large string ensemble

                                            not iss. / Mesa

Jan 94. (cd) *<79060>* **CLOUDS OVER EDEN**
– Within these walls / Paper airplane / Forbidden / Nobody knows me / Clouds over Eden / Waiting for the train / Miss Jean / Beautiful human / Standing in the line / Law of the jungle / Within these walls (reprise).

                                            Line / not iss.

Sep 94. (cd) *(LICD 901289)* **BETWEEN HEAVEN AND CELLO (live)**
– Certain harbours / Guinevere / Miss Jean / Before you were born / Forbidden / Before you were born / Tangled in your web / Numbers with wings (instrumental) / To the pure . . . / Beautiful human / Barbarella / Ballrooms of Mars / Standing in the line / Under someone's spell.

– compilations, etc. –

2000. (3xcd-box) *Line:* **THE BIG THREE** — German
– (COOL BLUE HALO / PRIMAL DREAM / CLOUDS OVER EDEN)

BONGWATER

Formed: New York, USA... 1987 by MARK KRAMER and actress ANN MAGNUSON, who he had met while working in the latter's PULSALLAMA band. KRAMER founded his new indie label, 'Shimmy Disc', releasing the mini-lp, 'BREAKING NO NEW GROUND'. This featured a cover of The MONKEES' 'PORPOISE SONG' and avant-garde guitarist FRED FRITH. The 1988 follow-up, 'DOUBLE BUMMER' featured more inspired covers including GARY GLITTER's 'ROCK & ROLL PART 2', JOHNNY CASH's 'THERE YOU GO' and an outrageous version of LED ZEPPELIN's 'DAZED AND CONFUSED' (re-born/aborted as DAZED AND CHINESE). They satirized many styles and cultures, nobody (even DAVID BOWIE) being safe from their merciless humour. KRAMER moonlighted with other projects, producing just about anyone who was anyone (i.e. GALAXIE 500, URGE OVERKILL and DOGBOWL) from the US indie world, while also finding time to play with B.A.L.L. The albums, 'THE POWER OF PUSSY' (1991) and 'THE BIG SELL-OUT' (1992), showed KRAMER and MAGNUSON at their most wilfully perverse/diverse. The neo-narrative, seductive/soft-core vox of ANN lent a shimmering, psychedelic beauty to proceedings, even on their version of FRED NEIL's 'EVERYBODY'S TALKIN'. Sadly, their partnership came to an abrupt halt, both taking off on solo flights. • **Songwriters:** KRAMER – music / MAGNUSON – lyrics (later a few with HUDSON), except RIDE MY SEE-SAW (Moody Blues) / WE DID IT AGAIN (Soft Machine) / JUST MAY BE THE ONE (Monkees) / SPLASH 1 (13th Floor Elevators) / THE DRUM (Slapp Happy) / KISSES SWEETER THAN WINE (Newman – Campbell) / BEDAZZLED (from the film) / ONE SO BLACK (Dogbowl) / LOVE YOU TOO + RAIN (Beatles) / REAGANATION (Fugs) / Kramer: YOU'VE GOT TO HIDE YOUR LOVE AWAY (Beatles). • **Trivia:** ANN's acting C.V. included a TV sitcom, 'Anything But Love', and a film, 'Making Mr Right'.

Album rating: BREAKING NO NEW GROUND! mini (*5) / HAPPINESS FINALLY CAME TO THEM – Kramer with Carney & Hild (*4) / DOUBLE BUMMER (*6) / TOO MUCH SLEEP (*6) / THE POWER OF PUSSY (*7) / THE BIG SELL-OUT (*8) / Kramer: THE GUILT TRIP (*6) / THE SECRET OF COMEDY (*5) / BLACK POWER with Carney & Hild (*5) / RUBBER HAIR with Daved Hild (*4) / LET ME EXPLAIN SOMETHING TO YOU ABOUT ART (*5) / SONGS FROM THE BIG DEATH (*4)

MARK KRAMER (b. 1958) – guitar, other instruments, vocals (of-B.A.L.L., ex-SHOCKABILLY, ex-BUTTHOLE SURFERS) / **ANN MAGNUSON** – vocals / guest **FRED FRITH** – guitar (ex-HENRY COW)

Shimmy Disc / Shimmy Disc

Feb 88. (m-lp) (SHIMMY 002) **BREAKING NO NEW GROUND!** Nov87
– Ride my see-saw / Barely coping / Sticks / U.S.O. / His new look / Julia.

— the duo added **DAVE RICK** – guitar (was part-time) / **DAVID LICHT** – drums, percussion

Feb 89. (d-lp) (SDE 8801) (SHIMMY 011) **DOUBLE BUMMER**
– Lesbians of Russia / Frank / We did it again / Homer / Joy ride / Decadent Iranian country club / David Bowie wants ideas / Rock & roll (part 2) / Just may be the one / There you go / Shark / Jimmy / Crime / Pornography / Dazed and Chinese / Bullaby / So help me God / His old look / Stone / Number / Love you too / Reaganation / Double birth / Bruce / Pool / Rain. (d-cd-iss. Nov97 on 'Shimmy Disc'; SHIMMY 011CD)

— In 1989, he and JAD FAIR (of HALF JAPANESE) released album 'ROLL OUT THE BARREL' (SDE 8802)

Apr 90. (lp/cd) (SDE 9017/+CD) <SHIMMY 031/+CD> **TOO MUCH SLEEP** Nov89
– The living end / The drum / Mr & Mrs Hell / Too much sleep / Talent is a vampire / Psychedelic sewing room / Slash one / He loved the weather / Teena stays the same / One hand on the road / Khomeini died tonight / One so black / No trespassing. (cd/lp re-iss. Sep99/Aug00; same as US)

— Late in 1990, KRAMER and REBBY SHARP issued 'IN ONE MOUTH AND OUT THE OTHER' (SHIMMY 033)

Feb 91. (lp/cd) <(SHIMMY 040/+CD)> **THE POWER OF PUSSY**
– The power of pussy / Great radio / What if? / Kisses sweeter than wine / Chicken pussy / White rental car blues / Nick Cave dolls / Bedazzled / Obscene and pornographic art / Connie / What kind of man reads Playboy / I need a new tape / Women tied up in knots / Junior / Mystery hole / Time is coming / Polar song. (re-iss. Mar98; same) (cd re-iss. Dec99; SHM 5040)

— **RANDOLPH A. HUDSON III** – guitars, devices, repl. DAVE RICK

— **DOGBOWL** also provided live guitar

Mar 92. (lp/cd) (SDE 9239/+CD) <SHIMMY 050CD> **THE BIG SELL-OUT**
– Ye olde backlash / The real thing / Free love messes up my life / You're like me now / I wanna talk about it now / What's big in England now? / Schmoozedance / Celebrity compass / When Johnnie dies / The big sell-out / Over the credit line / Flop sweats / Holding hands / Flute of shame / On the cusp of 1970 / Her litigious nature / Love song / Everybody's talking. (cd re-iss. Nov97; same)

— dropped out of scene; ANN signed a solo contract with 'Geffen'. This allegedly led to a bitter lawsuit between her and the now solo KRAMER and to his label folding

– compilations, etc. –

Nov 98. (5xcd-box) *Shimmy Disc*; <(SHM 5555)> **THE COMPLETE BONGWATER COLLECTION**
(re-iss. Jan02; same)

KRAMER

— next with **RALPH CARNEY** – saxophone, clarinet (ex-TIN HUEY, + of TOM WAITS) + **DAVED HILD**

Shimmy Disc / Shiloh

1988. (lp; by CARNEY / HILD / KRAMER) (SHIMMY 007) <SH 9027> **HAPPINESS FINALLY CAME TO THEM** 1987

— In 1991, KRAMER & JOHN S HALL (of KING MISSILE) released the album, 'REAL MEN' (SHIMMY 042CD)

— in 1992, KRAMER & DAEVID ALLEN (of GONG) released a collaborative work, 'WHO'S AFRAID'.

— with **RANDOLPH HUDSON III** – guitar / **DAVID LICHT** – percussion

Jun 93. (d-cd/d-c/d-lp) (SHIMMY 055 CD/MC/LP) **THE GUILT TRIP**
– Overture / Stupid summer / Got what I deserved / Wish I were in Heaven / Not guilty / Wisdom sits / Stubb's hallucination / The drowning heart / Welcome home / Swallow up Jonah / Hello music / The murder of God / You don't know / The wall of sleep / The guilt trip / Wait for the hate / Natasha disappears / Big of you / My friend Daniel / The Maximus poems / The seven seizures / Thank you music / Kathleen I'm sorry / God will see you / I'm your fan / The bosom friend / I love you / Next time try compassion / Charlotte's brain / Mudd Hutt four / The well hung jury / Won't get far without me / Ball five / She won't let go / I've seen the end / Coda.

— **BILLY BACON** – percussion, drums; repl. LICHT

Aug 94. (lp/cd) <(SHIMMY 075/+CD)> **THE SECRET OF COMEDY**
– Nine minus seven is two / The secret of suicide / Midnight / Strings / The secret of philosophy / I can watch / Who are you today? / My rock'n'roll / The secret of the band / Sounds like? / Wishing well / Second coda.

May 95. (cd; as CARNEY / HILD / KRAMER) <(SHIMMY 087CD)> **BLACK POWER**
– Tears come down / Speed shotting / Speaker of the house / Sweetheart / Wish / Infrared asylum green / The ballad of soap / These foolish things / The ballad of Jim Jones / Thanks for the tinklers / The ballad of Florida / Dangerous cult following / Hands / Telephone / Clown / Nothing / Slowly / Wanda / Larry / Name / Turkeyfaced / Javalena / End.

Mar 97. (cd; KRAMER & DAVED HILD) <(SHIMMY 087CD)> **RUBBER HAIR**
– Photograph / The cat in the window / Masonic hardware / The Veronic building / Bargains night bargains / Cold air / Vegetables do / Mr. Ryder on the beach / X is the sign / Distress in the Dixie girls / The ballad of veal / Rubber hair.

— KRAMER now with **DENI BONET** – violin, accordion, viola

Tzadik / Tzadik

Dec 97. (cd) <(TZA 7119)> **LET ME EXPLAIN SOMETHING TO YOU ABOUT ART**
– Umberto D. / Odds against tomorrow / Jupiter and the infinite.

— now with **SEAN EDEN** – guitar (of LUNA) / **DAMON KRUKOWSKI** – drums (ex-GALAXIE 500)

Knitting Factory / Knitting Factory

Mar 98. (cd) <(KNFR 502)> **SONGS FROM THE PINK DEATH** Feb98
– The funny scene / Buddy Holly will never die / The opium wars have long ceased / Don't come around / The parasite song / The pink death song of love / It never stops being absurd / Eddie called back on the carphone / You've got to hide your love away / The hot dog song / It's alright if she don't love you.

Simon BONNEY
(see under ⇒ CRIME & THE CITY SOLUTION)

BOOTS FOR DANCING

Formed: Edinburgh, Scotland... late 1979 by the songwriting pair of DAVE CARSON and GRAHAM HIGH, who enlisted the rhythm section of DOUGIE BARRIE and STUART WRIGHT. Influenced by the quirky/manic dance-punk rhythms of GANG OF FOUR or The POP GROUP, BOOTS FOR DANCING enjoyed a bit of airplay on the John Peel Radio One show. The quartet signed to 'Pop Aural' (also the launching pad for The FIRE ENGINES) and released their debut platter, the eponymous 'BOOTS FOR DANCING' single in 1980. They were subsequently dogged by numerous personnel changes initiating with a brief stint from ex-REZILLOS man, ANGEL PATERSON, who left to join TV21 (two drummers/percussionists were introduced, JAMO STEWART and DICKIE FUSCO). HIGH was also to take off, his replacement being another REZILLOS ex, JO CALLIS who was joined by MIKE BARCLAY. After a year long spell without a record, BFD were back with the follow-up, 'RAIN SONG', although this was certainly not as good as their debut. When CALLIS departed to take up a post in the HUMAN LEAGUE, the quintet were to release their third and last effort, 'OOH BOP SH'BAM', before CARSON became the only surviving original, he and BARCLAY having recruited SIMON TEMPLAR (another ex-REZILLOS and SHAKE member) and RONNIE TORRANCE (ex-JOSEF K).

DAVE CARSON – vocals / **GRAHAM HIGH** – guitar / **DOUGIE BARRIE** – bass / **STUART WRIGHT** – drums

Pop Aural / not iss.

Apr 80. (12"ep) (POP 002) **BOOTS FOR DANCING / PARACHUTE. / GUITARS / GIRL TROUBLE** -

— **JAMO STEWART** – drums + **DICKIE FUSCO** – percussion; repl. ANGEL PATERSON (ex-SHAKE, ex-REZILLOS) who repl. WRIGHT

— **MIKE BARCLAY** – guitar (ex-THURSDAYS) repl. HIGH who joined DELTA 5

— added **JO CALLIS** – guitar, vocals (ex-SHAKE, ex-REZILLOS)

Mar 81. (7") (POP 006) **RAIN SONG. / HESITATING** -

— trimmed to a quintet when CALLIS left to join HUMAN LEAGUE

Re-Pop X / not iss.

Feb 82. (7") (WAY 100) **OOH BOP SH'BAM. / MONEY IS THIN ON THE GROUND** -

— **SIMON TEMPLAR** (b. BLOOMFIELD) – bass (ex-FLOWERS, ex-SHAKE, ex-REZILLOS) repl. BARRIE

BOOTS FOR DANCING (cont)

— **RONNIE TORRANCE** – drums (ex-JOSEF K) repl. FUSCO + STEWART (the latter formed The SYNDICATE

— hung up their footwear some time in '82.

BORED GAMES (see under ⇒ STRAITJACKET FITS)

BOURGIE BOURGIE (see under ⇒ QUINN, Paul)

David BOWIE

Born: DAVID ROBERT JONES, 8 Jan'47, Brixton, London. In 1964 he formed The KING BEES with schoolmate GEORGE UNDERWOOD but after one single they split when BOWIE joined The MANNISH BOYS. They also lasted half a year, DAVID going solo with backing from The LOWER THIRD. In early 1966, he became DAVID BOWIE and signed to 'Pye' although commercial success continued to elude him. After three years of trying, he finally charted with 'SPACE ODDITY', a classic that introduced his "MAJOR TOM" character. That year (1969) his father died, but he was compensated by the introduction to ANGIE, his future wife. Although he was regarded as one of the top newcomers to the rock/pop scene, it took him until 1972 to finally establish himself as *the* rock star. He formed his now famous backing band, The SPIDERS, and announced his bisexuality to the music press. The single, 'STARMAN', and parent album, 'ZIGGY STARDUST' (an archetype alter-ego), were to hit the UK top 10. By this stage he'd come a long way from being a 60's ANTHONY NEWLEY copyist, innovating a risqué, glam rock style and pioneering the 'feathercut', make-up for men and stage-mime (the latter being learnt from LINDSEY KEMP). Signed to 'R.C.A.', the company duly re-issued his past three albums which all broke into the UK charts and 'ALADDIN SANE' (1973) was the first of his many No.1 albums. 'DIAMOND DOGS' (1974) represented the finale of his futuristic concept work and bore the hit single, 'REBEL, REBEL',

Album rating: DAVID BOWIE (*4) / MAN OF WORDS, MAN OF MUSIC aka SPACE ODDITY (*6) / THE MAN WHO SOLD THE WORLD (*8) / HUNKY DORY (*9) / THE RISE AND FALL OF ZIGGY STARDUST . . . (*10) / ALADDIN SANE (*8) / BOWIE PIN-UPS (*5) / DIAMOND DOGS (*6)

DAVID BOWIE – vocals, acoustic guitar / with session people

			Vocalion	not iss.
Jun 64.	(7"; as DAVIE JONES with The KING BEES) (*Pop V 9221*) **LIZA JANE. / LOUIE LOUIE GO HOME** (re-iss. Sep78 on 'Decca'; F 13807)			–
			Parlophone	not iss.
Mar 65.	(7"; as The MANNISH BOYS) (*R 5250*) **I PITY THE FOOL. / TAKE MY TIP**			–
Aug 65.	(7"; as DAVY JONES) (*R 5315*) **YOU'VE GOT A HABIT OF LEAVING. / BABY LOVES THAT WAY**			–
			Pye	Warners
Jan 66.	(7"; as DAVID BOWIE with The LOWER THIRD) (*7N 17020*) <*5814*> **CAN'T HELP THINKING ABOUT ME. / AND I SAID TO MYSELF**			–
Apr 66.	(7") (*7N 17079*) **DO ANYTHING YOU SAY. / GOOD MORNING GIRL**			–
Aug 66.	(7") (*7N 17157*) **I DIG EVERYTHING. / I'M NOT LOSING SLEEP**			–
			Deram	Deram
Dec 66.	(7") (*DM 107*) **RUBBER BAND. / THE LONDON BOYS**			–
Feb 67.	(7") <*85009*> **RUBBER BAND. / THERE IS A HAPY LAND**	–		
Apr 67.	(7") (*DM 123*) **THE LAUGHING GNOME. / THE GOSPEL ACCORDING TO TONY DAY** (re-iss. Sep73; same); hit UK No.6 (re-iss. Jun82)			–
Jun 67.	(lp; mono/stereo) (*DML/SML 1007*) **DAVID BOWIE** – Uncle Arthur / Sell me a coat / Rubber band / Love you till Tuesday There is a happy land / We are hungry men / When I live my dream / Little bombadier / Silly boy blue / Come and buy me toys / Join the gang / She's got medals / Maids of Bond Street / Please Mr. Gravedigger. (re-iss. Nov69 on 'Philips'; SBL 7912) (re-iss. Aug84 lp/c; DOA 1) (cd-iss. Oct88; 800 087-2)			–
Jul 67.	(7") (*DM 135*) <*85016*> **LOVE YOU TILL TUESDAY. / DID YOU EVER HAVE A DREAM**			–

— (Jul68-Feb69) **BOWIE** formed FEATHERS with girlfriend **HERMOINE FARTHINGALE + JOHN HUTCHINSON** – bass. BOWIE went solo, recording solo album with session players **RICK WAKEMAN** – keyboards

		Philips	Mercury
Jul 69.	(7") (*BF 1801*) <*72949*> **SPACE ODDITY. / THE WILD EYED BOY FROM FREECLOUD**	5	
Nov 69.	(lp) (*SBL 7912*) **DAVID BOWIE – MAN OF WORDS MAN OF MUSIC** – Space oddity / Unwashed and somewhat slightly dazed / Letter to Hermione / Cygnet committee / Janine / An occasional dream / The wild eyed boy from Freecloud / God knows I'm good / Memory of a free festival. (re-iss. Nov72 as 'SPACE ODDITY' on 'RCA' lp/c; LSP/PK 4813) (hit No.17 UK + No.16 US; <ST 61246>) (re-iss. Oct84 on 'RCA' lp/c/cd; PL/PK/PD 84813) (re-iss. Apr90 on 'EMI' cd/c/lp; CD/TC+/EMC 3571) (+=) – Conversation piece / Don't sit down. (hit UK No.64) (cd re-iss. Sep97 on 'Premier-EMI'; CDP 791835-2)	–	–

— **BOWIE** formed backing band **HYPE** with **TONY VISCONTI** – bass / **MICK RONSON** – guitar / **JOHN CAMBRIDGE** – drums

		Mercury	Mercury
Mar 70.	(7") (*MF 1135*) **THE PRETTIEST STAR. / CONVERSATION PIECE**		–

— **MICK 'Woody' WOODMANSEY** – drums repl. CAMBRIDGE

Jun 70.	(7") (*6052 026*) <*73075*> **MEMORY OF A FREE FESTIVAL (part 1). / (part 2)**		
Jan 71.	(7") (*6052 049*) **HOLY HOLY. / BLACK COUNTRY ROCK**		
Apr 71.	(lp) (*6338 041*) <*61325*> **THE MAN WHO SOLD THE WORLD** – The width of a circle / All the madmen / Black country rock / After all / Running gun blues / Saviour machine / She took me cold / The man who sold the world / The supermen. (re-iss. Nov72 on 'RCA' lp/c; LSP/PK 4816) (hit No.26 UK) (re-iss. Apr83 on 'RCA' lp/c; INTS/INTK 5237) (hit UK 64) (re-iss. Oct84 on 'RCA Int.' lp/c/cd; NL/NK/PD 84654) (re-iss. Apr90 on 'EMI' cd/c/lp; CD/TC+/EMC 3573) (+=) – Lightning frightening / Moonage daydream / Holy holy / Hang on to yourself. (hit UK No.66) (cd re-iss. Sep97 on 'Premier-EMI'; CDP 791837-2)		
Jun 71.	(7") <*73175*> **ALL THE MADMEN.**	–	–

— Became **SPIDERS FROM MARS** (BOWIE, RONSON, WOODMANSEY), **TREVOR BOULDER** – bass repl. VISCONTI

		R.C.A.	R.C.A.
Dec 71.	(lp/c) (*SF/PK 8244*) <*AFL-1 4623*> **HUNKY DORY** – Changes / Oh! you pretty things / Eight line poem / Life on Mars? / Kooks / Quicksand / Fill your heart – Andy Warhol / Song for Bob Dylan / Queen bitch / The Bewlay Brothers. (re-dist.Sep72 reached No.3 UK) (re-iss. Jan81 lp/c; INTS/INTK 5064) (hit No.32 UK) (pic-lp Apr84; BOPIC 2) (re-iss. Oct84 on 'RCA Int.' lp/c/cd; NL/NK/PD 83844) (re-iss. Apr90 on 'EMI' cd/c/lp; CD/TC+/EMC 3572) (+=) – Bombers / The supermen (alt.) / Quicksand (demo) / The Bewlay Brothers (alt.). (hit UK No.39) (cd re-iss. Sep97 on 'Premier-EMI'; LPCENT 21) (lp re-iss. Nov97 on 'E.M.I.'; CDP 791843-2)		93
Jan 72.	(7") (*RCA 2160*) <*74-0605*> **CHANGES. / ANDY WARHOL** (re-iss. Dec74; same); reached No.41 UK		66 Apr72
Apr 72.	(7") (*RCA 2199*) <*74-0719*> **STARMAN. / SUFFRAGETTE CITY**	10	65 Jun72
Jun 72.	(lp/c) (*SF/PK 8267*) <*AFL-1 4702*> **THE RISE AND FALL OF ZIGGY STARDUST AND THE SPIDERS FROM MARS** – Five years / Soul love / Moonage daydream / Starman / It ain't easy / Lady Stardust / Star / Hang on to yourself / Ziggy Stardust / Suffragette city / Rock'n'roll suicide. (re-iss. Jan81 lp/c; INTS/INTK 5063) (hit No.33 UK) (pic-lp Apr84; BOPIC 3) (re-iss. Oct84 on 'RCA Int.' lp/c/cd; NL/NK/PD 83843) (re-iss. Apr90 on 'EMI' cd+=/c+=/lp; CD/TC+/EMC 3577) <re-iss. Jun90 on 'Rykodisc'+=; 10134>; hit No.93. – John, I'm only dancing (demo) / Velvet goldmine / Sweet head / Ziggy Stardust (demo) / Lady Stardust (demo). (hit UK No.25) (re-iss. Feb97 on 'E.M.I.'; LPCENT 4)	5	75
Sep 72.	(7") (*RCA 2263*) **JOHN, I'M ONLY DANCING. / HANG ON TO YOURSELF**	12	–
Nov 72.	(7") (*RCA 2302*) **THE JEAN GENIE. / ZIGGY STARDUST**	2	–
Nov 72.	(7") <*74-0838*> **THE JEAN GENIE. / HANG ON TO YOURSELF**	–	71
Jan 73.	(7") <*74-0876*> **SPACE ODDITY. / THE MAN WHO SOLD THE WORLD**	–	15
Apr 73.	(7") (*RCA 2352*) **DRIVE-IN-SATURDAY. / ROUND AND ROUND**	3	–

— with guests **MIKE GARSON** – piano / **KEN FORDHAM** and **BUX** – saxophone, flute

Apr 73.	(lp/c) (*RS/PK 1001*) <*AFL-1 4852*> **ALADDIN SANE** – Watch that man / Aladdin Sane (1913-1938-197?) / Drive-in Saturday / Panic in Detroit / Cracked actor / Time / The prettiest star / Let's spend the night together / The Jean genie / Lady grinning soul. (re-iss. Feb81 on 'RCA Int.' lp/c; INTS/INTK 5067) (hit No.49 UK Feb82) (re-iss. Mar84 on 'RCA Int.' lp/c; NL/NK 83890) (pic-lp Apr84; BOPIC 1) (cd-iss. Jun85; PD 83890) (re-iss. Jul90 on 'EMI' cd/c/lp; CD/TC+/EMC 3579) (+=) – (other rare tracks). (hit UK No.43) (cd re-iss. Sep97 on 'Premier-EMI'; CDP 794768-2)	1	17 May73
Jun 73.	(7") <*APBO 0001*> **TIME. / THE PRETTIEST STAR**	–	–
Jun 73.	(7") (*RCA 2316*) **LIFE ON MARS. / THE MAN WHO SOLD THE WORLD**	3	–
Aug 73.	(7") <*APBO 0028*> **LET'S SPEND THE NIGHT TOGETHER. / LADY GRINNING SOUL**	–	–

— **AYNSLEY DUNBAR** – drums repl. WOODY

Oct 73.	(7") (*RCA 2424*) <*APBO 0160*> **SORROW. / AMSTERDAM**	3	Nov73
Oct 73.	(lp/c) (*RS/PK 1003*) <*AFL-0 0291*> **PIN-UPS** – Rosalyn / Here comes the night / I wish you would / See Emily play / Everything's alright / I can't explain / Friday on my mind / Sorrow / Don't bring me down / Shapes of things / Anyway anyhow anywhere / Where have all the good times gone!. (re-iss. Sep81 lp/c; RCA LP/K 3004) (re-iss. Mar84 on 'RCA Int.' lp/c; INTS/INTK 5236) (hit UK 57) (pic-lp Apr84; BOPIC 4) (re-iss. Jul90 on 'EMI' CD/TC+/EMC 3580) (hit No.52)	1	23

— DUNBAR and **TONY NEWMAN** – drums / **HERBIE FLOWERS** – bass / **MIKE GARSON** – keyboards

Feb 74.	(7") (*LPBO 5009*) **REBEL REBEL. / QUEEN BITCH**	5	–
Apr 74.	(7") (*LPBO 5021*) **ROCK'N'ROLL SUICIDE. / QUICKSAND**	22	–
May 74.	(7") <*APBO 0287*> **REBEL REBEL. / LADY GRINNING SOUL**	–	64
May 74.	(lp/c; as BOWIE) (<*APL/APK 1-0576*>) **DIAMOND DOGS** – Future legend / Diamond dogs / Sweet thing / Candidate / Sweet thing (reprise) / Rebel rebel / Rock'n'roll with me / We are the dead / 1984 / Big brother (including 'Chant of the ever circling skeletal family'). (re-iss. Feb81 on 'RCA Int.' lp/c; INTS/INTK 5068) (hit UK 60 in May83) (re-iss. Mar84 on 'RCA Int.' lp/c/cd; NL/NK/PD 83889) (pic-lp Apr84; BOPIC 5) (re-iss. Jun90 on 'E.M.I.' cd/c/lp; CD/TC+/EMC 3584) (+=) – Dodo / Candidate. (hit UK No.67)	1	
Jun 74.	(7") (<*APBO 0293*>) **DIAMOND DOGS. / HOLY HOLY**	21	

BOW WOW WOW

Formed: London, England . . . late '79 by extrovert entrepreneur and former SEX PISTOLS mastermind, MALCOLM McLAREN, who cannily matched up ADAM ANT's former backing band of MATTHEW ASHMAN, LEROY GORMAN and DAVE BARBAROSSA with a 14-year old Burmese schoolgirl, ANNABELLA LWIN. He'd apparently recruited her after hearing her sing

BOW WOW WOW (cont) — THE GREAT INDIE DISCOGRAPHY — The 1980s

in a North London launderette. If that sounds like a typically opportunistic McLAREN-esque scenario, then the debut single was straight out of the rock'n'roll swindle handbook; a bouncy little ditty entitled 'C'30, C'60, C'90', the song's calculated celebration of home taping (remember the skull & crossbones?) earned BOW WOW WOW instant infamy and a Top 40 placing. Music wise, the band were touting a suspiciously similar Burundi-drumming guitar-pop style to the revamped ADAM & THE ANTS, adopting a kind of primitive savage image in contrast to ADAM's pirates. McLAREN's next brainwave was for a cassette only EP, 'YOUR CASSETTE PET' (1980), featuring such provocative material as 'SEXY EIFFEL TOWERS'. While LWIN's yelp was perhaps something of an acquired taste there was no doubting her smouldering adolescent appeal and of course it was milked for all it was worth. In a move reminiscent of his 'PISTOLS tactics, McLAREN took the band from 'E.M.I.' to 'R.C.A.' and after a further couple of minor hits, a long awaited debut album, 'SEE JUNGLE! SEE JUNGLE!...' was finally unveiled in late '81. Boasting a decidedly risqué cover shot of LWIN (then still only 15) er... at one with nature (a mock-up of Monet's 'Dejeuner sur l'herbe'), the record was a three-chord teen-frenzy revelling in its own trashiness. Not exactly one-hit wonders, BOW WOW WOW would nevertheless struggle to come up with anything quite as infectious and exuberant as 'GO WILD IN THE COUNTRY', their first and most famous Top 10 hit. With constant hassle from LWIN's mother (who was none too happy about her daughter posing in the curly-headed one's teen mag, 'Chicken'), McLAREN almost replaced her with a certain Lieutenant Lush; perhaps he should've done, Lush later resurfaced as BOY GEORGE in CULTURE CLUB. Save for a last gasp Top 10 hit with a tepid cover of The Strangeloves' 'I WANT CANDY', BOW WOW WOW, meanwhile, were rapidly spiralling into pop oblivion. A follow-up album 'WHEN THE GOING GETS TOUGH, THE TOUGH GET GOING' (1983) was generally ignored amid critical meltdown and the band folded later that year. The backing boys, ASHMAN, GORMAN and BARBAROSSA carried on as CHIEFS OF RELIEF to little avail, while LWIN eventually surfaced in the mid 80's with a couple of flop singles and an album, 'FEVER'. She also had the dubious honour of releasing the first ever mini-disc single, 'CAR SEX', after signing to 'Sony' almost a decade later. • **Covers:** FOOLS RUSH IN (Brook Benton) / FEVER (Peggy Lee).

Album rating: YOUR CASSETTE PET mini/cassette (*8) / SEE JUNGLE! SEE JUNGLE! GO JOIN YOUR GANG YEAH! CITY ALL OVER, GO APE CRAZY! (*6) / I WANT CANDY compilation (*7) / WHEN THE GOING GETS TOUGH, THE TOUGH GET GOING (*4) / GO WILD – THE BEST OF BOW WOW WOW compilation (*7)

ANNABELLA LWIN (b. MYANT MYANT AYE, 31 Oct'65, Rangoon, Burma) – vocals / **MATTHEW ASHMAN** – guitar / **LEROY GORMAN** – bass / **DAVE BARBAROSSA** – drums (all 3 men ex-ADAM & THE ANTS)

		E.M.I.	not iss.
Jul 80.	(7") (EMI 5088) **C'30, C'60, C'90, GO. / SUN, SEA & PIRACY**	34	-
Nov 80.	(c-ep) (WOW 1) **YOUR CASSETTE PET**	58	-
	– Louis Quatorze / Gold he said / Fools rush in / Giant sized baby thing / I want my baby on Mars / Uomo sex al Apache / Sexy Eiffel towers / Radio G-string. (cd-iss. Oct93; CDP 827223-2)		
Mar 81.	(c-s/7") (TC+/EMI 5153) **W.O.R.K. (NO NAH NO NO NO MY DADDY DON'T). / C'30, C'60, C'90, GO . . . ANDA!**	62	-

— added 2 female backing vocalists around 1981

		R.C.A.	R.C.A.
Jul 81.	(7") (RCA 100) **PRINCE OF DARKNESS. / ORANG UTAN**	58	-
	(12") (RCAT 100) – ('A'side) / Sinner! sinner! sinner! (Prince of darkness).		
Oct 81.	(7"/12") (RCA/+T 144) **CHIHUAHUA. / GOLLY! GOLLY! GO BUDDY**	51	-
Oct 81.	(lp/c) (RCA LP/K 3000) <4147> **SEE JUNGLE! SEE JUNGLE! GO JOIN YOUR GANG YEAH! CITY ALL OVER, GO APE CRAZY!**		26
	– Jungle boy / Chihuahua / Sinner! sinner! sinner! (Prince of darkness) / Mickey put it down / (I'm a) T.V. savage / Elimination dancing / Golly! golly! go buddy! / King Kong / Go wild in the country / I am not a know it all / Why are babies so wise? / Orang-utang / Hello, hello daddy (I'll sacrifice you). (c+=) – The joy of eating raw flesh. (re-iss. Jul90 on 'Great Expectations' lp/cd+=; PIP LP/CD 013) – Orang utan / El boss dicho. (cd re-iss. Jun97 on 'One Way'; OW 34502)		
Jan 82.	(7"/ext.12") (RCA/+T 175) **GO WILD IN THE COUNTRY. / EL BOSS DICKO**	7	-
Apr 82.	(7"/ext.12") (RCA/+T 220) **SEE JUNGLE (JUNGLE BOY). / T.V. SAVAGE**	45	-
May 82.	(7") <13204> **I WANT CANDY. / ELIMINATION DANCING**	-	62
May 82.	(m-lp) <4314> **THE LAST OF THE MOHICANS**	-	67
	– Cowboy / Louis Quatorze / I want candy / Mile High club.		
May 82.	(7"etched) (RCA 238) **I WANT CANDY**	9	-
	(7"+=) (RCA 238) – King Kong.		
	(ext.12"+=) (RCAT 238) – Cowboy.		
Jul 82.	(7") (RCA 263) **LOUIS QUATORZE. / THE MILE HIGH CLUB**	66	
Feb 83.	(7"pic-d) (RCA 314) <13467> **DO YOU WANNA HOLD ME? / WHAT'S THE TIME (HEY BUDDY)**	47	77
	(12"+=) (RCAT 314) – Biological phenomenon.		
Feb 83.	(lp/c) (RCA LP/K 6068) <4570> **WHEN THE GOING GETS TOUGH, THE TOUGH GET GOING**		82
	– Aphrodisiac / Do you wanna hold me? / Roustabout / Lonesome tonight / Love me / What's the time (hey buddy) / Mario (your own way to Paradise) / Quiver (arrows in my) / Rikki Dee / Tommy Tucker / Love, peace and harmony. (re-iss. Nov90 on 'Great Expectations' lp/cd; PIP LP/CD 022) (cd re-iss. Jun97 on 'One Way'; OW 34503)		

— disbanded mid '83 when ANNABELLA opted for a solo career (one solitary album, 'FEVER' appeared in '86). ASHMAN formed CHIEFS OF RELIEF with ex-SEX PISTOLS. Sadly he was to die on 21st Nov'95 of complications due to his diabetes.

– compilations, others, etc. –

Jul 82.	(lp/c) E.M.I.; (EMC 3416) / R.C.A.; <4375> **I WANT CANDY**		Sep82
	– I want Candy / Cowboy / Louis Quatorze / Mile high club / W.O.R.K. (ne no my daddy oh) / Fools rush in / I want my baby on Mars / Gold he said / Sexy Eiffel Towers / Radio G-string / C-30, C-60, C-90, go / Sun, sea & piracy / Uomo sex al apache / Giant sized baby thing / C-30, C-60, C-90, anda (Spanish version). (re-iss. Nov90 on 'Great Expectations' lp/cd; PIP LP/CD 021)		
Sep 82.	(7") E.M.I.; (EMI 5344) **FOOLS RUSH IN. / UOMO SEX AL APACHE**		-
May 83.	(c-ep) R.C.A.; (RCXK 004) **I WANT CANDY / SEE JUNGLE (JUNGLE BOY). / GO WILD IN THE COUNTRY / CHIHUAHUA**		-
Nov 86.	(7") Old Gold; (OG 9638) **GO WILD IN THE COUNTRY. / I WANT CANDY**		-
Aug 89.	(lp/cd) Receiver; (RR LP/CD 116) **THE BEST OF BOW WOW WOW**		-
	(re-iss. Jul93; same)		
Jun 94.	(cd) Arista; (74321 21336-2) **GO WILD – THE BEST OF BOW WOW WOW**		
	– I want candy / Go wild in the country / Prince of darkness / Cowboy / Baby, oh no / Do you wanna hold me / Golly! Golly! go buddy / Louis Quatorze / What's the time? (hey buddy) / Joy of eating raw flesh / Elimination dancing / Aphrodisiac / The mile high club / T.V. savage / See jungle (see jungle boy) / Chihuahua (12" version) / Go wild in the country (12"version) / Chihuahua.		
Oct 96.	(cd) Camden-RCA; (74321 41967-2) **APHRODISIAC (THE BEST OF BOW WOW WOW)**		-
Feb 97.	(cd) Receiver; (RRCD 233) **LIVE IN JAPAN (live)**		-
Jan 99.	(cd) Cleopatra; (CLEO 4242) **WILD IN AMERICA**		-

BOX

Formed: Sheffield, England . . . 1982 by ex-CLOCKDVA members, PAUL WIDLER, CHARLIE COLLINS and ROGER QUAIL, alongside frontman PETER HOPE and bass player TERRY TODD. Becoming the first band to sign for indie imprint, 'Go! Discs' (later the home of HOUSEMARTINS, PAUL WELLER, etc), The BOX debuted early the following year with a 12" EP, 'NO TIME FOR TALK'. While ADI NEWTON took CLOCKDVA into darker but more popular territories, The BOX opened up further experimental possibilities in the spirit of The POP GROUP or The BIRTHDAY PARTY. Bass-heavy, saxy, discordant and jerkily rhythmic, The BOX's unconventional sound was topped off by HOPE's strangulated larynx, an approach that won them a marginal underground following but next to no mainstream coverage. Their debut album, 'SECRETS OUT' was unveiled in mid '83, tracks such as 'WATER GROWS TEETH', 'OLD STYLE DROP DOWN' and a guest appearance from STEPHEN MALLINDER (of CABARET VOLTAIRE), partly rescuing it from a critical savaging. A second set, 'GREAT MOMENTS IN BIG SLAM', was delivered exactly a year later, although 'Go! Discs' subsequent move into more commercial indie waters found The BOX on the CABS' 'DoubleVision' label for a swansong live lp, 'MUSCLE OUT' (1985). By this time, HOPE had begun the first of his numerous collaborations, a single with DAVID HARROW entitled 'TOO HOT'. The other half of CABARET VOLTAIRE, RICHARD H. KIRK was next to lend his services, their 'LEATHER HANDS' also surfacing later in '85; they would go on to work with each other on future projects. Early in 1987, the singer showcased a further collaborative sojourn, PETER HOPE & THE JONATHAN S. PODMORE METHOD, with an album, 'DRY HIP ROTATION'; HOPE reunited with saxman, CHARLIE COLLINS to form the short-lived BONE ORCHESTRA. • **Note:** Another outfit (a French one!) used the moniker in the late 80's after this group's demise.

Album rating: SECRETS OUT (*5) / GREAT MOMENTS IN BIG SLAM (*6) / MUSCLE OUT (*4) / Peter Hope & The Jonathan S. Podmore Method: DRY HIP ROTATION (*5)

PETER HOPE – vocals, percussion / **PAUL WIDLER** – guitar (ex-CLOCKDVA) / **CHARLIE COLLINS** – saxophone (ex-CLOCKDVA, ex-BONGOS guest) / **TERRY TODD** – bass / **ROGER QUAIL** – drums (ex-CLOCKDVA)

		Go! Discs	not iss.
Jan 83.	(12"ep) (VFM 1) **NO TIME FOR TALK**		-
	– Burn down that village / Unstable / Limpopo / Hazard.		
May 83.	(7") (VFM 2) **OLD STYLE DROP DOWN. / MOMENTUM**		-
	(12"+=) (VFM 3) –		
Jun 83.	(lp) (VFM 4) **SECRETS OUT**		-
	– Water grows teeth / Skin, sweat and rain / Something beginning with "L" / Strike / The hub / Hang your hat on that / I give protection / No sly moon / Slip and slant / Old style drop down / Swing / Out.		
Jun 84.	(lp/c) (VFM/ZVFM 5) **GREAT MOMENTS IN BIG SLAM**		-
	– Walls come down / Flatstone / Big slam / Stop / Low line / Breaking strain / Small blue car / Still in the woodwork.		

		DoubleVision	not iss.
Jan 85.	(12") (DVR 10) **MUSCLE IN. /**		-
Aug 85.	(lp) (DVRP 3) **MUSCLE OUT (live)**		-

— disbanded some time in '85 with TERRY joining The IAN ELLIOTT BAND after briefly co-forming WORKFORCE.

PETER HOPE

— worked on a series of collaborative work

		Ink	not iss.
Jun 85.	(12"ep; as PETER HOPE & DAVID HARROW with PINKIE McCLURE) (INK12 11) **TOO HOT. /**		-

— in Oct'85, PETER HOPE linked with RICHARD H. KIRK (of CABARET VOLTAIRE) on a 12", 'LEATHER HANDS'

		Native	not iss.
Oct 85.	(12"; as CHAIN) *(NTV 2)* **BANGING ON THE HOUSE. / CHAINS**	□	-
Feb 87.	(7"; by PETER HOPE & THE JONATHAN S. PODMORE METHOD) *(NTV 13)* **KITCHENETTE. / THE UNKNOWN INDUSTRIAL FATALITY**	□	-
	(12"+=) *(NTV12 13)* – ('A' version).		
Feb 87.	(lp; by PETER HOPE & THE JONATHAN S. PODMORE METHOD) *(NTVLP 14)* **DRY HIP ROTATION**	□	-
	– Kitchenette / Canal / 217 / Dry bone / Haulage / Dog eared pictures of birdwing cars / Needleheat / Hypnosis / Knife / Scurry bug / The unknown industrial fatality.		

— once again, HOPE and KIRK collaborated, this time on the 'HOODOO TALK' (1987) album, which spawned the following year's 'SURGEONS' 12"

— HOPE and COLLINS subsequently reunited in the short-lived, BONE ORCHESTRA

B-PEOPLE

Formed: Los Angeles, California, USA ... March 1979 out of various punk outfits by PAT DELANEY (ex-DEADBEATS; one mid'78 EP exists, 'KILL THE HIPPIES' for 'Dangerhouse' IQ 29), ALEX GIBSON, FREDRIK NILSEN and TOM RECCHION (the latter both ex-DOO DOOETTES; some recordings exist from 1976). The early 80's saw B-PEOPLE release their only two EP's, 'YOU AT EIGHT' and the eponymous 'B-PEOPLE', the band's provocatively experimental material later collected together for posterity on the 1986 compilation, 'PETRIFIED CONDITIONS 1979-1981'. Before their split they did manage to appear on V/A compilation, 'Let Them Eat Jellybeans', with the track 'PERSECUTION – THAT'S MY SONG'. MICHAEL GIRA (later SWANS) and PAUL CUTLER were said to have been part of the band prior to their demise.

Album rating: PETRIFIED CONDITIONS 1979-1981 compilation (*6)

PAT DELANEY – synthesizer, saxophone (ex-DEADBEATS) / **ALEX GIBSON** – guitar, vocals / **FREDRIK NILSEN** – bass, vocals, saxophone (ex-DOO DOOETTES) / **TOM RECCHION** – drums (ex-DOO DOOETTES)

		not iss.	Faulty
May 81.	(7"m) *<FP 03>* **YOU AT EIGHT. / WEATHER TO WORRY / M.C.P.D.**	-	□
Sep 81.	(12"ep; by ALEX GIBSON) *<FEP12 01>* **PASSIONNEL**	-	□
Feb 82.	(12"ep) *<FEP 1300>* **B-PEOPLE**	-	□

— MICHAEL GIRA and PAUL CUTLER could well have been members before they split. In 1984, ALEX GIBSON scored the soundtrack for the film, 'SUBURBIA', which was released by 'Enigma' in the US-only.

– compilations, etc. –

1986.	(lp) *Restless; <72029-1>* **PETRIFIED CONDITIONS 1979-1981**	-	□

BRADFORD

Formed: Blackburn, England ... 1987 by IAN MICHAEL HODGSON, MARK ANDREW MCVITIE, JOS MURPHY and STUART. Originally touted as the answer to the vacuum left by the recently disbanded SMITHS, the soulful skinhead band had much in common with the Mancunian legends of morose rock; although they also shared many similarities with the likes of ELVIS COSTELLO, thus it was wrong to just hail them as imitators of the MORRISSEY/MARR legacy. BRADFORD debuted in 1988 with the competent single, 'SKIN STORM', which also had the noteworthy record collector appeal of being the first debut single to be issued on the CD format. The same year the band also had the honour of supporting the great MORRISSEY at his first solo show (at Wolverhampton Civic Hall) following his erstwhile band's split. The links between them were even greater as MOZ covered their initial release as a B-side to his 1991 single, 'Pregnant For The Last Time'. Fellow MORRISSEY collaborator and producer, STEPHEN STREET, was reputed to be the man who discovered BRADFORD. He worked on their one and only album proper, 'SHOUTING QUIETLY' (1990), issued on the influential 'Sire' imprint in the States. However, the band did make the news again in the millennium, when drummer McVITIE was arrested and charged with possessing child pornography in his then position as English Language tutor at Blackburn College. Yet apart from this ugly incident the band seemed to have been relegated to the lower levels of music history.

Album rating: BRADFORD (*5) / SHOUTING QUIETLY (*6)

IAN H. (b. IAN MICHAEL HODGSON) – vocals, some guitar / **STUART** – guitar / **JOS MURPHY** – bass / **MARK McVITTIE** – drums

		Village	not iss.
Feb 88.	(7") *(VILS 101)* **SKIN STORM. / GATLING GUN**	□	-
	(12"+=) *(VILT 101)* – Dodging around in cars.		
	(cd-s+=) *(VILSCD 101)* – Lust roulette.		
Nov 88.	(7") *(VILS 104)* **TATTERED, TANGLED & TORN. /**	□	-
	(12"+=) *(VILT 104)* –		

		Midnight Music	not iss.
Feb 89.	(m-lp; w/drawn) *(CHIME 043M)* **BRADFORD**	-	-

— **EVAN BUTLER** – guitar + **JOHN BAULCOMBE** – keyboards, some guitar; repl. STUART

		Foundation	Sire
Jul 89.	(7") *(TFL 1)* **IN LIVERPOOL. / BOYS WILL BE BOYS**	□	-
	(12"+=/cd-s+=) *(TFL 1 T/CD)* – Everywhere I turn.		
Sep 89.	(12"m) *(TFL 4T)* **ADRIFT AGAIN. / THE LOSS / TATTERED, TANGLED & TORN**	□	-
Feb 90.	(12"m) *(TFL 5T)* **GANG OF ONE. / A PINT OF BITTERNESS / QUALITY OF MERCY**	□	-
Feb 90.	(lp/c/cd) *(FOUND 1/+C/CD) <26222-2>* **SHOUTING QUIETLY**	□	-
	– Greed and peasant land / To have and to hurt / Gang of one / Always torn / Lust roulette / Adrift again / Radio Edna / Everything at once / Gary's going down / Skin storm / A wounding. *(lp w/free 7")*		

— disbanded after JOE joined the circus of Zippo's. IAN formed the short-lived AFTERGLOW, but really all have retired from music biz.

Billy BRAGG

Born: STEVEN WILLIAM BRAGG, 20 Dec'57, Barking, Essex, England. Inspired by The CLASH, he formed Peterborough-based R&B/punk band, RIFF RAFF, in 1977. After releasing a string of indie 7" singles, (including the wonderfully titled 'I WANNA BE A COSMONAUT'), the band split in 1981, BILLY incredibly going off to join the army. Thankfully, a career in the military wasn't to be though, and he bought himself out after only 90 days. Complete with amplifier and guitar, he busked around Britain, finally furnished with some studio time in 1983 courtesy of 'Charisma' indie subsidiary, 'Utility'. The result was 'LIFE'S A RIOT WITH SPY VS SPY', and with the help and distribution of new label 'Go! Discs', the record finally hit the UK Top 30 in early '84. BRAGG's stark musical backdrop (for the most part, a roughly strummed electric guitar) and even starker vocals, belied a keen sense of melody and passionate, deeply humane lyrics. 'THE MILKMAN OF HUMAN KINDNESS' was a love song of the most compassionate variety which illustrated that BRAGG approached politics from a humanist perspective rather than a soapbox. After seeing firsthand how Thatcher had decimated mining communities, BRAGG's songs became more overtly political. 'BREWING UP WITH BILLY BRAGG' (1984) opened with the fierce 'IT SAYS HERE', but again the most affecting moments were to be found on heartfelt love songs like the wistful 'ST. SWITHIN'S DAY'. It would be another two years before he released a new album, in the interim taking time to make his Top Of The Pops debut and play a lead role in the 'Red Wedge' campaign. A well intentioned but ultimately hopeless initiative to persuade people to vote Labour, BRAGG toured alongside The STYLE COUNCIL, MADNESS, The COMMUNARDS and MORRISSEY. As the Conservatives romped home to another sickening victory, BRAGG licked his wounds and bounced back with a third album, 'TALKING WITH THE TAXMAN ABOUT POETRY' (1986). His most successful and accomplished release to date, the record spawned the classic single, 'LEVI STUBBS' TEARS' as well as the JOHNNY MARR collaboration, 'GREETINGS TO THE NEW BRUNETTE'. And of course, who could argue with the sentiments of 'HELP SAVE THE YOUTH OF AMERICA'?! Not content with saving our Transatlantic cousins, BRAGG also did his bit for kids back in Blighty. Recording a cover of 'SHE'S LEAVING HOME' with CARA TIVEY, BRAGG found himself at No.1 when the song was released as the B-side to WET WET WET's cover of 'WITH A LITTLE HELP FROM MY FRIENDS', the not inconsiderable proceeds going to the Childline charity. BRAGG's next album, 'WORKER'S PLAYTIME' (1988), saw a move away from the sparse accompaniment of old, while lyrically the record focused more on matters of the heart than the ballot box. 'THE INTERNATIONALE' (1990), meanwhile, was BRAGG's most political work to date, with the likes of 'NICARAGUITA' and 'THE RED FLAG'. On 'DON'T TRY THIS AT HOME' (1991), BRAGG enlisted a cast of musicians to flesh out the sound, a tactic that elicited mixed results. His stance with CND and anti-apartheid, anti-poll tax, etc, often saw him on wrong side of the law. For the 90's it looked as though he would become a bit more cosmopolitan but still ungagged. In 1998, BILLY and the alt-country group WILCO decided to do a tribute album dedicated to their dustbowl hero, WOODY GUTHRIE. 'MERMAID AVENUE' (a street in Coney Island where WOODY lived with his family in the late 40's and early 50's) was the title, the lyrics seemingly found in an attic while messers BRAGG and WILCO set them to tunes. From the bawdy, singalong raucousness of opener 'WALT WHITMAN'S NIECE' to the gorgeous, yawning back porch swing of 'CALIFORNIA STARS' and the desolate fragility of 'BIRDS AND SHIPS' (featuring a heart-stopping guest vocal by NATALIE MERCHANT), this ranked among the cream of both artists' back catalogues. While they each interpreted the material in their own way – BRAGG obviously coming closer to the mould of GUTHRIE's worldly, open hearted troubadour – both WILCO and BRAGG brought their own personality to bear on WOODY's words of wisdom. As well as being a great record in its own right – surely a contender for album of the year – this collection served to underline just how unceasingly prolific and inventive a songwriter GUTHRIE really was. The spirit of this work cut to the heart of popular music's foundations, no argument. Inevitably, 'MERMAID AVENUE VOL.2' (2000) couldn't quite match that high standard but was nevertheless an enjoyable companion piece to its predecessor. • **Covered:** WALK AWAY RENEE (Four Tops) / SHE'S LEAVING HOME + REVOLUTION (Beatles) / JEANE (Smiths) / SEVEN AND SEVEN IS (Love) / THERE IS POWER IN A UNION (trad.new words) / THINK AGAIN (Dick Gaughan) / CHILE YOUR WATERS RUN RED THROUGH SOWETO (B.Johnson Reagan) / TRAIN TRAIN (Z.Delfeur) / DOLPHINS (Fred Neil) / EVERYWHERE (Sid Griffin-Greg Trooper) / JERUSALEM (William Blake) / WHEN WILL I SEE YOU AGAIN (Three Degrees) / NEVER HAD NO ONE EVER (Smiths).

Album rating: LIFE'S A RIOT WITH SPY VS. SPY mini (*7) / BREWING UP WITH BILLY BRAGG (*8) / TALKING WITH THE TAXMAN ABOUT POETRY (*8) / BACK TO BASICS compilation (*7) / WORKERS PLAYTIME (*7) / THE INTERNATIONALE (*5) / DON'T TRY THIS AT HOME (*8) / WILLIAM BLOKE (*7) / BLOKE ON BLOKE (*6) / MERMAID AVENUE with Wilco (*8) / REACHING TO THE CONVERTED (MINDING THE GAPS) collection (*7) / MERMAID AVENUE VOL.II with Wilco (*6) / ENGLAND, HALF ENGLISH (*5)

RIFF RAFF

BILLY BRAGG – vocals, guitar and other members

			Chiswick	not iss.
May 78.	(7"ep)	(SW 34) **I WANNA BE A COSMONAUT**		-

– Cosmonaut / Romford girls / What's the latest? / Sweet as pie.

			Geezer	not iss.
Oct 80.	(7")	(GZ 1) **EVERY GIRL AN ENGLISH ROSE. / U SHAPED HOUSE**		-
Oct 80.	(7")	(GZ 2) **KITTEN. / FANTOCIDE**		-
Oct 80.	(7")	(GZ 3) **LITTLE GIRLS KNOW. / SHE DON'T MATTER**		-
Oct 80.	(7")	(GZ 4) **NEW HOME TOWN. / RICHARD**		-

BILLY BRAGG

			Utility	not iss.
Jun 83.	(m-lp)	(UTIL 1) **LIFE'S A RIOT WITH SPY VS. SPY**	30	-

– The milkman of human kindness / To have and have not / A new England / The man in the iron mask / The busy girl buys beauty / Lover's town revisited / Richard. *(re-iss. Jan84 on 'Go! Discs' lp/c; UTIL/+C 1) (cd-iss. Sep96 on 'Cooking Vinyl'; COOKCD 106)*

──── added for back-up **KENNY CRADDOCK** – organ / **DAVE WOODHEAD** – trumpet

			Go! Discs	Elektra
Oct 84.	(lp/c)	(A/Z GOLP 4) **BREWING UP WITH BILLY BRAGG**	16	-

– It says here / Love gets dangerous / The myth of trust / From a Vauxhall Velox / The Saturday boy / Island of no return / St. Swithin's Day / Like soldiers do / This guitar says sorry / Strange things happen / A lover sings. *(cd-iss. Sep96 on 'Cooking Vinyl'; COOKCD 107)*

Feb 85.	(7") **ST. SWITHIN'S DAY. / A NEW ENGLAND**	-	- Euro
Mar 85.	(7"ep) (AGOEP 1) **BETWEEN THE WARS**	15	-

– Between the wars / Which side are you on? / World turned upside down / It says here.

| Dec 85. | (7"m) (GOD 8) **DAYS LIKE THESE. / I DON'T NEED THIS PRESSURE RON / SCHOLARSHIP IS THE ENEMY OF ROMANCE** | 43 | - |

──── + guests **JOHNNY MARR** – guitar / **KIRSTY MacCOLL** – b.vocals / **KENNY JONES** – drums, co-producer / **JOHN PORTER** – bass, co-producer / **SIMON MORTEON** – percussion / **BOBBY VALENTINO** – violin

| Jun 86. | (7"m) (GOD 12) **LEVI STUBBS' TEARS. / THINK AGAIN / WALK AWAY RENEE** | 29 | - |

(12"+=) (GODX 12) – Between the wars (live).

| Sep 86. | (lp/c) (A/Z GOLP 6) **TALKING WITH THE TAXMAN ABOUT POETRY** | 8 | - |

– Greetings to the new brunette / Train train / The marriage / Ideology / Levi Stubbs' tears / Honey, I'm a big boy now / There is power in a union / Help save the youth of America / Wishing the days away / The passion / The warmest room / The home front. *(cd-iss. May87; AGOCD 6) (cd re-iss/Sep96 on 'Cooking Vinyl'; COOKCD 108)*

| Nov 86. | (7") (GOD 15) **GREETINGS TO THE NEW BRUNETTE. / DEPORTEES / THE TATLER** | 58 | - |

(12"+=) (GODX 15) – Jeane / There is power in a union (instrumental).

──── Oct'87, BRAGG is credited with OYSTER BAND backing **LEON ROSSELSON** on his single **BALLAD OF A SPYCATCHER** (Upside Down records)

──── May'88, he's credited with **CARA TIVEY** on 45 **SHE'S LEAVING HOME** the B-side of **WET WET WET** – With A little Help From My Friends. This UK No.1 single issued on 'Childline' gave all proceeds to children's charity, with backing including his usual friends.

			Go! Discs	Elektra
May 88.	(12"ep/cd-ep) (A/ZA GOLP 1) <960-787-2> **HELP SAVE THE YOUTH OF AMERICA (LIVE AND DUBIOUS)**		

– Help save the youth of America / Think again / Chile your waters run red through Soweto / Days like these (DC mix) / To have and have not / There is power in a union (with The PATTERSONS).

| Aug 88. | (7"m) (GOD 23) **WAITING FOR THE GREAT LEAP FORWARD. / WISHING THE DAYS AWAY / SIN CITY** | 52 | |
| Sep 88. | (lp/c/cd) (AGOLP/ZGOLP/AGOCD 15) <60824> **WORKER'S PLAYTIME** | 17 | |

– She's got a brand new spell / Must I paint you a picture / Tender comrade / The price I pay / Little timb-bomb / Rotting on demand / Valentine's day is over / Life with the lions / The only one / The short answer / Waiting for the great leap forward. *(cd re-iss. Sep96 on 'Cooking Vinyl'; COOKCD 109)*

| Nov 88. | (7") (GOD 24) **SHE'S GOT A BRAND NEW SPELL. / MUST I PAINT YOU A PICTURE** | | |

──── In Jul'89, BRAGG was credited on a NORMAN COOK Top 30 single 'Won't Talk About it'.

| May 90. | (m-lp/m-c/m-cd; on 'Utility') (UTIL/+C/CD 011) <60960> **THE INTERNATIONALE** | 34 | Jun90 |

– The internationale / I dreamed I saw Phil Ochs last night / The marching song of the convent battalions / Jerusalem / Nicaraguita / The red flag / My youngest son came home today.

──── still holding on to **MARR, MacCOLL, TIVEY** (keyboards) and **WOODHEAD** plus **WIGGY** – guitar, bass / **J.F.T. HOOD** – drums / **AMANDA VINCENT** – keyboards / etc.

| Jun 91. | (7") (GOD 56) **SEXUALITY. / BAD PENNY** | 27 | - |

(12"+=/cd-s+=) (GOD X/CD 56) – (2 'A'mixes).

| Aug 91. | (7") (GOD 60) **YOU WOKE UP MY NEIGHBOURHOOD. / ONTARIO, QUEBEC AND ME** | 54 | - |

(12"+=/cd-s+=) (GOD X/CD 60) – Bread and circuses / Heart like a wheel. (above single 'A'featured **MICHAEL STIPE and PETER BUCK (R.E.M.)** with first 12"extra track with **NATALIE MERCHANT** (10,000 MANIACS) – also backing vocals

| Sep 91. | (cd/c/d-lp)(8x7"box) (828279-2/-4/-1) <61121> **DON'T TRY THIS AT HOME** | 8 | |

– Accident waiting to happen / Moving the goalposts / Everywhere / Cindy of a thousand lives / You woke up my neighbourhood / Trust / God's footballer / The few / Sexuality / Mother of the bride / Tank park salute / Dolphins / North sea bubble / Rumours of war / Wish you were here / Body of water. *(re-iss. Nov93 & Apr98 on 'Cooking Vinyl' lp/c/cd; COOK/+C/CD 062) (cd re-iss. Sep96; COOKCD 110)*

| Feb 92. | (7"ep) (GOD 67) **ACCIDENT WAITING TO HAPPEN (Red Star version) / SULK. / THE WARMEST ROOM (live) / REVOLUTION** | 33 | - |

(12"+=/cd-s+=) (GOD X/CD 67) – ('A'live version) / Levi Stubbs' tears / Valentine's day is over / North Sea bubble.

			Cooking Vinyl	Elektra
Aug 96.	(7"/c-s) (FRY/+C 051) **UPFIELD / THATCHERITES**	46	-

(cd-s+=) (FRYCD 051) – Rule nor reason.

| Sep 96. | (lp/c/cd) (COOK/+C/CD 100) <61935> **WILLIAM BLOKE** | 16 | |

– From red to blue / Upfield / Everybody loves you babe / Sugardaddy / A Pict song / Brickbat / The space race is over / Northern industrial town / The fourteenth of February / King James version / Goalhanger.

| May 97. | (7") (FRY 064) **THE BOY DONE GOOD. / SUGARDADDY** | 55 | - |

(cd-s+=) (FRYCD 064) – Just one victory / Qualifications.
(cd-s+=) (FRYCDX 064) – Never had no one ever / Run out of reasons.

| Jun 97. | (cd) (COOKCD 127) **BLOKE ON BLOKE** | 72 | - |

– The boy done good / Just one victory / Qualifications / Sugar daddy / Never had no one ever / Run out of seasons / Rule nor reason / Thatcherites.

BILLY BRAGG & WILCO

──── **WILCO** were **JEFF TWEEDY** and Co

			Elektra	Elektra
Jun 98.	(cd/c) (<7559 62204-2/-4>) **MERMAID AVENUE**	34	90

– Walt Whitman's niece / California stars / Way over yonder in the minor key / Birds and ships / Hoodoo voodoo / She came along to me / At my window sad and lonely / Ingrid Bergman / Christ for President / I guess I planted / One by one / Eisler on the go / Hesitating beauty / Another man's done gone / The unwelcome guest.

| Nov 98. | (7"/c-s) (E 3798/+C) **WAY OVER YONDER IN THE MINOR KEY. / MY THIRTY THOUSAND** | | |

(cd-s+=) (E 3798CD) – Bug-eyed Jim.

| May 00. | (cd/c) <7559 62522-2/-4> **MERMAID AVENUE VOL.II** | 61 | 88 |

– Airline to Heaven / My flying saucer / Feed of man / Hot rod hotel / I was born / Secret of the sea / Stetson Kennedy / Remember the mountain bed / Blood of the lamb / Against th' law / All you fascists / Joe Dimaggio done it again / Meanest man / Black wind blowing / Someday some morning sometime.

BILLY BRAGG AND THE BLOKES

with **IAN McLAGAN** – keyboards, accordion / **MARTYN BARKER** – drums, percussion / **SIMON EDWARDS** – bass / **BEN MANDELSON** – bouzouki, mandolin, guitars / **DAVE WOODHEAD** – trumpet / **LU** – guitars

			Cooking Vinyl	Elektra
Feb 02.	(cd-s) (FRYCD 120) **ST. MONDAY / ENGLAND, HALF ENGLISH**		-
Mar 02.	(lp/cd) (COOK/+CD 222) <62743> **ENGLAND, HALF ENGLISH**	51	

– St. Monday / Jane Allen / Distant shore / England, half English / Npwa / Some days I see the point / Baby Faroukh / Take down the Union Jack / Another kind of Judy / He'll go down / Dreadbelly / Tears of my tracks.

| May 02. | (cd-s) (FRYCD 131) **TAKE DOWN THE UNION JACK / MYSTERY SHOES / ENGLAND, HALF ENGLISH (7" remix)** | 22 | |

(cd-s) (FRYCD 131X) – ('A'-band version) / Yarra song / England, half English (12" remix).
(cd-s) (FRYCD 131XX) – ('A'side) / You pulled the carpet out / England, half English (ambient remix) / ('A'video).

– compilations, etc. –

| May 87. | (12"ep) Strange Fruit; (SFPS 027) **THE PEEL SESSIONS** | | - |

– A new England / Strange things happen / This guitar says sorry / Love gets dangerous / A13 trunk road to the sea / Fear . . . *(cd-iss. 1988; SFPSCD 027)*

| Jun 87. | (d-lp/d-cd) Go! Discs; (AGOLP/ZGOLP/AGOCD 8) **BACK TO BASICS** (best 83-85 material) | 37 | - |

(re-iss. Apr98 on 'Cooking Vinyl' d-lp/c/cd; COOK/+C/CD 060)

| Feb 92. | (cd/c/lp) Strange Fruit; (SFR CD/MC/LP 117) **THE PEEL SESSIONS ALBUM** | | |

(cd with extra tracks)

| Nov 93. | (d-lp/c/cd) Cooking Vinyl; (COOK/+C/CD 061) **VICTIM OF GEOGRAPHY** | | |

– Greetings to the new brunette / Train train / Marriage / Idealogy / Levi Stubbs' tears / Honey I'm a big boy now / There is a power in a union / Help save the youth of America / Wishing the days away / Passion / The warmest room / She's got a new spell / Must I paint you a picture / Tender comrade / The price I pay / Little time bomb / Rotting on demand / Valentine's day is over / Life with the lions / The only one / Short answer / Waiting for the great leap forward. *(re-iss. Apr98 cd/c; same)*

| Aug 99. | (cd/c/lp) Cooking Vinyl; (COOK CD/MC/LP 186) / Rhino; <75962> **REACHING TO THE CONVERTED (MINDING THE GAPS)** | 41 | |

– Shirley / Sulk / Accident waiting to happen / Boy done good / Heart like a wheel / Bad penny / Ontario Quebec and me / Walk away Renee / Rule nor reason / Days like these / Think again / Scholarship is the enemy of romance / Wishing the days away (ballad version) / Tatler / Jeane / She's leaving home.

Glenn BRANCA

Born: 6 Oct'48, Harrisburg, Pennsylvania, USA. He left college in Boston to set up home in New York, where he formed theatre/No Wave outfits, STATIC and THE THEORETICAL GIRLS. During the rest of the 70's, he composed and conducted an array of musicians on tour including Y PANTS, KONK, NYC NOISE and LIQUID LIQUID. A few other musicians, LEE RANALDO and THURSTON MOORE, played guitar on his debut 45 'LESSON No.1'. He finally issued his first album 'THE ASCENSION', which was to sell independently around 10,000 copies. BRANCA resurrected the avant-garde in one fell swoop, generating repetitive rhythms from several guitarists, backed with heavy percussion. In 1982, he contributed 'BAD SMELLS' to poet JOHN GIORNO's 'WHO YOU STARING AT?', which also featured experimental dance piece choreographed by TWYLA THARP. He then formed the 'Neutral' label, which after his 'SYMPHONY No.1 (TONAL PLEXUS)' album (recorded July 16-19, 1981); became the platform for RANALDO & MOORE's splinter outfit SONIC YOUTH. In 1986, his film score for PETER GREENAWAY's 'The Belly Of An Architect' was rejected in favour of WIM MERTEN's, although several minutes of BRANCA can be heard. In 1989, he was back on record with 'SYMPHONY No.6 (DEVIL CHOIRS AT THE GATES OF HEAVEN)', which added many more guitarists alongside other musicians. He turned up a few times in the 90's, and in February '94, premiered in the UK 'SYMPHONY No.10 FOR MASSED GUITARS'. Over the last decade or so, BRANCA had quickly shifted from minimal symphonic "No Wave" music to PHILIP GLASS-like experimental classical music with heavenly crescendos of guitars.

Album rating: LESSON No.1 mini (*6) / THE ASCENSION (*7) / WHO YOU STARING AT?; with John Giorno (*5) / SYMPHONY NO.1 – TONAL PLEXUS (*6) / SYMPHONY NO.3 – GLORIA (*6) / SYMPHONY NO.6 – DEVIL CHOIRS AT THE GATES OF HEAVEN (*7) / THE WORLD UPSIDE DOWN (*6) / SYMPHONY NO.2 (THE PEAK OF THE SACRED) (*6) / SYMPHONY NOS. 8 & 10 – THE MYSTERY (*6) / SYMPHONY NO.9 (*5) / SELECTION FROM THE SYMPHONIES collection (*7)

THEORETICAL GIRLS

GLENN BRANCA – guitar, vocals / **MARGARET DEWYS** – bass, organ / **JEFFREY LOHN** – keyboards, bass / **WHARTON TIERS** – drums

not iss.   Theoretical

Oct 78. (7") <TR 01> **U.S. MILLIE. / YOU GOT ME**

— split early the following year, DEWYS later joined PINK PONG

STATIC

— **BRANCA** with **BARBARA ESS** – bass (ex-DAILY LIFE, ex-Y PANTS, ex-DIS BAND) / **CHRISTINE HAHN** – drums (ex-DAILY LIFE, ex-LUXUS)

Jun 79. (7") <TR 02> **MY RELATIONSHIP. / DON'T LET ME STOP YOU**

— when they split CHRISTINE joined MALARIA

GLENN BRANCA

— with the GUITAR ARMY; **LEE RANALDO, NED SUBLETTE, DAVID ROSENBLOOM** – guitars / **JEFFREY GLENN** – bass / **STEPHAN WISCHERTH** – drums

not iss.   99

Jul 80. (m-lp) <99-01> **LESSON No.1**
– Lesson No.1 for electric guitar / Dissonance. <cd-iss. 1999 on 'Robi Droli-New Tone'; RDC 5032>

Nov 81. (lp) <99-001> **THE ASCENSION**
– Lesson No.2 / The spectacular commodity / Structure / Light field (in consonance) / The ascension. <cd-iss. May02 on 'Felmay'; RDC 5021>

— added **THURSTON MOORE** – guitars

not iss.   Giorno Poetry Systems

1982. (lp; with JOHN GIORNIO) <none> **WHO YOU STARING AT?**
– Music for bad smells / Stretching it wider / We got here yesterday, we're here now . . .

not iss.   ROIR

1983. (lp) <A 125> **SYMPHONY No.1 (TONAL PLEXUS)**
– Movements 1-4. (UK-iss.1988; same) (cd-iss. Nov94 & Aug98; RE 125CD)

— now without RANALDO and MOORE who were sacked when they moonlighted as SONIC YOUTH on his tour

not iss.   Neutral

1984. (lp) **SYMPHONY No.3 (GLORIA)**
– First movement / Second movement / Third movement. (UK-iss.Aug93 on 'Atavistic'; ALP 8CD) (cd-iss. Apr94 on 'Barooni'; DEALP 05)

— in 1987, BRANCA was commissioned to score Peter Greenaway's 'The Belly Of An Architect'; released on 'Crepescule'

— now with several guitarists including **ALGIS KIZYS** (of SWANS)

Blast First   Restless

Apr 89. (lp/c/cd) (BFFP 39/+C/CD) <771426> **SYMPHONY No.6 (DEVIL CHOIRS AT THE GATES OF HEAVEN)**
– First movement / Second movement / Third movement / Fourth movement / Fifth movement. <cd re-iss. 1994 on 'Atavistic'; ALP 10CD>
below with The NEW YORK CHAMBER SINFONIA

Crepescule   Atavistic

Sep 92. (cd) (TWI 9102) <ALP 16CD> **THE WORLD UPSIDE DOWN**
– First movement (the temple of Venus, part 1) / Second movement (The temple of Venus, part 2) / Third movement / Fourth movement / Fifth movement / Sixth movement (fluid density) / Seventh movement (polyhymnia).

Blast First   Atavistic

Oct 96. (cd) (BFFP 106CD) <ALP 12CD> **SYMPHONY NOS. 8 & 10 (THE MYSTERIES)**   1995
– Symphony No.8 (The mystery): First movement (The passage) – Second movement (Spiritual anarchy) / Symphony No.10 (The mystery part 2): First movement (The final problem) – Second movement (The horror).

not iss.   Point Music

1996. (cd) <446505-2> **SYMPHONY No.9 (L'EVE FUTURE)**
– Glenn Branca symphony No.9 (L'eve future) / Freedom.

– compilations, etc. –

Aug 93. (cd) Atavistic; <(ALP 5CD)> **SYMPHONY No.2 (THE PEAK OF THE SACRED) (live at St. Mary's Church, 14 May, 1981)**
– First movement – Slow mass / Second movement – Radioactive poltergeist kitchen 1955 / Third movement – Melodrama and nuclear physics in the global theater / Fourth movement – Sacred field / Fifth movement – In the late 20th Century the impossible becomes possible.

Jun 96. (cd) Atavistic; <ALP 15CD> **SYMPHONY No.5 – DESCRIBING PLANES OF AN EXPANDING HYPERSPHERE**
– First movement / Second movement / Third movement / Fourth movement / Fifth movement (parts I-III) / Sixth movement. (UK-iss.May02 on 'Felmay'; FY 7007)

Dec 97. (cd) Atavistic; <(ALP 35CD)> **SELECTION FROM THE SYMPHONIES**   Oct96
– Symphony No.2: Second movement (excerpt) / Symphony No.3: Second movement (excerpt) / Symphony No.5: Fourth movement / Symphony No.6: Fourth movement / Symphony No.6: Fifth movement / Symphony No.8: First movement (excerpt) / Symphony No.10: Second movement.

Kirk BRANDON'S 10:51
(see under ⇒ SPEAR OF DESTINY)

BREAKING CIRCUS (see under ⇒ RIFLE SPORT)

BREATHLESS

Formed: London, England . . . 1983 by DOMINIC APPLETON, GARY MURRAY, ARI NEUFELD and MARTYN WATTS. Releasing records on their own 'Tenor Vossa' imprint, BREATHLESS became noted for APPLETON's unique vocal chords. After a few platters, notably the '2 DAYS FROM HEAVEN' 12"ep in 1985, DOMINIC moonlighting in IVO's '4 a.d.' supergroup, THIS MORTAL COIL (three tracks, 'The Jeweller', 'Tarantula' and 'Strength Of Strings' from the album, 'Filigree & Shadow', to be precise). During this period, BREATHLESS released their own debut (named after a Herman Hesse novel), 'THE GLASS BEAD GAME' (1986), a somewhat disappointing effort that was followed a year later by a second, 'THREE TIMES AND WAVING'. In 1989, a further set, 'CHASING PROMISES', was another lacklustre affair, DOMINIC and Co. finally running out of steam late in 1991 after 'BETWEEN HAPPINESS & HEARTACHE'. • Note: Not to be confused with a similarly titled band who released 'OH YOU BABE' and another BREATHLESS on 'E.M.I.' who issued 'TWILIGHT ZONE' in '89.

Album rating: THE GLASS BEAD GAME (*4) / THREE TIMES AND WAVING (*4) / CHASING PROMISES (*4) / BETWEEN HAPPINESS & HEARTACHE (*4)

DOMINIC APPLETON – vocals / **GARY MURRAY** – guitar / **ARI NEUFELD** – bass / **MARTYN WATTS** – drums (ex-DANIELLE DAX)

Tenor Vossa   not iss.

Apr 84. (7") (BREATH 1) **WATERLAND. / SECOND HEAVEN**
Nov 84. (7") (BREATH 2) **AGELESS. /**
Aug 85. (12"ep) (BREATH 3) **2 DAYS FROM HEAVEN.**
– Stone harvest / Pride / Across the water / Like knives.

Jun 86. (lp) (BREATHLP 4) **THE GLASS BEAD GAME**
– Across the water / All my eye and Betty Martin / Count on angels / Monkey talk / Every road leads home / Touchstone / Sense of purpose / See how the land lies.

Nov 86. (12") (BREATH 5) **NAILING COLOURS TO THE WHEEL. / BAD BLOOD**

Nov 87. (lp/c) (BREATH LP/CAS 6) **THREE TIMES AND WAVING**
– Sold down the river / Is it good news today / Three times and waving / Into the fire / Working for space / Waiting on the wire / Pizzy life / Say September sings / Let's make a night of it.

Apr 89. (lp/cd) (BREATH LP/CD 7) **CHASING PROMISES**
– Compulsion / Here by chance / Better late than never / Heartburst / Moment by moment / Smash package / Sometimes on Sunday / Glow.

Oct 89. (12"ep) (BREATH 8) **I NEVER KNOW WHERE YOU ARE. / MOMENT BY MOMENT / HEARTBURST**

Jul 90. (7") (7BREATH 9) **ALWAYS. / FLOWERS DIE**
(12"+=) (BREATH 9) – ('A'extended).

Nov 91. (cd/lp) (BREATH CD/LP 10) **BETWEEN HAPPINESS & HEARTACHE**
– I never know where you are / Over and over / Wave after wave / You can call it yours / All that matters now / Clearer than daylight / Flowers die / Help me get over it.

Mar 92. (cd-s) (BREATHCD 11) **OVER AND OVER / ALL THAT MATTERS NOW**

Jun 93. (cd-s) (BREATHCD 12) **DON'T JUST DISAPPEAR / EVERYTHING I SEE / DON'T JUST DISAPPEAR (mix)**

May 94. (cd) (BREATHCD 13) **HEARTBURST** (compilation)
– Don't just disappear (radio edit) / You can call it yours / Never know where you are / All that matters now / Always / Over and over / Waiting on the wire / Wave after wave / Ageless / Pride / All my eye and Betty Martin / Touchstone / Don't just disappear.

— had already disbanded some time in '93

Jacques BREL

Born: 8 Apr'29, Brussels, Belgium. Reared in a conservative middle-class environment, BREL went on to study law before entering the family business. He soon tired of a conventional lifestyle and instead relocated to Paris where he thought he'd try his hand at songwriting. Despite an awkward gait and buck-teeth, he soon graduated to performing his own compositions, appearing regularly at the Theatre Des Trois Baudets. BREL enthralled fans with a magnetic stage presence and a gift for dramaticism that helped define his vision of the doomed romantic, translating this to the wider record buying public with his first French hit, 'QUAND ON N'A QUE L'AMOUR'. Signed to 'Barclay' in France, BREL proceeded to release a string of singles which documented the dark underbelly of modern society in shrewdly observed style. A one-off album for 'C.B.S.', the self explanatory 'AMERICAN DEBUT' (1957), introduced BREL's literate genius to a whole new English speaking audience and influenced a host of future stars; while the likes of LEONARD COHEN would incorporate the spirit of BREL into his dark balladry, The KINGSTON TRIO interpreted him more literally, transforming 'LE MORIBUND' into the sentimental 'Seasons In The Sun' (later a UK hit for TERRY JACKS). British artists influenced by his work include SCOTT WALKER, DAVID BOWIE, RAY DAVIES, MARC ALMOND, MOMUS and The SENSATIONAL ALEX HARVEY BAND who covered 'NEXT' (a track centering on an army base brothel) as the title track to a 1973 album (mainman ALEX HARVEY had heard the track in a cult continental film, 'Jacques Brel Is Alive And Well And Living In Paris'). A hugely popular and hard working live performer, BREL had sold out both New York's Carnegie Hall and London's Royal Albert before giving up performing for good in the late 60's; he'd already stated his intention to boycott the USA after they became involved in the Vietnam war. He subseqently retired to French Polynesia from where he'd make sporadic recording trips back to Paris. Diagnosed with cancer in the mid-70's, BREL succumbed to the disease on the 10th of October 1978. Despite his dearth of either British or American chart success, he remains one of the last century's most influential songwriters.

Best CD compilation: QUINZE ANS D'AMOUR (*8)
for the complete discography, see THE GREAT ROCK DISCOGRAPHY

BRILLIANT CORNERS

Formed: Avonmouth, Bristol, England ... 1983 out of The HYBRIDS by DAVEY WOODWARD, who took the BRILLIANT CORNERS moniker from a THELONIUS MONK track. He recruited other likeminded indie minstrels, CHRIS GALVIN, WINSTON, BOB MORRIS and DAN, before setting up their own label, 'SS20' and releasing debut single, 'SHE'S GOT FEVER'. After several singles and a few mini-sets, 'GROWING UP ABSURD' (1985) and 'WHAT'S IN A WORD' (1986), went barely noticed, they came up with their finest and most comical three minutes in 'BRIAN RIX' (a parody of the English "King of farce" actor), its video appearance on 'The Tube' – featuring DAVEY running RIX-like around a couch with his trousers around his ankles accompanied by a trumpeter – helping raise the band's profile. The following year, the band initiated another label, 'McQueen', for the release of their first full-length set, 'SOMEBODY UP THERE LIKES ME' (1988). More fun-loving indie fare was to surface in the shape of 'EVERYTHING I EVER WANTED' (compilation 1988), mini 'JOY RIDE' (1989), 'HOOKED' (1990) and 'A HISTORY OF WHITE TRASH' (1993), although none were given full consideration by the press. Unperturbed, DAVEY and CHRIS (and initially CORIN) burst back onto the scene courtesy of a new studio project, The EXPERIMENTAL POP BAND. For the latter half of the 90's, EPB unleashed a plethora of singles and a handful of albums, highlights being Melody Maker SOTW, 'BOUTIQUE IN MY BACKYARD' from '96 and the following year's "eclectic boho-pop" set, 'DISCGROTESQUE'. However, tragedy was to hit the group when the terminally ill CHRIS GALVIN finally died of cancer on the 22nd of December, 1998. DAVEY continued later the following year, releasing some of the work ('HOMESICK') he and CHRIS were producing before his untimely death. In 2001, The EXPERIMENTAL POP BAND resurfaced once more with the JOHN PARISH-produced 'THE TRACKSUIT TRILOGY', an album of diverse leanings as far apart as BACHARACH to BECK. • **Note:** The BRILLIANT CORNERS who released 'Two Roads' in '98 were not the same.

Album rating: GROWING UP ABSURD mini (*5) / WHAT'S IN A WORD mini (*5) / SOMEBODY UP THERE LIKES ME (*7) / EVERYTHING I EVER WANTED compilation (*6) / JOY RIDE mini (*6) / HOOKED (*6) / CREAMY STUFF compilation (*7) / A HISTORY OF WHITE TRASH (*6) / Experimental Pop Band: WOOF (*6) / DISCGROTESQUE (*7) / HOMESICK (*5) / THE TRACKSUIT TRILOGY (*7)

DAVEY WOODWARD (b. 1966) – vocals, guitar / **CHRIS GALVIN** (b. 1959) – bass / **WINSTON** – percussion, vocals / **BOB MORRIS** – drums / **DAN** – guitar, occasional keyboards

SS20 — not iss.

Jan 84. (7") *(SS21)* **SHE'S GOT FEVER. / BLACK WATER**
Jun 84. (7") *(SS22)* **BIG HIP. / TANGLED UP IN BLUE**
Oct 84. (12"m) *(SS23T)* **MY BABY'S IN BLACK. / ROPE IN MY HAND / SIXTEEN YEARS**
Oct 85. (m-lp) *(SS24)* **GROWING UP ABSURD**
– Rambling Rose / A girl called property / Growing up absurd / Southern mystery / One of these days / Mary.
May 86. (7"ep/12"ep) *(SS25/+T)* **THE FRUIT MACHINE**
– Meet me on Tuesdays / Jim's room / The funniest thing / Everything I ever wanted.
Nov 86. (m-lp) *(SS26)* **WHAT'S IN A WORD**
– Laugh I could have cried / Brian Rix / I never said that / Delirious / A very easy death / Sweet Brandan / Egostistical me / Boy and the cloud. (re-iss. Jul88 on 'McQueen'; MCQLP 2)

— added trumpeter

Apr 87. (7") *(SS27)* **BRIAN RIX. / TRUDY IS A SEQUEL**
Oct 87. (7") *(SS28)* **DELILAH SANDS. / IS THERE ANYBODY HOME?**
(12"+=) *(SS28T)* – Please please please.

— when DAVEY broke his arm, he was briefly replaced by guitarist PHIL
— **ANTHONY FORBES** became guitarist around this time

McQueen not iss.

Mar 88. (7") *(MCQ 1)* **TEENAGE. / I DON'T WANT TO TALK TO YOU**
(12"+=) *(MCQ 1T)* – How embarrassing to dance like that.
Apr 88. (lp/cd) *(MCQ LP/CD 1)* **SOMEBODY UP THERE LIKES ME**
– Somebody up there likes me / Teenage / Friday Saturday Sunday Monday / She's dead / Never a young girl / Oh! / Your feet never touched the ground / Like father like sun / Trust me / Forever / I can't wait that long / With a kiss. (cd+=) – I don't want to talk to you / How embarrassing to dance like that / All for the good.
Oct 88. (7") *(MCQ 2)* **WHY DO YOU HAVE TO GO OUT WITH HIM WHEN YOU COULD GO OUT WITH ME. / SHANGRI LA**
(12"+=) *(MCQ 2T)* – Things will get better / Goodbye.
Oct 88. (lp/cd) *(MCQ LP/CD 3)* **EVERYTHING I EVER WANTED** (compilation)
– Rambling Rose / A girl called property / Growing up absurd / Southern mystery / One of these days / Mary / Meet me on Tuesdays / Jim's room / The funniest thing / Everything I ever wanted / Under the bridge / Trudy is a sequel.
May 89. (m-lp/m-cd) *(MCQ LP/CD 4)* **JOY RIDE**
– You don't know how lucky you are / This girl / Grow cold / I didn't see you / Emily / Nothing / Hemingway's back / Accused by the angels.
Mar 90. (12"ep) *(MCQ 3)* **LOVE IT I LOST IT / WHITE GATES. / I CRIED / LOVES LIKE THIS**
Sep 90. (7") *(MCQ 4)* **THE POPE, THE MONKEY AND THE QUEEN. / GHOST OF A YOUNG MAN**
(12"+=) *(MCQT 4)* – When the blossom falls / Silias.
Oct 90. (cd/lp) *(MCQ CD/LP 5)* **HOOKED**
– Long long way to go / Where are the Supremes tonight / The pope, the monkey and the queen / SAndy knows / Gone / Positively lips / Sam / Desperate situation blues song / Heaven inside her / Take the gun / Subtle as the bomb / Love is over.
Aug 91. (cd/lp) *(MCQ CD/LP 6)* **CREAMY STUFF** (compilation 84-90)
– She's got fever / angled up in blue / Big hip / My baby's in black / Sixten years / Meet me on Tuesdays / Jim's room / Brian Rix / Trudy is a squeal / Please please please / Delilah sands / Teenage / I don't want to talk to you / Why do you have to go out with him when you could go out with me / Shangri-la / Love it I lost it / The pope, the monkey and the queen / The ghost of a girl.

C.M.P. not iss.

Mar 93. (cd/lp) *(CMP CD/LP 005)* **A HISTORY OF WHITE TRASH**
– Get it up / Around the bend / You make the day seem longer / Death of a protest singer / I like it here / Gushing / Electric slam / La / Jukebox junk / He looks to be with you / Closer / Always on a Sunday / Electric slam No.6.

— disbanded later in '93

– compilations, etc. –

Nov 00. (cd/lp) *Vinyl Japan; (ASK CD/LP 117)* **THE BBC SESSIONS**

EXPERIMENTAL POP BAND

DAVEY WOODWARD – vocals, guitars / **CHRIS GALVIN** – bass, vocals / **CORIN** (a brief member who joined ALPHA)

Swarf Finger — not iss.

Aug 96. (12"ep) *(SF 005T)* **THE LOUNGE EP**
Aug 96. (12"ep) *(SF 008T)* **BOUTIQUE IN MY BACKYARD EP**
Jan 97. (cd) *(SF 009CD)* **WOOF** (compilation of 2 above)
– Skinny / Twentieth century tack / James remains / Les chanteurs et le grand orchestre / Universe / Black Elvis / Sunshine ices / California farm / Instrumental James / Boutique in my backyard / Oslo / Kickers / Terrible terrible pain / Skinny (Smith + Mighty remix) / Skinny (Ratman + B23 remix) / Twentieth century tack (ariel remix) / E.L.L.A. (pet project mix) / (untitled).
Jun 97. (cd) *(SF 017CD)* **DISCGROTESQUE**
– Chewing gum friends / Watch you cry / Mental health out patients clinic / By myself / Girlfriends story / Rocky path / Frisbee / London pregnancy test 1976 / Day / Desgrotesque / Piccadilly / Dead sea.

Cup Of Tea not iss.

Oct 98. (12"ep/cd-ep) *(COT 061)* **FORTY GREATEST HITS**
– Forty greatest hits / Futureless / For dancers only / Superfly.

— CHRIS died of cancer (aged 39) on the 22nd of December 1998 (he appeared on below recordings in '99)

Feb 99. (7") *(COT 064)* **FROZEN HEAD. / SPINNING AROUND**
(cd-s+=) *(COT 064CDS)* – Somethingsaremoreimportantthanmusic / Track 13.

— **DAVEY** now recruited **JOE ROONEY** – keyboards / **MARK BARBER** – bass / **KEITH BAILEY** – drums

City Slang not iss.

May 99. (7") *(08720-7)* **PUNK ROCK CLASSIC. / SOFT ROCK CLASSIC**
(cd-s+=) *(08720-2)* – Sisters / Extricate.

BRILLIANT CORNERS (cont)

Jun 99. (cd/lp) *(08721-2/-1)* **HOMESICK**
– Forty greatest hits / Punk rock classic / Carnival / For dancers only / Stop / Archive / Civil rights / Cocaine cowboy / Frozen head / Little Russia / Everything's easy / Give a little love / Homesick / Theme from the modern lover.
Feb 01. (cd-s) *(20166-2)* **BANG BANG YOU'RE DEAD / BANG BANG YOU'RE DEAD (unforscene reinterpretation) / THEME FROM EXPERIMENTAL POP BAND**
(12") *(20166-6)* – ('A'-Unforscene reinterpretation mix & dub) / ('A'-Fauna flash mix).
Mar 01. (cd) *(20170-2)* **THE TRACKSUIT TRILOGY**
– Bang bang you're dead / Emotion / Narcotic days / Hard enough / Remember / Somethingsaremoreimportantthanmusic / Satan's friends / I like it / All hang out / Casual sex / Bereaved / Alcudia / When the music ends.
Jun 01. (cd-s) *(20180-2)* **HARD ENOUGH**

BUILDERS/BILDERS (see under ⇒ DIREEN, Bill)

Mark BURGESS (see under ⇒ CHAMELEONS)

BUSH TETRAS

Formed: New York City, New York, USA ... 1979 by Chicago-born guitarist, PAT PLACE, who, after a musical apprenticeship with JAMES CHANCE's CONTORTIONS, began rehearsals with fellow compadres ADELE BERTEI, JIMMY ULIANO and DEE POP. Retaining only DEE, she formed THE BUSH TETRAS, enlisting "No Wave" students, LAURA KENNEDY and CYNTHIA SLEY, former classmates at the Cleveland Institute Of Art. Early in 1980, the 3-girl/1-guy quartet released a debut EP, 'TOO MANY CREEPS', which was issued on the '99' label. Subsequently signed to UK label, 'Fetish' (also home of another American outfit, The BONGOS), they hit the US dance charts late in 1981 with the TOPPER HEADON-produced follow-up, 'RITUALS'. Intentionally amateurish, the band's funky "No Wave" non-conformist jungle-rock was something of an anomaly on the early 80's post-punk scene. A cassette-only album finally reached the shops in 1983; entitled 'WILD THINGS', this was basically a collection of live recordings, the 'TETRAS having already ventured into other projects. Back due to popular demand, the original line-up re-united in 1995 (after having previously got back together for live gigs in '92) to record a one-off set of new material, 'BEAUTY LIES' (1996). • **Covered:** WILD THING (Troggs) / COLD TURKEY (John Lennon).
• **Trivia:** SLEY once designed clothes for LYDIA LUNCH (Teenage Jesus) and JUDY NYLON (Snatch).
Album rating: WILD THINGS compilation (*5) / BETTER LATE THAN NEVER compilation (*6) / BOOM IN THE NIGHT compilation (*5) / BEAUTY LIES (*6) / TETRAFIED compilation (*5)

PAT PLACE (b. 1964, Chicago, Illinois) – guitar (ex-JAMES CHANCE & THE CONTORTIONS) / **CYNTHIA SLEY** (b. 3 May'57, Cleveland, Ohio) – vocals, percussion / **LAURA KENNEDY** (b.30 May'57, Cleveland, Ohio) – bass / **DEE POP** (b.14 Mar'56, Queens, N.Y.) – drums

	not iss.	99
Sep 80. (7"ep) <99-02> **TOO MANY CREEPS. / SNAKES CRAWL / YOU TASTE LIKE THE TROPICS**	–	99
	Fetish	Stiff
May 81. (7") (FET 007) **THINGS THAT GO BOOM IN THE NIGHT. / DAS AH RIOT**		–
1981. (7"w/drwn) (FE 15) **CAN'T BE FUNKY**		–
Dec 81. (12"ep) (FET 16) **RITUALS** – Can't be funky (2 versions) / Too many creeps / Cowboys in Africa.		–
	R.O.I.R.	R.O.I.R.
Jan 83. (c) <(A 119)> **WILD THINGS** – Cowboys in Africa / Making a mistake / Stare / Rituals / Enemies / Wild thing / Boom / Damned / Submerging nations / Too many creeps / Can't be funky / Voodoo / Jaws.		

—— split; DEE POP formed FLOOR KIS, DEERFRANCE before joining GUN CLUB, etc. SLEY formed MAD ORPHAN (later LOVELIES) with then-husband IVAN JULIAN (ex-RICHARD HELL & THE VOID-OIDS). In the 90's, she was in 1-800-BOXX, before she briefly re-united BUSH TETRAS in 1992 for live gigs.

	not iss.	Tim/Kerr
Oct 96. (c-s) <139> **PAGE 18 / FIND A LIE / SATAN IS A BUMMER**	–	
	not iss.	Polygram
Dec 96. (cd) <830149> **BEAUTY LIES** – Mr. Love song / Page 18 / Dirty little secret / Beauty lies / Color green / Satan is a bummer / Silver chain / Ballad / Mental mishap / Find a lie / Basement babies / World / World dub.	–	

– compilations, etc. –

1989. (c) R.O.I.R.; <A 163> **BETTER LATE THAN NEVER, 1980-1983** – Too many creeps / Snakes crawl / You taste like the tropics / Things that go boom in the night / Das ah riot / You can't be funky / Funky (instrumental) / Rituals / Cowboys in Africa / Making a mistake / Stand up and fight / Dum dum / Moonlite / Who's gonna pay / It's so weird.	–	
Feb 96. (cd) ROIR USA; <(RUSCD 8218)> **BOOM IN THE NIGHT: ORIGINAL STUDIO RECORDINGS 1980-1983** – Cowboys in Africa / Things that go boom in the night / You can't be funky / Snakes crawl / Rituals / Moonlite / You taste like the tropics / Sad ah riot / Too many creeps / Dum dum / Stand up and fight / Who's gonna pay / It's so weird / Funky (instrumental).		Dec95
Apr 97. (cd) 2.13.61.; <21311-2> **TETRAFIED** (early demos, etc) – Punch drunk / Fess up / In mind a run / Ah dub / Dub in the night / Funky dub / Cowboys in Africa / Cold turkey / Boom lakka lakka / Make sure / Stare you down / Point that gun / Race for space / Dewback / Juana lagusta / Voodoo.	–	

BUTTHOLE SURFERS

Formed: San Antonio, Texas, USA ... 1980 originally as The ASHTRAY BABY HEELS by ex-accountant GIBBY (son of US children's TV presenter "Mr. Peppermint") and PAUL LEARY, who met at Trinity College, San Antonio. By 1983, they had signed to JELLO BIAFRA's (Dead Kennedys) label, 'Alternative Tentacles'. Around the mid-80's, they gigged heavily in Britain due to lack of Stateside interest, and this, together with radio play from John Peel, helped them make it into the UK indie charts. Heavy psychedelia mixing noise, confusion and futuristic art-punk, the manic GIBBY, (complete with loudspeaker, etc), was always offensive and disturbing while their weird stage act included the nude dancer, KATHLEEN. She covered herself in green jello, while GIBBY simulated sex with her! GIBBY was well-known for other stage antics; pissing in plastic baseball bats ('piss wands') and anointing the audience at the front. There were other obscenities, too rude to print here (no need to mention President Carter's creamy briefcase). In 1987, they unleashed the brilliantly crazed 'LOCUST ABORTION TECHNICIAN', complete with a parody of BLACK SABBATH's 'SWEET LEAF', the humourously titled 'SWEAT LOAF'. Also deep inside its nightmarish musical grooves was their gem, 'TWENTY TWO GOING ON TWENTY THREE', a track that made John Peel's Festive 50. A longer sojourn in Britain culminated in some riotous, oversubscribed London gigs. The follow-up, 'HAIRWAY TO STEVEN' (another piss-take; this time of LED ZEPPELIN – Stairway To Heaven), deliberately left the tracks nameless (instead using obscene looking symbols) as a twisted tribute to ZEPPELIN's "untitled" symbols album. 1990 saw them shift to a more commercial sound with 'PIOUHGD' (which means "pissed-off" in Red Indian), which featured a re-working of DONOVAN's 'HURDY GURDY MAN'. Having signed to 'Capitol' in 1992, they were back to their abrasive sound of old with the JOHN PAUL JONES-produced album, 'INDEPENDENT WORM SALOON'. This, together with their previous effort, had given them their first taste of chart success in Britain, this being well surpassed in 1996 when 'ELECTRICLARRYLAND' hit the US Top 30. It was due, no doubt, to a surprise domestic hit with 'PEPPER', and probably their "fiery" guest appearance on American mock talk show, 'The LARRY Sanders Show' in '97. Abandoning their trademark psychedelic noise for crazy electronica, insane synth sound effects and dance/techno beats, Texas' very own masters of the punk revolution had always been a little off-kilter, but with their most recent album 'WEIRD REVOLUTION' (2001), the group seemed to have taken things beyond the realm of anything to date. Like the MELVINS before them, GIBBY HAYNES and his LSD army began experimenting with electronica on the late eighties side-project group The JACK OFFICERS, who made unlistenable computer music on some old Apple Macs. This had really the same slant; oodles of weirdness poured from the speakers as breakbeats tore the bass into shreads and HAYNES' distorted vocal loops were something not to be reckoned with. The album was not all experimental and avant garde, however, 'THE SHAME OF LIFE' proved that they still had an ounce of pop sensibility, although those who cringed at the BECK pisstake/ripoff that was 'PEPPER' found themselves cringing again. What was missing was the rock and punk edge that had made the 'SURFERS music so appealing in the first place; gone was LEARY's swirling guitar to be replaced by droning effects and fuzzy electronic noise that would've sounded more at home on NEIL YOUNG's disastrous 'Trans' LP. The BUTTHOLE SURFERS: great band, fantastic legacy, but this album was no more important than a computer generated fart in the wind. • **Songwriters:** GIBBY and co., except AMERICAN WOMAN (Guess Who) / THE ONE I LOVE (R.E.M.). P covered DANCING QUEEN (Abba).
Album rating: BROWN REASONS TO LIVE mini (*6) / PSYCHIC ... POWERLESS ... ANOTHER MAN'S SAC (*7) / REMBRANDT PUSSYHORSE (*7) / LOCUST ABORTION TECHNICIAN (*8) / HAIRWAY TO STEVEN (*7) / DOUBLE LIVE (*4) / PHIOHGD (*6) / INDEPENDENT WORM SALOON (*7) / ELECTRICLARRYLAND (*7) / WEIRD REVOLUTION (*5)

GIBBY HAYNES (b. GIBSON JEROME HAYNES, 1957) – vocals / **PAUL LEARY** (b.1958) – guitar / **KING COFFEY** – drums repl. ? / **ALAN ?** – bass

	Alternative Tentacles	Alternative Tentacles
Apr 84. (m-lp) <(VIRUS 32)> **BUTTHOLE SURFERS** <'BROWN REASONS TO LIVE; US-title> – The Shah sleeps in Lee Harvey's grave / Hey / Something / Bar-b-que / Pope / Wichita cathedral / Suicide / The legend of Anus Presley. *(re-iss. Sep93 as 'BROWN REASONS TO LIVE' brown-lp; same)*		1983
Jan 85. (12"ep) <(VIRUS 39)> **LIVE PCPPEP (live)** – Cowboy Bob / Bar-b-q pope / Dance of the cobras / The Shah sleeps in Lee Harvey's grave / Wichita cathedral / Hey / Something.		

—— **TERENCE** – bass repl. ALAN (?)

	Fundam.	Touch & Go
Apr 85. (7") **LADY SNIFF. /**		–
Jul 85. (lp) (SAVE 5) <TGLP 05> **PSYCHIC ... POWERLESS ... ANOTHER MAN'S SAC** – Concubine / Eye of the chicken / Dum dum / Woly boly / Negro observer / Butthole surfer / Lady sniff / Cherub / Mexican caravan / Cowboy Bob / Gary Floyd. *(cd-iss. Jan88+=)* – CREAM CORN FROM THE SOCKET OF DAVIS *(cd re-iss. Jul99 on 'Latino Bugger'; LBV 003)*		

—— **MARK KRAMER** – bass (of SHOCKABILLY) repl. TREVOR who had repl. TERENCE

| Oct 85. (12"ep) (PRAY 69) <TG 14> **CREAM CORN FROM THE SOCKET OF DAVIS** – Moving to Florida / Comb – Lou Reed (two parter) / Tornados. | | |

BUTTHOLE SURFERS (cont)

	Red Rhino Europe	Touch & Go
Apr 86. (lp) (RRELP 2) <TGLP 8> **REMBRANDT PUSSYHORSE**	☐	☐

– Creep in the cellar / Sea ferring / American woman / Waiting for Jimmy to kick / Strangers die / Perry / Whirling hall of knives / Mark says alright / In the cellar. *(cd-iss. May88; RRECD 2) (cd re-iss. Jul99 on 'Latino Bugger'; LBV 004)*

—— JEFF 'TOOTER' PINKUS – bass; repl. KRAMER who formed BONGWATER

	Blast First	Touch & Go
Mar 87. (lp/c/cd) (BFFP 15/+C/CD) <TG 19/+C/CD> **LOCUST ABORTION TECHNICIAN**	☐	☐

– Sweat loaf / Graveyard 1 / Pittsburgh to Lebanon / Weber / Hay / Human cannonball / U.S.S.A. / Theoman / Kintz / Graveyard 2 / 22 going on 23 / The G-men. *(cd re-iss. Jul99 on 'Latino Bugger'; LBV 05)*

—— added THERESA NERVOSA (NAYLOR) – 2nd drummer / KATHLEEN – naked dancer (above with GIBBY, PAUL, COFFEY and PINKUS)

Apr 88. (lp/cd) (BFFP 29/+CD) <TG 29/+CD> **HAIRWAY TO STEVEN**	☐	☐

– Hairway part 1 / Hairway part 2 / Hairway part 3 / Hairway part 4 / Hairway part 5 / Hairway part 6 / Hairway part 7 / Hairway part 8 / Hairway part 9. *(9 tracks marked rude symbols as titles) (cd re-iss. Jul99 on 'Latino Bugger'; LBV 06CD)*

Aug 89. (12"ep/10"ep/cd-ep) (BFFP 41/+T/CD) <TG 50> **WIDOWERMAKER**	☐	☐

– Helicopter / Bong song / 1401 / Booze tobacco.

—— now without THERESA

	Rough Trade	Rough Trade
Nov 90. (7") (RT 240) **THE HURDY GURDY MAN. / BARKING DOGS**	☐	–

(12"+=/cd-s+=) (RTT 240/+CD) – ('A'-Paul Leary remix).

Feb 91. (cd/c/lp) (R 2081260-2/-4/-1) <RTE R2601> **PIOUHGD**	**68**	☐

– Revolution part 1 / Revolution part 2 / Lonesome bulldog / Lonesome bulldog II / The hurdy gurdy man / Golden showers / Lonesome bulldog III / Blindman / No, I'm iron man / Something / P.S.Y. / Lonesome bulldog, IV. *(cd+=)* – Barking dogs. *<(cd-iss. Dec94 on 'Danceteria'; DAN 069CD)>*

—— In Apr'92, GIBBY guested for MINISTRY on single 'Jesus Built My Hotrod'. PAUL LEARY had earlier issued a solo set, while DRAIN (COFFEY's outfit) delivered a further two albums.

	Capitol	Capitol
Mar 93. (cd/c/lp) (CD/TC+/EST 2192) <98798> **INDEPENDENT WORM SALOON**	**73**	☐

– Who was in my room last night? / The wooden song / Tongue / Chewin' George Lucas' chocolate / Goofy's concern / Alcohol / Dog inside your body / Strawberry / Some dispute over t-shirt sales / Dancing fool / You don't know me / The annoying song / Dust devil / Leave me alone / Edgar / The ballad of naked man / Clean it up.

May 96. (cd/c/d-lp) (CD/TC+/EST 2285) <29842> **ELECTRICLARRYLAND**	☐	**31**

– Birds / Cough syrup / Pepper / Thermador / Ulcer breakout / Jingle of a dog's collar / TV star / My brother's wife / Ah ha / The Lord is a monkey / Let's talk about cars / L.A. / Space.

Sep 96. (7") (CL 778) **PEPPER. / HYBRID**	**59**	☐

(cd-s+=) (CDCL 778) – Pepper (Butcha' Bros remix) / The Lord is a monkey.

—— now with HAYNES, LEARY + PINKUS

	not iss.	Hollywood
Aug 01. (cd) <162269> **WEIRD REVOLUTION**	–	☐

– The weird revolution / The shame of life / Dracula from Houston / Venus / Shit like that / Mexico / Intelligent guy / Get down / Jet fighter / The last astronaut / Yentel / They came in.

– compilations, others, etc. –

Jun 89. (d-lp/cd) *Latino Bugger; (LBV 01)* **DOUBLE LIVE** (live)	☐	–
Nov 94. (7"/7"pic-d) *Trance Syndicate; (TR 30/+PD)* **GOOD KING WENCENSLAUS. / THE LORD IS A MONKEY**	☐	☐
Apr 95. (cd) *Trance Syndicate; <(TR 35CD)>* **THE HOLE TRUTH & NOTHING BUTT!** (early demos)	☐	☐
Jun 02. (d-lp/cd) *Latino Bugger; <(LBV 07/+CD)>* **HUMPTY DUMPTY L.S.D.**	☐	☐

JACKOFFICERS

off-shoot with GIBBY, JEFF & KATHLEEN

	Naked Brain	Rough Trade
Dec 90. (lp/c/cd) (NBX 003/+C/CD) <ROUGHUS 100> **DIGITAL DUMP**	☐	☐

– Love-o-maniac / Time machine pt.1 & 2 / L.A.name peanut butter / Do it / Swingers club / Ventricular retribution / 6 / Don't touch that / An Hawaiian Christmas song / Flush.

P

formed 1993 by GIBBY + JOHNNY DEPP – bass, guitar (yes! the actor & beau of supermodel Kate Moss) / BILL CARTER – bass / SAL JENCO – drums

	Capitol	Capitol
Feb 96. (cd/c/lp) (CD/TC PCS 7379) <7243 8 32942-2/-4/-1> **P**	☐	☐

– I save cigarette butts / Zing Splash / Michael Stipe / Oklahoma / Dancing queen / Jon Glenn (megamix) / Mr Officer / White man sings the blues / Die Anne / Scrapings from ring / The deal.

PAUL LEARY

	Rough Trade	Rough Trade
Apr 91. (cd/c/lp) <(R 2081263-2/-4/-1)> **THE HISTORY OF DOGS**	☐	☐

– The birds are dying / Apollo one / Dalhart down the road / How much longer / He's working overtime / Indians storm the government / Is it milky / Too many people / The city / Fine home.

DRAIN

aka **KING COFFEY + DAVID McCREETH** (ex-SQUID)

	Trance Syndicate	Trance Syndicate
Apr 91. (7") <(TR 04)> **A BLACK FIST. / FLOWER MOUND**	☐	☐
Mar 92. (lp/cd) <(TR 11/+CD)> **PICK UP HEAVEN**	☐	☐

– National anthem / Crawfish / Martyr's road / Non compis mentis / Funeral pyre / Ozark monkey chant / Instant hippie / Flower mound / Every secret thing / The ballad of Miss Toni Fisher.

Apr 96. (cd) <(TR 49CD)> **OFFSPEED & IN THERE**	☐	☐

– Playground twist / Burma slowdrive / Return to Rosedale / Marrakesh: 3 a.m. / Bunch of guys about to turn blue / Helicopters are burning / Saipan murder mystery / Stop six / Wendy will win / Nitrous shuffle / In the Spring we eat cucumbers / Upright and in love.

BYRDS

Formed: Los Angeles, California, USA ... 1964 as The JETSET by JIM McGUINN, GENE CLARK and DAVID CROSBY. All three had come from folky backgrounds, McGUINN having toured with The CHAD MITCHELL TRIO as a teenager and CLARK already having proved an accomplished songwriter with The NEW CHRISTY MINSTRELS. CROSBY, meanwhile was an ambitious singer/songwriter who'd performed with LES BAXTER'S BALLADEERS. THE JETSET recorded a one-off flop single for 'Elektra', 'PLEASE LET ME LOVE YOU', under the pseudonym of The BEEFEATERS. Later the same year, they recruited expert bluegrass player CHRIS HILLMAN, previously of The HILLMEN, who'd incorporated his instrumental dexterity on the mandolin into his bass playing. Drummer MICHAEL CLARKE, with his chiselled, BRIAN JONES-esque looks, completed the line-up, initially playing on cardboard boxes when the band were too hard-up to afford a real drum-kit! Profoundly influenced by The BEATLES, they soon changed their name to The BYRDS (the mis-spelling a tribute to their heroes), and set about realising their vision of marrying the fab four's electric energy to the folk music which was their stock in trade. With the help of long-time manager JIM DICKSON and the unlikely recommendation of MILES DAVIS, the band signed to 'Columbia'. At the insistence of DICKSON and producer TERRY MELCHER, the reluctant BYRDS eventually agreed to re-work their earlier demo of 'MR. TAMBOURINE MAN' (this and other demos later surfaced on 'PREFLYTE'). It was a canny decision which did nothing less than change the course of pop/rock history. The resulting song's unforgettable euphoric rush charged DYLAN's lyrics with a youthful romanticism, encapsulating in 3 minutes, what it was to be young and have the world at your feet. It soon hit No.1 on both sides of the Atlantic and it still sounds as fresh today as it did then, a timeless slice of hypnotic, bittersweet pop with McGUINN's delivery forging an affecting DYLAN / LENNON hybrid. Much has since been made of the fact that only one BYRD, McGUINN, actually played on the record, with MELCHER hiring session musicians like LEON RUSSELL, LARRY KNECHTAL and HAL BLAINE. However, any doubts about The BYRDS' ability as a band were dispelled with the self-titled debut album, a folk-rock classic. It was a case of more of the same really, with the band turning in a dazzling string of DYLAN covers, making the songs distinctly their own. 'CHIMES OF FREEDOM' was a ringing, hippy call to arms, fuelled by a starry-eyed optimism and they even managed to transform the Welsh mining disaster ballad 'BELLS OF RHYMNEY', into an effervescent swirl. GENE CLARK was the band's chief songwriter at this stage, contributing the classic BEATLES-esque originals 'FEEL A WHOLE LOT BETTER', 'I KNEW I'D WANT YOU' and 'HERE WITHOUT YOU'. In the summer of '65, they played a residency at Ciro's nightclub on Sunset Strip, often cited as the origin of the L.A. hippy movement (described by The L.A. Times as being frequented by people who looked like they'd been dragged from Sherwood Forest!). They were back at No.1 by the end of 1965, when they managed to transform PETE SEEGER's Book Of Ecclesiastes-adaptation 'TURN! TURN! TURN!' into a classic pop record, a miracle of biblical proportions. Very early the next year, the second album boasted two more DYLAN covers, an uninspiring update of 'THE TIMES THEY ARE A-CHANGIN' and 'LAY DOWN YOUR WEARY TUNE', apparently the song that finally persuaded DYLAN that The BYRDS were doing something above and beyond mere imitation. McGUINN contributed two songs, one of which was his tribute to the assassinated JOHN F. KENNEDY, 'HE WAS A FRIEND OF MINE', while CLARK offered three originals, including the classic 'SET YOU FREE THIS TIME'. Recorded the previous January, 'EIGHT MILES HIGH' pioneered psychedelic rock, predating the efforts of The BEATLES, The BEACH BOYS and the San Franciscan bands. The JOHN COLTRANE-inspired track was promptly vetoed by radio stations on its spring '66 release, amid allegations that the song was an explicit account of an LSD trip. After the completion of the third album 'FIFTH DIMENSION', CLARK departed, citing his paranoia-fuelled fear of flying and CROSBY's digs regarding his tambourine playing. The new album heralded a move away from sparkling pop to a more complex, ambitious and intelligent sound. Influenced heavily by Indian sitar player RAVI SHANKAR, and modal jazz, the record didn't fulfil the promise of the preceding single but still contained some memorable moments. McGUINN's 'MR SPACEMAN' hinted at the country sound the band would later embrace. Just prior to releasing the fourth album, 'YOUNGER THAN YESTERDAY', the band issued 'SO YOU

WANT TO BE A ROCK'N'ROLL STAR', a sarcastic reaction to manufactured bands by a group that had fallen out of favour with the Hollywood set. The album was an assorted bag of styles, with HILLMAN emerging as a talented songwriter on the likes of 'TIME BETWEEN' and 'THOUGHTS AND WORDS', while CROSBY had his finest moment with the haunting 'EVERYBODY'S BEEN BURNED'. Despite the melange of styles, the album predated 'SGT PEPPER', once again proving that The BYRDS were ahead of their time. By the time of 'THE NOTORIOUS BYRD BROTHERS' in 1968, CROSBY's dictatorial manner had led to his ejection from the band, along with MICHAEL CLARKE. A contender for the The BYRDS best album, the record was again stylistically diverse but included possibly the band's finest moment in the GOFFIN/KING number, 'GOIN' BACK' (later a hit for DUSTY SPRINGFIELD). Its wistful musings on the passage from childhood to maturity were set against a backdrop of heavenly harmonies and celestial pedal steel while 'WASN'T BORN TO FOLLOW' (another GERRY GOFFIN-CAROLE KING cover), was a triumphant clarion call of phased, psychedelic country. With the addition of GRAM PARSONS and HILLMAN's cousin KEVIN KELLEY, the band steered radically away from the studio-enhanced sound of 'NOTORIOUS', straight into the heart of country, once again staying one step ahead of their peers and foreshadowing the country-rock boom of the early 70's. 'SWEETHEART OF THE RODEO', with its purist sound, confounded the hippies and despite playing a show at the Grand Ole Opry, and even, God forbid, cutting their hair! for the occasion, the country crowd remained suspicious of their druggy image, thereby ensuring little commercial success. Released in '68, PARSONS was the driving force behind the album, contributing beautiful songs like 'HICKORY WIND' and 'ONE HUNDRED YEARS FROM NOW', which sat majestically alongside covers of LOUVIN BROTHERS and DYLAN material. The gypsy-like PARSONS soon left, taking HILLMAN with him to form The FLYING BURRITO BROTHERS. McGUINN (who'd now changed his name to ROGER, following his immersion in the Indonesian religion, Subud) recruited country guitar maestro CLARENCE WHITE along with a cast of other musicians. The albums that followed were inconsistent, although they contained a few BYRDS classics and highlighted WHITE's virtuoso guitar playing. 'DR BYRDS & MR HYDE', featured the ironic stab at the country establishment, 'DRUG STORE TRUCK DRIVING MAN', while 'THE BALLAD OF EASY RIDER's gentle meandering title track was a minor classic. The half live/half studio set, 'UNTITLED', from 1970, included an impassioned performance from WHITE on 'LOVER ON THE BAYOU' and a lovely version of LOWELL GEORGE's 'TRUCK STOP GIRL'. Probably the strongest set of the latter day BYRDS, it also included the single 'CHESTNUT MARE', and the evocative McGUINN and JACQUES LEVY song 'ALL THE THINGS'. Much of McGUINN's songs during this period came from the abandoned 'Gene Tryp' project which he had begun with New York psychologist LEVY to chart the history of American music. The last few albums weren't quite as ambitious in their scope, but 'BYRDMANIAX' and 'FARTHER ALONG' were enjoyable despite having the weight of such an illustrious career on their shoulders. McGUINN did the right thing and called it a day at last in mid-72, later joining up with the original BYRDS for an uninspired album a year later. Two of the BYRDS most talented members died in separate incidents in the early 70's, CLARENCE WHITE killed by a drunken driver, GRAM PARSONS from a heroin overdose. CROSBY survived a descent into free-base cocaine addiction and a liver transplant to record songs in Nashville with McGUINN and HILLMAN in 1990. A proposed tour never happened but the tracks are included on the wonderful 'Columbia' boxed set released the same year. More recently, McGUINN was sighted running through some old numbers on 'Later With Jools (Holland)' in true troubadour style. An endless list of artists and bands (TOM PETTY, R.E.M., LONG RYDERS, SMITHS, PRIMAL SCREAM, RIDE, etc), have kept alive the spirit of The BYRDS in their own particular style, while the band's own recordings remain timeless treasures.

Album rating: MR. TAMBOURINE MAN (*8) / TURN! TURN! TURN! (*8) / FIFTH DIMENSION (*6) / YOUNGER THAN YESTERDAY (*8) / THE BYRDS' GREATEST HITS compilation (*10) / THE NOTORIOUS BYRD BROTHERS (*9) / SWEETHEART OF THE RODEO (*8) / DR. BYRDS & MR. HYDE (*5) / THE BALLAD OF EASY RIDER (*5) / UNTITLED (*6) / BYRDMANIAX (*4)

GENE CLARK (b. HAROLD EUGENE CLARK, 17 Nov'41, Tipton, Missouri, USA) – vocals, tambourine / **JIM McGUINN** (b.JAMES JOSEPH McGUINN, 13 Jul'42, Chicago, Illinois, USA) – guitar, vocals / **DAVID CROSBY** (b.DAVID VAN CORTLAND, 14 Aug'41, L.A.) – guitar, vocals

	Pye Inter.	Elektra
Nov 64. (7"; as BEEFEATERS) *(7N 25277)* <45013> **PLEASE LET ME LOVE YOU. / DON'T BE LONG**		Sep64

— added **CHRIS HILLMAN** (b. 4 Dec'42, L.A.) – bass, vocals (ex-HILLMEN) / **MICHAEL CLARKE** (b. 3 Jun'43, New York City) – drums

	C.B.S.	Columbia
Jun 65. (7") *(201765)* <43271> **MR. TAMBOURINE MAN. / I KNEW I'D WANT YOU**	1	1 May65
Aug 65. (7") *(201796)* <43332> **ALL I REALLY WANT TO DO. / I'LL FEEL A WHOLE LOT BETTER**	4	40 Jul65
Aug 65. (lp; stereo/mono) *(S+/BPG 62571)* <9172> **MR. TAMBOURINE MAN**	7	6 Jun65

– Mr. Tambourine man / I'll feel a whole lot better / Spanish Harlem incident / You won't have to cry / Here without you / The bells of Rhymney / All I really want to do / I knew I'd want you / It's no use / Don't doubt yourself, babe / Chimes of freedom / We'll meet again. *(re-iss. Jul77; CBS/40 31503) (cd-iss. May96 on 'Columbia'; 483705-2) (lp re-iss. Jul98 on 'Simply Vinyl'; SVLP 32) (lp re-iss. Jun99 on 'Sundazed'; SUNLP 5057)*

Oct 65. (7") *(202008)* <43424> **TURN! TURN! TURN!. / SHE DON'T CARE ABOUT TIME**	26	1
Feb 66. (7") *(202037)* <43501> **SET YOU FREE THIS TIME. / IT WON'T BE WRONG**		79 / 63
Mar 66. (lp; stereo/mono) *(S+/SPG 62652)* <9254> **TURN! TURN! TURN!**	11	17 Dec65

– Turn! Turn! Turn! / It won't be wrong / Set you free this time / Lay down your weary tune / He was a friend of mine / The world turns all around her / Satisfied mind / If you're gone / The times they are a-changin' / Wait and see / Oh! Susannah. *(re-iss. Jul77; CBS/40 31526) (cd-iss. May96 on 'Columbia'; 483706-2) (lp re-iss. Nov98 on 'Simply Vinyl'; SVLP 27) (lp re-iss. Jun99 on 'Sundazed'; SUNLP 5058)*

— trimmed to a quartet when GENE CLARK went solo

Apr 66. (7") *(202067)* <43578> **EIGHT MILES HIGH. / WHY?**	24	14
Jul 66. (7") *(202259)* <43702> **5D (FIFTH DIMENSION). / CAPTAIN SOUL**		44
Sep 66. (lp; stereo/mono) *(S+/BPG 62783)* <9349> **FIFTH DIMENSION**	27	24 Aug66

– 5D (Fifth Dimension) / Wild mountain thyme / Mr. Spaceman / I see you / What's happening?!?! / I come and stand at every door / Eight miles high / Hey Joe / John Riley / Captain Soul / 2-4-2 Foxtrot (the Lear jet song). *(re-iss. Jul83 lp/c; CBS/40 32284) (cd-iss. May96 on 'Sony'; 483707-2) (lp re-iss. Nov98 on 'Simply Vinyl'; SVLP 47) (lp re-iss. Jun99 on 'Sundazed'; SUNLP 5059)*

Oct 66. (7") *(202295)* <43766> **MR. SPACEMAN. / WHAT'S HAPPENING?!?!**		36 Sep66
Feb 67. (7") *(202559)* <43987> **SO YOU WANT TO BE A ROCK'N'ROLL STAR. / EVERYBODY'S BEEN BURNED**		29 Jan67
Apr 67. (lp; stereo/mono) *(S+/BPG 62988)* <9442> **YOUNGER THAN YESTERDAY**	37	24 Mar67

– So you want to be a rock'n'roll star / Have you seen her face / C.T.A. – 102 / Renaissance fair / Time between / Everybody's been burned / Thoughts and words / Mind gardens / My back pages / The girl with no name / Why. *(re-iss. Mar87 on 'Edsel' cd/c/lp; CD/C+/ED 227) (re-iss. Oct94 & May96 on 'Columbia' cd/c; 483708-2) (lp re-iss. Oct97 on 'Simply Vinyl'; SVLP 7) (lp re-iss. Jun99 on 'Sundazed'; SUNLP 5060)*

May 67. (7") *(2648)* <44054> **MY BACK PAGES. / RENAISSANCE FAIR**		30 Mar67
Jun 67. (7") <44157> **HAVE YOU SEEN HER FACE. / DON'T MAKE WAVES**	-	74
Sep 67. (7") <44230> **LADY FRIEND. / OLD JOHN ROBERTSON**	-	82
Sep 67. (7") *(2924)* **LADY FRIEND. / DON'T MAKE WAVES**		-
Oct 67. (lp; stereo/mono) *(S+/BPG 63107)* <9516> **THE BYRDS' GREATEST HITS** (compilation)		6 Aug67

– Mr. Tambourine man / I'll feel a whole lot better / Bells of rhymney / Turn! turn! turn! / All I really want to do / Chimes of freedom / Eight miles high / Mr.Spaceman / 5D (Fifth Dimension) / So you want to be a rock'n'roll star / My back pages. *(re-iss. Jan84; CBS/40 32068) (cd-iss. Jun89; CD 32068) (REMASTERED cd.Feb91; 467843-2) (cd re-iss. May96 on 'Sony'; 483705-2)*

— **GENE CLARK** – guitar, vocals returned to repl. DAVID who formed CROSBY, STILLS and NASH (JIM also changed name to ROGER McGUINN)

Dec 67. (7") *(3093)* <44362> **GOIN' BACK. / CHANGE IS NOW**		89 Nov67

(re-iss. Jun77; 5300)

Now a trio of **McGUINN, HILLMAN and CLARKE** (GENE continued solo career)

Apr 68. (lp; stereo/mono) *(S+/BPG 63169)* <9575> **THE NOTORIOUS BYRD BROTHERS**	12	47 Jan68

– Artificial energy / Goin' back / Natural harmony / Draft morning / Wasn't born to follow / Get to you / Change is now / Old John Robertson / Tribal gathering / Dolphin's smile / Space odyssey. *(re-iss. Aug88 on 'Edsel' cd/lp; CD+/ED 262) (cd re-iss. Mar97 on 'Columbia'; 486751-2)*

— **KEVIN KELLEY** (b.1945, California) – drums (ex-RISING SONS) repl. MICHAEL who joined DILLARD & CLARK. Also added **GRAM PARSONS** (b.INGRAM CECIL CONNOR III, 5 Nov'46, Winterhaven, Florida) – guitar, vocals, keyboards (ex-INTERNATIONAL SUBMARINE BAND) / guests on album – **SNEAKY PETE** – pedal steel guitar / **DOUG DILLARD** – banjo

May 68. (7") *(3411)* <44499> **YOU AIN'T GOING NOWHERE. / ARTIFICIAL ENERGY**	45	74
Sep 68. (lp) *(63353)* <9670> **SWEETHEART OF THE RODEO**		77 Aug68

– You ain't going nowhere / I am a pilgrim / The Christian life / You're still on my mind / Pretty Boy Floyd / You don't miss your water / Hickory wind / One hundred years from now / Blue Canadian Rockies / Life in prison / Nothing was delivered. *(re-iss. Jun87 on 'Edsel' cd/lp; CD+/ED 234) (cd re-iss. Mar97 on 'Columbia'; 486752-2) (lp re-iss. Nov98 on 'Simply Vinyl'; SVLP 57) (cd re-iss. Oct99 on 'Columbia'; MILLEN 6)*

Oct 68. (7") *(3752)* <44643> **PRETTY BOY FLOYD. / I AM A PILGRIM**		

— **CARLOS BERNAL** – guitar played on US tour replacing GRAM who joined FLYING BURRITO BROTHERS alongside HILLMAN and SNEAKY PETE. Soon McGUINN recruited entirely new members **CLARENCE WHITE** (b. 6 Jun'44, Lewiston, Maine, USA) – guitar, vocals (ex-NASHVILLE WEST) repl. BERNAL / **GENE PARSONS** (b. 9 Apr'44) – drums, vocals (ex-NASHVILLE WEST) repl. KELLEY / **JOHN YORK** – bass, vocals repl. HILLMAN

Mar 69. (7") *(4055)* <44746> **BAD NIGHT AT THE WHISKEY. / DRUG STORE TRUCK DRIVIN' MAN**		
Apr 69. (lp) *(63545)* <9755> **DR. BYRDS AND MR. HYDE**	15	Mar69

– This wheel's on fire / Old blue / Your gentle way of loving me / Child of the universe / Nashville West / Drug store truck drivin' man / King Apathy III / Candy / Bad night at the Whiskey / My back pages – B.J.blues – Baby what you want me to do. *(cd-iss. Aug91 on 'Beat Goes On'; BGOCD 107) (cd re-iss. Mar97 on 'Columbia'; 486753-2) (lp re-iss. Feb99 on 'Simply Vinyl'; SVLP 70)*

Jun 69. (7") *(4284)* <44868> **LAY LADY LAY. / OLD BLUE**		
Sep 69. (7") *(4572)* **WASN'T BORN TO FOLLOW. / CHILD OF THE UNIVERSE**		-
Oct 69. (7") <44990> **THE BALLAD OF EASY RIDER. / WASN'T BORN TO FOLLOW**	-	5
Jan 70. (lp) *(63795)* <9942> **THE BALLAD OF EASY RIDER**	41	36 Dec69

– The ballad of Easy Rider / Fido / Oil in my lamp / Tulsa County / Jack Tarr the sailor / Jesus is just alright / It's all over now, baby blue / There must be someone / Gunga Din / Deportee (plane wreck at Los Gatos) / Armstrong, Aldrin and Collins. *(cd-iss. Mar97 on 'Columbia'; 486751-2)*

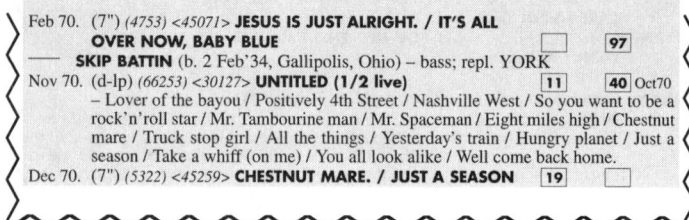

```
Feb 70.  (7") (4753) <45071> JESUS IS JUST ALRIGHT. / IT'S ALL
         OVER NOW, BABY BLUE                                    97
─── SKIP BATTIN (b. 2 Feb'34, Gallipolis, Ohio) – bass; repl. YORK
Nov 70.  (d-lp) (66253) <30127> UNTITLED (1/2 live)       11  40 Oct70
         – Lover of the bayou / Positively 4th Street / Nashville West / So you want to be a
         rock'n'roll star / Mr. Tambourine man / Mr. Spaceman / Eight miles high / Chestnut
         mare / Truck stop girl / All the things / Yesterday's train / Hungry planet / Just a
         season / Take a whiff (on me) / You all look alike / Well come back home.
Dec 70.  (7") (5322) <45259> CHESTNUT MARE. / JUST A SEASON  19
```

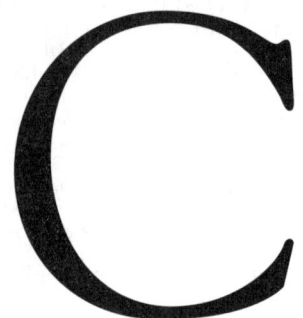

CAKEKITCHEN
(see under ⇒ THIS KIND OF PUNISHMENT)

CAMBERWELL NOW
(see under ⇒ THIS HEAT; 70's section)

CAMPER VAN BEETHOVEN

Formed: Redlands / Santa Cruz, California, USA ... 1983 by DAVE LOWERY and DAVID McDANIELS, who had relocated to college in Santa Cruz. Touted as one of the first real "alternative" acts to come out of America, CAMPER VAN BEETHOVEN were a reaction to the rigid conformity of the all-pervasive Californian hardcore scene, taking it upon themselves to brew up an exotic concoction of avant-folk-pop/cow-punk taking in elements of stone country, reggae, ska and even oompa-jazz. By the release of debut album, 'TELEPHONE FREE LANDSLIDE VICTORY' (1985), the line-up had stabilised around LOWERY, CHRIS MOLLA, VICTOR KRUMMENACHER, GREG LISHER and JONATHAN SEGAL (CHRIS PEDERSON was recruited later), the latter's strident violin flourishes adding the quintessential Eastern European flavour prevalent in much of the band's work. Ranging from the John Peel favourite, 'TAKE THE SKINHEADS BOWLING' to Cossack-style howdown's like 'BALALAIKA GAP' and 'VLADIVOSTOCK' and even an irreverent Black Flag cover, 'WASTED', the record's tongue-in-cheek humour and headlong eclecticism caused a major buzz on the US underground, even prompting R.E.M.'s MICHAEL STIPE to name it as one of his Top 10 albums of the year. A subsequent distribution deal with 'Rough Trade' saw the record gain a UK release yet both British and US sales weren't as high as expected and the group formed their own 'Pitch-A-Tent' label for the release of follow-up double set, 'CAMPER VAN BEETHOVEN II/III' (1986). The latter included one of their most infamous creations, 'ZZ TOP GOES TO EGYPT' alongside another hardcore makeover, Sonic Youth's 'I LOVE HER ALL THE TIME'. An eponymous third album and further couple of EP's, 'GOOD GUYS, BAD GUYS' and 'VAMPIRE CAN MATING OVEN', kept the band's profile high and a subsequent major label bidding war ended in a move to 'Virgin' in 1988. With the luxuries of a decent sized studio budget behind them, CVB made the record they'd probably always wanted to make in 'OUR REVOLUTIONARY SWEETHEART' (1988). Polishing off the rough edges but retaining the spontaneity, this should've been the record to propel them into the indie mainstream. In the event, crossover success proved out of reach and SEGAL bailed out for a solo career. The cracks were beginning to show on what proved to be the band's swansong set, 'KEY LIME PIE' (1990), a final split occurring later that year as PEDERSON, LISHER and KRUMMENACHER resurrected their MONKS OF DOOM, releasing their third album, 'THE INSECT GOD'; LOWERY eventually formed CRACKER. The aforementioned MONKS OF DOOM (with the addition of DAVID IMMERGLUCK) fused a type of BARRETT-meets-ZAPPA style incorporating jazz, world and the kitchen sink into several releases including career highlight, 89's 'THE COSMODEMONIC TELEGRAPH COMPANY'. KRUMMENACHER went on to record as a solo artist, releasing albums, 'OUT IN THE HEAT' (1995) and 'SAINT JOHN'S MERCY' (1998), on his own label (set up with SEGAL), 'Magnetic'.
• **Covers:** PHOTOGRAPH (Ringo Starr) / I'M NOT LIKE EVERYBODY ELSE (Kinks) / INTERSTELLAR OVERDRIVE (Pink Floyd) / PICTURES OF MATCHSTICK MEN (Status Quo). The MONKS OF DOOM covered; WHO ARE THE BRAIN POLICE? (Mothers Of Invention; Frank Zappa) / THE VIVIAN GIRLS (Snakefinger – Residents) / VOODOO VENGEANCE (Eugene Chadbourne).

Album rating: TELEPHONE FREE LANDSCAPE VICTORY (*7) / II & III (*6) / CAMPER VAN BEETHOVEN (*6) / VAMPIRE CAN MATING OVEN mini (*6) / OUR BELOVED REVOLUTIONARY SWEETHEART (*8) / KEY LIME PIE (*7) / CAMPER VANTIQUES compilation (*5) / TUSK (*6) / Monks Of Doom: BREAKFAST ON THE BEACH OF DECEPTION (*7) / THE COSMODEMONIC TELEGRAPH COMPANY (*6) / MERIDIAN (*5) / FORGERY (*5) / Victor Krummenacher: OUT IN THE HEAT (*6) / SAINT JOHN'S MERCY (*5)

DAVID LOWERY (b.10 Sep'60, San Antonio, Texas) – vocals, guitar, drums / **JONATHAN SEGAL** (b. 3 Sep'63, Marseilles, France) – keyboards, violin, mandolin, vocals / **GREG LISHER** (b.29 Nov'63, Santa Cruz) – guitar / **VICTOR KRUMMENACHER** (b. 7 Apr'65, Riverside, Calif.) – bass, vocals / **CHRIS MOLLA** – guitar, vocals, drums / **ANTHONY GUESS** – drums

not iss. — *Independents*

Oct 85. (lp) <IP 016> **TELEPHONE FREE LANDSCAPE VICTORY**
– Border ska / The day that Lassie went to the moon / Wasted / Yanqui go home / Oh no! / 9 of disks / Payed vacation: Greece / Where the hell is Bill? / Vladivostock / Skinhead stomp / Tina / Take the skinheads bowling / Mao reminisces about his days / I don't see you / Balalaika gap / Opi rides again – Club Med sucks / Ambiguity song. *(UK-iss.Apr87 on 'Rough Trade'; ROUGH 95) <cd-iss. Mar93 on 'I.R.S.'; X2 13208>*

— **CHRIS PEDERSEN** (b.16 Aug'60, San Diego, Calif.) – drums; repl. GUESS

not iss. — *Pitch A Tent*

Jan 86. (d-lp) <PITCH 1> **CAMPER VAN BEETHOVEN II/III**
– Abundance / Cowboys from Hollywood / Sad lovers waltz / Turtlehead / I love her all the time / No flies on us / Down and out / No krugerrands for David / (Don't you go to) Goleta / 4 year plan / (We're a) Bad trip / Circles / Dustpan / Sometimes / Chain of circumstances / ZZ Top goes to Egypt / Cattle (reversed) / From another stone / No more bullshit / Take the skinheads bowling / Epigram No.2 / Cowboys from Hollywood / At Kuda? / Epigram No.1 / Colonel Enrique Adolfo Bermudas. *(UK/German-iss.Nov87 on 'Full Blast'; FBLP 400320) <cd-iss. 1993 on 'I.R.S.'; 13209>*

below featured **EUGENE CHADBOURNE** – banjo (of SHOCKABILLY)

Rough Trade — *Pitch-A-Tent*

Dec 86. (lp) (ROUGH 109) <PITCH 2> **CAMPER VAN BEETHOVEN (THE THIRD LP)** Aug86
– Good guys & bad guys / Jo Stalin's Cadillac / Five sticks / Lulu land / Une fois / We saw Jerry's daughter / Surprise truck / Stairway to Heaven / The history of Utah / Still wishing to course / We love you / Hoe yourself down / Peace & love / Folly / Interstellar overdrive / Shut us down. *<cd-iss. 1993 on 'I.R.S.'; 13210>*

Mar 87. (12"ep) (RTT 161) **TAKE THE SKINHEADS BOWLING**
– Take the skinheads bowling / Cowboys from Hollywood (early version) / Epigram No.2 / At Kuda? / Colonel Enrique Adolfo Bermudez (a real bastard).

Nov 87. (m-lp/m-c) <PITCH 05> **VAMPIRE CAN MATING OVEN** (out-takes)
– Heart / Never go back / Seven languages / Six more miles (to the graveyard) [c-only] / Ice cream every day / Processional / Photograph. *(UK-iss.Oct87 as 'GOOD GUYS & BAD GUYS'+=; RTT 205)* – Good guys & bad guys (Peel session).

— In Feb 88, they teamed up with EUGENE CHADBOURNE on the lp, 'CAMPER VAN CHADBOURNE', on 'Fundamental' records.

— now without MOLLA

Virgin — *Virgin*

May 88. (cd/c/lp) (CD/TC+/V 2516) <90918> **OUR BELOVED REVOLUTIONARY SWEETHEART**
– Eye of Fatima (pt.1) / Turquoise jewelry / O death / She divines water / Devil song / One of these days / Waka / Change your mind / My path belated / Never go back / Eye of Fatima (pt.2) / Tania / Life is grand / The fool.

Sep 88. (7") (VS 1122) **LIFE IS GRAND. / LOVE IS A WEED**
(12"+=/cd-s+=) (VS T/CD 1122) – Harmony in my head / Wade in the water.

— **MORGAN FICHTER** – violin, vocals; repl. SEGAL who went solo

Virgin America — *Virgin*

Nov 89. (c-s) **PICTURES OF MATCHSTICK MEN / COME ON DARKNESS**

Jan 90. (cd/c/lp) (VUS CD/CM/LP 8) <91289> **KEY LIME PIE** Oct89
– Opening theme / Jack Ruby / Sweethearts / When I win the lottery / (I was born in a) Laundromat / Borderline / The light from a cake / June / All her favourite fruit / Interlude / Flowers / The humid press of days / Pictures of matchstick men / Come on darkness.

Jan 90. (7") (VUS 8) **PICTURES OF MATCHSTICK MEN. / JACK RUBY**
(12"+=/3"cd-s+=) (VUS T/CD 8) – Closing theme / The humid press of days.

— disbanded in Spring 1990; LOWERY formed CRACKER

— CAMPER VAN BEETHOVEN were back in 2002

– compilations, etc.

Mar 93. (cd,c) I.R.S.; <13211> **CAMPER VANTIQUES** (B-sides, rarities, etc)
– Heart / Never go back / Seven languages / Axe murderer song / SP37597 / Crossing over / Guardian angels / I'm not like everybody else / A.C. cover / Porpoise mouth / (We workers do not understand) Modern art / We eat your children / Six more miles to the graveyard / Ice cream everyday / Processional / Photograph / Om eye.

Oct 99. (cd) Knitting Factory; <(KFW 252)> **USED RECORD PILE**

Aug 02. (d-cd) Pitch-A-Tent; <(PITCH 12)> **TUSK** (covers the whole Fleetwood Mac album)

Oct 02. (5xcd-box) Cooking Vinyl; <(COOKCD 247)> **CIGARETTES AND CARROT JUICE – THE SANTA CRUZ YEARS**
– (the 4 Pitch-A-Tent albums + a live one)

MONKS OF DOOM

PEDERSON, LISHER + KRUMMENACHER with also **DAVID IMMERGLUCK** – guitar, vocals, piano (drummer of OPHELIAS)

not iss. — *Pitch A Tent*

Dec 87. (lp) <PITCH 6> **BREAKFAST ON THE BEACH OF DECEPTION** (soundtrack)
– In anticipation of the pope / Blues on Sunday / Facts about spiders / Ukranian technological faith dance / Lappish tea song / B-music / Fall from grace / Save me from myself / Visions from the acid couch / Insana and her manchild / Jim Gore and the ghost of Missouri / The haunting of an eastern man's mind / Eldridge street. *<cd-iss. Mar93 on 'IRS-Capitol'; X2-13213>*

Sep 89. (lp/c/cd) <PITCH 13/+C/CD> **THE COSMODEMONIC TELEGRAPH COMPANY**
– Vaporize your crystals / The Vivian girls / All in good time / Voodoo vengeance / Taste of tendon / Trapped / The evidence you hide / Unexplained murders / The beach of deception / Broadcast at midday. *<cd re-iss. Mar93 on 'IRS-Capitol'; X2-13214>*

not iss. — *Baited Breath*

1991. (cd) <4> **MERIDIAN**
– Cherry blossom baptism / Riverbed / Turn it on himself / Geode / Door to success / The traveler / Argentine dilemma / The better angels of our nature / Going south / Follow the queen / Hieroglyphic / The harbor incident / Miracle mile / Circassian beauty.

not iss. — *C/Z*

Jun 92. (cd-ep) <CZ 047> **THE INSECT GOD**
– Chang / Let's split / If it didn't kill me / Who are the brain police?

not iss. — *IRS-Capitol*

Sep 92. (cd/c) <X2/X4 13163> **FORGERY**
– Flint Jack / Flow / Tanguedia (for Astor Piazzolla) / Virtual lover / Queen of fortune / Dust / What does a man require? / A.O.A. / Cigarette man / Off on a comet / Tanguedia (reprise) / Chaos is not dead.

VICTOR KRUMMENACHER

with **CHRIS XEFOS, GREG LISHER, BRUCE KAPHAN, JOHN NELSON**, etc

not iss. — *Magnetic*

1995. (cd; as VICTOR KRUMMENACHER'S GREAT LAUGH) <0006> **OUT IN THE HEAT**
– All right / Clean as filth and finesse / Evangelina will sleep No.1 / Water gone to mist / '48 or '47 / Out in the heat / New Mexico / Insomniac / Foot on the pedal (instrumental) / Resurrection plant / Not an inch / Sweet talking Bill / Sister & me / Antebellum / As real as your dreams.

1996. (7") <007> **THE PRINCE OF LIES. / ROBERT**
1998. (cd) <0009> **SAINT JOHN'S MERCY**
– Tear-stained road / Nothing outside / Now that you're gone / Dreams die hard / No sin to wandering / Tierra o' Muerte / Expanse / Thunderhead / Quest sunset / Raven / Saint John's mercy / Long way home.

CANNANES

Formed: Sydney, Australia . . . late 1984 by STEPHEN O'NEIL, ANNABEL BLEACH, DAVID NICHOLS and namesake, MICHELLE CANNANE (who actually left early the following year!). A much celebrated band for their longevity, indie credentials and basic ability to write on the whole competent, and sometimes great, alternative melodious pop tunes. Another much noted point of interest was their revolving door policy on line-up; straight from the outset CANNANE, who gave the band their moniker, departed before the group even debuted. Replaced by FRANCES GIBSON, the CANNANES put out their initial single release, 'LIFE' under their own steam, in an extremely limited run of cassettes. Several years passed before the band got some time in the studio, recording the EP, 'BORED, ANGRY & JEALOUS' (1986), which gained them worthy acclaim, not the least of which was NME, branding it one of the best singles of the year. The following year saw the group put out their debut full-length outing, 'THE AFRICAN MAN'S TOMATO'. Due to extenuating circumstances, BLEACH's duties on the LP were fulfilled by RANDALL LEE (later of NICE and ASHTRAY BOY fame). This was to be LEE's only contribution for the Antipodean indie popsters. After some international touring and a near split the group came together again to record and deliver their sophomore LP, 'A LOVE AFFAIR WITH NATURE'. Paradoxically, although being hailed as the great Australian hope of the indie arena, the band were receiving far more praise abroad than in their homeland . . . a factor which set them on the course to get back in the studio. Disastrously the band lost the masters for what would have been their third set, but unperturbed they recruited new band member, NICK KIDD, to add brass to their sound, and set about putting down what became their third album, 'CAVEAT EMPTOR'. By the mid-nineties The CANNANES had also been joined by GAVIN ROY BUTLER, whose bass strummings were showcased on their fourth LP, 'SHORT POPPY SYNDROME'. Following this set, founding member NICHOLS bowed out to subsequently form BLAIRMAILER with his brother MICHAEL. The group as a whole paused for breath at this point and witnessed the departure of BUTLER. Lynch-pin members, O'NEIL and GIBSON, kept the spirit of the band alive as a duo, later employing the assistance of FRANCESCA and IVOR MOULDS. Several sets followed before FRANCESCA took maternity leave and was replaced by ANDREW COFFEY, with the added joy of strings provided by SALLY CAMERON. The CANNANES millennial release, 'COMMUNICATING AT AN UNKNOWN RATE', saw them billed alongside STEWARD (aka STEWART ANDERSON), who added a punkier edge to their sound. Not ones to sit around long, the group came out with their ninth full-length set, 'TROUBLE SEEMED SO FAR AWAY' (2002) in which they drafted in the skills of EXPLOSION ANDERSON (aka STEPHEN HERMANN), resulting in some of their best material for some time.

Album rating: THE AFRICAN MAN'S TOMATO (*7) / A LOVE AFFAIR WITH NATURE (*6) / CAVEAT EMPTOR (*6) / WITCHETTY POLE collection (*5) / SHORT POPPY SYNDROME (*4) / THE CANNANES (*6) / ARTY BARBECUE collection (*6) / COMMUNICATING AT AN UNKNOWN RATE (*6) / TROUBLE SEEMED SO FAR AWAY (*5)

STEPHEN O'NEIL – vocals, guitar / **ANNABEL BLEACH** – vocals, guitar / **FRANCIS GIBSON** – bass; repl. MICHELLE CANNANE / **DAVID NICHOLS** – drums

Happy Penis — *not iss.*

1985. (c-s) **LIFE / IT'S HARDLY WORTH IT** — Austra
1985. (c-ep) **THE CANNANES COME ACROSS WITH THE GOODS** — Austra

CANNANES (cont)

		Distant Violins	not iss.
1986.	(7"blue-ep) **BORED ANGRY & JEALOUS**	-	- Austra

— temp drummer, FOXY, until NICHOLS' return

— O'NEIL not at sessions, repl. by **RANDALL LEE** – vocals

		no label	not iss.
1987.	(lp) **AFRICAN MAN'S TOMATO**	-	- Austra
1987.	(7") **CARDBOARD. / WOE**	-	- Austra
1987.	(7") **I THINK THE WEATHER'S AFFECTED YOUR BRAIN. / STONES TO BE KEPT UNDER LOCK AND KEY**	- K	- Austra K
Jan 88.	(c-ep) <(KC 013)> **HAPPY SWING**		
Jan 88.	(7"ep) <(L 28202)> **NO ONE EP**		

— now without LEE, who formed NICE then ASHTRAY BOY

		no label	Feel Good All Over
1989.	(clear/white-lp) **A LOVE AFFAIR WITH NATURE**	-	1991

– I woke up / Take me to the hotel Johanna (and let's trash the joint) / Sound of the city / Nuisance / Seatbelt / Move some things around / Paper bag / 52 Linthorpe Street / Blue skies over the ocean / Vivienne. <US cd-iss. Jun95 on 'Ajax'+=; 45> – I think the weather's affected your brain / Cardboard / Don't let her ruin your life / Robert / Woe / Stories to be kept under lock and key / Countdown / Queen's hotel / Paper bag (live) / 1990 (single version) / Looking glass / Simon / Marco Polo suite: Marco Polo – Marco and his mother – Travelling to China – Don't believe him – Marco reprise.

— added **NICK KIDD** – French horn

1992.	(7"ep) **STUMPVISION**	-	

– Passionfruit / Another flight / Singing tp satellites.
(above issued on 'Ajax')

Sep 93.	(cd) <13> **CAVEAT EMPTOR**	-	

– White rabbit / Kitten on the keys / Candlesticks / Here is the blade / Beautiful names / 1991 / Last 3 weeks / Go and tell your father / Christmas tree / No visitors on Wednesdays / Say it again / Newcastle / Bottles / I met you as a baby / Green iguana / Some things happen.

		not iss.	K
1994.	(7"ep) **FRIGHTENING THING**	-	

– Frightening thing / King of Liliput / Ern Malley / Screaming.

		not iss.	Little Teddy
1994.	(7"ep) <704> **PROTOTYPE**	-	

– Prototype / Bad timing / Throw down the gauntlet / Empty channel.

— added **GAVIN ROY BUTLER** – bass

		Harriet	Ajax
May 94.	(cd) <AJAX 034> **SHORT POPPY SYNDROME**		

– Perfect light / Chosen one / Reckless child / Cocaine / Sydney 2000 / My dull surprise / Strange memories / Walking home / You're gorgeous / Cricket club porn night / Pearl / Red smoke across the square / History.

— added **FRANCESCA BUSSEY** – bass / **IVOR MOULDS** – drums

Feb 96.	(7"ep) <AJAX 047> **SIMPLE QUESTION**	-	

– Simple question / Fall / Dreadful / Outaside.

Mar 96.	(cd) <AJAX 048> **THE CANNANES**	-	

– Drug-induced delirium / Asleep / Caesar / Simple question / 3-way release / Ordinarily / Get on down / Matter of distinction / The promise / Pedagogy (the mystery of you) / Marching song / Swing, you little red devil.

1996.	(7"ep) split w/ **SLEEPY TOWNSHIP**	-	- Austra

– Price you pay / Tennyson / Platypus.
(above issued on 'H' records)

— O'NEIL + GIBSON continued when NICHOLS departed (he and his brother became BLAIRMAILER)

Jan 98.	(7"ep) (HARR 45) **IT'S A FINE LINE BETWEEN PLEASURE AND PAIN EP**		-

— **ANDREW COFFEY** – bass; repl. FRANCESCA who had a baby

— newcomer **SALLY CAMERON** – violin

		Chapter	not iss.
1998.	(cd) (CPM 31D) **LIVING THE DREAM**	-	- Austra

– Free bird / Japanese train station / Winding down again / Last resort / Defragmentation / Fuzzy at the tip / Overwhelmed / Population of two / In through the out door / Nearly there / Parade time.

		not iss.	Blackbean & Placenta
1998.	(12"ep) split w/ **TIMONIUM**	-	

– Lamington lane / Adelaide / Population.

		555 Record	Yo-Yo
May 98.	(m-cd) <9> **TINY FROWN**	-	

– Pillows / Angsty pants / Quite an education / Fuzzy (at the tip) / Tiny frown / Pacific gulls / Wherever you go.

2000.	(7"ep) <BBPTC 555> **AUSTRALIAN TOUR**		

(above issued on 'Blackbean & Placenta')

May 00.	(7") (555/24) **MISERABLE. / WILLIAM**		
Oct 00.	(12"pic-lp/cd; as The CANNANES AND STEWARD) (555LP 21) <1622> **COMMUNICATING AT AN UNKNOWN RATE**		

– Hey leopard / Mirage / Music and me / Clean forgot / Fragments / Not quite right / SDJ / Remembering the theremin / Sharpie / Kurrajong hotel / Oh yeah! / Astra / Savage.

Oct 00.	(cd-ep) **ELECTRO 2000**	-	- Austra

– You name it (Greg Wadley remix) / Postcard from Cuba / From the keyboard to your door / Solid / You're crazy.

— next with electronica guy **EXPLOSION ROBINSON** – keyboards

Oct 01.	(cd-ep) (555CD 32) **FELICITY EP** (split w/ STEWARD / EXPLOSION ROBINSON)		

– Felicity / I like cellos / Lost in darkness / L.O.V.E.

		not iss.	Slabco
May 02.	(cd; as The CANNANES with EXPLOSION ROBINSON) <50> **TROUBLE SEEMED SO FAR AWAY**	-	

– You name it / Felicity / This is the song / It's hopeless / Brand new craze / Radio Moscow / Ten stories / Sound of seduction / S.A.D. / Treading carefully / Western slowmotion / Trouble seems so far away.

– compilations, etc. –

Sep 94.	(cd) Feel Good All Over; <2> **WITCHETTY POLE**	-	

– (BORED, ANGRY & JEALOUS EP, HAPPY SWING EP, THE AFRICAN MAN'S TOMATO)

Mar 98.	(cd) Ajax; <AJAX 054> **ARTY BARBEQUE**	-	

– Frightening thing / King of Lilliput / Ern Malley / Screaming / Prototype / Bad timing / Throw down the gauntlet / Empty channel / Another fight / Passionfruit / Singing to satellites.

Jul 01.	(cd-ep) Blackbean & Placenta; <BBPTC 202> **CRANK IT UP!** (live summer 1999)	-	

– White rabbit / Anthem / I met you as a baby / 3-way release / Go and tell your father / Last resort / Parade time.

CAPTAIN BEEFHEART

Born: DON VAN VLIET, 15 Jan'41, Glendale, Los Angeles, California, USA. Started out as a child-prodigy sculptor who, between the ages of five and thirteen, had his clay animals featured on a weekly TV show hosted by Portuguese sculptor Augustino Rodriguez. An opportunity to develop his art skills were halted when his parents declined a scholarship on his behalf to study art in Europe, preferring instead to move to Lancaster in the Mojave desert. There, he met FRANK ZAPPA at the local high school, setting up a few local bands while ZAPPA started to write a script for a B-movie 'CAPTAIN BEEFHEART MEETS THE GRUNT PEOPLE'. When FRANK went to Los Angeles to form THE MOTHERS OF INVENTION, DON adopted the name CAPTAIN BEEFHEART and set about recruiting The MAGIC BAND. They signed to 'A&M' in 1964, releasing their version of BO DIDDLEY's 'DIDDY WAH DIDDY', which sold enough copies to encourage the label to buy studio time for an album. When completed, president Jerry Moss rejected the tapes, citing it too strange and anti-commercial. Undaunted, VAN VLIET and a new set of musicians, including RY COODER, re-recorded most of these masters, the album 'SAFE AS MILK' finally surfacing in 1967 on the 'Buddah' label. This was a masterpiece of its time, full of BEEFHEART on a HOWLIN' WOLF-style trip; the great tracks being 'ELECTRICITY', 'ABBA ZABA', 'AUTUMN CHILD' & 'ZIG ZAG WANDERER'. However, RY COODER departed for safer pastures when VAN VLIET/BEEFHEART left the stage halfway through their set at the 1967 Monterey Pop Festival, leaving the band to play to a bewildered but carefree hippy audience. BEEFHEART often showed signs of outlandish behaviour which split the band up as much as his personality. Late in 1968, they recorded another album, 'MIRROR MAN', although this was shelved until his popularity had grown in the early 70's. However, one album did appear that year, 'STRICTLY PERSONAL', which BEEFHEART slammed for its radical remix by producer BOB KRASNOW. This riled him so much that he signed a new contract with old friend ZAPPA who gave him complete artistic control on his new 'Straight' label. Having written about 30 songs in a day, BEEFHEART took his new bunch of weirdo musicians (ANTENNAE JIMMY SEMENS, DRUMBO, ART TRIPP III, ZOOT HORN ROLLO and THE MASCARA SNAKE) to rehearse in a house which was close-by an old friend JIMMY CARL BLACK (drummer for ZAPPA). They stayed there for a full eight months, only one of them at a time venturing out if the band was in need of food & drink, etc. This was VAN VLIET's tyrannical way of keeping the band tight, so as to establish virtuoso musicianship while he got on with the weird vocals. The resulting album (a double!) 'TROUT MASK REPLICA' was handed to ZAPPA, much to his surprise, after four and a half hours in the studio. When released at the turn of the decade, it was initially given the thumbs down by many critics and fans. Those hardy enough to give it a few tolerant spins, however, were convinced of its genius. The record surprisingly nearly made the UK Top 20, having been played to death on John Peel's Radio 1 night-time show. Its virtual insanity was literally not of this world, utilising the complex structures of jazz legend ORNETTE COLEMAN; the best tracks to break through – to the sane among us, were 'THE BLIMP', 'PENA', 'DALI'S CAR', 'ELLA GURU' & 'OLD FART AT PLAY'. It has since become regarded as a classic, although it should never be played to someone not of your generation. He returned a thank-you to ZAPPA, when he sang a track, 'WILLIE THE WIMP', on his 'Hot Rats' album, although their friendship was fraying with every meeting, two egos too big for one room. In 1970, he settled down to a more conventional avant-garde Delta-blues album 'LICK MY DECALS OFF, BABY' (compared their is, to their last). It was another excellent set; combing through the depths of his unearthly roots to find tracks such as 'DOCTOR DARK', 'I LOVE YOU, YOU BIG DUMMY' and the title track. 1972 saw another great album 'THE SPOTLIGHT KID', featuring the delights of 'CLICK CLACK', 'I'M GONNA BOOGLARIZE YOU BABY' & 'WHEN IT GROWS IT STACKS'. Their next, 'CLEAR SPOT' covered new territory on softer tracks like 'TOO MUCH TIME' & 'MY HEAD IS MY ONLY HOUSE UNLESS IT RAINS', tempting the MAGIC BAND to bail out and form their own outfit, MALLARD. The album did, however, include another powerful BEEFHEART special in the shape of 'BIG EYED BEANS FROM VENUS'. In 1974, with a new line-up, he signed to UK's 'Virgin' label but his work at this point, especially on the albums 'UNCONDITIONALLY GUARANTEED' & 'BLUEJEANS & MOONBEAMS', were just above average. He tried to escape yet another restrictive deal; it was said he would sign anything, and teamed up with his old pal FRANK ZAPPA and The MOTHERS. Their collaboration, 'BONGO FURY', set the ball rolling for a litigation battle between him and 'Virgin' UK, resulting in another deal!, this time with 'Warner Brothers' for the 1978

CAPTAIN BEEFHEART (cont)

album 'SHINY BEAST (BAT CHAIN PULLER)', a marked return to form on some tracks. Virgin won the rights to this album, which gained a UK release in early 1980. Two other records surfaced in the next two years; 'DOC AT RADAR STATION' and the considerably better 'ICE CREAM FOR CROW', the latter containing the excellent title track, his final epitaph. He retired from the music business and set up home with his wife JAN at a trailer park in the Mojave desert. Still an avid sculptor and painter, with the help of fan Julian Schnabel, he began exhibiting his primitive canvases which made him more money than his records ever did. In the mid-80's, a host of young British indie acts including STUMP, McKENZIES, The SHRUBS, etc, took on the mantle of the BEEFHEART sound. Always asked if he would return, BEEFHEART has repeatedly refused to get back on the bandwagon (having fallen into ill-health, both physically and mentally, a return to the recording studio is unlikely to say the least). A remarkable figure of his time, DON VAN VLIET exemplified the glory of not worrying about the exploitation of the music industry, only happy with his own, and of course the MAGIC BAND's work. Let's just hope he's around for several more years to enjoy whatever he creates. • Trivia: He also covered Jack Nitzsche's 'HARD WORKIN' MAN' on the 1978 film 'Blue Collar', which starred Harvey Keitel.

Album rating: SAFE AS MILK (*10) / STRICTLY PERSONAL (*6) / TROUT MASK REPLICA (*10) / LICK MY DECALS OFF, BABY (*8) / MIRROR MAN earlier recording (*7) / THE SPOTLIGHT KID (*8) / CLEAR SPOT (*8) / UNCONDITIONALLY GUARANTEED (*6) / BLUEJEANS & MOONBEAMS (*9) / BONGO FURY; with Frank Zappa (*5) / SHINY BEAST (BAT CHAIN PULLER) (*6) / DOC AT RADAR STATION (*6) / ICE CREAM FOR CROW (*7) / THE LEGENDARY A&M SESSIONS mini of early stuff (*5) / I MAY BE HUNGRY BUT I SURE AIN'T WEIRD collection (*6) / A CARROT IS AS CLOSE AS A RABBIT GETS TO A DIAMOND compilation (*8) / GROW FINS boxed set (*8) / MERSEYTROUT – LIVE IN LIVERPOOL 1980 (*7)

CAPTAIN BEEFHEART & HIS MAGIC BAND

DON VAN VLIET – vocals, harmonica, occasional guitar, wind instruments / **ALEX ST. CLAIRE SNOUFFER** – guitar / **DOUG MOON** – guitar / **JERRY HANDLEY** – bass / **PAUL BLAKELY** – drums

			A&M	A&M
1966.	(7") <794>	DIDDY WAH DIDDY. / WHO DO YOU THINK YOU'RE FOOLING	-	
1966.	(7") <818>	MOONCHILD. / FRYING PAN	-	
1968.	(7") (AMS 726)	MOONCHILD. / WHO DO YOU THINK YOU'RE FOOLING		-

— **JOHN FRENCH** (DRUMBO) – drums; repl. BLAKELY (MOON also departed) / **RY COODER** guested on 2 tracks below

			Pye Inter	Kama Sutra
Jan 68.	(7") (7N 25443)	YELLOW BRICK ROAD. / ABBA ZABA		-
Feb 68.	(lp) (NPL 28110) <BDS 5001>	SAFE AS MILK		Nov67

– Sure 'nuff 'n yes I do / Zig zag wanderer / Call on me / Dropout boogie / I'm glad / Electricity / Yellow brick road / Abba zaba / Plastic factory / Where there's woman / Plastic factory / Grown so ugly / Autumn child. (re-iss. 1968 on 'Marble Arch' 2 tracks less; MAL 1117) (re-iss. 1970 on 'Buddha' stereo; 623 171) (re-iss. Jan82 on 'P.R.T.'; NCP 1004) (re-iss. Jul85 on 'Buddah' lp/c; 252260-1/-4) (cd-iss. May91 on 'Castle'; CLACD 234) (cd re-mast.Sep99 on 'Buddha-RCA'+=; 74321 89175-2) – Safe as milk (take 5) / On tomorrow / Big black baby / Flower pot / Dirty blue Gene / Trust us (take 9) / Korn ring finger. (lp re-iss. Sep99 on 'Simply Vinyl'; SVLP 122)

— **JEFF COTTON** (ANTENNAE JIMMY SEMENS) – guitar; repl. COODER who went solo (HERB BERMANN co-contributed several songs)

			Liberty	Blue Thumb
Dec 68.	(lp; mono/stereo) (LBL/LBS 83172) <BTS 1>	STRICTLY PERSONAL		Oct68

– Ah feel like ahcid / Safe as milk / Trust us / Son of Mirror Man – Mere man / On tomorrow / Beatle bones 'n' smokin' stones / Gimme dat harp boy / Kandy korn. (re-iss. Nov79 lp/c; LBR/TCR 1006) (cd-iss. Aug94 on 'E.M.I.'; CZ 529) (lp re-iss. Dec99 on 'Simply Vinyl'; SVLP 157)

— The CAPTAIN retained DRUMBO and ANTANNAE plus new members **ZOOT HORN ROLLO** (b.BILL HARKLEROAD) – brass, narrator, guitar, flute / **ROCKETTE NORTON** (b.MARK BOSTON) – bass, narrator / **THE MASCARA SNAKE** (b.VICTOR HAYDEN) – clarinet; guest **DOUG MOON** returned

			Straight	Straight
Nov 69.	(d-lp) (STS 1053) <RS 2027>	TROUT MASK REPLICA	21	

– Frownland / The dust blows forward 'n dust blows back / Dachau blues / Ella guru / Hair pie: bake 1 / Moonlight on Vermont / Hair pie: bake 2 / Pena / Well / When big Joan sets up / Fallin' ditch / Sugar 'n spikes / Ant man bee / Pachuco cadaver / Bills corpse / Sweet sweet bulbs / Neon meate dream of an octafish / China pig / My human gets me blues / Dali's car / Orange claw hammer / Wild life / She's too much for my mirror / Hobo chang ba / The blimp (mousetrap replica) / Steal softly thru snow / Old fart at play / Veteran's day poppy. (re-iss. May75 on 'Reprise'; K 64026) (re-iss. cd Sep94 & Jul00 on 'WEA'; K 927196-2)

— **ED MARIMBA** (ART TRIPP) – marimba (ex-MOTHERS OF INVENTION) repl. THE MASCARA SNAKE

Jan 71.	(lp) (STS 1063) <RS 6240>	LICK MY DECALS OFF, BABY	20	

– Lick my decals off, baby / Doctor Dark / I love you, you big dummy / Peon / Bellerin' plain / Woe-is-uh-me-bop / Japan in a dishpan / I wanna find a woman that'll hold my big toe till I have a go / Petrified forest / One rose that I mean / The Buggy boogie woogie / The Smithsonian Institute blues (or the big dig) / Space-age couple / The clouds are full of wine (not whiskey or rye) / Flash Gordon's ape. (re-iss. Jul73 on 'Reprise') <US cd-iss. 1990 on 'Enigma'; >

CAPTAIN BEEFHEART

— **THE WINGED EEL FINGERLING** (r.n. ELLIOT INGBER) – guitar, etc. (ex-MOTHERS etc.) repl. SEMENS who had already formed MU

			Reprise	Reprise
Jan 72.	(7") <1068>	CLICK CLACK. / I'M GONNA BOOGLARIZE YOU BABY	-	
Feb 72.	(lp) (K 44162) <RS 2050>	THE SPOTLIGHT KID	44	

– I'm gonna booglarize you baby / White jam / Blabber 'n smoke / When it blows its stacks / Alice in Blunderland / The spotlight kid / Click clack / Grow fins / There ain't no Santa Claus on the evenin' stage / Glider.

CAPTAIN BEEFHEART
and the MAGIC BAND

— **ROY 'OREJON' ESTRADA** – bass (ex-LITTLE FEAT, ex-MOTHERS OF INVENTION) repl. INGBER / augmented by backing vocals The **BLACKBERRIES** / **RUSS TITELMAN** – guitar (guested, as he did on "Safe as Milk")

Nov 72.	(lp) (K 54007) <MS 2115>	CLEAR SPOT		

– Low yo yo stuff / Nowadays a woman's gotta hit a man / Too much time / Circumstances / My head is my only house unless it rains / Sun zoom sparks / Clear spot / Crazy little thing / Long neck bottles / Her eyes are a blue million miles / Big eyed beans from Venus / Golden birdies.

Mar 73.	(7") (K 14233) <1133>	TOO MUCH TIME. / MY HEAD IS MY ONLY HOUSE UNLESS IT RAINS		

— **ALEX SAINT CLAIRE** – guitar; returned to repl. ROY

— added **MARK MARCELLINO** – keyboards

			Virgin	Mercury
Apr 74.	(lp) (V 2015) <SRM1 709>	UNCONDITIONALLY GUARANTEED		

– Upon the my-o-my / Sugar bowl / New electric ride / Magic be / Happy love song / Full moon, hot sun / I got love on my mind / This is the day / Lazy music / Peaches. (re-iss. Aug82 + Aug85 on 'Fame' lp/c; FA/TCFA 3034) (re-iss. Aug88; OVED 66) (cd-iss. Jun88; CDV 2015)

| Apr 74. | (7") (VS 110) | UPON THE MY-O-MY. / MAGIC BE | | - |
| Apr 74. | (7") <73494> | UPON THE MY-O-MY. / I GOT LOVE ON MY MIND | - | |

— **IRA INGBER** – bass; repl. SAINT CLAIRE / added new session men **MARK GIBBONS** – keyboards / **MICHAEL SMOTHERMAN** – keyboards, vocals / **JIMMY CARAVAN** – keyboards / **DEAN SMITH** – guitar / **BOB WEST** – bass / **GENE PELLO** – drums / **TY GRIMS** – percussion

Nov 74.	(lp) (V 2123) <SRM1 1018>	BLUEJEANS & MOONBEAMS		

– Party of special things do / Same old blues / Observatory crest / Pompadour swamp / Captain's holiday / Rock'n'roll's evil doll / Further than we've gone / Twist ah luck / Bluejeans and moonbeams. (re-iss. Mar84; OVED 19) (cd-iss. Jun88; CDV 2023)

— Late '75 BEEFHEART collaborated with FRANK ZAPPA on "BONGO FURY" album. This was a near live album with 2 studio tracks.

— His new touring band featured past members **ELLIOT, INGBER** and **JOHN FRENCH** plus **DENNY WHALLEY** – slide guitar / **BRUCE FOWLER** – trombone (both on bongos)

— His '76 band were DRUMBO, WHALLEY, **JEFF MORRIS TEPPER** – slide guitar, guitar + **JOHN THOMAS** – piano (they recorded first sessions for the next album)

— **ERIC DREW FELDMAN** – synthesizer; repl. THOMAS / **ROBERT ARTHUR WILLIAMS** – drums; repl. DRUMBO / **RICHARD REDUS** – slide guitar, guitars. accordion, fretless bass; repl. WHALLEY / **ART TRIPP III** – marimba, percussion; returned from MALLARD **BRUCE LAMBOURNE FOWLER** also returned

			Virgin	Warners
Feb 80.	(lp) (V 2149) <BSK 3256>	SHINY BEAST (BAT CHAIN PULLER)		1979

– The floppy boot stomp / Tropical hot dog night / Ice rose / Harry Irene / You know you're a man / Bat chain puller / When I see mommy I feel like a mummy / Owed t' Alex / Candle mambo / Love lies / Suction prints / Apes-ma. (re-iss. Aug88; OVED 67) (cd-iss. Jun87; CDV 2149)

— **GARY LUCAS** – french horn, guitar (on 1); repl. REDUS

— **DRUMBO (JOHN FRENCH)** also returned

			Virgin	Virgin
Aug 80.	(lp) (V 2172) <13148>	DOC AT RADAR STATION		

– Hot head / Ashtray heart / A carrot is as close as a rabbit gets to a diamond / Run paint run run / Sue Egypt / Brickbats / Dirty blue Gene / Best batch yet / Telephone / Flavor bud living / Sheriff of Hong Kong / Making love to a vampire with a monkey on my knee. (re-iss. Aug88; OVED 68) (cd-iss. Jun88; CDV 2172)

— The CAPTAIN brought in **RICHARD 'MIDNIGHT HAT SIZE' SNYDER** – guitar, bass, marimba, viola / **CLIFF R. MARTINEZ** – drums, percussion, etc / to add to TEPPER + LUCAS FELDMAN remained a guest

| Aug 82. | (12") (VS 534-12) <03190> | LIGHT REFLECTED OFF THE OCEANS OF THE MOON. / ICE CREAM FOR CROW | | - |
| Sep 82. | (lp) (V 2237) | ICE CREAM FOR CROW | 90 | - |

– Ice cream for crow / The host the ghost the most holy-o / Semi-multicoloured caucasian / Hey Garland, I dig your tweed coat / Evening bell / Cardboard cutout sundown / The past sure is tense / Ink mathematics / The witch doctor life / "81" poop hatch / The thousandth and tenth day of the human totem pole / Skeleton makes good. (re-iss. Aug88; OVED 121) (cd-iss. Apr88; CDV 2237) <US cd-iss. 1990 on 'Caroline'; CAROL 1632-2>

— BEEFHEART retired from the music business to concentrate on painting/sculpting in his recently bought Mojave desert home.

– compilations etc. –

Jul 70.	(lp) Buddah; (2349 002)	DROPOUT BOOGIE		-

(a re-iss. of "SAFE AS MILK" 2 tracks less)

| May 71. | (lp) Buddah; (2365 002) <BDS 5077> | MIRROR MAN (rec.1967; not one night in 1965 as stated on sleeve!) | 49 | |

– Tarotplane / Kandy korn / 25th century Quaker / Mirror man. (re-iss. May82 on 'P.R.T.'; NCP 1006) (re-iss. Apr86 on 'Edsel'; ED 184) (cd-iss. May91 on 'Castle'; CLACD 235) (cd re-iss. Sep99 as 'THE MIRROR MAN SESSIONS' on 'Buddha-RCA'+=; 74321 69174-2) – Trust us (take 6) / Safe as milk (take 12) / Beatle bones n' smokin' stones / Moody Liz (take 8) / Gimme dat harp boy. (lp re-iss. Nov99 on 'Simply Vinyl'; SVLP 143)

CAPTAIN BEEFHEART (cont) — THE GREAT INDIE DISCOGRAPHY — The 1980s

Date	Format / Label / Cat# / Title
1975.	(lp) *WRMB;* **WHAT'S ALL THIS BOOGA-BOOGA MUSIC** (live)
Aug 76.	(d-lp) *Reprise;* (K 84006) **TWO ORIGINALS OF . . .** – (LICK MY DECALS OFF, BABY / THE SPOTLIGHT KID)
Nov 77.	(d-lp/d-c) *Pye;* (FILD/ZCFILD 008) **THE CAPTAIN BEEFHEART FILE** (first 2-lp's)
1978.	(d-lp) *Impossible;* **EASY TEETH**
Jan 78.	(7") *Buddah;* (BDS 466) **SURE 'NUFF 'N' YES I DO. / ELECTRICITY**
May 78.	(7") *M.C.A.;* (MCA 366) **HARD WORKIN' MAN** (by Jack Nitzsche featuring Captain Beefheart). / **Coke Machine** (by Jack Nitzsche) — above also features RY COODER – on guitar
1978.	(7"pic-ep) *Virgin;* (SIXPACK 1) **SIX-PACK / SIX TRACK** – Sugar bowl / Same old blues / Upon the my-o-my / Magic be / Rock'n'roll's evil doll / New electric ride.
Jul 83.	(10"lp/c) *P.R.T.;* (DOW/ZCDOW 15) **MUSIC IN SEA MINOR**
Jul 84.	(lp/pic-lp) *Design;* (PIL/+P 4) **TOP SECRET**
Oct 84.	(m-lp) *A&M;* (AMY 226) **THE LEGENDARY SESSIONS** – Diddy wah diddy / Who do you think you're fooling / Moonchild / Frying pan / Here I am, I always am. *(re-iss. Oct86 on 'Edsel'; BLIMP 902) (cd-iss. Mar92; BLIMPCD 902)*
Jun 88.	(d-lp/c/d-cd) *That's Original;* (TFO LP/MC/CD 11) **SAFE AS MILK / MIRROR MAN** *(re-iss. d-cd.May91 on 'Castle')*
Feb 91.	(d-cd) *Reprise;* (7599 26249-2) **THE SPOTLIGHT KID / CLEAR SPOT**
Jul 91.	(cd) *The Collection;* (ORO 146) **ZIG ZAG WANDERER** *(re-iss. Nov96 & Oct98 on 'Wooded Hill'; HILLCD 6)*
Jun 92.	(cd) *Sequel;* (NEXCD 215) **I MAY BE HUNGRY BUT I SURE AIN'T WEIRD – THE ALTERNATIVE CAPTAIN BEEFHEART**
Jun 93.	(cd) *Virgin Universal;* (CDVM 9028) <88303-2> **A CARROT IS AS CLOSE AS A RABBIT GETS TO A DIAMOND** – Sugar bowl / The past sure is tense / Happy love song / The floppy boot stomp / Bluejeans and moonbeams / Run paint run run / This is the day / Tropical hot dog night / Observatory crest / The host the ghost the most holy o / Harry Irene / I got love on my mind / Pompadour swamp / Love lies / Sheriff of Hong Kong / Further than we've gone / Candle mambo / Light reflected off the oceans of the Moon / A carrot is as close as a rabbit gets to a diamond.
Nov 93.	(cd) *Movieplay Gold;* (MPG 74025) **LONDON 1974** (live)
Jan 98.	(cd) *Camden-RCA;* (74321 55846-2) **ELECTRICITY**
Nov 98.	(7") *Table Of Elements;* <(TOE 759)> **SPITBALL SCALPED UH BABY. /**
Nov 98.	(cd+book) *Sonic Book;* (SB 1) **PEARLS BEFORE SWINE** (poems, paintings, aphorisms & discography)
May 99.	(5xcd-box) *Revenant;* (REV 210) **GROW FINS** (rarities 1965-1982)
May 99.	(d-lp) *Xeric;* <(XERLP 96)> **GROW FINS VOL.1 – JUST GOT BACK FROM THE CITY 1965-1967 / ELECTRICITY 1968**
Sep 99.	(d-lp) *Xeric;* <(XERLP 97)> **GROW FINS VOL.2 – THE TROUT MASK REPLICA HOUSE SESSIONS 1969**
Oct 00.	(cd) *Ozit;* <(BF 4003)> **MERSEYTROUT – LIVE IN LIVERPOOL 1980** (rec. 29 October 1980) – Toaster (bass solo) / Nowadays a woman's gotta hit a man / Abba zabba / Hothead / Dirty blue Jean / Best batch yet / One man sentence (poem) / Safe as milk / Flavour bud living / Her eyes are a million miles / One red rose that I mean / Doctor Dark / Bat chain puller / My human gets me blues / Sugar 'n' spikes / Veterans' day poppy / Dropout boogie / Sheriff of Hong Kong / Kandy korn / Suction prints / Big eyed beans from Venus.
May 01.	(d-lp) *Table Of Elements;* <(TOELP 52)> **GROW FINS VOL.3**

CAPTAINS OF INDUSTRY
(see under ⇒ WRECKLESS ERIC; 70's section)

CARDIACS

Formed: Carshalton, Surrey, England . . . 1978 as PHILIP PILF AND THE FILTH by songwriter, TIM SMITH, brother JIM, PETER TAGG and MICK PUGH. Not surprisingly they soon changed their name to CARDIAC ARREST, recruiting COLVIN MYERS in the process and releasing a low-key 45, 'A BUS FOR A BUS ON A BUS'. With MARK CAWTHRA replacing TAGG, The CARDIACS (as they were now called) began the 80's by self-financing (through their own 'Alphabet' outlet) a series of cassette-only releases, namely 'THE OBVIOUS IDENTITY' (1980) – still as CARDIAC ARREST, 'TOY WORLD' (1981) and the fan club compilation 'ARCHIVE CARDIACS' (1983). With PUGH and MYERS leaving to join The SOUND, it was down to the SMITH brothers to recruit an entire new line-up. This comprised SARA SMITH, WILLIAM D. DRAKE, DOMINIC LUCKMAN and TIM QUY, the band's condition remaining stable over the ensuing six years, at least in terms of personnel. A manic rock show parody outfit akin to HALF MAN HALF BISCUIT meeting the BONZOS, The CARDIACS found a sitting duck target in the shape of MORRISSEY, The SMITHS (TIM and JIM, that is!) showering the crowd with flour (as opposed to flowers/gladioli). Musically their ingredients were more varied, to say the least, chucking in handfuls of off-beat, dated punk, vintage Prog-rock and Cockney barrow-boy psychedelia. Virtually ignored by a hostile press, they continued their madcap malarky regardless over an unceasingly prolific release schedule that included fans favourite, 'IS THIS THE LIFE' (apparently loved by DAMON ALBARN), a near chart hit lifted from the equally impressive 'A LITTLE MAN, A HOUSE & THE WHOLE WORLD WINDOW' (1988). A relatively short-lived replacement for the departing trio of QUY, DRAKE and SARA SMITH, was found in the shape of CHRISTIAN 'BIC' HAYES (future LEVITATION), who played with them after the much loved 1989 album, 'ON LAND AND IN THE SEA'. Proper indie stardom looked to be on the cards with the scheduled 'HEAVEN BORN AND EVER BRIGHT'; in the event, however, a proposed deal with 'Rough Trade' fell through and the album eventually appeared as the 17th(!) release on 'Alphabet'. Despite the continuing media antipathy, TIM SMITH had become a much in-demand producer, working with the likes of EAT, LEVITATION and SIDI BOU SAID, while even BLUR were to sing the band's praises and include them as support act on their landmark Mile End Stadium show. Needless to say, studio activity continued apace with a slew of releases culminating in 1996's 'SING TO GOD' (available as both a double CD and two single discs).

Album rating: ARCHIVE CARDIACS first two cassettes compiled (*6) / THE SEASIDE (*5) / MR & MRS SMITH AND MR DRAKE (*5) / BIG SHIP mini (*5) / RUDE BOOTLEG – LIVE AT READING ROCK FESTIVAL 1986 (*5) / A LITTLE MAN, A HOUSE & THE WHOLE WORLD WINDOW (*7) / CARDIACS LIVE (*5) / ON LAND AND IN THE SEA (*6) / SONGS FOR SHIPS AND IRONS compilation (*7) / HEAVEN BORN AND EVER BRIGHT (*7) / ALL THAT GLITTERS IS A MARE'S NEST (*5) / EXTRA SPECIAL OCEANLAND WORLD by Tim Smith (*5) / SEA NYMPHS by Sea Nymphs (*5) / SING TO GOD double (*6) / GUNS (*6) / GREATEST HITS compilation (*7)

CARDIAC ARREST

MICK PUGH (b.21 Sep'58, Kingston, Surrey, England) – vocals (aka PETER "ZIP" BOKER) / **TIM SMITH** (b. 3 Jul'61) – guitar, vocals, synth (aka PHILIP PILF) / **JIM SMITH** (b.14 Apr'58) – bass (aka PATTY PILF) / **PETER TAGG** (b. London, England) – drums (aka RICHARD TARGETT) / **COLVIN MYERS** (b. London) – vocals, synth (aka MAX CAT + DUNCAN TOILET) / + 6th member **RALPH CADE** – saxophone (aka RAPHAEL CADD)

		Tortch	not iss.
1979.	(7"ep) *(TOR 002)* **A BUS FOR A BUS ON A BUS EP** – A bus for a bus on a bus / A cake for Bertie's party / Food on the wall.		

MARK CAWTHRA – drums (aka LITTLE BOBBY SHATTOCKS); repl. TAGG who later formed The TRUDY (CADE also departed)

		Private	not iss.
Jun 80.	(c) *(none)* **THE OBVIOUS IDENTITY** – The obvious identity / Visiting hours / Pip as Uncle Dick but Peter spoilt it / To go off and things / Rock around the clock / Leaf scrapings / A game for Bertie's party / Cameras / Bite 3/a / Pilf / Let alone my plastic doll / A balloon for Bertie's party.		mail-o

— they changed their name when another CARDIAC ARREST group came out with 'RUNNING IN THE STREET'

CARDIACS

Feb 81.	(c) *(none)* **TOY WORLD** – Aukamacic / Over (outtake) / Icky qualms / Over and over and over and over / Dead mouse / Big noise in a toy world / Trademark / Scratching crawling scrawling / As cold as can be in an English sea / Is this the life? / Nurses whispering verses / A time for rejoicing.		mail-o

		Alphabet	not iss.
1983.	(c) *(ALPH 000)* **ARCHIVE CARDIACS** (a fan club compilation) – Aukamacic / Icky qualms / Piffol four times / Scratching crawling scrawling / As cold as can be in an English sea / T.V.T.V. / My trademark / The obvious identity / Piffol one time / A game for Bertie's party / Piffol three times / Rock around the clock. *(cd-iss. May95; ALPHCD 013)*		

— PUGH and MYERS also left to join The SOUND; The **SMITH** brothers recruited **SARA SMITH** (b.30 Nov'60, Coleford, England) – saxophone / **WILLIAM D. DRAKE** (b. 7 Feb'62, Essex, England) – keyboards / **DOMINIC LUCKMAN** (b.29 Nov'61, Brighton, England) – drums / **TIM QUY** (b.14 Aug'61, Brixton, England) – percussion

1984.	(c) *(ALPH 001)* **THE SEASIDE** – Jibber and twitch / Gena Lollabridgida / Hello Mr. Sparrow / It's a lovely day / A wooden fish on wheels / Nurses whispering verses * / Is this the life? / A little man and a house * / Hope day / Dinner time * / Ice a spot and a dot on the dog / R.E.S. / To go off and things. *(re-iss. 1990 lp/c/cd; ALPH LP/MC/CD 013)* – (w/out *). *(re-iss. cd May95; ALPHCD 013)* – (w/out *).
May 86.	(12"ep) *(ALPH 002)* **SEASIDE TREATS EP** – A little man and a house / Hope day / R.E.S. / To go off and things.
Sep 86.	(c) *(ALPH 003)* **MR & MRS SMITH AND MR DRAKE** – Little creations / Camouflage / The collar / In a waiting room / All the string / Summer is a coming in / Too many colours / Your removal of me / A treat from Mr Smith / To my piano from Mr Drake / Dergo / That's all. (above with only TIM, SARAH + WILLIAM; aka the SEA NYMPHS)
Jan 87.	(m-lp) *(ALPH 004)* **BIG SHIP** – Big ship / Tarred and feathered / Burn your house down / Stoneage dinosaurs / Plane plane against the grain.
1987.	(lp/c) *(ALPH 005/MC005)* **RUDE BOOTLEG – RECORDED LIVE AT READING ROCK FESTIVAL 1986** (live) – The icing on the world / To go off and things / In a city lining / Tarred and feathered / Big ship / I'm eating in bed / Is this the life / The whole world window. *(cd-iss. May95; ALPHCD 005)*
Aug 87.	(12"ep) *(ALPH 006)* **THERE'S TOO MANY IRONS IN THE FIRE EP** – There's too many irons in the fire / All spectacular / Loosefish scapegrace.
Mar 88.	(lp/c) *(ALPH/+MC 007)* **A LITTLE MAN, A HOUSE & THE WHOLE WORLD WINDOW** – A little man and a house / In a city lining / Is this the life / Interlude / Dive / The icing on the world / The breakfast line / Victory egg / R.E.S. / The whole world window. *(cd-iss. on 'Torso'+=; TORSOCD 060)* – Goosegash / Loosefish scapegrace / I'm eating in bed / There's too many irons in the fire / All spectacular. *(re-iss. cd – original tracks – May95; ALPHCD 007)*
Mar 88.	(7") *(ALPHSP 008)* **IS THIS THE LIFE. / I'M EATING IN BED** (12"+=) *(ALPHT 008)* – Goosegash.

CARDIACS (cont)

Sep 88. (7") *(ALPH 009)* **SUSANNAH'S STILL ALIVE. / BLIND IN SAFETY AND LEAFY IN LOVE**
(12"+=) *(ALPH 009T)* – All his geese are swans.

Oct 88. (lp/cd) *(ALPH LP/CD 010)* **CARDIACS LIVE (at the Paradiso, Amsterdam)**
– The icing on the world / To go off and things / In a city lining / Gina Lollabridgida / There's too many irons in the fire / Tarred and feathered / Goosegash / Loosefish scapegrace / Cameras / Is this the life / Big ship. *(cd re-iss. May95; same)*

Apr 89. (7") *(ALPH 011)* **BABY HEART DIRT. / I HOLD MY LOVE IN MY ARMS**
(12"+=) *(ALPH 011T)* – Horsehead / The safety bowl.

Apr 89. (lp/c/cd) *(ALPH LP/MC/CD 012)* **ON LAND AND IN THE SEA**
– Two bites of cherry / Baby heart dirt / The leader of the starry skies / I hold my love in my arms / The duck and Roger the horse / Arnald / Horse head *[cd-only]* / Fast Robert / Mare's nest / The stench of honey / Buds and spawn / The safety bowl / The everso closely guarded bit. *(re-iss. cd May95; same)*

—— (1990) **BIC HAYES** (b. CHRISTIAN HAYES, 10 Jun'64, London) – guitar (+ JON POOLE); repl. SARA, TIM + WILLIAM

Nov 91. (12"ep/cd-ep) *(ALPH 015/+CD)* **DAY IS GONE EP**
– Day is gone / No bright side / Ideal / Joining the plankton.
(free 7" w/above by the SEA NYMPHS – 'APPEALING TO VENUS' / 'TREETOPS HIGH'; ALPH 016SP)

—— (now 4-piece) **JON POOLE** repl. BIC HAYES who joined LEVITATION
(below was to have appeared Nov'91 on 'Rough Trade')

May 92. (cd/lp) *(ALPH CD/LP 017)* **HEAVEN BORN AND EVER BRIGHT**
– The alphabet business concern (home of the fadeless splendour) / She is hiding behind the shed / March / Goodbye Grace / Anything I can't eat / Helen and Heaven / Bodysbad / For good and all / Core / Day is gone / Snakes-a-sleeping. *(re-iss. cd May95; same)*

—— **TIM, JIM + JON** recruited **BOB LEITH** – drums; repl. LUCKMAN

Apr 95. (cd-ep) *(ORGAN 011CD)* **BELLYEYE EP**
– Bellyeye / A horse's tail / No gold.
(above issued on 'Organ')

—— added guest **CLAIRE LEMMON** – backing vocals

Jul 96. (d-cd) *(ALPHCD 022)* **SING TO GOD**
Jul 96. (cd) *(ALPHCD 023)* **SING TO GOD PART ONE**
– Eden on the air / Eat it up worms hero / Dog like Sparky / Fiery gun hand / Insect hoofs on Lassie / Fairy Mary bag / Bellyeye / A horse's tail / Manhoo / Wireless.

Jul 96. (cd) *(ALPHCD 024)* **SING TO GOD PART TWO**
– Dirty boy / Billion / Odd even / Bell stinks / Bell clinks / Flap off you beak / Quiet as a mouse / Angelworm angel / Red fire coming out from his gills / No gold / Nurses whispering verses / Foundling.

Aug 96. (cd-s) *(ALPHCDS 025)* **MANHOO / SPINNEY / WHAT PARADISE IS LIKE**

Nov 96. (cd-s) *(ALPHCDS 026)* **ODD EVEN / HURRICANE / DEVILS**

—— added guest **SHARON SHADDINGTON** – backing vocals

Jun 99. (cd) *(ALPHCD 027)* **GUNS**
– Spell with a shell / There's good cud / Wind and rains is cold / Cry wet smile dry / Jitterbug (Junior is a) / Sleep all eyes open / Come back clammy Lammy / Clean that evil mud out your soul / Ain't he messy though / Signs / Song of a dead pest / Will bleed amen.

Jul 99. (cd-ep; split) *(ORG 056CD)* **CARDIACS MEET CAMP BLACKFOOT**
– Sleep all eyes open / Dirty boy / Foundling / Insect hoofs on Lassie (instrumental) / (other 3 by CAMP BLACKFOOT)
(above issued on 'Organ')

Aug 99. (cd-s) *(ALPHCD 028)* **SIGNS / SANG ALL AWAY AWAY / DOG LIKE SPARKY (instrumental).**

– compilations, others, etc. –

on 'Alphabet' unless stated otherwise

Sep 88. (12"ep) *Nighttracks; (SFNT 013)* **RADIO ONE SESSIONS**
(29.11.87)
– R.E.S. / Buds and spawn / In a city lining / Cameras – Is this the life?

Oct 91. (cd/lp) *(ALPH CD/LP 014)* **SONGS FOR SHIPS AND IRONS**
(compilation of 'BIG SHIP' and 'THERE'S TOO MANY IRONS . . .')
(re-iss. cd May95; same)

May 95. (cd/lp) *(ALPH CD/LP 018)* **ALL THAT GLITTERS IS A MARE'S NEST (live 30.6.90)**
– To duck and Roger the horse / There's too many irons in the fire / It's a lovely day / Everything is easy / Two bites of cherry / I hold my love in my arms / Arnald / Baby heart dirt / All spectacular / To go off and things / The leader of the starry skies / Tarred and feathered / Fast Robert / Big ship / Visiting / R.E.S. / Is this the life.

May 95. (cd) *(ALPHCD 019)* **CARDIACS SAMPLER**
– Is this the life / Angelworm angel / Burn your house down / Goodbye Grace / Piffol four times / Two bites of cherry (live) / Tarred and feathered (live) / Blind in safety and leafy in love / Big ship (live) / Veronica in ecstasy / Christ alive / The everso closely guarded line / To go off and things.

May 95. (cd; as THE SEA NYMPHS) *(ALPHCD 021)* **THE SEA NYMPHS** (private rec. from 1992)
– The spirit spout / Shaping the river / Nil in the nest / A thousand strokes and a rolling suck / Christ alive / Big heart / Lucky Lucy / Gods box / Piano interlude / Up in Annie's room / Mr. Drake's big heart reprise / The psalm of life / In the corner of sin / Tree tops high / Dog eat spine / Sarah on a worm / Lilly White's party / Appealing to Venus / Abade.

Jun 96. (cd; by TIM SMITH) *(ALPHCD 020)* **EXTRA SPECIAL OCEANLAND WORLD** (recorded 1989-1991)
– Exploded / Rat mice lice time / This grounds town / Savour / Swimming with the snake / England's / Ocean shipwreck / Bug from Heaven / Veronica in ecstasy / Ocean Heaven.

Aug 98. (cd-ep; as The SEA NYMPHS) *Organ; (ORG 044CD)* **APPEALING TO VENUS EP**
– Appealing to Venus / God's box / Up in Annie's room / Shaping the river / Little creations / Camouflage.

Nov 99. (cd) *(ALPHCD 029)* **GREATEST HITS**
– There's good cud / Manhoo / Buds and spawn / Core / Fairy Mary mag / Odd even /

She is hiding behind the shed / The breakfast line / Mare's nest / Wind and rain is cold / Faster than snakes with a ball and a chain / Victory egg / Dirty boy / Plane plane against the grain.

Jul 01. (cd; as CARDIACS AND AFFECTIONATE FRIENDS) *Organ; (ORG 228CD)* **A REMORSELESS AND INSOUCIANT COMPENDIUM OF SONGS BY CARDIACS AND AFFECTIONATE FRIENDS**

CARE (see under ⇒ WILD SWANS)

CARETAKER RACE

Formed: East London, England . . . 1987 by rock journo (for the Record Mirror) and former LOFT guitarist, ANDY STRICKLAND; his former LOFT compadre, PETER ASTOR, found more success with The WEATHER PROPHETS. Recruiting SALLY WARD, HENRY HERSOM and DAVE MEW, STRICKLAND and his CARETAKER RACE issued a couple of self-financed singles, 'SOMEWHERE ON SEA' and 'ANYWHERE BUT HOME', the leader's strong songwriting skills drawing comparisons to such antipodean critical luminaries as The GO-BETWEENS and The TRIFFIDS. The 'Foundation' label took over the reins in '89, although that year's solitary effort, 'I WISH I'D SAID THAT', was the last to feature HERSOM, who was replaced by ex-FLATMATES keyboard player, JACKIE CARRERA. A fourth single, 'MAN OVERBOARD', was followed by the long-awaited debut set, 'HANGOVER SQUARE' (1990), although STRICKLAND wasn't able to turn press support into sales figures; the split was imminent when SALLY departed for a job in teaching.

Album rating: HANGOVER SQUARE (*5)

ANDY STRICKLAND (b.16 Aug'59, Newport, Isle Of Wight, England) – vocals, guitar (ex-LOFT) / **SALLY WARD** (b.Preston, England) – keyboards / **HENRY HERSOM** – bass / **DAVE MEW** (b.11 May'59, Epping, Essex, England) – drums

Roustabout   not iss.

Oct 87. (12"ep) *(RST 1T)* **SOMEWHERE ON SEA / ALL LOVE OFFERS. / ANGELA'S BABY / MAN OVERBOARD (demo)**

Jul 88. (7"promo) *(RST 4)* **ANYWHERE BUT HOME. / GILDA**
(12"+=) *(RST 004T)* – Things that matter.

Foundation   not iss.

Jul 89. (12"ep) *(TFL 2T)* **I WISH I'D SAID THAT / FIRE IN THE HOLD. / ONE RUNG DOWN / HER SHINING ROOM**

—— (early 1990) **JACKIE CARRERA** (b. 6 Jun'64) – keyboards (ex-FLATMATES) repl. HERSOM who joined the group BOB

Jul 90. (12"ep) *(TFL 6T)* **MAN OVERBOARD. / GREY GARDENS / SQUIRREL FACE SHOES**

—— (on some of album) **ANDREW DEEVEY** – guitar; repl. WARD

Aug 90. (lp/cd) *(FOUND 2/+CD)* **HANGOVER SQUARE**
– All love offers / I've seen a thing or two / Two steel rings / Anywhere but home / Fire in the hold / Gun metal / Two minutes by train / Borrow my car / I wish I'd said that / You always hurt (the one you love) / Man overboard.

Oct 90. (12"ep/cd-ep) *(TFL 8 T/CD)* **TWO STEEL RINGS / ALL LOVE LETTERS. / YOUR BLACK HEART / BRIGHTEST STAR**

—— split later in 1990

Cath CARROLL

Born: 25 Aug'60, Chipping Sodbury, Avon, England; although raised in Greater Manchester. Moving to London and securing a job as a scribe for the NME, CARROLL initially turned her hand to singing as vocalist of the GLASS ANIMALS, then MIAOW alongside STEVE McGUIRE, RON CAINE and CHRIS FENNER. The band's vinyl debut came via a contribution – 'SPORT MOST ROYAL' – to the NME's fabled C86 compilation, a SMITHS-style rockabilly jangle framing CARROLL's fluid, almost DEBBIE HARRY-esque vocals. This was followed up with 'BELLE VUE' (the anti-Thatcher anthem, 'GROCER'S DEVIL DAUGHTER' appearing as an extra track on the 12") and a single for 'Factory', 'WHEN IT ALL COMES DOWN'. Still without an album to their name, the band split after a final single, 'BREAK THE CODE', CARROLL subsequently marrying BIG BLACK guitarist, SANTIAGO DURANGO and going on to pursue a solo career. Sticking with 'Factory', she set to work on a debut album with an exotic cast of musicians including her husband and former BIG BLACK mainman, STEVE ALBINI. Rich in electronically enhanced samba rhythms, 'ENGLAND MADE ME' (1991) illustrated how much CARROLL had been influenced by her time in South America, drawing almost universal praise from the press. Following the collapse of 'Factory', CARROLL cut an album, 'TRUE CRIME MOTEL' (1995) for US indie label, 'Teenbeat', the singer now actually living in Chicago.

Album rating: ENGLAND MADE ME (*6) / TRUE CRIME MOTEL (*5)

MIAOW

CATH CARROLL – vocals, guitar / **CHRIS FENNER** – drums, percussion / **RON CAINE** – bass, guitar / **STEVE McGUIRE** – guitar

Venus   not iss.

Dec 85. (7") *(VENUS 1)* **BELLE VUE. / FATE**
(12"+=) *(VENUS 1T)* – Grocer's devil daughter.

Factory   not iss.

Feb 87. (7") *(FAC 179)* **WHEN IT ALL COMES DOWN. / DID SHE**
(12"+=) *(FAC 179T)* – ('A'-Cotechism mix).

— JOE KORNER – keyboards; repl. STEVE
Oct 87. (7") *(FAC 189)* **BREAK THE CODE. / STOLEN CARS**
— disbanded when CATH augmented The HIT PARADE

CATH CARROLL

— with **MARK BRYDON** – guitar (ex-CHAKK) / **SIM LISTER** – sax, drums, keyboards (ex-CHAKK) / **ANTENOR SOARES GANDRA NETO** – guitar / **VINCENTE DA PAULA SILVA** – piano / **OSWALDINHO DA CUICA** – congas / **DIRCEU SIMOES DE MEDEIROS** – drums / **STEVE ALBINI** – guitar / **SANTIAGO DURANGO** – guitar

Factory   not iss.

Jun 91. (lp/c)(cd) *(FACT 210/+C)(FACD 210)* **ENGLAND MADE ME**
– To close your eyes forever / Unforgettable / Moves like you / Watching you / Beast on the streets / Subtitled / Next time (he's mine) / England made me / Send me over / Train you're on. *(cd re-iss. Jul02 on 'Les Tempes Modernes'; LTMCD 2348)*

— now with new set of musicians

Teenbeat   Teenbeat

May 94. (7") *(TB 137)* **MY COLD HEART. / INTO DAY**
Aug 95. (cd/lp) *(<TB 167-2/-1>)* **TRUE CRIMES MOTEL**
– Easter bunny song / Into day / True crime motel / Mississippi river factory town / Jimmy's candy / Just once / L'amour c'est ca / Lullaby for a steepleback / Breathe for me.
Sep 95. (cd-s) **BAD STAR / MISSISSIPPI RIVER FACTORY TOWN**

Chris CARTER (see under ⇒ CHRIS AND COSEY)

CASSANDRA COMPLEX

Formed: Leeds, England . . . 1984 by main songwriter, RODNEY ORPHEUS, PAUL DILLON and ANDY BOOTH. In 1985, they issued a self-financed debut single, 'MARCH' (actually released that month), which, after a live cassette, led to a signing for small local independent, 'Rouska'. An electro-industrial art-rock outfit featuring percussive treatments fused with a HAPPY MONDAYS feel, CASSANDRA COMPLEX nevertheless had a tendency to indulge in pseudo-intellectual lyrics. Two subsequent albums, 'GRENADE' (1986) and 'HELLO AMERICA' (1987), helped win them a healthier contract for Belgian-based label, 'Play It Again Sam' in 1987, their slightly contrived sound winning more fans on the continent where they were now living. First up for the label, bar a single 'KILL YOUR CHILDREN', was the live opus, 'FEEL THE WIDTH', which featured a faithful renditions of 'SOMETHING CAME OVER ME' by industrial forebears Throbbing Gristle and 'GHOST RIDER' by Suicide. In 1988, CASSANDRA COMPLEX delivered PAUL and ANDY's swansong, 'THEOMANIA', before RODNEY enlisted an all new cast including JOHN GALVIN and JURGEN JANSEN. Alongside additional members, PATRICK GORDEN and ALAN WILKINSON, the new line-up made its debut on 1989's 'SATAN, BUGS BUNNY AND ME', appropriately covering noneother than the Rolling Stones' 'SYMPATHY FOR THE DEVIL'. The turn of the decade saw GAZ WILSON replacing GALVIN on the 'CYBERPUNX' (1990) set, while prior to their following album, 'THE WAR AGAINST SLEEP' (1991), WILKINSON and WILSON had made way for VOLKER ZAPHOR ZACHARIAS and the returning ANDY BOOTH. Confusingly enough, the song 'THE WAR AGAINST SLEEP' actually appeared on 1993's last effort for some time, 'SEX & DEATH', a record that also featured another Suicide classic, 'FRANKIE TEARDROP' and John Cage's '4"33'. In 2000, the CASSANDRA's made their long-awaited comeback, 'WETWARE' featuring a cover of Borghesia's (from Yugoslavia) 'N.U.D.'. • **Note:** Late 80's side project outfit, WMTID, consisted of BOOTH, ORPHEUS, DILLON, SEAN ALBIEZ, MARTIN KELLY and RICHARD ROUSKA – one set, 'THE ELECTRIC CHURCH'. ORPHEUS was also behind the SUNGOD (one-set in '95) project with MARCUS GILTJES and PATRICIA NIAGHAVI.

Album rating: GRENADE (*6) / HELLO AMERICA (*6) / FEEL THE WIDTH (*7) / THEOMANIA (*6) / 30 MINUTES OF DEATH mini (*5) / SATAN, BUGS BUNNY AND ME (*6) / CYBERPUNX (*5) / THE WAR AGAINST SLEEP (*5) / BEYOND THE WALL OF SLEEP (*6) / SEX & DEATH (*5) / WORKS 1.0 compilation (*7) / WETWARE (*5)

RODNEY ORPHEUS – vocals / **PAUL DILLON** – keyboards / **ANDY BOOTH** – guitar

Complex   not iss.

Mar 85. (12") *(CXD 001)* **MARCH. / PICKUP (live) / HCOMA**
Apr 85. (c) *(CXC 004)* **LIVE IN LEATHER**

Rouska   not iss.

Sep 85. (12") *(COME 2T)* **MOSCOW IDAHO / BEYOND BELIEF. / DAVID VENUS**

— now without DILLON; he was repl. by **JEZ WILLIS** – keyboards, bass (of MDMA) / **KEITH LANGLEY** – guitar (of MDMA) / **JOHN MARCINI** – sax, bass

Jul 86. (12") *(COME 5T)* **DATAKILL. / WINTRY WEATHER SONG / THREE CITIES**
Sep 86. (lp/c) *(CXRA/+C 1)* **GRENADE**
– March '86 / Wonderworld / Presents (come of age) / Pickup / Power / Report from the back / Prairie bitch / Motherad. *(cd-iss. 1987 on 'Play It Again Sam'; CXM 1001)*
May 87. (lp) *(CXRA 2)* **HELLO AMERICA**
– Moscow idaho / Beyond belief / Datakill / Clouds / Fragile / Wintry weather song / David Venus / Three cities. *(cd-iss. May88 +=; CXRA 2CD)* – Something came over me / Angels in the sky / Kill your children.

Play It Again Sam   not iss.

Oct 87. (7") *(BIAS 064)* **KILL YOUR CHILDREN. / SOMETHING CAME OVER ME**
(12"+=) *(12BIAS 064)* – Angels in the city.

Nov 87. (lp/cd) *(BIAS/CDBIAS 068)* **FEEL THE WIDTH (live)**
– Report from the black * / Presents (come of age) * / Clouds / Wonderworld / Three string blues / Prairie bitch / Datakill / Power / Pickup / Something came over me / Moscow Idaho / March / David Venus / Moby Keitho * / Motherad * / Ghost rider. *(cd+= *)*

— guest **DAVE WILSON** – guitar; repl. WILLIS + LANGLEY

Apr 88. (lp/cd) *(BIAS/CDBIAS 088)* **THEOMANIA**
– God John / Oz / Too stupid to sin / Honeytrap / One millionth happy customer / Ground / Second shot / Defcon 1.
Jan 89. (m-lp/m-cd) *(BIAS/CDBIAS 112)* **30 MINUTES OF DEATH**   Belgium
– Gunship / Moments before impact.

— **ORPHEUS** brought in **JOHN GALVIN** – bass, guitar + **JURGEN JANSEN** – keyboards, computer / others **PATRICK GORDEN** – computers, percussion / **ALAN WILKINSON** – sax

Apr 89. (lp/cd) *(BIAS/CDBIAS 118)* **SATAN, BUGS BUNNY, AND ME**
– What can you say? / E.'O.'D. / Symphony for the Devil / Forever / Kill the christian swine / City of dreams / (In search of) Penny Century.
Sep 89. (7") *(BIAS 136-7)* **(IN SEARCH OF) PENNY CENTURY. / (IN SEARCH OF) PENNY CENTURY (extended)**   Belgium
(12"+=/cd-s+=) *(12/CD BIAS 136)* – Beyond belief (revisited) / Something came over me . . . you've lost that loving feeling / Oz.

— **GAZ WILSON** – guitar repl. GALVIN

Jan 90. (lp/cd) *(BIAS 148/+CD)* **CYBERPUNX**
– Nice work (if you can get it) / Let's go to Europe / Happy days (war is here again) / Jihad girl / Sunshine at midnight / I want you / Sleeper / Nightfall (over E.C.) / Into the heart / I believe in free everything / What turns you on? / Ugly.
Jan 90. (12"ep/cd-ep) *(BIAS 151/+CD)* **FINLAND**
– I believe in free everything (Charlie Victor) / Let's go to Europe / What turns you on? (plastic mix) / Fire & forget / Forests.
May 90. (12"/cd-s) *(BIAS 164/+CD)* **NICE WORK (mace mix) / I WANT YOU (Metropol mix). / NICE WORK (cellphone mix) / SLEEPER (dreamless mix)**

— **ANDY BOOTH** returned with new member **VOLKER ZAPHOR ZACHARIAS** – guitar, keyboards; repl. WILSON + WILKINSON

Nov 91. (lp/cd) *(BIAS 195/+CD)* **THE WAR AGAINST SLEEP**
– What can I do for you? / Dr. Adder / And you say / Why? / She loves me / Awake all night – When love comes / Tell me / Lullaby for the first born in Outer Space / Lakeside. *(cd w/free 3"cd-ep; BIAS 195CDX)* **GNOSTIC CHRISTMAS EP** – Sophia / Children / Mind machine.
Nov 92. (d-cd) *(BIAS 230DCD)* **BEYOND THE WALL OF SLEEP (live)**   Belgium
– When love comes / Kill your children / Into the heart / One millionth happy customer / Dr. Adder / And you say / Tell me / She loves me / What can I do for you / March / Sophia // Angels in the sky / Honeytrap / Datakill / Too stupid to sin / Why / Nightfall / Ground / Beyond belief / Let's go to Europe / Power / Oz / Second shot / (In search of) Penny century / Something came over me / What turns you on.
Nov 93. (cd) *(BIAS 255CD)* **SEX & DEATH**
– Kneel (to the boss) / Mouth of Heaven / The war against sleep / Come out / Satisfy me / Give me what I need / Devil's advocat / You make me sick / Voices / Realm of the senseless / Frankie Teardrop / 4"33; In memoriam JC / You still make me sick.
May 94. (cd-s) *(BIAS 258CD)* **GIVE ME WHAT I NEED (mixes; looking good / original / looking bad) / YOU STILL MAKE ME FEEL SICK**
Nov 95. (cd) *(BIAS 276CD)* **WORKS 1.0 (compilation)**
– Moscow idaho / Datakill / March '86 / Power / Kill your children / One millionth happy customer (EBM mix) / Defcon 1 / (In search of) Penny century / Let's go to Europe / Nightfall (over E.C.) / Why? / She loves me / Mouth of Heaven / The war against sleep / You make me sick.

S.P.V.   not iss.

Jun 00. (cd-s) *(SPV 055-62553)* **TWICE AS GOOD (mixes; LP / Apoptygma Berzerk / Front 242) / NOTHING PERSONAL**   German
Jul 00. (cd) *(SPV 085-62522)* **WETWARE**
– V.A.L.I.S. / Twice as good / N.U.D. / Bad faith / Phoenix / Theme from "The Invisibles" / When I fall in love / My possession / Dion fortune / Never / Blood vessel / It's ok.

CATERAN

Formed: Inverness, Scotland . . . mid-80's by vocalist SANDY MacPHERSON, CAMERON FRASER, MURDO MacLEOD, KAI DAVIDSON and ANDY MILNE. Influenced by HUSKER DU and the DEAD KENNEDYS (SANDY was indeed a self-styled clone of GRANT HART and JELLO BIAFRA) backed by cod-Ska pop rhythm, they were one of the many Caledonian outfits to sign for a 'Fast Forward' cartel (i.e. 'D.D.T.'). With production credits going to Pete Haigh, The CATERAN delivered their first vinyl offering in 1986, the mini-set 'LITTLE CIRCLES', a record promoted by several gigs alongside the young PROCLAIMERS. Further album releases included 1988's 'BITE DEEPER', 1989's 'ACHE', while a support slot to GRANT HART (having recently split from HUSKER DU) kept up their Punky profile. When Grunge came on to the music scene in the early 90's, The CATERAN were in trouble, although MURDO (and initially KAI) plus a new gang of cohorts, JOYRIDERS, tried once again with the 'KING OF GASOLINE' EP in 1992. • **Covered:** TIRED OF WAITING FOR YOU (Kinks).

Album rating: LITTLE CIRCLES (*5) / BITE DEEPER (*5) / ACHE (*4)

SANDY MacPHERSON – vocals / **CAMERON FRASER** – guitar / **MURDO MacLEOD** – guitar / **KAI DAVIDSON** – bass / **ANDY MILNE** – drums

D.D.T.   not iss.

Jul 86. (m-lp) *(DISPLP 005)* **LITTLE CIRCLES**
– Belting out the truth / Who's clever now / Gracious smile / Little circles / Its your mistake, not mine / Cold comfort / Desperate planning time / Brand new refugee.
Jan 87. (7") *(DISP 006)* **LAST BIG LIE. / DIFFICULT DAYS**

CATERAN (cont)

		Vinyl Solution	not iss.
Mar 88.	(lp) (SOL 9) **BITE DEEPER**		-

– Don't like what I do / She doesn't say much / A bit put out / Small dark hand / Surplus to need / Mirror / Love scars / This is what becomes of the broken ... / Knowing what I am / Strung along.

		Imaginary	not iss.
Dec 88.	(7"ep) (MIRAGE 666) **THE BLACK ALBUM EP**		-

– Teach yourself / Tired of waiting for you.

		What Goes On	not iss.
May 89.	(lp) (GOESON 30) **ACHE**		-

– Ache / Kitten / Early old / Tina / Hateable / Cage / Love or confusion / Someone else's sun / Traffic drone / Storm 7.

Mar 90.	(12"ep) (WHATGOES 17T) **DIE TOMORROW**		-

– Die tomorrow / Virgil's way / (+2)

—— split early '91 ...

JOYRIDERS

—— **MURDO** now lead vocals, guitar / **DUNSY** (DUNSMORE) – guitar, vocals / **CRAIG SMITH** – bass; repl. DAVIDSON / **RICK HELLER** – drums

		Avalanche	not iss.
1992.	(12"ep) (AVA 002) **KING OF GASOLINE EP**		-

– King of gasoline / Overboard / Here it comes / Moving on.

		Incredible Shrinking	not iss.
1995.	(cd-s) (SHRINK 002) **DON'T ASK ME / BEST FRIEND / HOME**		-

—— after they split, DUNSY would join Human Condition band, CHICKWEED

CAT HEADS

Formed: San Francisco, California, USA ... 1985 by MARK ZANANDREA, along with SAM BABBIT, ALAN KORN and MELANIE CLARIN, all seasoned Bay Area alternative writers/musicians. Signing to 'Enigma', the quartet debuted in '87 with 'HUBBA' (produced by RAIN PARADE's MATT PIUCCI), an anarchic ragbag of rootsy retro-rock, punk and off-beat humour. Of their contemporaries, CAMPER VAN BEETHOVEN were closest in spirit and it came as little surprise when the latter outfit's DAVID LOWERY offered his production services for 1988's more focused follow-up, 'SUBMARINE'. The band virtually split in two soon after, only BABBIT and KORN remaining for one further CAT HEADS platter, 'OUR FRISCO' (1989), although (alongside newcomers BARRY HALL and JOHN STUART) MELANIE did make a guest appearance. In the mid-90's, two pairings of the original quartet surfaced, MARK and MELANIE in IT THING while MARK and SAM became the ANDROGYNAUTS; the final CAT HEADS line-up was to re-emerge as the MUDSILLS.

Album rating: HUBBA (*6) / SUBMARINE (*7) / OUR FRISCO (*5)

MARK ZANANDREA – vocals, guitar (ex-LOVE CIRCUS, ex-LEACHES) / **SAM BABBIT** – guitar (ex-OPHELIAS) / **ALAN KORN** – bass (ex-X-TAL) / **MELANIE CLARIN** – drums, vocals (also of DONNER PARTY)

		Enigma	Restless
May 87.	(lp) (ENIG 2195-1) <9-71195> **HUBBA**		

– Hangin' around / Voyeur in the balcony / I would kill for Suzy / Victim / Final letter / Hubba part 1 / Golden Gate park / Power love and pizza / Need to know / Lego down / Saved by the bottle / New white things / Lullaby.

1988.	(lp/c) <72236-1/-4> **SUBMARINE**	-	

– Little less of me / Apologize / Grass / Hallelujah dance / Alice on the radio / Postcard / Upside down / Sister Tabitha / Juggy saw dust – Gumshoe / Paradise / Bisho / Crash landing.

—— **BABBIT + KORN** recruited new members **BARRY HALL** – multi / **JOHN STUART** – drums (of FLYING COLOR) / **MELANIE** (guested) vox (she and MARK became part of IT THING, while the latter re-united with SAM in mid-90's act, ANDROGYNAUTS; SAM and ALAN were now in MUDSILLS)

		not iss.	Twitch City
1989.	(lp; as ex CAT HEADS) <001> **OUR FRISCO**	-	

C-CAT TRANCE

Formed: Nottingham, England ... 1983 by JOHN REES LEWIS and NIGEL KINGSTON STONE, actually former members of late 70's/early 80's quintet, MEDIUM MEDIUM. The latter outfit (who also included ANDY RYDER, ALLAN TURTON and soundman, GRAHAM SPINK) appeared on the 'Hicks From The Sticks' V/A compilation (in 1979) and issued a couple of singles plus a solitary album for 'Cherry Red', 'THE GLITTER HOUSE' (1981). LEWIS and STONE had already gone AWOL almost immediately after the album's completion, the pair finally releasing their C-CAT TRANCE debut 12", 'DREAMS OF LIVING', in the Spring of '84. Now into Third World funk, this outfit stuttered commercially and found it hard to claw their way out of the second division indie scene. Three albums (one a year) appeared on Red Flame outlet, 'Ink' between 1985 and 1987, although neither 'KHAMU', 'ZOUAVE' or 'PLAY MASENKO COMBO' made any lasting impression on critic or public. Their most interesting release, 'ISHTA BIL HABUL', arrived in '87, a 12"/single which found C-CAT TRANCE augmented by The St. Louis Symphony Orchestra and conducted by Statkin.

Album rating: Medium Medium: THE GLITTER HOUSE (*5) / C-Cat Trance: C-CAT TRANCE mini (*4) / KHAMU (*4) / ZOUAVE (*4) / PLAY MASENKO COMBO (*4)

MEDIUM MEDIUM

JOHN LEWIS – saxophones, horns, vocals / **ANDY RYDER** – guitar, vocals / **ALLAN TURTON** – bass / **NIGEL STONE** – drums / **GRAHAM SPINK** – sound

		Apt	not iss.
Nov 78.	(7") (SAP 01) **THEM OR US. / FREEZE**		-

		Cherry Red	Cachalot
Feb 81.	(7") (CHERRY 18) **HUNGRY, SO ANGRY. / NADSAT DREAM**		-
Aug 81.	(12"ep) <BIG 1> **HUNGRY, SO ANGRY / HUNGRY, SO ANGRY (version). / FURTHER THAN FUNK DREAM / NADSAT DREAM**	-	
Oct 81.	(lp) (BRED 19) <CA 127> **THE GLITTER HOUSE**		Nov81

– Hungry, so angry / Nadsat dream / The glitter house / Guru maharaja / Further than funk dream / Nice or monsters / That Haiku.

—— **STEVE HARVEY** – drums, percussion; repl. STONE (see below)

—— **LES BARRETT** – keyboards; repl. SPINK + LEWIS (see below)

—— this quartet had a CD Dutch release, 'LIVE IN HOLLAND', issued in '88

– compilations, etc. –

Apr 01.	(cd) Cherry Red; (CDMRED 182) **HUNGRY, SO ANGRY**		-

– Hungry, so angry / Nadsat dream / 7th floor / Serbian village / Hidden fears / Further than funk dream / Splendid isolation / You've got me dangling on a string / Stir me up / Full of secrecy / Praying / Them or me / Frightened child / Guru maharaja / The glitter house / Hungry, so angry (video).

C-CAT TRANCE

—— **JOHN REES LEWIS** – saxophone, vocals, etc / **NIGEL KINGSTON STONE** – drums, percussion

		Red Flame	not iss.
1983.	(m-lp) (RFM 19) **C-CAT TRANCE**		-

– Hypnotised / My tattoo / Railway magazine / Let me sleep / Untitled / Dangling on a string.

		Ink	not iss.
Mar 84.	(12") (INK12-3) **DREAMS OF LIVING. / DANGLING ON A STRING**		-
Apr 85.	(12") (INK12-6) **SHE STEALS CARS. / RATTLING GHOSTS**		-
May 85.	(lp) (INKLP 6) **KHAMU (SHE SLEEP WALKS)**		-

– Puritanes / Barefoot doctor / The new Hassan / (Screaming) To be with you / Rattling ghosts / The old man / Simple Helen / Miss manners. (cd-iss. Oct93 as 'LES INVISIBLES'; INKCD 6)

—— added 3 members (unknown)

May 86.	(12") (INK12-20) **SHAKE THE MIND (mixes)**		-
Oct 86.	(12"m) (INK12-23) **SCREAMING (TO BE WITH YOU) (Volta Rouge mix). / LET ME SLEEP / DANCING ON A STRING (instrumental)**		-
Nov 86.	(lp) (INKLP 20) **ZOUAVE**		-

– Wind howl / Betty / He's crazy / Taksim / Ishta Bil Habul / If you steal / Take me to the beach / You've lost that loving feeling / Shake the mind. (cd-iss. Jun88; INKCD 20)

Apr 87.	(12"ep) (INK12-27) **ISHTA BIL HABUL (CREAM GALORE!). / ('A'dance mix) / ('A'edit)**		-
Dec 87.	(lp) (INKLP 33) **PLAY MASENKO COMBO**		-

– Dalbouka / They made them up / She ever does / Jamais / I looked for you / Cold / Two words / My tattoo / Railway magazine / Let me sleep / Untitled / Dangling on a string. (cd-iss. Jun88; INKCD 33)

Sep 88.	(12") (INK12-35) **YINNIYA (mixes)**		-

—— split in the late 80's

CELIBATE RIFLES

Formed: Sydney, Australia ... New Years Day 1982 by DAVE MORRIS and KENT STEEDMAN alongside DAMIEN LOVELOCK, PAUL DARROCH and PHIL JACQUET. Following in the musclebound, turbo R&B charged tradition of Aussie punks like RADIO BIRDMAN and The SAINTS, The CELIBATE RIFLES fired their initial vinyl shots on domestic label, 'Hot'. First up was an EP, 'BUT JACQUES, THE FISH?', followed by a debut album, 'SIDEROXYLON' (1983) and an eponymous follow-up in '84. By the release of the band's first UK-available long player, the cheerily titled 'THE TURGID MIASMA OF EXISTENCE' (1986), DARROCH had been killed in a car accident and the record was dedicated to his memory; prior to his untimely death DARROCH had formed EASTERN DARK, who released one obscure EP, 'LONG LIVE THE NEW FLESH'. 'THE TURGID MIASMA OF EXISTENCE' found the 'RIFLES broadening their musical palate while lyrically, an environmento-political bent was increasingly evident alongside the trademark caustic humour. Recorded at New York's infamous CBGB's, 'KISS KISS BANG BANG' was a raucous blast of Sydney's finest live in the raw and served as their first release to be distributed in the USA (on 'Homestead'). Although they also supported their heroes, The RAMONES, on the Stateside jaunt, a hostile reaction from the music press saw them concentrate future efforts on their Antipodean homeland. The latter set gained a UK release on the 'What Goes On' label, also home to their final release of the 80's, the smoking 'ROMAN BEACH PARTY'. By the turn of the decade, JIM LEONE had replaced RUDI (who in turn had previously replaced COUVRET) and PAUL LARSEN came in for the departing JACQUET, the new look rhythm section maintaining the high velocity of old on 1990's uncompromising 'BLIND EAR' album. Their most politically pointed and musically mature work to date, the record was nevertheless their last album to gain a release in America. Punk may have been long dead but the Aussie bruisers were dedicated to guarding the flame, signing a new deal with 'Hot' and continuing to release albums into the 90's, the last for some time being 1996's acoustic 'ON THE QUIET'. After family commitments took over the day-to-day slog of playing rock'n'roll, the 'RIFLES took their own time to come up with a follow-up. 2001's long-awaited 'A MID-STREAM OF CONSCIOUSNESS', was to the bulk of their fanbase, a return to basics, punk-rock basics that is, with LOVELOCK's laconic drawl evident on numbers such as 'I SHOULDA' and 'THE PADDO SHARPS'. • **Covers:** CITY OF FUN (Only Ones) / BURN MY EYE (Radio Birdman) / DANCING BAREFOOT (Patti Smith) / BABY PLEASE DON'T GO (Big Joe Williams) / 2000 LIGHT YEARS FROM HOME + CHILD OF THE MOON (Rolling Stones) / I WILL DARE (Replacements) / JOURNEY BY SLEDGE (Visitors) / etc.

Album rating: SIDEROXYLON (*6) / THE CELIBATE RIFLES (aka '5 LANGUAGES') (*6) / QUINTESSENTIALLY YOURS compilation (*5) / THE TURGID MIASMA OF EXISTENCE (*7) / MINA MINA MINA compilation (*5) / KISS KISS BANG BANG (*5) / ROMAN BEACH PARTY (*7) / BLIND EAR (*7) / PLATTERS DU JOUR collection (*6) / HEAVEN ON A STICK (*6) / YIZGARNNOFF (*6) / SOFA compilation (*6) / SPACEMAN IN A SATIN SUIT (*7) / ON THE QUIET (*5) / A MID-STREAM OF CONSCIOUSNESS (*6)

DAMIEN LOVELOCK – vocals / **DAVE MORRIS** – guitar / **KENT STEEDMAN** – guitar / **PAUL DARROCH** – bass / **PHIL JACQUET** – drums

	Custom	not iss.
Nov 82. (12"ep) *(HOT 702)* **BUT JACQUES, THE FISH?**	-	- Austra
(re-iss. Mar83 on 'Hot'; HOT 702)		
	Hot	not iss.
Apr 83. (lp) *(HOT 1001)* **SIDEROXYLON**	-	- Austra

– Killing time / Society / Tick tock / Anthem / Back on the corner / You're gonna cry / Where do I go / Ice blue / Gimme gimme gimme / God squad. *(cd-iss. Feb93; HOR 1001CD)*

Apr 84. (lp) *(HOT 1007)* **THE CELIBATE RIFLES** (aka '5 LANGUAGES') – - Austra
 – Wild desire / Kiss me deadly / Pretty colours / Back in the red / Darlinghurst confidential / Thank you America / Rainforest / Netherworld / Electric snake river. *(cd-iss. Feb93; HOT 1007CD)*

--- **MICHAEL COUVRET** – bass; repl. DARROCH who formed EASTERN DARK (however, he died in a car crash, 1986)

Jun 86. (lp) *(HOT 1024)* **THE TURGID MIASMA OF EXISTENCE** – -
 – Bill Bonney regrets / Conflict of instinct / Temper temper Mr. Kemper / Sentinel / Some kind of feeling / Glasshouse / Sometimes / No sign / Eddie / J.N.S. / New mistakes. *(w/ free 7")* – Eddie / Ice blue / Thank you America. *(cd-iss. Feb93; HOT 1024CD)*

	Shigaku	not iss.
Apr 87. (7") *(SHIGS 2)* **PRETTY PICTURES. / KENT THEME**	-	-
	What Goes On	Homestead
Apr 87. (lp) *(GOES ON 8)* **KISS KISS BANG BANG** (live at the CBGB's, New York City on 12th July 1986)	-	-

– Back in the red / Temper temper / J.N.S. / Pretty colours / Netherworld / Some kinda feeling / New mistakes / Carmine vatelly (N.Y.N.Y.C.) / City of fun / Conflict of instinct / Sometimes / Burn my eye / S.O.S. *(cd-iss. Feb93 & Jan01 on 'Hot'; HOT 1029CD)*

--- **RUDY MORABITO** – bass; repl. COUVRET
--- **PAUL LARSEN** – drums; repl. JACQUET

	Hot	not iss.
Oct 87. (lp) *(HOT 1030)* **ROMAN BEACH PARTY**	-	-

– Jesus on TV / The more things change / Downtown / Oceanshore / Circle sun / A word about Jones / Strange day, stranger nights / (It's such a) Wonderful life / I still see you / Invisible man / Frank Hyde (slight return). *(cd-iss. Feb93; HOT 1030CD)*

Jul 88. (12"ep) *(HOT12-33)* **DANCING BAREFOOT / JESUS ON TV** (live) / (+2) – -

--- **JIM LEONE** – bass, percussion, vocals; repl. RUDY

	Rattlesnake	True Tone-EMI
Aug 90. (cd) *(RAT 503)* **BLIND EAR**	-	Nov89

– Johnny / World keeps turning / Electravision mantra / Dial om / Wonderful life '88 / Sean O'Farrell / Belfast / Cycle / They're killing us all (to make the world safe) / O salvation / Fish and trees. *(re-iss. Oct94 on 'Hot'; HOT 1046CD)*

--- **NIK REITH** – drums; repl. LARSEN

	Hot	not iss.
Jul 92. (cd) *(HOT 1038CD)* **HEAVEN ON A STICK**	-	-

– Light of life / Cold wind / Happy house / Excommunication / S&M TV / Contemplating R.D. Laing (and the bird of paradise) / G.D. absolutely / Dream of night / Groovin' in the land of love / Electric flowers / Compared to what / Outside my window / Wild child. *(re-iss. Aug95; same)*

Aug 93. (cd) *(HOT 1041CD)* **YIZGARNNOFF** – -
 – Brickin' around / A word about Jones / Cycle / Downtown (street radio mix) / Johnny / Happy house / Dream of night / Groovin' in the land of love / S&M TV / Electravision mantra / 2000 light years from home / The more things change / Tubular greens / Invisible man / Glasshouse / O salvation / Oceanshore / Baby please don't go. *(re-iss. Aug95; same)*

May 94. (cd) *(HOT 1047CD)* **SPACEMAN IN A SATIN SUIT** – -
 – Spirits / Kev the head / Brickin' around / Living what I dream / City of hope / Seams / Big world / Whatever you want / Kathy says / Diamond sky / Cuttin' it fine / This gift / Let's do it again / Spaceman in a satin suit. *(re-iss. Apr96; same)*

Sep 96. (cd) *(HOT 1067CD)* **ON THE QUIET** (acoustic) – -
 – Netherworld / Back on the corner / Sentinel / Electric flowers / This gift / No sign / Electric snake river / Jesus on TV / Boys (what did the detectives say) / Astral wally / Hot generation / Hindu gods of love. *(lp-iss.Mar97 on 'Munster'; MR 115)*

	Oracle	Real-o-mind
Jul 01. (cd) *(ODCD 0303)* <005> **A MID-STREAM OF CONSCIOUSNESS**	-	2002

– Storm / The paddo sharps / I shoulda / G's gone / Child of mine / Wake up / Hammer (consolation prizes) / Dark city / Me and Slick and Willie / Talk back saviour / Tripping at the mall (i saw your cousin, she was . . .). *(some cd's+=)* – Child of the Moon / I will dare / Journey by sledge.

--- (2001) **MORRIS, LOVELOCK + STEEDMAN** brought back **COUVRET + LARSEN**

– compilations, etc. –

Jul 85. (m-lp) *What Goes On; (RIFLE 1)* **QUINTESSENTIALLY YOURS** – -
 – Let's get married / 24 hours / Tubular greens / This week / Killing time / Gonna cry / Ice blue / God squad.

Aug 86. (lp) *What Goes On; (GOES ON 5)* **MINA MINA MINA** – -
 – Back in the red / Pretty colours / Tick tock / Kiss me deadly / Rainforest / Back on the corner / Wild desire / Netherworld / Darlinghurst confidential / Where do I go / Thank you America / Gimme gimme gimme.

Dec 90. (cd) *Rattlesnake; (<RAT 504>)* **PLATTERS DU JOUR** – -
 – Kent's theme / Let's get married / 24 hours (S.O.S.) / Tubular greens / Pretty pictures / Out in the west again / Summer holiday blues / Merry xmas blues / Wild desire / I'm waiting for the man / Sometimes / E=Mc2 / Six days on the road / Groupie girl / Eddie (acoustic version) / Ice blue / Thank you America / Back in the red / Rain forest / Dancing barefoot / Jesus on TV / The more things change / Junk. *(cd re-iss. Oct94 on 'Hot'; HOT 1033/34CD)*

Jan 94. (cd) *Hot; (HOT 1043CD)* **SOFA** – -
 – Killing time / Wild desire / Sometimes / Bill Bonney regrets / Jesus on T.V. / Johnny / Electravision mantra / Wonderful life / More things change / Oceanshore / New mistakes / Back in the red / Ice blue / This week / Netherworld / Glasshouse / Frank Hyde (slight return) / Darlinghurst confidential / Pretty pictures / Gonna cry. *(re-iss. Aug95; same)*

--- In 1988, DAMIEN LOVELOCK (with some CELIBATE's and members of the band, The CHURCH – RICHARD PLOOG + PETER KOPPES) released a 'Hot' solo set, 'IT'S A WIG, WIG, WIG, WIG WORLD', while two years later, CRENT (i.e. KENT STEEDMAN + another) issued an eponymous album for 'Waterfront'.

Guy CHADWICK (see under ⇒ HOUSE OF LOVE)

Ken CHAMBERS (see under ⇒ MOVING TARGETS)

CHAMELEONS

Formed: Middleton, North Manchester, England … 1981 by MARK BURGESS, DAVE FIELDING and REG SMITHIES. The latter two, with drummer CHRIS SEDDON, had been part of The YEARS, who released one single, 'COME DANCING' / 'RED CHEVY' / 'DON'T LEAVE' on their own 'Tuff Going' label. As The CHAMELEONS, they sent a demo to Radio One DJ, John Peel, who was impressed enough to give them a session, the band's line-up now completed by JOHN LEVER. After a brief, disastrous spell with 'Epic' in 1982, they signed to 'Virgin' subsidiary, 'Statik'. Filling the huge gap left by the demise of TEARDROP EXPLODES, The CHAMELEONS championed a distinctive brand of power rock characterised by subtle shadings of mood and atmosphere. Oft sighted by many as one of the most criminally ignored bands in Manchester's chequered musical history, their acclaimed debut album, 'THE SCRIPT OF THE BRIDGE' (1983) went largely unnoticed despite glowing reviews for the near hour long set. A record that everyone should have in their collection, it contained the epic 'SECOND SKIN', the best song JULIAN COPE never wrote (and that's high praise indeed!). A belated follow-up, 'WHAT DOES ANYTHING MEAN? BASICALLY' (1985), was almost as strong and, with further critical plaudits, the album made the lower reaches of the chart. Their major break came later in the year, when new manager and 5th member TONY FLETCHER encouraged David Geffen to sign them to his label. Nevertheless, even major label US muscle couldn't help the band break the Top 40, 'SWAMP THING' and 'TEARS' highlights of a slightly patchy set, 'STRANGE TIMES' (1986). More grief was to follow when FLETCHER died of a heart attack the following year, the band finally throwing in the towel soon after. Various spin-off projects (including The SUN AND THE MOON and The REEGS) met with little success outside of their loyal fanbase. The CHAMELEONS (without LEVER) finally reunited in 2000, an acoustic set, 'STRIP' and their first proper studio album, 'WHY CALL IT ANYTHING?' (2001) – produced by DAVE ALLEN – unmistakable evidence to why thousands of fans wanted them out in the open again. While the acoustic set concentrated on past glories such as 'LESS THAN HUMAN' and 'PARADISO', the '…ANYTHING?' album adapted a deeper, melancholic and folk-structured charm, witnessed on tracks such as 'LUFTHANSA', 'ALL AROUND' and 'DANGEROUS LAND'; a second live reunion work, 'LIVE AT THE ACADEMY', was issued in 2002. • **Songwriters:** All penned by band, except JOHN, I'M ONLY DANCING + MOONAGE DAYDREAM (Bowie) / TOMORROW NEVER KNOWS (Beatles) / SPLITTING IN TWO (Alternative TV). REEGS covered; SEE MY FRIENDS (Kinks) / As The Three Imaginary Boys; THE LAST TIME (Rolling Stones). MARK BURGESS covered YOU ONLY LIVE TWICE (John Barry) / FACADES (Philip Glass) / SOMETHING FOR THE GIRL WITH EVERYTHING + MOON OVER KENTUCKY (Sparks).

Album rating: THE SCRIPT OF THE BRIDGE (*9) / WHAT DOES ANYTHING MEAN? BASICALLY (*6) / STRANGE TIMES (*7) / posthumous collections: THE FAN AND THE BELLOWS (*6) / TRIPPING DOGS (*5) / PEEL SESSIONS (*6) / HERE TODAY… COME TOMORROW (*5) / LIVE IN TORONTO (*6) / THE RADIO 1 EVENING SHOW SESSIONS (*5) / FREE TRADE HALL REHEARSAL (*4) / DALI'S PICTURE (*4) / NORTHERN SONGS (*5) / LIVE SHREDS (*5) / RETURN OF THE ROUGHNECKS – THE BEST OF THE CHAMELEONS (*8) / LIVE AT THE GALLERY CLUB, 1982 (*4) / reformed: STRIP (*6) / WHY CALL IT ANYTHING (*6) / LIVE AT THE ACADEMY (*5) / THIS NEVER ENDING NOW (*5) / Sun And The Moon: THE SUN AND THE MOON (*6) / Reegs: RETURN OF THE SEA MONKEYS (*6) / ROCK THE MAGIC ROCK (*6) / Mark Burgess: ZIMA JUNCTION (*6) / MANCHESTER, 1993 (*6) / SPRING BLOOMS TRA-LA-LA (*7) / PARADYNING (*6)

CHAMELEONS (cont)

MARK 'Birdy' BURGESS – vocals, bass (ex-CLICHES) / **DAVE FIELDING** – guitar, strings (ex-YEARS) / **REG SMITHIES** – guitar (ex-YEARS) / **JOHN LEVER** – drums, percussion (ex-POLITICIANS) repl. BRIAN SCHOFIELD

Epic / not iss.

Mar 82. (7") (EPCA 2210) **IN SHREDS. / LESS THAN HUMAN**

―― JOHN LEVER was repl. for a year by MARTIN JACKSON (ex-MAGAZINE)

Statik / not iss.

Feb 83. (7") (STAT 20) **AS HIGH AS YOU CAN GO. / PLEASURE AND PAIN**
(12"+=) (STAT 20-12) – Paper tigers.
Jun 83. (7") (TAK 6) **A PERSON ISN'T SAFE ANYWHERE THESE DAYS. / THURSDAY'S CHILD**
(12"+=) (TAK 6-12) – Prisoners of the sun.
Aug 83. (lp,pic-lp/c) (STAT LP/C 17) **SCRIPT OF THE BRIDGE**
– Don't fall / Here today / Monkeyland / Second skin / Up the down escalator / Less than human / Pleasure and pain / Thursday's child / As high as you can go / A person isn't safe anywhere these days / Paper tigers / View from a hill. (cd+=) – In shreds / Nostalgia. (cd-iss. Feb86; SCDT 17) (cd re-iss. Jun89; CDST 017) (cd re-iss. Jul95 on 'Dead Dead Good'; GOODCD 6)
Nov 83. (7") (TAK 11) **UP THE DOWN ESCALATOR. / MONKEYLAND** – / – German
(12"+=) (TAK 11-12) – Prisoners of the sun.
Feb 85. (7") (TAK 29) **IN SHREDS (live). / NOSTALGIA (live)**
(12"+=) (TAK 29-12) – Less than human (live).

―― added on stage ALISTAIR LEWTWAITE – keyboards, but he was replaced by ANDY CLEGG – keyboards (ex-MUSIC FOR ABORIGINES)

May 85. (lp/c) (STAT LP/C 22) **WHAT DOES ANYTHING MEAN? BASICALLY** 60 / –
– Silence, sea and sky / Perfume garden / Intrigue in Tangiers / Return of the roughnecks / Singing rule Britannia (while the walls close in) / On the beach / Looking inwardly / One flesh / Home is where the heart is / P.S. goodbye. (cd-iss. Feb86 +=; CDST 22) – In shreds / Nostalgia. (cd re-iss. Jul95 on 'Dead Dead Good'; GOODCD 7)
Aug 85. (7") (TAK 35) **SINGING RULE BRITTANIA (WHILE THE WALLS CLOSE IN). / SINGING RULE BRITTANIA (WHILE THE WALLS CLOSE IN) (Radio 1 'Saturday Live' session)**
(12"+=) (TAK 35-12) – Pleasure and pain (Radio 1 version).

Geffen / Geffen

Jun 86. (7") (GEF 4) **TEARS. / PARADISO**
(w/ free 7") (SAM 287) – SWAMP THING. / INSIDE OUT
(12"+=) (GEF 4T) – Inside out.
Sep 86. (lp/c) (<9 24119-1/-4>) **STRANGE TIMES** 44 / –
– Mad Jack / Caution / Soul in isolation / Swamp thing / Time – The end of time / Seriocity / In answer / Childhood / I'll remember / Tears. (cd-iss. Mar87; 924119-2) <US-iss.lp w/ free m-lp> – Tears (full arrangement) / Paradiso / Inside out / Ever after / John, I'm only dancing / Tomorrow never knows. (re-iss. d-cd Jul93; GFLDD 19207)
Sep 86. (7") (GEF 10) **SWAMP THING. / JOHN, I'M ONLY DANCING**
(12"+=) (GEF 10T) – Tears (original).

―― split late '86, after manager TONY FLETCHER died of a heart attack. MARK and JOHN formed The SUN AND THE MOON with ANDY CLEGG and ANDY WHITAKER. In 1993, MARK BURGESS formed his SONS OF GOD. FIELDING and SMITHIES formed The REEGS in '88.

SUN AND THE MOON

BURGESS + LEVER / + ANDY WHITAKER – keyboards (ex-MUSIC FOR ABORIGINES) / ANDY CLEGG – guitar (ex-MUSIC FOR ABORIGINES)

Geffen / Geffen

May 88. (lp/c/cd) (924 182-1/-4/-2) <24182> **THE SUN AND THE MOON**
– The speed of life / Death of imagination / Peace in our time / A matter of conscience / Dolphin / House on fire / The price of grain / Limbo-land / A picture of England / This passionate breed.
Jun 88. (7") (GEF 39-7) **THE SPEED OF LIFE. / DEATH OF IMAGINATION**
(12"+=) (GEF 39-12) – The boy who sees everything / I love you, you bastard.

Midnight Music / not iss.

Nov 88. (12"ep/cd-ep) (DONG 44/+CD) **ALIVE; NOT DEAD EP**
– Adam's song / C'est la vie / Arabs and Americans / Elected.

―― In 1991, LEVER, CLEGG + WHITAKER with ATKINSON formed WEAVEWORLD who released a 12"; DAVY JONES. / OUT AND DOWN / PATHETICAL TWAT for 'Sugarpussy'.

MARK BURGESS & THE SONS OF GOD

with BRIAN GLANCY

Imaginary / Pivot

Jul 93. (cd/lp) (ILLCD/ILLUSION 044) <003> **ZIMA JUNCTION** / May94
– World on fire / Waiting for a friend / Refugees / The great adventure / Beat the boat / When harmony comes / Our soul, dead soul, brother and fool / Happy new life / Up on the hill / Fascades / You only live twice.

―― added YVES ALTANA – guitar / KAREN LEATHEM – bass (of WONKY ALICE) / NEIL THIN – guitar (of THIN MEN)

Oct 94. (cd) <004> **MANCHESTER, 1993 (live)** – / –
– Swamp thing / A person isn't safe these days / Perfume garden / Soul in isolation / Paradiso / Caution / Refugees / Second skin / Happy new life / Don't fall.

Indigo / not iss.

Nov 94. (d-cd) (INDIGO 1174-2) **SPRING BLOOMS TRA-LA-LA (live)**
– The healer / Time / Soul in isolation / Perfume garden / Monkeyland / In shreds / Caution / World on fire / Tears / A person isn't safe anywhere these days / Happy new life / Second skin / Don't fall. (re-iss. Oct96; same)

MARK BURGESS & YVES ALTANA

Dead Dead Good / not iss.

Aug 95. (7") (GOOD 32) **SIN. / HOLLIN HIGH**
(cd-s+=) (GOOD 32CD) – Moon over Kentucky.
Sep 95. (7") (GOOD 33) **ALWAYS WANT. / STEPHANIE WEAVES**
(cd-s+=) (GOOD 33CD) – Something for the girl with everything.
Oct 95. (cd/lp) (GOOD CD/LP 8) **PARADYNING**
– Sin / Always went / Adrian be / Silver / Money won't save our soul / You opened my mind (then the acid kicked in) / Inhaling / World without end / Hi Joe / Stop talking.

REEGS

FIELDING + SMITHIES

Imaginary / not iss.

Apr 89. (12") (MIRAGE 006) **SEE MY FRIENDS. / IS THERE A MOTHER-IN-LAW IN THE CLUB / THIS SAVAGE GARDEN**
Aug 90. (12") (MIRAGE 012) **CHORUS OF THE LOST. / POND LIFE / START TO SEE (instrumental)**

―― added drum machine + GARY LAVERY – vocals

Jul 91. (cd/c/lp) (ILLCD/ILLCAS/ILLUSION 029) **RETURN OF THE SEA MONKEYS**
– See my friends / Is there a mother-in-law in the club / This savage garden / Chorus of the lost / Pond life / Start to see / These days / Turn it up / All tomorrow's parties.
Oct 93. (cd) (ILLCD 045) **ROCK THE MAGIC ROCK**
– JJ 180 / The blind denial / Goodbye world / The dream police / The nasty side / The dolphin's enemy / In disbelief / Oil and water / Running to a standstill / The nasty side (instrumental).

Columbus / not iss.

Jul 97. (cd-s) (THEMUS 001) **AS YOU LEAVE / JJ 180 / OUTER BODY EXPERIENCE**
Nov 97. (cd-s) (THEMUS 002) **YOU TOLD ME BEFORE / IS THERE A MOTHER-IN-LAW IN THE CLUB? / THE NASTYSIDE**

―― split . . . FIELDING became producer notably for The INSPIRAL CARPETS

CHAMELEONS

―― (or in the States, THE CHAMELEONS UK), re-formed with BURGESS, FIELDING + SMITHIES

Paradiso / not iss.

Jul 00. (cd) (PARADISOCD 01) **STRIP (live acoustic)**
– Less than human / Nathan's phase / Here today / Soul in isolation / Pleasure and pain / Paradiso / Caution / On the beach / Road to San Remo / Indian. (lp-iss.Mar01; PARADISOLP 01)

―― added the returning JOHN LEVER

Artful / Cleopatra

Jul 01. (cd) (ARTFULCD 39) <1195> **WHY CALL IT ANYTHING** / 2002
– Shades / Anyone alive? / Indiana / Lufthansa / Truth isn't truth anymore / All around / Dangerous land / Music in the womb / Miracles and wonders / Are you still there?

Paradiso / not iss.

Apr 02. (cd) (PARADISOCD 02) **LIVE AT THE ACADEMY (live)**
– A person isn't safe anywhere these days / Pleasure and pain / Perfume garden / Anyone alive? / Indiana / Caution / Up the down escalator / Lufthansa / Dangerous land / Second skin / Miracles and wonders / Shades / Swamp thing / Monkeyland / Splitting in two.
Sep 02. (cd) (PARADISOCD 03) **THIS NEVER ENDING NOW (live)**
– The fan and the bellows / Tears / Intrigue in Tangiers / Is it any wonder? / Seriocity / Swamp thing / All around / Second skin / Home is where the heart is / Miracles and wonders / View from a hill / Moonage daydream.

– compilations, others, etc. –

Mar 86. (ltd-lp) Hybrid; (CHAMLP 1) **THE FAN AND THE BELLOWS**
(most recorded 1981)
– The fan and the bellows / Nostalgia / Less than human / In shreds / Prisoners of the Sun / Turn to the vices / Nathan's phase / Endlessly falling / Everyday I'm crucified / Endlessly falling / Nathan's phase. <US-iss.1989 on 'Caroline' lp/cd; CAROL 1332/+CD> (cd-iss. Sep96 on 'Dead Dead Good'; GOODCD 9)
Oct 90. (cd-ep; w-drawn) Glass Pyramid; (EMC 1) **TONY FLETCHER WALKED ON WATER . . . LA LA LA LA LA – LA LA – LA LA** – / –
– Is it any wonder / Free for all / The healer / Denims and curls. (finally issued 1994) (re-iss. May97 on 'Dead Dead Good'; GOOD 39CD)
Oct 90. (cd/lp) Glass Pyramid; (CD+/EMC 2) **TRIPPING DOGS**
– Singing rule Britania / A person isn't safe / Here today / Pleasure and the pain / Bobby Moore's wine / Less than human / Thursday's child / In answer / Return of the roughnecks / Second skin / One flesh / Home is where the heart is.
Nov 90. (cd/lp) Strange Fruit; (SFR CD/LP 114) / Dutch East India; <DEI 8114-2> **PEEL SESSIONS** / 1991
– The fan & the bellows / Here today / Looking inwardly / Things I wish I'd said / Don't fall / Nostalgia / Second skin / Perfume garden / Dust to dust – Return of the roughnecks / One flesh / Intrigue in Tangiers / P.S. goodbye.
Jun 92. (cd/c/lp) Imaginary; (ILLCD/ILLCASS/ILLUSION 035) **HERE TODAY . . . GONE TOMORROW**
– String quartet / Home is where the heart is / In answer / Bobby Moore's wine / Sally / In shreds / Nathan's phase / Up the down escalator / On the beach / Dear dead days / Things I wish I'd said / String quartet.
Jun 92. (cd/c/lp) Imaginary; (ILLCD/ILLCASS/ILLUSION 036) **LIVE IN TORONTO (live '87)**
– Swamp thing / A person isn't safe anywhere these days / Monkeyland / Pleasure and pain / Singing rule Brittania (while the walls close in) / In shreds / Less than human / Paradiso / Home is where the heart is / Soul in isolation / Second skin / Caution / Splitting in two.
Jun 92. (d-cd/d-lp) Imaginary; (ILLCD/ILLUSION 037) **HERE TODAY . . . GONE TOMORROW / LIVE IN TORONTO**
Jan 93. (cd) Nighttracks; (cdnt 001) **THE RADIO 1 EVENING SHOW SESSIONS**
– Thursday's child / Pleasure and pain / Monkeyland / Singing rule Brittania / On the beach / View from a hill / Nathan's phase / Up the down escalator / Home is where the heart is / View from a hill.

Feb 93. (pic-cd) *Imaginary; (ILLCD 039P)* **FREE TRADE HALL REHEARSAL (live)**
– Singing rule Britannia (while the walls close in) / A person isn't safe anywhere these days / Here today / Pleasure and pain / Bobby Moore's wine / Less than human / Thursday's child / In answer / Return of the roughnecks / Second skin / One flesh / Home is where the heart is / Tomorrow never knows.

May 93. (cd/lp) *Imaginary; (ILLCD/ILLUSION 041)* **DALI'S PICTURE**
– Everyday and crucified / Monkeyland / Dreams in celluloid / Love is / The fan, the bellows / Looking inwardly / Dali's picture / Nostalgia / Less than human / Things I wish I'd said. *(d-cd; with free-cd; ILLCD 042)* **LIVE IN BERLIN** – Less than human / Paper tigers / Monkeyland / Thursday's child / Second skin / Pleasure and pain / Singing rule Britannia / Perfume garden / One flesh / In shreds / Splitting in two.

Nov 94. (cd) *Bone Idol; (BONE 001L)* **NORTHERN SONGS**
– Up the down escalator / On the beach / In shreds / Monkeyland / Looking inwardly / Second skin / Home is where the heart is / Dreams in celluloid / Less than human / Is it any wonder / Free for all / The healer / Denims and curls.

Apr 96. (cd) *Cleopatra; <CLP 9722-2>* **LIVE SHREDS (live 1983 . . .)**
– Paper tigers / Pleasure and pain / Men of steel / Years ago / In shreds / Don't fall / Second skin / Up the down escalator / Monkeyland / As high as you can go.

May 97. (cd) *Dead Dead Good; (GOODCD 12)* **RETURN OF THE ROUGHNECKS – THE BEST OF THE CHAMELEONS**
– Silence / Sea and sky / Swamp thing / In shreds / Home is where the heart is / A person isn't safe anywhere these days / Mad Jack / Don't fall / Caution / Second skin / Perfume garden / Tears (original) / Monkeyland / Nostalgia / View from a hill. *(re-iss. Oct99 d-cd; GOODCD 12X)* – TONY FLETCHER WALKED ON WATER tracks

Feb 99. (cd) *Visionary; (VICD 007) / Cleopatra; <263>* **LIVE AT THE GALLERY CLUB 1982 (live)** May 98
– Paper tigers / Nathan's phase / Don't fall / Pleasure & pain / Here today / In shreds / Up the down escalator / Second skin / Monkeyland / As high as you can go / Things I wish I'd said / A view from a hill. *(re-iss. Oct01 on 'Cherry Red'; CDMRED 198)*

CHARLOTTES

Formed: Huntingdon, Cambridgeshire, England . . . 1988 originally as The GIANT POLAR BEARS by PETRA RODDIS, DAVID WADE, GRAHAM GARGIULO and SIMON SCOTT. Another into the shoegaze faze around at the turn of the 80's/90's (i.e. MY BLOODY VALENTINE, LUSH and BLEACH), The CHARLOTTES with their fey singer PETRA down to their power-force drummer SIMON, were bubbling under the premier division of indie-pop at the time. After a breezy single, 'ARE YOU HAPPY NOW?', the willowy quartet delivered their debut long-player, 'LOVEHAPPY', in 1989. Subsequently signing to 'Cherry Red' records, the band made one more attempt at breaking through via sophomore set, 'THINGS COME APART' (1991), an embracing, blissful record that opened with their previous single, 'LIAR' (the B-side, 'VENUS' was a Shocking Blue cover). SIMON went on to have greater success as a member of SLOWDIVE. • **Note:** not the same group as another more modern act on 'Phantom' records.
Album rating: LOVEHAPPY (*6) / THINGS COME APART (*6)

PETRA RODDIS – vocals / **GRAHAM GARGIULO** – guitar / **DAVID WADE** – bass / **SIMON SCOTT** – drums

Molesworth not iss.
Oct 88. (7") *(HUNTS 5)* **ARE YOU HAPPY NOW? / HOW CAN YOU SAY**

Subway Org not iss.
Jul 89. (lp) *(SUBORG 12)* **LOVE HAPPY**
– Are you happy now / Cold / Keep me down / Stubborn / See the danger shine / Everything to me / In my hair / Lovehappy.
Apr 90. (12"ep) *(SUBWAY 27T)* **LOVE IN THE EMPTINESS**
– Love in the emptiness / Be my release / Could there ever be.

Cherry Red not iss.
Nov 90. (12"ep) *(12CHERRY 113)* **LIAR. / BLUE / VENUS**
(cd-ep+=) *(CDCHERRY 113)* – See me feel.
Mar 91. (cd/lp) *(CD+/BRED 92)* **THINGS COME APART**
– Liar / Prayer song / See me feel / By my side / Mad girl's love song / Beautify / Love in the emptiness / We're going wrong. *(cd+=)* – Blue / Venus.

— split after above; SCOTT joined SLOWDIVE (and later INNER SLEEVE), GRAHAM later formed BAREFOOT CONTESSA

Paul CHASTAIN
(see under ⇒ VELVET CRUSH; 90's section)

CHE (see under ⇒ MODERN EON)

CHEAP (see under ⇒ ADVERTS; 70's section)

CHEMICAL PEOPLE

Formed: Los Angeles, California, USA . . . mid-80's by DAVE NAZWORTHY, ED ULRIK, JAIME PINA and BLAIR JOBE, the latter bailing out prior to the recording of their 1988 debut set, 'SO SEXIST!'; he however, did contribute several of the songs. These porn-obsessed alternative/pop rockers had the output and background to compete with other stalwarts of their genre, although they unfortunately took a sabbatical just when the mainstream record-buying public began to take an interest in skatepark-favoured punk-pop music. CP's aforementioned debut release established their musical kudos, as well as forefronting a major theme in their work-porn; of the hardcore variety. With NAZWORTHY now on vocals, the trio released their second full-length outing, 'TEN-FOLD HATE' (1989), which again showed them wearing their skin-flick passions on their sleeves, or more accurately, album sleeve, which featured a photo of famed blue-movie star, Taija Rae. The following year saw the release of a third set, 'THE RIGHT THING', notable for the fact that although the boys may not have matured, their music certainly had. Though it must be said CP's interest in porn was not just voyeuristic, as they lent their artistic help to several movies of the genre in the form of musical accompaniment. Luckily for any puritans in their fanbase there was no need to search out the offending films as CP's movie material was released on the aptly-titled album, 'SOUNDTRACKS' (1992). The same year also saw the release of the 'CHEMICAL PEOPLE' album, which was made with new recruit ROBERT HECKER, from REDD KROSS, who had replaced the recently departed PINA. This release also marked a break for the band which was to last five years. An unfortunate time to take a long holiday as it coincided with the huge rise in popularity of this genre of music exemplified by similar acts like GREEN DAY and OFFSPRING. CP did bounce back though – although arguably half a decade late – with another long-player 'ARPEGGIO MOTORCADE' (1997). • **Covered:** SHOCK ME (Kiss) / VACATION (Go-Go's) / ASK THE ANGELS (Patti Smith) / etc.
Album rating: SO SEXIST! (*2) / TEN-FOLD HATE (*3) / THE RIGHT THING compilation (*6) / OVERDOSED ON . . . compilation (*6) / ANGELS 'N' DEVILS mini (*3) / SOUNDTRACKS (*4) / CHEMICAL PEOPLE (*4) / ARPEGGIO MOTORCADE (*5)

DAVE NAZWORTHY – vocals, drums, guitar / **JAIME PINA** – guitar / **ED URLIK** – bass / (vocalist/guitarist BLAIR JOBE left after contributing half the debut's songs)

Cruz Cruz
1988. (lp/c/cd) *<CRZ 002/+C/CD>* **SO SEXIST!**
– Don't tell me / Human fear / Submarine dream / The good, the bad and the ugly / Times will change / Henry Whitpenn / Find out / Donut-run / Shock me / Diet koke / Funky time / Those young girls. *(UK-iss.Jan90; same as US) <(re-iss. Sep95; same)*
Jan 90. (lp/c/cd) *<(CRZ 007/+C/CD)>* **TEN-FOLD HATE** 1989
– New food / Aquaman / Old habits / Strange taste / She's got a bad case / Ed intro / Cherry / Intro / All the best things / Nudist camp / Metallica / Cop a feel / Moodchanger / Vacation / Outrage / Black throat.
Aug 90. (lp/c/cd) *<CRZ 013/+C/CD>* **THE RIGHT THING** (compilation)
– Captain / The right thing / A pornography / Duck song / A different scene / Some other time / Unanswered question / Aqua II / Overdosed / Nutro / Cheri love affair / The jam / Ultramental.
Dec 90. (m-lp/m-c/m-cd) *<CRZ 019/+C/CD>* **ANGELS 'N' DEVILS**
– Ask the angels / Been here / Faust / Rap / Blo me fatti / 1490. *(UK-iss.May93; same as US)*
Apr 91. (lp/c/cd) *<CRZ 020/+C/CD>* **SOUNDTRACKS**
– Seventy six / Funk-K / Miami blues / Way we die now / Cockfighter / Noize jam / New wave theme / Sideswipe / Woman chaser / Black mass of Brother Springer / Baptismal / New wave reprise. *(UK-iss.May93 & Sep95; same as US)*

— **ROBERT HECKER** – guitar (of REDD KROSS) repl. PINA
May 92. (lp/c/cd) *<CRZ 023/+C/CD>* **CHEMICAL PEOPLE**
– Never was / When they're gone / Let it go / Two years / Mid air / Following / I don't mind / Won't do / I gotta know / Drift away. *(UK-iss.May93 & Sep95; same as US)*
Jul 92. (12"/c-s/cd-s) *<(CRZ 025/+C/CD)>* **LET IT GO. / MID AIR**

— DAVE NAZ and co took a long break (he now added tenor sax!)
Oct 97. (cd) *<(CRZ 040CD)>* **ARPEGGIO MOTORCADE** Aug97
– Counting days / Last one / I hope you're there / Can't see your face / Tables turn / No reason why / No hope / Waiting / It's up to you / Forgot about.

– compilations, etc. –

issued on 'Vinyl Solution' unless stated otherwise
Sep 90. (lp/cd) *(SOL 24/+CD)* **OVERDOSED ON . . .**
– All the best things / Aquaman / Who killed Marilyn / Hate / Overdosed / X-feminist / Automatic / Tonight I'm gonna rock you / Midnight madness / Shit on my dick / My tattoo / Walking down the street / Bye bye girl / Aqua II / Overdosed / Assface / Ultramental / Henry Whitpenn / All the best things / Find out / Cheri love affair / Your song / Old habits / Rip it out.
Apr 93. (7") *(VS 13)* **ASK THE ANGELS. /**
1990's. (cd) *Two Inch Pecker; <1>* **SINGLES**

CHESTERFIELDS

Formed: Yeovil, Somerset, England . . . summer 1985 by DAVID GOLDSWORTHY, SIMON BARBER, DOMINIC MANNS and BRENDAN HOLDEN. Recalling the heady days of the 'Postcard' era, The CHESTERFIELDS were initially associated with the C-86 scene, showcasing their charming but raw appeal via a debut EP, 'A GUITAR IN YOUR BATH' (hopefully the unplugged version!) on the 'Subway Organisation' label. Two further 45's, 'COMPLETELY AND UTTERLY' and 'ASK JOHNNY DEE', appeared over the course of the next year, although by the release of their summer '87 debut album, 'KETTLE', BRENDAN had been replaced by RODNEY ALLEN. He, in turn, found more fame in the BLUE AEROPLANES, his temp, ANDY STRICKLAND (from the CARETAKER RACE) filling in until the arrival of MARK BARBER. Subsequently initiating their own label, 'Household Name', The CHESTERFIELDS found a sympathetic ally in Radio One DJ, Janice Long, a live session followed by the release of a couple of singles and a follow-up set, 'CROCODILE TEARS' (1988). With GOLDSWORTHY and MANNS now out of the picture, the remaining BARBER brothers persevered, although only one single surfaced before SIMON formed BASINGER (and later GRAPE). The CHESTERFIELDS were back again in 1994 with the album, 'FLOOD'. • **Covered:** HOLIDAY HYMN (Vic Godard). • **Note:** Another group called The CHESTERFIELDS were around from the 50's; doo-wop.

CHESTERFIELDS (cont)   THE GREAT INDIE DISCOGRAPHY   **The 1980s**

Album rating: KETTLE (*6) / WESTWARD HO! compilation (*6) / CROCODILE TEARS (*5) / FLOOD (*5) / Grape: IN THE FAMILY OF DREAMS (*4) / Gear: BED & BREAKFAST (*4)

DAVID GOLDSWORTHY – vocals, guitar / **BRENDAN HOLDEN** – guitar / **SIMON BARBER** – bass, vocals / **DOMINIC MANNS** – drums

Subway Org. / not iss.

May 86. (7"ep) *(SUBWAY 3)* **A GUITAR IN YOUR BATH**
– Sweet revenge / What's your perversion / Love mountain / Best of friends.
Nov 86. (7") *(SUBWAY 7)* **COMPLETELY AND UTTERLY. / GIRL ON A BOAT**
Mar 87. (7") *(SUBWAY 11)* **ASK JOHNNY DEE. / POP ANARCHY!**

—— **RODNEY ALLEN** – guitar; repl. BRENDAN

Jul 87. (lp) *(SUBORG 003)* **KETTLE**
– Nose out of joint / Ask Johnny Dee / Two girls and a treehouse / Shame about the rain / Everything a boy could ever need / Kiss me stupid / The thumb / Storm Nelson / Holiday yhmn / Oh Mr. Wilson / The boy who sold his suitcase / Completely and utterly. *(cd-iss. Sep93 on 'Vinyl Japan'+=; ASKCD 030)* – Sweet revenge / What's your perversion? / Love mountain / Best of friends / Girl on a boat / Pop anarchy! / Cupid's outlaw / Sob sob story.
Dec 87. (lp) *(SUBORG 005)* **WESTWARD HO!** (compilation)
– Sweet revenge / What's your perversion / Love mountain / Best of friends / Completely and utterly / Girl on a boat / Ask Johnny Dee / Pop anarchy!

—— temp. **ANDY STRICKLAND** – guitar (of CARETAKER RACE) repl. RODNEY who joined the BLUE AEROPLANES
—— (Jul'87) **MARK BARBER** – guitar; repl. ANDY

Household Name / not iss.

Mar 88. (12") *(HOLD 1T)* **GOODBYE GOODBYE. /**
Aug 88. (7") *(HOLD 3)* **BLAME. /**
(12"+=) *(HOLD 3T)* –
Sep 88. (lp/cd) *(HOLD 4 LP/CD)* **CROCODILE TEARS**
– Lunchtime for the wild youth / Alison wait / When it all comes down / Hopes for Lauren or Joseph / Get some religion / Let it go / Twintown / Goodbye goodbye / Besotted / Blame / Male bimbo / Better smile / Last train to Yeovil / I've got to hand it to you.

—— GOLDSWORTHY and MANNS departed later in '88 and although SIMON and MARK carried on with evolving line-up

Apr 89. (12"ep) *(HOLD 5T)* **FOOL IS A MAN. / (+3)**

—— split in the summer of '89; SIMON formed BASINGER and MARK joined the Bristol-based GRAPE

BASINGER

SIMON BARBER with others

West / not iss.

Nov 90. (7") **SOMETHING. /**

Wilde Club / not iss.

Apr 92. (12"ep) **BOOMERANG EP**

Hair / not iss.

Mar 93. (7") *(HAIR 1)* **HANDSOME. / AMERICA**

GEAR

—— were formed by **SIMON**
Sep 93. (7") *(HAIR 3)* **HAIR. / SAY YEAH**
Feb 96. (cd) *(HAIR 7)* **BED & BREAKFAST**

GRAPE

MARK BARBER with others

Pencil Toast / not iss.

1991. (7") *(PENT 001)* **BABY IN A PLASTIC BAG. / LISTEN TO YOUR HEART**

Vinyl Japan / not iss.

Oct 92. (12"ep/cd-ep) *(TASK 15/+CD)* **MATHS & PASSION**
– Back again / Bane / Playground / All the way / Baby in a plastic bag / Listen to your heart.
Jul 93. (12"ep/cd-ep) *(TASK 20/+CD)* **PERFUME**
– Perfume / Real cheese / Virile but dead / Toilet.
Jan 94. (cd/lp) *(ASK CD/LP 33)* **IN THE FAMILY OF DREAMS**
– Family of dreams / Blzpub / Hallowed be / Another baby / Consumerama / With a woman / Break / God (sic) / Handshake from Hell / Doris Day / Man of wisdom / These dreams.

CHESTERFIELDS

—— re-formed in 1994 with **DAVID, SIMON, MARK + RICHARD CHANT** – drums

Vinyl Japan / not iss.

May 94. (12"ep/cd-ep) *(TASK/+CD 26)* **DOWN BY THE WISHING POOL**
– Down by the wishing pool / Balcony striptease / I don't know you now / The Berlin walk.
Aug 94. (cd) *(ASKCD 41)* **FLOOD**
– Fountain of youth / Glad for you / Controversial / Hangover eve / Slippery / Not gone but waiting to go / All the way / Ceiling / Oonagh Uma / High tide / Something happening / Flood.
Jan 95. (cd-ep) *(TASKCD 35)* **LET'S SPLIT EP**
– Open to persuasion / Where's the map? / (split with JOHNNY DEE): I wanna bang on the drum / Love plays cruel game.

—— DAVID was to form FURNT

– compilations, etc. –

Dec 87. (12"ep) *Nightracks; (SFNT 003)* **JANICE LONG SESSION** (17/12/86)
– Two girls and a treehouse / What's your perversion / Oh Mr. Wilson / Love mountain.

CHILDREN'S HOUR (see under ⇒ **HEADLESS CHICKENS**)

CHILLS

Formed: Dunedin & Christchurch, New Zealand ... October 1980 as a vehicle for singer-songwriter, MARTIN PHILLIPPS. Materialising around the ashes of Kiwi punk band, The SAME, The CHILLS initial line-up featured PHILLIPPS, his sister RACHEL and future VERLAINES musician, JANE TODD. Over the course of the ensuing decade the band would undergo almost continual personnel comings and goings (enough to give Pete Frame – of Rock Family Trees fame – nightmares!), usually from fellow 'Flying Nun' acts like the aforementioned VERLAINES and The CLEAN. One such member was MARTYN BULL, who briefly played with The CHILLS before succumbing to leukaemia in July 1983. The ghostly strains of 'PINK FROST' served as a memorial, the track being one of the most impressive to surface from their string of domestic EP and singles releases throughout the early to mid-80's. In 1985, The CHILLS played a handful of London dates as well as recording a session for John Peel. 'Creation', meanwhile, released a compilation, 'KALEIDOSCOPE WORLD' (1986), featuring the cream of their work to date. Ranging from the atmospheric VELVETS-esque charm of 'SATIN DOLL' to the harmony-driven pop of the title track and moody 'PINK FROST', The CHILLS' sound was characterised by a retro-psych melange of swirling organ, jangling guitars and chugging bass, a recipe also followed by the band's 'Paisley Underground' compatriots in the States. A long awaited debut album proper, the MAYO THOMPSON-produced 'BRAVE WORDS' (1987), was regarded as a half-baked affair by fans and critics alike, PHILLIPPS struggling to realise his unique musical vision over the course of a whole set. Nevertheless, the band secured a major label deal with 'Slash/Warners' and released a more palatable follow-up set, 'SUBMARINE BELLS', at the turn of the decade. Despite a cleaner, more accessible sound, The CHILLS – like most of their NZ brethren – remained an acquired taste, a less than prolific release schedule (1992's 'SOFT BOMB' being last album to date) not helping the transition to a wider market. However, mainman MARTIN PHILLIPPS & THE CHILLS (with a new UK-based formation including DAVE MATTACKS and DAVE GREGORY) delivered a new Craig Leon-produced effort in 1996, 'SUNBURNT', while a solo set of home demos, 'SKETCH BOOK VOL.1', hit the shops a few years later. • **Trivia:** MARTIN played keyboards on The CLEAN's debut Flying Nun 45, 'Tally Ho'.

Album rating: KALEIDOSCOPE WORLD compilation (*8) / BRAVE WORDS (*6) / SUBMARINE BELLS (*7) / SOFT BOMB (*6) / HEAVENLY POP HITS compilation (*7) / Martin Phillipps: SUNBURNT (*5) / SKETCH BOOK, VOL.1 (*5)

MARTIN PHILLIPPS (b. 2 Jul'63) – vocals, guitar / **PETER GUTTERIDGE** (b.19 May'61) – guitar (ex-CLEAN) / **ALAN HAIG** (b. 5 Aug'61) – drums (ex-RED TAPE) / **FRASER BATTS** (b.14 Apr'64) – keyboards, guitar (ex-BORED GAMES) repl. RACHEL PHILLIPPS / **TERRY MOORE** (b.27 Oct'61, England) – bass (ex-BORED GAMES) repl. PETER + JANE DODD (the latter joined The VERLAINES)

Flying Nun / not iss.

Jan 82. (d12"ep) *(FNDUN 1/2)* **DUNEDIN DOUBLE EP** — New Z.
– Kaleidoscope world / Satin doll / Frantic drift / (+ 10 other tracks by NZ groups The VERLAINES, The STONES + The SNEAKY FEELINGS).

—— **RACHEL PHILLIPPS** (b.17 Jun'65) – keyboards; returned to replace FRASER
—— **MARTYN BULL** (b. 6 Mar'61) – drums; repl. HAIG who joined CLEAN

May 82. (7"m) *(FNCOLD 001)* **ROLLING MOON. / BITE / FLAME THROWER** — New Z.

—— **PETER ALLISON** (b. 7 Jun'60) – keyboards; repl. RACHEL
Jul 82. (7") *(FNCOLD 002)* **PINK FROST. / PURPLE GIRL** — New Z.

—— **ALAN HAIG** – drums; returned to repl. MARTYN BULL who died on the 18th July '83 (DAVID KILGOUR was briefly a member)
—— **MARTIN KEAN** (b.17 Jun'61) – bass; repl. TERRY
Jan 84. (7") *(FNCOLD 003)* **DOLEDRUMS. / HIDDEN BAY** — New Z.

—— **MARTIN PHILLIPPS, PETER ALLISON + ALAN HAIG** brought back **TERRY MOORE** – bass, to repl. KEAN
Dec 84. (7") *(FNCOLD 004)* **THE LOST EP** — New Z.
– This is the way / Never never go / Dream by dream. *(UK-iss.Mar86; same)*

Creation / Homestead

Feb 86. (m-lp) *(CRELP 008)* <HMS 139> **KALEIDOSCOPE WORLD** (compilation) 1989
– Kaleidoscope world / Satin doll / Frantic drift / Rolling moon / Bite / Flame thrower / Pink frost / Purple girl. *(re-iss. Dec87 on 'Flying Nun'; FNE 13) (w/free 7"ep)* **THE LOST EP** *(cd-iss. Nov92 +=; FNE 13CD)* – This is the way / Never never go / Don't even know her name / Bee bah bee bah bee boe / Whole weird world / Dream by dream / Doledrums / Hidden bay / I love my leather jacket / The great escape.

—— **MARTIN PHILLIPPS** enlisted an entire new band **CAROLINE EASTER** (b.30 Nov'58) – drums repl. ALAN HAIG / **ANDREW TODD** (b.15 Dec'58) – keyboards, vocals / **JUSTIN HARWOOD** (b. 6 Jul'65) – bass, vocals

Flying Nun / Homestead

Mar 87. (12") *(FNUK 07)* **I LOVE MY LEATHER JACKET. / THE GREAT ESCAPE**
Aug 87. (12") *(FNUK 11T)* **THE HOUSE WITH A HUNDRED ROOMS. / LIVING IN A JUNGLE**
Sep 87. (lp) *(FN 090 – FNUK 12)* <HMS 103-1> **BRAVE WORDS**
– Push / Rain / Speak for yourself / Look for the good in others and they'll see the good in you / Wet blanket / Ghosts / Dan Destiny and the Silver Dawn / Night of the chill blue / 16 heart-throbs / Brave words / Dark carnival / Creep. *(cd-iss. Sep89 & Nov92 +=; FNE 12CD)* – Party in my heart / House with a hundred rooms / Living in a jungle.

1987.	(12") *(FN 097)* **WET BLANKET. /**	–	– NewZ
1987.	(12") *(FN 101)* **WET BLANKET. / THINK I THOUGHT**	–	– NewZ
1987.	(12") *(FN 103)* **WET BLANKET. /**	–	– NewZ
1988.	(7"; /drawn) *(FN 115)* **PART PAST PART FICTION. /**	–	– NewZ

— **JAMES STEVENSON** (b.17 May'70) – drums; repl. CAROLINE

Slash / Slash

Mar 90. (7") *(LASH 22)* **THE HEAVENLY POP HIT. / WHOLE LOT OF NONE**
(12"+=/cd-s+=) *(LAS HX/CD 22)* – Ways watching / Water wolves. *(above also; FN 157/158)*

Mar 90. (cd/c/lp) *(828 191-2/-4/-1)* <26130-1> **SUBMARINE BELLS**
– The Heavenly pop hit / Tied up in chain / The oncoming day / Part past part fiction / Singing in my sleep / I soar / Dead web / Familiarity breeds contempt / Don't be a memory / Efforence and deliquence / Sweet times / Submarine bells. *(NZ-iss. on 'Flying Nun'; FN 148)*

Oct 90. (7") *(FN 178)* **PART PAST PART FICTION. / WATER WOLVES** – – NewZ

— **GILLIAN DEMPSTER** (b.26 Apr'70) – keyboards; repl. TODD

— **TERRY MOORE** returned to repl. JUSTIN HARWOOD who joined LUNA with former GALAXIE 500 member, DEAN WAREHAM. He later appeared in supergroup, TUATARA with R.E.M. member, PETER BUCK

— **PHILLIPPS + MOORE** recruited **LISA MEDNICK** (b.27 Jun'57, USA) – keyboards / **STEVEN SCHAYER** (b.12 Feb'65, USA) – guitar / **EARL ROBERTSON** (b.15 Apr'62, USA) – bass

Aug 92. (cd/c/lp) *(828 322-2/-4/-1)* <26787-2/-4/-1> **SOFT BOMB**
– The male monster from the Id / Background affair / Ocean ocean / Soft bomb / There is no harm in trying / Strange case / Soft bomb II / So long / Song for Randy Newman etc / Sleeping giants / Double summer / Sanctuary / Halo fading / There is no point in trying / Entertainer / Water wolves / Soft bomb III. *(NZ-iss.on 'Flying Nun'; FNCD 234)*

Sep 92. (c-s/cd-s) *(FN 240)* **MALE MONSTER FROM THE ID / I WISH I COULD DO WITHOUT YOU / BIG DARK DAY** – – NewZ

Oct 92. (c-s/cd-s) *(FN 243)* **DOUBLE SUMMER / HALO FADING (demo) / SANCTUARY (demo)** – – NewZ

— **CRAIG MASON** (b.28 Jul'61) – drums; repl. ROBERTSON

— disbanded when it looked like PHILLIPPS would go solo

MARTIN PHILLIPPS & The CHILLS

with **DAVE GREGORY** – bass (ex-XTC) / **DAVE MATTACKS** – drums (ex-FAIRPORT CONVENTION)

Flying Nun / not iss.

Oct 96. (cd) *(FNCD 303)* **SUNBURNT**
– As far as I can see / Premonition / Surrounded / Come home / Sunburnt / The big assessment / Swimming in the rain / Dreams are free / You can understand me / Lost in future ruins / New millennium / Walk on the beach / Secret garden.

1997. (7") *(FN 340)* **COME HOME. / THE STREETS OF FORGOTTEN COOL** – – NewZ
(cd-s+=) *(FNCD 340)* – How much this place has changed / Lies, lies, lies.

1997. (7") *(FN 365)* **SURROUNDED. / YABBA DABBA DOO** – – NewZ
(cd-s+=) *(FNCD 365)* – (Please don't say we'll be) Friends again / Stupid way to go.

MARTIN PHILLIPPS

1998. (cd) *(FNCD 415)* **SKETCH BOOK, VOL.1** – – NewZ
– Evadene / February / No more tigers / Residential green cell / Haunt me / Evermore / Crow / Spring (segment) / Carabela / Warm / Secret garden / Bad dancer / Small spark / Witch's hat / Martini / Sleep sirens / Hawea.

– (CHILLS) compilations, etc –

1996. (lp/cd) *Flying Nun; (FN/+CD 306)* **HEAVENLY POP HITS**
– Heavenly pop hit / I love my leather jacket / Doledrums / Double summer / Oncoming day / Rolling moon / I'll only see you alone again / Never never go / Wet blanket / Pink frost / Kaleidoscope world / Look for the good in others and they'll see the good in you / House with 100 rooms / Part past part fiction / The male monster from the Id / This is the way. *(re-iss. Jan00; same)*

Alex CHILTON (see under ⇒ BIG STAR)

CHOIR INVISIBLE

Formed: Pasadena, California, USA ... late 70's as The FLYBOYS, by THAMES SINCLAIR, SCOTT 'TOWERS' LASKIN, JON BOY CURRIE and DENNY WALSH. After one EP in 1980, 'CRAYON WORLD', WALSH joined The CROWD, his replacement being DANNY BENAIR, a seasoned new waver from The WEIRDOS. They only managed to complete one U2-esque eponymous set in '81 before DANNY (who subsequently served a stint with The SALVATION ARMY i.e. THREE O'CLOCK) in turn, was substituted by DON DOMINE, although only one EP, 'SEA TO SHINING SEA' was forthcoming before they quietly disappeared.

Album rating: CHOIR INVISIBLE (*4)

JON BOY CURRIE – vocals, guitar / **THAMES SINCLAIR** – guitar, vocals / **SCOTT 'TOWERS' LASKIN** – bass, vocals / **DENNY WALSH** – drums

not iss. / Frontier

1980. (m-lp; as FLYBOYS) <*FLP 1001*> **FLYBOYS** – –
– Crayon world / Square city / Flyboys.

— **DANNY BENAIR** – drums (ex-QUICK, ex-WEIRDOS) repl. DENNY WALSH who joined The CROWD

1981. (lp) <*FLP 1006*> **CHOIR INVISIBLE** – –

— **DON DOMINE** – drums; repl. BENAIR who the SALVATION ARMY group before going on to THREE O'CLOCK

not iss. / P.V.C.

1984. (12"ep) **SEA TO SHINING SEA EP** – –

— SINCLAIR formed WONDERWALL and CHOIR INVISIBLE split

CHOO CHOO TRAIN (see under ⇒ VELVET CRUSH; in 90's section)

CHRIS (ECKMAN) & CARLA (see under ⇒ WALKABOUTS)

CHRIS AND COSEY

Formed: London, England ... 1981 by former THROBBING GRISTLE members, CHRIS CARTER and COSEY FANNI TUTTI. Just prior to the duo getting together again, CARTER released a solo outing, 'THE SPACE BETWEEN' on cassette (Industrial; IRC 32 – cd-iss. Jan92 on 'Grey Area'; ICC 1CD). The pair's debut album for 'Rough Trade', 'HEARTBEAT' was well received by the underground press, as was their 1982 follow-up, 'TRANCE'. Pioneers of trance-dance musak, CHRIS & COSEY mixed electronic rhythms with dark, subversive undertones that extended the foundations laid by THROBBING GRISTLE. In the Autumn of '83, C&C unveiled their first single, 'OCTOBER (LOVE SONG)', a track that bordered on mainstream Euro-rock territory without losing the sinister edge. A third set, 'SONGS OF LOVE AND LUST' was released simultaneously in late summer '84 with the first batch of material from off-shoot project and label, CTI (CREATIVE TECHNOLOGY INSTITUTE). This included the EP, 'CONSPIRACY INTERNATIONAL' and the lp/video, 'EUROPEAN RENDEZVOUS'. An unlikely collaboration with top synth popsters, the EURYTHMICS was next on the agenda, the resulting 'SWEET SURPRISE' single nevertheless failing to raise CHRIS & COSEY above cult status. The duo's final album for 'Rough Trade', 'TECHNO PRIMITIV', was issued in early '86, a subsequent move to Belgian label, 'Play It Again Sam' coming about the following year. Several albums appeared over the course of the next half decade, the likes of 1987's 'EXOTIKA' to 1992's 'MUSIK FANTASTIQUE!' were more geared towards the continental alternative dance contingent that also included industrial meisters, FRONT 242. The mid-90's, meanwhile, saw CHRIS & COSEY reactivating the dormant CTI via the associated 'Conspiracy' label, a plethora of cd's culminating in 1998's 'POINT SEVEN'.

Album rating: HEARTBEAT (*5) / TRANCE (*8) / SONGS OF LOVE AND LUST (*6) / EUROPEAN RENDEZVOUS (*6) / TECHNO PRIMITIV (*4) / ACTION! (*5) / EXOTIKA (*6) / CHRIS & COSEY (*7) / TRUST (*6) / PAGAN TANGO (*6) / MUSIK FANTASTIQUE! (*5) / METAPHYSICAL (*4) / CHRONOMANIC (*4) / IN CONTINUUM (*5) / SKIMBLE SKAMBLE (*4) / POINT SEVEN (*5) / UNION (*6) / THE ESSENTIAL CHRIS & COSEY COLLECTION compilation (*7) / Chris Carter: THE SPACE BETWEEN (*6) / MONDO BEAT (*5) / DISOBEDIENT (*5) / SMALL MOON (*5) / Cosey Fanni Tutti: TIME TO TELL (*5)

CHRIS CARTER – synthesizers, electro-percussion / guitar, vocals / **COSEY FANNI TUTTI** – synthesizers, tapes, vocals (with guest on debut before he joined PSYCHIC TV) **ALEX FERGUSSON** – guitar

Rough Trade / not iss.

Nov 81. (lp)(c) *(ROUGH 34)(COPY 008)* **HEARTBEAT**
– Put yourself in Los Angeles / Just like you / Voodoo / Moorby / Radio Void / This is me / Pressure drop *[c-only]* / Manic melody (hairy beary) / Useless information / Moving still / Bust stop / Heartbeat / Tight fit *[c-only]*. *(cd-iss. Jul88 on 'Conspiracy'; CTICD 004) <US cd-iss. 1990 on 'Wax Trax'; WAXCD 7122>*

May 82. (lp) *(ROUGH 44)* **TRANCE**
– Cowboys in Cuba / Lost / The giants feet / Impulse / Secret / Re-education through labour / Until / The gates of ancient cities. *(cd-iss. Jul88 on 'Conspiracy'+=; CTICD 005)* – Yes know / Nikki.

— (In 1982, COSEY FANNI TUTTI released C-30 cassette 'TIME TO TELL' for 'Flow Motion', re-iss. Sep88 on 'Cathexis')

Oct 83. (7") *(RT 078)* **OCTOBER (LOVE SONG). / LITTLE HOUSES** – –
(12") *(RTT 078)* – (mixes:- vocal, long / instrumental / dance / vocal, short).

Aug 84. (lp) *(ROUGH 64)* **SONGS OF LOVE AND LUST**
– Love cuts / Walking through Heaven / Lament / Talk to me / Gardens of the pure / Raining tears of blood / Chiron / Tantalize. *(cd-iss. Jul88 on 'Conspiracy'+=; CTICD 006)* – October love song / Little houses.

DoubleVision / not iss.

Sep 84. (lp,video; as CTI) *(DVR 7)* **ELEMENTAL 7** – –
– Temple bar / Dancing ghosts / Meeting Mr. Evans / Invisible spectrum / Sidereal / Well spring of life / The final calling.

Oct 84. (lp,video; as CTI) *(DVR 8)* **EUROPEAN RENDEZVOUS – CTI LIVE 1983 (live)** – –
– Intro / Mary / Funky / The need / Loop / Sequencer / Slow / Thy gift of tongues / Voice echo.

— next featured **GLENN WALLIS** (of KONSTRUKTIVIST)

C.T.I. / not iss.

Nov 84. (12"; as CONSPIRACY INTERNATIONAL ONE) *(CTI 1)* **HAMMER HOUSE. / CONQUEST / CRASH** – –

— now featured **BRIAN WILLIAMS** (of LUSTMORD)

Jan 85. (12"; as CONSPIRACY INTERNATIONAL TWO) *(CTI 2)* **THY GIFT OF TONGUES. / THE NEED** – –
below featured EURYTHMICS duo

CHRIS AND COSEY (cont)

Rough Trade / not iss.

Feb 85. (12") (RTT 148) **SWEET SURPRISE 1 (1984). / SWEET SURPRISE 2 (1985)**
Jan 86. (lp) (ROUGH 84) **TECHNO PRIMITIV**
– Hazey daze / Misunderstandings / Morning / Haunted heroes / Stolen kisses / Shivers / He's an Arabian / Last exit / Do or die / Techno primitiv. *(cd-is.Sep88 on 'Conspiracy'+=; CTICD 003)* – Silent cry / Sweet surprise.

Licensed / Nettwerk

Feb 87. (12"ep) (LD 874) <NMT 6302> **TAKE FIVE**
– Irama / Relay / Smell the roses / Love cuts / Send the magick down.
Apr 87. (lp) (LD 875) **ACTION! (live)**
– Akshyn / Talk to me / Relay / Send the magick down / Do or die / Love cuts / Shivers / Delerium.

Dragon / not iss.

Jul 87. (lp) (DRLP 109) **SWEET SURPRISE**

Play It Again Sam / Nettwerk

Jul 87. (12") (BIAS 054) **OBSESSION (12" mix) / OBSESSION (shortmix). / METROEME / 47 SOUND**
Oct 87. (12") <NT12 3007> **OBSESSION (remix). / 47 SOUND**
Oct 87. (lp/cd) (BIAS/CDBIAS 069) <NTL 30016> **EXOTIKA**
– Confession / Arcade / Exotika / Vengeance / Dr. John (sleeping Stephen) / BeatBeatBeat / Dancing on your grave. *(cd+=)* – Irama. *(cd re-iss. Jan99 on 'Conspiracy'+=; CC 1198)* – TAKE FIVE
Jan 88. (12") (BIAS 075) **EXOTIKA. / WORKOUT / BEATBEATBEAT**
Jun 88. (12") <NT12 3013> **EXOTIKA (extended re-mix). / BEATBEATBEAT (live)**
Nov 88. (12") (BIAS 105) <WI 3024> **RISE (vocal remix). / HYPNOTIKA**
Feb 89. (lp/cd) (BIAS/CDBIAS 124) <WI 30026> **TRUST**
– Deep velvet / Illusion / The ring / Percusex / Rise / Watching you / Enfectus / Trust. *(cd+=)* – Rise / Hypnotika.
Mar 91. (cd-s/12") (CD+/BIAS 186) <WAX 559153> **SYNAESTHESIA (Daniel Miller mix) / SYNAESTHESIA (C&C mix) / SYNAESTHESIA (Daniel Miller instrumental) / RETRODECT**
Apr 91. (lp/cd) (BIAS 179/+CD) <WAXCS 7150> **PAGAN TANGO**
– In ecstasy / Synaesthesia / I belong to me / Take control / Face to face / Feel to me / Go-go Latino / Pagan tango / Cords of love / Balfigore (before the feast). *(cd+=)* – Sacred silence.
Oct 92. (cd) (BIAS 221CD) **MUSIK FANTASTIQUE!**
– Fantastique / Sound of sound / Masqued / Apocalypso / Afrakira / Hidden man / Visions love / Loves lost immortal / Eternal / Neverneverland / Melancholia.

World Serpent / not iss.

1992. (7"etched) (WS7 004) **PASSION**
1993. (cd; as CTI) (CTI 93001) **METAPHYSICAL: LIBRARY OF SOUND – EDITION ONE**
– Fire trance / Invision / The end moment / Soul of souls / Bridge of sighs / No mans land / Nothing exists / Inner faint light.
1994. (cd; as CTI) (CTI 93002) **CHRONOMANIC: THE LIBRARY OF SOUND – EDITION 2**
– Syndromedia / Flames of Beltrane / Devash / Sysdome / Chronomanic / Eve of Samaine / The kissing bowl / Astrony.
1995. (cd; as CTI) (CTI 95003) **IN CONTINUUM: THE LIBRARY OF SOUND – EDITION 3**
– Subondare / Gamelal / Invision / Audio lava / Teche / Spectrophilia.
Jan 97. (cd) (CC 1096) **SKIMBLE SKAMBLE**
– Tachycardia / Real time / Vivid / Intoxicating / One minute more / Endless rain / Hybrid 'C' / Skimble skamble.
Feb 98. (cd; as CTI) (CTI 98004) **POINT SEVEN: LIBRARY OF SOUND EDITION FOUR**
– Alliz / Pausal / Hipspa / Restless / Repose / Daspooki / Reflux / Azimuth / Cell(f).
Aug 99. (cd) (CTI 0999) **UNION (live at The Unuin Chapel, 30th May 1999)**
– Gamelal / Subondare / Fire trance / Dr. John / Invision / Spectrophelia / Driving blind / Vivid / Exotika / Deep velvet / Dancing on your grave.

– compilations, etc. –

Sep 89. (cd) Conspiracy; (CTICD 1) **COLLECTIV ONE**
– (MONDO BEAT: Chris Carter / HAMMER HOUSE / THY GIFT OF TONGUES).
Sep 89. (cd) Conspiracy; (CTICD 2) **COLLECTIV TWO – THE BEST OF CHRIS & COSEY**
– Put yourself in Los Angeles / Cowboys in Cuba / Just like you / Dancing ghosts / October (love song) / Driving blind / Sweet surprise / Walking through Heaven / Haunted heroes / Misunderstandings / Raining tears of blood / Stolen kisses / Love cuts / Silent cry / Sending the magick down.
Jul 90. (cd) Staalplaat; (STCD 002) **ALLOTROPY** (rec.1987)
Sep 90. (cd) Conspiracy; (CTICD 7) **COLLECTIV THREE – AN ELEMENTAL RENDEVOUS**
– (ELEMENTAL 7 + EUROPEAN RENDEZVOUS minus 3 tracks).
Sep 90. (cd) Conspiracy; (CTICD 8) **COLLECTIV FOUR – ARCHIVE RECORDINGS**
– City of spirits / Devil god / Pressure drop / Junk jive / Night shift / Little vhouses / Yes know / Tight fit / Look down (Jehova) / Sweet surprise 2 / October love song (dance mix) / Nicki single.
Apr 02. (d-cd) World Serpent; (CC 1101 A/B) **THE ESSENTIAL CHRIS & COSEY COLLECTION**
– Exotika / Obsession / Deep velvet / Impulse / Dancing on your grave / Manic melody (hairy beary) / Love cuts / Vengeance / Driving blind / Infectus / Take control / October love song / Intoxicating / Pagan tango / Fantastique // Cords of love / One minute more / In ecstasy / Raining tears of blood / Cowboys in Cuba / Haunted heroes / Eternal / Silent cry / Walking through Heaven / I belong to me / Dr. John (sleeping Stephen) / Percusex / Synaesthesia / Sound of sound / Tantalize / To put yourself in Los Angeles.

CHRIS CARTER

Industrial / not iss.

1981. (c) (IRC 32) **THE SPACE BETWEEN**
– Beat / Outreach / Electrodub 1 / Clouds / Reprise / Electrodub 2 / Poptone / Slomo /

Walkabout / Maybe / Falling / Solidit / Snap / Interloop / Resonance. *(cd-iss. 1991 on 'Grey Area'; CC 1CD) <US cd-iss. 1991 on 'Mute-Elektra'; 961245-2> (cd re-mixed Apr02 as 'ELECTRONIC AMBIENT REMIXES: ONE' on 'CTI'; CTIEAR 1)*

Conspiracy / not iss.

Feb 85. (lp) (CTILP 3) **MONDO BEAT**
– Mondo B. / Nobadhairdo / Beyond temptation / Moonlight / Real life / Noevil.
Dec 98. (cd) (CTI 98CC2) **DISOBEDIENT**
– Pantavistiq / Pulseq / Solomo / Lixiez / YVX / Chautut / Versix / Sublev / Domank.
Jul 99. (cd) (CTI 99CC2) **SMALL MOON**
– Arcadia / Praxiz / Klypp'd / Non-pop / Reazymn / Soho . . . 3am.

— In Jul'00, (IAN) BODDY & CARTER collaborated on the 'CAGED' set

C.T.I. / not iss.

Apr 02. (cd) (CTIEAR 3) **ELECTRONIC AMBIENT REMIXES VOL.3**
– The world as a war film / Convincing people / Heathen mirth / Indisciplined / Hot on the heels of love / Someone came over me / Still talking / Generic terrorists / The old man died / What is today / Hamburger man / Dread head.

COSEY FANNI TUTTI

Flowmotion / not iss.

1983. (c; C-30) *(none)* **TIME TO TELL**
– The secret touch / Time to tell / Ritual awakening. *(lp-iss.Sep88 on 'Cathexis'; CRL 22-24) (cd-iss. 1993 & 2000 on 'World Serpent'+=; CTI 93004)* – Such as life. *(cd re-mixed Apr02 as 'ELECTRONIC AMBIENT REMIXES – TWO'; CTIEAR 2)*

CHRYSANTHEMUMS
(see under ⇒ DEEP FREEZE MICE)

CHUMBAWAMBA

Formed: Burnley / Barnsley, Yorkshire, England . . . 1980 by vegan sextet, ALICE NUTTER, BOFF, LOU, MAVIS, HARRY and DANBERT NOBACON, who shacked up in a Leeds commune. In 1982, they appeared as SKIN DISEASE on a single 'BACK ON THE STREETS', and toured as CHUMBAWAMBA a year later with CRASS, while releasing three cassettes independently. In 1985/86, they caused a little controversy by issuing records arguing the merits of the BAND/LIVE AID charity causes. Needless to say, these were banned from radio airplay. More publicity surrounded them around this time, when they poured red paint over The CLASH, after the one-time punks arrived in Leeds for their 'Busking Britain Tour'. 1987's 'NEVER MIND THE BALLOTS: HERE'S THE REST OF YOUR LIFE', meanwhile, berated all parties in the forthcoming general election although obviously the Tories came in for the most disdain, 'MR HESELTINE MEETS HIS PUBLIC'. The same year, CHUMBAWAMBA railed against tabloid hypocrisy when they released 'LET IT BE' under the moniker of SCAB AID. Perhaps as a reaction to yet another Conservative victory, the band released an album of traditional folk protest songs, 'ENGLISH REBEL SONGS 1381-1914' (1988), their MADDY PRIOR (Steeleye Span) meets CRASS sound rising with ease to the challenge. Discovering the subversive possibilities in the emerging rave culture, the band turned in the dancefloor-friendly 'SLAP!' in summer 1990, although it took a pair-up with agit-hip hoppers CREDIT TO THE NATION for CHUMBAWAMBA to finally get their message across to a wider audience. Now signed to 'One Little Indian', the track in question, 'ENOUGH IS ENOUGH', gave the band a minor UK chart hit. Its call to challenge the rise of right-wing activism was echoed in a similarly successful follow-up, 'TIMEBOMB'. The attendant album, 'ANARCHY', made the British Top 30. Unimaginable ten years earlier, the once crustie band signed to conglomorate, 'E.M.I.' in the mid-90's, obviously deciding to subvert the pop world from within (a likely story!). Not only did they come pretty damn close with the annoyingly infectious 'TUBTHUMPING' (a No.2 UK hit!), but they broke the normally impenetrable American market. The accompanying album, 'TUBTHUMPER' (1997) made the US Top 5 (having earlier made UK Top 20), proving that patience is a virtue, even for those committed to radical social change. Love them or loathe them (and there's never usually any waverers!), CHUMBAWAMBA are now something of an institution, their newfound pop/MTV-friendly sound ushering in a new era of chart topping protest, er, possibly . . . The faux anarchs were back in 2000 with a US album 'WYSIWYG' (What You See Is What You Get), a rambling, disjointed effort which saw no-one in particular pay attention. After the release of compilation 'UNEASY LISTENING' (2000), CHUMBAWAMBA issued the pretty dismal 'READYMADES' (2002), an album full of songs but not much soul. • **Songwriters:** Group, except some traditional Hungarian folk tunes. Also sampled JOHN LENNON (Imagine), ELVIS, ALTERNATIVE TV, GANG OF FOUR, CRASS, FALL, X-RAY SPEX, STIFF LITTLE FINGERS, DAGMAR KRAUSE and GERSHWIN!. The lp tracks on 'ENGLISH REBEL SONGS' were all traditional. Covered on 'JESUS H CHRIST'; ALRIGHT NOW (Free) / MONEY, MONEY, MONEY (Abba) / SOLID GOLD EASY ACTION (T.Rex) / HEY YOU GET OFF MY CLOUD (Rolling Stones) / STAIRWAY TO HEAVEN (Led Zeppelin) / BIGMOUTH STRIKES AGAIN (Smiths) / I SHOULD BE SO LUCKY (Kylie Minogue) / MANNEQUIN (Wire) / HUNCHBACK OF NOTRE DAME (Frantic Elevators; Mick Hucknall) / NEW YORK MINING DISASTER 1941 (Bee Gees). • **Trivia:** In 1982, track 'THREE YEARS LATER' appeared on 'Crass' label album 'BULLSHIT DETECTOR 2'. ALICE NUTTER was named after a 17th century witch. DANBERT NOBACON released a single before he joined them, which featured a picture of his utensil on the cover!. 'NEVER SAY DI' single (proceeds to charity) was surprisingly in support of Princess Diana, as

CHUMBAWAMBA (cont)

they were anti-royalists. 'BEHAVE!' was a tribute ha!, about 'The Hit Man And Her' (aka PETE WATERMAN & MICHAELA).

Album rating: PICTURES OF STARVING CHILDREN SELL RECORDS: CHARITY, LIES AND TRADITION (*7) / NEVER MIND THE BALLOTS: HERE'S THE REST OF YOUR LIFE (*7) / ENGLISH REBEL SONGS 1381-1914 mini (*5) / SLAP! (*6) / SHHH (*8) / ANARCHY (*9) / SHOWBUSINESS! CHUMBAWAMBA LIVE (*5) / SWINGIN' WITH RAYMOND (*5) / TUBTHUMPER (*6) / UNEASY LISTENING compilation (*7) / WYSIWYG (*6) / READYMADES (*7)

ALICE NUTTER – vocals / **BOFF** (b. BILLY McCOID) – guitar, vocals, clarinet / **LOU** (b. LOUISE MARY WATTS) – vocals, guitar / **MAVE DILLAN** – bass, trumpet, French horn / **HARRY** (b. DARREN HAMER) – drums / **DANBERT NOBACON** (b. ALAN WHALEY) – vocals / with **SIMON COMMONKNOWLEDGE** – keyboards, accordion, piano

—— (released 3 cassettes before the mid-80's)

Agit Prop   not iss.

Sep 85. (7"ep) *(AGIT 001)* **REVOLUTION EP** □ -
 – Unity / Stagnation / Natural response / Adversity.
Apr 86. (7") *(AGIT 002)* **WE ARE THE WORLD. / A STATE OF MIND** □ -
 —— In '86, they issued DESTROY FASCISM as The ANTIDOTE; alongside The EX
Oct 86. (lp) *(PROP 001)* **PICTURES OF STARVING CHILDREN SELL RECORDS: CHARITY, LIES AND TRADITION** □ -
 – (prologue) / How to get your band on television / British colonialism and the BBC / Flickering pictures hypnotise / Commercial break / Unilever / More whitewashing / ... An interlude. Beginning to take it back / Dutiful servants and political masters / Coca- colanisation / ... And in a nutshell "food aid is our most powerful weapon" / Invasion.
Jul 87. (lp) *(PROP 002)* **NEVER MIND THE BALLOTS: HERE'S THE REST OF YOUR LIFE** □ -
 – Always tell the voter what the voter wants to hear / Come on baby (let's do the revolution) / The wasteland / Today's sermon / Ah-men / Mr. Heseltine meets his public / The candidates find common ground / Here's the rest of your life.
 —— under the name SCAB AID, they issued 'Let It Be' on the 'Scum' label.
Jul 88. (7") *(AGIT 003)* **FIGHT THE ALTON BILL. / SMASH CLAUSE 29!** □ -
Oct 88. (10"m-lp) *(PROP 003)* **ENGLISH REBEL SONGS 1381-1914** □ -
 – The Cutty wren / The diggers song / Colliers march / The triumph of General Ludd / Chartist anthem / Song of the times / Smashing of the van / World turned upside down / Poverty knock / Idris strike song / Hanging on the old barbed wire / The Cutty wren (reprise). *(re-iss. Feb93 lp/cd; PROP 3/+CD) (re-iss. Feb95 on 'One Little Indian' lp/c/cd; TPLP 64/+C/CD) <US cd-iss. Jun98 on 'Imprint'; 8769>*
 —— In Dec'89; they appeared on 'Agit Prop' Various Artists (SPORTCHESTRA) lp '101 SONGS ABOUT SPORT' *PROP 004*. Another Various 'THIS SPORTING LIFE' was iss.Aug'90.
 —— added **DUNST** (b. DUNSTON BRUCE) – vocals, percussion, soprano sax / **COBIE** – live sound / + others
Jul 90. (cd/lp) *(CD+/PROP 7)* **SLAP!** □ -
 – Ulrike / Tiananmen Square / Cartrouble / Chase PC's flee attack by own dog / Rubens has been shot! / I never gave up: Rappoport's testament / Slap! / That's how grateful we are / Meinhof. *(re-iss. Feb95 & Jan99 on 'One Little Indian' lp/c/cd; TPLP 65/+C/CD)*
 —— In Mar'91, CHUMBAWAMBA AND OTHER SUBVERSIVES released 7"; GREATEST HITS for 'Peasant Revolt'. At the same time ALICE and LOUISE (I think?) as The PASSION KILLERS released mail-order EP 'FOUR WAR IS SHIT SONGS' featuring tracks 'Shipbuilding', 'Reuters' + 2 for 'Rugger Bugger' records.
 —— added **MATTY** (MC FUSION / MATTHEW HANSON) – vocals (of CREDIT TO THE NATION) / **NEIL FERGUSON** – guitar, keyboards / **GEOFF SLAPHEAD** – fiddle / **HOWARD STOREY** – vocals
Jan 92. (12"ep/cd-ep) *(AGIT 5)* **I NEVER GAVE UP** □ -
 – (Rondo mix) / (Cass mix) / Laughing nevere stopped (mix). *(re-iss. Jul94 on 'Southern'; 18521-1/2)*
Mar 92. (cd/c/lp) *(001)* **JESUS H CHRIST** w- drawn
 (above was to have been issued on 'Tragic Flop')
Jun 92. (cd/c/lp) *(CD/TC+/PROP 11)* **SHHH** □ -
 – Shhh / Big mouth strikes again / Nothing that's new / Behave! / Snip snip snip / Look! no strings! / Happiness is just a chant away / Pop star kidnap / Sometimes plunder / You can't trust anyone nowadays / Stitch that. *(re-iss. Nov94 & Sep97 on 'Southern' cd/c/lp; 18515-2/-4/-1)*
Jul 92. (7") *(none)* **NEVER SAY DI. / FOR THE LOVE OF A PRINCESS** - -
 (above was actually a hoax & never quite made it to recording stage)
Nov 92. (12"/cd-s) *(AGIT 666/+CD)* **SOMEONE'S ALWAYS TELLING YOU HOW TO BEHAVE! / (2-'A'mixes by PAPA BRITTLE)** □ -

One Little Indian   E.M.I.

Sep 93. (12"ep/c-ep/cd-ep; CHUMBAWAMBA & CREDIT TO THE NATION) *(79 TP 7C/12/7CD)* **ENOUGH IS ENOUGH. / HEAR NO BULLSHIT (on fire mix) / THE DAY THE NAZI DIED (1993 mix)** 56 -
Nov 93. (12"ep/c-ep/cd-ep) *(89 TP 12/7C/7CD)* **TIMEBOMB. / TECHNO THE BOMB / THE WORLD TURNED UPSIDE DOWN** 59 -
May 94. (lp/c/cd) *(TPLP 46/+C/CD) <40903>* **ANARCHY** 29 Jun98
 – Give the anarchist a cigarette / Timebomb / Homophobia / On being pushed / Heaven – Hell / Love me / Georgina / Doh! / Blackpool rock / This year's thing / Mouthful of shit / Never do what you are told / Bad dog / Enough is enough / Rage.
May 94. (12"ep/c-ep/cd-ep) *(119 TP 12/7C/7CD)* **HOMOPHOBIA (with The Sisters of Perpetual Indulgence). / MORALITY PLAY IN THREE ACTS / ('A'acappella mix) / SONG FOR DEREK JARMEN** □ -
 (cd-ep) *(119 TP7CDL)* – ('A'side) / Enough is enough (with CREDIT TO NATION) / The day the Nazi died (with CREDIT TO NATION) / Morality play in three acts.
Mar 95. (lp/c/cd) *(TPLP 56/+C/CD)* **SHOWBUSINESS! CHUMBAWAMBA LIVE (live)** □ -
 – Never do what you are told / I never gave up / Give the anarchist a cigarette / Heaven-Hell / That's how grateful we are / Homophobia / Morality play in three acts / Bad dog / Stitch that / Mouthful of shit / The day the Nazi died / Timebomb (Jimmy Echo vocal) / Slag aid.

Oct 95. (7"/c-s) *(139 TP7/+C)* **UGH! YOUR UGLY HOUSES! / THIS GIRL** □ -
 (cd-s+=) *(139 TPCD)* – Mannequin / Hunchback of Notre Dame.
Oct 95. (d-lp/c/d-cd) *(TPLP 66/+C/CD)* **SWINGIN' WITH RAYMOND** 70
 – This girl / Never let go / Just look at me now / Not the girl I used to be / The morning after (the night before) / Love can knock you over / All mixed up / This dress kills / Salome (let's twist again) / Oxymoron / Waiting, shouting / Hey you! outside now! / Ugh! your ugly houses!

E.M.I.   Republic

Aug 97. (c-s) *(TCEM 486) <56146>* **TUBTHUMPING / (Buttthumping mix) / (Danny Boy mix)** 2 6
 (cd-s+=) *(CDEM 486)* – ('A'-Mawr mix: Pablo & Lawrie) / ('A'-Timeshard mix) / ('A'-Gunshot mix).
 (7"red) *(EM 486)* – ('A'side) / Farewell to the Crown (featuring The OYSTER BAND) / Football song ("Shit ground, no fans").
Sep 97. (cd/c *TCEM EMC 3773) <53099>* **TUBTHUMPER** 19 3
 – Tubthumping / Amnesia / Drip drip drip / Big issue / Good ship lifestyle / One by one / Outsider / Creepy crawling / Mary Mary / Small town / I want more / Scapegoat. *(re-iss. Jun98 cd+=/c+=; 495238-2/-4)* – Top of the world (ole, ole, ole).
Jan 98. (c-s) *(TCEM 498)* **AMNESIA / AMNESIA (Zion Train 359 Amherst Road mix) / TUBTHUMPING (Escape From New York mix)** 10
 (cd-s) *(CDEM 498)* – (first 2 tracks) / ('A'-Done Lying Down mix) / ('A'-Jimmy Echo version) / ('A'-Decontrol mix).
 (cd-s) *(CDEMS 498)* – (first & third tracks) / Tubthumping (original) / Tubthumping (Tin Tin Out mix).
May 98. (c-s) *(TCEM 511)* **TOP OF THE WORLD (OLE, OLE, OLE) / I'M A WINNER BABY / STRIKE! (Barnsley 3, Man Utd 2 mix)** 21 -
 (cd-s) *(CDEM 511)* – (first 2 tracks) / The best is yet to come (acoustic) / The best is yet to come.
Feb 99. (cd) *(499231-2)* **UNEASY LISTENING** (compilation) □ -
 – ...And in a nutshell / Mouthful of shit / Behave / Timebomb / Morality play in three acts / Enough is enough / On being pushed / Hanging on the old barbed wire / Ugh! your ugly houses! / Look! no strings! / Big mouth strikes again / This girl / Smash clause 29! / Georgina / Waiting, shouting / Song of the mother in debt... / On the day the Nazi died / Give the anarchist a cigarette / Nothing knocks me over / We don't go to God's house anymore.
Apr 99. (cd-s; with NEGATIVLAND) *<(SEELAND 020CD)>* **THE ABC'S OF ANARCHISM / SMELLY WATER / c. IS FOR STUPID (ABC remix by DJ Dr.J Land)** □ -
 (above issued on 'Seeland')
Mar 00. (c-s/cd-s) *(TC/CD EMS 563)* **SHE'S GOT ALL THE FRIENDS MONEY CAN BUY / LEST WE FORGET / PASSENGER LIST FOR DOOMED FLIGHT No.1721** □ -
 (cd-s) *(CDEM 563)* – ('A'mixes).
Apr 00. (cd) *(525584-2) <157521>* **WYSIWYG** □ -
 – I'm with stupid / Shake baby shake / Pass it along / Hey hey we're the junkies / The health & the happiness show / I'm coming out / I'm in trouble again / Social dogma / www.dot / New York mining disaster 1941 / I not sorry, I was having fun / Jesus in Vegas / The standing still / She's got all the friends money can buy / Ladies for compassionate lynching / Celebration, Florida / Moses with a gun / The physical impossibilty of death in the mind of Jerry Springer / Smart bomb / Knickers / Lie lie lie lie / Dumbing down.

Mutt   Republic

Aug 02. (cd) *(MUTTCD 001) <018071>* **READYMADES** □ Jun02
 – Salt fare, North Sea / Jacob's ladder / All in vain / Home with me / If it is to be, it is up to me / Don't try this at home / Song for Len Shackleton / Without rhyme or reason (the killing of Harry Stanley) / Don't pass go / One way or the other / When I'm bad / Sewing up crap / After Shelley.
Sep 02. (cd-s) *(MUTTCDS 088)* **HOME WITH ME** □ -

– compilations, others, etc. –

Feb 92. (lp/cd) *Agit Prop; (PROP 4)* **FIRST 2** □ -
 – (as said 1st 2 albums, originally Aug89 as '100 SONGS ABOUT SPORT'; *PROP 004) (re-iss. Feb95 on 'One Little Indian' d-lp/c/cd; TPLP 63/+C/CD)*
Apr 96. (cd+book) *One Little Indian; (EYE 1)* **PORTRAITS OF ANARCHISTS** □ -
Jan 99. (cd) *One Little Indian; (TPLP 65CD)* **LOVE / HATE** □ -

DANBERT NOBACON

Rugger Bugger   not iss.

Mar 98. (cd) *(SEEP 16CD)* **THE UNFAIRYTALE** □ -
 – Does God go to the toilet – Wormkind – Lying in the dirt – The tree of knowledge – Comic-tragic-magic / Babbernation – Lay people – A fairy tale – House plants – Jack Horner – Catastrophe reality / Man papers his crack – All the king's men – Nodzeroon el Babo – The ba llad of peoplekind – Declaring peace – Insectkind – Scare city – Jungl E smells – One way system / Sugar daddy – Martini people – Thorn-EMI lightning – A psalm – Asleep – Awake – Times of crisis / Somebody else – In the thick of it – Disagreement – Saying no – Act wi th mother / Bigger than Jesus: a) Flesh and blood and feelings, b) Because I'm a he / Why are we still in Ireland?: a) Why are we still in Ireland (part one), b) The Birmingham six.

CHURCH

Formed: Sydney, Australia ... 1980 by English-born STEVE KILBEY along with PETER KOPPES, MARTY WILLSON-PIPER and NICK WARD. Initially signing to the Aussie arm of 'Parlophone', the quartet garnered much homeland acclaim for their jangling 60's-rooted New Wave sound as heard on their debut album, 'OF SKIN & HEART' (1981); but for a few tracklisting differences, this was virtually re-released in its entirety by 'Carrere' ('Capitol' in the US) as an eponymous set the following Spring. By this point, RICHARD PLOOG had taken the place of WARD, the drummer making his debut on the follow-up album, 'THE BLURRED CRUSADE', later that year. Breaking away from the trademark BOWIE meets RICHARD BUTLER

(PSYCHEDELIC FURS) vocal style and Paisley psyche meandering over the course of three mid 80's albums ('SEANCE', 'REMOTE LUXURY' and 'HEYDAY'), KILBEY and his disciples finally broke into the mainstream after signing worldwide to 'Arista'. 1988 saw a US Top 30 single, 'UNDER THE MILKY WAY', taken from a top-selling accompanying Woody Watchel-produced album, 'STARFISH', the band also taking the opportunity to branch out in their own right with individual solo projects. Although not nearly as successful, two early 90's albums, 'GOLD AFTERNOON FIX' (1990) and 'PRIEST = AURA' (1992) found The CHURCH sticking faithfully to their wordy, atmospheric soundscapes in the face of the grunge revolution. Having already lost PLOOG in '91, KILBEY and WILLSON-PIPER became the sole founding members following the subsequent departure of KOPPES. Augmented by a cast of session players, the pair recorded the self-indulgent 'SOMETIME ANYWHERE' (1994), making no concessions to commerciality and subsequently finding themselves minus a deal. Having previously cut an eponymous album in 1991 as JACK FROST (with ex-GO-BETWEENS mainman, GRANT McLENNAN), KILBEY again took on the JF mantle for 1996's 'SNOW JOB'; KILBEY had also previously sidelined with DONETTE THAYER (of GAME THEORY), releasing two albums as HEX. Moving back to the independent sector, The CHURCH followed their spiritual bent with two further albums, 'MAGICIAN AMONG THE SPIRITS' (1997) and 'HOLOGRAM OF BAAL' (1998). The former introduced drummer/songwriter TIM POWLES full-time, the CHURCH's melan-college rock as always lush and beautifully arranged, while the latter returned to a more plaintive style. 1999's covers set, 'A BOX OF BIRDS', ran over a gamut of neo-psychedelia dug up from the 60's and 70's (see below). Album No.14 or 15 (depending on your origin), 'AFTER EVERTHING NOW THIS' (2002), was a little too formulaic and staid for its own good, tracks such as 'CHROMIUM' and 'THE AWFUL ACHE' the exception to the rule. Nevertheless, if you were a CHURCH go'er, the set was full of relaxing picturesque ballads, just the thing for a Sunday morning after a night out; a subsequent remix set of sorts, 'PARALLEL UNIVERSE', losing their religion by the bucketload. • **Covered:** THE FAITH HEALER (Sensational Alex Harvey Band) / IT'S ALL TOO MUCH (George Harrison) / HIROSHIMA MON AMOUR (Ultravox) / THE PORPOISE SONG (hit; Monkees) / DECADENCE (Kevin Ayers) / THE ENDLESS SEA (Iggy Pop) / FRICTION (Television) / ALL THE YOUNG DUDES (Mott The Hoople) / SILVER MACHINE (Hawkwind) / CORTEZ THE KILLER (Neil Young).

Album rating: OF SKIN AND HEART or THE CHURCH (*7) / THE BLURRED CRUSADE (*6) / SEANCE (*6) / REMOTE LUXURY (*7) / HEYDAY (*7) / STARFISH (*7) / GOLD AFTERNOON FIX (*6) / PRIEST: AURA (*4) / SOMETIME ANYWHERE (*5) / CONCEPTION compilation (*7) / QUICK SMOKE AT POTS compilation (*6) / MAGICIAN AMONG THE SPIRITS (*6) / HOLOGRAM OF BAAL (*5) / A BOX OF BIRDS (*5) / AFTER EVERYTHING NOW THIS (*5) / PARALLEL UNIVERSE (*4) / Steve Kilbey: UNEARTHED (*5) / EARTHED (*5) / THE SLOW CRACK (*5) / REMINDLESSNESS (*4) / GILT TRIP (*5) / NARCOSIS + (*6) / ACOUSTIC & INTIMATE (*5) / DABBLE (*5) / Peter Koppes: MANCHILD & MYTH (*7) / FROM THE WELL (*5) / WATER RITES by The Well (*5) / LOVE ERA – IRONY (*5) / SIMPLE INTENT (*5) / Marty Willson-Piper: IN REFLECTION (*5) / ART ATTACK (*6) / RHYME (*5) / SPIRIT LEVEL (*6) / HANGING OUT IN HEAVEN (*6) / LIVE AT THE FINE LINE CAFE (*5) / LIVE AT THE KNITTING FACTORY (*4)

STEVE KILBEY (b.13 Sep'60, Welwyn Garden City, England) – vocals, bass, occasional keyboards / **PETER KOPPES** (b.1959) – guitar / **MARTY WILLSON-PIPER** (b. 7 May'59, Stockport, England) – guitar / **NICK WARD** – drums, percussion

		Parlophone	not iss.
1981.	(7") *(A367)* **SHE NEVER SAID. / IN A HEARTBEAT**	-	- Austra
1981.	(lp) *(PCS 07583)* **OF SKINS AND HEART**	-	- Aust.

– For a moment we're strangers / Chrome injury / Unguarded moment / Memories in future tense / Bel-Air / Is this where you live / She never said / Fighter pilot * / Korean war * / Don't open the door to strangers. *(UK-iss.Sep87 on 'Arista'+=*)* / Too fast for you / Tear it all away / Sisters. *(cd-iss. Sep02 on 'EMI Australia'; 539479-0)*

			Carrere	Capitol
1981.	(d7") *(A536-A525)* **TWO FAST FOR YOU. / SISTERS // TEAR IT ALL AWAY. / YOU'VE GOT TO GO / FRAULEIN**		-	- Austra
Mar 82.	(7") *(CAR 212)* **UNGUARDED MOMENT. / BUSDRIVER**			
Mar 82.	(lp) *(CAL 130) <ST 12193>* **THE CHURCH**			

– (same as 'OF SKINS AND HEART' except 'Tear it all away' repl. * above) *(re-iss. Apr85; same) (cd-iss. May88; CDCAL 130)*

Sep 82. (7") *(CAR 247)* **ALMOST WITH YOU. / LIFE SPEEDS UP**

RICHARD PLOOG (b.1959) – drums (on most tracks) repl. WARD

Oct 82. (lp) *(CAL 140)* **THE BLURRED CRUSADE**
– Almost with you / When you were mine / Field of Mars / An interlude / Secret corners / Just for you / A fire burns / To be in your eyes / You Took / Don't look back. *(re-iss. Mar85; same) (cd-iss. Aug88; CDCAL 140) (cd re-iss. Sep02 on 'EMI Australia'; 539496-0)*

Nov 82. (7"m) *(CAR 257)* **UNGUARDED MOMENT. / INTERLUDE / GOLDEN DAWN**
(10"ep+=) *(CAREP 257)* – Sisters.

Mar 83. (7") *(CHURCH R5A)* **A DIFFERENT MAN. / I AM A ROCK**
(12"ep+=) *(CHURCH 5)* **SING SONGS** – Ancient history / Night is very soft / In this room. *(released on 'Capitol')*

		Carrere	Arista
May 84.	(lp)<cd> *(CAL 201) <ARCD 8565>* **SEANCE**		

– Fly / One day / Electric / It's no reason / Travel by thought / Disappear? / Electric lash / Now I wonder why / Dropping names / It doesn't change. *(re-iss. May85; same) (cd-iss. Sep02 on 'EMI Australia'; 539480-0)*

Jun 84. (7") *(CAR 336)* **IT'S NO REASON. / SOMEONE SPECIAL**
(12"+=) *(CART 336)* – Autumn soon.

Feb 85. (lp) *(CAL 213)* **REMOTE LUXURY**
– Constant in opal / Violet town / No explanation / 10,000 miles / Maybe these boys / Into my hands / A month of Sundays / Volumes / Shadow cabinet / Remote luxury. *(re-iss. Mar89 on 'Arista' lp/c/cd; 209/409/259 649)*

— (note: they were still signed to 'Parlophone' Australia)

		E.M.I.	Warners
Feb 86.	(7") **COLUMBUS. / AS YOU WILL**	-	
May 86.	(7") *(EMI 5557)* **TANTALIZED. / THE VIEW.** (12"+=) *(EMI12 5557)* – As you will.		
Jun 86.	(lp/c/cd) *(EMC/TCEMC/CDEMC 3508) <25370>* **HEYDAY**		

– Myrrh / Tristesse / Already yesterday / Columbus / Happy hunting ground / Tantalized / Disenchanted / Night of light / Youth worshipper / Roman. *(c-s+=/cd-s+=)* – As you will / The view. *(cd re-iss. Oct97 on 'Axis'; 746526-2) (cd re-iss. Sep02 on 'EMI Australia'+=; 539863-0)* – (videos).

		Parlophone	Warners
Sep 86.	(7") *(R 6139)* **DISENCHANTED. / TRANCE ENDING** (12"+=) *(12R 6139)* – You've got to go.		

		Arista	Arista
Feb 88.	(7") *(109 778) <9637>* **UNDER THE MILKY WAY. / MUSK** (12"+=/cd-s+=) *(609/659 778)* – Warm spell.		24
Mar 88.	(lp/c/cd) *(208/408/258 895) <8521>* **STARFISH**		41

– Destination / Under the Milky Way / Blood money / Lost / North, south, east and west / Spark / Antenna / Reptile / A new season / Hotel womb. *(free 12"w/ lp)* **ANNA MIRANDA / MUSK. / PERFECT CHILD / FROZEN AND DISTANT / TEXAS MOON**

Mar 90. (cd/c/lp) *(260/410/210 541) <8579>* **GOLD AFTERNOON FIX** 66
– Pharaoh / Metropolis / Terra Nova Cain / City / Russian Autumn heart / Essence / You're still beautiful / Disappointment / Transient / Fading away / Grind. *(cd+=)* – Monday morning / Laughing.

Apr 90. (7") *(113 086)* **METROPOLIS. / MONDAY MORNING**
(12"+=/cd-s+=) *(613/663 086)* – Much too much.

Jun 90. (cd-ep) **RUSSIAN AUTUMN HEART / HUNTER / FEAST / DESERT / RIDE INTO THE SUNSET** -

— **JAY DEE DAUGHERTY** (b.22 Mar'56, Santa Barbara, Calif.) – drums (ex-PATTI SMITH GROUP) repl. PLOOG / **WILLSON-PIPER** joined ALL ABOUT EVE in 1990.

Mar 92. (cd/c/lp) *(262/412/212 643) <18683>* **PRIEST = AURA**
– Aura / Ripple / Paradox / Lustre / Swan lake / Feel Mistress / Kings / Dome / Witch hunt / The disillusionist / Old flame / Chaos / Film.

— now a basic duo of **KILBEY + WILLSON-PIPER** plus **TIM POWLES** – drums / **LINDA NEIL** – violin / **SANDY CHICK** – female voice / **CAROL BROCA-WANDER** – French female voice / **BORIS GOUDENOV** – drumloops / **DARREN RYAN** – loops, + drums on 1

May 94. (d-cd/c/lp) *(<07822 18727-2/-4/-1>)* **SOMETIME ANYWHERE**
– Days of the dead / Lost my touch / Loveblind / My little problem / The maven / Angelica / Lullaby / Eastern / Two places at once / Business woman / Authority / Fly home / The dead man's dream. *(d-cd+=)* – Drought / The time being / Leave your clothes on / Cut in two / The myths you made / Freeze to burn / Macabre tavern.

— **KOPPES** returned to the fold (sporadically at first)

		Festival	Deep Karma
Feb 97.	(cd) *(D 31562)* **MAGICIAN AMONG THE SPIRITS**		

– Welcome / Comedown / Ritz / Grandoise / Ladyboy / It could be anyone / Further adventures of the time being / Romany caravan / Magician among the spirits / Afterimage. *(re-iss. Jan99 on 'Cooking Vinyl'; COOKCD 168)*

			-
Aug 98.	(cd-s) *(D 1742)* **LOUISIANA / ANYWAY / LIZARD**		

		Cooking Vinyl	Thirsty Ear
Aug 98.	(d-cd) *(COOKCD 155) <57054>* **HOLOGRAM OF BAAL**		

– Anaesthesia / Ricochet / Louisiana / The great machine / No certainty attached / Tranquility / Buffalo / This is it / Another earth / Glow-worm // Bastard universe / Movements (stage 1-6).

Aug 99. (cd) *(COOKCD 183) <57073>* **A BOX OF BIRDS**
– The faith healer / It's all too much / Hiroshima mon amour / The porpoise song / Decadence / The endless sea / Friction / All the young dudes / Silver machine / Cortez the killer.

— line-up:- **KOPPES + KILBEY, WILLSON-PIPER + POWLES**

Jan 02. (cd) *(COOKCD 209) <57116>* **AFTER EVERYTHING NOW THIS**
– Numbers / After everything / The awful ache / Song for the asking / Chromium / Radiance / Reprieve / Night flowers / Seen it coming / Invisible.

Nov 02. (d-cd) *(COOKCD 248) <57126>* **PARALLEL UNIVERSE**
– Intro-MC / Seen it @ the Feelmore / Stay all night / Radiant 1934 (remix) / Replated – Chromium / Distant X unseen / Let X=X / Sleepless.night@reality.net / Earthfriend (version) / Down: nostalgia and everything after / The deep ache mix // live:- 1st woman on the Moon / Espionage / Reward / There you go / Night flower / Twin star.

– compilations, others, etc. –

Apr 88. (lp/c/cd) Carrere; *(CAL/CAC/CDCAL 229)* **CONCEPTION** -
– When you were mine / Chrome injury / A different man / To be in your eyes / Is this where you live / Unguarded moment / Just for you / Memories and future tense / Almost with you / You took.

May 88. (7") Carrere; *(CAR 425)* **UNGUARDED MOMENT. / BEL-AIR**
(12"+=) *(CART 425)* – ('A'side) / Temperature drop / Downtown / Winterland.

Dec 88. (d-cd) E.M.I.; *(838254)* **HINDSIGHT** - - Austra
(re-iss. Sep02; same)

Jan 95. (cd) Raven; (cd) *(RVCD 43)* **ALMOST YESTERDAY 1981-1990**

1996. (cd) Mushroom; *(D 32380)* **QUICK SMOKE AT POTS** (some later B-sides) - - Austra

Jun 00. (3xcd-box) Mushroom; *(MUSH 33275-2)* **BOX SET**
– (GOLD AFTERNOON FIX / PRIEST = AURA / SOMETIME ANYWHERE)

Sep 02. (cd) EMI Australia; *(535583-2)* **SING SONGS / REMOTE LUXURY / PERSIA** - -

STEVE KILBEY

— solo, with brother **RUSSELL** and fiancee **KARIN JANSSON**

E.M.I.	not iss.

1986. (7"m) *(A 1516)* **THIS ASPHALT EDEN. / NEVER COME BACK / SHELL** – – Austra
(re-iss. 1987 on 'Red Eye'; RED 13)

Enigma	Rykodisc

Aug 87. (lp/cd) *(3297-1/-2) <73207>* **UNEARTHED**
– Out of this world / Guilty / Pretty ugly, pretty sad / Swampdrome / Judgement day / Rising son / Tyrant / Transference / My birthday the moon festival / Design error / Nothing inside / Other time / Heliopolis / Famine.

Red Eye	Rykodisc

Nov 87. (lp)<cd> *(REDLP 2) <RCD 90043>* **EARTHED** (instrumental) – – Austra
– The dawn poems / Dreambeings / Memory / The white plague / A love letter from Sydney / City of women / Carthage / Hotel / The empire mourns her sun without tears / Cornucopia / Aphrodite / Sad little piano piece / The reality generators malfunctioned / Napoleon's army, Christmas eve, outside Moscow / Atlantis / Pan / The woman who was married to love / Agog / Earthed. *(cd-iss. Mar94 on 'Rykodisc';)*

1988. (7") *(RED 14)* **FIREMAN. / FORGETFULNESS / NONAPOLOGY** – – Austra
1989. (m-lp) *(RED 15)* **THE SLOW CRACK** – – Austra
– Fireman / Woman with reason / A favourite pack of lies / Something that means something / Ariel sings / A minute without you / Surrealist woman blues. *<US-iss.1990 on 'Rough Trade' lp/c/cd+=; ROUGHUS 70/+C/CD>* – TRANSACTIONS
1989. (12"ep) *(RED 19)* **TRANSACTIONS** – – Austra
– Transaction / Consider yourself conquered / Song of Solomon / Starling St.
1990. (d-lp/cd) *(RED LP/CD 11)* **REMINDLESSNESS** – – Austra
– The neverness hoax / Vanishing act / Life's little luxuries / She counts up the days / The amphibian / Liquid / Goliath / Some lysergic Africa / Gloriana / Danielle / Excerpt from 'Charlotte Bay Pde.' / Music from commercial for 'Eternity Inc.' / No such thing / Soul sample / Celebration of the birthday of the elephant god / Reminidlessness.
1990. (cd-ep) *(REDCDEP 20)* **TRANSACTION / RANDOM PAN / PAIN IN MY TEMPLES / NO SUCH THING** – – Austra

Polydor	not iss.

Jul 91. (cd-ep) *(511647-2)* **NARCOSIS** – – Austra
– Somna / Limbo / Sleep with me / Fall in love / Space. *(cd-iss. Jun97 as 'NARCOSIS +' on 'Vicious Sloth'+=; VSC 005)* – The Egyptian / Midnite in America / Linda Wong / English kiss.

Vicious Sloth	not iss.

Jun 97. (cd; by STEVE & RUSSELL P. KILBEY) *(VSC 004)* **GILT TRIP** – –
– Gilt trip / The onset / Tragic Mandarin love story / Eyes smeared with the ointment of love / Neither sun, nor moon, nor electricity / Darkness and gardens of steel / Dress circle seats for creation / Blowing through the mansion of a 1930s film star / Happy endings.

Karmic Hit	not iss.

Aug 00. (cd) *(KH 007)* **ACOUSTIC AND INTIMATE (live)** – –
– Providence / Mistress / Buffalo / My little problem / Nonapology / Limbo / Hotel womb / Othertime / Under the Milky Way / September 13 / Almost with you / Tristesse / An arrangement / SK's first song (excerpt) / Don't rely on your friends (excerpt) / Skyscraper carnivore (excerpt).
Oct 01. (cd) *(KH 009)* **DABBLE** – – Austra
– Blessed one / Keeper / Silencer / China / Loki / Selfish portrait / No time at all / Aloha Biggles and Starr / Untitled one / Stagefright / Untitled too / Seasick / The temptation of St. Anthony / Time to say goodbye.

HEX

KILBEY + DONETTE THAYER (of GAME THEORY)

Demon	Rykodisc

Mar 90. (lp/cd) *(FIEND/+CD 156) <RCD 10184>* **HEX** – Nov89
– Diviner / Hermaphrodite / Ethereal message / Mercury towers / Out of the pink / Fire island / In the net / Silvermine / Elizabeth Green / An arrangement.

— added **JIM McGRATH** – percussion

Feb 91. (lp/cd) *<RCD 10186>* **VAST HALOS**
– Monarch / Shelter / March / Centaur / Antelope / Hollywood in winter / Orpheus circuit / Aquamarine / Hell / Vast halos.

— a different HEX released stuff for the 'Ninja Tune' label

JACK FROST

— formed by **STEVE KILBEY + GRANT McLENNAN** (ex-GO-BETWEENS) with **PRYCE SURPLICE** – drums, computers

Arista	Arista

Mar 91. (cd/c/lp) *(261/411/211 354) <ARCD 8667>* **JACK FROST**
– Every hour God sends / Birdowner (as seen on TV) / Civil war lament / Geneva 4 a.m. / Trapeze boy / Providence / Thought I was over you / Threshold / Number eleven / Didn't know where I was / Even as we speak *[cd-only]* / Rauble / Everything takes forever.

Red Eye	not iss.

Apr 91. (7") *(879 262-7)* **EVERY HOUR GOD SENDS. / EVEN AS WE SPEAK / JACK'S DREAM** – – Austra
Jun 91. (7") *(879 857-7)* **THOUGHT THAT I WAS OVER YOU. / DUB THRESHOLD (nightmare mix)** – – Austra
(cd-s+=) n(879 857-2) – Jack's dream.

— PRYCE was repl. by **RUSSELL KILBEY** – organ, vocals + **TIM POWLES** – drums, percussion

Beggars Banquet	Beggars Banquet

Apr 96. (cd) *(BEGL 183CD) <80183>* **SNOW JOB** Aug96
– Jack Frost blues / Aviatrix / Running from the body / Shakedown / You don't know / Weightless and wild / Pony express / Cousin – Angel / Little song / Empire / Angela Carter / Haze / Dry dock.

PETER KOPPES

solo, featuring his wife **MELODY, KILBEY + PLOOG**

E.M.I.	not iss.

1984. (7") *(A 1249)* **LOVE CAN'T IMAGINE. / SHOW ME THAT** – – Austra

Session	Rykodisc

1987. (12"ep) *(SREP 001)* **WHEN REASON FORBIDS: A REQUIEM** – – Austra
– When reason forbids / At the castle / Air.
May 88. (lp) *(SRLP 002) <RLP 20046>* **MANCHILD & MYTH**
– Take a vow / These three things / The wise and the wicked / What's the matter? / Quest / Comes as no surprise / Opus / Sahara / The Colosseum / A drink from the cup / Into the bright light / Let you walk away / Our love. *(cd-iss. Mar94 on 'Rykodisc'; RCD 20046)*

not iss.	T.V.T.

Oct 89. (lp/c/cd) *<TVT 2460-1/-4/-2>* **FROM THE WELL** –
– In the wake / Her mark / Only wait / Horses in the sand / The lost peace / Pyramid building (she's leaving) / I wonder / Lullaby / Desert flower bride / Nursery fugue / Testing 3.2.1. / Aural garden / Anthem.

— The WELL:- **KOPPES, RICHARD PLOOG, ANTHONY SMITH, JIM LEONE, PETER PIX, SONIA CHEMARIN, MARK WOOD, MANNY LIEBER, ROBIEN HAIDER**, etc

Worldwater	not iss.

1995. (cd; aka as The WELL) *(WW 1)* **WATER RITES** – – Austra
– Caravan / Finest hour / Sublimation / Arabia / House afire / Spirit march / Brave / Liberation dance / Faith / Wolf run / On wings of love. *(UK-iss.Jan98; same)*

Phantom	not iss.

1990's. (12"blue-ep; as PETER KOPPES & THE WELL) *(PH12-49)* **IRIDESCENCE** – – Austra
– Peak to peak / Her mark / The destroyer.

— next feat. **TIM POWLES** – drums, percussion + **SONIA CHEMARIN** – vocals / + guests

Immersion	not iss.

Jan 98. (cd) *(IMM 001CD)* **LOVE ERA / IRONY** – –
– Celebration / Thankyou / Two in a million / Come a day / Sound / Apex farmer / Oblivion & beyond / Message / Make a move / Luminous / Esoterica.
Aug 02. (cd) *(IMMCD 5CD)* **SIMPLE INTENT** – – Austra
– Naked soul / Blame / Dedication / Drink? / Leaving / Het her today / Natural / Sleeping in my heart / Voyager / Walk with you / Winter.

MARTY WILLSON-PIPER

with various session people

Chase	not iss.

1987. (lp) *(451038-1)* **IN REFLECTION** – – Austra
– I know I won't / Art on the run / Night is over / Velvet fuselage / Sleepy metal box / Hamburg / How come they don't touch the ground / Winter splinter bay / The lantern / Volumes / Soft murder / Travelling through the sea of sun machines / The width and the height. *(cd-iss. 1999 on 'Phantom'; UM-7)*

Survival	Rykodisc

1988. (7") *(652891.7)* **SHE'S KING. / FRIGHTENED JUST BECAUSE OF YOU**
1988. (lp) *(462450.1) <RLP 0042>* **ART ATTACK** – – Austra
– O'Stockholm / Water / She's king / Too round to be square / You whisper / Fear / Evil Queen of England / On the tip of my tongue / Listen – Space / Frightened just because of you / White spots on my finger, Jupiter blue on my white shirt / Word / Ah Stockholm. *(<cd-iss. Mar94 on 'Rykodisc'+=; RCD 10042>)* – Winter splinter bay / The lantern / I know I won't / Night is over / Velvet fuselage / How come they don't touch the ground.

Borderline	Rykodisc

1989. (lp) *(BL 001) <RLP 10114>* **RHYME**
– St. Germain / Melancholy girl / Questions without answers / Melody of the rain / Idiots / Forever (with BOBBY WOMACK) / Say / Time is imaginary / How can I help it / Melancholy god / To where I am now / Cascade. *(<cd-iss. Mar94 on 'Rykodisc'; RCD 10114>)*

Festival	not iss.

1989. (7"/c-s) *(K/C 10009)* **QUESTIONS WITHOUT ANSWERS. / NEW YORK BUDDHA** – – Austra
1989. (7") *(K 10226)* **MELANCHOLY GIRL. / ON THE TIP OF MY TONGUE (live)** – – Austra

Rykodisc	Rykodisc

Jul 92. (cd-s) *<(RCD 51025)>* **I CAN'T CRY / LUSCIOUS GHOST**
Jul 92. (cd) *<(RCD 10197)>* **SPIRIT LEVEL**
– I can't cry / Will I start to bleed / Turn away to the stars / Luscious ghost / Scandinavian stare / Can't ever risk an openess with you / Even though you are my friend / Adelle Yvonne / The saddest house in Stockholm / Kiss you to death / Melts my heart.
1993. (cd-s) *<RCD5 1025>* **LUSCIOUS GHOST / IN CIRCLES / LUSCIOUS GHOST (unfinished version)**

not iss.	Heyday

2000. (cd) *<HEY 046-2>* **HANGING OUT IN HEAVEN** –
– Forget the radio / Swan / Wondering / Sanctuary / Waves towards the Moon / Goodbye / I don't think so / Watching us / You bring your love to me / After eight / All those wires / 1929 vintage wine / Wreck (a sea shanty) / What is her name / All that remains.
2000. (cd) *<HEY 047-2>* **LIVE AT THE FINE LINE CAFE (live in Minneapolis, Minnesota, 15 February, 2000)** –
– St. Germain / Frightened just because of you / Water / Melody of the rain / I can't cry / 10,000 miles / You whisper / Questions without answers / Time is imaginary / To where I am now / On the tip of my tongue / Here come the tears.
2000. (cd) *<HEY 048-2>* **LIVE AT THE KNITTING FACTORY (live New York City, 1998)** –
– I know I won't / St. Germaine / Evil Queen of England / She's king / The air between us / 10,000 miles / You whisper / Say / Spark / Time is imaginary.

CINdYTALK

Formed: London, England ... 1982 as a studio outfit by vocalist, GORDON SHARP and guitarist, DAVID CLANCY, both fresh from young Edinburgh punk outfit, The FREEZE. After only a few independently released singles (namely 'IN COLOUR' and 'CELEBRATION'), they broke up – with SHARP subsequently lending his services to '4 a.d.' outfits the COCTEAU TWINS and THIS MORTAL COIL. Around the same time (1984), he and CLANCY (alongside JOHN BYRNE and KINNISON) resurfaced with a brand new venture, CINdYTALK, a debut album, 'CAMOUFLAGE HEART', being poorly received by critics and public alike due to its impenetrable CLOCKDVA-esque experimentation. However, SHARP did return to the studio after a three year absence, completing the much improved follow-up double-set, 'IN THIS WORLD' (1988). ALIK and DEBBIE WRIGHT had now taken the place of CLANCY and KINNISON, the new line-up progressing to a refined ambient atmospheric sound incorporating SHARP's distinctive harsh vocal incantations. An album in 1991, 'THE WIND IS STRONG' was another marked progression, although this in turn was surpassed with the long awaited 1996 effort, 'WAPPINSCHAW'. The album was a return to his Scottish roots and featured readings by long-time SNP affiliated novelist, Alasdair Gray, while references were made to outsider heroes like Sitting Bull and Wolfe Tone among others. Of late, GORDON has become BAMBULE (which means "dance" or "riot"), a trip acidy combo who've released two limited edition 12" EP's. • **Songwriters:** SHARP except traditional, 'HUSH'. • **Trivia:** SHARP (along with ROBIN GUTHRIE, DAVID ROS, JAY AHERN + NADIA LANMAN) went under the moniker of MacBETH and contributed a cover of Mary Margaret O'Hara's 'HELP ME LIFT YOU UP' to the V/A comp, 'Volume 5'.

Album rating: CAMOUFLAGE HEART (*4) / IN THIS WORLD (*5) / THE WIND IS STRONG (*5) / WAPPINSCHAW (*6)

FREEZE

GORDON SHARP – vocals / **DAVID CLANCY** – guitar, vocals / **KEITH GRANT** – bass, vocals / **GRAEME RADIN** – drums

A1 / not iss.

Aug 79. (7"ep) *(A 11)* **IN COLOUR**
 – Paranoia / For J.P.S. (with love & loathing) / Psychodalek nightmares.
Apr 80. (7") *(A 11 S1)* **CELEBRATION. / CROSS-OVER**

— **MIKE MORAN** – bass; repl. GRANT

— **NEIL BRAIDWOOD** – drums, keyboards; repl. RADIN

— split late in 1981. A few years later, SHARPE guested for 4ad conglomerate THIS MORTAL COIL. He provided vox for the track 'KANGAROO' (a cover taken from BIG STAR) on album 'It'll End In Tears'.

CINdYTALK

GORDON SHARP – vocals, piano / **DAVID CLANCY** – guitar / **JOHN BYRNE** – bass / **KINNISON** – drums

Midnight Music / not iss.

Sep 84. (lp) *(CHIME 00.065)* **CAMOUFLAGE HEART**
 – It's luxury / Instinct (backtosense) / Under glass / Memories of skin and snow / The spirit behind the circus dream / The ghost never smiles / A second breath / Everybody is Christ / Disintegrate ... *(cd-iss. 1988; CHIME 006CD) (cd re-iss. Oct96 on 'Touch'; TOUCH 3CD)*

— **SHARP** with **BYRNE** – instruments / **ALIK WRIGHT** – instruments / **DEBBIE WRIGHT** – vocals, instruments

Mar 88. (d-lp/c/cd) *(CHIME 027/028CD)* **IN THIS WORLD**
 – In this world / Janey's love / Gift of a knife / Playtime / The room of delight / Touched / Circle of shit / My sun / The beginning of wisdom / No serenade / Sight after sight / Angels of ghosts / Through water / Cherish / Homeless / Still whisper / In this world. *(cd re-iss. Oct96 on 'Touch'; TOUCH 2CD)*
Jan 91. (lp/c/cd) *(CHIME 103/+CC/CD)* **THE WIND IS STRONG**
 – Landing / First sight / To the room / Waiting / Through flowers / Second sight / Through the forest / Arrival / Is there a room for hire / Choked I / Choked II / Dream ritual / Fuck you Mrs. Grimace / On snow moor / Angel wings.
Jan 94. (12"/cd-s) *(DONG 76/+CD)* **SECRETS & FALLING**
 – Song of changes / The moon above me / In sunshine / Empty hand.

— **SHARP** now with **PAUL MIDDLETON** – drums / **PAUL JONES** – guitar / **ANDREA BROWN** – bass / **MARK STEPHENSON** – samples, keyboards, electronics

Touched / not iss.

Oct 96. (7") *(FEEL 001)* **PRINCE OF LIES. / MUSTER**
Oct 96. (lp/cd) *(TOUCH/+CD 1)* **WAPPINSCHAW**
 – A song of changes / Empty hand / Return to pain / Wheesht / Snow kisses / Secrets and falling / Disappear / Traum lose nacht / And now in sunshine / Prince of lies / Hush. *(hidden track+=)* – Muster.

BAMBULE

GORDON SHARP + SIMON CARMICHAEL (aka CUNNING)

Praxis / not iss.

1997. (d12"ep) *(Praxis 19)* **CUNNING MEETS BAMBULE**
 – Signal furies / Ascent. / Disco dum dum / Descent (alone) // Lockstep part 1 / Lockstep part 2. / Spin fracture / Ubu-ma

— **SHARP** with **RICHIE YOUNG, DALE LLOYD** (of LUCID) / **STUART ARENTZEN** (of LUCID) + **TYMOTHI LOVING** (of DELAYED SHOCK REACTION)

Nov 00. (12"ep; by BAMBULE & PHOTON) *(Praxis 29)* **VERTICAL INVASION / JOY IS THE AIM. / THIRDFORCE / TRIPPED WIRE**

CLAN OF XYMOX (see under ⇒ XYMOX)

Anne CLARK

Born: Croydon, London, England. An up and coming poet of the early 80's, ANNE issued her debut, German-only album 'THE SITTING ROOM' in 1982, a set that featured fellow wordsmith, PATRIK FITZGERALD as well as keyboard accompaniment from DOMINIC APPLETON (of BREATHLESS). Subsequently signing to 'Red Flame', CLARK enlisted the help of VINI REILLY (of DURUTTI COLUMN) and DAVID HARROW to augment her on her second set, 'CHANGING PLACES' (1983). Combining her poetic works with other more conventional songs, she went on to record for the Red Flame offshoot imprint, 'Ink', where she worked with the RAVISHING BEAUTIES (i.e. VIRGINIA ASTLEY, etc) on a mini-set, 'JOINED UP WRITING' (1984). With her haunting, emotive alternative-pop finally getting noticed by the major labels, CLARK moved up to Virgin offshoot, '10' for further sets, the JOHN FOXX-produced 'PRESSURE POINTS' (1985), 'HOPELESS CASES' (1987) and 'R.S.V.P.' (1988). More popular on the continent (especially Germany and Norway), the sultry blonde singer/poetess continued to record into the 90's without ever rising above cult status in her home country. Nevertheless she did form writing and musical partnerships with English peers, EYELESS IN GAZA and ANDY BELL (ex-RIDE), while also taking on covers of 60's standards, 'IF I COULD' and 'THE WINDMILLS OF YOUR MIND'.

Album rating: THE SITTING ROOM (*5) / CHANGING PLACES (*5) / JOINED UP WRITING mini (*4) / PRESSURE POINTS (*5) / HOPELESS CASES (*5) / R.S.V.P. (*4) / AN ORDINARY LIFE compilation (*6) / UNSTILL LIFE (*5) / PSYCHOMETRY (*4) / THE LAW IS AN ANAGRAM OF WEALTH (*4) / TO LOVE AND BE LOVED (*5) / THE NINETIES compilation (*5) / JUST AFTER SUNSET with Martyn Bates (*5)

ANNE CLARK – vocals, keyboards / with **DOMINIC APPLETON** – keyboards / **ANDREA LASCHETTI** – keyboards / **PATRIK FITZGERALD** – piano / **GARY MUNDY** – guitar, synthesizer, vocals

unknown / not iss.

1982. (lp) *(206865)* **THE SITTING ROOM** — German
 – The sitting room / Swimming / An ordinary life / Shades / Short story / The power game / All we have to be thankful for.

— now augmented by **DAVID HARROW** – keyboards / **VINI REILLY** – guitar (of DURUTTI COLUMN)

Red Flame / not iss.

Aug 83. (lp) *(RF 22)* **CHANGING PLACES**
 – Contact / Sleeper in Metropolis / Poem for a nuclear romance / Wallies / Lovers audition / Poets turmoil No.364 / Echoes remain forever / All night party / Pandora's box / Feel / The last emotion.

— now with **HARROW / + VIRGINIA ASTLEY** – keyboards, vocals / **JO WELLS** – keyboards, vocals, clarinet / **ANNE STEPHENSON** – violin / **NICK PRETZEL** – drums, electro-percussion / **NICK COOK** – vocals

Ink / not iss.

Sep 84. (m-lp) *(MINK 5)* **JOINED UP WRITING**
 – Nothing at all / Weltschmerz / Killing time / True love tales / Self destruct / Our darkness.
Nov 84. (12") *(INK12-5)* **OUR DARKNESS. / THE SITTING ROOM / THE SITTING ROOM (LATER ON)**
Jun 85. (12") *(INK12-13)* **SLEEPER IN METROPLOIS (extended). / SELF DESTRUCT**

— next with **ASTLEY, HARROW + CHARLIE MORGAN** – drums

10-Virgin / not iss.

Jul 85. (7") *(TEN 79)* **HEAVEN. / BURSTING**
Nov 85. (lp/c) *(XID/CXID 18)* **PRESSURE POINTS**
 – Heaven / Red sands / Alarm call / Tide / The interruption / The power game / World without warning / Bursting / Lovers retreat. *(cd-iss. Aug86; DIXCD 8)*
Feb 87. (lp/c/cd) *(DIX/CDIX/DIXCD 48)* **HOPELESS CASES**
 – Poem without words 1 – The 3rd meeting / Homecoming / Up / Cane Hill / This must be the verse / Now will you be good? / Hope road / Armchair theatre / Leaving / Poem without words 2 – Journey by night.
Apr 87. (7") *(TEN 167)* **HOPE ROAD (A-Z ROUTE). / POEM WITHOUT WORDS 1 – THE 3rd MEETING**
 (12"+=) *(TENT 167)* – Heaven (live).

— her live band were:- **MORGAN / + GORDON REANEY** – guitar, vocals / **RICK KENTON** – keyboards, bass / **NED MORANT** – percussion

May 88. (lp/c/cd) *(DIX/CDIX/DIXCD 72)* **R.S.V.P. (live)**
 – Up / Homecoming / Red sands / The power game / Cane hill / Leaving / Heaven / The last emotion / Killing time / Wallies / Our darkness / Now will you be good? / This is the verse / Sleeper in Metropolis.

— retained **MORGAN** and enlisted several musicians

S.P.V. / not iss.

May 91. (cd/c/lp) *(08836-2/-4/-1)* **UNSTILL LIFE**
 – The moment / Sognsvann / The spiining turning of the summer earth / Ice, moving (instrumental) / White silence / Makes me feel at ease / Empty me / Nida / Counter act / Abuse / Silent prayer / Closed circuit.
1993. (cd) *(SPV 084-89282)* **PSYCHOMETRY (live)** — German
 – Journey by night / World without warning / Unstill life / Come in / So quiet here / The sitting room / The spinning turning of the summer earth / This be the verse / Windmills of your mind / Improvisation / Swallow song / Dedication / Interlude / At midnight / That we have been here / Fragility / Killing time / Closed circuit / Echoes remain forever. *(UK-iss.Aug95; same)*
1994. (cd) *(SPV 084-92702)* **THE LAW IS AN ANAGRAM OF WEALTH** — German
 – Flight through sunlit clouds / So quiet here / At midnight / Lost to the world / Come in / Fragility / That we have been here / Longing stilled / Nightship / Seize the vivid sky / The haunted road / I of the storm. *(UK-iss.Aug95; same)*

Anne CLARK (cont)

Oct 95. (cd) *(SPV 085-89542)* **TO LOVE AND BE LOVED**
— Dream made real / Mundesley beach / Letter of tanks to a friend / Healing / Acropolis / Key / Painting / Athens / Virtuality / Elegy for a lost summer.
Jun 97. (cd) **WORDPROCESSING (THE REMIX PROJECT)** – German
1998. (cd; ANNE CLARK & MARTYN BATES) **JUST AFTER SUNSET – THE POETRY OF R.M. RILKE** – German
— Silent forces / Autumn / From the book of pilgrimage / Song of the sea / To music / Going blind / The garden of olives / Time and again / The panther / From the book of monastic life #2 / The fruit / Early spring / The apple orchard / From the book of monastic life #1 / Autumn day / Departure of the prodigal son / Sehnsucht. *(re-iss. Nov02; same)*

– compilations, others, etc. –

Sep 85. (12") *Ink; (INK12-16)* **WALLIES.** /
Mar 86. (12") *Ink; (INK12-18)* **TRUE LOVE TALES.** /
Aug 88. (cd) *Ink; (INKCD 001)* **TRILOGY**
— (CHANGING PLACES / THE SITTING ROOM / JOINED UP WRITING).
Nov 90. (cd/c/lp) *Great Expectations; (PIP CD/MC/LP 017)* **AN ORDINARY LIFE**
— Sleeper in Metropolis / Self destruct / Wallies / True love tales / Our darkness / The sitting room / All night party / Echoes remain forever (with BOBBY WOMACK) / An ordinary life / Shades / Killing time / Our darkness (alt.mix) / Weltschmerz / Nothing at all / Our darkness (12"mix).
Feb 97. (cd) *S.P.V.; (SPV 085-44632)* **THE NINETIES (A FINE COLLECTION)**
— Abuse / Counter act / Empty me / If I could / Windmills of your mind / Haunted road / Fragility / Seize the vivid sky / Elegy for a lost summer / Echoes remain forever / Dream made real / Letter of thanks to a friend / Our darkness / Sleeper in Metropolis.
Mar 01. (cd) *S.P.V.; (SPV 310-71110)* **TO LOVE AND BE LOVED / THE LAW IS AN ANAGRAM OF WEALTH**

Jay CLARKSON

Born: Dunedin, New Zealand. Another to come out from under that proverbial musical rock called Dunedin and 'Flying Nun' records, JAY cut her teeth via some indifferent releases in the mid-80's under the billing of The EXPENDABLES (i.e. THEY WERE EXPENDABLE). Continuing her liaison with NZ indie specialists, 'Flying Nun', JAY and her band BREATHING CAGE released a number of low-key sets, the eponymous 'BREATHING CAGE' (i.e. 'MISERICORD') winning the prestigious Rhinebeck Rock Award at the turn of the decade. JAY resurfaced in '98/'99 with a new solo set, 'KINDLE', her dirge-like, peaceful, calming appeal evident from the opening 'WHEELING' to the last track, 'ABSOLUTE POVERTY'.

Album rating: JAY CLARKSON mini (*6) / BREATHING CAGE (*6) / PACKET compilation (*7) / KINDLE (*6)

EXPENDABLES

JAY CLARKSON with **MICHAEL KIME + ROBERT KEY**

Flying Nun   not iss.

1983. (12"ep; as THEY WERE EXPENDABLE) *(TWE 1/J1)* **BIG STRAIN** – NewZ
— Little Hitlers / Lukewarm vs hot / Big strain / Jazz thing / Posture / Putting the eye.
1984. (7") *(FN 025)* **THE FLOWER. / MAN WITH NO DESIRE** – NewZ
1985. (m-lp) *(FN 029)* **IN BETWEEN GEARS** – NewZ
— Say cheese / A different matter / Cain / No blame / Wrong key / Cargo / Head for the hills / In between gears.

— KEY (of The SOMBRETONES with PETER JEFFERIES) joined CAKE KITCHEN (with GRAEME JEFFERIES)

JAY CLARKSON

— (some with the BREATHING CAGE) incl. KIME
1986. (m-lp) *(FN 054)* **JAY CLARKSON** – NewZ
— Some kind of hurting / The boy with the sad hands / The wear and tear / A loose end / Penelope / Ghost of a life / Without decision / Gone.

— added **GREG MALCOLM** – guitar (now solo artist)
1991. (c-s; as BREATHING CAGE / JAY CLARKSON) *(FN 135)* **YOU AND ME AND THE OLD HILL / JUST HUMAN** – NewZ
1990. (lp; as BREATHING CAGE) *(FN 173)* **BREATHING CAGE** w-drawn
(Rheineck Award LP)
— Memory lane / Cheeky wings / More than an edge / Artful dodger / Man with no desire / Fly on the wall / Big life / Lucille / Chemistry / In spirit. *(cd-iss. 1991 as JAY CLARKSON BREATHING CAGE – 'MISERICORD' on 'Tall Poppy'; 130589)*
1992. (cd) *(FNCD 202)* **PACKET** (compilation) – NewZ
— The boy with the sad hands / Penelope / Say cheese / Loose end / Wear and tear / Liberal cad / Some kind of haunting / The flower / Big strain / No blame / Without decision / A ghost of a life. *(re-iss. 1993; FNCD 286)*

Arclife   not iss.

1999. (cd) *(Arclife 006)* **KINDLE** – NewZ
— Wheeling / Broken house / Walk away / This clown / Faint blue line of chalk / Whiskey priest / Time / Ricochet / Absolute poverty.

CLEAN

Formed: Dunedin, New Zealand . . . 1978 by DAVID KILGOUR, his brother HAMISH and PETER GUTTERIDGE. While the KILGOURS subsequently relocated to Auckland, GUTTERIDGE had already departed (he soon joined The CHILLS), the band were put on hold until DAVID met ROBERT SCOTT back in Dunedin. Eventually joined by HAMISH, the trio recorded a seminal debut single, 'TALLY HO', on the 'Flying Nun' label. Set up by a fan primarily to release the track, the imprint rapidly became an NZ institution. The fact that The CLEAN were one of the first bands to grace the label is a mark of their influence and, along with The CHILLS, KILGOUR & Co.'s organ-heavy garage-pop sound (memorably described as SONIC YOUTH conducting a choir of page boys) helped launch and inspire a scene that is still thriving today. For all that, The CLEAN's career was relatively brief, the band only releasing a further two mini-sets, 'BOODLE, BOODLE, BOODLE' and 'GREAT SOUNDS GREAT . . .' over the following two years before splitting. The former even breached the NZ Top 5 (!) despite the miniscule recording budget, a mark of the band's musical resourcefulness and instinct for quirky but effective pop. Following the departure of DAVID, SCOTT formed his own outfit, The BATS, although the KILGOUR brothers soon reunited under the banner of The GREAT UNWASHED, GUTTERIDGE returning to the fold as the line-up came full circle. Yet the new material was rootsier than The CLEAN (collected on album 'CLEAN OUT OF OUR MINDS'), bassist ROSS HUMPHRIES was brought in to allow a twin guitar format courtesy of KILGOUR and GUTTERIDGE. This proved to be another short-live venture, however, HAMISH later forming BAILTER SPACE with ALISTER PARKER and JOHN HALVORSEN while GUTTERIDGE formed the J&MC-esque SNAPPER. To the delight of many British fans, the KILGOUR brothers and ROBERT SCOTT reformed The CLEAN in 1988 and perfomed in London, a recording of the gig at Fulham's Greyhound venue released in Spring '89 as an EP, 'IN'N'NER LIVE'. The record's positive reception led to the band undertaking a full world tour and, at long last, recording a full length album. The resulting 'VEHICLE' (1990) was a more straightforwardly conventional affair lacking the inspired rough edge of old but making up for it with a sterling set of indie pop songs. With HAMISH concentrating on BAILTER SPACE for most of the early 90's, it was 1995 before a further CLEAN album, ('MODERN ROCK'), was polished off; 1996's 'UNKNOWN COUNTRY' was their last effort for some time. In 2001, originals DAVID and HAMISH KILGOUR reunited with ROBERT SCOTT to produce a fresh CLEAN set, 'GETAWAY', loopy experimental space pop at its best. 'Merge' records also issued the 4th album proper, 'A FEATHER IN THE ENGINE' (2002), from the mercurial DAVID KILGOUR, his other three, 'HERE COME THE CARS' (1991), 'SUGAR MOUTH' (1994) and 'DAVID KILGOUR & THE HEAVY EIGHTS' (1997), fusing spasmodic Krautrock and The BYRDS well before anyone even thought about it. Meanwhile, brother HAMISH was concocting his own atmospheric pop under the banner of MAD SCENE and the watchful eye of 'Flying Nun'. 'A TRIP THRU MONSTERLAND' (1993) and 'SEALIGHT' (1995), saw the man work alongside band members LISA SIEGEL and DANNY MANETTO, to name but a few; ROBERT VICKERS of The GO-BETWEENS made an appearance on the latter set. In 1996, MAD SCENE covered Echo & The Bunnymen's 'PICTURES ON MY WALL' for the mini-set/EP, 'CHINESE HONEY'.

Album rating: GREAT SOUNDS GREAT . . . mini (*5) / Great Unwashed: CLEAN OUT OF OUR MINDS (*5) / COLLECTION compilation (*6) / Stephen: RADAR OF SMALL DOGS (*6) / Clean: COMPILATION collection (*7) / ODDITIES collection (*6) / ODDITIES 2 collection (*6) / VEHICLE (*6) / MODERN ROCK (*5) / UNKNOWN COUNTRY (*5) / GETAWAY (*5) / ANTHOLOGY double compilation (*8) / Great Unwashed: COLLECTION (*5) / David Kilgour: HERE COME THE CARS (*5) / SUGAR MOUTH (*6) / FIRST STEPS & FALSE ALARMS compilation (*4) / DAVID GILGOUR & THE HEAVY EIGHTS (*7) / A FEATHER IN THE ENGINE (*6) / Mad Scene: A TRIP THRU MONSTERLAND (*4) / SEALIGHT (*6) / CHINESE HONEY mini (*5)

DAVID KILGOUR (b. 6 Sep'61) – vocals, guitar / **HAMISH KILGOUR** – drums / **ROBERT SCOTT** – bass; repl. PETER GUTTERIDGE who joined The CHILLS / guest on debut **MARTIN PHILLIPPS** (b. 2 Jul'63) – keyboards (of The CHILLS)

Flying Nun   not iss.

Feb 81. (7") *(FN 002)* **TALLY HO! / PLATYPUS** – New Z
Dec 81. (m-lp) *(FN 003)* **BOODLE BOODLE BOODLE** – New Z
— Beatnik / Anything could happen / Point that thing somewhere else / (+2).
1982. (7") *(FNLAST 1 CLEAN)* **GETTING OLDER.** / – New Z
1982. (m-lp) **"GREAT SOUNDS GREAT, GOOD SOUNDS GOOD, SO-SO SOUNDS SO-SO, BAD SOUNDS BAD, ROTTEN SOUNDS ROTTEN" WITH THE CLEAN** – New Z

— split when SCOTT formed The BATS

GREAT UNWASHED

DAVID + HAMISH

Flying Nun   not iss.

1983. (m-lp) *(FNRIG 001)* **CLEAN OUT OF OUR MINDS** – NewZ

— added **PETER GUTTERIDGE** +
1984. (m-lp) *(DIRT 001)* **SINGLES** – New Z
— Can't find water / Born in the wrong time / Duane Eddy / Neck of the woods / Boat with no ocean.

— added **ROSS HUMPHRIES**

— PETER left to form SNAPPER, while HAMISH formed BAILTER SPACE with former members of The GORDONS

STEPHEN

were **DAVID GILGOUR** plus **ALF DANIELSON** – bass (ex-GOBLIN MIX) / **GEOFF HOANI** – drums

Flying Nun   not iss.

1986. (7"ep) *(FN 123)* **DUMB EP** – New Z

CLEAN (cont) — THE GREAT INDIE DISCOGRAPHY — The 1980s

1988. (lp) *(30973)* **RADAR OF SMALL DOGS**
– Loved by you / Little Audrey / Don't know why / Thinkin' about you / Tape machine / Windy day / Blowing / Crystal / Spins you 'round / Mary had a steamboat / Tender shoots / Glover / Relic / Hedgehogs. *(cd-iss. 1990's; FN 252)*

CLEAN

— DAVID + HAMISH re-formed in July 1988, **ROBERT SCOTT** (of The BATS) returned

Flying Nun / not iss.

Apr 89. (12"ep) *(FN 145 – FNE 029)* **IN'N'NER LIVE (live at Fulham Greyhound '88)**
– Flowers / Point that thing somewhere else / Whatever I do is right.

Rough Trade / Rough Trade

Feb 90. (lp/c/cd) *(ROUGH/+C/CD 143)* <*ROUGHUS 72*> **VEHICLE**
– Draw(in)g to a (w)hole / I wait around / Bye bye / The blue / Dunes / Someone / Home / Diamond shine / Getting to you / Big soft punch / Big cat / I can see / Gem. *(cd re-iss. Jun95 on 'Flying Nun'; FNCD 143)*

— HAMISH joined BAILTER SPACE (and MAD SCENE as a side project)

Flying Nun / Summershine

Feb 95. (lp/cd) *(FN/+CD 292)* <*19007*> **MODERN ROCK** — Oct95
– Starting point / Outside the cage / Linger longer / Wake up in the morning / 2 reasons / Safe in the rain / Secret place / Something I need / Different world / Stomp the guru / Too much violence / Phluke / Doing your thing / Ginger ale. *(cd re-iss. Sep98; same)*

1995. (7"flexi) *(FN 311)* **TRAPPED IN AMBER / LUDWIG** — New Z
Nov 96. (cd) *(FNCD 349)* **UNKNOWN COUNTRY**
– Wipe me, I'm lucky / Fallaway and misery / Changing your head / Balkans / Clutch / Franz Kafka at the zoo / Whisk / Indigo blue / Chumpy / Get the liquid / Happy lil fella / Tweezer / Rope / Twist top / Cooking water / Valley cab / Walk walk / Balkans.

not iss. / Dark Beloved Cloud

1990's. (7") <*DBC 020*> **LATE LAST NIGHT. / PSYCHEDELIC CLOWN**

Matador / Merge

Aug 01. (cd) *(OLE 527-2)* <*MRG 188*> **GETAWAY**
– Stars / Jala / Crazy / Golden crown / Cell block No.5 / E motel / Twilight agency / Poor boy / Silence on something else / Alpine madness / Circle canyon / Aho / Holdin' on / Reprise (1-4) / Complications.

– compilations, etc. –

on 'Flying Nun' unless mentioned otherwise

1986. (12"ep) *(LDC 001)* **LIVE DEAD CLEAN (live)** — New Z.
May 87. (lp) *(FNUK 3 – FN 154)* <*HMS 114*> **COMPILATION** — 1995
– Billy two / At the bottom / Tally ho / Anything could happen / Point that thing somewhere else / Flowers / Fish / Beatnik / Getting older / Slug song / Oddity / Whatever / Whatever I do (wherever I go). *(cd-iss. Nov88; FNE 3CD) (re-iss. Apr93 on 'Homestead'; HMS 114) (cd re-iss. Jun95 & Jan00; FNCD 154)*

Jan 88. (c) *(FNMCODD 001)* **ODDITIES**
– Oddity / Success story / Thumbs off / Getting older / Yellow man / End of my dream / Platypus / This guy / David Bowie / Mudchucker blues / At the bottom / Hold onto the rail / Inside out / Fats Domino / Sad eyed lady / Tell me why / In the back / Band that never was / Wheels of industry / Point that thing dub / Safety at home / Lemmings / Stylaphone music. *(cd-iss. Jun95; FNCD 223)* <*US-iss.cd 1995; 9901*>

1988. (c) *(FNMCODD 002)* **ODDITIES 2** — New Z
Jun 95. (cd; as The GREAT UNWASHED) *(FNCD 208)* **COLLECTION**
– Intro / Hello is Ray there? / Meanwhile / Small girl / Thru the trees / Yesterday was / Toadstool blues / What U should be now / It's a day / Hold on to the rail / What you're thinkin' now / Obscurity blues / Quickstep / What happened Ray? / Duane Eddy / Neck of the woods / Can't find water / Born in the wrong time / Boat with no ocean.

2001. (cd) *Arclife; (Arclife 015)* **SLUSH FUND (live)** — NewZ
– Rollo / Slush fund / Filling the hole / Caveman / Point that thing somewhere else / Wipe me I'm lucky / Fish / Quickstep.

Nov 02. (d-cd) *Flying Nun;* **ANTHOLOGY**

DAVID KILGOUR

— with **NOEL WARD** – bass / **TANE TOKONA** – drums

1991. (c-s) *(FN 219)* **YOU FORGET** — New Z
1991. (cd) *(FNCD 220)* **HERE COME THE CARS**
– Here come the cars / Fine / You forget / Shivering / Spasm / Splash your jewels / Sometimes / Kills all my fun / Spins you round / Blueprint / Uplift / Because it was you / Nothing Vol.1.

— **JANE KEMP** – backing vocals; repl. TOKONA

Oct 94. (lp/cd) *(FN/+CD 282)* **SUGAR MOUTH**
– No, no, no / Fallaway / 1987 / Filter / Beached / Nail in my foot / Waiting round on you / Crazy / Listen to the rain / Look at it / Recollection / Never end.

Oct 94. (cd-ep; with POP ART TOASTERS) *(FN 288)* **POP ART TOASTERS EP** — NewZ
– What am I going to do / Everyone's gonna wonder / I won't hurt you / Go ahead / Circles.

Dec 94. (cd-ep) *(FN 308/+CD)* **SPIRITUAL GAS STATION EP**
– No, no, no / Fine / Beached / Look at it (El Speedo version) / Uplift.

— **ROBERT KEY** – drums; repl. KEMP

Sep 97. (cd; as DAVID KILGOUR & THE HEAVY EIGHTS) *(FN 397)* **DAVID KILGOUR & THE HEAVY EIGHTS**
– Round the bend / Off my mind / Chop me in 1/2 / Locked in blue / Brown man / Seemingly Stranded / Wave boarder / My one / Hey you / Maybe / Diggin' for gold / Thumbaline.

— now totally solo

Merge / Merge

Jan 02. (cd) <*(MRG 197CD)*> **A FEATHER IN THE ENGINE**
– Sept '98 / Slippery slope / All the rest / The perfect watch / Instra 2 / I lost my train / Time to run / Today is gonna be mine / I caught you / Instra 2 (reprise) / Wooden shed / Which one / Backwards forwards. *(NZ-iss.on 'Arclife'; 016)*

– compilations, etc. –

Dec 95. (lp/cd) *Ajax; (<AJAX 040/+CD>)* **FIRST STEPS & FALSE ALARMS: (THE BEST OF THE WORST – HOME DEMOS OF DEMOS)** — Sep95
– The bootlegger / November / Tape machine / Shine all night / This chord / Scene two / Another echo downer / Way down / Here come the cars / Wooden floor / Untitled / Pop song / Landed / Dirty hallway / Ditch / September / Slow wind / Gone Mekico again / Wait at your door / Bucket of you.

2002. (m-cd) *Arclife; <017>* **CRACKS IN THE SIDEWALK** (demos from 1993-98)
– I lost my train / Henry / Rubato / The holy ghost / Little bird / Plastic space / Way down here.

MAD SCENE

HAMISH – multi / with **LISA SIEGEL** – multi / **DANNY MANETTO** – vocals, multi / **TONY DINOFF** – guitar / **JAY RAIBOURNE** – bass, noise

Homestead / Homestead

1992. (7"ep) <*HMS 172*> **FALLING OVER, SPILLING OVER**
– People to talk to / Paper plane / Falling over, spilling over.

not iss. / Flying Nun

1993. (cd) <*FNCD 191*> **A TRIP THRU MONSTERLAND**
– Falling over, spilling over / Paper plane / Aeroplane / People to talk to / Holding pattern / Eye / I know / What's going on / Halo / Tiny demon / Whole world / Bee / Busstop / Paper plane.

— HAMISH + LISA recruited various sessioners

Merge / Merge

1994. (cd-ep) <*MRG 072*> **THE GREATEST TIME! E.P.**
– The greatest time / Sealight / Balloon.

— added **ROBERT VICKERS** – acoustic guitar, bass (ex-GO-BETWEENS) + **BILL GERSTEL** – drums, percussion

Mar 95. (cd) <*(MRG 077CD)*> **SEALIGHT**
– Strange to be here / Transatlantic telephone conversation / Gotta get back (to something) / Here goes nothing / Black flye / Marching song / Silhouette / Birthday party / Spilled oranges / Choose / Hoping / You wear funny clothes / Watertanks / My dreams are losing their teeth / Starshine. <*d-10"lp-iss.Jun99 on 'Little Teddy'; BITE 014*>

1996. (cd-ep) <*MRG 106*> **CHINESE HONEY**
– The big setup / I met you in my dreams / Pictures on my wall / Change / Waiting for the rain / Cold sun / Chinese honey. <*7"-iss.1996 on 'Little Teddy'; 7-45*>

— **DANNY TUNICK** – drums; repl. BILL

not iss. / Rover

1997. (7") <*004*> **SHAMU KILLER WHALE EP**
– Shamu killer whale / Kokomo Joe / Mustard king / Boom!

CLEANERS FROM VENUS

Formed: Colchester, England ... 1980 by MARTIN NEWELL and LOL ELLIOTT, GILES SMITH replacing the latter in 1983 after a few (very) limited cassettes ('BLOW AWAY YOUR TROUBLES', 'ON ANY NORMAL MONDAY' and 'IN THE GOLDEN AUTUMN') were distributed by mail order. Although these were of varying amateur quality, they charted the development of NEWELL's 60's influenced songwriting style and often surreal sense of humour, earning him a reputation as the 80's equivalent of SYD BARRETT or RAY DAVIES. With newcomer GILES on board, the CLEANERS polished off two further cassettes, 'UNDER WARTIME CONDITIONS' (1984) and the much loved, 'LIVING WITH VICTORIA GREY' (1986). The following year, the duo (and guests) issued their first lp proper, 'GOING TO ENGLAND', fans unhappy with the slick production sheen that marred revamped versions of tracks from its predecessor. However, they found a willing audience in Germany where their final two 'R.C.A.' issued albums, 'TOWN AND COUNTRY' (1988) and 'NUMBER 13' (1990) hit the shops. In Britain meanwhile, The CLEANERS were signed to Captain Sensible's 'Deltic' imprint for the former and 'Man At The Off License' for the latter. After the duo's final split, GILES went on to write a novel, 'Lost In Music', promoting this in 1995 by co-guesting (with noneother than myself, MC STRONG) at a wine'n'pinkie-in-air book launch in Edinburgh. NEWELL, meanwhile, released a few solo sets (including one with the help of ANDY PARTRIDGE, 'THE GREATEST LIVING ENGLISHMAN') and later formed The BROTHERHOOD OF LIZARDS before becoming a scruffy "rock poet", writing his own novel, 'I Hank Marvinned'. Low-key as ever, "THE WAYWARD GENIUS" that was MARTIN NEWELL (as the 1999 compilation album confirmed), sent out two further sets, 'THE SPIRIT CAGE' (2000) and 'RADIO AUTUMN ATTIC' (2002), the witty balladeer showing as always he had a sense of fun.

Album rating: BLOW AWAY YOUR TROUBLES (*4) / ON ANY NORMAL MONDAY (*5) / IN THE GOLDEN AUTUMN (*6) / UNDER WARTIME CONDITIONS (*5) / LIVING WITH VICTORIA GREY (*6) / GOING TO ENGLAND (*4) / TOWN AND COUNTRY (*7) / NUMBER 13 (*7) / Martin Newell: THE GREATEST LIVING ENGLISHMAN (*7) / THE OFF WHITE ALBUM (*5) / THE WAYWARD GENIUS OF MARTIN NEWELL compilation (*5) / THE SPIRIT CAGE (*4) / RADIO AUTUMN ATTIC (*5)

MARTIN NEWELL

Off Street / not iss.

1980. (7") *(OSR 001)* **YOUNG JOBLESS. / SYLVIE IN TOYLAND**
(re-iss. Apr81 on 'Liberty'; BP 392)

CLEANERS FROM VENUS

MARTIN NEWELL – vocals, guitar / **LOL ELLIOTT** – drums

Man At The Off Licence / not iss.

Jun 81. (c) *(WOW 002)* **BLOW AWAY YOUR TROUBLES** — mail-o
– Swinging London / A blue wave / Union lads / Modern T.V. / Marilyn on a train / Kool of the night / Marathon / Urban jungle / Minimal animal / I fell in love with a cleaner / So this is jazz is it? / Wivenhoe bells / Change change change / Hey dreamer / Alien / At home with myself / Winter in the country / Helpless / University challenge. *(cd-iss. Jan00 on 'Jar Music'+=; JAR 039)* – The girls in the flat upstairs (live) / Call me Michael Moonlight (acoustic) / "a Cleaners episode" (spoken word).

Apr 82. (c) *(ROW 001)* **ON ANY NORMAL MONDAY** — mail-o
– Night starvation / Tukani (Monday is grey) / A girl with cars in her eyes / I can't stop (holding on) / Living on nerve ends / I wanna do that / European war / Hungry day / F.U.N. / Be an idiot pop star / Spirit of youth in flames. *(cd-iss. Aug99 on 'Jar Music'+=; JAR 037)* – My mind's eyes (live) / Straight to you boy (live) / Follow the plough (version).

— in 1982, the band released the cassette (rec.1980), 'SECRET DREAMS OF A KITCHEN PORTER' on 'Man At The Off Licence'; *NOW 004)*

Dec 82. (c) *(MAO 005)* **MIDNIGHT CLEANERS**
– This rainy decade / Time in vain / Only a shadow / Corridor of dreams / Wivenhoe bells II / Midnight Cleaners / Factory boy / A wretched street / Don't worry about the ads. *(cd-iss. Aug99 on 'Jar Music'+=; JAR 035)* – Ilya Kuryakin looked at me (live electric version) / Wunderbarmaid (live) / Bus stop (live).

Aug 83. (c) *(FRAU 006)* **IN THE GOLDEN AUTUMN** — mail-o
– Renee (who's driving your car?) / A Holloway person / Ghosts in doorways / The autumn cornfield / Don't step on my rainbow / Balloon drop shadow / Krugerand gladiators / Golden age Saturday / Marilyn on a train / Sandstorm in paradise / Victorian society / A fool like you. *(cd-iss. 2000 on 'Jar Music'+=; JAR 038)* – Goodnight country girl / She rings the changes / The iceberg and unicorn.

Dec 83. (c-s) *(007)* **WHEN FIRE BURNS DREAMS / AMATEUR PARANOIAC**

— **GILES SMITH** – piano, vocals / (plus several guests on each album) repl. LOL

May 84. (c) *(TAO 008)* **UNDER WARTIME CONDITIONS**
– Summer in a small town / Johnny the moondog is dead / Hand of stone / Drowning butterflies / Radio seven / Fracas on West Street / Lukewarm lovesong / A blue wave / Song for Syd Barrett / The Winter Palace. *(lp-iss.1986 on 'Acid Tapes'; TAB 001) (cd-iss. Aug99 +=; JAR 036)* – When fire burns dreams / Amateur paranoiac / Drowning butterflies (live acoustic).

Man At The Off Licence / not iss.

May 85. (c; by MARTIN NEWELL) *(009)* **SONGS FOR A FALLOW LAND**
– Sun comes to the wood / Julie Profumo / Soul Monday / Gamma ray blue / Heroin clones / Winter palace 2 / Golden lane / Stars are cold / Late night / Beyond . . .

1986. (c) *(0010)* **LIVING WITH VICTORIA GREY** — mail-o
– Victoria Grey / Ilya Kuryakin looked at me / Clara Bow / Follow the plough / Stay on / What's going on (in your heart)? / The mercury girl / Armistice girl / Pearl / Victoria Grey (2). *(re-iss. 1986 on 'Acid Tapes'; TAB 028)*

Ammunition not iss.

Feb 87. (lp) *(CLEANLP 1)* **GOING TO ENGLAND**
– Julie Profumo / Living with Victria Grey / Clara Bow / Follow the plough / Armistica day / What's going on in your heart / Girl on a swing / A mercury girl / Illya Kurayakin looked at me / You must be out of my mind.

Mar 87. (7") *(JANGLE 1)* **ILLYA KURAYAKIN LOOKED AT ME. / BLACK AND WHITE (AND BLUE ALL OVER)**
(12"+=) *(JANGLE 1T)* – Albion's daughter / ('A'extended).

— in April'87, NEWELL released cassette-EP, 'APRIL FOOL'; a month previously The CLEANERS FROM MARS issued the EP, 'MIND HOW YOU GO!'

Jun 87. (12") *(JANGLE 2T)* **LIVING WITH VICTORIA GREY. / SUNDAY AFTERNOON / SHE'S CHECKING YOU OUT**

Jan 98. (7") *(JANGLE 3)* **MERCURY GIRL. / GAMMA RAY BLUE**
(12"+=) *(JANGLE 3T)* – The iceberg and unicorn.

Deltic / R.C.A.

Oct 88. (lp/c) *(DELT LP/MC 1)* **TOWN AND COUNTRY**
– Let's get married / Blue swan / The beat generation and me / Felicity / Mad March hare / Tenpenny Hill / Dizzy girl / Denmark Street / I was a teenage idol dancer / I wasn't drinking / Cardboard town / The last club in the world.

Dec 88. (7") *(PB 41835)* **LET'S GET MARRIED. / GAMMA RAY BLUE** — German
(12"+=) *(PT 41836)* – Mercury girl / The iceberg and unicorn.

— The BROTHERHOOD OF LIZARDS were **NEWELL + NELSON**; they released a very ltd eponymous set in November 1988

Oct 89. (lp/c/cd; as BROTHERHOOD OF LIZARDS) *(DELT CD/MC/LP 5)* **LIZARDLAND**
– It could have been Cheryl / The world strikes one / The dandelion marine / Rusty iron sun / The happening guy / Clockwork train / The day after yesterday / Market day / Dear Anya / Love the Anglian way / Sand dragon / She dreamed she could fly / Carmosine. <US-iss.1993 on 'Play Hard'; LP 32>

Man At The Off Licence / not iss.

Jun 90. (lp) *(013)* **NUMBER 13**
– The jangling man / No go (for Louis MacNeice) / Mariette / A man of our time / Here she crashes / A street called prospect / Minesweeping memory lane / Germayne (like a cathedral) / Boys from the Home Counties / The tear collector / Christmas in suburbia. *(cd-iss1990 on 'Acid Tapes'+=; TAB 070)* – The jangling man (live) / A street called prospect (live) / Green-gold girl of the summer (live).

— disbanded after above until several gigs in Japan; **MARTIN NEWELL, DAVE GREGORY, CAPTAIN SENSIBLE, TIV, NELSON + GARRIE DREADFUL**

– compilations, etc. –

Mar 93. (7"red) *Singles Only Label; (SOL 237)* **SONG FOR SYD BARRETT. / BOY FROM THE HOME COUNTIES**

Jul 93. (cd) *Tangerine; (TANGCD 3)* **GOLDEN CLEANERS – 20 CLASSIC CUTS FROM THE LEGENDARY U.K. POP COMBO**
– Julie Profumo / Summer in a small town / Living with Victoria Grey / A mercury girl / I was a teenage idiot dancer / Girl on a swaing / Sunday afternoons / Follow the plough / Blue swan / Armistice day / Johnny the moondog is dead / Drowning butterflies / In kingdoms of the cool / Mad March hare / Albion's daughter / Clara Bow / Illya Kuryakin looked at me / Felicity / Song for Syd Barrett / Radio seven.

Apr 95. (ltd-blue-cd-ep) *(JAR 002)* **THE LEGENDARY THIRTEEN E.P.**
– A man for our time / Minesweeping memory lane / Here she crashes / Germayne (like a cathedral).

Oct 95. (cd) *Tangerine; (TANGCD 014)* **BACK FROM THE CLEANERS**
– Let's get married / Major Mandy / She's checking you our / Black and white (and blue all over) / Monochrome world / Cardboard town / All cats are grey / Hands of stone / Dizzy girl / Gamma ray blue / The beat generation and me / You must be out of my mind / The iceberg and unicorn.

Jul 01. (ltd-cd) *Jar Music; (JAR-043)* **LIVE IN JAPAN (OSAKA 1994) (live)**
– Wunderbarmaid / Former phonebox vandal / Before the hurricane / A street called prospect / She rings the changes / We'll build a house / The world strikes one / The jangling man / Straight to you, boy / Girl on a swing / The green-gold girl of the summer / An Englishman's home / What a crazy world we're living in / Bus stop / She rings the changes (early demo version).

MARTIN NEWELL

— first record featured **ANDY PARTRIDGE**

Humbug / Pipeline

Nov 93. (cd/d-cd) *(BAH 10/+X) <PIPE CD/C 002>* **THE GREATEST LIVING ENGLISHMAN**
– Goodbye dreaming fields / Before the hurricane / We'll build a house / The greatest living Englishman / She rings the changes / Home Counties boy / A street called Prospect / Christmas in suburbia / Straight to you, boy / The jangling man / The green-gold girl of the summer / An Englishman's home. *(lp-iss.Jul97 on 'Jar Music'; JAR 005) (<cd re-iss. Jun00 on 'Cherry Red'+=; CDMRED 171)* – (live tracks).

Aug 95. (cd-ep) *(HUM 001)* **LET'S KIOSK!**
– The jangling man / Former phonebox vandal / Wunderbarmaid / I will haunt your room.

Apr 96. (cd) *(BAH 25)* **THE OFF WHITE ALBUM**
– Call me Michael Moonlight / The world of Dandy Leigh / Arcadian boys / The blue beret / Ursula in the waiting room / When the damsons are down / Lions drunk on sunlight / Miss Van Houten's coffee shop / She was never drowning / Some girls are bigger than others / Queen Phyllis of Colchester / Goodnight country girl / The girls in the flat upstairs. *(lp-iss.Jul97 on 'Jar Music'; JAR 010) (re-iss. Oct02 on 'Cherry Red'+=; CDMRED 221)* – Leaving London (extract from This Little Ziggy) / Princess Miriam (excerpt) / Jangling man (video).

Cherry Red / Cherry Red

Feb 99. (cd) *(<CDMRED 154>)* **THE WAYWARD GENIUS OF MARTIN NEWELL** (compilation)
– Julie Profumo / Drowning butterflies / Living with Victoria Grey / Girl on a swing / Blue swan / The world strikes one / Summer in a small town / I will haunt your room / A mercury girl / She rings the changes / Clockwork train / Miss Van Houten's coffee shop / The dark lovely daughter of the trashman / Former phonebox vandal / The popular girl / Mad March hare / Johnny the Moondog is dead / It could have been Cheryl / Good-bye dreaming fields / Albion's daughter / Jangling man.

— In 1999, NEWELL released a music/soken word cassette, 'WILD MAN OF WIVENHOE and BLACK SHUCK: THE GHOST OF EASTERN ENGLAND'

Oct 00. (cd) *(<CDBRED 176>)* **THE SPIRIT CAGE** — Nov00
– Wake up and smell the offy / You slay me / Sugarcane / My old school / New Europeans / The boys of September / A smashing bird like Brenda / The high clouds of summer / Your winter garden / Days like these / My funeral / Lily's lullaby. *(lp-iss.Jan01 on 'Blueberry Blue'+= 7"; JAR 042 – BLUE 001)* – ANDROID NATION / CLARENDON LANE / RUBY MOON

Mar 02. (cd) *(<CDBRED 206>)* **RADIO AUTUMN ATTIC**
– The Duchess of Leylandia / The wicked witch / Beat street / Do you dream of the sea? / A woman and some whisky / World of the stars / Because she's driftwood / Life as a broken doll / Sailing to America / When we were a thing / The beer elves / Prende mi / Chocks away (I-VI).

Jar Music / not iss.

Aug 02. (cd-ep) *(JAR-048)* **SONGS FROM THE STATION HOTEL**
– The speed of a train / Tuscany row / Return to Tuscany row / The ghost parade / Horses up on the hill.

– compilations, etc. –

Sep 97. (d-cd+cd-ep) *Humbug; (BAH 33)* **MARTIN NEWELL'S BOX OF OLD HUMBUG**
– (THE GREATEST LIVING ENGLISHMAN + THE OFF WHITE ALBUM + LET'S KIOSK!)

Jul 00. (ltd-cd) *Jar Music; (JAR 041)* **MY BACK PAGES – A COLLECTION OF CLEANERS RARITIES**
– Crane driver / Gulf War song / Incident in a greatcoat / Bag of dust / Haunt your house / Drowning butterflies / Red guitars and silver tambourines / Everytime I go up / You should have called / Gate crashing oyster park / Stay litt / Bodecea Jones / Smash your watch / Arcadian boys (version) / Clara Bow / Princess of suburbia / Finding my own way home.

below recorded in September, 1996 with **NEWELL, MAX VOLUME, TONY PHILLIPS + STIX NATKANSKI**

Feb 01. (cd; as The STRAY TROLLEYS) *Jar Music; (JAR 039)* **BARRICADES AND ANGELS + SECRET DREAMS OF A KITCHEN PORTER**
– Secret dreams of a kitchen porter / A bluebeat kid / Governor's only daughter / New age dreamer / Stilleto love / Gunslinger / Love into action / Ten million years / Flamingo road / Finding out / Barricades and angels / No static (young & vicious) // Days of firebirds / Russian picture / Bontemps roulez / Mrs. Diller / Teenage gunmen / Five pieces written for an autumn art exhibition. *(cd has bonus tracks not from original limited issue)*.

CLOCKDVA

Formed: Sheffield, England ... 1979 by ADI NEWTON, former frontman of The FUTURE (which subsequently became The HUMAN LEAGUE). With a line-up featuring NEWTON, CHARLIE COLLINS, ROGER QUAIL, STEVEN 'JUDD' TURNER and DAVID J. HAMMOND, the outfit released a debut cassette-only affair, 'WHITE SOULS IN BLACK SUITS' (1980) on THROBBING GRISTLE's 'Industrial' label. Lead track, 'CONSENT', was an early classic, an experimental soundclash of avant-garde chaos and dirty industrial funk which had a spiritual cousin in The POP GROUP amongst others. COLLINS' searing, freeform sax work, in particular, would become a distinguishing feature of the CLOCKDVA experience while NEWTON's vocal was pitched somewhere between IGGY POP and IAN CURTIS, even if he did occasionally sound like he'd been force-fed a diet of red-hot gravel. PAUL WILDER subsequently replaced HAMMOND for the release of a follow-up set, 'THIRST' on the small 'Fetish' label, another helping of atmospheric, vaguely gothic jazz-art complete with squealing clarinet, sax, chunky bass and unsettling vocals. A period of upheaval ensued as TURNER met an early death, ADI the only surviving founder member as the rest of the band departed to form The BOX. Hooking up with former SIOUXSIE & THE BANSHEES man, JOHN VALENTINE-CARRUTHERS, alongside new recruits PAUL BROWSE and NICK SANDERSON, NEWTON carried on the CLOCKDVA name and signed to 'Polydor' in 1982. By all accounts, the resulting 'ADVANTAGE' (1983) album should have given ADI his first taste of success, featuring as it did such enduring tracks as 'BEAUTIFUL LOSERS' (a sound from which MATT JOHNSON possibly drew inpiration for his 'Infected' album masterpiece). It wasn't to be though and CLOCKDVA fell apart in early '84, NEWTON subsequently forming The ANTI-GROUP alongside MARK HOLMES, BRDL HIRDEN D.F. D'SILVA, D.A. HEPPENSTAU and ROBERT E.BAKER. This project further served as a vehicle for NEWTON's experimental research (particularly with regards to film; NEWTON's idea of creating a complete audiovisual live experience was later echoed by The SHAMEN), his interest in the interface between technology and human evolution becoming apparent on albums such as 'DIGITARIA' (1987) and 'AUDIOPHILE' (1988). When CLOCKDVA eventually reappeared in the late 80's (with a line-up of NEWTON, BROWSE and DENNIS), a series of singles on Chicago's 'Wax Trax' label suggested an entirely different musical proposition than the group's original incarnation. Obviously influenced by the burgeoning underground dance culture, NEWTON was now creating music of a decidedly electro/techno minimalist hue albeit in the context of his evolutionary philosophy; most of the CLOCKDVA releases henceforth came with a NEWTON essay on the possibilities of sound, consciousness etc., namechecking figures as diverse as Greek scribe, Homer, and arch occultist, Aliester Crowley. Subsequent albums on the Italian-based 'Contempo' label such as 'MAN AMPLIFIED' (1992) and the belated 'DIGITAL SOUNDTRACKS' (1993) traded in a more refined electronica. • **Covered:** BLACK ANGEL'S DEATH SONG (Velvet Underground).

Album rating: WHITE SOULS IN BLACK SUITS (*6) / THIRST (*8) / ADVANTAGE (*9) / BURIED DREAMS (*5) / TRANSITIONAL VOICES (*5) / MAN AMPLIFIED (*5) / DIGITAL SOUNDTRACKS (*5) / SIGN (*6) / BLACK WORDS ON WHITE PAPER (*5) / VOICE RECOGNITION TEST (*5) / ISO-EROTIC CALIBRATIONS (*5) / COLLECTIVE compilation (*7) / Anti-Group: THE DELIVERY – BERLIN 1985 (*5) / DIGITARIA (*5) / AUDIOPHILE compilation (*5) / MEONTOLOGICAL RESEARCH: TESTE TONES (*4)

ADI NEWTON (b. ADOLPHUS NEWTON) – vocals, clarinet, synths (ex-FUTURE) / **CHARLIE COLLINS** – saxophone, flute, percussion, etc. / **ROGER QUAIL** – drums, perc. / **STEVEN 'Judd' TURNER** – bass, treated guitar / **DAVID J. HAMMOND** – guitar; repl. TYNE

Industrial not iss.

Oct 80. (c) (IRC 31) **WHITE SOULS IN BLACK SUITS**
– Consent / Discontentment 1 & 2 / Still – Silent / Non / Relentless / Contradict / Anti-chance (soundtrack; keyboards assemble themselves at dawn). *(lp-iss.1983; IRLP 31) (re-iss. Jun92 on 'Contempo' cd/c/lp; CONTECD/CONTAPE/CONTE 157)*

—— **PAUL WIDLER** – guitar; repl. HAMMOND

Fetish not iss.

Jan 81. (lp) (FR 2002) **THIRST**
– Uncertain / Sensorium / White cell / Piano pain / Blue tone / North pole / 4 hours / Moments / Impressions of African winter. *(re-iss. Nov85 on 'Doublevision'; DVR 19) (cd-iss. Jan95 on 'Contempo'+=; CONTECD 192)* – 4 hours (original single edit) / Sensorium (original single edit).

May 81. (7") (FET 008) **4 HOURS (re-mixed). / SENSORIUM**
(re-iss. Nov85 on 'Doublevision'; DVR 18)

—— ADI was sole survivor when JUDD died; the others formed The BOX – he recruited **JOHN VALENTINE-CARRUTHERS** – guitar, bass (ex-SIOUXSIE & BANSHEES) / **PAUL BROWSE** – saxophone / **NICK SANDERSON** – drums

Polydor not iss.

May 82. (7"ep/12"ep) (POSP/+X 437) **PASSION STILL AFLAME**
– Son of sons / Theme from I.M.D. / Don't (it's taboo) / Noises in limbo.

Nov 82. (7"; as DVA) (POSP 499) **HIGH HOLLY DISCO MASS. / THE VOICE THAT SPEAKS FROM WITHIN (TRIUMPH OVER WILL) (part 1)**

—— added **DEAN DENNIS** – bass

Apr 83. (7"/12") (POSP/+X 578) **RESISTANCE. / THE SECRET LIFE OF THE BIG BLACKSUIT**

May 83. (lp/c) (POLS/+C 1082) **ADVANTAGE**
– Tortured heroine / Beautiful losers / Resistance / Eternity in Paris / The secret life of the big black suit / Breakdown / Dark encounter / Poem. *(re-iss. Jun89 on 'Interfish' lp/cd; EFA 1706/+CD)*

Aug 83. (7"/12") (POSP/+X 627) **BREAKDOWN. / BLACK ANGEL'S DEATH SONG**

—— disbanded early '84; CARRUTHERS rejoined SIOUXSIE & THE BANSHEES, while SANDERSON and DENNIS joined JEFFREY LEE PIERCE solo

ANTI-GROUP

—— were formed by **ADOLPHUS NEWTON** with **MARK HOLMES** – guitar / **D.F. D'SILVA** – saxophone / **BRDL HIRDEN** – bass / **D.A. HEPPENSTAU** – keyboards, computers / **ROBERT E. BAKER** – engineer

Atonal not iss.

Sep 85. (m-lp) **THE DELIVERY – BERLIN 1985 (live)** – German
– The delivery / Morpheus' baby / Zulu / Ocean / Love flowers in the desert. *(re-iss. Jul87 as 'LIVE IN BERLIN')*

Sweatbox not iss.

Oct 85. (12") (SOX 09) **HA. / ZULU**

Feb 87. (m-lp) (SOX 010) **ShT**
– Shgl / Sunset eyes through water / Po Ema / Further and evident meanings / Morpheus' baby / New upheaval.

Apr 87. (lp/cd) (SOX/SACD 012) **DIGITARIA**
– Blood burns into water / Dog star / Balag Anti / Chozzar over abyss / Pre-eval / Ghost cultures under collapse / Noosphere / Lux nox / Tzaddi / The abominable plateau of Leng / Sekhet. *(cd re-iss. Sep94 on 'Audioglobe')*

Jul 87. (7") (OX 011) **BIG SEX. / THE OCEAN**
(12"+=) (SOX 011) – ('A'version).

Feb 88. (lp) (SAX 030) **AUDIOPHILE** (virtually everything)
(re-iss. cd Sep94 on 'Anterior';)

Side Effects not iss.

Jul 88. (lp) (SER 12) **MEONTOLOGICAL RESEARCH: TESTE TONES**
– Test tone (40 hz) / Teste tones / E.P.M.D. / A.A.A. / Magnesia / Magnetic pharmacology / A.A.A.A. *(cd-iss. Sep94 on 'Anterior'; same)*

not iss. Wax Trax

1990. (12") **BROADCAST TEST**

CLOCKDVA

—— re-formed with **NEWTON, BROWSE & DENNIS**

Interfisch Wax Trax

Nov 88. (12") (EFA 1701) <WAX 068> **THE HACKER. / THE CONNECTION MACHINE**
(cd-s+=) (EFA 1701CD) – The hacker (hacked version).
(re-iss. Jun92 on 'Contempo'; 188MX + 189MX)

Jan 89. (12") (EFA 1708) <WAX 9071> **THE ACT. / SONOLOGY OF SEX**
(cd-s+=) (EFA 1708CD) – React / React II.
(re-iss. Jun92 on 'Contempo'; TEMPO 187MX)

Jun 89. (12"ep) (EFA 1713) <WAX 9105> **SOUND MIRROR EP** 1990
– Sound mirror (programme 5) / Sound mirror (programme 5) / The sonology of sex (le comtesse de sang). *(re-iss. Jun92 on 'Contempo'; TEMPO 190MX)*

Jul 89. (lp/cd) (EFA 01717-08/-26) <WAX 7094> **BURIED DREAMS**
– Buried dreams / Hide / Sound mirror / Velvet realm / The unseen / The reign / The act / The hacker. *(cd+=)* – The connection machine / The sonology of sex I / The sonology of sex II (Le contesse de sang) / The hacker (video mix). *(cd re-mast.Aug99 on 'Next Era'; ERA 9815-2)*

Jan 91. (lp/cd) (EFA 01718-08/-26) **TRANSITIONAL VOICES (live in Bologna, Italy, March 1990)**
– TRansitional voices / Sound mirror / Syntactic / N.Y.C. overload / Fractal 9 / Technogeist.

Contempo not iss.

Dec 91. (12") (TEMPO 173MX) **FINAL PROGRAM. / FINAL PROGRAM (decoded 1) / FINAL PROGRAM (decoded 2)**

Mar 92. (lp/cd) (CONTE/+CD 182) **MAN AMPLIFIED**
– Man-amplifiers / Techno geist / Axiomatic and heuristic / NYC overload / Transitional voices / Fractalize / Bitstream / Final program. *(cd+=)* – Dark attractor / Memories of motion.

Nov 92. (cd-ep/w-book) (DUCA 172CDS) **BLACK WORDS ON WHITE PAPER EP / 7DC / OTTO M**
(cd-iss. Sep93 +=) (DD 172CD) – Alien tapes / 1.23.

Feb 93. (cd/lp) (CONTECD 217) **DIGITAL SOUNDTRACKS**
– The sensual engine / Cycom / Sound sweep / The operators / E-wave / The inversion / Diminishing point / Stations of the mind. *(cd+=)* – The presence / Chemicals / Delta machines / Stills of emotion.

—— **ADI NEWTON + ROBERT E. BAKER** (BROWSE went on to work as VISIONS OF EXCESS while DEAN DENNIS released a solo set the same year, 2002)

Sep 93. (12") (TEMPO 183T) **BITSTREAM / VIRTUAL FLESH. / BITSTREAM (2 mixes)**
(cd-ep+=) (TEMPO 183CD) – (3 other 'A'versions).

Sep 93. (cd/c/lp) (CONTECD/CONTAPE/CONTE 225) **SIGN**
– Signal / Voice recognition test / The obsession intensifies / Two souls / Re-entry / Pool of shades / Return to blue / Eternity / Sign.

Sep 93. (12"/cd-s) (TEMPO 224 T/CD) **VOICE RECOGNITION TEST**
– Voice recognition test / Cypher / De-cyphered.

Nov 93. (cd-book) **VIRTUAL REALITY HANDBOOK**
– Virtual flesh (tele-existence mix).

Jul 94. (cd-s) (TEMP 266CDS) **ETERNITY / ETERNITY (deep space mix) / ENDLESS PHASE**

Hypnobeat Cleopatra

Sep 94. (cd) (04632) <CLEO 94822> **COLLECTIVE** (remixes & compilation & live 24 November 1993)
– The hacker (viral version) / The act (activated) / Hacker – Hacked (operation sundevil) / Soundmirror (reflected) / The sonology of sex 2 / Final program (thinking machine) / Bitstream (teledildonic version) / H.I.T. (bio) / Cybertone (exoskeleton) / Virtual flesh (electrosex) / Voice recognition test (cognitive) / Cypher (glyph) / Eternity (ballard) / Solaris (mimetoid). *(cd-box iss.Jan95 on 'Hyperium-Sub-Mission'+=; 391010629)* – The hacker (video mix) / The hacker (hacked version) / RE-act / Hacker – Hacked (reprogrammed 2) / Hacker – Hacked (reprogrammed 3) / Soundmirror 1 / Soundmirror 2 / Final program / Final program (decoded) / Bitstream / Voice recognition test / De-cyphered / Eternity // Soundmirror (live) / Pool of shades (live) / Endless phase.

—— disbanded after above ...

T.A.G.C. (THE ANTI-GROUP CONSPIRACY)

— were back; **ADI** etc

		Anterior	not iss.
Sep 94.	(cd) **ISO-EROTIC CALIBRATIONS**	□	□ German

– Iso-erotic calibrations / Union with sirens / Mercurius / Annals of sancity / Neurological engineering / Psychophnophilia / Ethemeral.

		Dark Vinyl	not iss.
Mar 95.	(cd) *(DFX 017CD)* **BURNING WATER** (soundtrack)	□	–

– So 36 / Ars electronica.

CLOSE LOBSTERS

Formed: Johnstone, Scotland ... 1985 by ANDY BURNETT, his brother BOB BURNETT, TOM DONNELLY, STUART McFADYEN and GRAHAM WILKINTON. These quirky but easy-going jingle-janglers got their break via the NME C86 tape (to which they contributed 'FIRESTATION TOWERS'), subsequently netting a deal with 'Fire' and releasing 'GOING TO HEAVEN TO SEE IF IT RAINS' as their debut single in Autumn '86. Support slots to the likes of the JESUS & MARY CHAIN helped raise their profile while a follow-up single, 'NEVER SEEN BEFORE', confirmed their indie credentials and paved the way for an endearingly titled debut album, 'FOXHEADS STALK THIS LAND' (1987). Vaguely akin to a Caledonian version of The WEDDING PRESENT (especially in vocal terms), The CLOSE LOBSTERS were also – along with DAVID GEDGE & Co. – beloved of the US college circuit and even undertook a spot of transatlantic touring to promote follow-up album, 'HEADACHE RHETORIC' (1989). The strain of such a venture proved too much, however and the band fell apart at the turn of the decade, uniting briefly in 1991 for live work only. WEDDING PRESENT subsequently covered their 'LET'S MAKE SOME PLANS' on a B-side. • **Covered:** HEY HEY MY MY (INTO THE BLACK) (Neil Young) / PAPER THIN HOTEL (Leonard Cohen).

Album rating: FOXHEADS STALK THIS LAND (*6) / HEADACHE RHETORIC (*6)

ANDY BURNETT (b.11 Feb'65) – vocals / **TOM DONNELLY** (b.29 Aug'62) – guitar / **GRAHAM WILKINTON** (b.22 Aug'65) / **BOB BURNETT** (b.11 Sep'62) – bass / **STUART McFADYEN** (b.26 Sep'65, Paisley, Scotland) – drums

		Fire	not iss.
Oct 86.	(7") *(BLAZE 15)* **GOING TO HEAVEN TO SEE IF IT RAINS. / BOYS AND GIRLS**	□	–

(12"+=) *(BLAZE 15T)* – Heaven / Pathetik trivia.

| Apr 87. | (7") *(BLAZE 20)* **NEVER SEEN BEFORE. / PIMPS** | □ | – |

(12"+=) *(BLAZE 20T)* – Firestation towers / Wide waterways.

— **PAUL BENNETT** – bass; repl. BOB

| Oct 87. | (lp) *(FIRE 9)* **FOXHEADS STALK THIS LAND** | □ | – |

– Just too bloody stupid / Sewer pipe dream / I kiss the flower in bloom / Pathetique / A prophecy / In spite of these times / Foxheads / I take bribes / Pimps / Mother of God. *(cd-iss. Mar88; FIRECD 9)* *(re-iss. Apr89 c/cd; D4/D2 73333)* *(cd re-iss. Apr02 on 'Fire'; SFIRE 030CD)*

| Nov 87. | (7") *(BLAZE 22)* **LET'S MAKE SOME PLANS. / IN SPITE OF THESE TIMES** | □ | – |

(12"+=) *(BLAZE 22T)* – Get what they deserve.

| Aug 88. | (7") *(BLAZE 25)* **WHAT IS THERE TO SMILE ABOUT? / FROM THIS DAY ON** | □ | – |

(12"+=) *(BLAZE 25T)* – Loopholes / The skyscrapers of St. Mirin.
(cd-s+=) *(BLAZE 25CD)* – Violently pretty face.

| Mar 89. | (7") *(BLAZE 34)* **NATURE THING. / NEVER SEEN BEFORE** (live) | □ | – |

(12"+=/cd-s+=) *(BLAZE 34 T/CD)* – Hey hey my my (into the black) / Paper thin hotel.

| Mar 89. | (lp/c/cd) *(FIRE LP/MC/CD 17)* **HEADACHE RHETORIC** | □ | – |

– Lovely little swan / Gunpowderkeg / Nature thing / My days are numbered / Gutache / Got apprehension / Words on power / Skyscrapers / Knee trembler.
(c+=/cd+=) – FOXHEADS STALK THIS LAND

		Caff	not iss.
Dec 89.	(ltd-7") *(CAFF 4)* **JUST TOO BLOODY STUPID. / ALL THE LITTLE BOYS AND GIRLS I KNEW**	□	–

— split for two years, although a return to the live circuit was brief

– compilations, etc. –

| Apr 88. | (12"ep) *Night Tracks; (SFNT 008)* **THE JANICE LONG SESSIONS** (29.6.86) | □ | – |

– Nothing really matters / Going to Heaven to see if it rains / Pathetic trivia / Never seen before. *(c-ep-iss.1993 on 'Dutch East India';)*

COCTEAU TWINS

Formed: Grangemouth, Scotland ... late 1981 when the (then) trio of ELIZABETH FRASER, ROBIN GUTHRIE and WILL HEGGIE visited London to hand DJ John Peel a demo tape. He booked them for sessions on his Radio One night time show and they subsequently signed to IVO WATT-RUSSELL's indie label, '4 a.d.'. The COCTEAUS' debut offering, 'GARLANDS', was hastily recorded, hitting the shops just over a week later and giving a hint of things to come with an interesting fusion of monochromatic rhythms, textured guitar distortion and sampling technology. Resisting many offers from the majors, they were back in the studio again for 1983's 'LULLABIES' EP and 'HEAD OVER HEELS' album. A mesmerising collage of irridescent guitar soundscapes and sheets of feedback perforated with FRASER's unintelligible but highly emotive warbling, the latter record was a blueprint for the best of The COCTEAU TWINS work. After a support slot to OMD, WILL HEGGIE departed, making the long trip back north to set up his own outfit, LOWLIFE. Around the same time ROBIN and LIZ hit No.1 in the indie charts when guesting for 'IVO/4 a.d.' ensemble, THIS MORTAL COIL on 'SONG TO THE SIREN'; it was mistakenly thought by many to be a COCTEAU TWINS off-shoot, rather than IVO's project. That idea was laid to rest after the album, 'IT'LL END IN TEARS', was issued in '84. Meanwhile, The COCTEAU TWINS were back with another blissed out masterpiece, 'TREASURE', introducing newcomer, SIMON RAYMONDE on bass and seeing LIZ explore hitherto uncharted vocal territory in a fascinating, enigmatic and occasionally unsettling language that communicated everything and nothing. It also marked their first taste of Top 30 success although they surpassed this with 1986's more inscrutably minimalist Top 10 effort, 'VICTORIALAND'. An abortive film project collaboration with HAROLD BUDD was issued at the end of the year as they headed towards an increasingly "New Age"-style sound. Two more classics, 'BLUE BELL KNOLL' and 'HEAVEN OR LAS VEGAS' were released over the next half decade, both finding a home in the US charts for 'Capitol' records. In 1992, they finally succumbed to signing for 'Fontana' in the UK, leading to a comeback album, 'FOUR CALENDAR CAFE' in '93. Many longtime fans were disappointed with what was surely the duo's most accessible, grounded album to date yet devoid of much of the mystery that made their earlier work so alluring. The following year saw LIZ guest on FUTURE SOUND OF LONDON's ambient venture, 'Lifeforms'; she would subsequently go on to perform on MASSIVE ATTACK's 'Teardrops' single in '98. After another 3-year hiatus, FRASER and GUTHRIE returned with 'MILK & KISSES' (1996), a typically COCTEAU-esque affair that moved some critics to suggest the band were treading water. ROBIN resurfaced towards the end of 2000 via VIOLET INDIANA. His working partner on this collaboration was former MONO diva, SIOBHAN DE MARE, a slightly less ethereal vocalist than FRASER, witnessed on their debut EP, 'CHOKE'. The material on the EP, and especially on the debut album 'ROULETTE' (2001), evoked a laid-back GALAXIE 500-esque wig-out with GUTHRIE's instrumentation quite similar to the spacey hypnotics of TRANSIENT WAVES or PIANO MAGIC. DE MARE's whispering vocals on 'ROULETTE' were awesome and she did manage to completely re-invent her voice on the stand-out track 'SUNDANCE' where she soars while GUTHRIE's guitar spirals out of control. The pair issued a single 'KILLER EYES' at the end of 2001, which featured some fantastic B-sides such as the sparse 'STORM' and the free-jazz influenced 'SAFE WORLD'. • **Trivia:** ROBIN has produced many '4.a.d.' outfits in addition to The GUN CLUB (1987). An item for some time, LIZ and ROBIN became parents in 1989. Early in 1991, LIZ was surprisingly but not undeservedly nominated for Best Female Vocalist at the 'Brit' awards.

Album rating: GARLANDS (*7) / HEAD OVER HEELS (*8) / TREASURE (*9) / VICTORIALAND (*8) / THE MOON AND THE MELODIES with Harold Budd (*5) / THE PINK OPAQUE compilation (*8) / BLUE BELL KNOLL (*7) / HEAVEN OR LAS VEGAS (*7) / FOUR CALENDAR CAFE (*6) / MILK & KISSES (*7) / THE BBC SESSIONS collection (*7) / STARS AND TOPSOIL compilation (*9*) / Violet Indiana: ROULETTE (*7)

ELIZABETH FRASER (b.29 Aug'63) – vocals / **ROBIN GUTHRIE** (b. 4 Jan'62) – guitar, drum programming, keyboards / **WILL HEGGIE** – bass

		4 a.d.	not iss.
Jul 82.	(lp) *(CAD 211)* **GARLANDS**	□	–

– Blood bitch / Wax and wane / But I'm not / Blind dumb deaf / Grail overfloweth / Shallow than halo / The hollow men / Garlands. *(c-iss.Apr84 +=; CADC 211)* – Dear heart / Blind dumb deaf / Hearsay please / Hazel. *(cd-iss. 1986 ++=; CAD 211CD)* – Speak no evil / Perhaps some other acorn. *<US cd-iss. 1991 on 'Alliance'; 96415>*

| Sep 82. | (12"ep) *(BAD 213)* **LULLABIES** | □ | – |

– It's all but an ark lark / Alas dies laughing / Feathers-Oar-Blades.

| Mar 83. | (7") *(AD 303)* **PEPPERMINT PIG. / LAUGH LINES** | □ | – |

(12"+=) *(BAD 303)* – Hazel.

— Trimmed to a duo when HEGGIE left to form LOWLIFE

| Oct 83. | (lp) *(CAD 313)* **HEAD OVER HEELS** | 51 | – |

– When mama won't mush / Sugar hiccup / In our anglehood / Glass candle grenades / Multifoiled / In the gold dust rush / The tinderbox (of a heart) / My love paramour / Musette and drums / Five ten fiftyfold. *(c-iss.Apr84 +=; CADC 313)* *(cd-iss. 1986 +=; CAD 313CD)* – SUNBURST AND SNOWBLIND EP *<US cd-iss. 1991 on 'Alliance'; 96416>*

| Oct 83. | (12"ep) *(BAD 314)* **SUNBURST AND SNOWBLIND** | □ | – |

– Sugar hiccup / From the flagstones / Because of whirl-Jack / Hitherto.

— added **SIMON RAYMONDE** (b. 3 Apr'62, London, England) – bass, keyboards, guitar (ex-DROWNING CRAZE)

| Apr 84. | (7") *(AD 405)* **PEARLY DEWDROPS DROP. / PEPPER-TREE** | 29 | – |

(12"+=) *(BAD 405)* – The spangle maker.

| Nov 84. | (lp/c) *(CAD/+C 412)* **TREASURE** | 29 | – |

– Ivo / Lorelei / Beatrix / Persephone / Pandora – for Cindy / Amelia / Aloysius / Cicely / Otterley / Donimo. *(cd-iss. 1986; CAD 412CD)* *<US cd-iss. 1991 on 'Alliance'; 96418>*

| Mar 85. | (7") *(AD 501)* **AIKEA-GUINEA. / KOOKABURRA** | 41 | – |

(12"+=) *(BAD 501)* – Rococo / Quiquose.

| Nov 85. | (12"ep) *(BAD 510)* **TINY DYNAMITE** | 52 | – |

– Pink orange red / Ribbed and veined / Sultitan Itan / Plain tiger.

| Nov 85. | (12"ep) *(BAD 511)* **ECHOES IN A SHALLOW BAY** | 65 | – |

– Great spangled fritillary / Melonella / Pale clouded white / Eggs and their shells *(cd-iss. Oct86 +=; BAD 510/511)* – TINY DYNAMITE

— **RICHARD THOMAS** – saxophone, bass *(of DIF JUZ)* repl. SIMON who fell ill

| Apr 86. | (lp/c/cd) *(CAD/+C 602)(CAD 602CD)* **VICTORIALAND** | 10 | □ |

– Lazy calm / Fluffy tufts / Throughout the dark months of April and May / Whales tales / Oomingmak / Little Spacey / Feet-like fins / How to bring a blush to the snow / The thinner the air. *<US cd-iss. 1991 on 'Alliance'; 96417>*

COCTEAU TWINS (cont)

— SIMON RAYMONDE returned repl.temp. RICHARD (back to DIF JUZ)

Oct 86. (7") (AD 610) **LOVE'S EASY TEARS. / THOSE EYES, THAT MOUTH** — 53 / —
(12"+=) (BAD 610) – Sigh's smell of farewell.

— next was a one-off collaboration with label new signing **HAROLD BUDD** – piano

4 a.d. Relativity

Nov 86. (lp/c)(cd; by HAROLD BUDD, ELIZABETH FRASER, ROBIN GUTHRIE, SIMON RAYMONDE) (CAD/+C 611)(CAD 611CD) <8143> **THE MOON AND THE MELODIES** — 46 / —
– Sea, swallow me / Memory gongs / Why do you love me? / Eyes are mosaics / She will destroy you / The ghost has no home / Bloody and blunt / Ooze out and away, one how.

4 a.d. Capitol

Sep 88. (lp/c/dat)(cd) (CAD/+C/T 807)(CAD 807CD) <90892> **BLUE BELL KNOLL** — 15 / —
– Blue bell knoll / Athol-brose / Carolyn's fingers / For Phoebe still a baby / The itchy glowbo blow / Cico buff / Suckling the mender / Spooning good singing gum / A kissed and red floatboat / Ella megablast burls forever.

Oct 88. (7") **CAROLYN'S FINGERS. / BLUE BELL KNOLL** — — / —

— In Apr'90, LIZ was heard on Ian McCulloch's (ex-ECHO & THE BUNNYMEN) 'Candleland' single.

Aug 90. (7"/c-s) (AD 0011/+C) **ICEBLINK LUCK. / MIZAKE THE MIZAN** — 38 / —
(12"+=/cd-s+=) (AD 0011 T/CD) – Watchiar.

Sep 90. (cd)(lp/c) (CAD 0012CD)(CAD/+C 0012) <C2/C1/C4 93669> **HEAVEN OR LAS VEGAS** — 7 / 99
– Cherry coloured funk / Pitch the baby / Iceblink luck / Fifty-fifty clown / Heaven or Las Vegas / I wear your ring / Fotzepolitic / Wolf in the breast / Road, river and rail / Frou-frou foxes in midsummer fires.

— on U.S. tour, augmented by **MITSUO TATE + BEN BLAKEMAN** – guitars

Fontana Capitol

Sep 93. (7"/c-s) (CT/+C 1) **EVANGELINE. / MUD AND LARK** — 34 / —
(12"pic-d+=/cd-s+=) (CT X/CD 1) – Summer-blink.

Oct 93. (cd/c/lp) (518259-2/-4/-1) <C2/C4/C1 99375> **FOUR CALENDAR CAFE** — 13 / 78
– Know who you are ate every age / Evangeline / Blue beard / Theft and wandering around lost / Oil of angels / Squeeze-wax / My truth / Essence / Summerhead / Pur.

Dec 93. (cd-s) (COCCD 1) **WINTER WONDERLAND. / FROSTY THE SNOWMAN** — 58 / —
(above festive tracks, deleted after a week in UK Top 60)

Feb 94. (7"/c-s) (CT/+C 2) **BLUEBEARD. / THREE SWEPT** — 33 / —
(12"+=) (CTX 2) – Ice-pulse.
(cd-s++=) (CTCD 2) – ('A'acoustic).

Sep 95. (7"/7"cd-ep) (CCT1/CT1/CTCD 3) <30548> **TWINLIGHTS** — 59 / Dec95
– Rilkean heart / Golden-vein // Pink orange red / Half-gifts.

Oct 95. (12"ep/cd-ep) (CT X/CD 4) <36240> **OTHERNESS** (An Ambient EP) — 59 / Dec95
– Feet like fins / Seekers who are lovers / Violaine / Cherry coloured funk.

Mar 96. (cd-ep) (CTCD 5) **TISHBITE / PRIMITIVE HEART / FLOCK OF SOUL** — 34 / —
(12"cd-ep) (CT X/DDD 5) – (title track) / Round / An Elan.

Apr 96. (cd/c/lp) (514 501-2/4/-1) <37049-2/-4/-1> **MILK & KISSES** — 17 / 99
– Violaine / Serpent skirt / Tishbite / Half-gifts / Calfskin smack / Rilkean heart / Ups / Eperdu / Treasure hiding / Seekers who are lovers. (also ltd.cd; 532 363-2)

Jul 96. (12") (CTX 6) **VIOLAINE. / ALICE** — 56 / —
(cd-s+=) (CTDD 6) – Circling girl.
(cd-s) (CTCD 6) – ('A'side) / Tranquil eye / Smile.

— towards the end of 2000, GUTHRIE worked as the duo VIOLET INDIANA (alongside SIOBHAN DE MARE, ex-MONO), releasing the 'CHOKE' EP for his 'Bella Union' imprint

– compilations, others, etc. –

Dec 85. (cd) *4 a.d.; (CAD 513CD) / Relativity; <ENC 8040>* **THE PINK OPAQUE** — — / Sep85
– The spangle maker / Millimillenary / Wax and wane / Hitherto / Pearly-dewdrops' drops (12" Version) / From the flagstones / Aikea-Guinea / Lorelei / Pepper-tree / Musette and drums.

Nov 91. (10xcd-ep-box) *Capitol; (CTBOX 1)* **THE SINGLES COLLECTION** — — / —
– (above featured previous 9 singles + new 1) (sold separately Mar92)

Sep 99. (d-cd) *Bella Union; (BELLACD 14)* **THE BBC SESSIONS** — — / —

Oct 00. (cd) *4 a.d.; (CAD2K 019CD) <370019>* **STARS AND TOPSOIL 1982-1990** — — / —
– Blind dumb deaf / Sugar hiccup / My love paramour / Pearly dewdrops drop / Lorelei / Pandora / Aikea guinea / Pink orange red / Pale clouded white / Lazy calm / Thinner the air / Orange appled / Cico buff / Carolyn's fingers / Fifty fifty clown / Iceblink luck / Heaven or Las Vegas / Watchiar.

VIOLET INDIANA

ROBIN GUTHRIE – guitars, etc. / **SIOBHAN DE MARE** – vocals (ex-MONO)

Bella Union Instinct

Nov 00. (cd-ep) (BELLACD 22) **CHOKE EP** — — / —
– Purr la perla / Busted / Silent / Torn up.

Apr 01. (cd) (BELLACD 24) <571> **ROULETTE** — — / May01
– Air kissing / Busted / Sundance / Powder river / Little echo / Angel / Poison gorgeous / Hiding / Rage days / Liar / Feline or famine / Killer eyes.

May 01. (cd-ep) (BELLACD 26) **KILLER EYES EP** — — / —
– Killer eyes / Storm / Safe word / Killer eyes (CD-Rom).

Oct 01. (cd-ep) (BELLACD 28) **SPECIAL EP** — — / —
– Jailbird / Poppy / Sky / Chapter 3.

Leonard COHEN

Born: 21 Sep'34, Montreal, Canada. Emerging from the tail end of the beatnik scene in the early 60's, COHEN was nearing his mid thirties and had already published several volumes of poetry as well as two novels when he came to record his debut album, 'SONGS OF LEONARD COHEN'. Released in 1968, the record is still regarded by many as his finest work and includes two of his best loved and well known songs in 'SUZANNE' and 'SISTERS OF MERCY'. Musically, the album was sparse, fragile acoustic guitar accompanying COHEN's highly distinctive, tortured sliver of a voice. All ravaged sophistication and doomed romance, COHEN was inevitably compared with the likes of JACQUES BREL, although the richness of the imagery he employed immediately set him apart. While the seemingly self-pitying, bedsit-friendly image saw him panned and parodied by critics, he found an appreciative audience among disillusioned hippies as the singer/songwriter movement began to gather strength. Always more popular in Britain and Europe than America, his debut album reached No.13 in the UK charts. The follow-up, 'SONGS FROM A ROOM' (1969) was almost as good, another opus cloaked in a melancholic intensity and an aching sense of loss, boasting such timeless COHEN fare as 'BIRD ON A WIRE', 'THE PARTISAN' and 'LADY MIDNIGHT'. The record reached No.2 in Britain and COHEN set off for Europe on an extensive round of touring that included an appearance at the Isle Of Wight festival in 1970. Following the release of 'SONGS OF LOVE AND HATE' (1971), the singer embarked on another sojourn to foreign shores, even playing for Israeli soldiers at various military bases, an experience that informed a large part of the lyrical themes on 'NEW SKIN FOR THE OLD CEREMONY' (1974).

Album rating: THE SONGS OF LEONARD COHEN (*8) / SONGS FROM A ROOM (*6) / SONGS OF LOVE AND HATE (*6) / LIVE SONGS (*4) / NEW SKIN FOR THE OLD CEREMONY (*5) / GREATEST HITS compilation (*9)

LEONARD COHEN – vocals, guitar (with various session people)

C.B.S. Columbia

Feb 68. (lp) (CBS 63241) <9533> **SONGS OF LEONARD COHEN** — 13 / 83
– Suzanne / Master song / Winter lady / The stranger song / Sisters of mercy / So long, Marianne / Hey, that's no way to say goodbye / Stories of the street / Teachers / One of us cannot be wrong. (re-iss. Nov91;)

Apr 68. (7") <44439> **SUZANNE. / HEY, THAT'S NO WAY TO SAY GOODBYE** — — / —

May 68. (7") (CBS 3337) **SUZANNE. / SO LONG, MARIANNE** — — / —

Apr 69. (lp) (CBS 63587) <9767> **SONGS FROM A ROOM** — 2 / 63
– Bird on the wire / Story of Isaac / Bunch of lonesome heroes / The partisan / Seems so long ago, Nancy / Old revolution / The butcher / You know who I am / Lady midnight / Tonight will be fine. (re-iss. Nov81; CBS 32074) (cd-iss. Feb88; CDCBS 63587) (re-iss. cd Jun90; CD 32074)

May 69. (7") (CBS 4245) <44827> **BIRD ON THE WIRE. / SEEMS SO LONG AGO, NANCY** — — / —

Mar 71. (lp) (CBS 69004) <30103> **SONGS OF LOVE AND HATE** — 4 / —
– Avalanche / Last year's man / Dress rehearsal rag / Diamonds in the mine / Love call you by your first name / Famous blue raincoat / Sing another song / Boys / Joan of Arc. (re-iss. Sep82 lp/c; CBS/40 32219) (re-iss. Jun94 on 'Columbia' cd/c; 476799-2/-4)

Jul 71. (7") (CBS 7292) **JOAN OF ARC. / DIAMONDS IN THE MINE** — — / —

Jul 72. (7"ep) (CBS 9162) **McCABE & MRS. MILLER** — — / —
– Sisters of mercy / Winter lady / The stranger song.

— w / **RON CORNELIUS** – guitar / **BOB JOHNSTON** – organ, guitar, harmonica / **CHARLIE DANIELS** – bass, fiddle / **ELKIN FOWLER** – banjo, guitar / **JENNIFER WARNES** – vocals / **PETER MARSHALL** – bass / **DAVID O'CONNOR** – guitar

Apr 73. (lp) (CBS 65224) <31724> **LIVE SONGS (live)** — — / —
– (minute prologue) / Passing through / You know who I am / Bird on the wire / Nancy / Improvisation / Story of Isaac / Please don't pass me by (a disgrace) / Tonight will be fine / Queen Victoria. (re-iss. Mar84 lp/c; CBS/40 32272) (cd-iss. May88; CDCBS 65224)

Apr 73. (7") <45852> **NANCY (live). / PASSING THROUGH (live)** — — / —

Jul 74. (7") (CBS 2494) **BIRD ON THE WIRE (live). / TONIGHT WILL BE FINE (live)** — — / —

— now w/ loads of sessioners

Aug 74. (lp) (CBS 69087) <33167> **NEW SKIN FOR THE OLD CEREMONY** — 24 / —
– Is this what you wanted / Chelsea hotel No.2 / Lover lover lover / Field Commander Cohen / Why don't you try / There is a war / A singer must die / I tried to leave you / Who by fire / Take this longing / Leaving Green sleeves. (c-iss.Jun86; CBS40 32660) (cd-iss. Jun88; CDCBS 69087) (cd re-iss. Apr96; CD 32660)

Nov 74. (7") (CBS 2699) **LOVER LOVER LOVER. / WHO BY FIRE** — — / —

Nov 75. (lp) (CBS 69161) <34077> **GREATEST HITS** (compilation) — — / —
– Suzanne / Sisters of mercy / So long, Marianne / Bird on the wire / Lady Midnight / The partisan / Hey, that's no way to say goodbye / Famous blue raincoat / Last year's man / Chelsea hotel No.2 / Who by fire / Take this longing. (re-iss. Apr85 lp/c; CBS/40 32644) (cd-iss. Jun88; CDCBS 69161; hit UK No.99) (re-iss. cd Jun89; CDCBS 32644)

273

COIL

Formed: London, England ... 1983 by JOHN BALANCE and PETER 'SLEAZY' CHRISTOPHERSON. The latter had been a graphic designer for Hypnosis (album sleeves for PINK FLOYD and LED ZEPPELIN) in the 70's, before becoming part of THROBBING GRISTLE and later co-founder of PSYCHIC TV (with TG mainman, GENESIS P. ORRIDGE). PETER had just departed from the latter to become a pop video maker but chose to return to the studio in 1984 to record with BALANCE, cutting the 17-minute single, 'HOW TO DESTROY ANGELS'. Soon after its release, they found CLINT RUIN (aka JIM 'FOETUS' THIRLWELL), who produced their debut album 'SCATOLOGY', aided by the expanded line-up of STEPHEN E. THROWER, GAVIN FRIDAY (Virgin Prunes) and ALEX FERGUSSON. Ritualistic industrial experimentation incorporating arcane sexual ambience, one of the record's highlights was the subsequent single, 'PANIC', backed by a cover of Gloria Jones' 'TAINTED LOVE' (more recently covered by SOFT CELL). In fact, they used MARC ALMOND on an accompanying video, which was widely banned. During this time, they had also worked with gay film-maker, Derek Jarman on soundtrack, 'The Angel Conversation'. In 1986, COIL shared a billing with BOYD RICE (NON) on the album, 'NIGHTMARE CULTURE'. STEPHEN was now a full-time member, working on two further 1986 releases, the 'THE ANAL STAIRCASE' EP and 'HORSE ROTORVATOR' album. The following year, the group worked on Clive Barker's soundtrack for the horror movie, 'HELLRAISER', releasing the out-takes as a 10" EP, 'THE CONSEQUENCES OF RAISING HELL'. BALANCE, SLEAZY and Co incorporated OTTO AVERY into the line-up for 'GOLD IS THE METAL' album, although little was heard from them until a compilation was released in 1990. In 1994, the veteran experimentalists were snapped up by TRENT REZNOR, who signed them to his new 'Eksaton' label, the group's sound having evolved into a darker edged techno/industrial sound; 1998's 'TIME MACHINE' showed how far they had come since their early 80's inception. • **Songwriters:** BALANCE – CHRISTOPHERSON, except WHO BY FIRE (Leonard Cohen). • **Note:** Not to be confused with late 70's COIL, who released the 'MOTOR INDUSTRY' single.

Album rating: SCATOLOGY (*6) / HORSE ROTORVATOR (*6) / THE CONSEQUENCES OF RAISING HELL (*8) / GOLD IS THE METAL (*6) / UNNATURAL HISTORY compilation (*6) / LOVE'S SECRET DOMAIN (*7) / BACKWARDS (*6) / BLACK LIGHT DISTRICT (*5) / TIME MACHINES (*5)

JOHN BALANCE – guitar, bass, vocals, piano (also of CURRENT 93) / **PETER 'SLEAZY' CHRISTOPHERSON** – drum programming (ex-PSYCHIC TV, ex-THROBBING GRISTLE)

L.A.Y.L.A.H. not iss.

Jun 84. (12"one-sided) *(LAY 5)* **HOW TO DESTROY ANGELS**
 (cd-iss. 1988+=; LAY 5CD) – Absolute elsewhere. *(cd re-iss. Oct96 on 'Threshold House'=; LOCICD 5)* – The sleeper / Remotely / The sleeper II / Tectonic plates / Dismal orb.

— added guests **STEPHEN E. THROWER** – clarinet, percussion (of POSSESSION) / **ALEX FERGUSSON** – guitar (of PSYCHIC TV) / **GAVIN FRIDAY** – vocals (of VIRGIN PRUNES) / **CLINT RUIN** – synthesizers

Force & Form/K422 not iss.

Feb 85. (lp) *(FKK 1)* **SCATOLOGY**
 – Ubu noir / Panic / At the heart of it all / Tenderness of wolves / The spoiler / Clap / Aqua regis / Restless day / Solar lodge / The S.W.B.P. / Godhead = deadhead / Cathedral in flames. *(cd-iss. Dec88; FKK 001CD)(+=)* – Tainted love.
May 85. (12",12"red) *(FFK 512)* **PANIC. / TAINTED LOVE / AQUA REGIS**

— In 1986, shared billing with BOYD RICE on album 'NIGHTMARE CULTURE'.

— added **STEPHEN E. THROWER** – wind, percussion

Dec 86. (12"ep,12"clear-ep) *(ROTA 121)* **THE ANAL STAIRCASE (a Dionysian remix). / BLOOD FROM THE AIR / RAVENOUS**
Jan 87. (lp) *(ROTA 1)* **HORSE ROTORVATOR**
 – The anal staircase / Slur / Babylero / Ostia / Herald / Penetralia / Circles of mania / Blood from the air / Who by fire / The golden section / The first five minutes after death. *(cd-iss. Jan88; ROTA 1CD)(+=)* – Ravenous.

Solar Lodge Torso

Jan 88. (lp) *(SL 1)* **MUSIC FOR COMMERCIALS**
Jun 88. (10"m-lp; some colrd) *(COIL 001)* **THE CONSEQUENCES OF RAISING HELL**
 – Hellraiser theme / The hellbound heart / Box theme / No new world / Attack of the Sennapods / Main title. *(re-iss. as 'HELLRAISER' Feb89 c/cd; COIL C/CD 001)(+=)* – MUSIC FOR COMMERCIALS

— added **OTTO AVERY**

Threshold House Torso

Sep 88. (lp,red-lp,clear-lp/cd) *(LOCI/+CD 1)* **GOLD IS THE METAL**
 – The last rites of spring / Paradisiac / Thump / For us they will / The broken wheel / Boy in a suitcase / Golden hole / Cardinal points / Red slur / ...Of free enterprise / Aqua regalia / Metal in the head / Either his, or yours / Chickenskin / Soundtrap / The first five minutes after violent death. *(cd+=)* – The wheal / Hellraiser. *(lp's w/ free 7")* – THE WHEAL. *(lp re-iss. 1990 on 'Normal' lp/cd; NORMAL/+CD 77)* *(lp w/ free 7")* – THE WHEAL. / KEEL HAULER *(re-iss. cd May94 on 'Normal'; same)* *(cd re-iss. Oct96; same)*
1990. (7") *(SX 002)* **WRONG EYE. / SCOPE**
 (above issued on 'Shock')
Dec 90. (12") *(LOCI 3)* **WINDOWPANE. / WINDOWPANE**

Torso Wax Trax!

May 91. (lp/cd) *(TORSO/+CD 181) <WAXCD 7143>* **LOVE'S SECRET DOMAIN** 1989
 – Disco hospital / Teenage lightning / Things happen / The snow / Dark river / Where even the darkness / Something to see / Windowpane / Further back and faster / Lorca not Orca / Love's secret domain.

Aug 91. (12"ep/cd-ep) *(TORSO/+CD 180)* **THE SNOW REMIXES**
 – (6 remixes from last album by JACK DANGERS + DREW McDOWELL)

— now without THROWER

1992. (7") **AIRBORNE BELLS. / IS SUICIDE A SOLUTION**
 above issued on 'Clawfist'
Nov 92. (cd) *(LOCICD 4)* **STOLEN AND CONTAMINATED KISSES**
 (cont. 'HOW TO DESTROY ANGELS') (cd re-iss. Oct96; same)
1994. (12"blue) *(LOCIS 1)* **THEMES FROM BLUE 1. / THEMES FROM BLUE 2**

Eskaton Nothing

1994. (12") *(ESKATON 001)* **NASA ARAB. / FIRST DARK RIDE**
1994. (12") *(ESKATON 002)* **BEAUTIFUL CATASTROPHE**
 – Protection / Glimpse / Crawling sirit / PHILM #1.
1995. (10"ep,10"clear-ep; by COIL & ELPH) *(ESKATON 003)* **PHILM. / STATIC ELECTRICIAN / RED SCRATCH**
1995. (cd/lp; as ELpH) *(ESKATON 006/007)* **WORSHIP THE GLITCH**
Oct 96. (cd/d-lp) *(ESKATON 008/009)* **BLACK LIGHT DISTRICT**
Jan 98. (cd) *(ESKATON 010)* **TIME MACHINES**
 – Telepathine / DOET-Hectate / 5 MeO DMT / Dimethylamino / Psilocybin.

– compilations, etc. –

Dec 89. (cd) *Threshold House; (LOCICD 2)* **UNNATURAL HISTORY**
1995. (d-cd) *Eskaton;* **THE SOUND OF MUSIC** *(film music)*
Oct 96. (cd) *Threshold House; (LOCICD 6)* **ANGELIC CONVERSATION**
Oct 96. (cd) *Threshold House; (LOCICD 7)* **WINDOWPANE / THE SNOW**
Oct 96. (cd) *Threshold House; (LOCICD 10)* **UNNATURAL HISTORY VOL.2**
Apr 97. (cd) *Threshold House; (LOCICD 12)* **UNNATURAL HISTORY VOL.3 (JOYFUL PARTICIPATION IN THE SORROWS OF THE WORLD)**
 – First dark ride / Baby food / Music for commercials / Panic / Neither his nor yours / Feeder / Wrong eye / Meaning what exactly / Scope / Lost rivers Of London.
Oct 97. (cd; COIL & ZOSKIA) *Threshold House; (LOCICD 13) / Imprint; <84870>* **TRANSPARENT** Feb99
 – Sicktone / Baptism of fire / Rape / Poisons / Truth / Sewn open / Silence et secrecy / Here to here (double headed secret) / Stealing the words / On balance.

Lloyd COLE

Born: 31 Jan'61, Buxton, England. In summer of '83, COLE and BLAIR COWAN formed LLOYD COLE & THE COMMOTIONS after a meeting at Glasgow University. They subsequently recruited some fellow students, NEIL CLARK, LAWRENCE DONEGAN (son of LONNIE) and STEPHEN IRVINE, signing with 'Polydor' and scoring almost immediately with the classic 'PERFECT SKIN' single, a Top 30 hit in Spring '84. This was followed up by 'FOREST FIRE' and by the time the band's seminal debut set, 'RATTLESNAKES' was released later that Autumn, the critics were already fawning over the group's subtle, intelligent retro pop/rock. They scored extra points for the intellectual ruminations and name dropping in the lyrics, COLE's languorous croon a model of detached cool inevitably drawing comparisons with LOU REED. An auspicious start to their career, the album sold well enough to guarantee a Top 20 placing for the following year's 'BRAND NEW FRIEND' single. More readily endearing, the track's lilting pop melancholy was characteristic of the general mood on 'EASY PIECES' (1985), although the blackly humourous 'LOST WEEKEND' upped the tempo and provided the band with another Top 20 hit. By this point, COLE and his COMMOTIONS, had graduated from being the darlings of the college circuit to achieve considerable crossover success and the future looked good. A third set, 'MAINSTREAM' (1987), sounded lacklustre in comparison, only 'SEAN PENN BLUES' partly recovering the sly wit of old. After a further flop EP and a relatively successful best of compilation, the band went their separate ways. COLE embarked on a solo career, taking COWAN and relocating to New York, where he recruited ex-LOU REED players, ROBERT QUINE and FRED MAHER. The resulting album, 'LLOYD COLE' (1990) achieved a respectable chart placing but a muted critical reception, despite some genuinely evocative moments. Subsequent sets, the more buoyant 'DON'T GET WEIRD ON ME BABE' (1991) and 'BAD VIBES' (1993) rather unfairly met a similar fate. 1995's 'LOVE STORY', on the other hand, saw something of a belated critical comeback, the classy single, 'LIKE LOVERS DO', COLE's biggest hit in years, with the singer proving that a midnight shadow and artful lyrics still had a place in the pop jungle. After an extended period of legal hassles with 'Mercury', COLE emerged with a new band, The NEGATIVES, and an eponymous millennial album released on French-based indie label, 'XIII Bis'. While the song, by and large, remained the same, highlights such as 'PAST IMPERFECT' (a suitably askance view of his 80's heyday) suggested the ageing intellectual wasn't quite ready to don his dad-rock slippers. All of which made the release of 'PLASTIC WOOD' (2001) perhaps a little less surprising than it might have been. For the first time in his career, COLE abandoned the rock format, confounding expectations with a whole album's worth of ambient electronica. While he resisted singing, he couldn't quite give up his acoustic strumming or his penchant for winsome melody, factors which only served to enhance the music's enchanting ebb and flow. In complete contrast, 'ETC.' (2001), released around the same time, gathered together odds and sods from the vaults. More familiar territory then, but of an unexpectedly high quality for cutting room floor material. Sympathetic covers of Karen Black's 'MEMPHIS' and Bob Dylan's 'YOU'RE A BIG GIRL NOW' hinted at an as yet untapped talent for interpretation. • **Covered:** GLORY (Television) / MYSTERY TRAIN (Elvis Presley) / I DON'T BELIEVE YOU + IF YOU GOTTA GO, GO NOW

(Bob Dylan) / CHILDREN OF THE REVOLUTION (T.Rex). • **Trivia:** 60's chanteuse/singer, SANDIE SHAW, had minor UK chart hit in 1986 with their 'ARE YOU READY TO BE HEARTBROKEN?'.

Album rating: RATTLESNAKES (*7) / EASY PIECES (*6) / MAINSTREAM (*5) / 1984-1989 compilation (*7) / LLOYD COLE (*5) / DON'T GET WEIRD ON ME, BABE (*5) / BAD VIBES (*4) / LOVE STORY (*5) / THE COLLECTION compilation (*7) / THE NEGATIVES (*6) / PLASTIC WOOD (*6) / ETC. (*6)

LLOYD COLE & THE COMMOTIONS

LLOYD COLE (b.31 Jan'61, Derbyshire, England) – vocals, guitar / **NEIL CLARK** (b. 3 Jul'55) – guitar / **BLAIR COWAN** – keyboards, vocals / **LAWRENCE DONEGAN** (b.13 Jul'61) – bass (ex-BLUEBELLS) / **STEPHEN IRVINE** (b.16 Dec'59) – drums

		Polydor	Geffen
Apr 84.	(7") (COLE 1) **PERFECT SKIN. / THE SEA AND THE SAND** (12"+=) (COLEX 1) – You will never be so good.	26	
Aug 84.	(7"/7"g-f) (COLE/+G 2) **FOREST FIRE. / ANDY'S BABY** (12"+=) (COLEX 2) – Glory.	41	
Oct 84.	(lp/c)(cd) (LCLP/LCMC 1)(823 683-2) <24064> **RATTLESNAKES** – Perfect skin / Speedboat / Rattlesnakes / Down on Mission Street / Forest fire / Charlotte Street / 2CV / Four flights up / Patience / Are you ready to be heartbroken? (cd+=) – The sea and the sand / You will never be no good / Sweetness / Andy's babies. (cd re-iss. Jan92; same)	13	
Oct 84.	(7") (COLE 3) **RATTLESNAKES. / SWEETNESS** (12"+=) (COLEX 3) – Four flights up.	65	
Aug 85.	(7") (COLE 4) **BRAND NEW FRIEND. / HER LAST FLING** (12"+=) (COLEX 4) – Speedboat (live) / 2CV (live).	19	
Oct 85.	(7"/10") (COLE/+T 5) **LOST WEEKEND. / BIG WORLD** (12"+=) (COLEX 5) – Never ends.	17	
Nov 85.	(lp/c)(cd) (LCLP/LCMC 2)(827 670-2) <24093> **EASY PIECES** – Rich / Why I love country music / Pretty gone / Grace / Cut me down / Brand new friend / Lost weekend / James / Minor characters / Perfect blue. (c+=) – Her last fling / Big world. (cd++=) – Never ends. (cd re-iss. Jan92; same) (re-iss. May93 on 'Spectrum' cd/c; 550035-2/-4)	5	
Jan 86.	(7") (COLE 6) **CUT ME DOWN (remix). / ARE YOU READY TO BE HEARTBROKEN? (live)** (12"+=) (COLEX 6) – Forest fire (live). (d7"++=) (COLEG 6) – Perfect blue (instrumental).	38	

—— trimmed to a studio quartet when COWAN became part-time (gigs only)

		Polydor	Capitol
Sep 87.	(7") (COLE 7) **MY BAG. / JESUS SAID** ('A'dance-12"+=/cd-s+=) (COL EX/CD 7) – Perfect skin.	46	-
Oct 87.	(lp/c)(cd) (LCLP/LCMC 3)(833 691-2) <90893> **MAINSTREAM** – My bag / From the hip / 29 / Mainstream / Jennifer she said / Mister malcontent / Sean Penn blues / Big snake / Hey Rusty / These days.	9	
Oct 87.	(7") <44253> **MY BAG. / LOVE YOUR WIFE**	-	
Jan 88.	(7"/7"g-f) (COLE/+G 8) **JENNIFER SHE SAID. / PERFECT BLUE** (12"+=) (COLEX 8) – Mystery train (live) / I don't believe you (live). (cd-s+=) (COLCD 8) – My bag (mix).	31	
Apr 88.	(7"ep/ext-12"ep/cd-ep) (COL E/EX/CD 9) **FROM THE HIP** – From the hip / Please / Lonely mile / Love you wife.	59	
Mar 89.	(lp/c/cd) (837 736-1/-4/-2) <92223> **1984-1989** (compilation) – Perfect skin / Are you ready to be heartbroken? / Forest fire / You will never be so good / Rattlesnakes / Perfect blue / Brand new friend / Cut me down / Lost weekend / Her last fling / Mr. Malcontent / My bag / Jennifer she said / From the hip.	14	Jun89
Apr 89.	(7") (COLE 10) **FOREST FIRE ('89 remix). / PERFECT BLUE** (12"+=/cd-s+=) – ('A'&'B'extended).		

—— DONEGAN left and subsequently became a journalist. The group folded in the Spring of '89.

LLOYD COLE

—— solo with **BLAIR COWAN** – keyboards / **DARYLL SWEET** – bass / **ROBEDRT QUINE** – guitar / **FRED MAHER** – drums, etc / **NICKY HOLLAND + PARKER DU LANY** – backing vocals / (on tour; **DAN McCARROLL** repl. MAHER / **DAVID BALL** repl. SWEET)

		Polydor	Capitol
Jan 90.	(7"/c-s) (COL E/CS 11) **NO BLUE SKIES. / SHELLY I DO** (10"+=/12"+=) (COL ET/EX/CD 11) – Wild orphan.	42	-
Feb 90.	(cd/c/lp) (841 907-2/-4/-1) <92751> **LLOYD COLE** – Don't look back / What do you know about love? / Loveless / No blue skies / Sweetheart / To the church / Downtown / A long way down / Ice cream girl / I hate to see you baby doing that shift / Undressed / Waterline / Mercy killing. (cd re-iss. Apr95;)	11	
Mar 90.	(7"/c-s) (COL E/CS 12) **DON'T LOOK BACK. / BLAME MARY JANE** (10"+=/12"+=/cd-s+=) (COL ET/EX/CD 12) – Witching hour.	59	-
Oct 90.	(7"/c-s) (COL E/CS 13) **DOWNTOWN. / A LONG WAY DOWN (live)** (12"+=/cd-s+=) (COL EX/CD 13) – Sweetheart (live).		-

—— COLE now with COWAN + CLARK

Aug 91.	(7"/c-s) (COL E/CS 14) **SHE'S A GIRL AND I'M A MAN. / WEIRD ON ME** (12"+=/cd-s+=) (COL EX/CD 14) – Children of the revolution.	55	-
Sep 91.	(cd/c/lp) (511093-2/-4/-1) <96077> **DON'T GET WEIRD ON ME BABE** -Butterfly / Theme for her / Margo's waltz / Half of everything / Man enough / What he doesn't know / Tell your sister / Weeping wine / To the lions / Pay for it / The one you never had / She's a girl and I'm a man.	21	
Oct 91.	(7"/c-s) (COL E/CS 15) **WEEPING WINE. / TELL YOUR SISTER** (12"+=/cd-s+=) (COL EX/CD 15) – Somewhere out in the east.		-
Mar 92.	(7"/c-s) (COL E/CS 16) **BUTTERFLY. / JENNIFER SHE SAID** (12"+=/cd-s+=) (COL EX/CD 16) – ('A'-The Planet Anne Charlotte mix).		-

		Fontana	Rykodisc
Sep 93.	(7"/c-s) (VIBE D1/C1) **SO YOU'D LIKE TO SAVE THE WORLD. / VICIOUS** (cd-s+=) (VIBE 1) – Mystic lady. (cd-s) (VIBE 1) – ('A'side) / For your pleasure for your company / 4 M.B.	72	-
Oct 93.	(cd/c/lp) (518318-2/-4/-1) <10306> **BAD VIBES** – Morning is broken / So you'd like to save the world / Holier than thou / Love you so what / Wild mushrooms / My way to you / Too much of a good thing / Fall together / Mister Wrong / Seen the future / Can't get arrested. (cd re-iss. Aug01; same)	38	Jan94
Nov 93.	(7"/c-s) **MORNING IS BROKEN. / RADIO CITY MUSIC HALL** (cd-s+=) – Radio City music hall / Eat your greens. (cd-s+=) – The slider / Mannish girl.		

above album w/ **ADAM PETERS, ANN CHARLOTTE VENGSGAARD, JOHN MICCO, JOHN CARRUTHERS, NEIL CLARK, MATTHEW SWEET, DAN McCARROLL, ANTON FIER, CURTIS WATTS, FRED MAHER, DANA VLCEK,** Lightning **BOB HOFFNAR + PETER MARK**

Sep 95.	(cd-s) (LCCD 1) **LIKE LOVERS DO / TRAFFIC / FOREST FIRE** (cd-s) (LCDD 1) – ('A'side) / I will not leave you alone / Rattlesnakes. (cd-s) (LCDC 1) – ('A'side) / Brand new baby blues (demo) / Perfect skin.	24	-
Sep 95.	(cd/c) (528529-2/-4) <10327> **LOVE STORY** – Trigger happy / Sentimental fool / I didn't know that you cared / Love ruins everything / Baby / Be there / The June bride / Like lovers do / Happy for you / Traffic / Let's get lost / For crying out loud.	27	
Nov 95.	(c-s) (LCMCC 2) **SENTIMENTAL FOOL / BRAND NEW FRIEND** (cd-s+=) (LCCD 2) – Lost weekend / Cut me down. (cd-s) (LCDD 2) – ('A'side) / Most of the time / Millionaire / Sold.	73	
Jan 96.	(c-s/cd-s) (LCCMC/LCCD 3) **BABY / MY BAG / JENNIFER SHE SAID / FROM THE HIP** (cd-s) (LCDD 3) – ('A'side) / The steady slowing down of the heart / Like lovers do.		

		Mercury	not iss.
Sep 98.	(c-s) (MERMC 511) **THAT BOY / IF YOU GOTTA GO, GO NOW** (cd-s+=) (MERCD 511) – Tie me down. (cd-s) (MERDD 511) – ('A'side) / Rain on the parade / Missing.		-

		XIII Bis	What Are?
Jun 01.	(cd; as LLOYD COLE & THE NEGATIVES) (15548-2) <60445> **THE NEGATIVES** – Past imperfect / Impossible girl / No more love songs / What's wrong with this picture / Man on the verge / Negative attitude / Vin ordinaire / Never felt so cold / Too much E / Tried to rock / That boy / I'm gone. (UK-only+=) – Artificial tears.		Nov00

		XIII Bis	Megaworld
Nov 01.	(cd) <13900-2> **PLASTIC WOOD** (rec.1999-2000) – Omni 7th / Sim trees / 4-train / Velvet / Headlights / Dry ice / Plastic wood / After before and after / B-mushroom / Out time / On ice / The beach / Glass jar / Manhattan chase / Park west / Afterthought / Post script / Machinist.	-	
Nov 01.	(cd) (05712) <13901-2> **ETC.** (demos from late 90's) – Backwoods / Old enough to know better / Another lover / 39 down / Sunburst / Memphis / You're a big girl now / Alright people / Santa Cruz / Love like this can't last / Went to Woodstock / Fool you are (demo) / Weakness / Backwoods (reprise).		

– compilations, etc. –

Jan 91.	(cd/c) Polydor; (847733-2/-4) **RATTLESNAKES / EASY PIECES**		-
Jan 99.	(cd/c) Universal TV; (538104-2/-4) **THE COLLECTION** – Are you ready to be heartbroken? / Perfect skin / Forest fire / Rattlesnakes / Brand new friend / Lost weekend / My bag / Jennifer she said / No blue skies / Don't look back / Downtown / Undressed / She's a girl and I'm a man / Butterfly / So you'd like to save the world / My way to you / Like lovers do / Baby / Fool you are / That boy.	24	-
Mar 01.	(cd) Spectrum; (549605-2) **AN INTRODUCTION TO LLOYD COLE & THE COMMOTIONS**		-

COLENSO PARADE

Formed: Belfast, N.Ireland ... 1984 by LINDA CLANDINNING, NEIL LAWSON, JACKIE FORGIE, ROBERT WAKEMAN and frontman, OSCAR. Setting up their own label, COLENSO PARADE released their debut single, 'STANDING UP', showcasing their CHAMELEONS-esque sound complete with elastic bass riffs. Relocating to London the following year, they replaced FORGIE with Englishman, TERRY BICKERS, the guitarist making his first appearance on the single, 'DOWN BY THE BORDER'. Subsequently signing for manager, Dave Bedford's 'Fire' records, the group released their third single, 'HALLELUJAH CHORUS', previewing their long-awaited debut album, 'GLENTORRAN', in the Autumn of '86. However, by the time of the album's release, BICKERS had chosen to join the more ambitious HOUSE OF LOVE, his replacement being JOHN WATT. Further personnel shuffles saw drummer OWEN HOWELL substitute WAKEMAN (who would later throw in his lot with SALAD), a parting single, 'FONTANA EYES' rewarding them with a bit of belated recognition before a proposed major label deal collapsed and the band finally split; OSCAR would later turn down an offer to replace IAN McCULLOCH in ECHO & THE BUNNYMEN.

Album rating: GLENTORRAN (*5)

OSCAR – vocals / **LINDA CLANDINNING** – keyboards / **JACKIE FORGIE** – guitar / **NEIL LAWSON** – bass / **ROBERT WAKEMAN** – drums

		Goliath	not iss.
Sep 84.	(7") (SLING 01) **STANDING UP. / SMOKEY FINGERED REMINDER**		-

—— **TERRY BICKERS** (b. Fulham, London) – guitar; repl. FORGIE

COLENSO PARADE (cont)

Apr 85.	(12"m) (SLING 02) **DOWN BY THE BORDER. / SEE RED / BORDER MIXES**	Fire	not iss.
Jan 86.	(12"ep) (FIRE 7) **HALLELUJAH CHORUS / THE PERFECT ADOPTERS. / TOO LATE FOR ANYTHING / SACRED LOVER**		
Aug 86.	(lp) (FIRELP 6) **GLENTORRAN**		

— **JOHN WATT** – guitar; repl. BICKERS who joined HOUSE OF LOVE (he was later to front LEVITATION)

— **OWEN HOWELL** – drums (ex-BIG SELF) repl. WAKEMAN who later re-surfaced in SALAD

Oct 86.	(7") (BLAZE 11) **FONTANA EYES. / HERE COMES THE NIGHT**
	(12"+=) (BLAZE 11T) – Anything / Our man in Havana.

— split soon after above; OSCAR declined an offer to take over IAN McCULLOCH's job in ECHO & THE BUNNYMEN, while NEIL became an aircraft photographer and LINDA a hairdresser

Edwyn COLLINS

Born: 23 Aug'59, Edinburgh, Scotland. COLLINS formed ORANGE JUICE in Glasgow, Scotland ... 1977 initially as the NU-SONICS with JAMES KIRK, STEPHEN DALY and ALAN DUNCAN, who was subsequently replaced by DAVID McCLYMONT. In 1979, ORANGE JUICE signed to local indie label 'Postcard', the hub of the burgeoning Glasgow indie scene masterminded by ALAN HORNE. In contrast to the post-punk miserabilism coming out of England, ORANGE JUICE were purveyors of studiedly naive, wide-eyed indie pop as best sampled on the brace of early 45's, 'FALLING AND LAUGHING', 'BLUE BOY', 'SIMPLY THRILLED HONEY' and 'POOR OLD SOUL' (later collected on 1993's retrospective, 'THE HEATHER'S ON FIRE'). They subsequently signed to 'Polydor' in 1981, releasing a debut album, 'YOU CAN'T HIDE YOUR LOVE FOREVER', early the following year. Though some of their die-hard fans inevitably accused them of selling out, the set almost made the UK Top 20, its charming guitar pop auguring well for the future. The band suffered internal ruction soon after the album's release, however, MALCOLM ROSS and ZEKE MANYIKA replacing KIRK and DALY respectively. The Nigerian-born MANYIKA injected a newfound rhythmic thrust into the follow-up album, 'RIP IT UP' (1982), the clipped funk of the title track providing the band with their only Top 40 hit, albeit a sizeable one. Despite this belated success, further tensions reduced the band to a duo of COLLINS and MANYIKA who recorded an impressive mini-set, 'TEXAS FEVER' (1984) under the production auspices of reggae veteran, DENNIS BOVELL. Later that year saw the release of swansong set, 'THE ORANGE JUICE – THE THIRD ALBUM', a far more introspective affair which found COLLINS at a low ebb. The singer had already released a cover of The Velvet Underground's 'PALE BLUE EYES', with PAUL QUINN and subsequently embarked on a solo career which remained low key for the ensuing decade. Initially signed to ALAN McGEE's "side" label, 'Elevation', his first two solo singles flopped and as the label went belly-up, COLLINS opted for 'Demon' records. He finally issued a long-awaited album, 'HOPE AND DESPAIR' in summer '89. An eclectic, rootsy affair borne of COLLINS' troubled wilderness years, the record was hailed by the same critics who so vehemently supported ORANGE JUICE. Yet despite the praise, it seemed COLLINS was destined for cult appeal; a second 'Demon' set, 'HELLBENT ON COMPROMISE' (1990) failed to lift his profile and COLLINS went to ground. Well, not completely, the singer honing his production skills for indie outfits such as A HOUSE and The ROCKINGBIRDS. The throaty-voxed singer finally re-emerged in 1994 with 'GORGEOUS GEORGE', the record he'd been threatening to make for years. Recorded on classic studio equipment, the record's organic feel coupled with COLLIN's mordant cynicism and razor sharp songwriting resulted in a massive worldwide hit, 'A GIRL LIKE YOU'. With its crunching, NEIL YOUNG-like riffing and infectious delivery, the record was initially released in Europe and Australia before eventually hitting the Top 5 in the UK a year on. Though 1997's 'THE MAGIC PIPER' (from the album 'I'M NOT FOLLOWING YOU') didn't quite match this commercial feat, COLLINS remains one of Scotland's most accomplished songwriters with a reliable line in caustic wit. In 2002, his brand of humour was taken a step further via the release of 'DOCTOR SYNTAX', an album which saw COLLINS, for the first time, use beats and samples courtesy of SEBASTIAN LEWSLEY. The set comprised COLLINS' trademark guitar-led love songs, but with an edgier, personalised production. 'THE BEATLES' was obviously a direct ode to his peers, although 'SPLITTING UP' exemplified COLLINS' songwriting abilities by ten. '20 YEARS TOO LATE' employed a retro-electro-synth feel accompanied by some strange rapping never before encountered on an EDWYN COLLINS record. • **Songwriters:** ORANGE JUICE: most written by COLLINS, some with MANYIKA. Note that KIRK was the writer of FELICITY, and ROSS provided PUNCH DRUNK. • **Covered:** L.O.V.E. (Al Green), while COLLINS solo tried his hand at MY GIRL HAS GONE (Smokey Robinson) + TIME OF THE PREACHER (Willie Nelson) / WON'T TURN BACK (Vic Godard).

Album rating: Orange Juice: YOU CAN'T HIDE YOUR LOVE FOREVER (*7) / RIP IT UP (*6) / TEXAS FEVER mini (*5) / THE ORANGE JUICE (*5) / THE ESTEEMED ORANGE JUICE (THE VERY BEST OF ORANGE JUICE) compilation (*9) / Edwyn Collins: HOPE AND DESPAIR (*6) / HELLBENT ON COMPROMISE (*6) / GORGEOUS GEORGE (*8) / I'M NOT FOLLOWING YOU (*6) / DOCTOR SYNTAX (*6) / A CASUAL INTRODUCTION 1981-2001 compilation (*8)

ORANGE JUICE

EDWYN COLLINS – vocals, guitar, occasional violin / **JAMES KIRK** – guitar, vocals / **DAVID McCLYMONT** – bass, synths; repl. ALAN DUNCAN / **STEPHEN DALY** – drums

		Postcard	not iss.
Feb 80.	(7") (80-1) **FALLING AND LAUGHING. / MOSCOW** (free 7"flexi) (LYN 7609) – FELICITY (live).		
Aug 80.	(7") (80-2) **BLUE BOY. / LOVE SICK**		
Dec 80.	(7") (80-6) **SIMPLY THRILLED HONEY. / BREAKFAST TIME**		
Mar 81.	(7") (81-2) **POOR OLD SOUL. / (part 2)**		
Jun 81.	(7"; w-drawn) (81-6) **WAN LIGHT. / YOU OLD ECCENTRIC**	Polydor	Polydor
Oct 81.	(7") (POSP 357) **L.O.V.E. LOVE. / INTUITION TOLD ME PT.2**	65	
	(12"+=) (POSPX 357) – Moscow.		
Jan 82.	(7") (POSP 386) **FELICITY. / IN A NUTSHELL**	63	
	(12"+=) (POSPX 386) – You old eccentric.		
Feb 82.	(lp/c) (POLS/+C 1057) **YOU CAN'T HIDE YOUR LOVE FOREVER**	21	
	– Falling and laughing / Untitled melody / Wan light / Tender object / Dying day / L.O.V.E. love / Intuition told me (part 1) / Upwards and onwards / Satellite city / Three cheers for our side / Consolation prize / Felicity / In a nutshell.		

— **MALCOLM ROSS** – guitar (ex-JOSEF K) + **ZEKE MANYIKA** (b. Nigeria) – percussion, vocals, synths; repl. KIRK DALY who subsequently formed MEMPHIS, releasing only one single for 'Swamplands', 'YOU SUPPLY THE ROSES', early 1985

Jul 82.	(7"/10") (POSP/+T 470) **TWO HEARTS TOGETHER. / HOKOYO**	60	-
Oct 82.	(7") (POSP 522) **I CAN'T HELP MYSELF. / TONGUES BEGIN TO WAG**	42	
	(12"+=) (POSPX 522) – Barbeque.		
Nov 82.	(lp/c) (POLS/+C 1076) **RIP IT UP**	39	
	– Rip it up / Breakfast time / A million pleading faces / Mud in your eye / Turn away / I can't help myself / Flesh of my flesh / Louise Louise / Hokoyo / Tenter hook. (cd-iss. Jul89; 839768-2)		
Feb 83.	(7") (POSP 547) **RIP IT UP (remix). / SNAKE CHARMER**	8	
	(some w/ live c-s+=) – The Felicity Flexi Session: The formative years – Simply thrilled honey / Botswana / Time to develop / Blue boy.		
	(d7"+=) (POSPD 547) – Sad lament / Lovesick.		
	(12") (POSPX 547) – ('A'side) / Sad lament / ('A'long version).		
May 83.	(7"/7"pic-d/ext.12") (OJ/OJP/OJX 4) **FLESH OF MY FLESH. / LORD JOHN WHITE AND THE BOTTLENECK TRAIN**	41	-

— basically now a duo of **COLLINS + MANYIKA** with session people replacing ROSS (who joined AZTEC CAMERA) and McCLYMONT (to The MOODISTS)

Feb 84.	(7") (OJ 5) **BRIDGE. / OUT FOR THE COUNT** (free 7"flexi w/ above) (JUICE 1) – Poor old soul (live).	67	-
	(12"+=) (OJX 5) – ('A'-Summer '83 mix).		
Feb 84.	(m-lp/c) (OJM LP/MC 1) **TEXAS FEVER**	34	-
	– Bridge / Craziest feeling / Punch drunk / The day I went down to Texas / A place in my heart / A sad feeling. (cd-iss. Mar98 +=; 539982-2) – Leaner period / Out for the count / Move yourself.		
Apr 84.	(7") (OJ 6) **WHAT PRESENCE?! / A PLACE IN MY HEART (dub)**	47	
	(free c-s w/ above) (OJC 6) – In a nutshell (live) / Simply thrilled honey (live) / Dying day (live).		
	(12"+=) (OJX 6) – ('A'extended).		
Oct 84.	(7") (OJ 7) **LEAN PERIOD. / BURY MY HEAD IN MY HANDS**	74	-
	(free 7"flexi w/ above) (JUICE 3) – Rip it up / What presence?!		
	(12"+=) (OJX 7) – ('A'extended).		
Nov 84.	(lp/c) (OJ LP/MC 1) **THE ORANGE JUICE – THE THIRD ALBUM**		-
	– Get while the goings good / Salmon fishing in New York / I guess I'm just a little sensitive / Burning desire / The artisan / Lean period / What presence?! / Out for the count / All that mattered / Seacharger. (re-iss. Aug86 lp/c; SPE LP/MC 102) (c+=remixes) – I can't help myself / Rip it up / Love struck / Flesh of my flesh / Out for the count / What presence?! / Lean period.		

— disbanded after above album; MANYIKA went solo, as did EDWYN COLLINS. He'd already (in Aug'84) hit UK No.72 with PAUL QUINN on 7"/12" 'PALE BLUES EYES' (a Velvet Underground cover) released on 'Swamplands'.

– compilations, others, etc. –

Jul 85.	(lp/c) Polydor; (OJ LP/MC 3) **IN A NUTSHELL**		-
	– Falling and laughing / Poor old soul (live) / L.O.V.E. / In a nutshell / Felicity / I can't help myself / Hokoyo / Rip it up / Flesh of my flesh / A place in my heart / Bridge / Out for the count / The artisans / What presence?! (w/free 7"flexi) – Felicity.		
Jan 91.	(cd/c) Polydor; (847 727-2/-4) **THE ORANGE JUICE / YOU CAN'T HIDE YOUR LOVE FOREVER**		-
Jul 92.	(cd) Polydor; (513618) **THE VERY BEST OF ORANGE JUICE (THE ESTEEMED ORANGE JUICE)**		Oct95
	– Falling and laughing / Consolation prize (live) / Old eccentric / L.O.V.E. love / Felicity / In a nutshell / Rip it up / I can't help myself / Flesh of my flesh / Tenterhook / Bridge / The day I went down to Texas / Punch drunk / A place in my heart / A sad lament / Lean period / I guess I'm just a little too sensitive / The artisans / Salmon fishing in New York / What presence?! / Out for the count. (re-iss. cd Sep95; same) – (extra track).		
Jul 92.	(lp/c/cd) Postcard; (DUBH 922/+MC/CD) **OSTRICH CHURCHYARD (live in Glasgow)**		-
	– Louise Louise / Three cheers for our side / To put it in a nutshell / Satellite city / Consolation prize / Holiday hymn / Intuition told me (parts 1 & 2) / Wan light / Dying day / Texas fever / Tender object. (cd+=/c+=) – Falling and laughing / Lovesick / Poor old soul / You old eccentric. (cd re-iss. Oct95; DUBH 954CD)		
May 93.	(7") Postcard; (DUBH 934) **BLUEBOY. / LOVESICK**		-
	(cd-s+=) (DUBH 934CD) – Poor old soul (French version) / Poor old soul (instrumental).		

EDWYN COLLINS

solo, with **DENNIS BOVELL, MALCOLM ROSS, ALEX GRAY + CHRIS TAYLOR**

Elevation not iss.

May 87. (7") *(ACID 4)* **DON'T SHILLY SHALLY. / IF EVER YOU'RE READY**
(12"+=) *(ACID 4T)* – Queer fish.

Elevation not iss.

Nov 87. (7") *(ACID 6)* **MY BELOVED GIRL. / CLOUDS (FOGGING UP MY MIND)**
(12"+=) *(ACID 6T)* – My (long time) beloved girl.
(7"box+=) *(ACID 6B)* – 50 shades of blue (acoustic) / What's the big idea.

—— now with **BERNARD CLARKE** – keyboards / **DENNIS BOVELL** – bass / **DAVE RUFFY** – drums

Demon not iss.

Jun 89. (lp/c/cd) *(FIEND/+C/CD 144)* **HOPE AND DESPAIR**
– Coffee table song / 50 shades of blue / You're better than you know / Pushing it to the back of my mind / The wheels of love / Darling, they want it all / The beginning of the end / The measure of the man / Testing time / Let me put my arms around you / The wide eyed child in me / Ghost of a chance. (c+=/cd+=) – If ever you're ready. (re-iss. cd Sep95)

Jul 89. (7") *(D 1064)* **THE COFFEE TABLE SONG. / JUDAS IN BLUE JEANS**
(12"+=) *(D 1064T)* – Out there.

Oct 89. (7") *(D 1065)* **50 SHADES OF BLUE (new mix). / IF EVER YOU'RE READY**
(12") *(D 1065T)* – ('A'extended) / Kindred spirit / Just call her name / Ain't that always the way.
(cd-s) *(D 1065CD)* – ('A'side) / Judas in blue jeans / Kindred spirit / Just call her name.

Oct 90. (lp/c/cd) *(FIEND/+C/CD 195)* **HELLBENT ON COMPROMISE**
– Means to an end / You poor deluded fool / It might as well be you / Take care of yourself / Graciously / Someone else besides / My girl has gone / Everything and more / What's the big idea? / Hellbent medley:- Time of the preacher – Long time gone. (re-iss. cd Oct95; same)

—— now with **STEVEN SKINNER** – guitar / **PHIL THORNALLEY** – bass / **PAUL COOK** – drums

Setanta Bar None

Aug 94. (cd/c/lp) *(SET CD/MC/LP 014) <058>* **GEORGEOUS GEORGE** Sep95
– The campaign for real rock / A girl like you / Low expectations / Out of this world / If you could love me / North of Heaven / Georgeous George / It's right in front of you / Make me feel again / You got it all / Subsidence / Occupy your mind. (re-iss. Jul95, hit UK No.8)

Oct 94. (c-ep) *(ZOP 001C)* **EXPRESSLY EP** 42
– A girl like you / A girl like you (Macrame remix by Youth).
(cd-ep+=) *(ZOP 001CD1)* – Out of this world (I hear a new world) (St.Etienne remix) / Occupy your mind.
(cd-ep) *(ZOP 001CD2)* – ('A'side) / Don't shilly shally (Spotters'86 demo) / Something's brewing / Bring it on back.

Mar 95. (12"ep) *(ZOP 002CD1)* **IF YOU COULD LOVE ME (radio edit). / IN A BROKEN DREAM / INSIDER DEALING / ('A'-MC Esher mix)**
(cd-ep) *(ZOP 002CD1)* – (first 3 tracks) / Hope and despair.
(cd-ep) *(ZOP 002CD2)* – ('A'side) / If ever you're ready / Come to your senses / A girl like you (the Victoria Spaceman mix).

Jun 95. (7") *(ZOP 0037)* **A GIRL LIKE YOU. / YOU'RE ON YOUR OWN** 4
(c-s+=) *(ZOP 003C)* – If you could love me (acoustic version).
(cd-s++=) *(ZOP 003CD)* – Don't shilly shally (Spotters '86 demo).

Oct 95. (c-s) *<58-1234>* **A GIRL LIKE YOU / IF YOU COULD LOVE ME** – 32
(above used on the film 'Empire Records')

Feb 96. (c-s) *(ZOP 004C)* **KEEP ON BURNING / IF YOU COULD LOVE ME (IN TIME AND SPACE)** 45
(cd-s+=) *(ZOP 004CD1)* – Lava lamp / The campaign for real rock.
(cd-s) *(ZOP 004CD2)* – Won't turn back / You've grown a beard / A girl like you (live) / White room.

Setanta Sony

Jul 97. (12") *(SET 041T)* **THE MAGIC PIPER. / A GIRL LIKE YOU (Makrame mix) / WELWYN GARDEN CITY** 32
(cd-s) *(SETCDA 041)* – ('A'side) / More than you bargained for / Red menace / It takes a little time.
(cd-s) *(SETCDB 041)* – ('A'side) / Who is it? / Who is it? (halterbacked by the Victorian spaceman / Welwyn Garden City.

Sep 97. (cd/c/lp) *(SET CD/MC/LP 039) <68716>* **I'M NOT FOLLOWING YOU** 55 Oct97
– It's a steal / The magic piper (of love) / Seventies night / No one waved goodbye / Downer / Keep on burning / Running away with myself / Country rock / For the rest of my life / Superficial cat / Adidas world / I'm not following you.

Oct 97. (7") *(SET 045)* **ADIDAS WORLD. / HIGH FASHION** 71
(cd-s+=) *(SETCDA 045)* – Mr. Bojangles / Talking 'bout the times.
(cd-s) *(SETCDB 045)* – ('A'side) / Episode 3 / Episode 5 / Episode 10 (no, no, no Adidas – Adilated by . . .).

Nov 97. (d12") *(ZOPPR 005)* **I HEAR A NEW WORLD (mixes; Red Snapper / Deadly Avenger Supershine / Red Snapper vocal / DOWNER (James Lavelle mix) // THE MAGIC PIPER (the Wiseguys sniper mix) / ADIDAS WORLD (adilated by Sebastian Lawsely) / DOWNER (James Lavelle vocal)**

—— in Apr'01, EDWYN collaborated with BERNARD BUTLER on the 'Setanta' single 'MESSAGE FOR JOJO'

Apr 02. (cd) *(SETCD 098)* **DOCTOR SYNTAX**
– Never felt like this / Should've done that / Mine is at / No idea / The Beathes / Back to the back room / Splitting up / Johnny Teardrop / 20 years too late / It's a funny thing / Calling on you.

Sep 02. (cd-s) *(SETCD 112)* **JOHNNY TEARDROP / NEVER FELT LIKE THIS / POSTER**

Oct 02. (cd) *(SETCD 113)* **A CASUAL INTRODUCTION 1981-2001** (compilation)
– A girl like you / What presence? (ORANGE JUICE) / Magic piper (of love) / Rip it up (ORANGE JUICE) / A sad lament (ORANGE JUICE) / Witch queen of New Orleans / Johnny teardrop / Gorgeous George / Ghost of a chance / Campaign for real rock / Hope and despair / Falling and laughing (ORANGE JUICE) / Keep on burning / Adidas world / Felicity (ORANGE JUICE) / Tenterhook (ORANGE JUICE) / Witchcraft / Graciously.

COLORBLIND JAMES EXPERIENCE

Formed: Rochester, New York, USA . . . 1987 by COLORBLIND JAMES (aka "CHUCK" CUMINALE) – ex-WHITECAPS – alongside PHILIP MARSHALL, BERNIE HEVERON and JIM McAVANEY. Initially given British exposure via John Peel Radio One airplay for the classic 'CONSIDERING A MOVE TO MEMPHIS' (which featured in the man's Festive 50), COLORBLIND JAMES and his pardners could be experienced in full on the eponymous debut album. Released on NYC indie label, 'Earring', in 1988, the record could only really be described as geek-hillbilly with elements of folk, MOSE ALLISON-style jazz-blues and rockabilly played out awkwardly against often hilariously dry lyrics (check out 'FIRST DAY OF SPRING'). There was even an attempt at student-polka on the awful 'WHY'D THE BOY THROW THE CLOCK OUT THE WINDOW', a track that would've fitted perfectly over an early episode of 'The Young Ones'. By the release of 1989's 'WHY SHOULD I STAND UP?' (released by 'Cooking Vinyl' in the UK), HEVERON had departed while JOHN EBERT, KEN FRANK and DAVE McINTYRE added a whole new dimension to the band's sound with such diverse instrumentation as violin, tuba, clarinet, sax etc. 1990's 'STRANGE SOUNDS FROM THE BASEMENT', meanwhile, saw the band metamorphose into COLORBLIND JAMES AND THE DEATH VALLEY BOYS, a more seriously rootsy proposition cutting to the heart of America's damned soul. 'SOLID! BEHIND THE TIMES' (1992) reverted back to their offbeat kind of unique polka-rock as did 1996's 'I COULD BE YOUR GUIDE' and 6th set 'THE CALL OF THE WILD' (1999), the latter an infectious potpourri delivery that introduced co-lead singer RITA COULTER. However, this was to be the group's last outing as mainman CHUCK died of a heart attack while swimming on the 10th of July, 2001.

Album rating: THE COLORBLIND JAMES EXPERIENCE (*7) / WHY SHOULD I STAND UP? (*6) / STRANGE SOUNDS FROM THE BASEMENT (*5) / SOLID! BEHIND THE TIMES (*5) / I COULD BE YOUR GUIDE (*5) / THE CALL OF THE WILD (*6) / GREATEST HITS! compilation (*8)

COLORBLIND JAMES (aka "CHUCK") (b. JAMES CUMINALE, 1952, Oswego, NY) – vocals, rhythm guitar, vibraphone / **PHILLIP MARSHALL** – lead guitar, vocals / **BERNIE HEVERON** – upright bass, vocals / **JIM McAVANEY** – drums

Fundam. Earring

May 88. (lp/cd) *(SAVE 050/+CD)* **COLORBLIND JAMES EXPERIENCE** 1987
– Why'd the boy throw the clock out the window? / The German girls / A diferent Bob / First day of Spring / Walking my camel home / Gravel road / Considering a move to Memphis / Fledgling circus / Dance critters / Great Northwest.

Oct 88. (12") *(PRAY 009)* **DANCE CRITTERS (remix). / YOU NEED SOMEBODY ON YOUR SIDE**

—— HEVERON was repl. by **KEN FRANK** – bass, violin, vocals / **JOHN EBERT** – trombone, tuba, vocals / **DAVE McINTYRE** – clarinet, saxophone, vocals

Cooking Vinyl Gold Castle

Oct 89. (lp/c/cd) *(COOK/+C/CD 028) <D2/D4 71356>* **WHY SHOULD I STAND UP?**
– Why should I stand up? / She'll break yours too / Buster Cornelius / Polka girl / Ride aboard / I'm a sailor / That's entertainment / He must have been quite a guy / Wedding at Cana / Rocking as fast as I can / Hi-fi alphabet / If nobody loves you in Heaven. (re-iss. Nov93 cd/c; same)

Feb 90. (7") *(FRY 015)* **THAT'S ENTERTAINMENT. /**
(12"+=) *(FRY 015T)* –

Nov 90. (cd/c/lp; by COLORBLIND JAMES & THE DEATH VALLEY BOYS) *(COOK/+C/CD 042)* **STRANGE SOUNDS FROM THE BASEMENT**
– Ribbon cutting time / Don't be so hard on yourself / Acorn girl / I think I know what you mean / Cloorblind's night out / Oh come now / Sidewalk sale / Strange sounds from the basement / Jesus at the still / O Sylvia / Two headed girl / Not for sale / Call me sometime. (re-iss. Nov93 cd/c; same)

not iss. Red House

Oct 92. (cd/c) *<RHR CD/MC 52>* **SOLID! BEHIND THE TIMES**
– In these days ahead / She took the ring off a dead man's finger / Glasses / Pictures on a stone / Talk to me / Four horsemen / Euphoria Jones / Solid! behind the times / The wives of the saints / Jonah and the whale / Funky west side / Daniel in the lion's den / Kojak chair / Death fears no man. (UK cd-iss. Oct95; same as US)

Scout not iss.

1996. (cd) **I COULD BE YOUR GUIDE** – German
– Guiding light / Stranger / You need somebody on your side / I saved your life / Back to life / Maybe I will / I could be your guide / I'll never get tired / Evil mask / See if I care / The pin boy's life / A little while / Please don't make me wait.

—— added **RITA COULTER** – lead/backing vocals

—— others **CHUCK, JOHN EBERT, JAMES McAVANEY** plus **GARY HOLT** – bass / **TOMMY TROMONTANA** – guitar / **CHARLES JAFFE** – keyboards

COLORBLIND JAMES EXPERIENCE (cont)

Jul 99. (cd) <1117> **THE CALL OF THE WILD** [not iss. / Death Valley]
– Dr. Negative / High street / Call of the wild / I want to know you / Let's go back / Colorblind's reel / Show me / Lock him up! / I hate this world sometimes / Prodigal son / 'Bye now, wish me luck.

—— frontman CHUCK was to die in July 2001

– compilations, etc. –

Oct 89. (12"ep/cd-ep) *Strange Fruit; (SFPS/+CD 076) / Dutch East India; <8311>* **PEEL SESSIONS**
– Polka girl / Hey Bernadette / Havoc theme / Wedding at Canaan.
Nov 00. (cd) *Stub Daddy; <002>* **GREATEST HITS!**
– Considering a move to Memphis / A different Bob / Fledgling circus / Buster Cornelius / That's entertainment / Wedding at Cana / Oh come now / Colorblind's night out / Call me sometime / She took the ring off a dead man's finger / Solid! behind the times / In these days ahead / I could be your guide / I'll never get tired / Stranger / Call of the wild / Colorblind's reel / I hate this world sometimes / Let's go back.

COMING UP ROSES (see under ⇒ DOLLY MIXTURE)

COMSAT ANGELS

Formed: Sheffield, England ... 1978 as RADIO EARTH by STEPHEN FELLOWS, MIK GLAISHER, ANDY PEAKE and KEVIN BACON. Following the release of a self-financed debut EP, 'THE RED PLANET', this doomy new wave quartet were one of the many such outfits signed to 'Polydor' at the dawn of the 80's. 'WAITING FOR A MIRACLE' (1980) was a promising debut showcasing the band's dark, synth-laced pop/rock sound and boasting one of their most enduring tracks, the infectious 'INDEPENDENCE DAY'. By the release of the following year's 'SLEEP NO MORE' opus, the group had adopted an even gloomier, almost gothic sound taking a leaf out of JOY DIVISION's book with a brooding bass rumble and funereal vocals, even if the likes of 'BE BRAVE' could still conceivably have been a Top 10 hit. 'FICTION' (1982) was another worthwhile release, the opening 'AFTER THE RAIN' moving across similarly intense synth-pop territory as that year's SIMPLE MIND's masterpiece, 'New Gold Dream', while the anthemic wail of 'JU JU MONEY' became a live favourite. Yet while the band could cut it with the best of the post-punk pack, chart success remained tantalisingly out of reach and The COMSAT's soon found themsleves label-less. A testament to their undoubted potential, the group were picked up by a further two major record companies, first 'Jive/CBS' – where they released 'LAND' (1983) and 'SEVEN DAY WEEKEND' (1985) – then 'Island', who rather unadvisedly hooked them up with ROBERT PALMER (in a production capacity) on the 'CHASING SHADOWS' (1987) album. The band's run of bad luck continued as they were faced with the threat of legal action by American communications conglomorate, 'Com Sat' and subsequently forced to trade under the clipped moniker of CS ANGELS. In Britain, meanwhile, they also changed name to the DREAM COMMAND (initially the HEADHUNTERS), a tactic which failed to turn around their ailing fortunes. The group eventually re-emerged in 1992 under their original name (although BACON had briefly bailed out), releasing 'MY MIND'S EYE' on 'Thunderbird'. By the release of 1995's 'THE GLAMOUR', BACON was off the menu for good, his replacements being SIMON ANDERSON and TERRY TODD. While FELLOWS carved out his low-key solo ambient set in '97, he also found time to take on (as manager) an up and coming neo-blues outfit, GOMEZ. BACON was already producing work for The LONGPIGS and FINLEY QUAYE and it looked near certain one day that The COMSAT ANGELS would embark on another group outing before flying off to that great gig in the sky. • **Covered:** I WANNA DESTROY YOU (Soft Boys).

Album rating: WAITING FOR A MIRACLE (*8) / SLEEP NO MORE (*6) / FICTION (*6) / LAND (*6) / 7 DAY WEEKEND (*5) / CHASING SHADOWS (*5) / FIRE ON THE MOON as Dream Command (*3) / MY MIND'S EYE (*5) / THE GLAMOUR (*5) / TIME CONSIDERED ... collection (*7) / UNRAVELLED compilation (*5) / FROM BEYOND ... compilation (*5)

STEVEN FELLOWS – vocals, guitar / **ANDY PEAKE** – keyboards, synthesizers / **KEVIN BACON** – bass / **MIC GLAISHER** – drums

Mar 79. (red-7"m) *(JUNTA 1)* **RED PLANET. / I GET EXCITED / SPECIMEN No.2** [Junta / not iss.]

May 80. (7"m) *(2059 227)* **TOTAL WAR. / WAITING FOR A MIRACLE / HOME ON THE RANGE** [Polydor / not iss.]
Jul 80. (7") *(2059 257)* **INDEPENDENCE DAY. / WE WERE**
Sep 80. (lp) *(2383 578)* **WAITING FOR A MIRACLE**
– Missing in action / Baby / Independence day / Waiting for a miracle / Total war / On the beach / Monkey pilot / Real story / Map of the world / Postcard. *(cd-iss. Jan96 on 'R.P.M.'+=; RPM 155)* – Home on the range / We were.
Mar 81. (7") *(POSP 242)* **EYE OF THE LENS. / AT SEA**
(d12"+=) *(POSPX 242)* – Another world / Gone.
Aug 81. (lp/c) *(POLS/+C 1038)* **SLEEP NO MORE** [51]
– Eye dance / Slep no more / Be brave / Gone / Dark parade / Diagram / Restless / Goat of the west / Light years / Our secret. *(cd-iss. Jan96 on 'R.P.M.'+=; RPM 156)* – Eye of the lens / Another world / At sea / Do the empty house / Red planet revisited.
Oct 81. (d7") *(POSP 359)* **DO THE EMPTY HOUSE. / NOW I KNOW // RED PLANET REVISITED**
May 82. (7") *(POSP 432)* **IT'S HISTORY. / ZINGER**

Aug 82. (lp/c) *(POLS/+C 1075)* **FICTION** [94]
– After the rain / Zinger / Now I know / Not a word / Ju ju money / More / Pictures / Birdman / Don't look now / What else. *(cd-iss. Jan96 on 'R.P.M.'+=; RPM 157)* – It's history / After the rain / Private party / Mass.
Oct 82. (7") *(POSP 513)* **AFTER THE RAIN. / PRIVATE PARTY**

Jul 83. (7") *(JIVE 46)* **WILL YOU STAY TONIGHT. / SHINING HOUR** [Jive / Jive-Novus]
(12"+=) *(JIVET 46)* – A world away.
Sep 83. (lp/c) *(HIP/+C 8) <JL8/JC8 8184>* **LAND** [91]
– Will you stay tonight / Alicia (can you hear me?) / A world away / Independence day / Nature trails / Mister memory / Island heart / I know that feeling / As above so below. *(cd-iss. Nov00 on 'Connoisseur'+=; VSOPCD 329)* – A world away (dub) / Shining hour / Island heart (dub) / Scissors and the stone / Intelligence.
Oct 83. (7"/12") *(JIVE/+T 51)* **ISLAND HEART. / SCISSORS AND STONES**
Jan 84. (7") *(JIVE 54)* **INDEPENDENCE DAY. / MISTER MEMORY** [71]
(12"+=) *(JIVET 54)* – Intelligence.
(d7"+=/d12"+=) *(JIVE/+T 54)* – Total war / After the rain.
May 84. (7") *(JIVE 65)* **YOU MOVE ME. / ESCAPE FROM WILLESDEN**
(12") *(JIVET 65)* – ('A'side) / Land / Eye of the lens (live).
Sep 84. (7") *(JIVE 73)* **DAY ONE. / WILL YOU STAY TONIGHT**
(12"+=) *(JIVET 73)* – Independence day.

—— added guest **PAUL ROBERTSON** – keyboards

Aug 85. (7") *(JIVE 87)* **I'M FALLING. / NEW HEART AND MIND**
(12"blue+=) *(JIVET 87)* – ('A'extended).
Sep 85. (lp/c) *(HIP/+C 29) <JL8 8279>* **7 DAY WEEKEND**
– Believe it / Forever young / You move me / I'm falling / Close your eyes / Day one / You're the heroine / High tide / New heart and hand / Still it's not enough. *(cd-iss. Nov00 on 'Connoisseur'+=; VSOPCD 330)* – Land / Citadel.
Oct 85. (7") *(JIVE 111)* **FOREVER YOUNG. / STILL IT'S NOT ENOUGH**
(12"+=) *(JIVET 111)* – Sign.

—— reverted to original quartet, when ROBERTSON departed

Jan 87. (lp/cd) *(ILPS/CID 9855)* **CHASING SHADOWS** [Island / not iss.]
– The thought that counts / The cutting edge / Under the influence / Carried away / You'll never know / Lost continent / Flying dreams / Pray for rain.
Feb 87. (7") *(IS 312)* **THE CUTTING EDGE. / SOMETHING'S GOT TO GIVE**
(12"+=) *(12IS 312)* – Our secret.
(live-12"+=) *(ISB 312)* – Flying dreams.

—— changed their moniker and were without BACON

Oct 90. (cd/c/lp; as DREAM COMMAND) *<846216-2/-4/-1>* **FIRE ON THE MOON**
– Celestine / Whirlwind / Sleepwalking / Reach for me / Ice sculpture / Venus hunter / Phantom power / Transport of delight / She's invisible / Mercury.

—— original COMSAT ANGELS line-up re-formed in 1992 (with BACON again). They signed to 'Crisis' (Benelux) & 'Normal' (Germany). FELLOWS had recently written several songs for the HARBOUR KINGS. They had emerged in 1990 as The HEADHUNTERS until this fell through.

Jun 92. (7") *(CSA7 001)* **DRIVING. / THERE IS NO ENEMY** [Thunderbird / Caroline]
(12"+=/cd-s+=) *(CSA 001 T/CD)* – My mind's eye / Driving (mix).
Sep 92. (cd/lp) *(CSA 101/201) <CAROL 1891>* **MY MIND'S EYE** [Sep93]
– Driving / Beautiful monster / Shiva descending / My mind's eye / I came from the sun / Field of tall flowers / Always hear / Route 666 / Mystery plane / And all the stars. *(cd re-iss. Aug98 & Mar01; CSAM 101)*
Jul 93. (7") *(CSA7 003)* **FIELD OF TALL FLOWERS (remix). / STORM OF CHANGE**
(12"+=/cd-s+=) *(CSA 003 T/CD)* – Too much time / ('A'acoustic).
1993. (cd-ep) **SHIVA DESCENDING / MAFONIA / JU-JU MONEY / GOAT OF THE WEST** [– / German]

—— now without BACON who was repl. by **SIMON ANDERSON** – guitar / **TERRY TODD** – bass

Jun 95. (cd) *(CSA 103)* **THE GLAMOUR**
– Psychedelic dungeon / The glamour / Audrey in denim / Oblivion / Web of sound / Breaker / SS100X / Sailor / Demon lover / Pacific ocean blues / Anjelica / Valley of the Nile / Spaced.

—— disbanded later in '95

– compilations, etc. –

Apr 84. (lp) *Polydor; (810735)* **ENZ** [– / Dutch]
– Independence day / Do the empty house / Total war / It's history / Another world / Eye of the lens / At sea / Mass / Home on the range / After the rain.
Nov 92. (cd) *R.P.M.; (RPM 106)* **TIME CONSIDERED AS A HELIX OF SEMI-PRECIOUS STONES: THE BBC SESSIONS 1979-1984)**
– At sea / Eye of the lens / Total war / Real story / Waiting for a miracle / Ju ju money / Independence day / Eye dance / Gone / Dark parade / Our secret / Now I know / Citadel / High tide / Mister memory / Island heart / You move me / Nature trails.
Jul 94. (cd) *R.P.M.; (RPM 123)* **UNRAVELLED – THE DUTCH RADIO SESSIONS**
– After the rain / Beautiful monster / The cuting edge / Field of all flowers / SS 100X / Our secret / Always near / Eye of the lens / Storm of change / Audrey in denim / Citadel.
Jun 00. (cd) *Cherry Red; (<CDMRED 170>)* **FROM BEYOND 1987-1995: THE BEST OF THE COMSAT ANGELS VOL.2**
– A sound / My mind's eye / I hear a new world / Mystery plane / Always near / Ice sculpture / Goddess / Valley of the Nile (mix) / Venus hunter / Shiva descending / I wanna destroy you / SAilor / Waves / Not yours / We must be mad.

Julian COPE

Born: 21 Oct'57, Deri, Caerphilly, Wales, although he was raised in Liverpool, England. His first foray into the music business was with The CRUCIAL THREE, alongside IAN McCULLOCH and PETE WYLIE. During the Autumn of '78, COPE formed The TEARDROP EXPLODES (originally named A SHALLOW MADNESS), with MICK FINKLER and PAUL SIMPSON. In late '78, a deal was inked with local UK indie label, 'Zoo,' and after three critically acclaimed singles, they transferred to the major label, 'Mercury,' in July 1980. Keyboard-biased TEARDROP EXPLODES were mostly influenced by 60's pop psychedelia, COPE sounding distinctly like a modern, post-new wave SCOTT WALKER. Their first hit came about via 'WHEN I DREAM', a classic lifted from their classic album, Top 30 'KILIMANJARO' (1980); early in 1981, they cashed-in when 'REWARD' delivered them a Top tenner. 'TREASON', the next 45, didn't emulate this feat, although it still managed a Top 20 placing. Their second album, 'WILDER' (1981), was another commercial success, although it lacked the bite of its predecessor. A few minor hits followed over the next year and a bit, but it was clear JULIAN was gearing up for a solo career. Remaining with 'Mercury' records, he released two albums in 1984, 'WORLD SHUT YOUR MOUTH' and 'FRIED', both receiving a lukewarm response from the music press. Onstage antics such as cutting his stomach (IGGY POP-like) and singing perched on a high pole, saw him develop a weird new character; often he performed through his alter-ego (SQWUBBSY a seven foot giant). COPE subsequently signed for 'Island' in 1985, leaving behind the unissued (until 1990) 'SKELLINGTON' LP. Around the same time he suffered a marriage break-up and drug problems, although he re-married in 1986. Re-emerging triumphantly in 1986, he charted with the Top 20 hit 45, 'WORLD SHUT YOUR MOUTH' (curiously enough, the song wasn't included on the 1984 album of the same name). The single was a taster for the following year's comeback album 'SAINT JULIAN', a record which almost gave him his first solo top ten hit. A disappointing pop album, 'MY NATION UNDERGROUND', dealt his street cred a bitter blow and he retreated somewhat with two (meant for mail-order) 1990 albums, the aforementioned 'SKELLINGTON' and 'DROOLIAN'. He returned in fine fashion a year later with the splendid double-set, 'PEGGY SUICIDE', a record that targeted pollution and even the dreadful Tory poll tax (something he protested against vehemently). In 1992, he brought back his old influences (CAN, FAUST, "Kraut-rock") with 'JEHOVAKILL'. Creatively, the album was an admirable effort although it bombed both commercially and critically. This was his last for 'Island', who dropped him unceremoniously after he recorded the 'RITE' CD-album for German release. In 1994, he signed with 'Echo' and returned with three varying albums, 'AUTOGEDDON' (1994), '20 MOTHERS' (1995) and 'INTERPRETER' (1996). With a much needed direction change, COPE opted to form a fresh post-millennium outfit, BLOOD DONOR (along loyal sidekick, THIGHPAULSANDRA). Their album 'LOVE, PEACE & FUCK' (2001), was Krautrock centered around lyrics inspired by Celtic, Viking and Druid folklore. • **Songwriters:** COPE penned except; READ IT IN BOOKS (co-with; Ian McCulloch). He wrote all material, except NON-ALIGNMENT PACT (Pere Ubu) / COPE covered FREE YOUR MIND AND YOUR ASS WILL FOLLOW (Funkadelic) / ARE YOU HUNG UP? (Mothers Of Invention). • **Trivia:** The album DROOLIAN, was released as part of a campaign to free from jail ROKY ERICKSON (ex-13th FLOOR ELEVATORS). In '90, COPE took part in the Anti-Poll tax march from Brixton to Trafalgar Square.

Album rating: Teardrop Explodes: KILIMANJARO (*9) / WILDER (*7) / EVERYBODY WANTS TO SHAG THE TEARDROP EXPLODES posthumous (*7) / PIANO (*6) / THE GREATEST HIT compilation (*7) / Julian Cope:

Album rating: WORLD SHUT YOUR MOUTH (*7) / FRIED (*7) / SAINT JULIAN (*7) / MY NATION UNDERGROUND (*8) / SKELLINGTON (*7) / DROOLIAN (*7) / PEGGY SUICIDE (*8) / JEHOVAHKILL (*5) / AUTOGEDDON (*6) / 20 MOTHERS (*8) / INTERPRETER (*5) / FLOORED GENIUS: THE BEST OF JULIAN COPE & THE TEARDROP EXPLODES 1979-1991 compilation (*8) / FLOORED GENIUS, VOL.2 (1983-91) compilation (*7) / Brain Donor: LOVE, PEACE & FUCK (*6)

TEARDROP EXPLODES

JULIAN COPE – vocals, bass / **PAUL SIMPSON** – keyboards / **MICK FINKLER** – guitar / **GARY DWYER** – drums

	Zoo	not iss.
Feb 79. (7"m) *(CAGE 003)* **SLEEPING GAS. / CAMERA CAMERA / KIRBY WORKERS' DREAM FADES**	☐	-

--- **GERARD QUINN** – keyboards; repl. SIMPSON who formed WILD SWANS

May 79. (7") *(CAGE 005)* **BOUNCING BABIES. / ALL I AM IS LOVING YOU**	☐	-

--- **DAVID BALFE** – keyboards (ex-LORI & THE CHAMELEONS, ex-BIG IN JAPAN, ex-THOSE NAUGHTY LUMPS) repl. QUINN who joined The WILD SWANS

Mar 80. (7") *(CAGE 008)* **TREASON (IT'S JUST A STORY). / READ IT IN BOOKS**	☐	-

--- **ALAN GILL** – guitar (ex-DALEK I) repl. FINKLER now (COPE, DWYER, BALFE + GILL)

	Mercury	Mercury
Sep 80. (7") *(TEAR 1)* **WHEN I DREAM. / KILIMANJARO**	47	-
Oct 80. (lp) *(6359 035) <4016>* **KILIMANJARO**	24	

– Ha ha I'm drowning / Sleeping gas / Treason (it's just a story) / Second head / Poppies in the field / Went crazy / Brave boys keep their promises / Bouncing babies / Books / Thief of Baghdad / When I dream. *(re-iss. Mar81 lp/c +=; 6359/7150 035)* – Reward. *(re-iss. Jul84 lp/c; PRICE/PRIMC 59) (re-iss. May89 & Jan96 lp/c/cd; 836 897-1/-4/-2) (cd re-mast.Nov00 ++=; 548322-2)* – Kilimanjaro / Strange house in the snow / Use me / Traison / Sleeping gas (live). (below trumpet by RAY MARTINEZ)

Jan 81. (7") *(TEAR 2)* **REWARD. / STRANGE HOUSE IN THE SNOW**	6	-
Apr 81. (7") *(TEAR 3)* **TREASON (IT'S JUST A STORY). / USE ME**	18	-

(12"+=) *(TEAR 3-12)* – Traison (c'est juste une histoire).

Jun 81. (7") *(TEAR 4)* **POPPIES IN THE FIELD. / HA HA I'M DROWNING**	☐	-

(d7"+=) *(TEAR 44)* – Bouncing babies / Read it in books.

--- **TROY TATE** – guitar, vocals (ex-INDEX, ex-SHAKE) repl. GILL

Sep 81. (7") *(TEAR 5)* **PASSIONATE FRIEND. / CHRIST VS. WARHOL**	25	-

--- on session/gigs **ALFIE ALGIUS** (b. Malta) – bass / **JEFF HAMMER** – keyboards

Nov 81. (lp/c) *(6359/7150 056) <4035>* **WILDER**	29	☐

– Bent out of shape / Colours fly away / Seven views of Jerusalem / Pure joy / Falling down around me / The culture bunker / Passionate friend / Tiny children / Like Leila Khaled said / ...And the fighting takes over / The great dominions. *(re-iss. Jun87 lp/c; PRICE/PRIMC 112) (re-iss. May89 & Jan96 lp/c/cd; 836 896-1/-4/-2) (cd re-mast.Nov00 +=; 548284-2)* – Window shopping for a new crown of thorns / East of the equator / Rachael built a steamboat / You disappear from view / Suffocate / Ouch monkeys / Soft enough for you / The in-psychlopedia.

Nov 81. (7") *(TEAR 6)* **COLOURS FLY AWAY. / WINDOW SHOPPING FOR A NEW CROWN OF THORNS**	54	-

(12"+=) *(TEAR 6-12)* – East of the equator.

--- **DAVID BALFE** returned

--- **RON FRANCOIS** – bass (ex-SINCEROS) repl. guests

Jun 82. (7"/7"g-f) *(TEAR 7/+G)* **TINY CHILDREN. / RACHAEL BUILT A STEAMBOAT**	44	-

(12"+=) *(TEAR 7-12)* – Sleeping gas (live).

--- now trio of COPE, DWYER + BALFE plus session man FRANCOIS

--- TROY TATE went solo and joined FASHION

Mar 83. (7") *(TEAR 8)* **YOU DISAPPEAR FROM VIEW. / SUFFOCATE**	41	-

(d7"+=/12"+=) *(TEAR 88/8-12)* – Soft enough for you / Ouch monkeys / The in-psychlopedia.

--- disbanded early '83; BALFE went into producing films and music; JULIAN COPE went solo augmented by DWYER

– compilations, others, etc. –

Jun 85. (7") *Mercury; (TEAR 9)* **REWARD (remix). / TREASON (IT'S JUST A STORY)**	☐	-

(12"+=) *(TEAR 9-12)* – Strange house in the snow / Use me.

Jan 90. (7") *Fontana; (DROP 1)* **SERIOUS DANGER. / SLEEPING GAS**	☐	-

(12"+=)(c-s+=/cd-s+=) *(DROP 1-12)(DRO MC/CD 1)* – Seven views of Jerusalem.

Mar 90. (cd/c/lp) *Fontana; (842 439-2/-4/-1)* **EVERYBODY WANTS TO SHAG THE TEARDROP EXPLODES** (long lost 3rd album)	72	-

– Ouch monkey's / Serious danger / Metranil Vavin / Count to ten and run forever / In-psychlopaedia / Soft enough for you / You disappear from view / The challenger / Not only my friend / Sex / Terrorist / Strange house in the snow.

Apr 90. (7") *Fontana; (DROP 2)* **COUNT TO TEN AND RUN FOR COVER. / REWARD**	☐	-

(12"+=)(cd-s+=) *(DROP 2-12)(DROCD 2)* – Poppies / Khaled said.

Nov 90. (cd/c/lp) *Document; (DCD/DMC/DLP 004)* **PIANO** (early material)	☐	-

– Sleeping gas / Camera camera / Kirkby workers dream fades / Bouncing babies / All I am is loving you / Treason / Books / Take a chance / When I dream / Kwalo Klobinsky's lullaby.

Dec 93. (cd/lp) *Windsong; (<WIN CD/LP 050>)* **BBC LIVE IN CONCERT** (live)	☐	Jan95
Aug 95. (d-cd) *Mercury; (528601-2)* **WILDER / KILIMANJARO**	☐	-
Oct 01. (cd) *Mercury; (586391-2)* **THE GREATEST HIT – THE BEST OF THE TEARDROP EXPLODES**	☐	-

– Reward / Passionate friend / Treason (it's just a story) / Ha ha I'm drowning / The culture bunker / Colours fly away / Sleeping gas / Suffocate / When I dream / Tiny children / ...And the fighting takes over / The in-psychlopedia / Christ vs. Warhol / You disappear from view / The great dominions.

Aug 02. (cd) *Spectrum; (544616-2)* **THE COLLECTION**	☐	-

JULIAN COPE

JULIAN COPE – vocals, guitar, keyboards / with **GARY DWYER** / **STEVE CREASE** + **ANDREW EDGE** – drums / **STEPHEN LOWELL** – lead guitar / **RON FRANCOIS** – bass / **KATE ST. JOHN** – oboe

	Mercury	not iss.
Nov 83. (7") *(COPE 1)* **SUNSHINE PLAYROOM. / HEY HIGH CLASS BUTCHER**	64	-

(12"+=) *(COPE 1-12)* – Wreck my car / Eat the poor.

Feb 84. (lp/c) *(MERL/+C 37)* **WORLD SHUT YOUR MOUTH**	40	-

– Bandy's first jump / Metranil Vavin / Strasbourg / An elegant chaos / Quizmaster / Kolly Kibber's birthday / Sunshine playroom / Head hang low / Pussy face / The greatness and perfection of love / Lunatic and fire pistol. *(cd-iss. 1986; 818 365-2)*

Mar 84. (7") *(MER 155)* **THE GREATNESS AND PERFECTION OF LOVE. / 24a VELOCITY CRESCENT**	52	-

(12"+=) *(MERX 155)* – Pussyface.

Nov 84. (lp/c) *(MERL/+C 48)* **FRIED**	87	-

– Reynard the fox / Bill Drummond said / Laughing boy / Me singing / Sunspots / Me singing / Bloody Assizes / Search party / O king of chaos / Holy love / Torpedo. *(cd-iss. 1986; 822 832-2) (lp re-iss. Sep98 +=; 532370-2)* – I went on a chourney / Mik mak mok / Land of fear.

Feb 85. (7") *(MER 182)* **SUNSPOTS. / I WENT ON A CHOURNEY**	☐	-

(d7"+=) *(MER 182-2)* – Mik mak mok / Land of fear.

--- COPE recruited Americans **DONALD ROSS SKINNER** – guitar / **JAMES ELLER** – bass / **DOUBLE DE HARRISON** – keyboards / **CHRIS WHITTEN** – drums

Julian COPE (cont)

		Island	Island
Sep 86.	(7") (IS 290) <99479> **WORLD SHUT YOUR MOUTH. / UMPTEENTH UNNATURAL BLUES**	19	84 Feb87

(d7"+=) (ISB 290) – ('A'-Trouble Funk remix) / Transportation.
(c-s+=) (CIS 290) – I've got levitation / Non-alignment pact.
(12"++=) (12IS 290) – (all extra above).

Jan 87. (7") (IS 305) **TRAMPOLENE. / DISASTER** □ -
(7"ep+=/12"ep+=) (ISW/12IS 305) – Mock Turtle / Warwick the kingmaker.

Feb 87. (m-lp) <90560> **JULIAN COPE** □ -
– World shut your mouth / Transportation / Umpteenth unnatural blues / Non-alignment pact / I've got levitation.

Mar 87. (lp/c/cd) (ILPS/ICT/CID 9861) <90571> **SAINT JULIAN** 11 □
– Trampolene / Shot down / Eve's volcano (covered sin in) / Spacehopper / Planet ride / Trampolene / World shut your mouth / Saint Julian / Pulsar NX / Space hopper / Screaming secrets / A crack in the clouds. (re-iss. Aug91 cd)(c; IMCD 137)(ICM 2023)

Apr 87. (7") (IS 318) **EVE'S VOLCANO (COVERED IN SIN). / ALMOST BEAUTIFUL CHILD** □ -
(12"+=) (12IS 318) – Pulsar NX (live) / Shot down (live).
(12"+=) (12ISX 318) – Spacehopper – Annexe / ('B'side; pt.II).
(cd-s++=) (CID 318) – (all 3 extra above).

— **DAVE PALMER** – drums (studio) / **MIKE JOYCE** – drums (tour) repl. WHITTEN / added **RON FAIR** – keyboards / **ROOSTER COSBY** – percussion, some drums

Sep 88. (7") (IS 380) **CHARLOTTE ANNE. / CHRISTMAS MOURNING** 35 -
(12"+=/12"pic-d+=/pic-cd-s+=) (12IS/12ISP/CIDP 380) – Books / A question of temptation.

Oct 88. (lp/c/cd) (ILPS/ICT/CID 9918) <91025> **MY NATION UNDERGROUND** 42 -
– 5 o'clock world / Vegetation / Charlotte Anne / My nation underground / China doll / Someone like me / Easter everywhere / I'm not losing sleep / The great white hoax. (re-iss. Aug91 cd)(c; IMCD 138)(ICM 9918)

Nov 88. (7") (IS 399) **5 O'CLOCK WORLD. / S.P.Q.R.** 42 -
(10"+=/12"+=/pic-cd-s+=) (10IS/12IS/CIDP 399) – Reynard in Tokyo (extended live).

Jun 89. (7") (IS 406) **CHINA DOLL. / CRAZY FARM ANIMAL** 53 -
(10"+=/10"pic-d+=/12"+=) (10IS/10ISP/12IS 406) – Desi.
(cd-s++=) (CID 406) – Rail on.

— COPE retained SKINNER & COSBY plus **J.D. HASSINGER** – drums / **TIM** – keyboards / **BRAN** – bass (both of Guernsey)

Jan 91. (7"/c-s) (IS/CIS 483) **BEAUTIFUL LOVE. / PORT OF SAINTS** 32 -
(12"+=/cd-s+=) (12IS/CID 483) – Love L.U.V. / Unisex cathedral.
(12"pink+=) (12ISX 483) – Love L.U.V. / Dragonfly.

Mar 91. (cd/c/d-lp) (CID/ICT/ILPSD 9977) <848338-2/-4> **PEGGY SUICIDE** 23 -
– Pristeen / Double vegetation / East easy rider / Promised land / Hanging out & hung up on the line / Safesurfer / If you loved me at all / Drive, she said / Soldier blue / You . . . / Not raving but drowning / Head / Leperskin / Beautiful love / Uptight / Western First 1992 CE / Hung up & hanging out to dry / The American Lite / Las Vegas basement. (cd re-iss. Aug94 & Apr02; IMCD 188)

Apr 91. (7"/c-s) (IS/CIS 492) **EAST EASY RIDER. / BUTTERFLY E** 51 -
(12"+=/cd-s+=) (12IS/CID 492) – Almost live / Little donkey.
(12"pic-d+=) (12ISX 492) – Easty Risin' / Ravebury stones.

Jul 91. (7"/c-s) (IS/CIS 497) **HEAD. / BAGGED – OUT KEN** 57 -
(12"+=/cd-s+=) (12IS/CID 497) – Straw dogs / Animals at all.

Oct 92. (7"/c-s) (IS/CIS 545) **FEAR LOVES THE SPACE. / SIZEWELL B.** 42 -
(12"pic-d+=) (12ISX 545) – I have always been here before / Gogmagog.

Oct 92. (cd/c/d-lp) (<514052-2/-4/-1>) **JEHOVAHKILL** 20 Dec92
– Soul desert / No harder shoulder to cry on / Akhenaten / The mystery trend / Upwards at 45° / Cut my friends down / Necropolis / Slow rider / Gimme back my flag / Poet is priest / Julian H Cope / The subtle energies commission / Fa-fa-fa-fine / Fear loves this place / Peggy Suicide is missing. (cd re-iss. Aug94; IMCD 189)

— Next was last in the 90's album trilogy about pollution. Its theme this time was the car, (coincidentally he had just passed his driving test). It featured usual musicians.

		Echo	American
Jul 94.	(cd/c/lp) (ECH CD/MC/LP 001) <45705> **AUTOGEDDON**	16	Aug94

– Autogeddon blues / Madmax / Don't call me Mark Chapman / I gotta walk / Ain't no gettin' round gettin' round / Paranormal in the West Country (medley): i) Paranormal pt.1, ii) Archdrude's roadtrip. iii) Kar-ma-kanik / Ain't but the one way / S.t.a.r.c.a.r. (cd re-iss. Mar99; same)

Aug 95. (7"yellow/c-s) (ECS/+MC 11) **TRY TRY TRY. / WESSEXY** 24 -
(cd-s+=) (ECSCD 11) – Baby, let's play vet / Don't jump me, mother.

Aug 95. (cd/c/d-lp) (ECH CD/MC/LP 005) **20 MOTHERS** 20 -
– Wheelbarrow man / I wandered lonely as a child / Try try try / Stone circles 'n' you / Queen – Mother / I'm your daddy / Highway to the sun / 1995 / By the light of the Silbury moon / Adam and Eve hit the road / Just like Pooh Bear / Girl-call / Greedhead detector / Don't take roots / Senile get / The lonely guy / Cryingbabiessleeplessnights / Leli B. / Road of dreams / When I walk through the land of fear.

		Echo	Cooking Vinyl
Jul 96.	(7"white-ep/cd-ep) (ECS/+CDX 022) **I COME FROM ANOTHER PLANET, BABY. / HOW DO I UNDERSTAND MY MOTORMAN? / IF I COULD DO IT ALL OVER AGAIN, I'D DO IT OVER YOU**	34	-

(cd-s) (ECSCD 022) – Ambulance: Weesex post-ambient therapy.

Sep 96. (7"white) (ECS 025) **PLANETARY SIT-IN. / CUMMER IN SUMMERTIME / TORCH** 34 -
(cd-s) (ECSCX 025) – ('A'-Radio sit-in mixes).

Oct 96. (cd/c/lp) (ECH CD/MC/LP 12) <9007> **INTERPRETER** 39 Feb97
– I come from another planet, baby / I've got my TV and my pills / Planetary sit-in / Since I lost my head, it's awl-right / Cheap new age fix / Battle for the trees / Arthur / Spacerock with me / Re-directed male / Maid of constant sorrow / Loveboat / Dust.

— look out for 'DISCOVER ODIN: JULIAN COPE AT THE BRITISH MUSEUM' a partly spoken-word CD on 'Head Heritage' released in US 2001

BRAIN DONOR

— aka **JULIAN COPE** with **THIGHPAULSANDRA** – synths

		Impresario	not iss.
Apr 01.	(7"/cd-s) (IMP/+CD 007) **SHE SAW ME COMING. / SHAMAN UFO**	□	-
Jul 01.	(7"/cd-s) (IMP/+CD 009) **GET OFF YOUR PRETTY FACE. / WHO WILL ENTERTAIN YOUR MORON**	□	-
Sep 01.	(cd/lp) IMPODD CD/LP 001) **LOVE, PEACE & FUCK**	□	-

– She saw me coming / Get off your pretty face / Pagan dawn / Odin's gift to his mother (theme from speed kills) / Hairy music / U-know! – You take the credit / Laghnasad / She's gotta have it. (lp re-iss. Jul02; same)

– (COPE) compilations, others, etc. –

Feb 85. (7"; as RABBI JOSEPH GORDON) Bam Caruso; (NRICO 30) **COMPETITION. / BELIEF IN HIM** □ -

May 90. (cd/lp) Copeco-Zippo; (JUCD/JULP 89) **SKELLINGTON** (1985 lost lp) □ -
– Doomed / Beaver / Me & Jimmy Jones / Robert Mitchum / Out of my mind on dope and speed / Don't crash here / Everything playing at once / Little donkey / Great white wonder / Incredibly ugly girl / No how, no why, no way, no where, no when / Comin' soon.

Jul 90. (cd/lp) Mofo-Zippo; (MOFOCO CD/LP 90) **DROOLIAN** □ -

Jul 92. (c-s/7") Island; (C+/IS 534) **WORLD SHUT YOUR MOUTH (remix). / DOOMED** 44 -
(12"+=/cd-s+=) (12/CD IS 534) – Reynard the fox / The elevators / Levitation.

Aug 92. (cd/c/d-lp) Island; (CID/ICT/ILPSD 8000) <512788> **FLOORED GENIUS – THE BEST OF JULIAN COPE AND THE TEARDROP EXPLODES 1981-1991** 22 Oct92
– Reward / Treason / Sleeping gas / Bouncing babies / Passionate friend / The great dominions (; all TEARDROP EXPLODES) / The greatness & perfection of love / An elegant chaos / Sunspots / Reynard the fox / World shut your mouth / Trampolene / Spacehopper / Charlotte Anne / China doll / Out of my mind on dope & speed / Jellypop perky Jean / Beautiful love / East easy rider / Safesurfer.

Nov 92. (d-cd) Island; (ITSCD 11) **SAINT JULIAN / MY NATION UNDERGROUND** □ -

Nov 93. (cd/lp) Nighttracks; (CD/LP NT 003) / Dutch East India; <DEI 8124> **BEST OF THE BBC SESSIONS 1983-91 (FLOORED GENIUS VOL.2)** □ Feb94
– The greatness and perfection of love / Head hang low / Hey, high class butcher / Sunspots / Me singing / Hobby / 24a Velocity Crescent / Laughing boy / O king of chaos / Reynard the fox / Pulsar / Crazy farm animal / Christmas mourning / Planet rider: transmitting / Soul medley: Free your mind and your ass will follow – Are you hung up? / You think it's love / Double vegetation. (cd re-iss. May98 on 'Strange Fruit;' SFRSCD 61)

Jun 97. (cd) Island; (IMCD 251) **THE FOLLOWERS OF SAINT JULIAN** □ -

Feb 99. (cd) Island; (IMCD 260) <524636> **LEPER SKIN (AN INTRODUCTION TO JULIAN COPE)** □ May99
– Shot down / World shut your mouth / Trampolene / Planet ride / Transporting / Books / Charlotte Anne / Crazy farm animal / Hanging out and hung up on the line / Soul desert / The mystery trend / Pristeen / Double vegetation / Upwards at 45 degrees / Safesurfer.

Sep 01. (cd) Spectrum; (544586-2) **THE COLLECTION** □ -

CORN DOLLIES

Formed: South London, England ... 1986 by STEVE MUSHAM, TIM SALES, STUART RIDDLER and JACK HOSER; they added 5th member JONOTHAN PODMORE prior to their self-financed debut single, 'FOREVER STEVEN'. Produced by ROBERT FORSTER of The GO-BETWEENS, these twangy indie popsters soon found a home at Andy Wood's 'Medium Cool' records for the release of follow-up 'BE SMALL AGAIN'. While 'FOREVER STEVEN' was being re-issued in early '88 and PODMORE moonlighted with PETER HOPE (ex-BOX) on a single 'THE INDUSTRIAL ROTATION . . . ', the band returned with their fourth single, 'SHAKE'. 'MAP OF THE WORLD' and 'NOTHING OF YOU' wrapped their tenure with 'Medium Cool', while 'Midnight Music' delivered their long-awaited eponymous LP in 1989. Tours of mainland Europe found them reasonably busy for the remainder of the 80's, while the following decade kicked off with another version of 'NOTHING OF YOU', a taster from parent sophomore set, 'WRECKED' (1990). A prestigious support slot to IAN McCULLOCH couldn't prevent the band splitting in '91; the release of their third long-player, 'PAST CARING', obviously shelved.

Album rating: THE CORN DOLLIES (*4) / WRECKED (*5)

STEVE MUSHAM – vocals, acoustic guitar / **TIM SALES** – guitar / **STUART RIDDER** – bass / **JACK HOSER** – drums / added **JONO PODMORE** – violin

		Farm	not iss.
Jul 87.	(7") (FARM 001) **FOREVER STEVEN. / ABOUT TO BELIEVE**	□	-
		Medium Cool	not iss.
Oct 87.	(7") (MC 008) **BE SMALL AGAIN. / IN BETHPAGE**	□	-

(12") (MC 008T) – ('A'side) / The big house.

Feb 88. (12"ep) (MC 009T) **FOREVER STEVEN / BIG CANE CALL. / SWEETHEART ROSE SPECIAL / ABOUT TO BELIEVE** □ -

Jul 88. (7") (MC 015) **SHAKE. / CLIMBING STAIRS** □ -
(12"+=) (MC 015T) – Gathered up.

Oct 88. (7") (MC 017) **MAP OF THE WORLD. / PEOPLE GONE** □ -
(12"+=) (MC 017T) – This is mine.
(cd-shared w/ The WALTONES)

Apr 89. (12"ep) (MC 020T) **NOTHING OF YOU / POLLY WEST. / WRECKED / BE SMALL AGAIN (mix)** □ -

		Midnight Music	Danceteria
Feb 89.	(lp/cd) (CHIME 00.44 S/CD) <Dan 445> **THE CORN DOLLIES**	□	-

– Map of the world / Mouthful of brains / Forever Steven / The big house / What do I ever / Gathered up / Be small again / Big cane call / Sweetheart rose special / About to believe / Climbing stairs / People gone / This is mine.

Jan 90. (7"; one-sided) (DING 52) **NOTHING OF YOU**
Nov 90. (lp/c/cd) (CHIME 00.59/+CC/CD) **WRECKED**
— In your hands / Submarine / Map of the world / Seven / Wrecked / Nothing of you / Jingo / Everything box / Mary Hopkin song / This is mine.
Jan 91. (12"ep/cd-ep) (DONG 65/+CD) **JOYRIDER / SLOW DEATH. / HAPPY / KOOL-AID (mix)**
—— now with NOKO – bass (ex-LUXURIA)
Sep 91. (cd/lp; w-drawn) (CHIME 119 CD/S) **PAST CARING**
—— had already split earlier in 1991

COSEY FANNI TUTTI
(see under ⇒ CHRIS AND COSEY)

Cathal COUGHLAN

Born: Cork, Ireland. Together with SEAN O'HAGAN, COUGHLAN made his first real steps into the music industry with alternative/indie outfit, MICRODISNEY. After trying out various stylistic combinations, the songwriting partners decided upon the tried and tested drums, bass, guitar, keyboards format and enlisted MICK LYNCH and ROB MacKAHEY to help them record a debut single, 'HELICOPTER OF THE HOLY GHOST'. Issued on indie label, 'Kabuki', and included – along with follow-up, 'FICTION LAND' and other early recordings – on the unambiguously titled '82-84: WE HATE YOU SOUTH AFRICAN BASTARDS' (1984), the track introduced MICRODISNEY's patented brand of laid-back but thought provoking sophisti-rock. Subsequently relocating to London, COUGHLAN and O'HAGAN recruited a new rhythm section in ED FLESH and TOM FENNER, securing a deal with 'Rough Trade'. The resulting 'EVERYBODY IS FANTASTIC' (1984) album revealed a more readily audible COUGHLAN and a talent for melodic subversiveness not too far removed from The SMITHS. An increasingly scathing lyrical commentator, COUGHLAN put in another sterling performance on the more accessible follow-up set, 'THE CLOCK COMES DOWN THE STAIRS' (1985), growing interest in MICRODISNEY's offbeat style leading to a deal courtesy of 'Virgin'. With STEVE PREGNANT replacing FLESH and JAMES COMPTON added on keyboards, their tenure in major label land got off to a promising start in early '87 as the 'TOWN TO TOWN' single almost threatened the Top 40. Sales wise, the accompanying album, 'CROOKED MILE' (1987) didn't live up to expectations despite continuing critical praise, COUGHLAN upping the lyrical ante with the band's final effort, '39 MINUTES'. Featuring 'SINGER'S HAMPSTEAD HOME', his infamous take on the fading fortunes of labelmate, BOY GEORGE, the album nevertheless proved to be MICRODISNEY's parting shot as COUGHLAN and O'HAGAN went their separate ways. While the former went on to air his lyrical bile in uncompromising fashion with FATIMA MANSIONS, the latter indulged his penchant for classic US West Coast pop with The HIGH LLAMAS. With a line-up comprising COUGHLAN, ANDREAS 'GRIMMO' O'GRUNIA, HUGH BUNKER, NICHOLAS ALLUM and ZAK WOOLHOUSE, FATIMA MANSIONS named themselves after a deprived Dublin housing scheme and proceeded to function as a sounding board for COUGHLAN's increasingly unrestrained muse. Debut album, 'AGAINST NATURE' (1989) revealed an equally unrestrained musical backing as COUGHLAN – with the help of O'GRUNIA's scathing guitar outbursts – marked his departure from the conventional rock/pop approach of MICRODISNEY. The singer's most savage political diatribe to date came in the shape of follow-up single, 'BLUES FOR CEAUCESCU', while 'VIVA DEAD PONIES' (1990) had critics falling over themselves to praise its breadth of musical vision, funereal humour and razor-sharp commentaries. Recorded on the back of a series of lone acoustic gigs, 'BERTIE'S BROCHURES' (1991) was a pared-down mini-set featuring covers of Richard Thompson's 'GREAT VALERIO', Scott Walker's 'LONG ABOUT NOW' and a gleeful brutalisation of R.E.M's 'SHINY HAPPY PEOPLE', the title track skirting around one of COUGHLAN's favourite topics, the relationship between Britain and Ireland. 1992, meanwhile, proved a vintage year as FATIMA MANSIONS witnessed their first chart action with the 'VALHALLA AVENUE' album (Top 60) and COUGHLAN used a U2 support slot in Milan to demonstrate exactly what he thought of the Pope. They also found themselves in the Top 10 singles chart, by default rather than design as another lesson in pop deconstruction – Bryan Adams' nauseating 'EVERYTHING I DO' knocked into shape this time around – found its way onto the B-side of 'Suicide Is Painless', MANIC STREET PREACHERS style. While 1993 saw the release of a compilation set, 'COME BACK MY CHILDREN', COUGHLAN busied himself with his side project, BUBONIQUE, working with comedian SEAN HUGHES (now a regular feature of BBC2's 'Never Mind The Buzzcocks') on the brilliantly titled '20 GOLDEN SHOWERS' (1993). His prolific output continued with a 1994 FATIMA MANSIONS album, 'LOST IN THE FORMER WEST' and a 1995 BUBONIQUE follow-up, 'TRANCE ARSE VOLUME 3'. Giving the 'MANSIONS a break in the mid-90's, the irrepressible Irishman turned his attention towards a solo career proper with the almost RADIOHEAD-like 'UNBROKEN ONES' single and 'THE GRAND NECROPOLITAN' (1996) album. Four years in the making, 'BLACK RIVER FALLS' (2000), was his sophomore outing. COUGHLAN – and his backing band, DAVE GREGORY and AINDRIAS O GRUAMA – centered this string-laden treasure on various haunts around the globe from Las Vegas to Swansea and all with his trademark cathartic brogue to boot. Album No.3 'THE SKY'S AWFUL BLUE' put COUGHLAN up there with the greatest. Comparisons to DYLAN and COHEN rolled off many a journalist's tongue, while songs such as 'THE DRUNKEN HANGMAN' and 'GOODBYE SADNESS' rolled out from his. One of the most undervalued songwriters in rock, COUGHLAN seems destined for eternal cultdom. • **FATIMA MANSIONS covered:** STIGMATA (Ministry) / LONG ABOUT NOW + NITE FLIGHTS (Scott Walker) / THE GREAT VALERIO (Richard Thompson) / PAPER THIN HOTEL (Leonard Cohen) / SHINY HAPPY PEOPLE (R.E.M.) / EVERYTHING I DO (Bryan Adams).

Album rating: Microdisney: EVERYBODY IS FANTASTIC (*5) / 82-84: WE HATE YOU SOUTH AFRICAN BASTARDS mini-compilation (*6) / THE CLOCK COMES DOWN THE STAIRS (*6) / CROOKED MILE (*5) / 39 MINUTES (*5) / BIG SLEEPING HOUSE ... FINEST MOMENTS compilation (*7) / Fatima Mansions: AGAINST NATURE (*6) / VIVA DEAD PONIES (*7) / BERTIE'S BROCHURE mini (*7) / VALHALLA AVENUE (*8) / COME BACK MY CHILDREN compilation (*7) / LOST IN THE FORMER WEST (*6) / Cathal Coughlan: THE GRAND NECROPOLITAN (*6) / BLACK RIVER FALLS (*7) / THE SKY'S AWFUL BLUE (*7)

MICRODISNEY

CATHAL COUGHLAN – vocals, keyboards / **SEAN O'HAGAN** – guitar, vocals, harmonica / **MICK LYNCH** – bass, vocals / **ROB MacKAHEY** – drums

Kabuki not iss.

Sep 82. (7") (KAMD 2) **HELICOPTER OF THE HOLY GHOST. / HELLO RASCALS**
May 83. (7") (KAMD 4) **FICTION LAND. / PINK SKINNED MAN**
—— **ED FLESH** – bass; repl. LYNCH who formed STUMP
—— **TOM FENNER** – drums, percussion; repl. MacKAHEY who formed STUMP

Rough Trade not iss.

May 84. (lp) (ROUGH 75) **EVERYBODY IS FANTASTIC**
– Idea / A few kisses / Escalator in the rain / Dolly / Dreaming drains / I'll be a gentleman / Moon / Sun / Sleepless / Come on over and cry / This liberal love / Before famine / Everybody is dead. (cd-iss. May96 on 'Creation Rev-Ola'; CREV 40CD)
Jun 84. (7") (RT 135) **DOLLY. / THIS LIBERAL LOVE**
(12"+=) (RTT 135) – Everbody Is Dead / Dear Rosemary.
Mar 85. (12"ep) (RTT 175) **MICRODISNEY IN THE WORLD**
– In the world / Loftholdingswood / Teddy dogs / 464.
Sep 85. (7") (RT 185) **BIRTHDAY GIRL. / HARMONY TUNES**
(12"+=) (RTT 185) – Money for the trams.
Oct 85. (lp) (ROUGH 85) **THE CLOCK COMES DOWN THE STAIRS**
– Horse overboard / Birthday girl / Past / Humane / Are you happy? / Genius / Begging bowl / A friend with a big mouth / Goodbye it's 1987 / And. (cd-iss. May96 on 'Creation Rev-Ola'; CREV 41CD)
—— **STEVE PREGNANT** – bass; repl. ED. Also added **JAMES COMPTON** – keyboards (to **COUGHLAN, O'HAGAN, FENNER**)

Virgin not iss.

Jan 87. (7") (VS 927) **TOWN TO TOWN. / LITTLE TOWN IN IRELAND** — 55
(12"+=) (VS 927-12) – Genius / Bullwhip road.
(d7") (VSD 927) **'PEEL SESSIONS' EP:** – Begging bowl / Loftholdingswood / Horse overboard.
Jan 87. (cd/c/lp) (CD/TC+/V 2415) **CROOKED MILE**
– Town to town / Angels / Our children / Mrs. Simpson / Hey hey Sam / Give me all your clothes / Armadillo man / Bullwhip road / And he descended into Hell / Rack / Big sleeping house / People just want to dream.
—— **CRAZY JOHNNY NANCY** – bass; repl. STEVE
Oct 87. (7") (VS 1014) **SINGER'S HAMPSTEAD HOME. / SHE ONLY GAVE INTO ANGER**
(12"+=) (VST 1014) – Brother Olaf.
Feb 88. (7") (VS 1044) **GALE FORCE WIND. / I CAN'T SAY NO (Betty Lou version)**
(c-s+=) (VSTC 1044) – Irish nationl anthem / Say "no I can't".
(12+=) (VST 1044) – No, I can't say (thank you for speaking to me Mustapha) / Can't I say no (Hackney aid).
(cd-s+=) (VSCD 1044) – ('A'-version) / Town to town.
Mar 88. (cd/c/lp) (CD/TC+/V 2505) **39 MINUTES**
– Singer's Hampstead home / High and dry / Send Herman home / Ambulance for one / Soul boy / Back to the old town / United colours / Gale force wind / Herr direktor / Bluerings.
—— (split around Spring '88). SEAN O'HAGAN formed the TWILIGHT before going solo in 1989 (later he forrmed the HIGH LLAMAS).

– compilations, etc. –

Oct 84. (m-lp) Rough Trade; (RTM 155) **82-84: WE HATE YOU SOUTH AFRICAN BASTARDS!**
– Helicopter of the holy ghost / Michael Murphy / Love your enemies / Fiction land / Pink skinned man / Patrick Moore says you can't sleep here / Hello rascals / Pretoria quickstep.
Dec 89. (lp/c/cd) Strange Fruit; (SFR LP/MC/CD 105) **DOUBLE PEEL SESSIONS**
(re-iss. Nov94; same)
Mar 95. (cd) Virgin; (CDOVD 452) **BIG SLEEPING HOUSE ... FINEST MOMENTS (A COLLECTION OF CHOICE CUTS)**
– Horse overboard / Loftholdingswood / Singer's Hampstead home / She only gave into her anger / Gale force wind / I can't say no (Betty Lou version) / Angels / Mrs. Simpson / Armadillo man / And he descended into Hell / Rack / Big sleeping house / Back to the old town / Send Herman home / Town to town / Begging bowl.
May 96. (cd) Creation Rev-Ola; (CREV 42CD) **LOVE YOUR ENEMIES**

FATIMA MANSIONS

CATHAL COUGHLAN – vocals, keyboards, composer with **ANDREAS 'GRIMMO' O'GRUNIA** – guitar / **ZAK** – keyboards / **HUGH BUNKER** – bass / **NICHOLAS TIOMPAN ALLUM** – drums, wind

Kitchenware not iss.

Nov 89. (lp/cd) (KW LP/CD 11) **AGAINST NATURE**
– Only losers take the bus / The day I lost everything / Wilderness on time / You won't get me here / 13th century boy / Bishop of Babel / Valley of the dead ass / Big madness – Monday club Carol.

Cathal COUGHLAN (cont)

Feb 90. (12"m) *(SKX 43)* **ONLY LOSERS TAKE THE BUS. / ('A'version) / WHAT?**
Jun 90. (7") *(SK 45)* **BLUES FOR CEAUCESCU. / 13th CENTURY BOY**
(12"+=/cd-s+=) *(SK X/CD 45)* – Suicide bridge.
Sep 90. (lp/c/cd) **VIVA DEAD PONIES**
– Angel's delight / Concrete block / Mr. Bailey / The door-to-door inspector / Start the week / You're a rose / Legoland 3 / Thursday / Ceaucescu flashback / Broken radio No.1 / Look what I stole for us darling / Farewell Ontario / The white knuckle express / Chemical cosh / Tima Mansio speaks / A pack of lies / Viva dead ponies / More smack vicar. *(re-iss. Mar91 on 'Radioactive' lp/c/cd; RAR/+C/D 10242) (re-iss. Sep94 cd/c; KWL CD/MC 19262)*
Feb 91. (12"ep) *(SK 50)* **HIVE / STIGMATA. / CHEMICAL COSH / THE HOLY MUGGER**
Apr 91. (7"/c-s) *(SK/+C 53)* **YOU'RE A ROSE. / BLUES FOR CEAUCESCU**
(cd-s+=) *(SKXD 53)* – Against nature.
(12"+=) *(SKX 53)* – Only losers take the bus.
Oct 91. (m-cd/m-lp) *(KW CD/LP 16)* **BERTIE'S BROCHURES** (acoustic)
– Behind the man / Bertie's brochures / Long about now / The great Valerio / Shiny happy people / VN (apology) / Mario Vargas Yoni / Smiling. *(re-iss. Sep94 cd/c; KWL CD/MC 19257)*

—— **DUKE O MALAITHE** – keyboards; repl. ZAK

Kitchenware not iss.

Apr 92. (12"m) *(SKX 56)* **EVIL MAN. / THE SCARECROW / EVIL MAN II** | 59 | - |
(12"m) *(SKXD 56)* – EVIL MAN I & II / Blues for Ceaucescu (mix) / Chemical cosh.
(d-cd-s) *(SKXXD 56)* – EVIL MAN I & II / Only losers take the bus (dump the dead) / Hive.
May 92. (cd/c/lp) *(KW CD/MC/LP 18)* **VALHALLA AVENUE** | 52 | - |
– Evil man / Something bad / Valhalla avenue / 1000% / North Atlantic wind / Purple window / Go home bible Mike / Perfumes of Paradise / Greyhair / C7 – breakfast with Bandog / Ray of hope, hope of rape / Be dead. *(re-iss. Sep94 cd/c; KWL CD/MC 19258)*
Jul 92. (12"m) *(SK 59)* **1,000 %. / HIVE (live) / 1,000,000%** | 61 | - |
(cd-s) *(SKXD 59)* – Paper thin hotel *[repl. 'Hive']*
(cd-s) *(SKXXD 59)* – Angel's delight *[repl. '1,000,000']*
(cd-s) *(SKZD 59)* – ('A'side) / Behind the Moon (live) / Evil man (live) / White knuckles express (live).

—— Sep'92, covered a version of Bryan Adams' 'EVERYTHING I DO' on B-side of MANIC STREET PREACHERS UK Top 10 hit version of 'Suicide Is Painless'

Feb 93. (cd/c) *(CGCC/+D 001)* **COME BACK MY CHILDREN** (compilation)
– Only losers take the bus / The day I lost everything / Wilderness on time / You won't get me home / 13th century you / Bishop of Babel / Valley of the dead cars / Big madness / What? / Blues for Ceaucescu / On Suicide Bridge / Hive / The holy mugger / Stigmata / Lady Godiva's operation.
Jul 94. (7"/c-s) *(SK/+MC 67)* **THE LOYALISER. / GARY NUMAN'S PORSCHE / ARNIE'S FIVE** | 58 | - |
(12"+=/cd-s+=) *(SK X/CD 67)* – Into thinner air with the loyaliser.
Sep 94. (cd/c/colrd-lp) *(KW CD/MC/LP 25)* **LOST IN THE FORMER WEST**
– Belong nowhere / The loyaliser / Popemobile to Paraguay / Walk yr. way / Bruneceling's song / Lost in the former west / Nite flights / Your world customer / Sunken cities / Brain blister / A walk in the woods / Humiliate me.
Oct 94. (c-s) *(SKMC 68)* **NITE FLIGHTS / IGNORANCE IS PISS**
(10"/cd-s) *(SK T/CD 68)* – ('A'side) / As I washed the blood off / Diamonds, fur coat, champagne / It's so cold . . . I think.

BUBONIQUE

CATHAL's alter-ego featuring Irish comedian **SEAN HUGHES**

Kitchenware not iss.

Mar 92. (12") *(SKX 52)* **SCREW. / MONOGAMY I'M GOING TO KICK YOUR HEAD IN**
Nov 92. (12") *(SKX 54)* **SUMMER THE FIRST TIME. / FREE CHARLES MANSON**
Apr 93. (cd) *(KWCD 24)* **20 GOLDEN SHOWERS**
– Summer the first time / Think you're cool / Play that funky music / Cop lover / Codsucker blues / My baby gave me rabies / Release the bats / Elvis '93 / Chicken arse (theme) / Iron child / Yoda lady / Anytime anyplace it's ok / 2 J.G. / Stock Hausen and Waterman / East sheep station / Love me deadly kiss me Headley / DLT 666 no idea / The bubonique America Top 10 / Frank is Frank / Jellypop porky Jean / Dildo neighbour / Love camp 7 / Nation of Bubonique / Closedown.
Sep 95. (cd) *(KWCD 28)* **TRANCE ARSE VOLUME 3**
– You can't fool the dead / Cod is love / The pianna / Truck Turner / The sermon / Freestyle masterclass 1; Sawing / Talkin' about talkin' about / Freebird / I've always liked hunting / Oi copper / Return of the nice age / What's e saying / Hey, handsome / Industrial woman / Rainbow buffalo cornwoman / Freestyle masterclass; Drilling / Q magazine / Kind of pue / 'George' aid suite / Abbaabortion / Swan of Newcastle.

CATHAL COUGHLAN

Kitchenware not iss.

May 96. (7") *(SK 69)* **UNBROKEN ONES. / ON THE PARISH**
Jul 96. (cd) *(KWCD 29)* **THE GRAND NECROPOLITAN**
– This building / Unbroken ones / On the parish / The new "Royale" / Eerin go braghag / We are the sinister world government / The big lukewarm / Straying away / Irrational falsifier / Two grotesques, embracing / Angry white snail / Free and worthless / Garrai na muic / The last lamplighter – The grand necropolitan promenade / Waiting for wood, captain.

—— next with **DAVE GREGORY** – guitar (of XTC) + **AINDRIAS O GRUAMA** – multi + guest **DAWN KENNY** – vocals

Cooking Vinyl not iss.

Mar 00. (cd) *(COOKCD 126)* **BLACK RIVER FALLS**
– The ghost of limehouse cut / Officer material / The bacon singer / Black river falls / Payday / Dark parlour / Out among the ruins / God bless Mr.X / Frankfurt cowboy yodel / N.C. / Whitechapel mound / Cast me out in my hometown.

Beneath not iss.

Jul 02. (cd) *(BNT 101)* **THE SKY'S AWFUL BLUE**
– And springtime followed summer / Denial of the right to dream / Three rusty reivers / Goodbye sadness / Toxic mother / Last of eternity / You turned me / Amused as hell / Pawnshop riches / White's academy / Drunken hangman / Female line.

COWBOY JUNKIES

Formed: Toronto, Canada . . . 1985 by MICHAEL TIMMINS, with younger brother PETER and sister MARGO; all inviting ALAN ANTON to the fold. In the late 70's and early 80's, MICHAEL had been in groups, HUNGER PROJECT and GERMINAL, before moving to New York and London in the process. In the mid-80's, The COWBOY JUNKIES recorded a debut lp, 'WHITES OFF EARTH NOW!!' in their garage, releasing it on their own Canadian indie label 'Latent'. By 1988, they were on the roster of 'R.C.A.', with 'Cooking Vinyl' licensing them in UK. That year's album, 'THE TRINITY SESSION' was famously cut in a Toronto Church with the most basic of recording equipment. Despite this, or more likely because of it, the album remains 'JUNKIES most enduring effort. Proving that at its heart, real country music really is a religious experience, the band drifted gracefully through perceptive covers and original material alike. Whether investing in Hank Williams' 'I'M SO LONESOME I COULD CRY' and Patsy Cline's 'WALKIN' AFTER MIDNIGHT' with latter day angst or re-inventing Lou Reed's 'SWEET JANE' with a languorous poignancy, The COWBOY JUNKIES' melancholic, minimalistic take on Americana was hypnotic and groundbreaking. Though they initially appealed to the college market, the group successfully crossed over with follow-up set, 'THE CAUTION HORSES' (1990). A slightly more robust album, it included one of the group's most affecting originals to date 'CAUSE CHEAP IS HOW I FEEL', while they even managed to transform NEIL YOUNG's classic 'POWDERFINGER', into a spectral lament. 'BLACK EYED MAN' (1992) was even better, JOHN PRINE and the late, lamented TOWNES VAN ZANDT guesting on an album which mined a rawer country seam. The record also marked the peak of their commercial success, the band playing a prestigious gig at London's Royal Albert Hall. Since then, the band have lost their momentum somewhat, despite a further couple of critically acclaimed albums, 'PALE SUN, CRESCENT MOON' (1993) and 'LAY IT DOWN' (1996). The latter marked their debut for 'Geffen', their tenure with 'R.C.A.' ending in the mid-90's. Now something of an institution, the COWBOY JUNKIES proved their genteel, bookish take on US roots/vaguely alternative rock was built to last with 'OPEN' (2001). Earthy song titles, enduring themes and the low-key but unmistakable vocals of MARGO TIMMINS made for another pleasant, reassuringly introspective listen. Hardly likely to win new fans but tailor made for their unerringly loyal fanbase. • **Songwriters:** MICHAEL wrote & produced most songs, except other covers BLUE MOON (hit; Elvis Presley) / SHINING MOON (Lightning Hopkins) / STATE TROOPER (Bruce Springsteen) / ME AND THE DEVIL + CROSSROADS (Robert Johnson) / DECORATION DAY + I'LL NEVER GET OUT OF THESE BLUES ALIVE + FORGIVE ME (John Lee Hooker) / BABY PLEASE DON'T GO (Bukka White) / COWBOY JUNKIES LAMENT + TO LIVE IS TO FLY (Townes Van Zandt) / IF YOU'VE GOTTA GO, GO NOW (Bob Dylan) / LOST MY DRIVING WHEEL (Wiffen) / THE POST (Dinosaur Jr).

Album rating: WHITES OFF EARTH NOW!! (*6) / THE TRINITY SESSION (*7) / THE CAUTION HORSES (*8) / BLACK EYED MAN (*6) / PALE SUN, CRESCENT MOON (*7) / 200 MORE MILES live 1985-1994 (*5) / LAY IT DOWN (*5) / MILES FROM OUR HOME (*5) / STUDIO compilation (*6) / OPEN (*5) / THE BEST OF COWBOY JUNKIES compilation

MICHAEL TIMMINS (b.21 Apr'59, Montreal, Canada) – guitar / **MARGO TIMMINS** (b.27 Jun'61, Montreal) – vocals / **PETER TIMMINS** (b.29 Oct'65, Montreal) – drums / **ALAN ANTON** (b. ALAN ALIZOJVODIC, 22 Jun'59, Montreal) – bass

not iss. Latent

Nov 86. (lp) **WHITES OFF EARTH NOW!!** | - | Canada |
– Shining moon / State trooper / Me and the Devil / Decoration day / Baby please don't go / I'll never get out of these blues alive / Take me / Forgive me / Crossroads. *(UK-iss.Feb91 on 'R.C.A.' cd/c/lp; PD/PK/PL 82380)*

Cooking Vinyl R.C.A.

Mar 89. (7") *(FRY 008)* **SWEET JANE. / 200 MORE MILES** | | Nov88 |
(12"+=) *(FRY 008T)* – Postcard blues.
Mar 89. (lp/c/cd) *(COOK/+C/CD 011) <8568>* **THE TRINITY SESSION** | 26 | Oct88 |
– Mining for gold / Misguided angel / Blue moon revisited (a song for Elvis) / I don't get in / I'm so lonesome I could cry / To love is to bury / 200 more miles / Dreaming my dreams with you / Working on a building / Sweet Jane / Postcard blues / Walking after midnight. *(cd re-iss. Feb94; 74321 18356-2) (lp re-iss. Jun99 on 'Simply Vinyl'; SVLP 80)*
May 89. (7") *(FRY 011)* **MISGUIDED ANGEL. / POSTCARD BLUES**
Jul 89. (7") *(FRY 011)* **BLUE MOON REVISITED (SONG FOR ELVIS). / TO LOVE IS TO BURY**
(12"+=/cd-s+=) *(FRY 011 T/CD)* – ('A'live version).
(10") *(FRY 011X)* – ('A'side) / You won't be loved again / Shining moon / Walking after midnight.

R.C.A. R.C.A.

Feb 90. (7") *(PB 49301)* **SUN COMES UP, IT'S TUESDAY MORNING. / WITCHES**
(12"+=) *(PT 49302)* – Powderfinger.
(cd-s++=) *(PD 49302)* – Misguided angel.
(c-s+=) *(PK 49302)* – Dead flowers.

COWBOY JUNKIES (cont)

Mar 90. (cd/c/lp) (PD/PK/PL 90450) <2058> **THE CAUTION HORSES** [33] [47]
– Sun comes up, it's Tuesday morning / 'Cause cheap is how I feel / Thirty summers / Mariner's song / Powderfinger / Where are you tonight / Witches / Rock and bird / Escape is so easy / You will be loved again. (cd re-iss. Feb94; 74321 18537-2)

Jun 90. (7") **'CAUSE CHEAP IS HOW I FEEL. / THIRTY SUMMERS**
(12"+=/cd-s+=) – Declaration day / State trooper / Take me.

Sep 90. (c-s) **ROCK AND BIRD /** [-]

Jan 92. (cd-ep) **SOUTHERN RAIN / MURDER, TONIGHT, IN THE TRAILER PARK / LOST MY DRIVING WHEEL / IF YOU'VE GOTTA GO, GO NOW**

Feb 92. (cd/c/lp) (PD/PK/PL 90620) <61049> **BLACK EYED MAN** [21] [76]
– Southern rain / Oregon hill / This street, that man, this life / A horse in the country / If you were the woman and I was the man / Murder, tonight, in the trailer park / Black eyed man / Winter's song / The last spike / Cowboy Junkies lament / Townes' blues / To live is to fly. (w/ free cd-ep) – DEAD FLOWERS / CAPTAIN KIDD / TAKE ME / 'CAUSE CHEAP IS HOW I FEEL (cd re-iss. Jun96; 74321 36913-2)

Mar 92. (7") **A HORSE IN THE COUNTRY. / OREGON HILL**
(cd-s+=) – Five room love story.

Nov 93. (cd/c) <74321 16808-2/-4)> **PALE SUN, CRESCENT MOON**
– Crescent moon / First recollection / Ring on the sill / Anniversary song / White sail / Seven years / Pale Sun / The post / Cold tea blues / Hard to explain / Hunted / Floorboard blues. (cd re-iss. Jun96; same)

Feb 96. (d-cd) <(74321 29643-2)> **200 MORE MILES (live)**
– Blue moon revisited (a song for Elvis) / 200 more miles / Me and the Devil / State trooper / Sun comes up, it's Tuesday morning / Oregon hill / Where are you tonight / 'Cause cheap is how I feel / Floorboard blues / Murder tonight in the trailer park / Sweet Jane / If you were the woman and I was the man / Pale sun / Hunted / Lost mny driving wheel / Forgive me / Misguided angel / I'm so lonesome I could cry / Walking after midnight.

Geffen   Geffen

Mar 96. (c-s) (GFSC 22117) **A COMMON DISASTER / COME CALLING (HER SONG)**
(cd-s+=) (GFSTD 22117) – In the long run.

May 96. (cd/c) <(GED/GEC 24952)> **LAY IT DOWN** [ ] [55] Mar96
– Something more besides you / A common disaster / Lay it down / Hold on to me / Come calling (his song) / Just want to see / Lonely sinking feeling / Angel mine / Bea's song (river song trilogy: part II) / Musical key / Speaking confidentially / Come calling (her song) / Now I know.

Aug 96. (cd-s) (GED 2216-2) **ANGEL MINE / NOW I KNOW / CARMELITA**

Sep 98. (cd/c) <(GED/GEC 25201)> **MILES FROM OUR HOME** [98] Jun98
– New dawn coming / Blue guitar / Miles from our home / Good Friday / Darkling days / Hollow as a bone / Someone out there / Summer of discontent / No birds today / Those final feet.

Cooking Vinyl   Latent

May 01. (cd) (COOKCD 216) <431020> **OPEN**
– I did it all for you / Dragging hooks / Bread and wine / Upon still waters / Dark hole again / Thousand year prayer / I'm so open / Small swift birds / Beneath the gate / Close my eyes.

– compilations, etc. –

Feb 98. (cd) R.C.A.; (07863 67412-2) **STUDIO** (selected studio recordings 1986-1995)
– Shining moon / Misguided angel / Blue moon revisited (a song for Elvis) / Sweet Jane / Sun comes up, it's Tuesday morning / 'Cause cheap is how I feel / Powderfinger / Southern rain / A horse in the country / This street, that man, this life / Anniversary song / Ring on the sill / A common disaster / Lost my driving wheel.

Oct 99. (cd) Latent; <(74321 16808-2)> **RARITIES, B SIDES AND SLOW SAD WALTZES**

2000. (cd) Latent; **WALTZ ACROSS AMERICA (live)** [-] [-]
– Good Friday / Southern rain / Bea's song (river song trilogy) part 3 / Townes' blues / Five room love story / I saw your shoes / Misguided angel / Sweet Jane / Hunted / Blue guitar / Hollow as a bone (revisited) / Dark hole again.

Sep 01. (cd) B.M.G.; <07863 68052-2> **THE BEST OF THE COWBOY JUNKIES** [-]
– Blue moon revisited (song for Elvis) / Sweet Jane / Misguided angel / I'm so lonesome I could cry / Rock and bird / Sun comes up, it's Tuesday morning / Escape it's so simple / 'Cause cheap is how I feel / To live is to fly / Murder, tonight, in the trailer park / Southern rain / Cowboy Junkies lament / Anniversary song / Cold tea blues / Ring on the sill / Hard to explain. (hidden track+=) – A horse 'n the country. (UK-iss.Nov02 on 'R.C.A.'; 74321 96669-2)

Jul 02. (cd) Strange Fruit; (SFRSCD 109) **THE RADIO 1 SESSIONS**

CRASH
(see under ⇒ ULTRA VIVID SCENE; 90's section)

CRAWLING CHAOS

Formed: Rotherham, England ... 1979 by drummer EDDIE FENN and a handful of mystery sidemen. One of the many acts to sign for Tony Wilson's stable of diverse alt/indie acts, 'Factory', CRAWLING CHAOS delivered their debut single, 'SEX MACHINE' (no, nothing to do with the JAMES BROWN classic!), a noisy non-formulaic affair that unsurprisingly went nowhere. Switching to the Belgian ('Benelux') arm of the label, the group released their debut set, 'THE GAS CHAIR' (1981), a very disappointing collection of FAUST-inspired punk chants, screeching organs and sex-obsessed lyrics; the porny cartoon sleevework probably didn't help its sales. FENN took off to join MARC RILEY & THE CREEPERS (and TOOLS YOU CAN TRUST) and subsequently became a producer of obscure acts like WATERFOOT DANDY and IMPLIES CONSENT. Meanwhile, CRAWLING CHAOS returned on their own 'Foetus' label in the mid-80's with two contrasting sets, 'C' (anti-Commercial in the extreme) and 'WAQQAZ', a surprisingly bright and intelligent avant-garde collection of part instrumentals. Tracks like 'TROUTY HOBIN' – although having a dangerously similar intro to The SPECIALS' 'International Jet Set' – and 'COMRADE DOLPHIN' were stand-out pieces.

Album rating: THE GAS CHAIR (*3) / 'C' (*2) / WAQQAZ (*5)

EDDIE FENN – drums, guitar / with

Factory   not iss.

Jun 80. (7") (FAC 17) **SEX MACHINE. / BERLIN**

Factory Benelux   not iss.

Feb 82. (lp) (FACBN 6) **THE GAS CHAIR** [-] [-] Belgian
– Macabre royale / Creamo coyl / Left hand path / Guinness / Arabesque / Harry / Disierta membra / Canadian Pacific / Breaking down.

RAM   not iss.

1983. (7"; as BLONDE ETHIOPIAN) (RAM 515) **SINEWS ARE A GIRLS BEST FRIEND EP**
– Neep heads / Throwing pins / Reel 1 / Nothin' / Horse bath / I got loofahs / Not transferable.

— FENN joined TOOLS YOU CAN TRUST and MARC RILEY (was he still a member?)

Foetus   not iss.

Mar 84. (lp) (FOETUS 3) **'C'**
– Gygno / Urbane encounter / Wee Jimmy (part II) / Worms / The Katrina syndrome / Friends / Jhonn's angel / The vulva boatman / Frauline le Moine / D.S.S. / Skaill.

Apr 85. (lp) (FOETUS 4) **WAQQAZ**
– Remocarpet / 1078-1082 / Oh blase / Fatso dies and likes it / Trouty Hobin / Comrade dolphin / Reg Vase / The white Sybil / Yoni Suchons / Curling sandwiches / Netwilf / Bosumptwi / I must be ambidextrous (I can smoke with both hands) / Comrade dolphin (reprise) / Me.

Dec 85. (c) **HOMUNCULUS EQUINOX** [-] [-] foreign
– What's your noise / Fuel for the blonde Ethiopian / Taste of honey / Mummy's tummy / Valium B / Ashen / Tom's bum (there's) / Stinging gnats / Heavy lovin' / The Mongolian steak bar / Voedoux / Tell me why / East of east alotment / Suck / One more peso.

— split from the music scene after above

CRAZYHEAD

Formed: Leicester, England ... 1986 by (IAN) ANDERSON, KEV REVERB, FAST DICK, PORK BEAST and ex-DOCTOR & THE MEDICS drummer, VOM. Lumped in with the media created "Grebo" scene along with POP WILL EAT ITSELF, GAYE BYKERS ON ACID and the early WONDER STUFF, CRAZYHEAD signed to EMI offshoot, 'Food', debuting the following year with the 12"er, 'WHAT GIVES YOU THE IDEA YOU'RE SO AMAZING BABY?'. Over the course of the next year or so, the grimy 5-piece released a string of singles, the last of which, 'RAGS', accompanied the 'DESERT ORCHID' album in Autumn '88. Moving upstairs to 'Parlophone', CRAZYHEAD scored their second minor hit single, 'HAVE LOVE, WILL TRAVEL', having previously entered the charts with 'TIME HAS TAKEN ITS TOLL ON YOU'. In March 1990, having played Romania, CRAZYHEAD were the only Western outfit to appear at Namibia's Independence Festival in front of 50,000 people. After failing to cross over into the alternative mainstream, the group were consigned to 'Revolver' where they released their PAT COLLIER-produced follow-up set, 'SOME KIND OF FEVER' (1990). In 1998, CRAZYHEAD made a vain attempt to claw back any sort of respect via the album, 'FUCKED BY ROCK'.

Album rating: DESERT ORCHID (*6) / SOME KIND OF FEVER (*4) / LIVE IN MEMPHIS (*3) / FUCKED BY ROCK (*4)

(IAN) ANDERSON – vocals / **KEV REVERB** (b. KEVIN BAYLISS) – guitar, piano, sitar / **FAST DICK** (b. RICHARD BELL) – guitar / **PORK BEAST** (b. ALEX PEACH) – bass / **VOM** (b. ROB MORRIS) – drums, percussion (ex-DOCTOR & THE MEDICS)

Food   EMI America

Mar 87. (12"ep) (SNAK 8) **WHAT GIVES YOU THE IDEA YOU'RE SO AMAZING BABY? / OUT ON A LIMB / SNAKE EYES**

Jul 87. (7") (FOOD 10) **BABY TURPENTINE. / THAT KIND OF LOVE**
(12"+=) (SNAK 10) – Bang bang / That sinking feeling.

Jun 88. (7") (FOOD 12) **TIME HAS TAKEN ITS TOLL ON YOU. / DOWN** [65]
(ext-12"+=) (12FOOD 12) – The ballad of Baby Turpentine.
(10"+=) (10FOOD 12) – Here comes Johnny.
(cd-s+=) (CDFOOD 12) – Bang bang.

Sep 88. (7") (FOOD 14) **RAGS. / RUB THE BUDDHA**
(12"+=) (12FOOD 14) – Screaming apple.
(12"++=/cd-s++=) (12FOODS/CDFOOD 14) – Fortune teller.

Oct 88. (lp/c/cd) (FOOD LP/TC/CD 1) <E1/E4 91035> **DESERT ORCHID**
– In the sun / Jack the scissorman / Time has taken its toll on you / Have love, will travel / What gives you the idea you're so amazing baby? / I don't want that kind of love / Dragon city / Buy a gun / Rags / Tower of fire / Cardinal Phink. (c+=) – Bang bang. (cd+=) – Out on a limb / Down / Time has taken its toll on you (extended). (cd re-iss. Mar89 on 'Parlophone'; CDP 791035-2)

Parlophone   not iss.

Feb 89. (7"ep/12"ep) (SGE/12SGE 2025) **HAVE LOVE, WILL TRAVEL EP** [68]
– Have love will travel / Out on a limb (live) / Baby Turpentine (live) / Snake eyes (live).
(cd-ep++=) (CDSGE 2025) – Here comes Johnny (live).

— In Dec'89, CRAZYHEAD also covered Diesel Park West's 'LIKE PRINCES DO' on the Various Artists 'THE FOOD CHRISTMAS EP', which hit No.63.

Revolver   not iss.

Aug 90. (12"m) (12REV 64) **EVERYTHING'S ALRIGHT. / DEATH RIDE TO OSAKA / I CAN ONLY GIVE YOU EVERYTHING**

Nov 90. (cd/c/lp) (REV XD/MC/LP 162) **SOME KIND OF FEVER**
– Big sister / Above these things / Everything's alright / Magic eye / I can do anything / Movie theme / Talk about you / Rome / Night train / Some kinda fever.

— disbanded for the rest of the 90's, until ...

CRAZYHEAD (cont)

		Snatch	not iss.
Dec 98.	(cd) *(GASH 3)* **FUCKED BY ROCK**	□	-

– Buy a gun / Every mother's monkey / Time has taken it's toll on you / Baltimore / Movie theme / Golden highway / Out on a limb / Do anything / Bang bang / Sweet sweet life / Pretty sick / Dragon city / Fish / Dragster girl / Long dark daze / The ballad of baby turpentine.

– compilations, etc. –

Jan 89.	(12"ep/cd-ep) *Strange Fruit; (SFNT/+CD 018)* **NIGHT TRACKS**	□	-
Sep 95.	(cd) *Pearls From The Past; <BOE 3>* **GRIND (live in Memphis)**	-	-
May 99.	(cd) *Snatch; (ATOG 1)* **13th FLOOR**	□	-

CREATURES
(see under ⇒ SIOUXSIE & THE BANSHEES; 70's section)

CRIME & THE CITY SOLUTION

Formed: Melbourne ... 1978 by Australian vocalist, SIMON BONNEY, although it wouldn't be until 1984 and the demise of The BIRTHDAY PARTY that the band would arrive fully formed with the latter act's remnants, MICK HARVEY and ROWLAND S. HOWARD, making up the numbers alongside ROWLAND's brother HARRY and BONNEY's wife and future songwriting partner, BRONWYN ADAMS. After a debut EP for 'Mute', 'THE DANGLING MAN', ex-SWELL MAPS drummer, EPIC SOUNDTRACKS was drafted in to complete a mini-album's worth of material, 'JUST SOUTH OF HEAVEN' (1985). Conjuring up an ambitious cinematic sound rooted in voodoo blues, the group's material was often compared to the atmospheric soundtrack mastery of ENNIO MORRICONE, BONNEY's brooding whiskey-throated vocals similar to JIM MORRISON or DAVID McCOMB. This unique chemistry was showcased on 1986's first full album, 'ROOM OF LIGHTS', an acclaimed set which featured 'SIX BELLS CHIME'; the track was subsequently performed by the band in Wim Wenders' cult film, 'Wings Of Desire', while they also contributed a track, 'THE ADVERSARY' to the filmaker's 'Until The End Of The World'. By the time of its premiere, ROWLAND, HARRY and EPIC had struck out on their own to form THESE IMMORTAL SOULS, leaving behind SIMON, BRONWYN and MICK (the latter also moonlighted with NICK CAVE & THE BAD SEEDS) to rebuild the group in Berlin with the help of new members, ALEXANDER HACKE (ex-EINSTURZENDE NEUBAUTEN), CHRISLO HASS (ex-DAF) and PHIL CALVERT (ex-PSYCHEDELIC FURS). This line-up worked on the underrated classic, 'SHINE' (1988), a moody masterpiece highlighting BRONWYN's violin and replacing the blues feel with a more abstract folky sound. 'THE BRIDE SHIP' (1989) meanwhile, saw THOMAS STERN come in for CALVERT, a record based around the theme of emigration that included a revamped version of 'THE DANGLING MAN'. The band's studio swansong set, 'PARADISE DISCOTHEQUE' (1990), was also a pseudo concept affair, with a song cycle based on the collapse of the Nicolae Ceaucescu dynasty in Romania. While HARVEY joined The BAD SEEDS full-time, SIMON developed a rootsier country feel for his debut solo album, 'FOREVER', a record that also featured his wife and an array of session people including J.D. FOSTER. A further four years went by before the release of a follow-up set, 'EVERYMAN' (1996); influenced by his permanent move to the States and evoking that nation's wide open spaces, the record moved even further into classic country.

Album rating: JUST SOUTH OF HEAVEN mini (*6) / ROOM OF LIGHTS (*8) / SHINE (*8) / THE BRIDE SHIP (*6) / PARADISE DISCOTHEQUE (*5) / THE ADVERSARY – LIVE (*5) / Simon Bonney: FOREVER (*6) / EVERYMAN (*5)

SIMON BONNEY (b. Tasmania, Australasia) – vocals, guitar / **ROWLAND S. HOWARD** – guitar, keyboards (ex-BIRTHDAY PARTY) / **HARRY HOWARD** – bass / **MICK HARVEY** – keyboards, guitar, percussion (ex-BIRTHDAY PARTY) / **EPIC SOUNDTRACKS** – drums (ex-SWELL MAPS)

		Mute	Mute
Jun 85.	(12"ep) *(12MUTE 36)* **THE DANGLING MAN**	□	□

– The dangling man / The last day / At the crossroads / Shakin' chill.

| Sep 85. | (m-lp) *(STUMM 22) <71248>* **JUST SOUTH OF HEAVEN** | □ | □ |

– Rose blue / The coal train / Stolen & stealing / Five stone walls / Trouble come this morning / The wailing wall.

| May 86. | (12"ep) *(12STUMM 46)* **THE KENTUCKY CLICK / ADVENTURE. / IT TAKES TWO TO BURN** | □ | □ |
| Oct 86. | (lp) *(STUMM 36) <71329>* **ROOM OF LIGHTS** | □ | □ |

– Right man wrong man / No money no honey / Hey sin killer / Six bells chime / Adventure / Untouchable / The brother song / Her room of lights. *(cd-iss. 1988+=; CDSTUMM 36)* – Rose blue / The coal train / Five stone walls / The wailing wall / Trouble come this morning / The dangling man.

— added **BRONWYN ADAMS** – violin

— split temporary when ROWLAND, HARRY + EPIC formed THESE IMMORTAL SOULS

— **SIMON, BRONWYN + MICK** re-united with **ALEXANDER HACKE** – guitar (ex-EINSTURZENDE NEUBAUTEN) / **CHRISLO HAAS** – synthesizers (ex-DEUTSCH AMERIKANISCHE FREUNDSCHAFT) / **PHIL CALVERT** – drums (ex-BIRTHDAY PARTY, ex-PSYCHEDELIC FURS) repl. THOMAS STERN (bass)

| Apr 88. | (12") *(12MUTE 76)* **ON EVERY TRAIN (GRAIN WILL BEAR GRAIN). / ALL MUST BE LOVE** | □ | - |
| Apr 88. | (cd/lp) *(CD+/STUMM 59) <71402>* **SHINE** | □ | □ |

– All must be love / Fray so slow / Angel / On every train (grain will bear grain) / Hunter / Steal to the sea / Home is far from here. *(cd+=)* – On every train (grain will bear grain) (12" version) / All must be love (early version).

Mar 89.	(12") *(12MUTE 94)* **THE SHADOW OF NO MAN. / THREE – FOUR / THE BRIDE SHIP**	□	-
	(cd-s+=) *(CDMUTE 94)* – On every train (grain will bear grain).		
Apr 89.	(cd/c/lp) *(CD/C+/STUMM 65) <71422>* **THE BRIDE SHIP**	□	□

– The shadow of no man / The greater head / Stone / The dangling man / Keepsake / The bride ship / Free world / New world / Three-Four / The bride ship.

		Mute	Mute-Elektra
Aug 90.	(12"/cd-s) *(12/CD MUTE 114)* **I HAVE THE GUN. / MOTHERLESS CHILD (dance mix) / I HAVE THE GUN (Woody Guthrie mix)**	□	-
Sep 90.	(cd/c/lp) *(CD/C+/STUMM 78) <60990-2>* **PARADISE DISCOTHEQUE**	□	□

– I have the gun / The sly persuaders / The dolphins & the sharks / The sun before darkness / Motherless child / The last dictator I-IV.

| Feb 91. | (10"ep/cd-ep) *(10/CD MUTE 127)* **THE DOLPHINS & THE SHARKS (instrumental) / THE SUN BEFORE DARKNESS. / ON EVERY TRAIN / THE BRIDE SHIP** | □ | - |

— disbanded around August 1991

– compilations, etc. –

| Oct 93. | (cd) *(CDSTUMM 110)* **THE ADVERSARY LIVE (live)** | □ | - |

– The adversary (studio) / Keepsake / All must be love / The last dictator part 1 / The last dictator part 2 / The dangling man / On every train (grain will bear grain) / Angel / The dolphins & the sharks / The bride ship / The free world / The sun before darkness.

SIMON BONNEY

with **BRONWYN** – violin, backing vox / **J.D. FOSTER** – guitars, mandolin / **JON-DEE GRAHAM** – steel guitar / **REINHOLD REIL** – keyboards / **GREGORY BOAZ** – bass / **HANS BEHRENDT** – percussion / **ARCHIE FRANCIS** – drums / **BIFF BAREFOOT SANDERS** – drums / **SALLY NORVELL, JAYNE KLIMEK, NIKKO WEIDEMANN + CARLA BOZULICH** – b.vocals

		Mute	Mute-Elektra
May 92.	(12"/cd-s) *(12/CD MUTE 141)* **THERE CAN ONLY BE ONE. / ('A'mixes) / THE SUN DON'T SHINE**	□	-
Jun 92.	(cd/lp) *(CD+/STUMM 99) <61328>* **FOREVER**	□	□

– Ravenswood / Forever / A part of you / Like Caesar needs a Brutus / Saw you falling / Someone loves you / There can only be one / Now that she's gone / The sun don't shine / Ravenswood (reprise).

— next also with **J.D. FOSTER**

| May 96. | (cd-ep) *(CDMUTE 167)* **DON'T WALK AWAY FROM LOVE / ALL GOD'S CHILDREN / FOREVER / EVERYMAN** | □ | - |
| May 96. | (cd) *(CDSTUMM 114) <60114>* **EVERYMAN** | □ | - |

– Everyman: Where was it begun / Don't walk away from love / Travelin' on / Everyman: Looking for a life I can explain / A white suit in Memphis / Ruby / Everyman: Ozarks waltz / All God's children / Everyman: But there's no place for everyman / Where trouble is easier to find / Goodtime Charlie's got the blues / Western lights / Everyman: Eve / Blue eyes crying in the rain / Everyman: This is what you made me.

CRISIS (see under ⇒ DEATH IN JUNE)

CRISPY AMBULANCE

Formed: Manchester, England ... late 1977 by ALAN HEMPSALL, ROBERT DAVENPORT, KEITH DARBYSHIRE and GARY MADELEY, who basically got together to perform HAWKWIND and MAGAZINE songs. Bass-heavy miserabilists in the classic Mancunian mould, CRISPY AMBULANCE played their first gig at Spurley Hey Youth Centre on the 1st of January, 1978 and progressed to the Band On The Wall and the Cyprus Tavern by the following year. They progressed even further with the release of their debut single, 'FROM THE CRADLE TO THE GRAVE' on their own 'Aural Assault' label in 1980. A chugging dirge with HEMPSALL sounding as if he was singing from the bottom of a particularly deep well (after a particularly heavy dose of mogodon), the track established the group as one of Manchester's most promising acts alongside kindred spirits, JOY DIVISION (HEMPSALL even stood in for doomed frontman, IAN CURTIS, after he'd suffered an epileptic fit). One fan was JOY DIVISION manager, Rob Gretton, who secured the band a contract with 'Factory'. The first release to appear on the label proper was the 10" single, 'UNSIGHTLY AND SERENE', a similarly experimental effort with HEMPSALL adopting a more throaty punk-style growl alongside his trademark doom mongering. Previous to this the 'LIVE ON A HOT AUGUST NIGHT' 12" (featuring the classic 'THE PRESENCE') appeared on Belgium's 'Factory Benelux', a (relatively!) more accessible offering and a primer for the band's one and only album, 'THE PLATEAU PHASE' (1982). With the addition of understated keyboard and the use of even more repetitive rhythms, the effect was akin to a kind of goth psychedelia that bizarrely enough recalled HAWKWIND at their jamming best. With CRISPY AMBULANCE finally crashing soon after the album's release, however, the band were destined for obscure cultdom. They did subsequently reform as RAM RAM KINO, releasing a solitary single on arch weirdo GENESIS P. ORRIDGE's 'Temple' imprint in the mid-80's. All four original CRISPY's reunited for a one-off gig at Manchester's Band On The Wall on the 5th of November, 1999 (I attended the gig and met ALAN). The sheer anticipation led to a great atmosphere, HEMPSALL complete with walking stick still managing to blow the knowledgeable crowd away with classics such as 'DEAF', 'ARE YOU READY' and the effervescent 'THE PRESENCE'. Mancunian bands were going through something of a revival and CRISPY AMBULANCE

CRISPY AMBULANCE (cont)

were no exception. Finally, the comeback was complete when 'Darla' records delivered comeback set, 'SCISSORGUN', in spring 2002. Augmented by old friend GRAHAM MASSEY (808 STATE) on controls, the quartet pulsated all the way through, tracks such as 'LOUPGAROU' and 'STEP UP!' reminiscent but not retro-fied of their past glories. Very underrated at the time, CRISPY AMBULANCE have since attained cult status, although some at the NME made them out to be one of worst 'Factory' groups ever! – listen again lads, eh! • **Songwriters:** Group compositions except UNITED (Throbbing Gristle).

Album rating: THE PLATEAU PHASE (*10) / LIVE ON A HOT AUGUST NIGHT 12" (*9) / FIN (*6) / ACCESSORY AFTER THE FACT (*7) / FROZEN BLOOD collection (*6) / SCISSORGUN (*7)

ALAN HEMPSALL – vocals, synthesizer / **ROBERT DAVENPORT** – guitar / **KEITH DARBYSHIRE** – bass, synthesizer / **GARY MADELEY** – drums

Aural Assault / not iss.

Mar 80. (7") (AAR 001) **FROM THE CRADLE TO THE GRAVE. / FOUR MINUTES FROM THE FRONT LINE**

Factory Benelux / not iss.

Mar 81. (12"ep) (facbn 4) **LIVE ON A HOT AUGUST NIGHT (live)**
– The presence / Concorde square.
Jun 81. (10") Factory; (fac 32) **UNSIGHTLY AND SERENE**
– Deaf / Not what I expected.
Feb 82. (lp) (facbn 12) **THE PLATEAU PHASE**
– Are you ready? / Travel time / The force and the wisdom / The wind season / Death from above / We move through the plateau phase / Bardo plane / Chill / Federation / Simon's escape. (cd-iss. Jun90 & Dec99 & May02 on 'L.T.M.'+=; LTMCD 2315>)
– The presence / Concorde Square / Sexus.
Mar 84. (12") (fbn 18) **SEXUS. / BLACK DETAIL-LIFE IS KNIFE**

— split after above, although they soon evolved into ...

RAM RAM KINO

— re-formed original CRISPYs with added members

Temple / not iss.

Dec 85. (12"ep) (TOPY 006) **ADVANTAGE – TANTRIC ROUTINES 1-4 / (Basket mix) / (Into The Bush mix) / (Special mix) / (other mix)**

CRISPY AMBULANCE

— on the 5th of November, 1999, CRISPY AMBULANCE played a one-off gig at Manchester's Band On The Wall (MC Strong was there!) – see below –

L.T.M. / not iss.

Jun 00. (cd) (LTMCD 2317) **ACCESSORY AFTER THE FACT** (live at the Band On The Wall, 5th November, 1999)
– Are you ready? / Deaf / Come on / Federation / Travel time / The presence / Lucifer rising / Choral / Nightfall ends the ceasefire / The plateau phase / United / Say shake / Open, gates of fire / Sound block.

Darla / Darla

Apr 02. (cd) (<DRL 126>) **SCISSORGUN**
– Step up! / Loupgarou / Metal grey / Re-animator / Heatwave / Parallex / The drop / End game / Even now in Heaven there are angels carrying savage weapons / Sound block.

– compilations etc. –

Nov 83. (ltd-c) C.A. Tapes; (CSBT 5-2) **BLUE AND YELLOW (OF THE YACHT CLUB)** (rare, sessions & live)
– Motorway boys / Suzie's in fragments / This perfect day / No surrender / (interview #1) / Opening theme / The presence / A sense of reason / Concorde Square / The Eastern Bloc / 3 minutes from the frontline / From the cradle to the grave / (interview #2) / Deaf / New violence / Come on / October 31st / Egypt / (interview #3) / Rain without clouds / The presence / Feedback pease / Drug user, drug pusher.
Nov 83. (ltd-c) C.A. Tapes; (CSBT 5-3) **OPEN, GATES OF FIRE** (live late '81 – mid '82)
– United / Chill / I talking – you talking / Federation / Travel time / Say shake (hip wind up) / Cult / Green light – white shirt (Deaf) / Brutal / The plateau phase / Choral / Nightfall ends the ceasefire / The poison.
Aug 85. (lp) Les Tempes Modernes; (LTMV:X) **FIN (live)**
– Rain forest / United / Choral / Green light – white shirt (aka Deaf) / Brutal / The plateau phase / Nightfall ends the ceasefire / Bardo plane / At the sounding of the Klaxon / Chill. (cd-iss. 1989 & Dec99 & Jul02 on 'L.T.M.'+=; LTMCD 2302) – Lucifer rising / Black death / From the cradle to the grave / Four minutes from the frontline.
Dec 00. (cd) L.T.M.; (LTMCD 2327) **FROZEN BLOOD** (rare John Peel & Piccadilly radio sessions, singles, live, etc)
– Not what I expected / Deaf / Come on / Drug user – drug pusher / October 31st / Egypt / A sense of reason / Eastern bloc / Concorde Square / The presence / Headhunters / Frozen blood / Turnbuckle / The gift of danger / Hollow points / The grind / Cult.

CROWD

Formed: Huntington Beach, California, USA ... late 70's by JIM 'TRASH' DECKER, his brother JAY DECKER, JAMES KAA and BARRY CUDA. Untypical of the harsher hardcore scene around them, The CROWD decked themselves out in bright coloured beach attire, their noisy surf punk-pop never really being taken seriously outside their Californian locality. The only product to emerge during their brief lifespan was a solitary 1980 album, 'A WORLD APART', although following their demise a few members became SEXTET.

Album rating: A WORLD APART (*4)

JIM 'TRASH' DECKER – vocals / **JAMES KAA** – guitar / **TRACY** – guitar / **JAY DECKER** – bass / **BARRY CUDA** – drums

— the tracks, 'SUZY IS A SURF ROCKER', 'LIVING IN MADRID', 'TRIX ARE FOR KIDS', 'MODERN MACHINE' and 'NEW CREW' all featured on 'Posh Boy' various artists album, 'Beach Blvd.' <PBS 102> in 1979.

— added **TRACY** – guitar

— the track, 'RIGHT TIME', appeared on 'Posh Boy' various artists collection, 'Rodney On The Rock' <PBS 106> in 1980

— **DENNIS WALSH** – drums, percussion (ex-FLYBOYS) repl. BARRY + TRACY

not iss. / Posh Boy

Jan 81. (lp/c) <PBS/PBC 108> **A WORLD APART**
– As you were / Can't talk / Desmond and Kathy / He / Melody hill / On my own / Pleasure seeker / Right time / Something said / What's in a name.

— split some time in '81, some joining SEXTET

CRUCIFUCKS (see under ⇒ LOUDSPEAKER)

CUD

Formed Leeds, England ... 1987 by CARL PUTTNAM, MIKE DUNPHY, WILLIAM POTTER and STEVE 'CUD' GOODWIN. Apparently initiated after the lads found an abandoned set of drums in a skip, CUD soon built up a local following almost as fanatical as fellow indie stragglers The WEDDING PRESENT, on whose label, 'Reception', they issued their earliest recordings. Something of an acquired taste, CUD's er... distinctive appeal was best witnessed in the live arena, while the 'Imaginary' label released their first two studio sets, 'WHEN IN ROME, KILL ME' (1989) and 'LEGGY MAMBO' (1990). The latter record found PUTTNAM and co. taking their musical abilities slightly more seriously and with a number of minor hit singles under their belt, the band soon found themselves with a major label deal courtesy of 'A&M'. The first fruits of this unlikely partnership emerged in the shape of the 'ASQUARIUS' (1992) album, an acclaimed set which nevertheless failed to catch on with the more straightahead pop punters. Just as well, perhaps, as the band were beginning to show worrying signs of going all sensible on us by the release of 1994's 'SHOWBIZ' set. It seemed with OASIS now taking on all comers, bands were biting the dust left, right and centre and CUD were no exception. Mostly all landed on their feet: before going solo CARL starred in TV commercial and had a bit part in Emmerdale; POTTER, meanwhile pursued a career in comics (art wise); GOODWIN is in LAZERBOY; DUNPHY is managing CUBE and MICK DALE is a member of EMBRACE. • **Songwriters:** Group compositions, except YOU SEXY THING (Hot Chocolate) / LIVING IN THE PAST (Jethro Tull) / PRICE OF LOVE (Everly Brothers) / DOWN DOWN (Status Quo).

Album rating: WHEN IN ROME, KILL ME (*5) / ELVIS BELT compilation (*7) / LEGGY MAMBO (*7) / ASQUARIUS (*6) / SHOWBIZ (*5)

CARL PUTTNAM (b.1967, Ilford, Essex) – vocals / **MIKE DUNPHY** (b.1967, Northumberland, England) – guitar, keyboards / **WILLIAM POTTER** (b.1968, Derby, England) – bass / **STEVE GOODWIN** (b.1967, Croydon, Surrey, England) – drums

Reception / not iss.

Oct 87. (12"ep) (REC 007) **YOU'RE THE BOSS / MIND THE GAP. / VAN VAN VAN / YOU'RE THE BOSS (Out To Lunch mix)**

Ediesta / not iss.

Apr 88. (12"ep) (CALC 049) **UNDER MY HAT. / PUNISHMENT-REWARD RELATIONSHIP / ART!**

Dug-Nightime / not iss.

Sep 88. (12"ep) (DUGNI 001T) **SLACK TIME. / I'VE HAD IT WITH BLONDES / MAKE NO BONES**

Imaginary / not iss.

Apr 89. (7") (MIRAGE 007) **LOLA. / THE DAY CRIME PAID**
Jun 89. (lp)(cd) (ILLUSION 5)(ILLCD 500) **WHEN IN ROME, KILL ME**
– When in Rome, kill me: (i) When in Rome, kill me (ii) Only a prawn in Whitby (iii) Bibi couldn't see (iv) Strange kind of love (v) Push and shove (vi) The day crime paid (vii) When in Rome, kill me again / I've had it with blondes / Van van van / Vocally speaking / Wobbly jelly / Alison springs / Epicurean's answer.
Sep 89. (12"ep) (MIRAGE 010) **ONLY A PRAWN IN WHITBY (other version) / LIVING IN THE PAST / EVERYBODY WORKS SO HARD**
May 90. (7"one-sided-ltd.) (MIRAGE 018) **HEYWIRE**
(12"+=/cd-s+=) (MIRAGE 018 T/CD) – Purple love baloon / Possession.
Sep 90. (7") (MIRAGE 021S) **ROBINSON CRUSOE. / PLANTATION ISLAND** — 86
(cd-s+=) (MIRACD 021) – L.O.P.H.E. / 'A'-Friday mix).
Oct 90. (cd/c/lp) (ILLCD/ILLC/ILLUSION 021) **LEGGY MAMBO**
– Now / Heart / Hey, boots / Love in a hollow tree / Love mandarin / Not exactly D L E R C / Robinson Crusoe / Eau water / Carl's 115th coach trip nightmare / Magic / Syrup and sour grapes / Brain on a slow train.
Mar 91. (7") (MIRAGE 027) **MAGIC (Farsley mix). / MAGIC (Stockport mix)** — 80
(12"+=/cd-s+=) (MIRAGE 027T/MIRACD 027) – Marjorie / Beyond hair.

A&M / A&M

Oct 91. (d7"ep/12"ep/cd-ep) (AM B/X/CD 829) **OH NO WON'T DO / ARIEL. / PROCESSION / PRICE OF LOVE** — 49
Nov 91. (cd-ep) <5380> **"THE CUD BAND" EP**
– Magic / Robinson Crusoe / Now / Hey, Boots / Magic.
Mar 92. (7") (AM 857) **THROUGH THE ROOF. / UNDOUBTABLY THOMAS** — 44
(12"+=/cd-s+=) (AM X/CD 857) – Prime cut.
May 92. (7"/7"pic-d) (AM/+P 871) **RICH AND STRANGE. / LOVE MANDARIN (acoustic)** — 24
(12"/cd-s) (AM X/CD 871) – ('A'side) / Do it again / A song called that.
Jun 92. (cd/c/lp) (395 390-2/-4/-1) **ASQUARIUS** — 30
– Rich and strange / Easy / Sometimes rightly sometimes wrongly / Spanish love story / Magic / Alex / Beyond hair / Pink flamingo / Possession / Through the roof / Soul food / Once again / No smoking. (re-iss. cd May95; same)

Jul 92.	(7"pic-d/c-s) (AM 0024/+C) **PURPLE LOVE BALLOON. / SPANISH LOVE SONG (acoustic)**	27	-
	(12"pic-d/cd-s) (AM 0024 T/CD) – ('A'side) / ('A'-Killer rabbit mix-omatosis) / ('A'-US mix) / Remember what it is that your love.		
Oct 92.	(7"/c-s) (AM 0081/+C) **ONCE AGAIN. / DAY BY DAY**	45	-
	(12"+=/cd-s+=) (AM 0081 T/CD) – Eau water (acoustic) / Soul food (acoustic).		
Jan 94.	(7"/c-s) (580 517-7/-4) **NEUROTICA. / MIDNIGHT RIDE**	37	-
	(cd-s) (580 517-2) – ('A'side) / Juicy eurela / I.W.G.S. / Brand name skin.		
	(12"++=) (580 517-1) – Neurotica (remix).		
Mar 94.	(7"/c-s) (580 546-7/-4) **STICKS AND STONES. / SKI BUM**	68	-
	(12"+=) (580 547-1) – My need to hurry.		
	(cd-s) (580 547-2) – ('A'side) / Down the plug / My keyhole don't keep secrets anymore.		
Apr 94.	(cd/c/lp) (540 211-2/-4/-1) **SHOWBIZ**	46	-
	– Somebody snatched my action / E.S.P. / Waving and drowning / Sticks and stones / Mystery deepens / Slip away / One giant love / I reek of chic / Not necessarily evil / You lead me / Tourniquet / Neurotica. (re-is.cd May95)		
Aug 94.	(c-s/cd-s) (580 729-4/-2) **ONE GIANT LOVE / LOOK ON UP AT THE BOTTOM / FIND IT**	52	-
	(12") (580 729-1) – ('A'side) / Robinson Crusoe (live) / Strange kind of love (live) / Purple love balloon (live).		
	(cd-s) (580 731-2) – ('A'live) / Slip away (live) / Magic (live) / Neurotica (live).		

— **MICHAEL (MICK) DALE** – bass; repl. POTTER who pursued a career in comics

— split early in 1996; GOODWIN joined LAZERBOY, PUTTNAM formed solo project CARL (signed to 'Polydor') with new EMBRACE member DALE and DUNPHY now manages CUBE

– compilations, others, etc. –

Jan 88.	(12"ep) Strange Fruit; (SFPS 045) **THE PEEL SESSIONS** (16.6.87) – Mind the gap / You're the boss / Don't bank on it / You sexy thing.		-
Jul 90.	(cd/c/lp) Imaginary; (ILLCD/ILLC/ILLUSION 013) **ELVIS BELT** (1989-1991)		-

CULTURE SHOCK (see under ⇒ SUBHUMANS)

CUPOL (see under ⇒ WIRE; 70's section)

CURRENT 93

Formed: London, England ... 1983 initially as an offshoot group by 23 SKIDOO members, DAVID TIBET and FRITZ HAAMAN, along with JOHN BALANCE (ex-PSYCHIC TV and a member of COIL) and former members of CRISIS (an outfit who subsequently evolved into DEATH IN JUNE). Obscure but nevertheless influential early players in the UK experimental industrial scene, CURRENT 93 set out combining medieval style choral chants with unsettling samples and hypnotic electronic percussion on albums such as 'WE SEE THE DECAY OF THE ANGEL THE MARCH' (1985) and 'IN MENSTRUAL NIGHT' (1986). Recording alternately for the tiny 'Laylah' and 'Maldoror' labels at a prolific rate throughout the latter half of the 80's, TIBET worked with whoever was available at the time (STEVEN STAPLETON of NURSE WITH WOUND, HILMAR ORN HILMARSON of PSYCHIC TV and ROSE McDOWELL, ex-STRAWBERRY SWITCHBLADE(!), among others), gradually evolving a stark folky sound no less spookier than his earliest work. Come the turn of the decade, CURRENT 93 (and all who sailed with her) began a new chapter in their career via the newly established 'Durtro' imprint, releasing new vinyl-only material as well as re-issuing their rare and extremely collectable 80's work on CD.

Album rating: WE SEE THE DECAY OF THE ANGEL THE MARCH (*4) / IN MENSTRUAL NIGHT (*4) / DOGS BLOOD RISING (*4) / IMPERIUM (*4) / NIGHTMARE CULTURE with Sickness Of Snake (*4) / CHRIST AND THE PALE QUEEN (*4) / CURRENT 93 PRESENT C.R. LAMA – TANTRIC NYING MA CHANT OF TIBET (*3) / EARTH COVERS EARTH mini (*3) / DAWN (*4) / SWASTIKAS FOR NOBODY (*4) / LIVE AT BAR MALDORER with Nurse With Wound (*4) / ISLAND (*3) / THUNDER PERFECT MIND (*3) / OF RUINE, OR SOME BLAZING STARRE (*3) / ALL THE PRETTY LITTLE HORSES (*3) / THE CERNE BOX SET with others (*4)

DAVID TIBET – vocals (ex-23 SKIDOO) / **FRITZ HAAMAN** – drums, percussion (of 23 SKIDOO) / **JOHN BALANCE** – instruments (of COIL, ex-THROBBING GRISTLE, ex-PSYCHIC TV)

		Benelux	not iss.
Feb 85.	(lp) **WE SEE THE DECAY OF THE ANGEL THE MARCH**	-	- Belgian

		United Dairies	not iss.
May 86.	(pic-lp) (UDO 22M) **IN MENSTRUAL NIGHT** – Sucking up souls / To feed the moon / etc. (re-iss. lp Mar88; UD 022) (cd-iss. Oct94 on 'Durtro'+=; 020CD) – Killykillkilly (a fire sermon).		-

		Laylah	not iss.
Apr 86.	(12") (LAY 001) **LASHTAL**		-
Apr 86.	(12"ep) (LAY 004) **NATURE UNVEILED** (re-iss. 1990 on 'Maldorer'; MAL 123)		-
Apr 86.	(lp) (LAY 008) **DOGS BLOOD RISING** (cd-iss. Oct88; LAY 008CD) (cd re-iss. Aug95 on 'Durtro'+=; 027CD) – Dogs blood rising.		-
Apr 88.	(d-lp) (LAY 014) **NIGHTMARE CULTURE** (w/ SICKNESS OF SNAKE) – Benediction (a fire sermon) / etc.		-
Jul 88.	(12") (LAY 018) **HAPPY BIRTHDAY PIGFACE CHRISTUS**		-
Feb 89.	(lp/cd) (LAY 020/+C) **SWASTIKAS FOR NOBODY** – Benediction / Blessing / North / Black Sun bloody Moon / Oh coal blacksmith / Panzer rune / Black flowers please / The final church / The summer of love / The nobody / Beausoleil / Scarlet woman / The stair song / Angel / Since yesterday / Valediction / Malediction.		-

		Maldorer	not iss.
Aug 87.	(lp) (MAL 777) **IMPERIUM**		-
Oct 87.	(12") (MAL 108) **CROWLEYMASS. / CHRISTMASSACRE / CROWLEYMASS (mix mix mix)**		-
Mar 88.	(12") (MAL 088) **RED FACE OF GOD. / THE BREATH AND THE PAIN OF GOD**		-
Mar 88.	(lp) (MAL 666) **CHRIST AND THE PALE QUEEN**		-
Oct 88.	(lp) (MAL 111) **CURRENT 93 PRESENT C.R. LAMA – TANTRIC NYING MA CHANT OF TIBET**		-
1989.	(lp) (MAL 093) **DAWN**		-

		Yangki	not iss.
Jul 88.	(7") (002) **FAITHS FAVOURITES (with NURSE WITH WOUND). / BALLAD OF THE PALE GIRL**		-

		United Dairies	not iss.
Oct 88.	(m-lp) (UD 029) **EARTH COVERS EARTH**		-

— early '89, they were credited on lp '93 DEAD SUN WHEELS' with DEATH IN JUNE.

		Harbinger	not iss.
1990.	(7") (001) **NO HIDING FROM THE BLACKBIRD. / (NURSE WITH WOUND: Burial of the stoned sardine)**		-

		Shock	not iss.
1990.	(7") (SX 003) **SHE IS DEAD AND ALL FALL DOWN. / GOD HAS THREE FACES AND WOOD HAS NO NAME**		-

— In 1990, they shared an lp (some coloured) '1888' with DEATH IN JUNE

— TIBET subsequently added **MICHAEL CASHMORE** – guitar

		United Durtro	not iss.
Dec 89.	(lp) (DURTRO 001) **LIVE AT BAR MALDORER** (first rel.1985 with NURSE WITH WOUND)		-
Dec 90.	(12") (DURTRO 004) **LOONEY RUNES**		-
1992.	(lp) (DURTRO 006) **ISLAND**		-
1992.	(d-lp) (DURTRO 011) **THUNDER PERFECT MIND**		-
1994.	(lp-blue) (DURTRO 018) **OF RUINE, OR SOME BLAZING STARRE**		-
1994.	(12"red) (DURTRO 019) **LUCIFER OVER LONDON**		-
1995.	(12",cd-s) (DURTRO 025) **TAMLIN. / HOW THE GREAT SATANIC GLORY FADED**		-
Feb 96.	(lp-clear) (DURTRO 026) **ALL THE PRETTY LITTLE HORSES**		-
1997.	(12"clear) (DURTRO 028) **WHERE THE LONG SHADOWS FALL**		-
Oct 96.	(cd) (DURTRO 031) **STARRES MARCHING SADLY HOME**		-

– others, compilations, etc

on 'Cerne' unless mentioned otherwise

1990.	(7"gig freebie) (004) **THIS AIN'T THE SUMMER OF LOVE (live with SOL INVICTUS)**		-
1990.	(3xlp-box) (1-2-3) **THE CERNE BOX SET** – HORSE lp / plus others by NURSE WITH WOUND + SOL INVICTUS)		-

CYNICS

Formed: Pittsburgh, Pennsylvania, USA ... early 1984 by MARK KERESMAN, GREGG KOSTELICH, BILL VON HAGEN and PAM. KOSTELICH set up his own 'Get Hip' label for the release of the band's debut single, '69', follow-up, 'PAINTED MY HEART', issued a year later. 1985 also saw the arrival of vocalist MICHAEL KASTELIC, a replacement for the departing KERESMAN who would become a stalwart throughout the band's changing fortunes and ever evolving personnel situation. Sticksman, TOM HAHN, was also in place for 1986's debut album, 'BLUE TRAIN STATION', an impressive set that drew on the garage tradition of the late 60's yet flitted between different genres with confident ease. 1988's 'TWELVE FLIGHTS UP', meanwhile, was the first and only CYNICS product to gain a UK issue (through the 'Resonance' label) while MIKE MICHALSKI had replaced PAM by the release of 1989's 'ROCK'N'ROLL. A one-off 7" on 'Sympathy For The Record Industry' found the band entering the 90's in style and paying homage to their heroes with covers of The Heartbreakers' 'BORN TO LOSE' and T. Rex's 'BUICK MACKANE'. The 'Get Hip' label was also reactivated for a string of albums in the early 90's, the most recent being 1994's 'GET OUR WAY'. A seven-year itch was all but scratched away with the release of a fresh fuzzed-out set, 'LIVING IS THE BEST REVENGE' (2002); they were to tour Spain early the following year. • **Covered:** GOIN' AWAY (Boss Tweeds) / GIRL, YOU'RE ON MY MIND (Mystic Eyes) / I GOT YOU BABE (Sonny & Cher). • **Note:** Not to be confused with an Alaskan band who released an EP in 1980, 'Beat The Cynics'; two out of the four tracks, 'Rock Apocalypse' & 'Fools In Hell', issued in the UK on 'Stickfoot' 1984.

Album rating: BLUE TRAIN STATION (*5) / TWELVE FLIGHTS UP (*6) / ROCK'N'ROLL (*4) / GET OUR WAY (*5) / LEARN TO LOSE (*5) / LIVING IS THE BEST REVENGE (*6)

MARK KERESMAN – vocals / **GREGG KOSTELICH** – guitar (ex-JETSONS, ex-PROTOTYPE) / **STEVE MAGEE** – bass / **BILL VON HAGEN** – drums

— **MICHAEL KASTELIC** – vocals (ex-WAKE – US, ex-BOAT PEOPLE, ex-DUB SEX, ex-24 MINUTES) repl. KERESMAN

		not iss.	Dionysus
1984.	(7") **PAINTED MY HEART. / SWEET YOUNG THING**	-	

CYNICS (cont)

Date	Format	Title
1985.	(7")	**NO PLACE TO HIDE. / HARD TIMES** <re-iss. 1989 on 'Get Hip'; GH 99> — not iss. / Get Hip
Jul 84.	(7")	**69. / FRIDAY NIGHT** — f/club

—— **TOM HOHN** – drums (ex-WAKE – US, ex-PROTOTYPE) repl. HAGEN

1986. (lp) <GH 1000> **BLUE TRAIN STATION**
 – Blue train station / On the run / Waste of time / No friend of mine / No way / Love me then go away / Hold me right / Soul searching / Why you left me / I can't get away from you / I want love / Road block. <cd-iss. 1994 as 'BLUE TRAIN SESSIONS' on 'Skyclad'+=; 2> – Get away girl / Lying all the time / Blues in D / Dancing on the wall / I got nightmares.

1986. (7") <GH 101> **NO WAY. / DANCING ON THE WALL** — Resonance / Get Hip

Apr 88. (lp) (R 3388-13) <GH 1010> **TWELVE FLIGHTS UP**
 – Creepin' / Yeah! / I know / Took her hand / I never loved / Erica / A basket of flowers / Abba / Nothin' / Useless / Gloria's dream / Blues in D *[lp-only]*. <cd-iss. 1994 as 'SIXTEEN FLIGHTS UP' on 'Skyclad'+=; 5> – I'm in Pittsburgh and it's raining (live) / Smoke rings (live) / Little girl (live) / Cat and mouse (live) / But now I find (live).

Jun 88. (7") <GH 106> **I'M IN PITTSBURGH AND IT'S RAINING. / (YOU CAN'T BLOW) SMOKE RINGS**

—— **MIKE MICHALSKI** – bass (ex-HALF LIFE, ex-HERETICS) repl. MAGEE

Nov 89. (7"red) <GH 113> **GET MY WAY. / GOIN' AWAY**

Jan 90. (lp) <GH 1020> **ROCK'N'ROLL**
 – Baby, what's wrong / Way it's gonna be / Girl, you're on my mind / Get my way / Tears are coming / Business as usual / Cry, cry, cry / You got the love / Close to me / Different worlds / Now I'm alone / What you get / Last time around / The room. <cd-iss. 1994 on 'Skyclad'+=; 25>

1990. (7"colrd) <GH 129> **I DON'T NEED YOU. / GIRL, YOU'RE ON MY MIND**

1991. (m-lp) <GH 1002> **VPRO RADIO BROADCAST (live in the Netherlands)**
 – (interview) / Took her hand / Close to me / On the run / Baby what's wrong? / No way / Love me then go away. <cd-iss. 1994 on 'Skyclad'; >

1993. (7") <GH 141> **RIGHT HERE WITH YOU. / LEARN TO LOSE**

1993. (cd) <GH 1008CD> **LEARN TO LOSE**
 – Never again / When you'd go / How could I / Right here with you / Someone like me / You must be a witch / Learn to lose / Haunted / I want it all / One day you'll come / Pressure / I want you.

1993. (7") <GH 150> **I GOT YOU BABE. / Frampton Brothers: BANG BANG**

1993. (7") <GH 162> **I LIVE ALONE. / HAND IN HAND**

1993. (7") **I'LL WAIT. / 13 O'CLOCK (instrumental)**
 (above issued on 'Munster')

1994. (colrd-lp/cd) <GH 1030CD> **GET OUR WAY**
 – No reason / Private suicide / Hand in hand / I'll wait / Lose your mind / That's how I feel / 13 o'clock daylight savings time / Don't shoot me down / And she said yeah / I live alone / Dave V's car / Love me now / All these streets / Time alone.

1994. (7") <GH 170> **PRIVATE SUICIDE. / ALL THESE STREETS** — not iss. / Mind Cure

1994. (7") **DIRTY TRICK. / LOSE YOUR MIND**

—— (re-formed 2000) **SMITH HUTCHINGS** – bass (ex-PLEASURE HEADS) repl. MIKE

Nov 02. (lp/cd) <GH 1050/+CD> **LIVING IS THE BEST REVENGE**
 – Turn me loose / Making deals / Marianne / The tone / Ballad of J.C. Holmes / She lives (in a time of her own) / Revenge / I got time / Let me know / You've never had it better / Last day / Shine.

– compilations, others, etc. –

Date	Format	Title	Label
1991.	(lp) Impossible; <017>	**STRANDED IN MADRID (live)**	Spain
1992.	(cd) 1+2; <015>	**CYNICISM (best of)**	Japan
1993.	(7") Sympathy For The Record Industry; <SFTRI 099>	**BUICK MACKANE. / BORN TO LOSE**	
1994.	(cd) Get Hip; <GH 1014CD>	**NO SIESTA TONITE (live in Madrid, 1990)**	

 – Intro / Baby what's wrong? / Girl you're on my mind / You got the love / Close to me / Now I'm alone / Yeah! / I never loved her / Angel of the morning / No way / Love me then go away / Blue train station / I want love / Shot down / Erica / Took her hand.

1990's. (7") Get Hip; **WAY IT'S GONNA BE. / ROADRUNNER (live)**

y CYRFF

Formed: Llanrwst, Wales... 1984 by MARK ROBERTS, BARRY CAWLEY, PAUL JONES and DYLAN HUGHES. A solid indie outfit who sang in Welsh (well before SUPER FURRY ANIMALS), Y CYRFF (aka THE BODY) delivered a series of singles including 'PETHAU ACHLYSUROL / HWYL FAWR HEULWEN', 'PUM MUNUD', 'TRWY'R CYMYLAU', 'Y TESTAMENT NEWYDD', 'YR ATGOFODI'. After the defection of DYLAN to ANHREFN and the recruitment of MARK KENDALL, Y CYRFF delivered a couple of full-length sets between 1991 and 1992. When songwriters ROBERTS and JONES formed CATATONIA (taking CAWLEY as a guitar technician), the John Peel fave split; the latter was tragically killed in a car crash in July 2000.

Album rating: LLAWENYDD HEB DDIWEDD (*6) / MAE DDOE YN DDOE compilation (*6)

MARK ROBERTS (b. 3 Nov'69, Colwyn Bay) – vocals, guitar / **BARRY CAWLEY** – guitar / **PAUL JONES** (b. 5 Apr'60, Colwyn Bay) – bass / **DYLAN HUGHES** – drums

—— see above biography for early Welsh singles

 Ankst / not iss.

1990. (7") (ANKST 09) **HWYL FAWR HEULWEN. /**
1990. (c-s) (ANKST 12) **AWDL O ANOBAITH**

—— **MARK KENDALL** – drums; repl. DYLAN who joined ANHREFN

May 91. (lp/c) (ANKST 16) **LLAWENYDD HEB DDIWEDD**
Oct 92. (cd/c) (ANK CD/ST 30) **MAE DDOE YN DDOE** (compilation)
Oct 92. (c-s) (ANST 31) **DAMWAIN MEWN FFATRI CYLLELL A FFYRC**

—— split after above

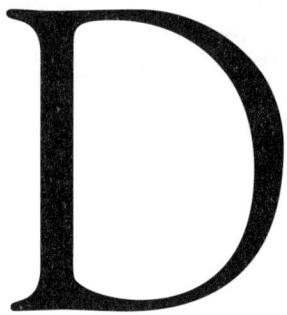

D.A.F.

Formed: Dusseldorf, Germany... 1979 as DEUTSCHE AMERIKANISCHE FREUNDSCHAFT by ROBERT GORL, who took the name from local posters depicting rosy German-US relations. Along with CHRISLO HAAS, MICHAEL KEHMER and WOLFGANG SPELMANS, he recorded a debut album, 'PRODUKT' (1979), for the domestic market before signing to DANIEL MILLER's newly formed 'Mute' label. Following the replacement of KEHMER with GABI DELGADO-(LOPEZ), recording sessions resulted in 1980's 'DIE KLEINEN UND DIE BOSEN' ('The Small And The Evil'), the record's teutonic experimentation following in the footsteps of sonic terrorists, SUICIDE, while also tracing the Kraut-rock lineage of forebears such as CAN and KRAFTWERK. Enjoying support from both John Peel and the underground club scene, DAF (now a duo of GORL and DELGADO) subsequently signed to 'Virgin', releasing a further three groundbreaking albums, 'ALLES IST GUT' (1981), 'GOLD UND LIEBE' (1981) and 'FUR IMMER' (1982). Yet DELGADO-LOPEZ's insistence on singing in German undoubtedly restricted their appeal, labelmates DEPECHE MODE going on to massive success while DAF's pioneering electro sounds and sexual claustrophobia were more influential on up and coming acts like FRONT 242 and NITZER EBB. Splitting in late '82, DELGADO-LOPEZ and GORL both recorded solo sets, 'MISTRESS' (1983) and 'NIGHT FULL OF TENSION' (1984) respectively. A brief mid-80's reformation led to a German-only album, '1st STEP TO HEAVEN' (1986), via 'Arista', while GORL re-emerged almost a decade later on German techno label, 'Disko B', releasing a couple of 12" singles and an album, 'THERAPIE' (1994). • **Trivia:** In 1981, DAF guested on the EURYTHMICS debut album, 'In The Garden'. ANNIE LENNOX returned the favour by contributing backing vox to GORL's 'DARLING DON'T LEAVE ME' single.

Album rating: EIN PRODUKT DER DEUTSCH AMERIKANISCHE FREUNDSCHAFT (*3) / DIE KLEINEN UND DIE BOSEN (*4) / ALLES IST GUT (*6) / GOLD UND LIEBE (*5) / FUR IMMER (*5) / D.A.F. compilation (*7) / 1st STEP TO HEAVEN (*5) / Robert Gorl: NIGHT FULL OF TENSION (*5) / PSYCHO THERAPIE (*4) / WATCH THE GREAT COPYCAT (*4) / SEXDROPS (*3) / FULL METAL PRALINES (*4) / Gabi Delgado: MISTRESS (*5)

DEUTSCHE AMERIKANISCHE FREUNDSCHAFT

ROBERT GORL – synthesizers, drums / **CHRISLO HAAS** – synthesizers, saxophone, bass / **WOLFGANG SPELMANS** – guitar / **MICHAEL KEHMER** – bass

Warning   not iss.

Nov 79. (lp) *(WR 001)* **EIN PRODUKT DER DEUTSCH AMERIKANISCHE FREUNDSCHAFT** – – German
– (22 untitled tracks). *(cd-iss. Jan00 on 'Grey Area'; DAF 0CD) <US cd-iss. Feb00 on 'Mute-Elektra'; 69117>*

—— **GABI DELGADO-**(LOPEZ) – vocals (ex-MITTAGSPAUSE); repl. KEHMER

Mute   not iss.

Mar 80. (7") *(MUTE 005)* **KEBAB TRAUME. / GEWALT (VIOLENCE)**
Aug 80. (lp) *(STUMM 1)* **DIE KLEINEN UND DIE BOSEN**
– Osten wahrt am langsten / Essen dann schlafen / Co co pino / Kinderfunk / Nachtarbeit / Ich gebe dir ein stuck von mir / Die panne / Gewalt / Gib's mir / Auf wiedersehen / Das ist liebe / Was ist eine Weele / Anzufassen und anzufassen / Volkstanz / Die lustigen stiefel / Die kleinen und die bosen / Ich bin die fesche Lola / El basilon / Y la gracia. *<cd-iss. Mar84; OVED 59> (cd-iss. Nov92 & Oct98; CDSTUMM 1) <US cd re-iss. 1998; 69082>*
Oct 80. (7") *(MUTE 011)* **DER RAUBER UND DER PRINZ. / TANZ MIT MIR**

—— trimmed to a duo of **DELGADO + GORL** when CHRISLO HAAS left, – later joined CRIME & THE CITY SOLUTION (SPELMANS also departed)

Virgin   not iss.

Mar 81. (lp) *(V 2202)* **ALLES IST GUT**
– Ich und die Wirklichkeit (Me and reality) / Als wars das letzte mal (As if it were the last time) / Verlier nicht den Kopf (Don't loose your head) / Alle gegen all (Everybody fights everybody) / Alles ist gut (Everything is good) / Sato-sato / Der Mussolini (The Mussolini) / Rote Lippen (Red lips) / Mein Herz macht bum (My heart goes boom) / Der rauber und der Prinz (The robber and the Prince). *(re-iss. Mar84; OVED 59) 1987; CDV 2202) (cd re-iss. Oct98 on 'Grey Area'; DAFCD 001) <US cd-iss. Oct98 on 'Mute-Elektra'; 69083>*
May 81. (12") *(VS 418-12)* **DER MUSSOLINI. / DER RAUBER UND DER PRINZ**
Nov 81. (12") *(VS 448-12)* **GOLDENES SPIELZEUG. / EL QUE**
Nov 81. (lp) *(V 2218)* **GOLD UND LIEBE**
– Liebe auf den ersten blick (Love at first sight) / El Que / Sex unter wasser (Sex under water) / Was ziehst du an heute nacht (What are you ?) / Goldenes spielzeug (Golden toy) / I want (I want) / Muskel (Muscle) / Absolute korperkontrolle (Absolute body control) / Verschwende deine Jugend (Waste your time) / Greif nach den Sternen (Reach for the stars). *(re-iss. Aug88; OVED 81) (cd-iss. Apr88 +=; CDV 2218) – Ich will / Sex unter wasser. (cd re-iss. Oct98 on 'Grey Area'; DAFCD 002) <US cd-iss. Oct98 on 'Mute-Elektra'; 69084>*
Feb 82. (12") *(VS 481-12)* **SEX UNTER WASSER. / KNOCHEN AUF KNOCHEN**
Sep 82. (12") **VERLIEB DICH IN MICH. / EIN BISSCHEN KRIEG**
Oct 82. (lp) *(V 2239)* **FUR IMMER**
– Im dschungel der liebe (In the jungle of love) / Ein bisschen krieg (A little bit of war) / Die gotter sind weiss (The gods are white) / Verlieb dich in mich (Fall in love with you) / Geheimnis (Secret) / Kebab traume (Kebab dreams) / Prinzessin (Princess) / Die lippe (The lip) / Verehrt euren haarschnitt (Honour your haircut) / Wer schon sein will mussleiden (If you want to be beautiful you must....). *(re-iss. Aug88 lp/c; OVED/+C 82) (cd-iss. Apr88; CDV 2239) (cd re-iss. Oct98 on 'Grey Area'; DAFCD 003) <US cd-iss. Oct98 on 'Mute-Elektra'; 69085>*

—— split late '82

GABI DELGADO

went solo with **RAOUL WALTON, STEPHAN WITTNER + EDWARD LOPEZ**

Mar 83. (7"/12") *(VS 579/+12)* **HISTORY OF A KISS. / SEX GODDESS**
Mar 83. (lp) *(V 2266)* **MISTRESS**
– Sex goddess / History of a kiss / Amor / Young lions / Victims / Mistress.. *(re-iss. Aug88; OVED 93)*
Jul 83. (12") *(VS 608-12)* **AMOR. / SEX AND SOUL**

ROBERT GORL

Mute   Elektra

Mar 83. (7") *(7MUTE 27)* **MIT DIR (WITH YOU). / BERUHRT VERFUHT**
Feb 84. (7") *(7MUTE 31)* **DARLING DON'T LEAVE ME. / IST WIEDER DA**
(12"+=) *(12MUTE 31)* – ('A'extended).
Mar 84. (lp/c) *(STUMM/CSTUMM 16)* **NIGHT FULL OF TENSION**
– Playtime / I love me / Charlie Cat / Gewinnen wir die beste der Frauen / Queen King / Love in mind / Darling don't leave me / Wind in hair. *(c+=)* – Mit dir (extended) / Beruhrt verfuhrt (remix) / Darling don't leave me (extended) / Ist wieder da / Eckhardt's party. *(cd-iss. Jun84; CDSTUMM 16) <US cd-iss. Oct98 on 'Mute-Elektra'; 60367>*

D.A.F.

—— **DELGADO + GORL** re-formed the duo

Illuminated   not iss.

Aug 85. (12") *(ILL 62-12)* **ABSOLUTE BODY CONTROL. / 1ST TRIP TO HEAVEN**
Nov 85. (7"/12") *(LEV/12LEV 65)* **BROTHERS (Robert's mix). / BROTHERS (Gabi's mix)**

Ariola   not iss.

Jan 86. (lp/c/cd) *(207/407/257 435)* **1ST STEP TO HEAVEN** – – German
– Voulez vous coucher avec moi (part 1) / Pure joy / Blond hair, dark brown hair / Sex up / Absolute body control / Voulez vous coucher avec moi (part 2) / Crazy crazy / Brothers (opium mix) / 1st step to Heaven (mix).

—— split again, although this was for the final time

– compilations etc. –

May 84. (c) *Music For Midgets; (MFM 40)* **LIVE IN BERLIN 1980** (live)
Jun 88. (cd/c/lp) *Virgin; (CD/TC+/V 2533)* **D.A.F. – THE BEST OF...**
– Verschwende deine jugend / Der Mussolini (remix) / Mein herz macht bum / El que / Mein ich und die wirklichkeit / Die gotter sind weiss / Der rauber und der prinz / Liebe auf der ersten blick (remix) / Im dschungel der liebe / Prinzessin / Greif nach den sternen / Kebab traume / Die lippe / Als wars das letzte mal.
Nov 98. (12"ep) *Grey Area; (12DAF 123)* **DER MUSSOLINI. / ALLE GEGEN ALLE. / VERSCHWENDE DEINE JUGEND / KEBAB TRAUME / CO CO PINO**

ROBERT GORL

not iss.   Hangman

1991. (cd-s) *<HGN 70-2>* **ELECTRIC MARILYN (mixes; radio / the B mix / repeat the beat Euromix / Schnapping)**

Disko B   Disko B

May 93. (12") *(15538)* **PSYCHO SAFE. /**
Aug 94. (2x12") *(EFA 12283-1)* **PSYCHO THERAPIE**
– Derja come / Eric's playing / Psychoring / Do we do we / M M / Psychofrau. *<US-iss.Jan98; 23>*
Feb 95. (12") *(EFA 122736)* **HAPPY GATHERING. /**
Mar 96. (cd/lp; ROBERT GORL & PETE NAMLOOK) *(PK 08109/08110)* **ELEKTRO**
(above issued on 'Fax' records)
May 96. (12") *(EFA12 2896)* **YIP YAP. /**
Sep 96. (cd/lp) *(EFA 12292-2/-6)* **WATCH THE GREAT COPYCAT**
– Insekter / Ali Baba / Wabe / Rund / Damonika / Rubber ritual / Yip yep / Have a bath / Bumba (a buddha) / Loop it baby 2 / Echt lollyzopf / End of a trip. *<US-iss.Jan98; 52>*
Jul 98. (2x12"/cd; as R.GORL) *(<EFAMS 294 68>)* **SEXDROPS**
– Dominatrix supreme / Pet teaser / Scoops / Deep intruder / Do it – Let's boogee / Triple dripping / Blue sex drops / Spanish bull / Call a loony.
Aug 98. (12"; as ROBERT GORL & KARL O'CONNOR) *(000)* **THE RIGHT SIDE OF REASON** – – German
(above issued on 'DN Test Series')
Jan 00. (cd/d-lp) *(EFA 29490-2/-6)* **FINAL METAL PRALINES**

Blag DAHLIA (see under ⇒ DWARVES)

DAINTEES (see under ⇒ STEPHENSON, Martin)

DALEK I LOVE YOU

Formed: Liverpool, England . . . late 1977 out of punk act, RADIO BLANK, by ALAN GILL and DAVID BALFE. Adding DAVE HUGHES and CHRIS 'TEEPEE' SHAW (MARTIN COOPER also p/t sax), the band signed to 'Vertigo' and released a debut single, 'FREEDOM FIGHTERS', in Spring '79. A well received slice of drum-machine backed experimental proto-electro pop, the track was followed by 'THE WORLD' later that year. The turn of the decade found the band setting up their own label, 'Back Door', initiating proceedings with an eponymous single in Spring 1980. The latter was backed with what was arguably the scousers' finest three minutes, 'EIGHT TRACK', an ice cool serving of indie electronica which was also one of the highlights on debut album, 'KUM'PAS (COMPASS)' (1980). A Top 60 success, the record cemented the band's reputation as more musically adventurous cousins to local lads, The TEARDROP EXPLODES. Subsequently reduced to what was basically ALAN GILL's one-man operation (BALFE having joined BIG IN JAPAN), only one further single, 'HEARTBEAT', was released in early '81 before GILL joined the aforementioned TEARDROP EXPLODES for a year. Furnished with a deal courtesy of 'Korova', he re-emerged under the DALEK I LOVE YOU banner in summer '82 with a new single, 'HOLIDAY IN DISNEYLAND'. Another extended gap followed, however, prior to the release of the singles, 'AMBITION', 'HORRORSCOPE' and a belated follow-up album, 'DALEK I LOVE YOU' (1983). Despite the ensuing critical acclaim, commercial success achieved by peers such as OMD seemed as far away as ever and GILL concentrated his efforts on writing the soundtrack to cult mid-80's movie, 'Letter To Brezhnev'. GILL also formed the small 'Bopadub' label, home to a final DALEK I LOVE YOU (cassette-only) album, 'NAIVE' (1985).

Album rating: KUM'PAS (*6) / DALEK I LOVE YOU (*5)

ALAN GILL – vocals, guitar, synthesizer / **DAVID BALFE** – bass, vocals, synthesizer (left before any releases) / **DAVE HUGHES** – keyboards, synthesizer (ex-SECRETS) / **CHRIS 'TEEPEE' SHAW** – synthesizer, bass / guest **MARTIN COOPER** – saxophone

			Vertigo	not iss.
May 79.	(7")	*(DALEK 1)* **FREEDOM FIGHTERS. / TWO CHAMELEONS**	☐	-
Sep 79.	(7")	*(DALEK 2)* **THE WORLD. / WE'RE ALL ACTORS**	☐	-

— now without BALFE who joined BIG IN JAPAN

			Back Door	not iss.
Apr 80.	(7")	*(CLOSE 1)* **DALEK I LOVE YOU. / EIGHT TRACK**	☐	-
May 80.	(12"ep; as DALEK I)	*(DOOR 5)* **DALEK I LOVE YOU (DESTINY). / HAPPY / THIS IS MY UNIFORM**	☐	-

— guests were **DAVID BATES** + **HUGH JONES** + **CHRIS HUGHES** + **KEN PEERS**

Jun 80.	(lp) *(OPEN 1)* **KUM'PAS (COMPASS)**	54	-

– The world / 8 track / Destiny (Dalek I love you) / A suicide / The kiss / Trapped / Two chameleons / Freedom fighters / You really got me / Mad * / Good times * / We're all actors / Heat / Missing 15 minutes. *(re-iss. Apr89 on 'Fontana' lp/c/cd; 836894-1/-4/-2)* – (omits 2 tracks =*).

— now basically just **ALAN GILL** when DAVE HUGHES joined OMD

Feb 81.	(7")	*(DOOR 10)* **HEARTBEAT. / ASTRONAUTS HAVE LANDED ON THE MOON**	☐	-

— GILL joined The TEARDROP EXPLODES for around a year

			Korova	not iss.
Jul 82.	(7"/12")	*(KOW 25/+T)* **HOLIDAY IN DISNEYLAND. / MARKS AND LICENSES**	☐	-
Sep 83.	(7"/12")	*(KOW 29/+T)* **AMBITION. / (I AM) HOT PERSON**	☐	-
Nov 83.	(7")	*(KOW 31)* **HORRORSCOPE. / THESE WALLS WE BUILD**	☐	-

(12"+=) *(KOW 31T)* – Heap big pow wow / The angel and the clown.

Nov 83.	(lp/c)	*(KODE/CODE 7)* **DALEK I LOVE YOU**	☐	-

– Holiday in Disneyland / Horrorscope / Health and happiness / Mouse that roared / Dad on fire / Ambition / Lust / 12 hours of blues / Sons of Sahara / Africa express.

— ALAN GILL was commissioned to write the soundtrack for the movie, 'Letter To Brezhnev', released in 1985 he briefly re-formed DALEK I and made one rare cassette-lp, 'NAIVE' for 'Bopadub'.

DALI'S CAR (see under ⇒ BAUHAUS)

DANCING DID

Formed: Evesham, Worcestershire, England . . . 1980 by TIM HARRISON, along with MARTIN DORMER, (trainee shepherd!) ROGER SMITH and CHRIS HOUGHTON. Taking their name from an antiquated term for travelling gypsies, the band set out to combine their love of rock/punk with the folk traditions of the English countryside. Setting up shop with their own 'Fruit & Veg' label, the lads released an eponymous debut single in October '79. Although not a novelty band in any sense of the term, DANCING DID were blessed with an often surreal sense of humour as heard on follow-up single, 'THE HAUNTED TEAROOMS'. A one-off 7" release, 'THE LOST PLATOON', followed on 'Stiff', while 1982 saw the release of a single, 'THE GREEN MAN AND THE MARCH OF THE BUNGALOWS' and debut album, 'AND DID THOSE FEET', their first effort for new label, 'Kamera'. Unsurprisingly perhaps, in an era more attuned to legwarmers and make-up, the band's pastoral Edwardian rockabilly didn't attract much more than a cult fanbase and after a single, 'BADGER BOYS', the various members went on to plough their own individual furrows. We also await the CD issue of their one and only set.

Album rating: AND DID THOSE FEET (*5)

TIM HARRISON – vocals / **MARTIN DORMER** (b. 1957) – lead guitar, synthesizer / **ROGER SMITH** – bass / **CHRIS HOUGHTON** – drums

			Fruit & Veg	not iss.
Oct 79.	(7")	*(F&V 1)* **DANCING DID. / LORRY PIRATES**	☐	-
1980.	(7")	*(F&V 0012)* **THE HAUNTED TEAROOMS. / SQUASHED THINGS ON THE ROAD**	☐	-

			Stiff	not iss.
Nov 81.	(7")	*(BUY 136)* **THE LOST PLATOON. / THE HUMAN CHICKEN**	☐	-

			Kamera	not iss.
May 82.	(7")	*(ERA 008)* **THE GREEN MAN AND THE MARCH OF THE BUNGALOWS. / A FRUIT PICKING FANTASY**	☐	-
Nov 82.	(lp)	*(KAM 009)* **AND DID THOSE FEET**	☐	-

– Wolves of Worcestershire / The rhythm section sticks together / On the roof / Squashed things / The headmaster and the fly / Ballad of a dying sigh / Charnel boy / Badger boys / The Dancing Did / Within the green green Avon o.

Feb 83.	(7")	*(ERA 017)* **BADGER BOYS. / THE WORLD'S GONNA END IN CHELTENHAM**	☐	-
May 83.	(7") *(w-drawn)*	**SIX WORD HEX. / HOUSE ON THE EDGE OF THE WOOD**	-	-

— split and all went back to their day jobs

DANCING HOOD (see under ⇒ SPARKLEHORSE; in 90's section)

Evan DANDO (see under ⇒ LEMONHEADS)

DANNY & DUSTY (see under ⇒ GREEN ON RED)

DANSE SOCIETY

Formed: Barnsley, England . . . early 80's as DANSE CRAZY by STEVE RAWLINGS, PAUL NASH, PAUL GILMARTIN and LYNDON SCARFE. Emerging from the ashes of Y? and LIPS-X, the group gained valuable exposure following a performance at the second Futurama Festival in Leeds. By the release of a limited edition debut single, 'THE CLOCK', on their own 'Society' label in summer '81, the band had changed their name and added bass player TIM WRIGHT. Following a further couple of singles on their manager's 'Pax' label, DANSE SOCIETY partially justified the hype surrounding them with the mini-set, 'SEDUCTION'. Part post-punk, part proto-goth, the outfit's dark synth swirls, pounding bass and brooding IAN CURTIS-esque vocals combined to striking effect on 'WAKE UP', the lead track on 'HEAVEN IS WAITING' (1984). The first fruits of their new deal with 'Arista', the album heralded a more immediately accessible, atmospheric style and even included a languid cover of The Rolling Stones' trippy classic, '2000 LIGHT YEARS FROM HOME'. With favourable critical reaction and continued support from DJ John Peel, the future looked bright; it wasn't to be, though, as internal ructions saw SCARFE replaced by DAVID WHITAKER and legal arguments with 'Arista' delayed the release of new material. Fans were less than impressed when they eventually resurfaced in '85 with the Stock, Aitken & Waterman-produced 'SAY IT AGAIN'. Such a sudden stylistic departure proved disastrous, however, and the band's second album was shelved by their record company. A split inevitably followed soon after, RAWLINGS following a more commercial path with SOCIETY while the rest of the band ploughed on in vain as JOHNNY IN THE CLOUDS.

Album rating: SEDUCTION mini (*6) / HEAVEN IS WAITING (*7) / LOOKING THROUGH (*4) / SEDUCTION – THE SOCIETY COLLECTION (*7)

STEVE RAWLINGS – vocals (ex-Y?) / **PAUL NASH** – lead guitar (ex-Y?) / **LYNDON SCARFE** – keyboards (ex-LIPS-X) / **PAUL GILMARTIN** – drums (ex-LIPS-X) / **PATRIC HERTZ** – guitar / **PAUL HAMPSHIRE** – bass

			I.F.K.	not iss.
1981.	(7")	*(SOC 3-81)* **THE CLOCK. / CONTINENT**	☐	-

(re-iss. Jul83 on 'IFK-Society'; SOC 2)

			Pax	not iss.
Aug 81.	(12"ep)	*(PAX 2)* **THERE IS NO SHAME IN DEATH. / DOLPHINS / THESE FRAYED EDGES**	☐	-

(re-iss. Jul83 on 'Society' blue-vinyl; SOC 12-1)

— **TIM WRIGHT** – bass; repl. HAMPSHIRE and PATRIC who joined 4 BE 2

Mar 82.	(7")	*(SOX 5)* **WOMAN'S OWN. / WE'RE SO HAPPY**	☐	-

(12"+=) *(POX 5)* – Belief / Continent.

(re-iss. Jul83 on 'Society'; SOC 12-3)

			Society	not iss.
Aug 82.	(m-lp)	*(SOC 882)* **SEDUCTION**	☐	-

– Godsend / My heart / Falling apart / Danse – Move / Ambition / In Heaven *(re-dist.Apr84 on 'Society-Arista'; same)*

Feb 83.	(7")	*(SOC 4)* **SOMEWHERE. / HIDE**	☐	-

(12"+=) *(SOC 12-4)* – The theme.

			Society-Arista	not iss.
Aug 83.	(7"/12")	*(SOC/+12 5)* **WAKE UP. / SEDUCTION**	61	-
Oct 83.	(7"pic-d)	*(SOC 6)* **HEAVEN IS WAITING. / LIZARD MAN**	60	-

(12"+=) *(SOC12 6)* – ('A'extended).

Feb 84.	(lp/c)	*(205/405 972)* **HEAVEN IS WAITING**	39	-

– Come inside / Wake up / Angel / Where are you now / Red light (shine) / Heaven is waiting / The hurt / 2000 light years from home / Valiant to vile / The night. *(re-iss. Jun91 on 'Great Expectations' cd/c/lp; PIP CD/MC/LP 024)* (<cd re-iss. Feb02 on 'Anagram'+=; CDMGOTH 14>) – Arabia / The seduction / The theme / Seen the light / Endless.

DANSE SOCIETY (cont)

Mar 84. (7") (SOC 7) **2,000 LIGHT YEARS FROM HOME. / SEEN THE LIGHT**
(12"light blue+=) (SOC12 7) – Angel (dub).
(d7"+=) (SOC 7-7) – Sway / Endless.

— DAVID WHITAKER – keyboards (ex-MUSIC FOR PLEASURE) repl. LYNDON

Jul 85. (7") (SOC 8) **SAY IT AGAIN. / FADE AWAY (SHE'S IN MY DREAMS)**
(12"+=) (SOC12 8) – ('A'extended).
(d12"+=) (SOC22 8) – Sensimilia / Treat me right.

Feb 86. (7") (SOC 9) **HOLD ON (TO WHAT YOU'VE GOT). / DANSE: MOVE**
(12"+=) (SOC12 9) – Heaven is waiting / ('A'dance mix).
(c-s+=) (SOCCS 9) – ('A'dance) / 2,000 light years from home / Wake up.

— (STEVE RAWLINGS solo); others formed JOHNNY IN THE CLOUDS

Aug 86. (lp; as DANSE SOCIETY INTERNATIONAL) (SOC 886) **LOOKING THROUGH**
– Looking through / All I want / Institution / Don't stop now / Sunset gun / Runaway / House of love / Midnight land.

Big Life / not iss.

Aug 87. (7"/12"; as SOCIETY) (BLR 001/+T) **SATURN GIRL. / LOVE IT**
(c-s) (BLR 1TCC) – (2-'B'versions).

— RAWLINGS retired from the music biz; over a decade later he and RAE DiLEO formed macabre ambient act, MERIDIAN DREAM

– compilations, etc. –

May 01. (cd) Anagram; (<CDMGOTH 6>) **SEDUCTION – THE SOCIETY COLLECTION**
– Clock / Continent / These frayed edges / We're so happy / Woman's own / Belief / Ambition / Godsend / My heart / Falling apart / Danse – Move / In Heaven (everything is fine) / Somewhere / Hide.

DARLING BUDS

Formed: Caerleon, Newport, Wales ... 1986 by ANDREA LEWIS and HARLEY FARR, who subsequently recruited CHRIS McDONAGH and BLOSS before relocating to Gwent, Wales. Fronted by blonde bombshell, Andrea, the band's feisty brand of indie pop/punk was first given an airing on a self-financed debut single, 'IF I SAID'. Subsequently signing with Doncaster based indie label, 'Native', the band released a string of 7"ers which won the favour of Radio One stalwart, John Peel. Playlisted almost nightly, the 'BUDS were soon snapped up by 'Epic', scoring a Top 50 hit with major label debut single, 'BURST'. 'HIT THE GROUND' performed even better, taking the band into the Top 30. While comparisons with BLONDIE may have been a mite too generous, the band notched up a deserved Top 30 placing for debut album, 'POP SAID' (1989). A more accurate comparison was The PRIMITIVES, a group who also arrived in a flurry of hype and acclaim only to fall from the media spotlight almost as quickly as they'd appeared. The signs weren't good for The DARLING BUDS as a further two singles, 'LET'S GO ROUND THERE' and 'YOU'VE GOT TO CHOOSE', scraped into the Top 50. Following the replacement of BLOSS with JIMMY HUGHES, they returned in 1990 with a more streamlined cutesy sound, notching up a minor hit with 'TINY MACHINE'. Another two singles and an accompanying album, 'CRAWDADDY' (1990), failed to chart, however, and The DARLING BUDS looked set for music business oblivion. Major label muscle made little difference as summer 1992's 'SURE THING' became their final (Top 75) hit and the 'EROTICA' (1992) album stiffed completely. As the record competed forlornly with MADONNA's opus of the same name, The DARLING BUDS split later that year. • **Songwriters:** ANDREA lyrics / HARLEY music.

Album rating: POP SAID (*6) / CRAWDADDY (*5) / EROTICA (*5) / SHAME ON YOU compilation (*6)

ANDREA LEWIS (b.25 Mar'67) – vocals / **HARLEY FARR** (b. 4 Jul'64, Singapore) – guitar / **SIMON** – bass / + drum machine

Darling Buds / not iss.

Feb 87. (7") (DAR 1) **IF I SAID. / JUST TO BE SEEN**

— **CHRIS McDONAGH** (b. 6 Mar'62) – bass; repl. SIMON / **BLOSS** – drums; repl. machine

Native / not iss.

Mar 88. (7") (NTV 21) **SHAME ON YOU. / VALENTINE**
(12"+=) (12NTV 21) – Uptight.
Jun 88. (7") (NTV 32) **THINK OF ME. / THAT'S THE REASON**
Jun 88. (7") (NTV 33) **IT'S ALL UP TO YOU. / THINK OF ME**
(ltd-7"flexi+=) (NTV 33L) – Spin.
(12"+=) (12NTV 33) – That's the reason.

Epic / Columbia

Sep 88. (7"/7"g-f/7"box) (BLOND/+Q/B 1) **BURST. / BIG HEAD** [50]
(12"+=/cd-s+=) (BLOND T/C 1) – Shame on you (slightlydelic version).
Dec 88. (7"/7"g-f) (BLOND/+Q 2) **HIT THE GROUND. / PRETTY GIRL** [27]
(12"+=/cd-s+=) (BLOND T/C 2) – ('A'extended) / If I said (re-recorded).
(10") (BLONDX 2) – ('A'side) / You've got to choose (live) / When it feels good (live).
Jan 89. (lp/c/cd) (462894-1/-4/-2) <45208> **POP SAID** [23]
– Hit the ground / Burst / Uptight / The other night / Big head / Let's go round there / She's not crying / Shame on you / You've got to choose / Spin / When it feels good / The things we do for love.
Mar 89. (7"/7"yellow) (BLOND/+V 3) **LET'S GO ROUND THERE. / TURN YOU ON** [49]
(12"+=/12"g-f/+=cd-s+=) (BLOND T/Q/C 3) – Different daze.
(7"ep++=) (BLONDE 3) – It's all up to you.

Jun 89. (7"/7"g-f/c-s) (BLOND/+G/M 4) **YOU'VE GOT TO CHOOSE. / MARY'S GOT TO GO / HIT THE GROUND (live)** [45]
(12"/cd-s) (BLOND T/C 4) – (first 2 tracks) / I'll never stop.

— **JIMMY HUGHES** (b. Liverpool, England) – drums (ex-BLACK) repl. BLOSS

May 90. (7"/7"box/c-s) (BLOND/+B/M 5) **TINY MACHINE. / SUGAR CITY** [60]
(12"+=/cd-s+=) (BLOND T/C 5) – ('A'-Hercules mix) / Me? satisfied?
Aug 90. (7") (BLOND 6) **CRYSTAL CLEAR. / TINY MACHINE (live at GLR)**
(12"+=) (BLONDT 6) – ('A'-mix amethyst).
(cd-s++=) (BLONDC 6) – Tripped up.
Sep 90. (c-s) <73662> **CRYSTAL CLEAR / YOU WON'T MAKE ME DIE**
Sep 90. (cd/c/lp) (467012-2/-4/-1) <46816> **CRAWDADDY**
– It makes no difference / Tiny machine / Crystal clear / Do you have to break my heart / You won't make me die / A little bit of Heaven / Fall / Honey suckle / So close / The end of the beginning.
Feb 91. (7"/c-s) (BLOND/+M 7) (656594-2) **IT MAKES NO DIFFERENCE. / OFF MY MIND**
(12"+=/cd-s+=) (BLOND T/C 7) – Love and death / If.

Epic / Chaos

Aug 92. (7"/c-s) (658215-7/-4) **SURE THING. / BABYHEAD** [71]
(12"+=/cd-s+=) (658215-6/-2) – Suffer / What goes around.
Sep 92. (cd/c/lp) (472151-2/-4/-1) <OK/OT/+/52913> **EROTICA**
– One thing leads to another / Sure thing / Off my mind / Gently fall / Please yourself / Angels fallen / Isolation / Long day in the universe / Wave / If.
Sep 92. (cd-ep) <42K 74446> **SURE THING / BABYHEAD / SUFFER / PLEASE YOURSELF**

— split later in 1992; drummer JON LEE (later of FEEDER) had guested

– compilations, etc. –

1989. (7"flexi) Flexi; (FLX 448) **VALENTINE (live). / THAT'S THE REASON (live)** – / – fanclub
Sep 90. (cd/c/lp) Native; (NTV CD/C/LP 44) **SHAME ON YOU**
Dec 90. (3x7"box) Native; (NTV 52) **SHAME ON YOU. / VALENTINE // IT'S ALL UP TO YOU. / SPIN // THINK OF ME. / THAT'S THE REASON**

DAS DAMEN

Formed: New York – from Arizona – USA ... mid 80's by JIM WALTERS, ALEX TOTINO, PHIL LEOPOLD VON TRAPP and LYLE HYSEN. After an initial eponymous release on 'Ecstatic Peace', they signed to 'SST', former home of HUSKER DU, MEAT PUPPETS and fIREHOSE. In 1987, they unleashed the sublime 'JUPITER EYE' album, a record of quasi-hardcore that touched on MC5-like garage psychedelia. This sound was even more pronounced on the follow-up album, 'TRISKAIDEKAPHOBE' and the EP 'MARSHMALLOW CONSPIRACY'. On the latter, the band ploughed through a manic re-working of The BEATLES' 'MAGICAL MYSTERY TOUR'. However, this was their last decent effort before signing to 'What Goes On', followed by 'City Slang' in the early 90's. • **Covered:** FRICTION (Television).

Album rating: DAS DAMEN (*6) / JUPITER EYE (*6) / TRISKAIDEKAPHOBE (*6) / MOUSETRAP (*6) / ENTERTAINING FRIENDS (*5) / HIGH ANXIETY mini (*5)

JIM WALTERS – vocals, guitar / **ALEX TOTINO** – guitar, vocals / **PHIL LEOPOLD VON TRAPP** – bass, vocals / **LYLE HYSEN** – drums, electronics

not iss. / Ecstatic Peace

1986. (lp) <004> **DAS DAMEN**
– Tsava / Trick question / Slave bird / House of mirrors / How do you measure / Behind my eyes. <US re-iss. 1988 on 'SST' lp/c; SST 040/+C>

S.S.T. / S.S.T.

1987. (lp/c) <(SST 095/+C)> **JUPITER EYE**
– Gray isn't black / Quarter after eight / Trap door / Where they all went / Name your poison / Impasse / Raindance / Do / Girl with the hair.
Aug 88. (lp) <(SST 190)> **TRISKAIDEKAPHOBE**
– Spiderbirds / Reverse into tomorrow / Pendant / Seven / Five five five / Firejoke / Bug / Siren plugs / Up for the ride / Ruby Woodpecker / Candy korn.
Dec 88. (12"ep/c-ep/cd-ep) <(SST/+C/CD 218)> **MARSHMALLOW CONSPIRACY EP**
– Bug / 555 / Sky yen.

What Goes On / Twin/Tone

1989. (cd) <89170> **MOUSETRAP**
– Noon daylight / Mirror leaks / Twenty four to zero / Somewhere, sometime / Demagnetized / Hey, angel / Sad mile / Please, please me / Click!
1989. (7") (GOES ON 16) **NOON DAYLIGHT. / GIVE ME EVERYTHING**

— **DAVID MOTAMED** – bass; repl. VON TRAPP

City Slang / Sub Pop

Sep 90. (lp) (EFA 0406108) **ENTERTAINING FRIENDS (live)**
– Reverse into tomorrow / Please please me / 555 / Somewhere sometime / Pendant / Demagnetized / Noon daylight / House of mirrors / Gray isn't black / Chaindrive / Click! / Friction.
Jul 91. (m-cd) (SLANG 10) <SP 111B> **HIGH ANXIETY**
– The promise / Chaindrive (a slight return) / The outsider / Thrilled to the marrow / Silence.

— disbanded after above; DAVID joined CELL

DATBLYGU

Formed: Aberteifi, Wales . . . 1982 by T. WYN DAVIES and DAVID R EDWARDS, two years later they were to be joined by PAT MORGAN and bringing up the rear, AL EDWARDS. Inspired by cult indie native countrymen, YOUNG MARBLE GIANTS, the band took on the mantle of a progressive Welsh-orientated stance, and along with the likes of Y CYRFF, TYNALL TYWYLL and FFLAPS, began a much needed tradition that inspired the next generation in the form of GORKY'S ZYGOTIC MYNCI and the SUPER FURRY ANIMALS. EDWARDS' lyrical compositons were almost entirely in the native tongue with the music being a post-punk mixture of electronica, country, folk-rock, and indie pop; the group dubbed themselves "non conforming non-conformists". DATBLYGU, whose moniker means 'Develop', first gained attention on the mid-80's genre-defining compilation, 'CAM O'R TYWYLLWCH', released by 'Anhrefn' records, although prior to this they had put out four tape-only pieces, 'AMHEUON CORFFOROL' (BODY DOUBTS), 'FI DU' (ME BLACK), 'TROSGLWYDDO'R GWIRIONEDD' (TRANSFERRING THE TRUTH) and 'CANEUON SERCH I BOBL SERCHOG' (LOVE SONGS FOR LOVERS). They also brought out their debut single, 'HWGR GRAWTH-OG' (1986) around this period. Gaining attention from the indie-spotter extraordinaire, Radio One's John Peel, the band sessioned for him in 1987, and began a tradition which would last five spots and the next 6 years. Out of these radio gigs came the 1992 compilation which collected three great pieces known as 'MAY 87 – NO AIDS', 'FEBRUARY 88 – NO SALMONELLA' and 'JANUARY 1991 – NO GULF WAR'. The band's initial full-length outing, 'WYAU', hit the shops in 1988, and was followed two years later by probably their career high-point, the LP 'PYST'. The ensuing year saw the issue of 'BLWCH TYMER TYMOR', evoking the fifties and sixties style of Christmas orientated releases, and included the stand-out track, 'GA I FOD SION CORN', roughly translated: 'Can I be Santa Claus'. EDWARDS extended his eclectic stance the following year with the collaborative set, 'LL.LLV T.G. MC DRE' which included the frontman doing a side each with native techno group TY GWYDR and progressive hip-hop dubmeisters LLWYBR LLAETHOG. Unfortunately for DATBLYGU, 1993 was to see their third and final full-length set, 'LIBERTINO', which again saw no stopping in the quality and lengths the band would take to do their own thing. Their last release came two years later with the 7", 'ALCOHOL' / 'AMNESIA' . . although for fans of these pioneers there was the final treat of the compilation, 'DATBLYGU 1985-1995', which was chock full of worthy material and included a written piece by SUPER FURRY ANIMALS frontman, GRUFF RHYS, a big fan, who had together with his band, covered 'Y TEIMLAD' on their Welsh language LP, 'Mwng' (2000).

Album rating: WYAU (*6) / PYST mini (*5) / LIBERTINO (*5) / THE PEEL SESSIONS mini (*6) / 1985-1995 compilation (*6)

DAVID R. EDWARDS – vocals / **PAT MORGAN** – guitars, **T. WYN DAVIES** – keyboards, bass / **AL EDWARDS** – drums

			Anhrefn	not iss.	
1986.	(c)	**AMHEUON CORFFOROL**	-	-	Welsh
1986.	(c)	**TROSGLWYDDO'R GWIRIONEDD**	-	-	Welsh
1986.	(c)	**FI DU**	-	-	Welsh
1986.	(c)	**CANEUON SERCH I BOBL SERCHOG**	-	-	Welsh
Feb 87.	(7")	(ANHREFN 008) **HUGR-GRAWTH-OG. /**			
Oct 88.	(lp)	(ANHREFN 014) **WYAU**			

– Paentio'r nenfwd: Efo f'ymenydd / Gwlad ar fy nghefn / Mynwent / 23 / Cristion yn y kibbutz / Cyfarth, cyfathrach / Pabell Len / Saith arch bach / Dafydd iwan yn y glaw / Gwenu dan bysiau / Tymer aspirin / Dwylo olew / Fanzine ynfytyn / Unrhywsgwrs / Babannod beichiog nawr / Hen ysgol cloff / Baban, nerfau mor rhydd / Blonegmeddyliau / Benjamin bore / Mas a lawr.

			Ofn	not iss.
1990.	(m-lp)	**PYST**		

– Cymryd mewn sioe / Am / Nofel o'r hofel / Ms. bara lawr / Dymuniadau da / Blwyddyn nesa efallai leukaemia / Ugain I un / Mae'r nyrs adref / Mwnci efo crach / Syrffedu / Rhawt / Nos da sgum.

			Ankst	not iss.
Dec 91.	(c)	<ANKST 021> **BLWCH TYMER TYMOR**		-
Feb 93.	(m-lp)	(ANKST 027) **THE PEEL SESSIONS**		-
Jun 93.	(cd/c)	(ANKST 037 CD/MC) **LIBERTINO**		-
Jan 95.	(7"ep)	(ANKST 054) **PUTSCH**		-

– Amnesia / Alcohol.

— disbanded after above

– compilations, etc. –

Sep 95.	(cd/c)	Ankst; (ANKST 060 CD/C) **WYAU / PYST**		-
Jul 00.	(cd)	Ankst; (ANKSTCD 086) **1985-1995**		-

– Y teimlad / Nefoedd putain prydain / Hollol, hollol, hollol / Yn symud I ddim / Braidd / Casserole efeilliad / Firws I frecwast / Mynd / Brechdanau tywod / Merch ty cyngor / Pop peth / Santa a Barbara / Sdim eisiau esgus / Sgorio Dafydd Iwan dyn eira / Ga I fod sion corn / Asid amino / 3 tabled doeth / Maes E / Amnesia / Alcohol.

Danielle DAX

Born: Southend, England. Following a one-off gig at Reading University as a member of AMY TURTLE & THE CROSSROADS, DAX made her first real foray into the music world alongside KARL BLAKE in his band The LEMON KITTENS. This partnership resulted in two avant-pop albums, 'WE BUY A HAMMER FOR DADDY' (1980) and 'THE BIG DENTIST' (1982), setting the scene for DAX's subsequent solo career. Things got off to an interesting start with 'POP-EYES' (1983; complete with gruesome sleeve artwork), wherein the pseudo-goth goddess treated listeners to her ethnic multi-instrumental skills and ear for the bizarre. A detour into acting – a bit part (all her bits in fact!) in Neil Jordan's 'The Company Of Wolves' – was followed by 1984's well received mini-set, 'JESUS EGG THAT WEPT'. The latter featured a one-off collaboration with BLAKE, 'OSTRICH', oft cited as one of her best tracks. It also kickstarted a renewed enthusiasm for live work as DAX recruited a backing band and began building up her profile in tandem with a series of singles on her own 'Awesome' label. Eventually coming to the attention of US alternative bigwig, Seymour Stein (after an appearance at Boston's New Music Seminar), DAX netted a major league deal with his 'Sire' label and proceeded to record the 'DARK ADAPTED EYE' (1988) album. Despite such increasingly accessible material as the DAX-goes-BILLY IDOL 'WHITE KNUCKLE RIDE', crossover success remained surprisingly out of reach. An ill-advised cover of The Beatles' 'TOMORROW NEVER KNOWS' seemed desperate and as the accompanying Stephen Street-produced album, 'BLAST THE HUMAN FLOWER' (1990) sank without trace, DAX returned to her independent roots. Setting up her own 'Biter Of Thorpe' (eh?!) label, the lady re-issued titles from her back catalogue although new material has been thin on the ground. • **Trivia:** Initially a painter/artist, she designed many album covers, including that of LEAGUE OF GENTLEMEN (a ROBERT FRIPP sideline).

Album rating: POP-EYES (*6) / JESUS EGG THAT WEPT (*6) / INKY BLOATERS (*6) / DARK ADAPTED EYE (*5) / BLAST THE HUMAN FLOWER (*5) / COMATOSE NON-REACTION: THE THWARTED POP CAREER OF... compilation (*6)

DANIELLE DAX – vocals, instruments

			Initial	not iss.
Jun 83.	(m-lp)	(IRC 009) **POP-EYES**		-

– Here comes the harvest burns / Bed caves / Tower of lies / Numb companions / Everyone squeaks gently / Kernow. (re-iss. Apr85 on 'Awesome'+=; AOR 2) – The wheeled wagon / The stone guest / The shamemen. (cd-iss. Dec92 on 'Reckless'+=;) (m-cd re-iss. Oct96 on 'Biter Of Thorpe'+=; BOT131 01CD) – (same extra tracks).

— now with **DAVE KNIGHT** – guitar, keyboards, percussion (of SHOCK HEADED PETERS) / **STEVE REEVES** – guitars / **IAN STURGESS** – bass, guitar / **MARTIN WATTS** – drums

			Awesome	Rough Trade
Oct 84.	(m-lp)	(AOR 1) **JESUS EGG THAT WEPT**		-

– Evil honky stomp / Pariah / Fortune cheats / Hammerheads / Ostrich / The spoil factor. (m-cd-iss. Oct96 on 'Biter Of Thorpe' BOT131 02CD)

— she continued to work with KNIGHT + STURGESS

Oct 85.	(7")	(AOR 3) **YUMMER YUMMER MAN. / BAD MISS "M"**		-
		(12"+=) (AOR 3T) – Fizzing human bomb.		
Sep 86.	(7")	(AOR 6) **WHERE THE FLIES ARE. / UP IN ARMS**		-
		(12"+=) (AOR 6T) – When I was young.		
May 87.	(lp/c/cd)	(AOR 13/+CS)(AORCD 13) **INKY BLOATERS**		-

– Flash back / Funtime / Inky bloaters / Sleep has no property / Bad Miss "M" / Big hollow man / Brimstone in a barren land / Where the flies are / Born to be bad / Fizzing human bomb. (cd re-iss. Oct96 on 'Biter Of Thorpe'+=; BOT131 04CD) – Yummer-yummer man.

Jun 87.	(7")	(AOR 10) **BIG HOLLOW MAN. / MUZZLES**		-
		(12"+=) (AOR 10T) – The passing of the third floor back.		
Apr 88.	(7")	(AOR 12) **CAT HOUSE. / TOUCH PIGGY'S EYES**		-
		(12"+=) (AOR 12T) – House-cat.		
Jan 89.	(lp/c/cd)	<CD 1290> **DARK ADAPTED EYE**	-	

– Cat house / Big hollow man / White knuckle ride / When I was young / Yummer yummer man / Fizzing human bomb / Whistling for his love / Inky bloaters / Brimstone in a barren land / Bad Miss "M" / Touch Piggy's eyes / House-cat / Bed caves / Sleep has no property.

Apr 89.	(7")	(AOR 23) **WHITE KNUCKLE RIDE. / WHISTLING FOR HIS LOVE**		
		(12"+=) (AOR 23T) – Cold sweat.		

			Sire	Sire
Oct 90.	(7"/c-s)	(921773-7/-4) **TOMORROW NEVER KNOWS. / KING CRACK**		
		(12"+=/cd-s+=) (921773-6/-2) – (3-'A'mixes).		
Jan 91.	(cd/c/lp)	(<7599 26126-2/-4/-1>) **BLAST THE HUMAN FLOWER**		

– The I.D. parade / Tomorrow never knows / Big blue '82 / Bayou / King crack / Daisy / Dead man's chill / The living and their stillborn / Jehovah's precious stone / 16 candles.

— nothing heard of her recently until . . . below

— now with **DAVID KNIGHT** – keyboards, electronics

			Biter Of Thorpe	not iss.
Oct 96.	(d-cd)	(BOT131 06CD) **COMATOSE NON-REACTION: THE THWARTED POP CAREER OF DANIELLE DAX** (compilation)		-

– Yummer yummer man / Bad Miss "M" / Fizzing human bomb / Where the flies are / Up in arms / When I was young / Muzzles / The passing of the third floor back / Music from the film "Axel" // Olamal (US mix) / Whistling for his love (US mix) / Cathouse / Touch Piggy's eyes / House cat / White knuckle ride / Cold sweat / Hate on sight (by SHOCK HEADED PETERS) / Defiled / Blight / Mongatron.

| Oct 96. | (7"ep/cd-ep) | (BOT131 07/+CDEP) **TIMBER TONGUE EP** | | - |

– Toygit / E.V.I.L. T / Timber tongue / Uru eu wau wau.

– compilations, etc. –

| Feb 88. | (12"ep) | Nighttracks; (SFNT 006) **THE EVENING SHOW SESSIONS** (1.12.85) | | - |

– Fizzing human bomb / Pariah / Ostrich / Numb companions.

DEAD C.

Formed: Dunedin, New Zealand ... 1986 by MICHAEL MORLEY (ex-WEEDS), BRUCE RUSSELL and ROBBIE YEATS. DEAD C's early career set them at the forefront of the Kiwi-rock circuit, and on their release to the US indie scene they became one of the more influential groups for the noise-rock experimental side of alternative rock and pop. Amongst their more discernible disciples are the likes of LOW, SONIC YOUTH and The HOOD, and the band themselves took on the mantle of such sonic pioneers as CAPTAIN BEEFHEART, CAN and JOHN CAGE. Prior to the glories of DC, MORLEY had already made a bit of a name for himself with the outfit WRECK SMALL SPEAKERS ON EXPENSIVE STEREOS, which he had formed in 1980 with RICHARD RAM in Dunedin. Their brand of drummerless post-punk sound investigation had been best experienced on the cult release EP 'RIVER FALLING LOVE' (1984) and to a lesser extent on the tape issue 'A CHILD'S GUIDE TO WRECK SMALL ... ' (1985). From here MORLEY moved to DEAD C and debuted with the cassette release 'DR503B' (1987), which displayed the punk credentials and love of lo-fi sensibilities. Following this issue came 'EUSA KILLS' (1989) which threw them to the top of their native music scene, although they were certainly not at odds with it, YEATS already having played with fellow antipodean line-up the VERLAINES. Their next two full-length outings, 'TRAPDOOR FUCKING EXIT' (1990) and 'HARSH 70'S REALITY' (1992) ranked as a peak time for the band, showcasing their ability to free themselves of the restraints of run-of-the-mill rock structure, but at the same time produce some remarkable pieces of understandable quality. What most appeals here is their hypnotic and adroit use of guitar fuzz and feedback. Throughout the rest of the decade the threesome were anything but lazy, dedicating their talents towards the goal of creating eclectic and thoughtful music, through releases such as 'WORLD PEACE HOPE ET AL' (1994), 'THE OPERATION OF THE SONNE' (1995) and 'WHITE HOUSE' (1995). Towards the latter part of the 90's, DC put out another masterpiece in the shape of LP 'TUSK' (1997) which showed that rock could be edgy, avant-garde and loud, and as well as exciting its listener could also be extremely contemplative and sonorous. The aural scientists were still going strong into the millennium with no let down in quality emphasized by the album 'NEW ELECTRIC MUSIC' in 2001. What was also most noteworthy was that quite apart from the phenomenal output of DC, its members also managed to find time for various exploratory side-projects. Most noteable of the bunch was MORLEY who, as well as playing in mid-90's band 2 FOOT FLAME with the giants of alternative rock in the shape of JEAN SMITH (of MECCA NORMAL) and PETER JEFFERIES (ex-THIS KIND OF PUNISHMENT), he also incredibly found time to work on his 'free noise' sideline, GATE. The various issues of this latter band saw MORLEY team up with others to continue to explore the outer regions of rock sound, employing guitars along with sampling and electronica, which saw their work being favourably compared to the jazz experimentaion of such greats as JOHN COLTRANE. GATE began around 1994 and kicked off with a year of touring which witnessed MORLEY along with the likes of SONIC YOUTH's THURSTON MOORE and LEE RANALDO, as well as influential Japanese guitarist KEIJI HAINO. The 'LIVE IN BOSTON / NYC 1994' (1995) release captures some of the more notable excursions of that year. Released the same year was the studio-based GATE set, 'LOUNGE', with MORLEY teaming up with brothers DAVID and SID MERRITT to create another slice of playful musical explorations. More releases followed, most notably 1996's album 'GOLDEN'. DEAD C's BRUCE RUSSELL was no less prolific in his other musical dabblings, creating the labels 'Xpressway' and 'Corpus Hermeticum', producing many local artists, writing on music and cultural theory in general, and forming the band HANDFUL OF DUST in the 90's. Although this output was mainly a solo one, he was well assisted by the likes of ALASTAIR GALBRAITH and PETER STAPLETON. As far as their sound was concerned HOD moved further into the uncharted waters of sound, using any technique to express the kind of innovative liberation from their structural shackles. Their output on the whole was of an extremely high calibre although evidently never to see the light of the mainstream charts. Most notable albums include 'PHILOSOPHICK MERCURY', showcasing the talents of violinist STAPLETON and 'MUSICA HUMANA' (1995), displaying RUSSELL's wide reading and knowledge of cultural history and thought. Even his work with the latter outfit did not seem to satisfy his appetite for experimentaion, thus he also issued work under his own name like his striking solo LP 'PAINTING THE PASSPORTS BROWN'.

Album rating: DR503 (*5) / HELEN SAID THIS mini (*5) / EUSA KILLS (*6) / TRAPDOOR FUCKING EXIT (*6) / HARSH 70s REALITY (*7) / CLYMA EST MORT (*5) / THE OPERATION OF THE SONNE (*5) / WORLD PEACE HOPE ET AL compilation (*5) / THE WHITE HOUSE (*7) / REPENT (*4) / TUSK (*7) / DR503c compilation (*5) / THE DEAD C (*5) / NEW ELECTRIC MUSIC (*5) / Wreck Small Speakers On Expensive Stereos: RIVER FALLING LOVE compilation (*5) / Gate: LOUNGE (*6) / LIVE IN BOSTON/NYC 1994 (*6) / GOLDEN compilation (*6) / MONOLAKE (*4) / THE PAVILLION OF FOOLS by Michael Morley (*5) / THE DEW LINE (*5) / THE WISHER TABLE (*5) / THE LAVENDER HEAD (*6) / A Handful Of Dust: THE PHILOSOPHIK MERCURY (*6) / NOW GODS, STAND UP FOR BASTARDS (*5) / JERUSALEM, STREET OF GRAVES (*5) / SPIRITUAL LIBERTINES compilation (*5) / Bruce Russell: PROJECT FOR A REVOLUTION IN NEW YORK (*5) / MAXIMALIST MANTRA MUSIC (*6) / PAINTING THE PASSPORTS BROWN (*5)

WRECK SMALL SPEAKERS ON EXPENSIVE STEREOS

MICHAEL MORLEY + RICHARD RAM

			Flying Nun	not iss.
1984.	(12"ep) *(FN 068)* **RIVER FALLING LOVE**		-	- NewZ

– Lots of hearts / Three shots / All of this / Torn. *<US-iss.1995 on 'Ajax'+=; AJAX 029>* – Alice in Wonderland / Oh and from the beach / Rain / Too late / Past (9:30 heartache).

―― added guest **DENISE ROUGHAN** – vocals

―― (MORLEY also spent some time in The WEEDS – members later peeling off to the STRAITJACKET FITS)

			Xpressway	not iss.
1988.	(c) *(X/WAY 03)* **A CHILD'S GUIDE TO . . .**		-	- NewZ

– Rain / Until I go / Together we sense / Shortwave / In your talk / Evenings / Why do I look at you that way / African fire / Sand shingle & stone / Over my skull (disco) / Try too / Oh and from the beach.

the DEAD C

BRUCE RUSSELL – vocals, bass, synthesizer (ex-XPRESSWAY) / **MICHAEL MORLEY** – guitar, vocals, synthesizer (ex-THIS KIND OF PUNISHMENT) / **ROBBIE YEATS** – drums, guitar (ex-VERLAINES)

			Flying Nun	not iss.
1987.	(lp) *(FN 092)* **DR503**		-	- NewZ

– Max Harris / Speed kills / The wheel / Mutterline / Country / I love this / Polio. *(cd-iss. 1992 on 'Feel Good All Over';)*

			Diabolic Root	not iss.
1987.	(c-s) *(DR 502)* **PERFORM MAX HARRIS**		-	- NewZ

– Max Harris / Beyond help > from Max Harris.

			Xpressway	not iss.
1988.	(c) *(X/WAY 01)* **THE LIVE DEAD C.**		-	- NewZ

– Crazy I know / Sun stabbed / Speed kills / The wheel / 3 years / Max Harris / This land is . . . / Bad politics / I love this / Polio.

| 1988. | (7"ep) *(X/WAY 07)* **THE SUNSTABBED EP** | | - | - NewZ |

– Bad politics / Crazy I know / Angel.

| 1989. | (c) *(X/WAY 012)* **PLAY 503b** | | - | - NewZ |

– (Beyond help from) Max Harris / (Turning) The wheel / 3 years / Mutterline (original) / Sunstabbed (fragment) / Angel / I love this / Fire / Speed kills.

			Flying Nun	not iss.
1989.	(lp/cd) *(FN/+CD 130)* **EUSA KILLS**		-	- NewZ

– Scarey nest / Call back your dogs / Alien to be / Phantom power / Now I fall / I was here / Children / Bumtoe / Glass hole pit / Maggot / Envelopment. *(UK cd-iss. Jan00; DFN 130)*

―― added guest **CHRIS HEAZLEWOOD** – guitar (ex-SFERIC EXPERIMENT)

			Precious Metal	not iss.
1990.	(c) *(01)* **RUNWAY**		-	- NewZ

– (12 untitled tracks).

| 1990. | (c) *(4)* **TRAPDOOR FUCKING EXIT** | | - | - NewZ |

– Heaven / Hell is now love / Mighty / Power / Bury / Bury (refutatio, omnium, haeresium) / Sky / Bone / Krossed / Calling slowly / Helen said this / Acoustico: Power – Bone – Mighty. *(<UK/US cd-iss. 1993 & Oct95 on 'Siltbreeze'; SB 021-2 /PM4>)*

			not iss.	Forced Exposure
1991.	(7"m) *<026>* **MIGHTY + PEACE. / POWER**		-	

			Siltbreeze	Siltbreeze
1990.	(12") *<002>* **HELEN SAID THIS. / BURY**			
1991.	(7") *<06>* **HELL IS NOW LOVE. / BONE**			
1992.	(d-lp) *<SB 11-22>* **HARSH 70s REALITY**			

– Driver UFO / Sky / Love / Suffer bomb damage / Sea is violet / Constellation / Baseheart / Hope. *(UK cd-iss. Apr98; same as US)* – (omits 2 tracks).

| 1992. | (lp/c) *<SB 16-1/-4>* **CLYMA EST MORT** (bootleg) | | | |

– Sunshine / Dirt for Harry / Sky / Electric / Power / Highway / Ein kampf, ein seig / World / Das fluten, das fluten (oh mama I can go).

| 1993. | (7"ep) *<SB 25>* **THE DEAD C. vs SEBADOH** | | | |

– Trust / I-you-love-it / Blind / River of Lethia / Lives of steel / Gate plaster moon / I-you-move-it-2 / Air (excerpt).

below added guests **ALASTAIR GALBRAITH** – violin

| 1994. | (7") *Precious Metal; <29>* **METALHEART 1. / METALHEART 2** | | - | |

(re-iss. Sep95; SILT 042) (re-iss. 1995 on 'Corpus Hermecitus'; HERMES 015)

| 1994. | (lp/c) *<SB 30-1/-4>* **THE OPERATION OF THE SONNE** | | - | |

– The marriage of reason and squalor / Mordant heaven / Air.

| Aug 95. | (cd/lp) *(<SB 40-2/-1>)* **THE WHITE HOUSE** | | | |

– Voodoo spell / The new snow / Your hand / Aime to prochain comme toi meme / Bitcher / Outside.

| Feb 97. | (cd) *(SB 66)* **REPENT** (live) | | | - |

– I / II / III / IV / V / VI.

| Oct 97. | (cd) *(<SB 64>)* **TUSK** | | | Jul97 |

– Plane / Head / Tuba / Half / Imaginary / Tusk.

			not iss.	Sub Pop
2000.	(7") *<SP 492>* **STEALTH. / FACTORY**		-	

			Language	not iss.
2000.	(d-cd) *(1&2)* **THE DEAD C**		-	- NewZ

– Accelerate / Dec / Pussyfooting / Speederbot / All channels open // One night / Realisation con slider / Fake electronics / Tuba is funny (slight return) / Drillbit / High original / Tidewater.

| 2001. | (cd) **NEW ELECTRIC MUSIC** | | - | - NewZ |

– Killer / Hush / Repulsion / Stand / Forever.

– compilations, etc. –

| 1994. | (cd) *Shock; (027)* **WORLD PEACE HOPE ET AL** | | - | - NewZ |

– Stars / Sun stabbed / Angel / Abschied / Fire / Puberty / Helen / Speed kills / This map / Communication with Heaven / Sea is violet / World / Peace / Hope.

| Nov 99. | (cd) *Flying Nun; (FNCD 443)* **DR503C** | | | - |

– Crazy I know / Speed kills / The wheel / Polio / Sun stabbed / Fire / Bad politics / 3 years / I love this / Max Harris / Angel.

GATE

MICHAEL MORLEY – synthesizer, guitar, vocals / **DAVID MERRITT** – guitar, vocals / + guest **SID MERRITT** – piano, accordion

			not iss.	Siltbreeze
1995.	(7") <SB 14> **PROPHET. / REBEL**		–	
			not iss.	Twisted
1995.	(7") <1023> **SUNSHINE. / IVES**		–	
Apr 95.	(cd) <1032> **LOUNGE**			

– Lounge / Lights burn / Asshole wanna-be / Touring nightmares slug #1 / Video hit masters / Crash bang fuck your head (F.Y.H.) / More than orphans / Uncle Jonah.

---- now with **LEE RANALDO** (of SONIC YOUTH) / **ZEENA PARKINS**

			not iss.	Poon Village
Dec 95.	(cd) <1> **LIVE IN BOSTON/NYC 1994 (live)**		–	

– Untitled / Untitled / Untitled / Untitled / Untitled / Untitled / Untitled.

			Precious Metal	not iss.
1996.	(d-lp) **THE LAVENDER HEAD**			– NewZ

– The blurred tree / Gasmask / Mary and Mars / Hands. (re-iss. 1998 on 'Hell's Half Halo'; HHH 04) (d-cd-iss. 2001 +=; HHH 04CD) – My dear sweet reluctant sweetheart / The lavender head.

---- **THURSTON MOORE** repl. ZEENA

			Krypton	Krypton
Mar 97.	(cd) <(KRYPTON 36)> **MONOLAKE**			

– Standing in fields / The hero tree / Sonora purring / To kiss the wall / Jennifer.

			Black Halo	not iss.
Jul 97.	(cd; by MICHAEL MORLEY) (BHC 004CD) **THE PAVILLION OF FOOLS**			–

– Parts I-VII.

			TableOfThe Elements	TableOfThe Elements
Sep 98.	(cd) <TOECD 22> **THE DEW LINE**		–	

– Millions / Needed all words / Have not / Autolevel / Venerable clouds / Dew line / Triphammer.

Nov 99.	(cd) <(TOECD 54)> **THE WISHER TABLE**			

– Center / Wail / Dark / Redux / Spirit / Faces / Hearts / Shimmer.

– compilations, etc. –

Apr 96.	(cd) I.M.D.; (IMD 10050) **GOLDEN**	–	– NewZ

– Wonderill / Tonken / Trig / Prophet / Rebel / I.O.M. (1967-1992) / Julian Dashper Gate experience I, II, III, IV / Sunshine / Ives / Mett / King.

A HANDFUL OF DUST

BRUCE RUSSELL + **ALASTAIR GALBRAITH** – violin / with guests **MICHAEL MORLEY** – guitar / + son **MAX RUSSELL**

			Corpus Hermeticum	Twisted Village
1992.	(7") <TW 1017> **A LITTLE AESTHETIC DISCOURSE**		–	

– Logopandocy / Titokowaru said.

1993.	(lp) (HERMES 001) <TW 1027> **CONCORD**		–	NewZ

– Come, breath upon these slain, that they may live / Squeezing Parson Foster's sponge / Truth's golden harrow / A brief apology (washing away & cleansing the stain of suspicion & infamy applied to the fraternity of the rosy cross with, as it were, a fludd of truth).

1994.	(cd) (HERMES 002) **THE PHILOSOPHIK MERCURY**	–	– NewZ

– Fama fraternitatis / God's love to his people Israel.

1994.	(c) (HERMES 003) **THE EIGHTHNESS OF ADAM QADMON**	–	– NewZ

– The oneness / The twoness / The threeness / The fourness / The fifthness / The sixness / The seventhness / The eighthness.

1994.	(7"one-sided) (HERMES 004) **THE SEVENTHNESS**	–	– NewZ
1994.	(cd) (HERMES 005) **MUSICA HUMANA** (compilation 1990-1993)	–	– NewZ

– The lonesome death of Albert Ayler / Logopandocy / Masonic inborn (parts 1 & 2) / Come, breath upon these slain, that they may live / Squeesing Parson Foster's sponge / Truth's golden harrow / Eulogy for a Riley / Titokoqru said / Calling Radio Ethiopia / A brief apology.

1994.	(7"ep) (HERMES 006) **THREE DANCES IN HONOUR OF SABBATAI SEVI, THE APOSTATE MESSIAH**	–	– NewZ

– The first dance in honour of Sabbatai Sevi / The second dance of Sabbatai Sevi / The third dance of Sabbatai Sevi.

---- added **PETER STAPLETON** – percussion; repl. guests

1994.	(7") (SB 038) **IN THE HOUSE OF VOLUNTARY POVERTY. / THE MIRROR OF SIMPLE SOULS (edit)**	–	– NewZ

(above issued on 'Siltbreeze')

1995.	(cd; as PIETERS / RUSSELL / STAPLETON) (HERMES 007) **LAST GLASS**	–	– NewZ

– Viper's widow / Last glass / Valerian / Gospelogy / Stoney verities / Auto violet reco.

---- PIETERS + STAPLETON were part of FLIES INSIDE THE SUN (ex-DADAMAH)

1995.	(7") (HERMES 008) **Michael Morley: RADIATION. / Bruce Russell: FOUR LETTERS**	–	– NewZ
1995.	(c) (HERMES 009) **FROM A SOUNDTRACK TO THE 'ANABASE' OF ST. JOHN PIERCE**	–	– NewZ

– He who eats the maggots of the palm tree / On the threshold of a land more chaste than death / The colour of grasshoppers crushed in their sap / And the sun is not names but named, but his power is amongst us / His heart savage and buzzing like a swarm of black flies / This world has more beauty than a rams skin painted red / A sort of saliva / Roses and bitumen, gift of song / Authority over all the signs of the earth.

(above without STAPLETON)

1995.	(7"one-sided) (HERMES 010) **AUTHORITY OVER ALL SIGNS OF THE EARTH**	–	– NewZ
1996.	(cd) (HERMES 013) **NOW GODS, STAND UP FOR BASTARDS**	–	– NewZ

– The book nature: chapter the first / Oration on the dignity of man / The expulsion of the triumphant beast / The Lullian art / The book nature: chapter the second / The dark lantern of reason.

---- in 1996-98, RUSSELL again recorded with PIETERS & STAPLETON on the album, 'SEX/MACHINE' (1999) – a single 'COLD SWEAT' was delivered in 2002 for 'Ecstatic Yod'.

1999.	(c) (HERMES 020) **TOPOLOGY OF A PHANTOM CITY**	–	– NewZ

– The city of the sun / The city of God / Negative Jerusalem.

2000.	(cd) (HERMES 029) **JERUSALEM, STREET OF GRAVES**	–	– NewZ

– Unreal city I / Unreal city II / Unreal city III / Unreal city IV / The city of God – Negative Jerusalem / I had not thought death had undone so many.

– compilations, etc. –

1997.	(cd) Crank Automotive; (C 6) **SPIRITUAL LIBERTINES**	–	– NewZ

– A peface to the hieroglyphic monad of Dr. John Dee / The first dance in honour of the Sabbatai Sevi / His heart savage and buzzing, like a swarm of black flies / Roses and bitumen, gift of song / The second dance in honour of the Sabbatai Sevi / This world has more beauty than a ram's skin painted red / The oneness of Adam Qadmon / The third dance in honour of the Sabbatai Sevi / And the sun is not named, but his power is amongst us / A single eye all light.

BRUCE RUSSELL

with **TOM LAX** + **PAUL TOOHEY**

			Siltbreeze	not iss.
Jun 98.	(lp) (SB 71) **PROJECT FOR A REVOLUTION IN NEW YORK**			–

– The erasers (live) / Recollections of the golden triangle.

			Crank	not iss.
1990's.	(cd) (CRANK 8) **MAXIMALIST MANTRA MUSIC**		–	– NewZ

– The war between desire and technology (cut up) / On certain obsolete notions (full length) / The air between desire and technology (tape version).

			Smalltown Supersound	not iss.
Feb 01.	(10"ep) (STS 044) **THE MOVEMENT OF THE FREE SPIRIT**		–	– Dutch

– The 1st movement / The 2nd movement.

			Corpus Hermeticum	not iss.
2001.	(cd) (HERMES 035) **PAINTING THE PASSPORTS BROWN**		–	– NewZ

– Black flies #1 / With Rimbaud in Abyssinia (ass backwards) / Black flies #2.

DEAD CAN DANCE

Formed: Melbourne, Australia . . . 1981 by multi-instrumentalist, BRENDAN PERRY and vocalist, LISA GERRARD, both of Anglo-Irish parentage. After initially immersing himself in the punk scene, PERRY became increasingly intrigued by the possibilities offered by electronic music, subsequently hooking up with GERRARD and two other early members, PAUL ERIKSON and SIMON MONROE. With a solitary homeland recording (very limited for 'Fast Forward' cassette mag) to their name, PERRY and GERRARD decided to take DEAD CAN DANCE to London where they fitted in perfectly among the avant-garde hopefuls at up and coming indie label, '4 a.d.'. At pains to point out that their name symbolised the energy inherent in apparently lifeless matter rather than the goth connotations many assumed, DEAD CAN DANCE were soon mesmerising critics and fans alike with their otherworldly synthesis of classical, ethnic and electronic music. An eponymous debut album emerged in 1984 and although its noisy dissonance only hinted at the sculpted aesthetics to come, highlights included 'A PASSAGE IN TIME', 'THE TRIAL' and 'THE FATAL IMPACT'. However, with a costly 15-piece ensemble in tow, they only selected a few venues for concerts and never toured consistently. 1985's 'SPLEEN AND IDEAL' was a more atmospheric, darkly intoxicating affair, introducing more varied instrumental textures and the wailing Middle Eastern, OFRA HAZA-style vocals of GERRARD on such compulsive tracks as 'THE CARDINAL SIN', 'MESMERISM', and every monk's favourite, 'DE PROFUNDIS (OUT OF THE DEPTHS OF SORROW)'. 'WITHIN THE REALM OF A DYING SUN' (1987) moved towards classical territory with a cast of violin, viola, etc, while 'SERPENT'S EGG' (1988) tackled medieval folk styles of Eastern Europe. PERRY and GERRARD moved even further into the past (or rather brought the past into the future) with their exploration of Renaissance era music – both spiritual and secular – on 1990's 'AION'. The early 90's found PERRY and GERRARD working on a variety of side projects including scoring music for a production of 'Oedipus Rex' and the soundtrack to the movie, 'Baraka'. DEAD CAN DANCE briefly emerged from the realm of cult obscurity and into the Top 50 (hovered under the US Top 100) in 1993 with their seventh album, 'INTO THE LABYRINTH'. LISA went on to release a few solo outings, one under the pseudonym of ELIJAH'S MANTLE, while DEAD CAN DANCE managed to capture the mystical allure of their studio work on live set, 'TOWARD THE WITHIN' (1994). With 1995's 'SPIRITCHASER', DEAD CAN DANCE nearly cracked the UK Top 40 while making the US Top 75, a mark of burgeoning popular appeal for a band who were already almost universally respected among fellow artists across the musical spectrum. DEAD CAN DANCE had been keeping uncharacteristically quiet, although LISA GERRARD (who'd debuted solo in 1995 with 'THE MIRROR POOL') released a collaborative set with PETER BOURKE (of SOMA) entitled 'DUALITY' (1998). Towards the end of the decade and with DCD now defunct, it would be BRENDAN's turn to go single-handed. 'EYE OF THE HUNTER' was a marked shift from his earlier goth-meets-baroque style rock in that he chose to virtually mimic his idols, SCOTT WALKER ('ARCHANGEL' & 'SATURDAY'S CHILD') and TIM BUCKLEY ('I MUST HAVE BEEN BLIND' – didn't he do this for '4ad' conglomerate THIS MORTAL COIL). However, the seriousness of his intentions came across quite well, although the world of opera might be getting ready for a new recruit – perhaps not! Inevitably perhaps, GERRARD's talent found a welcoming home in the world of film soundtracks, more specifically Ridley Scott's much praised 'Gladiator'. Co-writing with Hans Zimmer, the

DEAD CAN DANCE (cont)   THE GREAT INDIE DISCOGRAPHY   The 1980s

former DCD songstress was instrumental in shaping the film's wide ranging score. While the original CD soundtrack was released simultaneously with the film in Spring 2000, a second disc of excerpts rounded out the picture in early 2001. • **Songwriters:** GERRARD / PERRY (some w/ others and some trad folk samples). • **Trivia:** They also can be heard on '4 a.d.' amalgam THIS MORTAL COIL and also featured two tracks on various lp, 'Lonely As An Eyesore'.

Album rating: DEAD CAN DANCE (*7) / SPLEEN AND IDEAL (*6) / WITHIN THE REALM OF A DYING SUN (*8) / THE SERPENT'S EGG (*7) / AION (*8) / A PASSAGE IN TIME (*8) / INTO THE LABYRINTH (*7) / TOWARD THE WITHIN (*6) / SPIRITCHASER (*6) / Lisa Gerrard: THE MIRROR POOL (*6) / DUALITY with Peter Bourke (*6) / GLADIATOR with Hans Zimmer (*7) / Brendan Perry: EYE OF THE HUNTER (*6)

BRENDAN PERRY – multi-instrumentalist, vocals / **LISA GERRARD** – vocals, percussion / **PETER ULRICH** – percussion, drums, tapes with **JAMES PINKER** – timpani, mixer / **SIMON RODGER** – trombone; plus **MARTIN McCARRICK** + **GUY FERGUSON** – cello / **CAROLYN LOSTIN** – violin / **RICHARD AVISON** – trombone / **TONY AYERS** – timpani / **ANDREW NUTTER** – soprano vox

                                                                     4 a.d.   Rough Trade

Feb 84. (lp) *(CAD 404)* **DEAD CAN DANCE**
– The fatal impact / The trial / Frontier / Fortune / Ocean / East of Eden / Threshold / A passage in time / Wild in the woods / Musica eternal. *(cd-iss. Feb87; CAD 404CD)* – (includes below EP). *<US-iss.1994 on '4 a.d.-Reprise' cd,c; 45546>*

Sep 84. (12"ep) *(BAD 408)* **GARDEN OF ARCANE DELIGHTS**
– Carnival of light / In power we entrust the love advocated / The arcane / Flowers of the sea.

Nov 85. (lp/c)(cd) *(CAD/+C 512)(CAD 512CD)* **SPLEEN AND IDEAL**
– De profundis (out of the depths of sorrow) / Ascension / Circum radiant dawn / The cardinal sin / Mesmerism / Enigma of the absolute / Advent / Avatar / Indoctrination (a design for living). *(cd+=)* – This tide. *<US-iss.1994 on '4 a.d.-Reprise' cd,c; 45547>*

—— now a basic duo of **BRENDAN** + **LISA** when ULRICH departed (SIMON + JAMES formed HEAVENLY BODIES). Retained **FERGUSON** + **AVISON** and recruited **ALISON HARLING** + **EMLYN SINGLETON** – violin / **PIERO GASPARINI** – viola / **TONY GAMMAGE** + **MARK GERRARD** (bother) – trumpet / **RUTH WATSON** – oboe, bass trombone / **JOHN** + **PETER SINGLETON** – trombone / **ANDREW CAXTON** – tuba, bass trombone

Jul 87. (lp/c)(cd) *(CAD/+C 705)(CAD 705CD)* **WITHIN THE REALM OF A DYING SUN**
– Anywhere out of the world / Windfall / In the wake of adversity / Xavier / Dawn of the iconoclast / Cantara / Summoning of the muse / Persephone (the gathering of flowers). *<US-iss.1994 on '4 a.d.-Reprise' cd,c; 45577>*

—— **LISA** + **BRENDAN** brought in **DAVID NAVARRO SUST** (retained **ALISON** + **TONY**), new **REBECCA JACKSON** – violin / **SARAH BUCKLEY** + **ANDREW BEESLEY** – violas

Oct 88. (lp/c)(cd) *(CAD/+C 808)(CAD 808CD)* **THE SERPENT'S EGG**
– The host of Seraphim / Orbis de Ignis / Severance / Chant of the Paladin / The writing on my father's hand / Echolalia / In the kingdom of the blind, the one-eyed are kings / Song of Sophia / Mother tongue / Ullyses. *<US-ss.1994 on '4 a.d.-Reprise' cd,c; 45576>*

Jul 90. (cd)(lp/c) *(CAD 0007CD)(CAD/+C 0007)* **AION**
– The arrival and the reunion / Saltarello / Mephisto / The song of the Sibyl / Fortune presents gifts not according to the book / As the bell rings the maypole spins / The end of words / Black sun / Wilderness / The promised womb / The garden of Zephyrus / Radharc. *<US-iss.1994 on '4 a.d.-Reprise' cd,c; 45575>*

Sep 93. (cd)(c)(d-lp) *(CAD 3013CD)(CADC 3013)(DAD 3013) <45384>* **INTO THE LABYRINTH**   47
– Yulunga (spirit dance) / The ubiquitous Mr. Lovegrove / The wind that shakes the barley / The carnival is over / Ariadne / Saldek / Towards the within / Tell me about the forest (you once called home) / The spider's Stratagem / Emmeleia / How fortunate the man with none. *(d-lp+=)* – Bird / Spirit.

Oct 94. (cd)(d-lp/c) *(DAD 4015CD)(DAD/+C 4015) <45769>* **TOWARD THE WITHIN**
– Rakim / Persian love song / Desert song / Yulunga (spirit dance) / Piece for solo flute / The wind that shakes the barley / I am stretched on your grave / I can see now / American dreaming / Cantara / Oman / Song of the Sibyl / Tristan / Sanveen / Don't fade away.

Jun 96. (c/cd)(d-lp) *(CAD 6008/+CD)(DAD 6008) <46230>*
SPIRITCHASER   43   75
– Nierika / Song of the stars / Indus / Song of the dispossessed / Dedicaci outr / The snake and the Moon / Song of the Nile / Devorzhum.

– **compilations, etc.** –

Oct 91. (cd)(c) *4 a.d.; (CAD 1010CD)(CADC 1010) / Rykodisc; <RCD2/RACS 0215>* **A PASSAGE IN TIME** (part compilation)
– Saltarello / Song of Sophia / Ullyses / Cantara / The garden of Zephirus / Enigma of the absolute / Wilderness / The host of Seraphim / Anywhere out of the world / The writing on my father's hand / Severance / The song of the Sibyl (traditional version; Catalan 16th Century) / Fortune presents gifts not according to the book / In the kingdom of the blind the one-eyed are kings / Bird / Spirit.

Dec 91. (cd) *Emperion; (IMP 008)* **THE HIDDEN TREASURES** (out-takes, live, rare)
– Awakening / Reached from above / In power we entrust the love advocated / To the shore / Alone / Pray for dawn / Lartomento / The night we were lost / Lyndra / Isabella / Tune for Sheba / Cyndrill / The serpent's army / They don't even cry / Eyeless in Gaza / The endless longing of sea doves.

Nov 01. (3xcd-box) *Rhino; <(DCDBOX 1)>* **DEAD CAN DANCE 1981-1998**

LISA GERRARD

—— with The VICTORIAN PHILHARMONIC ORCHESTRA. She had worked on the scores for 'Oedipus Rex' and 'Baraku', while sidelining with ELIJAH'S MANTLE.

Aug 95. (cd)(c) *(CAD 5009CD)(CADC 5009) <45916>* **THE MIRROR POOL**
– Violina: The last embrace / La Bas: Song of the drowned / Persian love song: The silver gun / Sanvean / I am your shadow / The rite / Ajhon / Glorafin / Majhnavea's music box / Largo / Werd / Laurelei / Celon / Ventelas / Swans / Nilleshna / Gloradin. *(cd re-iss. Jul98; GAD 5009CD)*

—— next a collaboration with **PETER BOURKE** (of SOMA)

Apr 98. (cd; by LISA GERRARD & PETER BOURKE) *(CAD 8004CD) <46854>* **DUALITY**
– Shadow magnet / Tempest / Forest veil / The comforter / The unfolding / Pilgrimage of lost children / The human game / The circulation of shadows / Sacrifice / Nadir (synchronicity).

—— in May'00, HANS ZIMMER & LISA GERRARD collaborated on the soundtrack to hit (& UK No.17 / US No.66) chart album of 'GLADIATOR'

BRENDAN PERRY

with various musicians

Oct 99. (lp/cd) *<CAD 9015/+CD>* **EYE OF THE TIGER**
– Saturday's child / Voyage of bran / Medusa / Sloth / I must have been blind / The captive heart / Death will be my bride / Archangel.

DEAD FAMOUS PEOPLE

Formed: New Zealand . . . 1986 by DONNA SAVAGE, BIDDY LEYLAND, WENDY KJESTRUP, JENNY RENALS and ROBIN TEARLE. However, after minor homeland hits for who else, the 'Flying Nun' imprint, the 5-piece moved shop to England signing with 'Utility' (once home of BILLY BRAGG).

Album rating: ARRIVING LATE IN TORN AND FILTHY JEANS mini (*6)

DONNA SAVAGE – vocals / **BIDDY LEYLAND** – keyboards / **WENDY KJESTRUP** – guitar / **JENNY RENALS** – bass / **ROBIN TEARLE** – drums

                                         Craft   not iss.

1987. (7"flexi) *(BULL 1-0)* **DRIVE AWAY. / Screeming Custard!: RAFT**

                                          –   – NewZ
                                            Flying Nun not iss.

1987. (12"ep) *(FN 073)* **LOST PERSONS AREA**   –   – NewZ

—— **GILL MOON** – drums; repl. ROBIN TEARLE (partly on below set)

                                         Utility   not iss.

Jul 89. (m-lp/m-cd) *(UTIL 007/+CD)* **ARRIVING LATE IN TORN AND FILTHY JEANS**
– The girl with an attitude problem / Postcard from paradise / Evil child / Barlow's house / Traitor to the cause / Take your leather jacket off.

—— split in the summer of 1990, SAVAGE almost immediately guesting for SAINT ETIENNE on their version of The Field Mice's 'LET'S KISS AND MAKE UP'. She subsequently went solo, as did LEYLAND, returning to New Zealand in the process.

– **compilations, etc.** –

Jun 94. (cd) *La-Di-Da; (LADIDA 016CD)* **ALL HAIL THE DAFFODIL**
– With wings we'll soar the heavens / How to be kind / Little flashes of yesterday / Wild young ways / In praise of right now / Postcard from paradise / Life said to the boy / Gavin / Left / Go home stay home / All hail the daffodil.

DEAD MILKMEN

Formed: Philadelphia, Pennsylvania, USA . . . early 80's by RODNEY AMADEUS ANONYMOUS, JOE JACK TALCUM, DAVE BLOOD and DEAN CLEAN. Signed to 'Enigma', this bunch of punkoid piss-takers debuted with 1985's 'BIG LIZARD IN MY BACKYARD' album, no target too soft for their patented brand of adolescent high school humour. 'EAT YOUR PAISLEY!' continued in similar style the following year, the band's natural college campus fanbase lapping up the trashy likes of 'WHERE THE TARANTULA LIVES' and 'SWAMPLAND OF DESIRE'. Following the replacement of TALCUM and BLOOD with JASPER THREAD and LORD MANIAC respectively, the band offered up another trawl through the more satire-friendly aspects of American culture in the shape of 1987's 'BUCKY FELLINI'. Come the turn of the decade, The DEAD MILKMEN were still showing little sign of growing up with 'METAPHYSICAL GRAFFITI' (1990), featuring BUTTHOLE SURFER, GIBBY HAYNES on the YES-baiting 'ANDERSON, WALKMAN, BUTTHOLES AND HOW!'.

Album rating: BIG LIZARD IN MY BACKYARD (*7) / EAT YOUR PAISLEY! (*6) / BUCKY FELLINI (*7) / BEELZEBUBBA (*5) / METAPHYSICAL GRAFITTI (*4) / SOUL ROTATION (*3) / NOT RICHARD, BUT DICK (*4) / CHAOS RULES – LIVE AT THE TROCADERO (*4) / STONEY'S EXTRA STOUT (PIG) (*4)

RODNEY AMADEUS ANONYMOUS – vocals / **JOE JACK TALCUM** – guitar, vocals / **DAVE BLOOD** – bass / **DEAN CLEAN** – drums

                                          not iss.   Jerrock

1982. (c) *<none>* **A DATE WITH THE DEAD MILKMEN**
1983. (c) *<none>* **FUNKY FARM**
– Beach song / Labor day / Don't abort that baby / I'm going to purgatory / Watching Scotty die / I don't wanna / Taking retards to the zoo / Dance with me / Girl hunt / Stupid Mary Anne / Fillet of sole / Depression day dinner / Rastabilly.

1984. (c) *<none>* **DEATH RIDES A PALE COW**
– Labor day / I don't wanna, I don't wanna / Veterans of a fucked up world / Bitchin' Camaro / Plumb dumb / Laundromat song / Land of the shakers / Dance with me / Rastabilly / I hate myself / Ich bin ein junkie, was? / Beach party Vietnam / Milkmen stomp.

1984. (c) **THE DEAD MILKMEN TAKE THE AIRWAVES**
– Beach song / Dance with me / Labor day / Bitchin' Camaro / Plumb dumb / Swordfish / VCW (Veterans of a Censored World) / Spit sink / Laundromat song / Fillet of sole / I hate myself / I'm a junkie, so what? / Right Wing pigeons / Radio blast / Dean's dream / Rastabilly / Takin' retards to the zoo / Violent school / (extra snippets).

DEAD MILKMEN (cont)

1984. (c) <none> **SOMEONE SHOT SUNSHINE**
 – Serrated edge / Swordfish / Dean's dream / Takin' retards to the zoo / Surfin' cow / Gorrila girl / Nutrition / Spit sink / Whities gonna pay / Christmas party / Go tell it on the mountain.

<small>Enigma   Enigma</small>

1985. (lp/c/cd) <97105-1/-4/-2> **BIG LIZARD IN MY BACKYARD**
 – Tiny town / Beach song / Plum dumb / Swordfish / V.F.W. / Rastabilly / Serrated edge / Lucky / Big lizard / Gorilla girl / Bitchin' Camaro / Filet of sole / Spit sink / Violent school / Takin' retards to the zoo / Junkie / Right wing oigeons / Dean's dream / Laundromat song / Nutrition / Tugena. *(UK cd-iss. Mar98 on 'Restless'; 720542)*

Nov 86. (lp/c/cd) (2131-1) <97-131-1/-4/-2> **EAT YOUR PAISLEY!** <small>Aug86</small>
 – Where the tarantula lives / Air crash museum / KK suck 2 / Fifty things / Happy is / Beach party Vietnam / I hear your name / Two feet off the ground / The thing that only eats hippies / Sic days / Swampland of desire / Take me apart / Moron / The fez. *(cd+=)* – Vince Lombardi service center.

—— **JASPER THREAD** – guitar; repl. **JOE JACK TALCUM**
—— **LORD MANIAC** – bass; repl. **DAVE BLOOD**

Oct 87. (lp) (3260-1) <73260> **BUCKY FELLINI** <small>Jul87</small>
 – The pit / Take me to the specialist / I am the walrus / Watching Scotty die / Going to Graceland / Big time operator / Instant club hit (you'll dance to anything) / The badger song / Tacoland / City of mud / Rocketship / Nitro burning funny cars / Surfin' cow / Theme from 'Bloody Orgy Of The Atomic Fern') / Jellyfish heaven.

Nov 87. (cd-ep) <72231-2> **INSTANT CLUB HIT (YOU'LL DANCE TO ANYTHING) /** ('A'edit) / **BONER BEATS / ASK ME TO DANCE / TUGENA / VINCE LOMBARDI SERVICE CENTER**

<small>Enigma-Virgin   Enigma</small>

Dec 88. (lp/c/cd) (ENVLP/TCENV/CDENV 514) <73351> **BEELZEBUBBA**
 – Brat in the frat / RC's mom / Stuart / I walk the thinnest line / Sri Lanka sex hotel / Bad party / Punk rock girl / Bleach boys / My many smells / Smokin' banana peels / The guitar song / Born to love volcanos / Everybody's got nice stuff but me / I against Osbourne / Howard beware / Ringo buys a rifle / Life is shit.

Dec 88. (7") **PUNK ROCK GIRL. / DIZZY IN THE DAYLIGHT**
 (c-s+=) – Ringo buys a rifle.

Feb 89. (7") (ENV 8) **PUNK ROCK GIRL. / RINGO BUYS A RIFLE**
 (12"+=) (ENVT 8) – Life is shit.

<small>Restless   Enigma</small>

Sep 90. (cd/c/lp) (LS 93591) <D21S-73564-2/-4/-1> **METAPHYSICAL GRAFFITI** <small>Apr90</small>
 – Beige sunshine / Do the brown nose / Methodist coloring book / Part 3 / I tripped over the ottoman / The big sleazy / If you love somebody, set them on fire / Dollar signs in their eyes / In praise of Sha Na Na / Epic tales of adventure / I hate you, I love you / Now everybody's me / Little man in my head / Anderson, Walkman, Buttholes and How!

Jan 91. (cd-ep) <72546> **SMOKIN' BANANA PEELS (5 versions) / DEPRESSION DAY DINNER / PUKING SONG / I HATE MYSELF / GIRL HUNT / DEATH'S ALRIGHT WITH ME**

<small>not iss.   Hollywood</small>

Apr 92. (cd/c) <61294-2/-4> **SOUL ROTATION**
 – At the moment / The secret of life / Big scary place / Belafonte's inferno / The conspiracy song / How's it gonna be / All around the world / Silly dreams / Wonderfully colored plastic war toys / God's kid brother / If I had a gun / Here comes Mr. X / Shaft in Greenland.

Nov 92. (m-cd/m-c) <61409-2/-4> **IF I HAD A GUN**
 – If I had a gun / Bitchin' Camaro (the best thanksgiving ever) (live) / Silly dreams (live) / The conspiracy song (live) / Dolce.

Oct 93. (cd/c) <61564-2/-4> **NOT RICHARD, BUT DICK**
 – Leggo my ego / I dream of Jesus / Jason's head / Not crazy / Let's get the baby high / Little volcano / Nobody falls like / I started to hate you / The infant of Prague customized my van / The woman who was also a mongoose.

<small>not iss.   Restless</small>

Nov 94. (cd,c) <72793> **CHAOS RULES: LIVE AT THE TROCADERO (live)**
 – Tiny town / I walk the thinnest line / Smokin' banana peels / Surfin' cow / Bitchin' Camaro / Where the taratula lives / Nutrition / Big lizard / The thing that only eats hippies / I hate you, I love you / Lucky / V.F.W. / Rock girl / Rastabilly / Stuart / Right wing pigeons / Tacoland / Laundromat song / Swordfish.

Nov 95. (cd,c) <72798> **STONEY'S EXTRA STOUT (PIG)**
 – Peter Bazooka / Train I ride / The girl with the strong arm / I'm flying away / Helicopter interiors / The blues song / The man who rides the bus / Don't deny your inner child / When I get to Heaven / I can't stay awake / Crystalline / Chaos theory / Khrissy / Like to be alone / Big deal.

—— they split some time in '96

– compilations, etc. –

1993. (cd) *own label*; **NOW WE ARE 10**
Nov 97. (cd) *Restless*; <72945> **DEATH RIDES A PALE COW: THE ULTIMATE COLLECTION**
 – Milkmen stomp / Tiny town / Big lizard / Bitchin' Camaro / Nutrition / Dean's dream / Beach party Vietnam / The thing that only eats hippies / Big time operator / Instant club hit / Surfin' cow / Labor day / I walk the thinnest line / Stuart / Punk rock girl / Smokin' banana peels / Life is shit / If you love someone, set them on fire / Peter Bazooka / The girl with the strong arm / Big deal / The blues song.
Nov 98. (m-cd) *BMG Special*; <44841> **CREAM OF THE CROP: THE BEST OF THE DEAD MILKMEN**
 – Bitchin' Camaro / Punk rock girl / The thing that only eats hippies / Surfin' cow / Instant club hit (you'll dance to anything) / Smokin' banana peels / Stuart / Beach song / Dean's dream / Laundromat song.

DEATHFOLK
(see under ⇒ GERMS; 70's section)

DEATH IN JUNE

Formed: Guildford & Woking, Surrey, England ... 1981 out of CRISIS by DOUG PEARCE and TONY WAKEFORD. The latter post-punk combo released only three singles and a solitary album, 'HYMNS OF FAITH' (1980), before PEARCE and WAKEFORD teamed up with PATRICK LEAGAS and CHRIS JENNER. Signed to 'New European Records', DEATH IN JUNE released their debut EP in early 82; heavy goths in the mould of SISTERS OF MERCY or early DANSE SOCIETY, the band followed up with a debut album, 'THE GUILTY HAVE NO PRIDE' (1983). What set them apart from their peers was their use of militaristic electronic/percussive rhythms, although their sound did hint at influences as diverse as JOY DIVISION and SOFT CELL. Following WAKEFORD's departure to SOL INVICTUS, DIJ recruited RICHARD BUTLER, releasing follow-up set, 'BURIAL', in 1984. The more heavily electronic 'NADA' (1985), meanwhile, threw a bit of footstomping flamenco (incredibly calling to mind Miles Davis' 'SKETCHES OF SPAIN'!) into the mix with 'THE HONOUR OF SILENCE', while 'THE CALLING' could've been SPANDAU BALLET had they grown up in Sheffield! Like many "goth" bands, however, DEATH IN JUNE were something of an acquired taste, the doom-lord vocals and OTT arrangements occasionally descending into pretentiousness. While the band's prolific release schedule continued through the 80's and 90's on albums such as 'BROWN BOOK' – prior to which, DAVID TIBET replaced JENNER – 'WALL OF SACRIFICE' (1988) and 'ROSE CLOUDS OF HOLOCAUST' (1993), they failed to attract much more than the barest of cult underground publicity.

Album rating: THE GUILTY HAVE NO PRIDE (*6) / BURIAL (*5) / NADA (*5) / THE WORLD THAT SUMMER (*5) / LESSON 1 compilation (*5) / BROWN BOOK (*4) / THE WALL OF SACRIFICE (*4) / BUT, WHAT ENDS WHEN THE SYMBOLS SHATTER? (*4) / ROSE CLOUDS OF HOLOCAUST (*4) / SOMETHING IS COMING (*4) / Crisis: WE ARE ALL JEWS AND GERMANS compilation (*5)

CRISIS

DOUGLAS P.(EARCE) – rhythm guitar, vocals / **TONY WAKEFORD** – bass, vocals / **PHRAZER** – vocals / **LESTER JONES** – lead guitar, vocals / **THE CLEANER / INSECT ROBIN** – drums

<small>Peckham Action   not iss.</small>

Feb 79. (7"ep) (NOTH 1) **PC 1984. / HOLOCAUST / NO TOWN HALL**

<small>Ardkor   not iss.</small>

Dec 79. (7") (CRI 002) **UK '78. / WHITE YOUTH**
May 80. (m-lp) (CRI 003) **HYMNS OF FAITH**
 – On TV / Laughing / Back in the USSR / Afraid / Frustration / Red brigades / Kanada kommando.
Nov 81. (7"m) (CRI 004) **ALIENATION. / BRUKWOOD HOSPITAL**

—— last line-up **DEXTER** – vocals; repl. PHRAZER
—— **LUKE RENDALL** – drums; repl. THE CLEANER

- compilations, etc

Aug 82. (12"ep) *Crisis*; (NOTH 1) **HOLOCAUST UK EP**
Aug 84. (lp) *Bulleon*; (BULP 4) **ARMED TO THE TEETH**
Mar 97. (cd) *Crisis*; (CR 16) **WE ARE ALL JEWS AND GERMANS**
 (all material)

DEATH IN JUNE

TONY WAKEFORD – keyboards, bass / **DOUGLAS P** – guitar / **PATRICK LEAGAS** – drums / **CHRIS JENNER** – visuals

<small>N.E.R.   not iss.</small>

Feb 82. (12"ep) (SA 29634) **HEAVEN STREET. / WE DRIVE EAST / IN THE NIGHT TIME**
 (re-iss. Jan84 7"/12"; first 2 tracks only on 7")
Nov 82. (7") (SA 30634) **STATE LAUGHTER. / HOLY WATER**
Jun 83. (lp) (NER 6) **THE GUILTY HAVE NO PRIDE**
 – Till the living flesh is burned / All alone in her nirvana / State laughter / Nothing changes / Nation / Heaven street mk II / The guilty have no pride. *(re-iss. 1985; BADVC 3) (cd-iss. Dec90;)*

—— **RICHARD BUTLER** – keyboards; repl. WAKEFORD who joined SOL INVICTUS

Apr 84. (lp) (UBADVC 4) **BURIAL**
 – Death of the west / Fields / Nirvana / Sons of Europe / Black radio / Till the living flesh is burned / All done in her nirvana / Fields / We drive east / Heaven street. *(re-iss. Dec90 colrd-lp/cd;)*
Aug 84. (12"ep) (12BADVC 6) **THE CALLING. / SHE SAID DESTROY / DOUBT NOTHING**
Feb 85. (lp,pic-lp) (BADVC 13) **NADA!**
 – The honour of silence / The calling (mk.II) / Leper lord / Rain of despair / Foretold / Behind the rose (fields of rape) / She said destroy / Carousel / C'est un reve / Crush my love.
Mar 85. (12"m) (BADVC 69) **BORN AGAIN. / THE CALLING (Mk.II) / CAROUSEL (Bolt mix)**
 (re-iss. Oct88 on 'Cenaz' 12"pic-d; CENAZ 09)
Nov 85. (7") (BADVC 73) **COME BEFORE CHRIST AND MURDER LOVE. /** ('A'instrumental)
 (12") (12BADVC 73) – ('A'side) / Torture by roses.

—— **DAVID TIBET** – vocals (ex-23 SKIDOO, ex-PSYCHIC TV) repl. JENNER

Apr 86. (lp) (BADVC 726) **LESSON 1: MISANTHROPY** (early compilation)
 – Heaven Street / We drive east / In the night time / State laughter / Holy water / All alone in her nirvana / Till the living flesh is burned / The guilty have no pride / Fields / Death of the west.

DEATH IN JUNE (cont)

Jun 86. (d-lp) *(BADVC 9)* **THE WORLD THAT SUMMER**
– Rule again / Break the black ice / Rocking horse night / Blood victory / Blood of winter / Hidden among the leaves / Torture by roses / Come before Christ and murder love / Love murder / Death of a man / Reprise #1 / Reprise #2 / Reprise #3. *(cd-iss. Dec90;)*

—— added **ROSE McDOWELL** – vocals (ex-STRAWBERRY SWITCHBLADE)

May 87. (10"ep) *(BADVC 10)* **TO DROWN A ROSE. / EUROPA: THE GATES OF HEAVEN / ZIMMERIT**

Oct 87. (lp) *(BADVC 11)* **BROWN BOOK**
– Heilige Tod / Touch defiles / Hail! the white grain / Runes and men / To drown a rose / Red dog – Black dog / In the fog of the world / We are the lust / Punishment initiation / Brown book / Burn again.

Oct 88. (lp) *(BADVC 88)* **THE WALL OF SACRIFICE**
– The wall of sacrifice / Giddy giddy carousel / Heilige leben / Fall apart / Bring in the night / In sacrilege / Hullo angel / Death is a drummer. *(cd-iss. Jan90; BADVCCD 88)*

Jan 89. (m-lp) *(BADVC 93)* **93 DEAD SUNWHEELS** (with CURRENT 93)
– The torture garden / Last farewell / Doubt to nothing / Behind the rose (fields of rape) / C'est un reve / She said destroy.

Dec 90. (12"ep; shared with CURRENT 93) *(BADVC 693)* **1888 EP**
– Break the black ice / Fall apart (Rose mix) / Rule again (Tibet 93) / (CURRENT 93 tracks).

—— added **JAMES MANNOX**

Dec 91. (cd) *(BADVCCD 34)* **THE CATHEDRAL OF TEARS**
– Brown book (re-read) / Burn again / Death of a man / Rule again (instrumental) / Touch defiles / Hidden among the leaves / Red dog – Black dog / Blood victory (instrumental) / Brown book / Cathedral of tears / Blood victory.

Feb 92. (12"pic-d-ep) *(BADVC 8)* **CATHEDRAL OF TEARS (studio I) / CATHEDRAL OF TEARS (studio II). / TO DROWN A ROSE (Paris live) / THE FOG OF THE WORLD (Paris live) / EUROPA: THE GATES OF HELL (Paris live)**

1993. (lp/cd) *(BADVC/+CD 36)* **BUT, WHAT ENDS WHEN THE SYMBOLS SHATTER?**
– Death is the martyr of beauty / He's disabled / The mourner's bench / Because of him / Daedalus rising / Little black angel / The golden wedding of sorrow / The giddy edge of light / Ku ku ku / This is not paradise / Hollows of devotion / But, what ends when the symbols shatter? *(cd re-iss. Oct97; same)*

1993. (lp/cd) *(BADVC/+CD 38)* **ROSE CLOUDS OF HOLOCAUST**
– Lord winter / God's golden sperm / Omen filled season / Symbols of the sun / Jerusalem / Black / Luther's army / 13 years of carrion / Accidental protege / Rose clouds of holocaust / Lifebooks. *(re-iss. Oct97; same)*

—— added **SIMON NORRIS**

1993. (12"ep) *(BADVC 63)* **PARADISE RISING**
– This is not paradise / Ceci n'est pas le paradis / O paradis ... / Daedalus brise / Daedalus falling / Daedalus est tombe du nouvel age.

1994. (d-lp; 3 sides) *(BADVCCD 96)* **SOMETHING IS COMING (Crotia live!)**
– Death is the martyr of beauty / Hullo angel / Giddy giddy carousel / Hollows of devotion / Rocking horse night / He's disabled / Fall apart / Heaven Street / Break the black ice / Leper lord / Golden wedding of sorrow / Torture by roses / Little black angel / But what ends when the symbols shatter / Fields of rape / Ku ku ku / Zagreb stdio:- Giddy giddy carousel / Runes and men / The golden wedding of sorrow / Death is the martyr of beauty. *(re-iss. Oct97; same) (re-iss. 1996 d-lp; BADVC 96)*

1994. (7"ep) *(NERO 1)* **SUNDOGS**
– Rose clouds of holocaust / 13 years of Clarion.

– compilations, etc. –

Sep 87. (lp) *Eyas Media; (EYAS 011)* **OH, HOW WE LAUGHED**
– Knives / Nirvana / Heaven Street / Nothing changes / Nation / Holy water / State laughter / In the nightime / We drive east / How we laughed. *(cd-iss. Oct89; EYAS 1030) (re-iss. cd Aug93 on 'Trevor'; CDOS 1)*

Feb 89. (cd) *N.E.R.; (BADVCCD 007)* **THE CORN YEARS**
– Heilige! / Torture by roses / Love murder / Zimmerit / We are the lust / To drown a rose / Break the black ice / Behind the rose (fields of rape) / Punishment initiation / Rocking horse night / Break the black ice (instrumental) / Runes and men / Rule again / Hail! the white grain / Blood of winter / The fog of the world / Europa: the gates of Heaven / Come before Christ and murder love. *(re-iss. Oct97; same)*

1992. (red-lp) *Leprosy; (LEPER 2)* **NIGHT AND FOG**

1995. (7"box/10"box/12"box/cd-s-box) *N.E.R.;* **BLACK WHOLE OF LOVE**

Oct 96. (2xc-box) *N.E.R.; (SB 01)* **OSTENBRAUN / LES JOYAUX DE LA PRINCESSE**

DEATH OF SAMANTHA
(see under ⇒ COBRA VERDE; in 90's section)

DECORATORS

Formed: Manchester, England ... 1980 by MICHAEL BEVAN, JOHNNY GILANI, STEVE SANDOE, JOE SAX and ALLAN BOROUGHS. Moving to a communal London residence, the flatmates released a couple of singles on the 'New Hormones' imprint (debut, 'PENDULUM AND SWING' on offshoot, 'Red'), before nearly getting their big break from Island's Andrew Lauder. Unfortunately, he was to be snapped up by 'Demon' records and the now six-piece (with the addition of PETE SAUNDERS) found a home at 'Red Flame'. This is where they were to remain ('Virgin' in France), releasing two patchy, brassy MAGAZINE-esque sets, 'TABLETS' (1982) and the mini 'REBEL SONGS' (1983).

Album rating: TABLETS (*5) / REBEL SONGS (*4)

MICHAEL BEVAN – vocals, guitar / **JOHNNY GILANI** – guitar / **PETE SAUNDERS** – keyboards / **JOE SAX** – saxophone / **STEVE SANDOE** – bass / **ALLAN BOROUGHS** – drums

Mar 81. (7") *(RS 009)* **PENDULUM AND SWING. / RENDEZVOUS / STRANGE ONE**

Jul 81. (7") *(ORG 5)* **TWILIGHT VIEW. / REFLECTIONS**

—— added **PETE SAUNDERS** – keyboards

Jun 82. (7"/12") *(RF7/RF12 05)* **STRANGE ONE. / TABLETS**
Jul 82. (lp) *(RF 1)* **TABLETS**
– Strange one / We know it / Hidden hands / Headlights / Absent friends / Red sky over Wembley / American ways / Half world / Without you / We know it (part 2) / Curious.

Dec 83. (m-lp) *(RFM 208)* **REBEL SONGS**
—— disbanded some time the following year

Maurice DEEBANK (see under ⇒ FELT)

DEEP FREEZE MICE

Formed: Leicester, England ... 1979 by pop maverick ALAN JENKINS. Forming his own label, 'Mole Embalming', as a means of operating outwith the demands of the mainstream alternative scene, JENKINS – along with musical sidekicks SHERREE LAWRENCE and GRAHAM SUMMERS (MICHAEL BUNNAGE was a part-timer until 1980) – released the first DEEP FREEZE MICE album in 1979. Entitled 'MY GERANIUMS ARE BULLETPROOF', the record introduced the band's patented brand of psychedelic whimsy, often compared to SYD BARRETT, etc., but in reality more like HALF MAN HALF BISCUIT minus the fun. JENKINS' twee, Herbert-style vocals and off-kilter sense of humour (check out 'I VOTE CONSERVATIVE (BECAUSE I LOVE YOU)' and 'I MET A MAN WHO SPOKE LIKE AN UCCA FORM') can definitely be something of an acquired taste, while side-long slabs of tripped-out indulgence like the 26 minute 'THE OCTAGONAL RABBIT SURPLUS' are recommended only for the most iron-willed of old hippies. Still, if you didn't actually get past the first track, you could always amuse yourself with the chocolate mousse recipe on the lp's back cover. The sleeve also featured the adage, "If it's worth doing, it's worth overdoing". Quite. JENKINS maintained an impressively prolific release schedule throughout the 80's, releasing such inimitably titled albums as 'I LOVE YOU LITTLE BOBO WITH YOUR DELICATE GOLDEN LIONS' (1984) – the first release for the 'Cordella' label – 'WAR, FAMINE, DEATH, PESTILENCE AND MISS TIMBERLAKE' (1986) and 'THE TENDER YELLOW PONIES OF INSOMNIA' (1989). Under the guise of The CHRYSANTHEMUMS, JENKINS also released a trio of albums, namely 'IS THAT A FISH ON YOUR SHOULDER, OR ARE YOU JUST PLEASED TO SEE ME?' (1987), 'LITTLE FLECKS OF FOAM AROUND BARKING' (1988) and a wholesale reinvention of The ZOMBIES' 'ODYSSEY AND ORACLE' album. • **Covers:** Creams:- PALE BLUE EYES (Velvet Underground) / A WHITER SHADE OF PALE (Procol Harum) / THE BEAUTIFUL END (Calendar Dream) / THEY DON'T KNOW (Kirsty McColl) / BREAK ON THROUGH (Doors) / ANYTHING GOES (Cole Porter) / GENIE WITH A LIGHT BROWN LAMP (Shadows). • **Trivia:** In 1990, JENKINS privately published a booklet about the music business, 'HOW TO BE IN A POP GROUP'.

Album rating: MY GERANIUMS ARE BULLETPROOF (*6) / TEENAGE HEAD IN MY REFRIGERATOR (*6) / THE GATES OF LUNCH (*6) / SAW A RANCH HOUSE BURNING LAST NIGHT (*5) / I LOVE YOU LITTLE BOBO WITH YOUR DELICATE GOLDEN LIONS (*6) / HANG ON CONSTANCE LET ME HEAR THE NEWS (*5) / RAIN IS WHEN THE EARTH IS TELEVISION (*5) / WAR, FAMINE, DEATH, PESTILENCE AND MISS TIMBERLAKE (*5) / THE TENDER YELLOW PONIES OF INSOMNIA (*5)

ALAN JENKINS (b.16 Mar'59, Dudley, England) – guitar, clarinet, bass / **SHERREE LAWRENCE** (b.24 May'59, Rushden, England) – pianos, etc / p/t until follow-up lp- **MICHAEL BUNNAGE** (b.21 Dec'58, Romford, England) – bass, vocals (of STATICS) / **GRAHAM SUMMERS** (b.30 Jul'58, Wellingborough, England) – drums (of STATICS)

1979. (lp) *(MOLE 1)* **MY GERANIUMS ARE BULLETPROOF**
– Minstrel radio yoghurt / I vote Conservative / Emile Zola / Phylis is a protozoon actually / Embalming fluid fucha / I met a man who spoke like an UCCA form / The octagonal rabbit surplus. *(re-iss. May88 on 'Cordelia') (cd-iss. 1991 on 'Madagascar'+=; MADA 017)* – The octagonal rabbit surplus surplus.

1981. (lp) *(MOLE 2)* **TEENAGE HEAD IN MY REFRIGERATOR**
– I like digestive biscuits in my coffee / Dz / The letter song (scrib) / My geraniums are bulletproof / Peter Smith is a banana / Hegel's brain / Esther / Vera / God / Path to you / Dictatorship of the proletariat / Teenage head (in my refrigerator). *(re-iss. Jul88 on 'Cordelia') (cassette 'HEGEL'S BRAIN'; MOLE C2) (cd-iss. 1991 on 'Madagascar'+=; MADA 019)* – You took the blue one / Esther / Red light for the greens / Minstrel radio yoghurt.

1982. (lp) *(MOLE 3)* **THE GATES OF LUNCH**
– A red light for the greens / You might need me and this Winchester Curly / A ten legged beast (or an eight legged beast with feelers) / Fishing / I lay a green egg, it explodes on Tuesday / Bottles / The gates of lunch / Bottles / Brain dead baby / Godzilla loves me, I'm an ash-tray. *(re-iss. May88 on 'Cordelia') (cd-iss. 1991 on 'Madagascar'+=; MADA 018)* – You're going green / Careful with that axe / The damage / Polanski's dog / The rat dance / Hitler's knees.

Oct 83. (lp) *(MOLE 4)* **SAW A RANCH HOUSE BURNING LAST NIGHT**
– Under the cafe table / Down to a proton / The new emotional twist / Kiwis come in close / You took the blue one / You think I'm a car / Eat molten death / Hitler's knees / Funny monsters / Matter over mind / The damage / Ammonia suction / Everlasting lollipop / Sagittarians / Saw a ranch house burning last night. *(re-iss. May88 on 'Cordelia') (cd-iss. 1993 on 'Raffmond'+=; RAFF 042CD)* – Phylis #2 / I met a man who spoke in an UCCA form / Peter Smith is a banana / My geraniums

are bulletproof / The gates of lunch / A ten legged beast (or an eight legged beast with feelers) / Teenage head in my refrigerator / God / Ammonia suction / Thje new emotional twist.

— **PETER GREGORY** – drums; repl. SUMMERS

Cordelia not iss.

Jul 84. (d-lp) *(ERICAT 001)* **I LOVE YOU LITTLE BOBO WITH YOUR DELICATE GOLDEN LIONS**
– Something else instead / I love you little BoBo with your delicate golden lions / Why do you speak? / Most people aren't fit to live part one / Entropy of cubes / Most people aren't fit to live part two / Polanski's dog / Twenty three exceptions / O.P. 1 / O.P. 2 / Who's afraid of humans? / (untitled) / A trillion sprods / a) The dalmation – b) Natural forces – c) 186,000 endings per second / Thunderbirds / This is terrible / All through summer / Zoology / Whose afraid of humans? (reprise) / Roget's thesaurus / A motor throbbed above the rim of the brush / A trillion sprods (version). *(d-cd-iss. Jul97 on 'Jar Music'+=; JAR 011)* – Live at the Phoenix:- Reading an Agatha Christie / Under the cafe table / Roget's thesaurus / One of us / Most people aren't fit to live part two / Excerpts from a trillion sprods / These floors are smooth (single version).

1985. (ltd-12") *(ERICAT 002)* **ZOOLOGY. / THESE FLOORS ARE SMOOTH**

1985. (ltd-lp) *(ERICAT 004)* **HANG ON CONSTANCE LET ME HEAR THE NEWS**
– Green side up / Number five / The disappearance of the guard dog / The best thing in the entire world / Transparent evil plays / Reading an Agatha Christie / Irresistable moral force / Ahimperu-hissus / Is it safe? / Neuron music / The hero might as well be Jerry / A colony of sea birds / What more can I do? / Diagonally / Floccipaucinhillipilification / One of the people in this room is an animal / The unpronouncable Finn. *(cd-iss. 1998 on 'Jar Music'+=; JAR 020)* – Blue moon / No.9 / Dr. Z / Here comes the sun exploding / These floors are smooth / These floors are smooth (version) / Neuron music.

1986. (ltd-lp) *(ERICAT 013)* **RAIN IS WHEN THE EARTH IS TELEVISION**
– Minstrel radio yoghurt / I met a man who spoke like an UCCA form / Careful with that axe / A ten legged beast (or an eight legged beast with feelers) / Here comes the sun exploding / An eight sided thing / Peter Smith is a banana / The rat dance / Vera / Number 9 / Esther hit me with the marmalade / You're going green / You're going green pt.II / These floors are smooth / Phylis is a protozoa.

1987. (12"ep) *(ERICAT 016)* **NEURON MUSIC**
– Neuron music (a materialist anthem) / Why do you speak (by RIMARIMBA) / Most people aren't fit to live (by MR. CONCEPT) / God (by the JUNG ANALYSTS) / Blue moon.

1988. (lp) *(ERICAT 024)* **WAR, FAMINE, DEATH, PESTILENCE AND MISS TIMBERLAKE**
– Out-takes / I am big chief Radio Luxemburg / George Bailey lassoes a refrigerator / A kangaroo #1 / The Stockholm syndrome / A dead herring in the moonlight / Fish in the air – Birds in the sea / The time from Acurist (vorsprung durch webung) / It's snowing – parts one to five / A kangaroo #2 / In this area / The chocolate bar from hell / Something happened / Metamorphosis / The short Good Friday / The weasle under the cocktail cabinet.

Jul 89. (lp) *(ERICAT 027)* **THE TENDER YELLOW PONIES OF INSOMNIA**
– A (dog found a stick in the park with such magical powers that a bark caused a marvelous pie to drop out of the sky and the doggy would grin like a shark) / Ariadne metal cream pie / The postman's dry / The cake of conversation / Programme controller flowers / I don't have a horse / Poodle haddock: part one / Poodle haddock: part two / Conversation gap panic / Buzzing unobtrusively / The amphibious nun / Love you more / Janice / Into the valley of death rode the six hundred shouting "dig it" / Don't eat aluminium / To hell with it, let her keep the children (the postman's dryer).

Farce not iss.

1993. (ltd-7") *(GONERIL 04)* **SLOW SHINY BRICKS / GEORGE BAILEY LASSOES A REFRIGERATOR (remix). / BLANK**

— JENKINS concentrated on The CHRYSANTHEMUMS and The CREAMS

– compilations, etc. –

Mar 89. (lp) *Logical Fish; (LOGICAL FISH 1)* **LIVE IN SWITZERLAND (live)**
– I like digestive biscuits in my coffee / Dr. Z / Under the cafe table / Here comes the sun exploding / Reading an Agatha Christie / The gates of lunch / The disappearance of the guard dog / The unpronouncable Finn / Elephants that are disappearing / Ant men / In this area / My geraniums are bulletproof / Neuron music / Roget's thesaurus / All through the summer / American archeologists / I am big chief Radio Luxembourg (excerpt) / Teenage head in my refrigerator. *(cd-iss. 2000 on 'Jar Music'; JAR 026)*

CHRYSANTHEMUMS

— **ALAN JENKINS** – lead guitar, backing vocals, computers, etc / **YUKIO YUNG** – vocals, piano, etc / **VLADIMIR ZAJOWIECZ** – bass, bassoon, etc / **GERALDINE MINOU-SULLIVAN** – drums, etc.

Egg Plant not iss.

Mar 87. (7") *(ONE EGG)* **ANOTHER SACRED DAY. / MOUTH PAIN**

Jul 87. (7"flexi) *(EGGFLEXONE)* **extracts from 'IS THAT A FISH ON YOUR SHOULDER OR ARE YOU JUST PLEASED TO SEE ME**

— guest on below **JANE LAING** – backing vocals

Aug 87. (lp) *(TWO EGGS)* **IS THAT A FISH ON YOUR SHOULDER OR ARE YOU JUST PLEASED TO SEE ME?**
– Gloucestershire is just an illusion / Bullshit / Mouth pain / Geraldine / Logical fish / The pronouncable Finn / The holocaust parade / You are a Serbian (and I like you) / The ten foot high trim-phone / Another sacred day / The lawn / Geraldine (reprise) / I wish Marvin Gaye's father had shot me instead / Buzzing unobtrusively.

— added **R STEVIE MOORE** – tapes / **JONATHAN STAINES LEMON** – ukelele / + **ACTON HORNS**

Apr 88. (lp; one-sided etched) *(THREE EGGS)* **THE XXXX SESSIONS**
– Harold Melvin: the exorcist / Oh dear, what shall we do about the Americans? / The little dinosaurs, they sit in the trees like funny owls / Seven wild cucumbers / Bonus track / Larceny Nell flies in.

— **JENKINS, MINOU-SULLIVAN, MOORE, STAINES, LAING** plus **TERRY BURROWS** – vocals, keyboards, sax, acoustic guitar / **MARTIN HOWELLS** – bass, vocals / + **ACTON HORNS**

1988. (d-lp) *(FOUR EGGS)* **LITTLE FLECKS OF FOAM AROUND BARKING**
– The cheeping of the robot bees / Dream string / God and the Dave Clark 5 / The overseer on the indigo farm / The hygrometer song / And your dog can sing / Raymond Chandler / (They must have made it with their) Hats / I am a hen (Lucinda Lambton) / Irreversible syntax errors / The deathbed song / Light transforms the Peugeot dealers / Pigs and eagles / Double 'o' gauge dogs / The burning fascia / The hapless criminal / Love is for the astronauts / Josephine and Tchaikovsky / He's had his bears / The last great dogfight / Totally unacceptable (full of holes) / Spew forth frogs / Er / Life's not like that really (Yukio's dream #3) / Oh dear, what shall we do about the Christians (Harold Melvin: the heretic) / Climb aboard the groove tractor (pencils) / The fading memory of Mr Rose / Vulture culture / A big dog / The handkerchief man's last bonfire / Life's not like that really (Yukio's dream #3).

— **ALAN + YUKIO** only

1989. (12"ep) *(FIVE EGGS)* **PICASSO'S PROBLEM / (LIKE INDUSTRIOUS ELVES) WE STOPPED. / BUSH OF TROUSERS / ELECTRONS WILL / GOVERNMENT / SHOWROOM DUMMIES – ASCENSION**

— added **YUNG, MINOU-SULLIVAN + ZAJIKOWIECZ**

May 89. (cd) *(SIX EGGS)* **ODYSSEY AND ORACLE**
– Care of cell 44 / A rose for Emily / Maybe after he's gone / Beechwood park / Brief candles / Hung up on a dream / Changes / I want her she wants me / This will be our year / Butchers tale (Western Front 1914) / Friends of mine / Time of the season. *(re-iss. May91 on 'Madagascar' lp/cd; MAD 014/+CD)*

Madagascar not iss.

Sep 91. (12"/cd-s) *(MADA 016)* **PORCUPINE QUILLS (4 versions)**

— **ROBIN GIBSON** – drums; repl. SULLIVAN

Pink Lemon not iss.

Nov 95. (lp/cd) *(JAR 007)* **INSEKT INSEKT (live)**
– Porcupine quills / A big dead man / Followed by animals 1 / Followed by animals 2 / Electrons will / Harold Melvin: the exorcist / Robot bees / No-one went to Heaven / Happy birthday Blodwyn P-teabag / Double "O" gauge dogs / Mr. Neville / Glass hovercraft of the elven wizards / Big binoculars / World of interiors. *(lp w/ free 7")* – GLOUCESTERSHIRE IS JUST AN ILLUSION / I WISH MARVIN GAYE'S FATHER WOULD HAVE KILLED ME INSTEAD / THE HANDKERCHIEF MAN'S LAST BONFIRE *(re-iss. Oct97; same)*

Orgone not iss.

Nov 97. (cd) *(RG 001)* **BABY'S HEAD**

— (unsure if above set was actually the same group)

CREAMS

BLODWYN P. TEABAG – piano, oboe, synthesizers + **ARIADNE METAL-CREAM PIE** – guitar, viola / with **RUTH MILLER** – vocals; **JENKINS + STAINES/LEMON** were also involved

Cordelia not iss.

May 90. (lp/cd; as JODY AND THE CREAMS) *(ERICAT/CD 029)* **A BIG DOG-N**
– The queen #1 / Margery is dead / Moulted fur from a labrador / Three rings / Appleseed alley / Hi Felicity / Shropshire / N / The queen #2 / Blue moon / 11-20 more tunes which don't have titles (20 minutes).

Raffmond not iss.

1993. (d-lp/cd; as ALAN JENKINS AND THE CREAMS) *(none)* **IE**
– Overture / Best, banting, McLeod and their dog, Margery / Unusual calls / The metaphor list song / "Moonphase" for strings, percussion and woodwind / Why did the turkey boil his radio? / Investing a crime / No, I don't own any mechanical crushing equipment / Me and G.A.A.E. / If drum machines were fish / If fish were drum machines / Poems that are disappearing / The answering machine song / Hell with no sun cream / The eagle hates your poetry / The planted monogrammed handkerchief / Mr. Green was found outside your house / Ariadne dreams about big lobsters climbing up the world to get to the North Pole / ie / Metaphor list song reprise. *(d-lp+=)* – The ecological matador / I am rubber, you are glue / Carp / Glue, glue / Neville Chamberlain's head / Animent experimals (parts 1-4) / The emmental of the porcupine / Be my baby (probably Phil Spector and some other people) / Glass hovercraft of the elven wizards / They didn't believe me.

— **ALISON MACKINDER, PETER PENGWYN, BLODWYN P TEABAG, ALAN JENKINS, VLADIMIR ZAJIKOWIECZ + ROBYN GIBSON**

Pink Lemon not iss.

1994. (7") *(JAR 001.94)* **NOTHING'S GONNA CHANGE MY CLOTHES. / PALE BLUE EYES**

Raffmond not iss.

1994. (lp/cd) *(RAFF 008-1/-2)* **THE CREAMS AND NICO** German
– Electrons' will / Dream string / Hi Felicity / Followed by animals / Fortunately – 60 piano notes / How silly can you get / The Creams, the thief, his wife and her brother / Inside me / Oh dear, what shall we do about the Christians? / Busy bear organiser. *(cd tracks)* – The little list song / Stepford on sea / Milk and honey / Woman with magnet / The museum of the modern fly / Fish / Peter says / Metricious metonymy and the anachronistic quondam / 60 piano notes / Sit round a cigarette / Die yuppy scum / No other monkey / World of interiors / The Creams, the thief, his wife and her brother / Gloves and mittens / Followed by animals / Unusual blue moss / Fortunately / 60 more piano notes / Walk with me / Mice / Circus / Gingham girl meets plaid boy / Marlene Dietrich's make up man (parts 1 & 2) / The Creams are going to kill me.

1994. (7") *(RAFF 009-7)* **MICE. / BUZZING UNOBTRUSIVELY** German

1995. (7"; as KLAUS KORNFIELD AND THE CREAMS) *(RAFF 013-7)* **THE BEAUTIFUL END. / A WHITER SHADE OF PALE** German

1996. (cd) *(RAFF 019-2)* **PLUTO** German
– You've been standing in the middle of rooms / Captain Reasonable / Carrot cake / What would you do about it? / I want you (I'm so heavy) / Seriously / Nothing's gonna make me change my clothes / a) Break on through (to the other side) – b) Here today gone bad – c) They don't know – d) E331 and E104 – e) Just 16 – f) Screech – g) Doberman – h) Spencer Tracy's vacuum cleaner – i) Blind Muddy blues – j) The truth about soot – k) I remember you – l) You could be cuter / Sorry to phone you again / What's so interesting about actors? / Buzzing unobtrusively / Big binoculars / PYO / The beautiful end / First direct.

DEEP FREEZE MICE (cont)

JENKINS, TEABAG + GIBSON added DAWN LARDER, BAZZ LARDER + ANDY NICHOLLS

Little Teddy not iss.

1996. (ltd-7"m) *(LITE 737)* **THESE MAGIC BEANS (ARE BROWN) / SUB SUB. / ANYTHING GOES**

Pink Lemon not iss.

Jan 97. (ltd-7"ep) *(JAR 009)* **YOUR EYES ARE BETTER THAN MINE**
– Your eyes are better than mine / Nasty soap for dogs #9 / Drops / Tube guitar / The new animal / Bill's thought / Nasty soap for dogs #3 / HVSI // The dog and the television / The sandwich toaster / Murder ballad / Rats with a sausage / Less rats with a sausage / Things moving / Another HVSI.

—— HOWARD FAIRLEY repl. NICHOLLS

Oct 97. (d3"cd-ep) *(JAR 016)* **MALCOLM**
– Nasty soap for dogs #4 / Mostly crap / 70's tea room / Cupboard door / Echoes Myron / Nasty soap for dogs #5 / Genie with a light brown lamp // Nasty soap for dogs #7 / How much is the clock? / Wood / Victoria and Jane / Nasty soap for dogs #1 / Red dwarf / Comedy foxes from space.

—— now without the LARDER twins

Oct 97. (cd) *(JAR 018)* **ARE YOU REAL OR JUST SOME SORT OF DISGUSTING FRIDGE MAGNET** (live)
– Mostly crap / Something else instead / Gro Harlem Brundtland wants some fish / Me and the G.A.A.E. / Big binoculars / Your eyes are better than mine / The planted monogrammed handkerchief / The ecological matador / Mice / Nothing's gonna change my clothes / Sub sub / You've been standing in the middle of rooms / Echoes Myron / Hell with no sun cover / Marlene Dietrich's make-up man / Is this the dream? / What more can I do? / The little list song / Don't eat aluminium / I wish Marvin Gaye's father had shot me instead / The unpronouncable Finn / Hello Anne of Green Poplars / Unusual blue moss.

Nov 98. (d-cd) *(JAR 024)* **THE ALL NIGHT BOOKMAN**
– Beware / Little particle / Blitzkreig Bob / Big fat beautiful thighs / Here comes the snowy / No stories / The little green house / Reality control / Pretty thing / Passing stranglers / The dust and the pot-pourri / Four dozen monkeys / The Scottish track / Tarkovsky the otter / Robyn Gibson CBE / Kiss me son of God / Stubbs inflates a kangaroo / Tuesday, 30th June 1998 / Sideshow Margaret / Bag of moonshine / Non-U bee fur cannon plinth / Bursting (the bubble of love) // (Not an) Interflora van / Indication / Mr. Smith and his sarcastic cat / Ringing the bell on the chocolate / Walk don't run / Wretchedly arranged baskets / Sports casual is the way / Des Diables en Pierce / Why can't we hit these stupid porcupines? / Lovely and fart / Outdoors & indoors / Santa says / Sports casual samba / Mike Oldfield's Tubular Bells / The gas museum / Someone keeps moving my chair / Men with two heads / Alcoholics and beautiful girls / The brassica man / Civil disorder in bad rabbit.

– others, etc. –

1998. (ltd-cd; as JODY AND THE CREAMS) *Pink Lemon; (PINK 005)* **LORDS OF THE GROMET CANNING FACTORY** (rec. 1991)
– (part one) / (part two) / (18 untitled tracks).

1998. (cd-Rom) *n.UR-Kult; (bootleg)* **NET YANGERS FOR THE PIZZA FROY** (live)

1998. (cd-Rom) *(bootleg)* **FUCK MY ASS** (live)

RUTH'S REFRIGERATOR

RUTH MILLER, ALAN JENKINS, BLODWYN, ROBYN + TERRI LOWE

Madagascar not iss.

1990. (lp/cd) *(MADA 012)* **SUDDENLY A DISFIGURED HEAD PARACHUTED**
– She lies in state / Your dog is rich and your cat is good looking / Alan's refrigerator / He needs a dog / Picasso's problem / The red queen / Mind the paprika, Joe / Gro Harlem Brundtland wants some fish / On a western shore / Innocent boy / Hello Anne of Green Poplars / Examine the insects and kill them / Hi Felicity / Fish in the air birds in the sea.

1991. (cd) *(MADA 020)* **A LIZARD IS A SUBMARINE ON GRASS** (live at the Szere, Vienna – disguised as an American rock band)
– An improvisation / I don't have a horse / My head's on fire / Ducklings / Charlie & Charlie / Gosh what a lot of umbrellas / Barry baked bean is back / Bibbidi – bobiddi – boo / Accordian music / Accordian #2 / E / Ducklings #2 / Goodbye Joe / Examine the insects and hit them / Rain / Duck pond / What we waited for and where it was at / Moulted fur from a labrador / Mr. Misery / Accordian music #3 / Conversation gap panic / A science bar / And one more thing.

Gabi DELGADO (see under ⇒ D.A.F.)

DELMONAS
(see under ⇒ CHILDISH, Wild Billy; 70's section)

DELTA 5

Formed: Leeds, England … 1979 by JULZ SALE, ROS ALLEN, ALAN RIGGS, BETHAN PETERS and SIMON (the latter being replaced by KELVIN KNIGHT). This politicised femme-punk outfit cut a handful of singles for 'Rough Trade' beginning with 'MIND YOUR OWN BUSINESS' the same year. Propelled by a twin-bass funk groove behind a defiant female vocal, the record was repetitive, insidious and highly addictive, bringing enthusiasm from John Peel and drawing comparisons with post-punk experimentalists GANG OF FOUR. 1980 saw the release of another critically acclaimed single, 'YOU', along with a couple of Peel sessions for Radio One before the band took off for a US tour. Upon their return, DELTA 5 issued their third and final independent single, the double A-side 'TRY' and 'COLOUR', before securing a major label deal with Charisma subsidiary, 'Pre'. Boasting a polished-up sound with additional brass and keyboards, reviewers were sceptical and gave the debut album, 'SEE THE WHIRL' (1981) a thumbs down. By this point, SALE and PETERS were the only remaining original members (with newcomer, JACKI) and the group struggled to make any headway in the increasingly airbrushed alternative scene. With only one album to their name the band split (their record label also going under) although their influence has always been in inverse proportion to their recorded output.

Album rating: SEE THE WHIRL (*4)

JULZ SALE – vocals, guitar / ALAN RIGGS – guitar / ROS ALLEN – bass, vocals (ex-MEKONS) / BETHAN PETERS – bass, vocals / KELVIN KNIGHT – drums repl. SIMON

Rough Trade not iss.

Oct 79. (7") *(RT 031)* **MIND YOUR OWN BUSINESS. / NOW THAT YOU'VE GONE**

May 80. (7") *(RT 041)* **YOU. / ANTICIPATION**

Nov 80. (7") *(RT 061)* **TRY. / COLOUR**

—— JULZ + ALAN with different line-up JACKI (BETHAN joined FUN BOY THREE)

Pre not iss.

Jun 81. (7") *(PRE 16)* **SHADOW. / THE LEAVING**

Jul 81. (lp/c) *(PREX/PRICS 6)* **SEE THE WHIRL**
– Innocenti / Final scene / Circuit / Open life / Trail / Shadow / Delta 5 / Anticipation / Journey / Make up / Triangle / Waiting / Telephone / Different fun.

Jan 82. (7") *(PRE 24)* **POWERLINES. / THE HEART IS A LONELY PLACE TO BE**

—— split soon after above, JACKI formed The DELTONES

DEMON PREACHERS
(see under ⇒ ALIEN SEX FIEND)

DENTISTS

Formed: Chatham, Kent, England … 1983 by BOB COLLINS, along with MICK MURPHY, MARK MATTHEW and IAN SMITH. Trading in quintessential indie-pop bearing comparison to The HOUSEMARTINS, The SMITHS and occasionally even The PIXIES, The DENTISTS debuted with the 'SOME PEOPLE ON THE PITCH THINK IT'S ALL OVER … IT IS NOW' set and 'STRAWBERRIES ARE GROWING IN MY GARDEN' single in early '85, followed by similarly fruity EP, 'YOU AND YOUR BLOODY ORANGES'. By this point SMITH had been replaced by ALUN GWYNNE JONES, the latter replaced in turn by ROB L GRIGG the following year as the band released their well received 'DOWN AND OUT IN PARIS AND CHATHAM' EP. 1987 saw the release of a second four tracker, 'WRITHING ON THE SHAGPILE', while a follow-up album, 'BEER BOTTLE AND BANNISTER SYMPHPONIES', appeared on the 'Antler' label in 1988. The turn of the decade finally saw the band receiving some long overdue press interest with the 'HEADS AND HOW TO READ THEM' (1990) set, a more enthusiastic response from the American alternative market resulting in college radio airplay for tracks culled from the 'DRESSED' (1992) and 'POWDERED LOBSTER FIASCO' (1993) albums and an eventual major label deal with the 'East West' subsidiary of 'Atlantic' records. The resulting long player, 'BEHIND THE DOOR I KEEP THE UNIVERSE' (1994) kept up their penchant for long winded titles and delivered another fix of airy, spirited guitar pop, MURPHY's strangely feminine, vaguely PAUL HEATON-esque vocals floating over the jingle jangle chords on a carpet of ba-ba-ba backing vocals. The DENTISTS took a bow after the unappealing 'DEEP SIX' album in '95, leaving MICK, MARK, GRIGG and newcomer CHRIS FLACK to come up with a moniker, COAX. However, in the wake of the witty but disappointing 'FEAR OF STANDING STILL' album in 1998, the band took a runner.

Album rating: SOME PEOPLE ON THE PITCH THINK IT'S ALL OVER … IT IS NOW (*5) / BEER BOTTLE AND BANNISTER SYMPHONIES … compilation (*5) / HEADS AND HOW TO READ THEM (*5) / DRESSED compilation (*6) / POWDERED LOBSTER FIASCO (*5) / BEHIND THE DOOR I KEEP THE UNIVERSE (*5) / DEEP SIX (*5) / Coax: FEAR OF STANDING STILL (*4)

MICK MURPHY (b. 8 Oct'63, Bexley, Kent) – vocals, guitar / BOB COLLINS (b.12 Jun'65, Gillingham, Kent) – guitar, vocals / MARK MATTHEWS (b.15 May'65, Farnborough, Hampshire, England) – bass, vocals / IAN SMITH – drums

Spruck not iss.

Apr 85. (lp) *(SPR 001)* **SOME PEOPLE ON THE PITCH THINK IT'S ALL OVER … IT IS NOW**
– Flowers around me / I'm not the Devil / Tony Bastable v John Noakes / You make me say it somehow / Mary won't come out to play / I had an excellent dream / Kinder still / The little engineers set / Back to the grave / Tangerine / The arrow points to the spot / Everything in the garden / One of our psychedelic beakers is missing.

Jun 85. (7"m) *(SP 003)* **STRAWBERRIES ARE GROWING IN MY GARDEN (AND IT'S WINTERTIME). / BURNING THE THOUGHTS FROM MY SKIN / DOREEN**
(re-iss. Nov86; same)

Nov 85. (12"ep) *(SP 004)* **YOU AND YOUR BLOODY ORANGES**
– Pallino / The best of everything / I can see your house from up here / My friends in the best of circles / Something that will never happen / Where's my chicken, you bastard.

Tambourine not iss.

Jun 86. (12"ep) *(URINE 1)* **DOWN AND OUT IN PARIS AND CHATHAM**
– She dazzled me with basil / Peppermint dreams / Chainsaw the horse / You took me by surprise / Dawn overdone.

—— ALUN GWYNNE-JONES (b. 3 Feb'66) – drums; repl. SMITH

Jun 87. (12"ep) *(URINE 3)* **WRITHING ON THE SHAGPILE / JUST LIKE OLIVER REED. / A STRANGE WAY TO GO ABOUT THINGS / CALM YOU DOWN / THE TURQUISE CASTLE**

DENTISTS (cont)

					Antler	not iss.
Feb 88. (lp) *(ANT 072)* **BEER BOTTLE & BANNISTER SYMPHONIES: A COLLECTION OF SOME OF THE FINER MOMENTS OF DENTISTRY** (compilation)
– Writhing on the shagpile / You took me by surprise / A strange way to go about things / She dazzled me with Basil / Dawn overdone / I had an excellent dream / Strawberries are growing in my garden (and it's wintertime) / The turquoise castle / Calm you down / Chainsaw the horses / Peppermint dreams / Just like Oliver Reed.

Apr 88. (12"ep) *(ANT 077)* **THE FUN HAS ARRIVED / UGLY (1988 version). / KILLING ME / THERE WAS LOVE ON THE FLOOR, SO I WALKED ON THE CEILING**

	Integrity	Caroline

Jan 91. (7") *(IR 014-7)* **BEAUTIFUL DAY. / DELICIOUS**
Jan 91. (cd/lp) *(IR 014) <90014>* **HEADS AND HOW TO READ THEM**
– House the size of Mars / Beautiful day / Rivals for the hand of Isabel / Killing me / In the ocean / Butterfly / Crocodile tears / Daffodil scare / Eliza / Delicious / Have it your way. *(cd+=)* – Snapdragon / Pocket of silver / The fun has arrived / Around my room / There was love on the floor, so I walked on the ceiling.

1991. (7") *(IR 016-7)* **HOUSE THE SIZE OF MARS. / ELIZA**
1991. (7"m; shared) *(IR 018-7)* **HAVE IT YOUR WAY. /** (others by The Burtons and The Serenes)

	Independent Project	Independent Project

1991. (10"ep) *(IP 036) <ARCHIVE 5>* **NAKED** (rarities collection)
– Ugly / We thought we'd got to Heaven / Crimson skies again / The sun in the sands / Streets & houses / Reading the news / Naked.

	Me Two	Homestead

Aug 92. (cd) *(ME 2001) <HMS 180>* **DRESSED** (compilation)
– Strawberries are growing in my garden (and it's wintertime) / She dazzled me with Basil / I had an excellent dream / A strange way to go about things / Chainsaw the horse / Peppermint dreams / Just like Oliver Reed / The turquoise castle / I can see your house from up here / Pailino / Dawn overdone / Writhing on the shagpile / Flowers around me / I'm not the Devil / Tony Bastable v John Noakes / You make me say it somehow / Mary won't come out to play / Kinder still / The little engineers set / Tangerine / The arrow points to the spot / One of our psychedelic beakers is missing.

—— **ROB GRIGG** (b.28 Jul'68, Canterbury, Kent) – drums; repl. JONES

1992. (7"ep) *<HMS 187-7>* **SEE NO EVIL**
– Box of sun / I can see your house from up here (acoustic version) / See no evil (a poem written/performed by JOHN HEGLEY).

1992. (7"ep) *<IP 041>* **HEAR NO EVIL**
– Charms and the girl / Leave me alive / Hear no evil (a poem written/performed by JOHN HEGLEY).

<above issued on 'Independent Project', below on 'Bus Stop'>

1992. (7"ep) *<BUS 026>* **SPEAK NO EVIL**
– Outside your inside / All coming down / Speak no evil (a poem written/performed by JOHN HEGLEY).

—— in 1992, BOB COLLINS released the 7" for 'Hangman', 'JUST THE BIGGEST THING BY YE ASCOYNE D'ASCOYNES'

	Ball Product – Creation	Homestead

Jul 93. (cd) *(SHED 002CD) <HMS 203>* **POWDERED LOBSTER FIASCO**
– Pocket of silver / Charms and the girl / Outside your inside / Box of sun / Beautiful day / I can see your house from up here (acoustic version) / We thought we'd got to Heaven / Leave me alive / All coming down / Snapdragon.

1993. (3x7"box) *<7-98362>* **BIGBANGREDSHIFTBLACKHOLES**
– Gas / Tremendous many / This is not my flag / Faces on stone / Space man / Sorry is not enough / Apple beast / Water for a man on fire / Your kind of day (demo) / The quality of mercy / Ace of spades (rehearsal version) / Eyes (demo).

	East West	Atlantic

Mar 94. (cd/c) *(<7567 92288-2/-4>)* **BEHIND THE DOOR I KEEP THE UNIVERSE** | | Jan94
– This is not my flag / Space man / Sorry is not enough / In orbit / Faces on stone / A smile like oil on water / Tremendous many / Gas / Brittle sin and flowers / Apple beast / Water for a man on fire / The waiter.

	not iss.	Elektra

Apr 95. (cd) *<61767-2>* **DEEP SIX**
– Shining like a star / Slither / Weirdo (at 25,000 miles per hour) / My heart is like a town you moved / Kick start my body / Apetite / Hedonist / Not coming back / Agony in twelve fits / Whole world explode / Gradual / Good riddance / Orange gold / Electric train of thought.

—— split later in '95; MURPHY and the Dentists classic, 'STRAWBERRIES . . .' featured on the Lida Husik set, 'Joyride'

COAX

MURPHY, MATTHEWS + GRIGG added **CHRIS FLACK** – guitar

	Rainbow Quartz	Rainbow Quartz

Jun 96. (cd-ep) *<RQTX 007>* **HABERDASHERY**
– Orchestra / All brand new / Colors from the side show / Screaming reality / Warm day in the August sun (demo).

—— added **DAVE READ** – vocals, guitar

	Rainbow Quartz	Paradigm

May 98. (cd) *(RQTZ 010) <26>* **FEAR OF STANDING STILL** | | Feb98
– Orchestra / Turning to gold / Plates / Trophy wife / Rolling thunder / Rebecca in the presence of the enemy / Ringmaster goes down / Harrison fjord / Colours from the sideshow / Meatball heroes / Joe repairs cars.

Jun 98. (cd-s) *(RQTZ 011CD)* **ORCHESTRA / ROLLING THUNDER / MY NUMBER NINE**

—— COAX called it a day after above

DEPARTMENT S

Formed: London, England . . . 1980 out of the ashes of ska-punk outfit, GUNS FOR HIRE, by p/t 'Face' journo, VAUGHAN TOULOUSE, MICHAEL D. HERBAGE and TONY LORDAN. With the addition of EDDIE ROXY and MIKE HASLER, GFH issued one 1980 single, 'I'M GONNA ROUGH MY GIRLFRIEND'S BOYFRIEND UP TONIGHT', before metamorphosing into DEPARTMENT S. Taking the moniker from a cult 60's TV series and replacing MIKE and EDDIE with STUART MIZON and MARK TAYLOR, the group had a surprise near Top 30 hit courtesy of 'Demon' the following year with 'IS VIC THERE?'. A cool slice of catchy alternative pop, the single was backed with 'SOLID GOLD EASY ACTION', NOT actually a cover of the T.REX classic. Signing to 'Stiff' (through whom 'VIC' was given a US release), they scored a further minor hit, 'GOING LEFT RIGHT', although their chart luck ran out with 'I WANT'. With a proposed album subsequently shelved, DEPARTMENT S was permanently filed away, although TOULOUSE would later resurface as a solo artist while working for PAUL WELLER's STYLE COUNCIL. Sadly, the singer was to die of AIDS in August 1991 after suffering a long related illness.

Album rating: IS VIC THERE? compilation (*4)

VAUGHAN TOULOUSE (b. VAUGHAN COTILLARD, 30 Jul'59, St.Helier, Jersey, Channel Islands) – vocals / **MICHAEL D. HERBAGE** – guitar / **TONY LORDAN** – bass / **EDDIE ROXY** (b. EDWARD LLOYD BARNES) – keyboards / **MIKE HASLER** – drums (ex-INVADERS; aka MADNESS)

	Korova	not iss.

1980. (7"; as GUNS FOR HIRE) *(KOW 6)* **I'M GONNA ROUGH MY GIRLFRIEND'S BOYFRIEND UP TONIGHT. / I'M FAMOUS NOW**

—— **MARK TAYLOR** – synthesizer, keyboards; repl. EDDIE
—— **STUART MIZON** – drums; repl. MIKE

	Demon	not iss.

Mar 81. (7") *(D 1003)* **IS VIC THERE? / SOLID GOLD EASY ACTION** | 22 |

	Stiff	Stiff

Jun 81. (7") *<TEES7 02>* **IS VIC THERE? (remixed). / PUT ALL THE CROSSES IN THE RIGHT BOXES** | – | |
Jun 81. (7") *(BUY 118)* **GOING LEFT RIGHT. / SHE'S EXPECTING YOU** | 55 | –
(12"+=) *(BUY-IT 18)* – Is Vic there? (French version).
Oct 81. (7") *(BUY 128)* **I WANT. / MONTE CARLO** | | –
(12"+=) *(SBUY 128)* – Put all the crosses in the right boxes.

—— split after they flopped again and an album was shelved. VAUGHAN TOULOUSE worked as a DJ (MAIN T) before going solo and releasing a one-off summer '85 single, 'CRUISIN' THE SERPENTINE'. This was issued by PAUL WELLER's 'Respond' label, being at the same time part of the STYLE COUNCIL miner's charity outfit, COUNCIL COLLECTIVE.

– compilations, etc. –

Mar 93. (cd) *Mau Mau; (MAUCD 633)* **IS VIC THERE?**
– Of all the lost followers / Just pretend / Romany blood / I want / Fighting Irish / Is Vic there? / Going left right / Age concern / Somewhere between Heaven & Tesco's / Whatever happened to the blues / Ode to Koln / Clap now / Monte Carlo or bust / Put all the crosses in the right boxes / Is Vic there? (French version) / Is Vic there? (Italian version) / She's expecting you / Solid gold easy action.

DEPECHE MODE

Formed: Basildon, Essex, England . . . 1976 by VINCE CLARKE, MARTIN GORE and ANDY FLETCHER while still at school. The line-up was completed by frontman DAVE GAHAN, and by 1980 they had adopted the DEPECHE MODE moniker, immersing themselves in the London 'New Romantic' scene which spawned the likes of SPANDAU BALLET and VISAGE. After gigging around the capital and having a track, 'PHOTOGRAPHIC', included on the 'Some Bizzare Album' various artists collection, the band were picked up by the fledgling 'Mute' label. While their debut single, 'DREAMING OF ME', scraped the lower regions of the chart in 1981, a follow-up, 'NEW LIFE', almost made the Top 10. Dominated by synthesizers and drum machines, yet retaining a keen sense of melody, the band initially took their cue from KRAFTWERK. As evidenced on their insanely catchy Top 10 breakthrough, 'JUST CAN'T GET ENOUGH' (the first of 24 consecutive Top 30 hits), their lyrics weren't quite as enigmatic as their Teutonic heroes, although they improved with time. The success of the single (which no doubt still gets played ten times a night in French discos!) paved the way for the debut album, 'SPEAK AND SPELL' (1981), a promising collection of catchy synth-pop fare which made the UK Top 10. Chief songwriter VINCE CLARKE quit shortly after, going on to pastures new with YAZOO and then ERASURE, GORE taking up the pensmith chores for the follow-up album, 'A BROKEN FRAME' (1982). Shortly after its release, ALAN WILDER, who had previously toured with the band, was recruited as a full time replacement for CLARKE. Like its predecessor, 'CONSTRUCTION TIME AGAIN' (1983) failed to make any significant leap forward from the debut, musically at least, although it did contain the classic 'EVERYTHING COUNTS', GAHAN's voice summoning up as much portentous doom as he could muster. While the 'PEOPLE ARE PEOPLE' single gave the band valuable exposure in America, their real breakthrough came with 1984's 'SOME GREAT REWARD'. Featuring the likes of 'BLASPHEMOUS RUMOURS' and 'MASTER AND SERVANT', the album was palpably darker, the music more satisfyingly varied. 'BLACK CELEBRATION' (1986) was deliberately darker still, much of the material creeping along at a funereal pace. 'MUSIC FOR THE MASSES' (1987) was the band's biggest Stateside success to date, the material for the live album, '101' (1989) coming from the American leg of their 1988 sell-out world tour. 'VIOLATOR' (1990) was heralded as DEPECHE MODE's best work since 'SOME GREAT REWARD', spawning two of their better singles in 'PERSONAL JESUS' and the uncharacteristically emotional 'ENJOY THE SILENCE'. Never the warmest sounding band, with 'SONGS OF FAITH AND DEVOTION' (1993) their clinical sound was softened somewhat with a move towards more rock-centric territory. That's not to say the music was soft, at least not on the single, 'I FEEL YOU', a dirty great guitar riff grinding away relentlessly. Elsewhere, the album had something of a transcendent, redemptive quality about it on such powerful tracks as 'MERCY IN YOU' and 'ONE CARESS'. The record gave the band their first No.1, UK and US, although some longtime fans were understandably miffed at the band's new direction. The mid-90's brought the most turbulent period in the band's long career as GAHAN reportedly attempted suicide amid his battle with drug addiction. Add to that the departure of WILDER (who went to work on solo project RECOIL) and it seemed DEPECHE MODE had reached the end of the line. If nothing else, though, this band are doggedly determined, GAHAN beating his drug problem and enlisting BOMB THE BASS guru TIM SIMENON to help create an enticingly different sound on 1997's 'ULTRA'. No doubt overjoyed that their heroes had been resurrected, the group's staunch fanbase ensured the album would once again top the UK chart. The record was also a blueprint of sorts for 'EXCITER' (2001), maverick production touches supplied this time around by LFO man, MARK BELL. GAHAN's ongoing singing tuition reaped darkly alluring rewards, drawing the listener in to a late-night vigil of brooding acoustica and stained velour romance. • **Covered:** ROUTE 66 (Chuck Berry). • **Trivia:** MARTIN GORE's solo album contained six cover versions incl. NEVER TURN YOUR BACK ON MOTHER EARTH (Sparks). He later covered Leonard Cohen's COMING BACK TO YOU.

Album rating: SPEAK & SPELL (*6) / A BROKEN FRAME (*6) / CONSTRUCTION TIME AGAIN (*7) / SOME GREAT REWARD (*7) / THE SINGLES 1981-1985 compilation (*9) / BLACK CELEBRATION (*8) / MUSIC FOR THE MASSES (*7) / 101 (*5) / VIOLATOR (*7) / SONGS OF FAITH & DEVOTION (*7) / SONGS OF LOVE & DEVOTION LIVE (*3) / ULTRA (*6) / THE SINGLES 86>98 compilation (*7) / EXCITER (*6)

VINCE CLARKE (b. 3 Jul'60, South Woodford, England) – keyboards, synthesiser / **DAVID GAHAN** (b. 9 May'62, Epping, England) – vocals / **MARTIN GORE** (b.23 Jul'61) – keyboards, synthesizer, vocals / **ANDY FLETCHER** (b. 8 Jul'61, Nottingham, England) – guitar, synthesiser, drum machine

Mute Sire

Mar 81. (7") *(MUTE 013)* **DREAMING OF ME. / ICE MACHINE** [57] [ ]

Jun 81. (7") *(MUTE 014)* **NEW LIFE. / SHOUT!** [11] [ ]
(12") *(12MUTE 014)* – ('A'extended) / ('B'-Rio mix).

Sep 81. (7") *(MUTE 016)* **JUST CAN'T GET ENOUGH. / ANY SECOND NOW** [8] [-]
(12") *(12MUTE 016)* – ('A'-Schizo mix) / ('B'-altered).

Oct 81. (lp/c) *(STUMM/CSTUMM 5)* *<3642>* **SPEAK & SPELL** [10] [ ]
– New life / Just can't get enough / I sometimes I wish I was dead / Puppets / Boys say go / No disco / What's your name / Photographic / Tora! Tora! Tora! / Big Muff / Any second now. *(cd-iss. Apr88 +=; CDSTUMM 5)* – Dreaming of me / New life (extended) / Shout! (Rio mix) / Any second now (altered mix).

Nov 81. (7") **JUST CAN'T GET ENOUGH. / TORA! TORA! TORA!** [-] [ ]

— **ALAN WILDER** (b. 1 Jun'59, London, England) – electronics (ex-HITMEN) repl. VINCE who formed YAZOO

Jan 82. (7"/ext.12") *(MUTE/12MUTE 018)* **SEE YOU. / NOW, THIS IS FUN** [6] [ ] Aug82

Apr 82. (7") *(MUTE 022)* **THE MEANING OF LOVE. / OBERKORN (IT'S A SMALL TOWN)** [12] [ ]
(12") *(12MUTE 022)* – ('A'extended) / ('B'-Fairly odd mix).

Aug 82. (7") *(7BONG 1)* **LEAVE IN SILENCE. / EXCERPT FROM MY SECRET GARDEN** [18] [ ]
(ext.12"+=) *(12BONG 1)* – ('A'quieter version).

Sep 82. (lp/c) *(STUMM/CSTUMM 9)* *<23751>* **A BROKEN FRAME** [8] [ ]
– Leave in silence / My secret garden / Monument / Nothing to fear / See you / Satellite / The meaning of love / A photograph of you / Shouldn't have done that / The sun and the rainfall. *(cd-iss. Jul88; CDSTUMM 13)*

Feb 83. (7"/ext.12") *(7/12 BONG 2)* **GET THE BALANCE RIGHT. / THE GREAT OUTDOORS** [13] [ ]
(12") *(L12BONG 2)* – ('A'side) / My secret garden (live) / See you (live) / Satellite (live) / Tora! Tora! Tora! (live).

Jul 83. (7") *(7BONG 3)* **EVERYTHING COUNTS. / WORK HARD** [6] [ ]
(12") *(12BONG 3)* – ('A'-larger amounts) / ('B'-East End mix).
(12") *(L12BONG 3)* – ('A'side) / Boys say go (live) / New life (live) / Nothing to fear (live) / The meaning of love (live).

Aug 83. (lp/c) *(STUMM/CSTUMM 13)* **CONSTRUCTION TIME AGAIN** [6] [-]
– Love in itself / More than a party / Pipeline / Everything counts / Two minute warning / Shame / The landscape is changing / Told you so / And then . . . *(cd-iss. Jul88; CDSTUMM 13)*

Sep 83. (7") *(BONG 4)* **LOVE IN ITSELF. / FOOLS** [21] [ ]
(12") *(12BONG 4)* – Love in itself (3) / (4) / Fools (bigger).
(12") *(L12BONG 4)* – ('A'side) / Just can't get enough (live) / Photograph (live) / A photograph of you (live) / Shout! (live).

Mar 84. (7") *(7BONG 5)* *<29221>* **PEOPLE ARE PEOPLE. / IN YOUR MEMORY** [4] [13] May85
(12"+=) *(L12BONG 5)* – ('A'-On-U-Sound remix).
(12") *(12BONG 5)* – ('A'different mix) / ('B'-Slik mix).

Jul 84. (lp) *<25124>* **PEOPLE ARE PEOPLE** [-] [71]
– People are people / Everything counts / Get the balance right / Love in itself / Now this is fun / Leave in silence / Told you so / Work hard.

Aug 84. (7") *(7BONG 6)* *<28918>* **MASTER AND SERVANT. / SET ME FREE (RENOVATE ME)** [9] [ ] Aug85
('A'-Slavery whip mix-12"+=) *(12BONG 6)* – ('A'voxless).
('A'-On-U-Sound mix-12"+=) *(L12BONG 6)* – Are people people?.

Sep 84. (lp/c) *(STUMM/CSTUMM 19)* *<25194>* **SOME GREAT REWARD** [5] [51] Jan85
– Something to do / Lie to me / People are people / It doesn't matter / Stories of old / Somebody / Master and servant / If you want to / Blasphemous rumours. *(cd-iss. Sep87; CDSTUMM 19)*

Nov 84. (7") *(7BONG 7)* **BLASPHEMOUS RUMOURS. / SOMEBODY** [16] [ ]
(7"ep+=) *(7BONG 7E)* – Told you so (live) / Everything counts (live).
(12"+=) *(12BONG 7)* – Ice machine / Two minute warning / Everything counts (live).

May 85. (7"/remix-12") *(7/12 BONG 8)* **SHAKE THE DISEASE. / FLEXIBLE** [18] [ ]
(12") *(L12BONG 8)* – Edit the shake / Master and servant (live) / Flexible (deportation mix) / Something to do (metal mix).

Sep 85. (7"/remix-12") *(7/12 BONG 9)* **IT'S CALLED A HEART. / FLY ON THE WINDSCREEN** [18] [ ]
(ext.d12"+=) *(D12BONG 9)* – ('A'-slow mix) / ('A'-death mix).

Oct 85. (lp/c) *(MUTEL/CMUTEL 1)* *<25346>* **THE SINGLES 1981-1985** (compilation) <US-title 'CATCHING UP WITH DEPECHE MODE'> [6] [ ]
– People are people / Master and servant / It's called a heart / Just can't get enough / See you / Shake the disease / Everything counts / New life / Blasphemous rumours / Leave in silence / Get the balance right / Love in itself / Dreaming of me. *(c+=)* – (2 extra). *(cd-iss. Sep87; CDMUTEL 1)*

Feb 86. (7") *(7BONG 10)* **STRIPPED. / BUT NOT TONIGHT** [15] [ ]
(ext.12"+=) *(12BONG 10)* – Breathing in fumes / Fly on the windscreen (quiet mix) / Black day.

Mar 86. (lp/c) *(STUMM/CSTUMM 26)* *<25429>* **BLACK CELEBRATION** [4] [90]
– Black celebration / Fly on the windscreen – final / A question of tlust / Sometimes / It doesn't matter two / A question of time / Stripped / Here is the house / World full of nothing / Dressed in black / New dress. *(cd-iss. Sep87+=; CDSTUMM 26)* – But not tonight / Breathing in fumes / Black day.

Apr 86. (7") *(7BONG 11)* **A QUESTION OF LUST. / CHRISTMAS ISLAND** [28] [ ]
(free c-s. w/7") *(CBONG 11)* – ('A'-Flood mix) / If you want (live) / Shame (live) / Blasphemous rumours (live).
(ext.12"+=) *(12BONG 11)* – It doesn't matter (instrumental) / People are people (live) / A question of lust (minimal).

Aug 86. (7") *(7BONG 12)* **A QUESTION OF TIME. / BLACK CELEBRATION** [17] [ ]
(ext.12"+=) *(12BONG 12)* – Stripped (live) / Something to do (live).
(12") *(L12BONG 12)* – ('A'-Newtown mix) / ('A'live) / ('B'-Black tulip mix) / More than a party (live).

Apr 87. (7") *(7BONG 13)* *<28366>* **STRANGELOVE. / PIMPF** [16] [76]
('A'-Maximix-12"+=) *(12BONG 13)* – ('A'Midimix).
(cd-s++=) *(CDBONG 13)* – Agent orange.
('A'-Blind mix-12"+=) *(L12BONG 13)* – ('A'-Pain mix) / Agent orange.

Aug 87. (7") *(7BONG 14)* *<28189>* **NEVER LET ME DOWN AGAIN. / PLEASURE, LITTLE PLEASURE** [22] [63]
(12"/c-s) *(12/C BONG 14)* – ('A'-split mix) / ('B'-glitter mix) / ('A'-aggro mix).
(cd-s++=) *(CDBONG 14)* – To have and to hold (Spanish taster).
(12") *(L12BONG 14)* – ('A'-Tsangarides mix) / ('B'-join mix) / To have and to hold (Spanish taster).

Sep 87. (cd/d-c/lp,clear-lp) *(CD/C+/STUMM 47)* *<25614>* **MUSIC FOR THE MASSES** [10] [35]
– Never let me down again / The things you said / Strangelove / Sacred / Little 15 / Behind the wheel / I want you now / To have to hold / Nothing / Pimpf. *(cd+=)* – Agent orange / Never let me down again (aggro mix) / To have and to hold (Spanish) / Pleasure the treasure (glitter mix). *(d-c+=)* – BLACK CELEBRATION (album)

Dec 87. (7") *(7BONG 15)* *<27991>* **BEHIND THE WHEEL. / ROUTE 66** [21] [61]
(c-s+=/cd-s+=) *(C/CD BONG 15)* – ('A'-Shep Pettibone mix) / ('A'-lp version).
(12") *(12BONG 15)* – ('A'-Shep Pettibone mix) / ('B'-Beatmasters mix).
(12") *(L12BONG 15)* – ('A'-Beatmasters mix) / ('B'-Casualty mix).

May 88. (7"import) *(LITTLE 15)* **LITTLE 15. /** [60] [ ]

Sep 88. (7") *<27777>* **STRANGELOVE. / NOTHING** [-] [50]

Feb 89. (7") *(7BONG 16)* **EVERYTHING COUNTS (live). / NOTHING (live)** [22] [ ]
(12"+=/cd-s+=) *(12/CD BONG 16)* – Sacred (live) / A question of lust (live).
(remix-cd-s) *(CDLBONG 16)* – Strangelove (remix).
(3"cd-s) *(LCDBONG 16)* – ('A'-Tim Simenon & M. Saunders remix) / ('B'-Justin Strauss remix) / Strangelove (Tim Simenon & M. Saunders remix).
(12") *(L12BONG 16)* - **('A'-Bomb The Bass mix) / ('B'-Hijack mix).**
(10") *(10BONG 16)* – ('A'-Absolute mix) / ('B'-US mix) / ('A'-1983 mix).

Mar 89. (d-cd/d-c/d-lp) *(CD/C+/STUMM 101)* *<25853>* **101 (live)** [5] [45]
– Pimpf / Behind the wheel / Strangelove / Sacred * / Something to do / Blasphemous rumours / Stripped / Somebody / Things you said / Black generation / Shake the disease / Nothing * / Pleasure little treasure / People are people / A question of time / Never let me down again / A question of lust * / Master and servant / Just can't get enough / Everything counts *. *(c+=*/cd+=*)*

Aug 89. (7")<US-c-s> *(BONG 17)* *<19941>* **PERSONAL JESUS. / DANGEROUS** [13] [28] Nov89
(7"g-f+=/12"+=/c-s+=/cd-s+=) *(G/12/C/CD BONG 17)* – ('A'acoustic mix).
('A'pump mix-3"cd-s) *(LCDBONG 17)* – ('A'-Telephone stomp mix).

Feb 90. (c-s/7") *(C+/BONG 18)* *<19885>* **ENJOY THE SILENCE. / MEMPHISTO** [6] [8] Mar90
(cd-s+=) *(LCDBONG 18)* – ('A'-Bassline):- Bassline / Harmonium / Rikki Tick Tick / Memphesto.
(etched-12"/3"cd-s) *(XL12/XLCD BONG 18)* – ('A'-The quad: Final mix).

Mar 90. (cd/c/lp) *(CD/C+/STUMM 64)* *<26081>* **VIOLATOR** [2] [7]
– World in my eyes / Sweetest perfection / Personal Jesus / Halo / Waiting for the night / Enjoy the silence / Policy of truth / Blue dress / Clean.

May 90. (c-s/7") *(C+/BONG 19)* *<19842>* **POLICY OF TRUTH. / KALEID (remix)** [16] [15] Aug90
('A'-Trancentral mix; 12"+=/cd-s+=) *(LCDBONG 19)* – ('A'-Pavlov's dub mix).

Sep 90. (12"/cd-s/7") *(12/CD+/BONG 20)* *<19580>* **WORLD IN MY EYES. / HAPPIEST GIRL / SEA OF SIN** [17] [52] Nov90
(12") *(L12BONG 20)* – (first 2 tracks) / ('A'remix).
(c-s+=)(cd-s+=) *(CDLBONG 20)* – Meaning of love / Somebody.

DEPECHE MODE (cont)

Feb 93. (c-s/7") (C+/BONG 21) <18600> **I FEEL YOU. / ONE CARESS** — 8 / 37
 (12"+=)(cd-s+=) (12/CD BONG 21) – ('A'-Throb mix) / ('A'-Babylon mix).
 (12"/cd-s) (12L/CDL BONG 21) – ('A'side) / ('A'swamp mix) / ('A'-Renegade Soundwave mix) / ('A'-Helmut mix).
Mar 93. (cd/c/lp) (CD/C+/STUMM 106) <45243> **SONGS OF FAITH AND DEVOTION** — 1 / 1
 – I feel you / Walking in my shoes / Condemnation / Mercy in you / Judas / In your room / Get right with me / Rush / One caress / Higher love. (live version of album iss.Dec93; same)
May 93. (7"/c-s) (7C BONG 22) <18506> **WALKING IN MY SHOES. / MY JOY** — 14 / 69
 (12"+=/cd-s+=) (12/CD BONG 22) – ('A'-Grungy Gonads mix).
 (ext;12"/cd-s) (L12/LCD BONG 22) – ('A'-Random Carpet mix) / ('A'-Anandamidic mix) / ('A'-Mark Stent 12" Ambient Whale mix).
Sep 93. (7"/c-s) (7C BONG 23) **CONDEMNATION. / DEATH'S DOOR** (jazz mix) — 9 /
 (cd-s+=) (CDBONG 23) – Rush (spiritual mix) / Rush (amylnitrate mix).
 (12"+=) (12BONG 23) – Rush (mixes).
 (12"/cd-s) (L12/LCD 23) – ('A'live) / Personal Jesus (live) / Enjoy the silence (live) / Halo (live).
Dec 93. (cd) <45505> **SONGS OF FAITH AND DEVOTION – LIVE** (live) — – /
Jan 94. (c-s) (CBONG 24) **IN YOUR ROOM** (Zephyr mix) / **HIGHER LOVE** (Adrenaline mix) — 8 /
 ('A'-Jeep Rock mix; cd-s+=) (XLCDBONG 24) – ('A'-Apex mix).
 (12"++=) (12BONG 24) – ('A'-extended Zephyr mix).
 (cd-s) (CDBONG 24) – ('A'-Zephyr mix) / ('A'extended Zephyr mix) / Never let me down again / Death's door.
 (cd-s) (LCDBONG 24) – ('A'side) / Policy of truth / World in my eyes / Fly on the windscreen (final).
 (12"++=) (L12BONG 24) – Never let me down again / Death's door.

–––– ANDREW FLETCHER departed to take over groups' business affairs.
–––– On the 17th August '95, GAHAN was thought by the music press to have attempted suicide by cutting at his wrists after his wife left him. His record company however said this had been an accident and was over-hyped by the media.

Feb 97. (cd-s) (12BONG 25) <17409> **BARREL OF A GUN / PAINKILLER** ('A'-Underworld soft mix) / ('A'-One Inch Punch mix) — 4 / 47
 (12") (L12BONG 25) – ('A'-One Inch Punch mix) / ('A'-United mix) / Painkiller (Plastikman mix) / Painkiller.
 (cd-s) (LCDBONG 25) – ('A'-Underworld hard mix) / ('A'-United mix) / Painkiller (Plastikman mix).
 (12") (12BONG 25) – ('A'-Underworld hard mix) / ('A'-3 Phase mix) / ('A'-One Inch Punch mix) / ('A'-United mix).
Apr 97. (c-s) (CBONG 26) <43845> **IT'S NO GOOD / SLOWBLOW** — 5 / 38
 (cd-s+=) (CDBONG 26) – ('A'-Bass bounce mix) / ('A'-Speedy J mix).
 ('A'-Hardfloor mix; cd-s+=) (LCDBONG 26) – ('A'-Andrea Parker mix) / ('A'-Motor bass mix).
 (12") (12BONG 26) – ('A'-Hardfloor mix) / ('A'-Speedy J mix) / ('A'-Motor bass mix) / ('A'-Andrea Parker mix) / ('A'-Dom T mix).
Apr 97. (cd/c/lp) (CD/C+/Stumm 148) <46522> **ULTRA** — 1 / 5
 – Barrel of a gun / The love thieves / Home / It's no good / Uselink / Useless / Sister of night / Jazz thieves / Freestate / The bottom line / Insight.
Jun 97. (c-s) (CBONG 27) <17314> **HOME / IT'S NO GOOD** — 23 / 88 Nov97
 ('A'-Grantby mix; cd-s+=) (LCDBONG 27) – ('A'-Jedi Knights remix: Drowning in time) / Barrel of a gun.
 (12") (12BONG 27) – ('A'-Jedi Knights remix: Drowning in time) / ('A'-Grantby mix) / ('A'-Air around the golf remix) / ('A'-LFO mix).
 (cd-s) (CDBONG 27) – ('A'side) / ('A'-LFO mix) / ('A'-The Noodles and the damage done mix).
Oct 97. (cd-s) (CDBONG 28) **USELESS** / ('A'-Escape From Wherever parts 1&2) / ('A'-Cosmic Blues mix) / **BARREL OF A GUN** (video) — 28 /
 (12") (12BONG 28) – ('A'-The Kruder & Dorfmeister session) / ('A'-CJ Bolland funky sub mix) / ('A'-Air 20 mix).
 (cd-s) (LCDBONG 28) – ('A'-CJ Bolland ultrasonar mix) / ('A'-The Kruder & Dorfmeister session) / ('A'live) / It's no good (CD-rom).
Sep 98. (cd-s) (CDBONG 29) <44546> **ONLY WHEN I LOSE MYSELF / SURRENDER / HEADSTAR** — 17 / 61
 (12"/cd-s) (12/LCD BONG 29) – ('A'-Subsonic legacy remix) / ('A'-Dan The Automator remix) / Headstar (Luke Slater remix).
 (12") (L12BONG 29) – ('A'remixes) / Painkiller / Surrender.
 (cd-s+=) (XLCDBONG 29) – World in my eyes.
Sep 98. (d-cd/c/3x12") (CD/C+/MUTEL 5) <47110> **THE SINGLES 86>98** (compilation) — 5 / 38 Oct98
 – Stripped / A question of lust / A question of time / Strangelove / Never let me down again / Behind the wheel / Personal Jesus / Enjoy the silence / Policy of truth / World in my eyes / I feel you / Walking in my shoes / Condemnation / In your room / Barrel of a gun / It's no good / Home / Useless / Only when I lose myself / Little 15 / Everything counts (live).
Apr 01. (cd-s) (CDBONG 30) <44982> **DREAM ON / DREAM ON (Easy Tiger Bertrand Burgalat mix) / DREAM ON (A.S. Dragon version)** — 6 / 85
 (12") (12BONG 30) – ('A'-Bushwacka tough guy mix) / ('A'-Dave Clarke remix) / ('A'-Bushwacka blunt mix).
 (cd-s) (LCDBONG 30) – ('A'-Bushwacka tough guy mix) / ('A'-Dave Clarke acoustic) / ('A'-Octagon Man mix) / ('A'-Kid 606 mix).
May 01. (cd/c/lp) (CD/C+/STUMM 190) <47960> **EXCITER** — 9 / 8
 – Dream on / Shine / The sweetest condition / When the body speaks / The dead of night / Lovetheme / Freelove / Comatose / I feel loved / Breathe / Easy tiger / I am you / Goodnight lovers.
Jul 01. (cd-s) (CDBONG 31) **I FEEL LOVED / DIRT / I FEEL LOVED (extended instrumental)** — 12 / –
 (12"+=/cd-s+=) (12/LCD BONG 31) – ('A'-Tenaglia's labour of love mix) / ('A'-Thomas Brickman mix) / ('A'-Chamber's remix).
Nov 01. (cd-s) (CDBONG 32) **FREELOVE / ZENSTATION / STEREONERD** — 19 / –
 (12") (12BONG 32) – (first & third tracks) / ('A'-Console remix) / ('A'-DJ Muggs remix) / ('A'versions).
 (cd-s) (CDLBONG 32) – ('A'versions).
Feb 02. (12"/cd-s) (12/CD BONG 33) **GOODNIGHT LOVERS / WHEN THE BODY SPEAKS** (acoustic). / **THE DEAD OF NIGHT** (Electronicat remix) / **GOODNIGHT LOVERS** (isan falling leaf mix) — – / –

– compilations, others –

on 'Mute' unless otherwise mentioned
Nov 91. (6xcd-ep-box) (DMBX 1CD) **SINGLES BOX SET** — – / –
Nov 91. (6xcd-ep-box) (DMBX 2CD) **SINGLES BOX SET** — – / –
Nov 91. (6xcd-ep-box) (DMBX 3CD) **SINGLES BOX SET** — – / –
Jan 99. (cd/c) <47298> **THE SINGLES 81>85** — – / –

MARTIN L. GORE

 Mute / Sire
Jun 89. (m-cd/m-c/m-lp) (CD/C+/STUMM 67) <25980> **COUNTERFEIT** — 51 /
 – Smile in the crowd / Never turn your back on Mother Earth / Gone / Motherless child / Compulsion / In a manner of speaking.

DEUTSCHE AMERIKANISCHE FREUNDSCHAFT (see under ⇒ D.A.F.)

DEUX FILLES (see under ⇒ KING OF LUXEMBOURG)

DEVINE & STATTON (see under ⇒ LUDUS)

DIAGRAM BROS (see under ⇒ DISLOCATION DANCE)

DICKS (see under ⇒ SISTER DOUBLE HAPPINESS)

DIF JUZ

Formed: London, England . . . 1980 out of the ashes of LONDON PRIDE, by brothers DAVID and ALAN CURTIS, plus GARY BROMLEY and RICHARD THOMAS. Signed to the fledgling '4 a.d.' imprint early the following year, DIF JUZ began their recording career with two EP's in quick succession, namely 'HU/RE/MI/CS' and 'VIBRATING AIR'. Hardly your average post-punk outfit, the quartet delivered a type of sax-happy jazz-rock vaguely reminiscent of SOFT MACHINE / KING CRIMSON. Following a couple of low-key mini-sets, the first of which being 'WHO SAYS SO' (for 'Red Flame'), they were lured back to their original label, also home to the COCTEAU TWINS. In fact it was the husband and wife core of the latter act that augmented DIF JUZ on their debut album proper, 'EXTRACTIONS' (1985), ROBIN GUTHRIE producing and ELIZABETH FRASER contributing vocals on one track. Following a dismal remix album of early material, 'OUT OF THE TREES' (1986), the band went their separate ways, RICHARD THOMAS taking up an invitation to temporarily deputise for the unwell SIMON RAYMONDE in the COCTEAU TWINS.

Album rating: WHO SAYS SO mini (*6) / EXTRACTIONS (*6) / SOUNDPOOL compilation (*7)

DAVID CURTIS – guitar / **ALAN CURTIS** – guitar / **GARY BROMLEY** – bass / **RICHARD THOMAS** – drums, saxophone

 4 a.d. / not iss.
Jul 81. (12"ep) (BAD 109) **HU/RE/MI/CS** — – / –
 – Parts 1-4:- Hu / Re / Mi / Cs.
Oct 81. (12"ep) (BAD 116) **VIBRATING AIR** — – / –
 – Heset / Diselt / Gunet / Soarn.

 Red Flame / not iss.
Aug 83. (m-lp) (RFM 24) **WHO SAYS SO** — – / –
 – Roy's tray / So shy / Song with no name (pt.2) / Tabla piece / Swan-2 / Pass it on Charlie / Channel / The dub song.

 Pleasantly Surprised / not iss.
Feb 85. (c) (PS 009) **TIME CLOCK TURNS BACK** — – / –
 – Scottish express / Red tackle / The hole / Abroad / Adverts (clip slip) / Spy plane / Sea shanty / Bad tooth / Trance / Introducing Mrs. McCarthy / Obscure by face / Good bad the ugly.

 4 a.d. / not iss.
Aug 85. (lp) (CAD 505) **EXTRACTIONS** — – / –
 – Crosswinds / A starting point / Silver passage / The last day / Love insane / Marooned / Two fine days / Echo wreck / Twin and earth. (cd-iss. Feb87 +=; CAD 505CD)– VIBRATING AIR (EP). (cd re-iss. Jul98; GAD 505CD)

–––– guest on below SCOTT HODGES – trombone (ex-DEAD CAN DANCE)
Nov 86. (m-lp) (MAD 612) **OUT OF THE TREES** (remixes of earliest EP's) — – / –

–––– THOMAS having guested for The COCTEAU TWINS, joined the JESUS & MARY CHAIN before moving on to BUTTERFLY CHILD. DAVID joined WOLFGANG PRESS, while he and his NY bound brother were part of THIS MORTAL COIL.

– compilations, etc. –

Mar 99. (cd) 4 a.d.; (<GAD 109>) **SOUNDPOOL** (first 2 EP's) — – / –

Pat DiNIZIO (see under ⇒ SMITHEREENS)

DINOSAUR JR.

Formed: Amherst, Massachusetts, USA ... 1983 by J. MASCIS. Initially recording hardcore punk under the DEEP WOUND moniker, the band recruited PATRICK MURPHY and metamorphosed into DINOSAUR. Their self-titled debut album appeared in 1985, a raw blueprint for their distinctive candy-coated noise rock that was good enough to secure an American tour support slot with SONIC YOUTH. After protestations from aging West Coast rockers DINOSAUR, J.MASCIS' crew added the JR. to their name. Subsequently recording one album for 'SST', 'YOU'RE LIVING ALL OVER ME' (1987), the band further developed their melodic distortion although it was the 'FREAK SCENE' (1988) single, their debut for 'Blast First', which saw DINOSAUR JR. pressed to the cardigan-clad bosoms of the nation's pre-baggy indie kids. A wildly exhilarating piece of pristine pop replete with copious amounts of intoxicating noise pollution, MASCIS' go-on-impress-me vocals epitomised the word slacker when that dubious cliche was still gestating in some hack's subconscious. The follow-up album, 'BUG' (1988) was arguably the band's finest moment, perfectly crafted pop spiked with scathing slivers of guitar squall. BARLOW departed soon after the album's release, going off to form SEBADOH while MASCIS' mob came up with a wonderfully skewed cover of The CURE's 'JUST LIKE HEAVEN'. DON FLEMING (of GUMBALL fame) and JAY SPIEGEL featured on DINOSAUR JR.'s major label debut for 'WEA' subsidiary 'Blanco Y Negro', 'THE WAGON' (1991). Another slice of cascading noise-pop, the single raised expectations for the follow-up album 'GREEN MIND' (1991). More or less a MASCIS solo album, it failed to live up to its promise although by the release of 1993's 'WHERE YOU BEEN', MASCIS had found a permanent bassist in MIKE JOHNSON. Their most successful album to date, DINOSAUR JR. at last reaped some rewards from the grunge scene they'd played a major role in creating. With both JOHNSON and MASCIS releasing solo albums in 1996, the latter finally re-emerged late 2000 with the KEVIN SHIELDS-produced 'MORE LIGHT' (issued under J. MASCIS & THE FOG billing). Anyone expecting some kind of artistic rebirth or millennial rejuvenation was to be sorely disappointed as J delivered another set of ragged, tumbledown fuzz-pop. The slacker's slacker, MASCIS makes music that seemingly hangs together by only the seared threads of his own beleaguered vocal chords and that's not likely to change anytime soon. • **Songwriters:** MASCIS wrote all, except LOTTA LOVE (Neil Young) / QUICKSAND (David Bowie) / I FEEL A WHOLE LOT BETTER (Byrds) / GOIN' BLIND (Kiss) / HOT BURRITO 2 (Gram Parsons). J. MASCIS solo:- EVERY MOTHER'S SON (Lynyrd Skynyrd) / THE BOY WITH THE THORN IN HIS SIDE (Smiths) / ON THE RUN (Wipers) / ANTICIPATION (Carly Simon) / LEAVING ON A JET PLANE (John Denver). MIKE JOHNSON solo:- SECOND LOVERS SONG (Lynyrd Skynyrd) / LOVE AND OTHER CRIMES (Lee Hazlewood) / IF YOU'RE GONE (Gene Clark). • **Trivia:** In Jun'91, MASCIS moonlighted as a drummer with Boston satanic hard-core group UPSIDE DOWN CROSS, who made one self-titled album Autumn '91 on 'Taang!'. He also wrote songs and made a cameo appearance in the 1992 film, 'Gas, Food, Lodging'.

Album rating: DINOSAUR (*6) / YOU'RE LIVING ALL OVER ME mini (*7) / BUG (*8) / GREEN MIND (*7) / WHERE YOU BEEN (*8) / WITHOUT A SOUND (*5) / HAND IT OVER (*7) / J. Mascis: MARTIN AND ME (*6) / Mike Johnson: WHERE AM I? (*5) / YEAR OF MONDAYS (*5) / I FEEL ALRIGHT (*6) / J. Mascis & The Fog: MORE LIGHT (*6)

LOU BARLOW (b.17 Jul'66, Northampton, Mass.) – guitar / **J. MASCIS** (b. JOSEPH, 10 Dec'65) – drums / **CHARLIE NAKAJIMA** – vocals / **SCOTT HELLAND** – bass

		not iss.	Radiobeat
Dec 83.	(7"ep; as DEEP WOUND) <RB 002> **I SAW IT**	-	

– I saw it / Sisters / In my room / Don't need / Lou's anxiety song / Video prick / Sick of fun / Deep wound / Dead babies.

—— **J. MASCIS** – vocals, guitar, percussion / **LOU BARLOW** – bass, ukelele, vocals / added **MURPH** (b. EMMETT "PATRICK" MURPHY, 21 Dec'64) – drums (ex-ALL WHITE JURY)

		not iss.	Homestead
Jun 85.	(lp; as DINOSAUR) <HMS 015> **DINOSAUR**	-	

– Forget the swan / Cats in a bowl / The leper / Does it float / Pointless / Repulsion / Gargoyle / Several lips / Mountain man / Quest / Bulbs of passion.

| Mar 86. | (7"; as DINOSAUR) <HMS 032> **REPULSION. / BULBS OF PASSION** | - | |

(UK-iss.Apr97; same)

		S.S.T.	S.S.T.
Mar 87.	(12"ep) <SST 152> **DINOSAUR JR.**		

– Little fury things / In a jar / Show me the way. (cd-ep iss.Dec88; SSTCD 152)

| Jul 87. | (m-lp/c) <(SST/+C 130)> **YOU'RE LIVING ALL OVER ME** | | |

– Little fury things / Kracked / Sludgefeast / The lung / Raisans / Tarpit / In a jar / Lose / Poledo / Show me the way. (cd-iss. Oct95; same)

		Blast First	S.S.T.
Sep 88.	(7") <BFFP 30> **FREAK SCENE. / KEEP THE GLOVE**		

(US-iss.7",7"green; SST 220)

| Oct 88. | (lp/c/cd) <(BFFP 31/+C/CD)> <SST/+C/CD 216> **BUG** | | |

– Freak scene / No bones / They always come / Yeah we know / Let it ride / Pond song / Budge / The post / Don't. (cd re-iss. Feb99; SST 216CD)

—— **DONNA BIDDELL** – bass (ex-SCREAMING TREES) repl. BARLOW who formed SEBADOH

| Apr 89. | (7"/etched-12"/cd-s) <BFFP 47 S/T/CD> <SST 244> **JUST LIKE HEAVEN. / THROW DOWN / CHUNKS (A Last Rights Tune)** | 78 | Feb 90 |

(US version 12"ep+=/c-ep+=/cd-ep+=) (SST/+C/CD 244) – Freak scene / Keep the glove.

—— DONNA left and was repl. by **DON FLEMING** – guitar + **JAY SPIEGEL** – drums (both B.A.L.L.)

		Glitterhouse	Sub Pop
Jun 90.	(7"/7"white) (GR 0097) <SP 68> **THE WAGON. / BETTER THAN GONE**		

—— In Oct 90, J.MASCIS and other ex-DINOSAUR JR member FLEMING + SPIEGEL, made an album 'RAKE' as VELVET MONKEYS (aka B.A.L.L. + friends).

		Blanco Y Negro	Sire
Jan 91.	(7"/c-s) (NEG 48/+C) **THE WAGON. / THE LITTLE BABY**	49	-

(12"+=/cd-s+=) (NEG 48 T/CD) – Pebbles + weeds / Quicksand.

| Feb 91. | (lp/c/cd) (BYN 24/+C/CD) <26479> **GREEN MIND** | 36 | |

– The wagon / Puke + cry / Blowing it / I live for that look / Flying cloud / How'd you pin that one on me / Water / Muck / Thumb / Green mind.

| Aug 91. | (7"/c-s) (NEG 52/+C) **WHATEVER'S COOL WITH ME. / SIDEWAYS** | | - |

(12"+=/cd-s+=) (NEG 52 T/CD) – Thumb (live) / Keep the glove (live).

—— **MASCIS + MURPH** introduced new member **MIKE JOHNSON** (b.27 Aug'65, Grant's Pass, Oregon, USA) – bass (ex-MARK LANEGAN, ex-GEORGE LANE, ex-SNAKEPIT)

| Nov 92. | (7") (NEG 60) **GET ME. / HOT BURRITO #2** | 44 | - |

(c-s+=/12"+=/cd-s+=) (NEG 60 C/T/CD) – Qwest (live).

| Jan 93. | (7") (NEG 61) **START CHOPPIN'. / TURNIP FARM** | 20 | |

(10"+=/12"+=/cd-s+=) (NEG 61 TEP/T/CD) – Forget it.

| Feb 93. | (lp/c/cd) (BYN 28/+C/CD) <45108> **WHERE YOU BEEN?** | 10 | 50 |

– Out there / Start choppin' / What else is new? / On the way / Not the same / Get me / Drawerings / Hide / Goin' home / I ain't sayin'.

| Jun 93. | (7"/c-s/12") (NEG 63/+C/T) **OUT THERE. / KEEBLIN' (live) / KRACKED (live)** | 44 | |

(10"+=) (NEG 63TE) – Post.
(cd-s++=) (NEG 63CD) – Quest (live).
(cd-s) (NEG 63CDX) – ('A'side) / Get me / Severed lips / Thumb (radio sessions).

—— now without MURPH

| Aug 94. | (7"/c-s) (NEG 74/+C) **FEEL THE PAIN. / GET OUT OF THIS** | 25 | |

(10"etched+=/cd-s+=) (NEG 74 TE/CD) – Repulsion (acoustic).

| Sep 94. | (cd/c/lp) (4509 96933-2/-4/-1) <45719> **WITHOUT A SOUND** | 24 | 44 |

– Feel the pain / I don't think so / Yeah right / Outta hand / Grab it / Even you / Mind glow / Get out of this / On the brink / Seemed like the thing to do / Over your shoulder.

| Feb 95. | (7"green/c-s) (NEG 77 X/C) **I DON'T THINK SO. / GET ME (live)** | 67 | |

(cd-s+=) (NEG 77CD) – What else is new? / Sludge.

| Mar 97. | (c-s/12"/cd-s) (NEG 103 C/T/CD) **TAKE A RUN AT THE SUN. / DON'T YOU THINK IT'S TIME / THE PICKLE SONG** | 53 | |

| Mar 97. | (cd/c/lp) (0630 18312-2/-4/-1) <46506> **HAND IT OVER** | | |

– Take a run at the sun / Never bought it / Nothin's goin' on / I'm insane / Can't we move this alone / Sure not over you / Loaded / Mick / I know yer insane / Gettin' rough / Gotta know.

		Trade 2	not iss.
Sep 97.	(7") (TRDSC 009) **I'M INSANE. / I MISUNDERSTOOD**		-

– compilations, etc. –

| Aug 91. | (10"m-lp) S.S.T.; (SST 275) **FOSSILS** | - | |

– Little fury things / In a jar / Show me the way / Freak scene / Keep the glove / Just like heaven / Throw down / Chunks. <cd-iss. +UK May93 & Oct96; SST 276CD>

| Feb 99. | (cd) Strange Fruit; (SFRSCD 078) **THE BBC SESSIONS** | | - |

– Raisins / Does it float / Leper / Bulbs of passion / Keep the glove / In a jar / Get me / Keeblin / Budge / No bones.

MIKE JOHNSON

—— with **BARRETT MARTIN, AL LARSEN + DAVID KRUEGER**

		not iss.	Up
Nov 94.	(cd) <8> **WHERE AM I?**	-	

– Overland / Turn back alone / Save today / Separation / Untitled / Second lovers song / Down the line / Love and other crimes / See through / If you're gone / Carry on / 100% off / Atrophy.

—— now with his wife **LESLIE HARDY** – bass (of JUNED, who he produced) / **J. MASCIS, BARRETT MARTIN + MARK LANEGAN**

		Atlantic	Atlantic
Apr 96.	(cd/c) <(7567 92669-2/-4)> **YEAR OF MONDAYS**		Feb96

– Where am I? / One way out / The way it will be / Too far / Another side / Circle / Eclipse / Left in the dark / Hold the reins / Say it's so / Overdrive.

—— now with **KRUEGER, JOHN ATKINS, ELI BRADEN, DAN PETERS, TIFFANY ANDERS, CLAUDIA GROOM + BRETT ARNOLD**

		not iss.	Up
Aug 98.	(cd) <UP 057> **I FEEL ALRIGHT**	-	

– All there is / Turn around / I don't love you / Minor aversion / Not over yet / Leaving Greensleeves / I've got to have you / One liner / Message to pretty / Impatient and unwilling / Performer / Tradewinds.

J. MASCIS

		WEA	Warners
May 96.	(cd/c) <(46177)> **MARTIN + ME**		Apr96

– Thumb / So what else is new / Get me / Blowin' it / Repulsion / Goin' home / The boy with the thorn in his side / Not you again / On the run / Keeblin / Flying cloud / Anticipation / Drawerings / Every mother's son.

J. MASCIS & THE FOG

with **KEVIN SHIELDS**

City Slang / Artemis

Sep 00. (cd-s) (20171-2) **WHERE'D YOU GO / CAN I TELL U STORIES / TOO HARD**

Oct 00. (cd/lp) (20168-2/-1) <76665> **MORE LIGHT**
– Same day / Waistin' / Where'd you go / Back before you go / Grand me to you / Anmaring / All the girls / I not fine / Can I take this on / Does the kiss fit / More light.

Jun 01. (cd-s) (97745) **WAISTIN' / LEAVING ON A JET PLANE**

Bill DIREEN

Born: 1957, Christchurch, New Zealand. Influenced by the likes of LOU REED and ROKY ERICKSON, BILL formed his first group, VACUUM (later KAZA PORTICO), in 1980 with future PIN GROUP members STEPHEN COGLE and PETER STAPLETON. In the ensuing year or so, the vocalist/guitarist founded yet another short-lived cult outfit, SIX IMPOSSIBLE THINGS, although this time, a 7" single, 'SUMMER ON THE NULARBOR', was issued. When his SOLUBLE FISH ENSEMBLE floundered in '82, the man hooked up with ALLEN MEEK and MALCOLM GRANT (once again) to form The BUILDERS. Under various alternate name changes (the BILDERS was one!), the revolving-door ensemble issued a plethora of low-key releases. With his wife CAROL WOODWARD, he also chose to formulate a theatrical project, Blue Moon – FEAST OF FROGS in '83 were BILL and CAROL doing Boris Vian songs. BILL and his many chums subsequently attempted to generate their time, creating weird and wonderful recordings/compilations, a series of these included the excellent 'CUT' (1994).

Album rating: Bilders/Builders: BEATIN' HEARTS (*5) / SPLIT SECONDS (*4) / CoNCH3 (*5) / LET'S PLAY (*4) / DIVINA COMEDIA compilation (*6) / MAX QUITZ compilation (*5) / PYX compilation (*4) / CUT compilation (*6) / Bill Direen: HUMAN KINDNESS (*5)

BUILDERS

BILL DIREEN – vocals, guitar / **DEREK CHAMPION** – drums / + a host of others incl. **MALCOLM GRANT, CAROL WOODWARD, MIKE DOOLEY, ALLEN MEEK, ALISTAIR DOYLE, MARYROSE CROOK, STUART PAGE, SHARON CROSBIE, BRUCE MASON + IVAN ROGERS**

Sausage / not iss.

1981. (7"; as SIX IMPOSSIBLE THINGS) (none) **SUMMER ON THE NULARBOR. / ALIEN**

Prototype Productions / not iss.

1982. (7"ep; as SOLOMON'S BALL) (PR 1070) **SOLOMON'S BALL** – NewZ
– Dead heat / America / Strange nights / Son of Cronos.

1982. (12"ep) (PR 1084) **HIGH THIRTIES PIANO** – NewZ
– Dead heat (outro) / Magazine / L'union libre / Kicks / Payline / Bedrock bay / Avenue (live) / Avenue / Baby come back (backwards) / Outer date world / Dead heat.

Flying Nun / not iss.

1982. (7"ep; as Die BILDER) (FN 006) **SCHWIMMEN IN DER SEE EP** – NewZ
– Girl at night / I thought I knew you / Starry day / Russian rug.

—— next with GRANT, DOOLEY + CHRIS KNOX + CAMPBELL McLAY

Jan 83. (lp) (JAN 8) **BEATIN' HEARTS** – NewZ
– 1,000,000 hearts / Moderation Bedrock bay / Same old story / Heartbeats-a-go-go / Blue sand lonely / Dirty & disgusting / Alien / Accident / Wanganui with a white face / Magpies / Outer date world / Evidence / Inquest / Magazine / Kicks / Friend. *(cd-iss. 1993 as '... VOLUME 2'+=; FNCD 275)* – Red sky / On the beach last night.

South Indies / not iss.

1983. (c) (none) **LIVE AT THE GLADSTONE** (live) – NewZ

Prototype Publications / not iss.

1983. (c; as ABOVE GROUND) (013) **GONE AIWA**
– Outer date world / Dead heat (live) / To kill a bat / Gray goose.

1983. (7"ep; as FEAST OF FROGS) (PR 2025) **FEAST OF FROGS** – NewZ
– Snob / I drink / Monsieur le President / Hurt me Johnny.

Full Moon / not iss.

1983. (12"ep; as SOLUBLE FISH) (none) **DANCE OF DEATH EP** – NewZ
– Intro (Bill) / Play the game (Sarah) / Nose song (Charles) / Papa Kurl (Nicole) / Busker's song (Campbell) / Midnight dark (Liz) / Prison song (Carol).

1984. (lp; as BILDERINE) (001) **SPLIT SECONDS** – NewZ
– Baby cum back / Retail trade / Skulls / (Just like) All the rest / Girl at night / Avenue / Inside / Remember breaking up / Blenheim song No.28 / Crossword / Circle of blood / The spell / Surprise / Darling. *(cd-iss. 1993 by The BUILDERS as '... VOLUME 3' on 'Flying Nun'+=; FNCD 276)* – Sad but true / Serious / Iceberg / Wellington song / Envoi / Trees / Nutshell of love (jeopardy).

South Indies / not iss.

1985. (lp) (PRA 2301) **CoNCH3** – NewZ
– Black doors / Clifford flat / Look east / Lovers / Coalman / Bride of the wheel / Dublin / Nitric chatter / Alligator / Night / Holydays / Sunday news.

1986. (lp) (SINZ 11) **LET'S PLAY** – NewZ
– Rubbish in the city / Opium and gold / Magazine / Resting sleepwalker / Mouth of sound / Payline / Newspaper sleep / Johnny Devlin's shoes / Stand up / Friday / Kicks / Mehiko / Inquest.

1986. (7") (SINGL 001) **GINGER JAR. / WHAT A HOOMBAH** – NewZ

1987. (lp) (SOIN 3277) **LET'S PLAY** (version 2) – NewZ
– Rubbish in the city / Opium and gold / Magazine / Resting sleepwalker / Mouth of sound / Payline / Newspaper sleep / Aku aku / Opium and gold / Colors in the gutter / State of the play.

1987. (7"ep) (SOIN 5377) **CUP** – NewZ
– The cup / Chah hun ruh! / Sunday news update / Shortwave / Art in Heaven / Neither do I.

1987. (lp; as SOLUBLE FISH) (none) **SOUND CUES** – NewZ

1987. (lp) (SOIN 477) **DIVINA COMEDIA** (compilation) – NewZ
– Black doors / Clifford flat / Do the alligator / Buildings for crumbling / Retail trade / Hoombah hoombaba / At the solo man's ball / Girl at night / America / Wanganui with a white face / Alien / Dirty and disgusting / Russian rug / Friend.

1987. (m-lp; by BILL DIREEN & BARRY STOCKLEY) (SOIN 6242) **LIFE IN BARS** – NewZ
– Green shampoo / The drinker / Ahimsa / Dust / Jonny Hall / Fondness / You inhabit the wind / Life in bars / Green shampoo (reprise).

1989. (c) (none) **THE HAT** – NewZ

1990. (12"ep) (SOIN BILT 5) **WE ARE THE COOLEST CATS IN THE WORLD** – NewZ
– Gin trap / Chopin / Waxeye / Batter bad / Armchair / Neither do I / Chah hun run / Johny wobble / Next time / What eat / Julio / Grogblossom / Barina / Gin trap (return).

not iss. / Hecuba

1990's. (7") <HEX 03> **SKULLS. / ALIEN**

I.M.D. / not iss.

1994. (cd) (IMD 10030) **CUT** – NewZ
– No body / Snake / Nil nil / Fashion / Song of the snow / Repossessed / Worry / Swing / Looking up / Famous smile / C.B.A.Z.Y. / Let it go / Poke / Paint-fume / Glory / Close / Seaweed / Do you.

– compilations, etc. –

1993. (cd) (FN 274) **MAX QUITZ: VOL.1** – NewZ
– (HIGH THIRTIES PIANO + ABOVE GROUND + SCHWIMMEN IN DER SEE + SOLOMON'S BALL + SIX IMPOSSIBLE THINGS).

1994. (cd) (FN 277) **PYX: VOLUME 4 (1985-1988)** – NewZ
– Alligator song / Clifford flat / Payline / What shall we eat (at home) / What shall we eat (studio) / Next time / Holydays / Today's the day / One by one / Dublin / Cup / Grogblossom / Chipped Asian bowl / Shortwave (studio) / Shortwave (live) / Barina / Gin trap.

BILL DIREEN

Corazoo / not iss.

1998. (lp/cd) **HUMAN KINDNESS** – Swiss
– Out on the town / From Capp St to Langstr indirect / The way that I feel / Weapons bank / South into break-up / In the beauty house / The mettman medley: Pop whistle – 19:10 – Romeo's Offen song – Little time before / Pavlova flambe / Good while it lasted / Was a mighty fine horse but Alexander lost every town when he left it / Warm incarnadine drink of you / Go where the spirit takes you / My speech – Parched voice would fill with spittle / Gone / You're in the same situation.

DISLOCATION DANCE

Formed: Manchester, England ... December 1978 by frontman IAN RUNACRES, trumpeter ANDY DIAGRAM (also of The DIAGRAM BROS), bassist PAUL EMMERSON and drummer RICHARD HARRISON. Issued on The BUZZCOCKS' 'New Hormones' label, 1980's eponymous debut EP introduced the band's GANG OF FOUR-esque sound although it would be almost a year before a follow-up single, 'SLIP THAT DISC' (1981). A full length album, 'MUSIC MUSIC MUSIC' (1981) appeared a few months later, its sound embellished by new vocalist KATH WAY. A further series of singles followed over the next two years as the band emphasised the more free-floating, easy-jazz/pop elements of their sound, culminating in 1984's 'MIDNIGHT SHIFT' album. Reflecting this change, the latter set featured HERBIE RYAN guesting on sax, the man subsequently becoming a full-time member along with new recruit, Rochdale-born singer SONJA CLEGG. Her tenure was short-lived, however as the band split following a final single in late '85, 'WHAT'S GOING ON'. The track also featured a briefly returning DIAGRAM who had left a few years previous for The PALE FOUNTAINS, the man also having recorded material – including an album, 'SOME MARVELS OF MODERN SCIENCE' – in the early 80's as a member of The DIAGRAM BROTHERS. After a brief stint with The HONKIES in the late 80's, ANDY continued onwards with SPACEHEADS (alongside RICHARD HARRISON), recording two low-key efforts, 'PAY ME MONEY DOWN' 12" and 'HO! FAT WALLET' cassette at the turn of the decade. When 'Dark Beloved Cloud' records invited them into their roster in the mid-90's, things really got underway. An eponymous set in 1995 was followed by a live set a few years later (they had performed since 1993), which featured MTV fave video, 'SHOOT THE BOSS'. In 1999, while ANDY's attentions were somewhat in other directions (i.e. with DAVID THOMAS & THE PALE BOYS), the SPACEHEADS showcased their wares via US concerts and the start of a trio of albums, 'ANGEL STATION' (their first for 'Merge'). A collaboration with sound recordist MAX EASTLEY, 'THE TIME OF THE ANCIENT ASTRONAUT' (2001), was an avant-garde freeform rock trip that fell between the precipice between ambient and futuristic soundtrack scores. The third of these, 'LOW PRESSURE' (2002), broke into bebop and improv electronica territory, no doubt inspired by the works of MILES DAVIS or The APHEX TWIN. • **Covered:** WE CAN WORK IT OUT (Beatles).

Album rating: MUSIC MUSIC MUSIC (*5) / MIDNIGHT SHIFT (*4) / Diagram Brothers: SOME MARVELS OF MODERN SCIENCE (*4) / Spaceheads: HO! FAT WALLET (*6) / SPACEHEADS (*6) / ROUND THE OUTSIDE: LIVE IN THE U.S.A. (*5) / ANGEL STATION (*7) / THE TIME OF THE ANCIENT ASTRONAUT with Max Eastley (*6) / LOW PRESSURE (*6)

IAN RUNACRES – vocals, guitar / **ANDY DIAGRAM** – trumpet, vocals (also of the DIAGRAM BROS) / **PAUL EMMERSON** – bass / **RICHARD HARRISON** – drums

New Hormones / not iss.

Sep 80. (7"ep) (ORG 7) **DISLOCATION DANCE**
– It's so difficult / Familiar view / Birthday outlook / Perfectly in control.

DISLOCATION DANCE (cont)

Jul 81. (12"ep) (ORG 10) **SLIP THAT DISC EP**
– Spare concern / We can work it out / I'll see it / It's all . . . panic!
––– added **KATH WAY** – vocals
Oct 81. (lp) (ORG 15) **MUSIC MUSIC MUSIC**
– Stand me up / Don't knock me down / Yops course / Meeting mum and dad / Friendship / Take a chance (on romance) / . . . Have a dance / Roof is leaking / With a smile on your face and a frown in . . . / Vendetta (theme) / Narrow laughs / Footloose / Can't race time . . . and the mad killer / Wonder what I'll do tomorrow. (*<cd-iss. Jul00 on 'Vinyl Japan'+=; ASKCD 96>*) – Rosemary (7" version) / Shake / Can't race time . . . and the mad killer (alt. version) / You'll never know / You can tell.
Jun 82. (7") (ORG 19) **ROSEMARY. / SHAKE**
Oct 82. (7") (ORG 22) **YOU'LL NEVER KNOW. / YOU CAN TELL**
––– now without **ANDY DIAGRAM** who joined The PALE FOUNTAINS

The Music Label / *not iss.*

May 83. (7") (TML45 01) **VIOLETTE. / SAN MICHELLE**

Rough Trade / *not iss.*

Oct 83. (12"m) (RTT 142) **SHOW ME. / WE CAN WORK IT OUT / VENDETTA**
Aug 84. (lp) (ROUGH 63) **MIDNIGHT SHIFT**
– Show me / I'm doing fine / Here comes love / Remind me / Tyrannes of fun / Open cages / Baby blue / With a reason / Mr. Zak / Bottle of red wine / Midnight shift / San Michelle. (*<cd-iss. Mar00 on 'Vinyl Japan'+=; ASKCD 94>*) – Violette / Show me (12" mix) / Show me (alt. mix) / Vendetta / We can work it out.
––– **SONJA CLEGG** – vocals; repl. KATH
––– **DIAGRAM** returned as the group added **HERBIE RYAN** – sax (who appeared on the last album)

Slipped Discs / *not iss.*

Dec 85. (12") (SLIP12 1) **WHAT'S GOING ON. /**
––– split the following year with SONJA (augmented by IAN) going solo releasing the album, 'SOUL PRECIOUS' for 'Bop Cassettes' in '87. DIAGRAM rejoined The PALE FOUNTAINS and later teamed up with the band, JAMES.

– compilations, etc. –

Jun 99. (cd) *Vinyl Japan; (ASKCD 87)* **THE BBC SESSIONS**

DIAGRAM BROS

ANDY DIAGRAM – bass / **FRASER DIAGRAM** – vocals, guitar / **LAWRENCE DIAGRAM** – guitar / **SIMON DIAGRAM** – drums

Construct / *not iss.*

Oct 80. (7") (CON 1) **WE ARE ALL ANIMALS. / THERE IS NO SHOWER / I WOULD LOVE TO LIVE IN PRISON**

New Hormones / *not iss.*

Apr 81. (7") (ORG 9) **BRICKS. / POSTAL BARGAINS**
Nov 81. (lp) (ORG 17) **SOME MARVELS OF MODERN SCIENCE**
Jul 82. (10"ep) (ORG 21) **DISCORDO**
– I didn't get where I am today by being a right git (German version) / Discordo / Bricks.
––– ANDY was to later join JAMES, DAVID THOMAS and SPACEHEADS

SPACEHEADS

––– are **ANDY DIAGRAM** + **RICHARD HARRISON**

Big Biz Niz / *not iss.*

1990. (12"ep) **PAY ME MY MONEY DOWN**
– Pay me my money down / No zzzeds with those Spaceheads around / The golden age of Avarice / Change (stop the rot).

Bop / *not iss.*

1990. (c) **HO! FAT WALLET**
– Kalimpet / World upside down / (Seldom heard) Voices of discontent / The rulers are responsible for the gruesome conditions / Devil's claws / Love and bullets / Oh wow! look at the colours / Stuck in a storm / Slow life / Big waddle / Live in bed / Back to work (never going again). *<US cd-iss. 1998 on 'Dark Beloved Cloud'+=; DBC 212>* – PAY ME MY MONEY DOWN

Dark Beloved Cloud / *Dark Beloved Cloud*

1995. (cd) *<DBC 204>* **SPACEHEADS**
– Evacuate the planet / Bones / Whatever happened to Billy the comedian? / Eat the machine / Down in Outer Space (live) / Joyriding (live) / Parched (live) / Open my box / Gobsmacked! / Bella ciao / The whistle blower / Love the machine / What machine? (live).
Mar 97. (cd) *(<DBC 208CD>)* **ROUND THE OUTSIDE: LIVE IN THE U.S.A. (live)**
– Shoot the boss / Blowing monkeyshine / The blanket dancer / Grin of toast / Smash the God offensive / A.T.M.O. / Sideways steppers.

Power Tool / *Merge*

Apr 99. (cd) (PAN 032) <MRG 157> **ANGEL STATION**
– Electric gypsyland / One way system / Road sweeper / Black mirror / Magic in the Space Age / Trance figure / Psycho bubble / Angel station / Heads in orbit / Put me out / From now on the signs are no longer in the sky / Squat the idea / Pedalling power / Slow blind exit / Angel passing.

Bip Hop / *Merge*

Jun 01. (cd; as SPACEHEADS and MAX EASTLEY) (BLEEP 004) **THE TIME OF THE ANCIENT ASTRONAUT**
– The black drop of Venus / Life without gravity / Ghosts / Air as matter / The old moon in the young moons arms / Interstellar escalator / Hubble bath / Hail bop / Invisible nature / Generator X / Ancient astronauts.
Jul 02. (cd) (BLEEP 14) <MRG 30CD> **LOW PRESSURE**
– Low pressure / On a clear day / The Lugano affair / Astro temple / Pressure point / Fog / The hut / Storm force 8 / Red shift / Over the moon.

DIVINE HORSEMEN
(see under ⇒ FLESH EATERS; 70's section)

DOG FACED HERMANS

Formed: Edinburgh, Scotland . . . 1986 by MARION COUTTS, ANDY, COLIN and WILF. One of the weirdest and most experimental bands to come out of the capital, the DOG FACED HERMANS initially delivered their CHUMBAWAMBA-esque anarchist message via a single on their own 'Demon Radge' imprint. They subsequently appeared on the 'Alternative Tentacles' V/A album, 'Censorship Sucks' (a tribute set to raise funds for Jello Biafra's court case) while also releasing a trio of 45's for 'Calculus'. Towards the end of the decade, a debut LP, 'EVERYDAY TIME BOMB' finally appeared on 'Vinyl Drip', the 'HERMANS trading in the 'Burgh for the more liberal climes of Amsterdam. Finding a sympathetic Dutch recording home at 'Konkurrel' (in-house label of The EX), they released two sets, 'MENTAL BLOCKS FOR ALL AGES' (1991) and 'HUM OF LIFE' (1993), the last of which featured a cover of 8-Eyed Spy/Lydia Lunch's 'LOVE SPLIT WITH BLOOD' and Ornette Coleman's 'PEACE WARRIORS'. Renewing their relationship with San Francisco's 'Alternative Tentacles', DOG FACED HERMANS completed a further two sets of socially aware, post-feminist avant-punk in the shape of 'BUMP & SWING' (1994) and 'THOSE DEEP BUDS' (1994); they were now at home in the Netherlands.

Album rating: EVERYDAY TIME BOMB (*5) / MENTAL BLOCKS FOR ALL AGES (*5) / HUM OF LIFE (*5) / BUMP & SWING (*4) / THOSE DEEP BUDS (*4)

MARION COUTTS – vocals, trumpet, cowbells / **ANDY** – guitar / **COLIN** – bass / **WILF** – drums, saxophone / **GERT-JAN** – live sound

Demon Radge / *not iss.*

Feb 87. (7"ep) (RADGE 1) **UNBEND EP**
– Catbrain walk / Cruelty / Incineration.

Calculus / *not iss.*

Mar 88. (12"ep) (KIT 001) **HUMANS FLY**
– How much vegetation have you got? / Mary Houdini / Balloon girl / Cactus.
Sep 88. (7") (KIT 002) **NO PARTISAN. /**
Sep 88. (7") (KIT 003) **BELLA – CIAO. / MISS O'GRADY**

Vinyl Drip / *not iss.*

Jun 89. (m-lp/m-c) (SUK 007/+C) **EVERYDAY TIME BOMB**
– New shoots / Scottish block / Binding system / John Henry / Beautiful / Frock / Live action.

Konkurrel / *not iss.*

Nov 91. (lp/cd) (K 139/+CD) **MENTAL BLOCKS FOR ALL AGES**
– Punjabi monster beat / Fortune / Supressa / Astronaut / Bhopal / The running man / Body strategic / In a row / From the top of the mountain / It's time / Incineration / Big pot / The rain it raineth / El Doggo speaks / Catbrain walk / Bella ciao. (*cd+=*) – EVERYDAY TIME BOMB
Mar 93. (lp/cd) (K 147/+CD) **HUM OF LIFE**
– Jan 9 / Viva / Hook and the wire / How we connect / Love split with blood / Wings / White Indians / Hear the dogs / Love is the heart of everything / Madame la mer / Peace warriors.
(above 2 also issued on 'Project A-Bomb')

Compulsive / *not iss.*

Mar 93. (7") (CPS 2) **PEACE WARRIORS. / (track by Jonestown)**

Konkurrel / *Alternative Tentacles*

Aug 94. (cd) (K 153CD) <VIRUS 159CD> **BUMP & SWING (live)** Feb95
– Hear the dogs / Peace warriors / Viva / Love is the heart of everything / Transformation / Keep your laws – Off my body / Jan 9 / Human spark / Love split with blood / Fortune / The bride has feet of clay.
Oct 94. (lp/cd) (K 155/+CD) <VIRUS 151/+CD> **THOSE DEEP BUDS**
– Blessed are the follies / Volkswagen / Keep your laws – Off my body / Lie and swell / H tribe / Human spark / Les femmes et les filles vont danser / Virginia fur / Calley / Dream forever. (*cd re-iss. Apr00; same as US*)

––– disbanded some time in '95; MARION is a sculptor in London, ANDY joined The EX, WILF moved to Canada and joined RHYTHM ACTIVISM, while COLIN runs a record shop.

DOLLY MIXTURE

Formed: Cambridge, England . . . late 70's by all-girl trio of DEBSEY WYKES, RACHEL BOR and HESTER SMITH. More famous for having backed CAPTAIN SENSIBLE on a couple of his solo singles (including his No.1 smash, 'Happy Talk'), the DOLLY MIXTURE sweetened up the post-New Wave scene with their charmingly eccentric brand of girly pop-punk. Although they made a major label debut in 1980 with the single, 'BABY IT'S YOU' (a Shirelles cover), the trio subsequently disowned the track and complained they were being misrepresented by the company. Finding a more sympathetic home at PAUL WELLER's 'Respond' imprint, the girls released a further two 45's over the course of the early 80's. With all-female acts such as The MO-DETTES, The RAINCOATS and The MARINE GIRLS also making waves, DOLLY MIXTURE were primed for the top with an overload of media coverage and attendant expectation. After being out of the limelight for a while, the trio surprisingly returned with a self-financed double-set of home recordings released under the spartan title of 'DEMONSTRATION TAPES' (1983). Although virtually ignored at the time, the album was later re-issued by pop curator, BOB STANLEY (of SAINT ETIENNE). After their mid-80's demise, DEBSEY and HESTER re-united in a one-album project, COMING UP ROSES.

Album rating: DEMONSTRATION TAPES (*6) / Coming Up Roses: I SAID BALLROOM (*5)

RACHEL BOR (b.16 May'63, Wales) – cello, guitars / **DEBSEY WYKES** (b.21 Dec'60, London, England) – vocals, bass, piano / **HESTER SMITH** (b.28 Oct'60, West Africa) – drums, percussion

DOLLY MIXTURE (cont) — *THE GREAT INDIE DISCOGRAPHY* — **The 1980s**

		Chrysalis	not iss.
Sep 80.	(7") (CHS 2459) **BABY IT'S YOU. / NEW LOOK AWAY**		

		Respond	not iss.
Nov 81.	(7") (RESP 1) **BEEN TEEN. / HONKY HONDA AND ERNIE BALL**		-
Mar 82.	(7") (RESP 4) **EVERYTHING AND MORE. / YOU & ME ON THE SEASHORE**		-

— joined up as backing singers with CAPTAIN SENSIBLE

		Dead Good Dolly Platt.	not iss.
Dec 83.	(d-lp) (GOOD 1) **DEMONSTRATION TAPES** (demos)		

– Dream come true / Ernie Ball / He's so frisky / The didn't song / Will he kiss me tonight / Miss Candy twist / Shonay Shonay / How come you're such a hit with the boys, Jane? / Side street walker / Treasure hunt / Never let it go / Angel treads / Welcome to the perfect day / Step close now / Stareaway / In your eyes / Understanding / Never mind Sundays / Spend your wishes / Day by day / Wave away / Sorry to leave you / Winter seems fine / Grass is greener / Round the corner / Remember this / Whistling in the dark. *(cd-iss. Mar96 on 'Royal Mint'; RM 001CD)*

Jan 84. (7") (DMS 1) **REMEMBER THIS. / LISTENING PLEASURE**

		Cordelia	not iss.
May 86.	(12"ep) (ERICAT 017) **THE FIRESIDE E.P.**		

– Coriander – Let's cook! / Welcome home / Dilly dolly dally / Three o'clock rhapsody / Dolly medley / Borinda's lament.

— split in 1986 when RACHEL remained with CAPTAIN SENSIBLE and his band

COMING UP ROSES

— **DEBSEY + HESTER** with **NICKY BRODIE** – vocals, percussion (ex-SHILLELAGH SISTERS) / **PATRICIA O'FLYNN** – saxophone (ex-SHILLELAGH SISTERS) / **LEIGH LUSCIOUS** – guitar / **CLAIRE KENNY** – bass (ex-AMAZULU)

— (1987) **SOPHIE CHERRY** – bass; repl. CLAIRE

— (1989) **DEBSEY, HESTER + NICKY** recruited a new line-up of **TONY WATTS** – lead guitar / **MIDUS** – bass / **JANE KEAY** – saxophone (past members were also featured on the album)

		Utility	not iss.
Jul 89.	(m-lp/m-cd) (UTIL 005/+CD) **I SAID BALLROOM**		-

– Remember my name / I could fly / I don't know what it is / Black jean boy / I could have been your girlfriend (if you'd asked me to) / You kill me.

— split early in 1991; DEBSEY later helped form BIRDIE with EAST VILLAGE guy, PAUL KELLY

DOLPHIN BROTHERS
(see under ⇒ JAPAN; 70's section)

DOME (see under ⇒ WIRE; 70's section)

DONNER PARTY

Formed: San Francisco, California, USA . . . 1986 by singer-songwriter, SAM COOMES, who enlisted the aid of CAT HEADS drummer/singer, MELANIE CLARIN and bassist REINHOLD JOHNSON. Debuting with the eponymous 'THE DONNER PARTY' in '87 on their own 'Cryptovision' label, the trio garnered immediate underground acclaim for their wilfully naive and eccentric alt-pop folk, COOMES' vocals consistently drawing comparisons to the likes of JONATHAN RICHMAN and JAD FAIR. Spotted by CAMPER VAN BEETHOVEN man, DAVID LOWERY, the group signed to his 'Pitch-A-Tent' label where they issued another 'DONNER PARTY' album. This marked the end of the first chapter in the band's career as COOMES teamed up with ELLIOTT SMITH to form HEATMISER; SAM is now the mainman behind QUASI. That long-lost third DONNER PARTY album was finally ready for scrutiny courtesy of a retrospective 'COMPLETE RECORDINGS 1987-1989', which contained – as it suggested – all their work. • **Covered:** DASEN GR . . . (Swedish trad) / UP & DOWN (. . . Moss) / GOODNIGHT IRENE (Leadbelly) / SQUEEZE BOX (Who). • **Note:** The DONNER PARTY of the mid-90's on 'Infamous' records were not the same act.

Album rating: THE DONNER PARTY (*6) / THE DONNER PARTY (*6) / COMPLETE RECORDINGS 1987-1989 double compilation (*7)

SAM COOMES – vocals, guitar / **REINHOLD JOHNSON** – bass / **MELANIE CLARIN** – drums (of CAT HEADS)

		not iss.	Cryptovision
1987.	(lp) <1400> **THE DONNER PARTY**	-	

		not iss.	Pitch-A-Tent
1988.	(lp) <11> **THE DONNER PARTY**	-	

— after the recording of a shelved 3rd set, COOMES teamed up ELLIOTT SMITH in his band, HEATMISER; he subsequently formed MOTORGOAT then QUASI

– compilations, etc. –

Jun 00. (d-cd) *Innerstate;* <(7008)> **COMPLETE RECORDINGS 1987-1989**   Mar00

– Before too long / Halo / Are you in tune with yourself? / Godlike porpoise head of blue-eyed Mary / When you die your eyes pop out / The ghost / The owl of Minerva / Oh Esmeralda / John Wilkes Booth / That that is, is / Jeez Louise / Spiders / Surfin' to the Moon / Clean living / G-L-O-R-I-A / Why bother? / Sickness / Up & down / Try to imagine a terrible world / Boxful of bones / Mrs. Miserack / What a gush of matter into life is here / Treepig / Unfriendly / Trust in Henry / Friendly / Lost in Hoboken / Blue starch acid for baby's new tooth // Please don't listen / Would you like to have something to eat? / When I was a baby / Dasen GR Pa Svennsta ska / Chocolate shake / King Chico / Your mother / Harold Payne / Notker the stammere / Kore Cosmu / Goodnight Irene / Everyone is a girl / Nutty botty / The nixie / We cannot be happy / Birthday suit / Trepanned / Spiders / Friendly / Breakfast / Treepig (live) / Sickness (live) / Goodnight Irene (live) / When I was a baby / Squeeze box.

DOOR AND THE WINDOW
(see under ⇒ ALTERNATIVE TV; 70's section)

DOORS

Formed: Los Angeles, California, USA . . . July 1965 by RAY MANZAREK and JIM MORRISON. In 1966, after some personnel changes, they soon settled with JOHN DENSMORE and ROBBY KRIEGER and became The DOORS. They were released from a 'Columbia' recording contract, when ARTHUR LEE (of LOVE), recommended them to his 'Elektra' label boss Jac Holzman. Early in 1967, their eponymous debut album was issued, which soon climbed to US No.2 after an edited version of 'LIGHT MY FIRE' hit No.1 in July '67. The single and album showcased MORRISON's overtly sexual vocal theatrics against a backdrop of organ-dominated, avant-garde blues. The classic debut also contained two cover versions (see below), the lucid psychedelia of 'THE CRYSTAL SHIP', plus the extremely disturbing 11-minute epic, 'THE END' (which was later used on the soundtrack for the 1979 Francis Ford Coppola film, 'Apocalypse Now'). While other bands of the era were into peace and love, The DOORS found their salvation in a much darker vision, again in evidence on the follow-up (also in '67), 'STRANGE DAYS'. This was another classic, tracks like, 'LOVE ME TWO TIMES', 'YOU'RE LOST LITTLE GIRL' and 'PEOPLE ARE STRANGE' further enhancing the band's powerful mystique. As MORRISON's drink and drugs antics became increasingly problematic, he was arrested many times (on stage and off), mostly for lewd simulation of sexual acts and indecent exposure. Nevertheless, in the late summer of '68, they found themselves at the top of the US charts again with the 45, 'HELLO I LOVE YOU' and the album, 'WAITING FOR THE SUN'. A disappointing 4th album, 'THE SOFT PARADE' (1969), did, however, contain a classic US Top 3 hit, 'TOUCH ME'. More controversy was generated, when, in November '69, MORRISON was accused of interfering with an airline stewardess while a flight was in progress. He was later acquitted, but the following year, was given eights months hard labour after being found guilty of indecent exposure and profanity. He was freed on appeal and began work on 1970's, 'MORRISON HOTEL / HARD ROCK CAFE', a return to rawer, more basic rock'n'roll. After the recording of 'L.A. WOMAN', he relocated to Paris in the Spring of '71 with his girlfriend Pamela, amid rumours of an imminent split from the group. The aforementioned album was delivered in June, a masterpiece that carried on the re-evaluation of their blues roots. His over-indulgence in drugs and booze, had given his vocal chords a deeper resonance, showcased on such classics as, 'RIDERS ON THE STORM' (a Top 30 hit), 'LOVE HER MADLY', the JOHN LEE HOOKER cover 'CRAWLING KING SNAKE' and the freewheeling title track. Ironically, just as the band seemed to have found their feet again, JIM MORRISON was found dead in his bathtub on the 3rd of July 1971. Speculation was rife at the time, but it later became apparent he had died from a drugs/drink induced heart attack. He was also buried in Paris, his grave becoming a shrine to all but his parents, who disowned him in 1967. The others continued as a trio for the next two years, but sadly the public refused to acknowledge them as the real DOORS. The "god-like" cult of MORRISON has mushroomed to incredible proportions in the years following his death, rumours continuing, Elvis-like, to circulate that he is still alive. There have been many imitators over the last quarter of a century, although none have matched his/their dark majesty. • **Songwriters:** MORRISON – words/poetry (under the influence of explorative narcotics), Group/MANZAREK compositions. Covered; ALABAMA SONG (Brecht-Weill) / BACK DOOR MAN (Howlin' Wolf) / WHO DO YOU LOVE (Bo Diddley) / LITTLE RED ROOSTER (Willie Dixon) / BEEN DOWN SO LONG (J.B. Lenoir). • **Trivia:** In 1968, they featured on a UK TV documentary 'The Doors Are Open', which was later issued on video. In 1991, Oliver Stone released a feature film 'THE DOORS', with Val Kilmer playing the role of MORRISON.

Album rating: THE DOORS (*9) / STRANGE DAYS (*8) / WAITING FOR THE SUN (*6) / THE SOFT PARADE (*5) / MORRISON HOTEL – HARD ROCK CAFE (*8) / ABSOLUTELY LIVE (*6) / 13 compilation (*8) / L.A. WOMAN (*9) / OTHER VOICES (*4) / WEIRD SCENES INSIDE THE GOLDMINE compilation (*8) / FULL CIRCLE (*4) / AN AMERICAN PRAYER – JIM MORRISON exploitation (*4) / GREATEST HITS compilation (*8) / ALIVE, SHE CRIED exploitation (*4) / BEST OF THE DOORS compilation (*8) / LIVE AT THE HOLLYWOOD BOWL exploitation (*4) / THE DOORS soundtrack (*5) / IN CONCERT exploitation (*5) / GREATEST HITS compilation (*9) / THE COMPLETE STUDIO RECORDINGS boxed-set (*8)

JIM MORRISON (b. 8 Dec'43, Melbourne, Florida) – vocals / **RAY MANZAREK** (b.12 Feb'35, Chicago, Illinois) – keyboards, bass pedal / **ROBBY KRIEGER** (b. 8 Jan'46) – guitar / **JOHN DENSMORE** (b. 1 Dec'45) – drums / also guest **DOUG LUBAHN** – bass (of CLEAR LIGHT)

		Elektra	Elektra
Feb 67.	(7") (EKSN 45009) <45611> **BREAK ON THROUGH (TO THE OTHER SIDE). / END OF THE NIGHT**		Jan67
Mar 67.	(lp; mono/stereo) <(EKL/EKS 74007)> **THE DOORS**	1	Mar 67

– Break on through (to the other side) / Soul kitchen / The crystal ship / Twentieth century fox / Alabama song (whiskey song) / Light my fire / Back door man / I looked at you / End of the night / Take it as it comes / The end. *(re-iss. Nov71 lp/c; K/K4 42012) (cd-iss. Jan84; K2 42012) (re-iss. cd Feb89; 974007-2) (re-hit UK No.43 in Apr91)*

Apr 67. (7") (EKSN 45012) **ALABAMA SONG (WHISKEY BAR). / TAKE IT AS IT COMES**   -

305

DOORS (cont)

Date	Release	UK	US
Jul 67.	(7") (EKSN 45014) <45615> **LIGHT MY FIRE (edit). / THE CRYSTAL SHIP** (re-iss. Jul71; same)	49	1 Jun67
Sep 67.	(7") (EKSN 45017) <45621> **PEOPLE ARE STRANGE. / UNHAPPY GIRL**	–	12
Dec 67.	(lp; mono/stereo) <(EKL/EKS 74014)> **STRANGE DAYS**	–	3 Nov67

– Strange days / You're lost little girl / Love me two times / Unhappy girl / Horse latitudes / Moonlight drive / People are strange / My eyes have seen you / I can't see your face in my mind / When the music's over. (re-iss. Nov71 lp/c; K/K4 42016) (cd-iss. Jan86; K2 42016) (re-iss. Nov71 lp/c; K/K4 42016)

Dec 67.	(7") (EKSN 45022) <45624> **LOVE ME TWO TIMES. / MOONLIGHT DRIVE**	–	25
Apr 68.	(7") (EKSN 45030) <45628> **THE UNKNOWN SOLDIER. / WE COULD BE SO GOOD TOGETHER** (re-iss. Jun71; K 12004)	–	39 Mar68
Aug 68.	(7") (EKSN 45037) <45635> **HELLO, I LOVE YOU. / LOVE STREET**	15	1 Jul68

— **LEROY VINEGAR** – acoustic bass repl. LABAHN

| Sep 68. | (lp; mono/stereo) <(EKL/EKS 74024)> **WAITING FOR THE SUN** | 16 | 1 Aug68 |

– Hello I love you / Love street / Not to touch the Earth / Summer's almost gone / Wintertime love / The unknown soldier / Spanish caravan / My wild love / We could be so good together / Yes, the river flows / Five to one. (re-iss. Nov71 lp/c; K/K4 42041) (cd-iss. Jan86; K2 42041) (cd re-iss. Feb89; 974024-2)

Dec 68.	(7") (EKSN 45050) <45646> **TOUCH ME. / WILD CHILD**	–	3
May 69.	(7") (EKSN 45059) <45656> **WISHFUL SINFUL. / WHO SCARED YOU**	–	44 Mar69
Aug 69.	(7") (EKSN 45065) <45663> **TELL ALL THE PEOPLE. / EASY RIDE**	–	57 Jun69
Sep 69.	(lp) <(EKS 75005)> **THE SOFT PARADE**	–	6 Aug69

– Tell all the people / Touch me / Shaman's blues / Do it / Easy ride / Wild child / Runnin' blue / Wishful sinful / The soft parade. (re-iss. Nov71 lp/c; K/K4 42079) (cd-iss. Feb89; 975005-2)

| Sep 69. | (7") <45675> **RUNNIN' BLUE. / DO IT** | – | 64 |

— guest **LONNIE MACK** – bass repl. LUBAHN

Apr 70.	(7") <45685> **YOU MAKE ME REAL. / ROADHOUSE BLUES**	–	50
Apr 70.	(7") (2101 004) **YOU MAKE ME REAL. / THE SPY**	–	–
Apr 70.	(lp) <(EKS 75007)> **MORRISON HOTEL / HARD ROCK CAFE**	12	4 Mar70

– Land ho! / The spy / Queen of the highway / Indian summer / Maggie McGill / Roadhouse blues / Waiting for the sun / You make me real / Peace frog / Blue Sunday / Ship of fools. (re-iss. Nov71 lp/c; K/K4 42080) (cd-iss. Apr86; K2 42080) (re-iss. cd.Feb89; 975007-2)

| Jul 70. | (7") (2101 008) **ROADHOUSE BLUES. / BLUE SUNDAY** | – | – |
| Sep 70. | (d-lp) (2665 002) <9002> **ABSOLUTELY LIVE** (live) | 69 | 8 Aug70 |

– Who do you love medley: Alabama song – Back door man – Love hides – Five to one / Build me a woman / When the music's over / Close to you / Universal mind / Break on through (to the other side) / The celebration of the lizard / Soul kitchen. (re-iss. Nov71 d-lp; K 62005) (d-cd-iss. Mar87 w-drawn; 2665 002)

| Oct 70. | (7") <45708> **UNIVERSAL MIND. / THE ICEWAGON FLEW** | – | – |
| Mar 71. | (lp/c) (K/K4 42062) <74079> **13** (compilation) | – | 25 Dec70 |

– Light my fire / People are strange / Back door man / Moonlight drive / The crystal ship / Roadhouse blues / Touch me / Love me two times / You're lost little girl / Hello, I love you / Land ho / Wild child / The unknown soldier.

— guest **JERRY SCHEFF** – bass repl. MACK

| May 71. | (7") <(EK 45726)> **LOVE HER MADLY. / (YOU NEED MEAT) DON'T GO NO FURTHER** | – | 11 Apr71 |
| Jun 71. | (lp/c) (K/K4 42090) <75011> **L.A. WOMAN** | 26 | 9 May71 |

– The changeling / Love her madly / Been down so long / Cars hiss by my window / L.A. woman / L'America / Hyacinth house / Crawling King Snake / The wasp (Texas radio and the big beat) / Riders on the storm. (cd-iss. 1984; K2 42090) (cd re-iss. Feb89 & Apr91; 975011-2)

| Jul 71. | (7") (K 12021) <45738> **RIDERS ON THE STORM (edit). / THE CHANGELING** | 22 | 14 |

— **RAY** – vocals, ROBBIE and JOHN carried on when JIM MORRISON died 3rd Jul'71 of a mysterious heart attack. The trio continued on

– compilations, etc. –

Note; All on 'Elektra' until mentioned otherwise

| Mar 72. | (d-lp/d-c) (K/K4 62009) <6001> **WEIRD SCENES INSIDE THE GOLD MINE** | 50 | 55 Feb72 |

– Break on through (to the other side) / Strange days / Shaman's blues / Love street / Peace frog / Blue Sunday / The wasp (Texas radio and the big beat) / End of the night / Love her madly / Ship of fools / The spy / The end / Take it as it comes / Running blue / L.A. woman / Five to one / Who scared you? / Don't go no further / Riders on the storm / Maggie McGill / Horse latitudes / When the music's over.

Sep 74.	(lp/c) (K/K4 42143) <5035> **THE BEST OF THE DOORS**	–	–
Feb 76.	(7") (K 12203) **RIDERS ON THE STORM. / L.A. WOMAN**	33	–
Sep 76.	(7") (K 12227) **LIGHT MY FIRE. / THE UNKNOWN SOLDIER**	–	–
Sep 76.	(7") (K 12228) **LOVE HER MADLY. / TOUCH ME**	–	–
Nov 78.	(lp/c; by JIM MORRISON) (K/K4 52111) <502> **AN AMERICAN PRAYER** (poetry recorded 8 Nov'70 with some DOORS tapes)	–	54

– Awake / Ghost song / Dawn's highway / Newborn awakening / To come of age / Black polished chrome / Latino chrome / Angels and sailors / Stoned immaculate / The poet's dreams / The movie / Curses invocations / World on fire / American night / Roadhouse blues / Lament / The hitchhiker / An American prayer. (re-iss. May95 cd/lp;)

Jan 79.	(7") (K 12215) **LOVE ME TWO TIMES. / HELLO I LOVE YOU** (w/ free 7"+=) (SAM 94) – GHOST SONG. / ROADHOUSE BLUES	–	–
Jan 79.	(7") **ROADHOUSE BLUES. / AN AMERICAN PRAYER**	–	–
Jan 80.	(7")<12"> (K 12400) <ELK 22032> **THE END.** / (b-side 'Delta' not by The DOORS)	–	–
Oct 80.	(lp/c) (K/K4 52254) <515> **GREATEST HITS**	–	17

– Hello, I love you / Light my fire / People are strange / Love me two times / Riders on the storm / Break on through / Roadhouse blues / Touch me / L.A. woman / Love her madly / The ghost song / The end. (cd-iss. Oct95 cd/c; 7559 61860-2/-4)

Oct 80.	(7") **PEOPLE ARE STRANGE. / NOT TO TOUCH THE EARTH**	–	–
Oct 82.	(d-c) (K4 62034) **MORRISON HOTEL / L.A. WOMAN**	–	–
Oct 83.	(7") <60269> **GLORIA (live). / MOONLIGHT DRIVE (live)**	–	71
Oct 83.	(12") (E 9774T) **GLORIA (live). / LOVE ME TWO TIMES (live)**	–	–
Oct 83.	(lp/c) (960269-1/-4) <60269> **ALIVE SHE CRIED** (live)	36	23

– Gloria / Light my fire / You make me real / The wasp (Texas radio and the big beat) / Love me two times / Little red rooster / Moonlight drive. (cd-iss. Jul84; 960269-2)

Aug 84.	(d-c) (K4 62040) **THE SOFT PARADE / AN AMERICAN PRAYER**	–	–
Jun 85.	(lp/c) (EKT 9/+C) <60417> **CLASSICS**	–	–
Sep 85.	(7") Old Gold; (OG 9520) **RIDERS ON THE STORM. / LIGHT MY FIRE**	–	–
Nov 85.	(lp/c/cd) (EKT 21/+C/CD) <60345> **BEST OF THE DOORS**	–	–

– Break on through (to the other side) / Light my fire / The crystal ship / People are strange / Strange days / Love me two times / Five to one / Waiting for the Sun / Spanish caravan / When the music's over / Hello, I love you / Roadhouse blues / L.A. woman / Riders on the storm / Touch me / Love her madly / The unknown soldier / The end. (cd+=) – Alabama song (whiskey bar). (re-iss. Apr91 hit UK No.17 & US No.32) (re-iss. Mar98, hit UK No.37)

| Jun 87. | (m-lp/c)(cd) (EKT 40/+C)(960741-2) <60741> **LIVE AT THE HOLLYWOOD BOWL** (live) | – | – |

– Wake up / Light my fire / The unknown soldier / A little game / The hill dwellers / Spanish caravan.

Mar 91.	(lp/c)(cd) (EKT 85/+C)(961047) <61047> **THE DOORS: A FILM BY OLIVER STONE – MUSIC FROM THE ORIGINAL SOUNDTRACK**	11	8
Apr 91.	(7") (EKR 121) **BREAK ON THROUGH. / LOVE STREET** (12"+=/cd-s+=) (EKR 125 TW/CD) – Hello I love you / Touch me.	64	–
May 91.	(7") (EKR 125) **LIGHT MY FIRE. / PEOPLE ARE STRANGE** (ext; 12"+=/cd-s+=) (EKR 125 TW/CD) – Soul kitchen.	7	–
May 91.	(t-lp/d-c/d-cd) (EKT 88/+C/7559 61082) <61082> **THE DOORS: IN CONCERT** (live)	24	50
Jul 91.	(7") (EKR 131) **RIDERS ON THE STORM. / LOVE ME TWO TIMES** (live) (12"+=/cd-s+=) (EKR 131 TW/CD) – Roadhouse blues (live).	68	–
Jun 95.	(c-s; by JIM MORRISON & THE DOORS) (EKR 205C) **THE GHOST SONG. / (interview)** (cd-s+=) (EKR 205CD) – Love me two times (live) / Roadhouse blues (live).	–	–
Oct 97.	(4xcd-box) <(7559 62123-2)> **THE DOORS BOX SET**	–	65
Nov 99.	(cd) <(7559 62475-2)> **STONED IMMACULATE**	–	–
Nov 99.	(7xcd-box) <(7559 62434-2)> **THE COMPLETE STUDIO RECORDINGS**	–	–
Sep 00.	(cd/c) <(7559 62468-2/-4)> **THE BEST OF THE DOORS**	–	9

– Riders on the storm / Light my fire / Love me two times / Roadhouse blues (live) / Strange days / Break on through / Five to one / Moonlight drive / Alabama song / Love her madly / People are strange / Touch me / Backdoor man / The unknown soldier / L.A. woman / Hello I love you / The end. <(d-cd+=; 7559 62569-2)>

| Sep 01. | (cd) <79376> **THE VERY BEST OF THE DOORS** | – | 92 |
| Oct 01. | (4xcd-box) (7559 62716-2) **THE DOORS BOX SET** | – | – |

DOROTHY (see under ⇒ RAINCOATS; 70's section)

DOS (see under ⇒ MINUTEMEN)

DOUBLE HAPPYS (see under ⇒ STRAITJACKET FITS)

Graeme DOWNES (see under ⇒ VERLAINES)

DOWNY MILDEW

Formed: Los Angeles, California, USA ... mid 80's by main songwriter, CHARLIE BALDONADO, part co-writer, JENNY HOMER, NANCY McCOY and MIKE MARASSE. Initially signed to US indie label, 'Texas Hotel', the band debuted in 1986 with an eponymous 12" EP. Rooted in breezy West Coast 60's pop and psychedelia but delivered with an alternative edge, the DOWNY MILDEW sound was fairly typical of the era's loose Paisley Underground scene although the contrasting writing styles of BALDONADO and HOMER marked them out from the pack. A debut album, 'BROOMTREE', appeared in 1987, its folky pop sensibilities drawing comparisons with 10,000 MANIACS. Featuring new drummer JOHN HOFER and violinist, SALVADOR GARZA, follow-up set, 'MINCING STEPS' (1988), fleshed out the sound with atmospheric string flourishes while maintaining the songwriting flair. Replacing HOFER with ROB JACOBS and moving to Windham Hill's 'High Street' offshoot for 1992's Mitchell Froom-produced 'AN ONCOMING TRAIN', the band continued to prefect their retro sound while 1994's 'SLOW SKY' saw JANINE COOPER coming in for the pregnant McCOY. • **Covered:** 'TIL I DIE (Beach Boys) / LADY DAY AND JOHN COLTRANE (Gil Scott-Heron).

Album rating: BROOMTREE (*6) / MINCING STEPS (*6) / AN ONCOMING TRAIN (*7) / SLOW SKY (*5)

JENNY HOMER – vocals, guitar / **CHARLIE BALDONADO** – guitar, vocals / **NANCY McCOY** – bass / **MIKE MARASSE** – drums

		Glass	Texas Hotel
1986.	(12"ep) **DOWNY MILDEW**	–	–

– Experience in the far south west / The drive / Purple parlor / Bad dream.

May 87. (lp) *(GLALP 025)* **BROOMTREE**
- The frown song / The kitchen / Sally pt.III / Good dream / Hollow girl / Ocean motorkid / Burnt bridges / That's enough of that / Sally pt.II / Everybody's gone. *<re-iss. 1993 on 'High Street' cd+=/c+=; 10319-2/-4>* – DOWNY MILDEW EP

— **JOHN HOFER** – drums; repl. JACOBS

1988. (lp) *<10>* **MINCING STEPS**
- Offering / Turning yourself around / Tangled ladders / Six flights / Floorboard / Big surprise / Misfortune / Inside her house / Flower song / All is not well in this house. *<cd-iss. 1993 on 'High Street'; 10320>*

— **ROB JACOBS** – drums; repl. HOFER
— added **SALVADOR GARZA** – strings

not iss. High Street

1992. (cd-ep) *<19207>* **ELEVATOR**
- Elevator / Cool nights / Til I die / Lady Day and John Coltrane.

1992. (cd/c) *<10313-2/-4>* **AN ONCOMING TRAIN**
- An oncoming train / Borrowed chant / Trading jewels / Elevator / Twice told tale / Six months is a long time / Seconds protest / Melissa, I know the difference / Sleep! / Child.

— **JANINE COOPER** – bass (ex-PET CLARK) repl. NANCY

Mar 94. (cd/c) *<10321-2/-4>* **SLOW SKY**
- Your blue eye / Left foot down / Release / A polka dot-scarved woman / Girls by the lake / A liar needs a good memory / That he wrote / Them that dream / Machine / Sidewinding home / Don't change your mind / I remember yesterday.

— disbanded the following year

DR CALCULUS (see under ⇒ DUFFY, Stephen)

DREAM ACADEMY

Formed: London, England ... 1983 by NICK LAIRD-CLOWES and GILBERT GABRIEL along with KATE ST. JOHN. Unashamed psychedelic-lite revivalists, The DREAM ACADEMY floated into slush-pop consciousness circa 1985 with the much sampled 'LIFE IN A NORTHERN TOWN' single. A massive transatlantic Top 10 hit and a tribute to late, great English singer-songwriter, NICK DRAKE, the track's lilting melancholy (somewhat like PREFAB SPROUT), soaring vocals and nostalgic yearning for a bygone 60's era was a formula which The 'ACADEMY lived and breathed by but which brought predictable flak from the critics. Released as the first fruits of their deal with 'Warners', the band's eponymous debut album was characterised by graceful arrangements (enhanced by the classical expertise of ST. JOHN) and their self-professed love of adventurous pop, some reviewers taking issue with what they regarded as polished pastiche. Much was also made of the group's flamboyant retro clothing which hardly helped them defend themselves against throwback accusations. The DREAM ACADEMY remained studiously unperturbed, working with FLEETWOOD MAC maestro LINDSEY BUCKINGHAM on a follow-up set, 'REMEMBRANCE DAYS' (1987). Another collection of artfully refined pop, the record nevertheless failed to spawn a hit single never mind a success on the scale of their debut. Following 1991's swansong, 'A DIFFERENT KIND OF WEATHER' (which included the musical reincarnation of Hare Krishna devotee, POLY STYRENE, former X-RAY SPEX singer!), the group folded with ST. JOHN going on to undertake live work as part of VAN MORRISON's touring revue and subsequently writing for TV. NICK LAIRD-CLOWES was back again in the late 90's courtesy of TRASHMONK. Signed to 'Creation', they released one AOR-indie set, 'MONA LISA OVERDRIVE' (1999); Creation boss ALAN McGEE took the same album - with a few bonus tracks - to his new 'Poptones' imprint for release in 2001. • **Covers:** PLEASE, PLEASE, PLEASE, LET ME GET WHAT I WANT (Smiths) / EVERYBODY'S GOTTA LEARN SOMETIME (Korgis).

Album rating: THE DREAM ACADEMY (*6) / REMEMBRANCE DAYS (*4) / Trashmonk: MONA LISA OVERDRIVE (*5)

NICK LAIRD-CLOWES (b. 5 Feb'59) – vocals, acoustic guitar / **KATE ST. JOHN** (b. 2 Oct'57) – vocals, keyboards (ex-JULIAN COPE) / **GILBERT GABRIEL** (b.16 Nov'56) – keyboards, vocals

Blanco Y Negro Reprise

Mar 85. (7") *(NEG 10) <28841>* **LIFE IN A NORTHERN TOWN. / TEST TAPE NO.3** — 15 — 7 Nov85
(12"+=) *(NEG 10T)* – On the edge of forever.

Aug 85. (7") *(NEG 16) <28750>* **THE LOVE PARADE. / A GIRL IN A MILLION (FOR EDIE SEDGWICK)** — — 36 Apr86
(12"+=) *(NEG 16T)* – ('A'extended).

Oct 85. (lp/c) *(BYN/+C 6) <25265>* **THE DREAM ACADEMY** — 58 — 20
- Life in a northern town / The edge of forever / Johnny new light / In places on the run / This world / Bound to be / Moving on / The love parade / The party / One dream. *(cd-iss. Jul88; 925625-2) (cd re-iss. Mar96; 7599 25265-2)*

Nov 85. (7") *(NEG 20)* **PLEASE, PLEASE, PLEASE, LET ME GET WHAT I WANT. / IN PLACES ON THE RUN**
(12"+=) *(NEG 20T)* – The party.

Sep 87. (7") *(NEG 27)* **INDIAN SUMMER. / HEAVEN**
(12"+=) *(NEG 27T)* – ('A'extended).

Sep 87. (lp/c)(cd) *(BYN/+C 12)(925625-2) <25625>* **REMEMBRANCE DAYS**
- Indian summer / Lesson of love / Humdrum / Power to believe / Hampstead girl / Here / In the hands of love / Double minded / Ballad in 4-4 / Everybody's gotta learn sometime / In exile.

— split for a while until they added **POLY STYRENE** – vocals (ex-X-RAY SPEX) + **STEVE LAMBERT** –

Jan 91. (7"/c-s) *(NEG 46/+C)* **LOVE. / MORDECHAI VANUNU**
(12"+=) *(NEG 46T)* – ('A'extended).
(cd-s++=) *(NEG 46CD)* – The demonstration.

Feb 91. (cd)(lp/c) *(<7599 26307-2>)(BYN 23/+C)* **A DIFFERENT KIND OF WEATHER**
- L-O-V-E / Mercy killing / Lucy September / Gaby says / Waterloo / 12-8 angel / St. Valentine's day / It never happens again / Forest fire / Lowlands / Not for 2nd prize.

— split again after above. ST. JOHN now writes for various TV series

TRASHMONK

NICK LAIRD-CLOWES - vocals, guitars / with others

Creation not issued

Mar 99. (cd/lp) *(CRE CD/LP 212)* **MONA LISA OVERDRIVE**
- Girl I used 2 know / Polygamy / Sapphire / High times / Amarylis / All change / Inner Brownstone symphony / N.W.O. / It won't be long / Dying day / On the way home. *(cd re-iss.Sep01 on 'Poptones'+=; MC 5041CD)*- Furhat / Mr. Karma. *<US cd-iss.Feb02 on 'B.M.G.'; 66021>*

Poptones not issued

Aug 01. (7") *(MC 5041S)* **SAPPHIRE. / FURHAT**

DREAM SYNDICATE

Formed: Los Angeles, California, USA ... 1981 by STEVE WYNN and KENDRA SMITH. The former had previously cut his teeth with SID GRIFFIN in an embryonic LONG RYDERS. They soon completed the line-up with KARL PRECODA and DENNIS DUCK. After an untitled mini-lp back home, they caught the interest of UK indie, 'Rough Trade', in 1983, who released their debut full-length album 'THE DAYS OF WINE AND ROSES'. Cut from a distinctly rougher-hewn cloth than most of the band's 'Paisley Underground' contemporaries, the album's dark intensity caused enough of a stir to eventually get them snapped up by 'A&M'. By the release of their major label debut, 'MEDICINE SHOW' (1984), KENDRA SMITH had been replaced by DAVE PROVOST. Although more mainstream than its predecessor, the album still showed the ragged influence of NEIL YOUNG and THE VELVET UNDERGROUND and while it didn't accrue the success it was probably due, its critical acclaim paved the way for other majors to give them a shot at the big league. After a final album for 'A&M', the compilation of early live material, 'IT'S NOT THE NEW DREAM SYNDICATE ALBUM' (1985), the band released their next studio offering on 'Chrysalis', 1986's 'OUT OF THE GREY'. Despite the more commercial, straight ahead rock sound of the record, success continued to elude the band and they split in early 1989 after releasing a final well-received album for 'Enigma', 'GHOST STORIES'. With a vocal style more leaning towards NEIL YOUNG than LOU REED, STEVE WYNN embarked on a solo career at the turn of the decade. Albums such as 'KEROSENE MAN' (1990) and 'DAZZLING DISPLAY' (1991) set out his stall and further established the man as Paisley Underground's leader of the pack. From 1993 to 1995 he combined solo work alongside a new side project, GUTTERBALL (featuring BOB RUPE of The SILOS and ex-HOUSE OF FREAKS members), although this minor supergroup only delivered two sets, 'GUTTERBALL' and 'WEASEL'. In 2001, after a handful of unremarkable low-key sets ('PICK OF THE LITTER not even worthy of a British or American release), WYNN was back on song with 'HERE COME THE MIRACLES'. • **Songwriters:** Most written by WYNN, except covers CINNAMON GIRL (Neil Young) / BALLAD OF DWIGHT FRYE (Alice Cooper) / LET IT RAIN (Derek & The Dominoes) / SHAKE YOUR HIPS (Slim Harpo) / THE LONELY BULL (... Lake) / MR. SOUL (Buffalo Springfield). WYNN covered KOOL THING (Sonic Youth) / BONNIE & CLYDE (Serge Gainsbourg) / WATCHING THE RIVER FLOW (Bob Dylan) / VENUS (Shocking Blue) / TIGHTEN UP (Booker T & The MG's) / CRAZY FEELING (Lou Reed) / BOY IN THE BUBBLE (Paul Simon) / WHY DOES LOVE GOT TO BE SO SAD (Eric Clapton) / THE AIR THAT I BREATHE (Hollies) / GUTTERBALL mainly WYNN with HARVEY or McCARTHY.
• **Trivia:** Early '85, STEVE WYNN was also in DANNY & DUSTY duo alongside old cohort DAN STUART (of GREEN ON RED).

Album rating: THE DAYS OF WINE AND ROSES (*7) / THE MEDICINE SHOW (*7) / THIS IS NOT THE NEW DREAM SYNDICATE ALBUM (*4) / OUT OF THE GREY (*6) / 50 IN A 25 ZONE (*4) / GHOST STORIES (*5) / LIVE AT RAJI'S (*7) / TELL ME WHEN IT'S OVER: THE BEST OF DREAM SYNDICATE compilation (*8) / Steve Wynn: KEROSENE MAN (*6) / DAZZLING DISPLAY (*6) / TAKE YOUR FLUNKY AND DANGLE collection (*5) / FLUORESCENT (*5) / GUTTERBALL by Gutterball (*5) / WEASEL by Gutterball (*5) / MELTING IN THE DARK (*6) / SWEETNESS & LIGHT (*5) / MY MIDNIGHT (*6) / THE SUITCASE SESSIONS collection (*4) / PICK OF THE LITTER (*6) / HERE COMES THE MIRACLES (*7)

STEVE 'DUSTY' WYNN (b.21 Feb'60, Santa Monica, Calif.) – vocals / **KARL PRECODA** (b.1961) – guitar / **DENNIS DUCK** (b.25 Mar'53) – drums / **KENDRA SMITH** (b.14 Mar'60, San Diego, Calif.) – bass / guest on below; **TOM ZVONCHECK** – keyboards

not iss. Down There

Dec 82. (m-lp) *<VEX 10>* **THE DREAM SYNDICATE**
- Sure thing / Some kinda itch / That's what you always say / When you smile. *(UK-iss.Jun85 on 'Zippo'; ZANE 001) (cd-iss. Aug92; VEXCD 10)*

Rough Trade Ruby

Nov 83. (lp) *(ROUGH 53)* **THE DAYS OF WINE AND ROSES**
- Tell me when it's over / Definitely clean / That's what you always say / Then she remembers / Halloween / When you smile / Until lately / Too little, too late / The days of wine and roses. *(re-iss. Jan87 on 'Slash'; 23844-1) (cd-iss. Jan95 & Aug99 on 'Normal'; NORMAL 176CD) <(cd re-mast.Jul01 on 'Rhino'+=; 8122 79937-2)>*
– THE DREAM SYNDICATE ep tracks / (rehearsal/bonus tracks).

Dec 83. (12"ep) *(RTT 121)* **TELL ME WHEN IT'S OVER. / SOME KINDA ITCH (live) / MR. SOUL (live) / SURE THING (live)**

DREAM SYNDICATE (cont)   THE GREAT INDIE DISCOGRAPHY   The 1980s

—— **DAVE PROVOST** – bass repl. KENDRA (she joined RAINY DAY then OPAL) (appeared on live album early '84) and later went solo

A&M / not iss.
Jun 84. (lp/c) (AMLX/CXM 64990) **MEDICINE SHOW**
– Still holding on to you / Daddy's girl / Burn / Armed with an empty gun / Bullet with my name on it / The medicine show / John Coltrane stereo blues / Merrittville.

Feb 85. (lp) (AMLH 12511) **IT'S NOT THE NEW DREAM SYNDICATE ALBUM** (live)
– Tell me when it's over / Bullet with my name on it / Armed with an empty gun / The medicine show / John Coltrane stereo blues.

—— **PAUL B. CUTLER** (b. 5 Aug'54, Phoenix, Arizona) – lead guitar + **MARK WALTON** (b. 9 Aug'59, Fairfield, Calif.) – bass; repl. PRECODA + PROVOST

Chrysalis / Big Time
Jun 86. (lp/c) (CHR/ZCHR 1539) **OUT OF THE GREY**
– Out of the grey / Forest for the trees / 50 in a 25 zone / Boston / Slide away / Dying embers / Now I ride alone / Dancing blind / You can't forget. (cd-iss. 1987; CCD 1539) (re-iss. Oct87 on 'Big Time' lp/c; ZL/ZK 71457X) <US cd-iss. 1997 on 'Atavistic'+=; 66> (cd re-iss. Aug99 on 'Normal'+=; NORMAL 184CD) – Let it rain / Cinnamon girl / Ballad of Dwight Frye / Shake your hips / I won't forget / The lonely bull.

Sep 87. (12"ep) (ZT 41420) **50 IN A 25 ZONE. / DRINKING PROBLEM / BLOOD MONEY / THE LONELY BULL**

Enigma- / Enigma
Virgin
Sep 88. (lp/c/cd) (ENVLP/TCENV/CDENV 506) <73341-1/-4/-2> **GHOST STORIES**
– The side I'll never show / My old haunts / Loving the sinner, hating the sin / Whatever you please / Weathered and torn / See that my grave is kept clean / I have faith / Some place better than this / Black / When the curtain calls. (cd re-iss. Sep95 on 'Restless'; 72758-2)

Nov 88. (7") (ENV 6) **I HAVE FAITH. / NOW I RIDE ALONE**
(12"+=) (ENVT 6) – I ain't living long like this.

—— split early 1989, when WYNN decided to venture solo. He released a number of albums, the first two being 'KEROSENE MAN' and 'DAZZLING DISPLAY'. He also formed GUTTERBALL with Long Ryder; STEPHEN McCARTHY. WALTON would subsequently form The CONTINENTAL DRIFTERS.

– compilations etc. –
Jun 89. (lp/cd) Enigma-Virgin; (ENVLP/CDENV 531) / Restless; <72293-2> **LIVE AT RAJI'S** (live in Hollywood January '85)
– Still holding on to you / Forest for the trees / Until lately / That's what you always say / Burn / Merrittville / The days of wine and roses / The medicine show / Halloween / Boston / John Coltrane stereo blues. (re-iss. Jun90 on 'Demon' lp/cd; DFIEND/FIENDCD 176)

Sep 89. (lp) Another Cowboy; (ANOTHER 1) **IT'S TOO LATE TO STOP NOW**

Apr 90. (d-lp/cd) Demon; (FIEND/+CD 170) **LIVE AT RAJI'S / GHOST STORIES**

Jun 92. (cd/c) Rhino; <R2/R4 70373> **TELL ME WHEN IT'S OVER: THE BEST OF DREAM SYNDICATE**

Nov 93. (cd) Normal; (NORMAL 156CD) **THE LOST TAPES 1985-1988** (re-iss. Aug99; same)

STEVE WYNN

World / Rhino
Service
May 90. (lp/c/cd) (SERV 011/+MC/CD) <8122 70969-2> **KEROSENE MAN**   Apr90
– Tears won't help / Carolyn / The blue drifter / Younger / Under the weather / Here on Earth as well / Something to remember me by / Killing time / Conspiracy of the heart / Kerosene man / Anthem. (cd re-iss. Feb93 on 'Rhino'; same as US) <cd re-iss. Nov98 on 'Prima'+=; SID 009)> – demos:- Here on earth as well / Our little house / Under the weather / Killing time / Carolyn.

1991. (cd-ep) <74427> **KEROSENE MAN EP**
– Kerosene man / Something to remember me by / Kool thing / Boy in the bubble / Conspiracy of the heart.

Rhino / Rhino
Dec 91. (cd-ep) <PRO2 90114> **DRAG EP**
– Drag / Christine's tune / Younger (live) / How's my little girl.

Mar 93. (cd) <(8122 02832-2)> **DAZZLING DISPLAY**   Nov91
– Drag / Tuesday / When she comes around / A dazzling display / Halo / Dandy in disguise / Grace / As it should be / Bonnie and Clyde / 405 / Close your eyes / Light of hope. <(cd re-iss. Mar00 on 'Prima'+=; SID 012)> – Kool thing / Boy in the bubble / Conspiracy of the heart / Watching the river flow / Crazy feeling / The long goodbye.

—— next with an array of backing musos including JOHN WESLEY HARDING

Brake Out / Mute
Nov 94. (cd) (OUT 1162) <61652> **FLUORESCENT**   Mar94
– Follow me / Collision course / Carelessly / Carry a torch / Open the door / Order / Layer by layer / That's why I wear black / Wedding bells / The sun rises in the west / Look both ways / Never ending rain. (re-mast.May02 on 'Blue Rose'+=; BLUDP 285) <US on 'Innerstate', INNER 273> – Animation / Gospel No.1 / Counting the days / Closer / The subject was roses / Dead roses / Gospel No.2 / Our little house.

—— next with the group, COME

Brake Out / Zero Hour
Jul 96. (cd) (OUT 1242) <ZEROCD 1160> **MELTING IN THE DARK**
– Why / Sheeley's blues / What we call love / Drizzle / Angels / Epilogue / Silence is our only friend / Stare it down / Smooth / For all I care / The way you punish me / Down / Melting in the dark.

Zero Hour / Zero Hour
Sep 97. (cd) <(ZEROCD 2160)> **SWEETNESS AND LIGHT**
– Silver lining / Black magic / Sweetness and light / This strange effect / This deadly game / How's my little girl / Ghosts / Blood from a stone / In love with everyone / Great divide / That's the way love is / If my life was an open book.

—— again with CHRIS CACAVAS – keyboards + CHRIS BROKAW – guitar + **LINDA PITMAN** – drums / JOHN CONVERTINO + HOWE GELB

Mar 99. (cd) <(ZEROCD 3160)> **MY MIDNIGHT**
– Nothing but the shell / My favourite game / Cats & dogs / In your prime / Mandy breakdown / Lay of the land / Out of this world / My midnight / The mask of shame / We've been hanging on / 500 girl mornings. (w/ bonus cd on 'Blue Rose'+=; BLUCD 0082)

Glitterhouse / not iss.
Oct 99. (cd) **PICK OF THE LITTER**   German
– My family / Invisible / James river incident / Ladies and gentlemen / Smoke from a distant flame / Halfway to the afterlife / Don't be afraid / The air that I breathe / The impossible / Smoke from a distant flame #2 / Why does love got to be so sad.

Blue Rose / Innerstate
Jun 01. (d-cd/d-lp) (BLU DP/LP 237) <50063> **HERE COME THE MIRACLES**
– Here come the miracles / Shades of blue / Sustain / Blackout / Butterscotch / Southern California line / Morningside heights / Let's leave it like that / Crawling misanthropic blues / Drought / Death Valley rain / Strange new world / Sunset to the sea / Good and bad / Topanga Canyon freaks / Watch your step / Charity / Smash myself to bits / There will come a day.

Oct 01. (cd-ep) (BLUS 10268) **THERE WILL COME A DAY / live in Germany 2001:- DROUGHT / LET'S LEAVE IT LIKE THAT / DEATH VALLEY SUN / HALLOWEEN**

– his compilations, etc. –
Nov 94. (cd) Return To Sender; <(RTS 13)> **TAKE YOUR FLUNKY AND DANGLE** (unissued material rec.1987-1993)   Nov93
– Animation / Gospel #1 / How's my little girl / Counting the days / The subject was roses / Closer / Woodshed blues / Boxing song / AA / Gospel #2 / It only comes out at night. <(re-iss. Oct99 on 'Innerstate'; INNER 7002)> (lp-iss.Mar00 on 'Fruit Tree'; FT 805)

Aug 98. (cd) Return To Sender; (RTS 28) **THE SUITCASE SESSIONS**
– Why / Waiting like Mary / This cdeadly game / The difference between right and wrong / Make it up to you / The way you punish me / The actress / Venus / Draggin' the line / Tighten up / The blue drifter / John Coltrane stereo blues.

GUTTERBALL

STEVE WYNN – vocals, guitar / **BRYAN HARVEY** – guitar, vocals (ex-HOUSE OF FREAKS) / **STEPHEN McCARTHY** – guitar, vocals (ex-LONG RYDERS) / **JOHNNY HOTT** – drums, vocals (ex-HOUSE OF FREAKS) / **BOB RUPE** – bass, vocals (ex-SILOS)

Brake Out / Mute
Jan 94. (cd) (OUT 113-2) <61510> **GUTTERBALL**   Jun93
– Trial separation blues / Top of the hill / Lester Young / Motorcycle boy / One by one / When you make up your mind / Think it over / Falling from the sky / Please don't hold back / The preacher and the prostitute / Patent leather shoes / Blessing in disguise.

—— **ARMISTEAD WELLFORD** – bass, vocals; repl. RUPE

Brake Out / Brake Out
Apr 95. (cd/lp) <(OUT 119-2/-1)> **WEASEL**
– Transparency / Your best friend / Black and gold / Is there something I should know? / Hesitation / The firefly / Sugar fix / Maria / One-eyed dog / Tarzana, pt.2 / Angelene / California / Everything / Over 40 / Mickey's big mouth.

– compilations, etc. –
Aug 95. (cd) Return To Sender; <(RTS 17)> **TURNYOR HEDINKOV**

DR. FRANK (see under ⇒ MR. T EXPERIENCE)

DRINKING ELECTRICITY

Formed: Edinburgh, Scotland . . . 1980 by boy-girl pairing of ANNE-MARIE ROME and DAVID ROME, plus bassman PAUL EDGLEY. Having signed the brilliant FLOWERS and BOOTS FOR DANCING to his new 'Pop: Aural' stable, former boss of 'Fast Product' records, budding entrepreneur BOB LAST, took on this off-kilter trio. From the onset, it looked a bit dicey to say the least. With the similarly-minded SILICON TEENS fitting in quite nicely with 'Mute' and the cover-loving indie faction (there weren't that many!), the weirdly-named DRINKING ELECTRICITY generated nothing but diluted criticism. Three singles were unleashed in 1980, the first two were covers of Johnny Kidd's 'SHAKING ALL OVER' and the Flamin' Groovies 'SHAKE SOME ACTION', the third their own (I think!) 'CRUISING MISSILES'. The following year, the testing trio tried again, this time with 'Survival' records, although only two singles and an album, 'OVERLOAD' (1982), managed to see light of day.

Album rating: OVERLOAD (*4)

ANNE-MARIE ROME – vocals / **DAVID ROME** – guitar, vocals / **PAUL EDGLEY** – bass

Pop: Aural / not iss.
May 80. (7") (POP 004) **SHAKING ALL OVER. / CHINA**
Jul 80. (7") (POP 005) **SHAKE SOME ACTION. / (cheap version)**
Nov 80. (7") (POP 008) **CRUISING MISSILES. / SHAKING ALL OVER (dub)**

Survival / not iss.
Jul 81. (7") (SUR 001) **SUBLIMINAL. / RANDOM PARTICLES**
Feb 82. (lp) (SURLP 001) **OVERLOAD**
– Breakout / Discord dance / Good times / Colour coding / Fall / Breakout II / Count down / News peak / Twilight zone / Superstition / The promise.

Mar 82. (7") (SUR 005) **GOOD TIMES. / COLOUR CODING**
(12") (SUR12-1) – ('A'dance mix) / ('A'side) / Superstition.

May 82. (12") (SUR 122) **SUBLIMINAL (radical mix). / BREAKOUT (long version)**

—— split up later in 1982

DUET EMMO (see under ⇒ WIRE; 70's section)

Stephen DUFFY

Born: 1961, Birmingham, England. A founding member of DURAN DURAN, DUFFY left after six months i.e. before the hits and the attendant cash began rolling in. He was at least partly compensated (after a brief spell with The HAWKS) by solo success in the mid-80's, his club hit from two years previous, 'KISS ME', remixed and re-issued under the moniker of STEPHEN 'TIN TIN'

DUFFY. It duly made the UK Top 5, while the attendant album, 'THE UPS AND DOWNS' made the Top 40. Subsequent legal problems over the 'TIN TIN' part of his name led to DUFFY going back to the drawing board and after a mid-80's period with DR CALCULUS (with ex-PIGBAG trombonist ROGER FREEMAN) he resurfaced in 1987 with a new outfit, The LILAC TIME. Featuring DUFFY, his brother NICK, MICHAEL GIRI and MICKY HARRIS, the group named themselves after a line in a NICK DRAKE song and traded in a suitably pastoral, acoustic 60's pop sound first aired on the independently released, eponymous debut. 'Phonogram' were impressed enough to sign the band DUFFY amassing further critical plaudits but similarly poor sales with follow-up set, 'PARADISE CIRCUS' (1989). Despite the production clout of John Leckie, 1990's 'AND LOVE FOR ALL' again failed to kickstart the band's career and resulted in a move to 'Creation'. Lost amid the baggy debris and shoegazing feedback, 'ASTRONAUTS' (1991) was another non-starter; it also marked the end of the band's patience and in 1992 The LILAC TIME officially split. DUFFY kept a fairly profile, only a guest spot for SAINT ETIENNE indicating that he still had a finger in the music business pie. Come the mid-90's, the veteran popster had formed the band DUFFY along with US indie-strummers, VELVET CRUSH, signing to 'RCA'-offshoot, 'Indolent', and releasing an eponymous, MITCH EASTER-produced debut. A soothing tonic for Brit-pop overload, the record was generally regarded by longtime DUFFY observers as one of his finest efforts to date, combining as it did the man's charming way with a lyric and the subtle guitar interplay of the VELVET boys. Following another three year fallow period, DUFFY surprisingly re-emerged on the contemporary folk label, 'Cooking Vinyl', with 'I LOVE MY FRIENDS' (1998). Seven years of solo work was again temporarily abandoned as STEPHEN teamed up with his brother NICK again to re-form LILAC TIME. Remaining on 'Cooking Vinyl', the group took on a twee/SIMON & GARFUNKEL persona on worthy comeback set, 'LOOKING FOR A DAY IN THE NIGHT' (1999). 2001's 'LILAC6' was no slouch either, delivering another fling towards bright, summery folk-rock music. DUFFY came full circle in 2002 via a collaboration (The DEVILS) with old DURAN DURAN sparring partner, NICK RHODES. An album's worth of songs 'DARK CIRCLES', showed varying styles between Krautrock electropop to cutesy indie-pop.

Album rating: THE UPS AND DOWNS (*5) / BECAUSE WE LOVE YOU (*5) / Dr Calculus: DESIGNER BEATNIK (*5) / Lilac Time: THE LILAC TIME (*6) / PARADISE CIRCUS (*7) / AND LOVE FOR ALL (*6) / ASTRONAUTS (*7) / Stephen Duffy: MUSIC IN COLOURS (*6) / DUFFY (*6) / I LOVE MY FRIENDS (*5) / THE CALLED HIM TIN TIN compilation (*6) / Lilac Time: LOOKING FOR A DAY IN THE NIGHT (*6) / LILAC6 (*6) / Devils: DARK CIRCLES (*6)

HAWKS

STEVIE DUFFY – vocals / DAVE KUSWORTH – guitar / SIMON COLLEY – bass / PAUL ADAMS – guitar / DAVID TWIST – drums

Five Believers / not iss.

Jan 81. (7") *(FB 001)* **WORDS OF HOPE. / SENSE OF ENDING**

TIN TIN

STEPHEN 'TIN TIN' DUFFY – vocals, electronics

W.E.A. / W.E.A.

Oct 82. (7") *(TIN 1)* **KISS ME. / LOVE'S DUET**
(12") *(TIN 1T)* – ('A'dub) / ('B'dub).
Jun 83. (7") *(X 9763)* **HOLD IT. / BLOWING KISSES** — 55
(ext-d12"+=) *(X 9763T)* – ('A'instrumental) / Kiss me (US remix) / Love's duet / Kiss me (instrumental).
Mar 84. (12"m) *(X 9823T) <29790>* **KISS ME (US remix). / KISS ME (instrumental) / LOVE'S DUET** — Nov83

STEPHEN 'TIN TIN' DUFFY

10-Virgin / not iss.

Oct 84. (7") *(TEN 28)* **SHE MAKES ME QUIVER. / PUSH IT**
(12"+=) *(TEN 28-12)* – ('A'-M+M version).
Feb 85. (7"/7"pic-d/12") *(TIN/+P 2/TIN 2-12)* **KISS ME (1985). / IN THIS TWILIGHT** — 4
(d7"+=/d12"+=) *(TING 2/+12)* – Kiss me (1983) / Holes in my shoes.
Apr 85. (lp/c/cd) *(DIX/CDIX/DIXCD 5)* **THE UPS AND DOWNS** — 35
– Kiss me / She makes me quiver / A masterpiece / The darkest blues / But is it art? / Wednesday Jones / Icing on the cake / Be there / Believe in me / The world at large alone. *(re-iss. Jun88 lp/c; XID/CXID 5)*
May 85. (7") *(TIN 3)* **ICING ON THE CAKE. / BROKEN HOME** — 14
(d7"+=) *(TING 3)* – Hold it / She makes me quiver.
(d12"++=) *(TING 3-12)* – ('A'extended).
Aug 85. (7") *(TIN 4)* **UN KISS THAT KISS. / DONE FOR**
(12"+=) *(TIN 4-12)* – ('A'remix).
(d7"+=) *(TINd 4)* – Love's duet / Holes in my shoes (carry on version).

STEPHEN DUFFY

Feb 86. (7") *(TEN 91)* **I LOVE YOU. / LOVE IS DRIVING ME INSANE**
(w-drawn;12"+=) *(TEN 91-12)* – ('A'version).
— now with SANDII – vocals (ex-SANDII & THE SUNSETZ)
Apr 86. (7"; STEPHEN SANDII) *(TEN 105)* **SOMETHING SPECIAL. / THE DISENCHANTED**
(12"+=) *(TENT 105)* – Cocksure.
May 86. (lp/c/cd) *(XID/CXID/XIDCD 12)* **BECAUSE WE LOVE YOU**
– Something special / A lot of ink / Sunday supplement / When you go to bed / Why shouldn't I / Unkiss that kiss / I love you / Love station / We'll never argue / Julie Christie.

Aug 86. (7"ep)(10"ep/12"ep) *(TENEP 5)(TEN 5 10/12)* **I LOVE YOU / WEDNESDAY JONES (DIXIE). / ICING ON THE CAKE / KISS ME '82**

– compilations, etc. –

May 89. (7") *Old Gold; (OG 4121)* **KISS ME. / ICING ON THE CAKE**
Dec 98. (cd) *Virgin-VIP; (CDVIP 223)* **THEY CALLED HIM TIN TIN**

DR CALCULUS

DUFFY / + ROGER FREEMAN – trombone (ex-PIGBAG)

Apr 85. (7") *(TEN 32)* **PROGRAMME 7. / KILLED BY POETRY**
(12"+=) *(TEN 32-12)* – ('A'-mixed breve).
Jul 86. (7"/12") *(TEN 131/+12)* **PERFUME FROM SPAIN. / STRAIGHT TO STEREO**
Aug 86. (lp/c) *(XID/CXID 14)* **DESIGNER BEATNIK**
– Blasted with ecstasy / Programme 7 / Moments of being – interlude / Killed by poetry / Moments of being – reprisal / Man / Dream machine / Candyfloss pink / Just another honey / Designer beatnik / Perfume from Spain. *(cd-iss. Nov86; DIXCD 45)*

LILAC TIME

STEPHEN DUFFY – vocals, instruments / SAGAT GUIREY – guitar / MICKY HARRIS – bass / MICHAEL GIRI – drums, percussion / NICK DUFFY – bouzouki

Swordfish / not iss.

Feb 88. (7") *(LILAC 1)* **RETURN TO YESTERDAY. / TRUMPETS FROM MONTPARNASSE**
(12"+=) *(12LILAC 1)* – Railway bazar / Reunion ball.

Fontana / Mercury

May 88. (7") *(LILAC 2)* **RETURN TO YESTERDAY. / GONE FOR A BURTON**
(12"+=)(cd-s+=) *(LILAC 2-12)(LILCD 2)* – Rooftrees / Reunion ball.
Jun 88. (lp/c)(cd) *(SF LP/MC 006)(834 835-2) <836714-1/-4/-2>* **THE LILAC TIME**
– Black velvet / Rockland / Return to yesterday / Love becomes a savage / You've got to love / Together / Too sooner late than better / The road to happiness / Trumpets from Montparnasse. *(was to have been released on 'Swordfish' lp/cd; SWF LP/CD 6)*
Aug 88. (7") *(LILAC 3)* **YOU'VE GOT TO LOVE. / RAILWAY BAZAAR**
(12"+=) *(LILAC 3-12)(LILCD 3)* – Trumpets from Montparnasse.
Nov 88. (7") *(LILAC 4)* **BLACK VELVET. / BLACK DAWN**
(12"+=) *(LILAC 4-12)* – Tiger tea.
(cd-s+=) *(LILCD 4)* – Street corner.
Jul 89. (7"/c-s) *(LIL AC/MC 5)* **AMERICAN EYES. / WORLD IN HER ARMS**
(12"+=) *(LILAC 5-12)* – Crossing the line.
(cd-s++=) *(LILCD 5)* – Shepherd's plaid.
Sep 89. (7") *(LILAC 6)* **THE DAYS OF THE WEEK. / THE QUEEN OF THE HEARTLESS**
(12"+=)(cd-s+=) *(LILAC 6-12)(LILCD 6)* – Spin a cavalu.
Oct 89. (lp/c/cd) *(838 641-1/-4/-2)* **PARADISE CIRCUS**
– American eyes / The lost girl in the midnight sun / If the stars shine tonight / The beauty in your body / The days of the week / She still loves you / Paradise circus / The girl who waves at traffic / The last to know / Father mother wife and child / The rollercoaster song / Work for the weekend / Twilight beer hall.
Nov 89. (7") *(LIL AC/MC 7)* **THE GIRL WHO WAVES AT TRAINS. / IF THE STARS SHINE TONIGHT (acoustic)**
(12"+=) *(LILAC 7-12)* – Ounce of nails.
(cd-s++=) *(LILCD 7)* – American eyes (acoustic).
Apr 90. (7") *(LILAC 8)* **ALL FOR LOVE & LOVE FOR ALL. / BED OF ROSES**
(12"+=)(cd-s+=) *(LILAC 8-12)(LILCD 8)* – Rubovia / Night mail dirty armour.
May 90. (7"/c-s; w-drawn) *(LIL AC/MC 9)* **THE LAUNDRY. / ONLY PASSING THROUGH**
(12"+=) *(LILAC 9-12)* – Hurricane rice.
(cd-s++=) *(LILCD 9)* – Oeil biques a bacs.
Jul 90. (7") *(LILAC 10)* **IT'LL END IN TEARS. / JUKE WRITTEN ON THE FENCE**
(12"+=)(cd-s+=) *(LILAC 10-12)(LILCD 10)* – Cover.
Sep 90. (cd/c/lp) *(846 190-2/-4/-1)* **& LOVE FOR ALL**
– Fields / All for love & love for all / Let our land be the one / I went to the dance / Wait and see / Honest to God / The laundry / Paper boat / Skabackililio / It'll end in tears (I won't cry) / Trinity / And on we go. *(cd/c +free m-lp+=)* **RETURN 1 (GREATEST HITS)** – Black velvet / Return to yesterday / The beauty in your body / Together / The days of the week / American eyes / If the stars shine tonight / The girl who waves at trains.

Caff / not iss.

Sep 90. (7") *(CAFF 12)* **MADRESFIELD. / BIRD ON THE WIRE**

Creation / not iss.

May 91. (7") *(CRE 104)* **DREAMING. / THE DARKNESS OF HER EYES**
(12"+=) *(CRE 104T)* – ('A'version).
(cd-s++=) *(CRE 104CD)* – The rain falls deepest on the shortest haircut.
Aug 91. (cd/c/lp) *(CRE CD/MC/LP 098)* **ASTRONAUTS**
– In Iverna gardens / Hats off here comes the girl / Fortunes / A taste for honey / Grey skies and work things / Finistere / Dreaming / The whisper of your mind / The darkness of her eyes / Sunshine's daughter / North Kensington / Madresfield.

— split after above's release but re-formed briefly early '92

DUFFY

— with session people incl. NIGEL KENNEDY (!)

Parlophone / Parlophone

Apr 93. (c-s/7"; STEPHEN DUFFY) *(TC+/R 6339)* **NATALIE. / MAN WITHOUT A STAR**
(cd-s+=) *(CDR 6339)* – An angel gets his wings / C'est la vie, c'est la guerre.

May 93. (cd/c/lp; STEPHEN DUFFY) (CD/TC+/PCS 7361) <1423-2>
MUSIC IN COLOURS
– It sparkles / (transitoire) / Natalie / (transitoire II) / She wants to share her magic / (transitoire III) / Music in colours / Galaxy / (transitoire IV) / Totem / (transitoire V) / Holte and hotel / (transitoire VI) / Charlotte's conversation / (transitoire VII) / A fall from the sky. *(cd re-iss. Jun98 on 'E.M.I.'; 789420-2)*

—— recruited members of VELVET CRUSH:- **PAUL CHASTAIN, JEFFREY BORCHARDT + RIC MENCK**

	Indolent	Indolent

Jun 95. (7") (DUFF 001) **LONDON GIRLS. / YOU, ME & GOD / THE WAITRESS' STORY**
(cd-s+=) (DUFF 001CD) – The girl of the year.

Jul 95. (7"/c-s) (DUFF 002/+MC) **SUGAR HIGH. / TEMPUS FUGIT**
(cd-s+=) (DUFF 002CD) – The sugar on the pill / A vision of bliss.

Aug 95. (cd/c/lp; as DUFFY) (DUFF CD/MC/LP 003) <21113-2>
DUFFY
– London girls / Sugar high / She freak / Needle mythology / A child is waiting / The kids on every corner / Ghetto child / Starfit / Mr. Twentieth century man / Rachel / Smitten.

Jan 96. (7"/c-s) (DUFF 004/+MC) **NEEDLE MYTHOLOGY. / TWENTY THREE**
(cd-s+=) (DUFF 004CD) – Sugar high (slow version) / The world records her every thought.

May 96. (7") <shine-us 11> **STARFIT. / TEMPUS FUGIT**
(above issued on 'Summershine')

—— in Aug'96, STEPHEN, ALEX (of BLUR), JUSTIN (of ELASTICA) and CHARLIE BLOOR (aka ME ME ME) hit the charts with 'HANGING AROUND'.

Aug 97. (cd-s) (DUFF 006CD1) **17 / MAO BADGE / COMEDOWN / HEY KAT**
(cd-s) (DUFF 006CD2) – ('A'side) / House of flowers / Barbarellas / Hanging around.
(cd-s) (DUFF 006CD3) – ('A'side) / Holding hands with Grace / In the evening of her day / Darling who can't wait to taste you.

—— now without VELVET CRUSH who had their own album to do

	Cooking Vinyl	Cooking Vinyl

Apr 98. (cd-ep) (FRYCD 068) **17 / MAO BRIDGE / IN THE EVENING OF HER DAY / BARBARELLAS**

Apr 98. (cd) (<COOKCD 144>) **I LOVE MY FRIENDS**
– Tune in / Eucharist / 17 / You are / Lovers beware / The deal / She belongs to all / Autopsy / What if I fell in love with you? / Something good / Twenty three / The postcard / One day one of these fucks will change your life.

Jul 98. (cd-ep) (FRYCD 073) **YOU ARE / HOLDING HANDS WITH GRACE / COMEDOWN**

LILAC TIME

—— re-formed with **STEPHEN + NICK**

	Cooking Vinyl	SpinArt

Apr 99. (cd) (COOKCD 176) <77> **LOOKING FOR A DAY IN THE NIGHT** — Sep99
– Salvation song / The nursery walls / A dream that we all share / A day in the night / I won't die for you / Broken cloud / The family coach / Morning sun / All over again / Back in the car park / Mayfly too / Sleepy / The spirit moves. <US+=> – Reunion ball / Hard for her / Come down / Holding hands with grace / Ratoon.

	Cooking Vinyl	Cooking Vinyl

Oct 01. (cd-s) (FRYCD 110) **THIS MORNING /**
Oct 01. (cd) (COOKCD 220) <620> **LILAC6**
– Dance out of the shadows / This morning / Come home everyone / My forest brown / I want to be your man / Jupe longue / Jeans + summer / Wasted / Entourage / Foglights / The last man on the Moon / Junes buffalo.

– compilations, etc. –

Jul 01. (d-cd) *Mercury; (586151-2)* **COMPENDIUM - THE FONTANA TRINITY**

DEVILS

STEPHEN DUFFY + NICK RHODES (ex-DURAN DURAN)

	Tape Modern	import

Jul 02. (cd) (TPCD 001) <232730> **DARK CIRCLES** — Oct02
– Memory palaces / Big store / Dark circles / Signals in smoke / Come alive / Hawks do not share / Newhaven – Dieppe / World exclusive / Aztec moon / Lost decade / Barbarellas / The tinsel ritual.

DUKES OF STRATOSPHEAR
(see under ⇒ XTC; 70's section)

DURUTTI COLUMN

Formed: Manchester, England ... early 1978 by VINI REILLY, CHRIS JOYCE and DAVE ROWBOTHAM. That year, they signed to TONY WILSON's indie label, 'Factory', although they dramatically split in mid-'79 leaving skinny VINI to pick up the pieces. Taking their name from the 1930's art-terrorists, Situationiste Internationale, and given free time by label boss, WILSON, under the wing of producer MARTIN HANNETT, the guitarist finally came up with DURUTTI's debut 'THE RETURN OF ...' (1980). This was a brilliant introduction to his minimalist yet picturesque guitar improvisations, although its gimmick sandpaper sleeve was not exactly the toast of the record retailers who had to protect the rest of their stock from its glassy debris. He subsequently supported on tour fellow Mancunian, JOHN COOPER CLARKE, PAULINE MURRAY and even JOHN MARTYN,

while recording the follow-up, 'L.C.' (1981), another masterpiece that fused light jazz into barren but dreamy landscapes. However, not for the first time, ill-health was to dog VINI, and it took a few years to record 'ANOTHER SETTING' (1983). All the above albums featured eccentric percussionist BRUCE MITCHELL, he of former parody-rock outfit, ALBERTOS Y LOST TRIOS PARANOIAS, the man becoming a stalwart on all VINI/DURUTTI's further work. In 1986, VINI took a trip to California, where he invited punkette, DEBI DIAMOND, to sing on a version of JEFFERSON AIRPLANE's 'White Rabbit'. After the release of the 1987 album, 'GUITAR AND OTHER MACHINES', REILLY was invited by old fellow NOSEBLEEDS chum, MORRISSEY, to play guitar pieces on his 1988 solo debut, 'VIVA HATE'. In 1990, DURUTTI COLUMN returned in fine style with 'OBEY THE TIME', although this was the last for Factory, as the label went bankrupt in '92. Under the control of 'Polygram', the imprint was once again under way in 1994 as 'Factory Too', and a happier VINI unleashed another textured beauty, 'SEX AND DEATH'. REILLY resumed his intermittent recording schedule with low-key 'TIME WAS GIGANTIC ... WHEN WE WERE KIDS' (1998), a set featuring ELEY RUDGE on vocals. For 'REBELLION' (2001), the ageing guitar wunderkind crafting a markedly more accessible long player with an unprecedented ceding of leeway to the basic tenets of song structure. Thus one of the record's standouts is an inspired rendition of Irish folk standard (and Celtic fans' anthem), 'THE FIELDS OF ATHENRY', while a willingness to augment his work with contemporary elements served to showcase the man's still burning talent. • **Songwriters:** All composed by REILLY, except cover; I GET ALONG WITHOUT YOU VERY WELL (Hoagy Carmichael). • **Note:** On the 8th of November '91, original member, DAVE ROWBOTHAM, was axed to death.

Album rating: THE RETURN OF THE DURUTTI COLUMN (*9) / L.C. (*7) / ANOTHER SETTING (*6) / WITHOUT MERCY (*6) / DOMO ARIGATO (*7) / CIRCUSES AND BREAD (*5) / VALUABLE PASSAGES compilation (*8) / THE GUITAR AND OTHER MACHINES (*6) / VINI REILLY (*7) / OBEY THE TIME (*5) / DRY (*5) / SEX AND DEATH (*7) / FIDELITY (*5) / TIME WAS GIGANTIC ... WHEN WE WERE KIDS (*5) / REBELLION (*6)

VINI REILLY (b. Aug'53) – guitar (ex-NOSEBLEEDS, ex-V2) / **DAVE ROWBOTHAM** – guitar / **CHRIS JOYCE** – drums / **BRUCE MITCHELL** – percussion / also **TONY BOWERS** – bass / **PHIL RAINFORD** – vocals (left Jul78)

—— recorded for Various Artists EP – A FACTORY SAMPLER. Split mid'79, DAVE, CHRIS and TONY joined The MOTHMEN. **VINI REILLY** now brought in **MARTIN HANNETT** – switches, producer (ex-INVISIBLE GIRLS (JOHN COOPER CLARKE) with **PETER CROOKS** – bass / **TOBY** (b.PHILIP TOMANOV) – drums / **GAMMER** – melody

	Factory	not iss.

Feb 80. (lp) (FACT 14) **THE RETURN OF THE DURUTTI COLUMN**
– Sketch for Summer / Requiem for a father / Katherine / Conduct / Beginning / Jazz / Sketch for winter / Collette / In "D". (w/ free testcard flexi by MARTIN HANNETT) FIRST ASPECT OF THE SAME THING. / SECOND ASPECT OF THE SAME THING *(re-iss. Jul80 lp/c; FACT 14/+C) (cd-iss. DEc96 on 'Factory Too'; 828829-2)*

—— **VINI** on his own, featured **PHIL RAYNHAM** – vocals

Nov 80. (12") *Factory Benelux; (FACBN 2)* **LIPS THAT WOULD KISS (FORM PRAYERS TO BROKEN STONE). / MADELEINE** — Belgium
(re-iss. Mar81; FACBN 2-005) (re-iss. cd-ep Mar91 & Nov96; FBN 2CD)

Mar 81. (7"ltd) *Sordide Sentimentale; (SS 45-005)* **ENIGMA. / DANNY** — Italy

—— now just a duo when **VINI** – guitars, now on extra vocals & keyboards / added **BRUCE MITCHELL** – percussion (ex-ALBERTOS Y LOST TRIOS PARANOIAS)

Sep 81. (lp/c) (FACT 44/+C) **LC**
– Sketch for dawn 1 / Portrait for Frazier / Jacqueline / Messidor / Sketch for dawn 2 / Never known / The act committed / Detail for Paul / The missing boy / The sweet cheat gone. *(cd-iss. Dec96 on 'Factory Too'+=; 828827-2)* – For Mimi / Belgian friends / Self portrait / One Christmas for your thoughts / Danny / Enigma.

—— **VINI** now completely solo

1982. (7"ltd) *Factory Benelux; (FBN 100)* **FOR PATTI. / WEARINESS AND FEVER** — Belgium

Mar 82. (12"ep) *Factory Benelux; (FBN 10)* **DEUX TRIANGLES** — Belgium
– Favourite painting / Zinni / Piece for out of tune grand piano.

—— added guests **LINDSAY WILSON** – vocals / **MAUNAGH FLEMING** – cor anglais

Aug 82. (7") (FAC 64) **I GET ALONG WITHOUT YOU VERY WELL. / PRAYER**

—— **VINI** now augmented by **MERVYN FLETCHER** – saxophone / **TONY BOWERS** – bass / **CHRIS JOYCE** – drums / **TIM KELLETT** – trumpet (all ex-MOTHMEN)

Aug 83. (lp/c) (FACT 74/+C) **ANOTHER SETTING**
– Prayer / Bordeaux / The beggar / The response / For a western / Francesca / Smile in the crowd / Dream of a child / Spent time / You've heard it before / Second family. *(cd-iss. Sep98 on 'Factory Once'+=; 556041-2)* – (Portuguese versions).

—— **VINI** retained **MERVYN** and **TIM**. (TONY & CHRIS later joined SIMPLY RED with TIM). **BRUCE MITCHELL** rejoined (he had always been part of live set-up) / **MAUNAGH FLEMING** rejoined with new guests **CAROLINE LAVELLE** – cello / **RICHARD HENRY** – trombone / **BLAINE REININGER** – viola/violin (of TUXEDO MOON)

Dec 84. (lp/c) (FACT 84/+C) **WITHOUT MERCY**
– Without mercy / Goodbye / Room / Little mercy / Silence / EE / Hellow / All that love and maths can do / Sea wall. *(cd-iss. Sep98 on 'Factory Once'; 556039-2)*

—— now just basically **VINI** with **BRUCE** with old friends augmenting

Mar 85. (12"ep) (FAC 114) **SAY WHAT YOU MEAN, MEAN WHAT YOU SAY**
– Goodbye / The room / E.E. / A little mercy / Silence / Hello.

Aug 85. (video-cd) (FACD 144) **DOMO ARIGATO (live Japan)**
– Sketch for Summer / Mercy theme / Sketch for dawn / E.E. / Little mercy / Jacqueline / Dream of a child / Mercy dance / The room / Blind elevator girl / Tomorrow / Belgian friends / Missing boy / Self-portrait / (audience noise). *(cd-iss. Sep98 on 'Factory Once'+=; 556038-2)* – Our lady of the angels / White rabbit / Catos con guantos.

DURUTTI COLUMN (cont)

Mar 86. (7") *Factory Benelux; (FBN 51)* **TOMORROW. / TOMORROW (live)** — Belgium
(12"+=) *(FBN 51)* – All that love and maths can do.
Mar 86. (lp)(cd) *(FBN 36)(FACD 154)* **CIRCUSES AND BREAD**
– Pauline / Tomorrow / Dance 2 / For Hilary / Street fight / Royal infirmary / Black horses / Dance 1 / Blind elevator girl – Osaka. (cd+=) – (last 45). (cd-iss. Nov93 on 'Crepescule'; TWI 9882)

—— VINI with MITCHELL, KELLETT, JOHN METCALFE

Oct 86. (12") *Materiali Sonori; (MASO 70003)* **GREETINGS THREE** — Italy
– Florence sunset / All that love and maths can do / San Giovanni dawn / For friends in Italy.
Aug 87. (12"ep; w/ DEBI DIAMOND) *(FAC 184)* **THE CITY OF OUR LADY**
– Our lady of the angels / White rabbit* / Catos con guantes.
Dec 87. (cd-ep) *(FACD 194)* **OUR LADY OF THE ANGELS / CATOS CON GUANTAS / WHEN THE WORLD (Newson mix)**

—— VINI + BRUCE were joined by guests TIM KELLETT (of SIMPLY RED) (1 track.) / STANTON MIRANDA – vocals (solo artist – 2 tracks.) POL – vocals (3 tracks.) / STEPHEN STREET – bass (1 track.) JOHN METCALFE – viola (1 track.) / ROB GREY – mouth organ

Factory Venture

Nov 87. (lp/cd)(c/dat) *(FAC T/D 204)(FACT 204 C/D) <90887-1/-4/-2>* **THE GUITAR AND OTHER MACHINES**
– When the world / Arpeggiator / What is it to me (woman) / U.S.P. / Red shoes / Jongleur grey / Bordeaux sequence / Miss Haynes / Don't think you're funny / English tradition landscape / Pol in 'B'. (cd+=) – Dream topping / You won't feel out of place / 28 Oldham Street. (cd re-iss. Dec96 on 'Factory Too'+=; 828828-2)
– Otis / E.L.T. / Finding the sea / Bordeaux.
Dec 87. (7"flexi) *(FAC 214)* **THE GUITAR AND OTHER MARKETING DEVICES**
– Jongleur grey / Bordeaux sequence / English landscape tradition / U.S.P.

—— added ROBERT NEWTON plus DV8 PHYSICAL THEATRE

Apr 88. (cd-s-video) *(FACDV 194)* **WHEN THE WORLD (soundtrack) / WHEN THE WORLD (lp) / FINAL CUT / WHEN THE WORLD (video)**
Dec 88. (3"cd-ep) *(FACD 234)* **WOMAD LIVE (live)**
– Otis / English landscape tradition / Finding the sea / Bordeaux.
Mar 89. (lp/cd)(dat) *(FAC T/CD 244)(FACT 244D)* **VINI REILLY**
– Homage to Catalonia / Opera II / People's pleasure park / Pol in G / Love no more / Opera I / Finding the sea / Otis / They work every day / Requiem again / My country. (lp w/ free 7" with MORRISSEY) *(FAC 244+)* – I KNOW VERY WELL HOW I GOT MY NOTE WRONG (cd w/ free 3"cd-ep) *(FAC 244+)* – (above) / Red square / William B. (cd re-iss. Nov99 on 'Factory Too'; 828826-2)

—— Included sampled voices of OTIS REDDING, ANNIE LENNOX and TRACY CHAPMAN. VINI added PAUL MILLER

Dec 90. (cd/lp)(c/dat) *(FAC D/T 274)(FACT 274 C/D)* **OBEY THE TIME**
– Vino della easa Bianco / Fridays / Home / Art and freight / Spanish reggae / Neon / The warmest rain / Contra-indications / Vino della casa rosso. (cd re-iss. Sep98 on 'Factory Once'; 556040-2)
Feb 91. (12"ep/cd-ep) *(FAC/+D 284)* **THE TOGETHER MIX. / CONTRA INDICATIONS (version) / FRIDAYS (up-person mix)**
Jun 91. (cd)(lp) *Materiali Sonori; (CDMASO 90024)(33-065)* **DRY** — Italy
– Dry / Paradise passage road / Rope around my neck / Short / Boat people / Boat people / Our lady / Grade 2 duet / Octaves / Out of the blue / Otis / English language tradition / Finding the sea / Bordeaux / Beggar. (cd+=) – WOMAD LIVE (tracks). *(UK cd-iss. Mar00; same)*

—— VINI, BRUCE w / guests PETER HOOK – bass (of NEW ORDER) + MARTIN JACKSON – keyboards (ex/of-SWING OUT SISTER)

Factory Too Factory Too

Nov 94. (cd) *(FACD 201) <697-124 043-2>* **SEX AND DEATH**   Mar95
– Anthony / The rest of my life / For Colette / The next time / Beautiful lies / My irasable friend / Believe in me / Fermina / Where I should be / Fado / Madre mio / Blue period.

Crepescule not iss.

May 96. (cd) *(TWI 976-2)* **FIDELITY**   May01
– Fidelity / For Suzanne / Future perfect / Abstract of expressio / G and T / Remember me / Sanko / Grace / Guitar for Steve / Storm for Steve.

—— next with ELEY RUDGE – vocals

Factory Once not iss.

Sep 98. (cd) *(558330-2)* **TIME WAS GIGANTIC . . . WHEN WE WERE KIDS**
– Organ donor / Pigeon / I B yours / Twenty trees / Abuse / Drinking song / Sing to me / My last kiss / For Rachel / Highfield choir / Epilogue.

Artful not iss.

Jun 01. (cd) *(ARTFULCD 40)* **REBELLION**
– 4 Sophia / Longsight romance / Ceh cak af en yam / The fields of Athenry / Overload (part 1) / Falling / Voluntary arrangement / Mello (part 1) / Mello (part 2) / Protest song / Meschugana.

– compilations, etc. –

Jun 83. (lp) *V.U.; (VINI 1)* **LIVE AT THE VENUE (live VINI & BRUCE)**
– Sketch for summer / Conduct / Never known / Jacqueline / Party / etc.
Dec 85. (lp) *Fundacao Atlantica; (1652071)* **AMIGOS EM PORTUGAL / DEDICATIONS FOR JACQUELINE** — Portu
– Friends in Portugal / Small girl by a pool / Crumpled dress / Sara and Tristana / Nighttime Estoril / Lisbon / To end with / Wheels turning / Favourite descending intervals / Saudade / Games of rhythm / Lies of mercy.
Dec 86. (lp/cd)(d-c) *Factory; (FAC T/D 164)(FACT 164C) / Relativity; <88561 8123-1/-4/-2>* **VALUABLE PASSAGES**
– Sketch for summer / Conduct / Sketch for winter / Lips that would kiss / Belgian friends / Danny / Piece for out-of-tune piano / Never know / Jacqueline / Missing boy / Prayer / Spent time / Without mercy stanzas 2-8 & 12-15 / Room / Blind elevator girl / Tomorrow / LFO MOD.
Nov 87. (c) *R.O.I.R.; (A-152)* **THE DURUTTI COLUMN LIVE AT THE BOTTOM LINE, NEW YORK (live)**
– Prayer / Arpeggiator / Our lady of the angels / Pol in B / Miss Haymes / For mother / Requiem / Jaqueline / Elevator sequence / Missing boy / U.S.P. / Tomorrow. *(<re-iss. May93 & Feb95 cd/c; A-152 CD/C>) (<cd re-iss. Oct99 as 'A NIGHT IN NEW YORK' on 'R.O.I.R.'; RUSCD 8255>)*
Mar 88. (4xcd-box) *Factory; (FACD 224)* **THE DURUTTI COLUMN – THE FIRST FOUR ALBUMS**
Dec 89. (ltd-cd) *Spore; (CD 1)* **THE SPORADIC RECORDINGS**
Sep 94. (cd) *Materiali Sonori; (MASO 90037)* **RED SHOES**
Jul 02. (cd) *Kooky; (KOOKYDISC 018)* **RETURN OF THE SPORADIC RECORDINGS / THE SPORADIC RECORDINGS**

DUSTDEVILS

Formed: Leeds, England ... mid-80's by MICHAEL DUANE, along with Australian-born JAQI DULANY. One of Britain's most promising acts, DUSTDEVILS delivered a series of SONIC YOUTH-meets-THALIA ZEDEK-meets-CHRISSIE HYNDE-ish releases (including LP's 'RHENYARD'S GRIN' and 'GUTTERLIGHT') for UK independent imprint, 'Rouska'; a deal with 'Fundamental' was subsequently shelved. However, disillusioned with England the 'DEVILS took off to New York City (early '89), where they met future PAVEMENT bass man, MARK IBOLD. A one-off EP, 'IS BIG LEGGY' (for 'TeenBeat' records and produced by KRAMER), was superseded by a deal with 'Matador' and the 12", 'GEEK DRIP', in 1990; the band looked to have turned the corner. Their first post-trip, Wharton Tiers-produced set, 'STRUGGLING, ELECTRIC AND CHEMICAL' (1991), kicked off with a rendition of The Fall's 'HIP PRIEST', while the anthemic 'THROW THE FULL BOTTLE', progressed the band leaps and bounds. However, the shape of the duo/trio/band bordered on sheer chaos with its mish-mash of revolving-door musicians, including MARTIN KOB (LOUDSPEAKER), SASHA FRERE-JONES (Ui), GERARD COSLOY ('Matador' head) and DAVE REID (GLENN BRANCA sidekick). Worse was to come, when, after the split of JAQI and MICHAEL (c. 1993), the former took off, leaving the man to employ replacement singers, JACKIE NEMITZ (ex-STP) and then the late JON EASLEY (CROWN HEIGHTS); sessions came out as the weird 'EXTANT' EP. With the 'DEVILS clearly out of the way, JAQI teamed up with KEITH GREGORY (ex-WEDDING PRESENT) – who'd sessioned for the early DUSTDEVILS – to form the cross-Atlantic duo, CHA CHA COHEN.

Album rating: RHENYARD'S GRIN (*4) / GUTTERLIGHT (*4) / GEEK DRIP (*4) / STRUGGLIN' ELECTRIC AND CHEMICAL (*5)

JAQI DULANY – vocals, guitar / MICHAEL DUANE – guitar / guest KEITH GREGORY – bass (of WEDDING PRESENT)

Rouska not iss.

Jul 86. (12") *(COME 6T)* **SEEDS OF THE SPOIL**
Mar 87. (lp) *(PROPHANE 9)* **RHENYARD'S GRIN**
– Encient / Life garden / The lost divide / Hard rough force / Mouth full of stars / Dort of days / In it's own right / Pressed / Another hit / Real hate work.
1987. (7"flexi) *(PROFANE 008)* **MOTHER SHIPTON**
1987. (12"ep) *(PROFANE 036)* **THE DROPPING WELL**
Mar 88. (lp) *(CONCORDE 008)* **GUTTERLIGHT**

—— they relocated to New York City

—— added MARK IBOLD – bass / REED (b. SAM LOHMAN) – drums

not iss. Teenbeat

Sep 89. (7"ep) *<TEENBEAT 38>* **IS BIG LEGGY EP**
– Encient / King Woody / Seen heat.

not iss. Matador

Apr 90. (12"ep) *<OLE 003>* **GEEK DRIP**
– Stripper / Feeding fat city / Mack.

—— MARTIN KOB – drums (of LOUDSPEAKER) repl. REED who joined NIMROD / added p/t JAMES KAVOUSSI – guitar + SASHA FRERE-JONES, GERARD COSLOY served time

Mar 91. (cd/c/lp) *<OLE 014-2/-4/-1>* **STRUGGLIN' ELECTRIC AND CHEMICAL**
– Hip priest / The revenge of Cruiser Gurner / Feet head high / When gravity hits / Head of Kurtz / Love you like a rock / Neck surfing / Throw the bottlefull / Free born man / Slope / They don't sleep 8 hrs. a night. *<cd-iss. 1994; OLE 014CD>*

—— IBOLD joined PAVEMENT

Aug 96. (7"ep/cd-ep) *<OLE 065-7/-2>* **EXTANT EP**

Blood not iss.

Aug 96. (12"ep) *(BLOOD 4)* **BURN EP**

—— split after 'EXTANT'; JACQUI later surfaced with CHA CHA COHEN

DWARVES

Formed: Chicago, Illinois, USA ... 1985 out of The SUBURBAN NIGHTMARE (one album, 'A HARD DAY'S NIGHTMARE' for 'Midnight') by SIGH MOAN, SALT PETER, JULIUS SEIZURE, PETE VIETNAMACHEQUE and WHITE SLAMBEAU. Following in the filth encrusted wake of GG ALLIN, this grossly offensive hardcore punk outfit make local bad boys The JESUS LIZARD look like HANSON! Debuting in 1986 with 'HORROR STORIES', the pseudonymous jokers caused outrage wherever they deemed to inflict their music on the local populace, indulging freely in such time honoured rock'n'roll pastimes as self-mutilation, on-stage sex and hard drugs. After a second set, 'TOOLIN' FOR A WARM TEABAG' (1988), SALT PETER, SEIZURE (now named BLAG DAHLIA) and PETE (now as HEWHOCANNOTBENAMED) recruited drummer VADGE MOORE. The DWARVES career reaching a climax of sorts with their

DWARVES (cont)

outrageously titled 'Sub Pop' debut, 'BLOOD GUTS & PUSSY' (1990) – featuring an equally disgusting sleeve pic that again found them coming under severe flak from feminists. After a further two albums, 'THANK HEAVEN FOR LITTLE GIRLS' (1991) and 'SUGAR FIX' (1993), the grunge bastion finally cracked when the band falsely announced the death of HEWHOCANNOTBENAMED. Just when parents were breathing a sigh of relief, the dreaded DWARVES re-emerged in 1997 with a belated sixth album, 'THE DWARVES ARE YOUNG AND GOOD LOOKING' (on 'Epitaph'); if you believe that you'll believe anything! If you liked your punk lyrically shocking and thrashy, The DWARVES again pulled no punches on follow-up, 'COME CLEAN' (2000), er . . . a mini set featuring two soapy naked females and a "real" dwarve (sic!). • **Trivia:** In 1995, BLAG DAHLIA was the man (aka EARL LEE GRACE) behind a bluegrass meets indie rock set, 'BLACKGRASS'. • **Covered:** HURRICANE FIGHTER PILOT (Red Crayola) / THAT'S ROCK'N'ROLL (Shaun Cassidy) / I'M A MAN (Bo Diddley) / BIG BALLS (Ac/Dc) / SLUTS IN THE CITY (GG Allin).

Album rating: A HARD DAY'S NIGHTMARE mini; as the Suburban Nightmare (*4) / HORROR STORIES (*5) / TOOLIN' FOR A WARM TEABAG (*3) / BLOOD GUTS AND PUSSY (*7) / THANK HEAVEN FOR LITTLE GIRLS (*5) / SUGAR FIX (*5) / THE DWARVES ARE YOUNG AND GOOD LOOKING (*4) / COME CLEAN mini (*5) / Earl Lee Grace: BLACKGRASS (*5)

SUBURBAN NIGHTMARE

JULIUS SEIZURE / **HERR PETE** / **HAL LOW** / **FEISTER FAMINE** / **PETE REALGONACHECK**

not iss. Midnight

1985. (m-lp) <*MIRLP 109*> **A HARD DAY'S NIGHTMARE**
 – You need love / Mad (+ kind of sad) / Brand new Cadillac / Love makes me a monster / 6" / Every night / Suburban bonus.

DWARVES

SIGH MOAN – vocals, percussion / **SALT PETER** – bass, vocals / **JULIUS SEIZURE** – guitar, vocals / **PETE VIETNAMACHEQUE** – keyboards / **WHITE SLAMBEAU** – drums

not iss. Voxx

Jun 86. (lp) <*VOXX 200.037*> **HORROR STORIES**
 – In & out / Oozle / Don't love me / Monday blues / Mined expanders / I'm a living sickness / College town / Be a caveman / Get out of my life / Eat my dinner *[lp-only]* / Sometimes gay boys don't wear pink (aka Queen of the surf) / Stop and listen *[lp-only]* / Lick it *[re-lp-only]* / Love gestapo. (*UK cd-iss. Dec90 & Jul92 +=; VOXXCD 200.037*) – Underwater / Lick it (alt.take) / Nothing.

Ubik not iss.

Aug 88. (7") (*CRASH 001*) **LICK IT. / NOTHING**

not iss. Nasty Gash

Dec 88. (lp) <*NG-001*> **TOOLIN' FOR A WARM TEABAG**
 – Eat you to survive / It's your party (die if you want to) / Fukking life / Free cocaine / Dead brides in white / Let's get pregnant / I'm in a head.

not iss. own label

1989. (c-ep) <*demo*> **LUCIFER'S CRANK EP**
 – Free cocaine / She's dead / Dead brides in white / I wanna kill your boyfriend / Fuckhead / Eat you to survive / Fucking life / I'm in a head. <*7"ep-iss.1991 on 'Rough Trade-No.6'; KAR 13-7*> – Free cocaine / Dead brides / Get pregnant / Fukkin life / Eat you to survive / She's dead / I'm in a head / Nobody like me / Hurricane fighter pilot.

1989. (c-ep) <*demo*> **WE KILL COCK THROBBIN**
 – Free cocaine / Dead brides / Mother fukker / Fukhead.

— **SALT PETER** + **BLAG DAHLIA** (aka SEIZURE) + **HEWHOCANNOTBENAMED** (aka PETE VIETNAMACHEQUE) recruited **VADGE MOORE** – drums

— added **CRASH LANDON** (b. KONIK) – guitar

Sub Pop Sub Pop

Apr 90. (7",7"white) <*SP 50*> **SHE'S DEAD. / FUCKHEAD** Feb00

Jul 90. (lp,red-lp,pic-lp/c/cd) <*SP 67/+A/B*> **BLOOD, GUTS AND PUSSY**
 – Back seat of my car / Detention girl / Let's fuck / Drug store / Skin poppin' slut / Fuck you up and get high / Insect whore / Flesh fantrum / SFVD / What hit you / Gash wagon *[lp-only]*. (*cd/c+=*) – Astro boy / Motherfucker / Fuckhead / Bitch. (*lp re-iss. Aug00; same*)

Oct 90. (7"ep,7"purple-ep) <*SP 81*> **DRUG STORE / DETENTION GIRL. / ASTRO BOY / MOTHERFUCKER**

Jan 92. (7"m) <*SP 21/163*> **LUCKY TONIGHT. / SPEED DEMON / DAIRY QUEEN**

Feb 92. (lp/c/cd) <*SP 166/+C/CD*> **THANK HEAVEN FOR LITTLE GIRLS**
 – Satan / Johnny glue *[lp-only]* / Speed demon / Blood brothers revenge / Blag the ripper / Lucky tonight / Who's fucking who / Fuck 'em all / Anybody but me / Three seconds / Fuck around. (*c+=/cd+=*) – Dairy queen.

Jan 93. (5"orange,7"yellow) <*SP 183*> **UNDERWORLD. / LIES**
 (*cd-s+=*) <*SP 183CD*> – Down by the river.

Jun 93. (7") (*SP 84/254*) **ANYBODY OUT THERE. / WHO CARES** German
 (*cd-s+=*) <*SPCD 63/230*> – Underworld / Lies / Down by the river.

Jul 93. (lp/cd) <*SP/+CD 76/243*> **SUGAR FIX**
 – Anybody out there / Evil primeval / Reputation / Lies / Saturday night / New Orleans / Action man / Smack city / Cain novacaine / Underworld / Wish that I was dead. <*cd re-iss. Feb99 +=; SPCD 456*> – THANK HEAVEN FOR LITTLE GIRLS

not iss. Man's Ruin

May 95. (7"pic-d-ep) <*MR 005*> **GENTLEMEN PREFER BLONDES (BUT BLONDES DON'T LIKE CRIPPLES)**
 – Drugstore (live) / Dairy queen (live) / Goodnite Tacoma / Radio #2.

Feb 97. (7"m) <*REP 018*> **I WILL DENY YOU. / THE DWARVES ARE YOUNG AND GOOD LOOKING / ONE LIFE TO LIVE**
 (*UK-iss.Mar01; same*)
 (above issued on 'Reptilian')

Mar 97. (7") <*MR 051*> **WE MUST HAVE BLOOD. / SURFING THE INTERCOURSE BARN**

— **WHOLLY SMOKKES** (b. MIKE FOX) – guitar; repl. KONIK + PETE

— **GASH MONEY** – bass; repl. SALT

Epitaph Theologian

Nov 97. (cd/c/lp) (*6512-2/-4/-1*) <*TH 53*> **THE DWARVES ARE YOUNG AND GOOD LOOKING** Mar97
 – Unrepentant / We must have blood / I will deny / Demonica / Everybodies girl / Throw that world away / Hits / The ballad of Vadge Moore / One time only / Pimp / The crucifixion is now / You gotta burn. <*US cd re-pressed on 'Epitaph'; same as UK*>

— bassist at the time **STEVE BORGERDING** subsequently joined GRAND MAL (BILL WHITTEN formerly of ST*JOHNNY mid-late 90's outfit)

Epitaph Epitaph

Feb 00. (m-cd/m-lp) <(*6575-2/-1*)> **COME CLEAN**
 – How's it done / River city / Over you / Way out / Come where the favour is / Deadly eye / Better be women / I want you to die / Johnny on the spot / Accelerator / Act like you know / Production value. (*pic-lp Jul00 on 'Cold Front'; CF 046*)

– compilations, etc. –

on 'Sympathy For The Record Industry' unless mentioned otherwise

1991. (7"colrd) <(*SFTRI 132*)> **I WANNA KILL YOUR BOYFRIEND (by Seizure). / SIT ON MY FACE**
 (above recorded in 1987 and below April 1990)

1994. (7") <*SFTRI 280*> **THAT'S ROCK'N'ROLL. / I'M A MAN**

Feb 97. (lp/cd) *Recess*; <(*RECESS 32/+CD*)> **TOOLIN' FOR LUCIFER'S CRANK**

Feb 99. (m-cd) *Recess*; <(*RECESS 51*)> **FREE COCAINE** (early bites) Mar99

Mar 99. (cd) *Recess*; <(*RECESS 52*)> **LICK IT: THE PSYCHEDELIC YEARS** (earliest material)

BLAG DAHLIA

— **PENETRATION MOON** are **BLAG** as JUNIOR HIGH with **SPIDER HARLEY** – guitar / **PINKY SLIM** – guitar / **MUFF BRANDEYWINE** – bass / **BJORN LUZER** – drums

not iss. Sympathy..

1991. (7"; by PENETRATION MOON) <*SFTRI 131*> **FIFTH A DAY. / I'M TRASH**

— next with **VADGEAMORE** + **REX EVERYTHING** – bass (aka NICK OLIVERI of KYUSS) / **WHOLLY SMOKKES** (HEMI) – guitar

1994. (7") <*SFTRI 284*> **LET'S TAKE A RIDE. / LORD OF THE ROAD**

not iss. Atavistic

Oct 95. (m-cd) <*ALP 19*> **VENUS WITH ARMS**
 – Let's take a ride / The wicked / Haunt me / The crucifixion is now / Theme from the Vicelords.

not iss. Sympathy..

1995. (cd; as EARL LEE GRACE) <*SFTRI 317*> **BLACKGRASS**
 – Saturday night / Every girl in the world / Viodinah / Together / Riding on the road / Coyote ridge / Sharon needles / Long, long time / 7-11 / Kitchen girl / Big Vics / So good / Sunday morn.

not iss. Man's Ruin

Sep 96. (7") <*MR 006*> **HAUNT ME. / LET'S TAKE A RIDE**

Bob DYLAN

But DYLAN really hit his stride with 'THE TIMES THEY ARE A-CHANGIN' the following year, an album that represented his most pointed protest writing. On subsequent albums, DYLAN shied away from direct missives like 'WITH GOD ON OUR SIDE' and 'ONLY A PAWN IN THEIR GAME'. 'ANOTHER SIDE OF BOB DYLAN' (1964) was contrastingly personal in tone, 'I DON'T BELIEVE IN YOU' and 'IT AIN'T ME BABE' venting DYLAN's spleen on matters of the heart rather than the soapbox. The lyrics also began to assume an air of enigmatic suggestiveness, 'MY BACK PAGES' and 'CHIMES OF FREEDOM' boasting striking, lucid imagery which The BYRDS would later complement with their incandescent, chiming guitars and ringing harmonies. Influenced by the British R&B boom (especially The BEATLES), DYLAN stunned folk purists with the half electric/half acoustic 'BRINGING IT ALL BACK HOME' (1965). The newly plugged in DYLAN was a revelation and with the likes of the stream-of-consciousness 'SUBTERRANEAN HOMESICK BLUES', the album influenced in turn the bands DYLAN had taken his cue from. The acoustic tracks on the second side such as 'MR. TAMBOURINE MAN' and 'IT'S ALL OVER NOW BABY BLUE' rank among DYLAN's finest, the former giving The BYRDS their breakthrough hit. While the folk faithful dissed DYLAN at that summer's Newport Festival, he wowed the rock world with the masterful 'LIKE A ROLLING STONE' single and followed it up with the seminal 'HIGHWAY 61 REVISITED' (1965). A free flowing hybrid of blues, folk and R&B that used such esteemed musicians as AL KOOPER and PAUL BUTTERFIELD, rock music had never been graced with such complex, expansive lyrics. Backed by members of The HAWKS (who'd supported DYLAN on his recent tour and later become The BAND) and a posse of crack Nashville sessioneers, DYLAN recorded another rock milestone with 'BLONDE ON BLONDE' (1966). 'VISIONS OF JOHANNA' was DYLAN at his most lysergic, casting surreal lyrical spells with hypnotic ease. After a motorcycle accident that summer he

Bob DYLAN (cont)

sustained severe neck injuries and went into semi-retirement, looking after his family and holing up in Woodstock with The BAND.
Album rating: THE TIMES THEY ARE A-CHANGIN' (*7) / ANOTHER SIDE OF BOB DYLAN (*8) / BRINGING IT ALL BACK HOME (*9) / HIGHWAY 61 REVISITED (*10) / BLONDE ON BLONDE (*10) / GREATEST HITS compilation (*10)

Jun 64.	(lp; stereo/mono) *(S+/BPG 62251)* <8905> **THE TIMES THEY ARE A-CHANGIN'**		20	20 Mar64

– The times they are a-changin' / Ballad of Hollis Brown / With God on our side / One too many mornings / North country blues / Only a pawn in their game / Boots of Spanish leather / When the ship comes in / The lonesome death of Hattie Carroll / Restless farewell. *(re-dist.Apr65, hit No.4) (re-iss. Mar81 lp/c; CBS/40 32021) (cd-iss. Nov89; CD 32021)*

Nov 64.	(lp; stereo/mono) *(S+/BPG 62429)* <8993> **ANOTHER SIDE OF BOB DYLAN**		8	43 Sep64

– All I really want to do / Black crow blues / Spanish Harlem incident / Chimes of freedom / I shall be free No.10 / To Ramona / Motorpsycho nitemare / I don't believe you / Ballad in plain D / It ain't me babe. *(re-iss. Mar81 lp/c; CBS/40 32034) (cd-iss. Nov89; CD 32034)*

Mar 65.	(7") *(201751)* **THE TIMES THEY ARE A-CHANGIN'. / HONEY, JUST ALLOW ME ONE MORE CHANCE**		9	–

(re-iss. May82; 1751)

— with **BOBBY GREGG** – drums / **JOHN SEBASTIAN** – bass / **BRUCE LANGHORNE** – guitar

Apr 65.	(7") *(201753)* <43242> **SUBTERRANEAN HOMESICK BLUES. / SHE BELONGS TO ME**		9	39 Mar65
May 65.	(lp; stereo/mono) *(S+/BPG 62515)* <9128> **BRINGING IT ALL BACK HOME**		1	6 Apr65

– Subterranean homesick blues / She belongs to me / Maggie's farm / Love minus zero – No limit / Outlaw blues / On the road again / Bob Dylan's 115th dream / Mr. Tambourine man / Gates of Eden / It's alright, ma (I'm only bleeding) / It's all over now, baby blue. *(re-iss. Jul83 lp/c; CBS/40 62515) (cd re-iss. Jul89 as 'SUBTERRANEAN HOMESICK BLUES'; CD 32344)*

Jun 65.	(7") *(201781)* **MAGGIE'S FARM. / ON THE ROAD AGAIN**		22	–

— now with **AL KOOPER** – organ / **PAUL BUTTERFIELD** – guitar / **PAUL GRIFFIN** – keyboards / **CHARLIE McCOY** – guitar / **RUSS SAVAKUS** – bass

Aug 65.	(7") *(201811)* <43346> **LIKE A ROLLING STONE. / GATES OF EDEN**		4	2 Jul65

(re-iss. May82; 1811)

Sep 65.	(lp; stereo/mono) *(S+/BPG 62572)* <9189> **HIGHWAY 61 REVISITED**		4	3

– Like a rolling stone / Tombstone blues / It takes a lot to laugh, it takes a train to cry / From a Buick 6 / Ballad of a thin man / Queen Jane approximately / Highway 61 revisited / Just like Tom Thumb's blues / Desolation row. *(re-iss. Dec85 lp/c; CBS/40 62572) (cd-iss. Nov89; CD 62572)*

Oct 65.	(7") *(201824)* <43389> **POSITIVELY 4th STREET. / FROM A BUICK 6**		8	7 Sep65
Jan 66.	(7") *(201900)* <43477> **CAN YOU PLEASE CRAWL OUT YOUR WINDOW? / HIGHWAY 61 REVISITED**		17	58 Dec65
Apr 66.	(7") *(202053)* <43541> **ONE OF US MUST KNOW (SOONER OR LATER). / QUEEN JANE APPROXIMATELY**		33	Feb66

— Now augmented by members of The **BAND**:- **ROBBIE ROBERTSON** – guitar / **RICHARD MANUEL** – keyboards / **LEVON HELM** – drums / **RICK DANKO** – bass / **GARTH HUDSON** – keyboards plus also **KENNY BUTTREY** – drums

May 66.	(7") *(202307)* <43592> **RAINY DAY WOMEN NOS.12 & 35. / PLEDGING MY TIME**		7	2 Apr66
Jul 66.	(7") *(202258)* <43683> **I WANT YOU. / JUST LIKE TOM THUMB'S BLUES (live)**		16	20 Jun66
Aug 66.	(d-lp; stereo/mono) *(S+/66012)* <841> **BLONDE ON BLONDE**		3	9 Jul66

– Rainy day women Nos.12 & 35 / Pledging my time / Visions of Johanna / One of us must know (sooner or later) / Most likely you go your way (and I'll go mine) / Temporary like Achilles / Absolutely sweet Marie / 4th time around / Obviously 5 believers / I want you / Stuck inside of Mobile with the Memphis blues again / Leopard-skin pill-box hat / Just like a woman / Sad eyed lady of the lowlands. *(re-iss. May82 d-lp/d-c; CBS/40 22130) (d-cd-iss. Jul87; CD 66012) (d-cd re-iss. Jun89; CD 22130) (d-cd re-iss. Feb95; CK 64411)*

Sep 66.	(7") <43792> **JUST LIKE A WOMAN. / OBVIOUSLY 5 BELIEVERS**		–	33
Jan 67.	(lp; stereo/mono) *(S+/BPG 62847)* <9463> **BOB DYLAN'S GREATEST HITS** (compilation) <US diff.tracks>		6	10 Apr67

– Blowin' in the wind / It ain't me babe / The times they are a-changin' / Mr. Tambourine man / She belongs to me / It's all over now, baby blue / Subterranean homesick blues / One of us must know (sooner or later) / Like a rolling stone / Just like a woman / Rainy day women Nos. 12 & 35. *(re-iss. Mar88; 460907) (cd-iss. Nov89; 450882-2) (re-iss. Feb91 & Apr97 on 'Columbia'; 460907-2) (re-iss. cd Oct94 as 'BEST OF...';)*

May 67.	(7") *(202700)* <44069> **LEOPARD-SKIN PILL-BOX HAT. / MOST LIKELY YOU GO YOUR WAY (AND I'LL GO MINE)**			81

EASTERHOUSE

Formed: Manchester, England ... mid-80's by brothers ANDY (the lyricist) and IVOR PERRY, the initial line-up completed by PETER VANDEN, GARY ROSTOCK and MIKE MURRAY. Naming themselves after Glasgow's most infamous housing scheme, the band espoused a defiant left-wing philosophy against an atmospheric, finely textured alternative rock/pop backdrop. Hardly unique during the 80's, yet EASTERHOUSE were more convincing than most, winning over cynical critics and enjoying the patronage of MORRISSEY amongst others. Signed to 'Rough Trade', the band laid out their manifesto in impressive style with 1986's revered 'CONTENDERS' album. Despite the subsequent widespread acclaim, internal ructions led to IVOR departing to form his own outfit, The CRADLE. By the late 80's, ANDY had recruited a whole new cast of musicians – namely NEIL TAYLOR, LANCE SABIN, DAVID VERNER and co-producer STEVE LOVELL. The resultant follow-up set, 'WAITING FOR THE RED BIRD' (1989) strayed too far into chest-beating SIMPLE MINDS territory for many tastes yet the political commitment was as heartfelt as ever. The attendant single, 'COME OUT FIGHTING', had hit written all over it, quite why it wasn't remains a mystery. Moreover, in contrast to many of the far left doom-mongers, PERRY's vision was a generally positive one as outlined on the likes of 'HOPE AND GLORY'. The interest just wasn't there, however and EASTERHOUSE were soon confined to the more obscure annals of Manchester's musical history.

Album rating: CONTENDERS (*8) / WAITING FOR THE REDBIRD (*7)

ANDY PERRY – vocals / **IVOR PERRY** – guitar / **PETER VANDEN** – bass / **GARY ROSTOCK** – drums; repl. drum machine

		Easterhouse	not iss.
Mar 85.	(12"ep) *(EIREX 1)* **IN OUR OWN HANDS**		–

– Coming up for air / Endless march / Man alive / One more time.

— added **MIKE MURRAY** – rhythm guitar

		Rough Trade	Columbia
Jan 86.	(7") *(RT 164)* **WHISTLING IN THE DARK. / AIN'T THAT ALWAYS THE WAY**		–

(12"+=) *(RTT 164)* – Confrontation.

Mar 86.	(7") *(RT 174)* **INSPIRATION. / JOHNNY I HARDLY KNEW YOU**		–

(12"+=) *(RTT 174)* – Easter rising / Nineteen sixty nine.

Jun 86.	(lp/c) *(ROUGH/+C 94)* <CK 40469> **CONTENDERS**		

– Out on your own / Whistling in the dark / Nineteen sixty nine / Cargo of souls / Lenin in Zurich / Get back to Russia / To live like this / The boy can sing / Estates. *(lp w/ free 7")* **GET BACK TO RUSSIA** *(RDJ 94) (cd-iss. May87; ROUGHCD 94)* (+=) – Inspiration / Johnny I hardly knew you / Easter rising. *(cd re-iss. Jul01 on 'Cherry Red'+=; CDMRED 185)* – Ain't that always the way.

— they split after an argument; IVOR joined The CRADLE

— **ANDY** retained group name and completed line-up by bringing in **NEIL TAYLOR** – lead guitar / **DAVE VERNER** – drums / **STEVE LOVELL** – bass / **LANCE SABIN** – rhythm guitar

Feb 89.	(7") *(RT 204)* <68552> **COME OUT FIGHTING. / NEW WORLD IN THE MORNING**		82

(12"+=/3"cd-s+=) *(RTT/CDRT 204)* – (2 tracks).

Mar 89.	(lp/c/cd) *(ROUGH/+C/CD 124)* <CK/PCT 44467> **WAITING FOR THE REDBIRD**		

– Waiting for the redbird / You're gonna miss it (when it's gone) / Stay with me (death on the dole) / Come out fighting / America / Hope and glory / Say yes / This country / Sweatshop.

May 89.	(7") **YOU'RE GONNA MISS IT (WHEN IT'S GONE). /**		–

(12"+=/cd-s+=) –

— disbanded after above

EAST VILLAGE

Formed: London, England ... late 80's as EPISODE FOUR by brothers PAUL and MARTIN KELLY. A case of being in the wrong place at the wrong time, EAST VILLAGE were playing music inspired by groups such as The BYRDS and BIG STAR a few years before TEENAGE FANCLUB were music media darlings for doing the self same thing. After enlisting JOHNNY WOOD and SPENCER SMITH, the group recorded two singles and a self-financed album; however they struggled to find anybody willing to publish such unfashionable music. The album 'DROP OUT' was eventually released in 1993, unfortunately by this time the band had broken up. PAUL KELLY resurfaced in the late 90s with the group BIRDIE alongside ex-DOLLY

MIXTURE singer, DEBORAH WYKES. BIRDIE released their debut 'SOME DUSTY' in 1999. Both KELLY and WYKES had served stints in SAINT ETIENNE and the music of BIRDIE shared the same sweet pop sensibilities.

Album rating: DROPOUT (*5) / Birdie: SOME DUSTY (*6) / TRIPLE ECHO (*7)

MARTIN KELLY – vocals, guitar / **PAUL KELLY** – guitar

		Lenin And McCarthy	not iss.
1987.	(12"ep; as EPISODE FOUR) **STRIKE UP MATCHES**		-
	– Why / Doctor P / Strike up matches / Again and again.		
		Sub Aqua	not iss.
Jun 88.	(12"ep) (AQUA 2-12) **CUBANS IN THE BLUEFIELDS**		-
	– Cubans in the bluefields / Break your neck / Strawberry window / Kathleen.		
Oct 88.	(12"ep) (AQUA 4-12) **BACK BETWEEN PLACES**		-
	– Back between places / Her father's son / Precious diamond tears.		
		Caff	not iss.
1989.	(7"flexi) (CAFF 1) **FREEZE OUT**		-
		Heavenly	Summershine
Jan 91.	(7") (HVN 006) **CIRCLES. / HERE IT COMES**	-	-
Nov 91.	(7") <SHINE 014> **VIBRATO. /**	-	- Austra
1993.	(cd) <SHINELP 006> **HOTROD HOTEL**	-	- Austra
	– Her father's son / Vibrato / Cubans in the bluefields / Break your neck / Precious diamond tears / Kathleen / Meet the wife / Go and see him / Strawberry window / Here it comes. *(hidden track+=)* – Back between places.		
Nov 93.	(lp/cd) (HVNLP 003/+CD) <SHINELP 009> **DROPOUT**	-	1994
	– Silver train / Shipwrecked / Here it comes / Freeze out / Circles / When I wake tomorrow / Way back home / What kind of friend is this / Black autumn / Everybody knows.		
Nov 93.	(7") <SHINE 037> **SILVER TRAIN. / MOTORCYCLE THEME**	-	

BIRDIE

DEBSEY WYKES – vocals (ex-DOLLY MIXTURE) / **PAUL KELLY** – guitar / + various band members

		not iss.	Summershine
1997.	(7") <SHINEUS 18> **SPIRAL STAIRCASE. / PORT SUNLIGHT**	-	-
		In The Red	Kindercore
Aug 99.	(7") (ITRV 002) **FOLK SINGER. / PORT SUNLIGHT**		-
Aug 99.	(cd/lp) (ITR CD/LP 002) <KC 056CD> **SOME DUSTY**		Oct00
	– Laugh / Dusty morning / Let her go / One two five / Lazy day / Folk singer / Port sunlight / Blue dress / Linus / I can't let go. *(re-iss. Oct00 on 'Kindercore'+=; same as US)* – Thanks for the birthday card. *(re-iss. Oct00 on 'Elefant'; ER 1074CD)*		
Nov 99.	(7") (ITRV 004) **LET HER GO. / THANKS FOR THE BIRTHDAY CARD**		-
	(cd-s+=) (ITR 004) – Folk singer (CD-rom).		
Dec 00.	(7") (ITRV 009) **SUCH A SOUND. / THEME FROM TIRED**		-
	(cd-s) (ITR 009) – ('A'side) / Linus (version).		
Jul 01.	(7") (ITRV 011) **SIDEWALK. / SEND AND RECEIVE**		-
	(cd-s) (ITR 011) – ('A'side) / Natural star / Lift up the sun.		
Oct 01.	(cd/lp) (ITR CD/LP 005) **TRIPLE ECHO**		-
	– Original strand / Such a sound / Rosie's drug store / Sidewalk / Poster / Blue eyed son / Silver line / Twin / Monday / Hammond / Blue eyed son (reprise).		

EAT

Formed: Bath, Avon, England ... 1986 by ANGE DOLITTLE, brothers PAUL and MAX NOBEL, TIM SEWELL and PETE HOWARD. Relocating to the King's Cross area of North London, the band immersed themselves in the squat culture and warehouse party scene of the late 80's. Securing a deal with Polydor offshoot, 'Fiction', they released the 'AUTOGIFT' EP in early '89. This was closely followed by a debut album, 'SELL ME A GOD' (1989), the mutant grebo-funk/blues contained within confirming the band's position as spiritual southern cousins of Midlands wide boys POP WILL EAT ITSELF and The WONDER STUFF. DOLITTLE's offbeat, often half-spoken commentaries on life in the Big Smoke and other random subjects were powered along by blasting harmonicas, burbling bass and apparently whatever noise came to hand; not exactly easy listening but fun if you're in the mood. Despite positive reviews and the radio support of John Peel, however, inter-band instability led to the departure of the NOBEL brothers (both would go on to form UV RAY) and the end of EAT's first incarnation. DOLITTLE would subsequently re-form the band in 1991 with a line-up of SEWELL and HOWARD together with new members MAZ LAVILLA and JEM MOORSHEAD. A 1992 EP, 'GOLDEN EGG' (produced by TIM SMITH of The CARDIACS and CHRIS KIMSEY), was followed by a long awaited second album, 'EPICURE' (1993), a record which failed to significantly expand their fanbase despite critical praise. Inevitably, EAT splintered once more with DOLITTLE teaming up with ex-WONDER STUFF personnel to form WEKNOWWHEREYOULIVE in the mid-90's. • **Songwriters:** PAUL NOBLE until his departure, then group. Covered; SUMMER IN THE CITY (Lovin' Spoonful) / ON THE ROAD AGAIN (Canned Heat).

Album rating: SELL ME A GOD (*8) / EPICURE (*6)

ANGE DOLITTLE – vocals, (later added guitar) / **PAUL NOBLE** – guitar, percussion, vocals / **TIM SEWELL** – bass, synth, vocals / **PETE HOWARD** – drums, percussion / **MAX NOBLE** – guitar, percussion

		Fiction	not iss.
Jan 89.	(7"ep/12"ep/cd-ep) (WAN/+TX/CD 100) **THE AUTOGIFT EP**		-
	– Skin / Swampadelia / Red Moon.		
May 89.	(7"ep/12"ep/cd-ep) (CIF/+X/CD 1) **THE PLASTIC BAG EP**		-
	– Plastic bag / Baby boom / Mr. & Mrs. Smack / Little country.		
Aug 89.	(7") (CIF 2) **SUMMER IN THE CITY. / TWO NATIONS**		-
	(12"+=/cd-s+=) (CIF/+X/CD 2) – Gyrate (extended Jib mix).		
Sep 89.	(lp/c/cd) (838 944-1/-4/-2) **SELL ME A GOD**		-
	– Tombstone / Electric city / Fatman / Stories / Walking man / Skin / Red moon * / Insect head / Body bag / Things I need / Judgement train / Gyrate * / Summer in the city * / Mr. & Mrs. Smack. *(cd+= */c+= *)*		
Nov 89.	(7") (FICS 32) **TOMBSTONE. / SQUAT**		-
	(12"+=/cd-s+=) (FICS X/CD 32) – ('A'-Beyond the groove mix).		

—— MAX had already departed having formed WE ARE PLEBS

		Non-Fiction	not iss.
Sep 90.	(7") (YES 3) **PSYCHO COUCH. / ALIEN DETECTOR**		-
	(cd-s+=) (YESCD 3) – ('A'extended mixes).		
	(12") (YEST 3) – ('A'extended mixes).		

—— PETE HOWARD departed late 1990 and was repl. by **DANIEL NEWMAN**. PETE returned by mid-1991. PAUL formed UV RAY with brother and early EAT (then WE ARE PLEBS) member MAX NOBLE. (UV RAY other member PAUL O'NEILL – vocals, guitar)

—— Meanwhile mid'91 EAT re-formed and brought in **JEM MOORSHEAD** – guitar (ex-FLICK SPATULA) / **MAZ LaVILLA** – guitar

		Fiction	November
Jun 92.	(7"ep/12"ep/cd-ep) (FIC/+X/CD 38) **THE GOLDEN EGG EP**		-
	– Golden egg / Bellytown / Streets are full / Double bubble.		
	(12"ep+=) (FIXT 38) – Tombstone (live).		
Oct 92.	(7") (863754-7) **SHAME. / KNOCK ME DOWN**		-
	(12"+=/cd-s+=) (863754-0/-2) – On The road again / Out of line.		
May 93.	(7"ep/12"ep/cd-ep) (FICS/+X/CD 48) **BLEED ME WHITE. / HADDLYANNDAN / ICE POND**	73	-
	(cd-ep) (FICCD 48) – ('A'side) / How does it feel / Late gain.		
Jun 93.	(cd/c/lp) (519 103-2/4/-1) <NRD/NRC 1105> **EPICURE**		Feb94
	– Belly town / Shame / First time love song / Tranquilizer / Golden egg / Bottle blue / Fecund / Baby in flares / Fist / Bleed me white / Out people / Epicure.		

—— split when DOLITTLE joined WONDER STUFF splinter WEKNOWWHEREYOULIVE

ECHO & THE BUNNYMEN

Formed: Liverpool, England ... Autumn 1978 by IAN McCULLOCH, WILL SERGEANT and LES PATTINSON. McCULLOCH had once been in The CRUCIAL THREE alongside future stars, JULIAN COPE and PETE WYLIE, the former two starting up another low key act, A SHALLOW MADNESS, together writing 'READ IT IN BOOKS' (the b-side of E&TB's debut single, 'PICTURES ON MY WALL'). The BUNNYMEN, complete with drum machine ECHO, released the aforementioned 45 as a one-off for the local 'Zoo' label, before signing to 'WEA/Warners' subsidiary, 'Korova', late in '79. By the following year, they'd had a Top 20 album, 'CROCODILES', and were soon breaking into the singles chart with 'RESCUE'. Overtly melancholy and DOORS-influenced, their material contained a fresher up-tempo feel which combined powerful melodrama and McCULLOCH's ego-fuelled attitude. From 1981-84, their albums 'HEAVEN UP HERE', 'PORCUPINE' and 'OCEAN RAIN', solidified a Merseyside revival that even crossed successfully over the Atlantic. They split after their last gig on the 26th April '88, and it surprised everyone, not least the solo bound McCULLOCH (he had issued a single in '84, Kurt Weill's 'SEPTEMBER SONG'), when The BUNNYMEN decided to carry on without him. However, in June '89, PETE DE FREITAS was tragically killed in a motorcycle accident. In the early 90's, The BUNNYMEN (SERGEANT, PATTINSON, plus NOEL BURKE – vocals, JACK BROCKMAN – keyboards and DAMON REECE – drums) struggled without their moody frontman. A disappointing album, 'REVERBERATION' (1990), did little to excite the public, the group forming their own 'Euphoric' label after 'Korova/WEA' dropped them. McCULLOCH meanwhile, had been continuing his search for glory, releasing two albums, the Top 20 'CANDLELAND' (1989) and the Top 50, 'MYSTERIO' (1992), the last of which was poorly received. Late in '94, McCULLOCH and SERGEANT were back with a new rock-driven tour de force, ELECTRAFIXION, their sole album, 'BURNED' (1995), was well received by the music press, went Top 40 and enjoyed moderate sales. There was considerably more media interest over the reformation of the original ECHO & THE BUNNYMEN line-up in 1997. A strong comeback single, 'NOTHING LASTS FOREVER', and album, 'EVERGREEN', both made the UK Top 10, while the band proved they could still cut it live with a tour and a series of summer festival appearances. McCULLOCH and SERGEANT returned in 1999 with the eagerly awaited 'WHAT ARE YOU GOING TO DO WITH YOUR LIFE?', a short but very, very sweet album (its running time is around thirty eight minutes). The set was very similar to other ECHO releases, but less jaded and cynical than the previous 'EVERGREEN', with songs 'HISTORY CHIMES' and 'GET IN THE CAR' all displaying McCULLOCH's tenderness towards songwriting. Meanwhile SERGEANT, who had been dabbling in psychedelic electronica since the late seventies (anyone remember the soundtrack album 'THEMES FOR GRIND' from 1983) had been completing a musical manifesto all on his ownsome. Named GLIDE, SERGEANT issued both live albums 'SPACE AGE FREAK OUT' ('97) and 'PERFORMANCE' along with a lost classic from 1978 called 'WEIRD AS FISH', both in 2000. All albums sounded similar to the Krautrock movement or BRIAN ENO in his better experimental stages. Lashings of psychedelia and weirdness was born from somebody who used to be a post-punk rocker, but that didn't diminish the originality of the albums. ECHO AND THE BUNNYMEN returned in 2001 with another accomplished set, 'FLOWERS'. Although considerably mellower than previous ECHO works, the album acted as a Part 2 to the fantastic 'WHAT ARE YOU GOING TO DO ...?'. Mixing pop rock with classy melancholy, songs such as 'EVERYBODY KNOWS' and 'HIDE AND SEEK' had set the standards for future records by a band who were quite happy spending a third decade

ECHO & THE BUNNYMEN (cont)

together. • **Songwriters:** Mainly group compositions, except covers PEOPLE ARE STRANGE (Doors) / PAINT IT BLACK (Rolling Stones) / ALL YOU NEED IS LOVE + TICKET TO RIDE (Beatles) / FRICTION (Television) / RUN RUN RUN (Velvet Underground) / SHIP OF FOOLS (John Cale). McCULLOCH covered: RETURN TO SENDER (hit; Elvis Presley) / LOVER, LOVER, LOVER (Leonard Cohen). • **Trivia:** DAVE BALFE (of DALEK I LOVE YOU) played keyboards on their first JOHN PEEL session in August 1979.

Album rating: CROCODILES (*9) / HEAVEN UP HERE (*9) / PORCUPINE (*7) / OCEAN RAIN (*7) / SONGS TO LEARN AND SING compilation (*9) / ECHO & THE BUNNYMEN (*8) / BALLYHOO: THE BEST OF ECHO & THE BUNNYMEN compilation (*8) / EVERGREEN (*7) / WHAT ARE YOU GOING TO DO WITH YOUR LIFE? (*8) / FLOWERS (*6) / LIVE IN LIVERPOOL (*5) / Ian McCulloch: CANDLELAND (*6) / MYSTERIO (*5) / Electrafixion: BURNED (*6) / Will Sergeant: THEMES FOR GRIND (*3)

IAN McCULLOCH (b. 5 May'59) – vocals, guitar (ex-CRUCIAL THREE) **WILL SERGEANT** (b.12 Apr'58) – lead guitar / **LES PATTINSON** (b.18 Apr'58) – bass (& 'ECHO' a drum machine)

		Zoo	not iss.
Mar 79.	(7") (CAGE 004) **PICTURES ON MY WALL. / READ IT IN BOOKS** (re-iss. Mar91 on 'Document' 12"/cd-s; DC 3/+CD)		–

— **PETE DE FREITAS** (b. 2 Aug'61, Port Of Spain, Trinidad) – drums repl. 'ECHO'

		Korova	Sire
Apr 80.	(7") (KOW 1) **RESCUE. / SIMPLE STUFF** (12"+=) (KOW 1T) – Pride.	62	–
Jul 80.	(lp/c) (KODE/CODE 1) <6096> **CROCODILES** – Going up / Stars are stars / Pride / Monkeys / Crocodiles / Rescue / Villier's terrace / Pictures on my wall / All that jazz / Happy death men. (re-iss. Nov80 w/ free 7"; SAM 128) DO IT CLEAN. / READ IT IN BOOKS (re-iss. 1989 on 'WEA' lp/c/cd; same/same/2423162)	17	
Sep 80.	(7") (KOW 11) **THE PUPPET. / DO IT CLEAN**		
Apr 81.	(12"ep)(c-ep) (ECHOZ 1)(ECHO 1M) **SHINE SO HARD (live)** – Crocodiles / Zimbo / Over the wall / All that jazz.	37	–
May 81.	(lp/c) (KODE/CODE 3) <3569> **HEAVEN UP HERE** – Show of strength / With a hip / Over the wall / It was a pleasure / A promise / Heaven up here / The disease / All my colours / No dark things / Turquoise days / All I want. (cd-iss. Jul88 on 'WEA'; 2432173)	10	
Jul 81.	(7"/12") (KOW 15/+T) **A PROMISE. / BROKE MY NECK**	49	–
May 82.	(7") (KOW 24) **THE BACK OF LOVE. / THE SUBJECT** (12"+=) (KOW 24T) – Fuel.	19	–
Jan 83.	(7") (KOW 26) **THE CUTTER. / WAY OUT AND UP WE GO** (w/ free c-ep+=) (KOW 26C) – The cutter / Villier's terrace / Ashes to ashes (stars are stars) / Monkeys / Read it in books. (12"+=) (KOW 26T) – Zimbo (live).	8	–
Jan 83.	(lp/c) (KODE/CODE 6) <23770> **PORCUPINE** – The cutter / The back of love / My white devil / Clay / Porcupine / Heads will roll / Ripeness / Higher hell / Gods will be gods / In bluer skies. (free ltd.c-ep w/ above lp) – 'JOHN PEEL SESSIONS' (re-iss. Jul88 on 'WEA' lp/c/cd; same/same/K 400 272)	2	
Feb 83.	(7") **THE CUTTER. / GODS WILL BE GODS**	–	–
Jul 83.	(7") (KOW 28) **NEVER STOP. / HEADS WILL ROLL** (12"+=) (KOW 28T) – ('A'-Discotheque) / ('B'-Summer version) / The original cutter (A drop in the ocean).	15	–
Jan 84.	(7") (KOW 32) **THE KILLING MOON. / DO IT CLEAN** (12"+=) (KOW 32T) – ('A'-All night version).	9	–
Jan 84.	(m-lp) <23987> **ECHO AND THE BUNNYMEN** – Back of love / Never stop / Rescue / The cutter / Do it clean.	–	
Apr 84.	(lp/c)(cd) (KODE/CODE 8)(K 240388-2) <25084> **OCEAN RAIN** – Silver / Nocturnal me / Crystal days / The yo yo man / Thorn of crowns / The killing moon / Seven seas / My kingdom / Ocean rain.	4	87 Jun84
Apr 84.	(7") (KOW 34) **SILVER. / ANGELS AND DEVILS** (12"+=) (KOW 34T) – Silver (Tidal wave).	30	–
Jun 84.	(7") (KOW 35) **SEVEN SEAS. / ALL YOU NEED IS LOVE** (12"+=/d7"+=) (KOW 35 T/F) – The killing Moon / Stars are stars (acoustic) / Villier's terrace (acoustic).	16	–
Oct 85.	(7"/7"pic-d) (KOW 43/+P) **BRING ON THE DANCING HORSES. / OVER MY SHOULDER** (ext.12"+=) (KOW 43T) – Beds, bugs and ballyhoo. (d7"+=) (KOW 43F) – Villier's terrace / Monkeys.	21	–
Nov 85.	(lp/c)(pic-lp)(cd) (KODE/CODE 13)(KODE 13P)(240 767-2) <25360> **SONGS TO LEARN AND SING** (compilation) – Rescue / The puppet / Do it clean / The promise / The back of love / The cutter / Never stop / The killing moon / Silver / Seven seas / Bring on the dancing horses. (c+=/cd+=) – Pride / Simple stuff / Read it in books / Angels and devils. (free ltd.c-s w/ same extra tracks)	6	

— (Feb86) temp. **MARK FOX** – drums (ex-HAIRCUT 100) repl. DE FREITAS until return Sep'86.

		WEA	Sire
Jun 87.	(7") (YZ 134) **THE GAME. / SHIP OF FOOLS** (12"+=/12"w poster+=) (YZ 134T/+W) – Lost and found.	28	–
Jul 87.	(lp/c)(cd) (WX 108/+C)(242 137-2) <25597> **ECHO AND THE BUNNYMEN** – The game / Over you / Bedbugs and ballyhoo / All in your mind / Bombers bay / Lips like sugar / Lost and found / New direction / Blue blue ocean / Satellite / All my life. (re-iss. cd Nov94)	4	51
Jul 87.	(7"/7"gf/7"box) (YZ 144/+V/B) **LIPS LIKE SUGAR. / ROLLERCOASTER** (12"+=) (YZ 144T/+X) – People are strange.	36	–
Feb 88.	(7"/c-s) (YZ 175/+C) **PEOPLE ARE STRANGE. / RUN RUN RUN (live)** (12"+=) (YZ 175T) – Paint it black / Friction. (re-iss. Feb91 7"/c-s; YZ 567/+C /12"/cd-s; YZ 567 T/CD) – hit UK No.34	29	–

— They split some unofficial time in '88. Re-formed after McCULLOCH went solo.

PETE DE FREITAS joined SEX GODS. He died in motorcycle accident 14 Jun '89.

— **SERGEANT** and **PATTINSON** reformed group early 1990, with newcomers **NOEL BURKE** (b.Belfast, N.Ireland) – vocals (ex-St. VITAS DANCE) / **JACK BROCKMAN** – keyboards / **DAMON REECE** – drums

		Korova	Sire
Oct 90.	(7"/c-s) (9031 72796-7/-4) **ENLIGHTEN ME. / LADY, DON'T FALL BACKWARDS** (12"+=/cd-s+=) (9031 72796-1/-2) – ('A'extended).		–
Nov 90.	(cd)(c/lp) (9031 72553-2)(CODE/KODE 14) <26388> **REVERBERATION** – Freaks dwell / Cut and dried / Revilement / Flaming red / Salvatore / Fine thing / Gone, gone, gone / Enlighten me / King of your castle / Senseless / Thick skinned world. (cd+=) – False goodbyes.		Dec90

		Euphoric	not iss.
Oct 91.	(12"ep/cd-ep) (E 001 T/CDS) **PROVE ME WRONG. / FINE THING / REVERBERATION (live)**		–
Mar 92.	(12"/cd-s) (K 002 T/CD) **INSIDE ME, INSIDE YOU. / WIGGED OUT WORLD**		–

— The BUNNYMEN disbanded soon after the above and LES joined TERRY HALL'S backing group.

WILL SERGEANT

		WEA	not iss.
Jul 82.	(7") (K 19238) **FAVOURITE BRANCHES. / (b-side by Ravi Shankar & Bill Lovelady)**		–

		92HappyC.	not iss.
Mar 83.	(lp) (HAPLP 1) **THEMES FOR "GRIND"** – Grind starts the generator / The wheel turns / The small screen flickers. (cd-iss. Jan98 +=; HAPSCD 1) – Theme / Favourite branches / Aquarius dub.		–

		Ochre	not iss.
1995.	(7"orange) (OCH 003) **COSMOS. / VENUS IN FLARES**		–

— WILL went on to form project, GLIDE – (see Alt & Indie II book-only)

Ian McCULLOCH

IAN McCULLOCH – vocals while still a member of The BUNNYMEN

		Korova	not iss.
Nov 84.	(7"/10") (KOW 40/+L) **SEPTEMBER SONG. / COCKLES & MUSSELS** (12"+=) (KOW 40T) – ('A'extended).	51	–

— Now solo his back-up came from **RAY SHULMAN** – keyboards, programmer, bass, producer / plus guests **MICHAEL JOBSON** – bass / **BORIS WILLIAMS** – drums / **OLLE REMO** – drum programmer / **LIZ FRASER** – vox (of COCTEAU TWINS)

		WEA	Sire
Aug 89.	(7"/7"box/c-s) (YZ 417/+B/C) **PROUD TO FALL. / POTS OF GOLD** (12") (YZ 417T) – ('A'extended) / ('A'side) / The dead end. (cd-s) (YZ 417CD) – (above 3 tracks) / ('A'version). (12") (YZ 417TX) – ('A'side) / Everything is real / The circle game.	51	–
Sep 89.	(lp/c)(cd) (WX 303/+C)(2292 46225-2) <26012> **CANDLELAND** – The flickering wall / The white hotel / Proud to fall / The cape / Candleland / Horse's head / Faith and healing / I know you well / In bloom / Start again.	18	
Nov 89.	(7"/c-s) (YZ 436/+C) **FAITH AND HEALING (remix). / TOAD** ('A'mix-12"+=) (YZ 436T) – Fear of the known. (cd-s++=) (YZ 436CD) – Rocket ship. (12") (YZ 436TX) – ('A'side) / Fear of the known / Rocket ship.		–
Apr 90.	(7"/c-s) (YZ 436/+C) **CANDLELAND (THE SECOND COMING). / THE WORLD IS FLAT** (12"+=/12"gf+=/cd-s+=) (YZ 452 T/TG/CD) – Big days / Wassailing in the night.	75	–

— His backing band from late '89, were The PRODIGAL SONS; **MIKE MOONEY** – guitar / **JOHN McEVOY** – guitar, keyboards / **EDGAR SUMMERTIME** – bass / **STEVE HUMPHRIES** – drums

		East West	Warners
Feb 92.	(7"/c-s) (YZ 643/+C) **LOVER, LOVER, LOVER. / WHITE HOTEL (acoustic) / THE GROUND BELOW** ('A'-Indian Dawn remix-12"+=/cd-s+=) (YZ 643T) – Vibor blue (acoustic).	47	–
Apr 92.	(lp/c)(cd) (WX 453/+C)(<9031 76264-2>) **MYSTERIO** – Mayreal world / Close your eyes / Dug for love / Honeydrip / Damnation / Lover, lover, lover / Webbed / Pomegranate / Vibor blue / Heaven's gate / In my head.	46	–
Apr 92.	(7"/c-s) (YZ 660/+C) **DUG FOR LOVE. / POMMEGRANITE (live)** (12"+=)(cd-s+=) (YZ 660 T/CD) – Do it clean (live) / In my head (live).		–

ELECTRAFIXION

— **IAN McCULLOCH** – vocals, guitar / **WILL SERGEANT** – guitar / **LEON DE SYLVA** – bass / **TONY McGUIGAN** – drums

		WEA	Warners
Nov 94.	(c-ep/12"ep/cd-ep) (YZ 865 C/T/CD) **THE ZEPHYR EP** – Zephyr / Burned / Mirrorball / Rain on me.	47	–
Sep 95.	(7"red/c-s) (YZ 977 X/C) **LOWDOWN. / HOLY GRAIL** (cd-s+=) (YZ 977CD) – Land of the dying sun / Razors edge.	54	–
Sep 95.	(cd/c) (0630 11248-2/-4) <61793> **BURNED** – Feel my pulse / Sister pain / Lowdown / Timebomb / Zephyr / Never / Too far gone / Mirrorball / Who's been sleeping in my head? / Hit by something / Bed of nails.	38	Oct95
Oct 95.	(c-s) (WEA 022C) **NEVER / NOT OF THIS WORLD** (cd-s+=) (WEA 022CD) – Subway train / Lowdown (rest of the trash mix). (cd-s) (WEA 022CDX) – ('A'side) / Work it on out / Never (Utah Saints blizzard on mix) / Sister pain.	58	–
Mar 96.	(cd-ep) (WEA 037CD1) **SISTER PAIN / FEEL MY PULSE / ZEPHYR / LOWDOWN (live)** (cd-ep) (WEA 037CD2) – ('A'side) / Burned / Loose (live) / Who's been sleeping	27	–

ECHO & THE BUNNYMEN

— the original trio (McCULLOCH, SEARGEANT + PATTINSON) re-formed

		London	London
Jun 97.	(7") *(LO 396)* **NOTHING LASTS FOREVER. / WATCHTOWER**	8	–
	(cd-s+=) *(LONCD 396)* – Polly.		
	(cd-s) *(LONCDP 396)* – ('A'side) / Colour me in / Antelope.		
Jul 97.	(cd/c/lp) *(828905-2/-4/-1)* **EVERGREEN**	8	–

– Don't let it get you down / In my time / I want to be there (when you come) / Evergreen / I'll fly tonight / Nothing lasts forever / Baseball Bill / Altamont / Just a touch away / Empire state halo / Too young to kneel / Forgiven. *(d-cd-iss. Nov97; 828980-2)* *(cd re-iss. Sep99; 3984 29642-2)*

Aug 97.	(cd-s) *(LOCD 399)* **I WANT TO BE THERE (WHEN YOU COME) / THE KILLING MOON (session) / NOTHING LASTS FOREVER (session)**	30	–
	(cd-s) *(LOCDP 399)* – ('A'side) / Lips like sugar (live acoustic) / ('A'-live acoustic).		
Oct 97.	(cd-s) *(LOCD 406)* **DON'T LET IT GET YOU DOWN / BACK OF LOVE (live) / OVER THE WALL (live)**	50	–
	(cd-s) *(LOCDP 406)* – ('A'side) / Rescue / Altamont.		

— In Jun'98, McCULLOCH provided ENGLAND UNITED with their World Cup song, '(HOW DOES IT FEEL TO BE) ON TOP OF THE WORLD' which hit Top 10.

— a few months later, a joint single, 'GET IN THE CAR' with The FUN LOVIN' CRIMINALS, was withdrawn from release

Mar 99.	(7") *(LO 424)* **RUST. / THE FISH HOOK GIRL**	22	–
	(cd-s+=) *(LOCD 424)* – See the horizon.		
	(cd-s) *(LOCDP 424)* – ('A'side) / Sense of life / Beyond the green.		
Apr 99.	(cd/c) *(<556080-2/-4>)* **WHAT ARE YOU GOING TO DO WITH YOUR LIFE?**	21	Jun99

– What are you going to do with your life? / Rust / Get in the car / Baby rain / History chimes / Lost on you / Morning sun / When it all blows over / Fools like us.

— **McCULLOCH + SERGEANT** brought in **CERI JAMES** – keyboards, synths

		Cooking Vinyl	Cooking Vinyl
Apr 01.	(7") *(FRY 104)* **IT'S ALRIGHT. / SUPERMELLOW MAN (instrumental)**	41	–
	(cd-s) *(FRYCD 104)* – ('A'side) / Marble towers / Rescue (Mindwinders remix).		
	(cd-s) *(FRYCD 104X)* – ('A'side) / Scratch the past / A promise (lo-fi lullaby #1) / ('A'-video).		
May 01.	(lp/cd) *(COOK/+CD 208)* *<608>* **FLOWERS**	56	

– King of kings / Supermellow man / Hide and seek / Make me shine / It's alright / Buried alive / Flowers / Everybody knows / Life goes on / An eternity turns / Burn for me.

Aug 01.	(cd-s) *(FRYCD 112)* **MAKE ME SHINE / TICKET TO RIDE / NOTHING LASTS FOREVER (live)**		

— added **STEVE FLETT** – bass / **VINNY JAMIESON** – drums

Feb 02.	(cd) *(COOKCD 223)* *<623>* **LIVE IN LIVERPOOL (live August 2001)**		

– Rescue / Lips like sugar / King of kings / Never stop / Seven seas / Buried alive / Supermellow man / My kingdom / Zimbo / All the jazz / An eternity turns / The back of love / The killing moon / The cutter / Over the wall / Nothing lasts forever / Ocean rain.

– compilations, others, etc. –

Nov 88.	(12"ep/cd-ep) *Strange Fruit; (SFPS/+CD 060)* **THE PEEL SESSIONS (15.8.79)**		–

– Read it in books / Stars are stars / I bagsy yours / Villier's terrace. *(re-iss. cd-ep Dec94; same)*

Jul 90.	(7") *Old Gold; (OG 9939)* **THE KILLING MOON. / SEVEN SEAS**		–
Jul 90.	(7") *Old Gold; (OG 9941)* **THE CUTTER. / THE BACK OF LOVE**		–
Nov 91.	(cd/lp) *Windsong; (WIN CD/LP 006)* **BBC RADIO 1 LIVE IN CONCERT (live)**		
Mar 93.	(cd/c) *Pickwick-WEA; (4509-91886-2/-4)* **THE CUTTER** *(re-iss. Sep95 on 'Warners'; same)*		
Jun 97.	(cd/c) W.E.A.; *(0630 19103-2/-4)* **BALLYHOO – THE BEST OF ECHO & THE BUNNYMEN**	59	

– Rescue / Do it clean / Villier's terrace / All that jazz / Over the wall / A promise / The disease / The back of love / The cutter / Never stop / The killing moon / Silver / Seven seas / Bring on the dancing horses / People are strange / The game / Lips like sugar / Bedbugs & ballyhoo.

Aug 01.	(4xcd-box) *Rhino; (<8122 74263-2>)* **CRYSTAL DAYS 1979-1999**		

ED GEIN'S CAR

Formed: New York, USA … 1982 by ERIC HEDIN and TIM CARROLL who found SCOTT WEISS and filled the drumstool with a succession of temp sticksmen (the group moniker came via a character in the cult horror movie, 'Texas Chainsaw Massacre'). Poo-pooing the po-faced sincerity of the hardcore scene, the smart-arsed quartet joked their way onto vinyl with 1984's debut single, 'BRAIN DEAD', following it up with a full-length album, 'MAKING DICK DANCE' (1985). Blessed/cursed with the same un-PC adolescent humour as The BEASTIE BOYS would later make their name with, ED GEIN'S CAR were a regular fixture at the infamous CBGB's where their sarcastic stage antics went down a storm; the highlights of this period were captured for posterity on the swansong 1987 set, 'YOU LIGHT UP MY LIVER'. The same year saw WEISS continue his bad taste comedy crusade with the short-lived IRON PROSTATE.

Album rating: MAKING DICK DANCE (*5) / YOU LIGHT UP MY LIVER (*6)

ERIC HEDIN – guitar / **TIM CARROLL** – bass / **SCOTT WEISS** – vocals

		not iss.	Ed Gein's Car
1984.	(7"ep) *<egc 3355>* **BRAIN DEAD BABY. / TOO OLD TO DIE YOUNG / WAIT 'TIL YOUR FATHER GETS HOME**	–	
1985.	(lp) *<egc 1201>* **MAKING DICK DANCE**	–	

– Bars and brick / Go down on my dog / Kiss daddy goodnight / Annette / Boo hoo / Progress / A girl just like you / Selby / R.A.P.E. / Cream of wheat / Middle (r)age / Die like you really mean it / Making Dick dance.

		not iss.	Celluloid
1987.	(lp) *<cbgb 1002>* **YOU LIGHT UP MY LIVER (live at CBGB'S 1986)**	–	

– R.A.P.E. / My choice / Too old to die young / The petting zoo / Middle (r)age / My life's a game / Selby / Last caress / A girl just like you / Forever / Boo fuckin' hoo / Bars and brick / Surf Nazis / We're not you're world / Brain dead baby / Father gets home / Progress / Ay-ay. *<cd-iss. 1987 on 'Enigma'; 97295-2>*

		not iss.	Vital Music
1991.	(7"pink) *<vms 8>* **NAKED MAN. / CONSIDER BEING TRUE**	–	

— disbanded after above

8 EYED SPY
(see under ⇒ LUNCH, Lydia; 70's section)

EINSTURZENDE NEUBAUTEN

Formed: Berlin, Germany … 1st April 1980, when this arty industrial conglomerate played their first live gig. They issued a few singles for Germany's 'Zick Zack', before unleashing 'KOLLAPS' at the end of '81. A few more arrived (signed to UK label 'Some Bizzare'), before they settled with the line-up of BLIXA BARGELD, N.U. UNRUH, MUFTI and new mid-80's members ALEX HACKE and MARC CHUNG. By this time, most of them were finding moonlighting work, mainly BARGELD who had joined NICK CAVE & THE BAD SEEDS. HACKE joined CRIME & THE CITY SOLUTION, while FM EINHEIT went solo (backed by STEIN ('STONE') for the early 90's. EINSTURZENDE NEUBAUTEN subsequently released the album, 'STEIN', in 1990 and three years later, 'PROMETHEUS LEAR', although always intending to split during this period. Pioneers of experimental industrial power-metal, picking up any object to make a barrage of sound (from either power tools, metal piping, large hammers, steel girders and anything that could cut metal). The band were prone to just basically strip to the waist, wear hard hats and get on with the job. Incredibly for such an avant-garde outfit, EINSTURZENDE NEUBAUTEN were still going strong come the new millennium, twenty years on from their first blast of cochlea-collapsing noise. As the title might suggest, 'SILENCE IS SEXY' (2000) tended to forego the gratuitous sonic excess which characterises much of the band's work, instead opting for a more subtle yet just as disturbing line in musical subversion.
• **Trivia:** BARGELD featured alongside The BAD SEEDS in the 1988 Wim Wenders film 'Angels Uber Berlin'.

Album rating: KOLLAPS (*4) / PORTRAIT OF PATIENT O.T. (*5) / STRATEGIES AGAINST ARCHITECTURE compilation (*6) / 2x4 (*5) / HALBER MENSCHE (*5) / HANS DER LUEGE (*4) / STRATEGIES AGAINST ARCHITECTURE, VOL.2 compilation (*7) / TABULA RASA (*7) / ENDE NEU (*5) / SILENCE IS SEXY (*6)

BLIXA BARGELD (b.12 Jan'59) – vocals, guitar, percussion / **N.U. UNRUH** (b. ANDREW, 9 Jun'57, New York City) – vocals, bass, percussion / **BEATE BARTEL** – also industrial percussion / **GODRUN GUT** – industrial percussion / soon added **ALEXANDER VAN BORSIG** – percussion

		Mongam	not iss.
Nov 80.	(7") *(005)* **FUR DEN UNTERGANG. / STAHLVERSION**	–	– German

— (STUART) **MUFTI** (aka F.M. EINHEIT) (b.18 Dec'58, Dortmund, Germany) – industrial percussion (ex-ABWARTS) repl. BARTEL and GUT, who formed MANIA D and MATADOR

		Zick Zack	not iss.
Aug 81.	(d7"ep) *(ZZ 40)* **DURSTIGES TIER**	–	– German

– Kalte sterne / Aufrecht gehen / Erlicher stein & pygmaen / Schwarz.
above featured BIRTHDAY PARTY and LYDIA LUNCH

Dec 81.	(lp) *(ZZ 65)* **KOLLAPS**	–	– German

– Kollaps / Sehnsucht / Vorm krieg / Hirnsaege / Abstieg & zerfall / Helga / Tanz debil / Steh auf Berlin / Negativ nein / U-haft muzak / Draussen ist feindlich / Horen mit schmerzen / Jet'm. *(re-iss. Dec88 lp/cd; EFA 2517/+CD)* *(UK-iss.Oct96 on 'Strange Ways' cd/lp; INDIGO 2517-2/-1)* *(cd re-iss. Mar98 on 'Spalax'; 14537)*

— added **MARC CHUNG** (b. 3 Jun'57, Leeds, England) – bass (ex-ABWARTS)

		Some Bizarre	Ze-PVC
Nov 83.	(lp) *(SBVART 2) <PVC 9902>* **PORTRAIT OF PATIENT O.T.**		

– Vanadium-I-Ching / Hospitalistische kinder-engel der vernichtung / Abfackeln / Neun arme / Herde / Merle / Zeichnungen des patienten O.T. / Finger und zaehne / Falschgeld / Styropor / Armenia / Die genaue zeit. *<cd-iss. 1195 on 'Thirsty Ear'; 57011>*

— added **ALEXANDER HACKE** (b.11 Oct'65) – guitar, electronics

Mar 85.	(12") *(BART 12)* **YU-GUNG. / SEELEBRENNT / SAND**		–

EINSTURZENDE NEUBAUTEN (cont) — THE GREAT INDIE DISCOGRAPHY — The 1980s

Oct 85. (lp) (BART 331) **HALBER MENSCH** (HALF MEN)
– Halber mensch / Yu-gung (futter mein ego) / Trinklied / Z.N.S. / Seelebrennt / Sehnsucht / Der tod ist ein dandy / Letztes biest / Das schaben / Sand. (cd-iss. Jan87; BART 331CD) (re-iss. Oct96 on 'Strange Ways'; INDIGO 26141) <cd-iss. 1995 on 'Thirst EAr'; TE 57010>

Jul 87. (lp/c/cd) (BART 332/+C/CD) **FUNF AUF DER NACH OBEN OFFENEN RICHTERSKALA** (means 'FIVE ON THE OPEN-ENDED RICHTER SCALE')
– Zerstorte zell / Morning dew / Ich bin's / Modimidofraso / Zwolf stadte / Keine schonheit ohne gefahr / Kein bestandteil sein. <cd-iss. 1995 on 'Thirsty Ear'; TE 57016>

                                                                  Some Bizzare | Rough Trade
Sep 89. (lp/c/cd) (BART 333/+C/CD) <ROUGHUS 71/+C/CD> **HANS DER LUEGE**
– Prolog / Feurio / Ein stuhl in der Holle / Haus der luge / Epilog / Fiat lux / Maifestspiele / Himlego / Schwindel / Der kuss. <cd re-iss. 1995 on 'Thirsty Ear'; TE 57017>

                                                                  Beton-Mute | Mute-Elektra
Jan 93. (12"ep/cd-ep) (BETON 205/+CD) <61509> **INTERIM**
– Interimlovers / Salamandrina / 3 thoughts / Ring my bell / Rausch – Die interimsliebenden.

Feb 93. (lp/c/cd) (BETON 106/+MC/CD) <61458> **TABULA RASA**
– Die interimsliebenden / Zebulon / Blume / 12305 (te nacht) / Sie / Wuste / Headcleaner.

Apr 93. (lp/cd) (BETON 206/+CD) **MALADICTION**
– Blume (French version) / Blume (English version) / Blume (Japanese version) / Ubique media version / 3 thoughts / Ein gansz kleines loch in einem / Diapositiv / Ring my bell.

                                                                  Rough Trade | Revolver
Mar 94. (cd) (1971208) <1208-2> **HEINER MULLER: HAMLETMASCHINE**
– Soll ich / Weils brauch ist ein stuck eisen stecken ist in / Das nachste Fleisch oder ist in uberachste / Mich dran zu halten weil sich die welt sich dreht / Herr brich mir das Genick im sturz von einer / Bierbank. <re-iss. 1996 on 'Grey Area-Ego'; EGO 111>

                                                                  Ego-Grey Area | Elektra
Feb 96. (cd) (EGO 501) <69021> **FAUSTMUSIK**   May96
– Tische / Monolog / Besetzt / Burokratie / Burleske / Walpurgisnachtfestchen / Orchestrion / Still am abend / Letztes bild.

—— next featured JON SPENCER + ALEC EMPIRE (+ now without CHUNG)

Jul 96. (cd-ep) (BETON 503CD) <EGO 503> **STELLA MARIS (mixes)**
                                                                  Beton-Mute | Beton-Mute
Jul 96. (lp/cd) (<BETON 504/+CD>) **ENDE NEU**
– Was ist ist (What is it) / Stella maris / Die explosion im festspielhaus / Installation No.1 / Nnnaaammm / Ende neu (Ending new) / The garden / Der schacht von babel (shaft of . . .).

Jul 97. (12"ep) (<BETON 601>) **THE DARK WELCOME / SIDE GRINDER. / AMBIENT GUILLOTONE / STRAIGHT TO THE PLAIN**
(cd-ep) (<BETON 601CD>) – Nnnaaammm remixes (by DARKUS) / (Trilogy & Side Grinder).

Sep 97. (d-lp/cd) (BETON 602/+CD) **ENDE NEU REMIXED**
Aug 99. (cd-s) **TOTAL ECLIPSE OF THE SUN / SONNENBARKE / HELIUM / TOTAL ECLIPSE OF THE SUN**
                                                                  Mute | Orchard
Apr 00. (d-cd) (CDSTUMM 182) <2> **SILENCE IS SEXY**   May00
– Sabrina / Silence is sexy / In circles / Newton's gravitalnichkeit / Zampano / Heaven is of honey / Beauty / Die befindlichkeit des landes / Sonnebarke / Musentango / Alles / Redukt / Dingsaller / Total eclipse of the sun / Pelikanol.

– compilations, etc. –

Jan 84. (lp) Mute; (Stumm 14) / Homestead; <HMS 063> **80-83 STRATEGIES AGAINST ARCHITECTURE**
– Tanz debil / Schmerzen hoeren / Mikroben / Krieg in den staedten / Zum tier machen / Stahlversion / Schwarz / Negativ nein / Kalte sterne / Spaltung / U-haft muzak / Gestohlenes band (ORF) / Schwarz (mutiert). (cd-iss. Apr88 + Nov92; CDStumm 14) <US cd-iss. 1995 on 'Elektra'; 61677>

Dec 84. (c) R.O.I.R.; (<A 133>) **2 x 4**
– Fleisch 'Blutihaut' knochen / Sehnsucht (nie mehr) / Womb / Krach der schlegenden herzen / Armenisch bitter / Zum tier machen / Sehnsucht (still stehend) / Durstige tiere. (cd-iss. Nov97; RUSCD 8235)

May 91. (d-cd/d-c) Mute; / Mute-Elektra; <61100-2/-4> **STRATEGIES AGAINST ARCHITECTURE II**
– Abfackeln! / Partynummer (live) / Z.N.S. / Die elektrik (Merle) / Intermezzo – Yu-gung (live) / Seelebrennt / Blutvergiftung / Sand / Kangolicht / Armenia (live) / Ein stuhl in der holle / Vanadium I-Ching / Leid und elend (live) / DNS wasserturm / Armenia II (live) / Fackeln! / Ich bin's / Hirnlego / Wardrobe / Bildbeschreibung / Haus der luege (live) / Jordache / Kein bestandteil sein (alternative ending).

Dec 94. (3xcd-box) Beton-Mute; (BETONBOX 1) **TRI SET**

Mark EITZEL (see under ⇒ AMERICAN MUSIC CLUB)

ELEVENTH DREAM DAY

Formed: Chicago, Illinois, USA . . . 1983 by RICK RIZZO and JANET BEVERIDGE BEAN. The couple met at Lexington University, discovering a shared musical appreciation of NEIL YOUNG and raw punk. Subsequently relocating to Chicago, they initiated ELEVENTH DREAM DAY with the addition of SHU SHABAT (soon replaced by DOUG McCOMBS) and BAIRD FIGI, gigging hard prior to the release of their eponymous 1987 mini-set on the small 'Amoeba' label. 1988 saw RIZZO and BEAN tying the knot while a DIY debut album proper, 'PRAIRIE SCHOOL FREAKOUT', was sufficiently impressive to secure a major label deal with 'Atlantic'. 1989's 'BEET' was a tentative step up to the glare of major label exposure, the band's incisive rootsiness betraying traces of YOUNG, DINOSAUR JR., The PIXIES etc., while carving out their own emotionally charged alt-rock niche. 'LIVED TO TELL' (1991), meanwhile, fulfilled at least some of EDD's promise although it somehow missed out on the buzz surrounding a re-energised alternative scene ripe for the picking. Similarly, the failure of the admittedly more subdued 'EL MOODIO' was equally perplexing, the band unceremoniously shunted from the Atlantic roster and moving on to 'City Slang' ('Thrill Jockey' in the US) for the JOHN McENTIRE-produced 'URSA MAJOR'. Ironically, it would be his moonlighting work in TORTOISE (alongside McENTIRE) and PULLMAN that would bring McCOMB most recognition. In fact, by the release of the latter outfit's critically acclaimed 'Turnstyles And Junkpiles', EDD had already signed off with a 7th set, entitled 'EIGHTH'! BEAN also attracted more column inches in her own right as a founding member of FREAKWATER, a country/folk roots outfit comprising BEAN, CATHERINE ANN IRWIN and DAVE GAY. Initiated in the late 80's just as ELEVENTH DREAM DAY were being groomed for the big time, the project was EDD's alter ego, dealing in the kind of skeletal, down-to-the-wire country that CMTV wouldn't touch with a bargepole (and that can't be a bad thing!). Following 1989's eponymous debut and 1991's 'DANCING UNDER WATER', the group also signed up to 'City Slang'/'Thrill Jockey', releasing 'FEELS LIKE THE THIRD TIME' in 1995. With the rise and rise of the US alt-country scene, FREAKWATER attracted increasing attention throughout the 90's, albums such as 'OLD PAINT' (1995) and 'SPRINGTIME' (1998) actually garnering more attention in Europe than the States despite their high lonesome sounds. Be warned, though, FREAKWATER may be on an alternative label but their desperately mournful country is as about as authentic as it comes and in reality, this lot have more in common with GILLIAN WELCH than WILCO. IRWIN and BEAN collected their thoughts on yet another superb FREAKWATER set, 'END TIME' (1999), complete with a new acquisition, a drumkit, and a trio of strings. Meanwhile, ELEVENTH DREAM DAY were planning their next assault, 'STALLED PARADE' (2000), a CRAZY HORSE-flavoured delivery that saw McCOMBS, RIZZO, BEAN, etc., being augmented once again by TORTOISE general JOHN McENTIRE. • **Songwriters:** RIZZO or BEAN or FIGI (until latter's departure). SOUTHERN PACIFIC (Neil Young) / I GOT A THING . . . (Funkadelic) / FREAKWATER covered OUT OF THIS WORLD (Loudon Wainwright III) / PUT MY LITTLE SHOES + LITTLE BLACK TRAIN (Woody Guthrie) / PALE HORSE (Bailes-Stagg) / YOU'VE NEVER BEEN THIS FAR BEFORE (Conway Twitty) / AMELIA EARHART (D. McEnry) / YOU MAKE LOVE (Nick Lowe) / RANK STRANGERS (A. Brumley) / LITTLE GIRL AND THE DREADFUL SNAKE (Bill Monroe) / ANNABELLE LEE (Bob Neuwirth) / MY ONE DESIRE (Dorsey Burnette) / BURYING GERALDINE + TWISTED WIRE (Sean Garrison) / BLUE EYES CRYING IN THE RAIN (Willie Nelson) / CHILDISH LOVE + CRAZY MAN + KENTUCKY (Louvin Brothers) / SOUTH OF CINCINNATI (Dwight Yoakam) / WAR PIGS (Black Sabbath) / WILD AND BLUE (J. Sherill) / DARK AS A DUNGEON (M. Travis) / YOU'RE STILL ON MY MIND (L. Payne) / LOVER'S RETURN (Carter Family) / OUT AMONG THE STARS (Adam Mitchell) / DOLLAR BILL BLUES (Townes Van Zandt) / etc. • **Trivia:** RIZZO and BEAN guested on TARA KEY's band's ANTIETAM album, 'Bourbon Country'.

Album rating: ELEVENTH DREAM DAY mini (*5) / PRAIRIE SCHOOL FREAKOUT (*6) / BEET (*6) / LIVED TO TELL (*7) / EL MOODIO (*7) / URSA MAJOR (*6) / EIGHTH (*7) / STALLED PARADE (*6) / Freakwater: FREAKWATER mini (*5) / DANCING UNDER WATER (*8) / FEELS LIKE THE THIRD TIME (*6) / OLD PAINT (*7) / SPRINGTIME (*7) / END TIME (*7)

RICK RIZZO (b. 4 Jul'57) – vocals, guitar, harmonica / **JANET BEVERIDGE BEAN** (b.10 Feb'64, Louisville, Kentucky) – drums, vocals / **DOUG McCOMBS** (b. 9 Jan'62) – bass, guitar; repl. SHU SHABAT / **BAIRD FIGI** – guitar

                                                                  New Rose | Amoeba
1987. (m-lp) <A 002> **ELEVENTH DREAM DAY**
– Walking through the barrel of a gun / Vein of gold / Not the ballad of a girl / Liz Beth / The arsonist / Cascade. (re-iss. Oct89 on 'Fan Club'; FC 056)

May 89. (lp/cd) (ROSE 159/CD) <A 003> **PRAIRIE SCHOOL FREAKOUT**   Nov88
– Watching the candles burn / Sweet smell / Coercion / Driving song / Tarantula / Among the pines / Through my mouth / Beach miner / Death of Albert C. Sampson / Life on a string. (cd+=) – Tenth leaving train. (cd re-iss. May94; 422128)

Oct 89. (12"ep) <A 006> **AWAKE EP**
– Go / Southern Pacific / Tenth leaving train.

—— also in 1989, the track 'AWAKE I LIE' was a 7" free with Bucketful Of Brains issue #29 (other side by Kalaidoscope)

                                                                  Atlantic | Atlantic
Mar 90. (cd/c/lp) <(7567 82053-2/-4/-1)> **BEET**   Nov89
– Between here and there / Testify / Baghdad's last ride / Awake I lie / Road that never winds / Axle / Michael Dunne / Bomb the Mars Hotel / Teenage pin queen / Love to hate to love / Go (slight return). (cd+=) – Seiche. (cd re-iss. Jul01 on 'Collectors Choice'; CCM 0214-2)

Jun 91. (cd/c/lp) <(7567 82179-2/-4/-1)> **LIVED TO TELL**   Jan91
– Rose of Jericho / Dream of a sleeping sheep / I could be lost / It's not my world / You know what it is / Frozen mile / Strung up and/or out / North of wasteland / It's all a game / Trouble / There's this thing / Daedalus / Angels spread your wings. (cd re-iss. Jul01 on 'Collectors Choice'; CCM 0215-2)

—— (early '91) **MATTHEW "WINK" O'BANNON** (b.22 Jul'56) – guitar repl. FIGI who formed The DOORMATS (released a 7"ep)

                                                                  City Slang | Atlantic
Dec 92. (12"ep/cd-ep) (EFA 04904/+CD) **TWO SWEETIES EP**
– Makin' like a rug / Sunflower / Honeyslide.

Apr 93. (cd/c) <(7567 82480-2/-4)> **EL MOODIO**
– Makin' like a rug / Figure it out / After this time is gone / Murder / Honeyslide / That's the point / Motherland / The raft / Bend bridge / Rubberband.

—— now aided by the production of JOHN McENTIRE (of TORTOISE) + now without WINK (JANET BEAN more into FREAKWATER)

ELEVENTH DREAM DAY (cont)

				City Slang	Atavistic
Sep 94.	(7",7"orange) (EFA 04941-7) **ORANGE MOON. / I GOT A THING, YOU GOT A THING, EVERYBODY'S GOT A THING**			-	-
Jan 95.	(cd/lp) (EFA 04943-2/-1) <13> **URSA MAJOR**				Dec94

– History of brokeback / Occupation or not / Flutter / Orange moon / Taking leave / Bearish on high / Nova Zembla / The blindside / Exit right.

— McCOMBS still in this operative, although he concentrated more on his other co-project, TORTOISE. O'BANNON departed to form BODECO.

		City Slang	Thrill Jockey
Feb 97.	(cd) (EFA 94989-2) <THRILL 37> **EIGHTH**		

– For a king / Writes a letter home / Two smart cookies / Insomnia / View from the rim / April / Motion sickness / Last call.

— McCOMBS helped to initiate yet another offshoot outfit, PULLMAN

		Thrill Jockey	Thrill Jockey
Sep 00.	(lp/cd) <(THRILL 085/+CD)> **STALLED PARADE**		

– Stalled parade / Ice storm / On ramp / Interstate / Valrico 74 / In the style of . . . / Ground point zero / Bite the hand / Way too early on a Sunday morning.

— RIZZO subsequently joined CHESTNUT STATION

FREAKWATER

JANET BEAN – guitar + **CATHERINE ANN IRWIN** – guitar, vocals / **DAVE GAY** – upright bass / with **JOHN RICE** – fiddle, mandolin, pedal steel guitar

		not iss.	Amoeba
1989.	(m-lp) <A 007> **FREAKWATER**	-	

– Miner song / Childish love / Lonesome sound / Family tradition / Great Titanic / Blue eyes / Ballad of Freakwater / A mile away / Albert C. Samson.

| 1990. | (7") <1 1/4 York 002> **YOUR GODDAMNED MOTH. / WAR PIGS** | - | |

(above issued on '1 1/4 York')

| 1991. | (cd) <A 009> **DANCING UNDER WATER** | - | |

– A song you could cry for / Great potential / Rank strangers / Blood and fire / Selfishness in man / Fill my thermos / You're still on my mind / Your goddamn mouth / Little girl and the dreadful snake / Scratches on the door / Wild and blue / Annabelle Lee / Dark as a dungeon. <(UK + re-iss. May97 on 'Thrill Jockey' lp/cd; THRILL 040/+CD)>

		City Slang	Thrill Jockey
May 93.	(7") <THRILL 009> **MY OLD DRUNK FRIEND. / KENTUCKY**		
Nov 93.	(cd/lp) (EFA 04920-2/-1) <THRILL 010CD> **FEELS LIKE THE THIRD TIME**		May93

– My old drunk friend / Put my little shoes / Crazy man / Pale horse / You make me / You've never been this far before / Dream girl / Sleeping on hold / Amelia Earhart / Are you ready / Lullaby. (cd re-iss. Feb98 on 'Thrill Jockey'; same US)

— in 1994, JANET BEAN and JEFF LESCHER (of GREEN) released the Gram Parsons tribute set, 'JESUS BUILT A SHIP TO SING A SONG TO', for 'Kokopop'

| Oct 95. | (cd/lp) (EFA 04965-2/-1) <THRILL 022/+CD> **OLD PAINT** | | |

– Gravity / Smoking daddy / Gone to stay / Little black train / Waitress song / My one desire / White rose / Out of this world / Kentucky house / Hero – Heroine / Ugly man / Burying Geraldine. (cd re-iss. Apr98 on 'Thrill Jockey'; same US)

| Dec 95. | (7") <THRILL 027> **SOUTH OF CINCINNATI. / COUNT ME OUT** | | |

— **MAX KONRAD JOHNSON** – banjo, guitar, fiddle, dobro; repl. RICE

		Thrill Jockey	Thrill Jockey
Feb 98.	(cd) <(THRILL 047CD)> **SPRINGTIME**		Jan98

– Picture in my mind / Louisville lip / Twisted wire / Washed in the blood / Binding twine / One big union / Harlan / Jesus year / Scamp / Lorraine / Slowride / Heaven / Flat hand.

| Sep 99. | (lp/cd) <(THRILL 066/+CD)> **END TIME** | | |

– Good for nothing / Cloak of frogs / Sick, sick, sick / Cheap watch / My history / When the leaves begin to fall / Written in gold / Dog gone wrong / Queen bee / Raised skin / All life long.

| Jul 00. | (7") <(THRILL 078-7)> **HELLBOUND. / LORRAINE** | | |

— CATHERINE has since guested for The SADIES and BONNIE PRINCE BILLY (aka WILL OLDHAM); she has since released a solo set, 'CUT YOURSELF A SWITCH' for 'Thrill Jockey' in 2002. JANET appeared for the PINE VALLEY COSMONAUTS while DAVID hooked up with The UNHOLY TRIO

EMBARRASSMENT

Formed: Wichita, Kansas, USA . . . 1979 by JOHN NICHOLS, BILL GOFFRIER, RON KLAUS and BRENT GIESSMANN. Taking their cue from the best of British and American punk but fashioning their own distinctive brand of edgy alternative rock, the band's sound was characterised by GOFFRIER's elaborate guitar work while the lyrics displayed a talent for wry observation. After debuting in summer 1980 with the caustic 'PATIO SET' single, they released an eponymous EP the following year, accruing much underground acclaim for their cutting lyrical portraits and original style. Label hopping once more, they cut a swansong set, 'DEATH TRAVELS WEST' (1983), a pseudo-concept affair. And that was that, save for a posthumously issued eponymous album combining new and previously available material. While GIESSMANN joined the DEL FUEGOS, GOFFRIER formed BIG DIPPER with GARY WALEIK, STEVE MICHENER and JEFF OLIPHANT, releasing a series of albums on 'Homestead', 'BOO-BOO' (a mini-set/EP), 'CRAPS' and 'HEAVENS'. Come the late 80's, The EMBARRASSMENT re-formed on a part-time basis, eventually getting round to recording a one-off US-only album, 'GOD HELP US', for the 'Bar/None' label in 1990. With continuing interest in the band, the latter label released a thorough EMBARRASSMENT retrospective in 1995 entitled 'HEYDAY'. • **Covered:** DON'T STOP TILL YOU GET ENOUGH (Michael Jackson) / IMMIGRANT SONG (Led Zeppelin) / MAYBE BABY (Buddy Holly) / TIME HAS COME TODAY (Chambers Brothers) / OH PRETTY WOMAN (Roy Orbison) / PUSHIN' TOO HARD (Seeds) / I WANNA BE YOUR DOG (Leiber-Mann-Stoller-Weil) / NO REPLY (Beatles) / FUNTIME (Iggy Pop) / BURNIN' LOVE (Elvis Presley). BIG DIPPER covered ALL THE WAY FROM MEMPHIS (Mott The Hoople).

Album rating: DEATH TRAVELS WEST (*7) / GOD HELP US (*7) / HEYDAY 1979-1983 compilation (*8) / BLISTER POP compilation (*5) / Big Dipper: BOO-BOO mini (*5) / HEAVENS (*7) / CRAPS (*5) / SLAM (*3)

JOHN NICHOLS – vocals, keyboards / **BILL GOFFRIER** – guitar, vocals / **RON KLAUS** – bass / **BRENT GIESSMANN** – drums

		not iss.	Big Time
Jul 80.	(7") <BT 001> **PATIO SET. / SEX DRIVE**	-	
		not iss.	Cynykl
May 81.	(12"ep) <001> **THE EMBARRASSMENT EP**	-	

– Celebrity art party / Elizabeth Montgomery's face / (I'm a) Don Juan / Don't choose the wrong song / Wellsville.

		not iss.	Fresh Sounds
Mar 83.	(lp) <FS 204> **DEATH TRAVELS WEST**	-	

– Careen / Viewmaster / Drive me to the park / Lewis and Clark / D-rings / Chapter 12 / Hip and well read.

— disbanded after above; GIESSMANN joined the DEL FUEGOS

BIG DIPPER

— were formed by **BILL GOFFRIER** – vocals / **GARY WALEIK** – guitar (ex-VOLCANO SONS) / **STEVE MICHENER** – bass (ex-VOLCANO SONS) / **JEFF OLIPHANT** – drums (ex-DUMPTRUCK)

		Demon	Homestead
Apr 87.	(m-lp) <HMS 077> **BOO-BOO**		

– Faith healer / San Quentin, CA / What's in Sam Hill? / Wrong in the charts / Ancers / Loch Ness monster.

| Oct 88. | (lp/cd) (FIEND/+CD 132) <HMS 122/+CD> **CRAPS** | | Sep88 |

– Meet the witch / Ron Klaus wrecked his house / The insane girl Semjase / Stardom because / Bonnie / Hey! Mr. Lincoln / The bells of love / A song to be beautiful.

| Feb 89. | (lp) (FIEND 136) <HMS 086> **HEAVENS** | | Dec87 |

– She's fetching / Man o' war / Easter eve / Humanson / Lunar module / All going out together / Younger bums / When men were trains / Wet weekend / Mr. Woods.

		not iss.	Epic
1990.	(lp/cd) <E/EK 46063> **SLAM**	-	

– Love barge / The bond / Another life / Slam / Bony knees of nothing / Baby blue / Picnic / The monsters of jazz / Impossible things / Blood pact / Father's day / Baby doll / Life inside the cemetery / All the way from Memphis.

— split soon after above, although EMBARRASSMENT (original line-up) attempted once more (this time as a sideline)

EMBARRASSMENT

		not iss.	Bar/None
Nov 89.	(7") **TRAIN OF THOUGHT. / AFTER THE DISCO**	-	
Jan 90.	(cd/c/lp) <72635-2/-4/-1> **GOD HELP US**	-	

– Train of thought / Beautiful day / After the disco / Lifespan / Horror of the fire / Podmen / Albert / Burnin' love / Sex drive / . . .The train reprise / Vision of '61.

– compilations, etc. –

| 1984. | (c) Fresh Sounds; <Fresh Tape 104> **RETROSPECTIVE** (1979-1983) | - | |

– studio:- Sex drive / Berliner's night out / Two-week vacation / Can't forget / Special eyes / Sexy singer girl / Age five / She's one / live:- Podman / Lifespan / Celebrity art party / Don't stop (til you get enough) / Pushin' too hard / Woods of love / Time has come today / I only want a date / Casual man.

| 1987. | (lp) Time To Develop; <001> **THE EMBARRASSMENT** | - | |

– (THE EMBARRASSMENT EP tracks) / Rhythm line / Picture women / Special eyes / Jazzface / Age five / Woods of love / Out of town.

| Oct 95. | (d-cd) Bar None; <59> **HEYDAY 1979-1983** | - | |

– Sex drive / Patio set / Celebrity art party / Elizabeth's Montgomery's face / (I'm a) Don Juan / Don't choose the wrong song / Wellsville / Two cars / Careen / Viewmaster / Drive me to the park / Lewis & Clark / D-rings / Chapter 12 / Hip and well read / Death travels west / Rhythm line / Picture women / Special eyes / Jazzface / Age five / Woods of love / Out of town // Berliner's night out / After the disco / Dress like a man / Two-week vacation / The man with extra special eyes / Lifespan / Sound of wasps / Can't forget / Sexy singer girl / Sex drive – Pants down – Gibberish / Dino in the Congo / Godfrey Harold Hardy / D-rings / Chapter 12 / Jazzface / Don't stop till you get enough / Casual man / Immigrant song / She's one of the other kind.

| Mar 01. | (cd) My Pal God; <39> **BLISTER POP** | - | |

– Intro / Podmen / Proof / Time has come today / Oh pretty woman / You're not you anymore / Only want a date / Elizabeth Montgomery's face / Faith healer / Maybe baby / It's like it's what you like / The man makes the clothes / Song for Val / Pushin' too hard / On Broadway / I wanna be your dog / Nothing to eat / No reply / Play / Funtime.

EMBRACE

Formed: Washington, D.C., USA . . . 1985 by legendary hardcore brothers IAN and ALEC MACKAYE, along with MICHAEL HAMPTON, IVOR HANSON, and CHRIS BALD. IAN having left pioneering hardcore outfit, MINOR THREAT, teamed up with his brother, ALEC and the other forementioned members of his erstwhile band, The FAITH, to form EMBRACE. ALEC MACKAYE's old group, had begun around 1983, as a competent, fairly straight down the line hardcore quartet, releasing their debut LP, 'SUBJECT TO CHANGE', the same year. They did not survive for long before they disbanded in name only, and became EMBRACE, their only other release, 'FAITH / VOID' (1995), being a posthumously released shared

LP with hardcore brethren, The VOID. This latter release was aided by the production skills of DON ZIENTARA, who had also twiddled the knobs on EMBRACE's only eponymous LP released by 'Dischord' in '87. Although the group had only one release, and had already spilt by the time of its delivery, it has since become critically acclaimed and a forerunner of the emocore sound. 'EMBRACE' showcased a slower hardcore sound, with a greater emotional depth, but with no less power. After the band's speedy demise, IAN continued to run his trailblazing label, and went on to form, the equally groundbreaking, FUGAZI. HAMPTON also continued his musical whims, forming and disbanding the equally short-term band, ONE LAST WISH. They released one album before getting back together with old pal, HANSON, and BERT QUEIROZ, to form MANIFESTO in the early nineties. A bit of a poppier departure for the former hardcore boys, MANIFESTO released only one LP, the eponymous 'MANIFESTO' in 1991, before taking the customary bow a year later.

Album rating: The Faith: SUBJECT TO CHANGE mini (*6) / Embrace: EMBRACE (*5) / Manifesto: MANIFESTO (*7)

FAITH

MICHAEL HAMPTON – guitar (ex-STATE OF ALERT) / **ALEC MacKAYE** – vocals (ex-UNTOUCHABLES) / **CHRIS BALD** – bass / **IVOR HANSON** – drums

		not iss.	Dischord
Dec 83.	(m-lp) <DIS 11> **SUBJECT TO CHANGE**	-	

– Aware / Say no more / Limitations / No choice / Untitled / Subject to change / More of the same / Slowdown.

– others, etc. –

| Sep 95. | (lp/c/cd) <DIS 87/+C/CD> **THE FAITH / THE VOID split** | - | |

– It's time / Face to face / Trapped / In control / Another victim / What's wrong with me / What you think / Confusion / You're X'd / Nightmare / Don't tell me / In the black / (others by The VOID). <cd+=> – SUBJECT TO CHANGE

EMBRACE

— **IAN MacKAYE** – vocals; repl. ALEC

		Dischord	Dischord
Nov 87.	(lp) <(DIS 24)> **EMBRACE**		

– Give me back / Dance of days / Building / Past / Spoke / Do not consider yourself free / No more pain / I wish I / Said gun / Can't forgive / Money / If I never thought about it / End of a year / Last song. <(re-iss. Jun02 lp/cd+=; DIS 24/+CD)> – Money (alt.take) / Dance of days (alt.take).

— after they split, IAN MacKAYE joined MINOR THREAT (later FUGAZI); HAMPTON formed ONE LAST WISH alongside future FUGAZI team mates; the latter would also form Brit-pop act, MANIFESTO, with IVOR

MANIFESTO

— **MICHAEL HAMPTON** – vocals, guitar / **BERT QUEIROZ** – bass / **IVOR HANSON** – drums

		Fire	Atlantic
Feb 92.	(12"m) (BLAZE 44050) **WALKING BACKWARDS.** / (+2)		
Apr 92.	(cd) (FIRE 33030) <92239> **MANIFESTO**		

– Pattern 26 / Different day / Gravity / E dub / Matter of time / Long time / Down the line / Always / Sugar / Walking backwards.

| Jun 92. | (one-sided-7") (66055) **PATTERN 26** | | - |
| Jul 92. | (one-sided-7") (BLAZE 66056) **GRAVITY** | | - |

— disbanded after above

EPILEPTICS
(see under ⇒ FLUX OF PINK INDIANS)

Roky ERICKSON
(see under ⇒ 13th FLOOR ELEVATORS)

ESSENCE

Formed: Netherlands ... 1984 by frontman/musician HANS DIENER, along with rhythm section JEROEN "JERRY" GEERTSMA and OLAF WILLEMSEN. To describe The ESSENCE as CURE copyists or clones would be an understatement in the extreme, DIENER's ROBERT SMITH-like sound, whether in vox or swirling guitar, made them popular in any place that The CURE wasn't big. These indie CURE-meisters delivered their first single, 'ENDLESS LAKES', for 'Midnight Music' in the summer of 1985, while parent album 'PURITY', hit the shops a few months later. Sophomore set 'A MONUMENT OF TRUST' (1987) featured a surprise Spanish hit single, 'A MIRAGE' (ahmm, 'A Forest', anyone), building up a strong cult reputation with goths in and around mainland Europe and parts of the US; the aforementioned track even hit the charts for Spaniards ESQUEMA in '95. AKKI was to supersede JEROEN for The ESSENCE's third long-player, 'ECSTACY' (1988), while DIENER found new recruits after the 'NOTHING LASTS FOREVER' (1991) album, until their break-up in the mid 90's.

Album rating: PURITY (*5) / A MONUMENT OF TRUST (*6) / ECSTACY (*5) / NOTHING LASTS FOREVER (*4) / GLOW (*4) / DANCING IN THE RAIN" THE BEST OF ESSENCE compilation (*6)

HANS DIENER – vocals, guitar, piano, synthesizer / **JEROEN "JERRY" GEERTSMA** – bass / **OLAF WILLEMSEN** – drums

		Midnight Music	not iss.
Jul 85.	(12"m) (DONG 14) **ENDLESS LAKES. / FROM MY MOUTH / THE SWAYING WIND**		-
Sep 85.	(lp) (CHIME 00.11S) **PURITY**		-

– The last preach / A reflected dream / The cat / The blind / Never mine / Endless lakes / Forever in death / Salivation / The waving girl / Purity / Confusion / From my mouth / The swaying wind. (cd-iss. May88; CHIME 00.11CD) (cd re-iss. Sep95 & Feb01 on 'Anagram'; CDMGRAM 95) <US cd-iss. 1999; same as re-UK>

| Jun 86. | (12"ep) (DONG 24) **THE CAT (remix) / CONFUSION / THE HAPPINESS / THE CAT (extended version)** | | - |
| 1987. | (lp/cd) (CHIME 00.12/+CD) **A MONUMENT OF TRUST** | | - |

– A mirage / Drifting / In tears / Nothing / The waves of death / The happiness / Lollipop / Years of doubt / Fire / The death cell / A monument of trust. (cd re-iss. Sep95 & Feb01 on 'Anagram'+=; CDMGRAM 96) – A mirage (extended). <US cd-iss. 1999+=; same as re-UK>

| Feb 88. | (12"ep) (DONG 33) **A MIRAGE / A MIRAGE (remix). / TRICKED / LOLLIPOP / UN ESPEJISMO (extended version)** | | - |

— **AKKI** – bass; repl. JEROEN

| Oct 88. | (lp/c/cd) (CHIME 00.39 S/C/CD) **ECSTACY** | | - |

– Burned in Heaven / Only for you / Like Christ / Angelic / Ice / The afterworld / So gorgeously / Despair / One more wasted night. (cd+=) – Sleeping / Jump and fall / Understand why.

Oct 88.	(12"m) (DONG 41) **ONLY FOR YOU. / JUMP AND FALL / ANGELIC**		-
Nov 88.	(12"ep) (DONG 40) **A REFLECTED DREAM / SLEEP (IS FOR EVERYONE). / (same tracks by SAD LOVERS AND GIANTS)**		-
1990.	(12"ep/cd-ep) (DONG 64/+CD) **LIKE CHRIST. / TIME / THE WORLD COLLAPSED**		-
1991.	(12"ep/cd-ep) (DONG 69/+CD) **OUT OF GRACE / IN YOUR HEART. / I COULD NEVER TAKE THE PLACE OF YOUR MAN / ICE (live)**		-
Nov 91.	(cd/c/lp) (CHIME 01.14 CD/C/S) **NOTHING LASTS FOREVER**		-

– Separation / How you make me hate / September / Out of grace / Everything / Never let go / Air / Thirtysecondsong / All is empty.

— The ESSENCE were now **HANS** plus **MARK** – keyboards / **JOS** – bass / **GEORGE** – drums

		CNR Music	not iss.
1995.	(cd-s) **GONE**	-	- Dutch
1995.	(cd) **GLOW**	-	- Dutch

– Taking on the world / Gone / Mary my prayer / Right or wrong / Only for you / Up / Crack / Out of grace / The one / Through the years / Bleed.

| 1995. | (cd-s) **TAKING ON THE WORLD / GONE** | - | - Dutch |

— finally disbanded in 1995

– compilations, etc. –

| Aug 94. | (cd) Anagram; (<CDMGRAM 82>) **DANCING IN THE RAIN: THE BEST OF THE ESSENCE** | | 1995 |

– Out of grace / Like Christ / Only for you / The cat / Everything / Dridting / A mirage / In your heart / Time / Forever in death / The waves of death / Burned in Heaven / Endless lakes / Ice / Everything (remix) / U 4 life / Angelic / How you make me hate / A mirage '94 / The afterworld / Thirtysecondsong.

| Sep 94. | (cd-s) Anagram; **A MIRAGE '94 – THE MIXES** | | - |
| Mar 96. | (cd) Anagram; (<CDMGRAM 103>) **ECSTACY / NOTHING LASTS FOREVER** | | 2000 |

ETON CROP

Formed: Kuderstaadt, Amsterdam, Netherlands ... 1979 by songwriter CORNE BOS, ERWIN BLOM, RON BAARS, PETER VERSCHUEREN and ED TUYL (PETER DE KWAASTENIET and SUSIE HONEYMAN were later members). Following a Dutch-only debut 12", 'TIMMY BARKER IS A COWARD', The ETON CROP made their UK debut with 'GAY BOYS ON THE BATTLEFIELD', John Peel lending his vocal support and inviting them on to his Radio One show for a session (subsequently issued on the 'Strange Fruit' imprint). One of the tracks, 'IT'S MY DOG, MAESTRO', served as the title of their inaugural long-player, a surprisingly English sounding (especially the atonal vocals) indie-rock affair lumberingly reminiscent of MARC RILEY & THE CREEPERS or The WEDDING PRESENT. Later that year (1986), the band continued minus HONEYMAN (who later turned up with The MEKONS), signing to 'Ediesta' and releasing mini-set, 'YES PLEASE, BOB'. ETON CROP's final term report came in the shape of a swan song full-set, 'AND THE UNDERWATER MUSIC GOES ON' (1987), basically nothing to write home about you could say.

Album rating: IT'S MY DOG, MAESTRO (*5) / YES PLEASE, BOB mini (*4) / AND THE UNDERWATER MUSIC GOES ON (*4)

ERWIN BLOM – vocals, guitar / **CORNE BOS** – bass / **PETER VERSCHUEREN** – keyboards / **RON BAARS** – guitar / **ED TUYL** – drums

		Plahadima	not iss.
1980.	(7") **TIMMY BARKER IS A COWARD.**	-	- Dutch
1983.	(m-lp) **SIX SILHOUETTE ROMANCES**	-	- Dutch

— **PETER DE KWAASTENIET** – guitar; repl. BAARS

— also **SUSIE HONEYMAN** – violin / **MICHAEL HARDING** – trumpet / **FRANZ VREEKE**

		Bigger Bank	not iss.
May 84.	(12"ep) (BALANCE 1) **GAY BOYS ON THE BATTLEFIELD. / ROGER TROUDMAN / WE DIDN'T SAY ANYTHING**		-

— **ED SEROOS** – drums; repl. HONEYMAN, HARDING + 2 backers

ETON CROP (cont)

	Grunt Grunt A Go Go	not iss.
Jan 86. (lp) (ggagg 2) **IT'S MY DOG, MAESTRO**	☐	-

– It's my dog maestro / Loads of beer / Mind manipulation / Wart on a wanker's hand / You won't get me out in the rain / Get something for doing nothing / Live aid / Boy meets tractor / Harry Nelson Pillsbury / I only want to talk about the weather / Rocking the chessboard.

	Ediesta	not iss.
Nov 86. (12") (CALC 12) **YES PLEASE, BOB.** /	☐	-
Dec 86. (m-lp) (CALCMLP 13) **YES PLEASE, BOB**		
Apr 87. (12"ep) (CALC 20) **A BUNDLE OF BUCKS (FOR A DEAD DOG IS A BARGAIN). / BANANA BATTLE / COLOURLESS IDEAS (SLEEP FURIOUSLY) / PARAFFIN BRAIN**	☐	-
Dec 87. (lp) (CALCLP 33) **AND THE UNDERWATER MUSIC GOES ON**	☐	-

—— BOS + BLOM recruited LEONIEKE 'SPIKE' DAALDER – synthesizer

| 1991. (cd-s) **NOISY TOWN** (mixes; urban shortcut / booming basslines / rowdy rhythms / raw riffs) | - | - Dutch |

—— split some time in 1991; some members formed EC GROOVE SOCIETY

– compilations, etc. –

| Nov 88. (12"ep) Strange Fruit; (SFPS 063) **THE PEEL SESSIONS** (1.10.85) | ☐ | - |

– Cocacolanization / It's my dog, maestro / You won't get me out in the rain / Harry Nelson Pillsbury.

EVEREST THE HARD WAY
(see under ⇒ FIRE ENGINES)

EVERYTHING BUT THE GIRL

Formed: Hull, England ... mid-1982 by ex-Hull university graduates TRACEY THORN (ex-MARINE GIRLS) and BEN WATT. They both had recorded solo efforts ('A DISTANT SHORE' and 'NORTH MARINE DRIVE' respectfully) for indie label 'Cherry Red', before venturing onto 'WEA' (in 1983) subsidiary 'Blanco Y Negro' (run by Geoff Travis & Mike Alway). They almost immediately struck gold, with 'EACH AND EVERY ONE' (1984), making the UK Top 30, while its parent album, 'EDEN', hit the Top 20. A publicly shy, melancholy duo, EBTG blended together light jazz, folk and agitpop, their influences ranging from COLE PORTER to the modern day JOHN MARTYN. The following year's 'LOVE NOT MONEY', however, was a more conventional indie affair which breached the UK Top 10, although the band went for an orchestrated country sound on 'BABY THE STARS SHINE BRIGHT' (1986), having been influenced by America's grassroots music scene while touring there. Thus far, EBTG's career had been grounded in album sales, their loyal student following ensuring a respectable placing for each successive release; no one really expected their tender cover of Danny Whitten's heartbreaking 'I DON'T WANT TO TALK ABOUT IT' to make the Top 3 in summer '88. The attendant album, 'IDLEWILD' (1988), considered by many to be their finest hour, made the Top 20, although no further singles were forthcoming. Employing yet another ensemble of classy musicians, the band cut the more overtly jazzy 'THE LANGUAGE OF LIFE' (1990) at the turn of the decade. The early 90's saw the pair scoring with covers of The Everly Brothers' 'LOVE IS STRANGE' and Simon & Garfunkel's 'THE ONLY LIVING BOY IN NEW YORK', although WATT was still recovering from a rare, life threatening illness (something he later documented in his book). THORN, meanwhile, found a perfect vehicle for her languourous vocal stylings with trip hop pioneers, MASSIVE ATTACK, the singer's contribution resulting in two of the best songs on their 1994 set, 'Protection' i.e. 'Better Things' and the title track. With contributions from such stalwarts as RICHARD THOMPSON, DAVE MATTACKS and the ubiquitous DANNY THOMPSON, 'AMPLIFIED HEART' (1994) was a return to form, showing the duo more willing to experiment with sound and atmosphere. One of the album's tracks, 'MISSING', was given an unlikely remix by house DJ, TODD TERRY; the result was a stunning combination of dancefloor dynamics and raw emotion which captured the imagination of record buyers around the world in late '95 (also a transatlantic Top 5). Suddenly, EBTG were big news, a hip name to drop in dance circles; the following year's 'WALKING WOUNDED' album took the logical next step and paired the duo's stripped down melancholy with cutting edge drum 'n' bass textures. Critically acclaimed by both dance critics and the mainstream rock media, the record became one of the biggest selling EBTG albums to date, spawning two Top 10 singles in 'WRONG' and the title track. BEN and TRACEY were cutting the rug once more with a fresh set of songs courtesy of 1999's 'TEMPERAMENTAL', this critically lambasted bedsit musak for the New Labour yuppie becoming a bit trite for the more discerning rock ear. • **Songwriters:** Most written by duo or individually, except the covers; NIGHT AND DAY (Cole Porter) / KID (Pretenders) / ALFIE (hit; Cilla Black) / DOWNTOWN TRAIN (Tom Waits) / I FALL TO PIECES (Patsy Cline) / TAKE ME (Womack And Womack) / ON MY MIND (?) / NO PLACE LIKE HOME (from 'Wizard Of Oz') / LOVE IS STRANGE (Everly Brothers) / TOUGHER THAN THE REST (Bruce Springsteen) / TIME AFTER TIME (Cyndi Lauper) / ALISON (Elvis Costello) / MY HEAD IS MY ONLY HOUSE UNLESS IT RAINS (Captain Beefheart) / THESE DAYS (Jackson Browne) / CORCOVADO (Antonio Carlos Jobim) / SINGLE contains a sample of Tim Buckley's (SONG TO THE SIREN). TRACEY THORN solo:- FEMME FATALE (Velvet Underground). • **Trivia:** EVERYTHING BUT THE GIRL was the name of a local second hand store in Hull.

Album rating: Tracey Thorn: A DISTANT SHORE mini (*6) / Ben Watt: NORTH MARINE DRIVE (*6) / Everything But The Girl: EDEN (*7) / LOVE NOT MONEY (*5) / BABY, THE STARS SHINE BRIGHT (*5) / IDLEWILD (*6) / THE LANGUAGE OF LIFE (*5) / WORLDWIDE (*5) / AMPLIFIED HEART (*6) / HOME MOVIES – THE BEST OF EVERYTHING BUT THE GIRL compilation (*8) / WALKING WOUNDED (*7) / TEMPERAMENTAL (*4) / LIKE THE DESERTS MISS THE RAIN compilation (*7)

TRACEY THORN

	Cherry Red	not iss.
Aug 82. (m-lp) (MRED 35) **A DISTANT SHORE**	☐	-

– Smalltown girl / Simply couldn't care / Seascape / Femme fatale / Dreamy / Plain sailing / New opened eyes / Too happy. (cd-iss. Jun87 + Aug93; MRED 35CD)

| Dec 82. (7") (CHERRY 53) **PLAIN SAILING. / GOODBYE JOE** | ☐ | - |

BEN WATT

	Cherry Red	not iss.
Jun 81. (7"m) (CHERRY 25) **CANT. / AUBADE / TOWER OF SILENCE**	☐	-
Apr 82. (12"ep; by BEN WATT & ROBERT WYATT) (12CHERRY 36) **SUMMER INTO WINTER**	☐	-

– Walter and John / Aquamarine / Slipping slowly / Another conversation with myself / A girl in winter.

| Feb 83. (7") (CHERRY 55) **SOME THINGS DON'T MATTER. / ON BOX HILL** | ☐ | - |
| Feb 83. (lp) (BRED 40) **NORTH MARINE DRIVE** | ☐ | - |

– On Box hill / Some things don't matter / Lucky one / Empty bottles / North Marine Drive / Waiting like mad / Thirst for knowledge / Long time no sea / You're gonna make me lonesome when you go. (cd-iss. Jun87 + Jul93 w/ SUMMER INTO WINTER EP; BRED 40CD)

EVERYTHING BUT THE GIRL

TRACEY THORN (b.26 Sep'62) – vocals, guitar / **BEN WATT** (b. 6 Dec'62, London, England) – vocals, guitar, piano

| Jun 82. (7"m) (CHERRY 37) **NIGHT AND DAY. / FEELING DIZZY / ON MY MIND** | ☐ | - |

(12"-iss.Dec85; 12CHERRY 37) (cd-s-iss.Mar89; CDCHERRY 37) (re-iss. Jul93)

—— with **SIMON BOOTH** – guitar (of WORKING WEEK, ex-WEEKEND) / **CHUCHO MERCHAN** – double bass / **CHARLES HAYWARD** – drums / **BOSCO DE OLIVEIRA** – percussion / **PETER KING** – alto saxophone / **NIGEL NASH** – tenor saxophone / **DICK PEARCE** – flugel trumpet

	Blanco Y Negro	Sire
Apr 84. (7") (NEG 1) **EACH AND EVERY ONE. / LAUGH YOU OUT THE HOUSE**	28	-

(12"+=) (NEG 1T) – Never could have been worse.

| Jun 84. (lp/c/cd) (BYN/+C 2)(<240-395-2>) **EDEN** | 14 | ☐ |

– Each and every one / Bittersweet / Tender blue / Another bridge / The spice of life / The dustbowl / Crabwalk / Even so / Frost and fire / Fascination / I must confess / Soft touch. (US-title 'EVERYTHING BUT THE GIRL'; 7599-25212-1>

| Jul 84. (7") (NEG 3) **MINE. / EASY AS SIN** | 58 | - |

(12"+=) (NEG 3T) – Gun cupboard love.

| Sep 84. (7") (NEG 6) **NATIVE LAND. / RIVERBED DRY** | 73 | - |

(12"+=) (NEG 6T) – Don't you go.
(12"++=) (NEG 6TX) – Easy as sin / Gun cupboard love.

—— now with **NEIL SCOTT** – guitars / **PHIL MOXHAM** – bass (ex-The GIST ex-YOUNG MARBLE GIANTS) / **JUNE MILES KINGSTON** – drums, vocals (ex-MODETTES, ex-FUN BOY THREE) and the wind section

| Mar 85. (7") (NEG 7) **WHEN ALL'S WELL. / HEAVEN HELP ME** | ☐ | - |

(12"+=) (NEG 7T) – Kid.

| Apr 85. (lp/c/cd) (BYN 3/+C)(<240-657-2>) **LOVE NOT MONEY** | 10 | ☐ |

– When all's well / Ugly little dreams / Shoot me down / Are you trying to be funny / Sean / Ballad of the times / Anytown / This love (not for sale) / Trouble and strife / Angel. (c+=) – Heaven help me / Kid.

| May 85. (7"m) (NEG 15) **ANGEL / PIGEONS IN THE ATTIC ROOM / CHARMLESS, CALLOW WAYS** | ☐ | - |

(12"+=) (NEG 15T) – Easy as sin.

—— now **BEN + TRACEY** used new session people below plus an orchestra **CARA TIVEY** – keyboards / **MICKEY HARRIS** – bass / **PETER KING** – alto sax / **ROBERT PETERS** – drums (ex-DANGEROUS GIRLS)

| Jul 86. (7") (NEG 21) **COME ON HOME. / DRAINING THE BAR** | 44 | - |

(12"+=) (NEG 21T) – I fall to pieces.

| Aug 86. (lp/c/cd) (BYN/+C 9)(<240-966-2>) **BABY, THE STARS SHINE BRIGHT** | 22 | ☐ |

– Come on home / Don't leave me behind / A country mile / Cross my heart / Don't let the teardrops rust your shining heart / Careless / Sugar Finney / Come hell or high water / Fighting talk / Little Hitler.

| Sep 86. (7") (NEG 23) **DON'T LEAVE ME BEHIND. / ALFIE** | 72 | - |

(12"+=) (NEG 23T) – Where's the playground, Susie?.
(d7"+=) (NEG 23F) – Come on home (acoustic) / Always on my mind (live).

| Feb 87. (7") **DON'T LEAVE ME BEHIND. / DRAINING THE BAR** | - | - |

—— **BEN and TRACEY** now with **PETER KING / IAN FRASER** – tenor saxophone / **STEVE PEARCE** – bass / **JAMES McMILLAN** – trumpet / **DAMON BUTCHER** – piano, synth.

| Feb 88. (7") (NEG 30) **THESE EARLY DAYS. / DYED IN THE GRAIN** | 75 | - |

(12"+=) (NEG 30T) – No place like home.
(12"ep+=/3"cd-ep+=) (NEG 30TX) – ('A'original demo) / Another day another dollar.

| Mar 88. (lp/c/cd) (BYN/+C 14)(<242-288-2>) **IDLEWILD** | 13 | ☐ |

– Love is here where I live / These early days / I always was your girl / Oxford Street / The night I heard Caruso sing / Goodbye Sunday / Shadow on a harvest moon / Blue moon rose / Tears all over town / Lonesome for a place I know / Apron strings. (re-iss. Jul88, hit UK No.21- lp/c/cd; BYN/+C 16)(243-840-2) (+=) – I don't want to talk about it. (re-iss. 2nd version cd Nov94)

Mar 88. (7") *(NEG 33)* **I ALWAYS WAS YOUR GIRL. / HANG OUT THE FLAGS** [ ] [-]
(12"+=) *(NEG 33T)* – Home from home.
(3"cd-s++=) *(NEG 33CD)* – Almost blue.
Jun 88. (7") *(NEG 34)* **I DON'T WANT TO TALK ABOUT IT. / OXFORD STREET** [3] [ ]
(12"+=) *(NEG 34T)* – ('A'instrumental) / Shadow on a harvest moon.
(3"cd-s+=) *(NEG 34CD)* – ('A'instrumental) / Come on home.
Sep 88. (7") *(NEG 37)* **LOVE IS HERE WHERE I LIVE. / LIVING ON HONEYCOMB** [ ] [-]
(12"+=) *(NEG 37T)* – How about me?.
(3"cd-s++=) *(NEG 37CD)* – Each and every one.
Dec 88. (7") *(NEG 39)* **THESE EARLY DAYS (Dave Bascombe remix). / DYED IN THE GRAIN** [ ] [-]
(12"+=) *(NEG 39T)* – No place like home.
(3"cd-s++=) *(NEG 39CD)* – Another day another dollar.

— duo now with **OMAR HAKIM** – drums / **JOHN PATITUCCI** – bass / **LARRY WILLIAMS** – synth, piano / **LENNY CASTRO** – percussion / **MICHAEL LANDAU** – guitar / etc.

Blanco Y Negro | Atlantic

Jan 90. (7"/c-s) *(NEG 40/+C)* **DRIVING. / ME AND BOBBY D** [54] [-]
(12"+=/cd-s+=) *(NEG 40 T/CD)* – Downtown train / ('A'extended).
(ext.12"gf+=) *(NEG 40TG)* – Easy as sin / I don't want to talk about it.
Feb 90. (cd)(lp/c) *(246-260-2)(BYN/+C 21) <82057>* **THE LANGUAGE OF LIFE** [10] [77]
– Driving / Get back together / Meet me in the morning / Take me / Me and Bobby D / The language of life / Imagining America / My baby don't love me / Letting love go / The road. *(re-iss. cd Feb95)*
Mar 90. (7"/c-s) *(NEG 44/+C)* **TAKE ME. / DRIVING (acoustic)** [ ] [-]
(12"+=/cd-s+=) *(NEG 44 T/CD)* – ('A'-Hamblin remix).

— now with **GEOFF GISCOYNE and STEVE PEARCE** – bass / **DICK OATTS** – saxophone / **RALPH SALMINS** – drums, percussion

Aug 91. (7"/c-s) *(NEG 51/+C)* **OLD FRIENDS. / APRON STRINGS (live)** [ ] [-]
(12"+=) *(NEG 51T)* – Politics aside (instrumental).
(cd-s+=) *(NEG 51CD)* – Back to the old house (live).
Sep 91. (cd)(lp/c) *(9031-75308-2)(BYN/+C 25)* **WORLDWIDE** [29] [ ]
– Old friends / Understanding / You lift me up / Talk to me like the sea / British summertime / Twin cities / Frozen river / One place / Politics aside / Boxing and pop music / Feel alright. *(re-iss. cd Feb92 +=; 9031-76583-2)* – Love is strange.
Nov 91. (7"/c-s) *(NEG 53/+C)* **TWIN CITIES (Wildwood remix). / MEET ME IN THE MORNING (live)** [ ] [-]
(12"+=) *(NEG 53T)* – ('A'-The green plains a cappella mix). (cd-s++=) *(NEG 53CD)* – Mine.
Feb 92. (7"ep/c-ep/12"ep/cd-ep) *(NEG 54/+C/T/CD)* **COVERS EP** [13] [-]
– Love is strange / Tougher than the rest / Time after time / Alison. (above issued in the US as 'ACOUSTIC' w/ extra; *7567-82395-2>*
Apr 93. (7"ep/c-ep/12"ep/cd-ep) *(NEG 62/+C/T/CD)* **THE ONLY LIVING BOY IN NEW YORK EP** [42] [-]
– The only living boy in New York / Gabriel / Birds / Horses in the room.
May 93. (cd)(lp/c) *(4509-92319-2)(BYN/+C 29)* **HOME MOVIES – THE BEST OF EVERYTHING BUT THE GIRL** (compilation) [5] [ ]
– Each and every one / Another bridge / Fascination / Native land / Come on home / Cross my heart / Apron strings / I don't want to talk about it / The night I heard Caruso sing / Driving / Imagining America / Understanding / Twin cities / Love is strange / I didn't know I was looking for love / The only living boy in New York.
Jun 93. (7"ep/c-ep/cd-ep) *(NEG 64/+C/CD)* **I DIDN'T KNOW I WAS LOOKING FOR LOVE EP** [72] [-]
– I didn't know I was looking for love / My head is my only house unless it rains / Political science / A piece of my mind.

— with **DAVE MATTACKS** – drums / **DANNY THOMPSON** – double bass (both ex-FAIRPORT CONVENTION) / **MARTIN DITCHAM** – percussion / (guests) **RICHARD THOMPSON** – guitar / **PETER KING** – alto sax / **KATE ST.JOHN** – cor anglais

May 94. (7"ep/c-ep/cd-ep) *(NEG 69/+C/CD)* **THE ROLLERCOASTER EP** [65] [-]
– Rollercoaster / Straight back to you / Lights of Te Touan / I didn't know I was looking for love (demo).
Jun 94. (cd/c) *(4509-96482-2/-4) <82605>* **AMPLIFIED HEART** [20] [46]
– Rollercoaster / Troubled mind / I don't understand anything / Walking to you / Get me / Missing / Two star / We walk the same line / 25th December / Disenchanted. *(re-iss. Nov95 & Jul00; 0603-10453-2)*
Aug 94. (c-ep/cd-ep) *(NEG 71 C/CD1)* **MISSING – THE LIVE EP** [69] [-]
– Missing / Each and every one (live) / I don't want to talk about it (live) / These days (live).
(12"ep/cd-ep) *(NEG 71 T/CD2)* **THE (FULL) REMIX EP** – ('A'side) / ('A'-Chris & James remix) / ('A'-Little Joey remix) / ('A'-Ultramarine remix).
Oct 95. (c-s) *(NEG 84C) <87124>* **MISSING (Todd Terry club mix) / ('A'-Amplified Heart album mix)** [3] [2] Jul95
(cd-s+=) *(NEG 84CD)* – ('A'-radio edit) / ('A'-Rockin' blue mix) / ('A'-Chris & James full on club mix) / ('A'-Todd Terry's piece).
(12") *(NEG 84T)* – (all above except 'B'side).

Virgin | Atlantic

Apr 96. (c-s/12"/cd-s) *(VS C/T/CDT 1577)* **WALKING WOUNDED (mixes; Spring Heel Jack / Omni Trio / Dave Wallace)** [6] [-]
May 96. (cd/c/lp) *(CD/TC+/V 2803) <82912>* **WALKING WOUNDED** [4] [37]
– Before today / Wrong / Single / The heart remains a child / Walking wounded / Flipside / Big deal / Mirrorball / Good cop bad cop / Wrong (Todd Terry remix) / Walking wounded (Omni Trio remix). *(lp re-iss. Apr01 on 'Simply Vinyl'; SVLP 321)*
Jun 96. (c-s/12"/cd-s) *(VS C/T/CDT 1589) <87059>* **WRONG (mixes; original / Todd Terry / Deep Dish / Mood II Swing)** [8] [68] May96
Sep 96. (c-s) *(VSC 1600)* **SINGLE / CORCOVADO** [20] [-]
(cd-s+=) *(VSCDT 1600)* – ('A'-Photek remix) / ('A'-Brad Wood Memphis remix).
(12"+=) *(VST 1600)* – (above except 'Corcovado') / Wrong (Todd Terry remix).
Feb 97. (c-s/cd-s) *(VSC/+DT 1624)* **BEFORE TODAY (mixes; album / Adam F / Darren Emerson 1 & 2 / Dilinja / Chicane)** [25] [-]

— in Sep'98, EBTG were credited on the DEEP DISH hit single, 'The Future Of The Future (Stay Gold)'.

Sep 99. (c-s/cd-s) *(VSC/+DT 1742)* **FIVE FATHOMS / FIREWALL** [27] [ ]
(12"/cd-s) *(VST/VSCDX 1742)* – ('A'mixes).
Sep 99. (cd/c/lp) *(CD/TC+/V 2892) <83214>* **TEMPERAMENTAL** [16] [65]
– Five fathoms / Low tide of the night / Blame / Hatfield 1980 / Temperamental / Compression / Downhill racer / Lullaby of clubland / No difference / Future of the future (stay gold).
Dec 99. (12"/cd-s) *(VST/VSCDT 1752)* **BLAME (mixes; album / Grooverider Jeep dub / Fabio / J Majik VIP)** [ ] [-]
Feb 00. (c-s/12") *(VSC/+T 1761)* **TEMPERAMENTAL / (DJ Spen & Karizmo mix) / (Ralph Rosario mix)** [72] [-]
(cd-s+=) *(VSCT/+D 1761)* – ('A'-CD-Rom).
(cd-s) *(VSCDX 1761)* – ('A'side) / (Hex Hector mix) / (Amanda Project mix).

V.C. | not iss.

Jan 01. (c-s/cd-s; as EBTG vs. SOUL VISION) *(VCR C/D 78)* **TRACEY IN MY ROOM / (Lazy Dog bootleg mix)** [34] [-]
(12"+=) *(VCRT 78)* – ('A'-Lazy Dog bootleg vocal & dub).

– compilations, etc. –

Oct 96. (cd/c) *Blanco Y Negro; (0630 16637-2/-4)* **THE BEST OF EVERYTHING BUT THE GIRL** [23] [ ]
Nov 96. (c-s) *Blanco Y Negro; (NEG 99C)* **DRIVING (remix) /** [36] [-]
(cd-s) *(NEG 99CD1)* – ('A'remixes).
(cd-s) *(NEG 99CD2)* – ('A'remixes).
Dec 01. (12") *Cosmic Flux; (EBTG 1)* **TEMPERAMENTAL** [ ] [-]
Nov 02. (cd/c) *Virgin; (CDV/TCV 2966) / E.M.I.; <542616>* **LIKE THE DESERTS MISS THE RAIN** [58] [ ]
– My head is my only house unless it rains / Rollercoaster / Corcovado / Each and every one / Before today (Chicane remix) / Mine / Protection / Single / Tracey in my room (Lazy Dog bootleg vocal mix) / Missing (Todd Terry mix) / Almost blue / No difference / Cross my heart / Mirrorball / Piece of my mind / Walking wounded.

the EX

Formed: Amsterdam, Netherlands ... 1977 by G.W. SOK and TERRIE HESSELS. Over the years, The EX brought in a sizeable cast of musicians and singers to complement each release. The first of these, 'DISTURBING DOMESTIC PEACE' (1980), found its way to British shores via import where it was playlisted by Radio One DJ, John Peel. This agit-prop punk collective were finally let loose on a UK label in 1984 courtesy of a shared EP, 'RED DANCE PACKAGE' with ALERTA. A brief stint on the 'Ron Johnson' imprint (with the double 7" EP, 'THE SPANISH REVOLUTION – 1936'), paved the way for the EX to set up their own self-titled indie late in 1987. Always ready to experiment with various musical genres, the left-wing musical activists subsequently worked with SONIC YOUTH's LEE RANALDO and THURSTON MOORE, while on 1990's 'DEAD FISH' set, they were produced by JON LANGFORD of The MEKONS. That year's 'STONE STAMPERS SONG' was adapted from composer, KURT TUCHOLSKY, the band also working with avant-garde violinist, TOM CORA on subsequent collaborative albums, 'SCRABBLING AT THE DOCK' (1991) and 'SHRUG THEIR SHOULDERS' (1993).

Album rating: DISTURBING DOMESTIC PEACE (*5) / HISTORY IS WHAT'S HAPPENING (*5) / TUMULT (*5) / BLUEPRINTS FOR A BLACKOUT (*5) / POKKEHERRIE (*6) / THE SPANISH REVOLUTION 1936 double-7"EP (*7) / TOO MANY COWBOYS (*5) / HANDS UP YOU'RE FREE (*5) / AURAL GUERILLA (*5) / JOGGERS AND SMOGGERS (*4) / DEAD FISH (*4) / SCRABBLING AT THE LOCK (*5) / SHRUG THEIR SHOULDERS (*4) / MUDBIRD SHIVERS (*4) / INSTANT (*5)

G.W. SOK – vocals / **TERRIE HESSELS** – guitar / **BASZ** – bass / **OME GUERT** – drums

Verrecords | not iss.

1980. (7"ep) *(EX 001)* **ALL CORPSES SMELL THE SAME EP** [-] [-] Dutch
1980. (7"flexi) *(EX 002)* **NEW HORIZONS IN RETAILING** [-] [-] Dutch
1980. (lp) *(EX 005)* **DISTURBING DOMESTIC PEACE** [-] [-] Dutch
– The sky is blue again / Map / Outlook-army / Sucking pig / Sense of tumour / Meanwhile / Rules / Squatalong / Warning-shot / New wars / Introduction / Human car / Punk / Horse. *(with free live-7") (UK cd-iss. Jun94 on 'Konkurrent'; EX 004-005D)*
Apr 81. (7") *(EX 006)* **WAR IS OVER (WEAPONS FOR EL SALVADOR). / DUST / NEW WARS II** [-] [-] Dutch
Jun 81. (7"flexi) *(EX 007)* **CONSTITUTIONAL STATE** [-] [-] Dutch

— **WIM** – drums; repl. OME

More DPM | not iss.

1982. (lp) **HISTORY IS WHAT'S HAPPENING** [ ] [-] Dutch
– Six of one and half a dozen of the other / Barricades / Life line / Machinery / E.M. why / Moving pictures / Shoes / Watch-dogs / Dutch disease / Blessed box at the back-seat / Who pays / Strong & muscled / Grey / Equals only / H'wood – W'ton / Sports / $ / Pep talk / Attacked / 148.

— over the next decade or so, **G.W. SOK + HESSELS** added **KARTIN BORNFELD + SABIEN WITTEMAN** – drums / **JOS KLEY** – vocals / **JOKE LAARMAN + LUC KLASSEN** – bass / **DOLF PLANTEYDT + TOM GREENE** – guitar / **WINEKE T. HART** – violin / **KEES VANDEN HAAK** – saxophone

Sneeleeer | not iss.

Jun 83. (7"ep) **GONNA ROB THE SPERMBANK** [-] [-] Dutch
– Soldier toy / etc.

C.N.T. | not iss.

Feb 84. (12"ep) *(CNT 017)* **RED DANCE PACKAGE** (shared w/ ALERTA) [ ] [-]
– EX:- Crap rap / Long live the aged / ALERTA:- Perk avenue / Violet days.

V.G.Z. | not iss.

Feb 84. (7"box) *(EX 010-013)* **DIGNITY OF LABOUR** [ ] [-]
– Sucked out Cnucked out (parts 1-8). *(cd-iss. Aug95 on 'Konkurrent'; EX 010-013D)*

F.A.I. | not iss.

Nov 83. (lp) *(EX 014)* **TUMULT** [-] [-] Dutch
– Bouquet of barbed wire / Fear / Hunt the hunters / Survival of the fattest / Red musak / Happy thoughts / Well-known soldier / Black and white statements / Squat! / Same old news / F.U.N.E.I.D.Y. / O.S.L. (new schvienhunt league) / Island race. *(UK-iss.May93 on 'Konkurrent'; EX 14D) <US cd-iss. 1994 on 'Fist Puppet'; 19>*

the EX (cont)

		Pig Brother	not iss.

Apr 84. (lp) *(EX 019)* **BLUEPRINTS FOR A BLACKOUT**
– Streetcars named Desire – Animal harmonies / Blueprints for a blackout / Rabble with a cause / Requiem for a rip-off / Pleased to meet you / Goodbuy to you / Swim / Boo hoo / U.S. hole / (Not) 2B continued / Grimm stories / Plague to survive / Rise of the Dutch republic / Kidnap connection / Fire and ice / Jack Frost is innocent / Love you till eh / Food on 45 / Scrub that scum. *(cd-iss. May93 on 'Konkurrel-Ex'; EX 19D) <US cd-iss. 1994 on 'Fist Puppet'; 13>*

	Pockabilly	not iss.

Nov 85. (d-lp) *(EX 024)* **POKKEHERRIE**
– Nurse / Soviet threat / Mmm crisis / 1,000,000 ashtrays / Rock / White liberals / Everything we never wanted / Friendly neighbors / Hit the headlines / Rumours of music (the original soundtrack). *(cd-iss. Aug95 on 'Konkurrel'; EX 024D)*

	Ron Johnson	not iss.

Jul 86. (d7"ep) *(ZRON 11)* **THE SPANISH REVOLUTION – 1936**
– They shall not pass / Al Carmela / People again / E tron Bundano. *(re-iss. Jan89 & Nov97 on 'Ex'; EX 028-029) (d-cd-s iss.Nov00 on 'Alternative Tentacles'; <(VIRUS 253)>*

	Mordam	not iss.

Jul 87. (d-lp) (5) **TOO MANY COWBOYS**
– Red and black / White shirts / Adversity / People again / Knock / Hands up! you're free / Ignorance / Butter or bombs / Dumbo / How can one sell the air / Business as usual / Olympigs / Choice / Job / Stupid / Oops / No fear / Vivisection / Piece of paper / They shal not pass. *<US cd-iss. 1994 on 'Fist Puppet'; 19>*

	Red	not iss.	
	Ex	– Dutch Homestead	

1987. (c) **LIVE IN WROCLAW** (live)

Apr 88. (lp) *(EX 035) <HMS 116>* **HANDS UP! YOU'RE FREE** ... Sep88
(compilation of John Peel sessions)

Jul 88. (lp) *(EX 036) <HMS 115>* **AURAL GUERRILLA**
– Headache by numbers / Fashionation / 2.2 / Carcass / Welcome to the asylum / Meanwhile at McDonna's / Shooting party / Evolution(?) / A motorbike in Afrika / Godgloeiendeteringklootzat. *<cd-iss. 1994 on 'Fist Puppet'; 21>*

	Ex	Fist Puppet

Oct 89. (d-lp/d-cd) *(EX 040/041) <05>* **JOGGERS & SMOGGERS** ... 1990
– Humm (the full house mumble) / At the gate / Pigs and scales / Coughing / Morning star / The wall has ears / Invitation to the dance / Tightly stretched / Ask the prisoner / To be clear / Gentlemen / Make that call / Buzzword medley / Shopping street / Crackle engines vrop vrop / Greetings from Urbania / Wired / Got everything? / Waarom niet / Courtyard / Burst! crack! split! / Brickbat / Hieronymus / Nosey Parker / People who venture / Watch the driver / Let's get sceptical / Tin gods / State of freedom / Provisionally untitled / Kachun-K pschuh / Early bird's worm / Catkin / Upstairs with Picasso.

May 90. (7") *(EX 043)* **STONE STAMPERS SONG.** /
Jun 90. (12"ep/cd-ep) *(EX 044/+CD)* **DEAD FISH EP**
– Elvis & I / White liberals / Blah blah / Mousetrap / Dead fish / No more cigars.

— In 1990, the EX also collaborated with the DOG FACED HERMANS on a cassette-only release, 'TREAT'.

Mar 91. (7") *(EX)* **SLIMY TOAD JAKE'S CAFE.** /
Mar 92. (lp/cd; The EX / TOM CORA) *(EX 051/+CD)* **SCRABBLING AT THE LOCK**
– State of shock / Hidegen fujnak a szelek / King commie / Crusoe / The flute's tale / A door / Propadada / Batium / Total preparation / 1993 / Fire and ice / Sukaina. *above was a collaboration with violin player* **TOM CORA**

May 92. (7") **THIS SONG IS IN ENGLISH.** /
(above issued on 'Palber')

Jul 92. (12") *(EX 066)* **EUROCONFUSION.** /
Sep 93. (cd; The EX / TOM CORA) *(EX 57CD)* **SHRUG THEIR SHOULDERS**
– Dere gellyor dere / The big black / What's the story / Lamp lady / One-liner from China / Everything & me / New clear daze / Oh puckerlips now / Empty V / Hickwall / War OD / Untitled. *(re-iss. Feb94 as 'AND THE WEATHERMEN SHRUG THEIR SHOULDERS' on 'Fist Puppet'; 15)*

Aug 95. (cd) *(EX 060D)* **MUDBIRD SHIVERS**
– Thunderstruck blues / Only if you want 3 / Ret Roper / Embarrassment / House carpenter / Newsense / Former reporter / Shore thing / Things most people think / Audible bacillus / Hunt hat.

Nov 95. (d-cd; The EX & GUESTS) *(EX 063-064D)* **INSTANT**
– If the hat fits the suit / Pu hyun hwa / Kloptimog twist / Baars vs. Karakeit / Keng lil surf / Duo triptych too / Lip up, stump / So low, solex? / Skoplje bop / Buildance / Bratunac / Horsemeal / Expoobident / Slow sleeper / Duo loom / Te-au-o-tonga // Travel on, poor Bob / What inflexibility?! / Bon-go tell you git-la-la / Duo variola / Meanwhile on in Ozone street / Smuiger / Rusticles / Atoll / Exile o'phonics / Danse maudit / Knit, knack & zoom / Oh muted foghorn / Duo tonebone & hitgit / The turtle the hare / Karreman's last measure / Thereweresonicbangsinthesong ...

	Touch & Go	Touch & Go

Oct 98. (cd) *(<TG 198>)* **STARTERS & ALTERNATORS**
– Frenzy / Let's panic later / I.O.U. (nought) / Art of losing / It's a sin / Two struck by the moon / Mother / Bee coz / Lump sum insomnia / Wildebeast / Nem ugy van most.

– others, etc. –

Aug 95. (12"ep) *Moonroof; <50015>* **WE MUST GO FREE**

EXPENDABLES (see under ⇒ CLARKSON, Jay)

EXPLODING WHITE MICE

Formed: Adelaide, Australia ... January 1985 by PAUL GILCHRIST, JEFF STEPHENS and GILES BARROW, the trio subsequently being joined by ANDY McQUEEN and CRAIG RODDA (the latter replaced by DAVID BUNNEY during initial recordings). Taking their musical cue from such veteran US punk icons as MC5, The STOOGES and the RAMONES, The EXPLODING WHITE MICE played muscular trash-rock in the best Australian tradition, debuting with that year's 'A NEST OF VIPERS', a mini-set of half covers/half original material that was given a UK release the following year. Preceding the HAPPY MONDAYS by a few years, the EWM dusted down John Kongos' 'HE'S GONNA STEP ON YOU AGAIN' for release as a single. In 1988, they delivered their first full-set, 'BRUTE FORCE & IGNORANCE', JACK JACOMOS subsequently coming in for BARROW shortly after. Despite a limited audience in the homeland and virtually no interest in Britain, the 'MICE received a sympathetic reaction in Germany where they released two further sets, an eponymous(e) partly live affair in 1990 and 'COLLATERAL DAMAGE' in '92.

Album rating: A NEST OF VIPERS (*5) / BRUTE FORCE AND IGNORANCE (*6) / EXPLODING WHITE MICE (*6) / COLLATERAL DAMAGE (*5) / WE WALK ALONE (*4)

PAUL GILCHRIST – vocals / **JEFF STEPHENS** – guitar, vocals / **GILES BARROW** – guitar, vocals / **ANDY McQUEEN** – bass, vocals / **DAVID BUNNEY** – drums; repl. RODDA

	Big Time	not iss.

May 86. (m-lp) *(BTA 010)* **A NEST OF VIPERS**
– Burning red / Bad little woman / Let the kids dance / Pipeline / Your claws / Dangerous. *(Australian-release 1985 on 'Greasy Pop'; GPR 115) (German-iss.1987 on 'Normal'+=; NORMAL 87)* – He's gonna step on you again / Blaze of glory.

1987. (7") *(GRP 128)* **HE'S GONNA STEP ON YOU AGAIN.** / **BLAZE OF GLORY**

	Festival	– Austra not iss.

1988. (7"red) *(K 539)* **FEAR (LATE AT NIGHT).** / **WITHOUT WARNING** ... – Austra
1988. (lp) *(L 38912)* **BRUTE FORCE AND IGNORANCE** ... – Austra
– Fear (late at night) / Goodbye gravity / Worry about nothing / Verbal abuse / The wheel / Surfing in a dust storm / Breakdown No.2 / Bury me / Uninvited / Sea of justice / Hit in the face / When I get off / Without warning. *(German-iss.on 'Normal'+=; NORMAL 88)* – A NEST OF VIPERS

JACK JACOMOS – guitar; repl. BARROW

	Normal	N.K.V.D.

Jul 90. (lp/cd) *(NORMAL 119/+CD)* **EXPLODING WHITE MICE** (some live)
– Sleepwalk / Intuition / Real tough guy / Do the crunch / You're losing me / I just want my fun / Misunderstood / Ain't it sad / Verbal abuse / Meet the creeper / Univited / Bangkok / King of the surf / Dangerous / First time is the best time. *(cd+=)* – Do the crunch.

— now a trio of **STEPHENS, McQUEEN + BUNNEY**

1992. (lp/cd) *(NORMAL 144/+CD) <NKVD 5>* **COLLATERAL DAMAGE** ... – German
– And stay out / Enemies / In your eyes / Imaginary world / Human garbage / Frozen alive / Shadow in the sky / Everybody's waiting / Empty T.V. / This is the news / When she walks / Falling on all sides / Tooth and nail / Hate mail.

	Au-Go-Go	not iss.

1994. (cd) *(ANDA 172)* **WE WALK ALONE** ... – Austra

— split after above

– compilations, etc. –

May 02. (cd) *Subway; <332>* **WE WALK ALONE**

EYELESS IN GAZA

Formed: based- London, England ... early 80's by MARTYN BATES and PETE BECKER. Taking their moniker from the Aldous Huxley novel of the same name, EYELESS IN GAZA signed to independent label, 'Cherry Red', releasing their debut album, 'PHOTOGRAPHS AS MEMORIES', in 1981. Definitely something of an acquired taste, the duo's wailing, often unintelligible vocals and repetitive, minimalist musical constructs nevertheless attracted a cult following among the post-punk fraternity. Whether utilising pulsing electronics or a more conventional alternative rock format, the material was consistently experimental and its creators nothing if not prolific; a follow-up set, 'CAUGHT IN FLUX' appeared later in '81 while the Norwegian-only set, 'PALE HANDS I LOVED SO WELL', followed in '82. The former featured some brooding avant-pop numbers, namely 'SKELETAL FRAMEWORK', 'SCALE AMISS' and 'ROSE PETAL KNOT', the record buyer also treated to a free 12" EP which included arguably their finest moment, 'STILL AIR'. A further two sets, 'DRUMMING THE BEATING HEART' and 'RUST RED SEPTEMBER' were released over the course of the next year before the group took an extended sabbatical from the recording front. During this period, EIG managed to squeeze out two 45's, the darkly romantic 'SUNBURSTS IN' and 'WELCOME NOW', the latter featuring guest drummer DAVE RUFFY (of AZTEC CAMERA). They returned in 1986 with JOBY PALMER, the new sticksman making his debut on 'BACK FROM THE RAINS'. Following the addition of singer, ELIZABETH S., EYELESS IN GAZA resurfaced as a trio in 1993 with the 'FABULOUS LIBRARY' album, subsequently touring with performance poet, ANNE CLARK. Duly signed to Belgian label, 'Antler', the cream of the band's 'Cherry Red' recordings were released as 'ORANGE ICE AND WAX CRAYONS' in 1992. The previous decade has also seen BATES juggling a prolific solo career with several albums – beginning with the 1982 mini-set, 'LETTERS WRITTEN' – under his belt. In the early 90's he teamed up with ex-PRIMITIVES member STEVE DULLAHAN to form short-lived project, HUNGRY I, the duo covering R.E.M.'s 'TWO STEPS FORWARD', in '91. The rest of the 90's saw BATES moving in different musical circles, a plethora of albums under various guises (including DRIFT with MICK HARRIS) saw the man as busy as ever, although it would be his solo work that took precedence. Of these, 'CHAMBER MUSIC

1' in 1994 was the most appealing, the record set to the work of James Joyce (c. 1902) and delivered in an ambient-esque form. Poetry and poets seemed to be generally involved with BATES' post-'GAZA works, ANNE CLARK (with her interpretation of Rainer Maria Rilke's pieces) collaborated on 1998's, 'JUST AFTER SUNSET', album. Of late, MARTYN BATES took the role of Tennyson, Yeats and Walter De La Mare in yet another collaborative ambient-folk duo, TEN THOUSAND DAYS; their albums, 'IN THE GARDEN OF WILD STARS' (2000) and 'THE DEVIL IN THE GRAIN' (2001), featured accomplice/producer ALAN TRENCH (of ORCHIS).

Album rating: PHOTOGRAPHS AS MEMORIES (*7) / CAUGHT IN FLUX (*7) / DRUMMING THE BEATING HEART (*6) / RUST RED SEPTEMBER (*6) / PALE HANDS I LOVED SO WELL (*5) / BACK FROM THE RAINS (*5) / KODAK GHOSTS RUN AMOK compilation (*7) / TRANSCIENCE BLUES collection (*6) / ORANGE ICE & WAX CRAYONS collection (*5) / VOICES: THE BEST OF EYELESS IN GAZA compilation (*7) / FABULOUS LIBRARY (*5) / SAW YOU IN REMINDING PICTURES (*5) / BITTER APPLES (*5) / ALL UNDER THE LEAVES, THE LEAVES OF LIFE (*5) / SONG OF BEAUTIFUL WANTON (*5) / SIXTH SENSE: SINGLES COLLECTION (*6) / Martyn Bates: LETTERS WRITTEN mini (*5) / THE RETURN OF THE QUIET (*5) / LOVE SMASHED ON A ROCK (*5) / LETTERS TO A SCATTERED FAMILY (*5) / STARS COME TREMBLING (*5) / CHAMBER MUSIC I (*6) / MYSTERY SEAS: LETTERS WRITTEN VOL.2 (*5) / CHAMBER MUSIC II (*5) / IMAGINATION FEELS LIKE POISON (*5) / DANCE OF HOURS mini (*5) / Drift: MURDER BALLADS (THE COMPLETE COLLECTION) (*5) / Twelve Thousand Days: IN THE GARDENS OF WILD STARS (*7) / THE DEVIL IN THE GRAIN (*6)

MARTYN BATES – vocals, keyboards, synthesizers / **PETE BECKER** – vocals, synths

Ambivalent Scale / not iss.

May 80. (7"m) (ASR 002) **KODAK GHOSTS RUN AMOK. / CHINA BLUE VISION / THE FEELING'S MUTUAL**

Cherry Red / not iss.

Feb 81. (lp) (BRED 13) **PHOTOGRAPHS AS MEMORIES**
 – Seven years / Fixation / A keepsake / Looking daggers / From A to B / Clear cut apparently / Speech rapid fire / John of Patmos / Knives replace air / Faceless / In your painting / A keepsake / Whitewash / No noise. (<cd-iss. Mar00 & Sep02; CDMRED 166>)

Apr 81. (7"m) (CHERRY 20) **INVISIBILITY. / THREE KITTENS / PLAGUE OF YEARS**

Sep 81. (lp) (BRED 18) **CAUGHT IN FLUX**
 – Sixth sense / Point you / Voice from the tracks / Scale amiss / The decoration / Continual / Soul on thin ice / Rose petal knot / Skeletal framework / See red / Half light / Every which way. (w/ free 12"ep) **THE EYES OF BEAUTIFUL LOSERS** – Still air / Out from the day-to-day / Keynote inertia. (<cd-iss. Sep97; CDMRED 145>)

Nov 81. (7"ep) (CHERRY 31) **OTHERS / JANE DANCING. / EVER PRESENT / AVENUE OF TREES**

Sep 82. (lp) (BRED 36) **DRUMMING THE BEATING HEART**
 – Transcience blues / Ill wind blows / One by one / Picture the day / Dreaming at rain / Veil like calm / Throw a shadow / Pencil sketch / At arms length / Lights of April / Before you go. (<cd-iss. Mar96 +=; CDMRED 127>) – PALE HANDS I LOVED SO WELL

Oct 82. (7") (CHERRY 47) **VEIL LIKE CALM. / TAKING STEPS**

May 83. (7") (CHERRY 63) **NEW RISEN. / BRIGHT PLAY OF EYES**
 (12"+=) (12CHERRY 63) – Scent on evening air / Drumming the beating heart.

Jun 83. (lp/c) (BRED/CBRED 50) **RUST RED SEPTEMBER**
 – Changing stations / Pearl and pale / New risen / September hills / Taking steps / Only whispers / Leaves are dancing / No perfect stranger / Corner of dusk / Bright plays of eyes / Stealing Autumn. (c+=) – Steven / Sun-like-gold / To Elizabeth S. / Lilt of music / Inky blue sky / Tell. (<cd-iss. Jun96 & Oct01 +=; CDMRED 111>)

—— next with guest **MARK ROWS** – trumpet

Jun 84. (7") (CHERRY 74) **SUNBURSTS IN. / LILT OF MUSIC**
 (12"+=) (12CHERRY 74) – Inky blue sky / Tell.

Apr 85. (lp) (U 004) **PALE HANDS I LOVED SO WELL** – – Norway
 – Tall and white nettles / Warm breath, soft and slow / Blue distance / Sheer cliffs / Falling leaf / Fading flower: goodbye to summer / Lies of love / To Ellen / Pale saints / Letter to one / Light sliding / Big clipper ship.
 (above lp rec.1982 released on 'Uniton')

—— next with guest **DAVE RUFFY** – drums (of AZTEC CAMERA)

Sep 85. (7") (CHERRY 92) **WELCOME NOW. / SWEET LIFE LONGER**
 (12"+=) (12CHERRY 92) – New love here.

—— added **JOBY PALMER** – drums (ex-SINATRAS, ex-IN EMBRACE) + guest **ELIZABETH S** – backing vocals

Jul 86. (12"ep) (12CHERRY 93) **KISS THE RAIN GOODBYE**
 – Back from the rains / Evening music / Far lands blue.

Jul 86. (lp/c) (BRED/CBRED 69) **BACK FROM THE RAINS**
 – Between these dreams / Twilight / Back from the rains / Lie still, sleep long / Catch me / Evening music / She moved through the fair / Sweet life longer / Welcome now / Your rich sky / Flight of swallows / My last, lost melody. (<cd-iss. Jul89 +=; CDBRED 69>) – New risen / Bright play of eyes / Scent on evening air / Drumming the beating heart.

—— split but re-formed in the early 90's

—— added **ELIZABETH S** – vocals

Orchid / not iss.

1993. (cd) (EYE 001) **FABULOUS LIBRARY** – – Europe
 – Slow train / Fabulous library / As far and deep as love / Be the teacher / Vivid (full-on) / She tries on the jewels / Stone smile / Stormy weather / Feel like letting go / Loves a sometime thing.

—— reverted back to a duo

Hive-Arc / not iss.

1994. (ltd-cd) (015) **SAW YOU REMINDING PICTURES**
 – Book / Full beautiful / Wild flower / Reminding pictures / Mock sun / Orchard and brandy / All yr pages / Streets I ran / Cornish claw / Day screaming reminiscence / Sennen Cove cliff path / Sea bed / Lizard / Drive the nail thru the snake / Many / Brilliant blue / Hunger song / Dwell.

Ambivalent Scale / not iss.

Jun 95. (cd-ep) (A-SCALE 016) **STREETS I RAN**
 – Streets I ran / Songs of living sons / History book / Up the walls of song / Twilights walking.

Dec 95. (cd) (A-SCALE 020CD) **BITTER APPLES**
 – Bushes and briars / To cry mercy / Year dot / No further than the shore / Jump to glory lane / Dear light / Returning over / Dust alphabet / To listen across the sands / Likeness of summer / Sorrow came / Earth (legend of two daughters) / Guide this night / Bitter apples / Sunset / Harps in Heaven / (3 untitled tracks).

Jul 96. (cd) (A-SCALER 021) **ALL UNDER THE LEAVES, THE LEAVES OF LIFE**
 – Monstrous joy / Marionette / Struck like Jacob mArley / Morning / Fracture / The leave of life – Seven virgins / Answer song and dance / Passing and distant view / Damning yourself broken / Three ships / As was.

SoleilMoon / not iss.

Mar 00. (cd) (SOL 94) **SONG OF BEAUTIFUL WANTON**
 – Among the blue flowers and the yellow / One light then / Dearsong / Staring / Less sky / Sorrow loves yr laughter / Lullay my liking / Mysterious traffic / The silkie / Lord Gregory / Old and cold and full of ghosts / The lovely watch / I will give my love an apple.

– compilations, etc. –

on 'Cherry Red' unless mentioned otherwise

Feb 87. (lp/c) (BRED/CBRED 73) **KODAK GHOSTS RUN AMOK**
 – Kodak ghosts run amok / Invisibility / No noise / Others / Pencil sketch / Veil like calm / Bright play of eyes / New risen / No perfect stranger / Sunbursts in / Welcome now / New love here / Back from the rains. (c+=) – CAUGHT IN FLUX

Jan 90. (cd) Integrity; (IR 006CD) / S.P.V.; <840357> **TRANSCIENCE IN BLUE**
 – Lilt of music / Transcience blues / Sixth sense / Stealing Autumn / Inky blue sky / Evening music / Still air / Sweet life longer / Tell / Blue distance / Scent on evening air / Every which way / Bright play of eyes / Lights of April / Drumming the beating heart.

Dec 92. (cd/lp) Document; (DCD/DLP 005) **ORANGE ICE & WAX CRAYONS** (unreleased material)
 – Ways of Rachel / Stay / What I want to know / Old lime quarry / All lone hours / Street lamps n' snow / Early empty lanes / From drawn blinds / Hours grow / Fear clutches / My lost melody / P.S. for Michael. (cd+=) – Great ocean liner / Dogs bark / Fever pitch and bite. (lp w/7"; FDLP 5) – MUSIC FOR PLAYGROUNDS. / EGG-BOX BASKET

Oct 93. (cd) (CDBRED 104) **VOICE – THE BEST OF EYELESS IN GAZA**
 – Kodak ghosts run amok / No noise / Seven years / From A to B / Speech rapid fire / Invisibility / Others / Rose petal knot / Out from the day-to-day / Transcience blues / Picture the day / Two / Veil like calm / One by one / Pencil sketch / Through east fields / Changing stations / Corner of dusk / Drumming the beating heart / New risen / Sunbursts in / Welcome now / Back from the rains / Lilt of music / Evening music / Between these dreams. (<re-iss. Jun96; same>)

Jun 02. (cd) (<CDMRED 207>) **SIXTH SENSE: SINGLES COLLECTION**

MARTYN BATES

Ambivalent Scale / not iss.

1980. (c-60) (ASR 001) **DISSONANCE / ANTAGONISTIC MUSIC**
 – Bird trapping wing (in steel bars) / Ship in distance with cerise backdrop / Child squashing frog / Planes in collision, falling / Mona Lisa's sister and subsequent burning / Figure amongst ruins / Dead seahorse with sky melting / Engine failing – Resultant crash / Church with new shoes squeaking.

Cherry Red / T.F.C.K.

Oct 82. (10"m-lp) (TRED 38) **LETTERS WRITTEN**
 – Morning singing / Cut like sunset / In June / Call of birds / Mirrored in me / After taste of old / Jagged tears of words / Letters from yesterday / Overflowing look / Hungry like sharp desire. (cd-iss. Oct96 +=; CDMRED 134)– THE RETURN OF THE QUIET

Oct 87. (7") (CHERRY 99) **THE LOOK OF LOVE. / ADAM & EVE & PINCH ME**
 (12"+=) (12CHERRY 99) – May 3rd.

Nov 87. (lp) (BRED 81) <tfck 88815> **THE RETURN OF THE QUIET**
 – Love fell silent / Last chapel picnic / At the return of quiet / She will know / You've got to farewell / July late afternoon / Sad song almost / The look of love / Etc. angel. <US cd+=> – Adam & Eve / Pinch me.

Integrity / S.P.V.

Jan 89. (lp) (IR 002) **LOVE SMASHED ON A ROCK**
 – I'd better mean it all now / Since I can't have you / You so secret / This is what I say to love / Dark's chorus / Love smashed on a rock / We won't begin to belong / Azure flag / She's on a pedestala / You're the spell (I can't break). (cd-iss. Jan90 +=; IR 002CD) – And I don't know how it will be / Down amongst the lonely.

Apr 89. (12"ep) (IR 004) **YOU SO SECRET. / AND I DON'T KNOW HOW IT WILL BE / BORN AND BEGINNING / WHEN YOU PRAISE HER**

Feb 90. (7"m) (IR 005-7) **ON THE DAY YOU CLIMB DOWN. / CITY / ALL THE STRANGERS**

Feb 90. (cd) (IR 005CD) <3242> **LETTERS TO A SCATTERED FAMILY**
 – On the day you climb down / Snow rages / City / Little days / Your jewled footsteps / For love / Waiting to die / Shuttered nights / First and last February / This one refrain / I'll wrap your hopes.

1990. (cd-ep+booklet) (SSMCD 02) **PORT OF STORMY LIGHTS**
 – 3 weeks and after / She waltzes by the window / Beaten gold / Ways of going.

Integrity / Integrity

Oct 90. (lp/cd) (<IR 011/+CD>) **STARS COME TREMBLING**
 – Fired high / Her and same heaven / The words of the haunted / Flashes of sun / The gift of lieing / End of sleep / Lightening following / Later war cries / Wintersky / Glow of sight.

Sub Rosa / Sub Rosa

Oct 94. (cd) (<SR 81CD>) **CHAMBER MUSIC I**
 – Strings in the earth and air / Dark leaves / Twilight turns from amethyst / Yellow keys / All that hour when all things have repose / When the sky star goes forth in Heaven / Lean out of the window, goldenhair / I would in that sweet bosom be /

EYELESS IN GAZA (cont) — THE GREAT INDIE DISCOGRAPHY — The 1980s

Sad austerities / My love is in a light attire / Who goes amid the green wood / Rich apparel / Winds of May, that dance on the sea / Silvery arches / Bright cap and streamers / Bid adieu / What counsel has the hooded moon / Go seek her out courteously / Nightdew / My dove, my beautiful one / From dewey dreams, my soul arise / The flowery bells of morn / O cool is the valley now / Thrushes calling / Because your voice was at my side / Stranger / O sweetheart, hear you.

Feb 96. (cd) (<SR 91CD>) **CHAMBER MUSIC II**
– Be not sad / In the dark pine wood / His love / He who hath glory lost / His companion / Of that so sweet imprisonment / This heart / Between kiss and kiss / Silently she's coming / On the drappled glass / Lightly come or lightly go / Thou leanest to the shell of the night / At ghosting hour / Though I thy mithridates were / Gentle lady, do not sing / Dear heart / Love came to us / O, it was out by Donnycarney / Bat / The rain has fallen / Now o now / The wind is whistling / Sleep now / Unquiet / All day I hear the noise of waters / I hear an army / Fluttering whips.

Ambilavent Scale / not iss.

1995. (cd) (A-SCALE 018CD) **MYSTERY SEAS: LETTERS WRITTEN 2**
– You, looking to me for a sign / Shorepoem / Calm of dark / Imagination feels like poison / Trade winds / Over the waters / Everywhere there's rain / Empty pages / Midday coming misty / On the beach at Fontana / Sky after all / Fragment (little star #1) / If I could see in everyone / Of night / Gift.

Apr 97. (cd) (ASR 022) **IMAGINATION FEELS LIKE POISON**
– Mock sun #1 / I can't look for you / Bones of your face / Years of salt / I forget you / The god on the tree / Full sail / Flanaghan / Fully bright / Mystery seas / This wayward love / Fantaccini playground / Ellen Massey / Letters to a scattered family / Silvery images / No-one spoke / The mountain tomb.

—— in May'98, MARTYN and ANNE CLARK collaborated on the album, 'JUST AFTER SUNSET' (Labor; 8313-2)

Apr 01. (m-cd) (NDN 27) **DANCE OF HOURS**
– Poems pennyeach / Wishing-songs / Stars above / War-like / Bethlehem / Alone reprise / Once blessed / The heart's song.

HUNGRY I

—— **MARTYN BATES + STEVE DULLAHAN** (ex-PRIMITIVES)

Nursery / not iss.

Jun 91. (12"ep/cd-ep) (12/CD NYS 3) **FALLING ORCHARD**
– Falling orchard / News of 13 / Enter shakin' / She exploded love.
Oct 91. (12") (NYS 5) **HER 1000 DAYS**
Nov 91. (12"ep) (NYS 6) **SECOND STEP**
– Sudden supernature / Er / April bring the sky down / Two steps forward / Um / Rose elegy.

DRIFT

MARTYN BATES + M.J. HARRIS

Musica Maxima / Musica Maxima

1994. (cd-ep) (eee 26) **MURDER BALLADS**
– The death of Polly / The fowler / Lucy wan / Long Lankin.
1997. (cd-ep) (eee 36) **MURDER BALLADS (PASSAGES)**
– The bramble briar / The cruel mother / The banks of Fordie / The murder of Maria Marten.
Jun 98. (cd-ep) (eee 40) **MURDER BALLADS (INCEST SONGS)**
– The bonny hind / Sheath and knife / The two brothers / Edward.

Invisible / not iss.

Nov 98. (cd) (inv 127) **MURDER BALLADS (THE COMPLETE COLLECTION)**

TWELVE THOUSAND DAYS

MARTYN BATES + ALAN TRENCH – keyboards (of ORCHIS)

Apr 00. (cd) (<eee 37>) **IN THE GARDENS OF WILD STARS** Oct00
– Let the evening in / Children of the winter house / Locksley hall / The moon is down / Garden of wild stars / Stricken fields / The yearling / Dun fox / Jennet (part 1) / Jennet (part 2) / Twelve thousand days / Wandering aengus / Burning incense / Sally free and easy / The grey cock / Let the evening in.

Ice Flowers / not iss.

Aug 01. (cd) (efa 16918-2) **THE DEVIL IN THE GRAIN**
– Song of the prophet / Beauty is fading / All in the may / Darkness rising / Dream of you / Whitestone day / Glistening praise / The devil in the grain / The hand of glory / Plea.

PETE BECKER

Mannequin / not iss.

Jan 82. (c) (none) **BY TRAIN TO COAST**

FAD GADGET

Formed: London, England ... late 70's by Irish-born FRANK TOVEY. Basically a vehicle for TOVEY's twisted electronica and performance art (he was known for plucking his pubic hair out on stage, possibly due to a tarred and feathered photo shoot!), FAD GADGET was the first group to sign to the 'Mute' label, releasing a debut single, 'BACK TO NATURE', in late '79. This was followed by 'RICKY'S HAND' and a debut album, 'FIRESIDE FAVOURITES' (1980), for which he enlisted the help of 'Mute' mainman, DANIEL MILLER along with ERIC RADCLIFFE, PAUL WAUCLAIRE, NICHOLAS CASH and JOHN FRYER. Hardly the stuff of Perry Como-style cosiness, the record married repetitive, often jarring synth rhythms to lyrics exploring life's darker, seedier side, occasionally letting it . . . er, all hang out as on the tortured fade-out of 'COITUS INTERRUPTUS'. Retaining FRYER and recruiting a new cast of collaborators including ROBERT GOTOBED of WIRE, TOVEY concocted an even more uncompromising electronic brew on follow-up set, 'INCONTINENT' (1981). The funereal 'SATURDAY NIGHT SPECIAL' (sadly/thankfully not a cover of the LYNYRD SKYNYRD chestnut! delete as appropriate) was released as a single in early '82, a third album, 'UNDER THE FLAG', appearing later that year. Dealing with the Falklands conflict, the likes of 'SCAPEGOAT' bore more than a passing resemblance to the territory later covered by labelmates DEPECHE MODE. Following 1984's 'GAG', TOVEY ditched the FAD GADGET moniker and, hooking up with American, BOYD RICE, cut a disappointing collaborative effort, 'EASY LISTENING FOR THE HARD OF HEARING' (1984). Two years on, 'SNAKES AND LADDERS' marked TOVEY's solo debut proper, the synth veteran increasingly couching his work in a more rock orientated context. TOVEY made an even more radical departure from his early work with 1989's folky 'TYRANNY AND THE HIRED HAND', subsequently teaming up with The PYROS, for 'GRAND UNION' (1991) and 'WORRIED MEN IN SECONDHAND SUITS' (1992). FRANK died of heart failure at his London home on 3rd of April, 2002; he'd apparently suffered from heart problems from a young age.

Album rating: FIRESIDE FAVOURITES (*5) / INCONTINENT (*7) / UNDER THE FLAG (*7) / GAG (*6) / THE FAD GADGET SINGLES compilation (*7) / THE BEST OF FAD GADGET compilation (*7) / Frank Tovey: SNAKES AND LADDERS (*6) / CIVILIAN (*5) / TYRANNY AND THE HIRED HAND (*5) / GRAND UNION (*5) / WORRIED MEN AND SECOND HAND SUITS (*5)

FRANK TOVEY (b. 8 Sep'56, Donegal, Ireland) – vocals, synthesizers, flute / **ERIC RADCLIFFE** – keyboards, guitar / **JOHN FRYER** – guitar, percussion / **PAUL WAUCLAIRE** – bass / **NICHOLAS CASH** – drums, percussion (ex-PRAG VEC) / **DANIEL MILLER** – drums, programming (ex-NORMAL)

Mute / not iss.

Oct 79. (7") (MUTE 002) **BACK TO NATURE. / THE BOX**
Mar 80. (7") (MUTE 006) **RICKY'S HAND. / HANDSHAKE**
Sep 80. (7") (MUTE 009) **INSECTICIDE. / FIRESIDE FAVOURITES**
Sep 80. (lp) (STUMM 3) **FIRESIDE FAVOURITES**
– Pedestraian / State of the nation / Salt Lake City Sunday / The box / Fireside favourites / Coitus interruptus / Newsreel / Insecticide / Arch of the aorta. (cd-iss. Jun91 & Jun96; CDSTUMM 3)
Mar 81. (7") (MUTE 012) **MAKE ROOM. / LADY SHAVE**

—— **PETER BAHNER** – bass, guitar (ex-SKI PATROL); repl. WAUCLAIRE
—— guests included **ROBERT GOTOBED** – drums (of WIRE) / **DAVID SIMMONDS** – keyboards / **BARBARA (BIJI) FRONT + ANNE CLIFT** – backing vocals

Dec 81. (lp/c) (STUMM/CSTUMM 6) **INCONTINENT**
– Saturday night special / Incontinent / Blind eyes / Swallow it / King of the flies / Innocent bystanders / Diminished responsibility / Manual dexterity. (cd-iss. Jun91 & Jun96 +=; CDSTUMM 6) – Plain clothes.
Jan 82. (7") (MUTE 017) **SATURDAY NIGHT SPECIAL. / SWALLOW IT (live)**
Apr 82. (7"/12") (MUTE/12MUTE 021) **KING OF THE FLIES. / PLAIN CLOTHES**

—— **DAVID SIMMONDS** now replaced RADCLIFFE who joined The ASSEMBLY

Sep 82. (7"/12") (MUTE/12MUTE 024) **LIFE ON THE LINE. / 4M**
Sep 82. (lp/c) (STUMM/CSTUMM 8) **UNDER THE FLAG**
– Under the flag I / Scapegoat / Love parasite / Plainsong / Wheels of fortune / Life on the line IV / The sheep look up / Cipher / For whom the bells toll / Under the flag II. (cd-iss. Jun91 & Jun96; CDSTUMM 8)
Jan 83. (7"/12") (MUTE/12MUTE 026) **FOR WHOM THE BELLS TOLL. / LOVE PARASITE**

—— TOVEY, SIMMONDS, CASH, FRONT added **JONI SACKETT** – backing vocals / **DAVID ROGERS** + guest **ROWLAND HOWARD** – drums

324

FAD GADGET (cont)

Oct 83. (7") *(7MUTE 028)* **I DISCOVER LOVE. / LEMMINGS ON LOVER'S ROCK**
(12"+=) *(12MUTE 028)* – Lemming's storm.
Jan 84. (7"/12") *(7/12 MUTE 30)* **COLLAPSING NEW PEOPLE. / SPOIL THE CHILD**
Feb 84. (lp/c) *(STUMM/CSTUMM 15)* **GAG**
– Ideal world / Collapsing new people / I discover love / Jump / Sleep / One man's meat / Spoil the child / Stand up / Speak to me – Breathe in the air / The ring (hypnotic seduction of Dale) / Ad nauseam. *(cd-iss. Jun91; CDSTUMM 15)*
May 84. (7") *(7MUTE 033)* **ONE MAN'S MEAT. / SLEEP**
(12"+=) *(12MUTE 033)* – Ideal world.

— in Nov'84, synth man BOYD RICE and TOVEY released their 1981 recorded work as 'EASY LISTENING FOR THE HARD OF HEARING' on 'Mute'; *(STUMM 20) (cd-iss. May96; CDSTUMM 20)*

FRANK TOVEY

with **SIMMONDS** / **E.C. RADCLIFFE** / **CASH** / **ROGERS** / **GUY EVANS** – vibes

Aug 85. (7"/12") *(7/12 MUTE 39)* **LUXURY. / BED OF NAILS**
Apr 86. (7") *(7MUTE 44)* **LUDDITE JOE. / CLEAN THIS ACT UP**
(12"+=) *(12MUTE 44)* – Small world.
May 86. (cd/c/lp) *(CDC+/STUMM 23)* **SNAKES AND LADDERS**
– The cutting edge / Snakes and ladders / Shot in the dark / Concrete / Collapsing new people / Luxury / Small world / Luddite Joe / Megalomaniac. *(cd+=)* – Coitus interruptus / The sheep look up / Ideal world.

— now w/ **MARK JEFFERY** – drums, co-producer / **RICO CONNING** – instruments

Apr 88. (7"/12") *(7/12 MUTE 79)* **BRIDGE ST. SHUFFLE. / BRACE OF SHAKES**
Jun 88. (cd/lp) *(CD+/STUMM 56)* **CIVILIAN**
– New Jerusalem / Ultramarine / From the city to the Isle Of Dogs / Bridge St. shuffle / The brotherhood / Diana / Unknown civilian / Desperate Dan.

— added **DAVID ASH** – guitars, piano / **PAUL RODDEN** – banjo / **NETO VAANDRAGER** – fiddle, violin / **JEAN-MARIE CARROLL** – acoustic guitar, mandolin, etc / **MOLLY McANALLY BURKE** – banjo, guitar, vocals

Jul 89. (12"/cd-s) *(12/CD MUTE 100)* **SAM HALL / RICKY'S HAND. / JOHN HENRY – LET YOUR HAMMER RING / HOUSE OF THE RISING SUN**
Aug 89. (cd/c/lp) *(CD/C+/STUMM 73)* **TYRANNY AND THE HIRED HAND**
– '31 depression blues / Hard times in the cotton mill / John Henry – Let your hammer ring / The Blantyre explosion / Money cravin' folks / All I got's gone / Midwife song / Sam Hall / Dark as a dungeon / Men of good fortune / Sixteen tons / North country blues / Buffalo skinners / Black lung song / Pastures of plenty / Joe Hill.

FRANK TOVEY & THE PYROS

with **PAUL RODDEN** – banjo, guitar / **JOHN CUTLIFFE** – banjo, guitar; plus **STEVE SMITH** – organ / **CHARLIE LLEWELLYN** – drums, percussion / **TRACEY BOOTH** – bodhran / **ELLIOT CARNEGIE** – harp / **TOZIE LYNCH** – bones

Apr 91. (12"/cd-s) *(12/CD MUTE 121)* **THE LIBERTY TREE. / VICTORIA FALLS**
May 91. (cd/c/lp) *(CD/C+/STUMM 84)* **GRAND UNION**
– Bad day in Bow Creek / When the victim takes the tyrants place / Passing through / Bethnal Green tube disaster / Cities of the plain / Fallen angel / I.K.B. (R.I.P.) / The liberty tree / One November morning / The great attractor.
Oct 92. (cd/lp) *(CD+/STUMM 107)* **WORRIED MEN IN SECOND HAND SUITS**
– Chasing the blues away / All that is mine / Just like other men / Only doing your job / Hey bailiff / Crow's nest blues / Opportunity's knocking / The hermit of Hermes Point / You won't get that from me / Doing time / Worried man.

— FRANK retired for a while, although he returned to gig in 2001; he sadly died on the 3rd April, 2002

– compilations, etc. –

on 'Mute' unless stated otherwise

Nov 86. (cd/c/lp; as FRANK TOVEY) *(CD/C+/STUMM 37)* **THE FAD GADGET SINGLES**
– Back to nature / The box / Ricky's hand / Fireside favourites / Lady shave / Saturday night special / King of the flies / Life on the line / For whom the bells toll / I discover love / Collapsing new people. *(cd+=)* – Insecticide / 4M / Love parasite / One man's meat.
Oct 01. (d-cd) *(<CDMUTEL 7>)* **THE BEST OF FAD GADGET**
– (the singles & b-sides) // (12"mixes).

FAITH (see under ⇒ EMBRACE)

Tav FALCO

Born: raised- Arkansas, USA ... moved to Memphis, Tennessee where he subsequently formed The PANTHER BURNS in the early 80's alongside former BOX TOPS and BIG STAR guru ALEX CHILTON. Signed to 'Rough Trade', the band (completed by JIM DUCKWORTH and RONALD MILLER) made their debut in late '81 with a cover of Johnny Burnette's 'TRAIN KEPT A ROLLIN'. An album's worth of "Wreck-abilly"-style dixie blues, 'BEHIND THE MAGNOLIA CURTAIN', followed a couple of months later, CHILTON employing his not inconsiderable production experience. A parting of the ways was imminent however, the latter going solo and being replaced by JIM SCLAVUNOS prior to the recording of 1982's 'BLOW YOUR TOP' EP. DUCKWORTH was the next to leave, his departure to The GUN CLUB resulting in a three year sabbatical for TAV. In 1985, CHILTON accompanied TAV FALCO'S PANTHER BURNS (as they were now called) to Sam Philips' Memphis studio, recording a comeback mini-set for the French-based 'New Rose' label, 'SUGAR DITCH REVISITED'. They continued to release the odd EP until 1987's covers album, 'THE WORLD WE KNEW', FALCO renowned for his wild interpretations of blues & R&B standards; the man was to issue a similar collection in the shape of 'RETURN OF THE BLUE PANTHER' (1990). The turn of the decade saw TAV strike out on his own for the 'LIFE SENTENCE' (1992) album although CHILTON and DICKINSON were present in a guest capacity. TAV and his PANTHER BURNS brigade are still active, their last album to date being the "unapproachable" 'PANTHER PHOBIA' in 2000.

Album rating: BEHIND THE MAGNOLIA CURTAIN (*5) / SUGAR DITCH REVISTED (*4) / THE WORLD WE KNEW (*4) / RED DEVIL (*4) / MIDNIGHT IN MEMPHIS (*5) / RETURN OF THE BLUE PANTHER (*4) / LIFE SENTENCE (*4) / SHADOW DANCER (*4) / DISAPPEARING ANGELS mini (*4) / LOVE'S LAST WARNING (THE BEST OF TAV FALCO'S PANTHER BURNS) compilation (*6) / PANTHER PHOBIA (*4)

PANTHER BURNS

TAV FALCO – vocals, guitar / **'LX' ALEX CHILTON** – guitar, drums, producer (ex-BIG STAR, ex-BOX TOPS) / **JIM DUCKWORTH** – guitar, drums / **RONALD MILLER** – bass

Rough Trade   Rough Trade

Oct 81. (7") *(RT 077)* **TRAIN KEPT A ROLLIN'. / RED HEADED WOMAN**
Dec 81. (lp) *(ROUGH 32) <ROUGH-US 16>* **BEHIND THE MAGNOLIA CURTAIN**
– Come on little mama / She's the one that got it / Hey high school baby / Brazil / You're undecided / Ooee baby / River of love / Snake drive / Blind man / Where the Rio de Rosa flows / Snatch it back / Bourgeois blues / St. Louis blues / Moving on down the line. *(re-iss. Aug87 by TAV FALCO'S PANTHER BURNS on 'Fan Club' lp/cd+=; FC 029/+CD)* – BLOW YOUR TOP *(cd re-iss. May94 on 'New Rose'; 422135) <US cd-iss. 1994 on 'TRiple X'; 51120>*

— **JIM SCLAVUNOS** – percussion, vocals; repl. CHILTON who went solo again

Nov 82. (12"ep) *(RT 114T)* **BLOW YOUR TOP**
– I'm on this rocket / Pantherman / Love is my business / Bertha Lou.

— they split for a couple of years, DUCKWORTH joined The GUN CLUB

Frenzi   not iss.

1984. (c) *(FZC 37)* **PANTHER BURNS NOW! LIVE (live)**
– Cuban rebel girl / Starkweather / 60 highway / Agitator blues / Jump suit / Hairdresser underground / Mississippi river blues. *(re-iss. 12"ep – 1988 on 'NBTFZ'; NBTFZ 001)*

TAV FALCO PANTHER BURNS

New Rose   New Rose

Nov 85. (m-lp) *(ROSE 73)* **SUGAR DITCH REVISITED**
– Money talks / Arkansas stomp / Working on a building / White silver sands / Lonely avenue / Time, the go-go queen. *(cd-iss. May94; 422137)*
Sep 86. (12"ep) *(NEW 78)* **SHAKE RAG EP** — French
– Warrior Sam / Shade tree mechanic / Jumper on the line / Cuban rebel girl. *(w/ free live EP+=; FREE 78)* – Cuban rebel girl / Starkweather / 61 highway / Agitator blues / Jump suit / Hairdresser underground / Mississippi river blues.
Mar 87. (7") *(NEW 86)* **DROP YOUR MASK. / TRAM**
Jun 87. (lp/c/cd) *(ROSE 113/+C/CD)* **THE WORLD WE KNEW**
– Dateless night / Do the robot / It's all your fault / Pass the hatchet / The world we knew / Drop your mask / Mona Lisa / She's a bad motorcycle / Doubtful of your love / Ditch digging / Big road blues. *(cd+=)* – SHAKE RAG EP *(cd re-iss. May94; 422140) <US cd-iss. 1994 on 'Triple X'; 51121>*
Jan 88. (7") *(NEW 128)* **MEMPHIS BEAT. / RED HEADED WOMAN**
Mar 88. (10"lp/cd) *(ROSE 140/+CD)* **RED DEVIL**
– Oh, how she dances / Drifting heart / Poor man / Two little puppies (and one old shaggy hound) / Tram / Ode to Shetar / Ditch digging / She's the one to blame / A little mixed up / Running wild. *(also iss.as 7"box; NR 335) (cd+=)* – SUGAR DITCH (tracks). *<US cd-iss. 1994 on 'Triple X'; 51122>*
Nov 88. (7") *(NEW 155)* **TORTURE. / GUARDA CHE LUNA**
Aug 89. (d-lp/c/cd) *(ROSE 185/+C/CD)* **MIDNIGHT IN MEMPHIS (live 10th Anniversary)**
– Oh, how she dances / Bertha Lou / Shade tree mechanic / With your love / Jungle rock / It's only make believe / Big road blues / Goldfinger / She's the one that's got it / Memphis beat / Love whip / The world we knew / Ditch diggin' / Girl after girl / Do the robot / Same thing / Drop your mask (tango) / Train kept a-rollin'. *(cd+=/c+=)* – Red headed woman / Bourgeois blues. *(cd re-iss. May94; 422141) <US cd-iss. 1994 on 'Triple X'; 51123>*

not iss.   Sympathy..

1990. (7") *<SFTRI 062>* **SURFSIDE DATE. / HAVE LOVE WILL TRAVEL / FUN MOB**
1990. (7"; as the TAV & GABBY SHOW) *<SFTRI 071>* **I CAN HELP. / GIRL FROM FIRENZE**

New Rose   Triple X

Jul 90. (lp/cd) *(ROSE 215/+CD) <51051-2>* **RETURN OF THE BLUE PANTHER** (covers)
– Mala femmina / You believe everyone but me / I'm movin' on / Knot in my pocket / I got a woman / Rock me baby / Surfside date / I got love if you want it / Girls on fire: a movie theme / Love whip / Fun mob / Mala femmina.

— now with a host of guests including CHILTON + DICKINSON

Feb 92. (lp/c/cd) *(ROSE 264/+C/CD) <51095-2>* **LIFE SENTENCE**
– My mind was messed up at the time / Torture / Vampire from Havana / Make me know you're mine / Go on home / Auto sapien / Guarda che luna / Oh, girls, girls / (I'm gonna) Dig myself a hole / Sent up / What's wrong / Why was I born / Only the lonely. *(re-iss. May94; 422136)*

Intercord   Upstart

Feb 96. (cd; as TAV FALCO PANTHER BURNS) *(IRS 993513CD) <CD 017>* **SHADOW DANCER** — Nov95
– Invocation of the shadow dancer / Funnel of love / Sway / Love's last warning / Lotus blossom / Cuando vedrai la mia raggazza / Born to cry / I'll take care of you / Have I the right / Music maestro please / Guarda che luna / Born too late / Shadow dancer. *(cd re-iss. Nov96 on 'Last Call'; 422246-2)*

Tav FALCO (cont)

Sep 96. (10"m-lp/m-cd) <(SFTRI 460/+CD)> **DISAPPEARING ANGELS** — Sympathy F / Sympathy F — Oct96
– Gentleman in black / Kiss of fire / Chains of love / He'll have to go / Endless sleep / Mississippi river blues / Tobacco road / Disappearing angel.

—— now with **ROSS JOHNSON** – drums / **KITTY FIRES** – guitar, tambourine, spoons / **ERIC HILL** – synthesizer

In The Red / In The Red

Oct 00. (lp/cd; as TAV FALCO & THE UNAPPROACHABLE PANTHER BURNS) <(ITR 069/+CD)> **PANTHER PHOBIA** Dec00
– Streamline train / She wants to sell my monkey / Going home / Once I had a car / The young psychotics / Cypress grove / Wild wild women / Cockroach / Mellow peaches / Panther phobia: manifesto! / This could go on forever.

– compilations, etc. –

1988. (4x7"box) *New Rose; (TAV 1-4)* **PANTHER BURNS** – / – French
– DRIFTING HEART. / POOR MAN // RUNNING WILD. / TWO LITTLE PUPPIES & ONE OLD SHAGGY HOUND // DITCH DIGGING. / SHE'S THE ONE TO BLAME // ODE TO SHETAR. / A LITTLE MIXED UP

Oct 92. (10"lp/cd) *Marilyn; (FM 1011/+CD)* **UNRELEASED SESSIONS** – / –
– Come on little mama / The bug / She's the one that got it / Big road blues / Bourgeois blues / Bothering that thing / Train kept a-rollin' / Red headed woman / Doubtful of your love / Bullcow blues / Little mixed up.

Apr 94. (10"lp/cd) *Marilyn; (USM/+CD 1026)* **DEEP IN THE SHADOWS**
– Running wild / Cuban rebel girl / Poor man / She's a bad motorcycle / Drifting heart / Tina, the go-go queen / Drop your mask / Working on a building / Lonely avenue / Brazil. (cd+=) – White silver sands.

Nov 96. (cd) *Last Call; (422088)* **LOVE'S LAST WARNING (THE BEST OF TAV FALCO'S PANTHER BURNS)**
– Love's last warning / Torture / My mind was messed up at the time / Drifting heart / Ditch digging / Oh, how she dances / Tina, the go-go queen / Lonely avenue / Money talks / The world we knew / Drop your mask / Doubtful of your love / Dateless night / Cuban rebel girl / Brazil / You're undecided / She's the one that's got it / Mala your love (live) / Goldfinger (live) / It's only make believe (live).

Mar 97. (cd) *Munster; <(MRCD 111)>* **SHADOW ANGELS AND DISAPPEARING DANCERS** (compilation of two 1995 sets)

1998. (7"ep) *Sympathy..; <SFTRI 477>* **SHE'S THE ONE TO BLAME / DATELESS NIGHT. / DROP YOUR MASK / TRAIN KEPT A ROLLING** –

FALSE PROPHETS

Formed: New York City, New York, USA ... June 1980 by frontman STEPHAN IELPI, who surrounded himself with like-minded hardcore punks, PETER CAMPBELL, STEVE WISHNIA and MATTY SUPERTY. One of the first wave US hardcore acts, the FALSE PROPHETS eschewed the hard-man approach favoured by BLACK FLAG etc, choosing instead an intellectually-based manifesto that sought to expose injustice in all its multifarious guises. Yet like many bands of their ilk, the line-up was in almost constant flux and by the mid-80's – by which point the band's vinyl output amounted to a solitary 7" single, 'BLIND OBEDIENCE' – IELPI was the only remaining founder member (newcomers being DEBRA DeSALVO, STEVEN TAYLOR, NICK MARDEN and BILLY ATWELL III). Securing a deal with the San Francisco-based 'Alternative Tentacles' label, the band re-emerged in 1986 with a long awaited eponymous debut album. This was followed up by 'IMPLOSION' just over a year later although a second extended sabbatical from the recording front meant that fans had to wait until 1990 for further new material. Featuring brass courtesy of new addition JAMES WHITE, 'INVISIBLE PEOPLE' was a much more adventurous affair combining the adrenaline rush of hardcore with the visceral thrill of Latin rhythms.

Album rating: FALSE PROPHETS (*5) / IMPLOSION (*5) / INVISIBLE PEOPLE (*6) / BLIND ROACHES AND FAT VULTURES compilation (*6)

STEPHAN IELPI – vocals / **PETER CAMPBELL** – guitar / **STEVE WISHNIA** – bass / **MATTY SUPERTY** – drums

not iss. / Worn Out Brothers

1981. (7") <WOB 001> **BLIND OBEDIENCE. / OVERKILL / ROYAL SLIME** –

—— IELPI was the solo survivor, the quartet having involved others **DEBRA DE SALVO** – guitar, vocals / **STEVEN TAYLOR** – guitar, vocals / **NICK MARDEN** – bass, vocals / **BILLY ATWELL III** – drums, vocals

Alternative Tentacles / Alternative Tentacles

Jul 86. (lp) <(VIRUS 48)> **FALSE PROPHETS**
Sep 87. (lp) <(VIRUS 58)> **IMPLOSION**

—— added **JAMES WHITE** – horns (ex-CONTORTIONS)
—— **BENJAMIN ORICK** – drums; repl. ATTWELL

Konkurrel / Patois

1990. (m-lp) <003> **INVISIBLE PEOPLE**
– Never again, again / Plenty of death for all / Shadow government / Invisible people / No deposit, no return / Limit of the limitless.

—— folded in the early 90's after a decade as a unit

– compilations, etc. –

Jun 00. (cd) *Alternative Tentacles; <(VIRUS 244CD)>* **BLIND ROACHES AND FAT VULTURES: PHANTASMAGORICAL BEASTS OF THE REAGAN ERA** (virtually the debut + others)
– Overkill / Blind obedience / Good clean fun / Royal slime / Suburbanites / 7 deadly sins / Somebody react / Scorched earth / Mental ghetto / Functional / Marat – Sade / Taxidermist / Baghdad stomp / Helplessly screaming / Faith / Banana split republic / Decade of decay / Creatures of the woodwork / Premediated suicide / Dear mom I'm dead / Pounding raw burgers.

FAMILY FODDER

Formed: London, England ... late 70's as a large unit of singers and musicians numbering main songwriter DOMINIQUE PEARCE, other conspirator ALIG LEVILLIAN, plus IAN HILL, FELIX FRIEDOROWICZ, MICK HOBBS, MARTIN FREDERICK, CHARLES BULLEN, RICK WILSON and JUDY CARTER. Weird and musically directionless, this percussion-heavy avant-pop ensemble made their official debut late in '79 with the single, 'PLAYING GOLF (WHILE MY FLESH CRAWLS)', although a pseudonymous EP, 'TE DEUM', was issued around the same time under the guise of FRANK SUMATRA AND THE MOB. A series of singles/EP's followed in quick succession, 'WARM', 'SUNDAY GIRLS' 12"ep, BLONDIE ode, 'DEBBIE HARRY' and DOMINIQUE's pouting French-language showcase, 'SAVOIR FAIRE'. FAMILY FODDER delivered their first full-length baby in the shape of 'MONKEY BANANA KITCHEN' (1981), a shambolic ragbag of competing sounds and influences that made few concessions to chart-friendly accessibility. By the following year, only ALIG, IAN and BAZ remained from the original line-up while new members LYNNE ALICE and GRAHAM PAINTING were found. A switch of labels from 'Fresh' to 'Jungle' led to the subsequent release of a disappointing but appropriately titled second set, 'ALL STYLES' (1983), the group signing off with a 'GREATEST HITS' collection a year later.

Album rating: MONKEY BANANA KITCHEN (*5) / ALL STYLES (*3) / GREATEST HITS compilation (*6)

DOMINIQUE PEARCE – vocals / **IAN HILL** – vocals, percussion / **ALIG LEVILLIAN** – guitars, keyboards, saxophone, vocals (ex-CUDDLY TOYS) / **FELIX FRIEDOROWICZ** – keyboards, bassoon, violin / **MICK HOBBS** – bass, organ / **MARTIN FREDERICK** – bass, vocals / **CHARLES BULLEN** – drums, guitar, viola, vocals / **RICK WILSON** – drums, vocals / **MIKE** – guitar / **JUDY CARTER** – backing vocals / **MARK DOFFMAN** – drums / **BAZZ SMITH** – drums / **JAN BEETLESTONE** – backing vocals

Small Wonder / not iss.

Oct 79. (12"ep; as FRANK SUMATRA AND THE MOB) *(TEENY 1)* **TE DEUM** –
– The story so far / Telstar 176 all out: W/Indies 180 for 3 declared / Tedium – the blues.

Parole / not iss.

Oct 79. (7") *(PURL 4)* **PLAYING GOLF (WHILE MY FLESH CRAWLS). / MY BABY TAKES VALIUM** –
(re-iss. Apr81 on 'Fresh'; FRESH 1)

Jan 80. (7") *(PURL 6)* **WARM. / DESIRE** –
(re-iss. Apr81 on 'Fresh'; FRESH 8)

Fresh / not iss.

Apr 80. (12"ep) *(FRESH 9)* **SUNDAY GIRLS EP** –
– Sunday girl 1 / Mine and Billy's head / Disco purge / Good times underwater / No man's land / Accapulco / Street credibility / Kisses / Grand merchant loup / Ragged wolf of my passions / Blue girls / Sunday girl 2.

Jul 80. (7") *(FRESH 15)* **DEBBIE HARRY. / (version)** –
Oct 80. (7") *(FRESH 22)* **SAVOIR FAIRE. / CARNAL KNOWLEDGE** –
Apr 81. (lp) *(FRESHLP 3)* **MONKEY BANANA KITCHEN** –
– Darling / Symbols / Savoir faire / Cold wars / Monkey / Wrong / Organ grinder / Love song / Bass adds bass / Philosophy / Cerf volant / Banana.
Jul 81. (7") *(FRESH 32)* **FILM MUSIC. / ROOM** –

—— now without MIKE

Sep 81. (12"ep) *(FRESH 37-12)* **SCHIZOPHRENIA PARTY** –
– Dinosaur sex / Emergency / Dazomo / Silence / Tea with Dolly / Better lies.
May 82. (7") *(FRESH 42)* **THE BIG DIG. / PLANT LIFE** –

—— remaining members **ALIG, IAN + BAZ** recruited **LYNNE ALICE** – guitar, vocals / **GRAHAM PAINTING** – keyboards, bass

Jungle / not iss.

Nov 82. (7") *(JUNG 4)* **CORAL. / FRUSTRATION** –
May 83. (d-lp) *(FREUD 02)* **ALL STYLES** –
– Disarm completely / Winter song / Malfunction / Ecstasy harmony / Falling in love again / Mack the knife / Windmills of your mind.

Crammed Discs / not iss.

Sep 83. (7") *(CRAM 245-7)* **SAVOIR FAIRE. / I'LL BE YOURS** –
Sep 84. (lp) *(CRAM 016)* **GREATEST HITS** (compilation) –
– Playing golf (while my flesh crawls) / Film music / Debbie Harry / Savoir faire / Der Leiermann / Cerf volant / No fear no sorrow / Kisses / Love song / Warm / Fragments / One person per suit.

—— disbanded before above was released

FANATICS
(see under ⇒ OCEAN COLOUR SCENE; in 90's section)

FARM

Formed: Liverpool, England ... early '83 by PETE HOOTEN and STEVE GRIMES. They appeared on BBC2 TV's 'Oxford Road Show' where they met MADNESS frontman, SUGGS McPHERSON, who subsequently produced their 1984 debut 45, 'HEARTS AND MINDS'. The group struggled early on and ultimately suffered tragedy when drummer, ANDY McVANN, died in a car crash late in '86. Replacing him initially with MICK HANRATTY and later ROY BOULTER (KEITH MULLEN and CARL HUNTER also replaced MELVIN and PHILIP respectively), the group ploughed on, moving away from their overtly political, brassy DEXYS/REDSKINS fixation and adopting an ill-advised synth orientated sound with the addition of keyboard player, BEN LEACH. The resulting single, 'BODY AND SOUL', was another flop and the band decided drastic measures were needed; initiating their own label, 'Produce', and securing the services of house guru TERRY FARLEY, they scored a sizeable club hit (and a Top 60 chart placing) with a dancefloor friendly makeover of The Monkees' 'ALL TOGETHER NOW'. Finally, everything clicked into place; The FARM found themselves at the epicentre of the indie/dance "baggy" scene in 1990 with the unstoppable momentum of 'GROOVY TRAIN' and penned one of the scene's anthems in 'ALL TOGETHER NOW', both becoming massive UK Top 10 hits (even heartthrob, Mike Dixon – from scouse soap, Brookside, was seen sporting a FARM T-shirt!). By the release of a belated debut album proper, 'SPARTACUS', the following year, the scene was fading fast; hardly the most glamourous band in the world, The FARM had always been a favourite target for music press jibes and the continual criticism certainly didn't help reverse the band's swift fall from grace. Though the album had gone straight in at No.1, surplus copies were to be found propping up record store bargain bins for the next three years. Despite a new deal with 'Sony' and a further UK Top 20 hit (an awful cover of The Human League's 'DON'T YOU WANT ME'), the insipid songwriting on 'LOVE SEE NO COLOUR' (1992) saw the album sink without trace. Even a third-time-lucky deal with 'Sire' couldn't halt the decline and the band after the failure of 1994's 'HULLABALOO' (which contained another cover, The Flamin' Groovies 'SHAKE SOME ACTION'). • **Miscellaneous:** In 1990, their live technician RAY TOOMEY, was jailed for 30 months for his part in the Risley Remand Centre rooftop protest.

Album rating: SPARTACUS (*6) / LOVE SEE NO COLOUR (*5) / HULLABALOO (*4) / PASTURES OLD AND NEW early compilation (*5)

PETE HOOTEN (b.28 Sep'62) – vocals / **STEVE GRIMES** (b. 4 Jun'62) – guitar / **JOHN MELVIN** – guitar / **PHILIP STRONGMAN** – bass / **ANDY McVANN** – drums / plus **TONY EVANS** – trombone / **GEORGE MAHER** – trumpet / **STEVE 'SNOWY' LEVY** – saxophone / and occasional live **JOE MUSKER** – percussion

Skysaw / not iss.

Nov 84. (12"ep) *(END 1)* **HEARTS AND MINDS. / ('A'dub version) / INFORMATION MAN / SAME OLD STORY**

Admiralty / not iss.

Nov 85. (7") *(PRA 1)* **STEPS OF EMOTION. / MEMORIES**
(12") *(PRAT 1)* – ('A'side) / Power over me / No man's land / Better / Living for tomorrow.

Fire / not iss.

Sep 86. (7") *(BLAZE 13)* **SOME PEOPLE. / STANDING TOGETHER**
(12"+=) *(BLAZE 13T)* – Sign of the times / The Moroccan.
Oct 86. (lp) *(REFIRE 3)* **PASTURES OLD AND NEW** (compilation of sessions)
– Hearts and minds / Information man / Same old story / Hearts and minds (dub) / Steps of emotion / Power over me / No man's land / Better / Worn out sayings / Some people / Little ol' wine drinker me. *(re-iss. Aug89 & Oct91; REF 11003)*

— (early '87) **MICK HANRATTY** – drums (on tour) repl. ANDY McVANN who died in a crash Dec86. Late 1987; **ROY BOULTER** (b. 2 Jul'64) – drums repl. HANRATTY and the horn section / **KEITH MULLEN** (DR. KEITH LOVE) (b.Bootle) – guitar repl. MELVIN / **CARL HUNTER** (b.14 Apr'65, Bootle, England) – bass repl. PHILLIP

— (early '89) HOOTEN, GRIMES, HUNTER, MULLEN + BOULTER added **BEN LEACH** (b. 2 May'69) – keyboards

Foresight / not iss.

Jul 89. (7") *(FR 2301)* **BODY AND SOUL. / COLONELS**
(12") *(FR 2301-12)* – ('A'side) / Colonels and heroes / Stuck on you.

Produce / Sire

Apr 90. (7"/ext.12") *(MILK 101/+T)* **STEPPING STONE (ghost dance mix). / FAMILY OF MAN** — 58 / -
Sep 90. (7"/c-s) *(MILK 102/+C)* **GROOVY TRAIN. / ('A'-3:30 a.m. mix)** — 6 / -
(ext.12"+=)(cd-s+=) *(MILK 102T)(CDMILK 102)* – ('A'-Bootle mix).
(below featured PETE WYLIE; WAH!)
Nov 90. (7"/c-s) *(MILK 103/+C)* **ALL TOGETHER NOW. / ('A'-Terry Farley mix)** — 4 / -
(12"+=)(cd-s+=) *(MILK 103T)(CDMILK 103)* – ('A'-Rocky & Diesel mix).

— added guest backing vocalist **PAULA DAVID**
Mar 91. (cd/c/lp) *(MILK CD/MC/LP 1) <26600>* **SPARTACUS** — 1 / Apr91
– Hearts and minds / How long / Sweet inspiration / Groovy train / Higher and higher / Don't let me down / Family of man / Tell the story / Very emotional / All together now. *(initial copies, incl.free remix lp)*
Apr 91. (7"/c-s) *(MILK 104/+C)* **DON'T LET ME DOWN. / ('A' Terry Farley mix)** — 36 / -
(12"+=)(cd-s+=) *(MILK 104T)(CDMILK 104)* – ('A'-Rocky & Diesel mix).
Aug 91. (7"/c-s) *(MILK 105/+C)* **MIND. / STEPPING STONE** — 31 / -
(12"+=)(cd-s+=) *(MILK 105T)(CDMILK 105)* – ('A'new mix).
Sep 91. (c-s) *<19209>* **GROOVY TRAIN / STEPPING STONE** — - / 41
Dec 91. (7"/c-s) *(MILK 106/+C)* **LOVE SEE NO COLOUR (Suggs mix). / ('A' Noel Watson mix)** — 58 / -
(d12"+=)(cd-s+=) *(MILK 106T)(CDMILK 106)* – (6 other remixes).

— In October 1991, KEITH MULLEN was attacked and stabbed needing over 80 stitches. 'ALL TOGETHER NOW' is used by The Labour Party in their General election campaign.

End Product-Sony / Sire

Jun 92. (7"/c-s) *(658 468-7/-4)* **RISING SUN. / CREEPERS** — 48 / -
(12"+=/cd-s+=) *(658 468-6/-2)* – ('A'-Mark Saunders mix) / ('A'-Steve Spiro mix).
Oct 92. (7"/c-s) *(658 468-7/-4)* **DON'T YOU WANT ME. / OBVIOUSLY** — 18 / -
(cd-s+=) *(658 468-6/-2)* – Groovy train (US mix).
Nov 92. (cd/c/lp) *(472 029-2/-4/-1) <26959>* **LOVE SEE NO COLOUR**
– Rising sun / Hard times / Words of wisdom / Mind / Been a long time / Don't you want me / Rain / Good morning sinners / Love see no colour / Suzy Boo.
Dec 92. (7"/c-s) *(658 868-7/-4)* **LOVE SEE NO COLOUR. / ALL TOGETHER NOW** — 35 / -
(12"+=) *(658 868-6)* – Anytown / (other 'A'side).
(cd-s) *(658 868-2)* – ('A'side) / ('A'original) / Rain / Don't you want me (mixes).

Produce / not iss.

Feb 93. (5x12"box)(cd-box-ep) **STEPPING STONE. / ALL TOGETHER NOW (mix)/ GROOVY TRAIN. / (mix)/ ALL TOGETHER NOW. / (mix)/ MIND. / (mix)/ DON'T LET ME DOWN. / (mix)**

Warners / Sire

Jul 94. (7"/c-s) *(W 0256/+C)* **MESSIAH. / ONE MORE FOOL**
(cd-s+=) *(W 0256CD)* – Somewhere (acoustic) / Love made up my mind.
Aug 94. (cd/c) *<9362 45588-2/-4>* **HULLABALOO** — May94
– Messiah / Shake some action / Comfort / The man who cried / Hateful / Golden vision / To the ages / All American world / Distant voices / Echoes.

— split after failure of above album

– compilations, etc. –

May 98. (cd) *Essential; (ESS 595)* **THE BEST OF THE FARM**
May 01. (cd) *Music Club; (MCCD 456)* **THE VERY BEST OF THE FARM**

FARMER'S BOYS

Formed: Norwich, England . . . early 80's originally as BANG GOES MY STEREO by BAZ, FROG, MARK and ANDY (the latter being replaced by STAN). Straight outta Norwich in the wake of The HIGSONS, this bunch of straw-chewing, fun loving bumpkins made their vinyl debut in Spring '82 with 'I THINK I NEED HELP'. This was followed with a further two equally impressive, independently released singles, 'WHATEVER IS HE LIKE' and 'MORE THAN A DREAM'. Akin to ORANGE JUICE with a brass section or a more soulful proto-HOUSEMARTINS, 'E.M.I.' deemed the latter track sufficiently chartworthy to re-issue it in early '83. Perhaps it was also EMI's idea to release 'MUCK IT OUT' in the hope of a WURZELS-style novelty hit, the record scraping into the Top 50. The lilting 'FOR YOU' was also a minor hit, previewing their debut album, 'GET OUT AMD WALK' (1983). While a geeky, happy-go-lucky charm characterised the bulk of their work, BAZ's DAVID BYRNE/MORRISSEY/EDWYN COLLINS vocal hybrid began to wear thin over the course of an album; even so, the record surely deserved more than its lowly Top 50 placing. Although EMI ultimately failed in their bid to make The FARMER'S BOYS the toast of city and country alike, a further two minor hits, 'PHEW WOW' and 'I BUILT THE WORLD', along with a follow-up album, 'WITH THESE HANDS' (1985) surfaced before the lads went on to pastures new; while FROG joined locals The HIGSONS, BAZ and MARK joined the short-lived AVONS. With their indie reputation taking an upsurge in credibility, the lads reunited in the late 90's, not as The FARMER'S BOYS but as The GREAT OUTDOORS. A pair of 7" singles on 'Fierce Panda', 'IT LOOKS SO EASY' and 'HEAD IN THE CLOUDS', set out their stall, although their comeback set, 'WHAT WE DID ON OUR HOLIDAYS' (2001) seemed to be exactly what it said on the tin (er, label).

Album rating: GET OUT AND WALK (*4) / WITH THESE HANDS (*5) / ONCE UPON A TIME IN THE EAST (THE EARLY YEARS 1981-1982) compilation (*5) / Great Outdoors: WHAT WE DID ON OUR HOLIDAYS (*6)

BAZ – vocals / **FROG** – keyboards, guitar, synth-drums / **STAN** – guitar; repl. ANDY who joined SERIOUS DRINKING / **MARK** – bass

Waap / not iss.

Apr 82. (7") *(WAAP 3)* **I THINK I NEED HELP. / SQUIT**
(ext-12"+=) *(12WAAP 3)* – More quit / Squittest.

Backs / not iss.

Jul 82. (7") *(NCH 001)* **WHATEVER IS HE LIKE? / I LACK CONCENTRATION**
Nov 82. (7") *(NCH 003)* **MORE THAN A DREAM. / THE COUNTRY LINE**

E.M.I. / not iss.

Jan 83. (7") *(EMI 5367)* **MORE THAN A DREAM. / THE COUNTRY LINE**
Mar 83. (7"/7"pic-d) *(EMI/+P 5380)* **MUCK IT OUT! / FUNKY COMBINE, JOHN** — 48 / -
(12"+=) *(12EMI 5380)* – ('A'extended).
Jul 83. (7") *(EMI 5401)* **FOR YOU. / T.O.S.D.** — 66 / -
(w/ free-7"+=) *(EMID 5401)* – Muck it out (demo) / Drinking and dressing up / Something that I ate / I don't know why I don't like all my friends.
(12"+=) *(12EMI 5401)* – I don't know why I don't like all my friends.
Oct 83. (lp/c) *(EMC/TC-EMC 107799-1)* **GET OUT AND WALK** — 49 / -
– Matter of fact / Probably one of the best investments I ever made / More than a dream / I woke up this morning / The way you made me cry / A promise you can't keep / Soft drink / For you / Torn in two / Who needs it? *(lp w/ free-12"ep+=)* – PROBABLY ONE OF THE BEST INVESTMENTS I EVER MADE / SOFT DRINK. / FOR YOU / MUCK IT OUT *(c++=)* – Muck it out! / Funky combine, John.
Apr 84. (7") *(FAB 1)* **APPARENTLY . . . / UNCLE FREDDIE**
(12"+=) *(12FAB 1)* – Apparently . . . (bigger).
Jul 84. (7"/7"pic-d) *(FAB/+P 2)* **IN THE COUNTRY. / MAMA NEVER TOLD ME** — 44 / -
(12"+=) *(12FAB 4)* – Matter of fact (remix).
Oct 84. (7") *(FAB 3)* **PHEW WOW! / PORTRAIT OF A LEGEND (part 1)** — 59 / -
(12"+=) *(12FAB 3)* – Portrait of a legend (part 2).

FARMER'S BOYS (cont)

Feb 85. (7") *(FAB 4)* **I BUILT THE WORLD. / SOMETIMES**
(12"+=) *(12FAB 4)* – Sport for all (live) / Probably one of the best investments I ever made (live).

Mar 85. (lp/c) *(FBLP/TC-FBLP 2)* **WITH THESE HANDS**
– In the country / I built the world / Sport for all / Art gallery / Something from nothing / Phew wow! / All of a sudden / Heartache / Walkabout / Whatever is he like? (*<re-iss. Jul01 on 'Vinyl Japan' cd/lp; ASK CD/LP 126>*)

— they split just after the above was finally released; FROG joined The HIGSONS. BAZ and MARK joined the AVONS who ad two releases for 'Letharge', the lp 'THREE RIVERS REACH' and the 12" 'DIRTY AND CONTROVERSIAL'.

– compilations, etc. –

Nov 02. (cd) *Backs; (NCHCD 19)* **ONCE UPON A TIME IN THE EAST (THE EARLY YEARS 1981-1982)**
– I lack concentration / Or what / Squit / Autumn / I don't know why I don't like all my friends / I think I need help / Squittest / Muck it out / Spring / Funny old Mr. Baz (Whatever is he like?) / With these hands I built the world / Description of the River Waveney at Wortwell / Soft drink / Drinking and dressing up / The country line / Funky combine, John / T.O.S.D. / More than a dream / Homo kino.

GREAT OUTDOORS

BAZ, MARK + STAN

Fierce Panda / not iss.

Jun 99. (7") *(NING 73)* **IT LOOKS SO EASY. / MOOD OF THE NATION**
(cd-s+=) *(NING 73CD)* – Out of my tree.

Nov 99. (7"m) *(NING 87)* **HEAD IN THE CLOUDS. / IT'S BLOODY DARK IN HERE / RED MOUNTAIN LAMENT**

Backs / not iss.

Feb 01. (7") *(NCH 118)* **MY HEART ALIVE. / HIGH TIDE**
Feb 01. (cd) *(NCHCD 18)* **WHAT WE DID ON OUR HOLIDAYS**
– Brave new girl / Rainy days / It looks so easy / My heart alive / 5 o'clock shadow / The sunrise coast / Welcome to my garden / Head in the clouds / Boys left home / Mood of the nation / Burn the bridges.

Oct 01. (cd-ep) *(NCHCDS 119)* **FADING FAST EP**
– Fading fast / Return of the Romeo uncle / Valerie's theme / The birds and the bees / Head in the clouds (acoustic version).

FASTBACKS

Formed: Seattle, Washington, USA ... 1980 by guitarist/vocalist LULU GARGUILO, bassist/vocalist KIM WARNICK, guitarist KURT BLOCH and drummer DUFF McKAGAN. This basic power-pop act delivered one single ('IT'S YOUR BIRTHDAY') in the early 80's before McKAGAN was whisked off to play guitar for seminal grunge act, 10 MINUTE WARNING. He more famously took up the bass for metal superstars, GUNS N' ROSES and stayed with them until he reformed 10MW in 1997. Meanwhile, The FASTBACKS replaced DUFF with RICHARD STUVERUD in '81, releasing a second effort (an unknown EP) the following year. They split not long after, although the Bristol imprint, 'Subway', released some new work in 1988/89, most notably the album, ' ... AND HIS ORCHESTRA'. LULU, KIM, KURT and an ever changing drummer continued to surface now and then in the early 90's and in 1992 they signed to the seminal 'Sub Pop' label, releasing three worthy albums, 'THE QUESTION IS NO' (1992), 'ZUCKER' (1993) and 'ANSWER THE PHONE, DUMMY' (1994). • **Covered:** EYES OF A CHILD (John Lodge) / SPACE STATION No.5 (Montrose) / SIGN OF THE TIMES (...Hatch) / RAMBLIN' ROSE (MC5). • **Trivia:** Said to be EDDIE VEDDER's fave band. BLOCH took up production work for GAS HUFFER, TAD and MUDHONEY.

Album rating: FASTBACKS AND HIS ORCHESTRA (*6) / VERY VERY POWERFUL MOTOR (*5) / ZUCKER (*7) / THE QUESTION IS NO (*5) / ANSWER THE PHONE, DUMMY (*5) / NEW MANSIONS IN SOUND (*6) / THE DAY THAT DIDN'T EXIST (*7)

LULU GARGUILO – vocals, guitar / **KIM WARNICK** – vocals, bass / **KURT BLOCH** – guitar / **DUFF McKAGAN** (b. MICHAEL) – drums

not iss. / No Threes

Jun 81. (7") *<N3-005>* **IT'S YOUR BIRTHDAY. / YOU CAN'T BE HAPPY**

— **RICHARD STUVERUD** – drums, repl. McKAGAN (see above)

Apr 82. (12"ep) *<N3-006>* **FASTBACKS EP**

— split but re-formed in the late 80's

Subway / not iss.

Oct 88. (7") *(SUBWAY 24)* **IN THE WINTER. / DREAM**
Jun 89. (7") *(SUBWAY 26)* **WRONG WRONG WRONG. /**
Jul 89. (lp) *(SUBORG 008)* **...AND HIS ORCHESTRA**
– Seven days / The light's on you / If you tried / Don't cry for me / In the winter / Wrong, wrong, wrong / K street / You will be the one / Call it what you want / Set me free / I need some help / Midnight confessions / See and say / Only at night / What will they all say? / In America / No lethal hope / Fast enough / Wait! / Whenever I'm walking. (cd-iss. Feb95 on 'Pop Llama'; PLCD 803)

Blaster / Blaster

Sep 90. (lp) *(BLATLP 001)* **VERY VERY POWERFUL MOTOR**
– In the summer / Apologies / Trouble sleeping / Better than before / What to expect / Dirk's car jam / Says who / Last night I had a dream I could fly / I won't regret / I guess / I'll be okay. *(UK-iss.Feb95 on 'Pop Llama'; PLCD 011)*

1991. (lp) *(BLATLP 003)* **NEVER FAILS ... NEVER WORKS**
– In America / No lethal hope / Fast enough / Wait / Whenever I'm walking / Only at night / What will they all say? / Midnight confessions / See and say / It's your birthday / You can't be happy / Was late. *(re-iss. Nov93; same)*

Sub Pop / Sub Pop

Jun 92. (cd) *<(SP 146B)>* **THE QUESTION IS NO**
(UK-iss.Mar94; same)

Jan 93. (lp/cd) *<(SP 231/+CD)>* **ZUCKER**
– Believe me never / Gone to the moon / Hung on a bad peg / Under the old lightbulb / Never heard of him / When I'm old / All about nothing / Bill challenger / Parts / A kind of game / They don't care / Please read me / Save room for me / That was.

Mar 93. (7") *<(SP 69-236)>* **GONE TO THE MOON. / GO ALL THE WAY**
(12"+=/cd-s+=) *<(SP/+CD 68-235)>* – Right thing / Fanfare.

Sep 94. (7") *(MR 705-7)* **WAIT IT OUT. / THE JESTER**
(above issued on 'Munster')

Nov 94. (lp/c/cd) *<(SP/+MC/CD 259)>* **ANSWER THE PHONE, DUMMY**
– Waste of time / On the wall / Went for a swim / Old address of the unknown / Back to nowhere / BRD "coated" / I found the star / And you / On your hands / I'm cold / Think / In the observatory / Trumpets are loud / Meet the author / Future right.

May 96. (10"m-lp/m-cd) *<(MR 087/+CD)>* **ALONE IN A FURNITURE WAREHOUSE SCARING YOU AWAY LIKE A HOTEL MATTRESS**
– No information / Ladders / Buried treasure was crap / Wait it out / Alone in a furniture warehouse / Eyes of a child / All in order / Sign of the times.
(above issued on 'Munster')

Jun 96. (cd) *<(SPCD 357)>* **NEW MANSIONS IN SOUND**
– Fortunes misery / Which has not been written / No information / I know / Weather perfectly clear / 555 (part one) / 555 (part two) / Stay at home / Bitter drink / Just say / Banner year / Is it familiar? Space station No.5 / Find your way / Girl's eyes.

Pop Llama / Pop Llama

Feb 98. (cd) *<(PLCD 6)>* **WIN LOSE OR BOTH**
– No music played / So wrong / Book of revelation / Used to belong / In the winter / On your hands / I know / I'm cold / Banneryear / 555 (part 2) / Gone to the moon / Always tomorrow / Ramblin' Rose.

Munster / SpinArt

Nov 99. (lp/cd) *(MR 164/+CD) <SRT 079>* **THE DAY THAT DIDN'T EXIST**
– One more hour / Goodbye, bird / Like today / As everything / New book of old / Defy's gravity / I was stolen / Dreams I.H.S. / Have you had enough / We can be / Maybe / What's the use? / My destiny / The day that didn't exist.

– compilations, etc. –

Apr 92. (lp/cd) *Lost & Found; <(LF 016/+CD)>* **IN AMERICA**
1994. (cd) *Lucky; <3>* **BIKE TOY CLOCK GIFT**
Aug 96. (cd) *Lance Rock; <24>* **HERE THEY ARE** (live at the Crocodile Cafe)
– Out of the charts / Run no more / Hung on a bad peg / The light's on you / On the wall / Went for a swim / Old address of the unknown / Under the old lightbulb / I'm cold / In the observatory / On your hands / They don't care / Save room for me / Rat race.

FATIMA MANSIONS (see under ⇒ COUGHLAN, Cathal)

FEELIES

Formed: Hoboken, New Jersey, USA ... late 1977 by songwriter, GLENN MERCER and BILL MILLION, who completed the line-up with KEITH CLAYTON and VINNIE DeNUNZIO. They emerged from the garage and played the CBGB's in the late 70's, leading to a one-off single, 'RAISED EYEBROWS', for the UK label, 'Rough Trade'. Early the following decade, with ANTON FIER replacing DeNUNZIO, The FEELIES unleashed their debut album, 'CRAZY RHYTHMS' (1980), a TALKING HEADS meets VELVET UNDERGROUND affair combining sparse two-chord harmonies and jerky pop energy. Issued for another Brit imprint, 'Stiff' and despite critical acclaim, it failed to generate much interest, the band's reluctance to publicise with a tour not helping any. The FEELIES' generally lackadaisical attitude towards self promotion subsequently led to their 5-album contract being torn up and the members went off into various side projects, only surfacing occasionally to play on holiday weekends. This hiatus resulted in MERCER and MILLION joining old high school mates, The TRYPES, who released the 1984 EP, 'THE EXPLORERS HOLD' on the FEELIES' new label, 'Coyote'. In 1983, they found fellow songwriter, DAVID WECKERMAN (of YUNG WU), who helped them write the score for the film 'Smithereens'. The following year, the pair featured as The WILLIES in Jonathan Demme's film, 'Something Wild', covering 'I'M A BELIEVER', 'FAME' and 'BEFORE THE NEXT TEARDROP FALLS'. In 1986, PETER BUCK heard they were back together, the ubiquitous R.E.M. man offering to produce their comeback album, 'THE GOOD EARTH'. To many fans and critics alike, it was definitely worth the six year wait, the reaction even spurring them on to a tour of Europe early the following year. In 1988, The FEELIES finally signed to a major ('A&M') and hit the lower regions of the US chart with their third album, 'ONLY LIFE'. The group recorded one further set before MERCER and WECKERMAN took off, the pair later surfacing as WAKE OOLOO. • **Covered:** EVERYBODY'S GOT SOMETHING TO HIDE + SHE SAID, SHE SAID (Beatles) / PAINT IT BLACK (Rolling Stones) / SEDAN DELIVERY + BARSTOOL BLUES (Neil Young) / WHAT GOES ON + WHITE LIGHT – WHITE HEAT (Velvet Underground) / REAL COOL TIME (Stooges) / DANCING BAREFOOT (Patti Smith) / EGYPTIAN REGGAE + NOW I WANNA SLEEP IN YOUR ARMS (Jonathan Richman) / the Yung Wu: BIG DAY (Eno-Manzanera) / CHILD OF THE MOON (Rolling Stones) / POWDERFINGER (Neil Young) / Wake Ooloo:- SO WANT TO BE A ROCK'N'ROLL STAR (Byrds).

Album rating: CRAZY RHYTHMS (*8) / THE GOOD EARTH (*7) / ONLY LIFE (*7) / TIME FOR A WITNESS (*4) / Yung Wu: SHORE LEAVE (*5) / Wake Ooloo: HEAR NO EVIL (*5) / WHAT ABOUT IT (*5) / STOP THE RIDE (*4)

FEELIES (cont)

GLEN MERCER – vocals, guitar, drums / **BILL MILLION** – guitar, percussion, vocals / **KEITH CLAYTON** – bass, drums, vocals / **VINNIE DeNUNZIO** – drums

Rough Trade / not iss.

Sep 79. (7") *(RT 24)* **RAISED EYEBROWS. / FA CE-LA**

— **ANTON FIER** – drums; repl. VINNIE who later formed CERTAIN GENERALS after a spell with RICHARD LLOYD / added guests **ARTHUR ADAMS + ROLAND BAUTISTA** – guitars

Stiff / not iss.

Jan 80. (7";w-drawn) *(BUY 65)* **EVERYBODY'S GOT SOMETHING TO HIDE. / ORIGINAL LOVE**
Jan 80. (lp/c) *(SEEZ/ZSEEZ 20)* **CRAZY RHYTHMS**
 – The boy with the perpetual nervousness / Fa ce-la / Loveless love / Forces at work / Original love / Everybody's got something to hide / Moscow nights / Raised eyebrows / Crazy rhythms. *(re-iss. Nov87 on 'Line' lp/cd; XILP4/LICD9 00168) <US-iss.1991 on 'A&M' cd+=/c; 75021-5319-2/-4>* – Paint it black.

— rested/split for a time when ANTON joined PERE UBU

TRYPES

JOHN BAUMGARTNER – vocals / **GLENN + BILL / + STAN DEMESKI** – drums / **BRENDA SAUTER** – bass, vocals

not iss. / Coyote

1984. (12"ep) *<COYEP 006>* **THE EXPLORERS HOLD**
 – (From the) Morning glories / Love you to / Music for neighbors / The undertow.

FEELIES

— **DAVE WECKERMAN** – percussion; repl. BAUMGARTNER who evolved the band into SPEED THE PLOUGH

Rough Trade Twin/Tone-Coyote

Sep 86. (lp) *(ROUGH 104) <TTC 8673>* **THE GOOD EARTH**
 – On the roof / The high road / The last roundup / Slipping (into something) / When company comes / Let's go / Two rooms / The good earth / Tomorrow today / Slow down. *(cd-iss. Nov87 on 'Line'+=; LICD 900428)* – She said, she said / Sedan delivery.
Nov 86. (12"ep) *(RTT 180)* **NO ONE KNOWS EP**
 – The high road / She said, she said / Slipping (into something) / Sedan delivery.

A&M Coyote-A&M

Apr 89. (lp/c/cd) *(AMA/AMC/CDA 5214) <SP 5214>* **ONLY LIFE** Nov88
 – It's only life / Too much / Deep fascination / Higher ground / The undertow / For a while / The final word / Too far gone / Away / What goes on.

— in 1989, the Bob magazine, (iss.#35) released 7"flexi, 'DANCING BAREFOOT'

Mar 91. (cd/lp) *(<75021 5344-2/-1>)* **TIME FOR A WITNESS**
 – Waiting / Time for a witness / Sooner or later / Find a way / Decide / Doin' it again / Invitation / For now / What she said / Real cool time.
Jan 93. (cd-s) *<CD 17675>* **HIGHER GROUND / EGYPTIAN REGGAE / EVERYBODY'S GOT SOMETHING TO HIDE EXCEPT ME AND MY MONKEY**

— disbanded in 1992. STANLEY joined LUNA 2 with former GALAXIE 500 member DEAN WAREHAM. SAUTER joined SPEED THE PLOUGH and later WILD CARNATION

YUNG WU

— **WECKERMAN** (lead vox), **MERCER, MILLION + SAUTER + DEMESKI** recruited for this offshoot **JOHN BAUMGARTNER** – keyboards

not iss. / Coyote

Oct 87. (lp/c) *<TTC 87119/+C>* **SHORE LEAVE**
 – Shore leave / The empty pool / Aspiration / Spinning / Big day / Eternal ice / Strange little man / Return to Zion / Child of the moon / Powderfinger / Modern farmer.

WAKE OOLOO

MERCER + WECKERMAN + RUSS GAMBINO – keyboards / **TROY MEISS** – bass

Houses In Motion / Pravda

Dec 94. (cd/c) *(EFA 26207-2) <PR 6349-2/-4>* **HEAR NO EVIL**
 – Time to go / Another song / Forty days / Rise / Nobody heard / Knocking on ever door / From afar / Effax / Grams of sand / Any Mindy.

— **JOHN DEAN** – bass; repl. MEISS

Jun 95. (cd) *(EFA 06197-2) <PR 6356-2>* **WHAT ABOUT IT**
 – Don't look now / Beautiful feeling / Anything / Too long gone / Age of reason / Fun to be happy / It's forgotten / Common sense / Nature of the beast / Hard to find / Down that road / Monday morning.

Konkurrent Pravda

Sep 96. (cd) *(K 171CD) <PR 6362-2>* **STOP THE RIDE** Jul96
 – Too many times / In the way / Stiff / Stop the ride / Like yesterday / Get caught up / Alive and waiting / Every other one / Final warning / Maybe next time / So you want to be a rock'n'roll star.

FELT

Formed: Birmingham, England ... 1979 by LAWRENCE HAYWARD. Following glowing reviews for a self-produced single, 'INDEX', HAYWARD recruited a full band – MAURICE DEEBANK, GARY AINGE and NICK GILBERT (who issued a solo single, 'NEWTRITION' / 'BLIMP' under The VERSATILE NEWTS moniker on 'Shanghai' in 1980) – in an attempt to realise his dreams of pop stardom. Signed to 'Cherry Red', the first chapter in the FELT story began with a series of early 80's singles (including the sublime 'PENELOPE TREE') and a couple of mini-sets, 'CRUMBLING THE ANTISEPTIC BEAUTY' (1982) and 'THE SPLENDOUR OF FEAR' (1984). Characterised by DEEBANK's resonating guitar sound – an often romantic combination of TOM VERLAINE, The BYRDS and Spanish classical – these early recordings alternated between atmospheric instrumentals and moody HAYWARD vocal cuts. With a highly affected singing style lying somewhere between LLOYD COLE and JARVIS COCKER (although these two were undoubtedly influenced by him rather than the other way around), HAYWARD wasn't the greatest of vocalists in a technical sense yet the combination of his voice and the dreamy backing created music of a strange beauty. He was also something of a demanding boss and by the release of a first album, 'THE STRANGE IDOLS PATTERN AND OTHER SHORT STORIES' (1984), the band had already gone through two bassists with a line-up constantly on the brink of collapse. It was into this precarious situation that hammond player, MARTIN DUFFY entered in the mid-80's as the band began work on 'IGNITE THE SEVEN CANNONS' (1985) with ROBIN GUTHRIE at the production helm. The accompanying single, 'PRIMITIVE PAINTERS', featured fellow COCTEAU TWINS, LIZ FRASER, on vocals, a sterling slice of swirling psychedelia which remains one of the band's few near misses with actual chart action. Despite the permanent departure of DEEBANK in 1985, the band continued to reap critical acclaim with the likes of 'FOREVER BREATHES THE LONELY WORD' (1986), their fourth album proper and their second for new label 'Creation'. While FELT were clearly capable of penning melodies with chart-hit written all over them, HAYWARD's penchant for willfully obscure lyrical fare and song titles significantly reduced their chances of commercial success. Releasing an album – 'TRAIN ABOVE THE CITY' (1988) – consisting solely of Fender Rhodes piano instrumentals wasn't exactly a shrewd move either, although by this point LAWRENCE had obviously resigned himself to eternal cultdom. The following year FELT bowed out with 'ME AND A MONKEY ON THE MOON' (1989), perhaps the most accessible album of their decade-long recording career. While MARTIN DUFFY joined PRIMAL SCREAM's rock'n'roll circus, LAWRENCE eventually resurfaced with DENIM, a self-consciously ironic glitter-pop revivalist project. Recorded with bonafide glam musos from the 70's, 'BACK IN DENIM' was released by the trendy 'Boy's Own' label in '92, the music press briefly reprising LAWRENCE for a new generation of indie kids. Issued at the height of the Britpop phenomenon, follow-up set, 'DENIM ON ICE' (1996) was given scant media attention compared to the column inches devoted to the likes of PULP, an irony that HAYWARD would no doubt savour. Understandably, the man regrouped his thoughts under the auspices/patronage of a new moniker, GO KART MOZART; mmm, very indie. Yes, it had been twenty years since HAYWARD released his first record as FELT and this long arduous journey had culminated in his new venture's 'INSTANT WIGWAM AND IGLOO MIXTURE' set in 1999. A slight change in direction once again, LAWRENCE flitted between clever indie pop to intricate and satiristic meanderings; check out 'HIP OP', a record inspired by the Queen Mother's hip operation. What's next? In early 2002, former FELT people MARCO THOMAS, GARY AINGE and MARTIN DUFFY (alongside MARTIN DAVIS), instigated their own Krautrock-esque outfit, FLY, releasing the well-received 'Put The Needle Down And Fly'.

Album rating: CRUMBLING THE ANTISEPTIC BEAUTY mini (*6) / THE SPLENDOUR OF FEAR (*6) / THE STRANGE IDOLS PATTERN AND OTHER SHORT STORIES (*7) / IGNITE THE SEVEN CANNONS (*7) / LET THE SNAKES CRINKLE THEIR HEADS TO DEATH (*6) / FOREVER BREATES THE LONELY WORD (*7) / POEM OF THE RIVER mini (*6) / THE PICTORIAL JACKSON REVIEW (*6) / TRAIN ABOVE THE CITY (*6) / ME AND A MONKEY ON THE MOON (*5) / ABSOLUTE CLASSIC MASTERPIECES compilation (*8) / BUBBLEGUM PERFUME compilation (*6) / Denim: BACK IN DENIM (*7) / DENIM ON ICE (*5) / Go Kart Mozart: INSTANT WIGWAM AND IGLOO MIXTURE (*6) / Maurice Deebank: INNER THOUGHT ZONE mini (*4)

LAWRENCE HAYWARD – guitar, vocals

Shanghai / not iss.

Sep 79. (7") *(SRTS 79-CUS 321)* **INDEX. / BREAK IT**

— added **MAURICE DEEBANK** – guitar / **GARY AINGE** – drums / **NICK GILBERT** – bass

Cherry Red / not iss.

Jul 81. (7") *(CHERRY 26)* **SOMETHING SENDS ME TO SLEEP. / RED INDIANS / SOMETHING SENDS ME TO SLEEP (version)**
Feb 82. (m-lp) *(MRED 25)* **CRUMBLING THE ANTISEPTIC BEAUTY**
 – Birdmen / Cathedral / I worship the sun / Templeroy / Fortune / Evergreen dazed. *(cd-iss. w/ next album Sep86; MREDCD 25)*

— NICK GILBERT decided to leave. Also DEEBANK left for a short while

Sep 82. (7") *(CHERRY 45)* **MY FACE IS ON FIRE. / TRAILS OF COLOUR DISSOLVE**

— added **MICK LLOYD** – bass and the returning **DEEBANK**

Jun 83. (7") *(CHERRY 59)* **PENELOPE TREE. / A PREACHER IN NEW ENGLAND**
 (12"+=) *(12CHERRY 59)* – Now summer's spread its wings again.
Feb 84. (m-lp/c) *(MRED/CRED 57)* **THE SPLENDOUR OF FEAR**
 – The stagnant pool / Red Indians / The world is as soft as lace / Mexican bandits / The optimist and the poet / Preacher in New England.
Mar 84. (7") *(CHERRY 78)* **MEXICAN BANDITS. / THE WORLD IS AS SOFT AS LACE**
Jul 84. (7") *(CHERRY 81)* **SUNLIGHT BATHED THE GOLDEN GLOW. / FORTUNE**
 (12"+=) *(12CHERRY 81)* – Sunlight strings.
Oct 84. (lp) *(BRED 63)* **THE STRANGE IDOLS PATTERN AND OTHER SHORT STORIES**
 – Roman litter / Sempiternal darkness / Spanish Louise / Vasco da Gama / Sunlight bathed the golden glow / Crucifix heaven / Whirlpool vision of shame / Dismantled King is off the throne / Imprint / Crystal ball. *(cd-iss. Feb93; CDBRED 63)*

FELT (cont)

— **MARTIN DUFFY** – organ repl. LLOYD (below b-side was above line-up) / **MARCO THOMAS** – bass guested with **ELIZABETH FRAZER** – vocals (COCTEAU TWINS) ROBIN GUTHRIE of The COCTEAUS produced 1985 material.

Aug 85. (12") *(12CHERRY 89)* **PRIMITIVE PAINTERS. / CATHEDRAL (rec.'84)**
(pic-cd-s iss.Aug88; CDCHERRY 89)

— Band consisted of interchanging lead guitarists LAWRENCE and MAURICE, MARTIN and LIZ on some vocals, MARCO on nearly all bass, plus GARY – drums

Sep 85. (lp) *(BRED 65)* **IGNITE THE SEVEN CANNONS**
– My darkest light will shine / The day the rain came down / Scarlet servants / I don't know which way to turn / Serpent shade / Primitive painters / Elegance of an only dream / Black ship in the harbour / Textile ranch / Caspian see / Southern state tapestry. *(c+=)* – (incl.previous lp). *(cd-iss. Jul89 with last album' BREDCD 65) (cd re-iss. May96 & Aug00; CDBRED 65)*

— guest **TONY WILLE** – guitar repl. MAURICE DEEBANK (MARCO now full member)

Creation   not iss.

May 86. (7") *(CRE 027)* **BALLAD OF THE BAND. / I DIDN'T MEAN TO HURT YOU**
(12"+=) *(CRE 027T)* – Candles in a church / Ferdinand Magellan.

Jun 86. (lp) *(CRELP 009)* **LET THE SNAKES CRINKLE THEIR HEADS TO DEATH**
– Song for William S. Harvey / Ancient city where I lived / The seventeenth century / The palace / Indian scriptures / The Nazca plain / Voyage to illumination / Jewel sky / Viking dress / Sapphire mansions. *(cd-iss. Mar91 & May94; CRECD 009)*

— **TONY WILLE** – guitars guested again

Sep 86. (7") *(CRE 032)* **RAIN OF CRYSTAL SPIRES. / I WILL DIE WITH MY HEAD IN FLAMES**
(12"+=) *(CRE 032T)* – Gather up your wings and fly / Sandman's on the rise again.

Oct 86. (lp/c) *(CRELP 011/+C)* **FOREVER BREATHES THE LONELY WORD**
– Down but not yet out / Hours of darkness have changed my mind / All the people I like are those that are dead / Grey streets / Gather up your wings and fly / Rain of crystal spires / A wave crashed on rocks / September lady. *(c+=)* – (includes previous lp). *(cd-iss. Oct90; CRECD 011)*

— added 6th guest member **NEIL SCOTT** – Fender jazzmaster retained guest **TONY WILLE** to augment LAWRENCE, GARY, MARTIN and MARCO

Jun 87. (m-lp) *(CRELP 017)* **POEM OF THE RIVER**
– Declaration / She lives by the castle / Riding on the equator / Stained glass windows in the sky / Dark red birds / Silver plane. *(cd-iss. Mar91 & May94; CRECD 017)*

— **FELT** are LAWRENCE, MARTIN DUFFY, MARCO THOMAS, GARY AINGE but album features 1. LAWRENCE with guest **RICHARD THOMAS** – soprano saxophone (of DIF JUZ) 2. DUFFY – solo / 3. LAWRENCE – solo guitar / 4. LAWRENCE with **MICK TRAVIS** – bass 5. LAWRENCE, DUFFY and TRAVIS – instrumental

Jul 87. (12"ep) *(CRE 048T)* **THE FINAL RESTING PLACE OF THE ARK / AUTUMN. / FIRE CIRCLE / THERE'S NO SUCH THING AS VICTORY / BURIED WILD BLIND**

— added **MICK BUND** – bass (MARCO now lead guitar & LAWRENCE added organ)

May 88. (lp) *(CRELP 030)* **THE PICTORIAL JACKSON REVIEW**
– Apple boutique / Ivory past / Christopher St. / Bitter end / Until the fools get wise / How spook got her man / Don't die on my doorstep / Under a pale light / Sending lady Lord / The darkest ending.

— Next album was down to just DUFFY and AINGE. Others were rested

Aug 88. (lp) *(CRELP 035)* **TRAIN ABOVE THE CITY**
– On Weegee's sidewalk / Train above the city / Run Chico run / Press softly on the brakes Holly / Seahorses on Broadway / Spectral morning / Book of swords / Teargardens. *(cd-iss. Oct88, with last album; CRELP 035CD)*

— Full group again, + **ROSE McDOWELL** – vocals (ex-STRAWBERRY SWITCHBLADE)

Oct 88. (7") *(CRE 060)* **SPACE BLUES. / TUESDAYS SECRET**
(12"+=) *(CRE 060T)* – Be still / Female star.

— **JOHN MOHAN** – guitar (ex-SERVANTS) repl. ROSE who was only guest.

El   not iss.

Oct 89. (7"free-flexi) *(GPO F44)* **GET OUT OF MY MIRROR**

Nov 89. (lp/cd) *(ACME/+CD 24)* **ME AND A MONKEY ON THE MOON**
– I can't make love to you anymore / Mobile shack / Free / Budgie jacket / Carton sky / New day dawning / Down an August path / Never let you go / She deals in crosses / Get out of my mirror. *(cd re-iss. Oct96; same)*

— they split late 1989 having been together for 10 years. LAWRENCE moved to New York, having flitted to Brighton a year earlier. DUFFY joined PRIMAL SCREAM.

– compilations, etc. –

Sep 87. (lp/c/cd) Cherry Red; *(BRED/CBRED/BREDCD 79)* **GOLDMINE THRASH**
(c+=) – (includes 7 extra tracks).

Jun 90. (cd/c/lp) Creation; *(CRE CD/MC/LP 069)* **BUBBLEGUM PERFUME**
– I will die with my head in flames / Stained glass windows in the sky / I Didn't mean to hurt you / Space blues / Autumn / Be still / There's no such thing as victory / Magellan / The final resting of the ark / Sandman's on the rise again / Don't die on my doorstep / A wave crashed on rocks / Book of swords / Declaration / Gather up your wings and fly / The darkest ending / Bitter end / Rain of crystal spires / Voyage of illumination / Ballad of the band.

Mar 92. (12"ep/cd-ep) Cherry Red; *(12/CD CHERRY 124)* **PRIMITIVE PAINTERS / DISMANTLED KING IS OFF THE THRONE. / SUNLIGHT BATHED THE GOLDEN GLOW**

Apr 92. (cd) Cherry Red; *(CDBRED 97)* **ABSOLUTE CLASSIC MASTERPIECES**
– Primitive painters / The day the rain came down / My darkest light will shine / Textile ranch / Sunlight bathed the golden glow / Crystal ball / Dismantled king is off the throne / Fortune / Dance of deliverance / The stagnant pool / Red Indians / The world is as soft as lace / Penelope Tree / Trails of colour dissolve / Evergreen dazed / Templeroy / Something sends me to sleep / Index. *(re-iss. Oct96 & May00; same)*

Jun 93. (4xcd-ep-box) Cherry Red; *(FELT BOX 1)* **THE FELT BOX SET**

Sep 93. (d-cd) Creation; *(CRECD 150)* **ABSOLUTE CLASSIC MASTERPIECES VOL.2**

May 96. (cd) Cherry Red; *(CDBRED 72)* **CRUMBLING THE ANTISEPTIC BEAUTY / THE SPLENDOUR OF FEAR**
(re-iss. Aug00; same)

DENIM

— were formed by **LAWRENCE** – vocals, guitar, keyboards with **SIOBHAN** – bass / **GERRY SHEPHERD** – drums (ex-GLITTER BAND)

Boys Own   not iss.

Nov 92. (cd/c/lp) *(82849-2/-4/-1)* **BACK IN DENIM**
– Back in denim / Fish and chips / Bubble head / Middle of the road / The Osmonds / I saw the glitter on your face / American rock / Livin' on the streets / Here is my song for Europe / I'm against the eighties.

Jan 93. (7"/c-s) *(BOI/+CS 12)* **MIDDLE OF THE ROAD. / APE HANGERS**
(12"+=/cd-s+=) *(BOI X/CD 12)* – Robin's nest / The great grape ape hangers.

Echo   not iss.

Feb 96. (cd/c/lp) *(ECH CD/MC/LP 008)* **DENIM ON ICE**
– Great pub rock revival / It fell off the back of a lorry / Romeo Jones in love again / Bumburger / Supermodels / Mrs Back-to-front and the bull ring thing / City synthesis / Drinkin' um bongo / Mrs Mills / Best song in the world / Synthesizers in the rain / Job centre / Council house / Glue and smack / Jane Suck in '77 / Grandad's false teeth / Silly rabbit / Don't bite too much out of the apple / Myriad of hoops / Denim on ice. *(cd re-iss. Feb01; same)*

Feb 96. (7"/c-s) *(ECS/+MC 017)* **IT FELL OFF THE BACK OF A LORRY. / I WILL CRY AT CHRISTMAS**
(cd-s+=) *(ECSCD 017)* – Snake bite / Internet curtains.

EMI Disc   not iss.

Aug 97. (c-s/7") *(TC+/DISC 009)* **SUMMER SMASH. / SUN'S OUT**
(cd-s+=) *(CDDISC 009)* – Seaside shuffle / ('A'-Denim mix).

GO KART MOZART

LAWRENCE HAYWARD

Cherry Red   Cherry Red

Dec 99. (lp/cd) *(<GLUM 1/+CD>)* **INSTANT WIGWAM AND IGLOO MIXTURE**   Feb00
– Mandrax for minx cats / We're selfish & lazy & greedy / Here is a song / Sailor boy / City synthesis / Drinkin' um bongo / Mrs Back-to-front and the bull ring thing / Hip op / Plead with the man / Wendy James / Plug-in city / Depleted soul / She tore it up and walked out / Today / Wear your fooghat with pride / Fluff on the mallow.

May 00. (cd-s) *(GLUMCD 1)* **WE'RE SELFISH & LAZY & GREEDY / HIP OP / DRINKIN' UM BONGO**

MAURICE DEEBANK

also released a solo album while a FELT member. Augmented by **JOHN A. RIVERS** – producer, keyboards, percussion / **DA'AVE ELSON** – bass

Cherry Red   not iss.

Aug 84. (m-lp) *(MRED 61)* **INNER THOUGHT ZONE**
– The watery song / Four corners of the Earth / Study No.1 / Golden hills / Silver mountain of Paradise Square / So serene. *(cd-iss. Nov92 & Nov99 +=; CDMRED 61)* – Dance of deliverance / Pavanne / A tale from Scriabins lonely trail / Maestoso con anima.

FIAT LUX

Formed: Wakefield, Yorkshire, England . . . mid '82 by drama college students STEVE WRIGHT and DAVID P. CRICKMORE, who were initially blessed with the patronage of BILL NELSON (ex-BE-BOP DELUXE and boss of his own independent label, 'Cocteau'). He, in turn, introduced his younger brother, IAN NELSON, a session sax/keyboard player who was invited to become a permanent fixture following the release of the FIAT LUX debut single, 'FEELS LIKE WINTER AGAIN'. Healthy reviews and a minor industry buzz led to a deal with 'Polydor', the band raising their profile with support dates to the likes of HOWARD JONES. A string of singles were issued over the next year, 'PHOTOGRAPHY', 'SECRETS' and 'BLUE EMOTION' (the latter two scraping into the lower regions of the chart) collected together on 1984's mini-set, 'HIRED HISTORY'. Subsequent single releases, 'HOUSE OF THORNS' and 'SOLITARY LOVERS' crashed, however, FIAT LUX finally consigned to the synth-pop scrapheap following the departure of first CRICKMORE and then NELSON.

Album rating: HIRED HISTORY (*5)

STEVE WRIGHT (b. SEBASTIAN BARBARO) – vocals / **DAVID P. CRICKMORE** – guitar, bass, keyboards / **IAN NELSON** – keyboards, saxophone

Cocteau   not iss.

Nov 82. (7") *(COQ 9)* **FEELS LIKE WINTER AGAIN. / THIS ILLNESS**
(re-iss. Mar85; same)

— added on tour **STEVE SMITH** – bass / **RAY MARTINEZ** – drums

Polydor   not iss.

Aug 83. (7") *(FIAT 1)* **PHOTOGRAPHY. / AQUA VITAE**
(12"+=) *(FIATX 1)* – ('A'extended).

Jan 84. (7") *(FIAT 2)* **SECRETS. / COMFORTABLE LIFE**   65
(12"+=) *(FIATX 2)* – Aqua vitae.

Mar 84. (7") *(FIAT 3)* **BLUE EMOTION. / SLEEPLESS NIGHTMARE**   59
(7"box+=/12"+=) *(FIAT B/T 3)* – ('A'version).

Aug 84. (m-lp/m-c) *(821 637-1/-4)* **HIRED HISTORY**
– Blue emotion / Secrets / Photography / Sleepless nightmare / Aqua vitae / Comfortable life.

FIAT LUX (cont)

Sep 84. (7") *(FIAT 4)* **HOUSE OF THORNS. / THREE'S COMPANY**
(12"+=) *(FIATX 4)* – Sally, free and easy.
Jan 85. (7") *(FIAT 5)* **SOLITARY LOVERS. / NO MORE PROUD**
(12"+=) *(FIATX 5)* – ('A' extended).

—— trimmed a duo when CRICKMORE departed, and when IAN joined his solo brother the group were finished

Anton FIER (see under ⇒ GOLDEN PALOMINOS)

54•40

Formed: Vancouver, British Columbia, Canada ... 1981 by BRAD MERRITT, NEIL OSBORNE and DARRYL NEUDORF, who took their unusual moniker from an historical "Fifty-Four Forty Or Fight" campaign to alter the border between Canada and the USA. Adding PHIL COMPARELLI in '84, this hard-gigging unit released a domestic debut album, 'SET THE FIRE' the same year, drawing favourable comparisons to up and coming rootsy alt-rock outfit, R.E.M. or the dB's. Prior to a worldwide signing with major label, 'Reprise', 54•40 replaced NEUDORF with drummer MATT JOHNSON (not that one!) and it was this line-up who surfaced from the studio with their well-received eponymous album in '86. Over the course of the next few years, the quartet released two further sets, 'SHOW ME' (1987) and 'FIGHT FOR LOVE', both respectable offerings which nevertheless failed to build on standards they had set. A move to 'Columbia' for 1992's 'DEAR DEAR' could have conceivably introduced the band to a wider audience although in the event they subsequently found themselves without an American label. Finding a sympathetic home at Sony's 'Tristar' (independent, 'Revolver' in the UK), 54•40 released another set of sturdy, all-rounder alternative-rock/pop in '94's 'SMILIN' BUDDHA CABARET', displaying the inevitable traces of post-Grunge fallout. OSBORNE and Co jangled back into contention via 1997 and 1998's respective sets 'TRUSTED BY MILLIONS' and 'SINCE WHEN', the latter a little disappointing than its predecessor; the track 'I COULD GIVE YOU MORE' probably said it all. 'CASUAL VIEWIN' (the one released in Canada 2000 that is) was another below par effort, and was even made worse when the Americans issued it a year later with several tracks replaced with old singles! One of them, 'I GO BLIND', had been covered by HOOTIE & THE BLOWFISH; pocket money for OSBORNE and Co, perhaps.

Album rating: SET THE FIRE (*4) / 54•40 (*7) / SHOW ME (*6) / FIGHT FOR LOVE (*5) / DEAR DEAR (*4) / SMILIN' BUDDHA CABARET (*5) / TRUSTED BY MILLIONS (*6) / THE SOUND OF TRUTH compilation (*6) / SINCE WHEN (*5) / CASUAL VIEWIN' (*4)

NEIL OSBORNE – vocals, guitar / **PHIL COMPARELLI** – guitar, steel guitar, vocals / **BRAD MERRITT** – bass / **DARRYL NEUDORF** – drums

		not iss.	Mo-Da-Mu
1981.	(12"ep; as THINGS ARE STILL) **COMING ASHDRE**	-	
	– Long goodbye / Anxious moments / One of us / Contagious.		
1982.	(12"ep) **SELECTION**	-	
	– Yank / He's got / Vows sobs tears & kisses / Selection / Re-in-living / (Jamming with) Lawrence.		
1984.	(lp) *<MDM 8>* **SET THE FIRE**	-	- Canada
	– Set the fire / A big deal / Around the bend / One place set / What to do now / Lost my hand / Sound of truth / Broken pieces.		

—— **MATT JOHNSON** – drums; repl. NEUDORF

		Warners	Reprise
1986.	(lp/c) *<1-/4-25440>* **54•40**	-	
	– Baby ran / I wanna know / I go blind / Being fooled / Take my hand / Grace and beauty / Me island / Holy cow / Alcohol heart / AH (reprise).		
Dec 87.	(lp/c) *<925572-1/-4>* **SHOW ME**		
	– One day in your life / Get back down / Walk in line / Standing in the way / Everyday / What's in a name / One gun / Come here / Because of you / Open fire / All the love is gone / Show me.		
Mar 89.	(lp/c/cd) *<925961-1/-4/-2>* **FIGHT FOR LOVE**	-	
	– Here in my house / Kissfolk / Over my head / Miss you / Baby have some faith / Fight for love / Laughing / Walk talk madly / Where is my heart / Journey.		

		Columbia	Columbia
Mar 93.	(cd/c/lp) *(472054-2/-4/-1) <5440>* **DEAR DEAR**		Nov92
	– She la / Music man / Nice to luv you / Lovers & losers / We are, we pretend / Apollo & me / Faithful / Inside the horn / You don't get away (that easy) / Book / Dear dear . . . (social work).		

		Revolver	TriStar-Sony
Nov 94.	(cd/c) *(REV XD/MC 1001) <67200>* **SMILIN' BUDDHA CABARET**		
	– Blame your parents / Radio luv song / Assoholic / Daisy / Once a killer / Punk grass / Lucy / Beyond the outsider / Don't listen to that / Ocean pearl / Higher / Friends end / What Buddy was / Save yourself. *<cd+=)>* – Nice to luv you / You don't get away (that easy) / She la.		
Sep 97.	(cd) *(REVXD 5440)* **TRUSTED BY MILLIONS**		Nov96
	– Cheer up Peru / Stick to Milly / Love you all / Crossing a canyon / Hooked on bliss / Couldn't be sorry / This is my haircut / Desperately seeking anyone / Frankyl's revenge / I love candy / Cry a little / Lies to me.		
Nov 98.	(cd) *<80336>* **SINCE WHEN**	-	
	– In your image / Lost and lazy / Since when / I could give you more / You should come over / Runaway John / Pay for living / Angel in my bed / Playground / Greatest mistake / Stormy / Last people on Earth.		
Nov 00.	(cd) **CASUAL VIEWIN'**	-	- Canada
	– Casual viewin' / Unbend / Blue sky / Sunday girl / Roll up rule / She's a Jones / It's alright / Watching you / Say my name / Speak what you feel / Someone's mind / You one / Big you up / Castles. *<US-iss.Aug01 + different tracks on 'Nettwerk'; 30224>*		

– compilations, etc. –

Nov 91.	(cd) *Warners; <30857>* **SWEETER THINGS – A COMPILATION**	-	
	– Miss you / Over my head / Laughing / Baby have some faith / Here in my house / Sweeter things / One day in your life / Get back down / One gun / Walk in line / Set the fire / Take my hand / I go blind / Baby ran / Alcohol heart / Me island / Don Quixote.		
Feb 98.	(cd) *Revolver; (REVXD 240) / Columbia; <80336>* **THE SOUND OF TRUTH (THE INDEPENDENT COLLECTION)**		-
	– Set the fire / Big idea / What to do now / Sound of truth / Around the bend / One place set / Cha cha / Lost my hand / Broken pieces / Yank / He's got / Vows sobs tears and kisses / Selection / Re-in-living / (Jamming with) Lawrence.		
1999.	(d-cd) ; **HEAVY MELLOW**	-	Canada
Apr 02.	(cd) *Sony; <CK 80763>* **RADIO LOVE SONGS: THE SINGLES COLLECTION**	-	
	– Love rush / Plenty emotion / Unbend / Casual viewin' / I go blind / Since when / Baby ran / Crossing a canyon / Lies to me / Love you all / One day in your life / Blame your parents / Radio luv song / Assoholic / Ocean pearl / One gun / She-la / Music man / Nice to luv you.		

FINITRIBE

Formed: Edinburgh, Scotland ... 1984 by CHRIS CONNELLY, JOHN VICK, DAVID MILLER and PHILIP PINSKY (ANDREW McGREGOR and SIMON McGLYNN made up the early sextet). Initially a conventional post-punk guitar outfit, the band released a debut EP, 'CURLING & STRETCHING' on their own 'Finiflex' label in summer '84, graduating to a John Peel session before rethinking their whole approach in the mid-80's. Tired of the conventional drums, bass, guitar set-up, they acquired a sampler and began experimenting with electronic music. The result was 'LET THE TRIBE GROW', an EP released on the 'Cathexis' label and featuring 'DE TESTIMONY', a seminal dancefloor anthem for the original Balearic/Acid House generation. Subsequently hooking up with Chicago industrial label, 'Wax Trax', the FINI's released a further couple of 12" singles, 'I WANT MORE' and 'MAKE IT INTERNAL', raising their profile in the States but failing to advance their cause at home. A disastrous tour in early '88 led to the departure of three members – including CONNELLY, who went on to join The REVOLTING COCKS – and a parting of the ways with 'Wax Trax'. This in turn resulted in a resurrection of the 'Finiflex' label for a long-awaited debut album, 'NOISE, LUST & FUN' (1988), featuring contributions from such minor luminaries as LITTLE ANNIE, WILF PLUM (of DOG FACED HERMANS) and JESS HOPKINS. A series of remix EP's proved their dancefloor credentials while a deal with 'One Little Indian' ran into controversy almost immediately with the 'ANIMAL FARM' EP. Subverting the nursery rhyme 'Old MacDonald', for the purposes of berating the similarly titled hamburger outlet, FINITRIBE (as they were now known) offered up a flavour of the anti-consumerist stance prevalent on new album, 'GROSSING 10K' (1989). The subsequent threat of legal action wasn't exactly helped by a "Fuck Off McDonalds" poster campaign, the group running into similar trouble in 1991 with the '101' single, released as FINITRIBE 101 and drawing the wrath of ELECTRIBE 101. The latter effort was culled from 1992's 'AN UNEXPECTED GROOVY TREAT', the FINIS' most accessible, successful album to date and home of groovy near-hit, 'FOREVERGREEN'. The same period also saw the development of the 'Finiflex' label and in-house production team with releases by the likes of JUSTIN ROBERTSON, EGE BAM YASI and even SPARKS, the group co-ordinating releases from their dockside studio in Leith. A deal with 'Ffrr' gave the operation more commercial viability and even led to a Top 75 FINITRIBE hit single with 1994's 'BRAND NEW' EP. Yet by early '95, MILLER and longstanding member PINSKY were in the process of splitting from fellow founder VICK, who still works with 'Finiflex'. The slimmed down FINITRIBE now operated from a bedroom studio in Portobello after the pressures of running 'Finiflex' became too much. The duo subseqently set up a new label, 'UGT', continuing to indulge in side projects such as GEKO and SOLARIZE. With rumours of a harder edged, more organic sound in the pipeline, the FINITRIBE worked on new material with the likes of PAUL HAIG, CHRIS CONNELLY and KATE MORRISON. By the late 90's, the young MORRISON was part of MILLER and PINSKY's darker version of FINI, 'SLEAZY LISTENING' in 1998 marked breakaway from their dance roots. In the summer of 2001, the trio finally got around to delivering their first product for three years, 'BORED'. • **Trivia:** Their group name derives from 'Finny Tribe', the collective name for the fish species known to the Rosicrucians in Ireland.

Album rating: NOISE, LUST AND FUN (*7) / GROSSING 10k (*6) / AN UNEXPECTED GROOVY TREAT (*8) / SHEIGRA (*6) / SLEAZY LISTENING (*6)

CHRIS CONNELLY – vocals, guitars, etc / **JOHN VICK** (b. 6 Nov'65) – keyboards / **DAVID MILLER** (b. 20 Jul'62, Moffat, Scotland) – guitar, vocals / **PHILIP PINSKY** (b.23 Mar'65, Appleton, Wisconsin, USA) – bass, guitar, programming / **ANDREW McGREGOR** – guitar / **SIMON McGLYNN** – drums

		Finiflex	not iss.
Jun 84.	(12"ep) *(LT 1001)* **CURLING & STRETCHING EP**		-
	– Cathedral / Curling theme / etc. *(re-iss. 1988; FT 001)*		

		Cathexis	not iss.
Oct 86.	(12"ep) *(CRF 611)* **LET THE TRIBE GROW**		-
	– De testimony (collapsing edit) / Throttle hearts (rising mix) / Adults absolved / Monimail. *(re-iss. Oct88 on 'Finiflex';)*		

FINITRIBE (cont)

		Wax Trax	Wax Trax
Oct 87.	(12"ep) (WAKUK 027) **I WANT MORE / IDIOT STRENGTH. / I WANT MORE (row, row, row the mix)**	□	-

— now without ANDREW

| Feb 88. | (12"ep) (WAXUK 028) **MAKE IT INTERNAL (integrity mix) / LITTLE VISITORS. / MAKE IT INTERNAL (here we go round the mulberry mix)** | □ | Nov90 |

— CONNELLY joined The REVOLTING COCKS before embarking on solo career

		Finiflex	not iss.
Oct 88.	(12"ep) (FT 002) **DE TESTIMONY EP** – The batter mix / Micromix / Pick'n'mix.	□	-
Nov 88.	(12"ep) (FT 003) **ZULUS EP** – The crunchy mix / The rhythmix / Noise (pick'n'mix).	□	-
Nov 88.	(lp) (FTLP 001) **NOISE, LUST & FUN** – Electrolux / Disturb / Swans / Finis / Throttlehearts / Zulus / Fluke / Electrolux / Swans / Disturb / Ultra. (cd-iss. Oct89 on 'One Little Indian'; TPLP 21CD)	□	-
Dec 88.	(12"ep) (FT 004) **ELECT-ROLUX EP** – Electrolux (pick'n'mix) / Electrolux (minimix) / Disturb (cement mix).	□	-

		One Little Indian	Rough Trade
Nov 89.	(12"ep) (31 TP12) **ANIMAL FARM EP** Chicken mix / Ouch ya ya (ouchtakes) / Monkey mix / Animal farm (meatymix).	□	-
Dec 89.	(lp/c/cd) (TPLP 24/+MC/CD) **GROSSING 10K** – Eyeball / Instant access / An Earth creature / Whale of a tail / Ask a silly question / Monster in the house / Asstrax / 3 AAA's / Put your trunk in it / Built in monster / Animal farm / Ouch ya go.	□	-
Mar 90.	(12"ep) (38 TP12) **MONSTER IN THE HOUSE EP** – Monster club / Monster in the wireless / Eyeball / Built in monsters	□	-

— trimmed to a trio of VICK, PINSKY + MILLER when CONNELLY took off to go solo (having already joined REVOLTING COCKS)

Jul 91.	(7"/cd-s; as FINITRIBE 101) (54 TP7/+CD) **101. / SONIC SHUFFLE (mixed by Andy Weatherall)**	□	-
	(12") (54 TP12L) – 101 (mixed by Graham Massey of 808 State).		
Nov 91.	(12"/cd-s) (64 TP 12/7CD) **ACE LOVE DEUCE (Steve Osbourne mix). / ('A'-Justin Robertson mix)**	□	-
Jun 92.	(12") (74 TP12F) **FOREVERGREEN (mixes)**	51	-
	(12") (74 TP12J) – (2 Justin Robertson mixes)		
	(12") (74 12TPY) – ('A'-Youth mixes) / ('A'-Andy Weatherall mix).		
	(cd-s) (74 TP7CD) – (all mixes).		
Sep 92.	(lp/c/cd) (TPLP 34/+C/CD) <52846> **AN UNEXPECTED GROOVY TREAT** – Forevergreen / 101 (sonic shuffle edit) / Come and get it / Mellowman / Yer crazy / Forevergreen (the lunar eclipse mix) / Bagomatix 2 (there can only be one) / Ace love deuce / Hypnopaedia / Glisten / An unexpected groovy treat / Forevergreen (forevermost excellent) / Ace love deuce / Forevergreen (foreverdreaming).	□	Feb93

		Ffrr-London	London
Nov 94.	(12"ep/c-ep/cd-ep) (FX/FCS/FCD 247) **BRAND NEW EP** – Tip top tune / Tip top.	69	-
	(12") (FXX 247) – (remixes).		
Mar 95.	(c-s) (FCS 258) **LOVE ABOVE / 'A'-Sheigra 5 mix)**	□	-
	(12"+=) (FX 258) – ('A'-Cheeky Vee half mix) / ('A'-Analogue mix).		
	(cd-s++=) (FCD 258) – ('A'-original mix).		
Apr 95.	(d-cd/c/d-lp) (828 615-2/-4/-1) **SHEIGRA** – Dark / Sunshine / Brand new (tip-top tune) / Mushroom shaped / Sheigra 5 / Truth / Catch the whistle / We have come / Mesmerise / Off on a slow one / Love above (Analogue mix).	□	-

— JOHN VICK left in October '95 (he is still alive and kicking around the 'Finiflex' studios)

— next featured **JASON BEARNE**

		Aura Surround Sounds	not iss.
Jun 96.	(12"/cd-s) (SUSSX/SUCD 33) **SQUELCH 1 (remixes; Misiah / original 1 / Wreckage Inc.)**	□	-
	(12") (SUSSY 33) – Squelch 2:- (remixes; Black metal dub II / original 2 / MaC's mangattack).		

		Infectious	not iss.
Aug 97.	(12") (INFECT 42T) **FLYING PEPPERS. / WALTZER (dark hard dub) / FRANTIC (Angel Park accapella edit)**	□	-
	(12") (INFECT 42TX) – ('A'-Furnace dub) / Chiller (heartbeats for the haunted dub).		

— PINSKY + MILLER recruited **KATE MORRISON** – vocals

Feb 98.	(12") (INFECT 51T) **FRANTIC (mixes; Scissorkicks gets Laidback / Cut La Roc / Microspeech mix / Laidback).**	□	-
	(cd-s+=) (INFECT 51CD) – ('A'-A1 People mix) / Witchman live jam.		
Mar 98.	(cd/lp) (INFECT 43 CD/LP) **SLEAZY LISTENING** – Sleazy rider / Mind my make-up / Frantic / Chiller / Waltzer / Flying peppers / The electrician / The bells / The shining / Oxbow incident / Theme.	□	-
Mar 98.	(12"/cd-s) (INFECT 54 T/CD) **MIND MY MAKE-UP (mixes; original / Dust Junkys / Dope Smuglaz O.D. dub / Diminished responsibility / De-composed bass / Mind my B-cup)**	□	-

— after a 3-year hiatus, FINITRIBE (MILLER, PINSKY + MORRISON) were back on record adding **CHRIS ROSS** – drums + **BETTY OFFERMAN** – piano

		North East South West	not iss.
Jul 01.	(cd-ep) (NEWSCD 001) **BORED** – Bored / Single skin / Ecstatic in nylon.	□	-

FIRE ENGINES

Formed: Edinburgh, Scotland ... 1979 out of The DIRTY REDS by DAVEY HENDERSON, MURRAY SLADE, GRAHAM MAIN and RUSSELL BURN. Taking their name from a particularly psychotic 13th FLOOR ELEVATORS track, The FIRE ENGINES caused a minor furore at the dawn of the 80's with their trashy, discordant punk-funk din, as heard on debut single, 'GET UP AND USE ME'. The combination of the POP GROUP/GANG OF FOUR-style rhythmic guitar mangling and HENDERSON's demented vocal was enough to get the music press foaming at the mouth, a largely instrumental, self-financed mini-set, 'LUBRICATE YOUR LIVING ROOM' (1981) working out their frustrations over seven breakneck tracks. Picked up by Bob Last's 'Pop Aural' label, the band came close to a conventional song structure with the infectious 'CANDY SKIN' single, HENDERSON's erm, "unique" vocal talents pushed centre stage. Acclaimed by the press and a sizeable indie hit, the band pushed the boat out for follow-up, 'BIG GOLD DREAM', even employing female backing vocals in a last gasp effort for pop stardom. It wasn't to be and the FIRE ENGINES were soon parked in the station for good, RUSSELL forming the short-lived EVEREST THE HARD WAY with IAN STODDART and future ALTERED IMAGES man, STEPHEN LIRONI. He then enjoyed a further spell with The DIRTY REDS before resurfacing in the mid-80's with HENDERSON and STODDART as sophisticated soul/funk-pop outfit, WIN. Signed to Alan Horne's new 'Swamplands' label, they released two singles, 'UNAMERICAN BROADCASTING' and the anthemic 'YOU'VE GOT THE POWER' (later gaining belated exposure as the musical backdrop for a McEwan's lager TV ad), before the label was taken over by 'London' records. The major label backing led to a Top 60 placing for their debut LP, 'UH! TEARS BABY (A TRASH ICON)' (1987), new members MANNY SCHONIVVA, WILLIE PERRY and SIMON SMEETON coming in as the band switched to 'Virgin'. Despite continuing critical acclaim and enthusuastic support from the press, a follow-up set, 'FREAKY TRIGGER' (1989) did nothing and WIN called it a day in 1989. While STODDART went on to play with semi-legendary Edinburgh funksters, CAPTAIN SHIFTY, SCHONIVVA hooked up with dance act, YO YO HONEY; HENDERSON and RUSSELL recorded for 'Creation' under the PIE FINGER billing. HENDERSON went on to create quirky pop material as NECTARINE No.9, signing to the reactivated 'Postcard' label and releasing a debut album, 'A SEA WITH THREE STARS' (1993). A series of EP's followed – including a collaborative effort with PAUL QUINN and Caledonian performance poet, JOCK SCOT – prior to '95's 'SAINT JACK' album.
• **Songwriters:** All written by HENDERSON, except FASCIST GROOVE (Heaven 17). NECTARINE No.9 covered INSIDE OF YOUR HEART (Velvet Underground) / FROWNLAND (Captain Beefheart) / PULL MY DAISY (Ginsberg-Kerouac) / THESE DAYS (Jackson Browne).
Album rating: FOND compilation (*9) / Win: UH! TEARS BABY WIN (*7) / FREAKY TRIGGER (*6) / Pie Finger: A DALI SURPRISE (*5) / Nectarine No.9: A SEA WITH THREE STARS (*6) / SAINT JACK (*7) / FRIED FOR BLUE MATERIAL (*6) / IT'S JUST THE WAY THINGS ARE JOE, IT'S JUST THE WAY THINGS ARE compilation (*7) / RECEIVED TRANSGRESSED AND TRANSMITTED (*6)

DAVEY HENDERSON – vocals, guitar (ex-DIRTY REDS) / **MURRAY SLADE** – guitar / **GRAHAM MAIN** – bass / **RUSSELL BURN** – drums

		Codex	not iss.
Dec 80.	(7") (CDX 1) **GET UP AND USE ME. / EVERYTHING'S ROSES**	□	-

		Accessory	Fast
Jan 81.	(m-lp) (ACC 001) <FPA 002> **LUBRICATE YOUR LIVING ROOM** <US title 'AUFGELADEN UND BEREIT FUR ACTION UNDER SPASS'> – Plastic gift / Get up and use me / Hungry beat / Lubricate your living room pt.1 & 2 / New thing in the cartons / Sympathetic anaesthetic / Discord.	□	Aug81

		Pop Aural	not iss.
May 81.	(7") (POP 010) **CANDY SKIN. / MEAT WHIPLASH**	□	-

— added guests **SIMON BEST** – keyboards / **HI-RAY** (b. HILARY MORRISON) – vocals (of FLOWERS) / **KAREN BROWN** – b. vocals

| Nov 81. | (7") (POP 013) **BIG GOLD DREAM. / SYMPATHETIC ANAESTHETIC** | □ | - |
| | (12"+=) (POP 013-12) – New thing in cartons. | | |

— folded on the last day of '81. DAVEY and HILARY formed HEARTBEAT. (1 track on NME-c)

– compilations, etc. –

| Aug 92. | (lp) Creation Rev-Ola; (CREV 001LP) **FOND** – (contained all their work) | □ | - |

EVEREST THE HARD WAY

— were formed by RUSSELL with others **IAN STODDART** – bass / **STEPHEN LIRONI** – guitar, keyboards (later ALTERED IMAGES)

		Do-It	not iss.
Apr 82.	(7"/12") (DUN 17) **TIGHTROPE. / WHEN YOU'RE YOUNG**	□	-

— split later that year. RUSSELL joined DIRTY REDS before forming below

WIN

DAVEY HENDERSON – vocals, guitar / **RUSSELL BURN** – drums / **IAN STODDART** – bass

		Swamplands	not iss.
Mar 85.	(7"/12") (SW/+X 5) **UNAMERICAN BROADCASTING (pt.1). / UNAMERICAN BROADCASTING (pt.2)**	□	-
Jun 85.	(7"/s7") (SWP/+P 8) **YOU'VE GOT THE POWER. / IN HEAVEN (LADY IN THE RADIATOR SONG)**	□	-
	(12"/s12") (SWX/+X 8) – ('A'side) / Unamerican broadcasting (pt.1 & 2).		
	(d7") (SWDX 8) – (all 4 tracks).		

		London	not iss.
Mar 86.	(7") (LON 85) **SHAMPOO TEARS. / EMPTY HOLSTERS**	□	-
	(12"+=) (LONX 85) – The slider / ('A'-dub version).		

Mar 87. (7") (LON 128) **SUPER POPOID GROVE. / BABY CUTTING** [63] [-]
(12"+=) (LONX 128) – You've got the power.
(d7"++=) (LONG 128) – In Heaven (the lady in the radiator song).
Apr 87. (lp/c)(cd) (LON LP/C 31) (828 047-2) **UH! TEARS BABY (A TRASH ICON)** [51] [-]
– Super popoid groove / Shampoo tears / Binding love spell / Unamerican broadcasting / Hollywood Baby too / Empty holsters / You've got the power / Charms of powerful trouble / It may be a beautiful sky tonight but it's only a shelter for a world at risk / Charms (reprise) / Baby cutting. (c+cd+=) – Shampoo tears (extended) / You've got the power (extended).

—— added **MANNY SCHONIVVA** – guitar / **WILLIE PERRY** – keyboards / **SIMON SMEETON** – guitar (appeared on last set alongside SCHONIVVA)

Virgin / not iss.

Nov 88. (7") (VS 1121) **WHAT'LL YOU DO TILL SUNDAY, BABY. / TRIGGER HAPPY**
(12"+=) (VST 1121) – ('A'-Johnson's Baby mix).
(cd-s++=) (VSCD 1121) – Peace on egg.
Jan 89. (7") (VS 1157) **LOVE UNITS. / SCARY SCARY**
(12"+=) (VST 1157) – ('A'-12"mix).
(cd-s++=) (VSCD 1157) – Pull my daisy.
Mar 89. (cd/c/lp) (CD/TC+/V 2571) **FREAKY TRIGGER**
– What'll you do til' Sunday baby / Taboo / Love units / Rainbow / Truckee river / How do you do / What's love if you can kill for chocolate / Mind the gravy / Dusty heartfelt / We can cover up the "C". (c+=/cd+=) – Love units (12"mix) / What's love if you can kill for chocolate (12"mix).
May 89. (7") (VS 1178) **DUSTY HEARTFELT. / PEACE ON EGG**
(12"+=/3"cd-s+=) (VST/VSCD 1178) – ('A'version).

—— disbanded late 1989; STODDART formed the APPLES

PIE FINGER

—— **DAVEY HENDERSON + RUSSELL BURN** with **NICK PRECOTT**

Creation / not iss.

Apr 92. (lp/cd) (CRELP/+CD 122) **A DALI SURPRISE**
– Jaggy jungle / Time will tell / Strictly planets (Jupiter) / A Dali surprise / Let them drip gold / Amazonia howl / Without a name / Re-possession mix / Jaggy pie seas.

NECTARINE No.9

—— **HENDERSON, SIMON SMEETON + IAIN HOLFORD** with also poet **JOCK SCOT**

Postcard / Shake The Record Label (Canada)

Feb 93. (lp/cd) (DUBH 931/+CD) **A SEA WITH THREE STARS**
– Pop's love thing / She's a nicer word to sing / The holes of Corpus Christi / Beautiful car / 22 blue / Peanut brain / Smiths new automatic / A sea with three stars / The No. you mean / Don't worry babe, you're not the only one awake / Trace nine / Chocolate swastika.
Oct 93. (cd-ep) (DUBH 939CD) **UNLOADED FOR YOU**
– Pop's new thing / Chocolate swastika / Going off someone / Don't worry babe you're not the only one awake.
Apr 94. (cd) Nighttracks-Postcard: (CDNT 004) **GUITAR THIEVES**
– Scandal / The No. you mean / American loop / Pull my daisy / Memories of a ritual / A sea with three stars / Frownland / Crazy pony / Inside of your heart / Trashslide / Don't worry babe, you're not the only one awake / Evening star thing / Going off someone / Smith snow loop No.2 / Unloaded for you / We have a rendezvous / 22 blue.
Jun 95. (cd-ep; PAUL QUINN / NECTARINE No.9 / JOCK SCOT)
(DUBH 952CD) **PREGNANT WITH POSSIBILITIES EP**
– Tiger tiger / Will I ever be inside of you / Just another fucked-up little druggy on the scene / Grunge girl groan.
Jul 95. (cd) (DUBH 951CD) <SALD 223> **SAINT JACK** [Feb96]
– Saint Jack / Curdled fragments / Fading memory babe / Can't scratch out / This arsehole's been burned too many times before / It's not my baby putting me down / My trapped lightning / Just another fucked-up little druggy on the scene / Couldn't phone potatoes / Dead horse arum / Firecrackers / Un-loaded for you / Clipped wings & flower stings / Tape your head on.
Jul 95. (cd) <SALD 214> **NIAGARA FALLS**
– Un-loaded for you / The holes of Corpus Christ / Crazy pony / She's a nicer word to sing / 22 blue / Don't worry baby, you're not the only one awake / Beautiful car / Peanut brain / This arsehole's been burned too many times before / Going off someone / Smith snow automatic / Pop's love thing / Trace nine / Chocolate swastika / Inside of your heart / These days. (UK-iss.Jun98; same)

—— in Apr'97, they teamed up with JOCK SCOT (once again!) on his single, 'Tape Your Head On'.

Creeping Bent / not iss.

Mar 98. (7") (bent 033) **THE PORT OF MARS. / Alan Vega & The Revolutionary Corps: WHO CARES WHO DIES**
Apr 98. (cd) (bent 035cd) **FRIED FOR BLUE MATERIAL**
– Stacey Keach dada message bag / Blue material / Strychnine vinaigrette / Adidas Francis Bacon / Walter Tevis / Central Deli Davis Jnr. / Boneless chops / Starthing / Friends of the cult sixties, POW / Fuzzy dice-Mahlersdog / Burnt nylon carseat cover flavour / The port of Mars / South of an imaginary line / Subtitles for the blind drunk / Soon be over, soon be over / Michelangelo.
May 98. (7") (ST7 1879) **ADIDAS FRANCIS BACON. / BURNT NYLON CARSEAT COVER FLAVOUR**
(above issued on 'Sano')
May 98. (cd-ep) (bent 037) **SOUTH OF AN IMAGINARY LINE EP**
– South of an imaginary line / A cold meat pie / Pregnant / Gay paean to Thierry Lacroix.
Aug 99. (7") (bent 042) **WALTER TEVIS (mix). / Secret Goldfish: YOU'RE FUNNY 'BOUT THAT, AREN'T YOU**
Sep 99. (cd) (bent 047cd) **IT'S JUST THE WAY THINGS ARE JOE, IT'S JUST THE WAY THINGS ARE** (compilation)
– Walter Tevis / Saint Jack / 22 blue / The port of Mars / My trapped lightning / Don't worry babe, you're not the only one awake / She's a nicer word to sing / South of an imaginary line / Going off someone / Chocolate swastika / Firecrackers / Pops love thing / Adidas Francis Bacon (unreleased version). (re-iss. Dec00; same)

Beggars Banquet / not iss.

Oct 00. (cd-ep) (BBQ 348CD) **CONSTELLATIONS OF A VANITY EP**
– Constellations of a vanity / Indelible marquer / Giant haystacks / Frozen peas.
Apr 01. (cd) (BBQCD 221) **RECEIVED TRANSGRESSED AND TRANSMITTED**
– Pong pt 6 / Susan identifier / Constellations of a vanity / Foundthings / It's raining for some cloudy reasons / Pocket radiodrops / Look at my sleeves they fall down / Sic / Lid / Fibrecane No.4 / Bongo Kong / Lazy crystal.

fIREHOSE (see under ⇒ MINUTEMEN)

FIRE PARTY

Formed: Washington DC, USA ... 1986 by the all-girl foursome of AMY PICKERING, NATALIE AVERY, KATE SAMWORTH and NICKY THOMAS. Charged up by European support slots to SCREAM then THAT PETROL EMOTION, FIRE PARTY unleashed their eponymous debut mini-set in 1988 for 'Dischord' (base of FUGAZI). The album showed an astonishingly fresh grunge sound fusing elements of NIRVANA, WIRE and SONIC YOUTH, although the following year's, 'NEW ORLEANS OPERA', lacked the debut's bite and the girls split.

Album rating: FIRE PARTY (*6) / NEW ORLEANS OPERA (*4)

AMY PICKERING – vocals / **NATALIE AVERY** – guitar / **KATE SAMWORTH** – bass / **NICKY THOMAS** – drums

Dischord / Dischord

May 88. (m-lp) <(DISCHORD 28)> **FIRE PARTY**
– Jerk / Basis / Cake / Drowning intentions / Walls of mind / Engine.
Oct 89. (m-lp/m-c) <(DISCHORD 37/+C)> **NEW ORLEANS OPERA**
– Make it quick / Bite / First course / Gethsemane / Prisoner / Fire / Only nine mottos / New Orleans opera.

—— fizzled out after above

– compilations, etc. –

Oct 96. (cd) Dischord; <DIS 103> **FIRE PARTY**
– (FIRE PARTY + NEW ORLEANS OPERA) + / Pilate / Basis / Are you on? / How to / Stray bullet.

FISH & ROSES (see under ⇒ RUN ON; 90's section)

Simon FISHER-TURNER (SFT) (see under ⇒ KING OF LUXEMBOURG)

Steve FISK (see under ⇒ PELL MELL)

FIVE GO DOWN TO THE SEA

Formed: Cork, Ireland ... 1982, taking their moniker from the series of Enid Blyton's children's books. Comprising vocalist MICK DONNELLY, RICKY, SMELLY, STACK and UNA, the group debuted with a 1983 EP, 'KNOT A FISH'. A year later, and moving from 'Kabuki' records (home of MICRODISNEY) to UK indie imprint, 'Abstract', the FIVE issued their follow-up, 'THE GLEE CLUB'. Incorporating a type of PERE UBU, avant-garde art jazz style, they found favour with 'Creation' boss, ALAN McGEE, who subsequently issued what was to become their third and final effort, the 'HAWKING' EP. The latter contained the controversial and much criticised 'SINGING IN BRAILLE'. DONNELLY went on to form the group, BEETHOVEN, although his choice of moniker proved foolhardy as there was of course a classical bod already in the public domain. Sadly, just like his new outfit's namesake before him, he passed away in 1989.

Album rating: never released any

MICK DONNELLY – vocals / **RICKY** – / **SMELLY** – / **STACK** – / **UNA** –

Kabuki / not iss.

Mar 83. (7"ep) (KAFIVE 5) **KNOT A FISH**
– Fishes for compliments / Elephants for fun and profit / Why wait until April / There's a fish on top of Sharden swears he's Elvis.

Abstract / not iss.

Sep 84. (12"ep) (12ABS 027) **THE GLEE CLUB**
– Jumping Joey / Often / What happened to your leg? / Boon for travellists.

—— new drummer on next EP

Creation / not iss.

Sep 85. (12"ep) (CRE 021T) **HAWKING EP**
– Singing in braille / Aunt Nelly / Silk brain worm / Women.

—— never went down to the sea again

FIVE OR SIX

Formed: London, England ... early 80's by DAVE HARPER, DANNY WHITLOCK, GRAHAM CASSIE, SIMON HARPER and DAVID KNIGHT. With a style not too dissimilar to a pastel but off-key MONOCHROME SET, FIVE OR SIX issued a few singles/EP's for the 'Cherry Red' imprint before releasing a debut set, 'A THRIVING AND HAPPY LAND' (1982).

Album rating: A THRIVING AND HAPPY LAND mini (*4)

FIVE OR SIX (cont)

DAVID HARPER – guitar, vocals / DANIEL WHITLOCK – guitar, vocals / GRAHAM CASSIE – bass, vocals / SIMON HARPER – drums / DAVID KNIGHT – drum machine, synthesizer

	Cherry Red	not iss.
Feb 81. (7") (CHERRY 19) **ANOTHER REASON. / THE TRIAL**		-

─── ASHLEY WALES – repl. CASSIE

Oct 81. (12"ep) (12CHERRY 23) **POLAR EXPOSURE EP**		-

– Polar exposure / Inclination / Building kind / Dreams I cannot keep / Mud, clay and sticks / Concoction.

Sep 82. (m-lp) (FRIZBEE 2) **A THRIVING AND HAPPY LAND**		-

– Exhibit A / In construction / 22 hours / An occurance at hand / Dave's song / Anchors / Consider this.

Oct 82. (12"ep) (12CHERRY 43) **FOUR FROM FIVE OR SIX EP**		-

– This is for the moment / Rusties / Think / Theme.

─── a follow-up album, 'CANTAME ESA CANCION QUE DI YEAH YEAH YEAH' was shelved when they split in February '83. KNIGHT joined SHOCK HEADED PETERS

FIVE THIRTY

Formed: Reading, England ... 1985 by TARA MILTON and PAUL BASSETT, who released their first single, 'CATCHER IN THE RYE' not long after leaving school. However little was heard of them until 1990, when they moved to North London, drummer PHIL HOPPER being added to the all-male trio in the process. Signed to 'East West' and managed by ALAN McGEE of Creation records, FIVE THIRTY finally issued their follow-up 45, 'ABSTAIN', an adrenaline fuelled neo-Mod affair that was hardly in keeping with the blissed out spirit of the times. It was also their first of four minor hits, all taken from their one and only full-length set, 'BED' (1991), an impressive debut that brought comparisons with The JAM. A couple of years too early for the Brit-pop retro-revival, FIVE THIRTY were a talented band out of time, PHIL hastening their inevitable demise by taking up acting; TARA would subsequently form The NUBILES while PAUL formed ORANGE DELUXE with his brother ROB. The latter signed to 'Dead Dead Good' records (home to The CHARLATANS) and with two other members, COPE and KEITH McCUBBIN, they released several singles and two EAT-meets-MANSUN-esque sets, 'NECKING' (1995) and 'VODKA, DOUGHNUTS AND DOLE' (1996). • **Songwriters:** MILTON – BASSETT except COME TOGETHER (Beatles).

Album rating: BED (*7) / Orange Deluxe; NECKING (*6) / VODKA, DOUGHNUTS AND DOLE (*5)

TARA MILTON – vocals, bass / PAUL BASSETT – vocals, guitar

	Other	not iss.
Oct 85. (12"ep; as 5:30!) (120TH 2) **CATCHER IN THE RYE**		-

– Weight of the world / Catcher in the rye / Mood suite / Suburban town.

─── added PHIL HOPPER – drums

	East West	Atco
Jul 90. (7") (YZ 530) **ABSTAIN. / YOU**	75	-
(12"+=/cd-s+=) (YZ T/CD 530) – Catcher in the rye / Coming up for air.		
Nov 90. (7") (YZ 543) **AIR CONDITIONED NIGHTMARE. / JUDY JONES**		-
(12"+=/cd-s+=) (YZ T/CD 543) – Mistress daydream / The things that turn you on.		
May 91. (7") (YZ 577) **13th DISCIPLE. / HATE MALE**	67	-
(12"+=/cd-s+=) (YZ T/CD 577) – Out to get in / Come together.		
Jul 91. (7") (YZ 594) **SUPER NOVA. / STILL LIFE**	75	-
(12"+=/cd-s+=) (YZ T/CD 594) – Something's got to give.		
Aug 91. (cd)(lp/c)(9031 75304-2)(WX 530/+C) <91757> **BED**	57	

– Supernova / Psycho cupid / Junk male / 13th disciple / Strange kind of urgency / You / Songs and paintings / Womb with a view / Automations / Wrapped in blue. (cd+=/c+=) – Abstain / Catcher in the rye.

Oct 91. (7"ep/c-ep/12"ep/cd-ep) (YZ/+C/T/CD 624) **YOU ep**	72	-

– You / Cuddly drug / Slow train into the ocean.

─── virtually disappeared for a while after HOOPER became an actor. BASSETT resurfaced in ORANGE DELUXE, while MILTON formed The NUBILES

ORANGE DELUXE

PAUL BASSETT – vocals, guitar / COPE – guitar, vocals, keyboards / ROB BASSETT – bass / KEITH McCUBBIN – drums, percussion

	Dead Dead Good	not iss.
Oct 94. (7") (GOOD 27) **THE STRIPPER. / PLUSH ABATTOIR**		-
(cd-s+=) (GOOD 27CD) – Dreaming of a friend.		
Feb 95. (7") (GOOD 29) **LOVE 45. / SWIMMING POOL CULTURE**		-
(cd-s+=) (GOOD 29CD) – Ghost dance.		
Apr 95. (cd/d-lp) (GOOD CD/LP 4) **NECKING**		-

– The stripper / Love 45 / Soft control / Turkey breast / Bewitched / There goes my summer / Angelique / Pure grunt / Memoirs / Delectable / Hot lung / Atomic junkie / Anti-gravity blues.

May 95. (7") (GOOD 31) **DELECTABLE. / STEP IT UP**		-
(cd-s+=) (GOOD 31CD) – Me against the world / Step it up (remix).		
May 96. (cd-ep) (GOOD 35CD) **JUPITER'S EYE / BRAND NEW STONE-AGE MAN / SWOON**		-
Jul 96. (cd-ep) (GOOD 38CD) **ANDREX PUPPY LOVE / LOVE SLUG / SPECIAL K'ING / LOVELESS MAN**		-
Aug 96. (cd/lp) (GOOD CD/LP 10) **VODKA, DOUGHNUTS AND DOLE**		-

– Uncle Charles (friend of the stars) / 21st century / Jupiter's eye / LOve slug / Not giving up on you / Jelly shoe and liquid ether / Whole Sioux nation / Lexy's disappearing act / (Mr Helium) / Brand new stone-age man / Stevie's kid brother / (tape wind) / Andrew puppy love.

─── disbanded after above

FIZZBOMBS
(see under ⇒ JESSE GARON & THE DESPERADOES)

FLAMING LIPS

Formed: Oklahoma City, Oklahoma, USA ... 1983 by the COYNE brothers WAYNE and MARK, who reputedly stole instruments from a church hall to get their act off the ground. After a rare and weird EP in 1985, MARK left brother WAYNE to recruit new members for the 'Enigma' album, 'HEAR IT IS'. Their next, 'OH MY GAWD!!!', in '87, saw them strike with many poetic assaults, including the near 10-minute track 'ONE MILLION BILLIONTH OF A MILLISECOND ON A SUNDAY MORNING'. Their reputation grew, with wild, climactic live appearances, highlighting albums 'TELEPATHIC SURGERY' and 'IN A PRIEST-DRIVEN AMBULANCE (WITH SILVER SUNSHINE STARES)'. Phew!!!. Signed to 'Warners' in 1992, and between appearing at the Reading Festival, they released 'HIT TO DEATH IN THE MAJOR HEAD' and the US No.108 (!) album 'TRANSMISSIONS FROM THE SATELLITE HEART'. By the mid-90's, they had secured weirdo posterity, after giving birth to the drug-orientated, narrative track, 'WATERBUG'. Their avant-garde psychedelic (BARRETT / FLOYD) approach was now well behind them, their barrage of sound, once described as The JESUS & MARY CHAIN meeting BLACK FLAG or The DEAD KENNEDYS, took a sharp detour and ended up in DAVE FRIDMANN's (of MERCURY REV) up state New York studio, where the LIPS (now consisting of only three; WAYNE COYNE, STEVE DROZD and MICHAEL IVINS) recorded the spooky but highly commercial 'THE SOFT BULLETIN' (1999) for 'Warners'. The album spawned two hit singles, 'RACE FOR THE PRIZE' and the echo fronted 'WAITIN' FOR A SUPERMAN', which was their most pop orientated work since the 1995 release 'BAD DAYS'. 'THE SOFT BULLETIN' marked the work of a band who had matured in age and in sound. Adding the FRIDMANN formula, the album sounded similar to MERCURY REV's 'Deserter's Songs', although relying largely on its YES-type chord changes/structures and BEACH BOYS harmonies with COYNE attempting to sing in tune (possibly for the very first time). The group returned three years later with an album just as stunning and as beautiful as 'THE SOFT BULLETIN', influenced by Japanese counter-culture named 'YOSHIMI BATTLES THE PINK ROBOTS' (it's a concept album, kind of). From the lush title track, with its swirling analogue synth to the emotionally sweeping 'DO YOU REALIZE', 'YOSHIMI ...' could be categorized easily alongside GRANDADDY's 'The Sophtware Slump' and RADIOHEAD's 'Kid A', although it seems that The FLAMING LIPS had a lot more fun. • **Songwriters:** Group except; SUMMERTIME BLUES (Eddie Cochran) / WHAT'S SO FUNNY 'BOUT PEACE, LOVE & UNDERSTANDING (Brinsley Schwarz) / THANK YOU + COMMUNICATION BREAKDOWN (Led Zeppelin) / DEATH VALLEY '69 (Sonic Youth & Lydia Lunch) / STRYCHNINE (Sonics) / AFTER THE GOLD RUSH (Neil Young) / ALL THAT JAZZ + HAPPY DEATH MEN (Echo & The Bunnymen) / LIFE ON MARS (David Bowie) / WHAT A WONDERFUL WORLD (Nat King Cole) / ICE DRUMMER (Suicide) / CHOSEN ONE + LITTLE DRUMMER BOY (Smog) / CAN'T GET YOU OUT OF MY HEAD (Kylie Minogue; hit).

Album rating: HEAR IT IS (*5) / OH MY GAWD!!! ... THE FLAMING LIPS (*7) / TELEPATHIC SURGERY (*5) / IN A PRIEST-DRIVEN AMBULANCE (*6) / HIT TO DEATH IN THE FUTURE HEAD (*6) / TRANSMISSIONS FROM THE SATELLITE HEART (*8) / CLOUDS TASTE METALLIC (*7) / ZAIREEKA (*7) / THE SOFT BULLETIN (*9) / YOSHIMI BATTLES THE PINK ROBOTS (*8)

MARK COYNE – vocals / WAYNE COYNE – guitar / MICHAEL IVINS – bass / RICHARD ENGLISH – drums

	not iss.	Lovely Sorts Of Death
1985. (7"green-ep) <L-19679> **THE FLAMING LIPS E.P.**		

– Bag full of thoughts / Out for a walk / Garden of eyes – Forever is a long time / Scratching the door / My own planet. (re-iss. 1986 red-ep; same) (re-iss. 1987 on 'Pink Dust' 7"ep/c-ep; 731851-1/-4)

─── WAYNE now on vox, when MARK departed

	Enigma	Restless
Nov 86. (white-lp,lp/c/cd) <72173-1/-4/-2> **HEAR IT IS**	-	

– With you / Unplugged / Trains, brains and rain / Jesus shootin' heroin / Just like before / She is death / Charles Manson blues / Man from Pakistan / Godzilla flick / Staring at sound – With you. (cd+=) – Bag full of thoughts / Out for a walk / Garden of eyes – Forever is a long time / Scratching the door / My own planet / Summertime blues. (cd re-iss. Jul99; same)

Nov 87. (clear-lp,lp/c/cd) <72207-1/-4/-2> **OH MY GAWD!!! ... THE FLAMING LIPS**	-	

– Can't exist / Can't stop the spring / Ceiling is bending / Everything's explodin' / Love yer brain / Maximum dream for Evil Knievel / Ode to CC / One million billionth / Prescription: Overkill / Thank.

Feb 89. (lp/c/cd) (ENVLP/TCENV/CDENV 523) <72350-1/-4/-2> **TELEPATHIC SURGERY**		-

– Drug machine / Michael time to wake up / Miracle on 42nd Street / UFO story / Shaved gorilla / Begs and achin' / Right now / Hare Krishna stomp wagon / Chrome plated suicide / Redneck school of technology / Spontaneous combustion of John / The last drop of morning dew. (cd re-iss. Jul99 on 'Restless'; same as US)

─── JONATHAN PONEMANN – guitar + JOHN DONAHUE – guitar

FLAMING LIPS (cont)

Jun 89. (7"m) (EFA 40153) <SP-28> **DRUG MACHINE / STRYCHNINE. / ('WHAT'S SO FUNNY ABOUT) PEACE, LOVE AND UNDERSTANDING** — / Jan89 (City Slang / Sub Pop)

—— NATHAN ROBERTS – drums repl. ENGLISH

Jan 91. (12"ep) (EFA 04063-05) **UNCONSCIOUSLY SCREAMIN' EP** (City Slang / Atavistic)
 – Unconsciously screamin' / Lucifer rising / Ma, I didn't notice / Let me be it.

Feb 91. (pink-lp,lp/c/cd) (SLANG 005/+C/CD) <72359> **IN A PRIEST-DRIVEN AMBULANCE (WITH SILVER SUNSHINE STARES)** — / Sep90 (City Slang / Restless)
 – Shine on sweet Jesus – Jesus song No.5 / Unconsciously screamin' / Rainin' babies / Take me to Mars / Five stop Mother Superior rain / Stand in line / God walks among us now / Jesus song No.6 / There you are / Jesus song No.7 / Mountain song / What a wonderful world. (cd re-iss. Sep96 on 'Restless'; 72359-2)

Jul 92. (cd-ep) <40244> **…WASTIN' PIGS IS STILL RADICAL** (Warners / Warners)
 – Talkin' 'bout the smiling deathporn immorality blues (everyone wants to live forever) / All that jazz – Happy death men / Jets (Cupid's kiss vs. the psyche of death).

Aug 92. (cd/c/lp) <(7599 26838-2/-4/-1)> **HIT TO DEATH IN THE MAJOR HEAD**
 – Talkin' about the smiling deathporn immorality blues (everyone wants to live forever) / Hit me like you did the first time / The Sun / Felt good to burn / Gingerale afternoon (the astrology of a Saturday) / Halloween on the Barbary Coast / The magician vs. the headache / You have to be joking (autopsy of the Devil's brain) / Frogs / Hold your head. (re-iss. Apr95; same)

—— RONALD JONES – guitar repl. JOHN who joined MERCURY REV
—— STEVEN DROZD – drums repl. NATHAN

Jun 93. (cd/c/lp) <(9362 45334-2/-4/-1)> **TRANSMISSIONS FROM THE SATELLITE HEART**
 – Turn it on / Pilot can at the queer of God / Oh my pregnant head (labia in the sunlight) / She don't use jelly / Chewin' the apple of your eye / Superhumans / Be my head / Moth in the incubator / Plastic Jesus / When yer twenty-two / Slow nerve action.

Aug 94. (7"/c-s) (W 0246/+C) <9362 18131-2> **SHE DON'T USE JELLY. / TURN IT ON (bluegrass version)** — / 55 Nov94
 (cd-s+=) (WO 246CD) – Translucent egg.
 (cd-s) (WO 246CDX) – ('A'side) / The process / Moth in the incubator.

Apr 95. (cd-s) <9362 43509-2> **TURN IT ON / PUT THE WATERBUG IN THE POLICEMAN'S EAR / SHE DON'T USE JELLY (demo)** — / -

Jul 95. (m-cd) <9362 45748-2> **PROVIDING NEEDLES FOR YOUR BALLOONS** — / -
 – Bad days / Jets part 2 (my two days as an ambulance driver) / Ice drummer / Put the waterbug in the policeman's ear / Chewin the apple of yer ear / Chosen one / Little drummerboy / Slow nerve action.

Sep 95. (cd/c) <(9362 45911-2/-4)> **CLOUDS TASTE METALLIC**
 – The abandoned hospital ship / Psychiatric explorations of the fetus with needles / Placebo headwood / This here giraffe / Brainville / Guy who lost a headache and accidentally saves the world / When you smile / Kim's watermelon gun / They punctured my yolk / Lightning strikes the postman / Christmas at the zoo / Evil will prevail / Bad days (aurally excited version).

Dec 95. (c-s) (W 0322C) **BAD DAYS / GIRL WITH HAIR LIKE AN EXPLOSION**
 (cd-s+=) (W 0322CD) – She don't use jelly / Giraffe (demo).
 (cd-s) (W 0322CDX) – ('A'side) / Ice drummer / When you smiled I lost my only idea / Put the water bug in the policeman's ear.

Mar 96. (cd-s) (W 0335CD) **THIS HERE GIRAFFE / JETS pt.2 (MY TWO DAYS AS AN AMBULANCE DRIVER) / LIFE ON MARS** 72 / -
 (c-s/c/cd-s) (W 0335 C/CDX) – ('A'side) / The sun / Hit me like you did the first time. above was the first ever shaped cd single.

Aug 96. (3D-cd-s) (W 0370CD) **BRAINVILLE / EVIL WILL PREVAIL (live) / WATERBUG (live)**
 (c-s/c-cd-s) (W 0370 C/CDX) – ('A'side) / Brainville (live) / Raindrops keep falling on my head.

Oct 97. (4xcd-box) <(9362 46804)> **ZAIREEKA**
 – Okay I'll admit that I really don't care / Riding to work in the year 2025 (your invisible now) / Thirty-five thousand feet of despair / Machine in India / The train runs over the camel but is … / How will we know? (futuristic crashendos) / March of the rotten vegetables / Big ol' bug is the new baby now.
 (above was an unusual concept in that you needed 4 separate CD players to hear the simultaneous recordings at its full potential)

—— now down to a trio of WAYNE COYNE, STEVEN DROZD + MICHAEL IVINS

May 99. (cd/c) <(9362 47393-2/-4)> **THE SOFT BULLETIN** 39 /
 – Race for the prize / A spoonful weighs a ton / The spark that bled / Slow motion / What is the light? / The observer / Waitin' for a superman / Suddenly everything has changed / The gash / Feeling yourself disintegrate / Sleeping on the roof / Race for the prize (remix) / Waitin' for a superman (remix) / Buggin' (remix). <lp-iss.Aug02 on 'PIAS USA'; PIASA 09LP)>

Jun 99. (cd-s) (W 494CD1) **RACE FOR THE PRIZE / RIDING TO WORK IN THE YEAR 2025 (YOUR INVISIBLE NOW) (from 'Zaireeka' disc 1 / THIRTY THOUSAND FEET OF DESPAIR (from 'Zaireeka' disc 1)** 39 / -
 (cd-s) (W 494CD2) – ('A'side) / (same B's except from 'Zaireeka' disc 2).

Nov 99. (c-s/cd-s) (W 505 C/CD) <44793> **WAITIN' FOR A SUPERMAN / RIDING TO WORK IN THE YEAR 2025 / YOU'RE INVISIBLE / 35,000 FEET OF DESPAIR** — / Feb00
 (cd-s) (W 505CD1) – ('A'mixes).

Jul 02. (cd) <(9362 48141-2)> **YOSHIMI BATTLES THE PINK ROBOTS** 13 / 50
 – Fight test / One more robot – 3000-21 / Yoshimi battles the pink robots (part 1) / Yoshimi battles the pink robots (part 2) / In the morning of the magicians / Ego tripping at the gates of Hell / Are you a hypnotist? / It's summertime / Do you realize? / All we have is now / Approaching pavonis mons by balloon (utopia planitia). <lp-iss.Aug02 on 'PIAS USA'; PIASA 101LP>

Aug 02. (cd-s) (W 586CD1) **DO YOU REALIZE? / IF I GO MAD – FUNERAL IN MY HEAD / SYRTIS MAJOR** 32 / -
 (cd-s) (W 586CD2) – ('A'side) / Up above the daily hum / Zanthe terra.

Aug 02. (7"pic-d) <RE-1> **DO YOU REALIZE? / UP ABOVE THE DAILY HUM** — / -

– compilations, etc. –

Oct 98. (cd) Restless; <(RST 72963)> **A COLLECTION OF SONGS REPRESENTING AN ENTHUSIASM FOR RECORDING … BY AMATEURS** (1984-1990) — / Sep98
 – Bag full of thoughts / Jesus shootin' heroin / One million billionth / Chrome plated suicide / Michael time to wake up / Hell's angels cracker factory / Unconsciously screamin' / God walks among us now / Stychnini – Peace, love and understanding / Death valley '69 / Thank you / Ma, I didn't notice / After the gold rush / I want to kill my brother: The cymbal.

Sep 02. (3xcd-box) Restless; <(REST 73764)> **FINALLY, THE PUNK ROCKERS ARE TAKING ACID**
 – (THE FLAMING LIPS ep / HEAR IT IS / OH MY GAWD!!! / TELEPATHIC SURGERY / others).

Sep 02. (2xcd-box) Restless; <(REST 73765)> **THE DAY WE SHOT A HOLE IN THE JESUS EGG**
 – (IN A PRIEST DRIVEN AMBULANCE / DRUG MACHINE / UNCONSCIOUSLY SCREAMIN' / etc.)

FLATMATES

Formed: Bristol, England … mid 1985 by head of the household, MARTIN WHITEHEAD – the mastermind of up and coming indie label, 'Subway Organization' – together with fellow residents DEBBIE HAYNES, SARAH FLETCHER (who replaced KATH BEACH) and ROCKER. Joining the so-called jingle-jangle "anorak brigade" alongside The RAZORCUTS, etc, they fused BUZZCOCKS with The SHANGRI-LA'S on a series of mid-late 80's singles beginning with 'I COULD BE IN HEAVEN' in late '86. Flat harmony proved a problem throughout their sporadic recording career, members coming and going as they pleased (i.e. before the 3rd 45, JOEL O'BIERNE taking up ROCKER's empty room and on the group's final outing, 'HEAVEN KNOWS', SARAH handing over her lease to JACKIE CARRERA). Still without an album to their name, The FLATMATES temporarily moved out of the music biz in 1989, WHITEHEAD and relative newcomer TIM RIPPINGTON coming to blows on stage. For anyone who missed the singles first time round, the retrospective 'LOVE AND DEATH' album collected all their material in one package.

Album rating: LOVE AND DEATH (1986-1989) compilation (*6)

MARTIN WHITEHEAD – guitar / DEBBIE HAYNES – vocals / SARAH FLETCHER – bass; repl. KATH BEACH / ROCKER – drums

Subway Org / not iss.

Oct 86. (7") (SUBWAY 6) **I COULD BE IN HEAVEN. / TELL ME WHY / SO IN LOVE WITH YOU** — / -

Apr 87. (7") (SUBWAY 9) **HAPPY ALL THE TIME. / I DON'T CARE** — / -
 (12"+=) (SUBWAY 9T) – You're gonna get hurt / Thinking of you.

—— JOEL O'BIERNE – drums; repl. ROCKER who joined The ROSEHIPS

Nov 87. (7") (SUBWAY 14) **YOU'RE GONNA CRY. / LIFE OF CRIME** — / -
 (12"+=) (SUBWAY 14T) – Barbarella blue / Sportscar girl.

—— added TIM RIPPINGTON – guitar, keyboards

Mar 88. (7") (SUBWAY 17) **SHIMMER. / ON MY MIND** — / -
 (12"+=) (SUBWAY 17T) – If not for you / Bad.

—— JACKIE CARRERA – bass; repl. SARAH

Sep 88. (7") (SUBWAY 21) **HEAVEN KNOWS. / DON'T SAY IF** — / -
 (12"+=/cd-s+=) (SUBWAY 21 T/CD) – Turning you blue / My empty head.

—— split late in '88 after a fight with WHITEHEAD and RIPPINGTON. CARRERA joined The CARETAKER RACE, while WHITEHEAD and O'BIERNE formed the SWEET YOUNG THINGS

– compilations, etc. –

May 88. (12"ep) Night Tracks; (SFNT 011) **JANICE LONG SESSIONS** (1.3.87)
 – My empty head / I want to be with him / Everyday / When I'm with you.

Feb 90. (lp/cd) Subway; (SUBORG 14/+CD) **LOVE AND DEATH (1986-1989)**
 – I could be in heaven / So in love with you / Tell me why / Happy all the time / I don't care / You're gonna cry / Life of crime / Shimmer / On my mind / Heaven knows / Don't say if / This thing called love / Is it me? / Never coming down. (cd+=) – Thinking of you / Turning you blue / Love cuts / When I'm with you / My empty head.

FLESH FOR LULU

Formed: Brixton, London, England … early 80's by NICK MARSH and JAMES MITCHELL along with GLEN BISHOP and ex-WASTED YOUTH member ROCCO BARKER. Signed to 'Polydor', the band released their debut single, 'ROMAN CANDLE', in late '83, following it up with the infectious 'SUBTERRANEANS' and 'RESTLESS' in summer '84. After the release of an eponymous debut album later that year, BISHOP was replaced by KEVIN MILLS while keyboard player, DEREK GREENING completed the line-up. While the record lacked any coherent musical direction (although there was a loose strand of flashy garage rock akin to IGGY POP, LOU REED or GENERATION X), there were some interesting ideas and it's a fair bet that

The PIXIES copped an earful of the distinctive guitar sound. The record's commercial failure led to the end of their major label deal and the band released the decidedly more lo-fi 'BLUE SISTERS SWING' mini-set on the small 'Hybrid' imprint. Generating more publicity for its controversial cover (two nuns locked in an embrace) than its musical content, FLESH FOR LULU recorded their most accessible material to date in the shape of the 'BIG FUN CITY' (1985) album. Kicking off with the singalong 'BABY HURRICANE', the record displayed a quantum leap in confidence, from the itchy funk-rock of 'CAT BURGLAR' to the TOM PETTY-esque 'LET GO'. Moving on to 'Beggars Banquet', the band moved in an increasingly commercial direction with subsequent albums, 'LONG LIVE THE NEW FLESH' (1987) and 'PLASTIC FANTASTIC' (1990), their efforts unfortunately not reciprocated in sales terms. Dropped again, the band finally threw in the towel in the early 90's.

Album rating: FLESH FOR LULU (*6) / BLUE SISTERS SWING mini (*5) / BIG FUN CITY (*6) / LONG LIVE THE NEW FLESH (*5) / PLASTIC FANTASTIC (*5)

NICK MARSH – vocals, guitar / **ROCCO BARKER** – guitar, vocals (ex-WASTED YOUTH) / **POPE GLEN BISHOP** – bass / **JAMES MITCHELL** – drums

Polydor / not iss.

Nov 83. (7") *(POSP 653)* **ROMAN CANDLE. / COMING DOWN**
  (12"+=) *(POSPX 653)* – Lame train/ The power of suggestion.
May 84. (7") *(FFL 1)* **SUBTERRANEANS. / WHY ME?**
  (12"+=) *(FFLX 1)* – Gurl at the bar.
  (d7"+=) *(FFLD 1)* – Endless sleep / Ten foot tall.
Aug 84. (7"/12") *(FFL/+X 2)* **RESTLESS. / CAT BURGLAR**
  (d7"+=) *(POSP 653)* – Roman candle / Coming down.
Oct 84. (lp) *(POLD 5165)* **FLESH FOR LULU**
  – Restless / Dog dog dog / Hyena / Coming down / Jigsaw puzzle / Subterraneans / Brainburst (darling dissarray) / Peace and love / So strong / Heavy heavy angel.

–––– **KEVIN MILLS** – bass (ex-SPECIMEN) repl. BISHOP who joined UNDER TWO FLAGS / added **DEREK GREENING** – keyboards

Hybrid / not iss.

May 85. (m-lp) *(RIB 3)* **BLUE SISTERS SWING**
  – Seven hail Marys / Death shall come / I may have said you're beautiful, but you know I'm just a liar / Who's in danger / Black tattoo.

Statik / not iss.

Oct 85. (7") *(TAK 37)* **BABY HURRICANE. / ANTI-SOCIAL**
  (12"+=) *(TAK 37-12)* – 1970 (I feel alright).
Oct 85. (lp/c) *(STAT LP/C 28)* **BIG FUN CITY**
  – Baby Hurricane / Cat burglar / Let go! / Vaguely human / Rent boy / Golden handshake girl / In your smile / Blue / Laundromat kat / Just one second. *(cd-iss. Dec86 +=; CDST 28)* – BLUE SISTERS SWING *(cd re-iss. Aug01 on 'Anagram'; CDMGOTH 10)* – BLUE SISTERS SWING

Beggars Banquet / Capitol

Nov 86. (7") *(BEG 177)* **IDOL. / SLEEPING DOGS**
  (12"+=) *(BEG 177T)* – Life of crime / Spaceball ricochet.
Mar 87. (7") *(BEG 184)* **SIAMESE TWIST / THE DUMBEST THING**
  (c-s+=/12"+=) *(BEG 184 C/T)* – Blue sky / Idol.
May 87. (lp/cd)(c) *(BEGA 82/+CD)(BEGC 82) <48217>* **LONG LIVE THE NEW FLESH**
  – Lucky day / Postcards from Paradise / Hammer of love / Siamese twist / Sooner or later / Good for you / Crash / Way to go / Sleeping dogs / Dream on cowboy. *(re-iss. Feb90 & Jul91 lp/c/cd; BBL/+C 82/+CD)*
Jul 87. (7") *(BEG 193)* **POSTCARDS FROM PARADISE. / I'M NOT LIKE EVERYBODY ELSE**
  (12"+=) *(BEG 193T)* – Sometimes good guys don't wear white.
Oct 88. (7") *(BEG 221)* **I GO CRAZY. / CRASH**
  (12"+=) *(BEG 221T)* – Baby, baby, baby, baby, baby.

–––– **MIKE STEED** – bass + **HANS PERRSON** – drums; repl. MILLS (to NEWSBOYS and WHITEHEART) + MITCHELL

Jan 90. (7") *(BEG 240)* **TIME AND SPACE. / DECLINE AND FALL**
  (12"+=/cd-s+=) *(BEG 240 T/CD)* – Bloodshot moon.
Feb 90. (lp/cd)(c) *(BEGA 100/+CD)(BEGC 100) <90232>* **PLASTIC FANTASTIC**   Sep89
  – Decline and fall / House of cards / Time and space / Every little word / Slowdown / Highwire / Slide / Day one / Choosing you / Stupid on the street / Avenue / Plastic fantastic.

–––– **DEL STRANGE FISH** – guitar, keyboards; repl. GREENING

–––– disbanded when their label dropped them

FLIPPER

Formed: San Francisco, California, USA . . . 1979 out of NEGATIVE TREND by WILL SHATTER and STEVE DePACE. Following the departure of the latter act's original singer, ROZZ, the pair recruited RICKIE WILLIAMS, who in turn thought up the FLIPPER moniker. He was soon replaced himself with the wonderfully named BRUCE LOOSE alongside fourth member, TED FALCONI, the raggedy-assed punk renegades attracting a cult following in the Bay Area with their painfully slow, monolithically rhythmic noise-grind. Signed to the newly inaugurated 'Subterranean', the FLIPPER crew made their vinyl debut with a track on the 1979 label sampler, 'SF Underground', while they also popped up on a local v/a album, 'Live At Target'. A belated debut single, 'LOVE CANAL', eventually appeared in 1980 on the tiny 'Thermidor' label while a first single for 'Subterranean', the marathon one (two at a push!) chord screamathon, 'SEX BOMB BABY', previewed the definitive debut set, 'ALBUM-GENERIC FLIPPER' (1982). Seemingly dredged up from the blackest studio murk, this lumbering, deceptively basic collection of inspired hardcore sloppiness set the scene for all manner of SF weirdness to come (i.e. PRIMUS etc.), its malign influence winding its way right up the coast to Seattle where the likes of TAD and NIRVANA would later incorporate at least the spirit of FLIPPER into their work. Yet by the release of the cleaned-up but demented follow-up, 'GONE FISHIN' (1984), FLIPPER had done just that, posthumous live releases following in the shape of 'BLOWING CHUNKS' (1984) and double set, 'PUBLIC FLIPPER LTD.' (1987). Tragically, any possibilities of a full reunion were cut short when WILL SHATTER died of an accidental heroin overdose in late '87. Nevertheless, the patronage of many leading figures in the 90's grunge scene (and KURT COBAIN in particular) led to a belated re-formation with new member, JOHN DOUGHERTY. A surprise signing to Rick Rubin's 'Def American' label, FLIPPER were afloat once again with comeback album, 'AMERICAN GRAFISHY' (1993). Despite being given a cautious thumbs up by FLIPPER commentators, many mourned the noisy abandon of old as it became clear the guys had actually been practising in their absence! More tragedy struck around the same time when BRUCE damaged his spine in a car crash, while even worse was the death of DOUGHERTY on the 31st of October, 1997. • **Songwriters:** SHATTER – LOOSE.

Album rating: GENERIC FLIPPER (*8) / GONE FISHIN' (*7) / BLOW'N'CHUNKS: LIVE (*4) / PUBLIC FLIPPER LIMITED (*5) / SEX BOMB BABY (*6) / AMERICAN GRAFISHY (*4)

NEGATIVE TREND

WILL SHATTER (b. RUSSELL WILKINSON, 1956) – bass / **STEVE DePACE** (b.29 Jan'57) – drums / **MIKAL WATERS** – vocals / **CRAIG GRAY** – guitar

not iss. / Heavy Manners

Sep 78. (d7"ep) *<HM 1/2>* **WE DON'T PLAY, WE RIOT**
  – Mercenaries / Meathouse / Black and red / How ya feelin. *<12"ep-iss.Sep84 on 'Subterranean'; SUB 32>*

FLIPPER

–––– **SHATTER + DEPACE** plus **TED FALCONI** (b. LAURENCE FALCONI, 2 Sep'47, Bryn Mawr, Penns.) – guitar (ex-RAD COMMAND) / **BRUCE LOOSE** (b. BRUCE CALDERWOOD, 6 Jun'59, Fresno, Calif.) – bass, vocals

not iss. / Thermidor

1980. (7") *<T 1>* **LOVE CANAL. / HA HA HA**
  <re-iss. Feb81 on 'Subterranean'; SUB 7> (UK-iss.Jan82 on 'Alternative Tentacles'; VIRUS 8)

Alternative Tentacles / Subterranean

Apr 82. (7"red) *(VIRUS 18) <SUB 23>* **SEX BOMB. / BRAINWASH**   Nov81
Apr 82. (lp) *<SUB 25>* **ALBUM – GENERIC FLIPPER**
  – Ever / Life is cheap / Shed no tears / (I saw you) Shine / Way of the world / Life / Nothing / Living for the depression / Sex bomb. *(UK-iss.Aug93 on 'Def American' cd/lp; DAB CD/LP 3)*
Jun 83. (7") *<SUB 35>* **OLD LADY. / GET AWAY**
Dec 83. (7"; by BRUCE LOOSE) *<SUB 38>* **WHAT'S YOUR NAME. / WAKING TO SLEEP**
Aug 84. (lp) *<SUB 42>* **GONE FISHIN'**
  – The lights, the sound, the rhythm, the noise / First the heart / In my life friends / Survivors of the plague / Sacrifice / Talk's cheap / You nought me / One by one. *(UK-iss.Mar87 on 'Fundamental'; SAVE 017)*

–––– On the 9th Dec'87, SHATTER died of an accidental heroin overdose. They decided to split, although they re-formed early '91 with new member JOHN DOUGHERTY (b.20 Apr'61, Oakland, Calif.) – bass

Jan 91. (7") *<SUB 70>* **SOME DAY. / DISTANT**

not iss. / Matador

Dec 92. (7") *<OLE 048>* **FLIPPER TWIST. / SO FUCKED UP**

American / American

Jun 93. (cd/lp) *(DABCD/LP 1) <45120>* **AMERICAN GRAFISHY**   Jan93
  – Someday / Flipper twist / May the truth be known / We're not crazy / Fucked up once again / Exist or else / Distant illusion / Telephone / It pays to know / Full speed ahead.

–––– disbanded when BRUCE suffered back injuries in a car crash (c. 1993); DOUGHERTY was to die four years later

– compilations, etc. –

Feb 84. (c) *R.O.I.R.; <A 126>* **BLOW'N CHUNKS (live)**
  – Way of the world / The light, the sound, the rhythm, the . . . / Shed no tears / Love canal / Ha ha ha / In your arms / Life is cheap / In life my friend / Get away. *(UK cd-iss. Nov94; RE 126CD) (<cd re-iss. Mar01; RUSCD 8271>)*
Feb 87. (d-lp) *Fundamental; (SAVE 015/016) / Subterranean; <SUB 53>* **PUBLIC FLIPPER LTD. (live 1980-82)**   Nov86
  – Nuru nuru / Hard cold world / I'm fighting / The game's gotta price / Love canal / Oh oh ay oh / We don't understand / If I can be drunk / Sex bomb / Brainwash / Shy / Southern California / Life / The whel / Flipper blues.
Sep 88. (lp) *Subterranean; <SAVE 059>* **SEX BOMB BABY**
  – Sex bomb / Love canal / Ha ha ha / Sacrifice / Falling / Ever get away / Earthworm / The games got a price / The old lady who swallowed a fly / Brainwash / Lowrider / End the game. *(UK cd-iss. Oct95 on 'Infinite Zero-BMG'; 74321 29898-2)*
Jul 97. (cd) *Overground; (OVER 63CD)* **LIVE AT CBGB'S 1983 (live)**

FLOAT UP CP (see under ⇒ RIP, RIG + PANIC)

FLOUR (see under ⇒ RIFLE SPORT)

FLOWERS

Formed: Edinburgh, Scotland . . . late 1978 by HILARY MORRISON, SIMON BEST, ANDY COPELAND and FRASER SUTHERLAND. The quartet initially bloomed on Bob Last's 'EARCOM 1' 12"ep (a various artists collection), performing two numbers, 'CRIMINAL WASTE' and 'AFTER DARK', the second of which became a B-side of their 1979 debut single for 'Pop Aural', 'CONFESSIONS'. Lying somewhere between DELTA 5 and stablemates The FIRE ENGINES, The FLOWERS completed only one more bop-friendly indie single, 'THE BALLAD OF MISS DEMEANOR', before calling it a day in 1980.

HILARY (MORRISON) – vocals / **ANDY COPELAND** – guitar / **FRASER SUTHERLAND** – bass / **SIMON BEST** – drums

                                         Pop Aural not iss.

Dec 79. (7") *(POP 001)* **CONFESSIONS. / (LIFE) AFTER DARK**
May 80. (7") *(POP 003)* **THE BALLAD OF MISS DEMEANOR. / FOOD / TEAR ALONG**

— after their split, FRASER joined SO YOU THINK YOU'RE A COWBOY issuing one 'Cheatin' Heart' single in 1984, 'DON'T NEED YOU'; he subsequently joined the group, The SYNDICATE, while HILARY (HI RAY) joined HEARTBEAT with an ex-FIRE ENGINE (a band SIMON also made guest appearances for)

Gary FLOYD
(see under ⇒ SISTER DOUBLE HAPPINESS)

FLUID

Formed: Denver, Colorado, USA ... 1986 by JOHN "JR" ROBINSON, JAMES CLOWER, RICK KULWICKI, MATT BISCHOFF and GARRETT SHAVLIK. Yet another outfit to base their sound on the proto-punk blueprint of The STOOGES and MC5, the FLUID first made it on to vinyl via a self-financed album, 'PUNCH N JUDY' (1986). Picked up by the fledgling 'Sub Pop' label, the grungey retro-rockers subsequently toured with labelmates, TAD, while promoting their second set, 'CLEAR BLACK PAPER' (1988), issued in the UK a year later as 'FREAK MAGNET'. 'ROADMOUTH' (1989) was another transitional set, honing their chops for 1990's mini-album, 'GLUE'. Next on the agenda was a shared 7" with the soon-to-be massive NIRVANA, the FLUID's 'CANDY' back to back with COBAIN and Co's cover of The VASELINES' 'Molly's Lips'. One of the original grunge pioneers, the FLUID had evaporated by the time the Seattle scene really took off, ROBINSON, CLOWER, etc (having now signed to 'Hollywood') quitting while on top after recording the best album of their career, 'PURPLEMETALFLAKEMUSIC'.

Album rating: PUNCH N JUDY (*4) / CLEAR BLACK PAPER (*5) / ROADMOUTH (*5) / GLUE mini (*6) / PURPLEMETALFLAKEMUSIC (*7)

JOHN "JR" ROBINSON – vocals / **JAMES CLOWER** – guitar / **RICK KULWICKI** – guitar / **MATT BISCHOFF** – bass / **GARRETT SHAVLIK** – drums, vocals

                                        not iss. Rayon

1986. (lp) **PUNCH N JUDY**

                                        Glitterhouse Sub Pop

May 88. (lp/c) *(GR 0026)* <SP 16/+A> **CLEAR BLACK PAPER**
– Cold outside / Nick of time / Lonely one / Just another day / Nashville nights / Tell me things / Today I shot the Devil / Much too much / Your kinda thing / New questions.
May 89. (m-lp) *(GR 0041)* **FREAK MAGNET**
Oct 89. (lp/cd) *(efa 4489)* <SP 36/+B> **ROADMOUTH**   Jun89
– Hooked / Human mill / Big brother / Girl bomb / Leave it / Fools rule / Cop a plea / Ode to Miss Lodge / Twisted & pissed / Is it day / What man / Saccharin rejection.
Mar 90. (7"orange,7"yellow) <SP 57> **TIN TOP TOY. / TOMORROW**
Apr 90. (m-lp/m-c/m-cd) <SP 64/+B/A> **GLUE**
– Our love will still be there / Black glove / Closet case / Candy / Pretty mouse / Wasted time. *<cd+=/c+=>* – ROADMOUTH
Jan 91. (7"/7"green) <SP 97> **CANDY (live). / (b-side by Nirvana)**

                                        not iss. Hollywood

Apr 93. (c/cd) *<1+/61445>* **PURPLEMETALFLAKEMUSIC**
– My kind / One eye out / She don't understand / 7/14 / Pill / Wasn't my idea / On my feet / Lies / Mister Blameshifter / Said that I'm through / Change / Hand in hand.

— disbanded some time in 1993; SHAVLIK formed SPELL

FLUX OF PINK INDIANS

Formed: Bishop Stortford, England ... 1978 as The EPILEPTICS by DEREK BIRKETT and COLIN LATTER. Unsurprisingly, complaints from The British Epilepsy Association led to them changing their moniker to EPI-X or The LICKS. It would be the latter incarnation under which their debut EP, '1970s' would surface at the turn of the decade. An EPILEPTICS single, meanwhile, 'LAST BUS TO DEBDEN', surfaced a few years later although its release was overshadowed by the new line-up of FLUX OF PINK INDIANS, who unleashed the 'NEU SMELL' EP (featuring the definitive 'TUBE DISASTERS'); the record was actually issued by the in-house label of fellow anarcho subversives, CRASS, whom FOPI had recently supported on tour. In 1982, they set up their own independent label, 'Spiderleg', notching up a small victory in early 1983 with the non-tunes and militant politicism of debut album, 'STRIVE TO SURVIVE'. Eighteen months later, in a follow-up, the uncompromising troopers issued what must surely be a contender for the most bluntly (to put it lightly!) titled album in the history of rock, 'THE FUCKING CUNTS TREAT US LIKE PRICKS'. Predictably, this piece of fractured, barely listenable noise caused uproar among retailers such as HMV who immediately banned it. The Eastern Bloc record shop in Manchester was even charged for daring to display the album sleeve, seeing their stock seized by the Greater Manchester police under the obscene articles for publication law. 1987's more subdued 'UNCARVED BLOCK', meanwhile, was released on BIRKETT's new label project, 'One Little Indian', replacing the seething mess of noise with a caustic brand of free-funk influenced by the likes of ACR and 23 SKIDOO and produced by dubmeister, ADRIAN SHERWOOD. BIRKETT's label went on to become one of the main players in the indie scene, signing The SUGARCUBES, The HEART THROBS and The SHAMEN while 1990 saw the man return in his own right with new project, HOTALACIO.
• **Songwriters:** BIRKETT (+ COLIN).

Album rating: STRIVE TO SURVIVE (*7) / THE FUCKING CUNTS ... (*2) / UNCARVED BLOCK (*6)

LICKS

COLIN 'Colsk The Terrible' LATTER – vocals / **KEVIN HUNTER** – guitar / **DEREK BIRKETT** (b.18 Feb'61, London, England) – bass / **MARTIN WILSON** – drums

                                        Stormbeat not iss.

Nov 79. (7"ep) *(BEAT 8)* **1970'S E.P.**
– 1970's have been made in Japan / System rejects / Hitler's still a Nazi / War crimes. *(re-iss. Jan82 by EPILEPTICS on 'Spiderleg'; SDL 1)*

EPILEPTICS

(same line-up)

                                        Spiderleg not iss.

Oct 81. (7"ep) *(SDL 2)* **LAST BUS TO DEBDEN**
– Tube disasters / Two years too late / Target on my back / What've you got.

FLUX OF PINK INDIANS

COLIN + DEREK / + ANDY – guitar / **SID ATTION** (b.18 Apr'60, Sutton Coalfield, England) – drums

                                        Crass not iss.

Oct 81. (7"ep) *(321984-2)* **NEU SMELL EP**
– Neu smell / Tube disasters / Poem: Sick butchers / Background of malfunction. *(re-iss. Aug87 on 'One Little Indian' 12"ep; 12T PEP 1)*

— **DAVE 'BAMBI'** – drums (ex-DISCHARGE) repl. SID who joined RUBELLA BALLET / **SIMON** – guitar repl. ANDY repl. NEIL PINCHER

— **KEVIN HUNTER + MARTIN WILSON** returned to repl. SIMON + BAMBI who went back to INSANE

                                        Spiderleg not iss.

Jan 83. (lp) *(SDL 8)* **STRIVE TO SURVIVE CAUSING THE LEAST SUFFERING POSSIBLE**   79
– Song for them / Charity hilarity / Some of us scream, some of us shout / Take heed / TV dinners / Tapioca surprise / Progress / They lie, we die / Blinded by justice / Myxamatosis / Is there anybody there? / The fun is over. *(re-iss. Jun87 on 'One Little Indian'; TPLP 2) (cd-iss. Jun88 & Oct98; TPLP 2CD)*
Sep 84. (d-lp) *(SDL 13)* **THE FUCKING CUNTS TREAT US LIKE PRICKS**
– Punk / Mind fuckers fucking minds / Hard sell / Love song / Mickey Tuneoil / Desire / Blood lust rite / The Falklands war / Punk / Life we make / Trouble at the heart / The sun / Shadow of abuse / Very funny / Cure for the coprlite. *(re-iss. Jun87 on 'One Little Indian'; TPLP 3) (cd-iss. Jan89 & Oct98; TPLP 3CD) (+=)* – TAKING A LIBERTY EP

FLUX

Mar 85. (7"ep) *(SDL 16)* **TAKING A LIBERTY EP**
– Taking a liberty / Pass me another issue / For the love of beauty.

                                      One Little Indian not iss.

Jan 87. (lp) *(TP 1)* **UNCARVED BLOCK**
– Value of nothing / Youthful immortal / Just is / Children who know / Back word / Footprints in the snow / Nothing is not done / The stonecutter. *(re-press.Aug87; TPLP 1) (cd-iss. Jun88 & Oct98; TPLP 1CD)*
Mar 87. (12") *(12TP 6)* **NEU SMELL. / TAKING A LIBERTY**
May 87. (12") *(12TP 9)* **VISION. /**

– compilations, etc. –

Nov 97. (lp/cd) *Overground; (OVER 67/+CD)* **NOT SO BRAVE**
(re-iss. Aug02; same)
Sep 00. (cd/lp) *Overground-Voiceprint; (<OVER 87 VPCD/VPLP>)* **LIVE STATEMENT**
(re-iss. Apr02; same)

HOTALACIO

BIRKETT / TIM KELLY / COAL (ex-FLUX) / **LYDIE** (b. France) – drums / **KEITH LeBLANC** – producer (of TACKHEAD)

                                        Big Kiss not iss.

Mar 90. (7") **TALKIN' OUT THE SIDE OF YOUR NECK**
Sep 90. (lp) *(KISS 5)* **SURVEILLANCE**
– Talkin' out the side of your neck / Take me for a ride / How ya livin / Bass hell / Why d'ya lie? / Big boss boys / Don't kick me / Why July / Imagination / Deconstruction.

— DEREK now concentrated on his record company

FLYING COLOR

Formed: San Francisco, California, USA ... 1984 by DALE DUNCAN, HECTOR PENALOSA, RICHARD CHASE and JOHN STUART. Stemming from various Bay Area outfits, FLYING COLOR were heavily influenced by their harmonious West Coast forebears and traded in a similar, if less adventurous rootsy jangle to Georgia's R.E.M. A one-off 7" single, 'DEAR FRIEND', was their sole output in '85; prolific they weren't as it would take a further two years for the band to release their eponymous debut album.

Drawing comparisons with The BEATLES with regard to their interchangeable songwriting abilities and pristine melodies, FLYING COLOR had recorded a minor gem. Unfortunately, they didn't stick around long enough to reap the rewards, CHRIS VON SNEIDERN coming in briefly for CHASE before their early demise. In 1996, a CD-issue of the aforementioned album rekindled interest, inspiring DUNCAN, STUART and VON SNEIDERN to re-form.

Album rating: FLYING COLOR (*7)

DALE DUNCAN – guitar (ex-LOVE CIRCUS) / **RICHARD CHASE** – guitar / **HECTOR PENALOSA** – bass (ex-ZEROS) / **JOHN STUART** – drums

			Sound & Shigaku	Cryptovision
1987.	(7") <(SHIGS 1)> **DEAR FRIEND. / LOOK MY WAY**			1985
			not iss.	Frontier
Sep 87.	(lp/c) <FLP/+C 1022> **FLYING COLOR**			

– Dear friend / It doesn't matter / One Saturday / Through different eyes / Tumble / Believe, believe / Farewell song / Bring back the rain / I'm your shadow / Wise to her ways. *(cd-iss. 1997 on 'Munster'+=;)* – The road we're on / By the fire / Love is on its way.

— **CHRIS VON SNEIDERN** – guitar; repl. CHASE

— disbanded in 1990 (all went on own projects) but re-formed in '96' VON SNEIDERN has now released several jangle-pop albums

FOLK DEVILS (see under ⇒ LOWERY, Ian)

FOR AGAINST

Formed: Lincoln, Nebraska, USA . . . 1985 by JEFFREY RUNNINGS, HARRY DINGMAN III and GREG HILL. Their sound wore its influences of British post-punk bands in the shape of JOY DIVISION and TEARDROP EXPLODES on it sleeve, but weaved in with this a heightened sense of atmospherics and chilled ambience which created a dream indie pop sound analogous to EVERYTHING BUT THE GIRL and LUSH. Unfortunately FOR AGAINST never achieved the heights of fame of its predecessors or peers due mainly to a lack of live exposure and record industry ignorance. The band's debut album, 'ECHELONS', was released in 1987 and was closely followed with 'DECEMBER' in 1988, arguably one of their best sets. An aptly titled production RUNNING'S vocals expertly convey frosty dark emotions with the melancholic guitar sounds from DINGMAN and passionate rhythym provided by HILL and RUNNINGS. After this outing DINGMAN and HILL handed in their resignation and moved on to new musical pastures with the formation of The MILLIONS; STEVEN 'MAVE' HINRICHS and PAUL ENGELHAND moved in to take up their places. The new line-up set about recording their third full-length offering, 'APERTURE', also aided by JEFF GASKINS' bass doodlings. Recorded in the early 90s, it did not see the light of the record shops until 1993, by which time its sound had been surpassed by its makers and the indie scene around it. Nevertheless, with record industry problems put aside the band moved on with the release of fourth LP, 'MASON'S CALIFORNIA LUNCH ROOM' (1995). This set displayed an outfit that were maturer and back to their former 'DECEMBER' glories. This peak was retained on into the album, 'SHELF LIFE' (1997), which alongside their own gems featured for the first time two covers in the shape of 'SEASCAPE' by Everything But The Girl and 'TIMES SQUARE GO-GO BOY' by Eat River Pipe, which both rank up there with the originals in their loving interpretation. Again FA suffered at the hands of the record industry beast meaning that their sixth full-set, 'COALESCED', did not appear until 2002.

Album rating: ECHELONS (*4) / DECEMBER (*7) / APERTURE (*5) / MASON'S CALIFORNIA LUNCH ROOM (*6) / SHELF LIFE (*6) / COALESCED (*6)

JEFFREY RUNNINGS – vocals, bass / **HARRY DINGMAN** – guitar / **GREG HILL** – drums

		not iss.	Independent Project
1985.	(7") **AUTOCRAT. / IT'S A LIE**	-	
1987.	(lp/c) <IP/+C 19> **ECHELONS**	-	

– Shine / Daylight / Get on with it / Echelons / It's a lie / Autocrat / Forget who you are / Loud and clear / Broke my back.

		not iss.	Chameleon
1988.	(lp/c/cd) <D1/D4/D2 74781> **DECEMBER**	-	

– Sabres / Stranded in Greenland / Svengali / They said / The effect / December / The last laugh / Paperwhites / Clandestine high holy.

| 1990. | (10"ep) <IPR 000029> **IN THE MARSHES** (rec. 1986) | - | |

– Tibet / Amnesia / The purgatory salesman / Amen Yves / Fate / In the marshes.

— (1989) **STEVEN "MAVE" HINRICHS** – guitar + **PAUL ENGELHARD** – drums; repl. DINGMAN + HILL who formed The MILLIONS; they released two albums, 'M Is For Millions' (1991) + 'Raquel' (1994)

		not iss.	Part Trance
1993.	(7") <005> **YOU ONLY LIVE TWICE. / TODAY TODAY**	-	

— added **JEFF GASKINS** – bass (RUNNINGS switched to guitar)

| 1993. | (7"ep) <IP 40> **DON'T DO ME ANY FAVORS EP** | - | |

– Don't do me any favors / Breathless / Spent.

| Aug 93. | (cd) <IPCD 45> **APERTURE** | - | |

– Don't do me any favors / Breathless / Nightmare life / Spent / Mindframed / I wish / Unspeakable / Over Nepal / You only live twice / Today today / Memorial.

— reverted to a trio (GASKINS left) – RUNNINGS – (+) bass, organ

		not iss.	Rainbow Quartz
Jul 95.	(cd) <RQTZ 003> **MASON'S CALIFORNIA LUNCH ROOM**	-	

– Seesick / Vacuum / Crossed / Tagalong / Hindsight / Coursing / Vista / Infamous / Reinventing the wheel / Mirage / Blow.

		World Domination	World Domination
Mar 98.	(cd) <(WDM 10072-2)> **SHELF LIFE**		Nov97

– Shadow / Wintersong / Starblind / Lost / Profile / Lilacs / Harbor / Forever / Times Square go-go boy / Seascape.

		not iss.	Words On Music
2000.	(cd) <11> **COALESCED**	-	

– Medication / So long / Fuel / Coalesced / Outside a heart / Shelflife / Love you.

Robert FORSTER (see under ⇒ GO-BETWEENS)

FORTUNATE SONS (see under ⇒ BARRACUDAS)

14 ICED BEARS

Formed: Brighton, England . . . 1985 by ROB SEKULA, NICK EMERY and ALAN WHITE. This initial line-up only lasted for a short time as WHITE was replaced with DOMINIC MINQUES and KEVIN CANHAM, prior to their debut EP, which led with the track, 'INSIDE'. Line-up changes continued to dog the band to the extent that by the time they'd got round to recording a debut album, SEKULA was the only remaining founder member (joined at this point by WILL TAYLOR and GRAHAM DURRANT). Released on 'Sarah' records in 1988, the eponymous set moved away from the amateurish jangle of their early singles to a more focused retro sound. After a further series of singles and a contribution (a near comotose reading of 'Grease' classic, 'SUMMER NIGHTS') to anti-Poll Tax compilation, 'Alvin Lives In Leeds', the band released a belated follow-up set, 'WONDER' (1991). Characterised by spiralling guitars and a pseudo-psychedelic eastern feel, the record was well timed to coincide with the interest in all things "Shoegazing" yet failed to attract anything more than the usual minimal press coverage.
• **Covered:** BOUNCING BABIES (Teardrop Explodes) / INTERSTELLAR OVERDRIVE (Pink Floyd).

Album rating: 14 ICED BEARS (*4) / PRECISION compilation (*5) / WONDER (*5) / LET THE BREEZE OPEN YOUR HEARTS (*5)

ROB SEKULA (b.12 Dec'63, Camberwell, Surrey, England) – vocals, guitar / **DOMINIQUE MINQUES** – bass; repl. ALAN WHITE who formed PLEASURE SPLINTERS / **NICK EMERY** – drums / **KEVIN CANHAM** (b.10 Oct'64, Aldershot, England) – guitar

		Frank	not iss.
Nov 86.	(12"ep) (COPPOLA 101) **INSIDE. / BLUESUIT / CUT**		-

— added **NICK ROUGHLEY** – keyboards

| Feb 87. | (12"ep) (CAPRA 202) **LIKE A DOLPHIN / BALLOON SONG. / TRAIN SONG / LIE TO CHOOSE** | | - |

— now without ROUGHLEY who joined BLOW UP

		Penetration	not iss.
1987.	(7"flexi) (001) **LIE TO CHOOSE. / (other track by Splendour In The Grass)**		-

— **STEVE ORMSBY** – bass; repl. MINQUES

— **BILL COX** – drums; repl. EMERY

		Sarah	not iss.
Apr 88.	(7"m) (SARAH 005) **COME GET ME. / UNHAPPY DAYS / SURE TO SEE**		-

— SEKULA + CANHAM then recruited newcomers **WILL TAYLOR** (b.23 Aug'68) – bass / **GRAHAM DURRANT** (b.10 Oct'63, Camberwell) – drums

		Thunderball	not iss.
Nov 88.	(lp) (TBLP 001) **14 ICED BEARS**		-
Apr 89.	(12"; w-drawn) (7TBL 2) **MOTHER SLEEP.**		-
Nov 89.	(7") (7TBL 5) **WORLD I LOVE.**		-
Mar 90.	(lp) (TBLP 002) **PRECISION** (compilation)		-

— **TIM WHITE** (b.30 Mar'67, Essex, England) – bass; repl. TAYLOR who also joined BLOW UP

| 1990's. | (ltd-7"ep) (Surfacer 002) **FALLING BACKWARDS / WORLD I LOVE. / (other tracks by Crocodile Ride)** | | |

		Borderline	not iss.
1991.	(12"m) (BORD12 001) **HOLD ON. / SUMMER NIGHTS / IN THE MORNING**		
1991.	(cd; as FOURTEEN ICED BEARS) (BORD 002) **WONDER**		

– Hold on / Heaven star / Smooth in the sun / These are the things / When it comes / Rare (like you are) / Love on a sugar mountain / Eyes / RED NOW.

— **ROB COLLEY** (b.27 Jun'63) – bass (ex-WHIRL) repl. TIM WHITE

— they finally split for good after above

– compilations, etc. –

| Jan 99. | (cd) Overground; (OVER 78CD) **LET THE BREEZE OPEN OUR HEARTS** | | - |

– Rise / Beautiful child / World I love / Falling backwards / Coming down / Mother sleep / Florence / Spangle / Dust remains / Cut / Surfacer / Take it / Holland / Train song / Moths / Hay fever / If I said / Inside (live) / Bouncing babies (live) / Interstellar overdrive (live). *(re-iss. Aug02; same)*

| Jul 01. | (7") Slumberland; (WISH 009) **INSIDE. / BALLOON SONG** | | - |
| 2001. | (cd) Slumberland; <65> **IN THE BEGINNING** | | - |

– Balloon song (Peel session) / Balloon song / Blue suit / Come get me / Cut (Peel session) / Cut / Gave you my coat / Hay fever / I don't know why / If I said / Inside / Jumped in a puddle / Lie to choose / Like a dolphin / Miles away / Ring the far bell / Shy like you / Spangle / Sure to see / Train song (Peel session) / Train song / Unhappy days.

Kim FOWLEY

Born: 21 Jul'42, Manila. Based himself in Los Angeles in the late 50's, where he worked with PHIL SPECTOR and sang in black doo-wop outfit The JAYHAWKS. Soon turned to DJ work in Boise before producing PAUL REVERE & THE RAIDERS. Others groups to ask for his services were The HOLLYWOOD ARGYLES ('Alley Oop'), RIVINGTONS ('Papa Oom Mow Mow'), B.BUMBLE & THE STINGERS ('Nut Rocker'), girl-group The MURMAIDS No.1 ('Posicles And Icicles'). In 1966 while initiating a solo career, he worked on NAPOLEON XIV ('They're Coming To Take Me Away'), The FREAKS OF NATURE, plus FRANK ZAPPA's album 'Freak Out' on which he also sang back-up. In the 70's he produced GENE VINCENT, JOHNNY WINTER and SLADE. He was also the man behind new wave girl-group The RUNAWAYS, plus more production work with JOHN CALE for JONATHAN RICHMAN & THE MODERN LOVERS. • **Trivia:** Son of actor DOUGLAS FOWLEY and grandson of composer RUDOLF FRIMI.

Best Compilation: OUTRAGEOUS (*6)

KIM FOWLEY – vocals, keyboards, with **MICHAEL LLOYD** – multi instruments

C.B.S. / Columbia

- Aug 66. (7") *(202243)* **THEY'RE COMING TO TAKE ME AWAY HA-HAAA!. / YOU GET MORE FOR YOUR MONEY ON THE FLIP SIDE OF THIS RECORD TALKING BLUES**
- Oct 66. (7";w-drawn) *(202338)* **LIGHTS (THE BLIND CAN SEE). / SOMETHING NEW AND DIFFERENT**

Parlophone / not iss.

- Oct 66. (7") *(R 5521)* **LIGHTS. / SOMETHING NEW AND DIFFERENT**

not iss. / Tower

- 1967. (lp) *<T 5080>* **LOVE IS ALIVE AND WELL**
  – Love is alive and well / Flower city / Flower drum drum / This planet love / War game / Reincarnation / See how the other half love / Flowers / Super flower / Me.

—— with various session people

not iss. / Imperial

- 1968. (lp) *<12413>* **BORN TO BE WILD**
- Apr 69. (lp) *<12423>* **OUTRAGEOUS**
  – Hide and seek / Wildfire / Animal man / Chinese water torture / Nightrider / Inner space discovery / Bubble gum / Barefoot country boy / Up / Caught in the middle / Down / California hayride.
- 1969. (lp) *<12443>* **GOOD CLEAN FUN**
  – One man band / Ode to sweet sixteen / Good clean fun / Search for a teenage woman / Energy / Baby rocked her dolly / Motorcycle / Kangaroo / Lights (the blind can see) / Good to be around / The great telephone robbery / I'm not young anymore.

M.N.W. / not iss.

- 1970. (lp) *(MNWL 7P)* **THE DAY THE EARTH STOOD STILL**
  (UK cd-iss. Feb97 on 'Spalax'; 14260) —— Spain

Action

- Aug 72. (7") *(ACT 4606)* **BORN TO MAKE YOU CRY. / THUNDER ROAD**

Capitol / Capitol

- 1972. (lp) *<E-ST 11075>* **I'M BAD**
  – Queen of stars / Forbidden love / Man of God / Human being blues / I'm bad / California gypsy man / It's great to be alive / Red China / Gotta get close to you / Let it loose.
- 1973. (lp) *<E-ST 11159>* **INTERNATIONAL HEROES**
  – International heroes / E.S.P. reader / King of love / Ugly stories about rock stars and the war / I hate you / Something new / Born dancer / So good, wish you would / World wide love / Dancing all nite.
- Feb 73. (7") *(CL 15743)* **INTERNATIONAL HEROES. / E.S.P. READER**

Skydog / Capitol

- 1974. (lp) *(SG-KF 001)* *<24636>* **ANIMAL GOD OF THE STREET** —— France
  – Night of the hunter / Long live rock'n'roll / Werewolf dynamite / Is America dead / Rumble / California swamp dance / Hobo wine / Dangerous vision / Ain't got no transportation. (UK cd-iss. May97 on 'Skydog'; 622482)

Mercury / Mercury

- Feb 78. (7") *(6005 009)* **CONTROL. / RUBBER RAINBOW**

Sonet / not iss.

- Aug 78. (lp) *(SNTF 755)* **LIVING IN THE STREETS**
  – Motorboat / 25 hours a day / Big bad Cadillac / Man without a country / California summertime / Hollywood nights / Born to make you cry / Thunder road / Summertime frog / Love bomb / Living in the streets / Sex, dope and violence.

Illegal / P.V.C.

- Jan 79. (lp) *(ILP 002)* *<7906>* **SUNSET BOULEVARD**
  – The top / Rubber rainbow / Nightingale / Negative / In my garage / Sunset boulevard / North American man / Teenage death girl / Control / Love is a game / Black camels of Lavender Hill / Blow up.

Island / Antilles

- 1979. (7") *(ILS 12)* **RUBBER RAINBOW. / IN MY GARAGE**
- Dec 79. (lp) *(ILPS 9572)* *<7075>* **SNAKE DOCUMENT MASQUERADE**
  – 1980: Run for your life / 1981: Black Christmas / 1982: Stranded in the future / 1983: Don't feed the animals / 1984: The saga of Hugo X / 1985: Physical lies / 1986: Snake document masquerade / 1987: Lost like a lizard in the snow / 1988: Searching for human in tight blue jeans / 1989: Waiting around for the next ten years.
- Jan 80. (7") *(WIP 6555)* **1989: WAITING FOR THE NEXT TEN YEARS. / 1987: LOST LIKE A LIZARD IN SNOW**

Sonet / not iss.

- Jul 84. (lp) *(SNTF 918)* **FRANKENSTEIN AND MONSTER BAND**

Line / Bomp

- Jun 87. (lp) *(400 330)* *<40050>* **VAMPIRES FROM OUTERSPACE** —— German

Revola-Creation / Rykodisc

- Nov 95. (cd) *(CREV 36CD)* **MONDO HOLLYWOOD**

— compilations, others, etc. —

- Sep 77. (7") *Island;* *(WI 278)* **THE TRIP. / BEAUTIFUL PEOPLE**
- Jan 78. (lp) *Capitol;* *(E-ST 24636)* **VISIONS OF THE FUTURE**
  – Hollywood confidential / Shine like a radio / Visions of the future / California gypsy man / It's great to be alive / E.S.P. reader / World wide love / Forbidden love / Something new / Save my love for a rainy day / International heroes / Film maker / Mom and dad / Red China.
- 1988. (lp) *GNP Crescendo;* *(GNPS 2132)* **HOLLYWOOD CONFIDENTIAL**
- Jan 93. (cd/lp) *Marilyn;* *(USM CD/LP 1013)* **HOTEL INSOMNIA**
- Jul 93. (cd/lp) *Marilyn;* *(USM CD/LP 1022)* **WHITE NEGROES IN DEUTSCHLAND (featuring CHRIS WILSON & HIS DAWG GUITAR)**
- Feb 95. (cd) *Rev-ola;* *(CREV 033CD)* **OUTRAGEOUS / GOOD CLEAN FUN**
- Jul 95. (cd; as KIM FOWLEY & BEN VAUGHN) *Sector 2;* *(SECTOR2 10014)* **KINGS OF SATURDAY NIGHT**
- Aug 95. (cd) *Receiver;* *(RRCD 203)* **LET THE MADNESS IN**
- Mar 97. (cd; KIM FOWLEY & BMX BANDITS) *Receiver;* *(RRCD 231)* **HIDDEN AGENDA AT THE 13th NOTE**
  – Jaded / Ugly dream / Crabmeat / Ballad of a suicidal teenager / Medicine girl / Secret and sometimes cunning exploits of a Glaswegian mortua (up in flames) / Volcano / Sleep / Alice Cooper's roadie lovechild / Dancing with death on the lilac / Super highway / Tokyo summertime love affair number 69 / Susan was bleeding / Do you want to dance / It's my party / Peaches / Vampire scarecrow / Kimotronix / Sight surfing.

John FOXX

Born: DENNIS LEIGH, Chorley, Lancashire, England. After dramatically leaving new wave ouftit, ULTRAVOX! (who subsequently split for a time after his departure in March '79), he concentrated on a solo career. The "quiet man" (nicknamed as such from a past ULTRAVOX number) created a new label, 'Metal Beat' (through 'Virgin'), releasing his debut 45, 'UNDERPASS', which nearly cracked the UK Top 30 early in 1980. A compulsive, brooding slice of proto-electro, the single's minor chart success helped push the accompanying debut album, METAMATIC' into the Top 20. Although his previous act, ULTRAVOX, were doing a lot better commercially with new frontman, MIDGE URE ('Vienna', etc.), FOXX's cult following ensured Top 30 placing for subsequent sets, 'THE GARDEN' (1981) and 'THE GOLDEN SECTION' (1983). Finally, after the commercially disappointing 'IN MYSTERIOUS WAYS' (1985), the "mannequin of rock" who made the KRAFTWERK look energetic in comparison, retired from the music business, working on his book, 'The Quiet Man' (what else!?). Surprisingly, he was back early in 1997 with two simultaneously released sets of new ambient/electro-type material, 'CATHEDRAL OCEANS' and 'SHIFTING CITY' (the latter with LOUIS GORDON). Fitting nicely between 80's NUMAN or KRAFTWERK, FOXX ventured into the studio post-millennium for another pared-down, arty-rock piece, 'THE PLEASURES OF ELECTRICITY' (2002); keeping it light, eh JOHN.

Album rating: METAMATIC (*7) / THE GARDEN (*6) / THE GOLDEN SECTION (*5) / IN MYSTERIOUS WAYS (*4) / ASSEMBLY compilation (*7) / SHIFTING CITY (*5) / CATHEDRAL OCEANS (*6) / MODERN ART – THE BEST OF JOHN FOXX compilation (*8) / THE PLEASURES OF ELECTRICITY (*5)

JOHN FOXX – vocals, synthesizers, guitar, drum machine (ex-ULTRAVOX!) with **JOHN BARKER** – synth-drums / **JAKE DURANT** – bass / **ED CASE** – drums (*on 2nd lp*)

Virgin / not iss.

- Jan 80. (7") *(VS 318)* **UNDERPASS. / FILM 1** — 31 / —
- Jan 80. (lp/c) *(V/TCV 2146)* **METAMATIC** — 18 / —
  – Plaza / He's a liquid / Underpass / Metal beat / No one driving / A new kind of man / Blurred girl / 030 / Tidal wave / Touch and go. (re-iss. Mar84 lp/c; (OVED/+C 46) (cd-iss. Apr93; CDV 2146) (<cd re-iss. Aug01 on 'Edsel'+=; EDCD 702>) – Film 1 / Glimmer / Mr. No / This city / 20th century / Burning car.
- Mar 80. (d7") *(VS 338)* **NO ONE DRIVING. / GLIMMER / MR. NO. / THIS CITY** — 32 / —
- Jul 80. (7"pic-d) *(VS 360)* **BURNING CAR. / 20th CENTURY** — 35 / —
- Oct 80. (7") *(VS 382)* **MILES AWAY. / A LONG TIME** — 51 / —

—— **ROBIN SIMON** – guitar + **JO DWORNIAK** – bass repl. BARKER

- Aug 81. (7") *(VS 393)* **EUROPE AFTER THE RAIN. / THIS JUNGLE** — 40 / —
- Sep 81. (lp/c) *(V/TCV 2194)* **THE GARDEN** — 24 / —
  – Europe after the rain / Systems of romance / When I was a man and you were a woman / Dancing like a gun / Pater noster / Night suit / You were there / Fusion – Fission / Walk away / The garden. (re-iss. Mar84 lp/c; OVED/+C 47) (cd-iss. Apr93; CDV 2194) (<cd re-iss. Aug01 on 'Edsel'+=; EDCD 703>) – A long time / This jungle / Swimmer 2 / SWimmer 1 / Young man.
- Oct 81. (7") *(VS 459)* **DANCING LIKE A GUN. / SWIMMER 2**
  (12"+=) *(VS 459-12)* – Swimmer 1.

—— **PAUL WICKENS** (WIX) – drums, keyboards; repl. DURANT

- Jul 82. (7"pic-d) *(VS 543)* **ENDLESSLY. / YOUNG MAN** — 66 / —
  (d7"++=) *(VSY 543)* – Dance with me / A kind of love.
- Aug 83. (7") *(VS 615)* **YOUR DRESS. / WOMAN OF THE STAIRWAY** — 61 / —
  (12"+=) *(VS 615-12)* – The Garden.
  (d7"+=) *(VSY 615)* Lifting sky / Annexe.
- Oct 83. (lp/c) *(V/TCV 2233)* **THE GOLDEN SECTION** — 27 / —
  – My wild love / Someone / Your dress / Running across thin ice with tigers / Sitting at the edge of the world / Endlessly / Ghosts on water / Like a miracle / The hidden man / Twilight's last gleaming. (c+=) – Dance with me / The lifting sky / Annexe / Wings and a wind / A kind of wave / A woman on the stairway. (re-iss. Aug88 lp/c; OVED/+C 120) (<cd-iss. Aug01 on 'Edsel'++=; EDCD 704>)
- Oct 83. (7"sha-pic-d) *(VSP 645)* **LIKE A MIRACLE. / WING AND A WIND**
  (12"+=) *(VS 645-12)* – ('A'extended).
- Jun 85. (7"/12") *(VS 771/+12)* **THE STARS ON FIRE. / WHAT KIND OF GIRL**
  (free 7"with the 7")

John FOXX (cont)

Sep 85. (lp/c) (V/TCV 2355) **IN MYSTERIOUS WAYS** 85 –
– The stars on fire / Lose all sense of time / What kind of girl / Shine on / Enter the angel / In mysterious ways / This side of Paradise / Stepping softly / Morning glory / Enter the angel II. (cd-iss. Jul87; CDV 2355) (re-iss. Aug88 lp/c; OVED/+C 189) (<cd-iss. Aug01 on 'Edsel'+=; EDCD 705>) – Stairway.

Sep 85. (7"/12") (VS 814/+12) **ENTER THE ANGEL. / STAIRWAY**

―― FOXX retired from music biz, until he astonishing released two sets in 1997

                                                     Metamatic not iss.

Mar 97. (cd) (META 001CD) **CATHEDRAL OCEANS**
– Cathedral oceans / City as memory / Summer rooms / Geometry and coincidence / If only . . . / Shifting perspective / Floating islands / Infinite in all directions / Avenham collanade / Sunset rising / Invisible architecture. (re-iss. Mar02; same)

Mar 97. (cd; JOHN FOXX & LOUIS GORDON) (META 002) **SHIFTING CITY**
– Crash / Noise / Here we go / Shadow man / Through my shadow / Forgotten years / Everyone / Shifting city / Concrete / Bulletproof / Invisible / Ocean we can breathe. (re-iss. Mar02; same)

Feb 02. (cd) (META 004CD) **THE PLEASURES OF ELECTRICITY**
– A funny thing / Night life / Camera / Invisible women / Cities of light 5 / Uptown – Downtown / When it rains / Automobile / The falling room / Travel / Quiet city.

– compilations, etc. –

1988. (cd) Virgin; (COMCD 6) **ASSEMBLY**
– A new kind of man / Underpass / Burning car / This city / Twilight's last gleaming / Ghosts on water / This jungle / Endlessly / Someone / Sitting at the edge of the world / In mysterious ways / Morning glory / Europe after the rain / Systems of romance / Walk away / When I was a man and you were a woman / Pater noster / The garden. (re-iss. Jun92; CDVM 9002)

May 01. (cd) Music Club; (<MCCD 454>) **MODERN ART – THE BEST OF JOHN FOXX**
– Underpass / No-one driving / Burning car / 20th century / Miles away / Europe after the rain / Dancing like a gun / Endlessly / Your dress / Like a miracle / Stars on fire / Enter the angel / Sunset rising / The noise / Nightlife / Shifting city / My face / He's a liquid.

Roddy FRAME (see under ⇒ AZTEC CAMERA)

FRANK CHICKENS

Formed: London, England . . . 1982 by KAZUKO HOHKI and KAZUMI TAGUCHI (augmented by NORIKO IWATSUBO until late 1983), who met while helping out at the Japanese/American Toy Theatre. They first got their recording break when BILL NELSON invited them to sing on his 'Invisibility Exhibition' early in '83, the girls receiving publicity through a wacky promotional appearance on Channel 4's (then) flagship pop show, 'The Tube'. While their work may have benefitted from the attendant novelty factor, The FRANK CHICKENS were nevertheless attempting to present a more positive, proto girl-power portrait of the Japanese female (i.e. their first 45, 'WE ARE NINJA' (NOT GEISHA)'). With the support of airplay from John Peel, the pigeon-English funsters became a mid-80's cult phenomenom, the independent 'Kaz' label unleashing their long-playing debut album, 'WE ARE . . .', in 1984. Three years on, KAZUKO and KAZUMI launched their own 'Flying Lecords' rabel (sorry, label!), releasing a follow-up set, 'GET CHICKENIZED', before helping to introduce the Karaoke craze to Britain via their own zany celebrity-singing TV show. In the 90's, the 'CHICKENS scratched a living around the capital's cabaret circuit, one of their only recording ventures being 1996's 'UNDERFLOOR WORLD'.

Album rating: WE ARE FRANK CHICKENS (*6) / GET CHICKENIZED (*5)

KAZUKO HOHKI – vocals / **KAZUMI TAGUCHI** – vocals / with a plethora of session people including STEVE BERESFORD, DAVID TOOP, LOL COXHILL, ELIZABETH PERRY, ANNIE WHITEHEAD, ROBERT PIA, BOSCO DeOLIVERA, TONY COE, ALEX BALANESCU + CLIVE BELL

                                            Kaz not iss.

Jan 84. (7") (KAZ 10) **WE ARE NINJA (NOT GEISHA). / FUJIYAMA MAMA**
(12"+=) (KAZT 10) – Shellfish bamboo.

Oct 84. (lp) (RPS 8282) **WE ARE FRANK CHICKENS**
– Cheeba cheeba chimpira / Mothra / Green banana / Madam fatal / We are Ninja (not Geisha) / Yellow detective / Shellfish bamboo / Nichon fatal / Pikadon / We are Frank Chickens / Sake ballad. (cd-iss. Jul89 as 'THE BEST OF FRANK CHICKENS'+=; KAZCD 2) – Fujiyama mama / Blue canary / China night / Japanese rhumba / Ari Lang.

Oct 85. (7") (KAZ 20) **BLUE CANARY / WE ARE FRANK CHICKENS**
(12"+=) (KAZT 20) – China night / Japanese rumba.

                                          Flying Flying
                                          Lecords Lecords

Aug 87. (12"m) (SYZZLE 1-12) **YELLOW TOAST. / ONE MILLION HAMBURGERS / MONSTER**

Oct 87. (lp/cd) (<STIR/+D 1>) **GET CHICKENIZED**
– We say you say / Sacred marriage / Street angels, Tokyo / Two little ladies / Solid life / Japanese girl / Island inside island / Young summer / Chicken ondo / Yellow toast. (cd re-iss. Aug98 & Jun00 on 'Resurgence'; RES 136CD)

―― the duo were augmented by musicians **CLIVE BELL + JUSTIN ADAMS**

Dec 88. (lp/cd) (<STIR/+D 2>) **CLUB MONKEY**
– Club Monkey / Waiting for a dog / Burn that body / Revolution / Night drain / Feed me / Jackie Chan / Shaken by God's hand / M.Y.T.H. / Hey dead / Club Monkey reprise. (re-mixed+=; STIR 2X) – Do the karaoke. (cd re-iss. Aug98 & Jun00 on 'Resurgence'; RES 137CD)

Jun 89. (7") (SYZZLE 2) **DO THE KARAOKE. / JACKIE CHAN**

―― added **ATSUKO KAMURA** – vocals

                                        own label not iss.

1992. (cd) **PRETTY FRANK CHICKENS** – | Japan
– Yummy yummy yummy / Robot love / My resistance is low / Sayonara Rockefeller / Living in Tottenham / Werewolf woman / Total recall / Mister limbo / Surfin' Albania / Megalomaniacs.

                                        Creative Toys
                                        Man Factory
                                          (Japan)

Jun 96. (cd) (CMCD 009) **UNDERFLOOR WORLD** – | 1994
– One step / Different / Madman in Manchester / Time is a passerby (in Tokyo) / Johnny reggae / Miniature whale / Annabella / Thunderwing / Ring road / Yukasita – Underfloor world / Welcome to the space.

―― KAZUKO HOHKI also released two Japanese-only sets, '. . .CHANTE BRIGITTE BARDOT' (1991) and 'LOVE IN RAINY DAYS' (1992) for 'Chabada'.

FRAZIER CHORUS

Formed: Brighton, England . . . mid 80's as PLOP by songwriter/vocalist/pianist, TIM FREEMAN, with others MICHELE ALLARDYCE, KATE HOLMES and CHRIS TAPLIN. Initially signed to '4 a.d.', FRAZIER CHORUS unveiled their deliciously different amalgam of dreamy instrumental textures, infectious pop hooks and whispered vocals with the 'SLOPPY HEART' single. Moving on to 'Virgin', the quartet released their widely acclaimed but criminally overlooked debut album, 'SUE' (1989), critics salivating over such subtle, knowing snippets of domestic drama as 'KITCHEN' and 'TYPICAL', both tracks coming within shouting (make that whispering) distance of the Top 40. And therein lay the problem with this band, close but no cigar led to a change in musical direction as they embraced the all-pervasive dance culture. With ALLARDYCE departing midway through sessions for follow-up set, 'RAY' (1991), the group were reduced to a trio by the time of the album's release, its more dance-orientated feel dividing reviewers and fans. Yet major chart success still proved elusive and even a revamped version of the near-classic, 'CLOUD 8', failed to penetrate the Top 40, the group finally going their separate ways after a further couple of minor hits and a disappointing follow-up set, 'RAY' (1991). It took four years for FRAZIER CHORUS (now reduced to TIM and a handful of musicians) to return; TAPLIN had earlier formed dance-pop outfit ESPIRITU. The comeback album in question, 'WIDE AWAKE', was issued in the summer of '95.

Album rating: SUE (*6) / RAY (*4) / WIDE AWAKE (*5)

TIM FREEMAN – vocals / **KATE HOLMES** – flute / **MICHELE ALLARDYCE** – percussion / **CHRIS TAPLIN** – clarinet, keyboards

                                          4 a.d. not iss.

Oct 87. (12"m) (BAD 708) **SLOPPY HEART. / TYPICAL / STORM**

                                          Virgin Charisma

Jan 89. (7") (VS 1145) **DREAM KITCHEN. / DOWN** 57 –
(12"+=) (VST 1145) – ('A'extended).
(3"cd-s++=) (VSCD 1145) – 40 winks (extended).

Mar 89. (7") (VS 1174) **TYPICAL. / STRING** 53 –
(12"+=) (VST 1174) – Born with a headache
(cd-s) (VSCD 1174) – ('A'side) / Dream kitchen / ('A'extended) / Born with a headache.
(10") (VSX 1174) – ('A'extended) / Storm (live) / Typical (live).

May 89. (cd/c/lp) (CD/TC+/V 2578) **SUE** 56 –
– Dream kitchen / Storm / Forty winks / Ha-ha-happiness / Sloppy heart / Living room / Sugar high / Forgetful / Typical / Ski-head. (cd+=) – Little chef.

Jun 89. (7") (VS 1192) **SLOPPY HEART. / ANARCHY IN THE UK** 73 –
(12"+=) (VST 1192) – Spoonhead.
(12"+=) (VSTX 1192) – Living room (demo) / 40 winks (demo).
(3"cd-s+=) (VSCD 1192) – String / Typical.

May 90. (7") (VS 1252) **CLOUD 8. / LE CHANGE EST MAGNIFIQUE** 52 –
(cd-s+=) (VSCD 1252) – ('A'-raid mix) / The window.
(12") (VST 1252) – ('A'side) / ('A'-swing machine vocal mix) / ('A'-Richie Rich reconstruction).
(12") (VSTX 1252) – ('A'-The Paul Oakenfold remixes; raid / future).

Aug 90. (7") (VS 1284) **NOTHING. / LITTLE PIECE OF HELL** 51 –
(cd-s) (VSCD 1284) – ('A'side) / ('A'-Land of Oz mix) / Cloud 8 (future mix) / Blistered.
(12") (VST 1284) – ('A'-Chad Jackson remixes; nothing has been proved / instrumental / beats).
(12") (VSTX 1284) – ('A'-raid mix) / ('A'-Land of Oz mix).

Dec 90. (7"; w/drawn) (VS 1309) **HEAVEN. / HEAVEN (God like edit)** – –

Feb 91. (cd-ep) <2-96378> **CLOUD 8 (future mix) / CLOUD 8 (raid mix) / DREAM KITCHEN / TYPICAL (12"mix) / ANARCHY IN THE UK**

Feb 91. (7") (VS 1330) **WALKING ON AIR. / (album version)** 60 –
(cd-s+=) (VSCD 1330) – ('A'extended) / 40 winks (extended mix).
(12") (VST 1330) – ('A'side) / ('A'-Maharishi Yogi mix) / ('A'-18 Doc Marten mix).
(12") (VSTX 1330) – ('A'extended) / ('A'-dub instrumental).

Mar 91. (cd/c/lp) (CD/TC+/VFC 2654) <2-/4-91641> **"RAY"** 66
– Cloud 8 / Heaven / We love you / Never wake up / All the air / Walking on air / Nothing / The telephone / Here he comes again / Prefer you dead. (c+=/cd w/free cd+=) **THE BABY ALBUM** – Cloud 8 (raid mix) / Nothing (raid mix) / Heaven (God like instrumental) / Walking on air (dub instrumental).

―― ALLARDYCE departed during recording of above; were now basically **TIM + KATE** who tried their luck in the States – TAPLIN formed ESPIRITU in 1992 with VANESSA QUINENES

―― FRAZIER CHORUS re-formed with TIM recruiting **JAMIE FREEMAN** – guitars / **MAX MORE** – keyboards / **BENNY DIMASSA** – drums / **JOHNNY KNOWLES** – horns / **GENERAL DE GAULLE** – accordian

Jul 95. (cd) (PINKCD 1) <642310> **WIDE AWAKE** Pinkerton / Pure Jun96
– Wide awake / If the weather was up to me / Bye-bye little bird / Here we are / Take us away / Driving / Lie, mimic and mime / Sound asleep. <US+=> – Next to no-one / Funny thing / Thankyou.
May 96. (cd-ep) <002> **WIDE AWAKE / HERE WE ARE / TAKE US AWAY / SOUND ASLEEP**
(above issued on 'Seedy')
Aug 96. (cd-s) <00364 2311-2> **DRIVING (mixes; single / original / scenic route / mass transit)**
—— a fan club EP, 'MONKEY SPUNK' was issued in 1998
—— FRAZIER CHORUS are no longer

FREEZE (see under ⇒ CINdYTALK)

FREIWILLIGE SELBSTKONTROLLE

Formed: Munich, Germany ... 1980 by THOMAS MEINECKE, JUSTIN HOFFMAN, MICHAELA MELIAN and WILFRIED PETZI; FRANZ WAGNER and CARL OESTERHELT were also part of the evolving line-up. The group originally began as a straightforward punk outfit, however, by the mid 1980's they had began to fuse elements of folk, country & western, electronica and even a little yodelling. Their increasingly eclectic sound soon had DJ John Peel championing them, which brought them to the attention of CRACKER member DAVID LOWERY who became an occasional member and producer of the band (the MEKONS' KEVIN LYCETT had the controls in 1987). Aside from a number of 'Peel Sessions' much of the group's earlier albums were restricted to distribution in Germany only, however, a 1995, 44-song compilation, 'BEI ALFRED' allowed the rest of the world to experience the extreme music of FREIWILLIGE SELBSTKONTROLLE. The group's output was as prolific as it was inconsistent. Albums such as 'SON OF KRAUT' (1991), 'THE GERMAN AMERICAN OCTET' (1994), 'SOUND OF MUSIC' (1995) and 'INTERNATIONAL' (1996) all had their moments of brilliance, but were let down by poor production and misfiring eccentricities. The band's 1998 release 'TEL AVIV AND EIGHT OTHER ORIGINALS' did have a little more shape to it than previous efforts although there were still many unnerving absurdities. Both compelling and horrific, FSK are a musical equivalent to watching a car crash. • **Trivia:** Means VOLUNTARY SELF-CONTROL to the non-German-speaking among you.

Album rating: STURMER (*6) / CA C'EST LA BLUES (*5) / CONTINENTAL BREAKFAST (*5) / IN DIXIELAND (*5) / PARTY (*4) / ORIGINAL GASMAN BAND (*5) / SON OF KRAUT (*5) / THE SOUND OF MUSIC (*5) / THE GERMAN-AMERICAN OCTET (*2) / BEI ALFRED compilation (*7) / INTERNATIONAL (*5) / TEL AVIV AND 11 OTHER ORIGINALS (*6) / X (*5)

JUSTIN HOFFMAN – guitar, xylophone, vocals, etc / **WILFRIED PETZI** – guitar, melodian, vocals, etc / **THOMAS MEINECKE** – guitar, percussion, melodian, vocals, etc / **MICHAELA MELIAN** – bass, cello, violin, vocals, etc

Zick Zack / not iss.
1980. (7"ep) (ZZ 6) **FREIWILLIGE SELBSTKONTROLLE** – German
– Herz aus stein / Westberlin tanzparty / Moderne welt / Deutschland Deutschland.
1981. (7"ep) (ZZ 27) **TEILNEHMENDE BEOBACHTUNG** – German
– Im westen nix neues / Im rhythmus der zeit / Tagesschau / Tu den strand / Kaufhalle / Gudrun E. / Rita sagt.
1982. (12"ep) **MAGIC MOMENTS** – German
– Wir steigen ein / Trink wie ein tier / Herzschun melodie / Viel zu viel.
1982. (lp) (ZZ 80) **STURMER** – German
– Hallo wie gehts / Otto Hahn in Stahlgewittern / Ab nach Indien / Frau mit Stiehl / In Mogadishow / Das hilde ich gut / Liebe tut weh / Leserzirkel melodie / Ostblock girl / Tu den Hammelsprung / Verbotene Fruechte / Wir gehen in den zoo / Was kostet die welt / Kinderparty / Gesundheit / Kleiner polizist / Ich habe migraene / Mein erster freund / Ein kind fur Helmut.
1983. (12"ep) **LAST ORDERS (THE JOHN PEEL SESSIONS)** – German
– Drunk / Lieber ein glas zuviel / Trink wie ein tier / A swingin' safari.
1984. (lp) (ZZ 2001) **CA C'EST LA BLUES** – German
– Faire le chicken / Hol dir die Bundeslade / Lieve im hotel / Mit der tuer ins haus / Figaros hochzeit / My funny valentine / Bokassa in San Francisco / Mein kleiner sohn / Blues fur Harald / Move ahead / Hymne / Fragen der philosophie (volkerball).
1985. (lp) (ZZ 1789) **GOES UNDERGROUND** – German
– Batgirl / Lob der kybernetik / Did you see Jackie Robinson hit that ball / Big Ben / La strada / Blue yodel fur Herbert Wehner / Venus im Pelz #2 / Kansas City / Frau mit stiel / Dancing in the dawn / Coda.

Ediesta / not iss.
Jun 87. (lp; as FSK) (CALCLP 016) **CONTINENTAL BREAKFAST**
(compilation 1983-1985)
Oct 87. (12"ep) (CALC 032) **AMERICAN SECTOR**
– (I wish I could) Sprechen sie Deutsch / Lotse an bord / Salt Lake City / (I've got to get over) The wall.
Jan 88. (lp) (CALCLP 042) **IN DIXIELAND**
– Heidi high / Blue yodel fur lino ventura / Das licht der welt / Rock'n'Rolls Royce / Bahnsteig walzer / Recreation bounce / Mein funky Ballentine's / Ave Caesar / Striptease blues / Yankee goes home. (cd-iss. 1988 on 'Zick Zack'+=; ZZ 1987) – MAGIC MOMENTS
Jul 88. (12") (CALC 057) **CANNONBALL YODEL. /**

Strikeback / not iss.
1989. (lp) (SBR 30LP) **PARTY**

F.S.K.
1989. (lp/cd) (SBR 36 LP/CD) **ORIGINAL GASMAN BAND**
– Biergarten polka / Jack Lemmon O.M.U. / Mendocino / Jodler fur Sonny Sharrock / Die erfindung des blues / Walzer fur Charles Sealsfield / The saints / Musikaner 3-4-go / Jole blon / Lasky Jedne Plavovlasky / Petticoat schottische / "M" wie Munchen /

Pennsylfawnisch schnitzelbank / (I wish I could) Spechen sie Deutsch / Lotse an bord / Saly Lake City / (I've got to get over) The wall.
1990. (7") **BUDWEISER POLKA. / CANNONBALL YODEL** – German
—— added **DAVID LOWERY** – guitar, vocals, producer (ex-CAMPER VAN BEETHOVEN) / **CARSON HUGGINS** – drums, vocals

Sub-Up / Flying Fish
Dec 91. (lp/cd; as FREIWILLIGE SELBST-KONTROLLE)
(SUBCD 12) **SON OF KRAUT**
– Nationalhymne der DDR / Hitler lives / Die Englischen fraulein / Fraulein / Freddy Fender's sohn / (Some talking) / When it rains in Texas (it snows on the Rhine) / Patrona namibiae / Vatikan Oberek / Wooden heart (muss I denn) / The wall / Rastatt redemption Schottische / 504 / Oh Celine / Southern boys.
—— LOWERY had now joined CRACKER
Dec 93. (cd) (efa 15545-2) <70646> **THE SOUND OF MUSIC** 1995
– The transatlantic feedback / Unter dem doppeladler – Under the double eagle / Unter dem Rhein / Die original Trapp familie (John Coltrane) / Franz Joseph Strauss / Josh's accordion intermezzo / Flagge verbrennen (regierung ertranken) / Nicht die hand / Jazz im dritten reich / Red Sonja / (David talks to Music audience, 1987) / Shiner song / Diesel Oktoberfest / (Michaela talks to John Peel, 1992) / Hobo zwiefacher / Lonely river Rhine / Elke Sommer's territory band / Distant drums / (A.G.I.'s Germany, 1962) / Im naturtheater von Oklahoma / Dr. Bernice (live).
Jun 94. (cd) (RTS 8) **THE GERMAN-AMERICAN OCTET** (covers)
– Ramblin' man / California blues / Fraulein / She's about a mover / Drunk / Shiner song / Last fair deal / Jodler fur Sonny Sharrock / Derailed / Gold watch and chain / Dallas / Hobo zwiefacher / Sleep walk / Long tall Texan / (Packing for Austria).
(above issued on 'Return To Sender')
Mar 96. (cd/lp) (efa 15548-2/-1) **INTERNATIONAL**
– Roxy Munich / Die Kaiser Wilhelm / El pastor aleman / Olympaiturm '72 / I want out of the circus / El pit bull / She acts like a woman should / Mark Twain in Heidelberg / Mein kubano girl / The moog banjo revival / Euro-trash girl (Japanese yodel mix) / Karl-Eluard von schnitzler polka / When Amish go bad / Amon Duul discographie / Das schlechstein land der welt / Jane Fonda lied / Josh's melodica intermezzo / Dachshund walzer / To the other woman / 1+1=3 / Medley: Was kostet die welt – Kleiner Polizist / Roxy Munich 2.
1997. (12"ep) **4 INSTRUMENTALS** – German
– Tel Aviv / Peki d'Oslo / Jaques Rivette of Paris / Odenwald.
1998. (cd) (14831l) **TEL AVIV AND 11 OTHER ORIGINAL** – German
– Taunus anlage / Odenwald / Stilleben / Kuckkucksnest komplex / Jazz lexikon / Jaques Rivette of Paris / Altneuland / Rote sonne / Peki d-Oso / Ich als text / Tel Aviv / Lost in munich.
2000. (cd) **X** – German
– The key of Busta Rhymes / Westdeutscher rundfunk / Lido / Romantische strasse / Berliner ensemble / The Charlestoun maschine / Casino / Grosser arber / Haus der kunst.

– compilations, etc. –

1989. (m-lp) Strange Fruit; (SFPMA 204) **THE PEEL SESSIONS**
(3.8.86) (21.5.87)
– I wish I could sprechen sie Deutsch / Die musik finik findet nach haus / Dr. Arnold Fanck / Am tafelberg von kapstadt / Komm gib mir deine hand / Girl / **irthday / Don't pass me by.**
1995. (d-cd) Zick Zack; (1995) **BEI ALFRED** – German

Gavin FRIDAY (see under ⇒ VIRGIN PRUNES)

F.S.K.
(see under ⇒ FREIWILLIGE SELBSTKONTROLLE)

FUGAZI

Formed: Arlington, Virginia, USA ... 1987 by IAN MacKAYE (now of Washington DC), who had the previous year featured on an album by EMBRACE (not the more recent outfit!). MacKAYE and drummer JEFF NELSON subsequently founded the 'Dischord' label, a bedrock of the Washington DC hardcore scene and an outlet for the pair's new band, MINOR THREAT. Completing the line-up with LYLE PRESLAR and BRIAN BAKER, this highly influential outfit released two singles in 1981, before they added STEVE HANSEN to boost their minimalist sound on the album, 'OUT OF STEP' (1983). A further album, the eponymous 'MINOR THREAT', contained the track 'STRAIGHT EDGE', a term which would be adopted by a generation of fans who followed MacKAYE and Co.'s example of abstinence and individual responsibility. Following their split, mainman MacKAYE formed FUGAZI, sharing vocal and songwriting duties with GUY PICCOTTO (ex-leader of RITES OF SPRING and INSURRECTION – the latter outfit having released a self-titled effort for 'Peaceville'). With the FUGAZI line-up crystallising around BRENDAN CANTY and JOE LALLY, they released two HENRY ROLLINS-produced mini-sets, the eponymous 'FUGAZI' and 'MARGIN WALKER' (1989), before fully realising their aggressively economical sound on the acclaimed 'REPEATER' (1990) album. Bringing to mind the once wilfully obscure vocals of DAVID THOMAS (PERE UBU) backed by the hardcore of NO MEANS NO, FUGAZI delivered a fourth set, 'STEADY DIET OF NOTHING' (1991), their perseverance paying off with a minor placing in the UK charts. Two years later, 'IN ON THE KILLTAKER' scored a deserved UK Top 30 and dominated the indie charts for months; despite persistent major label interest, FUGAZI have admirably refused to play the corporate game (how many bands can you say that about?). The mid 90's saw the release of 'RED MEDICINE', the album taking the staunchly independent hardcore crusaders into previously uncharted territory, i.e. the UK Top 20 (appropriately enough, the commercial behemoth that is the American music industry has so far prohibited the band's domestic success). MacKAYE, PICCIOTTO and crew were back in '98, although 'END HITS' (not a compilation) suffered a little commercially due to their long

FUGAZI (cont)

absence. Unperturbed, FUGAZI worked on a soundtrack album. Jem Cohen's docu-film, 'INSTRUMENT', was delivered the following Spring, the music (with sparse vocals!) a return of sorts to their abrasive best. Now with the addition of second sticksman, JERRY BUSHER, FUGAZI returned via the 2001 set, 'THE ARGUMENT', a record that even boasted a minor UK hit single, 'FURNITURE' and the classic 'CASHOUT'. • **Covered:** 12XU (Wire). • **Trivia:** MacKAYE produced the early '89 BEEFEATER single, 'House Burning Down'.

Album rating: 13 SONGS compilation (*8) / REPEATER (*8) / STEADY DIET OF NOTHING (*7) / IN ON THE KILLTAKER (*7) / RED MEDICINE (*6) / END HITS (*6) / INSTRUMENT soundtrack (*7) / THE ARGUMENT (*&) / Minor Threat: COMPLETE DISCOGRAPHY compilation (*8)

MINOR THREAT

IAN MacKAYE (b.1963) – vocals, guitar / **LYLE PRESLAR** – guitar / **BRIAN BAKER** – bass (ex-GOVERNMENT ISSUE) / **JEFF NELSON** – drums

			Dischord	Dischord
Jun 81.	(7"ep) <Dischord 3> **MINOR THREAT EP**		-	
	– Out of step (with the world) / Guilty of being white / Steppin' stone.			
Dec 81.	(7",7"red) <Dischord 5-Limp 41> **IN MY EYES. / STAND UP / 12XU**		-	
—	added **STEVE HANSEN** – bass (BAKER now on second guitar)			
1983.	(lp/c) <(DISCHORD 10/+C)> **OUT OF STEP**			
	– Betray / It follows / Think again / Look back and laugh / Sob story / No reason / Little friend / Out of step.			
Jun 84.	(lp/c) <(DISCHORD 12/+C)> **MINOR THREAT**			
	– Filler / I don't wanna hear it / Seeing red / Straight edge / Small man, big mouth / Screaming at a wall / Bottled violence / Minor threat.			
Aug 85.	(7"ep) <(DISCHORD 15)> **SALAD DAYS / GOOD GUYS (DON'T WEAR WHITE). / STUMPED / CASHING IN**			
Mar 90.	(cd) <(DISCHORD 40)> **COMPLETE DISCOGRAPHY** (compilation)			

FUGAZI

IAN MacKAYE – vocals, guitar (ex-MINOR THREAT, ex-TEEN IDES, ex-EMBRACE) / **GUY PICCIOTTO** (b.1966) – vocals (ex-INSURRECTION, ex-RITES OF SPRING, ex-ONE LAST WISH) / **JOE LALLY** (b.1964, Rockville, Maryland) – bass / **BRENDAN CANTY** (b.1967) – drums

			Dischord	Dischord
Dec 88.	(m-lp/m-c) <(DISCHORD 30/+C)> **FUGAZI**			
	– Waiting room / Bulldog front / Bad mouth / Burning / Give me the cure / Suggestion / Glue man. (re-iss. Oct89; same)			
Jul 89.	(m-lp/m-c) <(DISCHORD 35/+C)> **MARGIN WALKER**			
	– Margin walker / And the same / Burning too / Provisional / Lockdown / Promises. (cd-iss. Oct89 as '13 SONGS'+=; DIS 36) – FUGAZI (re-iss. Apr98; same)			
Feb 90.	(7",7"green) <(DISCHORD 43)> **JOE #1. / BREAK IN / SONG #1**			
Mar 90.	(lp/c/cd) <(DISCHORD 44/+C/CD)> **REPEATER**			
	– Turnover / Repeater / Brendan /1 / Merchandise / Blueprint / Sieve-fisted grind / Greed / Two beats off / Styrofoam / Reprovisional / Shut the door. (cd+=) – Song #1 / Joe /1 / Break in. (re-iss. Apr98; same)			
Aug 91.	(lp/c/cd) <(DISCHORD 60/+C/CD)> **STEADY DIET OF NOTHING**		63	
	– Exit only / Reclamation / Nice new outfits / Stacks / Latin roots / Steady diet / Long division / Runaway return / Polish / Dear justice letter / K.Y.E.O. (re-iss. Apr98; same)			
Jun 93.	(m-lp/m-c/m-cd) <(DIS 70/+C/D)> **IN ON THE KILLTAKER**		24	
	– Facet squared / Public witness program / Returning the screw / Smallpox champion / Rend it / 23 beats off / Sweet and low / Cassavetes / Great cop / Walken's syndrome / Instrument / Last chance for a slow dance. (re-iss. Apr98; same)			
May 95.	(lp/cd) <(DIS 90/+CD)> **RED MEDICINE**		18	
	– Do you like me / Bed for the scraping / Latest disgrace / Birthday pony / Forensic scene / Combination lock / Fell, destroyed / By you / Version / Target / Back to base / Downed city / Long distance runner. (re-iss. Apr98; same)			
—	FUGAZI were put in backburner until their return below			
Apr 98.	(cd/c/lp) <(DIS 110 CD/C/V)> **END HITS**		47	
	– Break / Place position / Recap modotti / No surprise / Five corporations / Caustic acrostic / Closed captioned / Floating boy / Foreman's dog / Arpeggiation / Guilford fall / Pink frosty / F/D.			
Apr 99.	(cd/c/lp) <(DIS 120 CD/C/V)> **INSTRUMENT** (soundtrack)			
	– Pink frosty (demo) / Lusty scripps / Arpeggiator (demo) / Afterthought / Trio's / Turkish disco / Me and Thumbelina / Floating boy (demo) / Link track / Little Debbie / H.B. / I'm so tired / Rend it (demo) / Closed caption (demo) / Guilford fall (demo) / Swingset / Shaken all over / Slo crostic.			
—	now with second drummer **JERRY BUSHER**			
Oct 01.	(7"/cd-s) <(DIS 129/+CD)> **FURNITURE. / NUMBER / HELLO MORNING**		61	
Oct 01.	(cd/lp) <(DIS 130 CD/V)> **THE ARGUMENT**		63	
	– Untitled / Cashout / Full disclosure / Epic problem / Life and limb / The kill / Strangelight / Oh / Ex-spectator / Nightshop / Argument.			

FURNITURE

Formed: London, England ... 1981 by JIM IRVIN, TIM WHELAN and HAMMY LEE. Following the release of a mini-set, 'WHEN THE BOOM WAS ON' (1983) on their own label ('The Guy From Paraguay'), the band signed to the small 'Survival' imprint as the ranks swelled with the arrival of MAYA GILDER and SALLY STILL. A further series of singles followed, collected together on a Japan-only long player, 'THE LOVEMONGERS'. The band's mid-80's signing to 'Stiff' looked set to thrust them into the limelight as the stark but casual pop genius of the 'BRILLIANT MIND' single saw FURNITURE narrowly miss the UK Top 20. Disaster struck, however, as 'Stiff' went into liquidation and a follow-up single – a revamped version of 'LOVE YOUR SHOES' – fell by the wayside. The attendant album, 'THE WRONG PEOPLE' (1986) fared little better as 'Z.T.T.' took up the reins and deleted the record after pressing an initial 30,000 copies. An extended bout of legal jousting ensued with FURNITURE eventually extricating themselves from the label and signing to 'Arista'. The resulting 'FOOD, SEX AND PARANOIA' (1989) album brought further critical praise although by this point the momentum from their earlier success had long since dissipated, strained record company relations developing yet again as the record sank without trace. The subsequent departure of GILDER was followed by a wholesale split in the early 90's with IRVIN and STILL both diversifying into music journalism while WHELAN and LEE formed TRANSGLOBAL UNDERGROUND. Victims of bad timing and even worse luck, FURNITURE were one of the 80's hidden gems, their off-beat charm fairly represented by 1991's compilation, 'SHE GETS OUT THE SCRAPBOOK'.

Album rating: WHEN THE BEAT WAS ON mini (*5) / THE WRONG PEOPLE (*5) / FOOD, SEX AND PARANOIA (*4) / SHE GETS OUT THE SCRAPBOOK compilation (*6) / Because: MAD SCARED DUMB AND GORGEOUS (*4)

JIM IRVIN (b.20 Jul'59, Chiswick, London) - **vocals** / **TIM WHELAN** (b.15 Sep'58) – guitar / **HAMMY LEE** (b. HAMILTON, 7 Sep'58) – drums

			The Guy From Paraguay	not iss.
Oct 80.	(7") (PARA 1) **SHAKING STORY. / TAKE A WALK DOWN TOWN**			-
—	added **MAYA GILDER** (b.25 Apr'64, Poonak, India) – keyboards / **SALLY STILL** (b. 5 Feb'64) – bass			

			Survival	not iss.
Aug 83.	(m-lp) (4C 1) **WHEN THE BOOM WAS ON**			-
	– Transatlantic cable / They're on me / Robert Nightman's story / I miss you / Why are we in love / A letter to myself.			
Apr 84.	(7"/ext-12") (SUR/+12 023) **DANCING THE HARD BARGAIN. / ROBERT NIGHTMAN'S STORY**			-
Sep 84.	(7"/ext-12") (SUR/+12 028) **YOUR BRILLIANT MIND. / ROBERT NIGHTMAN'S STORY**			-

			Premonition	not iss.
Nov 84.	(7") (PREM 2) **LOVE YOUR SHOES. / THROW AWAY THE SCRIPT** (instrumental)			-
	(12"+=) (12PREM 2) – Escape into my arms.			
Jun 85.	(12"ep) (PREM 3) **I CAN'T CRACK. / SWITCH OFF / PAUSE / I CAN'T CRACK** (broken mix)			-
Jan 86.	(7") (PREM 5) **THE LOVEMONGERS. / TALKING KITTENS**			-
	(12"+=) (12PREM 5) – I can't crack.			
Jun 86.	(lp; cancelled) (PREM 6) **THE LOVEMONGERS**		-	-
	– The lovemongers / Throw away the script / Love your shoes / Escape into my arms / What the fog said / Dancing the hard bargain / Bullet / Talking kitten / Sang Froid / I can't crack.			

			Stiff	not iss.
May 86.	(7") (BUY 251) **BRILLIANT MIND. / TO GUS**		21	-
	(12"+=) (BUYIT 251) – ('A'extended).			
Oct 86.	(7") (BUY 254) **LOVE YOUR SHOES. / TURNUPSPEED**			-
	(12"+=) (BUYIT 254) – ('A'extended) / Me and you and the name.			
Nov 86.	(lp/c) (SEEZ/ZSEEZ 64) **THE WRONG PEOPLE**			-
	– Shake like Judy says / Love your shoes / Brilliant mind / She gets out the scrapbook / I miss you / Make believe I'm him / Let me feel your pulse / The sound of the bell / Escape into my arms / Answer the door / Pierre's fight.			

			Arista	not iss.
Sep 89.	(7") (112 648) **SLOW MOTION KISSES. / 40 HOURS IN A DAY**			-
	(ext-12"+=) (612 648) – Brlliant mind.			
	(cd-s+=) (662 648) – She gets out the scrapbook.			
Feb 90.	(7") (112 844) **ONE STEP BEHIND YOU. / IT CONTINUES**			-
	(ext-12"+=) (612 844) – ('A'club mix).			
	(cd-s+=) (662 844) – International people.			
Feb 90.	(cd/c/lp) (260/410/210 377) **FOOD, SEX AND PARANOIA**			-
	– One step behind you / Slow motion kisses / Swing tender / A taste of you / A plot to kill what was / On a slow fuse / Subway to the beach / Song for a Doberman / Love me / Friend of a friend / Hard to say. (c+=/cd+=) – Friend of a friend (extended).			
—	disillusioned by the music industry, they split Autumn 1990. IRVIN and STILL became journalists for The Melody Maker. GILDER went on to be part of the BBC, while LEE and WHELAN formed TRANSGLOBAL UNDERGROUND			

– compilations, etc. –

Aug 91.	(12") Survival; (SURT 53) **BRILLIANT MIND (extended) / BRILLIANT MIND (7" version). / ON A BUS WITH PETER NERO / BRILLIANT STRINGS**			-
Sep 91.	(cd/c/lp) Survival; (SUR CD/C/LP 013) **SHE GETS OUT THE SCRAPBOOK – THE BEST OF FURNITURE**			-
	– Brilliant mind / Make believe I'm him / Farewell / Song for a Doberman / Dancing the hard bargain / Love your shoes / Robert Nightman's story / Slow motion kisses / I miss you / How I've come to hate the moon / Bullet / Turnupspeed / One step behind you / She gets out the scrapbook.			

BECAUSE

— **IRVIN** duo with **COLIN INGHAM** – piano

			Haven	not iss.
May 92.	(cd/c/lp) (HAVEN CD/MC/LP 1) **MAD SCARED DUMB AND GORGEOUS**			-
	– Orientation / Her rhythm and her blues / A glass room / Song of all things / Archaeology / Love is coming / Stolen / Feast of Stephen / You don't forget / Mad scared dumb and gorgeous.			
—	IRVIN has since become editor for 'Mojo' magazine			

FUZZBOX (see under ⇒ WE'VE GOT A FUZZBOX . . .)

FUZZTONES

Formed: New York, USA . . . 1982 out of TINA PEEL, by RUDI PROTRUDI and DEB O'NAIR. In the closing years of the 70's, the aforementioned punk band (with rhythm section, JIM NASTICS and JACKSON PLUGS) released one self-financed US 7", 'FIFI GOES POP' / 'WEEKEND GEEK' and an EP, 'PYJAMA PARTY', before contributing to a string of various artists collections. With a line-up completed by ELAN PORTNOY, MICHAEL JAY and IRA ELLIOT (who replaced initial sticksman, MICHAEL PHILLIPS), The FUZZTONES made their UK vinyl debut in late '84 with the live set, 'LEAVE YOUR MIND AT HOME'. While they shared a similar trash aesthetic as fellow Americans, The CRAMPS, the group were more obsessed with garage-psych freakouts than 50's R'n'R and blues, as reflected in their choice of cover material. Follow-up studio set, 'LYSERGIC EMANATIONS', (1984) offered up more chemically enhanced nuggets although save for a further couple of singles, The FUZZTONES were put on hold in the mid-80's as RUDI, MICHAEL and MIKE CZEKAJ worked on an instrumental project, 'DRIVE IT HOME' (released in 1988 under the moniker of LINK PROTRUDI & THE JAYMEN). New FUZZTONES material eventually appeared in 1989 in the shape of the 'IN HEAT' album on Beggars Banquet offshoot, 'Situation 2', although PROTRUDI subsequently recruited an all-new line-up (featuring CZEKAJ, PHIL ARRIAGADA, RAHUL SARIPUTRA and even former LOVE genius, ARTHUR LEE in a guest capacity) for 1991's 'BRAINDROPS' album on the aptly titled 'Music Maniac' label. While PROTRUDI & Co. finally called a halt to proceedings the following year, the mysterious LINK PROTRUDI & THE JAYMEN reappeared with an EP in '97. • **Covers:** HIGHWAY 69 (Bob Dylan) / YOU'RE GONNA MISS ME (13th Floor Elevators) / PSYCHOTIC REACTION (Count Five) / 7 AND 7 IS (Love) / MY LITTLE RED BOOK (Bacharach-David) / HELLO I LOVE YOU (Doors) / 99th FLOOR (Moving Sidewalks) / JACK THE RIPPER (Screamin' Lord Sutch) / I CAN'T CONTROL MYSELF (Troggs) / etc.

Album rating: LEAVE YOUR MIND AT HOME (*4) / LYSERGIC EMANATIONS (*6) / LIVE IN EUROPE (*5) / CREATURES THAT TIME FORGOT (*5) / IN HEAT (*3) / BRAINDROPS (*4) / FLASHBACKS compilation (*6)

RUDI PROTRUDI – vocals, guitar (ex-TINA PEEL, ex-DEVIL DOGS) / **DEB O'NAIR** – organ (ex-TINA PEEL) / **ELAN PORTNOY** – guitar / **MICHAEL JAY** – bass / **IRA ELLIOT** – drums; repl. MICHAEL PHILLIPS

	Midnight Int.	not iss.
Nov 84. (m-lp) *(MIRLP 105)* **LEAVE YOUR MIND AT HOME** (live)		–
– Voices green and purple / Blackout at Cretely / No friend of mind / We're pretty quick / Flash on you / The bag I'm in / You burn me up and down.		

	A.B.C.	Pink Dust
Mar 85. (lp) *(ABCLP 4)* <*72123*> **LYSERGIC EMANATIONS**		
– 1-2-5 / Gotta get some / Journey to tyme / Ward 81 / Radar eyes / Cinderella / Highway 69 / Just once / Living sickness / She's wicked. *(pic-lp Sep88; ABCLP 4P)* *(re-iss. Feb91 on 'Music Maniac' lp/cd+=; MM LP/CD 036)* – (next singles).		
Jul 85. (7") *(ABCS 006)* **SHE'S WICKED. / EPITAPH FOR A HEAD**		–
(12"+=) *(ABCS 006T)* – Bad news travels fast.		
Jul 86. (12"ep) *(ABCS 011T)* **BAD NEWS TRAVELS FAST / GREEN SLIME. / STRYCHNINE / AS TIME'S GONE**		–

	Music Maniac	Head
Mar 87. (lp) *(MM 006)* **LIVE IN EUROPE** (live)		–
– Bad little woman / Blues theme / Cellar dweller / Love at psychedelic velocity / 1523 Blair / Run chicken run / 13 women / 7 and 7 is / Gotta get some / Journey to tyme / Human fly / Psychotic reaction / I'm loose.		
Jan 88. (lp; as LINK PROTRUDI & THE JAYMEN) *(MMLP 009)* **DRIVE IT HOME**		–
– Avalanche / Backfire / Chicken choke / The stroll / Slinky / Mr. Guitar / Commanche / No stopping / Orbit / Rawhide / Bodacious / Hanky panky / Psyclone / Bandito / Chaquita / Rumble. *(re-iss. Oct97 on 'Skoda'; 006)*		
above was instrumental featuring **RUDI, MICHAEL + MIKE CZEKAJ**		
Apr 88. (12"ep) *(MM 013S)* **NINE MONTHS LATER / GIRL YOU CAPTIVATE ME. / CHEYENNE RIDER / GREATEST LOVE IN THE WORLD**		–
(re-iss. Sep89 on 'Situation 2' 7"ep/10"ep/12"ep; SIT 061/+P/T)		
Feb 89. (lp) *(MMLP 020)* <*head 64cd*> **CREATURES THAT TIME FORGOT** (compilation)		
– 99th floor / Riot on Sunset Strip / Don't do it some more / Shooz wicked / The thing / Fabian lips / Brand new man / Action woman / Green slime / Bad news travels fast / Ward 81 / The witch.		

	Situation 2	Beggars Banquet
Jun 89. (7") *(SIT 058)* **HURT ON HOLD. / JACK THE RIPPER**		–
(12"+=) *(SIT 058T)* – I can't control myself.		
Jun 89. (lp/c/cd) *(SITU/+C/CD 23)* <*9808-1/-4/-2*> **IN HEAT**		
– In heat / Cheyenne rider / Black box / It came in the mail / Heathen set / What you don't know / Nine months later / Everything you got / Shame on you / Me Tarzan, you Jane / Hurt on hold / Charlotte's remains.		
Mar 90. (12"ep/cd-ep) *(SIT 069 T/CD)* **ACTION EP**		–
– Action speaks louder than words / I never knew / Yeah babe / My nothing.		

— **PROTRUDI** enlisted an entire new band **CHRIS HARLOCK** – bass / **"MAD" MIKE CZEKAJ** – drums (ex-LINK PROTRUDI & THE JAYMEN) / with back-up **PHIL ARRIAGADA** – guitar / **RAHUL SARIPUTRA** – sitar / + guest vocalists **ARTHUR LEE, SEAN BONNIWELL + JACQUI LYNN**

	Music Maniac	not iss.
Nov 91. (cd/lp) *(MM CD/LP 044)* **BRAINDROPS**		–
– Third times the charm / Skeleton farm / Romilar D / Fear / Rise / Ghost clinic / 7 and 7 is / Look for the question mark / I looked at you / The people in me / All the kings horses / Blackout.		

— split at the end of the year

– compilations, etc. –

1993.	(cd) *Music Maniac; (mmcd 8804)* **TEEN TRASH VOL.4**	–	– German
1994.	(cd) *Music Maniac; (mmcd 052)* **LYSERGIC EJACULATIONS, LIVE IN EUROPE 1991** (live)	–	– German
Nov 97.	(cd)(d-lp) *Sundazed;* <*(SC 11045)*>*(LP 5044)* **FLASHBACKS**		
	– 1-2-5 / Nine months later / Heathen set / I never knew / Bad news travels fast / Charlotte's remains / Ward 81 / Strychnine / In heat / All the kings horses / Rise / Down on the street / Look for the question mark / She's my witch / Blue's theme / Blood from a stone / Hurt on hold / Romilar D / I'm the wolfman / She's wicked / Cinderella.		
Sep 98.	(7"ep) *Sundazed; (SEP 139)* **ONE GIRL MAN. / I'M GONNA MAKE YOU MINE / YOU MUST BE A WITCH**		
May 02.	(7"ep) *Teen Sound; (TS 021EP)* **HELP MURDER POLICE EP**		
Jul 02.	(7") *Beard Of Stars; (BOSS 32)* **IDOL CHATTER. / WRISTBAND WATCH**		–

G

GADGETS (see under ⇒ THE THE)

Diamanda GALAS

Born: 29 Aug'55, San Diego, California, USA – although raised by Greek parents. A classically trained opera singer, GALAS' occult banshee glass-shattering vocal style (using a multi-mic stage set-up!) was supposedly based on the Schrei (shriek) opera of German expressionism. Finding a sympathetic home at 'Y Records' (home of PIGBAG), she made her UK vinyl debut with the characteristically intense 'THE LITANIES OF SATAN' (1982). In 1984 a German-only eponymous set – containing two more lengthy tales of historical human suffering – became her second release before she subsequently signed to UK's large independent, 'Mute'. GALAS' third set, 'DIVINE PUNISHMENT' (1986), was another morally challenging listen, the first of a trilogy, 'Masque Of The Red Death', written as a reaction to the spread of AIDS (her brother had recently died from the disease). Part two of the series, 'SAINT OF THE PIT', was premiered at Austria's ARS Electronica Festival on the 23rd June, 1986 and released on vinyl later that November. The final instalment, meanwhile, was unveiled two years later as 'YOU MUST BE CERTAIN OF THE DEVIL', GALAS also working with MAYO THOMPSON and SIMON TURNER on the scores for controversial films, 'Caravaggio' and 'The Last Days Of England'. The following decade saw the uncompromising tonsil-rupturing lady of avant-rock art deliver a further string of shock-goth albums with her trademark dark religious overtones and song titles that any black/death-metal group would DIE! for. Reportedly a good friend of ex-LED ZEPPELIN duo, PAGE and PLANT, GALAS also collaborated with JOHN PAUL JONES on a 1994 set, 'THE SPORTING LIFE'. Solo once again, "scary splice" GALAS performed her next project, 'SCHREI' (1996), both in the studio and on stage. Powerful, uncompromising and definitely theatrical, her voice was toned down a little for her next project/album, 'MALEDICTION AND PRAYER' (1998), a record that improvised cover versions (see below) sung in classical Greek, flamenco and classical stylings. • **Covered:** MY LOVE WILL NEVER DIE + INSANE ASYLUM (Willie Dixon) / I PUT A SPELL ON YOU (Screamin' Jay Hawkins) / REAP WHAT YOU SOW (Mike Bloomfield – Nick Gravenites) / WERE YOU THERE WHEN THEY CRUCIFIED MY LORD (Roy Acuff) / GLOOMY SUNDAY (Carter-Javor-Seress) / DARK END OF THE STREET (Moman-Penn) / IRON LADY (Phil Ochs) / THE THRILL IS GONE (BB King) / MY WORLD IS EMPTY WITHOUT YOU (hit; Supremes) / I'M GONNA LIVE THE LIFE (Lee Dosey) / 25 MINUTES TO GO (Shel Silverstein) / DEATH LETTER (. . . House) / KEIGOME KEIGOME (Gatsos-Xarhakos) / + a number of traditional work-outs LET MY PEOPLE GO + BALM IN GILEAD – SWING LOW, SWEET CHARIOT + SEE THAT MY GRAVE IS KEEP CLEAN.

Album rating: THE LITANIES OF SATAN (*4) / DIAMANDA GALAS (*6) / DIVINE PUNISHMENT (*5) / SAINT OF THE PIT (*5) / YOU MUST BE CERTAIN OF THE DEVIL (*5) / PLAGUE MASS (*5) / THE SINGER (*5) / VENA CAVA (*5) / THE SPORTING LIFE (*5) / SCHREI X (*5)

DIAMANDA GALAS – vocaaarrgghhls!!!

<small>Y   not iss.</small>

Mar 82. (lp) *(Y 18)* **THE LITANIES OF SATAN**
– The litanies of Satan / Wild women with steaknives (the homocidal love song for solo scream). *(re-iss. Apr89 on 'Fine Line' lp/cd; ISO/CDIS 001)* <US-iss.1989 on 'Restless-Mute' lp/c/cd; 71419-1/-4/-2>

<small>Metalanguagenot iss.</small>

Oct 84. (lp) **DIAMANDA GALAS**   German
– Panoptikon / Tragouthia apo to aima exoun fonos (song from the blood of those murdered).

<small>Mute   Restless</small>

Jul 86. (lp) *(STUMM 27)* **DIVINE PUNISHMENT**
– Deliver me from mine enemies:- I. This is the law of the plague – II. Deliver me from mine enemies – III. We shall not accept your quarentine – IV. Deliver me – V. Yiati o ozoe – VI. Psalm 22 / Free among the dead:- I. Free among the dead – II. Psalm 88 – III. Lamentations – IV. Sono l'Antichristo. <US-iss.1989 on 'Restless-Mute'; 71417>

Nov 86. (lp) *(STUMM 33)* **SAINT OF THE PIT**
– La trezieme revient (The thirteenth returns) / E-eaoyme [Deliver me] / l'Heautontimoroumenos (1857) [Self-tormentor] / Artemis (1854) / Cris d'Aveugle (1873) [Blind man's cry]. *(cd-iss. Apr88 +=; CDSTUMM 33) <US-iss.1989 on 'Restless-Mute' 71418>*

Apr 88. (12") *(12MUTE 75)* **DOUBLE-BARREL PRAYER. / MALEDICTION**

Jun 88. (cd/lp) *(CD+/STUMM 46) <71403>* **YOU MUST BE CERTAIN OF THE DEVIL**
– Swing low sweet chariot / Double-barrel prayer / Let's not chat about despair / Birds of death / You must be certain of the Devil / Let my people go / Malediction / The Lord is my shepherd.

<small>Mute   Mute</small>

Apr 91. (cd/lp) *(CD+/STUMM 83) <61034>* **PLAGUE MASS**
– There are no more tickets to the funeral / This is the law of the plague / I wake up and see the face of the Devil / Confessional (give me sodomy or give me death) / How shall our judgement be carried out upon the wicked? / Let us praise the masters of slow death / Consecration / Sono l'Antichristo / Cris d'Aveugle / Let my people go.

Apr 92. (cd/lp) *(CD+/STUMM 103) <61278>* **THE SINGER** (live)
– My love will never die / Reap what you sow / Were you there when they crucified my Lord? / Gloomy Sunday / Balm in Gilead – Swing low, sweet chariot / Insane asylum / I put a spell on you / Let my people go / See that my grave is kept clean / Judgement day.

Sep 93. (cd/lp) *(CD+/STUMM 119) <61459>* **VENA CAVA**
– Vena Cava (parts 1-8).

Aug 94. (cd-s; DIAMANDA GALAS & JOHN PAUL JONES) *(CDMUTE 171) <60171>* **DO YOU TAKE THIS MAN? (edit) / HEX (la diabla mix) / DO YOU TAKE THIS MAN? (lp version)**

Sep 94. (cd/lp; DIAMANDA GALAS & JOHN PAUL JONES) *(CD+/STUMM 127) <61276>* **THE SPORTING LIFE**
– Skotoseme / Do you take this man? / Dark end of the street / You're mine / Tony / Devil's rodeo / The sporting life / Baby's insane / Last man down / Hex.

Sep 96. (d-cd) *<(CDSTUMM 146)>* **SCHREI X**
– SCHREI X LIVE:- Do room / I – I am – Dreams / M dis I / O.P.M. / Abasement / Headbox / Cunt / Hepar / Coitum / Vein / M dis II / Smell / Hee shock die // SCHREI 27:- Do room / II / M dis I / O.P.M. / Headbox / Cunt / Hepar / Vein / M dis II / Smell / Hee shock die.

<small>Mute   Asphodel</small>

May 98. (cd/d-lp) *(CD+/STUMM 163) <984>* **MALEDICTION AND PRAYER** (live)
– Iron lady / The thrill is gone / My world is empty without you / Abel et Cain / Death letter / Supplica a mia madre / Insane asylum / Si la muerte / 25 minutes to go / Keigome keigome / I'm gonna live the life / Gloomy Sunday.

– compilations, etc. –

Jan 89. (d-cd) *Mute; (GALAS 001)* **MASQUE OF THE RED DEATH TRILOGY**
– (DIVINE PUNISHMENT / SAINT OF THE PIT / YOU MUST BE CERTAIN OF THE DEVIL)

Alastair GALBRAITH

Born: Dunedin, New Zealand. Hugely underrated antipodean singer/songwriter ALISTAIR GALBRAITH began his recording life in the early 1980's with ROBBIE MUIR in The RIP. The group released two EP's 'A TIMELESS PIECE' and 'STORMED POT' before disbanding. GALBRAITH resurfaced as a solo artist in 1990 with the EP 'GAUDY LIGHT' which showed he had lost none of his ability for penning dark, underground rock songs. The next year saw the release of GALBRAITH's first full album 'MORSE'. A four year silence followed before GALBRAITH issued a consistent string of releases. 'TALISMAN' (1995), singles collection 'SEELEY GIRN' (1996), 'MIRROR WORK' (1998), 'CRY' (2000) and 'LONG WIRES IN DARK MUSEUMS VOL.1' (2002) all enhanced GALBRAITH's reputation as a master of moody, two minute rock songs. The man was also part of A HANDFUL OF DUST, CAKEKITCHEN and a plethora of others (see list below).

Album rating: MORSE (*6) / TALISMAN (*5) / SEELEY GIRN compilation (*6) / MIRRORWORK (*6) / CRY (*7) / LONG WIRES IN DARK MUSEUMS VOL.1 mini with Matt De Gennaro (*5)

RIP

ALASTAIR GALBRAITH – vocals, violin / **ROBBIE MUIR** – instruments

<small>Flying Nun   not iss.</small>

1984. (12"ep) *(FN 023)* **TIMELESS PIECE EP**   –   – NewZ
– Holy room / Dr. Reszke and Dylan / Wow / Up and down.

1986. (12"ep) *(FN 069)* **STORMED PORT EP**   –   – NewZ
– River – Chasm / Starless road / Stormed port / Entropic Carol / Wrecked wee hymn.

—— added **PETER JEFFERIES** (ex-THIS KIND OF PUNISHMENT) although they split in '87; ALASTAIR would also join A HANDFUL OF DUST with BRUCE RUSSELL; MUIR issued a single with PETER JEFFERIES

ALASTAIR GALBRAITH

<small>Xpressway   not iss.</small>

1988. (c) *(X/WAY 04)* **HURRY ON DOWN**   –   – NewZ
– Indigo journeyman / Iron tender / Mavis grind / Swollow / Old screaming EEnie / Cranes / Mrs. Blucher / More than magnetic / Stormed port / Starless road / River chasm / Portrait of a lady / I don't get you / Many a one has / Yes jazz cactus / Timebomb / Ether.

1988. (7"; as ALASTAIR GALBRAITH & GRAEME JEFFERIES) *(X/WAY 10)* **TIMEBOMB. / BRAVELY, BRAVELY**   –   – NewZ

—— **PLAGAL GRIND** also included **PETER JEFFERIES, DAVID MITCHELL + ROBBIE MUIR**

1990. (12"ep; with PLAGAL GRIND) *(X/WAY 13)* **PLAGAL GRIND**   –   – NewZ
– Vincent / Midnight blue vision / Receivership / Yes jazz cactus / Marquesite lace / Starless road / Blackout.

—— next with **DAVID MITCHELL** – guitar (of 3Ds) / **DAVID SAUNDERS** – bass (of 3Ds) / **BRIAN JONES** – guitar

Alastair GALBRAITH (cont)

				not iss.	Siltbreeze
1991.	(7"ep) <SB 07> **GAUDY LIGHT**			-	

– John of the palsied eye / As in a blender / Gaudy light / Mrs. Blucher / Warden tie.

1992. (lp) <SB 22> **MORSE** – –
– Screaming E / Time please / Marcasite lace (with PLAGAL GRIND) / Fall / More than Magnetic / Hawks / Andalucia / Ivy bound / My bottom line / Bone idle / Semaphore / Portrait / Lit / Huxley / Vincent / R.D.S. / Stone / Cranes.

A Studio 13 Rushed   not iss.

1994. (c) *(none)* **2NDS CASSETTE** – – NewZ
– Pip proud / Black flame / As in a blender / O lucky man / I'm rich / Raining here / Water in my ears / Putty / Dark march / Platform / Semaphore / On Paul's imp / See how we seemed / Sugar mommy / R music / Policemen on ether / Hardly / Cemetry raga / Coast road / Mavis grind / Beehive / Anais / Nocturnal.

not iss.   Roof Bolt

1994. (cd-ep) <RB 001> **INTRO VERSION** – –
– Anais / Pendulum / Vinyl curtain / Hardly / Nocturnal.

1996. (7"; as ALASTAIR GALBRAITH & DEMARNIA LLOYD) <RB 003> **TAE KEENING EP** – –
– Tae keening / Flickering birds / Merry-go-round / Navajo.

Next Best Way   not iss.

1995. (lp) <NB 001> **TALISMAN** – – NewZ
– Talisman / Yuhahi / Carlos / Xtra I / Black flame / aits / Water in my ears / Anais / Cemetery raga / Welfare child / Mrs Meggary / I am rich / P.D. Lyte / Policemen on ether / Coast road / Allone / Lucid branches / Strong enough / Coded / Seamed.

Emperor Jones   Emperor Jones

Jun 98. (lp/cd) <(EJ 22/+CD)> **MIRRORWORK**
– For free / Doublet / Ludd / High & fired / Sob / Rivulets / Thoar / Song to the third / Filter / Ember / Blue room / Surrender / Moth / This hard / Star / Vinyl curtain / Raining here / Stealthy / Flickering birds / Frostfish / Hospice / Navajo / Favourite blue / Last air.

1999. (cd; by ALASTAIR GALBRAITH & MATT DE GENNARO) *(HERMES 031)* **WIRE MUSIC** – – NewZ
– Two wires and violin / Two wires / Two wires #1 / Two wires #2 / Two wires, loop and violin.
(above issued on 'Corpus Hermeticum') <below on 'Crawlspace'>

2000. (7") <SPACE 007> **HEAD SOUP DREAM. / FROM THE EMPIRE**

Sep 00. (cd) <(EJ 32CD)> **CRY**
– Bellbird / Charmed / Meatwork / Identical / Wish / Green dream / Full soup head / From the empire / In the Taieri / One method / Koterana / Lull and make it snow / Forest flower.

Jan 02. (m-cd; as ALASTAIR GALBRAITH & MATT DE GENNARO) <(EJ 39CD)> **LONG WIRES IN MUSEUMS VOL.1**
– Autahi / Rehua / Antares.

– compilations, etc. –

Sep 96. (cd) *Emperor Jones; (EJ 08CD)* **MORSE / GAUDY LIGHT**
Sep 96. (cd) *Feel Good All Over; <14>* **SEELEY GIRN** (singles)
– Screaming E / Huxley / Hawks / Mrs Blucher / Stormed port / Vincent / As in a blender / Warden tie / Midnight blue vision / Cranes / Iron tender / Marquesite lace / Portrait / Timebomb / Yes jazz cactus / Gentlemen it's time / Starless road / Bravely bravely / Indigo journeyman / Milky milo man / Mavis grind / Wrecked wee hymn.

GAME THEORY

Formed: Sacramento, California, USA . . . 1982 by main songwriter, SCOTT MILLER, along with NANCY BECKER, FRED JUHOS and MICHAEL IRWIN. MILLER had previously been part of ALTERNATE LEARNING, which numbered NANCY's brother JOZEF BECKER (later of TRUE WEST and THIN WHITE ROPE). Their extremely limited 1982 debut album, 'BLAZE OF GLORY', led MICHAEL QUERCIO (of THREE O'CLOCK) to produce a 1983 EP, 'DISTORTION'. Knob-twiddling was subsequently taken over by MITCH EASTER (button pusher for R.E.M. and dB's) on 1985's 'REAL NIGHTTIME', an album indebted to the ghost of BIG STAR and which established them as yet another contender in the Paisley underground power-pop stakes. Their next effort, 'THE BIG SHOT CHRONICLES' (1986), was surprisingly passed over by the buying public and throughout the remainder of the 80's the band were sadly content to tread water. In the early 90's, MILLER was back again with a new outfit, The LOUD FAMILY, a harder-edged 5-piece featuring ZACHARY SMITH and PAUL WIENEKE. Produced by MITCH EASTER (again), the band released a string of full-on albums starting with 1992's 'PLANTS AND BIRDS AND ROCKS AND THINGS' (a reference to AMERICA's 'A Horse With No Name'); others were 'THE TAPE OF ONLY LINDA' (1994), 'INTERBABE CONCERN' (1996), 'DAYS FOR DAYS' (1998), 'ATTRACTIVE NUISANCE' (2000) and the retrospective, live-in-concert set, 'FROM RITUAL TO ROMANCE' (2002). • **Covered:** YOU CAN'T HAVE ME (Big Star) / I WANT TO HOLD YOUR HAND (Beatles) / COULDN'T I JUST TELL YOU (Todd Rundgren) / SEATTLE (Hugo Montenegro) / Loud Family covered HERE COME THE WARM JETS (Eno) / DEBASER (Pixies) / WHEN YOU SLEEP (My Bloody Valentine).

Album rating: BLAZE OF GLORY (*4) / REAL NIGHTTIME (*6) / THE BIG SHOT CHRONICLES (*7) / LOLITA NATION (*7) / TWO STEPS FROM THE MIDDLE AGES (*4) / TINKER TO EVERS TO CHANCE (SELECTED HIGHLIGHTS 1982-1989) compilation (*8) / Loud Family: PLANTS AND BIRDS AND ROCKS AND THINGS (*7) / SLOUCHING TOWARDS LIVERPOOL mini (*6) / THE TAPE OF ONLY LINDA (*6) / INTERBABE CONCERN (*5) / DAYS FOR DAYS (*5) / ATTRACTIVE NUISANCE (*6) / FROM RITUAL TO ROMANCE (*6)

ALTERNATE LEARNING

SCOTT MILLER + others

not iss.   Rational

1979. (7") <RAT 001> **ALRN ep** – –
– Green card / What's the matter / Gumby's in a coma / When she's alone.

1981. (lp) <AT 100> **PAINTED WINDOWS** – –
– Another wasted afternoon / Sex war / The new you / Dark days / Occupation: unknown / Dresden / Beach state rocking / Ulysses / Painted windows / Let's not wait.

GAME THEORY

SCOTT MILLER – vocals, guitar, synthesizers / **NANCY BECKER** – keyboards / **FRED JUHOS** – bass, vocals / **MICHAEL IRWIN** – drums

not iss.   Rational

1982. (lp) <ION 003> **BLAZE OF GLORY** – –
– Something to show / Tin scarecrow / White blues / Date with an angel / Mary Magdalene / The young drug / Bad year at U.C.L.A. / All I want is everything / Stupid heart / Sleeping through Heaven / It gives me chills / T.G.A.R.T.G.

1983. (12"ep) <ONA 004> **POINTED ACCOUNTS OF PEOPLE YOU KNOW** – –
– Penny, things won't / Metal and glass exact / Selfish again / I wanna get hit by a car / Life in July / 37th day.

1984. (12"ep) <RGP 8405> **DISTORTION** – –
– Shark pretty / Nine lives to Rigel Five / The Red Baron / Kid Convenience / Too late for tears.

Enigma   Enigma

1985. (lp) <72002-1> **REAL NIGHTTIME**
– Here comes everybody / 24 / Waltz the halls always / I mean it this time / Friend of the family / If and when it all falls apart / Curse of the frontier land / Rayon Drive / She'll be a verb / Real nighttime / You can't have me / I turned her away. *(UK cd-iss. Feb94 on 'Alias'+=; A 047D)* – Any other hand / I want to hold your hand / Couldn't I just tell you.

–– **DONNETTE THAYER** – guitar, vocals, piano (ex-VEIL) + **GIL RAY** – drums; repl. JUHOS

Nov 86. (lp) <(3210-1)> **THE BIG SHOT CHRONICLES**
– Here it is tomorrow / Where you going Northern / I've tried subtlety / Erica's word / Make any vow / Regenisraen / Crash into June / Book of millionaires / The only lesson learned / Too closely / Never mind / Like a girl Jesus. *(cd-iss. Feb94 on 'Alias'+=; A 046D)* – Girl w/a guitar / Come home with me / Seattle / Linus and Lucy / Faithless.

Dec 87. (cd/d-lp) <(CDE/STB 73280-1/-2)> **LOLITA NATION**
– What's the frequency? / Not because you can / Shard / Go ahead, you're dying to / Dripping with looks / Exactly what we don't want to hear / We love you Carol and Alison / The waist and the knees / Nothing new / The world's easiest job / Look away / Slip / The real Sheila / Andy in ten years / Watch who you're calling space garbage meteor mouth pretty green card shark / Where they have to let you in / Turn me on dead man / Mammoth gardens / Little ivory / Museum of hopelessness / Toby Ornette / All clockwork and no bodily fluids . . . One more for St. Michael / Choose between two sons / Chardonnay / Last day that we're young / Together now, very minor.

–– **SHELLEY LA FRENIERE** – vocals, keyboards; repl. NANCY

–– **GILLAUME GASSAUN** – bass, repl. IRWIN

Oct 88. (cd/c/lp) <(CD/TC+/ENV 507)> <73350-1> **TWO STEPS FROM THE MIDDLE AGES**
– Room for one more, honey / What the whole world wants / The picture of agreeability / Amelia, have you lost / Rolling with the moody girls / Wyoming / In a Delorean / You drive / Leilani / Wish I could stand or have / Don't entertain me twice / Throwing the election / Initiation week.

–– **MILLER + RAY** (now guitar, keyboards) were joined by **QUERCIO + BECKER** (of THIN WHITE ROPE). THAYER went onto HEX with CHURCH singer STEVE KILBEY.

–– this line-up only lasted until the early 90's when, even MILLER left to form own outfit The LOUD FAMILY

– compilations, etc. –

1984. (lp) *Lolita; (5031B)* **DEAD CENTER** – – French
– Nine lives to Rigel Five / Penny, things won't / Dead center / The red baron / The letter / Shark pretty / Metal and glass exact / Selfish again / Too late for tears / 37th day.

Mar 90. (cd) *Enigma; <D21S-75351-2>* **TINKER TO EVERS TO CHANCE (SELECTED HIGHLIGHTS 1982-1989)** – –
– Beach state rocking (re-recording) / Bad year at U.C.L.A. (re-recording) / Sleeping through Heaven (re-recording) / Something to show / Penny, things won't (remix) / Metal and glass exact (remix) / Shark pretty / Nine lives to Rigel Five / The Red Baron / Curse of the frontier land / I turned her away / Regenisraen / Erica's word / Crash into June / Like a girl Jesus / We love you, Carol and Alison / The real Sheila / Together now, very minor / Room for one more, honey / Leilani / Throwing the election.

Feb 94. (cd) *Alias; <(A 048CD)>* **DISTORTION OF GLORY** (1982-1984)

LOUD FAMILY

SCOTT MILLER – vocals, guitar, etc / **PAUL WIENEKE** – synthesizer, guitar, vocals / **ZACHARY SMITH** – guitar, vocals / **R. DUNBAR POOR** – bass, effects / **JOZEF BECKER** – drums, percussion

Alias   Alias

Feb 93. (lp/cd) <(A 033/+D)> **PLANTS AND BIRDS AND ROCKS AND THINGS** Oct92
– He do the police in different voices / Sword swallower / Aerodeliria / Self righteous boy reduced to tears / Jimmy still comes around / Take me down (too halloo) / Don't all thank me at once / Idiot son / Some grand vision of motives and irony / Spot the setup / Inverness / Rosy overdrive / Slit my wrists / Isaac's law / The second grade applauds / Last honest face / Even you / Ballad of how you can all shut up / Give in world.

Sep 93. (7") <(A 043S)> **TAKE ME DOWN. / THE COME ON**

GAME THEORY (cont)

Dec 93. (m-lp/m-cd) <(A 055/+D)> **SLOUCHING TOWARDS LIVERPOOL**
– Take me down / The come on / Back of a car / Slit my wrists (live) / Aerodeliria (live) / Erica's word (live in studio).

Jan 95. (lp/cd) <(A 060/+D)> **THE TAPE OF ONLY LINDA** — Oct94
– Soul drain / My superior / Marcia and Etrusca / Hyde Street virgins / Baby hard-to-be-around / It just wouldn't be Christmas / Better nature / Still its own reward / For beginners only / Ballet hetero.

—— MILLER + WIENEKE recruited **KENNY KESSEL** – bass, vocals + **DAWN RICHARDSON** – drums

Sep 96. (cd) <(A 098D)> **INTERBABE CONCERN** — Aug96
– Sodium laureth sulfate / North San Bruno dishonor trip / Don't respond, she can tell / I'm not really a spring / Rise of the chokehold princess / Such little non-believers / The softest hip of her baby tongue / Screwed over by stylist introverts / Top dollar survivalist hardware / Not expecting both contempo and classique / I no longer fear the headlines / Hot rox avec lying sweet talk / Uncle Lucky / Just gone / Asleep and awake on the man's freeway / Where they go back to school but get depressed / Where they sell antique food / Where the flood waters soak their belongings / Where they walk over Sainte Therese.

—— MILLER + KESSEL brought in **GIL RAY** – drums, percussion + **ALISON FAITH LEVY** – keyboards, vocals

Aug 98. (cd) <(A 131CD)> **DAYS FOR DAYS** — May98
– Cortex the killer / Good, there are no lions in the street / Deee-pression / Way too helpful / Mozart sonatas / Businessmen are okay / Crypto sicko / Why we don't live in Mauritania / Sister sleep.

Apr 00. (cd) <(A 146CD)> **ATTRACTIVE NUISANCE** — Feb00
– 720 times happier than the unjust man / One will be the highway / Save your money / Nice when I want something / Years of wrong impressions / Blackness, blackness / Backwards century / Soul DC / The apprentice / No one's watching my limo ride / Controlled burn / Motion of ariel.

—— MILLER disbanded The LOUD FAMILY after above set

– compilations, etc. –

Sep 02. (cd) Innerstate; <(125-005)> **FROM RITUAL TO ROMANCE (live 5th October 1996 and 8th August 1998)** — Jun02
– Where the flood waters soak their belongings / Here come the warm jets / Spot the setup / Such little nonbelievers / Aerodeliria / Don't respond, she can tell / Sword swallower / (track 9 / Not because you can / Good, there are no lions in the street / (track 11) / (track 12) / Deee-pression / Debaser / Sodium laureth sulfate / Baby hard-to-be-around / Asleep and awake on the man's freeway / Curse of the frontier land / When you sleep / (outro)

GAYE BYKERS ON ACID

Formed: Leicester, England ... mid 80's by IAN GARFIELD HOXLEY (aka MARY MARY or MARY GOLIGHTLY) and TONE, along with KEVIN HYDE, ROBBER, and subsequently DJ, WILLIAM SAMUEL RONALD MONROE. A bizarre troupe of dayglo, grebo pseudo-bikers led by the cross-dressing, MARY MARY, GBOA made their album debut in 1987 with the 'Virgin' album (who else!), 'DRILL YOUR OWN HOLE'. Fans had to do just that as the record came minus a centre-punch, rendering it impossible to play. Though some might argue that was actually a blessing in disguise, the band atracted a cult following, gaining coverage mainly in the indie press. After a further major label set, 'STEWED TO THE GILLS' (1989), the band subsequently completed the independently issued 'GROOVEDIVESOAPDISH' the same year, before starting up their own label, 'Naked Brain'. The group folded after a few albums, various members going on to new projects, most notably MARY MARY, who surfaced in industrial "supergroup", PIGFACE, before co-forming HYPERHEAD. • Trivia: The band were at times complemented/augmented on stage by "drag-queen" DJ, ROCKET RONNIE, winner of 'The Alternative Miss Universe'.

Album rating: DRILL YOUR OWN HOLE (*6) / STEWED TO THE GILLS (*5) / GROOVEDIVESOAPDISH (*5) / CANCER PLANET MISSION (*4) / FROM TOMB OF THE YEAR (*4) / EVERYTHING'S GROOVY compilation (*6)

MARY MARY (b. IAN GARFIELD HOXLEY) – vocals / **TONE** (b. RICHARD ANTHONY HORSFALL) – guitar / **ROBBER** (b. IAN MICHAEL REYNOLDS) – bass / **KEVIN HYDE** (aka DR. JECKYL) – drums / plus **ROCKET RONNIE** (b. WILLIAM SAMUEL RONALD MONROE) – DJ

	In-Tape	not iss.
Nov 86. (7"/12") (IT/+TI 040) **EVERYTHING'S GROOVY. / T.V. CABBAGE**		–
May 87. (7") (IT 046) **NOSEDIVE KARMA. / DON'T BE HUMAN ERIC**		–
(10"+=) (IT 46-10) – Golf trek.		
(12"+=) (ITTO 46) – Delirium.		

	Virgin	Caroline
Oct 87. (7") (VS 1008) **GIT DOWN (SHAKE YOUR THANG). / TOLCHOCKED BY KENNY PRIDE**	54	–
(12"+=/12"s+=) (VS T/X 1008) – Go go in out, in out Garotschka.		
Nov 87. (cd/c/lp) (CD/TC+/V 2478) <CAROL 1347> **DRILL YOUR OWN HOLE**	95	
– Motorvate / Call me a liar / All hung up / Zen express / World War 7 blues / Git down / After suck there's blow / So far out / Drive-in salvation / T.V. cabbage.		
Dec 87. (7") (VS 1027) **ALL HUNG UP. / AFTERNOON TEA WITH DAVE GREENFIELD**		–
(12"+=/12"pic-d+=) (VS T/X 1027) – ('A'-Rough Rider mix) / ('A'-Reprisal mix).		
Jan 89. (7") (VS 1165) **HOT THING. / RAD DUDE**		–
(10"+=/12"+=) (VSA/VST 1165) – After there's blow there's suck.		
Feb 89. (cd/c/lp) (CD/TC+/V 2579) <CAROL 1376> **STEWED TO THE GILLS**		
– It is are you? / Better of dead / M.A.D. / Hot thing / Testicle of God (and was it good) / Ill / Mass gyrate / Harmonious murder / Shoulders / Hair of dog / Rad dude / Teeth / Floydrix / Bedlam a g-go / Fairway to Heaven / It is are you? (concept reprise).		

	Naked Brain	not iss.
Mar 90. (lp/c) (NBX 001/+MC) **CANCER PLANET MISSION**		–
– Welcome cancer planet mission / Face at the window / Hope ans psyche / Satyr naked / Catalytic converter / Advertise / Alive oh! / Mr. Muggeridge / Got is the kink / Demon seed / Bleed / Candle / Insomnia / Heavenly body. (cd-iss. Oct90; NBXCD 001)		
Dec 90. (lp/c/cd; as PFX) (NBX 2/+CD) **PERNICIOUS NONSENSE**		

—— when they split during this period, KEVIN formed G.R.O.W.T.H. with JEFF from The JANITORS. TONE formed The CAMP COLLECTION with BRAD BRADBURY.

– compilations, etc. –

Jan 89. (12"ep) Nighttracks; (SFNT 010) **THE JANICE LONG SESSIONS** — –
Nov 89. (m-lp/c/cd) Dry Communications; (MLP/DRY/DRYCD 002) **GROOVEDIVESOAPDISH** — –
Apr 93. (cd/lp) Receiver; (<RRCD/RRLP 160>) **G.B.O.A.** — May99
– Killer teens in New Orleans / S.P.A.C.E. / Radiation / John Wayne's a fag / Iguana trifle / What happened to Malcolm / Disinformation rise & shine / T.V. cabbage / Face at the window / Don't be human Eric – Let's be frank / Delirium / Everythings groovy baby.
May 93. (cd) Receiver; (<RRCD 162>) **FROM THE TOMB OF THE NEAR LEGENDARY** — Dec94
– Watch that roundabout Ben / Shit happens / Killer teens in New Orleans (a joy toy remix) / Why? / Space cadet / Nero fiddles / Animal farm / No justice, just us / S.P.A.C.E. (a joy toy remix).
Jun 01. (cd) Cherry Red; (<CDMRED 188>) **EVERYTHING'S GROOVY** —
– Everything's groovy / TV cabbage / Space rape / Nosedive karma / Don't be humam let's be frank / Delerium / Golf trek / All hanging up / Motorvate / Save your soul / Don't take me there / Leave your head alone / 007 / Getting down / Toytown / Toytown revisited.

GEE MR. TRACY

Formed: Norwich, England ... 1984 by TOM 'BRICK' SMITH and former TESTCARD-F member, VINCE ROGERS. Taking their moniker from a catchphrase used (by the character, Brains) on children's cult TV programme, 'Thunderbirds', GEE MR. TRACY embarked in their crusade to amuse (just slightly) the indie-pop world. Their simple electronic ditties matched the cronic lyrics/poetry of the bespectacled BRICK, his off-the-wall humour only matched by The VERY THINGS or even ALEXEI SAYLE. Surfacing on local label, 'Backs', GEE MR TRACY unleashed 'SHOOT ME THAT SHERBET HERBERT, STRAIGHT FROM THE FRIDGE POPS' (1985) to an unwitting public, a mini-set that featured their most outrageously mad track, 'THE DAY THE SHOES BIT BACK' (quite literally barking!). The quartet (the other gruesome twosome being REBECCA SLATER and er, ANT) carried on regardless but finally hit a "Brick" wall after the release of their second mini-set, 'HARMONY! RHAPSODY! DESTINY!' (1986).

Album rating: SHOOT ME THAT SHERBET HERBERT, STRAIGHT FROM THE FRIDGE POPS (*4) / HARMONY! RHAPSODY! DESTINY! (*3)

TESTCARD-F

VINCE ROGERS – keyboards / with a female vocalist + two others

	Backs	not iss.
Apr 83. (7") (NCH 004) **BANDWAGON TANGO. / UNFAMILIAR ROOM**		–
Mar 84. (7") (NCH 010) **THE THIRD STROKE. / IF ONLY IT WASN'T**		–

GEE MR. TRACY

TOM 'BRICK' SMITH – vocals, trumpet / **VINCE ROGERS** – keyboards / **REBECCA SLATER** – vocals / **ANT** – backing vocals

	Backs	not iss.
Mar 85. (7"m) (NCH 102) **YOU MAKE MY HOUSE SHINE. / GO SCUBA / FOR MY HONEY**		–
May 85. (m-lp) (NCHMLP 5) **SHOOT ME THAT SHERBERT HERBERT, STRAIGHT FROM THE FRIDGE POPS**		–
– The day the shoes bit back / Ooh bop sh'bam / Sorrowful / You make my house shine / When I lost my baby.		
Jul 85. (7") (NCH 103) **I WISH THE WHOLE DAMN WORLD WAS IN A BOTTLE. / HONEY, I'M OUT OF MY TREE**		–
Feb 86. (7") (NCH 106) **LAVA MAN. / MR. UNLUCKY**		–
Jun 86. (7") (NCH 108) **PERMANENT SWOON. / I FELL THROUGH THE FLOOR**		–
Oct 86. (m-lp) (NCHMLP 11) **HARMONY! RHAPSODY! DESTINY!**		–
– Permanent swoon / Lava man / etc		

—— the fun was over after above

Howe GELB (see under ⇒ GIANT SAND)

GENE LOVES JEZEBEL

Formed: Porthcawl, Wales ... 1981 by identical twins JAY and MICHAEL ASTON, a rhythm section of STEVE MARSHALL and DICK HAWKINS completing the line-up. Relocating to London, the group signed to the 'Situation 2' label and made their vinyl debut in Spring '82 with the 'SHAVING MY NECK' single. Bass-heavy tribal repetition and proto-goth posturing – albeit with a sense of humour – was the order of the day,

GENE LOVES JEZEBEL (cont)

the tortuous 'MACHISMO' showing the band at their most unlistenably experimental. While the twins formed the core of the outfit, a succession of people came and went as needed; future ALL ABOUT EVE frontwoman, JULIENNE REGAN, was a brief member while old school pal IAN HUDSON joined up prior to the recording of debut album, 'PROMISE' (1983). Promoted by the singles 'SCREAMING (FOR EMMALENE)' and 'BRUISES', the record's tarted-up goth grooves (well, image-wise anyway!) won them support from the likes of John Peel. The following year the band travelled to the States where they subsequently enjoyed greater success and even secured a contract with 'Geffen' in the mid-80's (funnily enough, The ASTONS' vocal bleatings could possibly, at a pinch, be described as a gothic AXL ROSE!). Back in Britain, meanwhile, more personnel upheaval saw PETER RIZZO and MARCUS GILVEAR take up the rhythm section reins for follow-up album, 'IMMIGRANT' (1985). A considerably more commercial and accessible affair, some tracks (eg. 'WORTH WAITING FOR') were even reminiscent of U2 in an ECHO & THE BUNNYMEN kinda way!? After a further US jaunt that resulted in the departure of HUDSON and recruitment of punk stalwart, JAMES STEVENSON, the 'JEZEBELS finally scraped the UK Top 75 in Spring '86 with 'THE SWEETEST THING' single. 'HEARTACHE' achieved a similar feat later that summer while a third set, 'DISCOVER' (1986) made the Top 40. The subsequent recruitment of ex-SPEAR OF DESTINY man, CHRIS BELL, preceded further minor hit singles and a fourth album, 'THE HOUSE OF DOLLS'. The turn of the decade brought major upheaval as MICHAEL ASTON emigrated to America and left his twin brother to take up the reins. Ironically enough, the subsequent single, 'JEALOUS' proved their biggest US hit, preceding the 'KISS OF LIFE' (1990) album. After a break of three years, GENE LOVES JEZEBEL resurfaced with yet another line-up – JAY ASTON, RIZZO, STEVENSON and ROBERT ADAM – and a new record deal with 'Savage-Arista'. The resulting album, 'HEAVENLY BODIES' (1993) failed to re-ignite their career and group subsequently split as STEVENSON defected to The CULT. The mid-90's saw another reformation with ASTON, STEVENSON and RIZZO, a live set, 'IN THE AFTERGLOW' (1995) appearing on the independent 'Pink Gun' label. Reminiscent of fellow goths, CHRISTIAN DEATH, GLJ split into two factions, both taking the group moniker. In 1999, there was JAY ASTON's GENE LOVE JEZEBEL and their anthem/folk rock set, 'LOVE LIES BLEEDING' and in 2001, MICHAEL's retro-psyche GENE LOVES JEZEBEL and their long-player, 'GIVING UP THE GHOST'. Make up lads, eh!

Album rating: PROMISE (*6) / IMMIGRANT (*6) / DISCOVER (*5) / THE HOUSE OF DOLLS (*5) / KISS OF LIFE (*5) / HEAVENLY BODIES (*5) / IN THE AFTERGLOW (*4) / FROM THE MOUTHS OF BABES compilation (*7) / VII (*4) / LIVE IN THE VOODOO CITY (*4) / LOVE LIES BLEEDING (*4) / GIVING UP THE GHOST (*5)

MICHAEL ASTON (b. 4 May'61) – vocals / **JAY ASTON** (b.JOHN) – guitar, vocals / **STEVE MARSHALL** – bass / **DICK HAWKINS** – drums

	Situation 2	Relativity
May 82. (7") *(SIT 18)* **SHAVING MY NECK. / SUN AND INSANITY**		–
(12"+=) *(SIT 18T)* – Machismo / Glad to be alive.		

— guests were **STEVE GOULDING** – saxophone / **JOHN MURPHY** – drums (ex-SPK, ex-ASSOCIATES)

Apr 83. (7") *(SIT 20)* **SCREAMING (FOR EMMALENE). / SO YOUNG (HEAVE HARD HEAVE HO)**		–
(12"+=) *(SIT 20T)* – No voodoo dollies.		

— on tour they used **JULIENNE REGAN** – bass (future ALL ABOUT EVE) / **ALBIO DE LUCA** – guitar (future FURYO)

Jul 83. (7") *(SIT 24)* **BRUISES. / PUNCH DRUNK**		–
(12"+=) *(SIT 24T)* – Brando bruises.		
Oct 83. (lp) *(SITU 7)* **PROMISE**		–
– Screaming (for Emmalene) / Bread from Heaven / Wraps and arms / Upstairs / Psychological problems / Scheming / Influenza / Punch drunk. *(re-iss. 1988 on 'Situation 2-Lowdown' lp/cd; SITL 7/+CD) <US-iss.1987 on 'Geffen'; 24165>*		
Mar 84. (7") *(SIT 31)* **INFLUENZA (RELAPSE). / WALKING IN THE PARK**		–
(12"+=) *(SIT 31T)* – Stephen.		
May 84. (7") *(SIT 35)* **SHAME (WHOLE HEART BOWL). / THIN THINGS**		–
(12"+=) *(SIT 35T)* – Gorgeous.		

— The **ASTON's** brought in **PETER RIZZO** – bass repl. MARSHALL / **MARCUS GILVEAR** – drums (ex-KLAXON 5) repl. HAWKINS who joined SKELETAL FAMILY. / added **I.C. HUDSON** – guitar (who had joined on earlier tours)

May 85. (7") *(SIT 36)* **COW. / ONE SOMEONE**		–
(12") *(SIT 36T)* – ('A' extended) / Weep for her (cow).		
Jun 85. (lp/c) *(SITU/SITC 14)* **IMMIGRANT**		–
– Worth waiting for / Shame / Stephen / The rhino plasty / Cow / Cole Porter / Always a flame / The immigrant / Deep south whale. *(cd-iss. Jan88; SITU 14CD)* *(re-iss. 1988 on 'Situation 2-Lowdown' lp/cd; SITL 14/+CD)*		

— **JAMES STEVENSON** – guitar (ex-CHELSEA, ex-GENERATION X) repl. HUDSON

Nov 85. (7") *(SIT 41)* **DESIRE. / FLAME (Steve Hurley mix)**		–
(12"+=) *(SIT 41T)* – The immigrant.		
Dec 85. (12"ep) *<8075>* **DESIRE EP**	–	
– Desire / Worth waiting for / Cow / Desire / Flame.		

	Beggars Banquet	Geffen
Mar 86. (7") *(BEG 156)* **THE SWEETEST THING. / PSYCHO II**	75	
(12"+=) *(BEG 156T)* – Sweetest Jezebel.		
Jun 86. (7") *(BEG 161)* **HEARTACHE. / BEYOND DOUBT**	71	
(12"+=) *(BEG 161T)* – Heartache I / Deli babies.		
Jul 86. (lp/cd)(c) *(BEGA 73/+CD)(BEGC 73) <24118>* **DISCOVER**	32	

– Heartache / Over the rooftops / Kick / White horse / Wait and see / Desire / Beyond doubt / The sweetest thing / Maid of Sker / Brand new moon. *(free-lp w/a)* **GLAD TO BE ALIVE (live)** – Upstairs / Over the rooftops / The rhino plasty / Worth waiting for / Cow / The immigrant / Brittle punches / Pop tarantula.

Oct 86. (7") *(BEG 173)* **DESIRE (COME AND GET IT). / SAPPHIRE SCAVENGER**		
(12"+=) *(BEG 173T)* – New horizons / Message.		
(c-s+=) *(BEG 173C)* – ('A'-US mix) / Message.		

— **CHRIS BELL** – drums (ex-SPEAR OF DESTINY, ex-THOMPSON TWINS, ex-SPECIMEN) repl. GILVEAR (he went to the States)

Aug 87. (d7"/d12") *(BEG 192 D/TD)* **THE MOTION OF LOVE. / A FRESH SLICE // BUGG'S BRUISES. / VAGABOND (A NEW ADVENTURE)**	56	–
Oct 87. (lp/cd)(c) *(BEGA 87/+CD)(BEGC 87) <24171>* **THE HOUSE OF DOLLS**	81	
– Gorgeous / The motion of love / Set me free / Suspicion / Every door / 20 killer hurts / Treasure / Message / Drowning crazy / Up there.		
Nov 87. (7"/7"g-f) *(BEG 202/+S)* **GORGEOUS. / SOMEONE ON THE 6TH FLOOR (AT THE JEZEBEL PALACE)**	68	
(12"+=/cd-s+=) *(BEG 202 T/CD)* – Suspicion / The motion of love / (Jezebel mixes).		
Jan 88. (7"/12";w-drawn) *(BEG 212/+T)* **EVERY DOOR.**		
Jan 88. (7") *<28183>* **THE MOTION OF LOVE. / BUGG'S BRUISES**	–	87
Apr 88. (7") **SUSPICION. / DROWNING CRAZY**	–	

— (mid'89) **JAY** now sole survivor, when twin emigrated to the US He brought in **RISINGHAM & RIZZO**

Jun 90. (7") *(BEG 236) <19688>* **JEALOUS. / LAST YEAR**		68
(12"+=/cd-s+=) *(BEG 236 T/CD)* – While you were there.		
Jul 90. (lp/cd)(c) *(BEGA 109/+CD)(BEGC 109) <24260>* **KISS OF LIFE**		
– Jealous / It'll end in tears / Kiss of life / Why can't I / Syzygy / Walk away / Tangled up in you / Two shadows / Evening star / I die for you.		
Dec 90. (12"ep/cd-ep) **TANGLED UP IN YOU**		
– Tangled up in you / Suspicion / Heartache / Stephen.		

— line-up; **JAY ASTON / RIZZO / STEVENSON + ROBERT ADAM**

— MICHAEL ASTON would released a solo set in '95, 'WHY ME WHY THIS WHY NOW' for 'Triple X'

	Savage-Arista	not iss.
May 93. (7"/c-s) *(74321 13152-7/-4)* **JOSEPHINA. / TOMORROW COLOURS**		–
(cd-s+=) *(74321 13152-2)* – ('A' extended).		
Jun 93. (cd/c) *(74785 50210-2/-4)* **HEAVENLY BODIES**		–
– American dreamer / Wild horse / Josephina / Any anxious colour / Break the chain / Down in a lonely place / Sweet sweet rain / Rosary / Heavenly bodies / Voice in the dark. *(<US+cd-iss. Apr00 on 'Robinson'; RRCD 0004>)*		

— split for a while when JAMES STEVENSON was poached by The CULT

— re-formed yet again with **ASTON / STEVENSON + RIZZO**

	Pink Gun	not iss.
Nov 95. (d-cd) *(PINKGCD 1)* **IN THE AFTERGLOW (live)**		–
– Gorgeous / The sweetest thing / Bugg's bruises / Coal porter / Set me free / Suspicion / Over the rooftops / Stephen / Every door / Heartache / The motion of love / 20 killer hurts / Desire / American dreamer / Sweet sweet rain / Suspicion / Wild horse / Any anxious colour / Why can't I / Kiss of life / Evening star / 20 killer hurts / Jealous / Josephina / Always a flame / Desire.		

— **JAY ASTON** with **PETE RIZZO** – bass / **CHRIS BELL** – drums

	Robinson	Robinson
Mar 99. (cd) *<RRCD 001>* **VII (live reunion)**	–	–
– Love keeps dragging me down / Who wants to go to Heaven? / Liquor man / The good bye girl / Uptown / Welcome to L.A. / Come naturally / Know I love you / When we were one / Switchblade memories / Heroine / Dream a big dream. *(UK-iss.Apr00; same)*		

— added **JAMES STEVENSON** – guitar

Sep 99. (cd) *<RRCD 0003>* **LIVE IN THE VOODOO CITY (live)**	–	–
– Josephina / Who wants to go to Heaven? / Come naturally / Sweet rain / Uptown / Kiss of life / So sad / Love keeps dragging me down / Jealous / Gorgeous / Desire (come and get it) / Upstairs / The motion of love. *(UK-iss.Apr00; same)*		

— meanwhile, **MICHAEL ASTON's GENE LOVES JEZEBEL**; another line-up **MICHAEL CIRAVOLO** – guitar, vocals / + **SVRDLAN** brothers rhythm section

	Triple X	Triple X
Aug 99. (cd) *(<TX 51261CD>)* **LOVE LIES BLEEDING**		
– Love lies bleeding / Give my regards to Ray / Who will survive you? / The lion in your eyes / Loving you is the best revenge / The prairie song / Joyrider 2000 / Alive within / Sorry (Suzan) / Necromancing the cunning linguist / Lifting the vale.		

— next with **POWELL, REYNOLDS + BRAHM**

Apr 01. (cd) *(<TX 51267CD>)* **GIVING UP THE GHOST**		
– Giving up the ghost / Phreque / Sly old fox / Nico superstar / Don't spoil my song / Push / Speak my language / Two boys and a wheelbarrow / Drive / Drowning and waving / Limey.		

– compilations, etc. –

Sep 95. (cd) *Avalanche; <21>* **SOME OF THE BEST OF GENE LOVES JEZEBEL: FROM THE MOUTHS OF BABES**	–	–
– Desire (come and get it) / Heartache / Jealous / Twenty killer hurts / Kiss of life / Suspicion / Upstairs / No sweat / Beyond dobt / Bread from Heaven / Body of soul.		
Oct 98. (cd) *Cleopatra; <377>* **DESIRE: GREATEST HITS REMIXED**	–	–
Mar 02. (cd) *Perris; <98>* **LIVE IN NOTTINGHAM**	–	

Lisa GERRARD (see under ⇒ DEAD CAN DANCE)

GHOST DANCE

Formed: Leeds, England ... 1985 by GARY MARX and ANNE-MARIE (NOVAK), both card-carrying goths with a top pedigree:- the former ex-SISTERS OF MERCY, the latter ex-SKELETAL FAMILY. Completing the line-up with a rhythm section of ETCH and PANDORA (actually a drum machine!), the group debuted on their own imprint, 'Karbon', the single, 'RIVER OF NO RETURN' selling well enough in Spring '86 to reach the higher rungs of the indie chart. A further handful of 45's haunted the shops over the course of the following year, collected together at the tail end of '87 as 'GATHERING DUST'. With the recruitment of second guitarist, RICHARD STEEL, the band signed a major record deal with 'Chrysalis', the resulting single, 'DOWN TO THE WIRE' (a minor UK hit) and album, 'STOP THE WORLD' (1989), treading an uncomfortable line between commerciality and underground credibility. While contemporaries such as the SISTERS, the MISSION and ALL ABOUT EVE, all found a way to combine artistic integrity and chart success, GHOST DANCE could only walk in their shadow, finding themselves unceremoniously dropped by their label midway through a European tour. The final nail in their proverbial coffin came early 1990 as ETCH signed up with rivals, The MISSION. • **Songwriters:** MARX except BOTH ENDS BURNING (Roxy Music) / HEART FULL OF SOUL (Yardbirds) / RADAR LOVE (Golden Earring) / CAN THE CAN (Suzi Quatro).

Album rating: GATHERING DUST compilation (*6) / STOP THE WORLD (*5)

ANNE-MARIE (NOVAK) – vocals (ex-SKELETAL FAMILY) / **GARY MARX** – guitar (ex-SISTERS OF MERCY) / **ETCH** – bass (ex-CITRON GIRLS) / drum machine PANDORA

		Karbon	not iss.
Apr 86.	(12"ep) *(KAR 602T)* **RIVER OF NO RETURN. / CELEBRATE. / YESTERDAY AGAIN / BOTH ENDS BURNING**	□	-
Oct 86.	(7") *(KAR 604)* **THE GRIP OF LOVE. / WHERE SPIRITS FLY**	□	-
	(12") *(KAR 604T)* – ('A'-Bombay mix) / Last train / A deeper blue / ('A'-Cheaper blues version).		
Dec 86.	(7") *(KAR 606)* **HEART FULL OF SOUL. / RADAR LOVE**	□	-
	(12"+=) *(KAR 606T)* – Can the can.		

— **JOHN GRANT** – drums repl. drum machine
— extra guitar players on tour **STEVE SMITH + PAUL SOUTHERN**

| Jul 87. | (12"ep) *(KAR 608T)* **A WORD TO THE WISE** – When I call / Fools gold / CRuel light / Holding on. | □ | - |
| Dec 87. | (lp) *(KARXL 303)* **GATHERING DUST** (compilation) – River of no return / Celebrate / Heart full of soul / Can the can / Last train / A deeper blue / Yesterday again / Both ends burning / The grip of love / Where spirits fly / Radar love. | □ | - |

— added **RICHARD STEEL** – guitar

		Chrysalis	not iss.
Jun 89.	(7") *(CHS/+MC 3376)* **DOWN TO THE WIRE. / BLOOD STILL FLOWS**	66	-
	(12") *(CHS12 3376)* – ('A'side) / Dr. Love / Gathering dust (live medley; The grip of love - Last train - Celebrate).		
	(cd-s) *(CHSCD 3376)* – ('A'side) / Mirror blind / Gathering dust (live medley; The grip of love - Last train - Celebrate).		
Sep 89.	(lp/c/cd) *(CHR/ZCHR/CCD 1706)* **STOP THE WORLD** – Down to the wire / Celebrate / Walk in my shadow / Cinder road / I will wait / Stop the world / Falling again / Heaven and beyond / The love I need / Spin the wheel. *(bonus-12"+=/c+=/cd+=)* – Stop the world (live) / The love I need (live) / Fools gold (live) / Turn to me (live).	□	-
Sep 89.	(7"/c-s) *(CHS/+MC 3402)* **CELEBRATE. / WHERE SPIRITS FLY (live) / WHEN I CALL (live)**	□	-
	(cd-s) *(CHSCD 3402)* – (first 2 tracks) / This way up / Nothing without you.		
	(12"/12"pic-d) *(CHS12 3402/+B)* – (first & third tracks) / This way up / Nothing without you.		

— split early 1990 and ETCH joined The MISSION, then LOUD

GIANT SAND

Formed: Tucson, Arizona, USA ... 1980 as GIANT SANDWORMS by singer-songwriter/multi-instrumentalist, HOWE GELB along with RAINER PTACEK, DAVE SEGER and BILLY SED. The original line-up recorded two EP's preceding a temporary relocation to New York. By the time they'd returned to Arizona, SEGER had departed for fellow desert-rockers NAKED PREY and had been replaced by SCOTT GARBER. A further EP followed before GELB sacked the whole band and basically operated GIANT SAND as a solo venture, using varying personnel according to the project in hand. The first such project was the 'VALLEY OF RAIN' (1986) album, utilising GERBER, NAKED PREY's TOM LARKINS and GREEN ON RED man, CHRIS CACAVAS. Released on 'Zippo' (the Clapham, London based record shop/label who were also instrumental in kickstarting the careers of GREEN ON RED and The LONG RYDERS), the record showcased GELB's brand of breakneck roots-rock and guitar manipulation/abuse (notably on 'BLACK VENETIAN BLIND') framing a vocal style lying somewhere between a preacher-like NEIL YOUNG exhortation and a LOU REED drawl. As prolific as he was restless, GELB filtered his acutely observed, sun-scorched vignettes through side projects such as THE BAND OF BLANKY RANCHETTE and bonafide solo ventures like 1991's 'DREADED BROWN RECLUSE'. GIANT SAND recordings continued to come thick and fast, 1986 seeing the release of a second album, 'BALLAD OF A THIN LINE MAN' (the last to feature GARBER, who went on to form LOS CRUZOS with former GS sticksman SED), while the blistering 'STORM' and the more composed 'THE LOVE SONGS' both surfaced in 1988; the latter saw GELB augmented by drummer JOHN CONVERTINO. 'LONG STEM RANT' was released at the turn of the decade while a link-up with EVAN DANDO resulted in touring ensemble, FRUIT CHILD LARGE. On the recording front, the Arizonian enigma continued to impress the critics and his cult following with a further series of GIANT SAND albums on various labels including 'RAMP' (1991), 'CENTER OF THE UNIVERSE' (1992) and 'STROMAUSFALL' (1994). Around the same time, GS delivered yet another masterpiece, 'GLUM' (1994), later returning to the studio with his GIANT SAND cohorts to record 'BACKYARD BARBECUE BROADCAST' (1996). HOWE subsequently worked with LISA GERMANO under the guise of OP8, releasing the 'SLUSH' (1997) album on Richard Branson's 'V2' imprint. CONVERTINO and other GIANT SAND sidekick, JOEY BURNS, subsequently hooked up to form minimalist, CALEXICO. In fact, the rise and rise of CALEXICO, with their unclassifiable but mesmerising melange of country, flamenco, mariachi, folk and ambient jazz, somewhat overshadowed the more level trajectory of GELB's work. While the half-finished sketches of 1998's 'HISSER' brought an end to his brief spell with 'V2', the more sympathetic environs of 'Thrill Jockey' resulted in the best GIANT SAND release in years, 'CHORE OF ENCHANTMENT' (2000). Heavy with the spirit of the late PTACEK (who'd died of cancer), the album's drifting desert laments were reassuringly opaque, setting the stage for 2001's 'CONFLUENCE'. While GELB's often contrary influences were – cryptically or otherwise – to the fore, the veteran songwriter gathered together an enticing selection of material for 2002's 'COVER MAGAZINE'. Marty Robbins' 'EL PASO', Goldfrapp's 'HUMAN' and Black Sabbath's 'IRON MAN' were just a few of the numbers upon which GELB trained his dessicated vocal chords, the latter in particular, coming in for a radical, low-key jazz reworking. • **Songwriters:** GELB except ALL ALONG THE WATCHTOWER + EVERY GRAIN OF SAND (Bob Dylan) / YOU CAN'T PUT YOUR ARMS AROUND A MEMORY (Johnny Thunders) / THE WEIGHT (Band) / IS THAT ALL THERE IS? (Lieber-Stoller) / GET READY (Rare Earth) / THE DOCK OF THE BAY (Otis Redding) + a THIN LIZZY tribute medley / I'M SO LONESOME I COULD CRY (Hank Williams) / YOU'RE SO VAIN (Carly Simon) / WELCOME TO MY WORLD (Winkler-Hatchcock) / I WISH YOU LOVE (Charles Trenet) / SEASHELLS (Farina Brothers) / SAND (Lee Hazlewood) / ROUND AND ROUND + MUSIC ARCADE (Neil Young) / CHANGE IS NOW (Byrds) / THE INNER FLAME (Rainer Ptacek) / Gelb solo:- CAN'T HELP FALLING IN LOVE (hit; Elvis Presley) / Band Of ... Blacky Ranchette covered: REVOLUTION BLUES (Neil Young) / TROUBLE MAN (Waylon Jennings) / YOU ARE MY SUNSHINE (Jimmy Davis).

Album rating: VALLEY OF RAIN (*7) / BALLAD OF A THIN LINE MAN (*6) / STORM (*6) / THE LOVE SONGS (*6) / LONG STEM RANT (*6) / SWERVE (*6) / RAMP (*7) / CENTER OF THE UNIVERSE (*6) / PURGE AND SLOUCH (*5) / GLUM (*8) / GIANT SONGS compilation (*7) / GIANT SONGS 2 compilation (*6) / GOODS AND SERVICES (*5) / BACKYARD BARBECUE BROADCAST (*5) / SLUSH as OP8 (*6) / CHORE OF ENCHANTMENT (*7) / COVER MAGAZINE (*5) / Howie Gelb: DREADED BROWN RECLUSE (*5) / HISSER (*4) / CONFLUENCE (*6) / The Band Of ... Blacky Ranchette: THE BAND OF BLACKY RANCHETTE (*5) / HEARTLAND (*6) / SAGE ADVICE (*5)

GIANT SANDWORMS

HOWE GELB – vocals, guitar, bass, keyboards, electronics / **DAVE SEGER** – bass, guitars, vocals / **RAINER PTACEK** – guitar / **BILLY SED** – drums, vocals

		not iss.	Boneless
Nov 80.	(7"ep) <WW 8006> **WILL WALLOW AND ROAM AFTER THE RUIN** – Electro-gospel / Mexican eyes / Me and my rocket / Lipstick criminals / Steadfast.	-	□

— **SCOTT GARBER** – bass, vocals; repl. PTACEK

		not iss.	Semi-Round
Apr 83.	(7"ep) <83031> **AN EVENING AT THE WILDCAT HOUSE + AN EVENING AT THE DEVIL HOUSE (live)** – Cross of wood / Coalwalker / CHRIS BURROUGHS & THE NATIONALS: Last call / Under the ladder.	-	- free
May 83.	(c) <demo> **ONE BIG TAPE** – Don't turn away / Mad city / Coalwalker / Tomorrow not today / I'm not romantic / Apache junction / Gallant are we.	-	-
Dec 85.	(7") One Big Guitar; (OBG 001) **DON'T TURN AWAY. / LONGSLEEVES** (above was rec. 1983) – SEGER formed NAKED PREY in 1984	□	-

GIANT SAND

— **GELB + GARBER** brought in **TOM LARKINS** – drums (ex-CHRIS BURROUGHS & THE NATIONALS + of NAKED PREY)

		New Rose	not iss.
Nov 85.	(7") *(ROSE 72)* **VALLEY OF RAIN. / TORTURE OF LOVE**	-	- French

— added **WINSTON A. WATSON Jr.** – drums / guests incl. **CHRIS CACAVAS** – piano (of GREEN ON RED)

		Zippo	Enigma
May 86.	(lp/c) *(ZONG/+CASS 008)* <72050> **VALLEY OF RAIN** – Down on town / Love's no answer / Black venetian blind / Curse of a thousand flames / Artists / Man of want / Valley of rain / Tumble and tear / October anywhere / Barrio / Death, dying and channel 5 / Torture of love. *(cd-iss. Jul90; ZONGCD 008)*	□	□ Nov85

— **PAULA JEAN BROWN** – guitar; repl. WINSTON (still a guest on 1)

| Sep 86. | (lp) *(ZONG 13)* **BALLAD OF A THIN LINE MAN** – Thin line man / All along the watchtower / Graveyard / Body of water / Last legs / You can't put your arms around a memory / A hard man to get to know / Who am I / The chill outside / Desperate man. *(cd-iss. Jul90; ZONGCD 013)* | □ | - |

GIANT SAND (cont)

— **NEIL HARRY** – pedal steel; repl. GARBER who joined SIDEWINDERS and eventually LOS CRUZOS

		Demon	What Goes On
Mar 88.	(7") <none> **UNEVEN LIGHT OF DAY. / BIG ROCK**		-

Apr 88. (lp/cd) (FIEND/+CD 115) <GOES ON 19> **STORM**
– Uneven light of day / Town where no town belongs / Back to black and grey / Bigger than that / Right makes right / Three 6ixes / Big rock / The replacement / Storm / War is a big word / Town with little or no pity / The weight. *(cd re-iss. Sep90; same)*

		Demon	Homestead
Dec 88.	(7") <HMS 128-7> **CHRISTMAS EVERYDAY (MAYBE IT'LL HELP). / MISH MASH SQUINTY SURPRISE**	-	

— **HOWE + PAULA** (now on bass) brought in **JOHN CONVERTINO** – drums / **CHRIS CACAVAS** – organ, accordian, acoustic guitar

Dec 88. (lp/cd) (FIEND/+CD 129) <HMS 129-1/-2> **THE LOVE SONGS**
– Wearing the robes of bible black / One man's woman – No man's land / Mad dog a man / Fingernail moon, barracuda and me / Mountain of love / Almost the politician's wife / The doors / Love like a train / Is that all there is? *(cd+=)* – Clump / Get ready / Murky red dew / Major glorious ending theme. *(cd re-iss. Sep90; same)*

— basically **GELB + CONVERTINO** with guests incl. **PAULA JEAN BROWN + CHRIS CACAVAS + JIM McGRATH** (percussion)

			Nov89
Jan 90.	(lp/cd) (FIEND/+CD 164) <HMS 148-1> **LONG STEM RANT**		

– Unfinished love / Sandman / Bloodstone / Searchlight / Smash jazz / Sucker in a cage / Patsy does Dylan / It's long 'bout now / Lag crow / Loving cup / Paved road to Berlin / Anthem / Picture shows / Drum & guitar / Get to leave. *(cd+=)* – Searchlight cha cha / Return of the big red guitar / Stuck dog / Real gone blue guitar / The jig "zup". *(re-iss. Jun93 on 'Homestead' cd/lp; same)*

— added more guests **MARK WALTON + STEVE WYNN + JULIANA HATFIELD**

		Demon	Restless
Nov 90.	(lp/cd) (FIEND/+CD 204) <72595-2> **SWERVE**		

– Trickle down system / Dream stay / Former version of ourselves / Angels at night / Can't find love / Swerver / Sisters and brothers / Swerving / Every grain of sand / Some kind of / Swervette / Final swerve.

— **GELB, CONVERTINO + BROWN** recruited **JOEY BURNS** – bass, vocals + **INDIOSA PATSY JEAN** – vocals (NEIL HARRY on steel)

		Rough Trade	Restless
Nov 91.	(cd/c/lp) (R 276-2/-4/-1) <72599-2> **RAMP**		

– Romance of falling / Warm storm / Wonder / Welcome to my world / Anti-shadow / Jazzer snipe / Shadow to you / Z.Z. quicker foot / Neon filler / Seldom matters / Resolver. *(cd+=/c+=)* – Nowhere / Always horses coming / Patsy's blues.

		not iss.	Jupa
1992.	(7") <JUPA 5> **BIG BEAR BORN SHADOW. / THIN LINE MAN NOT – NO MOUNTAIN NO LOVE**	-	

— **CHRIS CACAVAS** – organ; repl. INDIOSA

		Brake Out	Restless
Nov 92.	(cd/lp) (OUT 109-2/-1) <72731-2> **CENTER OF THE UNIVERSE**		Aug92

– Seeded ('tween bone and bark) *[cd-only]* / Pathfinder / Center of the universe / Off ramp man / Year of the dog / Live to tell / Thrust / Loretta and the insect world / Sonic drive in / Milkshake girl / Stuck / Thing like that / Return to fodder / Unwed and well sped / Solomon's ride. *<US cd+=>* – Goin' down to Mexico.

Feb 93. (7") (PELL 027) **SOLOMON'S RIDE. / GOIN' DOWN TO MEXICO**
(above issued on 'Capella')

— **MARK WALTON** – bass (ex-DREAM SYNDICATE) repl. PATSY

— **MALCOLM BURN** – guitar, bass; repl. CHRIS (HARRY still guest)

Nov 93. (cd/d-lp) (OUT 115-2) <72746-2/-1> **PURGE AND SLOUCH**
– Slander / Bender / Swamp thing / Santana, Castaneda & you / Blue lit rope / Overture (part 1) / Rice road rumba / Corridor *[US-only]* / Slice & dice blues / High lonesome curl / New carjack city blues / Howde owed / Overture (part 2) / Here on the planet / Elevator music / Song for the accountants / Dock of the bay / Tripping moon / Thin Lizzy tribute – Personality flaws – Last word Johnny *[US-only]* / Bed of nails *[US-only]* / Dance of the Cicadas / Disclaimer *[UK-only]* / Smokey Joe's deep blue pancakes *[UK-only]* / Overture (finale) *[US d-lp only]*.

— now down to **GELB, CONVERTINO + BURNS**

		Return To Sender	not iss.
Nov 93.	(cd) (RTSCD 7) **STROMAUSFALL (live)**	-	- German

– October anywhere / The Y stomp jumble / Steadfast / ...Robes of bible black / Mt. of love / The replacement / Severely altered on the hill / Dreamville, New Mexico / Seldom matters.

— added the returning **PAULA** (MALCOLM still a guest)

		not iss.	Imago
Mar 94.	(cd/c) <21037-2/-4> **GLUM**	-	

– Glum / Yer ropes / Happenstance / Frontage road / 1 helvakowboy song / Painted bird / Spun / Left / Faithful / Bird song / I'm so lonesome I could cry.

— added **BILL ELM** – steel guitar + **MIKE SEMPLE** – guitar

		Brake Out	Koch
Dec 95.	(cd) (OUT 122-2) **GOODS AND SERVICES**		

– Back to the black and grey / Opus – Solomon's ride – Opus / Good and gone / Bender / Occupied / Warm storm / You're so vain / Welcome to my world / Surfin' lean / Trickle down system.

Aug 96. (cd) (OUT 126-2) <KOC 2 7914-2> **BACKYARD BARBECUE BROADCAST** Jan96
– BBQ suite: a. World stands still – b. Good and gone – c. I wish you love – d. Romance of falling – e. Seashells / Mope-a-long / Lean / Get to leave / Lester lampshade / Blue waltz reprise. *(hidden track+=)* – Rolling Stones I am.

OP8

— **GELB + CONVERTINO + BURNS** featuring **LISA GERMANO** – violin, piano + vocals

		V2	Thirsty Ear
May 97.	(7"/cd-s) (VVR 500037-8/-3) **SAND. / CRACKLIN' WATER / LOST IN SPACE**		-
Jun 97.	(cd; as OP8 & LISA GERMANO) (VVR 100033-2) <57030> **SLUSH**		Feb97

– Sand / Lost in space / If I think of love / Leather / It's a rainbow / OP8 / Cracklin' water / Never see it coming / Tom, Dick and Harry / The Devil loves L.A. / Round and round.

GIANT SAND

— **GELB, CONVERTINO + BURNS** reunited with a plethora of friends

		Vinyl Junkie	Thrill Jockey
Mar 00.	(d-lp/cd) (VJCD 113) <THRILL 079/+CD> **CHORE OF ENCHANTMENT**		

– Overture / (Well) Dusted (for the millennium) / Under a punishing sun / X-tra wide / 1972 / Temptation of egg / Raw / Wolfy / Shiver / Dirty from the rain / Astonished (in Memphis) / No reply / Satellite / Bottom line man / Way to end the day / Shrine. *(d-lp iss.May00 on 'Thrill Jockey'+=; same as US)* – Astonished (in Tucson) / Dusted (in Tucson) / Shiver (in Tucson) / Punishing sun (in Tucson) / Bad.

		Thrill Jockey	Thrill Jockey
Mar 02.	(cd/lp) <(THRILL 104/+LP)> **COVER MAGAZINE**		

– El Paso / Out on the weekend / Johnny hit and run Pauline / Iron man / Human – Lovely head / The beat goes on / Plants and rags / Wayfaring stranger / Fly me to the Moon / Red right hand / King of the road / I'm leaving now (adios) / Blue marble girl / The inner flame / The beat goes on.

– compilations, etc. –

Jun 89. (lp)<cd> *What Goes On; (GOES ON 33) / Homestead; <HMS 134-2>* **GIANT SANDWICH**
– Wishing well / Tumble and tear / Reptillian / Hard man to get to know / Black venetian blind (Book II) / Thin line man / Artists / What you hate / October anywhere / Black venetian blind (Book I) / Code of the road / Underground train / Spinning room waltz / Accordian to Howe / Bad lands / Up on the hill / Heartland.

Jul 89. (cd) *Demon; (GSCD 1)* **GIANT SONGS: THE BEST OF – VOLUME ONE**
– Down on town – Love's no answer / Curse of a thousand flames / Valley of rain / Barrio / Thin line man / Graveyard / Body of water / Heartland / Moon over Memphis / Underground train / Uneven light of day / Bigger than that / Big rock / Wearing the robes of bible black / One man's woman – No man's land / Fingernail moon, barracuda and me / Mountain of love.

Aug 95. (cd) *Demon; <(GSCD 2)>* **GIANT SONGS 2 – THE BEST OF GIANT SAND VOLUME TWO**
– Can't find love / Get to leave / Town with little or no pity / Dreamville New Mexico / October anywhere / Almost the politician's wife / Badlands / Trickle down system / Love like a train / Sage advice / Sisters and brothers / Sandman / Death, dying and channel 5 / Who am I? / Sucker in a cage / Christmas everyday (maybe it'll help).

Feb 97. (cd) *Epiphany; (GSFANCD 1)* **BUILD YOUR OWN NIGHT, IT'S EASY (OFFICIAL BOOTLEG SERIES – VOLUME ONE)**
– No name guitars / Sled / Elevator music / Spit / Corridor of love / Mason card / Hank's rap city / Less the lie / Scorcher / Bed of nails / Crumb / T.W.'s forgotten chorus / Smokey Joe's deep blue pancakes.

Jun 97. (cd) *Diablo; (<831>)* **BALLAD OF A THIN LINE MAN / VALLEY OF RAIN**

2000. (cd) *Ow Om; <#1>* **THE ROCK OPERA YEARS (OFFICIAL BOOTLEG SERIES – VOLUME TWO)**
– Rock opera / Dusted (in Tucson) / Astonished (in Tucson) / Hard on things / Francoise / Punishing sun (in Tucson) / Chore of enchantment / Seldom matters again / Music arcade / Shiver (in Tucson) / Catapult / Dilemma / Not good.

Mar 01. (cd) *Vinyl Junkie; (VJCD 121)* **SELECTIONS CIRCA 1990-2000**
– Shiver / Temptation of egg / The inner flame / Sand / Music arcade / Remain distorted / Yer ropes / Corridor / Stuck / Center of the universe / Nowhere / Wonder / Burning desire / Change is now.

Nov 01. (cd) *Ow Om; <#5>* **UNSUNGGLUM (OFFICIAL BOOTLEG SERIES – VOLUME 3)**
– Glum / Yer ropes / Happenstance / Frontage road / 1 helvakowboy song / I'm so lonesome I could cry / Body's a boat / Remain distorted / Water fuels the fire / Occupy / Painted bird / Spun / Left / Faithful / Bird song / The professor.

The BAND OF... BLACKY RANCHETTE

GELB + PTACEK + LARKINS + JACOB MARTINEZ (bass)

		New Rose	not iss.
Jun 85.	(7") (NEW 62) **CODE OF THE ROAD. / NATURALLY LONESOME**		- French
Jun 85.	(lp) (ROSE 62) **THE BAND OF BLACKY RANCHETTE**		- French

– Code of the road / Blind justice / Revolution blues / Heartland / One more should do it / Play an old guitar / Up on the hill / Spinning room waltz / Evil / The wrong man. *(cd-iss. 1989 +=; ROSE 62CD)* – Naturally lonesome / Man on a string.

— added **NEIL HARRY** – pedal steel (+ PAULA as guest)

		Zippo	not iss.
Oct 86.	(lp) (ZONG 014) **HEARTLAND**		-

– Heartland / Moon over Memphis / All done in / Down on these badlands / Roof's on fire / Underground train / Nowhere / Steadfast / One way ticket / Change of heart.

		Demon	Demon
May 90.	(lp/cd) (FIEND/+CD 181) <72742> **SAGE ADVICE**		

– Loving cup / Burning desire / Trouble man / Dreamville, N.M. / Indiosa / Wild dog waltz / Sage advice / Outside an angel's reach (3 6ixes) / Shards of time / Still too far / Blanket of stars (Loving Cup: reprise) / You are my sunshine. *(cd+=)* – Heartland / Moon over Memphis / All done in / Roof's on fire / Underground train / Steadfast / Change of heart.

HOWE GELB

with **GARY SCHEUCH** – guitars, drums, bass / + others incl. **PTACEK + JACK MARTINEZ**

		not iss.	Left For Dead Tapes
1983.	(c) <0000001> **INCIDENTAL MUSIC**	-	

– Real love / The shot / Spinning room waltz / Steadfast / Chunk one / Chunk two / Chunk three / Chunk four.

— next with **CONVERTINO, BURNS, BROWN + PTACEK**

	Houses In Motion	Restless

Oct 91. (cd/lp) *(HIM 8907)* <72743-2/-1> **DREADED BROWN RECLUSE**   □   □ Oct93
– Spirit lie / Picture shows / Loretta and the insect world / Actually faxing Sophia / Cello of the city / Still too far / Warm storm / Always horses coming / Vigdis / Vienna two-step throw-away / Bible black, book II / Brown recluse / Wild dog waltz / Blanket for Tina / Victoria wisp. *(re-iss. Oct93; same)*

— **GELB** augmented by nearly all past GIANT SAND members

	V2	V2

Jun 99. (cd) *(VVR 100630-2)* <63881 27028-2> **HISSER**   □   □ Aug98
– Temptation of egg / 4 door maverick / This purple child / Shy of bumfuck / Propulsion / Catapult / Creeper / Tanks rolling into town / Halifax in a hurricane / Living on a waterfall / Like a store front display / Explore you / Nico's little opera / Thereminender / Hisser / Intro speak / Soldier of fortune / Lull / Short way to end the day. *(UK+=)* – No name guitar / Cracklin' water / Satellite.

— also unofficially issued two CD-R's 'DOWN HOME' in 1998/2000

	Vinyl Junkie	Thrill Jockey

Apr 01. (cd) *(VJCD 122)* <THRILL 097CD> **CONFLUENCE**   □   □ Mar01
– 3 sisters / Saint conformity / Pontiac slipstream / Sputter / Blue marble girl / Source / 2 rivers / Available space / Pedal steel and she'll / Cold / Can't help falling in love / Hatch / Shadow of where a river was / Vex (Paris) / Vex (Tucson) / Hard on things / Slide away.

— the usual GIANT SAND trio on below

	Ow Om	Ow Om

Oct 01. (cd) <(#4)> **LULL (SOME PIANO)**   □   □
– Do / You / See / What / Happens / When / None / Of / These / Tracks / Needed / To / Have / Names / But / Now / They / All / Do (2).

Michael GIRA (see under ⇒ SWANS)

GIRLS AT OUR BEST

Formed: Leeds, England ... 1979 out of S.O.S./BUTTERFLIES by JUDY 'JO' EVANS and three guys, JAMES 'JEZ' ALAN, GERARD 'TERRY' SWIFT and CHRIS OLDROYD. GAOB self-financed their debut single, 'GETTING NOWHERE FAST', the following Spring, a song which remains one of the band's finest three minutes and was later covered by Leeds' finest, The WEDDING PRESENT. A follow-up single, 'POLITICS', meanwhile, appeared on 'Rough Trade' later in 1980, their blend of RAINCOATS meets Baroque'n'roll one of the more interesting fusions of the post-punk era. JO's unique MADDY PRIOR-esque choral phrasing was meticulously enunciated in her characteristically Anglicised but off-key fashion, digging away at men in general on such proto-'Girl Power' ditties as 'FAST BOYFRIENDS'. The latter track actually previewed the group's one and only long-player, 'PLEASURE' (1981), a surprisingly impressive set of classy nursery rhyme punk which found a cult audience and a UK Top 60 placing; DARREN CARL HARPER had replaced OLDROYD by this point. Unfortunately, after a double-header, 'HEAVEN' / '£600,000' (both taken from the album), failed to hit the charts, they disbanded in the summer of '82, JEZ subsequently joined SEXBEAT (and later TALL BOYS). • **Trivia:** JUDY EVANS guested on THOMAS DOLBY's 1982 album, 'The Golden Age Of The Wireless'.

Album rating: PLEASURE (*8)

JUDY 'JO' EVANS – vocals / **JAMES 'JEZ' ALAN** – guitar / **GERARD 'TERRY' SWIFT** – bass / **CHRIS OLDROYD** – drums

	Record	not iss.

Apr 80. (7") *(RR 001)* **GETTING NOWHERE FAST. / WARM GIRLS**   □   –

	Rough Trade	Rough Trade

Nov 80. (7") *(RT 055)* <RR 2> **POLITICS. / IT'S FASHION**   □   □

— **DARREN CARL HARPER** – drums; repl. OLDROYD (to MUSIC FOR PLEASURE)

	Happy Birthday	not iss.

Jun 81. (7") *(UR 4)* **GO FOR GOLD. / I'M BEAUTIFUL NOW**   □   –

— **ROD JOHNSON** – drums; repl. HARPER (shared duties on album), guests incl. **THOMAS DOLBY** – synthesizer / **ALAN WAKEMAN** – clarinet / **DAVE FISHER** – piano

Oct 81. (lp) *(RULP 1)* **PLEASURE**   60   –
– Fast boyfriends / £600,000 / Pleasure / China blue / Heaven / I'm beautiful now / She's flipped / Waterbed babies / This train / Too big for your boots / Fun-city teenagers / Goodbye to that jazz. *(cd-iss. Oct94 on 'Vinyl Japan'; ASKCD 047)*

Oct 81. (7") *(UR 6)* **FAST BOYFRIENDS. / THIS TRAIN**   □   –

	God	not iss.

May 82. (7") *(GOD 1)* **HEAVEN. / £600,000**   □   –

— split 1982; JAMES ALAN joined SEXBEAT, and after only one single, 'PUMP', he joined The TALL BOYS

– compilations, etc. –

May 87. (12"ep) *Strange Fruit; (SFPS 029)* **THE PEEL SESSIONS (17.2.81)**   □   –
– China blue / This train / Getting nowhere fast / Warm girls.

GIST (see under ⇒ YOUNG MARBLE GIANTS)

GLAND SHROUDS (see under ⇒ BLAKE, Karl)

GLAXO BABIES

Formed: Bristol, England ... late 1977 by songwriter ROB CHAPMAN and DAN CATSIS (who also later moonlighted with The POP GROUP), the subsequent line-up also including TONY WRAFTER, TOMMY NICHOLS and the twin-drumming of GEOFF ALSOPP and CHARLES LLEWELLYN. Signing to Cherry Red subsidiary, 'Heartbeat', the freaky sextet issued their first John Peel Sessions in the shape of the 12"ep, 'THIS IS YOUR LIFE'. Later in 1979, a follow-up release, 'CHRISTINE KEELER', showed signs of danceability not unlike politico-punksters GANG OF FOUR and The MEKONS. The dawn of the 80's saw the release of their debut album, 'NINE MONTHS TO THE DISCO', recorded without lead singer, CHAPMAN and drummer, ALSOPP, the former having been replaced by a guy called AYLETT. Confusingly enough, a further album, 'PUT ME ON THE GUEST LIST', was released five months later although the recording stemmed from '78/'79. However, The GLAXO BABIES were forced to abandon the name after objections from the pharmaceutical company, Glaxo. In 1981, CATSIS, WRAFTER and LLEWELLYN adopted a new moniker, MAXIMUM JOY (after a GB track, 'MAXIMUM SEXUAL JOY'), taking on newcomers JANINE RAINFORTH and JOHN WADDINGTON (the latter ex-POP GROUP). Remaining with the GLAXO's last label, 'Y Records' (also home to SLITS and PIGBAG), MJ delivered a handful of 45's, the last of which, 'DO IT TODAY' (co-issued with 'Phonogram'), was aimed at the dance market. A disastrous attempt at a long-player, 'STATION MXJY' (co-produced by ADRIAN SHERWOOD), followed in 1982 and after an excursion into dance/DENNIS BOVELL-treated funk with a cover of Timmy Thomas' 'WHY CAN'T WE LIVE TOGETHER', the band finally split.

Album rating: NINE MONTHS TO THE DISCO (*4) / PUT ME ON THE GUEST LIST compilation (*5) / Maximum Joy: STATION MXJY (*3)

ROB CHAPMAN – vocals / **DAN CATSIS** – guitar, vocals / **TONY WRAFTER** – saxophone / **TOMMY NICHOLS** – bass, vocals / **GEOFF ALSOPP** – drums / **CHARLES LLEWELLYN** – drums

	Heartbeat	not iss.

Mar 79. (12"ep) *(12PULSE 3)* **THIS IS YOUR LIFE**   □   –
– This is your life / Stay awake / Because of you / Who killed Bruce Lee.

Aug 79. (7") *(PULSE 5)* **CHRISTINE KEELER. / NOVA BOSSANOVA**   □   –

— **AYLETT** – vocals; repl. CHAPMAN + ALSOPP

Apr 80. (lp) *(HB 2)* **NINE MONTHS TO THE DISCO**   □   –
– Maximum sexual joy / This is your vendetta / Seven days / Electric church / Nine months to the disco / Promised land / The tea master and the assassin / Free dem cells / Dinosaur disco meets the swampstomp / Conscience / Slim / Shake.

Jun 80. (7") *(PULSE 8)* **SHAKE THE FOUNDATIONS. / SHE WENT TO PIECES** (live)   □   –

Sep 80. (lp) *(HB 3)* **PUT ME ON THE GUEST LIST** (rec.1978-79 w/orig.line-up)   □   –
– Avoiding the issue / Because of you / This is your life / Police state / Who killed Bruce Lee / Stay awake / She went to pieces / Burning / Flesh / Puppet patrol.

— **JONES** – saxophone; repl. WRAFTER

	Y	not iss.

Dec 80. (7"ep) *(Y 6)* **LIMITED ENTERTAINMENT**   □   –
– There'll be no room for you in the shelter / Permission to be wrong / Limited entertainment / Dahij.

— altered their group moniker to ...

MAXIMUM JOY

— **CATSIS, LLEWELLYN + WRAFTER** recruited **JANINE RAINFORTH** – vocals, clarinet / **JOHN WADDINGTON** – guitar, vocals (ex-POP GROUP)

	Y Records	99 Records

Oct 81. (7"/12") *(Y 11/+T)* <99 08EP> **STRETCH. / SILENT STREET**   □   □

Feb 82. (7"/12") *(Y 15/+T)* **WHITE AND GREEN PLACE. / BUILDING BRIDGES**   □   –

— **KEV EVANS** – bass, piano, vocals; repl. CATSIS

Jul 82. (7"/12") *(Y 26/+T)* **IN THE AIR. / SIMMER TIL DONE**   □   –

Jul 82. (7") *(CLUB 1)* **DO IT TODAY. / TOUCHDOWN**   □   –
(above was co-issued with 'Phonogram')

Oct 82. (lp) *(Y 28LP)* **STATION MXJY**   □   –
– Dancing on my boomerang / Do it today / Let it take you there / Searching for a feeling / Where's Pete / Temple bomb twist / Mouse an' me / All wrapped up!

— **CATSIS** rejoined repl. EVANS

— guests on below were **PETA** – vocals / **DENNIS BOVELL** – production, vocals / **NELLY** – percussion

	Garage	not iss.

Apr 83. (7"/12") *(GAR 1/+12)* **WHY CAN'T WE LIVE TOGETHER. / MAN OF TRIBES**   □   –

— disbanded after the commercial failure of above

GLOVE (see under ⇒ SIOUXSIE AND THE BANSHEES)

Jeremy GLUCK (see under ⇒ BARRACUDAS)

GO-BETWEENS

Formed: Brisbane, Australia ... 1978 by ROBERT FORSTER (guitar, vocals) and GRANT McLENNAN (vocals, lead guitar, bass) with DENNIS CANTWELL on drums. After a debut Australian-only 7" single, 'LEE REMICK', CANTWELL was replaced with TIM MUSTAFA while organist MALCOLM KELLY was brought in briefly for the early classic, 'PEOPLE SAY', the band's second and final domestic release (were also on the books of

'Beserkley' UK for a few months). Finally settling with LINDY MORRISON on drums, The GO-BETWEENS recorded two singles for seminal Scottish indie label, 'Postcard', before settling in London and signing with 'Rough Trade'. Their debut, 'SEND ME A LULLABY' (1982), drew comparisons with The TALKING HEADS, although their root influences remained the classic songwriting of BOB DYLAN and The VELVET UNDERGROUND. Following the addition of ROBERT VICKERS on bass, allowing McLENNAN to switch to guitar, 'BEFORE HOLLYWOOD' (1983) was a marked improvement. The twin songwriting and singing strength of McLENNAN and FORSTER was developing apace, the former's 'CATTLE AND CANE' a yearning, melancholy highlight. Rave reviews abounded and the band were soon signed to the Warner Brothers-affiliated 'Sire' label. 'SPRING HILL FAIR' (1984) marked the GO-BETWEENS major label debut, their swooning melodies enhanced by a superior production on classics like 'BACHELOR KISSES'. Again the band were heralded by the press and adored by a cult following yet a commercial breakthrough proved elusive. The group switched labels yet again (moving to 'Beggar's Banquet') for 'LIBERTY BELLE AND THE BLACK DIAMOND EXPRESS' (1986), the band's most accessible, and probably finest effort of their career; it remains a mystery why the lush guitar-pop of 'SPRING RAIN' failed to breach the charts. With the addition of AMANDA BROWN (guitar, violin, oboe, keyboards), the band cut the more ambitious 'TALLULAH' (1987) and despite a couple of strong singles, were still confined to the indie margins. Understandably, the group were miffed at their lack of any real success and '16 LOVERS LANE' (1988), another sterling set of consummate, painstakingly crafted songs, proved to be their final effort. The record reached a lowly No.81 on the UK chart, The GO-BETWEENS finally going their own way with McLENNAN and FORSTER both embarking on solo careers. FORSTER's 1991 debut, 'DANGER IN THE PAST' was a fine effort, its sound not much of a departure from the later GO-BETWEENS albums. 'CALLING FROM A COUNTRY PHONE' (1993) was rootsier, employing such traditional instrumentation as banjo and mandolin. McLENNAN initially worked on the more avant-garde project, JACK FROST, with STEVE KILBEY of The CHURCH, before releasing 'WATERSHED' in 1991 as G.W. McLENNAN. Another two fine albums followed with 'FIREBOY' (1993) and 'HORSEBREAKER STAR' (1994), FORSTER releasing an album of covers the same year: I HAD A NEW YORK GIRLFRIEND'. 'BELLAVISTA TERRACE: THE BEST OF THE GO-BETWEENS' was issued as a sort of updated version of the lost and very rare '1978-1990', containing some of the group's best tracks that never made it into the charts (FORSTER's bitter linear notes are a tad tiresome). Yes, they was all there in their full glory: 'PART COMPANY', 'HEAD FULL OF STEAM' and the truly fantastic 'BYE BYE PRIDE' were some of the best singles that nobody heard for a long time. In a strange twist to the band's legacy, FORSTER and McLENNAN re-joined to split the songwriting credits on a brand new GO-BETWEENS album entitled 'FRIENDS OF RACHEL WORTH' (2000). Enlisting the help of SLEATER-KINNEY (the other members of the GO-B's refused to take part), the album sounded like it was recorded by LOU REED's mountain dwelling brother, with tracks such as 'GOING BLIND' and 'GERMAN FARMHOUSE' both returing back to the folksy, rock/pop sound that made the band so attractive in the beginning.

• **Songwriters:** All compositions by FORSTER and McLENNAN, with LINDY MORRISON contributing some. McLENNAN covered BALLAD OF EASY RIDER (Byrds). FORSTER covered; NATURE'S WAY (Spirit) / BROKEN HEARTED PEOPLE (...Clarke) / ECHO BEACH (Martha & The Muffins) / TELL ME THAT IT ISN'T TRUE (Bob Dylan) / 2541 (Bob Mould) / ANYTIME (... Nelson) / LOCKED AWAY (Richards-Jordan) / LOOK OUT HERE COMES TOMORROW (Neil Diamond) / ALONE (Kelly-Steinberg) / BIRD (...Hansoms) / FRISCO DEPOT (Mickey Newbury) / 3 A.M. (Anderson-Todd). • **Trivia:** In 1991, FORSTER and McLENNAN did support slot to LLOYD COLE on a Toronto gig, which prompted GO-BETWEENS reformation rumours.

Album rating: SEND ME A LULLABY (*7) / BEFORE HOLLYWOOD (*8) / SPRING HILL FAIR (*7) / LIBERTY BELLE AND THE BLACK DIAMOND EXPRESS (*7) / TALLULAH (*7) / 16 LOVERS LANE (*8) / THE GO-BETWEENS 1979-1990 compilation (*9) / Robert Forster: DANGER IN THE PAST (*6) / CALLING FROM A COUNTRY PHONE (*6) / I HAD A NEW YORK GIRLFRIEND (*5) / WARM NIGHTS (*5) / G.W. McLennan: WATERSHED (*7) / FIREBOY (*6) / HORSEBREAKER STAR (*7) / IN YOUR BRIGHT RAY (*6) / Go-Betweens: BELLAVISTA TERRACE compilation (*8) / THE FRIENDS OF RACHEL WORTH (*7)

GRANT McLENNAN (b.12 Feb'58, Rock Hampton, Australia) – vocals, lead guitar, bass / **ROB FORSTER** (b.29 Jun'57) – guitar, vocals / **DENNIS CANTWELL** – drums

Abel / not iss. / Austra

Oct 78. (7") *(AB 001)* **LEE REMICK. / KAREN**

— added **TIM MUSTAFA** – drums + **MALCOLM KELLY** – organ to repl. CANTWELL

Oct 79. (7") *(AB 004)* **PEOPLE SAY. / DON'T LET HIM COME BACK** — Austra
(above released UK Nov86 as 12"ep on 'Situation 2'; *SIT 44T*)

— **LINDY MORRISON** (b. 2 Nov'51) – drums (ex-ZERO) repl. TIM + MALCOLM

Postcard / not iss.

Nov 80. (7") *(80-4)* **I NEED TWO HEADS. / STOP BEFORE YOU SAY IT**

Jul 81. (7") *(81-9)* **YOUR TURN, MY TURN. / WORLD WEARY**
(*possibly not issued in UK, released on their Australian label, 'Missing Link'; MISS 29*)

Rough Trade / not iss.

Jun 82. (lp) *(ROUGH 45)* **SEND ME A LULLABY**
— Your turn, my turn / One thing can hold us / People know / The girls have moved / Midnight to neon / Eight pictures / Careless / All about strength / Ride / Hold your horses / Arrow in a bow / It could be anyone. <*US cd-iss. 1990 on 'Beggars Banquet'; 92702*> (*cd re-mast.Jun02 on 'Circus'+=; FYL 009*) – Sunday night / One word / I need two heads / Clowns are in town / Serenade sound / Hope / Stop before you say it / World weary / Distant hands / Undo what you did / Cracked wheat / After the fireworks / Your turn my turn (video).

Jul 82. (7") *(RT 108)* **HAMMER THE HAMMER. / BY CHANCE**

— added **ROBERT VICKERS** (b.25 Nov'59) – bass

Feb 83. (7") *(RT 124)* **CATTLE AND CANE. / HEAVEN SAYS**

Sep 83. (lp) *(ROUGH 54)* **BEFORE HOLLYWOOD**
— A bad debt follows you / Two steps step out / Before Hollywood / Dusty in here / Ask / Having it all / By chance / As long as that / On my block / That way. (*cd-iss. Jun90; LCD 54*) <*US cd-iss. 1990 on 'Beggars Banquet'; 92703*> (*cd re-mast.Jun02 on 'Circus'+=; FYL 010*) – Hammer the hammer / Heaven says / Just a king in mirrors / Peaceful wreck / Man o' sand to girl o' sea / Near the chimney / This girl black girl / Exception of deception / Cattle and cane (video).

Oct 83. (7") *(RT 114)* **MAN O' SAND TO GIRL O' SEA. / THIS GIRL BLACK GIRL**

Sire / not iss.

Jul 84. (7") *(W 9211)* **PART COMPANY. / JUST A KING IN MIRRORS**
(12"+=) *(W 9211T)* – Newton told me.

Sep 84. (lp) *(925 179-1)* **SPRING HILL FAIR**
— Bachelor kisses / Five words / The old way out / You've never lived / Part company / Slow slow music / Draining the pool for you / River of money / Unkind and unwise / Man o' sand girl o' sea. <*US cd-iss. 1990 on 'Beggars Banquet'; 82003*> (*cd re-mast.Jun02 on 'Circus'+=; FYL 011*) – Emperor's courtesan / Rare breed / Newton told me / Just right for him / Attraction / The power that I now have / Second hand furniture / Marco Polo Jr. / Sweet tasting hours / Unkind and unwise (instrumental) / Bachelor kisses (video).

Sep 84. (7") *(W 9156)* **BACHELOR KISSES. / RARE BREED**
(12"+=) *(W 9156T)* – Unkind and unwise (instrumental).

Beggars Banquet / Big Time

Feb 86. (7") *(BEG 155)* **SPRING RAIN. / LIFE AT HAND**
(12"+=) *(BEG 155T)* – Little Joe.

Mar 86. (lp/c) *(BEGA/BEGC 72)* <*6010*> **LIBERTY BELLE AND THE BLACK DIAMOND EXPRESS**
— Spring rain / The ghost and the black hat / The wrong road / To reach me / Twin layers of lightning / In the core of the flame / Head full of steam / Palm Sunday (on board the S.S.Within) / Apology accepted. (*re-iss. Feb89 on 'Beggars Banquet-Lowdown' lp/c)(cd; BBL/+C 72)(BBL 72CD*)

May 86. (7") *(BEG 159)* **HEAD FULL OF STEAM. / DON'T LET HIM COME BACK**
(12"+=) *(BEG 159T)* – The wrong road.

— added **AMANDA BROWN** (b.17 Nov'65) – keyboards, violin, guitar, oboe

Feb 87. (7") *(BEG 183)* **RIGHT HERE. / WHEN PEOPLE ARE DEAD**
(12"+=) *(BEG 183T)* – Don't call me gone.
(d7"++=) *(BEG 183D)* – A little romance (live).

May 87. (7") *(BEG 190)* **CUT IT OUT. / TIME IN DESERT**
(12"+=) *(BEG 190T)* – Doo wop in "A".

Jun 87. (lp/c/cd) *(BEGA/BEGC 81)(BEGA 81CD)* <*6042*> **TALLULAH** | 91 |
— Right here / You tell me / Someone else's wife / I just get caught out / Cut it out / The house that Jack Kerouac built / Bye bye pride / Spirit of a vampyre / The Clarke sisters / Hope then strife. (*re-iss. Feb90 on 'Beggars Banquet-Lowdown' cd)(c/lp; BEGA 81CD)(BEGC/BEGA 81*)

Aug 87. (7"/12") *(BEG 194/+T)* **BYE BYE PRIDE. / THE HOUSE THAT JACK KEROUAC BUILT**

— **JOHN WILSTEED** (b.13 Feb'57) – bass; repl. VICKERS

Beggars Banquet / Capitol

Jul 88. (7") *(BEG 218)* <*4BX 44262*> **STREETS OF YOUR TOWN. / WAIT UNTIL JUNE**
(12"+=) *(BEG 218T)* – Casanova's last words.
(cd-s++=) *(BEG 218CD)* – Spring rain / Right here.

Aug 88. (lp/c/cd) *(BEGA/BEGC 95)(BEGA 95CD)* <*91230*> **16 LOVERS LANE** | 81 |
— Love goes on / Quiet heart / Love is a sign / You can't say no forever / The Devil's eye / Streets of your town / Clouds / Was there anything I could do? / I'm alright / Dive for your memory.

Oct 88. (7") *(BEG 219)* **WAS THERE ANYTHING I COULD DO. / ROCK'N'ROLL FRIEND**
(12"+=) *(BEG 219T)* – Mexican postcard.
(cd-s++=) *(BEG 219CD)* – Bye bye pride.

— split on the day we moved into the 90's. FORSTER and McLENNAN went solo. The latter also being part of JACK FROST with STEVE KILBEY of The CHURCH. AMANDA formed CLEOPATRA WONG.

ROBERT FORSTER

— (solo, with MICK HARVEY – producer)

Beggars Banquet / Beggars Banquet

Sep 90. (7") *(BEG 245)* **BABY STONES. / THE LAND THAT TIME FORGOT**

Oct 90. (cd)(c/lp) *(BEGA 113CD)(BEGA/BEGC 113)* <*3028*> **DANGER IN THE PAST**
— Baby stones / The river people / Leave here satisfied / Heart out to tender / Is this what you call change / Dear black dream / Danger in the past / I've been looking for somebody / Justice.

Apr 93. (cd/c) *(BBQ CD/MC 127)* **CALLING FROM A COUNTRY PHONE**
— Atlanta lie low / 121 / The circle / Falling star / I want to be quiet / Cats life / Girl to a world / Drop / Beyond theit law / Forever & time. (*cd re-iss. Sep95 on 'Beggars Banquet-Lowdown'; BBL 127CD*)

— with **JOHN KEANE** – guitars, banjos, keyboards, bass, etc / **JOEL MORRIS** – drums / **STEVE VENZ** – bass / **ANDY CARLSON** – guitars, mandolin / **TIM WHITE & BILL HOLMES** – porga & piano / **DWIGHT MANNING** – oboe / **SYD STRAW** – backing vocals

		Beggars Banquet	Atlantic
Jul 94.	(cd-ep) *(BBQ 38CD)* **2541 / 3 a.m. / FREDDIE FENDER / DANGER IN THE PAST (live)**	□	-
Aug 94.	(cd/c) *(BBQ CD/MC 161) <92482>* **I HAD A NEW YORK GIRLFRIEND** – Nature's way / Broken hearted people / Echo beach / Tell me that it isn't true / 2541 / Anytime / Locked away / Look out loves comes tomorrow / Alone / Bird / Frisco depot / 3 a.m.	□	-

		Beggars Banquet	Beggars Banquet
Jul 96.	(cd-ep) *(BEG 300CD)* **CRYIN' LOVE / HALF THE WAY HOME / HYPNOTIZED**	□	-
Aug 96.	(cd)(lp) *(BEGL 185CD)(BEGA 185) <80185>* **WARM NIGHTS** – I can do / Warn nights / Cryin' love / Snake skin lady / Loneliness / Jug of wine / Fortress / Rock-n-roll friend / On a street corner / I'll jump.	□	Sep96

G.W. McLENNAN

		Beggars Banquet	Beggars Banquet
Mar 91.	(12"ep/cd-ep) *(BEG 247 T/CD)* **WHEN WORD GETS AROUND / BLACK MULE / SHE'S SO STRANGE / THE MAN WHO DIED IN RAPTURE**	□	-
May 91.	(12"ep/cd-ep) *(BEG 254 T/CD)* **EASY COME EASY GO. / MAKING IT RIGHT FOR HER / STONES FOR YOU (trumpet version)**	□	-
Jun 91.	(cd)(c/lp) *(BEGACD 118)(BEG/BEGC 118)* **WATERSHED** – When word gets around / Haven't I been a fool / Haunted house / Stones for you / Easy come easy go / Black mule / Rory the weeks back on / You can't have everything / Sally's revolution / Broadway bride / Just get that straight / Dream about tomorrow.	□	-

		Beggars Banquet	Atlantic
Jan 93.	(cd-ep) *(BBQ 2CD)* **FINGERS / WHOSE SIDE ARE YOU ON? / WHAT WENT WRONG (original)**	□	-
Feb 93.	(cd-ep) *(BBQ 11CD)* **LIGHTING FIRES / DARK SIDE OF TOWN / IF I SHOULD FALL BEHIND**	□	-
Mar 93.	(cd/c) *(BBQ CD/MC 127) <92387>* **FIREBOY** – Lighting fires / Surround me / One million miles from here / The dark side of town / Things will change / The pawnbroker / Whose side are you on? / Fingers / Signs of life / The day my eyes Came back / Bathe (in the water) / When I close my eyes / Riddle in the rain.	□	Jun94
Nov 94.	(d-cd/c) *(BBQ CD/MC 162)* **HORSEBREAKER STAR** – Simone & Perry / Ice in Heaven / What went wrong / Race day rag / Don't you cry for me no more / Put you down / Late afternoon in early August / Coming up for air / Ballad of Easy Rider / Open invitation / Open my eyes / From my lips / / Dropping you / Hot water / Keep my word / Do your own thing / That's that / If I was a girl / Head over heels / Girl in a beret / All her songs / No peace in the palace / I'll call you wild / Horsebreaker star. *(re-iss. d-cd Sep95 on 'Beggars Banquet-Lowdown'; BEGA 162CD)*	□	-
Jun 95.	(cd-ep) *(BBQ 57CD)* **SIMONE & PERRY / DON'T YOU CRY FOR ME NO MORE / BALLAD OF EASY RIDER / WHAT WENT WRONG (original)**	□	-
Jul 97.	(cd) *(BBQCD 192)* **IN YOUR BRIGHT RAY** – In your bright ray / Cave in / One plus one / Sea breeze / Malibu '69 / Who said love was dead / Room for skin / All them pretty angels / Comet scar / Down here / Lamp by lamp / Do you see the lights / Parade of shadows.	□	-

GO-BETWEENS

— re-formed with **FORSTER + McLENNAN** plus SLEATER-KINNEY:- **CORIN TUCKER, CARRIE BROWNSTEIN + JANET WEISS**

		Circus	Jetset
Sep 00.	(cd) *(CIRCUSCD 004) <TWA 31>* **THE FRIENDS OF RACHEL WORTH** – Magic in here / Spirit / The clock / German farmhouse / He lives my life / Heart and home / Surfing magazines / Orpheus beach / Going blind / When she sang about angels. *(lp-iss.on 'Clear Spot'; 054251) (re-mast.JUn02; FYL 003)*	□	□
Oct 00.	(cd-s) *(CIRCUSCDS 002) <TWA 32>* **GOING BLIND / WOMAN ACROSS THE WAY / THE LOCUST GIRLS**	□	□

– compilations, others, etc. –

1982.	(lp) *Man Made;* **VERY QUICK ON THE EYE – BRISBANE 1981 (demo)**		-
1985.	(lp) *P.V.C.; <PVC 8942>* **METAL AND SHELLS**	-	□
Oct 89.	(12"ep/cd-ep) *Strange Fruit; (SFPS/+CD 074) / Dutch East India; <8339>* **THE PEEL SESSIONS** – The power that I have now / Second hand furniture / Fire woods / Rare breed.	□	1991
Mar 90.	(cd)(c/d-lp) *Beggars Banquet; (BEGA 104CD)(BEGC/BEGA 104) / Capitol; <94681>* **THE GO-BETWEENS 1979-1990** – Hammer the hammer / I need two heads / Cattle and cane / When people are dead / Man o' sand to girl o' sea / Bachelor kisses / People say / Draining the pool for you / World weary / Spring rain / Rock and roll friend / Dusty in here / The Clarke sisters / Right here / Second-hand furniture / Bye bye pride / This girl, black girl / The house that Jack Kerouac built / Don't call me gone / Streets of our own town / Love is a sign / You won't find it again. *(c+=/d-lp+=)* – Karen / 8 pictures / The sound of rain / The wrong road / Mexican postcard.		
Apr 99.	(cd) *Tag; (TAGCD 002) / Jetset; <TWA 019>* **THE LOST ALBUM 1978-1979**		
May 99.	(d-cd) *Beggars Banquet; (BBL2 020CD) <82020>* **BELLAVISTA TERRACE: THE BEST OF THE GO-BETWEENS** – Was there anything I could do? / Head full of steam / That way / Part company / Cattle and cane / Draining the pool for you / The wrong road / Bye bye pride / Man o' sand to girl o' sea / The house that Jack Kerouac built / Bachelor kisses / Streets of your town / Spring rain / Dive for your memory.		

GOBLIN MIX / EXPLODING BUDGIES
(see under ⇒ 3Ds; 90's section)

GODFATHERS

Formed: London, England . . . 1983 as The SID PRESLEY EXPERIENCE by the COYNE brothers PETER and CHRIS, along with DEL BARTLE and KEVIN MOONEY. This basic post-punk aggregate released two singles, 'HUP TWO THREE FOUR' and a version of John Lennon's 'COLD TURKEY', before splintering early '85 into two factions that almost immediately fought over the group moniker. When the brothers lost out in the ensuing court battle to retain the group name, they chose The GODFATHERS instead, recruiting KRIS DOLLIMORE, MIKE GIBSON and GEORGE MAZUR and adopting a glowering, sharp-suited "Kray Twins" persona. After a clutch of fiery garage-punk/R&B singles on their own 'Corporate Image' imprint (namely 'LONELY MAN', 'THIS DAMN NATION', 'I WANT EVERYTHING' and 'LOVE IS DEAD'), they took the money and ran with 'Epic', the Brothers and Co finally issuing their first album proper in the shape of 'BIRTH, SCHOOL, WORK, DEATH' (early '88). Their second album for the label, 'MORE SONGS ABOUT LOVE AND HATE' (1989), cracked the UK Top 50 while, like its predecessor, the record made inroads into the US charts. With CHRIS BURROWS replacing DOLLIMORE, The GODFATHERS delivered a parting shot for 'Epic', in the shape of 'UNREAL WORLD' (1991), the label leaving the band to swim with the (indie) fishes after they'd failed to hit the sales target once again. Further personnel troubles dogged The GODFATHERS family when MAZUR and GIBSON went AWOL, leaving the inner core of the brothers to crack on with two 'Intercord' released sets, 'THE GODFATHERS aka ORANGE' (1993) and 'AFTERLIFE' (1996). • **Songwriters:** COYNE brothers, except; SUN ARISE (Rolf Harris) / BLITZKRIEG BOP (Ramones) / HOW DOES IT FEEL TO FEEL (Creation).

Album rating: HIT BY HIT mini compilation (*6) / BIRTH, SCHOOL, WORK, DEATH (*6) / MORE SONGS ABOUT LOVE AND HATE (*5) / UNREAL WORLD (*5) / DOPE, ROCK'N'ROLL AND FU**ING IN THE STREETS collection (*5) / THE GODFATHERS aka ORANGE (*4) / AFTERLIFE (*4) / BIRTH, SCHOOL, WORK, DEATH: THE BEST OF THE GODFATHERS compilation (*6)

SID PRESLEY EXPERIENCE

PETER COYNE – vocals / **DEL BARTLE** – guitar / **CHRIS COYNE** – bass / **KEVIN MOONEY** – drums

		I.D.	not iss.
May 84.	(7"/12") *(EYE/+T 4)* **HUP TWO THREE FOUR. / PUBLIC ENEMY NO.1**	□	-
		S.P.E.	not iss.
Dec 84.	(7") *(SPE 41)* **COLD TURKEY. / FIREWATER / 'F' FOR FAKE**	□	-

— split early '85. DEL and KEVIN formed The UNHOLY TRINITY (with bassist TIM ARROWSMITH), releasing a sole early '86 mini-set, 'RISE TO THE OCCASION' for 'Communique'.

The GODFATHERS

— were formed by the **COYNE** brothers **PETER + CHRIS** with also **MIKE GIBSON** (b. London) – guitar / **KRIS DOLLIMORE** (b.Isle Of Sheppey, Kent, England) – guitar / **GEORGE MAZUR** (b.Bradford, England) – drums

		Corporate Image	not iss.
Oct 85.	(7") *(GFTR 010)* **LONELY MAN. / I WANT YOU** (12"ep+=) **CAPO DI TUTTI CAPI** *(GFTR 010T)* – Sticks and stones.	□	-
Apr 86.	(12"m) *(GRFT 020)* **THIS DAMN NATION. / CAN'T LEAVE HER ALONE / JOHN BARRY**	□	-
Sep 86.	(7") *(GFTR 030)* **SUN ARISE. / I WANT EVERYTHING** (12"+=) *(GFTR 030T)* – I'm unsatisfied.	□	-
Nov 86.	(m-lp) *(GFTRLP 010)* **HIT BY HIT** (compilation) – I want everything / This damn nation / I want you / Can't leave her alone / Sun arise / Cold turkey / John Barry / Sticks & stones / I'm unsatisfied / Lonely man. *(re-iss. Dec87 c/cd+=; GFTR C/CD 010)* – Angela / Gone to Texas. *<US-iss.1987 on 'Link'; LINK 009>*	□	-
Feb 87.	(7") *(GFTR 040)* **LOVE IS DEAD. / ANGELA** (12"+=) *(GFTR 040T)* – ('A'remix) / Gone to Texas.	□	-

		Epic	Epic
Nov 87.	(7") *<34-07725>* **BIRTH, SCHOOL, WORK, DEATH (long). / BIRTH, SCHOOL, WORK, DEATH (short)**	-	□
Feb 88.	(7"/7"box) *(GFT Z/B 1)* **BIRTH, SCHOOL, WORK, DEATH. / IF I ONLY HAD TIME** (12"/12"s) *(GFT ZT/Q 1)* – ('A'-resurrection mix) / S.T.B. / Miss that girl.	□	-
Feb 88.	(lp/c/cd) *(460583-1/-4/-2) <40946>* **BIRTH, SCHOOL, WORK, DEATH** – Birth, school, work, death / If I only had time / Tell me why / It's so hard / When am I coming down / 'Cause I said so / The strangest boy / S.T.B. / Just like you / Obsession / Love is dead.	80	91
Jul 88.	(7"/7"pic-d) *(GFT/+P 2)* **'CAUSE I SAID SO. / WHEN AM I COMING DOWN (live)** (12"+=/cd-s+=) *(GFTT/CDGFT 2)* – I can only give you everything / Cold turkey (live).	□	-
Nov 88.	(7"/7"g-f/7"pic-d) *(GFT/+G/P 3)* **LOVE IS DEAD. / THOSE DAYS ARE OVER (live)** (12"+=/cd-s+=) *(GFTT/CDGFT 3)* – ('A'-Corporate Image version) / I'm satisfied (live).	□	-
Nov 88.	(12"ep) *<EAS 1377>* **LOVE IS DEAD / BIRTH, SCHOOL, WORK, DEATH. / COLD TURKEY (live) / THOSE DAYS ARE OVER (live) / WHEN AM I COMING DOWN (live)**	-	□
Apr 89.	(7"/7"box/7"pic-d) *(GFT/+B/P 4)* **SHE GIVES ME LOVE. / WALKING TALKING JOHNNY CASH BLUES** (12"+=/cd-s+=) *(GFTT/CDGFT 4)* – Just because you're not paranoid doesn't mean to say they're not out to get you!	□	-

GODFATHERS (cont)

May 89. (lp/c/cd) (463394-1/-4/-2) <45023> **MORE SONGS ABOUT LOVE AND HATE** `49`
– She gives me love / Those days are over / How low is low / Pretty girl / This is your life / I'm lost and then I'm found / I don't believe in you / Life has passed us by / Walking talking Johnny Cash blues / Halfway paralysed / Another you.

—— CHRIS BURROWS – guitar, vocals; repl. DOLLIMORE

Feb 90. (7") (GFT 5) **I'M LOST AND THEN I'M FOUND. / STILL ALONE**
(10") (GFTQT 5) – ('A'side) / Walking talking Johnny Cash blues / Blitzkrieg bop (live) / How low is low (live).
(12"/cd-s) **OUT ON THE FLOOR EP** (GFT T/C 5) – ('A'side) / Birth, school, work, death (extended) / She gives me love (Keith Le Blanc love mix) / She gives me love (mega dance authority mix).

Feb 91. (12"ep/cd-ep) (656648-6/-2) **UNREAL WORLD / SOMETHING GOOD ABOUT YOU. / THIS IS YOUR LIFE (live) / THIS DAMN NATION (live)**

Mar 91. (cd/c/lp) (466952-2/-4/-1) <46026> **UNREAL WORLD**
– Unreal world / Don't let me down / King of misery / Believe in yourself / I'll never forget what's his name / How does it feel to feel / Drag me down again / Something good about you / I love what's happening to me / Can't try harder / This is war.

—— MAZUR + GIBSON departed

                                                                                   Survival not iss.

1993. (cd-s) (SUR 719CD) **STRANGE ABOUT TODAY / THAT'S THE WAY I FEEL**

                                                                                   Intercord not iss.

Oct 93. (cd) (986974) **THE GODFATHERS aka ORANGE**
– Free yourself / Strange about today / World on fire / Trip on you / That's the way I feel / Help me now / Losing my mind / She said / The prisoner / Seven days / 21st century dreaming / Time is now. (re-iss. Apr96 as 'THE GODFATHERS – GOLDEN DELICIOUS' on 'I.R.S.'; 988874CD)

Nov 95. (cd-s) **THAT SPECIAL FEELING / I CAN'T HEAR YOU / YOU'RE MY FRIEND**

Feb 96. (cd) (IRS 845255CD) **AFTERLIFE**
– Love is real / Hear what I say / That special feeling / I can't hear you / You're my friend / Close to Jesus / I'm not well / Mother nicotine / Tim'e not on your side / Give me something / Afterlife.

—— the GODFATHERS have since broken up

– compilations etc. –

Feb 89. (12"ep/cd-ep) Strange Fruit – Night Tracks; (SFNT/+CD 019) / Dutch East India; <DEI 8011> **THE BBC SESSION**   Oct91
– If I only had time / I want everything / I'm unsatisfied / I want you.

Jun 92. (cd/c/lp) Corporate Image; (GFTR CD/MC/LP 020) **DOPE, ROCK'N'ROLL AND FU**ING IN THE STREETS (live)**
– Birth, school, work, death / She gives me love / Unreal world / I don't believe in you / Drag me down again / When am I coming down / Obsession / I love what's happening to me / If I only had time / Lonely man / Don't let me down / I want everything / 'Cause I said so / This damn nation / This is war / Cold turkey. (lp w/lp+=; GFTRX 020) – live at the Venue, London, Feb 14, 1992:- Walking Johnny Cash blues / This is your life / King of misery / Blitzkrieg bop.

Jul 96. (cd) Epic; (478423-2) <EK 64789> **BIRTH, SCHOOL, WORK, DEATH (THE BEST OF THE GODFATHERS)**   Apr96
– Birth, school, work, death / She gives me love / Unreal world / Just because you're not paranoid doesn't mean to say they're not going to get you! / Cause I said so / Angela / Walking talking Johnny Cash blues / Miss that girl / This is war / If I only had time / Love is dead / Another you / Gone to Texas / Don't let me down / Lonely man / When am I coming down / Cold turkey / Birth, school, work, death (extended remix).

GOD, MOTHER & COUNTRY
(see under ⇒ RIP, RIG + PANIC)

GOLDEN PALOMINOS

Formed: New York City, New York, USA ... 1981 by drummer ANTON FIER, formerly of Cleveland, Ohio art-rockers, PERE UBU. FIER and his fellow ex-LOUNGE LIZARDS sidekick set about recruiting an array of musicians drawn largely from the NY experimental scene including BILL LASWELL, FRED FRITH JOHN ZORN, NICKY SKOPELITIS, DAVID MOSS and JAMAALADEEN TACUMA to name but a few. Locating a sympathetic stable in the shape of France's 'Celluloid', The GOLDEN PALOMINOS unleashed their eponymous debut album in 1983, a bravely experimental soundclash of avant-funk characterised by LINDSAY's crazed vocals. Heavily imported into Britain and the States, the album's cult success generated much anticipation for a follow-up. This arrived in the shape of 1985's 'VISIONS OF EXCESS', FIER looking beyond NY and bringing in a wildly disparate cast of the hip and not so hip including RICHARD THOMPSON, JACK BRUCE, JOHN LYDON, MICHAEL STIPE, CHRIS STAMEY and unknown female singer, SYD STRAW; most of these (and future) revolving-door guests contributed lyrics to songs written by FIER and guitarist JODY HARRIS. The project took a rootsier turn with 'BLAST OF SILENCE' (1986), new collaborators MATTHEW SWEET, PETER BLEGVAD, SNEAKY PETE KLEINOW and T-BONE BURNETT steering the 'PALOMINOS down the dusty paths of folk, blues and country. A core of FIER, LASWELL, SKOPELITIS, ROBERT KIDNEY (from NUMBERS BAND) and AMANDA KRAMER (from INFORMATION SOCIETY), meanwhile, formed the musical basis for 1989's '- A DEAD HORSE', KRAMER coming into her own on the THROWING MUSES-esque 'DARKLANDS'. The outfit continued to evolve into the 90's, FIER and LASWELL now utilising the talents of MICHAEL STIPE, RICHARD THOMPSON, BOB MOULD and CARLA BLEY on, astonishingly, their first major UK/US effort, 'DRUNK WITH PASSION' (1991). A few years later, the seasoned thoroughbreds were back on track once more with 'THIS IS HOW IT FEELS' (1993), KRAMER being eclipsed in her lead vocal role by co-writer/singer, LORI CARSON. Another new female voice, LYDIA KAVANAUGH, could be heard alongside stalwarts FIER, LASWELL, SKOPELITIS and master funksters, BOOTSY COLLINS and BERNIE WORRELL. The darkly ethereal 'PURE', appeared in 1994 (the following year's 'NO THOUGHT, NO BREATH, NO EYES, NO HEART' was a remixed version), while FIER pared things down dramatically with 1996's 'DEAD HORSE', choosing to work solely with poet, NICOLE BLACKMAN. • **Songwriters:** FIER aided by others too numerous to mention. Covered OMAHA (Moby Grape) / I'VE BEEN THE ONE + BRIDES OF JESUS (Little Feat) / DIAMOND (Peter Holsapple).

Album rating: THE GOLDEN PALOMINOS (*7) / VISIONS OF EXCESS (*7) / BLAST OF SILENCE (*6) / – A DEAD HORSE (*6) / DRUNK WITH PASSION (*7) / THIS IS HOW IT FEELS (*6) / PURE (*6) / DEAD INSIDE (*6) / THE BEST OF THE GOLDEN PALOMINOS 1983-1989 compilation (*7) / RUN PONY RUN compilation (*6)

ANTON FIER (b.20 Jun'56, Cleveland, Ohio) – drums, programming (ex-PERE UBU, ex-FEELIES, ex-LOUNGE LIZARDS) / **ARTO LINDSAY** – vocals, guitar (ex-DNA, ex-LOUNGE LIZARDS) / **BILL LASWELL** – bass, piano (of MATERIAL) / **FRED FRITH** – guitar, violin / **DAVID MOSS** – percussion / **NICKY SKOPELITIS** – guitar / **JAMAALADEEN TACUMA** – bass / **JOHN ZORN** – saxophone / **M.E. MILLER** – vocals / **MICHAEL BEINHORN** – electronics / **PETER BLEGVAD** – vocals

                                                                    Celluloid Celluloid

Jul 85. (lp) (CEL 6662) <5002> **THE GOLDEN PALOMINOS**   – 1983
– Clean plate / Hot seat / Under the cap / Monday night / Cook out / I.D. / Two sided fist. (cd-iss. Dec96 on 'Charly'; CPCD 8198) (cd re-iss. Jan98 on 'Movieplay Gold'; MPG 74049)

—— ANTON, BILL, ARTO + NICKY added JODY HARRIS + RICHARD THOMPSON + HENRY KAISER + MIKE HAMPTON + CHRIS STAMEY – guitar / BERNIE WORRELL + CARLA BLEY – organ / SYD STRAW + MICHAEL STIPE + JOHN LYDON – vocals

Apr 86. (lp) <(CEL 6118)> **VISIONS OF EXCESS**   – French
– Boy (go) / Clustering train / Omaha / The animal speaks / Silver bullet / (Kind of) True / Buenos Aires / Only one party. (cd-iss. Nov95 on 'Charly'; CPCD 8151) (cd re-iss. Jan98 on 'Movieplay Gold'; MPG 74050)

Aug 87. (12") **BOY (GO).**   – – French

—— ROBERT KIDNEY – vocals, guitar (of NUMBERS BAND) / PETER BLEGVAD – vocals / T-BONE BURNETT – vocals, co-producer / DON DIXON – vocals, co-producer / ELLIOTT SHARP / SNEAKY PETE KLEINOW – pedal steel guitar

Oct 87. (lp/c/cd) <(CEL 6127/+CD)> **BLAST OF SILENCE**   – French
– I've been the one / Something becomes nothing / The push and the shove / (Something else is) Working harder / Angels / Diamond / Faithless heart / Work was new / Strong, simple silences / Brides of Jesus. (cd re-iss. Mar98 on 'Movieplay Gold'; MPG 74051)

—— line-up:- FIER, LASWELL, SKOPELITIS, KIDNEY / + AMANDA KRAMER – vocals (ex-INFORMATION SOCIETY) / + featuring BERNIE WORRELL / MICK TAYLOR – guitar (ex-ROLLING STONES) / JEFF BOVA + AIYB DIENG / CHUCK LEAVELL + LARRY SALTZMAN

Aug 89. (lp/c/cd) <(CEL 6138/+CD)> **- A DEAD HORSE**   – French
– Wild river / Shattered image / Angel of death / Lucky / Darklands / A letter back / Over. (re-iss. cd Jun96 on 'Charly'+=; CPCD 8185) – Simple silences / Brides of Jesus.

—— FIER, LASWELL, SKOPELITIS, KRAMER, BLEY, THOMPSON, KIDNEY + MICHAEL STIPE – vocals / BOB MOULD – vocals, guitar (ex-HUSKER DU) / AIYB DIENG

                                                                     Venture Nation – Charisma

Sep 91. (cd/c/lp) (CD/TC+/VE 905) <91745> **DRUNK WITH PASSION**
– Alive and living now / The haunting / When the kingdom cals / A sigh / Thunder cries / Hands of Heaven / Ding from the inside out / Begin to return.

—— FIER, LASWELL, SKOPELITIS, KRAMER, WORRELL plus BOOTSY COLLINS – bass / JEFF BOVA – keyboards / MATT STEIN – programmer / LORI CARSON + LYDIA KAVANAUGH – vocals

                                                                     Restless Restless

Nov 93. (cd-ep) <72749> **PRISON OF THE RHYTHM - THE REMIXES**

Dec 93. (cd) <(72735-2)> **THIS IS HOW IT FEELS**   Sep93
– Sleepwalk / Prison of the rhythm / I'm not sorry / This is how it feels / To a stranger / The wonder / Breakdown / These days / Rain holds / Twist the knife / Bird flying / A divine kiss.

—— In Apr'94, ANTON FIER released a solo album, 'DREAMSPEED' for 'Avant'; AVAN 009

—— KNOX CHANDLER – guitar; repl. WORRELL, STEIN and BOVA

—— KRAMER released her solo set, 'WINTERMASS' for 'Luminous' in '95

Oct 94. (cd) <(72761-2)> **PURE**
– Little suicides / Heaven / Anything / Wings / Pure / No skin / Gun / Break in the road / Touch you.

Dec 94. (12") <72786)> **NO SKIN - THE BANDALU REMIXES**

Mar 95. (cd) <(72790-2)> **NO THOUGHT, NO BREATH, NO EYES, NO HEART** (PURE remixes)
– Heaven (you have to in Hell to see Heaven) / No skin (tempting fate) / Gun – Little suicides (brown stain walls, red jelly corners) / No skin (cold spells) / No skin (aural circumcision) / No skin (funky hornsey).

Apr 95. (cd-ep) <72785> **HEAVEN (mixes)**

—— now only FIER + NICOLE BLACKMAN – poet, etc / KNOX CHANDLER – guitars / NICKY SKOPELITIS – wah wah guitar

Oct 96. (cd) <72907> **DEAD INSIDE**
– Victim / Belfast / Ride / Ambitions are / Drown / Holy / You are never ready / Metal eye / Thirst / Curses.

– compilations, etc. –

1991. (d-cd/d-c) Oceana; <4105-2/-4> **THUNDERING HERD: THE BEST OF THE GOLDEN PALOMINOS**

Sep 92. (cd) Mau Mau; (MAUCD 625) / Restless; <72651> **A HISTORY (1982-1985)**   Jul92
– Hot seat / Under the cap / Monday night / Cookout / I.D. / Two side fist / Boy (go) / Clustering train / Omaha / Animal speaks / Silver bullet / (Kind of) True / Buenos Aires / Only one party.

| Sep 92. | (cd) *Mau Mau; (MAUCD 626) / Restless; <72652>* **A HISTORY (1986-1989)** | | Jul92 |

– I've been the one / Something becomes nothing / The push and the shove / (Something else is) Working harder / Angels / Diamond / Faithless heart / Work was new / Strong, simple silences / Wild river / Shattered image / Angel of death / Lucky / Darklands / A letter black.

Oct 97.	(cd) *Music Club; <(MCCD 316)>* **THE BEST OF THE GOLDEN PALOMINOS 1983-1989**		
Oct 97.	(cd) *Charly; (CDNEW 112)* **THE BEST OF THE GOLDEN PALOMINOS**		-
Jun 00.	(cd) *Metrodome; <(METRO 429)>* **THE ANIMAL SPEAKS** <US-title 'SURREALISTIC SURFER'> (early work)		Jan01
Jun 02.	(cd) *Varese Sarabande; <(VAR 61205)>* **RUN PONY RUN: AN ESSENTIAL COLLECTION**		

– Boy (go) / Omaha / The animal speaks / (Kind of) True / Only one party / Wild river / Shattered image / Darklands / Over / I've been the one / (Something else is) Working harder / Faithless heart / Bridges of Jesus / Clean plate / Under the cap.

Mark GOLDTHORPE & Simon HINKLER
(see under ⇒ ARTERY)

GOODBYE MR MACKENZIE

Formed: Bathgate, Scotland ... 1984 by MARTIN METCALFE, JIMMY ANDERSON, RONA SCOBIE, SHIRLEY MANSON, FINLAY WILSON and DEREK KELLY. They recorded their first 45, 'DEATH OF A SALESMAN', via West Lothian College's 'Scruples' label before relocating to the thriving musical metropolis of Edinburgh. The band subsequently hooked up with Elliot Davis' (WET WET WET manager) 'Precious' label for the release of their debut single, 'THE RATTLER', in Autumn '86. A limited edition 12" follow-up, 'FACE TO FACE', was subsequently issued on the 'Mack' imprint, all proceeds going to the 'Rape Crisis' charity. With the addition of ex-EXPLOITED man and local legend, BIG JOHN DUNCAN, on guitar and a signing to 'Capitol' in 1988, the group looked set to follow in the footsteps of DEACON BLUE who'd broken big earlier that year. As intelligent and subtly creative as the latter outfit with a more alternative slant, GOODBYE MR MACKENZIE's sound hinged upon METCALFE's powerful BRUCE SPRINGSTEEN / NEIL DIAMOND-esque vocals and their knack for a rousing chorus. Continually tipped for the top, the band at last broke the Top 40 in early '89 with a re-recorded version of 'THE RATTLER', their much anticipated debut album, 'GOOD DEEDS AND DIRTY RAGS' making the Top 30 a few months later. Yet it wasn't to be, a flop set of live/rare tracks, 'FISH HEADS AND TAILS' (1989) and further clutch of minor hit singles no doubt convincing 'Capitol' to shelve a proposed follow-up album, 'HAMMER AND TONGS'. Help came in the form of M.C.A. subsidiary, 'Radioactive', who finally issued the record in Spring '91. By now, of course, much of the early buzz and momentum had been lost and the band drifted into obscurity. While various members went on to bigger and better things – DUNCAN as a roadie and sometime touring replacement with NIRVANA (these days he's a familiar face at Edinburgh's sterling Cafe Graffiti club) and MANSON with the massively successful GARBAGE – the remnants of the original line-up recorded albums such as 'FIVE' (1993) and 'JEZEBEL' (1995) to minimal interest. • **Songwriters:** All written by METCALFE-KELLY, except AMSTERDAM (Jaques Brel) / GREEN GREEN GRASS OF HOME (Engelbert Humperdinck) / HEROES (David Bowie) / CANDY SAYS (Velvet Underground) / FRIDAY'S CHILD (Lee Hazlewood) / THE WAY I WALK (J.Scott). • **Trivia:** METCALFE refused to pay his poll tax (community charge) early in 1990 due to the Scots being used as its guinea-pigs for the first year.

Album rating: GOOD DEEDS AND DIRTY RAGS (*7) / HAMMER AND TONGS (*6) / LIVE: ON THE DAY OF STORMS (*5) / FIVE (*5)

MARTIN METCALFE – vocals, guitar / **SHIRLEY MANSON** (b. 3 Aug'66, Edinburgh) – vocals, keyboards / **JIMMY ANDERSON** – guitar / **RONA SCOBIE** – keyboards, vocals / **FINLAY WILSON** – bass / (DEREK) **KELLY** – drums

Scruples   not iss.

| Nov 84. | (7") *(YTS 1)* **DEATH OF A SALESMAN. / (other track by Lindy Bergman)** | | - |

Precious   not iss.

| Sep 86. | (7") *(JEWEL 2)* **THE RATTLER. / CANDLESTICK PARK** (12"+=) *(JEWEL 2T)* – The end. | | - |

Clandestine   not iss.

| Oct 87. | (12"ltd) *(MACK 1)* **FACE TO FACE. / SECRETS. / GOOD DEEDS** | | - |

– (above proceeds went to Rape Crisis charity)

– BIG JOHN DUNCAN – guitar (ex-EXPLOITED, ex-BLOOD UNCLES) repl. ANDERSON

Capitol   Capitol

| Jul 88. | (7") *(CL 501)* **GOODBYE MR. MACKENZIE. / GREEN TURN RED** | 62 | - |

(ext.12"+=/ext.12"g-f+=)(ext.cd-s+=) *(12CL/+G 501)(CLCD 501)* – Knockin' on Joe.

| Nov 88. | (7"/7"g-f) *(CL/+G 513)* **OPEN YOUR ARMS. / SECRETS** | | - |

(ext.12"+=/ext.12"pic-d+=) *(12CL/+P 513)* – Amsterdam.
(ext.12"g-f+=/ext.cd-s++=) *(12CLG/CLCD 513)* – Pleasure search.

| Feb 89. | (7"/7"g-f) *(CL/+G 52)* **THE RATTLER. / HERE COMES DEACON BRODIE** | 37 | - |

(ext.12"+=) *(12CL 522)* – Calton Hill.
(12"w-poster++=/cd-s++=) *(12CLG/CLCD 522)* – Drunken sailor.

| Apr 89. | (lp/c/cd) *(EST/TCEST/CDEST 2089) <92638>* **GOOD DEEDS AND DIRTY RAGS** | 26 | |

– Open your arms / Wake it up / His master's voice / Goodwill city / Candlestick park / Goodbye Mr. Mackenzie / The rattler / Dust / You generous thing you / Good deeds. *(free-12"; GMM12 1) (c+=/cd+=)* – Amsterdam / Calton Hill / Secrets / Knockin' on Joe.

| Jul 89. | (7"/7"box/c-s) *(CL/CLX/TCCL 538)* **GOODWILL CITY. / I'M SICK OF YOU** | 49 | |

(ext.12"+=) *(12CL 538)* – What's got into you.
(ext.12"g-f++=/cd-s++=) *(12CLG/CLCD 538)* – Insidious thing.

| Oct 89. | (lp/c/cd) *(CAPS/TCCAPS/CDCAPS 2001) <3357>* **FISH HEADS AND TAILS** (live & rare compilation) | | |

– Amsterdam / Somewhere in China / Face to face / Knockin' on Joe / Sick of you / Green turn red / Pleasure search / Strangle your animal * / Mystery train / Here comes Deacon Brodie (live) *. *(cd+= *)

Parlophone   Capitol

| Apr 90. | (7"/c-s) *(R/TCR 6247)* **LOVE CHILD. / HEROES** | 52 | - |

(ext.12"+=) *(12R 6247)* – You generous thing you (live).
(dance.12"w-poster+=) *(12RX 6247)* – Goodwill city (Cava mix) / The rattler (live).
(cd-s) *(CDR 6247)* – ('A'side) / Goodwill city (live) / You generous thing you (live).

| Jun 90. | (7"/c-s) *(R/TCR 6257)* **BLACKER THAN BLACK. / GREEN GREEN GRASS OF HOME** | 61 | - |

(ext.12"+=) *(12R 6257)* – Mad cow disease.
(12"pic-d++=/cd-s++=) *(12RPD/CDR 6257)* – His masters voice.

Radioactive   M.C.A.

| Feb 91. | (7"/c-s) *(MCS/+C 1506)* **NOW WE ARE MARRIED. / FRIDAY'S CHILD** | | - |

(ext.12"+=/ext.12"g-f+=/cd-s+=) *(MCST/+G/D 1506)* – Candlestick Park II / Candy says.

| Mar 91. | (lp/c/cd) *(RAR/+C/D 10227) <10174>* **HAMMER AND TONGS** <US title 'GOODBYE MR MACKENZIE'> | 61 | |

– Blacker than black / Bold John Barleycorn / Diamonds / The burning / Now we are married / Sick baby / Down to the minimum / She's strong / Love child / Tongue-tied.

– (album was scheduled for release 1990 but dropped by 'Capitol')

| May 91. | (cd-ep) <54173> **THE RATTLER / OPEN YOUR ARMS / DOWN TO THE MINIMUM / FRIDAY'S CHILD / GOODBYE MR MACKENZIE** | - | |

Blokshok   not iss.

| Apr 93. | (12"ep/cd-ep) *(BLOK 001 T/CD)* **GOODWILL CITY LIVE E.P.** (live) | | - |

– Goodwill city / Mystery train / Open your arms / Working on the shoe-fly.

| May 93. | (cd/lp) *(BLOK CD/LP 001)* **LIVE: ON THE DAY OF STORMS** (live) | | - |

– Goodwill city / Blacker than black / Face to face / Diamonds / Pleasure search / Sick baby / Goodbye Mr. Mackenzie / Dust / HMV / Tongue tied / The rattler / What's got into you / Working on the shoe-fly. *(re-iss. Apr96; same)*

| Sep 93. | (12"ep/cd-ep) *(BLOK 002 T/CD)* **HARD / NORMAL BOY. / BAD DAY / ZOO** | | - |

(re-iss. Dec95; same)

| Nov 93. | (cd/lp) *(BLOK CD/LP 002)* **"FIVE"** | | - |

– Hard / Bam bam / The grip / Jim's killer / Niagara / Touch the bullseye / The day of storms / Yellouzeu / Bugdive / Normal boy / Hands of the receiver / Titanic. *(re-iss. Mar96; same)*

– METCALFE / WILSON / KELLY + DUNCAN (vox on track 1)

| Oct 94. | (12"ep/cd-ep) *(BLOK 003 T/CD)* **THE WAY I WALK / SUPERMAN. / SICK BABY ('94) / YOU WILL** | - | - |
| Jul 95. | (m-cd) *(BLOKCD 004)* **JEZEBEL** (rare) | - | - |

– Jezebel / Jim's killer / Good deeds are like dirty rags / Queen Christina / Friday's child / I see no devil / Dress rehearsal rag / Niagara (live in Belgium 1991).

– now without SHIRLEY MANSON, who joined GARBAGE in 1995, after being heard in ANGELFISH (a GOODBYE MR MACKENZIE off-shoot, with her as frontperson and relegating MARTIN to guitarist). BIG JOHN had moonlighted with NIRVANA, as tour replacement for wayward KURT COBAIN.

– compilations, others, etc. –

| Jul 98. | (cd) *Blokshok; (BLOKCD 003)* **THE GLORY HOLE** | | - |

– The ugly child / Smile trash it / She's got eggs / Troubling you / Space / Neurotic / Overboards / Concrete / Prince of Wales / Crew cut / House on fire / Neuromental.

ANGELFISH

– MANSON, METCALFE, WILSON + KELLY

not iss.   Wasteland

| Jun 93. | (c-ep/cd-ep) <WSLD 9200-4/-2> **SUFFOCATE ME / YOU CAN LOVE HER / KIMBERLEY / TRASH IT** | - | |

not iss.   Radioactive

| Feb 94. | (cd) <RARD 10917> **ANGELFISH** | - | |

– Dogs in a cage / Suffocate me / You can love me / King of the world / Sleep with me / Heartbreak to hate / The sun won't shine / / Mummy can't drive / Tomorrow forever / The end.

GOOD MISSIONARIES
(see under ⇒ ALTERNATIVE TV; 70's section)

GORDONS (see under ⇒ BAILTER SPACE)

Martin L. GORE (see under ⇒ DEPECHE MODE)

Robert GORL (see under ⇒ D.A.F.)

GO TEAM (see under ⇒ BEAT HAPPENING)

GRAB GRAB THE HADDOCK
(see under ⇒ MARINE GIRLS)

Dave GRANEY (see under ⇒ MOODISTS)

GREAT DIVIDE (see under ⇒ BIBLE)

GREAT LEAP FORWARD (see under ⇒ BIG FLAME)

GREAT UNWASHED (see under ⇒ CLEAN)

GREEN ON RED

Formed: Tucson, Arizona, USA ... 1979 by DAN STUART, CHRIS CACAVAS, JACK WATERSON and VAN CRISTIAN. The latter was replaced by ALEX MacNICOL prior to the release of their eponymous mini-lp for STEVE WYNN's 'Down There' label. Their debut album, 'GRAVITY TALKS' (1984), drew comparisons with NEIL YOUNG's more rocky outings, moving away from the ramshackle garage of their earlier releases. This influence was even more evident on their 1985 offering 'GAS FOOD LODGING', which featured the distinctive guitar style of the newly recruited CHUCK PROPHET. Signing to 'Mercury' the same year, they released the disappointing 'NO FREE LUNCH', an album that saw the band attempting a BYRDS-like country sound, and even included a WILLIE NELSON cover 'AIN'T IT FUNNY NOW'. After the similarly poor 'THE KILLER INSIDE ME' in 1987, the group disbanded although DAN and CHUCK re-formed, using session players to flesh out the sound. Always on the verge of a commercial breakthrough, they were dogged by label failures and by the time of 1989's 'HERE COME THE SNAKES', the band had signed to 'China' in the UK although the record, which showcased a bolshier, heavy guitar sound, was previously to have been issued in August '88 by the soon-to-be bust 'Red Rhino' records. Undaunted, the band played a blinding live set in London, documented on 'LIVE AT THE TOWN AND COUNTRY' (1989). The band issued another three albums (including AL KOOPER-produced 'SCAPEGOATS') to no commercial success and after the ironically titled 'TOO MUCH FUN' (1992), PROPHET and STUART went on to release well-received solo albums. • **More covers:** KNOCKIN' ON HEAVEN'S DOOR (Bob Dylan) / SMOKESTACK LIGHTNIN' (Howlin' Wolf) / RAINY DAYS AND MONDAYS (Carpenters).

Album rating: GREEN ON RED mini (*6) / GRAVITY TALKS (*7) / GAS FOOD LODGING (*8) / NO FREE LUNCH mini (*4) / THE KILLER INSIDE ME (*5) / HERE COME THE SNAKES (*7) / LIVE AT THE TOWN AND COUNTRY (*4) / THIS TIME AROUND (*6) / SCAPEGOATS (*5) / ROCK'N'ROLL DISEASE – THE BEST OF GREEN ON RED compilation (*7) / TOO MUCH FUN (*4) / Danny & Dusty: THE LOST WEEKEND (*5) / Dan Stuart: RETRONEUVO with Al Perry (*5) / CANO'WORMS (*5)

DAN STUART – vocals, guitar / **CHRIS CACAVAS** – keyboards, vocals / **JACK WATERSON** – bass / **ALEX MacNICOL** – drums; repl. VAN CRISTIAN who joined GIANT SAND

not iss. Private
Jul 81. (ltd-12"red-ep) <R-714> **TWO BIBLES**
– Two bibles / La vida muerta / New world / Not today / A tragedy.

not iss. Down There
Jul 82. (m-lp) <71026> **GREEN ON RED (UNTITLED)**
– Death and angels / Hair and skin / Black night / Illustrated crawling / Aspirin / Lost world / Apartment 6. (UK-iss.Jun85 on 'Zippo'; ZANE 002)

Slash Slash
Aug 84. (lp) (SR 207) <23964-1> **GRAVITY TALKS** 1983
– Gravity talks / Old chief / 5 easy pieces / Deliverance / Over my head / Snake bite / Blue parade / That's what you're here for / Brave generation / Abigail's ghost / Cheap wine / Narcolepsy. (re-iss. Jan87 lp/c; SLM P/C 16)

— added **CHUCK W. PROPHET** – steel guitar, vocals

Zippo Enigma
May 85. (lp/c) (ZONG/+CASS 005) <ST/4XT 73249> **GAS FOOD LODGING** 1986
– That's what dreams / Black river / Hair of the dog / This I know / Fading away / Easy way out / Sixteen ways / The drifter / Sea of Cortez / We shall overcome. (cd-iss. 1990 on 'Enigma'; D2-73249)

— **KEITH MITCHELL** – percussion repl. ALEX

Mercury Mercury
Oct 85. (m-lp/m-c) (MERM/+C 78) <82646-1> **NO FREE LUNCH** 99
– Time ain't nothing / Honest man / Ballad of Guy Fawkes / No free lunch / Funny how time slips away / Jimmy boy / Keep on moving. (c+=) – Smokestack lightning.
Nov 85. (7") (MER 202) **TIME AIN'T NOTHING. / NO FREE LUNCH**
Feb 87. (7") (GOR 1) **CLARKSVILLE. / NO DRINKIN'**
(12"+=) (GOR 1-12) – Broken.
Mar 87. (lp/c)(cd) (GOR LP/MC 1)(839122-2) <830912-2> **THE KILLER INSIDE ME**
– Clarksville / Mighty gun / Jamie / Whispering wind / Ghost hand / Sorry Naomi / No man's land / Track you down (his master's voice) / Born to fight / We ain't feee / The killer inside me. (cd+=) – NO FREE LUNCH (m-lp)
Jun 87. (7") (GOR 2) **BORN TO FIGHT. / DON'T SHINE YOUR LIGHT ON ME**
(ext.12"+=) (GOR 2-12) – While the widow weeps.

— Disbanded late 1987, DAN and CHUCK reformed and brought in new sessioners. WATERSON released an album 'WHOSE DOG' in 1988, while CHRIS CACAVAS & THE JUNKYARD LOVE released self-titled one in 1989.

China Restless
Apr 89. (7") (CHINA 16) **KEITH CAN'T READ. / THAT'S THE WAY THE WORLD GOES ROUND / VAYA CON DIOS**
(12") (CHINX 16) – (1st & 3rd tracks) / Tenderloin.

Apr 89. (lp/c/cd) (839294-1/-4/-2) <72351-1> **HERE COME THE SNAKES**
– Keith can't read / Rock and roll disease / Morning blue / Zombie for love / Broken radio / Change / Tenderloin / Way back home / We had it all / D.T. blues.
Aug 89. (ltd; 10"lp/c) (841013-0/-4) **LIVE AT THE TOWN & COUNTRY CLUB** (live)
– 16 ways / Change / DT blues / Fading away / Morning blue / Are you sure Hank done it this way / Zombie for love / Hair of the dog. (c+=) – Rock and roll disease / We had it all.

— duo now with **RENE COMAN** – upright bass, bass / **MIKE FINNEGAN** – keyboards / **DAVID KEMPER** – drums, percussion / plus **BERNIE LEADON** – mandolin, acoustic guitar (4) / **PAT DONALDSON** – bass (4) / **SPOONER OLDHAM** – piano (3)

China Catalina
Oct 89. (7") (CHINA 21) **THIS TIME AROUND. / FADING AWAY** (live)
(12"+=/cd-s+=) (CHINX/CHICD 21) – 16 ways (live).
Nov 89. (lp/c/cd) (841720-1/-4/-2) <841519-2> **THIS TIME AROUND**
– This time around / Cool million / Rev. Luther / Good patient woman / You couldn't get arrested / The quarter / Foot / Hold the line / Pills and booze / We're all waiting. (free-7"w.a.) – MORNING BLUE / ROCK AND ROLL DISEASE. (interview) (re-iss. Jul91 cd/c; WOL CD/MC 1019)
Dec 89. (7") (CHINA 22) **YOU COULDN'T GET ARRESTED. / BROKEN RADIO**
(ext.12"/ext.cd-s) (CHINX/CHICD 22) – Hair of the dog.

— DAN and CHUCK recruit **MICHAEL RHODES** – bass / **DAREN HESS** – drums

China China
Mar 91. (7") (WOK 2001) **LITTLE THINGS IN LIFE. / CHERRY KIND**
(12"+=/cd-s+=) (WOK 2001 T/CD) – Sun goes down / Waiting for love.
Mar 91. (cd/c/lp) <(WOL CD/MC/LP 1001)> **SCAPEGOATS**
– A guy like me / Little things in life / Two lovers (waitin' to die) / Gold in the graveyard / Hector's out / Shed a tear (for the lonesome) / Blowfly / Sun goes down / Where the rooster crows / Baby loves her gun.
Jun 91. (7") (WOK 2002) **TWO LOVERS (WAITIN' TO DIE). / KEITH CAN'T READ**
Sep 91. (cd/c/lp) (WOL/+MC/CD 1021) **THE BEST OF GREEN ON RED** (compilation)
– Time ain't nothing / Born to fight / Hair of the dog / Keith can't read / Morning blue / This time around / Little things in life / You couldn't get arrested / That's what dreams / Zombie for love / Baby loves her gun.

— added **J.D. FOSTER**
Oct 92. (cd-ep) (WOKCD 2029) **SHE'S ALL MINE / TWO LOVERS** (live) **/ BABY LOVES HER GUN** (live) **/ LITTLE THINGS IN LIFE** (live)
Oct 92. (lp/c/cd) <(WOL/+MC/CD 1029)> **TOO MUCH FUN**
– She's all mine / Frozen in my headlights / Love is insane / Too much fun / The getaway / I owe you one / Man needs woman / Sweetest thing / Thing or two / Hands and knees / Wait and see / Rainy days and Mondays.

– compilations, others, etc. –

Sep 91. (cd/c) Music Club; <(MC CD/TC 037)> **THE LITTLE THINGS IN LIVE** (live)
May 92. (cd) Mau Mau; <(MAUCD 612)> **GAS FOOD LODGING / GREEN ON RED** Jan96
Jun 94. (cd) China; <(WOLCD 1047)> **ROCK'N'ROLL DISEASE – THE BEST OF ...** 1995
– Rock'n'roll disease / This time around / 16 ways (live) / Fading away (live) / Hair of the dog / Keith can't read / Morning blue / Zombie for love / Change / Tenderloin / You couldn't get arrested / Little things in life / Two lovers (waitin' to die) / Hector's out / Baby loves her gun / The quarter / She's all mine / Frozen in my headlights / Too much fun. (re-iss. Jul99; 4509 96106-2)
Dec 97. (cd/lp) Corduroy; (CORD 026/+LP) **ARCHIVES VOL.1: WHAT WERE WE THINKING**
(cd re-iss. Aug99 on 'Normal'; NORMAL 194CD)
Dec 98. (cd) Edsel; (EDCD 591) **THIS TIME AROUND / TOO MUCH FUN**

— DAN STUART had also appeared on album below

DANNY & DUSTY

DUSTY being STEVE WYNN of DREAM SYNDICATE. Augmented by LONG RYDERS:- SYD GRIFFIN, TOM STEVENS + STEVE McCARTHY, plus DENNIS DUCK of DREAM SYNDICATE + CHRIS CACAVAS of GREEN ON RED

Zippo A&M
Nov 85. (lp) (ZONG 007) <5075> **THE LOST WEEKEND**
– Down to the bone / The word is out / Song for the dreamers / Miracle mile / Baby, we all gotta go down / The king of the losers / Send me a postcard / Knockin' on Heaven's door. <cd-iss. 1996 on 'Prima'; 6>

— DAN was also guest on two of NAKED PREY albums. CHRIS guested on the GIANT SAND album 'VALLEY OF RAIN' in Mar'86. In Sep'90, CHUCK PROPHET issued solo album 'BROTHER ALDO' for 'Fire'. In 1993 for 'China', he issued 'BALINESE DANCER' foolowed by in '95; 'FEAST OF HEARTS'. Meanwhile CACAVAS on 'Normal' released 'PALE BLONDE HELL' (1994) & 'NEW IMPROVED PAIN' (1995).

DAN STUART

— (on 1995 set) with **J.D. FOSTER, JON DEE GRAHAM, RANDY McREYNOLDS, JAMES VALENCIA, FERNANDO VALENCI, DAREN HESS + CRAIG SCHUMACHER**

Normal Monkey Hill
Jul 94. (cd; by AL PERRY & DAN STUART) (NORMAL 169CD) **RETRONEUVO**
– Daddy's girl / Hermit of Jerome / I could run / Little slant 6 / Sick and tired / Better than I did / Mamcita / Eyes of a fool / Empty chair / Lone wolf.
Jul 95. (cd) (NORMAL 189CD) <8131> **CANO'WORMS**
– Panhandler / Home after dark / La pasionara / Who needs more / What a day / Expat blues / Waterfall / In Madrid / Filipina stripped / Can't get through / The greatest.

GREEN TELESCOPE (see under ⇒ THANES)

Sid GRIFFIN (see under ⇒ LONG RYDERS)

GROOVE FARM
(see under ⇒ BEATNIK FILMSTARS; in 90's section)

GROOVY LITTLE NUMBERS

Formed: Bellshill, Lanarkshire, Scotland . . . mid-80's by JOE McALINDEN, multi-instrumentalist and part-time violinist with The BOY HAIRDRESSERS (who turned into TEENAGE FANCLUB without him!) and a BMX BANDIT. However, side-projects aside, JOE re-initiated his passion with everything BEATLES and reinstated co-founder CATHERINE STEVEN and future TEENAGE FANCLUB member GERARD LOVE; minor brass musicians also took their place, COLETTE WALSH, JOHN McRORIE, KEVIN McCARTHY, JAMES WOOD and MAIRI CAMERON. During the period 1987-1988, they recorded six worthy tracks and released them over a couple of 12"er's for '53rd & 3rd', 'YOU MADE MY HEAD EXPLODE' and 'HAPPY LIKE YESTERDAY'. JOE would later surface in his own SUPERSTAR after another spell with BMX BANDITS.

Album rating: THE 53rd & 3rd SINGLES mini compilation (*5)

JOE McALINDEN – multi-instruments / **CATHERINE STEVEN** – vocals / **GERARD LOVE** – bass, vocals / with **COLETTE WALSH** – tenor sax / **JOHN McRORIE** – alto sax / **KEVIN McCARTHY** – baritone sax / **MAIRI CAMERON + JAMES WOOD** – trumpets

		53rd & 3rd	not iss.
Jan 88.	(12"ep) (AGARR 013) **YOU MADE MY HEAD EXPLODE. / HEY HEY / WINDY**		-
Aug 88.	(12"ep) (AGARR 021) **HAPPY LIKE YESTERDAY. / SHOOT ME DOWN / A PLACE SO HARD TO FIND**		-

— McALINDEN would subsequently resurface with the BMX BANDITS and later formed his own outfit, SUPERSTAR

– compilations, etc. –

1998.	(m-cd/m-lp) Avalanche; (ONLY CD/LP 014) **THE 53rd & 3rd SINGLES**		-

GUADALCANAL DIARY

Formed: Marietta, Georgia, USA . . . 1981 by main songwriter MURRAY ATTAWAY and JEFF WALLS, along with RHETT CROWE and JOHN POE, naming themselves after a soldier's account of the WWII Guadalcanal operation. Trading in evocative countrified rock with a myriad of influences (although R.E.M. and the LONG RYDERS were the most prominent), GUADALCANAL DIARY issued the DON DIXON-produced debut single, 'WATUSI RODEO', in '83. A rootsy hoedown in the mould of DAVE EDMUNDS or NICK LOWE, the track featured on their inaugural album, 'WALKING IN THE SHADOW OF THE BIG MAN' (1984). Subsequently taken up by 'Elektra' on both sides of the Atlantic, the record was a fine example of 80's Americana with all the baggage that entails. Religion, war and the psychic landscape of the Yankee south were all familiar lyrical topics on 1986's follow-up, 'JAMBOREE', a patchwork of classic retro sounds stealthily rustled in a kinda cow-punk way from the likes of The BEATLES and The BYRDS. They finally managed to create something approaching greatness from the sum of their often derivative parts with the acclaimed '2x4' set in '87, a record that spent several weeks in the US Top 200. With a full commercial breakthrough seemingly just around the corner, GUADALCANAL DIARY struggled to live up to critical expectations with their slightly disappointing swansong, 'FLIP-FLOP' (1989), which also bubbled under the Top 100; ATTAWAY would find some work as a solo artist. Echoes of GUADALCANAL's musical ghost can be heard in the acoustic work of Seattle acts, the WALKABOUTS and NIRVANA; alternatively, try playing the chorus of 'SLEEPERS AWAKE' back to back with 'Penny Royal Tea'. • **Covered:** JOHNNY B GOODE (Chuck Berry) / AND YOUR BIRD CAN SING (Beatles).

Album rating: WALKING IN THE SHADOW OF THE BIG MAN (*7) / JAMBOREE (*6) / 2x4 (*8) / FLIP-FLOP (*6)

MURRAY ATTAWAY – vocals, electric guitar / **JEFF WALLS** – guitars, vocals / **RHETT CROWE** – bass / **JOHN POE** – drums

		not iss.	Entertainment On Disc
1983.	(7"ep) <EOD 102> **WATUSI RODEO EP** – Michael Rockefeller / Liwa Wechi / John Wayne / Dead eyes.	-	
		Hybrid	D.B.
Feb 85.	(lp) (HYBLP 2) <DB 73> **WALKING IN THE SHADOW OF THE BIG MAN** – Trail of tears / Fire from Heaven / Sleepers awake / Gilbert takes the wheel / Ghost on the road / Watusi rodeo / Why do the heathen rage? / Pillow talk / Walking in the shadow of the big man / Kumbayah. (re-iss. Aug85 on 'Elektra'; 60429-1/-2)		Nov84
		Elektra	Elektra
Aug 85.	(7"m) (EKR 23) **WATUSI RODEO. / SLEEPERS AWAKE / JOHNNY B. GOODE**		
Jul 86.	(lp/c) (960 478-1/-4) <60478-1/-4> **JAMBOREE** – Pray for rain / Fear of God / Jamboree / Michael Rockefeller / Spirit train / Lonely street / Country club gun / T.R.O.U.B.L.E. / I see Moe / Please stop me / Dead eyes / Cattle prod.		
Sep 87.	(lp/c/cd) (960 752-1/-4) <60752-1/-4/-2> **2x4** – Litany (life goes on) / Under the yoke / Get over it / Little birds / Things fall apart / Let the big wheel roll / And your bird can sing [cd+=] / Where angels fear to tread / Newborn / Winds of change / Say please / 3 a.m. / Lips of steel.		
Feb 89.	(lp/c/cd) (960 848-1/-4/-2) <60848-1/-4/-2> **FLIP-FLOP** – Look up! / Always Saturday / The likes of you / Barometer / Happy home / Whiskey talk / Pretty is as pretty does / Everything but good luck / Ten laws / Fade out / . . .Vista.		
Mar 89.	(7") <7-69316> **ALWAYS SATURDAY. / KISS OF FIRE**	-	

— split in '89; ATTAWAY went solo (and released 'IN THRALL' in 1993) while POE joined LOVE TRACTOR

– compilations, etc. –

Mar 99.	(cd) Guadco Merch; <1> **AT YOUR BIRTHDAY PARTY (live)** – Gilbert takes the wheel / Trail of tears / Country club gun / Pretty is as pretty does / The likes of you / Lips of steel / Newborn / Say please / I see Moe / Whiskey talk / Vista / Litany (life goes on) / Dead eyes / Cattle prod / Pau pau / Watusi rodeo.	-	

GUANA BATZ

Formed: Feltham, Middlesex, England . . . early '83 by MARK WHITE, PIP HANCOX, STUART OSBOURNE and DAVE TURNER. However, prior to the release of any material, co-founder WHITE was substituted by stand-up bass player, SAM SARDI. Psychobilly rockers in the vein of the METEORS, KING KURT and the STRAY CATS, the bequiffed GUANA BATZ signed to Chiswick off-shoot, 'Big Beat' and released a debut EP, 'YOU'RE SO FINE'. Next up was an appearance on compilation, 'Stompin' At The Klubfoot', an album that also premiered a host of similarly styled acts. Their inaugural long-player, 'HELD DOWN . . . AT LAST', finally saw the light of day in mid '85 and surprisingly nearly topped the indie charts. The record appeared on the 'I.D.' label, also home to an even better selling follow-up, 'LOAN SHARKS' (1986). The 'BATZ continued to sink their teeth into the heart of London's punkabilly scene over the latter half of the 80's, although bar a hardcore minority, the music scene had long since moved on by the turn of the decade. • **Covered:** I'M ON FIRE (Bruce Springsteen) / ENDLESS SLEEP (Joey Reynolds) / JOHNNY B. GOODE + NO PARTICULAR PLACE TO GO (Chuck Berry) / HIPPY HIPPY SHAKE (Swinging Blue Jeans) / YOU'RE MY BABY (Vacels) / + a plethora of others.

Album rating: HELD DOWN . . .AT LAST (*6) / LOAN SHARKS (*7) / LIVE OVER LONDON (*5) / ROUGH EDGES (*4) / ELECTRA GLIDE IN BLUE (*4) / GET AROUND (*3)

PIP HANCOX – vocals / **STUART OSBOURNE** – guitar / **SAM SARDI** – double bass; repl. MARK WHITE / **DAVE 'DIDDLE' TURNER** – drums

		Big Beat	not iss.
Nov 83.	(12"ep) (SW 89) **YOU'RE SO FINE / ROCKIN' IN MY COFFIN. / JUNGLE RUMBLE / GUANA ROCK**		-
Apr 84.	(7") (NS 96) **THE CAVE. / WEREWOLF BLUES**		-
		I.D.	not iss.
Jul 85.	(lp) (NOSE 4) **HELD DOWN . . . AT LAST** – Down on the line / Got no money / Can't take the pressure / Nightwatch / Lady Bacon / King Rat / You're my baby / Nightmare fantasy / Please give me something / Bust out. (cd-iss. Nov97 on 'Anagram'; CDMPSYCHO 18) (<cd re-iss. Jun02 on 'Harry May'; MAYOCD 511>)		-
Feb 86.	(12"ep) (EYET 6) **SEETHROUGH. / BATMAN THEME (live) / B SIDE BLUES**		-
Jul 86.	(7") (EYE 9) **I'M ON FIRE. /** (12"+=) (EYET 9) –		-
Oct 86.	(lp/c) (NOSE/KOSE 10) **LOAN SHARKS** – Pile driver boogie / My way / Slippin' in / Tiny minds / Radio Sweetheart / Life's a beach / Loan shark / Shake your moneymaker / I'm weird / Hippy hippy shake / Live for the day / No particular place to go / I'm on fire.		-
Dec 86.	(7") (EYE 12) **LOAN SHARKS. / RADIO SWEETHEART**		-
May 87.	(7") (EYE 13) **ROCK THIS TOWN. / JUST LOVE ME**		-
Jun 87.	(lp) (NOSE 14) **LIVE OVER LONDON (live)** – Can't take the pressure / Rockin' in the graveyard / My way / Live for the day / Rocky road / Seethrough / Loan shark / B side blues / Just love me / Baby blue eyes / I'm on fire / Dynamite / Rock this town / Endless sleep / King Rat / Shake your moneymaker – Tear it up / The overture. (cd-iss. Jun93 on 'Dojo'; DOJOCD 133)		-

— **GINGER** – drums (ex-METEORS) repl. TURNER

| Apr 88. | (lp/c/cd) (NOSE/KOSE/CDOSE 20) **ROUGH EDGES** – Streetwise / Open your mouth / One night / Good news / Rocking on Creek road / Fight back / Spy catcher / Love generator / Bring my Cadillac back / Rocking with Ollie Vee / Two shadows / You can run. | | - |

— **JOHNNY BOWLER** – drums (ex-GET SMART) repl. GINGER

		World Service	not iss.
Mar 90.	(12"one-sided) (SERT 001) **ELECTRA GLIDE IN BLUE**		-
Mar 90.	(lp/cd) (SERV/+CD 009) **ELECTRA GLIDE IN BLUE** – Electra glide in blue / Green eyes / Texas eyes / No matter how / Wonderous place / Katherine / Stylin' / Spector love / Self made prison / Who needs it / Lover man / Take a rocket.		-

— **MARK PENNINGTON** – bass (ex-CARAVANS) repl. SARDI

— continued to tour, but mainly in Europe where they were more popular

		Jappin' & Rockin'	not iss.
Mar 94.	(cd/lp) (JR CD/LP 008) **GET AROUND** – Every night and every day / Breakdown / Tell her / Native beat / Lady of the night / Heart of stone / Shake it up / She's neat / Soul disbeliever / Chill out blues / Don't take this to heart / Such a night / Hot stuff / Sunsets / You're my baby. (cd re-iss. Sep97; same)		-

– compilations, etc. –

Oct 88. (lp/cd) *Wrongco; (WRONG/+CD 001)* **THE BEST OF THE BATZ**
– King Rat / Nightmare fantasy / I'm on fire / You're my baby / Dynamite / Radio sweetheart / Streetwise / lease give me something / Seethrough / Baby blue eyes / Rock this town / Loan shark / Spy catcher / Bring my Cadillac back.

Jun 89. (cd) *I.D.; (CDOSE 4-10)* **LOAN SHARKS / HELD DOWN . . . AT LAST**
(re-iss. Apr93 on 'Loma'; LOMACD 13)

Dec 91. (cd) *Streetlink; (STRCD 020)* **GUANA BATZ 1985-1990**
(<re-iss. Mar93/Oct94 on 'Dojo'; DOJOCD 120>)

Oct 92. (cd) *Street Link; (STRCD 033)* **THE KLUB FOOT CONCERTS (live)**

May 93. (cd) *Loma; (LOMACD 14)* **ELECTRIC GLIDE IN BLUE / ROUGH EDGES**

Sep 95. (cd) *Anagram; (<CDMPSYCHO 07>)* **UNDERCOVER** Sep99
– You're mu baby / Please give me something / Bust out / My way / Slippin' in / Radio sweetheart / Shake your moneymaker / Hippy hippy shake / No particular place to go / I'm on fire / Baby blues eyes / Batman / One night / Bring my Cadillac back / Rock around with Ollie Vee / Wonderous place / Lights out / Johnny B. Goode / Joe 90 (live) / The train kept a-rollin' (live) / Devil's guitar (live) / Rockin' in the graveyard (live) / Rocky road blues (live) / Dynamite (live) / Rock this town (live) / Endless sleep (live). *(re-iss. Sep00; same)*

Dec 98. (cd) *Jappin' & Rockin'; (JRCD 36)* **THE PEEL SESSIONS**

Apr 00. (cd) *Harry May; (<MAYO 119>)* **CAN'T STAND THE PRESSURE**

Apr 01. (cd) *Jappin' & Rockin'; (JRCD 021)* **POWDER KEG**

Oct 01. (cd) *Anagram; (<CDMPSYCHO 24>)* **THE VERY BEST OF GUANA BATZ** Nov01

GUIDED BY VOICES

Formed: Dayton, Ohio, USA . . . mid-80's by ROBERT POLLARD; his brother JIM and TOBIN SPROUT soon became stable members after their initial release. Making their debut in 1986 with the 'FOREVER SINCE BREAKFAST' EP, GUIDED BY VOICES became something of a cult phenomenon via a series of independently released, limited edition albums. From 1987's 'DEVIL BETWEEN MY TOES' onwards, the band garnered a reputation for inaccessible lo-fi musings issued under such characteristically long-winded titles as 'SELF INFLICTED AERIAL NOSTALGIA' (1989) and 'SAME PLACE THE FLY GOT SMASHED' (1990). A subsequent deal with leading US indie label, 'Matador', led to a full British release for 1993's 'VAMPIRE ON TITUS', the band's increasing critical plaudits reaching a peak with the following year's 'BEE THOUSAND'. GBV's angular, surreal sketches sharing – in spirit at least – the same astral plane as MERCURY REV while drawing comparisons with fellow lo-fi pioneers such as PAVEMENT. Following on from live set, 'CRYING YOUR KNIFE AWAY' (1994), GUIDED BY VOICES kept up their unflaggingly prolific recording schedule with 'ALIEN LANES' (1995). Featuring a marathon 28 tracks on a single CD, the album veered from the CHRIS BELL/BEATLES-esque '(I WANNA BE A) DUMBCHARGER' to the almost TEENAGE FANCLUB-style harmonies of 'CIGARETTE TRICKS' and the soaraway pop brilliance of 'MOTOR AWAY'. The latter was an obvious choice for a single release while the sublime 'MY VALUABLE HUNTING KNIFE' was hailed as one of the finest songs POLLARD had yet penned. 1996's 'UNDER THE BUSHES UNDER THE STARS' moved in an increasingly accessible direction, the same year also seeing solo sets from both ROBERT POLLARD ('NOT IN MY AIRFORCE') and TOBIN SPROUT ('CARNIVAL BOY' and 'SUNFISH HOLY BREAKFAST' mini). Rumours of an imminent split between POLLARD and SPROUT were proved correct when 1997's 'MAG EARWHIG!' long-player featured just ROBERT POLLARD and punk band COBRA VERDE. POLLARD again continued on his moonlighting solo sojourn via bizarre but enlightening albums such as 'WAVED OUT' (1998), 'KID MARINE' (1999), 'SPEAK KINDLY OF YOUR VOLUNTEER FIRE DEPARTMENT' (a collaboration with DOUG GILLARD, 1999) and 'CHOREOGRAPHED MAN OF WAR' (with HIS SOFT ROCK RENEGADES; 2001). Always thought of as a fully paid-up member of GBV, the Michigan-based TOBIN also cracked on with his take on arty-pop with sets such as 'MOONFLOWER PLASTIC (WELCOME TO MY WIGWAM)' (1997), 'LET'S WELCOME THE CIRCUS PEOPLE' (1999) and 'SENTIMENTAL STATIONS' (2002), all receiving a glowing response from critics and public alike. Meanwhile, back at the GBV ranch, things were looking up via a fresh deal with major 'T.V.T.' records. The RIC OCASEK-produced set, 'DO THE COLLAPSE' (1999), was dismissed as a little amateurish and predictable, the album title a lttle too poignant for its own good. Getting back to basics with Rob Schnapf at the decks, POLLARD (and newcomers DOUG GILLARD and NATE FARLEY) was back to his songwriting best via 2001's 'ISOLATION DRILLS'. If POLLARD and SPROUT had completely fallen out, it wasn't apparent on their subsequent collaboration as AIRPORT 5, another lo-fi workout in the studio producing a couple of sets, 'TOWER IN THE FOUNTAIN OF SPARKS' (2001) and 'LIFE STARTS HERE' (2002). With a welcome mat put out by 'Matador' again, GBV once again hit the indie trail courtesy of 2002's 'UNIVERSAL TRUTHS AND CYCLES'. It lacked the coherence of their previous record but for immediate gems such as 'EUREKA SIGNS' and 'CHEYENNE'. With their album tally now well into double figures, GUIDED BY VOICES remain one of America's more enigmatic indie institutions. • **Covered:** INVISIBLE MAN (Breeders).

Album rating: DEVIL BETWEEN MY TOES (*5) / SANDBOX (*5) / SELF-INFLICTED AERIAL NOSTALGIA (*5) / SAME PLACE THE FLY GOT SMASHED (*5) / PROPELLER (*6) / I AM THE SCIENTIST (*5) / VAMPIRE ON TITUS (*6) / BEE THOUSAND (*7) / CRYING YOUR KNIFE AWAY (*6) / ALIEN LANES (*8) / UNDER THE BUSHES, UNDER THE STARS (*7) / SUNFISH HOLY BREAKFAST mini (*6) / MAG EARWHIG! (*7) / BOX compilation (*7) / DO THE COLLAPSE (*4) / ISOLATION DRILLS (*6) / UNIVERSAL TRUTHS AND CYCLES (*5) / Robert Pollard: NOT IN MY AIRFORCE (*6) / WAVED OUT (*5) / KID MARINE (*6) / SPEAK KINDLY OF YOUR VOLUNTEER FIRE DEPARTMENT with Doug Gillard (*6) / CHOREOGRAPHED MAN OF WAR (*6) / Tobin Sprout: CARNIVAL BOY (*6) / MOONFLOWER PLASTIC (WELCOME TO MY WIGWAM) (*7) / FIG.4 collection (*5) / LET'S WELCOME THE CIRCUS PEOPLE (*6) / DEMOS & OUTTAKES collection (*5) / SENTIMENTAL STATIONS mini (*5) / Airport 5: TOWER IN THE FOUNTAIN OF SPARKS (*4) / LIFE STARTS HERE (*5)

ROBERT POLLARD – vocals, guitar / **PAUL COMSTOCK** – guitar, piano / **MITCH MITCHELL** – bass / **PEYTON ERIC** – drums

not iss.   I Wanna

Jul 86. (12"ep) *<605058XB>* **FOREVER SINCE BREAKFAST EP**
– Land of danger / Let's ride / Like I do / Sometimes I cry / She wants to know / Fountain of youth / The other place.

—— **KEVIN FENNELL** – drums; repl. PEYTON + PAUL

—— added **JIM POLLARD** – guitar + **TOBIN SPROUT** – guitar, vocals (guested) / **STEVE WILBUR** – producer, guitar (guested)

not iss.   Schwa

Apr 87. (lp) *<gbv 001>* **DEVIL BETWEEN MY TOES**
– Old battery / Discussing Wallace Chambers / Cyclops / Crux / A portrait destroyed by fire / 3 year old man / Dog's out / A proud and booming industry / Hank's little fingers / Artboat / Hey hey, spaceman / The tumblers / Bread alone / Captain's dead.

not iss.   Halo

Dec 87. (lp) *<Halo 1>* **SANDBOX**
– Lips of steel / A visit to the creep doctor / Everyday / Barricade / Get to know the ropes / Can't stop / The drinking Jim Crow / Trap door soul / Common rebels / Long distance man / I certainly hope not / Adverse wind.

—— **WILBUR** was now a member + **PAYTON** returned

Apr 89. (lp) *<Halo 2>* **SELF-INFLICTED AERIAL NOSTALGIA**
– The future is in eggs / The great Blake St. canoe race / Slopes of big ugly / Paper girl / Navigating flood regions / An earful o' wax / White whale / Trampoline / Short on posters / Chief barrell belly / Dying to try this / The qualifying remainder / Liar's tale / Radio show (trust the wizard).

—— **ROBERT + JIM** recruited **GREG DEMOS** (aka FINGSTON REDWING) – bass + **DON THRASHER** – drums

not iss.   Rocket

Aug 90. (lp) *<#9>* **SAME PLACE THE FLY GOT SMASHED**
– Airshow '88 / Order for the new slave trade / The hard way / Drinker's peace / Mammoth cave / When she turns 50 / Club Molluska / Pendulum / Ambergris / Local mix-up / Murder charge / Starboy / Blatant doom trip / How loft am I?

—— added **TOBIN SPROUT** – guitar, vocals (guests were **MITCH MITCHELL** – guitar + **DAN TOOHEY** – bass)

not iss.   Rockathon

1992. (lp) *<ROCKATHON 001>* **PROPELLER**
– Over the Neptune – Mesh gear fox / Weed king / Particular damaged / Quality of armor / Metal mothers / Lethargy / Unleashed! the large-hearted boy / Red gas circle / Exit flagger / 14 cheerleader coldfront / Back to Saturn X radio report / Ergo space pig / Circus world / Some drilling implied / On the tundra. *<cd-iss. Nov96 on 'Scat'; SCT 49>*

—— **MITCH MITCHELL + KEVIN FENNELL** returned to repl. DEMOS + THRASHER

not iss.   Scat

Jan 93. (7"ep) *<SCT 28>* **THE GRAND HOUR**
– I'll get over it / Shocker in Gloomtown / Alien lanes / Off the floor / Break even / Bee thousand. *(UK-iss.Oct94; same)*

—— reverted to a trio (**ROBERT** (+ drums), **JIM** + **TOBIN**)

City Slang   Scat

Mar 93. (lp) *<SCT 31>* **VAMPIRE ON TITUS**
– "Wished I was a giant" / #2 in the model home series / Expecting brainchild / Superior sector janitor X / Donkey school / Dusted / Marchers in orange / Sot / World of fun / Jar of cardinals / Unstable journey / E-5 / Cool off kid kilowatt / Gleemer (the deeds of fertile Jim) / Wondering boy poet / What about it? / Perhaps now the vultures / Non-absorbing. *(re-iss. Oct94 on 'Matador' cd+=/lp; OLE 083-2/-1)* – PROPELLER

—— the trio added **MITCHELL, TOOHEY + FENNELL**

Nov 93. (7"ep) *(EFA 04939-7)* **STATIC AIRPLANE JIVE ep**
– Big school / Damn good Mr. Jam / Rubber man / Hey aardvark / Glow boy butlers / Gelatin, ice cream, plum . . . *<(cd-iss. May99 on 'Recordhead'; LUNA 15)>*

not iss.   Siltbreeze

Dec 93. (7"ep) *<SB 028>* **GET OUT OF MY STATIONS ep**
– Scalding creek / Mobile / Melted Pat / Queen of second guessing / Dusty bushworms / Spring tiger / Blue moon fruit. *(UK-iss.Sep97; same as US) (cd-ep; EAR 002CD)*

Domino   Luna

Feb 94. (7"ep/cd-ep) *(RUG 11/+CD)* *<LUNA 10>* **CLOWN PRINCE OF THE MENTHOL TRAIL ep** Nov93
– Matter eater land / Broadcaster house / Hunter complex / Pink gun / Scalping the guru / Grandfather Westinghouse / Johnny appleased.

—— were back to a trio; **THRASHER** returned to repl. JIM

not iss.   Anyway

Feb 94. (7"; split) *<#13>* **IF WE WAIT. / (other track by Jennie Mae Laeffel)**

—— **ROBERT, TOBIN, JIM, MITCH, DAN + KEVIN** (DON + GREG guested)

Matador   Scat

Jul 94. (cd/lp) *(OLE 084-2/-1)* *<SCT 35 CD/LP>* **BEE THOUSAND** Jun94
– Hardcore UFO's / Buzzards and dreadful crows / Tractor rape chain / Golden heart mountaintop queen directory / Hot freaks / Smothered in hugs / Yours to keep / Echos Myron / Awful bliss / Mincer Ray / A big fan of pigpon / Queen of cans and jars / Her psychology day / Kicker of elves / Ester's day / Demons are real / I am a scientist / Peep-hole / You're not an airplane. *(UK re-iss. Jun98; same as US)*

GUIDED BY VOICES (cont) — **THE GREAT INDIE DISCOGRAPHY** — **The 1980s**

Oct 94. (d-lp) <Lo-Fi 004> **CRYING YOUR KNIFE AWAY** (live at Stache's, Columbus, Ohio, June 18, 1994) — not iss. / Lo-Fi
– Postal blowfish / The closer you are the quicker it hits you / My valuable hunting knife / Gold star for robot boy / Lethargy / Striped white jets / Non-absorbing / The goldheart mountaintop / Shocker in Gloomtown / Motor away / Awful bliss / Tractor rape chain / Blimps go 90 / Exit flagger / I am a scientist / Quality of armor / Cruise / Unleashed! the large-hearted boy / Some drilling implied / If we wait / Weed king / Pimple zoo / Break even / Esters day. *(UK-iss.Aug98; same) (UK cd-iss. Nov99 on 'Simple Solution'; ss 016)*

—— for above live set:- ROBERT + TOBIN brought back MITCH, GREG + KEVIN (THRASHER joined SWEARING AT MOTORISTS)

Jan 95. (cd) <(SCT 38-CD)> **I AM THE SCIENTIST** — Scat / Scat Nov94
– I am a scientist / The curse of the black ass buffalo / Do the earth / Planet's own brand.

Feb 95. (cd-ep) <vroom 07> **FAST JAPANESE SPIN CYCLE ep** — Engine / not iss.
– 3rd World birdwatching / My impression now / Volcano divers / Snowman (showman?) / Indian fables / Marchers in orange / Dusted / Kisses to the crying cooks.

—— now down to ROBERT, TOBIN + JIM

Feb 95. (7"ep) <#2> **HEY, MR. SOUNDMAN** — not iss. / Now Sound
– Hey, Mr. Soundman / Announcers & umpires / Evil speaker B / Uncle Dave / I'm drunk (by The GRIFTERS).

Feb 95. (7") <#21> **ALWAYS CRUSH ME. / Believe: THE SILK KING** — not iss. / Anyway

—— ROBERT, TOBIN, JIM, MITCH, KEVIN + GREG added JIM GREER – bass

Apr 95. (cd/lp) <(OLE 123-2/-1)> **ALIEN LANES** — Matador / Matador
– A salty salute / Evil speakers / Watch me jumpstart / They're not witches / As we go up, we go down / (I wanna be a) Dumbcharger / Game of prick(s) / The ugly vision / A good flying bird / Cigarette tricks / Pimple zoo / Big chief Chinese restaurant / Closer you are / Auditorium / Motor away / Hit / My valuable hunting knife / Gold hick / King and Caroline / Stripped white jets / Ex-supermodel / Blimps go 90 / Strawdogs / Chicken blows / Little whirl / My son cool / Always crush me / Alright.

—— now without JIM POLLARD + GREG

Jun 95. (7") <(OLE 148-7)> **MOTOR AWAY. / COLOR OF MY BLADE**

Jul 95. (lp) <bootleg> **FOR ALL GOOD KIDS** (live at Maxwell's, Hoboken, NJ, 30 March 1995)
– Don't stop now / King and Caroline / Motor away / Gold star for roboy boy / Hot freaks / Game of pricks / Echos Myron / Redmen and their wives / Pimple zoo / Smothered in hugs / Johnny appleseed / Deathtrot and warlock riding a rooster / Weed king / Postal blowfish / Drinker's peace / Break even / The goldheart mountaintop queen directory.

—— JIM POLLARD returned

Nov 95. (7"ep) <(OLE 168-7)> **TIGERBOMB ep**
– My valuable hunting knife / Game of pricks / Mice feel nice (in my room) / Not good for the mechanism / Kiss only the important ones / Dodging invisible rays.

Jan 96. (7") <CH 4520> **THE OPPOSING ENGINEER (SLEEPS ALONE). / (other by NEW RADIANT STORM KING)**
(above issued on 'Chunk')

Feb 96. (7"ep/cd-ep) <(OLE 184-7/-2)> **THE OFFICIAL IRONMEN RALLY SONG / DEAF EARS. / WHY DID YOU LAND? / JUNE SALUTES YOU!**

Mar 96. (cd/d-lp) <(OLE 161-2/-1)> **UNDER THE BUSHES, UNDER THE STARS**
– Man called Aerodynamics / Rhine jive click / Cut-out witch / Burning flag birthday suit / The official ironmen rally song / To remake the young flyer / No sky / Bright paper werewolves / Lord of Overstock / Your name is wild / Ghosts of a diferent dream / Acorns & orioles / Look at them / The perfect life / Underwater explosions / Atom eyes / Don't stop now / Office of hearts / Big boring wedding / It's like soul man / Drag days / Sheetkickers / Redmen and their wives / Take to the sky. *(cd w/bonus cd)* – My valuable hunting knife / Game of pricks / Mice feel nice (in my room) / Not good for the mechanism / Kiss only the important ones / Dodging invisible rays / Delayed reaction brats / He's the uncle / The key losers.

May 96. (7"freebie) <#37> **BRIGHTON ROCKS (live)**
– Hot freaks / Game of pricks.
(above available with 'Fear & Lothing' mag)

Jun 96. (7"pic-d-ep) (OLE 218-7) **CUT-OUT WITCH / RHINE JIVE CLICK. / UNLEASHED! THE LARGE-HEARTED BOY / SOME DRILLING IMPLIED**

—— line-up now:- ROBERT, TOBIN, MITCH + KEVIN

Nov 96. (m-cd/m-lp) <(OLE 185-2/-1)> **SUNFISH HOLY BREAKFAST**
– Jabberstroker / Stabbing a star / Canteen plums / Beekeeper seeks truth / Cocksoldiers and their postwar stubble / A contest featuring human beings / If we wait / Trendspotter acrobat / The winter crows / Heavy metal country.

Nov 96. (7"ep) <(OLE 208-7)> **PLANTATIONS OF PALE PINK ep**
– Systems crash / Catfood on the earwig / The Who vs. Porky Pig / A life in finer clothing / The worryin' song / Subtle gear shifting.

—— ROBERT + TOBIN only

Jan 97. (cd) <ROCKATHON 002> **TONICS AND TWISTED CHASERS (SAY IT WITH ANGEL DUST)**
– Satellite / Dayton, Ohio – 19 something and 5 / Is she ever? / My thoughts are a gas / Knock 'em flyin' / The top chick's silver chord / Key losers / Ha ha man / Wingtip repair / At the farms / Inbaited vicar of scorched earth / Optional bases opposed / Look, it's baseball / Maxwell jump / The stir crazy pornographer / 158 years of beautiful sex / Universal nurse finger / Sadness to the end / Reptilian beauty secrets / Long as the block is black / Jellyfish reflector / The kite surfer / Girl from the sun / The candyland riots. *(UK-iss.May00; same as US)*
(above issued on 'Rockathon')

—— ROBERT + KEVIN added NICK SHULD – bass

Mar 97. (7"ep) <J 001> **WISH IN ONE HAND ep**
– Teenage FBI / Now I'm crying / Real.
(above on 'Jass') (below on 'Wabana')

Mar 97. (7") (ORE 10) **AIM CORRECTLY / ORANGE JACKET. / (other by Cobra Verde)**

—— ROBERT POLLARD now joined by COBRA VERDE:- DOUG GILLARD – guitars, piano / JOHN PETKOVIC – guitars, bass / DON DEPEW – guitars, synthesizer, bass, organ / DAVE SWANSON – drums, maracas / + on some:- MITCH, TOBIN, KEVIN + JIM POLLARD

May 97. (7"ep/cd-ep) <(OLE 217-7/-2)> **BULLDOG SKIN / THE SINGING RAZORBLADE. / NOW TO WAR (electric version) / MANNEQUIN'S COMPLAINT (WAX DUMMY MELTDOWN)**

May 97. (cd/lp) <(OLE 241-2/-1)> **MAG EARWHIG!**
– Can't hear the revolution / Sad if I lost it / I am a tree / The old grunt / Bulldog skin / Are you faster? / I am produced / Knock 'em flyin' / Not behind the fighter jet / Choking Tara / Hollow cheek / Portable men's society / Little lines / Learning to hunt / The finest joke is upon us / Mag earwhig! / Now to war / Jane of the waking universe / The colossus crawls west / Mute superstar / Bomb in the beehive.

Aug 97. (7"ep) <(OLE 264-7)> **I AM A TREE** — Jul97
– I am a tree / (I'll name you) The flame that cries / The ascended master's grogshop.
(cd-ep+=) <(OLE 264-2)> – Do they teach you the chase?

—— ROBERT, DOUG, GREG / + JIM MacPHERSON – drums

Jul 99. (7") <(TVT 1981-7)> **SURGICAL FOCUS. / FLY INTO ASHES** — T.V.T. / T.V.T. Jun99
Jul 99. (cd) <(16581 1980-2)> **DO THE COLLAPSE**
– Teenage FBI / Zoo pie / Things I will keep (for Jim Shepard) / Hold on hope / In stitches / Dragons awake / Surgical focus / Optical hopscotch / Mushroom art / Much better Mr. Buckies / Wormhole / Strumpet eye / Liquid Indian / Wrecking now / Picture me big time / An unmarketed product. *(re-iss. Sep99 on 'Creation' cd+=/lp; CRE CD/LP 251)* – Avalanche aminos. *(lp re-iss. Feb02 on 'TVT' TVT 1980-2)*

Sep 99. (7") (CRE 325) **TEENAGE F.B.I. / FLY INTO ASHES** — Creation / T.V.T.
(cd-s+=) (CRESCD 325) – Tropical robots.

Dec 99. (cd-ep) <1-888-4TV-TCDS> **PLUGS FOR THE PROGRAM** — — / mail-o
– Surgical focus (remix) / Sucker of pistol city / Picture me big time (demo).

Mar 00. (cd-ep) <TVT 1985-2> **HOLD ON HOPE ep**
– Underground initiations / Interest position / Fly into ashes / Tropical robots / A crick uphill / Idiot princess / Avalanche aminos / Do the collapse / Hold on hope.
(UK-iss.Feb02; same as US)

May 00. (7") (LUNA 22) <FCS 5> **DAYTON, OHIO – 19 SOMETHING AND 5 ep** — Apr00
– Dayton, Ohio – 19 something and 5 (live) / Travels / No welcome wagons / Selective service.
(above issued on 'Recordhead') <above issued on 'Fading Captain Series'>

Aug 00. (cd-s) (CRESCD 328) **HOLD ON HOPE / PERFECT THIS TIME / TEENAGE FBI**

—— JIM TOBIAS – bass + NATE FARLEY – guitar; repl. GREG

Oct 01. (cd) <(TVT 2160)> **ISOLATION DRILLS** — T.V.T. / T.V.T. Apr01
– Fair touching / Skills like this / Chasing Heather crazy / Frostman / Twilight campfighter / Sister I need wine / Want one? / The enemy / Unspirited / Glad girls / Run wild / Pivotal film / How's my drinking? / The brides have hit glass / Fine to see you / Privately. <(lp-iss.Feb02; TVT 2160-1)>

Feb 02. (7"blue) (TVT 2162) **CHASING HEATHER CRAZY. / ON WITH THE SHOW** — Mar01

—— Fading Captain Series / Fading Captain Series

May 02. (7") <(FCS 20)> **BACK TO THE LAKE. / DIG THRU' MY WINDOW**
May 02. (7") <(FCS 21)> **CHEYENNE. / VISIT THIS PLACE**
May 02. (7") <(FCS 22)> **EVERYWHERE. / ACTION SPEAKS VOLUMES**
May 02. (7") <(FCS 23)> **UNIVERSAL TRUTHS AND CYCLES. / BEG FOR A WHEELBARROW**

—— Matador / Matador

Jun 02. (cd-s) <(OLE 552-2)> **EVERYWHERE WITH HELICOPTER / PIPE DREAMS OF INSTANT WHIPPIT / KEEP IT COMING**
Jun 02. (cd/lp) <(OLE 547-2/-1)> **UNIVERSAL TRUTHS AND CYCLES**
– Wire greyhounds / Skin parade / Zap / Christian animation torch carriers / Cheyenne / Weeping bogeyman / Back to the lake / Love 1 / Storm vibrations / Factory of raw essentials / Everywhere with helicopter / Pretty bombs / Eureka signs / Wings of thorn / Car language / From a voice plantation / The Ids are alright / Universal truths and cycles / Father Sgt. Christmas card.

Aug 02. (cd-s) <(OLE 564-2)> **BACK TO THE LAKE / FOR LIBERTY / REQUEST PHARMACEUTICALS**

– compilations, etc. –

Feb 95. (5xcd-box/5xlp-box) Scat; <(SCT 040-2/-1)> **BOX**
– (DEVIL BETWEEN MY TOES + SANDBOX + SELF-INFLICTED AERIAL NOSTALGIA + SAME PLACE THE FLY GOT SMASHED + PROPELLER (on lp) / KING SHIT AND THE GOLDEN BOYS (on cd).

1996. (lp) none; <none> **BENEFIT FOT THE WINOS (live)** — — / —

Apr 97. (7"ep; split) Radiopaque; <RR 013> **8 ROUNDS ep (live in the studio at WHFS, Washington, DC)** — / —
– Unleashed! the large-hearted boy / Motor away / My valuable hunting knife / Shocker in Gloomtown – Some drilling implied / (others by GIRLS AGAINST BOYS).

Nov 97. (d-lp) Surefire; <(none)> **JELLYFISH REFLECTOR (live at The Patio Club, Indianapolis, February 17, 1996)**
– Man called aerodynamics / Rhine jive click / Cut-out witch / Burning flag birthday suit / The official ironmen rally song / Bright paper werewolves / Lord of overstock / Your name is wild / Look at them / Underwater explosions / Don't stop now / Office of hearts / Lethargy / Game of pricks / Melted Pat / Hot freaks / Postal blowfish / My son cool / King and Caroline / Motor away / Pimple zoo / Some drilling implied / Shocker in Gloomtown / A salty salute / Gold star for robot boy / Tractor rape chain / Yours to keep / Echos Myron / Weed king. *(cd-iss. Aug99 on 'Recordhead'; LUNA 1)*

Sep 00. (4xcd-box) Fading Captain Series; <(FCS 6)> **SUITCASE: FAILED EXPERIMENTS AND TRASHED AIRCRAFT**
(pseudonymous POLLARD songs from the last 25 years)
(re-iss. Oct02; same)

GUIDED BY VOICES (cont)

Sep 00. (ltd-lp) *Fading Captain Series; <FCS 7>* **SUITCASE ABRIDGED: DRINKS AND DELIVERIES** – / –

Mar 01. (ltd-blue-lp) *Fading Captain Series; <FCS 10>* **DAREDEVIL STAMP COLLECTOR: DO THE COLLAPSE B-SIDES** – / –

Nov 01. (m-cd) *Recordhead;* <*LUNA 48*> **SELECTIVE SERVICE: THE FADING CAPTAIN SINGLES** – / –
– Dayton, Ohio – 19 something and 5 / Travels / No welcome wagons / Selective service / Total exposure / Cold war water sports / The wheel hits the path (quite soon) / Stifled man casino / Peroxide / Eskimo clockwork / In the brain.

Aug 02. (m-cd) *Fading Captain Series;* <*FCS 24CD*> **PIPE DREAMS OF INSTANT PRINCE WHIPPET**
– Visit this place / Swooping energies / Keep it coming / Action speaks volumes / Stronger lizards / The pipe dreams of instant Prince Whippet / Request pharmaceuticals / For liberty / Dig through my window / Beg for a wheelbarrow.

AIRPORT 5

ROBERT POLLARD + TOBIN SPROUT

	Fading Captain Series	Fading Captain Series
May 01. (ltd-7"m) <FCS 11> **TOTAL EXPOSURE. / COLD WAR WATER SPORTS / THE WHEEL HITS THE PATH**	–	
Jul 01. (ltd-7"m) <LUNA 37> <FCS 12> **STIFLED MAN CASINO. / PEROXIDE / ESKIMO CLOCKWORK**		Jun01

(above issued on 'Recordhead' UK)

Aug 01. (ltd-cd) <FCS 13> **TOWER IN THE FOUNTAIN OF SPARKS** – / –
– Burns Carpenter, man of science / Total exposure / Subatomic rain / One more / Mission experiences / The cost of shipping cattle / Circle of trim / War & wedding / Stifled man casino / Up the nails / Tomorrow you may rise / Feathering clueless (the exotic freebird) / Mansfield on the sky / White car creek / Remain lodging. *(UK-iss.Oct02; same)*

Apr 02. (cd) <FCS 16CD> **LIFE STARTS HERE** – / Dec01
– Intro / We're in the business / Yellow wife No.5 / Wrong drama / Addiction / However young they are / Dawntrust guarantee / Forever since / Impressions of a leg / How brown / Natives approach our plane / I can't freeze anymore / Out in the world.

ROBERT POLLARD

with **JIM, KEVIN, DAN, STEVE, MITCH, TOBIN, MARK SWEENEY, JIM SHEPARD + STEVE WILBUR**

	Matador	Matador
Sep 96. (cd/lp) <*(OLE 215-2/-1)*> **NOT IN MY AIRFORCE**		

– Maggie turns to flies / Quicksilver / Girl named Captain / Get under it / Release the sunbird / John strange school / Parakeet troopers / One clear minute / Chance to buy an island / I've owned you for centuries / Ash gray proclamation / Flat beauty / King of Arthur avenue / Roofer's union fight song / Psychic pilot clocks out / Prom is coming / Party / Did it play? / Double standards Inc. / Punk rock gods / Meet my team / Good luck sailor.

— now with **DOUG GILLARD, JIM MacPHERSON, TOBIN + JOHNNY STRANGE**

Jun 98. (cd/lp) <*(OLE 316-2/-1)*> **WAVED OUT**
– Make use / Vibrations in the woods / Just say the word / Subspace biographies / Caught waves again / Waved out / Whiskey ships / Wrinkled ghost / Artificial light / People are leaving / Steeple of knives / Rumbling joker / Showbiz opera walrus / Pick seeds from my skull / Second step next language.

— **GREG DEMOS** – bass; repl. STRANGE

	Fading Captain Series	Fading Captain Series
Mar 99. (cd) <FCS 1> **KID MARINE**		

– Submarine teams / Flings of the waistcoat crowd / The big make-over / Men who create fright / Television prison / Strictly comedy / Far-out crops / Living upside down / Snatch candy / White gloves come off / Enjoy Jerusalem! / You can't hold your women / Town of mirrors / Powerblessings / Island crimes. <*(lp-iss.on 'Recordhead'; LUNA 14LP)*> (re-iss. Oct02; same)

	Recordhead	Recordhead
Dec 99. (lp/cd; by ROBERT POLLARD WITH DOUG GILLARD) <*(LUNA 19/+CD)*> **SPEAK KINDLY OF YOUR VOLUNTEER FIRE DEPARTMENT**		

– Frequent weaver who burns / Soul train college policeman / Pop Zeus / Slick as snails / So something real / Port authority / Soft smoke / Same things / And I don't (so now I do) / Tight globes / I get rid of you / Life is beautiful / Messiahs / Larger Massachusetts / And my unit moves. (cd re-iss. Oct02 on 'Fading Captain Series'; FCS 4)

— next with **GREG DEMOS, JIM MacPHERSON + JIM POLLARD**

	Fading Captain Series	Recordhead
Aug 01. (cd; by ROBERT POLLARD AND HIS SOFT ROCK RENEGADES) (FCS 14) <LUNA 40> **CHOREOGRAPHED MAN OF WAR**		Jun01

– I drove a tank / She saw the shadow / Edison's memos / 7th level shutdown / 40 yards to the burning bush / Aeriel / Citizen fighter / Kickboxer lightning / Bally hoo / Instrument beetle. (re-iss. Oct02; same)

— In Jun'02, ROBERT featured on The TROPIC OF NIPPLES mini-CD (a band fronted by RICHARD MELTZER, SMEGMA, ANTLER & VOM), 'THE COMPLETED SOUNDTRACK FOR THE TROPIC OF NIPPLES'

TOBIN SPROUT

with **ROBERT POLLARD**

	not iss.	AF4
1987. (ltd-lp) <#02002> **FIG.4**	–	

– Way way gone / Train brain / A hard place / Strangler / At bay / Fishin' / She loves her gown / Score / Naola / Contra koo. <*cd-iss. Mar98 on 'Recordhead'+=; LUNA 06*> – Jump now / Dig the catacombs / Sadder than you / Busy bodies / Bottle of the ghost of time / I'll buy you everything you own.

— now with **ROBERT POLLARD, KEVIN FENNELL + JOHN SHOUGH**

	Matador	Matador
Sep 96. (cd/lp) <*(OLE 216-2/-1)*> **CARNIVAL BOY**		

– The natural alarm / Cooler jocks / E's navy blue / The bone yard / Carnival boy / Martin's mounted head / Gas daddy gas / To my beloved Martha / White flyer / I didn't know / Gallant men / It's like soul man / Hermit stew / The last man well known to kingpin.

— with guest drummers

Aug 97. (cd/lp) <*(OLE 244-2/-1)*> **MOONFLOWER PLASTIC (WELCOME TO MY WIGWAM)**
– Get out of my throat / Moonflower plastic (you're here) / Paper cut / Beast of souls / A little odd / Angels hang their socks on the moon / All used up / Since I . . . / Back chorus / Curious things / Exit planes / Little bit of dread / Hit junky dives / Water on the boater's back.

	Recordhead	Recordhead
Dec 97. (7"ep) <LUNA 04> **POPSTRAM ep**		1996

– Toaster / Sadder than you / Bottle of the ghost of time.

— now with **JIM ENO** – drums

Jan 99. (cd-ep) <LUNA 12> **WAX NAILS ep** – / –
– Get your calcium / Cereal killer / Seed / The crawling backward man / In good hands / How's your house.

Mar 99. (cd) <LUNA 13> **LET'S WELCOME THE CIRCUS PEOPLE** / Feb99
– Smokey Joe's perfect hair / Digging up wooden teeth / Mayhem stone / And so on / Making a garden / Vertical insect (the lights are on) / Maid to order / Liquor bag / Who's adolescence / Lucifer's flaming hour / 100% delay / And then the crowd showed up.

Aug 01. (cd) <LUNA 35> **DEMOS & OUTTAKES** (collection) – / –
– Seven and nine / The lords of pretty things / To remake the young flyer / Jealous mantels / To my beloved Martha / Quarter turn here / Dusting coattails / E's navy blue / Little bit of dread / Hit junky dives / Sot #1 / Ketiling park / Slow flanges / Silicone slugs / Paper cut / Smokey Joe / Exit planes / Water on the boaters back / Hint #9 / Piano.

— next with **MacPHERSON + NICK KIZIRNIS** – guitar (of EYESINWEASEL)

Aug 01. (ltd-7") **LET GO OF MY BEAUTIFUL BALLOON. / SHIRLEY THE RAINBOW**
(above issued on 'Wigwam')

Sep 02. (m-cd) <LUNA 59> **SENTIMENTAL STATIONS** – / –
– Secret service / Branding Dennis / I think you would / Inside the blockhouse / Are you happening? / Doctor No.8 (piano version) / Sentimental stations.

GUN CLUB

Formed: Los Angeles, California, USA ... 1980 as CREEPING RITUAL by ex-'Splash' magazine editor, JEFFREY LEE PIERCE and KID CONGO POWERS; they subsequently changed their name at the suggestion of CIRCLE JERKS' KEITH MORRIS. 1981 saw the independent release of their red-raw CHRIS D (Flesheaters)-produced debut album, 'FIRE OF LOVE', 'Beggars Banquet' picking it up for UK release, while CHRIS STEIN (of BLONDIE) was impressed enough to sign the band to his 'Animal' label in '82. Trading in a low-slung fusion of punk and primal rockabilly/blues, the band were favourably compared with contemporaries The CRAMPS, PIERCE, like his counterpart LUX INTERIOR, equal parts damned preacher and demented sinner if not quite managing the same level of leering lasciviousness. Appropriately enough then, the band reinterpreted blues legend, Robert Johnson's 'PREACHIN' THE BLUES' (as well as Tommy Johnson's 'COOL DRINK OF WATER') alongside unhinged originals in the vein of 'SHE'S LIKE HEROIN TO ME', 'SEX BEAT' and the vicious 'JACK ON FIRE'. Although he had co-written the warped 'FOR THE LOVE OF IVY', guitarist POWERS had bailed out prior to the recording of the debut, WARD DOTSON recruited in his place. Despite being previewed by the dark, brooding malevolence of the 'WALKING WITH THE BEAST' single, follow-up set, 'MIAMI' (1982), didn't meet with such an enthusiastic critical reception and PIERCE struggled to keep the creative fires burning. The singer's battle with alcoholism was also a factor and although The GUN CLUB had established themselves as one of America's leading alternative acts, the first phase of the band's career stumbled to a halt following the more sophisticated 'THE LAS VEGAS STORY' (1984). PIERCE cut only one solo album, 'WILDWEED' (1985) before The GUN CLUB unexpectedly reformed in 1987 with KID CONGO back in the fold (he'd also returned briefly in the early 80's) alongside new members NICK SANDERSON and ROMI MORI. Setting themselves up in the UK, the group signed to indie label, 'Red Rhino', procuring the production services of COCTEAU TWIN, ROBIN GUTHRIE, for the resulting album, 'MOTHER JUNO' (1987). More experimental and considered than their previous output, the record saw The GUN CLUB briefly regain their popularity. PIERCE & co. switched to 'Fire' for the belated release of 'PASTORAL HIDE AND SEEK' (1990), while '91's 'DIVINITY' was a half live/half studio affair. It was also, finally, the band's epitaph, as KID CONGO went walkabout and PIERCE cut a further solo set, 'RAMBLIN' JEFFREY LEE & CYPRESS GROVE WITH WILLIE LOVE' (1992) before his health deteriorated inexorably. Sadly, on the 31st of March, 1996, PIERCE died of a brain clot; he was only 37. • **Songwriters:** PIERCE except; RUN THROUGH THE JUNGLE (Creedence Clearwater Revival) / etc.

Album rating: FIRE OF LOVE (*7) / MIAMI (*6) / THE BIRTH, THE DEATH, THE GHOST live collection (*4) / THE LAS VEGAS STORY (*5) / MOTHER JUNO (*7) / PASTORAL HIDE AND SEEK (*7) / DIVINITY (*6) / LUCKY JIM (*5) / Jeffrey Lee Pierce: WILDWEED (*6) / RAMBLIN' JEFFREY LEE . . . (*5)

JEFFREY LEE PIERCE (b.27 Jun'58, El Monte, Calif.) – vocals, guitar / **WARD DOTSON** – lead guitar repl. KID CONGO POWERS who joined The CRAMPS / **ROB RITTER** – bass / **TERRY GRAHAM** – drums (ex-BAGS)

GUN CLUB (cont) — THE GREAT INDIE DISCOGRAPHY — The 1980s

		Beggars Banquet	Ruby
May 82.	(lp/c) (BEGA/BEGC 37) <JRR 102> **FIRE OF LOVE**		Sep81

– Sex beat / Preachin' the blues / Jack on fire / She is like heroin to me / For the love of Ivy / Fire spirit / Ghost on the highway / Jack on fire / Black train / Promise me / Cool drink of water / Goodbye Johnny. *(re-iss. Jan86 on 'New Rose' blue-lp/c; ROSE 8/+CD) (cd re-iss. May94 on 'New Rose'; 42216-2) <US cd-iss. 1990 on 'Slash'; 828809> (cd re-iss. Apr01 on 'Wagram'; 3057172CD) <US cd-iss. 2001 on 'Slash-Rhino'; 79945>*

Jul 82. (7") (BEG 80) **SEX BEAT. / GHOST ON THE HIGHWAY**

		Chrysalis-Animal	Chrysalis-Animal
Aug 82.	(7") (CHCAT 2635) **WALKING WITH THE BEAST. / FIRE OF LOVE**		
Sep 82.	(lp) <(CHR 1398)> **MIAMI**		

– Carry home / Like calling up thunder / Brother and sister / Run through the jungle / A devil in the woods / Texas serenade / Watermelon man / Bad Indian / John Hardy / Fire of love / Sleeping in Blood city / Mother of Earth. *(cd-iss. 1990; X213065)*

— **KID CONGO POWERS** (b. BRIAN TRISTIAN) – guitar returned to repl. RITTER + DOTSON (latter formed PONTIAC BROTHERS)

— **PIERCE** recruited new members

— **JIM DUCKWORTH** – lead guitar (ex-TAV FALCO'S PANTHER BURNS) repl. KID CONGO who later formed FUR BIBLE / **DEE POP** – drum (ex-BUSH TETRAS) repl. TERRY GRAHAM

Apr 83. (7") (GUN 1) **DEATH PARTY. / HOUSE OF HIGHLAND AVENUE / THE LIE**
(12"+=) (GUN12 1) – Light of the world / Come back Jim.

— added **PATRICIA MORRISON** – bass

Jun 84. (lp) <(CHR 1477)> **THE LAS VEGAS STORY**
– The Las Vegas story / Walking with the beast / Eternally is here / The stranger in our town / My dreams / The creator was a master plan / My man's gone now / Bad America / Moonlight hotel / Give up the sun. *(cd-iss. 1990; X 213064)*

— Split late 1984. PATRICIA joined FUR BIBLE (released a one-off 12"EP in 1985 for 'New Rose', 'PLUNDER THE TOMBS') and later joined English goth outfit, The SISTERS OF MERCY

JEFFREY LEE PIERCE

— went solo with **MURRAY MITCHELL** – guitar / **JOHN McKENZIE** – bass / **ANDY ANDERSON** – drums

		Statik	not iss.
Apr 85.	(lp/c) (STAT LP/C 25) **WILDWEED**		–

– Love and desperation / Sex killer / Cleopatra dreams on / From temptation to you / Sensitivity / Hey Juana / Love Circus / Wildweed / From temptation to you / The midnight promise. *(cd-iss. Jun89 +=; CDST 25)* – The Fertility Goddess / Portrait of an artist in Hell / Love & Desperation (long) / Chris and Maggie meet Blind Willie McTell at . . . *(cd re-iss. Jan94 on 'Solid'; 527501220)*

— **PIERCE** brought in **HIROMI** – guitar / **DEAN DENNIS** – bass / **NICK SANDERSON** – drums (both ex-CLOCKDVA)

Aug 85. (7") (TAK 36) **LOVE AND DESPERATION. / THE FERTILITY GODDESS**
(12"+=) (TAK 36-12) – Portrait of an artist in Hell.

Nov 85. (12"ep) (STAB 5) **FLAMINGO (part 1 & 2). / GET AWAY / FIRE / NO MORE FIRE / LOVE AND DESPERATION**

GUN CLUB

— were reformed by PIERCE, KID CONGO + SANDERSON plus **ROMI MORI** – bass

		Red Rhino	Solid
Oct 87.	(lp/c/cd) (RED LP/C/CD 084) **MOTHER JUNO**		

– Breaking hands / Araby / Hearts / My cousin Kim / Port of souls / Bill Bailey / Thunderhead / Lupita screams / Yellow eyes. *(cd re-iss. Nov92 on 'Solid'; 527500420)*

Mar 88. (12"m) (REDT 089) **BREAKING HANDS. / CRABDANCE / NOBODY'S CITY**

— split again, KID CONGO went solo, but last line-up soon reformed

		Fire	Solid
Sep 90.	(12"ep/cd-ep) (BLAZE 47 T/CD) **THE GREAT DIVIDE. / CRABDANCE / ST. JOHN'S DIVINE (part 2)**		

(re-iss. Oct91; BLAZE 44047)

Oct 90. (cd/c/lp) (FIRE CD/MC/LP 28) **PASTORAL HIDE AND SEEK**
– Humanesque / The straits of love and hate / Emily's changed / I hear your heart singing / St.John's divine / The great divide / Another country's young / Flowing / Temptation and I. *(cd+=)* – Eskimo blue day. *(cd re-iss. Feb92 on 'New Rose'; NEW 162) (cd re-iss. Jun93 on 'Solid'; 52790020)*

		New Rose	Solid
Oct 91.	(cd/d-lp) (ROSE 262CD) **DIVINITY** (some live)	–	French

– Sorrow knows / Richard Speck / Keys to the kingdom / Black hole / Yellow eyes (live) / Hearts (live) / Fire of love (live). *(cd+=)* – St. John's divine. *(cd re-iss. Jun93 on 'Solid'; 527900020)*

		Triple X	Triple X
May 93.	(cd/lp) <(527001020)> **LUCKY JIM**		

– Lucky Jim / A house is not a home / Kamata / Hollywood city / Idiot waltz / Up above the world / Day turn the night / Blue moonspoons / Anger blues. *(cd+=)* – Desire.

– compilations etc. –

Feb 84. (lp/c) A.B.C.; (ABCLP/KAS 1) **THE BIRTH, THE DEATH, THE GHOST** (live 1983)
– Bo Diddley's a gunslinger / Railroad Bill / Seven miles with the Devil / Preachin' the blues / Goodbye Johnny / Black train / Walking with the beast / Bad mood / Not that much / Going down the red river / Willie Brown / Field Holler / Sex beat. *(cd-iss. Apr89; ABCD 1)*

Oct 84. (lp) Lolita; **SEX BEAT '81** (live)
Jul 85. (lp) Dojo; (JOJOLP 8) **TWO SIDES OF THE BEAST**
– Walking with the beast / Like calling up thunder / Mother of Earth / Run through the jungle / Eternally is here / The Las Vegas story / Death party / Seven miles with the Devil (live) / Bo Diddley's a gunslinger (live) / Preaching the blues (live) / Goodbye Johnny (live) / Going down the red river (live) / Sex beat (live). *(re-iss. Apr86; same)*

Nov 85. (lp) Eva; (OFFENCE 9002) **LOVE SUPREME** (live '82) – – French
Dec 85. (lp) Roadrunner; (MD 7979) **DANCE KALINDA BOOM** (live In Pandora's Box)
– Eternally is here / Bad America / Sytranger in town / Gila monster, New Mexico / Preaching the blues / Sleeping in Blood City / Goodbye Johnny / Give up the sun. *(cd-iss. Jun93 on 'Solid'; 527500120)*

May 89. (cd-ep) New Rose; (NEAT 1CD) **SEX BEAT / FOR THE LOVE OF IVY / BLACK TRAIN**
Aug 92. (cd) **IN EXILE**
– Breaking hands / Thunderhead / Lupita screams / Yellow eyes / Hearts / Port of souls / Pastoral hide 'n' seek / Straights of love and hate / Emily's changed / I hear your heart singing / St. John's divine (remix) / Another country's young / Flowing / Temptation and I / Richard Speck / Keys to the kingdom / Black hole / Sorrow knows.

Jun 93. (cd) Solid; (527500220) **AHMED'S WILD DREAM** (live)
– (The creator has a) Master plan / Walking with the beast / I hear your heart singin' / Another country's young / Sex beat / Lupita screams / Go tell the mountain / Preachin' the blues / Stranger in my heart / Goodbye Johnny / Port of souls / Black hole / Little wing / Yellow eyes.

May 94. (cd) New Rose; (89001-2) **DEATH PARTY** – –
May 98. (d-cd) Sympathy For The Record Industry; <(SFTRI 478)> **EARLY WARNING** Mar97

JEFFREY LEE PIERCE

		Solid	Solid
May 92.	(cd) (527901220) **RAMBLIN' JEFFREY LEE & CYPRESS GROVE WITH WILLIE LOVE**		

– Goin' down / Pony blues / Future blues / Long long gone / Bad luck and trouble / Alabama blues / Good times / Stranger in my heart / Go tell the mountain / Moanin' in the moonlight / Hardtime / Killin' floor blues

— On 31st March '96, PIERCE died of a blood clot to the brain

GYMSLIPS

Formed: East London, England . . . 1982 by the all-girl trio of PAULA RICHARDS, KAREN YARNELL and SUZANNE SCOTT. Lending a glam sheen to the austerity of the post-punk era, The GYMSLIPS debuted with a cover of Suzi Quatro's '48 CRASH', issued on 'Abstract' later that year. A follow-up, 'BIG SISTER', appeared in early '83, after which the girls took on KATHY BARNES as a full-time member (she'd already augmented the band at live gigs), the one and only album, ROCKIN' WITH THE RENEES' (1983), surfacing a few months later. Personnel upheavals led to sporadic releases, PAULA and SUZANNE recruiting LISA HINDLEY and SUE VICKERS for a final workout in '85, 'EVIL EYE'. RICHARDS subsequently joined The DELTONES until she and KAREN were back in the early 90's with short-lived new band, The RENEES.

Album rating: ROCKIN' WITH THE RENEES (*5)

PAULA RICHARDS (b. 1 Aug'63, Kent, England) – vocals, guitar / **SUZANNE SCOTT** – bass, vocals / **KAREN YARNELL** (b. 2 Apr'61) – drums, vocals

		Abstract	not iss.
Oct 82.	(7") (ABS 011) **48 CRASH. / MISS NUNSWEETA**		–
Jan 83.	(7") (ABS 014) **BIG SISTER. / YO-YO / PIE 'N MASH**		–

— added **KATHY BARNES** – keyboards (was already 4th live member)

May 83. (lp) (ABT 006) **ROCKIN' WITH THE RENEES**
– Drink problem / Barbara Cartland / Face lifts / Thinking of you / Angels / Robot man / Dear Marje / Wandering stars / Yo-yo / Some girls / Complications / Big sister / 48 crash. *(w/ free 7"ep; ABS 015F)* – SILLY EGG / TAKE AWAY. / PIE 'N MASH / MULTI COLOURED SUGAR *(cd-iss. Oct99 on 'Captain Oi'+=; AHOYCD 124)* – Miss Nunsweeta / Pie 'n mash / Multi coloured sugar / Take away / Evil eye / Wonderland / Don't lead me on / Call again / Love's not the answer / Slobadoddob / Silly egg / Valley girl / Renees' reprise.

Jul 83. (7") (ABS 016) **ROBOT MAN. / MULTI COLOURED SUGAR** –

— **LISA HINDLEY** – drums; repl. KAREN who joined SERIOUS DRINKING

— **SUE VICKERS** – keyboards; repl. KATHY

May 85. (7") (ABS 033) **EVIL EYE. / WONDERLAND** –
(12"+=) (ABS 033-12) – Don't lead me on.

— split in 1986 when PAULA joined The DELTONES then POTATO 5; PAULA + KAREN reunited in '91, enlisting also **JACQUI CALLIS** – vocals (ex-DELTONES) / **KATRINA SLACK** (b.14 Jul'62) – bass / **PAUL SEACROFT** – lead guitar (ex-POTATO 5) and delivered 'HE CALLED ME A FAT PIG (AND WALKED OUT ON ME)' for a female-only V/A comp, 'Postcard From Paradise'; an album 'HAVE YOU GOT IT!' was issued for 'Square' records.

THE GREAT INDIE DISCOGRAPHY | The 1980s

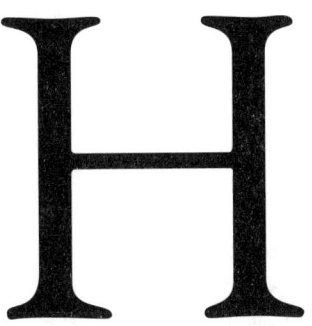

HAGAR THE WOMB

Formed: London, England ... 1983 by the largely pseudonymous sextet of MISS K. PENFOLD (aka JULIE), THE HON. RUTHLESS SAVAGE, EL JANETTI RAVIOLI, HASTA PAUL CENTIPEDE, COM. MITCH JAIL BATE (aka VEG) and MR. CHRIS ENGELBERT FUNKADINK. Early the following year, the 'orribly titled HAGAR THE WOMB made their debut on the heavy/protest label, 'Mortarhate' (home of CONFLICT), with the 'WORD OF THE WOMB' EP. Moving on to the more appropriate indie imprint, 'Abstract', the band came into their own with early '85 EP, 'FUNNERY IN A NUNNERY', a record characterised by an unusual hybrid of The BANSHEES behind DELTA 5 or the SLITS with chunky guitars chopping up "Essex-girl" chorus hooklines. Although this proved to be their final vinyl, four members, JULIE, VEG, PAUL and CHRIS resurfaced under a new, equally distasteful moniker, WE ARE GOING TO EAT YOU. Following the independently released debut single, 'I WISH I KNEW', they secured a longer-term deal with 'Big Cat' and released a follow-up, 'HEART IN HAND'. A subsequent appearance on BBC2's indie video show, 'Snub', led to serious major label A&R interest, although contractual hassles resulted in delays that effectively negated the buzz already created. While they did sign to 'TVT' in America, the group remained with 'Big Cat' for the UK release of debut album, 'EVERYWHEN', at the turn of the decade. The group then underwent a second metamorphosis as two members later re-emerged as the short-lived MELT, recording only one 1991 EP, 'NEVERLAND'.

Album rating: We Are Going To Eat You: EVERYWHEN (*4)

MISS K. PENFOLD (b. JULIE SORRELL) – vocals / **THE HON. RUTHLESS SAVAGE** – vocals / **EL JANETTI RAVIOLI** – guitar / **HASTA PAUL CENTIPEDE** (b. PAUL HARDING) – guitar / **COM. MITCH JAIL BATE** (b. PAUL VENABLES; aka VEG) – bass / **MR. CHRIS ENGELBERT FUNKADINK** (b. CHRIS KNOWLES) – drums

			Mortarhate	not iss.
Jan 84.	(12"ep) (MORT 2)	**WORD OF THE WOMB**	□	-
			Abstract	not iss.
Feb 85.	(12"ep) (12ABS 29)	**FUNNERY IN A NUNNERY**	□	-

– A song of deep hate / One bright spark / Come into the soul / Armchair observer / Once proud now dead.

WE ARE GOING TO EAT YOU

aka **CHRIS, VEG, PAUL + JULIE**

			All The Madmen	not iss.
Jul 87.	(12"ep) (MADT 16)	**I WISH I KNEW. / LET'S FLY. / FINE DAY / LET'S FLY (greedy mix)**	□	-
			Big Cat	T.V.T.
Nov 88.	(7") (ABB 07)	**HEART IN HAND. / JUST ANOTHER ONE (WHO GOT IT WRONG?)**	□	-

(12"+=) (ABB 07T) – What have the flowers got to do with it?

| Oct 89. | (12"ep) (ABB 12T) | **RIDE UPON THE TIDE. /** | □ | - |
| Jan 90. | (lp/c)(cd) (ABB 14/+C)(ABBCD 14) | **EVERYWHEN** | □ | - |

– If I could / Heart in hand / This conspiracy / Each life a mystery / Glory / Ride upon the tide / Eye to eye / On a day like this / Just another one / Here always / If you believe / Her dreamworld.

MELT

were formed by two of the group

| Apr 91. | (12"ep) (ABB 025T) | **NEVERLAND EP** | □ | - |

Paul HAIG (see under ⇒ JOSEF K)

HALF MAN HALF BISCUIT

Formed: Birkenhead, England ... 1984 by lyricist, NIGEL BLACKWELL and his brother SIMON, who enlisted NEIL CROSSLEY, DAVID LLOYD and PAUL WRIGHT (SIMON and the latter having previously played together with the WILDING brothers, ROY and MICHAEL, in late 70's act, ATTEMPTED MOUSTACHE; one single, 'SUPERMAN' / 'NO WAY OUT', appeared on 'Skeleton'). Late in '85, HALF MAN HALF BISCUIT stormed the bastions of good taste with debut album, 'BACK IN THE D.H.S.S', a record that re-introduced caustic wit and twisted humour back into the overly serious mid-80's rock/pop world; The BONZOS had shown the way in the 60's, The ALBERTOS carried the flame for the 70's, and now The 'BISCUITS were having a laugh at the expense of Britain's less glamourous TV celebs. Stalwart people's DJ, John Peel, took to them immediately, wearing out his stylus night after night on such eccentric post-punk (near-plagiarised) ditties as 'I HATE NERYS HUGHES – FROM THE HEART', 'FUCKIN' 'ELL, IT'S FRED TITMUS' and '99% OF GARGOYLES LOOK LIKE BOB TODD', while the tongue-in-cheek 'TIME FLIES BY (WHEN YOU'RE THE DRIVER OF A TRAIN)' took the Michael out of our long lost TV childhood. The following year, the album topped the indie charts for an extended period and even scraped into the national Top 60. Their indie imprint, 'Probe Plus', surely should have scored their first UK chart hit when the HMHB team unleashed their pastiche of a Kim Carnes number ('Bette Davies Eyes') in the shape of 'DICKIE DAVIES EYES', the accompanying thigh-slapping video parodying the Flake TV commercial with the long-haired beauty bearing a frightening resemblance to the moustachioed sports presenter in question! In fact, the band's love of sport, or at least football (they supprted Tranmere Rovers!), was a recurring theme in their work, obsessively expressed in the Subbuteo tribute, 'ALL I WANT FOR CHRISTMAS IS A DUKLA PRAGUE AWAY KIT'. Having amassed more acclaim than they could have dreamed of in their brief year long recording career, HMHB decided to abandon the game before any major crowd trouble. It wouldn't be until 1990 that the band re-emerged onto the musical pitch of that year's Reading Festival, their first single in four years being 'LET'S NOT'. The following Spring, the band enlisted the help of Northern sex symbol, MARGI CLARKE, to spice up their version of the Walker Brothers' 'NO REGRETS'. Virtually six years in the making, their follow-up album (barring exploitation sets), 'McINTYRE, TREADMORE AND DAVITT' (1991), inevitably failed to live up to the genius of its predecessor, although it did contain one throwback to their scathing past in 'OUTBREAK OF VITAS GERULAITIS'. Without exerting themselves too much, the Scouse chancers continued to document the duller side of British life with perverse enthusiasm over such albums as 'THIS LEADEN PALL' (1993), 'SOME CALL IT GODCORE' (1995), 'VOYAGE TO THE BOTTOM OF THE ROAD' (1997), 'FOUR LADS WHO SHOOK THE WIRRAL' (1998), 'TROUBLE OVER BRIDGWATER' (2000) and 'CAMMELL LAIRD SOCIAL CLUB' (2002). In the past decade there have also been a few personnel changes, although NIGEL and NEIL were always at the forefront of the band. • **Trivia for the uninitiated:** FRED TITMUS (former England cricketer) / BOB TODD (comic on Benny Hill show) / LEN GANLEY (snooker referee) / NERYS HUGHES (actress & children's TV presenter) / DEAN FRIEDMAN + ALBERT HAMMOND (US singers) / TED MOULT (TV presenter) / VITAS GERULAITIS (US tennis player).

Album rating: BACK IN THE D.H.S.S. (*9) / BACK IN THE D.H.S.S. AGAIN – ACD (*7) / McINTYRE, TREADMORE AND DAVITT (*5) / THIS LEADEN PALL (*5) / SOME CALL IT GODCORE (*7) / VOYAGE TO THE BOTTOM OF THE ROAD (*5) / FOUR LADS WHO SHOOK THE WIRRAL (*5) / TROUBLE OVER BRIDGWATER (*5) / CAMMELL LAIRD SOCIAL CLUB (*5)

NIGEL BLACKWELL – vocals, guitar / **NEIL CROSSLEY** – bass, vocals / **SIMON BLACKWELL** – lead guitar (ex-ATTEMPTED MOUSTACHE) / **DAVID LLOYD** – keyboards / **PAUL WRIGHT** – drums (ex-ATTEMPTED MOUSTACHE)

			Probe Plus	not iss.
Nov 85.	(lp) (PROBE 4)	**BACK IN THE D.H.S.S.**	59	-

– God gave us life / "Fuckin' 'ell, it's Fred Titmus" / Seal-clubbing / 99% of gargoyles look like Bob Todd / Time flies by (when you're the driver of a train) / I hate Nerys Hughes (from the heart) / The Len Ganley stance / Venus in flares / I love you because (you look like Jim Reeves) / Reflections in a flat. (c+=) – Busy little market town / I left my heart in Papworth General. (re-iss. Apr94 & Oct97 cd/c+=; PROBE 4 CD/C) – The TRUMPTON RIOTS

| Mar 86. | (7") (TRUMP 1-7) | **THE TRUMPTON RIOTS. / ALL I WANT FOR CHRISTMAS IS A DUKLA PRAGUE AWAY KIT** | □ | - |

(12"+=) (TRUMP 1) – Architecture, morality, Ted and Alice / 1966 and all that / Albert Hammond bootleg.

| Sep 86. | (7") (PP 21) | **DICKIE DAVIES EYES. / I LEFT MY HEART IN PAPWORTH GENERAL** | □ | - |

(12"+=) (PP 21T) – The bastard son of Dean Friedman.

| Feb 87. | (lp/c) (PROBE 8/+C) | **BACK IN THE D.H.S.S. AGAIN** (sessions & 12" singles) | □ | - |

– The best things in life / D'ye ken Ted Moult? / Reasons to be miserable (part 10) / Rod Hull is alive – why? / Dickie Davies eyes / The bastard son of Dean Friedman / I was a teenage armchair Honved fan / Arthur's farm / All I want for Christmas is a Dukla Prague away kit / The Trumpton riots (remix). (c+=) – I hate Nerys Hughes (from the heart) (live). (cd-iss. Feb89 as 'ACD'+=; PROBE 8CD) – Carry on cremating / Albert Hammond bootleg (live) / Reflections in a flat (live) / Sealclubbing (live) / Architecture and morality Ted and Alice (live) / Fuckin' 'ell, it's Fred Titmus (live) / Time flys by (when you're the driver of a train) (live). (cd re-iss. Apr94 & Oct97; same)

split late '86; re-formed in 1990

| Oct 90. | (7") (PP 26) | **LET'S NOT. / OUR TUNE** | □ | - |

(12"+=/cd-s+=) (PP 26 T/CD) – Ordinary to Enschede.

| Apr 91. | (7"/c-s; with MARGI CLARKE) (PP 28) | **NO REGRETS. / 1966 AND ALL THAT** (live) | □ | - |

(12"+=/cd-s+=) (PP 28 T/CD) – ('A'-long version).

| Oct 91. | (lp/c/cd) (PROBE 030/+C/CD) | **McINTYRE, TREADMORE AND DAVITT** | □ | - |

– Outbreak of Vitas Gerulaitis / Prag Veg at the Melkweg / Christian rock concert / Let's not / Yipps (my baby got the) / Hedley Verityesque / A lilac Harry Quinn / Our tune / Girlfriend's finished with him / Everything's AOR. (re-iss. Apr94 & Oct97; same)

NIGEL + NEIL + SIMON recruited **CARL ALTY** – drums

| Oct 93. | (lp/c/cd) (PROBE 036/+C/CD) | **THIS LEADEN PALL** | □ | - |

– M-6-ster / 4ad3dcd / Running order squabble fest / Whiteness thy name is Meltonian / This leaden pall / Turned up clocked on laid off / Improv workshop mimeshow gobshite / 13 Eurogoths floating in the Dead Sea / Whit week malarkey /

Doreen / Quality janitor / Floreat inertia / Malayan jelutong / Numanoid hang-glide / Footprints.

— **IAN JACKSON** – bass; repl. SIMON (NEIL now on guitar)

May 95. (lp/c/cd) *(PROBE 041/+C/CD)* **SOME CALL IT GODCORE**
 – Sensitive outsider / Fretwork homework / Faithlift / Song for Europe / Even men with steel hearts / £24.99 from Argos / Sponsoring the moshpits / Fear my wraith / Styx gig (seen with my mates coming out of a) / Friday night and the gates are low / I, Trog / Tour jacket with detachable sleeves.

— **KEN HANCOCK** – guitar; repl. IAN (NEIL bass again)
— **CARL HENRY** – drums; repl. ALTY who joined JOYRIDER

Aug 96. (7") *(PP 30)* **ENO COLLABORATION. /**
 (cd-s+=) *(PP 30CD)* – Get Kramer / Hair like Brian May blues. **C.A.M.R.A. MAN**

Jun 97. (lp/cd) *(PROBE 45/+CD)* **VOYAGE TO THE BOTTOM OF THE ROAD**
 – A Shropshire lad / Bad review / Eno collaboration (new version) / Dead men don't need season tickets / Deep house victims' minibus appeal / C.A.M.R.A. man / PRS yearbook (quick, the drawbridge) / Tonight Matthew I'm going to be with Jesus / The song of encouragement for the Orme ascent / Monmore hare's running / ITMA / He who would valium take / See that my bike's kept clean / Paintball's coming home.

Jun 98. (lp/cd) *(PROBE 46/+CD)* **FOUR LADS WHO SHOOK THE WIRRAL**
 – Children of apocalyptic techstep / Four skinny indie lads / You're hard / On reaching the Wensum / Moody chops / Turn a blind eye / Split single with happy lounge labelmates / A country practice / Secret gig / Soft verges / Multitude / Ready steady Goa / Keeping two Chevrons apart.

Sep 99. (cd-s) *(PP 31)* **LOOK DAD NO TUNES / ECLESIASTICAL PERKS / LOCK UP YOUR MOUNTAIN BIKES**

Apr 00. (lp/cd) *(PROBE 48/+CD)* **TROUBLE OVER BRIDGWATER**
 – Irk the purists / Uffington wassail / Third track main camera four minutes / Move on the sly / Ballad of Climie Fisher / Gubba look-a-likes / Mathematically safe / With goth on our side / Used to be in evil gazebo / Slight reprise / It's cliched to be cynical at Christmas / Visitor for Mr. Edmonds / Bottleneck at Capel Curig / Emerging from gorse / Look dad no tunes / Twenty four hour garage people.

Jun 01. (cd-ep) *(PP 32CD)* **EDITOR'S RECOMMENDATION**
 – Bob Wilson - anchorman / On passing lilac urine / Lark descending / Worried man blues / New York skiffle / Vatican broadside.

Sep 02. (cd) *(PROBE 52CD)* **CAMMELL LAIRD SOCIAL CLUB**
 – The light at the end of the tunnel (is the light of an oncoming train) / When the evening sun goes down / San Antonio foam party / Them's the vagaries / If I had possession over pancake day / The referee's alphabet / She's in Broadstairs / Tyrolean knockabout / Breaking news / 27 yards of dental floss / Paradise lost (you're the reason why) / Thy damnation slumbereth not / Stavanger toestub.

– compilations etc. –

Nov 88. (12"ep/cd-ep) *Strange Fruit; (SFPS/+CD 057) / Dutch East India; <DEI 8331>* **THE PEEL SESSIONS (10.11.85)**
 – D'ye ken Ted Moult / Arthur's farm / All I want for Christmas is a Dukla Prague away kit / Trumpton riots / Old Tiger.

John S. HALL (see under ⇒ KING MISSILE)

HALO OF FLIES

Formed: Minneapolis, Minnesota, USA ... 1985 by TOM HAZELMYER, who had previously been frontman for Seattle outfit, the U-MEN, after earlier enlisting for the US Marines. The brains behind the 'Amphetamine Reptile' label, TOM recruited a rhythm section of TIM 'MAC' McLAUGHLIN and JOHN ANGLIM, releasing 'RUBBER ROOM' as a debut single and the second release for that label. The latter track was issued as a strictly limited edition, as were subsequent 7"er's, 'SNAPPING BACK ROSCOE BOTTLES EP', 'CIRCLING THE PILE', 'RICHIE'S DOG', 'NO TIME' and 'LEDERHOSEN' (a collaboration with KILLDOZER's BILL HOBSON under the pseudonym, POGO THE CLOWN). Combining crazed rockabilly-based attitude with head-on crashing noise, HAZELMYER and Co continued to slash'n'burn their way through the alternative jungle, cutting a couple of EP's for 'Twin/Tone' ('GARBAGE ROCK' and 'HEADBURN'). Collected together as 'GARBAGEBURN', the records were licensed to 'What Goes On' for European release in 1988. A further two singles (including one in '91 shared with MUDHONEY) and a couple of compilation sets rounded up the band's career as HAZELMYER devoted more time to his ever growing 'Amphetamine Reptile'.

Album rating: GARBAGEBURN mini (*6) / SINGLES GOING NOWHERE compilation (*6) / MUSIC FOR INSECT MINDS compilation (*6)

TOM HAZELMYER – vocals, guitar / **JOHN ANGLIM** – drums / **TIM 'MAC' McLAUGHLIN** – bass

	What Goes On	Amphetam. Reptile
1986. (7") *<Scale 2>* **RUBBER ROOM. / THOUGHTS IN A BOOTH**	-	-
1986. (7") *<Scale 3>* **SNAPPING BLACK ROSCOE BOTTLES EP** – Can't touch her / D.D.T. Fin 13.		
1986. (7") *<Scale 4>* **CIRCLING THE PILE EP** – Sinner sings / Pipebomb / M.D. 20-20.	-	-
1987. (7") *<Scale 6>* **RICHIE'S DOG. / HOW DOES IT FEEL TO FEEL**		
1987. (c) *<Scale 9>* **FOUR FROM THE BOTTOM** – Rubber room / thoughts in a booth / Three more quarters / DDT fin 13 / Can't touch her / M.D. 20-20 / Pipebomb / Sinner sings / Richie's dog / How does it feel to feel / Drunk in Detroit.	-	
1988. (7") *<Scale 13>* **NO TIME. / YOU GET NOTHING**	-	
1988. (7"; as POGO THE CLOWN) *<Scale 15>* **LEDERHOSEN. / SESAME ST.** (above was TOM's collaboration with KILLDOZER's BILL HOBSON)	-	

1988. (m-lp) *(GOES ON 24)* **GARBAGEBURN** (a compilation of two 'Twin/Tone' EP's, 'GARBAGE ROCK' <TTR 87132> & 'HEADBURN') – Garbage rock / D.D.T. beat 69 / One barrel spent / I'm clean // Headburn / Easy or hard / Father paranoia / Drunk (in Detroit).		-

	not iss.	Forced Exposure
1990. (7") *<Scale 19>* **DEATH OF A FLY. / CLOWNS**	-	

	not iss.	Silt Breeze
1990. (12"ep) *<FE 019>* **WINGED EP**	-	
1991. (12"ep) **LIVE EP** (live)	-	

— HAZELMYER split the trio in 1991

– compilations, etc. –

on 'Amphetamine Reptile' unless otherwise mentioned
1990. (lp) *<001>* **SINGLES GOING NOWHERE**
1991. (7",7"maroon; shared with MUDHONEY) *<Scale 35/36>* **BIG MOD HATE TRIP EP**
 – Wasted time / Tired & cold / (others by MUDHONEY).
1991. (cd) *<002>* **MUSIC FOR INSECT MINDS**
 – Tired & cold / Wasted time / Death of a fly / Ain't no hell / Spit it out / Ballad of extreme hate / No time / You get nothing / Headburn / Easy or hard / Father paranoia / Drunk (in Detroit) / Garbage truck / D.D.T. beat 69 / One barrel spent / I'm clean / Richie's dog / How does it feel to feel / M.D. 20-20 / Pipebomb / Sinner sings / D.D.T. fin 13 / Can't touch her / Rubber room / Thoughts in a booth / Human fly / I'm a bug / Jagged time lapse / Clowns.

HAPPY FAMILY (see under ⇒ MOMUS)

HAPPY FLOWERS

Formed: Charlottesville, USA ... 1983 by Mr. ANUS (alias CHARLIE KRAMER) and Mr. HORRIBLY CHARRED INFANT (alias JOHN BEERS), who had previously met in the hardcore group The LANDLORDS (also run by bassman EDDIE JETLAG and TRISTAN PUCKETT on drums). ANUS had also been part of other early 80's outfit, The CHARLIE KRAMER BAND, while Mr. HCI featured in two bands, LOWEST COMMON DENOMINATOR and PSYCHODELIC TRASHCAN. The LANDLORDS issued one EP, 'OUR FAVORITE SONGS!' and an album, 'HEY! IT'S A TEENAGE HOUSE PARTY!', before a few members splintered into BIGFOOT (without Mr. ANUS and Mr. HCI). After a few EP's on 'Catch Trout' in the mid-80's, The HAPPY FLOWERS signed to 'Homestead' in 1987, releasing debut album, 'MY SKIN COVERS MY BODY', a basic attempt to resurrect the embryonic touches of SONIC YOUTH and DIY noise/punk and screeching non-tunes. A handful of 45's (the second 'BB GUN' their classiest) and albums ('I CRUSH BOZO', 'OOF' and 'LASTERDAY I WAS BEEN BAD') appeared in the late 80's/early 90's, before they unhappily went to ground. • **Covered:** BRING ON THE DANCING HORSES (Echo & The Bunnymen) / PENNY LANE (Beatles) / MRS. LENNON (Yoko Ono) / REAGANOMICS (DRI) / THIRTEEN (Big Star) / A POX ON YOU (Simeon-Taylor) / LOVE HURTS (Everly Brothers).

Album rating: MY SKIN COVERS MY BODY (*6) / I CRUSH BOZO (*7) / OOF (*5) / TOO MANY BUNNIES (NOT ENOUGH MITTENS) compilation (*7) / LASTERDAY I WAS BEEN BAD (*4) / FLOWERS ON 45: THE HOMESTEAD SINGLES compilation (*6)

MR. ANUS (b. CHARLIE KRAMER) – guitar / **MR. HORRIBLY CHARRED INFANT** (b. JOHN BEERS) – drums

	not iss.	Catch Trout
Feb 84. (7"ep) *<CT-52>* **SONGS FOR CHILDREN** – Mom, I gave the cat some acid / Meadowlands requests.	-	

— around the mid-80's, The LANDLORDS released the LP, 'HEY, IT'S A TEENAGE HOUSE PARTY' on 'Catch Trout'

Jul 86. (7"ep) *<CT-57>* **NOW WE ARE SIX** – Mom and dad like the baby more than me / All my toys hate me / Razors in my apple / Hush little baby / The vacuum ate Timmy / Daddy melted.	-	
Jul 87. (12"ep) *<CT-612>* **MAKING THE BUNNY PAY** (compilation of above tracks)	-	

	Homestead	Homestead
Jul 87. (lp/c) *<(HMS 085-1/-4)>* **MY SKIN COVERS MY BODY** – The sun that burns / Left behind / Jenny tried to kiss me at recess / Toastfire / Why didn't you tell me you were bringing home a baby / Mom, I gave the cat some acid (live) / Not fade away / I'm bored / Let me see your hand / Stop eating / I wet the bed again / If it was broken you'd be screaming / Love theme from KISS. *(c+=)*– Eruption / Under my bed.		
Jun 88. (7"m) *<(HMS 105)>* **THEY CLEANED MY CUT OUT WITH A WIRE BRUSH. / JUST WAIT TILL I'M BIGGER THAN YOU / MY MOTHER S A FISH**		
Jul 88. (lp/c) *<(HMS 106/+C)>* **I CRUSH BOZO** – Get me off of the broiler pan / I'm the stupid one / More mittens / Old relatives / Get Paul's head / Why don't I bleed / Fever dream / Wire brush / I've got the picnic disease / Jellyfish head / There's a worm in my hand / Know / Toenail fear / Mrs. Butcher / My frisbee went under a lawnmower / I saw my picture on a milk carton. *(c+=)* – Mom left me in the car / I crush Bozo.		
Apr 89. (7"m) *<(HMS 135)>* **BB GUN. / CHARLIE GOT A HAIRCUT / I ATE SOMETHING OUT OF THE MEDICINE CABINET**		
May 89. (lp/c/cd) *<(HMS 136-1/-4/-2)>* **OOF** (live) – Stop touching my food / Unhappy meal / Pickin' scabs / There's soft spot on the baby's head / Finger in my crackerjacks / Ain't got nothin' / I said I wanna watch cartoons / My evil twin / I'm gonna have an accident / Let's eat the baby (like my gerbils did) / BB gun / Let me out / I don't wanna go to school / Mrs. Lennon. *(c+=)* – My arm won't wake up / Charlie said the F-word again / Old McDonald.		
May 89. (cd) *<(HMS 137-2)>* **TOO MANY BUNNIES (NOT ENOUGH MITTENS)** (An Historical Perspective 1983-88) – Mom, I gave the cat some acid / Jenny tried to kiss me at recess / More mittens /		

Daddy melted / Left behind / I'm the stupid one / Bobby made me eat a frog / Just wait till I'm bigger than you / I saw my picture on a milk carton / BB gun / Stop touching my food / Not fade away / I've got the picnic disease / I want my tooth back / Charlie got a haircut / I said I wanna watch cartoons / Hush little baby / I don't need another enema / They cleaned my cut out with a wire brush / I crush Bozo / Know / I'm gonna have an accident / Fever dream / The vacuum ate Timmy / Why didn't you tell me you were bringing home a baby / Mom, I gave the cat some acid.

Jun 90. (7"m) *<HMS 159>* **CALL ME PUDGE. / CALL ME PUDGE (live) / GERMAN FOLK SONG (live)**

Jul 90. (cd/lp) *(HMS 160-2/-1)* **LASTERDAY I WAS BEEN BAD**
– We rock / Leave me alone / I don't want to share / Rock bottom / Not a happy birthday / Embryo / Simon / Call me Pudge / I shouldn't have eaten that stuff / Mr. Fuck / Thirteen / If this gun were real (I could shoot you and sleep in the big bed with mommy) / Pull off its head / A pox on you.

—— split after playing final show on 18 August, 1990 at Firenze Tavern, Philadelphia. However, they did play a reunion gig on 20 July 1991 at Fallout Shelter, Raleigh, North Carolina.

– compilations, etc. –

on 'Homestead' unless mentioned otherwise

Nov 91. (7"ep) *<(HMS 161-7>* **THE PEEL SESSIONS**
– My head's on fire / Mom and dad like the baby more than me / Ruckwerts Essen jetzt / I dropped my ice cream cone / These peas are so green.

Sep 92. (cd) *<(HMS 161-2)>* **FLOWERS ON 45: THE HOMESTEAD SINGLES**
– They cleaned my cut out with a wire brush / Just wait until I'm bigger than you / My mother is a fish / BB gun / Charlie got a haircut / I ate something out of the medicine cabinet / Call me Pudge / Call me Pudge (live) / German folk song (live) / My head's on fire / Mom and dad like the baby more than me / Ruckwerts Essen jetzt / I dropped my ice cream cone / These peas are so green / Bring on the dancing horses (live) / Penny Lane (live) / Reaganomics (live) / Love hurts (live) / I wanna BB gun (and some glass eyes) / I'm first on the swing / The big picture / Hitting / The butcher / The CHARLIE-CRAMER BAND:- Loser city / LOWEST COMMON DENOMINATOR:- Fish (I like . . .) / Joe hates work / PSYCHODELIC TRASHCAN:- Home in the jungle / BIGFOOT:- Avsnit Frya / Fleekor / Tak so meeka / The LANDLORDS:- Mrs. Butcher / Empty rhetoric / Press the bar / The strange house / Critical toast.

HAPPY MONDAYS

Formed: Salford, Manchester, England . . . 1984 by brothers SHAUN and PAUL RYDER. In 1985, with the help of A&R man and producer Mike Pickering, they signed a contract with Tony Wilson's 'Factory' records, issuing a debut 12", 'FORTY-FIVE'. With the addition of MARK BERRY aka BEZ on 'percussion', the band released the 'FREAKY DANCIN' single, as good a description as any for BEZ's onstage contortions. A JOHN CALE-produced debut album followed in 1987, the acclaimed mutant indie funk of 'SQUIRREL AND G-MAN . . .' winning the band many converts in the music press and the beginnings of a cult following. The early live shoes have been elevated to almost mythical status, SHAUN & Co. allegedly giving away drugs on the door to their own fans in true scally style. Despite sounding like it'd been recorded in a shed, the Martin Hannett-produced 'BUMMED' (1988) was a classic, a freewheeling groovy noise, punctuated intermittently by RYDER's stoned Mancunian slur. 'MAD CYRIL', 'LAZYITIS' and 'WROTE FOR LUCK' were all brilliant singles, the latter given a dance remix treatment by VINCE CLARKE (Erasure). 'Factory' supremo WILSON decided to take this a step further and set the band to work with the DJ/production team of PAUL OAKENFOLD and STEVE OSBORNE. The result was the pivotal 'MADCHESTER RAVE ON EP', a druggy mash-up of dance, indie, pop and funk that acted as a catylyst for the "Baggy" scene alongside The STONE ROSES' 'FOOL'S GOLD' single (spookily released exactly the same month), inspiring a whole string of bands in Manchester and beyond, some good, some not so good (just don't mention The FARM). Early the following year, The 'MONDAYS hit the Top 5 with their anthemic remake of JOHN KONGOS' 'He's Gonna Step On You Again', retitled 'STEP ON' and injected with typically laissez faire funk. 'KINKY AFRO' also made the Top 5, preceding the band's biggest success of their career, the 'PILLS 'N' THRILLS AND BELLYACHES' (1990) album. This time around there was a cleaner production and a melodic accessibility coating the trademark melange of dirty 'STONES'-style guitar, raggedy-assed funk and cheesy disco. In addition to the singles, the album's highlights included a tribute to 60's folk-popster DONOVAN, a leering piece of porn-funk, 'BOB'S YER UNCLE' and the classic 'GOD'S COP' (featuring the timeless RYDER line "God laid his E's all on me"). While much of the band's music sounded continuously on the point of collapse and live, The HAPPY MONDAYS often seemed as if they'd arrived onstage purely by accident, RYDER was no space cadet, his inimitable lyrical couplets sussed, sharp and dryly witty. Almost inevitably though, the backlash began in earnest with an NME interview painting RYDER and BEZ as dim witted homophobes. Whatever RYDER actually said, it's likely that his tongue was planted firmly in cheek, and besides, to expect The HAPPY MONDAYS to stand up as right-on, PC role models for student NME readers displays a naivety that beggars belief. Retreating to the Bahamas with Talking Heads' CHRIS FRANTZ and TINA WEYMOUTH at the production helm, the band struggled through sessions for the '. . .YES PLEASE!' album, amid tales of general strife, severe drug abuse and obligatory debauchery. The album, an expensive disaster (critically and commercially) that reputedly bankrupted 'Factory', eventually emerged in late '92. Generally ignored and panned by the press, the album nevertheless contained some stellar 'MONDAYS moments, not least the low-key brilliance of 'STINKIN' THINKIN' and the darkly hypnotic 'ANGEL', both tracks using female backing vocals to impressive effect. After a washout of a tour, The HAPPY MONDAYS drifted apart, a messy end for a band that were capable of true musical genius against all the odds. The loose limbed spirit of The 'MONDAYS lived on, though, in BLACK GRAPE, the band RYDER formed along with rapper KERMIT and JED from the RUTHLESS RAP ASSASSINS and a host of extras. SHAUN's brilliant return from oblivion was complete by summer 1995 when the storming 'REVEREND BLACK GRAPE' launched him back into the Top 10. The mouthiest, grooviest low-slung Manc rave-up to grace the charts since the 'MONDAYS' peak, the record pointed squarely in the direction where the party was really happening, bypassing completely the tedious Brit-pop posturing. As ever, RYDER and entourage were never far from controversy, both the song and video subsequently banned from TV as the Catholic church alleged the lyrics condoned Venezuelan terrorist, Carlos The Jackal (which also angered the New York based ADL – Anti-Defamation League). Another classic single, 'IN THE NAME OF THE FATHER', followed into the Top 10, funk rhythms and a sitar tinged intro previewing the eclecticism of the accompanying No.1 album, 'IT'S GREAT WHEN YOU'RE STRAIGHT . . . YEAH!'. Its title a reference to RYDER's clean living new ways (his inimitable cut 'n' paste lyrics apparently fuelled solely by Guinness!?), the record was compared favourably against The HAPPY MONDAYS' best work, and the second coming-style fuss over RYDER's critical rebirth seemed at least partly justified. Loping through a dayglo musical smarty pack of hip-hop, rock, indie-dance, soul and indeed, anything close to hand, RYDER proved his subversive genius was well intact, while KERMIT's hyperactive rapping assaults were a perfect foil for his stoned immaculate drawl. During this time, they were one of the successes at Hamilton Park's 'T In The Park' 2-day festival (near Glasgow), even though KERMIT broke his leg and had to sit out most of the gig on a speaker! During an eventful 1996 of regular touring and high profile press coverage, BEZ and RYDER finally parted ways, while KERMIT embarked on a side project, MAN MADE, the following year. A follow-up album, 'STUPID, STUPID, STUPID' finally emerged at the end of '97 amid furious interband disputes, claims and counter claims. The feuding saw the band cancel their New Year's Eve show at London's Alexandra Palace. SHAUN resurrected The HAPPY MONDAYS and in the meantime, BEZ was up to all sorts, including a TV spot on the Lee & Herring Sunday brunch show (dedicated to strange scientific happenings, mad for it, man). He also began writing an autobiography, no really man! The HAPPY MONDAYS (i.e. SHAUN, his brother PAUL, GAZ, 'WAGS', 'NUTS', ROWETTA and of course a reluctant BEZ!) were "smokin" once again when a new single, 'THE BOYS ARE BACK IN TOWN' (described as only inspired by the THIN LIZZY number!) hit the Top 30. However, after all the hype, the promise and the fuss, only an accompanying 'GREATEST HITS' package was supplied as a stop-gap to feed their fans; PAUL RYDER left on the 11th of August after the Eclipse '99 festival in Cornwall. By which time, SHAUN had paid off the taxman (and child maintenance) from his royalties, but really what did the 'MONDAYS give us during this spell apart from another chance to see the bleary-eyed singer trying to read a cue card on a stage monitor; you're answers please on the back of a postage stamp. In the month of July 2000, the most embarrassing sham on TV since the days of Oliver Reed and George Best when a sober-looking SHAUN was a guest on the Jim Davidson Friday show, er . . . singing 'BARCELONA' (yes, that one!) side by side with opera singer RUSSELL WATSON. • **Songwriters:** Group compositions except; DESMOND (Ob-la-di Ob-la-da; Beatles) / LAZYITIS (Ticket To Ride; Beatles) / TOKOLOSHE MAN (John Kongos). For BLACK GRAPE, SHAUN & KERMIT wrote alongside DANNY SABER, although in October '95, INTASTELLA members MARTIN WRIGHT and MARTIN MITTLER served a writ, claiming they co-wrote with SHAUN on early demos before they departed.

Album rating: SQUIRREL AND G-MAN TWENTY FOUR HOUR PARTY . . . (*8) / BUMMED (*8) / PILLS N' THRILLS AND BELLYACHES (*9) / LIVE (BABY BIG HEAD Bootleg album) (*4) / . . .YES PLEASE (*6) / LOADS – THE BEST OF . . . compilation (*8) / Black Grape: IT'S GREAT WHEN YOU'RE STRAIGHT . . . YEAH! (*9) / STUPID, STUPID, STUPID (*7) / Happy Mondays: THE GREATEST HITS compilation (*8)

SHAUN RYDER (b.23 Aug'62) – vocals / **PAUL RYDER** (b.24 Apr'64) – bass / **MARK DAY** (b.29 Dec'61) – guitar / **PAUL DAVIS** (b. 7 Mar'66) – keyboards / **GARY 'GAZ' WHELAN** (b.12 Feb'66) – drums

Factory Rough Trade

Sep 85. (12"ep) *(FAC 129)* **FORTY-FIVE EP** -
– Delightful / This feeling / Oasis.

—— added **BEZ** (b. MARK BERRY, 18 Apr'64) – percussion, dancer

Jun 86. (7") *(FAC 142)* **FREAKY DANCIN'. / THE EGG** -
(ext.12"+=) *(FAC 142)* – ('A'live).

Mar 87. (12") *(FAC 176)* **TART TART. / LITTLE MATCHSTICK OWEN'S RAP** -

Apr 87. (lp) *(FACT 170)* **SQUIRREL & G-MAN TWENTY-FOUR HOUR PARTY PEOPLE PLASTIC FACE CARNT SMILE (WHITE OUT)** -
– Kuff dam / Tart tart / 'Enery / Russell / Olive oil / Weekends / Little matchstick Owen / Oasis / Desmond * / Cob 20. *(re-iss. Nov88; same)(track * repl. by)* – Twenty four hour party people. *(cd-iss. Mar90 +=; FACD 170)* – Little matchstick Owen's rap. *(cd re-iss. May99 on 'London'; 520012-2)*

Oct 87. (12") *(FAC 192)* **TWENTY FOUR HOUR PARTY PEOPLE. / YAHOO / WAH WAH (THINK TANK)** -

Nov 88. (7") *(FAC 212-7)* **WROTE FOR LUCK. / BOOM** -
(12"+=/cd-s+=) *(FAC/+D 212)* – ('A'dance mix) / ('A'club mix).

Nov 88. (lp/cd)(d/dat) *(FACT/FACD 220)(FACT 220 C/D)* **BUMMED** -
– Country song / Moving in with / Mad Cyril / Fat lady wrestlers / Performance / Brain dead / Wrote for luck / Bring a friend / Do it better / Lazyitis. *(hit UK 59 UK Jan90) (cd re-iss. May99 on 'London'; 520013-2)*

HAPPY MONDAYS (cont)

May 89. (12"/7"/c-s; as HAPPY MONDAYS & KARL DENVER) (FAC 222/+7/C) **LAZYITIS - ONE ARMED BOXER. / MAD CYRIL – HELLO GIRLS** — 85 / –
(re-iss. May90; same); hit No.46)

Sep 89. (12"/7") (FAC 232/+7) **WFL** (Vince Clarke mix). / **WFL – THINK ABOUT THE FUTURE** (the Paul Oakenfold mix) — 68 / –
(cd-s+=) (FACD 232) – Lazyitis - one armed boxer.

Nov 89. (7"clear/12"clear) **MAD CYRIL – HELLO GIRLS. / DO IT BETTER** — – / –

Nov 89. (12"ep/cd-ep)(7"ep/c-ep) (FAC/+D 242)(FAC 242-7/-C) **MADCHESTER RAVE ON EP** — 19 / –
– Hallelujah / Holy ghost / Clap your hands / Rave on.
(7") (FAC 242R-7) – Hallelujah (the MacColl mix) / Hallelujah (in out mix).
(c-s)(12"/cd-s) (FAC 242RC)(FAC/+D 242R) – ('A'club mix) / Rave on (club mix).

— added guest ROWETA – backing vocals to repl. other guest KIRSTY MacCOLL

Factory / Elektra

Mar 90. (12"/7") (FAC 272/+7) <64899> **STEP ON** (stuff it in mix). / ('A'-One louder mix) — 5 / 57 Feb91
(c-s+=)(cd-s+=) (FAC 272C)(FACD 272) – 'A'-Twistin' my melons mix.

Oct 90. (12"/7"/c-s) (FAC 302/+7/C) **KINKY AFRO. / KINKY AFRO** (live) — 5 / –
(cd-s+=) (FACD 302) – 'A' radio edit.

Nov 90. (cd/lp)(c) (FACD/FACT 320)(FAC 320C) <60986> **PILLS 'N THRILLS AND BELLYACHES** — 4 / 89
– Kinky Afro / God's cop / Donovan / Grandbag's funeral / Loose fit / Dennis & Lois / Bob's your uncle / Step on / Holiday / Harmony. (cd re-iss. May99 on 'London'; 828223-2) (re-hit.Jul02 at No.47)

Feb 91. (12"/7"/c-s) (FAC 312/+7/C) **LOOSE FIT. / BOB'S YOUR UNCLE** — 17 / –
(cd-s+=) (FACD 312) – Kinky Afro (Euro mix).

Sep 91. (cd/d-lp)(c) (FACD/FACT 322)(FAC 322C) **LIVE** (live BABY BIG HEAD Bootleg album) — 21 / –
– Hallelujah / Donovan / Kinky Afro / Clap your hands / Loose fit / Holiday / Rave on / E / Tokoloshe man / Dennis and Lois / God's cop / Step on / W.F.L. (d-lp+=)(c+=) – Bob's your uncle.

Nov 91. (12"/7"/c-s) (FAC 332/+7/C) **JUDGE FUDGE. / TOKOLOSHE MAN** — 24 / –
(cd-s+=) (FACD 332) – 'A' version.

Sep 92. (7"/c-s) (FAC 362 7/C) **STINKIN' THINKIN'. / ('A'-Boys Own mix)** — 31 / –
(12"+=/cd-s+=) (FAC/+D 362) – ('A'-Terry Farley mix) / Baby bighead.

Oct 92. (cd/lp)(c) (FACD/FACT 420)(FAC 420C) <61391> **. . . YES PLEASE!** — 14 / –
– Stinkin' thinkin' / Monkey in the family / Sunshine & love / Dustman / Angel / Cut 'em loose Bruce / Theme from Netto / Love child / Total Ringo / Cowboy Dave. (cd re-iss. May99 on 'London'; 520026-2)

Nov 92. (7"/c-s) (FAC 372 7/C) **SUNSHINE & LOVE. / STAYING ALIVE** (mix) / **TWENTY FOUR HOUR PARTY PEOPLE** (remix) — 62 / –
(12"+=/cd-s+=) (FAC/+D 372) – 'A' dance mix.

— they disbanded early '93, with SHAUN and other two briefly forming The MONDAYS which evolved into BLACK GRAPE

BLACK GRAPE

SHAUN RYDER + BEZ with **KERMIT** (b.PAUL LEVEREDGE) – rapper (ex-RUTHLESS RAP ASSASSINS) / **JED BIRTWHISTLE** – rapper (ex-RUTHLESS RAP ASSASSINS) / **WAGS** – guitar (ex-PARIS ANGELS) / **CRAIG GANNON** – guitar (ex-SMITHS who replaced INTASTELLA guitarists MARTIN WRIGHT + MARTIN MITTLER

Radioactive / Radioactive

May 95. (c-s) (RAXC 16) **REVEREND BLACK GRAPE / STRAIGHT OUT OF TRUMPTON (BASEMENT TAPES)** — 9 / –
(cd-s+=) (RAXTD 16) – ('A'-dark side mix).
(12") (RAXT 16) – ('A'side) / ('A'-dub collar mix) / ('A'-dark side mix).

Jul 95. (c-s) (RAXC 19) **IN THE NAME OF THE FATHER / LAND OF A THOUSAND KAMA SUTRA BABIES** — 8 / –
(cd-s+=) (RAXTD 19) – ('A'-chopper's mix) / ('A'-chopper's instrumental).
(12") (RAXT 19) – ('A'side) / (above 2).

Aug 95. (cd/c/lp) (<RAD/RAC/RAR 11224>) **IT'S GREAT WHEN YOU'RE STRAIGHT . . . YEAH** — 1 / –
– Reverend Black Grape / In the name of the father / Tramazi party / Kelly's heroes / Yeah yeah brother / Big day in the north / Shake well before opening / Shake your money / Little Bob.

Nov 95. (c-s) (RAXC 22) **KELLY'S HEROES / ('A'-The Milky Bar Kid mix)** — 17 / –
(cd-s+=) (RAXTD 22) – ('A'-The Archibald mix) / Little Bob (live).
(cd-s) (RAXXD 22) – ('A'live) / In the name of the father (live) / Fat neck.

— BEZ quit due to argument with SHAUN over his role in the group.

— On Channel 4's TFI Friday, SHAUN caused more controversy by adding loads of live f words on their version on SEX PISTOLS 'Pretty Vacant'.

May 96. (c-s) (RAXC 24) **FAT NECK / PRETTY VACANT** (live) — 10 / –
(cd-s+=) (RAXTD 24) – Yeah yeah brother (Outlaw Josey Wales mix).
(12") (RAXT 24) – ('A'-GOLDIE Beat the f*** down mix) / Yeah yeah brother (Clockwork Orange mix) / Yeah yeah brother (Dog day afternoon mix).

Jun 96. (c-s) (RAXC 25) **ENGLAND'S IRIE / (Pass the Durazac mix)** — 6 / –
(12"+=/cd-s+=) (RAXT/+D 25) – ('A'-Suedehead dub) / ('A'-Mel's L.A. Irie mix). above featured JOE STRUMMER and KEITH ALLEN

— In Oct'96, SHAUN moonlighted with The HEADS (ex-TALKING HEADS) on minor hit single 'Don't Take My Kindness For Weakness'.

Oct 97. (c-s/cd/cd-s) (RAX C/TD 32) **GET HIGHER / ('A'mixes)** — 24 / –
(cd-s) (RAXXD 32) – ('A'mixes).

Nov 97. (lp/c/cd) (RAR/+C/D 11716) **STUPID STUPID STUPID** — 11 / –
– Get higher / Squeaky / Marbles / Dadi was a badi / Rubber band / Spotlight / Tell me something / Money back guaranteed / Lonely / Words.

Feb 98. (cd-s) (RAXTD 33) **MARBLES** (remixes by R.I.P. and FABIO PARAS) / **MARBLES** (demo) — 46 / –
(12"+=) (RAXT 33) – ('A'-Tricky remix).
(cd-s) (RAXXD 33) – ('A'-Tricky remix) / Harry the dog / Get higher (uncensored video on CD-ROM).

HAPPY MONDAYS

— re-formed SHAUN + PAUL RYDER , GAZ WHELAN, PAUL 'WAGS' WAGSTAFF, 'NUTS', BEZ + ROWETTA

London / not iss.

May 99. (12") (LONX 432) **THE BOYS ARE BACK IN TOWN. / ('A'-Dirty mix)** — 24 / –
(cd-s) (LONCD 432) – ('A'side) / Kinky Afro / ('A'extended).
(cd-s) (LOCDP 432) – ('A'-Dirty mix) / Loose fit (Perfecto mix) / Bob's yer uncle (Perfecto mix).

May 99. (cd/c) (556105-2/-4) **GREATEST HITS** (compilation) — 11 / –
– Step on / WFL (Vince Clarke mix) / The boys are back in town / Kinky Afro (Perfecto mix) / Hallelujah (club mix) / Mad Cyril / Lazyitis (One Armed Boxer mix) / Loose fit (Perfecto mix) / Bob's yer uncle / Judge fudge / Stinkin' thinkin' / 24 hour party people / WFL (Think About The Future mix) / Stayin' alive / Step on (Twisting My Melon mix).

— in Jul'00, SHAUN RYDER er, collaborated on a version of 'BARCELONA' with opera singer RUSSELL WATSON (it hit UK No.68)

– compilations, etc. –

May 90. (12"ep/c-ep/cd-ep) Strange Fruit; (SFPS/+C/CD 077) / Dutch East India; <8306> **THE PEEL SESSION** — – / –
– Tart tart / Mad Cyril / Do it better. (cd-ep re-iss. Feb92; same)

Nov 91. (cd-ep) Strange Fruit; **THE PEEL SESSION (1986)** — – / –
– Freaky dancin' / Kuff dam / Olive Oil / Cob 20.

Sep 93. (cd,c) Elektra; <61543> **DOUBLE EASY: THE US SINGLES** — – / –

Oct 95. (cd/c) London; (520036-2/-4) **LOADS** — 41 / –
– Step on / W.F.L. / Kinky Afro / Hallelujah – MacColl mix / Mad Cyril / Lazyitis / Tokoloshe man / Loose fit / Bob's yer uncle / Judge fudge / Stinkin' thinkin' / Sunshine & love / Angel / Tart tart / Kuff dam / Twenty four hour party people. (some cd's w/ free cd+=) **LOADS MORE** – Lazyitis - one armed boxer mix / W.F.L. / Bob's yer uncle (Perfecto mix) / Loose fit (Perfecto mix) / Hallelujah (Deadstock mix) / Freaky dancing / Delightful.

May 02. (12") Londpn; (LONX 466) **24 HOUR PARTY PEOPLE (mixes)** — – / –

Pearl HARBOR & THE EXPLOSIONS

Formed: San Francisco, California, USA . . . late '78 by PEARL E. GATES. Of American-Filipino parentage, she was once a dancer/backing singer with The TUBES' live troupe before hooking up with fellow member, JANE DORNACKER, to form the musically similar LEILA & THE SNAKES. Subsequently acquiring the group's rhythm section, JOHN and HILARY STENCH, while also finding guitarist, PETER BILT, GATES initiated PEARL HARBOR & THE EXPLOSIONS. Their independently released debut single, 'DRIVIN', set the underground New Wave scene alight, leading to 'Warners' harnessing their potential and releasing an eponymous debut album late in '79. Its failure to reach the US Top 100 resulted in her band bailing out for more mainstream waters (although they did later work with CHROME), while PEARL based herself in London for the recording of a MICKEY GALLAGHER-produced solo set, 'DON'T FOLLOW ME, I'M LOST TOO' (1981). A few years laters, it emerged that the singer tied the knot with The CLASH's PAUL SIMONON, although this didn't help her musical fortunes as a final album for 'Island', 'PEARLS GALORE!' (1985), bombed!

Album rating: PEARL HARBOR & THE EXPLOSIONS (*5) / Pearl Harbor: DON'T FOLLOW ME, I'M LOST TOO (*4) / PEARLS GALORE! (*5) / HERE COMES TROUBLE (*3)

PEARL E. GATES (b. 1958, Germany) – vocals, percussion / **PETER BILT** – guitar, vocals / **HILARY STENCH** – bass, vocals / **JOHN STENCH** – drums, percussion

not iss. / 415 Records

1979. (7") <S 0003> **DRIVIN'. / RELEASE IT** — – / –

Warners / Warners

Dec 79. (7") <WBS 49143> **YOU GOT IT (RELEASE IT). / BUSY LITTLE B SIDE** — – / –

Jan 80. (lp) (K 56769) <BSK 3404> **PEARL HARBOR & THE EXPLOSIONS** — – / –
– Drivin' / You got it / Don't come back / Keep going / Shut up and dance / The big one / So much for love / Get a grip on yourself / Up and over.

Feb 80. (7") <WBS 49207> **DRIVIN'. / THE BIG ONE** — – / –

Apr 80. (7") (K 17554) **UP AND OVER. / BUSY LITTLE B SIDE** — – / –

— now without the STENCH brothers who joined VITAL PARTS (JORMA KAUKONEN). They later became part of CHROME (DAMON EDGE, HELIOS CREED)

PEARL HARBOR

— now apparently backed by producer, **MICKEY GALLAGHER** / **OTIS WATKINS** – keyboards (ex-SHAKIN' STEVENS) / **NIGEL DIXON**

Jan 81. (7") (K 17740) **FUJIYAMA MAMA. / NERVES** — – / –

Jan 81. (lp) (K 56885) <BSK 3515> **DON'T FOLLOW ME, I'M LOST TOO** — – / –
– Alone in the dark / Fujiyama mama / Everybody's boring but my baby / You're in trouble again / Do your homework / Cowboys & Indians / Losing to you / Filipino baby / Let's go upstairs / Rough kids / Out with the girls / Heaven is gonna be empty / At the dentist.

Pearl HARBOR & THE EXPLOSIONS (cont)

Apr 81.	(7") (K 17781) **COWBOYS & INDIANS. / YOU'VE GOT ME ALL WRONG**	not iss.	Test Press
Jan 82.	(7") <TPB 6> **VOODOO VOODOO. / YOU DON'T FOOL ME**	–	–

— next with THE MODS (Japanese band) + CHRIS SPEDDING – guitars

		Island	Island
Jul 84.	(7"/10") (IS/10IS 191) **HULA LOVE. / PLEASE COME HOME**		
Feb 85.	(lp) (ILPS 9824) **PEARLS GALORE!**		

– Killer Joe / He ain't so bad / Flirt / Spanish bop / Nerves / Get outta here / Out in the streets / Please come home / Run rhythm run / Hula love.

— PEARL E retired from the music biz

– compilations, etc. –

| 1996. | (cd) *Backtrip*; **HERE COMES TROUBLE** | – | |

HARD-ONS

Formed: Sydney, Australia . . . 1982 out of The PLEBS and The DEAD RATS, by PETER BLACK, RAY AHN and KEISH DE SILVA, all ex-patriots from Yugoslavia, Korea and Sri Lanka. Fun lovin', if not exactly PC, this bunch of Aussie ne'er do wells initially traded exclusively in the 7" single market, releasing such sniggeringly titled "classics" as 'SURFIN' ON MY FACE' and 'SUCK 'N' SWALLOW' (both from 1985). More toilet humour followed with a debut album, the enticingly named 'SMELL MY FINGER' (no relation to the GEORGE CLINTON album!), their primary school punk RAMONES meets The DEAD KENNEDYS rehashes predictably finding a loyal, largely male audience. The MACC LADS of three-chord hardcore carried on inflicting their "hilarious" compositions on a largely uninterested metal scene throughout the 80's with the likes of 'HOT FOR YOUR LOVE, BABY' (aka 'THE WORST OF THE HARD-ONS') (1987), 'DICKCHEESE' (1988), 'LOVE IS A BATTLEFIELD OF WOUNDED HEARTS' (1989), 'YUMMY!' (1991) and 'TOO FAR GONE' (1993). Apart from a split album with The STUPIDS, their most high profile outing was probably the collaboration with HENRY ROLLINS, a 1991 cover of AC/DC's 'LET THERE BE ROCK'.

Album rating: SMELL MY FINGER (*4) / HOT FOR YOUR LOVE, BABY (*4) / DICKCHEESE (*4) / LOVE IS A BATTLEFIELD OF WOUNDED HEARTS (*5) / YUMMY! (*6) / TOO FAR GONE (*4) / THE HARD-ONS AT THEIR BEST compilation (*6) / THIS TERRIBLE PLACE (*5)

KEISH DE SILVA – vocals, drums / **PETER BLACK** – guitar / **RAY AHN** – bass

		Vi-Nil	Big Time
1985.	(7"ep) **SURFIN' ON MY FACE EP**	–	Austra

– There was a time / Excuses / Surfin' on my face / Bye bye girl. (UK-iss.1987 on 'Waterfront'; DAMP 34)

| 1985. | (7"flexi) (LE-3) **BY MY SIDE. / I'LL COME AGAIN** | – | Austra |

(above issued for the 'Livin' End' fanzine)

		Waterfront	not iss.
1986.	(7") (DAMP 27) **GIRL IN THE SWEATER. / I HEARD HER CALL MY NAME**	–	Austra
1986.	(lp) <6040> **SMELL MY FINGER** <US title 'THE HARD-ONS'>		Austra

– Lollipop / Buddies / Squat house / Wog food / Dancing girls / Then I kissed her / Think about you everyday / I farted. (UK-iss.Sep87 on 'Waterfront'; DAMP 37)

| 1987. | (7") (DAMP 47) **ALL SET TO GO. / FERDI'S SONG** | – | Austra |
| 1988. | (7") (DAMP 50) **SUCK N SWALLOW. / BUSTED!** | – | Austra |

		Vinyl Solution	Taang!
Feb 88.	(lp) (SOL 8) **HOT FOR YOUR LOVE, BABY** (other title 'THE WORST OF THE HARD-ONS')		

– Long song for Cindy / Coffs harbour blues / School days / It's cold outside / Then I kissed her (Arabic) / By my side / I'll come again / Fifteen / Keish's new song / From my window / Rock'n'roll all nite.

| Apr 88. | (lp) (SOL 10) <TAANG 26> **DICKCHEESE** | | |

– Made to love you / What am I spose to do? / Oozin for pleasure / Everytime I do a fart / Get away / Pretty face / There was a time / Mickey juice / Figaro / Fuck society / Yuppies sick / Something about you / All washed up / Ache to touch you / Why don't you shut up / Nerds / Got a baby / Stairway to punchbowl.

| Oct 89. | (lp/cd) (SOL 19/+CD) <TAANG 35> **LOVE IS A BATTLEFIELD OF WOUNDED HEARTS** | | |

– Don't wanna see you cry / Rejected / Chitty chitty bang bang / Been had before / You're a tease / Who do you wanna fool? / Get wet / Rich scrag / Do it with you / Missing you missing me / Throw it in / Kill your mum. (cd+=) – Made to love you / What am I spose to do / Everytime I do a fart / Get away / Pretty face.

— in 1989, split an album with The STUPIDS; 'NO CHEESE! – THE HIGHWAY TO HELL TOUR EP' on 'Waterfront'

| 1989. | (7") (DAMP 94) **JUST BEING WITH YOU. / GROWING OLD** | – | Austra |
| 1989. | (7"ep) (DAMP 111) **GIVEAWAY ep** | – | Austra |

– Sick of being sick / Graham / F.O.C.F.

| 1990. | (7") (DAMP 145) **WHERE DID SHE COME FROM. / GET OUT OF MY HOUSE** | – | Austra |
| Feb 91. | (lp/c/cd) (SOL 26/+CD) **YUMMY!** | | |

– Where did she come from / Raining / Dull / Cool hand Luke / Something I don't want to do / Sit beside you / Jaye's song / On and on / Ain't gonna let you go / Me or you / Spew / Fade away / Little Miss Evil / Wait around / Feast on flesh / Stairway to Heaven.

| Jul 91. | (12"/cd-s/<7") HENRY ROLLINS & The HARD-ONS) (VS 30/+CD / CZ 035> **LET THERE BE ROCK. / CARRY ME DOWN** | | |
| Sep 91. | (12"ep/cd-ep) (DAMP 157) **DULL EP** | – | – |

– Dull / Sri Lanka / Just being with you / Growing old.

		Waterfront	not iss.
1992.	(d7"red/green-ep) (DAMP 170) **WHERE THE WILD THINGS ARE**	–	Austra

– Sorry / Lose it / (other 2 by CELIBATE RIFLES).

| 1992. | (m-cd) (DAMP 176) **DATELESS DUDES CLUB!** | – | –• Austra |

– She's a dish / Selfish / World / Hate so hard / Test / Raining / What am I sposed to do? / Suck 'n' swallow.

| 1993. | (cd-s) (DAMP 180) **CRAZY, CRAZY EYES / I'M DOWN / DESTROYER** | – | Austra |
| 1993. | (cd-s) (DAMP 183) **TEST / STAN THE ICE CREAM MAN / WISHING WELL / BURN IN HELL / SEE HER TONITE** (live with Jerry A) | – | Austra |

		Survival	Skene
Sep 93.	(lp/cd) (SUR 538/+CD) <29> **TOO FAR GONE**		

– Crazy, crazy eyes / Notice me / If it makes you happy / Carphone / Test / I do I do I do / Lost / The blade (vocals by JERRY A from POISON IDEA) / No one can stop you / Cat scan / If she only knew / Stressed out / Sleepy. (hidden track+=) above was their last release, although they shared a single with The CELIBATE RIFLES, 'WHERE THE THINGS ARE' on 'Waterfront'

— they re-formed prior to the new millennium

		One Way Street	not iss.
1999.	(cd-ep) (OWSEP 01) **YESTERDAY AND TODAY**	–	Austra

– Small talk / You disappointed me / Been had before / Got a baby.

		Radio Blast	not iss.
1999.	(ltd-7") (RBR 024) **YOU DISAPPOINTED ME. / SAY GOODBYE**	–	Austra

		Munster	not iss.
1999.	(ltd-7") (7129) **SHARK'S HEAD. / BIRTHDAY**	–	Austra

		Bad Taste	Bad Taste
Feb 01.	(cd) (<BTR 45>) **THIS TERRIBLE PLACE**		

– Fallen star / Strangers / Ice cream / First cut is the weakest / Time won't let me / Trouble trouble / Shark's head / Oyster sauce / Charger / I'm bringing you dead / Nosebleed / Sadly ever after / Birthday / I hate clubbers.

– compilations, etc. –

| Apr 99. | (d-cd/d-lp) *Citadel*; (CITCD 546) **THE HARD-ONS BEST** | | |

– Small talk / Raining / She's a dish / Something about you / Think about you everyday / Do it with you / Sorry / Where did she come from? / Suck 'n' swallow / Missing you, missing me / Get away / It's up to me / Girl in the sweater / Busted! / There was a time / On and on / Wishing well / All set to go / Lose it / Wog food / Don't wanna see you cry / I do I do I do / Just being with you / Simple love / Wait around / School days / Get wet / Surfin' on my face / What am I spose to do? / Throw it in // LIVE 1991:- Get wet / Sorry / Been had before / Suck n swallow / Simple love / Rejected / Hate so hard / Just being with you / Test / Sit beside you / Kill your mom / She's a dish / Raining / World / Wait around / Little Miss Evil / Spew / Feast on flesh / Where did she come from? / All washed up / Me or you / What am I spose to do? / Something about you / Feast on flesh / Dull.

Grant HART (see under ⇒ HUSKER DU)

HAWKS (see under ⇒ DUFFY, Stephen)

Michael HEAD (see under ⇒ SHACK)

HEADLESS CHICKENS

Formed: New Zealand . . . 1985 by CHRIS MATTHEWS and JOHNNY PIERCE (ex-CHILDREN'S HOUR), with drummer MICHAEL LAWRY. Originally the INTERNATIONAL HEADLESS CHICKENS, they debuted with a track on student radio compilation 'Outnumbered By Sheep', followed by the 'HEADLESS CHICKENS' EP, which landed them a support slot on tour with NICO. The tragic suicide of bassist PIERCE, in August 1986, prompted their expansion to a four-piece, with additions GRANT FELL (PIERCE's replacement), and RUPERT TAYLOR, formerly with BIRD NEST ROYS. A $60,000 first prize in a national rock music competition funded the recording of their debut LP, and a national tour. With two new members – former CHILDREN'S HOUR drummer BEVAN SWEENEY and multi-instrumentalist ANTHONY NEVISON – and popular releases like 45s 'DONKA' and 'EXPECTIN' TO FLY', they landed a deal with the 'Flying Nun' label. Mainstream success came via 1991's 'BODY BLOW, and the single 'CRUISE CONTROL', the CHICKENS' line-up now also featured vocalist FIONA McDONALD. Further single success ('DONDE ESTA LA POLLO' and 'JUICE'), and a 1994 European tour didn't manage to stabilize the line-up; NEVISON, McDONALD, LAWRY and FELL all departing along the way. • **Covered:** SUPER TROUPER (Abba) / USED TO (Wire).

Album rating: STUNT CLOWN (*5) / BODY BLOW (*6) / GREEDY (*5) / CHICKENSHITS compilation (*7)

CHILDREN'S HOUR

CHRIS MATTHEWS – vocals, guitar / **JOHNNY PIERCE** – bass / **GRANT FELL** – guitar / **BEVAN SWEENEY** – drums

		Flying Nun	not iss.
1984.	(12"ep) (FN C60) **FRESH**	–	NewZ

HEADLESS CHICKENS

— added **MICHAEL LAWRY** – drums

		Flying Nun	not iss.
Sep 86.	(m-lp) (FN 061) **HEADLESS CHICKENS**	–	NewZ

– Monkey jar / Axe / Slice / Hedge song / Totalling dad's car / Agitopop / Ghost of some cold street.

— PIERCE committed suicide in August 1986

— he was repl. by **GRANT FELL** – bass, keyboards (ex-CHILDREN'S HOUR)

— added **RUPERT TAYLOR** – (ex-BIRD NEST ROYS)

── BEVAN SWEENEY – drums (ex-CHILDREN'S HOUR) repl. RUPERT (LAWRY now on keyboards)
Feb 88. (7") *(FN 088)* **SOULCATCHER. / DONKA** — / — NewZ
May 88. (lp) *(FN 100)* **STUNT CLOWN** — / — NewZ
 – Expecting to fly / Soulcatcher / Frank / Do the headless chicken / Fish song / Donka / Run, sheep run / White out / Untitled / Cyclic / Star at night. *(cd-iss. 1992 on 'Flying Nun Europe' +=; FNE 24)* – HEADLESS CHICKENS EP / King in me.
── added **ANTHONY NEVISON** – multi
Jun 88. (12"ep) *(FN 102)* **EXPECTIN' TO FLY** — / — NewZ
 – Expectin' to fly (extended) / Do the headless chicken / Donka / King in me.
1989. (12") *(FN 131)* **GASKRANKINSTATION. / CRASH HOT** — / — NewZ
 (7"/c-s iss.1990 in Australia; FN 139/140)
── added **FIONA McDONALD** – vocals (ex-STRAWPEOPLE)
── **BEVAN LARSON** – bass; repl. NEVISON, KAWRY + FELL
Oct 91. (cd/c/lp) *(FN 206)* **BODY BLOW** — / — New Z
 – Donde esta la pollo / Cruise control / Crash hot / Railway surfing / Nose / Million dollar dream / Gaskrankinstation / Body blow / Road train.
Nov 91. (cd-s)(12",c-s) *(FN 207)(FN 208)* **CRUISE CONTROL / CRUISE CONTROL (Eros mix). / CRUISE CONTROL (SOB mix) / I'M TALKING TO YOU** — / — NewZ
1992. (c-s/12"/cd-s) *(FN 231)* **DONDE ESTA LA POLLO (mixes; album / Kentucky Freud / Hen party) / CRUISE CONTROL (mixes; House of Harrow / Karaoke)** — / — NewZ
1992. (c-s/cd-s) *(FN/+CD 255)* **JUICE / CHOPPERS / CHOPPERS (heli-bator mix) / PLAY IT AGAIN, KIRI** — / — New Z
 (12"iss.1995; FN 304)
1993. (c-s) *(FN 267)* **MR. MOON / INSIDE TRACK** — / — NewZ
 (cd-s+=) – Attack of the killer androids.
1993. (c-s/cd-s) *(FN 268)* **UNSOUNDTRACKS** — / — NewZ
1993. (c/cd) *(FN/+CD 269 – D 30939)* **BODY BLOW – SUPER V8** — / — Austra
 – Choppers (Koppelman mix) / Donde esta la pollo (Kentucky Freud mix) / Mr. Moon / Gaskrankinstation / Body blow / Juice / Cruise control / Million $ dream / Inside track / Railway surfing ('93 octane mix) / Nose / Donde etsa la pollo (cock rock mix) / Choppers (helibator mix). *(cd re-iss. 1994 +=; FNCD 287 – D 31293)* – Donde esta la pollo (original) / Donde esta la pollo (low so low dub) / Inside track (sushi mix) / Cruise control (dub mix) / Cruise control (eskimos In Egypt mix) / Cruise control (Eskimos In Egypt dub).

Mushroom not iss.
Aug 94. (7"/cd-s; w-drawn) *(S/D 11835)* **CHOPPERS** — / —
Oct 94. (7"ep/cd-ep) *(S/D 11836)* **CRUISE CONTROL (Eskimos In Egypt mix) / RAILWAY SURFING (octane mix). / CRUISE CONTROL (original) / INSIDE TRACK** □ / —
Oct 94. (m-cd/m-c) *(D/C 19853)* **HEADLESS CHICKENS** □ / —
 – Mr. Moon / Juice / Donde esta la pollo (Kentucky Freud mix) / Gaskrankinstation / Body blow / Choppers (helibator mix) / Cruise control (original mix).

Flying Nun not iss.
Dec 95. (7"ep/cd-ep) *(FN 359)* **SUPER TROUPER. / Garageland: DANCING QUEEN / Loves Ugly Children: HONEY HONEY** □ / □
Dec 96. (c-s/cd-s) *(FN 302)* **GEORGE / CRUISE CONTROL (Eskimos In Egypt mix) / BESTIARY / MILTON BABBIT'S RAROTONGAN HOLIDAY** — / — NewZ
Nov 97. (cd-ep) *(FNCD 319)* **MAGNET / SMOKING BIG TED / MONSTER / MAGNET (Browning version)** — / — NewZ
Nov 97. (cd) *(FNCD 320)* **GREEDY** — / — NewZ
 – Dark angel / Stalk of a cherry / Secondtime virgin / Cipher / Magnet / Fire / Electricity / Chicken Little / Smoking Big Ted / Black water rising / Escalator / Day of the locust / George.
Jul 98. (cd-ep) *(FNCD 408)* **SECONDTIME VIRGIN / STALK OF A CHERRY (Screaming Chickens version) / DUMBHEAD / CE4 / USED TO** — / — NewZ
── disbanded after above

– compilations, etc. –

Jul 02. (cd) *Flying Nun; (FNCD 467)* **CHICKENSHITS** — / — NewZ
 – Cruise control / George / Gaskrankinstation / Choppers (helibator mix) / Expecting to fly / Donde esta la pollo / Juice / Mr. Moon / Slice / Monkey jar / Do the headless chicken (original) / Magnet / Dark angel / Second time virgin / Donka (original) / Smoking Big Ted / Fish song. *(w/ bonus-cd)* **CHICKENSHITS UNPLUCKED** – Expecting to fly (Magik's back to the 80's mix) / Gaskrankinstation (Der Keine Kopf remixen) / George (Magik's electric mix) / Cruise control (Willa Jean's disco mix) / Juice (P&G Tips mix) / Chicken Little (player one remix) / Inside track (1993 sushi mix) / Cruise control (Eskimos In Egypt remix) / Juice (Olly J remix) / Cruise control (Eskimos In Egypt dub remix).

HEART THROBS

Formed: Reading, England … 1986 by ROSE CARLOTTI and fellow residential college student, STEPHEN WARD. The pair were subsequently joined by ROSE's sister, RACHAEL DeFREITAS and MARK SIDE, releasing the 'TOY' single as their debut for 'In-Tape' a year later. Moving on to 'Rough Trade', The HEART THROBS released a further two 45's, promoting the car crash-themed 'BANG' on a support jaunt to the JESUS & MARY CHAIN. Naming their own label, 'Profumo', after the infamous 60's political sex scandal, the seductive quartet self-financed another two singles, 'HERE I HIDE' and 'BLOOD FROM A STONE'; ROSE was controversially snapped CHRISTINE KEELER-like for promo shots! At the turn of the decade, however, ROSE and RACHAEL were to suffer tragedy when their brother, PETE DeFRIETAS (of ECHO & THE BUNNYMEN), died in a road accident. Happier times were ahead though, as the group signed a fresh record deal with 'One Little Indian' ('Elektra' in the States), their long awaited GIL NORTON-produced debut album, 'CLEOPATRA'S GRIP', finally arriving in 1990. By this time, guitarist ALAN BARCLAY had been added, although a further period of upheaval saw the band being dropped by both 'Elektra' and their successors 'A&M'. Former PARACHUTE MEN bassist, COLLEEN BROWNE, was drafted in to replace RACHEL, making her first appearance after the largely disappointing follow-up set, 'JUBILEE TWIST' (1992). Their third and final long-player, 'VERTICAL SMILE' (1993), was a marked improvement, its title apparently a genital reminder of The HEART THROBS' naughty and unique appeal. ROSE re-surfaced a few years later with one-off ANGORA which evolved into TOM PATROL. • **Covered:** PUMPING (MY HEART) (Patti Smith Group).
Album rating: CLEOPATRA GRIP (*6) / JUBILEE TWIST (*5) / VERTICAL SMILE (*6)

ROSE CARLOTTI (b. ROSEMARIE DeFREITAS, 16 Dec'63, Barbados) – vocals, guitar / **RACHAEL DeFREITAS** (b.25 May'66, Reading) – bass / **STEPHEN WARD** (b.19 Apr'63, Chelmsford, England) – guitar, vocals / **MARK SIDE** (b.24 Jun'69, Reading) – drums

In-Tape not iss.
Jul 87. (7") *(IT 043)* **TOY. / MAKE MY DAY** □ / —
 (12"+=) *(ITT 043)* – I, the jury.

Rough Trade not iss.
Oct 87. (12"m) *(RTT 211)* **BANG. / SICK AT HEART / NAKED BANG** □ / —
Jun 88. (7") *(RT 221)* **TOO MANY SHADOWS. / THINGS THAT LINGER** □ / —
 (12"blue+=) *(RT 221B)* – I see danger.

Profumo not iss.
Oct 88. (7") *(PROS 1)* **HERE I HIDE. / PALE FIRE** □ / —
 (12"+=) *(PROST 1)* – Come.
── added **ALAN BORGIA** (b. ALAN BARCLAY, 4 Apr'68, Singapore) – guitar
Feb 89. (7") *(PROS 2)* **BLOOD FROM A STONE. / CRY HARD CRY FAST** □ / —
 (12"+=) *(PROST 2)* – Smothered.

One Little Indian Elektra
Feb 90. (7") *(33 TP)* **I WONDER WHY. / CLEAR AS A BELL** □ / —
 (12"+=) *(12TP 33)* – Big commotion.
 (cd-s++=) *(33 TP7CD)* – Pale fire.
May 90. (7") *(39 TP)* **DREAMTIME. / DREAMTIME (mix)** □ / —
 (12"+=) *(12 39TP)* – This man / I see danger.
 (cd-s) *(39 TP7CD)* – ('A'side / I see danger / This man / White laughter (the angel alpha mix).
Jul 90. (lp/c/cd/pic-lp) *(TPLP 23/+C/CD/SP) <60961-2>* **CLEOPATRA'S GRIP** □ / □
 – Tossed away / Dreamtime / Big commotion / In vain / Slip and slide / Here I hide / Calavera / I wonder why / She's in a trance / Blood from a stone / Kiss me when I'm starving / White laughter.
── **NOKO** – bass (ex-LUXURIA) repl. DeFREITAS
── **STEVE MONTI** – drums; repl. SIDE
Oct 91. (12"ep/cd-ep) *(50 TP12/TP7CD)* **TOTAL ABANDON** □ / —
 – Turn away / Pumping (my heart) / Bright green day / Turn away (mix).
Mar 92. (7") *(60 TP7)* **HOOLIGAN. / SO FAR** □ / —
 (12"+=/cd-s+=) *(60 TP 12/7CD)* **SPONGY THING EP** – Laughing & falling / Kiss me when I'm starving (Mastodon mix).

One Little Indian A&M
May 92. (7") *(70 TP7)* **SHE'S IN A TRANCE. / SHE'S IN A TRANCE (remix)** □ / —
 (12"+=) *(70 TP12)* – ('A'side / The girl became the stairs (barefoot) / In vain (barefoot).
 (cd-s) *(70 TP7CD)* – ('A'-extended remix) / Kiss me when I'm starving Marvin (remix) / Arcadia toss remix / ('A'-Hannett "Toad" remix).
Jun 92. (lp/c/cd) *(TPLP 33/+C/CD) <75021 5399-1/-4/-2>* **JUBILEE TWIST** □ / □
 – Tiny feet / Winter came too soon / Hooligan / Outside / The girl became the stairs / So far / Bright green day / Too late / Tuna / Gone / Tiny feet (reprise).
── **COLEEN BROWNE** (b.25 Aug'66, Kelowna, Canada) – bass (ex-PARACHUTE MEN) repl. NOKO who joined APOLLO 440
── **STEVE BESWICK** – drums; repl. MONTI
Apr 93. (12"ep/cd-ep) *(80 TP12/TP7CD)* **WORSER / AVALANCHE. / WE CONNECT / VISIONARY SONG** □ / —
Jun 93. (lp/c/2xcd) *(TPLP 43/+C/CD)* **VERTICAL SMILE** □ / —
 – Perry said / Stunned / Worser / Love is stretching / Incense of you / Avalanche / Brood bitch / Apple pie / Tranquilised, naked and shy / Go / Solemn child.
── split after above; BROWNE subsequently joined The PALE SAINTS

ANGORA

ROSE CARLOTTI – vocals, guitar / **FARZANA FIAZ** – keyboards / **ANDY EDWARDS** – bass / **POL BURTON** – drums / + **AMELIA**

Shiksa not iss.
May 96. (7") *(ANGORA 1)* **PRETTY NOTHING. / SHATTERED** □ / —
── ANGORA became TOM PATROL
── added **STEVE BESWICK** – drums (POL now on guitar)

Jimi HENDRIX

With JIMI's reputation now spreading, he was seen by ex-ANIMALS bassman CHAS CHANDLER, who invited him to London. After auditions, they found a rhythm section of NOEL REDDING and MITCH MITCHELL, smashing their way into the UK Top 10 in early '67 with the 'Polydor' one-off 45, 'HEY JOE'. CHANDLER then set up a deal with Kit Lambert's new 'Track' label, and The

Jimi HENDRIX (cont)

JIMI HENDRIX EXPERIENCE exploded onto the scene. Their first Hendrix-penned 45, the thundering acid-fever of 'PURPLE HAZE', made the UK Top 3, as did the scintillating debut album, 'ARE YOU EXPERIENCED?'. This was released hot on the heels of their third Top 10 single, 'THE WIND CRIES MARY'. Hendrix was a revelation, a black super-freak whose mastery of the guitar was above and beyond anything previously heard. In fact, he virtually re-invented the instrument, duly illustrating various methods of on-stage abuse (i.e. biting it, playing it with his teeth, shagging it and even setting fire to it!). He was duly booked on the Monterey International Pop Festival bill, where he proceeded to play an orgasmic version of 'WILD THING'. From the sublime to the ridiculous, the following month saw a wholly inappropriate US support tour with The MONKEES, leaving both him and teenybop audiences baffled, but no doubt entertained for seven nights. After another classic UK hit, 'THE BURNING OF THE MIDNIGHT LAMP', he released his second LP, 'AXIS: BOLD AS LOVE', which made the Top 5 early in '68, and was the first to chart and hit the Top 3 in his native America. In the Autumn of '68, JIMI revived and transformed BOB DYLAN's 'ALL ALONG THE WATCHTOWER', a song that broke into the US Top 20 and UK Top 5. It was trailed by a superb British Top 10 (US No.1) double-LP, 'ELECTRIC LADYLAND', the record featuring the now infamous naked women sleeve (much to JIMI's displeasure), which some shops sold in a brown cover!

Album rating (selective): ARE YOU EXPERIENCED? (*10) / AXIS: BOLD AS LOVE (*9) / SMASH HITS compilation (*8) / ELECTRIC LADYLAND (*10)

JIMI HENDRIX – vocals, lead guitar (ex-CURTIS KNIGHT) with **NOEL REDDING** (b.DAVID REDDING, 25 Dec'45, Folkstone, Kent, England) – bass / **MITCH MITCHELL** (b.JOHN MITCHELL, 9 Jun'47, Ealing, London, England) – drums

		Polydor	Reprise
Dec 66.	(7"; as JIMI HENDRIX) *(56139)* **HEY JOE. / STONE FREE**	6	–
	(re-iss. Jul84 on 'Old Gold')		

		Track	Reprise
Mar 67.	(7") *(604 001)* **PURPLE HAZE. / 51ST ANNIVERSARY**	3	–
Mar 67.	(7") *<0572>* **HEY JOE. / 51st ANNIVERSARY**	–	–
May 67.	(7") *(604 004)* **THE WIND CRIES MARY. / HIGHWAY CHILE**	6	–
May 67.	(lp; mono/stereo) *(612/613 001) <6261>* **ARE YOU EXPERIENCED?**	2	5 Aug67
	– Foxy lady / Manic depression / Red house / Can you see me / Love or confusion / I don't live today / May this be love / Fire / Third stone from the sun / Remember / Are you experienced? *(re-iss. Nov70; 2407 010) (re-iss. Nov81; 612 001) (re-iss. Sep85 on 'Polydor' lp/c; SPE LP/MC 97) (cd-iss. Jun91 & Oct93 cd/c; 521036-2/-4) (re-iss. Apr97 on 'MCA' cd/c; MCD/MCC 11608)*		
Aug 67.	(7") *<0597>* **PURPLE HAZE. / THE WIND CRIES MARY**	–	65
Aug 67.	(7") *(604 007)* **THE BURNING OF THE MIDNIGHT LAMP. / THE STARS THAT PLAY WITH LAUGHING SAM'S DICE**	18	–
Dec 67.	(7"; by JIMI HENDRIX) *<0641>* **FOXY LADY. / HEY JOE**	–	67
Dec 67.	(lp; mono/stereo) *(612/613 003) <6281>* **AXIS: BOLD AS LOVE**	5	3 Feb68
	– Experience / Up from the skies / Spanish castle magic / Wait until tomorrow / Ain't no telling / Little wing / If six was nine / You've got me floating / Castles made of sand / She's so fine / One rainy wish / Little Miss Lover / Bold as love. *(re-iss. Nov70;) (re-iss. Aug83 on 'Polydor' lp/c; SPE LP/MC 71) (cd-iss. 1987 on 'Polydor'; 813 572-2) (re-iss. Jul91 & Oct93 on 'Polydor' lp/c/cd; 847243-1/-4/-2) (re-iss. Apr97 on 'MCA' cd/c; MCD/MCC 11601)*		
Feb 68.	(7") *<0665>* **UP FROM THE SKIES / ONE RAINY WISH**	–	82
Apr 68.	(lp; mono/stereo) *(612/613 004) <2025>* **SMASH HITS** (compilation)	4	6 Jul69
	– Purple haze / Fire / The wind cries Mary / Can you see me / 51st anniversary / Hey Joe / Stone free / The stars that play with laughing Sam's dice / Manic depression / Highway chile / The burning of the midnight lamp / Foxy lady. *(re-iss. Jun73 on 'Polydor'; 2310 268) (re-iss. Aug83 on 'Polydor' lp/c; SPE LP/MC 3) (cd-iss. Feb85; 813 572-2)*		
May 68.	(7") *<0728>* **FOXY LADY. / PURPLE HAZE**	–	–
Jul 68.	(7") *<0742>* **ALL ALONG THE WATCHTOWER. / CROSSTOWN TRAFFIC**	–	–

— JIMI now brought in old session campaigners **AL KOOPER** and **STEVE WINWOOD** – keyboards plus **JACK CASADY** – bass / **BUDDY MILES** – drums / (to repl. MITCHELL and REDDING)

Sep 68.	(7") *<0767>* **ALL ALONG THE WATCHTOWER. / BURNING OF THE MIDNIGHT LAMP**	–	20
Oct 68.	(7") *(604 025)* **ALL ALONG THE WATCHTOWER. / LONG HOT SUMMER NIGHT**	5	–
Nov 68.	(d-lp) *(613 008-9) <6307>* **ELECTRIC LADYLAND**	6	1 Oct68
	– And the gods made love / (Have you ever been to) Electric Ladyland / Crosstown traffic / Voodoo chile / Rainy day, dream away / 1983 (a merman I should turn to be) / Moon, turn the tide... / Come on / Gypsy eyes / The burning of the midnight lamp / Still raining still dreaming / House burning down / All along the watchtower / Voodoo chile (slight return). *(also iss.lp/lp; 613 010/017) (re-iss. Jun73 on 'Polydor'; 2657 012) (re-iss. Jan84 on 'Polydor'; 350011-2) (re-iss. Jul91 & Oct93 on 'Polydor' lp/c/cd; 847233-1/-4/-2) (re-iss. Apr97 on 'MCA' cd/c; MCD/MCC 11600) (hit UK No.47 in Aug97)*		
Apr 69.	(7") *(604 029) <0798>* **CROSSTOWN TRAFFIC. / GYPSY EYES**	37	52 Nov68

Kristin HERSH (see under ⇒ THROWING MUSES)

Boo HEWERDINE (see under ⇒ BIBLE)

HIGH FIVE

Formed: Liverpool, England . . . 1982 by ASA HAYES, MARK BRABEN, PHIL JONES and his brother ROB JONES (the latter from WAH!). A politically motivated indie-pop act, they toured supporting AZTEC CAMERA and The STYLE COUNCIL before unsuccessfully auditioning for 'E.M.I.' and subsequently securing a deal with 'Probe Plus' (later home to HALF MAN HALF BISCUIT). The HIGH FIVE's debut single, 'COLD STEEL GANG', was released towards the end of '83 and re-issued early in '86 to promote their first album, 'DOWN IN THE NO GO'. By this time, TIM O'SHEA had replaced MARK, although no other releases were forthcoming.

Album rating: DOWN IN THE NO GO (*4)

ASA HAYES – vocals, acoustic guitar / **MARK BRABEN** – guitar / **PHIL JONES** – bass / **ROB JONES** – drums (ex-WAH!)

		Probe Plus	not iss.
Nov 83.	(7") *(PP 8)* **COLD STEEL GANG. / ARE YOU HAPPY**		–

		Big Village	not iss.
Oct 84.	(7") *(BIGV 1)* **WORKING FOR THE MAN. / WALK BACK THEME**		–

— **TIM O'SHEA** – guitar (ex-SEND NO FLOWERS) repl. MARK

		No-Go	not iss.
Mar 86.	(7") *(GO 1)* **COLD STEEL GANG. / CONFESSIONS** (12"+=) *(12GO 1)* – Turn this car around / On the banks.		–
Apr 86.	(lp) *(lp/c) (GOLP/TC-GOLP 1)* **DOWN IN THE NO-GO** – Cold steel gang / If they come in the morning / etc		–

— split not long after above

HIGSONS

Formed: Norwich, England . . . 1980 by university students CHARLIE 'SWITCH' HIGSON, TEZ EDWARDS, STUART McGEACHIN, SIMON CHARTERTON and COLIN WILLIAMS (DAVE CUMMINGS was also an early member but left before any recordings). Trading in a wiry strand of eccentric indie/funk characterised by EDWARDS' bleating sax and CHARLIE's often surreal lyrics, The HIGSONS made their debut in summer '81 with 'I DON'T WANT TO LIVE WITH MONKEYS'. Released on the tiny 'Romans In Britain' label and backed with the similarly bizarre 'INSECT LOVE', the single was championed by Radio One DJ and alternative guru, John Peel. A further clutch of singles appeared over the early to mid 80's including a couple for the legendary '2-Tone' label ('TEAR THE WHOLE THING DOWN' and 'RUN ME DOWN'), while a cover of Andy Williams' recently resurrected 'MUSIC TO WATCH GIRLS BY' possibly proves that The HIGSONS were ahead of their time. This was followed by the band's one and only album, 'CURSE OF THE HIGSONS' (1984), their final effort save for a final single, 'TAKE IT', on 'EMI'-offshoot, 'R4'. Following the band's split in March '86, TERRY EDWARDS became part of YEAH JAZZ, having already released the 1983 single, 'ROGER WILSON SAID' under the NEW YORK NEW YORK moniker (later suffixing the word EXPERIENCE and becoming a 4-piece; one single, 'I WANNA BE LIKE YOU', surfaced in late '85). He subsequently worked with the 8-TRACK CARTRIDGE FAMILY before teaming up with MARK BEDDERS (of MADNESS) to form the BUTTERFIELD 8. This bunch released one 1988 album, 'BLOW' for 'Go! Discs', preceded by the obligatory single, a version of Herbie Hancock's 'WATERMELON MAN'. EDWARDS later issued two fun tribute EP's to The FALL and The JESUS & MARY CHAIN. Meanwhile, SIMON formed BRAZILIAN NIGHTMARE with PETE SAUNDERS and JEM MOORE (both ex-SERIOUS DRINKING, former ex-DEXY'S). CUMMINGS joined LLOYD COLE & THE COMMOTIONS before doing the same for DEL AMITRI. Mainman and all round genius, CHARLIE HIGSON, meanwhile, took up writing, penning comedy material for Harry Enfield and Vic Reeves as well as completing a series of novels. He was also one of the team (including Paul Whitehouse) behind BBC2's now legendary 'The Fast Show' and could be witnessed (1998) presenting a film guide on Channel 4 alongside actress, Kathy Burke. • **Covered:** THEM CHANGES (Buddy Miles).

Album rating: THE CURSE OF THE HIGSONS (*6) / THE ATTACK OF THE CANNIBAL ZOMBIE BUSINESSMEN compilation (*6)

CHARLIE 'SWITCH' HIGSON – vocals / **TERRY 'TEZ' EDWARDS** (b. Hornchurch, Essex, England) – guitar, saxophone, trumpet / **STUART McGEACHIN** – guitar / **COLIN WILLIAMS** – bass / **SIMON CHARTERTON** – drums

		Romans In Britain	not iss.
Jul 81.	(7") *(HIG 2)* **I DON'T WANT TO LIVE WITH MONKEYS. / INSECT LOVE**		–

		Waap	not iss.
Dec 81.	(7") *(WAAP 1)* **IT GOES WAAP. / THE LOST & THE LONELY** (12") *(12WAAP 1)* – ('A'-re-recorded) / Got to let this heat out.		–
Mar 82.	(7") *(WAAP 2)* **CONSPIRACY. / TOUCHDOWN**		–

		2-Tone – Chrysalis	not iss.
Oct 82.	(7") *(CHSTT 21)* **TEAR THE WHOLE THING DOWN. / YLANG YLANG**		–
Feb 83.	(7") *(CHSTT 24)* **RUN ME DOWN. / PUT THE PUNK BACK INTO FUNK (pts.I & II)** (ext-12"+=) *(CHSTT12 24)* – ('A'instrumental).		–

HIGSONS (cont)

	Waap	not iss.
Oct 83. (7") *(WAAP 4)* **PUSH OUT THE BOAT. / ROUND AND ROUND**		-
Dec 83. (7") *(WAAP 5)* **THE LOST AND THE LONELY.** / Virgin Prunes: JIGSAW MENTALLAMA		-

(above was originally given away with Vinyl mag in Dec81)

	Upright	not iss.
Sep 84. (7") *(UP 9)* **MUSIC TO WATCH GIRLS BY. / LYING ON THE TELEPHONE**		-

('A'-BOYS version;12"+=) *(12UP 9)* – Clanking my bucket (live) / I don't want to live with monkeys (live).

Sep 84. (lp) *(UPLP 6)* **THE CURSE OF THE HIGSONS**
– Where have all the club-a-go-go's went went? / The junk keeps piling up / Ice age / Heat / Push out the boat / One world / Music to watch girls by / Gangway / Born blind / Annie & Billy / Run me down. *(re-iss. Mar87; same) (cd-iss. Apr92 on 'Mixture'+=; SORT 2CD)* – MUSIC TO WATCH BOYS BY:- Put the funk back into funk (pts.1 & 2) / Lying on the telephone / Round and round / Music to watch boys by. *(cd re-iss. Jul99 on 'Workers Playtime'; PLAY 23CD) (cd re-iss. Feb02 on 'Sartorial'+=; REFIT 006)* – MUSIC TO WATCH BOYS BY

— **DAVE CUMMINGS** – guitar; returned to repl. STUART

	R4 – EMI	not iss.
Jun 85. (7") *(FOR 2)* **TAKE IT. / I WALK THE LAND (live)**		-

(12"+=) *(12FOR 2)* – ('A'instrumental).

— disbanded after above; CHARLIE became a writer/actor in 'Fast Show'

– compilations, etc. –

	J.S.H.	not iss.
Oct 87. (lp) Waap; *(WAAPLP 1)* **THE ATTACK OF THE CANNIBAL ZOMBIE BUSINESSMEN** (all the singles & more) *(cd-iss. Apr92 on 'Mixture'; SORT 3CD)*		-
May 98. (cd) Hux; *(<HUX 004>)* **IT'S A WONDERFUL LIFE** (BBC sessions)		Jan00

HINDU LOVE GODS (see under ⇒ R.E.M.)

HIT PARADE

Formed: London, England ... 1983 by former postman, JULIAN HENRY, virtually a one-man outfit with augmentation from producer RAYMOND WATTS on programming and keyboards. Setting up their own 'J.S.H.' record label, JULIAN and his small team of collaborators issued a string of jangly, indie-styled dance singles from 1984's 'FOREVER' and 'MY FAVOURITE GIRL' to 1987's 'I GET SO SENTIMENTAL' (which featured CATH CARROLL of MIAOW); a compilation, 'IN LOVE WITH ...' contained every one of these. After the turn of the decade, HENRY and the more prominent WATTS were joined by HEAVENLY's AMELIA FLETCHER on the flipside version of the festive single, 'CHRISTMAS TEARS'. Squeezed inbetween their tenure (early to mid 90's) with the legendary twee-indie label, 'Sarah', The HIT PARADE released an album for Japan's 'Polystar' records (actually a re-working of 'MORE POP SONGS', which was issued earlier on London-based 'Vinyl Japan' – confused?); 'Sarah' records 'THE SOUND OF ...' (1994) marked the final chapter of The HIT PARADE. • **Note:** Not to be mistaken with the HIT PARADE on the 'Crass' label.

Album rating: WITH LOVE FROM THE HIT PARADE compilation (*6) / MORE POP SONGS (*5) / LIGHT MUSIC (*5)

JULIAN S. HENRY – vocals, guitar / **RAYMOND WATTS** – producer, keyboards, programming

	J.S.H.	not iss.
Jun 84. (7") *(JSH 1)* **FOREVER. / STOP**		-
Oct 84. (7") *(JSH 2)* **MY FAVOURITE GIRL. / IT RAINED ON MONDAY AFTERNOON**		-
Apr 85. (7") *(JSH 3)* **THE SUN SHINES IN GERRARDS CROSS. / YOU HURT ME TOO**		-
Sep 85. (7") *(JSH 4)* **YOU DIDN'T LOVE ME THEN. / HUEVOS MEXICAN**		-
Aug 86. (7") *(JSH 5)* **SEE YOU IN HAVANA. / WIPE AWAY THE TEARS**		-
Apr 87. (7") *(JSH 6)* **I GET SO SENTIMENTAL. / SUE**		-
Jun 88. (lp) *(JPEW 1)* **WITH LOVE FROM THE HIT PARADE** (compilation)		-

– Forever / Stop / My favourite girl / It rained on Monday afternoon / The sun shines on Gerrards Cross / You hurt me too / Heuvos Mexicana / You didn't love me then / See you in Havana / Wipe away the tears / I get so sentimental / Sue / Sun in my eyes / Come and get me girl / You as just a memory. *(cd-iss. 1990 on 'Vinyl Japan'; ASKCD 2)*

	Vinyl Japan	not iss.
Jan 91. (lp/cd) *(ASK/+CD 05)* **MORE POP SONGS**		-

– In the hit parade / Hitomi / The Beatles in 1963 / When I close my eyes / Girlfriends / The streets of toytown / Christmas tears / It was meant to be / Groovy heart attack / You were mine / It doesn't matter now / What did you love me for? / Christmas tears (starring AMELIA) / If you see her.

	J.S.H.	not iss.
Nov 91. (7") **CHRISTMAS TEARS. / CHRISTMAS TEARS (version)**		-
	Sarah	not iss.
Dec 91. (7") *(SARAH 058)* **IN GUNNERSBURY PARK. / HARVEY**		-
	not iss.	Polystar
1992. (cd) **LIGHT MUSIC**	-	Japan

– The wrong side of the world / Are you scared to be happy / Familiar goodbye kiss / On the eve of greatness / Blue lagoon / When the stars are bright / The photo session / Alice in Wonderland / So said Kayo / The first time / Goodbye to Jane / Somewhere.

	not iss.	Minty Fresh
Jul 93. (7") *<MF 2>* **HITOMI. /**	-	
	Sarah	not iss.
Jun 94. (7") *(SARAH 090)* **AUTOBIOGRAPHY. / THE DISPOSSESSED**		-
(cd-s+=) *(SARAH 090CD)* – Now the holiday's over.		
Jul 94. (lp/cd) *(SARAH 622/+CD)* **THE SOUND OF THE HIT PARADE**		-

– On the road to Beaconsfield / As I lay dying / Grace darling / Hello Hannah hello / Walk away boy / Farewell my lido / The fool / House of Sarah / She won't come back / Crying / She's lost everything / So this is London.

— disbanded after above

HOLLY & THE ITALIANS

Formed: Los Angeles, California, USA ... 1978 by HOLLY BETH VINCENT, who recruited her Italians in the shape of MARK HENRY and STEVE YOUNG. Inspired by London's punk explosion, HOLLY relocated her troops to the UK capital and set about securing a record deal. Discovered by future GLR DJ, Charlie Gillett, and signed to his 'Oval' imprint, the trio released 'TELL THAT GIRL TO SHUT UP' (later covered by TRANSVISION VAMP) as their debut single in early 1980. After a series of low-key pub gigs, the band scored support slots to BLONDIE and The CLASH, raising their profile and landing them a deal with 'Virgin'. Two singles, 'MILES AWAY' and 'YOUTH COUP', introduced the band to an appreciative post-punk, new-wave crowd although a debut album, 'THE RIGHT TO BE ITALIAN' (1981) was perhaps too one-dimensional and stuck in a New York groove for many UK fans. Following a further single, 'JUST FOR TONIGHT', the band fell apart and HOLLY subsequently recorded with her mate, JOEY RAMONE, on a cover of Sonny & Cher's 'I GOT YOU BABE'. Confusingly enough, the singer went on to release a solo album, 'HOLLY & THE ITALIANS' (1982) as HOLLY BETH VINCENT, although the record's more thoughtful textures distanced it from her earlier work, HOLLY's retro influences showing through on a cover of Buffalo Springfield's 'FOR WHAT IT'S WORTH'. After a brief spell in The WAITRESSES, she later hooked up with WATERBOY, ANTHONY THISTLETHWAITE, on his side project, The WILD THINGS. More recently, HOLLY re-surfaced as a collaborator with CONCRETE BLONDE frontwoman, JOHNETTE NAPOLITANO, on 1995's 'VOWEL MOVEMENT'.

Album rating: THE RIGHT TO BE ITALIAN (*5) / Holly Beth Vincent: HOLLY & THE ITALIANS (*5)

HOLLY BETH VINCENT (b. Chicago, Illinois, USA) – vocals, guitar, synthesizer / **MARK HENRY** (b. SIDGWICK) – bass (ex-BOYFRIENDS, ex-TOYAH) / **STEVE YOUNG** – drums

	Oval	not iss.
Jan 80. (7") *(OVAL 1016)* **TELL THAT GIRL TO SHUT UP. / CHAPEL OF LOVE**		-

(re-iss. Jul82; HOLLY 16)

— added **PAUL SCHAFFER** – keyboards / **MIKE OSBORN** – drums

	Virgin	Virgin
May 80. (7") *(VS 341)* **MILES AWAY. / IT'S ONLY ME**		-
Feb 81. (7") *(VS 391)* **YOUTH COUP. / POSTER BOY**		-
May 81. (7") *(VS 411)* **I WANNA GO HOME. / FANZINE**		-
May 81. (lp) *(V 2186) <37359>* **THE RIGHT TO BE ITALIAN**		

– I wanna go home / Baby gets it all / Youth coup / Just young / Miles away / Tell that girl to shut up / Just for tonight / Do you say love / Means to a den / Rock against romance.

| Jun 81. (7") *(VS 429)* **JUST FOR TONIGHT. / BABY GETS IT ALL** | | |

— split in the summer '81 (next A-side a duet with JOEY RAMONE)

| Jan 82. (7"; HOLLY & JOEY) *(VS 478)* **I GOT YOU BABE. / ONE MORE DANCE** | | - |

HOLLY BETH VINCENT

— went solo augmented by **BOBBY VALENTINO** – violins, mandolin (ex-FABULOUS POODLES) / **BOBBY COLLINS** – bass / **KEVIN WILKINSON** – drums (ex-THOSE NAUGHTY LUMPS)

| Aug 82. (7") *(VS 539)* **HONALU. / REVENGE** | | |
| Sep 82. (lp/c) *(V/TCV 2234) <38287>* **HOLLY & THE ITALIANS** | | |

– Honalu / For what it's worth / Only boy / Revenge / Samurai and courtesan / Cool love / Uptown / We danced / Unoriginal sin / Just like me.

| Oct 82. (7"/12") *(VS 517-12)* **FOR WHAT IT'S WORTH. / DANGEROUSLY** | | - |

— she joined The WAITRESSES for a brief stint and subsequently became part of ANTHONY THISTLETWAITE's moonlight combo, The WILD THINGS. In the mid-90's, HOLLY collaborated with JOHNETTE NAPOLITANO (CONCRETE BLONDE) project, VOWEL MOVEMENT, who released one eponymous album in '95.

HOLY JOY (see under ⇒ BAND OF HOLY JOY)

HONEYMOON KILLERS

Formed: New York City, New York, USA ... 1984 by JERRY TEEL and LISA WELLS, taking their moniker from a 1970 film. Under their two founding members, the band, named after a B-movie horror (the genre being a bit of a fixation of the band), churned out their unique brand of punk informed rockabilly, a style dubbed rather accurately as 'psychobilly'. HK debuted in 1984 with the LP 'HONEYMOON KILLERS FROM MARS', on the indie imprint, 'Fur'. They were subsequently joined by SALLY BARRY who, not only added drums to the group's sound, but an extra lead voice. BARRY's talents were first showcased on their sophomore full-length set, 'LOVE AMERICAN STYLE' (1985), taken from a live gig from legendary punk and alternative club, CBGB's. The 'KILLERS continued to improve with their third LP 'LET IT BREED', released the following year. HK's star was definitely in the ascendancy when they were joined by CRISTINA MARTINEZ (of PUSSY GALORE fame), to make the trio up to a quartet. This strengthened the band's sound for their fourth and probably best set, 'TURN ME ON' (1988). HK were characterized by their line-up changes for the way it influenced their sound. This was again exemplified on their sixth LP 'HUNG FAR LOW' (1992) where they were joined by future indie leading lights JON SPENCER and RUSSEL SIMINS (also from JON SPENCER BLUES EXPLOSION), producing a hard bluesy sounding set. By 1994 the band was virtually no more, leading 'Sympathy for the Record Industry' imprint to release the extensive overview album, 'SING SING (1984-1994)' in 1997. • Covered: DAZED AND CONFUSED + TRAMPLED UNDERFOOT (Led Zeppelin) / WHO'S DRIVIN' YOUR PLANE? (Rolling Stones) / LOVE MY LIFE AWAY (Gene Pitney) / SHE'S WRONG (Sky Saxon) / LAUGH AT ME (Sonny Bono) / JUST DON'T KNOW (MC5) / UUM BOY, YOU'RE MY BABY (… Johnson) / LOVE IS ALL AROUND (Troggs) / LAW-LIGA (Hank Williams) / TROUBLE COMING EVERY DAY (Frank Zappa) / TEENAGE HEAD (Flamin' Groovies) / BACK DOOR SANTA (Carter-Daniel) / LOOKING FOR MONEY + GIMME SOME MONEY (Al Urban) / UBANGI STOMP (… Underwood) / WHAT YOU GONNA DO? (trad) / and a few by the Bee Gees / etc

Album rating: HONEYMOON KILLERS FROM MARS (*5) / LOVE AMERICAN STYLE (*5) / LET IT BREED (*5) / TURN ME ON (*5) / TAKE IT OFF! mini (*4) / 'TIL DEATH US DO PART mini (*4) / HUNG FAR LOW (*6) / SING SING (1984-1994) compilation (*7)

JERRY TEEL – guitar, piano, drums / **LISA WELLS** – bass / **MICHAEL O'NEILL** – guitar; repl. TONY LEE / **CLAIRE LAWRENCE-SLATER** – drums; repl. JUSTIN WILLIAMS

		Buy Our Records	Fur
1984.	(lp) <FUR 1> **HONEYMOON KILLERS FROM MARS**	-	

– Honeymoon killers / Cornbread fed / I love to eat it / Rooms of doom / Place in France / Ubangi stomp / Cat people / Who do you love / Shake.

SALLY EDROSO/BARRY – drums, bass, vocals, trash cans; repl. 2

1985.	(lp) <FUR 2> **LOVE AMERICAN STYLE (live)**	-	

– Why / Night after night / Wee dawgees / Boom like I like it / Batman / Pain is easy / Good 'n' cheap / Motor city / Here we all are.

1986.	(lp) <FUR 666> **LET IT BREED**	-	

– Power man / Injun Joe / Dr. Pain / Rich 'n' famous / Dip it in the gravy / Day of the dead / Zoo train / Brain dead bird brain / Face of a beast / Don Gato / Godzilla.

JUDAH BAUER – organ, guitars / **RUSSELL SIMINS** – drums; repl. SALLY

1988.	(lp) (BOR12 015) <FUR 69> **TURN ME ON**	-	1987

– Dolly w/ a dick / Choppin' mall / Flophausen / You thrill me / Dazed 'n' hazey / Fingerlickin' spring chicken / Das dum / Hot wad of clay / Octopussy.

CRISTINA MARTINEZ – guitar (was also a member at some time)

Oct 89.	(m-lp/m-cd) (BORE/+CD 8901) **TAKE IT OFF!**	-	-

– Love bandit / Hard life / I'm glad my baby's gone / Hanky panky [cd-only] / Smotherly love / Too much! / The sexorcist / Dazed 'n' hazey [cd-only].

		not iss.	Sub Pop
Dec 89.	(7") <SP 51> **GET IT HOT. / GETTIN' HOT**	-	
		not iss.	King Size
1990.	(m-lp) <KS 0011> **'TIL DEATH US DO PART**	-	

– Baby blew / Jump / Evil green / I can't wait for nothin' / Head twister / 970-lick.

JERRY + LISA recruited **DAN KROHA** – guitar / **HOLLIS QUEENS** – drums (around this time?) / **JON SPENCER** was also a part-time member and took BAUER + TIMINS to his own group

		not iss.	Insipid
1991.	(7") <IV-02> **KANSAS CITY MILKMAN. / NOTHIN'**		-
		not iss.	Fist Puppet
1991.	(lp) <FIST 002> **HUNG FAR LOW**		-

– Mad dog / Kansas City milkman / Mr. Big stuff / Vanna White (goddess of love) / You can't do that / Quittin' time / Devil's jump / Tanks a lot / Fannie Mae / Scootch says / Something's wrong / Madwoman blues / Whole lotta crap.

		not iss.	Munster
1991.	(7"ep) <7026> **LIVE! (live)**	-	

– Who's driving your plane? / Training wheels / Mad woman blues.

		not iss.	Sympathy..
1991.	(7") <SFTRI 125> **VANNA WHITE (GODDESS OF LOVE). / YOU CAN'T DO THAT**	-	

— as CHEERLEADER MOM, the band issued 7" bootleg, 'SMELLS LIKE BI-FI'

— disbanded in 1994, TEEL subsequently joining The CHROME CRANKS

– compilations, etc. –

Jan 97.	(d-cd) Sympathy For The Record Industry; <(SFTRI 369)> **SING SING**		

– Ubangi stomp / What thing? / Uum boy, you're my baby / Looking for money / Gimme some money / Boogie man boogie / Oh yeah! / Dazed and confused / Crazy Daisy / Basket case / Godzilla / Back door Santa / Dolly w/a dick / Puddin' cups / Too much / Hard life / Teenage head / Just don't know / Hawaiian boogie / Reflections on a plane trip home / Who's drivin' your plane? / Subway rider blues / Livin' in a basement / She's wrong / Laugh at me / Devil doll / Boogie man boogie reprise / Love my life away / World gone mad / What you gonna do? / Milt's the man / Honey do you love me? / Stoned again / Trampled underfoot / One fine day / Who's drivin' your plane? / Dead again / Sound of flowers / Suppertime blues / Trouble coming every day / All the time / Bringin' me down / My baby's alright / Thinkin' man blues / Trouble blues / Honey doo jam / Mad woman blues / Devil jump / Jonestown boogie / Quittin' time / Joe's house / Kaw-liga / Chicken pickin' / Love is all around / Come on.

HOODOO GURUS

Formed: Sydney, Australia … 1981 as LE HOODOO GURUS by singer/songwriter, DAVE FAULKNER, JAMES BAKER, ROD RADALJ and KIMBEL RENDALL. Following the release of debut single, 'LEILANI', CLYDE BRAMLEY and BRAD SHEPPARD replaced the latter pair and after a few minor homeland hits they inked a Stateside deal with 'A&M'. Already popular in American underground circles, 1984's debut album, 'STONEAGE ROMEOS' presented The HOODOO GURUS as garage-punk/pop connoiseurs touching all bases from the crypt-kicking CRAMPS-esque shockabilly of 'DIG IT UP' to the harmonica-stomping groove of '(LET'S ALL) TURN ON'. Like The CRAMPS, the band were also self confessed American trash culture junkies, dedicating the album to US sitcom luminaries, ARNOLD 'The Pig' ZIFFEL and LARRY STORCH (Who?!). Despite the subsequent departure of founding member, BAKER (replaced by MARK KINGSMILL), the band bounced back with 'MARS NEEDS GUITARS!' (1985), a more professional sounding effort (released on 'Chrysalis' in the UK and 'Elektra' in the States) which saw the band become a hit on US college radio. Although the sloppy charm of old might've been missing, their newfound accessibility saw the 'BITTERSWEET' single making the Top 20 back home in Australia. After tours of Europe and America, the band began work on 'BLOW YOUR COOL!' (1987), FAULKNER further refining his songwriting skills on an album that was even more mainstream-friendly with help from fellow 60's revivalists The BANGLES on singles, 'WHAT'S MY SCENE' and 'GOOD TIMES'. Although the turn of the decade saw the 'GURUS release two of their strongest efforts in 'MAGNUM CUM LOUDER' (1989) and the raucous 'KINKY' (1991), the long awaited commercial breakthrough consistently failed to materialise and by 1994's 'CRANK' (featuring guest ex-BANGLE, VICKI PETERSON) FAULKNER and co. were beginning to sound tired. • **Trivia:** In the early 90's, GROSSMAN (with MIDNIGHT OIL's ROB HIRST) had his own project, The GHOSTWRITERS. They released two albums, 'GHOSTWRITERS' (1991) for 'Virgin' and 'SECOND SKIN' (1996) for 'Mercury'. • **Covered:** WIMP (Zeros) / I GOT A RIGHT (Stooges).

Album rating: STONEAGE ROMEOS (*8) / MARS NEEDS GUITARS! (*7) / BLOW YOUR COOL (*7) / MAGNUM CUM LOUDER (*6) / KINKY (*5) / CRANK (*4) / BLUE CAVE (*5) / ELECTRIC SOUP: THE SINGLES COLLECTION compilation (*8) / GORILLA BISCUIT: THE B SIDES AND RARITIES compilation (*5)

DAVE FAULKNER (b. 2 Oct'54, Perth, Australia) – vocals, guitar (ex-VICTIMS, ex-SCIENTISTS) / **ROD RADALJ** – guitar (ex-SCIENTISTS) / **KIMBLE RENDALL** – guitar / **JAMES BAKER** – drums (ex-SCIENTISTS)

		not iss.	Phantom
1982.	(7") **LEILANI. / LEILANI (part 2)**	-	

BRAD SHEPHERD (b. 1 Feb'61) – lead guitar (ex-SUPER K) repl. ROD

CLYDE BRAMLEY – bass; repl. KIMBLE

		Mushroom	not iss.
1983.	(7") (D 1028) **I WANT YOU BACK. / WHO DO YOU LOVE (live)**	-	- Austra
1983.	(7") (D 1033) **MY GIRL. / BE MY GURU**	-	- Austra
1984.	(7") **BITTERSWEET. / MARS NEEDS GUITARS**	-	- Austra
1985.	(7") **LIKE WOW, WIPEOUT. / BRING THE HOODOO DOWN**	-	- Austra
		Demon	A&M
Dec 84.	(lp) (FIEND 32) <7502 15012-1> **STONEAGE ROMEOS**		1986

– (Let's all) Turn on / I want you back / Arthur / Death ship / Dig it up / My girl / Zanzibar / Leilani / Tojo / In the echo chamber / I was a kamikaze pilot. (<cd-iss. Jul02 on 'Acadia'; ACAM 8029>) (cd re-iss. Aug02 on 'Limburger'; FU 1)

MARK KINGSMILL (b. 4 Dec'56) – drums; repl. BAKER

		Chrysalis	Elektra
Oct 85.	(7") (CHS 2926) **BITTERSWEET. / BRING THE HOODOO DOWN**		-
	(12"+=) (CHS12 2926) – Turkey dinner.		
Oct 85.	(lp/c) (CHR/ZCHR 1520) <60485-1> **MARS NEEDS GUITARS!**		

– Bittersweet / Poison pen / In the wild / Death defying / Like wow – Wipeout / Hayride to Hell / Show some emotion / The other side of Paradise / Mars needs guitars! / She. (cd-iss. Jul86; CCD 1520) (cd re-iss. Aug02 on 'Limburger'; FU 2)

Apr 87.	(7") (CHS 3123) **WHAT'S MY SCENE. / HEART OF DARKNESS**		-
	(12"+=) (CHS12 3123) – Where nowhere is.		
May 87.	(lp/c) (CHR/ZCHR 1601) <60728-1> **BLOW YOUR COOL!**		

– Out that door / What's my scene / Good times / I was the one / Hell for leather / Where nowhere is / Middle of the road / Come on / My caravan / On my street / Party machine. (cd-iss. Aug02 on 'Limburger'; FU 3)

Jul 87.	(7") (CHS 3151) **GOOD TIMES. / ON MY STREET**		-
	(12"+=) (CHS12 3151) – Like wow – Wipeout.		

RICK GROSSMAN (b. 2 Nov'55) – bass (ex-DIVINYLS) repl. BRAMLEY

		R.C.A.	R.C.A.
Aug 89.	(7") (PB 49347) **COME ANYTIME. / CAJUN COUNTRY**		
	(12"+=/cd-s+=) (PT/PD 49350) – Hallucination.		
Aug 89.	(lp/c/cd) (PL/PK/PD 90362) <9781> **MUGNUM CUM LOUDER**		Jun89

– Come anytime / Another world / Axegrinder / Shadow me / Glamourpuss / Hallucination / All the way / Baby can dance parts 2-4) / I don't know anything / Where's that hit? / Death in the afternoon. (cd re-iss. Aug02 on 'Limburger'; FU 4)

Apr 91.	(cd/c/lp) (PD/PK/PT 90558) <3009 R13> **KINKY**		

– Head in the sand / A place in the sun / Castles in the air / Something's coming / Miss Freelove '69 / 1000 miles away / Desiree / I don't mind / Brainscan / Too much fun / Dressed in black. (cd re-iss. Aug02 on 'Limburger'; FU 5)

Jun 91.	(7"/c-s) (PB/PK 44577) **1000 MILES AWAY. / THINK YOU KNOW**		
	(12"+=/12"pic-d+=)(cd-s+=) (PT/P 44636)(PD 49196) – Stomp the tumba rumba.		

HOODOO GURUS (cont)

1991.	(cd-s) <2805-2> **MISS FREELOVE '69 / STOMP THE TUMBARUMBA / BRAINSCAN**		L.D.	Zoo
Aug 94.	(cd-s) <14169> **RIGHT TIME /**		-	
Sep 94.	(cd/c) (LD 9453 CD/MC) <31094> **CRANK** – The right time / Crosed wires / Quo Vadis / Nobody / From a circle / Fading slow / Gospel train / Less than a feeling / You open my eyes / Hypocrite blues / I see you / Judgement day / Mountain. (cd re-iss. Aug02 on 'Limburger'; FU 6)			

			Mushroom	Volcano-Zoo
Oct 96.	(cd) (TVD 93455) <31123> **BLUE CAVE** – Big deal / Down on me / Mine / Waking up tired / Please yourself / If only . . . Mind the spider / Why? / All i know / Get high! / Always something / Son-of-a-gun / The night must fall. (re-iss. Aug02 on 'Limburger'; FU 7)			Aug96

– compilations, etc. –

1992.	(cd) R.C.A.; (74321 10741-2) **ELECTRIC SOUP: THE SINGLES COLLECTION** – What's my scene / Bittersweet / Come anytime / My girl / 1000 miles away / Axegrinder / Generation gap / Death defying / A place in the sun / Tojo / In the middle of the land / Good times / Castles in the air / Leilani / Poison pen / Another world / Like wow – Wipeout / Miss Freelove '69.		-	- Austra
1993.	(cd) R.C.A.; (74321 10742-2) **GORILLA BISCUITS: B-SIDES AND RARITIES**		-	- Austra
Apr 98.	(d-cd) Mushroom; (33066) **ELECTRIC CHAIR**			
Feb 99.	(3xcd-box) Mushroom; (MUSH 33156-2) **BITE THE BULLET (live)**			
Sep 00.	(d-cd) Acadia; (<ACAD 800-2>) **AMPOLOGY**			Oct00

Peter HOPE (see under ⇒ BOX)

HOUSEHUNTERS
(see under ⇒ SWELL MAPS; 70's section)

HOUSEMARTINS

Formed: Hull, England ... late 1983 by PAUL HEATON and STAN CULLIMORE, CHRIS LANG and TED KEY soon completing the line-up. After local gigs, many of them for political causes (i.e. the miners & CND), they signed to Andy McDonald's new 'Go! Discs' label. With HUGH WHITAKER replacing LANG, they released their debut single, 'FLAG DAY', a record that left you in no doubt where the band's political loyalties lay. Although the single failed to chart, with the follow-up, 'SHEEP' (prior to which, NORMAN COOK replaced TED KEY) faring little better, The HOUSEMARTINS imprinted themselves on mid-80's consciousness with 'HAPPY HOUR'. An outrageously catchy single, this was Brit-pop before Brit-pop was even invented; shiny, happy melodies, chiming guitars and nifty footwork, as always with an underlying right-on message. The record reached No.3 in the UK charts, the debut album, 'LONDON 0 HULL 4' (1986) attaining the same position later that summer. An endearing collection of witty, finely crafted songs which, above all, had a big heart and a deep soul, attributes which were at a premium in those dark 80's days with the twin spectres of Thatcher and Stock, Aitken & Waterman never far away. That Christmas, the band became a household name when they scaled the charts with a lovely a cappella cover of ISLEY JASPER ISLEY's 'CARAVAN OF LOVE'. The following Spring, WHITAKER was replaced by DAVE HEMMINGWAY, the band releasing their follow-up album later that year, 'THE PEOPLE WHO GRINNED THEMSELVES TO DEATH'. Even more politically pointed than the debut, the record nevertheless delivered its barbs in unerringly melodic packages, its highlight being the gorgeous gospel-pop of penultimate single, 'BUILD'. Yet the band had almost reached the end of their woefully short lifespan, HEATON and CULLIMORE agreeing from the start that it shouldn't exceed three years. Bowing out with a cover of Burt Bacharach's 'THERE'S ALWAYS SOMETHING THERE TO REMIND ME', The HOUSEMARTINS officially split in early '88. While HEATON went on to even greater success with The BEAUTIFUL SOUTH, the pseudo-Christian, Socialist sentiments he propounded in his earlier career seem a little hollow in light of his alleged penchant for soccer hooliganism. Working Class to the bone, eh mate? WHITAKER's subsequent conduct was little better, the man being sentenced to six years in prison in 1993 for assault and arson offences. NORMAN COOK, on the other hand, became a major player on the dance scene under various aliases, including BEATS INTERNATIONAL, PIZZAMAN and more recently the storming FATBOY SLIM. • **Songwriters:** Penned by HEATON-CULLIMORE except covers; HE AIN'T HEAVY, HE'S MY BROTHER (Hollies) / CARAVAN OF LOVE (Isley Jasper Isley). • **Trivia:** LONDON 0 HULL 4, stemmed from group's promotional hometown pride. They often described themselves as Hull's 4th best group. Who were better? RED GUITARS, EVERYTHING BUT THE GIRL and GARGOYLES?

Album rating: LONDON 0 HULL 4 (*8) / THE PEOPLE WHO GRINNED THEMSELVES TO DEATH (*7) / NOW THAT'S WHAT I CALL QUITE GOOD compilation (*8)

PAUL HEATON (b. 9 May'62, Bromborough, England) – vocals / **STAN CULLIMORE** (b.IAN, 6 Apr'62) – guitar, vocals / **TED KEY** – bass / **HUGH WHITAKER** – drums; repl. CHRIS LANG

			Go! Discs	Elektra
Oct 85.	(7") (GOD 7) **FLAG DAY. / STAND AT EASE** (12"+=) (GODX 7) – Coal train to Hatfield Main.		-	-
—	**NORMAN COOK** (b. QUENTIN COOK, 31 Jul'63, Brighton, England) – bass repl. TED KEY who formed GARGOYLES			

Mar 86.	(7"/7"pic-d) (GOD/+P 9) **SHEEP. / DROP DOWN DEAD** (d7"+=) (GOD 9/+7) – Flag day / Stand at ease. (12"+=) (GODX 9) – I'll be your shelter / Anxious / People get ready.		54	-
May 86.	(7"/7"sha-pic-d) (GOD/+P 11) <69515> **HAPPY HOUR. / THE MIGHTY SHIP** (12"+=) (GODX 11) – Sitting on a fence / He ain't heavy.		3	Sep86
Jun 86.	(lp/c)(cd) (A/Z GOLP 7)(CCD 1537) <60501> **LONDON 0 HULL 4** – Happy hour / Get up off our knees / Flag day / Anxious / Reverends revenge / Sitting on a fence / Sheep / Over there / Think for a minute / We're not deep / Lean on me / Freedom. (c+=) – I'll be your shelter. (cd++=) – People get ready / The mighty ship / He ain't heavy. (re-iss. Oct92 cd/c; same)		3	Feb87
Sep 86.	(7"/7"sha-pic-d) (GOD/+P 13) **THINK FOR A MINUTE. / WHO NEEDS THE LIMELIGHT** (12"+=) (GODX 13) – I smell winter / Joy joy joy / Rap around the clock.		18	-
Nov 86.	(7"/7"sha-pic-d) (GOD/+P 16) **CARAVAN OF LOVE. / WHEN I FIRST MET JESUS** (12"+=) (GODX 16) – We shall not be moved / So much in love / Heaven help us all. (7"box-set+=) (GODB 16) **THE HOUSEMARTINS CHRISTMAS BOX SET** – (all 4 singles +=; GOD 9) – I'll be your shelter. – hit No.84		1	-
Feb 87.	(7") <69491> **FLAG DAY. / THE MIGHTY SHIP**		-	
—	**DAVE HEMMINGWAY** (b.20 Sep'60) – drums; repl. WHITAKER who joined GARGOYLES full-time			
May 87.	(7") (GOD 18) **FIVE GET OVER EXCITED. / REBEL WITHOUT THE AIRPLAY** (c-s+=/12"+=) (XGOD/GODX 18) – So glad / Hopelessly devoted to them.		11	-
Aug 87.	(7") (GOD 19) **ME AND THE FARMER. / I BIT MY LIP** (c-s+=/12"+=) (XGOD/GODX 19) – He will find you out / Step outside.		15	-
Sep 87.	(lp/c) (A/Z GOLP 9) <60761> **THE PEOPLE WHO GRINNED THEMSELVES TO DEATH** – The people who grinned themselves to death / I can't put my finger on it / The light is always green / The world's on fire / Pirate aggro / We're not coming back / Me and the farmer / Five get over excited / Johannesburg / Bow down / You better be doubtful / Build. (re-iss. Oct92 cd/c; same)		9	Jan88
Nov 87.	(7") (GOD 21) **BUILD. / PARIS IN FLARES** (c-s+=)(10"+=/12"+=/cd-s+=) (ZGOD 21)(GOD X/T/CD 21) – Forwards and backwards / The light is always green (cheaper version).		15	-
Apr 88.	(7") (GOD 22) **THERE IS ALWAYS SOMETHING THERE TO REMIND ME. / GET UP OFF YOUR KNEES (live)** (12"+=/cd-s+=) (GOD X/CD 22) – Five get over excited (live) / Johannesburg (live).		35	-
Apr 88.	(d-lp/d-c/cd) (AGOLP/ZGOLP/AGOCD 11) **NOW THAT'S WHAT I CALL QUITE GOOD** (compilation) – I smell winter / Bow down / Think for a minute / There is always something there to remind me / The mighty ship / Sheep / I'll be your shelter / Five get over excited / Everybody's the same / Build / Step outside / Flag day / Happy hour / You've got a friend / He ain't heavy / Freedom / The people who grinned themselves to death / Caravan of love / The light is always green / We're not deep / Me and the farmer / Lean on me.		8	-
—	They had already decided to split up late '87. NORMAN COOK developed several solo projects including the unashamedly commercial BEATS INTERNATIONAL. HEATON and HEMMINGWAY formed The BEAUTIFUL SOUTH.			

HOUSE OF LOVE

Formed: Camberwell, London, England ... 1986 by vocalist GUY CHADWICK (ex-KINGDOMS), guitarist TERRY BICKERS (ex-COLENSO PARADE), guitarist ANDREA HEUKAMP, bassist CHRIS GROOTHIZEN and drummer PETE EVANS. Their demo tape soon caught the attention of Creation's ALAN McGEE who signed the act and released their debut single, the sublime and enigmatic 'SHINE ON'. The song was well-received although it didn't make the charts until 1990 when it went Top 20 in its remixed form. John Peel, in particular, was a great fan of the record and played it out over the course of the year. The follow-up, 'REAL ANIMAL' was rather underwhelming in comparison although a sample single for the band's PAT COLLIER (Vibrators)-produced debut album, 'CHRISTINE', picked up where 'SHINE ON' left off, all glistening guitar and darkly mysterious vocals. Sick of touring, HEUKAMP had departed the previous year, leaving the band to record the eponymous debut as a four piece. 'THE HOUSE OF LOVE' (1988) succeeded in living up to the band's early promise, a hypnotic VELVET UNDERGROUND/BYRDS/ONLY ONES hybrid that went down with The STONE ROSES' debut as one of the key releases of the decade. Touted as the future of British guitar music by the press, the band released a final single on 'Creation', 'DESTROY THE HEART', before being snapped up by the 'Polygram'-affiliated 'Fontana' label. A prolonged period of delays and problems ensued as the record company released the 'NEVER' single against the band's wishes in 1989 and the recording of the follow-up album went seriously awry. Another single, 'I DON'T KNOW WHY I LOVE YOU', lingered outside the Top 40 and the year ended with BICKERS departing on less than amicable terms to form his own act, LEVITATION. With SIMON WALKER replacing BICKERS, 'FONTANA' eventually emerged early in 1990 to a varied critical reception although it made the Top 10 and produced another minor Top 40 hit in 'BEATLES AND THE STONES'. A further round of touring followed and later that year ANDREA HEUKAMP returned to the fold. It was to be another year before any new material surfaced, 'THE GIRL WITH THE LONELIEST EYES' eventually being released in October '91. It was a classic CHADWICK composition and despite garnering critical favour again languished in the lower reaches of the charts. During the recording of the band's third album, 'BABE RAINBOW' (1992), WALKER departed, various personnel guesting on the album including WARNE LIVESAY (guitar, keyboards), CAROLE KENYON (vocals) and PANDIT DESH (tablas). Despite CHADWICK's pained deliberation in the studio the album failed to receive resounding critical acclaim and following a similarly underwhelming attempt to revive the band's earlier sound, 'AUDIENCE WITH THE MIND' (1993), CHADWICK called it a day. He eventually resurfaced in 1997, talking to the press about the drink and drug abuse, in-fighting and poor decisions that had marked the downfall of his band, shouldering the lion's share of the blame. Having inked a new deal with 'Setanta', he issued the mellow 'THIS STRENGTH' single in November, lifted from parent comeback album, 'LAZY, SOFT AND SLOW' (1998). • **Covered:** I CAN'T STAND IT (Velvet Underground) / PINK FROST (Chills) / IT'S ALL TOO MUCH (Beatles) / STRANGE BREW (Cream) / ROCK YOUR BABY (George McCrae).

Album rating: THE HOUSE OF LOVE (*8) / FONTANA (*7) / BABE RAINBOW (*6) / SPY IN THE HOUSE OF LOVE collection (*5) / AUDIENCE WITH THE MIND (*6) / THE BEST OF THE HOUSE OF LOVE compilation (*7) / Guy Chadwick: LAZY SOFT AND SLOW (*6)

GUY CHADWICK (b.21 Mar'56, Hanover, Germany) – vocals, guitar (ex-KINGDOMS) / **TERRY BICKERS** (b. 6 Sep'65) – guitar (ex-COLENSO PARADE) / **ANDREA HEUKAMP** (b.1965, Germany) – guitar, vocals / **CHRIS GROOTHUIZEN** (b. 8 Jul'65, Otahuhu, New Zealand) – bass / **PETE EVANS** (b.22 Oct'57, Swansea, Wales) – drums

	Creation	Creation
May 87. (12"m) (CRE 043T) **SHINE ON. / LOVE / FLOW**		
Sep 87. (12"m) (CRE 044T) **REAL ANIMAL. / PLASTIC / NOTHING TO ME**		

—— Now a quartet when ANDREA returned to Germany

Apr 88. (7") (CRE 053) **CHRISTINE. / LONELINESS IS A GUN**
(12"+=) (CRE 053T) – The hill.
May 88. (lp/cd) (CRELP 034/+CD) <88561 8245> **THE HOUSE OF LOVE**
– Christine / Hope / Road / Sulphur / Man to child / Salome / Love in a car / Happy / Fisherman's tale / Touch me. (lp w/ free 7") (CREFRE 01) – CHRISTINE (demo). / SHINE ON (demo) (re-iss. Aug94 cd/c;)
Aug 88. (7") (CRE 057) **DESTROY THE HEART. / BLIND**
(12"+=) (CRE 057T) – Mr Jo.

	Fontana	Polygram
Apr 89. (7") (HOL 1) **NEVER. / SOFT AS FIRE**	41	-
(12"+=/cd-s+=) (HOL 1-12/CD1) – Safe.		
Nov 89. (7") (HOL 2) **I DON'T KNOW WHY I LOVE YOU. / SECRETS**	41	-
(c-s+=)(12"+=) (HOLMC 2)(HOL 2-12) – I can't stand it.		
(cd-s++=) (HOLCD 2) – Clothes.		
(remix.12"+=) (HOLR 2-12) – Clothes / The spy.		
(7"g-f) (HOLG 2) – ('A'side) / Love II / Clothes.		

—— **SIMON WALKER** – guitar (of DAVE HOWARD SINGERS) repl. BICKERS

Jan 90. (7"/7"g-f) (HOL/+G 3) **SHINE ON (remix). / ALLERGY**	20	-
(c-s+=)(12"+=) (HOLMC 3)(HOL 3-12) – Scratched inside.		
(cd-s+=) (HOLCD 3-2) – Love III.		
(12"+=) (HOL 3-22) – Rosalyn.		
(cd-s++=) (HOLCD 3) – Rough.		
Feb 90. (cd/c/lp) (842 293-2/-4/-1) **FONTANA**	8	-
– Hannah / Shine on / Beatles and the Stones / Shake and crawl / Hedonist / I don't know why I love you / Never / Somebody's got to love you / In a room / Blind / 32nd floor / Se dest. (re-iss. Mar94; same)		
Mar 90. (7") (HOL 4) **BEATLES AND THE STONES. / LOVE IV**	36	-
(12"+=) (HOL 4-22) – Phone.		
(12"+=) (HOL 4-12) – Cut the fool down / Glorify me.		
(cd-s+=) (HOLCD 4-22) – Marble.		
(cd-s+=) (HOLCD 4) – Phone (extended) / Soft as fire.		
(7"pic-d) (HOLP 4) – ('A'side) / Love IV / Love V.		
Nov 90. (cd/c/lp) (846 978-2/-4/-1) **SPY IN THE HOUSE OF LOVE** (rare material, etc.)	49	-
– Safe / Marble / D song '89 / Scratched inside / Phone (full version) / Cut the fool down / Ray / Love II / Baby teen / Love III / Soft as fire / Love IV / No fire / Love V. (re-iss. cd Aug94; same)		

—— (Sep'90) added returning **ANDREA HEUKAMP** – guitar, vocals

Oct 91. (7"/c-s) (HOL/+MC 5) **THE GIRL WITH THE LONELIEST EYES. / PURPLE KILLER ROSE**	58	-
(12"+=)(cd-s+=) (HOL 5-12)(HOLCD 5) – Tea in the sun / Pink frost.		
Apr 92. (7") (HOL 6) **FEEL / IT'S ALL TOO MUCH**	45	-
(10"+=) (HOL 6-10) – Let's talk about you / Strange brew.		
(cd-s++=) (HOLCD 6) – Real animal.		

—— During recording of following album, SIMON left. He was succeeded by **SIMON MAWBEY** (b.24 Dec'60, Leicester, England) – guitar + album guests **ANDREA HEUKAMP** – guitar, vox / **WARNE LIVESEY** – guitar, keyboards, etc. / **CAROL KENYON** – vocals / **PANDIT DENESH** – tablas

Jun 92. (7") (HOL 7) **YOU DON'T UNDERSTAND. / SWEET ANATOMY**	46	-
(10"+=)(cd-s+=) (HOL 7-10)(HOLCD 7) – Kiss the mountain / Third generation liquid song.		
(cd-s+=) (HOLCD 7-2) – Destroy the heart / Blind / Mr Jo.		
Jul 92. (cd/c/lp) (512549-2/-4/-1) **BABE RAINBOW**	34	-
– You don't understand / Crush me / Crue / High in your face / Fade away / Feel / The girl with the loneliest eyes / Burn down the world / Philly Phile / Yer eyes. (re-iss. cd Aug94; same)		
Nov 92. (7") (HOL 8) **CRUSH ME. / LOVE ME**	67	-
(10"+=) (HOL 8-10) – Last edition of love / Skin 2 phase 2.		
(cd-s) (HOLCD 8) – ('A'side) / Christine / Ladies is a gun / The hitch.		
Jun 93. (cd/c/lp) (514880-2/-4/-1) <3145> **AUDIENCE WITH THE MIND**	38	
– Sweet anatomy / Audience with the mind / Haloes / Erosion / Call me / Shining on / Portrait in Atlanta / Corridors / Hollow / All night long / Into the tunnel / You've got to feel. (re-iss. Aug94 cd/c; same)		

—— CHADWICK was left with group name after the rest departed; he went solo in 1997

– compilations, etc.

Aug 95. (d-cd) *Fontana; (528602-2)* **HOUSE OF LOVE (FONTANA) / SPY IN THE HOUSE OF LOVE**		-
Aug 98. (cd) *Fontana; (<558323-2>)* **THE BEST OF THE HOUSE OF LOVE**		Sep98
– I don't know why I love you / Crush me / Destroy the heart / The girl with the loneliest eyes / Christine / Beatles and the Stones / Never / Shine on / Marble / Feel / Let's talk about you / SAfe / You don't understand / Yer eyes / Loneliness is a gun.		
Nov 00. (cd) *Strange Fruit;* (<*SFRSCD 096*>) **THE PEEL SESSIONS 1988-1989**		
Jun 01. (cd) *P.L.R.;* (*PLRCD 020*) **1986-1988 – THE CREATION RECORDINGS**		

GUY CHADWICK

	Setanta	Setanta
Nov 97. (cd-ep) (<*SETCD 052*>) **THIS STRENGTH / WASTED IN SONG / FAR AWAY**		
Feb 98. (cd) (<*SETCD 053*>) **LAZY SOFT AND SLOW**		May98
– Soft and slow / You've really got a hold of me / One of these days / In her heart / Song for Gala / Mirrored in her mind / Wasted in song / Fall in love with me / This strength / Crystal love song / Close your eyes.		
Apr 98. (7") (SET 048) **YOU'VE REALLY GOT A HOLD OF ME. / QUESTIONAIRE**		
(cd-s+=) (<*SETCD 048*>) – Laughter and honey / Slaughterhouse friend.		

HUGO LARGO

Formed: New York, USA . . . 1984 by music journalist TIM SOMMER and MIMI GOESE who enlisted two others in HAHN ROWE and ADAM PEACOCK. The group made a name for themselves in 1987, when MICHAEL STIPE produced, wrote and guested on the band's 'DRUM' EP (the track in question being 'HARPERS'), which contained a version of the Kinks' 'FANCY' and undoubtably their finest song ever, 'SECOND SKIN'. HUGO LARGO's atypical sound (with only a violin player, two bassists! and GOESE's scorching, at times hoarse vocals) attracted the ever watchful attention of BRIAN ENO, who re-issued the EP on his 'Opal' label the following year. 1989 saw the group plunge into the more mainstream 'METTLE' before evanescing into the musical wilderness. GOESE appeared some nine years later with the sullen DAVID BYRNE produced 'SOAK', which featured an inferior torch-esque version of Soundgarden's 'BLACK HOLE SUN'. • **Covered:** Screamin' Jay Hawkins' 'I PUT A SPELL ON YOU'.

Album rating: DRUM mini (*8) / METTLE (*8) / Mimi: SOAK (*6)

MIMI ROESE – vocals / **HAHN ROWE** – violin / **TIM SOMMER** – bass / **ADAM PEACOCK** – bass

	Land	Relativity
Jul 88. (m-lp/m-c/m-cd) (LAND/+C/CD 02) <8856 18167-1> **DRUM**		Aug87
– Grow wild / Eskimo song / Fancy / Harpers / Scream tall / Country / Eureka / Second skin. <se-iss. 1990 on 'Warners' cd/c; 2-/4-25768> <cd re-iss. Feb99 on 'Thirsty Ear'+=; 66037> – My favourite people. (cd re-iss. Mar99 on 'All Saints'+=; ASCD 038)		

	Land	Opal-Warners
Jan 89. (lp/c/cd) (LAND/+C/CD 05) <1-/4-/2-25847> **METTLE**		
– Turtle song / Hot day / Martha / Halfway knowing / 4 brothers / Ohio / Jungle Jim / Never mind. <cd re-iss. Feb99 on 'Thirsty Ear'; 66036> (cd re-iss. Mar01 on 'All Saints'; ASCD 39)		
1989. (c-s) <4-22851> **ARMS AKIMBO**	-	

—— split in the early 90's, HAHN ROWE later joined FIREWATER and SOMMER worked at 'Atlantic' records

MIMI

MIMI ROESE with HAHN ROWE, SAMM BENNETT, TONY MAIMONE, DAMIAN O'NEILL, PORL THOMPSON, HECTOR ZAZOU + DANIEL YVINEC

	not iss.	Luaka Bop-Warners
May 98. (cd) <46651> **SOAK**	-	
– Piece of cake / Fire and roses / Clues of you / I spy / Thrilled to pieces / Believer / Watch / Milky way / Black hole sun / Love is an island – Time to go home now. (UK-iss.Oct00 on 'Luaka Bop'; LBCD 22)		
Jun 98. (cd-ep) <9169> **SPELL ON YOU EP**	-	
– I put a spell on you / (+3)		

HULA

Formed: Sheffield, England . . . 1981 as the city's umpteenth industrial unit by MARK ALBROW, RON WRIGHT, ALAN FISH and ALAN WATT. Signing to Leeds-based 'Red Rhino', HULA delivered their debut EP, 'BLACK POP WORKOUT', an exercise in hard electro-funk that drew comparisons with 23 SKIDOO and CABARET VOLTAIRE. Having enlisted the services of CHAKK's MARK BRYDON (to replace WATT), the quartet unleashed their inaugural long-player, 'CUT FROM INSIDE' (1983), although personnel upheavals resulted in the subsequent departures of both BRYDON (briefly substituted by CHRIS BRANE) and FISH. Their respective replacements were JOHN AVERY and NORT, the more stable line-up cutting their finest three minutes in the shape of '(NO ONE LEAVES THE) FEVER CAR' and a slightly improved second set, 'MURMUR' (1984). Like many bands of their ilk, HULA livened up their stage show with the use of graphics and videos, their often enigmatic approach leaving them open to allegations of pretentiousness. From the release of the single, 'GET THE HABIT' onwards, the quartet experimented with jazzed-up dance rhythms and lost some of their underground kudos. Although they were now working from their home-built Sheffield studio, mid-80's albums, '1,000 HOURS' (1986) and 'SHADOWLAND' (1986), were made up largely of live material. Following the collapse of their label, 'Red Rhino', however, 1987's studio set, 'VOICE' proved to be their swansong (not counting compilation, 'THRESHOLD').

Album rating: CUT FROM INSIDE (*6) / MURMUR (*7) / 1,000 HOURS (*4) / SHADOWLAND (*4) / VOICE (*5) / THRESHOLD compilation (*6) / THE BEST OF HULA compilation (*6)

RON WRIGHT – vocals, guitar, clarinet, tapes / **MARK ALBROW** – keyboards, tapes / **ALAN FISH** – drums, percussion / **ALAN WATT** – bass

		Red Rhino	not iss.
Sep 82.	(12"ep) (REDT 018) **BLACK POP WORKOUT**		–
	– Feeding the animal / Ignoring the famine / Sacred serials.		

— **MARK BRYDON** – bass, percussion (of CHAKK) repl. WATT

Nov 83.	(lp) (REDLP 035) **CUT FROM INSIDE**		–
	– Flesh metal / Mother courage / Church juice / Murder in the clean states / Release the grip / Dirt talk / Stretch the attitude / Subliminal.		

— **NORT** – drums, percussion; repl. FISH (to CABARET VOLTAIRE)
— **JOHN AVERY** – bass; repl. CHRIS BRANE who repl. MARK BRYDON (the latter formed MOLOKO in 1994)

Sep 84.	(12"ep) (REDT 047) **(NO ONE LEAVES THE) FEVER CAR / BATS LOST. / BLOOD RUSH / HARD STRIPES / IN THE SHUTOUT**		–
Dec 84.	(lp) (REDLP 053) **MURMUR**		–
	– Ghost rattle / Invisible / Delirium / Pleasure hates language / Tear up / Hour by hour / Jump the gun / Red mirror / Cold kiss.		
Jun 85.	(12") (REDT 056) **GET THE HABIT. / BAD BLOOD**		–
Dec 85.	(12") (REDT 062) **WALKS ON THE STALKS OF SHATTERED GLASS. / WALK ON THE STALKS OF SHATTERED GLASS (version)**		–
Mar 86.	(d-lp) (REDLP 063) **1,000 HOURS** (half live at the Milky Way, Amsterdam)		–
	– The yesman / Bad blood / Hour by hour / Ghost rattle / Jump the gun / Baby doll / Hard stripes / Freeze out / Invisible / Ambient 2 / Tear up / The trouble with Benny // Big heat / Sour Eden / Hothouse / At the heart / Big car (both ways) / Bribery and winning ways / Gelsomina / Marnixstraat.		
Apr 86.	(12") (REDT 064) **FREEZE OUT** (club version). **/ FREEZE OUT** (radio version)		–

— added guest **ADAM BARNES**

Oct 86.	(lp) (REDLP 071) **SHADOWLAND** (live in Sheffield)		–
	– (untitled) / (untitled).		
Nov 86.	(12"ep) (REDT 072) **BLACK WALL BLUE. / STOCKY / 2 A.M.**		–

— added guests **ALAN FISH, JUSTIN BENNETT + DARRELL D'SILVA**

Mar 87.	(12") (REDT 074) **POISON. / POISON** (club mix)		–
May 87.	(lp/c) (RED LP/C 075) **VOICE**		–
	– Give me money (till it's crawling out of my face) / See you tomorrow / Cut me loose / Bush #2 / Cold stare / Clear water / Torn silk / Seven sleepers / Poison.		
Jul 87.	(12"ep) (REDT 080) **CUT ME LOOSE / CUT ME UP. / BURN IT OUT / INVISIBLE** (live) **/ WALK ON STALKS OF SHATTERED GLASS** (live)		–

— split when their label folded. NORT guested on an album with IAN ELLIOTT, while the others also kept busy in session work

– compilations, etc. –

Nov 87.	(lp/cd) Red Rhino; (RED LP/CD 083) **THRESHOLD**		–
Dec 87.	(c) Red Rhino; (REDC 085) **CUT FROM INSIDE / MURMUR**		–
Jun 94.	(cd) Anagram; (CDMGRAM 81) **THE BEST OF HULA**		–
	– (No one leaves the) Fever car / Get the habit / Freeze out (club mix) / Ghost rattle / Black wall blue / Big heat / Mother courage / Walk on stalks of shattered glass / Tear up / Hard stripes / Poison (club mix) / Seven sleepers / Junshi.		

Miles HUNT (CLUB) (see under ⇒ WONDER STUFF)

HUNTERS AND COLLECTORS

Formed: Melbourne, Australia . . . 1981 by MARK SEYMOUR, MARTIN LUBRAN, GEOFF CROSBIE, JOHN ARCHER, GREG PERANO, DOUG FALCONER, MICHAEL WATERS and live soundman, ROBERT MILES. After a couple of Australian-only released EP's, the ensemble speared their first major deal with 'Virgin' ('A&M' in the States) and unleashed an eponymous debut set early in '83. Featuring such marathon brooding gems as 'TALKING TO A STRANGER' and 'RUN RUN RUN' alongside 'SCREAM WHO' and 'TOW TRUCK', the record sounded like TOM BAILEY (of THOMPSON TWINS) fronting a more intense TALKING HEADS or GANG OF FOUR without forgetting their homeland's ethnic heritage. However, a rushed follow-up, 'THE FIREMAN'S CURSE' (1983), was something of a let-down which resulted in a move to 'Epic' records, who, in turn, released a third album, 'THE JAWS OF LIFE' (1984), a year later. A period of musical transition while the band were out of contract, resulted in the group issuing their own very rare white label set, 'THE WAY TO GO OUT' (1985). Subsequently signing to 'I.R.S.' the following year, H+C released a comeback album of sorts in 'HUMAN FRAILTY' (1986), revealing the more romantic side of the macho Aussie posse with a collection of radio-friendly pop rockers. Despite failing to shake off the cult listening tag, the group attracted an increasingly varied audience through constant touring, releasing 'FATE' (1988) as the creative pinnacle of this period. With CROSBIE, LUBRAN, PERANO and MILES out of the proverbial picture on 1990's 'GHOST NATION', a new band comprising BARRY PALMER, JACK HOWARD and JEREMY SMITH failing to find a focus. Going on musical safari, so to speak, over the next couple of years, HUNTERS & COLLECTORS eventually returned on 'Mushroom' records with two further albums, 'CUT' (1992) and 'DEMON FLOWER' (1994), although by this point, their mainstream sound wasn't so much dated as antique; a few live sets followed. • **Covered:** I'M SET FREE (Lou Reed) / DEBRIS (Ronnie Lane).

Album rating: HUNTERS + COLLECTORS (*7) / THE FIREMAN'S CURSE (*5) / THE JAWS OF LIFE (*6) / THE WAY TO GO OUT (*5) / HUMAN FRAILTY (*7) / FATE (*7) / GHOST NATION (*4) / COLLECTED WORKS compilation (*7) / CUT (*6) / DEMON FLOWER (*5) / LIVING IN LARGE ROOMS AND LOUNGES (*5) / JUGGERNAUT (*4) / UNDER ONE ROOF (*5)

MARK SEYMOUR – vocals, guitar / **MARTIN LUBRAN** – guitar / **GEOFF CROSBIE** – keyboards / **JOHN ARCHER** – bass / **DOUG FALCONER** – drums, percussion / **GREG PERANO** – percussion / **ROBERT MILES** – live sound / **MICHAEL WATERS** – trombone

		Festival	not iss.
1981.	(12"ep) (X 13078) **WORLD OF STONE**	–	– Austra
	– World of stone / Loinclothing.		
1982.	(7") (K 8754) **TALKING TO A STRANGER (Michael's version). / TALKING TO A STRANGER (our version)**	–	– Austra
1982.	(12"ep) (X 14002) **PAYLOAD EP**	–	– Austra
	– Towtruck / Droptank / Mouthtrap / Lumps of lead.		

		Virgin	A&M
Feb 83.	(7"/12") (VS 566/+12) **TALKING TO A STRANGER. / ALLIGATOR ENGINE**		–
Mar 83.	(12") <SP 12076> **TALKING TO A STRANGER. / TALKING TO A STRANGER (album) / RUN RUN RUN**	–	
Apr 83.	(lp) (V 2260) <SP 4973> **HUNTERS + COLLECTORS**		
	– Towtruck / Drop tank / Mouthtrap / Lumps of lead / Talking to a stranger / Scream who / Run run run. (re-iss. Aug88 lp/c; OVED/+C 92)		
Aug 83.	(7") (VS 616) **JUDAS SHEEP / MR. RIGHT**		–
	(12") (VS 616-12) – ('A'side) / Eggheart.		
Oct 83.	(lp) (V 2279) **THE FIREMAN'S CURSE**		–
	– (Slave, moan &) Sway / Judas sheep / Eggheart / Drinking bomb / Prologue / (The fireman's) Curse / Fish roar / Blind snake sundae / Mr. Right / Epilogue.		

		Epic	Slash
Aug 84.	(7") (A 4648) **CARRY ME. / THE UNBELIEVER**		–
	(12"+=) (TA 4648) – Follow me no more.		
Sep 84.	(lp/c) (EPC/40 26310) <25193-1/-4> **THE JAWS OF LIFE**		
	– 42 wheels / Holding down a "D" / The way to go out / I couldn't give it to you / It's early days yet / I believe / Betty's worry or the slab / Hayley's doorstep / Red lane / Carry me / Little Chalkie.		

		Festival	not iss.
Dec 84.	(7") (K 9539) **THROW YOUR ARMS AROUND ME. / THE UNBELIEVER**	–	– Austra
May 85.	(lp) (L 27148) **THE WAY TO GO OUT** (live)	–	– Austra
	– Throw your arms around me / The way to go out / Little Chalkie / Follow me no more / I couldn't give it to you / The slab / Carry me / I believe. (cd-iss. 1991; D 27148)		

		I.R.S.	I.R.S.
Aug 86.	(lp/c) (IRS/+C 5801) **HUMAN FRAILTY**		
	– Say goodbye / Throw your arms around me / Dog / Everything's on fire / Relief / Living daylight / Inside a fireball / January rain / The finger / 99th home positions / Is there anybody in there? / Stuck on you / This morning. <US cd-iss. Jul87 +=; IRSD 42024> – LIVING DAYLIGHT		
1987.	(12"ep) <IRS 36017> **LIVING DAYLIGHT**	–	
	– Inside a fireball / Living daylight / January rain / The slab (remix) / Carry me (remix).		
1987.	(lp/c) (RML/RMC 53253) **WHAT'S A FEW MEN?**		– Austra
	– Faraway man / Do you see what I see? / Around the flame / So long ago / Breakneck road / What are you waiting for? / Under the sun (where I come from) / Still hanging 'round / You can have it all / What's few men? / Give me a reason (above & below issued on 'Festival')		
1987.	(7")(12") (K 490)(X 13307) **STILL HANGING 'ROUND. / JOHN RILEY**	–	– Austra
Aug 88.	(7") (IRM 171) **DO YOU SEE WHAT I SEE? / WHAT'S A FEW MEN?**		–
	(12"+=) (IRMT 171) – Real world.		
Sep 88.	(lp/c/cd) (MIRF/MIRFC/DMIRF 1037) <IRSCD 42110> **FATE**		
	– Back on the breadline / Wishing well / You can have it all / Do you see what I see / Around the flame / Faraway man / Under the sun / What are you waiting for / So long ago / Real world / Something to believe in / Breakneck road / What's a few men.		
Nov 88.	(7") (IRM 177) **BACK ON THE BREADLINE. / BACK ON THE BREADLINE** (live)		–
	(12"+=/cd-s+=) (IRMT/DIRM 177) – Under the sun.		

— **BARRY PALMER** – guitar / **JACK HOWARD** – keyboards, trumpet / **JEREMY SMITH** – french horn, guitar, keyboards repl. PERANO, CROSBIE, LUBRAN + MILES

		Elektra	Atlantic
Apr 90.	(cd)(lp/c) (<7567 82096-2>)(WX 348/+C) <82096-2> **GHOST NATION**		
	– When the river runs dry / Blind eye / Love all over again / Crime passion / You stole my thunder / Ghost nation / The way you live / Gut feeling / Lazy summer day / Running water.		
May 90.	(7"/c-s) (A 7914/+MC) <87929> **WHEN THE RIVER RUNS DRY. / THE PRICE OF FREEDOM**		
	(12"+=/cd-s+=) (A 7914 T/CD) <86202-2> – Two roads.		

		Festival	not iss.
May 90.	(7"/c-s) (K/C 1120) **THE WAY YOU LIVE. / DO YOU SEE WHAT I SEE?** (acoustic)	–	– Austra
	(12"+=)(cd-s+=) (X 14756/D 1120) – Last summer day (acoustic).		
Nov 90.	(7"/c-s) (K/C 10260) **THROW YOUR ARMS AROUND ME. / SOMETHING TO BELIEVE ME / WHEN THE TRUTH COMES CALLING**	–	– Austra

		Mushroom	Attic
Sep 91.	(c-s/cd-s) (C/D 10493) **WHERE DO YOU GO? / WHEN THE RIVER RUNS DRY** (live) **/ LOVE ALL OVER AGAIN** (live) **/ DO YOU SEE WHAT I SEE?** (live)	–	– Austra

HUNTERS AND COLLECTORS (cont)   THE GREAT INDIE DISCOGRAPHY   The 1980s

Aug 92.	(cd-s) (D 11198) **HEAD ABOVE WATER / HEAR NO EVIL / HEAD ABOVE WATER (L.A. piece mix) / HEAD ABOVE WATER (extended)**	-	-	Austra
Sep 92.	(c-s/cd-s) (C/D 16038) **WE THE PEOPLE / MATTER OF TIME**	-	-	Austra
Oct 92.	(cd) (TVD 93364) <ACD 1373> **CUT**	-		Austra

– Head above water / Holy grail / Grindstone / True tears of joy / We the people / Hear no evil / Edge of nowhere / Love that I long for / Where do you go? / Imaginary girl / Angel of mercy. (UK-iss.Feb96; same)

Nov 92.	(c-s/cd-s) (C/D 12080) **TRUE TEARS OF JOY / ANOTHER ONE LIKE YOU**	- - Austra
Mar 93.	(cd-ep) (D 11579) **HOLY GRAIL / HEAD ABOVE WATER / TRUE TEARS OF JOY / GRINDSTONE**	- -
Aug 93.	(cd-s) (D 16071) **IMAGINARY GIRL / WHAT'S A FEW MEN? (live)**	- - Austra
Apr 94.	(cd-s) (D 11689) **EASY / PANIC IN THE SHADE / THE TRADE OFF**	- - Austra

                                                 Mushroom   Shake

May 94. (cd/c) (TVD/TVC 93401) <SACD 220> **DEMON FLOWER**   Jul95
– Easy / Panic in the shade / The one and only you / Mr Bigmouth / Courtship of America / Drop in the ocean / Newborn / Tender / Desert where her heart is / Betrayer / Ladykiller. (UK cd+=) – Holy grail.

Jun 94. (cd-s) (D 11788) **BACK IN THE HOLE / YES MAN / TOO GOOD LOOKING TO LOSE**   -   - Austra
Oct 94. (cd-s) (D 11862) **DROP IN THE OCEAN / I'M SET FREE / DEBRIS**   -   - Austra
Oct 95. (cd) (TVD 98017) **LIVING IN LARGE ROOMS AND LOUNGES (live at the Continental Cafe + in the pubs)**   -   - Austra
– The slab / Say goodbye / True tears of joy / Throw your arms around me / Easy / Courtship of America / Betrayer / Back in the hole / Ladykiller / The most unoriginal sin / Holy grail / When the river runs dry / Say goodbye // Holy grail / Easy / Stuck on you / Say goodbye / Chalkie / Blind eye / Everything's on fire / 42 wheels / Head above water / Mr. Bigmouth / Where do you go? / The one and only you / Do you see what I see?

Nov 95. (cd-ep) (D 1227) **LIVING SINGLE IN LARGE ROOMS AND LOUNGES (live)**   -   - Austra
– The slab (Continental) / Holy grail (Continental) / Say goodbye (Continental) / Say goodbye (the pubs) / 42 wheels (the pubs).

Jan 98. (cd-s) (MUSH 01750-2) **SUIT YOUR STYLE / WASTED IN THE SUN / POCKET**   -   - Austra
Jan 98. (cd) (MUSH 33081.2) **JUGGERNAUT**   -   - Austra
– True believers / Higher plane / When you fall / Wasted in the sun / Suit your style / Titanic / She's not fooling around / Good man down / Mother Hubbard / Human kind / Those days are gone / Long way to the water.

Nov 98. (cd) (MUSH 33176.2) **UNDER ONE ROOF (live on Friday the 13th March 1998)**   -   - Austra
– Where do you go? / Turn a blind eye / Head above water / What's a few men? / Talking to a stranger / 42 wheels / Back in the hole / True tears of joy / When the river runs dry / True believers / Say goodbye / Holy grail / The slab / Throw your arms around me / Inside a fireball / Struck on you / Do you see what I see?

   — disbanded in '98

– compilations, etc. –

May 91. (cd/c) I.R.S.; (<X2/X4 13053>) **COLLECTED WORKS**   Sep00
– Faraway man / Throw your arms around me / Inside a fireball / Dog / Everything's on fire / Do you see what I see? / Around the flame / Give me a reason / Whishing well / Stuck on you [UK-only] / Talking to a stranger (remix) [US-only] / Say goodbye / January rain / Back on the breadline / Is there anybody in there? / Still hanging 'round / Breakneck road.

Jul 91. (4xcd-box) Mushroom; (D 80932-5) **SKIN, BONE AND BOLTS: FOUR FROM THE ARCHIVES**   -   - Austra
– (HUNTERS AND COLLECTORS / THE FIREMAN'S CURSE / THE JAWS OF LIFE / THE WAY TO GO OUT).

Nov 98. (cd-s) Mushroom; (794) **TALKING TO A STRANGER**

HURRAH!

Formed: Newcastle, England ... early 80's briefly as the GREEN-EYED CHILDREN by main songwriters PAUL HANDYSIDE and TAFFY HUGHES, the pair enlisting ANTHONY PRICE and MARK SIM (the latter was soon to be replaced by DAMIEN MAHONEY). Opting for the punchier moniker, HURRAH!, the quartet were one of the first signings to local independent, 'Kitchenware' (others being PREFAB SPROUT, MARTIN STEPHENSON & THE DAINTEES and The KANE GANG), releasing their debut single, 'THE SUN SHINES HERE', in '82. It would be at least a year before HURRAH! followed it up with a second 7", 'HIP HIP' gaining some support in the music press and giving them an indie chart hit. DAVID PORTERHOUSE filled the shoes of the departing PRICE, while yet another two singles, 'WHO'D HAVE THOUGHT' and 'GLORIA', endeared them to fans of melodic mainstream jangle-pop but occasionally strayed too far into HAIRCUT 100 territory for comfort. Thankfully, HURRAH! celebrated their move (as part and parcel of Kitchenware's deal) to major label land ('Arista') with a shift towards a more rock-based sound on two singles, 'SWEET SANITY' and 'LOVE COULD KILL', and an accompanying UK Top 75 album, 'TELL GOD I'M HERE'. Appropriately enough, the lads secured a support slot with U2 (then going through their Messianic stage!) at the Wembley leg of their 'Joshua Tree' tour. Nevertheless, the party poopers remained under wraps as HURRAH! failed to make a breakthrough with 1989's 'THE BEAUTIFUL', ADRIAN EVANS substituting recent recruit STEVE PRICE for a final single and a posthumous live set entitled 'THE SOUND OF PHILADELPHIA' (1993). • **Covered:** SWEET JANE (Velvet Underground).

Album rating: BOXED compilation (*6) / TELL GOD I'M HERE (*5) / THE BEAUTIFUL (*4) / THE SOUND OF PHILADELPHIA (*5)

PAUL HANDYSIDE (b.28 Sep'60, Newcastle-Upon-Tyne, England) – vocals, guitar / **TAFFY HUGHES** (b. DAVID, 16 Mar'61, Southmoor, Northumberland, England) – guitar, vocals / **ANTHONY PRICE** – bass / **DAMIEN MAHONEY** – drums; repl. MARK SIM

                                               Kitchenware not iss.

Jun 82. (7") (SK 2) **THE SUN SHINES HERE. / I'LL BE YOUR SURPRISE**
Sep 83. (7") (SK 6) **HIP HIP. / FLOWERS**

   — **DAVE PORTERHOUSE** (b.17 Aug'61, Gateshead, England) – bass; repl. PRICE

Oct 84. (7") (SK 14) **WHO'D HAVE THOUGHT. / WHO'D HAVE THOUGHT (SLIGHT RETURN)**
(12"+=) (SKX 14) – Celtic (who wants to live by love alone).
May 85. (7") (SK 18) **GLORIA. / FUNNY DAY**
(12"+=) (SKX 18) – Tame / This boy.
Nov 85. (lp) (SKINT 1) **BOXED** (compilation)

   — trimmed to a trio for a while when MAHONEY joined the police force

   — added **STEVE PRICE** – drums; replaced him

                                            Kitchenware Arista

Oct 86. (7") (SK 28) **SWEET SANITY. / HEART AND HAND**
(12"+=) (SKX 28) – Don't need food.
Jan 87. (7") (SK 29) **IF LOVE COULD KILL. / TELL ME ABOUT YOUR PROBLEMS**
(12"+=) (SKX 29) – Girl of my dreams.
(d7"++=) (SKD 29) – Gloria.
Feb 87. (lp/c/cd) (208/408/258 201) **TELL GOD I'M HERE**   **71**
– I would if I could / Better times / Sweet sanity / Celtic (who wants to live by love alone) / A walk in the park / How many rivers? / If love could kill / Miss the kiss / How high the moon / Mr. Sorrowful. (also cd; KWCD 6)
May 87. (7") (SK 31) **HOW MANY RIVERS? / THREE WISHES**
(12"+=) (SKX 31) – If it rains.
Nov 88. (7") (111 911) **SWEET SANITY. / HEART AND HAND**
(12"+=/cd-s+=) (611/661 911) – Gloria / How many rivers?
Apr 89. (7") (SK 42 – 111 770) **BIG SKY. / SATURDAY'S TRAIN**
(12"+=/3"cd-s+=) (SK X/CD 42 – 611/661 770) – The secret life.
(10"pic-d+=) (SKPD 42 – 612 207) – A walk in the park.
Apr 89. (lp/c/cd) (SK LP/C/CD 10) **THE BEAUTIFUL**
– Big sky / Troubled brow / Wisdom waits / Diana Diana / Velveteen / Let it be her / Call for me / Sad but true / Girls of Janla / She said. (cd+=) – The secret life.

   — **ADRIAN EVANS** (b. 6 Mar'63, County Durham, England) – drums; repl. STEVE PRICE

Apr 91. (12"m) (SKX 51) **THAT DREAM'S OVER NOW. / SWEET JANE / ALIVE**

   — split up as their final unreleased single, 'MELT' might suggest, leaving behind . . .

                                            Creation Rev-Ola not iss.

Aug 93. (cd) (CREV 014CD) **THE SOUND OF PHILADELPHIA (live)**
– (live intro tape) / The sun shines here / I'll be your surprise / Don't need food / Saturday's train / Lonely room / Hip hip / Around and around (when in Rome) / If it rains / The point of perfection / Who'd have thought / Celtic (who wants to live by love alone) / Big sky / This boy / Gloria / Funny day / A walk in the park / Suffer and see / Sweet sanity / How many rivers? / Miss this kiss / If love could kill / I would if I could.

– compilations, etc. –

Mar 92. (cd) Insanity; **SOMETIME IN NEWCASTLE / CALIFORNIA DREAMING / ALIVE UNDERGROUND** (live bootlegs)

HUSKER DU

Formed: St. Paul, Minnesota, USA ... 1978 by MOULD, HART and NORTON. In 1980-82, they issued a few 45's and a live LP 'LAND SPEED RECORD', on their own label, 'New Alliance'. The record typified the band's early uncompromising hardcore which was often tediously workmanlike in its adherence to the steadfast confines of the genre. 'EVERYTHING FALLS APART' (1983) was also unflinching in its intensity and it was all the more surprising when the band showed glimmers of noise-pop greatness on their 1983 debut for 'SST', 'METAL CIRCUS'. They consolidated this by cross-fertilising the previously polarised psychedelia and hardcore punk on an electrifying cover of The BYRDS' 'EIGHT MILES HIGH' (1984). The follow-up double set, 'ZEN ARCADE' (1984) was a further giant step for hardcore-kind. A concept album no less, the twin songwriting attack of MOULD and HART was becoming sharper and even the sprawling, unfocused feel of the whole affair wasn't enough to blunt the edges of songs like 'WHATEVER' and 'TURN ON THE NEWS'. The songwriting on 'NEW DAY RISING' (1985) was even more trenchant, the band's adrenaline fuelled pop-core hybrid developing at breakneck speed. 'FLIP YOUR WIG' (1985), the band's last indie release, marked a stepping stone to their major label debut for 'Warners', 'CANDY APPLE GREY' (1986). While HART perfected HUSKER DU's melodic dischord on tracks like 'DEAD SET ON DESTRUCTION', MOULD showcased darkly introspective, acoustic elegies 'TOO FAR DOWN' and 'HARDLY GETTING OVER IT'. The more musically-challenged among HUSKER DU's following were none too taken with this new fangled unplugged business although the album was released to unanimous critical acclaim. The band's swansong, 'WAREHOUSE: SONGS AND STORIES' (1987) was the culmination of a decade's experimentation and possessed an unprecedented depth, clarity and consistency. By the time of its release, though, tension in the band was reaching breaking point and HUSKER DU was disbanded in 1987. While GRANT HART and BOB MOULD went on to solo careers, as well as respectively forming NOVA MOB and SUGAR, they were always better together and the magic of HUSKER DU is inestimable in its influence on a generation of alternative guitar bands. The new millennium saw HART return with a new set, 'GOOD NEWS FOR THE MODERN MAN' (1999). • **Songwriters:** MOULD-HART compositions except; SUNSHINE SUPERMAN (Donovan) / TICKET TO RIDE + SHE'S A WOMAN + HELTER SKELTER (Beatles) / EIGHT MILES HIGH (Byrds). NOVA MOB covered I JUST WANT TO MAKE LOVE TO YOU (Willie Dixon) / SHEENA IS A PUNK ROCKER (Ramones). Solo GRANT HART covered SIGNED D.C. (Love). • **Trivia:** HUSKER DU means DO YOU REMEMBER in Swedish.

Album rating: LAND SPEED RECORD mini (*6) / EVERYTHING FALLS APART (*5) / ZEN ARCADE (*9) / NEW DAY RISING (*9) / FLIP YOUR WIG (*9) / CANDY APPLE GREY (*7) / WAREHOUSE: SONGS & STORIES (*9) / THE LIVING END live compilation (*6) / Grant Hart: INTOLERANCE (*6) / Nova Mob: THE DAYS DAYS OF POMPEII (*6) / NOVA MOB (*6) / ECCE HOMO (*5) / Grant Hart: GOOD NEWS FOR THE MODERN MAN (*7)

BOB MOULD (b.12 Oct'61, Malone, New York) – vocals, guitar, keyboards, percussion / **GRANT HART** (b. GRANTZBERG VERNON HART, 18 Mar'61) – drums, keyboards, percussion, vocals / **GREG NORTON** (b.13 Mar'59, Rock Island, Illinois) – bass

not iss.   Reflex

Jan 81. (7") <38285> **STATUES. / AMUSEMENT (live)**

Alternative   New
Tentacles   Alliance

Jan 82. (m-lp) (VIRUS 25) <NAR 007> **LAND SPEED RECORD (live)**
– All tensed up / Don't try to call / I'm not interested / Big sky / Guns at my school / Push the button / Gilligan's Island / MTC / Don't have a life / Bricklayer / Tired of doing things / You're naive / Strange week / Do the bee / Ultracore / Let's go die / Data control. (re-iss. Nov88 on 'S.S.T.'; SST 195) (re-iss. cd/lp Oct95)

May 82. (7"m) <NAR 010> **IN A FREE LAND. / WHAT DO I WANT? / M.I.C.**

not iss.   Reflex

Jan 83. (lp; @45rpm) <D> **EVERYTHING FALLS APART**
– From the gut / Blah, blah, blah / Punch drunk / Bricklayer / Afraid of being wrong / Sunshine Superman / Signals from above / Everything falls apart / Wheels / Obnoxious / Gravity. (cd-iss. May93 on 'WEA'+=; 8122 71163-2) – In a free land / What do I want / M.I.C. / Statues / Let's go die / Amusement (live) / Do you remember?

S.S.T.   S.S.T.

Dec 83. (m-lp) <(SST 020)> **METAL CIRCUS**   Oct83
– Real world / Deadly skies / It's not funny anymore / Diane / First of the last calls / Lifeline / Out on a limb.

Apr 84. (7"colrd) <(SST 025)> **EIGHT MILES HIGH. / MASOCHISM WORLD**
(3"cd-s iss.Dec88; SST 025CD)

Sep 84. (d-lp) <(SST 027)> **ZEN ARCADE**   Jul84
– Something I learned today / Broken home, broken heart / Never talking to you again / Chartered trips / Dreams reoccurring / Indecision time / Hare Krishna / Beyond the threshold / Pride / I'll never forget you / The biggest lie / What's going on / Masochism world / Standing by the sea / Somewhere / One step at a time / Pink turns to blue / Newest industry / Monday will never be the same / Whatever / The tooth fairy and the princess / Turn on the news / Reoccurring dreams. (cd-iss. Oct87; SST 027CD) (re-iss. cd/c/d-lp Oct95 & Jun97; same)

Feb 85. (lp) <(SST 031)> **NEW DAY RISING**   Jan85
– New day rising / Girl who lives on Heaven Hill / I apologize / Folklore / If I told you / Celebrated summer / Perfect example / Terms of psychic warfare / 59 times the pain / Powerline / Books about UFO's / I don't know what you're talking about / How to skin a cat / Watcha drinkin' / Plans I make. (cd-iss. Oct87; SST 031CD) (re-iss. cd/c/lp Oct95; same)

Aug 85. (7") <(SST 051)> **MAKE NO SENSE AT ALL. / LOVE IS ALL AROUND (MARY'S THEME)**

Oct 85. (lp) <(SST 055)> **FLIP YOUR WIG**   Sep85
– Flip your wig / Every everything / Makes no sense at all / Hate paper doll / Green eyes / Divide and conquer / Games / Find me / The baby song / Flexible flyer / Private plane / Keep hanging on / The wit and the wisdom / Don't know yet. (cd-iss. Oct87; SST 055CD) (re-iss. cd/c/lp Oct95; same)

Warners   Warners

Feb 86. (7") (W 8746) **DON'T WANT TO KNOW IF YOU ARE LONELY. / ALL WORK NO PLAY**
(12"+=) (W 8746T) <20446-0> – Helter skelter (live).

Mar 86. (lp/c) (WX 40/+C) <25385> **CANDY APPLE GREY**
– Crystal / Don't want to know if you are lonely / I don't know for sure / Sorry somehow / Too far down / Hardly getting over it / Dead set on destruction / Eiffel Tower high / No promises have I made / All this I've done for you. (cd-iss. Nov92; 7599 25385-2)

Sep 86. (7") (W 8612) **SORRY SOMEHOW. / ALL THIS I'VE DONE FOR YOU**
(d7+=/12"+=) (W 8612 F/T) – Flexible flyer / Celebrated summer.

Jan 87. (7") (W 8456) **COULD YOU BE THE ONE. / EVERYTIME**
(12"+=) (W 8456T) – Charity, chastity, prudence, hope.

Jan 87. (d-lp/d-c) (925544-1/-4) <25544> **WAREHOUSE: SONGS & STORIES** | 72 |
– These important years / Charity, chastity, prudence and hope / Standing in the rain / Back from somewhere / Ice cold ice / You're a soldier / Could you be the one? / Too much spice / Friend, you've got to fall / Visionary / She floated away / Bed of nails / Tell you why tomorrow / It's not peculiar / Actual condition / No reservations / Turn it around / She's a woman (and now he is a man) / Up in the air / You can live at home. (cd-iss. Oct92; 7599 25544-2)

Jun 87. (7") (W 8276) **ICE COLD ICE. / GOTTA LETTA**
(12"+=) (W 8276T) – Medley.

—— disbanded in '87 after manager DAVID SAVOY Jr. committed suicide. GRANT HART went solo as did BOB MOULD; in 1992 the latter formed SUGAR

– compilations, etc. –

May 94. (cd/c) Warners; <(9362 45582-2/-4)> **THE LIVING END (live)**   Apr94
– New day rising / Heaven Hill / Standing in the rain / Back from somewhere / Ice cold ice / Everytime / Friend you're gonna fall / She floated away / From the gut / Target / It's not funny anymore / Hardly getting over it / Terms of psychic warfare / Powertime / Books about UFO's / Divide and conquer / Keep hangin' on / Celebrated summer / Now that you know me / Ain't no water in the well / What's goin' on / Data control / In a free land / Sheena is a punk rocker.

GRANT HART

S.S.T.   S.S.T.

Oct 89. (7"ep/cd-ep) (SST 219/+CD) **2541. / COME HOME / LET'S GO**

Nov 89. (lp/cd) <(SST 215/+CD)> **INTOLERANCE**
– All of my senses / Now that you know me / The main / Roller risk / Fanfare in D major (come, come) / You're the victim / 2541 / Anything / She can see the angels coming / Reprise.

May 90. (12"ep/cd-ep) (SST 262/+CD) **ALL OF MY SENSES. / THE MAIN (edit) / SIGNED D.C.**

NOVA MOB

(GRANT HART) & his group:- **TOM MERKL** – bass / **MICHAEL CRECO** – drums

Rough Trade   Rough Trade

Feb 91. (cd/c/lp) <(R 2081261-2/-4/-1)> **THE LAST DAYS OF POMPEII**
– Introduction / Woton / Getaway (gateway) in time / Admiral of the sea (79 a.d. version) / Wernher Von Braun / Space jazz / Where you grave land (next time you fall off of yo) / Over my head / Admiral of the sea / Persuaded / Lavender and grey / Medley:- The last days of Pompeii / Benediction.

Feb 91. (12"ep/cd-ep) (RTT/RCD 267) **ADMIRAL OF THE SEA (first avenue mix) / ('A' milk off mix) / THE LAST DAYS OF POMPEII (mix) / GETAWAY IN TIME (instrumental) / I JUST WANT TO MAKE LOVE TO YOU (live)**

—— **MARK RELISH** – drums; repl. CRECO

Southern   Big Store

Jul 92. (cd-ep) <EFA 04669CD> **SHOOT YOUR WAY TO FREEDOM / BALLAD NO.19 / OH! TO BEHOLD / CHILDREN IN THE STREET**

—— **HART** with **CHRIS HENSLER** – guitar / **TOM MERKL** – bass / **STEVE SUTHERLAND** – drums

World
Service   Restless

May 94. (cd/lp) (1571744-2/-1) <72762> **NOVA MOB**
– Old empire / Shoot your way to freedom / Puzzles / Buddy / See and feel and know / Little Miss Information / I won't be there anymore / Please don't ask / The sins of their sons / Beyond a reasonable doubt / I was afraid – Coda.

Jul 94. (cd-ep) (461507) **OLD EMPIRE / PLEASE DON'T ASK / LITTLE MISS INFORMATION / BEYOND A REASONABLE DOUBT**

GRANT HART

World
Service   Pachyderm

Dec 95. (cd) (RTD 1573096-2) **ECCE HOMO (live)**
– Ballad No.19 / 2541 / Evergreen memorial drive / Come come / Pink turns to blue / She floated away / The girl who lives on Heaven hill / Admiral of the sea / Back somewhere / Last days of Pompeii / Old Empire / Never talking to you again / Please don't ask / The main.

Jan 00. (cd) (1573717-2) <5> **GOOD NEWS FOR THE MODERN MAN**   Nov99
– Think if over now / Nobody rides for free / Run run run to the centre Pompidou / You don't have to tell me now / Teeny's hair / A letter from Anne Marie / In a cold house / Seka knows / Remains to be seen / Let Rosemary rock him, Laura-Louise / Little Nemo.

THE GREAT INDIE DISCOGRAPHY — The 1980s

ICICLE WORKS (see under ⇒ McNABB, Ian)

I, LUDICROUS

Formed: Finsbury, South London, England ... early 1985 by the duo of WILL HUNG and JOHN PROCTER, the pair having met at work four years previously; I, LUDICROUS is an anagram of ridiculous. Influenced by Mancunian punk poets such as JOHN COOPER CLARKE and er, well, MARK E. SMITH (of The FALL), WILL and JOHN procured a basic instrumental set-up of a Casio keyboard and a cheap guitar, securing an album deal with JOE FOSTER's 'Kaleidoscope' records on the strength of a few gigs. The band's first release however, came via a free fanzine ('Blah Blah Blah') flexi-disc in the Spring of '87, the track in question, 'PREPOSTEROUS TALES', showcasing their quirky, DIY narrative style and later turning up on John Peel's Festive 50. After being invited by the DJ to record a Radio One session, I, LUDICROUS finally delivered their debut lp, 'IT'S LIKE EVERYTHING ELSE' (1987), critics divided over its merits. After a further single for the label, 'QUITE EXTRAORDINARY', they were forced to move on to the smaller indie imprint, 'Rodney, Rodney!', where they welcomed in the new decade with two albums, 'A WARNING TO THE CURIOUS' and 'LIGHT AND BITTER' (an official release of 'PREPOSTEROUS TALES' was also on the cards). A few years later, they re-emerged with a surprise NME Single Of The Week in the shape of 'WE STAND AROUND', lifted from the accompanying self-financed album, 'IDIOTS SAVANTS' (1992). A further one-off 7" in 1994, 'HATS OFF TO ELDORADO', was their final instalment of off-the-cuff humour, the pair parting ways that year.

Album rating: IT'S LIKE EVERYTHING ELSE (*6) / A WARNING TO THE CURIOUS (*5) / LIGHT AND BITTER (*5) / IDIOTS SAVANTS (*5)

WILL HUNG (b. DAVID RIPPINGALE, 4 Nov'56) – vocals / **JOHN PROCTER** (b. 9 May'57, Epsom) – keyboards, guitar

	Blah Blah Blah	not iss.
Apr 87. (7"flexi) *(none)* **PREPOSTEROUS TALES. / THREE ENGLISH FOOTBALL GROUNDS**		–

	Kaleidoscope	not iss.
Sep 87. (lp) *(KSLP 004)* **IT'S LIKE EVERYTHING ELSE**		–
– Trevor Barker / A pop fan's dream / My baby's got jetlag / Three English football grounds / Preposterous tales / Fabulous / Ludicrous / Are you turning round and telling me.		
Apr 88. (7") *(KS 707)* **QUITE EXTRAORDINARY. / AT THE END OF THE DAY**		–
(12"+=) *(KS 107)* – Kick down the stumps / Mistakes.		

	Rodney Rodney!	not iss.
Oct 89. (lp/c) *(RODNEY 002/+C)* **A WARNING TO THE CURIOUS**		–
– Thirtysomething / Britische architect / House beautiful / Moynihan brings out the hooligan in me / Another beaten man / We will fall / Good evening / Stuck in a lift with Noel Edmonds.		
(above was scheduled in 1988 as 'I, LUDICROUS'; *KSLP 008*)		
Apr 90. (12"ep) *(RODNEY 003)* **PREPOSTEROUS TALES IN THE LIFE OF KEN MacKENZIE. / THREE ENGLISH FOOTBALL GROUNDS / SPOCK'S BRAIN**		–
Nov 90. (lp/cd) *(RODNEY 006/+CD)* **LIGHT AND BITTER**		–
– Manifesto / My favourite records / How much money should I give to charity? / Completely ratted / Last night / Bring out the Branson / Vix sinex / Duller than . . . / Your life's not over / Programmes for wealth.		

	Old King Lud	not iss.
Sep 92. (cd) *(LUD 001)* **IDIOTS SAVANTS**		–
– Oh, really / Carter, they're unstoppable / Richard Madeley / C2s in vans / We stand around / Bloody proud / When the computer engine comes / Cy Twombly / Non / Eastenders.		
Sep 92. (7"ep) *(LUD 002)* **WE STAND AROUND**		–
– We stand around / Quite extraordinary / Oh really / Spock's brain.		
Jul 93. (7"ep) *(LUD 003)* **HATS OFF TO ELDORADO / HACKEY'S WINE BAR. / MAN'S MAN / OUR MATES**		–
— (flipped over for release in Feb'97)		
Sep 00. (cd-s) *(LUD 2001)* **APPROACHING 40**		–
– Approaching 40 / Football, beer and a cigarette / Autobiography / Away from the rabble.		

— there were also a few self-released tapes from 1985-1998

I'M SO HOLLOW

Formed: Sheffield, England ... 1979 by ROD LEIGH and singer, JANE WILSON, alongside JOSEF SAWICKI and DAYTON MARSDEN. The quartet made their initial appearances on a handful of V/A releases including the EP, 'The First 15 Minutes' (on 'Neutron') and 'The Hicks From The Sticks' album (for 'Rockburgh'). The following year, I'M SO HOLLOW issued their debut 45, 'DREAMS TO FILL THE VACUUM', a post-punk favourite very much in the mould of ENO (c.1974) and MAGAZINE. The band's characteristic strained vocals and fuzz guitars were showcased on their one and only CABARET VOLTAIRE-produced album, 'EMOTION, SOUND, MOTION' (1981).

Album rating: EMOTION, SOUND, MOTION (*6)

JANE WILSON – vocals, synthesizer / **ROD LEIGH** – guitar, vocals / **DAYTON MARSDEN** – bass / **JOSEF SAWICKI** – hipercussion

	Hologram	not iss.
Jan 81. (7"clear) *(ISH 002)* **DREAMS TO FILL THE VACUUM. / DISTRACTION**		–

	Illuminated	not iss.
Oct 81. (lp) *(JAMS 5)* **EMOTION/SOUND/MOTION**		–
– Entrance / Which way? / Unbroken line / Touch / Collisions / Excitement = chance / The triangular hour / Emotion, sound, motion / Nosferatu / Distraction.		

— disappeared the following year

INCA BABIES

Formed: Manchester, England ... 1982 by BILL BONNEY, HARRY STAFFORD and vocalist/drummer PETE. A whirling, hard-hitting thrash-punk outfit in the grinding mould of LIVING IN TEXAS or a punkabilly BIRTHDAY PARTY, they formed their own 'Black Lagoon' label and proceeded to release a string of well-received (in indie circles at least) 45's beginning with 1983's 'THE INTERIOR'. Two full albums, 'RUMBLE' and 'THIS TRAIN', also surfaced in the mid 80's, although the INCA BABIES would be best remembered for the presence of CLINT BOON (later of The INSPIRAL CARPETS), who played on their final effort, 'EVIL HOUR' (1988).

Album rating: RUMBLE (*5) / THIS TRAIN (*5) / OPIUM DEN mini (*4) / EVIL HOUR (*5)

PETE – vocals, drums / **HARRY STAFFORD** – guitar / **BILL BONNEY** – bass

	Black Lagoon	not iss.
Nov 83. (7") *(INC 001)* **THE INTERIOR. / SENSE OF LOSS**		–
Mar 84. (7") *(INC 002)* **GRUNT CADILLAC. / NO SACRED SOUND**		–
— added **MIKE LOVIS** – vocals, harmonica (PETE no vocals)		
May 84. (12"ep) *(INC 003)* **BIG JUGULAR**		–
– Big jugular / Jericho / The brain cruiser / Brother rat.		
Aug 84. (7") *(INC 004)* **THE JUDGE. / BUS BREAKER**		–
(12"+=) *(INC 004T)* – Cowboy song.		
Feb 85. (lp) *(INCLP 005)* **RUMBLE**		–
– She mercenary / The interior / Blind man (the chiller) / The diseased stranger's waltz / Leucotomy meat boss / Big jugular / 16 tons of fink / Cactus mouth informer / Greaseball mechanic.		
Oct 85. (12"ep) *(INC 007)* **SURFIN' IN LOCUSTLAND**		–
Mar 86. (7") *(INC 009)* **SPLATTER BALLISTICS COP. / BURY THE SWAGGER**		–
(12"+=) *(INC 009T)* – ('A'version).		
May 86. (lp) *(INCLP 010)* **THIS TRAIN**		–
– Plenty more mutants / Correction stack / Hole in the gulley / Candy mountain / Splatter ballistics cop / The depths / Backyard bones / Daniella / Call me enemy.		
Jun 87. (m-lp) *(INCMLP 012)* **OPIUM DEN**		–
– Opium den / Thirst / Devil in my room / Ramblin' man / Big Cyprus / A grim thought / Dresden.		
Oct 87. (7") *(CON! 00027)* **BUSTER'S ON FIRE. /**	–	– German
(above issued for 'Constrictor')		

— **HARRY + BILL** recruited newcomers **TONY CLARKE** – drums / **CLINT BOON** – keyboards / **DIRK BULLOWS + SIMON HINSON**

May 88. (lp) *(INCLP 013)* **EVIL HOUR**		–
– Evil hour / Long uphill trek / Partisan's river / A madman's demise / Bad hombre / Artillery switchback / Two rails to nowhere / Volts / Burning town / Young blood.		
(re-iss. Oct88 on 'Vinyl Drip'; SUK 002) (cd-iss. Jan89 on 'Communion'; COMM 6CD)		

— split after above, CLINT joined The INSPIRAL CARPETS

INDIANS IN MOSCOW

Formed: Hull, England ... 1981 by ADELE NOZEDAR, a shaven-headed, seemingly schitzoid punk-angel/she-devil, akin to the third cousin thrice removed of ALTERED IMAGES lass, CLARE GROGAN. Early the following year, this post-punk act were initially heard on a V/A double-lp collection, 'Your Secret's Safe With Us', although the public were still blissfully unaware of ADELE's brutal image. Given exposure on Channel 4's pop/rock programme, 'The Tube', their debut single, 'NAUGHTY MIRANDA' (in which she took on the role of the wicked MIRANDA), hit the top of the indie charts at the turn of '83/'84. By the time of their follow-up, 'I WISH I HAD', a posse was sent out for the rest of the INDIANS IN MOSCOW (STUART WALTON, RICH HORNBY + PETE RICHES) who had gone AWOL for a while. Early in 1985, ADELE's body was witnessed painted purple on the sleeve of the group's Nigel Gray-produced eponymous album, their last release before she formed another 4-piece, The FEVER TREE.

Album rating: INDIANS IN MOSCOW (*5)

ADELE NOZEDAR – vocals / **STUART WALTON** – keyboards / **PETE RICHES** – keyboards / **RICH HORNBY** – drums

Kennick / not iss.

Nov 83. (7"/12") (KNK 1002/+T) **NAUGHTY MIRANDA. / MIRANDA**

—— not sure if her band stayed on at this point after a disagreement

Mar 84. (7"/12") (KNK 1003/+T) **I WISH I HAD. / SLICE**
Jun 84. (7"/12") (KNK 1004/+T) **JACK PELTER AND HIS SEX-CHANGE CHICKEN. / SALT**
Sep 84. (7") (KNK 1005) **BIG WHEEL. / DESIRE**
 (12"+=) (KNK 1005T) – Price of love / Indians in Moscow.
Feb 85. (lp/c) (KLNK/KCNK 1) **INDIANS IN MOSCOW**
 – Big wheel / Meeting place / Witches & heroes / Howard's at lunch / Puppet dance / Square dance in the republic / Love song / I wish I had / Singing to French / Naughty Miranda / Jack Pelter and his sex-change chicken.

—— ADELE decided to form a new band, The FEVER TREE, although only one single, 'THE PIXIE SHOP' / 'HIS HANDS GIVE HIM AWAY' came out late '85

IN EMBRACE

Formed: London, England . . . 1981 by Coventry lads CAMERON LINDO and GARY KNIGHT. Possibly a precursor to mid-80's TALK TALK, IN EMBRACE made their vinyl debut in '82 with a 5-track EP on 'Glass' records, 'INITIAL CARESS'. Adding ex-SINATRAS drummer, JOBY PALMER and temp vocalist CLAIRE JOHNSON, the duo really got things underway with an inaugural long-player, 'PASSION FRUIT PASTELS' (1983), an appropriately-titled collection of post-New Wave romantic, awkwardly funky piano'n'drums that could have easily passed for a softer EYELESS IN GAZA. Later in the year, LINDO was replaced by RICHARD FORMBY, the follow-up, 'TOO' (1983) also illustrating their ability to combine stark, melancholic piano with the EDWYN COLLINS-esque vocal chords of KNIGHT. He, in turn, enlisted yet another partner, CLIVE DOVE, their subsequent singles appearing on 'Cherry Red'. However, a last ditch long-playing effort for 'Glass' (recorded with who else but EYELESS IN GAZA's PETE BECKER), 'SONGS ABOUT SNOGGIN' (1987) only served to underline that the band's time had come and gone.

Album rating: PASSION FRUIT PASTELS (*5) / TOO (*5) / SONGS ABOUT SNOGGIN' (*4) / WANDERLUST 82-84 mini compilation (*5)

GARY KNIGHT – vocals, keyboards, guitar / **CAMERON LINDO** – bass

Glass / not iss.

May 82. (12"ep) (GLASS 019) **INITIAL CARESS EP**
 – Breathless with passion explicit / For lovers / Clutching / The air inbetween / Precious.

—— added **JOBY PALMER** – drums, percussion (ex-SINATRAS)
—— added **CLAIRE JOHNSON** – vocals

Feb 83. (7") (GLASS 024) **SUN BRINGS SMILES. / PLAY IN LIGHT**
Mar 83. (lp) (GLALP 001) **PASSION FRUIT PASTELS**
 – Tears turn fresh / Half-awake (mountains) / We fail each other / Our star drawn through planes / The ball rolling / Sun brings smiles / At east / (Sigh!) / Tickling the ivanes / To friends (an open letter) / Caroline beginning.

—— **RICHARD FORMBY** – guitar, keyboards (ex-RELIGIOUS OVERDOSE) repl. CAMERON LINDO

Sep 83. (7") (GLASS 030) **LIVING DAYLIGHTS. / BLUE BEACH / MAKE**
Oct 83. (lp) (GLALP 004) **TOO**
 – Embrace the base on Sunday / Love among the crumbs / Trying too hard / Under the skin / Emotional punchbags / With a satin finish / Uniform & unicorn / If we choose / Stretch / Pine needles / Kiss a cold shoulder.

—— added **STEPHAN REES** – bass

Mar 84. (7") (GLASS 034) **YOU'RE HEAVEN SCENT (PLAYS HELL WITH ME). / FLUID**
 (12") (GLASS12 034) – ('A'side) / The newer living daylights / The longer living daylights / Liquid / Trying too hard.

—— sole original **KNIGHT** added **CLIVE DOVE** – keyboards, guitar

Cherry Red / not iss.

Feb 85. (7") (CHERRY 84) **SHOUTING IN CAFES. / CHOCOLATES FOR BREAKFAST**
Oct 85. (7") (CHERRY 90) **THIS BRILLIANT EVENING. / THE DARKEST HORSE**
 (12"+=) (12CHERRY 90) – ('A'instrumental).

—— added **AMANDA LYDON** – vocals / **PETER BECKER** – keyboards, bass, drum machine (of EYELESS IN GAZA)

Glass / not iss.

Dec 86. (7") (GLASS 051) **A ROOM UPSTAIRS. / ('A'version)**
 (12") (12GLASS 051) – ('A'side) / My worst behavoir / Red blue eyes.
May 87. (lp) (GLALP 022) **SONGS ABOUT SNOGGIN'**
 – Mirror mirror / Perfect stranger / What's got into me / You can laugh / Bedtime / A room upstairs / Shipwrecks / Somebodys / Stay here / Wallpaper, bathroom, perfume & God / Lovelorn.
Jul 87. (7"ep) (GLAEP 106) **WHAT'S GOT INTO ME**

—— disbanded after above

– compilations, etc. –

May 86. (m-lp) *Glass;* **WANDERLUST 82-84**

IN THE NURSERY

Formed: Sheffield, England . . . 1982 by two sets of twins, NIGEL and KLIVE HUMBERSTONE alongside ANT and DOLORES BENNETT. Specialising in military marching drum effects mixed with COCTEAU TWINS/DEAD CAN DANCE-esque vocals and guitars mellowed down by romantic cello (bow on bass), this lot issued a string of low-key releases beginning with '83's mini-set, 'WHEN CHERISHED DREAMS COME TRUE'. Unfortunately, the group ran into a few problems with their follow-up 7", 'WITNESS TO A SCREAM', the artwork printed wrongly and John Peel uncharacteristically fading the record out due to its poor quality. 'New European Records' (home of DEATH IN JUNE) took them on for a one-off 12", 'SONORITY', this, and subsequent releases taking on a more orchestrated feel. During the second half of the 80's, IN THE NURSERY brushed aside charges of Fascist sympathies and concentrated on a prolific release schedule for the 'Sweatbox' imprint. By the time of 1990's 'Third Mind' ('Wax Trax' US) album, 'L'ESPRIT', ITN had fused their industrial sound with MORRICONE-type atmospherics, while 1992's 'DUALITY', saw them sampling the voice of actor, Richard Burton. With music press recognition seemingly as far off as ever, the band continued to deliver an album a year before founding their own 'ITN Corporation' label in the mid 90's.

Album rating: TWINS (*4) / KODA (*4) / COUNTERPOINT compilation (*5)

NIGEL HUMBERSTONE – bow on bass, vocals, etc / **KLIVE HUMBERSTONE** – drum machine, vocals, etc / **ANT BENNETT** – guitar / **DOLORES BENNETT** – vocals

Paragon / not iss.

Jul 83. (m-lp) (VIRTUE 2) **WHEN CHERISHED DREAMS COME TRUE**
Mar 84. (7") (VIRTUE 5) **WITNESS TO A SCREAM. / 1984**

New Europ. Records / not iss.

Mar 85. (12"ep) (BADVC 55) **SONORITY – A STRENGTH**
 – Deus / Ex machina / Lost prayer / And your eyes.

Sweatbox / efa

Nov 85. (12"ep) (SOX 008) **TEMPER. / BREACH BIRTH / JOAQUIN / ARM ME AUDACITY**

—— ANT + DOLORES were repl. by **GUS FERGUSON** – cello / **ELAINE McLEOD** – vocals

Sep 86. (lp) (SAX 014) **TWINS**
 – Timbre / Twins / Workcorps / Profile 63 / Huntdown / Outsider / Judgement of music / Joaquin / Intertwine. (cd-iss. 1988; SAX 014CD) (cd re-iss. Jun95 on 'ITN Corporation'; CORP 009CD)
May 87. (12"ep) (SOX 019) **TRINITY: ELEGY. / TRINITY: ELEGY (reprise) / BLIND ME**
Jul 87. (lp/c) (SAX/+C 021) **THE STORY HORSE**
 (cd-iss. Feb88 +=; SAX 021CD) – Trinity: elegy / Trinity: elegy (reprise) / Blind me.
Nov 87. (12") (SOX 027) **COMPULSION. / LIBERTAIRE**
Nov 88. (lp/cd) (SAX 034/+CD) **KODA**
 – Rites / Maiden / Te deum / Triumph / Burnished days / Ascent / Scherzo / Guarded rites / Suspire / Kotow / The seventeenth parallel. (cd+=) – Compulsion / Libertaire. (cd re-iss. Jun95 on 'ITN Corporation'; CORP 008CD)

Third Mind / Wax Trax

Feb 90. (cd/lp) (TMCD/TMLP 48) <WAX 7120> **L'ESPRIT**
 – To the faithful / At first sight / Sesudient / Azure wings / Soeurette / Inamorata / Retaliation / Scenes of childhood / The pearl / L'esprit / Reverie / Alluvion / Across the ruins / To the faithful (reprise). (cd re-iss. Jun95 on 'ITN Corporation'; CORP 010CD)
Jul 90. (12") **SESUDIENT. /**

—— featured the vox of **DOLORES (MARGUERITTE)**

Sep 91. (cd) (TM 9271-2) **SENSE**
 – Blue religion / A rebours / Boy behind the curtain / Temporis / Syntonic / Sense / Epigraph / Memoirs / Angelchrome / Sinistroi / Sense datum / Contre – coeur. (cd re-iss. Jan98 on 'ITN Corporation'; CORP 018CD)
Jun 92. (cd) (TM 9163-2) **DUALITY**
 – Belle epoque / Always / Red harvest / Duality / Corruption: (I) thorns – (II) Pulse – (III) Valediction / Universe / The engraver / Mecciano.
Nov 93. (cd) (TM 9038-2) **AN AMBUSH OF GHOSTS (soundtrack)**
 – After great pain / Sedation / Lipstick / Disorientated / Atchaize / White robe / Cop shed / Running scene / Christian returns / Christian decides / Silk robe / Sedation 2 / Cop house / Funeral (part 1) / Funeral (part 2) / Dear Grover / Casus Belli / Syntonic / The hidden fortress / Hallucinations.
May 94. (12"/cd-s) (TM 2369-6/-3) **HALLUCINATIONS**
Oct 94. (cd) (TM 8976-2) **ANATOMY OF A POET** *Feb98*
 – Bombed / Anatomy of a poet / In perpetuum / Motive / Hallucinations? (dream world mix) / Blue lovers / Paper desert / Byzantium / The seventh sea / The golden journey / Touched with fire / Hallucinations – The tower III / November trees / Hallucinations? – A sense of reality. (re-iss. Jun95 on 'ITN Corporation'; CORP 012)

ITN Corporation / EFA

Jun 95. (cd) (CORP 011CD) **SCATTER**
 – Libertaire / Belle epoque / Mystere / Huntdown / Pearl / Tempest / Twins / Epitaph / To the faithful / Painter / Seraphic / 17th parallel / Sixth sense / Workcorps / Haunted dancehall / Miracle of the rose II.
May 96. (cd) (CORP 014CD) <70114> **DECO** *Jun96*
 – Deco / Precedent / Syracuse / Mallarme / Woman / Cedione / Caprice / Mandra / Bassilica / Harmonica / Moreau.
Nov 96. (cd) (CORP 015CD) **IN THE CABINET OF DR. CAGLIARI**
Oct 97. (cd) (CORP 017CD) <70117> **ASPHALT** *Jan98*
 – Asphalt / Sobriety / Bergen's / Precious / Metropole / Entrapment / Seduction / Sobriety II / Underworld / De-Luxe / Opulence / Reflux / Necessity / Crime passionel / Judgement walk.
Apr 98. (cd) (CORP 019CD) <70119> **LINGUA** *Jul98*
 – Poema / Mute harmony / A ask for grace / Profundus / Living tongue / Shonen no hi / Biello dumlo / Salient / El secreto.

– compilations, etc. –

Nov 88. (lp/cd) Normal; (NORMAL 74/+CD) **PRELUDE**
(cd re-iss. Jun95 on 'ITN Corporation'; CORP 007CD)
May 89. (lp/cd) Sweatbox; (SAX 042/+CD) **COUNTERPOINT**
(compilation)
– Breach birth / Compulsion / Workcorps / Twins / Iskra / Arm me audacity / Sentiment / Blind me / Libertaire / Elegy / Joaquin / Butyrki / Breach birth (inception mix).
Apr 97. (cd) EFA; **COMPOSITE – THE BRASILIAN ISSUE**
– Libertaire / Belle epoque (scatter mix) / The pearl / Harmonia / A rebours / To the faithful / Te deum / Retaliation / Judgement of Paris / Miracle of the rose II / Triumph / Burnished days / Sedudient / Elegy / Always (strive to be) / Anatomy of a poet (instrumental).

INTO A CIRCLE

Formed: Yorkshire, England ... mid '85 from the ashes of SOUTHERN DEATH CULT offshoot band, GETTING THE FEAR (other two members being BUZZ and AKY) by BARRY JEPSON and BEE. The latter RCA-signed pop-goth outfit only managed to unveil one solitary flop single, 'LAST SALUTE', before BUZZ and AKY took off to form JOY. Meanwhile, BARRY and BEE (aka EDDIE TEMPLE MORRIS), drafted in BILLY MORRISON and PASQUELLE, almost immediately releasing the 12"EP, 'RISE' (as IN TWO A CIRCLE). Moving from their own 'Arcadia' imprint to the more experienced and credible 'Abstract' label, INTO A CIRCLE delivered a follow-up EP, 'INSIDE OUT'. 1987 looked promising for the duo when their producer, Larry Steinbeck, booked former STRAWBERRY SWITCHBLADE chanteuse, ROSE McDOWELL, to take on the vocal duties for single, 'FOREVER'. She subsequently became an integral part of the group and appeared on their debut album, 'ASSASSINS' (1988), although this was the last we heard of the act.

Album rating: ASSASSINS (*4)

BARRY JEPSON – bass (ex-SOUTHERN DEATH CULT, ex-GETTING THE FEAR) / **BEE** (b. EDDIE TEMPLE MORRIS) – instruments (ex-GETTING THE FEAR, ex-DANSE SOCIETY) / **BILLY MORRISON** – guitar / **PASQUALE I SERNIA** – drums (ex-UNDER TWO FLAGS)

Arcadia   not iss.

Jan 86. (12"ep; as IN TWO A CIRCLE) (ARC 001) **RISE. / AND IN FLAMES / GABRIEL**

Abstract   not iss.

Nov 86. (12"ep) (12ABS 42) **INSIDE OUT**
– Inside out / Reward / Flow / Field of sleep.
— now with **ROSE McDOWELL** – vocals (ex-STRAWBERRY SWITCHBLADE)
Jul 87. (7") (ABS 44) **FOREVER. / O SIREN**
(12"+=) (12ABS 44) – ('A'-12"mix).
Mar 88. (7") (ABS 50) **EVERGREEN. / BEIRUT (THE AMAHL OF YOUTH)**
(12"+=) (12ABS 50) – ('A'-12"mix).
Jun 88. (lp) (ABT 018) **ASSASSINS**
– Beneath Mikhail / Over and over / The swinging tree / 'Elim / Forever / Allah Akhbar / Tender skin / Evergreen / Assassins / Seraphin twin.
— split the circle after above; ROSE joined DEATH IN JUNE

IT'S IMMATERIAL

Formed: Liverpool, England ... 1980 by JOHN CAMPBELL, HENRY PRIESTMAN, MARTIN DEMPSEY and PAUL BARLOW. All but BARLOW were ex-members of art-popsters, The YACHTS, and there was certainly something of the latter outfit's quirkiness in IT'S IMMATERIAL unassuming strum and droll humour. The band's erratic output remains strewn across a variety of indie labels, the wryly titled 'YOUNG MAN (SEEKS INTERESTING JOB)' the first in a series of singles which found a comfortable niche but hardly troubled the mainstream charts. Pared down to a duo of CAMPBELL and WHITEHEAD following PRIESTMAN and BARLOW's mid-80's departure (the latter two both decamped to fellow scousers, The MIGHTY WAH!), IT'S IMMATERIAL enjoyed some belated Top 20 chart success with the low-key brilliance of 'DRIVING AWAY FROM HOME (JIM'S TUNE)'. Yet despite a re-released 'ED'S FUNKY DINER' scraping into the Top 75 and a fine (if long awaited), similarly placed debut album, 'LIFE'S HARD AND THEN YOU DIE' (1986), the group's eccentric musings seemed doomed to cult appeal. Although PRIESTMAN was still working with the band on a casual, part-time basis, he subsequently became a full-time member of The CHRISTIANS in the late 80's. CAMPBELL and WHITEHEAD meanwhile, returned in 1990 with a follow-up album, 'SONG', only their second in a decade. Sadly, afficionados of thinking man's pop have since had to look elsewhere for understated thrills, the duo finally throwing in the towel in the early 90's.

Album rating: LIFE'S HARD AND THEN YOU DIE (*6) / SONG (*4)

JOHN 'JJ' CAMPBELL – vocals, bass (ex-YACHTS) / **HENRY PRIESTMAN** – keyboards (ex-YACHTS, of WAH!) / **MARTIN DEMPSEY** – guitar (ex-YACHTS, ex-PINK MILITARY) / **PAUL BARLOW** – drums

Hit Machine   not iss.

Jul 80. (7") (HIT 001) **YOUNG MAN (SEEKS INTERESTING JOB). / DOOSHA (A SUCCESS STORY)**

Inevitable   not iss.

Jul 81. (7") (INEV 9) **A GIGANTIC RAFT (IN THE PHILLIPINES). / NO PLACE FOR A PROMTER**
(re-iss. Oct82 on 'Wonderful World Of'; WW 4)

I.H.M.   not iss.

Nov 81. (7") (IHM 002) **IMMITATE THE WORM. / THE WORM TURNS**

— **JARVIS WHITEHEAD** (b.Newcastle, England) – guitar; repl. DEMPSEY who joined MEL-O-TONES

Eternal   not iss.

Oct 83. (7") (JF 2) **WHITE MAN'S HUT. / THE WORM TURNS**
(12"+=) (JF 2T) – Solid piles of food.
Feb 84. (7"/12") (JF 4/+T) **A GIGANTIC RAFT (IN THE PHILLIPINES). / THE MERMAID**

— trimmed to a duo of **CAMPBELL + WHITEHEAD** when PRIESTMAN + BARLOW joined The MIGHTY WAH!

Ark   not iss.

Mar 85. (12"ep) (DOVE 3) **FISH WALTZ EP**
– Fish waltz / Several brothers / The better idea / Lullaby.

— the duo added backing musicians **HENRY PRIESTMAN, The CHRISTIANS, RODDY LORIMER, STEVE WICKHAM, BRENDA KENNY, GILLIAN MILLER, MERRAN LAGINESTRA** + 70 year-old **TARRANT BAILEY JNR** – banjo (on 'Rope')

Siren   A&M

Oct 85. (7") (SIREN 8) **ED'S FUNKY DINER. / WASHING THE AIR**
(12") (SIREN 8-12) – ('A'-remix) / Driving away from home / Only the lonely.
Mar 86. (7") (SIREN 15) **DRIVING AWAY FROM HOME (JIM'S TUNE). / TRAINS, BOATS, PLANES**   18
(12"+=) (SIREN 15-12) – ('A'-Wicked Weather For Walking mix) / A crooked tune.
Jul 86. (7") (SIREN 24) **ED'S FUNKY DINER (FRIDAY NIGHT, SATURDAY MORNING). / ONLY THE LONELY**   65
(12"+=) (SIREN 24-12) – Driving away from home (I mean after all it's only Dead Man's Curve).
(d7"++=) (SIREN 24) – We'll turn things upside down.
Sep 86. (lp/c/cd) (SRNLP/SRNMC/CDSRN 4) <5169> **LIFE'S HARD AND THEN YOU DIE**   62
– Driving away from home (Jim's tune) / The sweet life / Lullaby / Happy talk / Festival time / Hang on sleepy town / Rope / Ed's funky diner / The better idea / Space. (re-iss. Apr90 on 'Virgin' lp/c; OVED/+C 289)
Oct 86. (7") (SIREN 34) **SPACE. / WASHING THE AIR (rub a dub mix)**
(12") (SIREN 34-12) – Space, he called from the kitchen / Hereby hangs a tale / Jazz Bo's holiday transatlantique.
Feb 87. (7") (SIREN 38) **ROPE. / FESTIVAL TIME**
(12"+=) (SIREN 38-12) – Very.

— part-timer PRIESTMAN joined The CHRISTIANS
Jun 90. (cd/c/lp) (SRN CD/MC/LP 27) **SONG**
– New Brighton / Endless holiday / An ordinary life / Heaven knows / In the neighbourhood / Missing / Homecoming / Summer winds / Life on the hill / Your voice.
Aug 90. (7") (SIREN 129) **HEAVEN KNOWS. / RIVER**
(12"+=/cd-s+=) (SIREN 129 12/CD) – Faith / Driving away from home (I mean after all it's only 'Dead Man's Curve').

— the duo split soon after above

– compilations, etc. –

Nov 88. (3"cd-ep) Virgin; (CDT 26) **DRIVING AWAY FROM HOME (JIM'S TUNE) / ED'S FUNKY DINER / DRIVING AWAY FROM HOME (I MEAN AFTER ALL IT'S ONLY 'DEAD MAN'S CURVE'**

THE GREAT INDIE DISCOGRAPHY — The 1980s

David J (see under ⇒ BAUHAUS)

JACOBITES (see under ⇒ SWELL MAPS; 70's section)

JAMES

Formed: Manchester, England ... 1982 by JIM GLENNIE, TIM BOOTH, LARRY GOTT and GAVAN WHELAN. In 1983 they signed to Tony Wilson's 'Factory' label, issuing a debut 3-track, the 'JIMONE EP'. Their folksy idiosyncracy and wilful weirdness was beloved of the music press almost from the off and their cult standing increased considerably after their 2nd classic 45, 'HYMN FROM A VILLAGE', topped the indie chart early in '85. They were soon snapped up by Seymour Stein's 'Sire', legendary underground mover and shaker Lenny Kaye producing the debut album, 'STUTTER'. BOOTH's overtly accented vocals were the primary focus of the band's often erratic and unorthodox, cerebral, improvisation-driven indie rock/folk and this bizarre combination made the band a compelling live act. However, financial difficulties led to the band moving label to WEA subsidiary 'Blanco Y Negro', where they released 'STRIP MINE' (1988). In 1990, after a change of personnel and a spell on 'Rough Trade', JAMES had their first Top 40 hit on 'Fontana' with 'HOW WAS IT FOR YOU?'. It was soon followed by a Top 20 album, 'GOLD MOTHER', that when re-promoted early 1991 with No.2 hit, the outrageously anthemic and subsequently tediously annoying 'SIT DOWN', also hit No.2. Suddenly the band were riding on the frayed, flared coat-tails of the baggy scene alongside fellow Manchester bands like The HAPPY MONDAYS and The STONE ROSES. Their obstinately obscure sound of old had now been bolstered by chant-along choruses of almost terrace proportions and the ubiquitous JAMES t-shirt was de rigeur for fresher students up and down the country. The band were now playing to stadium-sized audiences and they made their follow-up, 'SEVEN' (1992), to match, all big production and bombast that went down like a lead balloon with critics. With 'LAID' (1993), the band roped in BRIAN ENO, and went for a more opaque, stripped-down sound that recalled their experimental, earlier work. Lyrically, the album was as complex and as vivid as ever while the gorgeous 'SOMETIMES' gave the band their first Top 20 hit since early '92. The ENO sessions also provided the material for the 'WAH WAH' (1994) album, a collection of ambient improvisations with the aging electronic wizard. Of late, TIM BOOTH teamed up with ANGELO BADALAMENTI (he of 'Twin Peaks' fame) and ex-SUEDE guitarist, BERNARD BUTLER to release one-off set, 'BOOTH AND THE BAD ANGEL' (1996). Last year (1997), JAMES were again in the UK Top 10, the single 'SHE'S A STAR' and its parent album, 'WHIPLASH', both achieving the feat. Of late, a stop-gap 'best of' package was treated well by the fans (who made it UK No.1) but 'MILLIONAIRES' (1999) fell short of requirements. Although the near chart-topping record featured hit singles, 'I KNOW WHAT I'M HERE FOR' and 'JUST LIKE FRED ASTAIRE', it had none of the zip and lyrical sparkle of old. Ten albums in and JAMES were showing little sign of middle age spread although 'PLEASED TO MEET YOU' (2001) imparted the wisdom of maturity rather than the arrogance of youth. Although the album didn't quite make the Top 10 and 'GETTING AWAY WITH IT' should've been a bigger hit, the veteran Mancunians proved that mid-life musical crisis is all in the mind. Unfortunately, a few months later, JAMES were no more. • **Songwriters:** TIM BOOTH penned, except SUNDAY MORNING (Velvet Underground) / CHINA GIRL (Iggy Pop & David Bowie).

Album rating: STUTTER (*6) / STRIP MINE (*6) / ONE MAN CLAPPING (*6) / GOLD MOTHER (*8) / SEVEN (*8) / LAID (*7) / WAH WAH (*6) / WHIPLASH (*6) / THE BEST OF JAMES compilation (*8) / MILLIONAIRES (*5) / PLEASED TO MEET YOU (*6) / Booth & The Bad Angel: BOOTH & THE BAD ANGEL (*5)

TIM BOOTH (b. 4 Feb'60) – vocals / **LARRY GOTT** (b. JAMES GOTT) – guitar / **JIM GLENNIE** (b.10 Oct'63) – bass / **GAVAN WHELAN** – drums

		Factory	not iss.
Sep 83.	(7") *(FAC 78)* **JIMONE**		–
	– What's the world / Fire so close / Folklore.		
Feb 85.	(7") *(FAC 119)* **JAMES II**		–
	– Hymn from a village / If things were perfect.		
Jun 85.	(12"ep) *(FAC 138)* **VILLAGE FIRE**		–
	– What's the world / Fire so close / Folklore / Hymn from a village / If things were perfect.		

		Sire	Warners
Feb 86.	(7") *(JIM 3)* **CHAIN MAIL. / HUP STRINGS**		–
	(12"+=) *(JIM 3T)* **SIT DOWN EP** – Uprising.		
Jul 86.	(7") *(JIM 4)* **SO MANY WAYS. / WITHDRAWN**		–
	(12"+=) *(JIM 4T)* – Just hipper.		
Jul 86.	(lp/c) *(JIM LP/C 1)* **STUTTER**	68	–
	– Skullduggery / Scarecrow / So many ways / Just hip / Johnny Yen / Summer song / Really hard / Billy's shirts / Why so close / Withdrawn / Black hole. *(cd-iss. Nov91; 7599 25437-2)*		

		Blanco Y Negro	Sire
Sep 87.	(7") *(NEG 26)* **YAHO. / MOSQUITO**		–
	(12"+=) *(NEG 26T)* – Left out of her will / New nature.		
Mar 88.	(7") *(NEG 31)* **WHAT FOR. / ISLAND SWING**		–
	(c-s+=/12"+=) *(NEG 31 C/T)* – Not there.		
Sep 88.	(lp/c)(cd) *(JIM LP/C 2)(925657-2)* **STRIP MINE**	90	
	– What for / Charlie Dance / Fairground / Are you ready / Yaho / Medieval / Not there / Riders / Vulture / Strip mining / Refrain. *(re-iss. Jul91; same) (cd re-iss. Feb95; 925657-2)*		

		Rough Trade	not iss.
Mar 89.	(lp/c/cd) *(ONEMAN 001/+C/CD)* **ONE MAN CLAPPING (live in Bath)**		–
	– Chain mail / Sandman (hup strings) / Whoops / Riders / Why so close / Leaking / Johnny Yen / Scarecrow / Are you ready / Really hard / Burned / Stutter. *(cd+=)* – Yaho.		

— **DAVE BAYNTON-POWER** – drums repl. WHELAN / added **SAUL DAVIS** – violin, percussion, guitar / **MARK HUNTER** – keyboards

Jun 89.	(7") *(RT 225)* **SIT DOWN. / SKY IS FALLING**		–
	(12"+=/3"cd-s+=) *(RTT 225/+CD)* – Goin' away / Sound investment.		

— added **ANDY DIAGRAM** – trumpet (ex-PALE FOUNTAINS, ex-DIAGRAM BROS)

Nov 89.	(7") *(RT 245)* **COME HOME. / PROMISED LAND**		–
	(12"+=/cd-s+=) *(RTT 245/+CD)* – ('A'extended) / Slow right down (demo).		

		Fontana	Mercury
May 90.	(7") *(JIM 5)* **HOW WAS IT FOR YOU? / WHOOPS (live)**	32	–
	(12") *(JIM 5-12)* – ('A'side) / Hymn from a village (live) / Lazy.		
	(cd-s) *(JIMCD 5)* – ('A'side) / Hymn from a village (live) / Undertaker.		
	(12") *(JIMM 5-12)* – ('A'side) / ('A'different mix) / Lazy / Undertaker.		
Jun 90.	(cd/c/lp) *(<846189-2/-4/-1>)* **GOLD MOTHER**	16	Aug90
	– Come home / Government walls / God only knows / You can tell how much suffering (on a face that's always smiling) / How was it for you? / Crescendo / Hang on / Walking the ghost / Gold mother / Top of the world. *(re-iss. Apr91 cd/c/lp; 848595-2/-4/-1); hit No.2) (cd+=)* – Sit down / Lose control. *(cd re-iss. Dec01 ++; 548785-2)* – Come home (skunk weed skank mix) / Lose control (live) / Sit down (live) / Gold mother (remix).		
Jul 90.	(7"/c-s) *(JIM/+C 6)* **COME HOME (Flood mix). / DREAMING UP TOMORROW**	32	–
	(12") *(JIM 6-12)* – ('A'extended) / Stutter (live) / Fire away.		
	(cd-s) *(JIMCD 6)* – ('A'side) / ('A'extended) / Gold mother (remix) / Fire away.		
	(12") *(JIMM 6-12)* – ('A'live) / Gold mother (Warp remix) / 'A'-Andy Weatherall Boys own remix).		
Nov 90.	(7"/c-s) *(JIM/+C 7)* **LOSE CONTROL. / SUNDAY MORNING**	38	–
	(ext.12"+=/ext.cd-s+=) *(JIM 7-12/CD7)* – Out to get you.		
Mar 91.	(7"/c-s) *(JIM/+C 8)* **SIT DOWN. / ('A'live)**	2	–
	(12"+=/cd-s+=) *(JIM 8-12/CD8)* – Tonight.		
Nov 91.	(7"/c-s) *(JIM/+C 9)* **SOUND. / ALL MY SONS**	9	–
	(12"+=/cd-s+=) *(JIM 9-12/CD9)* – ('A'extended) / Come home (Youth mix).		
Jan 92.	(7"/c-s) *(JIM/+C 10)* **BORN OF FRUSTRATION. / BE MY PRAYER**	13	–
	(12"+=/cd-s+=) *(JIM 10-12/CD10)* – Sound (mix).		
Feb 92.	(cd/c/lp) *(<510932-2/-4/-1>)* **SEVEN**	2	Mar92
	– Born of frustration / Ring the bells / Sound / Bring a gun / Mother / Don't wait that long / Live a life of love / Heavens / Protect me / Seven. *(cd+=/c+=)* – Next lover. *(re-iss. Aug98; same) (cd re-iss. Dec01 +=; 548786-2)* – live:- Protect me (acoustic) / Sound / Heavens / Don't wait that long.		
Mar 92.	(7"/c-s) *(JIM/+C 11)* **RING THE BELLS. / FIGHT**	37	
	(12"+=/cd-s+=) *(JIM 11-12/CD11)* – The skunk weed skank / Come home (live dub version).		
	(12"++=) *(JIM 11-122)* – Once a friend.		
Jul 92.	(7"ep/c-ep/cd-ep) *(JIM/+C/CD 12)* **SEVEN (remix) / GOALIES BALL. / WILLIAM BURROUGHS / STILL ALIVE**	46	–
Sep 93.	(7"/c-s) *(JIM/+C 13)* **SOMETIMES. / AMERICA**	18	
	(12"+=/cd-s+=) *(JIM 13-12/CD13)* – Building a charge.		
Sep 93.	(cd/c/lp) *(<514943-2/-4/-1>)* **LAID**	3	72 Oct93
	– Out to get you / Sometimes (Lester Piggott) / Dream thrum / One of the three / Say something / Five-o / P.S. / Everybody knows / Knuckle too far / Low, low / Laid / Lullaby / Skindiving. *(re-iss. Aug98; same) (cd re-iss. Dec01 +=; 548787-2)* – live at the BBC:- Laid / Sometimes / Five-O / Say something (live).		
Nov 93.	(7"/c-s) *(JIM/+C 14)* */858217>* **LAID. / WAH WAH KITS**	25	61 Jan94
	(cd-s+=) *(JIMCD 14)* – The lake / Seconds away.		
	(cd-s) *(JIMDD 14)* – ('A'live) / Five-O / Say something / Sometimes.		
Mar 94.	(c-s) *(JIMMC 15)* **JAM J / SAY SOMETHING**	24	
	(12"+=)(cd-s+=) *(JIMX 15/JMCD 15)* – Assassin / ('B'-version).		
	(cd-s) *(JIMCD 15)* – JAM J – James vs The Sabres Of Paradise (i) Arena dub (ii) Amphetamine pulsate / JAM J – James vs The Sabres Of Paradise (i) Sabresonic tremolo dub (ii) Spaghetti steamhammer.		
Sep 94.	(cd/c/d-lp;ltd) *(<314 526 408-2/-4/-1>)* **WAH WAH** (w / BRIAN ENO)	11	Oct94
	– Hammer strings / Pressure's on / Jam J / Frequency dip / Lay the law down / Burn the cat / Maria / Low clouds (1) / Building a fire / Gospel oak / DVV / Say say something / Rhythmic dreams / Dead man / Rain whistling / Low clouds (2) / Bottom of the well / Honest Joe / Arabic agony / Tomorrow / Laughter / Sayonara.		

— **ADRIAN OXAAL** – repl. DIAGRAM

Feb 97.	(cd-s) *(JIMED 16)* **SHE'S A STAR / STUTTER (live) / JOHNNY YEN (live)**	9	–
	(cd-s) *(JIMDD 16)* – ('A'side) / Chunney chops / Fishknives / Van Gogh's dog.		
	(cd-s) *(JIMCD 16)* – ('A'-Dave Angel mix) / ('A'-Biosphere mix) / Come home (Weatherall mix).		

378

Date	Format	Cat. No.	Title	Chart	
Mar 97.	(cd/c/lp)	(<534354-2/-4/-1>)	**WHIPLASH**	9	

- Tomorrow / Lost a friend / Waltzing along / She's a star / Greenpeace / Go to the bank / Play dead / Avalanche / Homeboy / Watering hole / Blue pastures. *(cd re-iss. Dec01 +=; 548788-2)* – LOst a friend (live) / Greenpeace (live) / Homeboy (live) / Waltzing along (Flytronic mix).

Apr 97.	(cd-ep)	(JIMCD 17)	**TOMORROW / GONE TOO FAR / HONEST PLEASURE / ALL ONE TO ME**	12	-

(cd-s) *(JIMDD 17)* – ('A'side) / Lost a friend (session) / Come home (session) / Greenpeace (session).
(cd-s) *(JIMED 17)* – ('A'mixes; Fila Brazilia / Archive / Dirty Beatnik).

Jun 97.	(cd-s)	(JIMCD 18)	**WALTZING ALONG / ('A'mix)**	23	-

(cd-s) *(JIMED 18)* – ('A'side) / ('A'live).
(cd-s) *(JIMED 18)* – ('A'remixes by; Midfield General & Flytronix).

Mar 98.	(cd-ep)	(JIMCD 19)	**DESTINY CALLING / GOALIE'S BALL / ASSASSIN / THE LAKE**	17	-

(cd-ep) *(JIMED 19)* – ('A'side) / Jam J (live) / Honest Joe (live) / Sound (live).
(cd-s) *(JIMED 19)* – ('A'side) / She's a star (CD-Rom video).

Mar 98.	(cd/c)	(<536898-2/-4>)	**THE BEST OF** (compilation)	1	

- Come home / Sit down / She's a star / Laid / Waltzing along / Say something / Tomorrow / Born of frustration / Destiny calling / Out to get you / Runaground / Lose control / How was it for you? / Seven / Sound / Ring the bells / Sometimes / Hymn from a village. *(also d-cd-iss. ; 558173-2)*

May 98.	(cd-ep)	(JIMCD 20)	**RUNAGROUND / CRESCENDO / HANG ON / BE MY POWER**	29	-

(cd-ep) *(JIMED 20)* – ('A'side) / Say something (live) / Laid (live) / Lose control (live).
(cd-ep) *(JIMED 20)* – ('A'side) / ('A'remix) / Egoiste / Lost a friend (Aloof remix).

Nov 98.	(cd-s/cd-s)	(JIM MC/CD 21)	**SIT DOWN (1998 remix) / ('A'-Apollo 440 remix)**	7	-

(cd-s) *(JIMDD 21)* – China girl (radio 1 Iggy Pop tribute).

Jul 99.	(c-s)	(JIMC 22)	**I KNOW WHAT I'M HERE FOR / ALL GOOD BOYS**	22	

(cd-s+=) *(JIMCD 22)* – Imagine ourselves.
(cd-s) *(JIMDD 22)* – ('A'side) / Downstairs / Stolen horses.

Oct 99.	(c-s)	(JIMC 23)	**JUST LIKE FRED ASTAIRE / I DEFEAT**	17	

(cd-s+=) *(JIMCD 23)* – Long to see.
(cd-s) *(JIMDD 23)* – ('A'side) / Mary / Goal, goal, goal.

Oct 99.	(cd/c)	(<546386-2/-4>)	**MILLIONAIRES**	2	

- Crash / Just like Fred Astaire / I know what I'm here for / Shooting my mouth off / We're going to miss you / Strangers / Hello / Afro lover / Surprise / Dumb jam / Someone's got it in for me / Vervaceous. *(also d-cd+=; 546789-2)* – (live):- I know what I'm here for / Crash / Destiny calling / Someone's got it in for me / Just like Fred Astaire / I know what I'm here for (video) / Just like Fred Astaire (video).

Dec 99.	(c-s)	(JIMMC 24)	**WE'RE GOING TO MISS YOU / WISDOM OF THE THROAT**	48	

(cd-s+=) *(JIMCD 24)* – Top of the world (live).
(cd-s) *(JIMDD 24)* – ('A'side) / Pocketful of lemons ('A'-Eno's version).

— now without OXAAL

Jun 01.	(cd-s)	(JIMCD 25)	**GETTING AWAY WITH IT (ALL MESSED UP) / MAKE IT ALRIGHT / SO SWELL (ambient mix)**	22	-

(cd-s) *(JIMDD 25)* – ('A'side) / Stand / Shining (live).

Jul 01.	(cd)	(<586146-2>)	**PLEASED TO MEET YOU**	11	-

- Space / Falling down / English beefcake / Junkie / Pleased to meet you / The shining / Senorita / Give it away / Fine / Getting away with it (all messed up) / Alaskan pipeline.

— JAMES disbanded in December 2001

- compilations, etc. -

Dec 01.	(cd)	*Fontana; (548440-2)*	**ULTRA** (B-sides)		-
JUn 02.	(d-cd)	*Sanctuary; (SANDD 119)*	**GETTING AWAY WITH IT (live)**		

BOOTH AND THE BAD ANGEL

— **TIM BOOTH** / **ANGELO BADALAMENTI** / + **BERNARD BUTLER** (ex-Suede)

				Fontana	Mercury
Jun 96.	(c-s)	(BBMC 1)	**I BELIEVE (edit) / I BELIEVE (long version)**	25	-

(cd-s+=) *(BBCD 1)* – When you smiled.
(cd-s+=) *(BBDD 1)* – Melting away.

Jul 96.	(cd/c)	(<526 852-2/-4>)	**BOOTH AND THE BAD ANGEL**	35	

- I believe / Dance of the bad angels / Hit parade / Fall in love with me / Old ways / Life gets better / Heart / Rising / Butterfly's dream / Stranger / Hands in the rain. (below lifted from the film 'Martha Meet Franky, Daniel & Laurence').

Jun 98.	(c-s)	(MERMC 503)	**FALL IN LOVE WITH ME (live) / I BELIEVE (live)**	57	-

(cd-s+=) *(MERCD 503)* – Hit parade (live).
(cd-s) *(MERDD 503)* – ('A'side) / Butterfly's dream (live) ('A'live).

JAMIE WEDNESDAY (see under ⇒ CARTER THE UNSTOPPABLE SEX MACHINE; in 90's section)

JANE (& BARTON) (see under ⇒ MARINE GIRLS)

JANITORS

Formed: Sunderland & Newcastle, England . . . late 1984 by DENTOVER, CRAIG HOPE, SIMON HARRIES and TIM. Signing to John Grayland's (YEAH YEAH NOH) imprint, 'In-Tape', they released a couple of singles in the mid-80's, 'CHICKEN STEW' and 'GOOD TO BE KING', both a mixture of MEMBRANES meeting CAPTAIN BEEFHEART. In the summer of '86, The JANITORS worked with producer, JON LANGFORD (MEKONS/THREE JOHNS) on their debut 12", 'THUNDERHEAD', their last for the label before moving to 'Abstract'. A year later and side by side with a new single, 'FAMILY FANTASTIC', CRAIG and DENTOVER teamed up as BIG ZAP with MARY GOLIGHTLY (of GAYE BYKERS ON ACID), SARAH CORINA (BOMB PARTY) and DJ/producer, STEVE McINTOSH on a version of The Temptations' 'PSYCHEDELIC SHACK' (B-side, 'ZAP ATTACK'). The JANITORS returned to their own playground in 1988 with a single, 'MOONSHINE', taken from their first album proper, 'DEAFHEAD' (produced by Pat Collier), although their return was short-lived.

Album rating: DEAFHEAD (*5)

DENTOVER (b. DENTON) – vocals / **CRAIG HOPE** – guitar, keyboards / **SIMON HARRIES** – bass / **TIM** – drums

				In-Tape	not iss.
Jul 85.	(7")	(IT 017)	**CHICKEN STEW. / THE DEVIL'S GONE TO WHITLEY BAY**		-
May 86.	(7")	(IT 031)	**GOOD TO BE KING. / WALL STAR**		-
Aug 86.	(m-lp)	(IT 028)	**THUNDERHEAD**		

- Thunderhead Johnny / Wall star / Long neck bottles / Mexican kitchen.

— **PETE** – bass; repl. SIMON

				Abstract	not iss.
Jun 87.	(7")	(ABS 045)	**FAMILY FANTASTIC. /**		

(12"+=) *(12ABS 045)* –

Mar 88.	(7")	(ABS 047)	**MOONSHINE. / ONLY ONE**		

(12"+=) *(12ABS 047)* –

Jun 88.	(lp)	(ABT 019)	**DEAFHEAD**		-

- Moonshine / Spin / Only one / Halfway to a happening / Get a load (get a job) / Happy / What can I say / The country song / Proud Mary / Time goes on / Going to be.

Dec 88.	(7")	(ABS 054)	**HALFWAY TO A HAPPENING. / DEAD SET ON DESTRUCTION / HUBBA HUBBA (SHE'S A WEIRD ANIMAL)**		

— disbanded after above

JARBOE (see under ⇒ SWANS)

JASMINE MINKS

Formed: Aberdeen, Scotland . . . 1983 by young lads ADAM SHEPHERD, TOM SANDERSON, JIM BALE and MARTIN ALVEY, as a 60's nostalgia outfit into BYRDS-esque jangle-pop psychedelia and influenced by the geographical proximity of Glasgow's 'Postcard' scene. Signing to Alan McGee's 'Creation' label, The JASMINE MINKS released a couple of decent 45's and an lp, '1,2,3,4,5,6,7, ALL GOOD PREACHERS GO TO HEAVEN' (1984), before the band moved down south to London; DAVE MUSKER was subsequently drafted in for one single, 'COLD HEART'. By the release of the 'ANOTHER AGE' album in '88, The 'MINKS had sharpened up their melodies, hooklines and overall approach, as heard on the likes of 'CUT ME DEEP', also one of the standout tracks on 'Creation' V/A sampler, 'Doing It For The Kids'. Having released the very low key, 'VERITAS' (in 2000), The JASMINE MINKS returned triumphantly with McGee's newly set up 'Poptones' imprint. The comeback single in question, 'DADDY DOG', featured Scottish Socialist MSP, Tommy Sheridan and was issued in the spring of 2001 prior to their brilliant follow-up album 'POPARTGLORY'. Fresh and dazzling, the group returned to their mid-80's roots while managing to add in funky basslines, and some seriously strange head-trip psychedelica. The set seemed to impress MINKS followers, and it's certain that McGee was glad to have them back on board (for a short-time!).

Album rating: 1,2,3,4,5,6,7 ALL GOOD PREACHERS GO TO HEAVEN mini (*5) / JASMINE MINKS (*5) / SUNSET compilation (*6) / ANOTHER AGE (*4) / SCRATCH THE SURFACE (*5) / SOUL STATION compilation (*6) / VERITAS (*5) / POPARTGLORY (*7)

ADAM SHEPHERD – guitar, vocals / **TOM SANDERSON** – vocals, guitar / **JIM BALE** – bass / **MARTIN ALVEY** – drums

				Creation	not iss.
Mar 84.	(7")	(CRE 004)	**THINK! / WORK FOR NOTHING**		-
Aug 84.	(7")	(CRE 008)	**WHERE THE TRAFFIC GOES. / MR. MAGIC**		-
Dec 84.	(m-lp)	(CRELP 003)	**1,2,3,4,5,6,7 ALL GOOD PREACHERS GO TO HEAVEN**		-

- The thirty second set up / What's gone wrong / Somers town / Ghost of a young man / Mr. Magic / Where the traffic goes.

Jul 85.	(7")	(CRE 018)	**WHAT'S HAPPENING. / BLACK AND BLUE**		

— added guest **DAVE MUSKER** – organ (ex-TV PERSONALITIES)

Apr 86.	(7")	(CRE 025)	**COLD HEART. / WORLD'S NO PLACE**		

(12"+=) *(CRE 025T)* – Forces network (AFM version) / You got me wrong.

— MUSKER left to form SLAUGHTER JOE

Jun 86.	(lp)	(CRELP 007)	**JASMINE MINKS**		-

- I don't know / Cold heart / Choice / The ballad of Johnny Eye / Work / Forces network / Like you / Painting / You take my freedom / Cry for a man. *(cd-iss. Oct90 +=; CRECD 007)* – The thirty second set up / What's gone wrong / Somers town / Ghost of a young man / Mr. Magic / Where the traffic goes.

Oct 86.	(lp)	(CRELP 013)	**SUNSET** (compilation)		

- Think / Work for nothing / Where the traffic goes / Ghost of a young man / Sunset / What's happening / Black and blue / Cold heart / World's no place / Forces network / Mr. Magic.

— **ED DE FLAM** – guitar; repl. ADAM

Nov 87.	(7"ep)	(PACE 1)	**PURE EP (live)**		-

(above issued on 'Esurient Communications')

Jan 88. (lp) (CRELP 025) **ANOTHER AGE**
– Veronica / Still waiting / Summer! where? / Follow me away / Cut me deep / Living out your dreams / Don't wait too long / Nothing can stop me / Soul station / Time for you / Another age / Sad.

Feb 89. (lp/cd) (CRELP 044/+CD) **SCRATCH THE SURFACE**
– Lost and living / Little things / I've lost her / Marcella / Misery / Can you hear me? / Take / Reaching out / Too young (my home town) / Shiny and black / Scratch the surface / Playing for keeps.

— folded after above . . . but re-formed towards the end of the decade

— **JIM SHEPHERD** with **TOM REID** – drums / + others

Genius Move / not iss.

2000. (cd) (GENMOVCD 1) **VERITAS**
– Easyblue / I heard 'I Wish It Would Rain' / February / Learn to suffer / Blown away / Toy story / Bloored CCR / Bad moon / Stress / Salvage / Suffer instrumental / Radio fuzz / Raving / Mother nature / On ice / Tough old birds.

Poptones / not iss.

Mar 01. (7"; JASMINE MINKS featuring TOMMY SHERIDAN) (MC 5025S) **DADDY DOG. /**

Sep 01. (cd) (MC 5025CD) **POPARTGLORY**
– Popartglory / 3b48 / Soul children / Daddy dog / Freefall / Midnight and I / Bloored OCR / Running ahead / On a Saturday / Ken's korubo / Keepin' hold of you / Angel / 2001 a mink odyssey / Red sky.

– compilations, etc. –

Oct 91. (cd/lp) *Creation*; (CRE CD/LP 112) **SOUL STATION**
– Cold heart / Forces network / Veronica / Somers town / Think! / Where the traffic goes / The thirty second set up / Ghost of a young man / Still waiting / Cut me deep / The ballad of Johnny Eye / Soul station.

JAYHAWKS

Formed: Minneapolis, Minnesota, USA . . . 1985 by MARK OLSON and GARY LOURIS, who formed the core of the band through an ever changing series of line-ups. After two American-only albums of rough-hewn country rock, 'THE JAYHAWKS' (1986) and 'BLUE EARTH' (1989), the band were taken under the wing of producer GEORGE DRAKOULIAS. In a well-thumbed tale, they were signed to Rick Rubin's 'Def American' label after roots maestro DRAKOULIAS allegedly phoned 'Twintone' mainman DAVE AYERS and heard a JAYHAWKS tape playing in the background. He was immediately spellbound, as were the country rock faithful among the record buying public when they heard the band's debut for 'Def American', the seminal 'HOLLYWOOD TOWN HALL' (1992). While many fans were under the impression this was the band's first album, the pristine harmonies of OLSON and LOURIS suggested otherwise. Like a fine malt whisky, The JAYHAWKS's songwriting and harmonising had been maturing over almost a decade and the result was something to savour. There wasn't a duff track in sight, and with veteran piano player NICKY HOPKINS on board, this was an essential purchase. Following its release, the band embarked on a heavy round of touring, sparking, along with peers like UNCLE TUPELO, a mini country-rock revival. Expectations were high for the follow-up, 'TOMORROW THE GREEN GRASS' (1995), the band bypassing the dilemma of matching 'HOLLYWOOD's perfection by going for a more eclectic approach. The crystal clear harmonising was still intact, the single 'BLUE' perhaps the JAYHAWKS' finest moment, as affecting a piece of resigned melancholy as ever graced a slab of vinyl. After a further tour, OLSON left and, after a long period of uncertainty and personal crisis, The JAYHAWKS re-emerged, albeit in a radically altered form. 'THE SOUND OF LIES' (1997) was a decidedly low-key affair and despite receiving a 'Masterpiece' award from retro music mag Mojo, the record has largely gone unnoticed. Something of a departure musically and lyrically, the album was downbeat and edgy, not as immediate as the older material but well worth persevering with; the likes of 'TROUBLE' and 'DYING ON THE VINE' the sound of a band exorcising their demons, coming through bruised but wiser. 'SMILE' (2000), meanwhile, suggested that The JAYHAWKS also wanted to exorcise some of their deep running country roots, opting instead for a more contemporary percussive kick and power pop sheen which strived to shake off the melancholy of their last album without leaving longtime fans in the lurch. • **Songwriters:** OLSON-LOURIS except; REASON TO BELIEVE (Tim Hardin). In 1996 LOURIS co-wrote with other members after OLSON left. • **Trivia:** OLSON and LOURIS can also be heard on sessions for MARIA McKEE, COUNTING CROWS and former stablemates SOUL ASYLUM. The latter's DAN MURPHY and DAVE PIRNER (latter part-time) were in the offshoot band, GOLDEN SMOG, which featured LOURIS and PERLMAN.

Album rating: THE JAYHAWKS (*6) / BLUE EARTH (*6) / HOLLYWOOD TOWN HALL (*8) / TOMORROW THE GREEN GRASS (*7) / THE SOUND OF LIES (*6) / SMILE (*5)

MARK OLSON – vocals, guitar, harmonica / **GARY LOURIS** – vocals, electric guitar / **MARC PERLMAN** – bass / **NORM ROGERS** – drums

not iss. / Bunkhouse

1986. (lp) <7001> **THE JAYHAWKS**
– Falling star / Tried and true / Let the critics wonder / Let the last night be the longest / Behind bars / Cherry pie / The liquor store came first / People in this place on every side / Misery tavern / (I'm not in) Prison / King of kings / Good long time / Six pack on the dashboard. <US cd-iss. 2001>

THAD SPENCER – drums; repl. NORM who joined The COWS

not iss. / Twin/Tone

Oct 89. (lp/cd) <TTR 89151-1/-2> **THE BLUE EARTH**
– Two angels / She's not alone anymore / Will I be married / Dead end angel / Commonplace streets / Ain't no end / Five cups of coffee / The Baltimore sun / Red firecracker / Sioux City / I'm still dreaming now I'm yours / Martin's song. (UK-iss.cd Jul95; same) (cd re-iss. Sep98 on 'R.C.A.'; 74321 60575-28)

— **KEN CALLAHAN** – drums; repl. THAD

— session **NICKY HOPKINS** – keyboards (ex-JEFF BECK GROUP, etc)

Def American / Def American

Sep 92. (cd/c/lp) (512 986-2/-4/-1) <26829> **HOLLYWOOD TOWN HALL**
– Waiting for the sun / Crowded in the wings / Clouds / Two angels / Take me with you / Sister cry / Settled down like rain / Wichita / Nevada, California / Martin's song. (re-iss. cd Apr95 on 'American-RCA'; 74321 23994-2) (cd re-iss. Apr00 on 'Columbia'; 491794-2)

Aug 93. (7"/c-s) (DEFA/MC 28) **SETTLED DOWN LIKE RAIN. / SISTER CRY**
(cd-s+=) (DEFCD 28) – Live medley: Settled down like rain – Martin's song.

Nov 93. (7"/c-s) (DEFA/MC 25) **WAITING FOR THE SUN. / MARTIN'S SONG**
(cd-s+=) (DEFCD 25) – Up above my head / Keith & Quentin.
(cd-s+=) (DEFCDX 25) – Reason to believe / Sister cry / Medley: Martin's song – Settled down like rain.
(cd-s) (DEFCDXX 25) – ('A'side) / Up above my head.

— added **KAREN GROTBERG** – keyboards

American-RCA / American-RCA

— drummers **DON HEFFINGTON** (studio) / **TIM O'REAGAN** (tour); repl. KEN

Feb 95. (cd/c) (74321 23680-2/-4) <43006> **TOMORROW THE GREEN GRASS** 41 / 92
– Blue / I'd run away / Miss Williams' guitar / Two hearts / Real light / Over my shoulder / Bad time / See him on the streets / Nothing left to borrow / Ann Jane / Pray for me / Red's song / Ten little kids. (cd re-iss. Jan99 on 'Columbia'; 491795-2)

Feb 95. (7"/c-s) (74321 25797-7/-4) **BLUE. / TOMORROW THE GREEN GRASS**
(cd-s+=) (74321 25797-2) – Darling today.

Jul 95. (7"/c-s) (74321 29163-7/-4) **BAD TIME. / LAST CIGARETTE** 70
(cd-s+=) (74321 29163-2) – Get the load out / Sing me back home.

— now without OLSON / line-up **LOURIS, PERLMAN, GROTBERG + O'REAGAN** plus **KRAIG JOHNSON + JESSY GREENE**

Apr 97. (cd/c) <(74321 46406-2/-4)> **SOUND OF LIES** 61
– The man who loved life / Think about it / Trouble / It's up to you / Stick in the mud / Big star / Poor little fish / Sixteen down / Haywire / Dying on the vine / Bottomless cup / Sound of lies / I hear you cry. (cd re-iss. Jan99 on 'Columbia'; 491796-2)

Jun 97. (c-s) (74321 48755-4) **BIG STAR / SLEEPYHEAD**
(cd-s+=) (74321 48677-2) – Dying on the vine / I'd run away.

— now without GREENE

Columbia / Columbia

May 00. (cd) (497971-2) <69522> **SMILE** 60
– Smile / I'm gonna make you love me / What led me to this town / Somewhere in Ohio / A break in the clouds / Queen of the world / Life floats by / Broken harpoon / Pretty thing / Mr. Wilson / (In my) Wildest dreams / Better days / Baby, baby, baby. (re-iss. Aug01; same)

Jul 00. (m-cd) (669689-2) **I'M GONNA MAKE YOU LOVE ME**
– I'm gonna make you love me / Somewhere in Ohio / What led me to this town / Waiting for the sun / Take me with you (when you go) / Blue / The man who loved life.

– compilations, etc. –

Sep 00. (cd) *Columbia*; (499876-2) **TOMORROW THE GREEN GRASS / HOLLYWOOD TOWN**

JAZZATEERS

Formed: Glasgow, Scotland . . . 1981 by MATTHEW WILCOX, IAN BURGOYNE, KEITH BAND and KENNY McDONALD. Being the last act to sign for the soon-to-be-defunct indie label, 'Postcard' (home of ORANGE JUICE, AZTEC CAMERA and JOSEF K), they found themselves in the unenviable position of having their debut single shelved. However, a year later the JAZZATEERS were on the books of 'Rough Trade', releasing their eponymous set and an accompanying single, 'SHOW ME THE DOOR', in the summer of '83. The album received some decent reviews with regards to the LOU REED/GORDON GANO-esque approach of lead singer, WILCOX. Unfortunately, the frontman's services were no longer required when the band metamorphosed into minor hitmakers, BOURGIE BOURGIE, their new vocalist being the crooning great, PAUL QUINN. The JAZZATEERS story was not yet over though, as WILCOX and BAND reformed the group in '85, recruiting MICK SLAVEN and COLIN AULD to record a self-financed one-off single, 'PRESSING ON'. Over a decade later – after WILCOX and BAND had spent the late 80's/early 90's in The WILD ANGELS – The JAZZATEERS released the posthumous compilation, 'I SHOT THE PRESIDENT' (1997).

Album rating: JAZZATEERS (*6) / I SHOT THE PRESIDENT compilation (*5)

MATTHEW WILCOX – vocals / **IAN BURGOYNE** – guitar / **KEITH BAND** – bass / **KENNY McDONALD** – drums

Postcard / not iss.

Jan 82. (7"; w-drawn) (81-14) **SINGLE. /**

Rough Trade / not iss.

Jul 83. (7") (RT 138) **SHOW ME THE DOOR. / SIXTEEN REASONS**

Jul 83. (lp) (ROUGH 46) **JAZZATEERS**
– Nothing at all / Sixteen reasons / Heartbeat / Looking for a girl / Something to prove / Baby this a no no / Once more with feeling / Texan / Show me the door / Here comes that feeling / First blood.

— all but WILCOX took off to form BOURGIE BOURGIE (⇒) with PAUL QUINN

— **WILCOX + BAND** re-formed The JAZZATEERS with **MICK SLAVEN** – guitar / **COLIN AULD** – drums

JAZZATEERS (cont)

Jun 85. (12") (STAMP 1) **PRESSING ON. / SPIRAL** *(Stampede / not iss.)*
— after their demise, SLAVEN joined DEL AMITRI while AULD joined FRUITS OF PASSION

– compilations, etc. –

Apr 97. (7") Marina; (MAR 29) **HERE COMES THAT FEELING. / TEXAN**
May 97. (cd) Marina; (MA 30) **I SHOT THE PRESIDENT** (rare & demos)
— Nothing at all / Sixteen reasons / Heartbeat / Looking for a girl / Something to prove / Baby that's a no no / Once more with feeling / Texan / Show me the door / Here comes that feeling / Religious me / Blood is sweeter than honey / Up to my eyes / Holding court / Cowboy mouth / Pressing on / Coastline / She's black and white / Don't let your son grow up to be a cowboy.

WILD ANGELS

— were formed by **WILCOX + BAND** plus **STEPHEN LIRONI** – keyboards (ex-ALTERED IMAGES, ex-FLESH) / **DOUGLAS McINTYRE** – guitar (ex-BATHERS, ex-WHITE SAVAGES, ex-FLESH)

Jul 87. (12") (EDITION 87.13) **SHE'S BLACK AND WHITE. / DON'T LET YOUR SON GROW UP TO BE A COWBOY** *(Supreme / not iss.)*
Jul 88. (cd) (VALD 8060) **ROCKIN' ON THE RAILROAD** *(Valentine / not iss.)*
— Rockin' on the railroad / Don't leave me now / Miss Froggie / Weekend / Boogie woogie country boy / It'll be me / Old black Joe / Lights out / Blue Monday / Moonshine boogie / Ballad of a teenage queen / There's a fight going on / Little G.T.O. / Break up / Lucille / The sledgehammer strikes back.

JAZZ BUTCHER

Formed: Oxford, England ... 1982 as an outlet for the off-beat but acute musical observations of PAT FISH (real name PATRICK HUNTRODS), the multi-instrumentalist/singer-songwriter having played in various outfits (including WOW FEDERATION) during his time as a student in Oxford. Securing a deal with the 'Glass' label, FISH rounded up former colleague MAX EIDER – who'd remain a pivotal part of the JAZZ BUTCHER operation for the next five years – and proceeded to record a debut album, 'BATH OF BACON'. More successful was 1984's 'SCANDAL IN BOHEMIA' (which saw the addition of ex-BAUHAUS man, DAVID J.), the record drawing cult underground acclaim with its droll cabaret-pop humour and eclectic array of musical styles (JONATHAN RICHMAN, LOU REED, FAD GADGET and MONOCHROME SET come to mind). Another fine offering surfaced the following year in the shape of mini-set, 'SEX AND TRAVEL', FISH taking a more relaxed but even more sardonic approach on the priceless 'HOLIDAY' and coming on like a Home Counties NICK CAVE on 'WALK WITH THE DEVIL'. Yet enthusiasm from the music press and public alike remained muted and FISH concentrated on building up a fanbase in Europe and America, this mid-80's period of instability seeing the departure of both DAVID J. and EIDER. After a final, poorly received album, 'DISTRESSED GENTLEFOLK' (1986; released under the moniker of JAZZ BUTCHER CONSPIRACY) for 'Glass', FISH re-emerged via a new deal with 'Creation' in 1988. The resulting album, 'FISHCOTHEQUE', saw him working with new guitarist KIZZY O'CALLAGHAN, a revised line-up subsequently forming around the pair and comprising ALEX GREEN, LAURENCE O'KEEFE and PAUL MULREANY. Under Alan McGee's benevolent wing, FISH & Co. were free to experiment to their heart's content, turning out a further series of highly individual albums including 'CULT OF THE BASEMENT' (1990) and 'CONDITION BLUE' (1991). Despite continuing success in the US alternative market, The JAZZ BUTCHER finally tired of domestic indifference and shut up shop following the release of 1995's 'ILLUMINATE'. • **Covered:** SPEEDY GONZALES (Pat Boone) / KNOCKIN' ON HEAVEN'S DOOR (Bob Dylan) / etc.

Album rating: IN BATH OF BACON (*7) / A SCANDAL IN BOHEMIA (*6) / SEX AND TRAVEL mini (*5) / DISTRESSED GENTLEFOLK (*6) / FISHCOTHEQUE (*6) / BIG PLANET SCAREY PLANET (*5) / CULT OF THE BASEMENT (*6) / BLACK EG (*5) / CONDITION BLUE (*5) / WESTERN FAMILY (5) / EDWARD'S CUPBOARD compilation (*6) / WAITING FOR THE LOVE BUS (*5) / ILLUMINATE (*5) / DRAINING THE GLASS 1982-86 compilation (*6) / GLORIOUS & IDIOTIC (*6) / ROTTEN SOUL (*6) / CAKE CITY compilation (*6)

PAT FISH (b. PATRICK HUNTRODS) – vocals / **MAX EIDER** – lead guitar / **FELIX RAY** – bass / **MR. O.P. JONES** – drums / guests incl. **ROLO + ALICE** (future WOODENTOPS)

(Glass / Big Time)

Aug 83. (lp) (GLALP 002) **IN BATH OF BACON**
— Gloop jiving / Jazz Butcher theme / Party time / Bigfoot motel / Sex engine thing / Chinatown / Zombie love / Grey flannellette / La mer / Poisoned by food / Love kittens / Bath of Bacon / Girls who keep goldfish. (re-iss. Feb85; same) (cd-iss. Aug88; GLACD 002)
Sep 83. (7") (GLASS 027) **SOUTHERN MARK SMITH. / JAZZ BUTCHER MEETS COUNT DRACULA**
Mar 84. (7") (GLASS 033) **MARNIE. / CAROLINE WHEELER'S BIRTHDAY PRESENT (bedroom version)**
(12") (GLASS 12-033) – ('A'extended) / Zombie love / Girls who keep goldfish / Sweet Jane / Cowgirl fever.
Jul 84. (7") (GLASS 040) **ROADRUNNER. / RAIN**
(ext.12"+=) (GLASS 12-040) – Drink.
— guests incl. **DAVID J + KEVIN HASKINS** (ex-BAUHAUS)
Nov 84. (lp) (GLALP 009) **A SCANDAL IN BOHEMIA**
— Southern Mark Smith (big return) / Real men / Soul happy hour / I need meat / Just like Betty Page / Marnie / Caroline Wheeler's birthday present / Mind like a playgroup / Girlfriend / My desert. (cd-iss. Sep88; GLACD 009) (cd re-iss. Sep01 on 'Vinyl Japan'; ASKCD 129)
Feb 85. (7") (GLASS 041) **REAL MEN. / THE JAZZ BUTCHER VS THE PRIME MINISTER**
(12"+=) (GLASS 12-041) – Southern Mark Smith (original).
Mar 85. (lp) (GLEX 101) **THE GIFT OF MUSIC** (compilation)
— Southern Mark Smith / Roadrunner / Real men / Jazz Butcher meets Count Dracula / Zombie love / Goldfish / Sweet Jane / Jazz Butcher vs the prime minister / Party time / Lost in France / Drink. (cd-iss. Jun88; GLEXCD 101)
Jun 85. (m-lp) (GLAMP 101) **SEX AND TRAVEL**
— Big Saturday / Holiday / Red pets / Only a rumour / President Reagan's birthday present / What's the matter, boy? / Walk with the Devil / Down the drain.
Aug 85. (7") (GLASS 043) **THE HUMAN JUNGLE. / DEATH DENTIST**
(ext.12"+=) (GLASS 12-043) – Mersey.
Feb 86. (7") (GLASS 046) **HARD. / GROOVIN' IN THE BUS LANE**
(ext.12"+=) (GLASS 12-046) – Vienna song / Thing.
Jun 86. (7"ep; as JAZZ BUTCHER VS MAX EIDER) (GLAEP 104) **THE CONSPIRACY EP**
— Conspiracy / A joy forever / Peter Lorre / Big old wind.
Jun 86. (lp) <6007> **BLOODY NONSENSE** (compilation of recent singles, etc)

— **FISH + KIZZY O'CALLAGHAN** – guitar / **LAURENCE O'KEEFE** – bass / **PAUL MULREANY** – drums / **ALEX GREEN** – saxophone

Sep 86. (7"; as JAZZ BUTCHER CONSPIRACY) (GLASS 049) **ANGELS. / REBECCA WANTS HER BIKE BACK**
(12"+=) (GLASS 12-049) – Mersey.
Oct 86. (lp/c) (GLA LP/MC 020) <6021> **DISTRESSED GENTLEFOLK**
— Falling in love / Big bad thing / Still in the kitchen / (Too much) Falling in love / Czechoslovakian love song / The new world / South America / Who loves you now? / Domestic animal / Buffalo shame / Nothing special / Angels. (cd-iss. 1990's; GLACD 20) (cd re-iss. Sep01 on 'Vinyl Japan'; ASKCD 130)

— MAX EIDER went solo and released 1987 album 'THE BEST KISSER IN THE WORLD' for 'Big Time'.

Apr 87. (lp) (GLASS 023) **BIG QUESTIONS (THE GIFT OF MUSIC VOL.2)** (compilation)
— The human jungle / Hard / Death dentist / South America / Groovin' in the bus lane / Mersey / Conspiracy / Thing / Peter Lorre / Vienna song / Olof Palme / Rebecca wants her bike back / City of night / The hairbrush & the tank / Big old wind / Forever. (w/ free 7"ep) **BIG QUESTIONS EP** – Speedy Gonzales / Knockin' on Heaven's door / May I? / Over you. (cd-iss. Aug88; GLACD 023)

— added guests **GREENWOOD GOULDING** – bass / **DAVE MORGAN** – drums / **ERAL SULLEYMAN** – bass / **BLAIR MacDONALD** – drums

(Creation / Combat)

Feb 88. (lp/cd) (CRELP 027/+CD) <8223> **FISHCOTHEQUE**
— Next move sideways / Out of touch / Get it wrong / Living in a village / Swell / Looking for lot 49 / The best way / Chickentown / Susie / Keeping the curtains closed. (re-iss. lp May94; same)
Sep 88. (7") (CRE 059) **SPOOKY. / BLAME**
(12"+=) (CRE 059T) – The best way.

(Creation / Genius)

Jul 89. (lp/c/cd) (CRELP/+C/CD 49) <GENI 008/+C/CD> **BIG PLANET SCARY PLANET**
— New invention / Line of death / Hysteria / The word I was looking for / Bicycle kid / Burglar of love / Nightmare being / Do the bubonic plague / Bad dream lover / The good ones.
Oct 89. (12") (CRE 069T) **NEW INVENTION. / DO THE BUBONIC PLAGUE / ALMOST BROOKLYN**

(Creation / Rough Trade)

May 90. (cd-ep) (CRESCD 077) **GIRL-GO / EXCELLENT! / BURGLAR OF LOVE (live) / GIRL-GO (live)**
Jun 90. (lp/c/cd) (CRELP/+C/CD 62) <ROUGHUS 83> **CULT OF THE BASEMENT**
— The basement / She's on drugs / Pineaple Tuesday / The onion field / Daycare nation / My zeppelin / Mr. Odd / After the great Euphrates / Panic in room 109 / Girl-go / Turtle bait / Sister death.
Nov 90. (12"; as J.B.C.) (CRE 083T) **WE LOVE YOU (554 vmix). / WE LOVE YOU (one for the band) / WE LOVE YOU (the great awakening)**
Feb 91. (cd/lp)(c) (CRE CD/LP 078)(C-CRE 078) **EDWARD'S CUPBOARD** (compilation)
— Mr. Odd / The best way (Edgar Wallace mix) / Spooky / Pineapple Tuesday / Keeping the curtains closed / She's on drugs / Line of death / Girl go / Susie / The good ones.

— PAT FISH now with **ALEX LEE + RICHARD FORMBY** – guitar / **ALEX GREEN** – saxophones / **JOE ALLEN** – bass / **PETER PAUL MULREANY** – drums (all under pseudonyms)

Jul 91. (cd/lp; by BLACK EG) (CRE CD/LP 086) **BLACK EG**
— Just Vincent / British gas makes it alright / The good, the bad and the ugly / Get a job / My radio / The Mi-Lai hotel / African disease / Drugs / Monster man / Jesus right now / The twilight zone / So easy (no New York).

(Creation / Skyclad)

Aug 91. (cd/c/lp) (CRECD/C-CRE/CRELP 110) <5080> **CONDITION BLUE** *(Jan92)*
— Girls says yes / Our friends the filth / Harlan / Still all / Monkeyface / She's a yo-yo / Honey / Shirley MacLaine / Racheland.
Nov 91. (cd-s) <7-5081-2> **SHE'S A YO-YO. / (mix)**
Feb 93. (cd) (CRECD 148) **WESTERN FAMILY (live)**
— Southern Mark Smith / Shirley MacLaine / Sister death / Still all all / Pineapple Tuesday / Angels / Beautiful snow-white hair / She's on drugs / Girl go / She's a yo-yo / Racheland / Everybody's talkin' / Tugboat captain / Over the rainbow.

the JAZZ BUTCHER CONSPIRACY

— **PAT FISH** with **RICHARD FORMBY** – guitars, prog/tapes / **DOOJ WILKINSON** – bass, vocals / **NICK BURSON** – drums / **PETER CROUCH** – guitars, keyboards / **PASCAL LEGRAS + MARK BOWN** – whatever?

JAZZ BUTCHER (cont) — THE GREAT INDIE DISCOGRAPHY — The 1980s

Aug 93. (cd) (CRECD 156) <57563> **WAITING FOR THE LOVE BUS**   Creation / TriStar — Mar94
- Rosemary Davis world of sound / Bakersfield / Kids in the mall – Kaliningrad / Whaddya? / Sweet water / Ghosts / Baltic / Killed out / Ben / Penguins / President Chang / Angel station / Rosemary Davis world of sound (reprise).

— FISH + DOOJ recruited GABRIEL TURNER + DAVE HENDERSON

Mar 95. (7") (CRE 167) **SIXTEEN YEARS. / TRUCK OF FEAR**
(cd-s+=) (CRESCD 167) – Surf gear in Idaho / Waiting for sumo.

— added ALEX LEE – saxophones

Apr 95. (cd/lp) (CRE CD/LP 182) **ILLUMINATE**
- A great visitation of elephants / Sixteen years / Cute submarines / Lulu's nightmare / Beetle George / Truck of fear / Old Snakey / Blues for Dean Read / When Eno sings / Waiting for sumo / The ugliest song in the world / Scarlett / Cops and hospitals / Surf gear in Idaho / Land / True stories.

— FISH + EIDER w/ OWEN JONES, PAT BIERNE + CURTIS E. JOHNSON

Mar 00. (cd) (<RUSCD 8260>) **GLORIOUS AND IDIOTIC (live in Hamburg February 1999)**   R.O.I.R. / R.O.I.R. — Jan00
- Partytime / Raking up the leaves / Just like Betty Page / Baby, it's you / Drink / The long night starts / The human jungle / Who loves you now? / Old Snakey / Rain / Caroline Wheeler's birthday present / Bigfoot motel / Roadrunner.

— PETER CROUCH – guitar; repl. CURTIS

Aug 00. (cd) (<ASKCD 114>) **ROTTEN SOUL**   Vinyl Japan / Vinyl Japan
- Big cats / Come on, Marie / Baby, it's you / Mother Siberia / Tough priest / Sleepwalking / Niagara / The one you adore / The ballad of Tiny and Clyde / I hate love / Call me / Diamorphine.

Aug 01. (cd/lp) (ASK CD/LP 128) **CAKE CITY** (compilation)
- Girlfriend / Soul happy hour / What's the matter boy / The human jungle / Who love's you know / Nothing special / Caroline Wheeler's birthday present / Big bad thing / Love kittens / Roadrunner / Big old wind / City of night / Sweet Jane / Knocking on Heaven's door.

– compilations, etc. –

Dec 85. (lp) Rebel; (RE 0010) **THE JAZZ BUTCHER AND THE SIKKORSKIS FROM HELL – HAMBURG – A LIVE ALBUM**
- Bath of Bacon / Soul happy hour / Death dentist / Walk with the Devil / Rain / Roadrunner / The Jazz Butcher meets Count Dracula / Bigfoot motel / Only a rumour / Real men / Girlfriend / Sweet Jane.

Aug 96. (cd) Nectar; (NTMCD 529) **DRAINING THE GLASS (THE JAZZ BUTCHER CONSPIRACY) 1982-86**
(re-iss. Jun98 on 'Reactive'; REMCD 527)

JEAN-PAUL SARTRE EXPERIENCE

Formed: Christchurch, New Zealand... 1984 when DAVE YETTON, GARY SULLIVAN met guitarist DAVE MULCAHY. After a year of local gigging (and the recruitment of additional guitarist JIM LAING), the group performed on the 'Flying Nun' stage at a festive gathering for the low-key indie label. They managed to secure enough money to record and release their debut eponymous EP which was issued in 1986 on the aforementioned imprint. The JPS EXPERIENCE delivered the standard pop/rock album 'LOVE SONGS' the following year (a different US version including the debut EP tracks was issued on 'Communion') featuring, yep, you guessed it (!) tiresome songs about love and loss, played in key by YETTON's rich vocals. 'THE SIZE OF FOOD' set was issued three years later just as the group were attracting a cult following in their native land. RUSSELL BAILLIE was added to the fold for a short stint, but retired after the release of two EPs, while the remaining members of the group were being legally threatened by the Estate of Jean-Paul Sartre. A quick change of name (now the JPS EXPERIENCE) and the quirky pop troupe were back on form for the release of The 'BLEEDING STAR' album, which mixed PIXIES harmonics while taking a cool lesson in trashy garage from label mates THE BATS. MULCAHY subsequently departed, and SOLID GOLD HELL guitarist MATT HEINE was added as a temporary replacement. However, the group of star-crossed divas were to meet their bitter end when, due to musical differences, they called it a day. YETTON later pursued a solo career but brought in various Kiwis to feature on a few sets by his band The STEREO BUS.

Album rating: LOVE SONGS (*5) / THE SIZE OF FOOD (*7) / ELEMENTAL mini (*5) / BLEEDING STAR (*6) / Stereo Bus: THE STEREO BUS (*5) / BRAND NEW (*4)

DAVID YETTON – vocals, bass / **DAVE MULCAHY** – guitar / **JIM LAING** – guitar / **GARY SULLIVAN** – drums

Flying Nun / Communion

Jan 87. (12"ep) (FN 057) **JEAN-PAUL SARTRE EXPERIENCE EP** — New Z
- Fish in the sea / Own two feet / Walking wild in your firetime / Grey parade / The loving grapevine.
1987. (lp) (FNE 04 – FN 078) **LOVE SONGS**
- Einstein / All the way down / Jabberwocky / Crap rap / Let that good thing grow / Grey parade / I like rain / Transatlantic love song / Let there be love.
1987. (7") (FN 083) **I LIKE RAIN. / BO DIDDLEY** — NewZ
1987. (lp) <COMM 2> **LOVE SONGS**
- Fish in the sea / Own two feet / Walking wild in your firetime / Grey parade / The loving grapevine / Let that good thing grow / I like rain / Einstein / Flex / All the way down / Bo Diddley. <cd-iss. 1995; COMM 2CD>
1990. (lp/cd) (FN/+CD 122) <COMM 10/+CD> **THE SIZE OF FOOD** — New Z
- Inside and out / Elemental / Slip / Shadows / Get my point / Gravel / Thrills / Window. (UK cd-iss. Jun95 & Jul96 on 'Flying Nun'; FNCD 122)

1990. (m-cd) <COMM 24CD> **ELEMENTAL**
- Elemental / Flex / Transatlantic love song / Jabberwocky / Crap rap.

JPS EXPERIENCE

— added RUSSELL BAILLIE – keyboards

Flying Nun / Matador

Oct 92. (c-ep/cd-ep) (FNMC/FNCD 212) **PRECIOUS EP**
- Precious / Crush / Slip.
Jul 93. (cd-ep) (FNCD 244) **MASKED AND TAPED EP** — NewZ
- Waste of time / Peaches and cream / Suzi lustlady / Fly / Fatness.
Aug 93. (cd-ep) (FNCD 245) **BREATHE EP**
- Breathe / Up in the sky / Kickback / Block.

— now without BAILLIE

Sep 93. (cd/c) (FNCD/FNMC 246) <OLE 057> **BLEEDING STAR**
- Intro / Into you / Ray of shine / I believe in you / Spaceman / Still can't be seen / Bleeding star / Breathe / Modus vivendi / Block / Angel.

— MULCAHY left during the recording of above (he formed MONSTER, who later became SUPERETTE)

MATT HEINE – guitar (of SOLID GOLD HELL)

Dec 93. (cd-s) (FNCD 253) **RAY OF SHINE / SHIVER**
Apr 94. (cd-ep; as JPSE) (FNCD 271) **INTO YOU EP**
- Into you (freegard mix) / Into you (stars on mix) / Disappear / Hold tight / Own two feet (live).

— disbanded later in '94, YETTON had a brief solo sojourn and he joined The MUTTON BIRDS. SULLIVAN joined SOLID GOLD HELL (featuring ex-S.P.U.D. members)

– compilations, etc. –

Jun 95. (cd) Flying Nun; (FNCD 078) **THE JEAN-PAUL SARTRE EXPERIENCE**
- Fish in the sea / Own two feet / Firetime / Grey parade / Loving grapevine / Let there be love / Transatlantic love song / Einstein / All the way down / Jabberwocky / Crap rap / I like rain / Flex / Let the good thing grow.

STEREO BUS

DAVE YETTON plus **GARY SULLIVAN, DAVID PINE, ALAN GREGG + ROSS BURGE**

Beats Bodega / not iss.

Mar 97. (cd) (BEATS 005) **THE STEREO BUS** — NewZ
- Shallow / Don't open your eyes / Wash away / Mirror / Be a girl / Tell / Lie in the arms / Waste of time / Bright lights / Fade / God's fingers / Far away.

E.M.I. / not iss.

Oct 99. (cd) (522609-2) **BRAND NEW** — NewZ
- Hey thank you / Touchdown / Pretty boys and girls / Birthday / Brand new / Quiet rose / Caramel / Nova Scotia / Let it flow / Hold you close / Burning alcohol.

JESSE GARON & THE DESPERADOES

Formed: Edinburgh, Scotland... 1986 by FRAN SCHOPPLER, ANGUS McPAKE and two ROTE KAPELLE members, ANDREW TULLY and MARGARITA VASQUEZ-PONTE (in fact this drummer/vocalist also moonlighted for a third "Burgh" act, The FIZZBOMBS, alongside the aforementioned ANGUS). ROTE KAPELLE – who also included CHRIS HENMAN, IAN DUNN, MALCOLM KERGAN and JONATHAN WIND – evolved a few years earlier, releasing their debut EP, 'THE BIG SMELL DINOSAUR', towards the end of '85. Signing with MARC RILEY's 'In-Tape' label, they issued a handful of other indie-pop releases, notably the JON LANGFORD-produced 'FIRE ESCAPE' single in the Spring of '88. Meanwhile, the 'Narodnik' stable (run by part-timer, EDDY) was home for JESSE GARON & THE DESPERADOES (confusingly enough, there wasn't actually a JESSE GARON in the band!), a country-tinged, fun-loving bunch of indie-rockers who made their first break for the border late in '86 with the DOUGLAS HART-produced 45, 'SPLASHING ALONG'. They also delivered a string of 45's before finally getting around to their full-set proper (a compilation, 'A CABINET FULL OF CURIOSITIES', had already hit the shops in '88) at the turn of the decade with 'NIXON'. Released discreetly on TULLY's own 'Avalanche' records, the lp was followed by what was to be their last offering, 'HOLD ME NOW', a mini-set that featured covers of Bachman Turner Overdrive's 'YOU AIN'T SEEN NOTHING YET' and Lulu's 'LOVE LOVES TO LOVE LOVE'.

Album rating: A CABINET OF CURIOSITIES compilation (*6) / NIXON (*5) / Fran Schoppler: 1 2 3 4 5 6 7 8 9 (*4)

FRAN SCHOPPLER – vocals / **ANDREW TULLY** – vocals, guitar / **ANGUS McPAKE** – bass / **MARGARITA VASQUEZ-PONTE** – drums / **KEVIN + STUART** – guitars

Narodnik / not iss.

Oct 86. (7") (NRK 001) **SPLASHING ALONG. / PRESENCE DEAR**
Mar 87. (7") (NRK 002) **THE RAIN FELL DOWN. / I'M UP HERE**

— **BRUCE HOPKINS + JOHN ROBB** – guitars; repl. KEVIN + STUART

May 87. (12"ep) (NRK 005T) **THE BILLY WHIZZ EP**
- Blacker than blue / Thursday feels fine / This town is falling down / Wealth of nations.

— **MICHAEL KERR** – lead guitar (of MEAT WHIPLASH) repl. BRUCE + JOHN

Wild Rumpus / not iss.

1987. (7"flexi) (SHEP 001) **HANK WILLIAMS IS DEAD. / Fizzbombs: YOU WORRY ME**

JESSE GARON & THE DESPERADOES (cont)   **THE GREAT INDIE DISCOGRAPHY**   **The 1980s**

			Velocity	Fast Forward
Jan 88.	(7")	(SPEED 001) **THE ADAM FAITH EXPERIENCE. / LAUGHING AND SMILING** (12"+=) (SPEEDT 001) – Just for a while (if ever).	☐	-
Jun 88.	(7")	(SPEED 002) **YOU'LL NEVER BE THAT YOUNG AGAIN. / AND IF THE SKY SHOULD FALL**	☐	-
Jan 89.	(lp)	(SPEEDLP 111) <FFUS 3302> **A CABINET FULL OF CURIOSITIES** (singles compilation) – Splashing along / I'm up here / The rain fell down / The Adam Faith experience / Laughing and smiling / Just for a while (if ever) / And if the sky should fall / You'll never be that young again / Blacker than blue / Thursday feels fine / This town is falling down / Wealth of nations. (re-iss. Aug90 on 'Avalanche'; ONLYLP 004)	☐	-

— now without KERR who joined the DARLING BUDS on tour

			Avalanche	not iss.
Mar 90.	(cd/lp)	(ONLY CD/LP 001) **NIXON** – Grand hotel / Goodbye misery / Her eyes closed / Heaven and a higher place / Love loves to love love / She falls from me / Hold me now / Bury me deep / Stand up / Eight lane freeway / Deliverance / Eden.	☐	-
Oct 90.	(12"ep)	(AGAP 004T) **HOLD ME NOW (remix) / GRAND HOTEL. / YOU AIN'T SEEN NOTHING YET / HEAVEN IN YOUR HANDS / UNTITLED (gentle mix) / CALIFORNIA GIRL (live)**	☐	-

— disbanded towards the end of 1990

ROTE KAPELLE

ANDREW TULLY – vocals / **MARGARITA VASQUEZ-PONTE** – vocals / **CHRIS HENMAN** – guitar / **IAN DINN** – keyboards (also of The STAIRCASE) / **MALCOLM KERGAN** – bass / **JONATHAN WIND** – drums

			Big Smell Dinosaur	not iss.
Dec 85.	(7"ep)	(SMELL 1) **THE BIG SMELL DINOSAUR** – King Mob / Evolution / Fergus! the sheep! / A gas fire.	☐	-

			In-Tape	not iss.
Oct 86.	(7")	(IT 037) **THESE ANIMALS ARE DANGEROUS. / SUNDAY**	☐	-
Aug 87.	(12"ep)	(IT 044) **IT MOVES BUT DOES IT SWING?** (John Peel Sessions) – Marathon man / Jellystone park / Acid face baby / Sunday / You don't know.	☐	-
Apr 88.	(7")	(IT 051) **FIRE ESCAPE. /**	☐	-
Jun 88.	(12"ep)	(IT 054) **SAN FRANCISCO AGAIN EP** – San Francisco again / Preacher man aural / You don't know / Fire escape (non-dance version).	☐	-
1990.	(lp)	**NO MORE BRITON**	☐	-

— they disbanded later in the year, MARGARITA having joined another indie outfit, the re-formed SHOP ASSISTANTS. TULLY became part of the short-lived BRIDGE HOPPER and ran 'Avalanche' records.

FIZZBOMBS

KATY McCULLARS – vocals / **MARGARITA + ANGUS** with **ANN DONALD** – drums (ex-SHOP ASSISTANTS)

			Narodnik	not iss.
Apr 87.	(7")	(NRK 003) **SIGN ON THE LINE. / THE WORD THAT**	☐	-

— SARAH – vocals, bass; repl. KATY who later resurfaced (mid-90's) in The SECRET GOLDFISH along with ex-MACKENZIES

			Calculus	not iss.
Mar 88.	(7"ep/12"ep)	(KIT 002/+T) **THE SURFIN' WINTER EP** – Surfaround / Beach party / Blue summer.	☐	-

— short-lived due to other commitments (see above)

FRAN SCHOPPLER

— took her time to get back to singing; augmented by **MICK COOKE** – trumpet, flugel (of BELLE & SEBASTIAN) / double bass – **ROY HUNTER**

| Dec 00. | (cd) | (none) **1 2 3 4 5 6 7 8 9** – Given up on love / Superman / Rain / Breathe / Snow queen / Tell him to go / Provincial town / Under your wing / Crush. | ☐ | - |

JESUS & MARY CHAIN

Formed: East Kilbride, Scotland ... 1983 by brothers WILLIAM and JIM REID, who took their name from a line in a Bing Crosby film. After local Glasgow gigs, they moved to Fulham in London, having signed for Alan McGhee's independent 'Creation' label in May'84. Their debut SLAUGHTER JOE-produced 45, 'UPSIDE DOWN', soon topped the indie charts, leading to WEA subsidiary label, 'Blanco Y Negro', snapping them up in early 1985. They hit the UK Top 50 with their next single, 'NEVER UNDERSTAND', and they were soon antagonising new audiences, crashing gear after 20 minutes on set. Riots ensued at nearly every major gig, and more controversy arrived when the next 45's B-side 'JESUS SUCKS', was boycotted by the pressing plant. With a new B-side, the single 'YOU TRIP ME UP', hit only No.55, but was soon followed by another Top 50 hit in October, 'JUST LIKE HONEY'. A month later they unleashed their debut album, 'PSYCHOCANDY', and although this just failed to breach the UK Top 30, it was regarded by many (NME critics especially) as the album of the year. Early in '86, BOBBY GILLESPIE left to concentrate on his PRIMAL SCREAM project and soon after, JAMC hit the Top 20 with the softer single, 'SOME CANDY TALKING'. In 1987 with new drummer JOHN MOORE, the single 'APRIL SKIES' and album 'DARKLANDS' both went Top 10. Later that year, they remixed The SUGARCUBES' classic 'Birthday' single. 'BARBED WIRE KISSES' (1988)

was a hotch-potch of B-sides and unreleased material, essential if only for the anarchic trashing of The Beach Boys' 'SURFIN' U.S.A.'. By the release of the 'AUTOMATIC' album in 1989, the Reid brothers had become the core of the band, enlisting additional musicians as needed. The record sounded strangely muted and uninspired although the 'ROLLERCOASTER' EP and subsequent tour (alongside MY BLOODY VALENTINE and a pre-'PARKLIFE' BLUR) were an improvement. True to controversial style, the band returned to the singles chart in 1992 with the radio un-friendly, post-industrial mantra, 'REVERENCE'. Perhaps the last great piece of venom-spewing noise the 'MARY CHAIN produced, the follow-up album, 'HONEY'S DEAD', was tame in comparison. No surprise then, that it received mixed reviews although there were a few low key highlights, notably the melodic bubblegum grunge of 'FAR GONE AND OUT'. After 1993's 'SOUND OF SPEED' EP, the band hooked up with MAZZY STAR'S Hope Sandoval for 'STONED AND DETHRONED', a mellow set of feedback free strumming. While still echoing the brooding portent of the THE VELVETS, the style of the record was more 'PALE BLUE EYES' than 'SISTER RAY'. Predictably, the band were seen as having 'sold out' by Indie-Rock dullards and a 1995 single, 'I HATE ROCK'N'ROLL', didn't even scrape the Top 50. 1998's comeback set, 'MUNKI', peaked at only No.47 in the charts; tension had been reported from other band members as WILLIAM and JIM fought out their differences. With the latter working on something solo (and Alan McGee's label coming to a close) it was inevitable that the brothers would split the 'CHAIN late in '99. WILLIAM had already delivered his first solo outing a year earlier, 'TIRED OF FUCKING' very low key. LAZYCAME's 'SATURDAY THE FOURTEENTH' finally featured his rejected penis sleeve (from creation days) and FREEHEAT (JIM's project) comprised of BEN LURIE (guitar), ROMI MORI (bass & ex-GUN CLUB) and NICK SANDERSON (drums of EARL BRUTUS) • **Songwriters:** All written by JIM and WILLIAM except; VEGETABLE MAN (Syd Barrett) / SURFIN' USA (Beach Boys) / WHO DO YOU LOVE (Bo Diddley) / MY GIRL (Temptations) / MUSHROOM (Can) / GUITAR MAN (Jerry Lee Hubbard) / TOWER OF SONG (Leonard Cohen) / LITTLE RED ROOSTER (Willie Dixon) / (I CAN'T GET NO) SATISFACTION (Rolling Stones) / REVERBERATION (13th Floor Elevators) / GHOST OF A SMILE (Pogues) / ALPHABET CITY (Prince) / NEW KIND OF KICK (Cramps). • **Trivia:** Their 1986 single 'SOME CANDY TALKING' was banned by Radio 1 DJ Mike Smith, due to its drug references. The following year in the States, they were banned from a chart show due to their blasphemous name.

Album rating: PSYCHOCANDY (*9) / DARKLANDS (*8) / BARBED WIRE KISSES collection (*7) / AUTOMATIC (*7) / HONEY'S DEAD (*8) / THE SOUND OF SPEED compilation (*7) / STONED AND DETHRONED collection (*6) / I HATE ROCK N ROLL (*5) / MUNKI (*5) / 21 SINGLES compilation (*9) / Lazycame: FINBEGIN (*8)

JIM REID (b.29 Dec'61) – vocals, guitar / **WILLIAM REID** (b.28 Oct'58) – guitar, vocals / **MURRAY DALGLISH** – drums (bass tom & snare) / **DOUGLAS HART** – bass

			Creation	not iss.
Nov 84.	(7")	(CRE 012) **UPSIDE DOWN. / VEGETABLE MAN** (12"+=) (CRE 012T) – ('A' demo).	☐	-

— **BOBBY GILLESPIE** – drums (ex-WAKE, of PRIMAL SCREAM) repl. DALGLISH who formed BABY'S GOT A GUN

			Blanco Y Negro	Reprise
Feb 85.	(7")	(NEG 8) **NEVER UNDERSTAND. / SUCK** (12"+=) (NEGT 8) – Ambition.	47	-
Jun 85.	(7")	(NEG 13) **YOU TRIP ME UP. / JUST OUT OF REACH** (12"+=) (NEGT 13) – Boyfriend's dead.	55	-
Oct 85.	(7")	(NEG 017) **JUST LIKE HONEY. / HEAD** (12"+=) (NEGT 17) – Just like honey (demo) / Cracked. (d7"+=) (NEGF 17) – ('A'demo) / Inside me.	45	-
Nov 85.	(lp/c)	(BYN/+C 11) <25383> **PSYCHOCANDY** – Just like honey / The living end / Taste the floor / Hardest walk / Cut dead / In a hole / Taste of Cindy / Never understand / It's so hard / Inside me / Sowing seeds / My little underground / You trip me up / Something's wrong. (cd-iss. Aug86 & Jan97 +=; K 242 000-2) – Some candy talking.	31	

— **JOHN LODER** – drums (on stage when BOBBY was unavailable)

| Jul 86. | (7") | (NEG 19) **SOME CANDY TALKING. / PSYCHO CANDY / HIT** (12"+=) (NEGT 19) – Taste of Cindy. (d7"+=) (NEGF 19)(SAM 291) – Cut dead (acoustic) / You trip me up (acoustic) / Some candy talking (acoustic) / Psycho candy (acoustic). | 13 | - |

— now basic trio of JIM, WILLIAM and DOUGLAS brought in **JOHN MOORE** (b.23 Dec'64, England) – drums repl. GILLESPIE (who was busy with PRIMAL SCREAM) / **JAMES PINKER** – drums (ex-DEAD CAN DANCE) repl. MOORE now on guitar

| Apr 87. | (7") | (NEG 24) **APRIL SKIES. / KILL SURF CITY** (12"+=) (NEGT 24) – Who do you love. (d7"+=) (NEGF 24) – Mushroom / Bo Diddley is Jesus. | 8 | - |
| Aug 87. | (7") | (NEG 25) **HAPPY WHEN IT RAINS. / EVERYTHING IS ALRIGHT WHEN YOU'RE DOWN** (ext.12"+=) (NEGT 25) – Happy place / F-Hole. (ext.10"+=) (NEGTE 25) – ('A'demo) / Shake. | 25 | - |

— trimmed to basic duo of REID brothers

| Sep 87. | (lp/c)(cd) | (BYN/+C 25)(K 242 180-2) <25656> **DARKLANDS** – Darklands / Deep one perfect morning / Happy when it rains / Down on me / Nine million rainy days / April skies / Fall / Cherry came too / On the wall / About you. (cd re-iss. Nov94; K 242 180-2) | 5 | ☐ |
| Oct 87. | (7"/7"g-f) | (NEG/+F 29) **DARKLANDS. / RIDER / ON THE WALL (demo)** (12"+=/12"g-f+=) (NEGTF 29) – Surfin' U.S.A. (10"+=/cd-s+=) (NEG TE/CD 29) – Here it comes again. | 33 | - |

383

JESUS & MARY CHAIN (cont)

— DAVE EVANS – rhythm guitar repl. MOORE who formed EXPRESSWAY

Mar 88. (7") *(NEG 32)* **SIDEWALKING. / TASTE OF CINDY (live)** — 30 / -
(12"+=) *(NEGT 32)* – ('A'extended) / April skies (live).
(cd-s++=) *(NEGCD 32)* – Chilled to the bone.

Apr 88. (lp/c)(cd) *(BYN/+C 29)(K 242 331-2) <25729>* **BARBED WIRE KISSES** (part compilation) — 9 / -
– Kill Surf City / Head / Rider / Hit / Don't ever change / Just out of reach / Happy place / Psychocandy / Sidewalking / Who do you love / Surfin' USA / Everything's alright when you're loved / Upside down / Taste of Cindy / Swing / On the wall. (c+=/cd+=) – Cracked / Here it comes again / Mushroom / Bo Diddley is Jesus. (cd re-iss. Jan97; same)

— In Nov'88, DOUGLAS HART moonlighted in The ACID ANGELS, who released 7"promo 'SPEED SPEED ECSTASY' on 'Product Inc.'; *FUEL 1)*

Nov 88. (7") *<27754>* **KILL SURF CITY. / SURFIN' USA (summer mix)** — - / -

— Basically REID brothers, HART and EVANS. (added **RICHARD THOMAS** – drums) / **BEN LURIE** – rhythm guitar repl. EVANS

Sep 89. (7") *(NEG 41)* **BLUES FROM A GUN. / SHIMMER** — 32 / -
(10"+=) *(NEG 41TE)* – Break me down / Penetration.
(12"+=/c-s+=) *(NEG 41 T/C)* – Penetration / Subway.
(3"cd-s+=) *(NEG 41CD)* – Penetration / My girl.

Oct 89. (lp/c)(cd) *(BYN/+C 20)(K 246 221-2) <26015>* **AUTOMATIC** — 11 / -
– Here comes Alice / Coast to coast / Blues from a gun / Between planets / UV ray / Her way of praying / Head on / Take it / Halfway to crazy / Gimme hell. *(cd re-iss. Jan97; same)*

Nov 89. (7") *(NEG 42)* **HEAD ON. / IN THE BLACK** — 57 / -
(12"+=) *(NEG 42T)* – Terminal beach.
(3"cd-s++=) *(NEG 42CD)* – Drop (acoustic re-mix).
(7") *(NEG 42XB)* – ('A'side). / DEVIANT SLICE
(7") *(NEG 42Y)* – ('A'side). / I'M GLAD I NEVER
(7") *(NEG 42Z)* – ('A'side). / TERMINAL BEACH

Mar 90. (7") *<19891>* **HEAD ON. / PENETRATION** — - / -

Aug 90. (7") *(NEG 45)* **ROLLERCOASTER. / SILVER BLADE** — 46 / -
(12"+=) *(NEG 45T)* – Tower of song.
(7"ep++=/cd-ep++=) *(NEG 45 D/CD)* – Low-life.

— Trimmed again, when THOMAS joined RENEGADE SOUNDWAVE on U.S.tour. HART became video director. The **REID** brothers and **BEN** recruited **MATTHEW PARKIN** – bass + **BARRY BLACKER** – drums (ex-STARLINGS)

Blanco Y Negro / American

Feb 92. (7") *(NEG 55)* **REVERENCE. / HEAT** — 10 / -
(12"+=/cd-s+=) *(NEG 55 T/CD)* – ('A' radio remix) / Guitar man.

Mar 92. (cd/c/lp) *(9031 76554-2/-4/-1) <26830>* **HONEY'S DEAD** — 14 / -
– Reverence / Teenage lust / Far gone and out / Almost gold / Sugar Ray / Tumbledown / Catchfire / Good for my soul / Rollercoaster / I can't get enough / Sundown / Frequency. *(cd re-iss. Jan97; same)*

Apr 92. (7") *(NEG 56)* **FAR GONE AND OUT. / WHY'D YOU WANT ME** — 23 / -
(12"+=/cd-s+=) *(NEG 56 T/CD)* – Sometimes you just can't get enough.

Jun 92. (7") *(NEG 57)* **ALMOST GOLD. / TEENAGE LUST (acoustic)** — 41 / -
(12"+=) *(NEG 57T)* – Honey's dead.
(gold-cd-s+=) *(NEG 57CD)* – Reverberation (doubt) / Don't come down.

Jun 93. (7"ep/c-ep/10"ep/cd-ep) *(NEG 66/+C/TE/CD)* **SOUND OF SPEED EP** — 30 / -
– Snakedriver / Reverence / I can't have / White record release blues / Little red rooster.

Jul 93. (cd/c/lp) *(4509 93105-2/-4/-1)* **THE SOUND OF SPEED** (part comp '88-'93) — 15 / -
– Snakedriver / Reverence (radio mix) / Heat / Teenage lust (acoustic version) / Why'd you want me / Don't come down / Guitar man / Something I can't have / Sometimes / White record release blues / Shimmer / Penetration / My girl / Tower of song / Little red rooster / Break me down / Lowlife / Deviant slice / Reverberation / Sidewalking (extended version). *(cd re-iss. Jan97; same)*

— next album feat. guest vox HOPE SANDOVAL (Mazzy Star) + SHANE MacGOWAN / **STEVE MONTI** – drums repl. BLACKER

Jul 94. (7"/c-s) *(NEG 70/+C)* **SOMETIMES ALWAYS. / PERFECT CRIME** — 22 / -
(10"+=/cd-s+=) *(NEG 70 TE/CD)* – Little stars / Drop.

Aug 94. (cd/c/lp) *(4509 93104-2/-4/-1) <45573>* **STONED AND DETRONED** — 13 / 98
– Dirty water / Bullet lovers / Sometimes always / Come on / Between us / Hole / Never saw it coming / She / Wish I could / Save me / Till it shines / God help me / Girlfriend / Everybody I know / You've been a friend / These days / Feeling lucky. *(cd re-iss. Jan97; same)*

Oct 94. (c-s) *<18078>* **SOMETIMES ALWAYS / DROP** — - / 96

Oct 94. (7"/c-s) *(NEG 73/+C)* **COME ON. / I'M IN WITH THE OUT-CROWD** — 52 / -
(cd-s+=) *(NEG 73CD)* – New York City / Taking it away.
(cd-s) *(NEG 73CD)* – ('A'side) / Ghost of a smile / Alphabet city / New kind of kick.

Jun 95. (c-ep/12"ep/cd-ep) *(NEG 81 C/TEX/CD)* **I HATE ROCK N ROLL / BLEED ME. / 33 1-3 / LOST STAR** — 61 / -

Sep 95. (cd,c) *<43043>* **HATE ROCK N ROLL** (compilation of B-sides & rarities) — - / -
– I hate rock'n'roll / Snakedriver / Something I can't have / Bleed me / Thirty three and a third / Lost star / Penetration / New York City / Taking it away / I'm in with the out crowd / Little stars / Teenage lust / Perfect crime.

— **JIM, WILLIAM + BEN** were joined by **NICK SANDERSON** – drums / **TERRY EDWARDS** – horns / + guests vocalists HOPE SANDOVAL + SISTER VANILLA (PAUL KING was also a member late '97)

Creation / Sub Pop

Apr 98. (7") *(CRE 292)* **CRACKING UP. / ROCKET** — 35 / -
(cd-s+=) *(CRESCD 292)* – Hide myself / Commercial.

May 98. (7"/c-s) *(CRE/+CS 296)* **I LOVE ROCK N ROLL. / EASYLIFE, EASYLOVE** — 38 / -
(cd-s+=) *(CRESCD 296)* – 40,000k / Nineteen 666.

Jun 98. (cd/c/d-lp) *(CRECD/CCRE/CRELP 232) <SP 426>* **MUNKI** — 47 / -
– I love rock n roll / Birthday / Stardust remedy / Fizzy / Moe Tucker / Perfume / Virtually unreal / Degenerate / Cracking up / Commercial / Supertramp / Never understood / I can't find the time for times / Man on the moon / Black / Dream lover / I hate rock n roll. *(cd re-iss. Jan01; same)*

— they disbanded in October '99

– compilations, etc. –

Sep 91. (m-lp/m-c/m-cd) *Strange Fruit; (SFP MA/MC/CD 210)* **THE PEEL SESSIONS (1985-86)** — - / -
– Inside me / The living end / Just like honey / all / Hapy place / In the rain.

Jun 94. (cd+book) *Audioglobe;* **LIVE** (live) — - / -

Jul 01. (lp) *Strange Fruit; (SFRSLP 092)* **THE COMPLETE JOHN PEEL SESSIONS** — - / -

May 02. (cd) *Blanco Y Negro; (0927 46141-2) / Rhino; <78256>* **21 SINGLES** — - / Jul02

LAZYCAME

WILLIAM REID – solo

Creation / not iss.

Apr 98. (cd-ep; as WILLIAM) *(CRESCD 295)* **TIRED OF FUCKING EP** — - / -
– Tired of fucking / Lucibelle / Kissaround / Hard on.

Hot Tam / not iss.

Oct 99. (7"ep) *(HTAM 001)* **TASTER EP** — - / -
– Muswileclouds / Stevinik / Dement / Engine8.
(cd-ep+=) *(HTAM 001CD)* – God / Complicated.

Dec 99. (cd) *(HOTTAMCD 002)* **FINBEGIN** — - / -
– God / Complicated / Five one zero lovers / Rokit / Go get find / Fornicate / Unfinished business / Blue June / Naturallow / McIntosh lost.

May 00. (cd) *(HOTTAMCD 003)* **SATURDAY THE FOURTEENTH** — - / -
– Drizzle / Last days of Creation / Lo Fi Li / Fuck you genius / You don't belong / Kill kool kid / Kissaround / Muswil clouds / Tired of fucking / Mayhem / Everyone knows / Dement / Unamerican.

Guided Missile / not iss.

Apr 00. (7"ep) *(GUIDE 41)* **YAWN! EP** — - / -
– Drizzle / K to be lost.
(cd-ep+=) *(GUIDE 41CD)* – Who killed Manchester? / Male wife / Commercial.

FREEHEAT

JIM REID – vocals, guitar / **BEN LURIE** – guitar / **ROMI MORI** – bass (ex-GUN CLUB) / **NICK SANDERSON** – drums (ex-EARL BRUTUS)

Outafocus / Hall Of Records

Nov 00. (cd-ep) *<1104>* **DON'T WORRY, BE HAPPY** — - / -
– Two of us / Facing up to the facts / Shine on little star / Nobody's gonna trip my wire.

Feb 02. (cd-ep) *(OUTA 4CD)* **RETOX** — - / -
– DON'T WORRY, BE HAPPY + / Long goodbye.

JESUS LIZARD

Formed: Austin, Texas, USA ... late 80's by DAVID YOW and DAVID SIMS, who had just folded SCRATCH ACID. This band, who also had in their ranks, BRETT BRADFORD, REY WASHAM and brief frontman STEVE ANDERSON, released a clutch of demented hardcore punk releases including the eponymous 'SCRATCH ACID' (1984), 'JUST KEEP EATING' (1986) and 'BERSERKER' (1986) before WASHAM joined STEVE ALBINI in RAPEMAN. YOW and SIMS subsequently recruited Chicago-born DUANE DENISON and MAC McNEILLY to complete the JESUS LIZARD formation, embarking on extensive US and UK tours. Roping in the ubiquitous ALBINI to produce their debut release, 'PURE' (a 1989 mini-set), YOW delivered a ferocious fusion of howling punk metallic blues that called to mind prime(evil) BIRTHDAY PARTY, IGGY POP and The BUTTHOLE SURFERS. Live, the JESUS LIZARD experience was a psychotic, apocalyptic cabaret with the bare-chested YOW a deranged focal point. He was renowned for launching himself into the audience mid set, at times disappearing from view, other times crowd-surfing while remarkably still managing to sing! In the early 90's, the group released a series of uncompromising, lyrically disturbing albums for 'Touch & Go', the last of these 'LIAR' (1992) omitting possibly their most gross track/single to date, a cover of The Dicks' 'WHEELCHAIR EPIDEMIC'. YOW and Co. enjoyed an unexpected taste of success (UK Top 20) the following year when they shared a split 45 with NIRVANA, JESUS LIZARD contributing the lovely 'PUSS'. The group released an unofficial live affair before leaving their label with a final effort, 'DOWN', an album that witnessed them at their grimy, bass-heavy best. Surprisingly signing a lucrative deal with 'Capitol' records (having earlier rejected 'Atlantic'), they signalled that their twisted musical vision remained resolutely uncommercial with the 1996 'SHOT' album. • **Covered:** SUNDAY YOU NEED LOVE + ANNA (Trio).

Album rating: Scratch Acid: SCRATCH ACID (*6) / JUST KEEP EATING (*6) / BERSERKER (*6) / Jesus Lizard: PURE mini (*5) / HEAD (*6) / GOAT (*7) / LIAR (*7) / SHOW (*5) / DOWN (*6) / SHOT (*7) / BLUE (*7) / Denison – Kimball Trio: WALLS IN THE CITY (*6) / SOUL MACHINE (*5) / NEUTRONS (*5)

SCRATCH ACID

DAVID YOW – vocals, bass / **BRETT BRADFORD** – guitar, vocals / **DAVID WILLIAM SIMS** – bass, guitar / **REY WASHAM** – drums, piano (ex-BIG BOYS)

Fundam. / Rabid Cat

Apr 86. (lp) *(HOLY 1)* **SCRATCH ACID** — - / -
– Cannibal / Greatest gift / Monsters / Owners lament / She said / Mess / El spectro / Lay screaming.

Jul 86. (m-lp) *(SAVE 012)* **JUST KEEP EATING**
– Crazy Dan / Eyeball / Big bone lick / Unlike a beast / Damned for all time / Ain't that love / Holes / Albino slug / Spit a kiss / Amicus / Cheese plug.
Mar 87. (lp) *(HOLY 2)* **BERSERKER**
– Mary had a little drug problem / For crying out loud / Moron's moron / Skin drips / Thing is bliss / Flying houses.

—— In 1988, YOW joined RAPEMAN alongside STEVE ALBINI (BIG BLACK). WESHAM joined TAD.

– compilations, etc. –

Oct 91. (lp/cd) *Touch & Go;* <*(TG LP/CD 76)*> **THE GREATEST GIFT**

JESUS LIZARD

—— **DAVID YOW** – vocals / **DUANE DENISON** – guitar / **DAVID WILLIAM SIMS** – bass / **MAC McNEILLY** – drums

	Touch & Go	Touch & Go
Feb 89. (m-lp) <*TGLP 30*> **PURE**	-	

– Blockbuster / Bloody Mary / Rabid pigs / Starlet / Happy bunny goes fluff fluff along. *(UK-iss.Jul93; same)*
Feb 90. (7") <*TG 53*> **CHROME. / 7 vs. 8**
May 90. (lp) <*(TGLP 54)*> **HEAD**
– One evening / S.D.B.J. / My own urine / If you had lips / 7 vs 8 / Pastoral / Waxeater / Good thing / Tight 'n' shiny / (None other than) Killer McHann. *(cd-iss. Jul93+=; TGCD 54)* – PURE
Nov 90. (7") <*TG 66*> **MOUTH BREATHER. / SUNDAY YOU NEED LOVE**
Feb 91. (lp/cd) <*(TG 68/+CD)*> **GOAT**
– Then comes Dudley / Mouth breather / Nub / Monkey trick / Karpis / South mouth / Lady shoes / Rodeo in Joliet / Seasick. *(re-iss. Apr94; same)*

—— In Apr'91, YOW featured for super techno-punks PIGFACE on their 'GUB' album
May 92. (7") <*TG 87*> **WHEELCHAIR EPIDEMIC. / DANCING NAKED LADIES**
1992. (7"blue) <*IV-12*> **GLADIATOR. / BOILERMAKER** –
(above issued on 'Insipid')
Oct 92. (lp/c/cd/pic/cd) <*TG 100/+C/CD/P)*> **LIAR**
– Boilermaker / Gladiator / The art of self-defense / Slave ship / Puss / Whirl / Rope / Perk / Zachariah / Dancing naked ladies.
Feb 93. (7"/cd-s) <*(TG 83/+CD)*> **PUSS. / (b-side by NIRVANA)**   12
Jun 93. (cd/lp) <*none*> **SHOW** (live atr CBGB's)
– Glamorous / Deaf as a bat / Sea sick / Bloody Mary / Mistletoe / Nub / Elegy / Killer McHann / Dancing naked ladies / Fly on the wall / Boilermaker / Puss / Gladiator / Wheelchair epidemic / Monkey trick. *(imported into UK Jul94 on 'Collision Arts-Giant')*
Jul 93. (7") <*TG 110*> **GLADIATOR (live). / SEASICK (live)**   –   – gig
Sep 93. (3x7"/cd-ep) <*TG 121/+CD*> **LASH**
– Glamorous / Deaf as a bat / Ladyshoes (live) / Killer McHann (live) / Bloody Mary (live) / Monkey trick (live).
Nov 93. (7"/cd-s) <*(TG 128/+CD)*> **(FLY) ON (THE WALL). / WHITE HOLE**
Aug 94. (lp/c/cd) <*(TG 131/+C/CD)*> **DOWN (live)**   64
– (Fly) On (the wall) / Mistletoe / Countless backs of sad losers / Queen for a day / The associate / Destroy before reading / Low rider / 50 cents / American BB / Horse / Din / Elegy / The best parts.

	Capitol	Capitol
May 96. (cd/c/lp) <*(CD/TC+/EST 2284)*> **SHOT**		

– Thumper / Blue shot / Thumbscrews / Good riddance / Mailman / Skull of a German / Trephination / More beautiful than Barbie / Too bad about the fire / Churl / Now then / Inamorata / Pervertedly slow.

—— **JIM KIMBALL** – drums (ex-MULE, ex-LAUGHING HYENAS) repl. MAC
Feb 98. (ltd-10"/cd-s) *(TWA 10/+CD)* **THE JESUS LIZARD**
– Cold water / Inflicted by humans / Eyesore / Valentine / Needles for teeth.
(above issued on 'Jet Set'; as was below on lp; *TWA 12LP*)
Mar 98. (cd-s) *(882656-2)* **THUMPER EP**   –
– Thumper / Good riddance / Shut up.
Apr 98. (cd) <*8 59266-2*> **BLUE**
– I can learn / Horse doctor man / Eucalyptus / A tale of two women / Cold water / And then the rain / Postcoital glow / Until it stopped to die / Soft damage / Happy snakes / Needles for teeth / Terremoto. *(lp-iss.May98 on 'Jetset'; TWA 12LP)*

—— disbanded in July 1999

– compilations, etc. –

Feb 00. (cd) *Touch & Go;* <*(TG 207CD)*> **BANG**   Jan00
– Chrome / 7 vs 8 / Gladiator / Seasick / Wheelchair epidemic / Dancing naked ladies / Mouth breather / Sunday you need love / Glamorous / Deaf as a bat / Lady shoes / Killer McHann / Monkey trick / Uncommonly good / Test / Blockbuster / Fly on the wall / White hole / Anna.

DENISON / KIMBALL TRIO

—— aka **DUANE + JAMES** on a soundtrack for a film starring YOW

	Skin Graft	Skin Graft
Oct 94. (lp/cd) <*(GR 16/+CD)*> **WALLS IN THE CITY**		

– Prelude / Cold light of day / Walk away / Reunion / Harry's theme / One if by land . . . / Romantic interlude / Separate checks / Blue corridor / Postlude / . . . Two if by sea.
May 95. (m-cd) <*(GR 22CD)*> **SOUL MACHINE**
– Terminal 2 / Soul machine / Ad infinitum / Lonely woman / Factory loop / Framed / Passing blue / Blueball avenue / Trans-mission / Solitaire.

	Quarter Stick	Quarter Stick
Aug 97. (cd/lp) <*(QS 48 CD/LP)*> **"NEUTRONS"**		

– Downriver / Landshark pt.2 / Monte's casino / Heavy water / Traveling salesman / Neutrons / Issa / Lullaby.

—— DENISON + KIMBALL became part of TOD A's (COP SHOOT COP) ensemble, FIREWATER

JOHN AND MARY (see under ⇒ 10,000 MANIACS)

Daniel JOHNSTON

Born: Sacramento, California, USA. A tortured, troubled but incredibly gifted and prolific legend of the US underground, DANIEL JOHNSTON has spent a lifetime balancing the unpredictable demands of mental illness with a recording career. Presumably self taught, JOHNSTON issued a series of early cassette-only releases on his own 'Stress' label, beginning with 1980's self-explanatory 'SONGS OF PAIN'. Hardly musical genius, the appeal lay in the heart-rending emotional nakedness of JOHNSTON's amateur guitar strumming, keyboard plonking and singing, his lyrics focusing on the day to day difficulties, heartaches and small victories of JOHNSTON's world. Having based himself in Austin, Texas, he finally broke from obscurity after MTV filmed him as part of a profile on the city's thriving alternative music scene. While his name soon became more famous than his music, 'Homestead' redressed the balance in the late 80's by re-issuing 'YIP JUMP MUSIC', an acclaimed set featuring heartfelt tributes to The BEATLES and cartoon legend, Caspar The Friendly Ghost against a backdrop of skeletal organ. The late 80's also found DANIEL collaborating with fellow maverick, JAD FAIR, on an eponymous album for the latter's '50 Skidillion Watts' label. By this point, JOHNSTON had already survived two periods of hospitalisation yet his work rate showed no sign of slowing. A move to KRAMER's 'Shimmy Disc' in the early 90's resulted in the appropriately titled '1990' and 'ARTISTIC VICE' (1992). Around the same time, DANIEL performed an acappella version of his classic 'SPEEDING MOTORCYCLE' (later covered by Scots shamblers, The PASTELS) down a transatlantic phoneline to John Peel, one of the more memorable moments from the veteran DJ's Radio One show in recent times. Against all the odds, the irrepressible troubadour subsequently signed a major label deal with 'Atlantic', releasing the well received 'FUN' in 1994. With production assistance from BUTTHOLE SURFER, PAUL LEARY, the record displayed a marked leap in confidence with a strong set of songs which brought widespread critical plaudits. JOHNSTON, who was unceremoniously dropped by 'Atlantic', spent many years in the wilderness overcoming his battle with chronic depression and writing material for his new album 'REJECTED UNKNOWN' (2001) – the title, a dig at the major labels, perhaps? The set, which consisted of JOHNSTON's trademark lo-fi ramblings, coupled with a shambolic production and some nifty musical noodlings, once again established a true American songwriting genius. DJ sounded like a really upset child, forced to go up on stage and sing broken down renditions of Beatles songs, while the audience slyly sniggered and his teacher (on the piano, of couse) gave him reassuring nods. 'DAVINARE', which stole the melody from The Police's 'Every Breath You Take', is a downright classic, with DJ singing "I'm a worthless bum, says I!" Elsewhere, on the 'Rocky Horror'-esque 'THRILL', a congregation appeared and it marked the advent of JOHNSTON's first stonking musical jam. But the jumped-up Ska (no, really) of 'LOVE FOREVER' was the overall highlight, silencing those who claimed he was not a proper songwriter. Anyway, BOWIE said he was, so he must be!

Album rating: YIP – JUMP MUSIC (*6) / HI, HOW ARE YOU (*6) / CONTINUED STORY (*5) / 1990 (*6) / ARTISTIC VICE (*6) / FUN (*7) / REJECTED UNKNOWN (*5) / DANIEL JOHNSTON AND THE HYPERJINX TRICYCLE (*6)

DANIEL JOHNSTON – vocals, guitar, keyboards

	not iss.	Stress
1980. (c) **SONGS OF PAIN**	-	
1981. (c) **MORE SONGS OF PAIN**	-	
1982. (c) **THE WHAT OF WHOM**	-	
1982. (c) **DON'T BE SCARED**	-	
1983. (c) **THE LOST RECORDINGS I** (compilation)	-	
1983. (c) **THE LOST RECORDINGS II** (compilation)	-	
1984. (c) **RETIRED BOXER**	-	
1985. (c) **RESPECT**	-	

– No love in town / An angel cry / Have respect / Dream / I know what I want / Merry-go-round / A little bit of soap / Loneliness / Good morning you / Go / Car crash / Just like a widow / Heartbreak hotel / I know my baby / You are a writer / Go some more / Theme from Respect. <*re-iss. 1993 on 'Ay Carramba' as 10"lp; EL BARTO 001*>

	Furthur	Homestead
Oct 88. (lp/c) *(FU 4)* <*HMS 117/+C*> **HI, HOW ARE YOU?**		
1989. (d-lp/cd) <*HMS 142-1/-2*> **YIP / JUMP MUSIC**	-	

– Chord organ blues / The Beatles / Sorry entertainer / Speeding motorcycle / Caspar the friendly ghost / Don't let the sun down on your grievances / Danny don't rapp / Sweet heart / King Kong / The creature – 3rd chair / I live for love / Almost got hit by a truck / Worried shoes / Dead lover's twisted heart / Rocket ship / God / Love defined / Museum of love / Rarely / I remember painfully. *(UK-iss.Nov94; same)*
1989. (lp/cd) <*HMS 155-1/-2*> **CONTINUED STORY**   –
– It's over / Ain't no woman gonna make a George Jones outta me / The dead laughing in the cloud / Funeral home / Her blues / Running water revisited / I saw her standing there / Casper / Ghost of our love / Fly eye / Etiquette / A walk in the wind / Dem blues / Girls.

—— In 1989, he collaborated with JAD FAIR (ex-HALF JAPANESE) on the album, 'JAD FAIR & DANIEL JOHNSTON', released on '50 Skadillion Watts'.

	not iss.	Stress
1990. (c) **LIVE AT S x SW** (live)		

	Shimmy Disc	Shimmy Disc
Nov 90. (lp) *(SDE 9015LP)* <*SHIMMY 028*> **1990**		

– Devil town / Spirit world rising / Held the hand / Lord give me hope / Some things last a long time / Tears stupid tears / Don't play cards with Satan / True love will find you in the end / Got to get you into my life / Careless soul / Funeral home / Softly and tenderly. *(cd-iss. Apr98; SHIMMY 028)*

Daniel JOHNSTON (cont)

1991. (7") *(sol-911-7)* **SPEEDING MOTORCYCLE! / DO YOU REALLY LOVE ME? (live)**
(above issued on 'Vinyl Solution' & shared with YO LA TENGO)

Mar 92. (lp) *<(SDE 9237)>* **ARTISTIC VICE**
– My life iis starting over / Honey I sure miss you / I feel so high / A ghostly story / Tell me now / Easy listening / I know Casar / The startling facts / Hoping / It's got to be good / Happy soul / The dream is over / Love of my life / I killed the monster / Laurie / Fate will get done.

Seminal Twang / not iss.

1991. (7"ep) *(twang 5)* **BIG BIG WORLD**
– Big big world / I stand horrified / December blues.

1992. (7"ep) *(twang 13)* **LAURIE ep**
– Laurie / The monster inside of me / Whiz kid / The Lennon song.

Seed / Atlantic

Sep 94. (7"red-ep) *(seed 10)* **HAPPY TIME EP**
– Happy time / Come see me tonight / Rock'n'roll – Ega / Love me do.

Sep 94. (cd,c) *<82659>* **FUN**
– Love wheel / Life in vain / Crazy love / Catie / Happy time / Mind contorted / Jelly beans / Foxy girl / Sad sac + Tarzan / Psycho nightmare / Silly love / Circus man / Love will see you through / Lousy weekend / Delusion + confusion / When I met you / My little girl / Rock'n'roll – Ega.

Pickled Egg / Gammon

Oct 98. (7",7"white) *(EGG 6)* **DREAM SCREAM. / FUNERAL GIRL**

—— in 1999, a proposed set, 'REJECTED', was withdrawn by 'Tim/Kerr'

Jun 00. (d-lp/cd) *(EG 22/+CD) <2100>* **REJECTED UNKNOWN**   Oct01
– Impossible love / Funeral girl / Dream scream / Love forever / Cathy Cline / Davinare / Party / The spook / Girl of my dreams / Billions – Rock / Thrill / Favorite darling girl / Some time spent in Heaven / Wedding ring bell blues / I lose.

Sep 01. (7"blue) *<IMPREC 001>* **IMPOSSIBLE LOVE. / FAVORITE DARLING GIRL / THE SPOOK**

Jan 02. (7"m; by DANIEL JOHNSTON & SLOW DEATH vs The INSTANT COFFIN) *(EGG 33)* **SHINING IS EASY. / I WANT YOU BACK INTO MY LIFE / A PRAYER FROM THE DEPTHS**

DANIEL JOHNSTON AND THE HYPERJINX TRICYCLE

aka **JOHNSTON** with **RON ENGLISH + JACK MEDICINE**

Soft Skull Software / Important

May 02. (cd) *(SSS 9060) <IMPREC 006>* **DANIEL JOHNSTON AND THE HYPERJINX TRICYCLE**
– Face yourself / Starship / Reality / Greg the bunny / UFO / Keep your feelings to yourself / Wasted life / Happy Springfield (for Matt Groening) / Slice of life / Road to Heaven / Disney movie / Merry Christmas Oblio / Seasons in the sun. *(UK-iss.Oct02; same as US)*

Important / Important

May 02. (7"colred-ep) *(IMPREC 003)* **LONG LOST LOVE**
– Long lost love / Mystery song #1 / Here I am / Greg the bunny (alt).

JOOLZ

Born: Bradford, England. A socially aware and extreme feminist punk poetess, the tattooed and sultry JOOLZ recited her work on stage, pricking the conscience of laddish men looking for a night on the town. Finding an outlet for her work via 'Abstract' records (through her live-in boyfriend, SLADE THE LEVELLER of NEW MODEL ARMY), she released a couple of EP's and a mini-album, 'NEVER NEVER LAND' (1985), a set that included the poignant 'JACKANORY'. When NEW MODEL ARMY made it big time by signing to 'E.M.I.', she was also invited to step up to the majors, although this unsteady partnership only produced a handful of 45's and a much delayed first album proper, 'HEX' (1987); the record was to have been issued a year earlier as 'MUSKET, FIFE AND DRUM'. Ten years or so onwards, JOOLZ was extremely busy working all over the world, reading poetry in New Zealand, Slovenia, Canada, Holland and the Edinburgh Fringe Festivals. In 1998, she was awarded New Crimewriter Of The Year for her novel, 'Stone Baby', while the media beckoned for her sharp wit on programmes such as 'Toksvig!', 'Later With Jools Holland – Live' and Radio One's Mark Radcliffe Show.

Album rating: NEVER NEVER LAND mini (*4) / HEX (*5) / WEIRD SISTER (*4) / RECORDED 1983-85 compilation (*5)

JOOLZ – words / with **JAH WOBBLE** – dub effects

Abstract / not iss.

Oct 83. (12"ep) *(12ABS 018)* **WAR OF ATTRITION**
– War of attrition / Denise / Latest craze / Protection.

—— added guest **OLLIE MARLAND** – saxophone

Jul 84. (12"ep) *(12ABS 025)* **THE KISS. / THE KISS (dub) / PAVED WITH GOLD**

Jun 85. (m-lp) *(ABT 011)* **NEVER NEVER LAND**
– Home sweet home / Seventeen / At dawn / Housewives choice / Never never land / Jackanory / Relax . . . don't do it! / Jerusalem.

—— now with **SLADE THE LEVELLER** – backing

E.M.I. / not iss.

Nov 85. (7") *(JLZ 1)* **LOVE IS (SWEET ROMANCE). / MUSKET, FIFE AND DRUM**
(12"+=) *(12JLZ 1)* – Fury.

Aug 86. (7") *(EMI 5582)* **MAD, BAD AND DANGEROUS TO KNOW. / LEGEND**
(12"+=) *(12EMI 5582)* – Babies.

Oct 87. (7") *(JLZ 3)* **PROTECTION. / A DAY IN THE LIFE OF . . .**

Columbia / not iss.

Oct 87. (lp/c)(cd) *(SCX/TC-SCX 6711)(CDP 748537-2)* **HEX**
– Protection / The cat / Facade / Love is (sweet romance) / The stand / Storm / Mummy's boy / Ambition / House of dreams / Requiem. *(cd+=)* – Musket, fife and drum / Legend / Mad, bad and dangerous to know. *(<re-iss. Apr90 & Mar01 on 'Anagram' cd+=/lp; CD+/GRAM 44>)*

Intercord / not iss.

Feb 92. (lp) *(IRS 951946)* **WEIRD SISTER**
– The game / Tracy / The ballad of Steve & Joe / The boy next door but one / Bad blood / Fuel to the flame / Vendetta / The wait / Pandora / May / Miami / Treasure in the heart / Pamela.

—— she again retired from solo studio work

– compilations, etc. –

Jun 93. (cd) *Get Back; (GBR 004CD)* **RECORDED 1983-85**

JOSEF K

Formed: Edinburgh, Scotland . . . 1979 by PAUL HAIG, MALCOLM ROSS, DAVID WEDDELL and RONNIE TORRANCE. Named after the main character from one of Franz Kafka's darkly paranoid novels and influenced by New York "No Wave" bands like TALKING HEADS, HAIG & Co. debuted in late '79 with the self-financed 'ROMANCE'. Subsequently signed to Alan Horne's ultra-hip Glasgow-based 'Postcard' label, the band were heralded as "The Sound Of Young Scotland" alongside labelmates ORANGE JUICE and AZTEC CAMERA. A string of singles, including 'RADIO DRILL TIME' and the low-end lurch of 'SORRY FOR LAUGHING', brought fawning press acclaim with one critic moved to describe their awkward, indie-noir sound as a "cross between CAPTAIN BEEFHEART and CHIC". Problems arose, however, with a proposed debut album, 'SORRY FOR LAUGHING', the band unhappy with the production and scrapping it at the last minute; some copies did filter through, mint editions now change hands for over £100. Recorded in Belgium, 'THE ONLY FUN IN TOWN' eventually surfaced as their debut long player in summer '81. Yet no sooner was the record out than HAIG, sticking rigidly by one of punk's guiding principles, decided that they'd reached an artistic peak and had to split. After a final single, 'THE MISSIONARY', JOSEF K disbanded in early '82, TORRANCE and WEDDELL forming HAPPY FAMILY while ROSS joined ORANGE JUICE and later AZTEC CAMERA. HAIG, meanwhile, embarked on a solo career via Belgian label, 'Crepescule', following an ill-advised, vaguely SIMPLE MINDS-ish synth-pop/rock direction with 1983's 'RHYTHM OF LIFE' album. The singer continued releasing albums throughout the 80's, never drawing more than minor cult acclaim and modest sales; while HAIG's influence was apparent in the more commercially successful material of LLOYD COLE, for instance, the man himself had to make do with recognition on the continent. • **Covered:** APPLEBUSH (Alice Cooper).

Album rating: THE ONLY FUN IN TOWN (*6) / YOUNG AND STUPID compilation (*8) / Paul Haig: RHYTHM OF LIFE (*7)

PAUL HAIG (b.1960) – vocals, guitar / **MALCOLM ROSS** (b.31 Jul'60) – guitar, keyboards / **DAVID WENDELL** – bass; repl. GARY McCORMACK who later joined The EXPLOITED / **RONNIE TORRANCE** – drums

Absolute / not iss.

Dec 79. (7") *(ABS 1)* **ROMANCE. / CHANCE MEETING**

Postcard / not iss.

Aug 80. (7") *(80-3)* **RADIO DRILL TIME. / CRAZY TO EXIST (live)**
Dec 80. (7") *(80-5)* **IT'S KINDA FUNNY. / FINAL REQUEST**
Jan 81. (lp; w-drawn) *(81-1)* **SORRY FOR LAUGHING**
Feb 81. (7") *(81-4)* **SORRY FOR LAUGHING. / REVELATION**
May 81. (7") *(81-5)* **CHANCE MEETING. / PICTURES (OF CINDY)**
Jun 81. (lp) *(81-7)* **THE ONLY FUN IN TOWN**
– Fun 'n' frenzy / Revelation / Crazy to exist / It's kinda funny / The angle / Forever drone / Heart of song / 16 years / Citizens / Sorry for laughing. *(cd-iss. Sep90 on 'Les Tempes Modernes'+=; LTMCD 2305)* – (w/ shelved album 'SORRY FOR LAUGHING')

Operation Twilight / not iss.

Feb 82. (7") *(7TWI 053)* **MISSIONARY. / ONE ANGLE / SECOND ANGLE**

—— split early '82 when MALCOLM joined ORANGE JUICE (later AZTEC CAMERA). TORRANCE joined BOOTS FOR DANCING and subsequently teamed up with DAVID to form The HAPPY FAMILY. In 1992, MALCOLM reunited with DAVID forming the MAGIC CLAN in the process.

– compilations, etc. –

Mar 87. (12") *Supreme; (87-7)* **HEAVEN SENT / RADIO DRILL TIME (demo). / HEADS WATCH / FUN 'N' FRENZY**

Jun 87. (lp) *Supreme; (87-6)* **YOUNG AND STUPID**
– Heart of song / Endless soul / Citizens / Variation of scene / It's kinda funny / Sorry for laughing / Chance meeting / Heaven sent / Drone / Sense of guilt / Revelation / Romance. *(re-iss. Mar89 as 'ENDLESS SOUL'; same) (cd-iss. Sep90 on 'Les Tempes Modernes'; LTMCD 2307)*

PAUL HAIG

—— (solo) – vocals, guitar with the **RHYTHM OF LIFE** band:- **JAMES LOCKE, DAVID GRAHAM + STEPHEN HAINES** (ex-METROPAK)

1982. (c) *(none)* **DRAMA**   – / – gigs

Operation Twilight / not iss.

May 82. (7") *(OPT 03)* **RUNNING AWAY. / TIME**

Crepescule / not iss.

Sep 82. (7") *(OPT 001)* **CHANCE. / JUSTICE**

JOSEF K (cont)

Dec 82. (12") *(TWI 106)* **BLUE FOR YOU. / BLUE FOR YOU (version)**
  Crepescule-Island / *not iss.*

May 83. (7"/ext-12") *(IS/12IS 111)* **HEAVEN SENT. / RUNNING AWAY, BACK HOME** — 74 / -
Jul 83. (7"/ext-12") *(IS/12IS 124)* **NEVER GIVE UP (PARTY, PARTY). / HEARTACHE (Party mix)**
Oct 83. (lp/c) *(ILPS/ICT 9742)* **RHYTHM OF LIFE** — 82 / -
  – Heaven sent / Never give up (party, party) / Adoration / Stolen love / Don't rush in / Blue for you / In the world / Justice / Work together.
Oct 83. (7") *(IS 138)* **JUSTICE. / ON THIS NIGHT OF DECISION**
  (12"+=) *(12IS 138)* – Justice '82.
Sep 84. (7") *(IS 198)* **THE ONLY TRUTH. / GHOST RIDER**
  (12"+=) *(ISX 198)* – ('A'-US remix).

—— with **ALAN RANKINE** – lead guitar / **MIKE McCANN** – bass / **JAMES LOCK** – drums
  Operation Twilight / *not iss.*

Sep 85. (7") *(OPA 2)* **HEAVEN HELP YOU NOW. / WORLD RAW**
  (ext-12"+=) *(12OPA 2)* – Chance.
  (re-iss. Aug88; TWI 624)
Nov 85. (lp) *(OPA 3)* **THE WARP OF PURE FUN**
  – Silent motion / Heaven help you now / Love eternal / This dying flame / Sense of fun / Scare me / Big blue world / The only truth / One lifetime away / Love and war. *(re-iss. Feb87 on 'Crepescule' lp/cd; TWI 669/+CD)*
Feb 86. (7") *(OPA 4)* **LOVE ETERNAL. / TRUST**
  (12"+=) *(12OPA 6)* – Dangerous life.
  (re-iss. Sep88; TWI 660)
  Crepescule / *not iss.*
Jan 88. (lp)(cd) *(TWI 829)(IPCD 2018-36)* **EUROPEAN SUN: ARCHIVE COLLECTION 1982-1987**
  – Running away / Chance / Justice / Swinging for you / Shining hour / Fear and dancing / Blue for you / Ghost rider / Torchomatic / Endless song / Closer now / Dangerous life / The executioner / Psycho San Jose / On this night of indecision / World raw.
Mar 88. (12"ep) *(TWI 832)* **TORCHOMATIC. / BEAT PROGRAMME / CHASE MANHATTAN / WHITE HOTEL / SONG FOR**

—— now with **ALAN RANKINE** – keyboards, guitar, co-producer / **JOHN TURNER** – piano
  Circa / *not iss.*

Mar 89. (lp/c/cd) *(CIR CA/C/CD 7)* **CHAIN**
  – Something good / True blue / Communication / Swinging for you / Time of her life / Faithless / Times can change / Turn the vision / Sooner or later / Chained.
  (cd+=) – Ideal of living.
Jun 89. (7") *(YR 25)* **SOMETHING GOOD. / OVER YOU**
  (3"cd-s+=) *(YRCD 25)* – Free to go / Outback.
  (ext-12"+=) *(YRT 25)* – Free to go (technology) / ('A'radio).
  (remixed-12"g-f+=) *(YTRX 25)* – The last kiss / Free to go (public).
Sep 90. (cd-s) *(YRCD 47)* **I BELIEVE IN YOU / FLIGHT X (Long Flight mix) / I BELIEVE IN YOU (Life In A Dolphinarium mix)**
Feb 91. (12") *(YRTX 47)* **FLIGHT X (school mix). / FLIGHT X (Give the DJ a break mix)**
  (12") *(YRRR 47)* – ('A'-New school mix) / ('A'-Music School instrumental) / ('A'-Mantronik mix).
  Les Tempes Modernes / *not iss.*
Jan 92. (cd/c/lp) *(LTMCD 2309)* **CINEMATIQUE – THEMES FOR UNKNOWN FILMS, VOLUME ONE** — - / - Belgian
  – Black veil and gold / City of fun / Somewhere inbetween / The hunting party / Crime interlude / City of fun (slight return) / Lagondola 1 / Beauty / Highland / Deception / Intimacy / Lagondola 2 / Flashback / Eastworld / In-flight entertainment / Oil.
  Crepescule / *not iss.*
May 93. (cd-ep) *(TWI 989-2)* **SURRENDER / HEAVEN HELP YOU NOW ('93 remix) / COINCIDENCE VS FATE**
Nov 93. (cd) *(TWI 962-2)* **COINCIDENCE VS FATE**
  – I believe in you / Flight X / Born innocence / My kind / Si senorita / Right on line / Out of mind / Surrender / Stop and stare / The originator / 1959.

—— took a hiatus until his mid-90's recording with BILLY MACKENZIE
  Rhythm Of Life / *not iss.*

Jan 00. (cd; by PAUL HAIG & BILLY MACKENZIE) *(ROL 003)* **MEMORY PALACE**
  – Thuderstorm / Stone the memory palace / Beyond love / Transobsession / Trash 3 / Listen to me / Listen again / Take a chance / Give me time.
Mar 01. (cd) *(ROL 004)* **CINEMATIC VOL.2**
  – Paradise angel / Syncro firefly / Wild sync lair / Apple corr / Corr (part 2) / Oyster world / Looking / I.D. / Jewel divine / Spirit.

– compilations, etc. –

on 'Operation Twilight' unless mentioned otherwise
Jun 84. (7"/12") *(TWI 230/231)* **BIG BLUE WORLD. / GHOST RIDER / ENDLESS SONG**
Jun 84. (7"ep) *(7TWI 240)* **HEAVEN SENT EP (remixes)**
  – Heaven sent / Blue for you / Never give up (party, party) / Stolen love / Justice.
Apr 85. (12"ep) *(TWI 094)* **SWING '82**
  – The song is you / All of you / Music and dance / Love me tender / The way you look tonight.

JOYRIDERS (see under ⇒ CATERAN)

JPS EXPERIENCE (see under ⇒ JEAN-PAUL SARTRE EXPERIENCE)

JUNE BRIDES

Formed: Coventry, England . . . 1983 out of INTERNATIONAL RESCUE by PHIL WILSON and SIMON BEESLEY, the pair recruiting FRANK SWEENEY, ADE CARTER and BRIAN ALEXIS before any recordings. Influenced initially by JOSEF K, the sextet's sound was also distinguished by the trumpet playing of JON HUNTER. Having signed a deal with Rough Trade offshoot, 'Pink', The JUNE BRIDES released a couple of effervescent indie-pop singles, the second of which, 'EVERY CONVERSATION' stood out. However, a full year passed (during which time CHRIS NINEHAM replaced BRIAN) before the band followed up with their debut 12", a mini-set comprising the aforementioned song and an unusual cover of The Radiators From Space's 'ENEMIES'. Further personnel changes blighted the band's career as PHIL WILSON was left to go it alone following a final couple of 45's. Signing to Alan McGee's 'Creation', WILSON pursued a short-lived solo career and later resurrected The JUNE BRIDES for a brief period in the mid 90's.

Album rating: THERE ARE EIGHT MILLION STORIES mini (*5) / FOR BETTER OR WORSE 1983-1986 compilation (*6)

PHIL WILSON – vocals, guitar / **SIMON BEESLEY** (b. Shrewsbury, England) – guitar, vocals / **FRANK SWEENEY** (b. Lewisham, England) – organ, viola, etc / **JON HUNTER** – trumpet / **ADE CARTER** – bass / **BRIAN ALEXIS** – drums
  Pink / *not iss.*

Jun 84. (7") *(PINKY 1)* **IN THE RAIN. / SUNDAY TO SATURDAY**
Sep 84. (7") *(PINKY 2)* **EVERY CONVERSATION. / DISNEYLAND**
  (12"ep of above two 45's iss.Apr86; PINKY 9)

—— **CHRIS NINEHAM** – drums; repl. BRIAN

—— FRANK left to join The RINGING (who also comprised of his brother NICK, plus JENNY BENWELL, DIRK HIGGINS and CHRIS BLAWAT), releasing one single early '85, 'CAPRICE' / 'DOCTOR' for 'Pinky' *(PINKY 3)*. FRANK subsequently formed YEAH JAZZ.

Sep 85. (m-lp) *(PINKY 5)* **THERE ARE EIGHT MILLION BRIDES**
  – Every conversation / Enemies / Sick tired and drunk / Sunday to Saturday / Have you heard / Instrumental.

—— **MARTIN PINK** – drums (of BATFISH BOYS) repl. CHRIS
  In-Tape / *not iss.*

Nov 85. (7") *(IT 024)* **NO PLACE LIKE HOME. / WE BELONG**
  (12"+=) *(ITT 024)* – On the rocks / Josef's gone.
May 86. (7"m/12"m) *(IT/+T 030)* **THIS TOWN. / COLD / JUST THE SAME**

—— they split after above with most going into session work

– compilations, etc. –

Apr 87. (12"ep) *Strange Fruit; (SFPS 023)* **PEEL SESSIONS** (22/10/85)
  – This town / Waiting for a change / We belong / One day.
Jan 95. (cd) *Overground; (OVER 40CD)* **FOR BETTER OR WORSE (1983-1986)**

PHIL WILSON

—— went solo
  Creation / *not iss.*

Feb 87. (7") *(CRE 036)* **WAITING FOR A CHANGE. / EVEN NOW**
  (12"+=) *(CRE 036T)* – A cowboy's lament.
  (d7"+=) *(CRE 036D)* – Down in the valley / Love in vain.
Jun 87. (7") *(CRE 046)* **TEN MILES. / JINGLE**
  (12"+=) *(CRE 046T)* – Jackson.
  Caff / *not iss.*
1989. (ltd-7") *(CAFF 3)* **BETTER DAYS. / YOU WON'T SPEAK**

—— PHIL retired from the indie limelight until a brief JUNE BRIDES reformation in the mid 90's

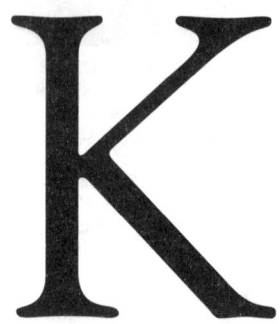

K

KALIMA (see under ⇒ A CERTAIN RATIO)

Nash KATO (see under ⇒ URGE OVERKILL)

Tara KEY (see under ⇒ ANTIETAM)

Steve KILBEY (see under ⇒ CHURCH)

David KILGOUR (see under ⇒ CLEAN)

KILLDOZER

Formed: Madison, Wisconsin, USA . . . 1983 by brothers BILL and DAN HOBSON alongside MICHAEL GERALD. Politically aware punks with an acute sense of humour/observation and a penchant for gritty country, KILLDOZER made their debut in 1984 with the wonderfully titled mini-set, 'INTELLECTUALS ARE THE SHOESHINE BOYS OF THE RULING ELITE'. Subsequently picked up by Chicago's 'Touch & Go' label, the band ran off a series of BUTCH VIG-produced records – 'SNAKEBOY' (1986), 'BURL' (1987) and 'LITTLE BABY BUNTIN'' (1988) – exploring the backwoods mentality of rural America from differing narrative perspectives. Occasionally unsettling and often highly amusing, the band's lyrical caricatures were put on hold for 1989's 'FOR LADIES ONLY', wherein the boys KILLDOZER-ed their way through a selection of prime 70's FM rock classics. Following the release of '12 POINT BUCK' later that year, the band entered a period of instability as BILL departed due to family commitments. After periods of sporadic touring, KILLDOZER finally re-emerged – complete with new guitarist, PAUL ZAGORES – in 1994 with 'UNCOMPROMISING WAR ON ART UNDER THE DICTATORSHIP OF THE PROLETARIAT'. While the latter set revisited the political sentiments of the band's debut, 1995's STEVE ALBINI-produced 'GOD HEARS PLEAS OF THE INNOCENT' and 1997's 'THE LAST WALTZ' saw the band bow out with some of the most skull-crushing music of their career. • **Covered:** FUNK #49 (James Gang) / CINNAMON GIRL (Neil Young) / RUN THROUGH THE JUNGLE (John Fogerty) / AMERICAN PIE (Don McLean) / GOOD LOVIN GONE BAD (Bad Company) / TAKE THE MONEY AND RUN (Steve Miller Band) / HUSH (Joe South) / EVERY CHRISTIAN HEARTED MAN WILL (Bee Gees) / CONQUISTADOR (Procol Harum) / AQUARIUS – LET THE SUNSHINE IN (Fifth Dimension) / POUR MAN (Lee Hazlewood) / WHEN THE LEVEE BREAKS + NO QUARTER + HOT DOG (Led Zeppelin) / I SAW THE LIGHT (Hank Williams) / etc.

Album rating: INTELLECTUALS ARE THE SHOESHINE BOYS OF THE RULING ELITE (*5) / SNAKEBOY (*5) / BURL mini (*5) / LITTLE BABY BUNTIN' (*6) / FOR LADIES ONLY (*7) / 12 POINT BUCK (*7) / UNCOMPROMISING WAR ON ART UNDER THE DICTATORSHIP OF THE PROLETARIAT (*6) / GOD HEARS PLEAS OF THE INNOCENT (*7) / THE LAST WALTZ (*5)

MICHAEL GERALD – vocals, bass / **DAN HOBSON** – guitar / **BILL HOBSON** – drums

                                                                not iss. Bone Air

1984. (m-lp) <*001*> **INTELLECTUALS ARE THE SHOESHINE BOYS OF THE RULING ELITE**
– Man of meat! / Pile driver! / Parade! / Farmer Johnson! / Ed Gein! / A man's gotta be a man . . .! / Dead folks! / Run through the jungle! <(re-iss. Oct89 on 'Touch & Go' lp/cd+=; T&G LP/CD 47)> – SNAKEBOY

                                                          Touch   Touch
                                                          & Go   & Go

Aug 86. (lp) <*TGLP 6*> **SNAKEBOY**   Nov85
– King of sex / Going to the beach / River / L.Y.L.L.Y.D.E. / Don't cry / Cinnamon girl / Gone to Heaven / Revelations / Burning house.

1987. (m-lp) <*TGLP 17*> **BURL**   Nov86
– Hamburger martyr / Cranberries / Slackjaw / Hot n' tot / One for the people / I'm not Lisa.

Mar 88. (lp) <*TGLP 26*> **LITTLE BABY BUNTIN'**   Feb88
– Little Baby Buntin' / Cotton bolls / The puppy / Hi there / Ballad of my old man / The rub / 3/4 inch drill bit / I am I said / Cyst / Never gave me a kiss / The noble art of self defence.

Apr 89. <(ltd-5x7")> <*TGLP 39*> **FOR LADIES ONLY**
– Hush / Good lovin' gone bad / Burnin' love / You've never been this far before / One tin soldier / Take the money and run / American pie / Funk #49 . (re-iss. Sep90 lp/c/cd/pic-lp/pic-cd; T&GLP 39/+C/CD/PD/CP)

Mar 89. (7") <*TGLP 26*> **HER MOTHER'S SORROW. / SHORT EYES**
(above issued on 'Amphetamine Reptile' and feat. TOM HAZELMYER)

Jul 89. (7") <*TG 44*> **YOW**
– Lupus / Nasty.

Nov 89. (lp/cd) <(*TGLP/TGCD 48*)> **TWELVE POINT BUCK**   1988
– Twelve point buck / New pants and shirt / Space 1999 / Lupus / Richard / Man versus nature / Gates of Heaven / Pigfoot and bear / Seven thunders / Free love in Amsterdam / Ted Key beef. (cd+=) – LITTLE BABY BUNTIN'

— **PAUL ZAGORAS** – guitar; repl. GERALD who took accountancy exams until he returned in '93

Mar 94. (lp/c/cd) <(*TG 82/+C/CD*)> **UNCOMPROMISING WAR ON ART UNDER THE DICTATORSHIP OF THE PROLETARIAT**
– Final market / Knuckles the dog (who helps people) / Turkey shoot / Grandma Smith said a curious thing / Hot 'n' nasty / Peach pie / Enemy of the people / Earl Scheib / Das kapital / The pig was cool / Working hard, or hardly working?

Sep 94. (7") <*TG 122*> **THE PIG WAS COOL. / UNBELIEVABLE**

Feb 95. (lp/cd) <(*TG 139/+CD*)> **GOD HEARS PLEAS OF THE INNOCENT**
– A mother has a hard road / Porky's dead / Pour man / The buzzard / Paul doesn't understand jazz / Daddy's boy / The Nobbies (a sea chanty) / Big song of Hell / Cannonball run II '95 / I have seen grown men cry / Spork.

— **ERIK TUNISON** – drums (ex-DIE KREUZEN) repl. DAN

— added **JEFF DITZENBERG** – guitar (ex-POWER WAGON)

May 96. (7"ep/cd-ep; with ALICE DONUT) <(*TG 146/+CD*)> **MICHAEL GERALD'S PARTY MACHINE EP**   Apr96
– Every Christian lion hearted man will / Conquistador / Medley: Aquarius – Let the sunshine in.

                                                      Man's Ruin Man's Ruin

Sep 96. (12"ep) <*MR 007*> **WHEN THE LEVEE BREAKS. / NO QUARTER / HOT DOG**

Aug 97. (7") (*ism 27V*) **GO BIG RED**
– Sonnet '96 / I saw the light.
(above issued on 'Ismist')

Sep 97. (cd) <*MR 065CD*> **THE LAST WALTZ**
– Porky's dad / The nobbies (a sea shanty) / Man of meat / I've seen grown men cry / A mother's road / Space: 1999 / Richard / A Xmas song / Knuckles the dog / Cannonball run III '97 / Mama's boy / Way down in old Alabam' / Songs for grand folks. (re-iss. Aug00; same)

— KILLDOZER had already disbanded in 1996

KILLING JOKE

Formed: Notting Hill, London, England . . . 1979 by JAZ COLEMAN and PAUL FERGUSON, who subsequently added GEORDIE (K. WALKER) and YOUTH (MARTIN GLOVER). After borrowing money to finance a debut EP (contained three tracks including 'TURN TO RED'), the band were the subject of some interest to DJ John Peel who championed their alternative rock sound. This immediately led to KILLING JOKE signing a deal with 'Island', who virtually re-issued the aforementioned single/EP in abbreviated 7" form (A-side, 'NERVOUS SYSTEM'), adding a fourth track on the 12". While supporting the likes of JOY DIVISION and The RUTS, they released a follow-up double A-sided single, 'WARDANCE' / 'PSYCHE', resurrecting their own 'Malicious Damage' label in the process. The left-field 'E.G.' operation were quick to spot the group's potential, taking on both KILLING JOKE and their label. The first results of this partnership came in the form of 'REQUIEM', the single taken from their pioneering eponymous UK Top 40 album. Replacing the anger of punk with apocalyptic doom mongering, KILLING JOKE were akin to a sonically disturbing, industrialised BLACK SABBATH. Now regarded as a catalystic classic in metal circles, the album also inspired many US hardcore acts, as well as such big guns as METALLICA, MINISTRY, SOUNDGARDEN and NIRVANA. By the release of follow-up set, 'WHAT'S THIS FOR' (1981), KILLING JOKE had taken their occult punk-like chants/anthems to extreme new dimensions. Nevertheless, they retained a strange accessibility which saw the single, 'FOLLOW THE LEADERS' attaining a minor UK chart placing and incredibly, a hit on the American dancefloors! A third set, 'REVELATIONS' (1982), eased up a little on the intensity factor, although it peaked at No.12 having already spawned another hit single, 'EMPIRE SONG'. Convinced of imminent world destruction, the occult-fixated COLEMAN remained in Iceland after a tour, YOUTH initially returning home but later following his lead to the frozen north. He subsequently flew back to England, teaming up with FERGUSON and newfound friend, PAUL RAVEN to form BRILLIANT. However, both FERGUSON and RAVEN soon departed from YOUTH's group, taking off for Iceland in search of the missing COLEMAN. Eventually locating their frontman, all three returned to UK shores and re-entered the studio (GEORDIE also in tow) with a view to recording new KILLING JOKE material. The resulting album, 'FIRE DANCES' (1983), only managed to scrape into the Top 30, its lack of bite and experimentation possibly a hangover from their northern treks. The following year, KILLING JOKE released only two 45's, although one of them, 'EIGHTIES' (a minor hit), was showcased in all its eccentric glory on Channel 4's new pop show, 'The Tube'. Having overcome the mental obstacle of 1984 (and all of its apocalyptic implications), COLEMAN and Co. unleashed their most focused work to date in 'NIGHT TIME' (a near Top 10 album), the 'LOVE LIKE BLOOD' single preceding the set and breaking into the Top 20 in early '85. The latter half of the eighties weren't so kind, both critically and commercially, the albums, 'BRIGHTER THAN A THOUSAND SUNS' (1986) and 'OUTSIDE THE GATE' (1988), taking a more self-indulgent keyboard-orientated approach. Following major personnel upheavals, KILLING JOKE decided to take a brief sabbatical, COLEMAN finding time to release a collaborative album with ANNE DUDLEY (ex-ART OF NOISE), 'SONGS FROM THE VICTORIOUS CITY' (1990). The same year, COLEMAN, GEORDIE, RAVEN and newcomer MARTIN ATKINS,

KILLING JOKE (cont)

returned with the acclaimed 'EXTREMITIES, DIRT AND VARIOUS REPRESSED EMOTIONS' album. Having spent most of the early 90's globetrotting in various exotic locations, KILLING JOKE (now COLEMAN, GEORDIE and the returning YOUTH), were back with a vengeance on 1994's 'PANDEMONIUM'. Their biggest selling album to date, the record and the 'PANDEMONIUM' single from it both made the Top 30 (the previous 'MILLENNIUM' made Top 40), while also seeing an American release on the 'Zoo' label. Another, increasingly metallic/industrial set, 'DEMOCRACY' followed in 1996, although COLEMAN now spends the bulk of his time in New Zealand, where he is composer in residence for the country's Symphony Orchestra.

Album rating: KILLING JOKE (*9) / WHAT'S THIS FOR . . .! (*7) / REVELATIONS (*5) / HA! KILLING JOKE LIVE (*5) / FIRE DANCES (*7) / NIGHT TIME (*7) / BRIGHTER THAN A THOUSAND SUNS (*6) / OUTSIDE THE GATE (*6) / EXTREMITIES, DIRT AND VARIOUS REPRESSED EMOTIONS (*7) / LAUGH? I NEARLY BOUGHT ONE! compilation (*8) / PANDEMONIUM (*8) / DEMOCRACY (*6)

JAZ COLEMAN (b. JEREMY, 26 Feb'60, Cheltenham, England; raised Egypt) – vocals, keyboards / **GEORDIE** (b. K.WALKER, 18 Dec'58, Newcastle-upon-Tyne, England) – guitar, synthesizers / **YOUTH** (b. MARTIN GLOVER, 27 Dec'60, Africa) – bass, vocals (ex-RAGE) / **PAUL FERGUSON** (b.31 Mar'58, High Wycombe, England) – drums

Malicious Damage / not iss.

Oct 79. (10"ep) (MD 410) **ARE YOU RECEIVING ME. / TURN TO RED / NERVOUS SYSTEM**

Island / not iss.

Nov 79. (7") (WIP 6550) **NERVOUS SYSTEM. / TURN TO RED**
(12"+=) (12WIP 6550) – Almost red / Are you receiving me.

Malicious Damage / not iss.

Mar 80. (7") (MD 540) **WARDANCE. / PSYCHE**

E.G. – Malicious Damage / Editions

Sep 80. (7") (EGMD 1.00) **REQUIEM. / CHANGE**
(12"+=) (EGMX 1.00) – Requiem 434 / Change (version).
Oct 80. (lp/c) (EGMD/+C 545) **KILLING JOKE** [39]
– Requiem / Wardance / Tomorrow's world / Bloodsport / The wait / Complications / S.O. 36 / Primitive. (re-iss. Jan87 lp/c/cd; EG LP/MC/CD 57) <US cd-iss. 1987 on 'Caroline'; 1538>
May 81. (7") (EGMDS 1.01) **FOLLOW THE LEADERS. / TENSION** [55]
(10"+=) (EGMDX 1.010) – Follow the leaders – dub.
Jun 81. (lp/c) (EGMD/+C 550) <111> **WHAT'S THIS FOR . . .!** [42]
– The fall of Because / Tension / Unspeakable / Butcher / Follow the leaders / Madness / Who told you how? / Exit. (re-iss. Jan87 lp/c/cd; EG LP/MC/CD 58) <US cd-iss. 1987 on 'Caroline'; 1539>

E.G. / Caroline

Mar 82. (7") (EGO 4) **EMPIRE SONG. / BRILLIANT** [43]
— **GUY PRATT** – bass; repl. YOUTH who formed BRILLIANT
Apr 82. (lp/c) (EGMD/+C 3) **REVELATIONS** [12]
– The hum / Empire song / We have joy / Chop chop / The Pandys are coming / Chapter III / Have a nice day / Land of milk and honey / Good samaritan / Dregs. (re-iss. Jan87 lp/c/cd; EG LP/MC/CD 59) <US cd-iss. 1987 on 'Caroline'; 1540>
Jun 82. (7") (EGO 7) **CHOP CHOP. / GOOD SAMARITAN**
Oct 82. (7") (EGO 10) **BIRDS OF A FEATHER. / FLOCK THE B-SIDE** [64]
(12"+=) (EGOX 10) – Sun goes down.
Nov 82. (10"m-lp/m-c) (EGMD T/C 4) **HA – KILLING JOKE LIVE (live)** [66]
– Psyche / Sun goes down / The Pandys are coming / Take take take / Unspeakable / Wardance.
— **PAUL RAVEN** – bass (ex-NEON HEARTS) repl. PRATT who joined ICEHOUSE
Jun 83. (7") (EGO 11) **LET'S ALL GO (TO THE FIRE DANCES). / DOMINATOR** (version) [51]
(12"+=) (EGOX 11) – The fall of Because (live).
Jul 83. (lp/c) (EGMD/+P 5) **FIRE DANCES** [29]
– The gathering / Fun and games / Rejuvenation / Frenzy / Harlequin / Feast of blaze / Song and dance / Dominator / Let's all go (to the fire dances) / Lust almighty. (re-iss. Jan87 lp/c/cd; EG LP/MC/CD 60) <US cd-iss. 1987 on 'Caroline'; 1541>
Oct 83. (7") (EGOD 14) **ME OR YOU?. / WILFUL DAYS** [57]
(with free 7") (KILL 1-2) – ('A'side / Feast of blaze.
(d12"++=) (EGOXD 14) – Let's all go (to the fire dances) / The fall of Because (live) / Dominator (version).
Mar 84. (7") (EGO 16) **EIGHTIES. / EIGHTIES (Coming mix)** [60]
(12"+=) (EGOX 16) – ('A'-Serious dance mix).
Jun 84. (7") (EGO 17) **A NEW DAY. / DANCE DAY** [56]
(12"+=) (EGOX 17) – ('A'dub).
Jan 85. (7") (EGO 20) **LOVE LIKE BLOOD. / BLUE FEATHER** [16]
(12"+=) (EGOY 20) – ('A'-Gestalt mix).
(12"++=) (EGOX 20) – ('A'instrumental).
Feb 85. (lp/c) (EGMD/+C 6) <1531> **NIGHT TIME** [11]
– Night time / Darkness before dawn / Love like blood / Kings and queens / Tabazan / Multitudes / Europe / Eighties. (re-iss. Jan87 lp/c/cd; EG LP/MC/CD 61)
Mar 85. (7") (EGO 21) **KINGS AND QUEENS. / THE MADDING CROWD** [58]
(12"+=) (EGOX 21) – ('A'-Right Royal mix).
(12"+=) (EGOY 21) – ('A'-Knave mix).
Aug 86. (7") (EGO 27) **ADORATIONS. / EXILE** [42]
(d7"+=) (EGOD 27) – Ecstacy / ('A'instrumental).

E.G. / Virgin

Oct 86. (7") (EGO 30) **SANITY. / GOODBYE TO THE VILLAGE** [70]
(free c-s with-7") (above tracks) – Wardance (remix).
(12"+=) (EGOX 30) – Victory.
Nov 86. (lp/c/cd) (EG LP/MC/CD 66) <90568-1/-4/-2> **BRIGHTER THAN A THOUSAND SUNS** [54]
– Adorations / Sanity / Chessboards / Twilight of the mortal / Love of the masses / A new day / Wintergardens / Rubicon. (c+=/cd+=) – Goodbye to the village / Victory.

E.G. / Caroline

Apr 88. (7") (EGO 40) **AMERICA. / JIHAD (Beyrouth edit)**
(12"+=) (EGOX 40) – ('A'extended).
(cd-s++=) (EGOCD 40) – Change (original 1980 mix).
Jun 88. (lp/c/cd) (EG LP/MC/CD 73) <1378> **OUTSIDE THE GATE** [92]
– America / My love of this land / Stay one jump ahead / Unto the ends of the Earth / The calling / Obsession / Tiahuanaco / Outside the gate. (cd+=) – America (extended) / Stay one jump ahead (extended).
Jul 88. (7") (EGO 43) **MY LOVE OF THIS LAND. / DARKNESS BEFORE DAWN**
(12"+=) (EGOX 43) – Follow the leaders (dub) / Psyche.
(10"+=) (EGOT 43) – Follow the leaders (dub) / Sun goes down.
— **JAZ + GEORDIE** brought in new members **MARTIN ATKINS** (b. 3 Aug'59, Coventry, England) – drums (ex-PUBLIC IMAGE LTD.) repl. FERGUSON / **TAFF** – bass repl. ANDY ROURKE (ex-SMITHS) who had repl. RAVEN. Early 1990, JAZ COLEMAN teamed up with ANNE DUDLEY (see; ART OF NOISE)
— **KILLING JOKE** reformed (COLEMAN, GEORDIE, ATKINS + RAVEN)

Noise Int. / R.C.A.

Nov 90. (cd/c/lp) (AGR 054-2/-4/-1) <4828-2/-4> **EXTREMITIES, DIRT AND VARIOUS REPRESSED EMOTIONS**
– Money is not our god / Age of greed / Beautiful dead / Extremities / Inside the termite mound / Intravenus / Solitude / North of the border / Slipstream / Kalijuga struggle. (cd re-iss. Sep98 on 'F.A.D.'; FAD 5054)
Jan 91. (12"/cd-s) (AG 054-6/-3) **MONEY IS NOT OUR GOD. / NORTH OF THE BORDER**

Invisible / Invisible

Jul 93. (d-lp) (<INV 004>) **THE COURTHOLD TALKS**
– (spoken word with JAZ, GEORDIE & JAFF SCANTLEBURY on percussion)
— **YOUTH** returned to repl. RAVEN
— **GEOFF DUGMORE** – drums (ex-ART OF NOISE) repl. ATKINS (to PIGFACE, etc)

Butterfly / Volcano-Zoo

Mar 94. (10"ep/cd-ep) (BFL T/D 11) **EXORCISM. / ('A'live) / ('A'-German mix) / WHITEOUT (Ugly mix) / ANOTHER CULT GOES DOWN (mix) / ('A'-Bictonic revenge mix)**
Apr 94. (7"clear/c-s) (BFL/+C 12) **MILLENNIUM. / ('A'-Cybersank remix)** [34]
(12"+=/cd-s+=) (BFL T/D 12) – ('A'-Drum Club remix) / ('A'Juno Reactor remix).
Jul 94. (12"/c-s/cd-s) (BFL T/C/D 17) <14178> **PANDEMONIUM. ('A'mix)** [28] Oct94
(cd-s) (BFLD 17) – ('A'side) / Requiem (Kris Weston & Greg Hunter remix).
Jul 94. (cd/c/d-lp) (BFL CD/MC/LP 9) <31085> **PANDEMONIUM** [16] Aug94
– Pandemonium / Exorcism / Millenium / Communion / Black Moon / Labyrinth / Jana / Whiteout / Pleasures of the flesh / Mathematics of chaos.
— re-united originals **JAZ COLEMAN / GEORDIE + YOUTH**
Jan 95. (cd-ep) (BFLDA 21) **JANA (Youth remix) / JANA (Dragonfly mix) / LOVE LIKE BLOOD (live) / WHITEOUT** [54]
(12"ep/cd-ep+=) (BFL T/DB 21) – Jana (live) / Wardance (live) / Exorcism (live) / Kings and queens (live).
Mar 96. (cd-s) (BFLDA 33) <34262> **DEMOCRACY / DEMOCRACY (Rooster mix by Carcass) / MASS** [39]
(cd-s) (BFLDD 33) – ('A'-United Nations mix) / ('A'-Russian tundra mix) / ('A'-Hallucinogen mix).
Apr 96. (cd/c) (BFL CD/MC 17) <31127> **DEMOCRACY** [71]
– Savage freedom / Democracy / Prozac people / Lanterns / Aeon / Pilgrimage / Intellect / Medicine wheel / Absent friends / Another bloody election. (cd re-iss. Aug99; same)

– compilations, etc. –

on 'Virgin' unless mentioned otherwise
Sep 92. (12"/c-s) (VST/VSC 1432) **CHANGE. / REQUIEM**
(cd-s) (VSCDT 1432) – ('A'spiral tribe mix). / ('B'trash Greg Hunter mix).
(cd-s) (VSCDX 1432) – ('A'-Youth mix). / ('B'-Youth mix).
Oct 92. (cd/c) (CDV/TCV 2693) / Caroline; <1596> **LAUGH? I NEARLY BOUGHT ONE!**
– Turn to red / Psyche / Requiem / Wardance / Follow the leaders / Unspeakable / Butcher / Exit / The hum / Empire song / Chop-chop / The Sun goes down / Eighties / Darkness before dawn / Love like blood / Wintergardens / Age of greed.
May 95. (cd) (CDOVD 440) / Caroline; <1884> **WILFUL DAYS** (remixes)
Oct 95. (cd) Windsong; (WINCD 068) **BBC LIVE IN CONCERT** (live)
Apr 98. (12") Dragonfly; <48> **LOVE LIKE BLOOD. / INTELLECT**
Aug 99. (cd) Butterfly; (BFLCD 9) <114151> **WAR DANCE** (remix album) Aug98
Apr 01. (d-cd) Burning Airlines; <(PILOT 085)> **NO WAY OUT BUT FORWARD GO** (live 1985) May01
Nov 02. (cd) Brilliant; (BT 33087) **LOVE LIKE BLOOD**

KING BLANK (see under ⇒ LOWERY, Ian)

KING MISSILE

Formed: New York, USA . . . 1987 by wordsmith/poet/singer, JOHN S. HALL. A mainstay of NY's Lower East Side "anti-folk" scene, HALL began putting his crazed poetical mutterings to music with the addition of guitarist DOGBOWL and his girlfriend, REBECCA KORBETT (on the drumstool). Also roping in the services of harmonica player, ALEX DeLASZLO, HALL secured a deal with 'Shimmy Disc' and recorded a KRAMER-produced debut album, 'FLUTING ON THE HUMP' (1987). This was released under the moniker, KING MISSILE – DOG FLY RELIGION, as was the following year's set, 'THEY', a more musically adventurous opus that saw STEPHEN DANZIGER replace KORBETT. Further personnel shuffles (DAVID RICK replaced DOGBOWL while CHRIS XEFOS was added on bass) were effected prior to the release of 'MYSTICAL SHIT' (1989), a record that benefitted from the beefed-up alt-rock backing and featured the college-rock minor-classic, 'JESUS WAS WAY COOL'. Subsequently securing a deal with 'Atlantic', KING MISSILE aimed straight at the heart of the alternative market with major label debut, 'THE WAY TO SALVATION' (1992), another entertaining selection of surreal vignettes including 'THE BOY WHO ATE LASAGNE AND COULD JUMP OVER A CHURCH' and a tribute to that great land of heather 'n' haggis, 'SCOTLAND'. 1993's 'HAPPY HOUR', meanwhile, featured such toilet humour fantasies as 'THE VULVAVOID' and 'DETACHABLE PENIS', the latter scaling the college charts to bring KING MISSILE their closest brush with fame. A Daniel Ray-produced follow-up failed to build on this success and HALL subsequently put the band on hold before re-emerging on 'Shimmy Disc' as KING MISSILE III with the string-enhanced 'FAILURE'.

Album rating: FLUTING ON THE HUMP mini (*6) / THEY (*6) / MYSTICAL SHIT (*6) / REAL MEN by John S. Hall & Kramer (*6) / THE WAY TO SALVATION (*6) / HAPPY HOUR (*6) / KING MISSILE (*6) / John S. Hall: BODY HAS A HEAD (*5)

JOHN S. HALL – vocals / **DOGBOWL** – guitars / **ALEX DeLASZLO** – harmonica / **REBECCA KORBETT** – percussion

Shadowline   Shimmy Disc

Dec 87. (m-lp; as KING MISSILE – DOG FLY RELIGION) *(SR 6987)* <SHIMMY 003> **FLUTING ON THE HUMP**
 – Love you more / Fourthly / Lou / At Dave's / Muffy / Take stuff from work / Sensitive artist / Wuss / Heavy holy man / Fluting on the hump / Dick / That old dog.

—— **STEVE DANZIGER** – percussion; repl. REBECCA

Shimmy Disc   Shimmy Disc

Nov 88. (lp; as KING MISSILE – DOG FLY RELIGION) *(SHIMMY 015)* <SDE 9023> **THEY**
 – Now / I'm open / Mr. Johnson / She had nothing / He needed / The love song / Margaret's eyes / The bunny song / The blood song / Stonehenge / They / When she closed her eyes / Hemopheliac of love / The box / Fish / Leather clown / WW3 is a giant ice cream cone / Farm / As I walked thru queens / Hey Jesus / If only / Double fucked by 2 black studs.

—— In '89, the departing DOGBOWL issued his solo debut, 'Tit! An Opera'. Two years later, he made another, 'Cyclops Nuclear Submarine Captain'.

—— added **DAVE RICK** – guitar (ex-BONGWATER) / **CHRIS XEFOS** – multi (of WHEN PEOPLE WERE SHORTER)

Feb 90. (lp) <(SDE 9016LP)> **MYSTICAL SHIT**
 – Mystical shit / Rock'n'roll will never die / No point / Gary and Melissa / Frightened and freezing / How to remember your dreams / The fish that played the ponies / Jesus was way cool / Open / The sandbox / The neither world / She didn't want / Cheesecake truck / Equivalencies.

Atlantic   Atlantic

Aug 91. (12") <85974> **MY HEART IS A FLOWER (mixes). / JESUS WAS WAY COOL (live)**
Mar 92. (cd/c/lp) <(7567 82208-2/-4/-1)> **THE WAY TO SALVATION**
 – The way to salvation / Life / The boy who ate lasagna & could jump over a church / The story of Willy / Dinosaurs / I wish / The Indians / It's / My heart is a flower / Pickaxe / Sex with you / art two / Betrayal takes two / Listen to me / Come closer / Scotland / To walk among the pigs.
Feb 93. (cd/c) <(7567 82589-2/-4)> **HAPPY HOUR**
 – Sink / Martin Scorcese (Why are we) Trapped? / It's Saturday / The vulvavoid / Metanoia / Detachable penis / Take me home / Ed / Anywhere / The evil children / Glass / And / King Murdoch / I'm sorry / Happy hour.
Jun 94. (cd) <(7567 82589-2)> **KING MISSILE**
 – Love is / Let's have sex / Pigs will fly / Tongue / The dishwasher / Bloodletting / Socks / King David's dirge / What if / These people / Open up / Wind up toys / Delores / Lies / The commercial / Psalm / Happy note.

—— split but reformed as KING MISSILE III:- **HALL** / + **SASHA FORTE** – vocals, guitar, violin, viola, bass, bells / **BRADFORD REED** – vocals, multi / **JANE SCARPANTONI** – cello, synthesizer / **CHARLES CURTIS** – vocals, guitar, cello

Shimmy Disc   Shimmy Disc

Oct 98. (cd) <(SHM 5090)> **FAILURE**   Sep98
 – Failure / The boy made out of bone China / A good hard look / Up my ass / The little sandwich that got a guilt complex because he was the sole survivor of a horrible bus crash / Despair / Monks / Gay – not gay! / Happiness / Mr. Pomerantz / Juniper dog / Tour diary: Louisville / The adventures of Planky / I dare to hope.

—— KING MISSILE returned for an album in early 2003

JOHN S. HALL

Shimmy Disc   Shimmy Disc

1991. (cd; by JOHN S. HALL & KRAMER) <(SHIMMY 042CD)> **REAL MEN**
 – Enjoy your tea / Things / Clarity transcending choice / The birds / My life / How much longer / Mr. Story / Wind-up toys / Knowledge / Garbage party / The Spanish armada / Hide the knives / Shit / Everybody screams inside / Pain and pleasure / The party / Columbus day weekend / My personal life / Francis Bacon / Empty / The trees / The absolute / Real men / Water.

—— next with **SCARPANTONI + BRADFORD REED**, etc

Bob's Airport   Manifatture Criminal

Nov 96. (cd) *(BOB 104)* <4154> **BODY HAS A HEAD**
 – The bunny who wanted to be a rat / Punish him / A good hard look / On the metro north / The friendly man / Keep walking / My lover / Wizard / A little restraint / Clamsauce / Satan / Freyne / The angel / Nine wishes / Prophecy.

KING OF LUXEMBOURG

Formed: London, England... 1986 as the nom de plume for Dover-born child star/actor, sound designer and modern composer/songwriter, SIMON FISHER-TURNER. SIMON's pre-KING OF LUXEMBOURG was indeed surprisingly plentiful, his youthful musical beginnings (he was aged 17+ and the English version of DAVID CASSIDY) coming courtesy of JONATHAN KING in the early 70's. A barrage of cover singles, from Bowie's 'THE PRETTIEST STAR' to 'Stephen Stills' 'SIT DOWN I THINK I LOVE YOU', all flopped, and in the words of SIMON himself, better left dead and buried. Things took a turn for the better at the turn of the decade (having acted alongside Robert Mitchum and Joan Collins), when he was given the job of backing MATT JOHNSON and COLIN LLOYD TUCKER in indie act, The GADGETS. While the former would hit gold with the legendary THE THE, the latter remained at the helm of SIMON's next dual projects, DEUX FILLES (two French girls) and JEREMY'S SECRET (see discography for LP releases). During the mid-80's, and after a period serving the late Derek Jarman on his controversial film project, 'Caravaggio', FISHER-TURNER took on the persona of The KING OF LUXEMBOURG. Opening KOL's musical account in 1986 – on Mike Alway's 'El' records – with a cover of 'VALLERI' (once a minor hit for the Monkees), the debonair TURNER seemed to have finally found his niche. With the advent of twee indie pop through rights-of-passage C-86 bands, his KING OF LUXEMBOURG were beginning to make inroads into the minds and ears of trendy fashionable Londoners. However, after only two mooted sets, 'ROYAL BASTARD' (1987) and 'SIR' (1988), SIMON abandoned this project (and moonlighting project, BAD DREAM FANCY DRESS) to once again go solo. As SIMON TURNER (the same moniker he utilised in the early 70's), he recorded a solitary mini-album in spring 1990 for Alan McGee's 'Creation' imprint. His subsequent solo work was mainly of the soundtrack variety, although during the late 90's (having recorded for 'Mute' records), he branched out with The HANGOVERS, a group that featured GINA BIRCH of The RAINCOATS. Around the same period, 1999 to be exact, SIMON turned in some of his best work to date, the solo 'STILL, MOVING, LIGHT' and with his LOVELETTER project, 'BEETHOVEN CHOPIN KITCHEN FRAUD'. 2002 saw him return as SFT (he'd used this moniker for 1996's 'SCHWARMA' soundtrack) and his film collage compilations 'SWIFT', a part CD/part DVD release – yes, a man with vision.

Album rating: ROYAL BASTARD (*6) / SIR (*5) / Bad Dream Fancy Dress: CHOIRBOYS GAS (*4) / Simon Turner: SIMON TURNER (*5) / THE MANY MOODS OF ... collection (*5) / SEX APPEAL collection (*6) / Loveletter: BEETHOVEN CHOPIN KITCHEN FRAUD (*5) / Simon Fisher-Turner: STILL, MOVING, LIGHT (*5) / TRAVELCARD (*4)

SIMON FISHER-TURNER (b.21 Nov'54, Dover, England) – vocals, instruments

El   not iss.

Jul 86. (7") *(GPO 14)* **VALLERI. / SKETCHES OF LUXEMBOURG**
Mar 87. (12"ep) *(GPO 24T)* **A PICTURE OF DORIAN GRAY**
 – A picture of Dorian Gray / Hasta pronto / Lee Remick / Espedarte / Where are the prawns?
May 87. (lp) *(ACME 3)* **ROYAL BASTARD**
 – A picture of Dorian Gray / Valleri / The Rubens room / Mad / Poptones / Something / Baby / Wedding of Ramona Blair / Happy together (prelude) / Liar liar.
Sep 87. (lp; as SIMON FISHER-TURNER) *(ACME 6)* **CARAVAGGIO 1610** (soundtrack)
 – The hills of Abruzzi / Dog star / All paths lead to Rome / Fantasia, childhood memories / How blue sky was / Light and dark (from 'Missa Lux Et Orrigo') / Umber wastes / Cafe of the moors / Timeout and mind / In the still of the night / Michele of the shadows / The waters of forgetfullness / Running, running / Frescobaldi, the greatest organist of our time / Hourglass / I love you more than my eyes.
Oct 87. (7") *(GPO 32)* **TRIAL OF DR. FANCY. / ELUSIVE PIMPERNEL (LE CHEVALIER DE LONDRES)**
Aug 88. (7") *(GPO 38)* **FLIRT. / BLISS LOVE KISS**
Sep 88. (lp/cd) *(ACME 16/+CD)* **SIR**
 – Flirt / Personality parade / Walnut whirl / Sorry / Penny was a tomboy / Chateau Palmer '61 / Turban disturbance / Battle for beauty / The Queen of Luxembourg / Her eyes are a blue million miles / Virgin on the rocks / Trial of Dr. Fancy / Straits of Malacca / How to get on in society / Lee Remick. *(cd+=)* – ROYAL BASTARD

BAD DREAM FANCY DRESS

TURNER + DEAN BRODERICK + KEITH WEST plus **CALLY + KATZ**

Mar 88. (10") *(GPO 33T)* **CURRY CRAZY. / UP THE KING OF LUXEMBOURG**
Nov 88. (7") *(GPO 41)* **THE SUPREMES. / CHOIRBOYS GAS**
Nov 88. (lp) *(ACME 18)* **CHOIRBOYS GAS**
 – The Supremes / Lemon tarts / Choirboys gas / Where have all the schoolboys gone? / Foreign muck / Discotheque / Kick in the teeth / Dali's diet / Leigh-On-Sea / Curry crazy / Colour problem / Rave-up. *(<cd-iss. Jul00 on 'Richmond'+=; MONDE 10CD>)* – Up the King Of Luxembourg / Flair / You wind me up.
Sep 89. (7") *(GPO 42)* **FLAIR. / YOU WIND ME UP**
 (12"+=) *(GPO 42T)* – ('A'extended).

SIMON FISHER-TURNER

Creation   not iss.

Apr 90. (m-cd/m-c/m-lp; as SIMON TURNER) *(CRE CD/C/LP 64)* **SIMON TURNER**
 – Almost bliss / Warm melt / Dark melt / Muzak / Bliss / Pop shop (90).

Fine Line   not iss.

Jan 01. (cd) *(IONIC 5CD)* **THE GARDEN** (soundtrack)
 – Blue landscape / Drowned by time / Altars of peace / Fill the silence with false notes / My melancholy stones / Clock faced flower beds / Twelve apostles dance / Cool marble arms / Rushing forgotten secrets.

KING OF LUXEMBOURG (cont)

Nov 91. (cd; as SFT) (IONIC 8CD) **THE EDWARD II** (soundtrack) — Humbug / not iss.
May 93. (cd) (BAH 7) **LIVE IN JAPAN** (live)
Feb 94. (cd) (BAH 16) **REVOX**
– Scott / I just woke up man, is it too early / Miaw / Blackouts / Sappora sky / Pop song 93 / The fall / The boxer / Luch at Great Rissington / Recover / Where are we going / Iona / Stuck inside lady / Mr. Davidson's tube / Moist.

—— in 1994, SIMON provided the score for Jarman's film, 'Blue'

Mute / not iss.
Jun 95. (cd; as LIVE BLUE ROMA) (CDSTUMM 149) **THE ARCHAEOLOGY OF SOUND**
– Chapter I: The blue mood / Chapter II: Open your eyes / Chapter III: The further one goes / Chapter IV: Mind how you go / Chapter V: Black floaters / Chapter VI: Charity / Chapter VII: Youths of the sun / Chapter VIII: Pure blue / Chapter IX: Interference / Chapter X: Flares and dyes / Chapter XI: Kiss me again / Chapter XII: The indigo shores / Chapter XIII: Pearl fishers.
Apr 96. (cd) (IONIC 16CD) **NADJA** (soundtrack)
– The dead travel fast / Allergy to sunlight / No comfort in the bloody shadows / Isle of spices / Pixsmiles / Stake in the heart / Lunch at Great Rissington / Love, death, avoid it / Orchestrated gravel.
Sep 96. (cd; as SFT) (CDSTUMM 151) **SCHWARMA**
– Jazz / Classical piano / Young & beautiful / Lower / Cut / Bm / Dica – Whoa / Low / New song / Drum / Sequel / Gong – Echo / Last sky / Ski / Strung out / Endbang.

—— in 1997, he scored the soundtrack for Anna Campion's 'Loaded'
—— next was his collaboration with **ROSEMARY BUTCHER**

Cherry Red / not iss.
Mar 99. (cd) (CDBRED 153) **STILL, MOVING, LIGHT**
– Still / Peeling away / Fragment 21 / 2 white / Displace / Swallow line / The harder you look, the more you see / Recover / Change of speed / Pathway of the spine.

LOVELETTER

aka **SIMON**

Siesta / not iss.
Apr 99. (cd/lp) (SIESTA 96 CD/LP) **BEETHOVEN CHOPIN KITCHEN FRAUD**
– Forget that girl / Penelope / On days like these / Red chair fadeaway / Through spray coloured glasses / Apples & oranges / Sun / Dreamworld / Wind up toys / Mr Loveletter / Psychedelic love / Rose petals incense & a kitten / R.S.V.P. / Who is Penelope?

SIMON FISHER-TURNER

Mute / not iss.
May 99. (m-cd) (CDSTUMM 169) **OH VENUS**
– Dekaparts / Perfume / Eyes open / Pearl / Rose / Velcrose / Oh / Marlborough country / Min.

Sulphur / Beggars Banquet
Jul 00. (cd; as SIMON FISHER) (SULCD 005) <80006> **TRAVELCARD** — Sep00
– Hole entry / Phote / Slope / Twice two / Guitar pule / Filter / Sleeper drought / Close.

Mute / Mute
Aug 02. (cd; as SFT) (<CDSTUMM 197>) **SWIFT: A CD & DVD 50.21 TWENTY PIECES OF MUSIC, FILM & SILENCE** — Sep02
– Deum de Deo / So long, isolated sunshine / Youngtoolong / A difficult cat to pill / S-bahn / Hawthorn / Silentsurface / Strew / Tusalava / Glia / Fasika / Colourfaker / The blunted needle / Softplay / Senapsis / Pitanga / Microgroovers / Sandsong / Lastordersplease / Pebbledashed // (+ DVD tracks).

– compilations, etc. –

Oct 92. (cd) Richmond; (MONDE 7) **"SEX APPEAL": THE FANTASTIC WORLD OF SIMON TURNER**
– SIMON TURNER: The prettiest star / Wild thing / 17 / Love around / Sit down I think I love you / Shoeshine boy / I wanna love my life away / She was just a young girl / Sex appeal / I've been a bad bad boy / California revisited: Surf city / Simon talk // THE KING OF LUXEMBOURG: A picture of Dorian Gray / Valleri / The Rubens room / Smash hit wonder / Trial of Dr. Fancy / Lee Remick / Flirt / Personality parade / Straits of Malacca / Poptones. <US-iss.Nov99; same as UK>
1993. (cd) Richmond; (MONDE 14) **THE MANY MOODS OF SIMON TURNER**
– Isles of spice / Exotic hats / Esperanza / Caravaggio 1986 / Sloane Square / A gourmet's love song / Colours of my life / Violet crumble.

– SIMON's pre-KOL days –

SIMON TURNER

UK / not iss.
Nov 72. (7") (UK 20) **SHOESHINE BOY. / 17**
Mar 73. (7") (UK 33) **BABY. / LOVE AROUND**
Apr 73. (7") (UK 37) **BABY. / I WANNA LOVE MY LIFE AWAY**
Jun 73. (7") (UK 44) **THE PRETTIEST STAR. / LOVE AROUND**
Nov 73. (7") (UK 52) **CALIFORNIA REVISITED, SURF CITY. / FUN FUN FUN, ETC.**
Mar 74. (7") (UK 60) **SHE WAS JUST A YOUNG GIRL (NO WAY). / I'LL TAKE YOUR HAND**
Aug 74. (7") (UK 74) **SEX APPEAL. / LITTLE LADY**

—— in the early 80's, SIMON augmented MATT JOHNSON and COLIN LLOYD TUCKER in The GADGETS (a group which evolved into THE THE)

DEUX FILLES

SIMON FISHER-TURNER + COLIN LLOYD TUCKER

Mar 83. (lp) (PULP 31) **SILENCE & WISDOM**
– The letter / L'intrigue / Drinking at a stream / Oakwood green / Children of clay / Sur la plage / Her master's voice / The draw in room / She slides / Fleurs doll / Mortuary / The city sleeps / Birds / Silence and wisdom / Festival.
Jun 83. (7"; as JEREMY'S SECRET) (PULPTT 12) **THE KEY TO JEREMY'S SECRET**
Mar 84. (c-s) (T5) **DAY FOR NIGHT**
(above issued on 'Touch', below on 'Deep Six')
May 84. (lp; as JEREMY'S SECRET) (DEEP 001) **THE SNOWBALL EFFECT**
Oct 84. (lp) (PULP 32) **DOUBLE HAPPINESS**

SIMON FISHER-TURNER

Papier Mache / not iss.
Nov 85. (lp) (PULP 33) **BONE OF DESIRE**

KING OF THE SLUMS

Formed: Salford, Manchester, England ... mid 80's by writer/poet, CHARLEY KEIGHER along with electric violinist, SARAH CURTIS. The duo made their vinyl debut around Xmas '86 with the independently released 'SPIDER PSYCHIATRY', subsequently spending the following year locating a solid rhythm section and finally settling on JON CHANDLER and STUART OWEN (the latter replacing a succession of drummers after their early 1988 second EP, 'ENGLAND'S FINEST HOPES'). All the aforementioned tracks along with early 89's single and EP package, 'BOMBS AWAY ON HARPURHEY' and 'VICIOUS BRITISH BOYFRIEND', were collected together on that year's debut long-player, 'BARBAROUS ENGLISH FAYRE'. Avant-garde but danceable, the focal point of this unorthodox alternative act was KEIGHER's scathing lyrical diatribes against the British establishment and its inherent racism, class divide and nationalistic bent. Having already taken on a new bass and drum team of ADAM and CHARLIE, KEIGHER and CURTIS added guitarist GARY SPARKES and yet another bassist, JAMES CASHAN prior to the release of a debut album proper, 'DANDELIONS' (1989). Undergoing yet more personnel upheaval as PETE MASON replaced SPARKES, the band would move from 'Midnight Music' to 'Cherry Red' for what would turn out to be their swansong offering, 'BLOWZY WEIRDOS' (1991).

Album rating: BARBAROUS ENGLISH FAYRE (*6) / DANDELIONS (*7) / BLOWZY WEIRDOS (*5)

CHARLIE KEIGHER – vocals / **SARAH CURTIS** – electric violin

S.L.R. / not iss.
Dec 86. (7") (SLR 001) **SPIDER PSYCHIATRY. / THE LODGE / LOSING GROUND**

—— added **JON CHANDLER** – bass / drummers in the 80's; **TREVOR RISING, ROSS CAIN + GED O'BRIEN**

Play Hard / not iss.
Feb 88. (12"ep) (DEC 88) **ENGLAND'S FINEST HOPES**
– The Pennine splitter / England's leading light / Venerate me utterly / Bedevilment's favourite son.

—— **STUART OWEN** – drums (now more permanent)
Jan 89. (7") (DEC 13) **BOMBS AWAY ON HARPURHEY. / BIG GIRL'S BLOUSE**
Feb 89. (12"ep) (DEC 14) **VICIOUS BRITISH BOYFRIEND**
– Fanciable headcase / Leery bleeder / Hardcore pornography star / Bombs away on Harpurhey.

—— new rhythm for '89 **ADAM + CHARLIE**
Jun 89. (lp) (DEC 22) **BARBAROUS ENGLISH FAYRE**
– Simpering blonde bombshell / Bombs away on Harpurhey / England's leading light / Mere slip of a lad / The Pennine splitter / Up to the fells / Full speed ahead / Venerate me utterly / Bedevilment's favourite son / Leery bleeder / Fanciable headcase / Hardcore pornography star. (re-iss. Jan91 on 'Midnight Music' lp/cd; CHIME 109/+CD)

—— **JAMES CASHAN** – bass; repl. CHANDLER
—— added **GARY SPARKES** – guitar

Midnight Music / not iss.
Oct 89. (12"m) (DONG 57) **ONCE A PREFECT. / IDOLATOR / VENERATE ME UTTERLY**
Nov 89. (lp/c/cd) (CHIME 104/+C/CD) **DANDELIONS**
– Schooley / Armed robbery / Unfit mother / Violate nothing but the best / Up she rises / Barbarous superiors / Idolator / Ardent swains / Up the empire – Balls to the bulldog breed / Psycho motorbike ride / Bear wiv me.

—— **PETE MASON** – guitar; repl. SPARKES
Jul 90. (one-sided-12") (DONG 63) **IT'S DEAD SMART**
Sep 90. (12") (DONG 66) **BEAR WIV ME** (fluorescent mix)

Cherry Red / not iss.
Apr 91. (12"m) (12CHERRY 114) **JOY. / (+2)**
May 91. (cd/lp) (CD+/BRED 93) **BLOWZY WEIRDOS**
– Gone all weirdo / Smile so big / Casin' the joint / Hot pot shebeen / Keeping it all sweet / Clubland gangs / Joy / Rimo / Hard arse / Mood on / Blowzy luv of life. (cd+=) – Casin' the joint (rollin') / Gone all weirdo (reaper mix) / Joy (skunkweed) / Smiles (big smiles mix).

—— split later in 1991

KITCHENS OF DISTINCTION

Formed: Tooting Broadway, London, England... 1986 by the multicultural trio of PATRICK FITZGERALD, JULIAN SWALES and DANIEL GOODWIN. Named after a "fitted kitchen" ad slogan, this bunch achieved almost instantaneous acclaim when their self-financed debut single, 'LAST GASP DEATH SHUFFLE', was awarded an NME Single Of The Week award. Acclaimed for their innovative amalgam of indie guitar strumming, pre-shoegazing effects and dub-style dynamics, The KITCHENS continued to impress with a further two singles, 'THE PRIZE' and 'THE THIRD TIME WE OPENED THE CAPSULE' and a debut album, 'LOVE IS HELL' (1989) via a deal with Derek Birkett's (ex-FLUX OF PINK INDIANS) 'One Little Indian' label. Much was made of FITZGERALD's openly homosexual lyrical stance, hardly a common topic of discussion in indie/alternative circles, at least not since the heyday of TOM ROBINSON. Whether this affected the band's popularity is a moot point but there was no question that column inches weren't being matched by record sales despite another fine release in the 'ELEPHANTINE' EP. The trio's cult ascendancy slowed considerably with follow-up album, 'STRANGE FREE WORLD' (1991), a minor chart placing as near to mainstream success as The KITCHENS would ever come. Moreover, by the release of 1992's 'THE DEATH OF COOL', the band's dark appeal had become slightly diluted with an overblown, almost U2-esque "big rock" sound. Wider recognition was looking as unlikely as ever, 'One Little Indian' bailing out after 'COWBOYS AND ALIENS' (1994). Scaling down their ambitions, the band subsequently clipped their moniker to KITCHENS O.D. and signed to hip indie label, 'Fierce Panda', for a one-off single, 'FEEL MY GENIE'. FITZGERALD almost immediately became FRUIT for a solo project that spanned over one EP, 'WHAT IS FRUIT?' (featuring rough covers of Gershwin's 'THE MAN I LOVE' and 'Hammerstein-Rodgers' 'CLIMB EV'RY MOUNTAIN') and an album, 'HARK AT HER' (1997); the latter saw guest spots for DAVID McALMONT, ISABEL MONTIERO and MIKI BERENYI. Thinking on his feet again, FITZY took on the role of STEPHEN HERO (a name lifted from James Joyce's novel 'Portrait Of The Artist As A Young Man'), although SWALES and veteran drummer DAVE MORGAN were in tow. Two mini-sets, 'LANDED' and LULLBY' were issued in 2000 and 2001 respectively, while his/their first full-set, 'DARKNESS & THE DAY' (for 'Artful' records), came out in spring 2002; ex-MIRACLE LEGION leader MARK MULCAHY provided guest vocals on the track, 'THANKS, NO AFRAID'.

Album rating: LOVE IS HELL (*7) / STRANGE FREE WORLD (*8) / THE DEATH OF COOL (*7) / COWBOYS AND ALIENS (*6) / Fruit: HARK AT HER (*5) / Stephen Hero: LANDED mini (*6) / LULLABY mini (*6) / DARKNESS & THE DAY (*6)

PATRICK FITZGERALD (b. 7 Apr'64, Basel, Switzerland) – vocals / **JULIAN SWALES** (b.23 Mar'64, Gwent, Wales) – guitar / **DANIEL GOODWYN** (b.22 Jul'64, Salamanca, Spain) – drums (ex-AR KANE)

Goldrush / not iss.

Oct 87. (7") (GRR 3) **ESCAPE. / THE LAST GASP DEATH SHUFFLE**

One Little Indian / A&M

Oct 88. (12"ep) (12 TP12) **PRIZE. / CONCEDE / INNOCENT**
May 89. (12"ep) (19 TP12) **THE THIRD TIME WE OPENED THE CAPSULE / 4 MEN. / INTO THE SEA / PRIZE (demo)**
May 89. (lp/c/cd) (TP LP/C/CD 9) <31454 0098-2> **LOVE IS HELL** Feb90
– In a cave / Time to groan / Shiver / Prize / The 3rd time we opened the capsule / Her last day in bed / Courage, mother / Mainly mornings / Hammer.
Oct 89. (12"ep/cd-ep) (29 TP 12/7CD) **ELEPHANTINY / MARGARET'S INJECTION. / THE 1000st FAULT / ANVIL DUB**
Apr 90. (12"ep/cd-ep) (43 TP 12/7CD) **QUICK AS RAINBOWS. / MAINLY MORNINGS (live) / IN A CAVE (live) / SHIVER**
May 90. (cd-ep) <75021 7226-2> **GORGEOUS LOVE / PRIZE (demo) / CONCEDE / INNOCENT**
Aug 90. (12") <75021 7494-1> **DRIVE THAT FAST. / RAILWAYED**
 (cd-s) <75021 7488-2> – ('A'edit) / ('A'side).
Nov 90. (12"ep/cd-ep) <75021 7534-1/7536-2> **QUICK AS RAINBOWS / THESE DRINKERS / ELEPHANTINY / THREE TO BEAM UP**
Feb 91. (12"ep/cd-ep) (49 TP 12/7CD) **DRIVE THAT FAST / THESE DRINKERS. / ELEPHANTINY / THREE TO BEAM UP**
Mar 91. (cd/c/lp) (TP CD/C/LP 19) <75021 5340-2> **STRANGE FREE WORLD** 45
– Railwayed / Quick as rainbows / Hypnogogie / He holds her, he needs her / Polaroids / Gorgeous love / Aspray / Drive that fast / Within the days of passion / Under the sky, inside the sea.
1991. (3"cd-s) <RTD 199.0010-2> **CONCEDE / INNOCENT**
 (above issued on 'Rough Trade')
May 92. (12"ep) (59 TP12) **BREATHING FEAR / GOODBYE VOYAGER. / SMILING / WHEN IN HEAVEN**
 (12"/cd-s) (59 TP 12/CD) – (first two tracks) / Skin (instrumental) / Air shifting (instrumental).
Aug 92. (lp/c/cd) (TPLP 39/+C/CD) <75021 5402-2> **THE DEATH OF COOL** 72
– What happens now? / 4 men / On Tooting Broadway station / Breathing fear / Gone world gone / When in Heaven / Mad as snow / Smiling / Blue pedal / Can't trust the waves.
Sep 92. (12"ep/cd-ep) (69 TP 12/7CD) **WHEN IN HEAVEN / GLITTERY DUST. / DON'T COME BACK / SPACEDOLPHINS**
Oct 92. (cd-s) <31458 8038-2> **4 MEN / GOODBYE VOYAGER / SKIN**
Sep 94. (c-s/12"/cd-s) (111 TP 7C/12/7CD) **NOW IT'S TIME TO SAY GOODBYE. / JESUS NEVADA / WHITE HORSES / WHAT WE REALLY WANTED TO DO**
Sep 94. (lp/c/cd) (TPLP 53/+C/CD) <314 540227-4/-2> **COWBOYS AND ALIENS**
– Sand on fire / Get over yourself / Thought he had everything / Cowboys and aliens / Come on now / Remember me? / One of these sometimes is now / Here comes the swans / Now it's time to say goodbye / Pierced / Prince of Mars.
Oct 94. (cd-ep) <31458 8377-2> **COWBOYS AND ALIENS / JESUS NEVADA / WHITE HORSES / WHAT WE REALLY WANTED TO DO**

Fierce Panda / not iss.

May 96. (7"/cd-s; as KITCHENS O.D.) (NING 19/+CD) **FEEL MY GENIE. / TO LOVE A STAR**

—— the band split; PATRICK formed...

FRUIT

PATRICK FITZGERALD solo with **JULIAN SWALES** + **DAN GOODWIN** – drums, percussion / with guests **ISABEL MONTIERO** (of DRUGSTORE) / **MIKI BERENYI** (of LUSH) + **DAVID McALMONT**

One Little Indian / not iss.

Nov 96. (cd-ep) (TPCD 120) **WHAT IS FRUIT? / GENE K. / THE MAN I LOVE / CLIMB EV'RY MOUNTAIN**
Feb 97. (cd) (TPLPCD 75) **HARK AT HER**
– What is fruit? / Pleasure yourself / Vile / Sally's car / Starring relationship / Close personal friends / Prowler / Leather jacket / Reprise / Silver girl / Vienna weirdo / Soatter me.

—— PATRICK (+ JULIAN) later became STEPHEN HERO

STEPHEN HERO

PATRICK FITZGERALD – vocals, bass / **JULIAN SWALES** – guitar / **DAVE MORGAN** – drums, programmer (ex-PRIMAL SCREAM, ex-WEATHER PROPHETS)

Ragoora / not iss.

Oct 00. (m-cd) (RAG 001) **LANDED**
– Walden / Land / A howl? at 3 a.m. / Krave / The Nobel Prize is mine / Childhood poetry / Being brave.
May 01. (cd-ep) (RAG 002) **LULLABY**
– Lullaby for a broken dog / Lull 2 (Hamlet was a prince) / Lull 5 (Venus slipped) / Lull 3 (night fairy guide) / Lull 4 (I know who is sick) / Lull 1 (feed me on the banks of the River Nile afterlife).

Track & Field / not iss.

Mar 02. (7") (LANE 13) **CYCLE VARIATION** (split w/ CANE 141)

—— now without SWALES

Artful / not iss.

Apr 02. (cd) (ARTFULCD 44) **DARKNESS & THE DAY**
– Foolish things / Fall (let the water get close) / My beautiful one / Hexmass waltz / NYC / The dark dirt / Laughing gas / Making sense / She got fever / The sun shall walk us home / (The march home) / Thanks, not afraid / E flat.

Chris KNOX (see under ⇒ TALL DWARFS)

Peter KOPPES (see under ⇒ CHURCH)

KRAMER (see under ⇒ BONGWATER)

Victor KRUMMENACHER (see under ⇒ CAMPER VAN BEETHOVEN)

KUKL (see under ⇒ BJORK)

THE GREAT INDIE DISCOGRAPHY — The 1980s

Mark LANEGAN (see under ⇒ SCREAMING TREES)

Gerard LANGLEY & Ian KEAREY (see under ⇒ BLUE AEROPLANES)

LARD (see under ⇒ DEAD KENNEDYS; 70's section)

LA'S

Formed: Liverpool, England ... 1984 by songwriters MIKE BADGER (ex-KINDERGARTEN PAINTSET) and LEE MAVERS, along with drummer JOHN TIMSON; a limited V/A sampler 'A Secret Liverpool' exists of these times. When an inexperienced young bass player JOHN POWER joined the well-touted LA'S (alongside brief member PAUL HEMMINGS), things began to change, friction also set-in between BADGER and MAVERS, the former bailing out and disappearing into the world of sculpture and painting (he had been a great fan of CAPTAIN BEEFHEART!). Signing to 'Go! Discs' early in 1987, the new LA'S (with MAVERS at the helm) released the charming retro-pop debut single, 'WAY OUT'. The record was well received but failed to chart and replacing TIMSON with CHRIS SHARROCK, the band followed up the single with the seminal BYRDS-like pop genius of 'THERE SHE GOES', all soaring melodies and youthful vigour. Incredibly, the single failed to chart, although it later reached the Top 20 when it was re-released in 1990 at the same time as the eponymous debut. Over the two year period it took to record the album, MAVERS' friend BARRY SUTTON replaced SHARROCK on the drum stool while JAMES JOYCE was recruited for the departing POWER (who went on to form the highly successful CAST). CAMMY, another guitarist, was also added. Part of the problem was the notoriously perfectionist MAVERS who obsessed over every tiny detail of the recording process in his search for an 'authentic' sound. 'Go! Discs' became increasingly worried about the escalating cost of the project and decided to go ahead and release the album against MAVERS' wishes. He retaliated by criticising the company in press interviews and dismissed the debut as a collection of demos. In reality, the album was a seamless collection of post-baggy guitar pop, drawing comparisons with the STONE ROSES and garnering almost universal acclaim. After a tour of America and Japan in 1991, the band went to ground and little has been heard from them since, save a brief, disastrous appearance supporting PAUL WELLER in 1994. While rumours continue to abound, the band remain one of the greatest modern day musical enigmas. BADGER finally emerged as a solo artist (he had worked for SPACE on the cover of 'Tin Planet') at the beginning of 1999, an album 'VOLUME' (on his SPACE mate TOMMY SCOTT's new 'Viper' imprint and produced by new LIGHTNING SEEDS man PAUL HEMMINGS) was the missing piece in The LA's troubled rock'n'roll history. A subsequent tabloid grouch by the equally reclusive MAVERS on the worthiness of CAST frontman JOHN POWER was given short shrift – meanwhile SIXPENCE NONE THE RICHER (how well named) were high in the US charts with the LA'S classic, 'THERE SHE GOES'.

Album rating: THE LA'S (*8) / BREAKLOOSE (LOST LA'S 1983-86) (*6) / Mike Badger: VOLUME (*6)

LEE MAVERS (b. 2 Aug'62) – vocals, guitar / **JOHN TIMSON** – drums / added **JOHN POWER** (b.14 Sep'67) – bass

— (late '86) MIKE BADGER was repl. by **PAUL HEMMINGS** – guitar / **JOHN 'BOO' BYRNE** – guitar

	Go! Discs	London
Oct 87. (7") *(GOLAS 1)* **WAY OUT. / ENDLESS**		
(12"+=) *(GOLAS 1-12)* – Knock me down.		
(12"++=) *(GOLAR 1-12)* – Liberty ship (demo) / Freedom song (demo).		
— **CHRIS SHARROCK** – drums (ex-ICICLE WORKS) repl. TIMSON		
Nov 88. (7") *(GOLAS 2)* **THERE SHE GOES. / COME IN, COME OUT**	59	
(12"+=)(cd-s+=) *(GOLAS 2-12)(LASCD 2)* – Who knows / Man I'm only human.		
(7"ep+=) *(LASEP 2)* – Who knows / Way out (new version).		
May 89. (7";w-drawn) *(GOLAS 3)* **TIMELESS MELODY. / CLEAN PROPHET**	-	-
(10"+=; w-drawn) *(LASEP 3)* – All by myself / There she goes.		
(cd-s+=; w-drawn) *(LASCD 3)* – All by myself / Ride yer camel.		
— **NEIL MAVERS** (b. 8 Jul'71) – drums repl. SHARROCK / **JAMES JOYCE** (b.23 Sep'70) – bass repl. POWER who formed CAST / added **CAMMY** (b.PETER JAMES CAMELL, 30 Jun'67) – guitar (ex-MARSHMALLOW)		
Sep 90. (7"/c-s) *(GOLAS/LASMC 4)* **TIMELESS MELODY. / CLEAN PROPHET**	57	
(12"purple+=)(cd-s+=) *(GOLAS 4-12)(LASCD 4)* – Knock me down / Over.		
Oct 90. (cd/c/lp) *(<828 202-2/-4/-1>)* **THE LA'S**	30	
– Son of a gun / I can't sleep / Timeless melody / Liberty ship / There she goes / Doledrum / Feelin' / Way out / I.O.U. / Freedom song / Failure / Looking glass. *(cd re-iss. Sep99 on 'Polydor'; same) (cd re-mast.Jan01 on 'Universal'+=; 549566-2)* – All by myself / Clean prophet / Knock me down / Over (live) / IOU (alt.take).		
Oct 90. (7"/c-s) *(GOLAS/LASMC 5)* **THERE SHE GOES (new version). / FREEDOM SONG**	13	-
(12"+=)(cd-s+=) *(GOLAS 5-12)(LASCD 5)* – All by myself.		
Feb 91. (7"/c-s) *(GOLAS/LASMC 6)* **FEELIN'. / DOLEDRUM**	43	-
(12"+=)(cd-s+=)(7"ep+=) *(GOLAS 6-12)(LASCD 6)(GOLAB 6)* – I.O.U. (alt.version) / Liberty ship.		
Jun 91. (c-s) *<869 370-4>* **THERE SHE GOES / ALL BY MYSELF**	-	49

— had already disbanded just prior to above. In Apr'97 a various artists EP (taken from the movie, 'Fever Pitch', featured 'THERE SHE GOES' (issued on 'Blanco Yo Negro'; NEG 104 C/T/CD)

– compilations, etc. –

Sep 99. (cd-s) *Polydor; (561403-2)* **THERE SHE GOES / COME IN COME OUT / WHO KNOWS**	65	-
Oct 99. (cd/lp) *Viper; (VIPER 2 CD/LP)* **BREAKLOOSE (LOST LA'S 1984-1986)**		-
– Breakloose (live) / Open your heart / Sweet 35 / Trees and plants / Red deer stalk / Dovecot dub / Walk / Get down over / What do you do / I did the painting / My girl sits like reindeer / Money in your talk / You blue / Moonlight.		
Jul 01. (cd/lp) *Viper; (VIPER 8 CD/LP)* **CALLIN' ALL (LOST LA'S 1986-1987)**		-

LAUGHING APPLE (see under ⇒ McGEE, Alan)

LAUGHING CLOWNS

Formed: Sydney, Australia ... late 70's by former SAINTS guitarist/singer, EDMUND KUEPPER. Following his departure from the band in early '79, KUEPPER returned to his beloved Australia and, along with cousins DAN and BEN WALLACE-CRABBE, ROBERT FARRELL and JEFFREY WEGENER, formed The LAUGHING CLOWNS. Signed to Aussie label, 'Prince Melon', the group debuted in late 1980 with an EP, 'SOMETIMES ... THE FIRE DANCE', following it up with a second four-tracker, '3', early in '81. Avant-garde but surprisingly listenable, The LAUGHING CLOWNS sound was certainly a departure from the sweaty R&B of The SAINTS, employing often dense collages of screeching sax and trumpet (courtesy of new recruits PETER DOYLE and LOUISE ELLIOT), awkward rhythms, off-kilter time signatures and occasional bursts of eastern-tinged jazz improvisation. KUEPPER and Co. even made a foray into vaguely Afro-Cuban/mariachi territory with the melancholy brilliance of 'KNIFE IN MY HEAD', one of the standout tracks on the band's debut album, 'MR UDDICH SCHMUDDICH GOES TO TOWN' (1982). LAUGHING CLOWNS material finally saw a British release via an eponymous compilation on indie label, 'Red Flame', by which point the WALLACE-CRABBE brothers had departed. Despite the pockets of critical acclaim afforded a further two albums, 'LAW OF NATURE' (1984) and 'GHOSTS OF AN IDEAL WIFE' (1985) – the latter's title track featuring some nifty banjo playing from KUEPPER – The LAUGHING CLOWNS split in the mid-80's and KUEPPER set about carving a niche as solo artist. Generally more accessible than The LAUGHING CLOWNS, KUEPPER's solo career got underway with 1985's 'ELECTRICAL STORM' album, the atmospheric, widescreen guitar assault of the title track a long held favourite of KUEPPER obsessives. Playing most of the instruments himself with additional help from a revolving cast of musicians (of whom drummer MARK DAWSON has been the most prominent), KUEPPER kept fans and critics alike rapt by a succession of dazzling albums (almost one a year), displaying a chameleon-like ability to flit between different musical styles. While KUEPPER's striking originality makes any comparisons only a vague pointer, he has at various times sounded vaguely akin to THE THE, The SMITHS (especially on 'BLACK TICKET DAY', originally recorded for 1988's 'HAPPY AS HELL' EP), TEARDROP EXPLODES, JAMES and even R.E.M.. Critics have continually marvelled at KUEPPER's guitar technique (he can also blow a mean harmonica!), while his distinctive vocal is akin to a bastard cross between LLOYD COLE and MARK E SMITH! The archetypal cult hero, this enigmatic Aussie has gathered rave reviews without sales to match over the course of the next decade, albums such as 'ROOMS OF THE MAGNIFICENT' (1986), 'EVERYBODY'S GOT TO' (1988), 'TODAY WONDER' (1990), 'HONEY STEEL'S GOLD' (1991), 'BLACK TICKET DAY' (1992) and 'SERENE MACHINE' (1993) often featuring in the upper reaches of annual writers polls and even netting him a couple of awards back in Australia. Still going strong in the 90's, 'CHARACTER ASSASSINATION' (1994) and 'A KING IN THE KINDNESS ROOM' (1995) have shown little sign of KUEPPER mellowing, while his simultaneous career with The 'AINTS (so named as a reaction to the still-lumbering-on SAINTS) has produced a series of blistering guitar workouts via 'S.L.S.Q.' (1991), 'ASCENSION' (1991), 'AUTOCANNIBALISM' (1992) and 'AFTERLIFE' (1993), all available – as with KUEPPER's solo output – on Aussie indie label, 'Hot'. • **Songwriters:** KUEPPER except IF I WERE A CARPENTER (Tim Hardin) / WHITE HOUSES (Eric Burdon & The Animals) / HIGHWAY TO HELL (Ac/Dc) / BUILT FOR COMFORT (Willie Dixon) / CYPRUS GROVE BLUES (Elmore James) / INDIAN RESERVATION (J.D. Loudermilk) / MILK

COW BLUES (Billy Boy Arnold) / STEAM TRAIN (. . . Davies) / + a whole album worths in 'REFLECTIONS OF OL' GOLDEN EYE'.
Album rating: LAUGHING CLOWNS mini (*6) / REIGN OF TERROR – THRONE OF BLOOD (*6) / REIGN MR UDDICH SCHMUDDICH GOES TO TOWN (*6) / LAUGHTER AROUND THE TABLE (*6) / LAW OF NATURE (*5) / GHOSTS OF AN IDEAL WIFE (*5) / HISTORY OF ROCK'N'ROLL VOLUME ONE compilation (*7) / Ed Kuepper: ELECTRICAL STORM (*7) / ROOMS OF THE MAGNIFICENT (*6) / EVERYBODY'S GOT TO (*6) / TODAY WONDER (*7) / HONEY STEEL'S GOLD (*6) / BLACK TICKET DAY (*6) / LEGENDARY BULLY compilation (*6) / SERENE MACHINE (*7) / THE BUTTERFLY NET compilation (*7) / CHARACTER ASSASSINATION (*6) / A KING IN THE KINDNESS ROOM (*6) / SINGS HIS GREATEST HITS FOR YOU compilation (*6) / FRONTIERLAND (*5) / STARSTRUCK (*5) / THE WHEELIE BIN AFFAIR compilation (*5) / WITH A KNAPSACK ON MY BACK (*6) / CLOUDLAND (*5) / LIVE (*5) / REFLECTIONS OF OL' GOLDEN EYE covers compilation (*5) / 'Aints: ASCENSION (*5) / AUTOCANNIBALISM (*5) / S.L.S.Q. (*6) / AFTERLIFE (*5)

EDMUND KUEPPER (b. 1955, Germany) – vocals, guitar (ex-SAINTS) / **DAN WALLACE-CRABBE** – piano / **BEN WALLACE-CRABBE** – bass / **ROBERT FARRELL** – saxophone / **JEFFREY WEGENER** – drums

May 80. (m-lp) (MLB 001) **THE LAUGHING CLOWNS**   Missing Link / not iss. / – / – / Austra
 – Holy Joe / I want to scream / Lucky days / That's the way it goes / Eology / The laughing clowns.

Oct 80. (12"ep) (pm 01) **SOMETIMES . . . THE FIRE DANCE**   Prince Melon / not iss. / – / – / Austra
 – Sometimes (I can't live with anyone) / Crying dance / The fire might fall.

 added **PETER DOYLE** – trumpet

Jan 81. (12"ep) (pm 05) **3**   – / – / Austra
 – I don't know what I want / Collapse board / Ghost beat / Clown town / Mr. Ridiculous.

Jul 81. (lp) (pm 2000) **REIGN OF TERROR / THRONE OF BLOOD** (compilation)   – / – / Austra
 – The fire might fall / Crying dance / Sometimes / Collapse board / I don't know what I want / Ghost beat / Clown town / Mr. Ridiculous.

 LOUISE ELLIOT – saxophone; repl. BOB + DAN
 LESLIE MILLAR – bass; repl. BEN

Mar 82. (lp) (pm 5000) **MR UDDICH SCHMUDDICH GOES TO TOWN**   – / – / Austra
 – In front of your eyes / Come one, come all / Laughter around the table / Knife in the head / Theme from "Mad flies, mad flies" / A song of joy / Mr. Uddich Schmuddich goes to town / When what you see . . .

Aug 82. (7") (pm 020) **THEME FROM MAD FLIES, MAD FLIES. / MR. UDDICH SCHMUDDICH GOES TO TOWN**   – / –

Aug 82. (lp) (rf 14) **LAUGHING CLOWNS** (compilation)   Red Flame / not iss. / – / –
 – The fire might fall / Crying dance / I don't know what I want / Knife in the head / Mr. Ridiculous / Sometimes / Ghost beat / A song of joy / Come one, come all / Collapse board.

May 83. (12"ep) (rf 12-23) **EVERYTHING THAT FLIES (IS NOT A BIRD). / THE YEAR OF THE BLOATED GOAT / KNIFE IN THE HEAD**   – / –
 (above was also rel.in Australia; last track being repl. by 'NOTHING THAT HARMS' & 'EVERY DOG HAS ITS DAY')

Aug 83. (lp) (RTD 14) **LAUGHTER AROUND THE TABLE**   Rough Trade / not iss. / – / – / German
 – Everything that flies (is not a bird) / Nothing that harms / Every dog has its day / Laughter around the table / Theme from Mad Flies, Mad Flies / Sometimes . . . / Crying dance / The fire might fall / When what you see.

 KUEPPER + WEGENER recruited new members; **PETER MILTON-WALSH** – bass (ex-APARTMENTS). (repl. MILLAR who went solo making one eponymouse set in 1986 for 'Directional'; another lp, 'THE KEY – CONSUMOSOCIETY') / guest **CHRIS ABRAHAMS** – piano (of BENDERS)
 (below 'Hot' releases were issued months earlier in Australia)

Oct 84. (7") (HOT 719) **JUST BECAUSE I LIKE. / CRYSTAL CLEAR**   Hot / not iss. / – / – / Austra

Dec 84. (lp) (HOT 1004) **LAW OF NATURE**   – / – / Jun84
 – Monkey see monkey do / Law of nature / Eternally yours / Bride of Jesus / Possessions / Eating off the floor / Written in exile / As your bridges burn behind you / The year is more important / Stinking to high heaven. (cd-iss. Nov92; HOT 1004CD)

Jan 85. (12"m) (HOT12 001) **ETERNALLY YOURS. / POSSESSIONS / TIMES NOT HIT BUT MISSED BLUES**   – / Apr84

Aug 85. (lp) (HOT 1013) **GHOSTS OF AN IDEAL WIFE**   – / Feb85
 – Crystal clear / Diabolical creature / No words of honour / Winter's way / Ghosts of an ideal wife / The only one that knows / New bully in town / It gets so sentimental / The flypaper. (cd-iss. Nov93; HOT 1013CD)

 had already disbanded late in '84. MILTON-WALSH rejoined The APARTMENTS, while WEGENER guested for NICK CAVE & THE BAD SEEDS

– compilations, etc. –

Sep 84. (7") Hot; (HOT 714) **HOLY JOE. / SOMETIMES (I CAN'T LIVE WITH ANYONE)**   – / Austra

Oct 84. (12"m) Hot; (HOT12 005) **SOMETIMES (I CAN'T LIVE WITH ANYONE) / HOLY JOE. / I DON'T KNOW WHAT I WANT**   – / – / Austra

Sep 86. (lp) Hot; (HOT 1010) **HISTORY OF ROCK'N'ROLL VOLUME 1**   – / Oct84
 – Theme from "Mad flies, mad flies" / Every dog has its day / Holy Joe / Sometimes (I can't live with anyone) / The laughing clowns / Ghost beat / I want to scream / Clown town / Everything that flies (is not a bird) / Collapse board. (cd-iss. Mar93; HOT 1010CD)

Aug 95. (cd) Hot; (HOT 1055CD) **GOLDEN DAYS . . . WHEN GIANTS WALKED THE EARTH**   – / –
 – Eternally yours / Theme from "Mad Flies, Mad Flies" / Winter's way / Mr Uddich Smuddich / Holy Joe / I don't know what I want / Possessions / Eulogy / The flypaper / Every dog has its day.

ED KUEPPER

 with **PAUL SMITH** – bass / **MARK DAWSON** – drums / **CHRIS ABRAHAMS** – keyboards / + guest LOUIS TILLET – viola (on debut)
 (below material released months earlier on 'True Tone' Australia)

May 86. (lp) (HOT 1020) **ELECTRICAL STORM**   Hot / not iss. / – / Sep85
 – Car headlights / No more sentimental jokes / Master of two servants / A trick or two / When the sweet turns to sour / Another story / Electrical storm / Told myself / One small town / Palace of sin / Rainy night. (re-iss. Nov91; same) (cd-iss. Jan93; HOT 1020CD)

Oct 86. (7") **ALSO SPRACH THE KING OF EURODISCO. / WITHOUT YOUR MIRROR**   – / – / Austra
 (above issued on 'True Tone') (below unknown)

Jan 87. (7"; as ED KUEPPER & THE YARD GOES ON FOREVER) **I AM YOUR PRINCE. / SEA AIR**   – / – / Austra

Feb 87. (lp) (HOT 1027) **ROOMS OF THE MAGNIFICENT**   – / Nov86
 – Rooms of the magnificent / Also Sprach the king of Eurodisco / Sea air / The sixteen days / Without your mirror / No point in working / I am your prince / Spent five years / Show pony / Nothing you can do. (cd-iss. Feb93; HOT 1027CD)

 JIM BOWMAN – keyboards; repl. ABRAHAMS

Apr 87. (12"ep) (HOT 1231) **NOT A SOUL AROUND**   – / – / Austra
 – Not a soul around / Electrical storm / Also Sprach the king of Euro-disco / Without your mirror.

Sep 87. (7"; as ED KUEPPER & THE YARD GOES ON FOREVER) (TS 2025) **NOTHING CHANGES IN MY HOUSE. / AT TIMES, SO EMOTIONAL**   True Tone / not iss. / – / – / Austra
 (12"+=) (BUG 748636) – Not a soul around / (Queen of) Winter hotel.

Apr 88. (7") **(WHEN THERE'S) THIS PARTY. / ONE GOOD REASON**   – / – / Austra

Jun 88. (7") **TOO MANY CLUES. / SPARTAN SPIRITUALS**   – / – / Austra

Sep 88. (7"m) **BURNED MY FINGERS. / THE SIXTEEN DAYS / NO MORE SENTIMENTAL JOKES**   – / – / Austra

Jan 89. (12"ep) (ED 444) **HAPPY AS HELL**   – / – / Austra
 – Sometimes / Everything's fine / Ghost of an ideal wife / New bully in the town.

Jun 89. (cd/c/lp) (CD/TC+/EST 2099) <790513-2/-4/-1> **EVERYBODY'S GOT TO**   Capitol / Capitol / / Apr88
 – Everybody's got to / Too many clues / (When there's) This party / Standing in the cold, in the rain / Lonely paradise / Burned my fingers / Not a soul around / Nothing changes in my house / Spartan spirituals / No skin off your nose. (cd re-iss. Jun94 on 'Hot'; HOT 1044CD)

Nov 90. (lp/cd) (RAT 506/+CD) **TODAY WONDER**   Rattlesnake / not iss. / – / Jun90
 – Horse under water / Always the woman pays / Everything I've got belongs to you / What you don't know / I'd rather be the Devil / There's nothing natural / Medley: Pretty Mary – Eternally yours – If I were a carpenter. (cd re-iss. Sep93 on 'Hot'; HOT 1032CD) (cd re-mast.May02 +=; HOT 1032CDR) – live:- Intermission / Always the woman pays / What you don't know / Pretty Mary / Today wonder medley / Horse under water / I am your prince – Told myself / Everything I've got belongs to you.

Nov 91. (cd) (UFO 7CD) <72950> **HONEY STEEL'S GOLD**   UFO / Restless / / Jun95
 – King of vice / Everything I've got belongs to you / Friday's blue cheer – Libertines of Oxley / Honey steel's gold / The way I made you feel / Not too soon / Closer (but disguised) / Summerfield. (re-iss. Nov93 & Apr00 on 'Hot'; HOT 1036CD) (c-iss.Jun94; HOT 1036MC) (cd re-iss. Jan01 +=; HOT 1036R) – Indian reservation / Steamtrain / No wonder medley: No wonder – Built for comfort – Cyprus grove blues / Milk cow blues / The way I made you feel (part 2) / Everything I've got belongs to you (part 2).

Mar 92. (cd-ep) (HIT 1) **THE WAY I MADE YOU FEEL / EVERYTHING I GOT BELONGS TO YOU / PALACE OF SIN / ELECTRICAL STORM**

Jun 92. (cd-ep) (HIT 2) **REAL WILD LIFE / STEAM TRAIN / NO WONDER MEDLEY: NO WONDER – BUILT FOR COMFORT – CYPRUS GROVE BLUES / INDIAN RESERVATION**   Hot / Restless / – / –

Aug 92. (lp/cd) (HOT 1040/+CD) **BLACK TICKET DAY**
 – It's lunacy / Blind girl stripper / Real wild life / All my ideas run to crime / Black ticket day / Helps me understand / There's nothing natural / Walked thin wires. (c-iss.Jun94; HOT 140MC)

May 93. (cd-ep) (HIT 5) **SLEEPYHEAD (SERENE MACHINE) / NOT TO SOON / THERE'S NOTHING NATURAL / TODAY WONDER MEDLEY: TODAY WONDER – HEY GYP – WHITE HOUSES**

May 93. (cd) (HOT 1042CD) **SERENE MACHINE**   – / – / Austra
 – When she's down / Sleepy head (serene machine) / Who's been talkin' / It's happening before / I wish you were here / Maria Peripatetica / Sounds like mysterious wind / Reasons / This hideous place / (You) Don't know what to steal / You can't please everybody (Sweete reprise) / Married to my lazy life. (c-iss.Jun94; HOT 1042MC)

Jul 93. (cd) (HOT 1045CD) **THE BUTTERFLY NET** (compilation)
 – Not a soul around / At times, so emotional / Nothing changes in my house / Sometimes / Everything's fine / Also sprach the king of Euro-disco / Ghost of an ideal wife / New bully in the town / Sea air / Electrical storm / What you don't know / Black ticket day / The way I made you feel / Real wild life / Always the woman pays / It's lunacy / Honey steel's gold / Everything I've got belongs to you. (c-iss.Jun94; HOT 1045MC)

Mar 94. (cd-ep) (HIT 6) **IF I HAD A TICKET / IT'S STILL NOWHERE / CAR HEADLIGHTS / ETERNALLY YOURS**   – / – / Austra

Sep 94. (d-lp/c/cd) (HOT 1049/+MC/CD) <72953> **CHARACTER ASSASSINATION**
 – By the way / Little fiddle (and the ghost of Christmas past) / The cockfighter / My best interests at heart / Take it by the hand / La di doh / I'm with you / Ill wind / So close to certainty / A good soundtrack / Ring of fire / If I had a ticket / (some w/ free cd) **DEATH TO THE HOWDY-DOWDY** – By the way / Little fiddle (and the ghost of Xmas past) / The cockfighter / My best interests at heart / Take it by the hand / La di doh / I'm with you / Ill wind / So close to certainty / A good soundtrack (pushin' fear) / Ring of fire / Number ten.

LAUGHING CLOWNS (cont)

Jul 95. (cd) (HOT 1052CD) **A KING IN THE KINDNESS ROOM**
- Confessions of a window cleaner / Pissed off / Highway to Hell / Messin' (part 2) / They call me Mr Sexy / Sundown / Space pirate / Diving board.

Oct 95. (cd-s) (HIT 7) **I'M WITH YOU / WISH YOU WERE HERE / THERE'S NOTHING NATURAL / CLOSER (BUT DISGUISED)** — Austra

Mar 96. (cd) (HOT 1057CD) **SINGS HIS GREATEST HITS FOR YOU** (compilation)
- The way I made you feel / Pissed off / The real wild life / If I had a ticket / Sleepy head / This hideous place / La di doh / It's lunacy / Highway to Hell / I'm with you / Black ticket day / Everything I've got belongs to you / Confessions in Paradise / I wish you were here / Dark sad eyes.

Mar 96. (cd-s) (HIT 10) **WASN'T I PISSED OFF TODAY / KARAOKE VERSION** — Austra

Jul 96. (cd-s) (HIT 12) **FIREMAN JOE / EDMUND THE CONFESSOR / SOMEONE'S RESPONSIBLE / THE SWIMMING POOL HAUNTINGMAN** — Austra
(cd-s) (HIT 12X) – ('A'side) / The meaning of the word fear / Farewell Sparky the improviser / My girlfriend's house.

Oct 96. (cd) (HOT 1058CD) <89343> **FRONTIERLAND** Jan97
- All of these things / Fireman Joe / Weepin' willow / How would you plead / MDDP Limited / Pushin' fear / Roughneck blues / Someone told me / Poor Howard. (re-iss. Mar00; same) (some w/ free cd+=; SAMPLE 1058CD) **SAMPERLAND** – My best interest at heart / Confessions of a window cleaner / Sleepy head / Sad dark eyes / Lonely paradise / Maria peripatetica / There's nothing natural / Like an oil spill / Without your mirror / Messin' with the kid / Sometimes / Lit up by sexual gymnastics / Eternally yours / What you don't know / Car headlights / All of these things (demo).

May 97. (cd-ep) (HIT 14) **WEEPIN' WILLOW / ALL OF THESE THINGS / THE CHLORINE VENDOR / FRIEND OR LENDER**

Jul 97. (cd-ep) (HOT 13) **ALL OF THESE THINGS EP**
- All of these things / Hardhats and handbags / No.3 runaway / All of these things #2.
(cd-ep) (HOT 13X) – ('A'side) / Perry rests his case / Shushin' fear / More of those things.

Jul 97. (cd) (HOT 1064CD) <1/2> **STARSTRUCK: MUSIC FOR FILMS & ADVERTS** Hot Hot
- Lion to your lamb / Hardhats and handbags / No.3 runaway / The rape of Cornelius / Love and happiness / Eightball / The spook / Anne 1 / Spook strain / Spring is sprung / Rachel owns the creek / The favourite angel / Wenceslas' daughter / Too many things / Angel's lament / Messin' with the tall / The diving board / Love me splendour / The Christmas cake / Tom's theme / The green hat / Paul and Laurie have a party / Supermarket – Heaven / Everybody's got to / Pleading ignorance / International playboys vs. the 3rd Reich / Shushin' fear / Pennies from him.

Jul 98. (cd) (HOT 1065CD) **THE WHEELIE BIN AFFAIR** (compilation)
- Highway to Hell / Edmund the confessor / Steam train / No wonder – Built for comfort / It's still nowhere / Car headlights / The chlorine vendor / Indian reservation / Cyprus Grove blues / Wasn't I pissed off today sayeth Bing Bing the techno king / Milk cow blues / Someone's responsible / Lament for a lousy lover (parts 1 & 2) / Eternally yours / Romance in karaoke hell.

Jul 98. (cd) (HOT 1066CD) **WITH A KNAPSACK ON MY BACK (live)**
- Sleepy head / Sam Hall / Highway to Hell / All of these things / Little fiddle / Weepin' willow / I'm with you / Messin' (part 2) / La di doh / Eternally yours / Crowd rain chant / Poor Howard / When I first came to this land / I'd rather be the Devil / Sea air / Blind girl stripper.

Jul 98. (cd) (HOT 1069CD) **CLOUDLAND**
- Gun runnin' I / The three stigmata of James Ulmer / The last of the knucklemen / Delegatin' for the masses / Don't say, you don't say / My dog killed ma gurski's chook / The thickness of two planks / Bikie groupie, or the world Jones made.

Jul 98. (cd; as ED KUEPPER & HIS OXLEY CREEK PLAYBOYS) (HOT 1070CD) **LIVE (live)**
- Intro / Electrical storm / Honey's steel gold / Confessions of a window cleaner / Liddle fiddle / La di doh / My best interests at heart / Weeping willow blues / When I first came to this land / Black ticket day / Poor little fool.

Dec 98. (ltd-cd) (HOT 1071CD) **THE BLUE HOUSE** — Austra
- Black hole / A lot of nerve / I am right and you are wrong / World of chance / The drunken sailor / September the 4th is too late / Barefoot on the grass / The comedians / Marching along, singing a song / "Mr. Harry, ein Verbrecher!" / Duplex planet / Copper / Why call them back from Heaven? / Dispatch from the high castle / Half a mill' a week / The first final program / Big city.

Jan 00. (cd) (HOT 1072CD) **REFLECTIONS OF OL' GOLDEN EYE** (covers compilation)
- Camooweal / Ring of fire / Cyprus grove blues / Highway to Hell / The man who sold the world / If I were a carpenter / Sad dark eyes / Steam train / Built for comfort / Indian reservation / Do you love me / Sundown / If I had a ticket / When I was young / Teenage idol / Hunger.

Aug 00. (cd) (HOT 1073CD) **SMILE . . . PACIFIC**
- Sinnerman / Baby well I / I still call this failure / Without you / Fever / Everything in the world / Rue the day / Pay me my money down / Starstruck / Here to get my baby from jail.

– compilations, etc. –

Sep 93. (cd/c) Castle; (<CCS CD/MC 384>) **LEGENDARY BULLY** Oct94
- It's happened before / Not too soon / Everything I've got to belongs to you / Maria peripatetica / Blind girl stripper / This hideous place / Burned my fingers / Without your mirror / Medley: Today wonder – Hey Gyp – White houses / King of vice / Too many clues / Pretty Mary / No point in working / Helps me understand / I am your prince / Eternally yours.

Oct 95. (cd) Hot; <MAIL 1> **I WAS A MAIL ORDER BRIDEGROOM**
- When she's down / The way I made you feel / The cockfighter / Little fiddle / Electrical storm / I'm with you / There's nothing natural / Messin' with the kid / Ill wind / The seeker / Everything I've got belongs to you / La di doh / Ring of fire / Black ticket day / So close to certainty / Teenage idol. (UK-iss.Jan01; same)

Oct 95. (cd) Hot; <MAIL 2> **EXOTIC MAIL ORDER MOODS**
- Lights up / The man who sold the world / When I first came to this land / Lit up by sexual gymnastics (the like of which are not encountered outside of plain wrappers) / Sam Hall / Memories (as made of this) / When I was young / Stagolee / Stagolee II / The night is long / Do you love me / Cindy / Stagolee II / Lights down.

Jan 02. (cd) Hot; (HOT 1078CD) **OUT-TAKES, CASTAWAYS, PIRATE WOMEN AND TAKEAWAYS**

- Also Sprach 2001 / All of these things / CCR versus the 3rd Reich / If not for you / Eternally yours / Mona / Okie from Muskogee / Poor Howard / Horse under water / Kissin' cousins / Hunker down / La di doh (live) / Rough neck blues.

The AINTS!

ED KUEPPER – vocals, guitar / **KENT STEEDMAN** – bass / **TIM REEVES** – drums
UFO   not iss.

Nov 91. (lp/cd) (UFO 005/+CD) **ASCENSION**
- It's still nowhere / What's it like out there? / A good soundtrack / Like an oil spill / Both worlds / Ascension. (cd re-iss. Nov93 Aug95 & & May97 on 'Hot'; HOT 1035CD)
Hot   Restless

Dec 91. (cd-s) **I'M STRANDED (live) / NO TIME (live)** — Austra

Sep 92. (cd) (HOT 1037CD) **AUTOCANNIBALISM**
- You can't please everybody / Other side of the creek / Linda and Abilene / Ill wind / Red aces / The 'Aints go pop-camping. (re-iss. Aug95 & May97; same)

Apr 93. (cd) (AINTONECD) **S.L.S.Q. – VERY LIVE! (live SAINTS reworkings 1991)**
- Intro / This perfect day / Erotic neurotic / Runaway / Know your product / River deep, mountain high / Audience rain chant / Messin' with the kid / Nights in Venice. (re-iss. Aug95; same)

Aug 93. (cd-ep) (HIT 004CD) **CHEAP EROTICA**
- Erotic neurotic (live) / Like an oil spill / Ill wind / Audience rain chant / (I'm) Stranded (live).

Jul 95. (lp/cd) (HOT 1053/+CD) **THE MOST PRIMITIVE BAND IN THE WORLD (live from the Twilight Zone, Brisbane 1974)**
- Wild about you / Do the robot / One way street / Knock on wood / Erotic neurotic / River deep, mountain high / Lies / Misunderstood / Messin' with the kid / Stranded.

Aug 95. (cd) (HOT 1054CD) <72957> **SHELFLIFE UNLIMITED!! HOTTER THAN THE BLAZING PISTOLS!!!** (compilation)
- Like an oil spill / Ill wind / River deep, mountain high / It's still nowhere / Erotic neurotic / The Aints go pop-camping / What's it like out there? / Linda and Abilene.

LAUGHING HYENAS

Formed: Ann Arbor, Michigan, USA . . . 1985 by JOHN BRANNON and LARISSA STRICKLAND; her brother KEVIN STRICKLAND and JIM KIMBALL were found prior to theit first mini-set, 'MERRY-GO-ROUND' (1988). Calling up a hybrid of pre-punk blues and noisy dirge that drew a line through HOWLIN' WOLF, The 'STONES and IGGY POP, the LAUGHING HYENAS were, although not the greatest of their ilk, a template of the late 80's pre-grunge era. Their debut set in '89, 'YOU CAN'T PRAY A LIE', was unsettling to say the least, although by 1990's 'LIFE OF CRIME' (title track, once territory of the Weirdos), things were melodic and more mature. When KEVIN and JIM took off to form another 'Touch & Go' band, MULE, it looked like the LAUGHING HYENAS would be miserable once again. However, guitarist LARISSA and the hoarse one JOHN took up the reins for future work, ex-NECROS drummer TODD SWALLA and KEVIN REIS making up the numbers for the vastly improved comeback EP, 'CRAWL' (1992). With REIS making way for RON SAKOWSKI, the 'HYENAS made one last shout via 1995's 'HARD TIMES'.

Album rating: MERRY-GO-ROUND mini (*5) / YOU CAN'T PRAY A LIE (*3) / LIFE OF CRIME (*5) / CRAWL mini (*6) / HARD TIMES (*7)

JOHN BRANNON – vocals / **LARISSA STRICKLAND** – guitar / **KEVIN STRICKLAND** – bass / **JIM KIMBALL** – drums
Touch & Go   Touch & Go

Sep 88. (m-lp) <(TGLP 25)> **MERRY-GO-ROUND** Nov87
- Stain / Hell's kitchen / That girl / Gabriel / Playground / What tomorrow brings. <(cd-iss. Sep95+=; TGLP 25CD)> – Soul kiss / Candy / Dedications to the one I love / Don't bogue my high / Public animal #9.

Mar 89. (lp) <TGLP 38> **YOU CAN'T PRAY A LIE**
- Love's my only crime / Seven come eleven / Black eyed Susan / Lullaby and goodnight / Sister / Desolate son / Dedications to the one I love / New gospel.

Sep 90. (lp/c/cd) <TGLP 61/+C/CD> **LIFE OF CRIME**
- Everything I want / Hitman / Let it burn / Kick / Here we go again / Wild heart / Outlaw / Life of crime. <cd+=/c+=> – YOU CAN'T PRAY A LIE

Sep 90. (7") <TG 65> **HERE WE GO AGAIN. / CANDY**

TODD SWALLA – drums (ex-NECROS) repl. KIMBALL who joined MULE (KEVIN STRICKLAND also went that way) / added **KEVIN REIS** – bass

Oct 92. (m-lp/m-cd) <(TG 102/+CD)> **CRAWL**
- Crawl / Living in darkness / Walk / Girl.

RON SAKOWSKI – bass; repl. REIS

Feb 95. (lp/cd) <(TG 136/+CD)> **HARD TIMES**
- Just can't win / Hard time blues / You're so cruel / Stay / Slump / Home of the blues / Each dawn I die.

- disbanded after above

LAZY COWGIRLS

Formed: Los Angeles, California, USA . . . 1983 by Vincennes, Indiana lads PAT TODD, DD WEEKDAY (aka DOUG PHILLIPS), ALLEN CLARK, and KEITH TELLIGMAN. Their raucous blend of MC5 style garage rock, country honky-tonk, and original 70's punk attracted the ears of ex-FLESH EATERS vocalist, CHRIS DESJARDINS who assisted the band to ink a deal with 'Restless' records, the label issuing their eponymous debut LP, 'LAZY COWGIRLS', in 1984. Unfortunately the set failed to capture the sheer punk vitality of their much admired live work, and thus the band were unfairly

dropped from the label's roster. Unperturbed, the band went back to what they did best; 'kicking out the jams', until 'Bomp' gave them a deserved second chance, and put out their sophomore full-length outing, 'TAPPING THE SOURCE' (1987). An accurate title, as this set, unlike their former, managed to get down in the studio what the band were so adept at on the stage; banging upfront rock and roll. Their third album, 'RADIO COWGIRL' (1989), delivered a close approximation of their gig sound straight to the record buying public, being a live recording from a radio session on Santa Barbara based, KCSB-FM. It was also worthy of note for the fact that it was one of the first issues from soon to become hugely influential indie label 'Sympathy for the Record Industry'. The ensuing year saw the issue of their fourth long player, 'HOW IT LOOKS, HOW IT IS', which still remains one of their finest pieces to date. Unfortunately by 1991, the band were beginning to feel less sympathy for the record industry and the amount of effort it was taking to make little headway, culminating in the departure of CLARK and TELLIGMAN. The rumour in the West Coast punk rock scene was that the band had split altogether, but TODD and WEEKDAY plodded on with various line-ups, releasing a handful of 7" singles and EPs. Four years on with a rhythm section provided by ED HUERTA and LEONARD KERRINGER, plus second guitarist, MICHAEL LEIGH, LC put paid to the tittle-tattle with the issue of their fifth LP, 'RAGGED SOUL' (1995). An amazing comeback piece which lacked nothing of the punk spirit of their earlier releases, proving that time had not distilled their energy one iota. Sadly the succeeding year saw the departure of founding member WEEKDAY and newboy HUERTA, who was replaced by stickman BOB DEAGLE. Although it seemed almost impossible to replace the LC guitar sound which the erstwhile guitarist had established, ERIC CHANDLER did a more than passable job to emulate it on the sixth full-set release, 'A LITTLE SEX AND DEATH' (1997). By the turn of the millennium the boys were back up to form, with the return of earlier sit-in guitarist, LEIGH, empathised by the back-to-back release of 'RANK OUTSIDER' (1999) and 'SOMEWHERE DOWN THE LINE' (2000). At one stage conceived of as a double album, these two sets showcased the band's continuing punk rock vibrance, and the handful of acoustic tracks displayed their love of bluesy hoe-down honky tonk. After nigh-on two decades gigging TODD and the boys proved they still had balls of rock when it came to pleasing the fans, delivering the live set, 'HERE AND NOW: LIVE', the following year.
• Covered: YOU'RE GONNA MISS ME (13th Floor Elevators) / YAKETY YAK (Coasters) / JUSTINE (Don & Dewey) / HYBRID MOMENTS (Don & Dewey) / CARBONA NOT GLUE (Ramones) / KNOW YOUR PRODUCT (Saints) / SLOW DOWN (Larry Williams) / GREEN ACRES (Vic Mizzy) / HEARTACHE (Jim Reeves) / THAT MAKES IT TOUGH (Buddy Holly) / HOME OF THE BLUES (Johnny Cash) / THE MAGNIFICENT SEVEN (Bernstein) / ROUTE 66 (Bobby Troup) / GOODBYE TO YESTERDAY (Billy Joe Shaver) / LIVE IN THE PAST (Bill Monroe) / ROUTE 90 (Garlow-Rene).
Album rating: LAZY COWGIRLS (*5) / TAPPING THE SOURCE (*6) / THIRD TIME'S THE CHARM mini (*4) / RADIO COWGIRL (*5) / HOW IT LOOKS, HOW IT IS (*7) / RAGGED SOUL (*7) / A LITTLE SEX AND DEATH (*6) / RANK OUTSIDER (*6) / SOMEWHERE DOWN THE LINE (*6) / HERE AND NOW (LIVE!) (*4)

PAT TODD – vocals / **D.D. WEEKDAY** (b. DOUG PHILLIPS) – guitar / **KEITH TELLIGMAN** – bass / **ALLEN CLARK** – drums

not iss. Restless
1984. (lp) <72078-1> **LAZY COWGIRLS**
– Anymore / Rock of Gibraltar / Work / Jungle song / I'm talking to you / What are you talkin' 'bout baby? / Time / Tearful pillows / It hit me / Read that book / Dead stories / Drugs / You're gonna miss me.

Bomp! Bomp!
Nov 86. (7") <BMP 37> **SOCK IT TO ME, SANTA. / GODDAMN BOTTLE**
Aug 88. (lp) <(BLP 4025)> **TAPPING THE SOURCE**   Nov87
– Can't you do anything right? / Bullshit summer song / No name left / Heartache / Reacurrin' thang / Goddamn bottle / Yakety yak / Justine / Allen says Mr. Screwdriver. (cd-iss. Jan98 on '1+2'; 1+2CD 027)

not iss. Grown Up Wrong
1989. (m-lp) <Wrong 7> **THIRD TIME'S THE CHARM**
– Losin' your mind / Meat song / Dye 'n' red / A lot to learn / Reborn. (UK-iss.Jun92 as 'THIRD TIME'S THE CHARM – AGAIN' on 'Dog Meat' lp/cd+=; DOG 030/+CD) – Loretta / Hybrid moments / Rock of Gibraltar / Jungle song / Anymore / What are you talkin' 'bout baby? / Tearful pillows / I'm talking to you / Justine / Bullshit summer song.

not iss. Sympathy F
1989. (lp) <SFTRI 001> **RADIO COWGIRL (live at the KCSB, Santa Barbara)**
– Losin' your mind / Meat shop / Carbona not glue / Know your product / Slow down / Mr. Screwdriver / Goddamn bottle / Bullshit summer song / Green acres / You're gonna miss me. <cd w/free cd+=> – The long goodbye / Who are the mystery girls? / Crazy arms / Drugs II / Intellectual baby / The wayward wind / This is where I belong / Repeat after me.
1989. (7") <SFTRI 25> **THE LONG GOODBYE. / WHO ARE THE MYSTERY GIRLS? / CRAZY ARMS**
1989. (7") <SP 43> **LORETTA. / HYBRID MOMENTS**
(above issued on 'Sub Pop', below on 'Romilar-D')
1990. (7") <016> **ANYMORE. / WHAT ARE YOU TALKIN' 'BOUT BABY / TEARFUL PILLOWS**
1990. (lp) <SFTRI 039> **HOW IT LOOKS, HOW IT IS**
– How it looks, how it is / Sex kittens compare scratches / Cheap shit / One on the list / The long goodbye / When it all comes down / D.I.E. in Indiana / Alienation maybe / I've had enough of it / Danielle / Teenage Frankenstein / How long. <cd-iss. 1992 +=; SFTRI 039CD> – THIRD TIMES THE CHARM – AGAIN
1991. (7") <DOG 009> **JUNGLE ROCK. / ROCK OF GIBRALTAR**
(above issued on 'Dog Meat')

—— (1991) now without TELLIGMAN + CLARK
1992. (7") <SFTRI 93> **TEENAGE FRANKENSTEIN. / INTELLECTUAL BABY**
1992. (d7"ep) <SFTRI 122> **A NEW GIRL IN TOWN**
– The wayward wind / This is where I belong / Drugs II / Repeat after me.
1993. (10"ep) <SFTRI 219> **ANOTHER LONG GOODBYE**
– Another long goodbye / I can almost remember / You got a hard time coming / Let you behind (aka Losin' your mind).

Crypt Crypt
1993. (7"m) <CRYPT 037> **FRUSTRATION< TRAGEDY & LIES. / DON'T TEMPT ME / HERE I SIT**
—— (1995) **MICHAEL LEIGH** – rhythm guitar, vocals + **LEONARD KERINGER** – bass, vocals; repl. a series of bass players
—— **ED HUERTA** – drums; repl. drummer
Jul 95. (cd/lp) <(efa 11591-2/-1)> <CRYPT 061> **RAGGED SOUL**
– I can't be satisfied / Much too slow / Frustration, tragedy and lies / Who you callin' a slut / Everything you heard about me is true / Never got the chance / Too much – one more time / Time and money / Another long goodbye / Now that you're down on me / I can almost remember / Still on the losin' side (aka Snake Eyes) / Take it as it comes / Bought your lies.
—— **BOB DEAGLE** – drums; repl. HUERTA
—— **ERIC CHANDLER** – guitars, vocals; repl. LEIGH + WEEKDAY
Oct 97. (cd) <(efa 12895)> <CRYPT 083> **A LITTLE SEX AND DEATH**
– Here comes trouble / The end of the line / A little sex and death / Montana / I'll tell you why / World up for grabs (another emergency) / Bad news / Can you tell me / Sweet thing / Hittin' bottom / Name droppin' son of a bitch / The big restless / Your charmed life's fadin' fast.

Sympathy F Sympathy F
Nov 97. (7"pic-d) <SFTRI 465> **ROUTE 66. / I'LL TELL YOU WHY**
Aug 98. (cd-ep) <(SFTRI 538)> **BROKEN HEARTED ON VALENTINES DAY**
– Just the last goodbye / That makes it togh / Home of the blues / Broken hearted on Valentines Day.
1999. (7"yellow) <CH7-03> **DON'T COUNT ME OUT. / WHEN YOU FALL**
(above issued on 'Chatterbox', below issued on 'Sheep')
1999. (7",7"pink) <Kebab 012> **GOODBYE TO YESTERDAY. / GOODNIGHT AND GOODBYE**
—— **MICHAEL LEIGH** – guitar + **RICK JOHNSON**; repl. CHANDLER
Oct 99. (lp/cd) <(SFTRI 588/+CD)> **RANK OUTSIDER**
– Don't turn your back on me / Not a goddamn thing / Since you got here / When you fall / Sylvia / Bad time / Goodnight and goodbye / Rank outsider / That kinda trouble I can use / Your time is over / Grit and glamour / Here and gone.
Apr 00. (lp/cd) <(SFTRI 605/+CD)> **SOMEWHERE DOWN THE LINE**
– Another lost cause / Somewhere down the line / Bittersweet shit / Stripper blues / Leap of faith / But it's alright now / Lookin' back / Rawhide and steel / What I want / You have got religion now / Cold, cold world / Back down in the basement.
Jul 01. (cd) <SFTRI 661CD> **HERE AND NOW (LIVE!) (live)**
– The magnificent seven / Route 66 / Don't count me out / Goodbye to yesterday / Your charmed life's fadin' fast / Live in the past / Somewhere down the line / When it comes to you I've got no dreams to lose / Second cousin / Route 90 / You / Rock of Gibraltar / Bought your lies.

Paul LEARY (see under ⇒ BUTTHOLE SURFERS)

LEATHER NUN

Formed: Goreburg, Sweden ... 1979 by JONAS ALMQUIST, a DJ and fanzine editor with a penchant for the Godfather of Punk, IGGY POP. Coming into contact with GENESIS P. ORRIDGE (a member of THROBBING GRISTLE at the time) at a London gig, JONAS handed him a demo of the track, 'DEATH THREATS'. ORRIDGE subsequently released it (as part of the 'SLOW DEATH' EP) on his own 'Industrial' imprint after JONAS had returned from Sweden with a studio ready band drawn from punk group, the STRAIT JACKET (BENGT ARONSSON, FREDDIE WADLING and GERT CLAESSON). The following year, the re-hashed demo also found its way onto a cassette, 'LIVE AT SCALA CINEMA', which circulated at gigs around the same time. The gigs in question fuelled controversy after the band used background hardcore gay-pornography to provoke attention, although the focus was obviously peroxide blonde, ALMQUIST, an exotic post-punk clone of IGGY POP and LOU REED (circa '69) complete with cool wraparound shades. FREDDIE departed just after the recording of the long-awaited 'PRIMEMOVER' single in 1983, while a revamped version of 'SLOW DEATH' appeared on the similarly titled EP in '84, the record featuring guest slots by GENESIS P. and MONTE CAZAZZA. Adding NILS WOHLRABE and replacing recent member, HAKEN with ANDERS OLSSON, the LEATHER NUN finally came up with some fresh songs for the 'Wire' label in mid-85, the result being the appropriately titled 'ALIVE'. The band took a slightly more commercial turn the following year when they "un-covered" the ABBA pop classic, 'GIMME GIMME GIMME (A MAN AFTER MIDNIGHT)'. Such unsavoury albums as 'LUST GAMES' (1986) and 'STEEL CONSTRUCTION' (1987) found their way to the shops before Miles Copeland's 'I.R.S.' imprint took them on in early '88. Although they failed to convert many mainstream indie fans, their dark gospel was enthusiastically received by their cult following on two further albums, 'INTERNATIONAL HEROES' (1990) and 'NUN PERMANENT' (1991), the latter produced by MICK RONSON. A few years onward and ARONSSON was back under the banner of SISTER AARON and an album, 'PRIFICATION' (1993).
Album rating: ALIVE (*6) / LUST GAMES mini (*5) / STEEL CONSTRUCTION (*5) / FORCE OF HABIT compilation (*7) / INTERNATIONAL HEROES (*5) / NUN PERMANENT (*5) / A SEEDY COMPILATION (*6)

JONAS ALMQVIST – vocals / **BENGT ARONSSON** – guitar / **FREDDIE WADLING** – bass / **GERT CLAESSON** – drums

		Industrial	not iss.
Dec 79.	(7"ep) (IR 0006) **SLOW DEATH EP**		

– No rule / Death threats / Slow death / Ensam i natt.

		Sista Bussen	not iss.
1980.	(c) (IRC 027) **LIVE AT SCALA CINEMA** (live)		

		Subterranean	Obsession
1982.	(7"m) (SB 207) **ENSAM I NATT. / HERE COMES LIFE** (live) / **NO RULE** (live)	– Sweden	
Feb 84.	(7") (SUB 40) <OBS 1> **PRIMEMOVER. / F.F.A.**		Nov83

— **HAKEN** – bass; repl. FREDDIE

		Criminal Damage	not iss.
May 84.	(12"ep) (CRIMLP 113) **SLOW DEATH**		

– No rule / Slow death / Ensam I natt (full version) / Death threats / Slow death (live at Scala Cinema, featuring GENESIS P-ORRIDGE and MONTE CAZAZZA).
(re-iss. Aug86 on 'Wire'; WRMLP 100)

— added **NILS WOHLRABE** – guitar

		Wire	I.R.S.
Jul 85.	(12") (WRMS 005) **506. / FLY, ANGELS, FLY / I'M ALIVE**		–

— **ANDERS OLSSON** – bass; repl. HAKEN

| Dec 85. | (lp) (WRLP 002) **ALIVE** | | – |

– Prime mover / Fly, angels, fly / Son of a good family / I'm alive / Busted knee caps / F.F.A. / On the road / Here comes life / For the love of your eyes / Lollipop.

Feb 86.	(7") (WRS 007) **DESOLATION AVE. / ON THE ROAD**		–
	(12"+=) (WRMS 007) – Son of a good family.		
May 86.	(7") (WRS 009) **GIMME GIMME GIMME. / LOLLIPOP**		–
	(12"+=) (WRMS 009) – ('A'-Chopper mix).		
	(12") (WRXS 009) – ('A'+'B' versions) / ('A'-Chopper version).		
Oct 86.	(7") (WRS 010) **PINK HOUSE. / SPEED OF LIFE**		–
	(12"+=) (WRMS 010) – Lucky strike.		
Oct 86.	(m-lp) (WRMLP 200) **LUST GAMES**		–

– I can smell your thoughts / Jesus came driving along / Pink house / Pure heart / Have sex with me / For the love of your eyes.

May 87.	(7") (WRS 014) **I CAN SMELL YOUR THOUGHTS (remix). / FALLING APART**		–
	(12"+=) (WRMS 014) – 506 (re-visited).		
Aug 87.	(7") (WRS 016) **COOL SHOES. / I WISH**		–
	(12"+=) (WRMS 016) – Special agent.		
Aug 87.	(lp/c) (WR LP/TC 005) **STEEL CONSTRUCTION**		–

– Dance, dance, dance / Someone special like you / Lost and found / Ride to live / Just a hustler / Cool shoes / Summer's so short / Trail of pain / Godzilla is back / Let me be. (cd+=) – I wish / Special agent.

Oct 87.	(7") (WRS 020) **LOST AND FOUND. / SOMEONE SPECIAL LIKE YOU**		–
	(12") (WRMS 020) – ('A'side) / Dance dance dance / Ride like a Cheyenne.		
Jan 88.	(cd) (WRCD 008) <IRS 42053> **FORCE OF HABIT** (compilation)		

– I can smell your thoughts / Jesus came driving along / Pink house / For the love of your eyes / No rule [UK-only] / 506 / Desolation avenue / Gimme gimme gimme / Primemover / Death threats / Have sex with me / F.F.A. [UK-only] / Lollipop [UK-only] / Fly, angels, fly [UK-only] / On the road [UK-only]. (lp-iss.May88; WRLP 008)

| Oct 88. | (12") (WRMS 023) **DEMOLITION LOVE. / SHE SAID / DEMOLITION LOVE** (Tyson mix) | | – |

— ALMQVIST, ARONSSON, CLAESSON added **ULF VIDLUND** – bass

Nov 89.	(12") (WRMS 025) **A THOUSAND NIGHTS. / SOMEBODY / RED GUITARS (OF PLANET EARTH)**	–	– Sweden
Jun 90.	(12") (WRMS 028) **RIDE INTO YOUR TOWN. / LICK MY TATTOES / RED GUITARS (OF PLANET EARTH)**	–	– Sweden
Nov 90.	(cd/lp) (WIRE CD/LP 011) **INTERNATIONAL HEROES**		

– Ride into your town / How does it feel / A thousand nights / Whama-lama-bam-bam-boy / Waiting for your train / Reach out / Velvet sky / Hooked to your lips / Toxic darlings / She said / Red guitars.

— added **FREDRIK ADLERS** – keyboards / **MATS GRUNDSTROM** – guitar

| Oct 91. | (cd-s) (WRMS 034) **GIRLS / I AIN'T TURNING BACK / GIRLS** (long version) | – | – Sweden |
| Oct 91. | (cd/lp) (WIRE CD/LP 012) **NUN PERMANENT** | | |

– Take me home / At your doorstep / Girls / These eyes cannot lie / She's so bad / Big city / Desperation drive / She's had a past / Even a fool can learn to love / The sun still shines. (cd+=) – I ain't turning back.

— disbanded in the early 90's

– compilations, etc. –

| Nov 88. | (12"ep) Nighttracks; (SFNT 014) **RADIO ONE SESSIONS** (13.7.86) | | – |

– Lust for love / Pure heart / Desolation avenue / Primemover.

| 1994. | (cd) MNW Zone; (9824-2) **A SEEDY COMPILATION** | – | – Sweden |

– A thousand nights / Pink house / Ride into your town / She has a past / Girls / I can smell your thoughts / Take me home / Save my soul / Lost and found / At your doorstep / Bright lights / Demolition love / She said / Just a hustler / Primemover / Dance dance dance / Reach out / Ensam i natt / Gimme gimme gimme / Desolation Ave. / No rule / Big city / F.F.A. / I ain't turning back / Somebody.

LEAVING TRAINS

Formed: Los Angeles, California, USA … 1981 by FALLING JAMES (MORELAND), along with brothers MANFRED and TOM HOFER, SYLVIA JUNCOSA and HILLARY LADDIN. This was the line-up that contributed one track, 'VIRGINIA CITY', to the V/A compilation, 'Keats Rides A Harley', the aforementioned members, SYLVIA and HILLARY, making way for CHRIS CACAVAS and JASON KAHN prior to their full-length LP debut, 'WELL DOWN BLUE HIGHWAY' (1984). JAMES had previous form with late 70's L.A. punk bands such as The DOWNERS and The MONGRELS, and was at times a bit risqué on stage when he performed in a dress! (he subsequently married and divorced COURTNEY LOVE). The 'TRAINS (without CACAVAS who joined GREEN ON RED) were taken on board by the iconic 'S.S.T.', although personnel tribulations (see discography) left them stranded at the musical station, while bands such as HUSKER DU, MEAT PUPPETS and others were leaving them in their tracks; even FALLING JAMES hopped off a few times! Their albums, 'KILL TUNES' (1986), 'FUCK' (1987), 'TRANSPORTATIONAL D. VICES' (1989), 'SLEEPING UNDERWATER DEVICES' (1991), 'THE LUMP IN MY FOREHEAD' (1993) and 'THE BIG JINX' (1994), all had their moments, although the latter was marred by the subsequent accidental death of recently signed bassist CHAZ RAMIREZ. Mainman, JAMES (who'd spent some time in SLUTS FOR HIRE), took hold of the reins again, and with a new band (MELANIE VAMMEN, JIMMY GREEN and ALLEN CLARK), delivered The LEAVING TRAINS "farewell" long-player, 'SMOKE FOLLOWS BEAUTY' (1997). • **Covered:** PRIVATE AFFAIR (Saints) / THE HORSE SONG (Iggy Pop).

Album rating: WELL DOWN BLUE HIGHWAY (*5) / KILL TUNES (*7) / FUCK (*6) / TRANSPORTATIONAL D. VICES (*5) / SLEEPING UNDERWATER SURVIVORS (*4) / THE LUMP IN MY FOREHEAD (*6) / THE BIG JINX (*5) / SMOKE FOLLOWS BEAUTY (*3) / FAVORITE MOOD SWINGS (1986-1995) compilation (*6)

FALLING JAMES (MORELAND) – vocals, guitar (ex-DOWNERS, ex-MONGRELS) / **MANFRED HOFER** – guitar / **TOM HOFER** – bass / **CHRIS CACAVAS** – keyboards; repl. SYLVIA JUNCOSA (on most) / **JASON KAHN** – percussion, drums; repl. TERRY GRAHAM who repl. HILLARY LADDIN

		not iss.	Bemisbrain
1984.	(lp) <1108> **WELL DOWN BLUE HIGHWAY**	–	

– Bringing down the house / Leaving train / All my friends / All my friends / Always between wars / You can't see / I am in a world crash with you / Hometown blues / She knows the rain / Creeping coastline of lights / Virginia City / Going down to town.

— now without CACAVAS who joined GREEN ON RED

		S.S.T.	S.S.T.
1986.	(lp/c/cd) <SST 071/+C/CD> **KILL TUNES**	–	

– Light rain / She's looking at you / Private affair / Cigarette model / 10 Generations / Kinette / A drunker version of you / Black / Falling / Vicki / Terminal island / Warning track.

— FALLING JAMES recruited new band **SAM MERRICK** – guitar / **ERIC STRINGER** – bass / **BRUCE GUNNELL** – drums

| Nov 87. | (lp/cd) <(SST 114/+CD)> **FUCK** | | |

– Temporal slut / How can I explode? / What Cissy said / The horse song / Disasters / Walking with you / Sleep / With Dr. A.W.O.L. / 27 days / So fucked up / I don't know what I'm doing here / Violent sex / Welcome to New York / What the president meant to say.

— **DENNIS CARLIN** – drums (+ later keyboards); repl. GUNNELL

| Feb 89. | (lp/c/cd) <(SST 221/+C/CD)> **TRANSPORTATIONAL D. VICES** | | |

– Dude the cat / Love or die / Cement / Store / Diggin' you / You're never gonna love me anymore / Payday / Sue wants to sleep / Dead days / The worst / Any old time / Favorite bar / Bad mood / Black hole / Everybody loves a clown.

— added **BOBBY BELLTOWER** – guitar, vocals (ex-NYMPHS)

| Mar 91. | (lp/cd) <(SST 271/+CD)> **SLEEPING UNDERWATER SURVIVORS** | | |

– I love you, goodbye / Walk like a river / Suicide blues / Relapse, recover / What was left was red / Hurting world / Come / Room at the bottom / Extinction.

— after a short break (in which he formed The POWER OF SKY), JAMES returned with his/their co-songwriter **WHITEY SIMS** – bass / **LENNY MONTOYA** – drums / + BELLTOWER plus CHAZ RAMIREZ – bass, piano, etc

| Oct 91. | (7";w-drawn) <SST 283> **ROCK'N'ROLL MURDER. /** | – | – |

(UK-iss.May93 as 12"ep/cd-ep; same as US)

| Feb 92. | (10"ep/cd-ep) <SST 284/+CD> **LOSER ILLUSION Pt.0** | | |

– Kids wanna know / Fuck you, God! / Rock'n'roll murder / Bleach in the fishtank / Good for no reason / You don't need a doctor. (UK-iss.May93; same as US) (below 1991 recording was finally delivered …)

| May 93. | (lp/c/cd) <(SST 288/+C/CD)> **LUMP IN MY FOREHEAD** | | |

– Bob Hope / She's got bugs / Women are evil / Abnormal / 1-900 world / Gas, grass or ass (no one rides for free) / Heart / I'm o.k. / Clairevoyeur / Transposing heat.

— **DENNIS CARLIN** – drums, guitar, vocals; returned to repl. LENNY (on most cuts) / added **MARK PRITCHARD** – guitar

| Jul 94. | (lp/c/cd) <(SST 293/+C/CD)> **THE BIG JINX** | | Jun94 |

– The big jinx / Ice cream truck / Go a-fuckin' head / Nothing left / Woman's clouds / Stowaway / Sex war / Osmosis / Blacklist / Can't afford to die / Chloroformality.

| Apr 95. | (cd-ep) <SST 311CD> **DROWNED AND DRAGGED** | | |

– She'll be crushed / Submarine Y / Dream until you're sore / Die / We don't like you.

— when RAMIREZ died in a warehouse accident in '95, FALLING JAMES recruited new band **MELANIE VAMMEN** – guitar, vocals (ex-SLUTS FOR HIRE) / **JIMMY GREEN** – bass / **ALLEN CLARK** – drums

| Jan 97. | (cd) <SST 338CD> **SMOKE FOLLOWS BEAUTY** | – | |

– Legalize me / Now I'm mad / Bad dolly / Extra vagrant / Big star / I wanna be you / Smoke a fatty / Bash in your face / Dreams overboard / A long road, a long time / Smoke follows beauty / Go on strike / Party sluts hangout / Hey come on / Marijuana / Sugarcaning / Nobody home.

		Get Hip	Get Hip
Jan 97.	(7") <(GH 190)> **FIVE YEARS AHEAD OF MY TIME. / (other by COBRA VERDE)**		

— went off the rails after above US-only set

LEAVING TRAINS (cont)   THE GREAT INDIE DISCOGRAPHY   The 1980s

– compilations, etc. –

Nov 97. (cd) *S.S.T.; <(SST 334CD)>* **FAVORITE MOOD SWINGS (1986-1995)**   Oct97
– Cigarette motel / She's looking at you / A drunker version of you / Black / What Cissy said / With Dr. A.W.O.L. / 27 days / So fucked up / Temporal slut / Sue wants to sleep / The worst / Any old time / Dude the cat / I love you / Dream until you're sore / Submarine Y / Relapse, recover / Fuck you, God! / Gas, grass or ass (no one rides for free) / Bob Hope / Rock'n'roll murder / Kids wanna know / Ice cream truck / Osmosis / Stowaway.

LEGENDARY PINK DOTS

Formed: London, England . . . late 1980 by EDWARD KA-SPEL and PHILIP KNIGHT (aka THE SILVERMAN). This outfit released their debut album, 'BRIGHTER NOW' (1982), for the Birmingham-based indie label, 'In-Phaze', although they subsequently moved to the Netherlands a few years later after the disappointing reception afforded 'THE TOWER' album. Signing to Belgium's 'Play It Again Sam', they issued the first of several albums, 'FACES IN THE FIRE' (1984). Experimental and exploratory, this electro-psychedelic outfit were akin to FAUST or CAN meeting STEVE HILLAGE or SYD BARRETT, a less than commercial approach which left them as perennial alternative fringe players. Nevertheless, KA-SPEL moonlighted as a solo artist around the same time, releasing the first of many albums, 'LAUGH CHINA DOLL'. He also collaborated with SKINNY PUPPY on the TEARGARDEN project for the 1987 album, 'TIRED EYES SLOWLY BURNING'. Various LPD personnel came and went and, in the 90's they came up with their best efforts to date, 'THE MARIA DIMENSION' (1991) and 'SHADOW WEAVER' (1992). The latter was promoted by a US tour, KA-SPEL and Co. having previously been refused work permits due to the "lack of artistic merit" rule!

Album rating: BRIGHTER NOW (*5) / CURSE (*4) / THE TOWER (*7) / FACES IN THE FIRE (*5) / THE LOVERS (*5) / ASYLUM (*6) / ISLAND OF JEWELS (*5) / ANY DAY NOW (*7) / STONE CIRCLES compilation (*7) / THE GOLDEN AGE (*6) / CRUSHED VELVET APOCALYPSE (*5) / THE MARIA DIMENSION (*8) / THE SHADOW WEAVER (*7) / MALACHAI (*5) / 9 LIVES TO WONDER (*7) / FROM HERE YOU'LL WATCH THE WORLD GO BY (*5) / IT'S RAINING IN HEAVEN (*5) / NEMESIS ONLINE (*5) / Edward Ka-Spel: LAUGH CHINA DOLL (*6) / EYES! CHINA DOLL (*5) / TANITH AND THE LION TREE (*5) / DOWN IN THE CITY OF HEARTBREAK & NEEDLES (*6) / LYVV CHINA DOLL (*6) / THE SCRIPTURES OF ILLUMINA (*5) / DOWN IN THE CITY OF HEARTBREAKS, VOL.2 (*5)

EDWARD KA-SPEL (as D'ARCHANGEL) – vocals, instruments / **PHILIP KNIGHT** (as THE SILVERMAN) – keyboards, tapes, samples

                                         In-Phaze   not iss.

Jan 82. (lp) *(IPNER 1)* **BRIGHTER NOW**
– Red castles / Louder after six / The wedding / Apocalypse then / Legacy / City ghosts / Hanging gardens / Soma bath / Premonition four. *(re-iss. Jun86 on 'Terminal Kaleidoscope'; TK 001)*

— added **ROLAND CALLOWAY** (as PRUUMPTJE JUSTE) – bass / **STRET MAJEST** – guitars / **APRIL ILIFFE** – vocals, keyboards

Aug 83. (lp) *(PHA 2)* **CURSE**
– Love puppets / Wallpurges night / Lisa's party / Arzhklahh Olgevezh / Pruumptje kurss / Waving at the aeroplanes / Hiding / Doll's house / The palace of love / Stoned obituary. *(re-iss. Dec86 on 'Terminal Kaleidoscope'; TK 002) (cd-iss. Aug88; TK 002CD)*

— added **PAT PAGANINI** (aka WRIGHT) – violin, keyboards, vocals

May 84. (lp) *(PHA 3)* **THE TOWER**
– Black zone / Break day / Tower one / Vigil-anti / A lust for powder / Poppy day / Tower two / Astrid / Rope and glory / Tower three / Tower four / Tower five. *(cd-iss. Aug88 with 'BRIGHTER NOW' on 'Terminal Kaleidoscope'; TK 003CD)*

                                      Ding Dong   not iss.

Jan 85. (lp) *(DDD 3333)* **THE LOVERS**   Dutch
– MMMmmmmmmmmmm / Geisha mermaid / The heretic / Jungle / The lovers (part 1) / Silverture / Flowers for the silverman / The lovers (part 2). *(cd-iss. 1990 on 'Play It Again Sam'+=; CDBIAS 156)* – Curious guy / Premonition 16.

                                    Play It Again Sam   S.P.V.

Jun 84. (lp) *(BIAS 01)* **FACES IN THE FIRE**
– Blasto / Love in a plain brown envelope / Sleeso / Neon gladiators / Kitto / Eight minutes to live. *(cd-iss. Aug88; CDBIAS 001)*

— added **GRAHAM WHITEHEAD** – bass, guitar

Sep 85. (d-lp) *(BIAS 12)* **ASYLUM**
– Echo police / Gorgon Zola's baby / Fifteen flies in the marmalade / Femme mirage / The hill / Demonism / Prisoner / So gallantly screaming / I am the way, the truth, the light / Agape / Golden dawn / The last straw / A message from our sponsor / Go ask Alice / This could be the end. *(cd-iss. Mar88; CDBIAS 012)*

— added **HANS MEYER** – saxophone, flute, electronics / **BOB PISTOOR** – guitar, bass (to KA-SPEL, THE SILVERMAN)

Aug 86. (12") *(BIAS 030)* **CURIOUS GUY. / PREMONITION 16**
Nov 86. (lp) *(BIAS 041)* **ISLAND OF JEWELS**
– Tower six / The red and the black / The dairy / Emblem parade / Jewel on an island / Rattlesnake arena / The shock of contact / Jewel in the crown / Our lady in chambers / Our lady in Kharki / Our lady in darkness / The guardians of Eden. *(cd-iss. 1988; CDBIAS 041)*

Oct 87. (12"ep) *(BIAS 074)* **UNDER GLASS. / THE LIGHT IN MY LITTLE GIRL'S EYES / THE PLASMA TWINS**
Nov 87. (cd/lp) *(CD+/BIAS 080)* **ANY DAY NOW**
– Casting the runes / A strychnine kiss / Laguna beach / The gallery / Neon mariners / True love / The peculiar funfair / Waiting for the cloud / Cloud zero / Under glass / The light in my little girl's eyes / The plasma twins.

                                    Play It Again Sam   Play It Again Sam

Nov 88. (lp) *(BIAS 101) <BIUS 1001CD>* **STONE CIRCLES** (compilation)
– Love puppets / Black zone / Golden dawn / Curious day / The hanging gardens / Fifteen flies / Our lady in darkness / Apocalypse / Gladiators (version). *(cd-iss. Apr89; CDBIAS 101)*

Jul 89. (cd/c/lp) *(CD/C+/BIAS 103) <BIUS 1017CD>* **THE GOLDEN AGE**
– Maniac / The talent contest / The more it changes / Hotel noir / Stille nacht / The month after / Lisa's separation / The golden age? / Black castles / And even the vegetables screamed / Regression. *(cd+=)* – Blacklist / Methods / Our lady in Cervetori.

Oct 89. (12"ep/cd-ep) *(BIAS 109/+CD)* **BLACKLIST. / METHODS / OUR LADY OF CERVETORI**

Mar 90. (cd/c/lp) *(<CD/C+/BIAS 149>)* **CRUSHED VELVET APOCALYPSE**
– I love you in your tragic beauty / Green gang / Hellsville / Hellowe'en / The safe way / Just a lifetime / he death of Jack The Ripper / New tomorrow. *(cd+=)* – Princess Coldheart / The pleasure palace / The collector.

Jun 90. (12"ep/cd-ep) *(BIAS 153/+CD)* **PRINCESS COLDHEART / THE PLEASURE PALACE. / THE COLLECTOR / C.V.A.**

— KA-SPEL, KNIGHT + PISTOOR added **NIELS VAN HOORNBLOWER** – wind, bass

Mar 91. (cd/lp) *(<CD+/BIAS 184>)* **THE MARIA DIMENSION**
– Disturbance / Pennies for Heaven / Third secret / The grain kings / The ocean cried "blue murder" / Belladonna / A space between / Evolution. *(cd w/free cd-ep+=)* – I DREAM OF JEANNIE / LITTLE OYSTER / SHE GAVE ME AN APPLE / STIRRED BUT NOT SHAKEN / WHERE NO MAN *(cd+=)* – Cheraderama / Lilith / Fourth secret / Expresso noir / Home / Crushed velvet.

Sep 92. (cd) *(<BIAS 225CD>)* **THE SHADOW WEAVER**
– Zero zero / Guilty man / Ghosts of unborn children / City of needles / Stitching time / Twilight hour / The key to heaven / Laughing guest / Prague Spring / Leper colony.

— **RYAN MOORE** – bass (of TEARGARDEN) repl. PISTOOR

— added **MARTYN DE KLEER** – guitar

Mar 93. (cd) *(<BIAS 236CD>)* **MALACHAI** (SHADOW WEAVER PART 2)
– Joey the canary / Kingdom of the flies / Encore une fois / Wildlife estate / Pavane / Window of the world / On the boards / We bring the day / Paris 4 a.m.

— with drummer **CEVIN KEY** (of SKINNY PUPPY)

Mar 94. (cd) *(<BIAS 280CD>)* **9 LIVES TO WONDER**
– Madame Guillotine / On another shore / Softly softly / Crumbs on the carpet / Hotel Z / Oasis Malade / A crack in melancholy time / Siren / The angel trail / Nine shades to a circle / A terra firma welcome.

                                    Soleilmoon   Staalplaat

Sep 95. (cd) *(28) <STCD 099>* **FROM HERE YOU'LL WATCH THE WORLD GO BY**
– Clockwise / Citadel / Friend / A velvet resurrection / Kollusim / 1001 commandments / Remember me this way / This one-eyed man is king / Straight on 'til morning / Damien / This hollowed ground.

                                    Soleilmoon   Soleilmoon

Jan 96. (cd-ep) *(SOL 31CD)* **REMEMBER ME THIS WAY EP**
Sep 96. (cd) *(SOL 43CD)* **IT'S RAINING IN HEAVEN**
– Puppets apocalypse / Poppy day / A lust for powder / Only when I laugh / La cazza nova / Lyriex / Premonition 11 (full length version).

Jan 98. (cd-ep) *(SOL 56CD)* **STERRE**
– Sterre / Spike psychomix / Elefant's graveyard / Sterre.

Dec 98. (12"ep/cd-ep) *(SOL 74/+CD)* **PRE MILLENNIAL SINGLE EP**
– Hellsville '98 / Needles / Andromeda suite '98 / Abracadabra zzzz.

Dec 98. (lp/cd) *(<SOL 75/+CD>)* **NEMESIS ONLINE**
– Dissonance / Jasz / As long as it's purple and green / Under your wheels / Sunset for a swan / Is it something I said? / Zoo / Fate's faithful punchline / Cheating the shadow / Abracadabra / Slaapliedje.

– compilations, etc –

on 'Play It Again Sam' unless mentioned otherwise

Jul 83. (c) *Third Mind Tapes; (TMT 08)* **BASILISK**
Nov 88. (lp/cd) *Materiali Sonori; (MASO/+CD 70009)* **GREETINGS 9** (half live)   Italy
1985. (cd) *Bain Total; (K 24)* **PRAYER FOR ARCADIA** (rec. 1982)   French
1989. (3xlp-box/d-cd) *(BIAS 834/+CD)* **THE LEGENDARY PINK BOX**
1994. (ltd-cd) *Terminal Kaleidoscope; (TEKA 999)* **FOUR DAYS**
Aug 96. (cd) *(BIAS 325CD)* **CANTA MIENTRAS PUEDAS** ('90-'95)
– Belladonna / I love you in your tragic beauty / Green gang / Princess coldheart / Disturbance / The grain kings / Prague spring / A triple moon salute / Joey the canary / Siren / The angel trail / A velvet resurrection (version) / Friend (version).

Oct 96. (d-cd) *Terminal Kaleidoscope; (TEKA 834)* **CHEMICAL PLAYSCHOOL**
May 97. (cd) *R.O.I.R.; (RUSCD 8231)* **UNDER TRIPLE MOONS** (very early material)
– As if / Splash / Submerged / Amphitheatre / Digital / Dying for the emperor / Oceans of emotion / Small anthem / Intruder / Premonition 2 / Frosty / One for the pearl moon / Whore of Babylon / War of silence / Garlands / Lust for powder / Punishment / Down from the country / Premonition 1.

Aug 02. (lp) *Soleilmoon; (CAL 027)* **EL KALEIDOSCOPIO TERMINAL**
Oct 02. (cd) *Soleilmoon; (CAD 028) / R.O.I.R.; <RUSCD 8278>* **ALL THE KING'S MEN**   Nov02

LEMONHEADS

Formed: Boston, Massachusetts, USA . . . 1983 by EVAN DANDO. Raised by middle-class parents (they were divorced when he was 12), the singer was originally the band's drummer and in March '86 he was joined by one-time school-friend, jazz-bassist JESSE PORETZ. With BEN DEILY completing the line-up, this early incarnation of The LEMONHEADS released their debut EP, the amateurish indie squall of 'LAUGHING ALL THE WAY TO THE CLEANERS' on the recently formed Boston label, 'Taang!'. The band stayed with the label for their first three releases, belting out spirited melodic punk (drawing comparisons with DINOSAUR JR, HUSKER DU, REPLACEMENTS etc,) on 'HATE YOUR FRIENDS' (1987), 'CREATOR'

LEMONHEADS (cont)

(1988) and 'LICK' (1989), the latter the pick of the bunch with a beguiling cover of Suzanne Vega's 'LUKA'. 'Atlantic' records were sufficiently confident in the band's pop-grunge abilities to offer them a deal, the initial fruits of which, the well received 'LOVEY' (1990), saw DANDO take more of a leading role following the departure of DEILY. From this point on he steered the band in an increasingly mellow, country-flavoured direction (an area he'd already explored on his 1990 solo EP, 'FAVOURITE SPANISH DISHES') with a brilliant cover of Mike Nesmith's 'DIFFERENT DRUM', while 'LOVEY' featured a fairly faithful rendition of his hero Gram Parson's 'BRASS BUTTONS'. Yet the ever unpredictable DANDO split the band up after the major label debut, eventually reforming with the help of girlfriend JULIANA HATFIELD and DAVE RYAN, the latter having played on 'LOVEY'. A spell in Australia seemed to have further mellowed the singer and the resultant album, 'IT'S A SHAME ABOUT RAY', was the most accessible LEMONHEADS release to date, heavy on harmonies and melody. Despite a favourable critical reception, the album lingered in the lower reaches of the album chart and it was only when 'Atlantic' issued the band's power pop cover of Simon & Garfunkel's 'MRS. ROBINSON', that The LEMONHEADS became a household name. Re-released to include the track, 'IT'S A SHAME ABOUT RAY' enjoyed a commercial comeback, eventually making it into the UK Top 40. Suddenly DANDO's long-haired, slacker-extraordinaire visage was staring out from every magazine cover from NME to The FACE, although this sudden thrust into the limelight seemed to drive DANDO further into drug abuse, a follow-up album, 'COME ON FEEL THE LEMONHEADS', eventually surfacing in late 1993. The record was another mellow beauty, powering into the UK Top 5 on the back of a successful Love Positions' cover, 'INTO YOUR ARMS', and even featuring contributions from legendary pedal steel player, SNEAKY PETE KLEINOW. Predictably, the Yanks just didn't get it, preferring the bluster of PEARL JAM instead. Lack of success in his home country sent DANDO spiralling further into drug use, although he had apparently cleaned up by the end of the year, undertaking a solo acoustic tour of the US. However, after a much criticised appearance at the 1995 Glastonbury festival, DANDO went to ground, spending much of his time in Australia strung out on heroin and LSD. A shorn, torn and frayed DANDO eventually surfaced in October 1996 with 'CAR BUTTON CLOTH', the first LEMONHEADS album in four years, finding DANDO in reflective and world weary mood, the melancholy side of his songwriting more pronounced than ever. After a seemingly interminable wait, DANDO came in from the wilderness with 'LIVE AT THE BRATTLE THEATRE / GRIFFITH SUNSET' (2001), a half live/half studio covers affair which revisited old favourites like 'DOWN ABOUT IT' and 'MY DRUG BUDDY'. If it was hardly a high profile comeback, we shouldn't be too surprised; thankfully DANDO still sounds as if he's doing it all off the cuff with the kind of haphazard enthusiasm his druggy days might well have leached out of him. • **Songwriters:** DANDO, although DELLY or MADDOX were contributors early on. Covered; I AM A RABBIT (Proud Scum) / HEY JOE + AMAZING GRACE (trad.) / MOD LANG (Big Star) / STRANGE (Patsy Cline) / YOUR HOME IS WHERE YOU ARE HAPPY (C. MANSON) / PLASTER CASTER (Kiss) / SKULLS (Misfits) / GONNA GET ALONG WITHOUT YA NOW (Hoagy Carmichael) / STEP BY STEP (New Kids On The Block) / FRANK MILLS (from 'Hair' musical) / KITCHEN (Hummingbirds) / MISS OTIS REGRETS (Cole Porter) / FADE TO BLACK (Metallica) / LIVE FOREVER (Oasis) / KEEP ON LOVING YOU (Reo Speedwagon) / TENDERFOOT (Tom Morgan / Adam Young) / GALVESTON (Jimmy Webb) / PIN YR HEART (Jacobites). Between 1994-1996, he co-wrote 'PURPLE PARALLELOGRAM' with Noel Gallagher (Oasis) + 'IF I COULD TALK I'D TELL YOU' with Eugene Kelly (Eugenius). • **Trivia:** DANDO and JOHN STROHM appeared on BLAKE BABIES lp, 'Slow Learners'.

Album rating: HATE YOUR FRIENDS (*4) / CREATOR (*4) / LICK (*7) / LOVEY (*5) / IT'S A SHAME ABOUT RAY (*8) / COME ON FEEL THE LEMONHEADS (*7) / CAR BUTTON CLOTH (*6) / THE BEST OF THE LEMONHEADS compilation (*8) / Evan Dando: LIVE AT THE BRATTLE THEATRE ... (*5)

EVAN DANDO (b. 4 Mar'67) – vocals, guitar + some drums / **JESSE PERETZ** – bass / **BEN DEILY** – guitar, + some drums

not iss.   ArmoryArms

Jul 86. (7"ep) <*1-2-Huh-Bag 1*> **LAUGHING ALL THE WAY TO THE CLEANERS**
– Glad I don't know / I like to / I am a rabbit / So I fucked up.

―――― added **DOUG TRACHTON** – drums

World Service   Taang!

May 88. (lp)<US-lp some colrd> (*SERVM 001*) <*T 15*> **HATE YOUR FRIENDS**   Jun87
– I don't wanna / 394 / Nothing time / Second change / Sneakyville / Amazing Grace / Belt / Hate your friends / Don't tell yourself it's ok / Uhhh / Fed up / Rat velvet. *(US-cd 1989; same +=)* – Glad I don't know / I like to / I am a rabbit / So I fucked up / Ever / Sad girl / Buried alive / Gotta stop. *(re-iss. cd Mar93 with the extra tracks)*

―――― **EVAN**, on bass, also joined BLAKE BABIES in 1988, alongside girlfriend JULIANA HATFIELD. **JOHN STROHM** – drums (ex-BLAKE BABIES) repl. DOUG.

Sep 88. (lp)(c) (*SERV 001*) <*T 23*> **CREATOR**
– Burying ground / Sunday / Clang bang clang / Out / Your home is where you're happy / Falling / Die right now / Two weeks in another town / Plaster caster / Come to my window / Take her down / Postcard / Live without. *(US-cd 1989; same +=)* – Luka (live) / Interview / Mallo cup. *(re-iss. Sep92 on 'Taang!', with 6 extra live tracks included)* *(re-iss. cd Mar93 with all re-issued tracks + 2 acoustic)*

―――― **COREY LOOG BRENNAN** – guitar (ex-BULLET LAVOLTA) repl. JOHN STROHM

Apr 89. (7"colrd) <*T 31*> **LUKA. / STRANGE / MAD**
(scheduled UK Nov89 unissued 12"/cd-s; SEVS 010/+CD)
(UK-iss. 7"/12"/cd-s Apr93)

May 89. (lp/cd) (*SERV/+CD 007*) <*T 32*> **LICK**
– Mallo cup / Glad I don't know / 7 powers / A circle of one / Cazzo di ferro / Anyway / Luka / Come back D.A. / I am a rabbit / Sad girl / Ever. *(US-cd+=)* – Strange / Mad. *(re-iss. cd Mar93)*

―――― **MARK "BUDOLA"** – drums, toured until he checked out mid '89. (COREY also left to concentrate on his PhD)

Roughneck   not iss.

Jun 90. (7") (*HYPE 3*) **DIFFERENT DRUM. / PAINT**
(12"+=)(cd-s+=) *(12 HYPE 3)(HYPE 3CD)* – Ride with me. *(re-iss. Feb93 12"ep/cd-ep; HYPE 3 T/CD)*

Atlantic   Atlantic

Jun 90. (cd-ep) <*786088-2*> **FAVORITE SPANISH DISHES EP**
– Different drum / Paint / Ride with me / Skulls / Step by step.

―――― **DAVID RYAN** (b.20 Oct'64, Fort Wayne, Indiana) – drums repl. DEILY

Oct 91. (lp/c/cd) <(*7567 82137-2/-4/-2*)> **LOVEY**   Aug90
– Ballarat / Half the time / Year of the cat / Ride with me / Li'l seed / Stove / Come downstairs / Left for dead / Brass buttons / (The) Door. *(re-iss. cd/c/lp Nov93)*

―――― In Sep'90, DANDO recruited **BEN DAUGHTY** – drums (ex-SQUIRREL BAIT) repl. RYAN / **BYRON HOAGLAND** – bass (ex-FANCY PANTS) repl. PERETZ.

Sep 91. (7") (*A 7709*) **GONNA GET ALONG WITHOUT YA NOW. / HALF THE TIME**
(12"ep+=) *(TA 7709)* – PATIENCE AND PRUDENCE EP: Stove (remix) / Step by step.

―――― **DANDO, RYAN + JULIANA HATFIELD** (b. 2 Jul'67, Wiscasset) – bass, vocals (ex-BLAKE BABIES)

Jul 92. (cd/c/lp) <(*7567 82137-2/-4/-1*)> **IT'S A SHAME ABOUT RAY**   69   68
– Rockin' stroll / Confetti / Rudderless / My drug buddy / The turnpike down / Bit part / Alison's starting to happen / Hannah and Gaby / Kitchen / Ceiling fan in my spoon / Frank Mills. *(album hit UK No.33 Jan'93)* *(re-iss. Feb95)*

Oct 92. (7"/c-s) (*A 7423/+C*) **IT'S A SHAME ABOUT RAY. / SHAKEY GROUND**   70
(10"+=/cd-s+=) *(A 7423 TE/CD)* – Dawn can't decide / The turnpike down.

Nov 92. (7"/c-s) (*A 7401/+C*) **MRS. ROBINSON. / BEING AROUND**   19
(10"+=/cd-s+=) *(A 7401 TE/CD)* – Divan / Into your arms.

―――― 1993 line-up: **DANDO, RYAN, NIC DALTON** (b.14 Jun'64, Australia) although she did provide b.vox for 1993 releases. – bass HATFIELD formed own trio)

Jan 93. (7"/c-s) (*A 7430/+C*) **CONFETTI (remix). / MY DRUG BUDDY**   44
(10"+=/cd-s+=) *(A 7430 TE/CD)* – Ride with me (live) / Confetti (acoustic).

Mar 93. (c-s) (*A 5764C*) **IT'S A SHAME ABOUT RAY / ALISON'S STARTING TO HAPPEN**   31
(cd-s+=) *(A 5764CD)* – Different drum (Evan acoustic) / Stove (Evan acoustic).
(10"+=) *(A 5764TE)* – Different drum (acoustic) / Rockin' stroll (live).
(cd-s) *(A 5764CDX)* – ('A'live) / Confetti / Mallo cup / Rudderless (all 4 live).

Oct 93. (7"/c-s) (*A 7302/+C*) <*87294*> **INTO YOUR ARMS. / MISS OTIS REGRETS**   14   67
(10"+=/cd-s+=) *(A 7302 TE/CD)* – Little black egg / Learning the game.

Oct 93. (cd/c/lp) <(*7567 82537-2/-4/-1*)> **COME ON FEEL THE LEMONHEADS**   5   56
– The great big no / Into your arms / It's about time / Down about it / Paid to smile / Big gay heart / Style / Rest assured / Dawn can't decide / I'll do it anyway / Rick James style / Being around / Favourite T / You can take it with you / The jello fund. *(lp+=)* – Miss Otis regrets.

Nov 93. (7"/c-s) (*A 7296/+C*) **IT'S ABOUT TIME. / RICK JAMES ACOUSTIC STYLE**   57
(10"+=/cd-s+=) *(A 7296 TE/CD)* – Big gay heart (demo) / Down about it (acoustic). (above 'A'side was written about JULIANA. I'LL DO IT ANYWAY for BELINDA CARLISLE)

May 94. (c-ep/10"ep/cd-ep) (*A 7259 C/TE/CD*) **BIG GAY HEART / DEEP BOTTOM COVE. / HE'S ON THE BEACH / FAVORITE T (session)**   55

―――― Offending lyrics to above 'A'side, were changed; with Stroke & Brick.

―――― DALTON departed Sep '94

―――― **PATRICK MURPHY** – drums (ex-DINOSAUR JR) repl. RYAN

―――― other members with DANDO; **BILL GIBSON** – bass, guitar / **DINA WAXMAN** – bass / **KENNY LYON** – guitar / **RICH GILBERT** – pedal steel / **BRYCE GOGGIN** – vocals, keyboards / etc.

Sep 96. (c-s) (*A 5495C*) **IF I COULD TALK I'D TELL YOU /**   39
(cd-s) *(A 5495C)* – ('A'side) / How will I know (acoustic & electric version) / I don't want to go home / Seagulls aren't free.
(cd-s) *(A 5495CDX)* – ('A'side) / It's all true (acoustic – no drums) / Sexual bryceulidge.

Oct 96. (cd/c) <(*7567 92726-2/-4*)> **CAR BUTTON CLOTH**   28
– It's all true / If I could talk I'd tell you / Break me / Hospital / The outdoor type / Losing your mind / Something's missing / Knoxville girl / 6ix / C'mon daddy / One more time / Tenderfoot / Secular rockulidge.

Nov 96. (c-s) (*A 5635C*) **IT'S ALL TRUE / LIVE FOREVER**   61
(10"+=/cd-s+=) *(A 5635 C)* – Fade to black / Keep on loving you.

Mar 97. (c-s) (*A 5620C*) **THE OUTDOOR TYPE (remix) / PIN YR HEART**
(cd-s+=) *(A 5620CD)* – Losing your mind (live acoustic).

Aug 97. (7") (*AT 0012*) **BALANCING ACTS. / GALVESTON**

– compilations, etc. –

1990. (cd) *Taang!;* <*T 15/T23*> **CREATE YOUR FRIENDS**
– (HATE YOUR FRIENDS / CREATOR / LAUGHING E.P.)

Aug 98. (cd/c) *Atlantic;* <(*7567 80851-2/-4*)> **THE BEST OF THE LEMONHEADS**
– Confetti / Into the arms / Mrs. Robinson / Rudderless / It's a shame about Ray / The great big no / Ride with me (acoustic) / My drug buddy / Big gay heart / It's about time / The outdoor type / It's all true / If I could talk I'd tell you / Hospital / Rudy with a flashlight / Into your arms (acoustic) / Down about it (acoustic) / Being around / Rick James acoustic style.

EVAN DANDO

Dec 01. (d-cd) <(MODCD 017)> **LIVE AT THE BRATTLE THEATRE / GRIFFITH SUNSET (live)** — Modular / Modular — Nov01
– Down about it / The turnpike down / The outdoor type / My drug buddy / The same thing you thought hard about is . . . . / Ride with me / Frying pan / Excuse me mister / Thirteen / Stove / Half the time / Ba-de-da / Fraulein / Sam Stone / Nothin / My baby's gone / Tribute to Hank Williams / (untitled).

LEMON KITTENS (see under ⇒ BLAKE, Karl)

LEN BRIGHT COMBO (see under ⇒ WRECKLESS ERIC; 70's section)

LET'S ACTIVE

Formed: Winston-Salem, North Carolina, USA ... 1981 by multi-instrumentalist, MITCH EASTER, who'd set up a studio in the late 70's after playing alongside moonlighting members of the dB's in a group called The SNEAKERS. His first solo outing was heard on UK V/A compilation, 'Shake To Date' a record which featured other US artists. In 1983, his new group, LET'S ACTIVE (which included long-time girlfriend, FAYE HUNTER), debuted with mini-lp, 'AFOOT', released around the same time as he chanced upon the up and coming, R.E.M., who he subsequently produced and toured alongside; he also worked with PYLON and The dB's. LET'S ACTIVE were really up and running with 1984's DON DIXON-produced set, 'CYPRESS', a 60's fixated jingle-jangle rock/pop (likened to the KINKS, the MONKEES or the BEATLES) affair given the thumb down by music press. In 1986, they finally made a critical impact with album, 'BIG PLANS FOR EVERYBODY', although it would be three years before they were back again with 'EVERY DOG HAS HIS DAY' (1989). Although this proved to be their final album, EASTER's production pedigree ensured he was never short of work.

Album rating: AFOOT mini (*6) / CYPRESS (*4) / BIG PLANS FOR EVERYBODY (*6) / EVERY DOG HAS HIS DAY (*5)

MITCH EASTER (b.15 Nov'54) – vocals, guitar / **FAYE HUNTER** (b.13 Sep'53) – bass, vocals / **SARA ROMWEBER** (b.13 Feb'64, Indiana) – drums

I.R.S. / I.R.S.

Nov 83. (m-lp) <4497-70505> **AFOOT**
– Every word means no / Make up with me / Edge of the world / Room with a view / In between / Leader of men.

Sep 84. (lp/c) (IRSA 7047) <70648> **CYPRESS**
– Easy does / Waters part / Lowdown / Gravel truck / Crows on a phone line / Ring true / Blue line / Flags for everything / Prey / Co-star / Grey scale.

— **ERIC MARSHALL** (b.1962) – drums + **ANGIE CARLSON** (b.13 Sep'60, Minnesota) – backing vocals, guitar, keyboards

Jun 86. (7") (IRM 116) **IN LITTLE WAYS. / TWO YOU'S**
(12"+=) (IRMT 116) –

Jul 86. (lp/c) (MIRF/+C 1011) **BIG PLANS FOR EVERYBODY**
– In little ways / Talking to myself / Writing on the book of last pages / Last chance town / Won't go wrong / Badger / Fell / Still dark out / Whispered news / Reflecting pool / Route 67.

Apr 89. (lp/c) (EIRSA/+C 1001) **EVERY DOG HAS HIS DAY**
– Every dog has his day / Horizon / Sweepstakes winner / Orpheus in Hades lounge / Mr. Fool / Ten layers down / Too bad / Night train / Forty years / Bad machinery / I feel funny / Terminate.

— EASTER went back to production and subsequently returned to tour with VELVET CRUSH; ANGIE formed mid-90's outfit GROVER (one set in 1996, 'My Wild Life') – she became an editor for a North Carolina newspaper

LICKS (see under ⇒ FLUX OF PINK INDIANS)

LIGHTNING SEEDS

Formed: by IAN BROUDIE, 4 Aug'58, Liverpool, England. This seasoned Scouser had previously been an integral part of BIG IN JAPAN (Autumn 77-78), before joining The SECRETS and then London-based band, ORIGINAL MIRRORS, in late '78. The latter outfit cut one eponymous album (c. early 1980) for 'Mercury', although BROUDIE left soon after to go into production work, chosen by ECHO & THE BUNNYMEN, The WAH!, The FALL and ICICLE WORKS, amongst the many to request his services. He subsequently helped form The CARE in 1983, with ex-WILD SWANS leader PAUL SIMPSON, although they disbanded after around a year and three singles; one of them, 'MY FLAMING SWORD', hit No.48 in the UK charts. After production work (mainly Merseyside bands), BROUDIE resurfaced in 1989, when he and a few session people formed The LIGHTNING SEEDS. The group signed to new indie label 'Ghetto', immediately scoring with surely one of the most fey, quintessentially indie-pop yet swoonsomely gorgeous singles ever, 'PURE'. This and its parent album, 'CLOUDCUCKOOLAND' (1990), surprised many by also making the US lists in '91 and BROUDIE garnered enough interest for 'Virgin' to sign him up for 1992's 'SENSE' album. Despite another batch of pristine, gilt-edged pop nuggets, the album hung around tentatively on the fringes of the album chart like a shy kid at the playground gates. Only 'THE LIFE OF RILEY' single managed to dent the Top 30. Perhaps as a response, 'JOLLIFICATION' (1994) was more blatantly commercial. The change was very subtle, but it was definitely there; in the way every track sounded like a muso rerun of 'PURE', in the way BROUDIE's little-boy-lost vocals now seemed to grate rather than soothe and in the way that the whole shebang continually teetered on the verge of self-parody. The resultant live shows, with their cack-handed rock approach, confirmed that BROUDIE was now writing for 20-something couples who had grown too old to go down the indie disco. The final nail in the coffin was the utterly nauseating England Euro '96 football theme, 'THREE LIONS', a track that sounded even more limp-wristed than NEW ORDER's World Cup effort two years previously. They think it's all over . . . it is now (we live in hope!?). The LIGHTNING SEEDS were back in the music game by 1999, although their comeback album of-sorts, 'TILT', did nothing to seriously shake up the indie-pop world.

• **Songwriters:** BROUDIE obviously, except SOMETHING IN THE AIR (Thunderclap Newman) / HANG ON TO A DREAM (Tim Hardin) / LUCIFER SAM (Pink Floyd) / HERE TODAY (Beach Boys) / ANOTHER GIRL, ANOTHER PLANET (Only Ones) / WHOLE WIDE WORLD (Wreckless Eric) / OUTDOOR MINER (Wire) / YOU SHOWED ME (Byrds; minor hit Turtles). LUCKY YOU + FEELING LAZY + MY BEST DAY were co-written & sung w/ TERRY HALL + IAN McNABB + ALISON MOYET respectively. The track OPEN GOALS sampled; LOOK KA PY PY (Meters).

• **Trivia:** The track 'PERSUASION' featured IAN McCULLOCH (ex-ECHO & THE BUNNYMEN). He has also produced NORTHSIDE, PRIMITIVES and TERRY HALL.

Album rating: CLOUDCUCKOOLAND (*7) / SENSE (*6) / JOLLIFICATION (*6) / PURE LIGHTNING SEEDS compilation (*7) / DIZZY HEIGHTS (*7) / LIKE YOU DO ... THE BEST OF compilation (*7) / TILT (*5)

IAN BROUDIE – vocals, keyboards, guitar / with **PETER COYLE + PAUL SIMPSON** (ex-LOTUS EATERS + WILD SWANS)

Ghetto / M.C.A.

Jun 89. (7") (GTG 004) <53816> **PURE. / FOOLS** — 16 / 31 Apr90
(12"+=) (GTGT 004) – God help them.
(cd-s+=) (GTG 004CD) – All I want.

Aug 89. (lp/c/cd) (GHETTI/+C/CD 3) <MCA/+C/D 6404> **CLOUDCUCKOOLAND** — 50 / 46
– All I want / Bound in a nutshell / Pure / Sweet dreams / The nearly man / Joy / Love explosion / Don't let go / Control the flame / The price / Fools / Frenzy. (c+=/cd+=) – God help them. (re-iss. cd May92; CDOVD 436)

Oct 89. (7") (GTG 6) **JOY. / FRENZY**
(12"+=/cd-s+=) (GTGT/CDGTG 6) – Control The Flame.
(US cd-ep+=) – Hang on to a dream.

Apr 90. (7") (GTG 9) <24054> **ALL I WANT. / PERSUASION** — Aug90
(12"+=/cd-s+=) (GTGT/CDGTG 9) – ('A'extended).

— BROUDIE made appearance on WILD SWANS non-UK album 'SPACE FLOWER'.

Virgin / M.C.A.

Mar 92. (7")/c-s) (VS/VSC 1402) <54195> **THE LIFE OF RILEY. / SOMETHING IN THE AIR** — 28 / 98
(12"+=/cd-s+=) (VST/VSCDG 1402) – Marooned.
(US c-s) <54195> – ('A'side) / excerpts: Blowing bubbles – Sense – A cool place.

Apr 92. (cd/c/lp) (CDV/TCV/V 2690) <MCA D/C 10388> **SENSE** — 53
– Sense / The life of Riley / Blowing bubbles / A cool place / Where flowers fade / A small slice of heaven / Tingle tangle / Happy / Marooned / Thinking up, looking down.

May 92. (7"/c-s) (VS/VSC 1414) <54431> **SENSE. / FLAMING SWORD** — 31 / Jun92
(12"+=/cd-s+=) (VST/VSCDT 1414) – The life of Riley (remix) / Hang on to a dream.

May 92. (c-s) <54425> **SENSE / TINGLE TANGLE** — –
(cd-s) <54431> – ('A'side) / The life of Riley / Flaming sword / Lucifer Sam.

— BROUDIE added **SIMON ROGERS** – instruments, co-producer / **CLIVE LAYTON** – Hammond organ / **MARINA VAN RODY** – vocals (Why Why Why). The live band BROUDIE – vocals, guitar / with **ALI KANE** – keyboards / **MARTYN CAMPBELL** – bass / **CHRIS SHARROCK** – drums

Epic / Trauma-Interscope

Aug 94. (7"/c-s) (660 628-8/-4) <51002> **LUCKY YOU. / ('A'lunar mix)** — 43
(12"/cd-s) (660 628-6/-2) – ('A'hard luck mix) / ('A'lucky devil mix) / ('A'lunar cabaret mix).

— Above was co-written w/ **TERRY HALL**. They are now best known for contributing football theme to Match of the Day's 'Goal Of The Month'. ALISON MOYET wrote a track for the next album.

Sep 94. (cd/c/lp) (477237-2/-4/-1) <71008> **JOLLIFICATION** — 12 / Dec94
– Perfect / Lucky you / Open goals / Change / Why why why / Marvellous / Feeling lazy / My best day / Punch & Judy / Telling tales.

Jan 95. (7")(c-s) (660 986-7/-4) **CHANGE. / SAY YOU WILL** — 13 / –
(cd-s+=) (660 986-5) – Dust.
(cd-s) (660 986-2) – ('A'side) / The life of Riley (instrumental) / Lucky you (live).

Apr 95. (c-s) (661 426-4) **MARVELLOUS / LUCIFER SAM** — 24 / –
(cd-s+=) (661 426-5) – I met you.
(cd-s) (661 426-2) – ('A'side) / ('A'club mix) / ('A'dub mix) / All I want.

Jul 95. (c-s) (662 179-4) **PERFECT / HOWL** — 18 / –
(cd-s+=) (662 179-5) – ('A'acoustic) / Blowing bubbles (extended remix).
(cd-s) (662 179-5) – ('A'side) / Change (live) / Flaming sword (live).

Oct 95. (c-s) (662 518-4) **LUCKY YOU / LUCKY YOU (Lunar mix)** — 15 / –
(cd-s) (662 518-2) – ('A'side) / Life of Riley (live) / Pure (live) / Here today (live).
(cd-s) (662 518-5) – ('A'side) / Open your eyes / The likely lads.

Feb 96. (c-s) (662 967-4) **READY OR NOT / PUNCH AND JUDY (electric '96 version)** — 20 / –
(cd-s+=) (662 967-5) – Outdoor miner.
(cd-s) (662 967-2) – ('A'side) / Another girl, another planet / Whole wide world.

May 96. (7"/c-s; BADDIEL & SKINNER & The LIGHTNING SEEDS) (663 273-7/-4) **THREE LIONS (The Official Song Of The England Football Team) / ('A'-Karaoke version)** — 1 / –
(cd-s+=) (663 273-2) – ('A'-Jules Rimet extended version).
(the '98 World Cup version returned to No.1 in Jun'98)

LIGHTNING SEEDS (cont)

			Epic	Sony
Oct 96.	(c-s) (663863-4) **WHAT IF . . . / HERE TODAY (live)**		14	-

(cd-s) (663863-2) – ('A'side) / Never / The crunch / ('A'-Leuroj's slo'n'easy mix).
(cd-s) (663863-5) – ('A'side) / Lightning Seeds mix'n'match / ('A'-Leuroj's easy disco dub mix).

Nov 96. (cd/c) (486640-2/-4) <68054> **DIZZY HEIGHTS** — 11 / —
 – Imaginary friends / You bet your life / Waiting for today to happen / What if . . . / Sugar coated iceberg / Touch and go / Like you do / Wishaway / Fingers and thumbs / You showed me / Ready or not / Fishes on the line.

Jan 97. (c-s) (664043-4) **SUGAR COATED ICEBERG / THIS POWER** — 12 / —
 (cd-s+=) (664043-2) – S.F. sorrow is born / Porpoise song.
 (cd-s) (664043-5) – ('A'side) / Why why why / Telling tales.

Apr 97. (cd-s) (664328-2) **YOU SHOWED ME (mixes by Attica Blues / The Wiseguys & DJ Pulse)** — 8 / —
 (c-s+=) (664328-4) – (Todd Terry mix).
 (cd-s) (664328-5) – (Todd Terry mixes).

Nov 97. (cd/c) (<489034-2/-4>) **LIKE YOU DO . . . THE BEST OF** (compilation) — 5 / —
 – What you say / Life of Riley / Lucky you / You showed me / Change / Waiting for today to happen ('97 mix) / Pure / Sugar coated iceberg / Ready or not / All I want / Perfect / What if? / Sense / Marvellous / Three lions.

			Epic	Alex
Nov 97.	(c-s) (665367-4) **WHAT YOU SAY / BE MY BABY**		41	Apr98

(cd-s+=) (665367-2) <6090> – Weirdaway / Blue.
(cd-s) (665367-5) <6050> – ('A'-Psyche Beach trip pts.1-3) / ('A'mixes by Ballistic Brothers & Wiseguys).

Nov 99. (c-s) (668150-4) **LIFE'S TOO SHORT / EVERYDAY AND EVERYNIGHT** — 27 / —
 (cd-s+=) (668150-2) – ('A'-ATFC remix).
 (cd-s) (668150-5) – ('A'mixes by; 3 Jays & Way Out West).

Nov 99. (cd/c) (496263-2/-4) **TILT** — 46 / —
 – Life's too short / Sweetest soul sensations / If only / City bright lights / I wish I was in love / Happy satellite / Get it right / Cigarettes and lies / Crowdpleaser / Tales of the riverbank / Pussyfoot: reprise / All the things.

Mar 00. (c-s/cd-s) (668942-4/-2) **SWEETEST SOUL SENSATIONS / LIFE'S TOO SHORT – remix / SWOOSH** — 67 / —
 (cd-s) (668942-5) – ('A'side) / ('A'mixes; Underwolves mind games / Terminalhead).

— in June 2002, The LIGHTNING SEEDS were again involved with the Top 20 re-issued of '3 Lions '98'.

– compilations, etc. –

on 'Virgin' unless otherwise mentioned
May 96. (cd/c/lp) (CDV/TCV/V 2805) **PURE LIGHTNING SEEDS** — 27 / —
May 96. (VSC 1586) **LIFE OF RILEY / SOMETHING IN THE AIR** — — / —
 (cd-s+=) (VSCDT 1586) – Marooned.
 (cd-s) (VSCDX 1586) – ('A'side) / Control the flame / ('A'remix).
Sep 00. (cd) Epic; (500511-2) **JOLLIFICATION / DIZZY HEIGHTS** — — / —

LILAC TIME (see under ⇒ DUFFY, Stephen)

LILIPUT (see under ⇒ KLEENEX; 70's section)

LITTLE ANNIE (see under ⇒ ANXIETY, Annie)

Robert LLOYD (see under ⇒ NIGHTINGALES)

LOFT (see under ⇒ WEATHER PROPHETS)

LONG RYDERS

Formed: Paisley, Los Angeles, California, USA . . . March '82, out of The UNCLAIMED by SID GRIFFIN, BARRY SKANK, MATT ROBERTS and STEVE WYNN. The latter soon formed his own band, The DREAM SYNDICATE and was superseded by STEPHEN McCARTHY. This revised line-up made an EP for 'Moxie', which included the tracks, 'Time to Time' and 'Deposition Central'. As The LONG RYDERS (named so after the Walter Hill film, 'The Long Riders), they issued a debut album, '10-5-60' (a mini-set), on their own 'Jem' label, a distinctive hybrid of jagged garage rock, psychedelia and country. While the band were lumped in with their mates under the catch-all term, "Paisley Underground", The LONG RYDERS always wore their country influences more proudly. 'NATIVE SONS' (1984), their debut for 'Zippo', marked the fruition of that experimentation, a finely hewn tapestry of alternative country which featured GENE CLARK on the keening 'IVORY TOWER'. Heralded by the critics, the band signed to 'Island' in 1985 and recorded a further two albums, 'STATE OF OUR UNION' (1985) and 'TWO FISTED TALES' (1987). More overtly country and lyrically politically pointed than their previous efforts, the latter proved to be the band's swansong and they split the following year. SID GRIFFIN subsequently relocated to London where he concentrated on his band The COAL PORTERS. The man has also helped to keep the 'Cosmic American Music' flame burning by penning a GRAM PARSONS biog and he continues to write for various music mags. Of late, GRIFFIN initiated a new project, WESTERN ELECTRIC, who released one eponymous set at the turn of the millennium. • **Songwriters:** GRIFFIN-McCARTHY compositions, except YOU'RE GONNA MISS ME (13th Floor Elevators) / I SHALL BE RELEASED + MASTERS OF WAR (Bob Dylan) / DIRTY OLD TOWN (Ewan MacColl) / PRISONERS OF ROCK'N'ROLL (Neil Young) / ANARCHY IN THE UK (Sex Pistols) / PUBLIC IMAGE (P.I.L. w/ STEVE MACK of THAT PETROL EMOTION on vox). • **Trivia:** Will Birch produced them in 1985. SID, STEPHEN + TOM featured on 'Zippo' lp THE LOST WEEKEND by DANNY & DUSTY. They also guested on DREAM SYNDICATE album 'Medicine Show'.

Album rating: 10-5-60 (*6) / NATIVE SONS (*8) / STATE OF OUR UNION (*7) / TWO-FISTED TALES (*5) / METALLIC B.O. early stuff (*4)

SID GRIFFIN (b.18 Sep'55, Louisville, Kentucky) – vocals, guitar / **STEPHEN McCARTHY** (b.12 Feb'58, Richmond, Virginia) – steel guitar, vocals; repl. STEVE WYNN (to DREAM SYNDICATE) / **DES BREWER** – bass; repl. BARRY SKANK / **MATT ROBERTS** – drums

			not iss.	P.V.C.
1983.	(m-lp) <PVC 5906> **10-5-60**		-	

 – Join my gang / I don't care what's right, I don't care what's wrong / 105-60 / And she rides / Born to believe in you. (UK-iss.1985 on 'P.V.C.'; PVC 50) (re-iss. Nov85 on 'Zippo'+=; ZANE 004) – The trip. (cd-iss. Aug87 on 'Zippo'; CMCAD 31038)

— **TOM STEVENS** (b.17 Sep'56, Elkhart, Indiana) – drums repl. DON McCALL who had repl. DES BREWER

— **GREG SOWDERS** (b.17 Mar'60, La Jolla, Calif.) – drums, repl. ROBERTS

			Zippo	Frontier
Nov 84.	(lp) (ZONG 004) <4606-1> **NATIVE SONS**			1983

 – Final wild sun / Still by / Ivory tower / Run Dusty run / (Sweet) Metal revenge / Fair game / Tell it to the judge on Sunday / Too close to the light / Wreck of the 809 / Never get to meet the man / I had a dream. (cd-iss. Jan88; ZONGCD 003) – (w/ last m-lp tracks). (cd re-iss. Jun96 on 'Diablo'; DIAB 821)

Apr 85. (7") (ZIPPO 45-2) **I HAD A DREAM. / TOO CLOSE TO THE LIGHT (Buckskin mix)**

			Island	Island
Sep 85.	(7") (IS 237) **LOOKING FOR LEWIS & CLARK. / CHILD BRIDE**		59	

 (d7"+=/10"+=) (ISD/10IS 237) – Southside of the story / If I were a bramble and you were a rose.

Oct 85. (lp/c) (ILPS/ICT 9802) <422842863-1> **STATE OF OUR UNION** — 66 / —
 – Looking for Lewis & Clark / Lights of downtown / WDIA / Mason-Dixon line / Here comes that train again / Years long ago / Good times tomorrow, hard times today / Two kinds of love / You just can't ride the boxcars anymore / Capturing the flag / State of my union. (cd-iss. Mar95 on 'Prima'+=; SID 003) – If I were a bramble and you were a rose / Southside of the story / Child bride / Christmas in New Zealand.

Jun 87. (lp/c/cd) (ILPS/ICT/CID 9869) <422842864-1> **TWO FISTED TALES** — — / —
 – Gunslinger man / I want you bad / A stitch in time / The light gets in the way / Prairie fire / Baby's in toyland / Long short story / Man of misery / Harriet Tubman's gonna carry me home / For the rest of my life / Spectacular fall. (cd re-iss. cd Mar96 on 'Prima'+=; SID 005) – Ring bells / Time keeps travelling / State of our union (live) / Baby we've all got to go down (live).

Jun 87. (7") (IS 330) **I WANT YOU BAD. / RING BELLS** — — / —
 (12"+=) (12IS 330) – State of our union.

— They split New Year '88. In Spring '90, GRIFFIN formed country-rock band The COAL PORTERS, who released first album 'REBELS WITHOUT APPLAUSE' in 1992. McCARTHY later appeared in GUTTERBALL with STEVE WYNN. GRIFFIN released a solo album in 1997.

– compilations, others, etc. –

Jan 91. (cd) Overground; (OVER 16CD) **METALLIC B.O.** (covers) — — / —
 – You're gonna miss me / Route 66 / Brand new headache / Prisoners of rock'n'roll / Dirty old town / Billy Jean / Circle round the sun / Six days on the road / Anarchy in the U.K. / Masters of war / Sandwich man / Blues theme / P.I.L. theme / I shall be released. (re-iss. Dec94; same) (re-iss. Mar00 on 'Prima'; SID 001)

May 94. (cd) Windsong; (WINCD 058) **BBC RADIO 1 LIVE IN CONCERT (live)** — — / —

COAL PORTERS

SID GRIFFIN – vocals, guitar / **BILLY BLOCK** – drums; repl. GREG SOWDERS / **CHRIS BUESSEM** – guitar / **IAN THOMSON** – bass / added **ANDY KAULKIN** – keyboards

			Rubber	Rubber
Aug 92.	(cd) <(RUB 17)> **REBELS WITHOUT APPLAUSE**			

 – Roll Columbia roll / I tell her all the time / The light that shines within / Rhythm and blues angel / Stealin' horses / Sittin' in an isle of palms (live). (UK+=) – Stuck on an island / John F. Kennedy blues (live) / March of the tap-dancing rats.

— **GRIFFIN** retained **THOMSON** and added **PAT McGARVEY** – bass + **BOB STONE** – keyboards / (wife **KATE ST. JOHN** (ex-DREAM ACADEMY) guested

			Prima	Prima
Sep 94.	(cd) <(SID 002)> **THE LAND OF HOPE AND CROSBY**			

 – Imperial beach / Death like a valentine / She loved me / What am I doing? (in this thing called love) / How did we get this far? / You can see them there / Windy city / Playing dumb #1 / Everybody's fault but mine / What about tomorrow / All the colours of the world / The pipsqueaks theme.

Sep 95. (cd) <(SID 004)> **LOS LONDON**
 – Me, here at the door / Crackin' at the seams / Chasing rainbows / A woman to love / Apple tree / It happened to me / Santa Mira / After it's broken / A Jacobite at heart / Someone's gonna love you too / Help me / Ain't no way I'll be your cowboy.

Oct 98. (cd-ep) <SID 008> **EP ROULETTE** — — / —
 – Everything / Emily in ginger / Who'll stop the rain / Help me / Don't fence me in / Me, here at your door (live).

Mar 99. (cd) <(SID 010)> **THE GRAM PARSONS TRIBUTE CONCERT (live)**
 – Luxury liner / Hickory wind / One hundred years from now / Drug store truck driving man / Sweet mental revenge / Sin city / Return of the grevious angel / Wheels / In my hour of darkness / Older guys / Hot burrito #2 / Six days on the road / Apple tree.

Jul 01. (cd) <(SID 013)> **THE CHRIS HILLMAN TRIBUTE CONCERTS (live)**
 – (introduction) / My uncle / When the ship comes in / Summer wind / Draft morning / Older guys / Tim between / Wheels / The lost highway / Sin city / Cody, Cody / Brand new heartache / The girl with no name / I am a pilgrim / The fallen eagle / So you want to be a rock'n'roll star? / You ain't goin' nowhere.

SID GRIFFIN

May 97. (cd) <(SID 007)> **LITTLE VICTORIES**
– When I'm out walking with you / Jimmy Reed / Good times tomorrow, hard times today / Rate of exchange / I wish I was a mountain / Distant trains / Sailors and soldiers / Man who invented the blues / Monk's moods / Flak jacket / Alma mater / Jerusalem road.

WESTERN ELECTRIC

GRIFFIN + McGARVEY with a few others

		Munich	Gadfly
May 00. (cd) (MRCD 199) <261> **WESTERN ELECTRIC**			Mar01

– Everything / The power of glory / When I'm out walking with you / Emily in ginger / 10-4 faithless disciplewhirlwind / Memory captures time / Carousel days / Straight from the heart / (untitled) / (untitled).

LOOK BLUE GO PURPLE

Formed: Dunedin, New Zealand ... 1983 by DENISE ROUGHAN, KATHY BULL, KAREN WEBSTER, NORMA MALLEY and LESLEY PARIS, this all-female group released three EP's, 'BEWITCHED' (1985), 'LBGPEP2' (1986) and 'THIS IS IT' (1989) – on the 'Flying Nun' label – before disbanding. The music the band performed was barbed pop which was both inviting and confrontational. The inclusion of four singer/songwriters in the group also ensured a level of tonal variation. NORMA O'MALLEY resurfaced in 1991 as part of the band CHUG. The group released a number of singles many of which appeared on their debut EP 'KISSER' (1993). The next year saw the departure of guitarist STEPHEN KILROY and drummer ALAN HAIG who were replaced by SEAN O'REILLY and SHAUN BROADLEY respectively. The group then went on to release their debut album 'SASSAFRAS' in 1994, which introduced another new guitarist, DAVID MITCHELL, In 1996, they released the EP 'LITTLE THINGS' followed by the album 'METALON' the next year.

Album rating: COMPILATION collection (*6) / Chug: SASSAFRAS (*5) / METALON (*6)

NORMA O'MALLEY – vocals, organ, guitar, organ, harmonica / **DENISE ROUGHAN** – vocals / **KATH WEBSTER** – vocals, guitar / **KATHY BULL** – bass / **LESLEY PARIS** – drums

		Flying Nun	not iss.
1985.	(12"ep) (FNLBGP 001) **BEWITCHED EP**	–	– NewZ

– Safety in crosswords / As does the sun / 100 times / Winged rumour.

| 1986. | (12"ep) (FNLBGP 002) **LBGPEP2 EP** | – | – NewZ |

– Grace / Circumspect Penelope / Hiawatha / Cactus cat / Vain hopes.

| 1987. | (c) (FNLBGP 003) **LBGPEPs** | – | – NewZ |
| 1987. | (12"ep) (FN 117) **THIS IS THIS** | – | – NewZ |

– I don't want you anyway / In your favour / Year of the tiger / Conscious unconscious / Days of old.

––– split later in '87; NORMA formed CHUG, DENISE formed 3Ds and later the GHOST CLUB; LESLEY joined OLLA (later evolved into KING LOSER without her)

– compilations, etc. –

| 1991. | (cd/c) Flying Nun; (FN CD/C 171) **COMPILATION** (the 3 EP's) | – | –NewZ |

CHUG

NORMA O'MALLEY – vocals, multi / **ALF DANIELSON** – vocals, bass, guitar / **STEPHEN KILROY** – guitar / **ALAN HAIG** – drums

		own label	not iss.
1991.	(7") (none) **CHUG**		NewZ

		Flying Nun	Alias
1992.	(7") (FN 248) **FLOWERS. / GUNNERA**	–	NewZ
1993.	(cd-ep) (FN 263) **KISSER**	–	NewZ

– Oozing / Flowers / Iron maiden / Horses / Gunnera / Silver.

––– **SEAN O'RILEY** – guitar; repl. KILROY ho formed KING LOSER
––– **SHAUN BROADLEY** – drums; repl. HAIG

| Nov 94. | (lp/cd) (FN/+CD 300) <A 112> **SASSAFRAS** | | 1996 |

– Evel Knievel / Golden mile / Hey Jimmy / Sylvia / Sometimes / Long haul / Witches / Black Sedan / Mustang / Sassafras / Chan / Wimple.

| Nov 94. | (7") (FN 305) **GOLDEN MILE. / CONCORD** | | |

(cd-s+=) (FNCD 305) – Cosmos.

––– **DAVID MITCHELL** – guitar (of 3D's, ex-GOBLIN MIX, ex-PLAGAL GRIND, ex-EXPLODING BUDGIES) repl. O'RILEY

| 1996. | (7") (FN 379) **QUEEN BEE. / DENNIS POTTER** | | |

(cd-s+=)<10"ep> **LITTLE THINGS** – Metalon / Seam.

| May 97. | (cd) <A 117> **METALON** | – | |

– Strangleknot / Catbag / Queen bee / Blue rider / Easy beat / Water torture / Vynal / Detuned / Viva / Good morning midnight / Metalon.

––– **GARY SULLIVAN** – drums (ex-GOBLIN MIX, ex-JPS EXPERIENCE, ex-SOLID GOLD HELL) repl. SHAUN

––– NORMA and ALF continued writing together; SULLIVAN joined The STEREO BUS and later DIMMER, MITCHELL continued with the GHOST CLUB

LOOP

Formed: Croydon, London, England ... 1986 by ROBERT HAMPSON, who replaced the old rhythm section for JOHN WILLS and NEIL MacKAY. They issued their own releases on 'Head' records, their debut album seeing the light of day in November 1987. A ramshackle affair, it nevertheless sowed the seeds for 1989's 'FADE OUT'. Released on the small indie label, 'Cheree', the album showcased the band's queasily churning, endlessly repetitive riffs enveloping HAMPSON's brooooding vocals. The sound and atmosphere conjured up nothing less than a hallucinogenic fever and indeed, the band's alleged stated intention was to sonically reproduce an acid trip gone wrong. While their indie compadres were getting 'sorted' during the supposed second summer of love, Loop concerned themselves with darkness and despair and it was obvious they never really fitted with the mood of the times. Their swansong, 'A GILDED ETERNITY', was a distillation of their sound, a hypnotic trip to the scarier side of the human psyche. In early 1991 they finally split, with McKAY and WILLS going off to form the rockier HAIR AND SKIN TRADING COMPANY. HAMPSON and newcomer SCOTT DAWSON formed the tripped-out MAIN, releasing 'HYDRA' in November, the first of a series of long E.P.'s and mini-albums that were more sculptured trance-ambient than the SPACEMEN 3/MC5 hybrid of LOOP. Throughout the last half of 1995, their unique 'HERTZ' series demonstrated their continuing break from the rock world.
• **Songwriters:** All penned by HAMPSON and group, except MOTHER SKY (Can) / CINNAMON GIRL (Neil Young).

Album rating: ETERNAL – THE SINGLES compilation (*7) / A GILDED ETERNITY (*7) / Main:- FIRMAMENT (*6) / MOTION POOL (*7) / LIGATURE (*6) / FIRMAMENT II (*7) / FIRMAMENT III & IV (*5)

ROB 'Josh' HAMPSON – vocals, guitar / **JAMES** – guitar / **GLEN** – bass repl. PHILIP KING (ex-SERVANTS) / **JOHN WILLS** – drums (ex-SERVANTS)

		Head	Mute
Jan 87.	(12"m) (HEAD 5) **16 DREAMS. / HEAD ON / BURNING WORLD**		–
Jun 87.	(7"pic-d) (HEAD 7L) **SPINNING. / SPINNING (part 2)**		–

(12") (HEAD 7) – ('A'side) / Deep hit / I'll take you there.

| Nov 87. | (lp) (HEADLP 1) <61154> **HEAVEN'S END** | | |

– Soundhead / Straight to your heart / Forever / Heaven's end / Too real to feel / Fix to fall / Head on / Carry me / Rocket U.S.A. / Spinning / Brittle head girl. (cd-iss. Mar88; HEADCD 1) (re-iss. Jul91 & Mar94 on 'Reactor' cd/c/lp ; REACTOR CD/C/LP 001)

––– **NEIL MacKAY** – bass repl. GLEN / **SCOTT DOWSON** – guitar repl. JAMES

		Chapter 22	not iss.
Apr 88.	(7") (LCHAP 27) **COLLISION. / CRAWLING HEART**		–

(12"+=) (12CHAP 27) – Thief of fire / Thief.

		Cheree	Rough Trade
1988.	(7"flexi) (CHEREE 1) **SOUNDHEAD (live). / (other by The TELESCOPES)**		–

––– trimmed to trio when NEIL departed

| Dec 88. | (12"m) (12CHAP 32) **BLACK SUN. / CIRCLE GRAVE / MOTHER SKY** | | |
| Jan 89. | (2x12"lp/lp/c/cd) (CHAP LLP/LP/C/CD 34) <ROUGHUS 52/+C/CD> **FADE OUT** | 51 | |

– Black sun / This is where you end / Fever knife / Torched / Fade out / Pulse / Vision strain / Got to get it over / Collision / Crawling heart / Thief of fire / Thief (motherfucker) / Mother sky. (cd re-iss. Nov92 on 'Reactor'+=; REACTORCD 004) – Where you end.

		Situation 2	Beggars Banquet
Nov 89.	(7") (SIT 64) **ARC-LITE (SONAR). / ARC-LITE (RADIATED)**		–

(12"+=/cd-s+=) (SIT 64 T/CD) – Sunburst.

| Jan 90. | (cd)(c/2x12"m-lp) (SITU 27CD)(SIT C/U 27) <2061> **A GILDED ETERNITY** | 39 | |

– Vapour / Afterglow / The nail will burn / Blood / Breathe into me / From centre to wave / Be here now. (free-7"w/above) – SHOT WITH A DIAMOND. / THE NAIL WILL BURN (BURN OUT) (cd++=) – Arc-lite (sonar). (cd re-iss. Sep95 on 'Beggars Banquet'; BBL 27CD)

––– Disbanded early in 1991; WILLS founded HAIR & SKIN TRADING CO (with McKAY)

– compilations, others, etc. –

| Aug 88. | (lp)<cd/c> Head; (HEADLP 2) / Mute; <61155-2/-4> **THE WORLD IN YOUR EYES** | | |

– 16 dreams / Head on / Burning world / Rocket U.S.A. / Spinning / Deep hit / I'll take you there / Brittle head girl / Burning prisma / Spinning (spun out). (re-iss. Jul91 & Mar94 on 'Reactor' cd/c/lp; REACTOR CD/C/LP 002)

| Nov 89. | (lp) Chapter 22; (CHAPLP 44) **ETERNAL – THE SINGLES 1988** | | |

(all Chapter 22 singles)

| May 91. | (cd/c/2x12"m-lp) Reactor; (REACTOR CD/C/LP 003) **WOLF FLOW** (The John Peel sessions 1987-91) | | – |

– Soundhead / Straight to your heart / Rocket U.S.A. / Pulse / This is where you end / Collision / From centre to wave / Afterglow / Sunburst. (re-iss. Mar94 on 'Reactor'; same)

| Mar 94. | (cd/lp) Reactor; (REACTOR CD/LP 5) **DUAL** | | – |

MAIN

were founded by **HAMPSON + DOWSON**

		Situation 2	not iss.
Nov 91.	(12"ep) (SIT 83T) **HYDRA**		–

– Flametracer / Time over (dub) / Suspension.

| May 92. | (12"ep) (SIT 89T) **CALM** | | – |

– There is only light / Remain / Feed the collapse / Sever.

(cd-ep+=) (SITL 89CD) – Thirst.

––– HAMPSON joined GODFLESH, when MAIN split temporarily.

		Beggars Banquet	Beggars Banquet
Jul 93.	(12"ep/cd-ep) (BBQM 18 T/CD) **DRY STONE FEED**		–

– Cypher / Above axis / Blown / Pulled from the water / Dry stone feed.

| Aug 93. | (12"ep) (BBQ 19CD) **FIRMAMENT (cloudscape). / CYPHER (pentode) / HEAT REALM (shortwave) / SUSPENSION (hyaline) / CODE RAYS** | | – |

(re-iss. Oct94; 12"ep/cd-ep as 'LIGATURE'; BBQM 43 T/CD)

LOOP (cont) THE GREAT INDIE DISCOGRAPHY The 1980s

Apr 94. (cd/3x12"m-lp) *(BBQ CD/LP 148)* <*92382*> **MOTION POOL**
– VII / Rail / Crater star / Core / Spectra decay / Rotary eclipse / Reformation / Heat realm / VIII / Liquid reflection.
Nov 94. (cd) *(BBQCD 168)* <*92512*> **FIRMAMENT II** – (part IX, X)
Jun 95. (cd-ep) *(HERTZ 1)* **CORONA** – (part I & II)
Aug 95. (cd-ep) *(HERTZ 2)* **TERMINUS** – (part I, II & III)
Sep 95. (cd-ep) *(HERTZ 3)* **MASER** – (part I, II, III & IV)
Oct 95. (cd-ep) *(HERTZ 4)* **HALOFORM** – (part I, II, III)
Nov 95. (cd-ep) *(HERTZ 5)* **KAON** – (part I, II, III, IV & V)
Dec 95. (cd-ep) *(HERTZ 6)* **NEPER** – (part I, II & III)
Jan 96. (cd/d-lp) *(HERTZ 16 CD/LP)* <*84016*> **HZ**   May96
– (the 'HERTZ' singles) *(re-iss. Jan98; same)*
Nov 96. (cd) *(BBQCD 179)* **FIRMAMENT III**
Aug 97. (cd) *(BBQCD 196)* **DELIQUESCENCE** (live)
– Particle suspension / Phase space / Outer Corona / Carrier wave / Cavitation / Valency.
May 98. (cd) *(BBQCD 202)* **FIRMAMENT IV**
Sep 98. (cd) <*80202*> **FIRMAMENT III & IV**
– XI / XII / XIII / XIV / XV / XVI / XVII / XVIII / XIX / XX / XXI / XXII / XXIII / XXIV / XXV / XXVI.

K031 not iss.

May 02. (cd) *(KRAAK 3)* **TAU**

LORDS OF THE NEW CHURCH
(see under ⇒ DEAD BOYS; 70's section)

LORI & THE CHAMELEONS

Formed: Liverpool, England . . . 1979 by art college student, LORI LARTY alongside DAVE BALFE and BILL DRUMMOND. Basically a studio outfit for 'Zoo' (label) keeper and ECHO & THE BUNNYMEN manager, DRUMMOND, LORI and Co only managed to scrape out four tracks in their short musical lifetime. Spread over three singles starting with the minor hit, 'TOUCH', LORI's sensuous voice should have been reason enough to secure a wider audience. An OMD-influenced/JAMES BOND movie sampling second single, 'THE LONELY SPY' (released on 'Korova' in 1980), was followed by a double header of both the aforementioned indie favourites, although this proved to be their final outing.

Album rating: didn't release any

LORI LARTY – vocals / **DAVE BALFE** – keyboards (of TEARDROP EXPLODES) / **BILL DRUMMOND** – guitar, vocals (ex-BIG IN JAPAN) / with **TIM WHITAKER** – drums (ex-DEAF SCHOOL, ex-PINK MILITARY)

Zoo not iss.

Oct 79. (7") *(CAGE 006)* **TOUCH. / LOVE ON THE GANGES**
(re-iss. Nov79 on 'Sire' SIR 4025) – (hit No.70)

Korova not iss.

Apr 80. (7") *(KOW 5)* **THE LONELY SPY. / PERU**

— **GARY DWYER + RAY MARTINEZ** – drums; repl. TIM

Oct 81. (7") *(KOW 20)* **TOUCH. / THE LONELY SPY**
(12"+=) – *(KOW 20T)* – Love on the ganges.

— split after above, DRUMMOND went solo and created JUSTIFIED ANCIENTS OF MU MU and KLF. BALFE was already part of DALEK I LOVE YOU. He later formed the label, 'Food'.

LOTUS EATERS (see under ⇒ WILD SWANS)

LOUDSPEAKER

Formed: New York City, New York, USA . . . 1986 out of 'Alternative Tentacles' combo, The CRUCIFUCKS (singer – DOC CORBIN DART), a controversially named hardcore/punk act with subsequent LOUDSPEAKER hailers, MATT BORRUSO and CHRISTOPHER DOUGLAS. Enlisting former PUSSY GALORE member, KURT WOLF and JENS JURGENSEN, the band delivered a one-off 1990 debut single for 'Sympathy For The Record Industry', 'PRAY' (not as suggested in my last edition on UK's 'One Little Indian' in '87 as this was a different LOUDSPEAKER). Resurfacing in the early 90's with ex-RHYTHM & NOISE merchant, CHARLES HANSON replacing JENS, LOUDSPEAKER subsequently delivered their long-awaited debut album, entitled 'RUBBERNECKERS VS. TAILGATERS' (1994). However, the group went AWOL yet again, only to return with the 1996 follow-up, 'RE-VERTEBRATE'.

Album rating: RUBBERNECKERS VS. TAILGATERS (*6) / RE-VERTEBRATE (*5) / Crucifucks: THE CRUCIFUCKS (*4) / WISCONSIN (*6)

CRUCIFUCKS

DOC CORBIN DART – vocals / **JAKE** – guitar / **MATT BORRUSO** – bass / **CHRIS DOUGLAS** – drums

Alternative Alternative
Tentacles Tentacles

Dec 84. (lp) <*(VIRUS 38)*> **THE CRUCIFUCKS**
– Democracy spawns bad taste / Go bankrupt and die / You give me the creeps / Marching for trash / Legal genocide / I am the establishment / Cops for fertilizer / Hinkley had a vision / By the door / Oh where, oh where? / I was / Similar items / Official terrorism / No one can make me play along with this / Down on my kness.

— **CHRIS DOUGLAS** – drums; repl. SHELLEY who joined SONIC YOUTH

Dec 85. (lp) <*(VIRUS 53)*> **WISCONSIN**
– Annual report – Intro / Mountain song / Washington / Resurrection / Earth by invitation only / Laws against laughing / Pig in a blanket / When the top comes off / Concession stand / Wisconsin / Artificial competition / Holiday parade / Savior.
Feb 92. (cd) <*(VIRUS 111)*> **OUR WILL BE DONE** (compilation of above albums)

— DART released a solo set, 'PATRICIA', in 1990

LOUDSPEAKER

— **MATT + CHRISTOPHER** plus **KURT WOLF** – guitar (ex-PUSSY GALORE) / **JENS JURGENSEN** – bass

not iss. Sympathy F

1990. (7") <*SFTRI 105*> **PRAY. / PULP**

— **CHARLES HANSON** – bass (ex-RHYTHM & NOISE) repl. JENS

not iss. Lungcast

1991. (7") <*organ 002*> **KING. / LUCKY 13**

not iss. Sympathy F

1993. (7") <*SFTRI 218*> **KNOCKOUT. /**
(UK-iss.Jul98; same)
Apr 95. (cd) <*SFTRI 285*> **RUBBERNECKERS VS. TAI**
– 5 a.m. / Low obsessor / Superbait / Vertigo / Six fingered son / Stripmind / Ape king supreme / Hunchback tragedy / Crime scene / Inflator.

— **MATT BORRUSO** recruited **CHRISTIAN BONGERS** – bass + **MARTIN KOB** – drums
Dec 95. (7") <*SFTRI 399*> **LIT. / SEW THEIR EYES SHUT**

not iss. I.F.A.

1996. (7"purple) <*IFA 008*> **X-RAY. /**

Another Another
Planet Planet

Jul 96. (cd) <*(AP 6020-2)*> **RE-VERTEBRATE**
– California son / Vaporize / Scientific / (Don't) Kill the messenger / Rerun / Supermantra / Lit / April fool / X-ray / The twin / Bassman 10.

CRUCIFUCKS

— re-formed with DART + BREHER

Alternative Alternative
Tentacles Tentacles

Sep 96. (m-cd/m-lp) <*VIRUS 186*> **L.D. EYE**
– The L.D. eye theme / Lights over Baghdad / The story of Thomas McElwee / Suicide / Officer Powell / Artificial girl / Jeanetta Jones.

LOVE AND ROCKETS (see under ⇒ BAUHAUS)

LOVE TRACTOR

Formed: Athens, Georgia, USA . . . 1980 by MIKE RICHMOND, ALFREDO VILLAR and KIT SCHWARTZ, all three seasoned players in their own respective groups, The METHOD ACTORS, The FANS and The SIDE EFFECTS. ARMISTEAD WELLFORD and MARK CLINE, were subsequently added although VILLAR had departed following the release of their eponymous 1982 debut album. Routinely compared to labelmates, PYLON, this initially instrumental band made their mark with 1983's 'AROUND THE BEND', MIKE RICHMOND taking on some vocal chores. The 'TRACTOR crew continued to plough their unorthodox furrow of hip-shaking alternative pop throughout the 80's with albums such as 'TILL THE COWS COME HOME' (1984), 'WHEEL OF PLEASURE' (1984) and 'THIS AIN'T NO OUTER SPACE SHIP' (1987), the latter featuring a cover of the Gap Band's 'PARTY TIME'. By this point the beat farmers of Athens had signed to 'Big Time', although only one further set, 'THEMES FROM VENUS' (1989) would surface; WELLFORD went on to sow his musical oats with GUTTERBALL alongside one-time DREAM SYNDICATE mainman, STEVE WYNN and BOB RUPE. • **Covered:** NEON LIGHTS (Kraftwerk).

Album rating: LOVE TRACTOR (*5) / AROUND THE BEND (*6) / TILL THE COWS COME HOME (*5) / WHEEL OF PLEASURE (*6) / THIS AIN'T NO OUTER SPACE SHIP (*6) / THEMES FROM VENUS (*7) / THE SKY AT NIGHT (*5)

MIKE RICHMOND – guitar (bassist of METHOD ACTORS) / **ALFREDO VILLAR** – keyboards (bassist of FANS) / **KIT SCHWARTZ** – drums (guitarist of SIDE EFFECTS) / **ARMISTEAD WELLFORD** – guitar / **MARK CLINE** – bass / + guest **ANDREW CARTER** – guitars, drums

DB DB

1982. (lp) <*DB 60*> **LOVE TRACTOR**
– Buy me a million dollars / Sixty degrees below / Motorcade / Festival / Cowboy songs / Hairy beat / Tropical / Wheel of pleasure.

— RICHMOND (some vocals) (WELLFORD + CLINE swopped instruments)
1983. (lp) <*DB 67*> **AROUND THE BEND**
– Highland sweetheart / Cutting corners / Spin your partner / Pretty / Fat birds / Paint (your face and stand in the mirror) / Slum dungeon / J.E.B. Pharoahs / Timberland. <*cd-iss. 1997 on 'Ichiban'; 4548*>
1984. (lp,cd) <*DB 71*> **TILL THE COWS COME HOME**
– Chilly damn Willy / Seventeen days / Fun to be happy / Neon lights / March / Cutting corners / Greedy dog / Seventeen days. <*cd+=*> – LOVE TRACTOR <*cd re-iss. 1997 on 'Ichiban'; 4547*>
Nov 84. (lp) <*DB 74*> **WHEEL OF PLEASURE**
– Neon lights / March / Jeb Pharoah's / Fun to be happy / Highland sweetheart / Spin your partner / Wheel of pleasure / Chilly damn Willy / Slum dungeon / Seventeen days / Paint / Timberland.

Big Time Big Time

Jun 87. (lp/c) *(ZL/ZK 71273)* <*6015-1/-4*> **THIS AIN'T NO OUTER SPACE SHIP**
– Cartoon kiddies / Small town / Chili part two / Night club scene / Outside with ma / Rudolf Nureyev / Beatle boots / Amusement park / Party train / We all loved each other so much. <*cd-iss. Nov00 on 'Razor & Tie'+=; RE 82217-2*> – Country club / Llama.

LOVE TRACTOR (cont)   THE GREAT INDIE DISCOGRAPHY   The 1980s

Oct 87. (7") (ZB 41421) **PARTY TRAIN. / RUDOLF NUREYEV**
(12"+=) (ZT 41422) – Got to give it up.

                                                  not iss.   DB

1989. (lp,c,cd) <DB 92> **THEMES FROM VENUS**
– I broke my saw / Themes from Venus / Crash / Satan / Crystal world / Venice / Hey mess / Nova express / Fantasy / Here comes the cops / Crash / Satan.

–––– disbanded and WELLFORD subsequently joined GUTTERBALL (with STEVE WYNN, ex-DREAM SYNDICATE and BOB RUPE, ex-HOUSE OF FREAKS)

–––– **CLINE, RICHMOND + WELLFORD** re-formed LOVE TRACTOR

                                     Razor & Tie   Razor & Tie

Mar 01. (cd) <(RE 82861-2)> **THE SKY AT NIGHT**
– Tree / Christ among the children / Bright / Palace of illusion / Birthday of time / The sky at night / Us desert / Balthus (the old clotheshine) / Antarctica (widespread panic) / Elevator / And the ship salts on / Float on / The red balloon.

Ian LOWERY

Born: London, England. Initially the singer with 'Small Wonder' outfit, The WALL (on two singles), LOWERY subsequently formed his own outfit, SKI PATROL, alongside NICK CLIFT, PETER BALMER and BRUCE ARCHIBALD. The latter was replaced after their debut 45, 'EVERYTHING IS TEMPORARY', by drummer ALAN COLE, a man who would join LOWERY's next outfit, The FOLK DEVILS. Formed in 1983, they released a few platters on their own 'Ganges' imprint, the first of which, 'HANK TURNS BLUE', was a thrashy rock'n'roll number not unlike the early DOORS. Quarrelling and personnel changes dogged this outfit and by late 1987, LOWERY was fronting yet another group, KING BLANK. Signing to 'Situation 2', LOWERY finally issued his/their first album proper (not including compilations), 'THE REAL DIRT', in 1988. Confusingly, the man returned the following year with the IAN LOWERY GROUP, releasing the 'KING BLANK TO . . .' album; the record proved to be his swansong effort as nothing's been heard of him since.

Album rating: King Blank: THE REAL DIRT (*5) / Ian Lowery Group: KING BLANK TO . . . (*5)

SKI PATROL

IAN LOWERY – vocals (ex-WALL) / **NICK CLIFT** – guitar / **PETER BALMER** – bass, vocals / **BRUCE ARCHIBALD** – drums

                                Clever Metal   not iss.

Apr 80. (7") (VIN 1) **EVERYTHING IS TEMPORARY. / SILENT SCREAMS**

–––– **ALAN COLE** – drums; repl. BRUCE

                               Malicious Damage   not iss.

Nov 80. (7") (MD 2) **AGENT ORANGE. / DRIVING**
Jul 81. (7") (MD 3) **FAITH IN TRANSITION. / CUT**

–––– disbanded in mid-81 when IAN formed the short-lived, F FOR FAKE

–––– re-formed with **NICK CLIFT** taking over all instruments (LOWERY still in there; BALMER joined FAD GADGET, COLE to FOLK DEVILS)

–––– new recruits:- **TRINA WILSON + TRACY HALL** – vocals / **MATTHEW FOX** – saxophone

                              Clever Metal   not iss.

Sep 82. (7") (VIN 2) **BRIGHT SHINY THINGS. / ELECTRIC BELLS GIRLS**

FOLK DEVILS

IAN LOWERY – vocals, acoustic guitar, piano / **ALAN COLE** – drums / **KRIS JOZAJTIS** – guitar, vocals / **WHITELY** – bass

                               Ganges   not iss.

Mar 84. (7") (RAY 1) **HANK TURNS BLUE. / CHEWING THE FLESH**
Aug 84. (7") (RAY 2) **BEAUTIFUL MONSTER. / NICE PEOPLE**
(12") (RAY 2T) – ('A'side) / Brian Jones.

                               Karbon   not iss.

Jul 85. (12"ep) (KAR 601T) **FIRE & CHROME**
– Evil eye / Where the buffalo roam / Wait / English disease.
Oct 85. (7";w-drawn) **IT DRAGS ON. /**

–––– now a 5-piece, newcomers being **JOHN HAMILTON** – bass / **ROB JONES** – drums (ex-WAH!, ex-HIGH FIVE)

                               Situation 2   Beggars Banquet

Jun 87. (12"m) (SIT 47T) **THE BEST PROTECTION. / YOUR MISTAKE / THE THIRD STROKE**
Oct 87. (lp/c) (SIT UP/CP 19) **GOODNIGHT IRONY** (compilation)

KING BLANK

–––– **LOWERY + JOZAJTIS** plus **NIGEL PULSFORD** – guitar, keyboards / **HUGH GARRETY** – bass / **KEVIN ROONEY** – drums

May 88. (7") (SIT 51) **MOUTH OFF. / DRUNK ON TEARS**
(12"+=) (SIT 51T) – Bagman.
Jul 88. (12"m) (SIT 53T) **BLIND BOX. / THOUGHT I WAS WELL / FILL ME UP**
Jul 88. (lp/c)(cd) (SITU/SITC 21)(SITU 21CD) **THE REAL DIRT**
– Howl upside down / Blind box / The real dirt / Big pink bang / Guilty as hell / Map of pain / Shot full of holes / Killer in the rain / Uptight / Bulletproof (cross symbol). (re-iss. 1989 on 'Situation 2-Lowdown' lp/c; SITL 21/+CD)
Oct 88. (7") (SIT 55) **UPTIGHT. / HOWL UPSIDE DOWN**
(12"+=) (SIT 55Z) – Slack jaw man.

IAN LOWERY GROUP

–––– nearly the same as above

Jul 89. (7") (SIT 57) **BEED. / SAILOR ON HORSE**
(12"+=) (SIT 59T) – 13th floor.
Aug 89. (lp/c/cd) (SITU 24/+C/CD) <9992-1/-4/-2> **KING BLANK TO . . .**
– Need / I said skin / A kind of loathing / Sick little minds / Wild times / You're gonna pay / Beach fire / Never trust me / Driver's arrived / The party / One last blast. (cd+=) – Jack dust. (re-iss. Nov91 on 'Situation 2-Lowdown' lp/c)(cd; SITL/+C 24)(SITL 24CD)

–––– LOWERY looks to have retired in the 90's

LOWLIFE

Formed: Grangemouth, Scotland . . . 1985 from the ashes of The DEAD NEIGHBOURS. Comprising ex-COCTEAU TWINS bassist WILL HEGGIE, GRANT McDOWELL, CRAIG LORENTSON, ALEX BURNETT and DAVY STEELE and having given up on punk monikers The IDIOCS, The AVOIDED and SOCIAL SECURITY, the early to mid 80's punk outfit released a couple of LP's, 'HARMONY IN HELL' (1984) and 'STRANGE DAYS, STRANGE WAYS' (1985). GRANT, WILL and CRAIG subsequently recruited guitarist STUART EVEREST and set about forming their own 'Nightshift' label. LOWLIFE debuted early in '86 with the mini-set, 'RAIN', following it up with first album proper, 'PERMANENT SLEEP' (1986). However, it was 1987's 'DIMENUENDO' which best captured their deep, atmospheric, vaguely gothic alt-rock sound, further albums failing to progress and leaving the band sounding increasingly dated. This was particularly evident on 1991's 'SAN ANTORIUM', recorded without the talents of EVEREST and McDOWELL (the latter is currently head of C.I.D. – not a group!). After going to ground for almost four years, LORENSTON, HEGGIE and Co resurfaced with a much-improved new album, 'GUSH' (1995), the sound lent an added edge by the presence of new secondary vocalist, JENNIFER BACHEN.

Album rating: PERMANENT SLEEP (*4) / DIMINUENDO (*6) / FROM A SCREAM TO A WHISPER compilation (*6) / GODHEAD (*4) / SAN ANTORIUM (*4) / GUSH (*6)

DEAD NEIGHBOURS

CRAIG LORENTSON – vocals / **WILL HEGGIE** – rhythm guitar, vocals (ex-COCTEAU TWINS) / **DAVY STEELE** – lead guitar / **ALEX BURNETT** – bass / **GRANT McDOWELL** – drums

                               Sharko   not iss.

Aug 84. (lp) (BITE 1) **HARMONY IN HELL**
Mar 85. (lp) (TUFT 2) **STRANGE DAYS, STRANGE WAYS**
1988. (lp) (TUFT 003) **WILD WOMAN VS. RUBBER FISH**

–––– I think their last set just comprised DAVY, ALEX + ROBBIE BUCHANAN. They became GRIM BISCUITS; ROBBIE is now deceased.

LOWLIFE

CRAIG LORENTSON – vocals / **STUART EVEREST** – guitar, keyboards / **WILL HEGGIE** – bass, keyboards, sampling (ex-COCTEAU TWINS) / **GRANT McDOWELL** – drums

                               Nightshift   not iss.

Jan 86. (12"ep) (LOLIF 1) **RAIN**
– Sometime something / Gallery of shame / Reflections of 1 (for Kelly) / Sense of fondness / Hail ye / Again and again.
Oct 86. (lp/cd) (LOLIF 2/+CD) **PERMANENT SLEEP**
– Cowards way / As it happens / Mother tongue / Wild swan / Permanent sleep / A year past July / The betting and gaming act 1964 / Do we party?.
Jan 87. (12"ep) (LOLIF 3T) **VAIN DELIGHTS**
– Vain delights / Hollow gut / Permanent sleep (steel mix) / From side to side.
Mar 87. (lp/cd) (LOLIF 4/+CD) **DIMINUENDO**
– Off pale yellow / Given to dreaming / A sullen sky / Big uncle ugliness / From side to side / Ragged rise to Tumbledown / Wonders will never cease / Tongue tied and twisted / Licked ones words.
Nov 87. (7"/12") (LOLIF 5-7/5T) **ETERNITY ROAD. / OFF PALE YELLOW**
Jan 88. (12"ep) (LOLIF 6T) **SWIRL, IT SWINGS EP**
– Swing / Colours blue / Ramified / Eternity road.
Feb 89. (lp/cd) (LOLIF 7/+CD) **FROM A SCREAM TO A WHISPER**
(a retrospective 85-88)
– Ramified / Sometime something / Cowards way / Big uncle ugliness / Wild swan / Hollow gut / Again and again / A sullen sky / Eternity road / Swing / From side to side.
Jul 90. (lp/cd) (LOLIF 8/+CD) **GODHEAD**
– In thankful hands / Where I lay, I'll lie / Marjory's dream / I don't talk to me / Drowning leaves / Bittersweet / River of woe / I the cheated / Mising the kick / Forever filthy / Never ending shroud.

–––– **HUGH DOUGIE** – guitar / **CALUM MacLEAN** – programming, guitars, bass; repl. EVEREST + McDOWELL

Sep 91. (lp/cd) (LOLIF 9/+CD) **SAN ANTORIUM**
– Jaw / Inside in / My mothers fatherly father / Big fat funky whale / Good as it gets / Suddenly violently random / June Wilson / Give up giving up / Bathe / As old as new.

–––– without CALUM but added; **JASON TAYLOR** – guitar, bass, keyboards, sampling / **JENNIFER BACHEN** – backing vocals

Nov 95. (cd) (LOLIF 10CD) **GUSH**
– Bleach / Kiss me kick / Former comrade / Truth in needles / Tocopherol / Loaded. primal / And pulled / Wicked papa / Tantalus / Petricide / Swell.

–––– disbanded the following year

LUDUS

Formed: Manchester, England … 1978 by vocalist LINDER (aka LINDA MULVEY or STERLING), along with ARTHUR CADMAN, WILLIE TROTTER and PHIL 'TOBY' TOLMAN. Managed by Richard Boon, they subsequently signed to the 'New Hormones' imprint (former DIY home of The BUZZCOCKS; LINDER was also then girlfriend of their original frontman, HOWARD DEVOTO) and debuted early 1980 with the EP, 'THE VISIT'; prior to this however, co-writer IAN DEVINE replaced ARTHUR CADMON. TROTTER was also to leave during a period in which LINDER might have secured a better mainstream following, although their indie-jazz experimentation (likened to RED CRAYOLA or ESSENTIAL LOGIC) failed to secure more than a cult audience. Several years later, DEVINE was to form a duet with another Welsh-born indie luminary, ALISON STATTON (ex-YOUNG MARBLE GIANTS), the pair recording two albums at the turn of the decade, 'THE PRINCE OF WALES' (1989) – with a cover of New Order's 'BIZARRE LOVE TRIANGLE' – and 'CARDIFFIANS' (1991).

Album rating: PICKPOCKET (*6) / THE SEDUCTION (*5) / DANGER CAME SMILING (*5) / RIDING THE BAG (*5) / Devine & Statton: THE PRINCE OF WALES (*5) / CARDIFFIANS (*4)

LINDER (b. LINDA MULVEY, 1954, Liverpool, England) – vocals / **IAN DEVINE** (b. IAN PINCOMBE, Cardiff, Wales) – guitar, vocals repl. ARTHUR CADMAN (b. PETER SADLER) / **WILLIE TROTTER** (b. 1959) – bass / **TOBY** (b. PHIL TOLMAN) – drums (ex-ED BANGER & THE NOSEBLEEDS, also of DURUTTI COLUMN)

		New Hormones	not iss.
Feb 80.	(12"ep) (ORG 4) **THE VISIT (4 COMPOSITIONS)**	□	–
	– Lullaby cheat / Unveil / Sightseeing / I can't swim, I have nightmares.		
Aug 80.	(7") (ORG 8) **MY CHERRY IS IN SHERRY. / ANATOMY IS NOT DESTINY**	□	–

— **DIDS** – drums, synthesizers; repl. TROTTER

May 81.	(c) (CAT 1) **PICKPOCKET**	□	–
	– Patient / The fool / Hugo Blanco / Mutilate / Box / Mouthpiece.		
Jul 81.	(7") (ORG 12) **MOTHER'S HOUR. / PATIENT**	□	–
Dec 81.	(2x12"ep) (ORG 16) **THE SEDUCTION**	□	–
	– Seduction (unveiled) / A woman's travelogue / My cherry is in Sherry / See the keyhole / Her story.		

— **LINDER + IAN** recruited guests LEE BUICK, GRAHAM REVELL, MICHAEL ADCOCK + MICHAEL PINCOMBE

Sep 82.	(lp) (ORG 20) **DANGER CAME SMILING**	□	–
	– Foaming at the bit / Howling comique / You open my legs like a book / Flogging cully / Mememormee / Invasion of compulsory sex morality / I stabbed at the sheep / Mistresspiece / Bloody chamber / Would you rather dancing be? / Wonder-wounded / Savasana / Bitch party / Modju / Palace of thieves / Redress / Crinkum crankum / Centuries.		
1983.	(lp) **RIDING THE BAG**	–	– Europe
	– I can't swim, I have nightmares / My cherry is in sherry / Inheritance / The escape artist / How high does the sky go? / See the keyhole / The fool / Hugo Blanco / Patient.		

		Sordide Sentimental	not iss.
1983.	(7") (SS45 008) **BREAKING THE RULES. / LITTLE GIRLS**	–	– Italy

– compilations, etc. –

Jan 88.	lp) *Interior;* (IM 013) **NUE AU SOLEIL**	□	–
	– How high does the sky go? / I can't swim, I have nightmares / SheShe / Patient / Nue au soleil / My cherry is in Sherry / Lullaby cheat / Unveil / Unveiled / Howling consigne / Let me go where my pictures go.		
	(above was to have been issued in 1985 as 'LET ME GO WHERE THE PICTURES GO' for 'Les Disques Du Crepescule')		
Oct 02.	(cd) *L.T.M.;* (itmcd 2338) **PICKPOCKET / DANGER CAME SMILING**	□	–

DEVINE & STATTON

IAN DEVINE + ALISON STATTON – vocals (ex-WEEKEND, ex-YOUNG MARBLE GIANTS) / with session people

		LesDisques	not iss.
Jan 89.	(7") (TWI 878) **UNDER THE WEATHER. /**	□	–
Mar 89.	(lp/cd) (TWI 873-1/-2) **THE PRINCE OF WALES**	□	–
	– Under the weather / Friend of the family / Bizarre love triangle / We deserve it / Not coming back / I wish I was / You're almost there / Like a blind man / Break up your heart / Comprehensible / Turn the aerials away from England / Ugly town.		
Jun 89.	(7") (TWI 895) **DON'T IT MAKE MY BROWN EYES BLUE. /**	□	–
Nov 89.	(12") (TWI 891-12) **BIZARRE LOVE TRIANGLE**	□	–
Jun 90.	(7") (TWI 908) **HIDEAWAY. /**	□	–
	below with guest ROBERT FRIPP – guitar (of KING CRIMSON)		
Jan 91.	(lp) **CARDIFFIANS**	□	–
	– Hideaway / Lovers get in the way / Crestfallen / A fact of life / Regina & Michael / Silence / Enough is enough / In the rain / Green & pleasant land / A right to be lazy / Don't make my brown eyes blue / Last days.		

LUXURIA (see under ⇒ MAGAZINE; 70's section)

LYRES

Formed: Boston, Massachusetts, USA … 1979 by (MONOMAN) JEFF CONOLLY (ex-DMZ), RICK CARMEL, RICK CORACCIO and PAUL MURPHY. Initially a surfadelic/garage trio in the mould of early LOVE, the MISUNDERSTOOD and the TROGGS, The LYRES surfaced in September that year with a debut 7", 'HOW DO YOU KNOW'. Two years on, CONOLLY and Co were back with an eponymous 12" EP, although it would be some time before The LYRES were plucking garage fans' musical heartstrings again. Eventually picked up by the French-based 'New Rose' label, the retro-fixated Farfisa freaks re-emerged with the blistering 'ON FYRE' (1984), a record that burned up reverberating semi-recycled guitar riffs (borrowing a couple of RAY DAVIES songs in the process), crazed vocals and general sonic mayhem on such stand-out tracks as 'HELP YOU ANN' and 'I'M TELLING YOU GIRL'. 1986 saw The LYRES mellowing out (in relative terms) with 'LYRES, LYRES', although their fire'n'brimstone approach to garage-punk remained undimmed. After a change of label to 'Fundamental' (US home of EUGENE CHADBOURNE, etc) for third set, 'A PROMISE IS A PROMISE' (1988), the band finally imploded, although a resurgence of interest saw CONOLLY re-form his troops for a last ditch effort on 'Taang!', 'NOBODY BUT ME' (1993). Of late, younger audiences have been catching up on what they've missed via a 'Matador' re-issue programme while another label, 'Sundazed', have re-activated 'HELP YOU ANN'.

Album rating: ON FYRE (*7) / LYRES, LYRES (*5) / A PROMISE IS A PROMISE (*5) / NOBODY TOLD ME (*5) / SOME LYRES compilation (*6)

(MONOMAN) JEFF CONOLLY – vocals, organ (ex-DMZ) / **RICK CARMEL** – guitar / **RICK CORACCIO** – bass / **PAUL MURPHY** – drums

		not iss.	Sounds Intriguing
Sep 79.	(7") <SI45 002> **HOW DO YOU KNOW. / DON'T GIVE IT UP NOW**	–	□

— **CONOLLY** now with **PETER GREENBERG** – guitar / **MIKE LEWIS** – bass / **HOWIE FERGUSON** – drums

		not iss.	Ace Of Hearts
1981.	(12"ep) <AHS 1005> **LYRES EP**	–	□
	– Buried alive / In motion / High on yourself / What a girl can't do. (UK-iss.Aug86 on 'Fan Club'; FC 016) <(cd-iss. Jun98 on 'Matador'+=; OLE 302-2)> – Help you Ann / I really want you right now / Ain't going nowhere / 100cc's (pure thrust) / She pays the rent / High on yourself / What a girl can't do / Buried alive / In motion.		
1983.	(7") <AH 105> **HELP YOU ANN. / I REALLY WANT YOU RIGHT NOW**	–	□

— there were a few more acetate singles; not on general release

— **CONOLLY** brought back **CORACCIO + MURPHY** + newcomer **DANNY McCORMACK** – guitar

		New Rose	not iss.
Jul 84.	(lp) (ROSE 35) **ON FYRE**	□	–
	– Don't give it up now / Help you Ann / I confess / I'm telling you girl / Love me till the sun shines / I really want you right now / Tired of waiting / Dolly / Soapy / The way I feel about you / Not like the other one. (cd-iss. Sep84 +=; ROSE 35CD) – Never met a girl like you / How could I have done all these things / Swing swift / Trying to please you / Busy body / Someone who'll treat you right now / She pays the rent / You've been wrong / I'll try anyway.		
Dec 85.	(12"ep) (NEW 60) **SOMEONE WHO'LL TREAT YOU RIGHT / SHE PAYS THE RENT. / YOU'VE BEEN WRONG / I'LL TRY ANYWAY**	□	–

— **JOHN BERNANDO** – drums; repl. MURPHY

Nov 86.	(lp/cd) (ROSE 103/+CD) **LYRES, LYRES**	□	–
	– Not looking back / She pays the rent / You'll never do it baby / I love her still, I always will / No reason to complain / Only think / Stacey / How do you know / You won't be sad anymore / If you want my love / Busy men / Teach me to forget you / Stormy. (cd re-iss. Jun98 on 'Matador'; OLE 304-2)		
Dec 87.	(7") (NEW 97) **HOW DO YOU KNOW. / STACY** (7"pink)	□	– French
Feb 88.	(NEW 116) **TOUCH. / JEZEBEL (live) / GO-GO-GIRL (live)**	□	–

— **CONOLLY** now with **JACK HICKEY** – guitar / **MATT MIKLOS** – bass / **JOHN SMITH** – drums

		Fundam.	Fundam.
Jun 88.	(12"m) (PRAY 008) **HERE'S A HEART (with STIV BATOR). / TOUCH (with WALLY TAX) / SHE'S GOT EYES THAT TELL LIES**	□	□
Jul 88.	(lp/cd) (SAVE 059/+CD) **A PROMISE IS A PROMISE**	□	□
	– A promise is a promise / Here's a heart (on fyre) / Every man for himself / Feel good / I'll try anyway / Worried about nothing / Touch / Running through the night / She's got eyes that tell lies / Jagged time lapse / Knock my socks off / Sick and tired / Trying just to please / Witch. (also on 'New Rose'+=; ROSE 153/+CD) – (French version inc. extras).		

— split around the late 80's, although they re-formed for below

		Taang!	Taang!
Jan 93.	(m-lp/m-cd) <(TAANG 58/+CD)> **NOBODY BUT LYRES**	□	□
	– Nobody but me / How can I make her mine / Happy now / Here's a heart (w/ STIV BATORS) / Baby / We sell soul.		

– compilations, etc. –

Jan 86.	(lp) *New Rose;* (LYRES 001) **THE BOX SET**	□	□
Aug 94.	(lp/cd) *Taang!;* <(TAANG 82/+CD)> **SOME LYRES**	□	□
Apr 97.	(cd) *Crypt;* (EFA 11578) **THE EARLY YEARS**	□	□
Sep 98.	(7") *Sundazed;* (LSD 6) **HELP YOU ANN. / (other track by The Chesterfield Kings)**	□	□

THE GREAT INDIE DISCOGRAPHY — The 1980s

Billy MACKENZIE (see under ⇒ **ASSOCIATES**)

MacKENZIES
(see under ⇒ **SECRET GOLDFISH**; in 90's section)

MAGNOLIAS

Formed: Minneapolis, Minnesota, USA . . . December 1984 by JOHN FREEMAN and his various cohorts. The group made their startling debut in 1986 with the GRANT HART (HUSKER DU) produced 'CONCRETE PILLBOX', which was issued through 'Twin/Tone' records. The noisy, battered and raw edged punk rock album was followed up by 'FOR RENT' (1988) and the inferior (but brilliantly titled) 'DIME STORE DREAM', which marked the band's last work of the 80's. Veering more towards the mainstream audiences in early '92, the fourth set, 'OFF THE HOOK', saw FREEMAN and his team of downtrodden degenerates pulling off catchy, powerchord punk, which would provide inspiration for the then up-and-coming GREEN DAY and NOFX. Surprisingly enough, after this extremely successful release, the group disappeared, providing column inches written mostly by sceptical critics and worried fans. It was refreshing to see the MAGNOLIAS arise again in 1996 when they delivered the uncompromising 'STREET DATE TUESDAY', with FREEMAN (in tradition) remaining as the only original member. • **Covered:** WAY OUT (Barbera-Hanna) / LAST TRAIN TO CLARKSVILLE (Monkees) / STOLE YOUR LOVE (. . . Stanley).

Album rating: CONCRETE PILLBOX (*5) / FOR RENT (*7) / DIME STORE DREAM (*4) / OFF THE HOOK (*8) / STREET DATE TUESDAY (*6)

JOHN FREEMAN – vocals, rhythm guitar / **TOM LISCHMANN** – lead guitar / **JOHN PAUL JOYCE** – bass / **RON ANDERSON** – drums

		not iss.	Twin/Tone
Sep 86.	(lp) <TTR 8683> **CONCRETE PILLBOX**	-	

— **KYLE KILLORIN** – bass; repl. JOYCE

| Apr 88. | (lp/c) <TTR 88129/+C> **FOR RENT** | - | |

– Walk a circle / Glory hop / Goodbye for now / Down and out / Gangs in my town / Halfway down the road / Illusion / Bring it back / East Coast, West Coast girl / A little more / Pale horse / Nothin' much to do.

— **TOM COOK** – drums; repl. ANDERSON

| Oct 89. | (cd/c) <TTR 89159 CD/C> **DIME STORE DREAM** | - | |

– Asking the time / Pardon me / Flowin' thru / Shirley's looking down / Don't see tat girl / Coming on too strong / Folks on the block / Fathers and sins / I've been gone / In my nightmare / Red light district / Leave ya at the morgue / Bouncing ball.

— **FREEMAN + COOK** enlisted **CALEB PALMITER** – bass / **KENT MILITZER** – guitar, vocals

		Alias	Alias
Jun 92.	(lp/c/cd) <(A 024/+C/D)> **OFF THE HOOK**		Apr92

– Hello or goodbye / Don't pack it in / Matter of time / My little flame / Never lasts / Tear up this town / Take me away / Up the ladder / When I'm not / Time bomb / Complicated fun / Playing to win.

| Oct 92. | (cd-ep) <(A 031CD)> **HUNG UP ON THE MAGNOLIAS EP** | | |

– When I'm not / Hello or goodbye / Way out / Fathers and sins / Last train to Clarksville / Stole your love.

— **FREEMAN** recruited **ERIC KASSEL** – guitar, vocals / **JOHNNY O'HALLORAN** – bass / **DAVE WIEGART** – drums

		not iss.	Twin/Tone
Sep 96.	(cd) <89339> **STREET DATE TUESDAY**	-	

– Hello Belinda / Beat skip jump & walk / Dropping blood and names / Old news / Bullet for a badman / Polecat creek / Weather couldn't get any better / Even without you / Sara the driver / In your eye / Trashbin / My heart / On & on.

— shunned the limelight for a quieter existence

MALARIA!

Formed: Berlin, Germany . . . 1980 by the all-female crew of BETTINA KOESTER, MANON DUURSMA, GUDRUN GUT, SUSANNE KUHNKE and New Yorker CHRISTINE HAHN. Although not around for that long (until 1983, to be exact!), MALARIA! have been influential – alongside the likes of KLEENEX and The RAINCOATS – for many all-girl post-punk groups such as CHICKS ON SPEED, etc. Following their eponymous EP debut in 1980, they signed to Belgium's 'Les Disques Du Crepuscule', releasing 'HOW DO YOU LIKE MY NEW DOG' and 'WHITE WATER', towards the end of '81 and spring '82 respectively. If you liked your New Wave noisy, well MALARIA were for you.

Album rating: EMOTION (*7) / MALARIA! . . .REVISITED (*5)

BETTINA KOESTER – vocals, saxophone (ex-MANIA D) / **MANON DUURSMA** – guitar / **GUDRUN GUT** – drums, guitar, vocals (ex-MANIA D) / **CHRISTINE HAHN** – drums, organ (ex-STATIC, ex-LUXUS, ex-PINK PONG) / **SUSANNE KUHNKE** – synthesizer

		Marat	not iss.
Nov 80.	(12"ep) (006) **MALARIA!**	-	- German

– Laufen / Verfuhrung / I will be your only one / Kampfen und siegen / Dabo.

		Operation Twilight	not iss.
Jan 82.	(7") (TWI 033) **HOW DO YOU LIKE MY NEW DOG? / PERNOD**	-	-

		Crepuscule	not iss.
Apr 82.	(12"ep) (TWI 067) **WHITE WATER, WHITE SEA**	-	-

– Weisser himmer, weiser hair / White water, white sea / Kaltes 2 klares wasses.

| Aug 82. | (lp) (TWI 077) **EMOTION** | | |

– Geld / Leidenschaft / Eifersucht / Einsam / Macht tod / Mensch / Slave / Traum / Gewissen.

		Jungle	not iss.
Nov 82.	(12"ep) (JUNG 3) **NEW YORK PASSAGE**		

– Your turn to run / Zarah / Duschen.

— disbanded in 1983

– **compilations, etc.** –

| May 83. | (c) R.O.I.R.; <A 123> **MALARIA! . . .REVISITED (live)** | - | |

– Kaltes klares wasser (Cold clear water) / Duschen (Take a shower) / White sky, white sea / Jealousy / Leidenschaft (Passion) / Macht (Might) / You / Thrash me / Meeting place / Tod (Death) / Slave. <(UK cd-iss. Jul97 on 'Danceteria'; DANCD 083)>

| 1985. | (cd) Rebel; <SPV 08-1429> **BEAT THE DISTANCE** | - | - German |

– You you / Jealousy / You you / Meeting place / Thrash me / Lone some / Tod.

MAN FROM DELMONTE

Formed: Manchester, England . . . mid 80's when local art school student MARTIN met classical pianist and budding bassist SHEILA. However, the band were not complete until they found Australian-born songsmith MIKE WEST and rusty drummer HOWARD (the latter hadn't used his sticks for several years!). Choosing to rehearse in SHEILA's living room, they finally surfaced with several jangly, twee-like pop numbers and a group name, THE MAN FROM DELMONTE (Del Monte being a tinned-fruit brand name with the well-versed TV ad catch phrase, "the man from Del Monte, he say yes!"). In spring '87, their first record, 'DRIVE DRIVE DRIVE', for the newly-formed 'Ugly Man' records (once home to BLACK), was in the can, so to speak. Backed by a cheap video, the follow-up singles 'WATER IN MY EYES' and 'WILL NOBODY SAVE LOUISE' repeated the formula and things looked up for the band. Early in '89 and signed to 'Bop Cassettes', they delivered their first long-player, 'BIG NOISE', although only two further singles/EP's were completed before they returned to their day jobs; MIKE WEST currently records with MYSKIN.

Album rating: BIG NOISE (*6) / THE GOOD THINGS IN LIFE collection (*6)

MARTIN – vocals / **SHEILA** – bass, piano / **MIKE WEST** – guitar, vocals / **HOWARD** – drums

		Ugly Man	not iss.
Apr 87.	(7") (UGLY 3) **DRIVE DRIVE DRIVE, TWENTY TWO AND STILL IN LOVE WITH YOU. / SUN SERIOUS**		-
Aug 87.	(7") (UGLY 5) **WATER IN MY EYES. / BORED BY YOU** (12"+=) (UGLY 5T) – The country.		-
Mar 88.	(7") (UGLY 7) **WILL NOBODY SAVE LOUISE. / THE GOOD THINGS IN LIFE** (12"+=) (UGLY 7T) – Like a millionaire.		-

		Bop Cassettes	not iss.
Jan 89.	(12"ep) (BIP 502) **MONDAY MORNING AFTER**		-

– Waiting for Ann / Australia fair / M.I.C.H.A.E.L. / Ascension day.

| Feb 89. | (lp) (BIP 503V) **BIG NOISE (live from the Boardwalk, Manchester)** | | - |

– The good things in life / Louise and I / The country / Bored by you / Casual friends / M.I.C.H.A.E.L. / Monday morning after / Water in my eyes / Sun serious / My girl / Big noise / Louise / Mathematically speaking / Lasha me. (<re+US-iss.Jul00 on 'Vinyl Japan' lp/cd; ASK LP/CD 101>)

| Jul 89. | (12"ep) (BIP 701) **MY LOVE IS LIKE A GIFT YOU CAN'T RETURN** | | - |

– My love is like a gift you can't return / Armchair Valentino / I don't go out with her anymore, but / Lasha me.

— split in 1990, some became SURFURBIA who released 'THE NEIGHBOURHOOD' 12" EP in 1992

– **compilations, etc.** –

on 'Vinyl Japan' unless mentioned otherwise

| Nov 99. | (cd) (<ASKCD 102>) **THE GOOD THINGS IN LIFE** | | Jun00 |
| Jan 00. | (cd) (<ASKCD 103>) **THE GOOD THINGS IN LIFE VOL.1** | | Jun00 |

– Drive drive drive / Sun serious / Water in my eyes / Bored by you / Take me to the country / Will nobody save Louise / Casual friends / Patient / Ascension day / The good things in life / Like a millionaire / Waiting for Annie / Australia fair.

| Jan 00. | (cd) (<ASKCD 104>) **THE GOOD THINGS IN LIFE VOL.2** | | Jun00 |

– M.I.C.H.A.E.L. / Stand by my man / Mathematically speaking / My love is like a gift you can't return / Armchair Valentino / Big noise / I don't go out with her anymore, but / Lasha me / Stop / Lebanese American / Patient / Australia fair / Big noise / Like a millionaire.

Barbara MANNING

Born: 12 Dec'64, San Diego, California, USA. Beginning her career with local folk-rock act, 28TH DAY (who also comprised COLE MARQUIS and MIKE CLOWARD), MANNING recorded a solitary eponymous mini-set in 1985 – covering Pete Seeger's 'THIS TRAIN' – before embarking on a solo career. Subsequently basing herself in San Francisco, the singer/songwriter/guitarist cut two albums worth of her own material, 'LATELY I KEEP SCISSORS' (1989) and 'ONE PERFECT GREEN PLANET' (1991). The former found MANNING backed by the WORLD OF POOH (featuring ex-CAT HEADS member, MELANIE CLARIN and KIM OSTERWALD) while the latter saw her working with the TABLESPOONS, an act that numbered MICHELLE CERNUTO and LINCOLN ALLEN alongside two future members (the aforementioned MELANIE and KIM), of her soon-to-be-formed outfit, S.F. SEALS. Still based in the Bay Area, the experimental, retro-pop influenced trio signed to hip US indie label, 'Matador', debuting late in 1993 with a homage to three of their World Series heroes in the shape of the 'BASEBALL TRILOGY' EP. The band (with additional personnel including MARGARET MURRAY and BENTLEY PUSSER) went on to record two full sets, 'NOWHERE' (1994) and 'TRUTH WALKS IN SLEEPY SHADOWS' (1995), while MANNING herself found time to fit in another solo album, '... SINGS WITH THE ORIGINAL ARTISTS' (1995), a collaborative effort with English post-punk stalwarts, The MEKONS. A few years later, the indie-roots maverick returned with a surprisingly strong set of songs in '1212' (1997), named so due to her birth day/month and originally mooted for a SF SEALS project. In 1999, she teamed up with Kiwi indie legends such as CHRIS KNOX, GRAEME DOWNES, ROBERT SCOTT, DAVID KILGOUR and DENISE ROUGHAN (along with CALEXICO's JOEY BURNS and JOHN CONVERTINO, er, from the States) to record one unique, transpacific set of an album, appropriately titled 'IN NEW ZEALAND'. Not content with just playing the solo game, MANNING subsequently worked with The GO-LUCKYS! (FABRIZIO and FLAVIO STEINBACH) on two further collaborative works, 'HOMELESS IS WHERE THE HEART IS' (1999) and 'YOU SHOULD KNOW BY NOW' (2001). • **Covered:** DON'T LET IT BRING YOU DOWN (Paul McCartney) / THESE DAYS (Jackson Browne) / BABY, WE'RE REALLY IN LOVE (Hank Williams) / I LOVE YOU 1000 WAYS (Lefty Frizzell) / CAKE WALKING (Young Marble Giants) / YOU'VE GOT TO HIDE YOUR LOVE AWAY (Beatles) / etc.

Album rating: 28th Day: 28th DAY mini (*5) / Barbara Manning: LATELY I KEEP SCISSORS (*6) / ONE PERFECT GREEN PLANET compilation (*6) / ... SINGS WITH THE ORIGINAL ARTISTS (*5) / 1212 (*7) / IN NEW ZEALAND (*6) / HOMELESS IS WHERE THE HEART IS with the Go-Luckys! (*6) / UNDER ONE ROOF: SINGLES AND ODDITIES collection (*6) / YOU SHOULD KNOW BY NOW with The Go-Luckys! (*5) / S.F. Seals: NOWHERE (*6) / TRUTH WALKS IN SLEEPY SHADOWS (*6)

28th DAY

BARBARA MANNING – vocals, guitar / **COLE MARQUIS** – guitar / **MIKE CLOWARD** – drums

		not iss.	Enigma
1985.	(m-lp/m-c) <72047-1/-4> **28th DAY** – 25 pills / Where the bears sing / This train / I'm only asking / Dead sinner / Pages turn / Lost. <cd-iss. 1991 on 'Skyclad'+=; 128> – Burnsite / Instrumental #1 / Holiday / Stones of judgement / Pages turn (alt.take) / Life story.	-	

— MANNING and CLOWARD split up, with the latter and MARQUIS forming SUN BIRDS. MARQUIS subsequently joined The DOWNSIDERS and later the SNOWMEN.

BARBARA MANNING

- vocals, guitar, cello, bass / with **BRANDON KEARNEY** – clarinet / also her band **WORLD OF POOH** (who made one set, 'Land Of Thirst')

		Heyday	Heyday
May 89.	(lp) <(HEY 002)> **LATELY I KEEP SCISSORS** – Scissors / Breathe lies / Somewhere soon / Talk all night / Make it go away / Never park / Every pretty girl / Mark E. Smith and Brix / Something you've got (isn't good) / Prophecy written.		Nov88
		not iss.	Forced Exposure
1990.	(7") **DON'T LET IT BRING YOU DOWN. / HAZE IS FREE**	-	

— now with her group the **TABLESPOONS** including **KIM OSTERWALD + MELANIE CLARIN + MICHELLE CERNUTO + LINCOLN ALLEN**

Sep 91.	(cd/c/lp) <(HEY 018 CD/CS/LP)> **ONE PERFECT GREEN PLANET** – Straw man / Smoking her wings / Don't rewind / Sympathy wreath / Green / Lock yer room (uptight) / Someone wants you dead / Sympathy wreath (reprise). (cd re-iss. Mar94 on 'Normal'+=; NORMAL 138CD) – LATELY I KEEP SCISSORS		
		not iss.	TeenBeat
Jun 93.	(7") <TEENBEAT 102> **B4 WE GO UNDER. / LOVE YOU 1000 WAYS**	-	

— In 1993, BARBARA augmented STUART MOXHAM & THE ORIGINAL ARTISTS (aka The MEKONS) on an album, 'SIGNAL PATH'.

S.F. SEALS

— **BARBARA MANNING** with **MELANIE CLARIN** – drums, accordion, vocals / **KIM OSTERWALD** – cello / also with 4th member **MARGARET MURRAY** – bass (ex-U.S. SAUCER) / toured with **CHRIS MILNER** – bass (of MOLECULES) / **JAY PAGE** – drums

		not iss.	Sub Pop
1993.	(7") <SP 204> **NOWHERICA. / BEING CHEATED**		
		Matador	Matador
Dec 93.	(7"ep/cd-ep) <(OLE 064-7/-2)> **BASEBALL TRILOGY** – Joltin' Joe DiMaggio / The ballad of Denny McLain / Dock Ellis.		

— added 5th member **BRENTLY PUSSER** – guitar (of 3-DAY STUBBLE)

May 94.	(7") <(OLE 088-7)> **STILL? / DON'T UNDERESTIMATE ME**		
Jun 94.	(cd/lp) <(OLE 089-2/-1)> **NOWHERE** – Back again / Don't underestimate me / 8's / Janine's dream / Still / Day 12 / Winter song / Baby blue / Demons on the corner / Missing.		
Sep 95.	(cd/lp) <(OLE 162-2/-1)> **TRUTH WALKS IN SLEEPY SHADOWS** – S.F. Sorrow / Ladies of the sea / Ipecac / Locked out / Bold letters / Flashback Caruso / Pulp / Soul of Patrick Lee / Kid's pirate ship / How did you know / Stellar lullabye.		
Nov 95.	(7") <(OLE 176-7)> **IPECAC. / HOW DID YOU KNOW**		

BARBARA MANNING

— with The MEKONS, etc

		not iss.	Feel Good All Over
1995.	(cd) <FGAO 7001> **BARBARA MANNING SINGS WITH THE ORIGINAL ARTISTS** – My first gun / Gold brick / When I dream / Here comes love / Daddy bully / Untitled #2 / Optimism is it's own reward / Martian man / Big eye / Cry me a river / You were the one.	-	

— with **JIM O'ROURKE, JOHN CONVERTINO, JOEY BURNS, CRAIG SCHUMACHER**

		Matador	Matador
Jun 97.	(cd/d-lp) <(OLE 221-2/-1)> **1212** – The arsonist story: Fireman – Evil plays piano – Evil craves attention.... – Trapped and drowning / End of the rainbow / Blood of feeling / Rickity tikity tin / Stain on the sun / Isn't lonely lovely? / That kid / First line (seven the row) / Marcus Leid / Stammtisch.		

— next with **JOEY BURNS + JOHN CONVERTINO** (of CALEXICO) / **DAVID KILGOUR** (of the CLEAN) / **GRAEME DOWNES** (of VERLAINES) / **CHRIS KNOX** (of 3-D's) / **ROBERT SCOTT** (of BATS) + **DENISE ROUGHAN**

		Communion	Communion
Oct 98.	(cd) <(COMM 50CD)> **IN NEW ZEALAND** – Everything happens by itself / Lover's leap / Walking stick / Your pies / Patience is gone / Whatever I do is right/wrong / Aramsana.		Dec99

BARBARA MANNING AND THE GO-LUCKYS!

— with **FABRIZIO + FLAVIO STEINBACH** / **+ JEFF PALMER** – musical saw

		Naive	Naive
Nov 99.	(m-cd/m-lp) <(NAIVEP 1990920 CD/V)> **HOMELESS IS WHERE THE HEART IS** – Life – Luck / Long distance / Soundtracks / Old woman / Hanging by strands / Isn't lonely lovely?		Jan00
		Innerstate	Innerstate
Jun 01.	(cd/lp) <(7010-2/-1)> **YOU SHOULD KNOW BY NOW** – Don't neglect yourself / You knock me out / I insist / Time to B. / Goof on the roof / Boston song / Buds won't bud / Rhombus / Never made love / Incapable.		May01

– compilations, etc. –

Aug 00.	(cd) *Innerstate*; <(7009-2)> **UNDER ONE ROOF: SINGLES AND ODDITIES** – Don't let it bring you down / Haze is free (mounting a broken ladder) / These days / Someone wants you dead / Baby, we're really in love / I love you 1000 ways / B4 we go under / Joed out / Damned lucky / Being cheated / Don't rewind / Cake walking / You've got to hide your love away / The blood of feeling / Slip into the ocean / Hummingbird / The shalala song / I can't watch you play drums.		

MARC & THE MAMBAS (see under ⇒ ALMOND, Marc)

MARCH VIOLETS

Formed: Leeds, England ... late 1981 by SIMON DENBIGH and LOZ ELLIOT. Featuring a line-up completed by guitarist HUGH and secondary vocalist, ROSIE GARLAND, this fledgling goth outfit emerged from the same scene that spawned The SISTERS OF MERCY, releasing the cheesy 'RELIGIOUS AS HELL' as their debut single on the latter outfit's 'Merciful Release' imprint in summer '82. Like the SISTERS, they also powered their rhythm section with a tinny drum machine for that quintessential 80's sound. After a further single, 'GROOVING ON GREEN', the band signed to the 'Rebirth' label, subsequently bringing in TOM ASHTON as a replacement for HUGH. This served to bolster the sound and by the release of early '84's classy 'SNAKE DANCE', the band had progressed to a kind of CULT-esque groove with GARLAND providing far more effective backing vocals. Later that year, the 'NATURAL HISTORY' compilation collected together the cream of the band's work to date although the departure of founding member DENBIGH (to form The BATFISH BOYS) reduced The MARCH VIOLETS to a trio of newcomer CLEO MURRAY, ELLIOT and ASHTON. Fresh material finally surfaced in the shape of Spring '85's 'DEEP' single and its 1986 follow-up, 'TURN TO THE SKY', although unlike their more famous contemporaries, the MARCH VIOLETS failed to effect a major critical and commercial coup.

Album rating: NATURAL HISTORY compilation (*6) / ELECTRIC SHADES compilation (*6) / THE BOTANIC VERSES compilation (*7)

SIMON DENBIGH – vocals / **LOZ ELLIOT** – bass / **HUGH** – guitar / **ROSIE GARLAND** – vocals

MARCH VIOLETS (cont)

		Merciful Release	not iss.
Aug 82.	(7"ep) (MR 013) **RELIGIOUS AS HELL. / FODDER. / CHILDREN ON STUN / BON BON BABIES**	☐	-
Nov 82.	(7") (MR 017) **GROOVING IN GREEN. / STREAM**	☐	-

		Rebirth	Relativity
May 83.	(7") (RB 18) **CROW BABY. / ONE TWO I LOVE YOU** (12"=Mar85+=) (RB 18-12) – Long pig / Crow bait.	☐	-

— TOM ASHTON – guitar; repl. HUGH

Jan 84.	(7") (RB 21) **SNAKE DANCE. / SLOW DRIP LIZARD** (12"+=) (RB 21-12) – It's hot / ('A'extended).	☐	-
May 84.	(7") (RB 23) **RESPECTABLE. / MICROWAVES**	☐	-
Jul 84.	(7") (VRB 24) **WALK IN THE SUN. / LIGHTS GO OUT** (12"+=) (VRB 24-12) – Essence.	☐	-
Oct 84.	(lp) (VRB 25) **NATURAL HISTORY** (compilation)	☐	-

— now without ROSIE + SIMON D (the latter formed the BATFISH BOYS)
— Autumn '84, both were repl. by CLEO – vocals
— late '84 – briefly added TRAVIS – drums to repl. drum machine
— now a trio of CLEO + TOM + LOZ

Apr 85.	(7") (VRB 26) **DEEP. / ELDORADO** (12"+=) (VRB 26-12) – Electric shades.	☐	-
Jan 86.	(lp) <EMC 8039> **ELECTRIC SHADES** (compilation)	-	☐
Feb 86.	(7") (VRB 27) **TURN TO THE SKY. / NEVER LOOK** (12"+=) (VRBX 27) – Deep (deeper mix).	☐	-

— split after their latest failure

– compilations, etc. –

| Sep 93. | (cd) Jungle; (FREUDCD 42) / Cleopatra; <1030> **THE BOTANIC VERSES** | | Feb94 |

– Snake dance (extended) / Walk into the sun / Slow drip lizard / The lights go out / Essence / Crow baby / 1 2 I love you / Grooving in green / It's hot / Long pig / Steam / Fodder / Radiant boys / Bob bon babies / Religious as hell / Children on stun / Crow bait / Snake dance. (re-iss. Aug01; same)

MARINE GIRLS

Formed: Hatfield, Hertfordshire, England ... 1980 by TRACEY THORN, alongside sisters ALICE and JANE FOX. This quirky but charming post-New Wave trio issued their first official release in 1981, the cassette-only 'BEACH PARTY – Catch The Cod'. Subsequently re-issued on vinyl by TV PERSONALITY, DAN TREACY's 'Whaam!' imprint, the album showcased the girls' YOUNG MARBLE GIANTS-esque, cheap but effective pop minimalism with TRACEY THORN's sultry vocal rapidly blossoming among the mainly ALICE FOX-led 2-minutes tales of lovelorn angst. THORN, however, was to take the lead vocals on their debut single, 'ON MY MIND', its child-like simplicity no doubt persuading 'Cherry Red' to net their signatures. Having re-released the single and given THORN a solo shot ('A Distant Shore' mini-set), the MARINE GIRLS finally began making waves with the more widely distributed follow-up lp, 'LAZY WAYS', early in '83. However, by this time, TRACEY had met her beau, BEN WATT, at Hull University, the pair releasing their first joint recording, Cole Porter's 'NIGHT AND DAY' as EVERYTHING BUT THE GIRL in summer '83. Inevitably, THORN found it increasingly difficult to juggle two/three careers and opted to part ways with the FOX sisters later that year. JANE, too, was attempting to balance group and solo commitments, having already released the summer single, 'IT'S A FINE DAY', a starkly atmospheric, acappella gem which was radically overhauled by OPUS III for a massive disco hit nine years later. JANE subsequently found her "Ben Watt" in rhythm man, BARTON, the partnership extended to a mini-set, 'JANE AND BARTON' (1983). The following year, the dreamy singer was re-united with ALICE in another maritime-themed outfit, GRAB GRAB THE HADDOCK, although they only surfaced for a couple of 45's.

Album rating: BEACH PARTY (*6) / LAZY WAYS (*6) / Jane And Barton: JANE AND BARTON mini (*4)

ALICE FOX (b.1966) – vocals / **TRACEY THORN** (b.26 Sep'62) – guitar, vocals / **JANE FOX** (b.1963) – bass

		In-Phaze	not iss.
1980.	(ltd-c; various) (Tapes 001) **A DAY BY THE SEA**	☐	-
1981.	(c) (Tapes 002) **(BEACH PARTY – Catch The Cod)**	☐	-

– In love / Fridays / Tonight / Times we used to spend / Honey / Flying over Russia / Tuti lo sanno / Dishonesty / Promises / Silent red / He got the girl / All dressed up / Holiday song / Day-night dream / 20,000 leagues / Marine girls. (lp-iss.Dec81 on 'Whaam!-InPhaze'; COD 1) (re-iss. lp Apr87 on 'Cherry Red'; BRED 75)

| Mar 82. | (7") (COD 2) **ON MY MIND. / THE LURE OF THE ROCKPOOLS** (re-iss. May82 on 'Cherry Red'; CHERRY 40) | ☐ | - |

		Cherry Red	not iss.
Jan 83.	(7") (CHERRY 54) **DON'T COME BACK. / YOU MUST BE MAD**	☐	-
Mar 83.	(lp) (BRED 44) **LAZY WAYS**	☐	-

– A place in the sun / Leave me with the boy / Falling again / Love to know / A different light / Sunshine blue / Second sight / Don't come back / That fink, jazz-me-blues boy / Fever / Shell island / Lazy ways / Such a thing / You must be mad. (cd/c iss.Aug88 +=; CD/C MRED 44) – BEACH PARTY (cd+ re-iss. Jul01; CDMRED 189) <US cd+ iss.2001 on 'Cooking Vinyl'; COOKCD 402>

— TRACEY had already gone solo and formed EVERYTHING BUT THE GIRL with BEN WATT

JANE

— augmented by **BARTON** on rhythm

May 83.	(7") (CHERRY 65) **IT'S A FINE DAY. / OF ALL / LEAVES WERE FALLING** (cd-s iss.Jul93; CDCHERRY 65)	☐	-
Sep 83.	(7"; by JANE & BARTON) (CHERRY 69) **I WANT TO BE WITH YOU. / ('A'version)**	☐	-
Sep 83.	(m-lp; by JANE & BARTON) (MRED 53) **JANE & BARTON**	☐	-

– There is a man / It's a fine day / You are over there (part 1) / I want to be with you / You are over there (part 2) / Ha bloody ha.

GRAB GRAB THE HADDOCK

— **ALICE + JANE** plus **LESTER NOEL** – guitar + **STEVEN GOLLOWAY** – drums

| Sep 84. | (12") (12CHERRY 83) **I'M USED NOW. / NOTHING TO SAY** | ☐ | - |
| Apr 85. | (7"ep/12"ep) (CHERRY/12CHERRY 86) **THE LAST FOND GOODBYE / ONE BUT SMILING. / FOR ALL WE KNOW / THAT BIG WORD BUT** | ☐ | - |

— the sisters & co. retired from the music biz

Chris MARS (see under ⇒ REPLACEMENTS)

J. MASCIS (see under ⇒ DINOSAUR JR.)

MASS (see under ⇒ WOLFGANG PRESS)

MATCHING MOLE (see under ⇒ WYATT, Robert)

MAXIMUM JOY (see under ⇒ GLAXO BABIES)

McCARTHY

Formed: Barking Abbey, Essex, England ... 1984 by school mates MALCOLM EDEN, TIM GANE, JOHN WILLIAMSON and GARY BAKER; all attended the same school as BILLY BRAGG. Following a self-financed, limited edition debut single, 'IN PURGATORY', the band signed to the Rough Trade offshoot 'Pink' and released the acclaimed 'RED SLEEPING BEAUTY'; all guitar crescendos and rolling, tumbling drums, the track was a lullaby for socialism amid the rampant Thatcherism of the mid-80's. One of a string of overtly left-wing bands of the era – prior to the final nail in the coffin of the 1987 Conservative victory – McCARTHY came to greater prominence via the inclusion of the very SMITHS-esque 'CELESTIAL CITY' on the NME's C86 compilation tape. The following year saw the release of a debut album, 'I'M A WALLET' (1987), two further politically barbed sets, 'THE ENRAGED WILL INHERIT THE EARTH' and 'BANKING, VIOLENCE AND THE INNER CITY LIFE TODAY' emerging at the turn of the decade as the band hopped from label to label. With wider recognition seemingly as far off as ever and the political climate as stagnant as ever, McCARTHY finally split in 1990, GANE going on to cult hero status with avant-popsters, STEREOLAB. As well as being the latter outfit's home from home, GANE's 'Duophonic Super 45s' label also handled EDEN's solo venture, 'HERZFELD', while he made his home in Paris.

Album rating: I AM A WALLET (*8) / THE ENRAGED WILL INHERIT THE EARTH (*7) / BANKING, VIOLENCE AND THE INNER LIFE TODAY (*7) / THAT'S ALL VERY WELL BUT ... THE BEST OF McCARTHY compilation (*8) / Herzfeld: THE SACK mini (*5)

MALCOLM EDEN (b. 1 Sep'63, Ilford, Essex, England) – vocals, guitar / **TIM GANE** (b.12 Jul'64) – guitar / **JOHN WILLIAMSON** (b.28 Dec'63, Ilford) – bass / **GARY BAKER** (b. 8 Sep'63) – drums

		Wall Of Salmon	not iss.
Feb 86.	(7"m) (MAC 001) **IN PURGATORY. / THE COMRADE ERA / SOMETHING WRONG SOMEWHERE**	☐	-

		Pink	not iss.
Oct 86.	(7") (PINKY 12) **RED SLEEPING BEAUTY. / FROM THE DAMNED** (12"+=) (PINKY 12T) – The comrade era / For the fat lady.	☐	-
Mar 87.	(7") (PINKY 17) **FRANS HALS. / THE FALL (remix)** (12"+=) (PINKY 17T) – Kill, kill, kill, kill / ('A'version).	☐	-

		September	not iss.
Oct 87.	(7") (SEPT 1) **THE WELL OF LONELINESS. / ANTIAMERICANCRETIN / UNFORTUNATELY** (12"+=) (SEPT 1T) – Bad dreams / Someone worse off.	☐	-
Oct 87.	(lp) (SEPT 2) **I AM A WALLET**	☐	-

– An M.P. speaks / Monetaries / The international narcotics traffic / The way of the world / Antinature / Charles Windsor / The vision of Peregrine Worsthome / The well of loneliness / The wicked palace revolution / God made the virus / The funeral / A child soon in chains / In the dark times / The procession of popular capitalism. (re-iss. Jan89 on 'Midnight Music' lp/c/cd+=; CHIME 0045 S/CC/CD) – Unfortunately / Bad dreams / Someone worse off / Antiamericancretin.

| Feb 88. | (12"ep) (SEPT 4T) **THIS NELSON ROCKEFELLER / THE FALL. / THE FUNERAL / THE ENEMY IS AT HOME (FOR THE FAT LADY) / THE WAY OF THE WORLD** | ☐ | - |
| Apr 88. | (12"m) (SEPT 5T) **SHOULD THE BIBLE BE BANNED? / ST. FRANCIS AMONGST THE MORTALS / WE ARE ALL BOURGEOIS NOW** | ☐ | - |

			Midnight Music	not iss.
Feb 89.	(7"m/12"m)	*(DING/DONG 045)* **KEEP AN OPEN EYE OR ELSE. / TWO CRIMINALS POINT OF VIEW / THE NEW LEFT REVIEW #1**	☐	-
Mar 89.	(lp/c/cd)	*(CHIME 00.47 S/C/CD)* **THE ENRAGED WILL INHERIT THE EARTH**	☐	-

– Boy meets girl, so what / Governing takes brains / An address to the better off / Hands off or die / What our boys are fighting for / Two criminal points of view / The new left review / Keep an open mind or else / We are all born creeps / I'm not a patriot but . . . / The Home Secretary briefs the forces of law and order / Throw him out he's breaking my heart. (<cd re-iss. Apr98 on 'Cherry Red' +=; CDMRED 148)> – All your questions answered / New left review #2 / The lion will lie down with the lamb / St. Francis amongst the mortals / Nobody could care less about your private lives / Can the haves use their brains / With one eye on getting their pay / Boy meets girl, so what (single version).

| May 89. | (12"ep/cd-ep) | *(DONG 48/+CD)* **McCARTHY AT WAR** | ☐ | - |

– The lion will lie down with the lamb / The new left review #2 / All your questions answered / Boy meets girl, so what.

| Apr 90. | (cd/c/lp) | *(CHIME 01.05 CD/C/S)* **BANKING, VIOLENCE AND THE INNER LIFE TODAY** | ☐ | - |

– I'm on the side of mankind as much as the next man / And tomorrow the stock exchange will be the human race / Now is the time for an iron hand / The drinking song of the merchant bankers / Write to your M.P. today / Use a bank I'd rather die / I worked myself up from nothing / The well-fed point of view / Get a knife between your teeth / Take the shortest way with the men of violence / You'll have to put an end to them.

| Apr 90. | (7") | *(DING 61)* **GET A KNIFE BETWEEN YOUR TEETH** | ☐ | - |

(12"+=) *(DONG 61T)* – With one eye on getting their pay / Can the haves use their brains?

— disbanded after above and TIM quickly formed his complete diversion STEREOLAB; EDEN formed HERZFELD while studying literature. BAKER was last heard working as a radiographer.

– compilations, etc. –

| May 88. | (lp) | *Danceteria; (TUE 871)* **A LA GUILLOTINE** (first three singles/EPs) | ☐ | - |
| Jul 91. | (d-lp/c/cd) | *Midnight Music; (CHIME 41/+C/CD)* **THAT'S ALL VERY WELL BUT . . . – THE BEST OF McCARTHY** | ☐ | - |

– Red sleeping beauty / Should the bible be banned / An M.P. speaks / The fall / The funeral / We are all bourgeois now / Antinature / Kill, kill, kill, kill / Frans Hals / The myth of the north / Something wrong somewhere / This Nelson Rockefeller / Charles Windsor / From the damned / Child soon in chains / The enemy is at home (for the fat lady) / The well of loneliness / You're alive / Keep an open mind or else / I'm not a patriot but . . . / Comrade era / Should the bible be banned. (<cd re-iss. May96 & Jun01 on 'Cherry Red'; CDMRED 125>)

| Feb 97. | (cd) | *Cherry Red; (<CDMRED 138>)* **I AM A WALLET / VIOLENCE AND INTERNATIONAL NARCOTICS** | ☐ | Sep99 |

HERZFELD

MALCOLM EDEN + others

			Duophonic Super 45s	not iss.
Nov 93.	(7")	*(DS45 07)* **TWO MOTHERS. / WHO THE SCROUNGERS ARE**	☐	-
Nov 94.	(10"m-lp)	*(DS 33)* **THE SACK**	☐	-

– Do you want this job or not? / Old Winston / Reign of terror / Its your company too / Hang em high / The stock exchange speaks / He wasn't ill enough / Small businessman gone beserk.

— MALCOLM retired from the music biz

Scott McCAUGHEY
(see under ⇒ YOUNG FRESH FELLOWS)

Dave McCOMB (see under ⇒ TRIFFIDS)

Ian McCULLOCH
(see under ⇒ ECHO & THE BUNNYMEN)

Rose McDOWALL
(see under ⇒ STRAWBERRY SWITCHBLADE)

Alan McGEE

Born: 29 Sep'60, East Kilbride, Scotland. Moved down south to London in 1983 to become boss of up and coming indie imprint, 'Creation'. Named after 60's cult psych-pop combo, The CREATION (who recorded a track, 'BIFF BANG POW!'), the label was to become McGEE's most successful venture into the music business after years of low-key activities on the fledgling indie scene. His first outfit had been the LAUGHING APPLE, who issued a couple of 45's in the early 80's, a trial run for BIFF BANG POW!. The latter outfit's debut single, '50 YEARS OF FUN', appeared in '84, the man McGEE subsequently launching the careers of such influential acts as JESUS & MARY CHAIN, PRIMAL SCREAM and of course, OASIS. When he found the time, the flame-haired entrepreneur beavered away at BIFF BANG POW! material. Over the course of nearly a decade, McGEE indulged his love of psychedelia, punk and NEIL YOUNG with such albums as 'PASS THE PAINTBRUSH . . . HONEY!' (1985), 'LOVE IS FOREVER' (1988) and his final studio outing 'ME' (1991). Now a multi-millionaire, McGEE has always had an uncanny ability to spot innovative "indie" rock talent, the success of outfits like RIDE, BOO RADLEYS and initially MY BLOODY VALENTINE allowing him to loyally stand by less profitable artists such as EDWARD BALL. Talking of ED, he was paid tribute by noneother than ALAN's composer-cum-panel-beater dad, JOHN, who with his orchestra released 'SLINKY' (1997) – now there's a bit of trivia. Another bit was surely his £20,000 donation to New Labour's May 1997 election campaign. In 1999/2000 after 'Creation' were put out to pasture, McGEE opted for a new venture, 'Poptones' records; one of his first signings were Glasgow-based COSMIC ROUGH RIDERS.

Album rating: Biff Bang Pow!: PASS THE PAINTBRUSH . . . HONEY (*6) / THE GIRLS WHO RUNS THE BEAT HOTEL (*6) / OBLIVION (*6) / LOVE IS FOREVER (*6) / SONGS FOR THE SAD EYED GIRL (*6) / ME (*5) / L'AMOUR, DEMURE, STENHOUSEMUIR compilation (*6) / Chemical Pilot: JOURNEY TO THE CENTRE OF THE MIND (*5)

LAUGHING APPLE

ALAN McGEE – vocals, guitar / with others unknown

			Autonomy	not iss.
1981.	(7"ep)	*(AUT 001)* **HA HA HEE HEE**	☐	-
1981.	(7")	*(AUT 002)* **PARTICIPATE!. / WOULDN'T YOU**	☐	-
			Essential	not iss.
1982.	(7")	*(ESS 001)* **PRECIOUS FEELING. / CELEBRATION**	☐	-

— in 1983, the track, 'WOULDN'T YOU' appeared on a 7"flexi given away free to buyers of the LEGEND's 7" '73 IN '83' on 'Creation' (CRE 001).

BIFF BANG POW!

ALAN McGEE with **DICK GREEN** – guitar / **JOE FOSTER** – bass (aka SLAUGHTER JOE) / **KEN POPPLE** – drums

			Creation	not iss.
Feb 84.	(7")	*(CRE 003)* **50 YEARS OF FUN. / THEN WHEN I SCREAM**	☐	-
Jun 84.	(7")	*(CRE 007)* **THERE MUST BE A BETTER LIFE. / THE CHOCOLATE ELEPHANT MAN**	☐	-

— **DAVE EVANS** – bass; repl. FOSTER (who continued solo)
— **ANDREW INNES** – guitar, organ (became part-timer)

| Feb 85. | (lp) | *(CRELP 004)* **PASS THE PAINTBRUSH . . . HONEY** | ☐ | - |

– There must be a better life / Lost your dreams / Love and hate / The chocolate elephant man / Water bomb / Colin Dobbins / Wouldn't you? / A day out with Jeremy Chester.

| Mar 86. | (7") | *(CRE 024)* **LOVE'S GOING OUT OF FASHION. / IT HAPPENS ALL THE TIME** | ☐ | - |

(12"+=) *(CRE 024T)* – Inside the mushroom / In the afternoon.

| Nov 86. | (7") | *(CRE 034)* **SOMEONE STOLE MY WHEELS. / SUNNY DAYS** | ☐ | - |

(12"+=) *(CRE 034T)* – It makes you scared.
below credited the artist/painter, JC BROUCHARD

| Feb 87. | (7") | *(CRE 038)* **THE WHOLE WORLD IS TURNING BROUCHARD. / THE DEATH OF ENGLAND** | ☐ | - |
| Mar 87. | (lp) | *(CRELP 015)* **THE GIRL WHO RUNS THE BEAT HOTEL** | ☐ | - |

– Someone stole my wheels / Love's going out of fashion / She never understood / He don't need that girl / She shivers inside / The beat hotel / The happiest girl in the world / If I die / Five minutes in the life of Greenwood Goulding / The whole world is turning Brouchard. (cd/c-iss.May88 +=; CRECD/CCRE 015) – PASS THE PAINTBRUSH . . . HONEY.

| Jun 87. | (lp) | *(CRELP 020)* **OBLIVION** | ☐ | - |

– In a mourning town / There you go again / Seven seconds to Heaven / A girl called destruction / She's got diamonds in her hair / The only colour in the world is love / Baby sister / Then when I scream / I see the sun / I'm still waiting for my time.

| Feb 88. | (12"ep) | *(CRE 051)* **SHE HAUNTS / THE BEAT HOTEL. / SHE PAINTS / IT HAPPENS ALL THE TIME** | ☐ | - |
| Apr 88. | (lp) | *(CRELP 029)* **LOVE IS FOREVER** | ☐ | - |

– Miss California Toothpaste 1972 / She haunts / Searching for the pavement / She paints / Close / Ice cream machine / Electric sugar child / Dark in mind / Startripper / She went away to love / The beat hotel / It happens all the time.

| Jun 89. | (lp/cd) | *(CRE LP/CD 046)* **THE ACID HOUSE ALBUM** (compilation) | ☐ | - |

– I'm still waiting for my time / Love and hate / Someone stole my wheels / Love's going out of fashion / She haunts / 50 years of fun / She never understood / The beat hotel / In a mourning town / Then when I scream / She's got diamonds in her hair / The girl from Well Lane / There must be a better life.

| Jan 90. | (cd/c/lp) | *(CRECD/CCRE/CRELP 058)* **SONGS FOR THE SAD EYED GIRL** | ☐ | - |

– She kills me / The girl from Well Lane / Baby you just don't care / If you don't love me now, you never ever will / Someone to share my life with / Religious / Hug me honey. (cd+=) – OBLIVION (c+=) – LOVE IS FOREVER

| Nov 90. | (7") | *(CAFF 13)* **SLEEP. / (other by The TIMES)** | ☐ | - |

(above issued on 'Caff')

| Apr 91. | (cd/c/lp) | *(CRECD/CCRE/CRELP 071)* **ME** | ☐ | - |

– My first friend / Miss you / I'm burned / Song for a nail / She saved me / You just can't buy satisfaction / Sad eyes in velvet / Guilt ridden / Lovers / Baby you just make me strong.

| Nov 91. | (cd/c/lp) | *(CRECD/CCRE/CRELP 099)* **L'AMOUR, DEMURE, STENHOUSEMUIR** (compilation) | ☐ | - |

– She haunts / Someone to share my life with / Startripper / There must be a better life / She paints / Ice cream machine / Hug me honey / Miss you / She kills me / I'm waiting for my time / Someone stole my wheels / Song for a nail / Love's going out of fashion / Girl from Well Lane / Baby you just don't care / The chocolate elephant man / Tell Laura I love her / Searching for the pavement.

| Feb 92. | (cd/lp) | *(CRE CD/LP 125)* **DEBASEMENT TAPES** (compilation of out-takes, etc.) | ☐ | - |

– Long live Neil Young and all who sail in him / In bed with Paul Weller / It makes you scared / It happens all the time / The death of England / In the afternoon / Sleep / Back to the start / Inside the mushroom / Everybody wants to divorce her.

— McGEE decided to hang up his proverbial boots and sign on OASIS

– compilations, etc. –

| Apr 94. | (cd) | *Tristar;* **BERTULA POP** | - | ☐ |

CHEMICAL PILOT

ALAN McGEE + ED BALL

		Eruption	not iss.
Mar 98.	(12"/cd-s) *(ERUP T/SCD 004)* **ASTRAL DOMINOES** (mixes: Decoder / Matt Schwartz / Profound Noize)	□	-
Jul 98.	(12") *(ERUPT 006)* **MOVE A LITTLE CLOSER. / CLASSICAL FRUIT**	□	-
Oct 98.	(cd/d-lp) *(ERUP CD/LP 003)* **JOURNEY TO THE CENTRE OF THE MIND**	□	-

– Astral dominoes / Classical fruit / Alien abduction / Bye bye lover / Chemical gangsters / Anti-American / Move a little closer / Colours / Watch the target.

G.W. McLENNAN (see under ⇒ GO-BETWEENS)

Ian McNABB

Born: ROBERT IAN McNABB, 3 Nov'60, Liverpool, England. After a spell with CITY LIGHTS, then SUNSET BOULEVARD, he formed The ICICLE WORKS in 1979 with CHRIS LAYHE and CHRIS SHARROCK. A cassingle appeared on 'Probe' in 1981, followed a year later by their vinyl debut 'NIRVANA', the single surfacing on manager Tony Barwood's 'Troll Kitchen' label. After their classy 45, 'BIRDS FLY' won over numerous indie legions, they moved upstairs in 1983 to 'Beggars Banquet' and immediately made an impact in the Top 20 with 'LOVE IS A WONDERFUL COLOUR'. A re-issue of 'BIRDS FLY (WHISPER TO A SCREAM)', didn't fare as well, although it surprisingly broke them into the US Top 40. Their eponymous debut album also cracked the American market having already gone Top 30 in the UK. Still sounding SCOTT WALKER-ish at this early stage, McNABB (complete with attached microphone gadget) was a compelling frontman for this college circuit power-rock trio. Follow-up set, 'THE SMALL PRICE OF A BICYCLE' (1985), featured a number of good reasons ('SEVEN HORSES' and 'ALL THE DAUGHTERS' for starters) why they deserved promotion from Rock's second division, while 'IF YOU WANT TO DEFEAT YOUR ENEMY SING HIS SONG' (1987) finally gave them a UK Top 30 album. The following year, 'BLIND' also scraped into the Top 40, although this was their final effort for the label having signed to 'Epic'. Major label status did them no favours, the disappointing 'PERMANENT DAMAGE' seeing a slide in their popularity and leading to them being dropped. McNABB was virtually left in the cold, that is until 'Way Cool' released his debut solo single, 'GREAT DREAMS OF HEAVEN' in 1991. This was closely followed by another independently released 45, McNABB's deserved break coming the following year when ANDREW LAUDER signed him to his 'This Way Up' label. Early in 1993, McNABB was back in the album charts, 'TRUTH & BEAUTY' nearly making the UK Top 50. He subsequently realised one of his longheld musical dreams when he secured the services of the legendary CRAZY HORSE, initially for live work before going into the studio to record a whole album together. The resulting 'HEAD LIKE A ROCK' (1994), was short-listed for a Mercury Music Award, his critical rehabilitation now complete. In 1996, McNABB released his third solo set, 'MERSEYBEAST', his second consecutive Top 30 achievement and a worthy addition to his increasingly impressive back catalogue. After the latter's full-frontal roots-pop assault, the singer/songwriter stripped things right down to basics for the cannily titled 'A PARTY POLITICAL BROADCAST ON BEHALF OF THE EMOTIONAL PARTY' (1998). McNABB's most skeletal recording to date, the album found the singer concentrating on affairs of the heart. Given that the crowd noise was dubbed out, 'LIVE AT LIFE' (2001), ostensibly recorded for a fan-club release, retains a slightly similar feel although the set list, unsurprisingly, is composed of tried and tested McNABB favourites stretching way back to the early days of The ICICLE WORKS. His next set proper (i.e. studio set) was 2001's 'WAIFS AND STRAYS' while 'IAN McNABB' (2002), as its title might imply, was, if not a creative rebirth as such, at least a return to the livewire pop/rock sound he'd made his name with. As ever, the scouse troubadour's guiding musical light is NEIL YOUNG/CRAZY HORSE although for many fans, that's no bad thing, bearing in mind the fact that he's tended to rein in his muse in recent years. • **Songwriters:** Mostly McNABB compositions for ICICLE WORKS except; SEA SONG (Robert Wyatt) / NATURE'S WAY (Spirit) / COLD TURKEY (John Lennon) / INTO THE MYSTIC (Van Morrison) / YOU AIN'T SEEN NOTHIN' YET (Bachman-Turner Overdrive) / SHOULD I STAY OR SHOULD I GO (Clash) / ROCK'N'ROLL (Led Zeppelin) / PRIVATE REVOLUTION (World Party) / ROADHOUSE BLUES (Doors) / TRIAD – CHESTNUT MARE (Byrds) / MR SOUL + FOR WHAT IT'S WORTH (Buffalo Springfield). McNABB covered UNKNOWN LEGEND + THE NEEDLE AND THE DAMAGE DONE (Neil Young) / CAROLINE NO (Brian Wilson). • **Trivia:** In Aug'85, an ICICLE WORKS off-shoot MELTING POT, were supposed to have had a single 'IT MAKES NO DIFFERENCE' issued.

Album rating: Icicle Works: THE ICICLE WORKS (*6) / THE SMALL PRICE OF A BICYCLE (*7) / IF YOU WANT TO DEFEAT YOUR ENEMY SING HIS SONG (*6) / BLIND (*5) / PERMANENT DAMAGE (*5) / THE BEST OF THE ICICLE WORKS compilation (*8) / Ian McNabb: TRUTH & BEAUTY (*6) / HEAD LIKE A ROCK (*8) / MERSEYBEAST (*6) / A PARTY POLITICAL BROADCAST ON BEHALF OF THE EMOTIONAL PARTY (*5) / LIVE AT LIFE (*4) / WAIFS & STRAYS (*5) / IAN McNABB (*5) /

ICICLE WORKS

IAN McNABB – vocals, guitar, keyboards / **CHRIS LAYHE** – bass, keyboards, vocals / **CHRIS SHARROCK** – drums, percussion

		Probe	not iss.
Mar 81.	(c-ep) *(private)* **ASCENDING**	□	-

		Troll Kitchen	not iss.
Oct 82.	(7"m) *(WORKS 001)* **NIRVANA. / LOVE HUNT / SIROCCO**	□	-

		Situation2	not iss.
Jun 83.	(7") *(SIT 22)* **BIRDS FLY (WHISPER TO A SCREAM). / REVERIE GIRL** (12"+=) *(SIT 22T)* – Gunboys.	□	-

		Beggars Banquet	Arista
Oct 83.	(7"/7"pic-d) *(BEG 99/+P)* **LOVE IS A WONDERFUL COLOUR. / WATERLINE** (ext.12"+=/ext.12"pic-d+=) *(BEG 99 T/TP)* – In the dance the Shamen led. (d7"++=) *(BEG 99 + ICE 1)* – The Devil on horseback.	15	-
Mar 84.	(7") *(BEG 108)* **BIRDS FLY (WHISPER TO A SCREAM). / IN THE CAULDRON OF LOVE** (12"+=) *(BEG 108T)* – Ragweed campaign / Scarecrow. (12"+=) *(BEG 108TD)* – ('A'-Frantic mix).	53	-
Mar 84.	(lp/c) *(BEGA/BEGC 50)* <8202> **THE ICICLE WORKS** – Chop the tree / Love is a wonderful colour / Reaping the rich harvest / As the dragonfly flies / Lover's day / In the cauldron of love / Out of season / A factory in the desert / Birds fly (whisper to a scream) / Nirvana. (cd-iss. Jul86; BEGA 50CD) (re-iss. Jul88 lp/c/cd; BBL/+C 50/+CD)	24	40
Mar 84.	(7") <9155> **BIRDS FLY (WHISPER TO A SCREAM). / IN THE DANCE THE SHAMEN LED**	-	37
Sep 84.	(7") *(BEG 119)* **HOLLOW HORSE. / THE ATHEIST** (12"+=) *(BEG 119T)* – Nirvana (live). (12"+=) *(BEG 119TR)* – ('A' remix).	□	-
May 85.	(7") *(BEG 133)* **ALL THE DAUGHTERS (OF HER FATHER'S HOUSE). / A POCKETFUL OF NOTHING** (12"+=) *(BEG 133T)* – Mr. Soul.	□	-
Jul 85.	(7") *(BEG 142)* **SEVEN HORSES. / SLINGSHOT** (d7"+=) *(BEG 142D)* – Beggars legacy / Goin' back. (12") *(BEG 142T)* – ('A'-American) / ('B'side) / Beggars legacy.	□	-
Sep 85.	(lp/c) *(BEGA/BEGC 61)* **THE SMALL PRICE OF A BICYCLE** – Hollow horse / Perambulator / Seven horses / Rapids / Windfall / Assumed sundown / Saint's sojourn / All the daughter's (of her father's horse) / Book of reason / Conscience of kings. (re-iss. Jan89 lp/c/cd; BBL/+C 61/+CD)	55	-
Oct 85.	(7") *(BEG 151)* **WHEN IT ALL COMES DOWN. / (LET'S GO) DOWN TO THE RIVER** ('A' unabridged-12"+=) *(BEG 151T)* – Cold turkey.	□	-
Feb 86.	(m-lp/c) *(BEGA/BEGC 71)* **SEVEN SINGLES DEEP** (compilation) – Hollow horse / Love is a wonderful colour / Birds fly (whisper to a scream) / All the daughters (of her father's house) / When it all comes down / Seven horses / Rapids. (c+=) – I never saw my hometown 'til I went around the world / (Let's go) Down to the river / Slingshot / The atheist / Into the mystic / A pocketful of nothing / Goin' back. (re-iss. Sep88 lp/c/cd; BBL/+C 71/+CD) (cd+=) – Perambulator / Lover's day / Out of season / Saints sojourn / Nirvana / Conscience of kings.	52	-

		Beggars Banquet	Beggars Banquet
Jun 86.	(7") *(BEG 160)* **UNDERSTANDING JANE. / I NEVER SAW MY HOMETOWN 'TIL I WENT AROUND THE WORLD** (12"+=) *(BEG 160T)* – Into the mystic. (d7"+=) *(BEG 160 + ICE 3)* – Hollow horse (live) / You ain't seen nothin' yet (live). (c-s+=) *(BEG 160C)* – Seven horses (live) / Perambulator (live) / Rapids (live).	52	-
Sep 86.	(7") *(BEG 172)* **WHO DO YOU WANT FOR YOUR LOVE. / UNDERSTANDING JANE (live)** (w/ free c-s+=) *(BEG 172F)* – John Geoffrey Muir shopkeeper / Impossibly three lovers. (12"+=) *(BEG 172T)* – Should I stay or should I go (live) / Roadhouse blues (live).	54	-
Dec 86.	Situation2; (12"ep) *(SIT 45T)* **UP HERE IN THE NORTH OF ENGLAND. / SEA SONG (Ian McNabb) / NATURE'S WAY / IT MAKES NO DIFFERENCE / WAYLAID (Chis Layhe)**	□	-
Jan 87.	(7") *(BEG 181)* **EVANGELINE. / EVERYBODY LOVES TO PLAY THE FOOL** (12"+=) *(BEG 181T)* – Waiting in the wings / ('A'demo). (c-s+=) *(BEG 181C)* – It makes no difference / Nature's way / Sea song.	53	-
Mar 87.	(lp/c)(cd) *(BEGA/BEGC 78)(BEGA 78CD)* <6447> **IF YOU WANT TO DEFEAT YOUR ENEMY SING HIS SONG** – Hope springs eternal / Travelling chest / Sweet Thursday / Up here in the north of England / Who do you want for your love / When you were mine / Evangeline / Truck driver's lament / Understanding Jane / Walking with a mountain. (c+=) – Everybody loves to play the fool / Don't let it rain on my parade. (cd++=) – I never saw my hometown 'til went around the world / Into the mystic. (re-iss. Feb90 lp/c/cd; BBL/+C 78/+CD)	28	-
Nov 87.	(7"/s7") *(BEG 203/+S)* **HIGH TIME. / BROKEN HEARTED FOOL** (12"+=) *(BEG 203T)* – Travelling chest (live) / Private revolution (live).	□	-
Feb 88.	(7") *(BEG 208)* **THE KISS OFF. / SURE THING** (12"ep/c-ep+=/cd-ep+=) *(BEG IW/+C/CD)* – THE NUMB EP – High time (acoustic) / Whipping boy.	□	-
Apr 88.	(7") *(BEG 220)* **LITTLE GIRL LOST. / TIN CAN** (12"+=/pic-cd-s+=) *(BEG 215 T/CD)* – Hot profit gospel / One time.	59	-
May 88.	(lp/c)(cd) *(IWA/IWC 2)(IWA 2CD)* <8424> **BLIND** – (intro) Shit creek / Little girl lost / Starry blue-eyed wonder / One true love / Blind / Two two three / What do you want me to do? / Stood before Saint Peter / The kiss off / Here comes trouble / Walk a while with me.	40	-
Jun 88.	(7") *(BEG 220)* **HERE COMES TROUBLE. / STARRY BLUE-EYED WONDER** (12"+=)(12"box) *(BEG 220T)(IW 3)* – Rock'n'roll (live) / For what it's worth (medley live).	□	□

— **ZAK STARKEY** (b.13 Sep'65, London, England, son of RINGO) – drums repl. LAYHE SHARROCK who joined WILD SWANS + The LA'S / added **DAVE GREEN** – keyboards / **ROY CORKHILL** – bass (both ex-BLACK)

Ian McNABB (cont)

— (1989) **IAN** and **ROY** brought in **DAVE BALDWIN** – keyboards / **MARK REVELL** – guitar, vocals / **PAUL BURGESS** – drums

			Epic	Work-Epic
Mar 90.	(7") *(WORKS 100)* **MOTORCYCLE RIDER. / TURN ANY CORNER**		73	
	(12"+=/12"etched+=) *(WORKS T/E 100)* – People change.			
	(cd-s++=) *(WORKS C100)* –			
	(12") *(WORKS Q100)* – ('A'side) / Let's get loaded / Red lightning.			
May 90.	(cd/c/lp) *(466 800-2/-4/-1)* **PERMANENT DAMAGE**			-
	– I still want you / Motorcycle rider / Melanie still hurts / Hope street rag / I think I'm gonna be OK / Baby don't burn / What she did to my mind / One good eye / Permanent damage / Woman on my mind / Looks like rain / Dumb angel.			
May 90.	(7") *(WORKS 101)* **MELANIE STILL HURTS. / WHEN THE CRYING'S DONE**			-
	(12"+=) *(WORKS T101)* – Mickey's blue.			
	(7"ep++=/cd-ep++=) *(WORKS Q/C 101)* – I dreamt I was a beautiful woman.			
Jul 90.	(7"/c-s) *(WORKS/+M 102)* **I STILL WANT YOU. / I WANT THAT GIRL**			-
	(12"+=) *(WORKST 102)* – It's gonna rain forever.			
	(10"++=/cd-ep++=) *(WORKS Q/C 102)* – Sweet disposition.			

— McNABB joined the WILD SWANS briefly before going solo.

– compilations, etc. –

Nov 88.	(12"ep) *Nighttracks; (SFNT 015)* **THE EVENING SHOW SESSIONS** (14.11.82)		-
	– Birds fly (whisper to a scream) / Lover's day / Love hunt / As the dragonfly flies.		
Jan 90.	(7") *Old Gold; (OG 9918)* **LOVE IS A WONDERFUL COLOUR. / BIRDS FLY (WHISPER TO A SCREAM)**		-
Aug 92.	(cd)(c) *Beggars Banquet; (BEGA 124CD)(BEGC 124)* **THE BEST OF THE ICICLE WORKS**	60	-
	– Hollow horse (long version) / Love is a wonderful colour / Birds fly (whisper to a scream) / Understanding Jane ('92 version) / Shit creek / High time (acoustic) / Who do you want for your love? / Evangeline / Little girl lost / When it all comes down ('92 version) / Starry blue eyed wonder / Out of season / The kiss off / Up here in the North of England / Firepower / Blind. *(ltd. w/ free cd 'BEST KEPT SECRET'; BEGA 124CD2) (re-iss. cd Sep95; BBL 124CD)*		
Aug 92.	(7") *Beggars Banquet; (BEG 262)* **UNDERSTANDING JANE '92. / LITTLE GIRL LOST**		-
	(12"+=) *(BEG 262T)* – When it all comes down '92 / Firepower.		
	(cd-s+=) *(BEG 262CD)* – Solid ground / Like weather.		
Mar 94.	(cd) *Windsong; (<WINCD 053>)* **BBC RADIO 1 LIVE IN CONCERT** (live)		
Jul 97.	(cd) *Dutch East India; <8004>* **THE PEEL SESSIONS**	-	

IAN McNABB

		Way Cool	not iss.
Jun 91.	(12"ep/cd-ep) *(WAYCOOL 14 T/CD)* **GREAT DREAMS OF HEAVEN / THAT'S WHY I BELIEVE. / MAKE LOVE TO YOU / POWER OF SONG**		-
		Fat Cat	not iss.
Oct 91.	(12"ep/cd-ep) *(FC 001/+CD)* **THESE ARE THE DAYS. / TRAMS IN AMSTERDAM / GREAT DREAMS OF HEAVEN (acoustic)**		-
		This Way Up	not iss.
Jan 93.	(7") *(WAY 211)* **IF LOVE WAS LIKE GUITARS. / TRAMS IN AMSTERDAM**	67	-
	(cd-s+=) *(WAY 233)* – Great dreams of Heaven.		
Jan 93.	(cd/c/d-lp) *(514 378-2/-4/-1)* **TRUTH AND BEAUTY**	51	-
	– (I go) My own way / These are the days / Great dreams of Heaven / Truth and beauty / I'm game / If love was like guitars / Story of my life / That's why I believe / Trip with me / Make love to you / Presence of the one. *(re-iss. cd/c Apr95; same)*		
Mar 93.	(7"/c-s) *(WAY 811/844)* **GREAT DREAMS OF HEAVEN. / UNKNOWN LEGEND**		-
	(12"+=/cd-s+=) *(WAY 822/833)* – I'm game / Caroline no.		
Jun 93.	(7") *(WAY 1211)* **I'M GAME. / A PIRATE LOOKS AT FORTY**		-
	(cd-s+=) *(WAY 1233)* – ('A'side) / What's it all about / ('A'version).		
Sep 93.	(7"/c-s/cd-s) *(WAY 1611/1644/1655)* **(I GO) MY OWN WAY / PLAY THE HAND THEY DEAL YOU**		-
	(10"+=/cd-s+=) *(WAY 1688/1633)* – If my daddy could see me now / For you, angel.		

— with **RALPH MOLINA + BILLY TALBOT** (of NEIL YOUNG's CRAZY HORSE) + **MIKE 'TONE' HAMILTON** (of SMITHEREENS)

Jun 94.	(7"/c-s) *(WAY 3111/3144)* **YOU MUST BE PREPARED TO DREAM. / THAT'S WHY THE DARKNESS EXISTS**	54	-
	(12"/cd-s) *(WAY 3122/3133)* – ('A'side) / Sometimes I think about you / Woo yer.		
	(cd-s) *(WAY 3199)* – ('A'side) / ('A'radio) / Love is a wonderful colour / When it all comes down (both acoustic).		
Jul 94.	(cd/c) *(522 298-2/-4)* **HEAD LIKE A ROCK**	29	-
	– Fire inside my soul / You must be prepared to dream / Child inside a father / Still got the fever / Potency / Go into the light / As a life goes by / Sad strange solitary Catholic mystic / This time is forever / May you always. *(cd re-iss. Sep96 on 'Island'; IMCD 233)*		
Aug 94.	(c-s) *(WAY 3644)* **GO INTO THE LIGHT / TIME YOU WERE IN LOVE**		-
	(cd-s+=) *(WAY 3633)* – For you, angel.		
	(12") *(WAY 3622)* – ('A'side) / ('A'-Celestial dub mix) / For you, angel.		
	(cd-s) *(WAY 3699)* – ('A'side) / I stood before St.Peter / Rock / ('A'-Celestial dub mix).		
Apr 96.	(7"/c-s) *(WAY 5011/5044)* **DON'T PUT YOUR SPELL ON ME. / DON'T PATRONISE ME**		-
	(cd-s+=) *(WAY 5033)* – What she did to my mind.		
May 96.	(cd/c/d-lp) *(524 215-2/-4/-1)* **MERSEYBEAST**	30	-
	– Merseybeast / Affirmation / Beautiful old mystery / Love's young dream / Camaraderie / Don't put your spell on me / Heydays / Little bit of magic / You stone my soul / Too close to the sun / They settled for less than they wanted / I'm a genius / Available light / Merseybeast (reprise). *(some cd's w/ free cd 'NORTH WEST COAST'; 524 240-2)*		
Jun 96.	(7") *(WAY 5211)* **MERSEYBEAST. / UP HERE IN THE NORTH OF ENGLAND** (demo Jan 86)	74	-
	(cd-s+=) *(WAY 5233)* – Permanent damage (demo Sept 88) / Merseybeast (demo March 95).		
	(cd-s) *(WAY 5266)* – ('A'side) / Pretty boys with big guitars / The slider / Snaked.		

— next with **MIKE SCOTT, ANTHONY THISTLETHWAITE + DANNY THOMPSON**

		Fairfield	not iss.
Oct 98.	(cd) *(FAIRCD 1)* **A PARTY POLITICAL BROADCAST ON BEHALF OF THE EMOTIONAL PARTY**		-
	– Sex with someone you love / A guy like me (and a girl like you) / Loveless age / You only get what you deserve / Bloom / The man who can make a woman laugh / Liverpool girl / Absolutely wrong / Little princess / Girls are birds. *(<re+US-iss.Aug01 on 'Castle'; CMRCD 307>)*		
		Castle	Castle
Aug 01.	(cd) *<CMRCD 306> <CMA 689>* **LIVE AT LIFE** (live fan club rec. December '99)		Jan01
	– Hollow horse / Sex with someone you love / Great dreams of Heaven / Permanent damage / Little girl lost / I'm a genius / One true love / Why are the beautiful so sad? / When it all comes down / A guy like me (and a girl like you) / Fire inside my soul / What she did to my mind / Merseybeast / Camaraderie / Reaping the rich harvest.		

— next with **GEOFF DUGMORE, HENRY PRIESTMAN + DANNY STRITTMATTER**

		Evangeline	Evangeline
Oct 01.	(cd) *(<GEL 4034>)* **WAIFS & STRAYS**		Nov01
	– Loveless age / Camaraderie / Fire inside my soul / Gak mummy No.1 / I'm a genius / Me and the Devil / Why are the beautiful so sad? / Misty meadows / Not lost enough to be rescued / Time of my time / Great dreams of Heaven / Nobody say nothin' to no one / You stole my soul / The new golden age.		
		Castle	not iss.
Apr 02.	(cd) *(CMRCD 440)* **IAN McNABB**		-
	– Livin' proof (miracles can happen) / Whatever it takes / What you wanted / Liverpool girl / If we believe what love can do / Alright with me / Hollywood tears / Open air / Nothin' less than the very best / Hotel stationary / Rockin' for Jesus / Friend of my enemy / Moment in the sun / I wish I was in California.		

MEAT PUPPETS

Formed: Tempe, Phoenix, Arizona, USA … 1980 by brothers CURT and CRIS KIRKWOOD. They were soon snapped up by rising US indie label 'SST' in 1981, after a debut on their own label. Their first recording for the company, 'MEAT PUPPETS 1' (1982), was a demanding blast of howling noise and twisted country that barely hinted at the compelling sound they'd invent with the follow-up 'MEAT PUPPETS II' (1983). A hybrid of mystical GRATEFUL DEAD-like psychedelia that short-fused hardcore punk rock and the country-boy slur of CRIS, the record was the blueprint for most of their subsequent output. 'UP ON THE SUN' (1985) was slightly more polished and saw the band garner snowballing critical acclaim. By the release of 'MIRAGE' (1987), the band had fully realised their desert-rock vision with a collection of weather beaten, psychedelic country classics; tracks like 'BEAUTY' and 'CONFUSION FOG' rank among the MEAT PUPPETS' best. Yet the record failed to sell and the band returned to a rawer, ZZ TOP-influenced sound on 'HUEVOS'. This album, together with the more mainstream 'MONSTERS' (1989) and continuing critical praise led to a deal with 'London'. Their major label debut, 'FORBIDDEN PLACES' (1991) was accomplished but lacked the high-noon intensity of their earlier work. After a step-up from KURT COBAIN (see below), the raw 'NO JOKE' (1995) album at last saw THE MEAT PUPPETS reaping some financial rewards, sales of the album going on to break the half million mark. Having relocated to Austin, Texas, KIRKWOOD finally re-emerged with a new-look MEAT PUPPETS – featuring ex-PARIAH members KYLE ELLISON and SHANDON SAHM along with ANDREW DUPLANTIS – and a belated album in the shape of 'GOLDEN LIES' (2000). MEAT-ier than most of the band's back catalogue, the album cranked up the amps for a set missing much of the sun-baked strangeness of old but at least partly making up for it with strong, memorable songwriting. • **Songwriters:** Most by CURT, some with CRIS or DERRICK. Covered TUMBLIN' TUMBLEWEEDS (Bob Nolan) / EL PASO CITY (Marty Robbins) / GOODNIGHT IRENE (Leadbelly) / PARANOID + SWEET LEAF (Black Sabbath). • **Trivia:** On 18 Nov'93, CURT & CRIS guested with NIRVANA's on an unplugged MTV spot. The tracks they performed were 'PLATEAU', 'OH ME' and 'LAKE OF FIRE'.

Album rating: MEAT PUPPETS mini (*5) / MEAT PUPPETS II (*8) / UP ON THE SUN (*9) / OUT MY WAY mini (*6) / MIRAGE (*8) / HUEVOS (*8) / MONSTERS (*7) / NO STRINGS ATTACHED compilation (*6) / FORBIDDEN PLACES (*6) / TOO HIGH TO DIE (*7) / NO JOKE! (*6) / LIVE IN MONTANA (*5) / GOLDEN LIES (*5) / LIVE (*6)

CURT KIRKWOOD (b.10 Jan'59, Amarillo, Texas) – guitar, vocals / **CRIS KIRKWOOD** (b.22 Oct'60, Amarillo) – vocals, bass, rhythm guitar / **DERRICK BOSTROM** (b.23 Jun'60, Phoenix) – drums

		not iss.	World Imitation
Sep 81.	(7"ep) *<PRC-1>* **IN A CAR / BIG HOUSE. / DOLPHIN FIELD / OUT IN THE GARDENER / FOREIGN LAWNS**	-	
	(cd-ep iss.Nov88 on 'S.S.T.'; SST 044CD)		
		S.S.T.	S.S.T.
Jan 82.	(m-lp) *<SST 009>* **MEAT PUPPETS**		-
	– Reward / Love offering / Blue green god / Walking boss / Melons rising / Saturday morning / Our friends / Tumblin' tumbleweeds / Milo, Sorghum and maize / Meat puppets / Playing dead / Litterbox / Electromud / The goldmine. *(re-iss. May93 lp/c/cd; SST 009/+C/CD) (<cd re-iss. Feb99 on 'Rykodisc'+=; RCD 10466>)* – In a car / Big house / Dolphin field / Out in the gardner / Foreign lawns / Meat puppets / Everybody's talkin' / H Elenore / Hair / I got a tight / I am a child / Franklin's tower / Milo, Sorghum and maize / Electromud / Lover offering / Saturday morning / Magic toy missing / Unpleasant / Walking boss (video).		

Apr 84. (lp) *<(SST 019)>* **MEAT PUPPETS II** 1983
– Split myself in two / Magic toy missing / Lost plateau / Aurora Borealis / We are here / Climbing / New gods / Oh, me / Lake on fire / I'm a mindless idiot / The whistling song. *(re-iss. May93 lp/c/cd; SST 019/+C/CD) <(cd re-iss. Feb99 on 'Rykodisc'+=; RCD 10467)>* – Teenager / I'm not here / New gods / Lost / What to do / 100% of nothing / Aurora borealis / New gods (video).

Apr 85. (lp) *<(SST 039)>* **UP ON THE SUN**
– Up on the sun / Maiden's milk / Away / Animal kingdom / Hot pink / Swimming ground / Buckethead / Too real / Enchanted porkfist / Seal whales / Two rivers / Creator. *(cd-iss. Sep87; SST 039CD) (re-iss. May93 cd/c; SST 039 CD/C) <(cd re-iss. Mar99 on 'Rykodisc'+=; RCD 10469)>* – Hot pink / Up on the sun / Mother American marshmallow / Embodiment of evil / Hot pink / Swimming ground (video).

Aug 86. (m-lp) *<(SST 049)>* **OUT MY WAY**
– She's hot / Out my way / Other kinds of love / Not swimming ground / Mountain line / Good golly Miss Molly. *(cd-iss. Sep87; SST 049CD) (re-iss. May93 cd/c; SST 049 CD/C) <(cd re-iss. Apr99 on 'Rykodisc'+=; RCD 10468)>* – I just want to make love to you / On the move / Burn the honky tonk down / Boyhood home / Backwards drums / Everything is green / Other kinds of love / Little wing (video).

Apr 87. (lp/cd) *<(SST 100/+CD)>* **MIRAGE**
– Mirage / Quit it / Confusion fog / The wind and the rain / Mighty zero / Get on down / Leaves / I am a machine / Beauty / A hundred miles / Love your children forever / Liquified: Mighty zero – I am a machine – Liquified – Rubberneckin'. *(re-iss. May93 cd/c; SST 100 CD/C) <(cd re-iss. May99 on 'Rykodisc'+=; RCD 10473)>* – Grand intro.

Oct 87. (lp/cd) *<(SST 150/+CD)>* **HEUVOS**
– Paradise / Look at the rain / Bad love / Sexy music / Crazy / Fruit / Automatic mojo / Dry rain / I can't be counted on at all. *(re-iss. May93 cd/c; SST 150 CD/C) <(cd re-iss. Apr99 on 'Rykodisc'+=; RCD 10470)>* – Baby what you want me to do / I can't be counted on / Sexy music / Automatic mojo / Paradise / Fruit / Automatic mojo (video).

Oct 87. (12") *<(PSST 150)>* **I CAN'T BE COUNTED ON AT ALL. / PARADISE**

Oct 89. (lp/cd) *<(SST 253/+CD)>* **MONSTERS**
– Attacked by monsters / Light / Meltdown / In love / The void / Touchdown king / Party till the world obeys / Flight of the fire weasel / Strings on your heart / Like being alive. *<(cd re-iss. May99 on 'Rykodisc'+=; (RCD 10471)>* – Wish upon a storm / Flight of the fire weasel / Flight of the fire weasel / Light (video).

Nov 90. (d-lp/cd) *<(SST 265/+CD)>* **NO STRINGS ATTACHED** (compilation)
– Big house / In a car / Tumblin' tumbleweeds / Reward / The whistling song / New gods / Lost / Lake of fire / Split myself in two / Up on the Sun / Swimming ground / Maiden's milk / Bucket head / Out my way / Confusion fog / I am a machine / Quit it / Beauty / Look at the rain / I can't be counted on at all / Automatic mojo / Meltdown / Like being alive / Attacked by monsters.

London London

Nov 91. (cd/c/lp) *<(828254-2/-4/-1)>* **FORBIDDEN PLACES**
– Sam / Nail it down / This day / Open wide / Another Moon / That's how it goes / Whirlpool / Popskull / No longer gone / Forbidden places / Six gallon pie.

Mar 94. (cd/c/lp) *<(828484-2/-4/-1)>* **TOO HIGH TO DIE** 62
– Violet eyes / Never to be found / We don't exist / Severed goddess head / Flaming heart / Shine / Backwater / Roof with a hole / Station / Things / Why / Evil love / Comin' down / Lake of fire.

Jul 94. (cd-ep) *<857553>* **BACKWATER / OPEN WIDE / ANIMAL / UP ON THE SUN / WHITE SPORT COAT** - 47

Dec 94. (10"ep) *<1109>* **RAW MEAT EP** -
– We don't exist / Up on the sun / El Paso city / White sport coat / Goodnight Irene.

Oct 95. (cd/c) *<(828665-2/-4)>* **NO JOKE!**
– Scum / Nothing / Head / Taste of the sun / Vampires / Predator / Poison arrow / Eyeball / For free / Cobbler / Inflamable / Sweet ammonia / Chemical garden.

— **CURT** recruited entire new band **KYLE ELLISON** – guitar, vocals (ex-PARIAH) / **ANDREW DuPLANTIS** – bass / **SHANDON SAHM** – drums (ex-PARIAH)

Atlantic Atlantic

Sep 00. (cd/c) *<(7567 83402-2/-4)>* **GOLDEN LIES**
– Intro / Armed and stupid / I quit / Lamp / Hercules / Batwing / Take off your clothes / You love me / Pieces of me / Push the button / Tarantula / Endless wave / Wipeout / Fat boy (Fat – Requiem).

not iss. D.C.N.

Apr 02. (cd) *<1003>* **LIVE** (at Maxwell's 2.08.01) -
– Intro / Armed and stupid / Wipe out / I quit / Hercules / Oh, me / Push the button / Lamp / Pieces of me / Up on the sun / Take off your clothes / Fatboy – Fat – Requiem / Lake of fire / Way that it are / You love me / Plateau / Touchdown king.

– compilations, etc. –

Feb 99. (cd) *Rykodisc; <(RCD 1047-2)>* **LIVE IN MONTANA (live December '88)**
– Touchdown king / Cotton candy land / Automatic mojo / Plateau / Maiden's milk / Lake of fire / I can't be counted on / Liquified / Dough-rey-mi / S.W.A.T. (get down) – Attacked by monsters / Party till the world obeys / The small hours – Paranoid – Sweet leaf.

MEAT WHIPLASH (see under ⇒ MOTORCYCLE BOY)

MECCA NORMAL

Formed: Vancouver, Canada … 1981 by DAVID LESTER and JEAN SMITH. The politically charged duo whose material, to a greater degree, was heavily concerned with a wide range of social issues, shot through the lenses of their more socialist vision. Their messages and vignettes about the world, were achieved through a combination of the PATTI SMITH-like vocalisation of JEAN SMITH, backed up by LESTER's skillful and wide-ranging use of the guitar. MC's self-titled debut, 'MECCA NORMAL', appeared on their own label, 'Smarten Up!' in 1986, and was later re-released by pioneering indie imprint, 'K'. This initial set exemplified that though their set up was extremely slimmed down, it was in no way limited, showcased by the virtuostic work of LESTER, managing to work styles (from folk to punk) into the pieces. Also worthy of note on this debut offering is the track, 'I WALK ALONE', which became an MC anthem. Their work continued to improve and please through the late eighties and early nineties, through sets such as 'WATER CUTS MY HANDS', 'DOVETAIL', 'FLOOD PLAIN' and 'JARRED UP'. The latter of these, although a collection of earlier singles, displayed in parts their willingness to expand and diversify their sound. This was further demonstrated on 1995's 'SITTING ON SNAPS', where the inclusion of Kiwi PETER JEFFERIES on piano added further body to the mix. While continuing to issue competent and politically-conscious sets throughout the 90s, the duo also extended their project with the setting up of publishing company, 'Get To The Point', which put out among other things, SMITH's own novels. The mid-point of the decade also saw SMITH branching out in other musical directions. The best of these was the formation of 2 FOOT FLAME, which included MC collaborator JEFFERIES and MICHAEL MORLEY (of DEAD C fame); aurally, a heavier punch than that of MECCA NORMAL, with first release, '2 FOOT FLAME', standing up to SMITH's previous work. SMITH also tried her hand at solo experimental work. The post-millennial self-titled outing, 'JEAN SMITH', although highly innovative, was a difficult listen for most fans. MC regrouped though for comeback set, 'THE FAMILY SWAN' (2001), and proved with this, that they were still as strong and strident as ever.

Album rating: MECCA NORMAL (*5) / CALICO KILLS THE CAT (*5) / WATER CUTS MY HANDS (*5) / DOVETAIL (*6) / JARRED UP compilation (*6) / FLOOD PLAIN (*5) / SITTING ON SNAPS (*6) / THE EAGLE AND THE POODLE (*5) / WHO SHOT ELVIS? (*5) / THE FAMILY SWAN (*5) / 2 Foot Flame: 2 FOOT FLAME (*6) / ULTRA DROWNING (*3) / Jean Smith: JEAN SMITH (*6)

JEAN SMITH – vocals, guitar / **DAVID LESTER** – guitar

not iss. Smarten Up!

1986. (lp) **MECCA NORMAL** -
– Who told you so? / Are you hungry Joe? / Not with me / Tolerate me / Sha la la la la / Scare in the hallway / I walk alone / Beaten down / Phone's unplugged / Women were king / Fight for a little. *<re-iss. Mar95 as 'MECCA NORMAL – 1st ALBUM' lp/cd; KLP 38/+CD>*

K K

1987. (7"ep) *(IPU 004)* **OH YES YOU CAN EP** -
– Strong white male / More more more / Man thinks "woman".

1989. (c) *<KLP 04>* **CALICO KILLS THE CAT** -
– Then / Blue TV / One woman / My first love song / Ancient fire / Don't shoot / I'm a bit confused / Joelle / 12 murders / Smile baby / Richard / I know a little bit / Will he change?

1990. (7") *<IPU 011>* **CARDBOARD BOX HOUSE OF LOVE** -
– Forlorn / He didn't say.

not iss. Matador

Apr 91. (m-cd/m-c/m-lp) *<OLE 011-2/-4/-1>* **WATER CUTS MY HANDS** -
– Taking the back stairs / 20 years – No escape / Water in a bucket / Not standing still / Water cuts my hands / Dead bird's feet / Lois wrote about the farm / Orange sunset / The dogs / Deep dark secret.

not iss. Smarten Up!

1991. (7") **I CAN HEAR ME FINE. /** -

1991. (7") **BRIGHT LIKE ICE. /** -

not iss. Harriet

Jan 92. (7") *<HARRIET 10>* **ORANGE. /** -

not iss. Sub Pop

Jan 92. (7"m; split w/ KREVISS) *<SP 149>* **YOU HEARD IT ALL. / BROKEN FLOWERS / GOING TO HELL** -

not iss. Kill Rock Stars

1992. (7"; by JEAN SMITH) **CARBONI ANGELS** (spoken word) -

not iss. Dionysus

1992. (7") *<ID 074539>* **FROM THE SURFACE. / UPSIDE DOWN FLAME** -

not iss. K

1992. (lp) *<KLP 14>* **DOVETAIL** -
– Throw silver / Held / Cherry flowers / This machine / Not yet / Once / Drilling / Clatter / Flashlight / Engine rain. *<cd-iss. May95 +=; KLP 14CD>* – Trapped against.

Jun 92. (7"m) *<IPU 28>* **THIS IS DIFFERENT. / ARMCHAIRS FIT THROUGH DOORWAYS / ACCIDENTALLY** -

Nov 92. (7") *<IPU 32>* **ROSE. / DAYS** -

1993. (lp) *<KLP 18>* **JARRED UP** (compilation 1987-1993) -
– Strong white male / Man thinks woman / Forlorn / He didn't say / Follow down / It's important / How many now? / Horse heaven hills / This is different / Armchairs fit (through doorways) / Accidentally / You heard it all / Days / Rose / Fan of sparks / Narrow / Broken flowers / Upside down flames / From the surface / More more more / Echo / One more safe. *<cd-iss. Jun95; KCD 18>*

1993. (lp) *<KLP 22>* **FLOOD PLAIN** -
– Ribbon / Current of agreement / Nobody's asking / A kind of a girl / Greater beauty / Waiting for Rudy / Straying to summer / Walking the walls / On the row of dials / Texada warns me / Museum of open windows. *<cd-iss. Jun95; KCD 22>*

not iss. Jettison

1993. (7") *<23>* **ECHO. / FAN OF SPARKS** -

Matador Matador

Feb 95. (cd/lp) *<(OLE 112-2/-1)>* **SITTING ON SNAPS** Jan95
– Vacant night sky / Something to be said / Crimson dragnet / Frozen rain / Only heat / Trapped inside your heart / Alibi / Pamela makes waves / Beppo's room / Cyclone / Gravity believes.

Oct 95. (7") *<(OLE 164-7)>* **THE BIRD THAT WOULDN'T FLY. / BREATHING IN THE DARK** Sep95

Apr 96. (cd/lp) *<(OLE 186-2/-1)>* **THE EAGLE AND THE POODLE**
– Breathing in the dark / Her ambition / The revival of cruelty / Rigid man in an ice age / When you build a house without doors / Prize arm / Mrs. McGillvary / Now that you're here / Kingdom without weather / Cave in / Drive at / Come on pink pearl / When you know.

1996. (7"m) <IPU 068> **PARIS IN APRIL. / TOWER ISLAND / INVISIBLE WEAPON**
(above issued on 'K' records)
Oct 97. (cd/lp) <(OLE 245-2/-1)> **WHO SHOT ELVIS?**
– Medieval man / Who shot Elvis? / Excalibur / The orbit / Step into my sphere / The way of love / All about the same thing / OK here we go / Don't heal me like a dog just to break me like a horse / In Canada.

2 FOOT FLAME

JEAN SMITH – vocals, guitar, drums / with **MICHAEL MORLEY** – guitar, synthesizer (of-the DEAD C) / **PETER JEFFERIES** – drums, piano, keyboards (ex-THIS KIND OF PUNISHMENT)

Matador Matador

Oct 95. (cd/lp) <(OLE 165-2/-1)> **2 FOOT FLAME**
– Lindauer / To the sea / Already waiting / Mr. H / Reinvention / Compass / The arbitrator / Cordoned off / Chisel.
Apr 97. (cd/lp) <(OLE 209-2/-1)> **ULTRA DROWNING**
– Sample stars / Resin box / Peacock coal / I think you're the weird one / Everwilling / Pipeline to vertigo / Ultra drowning / Salt doubt / The dance alone / Lunar intuition.

JEAN SMITH

— solo playing numerous instruments + singing

Kill Rock Stars Kill Rock Stars

Jun 00. (cd) <(KRS 361CD)> **JEAN SMITH**
– Ghost of understanding / Siamese hips / Root smooth sapling whips / Snippet from Hell / The story of history / A little black dress / (untitled) / Flesh freezes in less than a minute / Mobilized by loneliness / Halfway.

— in 1999, DAVID LESTER issued a solo guitar cassette

MECCA NORMAL

— **JEAN + DAVID**

Kill Rock Stars Kill Rock Stars

Aug 02. (cd) <(KRS 385CD)> **THE FAMILY SWAN**
– Is this you? / What about the boy? / Revolution pine / In January / Every wrong word / I hear you / The family swan / No mind's eye / Ice flows aweigh / Convince yourself.

MEGA CITY FOUR

Formed: Farnborough, England ... early 1987 by CHRIS JONES and ex-CAPRICORN members, GERRY BRYANT and brothers WIZ and DANNY BROWN. Taking their name from '2000 A.D.' comic hero/lawman, Judge Dredd's home city, MC4 never quite achieved the wild abandon or political influence of near-namesakes MC5 but nevertheless attempted to put the world to rights with their patented brand of late 80's melodic punk so beloved of the crusty scene. Along with hard-gigging peers like The SENSELESS THINGS, MC4 regularly traipsed the length and breadth of the country living out the back of a transit van. These were the experiences which informed their debut album, 'TRANZOPHOBIA' (1989), released on indie label 'Decoy' following a couple of acclaimed singles, 'DISTANT RELATIVES' and 'LESS THAN SENSELESS'. The album itself scaped into the UK Top 75 and topped the indie chart, the 'MEGA's regular features in the weekly music press pre-Madchester. As the admittedly more colourful 'baggy' scene came to dominate the media, the more worthy strains of thrash-pop weren't such hip currency and MC4's cause wasn't helped by a lacklustre production on follow-up set, 'WHO CARES WINS' (1990). Nevertheless, it was enough to get them signed up by happening label, 'Big Life', through whom they released the minor hit EP, 'WORDS THAT SAY' and their first Top 40 single, 'STOP'. The accompanying album, 'SEBASTOPOL RD' (1992) confirmed a newfound musical and lyrical maturity which combined intelligent comment with contagiously hook-laden buzz-pop. Yet it seemed the band had missed out yet again with the record frustratingly stalling just outside the Top 40. Unsurprisingly perhaps, WIZ's songwriting took a gradually more downbeat turn and 1993's 'MAGIC BULLETS' album generated even less interest. Subsequently parting company with 'Big Life', the band spent a couple of years in label limbo before signing to 'Fire' in 1995 and releasing a couple of singles, 'SKIDDING' and 'SUPERSTAR'. The following year saw the release of a comeback album (of sorts), 'SOULSCRAPER', although this did little to re-establish the band. WIZ gathered together another band, SERPICO, who delivered a mini-set, 'EVERYONE VS. EVERYONE', early in 2001; they are currently the trio IPANEMA. • **Covered:** DON'T WAN'T TO KNOW IF YOU ARE LONELY (Husker Du) / A HARD DAY'S NIGHT (Beatles).

Album rating: TRANZOPHOBIA (*8) / WHO CARES WINS (*7) / TERRIBLY SORRY BOB compilation (*7) / SEBASTOPOL RD (*6) / INSPIRINGLY TITLED – THE LIVE ALBUM (*5) / MAGIC BULLETS (*5) / SOULSCRAPER (*5) / Serpico: EVERYONE VS. EVERYONE mini (*6)

DARREN 'WIZ' BROWN – vocals, guitar / **DANNY BROWN** – guitar / **GERRY BRYANT** – bass / **CHRIS JONES** – drums (ex-EXIT EAST) repl. MARTIN

Primitive not iss.

Mar 88. (ltd-7") (PRIME 009) **MILES APART. / RUNNING IN DARKNESS**
(re-iss. Jul88 on 'Mega City'; MEGA 001)

Decoy not iss.

Nov 88. (7") (DYS 1) **DISTANT RELATIVES. / CLEAR BLUE SKY**
Feb 89. (7") (DYS 2) **LESS THAN SENSELESS. / DANCING DAYS ARE OVER**
May 89. (lp/cd) (DYL 3/+CD) **TRANZOPHOBIA** — 67
– Start / Pride and prejudice / Severe attack of the truth / Paper tiger / January / Twenty one again / On another planet / Things I never said / New years day / Occupation / Alternative arrangements / Promise / What you've got / Stupid way to die. (cd re-iss. Sep01 on 'Cherry Red'; CDMRED 197)
Oct 89. (7") (DYS 5) **AWKWARD KID. / CRADLE**
Mar 90. (7"ep/12"ep) (DYS 10/+T) **FINISH / SEVERANCE. / THANX / SQUARE THROUGH A CIRCLE**
Sep 90. (lp/cd/cd) (DYL 20/+C/CD) **WHO CARES WINS**
– Who cares? / Static interference / Rose coloured / Grudge / Me not you / Messenger / Violet / Rail / Mistook / Open / Revolution / No such place as home / Storms to come / Balance.
Apr 91. (lp/cd) (DYL 24/+CD) **TERRIBLY SORRY BOB** (compilation)
– Miles apart / Running in darkness / Distant relatives / Clear blue sky / Less than senseless / Dancing days are over / No time / Awkward kid / Cradle / Finish / Severance / Thanx / Square through a circle.

Big Life Caroline

Sep 91. (7"ep/7"green-ep/12"ep/cd-ep) (MEGA/+R/T/D 3) **WORDS THAT SAY / UNTOUCHABLE. / LIPSCAY / MANSION** — 66
(re-iss. Aug93 12"ep/cd-ep; same)
Jan 92. (7"red-ep/12"ep/cd-ep) (MEGA R/T/D 3) **STOP / DESERT SONG. / BACK TO ZERO / OVERLAP** — 36
(ltd.live-7"ep) (MEGA R3) – Stop / Revolution / Who cares / Finish / Props.
(re-iss. Aug93 7"ep/12"ep/cd-ep; same)
Feb 92. (cd/c/lp) (MEG CD/MC/LP 1) <CAROL 2800> **SEBASTOPOL RD** — 41
– Ticket collector / Scared of cats / Callous / Peripheral / Anne Bancroft / Prague / Clown / Props / What's up? / Vague / Stop / Wasting my breath. (re-iss. Sep93; same)
May 92. (7"ep/12"ep/cd-ep) (MEGA/+T/D 4) **SHIVERING SAND. / EVERYBODY LOVES YOU / DISTURBED** — 35
(ltd.live-7"ep) (MEGAL 4) – Shivering sand / Words that say / Callous / Don't want to know if you are lonely.
Nov 92. (cd/c/lp) (MEG CD/MC/LD 2) **INSPIRINGLY TITLED – THE LIVE ALBUM** (live)
– Who cares / Finish / Thanx / Shivering sand / Props / Messenger / Stop / Revolution / Words that say / Callous / Lipscar / Peripheral / Clown / Open / What've you've got / Don't want to know if you are lonely.
Apr 93. (7"ep/c-ep/10"ep/cd-ep) (MEGA/+C/T/D 5) **IRON SKY. / ON THE EDGE / SOMETIMES** — 48
May 93. (cd/c/lp) (MEG CD/MC/LP 003) **MAGIC BULLETS** — 57
– Perfect circle / Drown / Rainman / Toys / Iron sky / So / Enemy skies / Wallflower / President / Shadows / Underdog / Greener / Speck.
Jul 93. (7"/c-s) (MEGA/+C 6) **WALLFLOWER. / INAMORATA / WILDERNESS** — 69
(12"/cd-s) (MEGA T/D 6) – ('A'side) / Iron sky / Scared of cats / Rain.

Fire not iss.

Sep 95. (7") (BLAZE 93) **SKIDDING. / LAZERGAZE**
(cd-s+=) (BLAZE 93CD) – Stay dead.
Nov 95. (7") (BLAZE 97) **SUPERSTAR. / CHRYSANTH**
(cd-s+=) (BLAZE 97CD) – My own ghost.
Feb 96. (7") (BLAZE 102) **ANDROID DREAMS. / ST CATHERINE'S**
(cd-s+=) (BLAZE 102CD) – Skywide.
Mar 96. (cd/c/lp) (FIRE CD/MC/LP 54) **SOULSCRAPER**
– Android dreams / The dog lady / Skidding / I stop breathing / Creepy crawlies / Circles of one / I know where you live / Superstar / Walking-glass / Slow down / Picture perfect.

— split early in 1998; WIZ formed SERPICO

– compilations, others, etc. –

Nov 93. (cd) Strange Fruit; (SFRCD 124) / Dutch East India; <DEI 8415>
THE PEEL SESSIONS (rec.19/7/88 except *) — Mar94
– Clear blue sky / Alternative arrangements / Severe attack of the truth / January / Distant relatives / Stay dead / Clown / Prague / Slow down *.

SERPICO

WIZ – vocals, guitar / **SHAUN** – guitar, vocals / **RUSS** – drums

Boss Tunage Boss Tuneage

Jan 01. (m-cd) (<BOSTAGE 527>) **EVERYONE VS. EVERYONE** — Mar01
– Little star / Price of everything / Winter / King is dead / Next sound you hear / Don't lean on me.

— (late 2002) SERPICO evolved into IPANEMA

MELVINS

Formed: Aberdeen, Washington, USA ... early '85 by BUZZ OSBOURNE, who found LORI BECK and other floating members. Debuting early in 1987 with the patchy 'GLUEY PORCH TREATMENTS', they improved enough in the early 90's to sign for major label 'Atlantic'. In the interim period, this endearingly amateurish outfit (revered by KURT COBAIN, he had been their roadie!) graced a handful of largely ignored albums with their noisy BLACK SABBATH/SWANS fusions. Future MUDHONEY man, MATT LUKIN, appeared on their 1989 set, 'OZMA', before he was replaced by JOE PRESTON. In 1992, the three members simultaneously issued three solo EP's, much in the same way as KISS did in the late 70's. Still a long-time fan, KURT COBAIN worked with them on 1993's 'HOUDINI' set, although his continued patronage did little do much for their record sales. A couple of uninspiring albums surfaced during the next few years, the last of which, 'HONKY' was released on the 'Amphetamine Reptile' label. Perhaps the most influential Seattle band of them all, The MELVINS were still kicking out the sludgy jams come the end of the century. 'THE MAGGOT' (1999) marked the first release in a trilogy of albums recorded for MIKE PATTON's 'Ipecac' imprint, featuring an unmissable rendezvous with Peter Green's spine chilling 'GREEN MANALISHI'. 'THE BOOTLICKER' was marginally easier on the ear while 'THE CRYBABY' (2000) – the final part of the series – featured an array of carefully chosen guests including FOETUS' JIM THIRLWELL, HELMET's HENRY BOGNER and even HANK WILLIAMS III (you read that correctly); so, alongside a LEIF GARRET (no, seriously) reading of Nirvana's 'SMELLS LIKE TEEN SPIRIT' were trashings of HANK WILLIAMS' (the original) 'RAMBLIN' MAN' and Merle Haggard's much misunderstood 'OKIE FROM MUSKOGEE'. Continuing in uncharacteristically experimental mode, 'ELECTRORETARD' (2001) was a surprisingly listenable remix album wherein The MELVINS treated the cream of their back catalogue to an electronic going over as well as meting out cover treatment to Pink Floyd's 'INTERSTELLAR OVERRIVE', The Wiper's 'YOUTH OF AMERICA' and The Cows' 'MISSING'. With each release, The MELVINS turned out more acid-metal attacks and 2002's 'HOSTILE AMBIENT TAKEOVER' (which signed off with the 15-minute+ epic 'THE ANTI-VERMIN SEED'), was no exception to their headbanging rule. • **Songwriters:** OSBOURNE except; WAY OF THE WORLD + SACRIFICE (Flipper) / BALLAD OF DWIGHT FRY (Alice Cooper) / SWEET YOUNG THING AIN'T SWEET NO MORE (Mudhoney) / THE GREEN MANALISHI (Fleetwood Mac) / TEEN SPIRIT (Nirvana) / BLOCKBUSTER (Jesus Lizard) / RAMBLIN' MAN (Hank Williams) / OKEE FROM MUSKOGEE (Merle Haggard) / G.I. JOE (Mike Patton) / YOUTH OF AMERICA (Wipers) / MISSING (Cows) / INTERSTELLAR OVERDRIVE (Pink Floyd).

Album rating: GLUEY PORCH TREATMENTS (*5) / OZMA (*5) / BULLHEAD (*6) / LYSOL compilation (*7) / HOUDINI (*5) / PRICK (*5) / STONER WITCH (*5) / STAG (*5) / HONKY (*5) / THE MAGGOT (*4) / THE BOOTLICKER (*5) / THE CRYBABY (*5) / ELECTRORETARD (*5) / THE COLOSSUS OF DESTINY (*5) / HOSTILE AMBIENT TAKEOVER (*5)

BUZZ OSBOURNE (aka KING BUZZO) – vocals, guitar / **LORI BECK** – bass / **DALE CROVER** – drums

— note that The MELVINS had bootleg singles issued in the mid-late 80's

Feb 87. (lp) *(VM 103) <24>* **GLUEY PORCH TREATMENTS**
– Eye flys / Echo head – Don't piece me / Heater moves and eyes / Steve Instant Newman / Influence of atmosphere / Exact paperbacks / Happy grey or black / Leeech / Glow god / Big as a mountain / Heaviness of the load / Flex with you / Bitten into sympathy / Gluey porch treatments / Clipping roses / As was it / Over from under the excrement. *<cd-iss. Mar01 on 'Ipecac'; IPC 12)>*

Feb 90. (lp/cd) *(TUPLP 7) <BR 16/+CD>* **OZMA**
– Vile / Oven / At a glance / Let God be your gardener / Creepy smell / Kool legged / Green honey / Agonizer / Raise a paw / Love thing / Ever since my accident / Revulsion – We reach / Dead dressed / Cranky Messiah / Claude / My small percent shows most / Candy-O. *<cd+=> – GLUEY PORCH TREATMENTS*

Jul 90. (7"/12") *<BR 21>* **SWEET YOUNG THING AIN'T SWEET NO MORE. / (other by STEEL POLE BATH TUB)**

— **MATT LUKIN** – bass; repl. LORI

— **JOE PRESTON** – bass repl. LUKIN who joined MUDHONEY

Feb 91. (cd/lp) *(TUP CD/LP 26) <BR 25CD>* **BULLHEAD**
– Boris / Anaconda / Ligature / It's shoved / Zodiac / If I had an exorcism / Your blessened / Cow. *<cd re-iss. Jun99 on 'Boner'; same)>*

Sep 91. (10"ep/cd-ep) *(TUP EP/CD 31) <BR 28CD>* **EGGNOG**
– Wispy / Antitoxidote / Hog leg / Charmicarmicat.

Aug 92. (12"ep/cd-ep) *(TUP 39 1/-2) <BR 32/+CD>* **KING BUZZO**
– Isabella / Porg / Annum / Skeeter.

— BUZZO augmented by **DALE NIXON** – guitars, etc (on above)

Aug 92. (12"ep/cd-ep) *(TUP 40 1/-2) <BR 33/+CD>* **DALE CROVER**
– Hex me / Dead wipe / Respite / Hurter.

Aug 92. (12"ep/cd-ep) *(TUP 41 1/-2) <BR 34/+CD>* **JOE PRESTON**
– The eagle has landed / Bricklebrit / Hands first flower.

Nov 92. (cd/c/lp) *(TUP 42 2/4/1) <BR 35CD>* **LYSOL** (compilation of above 3)

Jun 92. (7") *<Scale 44)>* **NIGHT GOAT. / ADOLESCENT WET DREAM**

1993. (7") *<RR 76>* **HOOCH. / SKY PUP**

Sep 93. (cd/c) *<7567 82532-2/-4)>* **HOUDINI**
– Hooch / Set me straight / Sky pup / Joan of Arc / Pearl bomb / Spread eagle Beagle / Night goat / Lizzy / Going blind / Honey bucket / Hag me / Teet / Copache. *<cd re-iss. Apr02; same)>*

— **MARK DEUTROM** – bass; repl. JOE PRESTON

Nov 94. (cd/c/lp) *<7567 82704-2/-4/-1)>* **STONER WITCH**
– Skweetis / Queen / Sweet Willy Rollbar / Revolve / Goose freight train / Roadbull / At the stake / Magic pig detective / Shevil / June bug / Lividity. *<cd re-iss. Apr02; same)>*

Jul 96. (cd/c/lp) *<7567-82878-2/-4/-1)>* **STAG**
– The bit / Hide / Bar-X-the rocking M / Yacob's lab / The bloat / Tipping the lion / Black bock / Goggles / Soup / Buck Owens / Sterilized / Lacrimosa / Skin horse / Captain Pungent / Berthas / Cottonmouth. *<cd re-iss. Apr02; same)>*

May 97. (cd) *<AR 64>* **HONKY**
– They all must be slaughtered / Mombius Hibachi / Lovely butterfly / Pitfalls in serving warrants / Air breather in the arms of Morphius / Laughing with Lucifer at Satans's sideshow / How / Harry Lauders walking stick tree / Grin / In the freaktose the bugs are dying.

Aug 98. (cd-ep) *<AMREP 072CD)>* **MELVINS ALIVE AT F*CKER CLUB**
– Boris / It's shoved / Bar-X the rocking M / Antioxidote / The bloat / Lizzy / Mombius Hibachi.

May 99. (cd) *<(IPC 002CD)>* **THE MAGGOT**
– Amazon / We all love Judy / Manky / The green manalishi / The horn bearer / Judy / See how pretty, see how smart.

Aug 99. (cd) *<(IPC 003CD)>* **THE BOOTLICKER**
– Toy / Let it be me / Black Santa / We we / Up the dumper / Mary lady Bobby kins / Jew boy flower head / Lone rose holding now / Prig.

Feb 00. (cd) *<(IPC 006CD)>* **THE CRYBABY**
– Teen spirit / Blockbuster / Ramblin' man / G.I. Joe / Mine is no disgrace / Spineless / Divorced / Dry drunk / Okee from Muskogee / The man with the laughing hand is dead / Moon pie.

Nov 00. (t-lp) *<(IPC 011)>* **TRILOGY** (3 above)

Feb 01. (cd) *<(MR 2002)>* **ELECTRORETARD**
– Shit storm / Youth of America / Gluey porch treatment / Revolve / Missing / Lonely butterflies / Tipping the lion B / Interstellar overdrive.
(above issued on 'Man's Ruin').

Apr 01. (cd) *<(IPC 014)>* **THE COLOSSUS OF DESTINY**
– The colossus of destiny.

Apr 02. (cd) *<(IPC 020)>* **HOSTILE AMBIENT TAKEOVER**
– Intro / Black Stooges / Dr. Geek / Little Judas Chongo / The fool, the meddling idiot / The brain center at whipples / Foaming / The anti-vermin seed.

– compilations, others, etc. –

1990's. (7") Sympathy For The Record Industry; *<(SFTRI 81)>* **WITH YO HEART NOT YO HANDS. / FOUR LETTER WOMAN / ANAL SATAN**

Jan 92. (cd/c) *C/Z; <(CZ 002/+A)>* **MELVINS (live in 1986)**
– Easy as it was / Now a Limo / Grinding process / #2 pencil / At a crawl / Disinvite / Snake appeal / Show off your red hands / Over the underground / Crayfish.

Jan 92. (cd) *Your Choice; (YCR 012/+CD)>* **MELVINS** (early material)   Mar94

Nov 92. (5"clear-ep) *Scooby Doo; (SAH 13)* **LOVE CANAL. / CANAL**

Aug 94. (lp/cd) *Amphetamine Reptile; <(ARR/+CD 58-333)>* **PRICK**
– How about / Rickets / Pick it n' flick it / Montreal / Chief ten beers / Underground / Chalk people / Punch the lion / Pure digital silence / Larry / Roll another one.

Aug 97. (cd) *Amphetamine Reptile; <AR 63CD>* **1996, VOL.1-12**
– Lexicon devil / Pigtro / In the rain / Spread eagle / Leech / Queen / Way of the world / Theme / It's shoved / Forgotten principles / GGIIBBYY / Theresa screams / Poison / Double troubled / Specimen / All at once / Jacksonville / Dallas / Bloat / Fast forward / Nasty dogs and funky kings / HDYF / How – Walking stick tree / Brutal truth – Zodiac.

MEMBRANES

Formed: Preston, Lancashire, England ... 1977 by JOHN ROBB alongside MARK TILTON, MARTIN CRITCHLEY and MARTIN KELLY. Their first recording, 'ICE AGE', was for Various Artists compilation EP, 'BLACKPOOL ROX', released on 'Vinyl Drip'. With CRITCHLEY subsequently replaced by COOFY SID, The MEMBRANES gained instant notoriety in 1980 via their flexi-disc 45, 'FLEXIBLE MEMBRANE' and a debut single proper, 'MUSCLES'. Raved over by both the music press and John Peel, the track's cult success secured the band a deal with 'Rondolet' records through whom they released a follow-up track, 'PIN STRIPE HYPE', complete with extra guitarist STEVE FARMBRY. His tenure was brief, however, the group reverting to a three piece and signing to 'Criminal Damage' for 1984's 'PULP BEATING AND ALL THAT'. Featuring the infamous blast of cacophonous noise that was 'SPIKE MILLIGAN'S TAPE RECORDER', the record fully displayed ROBB's ability for subhuman wailing together with the band's talent for generating bass-crunching sonic chaos; a challenging listen to say the least, The MEMBRANES augmented their unholy racket with bleating sax on 1985's 'GIFT OF LIFE', their first and only effort for 'Creation'. Constant personnel changes blighted the band's career and as ROBB increasingly concentrated on a career in music journalism, The MEMBRANES gradually fell by the wayside. The STEVE ALBINI (of spiritual heirs, BIG BLACK)-produced 'KISS ASS GODHEAD' (1988) surfaced on US label, 'Homestead', while 1989's 'TO SLAY THE ROCK PIG' was to be The MEMBRANES' parting shot as ROBB became enmeshed in the emerging dance culture with SENSURROUND. One of the UK's more respected music scribes, ROBB went on to pen an acclaimed biography of The STONE ROSES as well as fronting rock'n'roll renegades, GOLD BLADE. Along with KEITH CURTIS (ex-A WITNESS), future BONE-BOX members JAY TAYLOR and ROB HAYNES, they released a couple of albums, 'HOME TURF' (1997) and 'DROP THE BOMB' (1998). • **Songwriters:** PENAL LANDSCAPE GARDENER (Dead Kennedys) / ICE CREAM FOR CROW (Captain Beefheart) / ANGIE (Rolling Stones) / VOODOO CHILE (Jimi Hendrix) / BIG DECISION (That Petrol Emotion).

Album rating: CRACK HOUSE mini (*5) / THE GIFT OF LIFE (*5) / GIANT (*4) / PULP BEATING AND ALL THAT compilation (*6) / SONGS OF LOVE AND FURY (*5) / KISS ASS ... GODHEAD! (*4) / TO SLAY THE ROCK PIG (*4) / THE BEST OF THE MEMBRANES compilation (*7) / Goldblade: HOME TURF (*5) / DROP THE BOMB (*5) / DO U BELIEVE IN THE POWER OF ROCK'N'ROLL? (*5)

JOHN ROBB (b. 4 May'61, Preston, England) – vocals, bass, dustbin lids / **MARK TILTON** – guitar, vocals / **T.P. KELLY** – guitar, keyboards / **COOFY SID (COULTHART)** – drums; repl. vocalist MARTIN CRITCHLEY

Dec 80. (7"flexi) *(VD 005)* **FLEXIBLE MEMBRANE**
– Fashionable junkies / Almost China.

Jan 82. (7") *(VD 007)* **MUSCLES. / ALL ROADS LEAD TO NORWAY**

May 82. (7"ep/12"ep) *(ROUND/12ROUND 19)* **MUSCLES / ALL ROADS LEAD TO NORWAY. / GREAT MISTAKE / ENTERTAINING FRIENDS**

— **STEVE FARMBRY** – guitar; repl. KELLY

MEMBRANES (cont)

Nov 82. (7"ep/12"ep) *(ROUND/12ROUND 28)* **PIN STRIPE HYPE**
– High St. Yanks / Funny old world / The hitch / Man from Moscow.

—— now a trio when STEVE departed

Criminal Damage — not iss.

Dec 83. (m-lp) *(CRIMLP 105)* **CRACK HOUSE**
– Get ahead / Myths and legends / Kafka's dad / The throat / Attraction for the easy life / The throat. *(re-iss. Jun85; same)*

Jun 84. (7") *(CRI 115)* **SPIKE MILLIGAN'S TAPE RECORDER. / ALL SKIN AND BONE**

Jan 85. (12"ep) *(CRI 12-125)* **DEATH TO TRAD ROCK**
– Shine on Pumpkin Moon / Myths and legends (re-recorded) / Big nose and the howling wind / The kite-man.

—— STAN BATCOW – bass, vocals, guitar; repl. TILTON who was still co-producer and part-time member until he joined The CREEPERS (MARC RILEY)

Creation — not iss.

Aug 85. (lp) *(CRELP 006)* **THE GIFT OF LIFE**
– Shot by my own gun / I am fisheye / Dreadful saint engine / Green and godless land / More skin and bone / Barbest snake fish thing / Chewing the fat / Typical male penis / Fire face / Gift of life.

In-Tape — not iss.

Mar 86. (7") *(IT 029)* **EVERYTHING'S BRILLIANT. / CLEANSED AGAIN**
(12"+=) *(ITT 029)* – ('A'mix) / New blood for young skulls / King Cotton Whiplash.

—— WALLAS TERROR – bass, vocals; repl. STAN

—— brought in guests TIM HYLAND – sax / NICK BROWN – violin, guitar / TED CHIPPINGTON – vocals (Solo artist) / KEITH CURTIS – guitar, bass / NOEL KILBRIDE – guitar

Oct 86. (lp) *(IT 038) (CON 00010)* **SONGS OF LOVE AND FURY**
– Big fun tonight / Kennedy '63 / Post detergent vacuum cleaner man / The day my universe changed / Bang! / Snaffleflatch / The murder of Sister George / Spaceships / 1986 / Thank heavens for the iron horse / Sleazeball / Phoney T.V. repair man / The Elvis I knew was no junkie / Everyone's going triple bad acid, yeah! / Jaw cracker fuzz.

—— NICK + KEITH were now added full-time

—— Early in '87, the group were credited on 'Past Caring' with PIG BROS.

1987. (7"orange) *(CON 00024)* **GROOVY F---ERS. / TIME WARP 1991 (mix) / GREAT MISTAKE**

Glass — Homestead German

Aug 87. (7") *(GLASS 052)* **TIME WARP 1991. / TOO FAST TO LIVE, TOO FAST TO DIE**
(12"+=) *(GLASS12 052)* – ('A'mix) / Groovy / Dragon fly.

Apr 88. (lp) *(GLALP 028) (CON 00034) <HMS 108>* **KISS ASS . . . GODHEAD!**
– Tatty seaside town / Love your puppy / Viva! Spanish turncoat / Bulbous love child / Electric storm / Fuck my old boots / John Robb's 91st nightmare / Long live the hooligan / Punk out baby / Corn dolly fear / The world acclaims eternal protein man / Let's take the death trip / Cheap male aggression / Cor blimey ain't England snidey / Bacon factory. *(cd-iss. Apr02 on 'Overground'+=; OVER 86VPCD)* – Time warp 1991 / Too fast to live / Groovy fuckers / Dragonfly.

—— PAUL MORLEY – bass, vocals (ex-SLUM TURKEYS) repl. WALLAS

Vinyl Drip — not iss.

Jul 89. (12"ep) *(SUK 8)* **EURO PIG VS. AUTO FLESH**
– Auto flesh / Tatty seaside town II / Voodoo smile / Hey Bryn Maer.

Nov 89. (lp/cd) *(SUK 9/+CD) <CON 00041>* **TO SLAY THE ROCK PIG**
– Auto flesh / Space hopper ignites / Caretaker mentality / Life, death and the scary bits inbetween / Tuff veggie aggro / More than a kiss (the freak remains high) / 24 hour drinking at northern prices / Vile antics of supa yob! / Missive from couch potato command / England expects every man to do his booty (Starfucker No.2) / Growling people.

Clawfist — not iss.

1991. (7") *(XPIG 6)* **BIG DECISION (SLIGHT RETURN). / (B-side by THAT PETROL EMOTION)**

—— disbanded when ROBB formed SENSURROUND (late GOLD BLADE); KEITH CURTIS was a member before The MEMBRANES folded

– compilations, etc. –

Apr 86. (lp) *Criminal Damage; (CRIMLP 130)* **PULP BEATING AND ALL THAT**
– Spike Milligan's tape recorder / Kafkas's dad / All skin and bone / Shine on pumpkin moon / Big nose and the howling wind / Myths and legends / The kite-man.

Jun 86. (lp) *Constrictor; (CON 00004)* **GIANT** *German*
– Sexy? big tongue! / Everything's brilliant / Mr. Charisma brain / King cotton whiplash / Gift of life (parts 1 & 2) / Shot by my own gun / Everyone's going, triple bad acid yeah! / New blood for young skulls / Chwing the fat.

Sep 86. (7") *Constrictor; (CON 9)* **SPIKE MILLIGAN'S TAPE RECORDER. / KENNEDY '63** *German*
(above featured PHILIP BOA)

Jun 87. (lp) *Vinyl Drip; (DRIPLP 1)* **THE VIRGIN MARY VERSUS PETER SELLERS – BACK CATALOGUE**

Jul 93. (cd) *A-Bomb / Constrictor; (13) / (CCON 001CD)* **WRONG PLACE AT THE WRONG TIME**

Jun 97. (cd) *Anagram; (CDMGRAM 112)* **THE BEST OF THE MEMBRANES**
– Ice age / Fashionable junkies / Muscles / High St. Yanks / Man from Moscow / Kafka's dad / Spike Milligan's tape recorder / Myths and legends / Shine on pumpkin moon / I am fish eye / Mr. Charisma brain / Everything's brilliant / Kennedy '63 / Spaceships / Everyone's going triple bad acid yeah / Time warp 1991 / Love your puppy / Electric storm / Tatty seaside town / Voodoo chile.

SENSURROUND

JOHN ROBB – bass, etc / **TRACEY CARMEN** – vocals / **GREG WILSON** – DJ (ex-manager of RUTHLESS RAP ASSASSINS) / **PATRICK + ADAM**

Ice Rink — not iss.

Jun 92. (12") *(DAV 2 12)* **BLIND FAITH / BLIND FAITH (Aloof mix). / PRETTY FACE / PRETTY FACE (remix)**

Apr 93. (12") *(DAV 5 12)* **WHEN I GET TO HEAVEN (mixes; 7" / regressive / 12" / red) / DEEP INSIDE YOUR LOVE (Hulme mix)**
(cd-s+=) *(DAV 5 CD)* – ('A'-smooth and silky mix).

GOLDBLADE

JOHN ROBB – vocals, guitar (ex-MEMBRANES, ex-SENSURROUND) / **ROBERT HAYNES** – drums / **WAYNE SIMMONS** – bass / **JAY TAYLOR** – guitars / **KEITH CURTIS** – guitar (ex-A WITNESS)

Ultimate — not iss.

Jul 96. (7"ep) *(Topp 047)* **INTRODUCING . . . GOLD BLADE**
– Soul power / Dirty hips / A little terror is good for the soul.

Oct 96. (7"clear) *(Topp 052)* **BLACK ELVIS. / GHOSTS OF THE DISTANT PAST**
(cd-s) *(Topp 052cd)* – ('A'side) / I love the city / Lord a' mercy.

Mar 97. (7"pink) *(Topp 056)* **STRICTLY HARDCORE. / SNAKE STYLE** | 64 |
(cd-s) *(Topp 056cd)* – ('A'side) / Sharp and angular / Sticks and stones.
(cd-s) *(Topp 056cdx)* – ('A'side) / Dirty hips / Bad day in Hell.

Apr 97. (cd/c/lp) *(Topp cd/mc/lp 058)* **HOME TURF**
– Strictly hardcore / Soul power / Genius is pain / Soul on fire / Feel my disease / Fastest man alive / Jackknife (meet thy saviour) / Black Elvis / Not even Jesus / Hail the people / Long slow fuck / Downtown (greed in my soul) / Saddest song / Canal street breakdown / 5 True believers.

Jun 97. (7") *(Topp 060)* **NOT EVEN JESUS. / STRICTLY HARDCORE (Ned Sherrin acoustic)**
(cd-s) *(Topp 060cd)* – ('A'side) / ('B'-Phil Mossman FU-11 mix) / ('A'-Papa mantra mix).
(cd-s) *(Topp 060cdx)* – ('A'side) / Shake shake shake / Death of the blue eyed soul brother / Oxfore union rant.

Jun 98. (7") *(Topp 067)* **16 TONS. / 4 REAL 4 EVER**
(cd-s) *(Topp 067cd)* – ('A'side) / Gold Blade make me wanna fuck / King o' the north.

Oct 98. (7") *(Topp 076)* **HAIRSTYLE. / MOHICAN**
(cd-s) *(Topp 076cd)* – ('A'side) / ('A'-why don't you rub it in my face? – Black Box Recorder remix) / ('A'-body 2 body – close shave version – Black Box Recorder remix).

Nov 98. (cd) *(Toppcd 071)* **DROP THE BOMB**
– Home turf / (R U ready 4) The 21st Century? / Living outside the capital / Rock'n'roll's a loser's game / 16 tons / Nu soul warriors / Hairstyle / Glam rock star / Let's see those hands / Float like a butterfly / Dream the vicious dream, baby / Carbohydrate of love (L.U.V.).

—— JAY TAYLOR would leave to form BONE-BOX (with ROB)

—— line-up now JOHN, ROB, KEITH plus JOHNY SKULLKNUCKLES – guitar / PETE G.O.R.G.E.O.U.S. – guitar / MARTIN – percussion

20 Stone Blatt — not iss.

May 02. (cd-s) *(BAMF 27CD)* **AC/DC / WE DON'T CARE / GOOD TASTE IS THE ENEMY OF THE REVOLUTION / LOST, LONELY AND VICIOUS**

Jul 02. (cd) *(BAMF 29CD)* **DO U BELIEVE IN THE POWER OF ROCK'N'ROLL?**
– Do U believe in the power of rock'n'roll? / Who was the killa? / AC/DC / Kiss my ass / This powerful intoxicant known as love / Mutha fukka / Punk rock! / Panic attack / Uranus / Square peg in a round hole (every prophet must get stoned) / What a life / Little baby satellite.

MEN THEY COULDN'T HANG

Formed: London, England . . . 1983 by former buskers, (PHIL) SWILL, his brother JOHN, PAUL SIMMONDS, STEPHAN CUSH and SHANNE HASLER, who got together for an impromptu performance at the Alternative Country Festival in London. Though they never intended to become a professional outfit, their performance was so well received that promoters were queuing up to offer them gigs and ELVIS COSTELLO was so impressed he signed them to his 'Imp' label. Though they were initially lumped in with the "cowpunk" scene (and compared to The POGUES, HASLER having been a member of The NIPPLE ERECTORS with SHANE MacGOWAN), the MTCH's hard-edged folk-rock/thrash was always more politically motivated, tracing the lineage of historical protest and choosing a cover of Scottish folkie, Eric Bogle's anti-war anthem, 'THE GREEN FIELDS OF FRANCE', as a debut single in late '84. One of their biggest fans was the evergreen John Peel, whose audience rated the song at No.3 in his Radio 1 Festive 50. A follow-up, 'IRONMASTERS', was even more frenetic and just as cutting, while the debut album, 'NIGHT OF A 1,000 CANDLES' (1985) brought widespread acclaim. A final, NICK LOWE-produced single for 'Imp' later that year, 'GREENBACK DOLLAR', preceded a major label deal with 'M.C.A.'. The resulting album, 'HOW GREEN IS MY VALLEY' (1986), was a disappointment in comparison, the band's material not translating well to big budget production values. Though it made the Top 75, the album failed to achieve the crossover success that their new label were obviously hoping for and the band duly found themselves dropped. Picking up where they left off with 'Magnet', the band eventually released the much improved 'WAITING FOR BONAPARTE' (1988), missing the UK Top 40 by a whisker. After being subjected to record company pressure for a name change, the band again parted company with their label. Subsequently finding a more sympathetic home at 'Silvertone', the band released the superior 'SILVERTOWN' (1989), a record which found SIMMONDS at his most lyrically scathing and provided them with the only Top 40 entry of their career. Finally, shortly after the release of

MEN THEY COULDN'T HANG (cont)

1990 set, 'THE DOMINO CLUB', the band called it a day, the concert set, 'ALIVE, ALIVE-O' (1991) a document of their final night at London's Town and Country Club and testament to the onstage intensity of these musical vagabonds. Surprisingly, The MEN THEY COULDN'T HANG came back to haunt the scene in late '96 with an EP on 'Demon'. This was followed by a full-length album, 'NEVER BORN TO FOLLOW' (1996) and mini-set, 'SIX PACK' (1997), although their profile remained low. • **Covered:** DONALD WHERE'S YOUR TROOSERS? (hit; Andy Stewart) / RAWHIDE (Link Wray) / MAN IN THE CORNER SHOP (Paul Weller) / GOODBYE T'JANE (Slade) / HARVEST MOON (Neil Young) / NEVER BORN TO FOLLOW (Goffin-KIng) / etc. • **Trivia:** GREENBACK DOLLAR was produced by NICK LOWE.

Album rating: FIVE GLORIOUS YEARS compilation (*7) / NIGHT OF 1,000 CANDLES (*8) / HOW GREEN IS MY VALLEY (*6)

PHIL 'SWILL' ODGERS – vocals, accoustic guitar, tin whistle, melodia / **PAUL SIMMONDS** – guitar, vocals, mandolin, keyboards / **STEFAN CUSH** (b.Wales) – guitar, vocals / **SHANNE HASLER** – bass (ex-NIPPLE ERECTORS, ex-NIPS) / **JON ODGERS** – drums, percussion

Imp-Demon / not iss.

Oct 84. (7") *(IMP 003)* **THE GREEN FIELDS OF FRANCE. / ('A'version)**
(12"+=) *(IMP 003T)* – Hush little baby.
Jun 85. (7") *(IMP 005)* **IRONMASTERS. / DONALD WHERE'S YOUR TROOSERS?**
(12"+=) *(IMP 005T)* – Rawhide.

Demon / not iss.

Jul 85. (lp/c) *(FIEND/+CASS 50)* **NIGHT OF A 1,000 CANDLES** [91]
– The day after / Jack Dandy / A night to remember / Johnny comes home / The green fields of France (no man's land) / Ironmasters / Hush little baby / Walkin' talkin' / Kingdom come / Scarlet ribbons. *(cd-iss. 1988; FIENDCD 50) (cd re-iss. Nov97 on 'Diablo'; DIAB 839)*
Nov 85. (7") *(D 1040)* **GREENBACK DOLLAR. / A NIGHT TO REMEMBER**
(12"+=) *(D 1040T)* – The bells.

M.C.A. / M.C.A.

Jun 86. (7") *(SELL 1)* **GOLD RUSH. / GHOSTS OF CABLE STREET**
(12"+=) *(SELLT 1)* – Walkin' talkin'.
Oct 86. (7") *(SELL 2)* **SHIRT OF BLUE. / JOHNNY COME HOME**
(12"+=) *(SELLT 2)* – Whiskey in me giro / Scarlet ribbons.
Oct 86. (lp/c) *(MCF/+C 3337)* **HOW GREEN IS MY VALLEY** [68]
– Gold strike / Gold rush / Ghosts of Cable Street / Dancing on the pier / The bells / Wishing well / Going back to Coventry / Shirt of blue / Rabid underdog / Tiny soldiers / The parade / Parted from you. *(cd-iss. Jan90; DMCF 1898) (re-iss. Nov92 cd/c; MCL D/C 19075)*
Mar 87. (7"/12") *(SELL/+T 3)* **GHOSTS OF CABLE STREET. / DREAM MACHINE**
(c-s+=) *(SELLC 3)* – Liverpool lullaby.

— **RICKY McGUIRE** – bass; repl. SHANNE

Magnet / Warners

Oct 87. (7"/7"pic-d) *(SELL/+P 5)* **ISLAND IN THE RAIN. / COUNTRY SONG**
(7"ep+=/12"ep+=) *(SELL E/T 5)* – Silver dagger / Restless highway.
Mar 88. (7") *(SELL 6)* **THE COLOURS. / RORY'S GRAVE** [61]
(12"+=) *(SELLT 6)* – Big iron.
(cd-s+=) *(CDSELL 6)* – ('A'-full remix).
Apr 88. (lp/c/cd) *(MAGL/MAGC/DMAG 5075)* **WAITING FOR BONAPARTE** [41]
– The crest / Smugglers / Dover lights / Bounty hunter / Island in the rain / The colours / Midnight train / Father's wrong / Life of a small fry / Mary's present. *(cd+=)* – The crest (12"version). *(c+=)* – Silver dagger / Restless highway / Country song. *(re-iss. May88 lp/c)cd; WX 183/+C)(242380-2)*

WEA / not iss.

Jun 88. (7"/12") *(YZ 193/+T)* **THE CREST. / TIME AT THE BAR**
(cd-s+=) *(YZ 193CD)* – Goodbye t'Jane / Ironmasters.

— added p/t **NICKY MUIR** – keyboards, accordion

Silvertone / not iss.

Feb 89. (7") *(ORE 4)* **RAIN, STEAM AND SPEED. / SHIRT OF BLUE**
(12"+=) *(ORET 4)* – Scarlet ribbons.
(cd-s+=) *(ORECD 4)* – Iron masters.
Apr 89. (lp/c/cd) *(ORE LP/MC/CD 503)* **SILVERTOWN** [39]
– Rosettes / A place in the sun / Home fires / Diamonds, gold & fur / Company town / Lobotomy gets 'em home / Blackfriar's bridge / Rain, steam and speed / Down all the days / Hellfire and damnation / Homefires / El vaquero. *(cd+=)* – A map of Morocco / Rain, steam and speed (12"mix).
May 89. (7") *(ORE 7)* **A PLACE IN THE SUN. / A MAP OF MOROCCO**
(12"+=) *(ORET 7)* – Scarlet ribbons.
(cd-s+=) *(ORECD 7)* – The day after (live).
Dec 89. (7") *(ORE 14)* **A MAP OF MOROCCO. / ROSETTES / THE DAY THE CLOCK WENT BACK**
(12"+=/12"s+=) *(ORE T/X 14)* – Rosettes (live).
(cd-s+=) *(ORECD 14)* – The iron men of rap (with ATTILA THE STOCKBROKER).
Jul 90. (7") *(ORE 19)* **GREAT EXPECTATIONS. / MARGARET PIE**
(cd-s+=) *(ORECD 19)* – Green fields of France.
(12"+=) *(ORET 19)* – (excerpts from forthcoming album below).
Aug 90. (cd/c/lp) *(ORE CD/MC/LP 512)* **THE DOMINO CLUB** [53]
– The lion and the unicorn / Great expectations / The family man / Handy man / Kingdom of the blind / Grave rosting in gig harbour / Industrial town / You're the one / Australia / Dog eyes, owl meat, man-chops / Billy Morgan / On the razzle. *(cd re-iss. May01; same)*
Oct 90. (10"/cd-s) *(ORE 22 10/CD)* **THE LION AND THE UNICORN. / KINGDOM OF THE BLIND**

— disbanded Feb '91 after some farewell gigs (& periodical one-offs)

Fun After All / not iss.

May 91. (cd/c/lp) *(CD/T+/AFTER 10)* **ALIVE, ALIVE-O** (live)
– The crest / Billy Morgan / You're the one / Home fires / Going back to Coventry / The colours / Ironmasters / Lobotomy, gets 'em home / Man in the corner shop / Australia / Night to remember / Scarlet ribbons.

LIBERTY CAGE

— **SIMMONDS + ODGERS / + DAVE KENT** – whistle, harmonica, trumpet, vocals / **NEIL SIMMONDS** – double bass, sax, bass, guitar

Line / not iss.

Sep 94. (cd) *(LICD 9.01293)* **SLEEP OF THE JUST**
– Everything's different now / Fires below / Throwing stones at the sea / On her majesty's service / Swimming against the tide / One for the road / Judgement day / You make my mind stand still / Mercy of the guards / Cat and mouse affair / Murder in cell #9 / C.D.C.

Kronk / not iss.

Sep 95. (cd-ep) **I'LL KEEP IT WITH MONE / THE RIVERS RUN DRY / SLIP AWAY GENTLY / HEAVEN'S PRISONERS**
(above a DYLAN song) **PAUL HOWARD** – guitar, c-vocals (ex-TENDER TRAP) repl. KENT, although they subsequently split after

MEN THEY COULDN'T HANG

— re-formed in 1996, **KENNY HARRIS** – drums, percussion; repl. JON

Demon / Demon

Oct 96. (cd-ep) *(D 2000)* **THE EYE / HARVEST MOON / PERRY BORDER / PIECES OF PARADISE**
Nov 96. (cd) *(<FIENDCD 788>)* **NEVER BORN TO FOLLOW**
– The eye / Glittering prize / Never born to follow / I survived / Contenders / Our day / Gangland / House of cards / Denis Law & Ali MacGraw / To have and to hold / The spell is broken / Jennifer Grey.

— **ANDY SELWAY** – drums, percussion; repl. HARRIS

Jul 97. (m-cd) *(<VEXCD 15>)* **SIX PACK**
– Nightbird / The wonder of it all / Moving on / Refugee / Come forward / Henry Krinkle: Alone inna ugly town.

– compilations, others, etc. –

Aug 88. (12"ep) *Strange Fruit; (SFNT 012)* **THE EVENING SHOW SESSIONS (15.6.86)**
– Dancing on the pier / Ghosts of Cable Street / Going back to Coventry / Tiny tin soldiers.
Apr 90. (cd/c/lp; w-drawn) *Silvertone; (ORE CD/MC/LP 509)* **FIVE GLORIOUS YEARS**
1992. (7"ep/12"ep/cd-ep) *(ORE 019/+T/CD)* **GREAT EXPECTATIONS (BIG DREAMS) / THE COLOURS (live). / GHOSTS OF CABLE STREET (live) / KINGDOM OF THE BLIND**
Apr 98. (cd) *Demon; (<FIENDCD 940>)* **MAJESTIC GRILL: THE BEST OF THE MEN THEY COULDN'T HANG**
– Ironmasters / Ghosts of Cable Street / Shirt of blue / Scarlet ribbons / The crest / Colours / Islands in the rain / Rosettes / Dogs' eyes / owl meat and man chop / Map of Morocco / Denis Law and Ali Maggraw / Australia / Eye / Our day / Nightbird / Green fields of France (no man's land).

MEN WITHOUT HATS

Formed: Montreal, Quebec, Canada . . . 1980 by brothers IVAN and JEREMIE ARROBAS. North America's premier electro-pop purveyors if only because of a dearth of any peers, these mad hatters issued two US-only 12"ers for the Stateside branch of 'Stiff', 'FOLK OF THE 80's' and 'NATIONALE 7'. However, these were the only two recordings to feature the brothers together, JEREMIE leaving his more talented sibling to recruit a full band (including brothers STEFAN and COLIN DOROSCHUK alongside ALLAN McCARTHY) and sign to 'Backstreet' ('Statik' in the UK). Initially the act struggled, two singles and an album failing to sell any significant quota while even the 'SAFETY DANCE' single made little impact the first time round. A quirky but irresistably infectious, post-PETER GABRIEL new wave pop classic, the latter track finally entered the US charts in the summer of '83. Promoted by an innovative video (with IVAN as the colourful court jester!) and featuring fashionable pre-1984/anti-nuclear sentiments, the single rocketed into the American Top 3 before making the Top 20 in both Britain and Europe. The aforementioned debut album, 'RHYTHM OF YOUTH' (1982/3), made Stateside inroads after being re-promoted, although this was their only long-playing success. Unfortunately, 'SAFETY DANCE', became the proverbial albatross around their necks with further singles and albums – 'FOLK OF THE 80's PART III' (1984) and 'POP GOES THE WORLD' (1987) – selling only moderately; the fact that 'WEIRD AL' YANKOVIC graced them with a parody certainly didn't help their cause. • **Covered:** I AM THE WALRUS (Beatles) / EDITIONS OF YOU (Roxy Music).

Album rating: RHYTHM OF YOUTH (*5) / FOLK OF THE 80'S PART III (*4) / POP GOES THE WORLD (*4) / ADVENTURES OF WOMEN & MEN WITHOUT HATE IN THE 21st CENTURY (*3) / SIDEWAYS (*3) / GREATEST HATS compilation (*6)

IVAN ARROBAS – vocals, synths / **JEREMIE ARROBAS** – drums, synths

not iss. / Stiff

1981. (12"ep) *<TEES12 01>* **FOLK OF THE 80'S**
– Modern(e) dancing / Utter space / Antartica / Security (everybody feels better with it).

— <above originally issued for 'Trend' in Canada; HATS 001>

1981. (12") *<TEES12 08>* **NATIONALE 7. / FREEWAYS** [-] ☐

— **IVAN** (now without JEREMIE) recruited **STEFAN DOROSCHUK** – guitar, violin + **ALLAN McCARTHY** – electronics, piano, percussion / plus **COLIN DOROSCHUK** – guitar / **ANNE DUSSAULT** – vocals / **DANIEL VERMETTE** – guitar / **MARTIN CARTIER** + **MICHEL JEROME** – percussion

Statik Backstreet

Mar 82. (7") *(STAT 13)* **ANTARTICA. / MODERN DANCING** ☐ ☐
Aug 82. (7") *(STAT 20)* **I GOT THE MESSAGE. / UTTER SPACE** ☐ ☐
Oct 82. (lp/c) *(STAT LP/C 10) <39002>* **RHYTHM OF YOUTH** ☐ [13] Jul83
– Ban the game / Living in China / The great ones remember / I got the message / Cocoricci (le tango des voleurs) / Safety dance / Ideas for walls / Things in my life / I like / The great ones remember – reprise. *(cd-iss. Oct85; CDST 10)* *<US cd-iss. 1997 on 'Oglio'+=; 81588>* – FOLK OF THE 80's
Mar 83. (7") *(TAK 1)* **SAFETY DANCE. / SECURITY** ☐ ☐
(12"+=) *(TAK 1-12)* – I got the message.
(re-iss. Sep83; same) – hit No.6
Jun 83. (7") *<52232>* **SAFETY DANCE. / LIVING IN CHINA** [-] [3]
Oct 83. (7") *<52293>* **I LIKE. / THINGS IN MY LIFE** [-] [84]
Jan 84. (7") *(TAK 3)* **LIVING IN CHINA. / COCORICCI (LE TANGO DES VOLEURS)** ☐ ☐
(12"+=) *(TAK 3-12)* – Modern dancing.

— now a 4-piece of **IVAN, ALLAN, STEFAN + COLIN** with guest ANNE

Jun 84. (7"/12") *(TAK 15/+12)* **WHERE DO THE BOYS GO? / EUROTHEME** ☐ ☐
Sep 84. (lp/c) *(STAT LP/C 18) <5487>* **FOLK OF THE 80'S (PART III)** ☐ ☐
– No dancing / Unsatisfaction / Where do the boys go? / Mother's opinion / Eurotheme / Messiahs die young / I know their name / Folk of the 80's / I sing last – Not for tears. *(cd-iss. Oct85; CDST 18)*

— **IVAN** recruited an entire new line-up **JOHNNY** – guitar / **JENNY** – bass / **J. BONHOMME** – drums

Mercury Mercury

Oct 87. (7") *(MER 257) <888859>* **POP GOES THE WORLD. / THE END (OF THE WORLD)** ☐ [20]
(12"+=/cd-s+=) *(MER X/CD 257)* – ('A'-dance mix).
Nov 87. (lp) *<832730>* **POP GOES THE WORLD** [-] [73]
– Intro / Pop goes the world / On Tuesday / Bright side of the sun / O sole mio / Lose my way / The real world / Moonbeam / In the name of angels / La valese d'Euge'nie / Jenny wore black / Intro – Walk on water / The end (of the world).
Oct 89. (lp/cd) *<842000-1/-2>* **ADVENTURES OF WOMEN & MEN WITHOUT HATE IN THE 21st CENTURY** [-] ☐
– In the 21st century / Hey men / You and me / Everybody's selling something / Here come the 90's / S.O.S. / All we do / I'm in love / Intro Louise – Louise and I / Underneath the rainbow / 21st century safety dance.
1991. (cd) *<848569-2>* **SIDEWAYS** [-] [-] Canada
– Sideways / Fall down gently / In the meadow / The Van Der Graaf generation blues / Nadine / Everybody wants to know / I am the walrus / KenBarbielove / Lost forever / Life after Diamond Head / Love (all over the world) / Harry Crews.
above was their final release

– compilations, etc. –

Feb 96. (cd) *Oglio; <81587>* **COLLECTION** [-] ☐
Nov 97. (cd) *Aquarius; <579>* **GREATEST HITS** [-] [-] Canada
– The safety dance / Living in China / Antartica / I got the message / I like / Where do the boys go? / Freeways (Euromix) / Pop goes the world / On Tuesday / Sideways / Editions of you / The safety dance (extended) / Where do the boys go? (extended).

METEORS

Formed: London, England . . . 1980 as RAW DEAL by alleged self-confessed Satanist, P. PAUL FENECH, alongside NIGEL LEWIS and MARK ROBERTSON. All veterans of the rockabilly/R'n'R scene (specifically the bands The SOUTHERN BOYS and ROCK THERAPY) despite their youthfulness, the trio made their vinyl debut via an appearance on 'Alligator' records' various artists compilation, 'Home Grown Rockabilly'. Subsequently adopting the METEORS moniker, the band released a debut EP, 'METEOR MADNESS', combining a rockabilly rebel stance with gothic punk in much the same fashion as the more outlandish CRAMPS, substituting the latter outfit's fetishism for a more Oi!-like gang mentality. This ethos was neatly summed up with 'WRECKIN' CREW' (1986), the title of the band's second album and a phrase associated with the band for the rest of their career. In the meantime, they'd released a debut set, 'IN HEAVEN' (1981) on their own 'Lost Souls' imprint, LEWIS later striking out to form his own outfit, The TALL BOYS. New members MICK WHITE, RUSSELL JONES and STEVE MEADHAM were in place for the galloping, lip-curling minor hit rendition of John Leyton's 'JOHNNY REMEMBER ME', one of the highlights on the aforementioned 'WRECKIN' CREW'. Issued on the 'I.D.' label, the record was confirmation of The METEORS' psychobilly credentials; by this point, the band's gigs had already become notorious for raucous activities as be-quiffed boot boys became as regular an 80's subcultural feature as punks and skinheads. More personnel changes ensued as WHITE also departed to form his own outfit, GUANA BATZ, a temporary replacement found in RICK ROSS before IAN CUBITT was brought in for the recording of the 'STAMPEDE' (1984) album. In keeping with their spirit as a live act, a couple of unoffical live sets appeared in 1986/87 before the band signed to 'Anagram' for the release of 'SEWERTIME BLUES' (1987). This lovingly titled METEORS artefact featured a cover of Jan & Dean's 'SURF CITY', adding to their extensive back catalogue of trademark interpretations which already included the likes of Creedence Clearwater Revival's 'BAD MOON RISING'. Albums such as 'DON'T TOUCH THE BANG BANG FRUIT' (1987), 'ONLY THE METEORS ARE PURE PSYCHOBILLY' (1988) and 'MUTANT MONKEY AND THE SURFERS FROM ZORCH' (1988) continued to please the faithful if not exactly offering up anything to tempt the casual listener save the usual cover material, The Ramones' 'SOMEBODY PUT SOMETHING IN MY DRINK' given the honours this time around. While they may have had a more fanatical following (obsessed fan, Mark Silman, turned into a mad psycho killer!) than The CRAMPS for example, The METEORS never enjoyed the same level of support from the press and while the latter act are still going fairly strong more than twenty years on, The METEORS seemed to have burned out at the dawn of the 90's. • **Covered:** GET OFF MY CLOUD (Rolling Stones) / GET ME TO THE WORLD ON TIME (Electric Prunes) / WIPEOUT (Surfaris) / WILD THING (Troggs) / GO BUDDY GO (Stranglers) / THESE BOOTS ARE MADE FOR WALKING (hit; Nancy Sinatra) / RAWHIDE (Link Wray) / PLEASE DON'T TOUCH (Johnny Kidd) / etc. • **Note:** Not to be confused with Dutch band of the early 80's (out of ALQUIN) who were on 'E.M.I.'.

Album rating: ONLY THE METEORS ARE PURE PSYCHOBILLY compilation (*7)

P. PAUL FENECH – vocals, guitar / **NIGEL LEWIS** – bass, vocals / **MARK ROBERTSON** – drums

Ace not iss.

Jul 81. (7"ep) *(SW 65)* **METEOR MADNESS** ☐ [-]
– Voodoo rhythm / Maniac rockers from Hell / My daddy's a vampire / You can't keep a good man down.
Jul 81. (m-lp) *(MAD 1)* **THE METEORS MEET SCREAMING LORD SUTCH** ☐ [-]
– (4 above) + tracks by SCREAMING LORD SUTCH (yes! that one!).

Chiswick not iss.

Nov 81. (7") *(CHIS 147)* **RADIOACTIVE KID. / GRAVEYARD STOMP** ☐ [-]

Upright not iss.

Dec 81. (7"; as CLAPHAM SOUTH ESCALATORS) *(UPYOUR 1)* **GET ME TO THE WORLD ON TIME. / LEAVE ME ALONE / CARDBOARD CUT OUTS** ☐ [-]

Lost Souls not iss.

Dec 81. (lp) *(LOSTLP 3001)* **IN HEAVEN** ☐ [-]
– In Heaven / Shout so loud / Earwigs in my brain / In the cards / Attack of the Zorch men / The crazed / Get off my cloud / Love you to death / Teenagers from outer space / Maniac / Into the darkness / Death dance / Psycho for your love / The room / Rockabilly psychosis. *(<cd-iss. Feb97 on 'Edsel'; ED 509>)*
Jan 82. (7") *(LOST 101)* **THE CRAZED. / ATTACK OF THE ZORCH MEN** ☐ [-]

— **FENECH** brought in **MARK WHITE** – bass to repl. LEWIS who joined The TALL BOYS

— **RUSSELL JONES** – drums repl. WOODY who repl. ROBERTSON

WXYZ not iss.

Aug 82. (7") *(ABCD 5)* **MUTANT ROCK. / THE HILLS HAVE EYES** ☐ [-]

— **STEVE 'Ginger' MEADHAM** – drums repl. JONES

I.D. not iss.

Dec 82. (7"/7"pic-d) *(EYE 1/+P)* **JOHNNY REMEMBER ME. / FEAR OF THE DARK / WRECKIN' CREW** [66] [-]
Jan 83. (lp) *(NOSE 1)* **WRECKIN' CREW** ☐ [-]
– Insane / I ain't ready / Johnny remember me / I don't worry about it / Axe attack / Zombie noise / Rattlesnakin' daddy / When a stranger calls / Phantom of the opera / Blue sunshine / Wreckin' crew / Sick things / Wild thing / I'm not mad / Get off my cloud. *(cd-iss. Dec91 on 'Streetlink';) (<re-iss. cd Apr93 on 'Dojo'; DOJOCD 121>) (cd re-iss. Jun01 on 'Receiver'; RRCD 315)*

— **RICK ROSS** – bass, vocals repl. WHITE who formed GUANA BATZ

Wreckin' not iss.

Nov 83. (lp) *(WRECK 1)* **THE METEORS LIVE (live)** ☐ [-]
– Wipe out / Maniac rockers from Hell / Lonesome train / I ain't ready / Ain't gonna bring me down / Sick things / Crazy love / When a stranger calls / Rawhide / I don't worry about it / Voodoo rhythm / You crack me up / Mutant rock / Graveyard stomp / Wreckin' crew / These boots were made for walking / Long blonde hair.

— **IAN 'Spider' CUBITT** – bass repl. ROSS who went to America

Mad Pig not iss.

Oct 84. (lp) *(CHOP 1)* **STAMPEDE** ☐ [-]
– Night of the werewolf / Ain't gonna bring me down / Electro / Stampede / I'm just a dog / In too deep / Cecil drives a combined harvester / Michael Myers / Out of the dark / Only a fury in my heart / Do the demolition / You're out of time. *(cd-iss. Jul89; CDCHOP 1)*
Oct 84. (7") *(PORK 1)* **I'M JUST A DOG. / YOU CRACK ME UP** ☐ [-]
(12"+=) *(PORK 1T)* – Ain't gonna bring me down.
(12") *(PORR 1)* – ('A'-Wild hog mix down) / Hoover rock / Electro rock.
May 85. (7") *(PORK 2)* **FIRE, FIRE. / LITTLE RED RIDING HOOD** ☐ [-]
(12"+=) *(PORK 2T)* – Stampede (King Ray bat scalator in the dark mix).

— **NEVILLE HUNT** – bass repl. CUBITT

Oct 85. (7") *(PORK 3)* **BAD MOON RISING. / RHYTHM OF THE BELL** ☐ [-]
(12"+=) *(PORK 3T)* – Hogs and cuties (What? another cover mix).
Nov 85. (lp) *(CHOP 2)* **MONKEY'S BREATH** ☐ [-]
– Ex man boogie / Power of steel / Hoover rock / Kick boy / Eat the baby / Maybe tomorrow / Hogs and cuties / Alligator man / Rhythm of the bell / Sweet love on my mind / Meat is meat / Take a ride / Just the three of us / Joba's snake.

Anagram not iss.

Aug 86. (7") *(ANA 31)* **SURF CITY. / THE EDGE** ☐ [-]
('A'-Has Beens From Outer Space mix-12"+=) *(12ANA 31)* – Johnny's here.
Dec 86. (lp/c) *(GRAM/CGRAM 27)* **SEWERTIME BLUES** ☐ [-]
– Ain't takin a chance / So sad / Here's Johnny / Mind over matter / Acid and psyam / Sewertime blues / Return of Ethel Merman / Deep dark jungle / Never get away / I bury the living / Vibrate / Surf city. *(cd-iss. Jul89 +=; CDGRAM 27)* – DON'T TOUCH THE BANG BANG FRUIT *(cd re-iss. Apr95 as above on 'Anagram'; CDMPSYCHO 03)*

— **TOBY 'Jug' GRIFFIN + AUSTIN H. JONES** – bass repl. NEVILLE

Jun 87. (7") *(ANA 35)* **GO BUDDY GO. / WILDKAT WAYS** ☐ [-]
('A'-Wonkey Donkey mix-12"+=) *(12ANA 35)* – You crack me up.

— **LE BROWN** – bass (ex-PHAROAHS) repl. above temp. bassists

METEORS (cont)

Sep 87. (lp/c) *(GRAM/CGRAM 30)* **DON'T TOUCH THE BANG BANG FRUIT**
– Go buddy go / Midnight people / Low livin' daddy / Your worst nightmare / Wildkat ways / Repo man / You crack me up / Shakey shakey / Psycho kat / Let's go / Revenge of El Trio Los Bastardos / Don't touch the bang bang fruit.
Oct 87. (7") *(ANA 39)* **DON'T TOUCH THE BANG BANG FRUIT. / DATELESS NITES**
(12"+=) *(12ANA 39)* – Corpse grinders.
Feb 88. (12") *(12ANA 41)* **SOMEBODY PUT SOMETHING IN MY DRINK**
Feb 88. (lp/c/cd) *(GRAM/CGRAM/CDGRAM 33)* **ONLY THE METEORS ARE PURE PSYCHOBILLY** (compilation)
– Voodoo rhythm / Graveyard stomp / Wreckin' crew / Sick things / Blue sunshine / Mutant rock / The hills have eyes / Fire, fire / Power of steel / Eat the baby / Rhythm of the bell / Surf city / Go buddy go / Somebody put something in my drink. *(cd-iss. Jan97 on 'Summit'; SUMCD 4089)*
Oct 88. (7") *(ANA 43)* **RAWHIDE. / SURFIN' ON THE PLANET ZORCH**
(12"+=) *(12ANA 43)* – Little Red Riding Hood.
Nov 88. (lp/cd) *(GRAM/CDGRAM 37)* **MUTANT MONKEY AND THE SURFERS FROM ZORCH**
– Swamp thing / Electro II (the revenge) / Side walk psycho / I'm invisible man / She's my baby again / Surfin' on the Planet Zorch / Spine bender / Dance crazy baby / Rawhide / Oxygen dog / Yellow zone / Meet me in the morgue / Little Red Riding Hood. *(<cd re-iss. Jun00; CDMPSYCHO 12>)*

—— MARK HOWE – drums; repl. MEADHAM

Sep 89. (lp/c/cd) *(GRAM/CGRAM/CDGRAM 43)* **UNDEAD, UNFRIENDLY AND UNSTOPPABLE**
– Razorback / Disneyland / My kind of rockin' / Lonesome train / Johnny God / I go to bed with the undead / Out of the attic / Brains as well / Charlie, Johnny, Redhead and me / Lies in wait / Surf mad pig / Please don't touch. *(cd re-iss. Apr95; CDMPSYCHO 02)*
Dec 89. (12"m) *(12ANA 51)* **PLEASE DON'T TOUCH. / DISNEYLAND / MY KINDA ROCKIN'**
May 90. (lp/c/cd) *(GRAM/CGRAM/CDGRAM 45)* **LIVE STYLES OF THE SICK AND SHAMELESS (live)**
– Ex-men boogie / Wipe out / Rattle snake daddy / Mutant rock / Maniac / Blue sunshine / Mind over matter / These boots are made for walking / Little Red Riding Hood / The hills have eyes / Wild thing / I go to bed with the undead / Voodoo rhythm / I ain't ready / Wreckin' crew. *(cd+=)* – Lonesome train / Rock bop / Ain't gonna bring me down / Graveyard stomp. *(cd re-iss. Mar97 on 'Summit'; SUMCD 4109) (cd re-iss. Oct01 on 'Anagram'; CDMPSYCHO 23)*

—— disbanded after above

– compilations, etc. –

Feb 85. (lp) *Dojo; (DOJOLP 2)* **THE CURSE OF THE MUTANTS**
– Mutant rock / Insane / Scream of the mutants / When a stranger calls / Fear of the dark / The hills have eyes / Wild thing / Get off my cloud / Wreckin' crew / Zombie noise / Johnny remember me / Phantom of the opera / Blue sunshine / I don't worry about it / Axe attack / Rattlesnakin' daddy.
Sep 85. (pic-lp) *Dojo; (DOJOLP 4P)* **LIVE**
(re-iss. Jan86; DOJOLP 4) (cd-iss. 1988; DOJOCD 4)
Apr 86. (lp) *Dojo; (DOJOLP 22)* **HORRIBLE MUSIC FOR HORRIBLE PEOPLE: LIVE VOL.2 (live)**
Jun 86. (lp/cd) *Big Beat; (WIKA/CDWIK 47)* **TEENAGERS FROM OUTER SPACE**
– Voodoo rhythm / Maniac rockers from Hell / My daddy is a vampire / You can't keep a good man down / Graveyard stomp / Radioactive kid / Leave me alone / Dog eat robot / Walter Mitty blues / Just the three of us / Blue sunshine insight / Attack of the Zorch men / Jupiter stroll. *(cd+=)* – Another half hour till sunrise / Island of the lost souls / The Napoleon solo / Get me to the world on time.
Aug 86. (12"ep) *Archive 4; (TOF 106)* **WRECKIN' CREW / JOHNNY REMEMBER ME. / I DON'T WORRY BOUT IT / WILD THING**
Sep 86. (7"green-ep/12"green or blue) *I.D.; (EYE/+T 10)* **MUTANT ROCK**
– Wreckin' crew / Scream of the mutants / The hills have eyes / Mutant rock.
Jul 87. (d-lp) *Anagram; (DCHOP 1)* **MONKEY'S BREATH / STAMPEDE**
(cd-iss. Oct95; CDMPSYCHE 09)
Nov 87. (pic-lp) *Dojo; (DOJOLP 56P)* **NIGHT OF THE WEREWOLF – LIVE ALBUM**
(cd-iss. Sep98 on 'Raucous'; RAUCD 309)
Dec 87. (lp) *Link; (LINK LP06)* **LIVE AND LOUD**
Sep 93. (cd) *Anagram; (CDGRAM 66)* **THE BEST OF THE METEORS**
Feb 95. (cd) *Dojo; <213>* **LIVE, LEARY & FUCKIN' LOUD!**
Apr 95. (cd) *Receiver; (<RRCD 217>)* **WELCOME TO THE WRECKIN' PIT**   May96
Sep 95. (cd) *Nectar; (NTMCD 508)* **GRAVEYARD STOMP (BEST OF THE METEORS)**
1995. (cd) *Cleopatra; <CLEO 9647>* **CORPSE GRINDER**
Oct 96. (cd) *Receiver; (<RRCD 230>)* **INTERNATIONAL WRECKERS 2: THE LOST TAPES OF ZORCH**   Nov96
Jan 97. (lp/cd) *Hellraiser; (<001/+CD>)* **BASTARD SONS OF A ROCK'N'ROLL DEVIL**   Sep97
Dec 97. (cd) *Anagram; (<CDMPSYCHO 17>)* **FROM ZORCH WITH LOVE: THE VERY BEST OF THE METEORS 1981-1987**   Sep99
Mar 99. (cd) *Raucous; (<RAUCD 044>)* **JOHN PEEL SESSIONS (1983-1985)**   Jun99
Sep 99. (cd) *Anagram; (CDGRAM 123) / Cleopatra; <CLEO 811>* **THE METEORS VS. THE WORLD**   Jan00
Feb 00. (lp) *Raucous; (RAUCLP 056)* **THE METEORS VS. THE WORLD VOL.1**
Feb 00. (lp) *Raucous; (RAUCLP 057)* **THE METEORS VS. THE WORLD VOL.2**
Mar 00. (cd) *Anagram; (<CDMPSYCHO 3>)* **SEWERTIME BLUES / DON'T TOUCH THE BANG BANG FRUIT**
Feb 01. (cd) *Anagram; (<CDMPSYCHO 20>)* **THE ANAGRAM SINGLES COLLECTION**

Mar 01. (cd) *Raucous; (<RAUCD 079>)* **PSYCHOBILLY REVOLUTION**   May01
Jul 01. (cd) *Anagram; (<CDGRAM 145>)* **PSYCHO DOWN** *(re-iss. Dec01 on 'Cleopatra'; CLP 1172CD)*
Jul 02. (cd) *Raucous; (<RAUCD 116>)* **LIVE VOL.1 & 2**
Jul 02. (cd/lp) *Raucous; (<RAU CD/LP 109>)* **THE FINAL CONFLICT (live)**
Nov 02. (d-cd) *Castle; (<CMDDD 628>)* **WRECKIN' LIVE**

MIAOW (see under ⇒ CARROLL, Cath)

MICRODISNEY (see under ⇒ COUGHLAN, Cathal)

MIGHTY LEMON DROPS

Formed: Dudley, Midlands, England . . . 1984 by PAUL MARSH, DAVID NEWTON, TONY LINEHAN and KEITH ROWLEY. All veterans of the local music scene, various band members had played alongside each other in ACTIVE RESTRAINT, this outfit releasing a one-off single, 'TERROR IN MY HOME', the previous year. Encouraged by the band's pedigree and no doubt hoping to cash in on the much hyped C-86 movement, 'Chrysalis' signed them following a one-off single, 'HAPPY HEAD' issued on the independent 'Dreamworld' label. A Stephen Street-produced debut album of the same name surfaced later in '86, developing the tinny guitar clatter of their first single. Despite their Midlands origins, the band's sound and image bore a heavy debt to Liverpool legends ECHO & THE BUNNYMEN, with MARSH's gloomy vocals in particular bearing comparison to IAN McCULLOCH. Despite generally favourable reviews, subsequent albums such as 'WORLD WITHOUT END' (1988) and 'LAUGHTER' (1989) proved too one dimensional for wider pop consumption, alternating between introspective laments and jingle/jangle indie fare. Popularity on America's college scene led to a brief dalliance with 'Sire' for 1991's 'SOUND . . . GOODBYE TO YOUR STANDARDS' album, their parting shot save for a posthumous live effort recorded in the States. • **Covered:** SPLASH #1 (13th Floor Elevators) / PAINT IT BLACK + WE LOVE YOU (Rolling Stones) / WHEN I DREAM (Teardrop Explodes) / ANOTHER GIRL, ANOTHER PLANET (Only Ones) / SOMETIMES GOOD GUYS DON'T WEAR WHITE (Standells).

Album rating: HAPPY HEAD (*6) / WORLD WITHOUT END (*5) / LAUGHTER (*5) / SOUND . . . GOODBYE TO YOUR STANDARDS (*5) / RICOCHET (*5) / ROLLERCOASTER compilation (*7)

ACTIVE RESTRAINT

PAUL MARSH – vocals / **DAVID NEWTON** – guitar / **TONY LINEHAM** – bass / **MARTIE GILKS** – drums

                                                                                       Sticky   not iss.
Nov 83. (7") *(PEEL OFF 3)* **TERROR IN MY HOME. / TURNS OUT ROSES**

MIGHTY LEMON DROPS

                                                                                       Dreamworld   not iss.
Nov 85. (12"ep) *(DREAM 005)* **LIKE AN ANGEL. / SOMETHING HAPPENS / SYMPATHISE WITH US**
Apr 86. (7") *(DREAM 006)* **LIKE AN ANGEL. / NOW SHE'S GONE**

—— **KEITH ROWLEY** – drums; repl. MARTIE who joined The WONDER STUFF

                                                                    Blue Guitar   Sire
Aug 86. (7") *(AZUR 1)* **THE OTHER SIDE OF YOU. / UPTIGHT**   51
(12"+=) *(AZURX 1)* – Pass you by.
Sep 86. (lp/c/cd) *(AZLP/ZAZLP/) <25532>* **HAPPY HEAD**   58
– The other side of you / My biggest thrill / Behind your back / All the way / Hypnotised / Like an angel / Pass you by / Take me up / On my mind / Something happens / Turn me around. *<US+=>* – Out of hand / Going under / Count me out / Splash #1 (now I'm home) / Rollercoaster / My biggest thrill / Hypnotised / The other side of you.
Oct 86. (7") *(AZUR 3)* **MY BIGGEST THRILL. / OPEN MIND**
(12"+=) *(AZURX 3)* – Take my heart.
Apr 87. (7"/12") *(AZUR/+X 4) <25595>* **OUT OF HAND. / GOING UNDER**   66
Jan 88. (7") *(AZUR 6)* **INSIDE OUT. / SHINE**   74
(12"+=) *(AZURX 6)* – Head on the block. *<US; b-side>*
Feb 88. (lp/c/cd) *(AZLP/ZAZLP/CDAZ 4) <25701>* **WORLD WITHOUT END**   34
– Inside out / One by one / In everything you do / Hear me call / No bounds / Fall down (like the rain) / Crystal clear / Hollow inside / Closer to you / Breaking down.
Apr 88. (7") *(AZUR 9)* **FALL DOWN (LIKE THE RAIN). / PAINT IT BLACK**
(c-s+=) *(ZAZURX 9)* – Laughter.
(12"++=/cd-s++=) *(AZUR X/CD 9)* – Happy head / Hollow inside (live).

—— **MARCUS WILLIAMS** – bass; repl. LINEHAM

Aug 89. (7"/7"s/c-s) *(AZUR/+B/MC 12)* **INTO THE HEART OF LOVE. / RUMBLETRAIN**
(ext; 12"+=/cd-s+=) *(AZUR X/CD 12)* – Sometimes good guys don't wear white.

                                                                    Chrysalis   Sire
Sep 89. (lp/c/cd) *(CHR/ZCHR/CCD 1733) <26017>* **LAUGHTER**
– At midnight / Into the heart of love / Where do you go from Heaven / The heartbreak thing / One in a million / Written in fiction / The real world / All that I can do / Second time around / Beautiful shame. *<US-only+=>* – Rumbletrain?
Oct 89. (7") *(AZUR 13)* **BEAUTIFUL SHAME. / AT MIDNIGHT (live club mix)**
(12"+=/cd-s+=) *(AZUR X/CD)* – Forever home at heart (live) / Like an angel (live).

	Sire	Sire
Apr 91. (12"m) (W 0032T) **TOO HIGH. / DISCONTENT / WE LOVE YOU**	☐	-
(cd-s+=) (W 0032CD) – You don't fast.		
May 91. (cd/c/lp) (<7599 26512-2/-4/-1>) **SOUND . . . GOODBYE TO YOUR STANDARDS**	☐	-

– Too high / Unkind / My shadow girl / Barry's poem / Always / Big surprise / Cold, cold heart / Annabelle / You don't appreciate anything / Colorful-loving-me / Ready, steady, no!.

Jun 91. (12"ep) (W 0046T) **UNKIND / ANOTHER GIRL, ANOTHER PLANET. / COLOURFUL-LOVING-ME (original demo version)** ☐ -

Feb 92. (cd/c/lp) <2-/4-26993> **RICOCHET** ☐ -
– Nothing / Into the sun / Sense / From the sky / (She's so) Out of touch / Falling deep / Reach out / Between the lines / More / Blues inside / Hallowed ground.

---- disbanded after above

– compilations, etc. –

Jul 87. (12"ep) Night Tracks; (SFNT 004) **THE EVENING SHOW SESSIONS** ☐ -
– The other side of you / Now she's gone / Waiting for the rain / When I dream.

Nov 93. (cd) Overground; <OVER 31CD> **ALL THE WAY – LIVE IN CINCINNATI** - ☐

Feb 97. (cd) Chrysalis; (CDCHRM 103) **ROLLERCOASTER (THE BEST OF THE MIGHTY LEMON DROPS 1986-1989)** ☐ ☐
– Happy head / Into the heart of love / My biggest thrill / Inside out / The other side of you / Out of hand / Like an angel / Fall down (like the rain) / Splash #1 (now I'm home) / Beautiful shame / Rollercoaster / In every thing you do / Uptight / Shine / Where do you go from Heaven / Count me out / Something happens / Sympathise with us / Now she's gone.

MIGHTY MIGHTY

Formed: Birmingham, England ... mid 80's by HUGH HARKIN, MICK GEOGHEGAN, brother PETER GEOGHEGAN, RUSSELL BURTON and DAVID HENNESSY. Having formed their own 'Girlie' label, MIGHTY MIGHTY released their debut single, 'EVERYBODY KNOWS THE MONKEY', around the same time as they contributed a track to the fresh-faced NME newcomers V/A compilation, C-86. Harkin' er, back to the golden era of 'Postcard' Scot-pop, HUGH and Co subsequently jangled their way onto the 'Chapter 22' label after a second self-financed release, 'IS THERE ANYBODY OUT THERE?'. Over the ensuing year and a half, the lads issued a string of largely uninspired singles, culminating in their debut album and swansong effort, 'SHARKS' (1988).

Album rating: SHARKS (*5) / A BAND FROM BIRMINGHAM compilation (*6) / THE GIRLIE YEARS compilation (*6) / AT THE BBC (*5)

HUGH HARKIN – vocals / **MICK GEOGHEGAN** – guitar / **PETER GEOGHEGAN** – organ / **RUSSELL BURTON** – bass, vocals / **DAVID HENNESSEY** – drums

	Girlie	not iss.
Mar 86. (7") (GAY 001) **EVERYBODY KNOWS THE MONKEY. / YOU'RE ON MY MIND**	☐	-
Jul 86. (12"ep) (XGAY 2) **IS THERE ANYBODY OUT THERE? / SETTLE DOWN. / LET'S CALL IT LOVE / MAN OR BOY**	☐	-

	Chapter 22	not iss.
Nov 86. (7") (CHAP 10) **THROWAWAY. / CEILING TO THE FLOOR**	☐	-
(12"+=) (12CHAP 10) – Lionheart.		
Mar 87. (7") (CHAP 12) **BUILT LIKE A CAR. / I DON'T NEED YOU ANYMORE**	☐	-
(12"+=) (12CHAP 12) – Twilight / Love so strong.		
Oct 87. (7") (CHAP 19) **ONE WAY. / LAW**	☐	-
(12"+=) (12CHAP 19) – I never imagined / Night after night.		
Jan 88. (7") (CHAP 21) **BORN IN A MAISONETTE. / POSITIVELY SESAME STREET**	☐	-
(12"+=) (12CHAP 21) – Precious moments / Loose end.		
Feb 88. (lp) (CHAPLP 24) **SHARKS**	☐	-

– Gemini smiles / Maisonette / Biddy Baxter / Little wonder / Settle down / Blue and green / One way / When you trusted me / Michael says not / Sulk / I'll get you back / Yours truly. (<re-iss. Jul00 on 'Vinyl Japan' cd/lp; ASK CD/LP 109>)

---- disbanded after above

– compilations, etc. –

on 'Vinyl Japan' unless mentioned otherwise

May 00. (cd/lp) (<ASK CD/LP 110>) **A BAND FROM BIRMINGHAM** ☐ ☐ Jun00
– Throwaway / Ceiling to the floor / Lionheart / Built like a car / I don't need you anymore / Twilight / Love so strong / One way / Law / I never imagined / Night after night / Maisonette / Positively Sesame Street / Precious moments / Loose end.

Mar 01. (cd/c) (<ASK CD/LP 120>) **THE GIRLIE YEARS** ☐ ☐ May01
– Everybody knows the monkey / You're on my mind / Yours truly / Is there anyone out there? / Settle down / Let's call it love / Man or boy / Throwaway / Sunday supplement girl / Lucky break / Oedipus and you / Four leave clover / Radio / I can't help it / The levitating man / Sixty seconds / Painted words / Touch of the sun.

May 01. (cd) (<ASKCD 123>) **AT THE BBC** ☐ ☐
– Throwaway / Is there anyone out there? / Ceiling to the floor / Settle down / I don't need you anymore / One way / Little wonder / Gemini smiles / I'll get you back / I never imagined / Yours truly / Built like a car / Maisonette / Blue and green / Law / Biddy Baxter.

Roger MILLER (see under ⇒ MISSION OF BURMA)

Ted MILTON (see under ⇒ BLURT)

MIMI (see under ⇒ HUGO LARGO)

MINNY POPS

Formed: Amsterdam, Netherlands ... September '78 by songwriter and er, "singer", WALLY VAN MIDDENDORP and his synthesized accomplice WIM DEKKER. A year on, the gruesome twosome released their debut single, 'KOJAK', following it up with a Dutch-only long-player, 'DRASTIC MEASURES, DRASTIC MOVEMENT' (1979). Fleshing out the minimalist sound with the addition of guitarist, GERARD WALHOF and bassist LION VAN ZOEREN, they delivered another heavy dose of mogadon electronica in the shape of the EP, 'LIVE 33'. One of its tracks, 'DOLPHIN SPURT', was seemingly interesting enough for 'Factory' boss, Tony Wilson to give it a full UK release. Thanks Tony! Further personnel shuffles were effected as P. MULDER substituted GERARD and LION, while the group were shunted onto Factory's continental branch 'Benelux' for a further two singles and album, 'SPARKS IN A DARK ROOM' (1982). Designed to make your party go with a bang (if you were playing Russian roulette with all barrels loaded, that is), this was possibly the most depressing material ever to be released by 'Factory' (and they've had some beauties, haven't they); imagine IAN CURTIS at 16 rpm inside a medieval monastery or alternatively an android on prozac and you're probably still nowhere near the full suicidal impact of the well named WALLY VAN MIDDENDORP's vocal drone.

Album rating: DRASTIC MEASURES, DRASTIC MOVEMENT (*4) / SPARKS IN A DARK ROOM (*3)

WALLY VAN MIDDENDORP – vocals / **WIM DEKKER** – synthesizer

	Plurex	not iss.
Mar 79. (7"ep) (005) **KOJAK. / FOOTSTEPS / NERVOUS**	-	- Dutch
Sep 79. (lp) (009) **DRASTIC MEASURES, DRASTIC MOVEMENT**	-	- Dutch

– Springtime 1 / Minny pops / Hologram / Total confusion / Dolphins spurt / Motor city / Springtime 2 / Monica / Flash goes the eyes / M.D. mania / R.U. 21 / Mono / New muzak. (re-iss. Dec81; same) (with free 7") – KOGEL. / STRALERS

---- added **GERARD WALHOF** – guitar / **LION VAN ZOEREN** – bass

Jun 80. (7"ep) (0016) **MINNY POPS – LIVE 33** - - Dutch
– Mental / Night out / Dolphin spurt.

	Factory	not iss.
Oct 80. (7") (FAC 31) **DOLPHIN SPURT. / GODDESS**	☐	-

---- **P. MULDER** – instruments; repl. GERARD + LION

	Factory Benelux	not iss.
Nov 81. (7"ep) (FACBN 11) **TIME. / TRANCE / NIGHT VISIT**	-	-
Nov 81. (7"flexi) (FACBN 13) **EEN KUS. / (other side by the band, MENTAL)**	-	- Dutch
Jul 82. (lp) (FBN 15) **SPARKS IN A DARK ROOM**	-	-

– Black eye / Dream / Night visit / A feeling / Crack / Tracking / Vital / Blue roses / Mountains.

	Plurex	not iss.
Oct 83. (lp) (3000) **POSTE RESTANTE**	-	- Dutch

– Koel / Wandelen / The sea / Drom / Achterlaten / Vreemde dagen, vreemde nachten / On our side / Piano / Raag / White wings.

	Les Tempes	not iss.
Jun 84. (7") (CSBT 4-5) **EEN KUS. / SON**	-	-

	Prime	not iss.
Mar 85. (lp) (none) **FOURTH FLOOR**	-	- Dutch

– Palm beach / Touch / Fighting man / Back / Wave of flames / Secure / West desert / East Cairo / State of mind.

---- had already split prior to above release; WALLY moonlighted with WHITE BIRDS, RAVING LUNATIC and The TITS

MINOR THREAT (see under ⇒ FUGAZI)

MINUTEMEN

Formed: San Pedro, California, USA ... 1979 originally as The REACTIONARIES, by D BOON and MIKE WATT (third member GEORGE HURLEY replaced FRANK TONCHE). The band featured on Various Artists US lp's on indie labels 'Radio Tokyo', 'New Alliance' and 'Posh Boy', before signing for 'S.S.T.' (home base of BLACK FLAG and MEAT PUPPETS). For five years they committed many songs (mostly hardcore/jazz! around a minute long!) to EP and LP before having to disband late in 1985 after the untimely death of BOON. From 'PARANOID TIME' to '3-WAY TIE (FOR LAST)', MINUTEMEN showcased their politically leftfield attacks on the establishment including RONNIE REAGAN and JOE McCARTHY. In 1986 the remaining two, MIKE WATT and GEORGE HURLEY re-formed as fIREHOSE alongside guitarist ED CRAWFORD. This trio debuted with an album, 'RAGIN' FULL ON' (1987), their sound slightly mellowing. After an acclaimed 1989 third album 'fROMOHIO', they shifted to 'Columbia', where they scored minor hit albums in the early 90's. • **Covered:** HEY LAWDY MAMA (Steppenwolf) / HAVE YOU EVER SEEN THE RAIN + GREEN RIVER (Creedence Clearwater Revival) / DOCTOR WU (Steely Dan) / THE RED AND THE BLACK (Blue Oyster Cult). fIREHOSE covered WALKING THE COW (Daniel Johnston) / SLACK MOTHERFUCKER (Superchunk). DOS covered PACIFIC COAST HIGHWAY (Sonic Youth) + DON'T EXPLAIN (Billie Holiday).

Album rating: PARANOID TIME (*5) / THE PUNCH LINE mini (*4) / WHAT MAKES A MAN START FIRES? (*7) / DOUBLE NICKELS ON THE DIME (*8) / 3-

MINUTEMEN (cont)   THE GREAT INDIE DISCOGRAPHY   The 1980s

WAY TIE (FOR LAST) (*6) / PROJECT: MERSH mini (*6) / BALLOT RESULTS (*7) / fIREHOSE: RAGIN', fULL-ON (*6) / fROMOHIO (*8) / FLYING THE FLANNEL (*6) / Mike Watt: BALL-HOG OR TUGBOAT? (*7) / CONTEMPLATING THE ENGINE ROOM (*6) / Dos: DOS (*6)

D BOON (b. DENNES DALE BOON, 1 Apr'58) – vocals, guitar / **MIKE WATT** (b.20 Dec'57, Portsmouth, Virginia) – bass (also of DOS) / **GEORGE HURLEY** (b. 4 Sep'58, Brockton, Massachusetts) – drums; repl. FRANK TONCHE

			S.S.T.	S.S.T.

Dec 80. (7"ep) <SST 002> **PARANOID TIME**
 – Untitled song for Latin America / Political song for Michael Jackson to sing / Validation / The maze / Definitions / Fascist / Joe McCarthy's ghost. *(UK-iss.Mar83, cd-ep iss.Nov88; same)*

Sep 81. (7"ep) <NAR 004> **JOY / BLACK SHEEP. / MORE JOY**

—— <above issued on 'New Alliance'>

Nov 81. (m-lp) <SST 004> **THE PUNCH LINE**
 – Search / Tension / Games / Boiling / Disguises / Struggle / Monuments / Ruins / Issued / The punch line / Song for El Salvador / History lesson / Fanatics / No parade / Straight jacket / Gravity / Warfare / Static. *<(cd/c-iss.May93; SST CD/C 004)>*

Feb 83. (lp) <SST 014> **WHAT MAKES A MAN START FIRES?**
 – Bob Dylan wrote propaganda songs / One chapter in the book / Fake contest / Beacon sighted through fog / Mutiny in Jonestown / East wind – Faith / Pure joy / '99 / The anchor / Sell or be sold / Only minority / Split red / Colors / Plight / Tin roof / Life as rehearsal / This road / Polarity. *(UK-iss.Aug91 & May93 cd/c; SST 014 CD/C)*

Nov 83. (m-lp) <SST 016> **BUZZ OR HOWL UNDER THE INFLUENCE OF HEAT**
 – Self-referenced / Cut / Dream told by Moto / Dreams are free, motherfucker! / Tow jam / I felt like a gringo / Product / Little man with a gun in his hand. *(UK-iss.May93 cd/c; SST 016 CD/C)*

Oct 84. (d-lp) <(SST 028)> **DOUBLE NICKELS ON THE DIME**
 – D's car jam – Anxious Mo-Fo / Theatre is the life of you / Viet nam / Cohesion / It's expected I'm gone / #1 hit song / Two beads at the end / Do you want new wave or do you want the truth? / Don't look now / Shit from an old notebook / Nature without man / One reporter's opinion / Political song for Michael Jackson to sing / Maybe partying will help / Toadies / Retreat / The big foist / God bows to math / Corona / The glory of man / Take 5, D. / My heart and the real world / History lesson – part II / You need the glory / The roar of the masses could be farts / ***** Mr Robot's holy orders / West Germany. <(cd-iss. Oct87 +=; SST 028CD)> – THE POLITICS OF TIME lp – The politics of time / Themselves / Please don't be gentle with me / Nothing indeed / No exchange / There ain't shit on TV tonight / This ain't no picnic / Spillage / Untitled song for Latin America / Jesus and tequila / June 16th / Storm in my house / Martin's story / Doctor Wu / Ain't talkin' about love / Little man with a gun in his hand / The world according to nouns / Love dance.

Jun 85. (12"ep) <(SST 034)> **PROJECT: MERSH**
 – Cheerleaders / King of the hill / Hey lawdy mama / Take our test / Tour-spiel / More spiel.

—— tragedy struck on the 23rd December '85 when D BOON was killed in a car crash

Jan 86. (lp) <(SST 058)> **3 WAY TIE (FOR LAST)**
 – The price of Paradise / Lost / The big stick / Political nightmare / Courage / Have you ever seen the rain? / The red and the black / Spoken word piece / No one / Stories / What is it? / Ack ack ack / Just another soldier / Situations at hand / Hittin' the bong / Bermuda. *(cd-iss. Aug87; SST 058CD)*

—— Broke-up early 1986. WATT guested for CICCONE YOUTH (aka SONIC YOUTH).

– compilations, etc. –

1984. (lp/cd) *New Alliance;* **THE POLITICS OF TIME** (early REACTIONARIES material)
Apr 85. (7"ep) *Reflex;* (REFLEX L) **TOUR SPIEL** (live)
Dec 86. (d-lp/cd) *S.S.T.;* <(SST 068)> **BALLOT RESULTS**
 – Little man with a black gun in his hand / Political song for Michael Jackson to sing / I felt like a gringo / Jesus and tequila / Courage / King of the hill / Bermuda / No one / Mr.Robot's holy orders / Ack ack ack / History lesson (part two) / This ain't no picnic / The cheerleaders / Time / Cut / Split red / Shit you hear at parties / Hell (second take) / Tour-spiel / Take our test / The punch line / Search / Bob Dylan wrote propaganda songs / Badges / Tension / If Reagan played disco / No! no! no! to draft and war – Joe McCarthy ghost. *(re-iss. May93)*
1987. (lp/cd) *S.S.T.;* <SST 138/+CD> **POST-MERSH, VOL.I**
 – THE PUNCH LINE ep / WHAT MAKES A MAN START FIRES lp *(re-iss. May93)*
1987. (lp/cd) *S.S.T.;* <SST 139/+CD> **POST-MERSH, VOL.II**
 – BUZZ OR HOWL UNDER THE INFLUENCE OF HEAT lp / PROJECT: MERSH ep *(re-iss. May93)*
Sep 87. (7"ep) *New Alliance;* **JOY / BLACK SHEEP. / MORE JOY**
 (re-iss. Feb90 on 'S.S.T.' 10"colrd; SST 214)
May 89. (cd) *S.S.T.;* <(SST 165)> **POST-MERSH, VOL.III**
Aug 98. (cd) *S.S.T.;* <(SST 363CD)> **INTRODUCING THE MINUTEMEN**

fIREHOSE

MIKE WATT – bass (also of CRIMONY, with **PAUL ROESSLER** – keyboards) / **GEORGE HURLEY** – drums / **ED CRAWFORD** (b.26 Jan'62, Steubenville, Ohio) – vocals, guitar (of COLUMBUS)

			S.S.T.	S.S.T.

Apr 87. (lp/c/cd) <(SST 079/+C/CD)> **RAGIN' fULL-ON**
 – Caroma / Mutiny / Perfect pairs / Chemical wires / Choose and memory / Relating dudes to jazz? / Another theory shot to shit on your… / Under the influence of the Meat Puppets / Locked in. / Brave captain. *(re-iss. Mar93; same)*

Mar 88. (lp/c/cd) <(SST 115/+C/CD)> **If'N**
 – Sometimes / Hear me / Honey, please / Backroads / From one cums one / Making the freeway / Anger / For the singer of R.E.M. / Operation solitaire / Windmilling / Me & you, remembering / In memory of Elizabeth Cotton / Soon / Thunder child. *(re-iss. Mar93; same)*

Jun 88. (12"ep) <(SST 131)> **SOMETIMES. / RHYMIN' SPILIN' / SHE PAINTS PICTURES**
 (re-iss. Aug93 cd-ep+=; SST 131CD) – For the singer of R.E.M.

Mar 89. (lp/c/cd) <(SST 235/+C/CD)> **fROMOHIO**
 – In my mind / Whisperin' while hollerin' / Mas cojones / What gets heard / Fiddle of the eighties / Time with you / If'n / Understanding / The softest hammer / Vastapol / Let the drummer have some / Liberty for our friend / Some things / Not that shit George.

		not iss.	New Alliance

1989. (lp,c,cd; as BOOTSTRAPPERS) <46> **BOOTSTRAPPERS**
 – Memory is a muscle / Spider baby / New boots / Taxita / Flicker / Third rail / Media dub / D-I-A-L-C-A-S-H / X – Delta / Their faces are green and their hands / Presidential apology / Mud / Indeed / Empty-vee / Long beach dub – Feen / Maneuvres.
 (above:- WATT + HURLEY with ELLIOTT SHARP)

		Columbia	Columbia

Oct 91. (cd/c/lp) (468422-2/-4/-1) <47839> **fLYIN' THE fLANNEL** — Apr91
 – Down with the bass / Up Finnegan's ladder / Can't believe / Walking the cow / Flyin' the flannel / Epoxy for example / O'er the town of Pedro / Too long / The first class / Anti-misogyny manoever / Toolin' song for Dave Alvin / Tienan man dream again / Lost colors / Towin' the line / Losers, boozers and heroes.

Feb 92. (m-cd) <74152> **THE LIVE TOTEM POLE EP**
 – The red and the black / Sophisticated bitch / Revolution part 2 / Slack motherfucker / What gets heard / Mannequin / Making the freeway safe for the freeway. *<re-iss. Feb95 as 'THE RED AND THE BLACK'; same>*

Mar 93. (cd/c/lp) (472967-2/-4/-1) <53208> **MR. MACHINERY OPERATOR** — Feb93
 – Formal introduction / Blaze / Herded into pools / Witness / Number seven / Powerful hankerin' / Rocket sled-fuel tank / Quicksand / Disciples of the 3-way / More famous quotes / Sincerely / Hell-hole / 4.29.92 / The cliffs thrown down.

1994. (m-cd) <5122> **BIG BOTTOM POW-WOW**
 – People, this is why (first spiel) / Witness / Sperm count theory (second spiel) / Revolution (part two) / What about Don Quixote? (third spiel) / Down with the bass / If you fail, you fall down (fourth spiel) / Blaze / Enough spiel? (final spiel) / Formal introduction.

—— disbanded on the 12th of February 1994 after playing a small unadvertised gig. MIKE WATT joined PORNO FOR PYROS after a solo album.

MIKE WATT

		Columbia	Columbia

Mar 95. (cd/c) (478375-2/-4) <67086> **MIKE WATT: BALL-HOG OR TUGBOAT?**
 – Big train / Against the 70's / Drove up from Pedro / Piss-bottle man / Chinese firedrill / Song for Madonna to sing / Tuff gnarl / Sexual military dynamics / Max and Wells / E-ticket ride / Forever – one reporter's opinion / Song for Igor / Tell 'em boy! / Sidemouse advice / Heartbeat / Maggot brain / Coincidence is either hit or miss.

—— now with **NELS CLINE** – guitar / **STEPHEN HODGES** – drums

Oct 97. (cd,c) <CK 68161> **CONTEMPLATING THE ENGINE ROOM**
 – In the engine room / Red bluff / The bluejackets' manual / Pedro bound! / The boilerman / Black gang coffee / Topsiders / No one says old man (to the old man) / Fireman Hurley / Liberty calls! / In the bunk room / Navy wife / Crossing the equator / Breaking the choke hold / Wrapping around the screw / Shore duty.

DOS

MIKE WATT + his wife **KIRA ROESSLER** – bass (ex-BLACK FLAG)

		not iss.	New Alliance

1986. (lp) <NAR 032> **DOS**
 – The fisherman & his wife / Forever / Funk one / Number four / Number one / Number three / Number two / The rabbit and the porcupine / Slow little turtle / Snapshot / Taking away the fire. *(UK cd-iss. May93; NAR 032CD)*

1989. (12"ep) <NAR 044> **NUMERO DOS**
 – Don't explain / Heartbeat / PCH / I worry, my son / Silence / Number six.

Aug 91. (cd) <NAR 061> **UNO CON DOS** (compilation of above 2)
 (UK-iss.May93; NAR 061CD)

		not iss.	Kill Rock Stars

Jun 96. (cd) <KRS 256> **JUSTAMENTE TRES**
 – Down in the dumps / Dream of San Pedro / Image that / Intense song for Madonna / 'Til the blood ran / Sidemouse advice / Excerpts from a captain's log / To each his dulcinea / Powerful hankerin' / Little doll / Willow weep for me / Even the pain has changed / Formal introduction / Angel face is the Devil's daughter / Number seven / Do you want new wave or do you want the truth? / Number five.

MIRACLE LEGION

Formed: Connecticut, USA ... 1984 by MARK MULCAHY, RAY NEAL, JEFF WIEDERSCHALL and JOEL. Yet another American act to emerge in the seismic wake of R.E.M., MIRACLE LEGION first marched onto the scene the following year with a mini-set, 'THE BACKYARD'. Subsequently picked up by 'Rough Trade', the band finally released a full length album, 'SURPRISE, SURPRISE, SURPRISE', in summer '87, their rickenbacker-ringing alterna-pop finding an audience among post-Paisley Underground fans. By this point, STEVEN WEST had replaced JOEL on bass although the band was subsequently reduced to a core of MULCAHY and NEAL for 1989's stripped down, rootsy acoustic effort, 'ME AND MR. RAY'. While they did recruit another rhythm section (in the shape of DAVE McCAFFREY and SCOTT BOUTLER) and even had IAN McLAGAN (ex-SMALL FACES) guesting for them, MULCAHY and NEAL disbanded MIRACLE LEGION after the country influenced 1992 album, 'DRENCHED'. MULCAHY took up a low-key solo career before he hooked up with NEAL once more to deliver a comeback set, 'PORTRAIT OF A DAMAGED FAMILY' (1997). The following year MULCAHY had the music press all hot and bothered over his 'FATHERING' solo set, sending journos into an orgasmic frenzy of superlatives with his patented brand of alternative sexual healing. TIM BUCKLEY, JOHN MARTYN and even VAN the man were the reference points as MULCAHY reconciled the sacred and the profane in a furtive clinch.

If the acoustic sparseness was something of a smokescreen for his wayward passion, the richer production on 'SMILESUNSET' (2001) served only to ripen his downbeat desire.

Album rating: THE BACKYARD mini (*5) / SURPRISE SURPRISE SURPRISE (*5) / ME AND MR. RAY (*5) / DRENCHED (*6) / PORTRAIT OF A DAMAGED FAMILY (*4) / Mark Mulcahy: FATHERING (*8) / SMILESUNSET (*7)

MARK MULCAHY – vocals (ex-DUMPTRUCK) / **RAY NEAL** – guitar / **JOEL** – bass / **JEFF WIEDERSCHALL** – drums

	Making Waves	Incas
Nov 85. (m-lp) (SPIN 302) **THE BACKYARD**		May85

– Butterflies / Steven, are you there? / The backyard / Closer to the wall / Just say hello / The heart is attached. <US re-iss. 1988 on 'Rough Trade'; ROUGH-US 31>

| Feb 86. (7") (SURF 112) **THE BACKYARD. / UNTIL SHE TALKS** | | |

---- **STEVEN WEST** – bass; repl. JOEL

	Rough Trade	Rough Trade
Jul 87. (lp/c) (ROUGH/+C 112) **SURPRISE, SURPRISE, SURPRISE**		

– Storyteller / Truly / Little man / Mr. Mingo / Crooked path / Paradise / Everyone in Heaven / Country boy / Wonderment / All for the best. <US-iss.May88 as 'GLAD'; ROUGHUS 34>

| Jan 89. (lp/c/cd) (ROUGH/+C/CD 136) <ROUGHUS 57> **ME AND MR. RAY** | | |

– The ladies from town / And then / Old & new / Sailors and animals / If she could cry / Pull the wagon / You're the one Lee / Even better / Cold shoulder balcony / Gigantic transatlantic trunk call.

| Feb 89. (7") (RT 226) **YOU'RE THE ONE LEE. /** (12"+=) (RTT 226) – | | |

---- (briefly before their split in 1991) **MARK + RAY** enlisted **DAVE McCAFFREY** – bass / **SCOTT BOUTLER** – drums

	not iss.	Morgan Creek
1992. (cd/c) <2959-20006-2/-4> **DRENCHED**	–	

– Sooner / Sea hag / Snacks and candy / So good / Everything is rosy / With a wait / Little blue light / Out to play / Velvetine / Waiting room / Maybelline.

	not iss.	Mezzotint
1992. (7") **OUT TO PLAY. /**	–	
Feb 97. (cd) <71321> **PORTRAIT OF A DAMAGED FAMILY**	–	

– You're my blessing / Screamin' / Homer / Say I had a lovely time / La muerte di gardenier / Accidentally on purpose / Please / 6 months / Madison park / I wish I was Danny Kaye / K.K.M. / 30.06 (you better watch out) / Good for her / Gone to bed at 21.

MARK MULCAHY

MARK – vocals, multi

	Vinyl Junkie	Mezzotint
May 99. (cd) (VJCD 109) <MEZZ 7132-2> **FATHERING**		1998

– Hey self defeater / Hurry, please hurry / I woke up in the Mayflower / Tempted / In the afternoon / Jason / Ciao my shining star / Apartment murders / Bill Jocko / Fathering / (untitled).

| Mar 01. (m-cd) <(MEZZ 7134)> **I JUST SHOT MYSELF IN THE FOOT AGAIN** | | |

– I just shot myself in the foot again / 900 yards away / Shipbuilding / Frisky said / We're not in Charleston (video).
(above on 'Mezzotint' UK)

| Apr 01. (cd/lp) (VJCD/VJLP 123) <MEZZ 1325> **SMILESUNSET** | | |

– Micon the icon / Just shot myself in the foot again / Alamo in Alabama / The quiet one / The way that she really is / Until I say no / We're not in Charleston anymore / Wake up whispering / The come on / Revolution No.1 / I hate to needy need you / A cup of tea and your insights.

MISSION

Formed: Leeds, England ... late 1985 by ex-SISTERS OF MERCY members WAYNE HUSSEY and CRAIG ADAMS. After falling out with the aforementioned band's singer ANDREW ELDRITCH, the pair recruited SIMON HINKLER (ex-ARTERY) and MICK BROWN (ex-RED LORRY YELLOW LORRY), forming a new band originally under The SISTERHOOD moniker. Calculated to annoy their former colleague, ELDRITCH retaliated by releasing a single under a similar name, HUSSEY and Co. subsequently switching to The MISSION. In Spring '86, the band signed to indie label, 'Chapter 22', releasing the enjoyably amateurish goth theatrics of the 'SERPENT'S KISS' single a couple of months later. Another single, 'GARDEN OF DELIGHT', appeared that summer before the band were snapped up by 'Mercury'. The debut album, 'GOD'S OWN MEDICINE', appeared towards the end of the year, almost making the UK Top 10. Given a bit of a rough ride by critics for its often overbearing goth pompousness, the record was nevertheless a fairly accomplished set of adult rock, a bit like what U2 might have sounded like had they been born in Leeds and developed a penchant for wearing pointy shoes and smearing their faces with flour. The grandiose 'WASTELAND' made No.11 when it was released as a single early the following year, staking The MISSION's claim as the new Goth messiahs and no doubt making ELDRITCH sick to his stomach. But much as they liked to be serious fellows on record, they liked to party hard behind the scenes, CRAIG ADAMS coming a cropper on a particularly gruelling US tour and briefly leaving the band. His temporary replacement was PETE TURNER who filled in for the remainder of the tour and also played at The MISSION's triumphant Reading Festival headlining appearance later that summer. With ADAMS back in the fold, the band began work on a new album with LED ZEPPELIN bassist JOHN PAUL JONES on production chores. The less than impressive result was 'CHILDREN' (1988), a No.2 hit despite its critical lashing. Preceded by the delicate 'BUTTERFLY ON A WHEEL', the 'CARVED IN SAND' album was eventually released to expectant fans in early 1990. More elegantly refined than their normal heavy handed approach, the set remains their most listenable effort, if not their most successful. The band resumed heavy touring following the album's release, HINKLER subsequently storming out on the American jaunt. His replacement for the remainder of the tour was another ex-RED LORRY YELLOW LORRY man, DAVID WOLFENDEN, the band eventually recruiting guitarist ETCH (PAUL ETCHELLS, ex-GHOST DANCE) as a semi-permanent fixture later that year. Following the ambitious 'MASQUE' (1992) set (which featured the violin playing of FAIRPORT CONVENTION's RIC SAUNDERS), MARK THWAITE (ex-SPEAR OF DESTINY) and RIK CARTER (ex-PENDRAGON) were brought in after the departure of ADAMS. Two further albums appeared on the band's own label, 'Equator', following the end of their tenure with 'Mercury', none making any substantial commercial headway. In 1996, The MISSION scraped into the charts with their new 'BLUE' set, although this was a sad swansong for a once enterprising outfit. HUSSEY and crew resurfaced in the late 90's to re-work many of their past faves via the album, 'RESURRECTION' (1999). Leeds' goth shock troops returned in 2001 with 'AURA', a reasonable attempt at reanimating the spell they held over the nation's black clad youth back in their 80's heyday. • **Songwriters:** HUSSEY penned, including LIKE A HURRICANE (Neil Young) / DANCING BAREFOOT (Patti Smith) / SHELTER FROM THE STORM (Bob Dylan) / OVER THE HILLS AND FAR AWAY (Led Zeppelin) / LOVE (John Lennon) / ATOMIC (Blondie). • **Trivia:** In 1991, HUSSEY was ushered off James Whale's late night TV show for being drunk and abusive to its ever-polite presenter!!

Album rating: GOD'S OWN MEDICINE (*7) / CHILDREN (*6) / CARVED IN SAND (*5) / GRAINS OF SAND out-takes (*5) / MASQUE (*5) / SUM AND SUBSTANCE compilation (*7) / NEVERLAND (*4) / BLUE (*4) / RESURRECTION – THE GREATEST HITS (*6) / AURA (*6)

WAYNE HUSSEY (b.26 May'59, Bristol, England) – vocals, guitar (ex-SISTERS OF MERCY, ex-DEAD OR ALIVE, ex-HAMBI & THE DANCE, ex-WALKIE TALKIES) / **CRAIG ADAMS** – bass (ex-SISTERS OF MERCY, ex-EXPELAIRES) / **SIMON HINKLER** – guitar (ex-ARTERY) / **MICK BROWN** – drums (ex-RED LORRY YELLOW LORRY)

	Chapter 22	not iss.
May 86. (7") (CHAP 6-7) **SERPENT'S KISS. / WAKE (R.S.V.)**	70	–
(12"+=) (CHAP 6) – Naked and savage.		
Jul 86. (7") (CHAP 7) **GARDEN OF DELIGHT. / LIKE A HURICANE**	50	–
(12"+=) (12CHAP 7) – Over the hills and far away / The crystal ocean.		
(12"+=) (L12CHAP 7) – Dancing barefoot / The crystal ocean.		

	Mercury	Mercury
Oct 86. (7") (MYSG 1) **STAY WITH ME. / BLOOD BROTHER**	30	–
(12"+=) (MYSGX 1) – Islands in a stream.		
Nov 86. (lp/c)(cd) (MERH/+C 102)(<830603-2>) **GODS OWN MEDICINE**	14	

– Wasteland / Bridges burning / Garden of delight (hereafter) / Stay with me / Blood brother * / Let sleeping dogs lie / Sacrilege / Dance on glass / And the dance goes on / Severina / Love me to death / Island in a stream *. (c+=/cd+=*)

Jan 87. (7") (MYTH 2) **WASTELAND. / SHELTER FROM THE STORM**	11	–
(12"+=) (MYTHX 2-1) – Dancing barefoot (live).		
('A'-Anniversary mix.12"+=) (MYTHX 2-2) – 1969 (live) / Wake (live).		
(d7") (MYTHB 2) – 1969 (live) / Serpent's kiss (live).		
Mar 87. (7"/7"s) (MYTH/+P 3) **SEVERINA. / TOMORROW NEVER KNOWS**	25	–
(12"+=) (MYTHL 3) – Wishing well.		

---- **PETE TURNER** – bass; took over on tour while ADAMS recovered from illness

---- **CRAIG ADAMS** was soon back after a 4 month lay-off.

Jan 88. (7") (MYTH 4) **TOWER OF STRENGTH. / FABIENNE**	12	–
(ext.12"+=) (MYTHX 4) – Dream on / Breathe (instrumental).		
(ext.cd-s+=) (MTHCD 4) – Dream on / Breathe (vocal).		
Mar 88. (lp/c)(cd) (MISH/+C 2)(<834263-2>) **CHILDREN**	2	

– Beyond the pale / A wing and a prayer / Fabienne * / Heaven on Earth / Tower of strength / Kingdom come / Breathe / Child's play / Shamera kye / Black mountain mist / Dream on * / Heat / Hymn (for America). (c+=/cd+= *)

Jul 88. (7") (MYTH 6) **BEYOND THE PALE. / TADEUSZ (1912-1988)**	32	–
('A'-Armageddon mix.12"+=) (MYTHX 6) – Love me to death / For ever more.		
('A'-Armageddon mix.cd-s+=) (MTHCD 6-2) – Tower of strength (Bombay edit).		
Nov 88. (7") (MYTH 7) **KINGDOM COME. / CHILD'S PLAY (live)**		–
(12"+=) (MYTHX 7) – The crystal ocean.		
(cd-s++=) (MTHCD 7) – Garden of delight (live).		

---- (all formats on above single withdrawn)

Jan 90. (7"/c-s) (MYTH/MTHMC 8) **BUTTERFLY ON A WHEEL. / THE GRIP OF DISEASE**	12	–
(12"+=/cd-s+=/box-cd-s+=)(10"+=) (MYTHX/MTHCD/MYCDB 8)(MYTH 8-10) – ('A'-Magni-octopus) / Kingdom come (forever and again).		
Feb 90. (cd/c/lp) (<842251-2/-4/-1>) **CARVED IN SAND**	7	

– Amelia / Into the blue / Butterfly on a wheel / Sea of love / Deliverance / Grapes of wrath / Belief / Paradise (will shine like the Moon) / Hungry as the hunter / Lovely.

Mar 90. (7"/c-s) (MYTH/MTHMC 9) **DELIVERANCE. / MR. PLEASANT**	27	–
(12"+=/cd-s+=/pic-cd-s+=)(10"+=) (MYTHX/MTHCD/MYCDB 9)(MYTH 9-10) – Heaven sends us.		
May 90. (7"/c-s) (MYTH/MTHMC 10) **INTO THE BLUE. / BIRD OF PARADISE**	32	–
(12"+=/cd-s+=) (MYTHX/MTHCD 10) – Divided we fall.		

---- **DAVID WOLFENDEN** – guitar (ex-RED LORRY YELLOW LORRY) repl. HINKLER.

---- (Oct'90) added **ETCH** – guitar (ex-GHOST DANCE)

| Oct 90. (cd/c/lp) (846937-2/-4/-1) **GRAINS OF SAND** (out-takes) | 28 | – |

– Hands across the ocean / The grip of disease / Divided we fall / Mercenary / Mr.Pleasant / Kingdom come (forever and again) / Heaven sends you / Sweet smile of a mystery / Love / Bird of passage. (c+=/cd+=) – Tower of strength (Casbah mix) / Butterfly on a wheel (Troubadour mix).

MISSION (cont) — THE GREAT INDIE DISCOGRAPHY — **The 1980s**

			Vertigo	Mercury
Nov 90.	(7"/c-s) (MYTH/MTHMC 11) **HANDS ACROSS THE OCEAN. / AMELIA / LOVE**		28	-
	(12"+=) (MYTHX 11) – Amelia (live) / Tower of strength (mix) / Mercenary.			
	(cd-s+=) (MTHCD 11) – Amelia (live) / Stay with me / Mercenary.			
Apr 92.	(7"/c-s) (MYTH/MTHMC 12) **NEVER AGAIN. / BEAUTIFUL CHAOS**		34	-
	(12"+=/cd-s+=) (MYTHX/MTHCD 12) – ('A'-F1 mix) / ('A'-Zero G mix.			
Jun 92.	(cd/c/lp) <(512121-2/-4/-1)> **MASQUE**		23	
	– Never again / Shades of green (part II) / Even you may shine / Trail of scarlet / Spider and the fly / She conjures me wings / Sticks and stones / Like a child again / Who will love me tomorrow? / You make me breathe / From one Jesus to another / Until there's another sunrise. (re-is.cd/c Aug94; same)			
Jun 92.	(7"/c-s) (MYTH/MTHMC 13) **LIKE A CHILD AGAIN (remix). / ALL TANGLED UP IN YOU**		30	-
	(12"+=/cd-s+=) (MYTHX/MTHCD 13) – ('A'-Mark Saunders remix) / Hush a bye baby (child again) (Joe Gibbs remix).			
Oct 92.	(7"/c-s) (MYTH/MTHMC 14) **SHADES OF GREEN. / YOU MAKE ME BREATHE**		49	-
	(cd-s) (MTHCD 14) – ('A'side) / Sticks and stones / Trail of scarlet / Spider and the fly.			
	(etched-12"+=) (MYTHX 14) – ('A'mix).			
—	(Nov'92) **MARK THWAITE** – guitar (ex-SPEAR OF DESTINY) repl. HINKLER + ADAMS. Note:- **RIC SAUNDERS** – violin (of FAIRPORT CONVENTION) on last lp			
Jan 94.	(7") (MYTH 15) **TOWER OF STRENGTH (Youth remix). / WASTELAND**		33	-
	(12"+=) (MYTHX 15) – Serpent's kiss.			
	(cd-s) (MYTCD 15) – ('A'mixes) / ('A'-East India Cairo mix) / Deliverance.			
Feb 94.	(cd/c/d-lp) <(518447-2/-4/-1)> **SUM AND SUBSTANCE** (compilation)		49	-
	– Never again / Hands across the ocean / Shades of green / Like a child again / Into the blue / Deliverance / Tower of strength / Butterfly on a wheel / Kingdom come / Beyond the pale / Severina / Stay with me / Wasteland / Garden of delight / Like a hurricane / Serpent's kiss / Sour puss / Afterglow.			
Mar 94.	(7") (MYTH 16) **AFTERGLOW. / SOUR-PUSS**		53	-
	(cd-s+=) (MYTCD 16) – Cold as ice / Valentine.			

			Equator	not iss.
Oct 94.	(7"ep/cd-ep) (HOOK S/CD 001) **MISSION 1 EP**			
	– Raising Cain / Sway / Neverland.			
Jan 95.	(7"ep/cd-ep) (HOOK S/CD 002) **MISSION 2 EP**		73	
	– Swoon / Where / Wasting away.			
	(cd-ep+=) (HOOKCDR 002) – ('A'-Resurrection mix).			
Feb 95.	(cd/c/lp) (SMEE CD/MC/LP 001) **NEVERLAND**		58	
	– Raising Cain / Sway / Lose myself / Swoon / Afterglow (reprise) / Stars don't shine without you / Celebration / Cry like a baby / Heaven knows / Swim with the dolphins / Neverland / Daddy's going to Heaven now.			
Jun 96.	(cd/c/lp) (SMEE CD/MC/LP 002) **BLUE**		73	
	– Coming home / Get back to you / Drown in blue / Damaged / More than this / That tears shall drown the wind / Black & blue / Bang bang / Alpha man / Cannibal / Dying room / Evermore & again.			
—	HUSSEY and Co called it a day after above; he revived the band with **GEOFF READING** – drums, etc.			

			Eagle	Cleopatra
Nov 99.	(cd) (EAGCD 055) <CLP 756> **RESURRECTION – GREATEST HITS** (re-workings)			
	– Prelude: Anniversary / Wasteland / Severina / Love me to death / Interlude: Never forever / Beyond the pale / Deliverance / Without you / Like a child again / Sacrilege / You make me breathe / Crystal ocean / Interlude: Infection / Hands across the ocean / 1969 / Resurrection.			

			Playground	Playground
Nov 01.	(12"/cd-s) (PGND/+CD 001) **EVANGELINE / ANYONE BUT YOU. / MELT / SWOON (reprise)**			-
Dec 01.	(lp/cd) (<PGND/+CD 002>) **AURA**			
	– Evangeline / Shine like the stars / (Slave to) Lust / Mesmerised / Lay your hands on me / Dragonfly / Happy / To die by your hand / Trophy – It never rains ... / The light pours from you / Burlesque / Cocoon / In denial. (d-cd-iss. Dec01 +=; PGNDCDX 002) – (bonus tracks).			
Mar 02.	(d7"red-ep/cd-ep) (PGND/+CD 003) **SHINE LIKE THE STARS. / NEVER LET ME DOWN // SPIDER & THE FLY (IN THE OINTMENT) / SORRY ...**			-
Oct 02.	(cd) (PGNDCD 004) **AURAL DELIGHT**			-
	– Amelia / Even you may shine / Spider in the fly (in the ointment) / Sorry ... / Anyone but you / Never let me down / Never again / Melt / Mesmerised (reprise) / Swoon / Dragonfly (demo) / Can't help falling in love with you.			

– compilations, others, etc. –

Jun 87.	(lp/c) Mercury; (MISH/+C 1) <832527-1/-4> **THE FIRST CHAPTER**		35	May88
	(cd-iss. May88; 832527-2)			
Jul 94.	(cd/lp) Nighttracks; (CDNT/LPNT 005) **SALAD DAZE**			-
Aug 95.	(d-cd) Mercury; (528805-2) **CHILDREN / CARVED IN SAND**			-
Feb 00.	(cd) Spectrum; (544228-2) **TOWER OF STRENGTH**			-
Aug 00.	(cd) Receiver; (RRCD 294) **EVER AFTER: LIVE**			-
	(<US + re-iss. Nov02 on 'Castle'; CMRCD 592>)			
Oct 02.	(cd) Delta; (CD 47100) **REVISITED**			-
Oct 02.	(cd) Armoury; (ARMCD 070) **SACRILEGE**			-

MISSION OF BURMA

Formed: Boston, Massachusetts, USA ... 1979 from the ashes of The MOVING PARTS by the classically trained ROGER MILLER and CLINT CONLEY. They subsequently completed the line-up with a further two members, backing tape man MARTIN SWOPE and PETE PRESCOTT, the pair supplying the rhythm behind their classic 1980 debut 45, 'ACADEMY FLIGHT SONG' (later covered by R.E.M.). At this stage of the career, MISSION OF BURMA were known for their uncomfortable wall-of-noise punk sound, likened to WIRE, HUSKER DU or MC5. A mini-set, 'SIGNALS, CALLS AND MARCHES' (1981), featured the seminal 'THAT'S WHEN I REACH FOR MY REVOLVER', a favourite among the US hardcore fraternity and later, much later, revived by ambient punkmeister, MOBY. Unfortunately, after an astounding debut album proper, 'VS.' (1982), the short-lived outfit had no choice but to retire due to MILLER's worsening tinnitus (a hearing disorder). Nevertheless, the frontman coped with his ailment as best he could throughout a prolific solo career (at times as NO MAN IS ROGER MILLER) which he pursued with another band project, BIRDSONGS OF THE MESOZOIC, but only until 1988. • **Covered:** HEART OF DARKNESS (Pere Ubu) / 1970 (Stooges).

Album rating: VS. (*7) / THE HORRIBLE TRUTH ABOUT BURMA (*5) / FORGET (*5) / MISSION OF BURMA compilation (*9)

ROGER MILLER (b.24 Feb'52, Ann Arbor, Michigan) – guitar, vox / **CLINT CONLEY** (b.16 May'55, Indianapolis, Indiana) – bass, vox / **PETE PRESCOTT** (b.26 Oct'57, Nantucket Island, Mass.) – drums (ex-MOLLS) / **MARTIN SWOPE** (b. 1 Jun'55, Ann Arbor) – tapes

			not iss.	Ace Of Hearts
Jun 80.	(7") <AHS 104> **ACADEMY FLIGHT SONG. / MAX ERNST**		-	
1981.	(m-lp) <AHS 10006> **SIGNALS, CALLS, AND MARCHES**		-	
	– That's when I reach for my revolver / Outlaw / Fame and fortune / This is not a photograph / Red / All world cowboy romance.			
1982.	(lp) <AHS 210> **VS.**		-	
	– Secrets / Train / Trem two / New nails / Dead pool / Learn how / Mica / Weatherbox / The ballad of Johnny Burma / Einstein's day / Fun world / That's how I escaped my certain fate / Ok – No way / Laugh the world away / Progress. <cd-iss. 1997 on 'Rykodisc'; 10340>			
—	split due to MILLER's tinnitus, although he did release quieter solo stuff and form BIRDSONGS OF THE MESOZOIC, with SWOPE. PRESCOTT had formed and continued to tour and record with The VOLCANO SUNS. CONLEY later produced YO LA TENGO.			

– compilations, etc. –

Nov 85.	(lp) New Rose; (ROSE 76) **THE HORRIBLE TRUTH ABOUT BURMA (live)**			-
	– That's when I reach for my revolver / Tremelo / Dumbells / Peking Spring / 1970 / Learn how / New disco / Dirt / Red / Heart of darkness / Them two / Blackboard / He is, she is / Go fun burn man. <cd-iss. 1997 on 'Rykodisc'; 10341>			
1987.	(m-lp) Taang!; (TAANG 20) **MISSION OF BURMA** (1979-1982 ...)			
	– This is not a photograph / Peking spring / Dumbells / Dirt / Sing-a-long / He is, she is / Blackboard / Go fun burn man / Nu disco / Foreign country. (UK cd-iss. Jun92; TAANG 20CD)			
1988.	(cd) Rykodisc: <RCD 40072> **MISSION OF BURMA**			-
	– Academy fight song / That's when I reach for my revolver / Outlaw / Fame and fortune / This is not a photograph / Red / All world cowboy romance / Forget / Laugh the world away / Ok no way / Secrets / Train / Trem two / New nails / Dead pool / Learn how / Mica / Weatherbox / The ballad of Johnny Burma / Einstein's day / Fun world / That's how I escaped my certain fate / Go fun burn man / 1970. (re-iss. Jun92 & Mar94 cd/c; RCD4/RACS 0072)			
Mar 89.	(lp) Taang!; <(TAANG 24)> **FORGET**			1987
	– Execution / Progress / Playland / House flaming / Eyes of men / Manic incarnation / Anti-aircraft warning / Active in the yard / Hunt again / Smoldering hammers / Head over head / Forget. (re-iss. Jan93 lp/cd; TAANG 024/+CD)			
Sep 90.	(cd) Emergo; (EM 94081) / Relix; <983608> **LET THERE BE BURMA**			
	– Execution / Progress / Playland / House flaming / Eyes of men / Manic incarnation / Anti-aircraft warning / Active in the yard / Hunt again / Smoldering hammers / Head over head / Forget / This is not a photograph / Peking spring / Dumbells / Dirt / Sing-a-long / He is – she is / Black board / Go fun burn man / Nu disco / Foreign country / Einstein's day.			

ROGER MILLER

			Fundam.	Fundam.
1988.	(lp) <(SAVE 054)> **THE BIG INDUSTRY**			
	– Portrait of a mechanical dog / Boil away / Hammers / Upon this boat in the sea / The age of reason / Groping hands / Manic depression / The big industry / We don't know why.			

NO MAN

— aka **MILLER + ANDREW DECKARD** – percussion, drums

			S.S.T.	S.S.T.
Jul 89.	(lp/c/cd) <(SST/+C/CD 243)> **WIN! INSTANTLY!**			
	– Run water, run water / No man's landing / Calling the animals / Scratch / This is not a photograph / The promised land / The quarry / Renegades / Volumptuous airplane.			
1990.	(7") <SST 912> **DIAMONDBACK.**			
Sep 90.	(lp/c/cd) <(SST/+C/CD 267)> **WHAMON EXPRESS**			
	– Oppression / Zelia / The man who sold the world / Red ants Iv / S.O.B. / Not enough / Diamondback / (I live on) Heaven Street / Save me / Goodbye paper / Floated – Overflow / Broke a string.			
—	added **RUSS SMITH** – guitar / **KEN WINOKUR** – percussion			
Dec 91.	(lp/c/cd; as NO MAN IS ROGER MILLER) <(SST/+C/CD 281)> **HOW THE WEST WAS WON**			
	– Cartoon, cartoon (where's the exit?) / Boomerang / How the west was won / Reach for the sun / Here we go / Set-up / Wounded world / Grabbed star / It's just a day / No warning / Call on me / (Astronomy engine).			
—	An entirely different NO MAN; the UK one featuring STEVEN WILSON of PORCUPINE TREE released stuff from 1989 onwards (mostly for 'One Little Indian' label).			

ROGER MILLER

		New Alliance	New Alliance
Apr 91.	(lp/c/cd) <(NAR/+C/CD 051)> **XYLYL & A WOMAN IN HALF**		

– Lampbase / Wheelstop / Childrum / Palmsandr / House rock compost / V-2 / Pecan box lope.

Apr 94. (cd) <(NAR 097CD)> **OH, GUITARS ETC**
– We grind open (in) / Meltdown man / Chinatown samba / Firetruck / Cosmic battle / You son of a bitch / War bolts / Fun world reductions / Space is the place / Forest / Kalgastak.

		S.S.T.	S.S.T.
Oct 94.	(cd/c; as ROGER MILLER'S EXQUISITE CORPSE) <(SST 307 CD/C)> **UNFOLD**		

– Entry / Dance in the poet's eye / Djinn / Mentabolism / Looney tunes / Mooche / Nothing what / Game #2 / Gargoyle / Owl / Machete hacker's boogie-woogie / Game #3 / Cheese and the worms / Prelude to the demolition of the teal / Dream interpretation No.1 / Exit (Bach).

Sep 95. (cd/c) <(SST 318 CD/CA)> **ELEMENTAL GUITAR** — Aug95
– Misunderstanding the time / Lost eyes / Repair / Dream interpretation No.7 / Warp zombie / Broken head / Off-On / Dream interpretation No.8 / Talamin Yarka / Are you experienced?

Jul 96. (cd) <SST 331> **THE BENEVOLENT DISPUPTIVE RAY** — -
– ...Then every winter would last one second / Dream interpretation No.9 / Peerd rail se / All the time in the world / Abruption / Float #517 / The fish, he laughs at his own commands / A catapult out of the box / The prisoner's guest / A call for all demons / Geometric transportation (part 1 & 2) / The reptilian system / The rarified dust on the underside of a teacup.

Aug 97. (cd) <SST 349> **THE BINARY SYSTEM LIVE AT THE IDEA ROOM** — -
– The fish, he laughs at his own commands / Peerd rail se / Plate glass w/ Tornado / Moon dance (Ra) / Machete Hacker's boogie-woogie / Abruption / What's up, Ched Voogis? / Djinn / Binary mechanics (Oct.4, 10:37 pm) / Turbo wheel (Oct.4, 10:58pm) / Tibet (Oct.5, 10:31pm) / Last oak king (Oct.4, 11:06pm).

MOB (see under ⇒ BLYTH POWER)

MOCK TURTLES

Formed: Manchester, England ... 1985 by former JUDGE HAPPINESS frontman, MARTIN COOGAN. The aforementioned outfit won a local Battle Of The Bands competition before releasing what proved to be a one-off single, 'HEY JUDGE'. COOGAN subsequently recruited STEVE GREEN, STEVE COWEN and KRZYSZTOF KORAB and adopted the name MOCK TURTLES, signing to Alan Duffy's indie label 'Imaginary' in the process. Summer '87's 'POMONA' (after the release of which they added MARTIN GLYN MURRAY) was the first of several 12"ep's for the label, many of them dented the higher regions of the indie charts. By the turn of the decade, ANDREW STEPHENSON and JOANNE GENT had replaced GREEN and KORAB, their psychedelic retro leanings now becoming more attuned to the prevailing indie dance movement. The long-awaited debut album, 'TURTLE SOUP' (1990), consolidated their jangly 60's influences – The BYRDS and the original TURTLES – and their love of BE-BOP DELUXE/BILL NELSON (the latter featuring on a 1989 B-side, 'TAKE YOUR TIME') with a newfound baggy groove. Although this wasn't an immediate recipe for success, the subsequent re-release of 'CAN YOU DIG IT?' by new label 'Siren', led to a UK Top 20 hit single and a minor resurgence in sales of the album; the essential compilation of their early work, '87-90', also benefitted from the fresh interest. Their most famous four minutes and latterly an albatross round their their necks, 'CAN YOU DIG IT?' was also – alongside other 1991 singles – the main attraction on their second album proper, the Top 40 entry, 'TWO SIDES'. However, the glare of the limelight proved too bright for The MOCK TURTLES and they ended up crawling back into their proverbial shells. While MURRAY found work as an actor (bit part in TV soap, 'Families'), COOGAN and his old muckers KORAB and GREEN formed mid 90's outfit, UGLI. • **Songwriters:** COOGAN wrote all, except covers; PALE BLUE EYES (Velvet Underground) / BIG-EYED BEANS FROM VENUS (Captain Beefheart) / BIG SKY (Kinks) / WHY (Byrds) / ARE YOU EXPERIENCED? (Jimi Hendrix) / NO GOOD TRYING (Syd Barrett) / THE WILLOW SONG (from film 'The Wicker Man').

Album rating: TURTLE SOUP (*7) / 87-90 compilation (*8) / TWO SIDES (*6)

MARTIN COOGAN – vocals, guitar / + unknown others

		Mynah	not iss.
1985.	(7"; as JUDGE HAPPINESS) (SCS 8501) **HEY JUDGE. / PIG IN PINK**		-

— **MARTIN** was joined by **KRZYSZTOF KORAB** – keyboards / **STEVE GREEN** – bass / **STEVE COWAN** – drums

		Imaginary	Relativity
Jun 87.	(12"ep) (MIRAGE 003) **POMONA**		-

– John O'War / Bathing in blue / Mary's garden / Watching the waning moon.

— added **MARTIN GLYN MURRAY** – guitar

May 89. (12"m) (MIRAGE 003) **WICKER MAN / THE WILLOW SONG. / ANOTHER JESUS WALKS ON WATER / FIONNUALA** — -

— **ANDREW STEPHENSON** – bass, viola, violin; repl. GREEN

Nov 89. (12"m) (MIRAGE 015) **AND THEN SHE SMILES. / CALM BEFORE THE STORM / SHANGRI-LA** — -

— **JOANNE GENT** – keyboards; repl. KORAB

Apr 90. (12"/cd-s) (MIRAGE 017/+CD) **LAY ME DOWN. / CAN U DIG IT?** — -

May 90. (cd/c/lp) (ILLCD/ILLCASS/ILLUSION 012) <1058> **TURTLE SOUP**
– Kathy come home / Head run wild / Lay me down / Another Jesus walks on water / Oh Helen how? / How does it feel? / And then she smiles / The willow song / Mary's garden / Can you dig it? / Wicker man. (re-dist.May91) – (hit No.54).

Oct 90. (7") (MIRAGE 022S) **MAGIC BOOMERANG. / TAKE YOUR TIME** — -
(12"+=/cd-s+=) (MIRAGE 022 T/CD) – ('A' version).

Mar 91. (cd/c/lp) (ILLCD/ILLCASS/ILLUSION 019) **87-90** (rare singles + demos for the label) — -
– John o'war / No good trying / Bathing in blue / Watching the waning moon / Big sky / Fionnuala / Oh Helen how / Shangri-la / Time between / Calm before the storm / Magic boomerang / Take your time.

		Siren	not iss.
Mar 91.	(7") (SRN 136) **CAN U DIG IT. / LOSE YOURSELF**	18	-

(12"+=/cd-s+=) (SRN T/CD 136) – Lay me down (live) / ('A'-yeah version).

Jun 91. (7") (SRN 139) **AND THEN SHE SMILES. / ANOTHER JESUS WALKS ON WATER (live)** 44 -
(12"+=/cd-s+=) (SRN T/CD 139) – How does it feel (live).

Jul 91. (cd/c/lp) (CDSRN/SRNMC/SRNLP 31) **TWO SIDES** 33 -
– Strings and flowers / And then she smiles / Shine on me / Baby and the stars / Words of wisdom / Pearls for my girl / Brush of a butterfly's wing / Can u dig it? / You move me / Deep down / Why must I share this air with foolish men?

Sep 91. (7") (SRN 144) **STRINGS AND FLOWERS. / SHE TOLD ME** — -
(12"+=) (SRNT 144) – ('A'-Steve Proctor mix).
(cd-s++=) (SRNCD 144) – Deep down (remix).

— MURRAY departed to become an actor (he played a bit part in the TV soap, 'Families'). COOGAN, KORAB and GREEN re-formed in the mid-90's as UGLI, although as yet they've released no records. Stop press:- due to a successful TV phone ad featuring 'CAN U DIG IT', the MOCK TURTLES will be active again in 2003; it also hit the charts

MODERN ENGLISH

Formed: Colchester, Essex, England ... 1979 by ROBBIE GREY, GARY McDOWELL, MICHAEL CONROY and RICHARD BROWN. Signed to '4 a.d.' after a debut single on the tiny 'Limp' label, the band were initially inspired by the post-punk morbidity of JOY DIVISION, as heard on their early singles and debut album, 'MESH AND LACE' (1981). However, it was a strikingly different MODERN ENGLISH which emerged in Spring '82 with follow-up set, 'AFTER THE SNOW', a far more accessible, keyboard heavy effort bringing to mind SIMPLE MINDS, PETER GABRIEL, DAVID DOWIE and perhaps even a more credible DURAN DURAN! With po-faced English pop all the rage in America at the time, MODERN ENGLISH actually made No.70 in the billboard chart, achieving a similar feat with the uncharacteristically jangly 'I MELT WITH YOU'. Relocating to New York, the band worked on third set, 'RICOCHET DAYS' (1984), another fine album which again made the US Top 100 and featured some subtle french horn touches amid an overall more mature sound. 'Sire', who had been handling the band's Stateside releases, took over completely from '4 a.d.' with 1986's disappointing 'STOP START'. Following the subsequent split, GREY later reappeared briefly with '4 a.d.' "supergroup", THIS MORTAL COIL, before re-forming MODERN ENGLISH for a one-off album, 'PILLOW LIPS' (1990) on US label, 'T.V.T.'. Half a decade on, ROBBIE and a revamped MODERN ENGLISH issued the US-only 'EVERYTHING IS MAD' (1996).

Album rating: MESH AND LACE (*5) / AFTER THE SNOW (*5) / RICOCHET DAYS (*4) / STOP START (*4) / PILLOW LIPS (*4) / EVERYTHING IS MAD (*4) / LIFE IN THE GLADHOUSE 1980-1984 compilation (*7)

ROBBIE GREY – vocals, guitar / **GARY McDOWELL** – guitar / **STEPHEN WALKER** – keyboards / **MICK CONROY** – bass / **RICHARD BROWN** – drums

		Limp	not iss.
Sep 79.	(7") (LMP 2) **DROWNING MAN. / SILENT WORLD**		-
		4 a.d.	Sire
Apr 80.	(7") (AD 6) **SWANS ON GLASS. / INCIDENT**		-
Oct 80.	(7") (AD 15) **GATHERING DUST. / TRANQUILITY OF A SUMMER MOMENT**		-
Apr 81.	(lp) (CAD 105) **MESH & LACE**		-

– Gathering dust / 16 days / Just a thought / Move in light / Grief / The token man / A viable commercial / Black houses / Dance of devotion (a love song) / Smiles and laughter / Mesh and lace . (cd-iss. Nov92 +=; CAD 105CD) – Tranquility of a summer moment / Home / Swans on glass / Incident. (cd re-iss. Jul98; GAD 105CD)

Aug 81. (7") (AD 110) **SMILES AND LAUGHTER. / MESH AND LACE** — -

Apr 82. (lp/c) (CAD/+C 206) <23821> **AFTER THE SNOW** 70 Feb83
– Someone's calling / Life in the gladhouse / Face of wood / Dawn chorus / I melt with you / After the snow / Carry me down / Tables turning. (cd-iss. Nov92 +=; CAD 206CD) – Someone's calling (version) / Life in the gladhouse (version) / I melt with you (mix) / The prize / The choicest view. (cd re-iss. Jul98; GAD 206CD)

Jun 82. (7") (AD 208) **LIFE IN THE GLADHOUSE (remix). / THE CHOICEST VIEW** — -
(12"+=) (BAD 208) – Fragments of fear / Legion.

Oct 82. (7") (AD 212) <29339> **I MELT WITH YOU. / THE PRIZE** 78 Mar83
Sep 83. (7"/12") (AD/BAD 309) **SOMEONE'S CALLING. / LIFE IN THE GLADHOUSE** — -

Jan 84. (7") (AD 401) **CHAPTER 12. / RINGING IN THE CHANGES** — -
(12"+=) (BAD 401) – Reflection.

Feb 84. (lp/c) (CAD/+C 402) <25066> **RICOCHET DAYS** 93
– Rainbow's end / Machines / Spinning me round / Ricochet days / Hands across the sea / Blue waves / Heart / Chapter 12 . (cd-iss. Nov92 +=; CAD 402CD) – Chapter 12 (extended) / Ringing in the change / Reflection / Breaking away.

		Sire	Sire
Mar 84.	(7") <29339> **HANDS ACROSS THE SEA. /**	-	91

Aug 86. (lp/c) (925343-1/4) <25343> **STOP START** Mar86
– The border / Ink and paper / Night train / I don't know the answer / Love breaks

MODERN ENGLISH (cont)

down / Breaking away / The greatest show / Love forever / Start stop – Stop start.

— future MARCH VIOLETS member **AARON DAVIDSON** – guitar, keyboards ; repl. McDOWELL + WALKER before they broke up in 1986. ROBBIE GREY joined THIS MORTAL COIL on some of their output.

— **GREY, DAVIDSON + CONROY** reformed in 1990 after moving to the States.

		not iss.	T.V.T.

Jun 90. (cd/c) <TVT 2810-2/-4> **PILLOW LIPS**
– I melt with you / Life's rich tapestry / Beauty / You're too much / Beautiful people / Care about you / Let's all dream / Coming up for air / Take me away / Pillow lips.

Jun 90. (c-s/cd-s) <TVT 2812-4/-2> **I MELT WITH YOU / BEAUTIFUL PEOPLE** — 76

— split in 1991. GREY formed ENGINE which was to become the re-formed MODERN ENGLISH (other two **TED MASON** – guitars, etc + **MATTHEW SHIPLEY** – keyboards

		not iss.	Imago

Mar 96. (cd/c) <23003> **EVERYTHING IS MAD**
– The planet / That's right / Waves (when I cum) / Heaven / I can't breathe / Here we go again / I don't know anything / Elastic / Film one / The killing screens.

– compilations, etc. –

Jun 83. (12"ep) *4 a.d.; (BAD 306)* **THE SINGLES**
– Gathering dust / Mesh and lace / Smiles and laughter / Swans on glass / Home.

Mar 01. (cd) *4 a.d.; (GAD 2K021CD)* <70021> **LIFE IN THE GLADHOUSE 1980-1984 – THE BEST OF MODERN ENGLISH**
– Sixteen days / Gathering dust / I melt with you / Mesh and lace / Black houses / After the snow / Rainbows end / Smiles and laughter / Ricochet days / Dawn chorus / Carry me down / Machines / Heart / Swans on glass / Blue waves / Life in the gladhouse.

MODERN EON

Formed: Liverpool, England … 1979 out of the LUGLO SLUGS by ALIX PLAIN and DANNY HAMPSON, who enlisted BOB WAKELIN, JOEY McKECHNIE and GED ALLEN (the latter was replaced by TIM LEVER). Thankfully abandoning earlier names such as TANK TIME, ONE-TWO and J&J MODERN EON, these Merseyside hopefuls were one of the many post-punk acts to emerge as part of the burgeoning Liverpool music scene. Appropriately enough, MODERN EON kicked off the new decade with a self-financed debut EP, 'PIECES', a very rhythmically militaristic, JOY DIVISION-esque affair, at least musically; vocally, the high-pitched but throaty PLAIN came across as an FM rock combination of JON ANDERSON and DON HENLEY! A follow-up single, 'EUTHENTICS' appeared towards the end of 1980 prior to the replacement of PASSAGE-bound McKECHNIE with CLIFF HEWITT and a subsequent signing to 'Dindisc'. Following the release of a revamped version of the aforementioned track, MODERN EON delivered their debut long-player, 'FICTION TALES' (1981), collecting together most of their vinyl repertoire to date and featuring forthcoming singles, 'CHILD'S PLAY' and 'MECHANIC'. Although this marked the end of the road for the band, LEVER went on to join DEAD OR ALIVE while various members resurfaced with BONE a decade on; they had posed as THIS TIME NEXT YEAR while PLAIN formed his own CHE outfit.

Album rating: FICTION TALES (*6) / Che: NARCOTIC (*5)

ALIX PLAIN (b. ALEX JOHNSON) – vocals, guitar, piano / **TIM LEVER** – guitar, saxophone; repl. GED ALLEN / **BOB WAKELIN** – keyboards, synthesizer, vocals / **DANNY HAMPSON** – bass / **JOEY McKECKNIE** – drums, percussion

		Modern Eon	not iss.

Jan 80. (7"ep) *(EON 001)* **PIECES**
– Second still / Special patrol / Choreography / The look a smack.

		Inevitable	not iss.

Nov 80. (7") *(INEV 3)* **EUTHENTICS. / WAITING FOR THE CAVALRY**

— **CLIFF HEWITT** – drums, timpani; repl. JOEY who joined The PASSAGE

		Dindisc	

Feb 81. (7") *(DIN 30)* **EUTHENTICS (new version). / CARDINAL SINS**

May 81. (lp) *(DID 11)* **FICTION TALES**
– Second still / The grass still grows / Playwrite / Watching the dancers / Real hymn / Waiting for the cavalry / High noon / Child's play / Choreography / Euthentics / In a strange way / Mechanic.

Jun 81. (7") *(DIN 31)* **CHILD'S PLAY. / VISIONARY**

Aug 81. (7") *(DIN 35)* **MECHANIC. / SPLASH**

— disbanded late 1981 and LEVER joined DEAD OR ALIVE. Two members formed BONE (aka THIS TIME NEXT YEAR) in 1990 and released ep 'AN ARM AND A LEG' for 'Belly Up'. HEWITT is now a member of APOLLO 440.

CHE

ALIX PLAIN + help from **ADRIAN SHERWOOD** (On-U-Sound team)

		DEsire	not iss.

Jan 84. (7"/12") *(WANT/+X 3)* **WHAT YOU'VE BEEN THROUGH IS LOVE (SCREAM LIKE A SWIFT). / ('A'version)**

		Siren	not iss.

Jun 89. (7"/12") *(SRN/+T 115)* **I WISH HE DIDN'T TRUST ME SO MUCH. / FIREFLIES IN SUMMER**

Jun 89. (lp/c/cd) *(SRNLP/SRNMC/CDSRN 16)* **NARCOTIC**
– Scream like a swift / Fireflies in summer / I wish he didn't trust me so much / Moving the silence / Imperfections / Be my powerstation / Jerusalem / View from a new perspective / Celebrating life.

MO-DETTES

Formed: London, England … 1979 by American-born ex-SLITS member, KATE KORUS along with Swiss frontwoman RAMONA CARLIER, JANE CROCKFORD and JUNE MILES-KINGSTON. Trading in a spiky new wave sound despite their moniker and the (then) current mod revival, this all-female outfit debuted the same year with the self-financed 'WHITE MICE' single. CARLIER's Euro-centric pronunciation and "hiccuping" vocal style was reminiscent of LENE LOVICH while the backing harmonies and handclaps added a retro touch to proceedings. A debut album, 'THE STORY SO FAR', followed in 1980 but failed to generate the anticipated interest and preceded a period of upheaval with both CARLIER and KORUS departing for pastures new in 1981. Despite the recruitment of respective replacements, SUE SLACK and MELISSA RITTER, the band came to a halt the following year amid yet more internal strife. MILES-KINGSTON went on to gain most recognition, initially as a member of FUN BOY THREE's backing band before going on to join The COMMUNARDS. She also released a one-off single for 'Go! Discs', while KORUS subsequently recorded a collaborative effort with BELLE STAR, JENNIE McKEOWN.

Album rating: THE STORY SO FAR (*6)

RAMONA CARLIER – vocals (ex-KLEENEX) (as REGULA SING) / **KATE KORRIS** – guitar (ex-SLITS) / **JANE CROCKFORD** – bass / **JUNE MILES-KINGSTON** – drums

		Mode – Rough Trade	not iss.

Dec 79. (7") *(MODE 1)* **WHITE MICE. / MASOCHISTIC OPPOSITE**

		Deram	not iss.

Jun 80. (7") *(DET-R-1)* **PAINT IT BLACK. / BITTA TRUTH** 42
(free ltd 7"flexi) *(MODE 1-2)* – TWIST AND SHOUT.

Oct 80. (lp) *(SML 1120)* **THE STORY SO FAR**
– White mouse disco / Fandango / Satisfy / Foolish girl / He's no rebel / Paint it black / The Kray twins / Bedtime stories / Norman / Dark park creeping / Masochistic opposite / Mi lord / The sparrow.

Oct 80. (7") *(DET 2)* **DARK PARK CREEPING. / TWO CAN PLAY**

Jun 81. (7") *(DET 3)* **TONIGHT. / WALTZ IN BLUE MINOR**

		Human	not iss.

Jul 81. (7") *(HUM 10)* **WHITE MICE. / THE KRAY TWINS (live)**

— **SUE SLACK** – vocals; repl. RAMONA

— **MELISSA RITTER** – guitar; repl. KATE who teamed up with JENNY (BELLE STARS)

— They split late 1982. JANE married someone from MADNESS. JUNE MILES-KINGSTON went solo after a spell with FUN BOY THREE.

MOFUNGO

Formed: New York City, New York, USA … 1980 by noisy guitarist, WILLIE KLEIN and JAMES POSNER, both formerly of the appropriately named BLINDING HEADACHE. The pair, along with ROBERT SIETSEMA and JEFF McGOVERN, set about dishing out (well, they did take their moniker from a Puerto Rican meal of mashed plantains and gravy!) from 1980's 12" EP, 'ELEMENTARY PARTICLES'. Ultimately "No-Wave", and subsequently augmented by 'S.S.T.' saxophonist and stalwart, ELLIOTT SHARP, the MOFUNGO quartet delivered all sorts of releases varying from the cassette, 'OUT OF LINE' (1983) to 1989's swansong effort, 'WORK'.

Album rating: END OF THE WORLD: ANTHOLOGY TAPE No.1 compilation (*5) / OUT OF LINE (*6) / FREDERICK DOUGLASS (*7) / MESSENGER DOG OF THE GODS (*5) / END OF THE WORLD No.2 compilation (*5) / BUGGED (*5) / WORK (*4)

WILLIE KLEIN – guitar, vocals (ex-BLINDING HEADACHE) / **JAMES POSNER** – guitar, bass, percussion (ex-BLINDING HEADACHE) / **ROBERT SIETSEMA** – bass, piano, percussion / **JEFF McGOVERN** – drums

		not iss.	Living Legends

1980. (12"ep) <LL 001> **ELEMENTARY PARTICLES**
– At the shop / Ya da / 5 G's / Gato perdido.

		not iss.	Mofungo

Nov 81. (c) <1> **END OF THE WORLD: ANTHOLOGY TAPE NO.1**
(compilation incl. BLINDING HEADACHE tracks)

— **A.C. CHUBB** – alto sax, violin / **SETH GUNNING** – drums; repl. POSNER

		Rough Trade	Zoar

Aug 82. (7"ep) *(RT 103)* **EL SALVADOR. / JUST THE WAY / GIMME A SASPARILLA**

— now augmented by **ELLIOTT SHARP** (b. 1 Mar'51, Cleveland, Ohio) – saxophone, clarinet (also a solo artist) / **CHRIS NELSON** – trombone / **ADRIANNE BRENTARI** – tenor sax / **DAVE SEWELSON** – baritone sax / **PHILIP JOHNSTON** – soprano sax / **ALEX DE LICA** – trombone

Nov 83. (lp) <ZOAR 13> **OUT OF LINE**
– Where do we get the money to save our souls / In your heart / Shortage / Migrant assembly line worker / Constance / F.B.I. informant (he sold his soul) / Break / Wage slave / Three / Watermark / Hunter gatherer / Boom boom / Chips / Happy man.

— **PHIL DRAY** – drums, percussion; repl. McGOVERN, CHUBB + GUNNING

— **SHARP + NELSON** were now fully-fledged members

		not iss.	TwinTone – Coyote

May 85. (lp) <TTC 8555> **FREDERICK DOUGLASS**

— added **HEATHER DRAKE** – vocals; repl. DRAY

		not iss.	TwinTone – Lost

Apr 86. (lp) <TTL 8675> **MESSENGER DOG OF THE GODS**

Nov 86. (12") <TT 8694> **45**

Jan 87. (12") <TT 8697> **LEMMINGS. /**

MOFUNGO (cont)

Mar 87. (lp) <TTL 87106> **END OF THE WORLD No.2** (compilation)

—— line-up now:- **KLEIN, SIETSEMA, SHARP + NELSON**

S.S.T. S.S.T.

Oct 88. (lp/c/cd) <(SST 191/+C/CD)> **BUGGED**
– No.1 for take-off / The pope is a potatoe / Hello Ollie / All I've got's gone / Hosting a war / My aluminium plate / Backwards Christian soldiers / The wit and the wisdom of Judge Bork / Forty cent meat / Long haired preachers / Sold again / Saviour impede me not / Guided tour.

May 89. (lp/c/cd) <(SST 240/+C/CD)> **WORK**
– Once it's gone / Two New York minutes – Voting is for suckers / Panama hat / Labor day / Memory / Big Mac attack / New west / Toadstool / Fattenin' frogs for snakes / Money craving folks / Scrape / Themselves / American way / Space filler.

—— split after above, SHARP continued his hard-working solo career

MOMUS

Born: NICHOLAS CURRIE, 1960, Paisley, Scotland. A kind of Scottish MORRISSEY with a wordy, occasionally pretentious penchant for painstakingly examining controversial subject material, especially with regards to sexual morality, CURRIE (ironically the cousin of JUSTIN CURRIE, mainman with coffee table chart-schmoozers DEL AMITRI) has courted more criticism than success (at least in Britain) over the course of his lengthy career. Initially the frontman of Scots alternative popsters The HAPPY FAMILY (who also numbered ex-JOSEF K members DAVE WENDELL and RONNIE TORRANCE), CURRIE split the group up after what he saw as "indifference" by their label, '4 a.d.', leaving behind a solitary album, 'THE MAN ON YOUR STREET' (1982). Relocating to Sloane Square in London and adopting the MOMUS moniker (a name taken from the god who was dismissed from Heaven and who inspired the modern day poet, Peter Porter), CURRIE's debut release came in the shape of the 'BEAST WITH NO BACKS' EP, issued by the 'El' label and quickly followed by an excellent but quickly forgotten debut album, 'CIRCUS MAXIMUS' (1986). An enthusiastic fan of French legends like JACQUES BREL and SERGE GAINSBOURG – obvious influences – CURRIE relied on mood, atmosphere and lyrical expression to capture the listener's attention, setting about lyrically ridiculing everything in sight, at times transfiguring himself into the past. His episodes of infidelity and injustice were romantically delivered in a vocal vein reminiscent of a cross between the fragility of NICK DRAKE and the effete camp of NEIL TENENT. Finding a welcoming home at 'Creation', MOMUS released 'THE POISON BOYFRIEND' album in 1987 but it was the following year's 'TENDER PERVERT' which really caused a stir. A compelling set of narratives centering on such cheery everyday topics as incest, paedophilia and bestiality, the album won him a cult following but predictably came in for flak from the usual quarters, as did 1991's 'HIPPOPOTAMOMUS', the NME famously awarding it a big round zero out of ten. In his defence, MOMUS argued that he was simply performing one of the basic functions of pop since its inception i.e. to help angst-ridden teenagers come to terms with their sexual identity. The album, which was dedicated to French pensmith SERGE GAINSBOURG, was initially removed from the record shops, due to its cover of the TV ad for the 'Michelin Man'! Whatever, the man continued to shock and delight throughout the 90's with albums such as 'THE ULTRACONFORMIST' (1992) – a mock-live affair which featured the sleazy BRECHT-WEILL-esque gems, 'THE MOTHER-IN-LAW' and 'THE LADIES UNDERSTAND' – and 'THE PHILOSOPHY OF MOMUS' (1995). No doubt having given up on winning over the sexually repressed British public long ago, MOMUS could content himself with the fact that he was big in Japan. He was even commissioned to pen a song for a Japanese cosmetics commercial; the result was the quasi-psychedelic BEATLES via BOOKER T. strangeness of 'GOOD MORNING WORLD', a Top 5 hit in the land of saki and one of the more interesting moments on the '20 VODKA JELLIES' (1996) album. The latter set also featured a number of songs apparently written during CURRIE's grunge phase, an interesting diversion – at least musically – from the usual wistful, intellectual forays into cabaret style alternative pop. Love him or loathe him, MOMUS should at least be given credit for having the courage to write about the stuff most people would rather sweep under the carpet. In early 1997, JACQUES was a new project, virtually a collaboration with ANTHONY REYNOLDS (of JACK); they managed to excrete one badly-thought-out set, 'HOW TO MAKE LOVE (VOLUME 1)'. Reverting to his MOMUS moniker, CURRIE took his music and SERGE GAINSBOURG-type wit further afield via four further albums, 'PING PONG' (1997), 'THE LITTLE RED SONGBOOK' (1998), 'STARS FOREVER' (1999) and 'FOLKTRONIC' (2001), all masterful pieces of eccentricity and thematic from Japanese culture to Smithsonian fanaticism.
• **Trivia:** MANFRED MANN'S EARTH BAND covered his 'COMPLETE HISTORY OF SEXUAL JEALOUSY' in the early 90's! He also composes for Japanese singers KAHIMI KARIE and NORIKO SEKIGUCHI, THE POISON GIRLFRIEND.

Album rating: Happy Family: THE MAN ON YOUIR STREET (*5) / Momus: CIRCUS MAXIMUS (*6) / THE POISON BOYFRIEND (*6) / THE TENDER PERVERT (*7) / DON'T STOP THE NIGHT (*4) / MONSTERS OF LOVE compilation (*7) / HIPPOPOTAMOMUS (*5) / THE ULTRACONFORMIST (*7) / VOYAGER (*6) / TIMELORD (*6) / PHILIOSOPHY OF MOMUS (*6) / SLENDER SHERBET (*6) / 20 VODKA JELLIES collection (*5) / PING PONG (*6) / THE LITTLE RED SONGBOOK (*6) / STARS FOREVER (*7) / FOLKTRONIC (*5)

HAPPY FAMILY

NICHOLAS CURRIE – vocals, guitar / **DAVE WENDELL** – bass, vocals (ex-JOSEF K)

4 a.d.   not iss.

Mar 82. (7"ep) (AD 204) **PURITANS. / INNERMOST THOUGHTS / THE MISTAKE**

—— added **RONNIE TORRANCE** – drums (ex-JOSEF K, ex-BOOTS FOR DANCING) / **NEIL MARTIN** – synthesizer / **PAUL MASON** – guitar

Nov 82. (lp) (CAD 214) **THE MAN ON YOUR STREET**
– The salesman / Letter from Hall / The luckiest citizen / Revenge / The courier / The man on your street / A night underground / Two of a kind / March in Turin. (cd-iss. Nov92 +=; CAD 214CD) – Puritans / Innermost thoughts / The mistake.

—— split in 1983, leaving behind last recordings below . . .

Les Tempes   not iss.

Oct 84. (c) **THE BUSINESS OF LIVING**

MOMUS

NICHOLAS CURRIE – vocals, guitar / with **NEIL MARTIN** / + on album only **JANE DAVIES** – vocals

El   not iss.

Oct 85. (12"ep) (el 5T) **THE BEAST WITH 3 BACKS**
– The ballad of the barrel-organist / Hotel Marquis de Sade / Third party, fire and theft.

Jan 86. (lp) (ACME 2) **CIRCUS MAXIMUS**
– Lucky like St. Sebastian / The lesson of Sodom (according to Lot) / John the Baptist Jones / King Solomon's song and mine / Little Lord Obedience / The day the circus came to town / The rape of Lucretia / Paper wraps rock / Rules of the game of quoits. (cd-iss. Jul89 & Jun97 +=; ACME 2CD) – Nicky / Don't leave / See a friend in tears.

Jun 86. (12"m) (GP 09T) **NICKY. / DON'T LEAVE / SEE A FRIEND IN TEARS**

—— with **DEAN KLERAT** – keyboards / **FEIN O'LOCHLAINN** – bass / **TERRY NEILSON** – drums / **ARUN G. SHENDURNIKAR** – percussion

Creation   not iss.

Mar 87. (12"ep) (CRE 037T) **MURDERERS, THE HOPE OF WOMEN. / ELEVEN EXECUTIONERS / WHAT WILL DEATH BE LIKE?**

Jul 87. (lp) (CRELP 021) **THE POISON BOYFRIEND**
– The gatecrasher / Violets / Islington John / Three wars / Flame into being / Situation comedy blues / Sex for the disabled / Closer to you. (cd-iss. Apr88 +=; CRELP 021CD) – Murderers, the hope of women / Eleven executioners / What will death be like?

Jul 88. (lp/cd) (CRELP 036/+CD) **THE TENDER PERVERT**
– The angels are voyeurs / Love on ice / I was a Maoist intellectual / The homosexual / Bishonen / A complete history of sexual jealousy (parts 17-24) / Ice king / In the sanatorium / The charm of innocence / The angels are voyeurs (reprise). (w/ free 7")

Apr 89. (7") (CRE 063L) **HAIRSTYLE OF THE DEVIL. / AMONGST WOMEN ONLY**
(ext-12"+=) (CRE 063LT) – Monsters of love.

Nov 89. (cd)(c/lp) (CRECD 59)(C+/CRE 59) **DON'T STOP THE NIGHT**
– Trust me, I'm a doctor / Right hand heart / Lord of the dance / Lifestyles of the rich and famous / How do you find my sister? / The hairstyle of the Devil * / Don't stop the night / Amongst women only / The guitar lesson / The cabriolet / Shaftesbury Avenue. (cd+= *)

Mar 90. (cd)(c/lp) (CRECD 59)(C+/CRE 59) **MONSTERS OF LOVE: SINGLES 85-89** (readings of my early years)
– Morality is vanity / Ballad of the barrel organist / Third party, fire and theft / Hotel Marquis de Sade / Murderers, the hope of women / What will death be like? / Eleven executioners / Gilda / The hairstyle of the Devil / Monsters of love.

Jul 91. (cd)(c/lp) (CRECD 97)(C+CRE 97) **HIPPOPOTAMOMUS**
– Hippopotamomus / I ate a girl right up / Michelin man / A dull documentary / Marquis of sadness / Bluestocking / Ventriloquists & dolls / The painter & his model / A monkey for Sallie / Pornography / Song in contravention.

May 92. (lp/cd) (MONDE 3/+CD) **THE ULTRACONFORMIST** (live whilst out of fashion)
– Sinister themes / Last of the window cleaners / The ladies understand / Cape and stick gang / The ultraconformist / The mother-in-law / La Catrina / The cheques in the post / Spy on the moon / Forests. (cd re-iss. Jun97; same)
above issued on 'Richmond-Cherry Red'.

Jun 92. (cd)(lp/c) (CRECD 113)(C+/CRE 113) **VOYAGER**
– Cibachrome blue / Virtual reality / Vocation / Conquistador / Spacewalk / Summer holiday 1999 / Afterglow / Trans Siberian express / Voyager / Momutation 3.

Sep 92. (12")(cd-s) (CRE 134T)(CRESCD 134) **SPACEWALK (Deja vu remix). / CONQUISTADIOR (Lovecut db remix) / MOMUTATION 3**

Nov 93. (cd/lp) (CRE CD/LP 151) **TIMELORD**
– Platinum / Enlightenment / You've changed / Landrover / Rhetoric / Suicide pact / Christmas on Earth / Breathless.

Cherry Red   Cherry Red

Apr 95. (cd-ep) (CDCHERRY 137) **THE SADENESS OF THINGS / LONDON 1888 / THE END OF HISTORY / AN INFLATABLE DOLL**

Jun 95. (cd) (CDBRED 119) **PHILOSOPHY OF MOMUS**
– Toothbrushead / The madness of Lee Scratch Perry / It's important to be trendy / Quark and charm, the robot twins / Girlish boy / Yokohama Chinatown / Withinity / K's diary / Virtual Valerie / Red pyjamas / The cabinet of Kuniyoshi Kaneko / Slide projector, lie detector / Microworlds / Complicated / I had a girl / The philosophy of Momus / The loneliness of lift music / Paranoid acoustic seduction machine / The sadeness of things.

Nov 95. (cd) (CDBRED 123) **SLENDER SHERBET – CLASSIC SONGS REVISITED** (readings of my early years)
– The complete history of sexual jealousy / The guitar lesson / Closer to you / The homosexual / Charm of innocence / Lucky like St. Sebastian / I was a Maoist intellectual / Lifestyles of the rich and famous / Angels are voyeurs / Hotel Marquis de Sade / The gatecrasher / Hairstyle of the Devil / Bi shonen / Angels (reprise).

Sep 96. (cd) (<CDMRED 133>) **20 VODKA JELLIES** (an assortment of curiosities and rarities)   Jan97
– I am a kitten / Vogue Bambini / The poisoners / Nikon 2 / Giapponese a Roma /

Paolo / The end of history / London 1888 / Streetlamp soliloquy / An inflatable doll / Saved / Someone / Howard Hughes / Three beasts / Good morning world / Germania / The girl with no body / Radiant night / Orgasm addict / Nobody.

Nov 97. (cd) (SATYR 001) <60004> **PING PONG** — Satyricon / Le Grand Magistery
- Ping pong with Hong Kong King Kong / His majesty the baby / My pervert doppleganger / I want you, but I don't need you / Professor Shaftenberg / Shoesize of the angel / The age of information / The sensation of orgasm / The anthem of Shibuya / Lolitapop dollhouse / Tamagotchi press officer / Space Jews / My kindly friend the censor / The animal that desires / How to get – and stay – famous / 2 p.m.
(re-iss. Jun99 on 'Cherry Red'; CDMRED 158)

Nov 98. (cd) (ANALOG 001CD) <60006> **THE LITTLE RED SONGBOOK** — Cherry Red / Le Grand Magistery
- Old friend, new flame / MC Escher / Who is Mr. Jones? / Harry K-Tel / Lucretia Borgia / How to spot an invert / Everyone I have ever slept with / Born to be adored / Coming in a girl's mouth / What are you wearing? / The new decameron / Walter Carlos / The symphonies of Betthoven / Tragedy and farce / Mrs.X, an ex-lover / A white Oriental flower. (d-cd; w/ extra karaoke tracks)

Aug 99. (d-cd) (ANALOG 002CD) <60010> **STARS FOREVER**
- Other music / Tinnitus / £D corporation / Akiko Masuda / Stefano Zarelli / Minty fresh / Jeff Koons / Milton Jacobson / Mai Noda / Robert Dye / Florence Manlik / Adam Green / Maf / Stephanie Pappas / Steven Zeeland / Mika Akutsu / Miles Franklin / Paolo Rumi / Karin Komoto // Reckless records / Kokoro Hirai / Indiepop list / Keigo Oyamada / Team Clermont / Brent Busboom / Natsuko Tayama / Girlie action / The Minus 5 / Noah Brill / Shawn Krueger / New flame, same old story / Not intended for children / Coming on an intern's dress / Nicky my friend / Mr. Jones / The taste of pink champagne / Onan the barbarian / Suggestion to jealous men.

Feb 01. (cd) (ANALOG 006CD) <60020> **FOLKTRONIC**
- Appalachia / Smooth folk singer / Mountain music / Simple men / Finnegan the folk hero / Protestant art / U.S. knitting / Jarre in Hicksville / Tape recorder man / Little apples / Robocowboys / Psychopathia sexualis / Folk me Amadeus / Handheld / The penis song / Heliogabalus / Going for a walk with a line / The lady of Shalott / Mistaken memories of medieval Manhattan / Pygmalism.

MONKS OF DOOM
(see under ⇒ CAMPER VAN BEETHOVEN)

Roy MONTGOMERY

Born: Christchurch, New Zealand. Guitar wizard MONTGOMERY formed his first group the PSYCHEDELICS in 1971, however, it would be another ten years before his talents gained any notable recognition. The PIN GROUP, which comprised MONTGOMERY, ROSS HUMPHRIES and PETER STAPLETON, came and went in the brief period between 1981 and '84. The group released a couple of singles and an EP of jangly guitar pop, almost embarrassingly similar to a bare-boned JOY DIVISION, before disbanding. A year later, MONTGOMERY received a $750 National Arts Council grant to form the SHALLOWS, who released the lone 1985 single, 'SUZANNE SAID'. Throughout the 1990's, MONTGOMERY collaborated on a number of different projects including the experimental groups DISSOLVE and HASH JAR TEMPO as well as reuniting with PETER STAPLETON in the band DADAMAH. Although MONTGOMERY continued collaborating with other artists, he released his solo debut 'SCENES FROM SOUTH ISLAND' in 1994. MONTGOMERY'S output was prolific, releasing 'TEMPLE IV' (1996), 'AND NOW THE RAIN SONDS LIKE LIFE IS FALLING DOWN THROUGH IT' (1998), 'ALLEGORY OF HEARING' (2000) and 'SILVER WHEEL OF PRAYER' in 2001, interspersed with a range of side-projects. MONTGOMERY's two decades as a musical journeyman saw him explore many musical avenues from post-punk to avant-garde twaddle and finally murky psychedelia and consequently he has emerged as a truly unique and intriguing artist. • **Covers:** PIN GROUP covered War's 'LOW RIDER' and Red Crayola's 'HURRICANE FIGHTER PILOT'. Roy covered USED TO (Wire). • **Trivia:** ROY also guested/collaborated on some releases by FLYING SAUCER ATTACK.

Album rating: Pin Group: A RETROSPECTIVE compilation (*6) / Dadamah: THIS IS NOT A DREAM (*7) / Dissolve: THAT THAT IS … IS (NOT) (*7) / THIRD ALBUM FOR THE SUN (*7) / TRUE as Roy Montgomery & Chris Heaphy (*6) / Roy Montgomery: SCENES FROM THE SOUTH ISLAND (*7) / TEMPLE IV (*6) / HARMONY POF THE SPHERES (*6) / AND NOW THE RAIN … (*7) / 324 E. 13th ST #7 collection (*7) / THE ALLEGORY OF HEARING (*7) / SILVER WHEEL OF PRAYER (*6) / Hash Jar Tempo: WELL OILED (*8) / UNDER GLASS (*7)

PIN GROUP

ROY MONTGOMERY – vocals, guitar / **ROSS HUMPHRIES** – bass, vocals / **RUSSELL BRICE** – keyboards / **PETER STAPLETON** – drums

			Flying Nun	not iss.	
1981.	(7") (FN 001)	**AMBIVALENCE. / COLUMBIA**	-	-	New Z
1982.	(7") (FN 004)	**COAT. / JIM**	-	-	New Z
1983.	(12"ep) (FN 1967)	**GO TO TOWN**	-	-	New Z

- Power / Long night / Ambivalence / When I tell you / A thousand sins.

— disbanded until 1993's reunion; ROY recorded as/with The SHALLOWS who released one single in 1985; 'SUZANNE SAID' / 'TRIAL SEPERATION'. HUMPHRIES joined The CLEAN and STAPLETON as with the VICTOR DIMISICH BAND which soon evolved into The TERMINALS (incl. HUMPHRIES).

– compilations, etc. –

Mar 97. (cd) Siltbreeze; (<SB 68>) **A RETROSPECTIVE** — Jun97
- Ambivalence / Columbia / Coat / Jim / Power / Long night / Ambivalence / When I tell you / A thousand sins / Low rider / Hurricane fighter pilot / Coat.

DADAMAH

ROY MONTGOMERY + PETER STAPLETON plus **KIM PIETERS** – vocals, bass / **JANINE STASS** – keyboards, vocals

			Majora	Kranky
1992.	(7") <U 31973>	**NICOTINE. / HIGH TIME**	-	
1992.	(7") <U 32904>	**SCRATCH SUN. / RADIO BRAIN**	-	
1992.	(cd) <KRANK 002>	**THIS IS NOT A DREAM**		May95

- Limbo swing / Papa Doc / Too hot to dry / Prove / Brian's children / High tension house / Nicotine / High time / Scratch sun / Radio brain / Replicant emotions.
(UK-iss.Mar97; same as US)

ROY MONTGOMERY

			Drunken Fish	Drunken Fish
Sep 95.	(cd) <DFR 22>	**SCENES FROM THE SOUTH ISLAND**	-	

- Along the main divide / A clear night port hills / Twilight conversation / Rainshadow over Christchurch / Rain receding / Escape velocity / The barracuda sequence / Downtown to Vesuvio / The road to Diamond Harbour / Winding it out in the high country / Nor wester head-on / The last Kakapo dreams of flying.

1996. (ltd-7"blue) <004> **CUMULUS FUGUE. / (other by AZUSA PLANE)** — —
(above issued on 'Colorful Clouds Of Acoustics')
below featured **LISA SIEGEL** – bass, vocals

Aug 96. (7"m) <(DFR 27)> **E.N.D. / INTERTIDAL / BOAT ON A WAVE**
1996. (7") **SOMETHING ELSE AGAIN. / ADRIFT** - -
1996. (7") **STRANGE ATTRACTOR. / ON THE ROAD**
(above 2 on 'Roof Bolt')

Nov 96. (7") (AJAX 051) **JUST MELANCHOLY. / USED TO** - -
(above issued on 'Ajax') (below issued on 'Enraptured')

Nov 96. (7") (RAPT45 09) **TWO TRAJECTORIES**
- Times three / Some other time.

— early in '97, ROY teamed up with FLYING SAUCER ATTACK on the 'Goodbye' EP

Feb 97. (7"/7"box) (SB 59/58) **LONG NIGHT EP** (rec. 1994) - -
- Submerged and colorful / Cousin song / Film as a subversive art / Long night / It's cold outside / German sister.
(above issued on 'Siltbreeze')

Mar 97. (cd) <(KRANK 009CD)> **TEMPLE IV** — Jan96
- She waits on Temple IV / Departing the body / Soul quietens / Passage of forms / Jaguar meets snake / Above the canopy / Jaguar unseen.
(above issued on 'Kranky') (below on 'Roof Bolt')

Dec 97. (10"ep) **WINTER SONGS EP** -
- Dawn fades over ocean / Sister clean / Strange attractor / Visions of Emma.

— late in '97, ROY featured on one side (with track 'FANTASIA ON A THEME BY SANDY BULL') from the 'Drunken Fish' Various Artists triple-LP, 'HARMONY OF THE SPHERES'

Apr 98. (cd) <(DFR 41)> **AND NOW THE RAIN SOUNDS LIKE LIFE IS FALLING DOWN THROUGH IT**
- No she never made it to Japan / In our own time / Opportunity passed in less than a minute / Down from that hill and up to the pond / And now the rain sounds like life is falling down through it / Kafka was correct / Catherine at Aldeburgh / Entertaining Mr. Jones / The small sleeper (for Jack) / Algeria 7 / A little soundtrack (for Epic) / Ill at home / In another time.

Jul 98. (7"white; as ROY MONTGOMERY with KIRK LAKE) (RGIRL 3) **LONDON IS SWINGING BY HIS NECK. / LONDON IS SWINGING BY HIS NECK** -
(above issued on 'Rocket Girl')

Aug 00. (cd) <(DFR 47)> **THE ALLEGORY OF HEARING**
- Ex cathedra / Rock, sea, muse, seek / As the Dali Lama was remarking I believe / Sounding the abyss / Where the belltower once stood / From a promontory / Resolution island suite: A vessel sublime – And but a gentle swell – Hubris fills the rash and young – Now the reef-dashed mariner – The sirens, they feel pity – Wind upon the sails, light upon the sea – Cast away the island, cruel so, fat / At the intersection of Herzog & Wenders / Above all, compassion.

			V.H.F.	V.H.F.
Feb 01.	(cd) <(VHF 49CD)>	**SILVER WHEEL OF PRAYER**		

- For the imperiled / For the disorientated / For the mortified / For the dispossessed / For the intense / For the circulation / For a small blue orb.

– compilations, etc. –

Nov 99. (cd) Drunken Fish; <(DF 28CD)> **324 E. 13th ST. #7**
- (the SHALLOWS single) / the LONG NIGHT EP / (Roof Bolt, Ajax + Drunken Fish 7" singles).

DISSOLVE

ROY MONTGOMERY – vocals, guitar / **CHRIS HEAPHY** – guitar

			Kranky	Kranky
May 95.	(cd) <KRANK 005CD>	**THAT THAT IS … IS (NOT)**	-	

- Strand / 8 wire / Dissong / 3 films / Blurred / The mortal pleasure of Wanda Lust / Encounter / See the world / S.T.P.P.

Aug 97. (cd) <(KRANK 018CD)> **THIRD ALBUM FOR THE SUN**
- Rogue satellite / Into the black / Presume too far / High on upper street / Street philosopher / Dream index / Sunflower search engine.

Oct 97. (12") (01) **EARTHBOUND** -
(above issued on 'Captain Mimmo') (below issued on 'Elevator')

Mar 98. (cd) (ELM 013CD) **DISMANTLE** -
- Dismantle / Sandblaster / The cleaner / Sunshine / Gabriel's wrench / Kill / Morbid self attention.

Apr 99. (cd; as ROY MONTGOMERY & CHRIS HEAPHY) <(KRANK 033CD)> **TRUE**
- Virtually so #1 / Virtually so #2 / Unfathomable #1 / Picnic time / Clouding over / Certainly / Spurious / Unfathomable #2.

HASH JAR TEMPO

ROY MONTGOMERY and the **BARDO POND** group

		Drunken Fish	Drunken Fish
Apr 97.	(cd) <(DFR 24)> **WELL OILED**	□	□
	– Movements 1-7.		
Mar 99.	(cd) <(DFR 44)> **UNDER GLASS**	□	□
	– Praludium und fugue D-moll / Labiomancy / Sources in Cleveland / Hymenoptera in amber crybaby / Gravitational lens opera / Atropine / In the cells of Walken's corti.		

MOODISTS

Formed: Mt. Gambier, Melbourne, Australia ... 1980 by DAVE GRANEY, formerly of the short-lived SPUTNIKS, who released one single, 'OUR BOYS' / 'SECOND GLANCE', in late '79. Joined by STEVE MILLER (no, not that one), MICK TURNER, CHRIS WALSH and CLARE MOORE, GRANEY instigated The MOODISTS, a longer term garage/psyche outfit that enjoyed much cult acclaim in their native Australia. After a couple of homegrown 45's, they secured a UK deal with the small independent, 'Red Flame', subsequently issuing a string of releases including two mini-sets, 'ENGINE SHUDDER' (1983) and 'DOUBLE LIFE' (1985) either side of a full-length album, 'THIRSTY'S CALLING' (1984). The mid-80's also saw the band (who were now without TURNER) release a one-off single, 'JUSTICE AND MONEY TOO', for Alan McGee's yet-to-be-massive 'Creation' label. Ex-ORANGE JUICE bassist, DAVID McCLYMONT, was soon to be drafted in for the departing WALSH, although two further singles rounded off their seven year career. GRANEY was to enjoy greater commercial success with his own outfit, DAVE GRANEY & THE CORAL SNAKES (who included another former ORANGE JUICE member, MALCOLM ROSS), his songwriting prowess and balladeering style seeing him elevated to the critical heights scaled by fellow countrymen, DAVE McCOMB, NICK CAVE and GRANT McLENNAN. Signed to UK 'Fire', GRANEY and Co delivered three albums between '89 and '92, namely 'WORLD FULL OF DAUGHTERS', 'MY LIFE ON THE PLAINS' and 'I WAS THE HUNTER ... AND I WAS THE PREY'. In 1993, he surpassed expectations with the much praised 'NIGHT OF THE WOLVERINE'; the album was given a belated UK release three years later by the astute 'This Way Up' label, who issued a 1995 set, 'THE SOFT 'N' SEXY SOUND', in 1996. DAVE has since formed The DAVE GRANEY SHOW (a self-titled album was issued in '98), mostly all featuring the loyal CLARE MOORE. • **GRANEY covered:** IN A MISTY MORNING (Gene Clark) / BRASS BUTTONS (Gram Parsons) / THE DOLPHINS (Fred Neil) / SHOWBUSINESS (Ac/Dc) / etc. • **Trivia:** CLARE MOORE is the younger sister of LINDY MORRISON (of The Go-Betweens).

Album rating: ENGINE SHUDDER mini (*5) / THIRSTY'S CALLING (*6) / DOUBLE LIFE mini (*4) / Dave Graney...: MY LIFE ON THE PLAINS (*6) / I WAS THE HUNTER ... AND I WAS THE PREY (*6) / THE LURE OF THE TROPICS (*6) / NIGHT OF THE WOLVERINE (*8) / YOU WANNA BE THERE BUT YOU DON'T WANNA TRAVEL (*6) / THE SOFT 'N' SEXY SOUND (*6) / THE DEVIL DRIVES (*5) / THE DAVE GRANEY SHOW (*6) / THE BADDEST compilation (*7) / KISS TOMORROW GOODBYE (*6) / HEROIC BLUES (*6)

DAVE GRANEY – vocals / **STEVE MILLER** – guitar / **MICK TURNER** – guitar / **CHRIS WALSH** – bass / **CLARE MOORE** – drums

		Au Go Go	not iss.
Sep 81.	(7") (ANDA 015) **WHERE THE TREES WALK DOWN HILL. / I SHOULD HAVE BEEN THERE**	□	□
Apr 82.	(7") (ANDA 018) **GONE DEAD. / CHAD'S CAR**	-	- Austra

		Red Flame	not iss.
Mar 83.	(7") (RF 721) **THE DISCIPLES KNOW. / SHE CRACKLES**	□	-
Jun 83.	(m-lp) (RFM 21) **ENGINE SHUDDER**	□	-
	– Gone dead / Chad's car / Kept spectre / Woken strength / The road is holy / Chatter shapes / The disciples know.		
Apr 84.	(lp) (RFA 39) **THIRSTY'S CALLING**	□	-
	– That's Frankie's negative / Bad cabin / Some kinda Jones / Do the door, friend / Runaway / Machine machine / Pure gold flesh / You could be his killer / Swingy George / Thirsty's calling / Boss shitkicker.		
May 84.	(7") (RFB 39) **RUNAWAY. / CHEVROLET ROSE**	□	-
	(12"+=) (RFB 39-12) – Busy splinters.		
Sep 84.	(7"/10") (RFB/10RFB 41) **ENOUGH LEGS TO LIVE ON. / CAN'T LOSE HER**	□	-

--- now without TURNER

Sep 85.	(m-lp) (RFM 44) **DOUBLE LIFE**	□	-
	– Double life / Enough legs to live on / Chevrolet rise / That's how you'll cry / Can't lose her / Six dead birds.		

		Creation	not iss.
Dec 85.	(12"ep) (CRE 023T) **JUSTICE AND MONEY TOO. / YOU'VE GOT YOUR STORY / TAKE US ALL HOME**	□	-

--- **DAVID McCLYMONT** – bass (ex-ORANGE JUICE) repl. CHRIS

		Tim	not iss.
Oct 86.	(12"ep) (12MOT 1) **TAKE THE RED CARPET OUT OF TOWN. / JACK OF DIAMONDS / EVERYBODY DON'T TELL HER**	□	-
May 87.	(7") (MOT 5) **HEY LITTLE GARY. / SOMEONE'S GOT TO GIVE**	□	-
	(12"+=) (12MOT 5) – Somebody to love / It takes a thief.		

DAVE GRANEY 'N' THE CORAL SNAKES

--- with **CLARE MOORE** + **ROD HAYWARD** + **GORDY BLAIR** + **ROBIN CASINADER** others in group **MALCOLM ROSS** – guitar (ex-ORANGE JUICE)

		Fire	Fire
Oct 88.	(12"ep) (BLAZE 32T) **AT HIS STONE BEACH**	□	□
	– Listen to her lovers sing / The greatest show in town / A deal made for somebody else / World full of daughters.		
Mar 90.	(cd/lp; as DAVE GRANEY WITH THE WHITE BUFFALOES) (<FIRE CD/LP 20>) **MY LIFE ON THE PLAINS**	□	□ Jul91
	– Nobody's gonna love you / Robert Ford on the stage / Take me for a ride / I'll set the scene / In a misty morning / Girl in the Moon / Brass buttons / I can't want you / Dolphins / The streets of Laredo / Listen to her lovers sing / A deal made for somebody else / World full of daughters / The greatest show in town.		
Nov 90.	(cd-ep) **CODINE** (live EP)	□	-
Feb 92.	(cd) (FIRE 33029) **I WAS THE HUNTER ... AND I WAS THE PREY**	□	-
	– $1,000,000 in a red velvet suit / You could be mine / I got myself a beautiful nightmare / Same place another time / A love that blinds a love / Somebody tryin' to hold you now / I was the hunter and I was the prey / I caught my head in a crack of time / We were going faster / Everybody does what they want to / Belong to you / Everything flies away / Codine / Jack of diamonds.		

		Torn And Frayed	not iss.
Jun 92.	(cd) **LURE OF THE TROPICS** (live)	-	- Austra
	– I caught my heel in a crack of time / A million dollars in a red velvet suit / Beautiful nightmare / You wanna be there but you don't wanna travel / Jesus what'd I do / Warren Oates / Robert Ford / The lure of the tropics / Everything flies away / Rave on / In the misty morning – My life on the plains / Morning dew / Just the bullshit.		

		Universal	not iss.
Jun 93.	(cd) **NIGHT OF THE WOLVERINE**	-	- Austra
	– You're just too hip baby / Mogambo / Night of the wolverine 1 / I'm just havin' one of those lives / I held the cool breeze / I remember you (you're the girl I love) / Three dead passengers in a stolen second hand Ford / That's the way it's gonna be / Maggie Cassidy / You need to suffer / Night of the wolverine 2 (could have stayed home – King of Adelaide – Make band laugh) / Out there (in the night of time). (UK-iss.May96; 532 129-2/-4)		
Jun 94.	(cd) (522 381-2) **YOU WANNA BE THERE BUT YOU DON'T WANNA TRAVEL**	-	- Austra
	– I'm gonna release your soul / There was a time / You wanna be loved / Warren Oates / Soul into time / Won't you ride with me / A new life in a new town / Livin' out your tomorrow (hard against yesterday) / Imagine if what you did on your weekend was your life / You wanna be there but you don't wanna travel / Let me tell you about yourself / The word is nah / The stars baby, the stars / We didn't have the words to say it (we didn't have the words to get around).		
Jun 95.	(cd/c) (528 416-2/-4) **THE SOFT 'N' SEXY SOUND**	-	- Austra
	– The birds and the goats / I'm gonna live in my own big world / Apollo 69 / I'm not afraid to be heavy / Deep inside a song / The pre-revolutionary scene / Rock'n'roll is where I hide / Salty girls / Outward bound / Scorched earth love affair / Morrison floorshow / Dandies are never unbuttoned. (UK-iss.Sep96; same)		
Apr 96.	(7"ep) (WAY 48-33) **YOU'RE JUST TOO HIP, BABY. / THAT'S THE WAY IT'S GONNA BE / 3220 BLUES**	□	-
	(above + below issued on 'This Way Up' UK)		
Jun 96.	(cd-s) (WAY 51-33) **3 DEAD PASSENGERS / CONFESSIONS OF SERGE GAINSBOURG / IT'S YOUR CROWD I HATE**	□	-
Jun 97.	(cd) **THE DEVIL DRIVES**	-	- Austra
	– The oblivion seekers / My only regret (I opened my mouth) / I don't know you exist / Rackin' up some zeds / Everybody loves a mass killer / I dig the pioneers / The sheriff of Hell / Pianola roll / Land of the giants / I love your gravity / Biker in business class / A man on the make / Pascal et Caroline / The Devil drives / Feelin' kinda sporty.		

DAVE GRANEY SHOW

--- GRANEY with **CLARE MOORE** – drums, percussion, keyboards / **BILL MILLER** – guitars, vocals **ADELE PICKVANCE** – bass, vocals **STUART PERERA** – guitar

		Festival	not iss.
Nov 98.	(cd) **THE DAVE GRANEY SHOW**	-	- Austra
	– Lt. Colonel, calvary / Your masters must be pleased with you / I'm a commander / Aristocratic jive / Am I wearing something of yours? / No pockets in a jumpsuit / Speak to my medium / Twixt this world and the next / I'm gonna do ya slowly / Driving through his mythic country, whistling / Between times / They wanted to be player / Smile and wave.		

		Cockaigne	not iss.
May 00.	(cd) (Cock 001) **KISS TOMORROW GOODBYE**	-	- Austra
	– The stuff that night is made of / Death by a thousand sucks / Don't be true / Street dreams / Drugs are wasted on the young / Vengeance is on its way (don't worry) / Out of the loop / Have you heard about the Melbourne mafia? / I need some scratch / Mind full of leather / You're on your own, now / Outing the suits / Kiss tomorrow goodbye. (UK-iss.Nov00 on 'Cooking Vinyl'; COOKCD 206)		
Jul 02.	(cd) (Cock 005) **HEROIC BLUES**	-	- Austra
	– Don't mess with the blood / Anchors aweigh / Son of Maggie Mae / Leavin' the Mount / Clingin' to the coast / I will always hate you / Heroic blues / I don't know anything / Eye o' the vibe.		

– compilations, etc. –

Oct 99.	(cd) Universal; (153 754-2) **THE BADDEST**	-	- Austra
	– The sheriff of Hell (hang 'em high mix) / Showbusiness / A million dollars in a red velvet suit / Warren Oates / You're just too hip, baby / Night of the wolverine / You wanna be love / I'm gonna release your soul / The stars, baby, the stars / The confessions of Serge Gainsbourg / I'm not afraid to be heavy / Morrison floorshow / Rock'n'roll is where I hide / The Devil drives / Feelin kinda sporty / I dig the pioneers.		

MOOD SIX

Formed: Margate, England ... 1981 by SIMON SMITH, songwriter TONY CONWAY, ANDY GODFREY, PAUL SHUREY, GUY MORLEY and PHIL WARD. Although most members were from Mod backgrounds, The MOOD SIX chose retro psychedelia as the inspiration for their new style, making their vinyl debut in 1982 on WEA's V/A compilation, 'A Splash Of Colour'. The two featured MOOD SIX tracks ('JUST LIKE A DREAM' and 'PLASTIC

MOOD SIX (cont)

FLOWERS') were certainly highlights, resulting in an interview on BBC-TV's 'Nationwide' news programme. They subsequently secured a deal with 'E.M.I.' and debuted with the single, 'HANGING AROUND' (soon to be covered by US pop star, TONI BASIL), a sales flop that did little to further their relationship with the label. Finally dropped after the withdrawal of their follow-up, 'SHE'S TOO FAR (OUT)', the group took a lengthy sabbatical while SMITH went off to join The TIMES. By the time of his return, CHRIS O'CONNOR had been chosen to replace PAUL and GUY, a long-awaited debut album, 'THE DIFFERENCE IS . . .', finally hitting the racks in early '85. The following year, The MOOD SIX found a new home at 'Cherry Red', through whom they released a second album, 'A MATTER OF!' (1986), the last recording to feature O'CONNOR who was substituted with SIMON TAYLOR. Following the collapse of Cherry Red, it would be several years before loyal fans were furnished with a third and final set, 'AND THIS IS IT' (1993), by which point WARD had made way for GERRY O'SULLIVAN.

Album rating: THE DIFFERENCE IS . . . (*6) / A MATTER OF! (*7) / AND THIS IS IT (*5) / THE BEST OF MOOD SIX: SONGS FROM THE LOST BOUTIQUE compilation (*6)

PHIL WARD – vocals / **TONY CONWAY** (b.28 Feb'58, Newbury, England) – guitar / **PAUL SHUREY** – (ex-V.I.P's) / **GUY MORLEY** – (ex-V.I.P.'s) / **ANDY GODFREY** (b.28 Dec'57, Ilford, Essex, England) – bass (ex-SECURITY RISK) / **SIMON SMITH** (b. 3 Dec'58, Merton Park, London) – drums (ex-MERTON PARKAS)

	E.M.I.	not iss.
May 82. (7") (EMI 5300) **HANGING AROUND. / MOOD MUSIC**		
Sep 82. (7"w/drawn) (EMI 5336) **SHE'S TOO FAR (OUT). / VENUS**	-	-

—— **CHRIS O'CONNOR** – keyboards repl. PAUL SHUREY + GUY MORLEY

	Psycho	not iss.
Feb 85. (lp) (PSYCHO 33) **THE DIFFERENCE IS . . .**		-

– She's too far (out) / Party time / It's your life / Victim / Hanging around / Plastic flowers / Brief encounter / Stay this way / The rain falls on Mary / The difference is . . .

Apr 85. (7") (PSYCHO 2001) **PLASTIC FLOWERS. / IT'S YOUR LIFE** | | - |
(12"+=) (PSYCHO 4001) **PLASTIC FLOWERS EP** – Is it right? / I wanna destroy you / Starting points.

	Cherry Red	not iss.
Aug 86. (12") (12CHERRY 94) **WHAT HAVE YOU EVER DONE. /**		-
Sep 86. (lp/c) (BRED/CBRED 71) **A MATTER OF!**		-

– The contemporary scene / The voice of reason / Eternal / Back to the day / The life that Jack built / A matter of! / What have you ever done? / Love of money / Far away / When the time came / The perfect life / Game show.

—— **SIMON TAYLOR** (b.28 Dec'60, Redhill, Surrey) – keyboards repl. O'CONNOR
May 87. (7") (CHERRY 97) **I SAW THE LIGHT. / FLOWERS AND BOXES** | | - |
(12"+=) (12CHERRY 97) – Light music / Theme from 'The Chase'.

—— not much happened after 'Cherry Red' went bust; re-formed in 1993

—— **GERRY O'SULLIVAN** (b.25 Mar'63, Paddington, London) – vocals repl. WARD

	Lost Recording Co.	not iss.
1993. (cd) **AND THIS IS IT**		-

—— SIMON SMITH would subsequently join SMALLTOWN PARADE

– compilations, etc. –

Mar 97. (cd) Cherry Red; (<CDMRED 141>) **THE BEST OF MOOD SIX: SONGS FROM THE LOST BOUTIQUE** | | - |
– Hanging around / She's too far (out) / The rain falls on Mary / It's your life / Plastic flowers / Party time / Victim / I wanna destroy you / What have you ever done? / The intruder / The contemporary scene / When the time comes / The voice of reason / Game show / I saw cthe light / You could be my soul / I'll keep on holding on / Mad about the boy / Flowers and boxes / Look at me now / Shake some action / Somebody.

Thurston MOORE (see under ⇒ SONIC YOUTH)

MORRISSEY

Born: STEPHEN PATRICK MORRISSEY, 22 May'59, Manchester, England. After his bust-up with SMITHS guitarist JOHNNY MARR in August '87, MORRISSEY, one of rock music's most intellectually incisive wordsmiths, hastily embarked upon a relatively successful solo career. Remaining with 'E.M.I.', his debut effort, 'VIVA HATE', was subsequently released on the re-activated 'H.M.V.' imprint in Spring '88. With the music co-written by his new producer, STEPHEN STREET, and a backing band that numbered VINI REILLY (guitar, keyboards; ex-DURUTTI COLUMN) and ANDREW PARESI (drums), the album was a strong start, reaching No.2 in the UK charts on the back of the catchy SUEDEHEAD single (incredibly, the singer's first ever Top 5 hit single). Another stand-out track was the lavish melancholy of 'EVERYDAY IS LIKE SUNDAY', arguably his best solo track to date and a song which gave him another Top 10 hit later that summer. Though the album received a relatively warm critical reception, it was, as ever, not without controversy. 'BENGALI IN PLATFORMS' was an ambiguous address to immigrants which he later unsuccessfully attempted to play down while 'MARGARET ON THE GUILLOTINE' was self explanatory, no doubt meeting with a little more empathy. Recruiting a new band composed of NEIL TAYLOR (guitar) and ex-SMITHS', CRAIG GANNON, ANDY ROURKE and MIKE JOYCE, MORRISSEY returned the following year with another couple of fine singles, the playfully coy 'LAST OF THE INTERNATIONAL PLAYBOYS' and 'INTERESTING DRUG', both records going Top 10. The line-up didn't last, however, and he brought in a completely new cast for his next single 'OUIJA BOARD, OUIJA BOARD', a song that suffered scathing reviews in the music press and barely made the Top 20. The following year, a projected album was scrapped although its title, 'BONA DRAG', was retained for an impressive career resume that appeared in late 1990. The collection also contained some new material, notably the grim 'NOVEMBER SPAWNED A MONSTER' and the contentious narrative, 'PICCADILLY PALARE', both released as singles. With a fresh backing group that included ex-MADNESS bassist BEDDERS and MORRISSEY's new writing partner, MARK E. NEVIN (ex-FAIRGROUND ATTRACTION), the singer cut the 'KILL UNCLE' opus. Released in 1991 to mixed reviews, the album failed to deliver on the promise of the earlier singles, although MORRISSEY subsequently recruited a rockabilly backing band: ALAIN WHYTE (guitar), GARY DAY (bass), BOZ BOORER (guitar, ex-POLECATS) and SPENCER COBRIN (drums), touring the album around the world, his first live appearances since the prime of The SMITHS. The tour was largely a success and, enlivened and inspired, MORRISSEY cut the 'YOUR ARSENAL' (1992) set. Produced by MICK RONSON and co-penned with WHYTE, the album took the watered down glam-rock of 'KILL UNCLE' and kickstarted it with some raw rockabilly, resulting in MORRISSEY's highest chart placing for years (No.4). Though the record failed to spawn any major hits, it contained such thoughtful material as 'I KNOW IT'S GONNA HAPPEN SOMEDAY' and 'YOU'RE THE ONE FOR ME, FATTY', the former subsequently covered by DAVID BOWIE, another of MORRISSEY's idols. The same year, MORRISSEY hit the headlines with his scathing criticism of Johnny Rogan, author of the SMITHS biography, 'Morrissey & Marr: The Severed Alliance'. It wasn't the last time the 'Oscar Wilde of Rock' would be in the news, MORRISSEY subsequently losing a well publicised court battle with MIKE JOYCE over unpaid SMITHS royalties. More controversy surrounded the singer following his disastrous appearance at the 1993 'Madstock' concert in London's Finsbury Park. Supporting headliners MADNESS, MORRISSEY was given an extremely hostile reception after coming out draped in a Union Jack, further fuelling debate over the perceived ambiguity of his motivations. Following all this strife, 'VAUXHALL AND I' (1994) resurrected MORRISSEY's career, a sympathetic production by STEVE LILLYWHITE setting the scene for his most considered and consistent album to date. The record was also MORRISSEY's first No.1, a critically acclaimed opus that was marked by more emotionally-charged lyrics, laying off the trademark caustic barbs. Moving to 'R.C.A.', MORRISSEY released 'SOUTHPAW GRAMMER' almost a year later, a bizarre album that focussed on the singer's apparent boxing fixation. Unsurprisingly, the record met with bewilderment from critics, though it consolidated his position as one of rock's few genuine mavericks. In 1997, MORRISSEY once again shifted stables, this time to 'Island' who got their chance to showcase the bard on some new work, 'MALADJUSTED'. Without a contract for around five years, MORRISSEY looked to have retired to his L.A. bachelor pad, until that is, 'Sanctuary' records signed him for a return in 2003. • **Covered:** THAT'S ENTERTAINMENT (Jam) / SKIN STORM (Bradford) / MOON RIVER (Henry Mancini). • **Trivia:** In the late 80's, MORRISSEY made a cameo appearance in Channel 4's 'Brookside' off-shoot, 'South'.

Album rating: VIVA HATE (*9) / BONA DRAG collection (*7) / KILL UNCLE (*8) / YOUR ARSENAL (*8) / BEETHOVEN WAS DEAF (*5) / VAUXHALL AND I (*9) / WORLD OF MORRISSEY part compilation (*7) / SOUTHPAW GRAMMAR (*6) / MALADJUSTED (86) / SUEDEHEAD (THE BEST OF . . .) compilation (*7)

MORRISSEY – vocals; with **STEPHEN STREET** – guitar, bass, producer, co-writer / **ANDREW PARESI** – drums / **VINI REILLY** – guitar, keyboards (of DURUTTI COLUMN)

	H.M.V.	Sire
Feb 88. (7") (POP 1618) **SUEDEHEAD. / I KNOW VERY WELL HOW I GOT MY NAME**	5	-

(12"+=) (12POP 1618) – Hairdresser on fire.
(c-s++=/cd-s++=) (TC/CD POP 1618) – Oh well, I'll never learn.

| Mar 88. (cd/c/lp) (CD/TC+/CDS 3787) <25699> **VIVA HATE** | 2 | 48 |

– Alsatian cousin / Little man, what now? / Everyday is like Sunday / Bengali in platforms / Angel, angel, down we go together / Late night, Maudlin Street / Suedehead / Break up the family / The ordinary boys / I don't mind if you forget me / Dial-a-cliche / Margaret on the guillotine. (re-iss. Mar94 on 'Parlophone' cd/c; same) (cd re-iss. Mar97 on 'E.M.I.' +=; CDCNTV 2) – Let the right one slip in / Pashernate love / At amber / Disappointed (live) / Girl least likely to / I'd love to / Michael's bones / I've changed my plea to guilty. (lp re-iss. Aug00 on 'Simply Vinyl'; SVLP 233)

| Jun 88. (7") (POP 1619) **EVERYDAY IS LIKE SUNDAY. / DISAPPOINTED** | 9 | - |

(12"+=) (12POP 1619) – Sister I'm a poet.
(c-s++=/cd-s++=) (TC/CD+/POP 1619) – Will never marry.

—— MORRISSEY only retained STREET. He brought in **NEIL TAYLOR** – guitar and re-united with (ex-SMITHS):- **CRAIG GANNON, ANDY ROURKE + MIKE JOYCE**

| Feb 89. (7") (POP 1620) **THE LAST OF THE FAMOUS INTERNATIONAL PLAYBOYS. / LUCKY LIPS** | 6 | - |

(12"+=/cd-s+=) (12/CD POP 1620) – Michael's bones.

| Apr 89. (7"/etched-12") (POP/12POPS 1621) **INTERESTING DRUG. / SUCH A LITTLE THING MAKES SUCH A BIG DIFFERENCE** | 9 | - |

(c-s+=/12"+=/cd-s+=) (TC/12/CD POP 1621) – Sweet and tender hooligan (live).

—— He brought in complete new line-up:- **KEVIN ARMSTRONG** – guitar / **MATTHEW SELIGMAN** – bass / **STEVE HOPKINS** – drums and returning **ANDREW PARESI** – keyboards

| Nov 89. (7") (POP 1622) **OUIJA BOARD, OUIJA BOARD. / YES, I AM BLIND** | 18 | |

(c-s+=/12"+=/cd-s+=) (TC/12/CD POP 1622) <21424> – East west.

—— **ANDY ROURKE** returned to repl. SELIGMAN + HOPKINS / added guest **MARY MARGARET O'HARA** – vocals (up & coming solo artist)

Apr 90. (c-s/7") (TC+/POP 1623) **NOVEMBER SPAWNED A MONSTER. / HE KNOWS I'D LOVE TO SEE HIM** | 12 | |
(12"+=/cd-s+=) (12/CD POP 1623) <21529> – The girl least likely to.

Oct 90. (c-s/7") (TC+/POP 1624) **PICCADILLY PALARE. / GET OFF THE STAGE** | 18 | – |
(12"+=/cd-s+=) (12/CD POP 1624) – At amber.

Oct 90. (cd/c/lp) (CD/TC/CSD 3788) <26221> **BONA DRAG** | 9 | 59 |
– Piccadilly palare / Interesting drug / November spawned a monster / Will never marry / Such a little thing makes such a big difference / The last of the famous international playboys / Ouija board, ouija board / Hairdresser on fire / Everyday is like Sunday / He knows I'd love to see him / Yes, I am blind / Lucky lisp / Suedehead / Disappointed. (re-iss. Mar94 on 'Parlophone'; same)

—— He now retained **ANDREW PARESI**. Newcomers were **BEDDERS** – bass (ex-MADNESS) / **MARK E.NEVIN** – guitars, co-composer (ex-FAIRGROUND ATTRACTION) plus **STEVE HEART + SEAMUS BEAGHAN** – keyboards / **NAWAZISH ALI KHAN** – violin

Feb 91. (c-s/7") (TC+/POP 1625) **OUR FRANK. / JOURNALISTS WHO LIE** | 26 | |
(12"+=/cd-s+=) (12/CD POP 1625) <40043> – Tony the pony.

Feb 91. (cd/c/lp) (CD/TC+/CSD 3789) <26514> **KILL UNCLE** | 8 | 52 | Mar91
– Our Frank / Asian rut / Sing your life / Mute witness / King Leer / Found found found / Driving your girlfriend home / The harsh truth of the camera eye / (I'm) The end of the family line / There's a place in Hell for me and my friends.

—— His tour band Spring '91; **ALAIN WHYTE** – guitar / **GARY DAY** – bass / **BOZ BOORER** – guitar (ex-POLECATS) / **SPENCER COBRIN** – drums

Apr 91. (c-s/7") (TC+/POP 1626) **SING YOUR LIFE. / THAT'S ENTERTAINMENT** | 33 | |
(12"+=/cd-s+=) (12/CD POP 1626) <40084> – The loop.

Jul 91. (c-s/7") (TC+/POP 1627) **PREGNANT FOR THE LAST TIME. / SKIN STORM** | 25 | – |
(12"+=/cd-s+=) (12/CD POP 1627) – Cosmic dancer (live) / Disappointed (live).

Oct 91. (c-s/7") (TC+/POP 1628) **MY LOVE LIFE. / I'VE CHANGED MY PLEA TO GUILTY** | 29 | |
(12"+=/cd-s+=) (12/CD POP 1628) <40163> – There's a place in Hell for me and my friends.

Oct 91. (cd-ep) <40184> **AT KROQ (live)** | – | |
– There's a place in Hell for my friends / My love life / Sing your life.

May 92. (c-s/7") (TC+/POP 1629) **WE HATE IT WHEN OUR FRIENDS BECOME SUCCESSFUL. / SUEDEHEAD** | 17 | |
(12"+=) (12POP 1629) – Pregnant for the last time.
(cd-s+=) (CDPOP 1629) <40560> – I've changed my plea to guilty.

Jul 92. (c-s/7") (TC+/POP 1630) **YOU'RE THE ONE FOR ME, FATTY. / PASHERNATE LOVE** | 19 | – |
(12"+=/cd-s+=) (12/CD POP 1630) – There speaks a true friend.

Jul 92. (cd/c/lp) (CD/TC/CSD 3790) <26994> **YOUR ARSENAL** | 4 | 21 |
– You're gonna need someone on your side / Glamorous glue / We'll let you know / The National Front disco / Certain people I know / We hate it when our friends become successful / You're the one for me, Fatty / Seasick, yet still docked / I know it's gonna happen someday / Tomorrow. (lp re-iss. Sep00 on 'Simply Vinyl'; SVLP 244)

Sep 92. (cd-s) <40580> **TOMORROW / LET THE RIGHT ONE SLIP IN / PASHERNATE LOVE** | – | – |

Dec 92. (c-s/7") (TC+/POP 1631) **CERTAIN PEOPLE I KNOW. / JACK THE RIPPER** | 35 | |
(12"+=/cd-s+=) (12/CD POP 1631) – You've had her.

Parlophone E.M.I.

May 93. (cd/c/lp) (CD/TC+/CSD 3791) <89061> **BEETHOVEN WAS DEAF (live)** | 13 | |
– You're the one for me, Fatty / Certain people I know / National Front disco / November spawned a monster / Seasick, yet still docked / The loop / Sister I'm a poet / Jack the ripper / Such a little thing makes such a big difference / I know it's gonna happen someday / We'll let you know / Suedehead / He knows I'd love to see him / You're gonna need someone on your side / Glamorous glue / We hate it when our friends become successful. (re-iss. Sep94 on 'Parlophone' cd/c; same)

—— **BOZ BOORER + ALAIN WHYTE** – guitars / **JONNY BRIDGEWOOD** – bass / **WOODIE TAYLOR** – drums

Parlophone Sire

Mar 94. (c-s/7") (TCR/R 6372) <18207> **THE MORE YOU IGNORE ME, THE CLOSER I GET. / USED TO BE A SWEET BOY** | 8 | 46 |
(12"+=/cd-s+=) (12R/CDR 6372) – I'd love to.

Mar 94. (cd/c/lp) (CD/TC/PCSD 148) <45451> **VAUXHALL AND I** | 1 | 18 |
– Now my heart is full / Spring-heeled Jim / Billy Budd / Hold on to your friends / The more you ignore me, the closer I get / Why don't you find out for yourself / I am hated for loving / Lifeguard sleeping, girl drowning / Used to be a sweet boy / The lazy sunbathers / Speedway.

Jun 94. (c-s/7") (TCR/R 6383) **HOLD ON TO YOUR FRIENDS. / MOONRIVER** | 47 | |
(12"/cd-s) (12R/CDR 6383) – (extended versions).

Aug 94. (c-s/7"; by MORRISSEY and SIOUXSIE) (TCR/R 6365) **INTERLUDE. / ('A'extended)** | 25 | |
(12"+=/cd-s+=) (12R/CDR 6365) – ('A'mix).

Aug 94. (cd-s) <41700> **NOW MY HEART IS FULL / MOON RIVER / JACK THE RIPPER** | – | |

Jan 95. (c-s/7") (TC+/R 6400) **BOXERS. / HAVE-A-GO MERCHANT** | 23 | |
(12"+=/cd-s+=) (12/CD R 6400) <41914> – Whatever happens, I love you.

Feb 95. (cd/c/lp) (CD/TC/PCSD 163) <45879> **WORLD OF MORRISSEY** (part compilation) | 15 | |
– Whatever happens, I love you / Billy Budd / Jack the ripper (live) / Have-a-go merchant / The loop / Sister I'm a poet (live) / You're the one for me, Fatty (live) / Boxers / Moon river (extended) / My love life / Certain people I know / The last of the famous international playboys / We'll let you know / Spring-heeled Jim. (cd re-iss. Mar99 on 'EMI Gold'; CDPCSD 163)

—— **SPENCER JAMES COBRIN** – drums; repl. WOODIE

RCA Victor RCA Victor

Aug 95. (7"/c-s) (74321 29980-7/-4) **DAGENHAM DAVE. / NOBODY LOVES US** | 26 | – |
(cd-s+=) (74321 29980-2) – You must please remember.

Aug 95. (cd/c/lp) (74321 29953-2/-4/-1) <45939> **SOUTHPAW GRAMMAR** | 4 | 66 |
– The teachers are afraid of the pupils / Reader meet author / The boy racer / The operation / Dagenham Dave / Do your best and don't worry / Best friend on the payroll / Southpaw.

Nov 95. (7") (74321 33294-7) **THE BOY RACER. / LONDON (live)** | 36 | – |
(cd-s+=) (74321 33294-4) – Billy Budd (live).
(cd-s) (74321 33294-2) – ('A'side) / Spring heeled Jim (live) / Why don't you find out for yourself (live).

Parlophone Capitol

Dec 95. (c-s/7") (TC+/R 6243) **SUNNY. / BLACK-EYED SUSAN** | 42 | – |
(cd-s+=) (CDR 6243) – A swallow on my neck.

Island Polygram

Jul 97. (c-s/7") (C+/IS 667) **ALMA MATTERS. / I CAN HAVE BOTH** | 16 | – |
(12"+=/cd-s+=) (12IS/CID 667) – Heir apparent.

Aug 97. (cd/c/lp) (CID/ICT/ILPS 8059) <536036> **MALADJUSTED** | 8 | 61 |
– Maladjusted / Alma matters / Ambitious outsiders / Trouble loves me / Papa Jack / Ammunition / Wide to receive / Roy's keen / He cried / Satan rejected my soul.

Oct 97. (c-s/7") (C+/IS 671) **ROY'S KEEN. / LOST** | 42 | – |
(12"+=/cd-s+=) (12IS/CID 671) – The edges are no longer parallel.

Dec 97. (c-s/7") (C+/IS 686) **SATAN REJECTED MY SOUL. / NOW I AM I WAS** | 39 | – |
(cd-s+=/12"+=) (CID/12IS 686) – This is not your country.

– compilations, etc. –

on 'E.M.I.' unless mentioned otherwise

Sep 97. (cd/c/lp) (<CD/TC+/EMC 3771>) **SUEDEHEAD (THE BEST OF MORRISSEY)** | 26 | – |
– Suedehead / Interesting drug / Boxers / Last of the famous international playboys / Sunny / Tomorrow / Interlude / Everyday is like Sunday / Hold on to your friends / My love life / Our Frank / Piccadilly palare / Ouija board, ouija board / You're the one for me, fatty / We hate it when our friends become successful / Pregnant for the last time / November spawned a monster / The more you ignore me, the closer I get / That's entertainment. (special edition; CDEMCX 3771)

Jun 00. (10xcd-s-box) (887293-2) **THE CD SINGLES 1988-1991** | | – |
Sep 00. (3xcd-box) (528376-2) **BONA DRAG / KILL UNCLE / VAUXHALL AND I** | | – |
Sep 01. (9xcd-s-box) (879745-2) **THE CD SINGLES 1991-1995** | | – |
Dec 01. (cd) Rhino/Warners-Sire; <R2 78375> **THE BEST OF . . .** | – | |
– The more you ignore me, the closer I get / Suedehead / Everyday is like Sunday / Glamorous glue / Do your best and don't worry / November spawned a monster / The last of the famous international playboys / Sing your life / Hairdresser on fire / Interesting drug / We hate it when our friends become successful / Certain people I know / Now my heart is full / I know it's gonna happen someday / Sunny / Alma matters / Hold on to your friends / Sister I'm a poet / Disappointed / Tomorrow / Lost.

Oct 02. (d-cd) (543151-2) **BONA DRAG / YOUR ARSENAL** | | – |

MOTHMEN

Formed: Manchester, England . . . 1979 by former ALBERTOS Y LOST TRIOS PARANOIAS members; TONY BOWERS and BOB HARDING, plus DAVE ROWBOTHAM and CHRIS JOYCE. Virtually the stamping ground for SIMPLY RED (albeit without Mr. HUCKNALL), The MOTHMEN were something of an oddity in the ever-changing early 80's world of post-New Wave. A handful of singles and two mediocre sets, including their 'On-U-Sound' debut 'PAY ATTENTION' (1981), did little to challenge the alt/indie scene.

Album rating: PAY ATTENTION (*4) / ONE BLACK DOT (*5)

TONY BOWERS – vocals, guitar, bass / **BOB HARDING** – guitar, bass / **DAVID ROWBOTHAM** – guitar, bass / **CHRIS JOYCE** – drums (of PINK MILITARY)

Absurd not iss.

Jun 79. (7") (ABSURD 6) **DOES IT MATTER IRENE? / PLEASE LET GO** | | – |

On-U-Sound not iss.

Jan 81. (lp) (ON-U LP 2) **PAY ATTENTION** | | – |
– Afghan farmer driving cattle / Animal animaux / Not moving / Factory – Tea point – Factory / Please let go / Tardis (Sweep is dead, long live Sweep) / Mothman.

Do-It not iss.

Jul 81. (7"/12"; deleted after 1 day) (DUN/+IT 12) **SHOW ME YOUR HOUSE AND CAR. / PEOPLE PEOPLE** | | – |
Oct 81. (7") (DUN 14) **TEMPTATION. / PEOPLE PEOPLE** | | – |
Jan 82. (lp) (RIDE 9) **ONE BLACK DOT** | | – |
– Wadada / Temptation / One more weapon / Let's talk about it / No rest / One black dot / Weekend / House and car / Home sweet home / Thank you I like it.

Mar 82. (7") (DUN 19) **WADADA. / AS THEY ARE** | | – |

—— disbanded when the ALBERTOS re-formed, although all of them joined MICK HUCKNALL in SIMPLY RED

MOTOR BOYS MOTOR
(see under ⇒ SCREAMING BLUE MESSIAHS)

MOTORCYCLE BOY

Formed: East Kilbride, Scotland . . . early 1985 as MEAT WHIPLASH (named after a FIRE ENGINES b-side!) by PAUL McDERMOTT, MICHAEL KERR (also part-time with JESSE GARON & THE DESPERADOS), EDDY CONNOLLY and STEPHEN McLEAN. They signed to Alan McGee's 'Creation' independent, supporting The JESUS & MARY CHAIN while the REID brothers produced their one and only single, 'DON'T SLIP UP'. All but STEPHEN resurfaced as MOTORCYCLE BOY (after the hero in cult film, 'Rumblefish') a few years later and, with the recruitment of female, ALEX TAYLOR (ex-SHOP ASSISTANTS) on vocals and SCOTTIE on aggressive guitar, they became a big signing for 'Rough Trade'. However, the band moved on up to 'Chrysalis', having only issued one single, 'BIG ROCK CANDY MOUNTAIN', in 1987. For a few years little was heard from ALEX's wonderful vocals until 1989 brought forth two singles, 'TRYING TO BE KIND' and 'YOU AND ME AGAINST THE WORLD', both were to be taken from their one and only album, 'SCARLET', which was shelved. Stop press:- the album might see light of day via 'Cherry Red' in 2003.

Album rating: never actually issued any

MEAT WHIPLASH

PAUL McDERMOTT – vocals, percussion / **MICHAEL KERR** – guitar / **EDDY CONNOLLY** – bass / **STEPHEN McLEAN** – drums

Creation / not iss.

Sep 85. (7") *(CRE 020)* **DON'T SLIP UP. / HERE IT COMES**

MOTORCYCLE BOY

— added **ALEX TAYLOR** – vocals (ex-SHOP ASSISTANTS)
— **SCOTTIE** (b. DAVID SCOTT) – guitar; repl. STEPHEN

Rough Trade / not iss.

Sep 87. (7") *(RT 210)* **BIG ROCK CANDY MOUNTAIN. / ROOM AT THE TOP**
(12"+=) *(RTT 210)* – ('A'-Velocity dance mix) / His latest flame.

Chrysalis / not iss.

Jun 89. (7") *(CHS 3310)* **TRYING TO BE KIND. / THE WORLD FALLS INTO PLACE**
(ext-12"+=) *(CHS12 3310)* – ('A'-1000cc version) / Will you love me tomorrow.
Sep 89. (7") *(CHS 3398)* **YOU AND ME AGAINST THE WORLD. / UNDER THE BRIDGE**
(12"+=) *(CHS12 3398)* – Some girls / ('A'extended).
Sep 89. (lp/c/cd; w-drawn) *(CHR/ZCHR/CCD 1689)* **SCARLET**

Nym. Pink Sensation / not iss.

Apr 90. (12"ep) *(NPST 001)* **THE ROAD GOES ON FOREVER**
– Starlight – Starlight (paradise a go-go mix) / The road goes forever (overdrive karma mix) / Salvation / The road goes on forever.
Oct 90. (12") *(NPST 002)* **HERE SHE COMES. / EVERYTHING I SEE / THE ROAD GOES ON FOREVER (live)**
— added **FITZPATRICK**
Jan 91. (12"ep; as ONE NOTE JAM) *(NPST 003)* **WARP EIGHT IN ELECTRAGLIDE (ONLY YOU). / WARP NINE IN ELECTRAGLIDE (ONLY YOU)**

— split the following year, TAYLOR became a "real" shop assistant

Bob MOULD (see under ⇒ HUSKER DU)

MOVING TARGETS

Formed: Ipswich, Massachusetts, USA . . . early 80's as the brainchild of KEN CHAMBERS. MOVING TARGETS first made it onto vinyl by contributing a handful of tracks to local V/A album sampler, 'Bands That Would Be God', although it would be some time before the band would record in their own right. Eventually securing a deal with fledgling US indie, 'Taang!', CHAMBERS and Co showcased their blistering punk wares on 1986's 'BURNING IN WATER, DROWNING IN FLAMES'. Despite a positive reception, KEN would pursue a number of side projects, BULLET LAVOLTA being the most high profile. CHAMBERS later reassembled MOVING TARGETS with a new line-up that included guitarist, PAT LEONARD, the band slightly off the mark with a belated follow-up set, 'BRAVE NOISE' (1989). The 'TARGETS mainman began a new decade with yet another line-up that boasted the former rhythm section of JONES VERY, JEFF GODDARD and JAMIE VAN BRAMER, along with guitarist BEN SEGAL (prior to the next recording, 'FALL', another backing team were used). Although CHAMBERS continued to record into the 90's, he gradually phased out the MOVING TARGETS name, releasing 'NO REACTION' (1994) in a solo capacity.

Album rating: BURNING IN WATER, DROWNING IN FLAMES (*7) / BRAVE NOISE (*6) / FALL (*5) / Ken Chambers: TAKE THIS RIDE (*5) / NO REACTION (*4)

KEN CHAMBERS – vocals, lead guitar / **unknown**

What Goes On / Taang!

May 88. (lp) *(GOES ON 14) <TAANG 11>* **BURNING IN WATER, DROWNING IN FLAMES** — 1986
– The other side / Faith / Let me know why / Shape of somethings / Less than gravity / Almost calling – Drone / Urban dub / Always calling / Underground / MTV / Funtime / This world / Squares and circles. *(re-iss. Nov92 on 'Taang!'; TAANG 11LP)*

— CHAMBERS also went into other projects, DRED FOOLE & THE DIN, The GROINOIDS and BULLET LAVOLTA (latters' albums 'THE GIFT' 1989 and 'THE GUN DIDN'T KNOW I WAS LOADED' (1992)

— **PAT LEONARD** – bass; returned to repl. CHUCK FREEMAN

1989. (lp/cd) *<TAANG 30/+CD>* **BRAVE NOISE**
– Falling / Brave noise / Nothing changes / Things are going by / Car crash / Separate hearts / Instrumental No.3 / In the way / 2500 club / Into the forest / June 7th / Through the door / Lights. *(UK-iss.Mar93; same as US)*

— **CHAMBERS** recruited **JEFF GODDARD** – bass / **JAMIE VAN BRAMER** – drums (both ex-JONES VERY) **BEN SEGAL** – guitar

— now **CHAMBERS, LEONARD + PAT BRADY** – drums / **CHUCK FREEMAN** – bass

Taang! / Taang!

1990. (7") *<(TAANG 43)>* **AWAY FROM ME. /**

Roadrunner / Taang!

May 91. (cd/lp) *(TG 9304-2/-1) <TAANG 54>* **FALL**
– Taang intro / Only fun in life / Fumble / Answer / Can you blame me / Travel music / Away from me / No soul / Blind / Once upon a time / Overrated / Awesome sky / Fake it.
Jun 93. (cd-ep) *<TAANG 72>* **LAST OF THE ANGELS EP**
– Last of the angels / Babble / No quarter / Answer II.

KEN CHAMBERS

— now with **PAT** + new drummer **J. ARCARI**

City Slang / City Slang

Dec 92. (7") *<(efa 0490645)>* **BLOOD & FLOWERS. /**

Plastic Head / Plastic Head

Apr 93. (7") *<(PHD 001)>* **TAKE THIS RIDE. /**

Taang! / Taang!

Jun 93. (lp/cd/cd) *<(TAANG 73/+MC/CD)>* **TAKE THIS RIDE**
– Last of the angels / Story / A thousand times / Unwind / The right way / Take this ride / Alright / Reason to believe / Take that away / Answer II / Erase / Drown it out.
Aug 94. (7") *<(TAANG 83)>* **ABOVE YOU. / TEMPTATION**
(cd-s+=) *<(TAANG 83CD)>* – Jesus Christ superstar / Wiped out / Above you (demo).
— with **JEFF GODDARD** – bass / **GLENN FOSTER BROWN** – keyboards
Nov 94. (cd) *<(T 84CD)>* **NO REACTION**
– Smile / No reaction / In between / Above you / Temptation / Too hard to wait / Here and gone / Operation / No sin / Play the blues / Wintergreen.
— KEN continued with BULLET LAVOLTA

Stuart MOXHAM & THE ORIGINAL ARTISTS (see under ⇒ YOUNG MARBLE GIANTS)

MR. T EXPERIENCE

Formed: Berkeley/East Bay Gilman Street, California, USA . . . mid-80's by DR. FRANK (PORTMAN) and an ever revolving sequence of rhythm players. Evolving from the same terrain as megabucks superstars, GREEN DAY and RANCID, the original punk popsters have influenced a generation of gob-slobbering thrashy misfits. RAMONES-esque (in every sense of the description), the quirky ensemble debuted in 1986 with the "so-underground-it's-six-foot-deep", 'EVERYBODY'S ENTITLED TO THEIR OWN OPINION'; later re-issued by 'Lookout!', who else. After a second (and equally as poor as the first) set, MTX made their semi-cult debut for 'Lookout!' with the 'MAKING THINGS WITH LIGHT' (1990) long-player, which helped them gain acknowledgment in the San Francisco neighbourhood. GREEN DAY, who were taken aback by the combo, described themselves as "the little brothers of MTX" when they started to promote their punky antics in the area. Very much like their musical siblings, MTX defined the cartoon punk ethics with their shouty, power chord rock'n'roll that has been very much the same throughout all their releases including such albums as 'MILK, MILK, LEMONADE' (1992), 'OUR BODIES, OUR SELVES' (1994), 'LOVE IS DEAD' (1995) and arguably their best, 'REVENGE IS SWEET AND SO ARE YOU' (1997). The band's latest set (with 'God knows who' in the line up, as it changed so many times that FRANK wittily suggested re-forming as MTX STARSHIP) 'ALCATRAZ', finally gained the post-punk credit it deserved when released on these shores in 1999. One only wonders, however, why GREEN DAY are selling out stadiums when it should be the work of their big brother. • **Covered:** PLEASANT VALLEY SUNDAY (hit; Monkees) / NO MILK TODAY (Herman's Hermits) / I FEEL LOVE (Donna Summer) / UP AND DOWN (. . . Moss) / FLYING JELLY ATTACK (. . . Yomano) / SEX OFFENDER (Blondie) / SOMEBODY WANTS TO LOVE YOU (Appel-Cretecos-Farrell) / SPIDERMAN (Harris-Webster) / CAN'T GET THERE FROM HERE (R.E.M.) / SPEED RACER (Shonen Knife) / DON'T GO AWAY GO GO GIRL (Radcliffe-Scott) / etc

Album rating: EVERYBODY'S ENTITLED TO THEIR OWN OPINION mini (*4) / NIGHT SHIFT AT THE THRILL FACTORY (*5) / MAKING THINGS WITH LIGHT (*6) / MILK, MILK, LEMONADE (*7) / OUR BODIES, OUR SELVES (*6) / LOVE IS DEAD (*6) / BIG BLACK BUGS BLEED BLUE BLOOD compilation + mini-set (*6) / REVENGE IS SWEET AND SO ARE YOU (*5) / ALCATRAZ (*6) / . . .AND THE WOMEN WHO LOVE THEM compilation + mini-set (*6) / Dr. Frank: SHOW BUSINESS IS MY LIFE (*5)

DR. FRANK (PORTMAN) – vocals, guitar / **JON VON** – rhythm guitar, vocals / **AARON ELLIOTT** – bass / **ALEX** – drums, vocals

not iss. / Disorder

1986. (m-lp) **EVERYBODY'S ENTITLED TO THEIR OWN OPINION**
– One big lie / Just your way of saying no / Marine recruiter / Sheep / Surfin' Mozart / Danny Partridge / Scientific / Disconnection / Surfin' cows / I'm in love with Paula Pierce / Big mistake / Pleasany valley Sunday / Mary Mary / Empty experience. *<cd-iss. 1990 on 'Lookout' cd+=; LOOKOUT 39CD>* (UK-iss.Jul95 on 'Lookout' cd/lp; same as US)

not iss. / Rough Trade

1987. (lp) **NIGHT SHIFT AT THE THRILL FACTORY**
– Now we are twenty-one / Don't know what I'll do if you don't / Predictable / Mind is a terrible thing / Skatin' cows / Go away / What is punk? / The history of the concept of the soul / Say goodnight / Velveeta / She did me in / Wearing out / No milk today / Slagbag / A zillion years / Itching powder in sleeping bags / Dick with ears / I ain't gonna be history / Kenny smokes cloves / Time for your medicine / Boredom zone / At Gilman Street. *<(UK+re-iss. Aug96 on 'Lookout' cd+=/lp; LOOKOUT 144 CD/LP)>*

MR. T EXPERIENCE (cont)

				Lookout	Lookout
1989.	(m-lp/m-c) <ROUGH-US 68/+C> **BIG BLACK BUGS BLEED BLUE BLOOD**			-	

– Super sonic / Up and down / On the team / At Gilman Street / Dictionary girl / End of the Ramones / Song about a girl who went shopping.

				Lookout	Lookout
1990.	(7") <L 023> **SO LONG SUCKER. / ZERO**			-	
1990.	(cd/lp) <LOOKOUT 37 CD/LP> **MAKING THINGS WITH LIGHT**			-	

– What went wrong / She's no rocket scientist / What's in the cuckoo clock / I don't get it / Zero / Pig Latin / Parasite / I'm breaking out / So long, sucker / Weekend in Hogboro / Psycho girl / The girl who still lives at home / Send me a postcard / Untitled spoken word piece / Now we are twenty-one / Danny Partridge got busted / Marine recruiter / Slagbag / Velveeta / A zillion years / The history of the concept of the soul / Flying jelly attack. *(UK-iss.Jul95; same as US)*

1991. (one-sided-7") <L 045> **LOVE AMERICAN STYLE**

Jan 92. (cd/lp) <LOOKOUT 49 CD/LP> **MILK, MILK, LEMONADE**
– Book of revelation / What do you want? / Ready set go / Two-minute itch / There's something wrong with me / Master of the situation / What difference does it make / Last time I listened to you / Love American style / Christine bactine / I love you, but you're standing on my foot / Makeup / See it now.

1993. (7"ep) <L 068> **GUN CRAZY EP**
– More than toast / Swallow everything / Together tonight.

Jan 94. (cd/lp) <LOOKOUT 80 CD/LP> **OUR BODIES, OUR SELVES**
– Somebody who cares / Love manifesto / The dustbin of history / Personality seminar / Are you there God? it's me Margaret / Martyr / Even Hitler had a girlfriend / Bridge to Taribithia / I feel love / More than toast / Swallow everything / Not guilty / Game over / Will you still love me when I don't love you? / Together tonight / God bless America. *(UK cd-iss. Jul95; same as US)*

Mar 95. (cd-ep) <LOOKOUT 106CD> **... AND THE WOMEN WHO LOVE THEM**
– Tapin' up my heart / My stuped life / I believe in you / All my promises / Checkers speech / We hate all the same things / Now that you are gone.

Jun 95. (7"ep/cd-ep; shared w/ GOOBER PATROL) <(PAD 001/+CD)> **FROM OUT OF SPACE E.P.**
(above issued on 'Punk As Dunk')

Sep 95. (7") <(LOOKOUT 126)> **ALTERNATIVE IS HERE TO STAY. / NEW GIRLFRIEND** *Aug95*
(cd-s+=) <(LOOKOUT 126CD)> – You today / ('A'-alt. version).

Jan 96. (lp/cd) <(LK 134/+CD)> **LOVE IS DEAD**
– Sackcloth and ashes / Ba ba ba ba ba / I just wanna do it with you / Somebody's song / Thank you (for not being one of them) / Dumb little band / Hangin' on to you / The future ain't what it used to be / I fell for you / Deep deep down / Can I do the thing? / I'd do anything for you / Semi-ok / I'm like yeah, but she's all no / That prozac moment / You're the only one.

—— **JOEL** – bass / **JYM** – drums (joined **DR. FRANK**)

Aug 97. (7"m) <LK 164> **...AND I WILL BE WITH YOU. / DON'T GO BREAKING MY HEART / YOU ALONE** *Jul97*

Sep 97. (cd/lp) <LK 180 CD/LP> **REVENGE IS SWEET AND SO ARE YOU** *Aug97*
– Here she comes / She's coming (over tonight) / Love is dead / Hell of dumb / Lawnmower of love / With my looks␣your brains / The weather is here, wish you were beautiful / Another yesterday / Swiss army girlfriend / ...And I will be with you / Who needs happiness (I'd rather have you) / When I lost you / I don't need to know / Our love will last forever and ever / Some foggy mountain top / You you you.

Sep 99. (cd/lp) <LK 232 CD/LP> **ALCATRAZ**
– I wrote a book about rock and roll / Naomi / Self-pity / Hey Emily / Tomorrow is a harsh mistress / The two of us / Our days are numbered / We're not no one / Re-activate your heart / Perhaps / She's my Alcatraz / I feel for you / We'll get by.

—— **GABE MELINE** – bass; repl. AARON

—— added **ERIC NOYES** – keyboards

Oct 00. (cd-ep) <LK 254> **THE MIRACLE OF SHAME** *Sep00*
– Spy vs. spy / Leaving the thinking to the smart people / Mr. Ramones / I don't know where Dan Treacy lives / Stephanies of the world unite.

– compilations, others, etc. –

May 97. (10"lp/cd) *Lookout;* <(LOOKOUT 145/+CD)> **BIG BLACK BUGS BLEED BLUE BLOOD**
– (the EP tracks) / Flying jelly attack / So long sucker / Zero / Psycho girl / Fill in the blank / How I made a million in a punk rock band / Look back and crack / Sex offender / Last time I listened to you / Love American style / Somebody wants to love you / Spiderman / Can't get there from here / God bless America / Let's be together tonight / Merry fucking Christmas / Speed racer / T-shirt commercial / Vive le France / More than toast / Swallow everything / God bless Lawrence Livermore / Don't go away go go girl / Hello Kitty Menendez.

Feb 02. (cd) *Lookout;* <(LK 273CD)> **...AND THE WOMEN WHO LOVE THEM**
– Tapin' up my heart / My stupid life / I believe in you / All my problems / Checkers speech / We hate all the same things / Now that you're gone / How'd the date end? / Alternative is here to stay / You today / New girlfriend / Yeah, yeah, yeah, yeah / Unpack your adjectives / Sackcloth and ashes (demo) / Is there something I should know? / We are the future people of tomorrow / Whistle bait / Crash / Another yesterday / You alone / Don't go breakin' my heart / As life goes on, you get more and more out of it / King Dork / I was losing you all along.

DR. FRANK

with **KEVIN ARMY** – guitar / **AARON COMETBUS** – bass, drums / **EVAN EUSTIS** – bass

		Lookout!	Lookout!
May 99.	(cd/lp) <LK 222 CD/LP> **SHOW BUSINESS IS MY LIFE**		Apr99

– She turned out to be crazy / I made you and I can break you / Knock-knock (please let me in) / Suicide watch / Bitter homes and gardens / She all right / Ask Beth / Population: Us / Thinking of you / I'm in love with what's-her-name / Two martinis from now / Sad, sad shadow / This isn't about you anymore.

MUDHONEY

Formed: Seattle, Washington, USA ... 1988 by MARK ARM (vocals, guitar), STEVE TURNER (guitar), MATT LUKIN (bass) and DAN PETERS (drums). A band boasting impeccable credentials, ARM and TURNER had both graduated from the seminal GREEN RIVER (and The THROWN UPS), while LUKIN had previously been a member of Seattle noisemongers, The MELVINS. With as much a claim to the 'Godfathers of Grunge' crown as labelmates NIRVANA, MUDHONEY released the definitive 'Sub Pop' single in 1988 with 'TOUCH ME I'M SICK'. Arguably one of the few tracks to ever match the primal howl of The STOOGES, the single was a revelation, a cathartically dumb three chord bludgeon with ARM shrieking over the top like a man who was, erm, very sick indeed. A mini-album followed shortly after, the wonderfully titled 'SUPERFUZZ BIGMUFF' (rather disappointingly named after STEVE TURNER's favourite effects pedals, apparently). Visceral, dirty, fuzz-drenched rock'n'roll, this was one of the seminal records of the 80's and the blueprint for "grunge", a term that would later become bastardised to represent a glut of snooze-worthy, sub-metal toss. There was also a deep, underlying sense of unease and melancholy to these songs (especially 'NO ONE HAS' and 'NEED') that gave MUDHONEY an edge over most of their contemporaries, a subsequent cover of SONIC YOUTH'S 'HALLOWEEN' (released as a split single with SONIC YOUTH covering 'TOUCH ME..') sounding positively evil. Given all this, then, the debut album proper, 'MUDHONEY', was regarded as something of a disappointment when it was finally released in late '89. Nevertheless, 'THIS GIFT' and 'HERE COMES SICKNESS' were worth the price of admission alone. By summer '91, MUDHONEY had modified their sound somewhat, releasing the 'LET IT SLIDE' EP as a taster for the forthcoming 'EVERY GOOD BOY DESERVES FUDGE' album (a UK Top 40 hit). The intensity of the EP harked back to 'SUPERFUZZ..', this time with more of a retro garage-punk feel on the blistering 'PAPERBACK LIFE' and 'OUNCE OF DECEPTION'. The album continued in this direction, adding funky (in the loosest sense of the term) hammond organ and harmonica to the mutant guitar buzz. Hell, they even came close to a pop song with 'GOOD ENOUGH'. Following a financial dispute with 'Sub Pop', MUDHONEY followed NIRVANA into the big league, signing with 'Reprise' and releasing the lacklustre 'PIECE OF CAKE' (1992). Having sold their souls to the corporate 'devil', it seemed MUDHONEY had had the life sucked out of them, the rough edges smoothed into a major production gloss. The mini-album, 'FIVE DOLLAR BOB'S MOCK COOTER STEW' (1993) was an improvement but it took Seattle legend, Jack Endino to summon forth the raw spontaneity of old on 'MY BROTHER THE COW' (1995), a return to form of sorts, notably on 'INTO YOUR SCHTIK' and 'GENERATION SPOKESMODEL'. MUDHONEY subsequently took a few years hiatus in which ARM went on tour with his side-project, BLOODLOSS, while TURNER continued with his label, 'Super-Electro' (MUDHONEY were allowed dual output for the imprint) and PETERS guested for solo MIKE JOHNSON (DINOSAUR JR). In the Autumn of '98, the quartet were back once again, although the album, TOMORROW HIT TODAY', disappointed most of their hardcore fanbase. Recorded in just over a week, emboldened by blasts of neo-free jazz horns and adrenalised by an undertow of twisted gutter-funk, 'SINCE WE'VE BECOME TRANSLUCENT' (2002) was the sound of MUDHONEY rediscovering that mutant garage gene that made them so seminal in the first place. • **Covers:** HATE THE POLICE (Dicks) / EVOLUTION (Spacemen 3) / OVER THE TOP (Motorhead) / PUMP IT UP (Elvis Costello) / TONIGHT I THINK I'M GONNA GO DOWNTOWN (Jimmie Dale Gilmore) / BUCKSKIN STALLION BLUES (Townes Van Zandt). MARK ARM solo:- MASTERS OF WAR (Bob Dylan).

Album rating: SUPERFUZZ BIGMUFF mini (*7) / MUDHONEY (*6) / BOILED BEEF & ROTTING TEETH (*6) / EVERY GOOD BOY DESERVES FUDGE (*7) / PIECE OF CAKE (*5) / MY BROTHER THE COW (*5) / TOMORROW TODAY (*5) / MARCH TO FUZZ compilation (*7) / SINCE WE'VE BECOME TRANSLUCENT (*6) / Monkeywrench: CLEAN AS A BROKE-DICK DOG (*6) / ELECTRIC CHILDREN (*7)

MARK ARM (b.21 Feb'62, California) – vocals, guitar (ex-GREEN RIVER, ex-THROWN UPS) / **STEVE TURNER** (b.28 Mar'65, Houston, Texas) – guitar (ex-GREEN RIVER, ex-THROWN UPS) / **MATT LUKIN** (b.16 Aug'64, Aberdeen, Washington) – bass (ex-MELVINS) / **DAN PETERS** (b.18 Aug'67) – drums

		Glitterhouse	Sub Pop
Aug 88.	(7",7"brown) <SP 18> **TOUCH ME I'M SICK. / SWEET YOUNG THING AIN'T SWEET NO MORE**	-	
Oct 88.	(12"ep) (GR 0034) <SP 21> **SUPERFUZZ BIGMUFF** – No one has / If I think / In 'n' out of grace / Need / Chain that door / Mudride. (cd-iss. Mar00; same as US)		
Jan 89.	(7",7"clear) <SP 26> ('A'side by 'Sonic Youth'). / **TOUCH ME I'M SICK**		-
Jun 89.	(7",7"white) (GR 060) <SP 33> **YOU GOT IT (KEEP IT OUTTA MY FACE). / BURN IT CLEAN / NEED (demo)** *(re-iss. May93; same)*		
Oct 89.	(7",7"purple,12") (GR 0070) <SP 44AA> **THIS GIFT. / BABY HELP ME FORGET / REVOLUTION** *(re-iss. May93; same)*		
Oct 89	(lp/c/cd) (GR 0069) <SP 44/+A/B> **MUDHONEY** – This gift / Flat out f***ed / Get into yours / You got it / Magnolia caboose babyshit / Come to mind / Here comes sickness / Running loaded / The further I go / By her own hand / When tomorrow hits / Dead love. (cd re-iss. Mar00; same as US)		
Jun 90.	(7",7"pink) (GR 0102) <SP 63> **YOU'RE GONE. / THORN / YOU MAKE ME DIE** *(re-iss. May93; same)*	60	

431

MUDHONEY (cont)

		Sub Pop	Sub Pop
Jul 91.	(7",12"grey) *(SP 15154)* <SP 95> **LET IT SLIDE. / OUNCE OF DECEPTION / CHECKOUT TIME**	60	
	(cd-s+=) *(SP 95B)* – Paperback life / The money will roll right in.		
Aug 91.	(lp/c/cd) <(SP 160/+A/B)> **EVERY GOOD BOY DESERVES FUDGE**	34	
	– Generation genocide / Let it slide / Good enough / Something so clear / Thorn / Into the drink / Broken hands / Who you drivin' now / Move out / Shoot the Moon / Fuzzgun '91 / Poking around / Don't fade IV / Check out time.		
1991.	(7") *<scale 36>* **MOD SHOWDOWN!**	-	
	– She's just fifteen / (track by HALO OF FLIES) (above issued on 'Amphetamine Reptile' + below on 'eMpTy')		
1991.	(7") *<MT 166>* **YOU STUPID ASSHOLE.** (w/ Gas HUFFER)	-	

— MARK + STEVE took up time in MONKEYWRENCH, and DAN joined SCREAMING TREES, after below album.

		Warners	Reprise
Oct 92.	(7"/c-s) *(W 0137/+C)* **SUCK YOU DRY. / DECEPTION PASS**	65	-
	(12"+=/cd-s+=) *(W 0137/TCD)* – Underride / Over the top.		
Oct 92.	(cd/c) *(4509 90073-2/-4)* **PIECE OF CAKE**	39	
	– No end in sight / Make it now / Suck you dry / Blinding sun / Thirteenth floor opening / Youth body expression explosion / I'm spun / Take me there / Living wreck / Let me let you down / Ritzville / Acetone.		
Jan 93.	(cd-ep) *(40741)* **BLIDING SUN / DECEPTION PASS / KING SANDBOX / BABY O BABY**	-	
Oct 93.	(m-cd/m-c/m-lp) *(9362 45439-2/-4)* **FIVE DOLLAR BOB'S MOCK COOTER STEW**		
	– In the blood / No song III / Between you & me kid / Six two one / Make it now again / Deception pass / Underide.		

— In Mar'94, MUDHONEY released a collab with JIMMIE DALE GILMOUR; 7"yellow/cd-ep 'BUCKSKIN STALLION BLUES' for 'Sub Pop' (SP 124/305/+CD) Also a single, 'PUMP IT UP, was released by 'Fox' in April '94

		Reprise	Reprise
Mar 95.	(cd/c/lp) *(9362 45840-2/-4/-1)* **MY BROTHER THE COW**	70	
	– Judgement, rage, retribution and thyme / Generation spokesmodel / What moves the heart? / Today, is a good day / Into yer schtik / In my finest suit / F.D.K. (Fearless Doctor KIllers) / Orange ball-pen hammer / Crankcase blues / Execution style / Dissolve / 1995.		
Apr 95.	(7") *(SE 708)* **INTO YOUR SCHTIK. / YOU GIVE ME THE CREEPS**		
	(above single on 'Super Electro')		
May 95.	(7"colrd/c-s) *(W 0292/+C)* **GENERATION SPOKESMODEL. / NOT GOING DOWN THAT ROAD AGAIN**		
	(cd-s+=) *(W 0292CD)* – What moves the heart live) / Judgement, rage, retribution and thyme (live).		

		Amphetam. Reptile	Amphetam. Reptile
Aug 95.	(7") *<scale 76>* **GOAT CHEESE.** / (w/ Strapping Fieldhands)		
	(above on 'Amphetamine Reptile' and below on 'Super Electro')		
May 98.	(ltd-7") *(SE 716)* **NIGHT OF THE HUNTED. / BRAND NEW FACE**		
Sep 98.	(cd) <(9362 47054-2)> **TOMORROW HIT TODAY**		
	– A thousand forms of mind / I have to laugh / Oblivion / Try to be kind / Poisoned water / Real low vibe / This is the life / Night of the hunted / Move with the wind / Ghost / I will fight no more forever / Beneath the valley of the underdog.		

— MATT LUKIN departed in '99; **GUY MADDISON** – bass (replaced him)

		Sub Pop	Sub Pop
Aug 02.	(lp/cd) <(SP 555/+CD)> **SINCE WE'VE BECOME TRANSLUCENT**		
	– Baby, can you dig the light / The straight life / Where the flavor is / In the winner's circle / Our time is now / Dyin' for it / Inside job / Take it like a man / Crooked and wide / Sonic infusion.		
Sep 02.	(7") *(SP 603)* **SONIC INFUSION. / A LONG WAY TO GO**		-

– compilations, etc. –

Nov 89.	(cd-ep) *Tupelo; (TUPCD 009) / Sub Pop; <SP 62>* **BOILED BEEF AND ROTTING TEETH**		
Jan 00.	(cd) *Strange Fruit; (SFRSCD 090)* **THE RADIO SESSIONS**		
Mar 00.	(t-lp/d-cd) *Sub Pop; <(SP/+CD 500)>* **MARCH TO FUZZ**		
	– In 'n' out of grace / Suck you dry / I have to laugh / Sweet young thing ain't sweet no more / Who you drivin' now / You got it / Judgement, rage, retribution and thyme / Into the drink / A thousand forms of mind / Generation genocide / If I think / Here comes sickness / Let it slide / Touch me I'm sick / This gift / Good enough / Blinding sun / Into your shtik / Beneath the valley of the underdog / When tomorrow hits / Make it now again / Hate the police / Hey sailor / Twenty four / Baby help me forget / Revolution / You stupid asshole / Who is who / Stab yor back / Pump it up / The money will roll right in / Fix me / Dehumanized / She's just 15 / Baby o baby / Over the top / You goive me the creeps / March to fuzz / Ounce of deception / Paperback life / Bushpusher man / Fuzzbeater / Overblown / Run shithead run / King sandbox / Tonight I think I'm gonna go downtown / Holden / Not going down that road again / Brand new face / Drinking for two / Butterfly stroke / Editions of you.		

THROWN UPS

STEVE TURNER + MARK ARM + ED FOTHERINGHAM – vocals + **LEIGHTON BEEZER** – bass

		not iss.	Amphetam. Reptile
1987.	(ltd-7"ep) *<Scale 5>* **FELCH / LARD BUTT. / YER BAND SUCKS / SHE'S FAT**		-
1988.	(ltd-7"ep) *<Scale 7>* **SMILING PANTIES. / ELEPHANT CRACK / MY COCK IS THE COIN**		-
1989.	(ltd-7"ep) *<Scale 10>* **EAT MY DUMP / FLUBBERMATE. / LADIES LOVE ME / SCABBY LIKE MY LOVE**		-
1990.	(3x7"box) *<Scale 26>* **MELANCHOLY GIRLHOLE** (3 singles boxed)		-
Jan 97.	(cd) *<AR 55>* **SEVEN YEARS GOLDEN** (compilation)		-
	– Yer band sucks / She's fat / Eat my dump / Flubbermate / Bucking retards / Dude pump / The person in my bowel (is sad) / Fleshy web pit / Elephant crack / My cock is the coin / Hairy crater man / Sparse tits / Smiling panties / Be correct / Melancholy girlhole / Stock boy, superhero / Felch / Lard Butt / Sloppy pud love / Hot lunch / Ladies love me / Scabby like my love / My love is simple / R ladies R bitches / Patty has a problem / Slick lip / Thorp, Thorp.		

THE FREEWHEELIN' MARK ARM

		Sub Pop	Sub Pop
Feb 91.	(7",7"red,7"green) <(SP 87)> **MASTERS OF WAR. / MY LIFE WITH RICKETS**		Dec90

MONKEYWRENCH

— **MARK + STEVE** plus **TOM PRICE, TIM KERR + MARTIN BLAND**

		Sub Pop	Sub Pop
Jan 91.	(7") *<SP 139>* **BOTTLE UP AND GO. / COLD COLD WORLD (WITHOUT ORGAN) / OUT OF FOCUS**		-
Jan 92.	(lp/c/cd) *<SP 129/+C/CD>* **CLEAN AS A BROKE-DICK DOG**		
	– I call my body home / Angelhead / Cold cold world / Codine / From you / Doubled over again / Great down here / Look back / Bottle up & go / The story as I was told / Notes & chords mean nothing to me / Stop this world / I'm blown.		

		not iss.	Dutch East
1995.	(7") *<DEI 9037-7>* **SHUTDOWN.** / (track by Holez)	-	

		not iss.	Estrus
Mar 00.	(7") *<ES 7149>* **SUGAR MAN. / THE PUSHER**	-	
Apr 00.	(lp) *<(ES 126-9)>* **ELECTRIC CHILDREN**		
	– Solar revelations / The empty place / Thirteen nights / Love is a spider / In the city tonight / The weasel's in the barn / Cherry red / Bring on the judgement day / From now on / Around again / Day trader shuffle / Sugar man / In the days of the five. (cd-iss. on 'Sweet Nothing'; SNCD 005)		

Mark MULCAHY (see under ⇒ MIRACLE LEGION)

Peter MURPHY (see under ⇒ BAUHAUS)

MUSIC FOR PLEASURE

Formed: Leeds, England . . . 1980 by MARK COPSON, DAVE WHITAKER and MARTIN KING, the trio adding ex-GIRLS AT OUR BEST drummer, CHRIS OLDROYD, following the release of their debut 45, 'THE HUMAN FACTOR.' Very much part of the uptempo-electro-pop-with-droning-vocals brigade, MFP delivered a similarly themed follow-up single, 'FUEL TO THE FIRE', before signing a major label deal with 'Polydor'. In 1982, with KING having made way for IVAN ROBERTS, the synth crew issued an inaugural long-player, 'INTO THE RAIN', a more reflective effort mapping out similar territory to OMD and early SIMPLE MINDS. Moving back to the more sympathetic climes of the indie sector, MUSIC FOR PLEASURE began recording for the tiny 'Whirlpool' imprint, releasing a few singles and a mini-album, 'BLACKLANDS' (1986), before calling it a day. Two of their members, WHITAKER and OLDROYD, took up more high profile posts with DANSE SOCIETY and RED LORRY YELLOW LORRY respectively.

Album rating: INTO THE RAIN (*6) / BLACKLANDS mini (*4)

MARK COPSON – vocals / **DAVE WHITAKER** – keyboards, synthesizer / **MARTIN KING** – bass / . . . **PEACE** – guitar / . . . **LEWIS** – drums

		Rage-DJM	not iss.
Nov 80.	(7") *(RAGE 1)* **THE HUMAN FACTOR. / MURDER AT THE MISSION**		-

— **CHRIS OLDROYD** – drums (ex-GIRLS AT OUR BEST) repl. LEWIS + PEACE

Feb 81.	(7") *(RAGE 2)* **FUEL TO THE FIRE. / DEBRIS**		-

— **IVAN ROBERTS** – bass; repl. KING

		Polydor	not iss.
Jul 82.	(7") *(POSP 464)* **SWITCHBACK. / I RECALL**		-
Aug 82.	(lp/c) *(POLS/+C 1070)* **INTO THE RAIN**		-
	– Light / Switchback / Nostalgia / Time / New day / Lost detail / Winterscene / Aim to life / Warehouse / Underworld.		
Oct 82.	(7") *(POSP 533)* **LIGHT. / MALEFICE**		-
	(12") *(POSPX 533)* – ('A'side) / Nostalgia.		
Jan 83.	(7") *(POSP 553)* **TIME. / SLIDE**		-
	(12") *(POSPX 553)* – ('A'side) / Switchback.		
May 83.	(7") *(POSP 594)* **DARK CRASH. / URBAN POISON**		-
	(12"+=) *(POSPX 594)* – Blacklands.		

		Whirlpool	not iss.
Jan 84.	(7") *(WH 1)* **DISCONNECTION. / WHIPLASH CARESS**		-
May 84.	(12"ep) *(WH 4)* **CHROME HIT CORROSION**		-
	– Pleasure ride / Grey parade / Walking / The rise.		
Jan 86.	(m-lp) *(WHLP 6)* **BLACKLANDS**		-
	– Remember the sun / Disconnection (part 1) / Look around you / Blue / Whiplash caress / Grey parade / Disconnection (part 2) / Drive.		

— had already disbanded before above. WHITAKER joined DANSE SOCIETY while OLDROYD was snapped up by RED LORRY YELLOW LORRY

MY DAD IS DEAD

Formed: Cleveland, Ohio, USA ... summer 1984 by sticksman-cum-guitarist, MARK EDWARDS, the man recently departing from RIOT ARCHITECTURE. MY DAD IS DEAD was essentially MARK EDWARD'S solo project with an ever changing succession of backing musicians. The early output of MDID beginning with debut 'AND HE'S NOT GONNA TAKE IT' (1986), 'PEACE LOVE AND MURDER' (1987), 'LET'S SKIP THE DETAILS' (1988) – which featured JOHN McENTIRE (later of TORTOISE) and 'THE BEST DEFENSE' (also released in 1988) were largely experimental and self-indulgent lacking any real direction. It was not until the release of 'THE TALLER YOU ARE, THE SHORTER YOU GET' that the music began to show signs of cohesion. EDWARDS' prolific output continued throughout the 90s releasing the 'SHINE' EP at the turn of the decade followed by 'CHOPPING DOWN THE FAMILY TREE' (1991) and 'OUT OF SIGHT OUT OF MIND' two years later. It was the release of 'FOR RICHER FOR POORER' in 1995 that saw the band's full potential realised with the inclusion of SCOTT PICKERING and MATT SWANSON, EDWARDS had finally constructed a band who could accommodate his starkly moving lyrics and limited vocal range. This promising new direction continued on the 1997 follow up 'EVERYONE WANTS THE HONEY BUT NOT THE STING' which established EDWARDS as one of the better underground lyricists. With a new drummer, SHAYNE IVY, MDID delivered their comeback set, 'THE ENGINE OF COMMERCE' (2002).

Album rating: THE BEST DEFENSE compilation 1986/87 (*5) / LET'S SKIP THE DETAILS (*6) / THE TALLER YOU ARE, THE SHORTER YOU GET (*7) / SHINE(R) mini (*4) / CHOPPING DOWN THE FAMILY TREE (*5) / OUT OF SIGHT, OUT OF MIND; as MDID (*5) / FOR RICHER, FOR POORER (*5) / EVERYONE WANTS THE HONEY BUT NOT THE STING (*3) / THE ENGINE OF COMMERCE (*5)

MARK EDWARDS – vocals, guitar (ex-RIOT ARCHITECTURE) with a drum machine

		not iss.	St. Valentine
May 86.	(lp) **AND HE'S NOT GONNA TAKE IT ANYMORE**	-	
		not iss.	Birth
May 87.	(lp) **PEACE, LOVE AND MURDER**	-	

— helped by **CHRIS BURGESS** – bass, vocals

		Homestead	Homestead
Jul 88.	(lp/c/cd) <(HMS 109/+C/CD)> **LET'S SKIP THE DETAILS**		May88

– Baby's got a problem / Put it away / Lay down the law / Boiling over / Not a pretty sight / Five minutes / The escape artists / On holy ground / The water's edge / Bad judgement day.

Dec 88. (lp/c/cd) <HMS 127/+C/CD> **THE BEST DEFENSE** (compilation from first two albums) | - | |
– In the mourning / When elephants fight, the grass gets / Anti-socialist 2 / For your trouble / Pile it on / Cut out / It's not what you said / Chopsticks / Hole in my eye / The best defense.

— added **JEFF CURTIS** – bass / **JOHN McENTIRE** – drums

— after a few sessions, McENTIRE joined BASTRO – and later TORTOISE – (CURTIS also shirked touring) **CHRIS BURGESS + SCOTT PICKERING** (of PRISONSHAKE) took over their duties

Dec 89. (d-lp/c/cd) <HMS 146/+C/CD> **THE TALLER YOU ARE, THE SHORTER YOU GET** | - | |
– For lack of a better word / The big picture / Seven years / Too far gone / Planes crashing / Boundaries / Can't get started / Only one / World on a string / What can I do / Whirlpool / Nothing special / Man possessed / So much to lose.

		Houses in Motion	Scat
Apr 90.	(m-lp) **SHINE(R)**	-	

– Weatherman / Nothing special / Red eye / 20 yards deep / Morning after / Like a vise / Sabotage / Beg borrow steal / Gone gonna rise / Dreamland / Pillow talk / Empty glass / All my strength / Only one / Taxi driver / Always and forever / Bittersweet / In your mind / Babe in the woods / Babe. <(UK cd+re-iss. Jun96 on 'Emperor Jones'; EJ 05CD)>

1990. (7") **FLESH COLORED HOUSE. / (split w/ BASTRO)** | - | |
(above issued on 'Clawfist')

— added **TIM GILBRIDE** – guitar / **DOUG GILLARD** – guitar (below album also featured past members)

Feb 92. (lp/cd) (efa 06178/+CD) <SCAT 22/+CD> **CHOPPING DOWN THE FAMILY TREE** | | Oct91 |
– Cool rain / Deliver me home / Chopping down the family tree / Journey / Know how to run / Come to me / Without a doubt / Shine / The last time / Walk on water / Outside my window / Don't burn down the bridge.

— **MATT SWANSON** – bass; repl. BURGESS who remained the engineer (PICKERING also moved on)

Oct 93. (cd; as MDID) <SCAT 32CD> **OUT OF SIGHT, OUT OF MIND** | - | |
– Untitled / She's in love / Had to laugh / Legacy / Never was / Razor sharp / Sight unseen / Racing heart / Prisoner / You are the one.

		Emperor Jones	Emperor Jones
Nov 95.	(cd) <(EJ 01CD)> **FOR RICHER, FOR POORER**		May95

– Evolution / Heirloom / Coat of armor / I had a dream / Play the game / Crazy world / Something more / I think I should / Way too wise / Recharge / Chasing shadows / Deja vu / Nasty little habit.

Oct 97. (cd/lp) <(EJ 16 CD/LP)> **EVERYONE WANTS THE HONEY BUT NOT THE STING** | | |
– Don't look now / Statistician's day off / King is dead / Lesson #1 / Deer on the highway / Year of loss / Two pills in the water / Harvesting / Two clean slates / Ghost attack / Million questions.

— new drummer **SHAYNE IVY**

		not iss.	Vital Cog
2002.	(cd) <COG 226-2> **THE ENGINE OF COMMERCE**	-	

– All we want / Sleight of hand / Finger on the pulse / Stories left untold / Urgency / The engine of commerce / Labor of love / Strange highway / In command / Physical fitness / On my way / Out of the mouths of babes / Let's be DIY / Nobody else but you / Winners and losers / Memory of your kiss.

THE GREAT INDIE DISCOGRAPHY — The 1980s

NAKED PREY

Formed: Tucson, Arizona, USA . . . 1981 by ex-SERFERS and KRELS frontman, VAN CHRISTIAN, alongside DAVID K. SEGER, RICHARD BADENIOUS and SAM BLAKE. Part of the early-mid 80's roots/retro US rock revival that also included DREAM SYNDICATE, GREEN ON RED and GIANT SAND, NAKED PREY were first given a break by the scene's pivotal but tiny 'Down There' label. The eponymous DAN STUART (GREEN ON RED)-produced mini-set (in '84) showed a lot of promise, enough for 'Frontier' records ('Zippo' in the UK) to take them on for a debut album proper, 'UNDER THE BLUE MARLIN', a few years later. Galloping desert-rock fusing NEIL YOUNG & CRAZY HORSE-esque dirgy guitar solos with sun-parched, whiskey-throated vocals, the record was a far more metallic – in a LYNYRD SKYNYRD kind of way – affair than the material offered by their aforementioned peers. Having already covered the Stooges 'DIRT' on the latter set, NAKED PREY swooped on the Rolling Stones' 'SILVER TRAIN' and Jim Webb's 'WICHITA LINEMAN', for the otherwise disappointing mini-set, '40 MILES FROM NOWHERE' (1987). Having never quite made the breakthrough they had threatened early on, NAKED PREY were fed to the critical vultures with what was supposed to be their final studio set, 'KILL THE MESSENGER', in 1989. However, CHRISTIAN and Co did recover enough to return to the studio for one more long-player, 'AND THEN I SHOT EVERYONE' (1995). • **Covered:** BILLY THE KID II (Bob Dylan) / UNDER MY WHEELS (Alice Cooper).

Album rating: NAKED PREY mini (*6) / UNDER THE BLUE MARLIN (*7) / 40 MILES FROM NOWHERE mini (*4) / KILL THE MESSENGER (*4) / AND THEN I SHOT EVERYONE (*5)

VAN CHRISTIAN – vocals, guitar / **DAVID K. SEGER** – guitar, vocals / **RICHARD BADEN(IOUS)** – bass, vocals / **SAM BLAKE** – drums

			not iss.	Down There
Nov 84.	(m-lp/m-c) <E 1126/+C> **NAKED PREY**		-	

– Flesh on the wall / Take the word / The story never ends / Freezin' steel / No place to be / Hour glass / Billy The Kid II. *(m-c+=)* – Million rifles.

— **TOM LARKINS** – drums; repl. BLAKE

		Zippo	Frontier
Jun 86.	(lp/c) (ZONG/+CASS 011) <FLP/FCX 1016> **UNDER THE BLUE MARLIN**		

– The ride / A stranger (never says goodbye) / Dirt / Train whistle / How I felt that day / Come on down / Rawhead / Voodoo godhead / Fly away / What price for freedom. *(c+=)* – Under my wheels.

Jan 88.	(m-lp) (ZANE 006) <FLP 1024> **40 MILES FROM NOWHERE**		

– 40 miles from nowhere / Ill. central *[US-only]* / Another day *[US-only]* / I'm coming home *[US-only]* / Find my way / Silver train / Sweet Marie *[US-only]* / The carnival / Rodeo *[US-only]* / Wichita lineman / Too far gone *[UK-only]*.

		Fundam.	Fundam.
Jul 89.	(lp/cd) <(SAVE 073/+CD)> **KILL THE MESSENGER**		

– One even stand / Yardman / Dr. Brown / Blue tick hound / Plastic Jesus / Ike on Mars / I saw the light / Road rash / Blind man (live in Tucson) / Night crew.

May 90.	(m-lp/m-cd) (NR 300/+CD) **LIVE IN TUCSON (live)**	-	-	Dutch

– Stalker / Rawhead / Forsaken / Blind man / The bitter end.

— VAN CHRISTIAN and p/t NAKED PREY member BILL ELM helped form FRIENDS OF DEAN MARTINEZ

— **VAN CHRISTIAN, TOM LARKINS, CHRIS CACAVAS, PAUL B CUTLER + PETE HOLMES** (guitar) + **JIM BLACKHALL** (bass)

1992.	(cd) (BOOK 1) **JUMBO'S SHINEBOX**	-	

– Touch the ground / Love letters / Automotive tips from the master / Souvenir / Beside me / It's alright / Why'd ya do it Jimmy / Edge of a knife / Lizard car / The sensitive number.

— **VAN C + LARKINS** brought in **JOHN VENET** – guitar / **DAVID HERBERT** – bass / **CRAIG SCHUMACHER** – keyboards / **RAINER PTACEK** – guitar / **RANDY McREYNOLDS** – guitar, organ, vocals / + **JOEY BURNS + CHUCK PROPHET + JOHN CONVERTINO + BRUCE HALPER** etc.

		not iss.	Epiphany
Oct 95.	(cd) <1005> **AND THEN I SHOT EVERYONE**	-	

– El grande market / Fortune teller / Now I know / Love me to death / Lucky lager / Space / It's on me / That's how much I love you / Mop it up / The bitter end / Dillonious skunk.

NAKED RAYGUN

Formed: (based) Chicago, Illinois, USA . . . 1981 by JEFF PEZZATI, his brother MARCO PEZZATI (who was almost immediately replaced by CAMILO GONZALEZ) and future BIG BLACK member, SANTIAGO DURANGO (who in turn was substituted by JOHN HAGGERTY) with subsequent addition of drummer JIM COLAO. Having garnered an early live reputation for raw (the lads played with their boots on – and nothing else!) hardcore, their first vinyl outing came in the shape of four tracks, 'BOMB SHELTER', 'LIBIDO', 'PARANOIA' and 'WHEN THE SCREAMING STOPS', featured on an Autumn 1981 V/A compilation, 'Busted At Oz' (alongside the EFFIGIES and STRIKE UNDER). With ERIC SPICER newly installed on the drumstool, NAKED RAYGUN fired out a debut EP, 'BASEMENT SCREAMS' before signing to 'Homestead' (stamping ground of DINOSAUR JR and SONIC YOUTH) for whom they released debut album, 'THROB THROB' (1984). Following the replacement of GONZALEZ with PIERRE KEZDY, the band established themselves as one of the Windy City's premier guitar assault units (alongside STEVE ALBINI's noisemongers, BIG BLACK) with 1985's sophomore album, 'ALL RISE'. After parting company with 'Homestead', NAKED RAYGUN initiated their own short-lived imprint, 'Sandpounder' – only a one-off 45, 'VANILLA BLUE', would materialise – before signing to 'Caroline' for 1988's 'JETTISON', which featured a rousing cover of Stiff Little Finger's 'SUSPECT DEVICE'. In '89, they released the follow-up, 'UNDERSTAND?', an album that disappointed many for its occasional ordinariness. One further personnel change (BILL STEPHENS for HAGGERTY) was effected prior to the band's below par swansong set, 'RAYGUN . . . NAKED RAYGUN', in 1990. • **Covered:** I DON'T MIND (Buzzcocks) / TWENTIETH CENTURY BOY (T.Rex).

Album rating: THROB THROB (*5) / ALL RISE (*7) / JETTISON (*7) / UNDERSTAND? (*4) / RAYGUN . . . NAKED RAYGUN (*4)

JEFF PEZZATI – vocals, guitar / **SANTIAGO DURANGO** – lead guitar, vocals / **CAMILO GONZALEZ** – bass; repl. MARCO PEZZATI / **JIM CALAO** – drums

		not iss.	Ruthless
1983.	(7"ep) <RRNR 03> **BASEMENT SCREAMS**	-	

– I lie / Bombshelter / Emperor Tojo / Swingo / Mofo / Potential rapist.

1983.	(7"ep) **FLAMMABLE SOLID**	-	

– Surf combat / Gear / Libido.

— **JOHN HAGGERTY** – guitar; repl. SANTIAGO DURANGO

		Homestead	Homestead
Mar 85.	(lp) <(HMS 008)> **THROB THROB**		Nov84

– Rat patrol / Surf combat / Gear / Metastasis / Leeches / Roller queen / On I don't know / Libido / Only in America / No sex / Stupid / Managua. *(cd-iss. Jul88 & Mar98; HMS 008CD)* <cd re-iss. Aug99 on 'Quarter Stick'; QS 84CD>

— **ERIC SPICER** – drums; repl. JIM COLAO
— **PIERRE KEZDY** – bass; repl. GONZALEZ

May 86.	(lp) <(HMS 045)> **ALL RISE**		Nov85

– Home of the brave / Dog at large / Knock me down / Mr. Gridlock / The strip / I remember / Those who move / The envelope / Backlash Jack / Peacemaker / New dreams. *(cd-iss. Jul88; HMS 045CD)* <cd re-iss. Aug99 on 'Quarter Stick'; QS 85CD>

		not iss.	Sandpounder
1987.	(7") <SR 001> **VANILLA BLUE. / SLIM**	-	

(UK-iss.Oct97; same)

		Caroline	Caroline
May 88.	(lp/c/cd) <CAROL 1348-1/-4/-2> **JETTISON**		

– Soldiers requiem / When the walls come down / Walk in cold / Jettison / Live wire / The mule / Coldbringer / Blight / Free nation / Hammer head / Ghetto mechanic / Suspect device / Vanilla blue. <re-iss. Aug99 on 'Quarter Stick'+=; QS 86CD)> – Roller queen (live) / The strip (live) / Backlash Jack (live).

Feb 89.	(lp/c) (CAR LP/C/CD 6) <CAROL 1371/+C/CD> **UNDERSTAND?**		

– Treason / Hips swingin' / Understand? / Entrapment / Bughouse / Wonder beer / Never follow / Too much of you / Vagabond dog / O.K. wait / The sniper song / Which side you're on. <cd-iss. Aug99 on 'Quarter Stick'+=; QS 87CD)> – Mr. Gridlock (live) / I don't know (live).

— **BILL STEPHENS** – guitar; repl. HAGGERTY who joined PIGBOY

1990.	(cd/c/lp) <CAROL 1642-2/-4/-1> **RAYGUN . . . NAKED RAYGUN**	-	

– Home / Fever island / The grind / Jazz gone bad / Prepare to die / The promise / Holding you / Strange days / In my head / Camarilla / Terminal. <cd re-iss. Aug99 on 'Quarter Stick'; QS 88CD>

— disbanded in 1991

– compilations, etc. –

Jan 98.	(cd) Dyslexic; <(DYS 21)> **THE LAST OF THE DEMOHICANS**		
1999.	(cd) Quarter Stick; <(QS 89CD)> **HUGE BIGNESS: SELECTED TRACKS FROM THE COLLECTED WORKS 1980-1992**		
Aug 01.	(cd) Haunted Town; <(HTR 011CD)> **FREE SHIT**		

– I don't know / The strip / Metastasis / Coldbringer / Dog at large / Backlash Jack / Peacemaker / Surf combat / Gear / Entrapment / Knock me down / Treason / Hips swingin' / Home / I don't mind / Vanilla blue / Hot atomics / NO sex / Twentieth Century boy / Rat patrol / Wonder beer / New dreams.

NAMES

Formed: Brussels, Belgium . . . late 1977 (out of Benelux New Wave outfit The PASSENGERS) by MARC DEPREZ and MICHEL SORDINIA; MIKE S. CHRISTOPHE DEN ZANDT, ROBERT FRANKSON and singer ISABELLE HANREZ were added in '78, although the latter two left shortly. After touring under the banner of N.I.M. (aka NAMES IN MUTATION), the group finally got underway with the release of a French-only EP,

'SPECTATORS OF LIFE'. Picked up by Manchester's 'Factory' records, the English-speaking/singing Belgians made their UK debut early in '81 with the single, 'NIGHTSHIFT'. Farmed out to 'Factory Benelux', the NAMES released a further track, 'POSTCARDS', prior to cutting a full-length album, 'SWIMMING' (1982) for homegrown imprint, 'Les Disques Du Crepuscule'. Vaguely reminiscent of early CURE and JOHN FOXX-era ULTRAVOX!, the record was swathed in mogadon-paced but atmospheric synth flourishes while the occasional discordant piano plonked away in the background. Accessible for 'Factory' but too obscure for many indie fans, the NAMES were struck off the register for good after a final single, 'THE ASTRONAUT', in 1983.

Album rating: SWIMMING (*5)

MICHEL SORDINIA – vocals, bass / **MARC DEPREZ** – guitar / **MIKE S. CHRISTOPHE DEN TANDT** – drums, synthesizer

		Celluloid WEA	not iss.
Oct 79.	(7"ep) *(18087)* **SPECTATORS OF LIFE** – Spectators of life / White life / The drive. *(re-iss. Nov79 on French 'Celluloid' 12"ep; CEL 2-6554)*	–	– Belgian

—— added **LUC CAPELLE** – drums

		Factory	not iss.
Jan 81.	(7") *(FAC 29)* **NIGHTSHIFT. / I WISH I COULD SPEAK YOUR LANGUAGE**		–

		Factory Benelux	not iss.
Oct 81.	(7"/12") *(FACBN 9/+12)* **POSTCARDS. / CALCUTTA** below was actually by **SORDINIA** alone		–

		Crammed Discs	not iss.
Dec 81.	(7"; as BY CHANCE) *(CRAM 545)* **SOUL KITCHEN. / REVENGE**		–

		Crepuscule	not iss.
Apr 82.	(lp) *(TWI 065)* **SWIMMING** – (This is) Harmony / Shanghai gesture / Leave her to Heaven / Light / Discovery / Floating world / The fire / Life by the sea. *(cd-iss. Jan91 on 'Factory Benelux'+=; FBN 9CD)* (+ Jun00 on 'L.T.M.'+=; LTMCD 2324) – Nightshift / I wish I could speak your language / The astronaut / Cat / I wish I could speak your language (pre-mix).		–

—— **MICHEL SILVERSTEIN** – drums; repl. the injured LUC

		Operation Twilight	not iss.
Oct 83.	(12") *(TWI 111)* **THE ASTRONAUT. / SHINING HOURS / REVENGE**	–	– Belgian

—— disbanded around this time

– compilations, etc. –

Nov 85.	(c) *Les Tempes Modernes; (LTM V:XII)* **POSTCARD VIEWS** – Music for someone / Tokyo twilight / Nightshift / I wish I could speak your language / Cat / Life by the sea / Shanghai gesture / (This is) Harmony / Discovery / Revenge / Leave her to Heaven (live) / Music for someone (live) / Calcutta (live) / Life by the sea (live) / Postcards (live) / Shanghai gesture (live) / Secrets (live) / Nightshift (live) / Light (live) / (This is) Harmony (live).	–	– Belgian

NATIVE HIPSTERS

Formed: London, England . . . late 70's by WILLIAM WILDING and South African-born BLATT (aka NANETTE GREENBLATT). Setting up their own 'Heater Volume' imprint while recruiting ROBERT CUBITT and TOM FAWCETT, The WILDINGS – as they were then known – released a solitary album, 'WHY DID I BUY THOSE PYJAMAS', at the turn of the decade. After issuing a one-off 45 as The PATTERNS, the group changed their moniker once again, this time releasing an EP, 'THERE GOES CONCORDE AGAIN', as (AND THE) NATIVE HIPSTERS. Enthusiastically playlisted by noneother than John Peel, the track's whimsical novelty factor saw it cruise into the upper reaches of the indie charts. With CUBITT subsequently out of the picture, the band's line-up was bolstered by three extra members, MICK LOUGHRAN, LUCINDA VAN DER SMAN and YUM YUM MOSELEY (the latter two both sax players). A further couple of singles, 'TENDERLY HURT ME' and 'LARRY'S COMING BACK', never caught the public imagination in quite the same way although their maverick musical hotch-potch attracted an underground following.

Album rating: BLATT ON THE LANDSCAPE compilation cassette (*6)

WILLIAM WILDING (b.18 May'53, Romford, Essex, England) – vocals, bass / **BLATT** (b. NANETTE GREENBLATT, 9 Mar'52, Cape Town, South Africa) – vocals / **ROBERT CUBITT** – guitar, tapes, sax / **TOM FAWCETT** – guitar, synthesizer, trombone

		Heater Volume	not iss.
Dec 79.	(lp; as The WILDINGS) *(HVR 001)* **WHY DID I BUY THOSE PYJAMAS**		–
Aug 80.	(7"; as The PATTERNS) *(HVR 002)* **THE BISHOP'S IN THE FRIDGE (part 2). / NO VIOLENT PACING**		–
Oct 80.	(7"ep; as AND THE NATIVE HIPSTERS) *(HVR 003)* **THERE GOES CONCORDE AGAIN . . . / STANDS STILL THE BUILDING / I WANNA BE AROUND (PAUL)**		–

—— **LUCIANA VAN DER SMAN + YUM YUM MOSELEY** – sax + **MICK LOUGHRAN** – guitar; repl. CUBITT

		Illuminated Glass	not iss.
Feb 82.	(12"ep) *(MAP 1)* **TENDERLY HURT ME EP** – Tenderly hurt me / Stuck / Poor prince / Hang ten.		–

		Plattekop	not iss.
Jul 83.	(7") *(KOP 1)* **LARRY'S COMING BACK. / EMMA KALEMMA**		–

—— **WILDING + BLATT** recruited a host of backers, namely **LESTER SQUARE** – guitar (ex-MONOCHROME SET) / **SIMON DAVIDSON** – piano / **ANNIE WHITEHEAD** – trombone / **CHRIS CORNETTO** – cornet

		own	not iss.
1988.	(c) **BLATT ON THE LANDSCAPE**		–

NEGATIVE TREND (see under ⇒ FLIPPER)

NEGATIVLAND

Formed: Berkeley, California, USA . . . 1979 by MARK HOSLER, DAVID WILLS and RICHARD LYONS (PETER DAYTON was part-time member). Taking their name from a track by Kraut-rockers, NEU!, these suburban experimentalists initially began mixing 'n' matching disparate material in the early 80's, both with vinyl LP's, 'NEGATIVLAND' (1980), 'POINTS' (1981), 'A BIG 10-8 PLACE' (1983) and their own radio show, 'OVER THE EDGE, VOL.1: JAM CON '84' (1985). 1987's debut for 'S.S.T.', 'ESCAPE FROM NOISE' kicked up a storm of controversy as the band fooled the media into believing the track, 'CHRISTIANITY IS STUPID', had inspired a brutal inter-family murder. Outrage aside, the record's media-manipulating sonic terrorism was created with the help of such anti-establishment luminaries as The RESIDENTS, JELLO BIAFRA, FRED FRITH, JERRY GARCIA, HENRY KAISER and er, DEVO's MARK MOTHERSBAUGH. Come the turn of the decade, NEGATIVLAND turned their satirical sights on America's redundant MOR history with a full album's worth of chestnut send-ups, 'HELTER STUPID' (1989). The latter's title was perhaps a reference to U2 whom they ripped to shreds with the EP, 'THE LETTER U AND THE NO.2', sending up their pomp-rock classic, 'I Still Haven't Found What I'm Looking For'. Needless to say, BONO and Co weren't amused, dispatching their legal team to tackle the copyright breach; U2 subsequently dropped the case although the incident didn't discourage the NEGATIVLAND posse from further risky shenanigans.

Album rating: NEGATIVLAND (*5) / POINTS (*5) / A BIG 10-8 PLACE (*5) / OVER THE EDGE, VOL.1: JAM CON '84 (*5) / ESCAPE FROM NOISE (*6) / HELTER STUPID (*6) / FREE (*4) / DISPEPSI (*5) / HAPPY HEROES (*4)

MARK HOSLER – keyboards, bass, guitar, tapes, etc / **DAVID WILLS** – synthesizer, keyboards, vocals, etc / **RICHARD LYONS** – clarinet, keyboards, etc / 4th member **PETER DAYTON** – bass, guitar

		not iss.	Seeland-Optional
1980.	(lp) *<OPTLP 001>* **NEGATIVLAND** *<US re-iss. 1991 on 'SST'; 272>*	–	
1981.	(lp) *<OPTLP 002>* **POINTS** – Harry to the ferry / The answer is . . . / Scolding box / That darn keet / Dear Mary / Clutch cargo '81 / BABAC D'BABC . . . / Nice place to live / Bee fly / No hands / Potty air.	–	
1983.	(lp) *<OPTLP 003>* **A BIG 10-8 PLACE** – Theme from a big place / A big 10-8 place (pt.1) / Clowns and ballerinas / Introduction / Four fingers / 180-G, a big 10-8 place (pt.2). *<cd-iss. Mar01 on 'Seeland'; SEELAND 003>*	–	
1985.	(cd) *<OPTCD 004>* **OVER THE EDGE, VOL.1: JAM CON '84 (radio compiled)** – Introduction / JamJamJam – A little history – Jam this guy: An interview with W6DR – Jamming the "S / Crosley Bendix reviews JamArt and cultural jamming / The worst programming ever – Mind jamming – A report by Rex Everything / C. Eliot Friday's presidential campaign shortwave broadcast (live from Howland Island) / Two or three people listening – You motherfucking son of a sack of piece of shit – Attempts to jam / Introduction to the show – Parade of condiments – Walking and driving and hiking to the picnic / Stockholders' meeting (with Crosley Bendix) – Insects in your pop bottle – An abrupt ending / Body English. *<(c-iss.Mar89 on 'S.S.T.'; SSTC 233)>*	–	

—— DAYTON repl. by **DON JOYCE** – tapes, synthesizer / **CHRIS GRIGG** – drums, synthesizer, computers

		Recommended	S.S.T.
Dec 87.	(lp) *(REC 017) <SST 133>* **ESCAPE FROM NOISE** – Announcement / Quiet phone / Michael Jackson / Escape from noise / The Playboy channel / Stress in marriage / Nesbitt's lime soda song / Over the hiccups / Sycamore / Car bomb / Methods of torture / Yellow black and rectangular / Backstage pass / Christianity is stupid / Time zones / You don't even live here / The way of it / Endscape. *(cd-iss. Jun93; RECDEC 17) <(cd re-iss. Nov99 on 'Seeland'; SEELAND 006CD)>*		

		S.S.T.	S.S.T.
Nov 89.	(c) *<(SST 901)>* **OVER THE EDGE, VOL.2 – PASTOR DICK: MURIEL'S PURSE FOUND (radio compiled)** – Thrilling choice / Dayle Embree / Ask Pastor Dick – Muriel's purse found / Hell car / The men's continental breakfast / Christianity and the cults / Joseph / I love my B.I.B.L.E. – More bible / Whisper a prayer / Drunk at last – A date with ham – etc / Forty-three fuck you's – Sign off. *(c-iss. May93; SST 901)*		
Nov 89.	(c) *<(SSTC 902)>* **OVER THE EDGE, VOL.3: THE WEATHERMAN (radio compiled)** – One of them / Clorox cowboy. *<US cd-iss. Aug98 on 'Seeland'; SEE 19>*		

		Recommended	S.S.T.
Apr 90.	(lp/c/cd) *(REC 029) <SST 252/+C/CD>* **HELTER STUPID** – Prologue / Helter stupid / The perfect cut (Canned music) / The perfect cut (Rooty poops) / The perfect cut (Good as gold) / The perfect cut (Piece of meat) / The perfect cut (White rabbit – Dog named Gidget) / The perfect cut (11 minutes) / The perfect cut (48 hours). *(re-iss. May93 lp/c/cd; SST 252/+C/CD) (cd-iss. Jul93 as 'HELTER STUPID: THE PERFECT CUT'; RECDEC 29)*		Nov89
1990.	(c-ep) *<SSTC 904>* **DICK VAUGHN**	–	
Aug 91.	(12") *<SST 272>* **U2** – I still haven't found what I'm looking (1991 a capella mix) / I still haven't found what I'm looking (special radio mix). *(re-iss. May93; SEE 008CD)*	–	
Feb 92.	(12"ep/c-ep/cd-ep) *<SST/+C/CD 291>* **GUNS EP** – Then / Now.	–	

NEGATIVLAND (cont)

Sep 92. (m-lp) *(REC 051)* **THE LETTER U AND THE NUMERAL 2**
(cd-iss. Jul93; RECDEC 51)

                                                                Seeland   Seeland

Jun 93. (cd) <*(SEE 9CD)*> **FREE**
– Freedom's waiting / Cityman / The gun and the bible / Truck stop drip drop / The bottom line / Crumpled farm / Happy the harmonica / Pip digs Pep / We are driven / View to the sun / I am God / Our national anthem.

Oct 93. (cd) *<SEE 10>* **OVER THE EDGE, VOL.5: CROSLEY BENDIX RADIO REVIEWS** (radio compiled)

Mar 94. (cd) *<SEE 11>* **OVER THE EDGE, VOL.6: THE WILLSAPHONE STUPID SHOW** (radio compiled)

1994. (d-cd) *<SEE 12>* **OVER THE EDGE, VOL.7: TIME ZONES EXCHANGE PROJECT** (radio compiled)
– Executive window – Memo to Friday – Memo from the future – Dickie Diamond and the media shifter / The piddle diddle report 1: Sandamanians – Transinfiltration – Nothing is too wonderful to be true / The piddle diddle report 2: Human values – Where is Friday? – Call from Howland Island and the priest / The piddle diddle report 3: Stike it rich – This fabled island – Cary Grant tapes a ghost / The piddle diddle report 4: After the rain – Let's take a few calls – Photos of Mrs. Gorbachev – Com / The piddle diddle report 5: Sergio Caracus – Frankenstein meets cyclops – What was on the island? / The piddle diddle report 6: A future confronting the past which is our future – Last call from Howl / A unique cultural simulcast / Cubulax guidelines / Dickie Diamond grabs the gusto / Russian nationa / Americo-Soviet free market osmosis – Mertz – Intercontinental phone mess / Russian factoids – Natural woman – Tiolet paper ads and smiles / Hey you-buy this! – Innovation – Shilling for attention / Mertz – A force of nature / Hard and soft thinking – The good life – Cars / One bar of soap – Rubles – Mertz – It's as if we never left home – Negativ thoughts – Nuts-oh-nuts! / Passage to the 4th dimension – Memo to Howland – Calling Radio Moscow / A presidential campaign shortwave broadcast by C. Eliot Friday / The piddle report 7: What's to come – The quantum edge – Fiber optics – Experimental sharpner / A place in time to put time in it's place – Do you have a job? – Das vedanya – Mertz – Credits – So.

Feb 95. (cd) *<SEE 13>* **FAIR USE THE STORY OF THE LETTER U AND THE NUMERAL 2**

Jul 95. (cd) *<SEE 14>* **OVER THE EDGE, VOL.1 1/2: STARTING LINE** (radio compiled)
– The drive line: World's most beloved & exalted status symbol – Metallic root beer – Lada – etc / Stir the stumps: Answer man – Hitler's staff car – Chappaquiddick – Transient peaks – Carnuba wax – etc / Receptacle programming – Fear of freeways mix – Defend the fuel – Total asshole – etc / Auto trivia: Cool cars – Cheaper cheese – Limousines of Pope Paul VII – etc / Chevy innovation and JamJamJam / It fell from Port Costa – Rototiller mix – Bottlebrush bushes – etc / Phone-in singalong – Song list – What the world needs now / Tammy / Drug free / Transient peaks – etc / This disco's out of sight – A lot about mucus – Sammy the whammy – A prayer to O.T.E. – Life's unanamous / Pure full stereo rototiller and so long.

Nov 95. (cd) *<SEE 14>* **OVER THE EDGE, VOL.8: SEX DIRT** (radio compiled)

Jul 97. (cd) *<SEE 17>* **DISPEPSI**
– A smile you can't hide / Drink it up / Why is this commercial? / Happy hero / A most successful formula / The greatest taste around / Hyper real / All she called about / I believe it's L / Humanitarian effort / Voice in my head / Aluminium or glass: the memo / Bite back.

May 98. (m-cd) *<SEE 18>* **HAPPY HEROES**
– Mertz #1 / Jolly green giant / Mertz #2 / Chicken diction / Black hole tube / O.J. and his personal trainer kill Ron and Nicole / Happy hero: the remedia megamix / Mertz end.

– compilations, etc. –

Jan 94. (d-cd) *ReR; (CD 1806)* **NEGATIV CONCERT LAND**
1994. (lp) *Knitting Factory; <128>* **LIVE AT THE KNITTING FACTORY** (live)
Jun 97. (7") *Eerie Materials; <(EM 01)>* **TRUTH IN ADVERTISING. /**
Aug 97. (cd) *S.S.T.; <355>* **LIVE ON TOUR** (live)
– Christianity is stupid / Murder and music / Escape from noise / Time / Fourfingers / Record industry / Christianity is stupid (part 2).

Oct 01/ (cd) *Seeland; <(SEELAND 021CD)>* **THESE GUYS ARE FROM ENGLAND AND WHO GIVES A SHIT**
Nov 01. (cd) *Seeland; <(SEELAND 022CD)>* **OVER THE EDGE VOL.4**

NEUROTICS (see under ⇒ NEWTOWN NEUROTICS)

Martin NEWELL
(see under ⇒ CLEANERS FROM VENUS)

NEW MODEL ARMY

Formed: Bradford, England … 1980 by SLADE THE LEVELLER (aka JUSTIN SULLIVAN) alongside STUART MORROW and ROBB HEATON, taking their name from Oliver Cromwell's forces in the 17th century English civil war. Following a one-off release, 'BITTERSWEET', on the small 'Quiet' label, the band moved on to the larger independent operation, 'Abstract'. By the release of a debut mini-set, 'VENGEANCE' (1984), the group had attracted a notoriously partisan, clog-footed following, their uncompromising anti-Thatcherite stance and crusty-punk musical assault endearing them to those actively dropping out of the prevailing 80's ethos. Songs such as 'NO MAN'S LAND', 'SPIRIT OF THE FALKLANDS' and the raging title track laid out their political agenda in bruising style, NEW MODEL ARMY's growing popularity subsequently leading to a deal with 'E.M.I.'. The irony of signing with a multi-national corporation wasn't wasted on the band's more scathing critics, although the fact that their music was now more widely available than ever before was no doubt justification enough for such a move; a major label debut single, 'NO REST' / 'HEROIN' (the latter's subject matter resulting in an IBA ban), made the UK Top 30, while a full-length follow-up album, 'NO REST FOR THE WICKED' (1985), almost made the Top 20. In light of this chart success, a ban from performing in America – reputedly on the grounds of poor artistic quality – looked all the more untenable. With JASON 'MOOSE' HARRIS replacing MORROW, the band continued to kick against the pricks throughout the latter half of the 80's on such grimly defiant albums as 'THE GHOST OF CAIN' and 'THUNDER AND CONSOLATION' (1989). In line with the new age travelling movement's increasing concern with environmental matters and the rise of bands like The LEVELLER's, NEW MODEL ARMY gradually moved away from jackboot punk towards a more traditional folky approach, the tellingly titled 'THE LOVE OF HOPELESS CAUSES' (1993) marking the first fruits of a new deal with 'Epic'. Never strangers to controversy, there was a minor storm over the attendant 'HERE COMES THE WAR' single, its enclosed instructions on how to construct a nuclear device typical of NEW MODEL ARMY's militantly subversive approach. After an extended hiatus, the band returned in 1998 with the independently released, string-enhanced 'STRANGE BROTHERHOOD' album. The mail order-only 'EIGHT' followed in 2000, SULLIVAN proving himself a master of foreboding, acoustic atmospherics when not railing full pelt against his chosen targets. • **Songwriters:** All written by SULLIVAN / HEATON. • **Trivia:** SULLIVAN and HEATON played back-up to the former's girlfriend poet JOOLZ on many stage shows.

Album rating: VENGEANCE (*7) / NO REST FOR THE WICKED (*6) / THE GHOST OF CAIN (*5) / THUNDER AND CONSOLATION (*6) / IMPURITY (*6) / RAW MELODY MEN (*5) / HISTORY THE SINGLES compilation (*7) / THE LOVE OF HOPELESS CAUSES (*5) / STRANGE BROTHERHOOD (*4) / EIGHT (*4)

SLADE THE LEVELLER (b. JUSTIN SULLIVAN, 1956) – vocals, guitar / **STUART MORROW** – bass / **ROBB HEATON** (b.1962) -drums

                                                             Quiet   not iss.

May 83. (7"m) *(QS 002)* **BITTERSWEET. / BETCHA / TENSION**
(w/free flexi-7") – FASHION / CAUSE.

                                                         Abstract   not iss.

Nov 83. (7") *(ABS 0020)* **GREAT EXPECTATIONS. / WAITING**
(re-iss. Feb90 – 7"blue; ABS 090)

Apr 84. (m-lp) *(ABT 006)* **VENGEANCE**   73
– Christian militia / Notice me / Smalltown England / A liberal education / Vengeance / Sex (the black angel) / Running / Spirit of the Falklands. *(c-iss.Nov85; ABTC 006) (cd-iss. Jun87 +=; ABT 006CD)* – Great expectations / Waiting / The price / 1984 / No man's land. *(blue-lp iss.Nov87 with 6xlp-box-set of 'Abstract' label records: 'SIX DISQUES BLEU')*

Oct 84. (7") *(ABS 0028)* **THE PRICE. / 1984**
(12"+=) *(12ABS 0028)* – No man's land / Notice me / Great expectations.

                                                         E.M.I.   Capitol

Apr 85. (c-s/7") *(TC+/NMA 1)* **NO REST. / HEROIN**   28
(d12"+=) *(12NMA 1 – PSLP 387)* – Vengeance (live) / The price (live) / No greater love (live).

May 85. (lp/c) *(EJ 240335-1/-4) <12432>* **NO REST FOR THE WICKED** 22
– Frightened / Ambition / Grandmother's footsteps / Better than them / My country / No greater love / No rest / Young, gifted & skint / Drag it down / Shot 18 / The attack. *(re-iss. May88 on 'Fame' lp/c; FA/TC-FA 3198) (cd-iss. Jul89; CDFA 3198)*

Jun 85. (d7") *(NMA 2)* **BETTER THAN THEM. / NO SENSE // ADRENELIN. / TRUST**   49
(7"ep)(12"ep) *(NMAD – NMA 22)(12NMA 2)* – THE ACOUSTIC EP

JASON 'MOOSE' HARRIS repl. MORROW

Nov 85. (7") *(NMA 3)* **BRAVE NEW WORLD. / R.I.P.**   57
(12"+=) *(12NMA 3)* – Brave new world 2.
(d12"+=) *(12NMA 3 – PSLP 395)* – Young, gifted & skint (live) / Sex (the black angel) (live)

Sep 86. (lp/c) *(EMC/TC-EMC 3516) <46695>* **THE GHOST OF CAIN** 45
– The hunt / Lights go out / 51st state / All of this / Poison street / Western dream / Love songs / Heroes / Ballad / Master race. *(cd-iss. Jul89; CDP 746695-2) (re-iss. Jul90 on 'Fame' cd/c/lp; CD/TC+/FA 3237)*

Oct 86. (7") *(NMA 4)* **51st STATE. / TEN COMMANDMENTS** 71
(d12"+=) *(12NMA 4 – PSLP 348)* – A liberal education (live) / No rest (live) / No man's land (live).

Feb 87. (7",7"red) *(NMA 5)* **POISON STREET. / COURAGE** 64
(12"+=) *(12NMA 5)* – ('A'extended version).
(d12"+=) *(12NMA 5 – PSLP 1002)* – All of this (live) / My country (live).

Jun 87. (7"ep/12"ep) *(NMA/12NMA 6)* **WHITE COATS / THE CHARGE. / CHINESE WHISPERS / MY COUNTRY** 50

Dec 88. (m-lp/m-c) *<CLP/C4P 46928>* **SEVEN SONGS**
– My country (live) / Waiting / 51st state / The hunt (live) / White coats / The charge / Chinese whispers.

Jan 89. (7"/7"g-f) *(NMA/+G 7)* **STUPID QUESTIONS. / NOTHING TOUCHES**   31
(12") *(12NMA 7)* – ('A'extended) / Betcha (live).
(cd-s++=) *(CDNMA 7)* – 51st state.

Feb 89. (cd/c/lp) *(CD/TC+/EMC 3552) <91317>* **THUNDER AND CONSOLATION**   20   Mar89
– I love the world / Stupid questions / 225 / Inheritance / Green and grey / Ballad of Bodmin Pill / Family / Family life / Vagabonds / Archway towers. *(re-iss. Aug91 on 'Fame' cd+=/c/lp; CD/TC+/FA 3257)*– The charge / Chinese whispers / Nothing changes / White coats.

Feb 89. (7"/7"g-f/7"pic-d) *(NMA/+G/P 8)* **VAGABONDS. / DEAD EYE**   37
(12"+=) *(12NMA 8)* – ('A'extended) / White coats (live).
(cd-s++=) *(CDNMA 8)* – Lights go out (extended).

Jun 89. (7"/7"pic-d) *(NMA/+P 9)* **GREEN AND GREY. / THE CHARGE (live)**   37
(12") *(12NMA 9)* – ('A'side) / Family life (live) / 125 mph (live).
(cd-s+=) *(CDNMA 9)* – Green and grey (live).

NELSON – bass (ex-HIDING PLACE) repl. JASON

Aug 90. (7") *(NMA 10)* **GET ME OUT. / PRISON**   34
(10"+=) *(10NMA 10)* – ('A'extended) / Waiting (live).
(12"+=) *(12NMA 10)* – ('A'extended) / White coats (live).
(cd-s+=) *(CDNMA 10)* – White coats (live) / Waiting (live).

Sep 90.	(cd/c/lp) (CD/TC+/EMC 3581) **IMPURITY**		23	-

 – Get me out / Space / Innocense / Purity / Whirlwind / Lust for power / Bury the hatchet / 11 years / Lurkstop / Before I get old / Vanity. *(cd+=)* – Marrakesh. *(re-iss. Oct92 & Jul98 on 'Fame' cd/c; CD/TC FA 3273)*

Oct 90.	(c-s/7") (TC+/NMA 11) **PURITY (IS A LIE). / CURSE**		61	-

(12"+=/cd-s+=) (12/CD NMA 12) – ('A'extended) / Vengeance (live).

May 91.	(c-s/7") (TC+/NMA 13) **SPACE (live). / FAMILY LIFE**		39	-

(12") (12NMA 13) – ('A'side) / No rest (live) / Stupid questions (live).
(cd-s) (CDNMA 13) – ('A'side) / 225 (live) / Ambition (live).
(10") (10NMA 13) – ('A'side) / Bury the hatchet (live) / Stupid questions (live).

Jun 91.	(cd/c/lp) (CD/TC+/EMC 3595) **RAW MELODY MEN (live)**		43	-

 – Whirlwind / The charge / Space / Purity / White coats / Vagabonds / Get me out / Lib. fol / Better than them / Innocense / Love songs / Innhstaap / Archway towers / Smalltown England / Green & grey / The world. *(re-iss. Jun93 on 'Fame' cd/c; CD/TC FA 3296)*

Apr 92.	(cd/c/lp) (CD/TC+/EMC 3622) **HISTORY THE SINGLES 1985-91** (compilation)			-

 – No rest / Better than them / Brave new world / 51st state / Poison street / White coats / Stupid questions / Vagabonds / Green and grey / Get me out / Purity / Space (live). *(incl.free 12"*)* – Far Better Thing * / Higher Wall * / Adrenalin (version) Luurstaap (acoustic). *(cd+=/c+=)* – (2 extra tracks *) *(cd re-iss. Apr01; CDP 798954-2)*

 —— Jun'92, JUSTIN was nearly killed when he was electrocuted on stage.

		Epic	Epic
Jan 93.	(7") (658 935-7) **HERE COMES THE WAR. / MODERN TIMES**	25	-

(12"+=/cd-s+=) (658 935-6/-2) – Ghost of your father.

Mar 93.	(cd/c/lp) (473 356-2/-4/-1) **THE LOVE OF HOPELESS CAUSES**		22	-

 – Here comes the war / Fate / Living in the rose / White light / Believe it / Understand U / My people / These words / Afternoon song / Bad old world. *(cd re-iss. Jan02 on 'Sony'; 506066-2)*

Jul 93.	(12"ep/cd-ep) (659 244-6/-2) **THE BALLADS EP**		51	-

 – Living in a rose / Drummy B / Marry the sea / Sleepwalking.

 —— split around 1994, although they arrived back four years later. Line-up: **SULLIVAN, HEATON, NELSON** plus **DAVE BLOMBERG** – guitar, keyboards, vocals / **DEAN WHITE** – keyboards, clarinet / plus a string & brass section

		Eagle	not iss.
Apr 98.	(cd/c) (EAG CD/MC 021) **STRANGE BROTHERHOOD**	72	-

 – Wonderful way to go / Whites of their eyes / Aimless desire / Over the wire / Queen of my heart / Gigabyte wars / Killing / No pain / Headlights / Big blue / Long goodbye / Lullaby. *(cd re-iss. Mar02; same)*

Apr 98.	(c-s) (EAGCS 021) **WONDERFUL WAY TO GO / REFUGEE**			-

(cd-s+=) (EAGXA 021) – South west / ('A'-radio edit).
(cd-s) (EAGXS 021) – ('A'side) / F?NY / BD7 / Ballad of Bodmin Pill.

		Attack Attack	not iss.
Jan 00.	(cd) (ATK 2304) **EIGHT**		-

 – Flying through the smoke / You weren't there / Orange tree roads / Someone like Jesus / Stranger / R&R / Snelsmore Wood / Paekakariki beach / Leeds road 3 a.m. / Mixam / Wipe out. *(re-iss. Dec01; same)*

 —— JUSTIN SULLIVAN has since went solo

– compilations, others, etc. –

on 'Abstract' unless mentioned otherwise

Apr 88.	(m-lp/cd) (ABT 017/+CD) **RADIO SESSIONS (1983-1984 rare)**			-
	(cd re-iss. Mar02; ABT 5002CD)			
Dec 93.	(cd) Windsong; (WINCD 051) **BBC RADIO 1 LIVE IN CONCERT (live)**			-
Sep 94.	(cd) E.M.I.; (CDEMC 3688) **B SIDES AND ABANDONED TRACKS**			-
Oct 94.	(12"ep/cd-ep) **VENGEANCE 1994.** / ('A'-Zion Train mix) / ('A'-The Headman mix) / ('A'-Pressure Of Speech mix)			-
Jun 95.	(d-cd) (NMA 001CD) **VENGEANCE / RADIO SESSIONS**			-
Jul 97.	(d-cd) Snapper; (SMDCD 129) **SMALL TOWN ENGLAND**			-
Apr 99.	(cd) EMI; (499678-2) **ALL OF THIS: THE "LIVE" RARITIES (live)**			-

 – Vengeance / Young gifted and skint / A liberal education / No rest / No mans land / My country / All of this / Waiting / 57th state / The hunt / 125 mph / 225 / Ambition / Betcha.

Aug 99.	(cd) Abstract; (ABT 008CD) **VENGEANCE – THE INDEPENDENT STORY**			-
	(re-iss. Mar02; ABT 5001CD)			
Aug 99.	(d-cd) Attack Attack; (ATK 2303) **AND NOBODY ELSE**			-
	(re-iss. Dec01; same)			
Sep 00.	(3xcd-box) EMI; (528374-2) **GHOST OF CAIN / THUNDER AND CONSOLATION / RAW MELODY MEN**			-
Feb 02.	(d-cd) Attack Attack; (ATK 2305) **LOST SONGS**			-
Oct 02.	(cd; by JUSTIN SULLIVAN & DAVE BLOMBERG) Attack Attack; (WOOLCD 1) **BIG GUITARS IN LITTLE EUROPE (live in 1994)**			-

NEW ORDER

Formed: Manchester, England ... mid 1980, from the fragments of JOY DIVISION following the death of frontman IAN CURTIS on the 18th of May 1980. The remaining JOY DIVISION members, vocalist/guitarist BERNARD ALBRECHT (now SUMNER), bassist PETER HOOK and drummer STEPHEN MORRIS remained with 'Factory' records, subsequently adopting the NEW ORDER moniker at the suggestion of manager Rob Gretton. With SUMNER taking over vocal duties, the group gigged around Manchester, eventually releasing a debut single, 'CEREMONY' in 1981. This broke the Top 40, as did the Martin Hannett-produced follow-up, 'PROCESSION' / 'EVERYTHING'S GONE GREEN' although in reality, these releases weren't much of a departure from the rumbling, melodic bass sound of old, critics unimpressed with SUMNER's weak vocals. With their debut album, 'MOVEMENT' (1981), however, NEW ORDER were beginning to crystallise their own unique sound, new recruit GILLIAN GILBERT embellishing the music with cutting keyboard swathes. A subtle dance feel was also edging it's way in and with the release of 'TEMPTATION' the following year, NEW ORDER had begun experimenting openly with sequencing technology. The single married the raw cut 'n' thrust of alternative rock to danceable rhythms, echoing hip-hop's similar experimentation with European electronica (see AFRIKA BAMBAATAA's seminal KRAFTWERK-sampling 'Planet Rock') and creating sonic waves that are still rippling through the eclectic musical free-for-all of the 90's. Fittingly then, NEW ORDER's tour de force, 'BLUE MONDAY' was produced by cult US hip-hop producer, Arthur Baker. The best selling 12 inch single in the history of rock, the record was dominated by compelling, almost militaristic dancefloor beats behind SUMNER's moodily introspective, melancholy vocal musings and HOOK's insidious bass melody. A true crossover single, the record appealed to indie fans, B-boys and club posers alike, cementing NEW ORDER's reputation as one of the UK's most street-cred acts. The accompanying album (an inferior demo version of 'BLUE MONDAY', '5-8-6' was included at the expense of the original single), 'POWER, CORRUPTION AND LIES' (1983) made the Top 5, confirming NEW ORDER's commitment to electronic experimentation via a hypnotic, slightly hazy set. A further Arthur Baker-produced 12 inch single followed, 'CONFUSION', the New Yorker also collaborating on the 1984 follow-up, 'THIEVES LIKE US'. But it wasn't until the acclaimed 'LOW LIFE' the following year that NEW ORDER successfully integrated the various strands which made up their inimitable sound. Previewed by the affecting 'PERFECT KISS' single and arguably the most consistently listenable NEW ORDER long player, the record convincingly welded driving, bass-heavy rock onto dance rhythms as well as featuring some interesting stylistic diversions. 'BROTHERHOOD' (1986) was a harder-edged affair, enjoyable enough and boasting the brilliant 'BIZARRE LOVE TRIANGLE', although hardly breaking new ground. 'TRUE FAITH' was another landmark NEW ORDER single; co-written and produced by STEPHEN HAGUE (who'd worked wonders on the PET SHOP BOYS' early material), the single was a hauntingly infectious piece of dance-pop, possibly the most commercial material NEW ORDER had ever released. Following the release of the best selling compilation, 'SUBSTANCE (1980-1987)' later that summer, the band went to ground, finally resurfacing in 1989 with 'TECHNIQUE' and quashing rumours of an imminent split. Heavily influenced by the house explosion of the late 80's and partly recorded on the Balearic Island of Ibiza, the album fully indulged the band's dancier leanings with a verve and passion that's missing from much of their later work. Deservedly, the album rode into the No.1 spot on the back of the club zeitgeist, a scene NEW ORDER had a major hand in creating. The single, 'FINE TIME', almost made the Top 10, an uncharacteristically humorous ditty featuring parodic mock-medallion man, BARRY WHITE-esque vocal rumblings. The following year, NEW ORDER were back at No.1 with their World Cup theme tune, 'WORLD IN MOTION'. Nationalist prejudice aside, this song seemed to set the trend for the nauseous, 'Engerland' limp-wristed crap that the LIGHTNING SEEDS would update six years later for the European championships. Maybe NEW ORDER felt the same way, as the various members soon drifted away to their respective side projects; HOOK to the muscular REVENGE (subsequently stiffing with the 'ONE TRUE PASSION' album), GILBERT and MORRIS to The OTHER TWO (1993's 'THE OTHER TWO AND YOU' album getting lost in the ether when 'Factory' went belly-up) and SUMNER hooking up with JOHNNY MARR (ex-SMITHS) and occasionally NEIL TENNANT (PET SHOP BOYS) to form ELECTRONIC. By far the most successful NEW ORDER-offshoot, the group scored three Top 20 hit singles, including the pop wistfulness of 'GETTING AWAY WITH IT'. They also narrowly missed No.1 with their 1991 eponymous album, their sound akin to a breezier NEW ORDER, fusing house and indie-pop with wry, intelligent lyrics. With 'Factory' going bust following HAPPY MONDAYS' bank-breaking 'SUNSHINE AND LOVE' debacle, a belated NEW ORDER follow-up, 'REPUBLIC' (1993), was subsequently released on 'London' records. A strangely muted collection, the record nevertheless spawned a succession of Top 30 singles including the aptly named Top 5 hit, 'REGRET'. Rumours of tensions within the group persisted and after a final appearance at the 1993 Reading Festival, the various members soon went off to do their own thing once more. ELECTRONIC charted with another set, 'RAISE THE PRESSURE' in 1996 and HOOK came up with the highly-NEW ORDER-esque MONACO project (with SUMNER-like DAVID POTTS) the following year. In 1999, ELECTRONIC returned with a third set, 'TWISTED TENDERNESS' – featuring the UK hit 'VIVID' – while MONACO again delighted the pop world with their eponymous follow-up in 2000. Few could've predicted NEW ORDER would return at all, never mind return with as good an album as 'GET READY' (2001). Rather than cater to the whims of contemporary club tastes, SUMNER, HOOK et al unashamedly made a record on their own terms. As a taster single, 'CRYSTAL' was perfect, a keening slice of classic NEW ORDER with the constituent parts (HOOKY's all-consuming bassline, SUMNER's little boy lost vocals, a melody to die for) all present and correct. Even the collaborative efforts of BOBBY GILLESPIE and BILLY CORGAN were subsumed under the record's driving focus. • **Songwriters:** All group compositions except; TURN THE HEATER ON (Keith Hudson). • **Trivia:** In 1987, they contributed some tracks to the movie, 'Salvation'.

NEW ORDER (cont) — THE GREAT INDIE DISCOGRAPHY — The 1980s

Album rating: MOVEMENT (*8) / POWER, CORRUPTION AND LIES (*9) / LOW-LIFE (*8) / BROTHERHOOD (*8) / SUBSTANCE 1980-1987 compilation (*10) / TECHNIQUE (*9) / REPUBLIC (*6) / ? (THE BEST OF) compilation (*9) / THE REST OF NEW ORDER compilation (*7) / GET READY (*6) / Electronic: ELECTRONIC (*8) / RAISE THE PRESSURE (*6) / TWISTED TENDERNESS (*6) / Revenge: ONE TRUE PASSION (*5) / Monaco: MUSIC FOR PLEASURE (*6) / MONACO (*7) / Other Two: THE OTHER TWO AND YOU (*5) / SUPER HIGHWAYS (*5)

BERNARD SUMNER (b. BERNARD DICKEN, 4 Jan'56) – vocals, guitar / **PETER HOOK** (b.13 Feb'56) – bass / **STEPHEN MORRIS** (b.28 Oct'57, Macclesfield, England) – drums

		Factory	Streetwise
Mar 81.	(7"/ext.12") *(FAC 33/+T)* **CEREMONY. / IN A LONELY PLACE** *(re-iss. Jul81 re-recorded; FAC 33-12)*	34	-

— added **GILLIAN GILBERT** (b.27 Jan'61) – keyboards, synth.

Sep 81.	(7") *(FAC 53)* **PROCESSION. / EVERYTHING'S GONE GREEN**	38	-
Nov 81.	(lp) *(FACT 50)* **MOVEMENT** – Dreams never end / Truth / Senses / Chosen time / I.C.B. / The him / Doubts even here / Denial. *(re-iss. Nov86 c/cd; FACT 50C)(FACD 50) (re-iss. Jul93 on 'Centredate' cd/c; 520018-2/-4)*	30	-
Dec 81.	Factory Benelux; (12"m) *(FBN 8)* **EVERYTHING'S GONE GREEN (extended). / MESH / CRIES AND WHISPERS** *(re-iss. cd-ep Jul90; FBN 8CD)*	-	- Belg.
May 82.	(7"/ext.12") *(FAC 63/+T)* **TEMPTATION. / HURT**	29	-
Nov 82.	Factory Benelux; (m-lp) *(FACTUS 8)* **NEW ORDER 1981-82** (compilation)	-	- Belg.
Mar 83.	(12") *(FAC 73)* **BLUE MONDAY. / THE BEACH**	9	
May 83.	(lp)(c) *(FACT 75)(FACTUS 12C) <25308>* **POWER, CORRUPTION AND LIES** – Your silent face / Ultraviolence / Ecstasy / Leave me alone / Age of consent / We all stand / The village / 5-8-6. *(re-iss. Nov86 c/cd; FACT 75C)(FAC 75CD)* – Blue Monday / The beach. *(re-iss. Jul93 on 'Centredate' cd/c; 520019-2/-4)*	4	
Aug 83.	(12"ep) *(FAC 93)* **CONFUSION. / CONFUSED BEATS / CONFUSION** (instrumental & Rough mixes)	12	
Apr 84.	(12") *(FAC 103)* **THIEVES LIKE US. / LONESOME TONIGHT**	18	
May 84.	Factory Benelux; (12") *(FBN 22)* **MURDER. / THIEVES LIKE US** (instrumental)	-	- Belg.

		Factory	Qwest
May 85.	(7") *(FAC 123)* **THE PERFECT KISS. / THE KISS OF DEATH** (12"+=) *(FAC 123-12)* – Perfect pit.	46	-
Jun 85.	(7") **THE PERFECT KISS. / PERFECT PIT**	-	-
May 85.	(lp/c)(cd) *(FACT 100/+C)(FACD 100) <25289>* **LOW-LIFE** – Sooner than you think / Sub-culture / Face up / Love vigilantes / Elegia / The perfect kiss / This time of the night / Sunrise. *(c+=)* – The perfect kiss / The kiss of death / Perfect pit. *(re-iss. Jul93 on 'Centredate' cd/c; 520020-2/-4)*	7	94
Nov 85.	(7"/ext.12") *(FAC 133/+T)* **SUB-CULTURE. / DUB-CULTURE**	63	-
Mar 86.	(7") *(FAC 143)* **SHELLSHOCK. / THIEVES LIKE US** (instrumental) (12") *(FAC 143T)* – ('A'extended) / Shellshock (dub).	28	-
Sep 86.	(ext.12"/7") *(FAC 153/+7)* **STATE OF THE NATION. / SHAME OF THE NATION**	30	-
Oct 86.	(lp/c/s-lp)(cd) *(FACT 150/+C/SP)(FACD 150) <25511>* **BROTHERHOOD** – Paradise / Weirdo / As it was when it was / Broken promise / Way of life / Bizarre love triangle / All day long / Angel dust / Every little counts. *(cd+=)* – State of the nation. *(re-iss. Jul93 on 'Centredate' cd/c; 520021-2/-4)*	9	
Nov 86.	(ext.12"/7") *(FAC 163/+7)* **BIZARRE LOVE TRIANGLE. / BIZARRE DUB TRIANGLE**	56	-
Mar 87.	(7") **BIZARRE LOVE TRIANGLE. / EVERY LITTLE COUNTS**	-	-
Jul 87.	(ext.12"/7") *(FAC 183/+7) <28271>* **TRUE FAITH. / 1963** (remix-12"+=) *(FAC 183R)* – True dub.	4	32 Oct87
Aug 87.	(d-lp/d-c)(d-cd) *(FACT 200/+C)(FACD 200) <25621>* **SUBSTANCE (1980-1987)** (compilation) – Ceremony / Everthing's gone green / Temptation / Blue Monday / Confusion / Thieves like us / Perfect kiss / Subculture / Shellshock / State of the nation / Bizarre love triangle / True faith. *(d-c+=)* – Procession / Mesh / Hurt / In a lonely place / The beach / Confused / Murder / Lonesome tonight / Kiss of death / Shame of the nation / 1963. *(cd++=)* – Cries and whispers / Dub culture / Shellcock / Bizarre dub triangle. *(re-iss. Jul93 on 'Centredate' cd/c; 520008-2/-4); hit UK No.32) (d-cd re-iss. Jun98; 520008-2)*	3	36
Dec 87.	(ext.12"/7") *(FAC 193/+7)* **TOUCHED BY THE HAND OF GOD. / TOUCHED BY THE HAND OF DUB** (cd-s) *(FACD 193)* – ('A'extended) / Confusion (dub '87) / Temptation (original).	20	-
Mar 88.	(7") **TOUCHED BY THE HAND OF GOD. / BLUE MONDAY 1988**	-	-
Dec 88.	(7") *(FAC 223-7)* **FINE TIME. / DON'T DO IT** (12"+=) *(FAC 223)* – Fine line. (cd-s+=) *(FACCD 223)* – ('A'-Silk mix) / ('A'-Messed around mix).	11	
Jan 89.	(cd)(lp/c/dat) *(FACD 275)(FACT 275/+C/D) <25845>* **TECHNIQUE** – Fine time / All the way / Love less / Round & round / Guilty partner / Run / Mr. Disco / Vanishing point / Dream attack. *(re-iss. Jul93 on 'Centredate' cd/c; 520011-2)*	1	32
Mar 89.	(ext.12"/7") *(FAC 263/+7) <27524>* **ROUND & ROUND. / BEST AND MARSH** (ext.& club-12"+=) *(FAC 263R)* – ('A'-Detroit mix). (cd-s+=) *(FACD 263)* – Vanishing point (instrumental 'Making Out' mix) / ('A'-12"mix). (3"cd-s) *(FACD 263R)* – ('A'-Detroit) / ('A'-12") / ('A'-club).	21	64
Sep 89.	(7") *(FAC 273-7)* **RUN 2. / MTO** (12"+=) *(FAC 273)* – ('A'extended) / ('B'-Minus mix).	49	-
May 90.	(12"/7"/c-s; as ENGLAND / NEW ORDER) *(FAC 293/+7/C)* **WORLD IN MOTION.... / THE B SIDE** (cd-s+=) *(FACD 293)* – No alla violenzia / ('A'-Subbuteo mix). (12") *(FAC 293R)* – ('A'-Subbuteo mix) / ('A'-Subbuteo dub) / No alla violenzia mix / ('A'-Carabinieri mix).	1	-

— Around the late 80's/early 90's, all members splintered to do own projects

		Centredate	Qwest
Apr 93.	(7"/c-s) *(NUO/+C 1) <18586>* **REGRET. / ('A'mix)** (cd-s+=) *(NUOCD 1)* – ('A'-Fire Island mix) / ('A'-Junior's dub mix). (12") *(NUOX 1)* – ('A'-Fire Island mix) / ('A'-Junior's dub mix) / (2-'A' Sabres mixes)	4	28
May 93.	(cd/c/lp) *(828413-2/-4/-1) <45250>* **REPUBLIC** – Regret / World / Ruined in a day / Spooky / Everyone everywhere / Young offender / Liar / Chemical / Times change / Special / Avalanche.	1	11
Jun 93.	(7"/c-s) *(NUO/+C 2)* **RUINED IN A DAY. / VICIOUS CIRCLE (mix)** (cd-s+=) *(NUOCD 2)* – ('A'mixes). (cd-s) *(NUOCDX 2)* – ('A'mixes). (12") *(NUOX 2)* – ('A'side) / World (the price of dub mix).	22	-
Aug 93.	(c-s) *(NUOC 3) <18432>* **WORLD (THE PRICE OF LOVE) / ('A'mixes)** (12"+=/cd-s+=) *(NUOX/NUOCD 3)* – ('A'-Perfecto + sexy club mixes). (cd-s) *(NUOCDX 3)* – ('A'-Brothers in rhythm mix) / ('A'dubstramental mix) / ('A'-World in action mix) / ('A'-Pharmacy dub).	13	-
Sep 93.	(c-s,cd-s) *<18432>* **WORLD (THE PRICE OF LOVE) / RUINED IN A DAY**	-	92
Dec 93.	(c-s/12"/cd-s) *(NUO MC/X/CD 4)* **SPOOKY. / (3 'A' mixes-magimix-minimix-moulimix)** (cd-s) *(NUCDP 4)* – ('A'-Out of order mix) / ('A'-Stadium mix) / ('A'-In Heaven mix) / ('A'-Boo-dub mix) / ('A'-Stadium instrumental).	22	-
Nov 94.	(7"/c-s) *(NUO/+MC 5)* **TRUE FAITH '94. / ('A'-Perfecto mix)** (12"+=) *(NUOX 5)* – ('A'-sexy disco dub mix) / ('A'-TWA Gim Up North mix). (cd-s++=) *(NUOCD 5)* – ('A'radio mix).	9	-
Nov 94.	(cd/c/d-lp) *(828 580-2/-4/-1) <45794>* **? (THE BEST OF)** (compilation) – True faith '94 / Bizarre love triangle '94 / 1963 / Regret / Fine time / The perfect kiss / Shellshock / Thieves like us / Vanishing point / Run (2) / Round and round '94 / World (price of love) / Ruined in a day / Touched by the hand of God / Blue Monday '88 / World in motion.	4	78
Jan 95.	(c-s) *(NUOMC 6)* **NINETEEN63 (Arthur Baker remix) / ('A'-'94 album version) / ('A'-Lionrock full throttle mix) / ('A'-Joe T Venelli remix)** (12") *(NUOX 6)* – ('A'-Lionrock & Joe T mixes / True faith (Eschreamer mix)/ ('A'-Eschreamer dub). (cd-s) *(NUOCD 6)* – ('A'-Arthur Baker remix) / Let's go/ Spooky (Nightstripper mix)/ True faith '87 (Shep Pettibone mix).	21	-
Jul 95.	(c-s) *(NUOMC 7)* **BLUE MONDAY '95 / ('A'-original)** (12"+=/cd-s+=) *(NUO X/CD 7)* – ('A'-Hardfloor mix) / ('A'-Jam & Spoon mix).	17	-
Jul 95.	(cd-ep) *<20546>* **BIZARRE LOVE TRIANGLE (2 mixes) / STATE OF THE NATION (2 mixes)**	-	98
Aug 95.	(cd/c) *(828 661-2/-4)* **THE REST OF NEW ORDER** (remixes, etc)	5	
Aug 01.	(cd-s) *(NUCDP 8)* **CRYSTAL / CRYSTAL (Digweed & Muir bedrock remixes)** (cd-s/d12") *(NUO CD/X 8)* – ('A'-Lee Coombs remix & dub) / ('A'-John Creamer & Stephane K mixes) / Behind closed doors. (12") *(NUOXX 8)* – (some 'A'-mixes above). (12") *(NUOXXX 8)* – (some 'A'-mixes above).	8	-
Aug 01.	(cd/c/lp) *(<8573 89621-2/-4/-1>)* **GET READY** – Crystal / 60 miles an hour / Turn my way / Vicious streak / Primitive notion / Slow jam / Rock the shack / Someone like you / Close range / Run wild.	6	41 Oct01
Nov 01.	(cd-s) *(NUOCD 9)* **60 MILES AN HOUR / SABOTAGE / SOMEONE LIKE YOU (Funk D'void mix)** (cd-s) *(NUODP 9)* – ('A'side) / ('A'-Supermen lovers remix) / Someone like you (James Holden dub) / Someone like you (Future Shock mix).	29	-
Dec 01.	(12") *(NUOX 10)* **SOMEONE LIKE YOU (mixes; futureshock vocal / Gabriel & Dresden 911 vocal / futureshock stripdown / Gabriel & Dresden voco-tech dub)** (12") *(NUOXX 10)* – ('A'-mixes; James Holden heavy dub / Funk d'Void).	-	-
Apr 02.	(cd-s; as NEW ORDER & THE CHEMICAL BROTHERS) *(NUOCD 11)* **HERE TO STAY / HERE TO STAY (mix) / PLAYER IN THE LEAGUE** (cd-s) *(NUCDP 11)* – ('A'mixes; radio / Felix Da Housecat – thee extended glitz / the scumfrog dub). (12") *(NUOX 11)* – ('A'mixes) / Crystal (original).	15	-
Jun 02.	(cd-s; as ENGLAND NEW ORDER) *(NUOCD 12)* **WORLD IN MOTION (mixes) / SUCH A GOOD THING**	43	-

– compilations, etc. –

Sep 86.	(12"ep) *Strange Fruit; (SFPS 001)* **PEEL SESSIONS (1.6.82.)** – Turn the heater on / We all stand / 586 / Too late. *(re-iss. Jul87 c-ep; SFPSC 001) (re-iss. Mar88 cd-ep; SFPSCD 001)*	54	-
Oct 87.	(12"ep) *Strange Fruit; (SFPS 039)* **PEEL SESSIONS (26.1.81.)** – Truth / Senses / I.C.B. / Dreams never end. *(re-iss. May88 cd-ep; SFPSCD 039)*	-	-
Mar 88.	(7"/12") *Factory; (FAC 73-7/R) / Qwest; <27979>* **BLUE MONDAY 1988. / BEACH BUGGY** (cd-s+=) *(FACD 73)* – ('A'original).	3	68
Sep 90.	(m-cd/m-c/m-lp) *Strange Fruit; (SFR CD/C/LP 110)* **PEEL SESSIONS** (2 ep's combined)	-	-
Feb 92.	(cd/c/lp) *Windsong; (WIN CD/MC/LP 011)* **BBC RADIO 1 LIVE IN CONCERT** (live June '87) – Touched by the hand of God / Temptation / True faith / Your silent face / Every second counts / Bizarre love triangle / Perfect kiss / Age of consent / Sister Ray.	33	-
Sep 97.	(12") *Touch; (502780314769)* **TOUCH TONE 7.1**	-	-

— In Mar'89, they issued two 5"cd-vids of TRUE FAITH + BLUE MONDAY '88

Jul 02.	(12") *Factory USA; (2054-6)* **BIZARRE LOVE TRIANGLE**	-	-
Nov 02.	(12") *Whacked; (WACKT 002)* **CONFUSION (2002 remixes; Koma & Bones / Larry T's)** (12") *(WACKT 002R)* – ('A'mixes; Junior Sanchez vocal / Arthur Baker / Asto's). (cd-s) *(WACKT 002CD)* – (all mixes above).	-	-
Dec 02.	(4xcd-box) *London; (0927 49499-2) <73834>* **RETRO**	-	-

ELECTRONIC

BERNARD SUMNER – vocals, guitar / **JOHNNY MARR** – guitar (ex-SMITHS) + both programmers / also with **NEIL TENNANT** – vocals (of PET SHOP BOYS)

		Factory	Warners
Dec 89.	(7"/c-s) *(FAC 257-7/-C)* <19880> **GETTING AWAY WITH IT. / LUCKY BAG**	12	38
	(12"+=/cd-s+=) *(FAC 257 T/CD)* – ('A'extended).		
	(12"+=) *(FAC 257X)* – ('A'extra mixes).		

—— added further guests **CHRIS LOWE, DONALD JOHNSON, DAVID PALMER, DENISE JOHNSON, HELEN POWELL + ANDREW ROBINSON** (on same track)

Apr 91.	(7"/c-s) *(FAC 287-7/-C)* **GET THE MESSAGE. / FREE WILL**	8	
	(cd-s+=) *(FACD 287)* – ('A'-DNA groove mix).		
	(12"+=) *(FAC-12 287)* – ('A' 2 other mixes).		
May 91.	(cd)(lp/c) *(FACD 290)(FACT 290/+C)* <26387> **ELECTRONIC**	2	
	– Idiot country / Reality / Tighten up / The patience of a saint / Gangster / Soviet / Get the message / Try all you want / Some distant memory / Feel every beat. *(re-iss. Feb94 on 'Parlophone' cd/c; FACT PRG 1012)*		
Sep 91.	(7"/c-s) *(FAC 328-7/-C)* **FEEL EVERY BEAT. / LEAN TO THE INSIDE**	39	
	(12"+=) *(FAC-12 328)* – ('A'dub version).		
	(cd-s+=) *(FACD 328)* – Second to none / ('A' DNA mix).		

—— next with NEIL TENNANT again

		Parlophone	Warners
Jun 92.	(c-s/7") *(TC+/R 6311)* **DISAPPOINTED. / IDIOT COUNTRY TWO**	6	
	(12"+=/cd-s+=) *(12R/CDR 6311)* – ('A'-808 State mix) / ('B'-Ultimatum mix).		
Jun 96.	(c-s/7") *(TC+/R 6436)* **FORBIDDEN CITY. / IMITATION OF LIFE**	14	
	(cd-s+=) *(CDR 6436)* – A new religion.		
Jul 96.	(cd/c) *(CD/TC+/PCS 7382)* <45955> **RAISE THE PRESSURE**	8	
	– Forbidden city / For you / Dark angel / One day / Until the end of time / Second nature / If you've got love / Out of my league / Interlude / Freefall / Visit me / How long / Time can tell.		
Sep 96.	(c-s) *(TCR 6445)* **FOR YOU / ALL THAT I NEED**	16	
	(cd-s+=) *(CDR 6445)* – I feel alright.		
	(cd-s) *(CDRS 6445)* – ('A'side) / Free will (12"mix) / Disappointed / Get the message (DNA mix).		
Feb 97.	(c-s) *(TCR 6455)* **SECOND NATURE / TURNING POINT**	35	
	(cd-s+=) *(CDRS 6455)* – Feel every beat (12"remix).		
	(cd-s) *(CDRS 6455)* – ('A'side) / ('A'-Plastik mix) / ('A'-Trance Atlantic dub) / ('A'-Sweet remix).		
Apr 99.	(12") *(12R 6514)* **VIVID. / PRODIGAL SON (mixes; Two Lone Swordsmen & Harvey's)**	17	-
	(cd-s) *(CDR 6514)* – ('A'side) / Radiation / Prodigal son (inch mix).		
	(cd-s) *(CDRS 6514)* – ('A'side) / Haze (alternative mix) / Prodigal son (Harvey's a star in your mind mix).		
Apr 99.	(cd/c) *(<498345-2/-4>)* **TWISTED TENDERNESS**	9	
	– Make it happen / Haze / Vivid / Vivid / Breakdown / Can't find my way home / Twisted tenderness / Like no other / Late at night / Prodigal son / When she's gone / Flicker.		
Jul 99.	(12") *(12R 6519)* **LATE AT NIGHT. / MAKE IT HAPPEN / MAKE IT HAPPEN (Darren Price mix)**		
	(cd-s) *(CDR 6519)* – ('A'side) / King for a day / Come down now (Cevin Fisher mix).		
	(cd-s) *(CDRS 6519)* – ('A'side) / Warning sign / Make it happen (Darren Price mix).		

REVENGE

PETER HOOK – bass / with **DAVE HICKS** – words, vocals / **C. JONES**

		Factory	Capitol
Nov 89.	(7") *(FAC 247-7)* **7 REASONS. / JESUS I LOVE YOU**		-
	(12"+=) *(FAC 247)* – Love you 2.		
	(cd-s+=) *(FACD 247)* – ('B'version) / Bleach boy.		
May 90.	(7"/c-s) *(FAC 267-7/-C)* **PINEAPPLE FACE. / 14K**		-
	(12"+=) *(FAC 267)* – ('A'-Revenge version).		
	(cd-s+=) *(FACD 267)* – ('A'-Last Lunge version).		
Jun 90.	(cd)(lp/c) *(FACD 230)(FAC 230/+C)* <94053> **ONE TRUE PASSION**		
	– Pineapple face / Big bang / Lose the chrome / Slave / Bleachman / Surf Nazi / Fag hag / It's quiet.		
Sep 90.	(7") *(FAC 279)* **I'M NOT YOUR) SLAVE. / AMSTERDAM**		-
	(12"+=/cd-s+=) *(FAC 279 T/CD)* – ('A'-II version) / Slave.		

—— DAVE HICKS departed Apr'91, replaced by **POTTSY**

Jan 92.	(12"ep/cd-ep) *(FAC 327 T/CD)* <98479> **GUN WORLD PORN**		Feb92
	– Deadbeat (remix) / Cloud nine / State of shock / Little pig.		

MONACO

PETER HOOK – bass (now departed from NEW ORDER) / **DAVID POTTS** – guitar, vocals

		Polydor	A&M
Mar 97.	(7"/c-s) *(573 190-7/-4)* **WHAT DO YOU WANT FROM ME? / BICYCLE THIEF**	11	-
	(cd-s+=) *(573 191-2)* – Ultra.		
May 97.	(c-s) *(571 054-4)* **SWEET LIPS / SHATTERED**	18	-
	(cd-s+=) *(571 055-2)* – ('A'-Tony De Vit mix) / ('A'-arley & Heller mix).		
	(cd-s) *(571 057-1/-2)* – ('A'side) / ('A'-Farley & Heller mix) / ('A'-Joey Negro mix).		
Jun 97.	(cd/c/lp) *(<537 242-2/-4/-1>)* **MUSIC FOR PLEASURE**	11	
	– What do you want from me? / Shine (someone who needs me) / Sweet lips / Buzz gum / Blue / Junk / Billy Bones / Happy Jack / Tender / Sedona.		
Sep 97.	(7"/c-s) *(571 418-7/-4)* **SHINE (SOMEONE WHO NEEDS ME). / (instrumental)**	55	-
	(cd-s+=) *(571 418-2)* – Comin' around again / Tender.		
		Papillion	Papillion
Aug 00.	(7") *(BTFLYS 0005)* **I'VE GOT A FEELING. / HEAVEN**		-
	(cd-s+=) *(BTFLYX 0005)* – Barfly.		
Aug 00.	(cd) *(<BTFLYCD 0005>)* **MONACO**		
	– I've got a feeling / A life apart / Kashmere / Bert's theme / Ballroom / See-saw / Black rain / It's a boy / End of the world / Marine.		

The OTHER TWO

STEPHEN + GILLIAN

		Parlophone	Warners
Oct 91.	(7"/c-s) *(FAC 329-7/-C)* **TASTY FISH (Pascal mix). / ('A'mix)**	41	-
	(12"+=/cd-s+=) *(FAC/+D 329)* – ('A'-Almond slice mix).		
		London	London
Oct 93.	(7"/c-s) *(TWO/+CD 1)* **SELFISH. / SELFISH (that pop mix)**	46	
	(12"+=/cd-s+=) *(TWO X/CD 1)* – ('A'-East Village vocal mix) / ('A'-Waterfront mix).		
Nov 93.	(cd/c/lp) *(<520028-2/-4/-1>)* **THE OTHER TWO AND YOU**		
	– Tasty fish / The greatest thing / Selfish / Movin' on / Ninth configuration / Feel this love / Spirit level / Night voice / Innocence. *(cd+=)* – Love it.		
Feb 99.	(c-s/cd-s) *(TWO CS/CD 2)* **SUPER HIGHWAYS / YOU CAN FLY (Cevin Fisher mile high club mix)**		-
	(cd-s) *(TWCDP 2)* – ('A'-Andy Votel mix).		
Mar 99.	(cd/c) *(566018-2/-4)* **SUPER HIGHWAYS**		-
	– You can fly / Super highways / The river / One last kiss / Voytek / Unwanted / New horizons / Cold feet / The grave / Hello / Ripple / Weird woman. *(cd-bonus+=)* – Super highways (Andy Votel mix) / You can fly (Cevin Fisher's mile high mix).		

NEW RACE
(see under ⇒ RADIO BIRDMAN; 70's section)

NEWTOWN NEUROTICS

Formed: Harlow, Essex, England ... mid 1978 by STEVE DREWETT, COLIN DREDD and TIGGY BARBER. Instigating their own 'No Wonder' label, these agit power-poppers struggled to make an impact at the turn of the decade with their first two 45's, 'HYPOCRITE' and 'WHEN THE OIL RUNS OUT'. With SIMON LOMOND having replaced TIGGY, the newlook trio returned with a harder hitting political agenda on 1982's 'KICK OUT THE TORIES!'. The campaign continued with a second single for 'C.N.T.' (then home to SISTERS OF MERCY), 'LICENSING HOURS', before the latter imprint went bust. A cover of the Ramones' 'BLITZKRIEG BOP', marked their debut for 'Razor' records, heralding a full-length album, 'BEGGARS CAN BE CHOOSERS' (1983); left-wing/social sentiments mixed with short-circuit guitars on a set that veered towards the overt politicism of The REDSKINS and NEW MODEL ARMY. The RAMONES influence resurfaced on 1984's solitary single, 'SUZI IS A HEARTBREAKER', while a subsequent name change to The NEUROTICS saw the band heading in a more lyrically militant but musically adept direction with the string-enhanced 'REPERCUSSIONS' (1985) mini-set. They continued in a similar vein with two further albums, 'KICKSTARTING A BACKFIRING NATION' (1986) and 'IS YOUR WASHROOM BREEDING BOLSHEVIKS?' (1988), before calling it a day in the late 80's as political pop lost its way.

Album rating: BEGGARS CAN BE CHOOSERS (*5) / Neurotics: REPERCUSSIONS mini (*5) / KICKSTARTING A BACKFIRING NATION (*5) / IS YOUR WASHROOM BREEDING BOLSHEVIKS? (*4) / 45 REVOLUTIONS PER MINUTE compilation (*5)

STEVE DREWETT – vocals, guitar / **COLIN DREDD** – bass, vocals / **TIGGY BARBER** – drums

		No Wonder	not iss.
Nov 79.	(7") *(CUS 363)* **HYPOCRITE. / YOU SAID NO**		-
Nov 80.	(7") *(NOW 4)* **WHEN THE OIL RUNS OUT. / OH NO**		-

—— **SIMON LOMOND** – drums; repl. TIGGY

		C.N.T.	not iss.
Jun 82.	(7") *(CNT 005)* **KICK OUT THE TORIES! / MINDLESS VIOLENCE!**		-
Dec 82.	(7") *(CNT 010)* **LICENSING HOURS. / NO SANCTUARY**		-
		Razor	not iss.
Aug 83.	(7"m) *(RZS 107)* **BLITZKRIEG BOP. / HYPOCRITE (new version) / I REMEMBER YOU**		-
Sep 83.	(lp) *(RAZ 6)* **BEGGARS CAN BE CHOOSERS**		-
	– Newtown people / Does anybody know where the march is? / Life in their hands / My death / Living with unemployment / Wake up / The mess / Get up and fight / No respect / Agony. *(cd-iss. Jan95 on 'Dojo'; DOLECD 111)*		
		No Wonder	not iss.
Oct 84.	(7"/12") *(NOW/+T 6)* **SUZI IS A HEARTBREAKER. / FOOLS**		-

NEUROTICS

—— same line-up, **STEVE, COLIN + SIMON**

		Jungle	not iss.
Jul 85.	(m-lp) *(FREUD 07)* **REPERCUSSIONS**		-
	– This fragile life / Screaming / Sects / Fighting times / The value of Maleriè / Bored policemen / Creatures from another world.		
Jul 86.	(7") *(JUNG 29)* **LIVING WITH UNEMPLOYMENT. / AIRSTRIP 1**		-
	(12"+=) *(JUNG 29T)* – My death / Oh no / Mindless violence / Porky the poet / Peter Campbell.		
Sep 86.	(lp/c) *(FREUD/+C 10)* **KICKSTARTING A BACKFIRING NATION**		-
	– Expletive deleted – Porky The Poet / The mess / No respect / Never hold your tongue / Does anyone know where the match is? / Airstrip one / The housewifes trial – The big J / Agony / Sects / Raspberry ripple – Peter Campbell. *(c+=)* – REPERCUSSIONS		

NEWTOWN NEUROTICS (cont)

—— PORKY THE POET + comedian PHIL JUPITUS
Mar 88. (12"ep) (JUNG 39T) **NEVER THOUGHT / SCREAMING (live) / STAND BY ME. / MIND OF VALERIE / SECTS / MY DEATH**
Jul 88. (lp) (FREUD 19) **IS YOUR WASHROOM BREEDING BOLSHEVIKS?**
– The loneliest jukebox / Inch away / Keep the faith / Angela / You must be mad / The winds of change / Never thought / Afrika / If only / Local news.
—— disbanded later in 1988, DREWETT later formed The UNSTOPPABLE FORCE

– compilations, etc. –

Nov 90. (cd) Jungle; (FREUDCD 31) **45 REVOLUTIONS PER MINUTE – THE SINGLES 1979-1984**
– Hypocrite / You said no / I get on your nerves / When the oil runs out / OhNo / Kick out the Tories / Mindless violence / No sanctuary / Suzi / Fools / When I need you / Andy is a corporatist.
Oct 92. (cd/lp) Terz; **HIS MASTER'S VOICE – THE VERY BEST OF THE NEUROTICS**
Mar 97. (cd) Anagram; (CDPUNK 91) **PUNK SINGLES COLLECTION** — German
– Hypocrite / You said no / When the oil runs out / Oh no / Kick out the Tories! / Mindless violence / Licensing hours / No sanctuary / Blitzkrieg bop / Hypocrite (new version) / I remember you / Suzi is a heartbreaker / Fools / Living with unemployment / Airstrip 1 / My death / Never thought / Screaming / Stand by me / Mind of Valerie / Sect / My death. (re-iss. Nov99; same)

NICO

Born: CHRISTA PAFFGEN, 16 Oct'38, Cologne, Germany. Her father died in a concentration camp, and, as a girl, she travelled throughout Europe with her mother. Developing a fondness for opera, she learned to play classical piano and harmonium. In 1959, while vacationing in Italy, she was introduced by new friends to film director Federico Fellini and following a bit-part in 'La Dolce Vita', she became a top model, appearing in Vogue magazine. In the early 60's, while working in films, she became the girlfriend of French actor Alain Delon. She later gave birth to his son, having already borne a daughter to actor/dancer Eric Emerson. In 1963, she fell in love with up and coming folk-star BOB DYLAN, who wrote a song for her, 'I'LL KEEP IT WITH MINE'. In 1965, at his suggestion, she moved to London and signed for Andrew Loog Oldham's new label, 'Immediate'. A single, 'I'M NOT SAYING' (written by GORDON LIGHTFOOT) was issued, although the record subsequently flopped, even after an appearance on 'Ready Steady Go'. She then moved to New York, where she met pop-artist ANDY WARHOL. He asked her to feature in an avant-garde film, 'Chelsea Girl', also asking her to join LOU REED, JOHN CALE, MO TUCKER, etc. in his managerial group, The VELVET UNDERGROUND. Together they made one glorious late 1966 album, 'THE VELVET UNDERGROUND AND NICO', NICO leaving soon after for a return to solo work. Decribed as 'The Edith Piaf of the Blank Generation', she was an avant-garde, moody songstress who was anti-pop music in every sense. After a liaison with BRIAN JONES of The ROLLING STONES, she became the opposite number of teenager and new pensmith JACKSON BROWNE who wrote songs for her debut 1968 album, 'CHELSEA GIRL' (notebly 'THESE DAYS'). Regarded as an artistic triumph, she nevertheless disagreed with producer Tom Wilson's string arrangements. Subsequently moving to Los Angeles, she started writing material for her follow-up 'Elektra' album, 'THE MARBLE INDEX'. She travelled constantly between America and Europe, starring in another underground film, 'La Cicatrice Interieupe' for Philippe Garrel. In 1971, she cut the JOHN CALE-produced 'DESERTSHORE', the track 'Le Petit Chevalier' featuring her son. Fleeing New York for France after she was involved in a bottle fight with a female Black Panther member, she later appeared at The Rainbow, London on 1st of June '74 alongside JOHN CALE, ENO and KEVIN AYERS. A track, 'THE END', was recorded, and 'Island' records promptly signed her for an album of the same name, with ENO and PHIL MANZANERA at the production helm. That year, she also contributed vocals to KEVIN AYERS' album, 'Confessions Of Dr. Dream', although she subsequently retired from music to live between Berlin, Los Angeles and Spain. In 1981, she made a comeback album, appropriately titled 'DRAMA OF EXILE', but after poor audience response on a SIOUXSIE & THE BANSHEES support slot, she again went AWOL, shacking up in Manchester, England with her live-in-boyfriend and poet JOHN COOPER CLARKE. After another dismissed vinyl return in 1985, she again retired, only to reappear at a 1987 ANDY WARHOL tribute. Tragically, on the 18th of July '88, on a holiday in Ibiza with CLARKE, she fell off her bike and died of a brain hemorrhage. • **Songwriters:** As said, and other covers; THE END (Doors) / DEUTSCHLAND UBER ALLES (German national anthem) / HEROES (David Bowie) / etc. Plus there are obviously a number of VELVET UNDERGROUND renditions littered about. • **Trivia:** In 1974, she joined LOU REED and JOHN CALE for a French filmed VELVET UNDERGROUND reunion.

Album rating: CHELSEA GIRL (*8) / THE MARBLE INDEX (*7) / DESERTSHORE (*7) / THE END (*5) / DRAMA OF EXILE (*4) / CAMERA OBSCURA (*4) / THE BLUE ANGEL collection (*6) / BEHIND THE IRON CURTAIN (*4) / LIVE IN TOKYO (*5) / posthumous:- HANGING GARDENS (*6) / HEROINE (*4) / INNOCENT & VAIN: AN INTRODUCTION TO NICO compilation (*7)

NICO – vocals (plus session people)

                                                                    Immediate   not iss.
Aug 65. (7") (IM 003) **I'M NOT SAYIN'. / THE LAST MILE**
    (re-iss. May82; IMS 003)
    (above 'B'side featured JIMMY PAGE as guitarist/writer)

—— In 1966, she teamed up with The VELVET UNDERGROUND on their eponymous lp. Breaking from them the following year, she returned to solo work, augmented by JOHN CALE + LOU REED. Her beau JACKSON BROWNE at the time also became her main songwriter.

                                                                    not iss.   Verve
Feb 68. (lp) <2353 025> **CHELSEA GIRL**
    – The fairest of the seasons / These days / Little sister / Winter song / It was a pleasure then / Chelsea girls / I'll keep it with mine / Somewhere there's a father / Wrap your troubles in dreams / Eulogy to Lenny Bruce. (UK-iss.Sep71 on 'MGM Select'; 2353 025) (re-iss. 1974 on 'Polydor'; same) (cd-iss. May88 & Apr94; 835 209-2)

—— Retained JOHN CALE as producer, etc.

                                                                    Elektra   Elektra
Jul 69. (lp) <(EKL 4029)> **THE MARBLE INDEX**
    – Prelude / Lawns of dawns / No one is there / Ari's song / Facing the wind / Julius Caesar (memento Hodie) / Frozen warnings / Evening of light. (cd-iss. Apr91 on 'WEA'+=; 7559 61096-2) – Roses in the snow / Nibelungen.

                                                                    Reprise   Reprise
Jan 71. (lp) <(RSLP 6424)> **DESERTSHORE**
    – Janitor of lunacy / Falconer / My only child / Le petit chevalier / Abschied / Afraid / Mutterlein / All that is my own. (re-iss. 1974; K 44102) (cd-iss. Apr91 on 'WEA'; 7599 25870-2)

—— She retained **CALE** and brought in **ENO** – synthesizer / **PHIL MANZANERA** – guitar / **STERLING MORRISON** – guitar

                                                                    Island   not iss.
Oct 74. (lp) (ILPS 9311) **THE END**
    – It has not taken long / Secret side / You forgot to answer / Innocent and vain / Valley of the kings / We've got the gold / The end / Das lied der Deutschen. (cd-iss. Apr94; IMCD 174)

—— now with **ANDY CLARKE** – keyboards / **MUHAMMED HADI** – guitar / **DAVEY PAYNE** – sax / **STEVE CORDONA** – drums / **PHILIPPE QUILICHINI** – bass

                                                                    Aura   not iss.
Jul 81. (lp) (AUL 715) **DRAMA OF EXILE**
    – Genghis Khan / Purple lips / One more chance / Henry Hudson / I'm waiting for the man / Sixty forty / The sphinx / Orly flight / Heroes. (cdiss.Mar88 on 'Line'; LILP 400106) (cd re-iss. Jul92 on 'Great Expectations'; PIPCD 037) (cd re-iss. Aug96 on 'See For Miles'; SEECD 449)

                                                                    Flicknife   not iss.
Sep 81. (7") (FLS 206) **VEGAS. / SAETA**

                                                                    Half   not iss.
Jul 82. (7") (1/2 1) **PROCESSION. / ALL TOMORROW'S PARTIES**
    (12"+=) (1/2 1-12) – Secret side (live) / Femme fatale (live).

                                                                    Aura   not iss.
Jun 83. (7") (AUS 137) **HEROES. / ONE MORE CHANCE**

—— with **JAMES YOUNG** – keyboards / **GRAHAM DIDS** – percussion

                                                                    Beggars
                                                                    Banquet   not iss.
Jun 85. (7"/12"; as NICO & THE FACTION) **MY FUNNY VALENTINE. / MY HEART IS EMPTY**
Jun 85. (lp/c/cd; as NICO & THE FACTION) (BEG A/C/CD 63) **CAMERA OBSCURA**
    – Camera obscura / Tananore / Win a few / My funny valentine / Das lied von einsamen Madchens / Fearfully in danger / My heart is empty / Into the arena / Konig. (re-iss. Jan89 on 'Beggars Banquet-Lowdown' lp/c)(cd; BBL/+C 63)(BBL 63CD)

—— added **ERIC RANDOM** – percussion, etc / **TOBY TOMAN** – drums

                                                                    Dojo   not iss.
Apr 86. (d-lp/c/cd) (DOJO LP/TC/CD 27) **BEHIND THE IRON CURTAIN (live 1985)**
    – All saints night from a Polish motorway / One more chance / Frozen warnings / The song of the lonely girl / Win a few / Konig / Purple lips / All tomorrow's parties / Fearfully in danger / The end / My funny valentine / 60-40 / Tananoori / Janitor of lunacy / My heart is empty / Femme fatale.
1987. (lp) (DOJOLP 50) **LIVE IN TOKYO, JAPAN (live)**
    – My heart is empty / Purple lips / Tananore / Janitor of lunacy / You forgot to answer / 60-40 / My funny valentine / Sad lied von einsannen madchens / All tomorrow's parties / Femme fatale / The end. (cd-iss. 1988 & Jun95; DOJOCD 50)

—— NICO died 18th Jul'88 (see info above)

– compilations, others, etc. –

1983. (c) R.O.I.R.; <A 117> **DO OR DIE**
    (cd-iss. May93 & Nov94; RE 117CD) <(cd re-mast.Apr00; RUSCD 8261)>
Sep 85. (lp/c/cd) Aura; (AU L/C/CD 731) **THE BLUE ANGEL** (best of)
    – Femme fatale / All tomorrow's parties / I'll keep it with mine / Chelsea girls / Janitor of lunacy / Heroes / One more chance / Sixty forty / Waiting for the man / The end.
Oct 85. (7") Aura; (AUS 147) **I'M WAITING FOR THE MAN. / PURPLE LIPS (live)**
Feb 87. (12"ep) Archive 4; (TOF 110) **LIVE (live)**
Mar 87. (pic-lp) V.U.; (NICO 1) **LIVE IN DENMARK (live)**
May 88. (c) Half; (1/2 CASS 2) **EN PERSONNE EN EUROPE**
Nov 88. (12"ep/cd-ep) Strange Fruit; (SFPS/+CD 064) / Dutch East India; <DEI 8314> **NICO / PEEL SESSIONS (2/2/71)**
    – Secret side / No one is there / Janitor of lunacy / Frozen warnings.
Jun 89. (lp/cd) Performance; (PERF 385/+CD) **LIVE HEROES (live)**
Nov 90. (cd/c/lp) Emergo; (EM 9349-2/-4/-1) **HANGING GARDENS**
Jul 92. (cd) Great Expectations; (PIPCD 039) **CHELSEA GIRL LIVE (live)**
    (re-iss. Jun94 on 'Cleopatra'; CLEO 61062) (cd re-iss. Nov96 on 'See For Miles'; SEECD 461)
Sep 94. (cd) Anagram; <(CDMGRAM 85)> **HEROINE (live)** — 1995
    (lp-iss.Oct00 on 'Get Back'; GET 68) (re-iss. Mar02; CDMGOTH 16)
Apr 96. (cd) Cleopatra; <CLP 9709> **ICON**
Sep 96. (cd) Visionary; (VICD 008) **JANITOR OF LUNACY**
    (re-iss. Jun01 on 'Anagram'; CDGOTH 7)

Sep 96. (cd) *S.P.V.; (SPV 0849620-2)* **NICO'S LAST CONCERT (FATA MORGANA – DESERTSOUNDS IN THE PLANETARIUM) (live)**
(<re-iss. Feb02; SPV 0769620-2>)
Sep 98. (cd) *Island; <565185>* **THE CLASSIC YEARS**
Aug 99. (cd) *Koch World; <(34042-2)>* **COSMOS**
Feb 02. (cd) *Verve; (589421-2)* **INNOCENT & VAIN: AN INTRODUCTION TO NICO**
– I'll keep it with mine / All tomorrow's parties / You forgot to answer / Wrap your troubles in dreams / Valley of the kings / Femme fatale / Eulogy to Lenny Bruce / Secret side / Little sister / It was a pleasure then / Innocent and vain / The end (live).
Apr 02. (cd) *Jungle; (FREUDCD 069)* **FEMME FATALE**

NIGHTINGALES

Formed: Birmingham, England . . . 1978 out of punk band, The PREFECTS, by mainman ROBERT LLOYD along with brother ANDY LLOYD, PAUL APPERLEY and JOW CROW. After one single, 'GOING THROUGH THE MOTIONS', they added EAMONN DUFFY. Now going under The NIGHTINGALES moniker, a follow-up single, 'IDIOT STRENGTH', appeared in Spring '81 (their second for 'Rough Trade'), benefitting from the continuing support of DJ John Peel – who had already recorded a PREFECTS session – and paving the way for a deal with the independent 'Cherry Red' label. By the recording of the band's first album, 'PIGS ON PURPOSE' (1982), CROW had been replaced by JOHN NESTOR. While the record displayed LLOYD's barbed lyrical wit on such slyly humourous ditties as 'USE YOUR LOAF', commentators criticised the lacklustre production. A move to Red Flame's 'Ink' provided a more vibrant showcase for the NIGHTINGALES' grating, angular approach with follow-up set, 'HYSTERICS' (1983) while the addition of new member, multi-instrumentalist PETE BYRCHMORE lent a new, more accessible dimension to the band's sound. Recorded with NICK BEALES in place of NESTOR, single/EP 'THE CRUNCH' appeared on the new 'Vindaloo' imprint in '84, LLOYD subsequently developing a roster that included the likes of WE'VE GOT A FUZZBOX . . . AND WE'RE GONNA USE IT and comedian TED CHIPPINGTON. The violin-enhanced (courtesy of MARIA COLLINS) 'IN THE GOOD OLD COUNTRY WAY' (1986) proved to be the NIGHTINGALES' swansong as the band's head honcho devoted his time to his label and a solo career (with his NEW FOUR SEASONS!). As vociferous in his support of the band as ever, John Peel added to his tally of NIGHTINGALES sessions by writing sleevenotes for the 1991 compilation, 'WHAT A SCREAM'. • **Note:** A different PREFECTS released two singles YOUNG WORLD + LOVE IS ALL AROUND in 1981 + 1982.

Album rating: PIGS ON PURPOSE (*5) / HYSTERICS (*4) / JUST THE JOB compilation (*6) / IN THE GOOD OLD COUNTRY WAY (*5) / WHAT A SCREAM compilation (*6) / PISSED AND POTLESS collection (*7) / Robert Lloyd & The New Four Seasons: ME AND MY MOUTH (*6)

ROBERT LLOYD (b. 1959, Cannock, Staffordshire) – vocals / **ANDY LLOYD** – guitar / **JOE 'Motivator' CROW** – bass / **PAUL APPERLEY** – drums

Rough Trade not iss.

Jun 80. (7"; as PREFECTS) *(RT 040)* **GOING THROUGH THE MOTIONS. / THINGS IN GENERAL**

—— added **EAMONN DUFFY** – guitar, bass
Apr 81. (7") *(RT 075)* **IDIOT STRENGTH. / SECONDS**

Cherry Red not iss.

Feb 82. (7"ep) *(CHERRY 34)* **USE YOUR LOAF EP**
– Use your loaf / Inside out / Under the lash.
Apr 82. (7") *(CHERRY 38)* **PARAFFIN BRAIN. / ELVIS, THE LAST TEN DAYS**
Jul 82. (12"ep) *(12CHERRY 44)* **4 PIECE SESSION** (John Peel sessions)
– Give 'em time / Which hi-fi? / My brilliant career / The son of God's mate.
Nov 82. (lp) *(BRED 39)* **PIGS ON PURPOSE**
– Blood for dirt / Start from scratch / One mistake / Well done underdog / The crunch / The hedonists sigh / It lives again / Make good / Don't blink / Joking apart / Yeah it's o.k. / Use your loaf / Blisters.

—— **JOHN NESTOR** – bass; had already repl. CROW who went solo
Feb 83. (7") *(CHERRY 56)* **URBAN OSPREYS. / CAKEHOLE**

—— **PETE BYRCHMORE** – guitar; repl. DUFFY

Ink not iss.

Nov 83. (7") *(INK 71)* **CRAFTY FAG. / HOW TO AGE**
Nov 83. (lp) *(INK 1)* **HYSTERICS**
– Big print / This / The happy medium / Nothing but trouble / The bending end / Lower than ever / Insurance / Whys of acknowledgement / Bachelor land / Crafty fag / Ponces all.

—— **NICK BEALES** – bass, guitar; repl. NESTOR

Vindaloo not iss.

May 84. (12"ep) *(YUS 1)* **THE CRUNCH EP**
– The crunch / All talk / Look satisfied / Not man enough.
Sep 84. (lp) *(VILP 1)* **JUST THE JOB** (compilation)
– The crunch / All talk / Look satisfied / Not man enough / Urban ospreys / Cakehole / Insurance / How to age.

—— **ROBERT, ANDY, PETE + PAUL** recruited **HOWARD JENNER** – bass to repl. BEALES who formed The PIG BROS
Feb 85. (7") *(UGH 9)* **IT'S A CRACKER. / HERE WE GO NOW**
Sep 85. (12"ep) *(YUS 4)* **WHAT A CARRY ON / CARRY ON CARRYING ON. / COMFORT AND JOY / FIRST MY JOB**
(free-7"flexi w.a.) – HOW TO AGE. / HEROIN

—— **MARIA COLLINS** – violin; repl. ANDY who formed LITTLE RED SCHOOL HOUSE / **RON COLLINS** – drums; repl. PAUL
Mar 86. (lp) *(YUS 7)* **IN THE GOOD OLD COUNTRY WAY**
– The headache collector / Down in the dumps / Leave it out / Comfort and joy / Coincidence / I spit in your gravy / The square circle / Part time moral England / How to age / No can do.

Vindaloo not iss.

Jul 86. (7"; as VINDALOO SUMMER SPECIAL) *(UGH 13)* **ROCKIN' WITH RITA (HEAD TO TOE). / LET'S SURF** | 56 | - |

—— disbanded later in '86; MARIA and PETE formed The CAPITOLS, MARIA also being part of RUMBLEFISH, who issued a trio of 45's, 'TUG BOAT LINE', 'MEDICINE' and 'DON'T LEAVE ME', before splitting summer '88

– compilations, etc. –

Apr 87. (12"ep; as the PREFECTS) *Strange Fruit; (SFPS 025)* **THE PEEL SESSIONS** (8.1.79)
– Faults / Motions / Barbarella's / Total luck.
Jul 88. (12"ep) *Strange Fruit; (SFPS 052)* **THE PEEL SESSIONS**
– Start from scratch / Butter bricks / Torn / 12 years.
Jun 91. (cd) *Mau Mau; (MAUCD 607)* **WHAT A SCREAM (1980-1986)**
– Bristol road leads to Dachau / Hark my love / Nowhere to run (alternative mix) / Blisters / Idiot strength / Seconds / Return journey / The crunch / The hedonists sigh / My brilliant career / Use your loaf / Which hi-fi? / Paraffin brain / Only my Opinion / Urban ospreys / This / Surplus and scarcity / Crafty fag / It's a cracker / Here we go now / Heroin / What a carry on / Faithful lump / At the end of the day.
Jul 01. (cd) *Cherry Red; (<CDMRED 187>)* **PISSED AND POTLESS (THE DEFINITIVE NIGHTINGALES COLLECTION)**
– Idiot strength / Use your loaf / Paraffin brain / Elvis, the last ten days / Which hi-fi? / Give 'em time / Joking apart / Urban ospreys / Cakehole / Crafty fag / How to age / The bending end / Insurance / The crunch / It's a cracker / What a carry on / Comfort & joy / Down in the dumps / Coincidence.

ROBERT LLOYD & The NEW FOUR SEASONS

—— ROBERT had early in 1986 released with VI SUBVERSA (of POISON GIRLS) the single 'KEEP LYING, I LOVE IT' for 'Vindaloo'.

In-Tape not iss.

Jul 88. (7") *(IT 056)* **SOMETHING NICE. / ALL THE TIME IN THE WORLD**
(12"+=) *(ITT 056)* – Of course you can't.
Oct 88. (7") *(IT 059)* **NOTHING MATTERS. / MAMA NATURE'S SKIN**
(12"+=) *(ITT 059)* – The race is on / Something nice.

Virgin not iss.

Mar 90. (7") *(VS 1196)* **FUNERAL STOMP. / STRAYED**
(12"+=) *(VST 1196)* – The last laugh.
(cd-s++=) *(VSCD 1196)* – All the time in the world.
May 90. (7"/c-s) *(VS/+TC 1256)* **NOTHING MATTERS. / MAMA NATURE'S SKIN**
(12"+=) *(VST 1256)* – The race is on.
(cd-s++=) *(VSCD 1256)* – Something nice.
Jun 90. (cd/c/lp) *(CD/TC+/V 2623)* **ME AND MY MOUTH**
– Cheap as sin / Nothing matters / Something nice / Top floor to let / Not forever / Sweet Georgia Black / Funeral stomp / Of course you can't / Man oh man / Hey Roberta / Better to have / The part of the anchor.

—— In 1992, ROBERT re-surfaced in TERMINAL HOEDOWN

NIRVANA

Formed: Aberdeen, Washington, USA . . . 1987 by singer/songwriter/guitarist KURT COBAIN and bassist KRIST NOVOSELIC. Recruiting drummer CHAD CHANNING, they soon became a talking point and pivotal band in nearby Seattle where the likes of SOUNDGARDEN and MUDHONEY were major players in the emerging grunge scene. Whereas those bands dealt in raw garage punk/metal, NIRVANA immediately stood out from the pack by dint of the subtle pop melodies which COBAIN craftily incorporated into his songs. They also fast gained a reputation for their ferocious live shows which drew comparisons with early WHO, if only for their sheer nihilistic energy, invariably ending in trashed equipment. Signing, of course, with the hub of the Seattle scene, 'Sub Pop', NIRVANA released their debut single, 'LOVE BUZZ' in October 1988, the album, 'BLEACH', following a year later. One of the seminal 'Sub Pop' releases alongside, MUDHONEY's 'SUPERFUZZ BIGMUFF' and TAD's 'GOD'S BALLS', this was a darkly brooding, often savagely angry collection, driven by bass and fuzz and interspersed with pockets of melody. The likes of 'SCHOOL' and the throbbing 'NEGATIVE CREEP' saw COBAIN lapse into his trademark howl, an enraged, blood curdling shriek, almost primal in its intensity. Conversely, 'ABOUT A GIRL' was an achingly melodic semi-acoustic shuffle, as steeped in hurt as the rest of the album but more resigned than angry. New guitarist JASON EVERMAN had contributed to the record's sonic bludgeon as well as paying for recording costs, although he soon parted ways (he went on to play with the much hyped MINDFUNK) with COBAIN and NOVOSELIC over the ever reliable, 'musical differences'. 'BLEACH' was heartily received by the indie/metal press, NIRVANA embarking on a heavy round of touring, first in the States, then Europe. Following the departure of CHANNING, MUDHONEY's DAN PETERS joined briefly and was involved with the 'SLIVER' single, a brilliant chunk of pop-noise which further enhanced NIRVANA's underground kudos and raised expectations for a follow-up album to fever pitch. 'NEVERMIND' (1991) let down no-one, except possibly the anally-retentive sad-kids who accused the band of selling out to a major label ('Geffen'). Released immediately after a blinding set at England's Reading festival (where NIRVANA, who probably drew the most frenetic crowd reaction of the day, had to make do with a paltry afternoon slot; the following year they'd be headlining), and with appetites whetted via import copies of 'SMELLS LIKE TEEN SPIRIT', the record was met with an ecstatic press reaction. While the album brought the grunge phenomenon into the mainstream, NIRVANA had already moved on to a blistering power pop/punk sound, best evidenced in the sardonic fury of the aforementioned 'SMELLS . . .'. Here was an anthem for the blank generation, for all the people who'd given up before even starting; COBAIN had condensed the collective frustration/despair/apathy into an incendiary slice of pop genius not witnessed since The SEX PISTOLS' heyday. 'COME AS YOU ARE' was another piece of semi-acoustic bruised beauty while 'TERRITORIAL PISSINGS' was as extreme as the record went, a rabid blast of hardcore punk introduced with a sarcastic send-up pilfered from The YOUNGBLOOD's 60's love 'n' peace classic, 'GET TOGETHER'. Most of the other tracks lay somewhere in between, COBAIN never letting up the intensity level for a minute, whether on the deceptively breezy 'IN BLOOM' or the stinging 'BREED'. For a three piece (the drum seat had now been filled by DAVE GROHL, ex-SCREAM), the group made one hell of a racket, but it was a racket which was never less than 100% focused, the GROHL/NOVOSELIC rhythmic powerhouse underpinning every track with diamond-edged precision. It's fair to say that 'NEVERMIND' literally changed the face of music, American indie bands coming to dominate the scene until the arrival of OASIS in the mid-90's. COBAIN was heralded as the spokesman of a generation, although it was a role he was both unwilling and unable to cope with. As the inevitable, punishing round of touring ensued, the singer's health began to suffer once more; never the healthiest of people, COBAIN suffered from a chronic stomach complaint as well as narcolepsy, a condition which causes the sufferer to sleep for excessive periods of time. What's more, he was concerned that the irony of his lyrics was lost on his growing legions of fans (which now included the macho 'jocks' whom COBAIN so despised) who now doted on his every word. Amid all this confusion, COBAIN was married to HOLE's COURTNEY LOVE on the 24th February '92, the couple almost losing custody of their newborn child, Frances, later that summer following revelations of drug abuse. The end of the year saw the release of a compilation of rare material, 'INCESTICIDE', including two storming VASELINES' (obscure but brilliant Scottish punk-popsters) covers, 'MOLLY'S LIPS' and 'SON OF A GUN'. Rumours of COBAIN's heroin abuse were rife, however, and the singer overdosed twice the following year. 'IN UTERO' (1993) reflected the turmoil, an uncompromising wall of noise (courtesy of STEVE ALBINI) characterising most of the album. The melodies were still there, you just had to dig deeper in the sludge to find them. Despite 'Geffen's misgivings, the record was a transatlantic No.1, its success engendering another round of live work. After a final American show in January, the group set off for Europe, taking a break at the beginning of March. COBAIN remained in Rome, where, on the 4th March, LOVE found him unconscious in their hotel room, the result of an attempted tranquilizer overdose. Although COBAIN eventually recovered, the tour was abandoned and the couple returned to their Seattle home. Though it didn't come as a complete surprise, the music world was stunned nonetheless when, on the 8th April, news broke that COBAIN had finally killed himself, blowing his own head off with a shotgun. The most widely mourned rock'n'roll death since JOHN LENNON, COBAIN's suicide even sparked off a series of 'copycat' incidents in America by obsessive fans. Posthumously released later that year, the acoustic 'UNPLUGGED IN NEW YORK' (1994) live set was heavy going, a tragic poignancy underpinning the spare beauty of tracks like 'DUMB' and 'PENNYROYAL TEA' (from 'IN UTERO') while the heart-rendingly resigned 'ALL APOLOGIES' sounds like COBAIN's final goodbye to a world that he could no longer bear to be a part of. Eventually picking up the pieces, GROHL formed The FOO FIGHTERS, turning his hand to guitar playing/songwriting and recruiting ex-GERM, PAT SMEAR. After time spent campaigning for his native, war torn Yugoslavia, NOVOSELIC returned with his own band, SWEET 75, a collaboration with diminutive Venezuelan lesbian folk-singer, YVA LAS VEGAS. They finally released one unstartling eponymous set in 1997, which just might be their only outing. • **Songwriters:** COBAIN wrote late 80's work. In the 90's, the group were credited with COBAIN lyrics. Covers; LOVE BUZZ (Shocking Blue) / HERE SHE COMES NOW (Velvet Underground) / DO YOU LOVE ME? (Kiss) / TURNAROUND (Devo) / JESUS WANTS ME FOR A SUNBEAM (Vaselines) / D7 (Wipers) / THE MAN WHO SOLD THE WORLD (David Bowie) / WHERE DID YOU SLEEP LAST NIGHT (Leadbelly).

Album rating: BLEACH (*8) / NEVERMIND (*10) / INCESTICIDE collection (*7) / IN UTERO (*10) / UNPLUGGED IN NEW YORK (*9) / FROM THE MUDDY BANKS OF THE WISHKAH (*8) / NIRVANA compilation (*10) / Sweet 75: SWEET 75 (*4)

KURT COBAIN (b.20 Feb'67, Hoquaim, Washington) – vocals, guitar / **CHRIS NOVOSELIC** (b.16 May'65) – bass / **CHAD CHANNING** (b.31 Jan'67, Santa Rosa, Calif.) – drums

Tupelo — Sub Pop

Oct 88. (7") *<SP 23>* **LOVE BUZZ. / BIG CHEESE** [–] [ ]

— Early '89, added **JASON EVERMAN** – guitar Also guest drummer on 2 tracks **DALE CROVER**

Aug 89. (lp,white or green-lp/cd) *(TUP LP/CD 6) <SP 34>* **BLEACH** [ ] [ ] Jun89
– Blew / Floyd the barber / About a girl / School / Paper cuts / Negative creep / Scoff / Swap meet / Mr.Moustache / Sifting / Big cheese. *(cd+=)* – Love buzz / Downer. *<US re-iss. Dec91 hit 89> (re-iss. Feb92 on 'Geffen'; GEFD 24433) (hit UK No.33) (c+=)* – Big cheese. *(re-iss. Oct95 on 'Geffen' cd/c; GFLD/GFLC 19291) (lp re-iss. Aug01 on 'Sub Pop';* **SP 34)** *(re-iss. Oct01 on 'Warners' cd/lp; 9878 40034-2/-1)*

Dec 89. (12"ep/cd-ep) *(TUP EP8/CD8)* **BLEW / LOVE BUZZ. / BEEN A SON / STAIN** [ ] [–]

— **DAN PETERS** – drums (of MUDHONEY) repl. CHANNING (Apr90)

Jan 91. (7",7"green) *(TUP 25)* **SLIVER. / DIVE** [ ] [ ] Sep 90
(12"+=) *(TUP EP25)* – About a girl (live). *(US-iss.7"blue; SP 72)*
(cd-s++=) *(TUP CD25)* – Spank thru (live).

Feb 91. (7",7"green) *<SP 97>* **MOLLY'S LIPS. / ('Candy' by FLUID)** [–] [ ]
not iss. — Communion

Mar 91. (7"colrd) *<Communion 25>* **HERE SHE COMES NOW. / ('Venus In Furs' by MELVINS)** [–] [ ]

— (Apr'91 trio) **DAVE GROHL** (b.14 Jan'69, Warren, Ohio) – drums, vocals (ex-SCREAM) repl. PETERS and EVERMAN, who joined MIND FUNK

Geffen — Geffen

Sep 91. (lp/c/cd) *<(DGC/+C/D 24425)>* **NEVERMIND** [7] [1]
– Smells like teen spirit / In bloom / Come as you are / Breed / Lithium / Polly / Territorial pissings / Drain you / Lounge act / Stay away / On a plain / Something in the way. *(cd+=)* – Endless nameless. *(lp re-iss. Nov98 on 'Simply Vinyl'; SVLP 38)*

Oct 91. (c-s/cd-s) *<19050>* **SMELLS LIKE TEEN SPIRIT / EVEN IN HIS YOUTH** [–] [6]

Nov 91. (7"/c-s) *(DGC/+C 5)* **SMELLS LIKE TEEN SPIRIT. / DRAIN YOU** [7] [–]
(12"pic-d+=) *(DGCTP 5)* – Aneurysm.
(cd-s++=) *(DGCCD 5)* – Even in his youth.
(12") *(DGCT 5)* – ('A'side) / Even in his youth / Aneurysm.

Mar 92. (c-s/cd-s) *<19120>* **COME AS YOU ARE. / DRAIN YOU (live)** [–] [32]

Mar 92. (7"/c-s) *(DGC/+C 7)* **COME AS YOU ARE. / ENDLESS NAMELESS** [9] [–]
(12"+=/12"pic-d+=) *(DGCT/+P 7)* – School (live).
(cd-s++=) *(DGCTD 7)* – Drain you (live).

Jul 92. (7"/c-s) *(DGCS/+C 9)* **LITHIUM. / CURMUDGEON** [11] [–]
(12"pic-d+=) *(DGCTP 9)* – Been a son (live).
(cd-s++=) *(DGCSD 9)* – D7 (Peel session).

Jul 92. (c-s,cd-s) *<19134>* **LITHIUM / BEEN A SON (live)** [–] [64]

Nov 92. (7"/c-s) *(GFS/+C 34)* **IN BLOOM. / POLLY** [28] [–]
(12"pic-d+=/cd-s+=) *(GFST P/D 34)* – Sliver (live).

Dec 92. (cd/c/lp) *<(GED/GEC/GEF 24504)>* **INCESTICIDE** (rare material) [14] [39]
– Dive / Sliver / Stain / Been a son / Turnaround / Molly's lips / Son of a gun / (New wave) Polly / Beeswax / Downer / Mexican seafood / Hairspray queen / Aero zeppelin / Big long now / Aneurysm.

— In Feb'93, NIRVANA's 'OH, THE GUILT' appeared on double'A'side with JESUS LIZARD's 'Puss'. Issued on 'Touch & Go' 7"blue/cd-s; *(TG 83/+CD)*. It had UK No.12, and crashed out of the Top 60 the following week!.

— GOODBYE MR MACKENZIE's BIG JOHN played guitar for them in mid'93.

— In Aug'93, KURT COBAIN and WILLIAM S.BURROUGHS narrated 'The Priest, They Call Him By' on 10"lp/cd 'Tim Kerr'; *(92 10/CD 044)*

Aug 93. (7"/c-s) *(GFS/+C 54)* **HEART-SHAPED BOX. / MARIGOLD** [5] [–]
(12"+=/cd-s+=) *(GFST/+D 54)* – Milk it.

Sep 93. (cd/c/lp)<clear-lp> *<(GED/GEC/GEF 24536)><DGC 24607>* **IN UTERO** [1] [1]
– Serve the servants / Scentless apprentice / Heart-shaped box / Rape me / Frances Farmer will have her revenge on Seattle / Dumb / Very ape / Milk it / Penny royal tea / Radio friendly unit shifter / Tourette's / All apologies. *(cd+=)* – Gallons of rubbing alcohol flow through the strip. *(lp re-iss. Nov98 on 'Simply Vinyl'; SVLP 48)*

Dec 93. (7"/c-s) *(GFS/+C 66)* **ALL APOLOGIES. / RAPE ME** [32] [–]
(12"+=/cd-s+=) *(GFST/+D 66)* – MV.

— On the 4th March '94, KURT overdosed while on holiday in Italy and went into a coma. A month later, on the 8th April he committed suicide, by shooting himself through the mouth. He was only 27, and this was certainly the biggest rock star death since JOHN LENNON. For more details see HOLE and the COURTNEY LOVE story.
below album featured **LORI GOLDSTON** – cello + **MEAT PUPPETS' Curt & Cris Kirkwood** on 3rd, 4th & 5th last songs.

Nov 94. (cd/c/white-lp) *<(GED/GEC/GEF 24727)>* **UNPLUGGED IN NEW YORK** (live acoustic) [1] [1]
– About a girl / Come as you are / Jesus doesn't want me for a sunbeam / Dumb / The man who sold the world / Pennyroyal tea / Polly / On a plain / Something in the way / Plateau / Oh me / Lake of fire / All apologies / Where did you sleep last night. *(lp re-iss. Nov98 on 'Simply Vinyl'; SVLP 53)*

— GROHL (now vox, guitar) formed The FOO FIGHTERS with ex-GERMS guitarist PAT SMEAR; meanwhile NOVOSELIC formed the trio SWEET 75

– compilations, etc. –

on 'Geffen' unless mentioned otherwise

Jul 95. (d-cd) *<(GES 00001)>* **BLEACH / INCESTICIDE** [ ] [ ]

Nov 95. (6xcd-s-box) *<(GED 24901)>* **6 CD SINGLE BOXED SET** [ ] [ ]

Oct 96. (cd/c/lp) *<(GED/GEC/GEF 25105)>* **FROM THE MUDDY BANKS OF THE WISHKAH (live)** [4] [1]
– Intro / School / Drain you / Aneurysm / Smells like teen spirit / Been a son / Lithium / Sliver / Spank thru / Scentless apprentice / Heart-shaped box / Milk it / Negative creep / Polly / Breed / Tourette's / Blew.

Oct 02. (cd) *Geffen; <(493507)>* **NIRVANA** [3] [3]
– You know you're right / About a girl / Been a son / Sliver / Smells like teen spirit / Come as you are / Lithium / In bloom / Heart-shaped box / Pennyroyal tea / Rape me / Dumb / All apologies (live) / The man who sold the world (live).

SWEET 75

KRIST NOVOSELIC – guitar (ex-NIRVANA) / **YVA LAS VEGAS** – vocals, bass / **ADAM WADE** – drums

Geffen — Geffen

Aug 97. (cd/c) *<(GED/GEC 25140)>* **SWEET 75** [ ] [ ]
– Fetch / Lay me down / Bite my hand / Red dress / La vida / Six years / Take another stab / Poor Kitty / Ode to Dolly / Dogs / Cantos de Pilon / Nothing / Japan trees / Oral health.

Danbert NOBACON (see under ⇒ CHUMBAWAMBA)

NOMADS

Formed: Solna, Stockholm, Sweden … 1983 by lynch-pin members NICK VAHLBERG, HANS OSTLUND, plus TONY CARLSSON, FRANK MINARIK and ED JOHNSSON; the nineties saw BORNE FROBERG and JOAKIM ERICSON joining to create a more stable line-up. The Scandanavian garage-rockers began as a devotee band of such luminaries as the SONICS, MC5, and the STOOGES; their first release, 'PSYCHO' (1981), a cover of the SONICS grungy classic. Continuing this theme, their sopohmore 7", 'NIGHT TIME', covered the STRANGELOVES tune. When they released their follow-up EP, 'WHERE THE WOLF BANE BLOOMS' (1984), they began to garner a little more respect, albeit mainly within their own country. Wider European and Stateside notice was taken with the release of the full-length, 'OUTBURST', which led to support slots with their idols, IGGY POP and RAMONES on European tour legs in the early nineties. 'POWERSTRIP' and 'COLD HARD FACTS OF LIFE' followed that decade and they widened the scope of their sound with the introduction of synthesizers and brass instruments, as well as dipping into other musical genres. Larger appeal throughout the world still remained small, but their longevity paid off with the post-millennial appearance of The STROKES and fellow Swedes The HIVES, putting the garage sound back to the forefront of the mainstream rock scene. Thus making their latest album, 'UP-TIGHT', find a hungrier and knowledgeable audience.
• **Covers:** PSYCHO + BOSS HOG + HE'S WAITIN' + HAVE LOVE WILL TRAVEL + CINDERELLA (Sonics) / OUT OF THE FRING PAN (Captain Beefheart) / 16 FOREVER + THE NEXT BIG THING (Dictators) / WIMP (Zeros) / GRAVEYARD (Dead Moon) / LOVE'S GONE BAD + LEAVING HERE (Supremes) / SHE WILL ALWAYS BE MINE (Customs). • **Note:** Watch out for other groups of the same name.
Album rating: WHERE THE WOLF BANE BLOOMS mini (*4) / TEMPTATION PAYS DOUBLE mini (*4) / OUTBURST! (*4) / HARDWARE (*4) / ALL WRECKED UP (*6) / SONICALLY SPEAKING (*5) / POWERSTRIP (*5) / RAW & RARE (*5) / BIG SOUND 2000 (*5) / UP-TIGHT (*5)

NICK VAHLBERG – vocals, rhythm guitar / **HANS OSTLUND** – lead guitar / **FRANK MINARIK** – organ / **TONY CARLSSON** – bass, vocals / **ED JOHNSSON** – drums

1981. (7") (SNS 811) **PSYCHO. / COME SEE ME** — Noon / not iss. (Amigo / not iss.)
1982. (7") (AMS 164) **NIGHT TIME. / BOSS HOSS** — Amigo / Dutch
1983. (m-lp) (AMMP 302) **WHERE THE WOLF BANE BLOOMS** — Dutch
 – The way you touch my hand / I'm 5 years ahead of my time / Lowdown shakin' chills / Rockin' all through the night / Downbound train / Milkcow blues.
1984. (m-lp) (AMMP 304) **TEMPTATION PAYS DOUBLE** — Dutch
 – Rat fink a boo-boo / Real gone lover / Where the wolf bane blooms / Stranger blues / Bangkok / I'm not like everybody else / Don't tread on me.
Dec 84. (lp) (GOES ON 01) <HMS 010> **OUTBURST!** — What Goes On / Homestead
 – The way you touch my hand / Where the wolfbane blooms / I'm 5 yearts ahead of my time / I'm not like everybody else / Real gone lover / Lowdown shakin' chills / Rat fink a boo-boo / Don't tread on me / Bangkok / Stranger blues / Milkcow blues / Sometimes good guys don't wear white.
1985. (7"split) (CL 0726) **E.S.P. / DRIVING SIDEWAYS ON A ONE WAY STREET** — Closer / not iss. (Wire / not iss.) French
Nov 85. (12"m) (TNMS 66) **SHE PAYS THE RENT. / MY LITTLE RUBY / NITROGLYCERINE SHRIEKS**

In 1986, 'Nineteen' issued the flexi (as SCREAMING DIZBUSTERS) 'ROCKIN' ALL THROUGH THE NIGHT'

May 87. (12") (WIMS 001) **16 FOREVER. / COME ON / YOU'RE GONNA MISS ME**
 (re-iss. Aug89 on 'Play It Again Sam'; LD 876)
May 87. (lp) (WILP 003) **HARDWARE**
 – Call off your dogs / Knowledge comes with deaths release / Surfin' in the bars / Jungle fever / (I can't use) The stuff I used to use / 16 forever / Temptation pays double / 10086 Sunset Boulevard / Swamp gal / Check your backdoor / Move it on over. (re-iss. Aug89 on 'Play It Again Sam'; LD 877)
1987. (7") (AMS 171) **16 FOREVER. / SALVATION BY DAMNATION** — Amigo / Dutch
1988. (7"; as The SCREAMING DIZBUSTERS) (NBT 4502) **THE NEXT BIG THING. / HE'S WAITING** (above issued on 'The Next Big Thing')
1989. (7") (AMS 174) **FIRE AND BRIMSTONE. / BEYOND THE VALLEY OF THE DOLLS** — Dutch
 (12"+=) (AMMS 503) – Solitary confinement.
1989. (7") (AMS 180) **MY DEADLY GAME. / I HAVE ALWAYS BEEN HERE BEFORE** — Dutch
Mar 91. (cd/lp) (AMCD/AMLP 2017) **ALL WRECKED UP** — Dutch
 – Holyhead / Twilight fades / I don't need no doctor / First you dream then you die / Beyond the valley of the dolls / My deadly game / Friendship / I'm gonna make you mine / Butcher baker nightmare maker / Outburst / Down by the river / I have always been here before / Cinderella / Fire and brimstone.
1991. (cd-s) (CD12T 10395) **SMOOTH / SHOWING PICTURES TO THE BLIND / CALL OFF YOUR DOGS** — Sonet / not iss. Dutch
Jan 92. (lp/cd) (SNTF/+CD 1048) **SONICALLY SPEAKING**
 – Can't keep you off my mind / Primordial ooze / Smooth / A certain girl / The goodbye look / Wasn't born to work / Rollercoaster / Long goodbye / Come on / Pair of deuces / Party till I die.
1992. (7"m) <SFTRI 189> **PRIMORDIAL OOZE. / SHOWING PICTURES TO THE BLIND / I'M BRANDED** (above issued on 'Sympathy For The Record Industry', below 'Munster')
1993. (7") <7047> **WIMP. / I REMEMBER**
1993. (7"m) (SHAKE 70) **WASN'T BORN TO WORK. / A CERTAIN GIRL / RAT FINK A BOO-BOO** (above issued on 'Shake It', below on 'Estrus')
1994. (7") <ES 754> **(I'M) OUT OF IT. / FAN CLUB**
1994. (cd-s) (CDS 10477) **KINDA CRIME / DIG UP THE HATCHET** — Dutch
1994. (cd-s) (CDS 10487) **BLIND SPOT / (I'M) OUT OF IT** — Dutch

VAHLBERG + OSTLUND recruited newcomers **BJORNE FROBERG** – bass + **JOAKIM ERICSON** – drums

Jun 94. (cd/lp) (157808-2/-1) <SFTRI 305> **POWERSTRIP** — World Service / Sympathy F 1995
 – (I'm) Out of it / Bad vibes / Better off dead / I don't know – I don't care / Sacred / Just lost / Kinda crime / Dig up the hatchet / Robert Johnson / In the doghouse / Glad to be in your past / Blind spot. (cd+=) – T.C.P. / The fire of love. (also lp-iss.Sep94 on 'Munster'; MR 056LP)
1996. (7") (45062) **DIG UP THAT HATCHET. / THE GOODBYE LOOK** — 1+2 / not iss. Lance Rock / Dutch
1996. (10"ep/cd-ep) (LRR 026 – Straight Edge; 96) **THE COLD HARD FACTS OF LIFE** — Dutch
 – Hard to cry / She ain't no use to me / Picture my face / Get away from it all / Who dat? / Nothin' / That's my girl (rotten to the core) / Been burnt.
1996. (7") (MR 023) **IRON DREAM. / EDVIN MEDVIND** — Man's Ruin / Dutch
1996. (7"split) (ES 002) **KINDA CRIME (demo)** — Explicit Sounds / Dutch
1997. (7") <ES7 104> **PACK OF LIES. / GRAVEYARD** — Bad Afro / Estrus
Nov 97. (7") (BA 03) **LOVE'S GONE BAD. / LEAVING HERE** — 1+2 / not iss.
Jan 98. (cd) (1+2CD 086) **MADE IN JAPAN (recorded in Sweden)**
 – Bad vibes / Primordial ooze / Surfin' in the bars / I'm 5 years ahead of my time / Better off dead / I don't know / I don't care / 16 forever / Fan club / Wasn't born to work / Bangkok / Real gone love / Fire and brimstone / She pays the rent / Blind spot / Rat fink a boo-boo / T.C.P. / Call off your dogs. (lp-iss.Jun98 on 'Munster'; MR 102)
1999. (7"m) (SCAP 059) **SHE'LL ALWAYS BE MINE. / I'M OUT OF IT / I'VE SEEN BETTER** — Screaming Apple / not iss. Bang / Dutch
1999. (7") (BANG 5) **TRUCKER SPEED. / (other by ROBERT JOHNSON AND THE PUNCHDRUNKS)** — White Jazz / Estrus
May 99. (cd/lp) (JAZZ 019 CD/LP) <ESD 1252> **BIG SOUND 2000** — Jul99
 – Don't pull my string / Ain't yet dead / Going down slow / Your main man / Some other crime / I've seen better / The king of the night train / The good stuff / The fast can't lose / Screaming / Worst case scenario / Another man's cross.
Jan 00. (7") (SP 021) **I'M GONE. / AIN'T YET DEAD** (above issued on 'Safety Pin')
Mar 00. (7"/cd-s) (7JAZZ 027/+CD) **THE KING OF THE NIGHT TRAIN. / TOP ALCOHOL**
Apr 01. (lp/cd) (JAZZ 040/+CD) **UP-TIGHT** — Jun01
 – Can't keep a bad man down / Crystal ball / Open up your door / In a house of cards / It's lonely down there too / To make a short story long / Top alcohol / Competitors in crime / My finest hour / I can't wait forever / You ain't gonna bring me down / The cold hard facts / Wish I was dumb.

– compilations, etc. –

1987. (7") Marilyn; **WHERE THE WOLF BANE BLOOMS. / RAT FINK A BOO-BOO** — French
1987. (lp) Marilyn; (M 014) **RAT FINK A BOO-BOO** — French
Oct 94. (d-cd) Amigo; (AMCD 2028/9) / Sympathy For The Record Industry; <SFTRI 333> **SHOWDOWN! (1981-1993)**
May 96. (cd) Estrus; <ES 112> **RAW & RARE (live)**
 – Lights out / Come back baby / Weekend on Mars / I wanna come back from the world of LSD / Double decker bus / Downbound train / My little ruby / Nitroglycerine shrieks / E.S.P. / I can't use the stuff I used to use.
Oct 02. (d-cd) White Jazz; (<JAZZCD 057>) **SHOWDOWN VOL.2: THE 90's**

NO MAN IS ROGER MILLER (see under ⇒ MISSION OF BURMA)

NOMEANSNO

Formed: Victoria, British Columbia, Canada … 1983 by the WRIGHT brothers ROB and JOHN (their name a reference to a woman's right to refuse sexual advances). Deliberately anti-image and fiercely independent from the beginning, NOMEANSNO delivered their debut set, 'MAMA', in 1983 on their own label, 'Wrong'. With darkly caustic social commentary and fragmented, avant-garde fuzzcore their forte, this trio (having recently added ANDREW KERR) certainly weren't in the game of rock stardom. They found a soul mate in JELLO BIAFRA, who subsequently signed/licensed them to the ever bulging roster of 'Alternative Tentacles' in 1984. Several albums followed through the 80's, namely 'SEX MAD' (1987), 'SMALL PARTS ISOLATED AND DESTROYED' (1988), 'WRONG' (1989) and '0+2=1' (1991). A year previously, they were one of the many acts to collaborate with BIAFRA, recording an album, 'THE SKY IS FALLING AND I WANT MY MOMMY' together. More recently, the trio have issued two

NOMEANSNO (cont)

further, equally barbed sets, 'WHY DO THEY CALL ME MR. HAPPY?' (1993) (Mr. HAPPY being ROB's solo alter-ego) and 'THE WORLDHOOD OF THE WORLD (AS SUCH)' (1995). The snappily titled 'DANCE OF THE HEADLESS BOURGEOISIE' arrived in 1998, confirming the veteran Canadian subversives as leaders in the – admittedly fairly undersubscribed – field of abrasive but curiously rhythmic avant-hardcore. Fittingly then, perhaps, the band even turned their hand to a cover (and there aren't that many around) of Miles Davis' fusion classic, 'BITCHES BREW', carried off in NOMEANSNO style along with The Ramones' 'BEAT ON THE BRAT'; both could be found nestled away in the closing section of 'ONE' (2000). • **Covers:** OH CANADUH (Subhumans) / NEW AGE (D.O.A.).

Album rating: MAMA (*6) / SEX MAD (*5) / SMALL PARTS ISOLATED AND DESTROYED (*6) / WHY DO THEY CALL ME MR. HAPPY? (*6) / WRONG (*5) / 0+2=1 (*6) / THE WORLDHOOD OF THE WORLD (AS SUCH) (*6) / DANCE OF THE HEADLESS BOURGEOISE (*6) / ONE (*5)

ANDREW KERR – guitar (joined after debut) / **ROB WRIGHT** – bass / **JOHN WRIGHT** – drums

                                                                        not iss.   no label
1980.   (ltd-7") <none> **LOOK, HERE COME THE WORRIES. / S.S. SOCIAL SERVICE**

1981.   (ltd-7"ep) <none> **BETRAYAL FEAR ANGER HATRED**
        – Try not to stutter / I'm all wet / Approaching zero / Forget your life. <(re-iss. 1991 on 'Wrong'; WRONG 2)>

1983.   (lp) <none> **MAMA**
        – Living is free / My roommate is turning into a monster / Red devil / Mama's little boy / We are the chopped / No sex / Rich guns / No rest for the wicked / Living in Detente. (UK-iss.Nov92 on 'Wrong' cd/c; WRONG 001 CD/C)

                                                                        not iss.   Undergrowth
1985.   (12"ep) <UG 1302> **YOU KILL ME**
        – Body bag / Stop it / Some bodies / Manic depression / Paradise (with BILLY & SARAH GAINES). <(re-iss. 1990 & Apr00 on 'Alternative Tentacles'+=; VIRUS 86)> – SEX MAD

                                                                        Alternative Alternative
                                                                        Tentacles   Tentacles
Jan 87. (lp) <(VIRUS 56)> **SEX MAD**
        – Sex mad / Dad / Obsessed / No fgcnuik / Hunt the she beast / Dead Bob / Long days / Metrognome / Revenge / Self pity. <cd-iss. Jun91 +=; VIRUS 56CD> – YOU KILL ME

Feb 88. (7") <VIRUS 60> **DAD. / REVENGE**

May 88. (12"ep) <(VIRUS 62)> **THE DAY EVERYTHING BECAME NOTHING**
        – Forget your life / Beauty and the beast / Brother rat / What Slayde said.

May 88. (lp/c/cd) <(VIRUS 63/+MC/CD)> **SMALL PARTS ISOLATED AND DESTROYED**
        – Brother rat / What Slayde says / Dark ages / Junk / And that's sad / Small parts isolated and destroyed / Victory / Teresa give me that knife / Real love / Lonely. (cd-iss. as 'THE DAY EVERYTHING BECAME ISOLATED AND DESTROYED', which included last ep)

Nov 89. (lp/c/cd) <(VIRUS 77/+MC/CD)> **WRONG**
        – It's catching up / The tower / Brainless wonder / Tired of waiting / Stocktaking / The end of all things / Big Dick / Two lips, two lungs, and one tongue / Rags and bones / Oh no! Bruno! / All lies. (cd+=) – Life in Hell / I am wrong.

Apr 90. (12"ep/cd-ep) <(VIRUS 81/+CD)> **THE POWER OF POSITIVE THINKING**
        – I am wrong / Manic depression / Life in Hell.

―――   early 1991, collaborated with JELLO BIAFRA (Dead Kennedys) on album 'THE SKY IS FALLING AND I WANT MY MOMMY'

1991.   (7") (ALLIED No.10) **OH CANADUH. / NEW AGE**
        (above issued on 'Plastic Head';, below 'Konkurrel' UK)

Jun 91. (d-lp/c/cd) (K 031-130) <VIRUS 97/+MC/CD> **LIVE + CUDDLY (live in Europe)**
        – It's catching up / Two lips, two lungs and one tongue / Rags and bones / Body bag / Brother rat, what Stayde says / Some bodies / Teresa, give me the knife // Victory / Dark ages / The end of all things / The everything became nothing / Dead souls / Metronome / No fucking.

Oct 91. (lp/c/cd) <(VIRUS 98/+MC/CD)> **0 + 2 = 1**
        – Now / The fall / 0 + 2 = 1 / The valley of the blind / Mary / Everyday I start to ooze / When putting it all in order ain't enough / The nothing became everything / I think you know / Ghosts / Joyful reunion.

―――   now without KERR who formed HISSANOL with their engineer, SCOTT HENDERSON

Jun 93. (lp/c/cd) <(VIRUS 123/+MC/CD)> **WHY DO THEY CALL ME MR. HAPPY?**
        – The land of the living / The river / Machine / Madness and death / Happy bridge / Kill everyone now / I need you (with TONYA WYNNE). (c+=/cd+=) – Slowly melting / Lullaby / Cats, sex and Nazis.

―――   added guitarist/keyboardist (TOMMY) and uncredited drummer

Nov 95. (cd/lp) <(VIRUS 171 CD/LP)> **THE WORLDHOOD OF THE WORLD (AS SUCH)**   Oct95
        – Joy / Humans / Angel or devil / He learned how to bleed / I've got a gun / My politics / Lost / Predators / Wiggley worm / Tuck it away / Victim's choice / State of grace / Jungle.

Nov 96. (12") <VIRUS 184> **WOULD WE BE ALIVE? / RISE**

May 97. (m-cd/m-lp) <(FIRSTFISH 1 CD/LP>) **IN THE FISHTANK**   May99
        – Would we be alive? / The river / Joy / You're not one / Big Dick. (above issued on 'Konkurrel')

Dec 97. (12"ep/cd-ep) <(VIRUS 207/+CD)> **WOULD WE BE ALIVE? / YOU ARE NOT THE ONE. / RISE / BIG DICK (alternate version)**

Jun 98. (lp/cd) <(VIRUS 215/+CD)> **DANCE OF THE HEADLESS BOURGEOISE**
        – This story must be told / Going nowhere / I'm an asshole / Disappear / Dance of the headless bourgeoisie / The world wasn't built in a day / I can't stop talking / The rape / Give me the push / One fine day.

Sep 00. (cd) <(VIRUS 248CD)> **ONE**
        – The graveyard shift / Under the sea / Our town / A little too high / Hello, goodbye / The phone call / Bitch's brew / Beat on the brat.

                                                                        Wrong   Wrong
May 01. (cd-ep) <(WRONG 21CD)> **GENERIC SHAME**
        – No big surprise / I get up in the morning and I go to bed at night / Sex is philosophy.

– compilations, etc. –

Oct 94. (cd) Wrong; <(WRONG 13)> **MR. RIGHT & MR. WRONG / ONE DOWN AND TWO TO GO** (material from 1980 to 1994)
        – Red on red / Who fucked who? / Pigs & dogs / Widget / More ICBMs / Blinding light / I'm doing well / This wound will never heal / Real love / Remember / Baldwang must die / Victoria (HANSON BROTHERS) / Sitting on top of the world / Canada is pissed / Burn.

NON

Formed: San Diego, California, USA ... 1977 by BOYD RICE. Although recording in his own name, RICE's solo efforts came mainly under his musical moniker, NON. His output, to a greater degree, sat pretty close to the far edge of avant-garde rock. Using both traditional instruments, as well as turntables, samples and tape loops, NON managed to create a body of provocative, disturbing, and depressive ambient soundscapes. It was not only his sonic stylings that kept him from the mainstream, but also his unpopular and offensive anti-semitic views and Nazi-style takes on Darwin's 'Origin of the Species'. He also built up a relationship with infamous cult-leader and life-serving prisoner, Charles Manson. As with most social aggrovators, RICE was a more complex character than one would believe, having a real propensity for mid sixties love ballads which he saw as the zenith of the pop style. RICE's self-titled debut, 'BOYD RICE', was delivered to the shops in 1981, although he had originally recorded this piece in the seventies, with the working title of 'THE BLACK ALBUM'. This LP showcased RICE's experimental, non-accessible stylings, using mainly tape loops to produce an alienating listen. The following year RICE took on the title of NON to release the full-length outing, 'PHYSICAL EVIDENCE', tracking this during the eighties with the LP, 'BLOOD AND FLAME' (1987). At this point, RICE took a break from the NON musical persona, signalling his label, 'Mute', to issue the compilation, 'EASY LISTENING FOR IRON YOUTH'. The eighties also saw NON collaborate with FRANK TOVEY on the odd, experimental percussion piece, 'EASY LISTENING FOR THE HARD OF HEARING' (1984). NON came back in 1992 with 'IN THE SHADOW OF THE SWORD'. Between this and the release of his 'MIGHT' (1995) full-length set, RICE collaborated with ROSE McDOWALL (of STRAWBERRY SWITCHBLADE fame), SOL INVICTUS' TONY WAKEFORD and DOUG PIERCE of DEATH IN JUNE to form SPELL. Having already worked with McDOWALL on the LP, 'MUSIC, MARTINIS AND MISANTHROPY' (1989), RICE and the strawberry one made a good partnership, and together with the others, SPELL, released the troubling covers album, 'SEASONS IN THE SUN'. McDOWALL continued her musical relationship with RICE, appearing on his NON release, 'GOD AND BEAST' (1997), which was also aided by the production skills of KEN THOMAS. Not to be stopped, NON continued with his off-kilter musical stylings into the millennium, releasing the haunting, yet competent, piece, 'CHILDREN OF THE BLACK SUN' in 2002.

Album rating: BOYD RICE (*5) / PHYSICAL EVIDENCE (*4) / EASY LISTENING FOR THE HARD OF HEARING with Frank Tovey (*5) / BLOOD AND FLAME (*6) / EASY LISTENING FOR IRON YOUTH – THE BEST OF NON compilation (*6) / IN THE SHADOW OF THE SWORD (*4) / SEASONS IN THE SUN as Spell (*5) / MIGHT! (*4) / GOD & BEAST (*6) / RECEIVE THE FLAME (*4) / CHILDREN OF THE BLACK SUN (*6)

BOYD RICE – synthesizers, multi instruments

                                                                        Non   Non
1978.   (one-sided-7"ep) (MR-00) **MODE OF INFECTION / KNIFE LADDER / SOUNDTRACKS**
                                                                        Mute   Grey Beat
1980.   (7"ep; shared with SMEGMA) (MUTE 7) **I CAN'T LOOK STRAIGHT / FLASH CARDS**

Feb 81. (lp; as BOYD RICE) (STUMM 4) **BOYD RICE**
        – Selections 1-9.

Apr 81. (7"ep) <PAGAN 1> **PAGAN MUZAK**
        – Soundtracks 1-3 / Mode of infection. (re-iss. Sep99)

Jan 82. (12"ep) (MUTE 015) **RISE / OUT OUT OUT. / ROMANCE FATAL / DENTRO DE UN ATO**
        <US-iss.Mar96; same as UK>

Sep 82. (lp/c) (STUMM/CSTUMM 10) **PHYSICAL EVIDENCE (live)**
        – The surface runs deep / Going, going, gone / Into thin air / Defenestration / Opening / There / That's that / In the room / Physical evidence / Man kills self while cleaning gun / Inside out / Carnis vale. (re-iss. Apr84; same)

Nov 84. (lp; by BOYD RICE & FRANK TOVEY) (STUMM 20) **EASY LISTENING FOR THE HARD OF HEARING**
        – Extractions 1-12.

                                                                        Mute   Elektra
Jan 87. (lp/cd) (STUMM/CDSTUMM 32) **BLOOD AND FLAME**
        – Fire in the organism / Make red / Sunset / A taste of blood / Kingdom come / King of beast / (Theme from) Dark shadows / Pillar of silence / Storm / Cruenta voluptas / Secret garden, secret fire / Blood stream / Only one / Rise below / And if thou will, remember / Operation Carnival. (cd+=) – Rise / And if thou will, forget / Inside out / Carnis vale. <US-iss.Mar96; same as UK>

Nov 89. (cd/lp) (CD+/STUMM 69) <61262> **EASY LISTENING FOR IRON YOUTH: THE BEST OF NON** (compilation)   Dec91
        – Iron destiny / Conflagration / Rise / Carnis vale / Cruenta voluptas / Tourist trap / Fire in the organism / Fathers day / Scorched earth / Predator – Prey / There was never a moment when evil was real / Eternal ice / Sunset / Cleanliness and order / Defenestration / Embers.

NON (cont) — THE GREAT INDIE DISCOGRAPHY — The 1980s

Oct 92. (cd/lp) *(CD+/STUMM 113)* **IN THE SHADOW OF THE SWORD**
– Introduction – Total war / Eternal ice / Sunrise / Fire in the organism – Vengeance / A world on fire / Without judgement / Scorched Earth / Invocation / Abraxas / Prey / The time will come / Number one law / A world on fire / Love and loves murder. <US-iss.Mar96; same>

— SPELL was actually BOYD + ROSE McDOWALL (of DEATH IN JUNE)

Nov 93. (cd; as SPELL) *(CDSTUMM 126)* **SEASONS IN THE SUN**
– Johnny remember me / Free now to roam / Stone is very very cold / Down from Dover / There's no blood in bone / Terry / Seasons in the sun / This little bird / Our own way / Big red balloon / Endless sleep / Rosemary's baby (lullaby part I). <US-iss.Dec95; 61616>

Oct 95. (cd/lp) *(<CD+/STUMM 139>)* **MIGHT!**
– No nirvana (prelude) / Ye who fall / Credo / Ultimatum / Force / Deletion / Warring atoms / Evolution / No nirvana / The immolation of man / Logic of the spheres / Great destroyers.

Nov 97. (cd) *(CDSTUMM 158) <69044>* **GOD & BEAST**   Dec97
– God & beast / Between Venus & Mars / Millstones / The coming forth / The law / Lucifer, the morning star / Out out out / Phoenix / Total war.

Dec 99. (cd) *(CDSTUMM 128) <9103>* **RECEIVE THE FLAME**   Jan00
– Alpha / Spectre / Everlasting fire / Solitude / Monism / Medici mass / Sangraal / Omega.

Aug 02. (cd) *(CDSTUMM 213) <9183>* **CHILDREN OF THE BLACK SUN**
– Arka / Black sun / Serpent of the heavens / Serpent of the abyss / The underground stream / The fountain of fortune / Son of the sun.

BOYD RICE & FRIENDS

— FRIENDS:- DEATH IN JUNE / CURRENT 93 / SOL INVICTUS / ROSE McDOWALL

New European / People Who

Jul 90. (lp; as BOYD RICE & FRIENDS) *(BADVC 1969)* **MUSICS, MARTINIS AND MISANTHROPY**
(cd-iss. Oct96; BADVCCD 1969)

Hierarchy / not iss.

Apr 96. (cd) *(H330 1CD)* **HATESVILLE!**
– Hatesville / Race riot / Dog / Daydream / What if they gave a love in…. / How God makes little girls / Let's hear it for violence towards women / Piss ant / Nation down for the count / Mr. Intolerance / I am man (sometimes I hate) / The wandering parasite / Love will change the world / Hatesville suicide hotline / Alone with the calm.

Oct 96. (cd) *(H330 3CD)* **BOYD RICE PRESENTS: DEATH'S GLADSOME WEDDING**
(above was actually performed by Transylvania's LEGIONARI)

World Serpent / not iss.

Oct 96. (cd) *(WSB 13)* **RAGNAROK RUNE**

Cacloavello / not iss.

Sep 00. (lp) *(CAL 4)* **THE WAY I FEEL**

— In 2001, BOYD and DOUGLAS PIERCE (off DEATH IN JUNE) released 'WOLF PACT' for 'Neroz'. Previously, a similar collaboration (under SCORPION WIND) issued 'HEAVEN SENT' (1996)

NOTHING BUT HAPPINESS
(see under ⇒ ULTRA VIVID SCENE; 90's section)

NURSE WITH WOUND

Formed: London, England… 1978 by STEPHEN STAPLETON, a graphic designer who resided in Ireland. Although he wrote and performed most of the material himself, he occasionally employed members of spiritual cousins, CURRENT 93, who shared releases with NWW. That year, STAPLETON and the 'United Dairies' imprint debuted with 'CHANCE MEETING ON A DISSECTING TABLE OF A SEWING MACHINE AND AN UMBRELLA', the first limited-edition album in a mindbogglingly prolific career that took in the whole of the 80's and most of the 90's. A tireless noise/sample experimentalist, STAPLETON utilised any sound he could get his hands on, the more humdrum or the more exotic the better. Unsurprisingly, his audience was restricted to those with an enquiring and patient mind, not to mention a healthy bank balance; many of NWW's early albums now fetch between £50 and £100 at record fairs. • **Trivia:** STAPLETON produced The LEGENDARY PINK DOTS among others.

Album rating: CHANCE MEETING… (*4) / + most others depending on your point of view averaging around the same

STEPHEN STAPLETON – instruments

United Dairies / not iss.

1979. (lp) *(UD 01)* **CHANCE MEETING ON A DISSECTING TABLE OF A SEWING MACHINE AND AN UMBRELLA**
1980. (lp) *(UD 03)* **TO THE QUIET MEN FROM A TINY GIRL**
1980. (lp) *(UD 04)* **MERZBILD SCHWET**
1981. (lp) *(UD 08)* **INSECT AND INDIVIDUALS SILENCED**
– Alvin's funeral / Absent old queen underfoot / Mutiles De Guerre.
Feb 84. (lp) *(YMR 03)* **OSTRANENIE 1913**
(above issued on 'Third Mind')
Jul 85. (lp) *(UD 012)* **HOMOTOPY TO MARIE**
May 86. (lp) *(UD 019)* **AUTOMATING VOL.1**
Jul 86. (lp) *(UD 020)* **A MISSING SENSE** (shared with ORGANUM)
Nov 86. (lp) *(TORSO 33-016)* **SPIRAL INSANA**
(above released on 'Torso')

— In 1987, they shared a single 'CRANK' with TERMITE QUEEN's 'Wisecrack' for 'Crystal-Wisewound' label; *WW 01*)
Nov 87. (lp) *(UD 025)* **DRUNK WITH THE OLD MAN OF THE MOUNTAINS**
Jun 88. (m-lp) *(UD 027)* **ALAS THE MADONNA DOES NOT FUNCTION**
– Cut glass poison /

— In 1988, shared 12" 'FAITH'S FAVOURITES' with CURRENT 93 on 'Yankhi' label; *YANKHI 002*)
Jun 89. (lp) *(UD 030)* **AUTOMATING II**
Sep 89. (12"ep/cd-ep) *(UD 031/+CD)* **SORESUCKER. / JOURNEY THROUGH CHEESE**
Dec 89. (lp/cd) *(UD 032/+CD)* **A SUCKED ORANGE**
– Paradise lost / Internal torment II / Autopsy / Stillborn / Deviated instinct / The resurrection encore / Doom / A means to an end / Confessor / Uncontrolled / Talion / Laws of retaliation / Electro hippies / Freddy's revenge (live) / Toranga / Dealers in death.

— In 1990, shared another single 'BURIAL OF THE STONED SARDINE' with CURRENT 93 for 'Harbinger' label; *001*)
Jan 91. (lp) *(UD 038)* **CREAKINESS** (with SPASM)
Apr 91. (lp/cd) *(UD 09/+CD)* **THE 150 MURDEROUS PASSIONS**
1992. (cd) **THUNDER PERFECT MIND**

Clawfist / not iss.

1992. (7") *(Clawfist 12)* **STEEL DREAM MARCH OF THE METAL MEN. / THE DADDA'S INTOXICATION**
1993. (10"ep) *(Clawfist 20)* **CRUMB DUCK** (shared with STEREOLAB)

World Serpent / not iss.

1993. (7") *(WS 7004)* **ALIEN. /**

– other releases, etc. –

Laylah / not iss.

Dec 84. (12") *(LAY 007)* **BRAINED BY FALLING MASONARY. / SHORT DIP IN THE GLORY HOLE**
Sep 85. (lp) *(LAY 015)* **SYLVIE & BABS HIGH-THIGH COMPANION**
(cd-iss. 1989; *LAY 015CD*)
Nov 89. (cd) *(LAY 030CD)* **GYLLENSKOLD**
(lp-iss.Mar90; *LAY 030*)

Idle Hole / not iss.

1988. (3xlp-box) *(MIRROR ONE)* **SOLILOQUY FOR LILITH**
1988. (lp) *(MIRROR 1C)* **SOLILOQUY FOR LILITH PTS 5/6**
1989. (lp) *(MIRROR TWO)* **PRESENTS THE SISTERS OF PATAPHYSICS**
1989. (12") *(MIRROR 003)* **COOLOORTA MOON. / GREAT EMPTY SPACE**

Shock / not iss.

1990. (7") *(SX 004)* **SINISTER SENILE: HUMAN HUMAN HUMAN. / PSYCHEDELIC UNDERGROUND**

Torso / Torso

Oct 97. (lp) *(TORSO 33016)* **SPIRAL INSANA**

THE GREAT INDIE DISCOGRAPHY — The 1980s

OFFHOOKS (see under ⇒ THANES)

OINGO BOINGO

Formed: Los Angeles, California, USA ... 1979 out of performance art/comedy collective, the MYSTIC KNIGHTS OF OINGO BOINGO, by frontman/songwriter, DANNY ELFMAN, who completed the line-up with STEVE BARTEK, KERRY HATCH and drummer DAVID EAGLE (a brass section of LEON SCHNEIDERMAN, SAM PHIPPS and DALE TURNER augmented the New Wave synth sound). Possibly America's answer to XTC, OINGO BOINGO mined a similar vein of surreal humour/downright quirkiness to Ohio-based spiritual cousins, DEVO, on their eponymous debut EP in 1980. After signing to 'A&M' and acquiring the services of fresh drummer, JOHNNY 'VATOS' HERNANDEZ, the increasingly electro-pop styled combo found some degree of success with their first full-set, 'ONLY A LAD' (1981). Subsequent albums, 'NOTHING TO FEAR' (1982) and the ROBERT MARGOULEFF (formerly of late 60's electronic experimentalists, TONTO'S EXPANDING HEADBAND)-produced 'GOOD FOR YOUR SOUL' (1983), also made appearances in the US Top 200, although ELFMAN and his spaced-out crew (HATCH having made way for JOHN AVILA) only really cracked the charts with the 1985 title track to teen movie, 'WEIRD SCIENCE'. By this point, the band had signed a long term deal with 'M.C.A.', going on to further left-field pop successes throughout the mid to late 80's. ELFMAN, however, was to garner greater acclaim for his TV/film soundtrack work, writing scores for such Hollywood blockbusters as 'Beetlejuice', 'Batman' and 'Dick Tracy'. More importantly, ELFMAN was the man behind the backing music for 'The Simpsons', all this activity putting BOINGO (as his outfit were now called) on ice until 1994 when they returned with a Top 75 eponymous album on 'Giant'.

Album rating: ONLY A LAD (*4) / NOTHING TO FEAR (*4) / GOOD FOR YOUR SOUL (*5) / DEAD MAN'S PARTY (*6) / BOI-NGO (*4) / BOINGO ALIVE: CELEBRATION OF A DECADE 1979-1988 (*4) / DARK AT THE END OF THE TUNNEL (*4) / SKELETONS IN THE CLOSET: THE BEST OF OINGO BOINGO compilation (*5) / BOINGO (*3) / FAREWELL: LIVE ... (*4) / ANTHOLOGY collection (*7) / Danny Elfman: also released solo material mainly soundtracks except '84's 'SO-LO'.

DANNY ELFMAN – vocals / **STEVE BARTEK** – lead guitar / **KERRY HATCH** – bass / **RICHARD GIBBS** – keyboards / **DAVID EAGLE** – drums / **LEON SCHNEIDERMAN** – saxophone / **SAM PHIPPS** – saxophone / **DALE TURNER** – trumpet

		I.R.S.	I.R.S.
Aug 80.	(10"ep) <SP 70400> **OINGO BOINGO EP**	-	-
	– Only a lad / Violent love / Ain't this the life / I'm so bad.		
Jun 81.	(7") (PFP 1002) **ONLY A LAD. / AIN'T THIS THE LIFE**		

— **JOHNNY 'VATOS' HERNANDEZ** – drums; repl. EAGLE

		A&M	A&M
Aug 81.	(lp) (AMLH 64863) <4863> **ONLY A LAD**		
	– Little girls / Perfect system / On the outside / Capitalism / You really got me / Only a lad / What you see / Controller / Imposter / Nasty habits.		
Aug 82.	(7") (AMS 8244) **PRIVATE LIFE. / WILD SEX**		
Sep 82.	(lp) (AMLH 64903) <4930> **NOTHING TO FEAR**		Aug82
	– Nothing to fear / Grey matter / Reptiles and Samurai / Insects / Whole day of / Islands / Running on a treadmill / Private life / Wild sex / Why'd we come.		
Sep 83.	(lp) (AMLH 64959) <4959> **GOOD FOR YOUR SOUL**		
	– Who do you want to be / Little guns / Nothing bad ever happens / Fill the void / Good for your soul / Cry of the Vatos / No spill blood / Wake up (it's 1984) / Pictures of you / Dead or alive / Sweat.		

— **JOHN AVILA** – bass; repl. HATCH

		M.C.A.	M.C.A.
Aug 85.	(7") <52633> **WEIRD SCIENCE. / (other track by Ira & The Geeks)**	-	45
	(above songs from the film of the same name)		
Nov 85.	(lp/c/cd) <(MCA/+C/D 5665)> **DEAD MAN'S PARTY**		98
	– Just another day / Dead man's party / Heard somebody cry / No one loves forever / Stay / Fool's paradise / Help me / Same man as I was before / Weird science.		
Jan 86.	(7") <52726> **JUST ANOTHER DAY. / DEAD MAN'S PARTY**	-	85

— **MIKE BACICH** – keyboards; repl. R.GIBBS

Mar 87.	(lp/c/cd) <(MCA/+C/D 5811)> **BOI-NGO**		77
	– Home again / Where do all my friends go / Elevator man / New generation / We close our eyes / Not my slave / My life / Outrageous / Pain.		
Oct 88.	(d-lp/d-cd) <MCA/+D 8030> **BOINGO ALIVE – CELEBRATION OF A DECADE 1979-1988 (live July '88)**	-	90

– Dead man's party / Dead or alive / No spill blood / Stay / Cinderella undercover / Home again / Help me / Just another day / Only makes me laugh / My life / Nothing to fear (but fear itself) / Not my slave / We close our eyes / Elevator man / Return of the dead man / Winning side / Wild sex (in the working class) / Grey matter / Private life / Gratitude / No one lives for ever / Mama / Capitalism / Who do you want to be / Sweat / Violent love / On the outside / Only a lad / Goodbye-goodbye / Country sweat / Return of the dead man 2.

— **CARL GRAVES** – keyboards, vocals; repl. BACICH

Mar 90.	(cd/c/lp) <MCA 6363> **DARK AT THE END OF THE TUNNEL**		72
	– When the lights go out / Skin / Out of control / Glory be / Long breakdown / Flesh 'n' blood / Run away (the escape song) / Dream somehow / Is this / Try to believe. (cd+=/c+=) – Right to know.		

— around this time ELFMAN concentrated writing scores for movies, namely 'Beetlejuice', 'Batman', 'Dick Tracy' and of course 'The Simpsons' TV series

		Giant	Giant
Oct 94.	(cd/c; as BOINGO) (74321 18971-2/-4) <24555> **BOINGO**		71 May94
	– Insanity / Hey! / Mary / Can't see (useless) / Pedestrian wolves / Lost like this / Spider / War again / I am the walrus / Tender lumplings / Change / Helpless.		
		not iss.	A&M
Apr 96.	(d-cd/d-lp) <540504> **FAREWELL – LIVE FROM THE UNIVERSAL AMPHITHEATRE, HALLOWEEN 1995 (live)**	-	
	– Insanity / Little girls / Cinderella undercover / Controller / Burn me up / Insects / No one lives forever / Hey! / Reptiles and Samurai / Water / I am the walrus / Piggies / We close our eyes / Mary / Can't see (useless) / Helpless / I'm so bad / Change / Stay / Who do you want to be / On the outside / Wild sex (in the working class) / Dead man's party / Nasty habits / Clowns of death / Ain't this the life / A whole day off / Grey matter / No spill blood / Only a lad.		

– compilations, etc. –

Feb 89.	(lp,cd) A&M; <5217> **SKELETONS IN THE CLOSET: THE BEST OF OINGO BOINGO**		
Nov 92.	(cd/c) M.C.A.; <MCA D/C 10424> **BEST O' BOINGO**	-	-
Nov 99.	(d-cd) Hip-O; <490494> **ANTHOLOGY**	-	-
	– Intro – Tender lumpings (live) / Ain't this the life / Nasty habits / On the outside / Only a lad / Little girls / Grey matter / Wild sex (in the working class) / Private life / No spill blood / Nothing bad ever happens / Sweat / Who do you want to be / Gratitude / It only makes me laugh / Everybody needs / Dead man's party / Weird science / Just another day / Stay / Not my slave / Where do all my friends go / Mama / Cinderella undercover / Flesh 'n blood / When the lights go out / Out of control / Insanity (medium version) / Mary / We close our eyes (live) / Whole day off (live) / Piggies (live) / Insects (live) / Goodbye, goodbye.		
Sep 02.	(cd) A&M; <113020> **THE BEST OF OINGO BOINGO**	-	

OMD (see under ⇒ ORCHESTRAL MANOEUVRES IN THE DARK)

100 FLOWERS (see under ⇒ URINALS; 70's section)

OPAL (see under ⇒ MAZZY STAR; in 90's section)

ORANGE (see under ⇒ STRAITJACKET FITS)

ORANGE JUICE (see under ⇒ COLLINS, Edwyn)

ORCHESTRAL MANOEUVRES IN THE DARK

Formed: West Kirby, Liverpool, England ... Autumn 1978, initially as The ID, by ANDREW McCLUSKEY and PAUL HUMPHREYS. After a one-off indie single, the coldly pulsing 'ELECTRICITY', for 'Factory', they signed to 'Virgin' subsidiary label, 'Dindisc'. Early in 1980, the group hit the UK Top 75 with 'RED FRAME – WHITE LIGHT', paving the way for an eponymous Top 30 parent album. Later that summer, they scored further chart successes with 'MESSAGES' and 'ENOLA GAY' (the name of the plane which dropped the Hiroshima bomb), the latter an infectiously melancholy swirl of electronica which belied its horrific subject matter. The song was also the highlight of the 'ORGANISATION' (1980) album, wherein the drum machines of previous recordings had been replaced with a live drummer, MALCOLM HOLMES. Heavily influenced by KRAFTWERK, OMD's cerebral electro-pop became progressively warmer and more commercial as the decade wore on. Beginning with the soporific lilt of 'SOUVENIR', McCLUSKEY and HUMPHREYS embarked upon the most successful period of their career, releasing a string of Top 5 hits and well-received albums, namely 'ARCHITECTURE & MORALITY' (1981), 'DAZZLE SHIPS' (1983), 'JUNK CULTURE' (1984) and 'CRUSH' (1985). O.M.D. were a constant feature in the singles chart through the early to mid 80's, like a more pretentious, less claustrophobic cousin to DEPECHE MODE, their biggest hit of the era being the breezy 'LOCOMOTION' (mercifully, not a cover of the LITTLE EVA number!), complete with horn stabs courtesy of the WEIR BROTHERS (NEIL & GRAHAM) who later joined the group as a permanent fixture. With the 'CRUSH' album, OMD enjoyed a brief flurry of Stateside success via the twee romanticism of the 'SO IN LOVE' and 'SECRET' singles, although by the release of the patchy 'PACIFIC AGE' (1986) the following year, the writing partnership of McCLUSKEY and HUMPHREYS was beginnning to falter. The latter eventually departed in 1989 to form The LISTENING POOL, while McCLUSKEY carried on with OMD as a solo project, resurfacing in

ORCHESTRAL MANOEUVRES IN THE DARK (cont)   **THE GREAT INDIE DISCOGRAPHY**   The 1980s

early '91 with the annoying 'SAILING ON THE SEVEN SEAS', a Top 3 hit. The subsequent album, 'SUGAR TAX' (1991) also made the Top 3 although the revamped OMD was clearly an entirely different beast, airbrushed pop lacking the mystery and romance of the early material. A further album, 'LIBERATOR', carried on in a similar vein. • **Songwriters:** All material written by McCLUSKEY & HUMPHREYS, until the latter's exit. Covered; I'M WAITING FOR THE MAN (Velvet Underground) / NEON LIGHTS (Kraftwerk). • **Trivia:** An ID track 'JULIA'S SONG', appeared on an 'Open Eye' indie compilation album, 'Street To Street' in 1978.

Album rating: ORCHESTRAL MANOEUVRES IN THE DARK (*7) / ORGANISATION (*6) / ARCHITECTURE & MORALITY (*7) / DAZZLE SHIPS (*5) / JUNK CULTURE (*6) / THE PACIFIC AGE (*4) / IN THE DARK – THE BEST OF OMD compilation (*8) / SUGAR TAX (*5) / LIBERATOR (*5) / UNIVERSAL (*5) / THE OMD SINGLES compilation (*7)

ANDREW McCLUSKEY (b.24 Jun'59, Wirral, England) – vocals, bass, synthesizers (ex-DALEK I) / **PAUL HUMPHRIES** (b.27 Feb'60, London, England) – keyboards, synths. (ex-The ID) with backing from computer 'Winston'.

		Factory	not iss.
May 79.	(7") *(FAC 6)* **ELECTRICITY. / ALMOST**	–	–
		Dindisc	not iss.
Sep 79.	(7") *(DIN 2)* **ELECTRICITY (re-recorded). / ALMOST**	–	–
Feb 80.	(7"/12") *(DIN 6/+12)* **RED FRAME – WHITE LIGHT. / I BETRAY MY FRIENDS**	67	–

— guests **DAVID FAIRBURN** – guitar / **MALCOLM HOLMES** – drums / **MARTIN COOPER** – sax

| Feb 80. | (2x12"lp/c) *(DID/+C 2)* **ORCHESTRAL MANOEUVRES IN THE DARK** | 27 | |

– Bunker soldiers / Almost / Mystereality / Electricity / The Messerschmit twins / Messages / Julia's song / Red frame – white light / Dancing / Pretending to see the future. *(re-iss. Aug84 on 'Virgin' lp/c; OVED/+C 96) (cd-iss. Jul87; DIDCD 2)*

| May 80. | (7") *(DIN 15)* **MESSAGES. / TAKING SIDES AGAIN** | 13 | – |

(ext-10") *(DIN 15-10)* – Waiting for the man.

— added **DAVID HUGHES** – keyboards (ex-DALEK I LOVE YOU, ex-SECRETS) and now f/t member **MALCOLM HOLMES** – drums (ex-CLIVE LANGER & THE BOXES, ex-ID)

| Sep 80. | (7"/ext.12") *(DIN 22/+12)* **ENOLA GAY. / ANNEX** | 8 | – |
| Oct 80. | (lp/c) *(DID/+C 6)* **ORGANISATION** | 6 | – |

– Enola Gay / 2nd thought / VCL XI / Motion and heart / Statues / The misunderstanding / The more I see you / Promise / Stanlow. *(free 7"ep)* – INTRODUCING RADIOS / PROGRESS. / DISTANCE FADES BETWEEN US / WHEN I WAS SIX *(re-iss. Aug88 on 'Virgin' lp/c; OVED/+C 147) (cd-iss. Jul87; DIDCD 6)*

— **MALCOLM COOPER** – saxophone, keyboards (ex-DALEK I LOVE YOU) repl. HUGHES

		Dindisc	Epic
Aug 81.	(7"/ext.10") *(DIN 24/+10)* **SOUVENIR. / MOTION AND HEART (Amazon version) / SACRED HEART**	3	–
Oct 81.	(7"/ext.12") *(DIN 36/+12)* **JOAN OF ARC. / THE ROMANCE OF THE TELESCOPE (unfinished version)**	5	–
Nov 81.	(lp/c) *(DID/+C 12) <37721>* **ARCHITECTURE & MORALITY**	3	

– New stone age / She's leaving / Souvenir / Sealand / Joan Of Arc (Maid of Orleans) / Architecture and morality / Georgia / The beginning and the end. *(cd-iss. 1988 on 'Virgin' lp/c; OVED/+C 276) (re-iss. Apr90; DIDCD 12) (cd re-iss. Jan95; CDIDX 12)*

| Jan 82. | (7") *(DIN 40)* **MAID OF ORLEANS (THE WALTZ JOAN OF ARC). / NAVIGATION** | 4 | |

(12"+=) *(DIN 40-12)* – Of all the things we've made. *(3"cd-s iss.Jan88; CDT 2)*

Jan 82.	(7") **SOUVENIR. / NEW STONE AGE**	–	
		Virgin	Epic-Virgin
Feb 83.	(7"/7"pic-d)(12") *(VS/+Y 527)<VS 527-12>* **GENETIC ENGINEERING. / 4-NEU**	20	–
Mar 83.	(lp/c) *(V/TCV 2261) <38543>* **DAZZLE SHIPS**	5	

– Radio Prague / Genetic engineering / ABC auto-industry / Telegraph / This is Helena / International / Dazzle ships / The romance of the telescope / Silent running / Radio waves / Time zones / Of all the things we've made. *(cd-iss. 1985; CDV 2261) (re-iss. 1987 lp/c; OVED/+C 106) (cd re-iss. Apr97 on 'Virgin-VIP'; CDVIP 170)*

Apr 83.	(7"/7"pic-d)(12") *(VS/+Y 580)(VS 580-12)* **TELEGRAPH. / 66 AND FADING**	42	–
May 83.	(7") **TELEGRAPH. / THIS IS HELENA**	–	
		Virgin	A&M
Apr 84.	(7"/7"sha-pic-d) *(VS/+Y 660)* **LOCOMOTION. / HER BODY IN MY SOUL**	5	Nov84

(ext.12") *(VS 660-12)* – The avenue. *(3"cd-s-iss.Jun88; CDT 12)*

| May 84. | (lp/c) *(V/TCV 2310) <5027>* **JUNK CULTURE** | 9 | Nov84 |

– Junk culture / Tesla girls / Locomotion / Apollo / Never turn away / Love and violence / Hard day / All wrapped up / White trash / Talking loud and clear. *(cd-iss. 1986; CDV 2310) (re-iss. Mar90 lp/c; OVED/+C 215) (cd re-iss. Aug98 on 'Virgin-VIP'; CDVIP 215)*

| Jun 84. | (7"/7"pic-d)(12") *(VS/+Y 685)(VS 685-12)* **TALKING LOUD AND CLEAR. / JULIA'S SONG** | 11 | – |
| Aug 84. | (7") *(VS 705)* **TESLA GIRLS. / TELEGRAPH (live)** | 21 | – |

(12"+=)(c-s+=) *(VS 705-12)(TVS 705)* – Garden city.

| Oct 84. | (7"/7"pic-d) *(VS/+Y 727)* **NEVER TURN AWAY. / WRAP-UP** | 70 | – |

(ext.12") *(VS 727-12)* – Waiting for the man.

| May 85. | (7") *(VS 766) <2746>* **SO IN LOVE. / CONCRETE HANDS** | 27 | 26 Aug85 |

(ext;12")(ext.12"pic-d) *(VS 766-13)(VSY 766-14)* – Maria Gallante.
(d7"+=) *(VS 766)* – White trash (live).

| Jun 85. | (lp)(c) *(V/TCV 2349) <5077>* **CRUSH** | 13 | 38 Jul85 |

– So in love / Secret / Bloc bloc bloc / Women III / Crush / 88 seconds in Greensboro / The native daughters of the west / La femme accident / Hold you / The lights are going out. *(cd-iss. Jan86; CDV 2349) (cd re-iss. Oct96 on 'Virgin-VIP'; CDVIP 155)*

| Jul 85. | (7") *(VS 796)* **SECRET. / DRIFT** | 34 | – |

(ext-d12"+=) *(VS 796-12)* – Red frame – white light / I betray my friends.

| Oct 85. | (7"/7"sha-pic-d) *(VS/+S 811)* **LA FEMME ACCIDENT. / FIREGUN** | 42 | |

(ext.d12"+=) *(VSD 811-12)* – Locomotion (live) / Enola Gay (live).

Nov 85.	(7") *<2794>* **SECRET. / FIREGUN**	–	63
Feb 86.	(7") *<2811>* **IF YOU LEAVE. / LA FEMME ACCIDENT**	–	4
Apr 86.	(7") *(VS 843)* **IF YOU LEAVE. / 88 SECONDS IN GREENSBORO**	48	

(12") *(VS 843-12)* – ('A'extended) / Locomotion (live).

— added The **WEIR BROTHERS** (NEIL & GRAHAM) (had guested on earlier songs)

| Aug 86. | (7"/7"pic-d) *(VS/+Y 888) <2872>* **(FOREVER) LIVE AND DIE. / THIS TOWN** | 11 | 19 |

(12"+=) *(VS 888-13)* – ('A'extended).

| Sep 86. | (lp/c/cd) *(CD/TC+/V 2398) <5144>* **THE PACIFIC AGE** | 15 | 47 Oct86 |

– Stay (the black rose and the universal wheel) / (Forever) Live and die / The Pacific age / The dead girls / Shame / Southern / Flame of hope / Goddess of love / We love you / Watch us fall.

| Nov 86. | (7") *(VS 911)* **WE LOVE YOU. / WE LOVE YOU (dub)** | 54 | |

(12"+=) *(VS 911-12)* – ('A'extended).
(d7"+=) *(VS 911)* – If you leave / 88 seconds on Greensboro.
(free c-s w7"+=) *(VSC 911)* – Souvenir / Electricity / Enola Gay / Joan of Arc.

| Apr 87. | (7") *(VS 938)* **SHAME (re-recorded). / GODDESS OF LOVE** | 52 | |

(12"+=) *(VS 938-12)* – ('B're-recorded version).
(cd-s+=) *(MIKE 938-12)* – (Forever) Live and die / Messages.

| Jan 88. | (7") *(VSG 987) <3002>* **DREAMING. / SATELLITE** | 50 | 16 Feb88 |

(ext.12"pic-d) *(VS 987-12)* – Gravity never failed.
(cd-s++=/3"cd-s++=) *(VDCD/+X 987)* – Dreaming. *(re-dist.Jun88, hit Uk No.60)*
(10") *(VS 987-10)* – ('A'side) / ('A'William Orbit mix) / Messages / Secret.

| Feb 88. | (pic-cd/cd/c/lp) *(CDP/CD/TC+/OMD 1) <5186>* **IN THE DARK – THE BEST OF O.M.D.** (compilation) | 2 | 46 |

– Electricity / Messages / Enola Gay / Souvenir / Joan of Arc / Maid of Orleans (Joan Of Arc waltz) / Talking loud and clear / Tesla girls / Locomotion / So in love / Secret / If you leave / (Forever) Live and die / Dreaming. *(cd+=)* – Telegraph / We love you (12"version) / La femme accident (12"version) / Genetic engineering. *(re-iss. Sep94; same)*

OMD

— **ANDY McCLUSKEY** now sole survivor after others left 1989. HUMPHREYS formed The LISTENING POOL in the early 90's. / added **STUART BOYLE** – guitar / **NIGEL IPINSON** – keyboards / **PHIL COXON** – keyboards / **ABE JUCKS** – drums

		Virgin	Virgin
Mar 91.	(7"/c-s) *(VS/+C 1310)* **SAILING ON THE SEVEN SEAS. / BURNING**	3	

(12") *(VS 1310-12)* – ('A'extended) / Floating on the seven seas.
(cd-s) *(VSCD 1310)* – ('A'extended) / Dancing on the seven seas / Big town.
(cd-s) *(VSCD 1310)* – ('A'side) / Floating on the seven seas / Dancing on the seaven seas (Larrabee mix) / Sugartax.

| May 91. | (cd/c/lp) *(CD/TC+/V 2648) <91715>* **SUGAR TAX** | 3 | |

– Sailing on the seven seas / Pandora's box / Then you turn away / Speed of light / Was it something I said / Big town / Call my name / Apollo XI / Walking on air / Walk tall / Neon lights / All that glitters.

| Jun 91. | (7"/c-s) *(VS/+C 1331)* **PANDORA'S BOX. / ALL SHE WANTS IS EVERYTHING** | 7 | |

(cd-s+=) *(VSCD 1331)* – ('A'-Constant pressure mix) / ('A'-Diesel fingers mix).
(12") *(VS 1331-12)* – (2-'A'mixes).
(cd-s) *(VSCDX 1331)* – (3-'A'mixes).

| Sep 91. | (7"/c-s) *(VS/+C 1368)* **THEN YOU TURN AWAY. / SUGAR TAX** | 50 | |

(cd-s+=) *(VSCD 1368)* – Area / ('A'-Inforce repeat mix).
(cd-s) *(VSCDG 1368)* – ('A'side) / ('A'-Repeat mix) / Sailing on the seven seas / Vox humana.

| Nov 91. | (7"/c-s) *(VS/+C 1380)* **CALL MY NAME. / WALK TALL** | 50 | |

(12") *(VS 1380-12)* – ('A'side) / Brides of Frankenstein.
(cd-s++=) *(VSCD 1380)* – ('A'side) / ('A'version) / Brides . . . (dub).

| May 93. | (7"/c-s) *(VS/+C 1444)* **STAND ABOVE ME. / CAN I BELIEVE YOU** | 21 | |

(cd-s+=) *(VSCDG 1444)* – ('A'-Transcendental mix) / ('A'-Hynofunk mix).
(12") *(VS 1444-12)* – ('A'side) / ('A'-Transcendental mix) / ('A'-10 minute version).

| Jun 93. | (cd/c/lp) *(CD/TC+/V 2715) <88225>* **LIBERATOR** | 14 | |

– Stand above me / Everyday / King of stone / Dollar girl / Dream of me (based on Love's theme) / Sunday morning / Agnus Dei / Love and hate you / Heaven is / Best years of our lives / Christine / Only tears. *(cd re-iss. Aug98 on 'VIP-Virgin'; CDVIP 217)*

| Jul 93. | (7"/c-s) *(VS/+C 1461)* **DREAM OF ME (BASED ON LOVE'S THEME). / ('A'mix)** | 24 | |

(cd-s+=) *(VSCDT 1461)* – Strange sensations / The place you fear the most.
(cd-s) *(VSCDX 1461)* – ('A'side) / Enola Gay / Dreaming / Call my name.

| Sep 93. | (7"/c-s) *(VS/+C 1471)* **EVERYDAY. / ELECTRICITY (live)** | 59 | |

(cd-s+=) *(VSCDT 1471)* – Walk tall (live) / Locomotion (live).

— **STUART KERSHAW** – drums; repl. JUCKS

| Aug 96. | (c-s/cd/cd-s) *(VSC/+DT 1599)* **WALKING ON THE MILKY WAY / MATTHEW STREET / NEW DARK AGE** | 17 | – |

(cd-s) *(VSCDG 1599)* – ('A'side) / Joan of Arc (live) / Maid of Orleans (live) / Walking on air (live).

| Sep 96. | (cd/c) *(CDV/TCV 2807)* **UNIVERSAL** | 24 | – |

– Universal / Walking on the Milky Way / The Moon & the Sun / The Black Sea / Very close to far away / The gospel of St Jude / That was then / Too late / The boy from the chemist is here to see you / If you're still in love with me / New head / Victory waltz.

| Oct 96. | (c-s) *(VSC 1606)* **UNIVERSAL / HEAVEN IS** | 55 | – |

(cd-s+=) *(VSCDT 1606)* – Messages (live).
(cd-s) *(VSCDG 1606)* – ('A'side) / King of stone (live) / Talking loud & clear (live) / ('A'-abum version).

| Sep 98. | (cd-s) *(VSCDT 1694)* **THE OMD REMIXES: ENOLA GAY (OMD vs SASHI) / ELECTRICITY (Micronauts mix) / SOUVENIR (Moby mix)** | 35 | – |

(12") *(VST 1694)* – (first mix) / Souvenir (hard house) / Souvenir (7am version).
(12") *(VSTX 1694)* – (first two mixes) / Apollo XI (Northern electric soul remix).

ORCHESTRAL MANOEUVRES IN THE DARK (cont)

Sep 98. (cd/c) (CDV/TCV 2859) <46520> **THE OMD SINGLES**
(compilation)   **16**   Nov98
– Electricity / Messages / Enola Gay / Souvenir / Joan of Arc / Maid of Orleans / Tesla girls / Locomotion / Talking loud and clear / So in love / If you leave / (Forever) Live and die / Dreaming / Sailing the seven seas / Pandora's box / Call my name / Dream of me (based on love's theme).

– compilations, etc. –

May 84. (lp) *Epic;* **ORCHESTRAL MANOEUVRES IN THE DARK**
– (compilation of first 2 albums)
Feb 89. (12") *Old Gold; (OG 4099)* **ENOLA GAY. / ELECTRICITY**
Mar 89. (12") *Old Gold; (OG 4109)* **SOUVENIR (extended). / TALKING LOUD AND CLEAR (extended)**
Feb 89. (12") *Virgin; (SP12 285)* **BRIDES OF FRANKENSTEIN (OMD megamixes: LOCOMOTION / SO IN LOVE / SECRET / IF YOU LEAVE / WE LOVE YOU)**
Nov 90. (3xpic-cd-box) *Virgin; (TPAK 7)* **CD BOXED SET**
– (first 3 albums)

ORCHIDS

Formed: Govan, Glasgow, Scotland ... by main songwriter, JAMES HACKETT, alongside MATTHEW DRUMMOND, CHRIS QUINN, JAMES MOODY and JOHN. A surprise signing to 'Sarah' records late in 1987, they released their first official debut, 'I'VE GOT A HABIT', early the following year having previously recorded a flexi-disc track for indie fanzine 'Sha La La'. A popsicle bedsit-land band with a sound similar to The BATHERS or The WEATHER PROPHETS, they released a series of singles, most of them appearing on their IAN CARMICHAEL (ONE DOVE)-produced debut set, 'UNHOLY SOUL' (1991). The ORCHIDS continued to flower over subsequent albums, namely 'EPICUREAN: A SOUNDTRACK' (1992) and 'STRIVING FOR THE LAZY PERFECTION' (1994), the latter being produced by ONE DOVE's IAN CARMICHAEL.

Album rating: UNHOLY SOUL (*5) / EPICUREAN: A SOUNDTRACK compilation (*6) / STRIVING FOR THE LAZY PERFECTION (*6)

JAMES HACKETT – vocals / **MATTHEW DRUMMOND** – guitar / **JOHN** – guitar / **JAMES MOODY** – bass / **CHRIS QUINN** – drums

Sha La La   not iss.

Jun 87. (7"flexi) *(Sha La La Ba Ba Ba 5)* **FROM THIS DAY. / Sea Urchins:- Summertime**

Sarah   not iss.

Feb 88. (7"ep) *(SARAH 002)* **I'VE GOT A HABIT EP**
– I've got a habit / Apologies / Give me some peppermint freedom.
Nov 88. (7"ep) *(SARAH 011)* **UNDERNEATH THE WINDOW, UNDERNEATH THE SINK EP**
– Defy the law / Underneath the window, underneath the sink / Tiny words / Walter.
Aug 89. (10"m-lp) *(SARAH 401)* **LYCEUM (live)**
– It's only obvious / A place called home / Caveman / The York song / Carole-Ann / Hold on / Blue light / If you can't find love.
Sep 89. (7"m) *(SARAH 023)* **WHAT WILL WE DO NEXT. / AS TIME GOES BY / YAWN**
Feb 90. (12"m) *(SARAH 029)* **SOMETHING FOR THE LONGING. / FAREWELL, DEAR BONNIE / ON A SUNDAY**
(below single on 'Caff')

––– DRUMMOND + MOODY were also part of The WAKE in the early 90's
Sep 90. (7"ltd) *(CAFF 11)* **AN ILL WIND THAT BLOWS. / ALL THOSE THINGS**
Feb 91. (12"ep) *(SARAH 042)* **PENETRATION**
– Bemused confused and bedraggled / Pelican blonde / Tropical fishbowl / How does that feel / Sigh.
May 91. (lp/cd) *(SARAH 605/+CD)* **UNHOLY SOUL**
– Me and the black and white dream / Women priests and addicts / Bringing you the love / Frank De Salvo / Long drawn Sunday night / Peaches / Dirty clothing / Moon lullaby / Coloured stone / The sadness of sex (part 1) / Waiting for the storm / You know I'm fine.
Sep 92. (7"/cd-s) *(SARAH 066/+CD)* **THAUMATURGY. / I WAS JUST DREAMING / BETWEEN SLEEPING AND WAKING**
Sep 92. (lp/cd) *(SARAH 611/+CD)* **EPICUREAN: A SOUNDTRACK**
(compilation)
– Peaches / A place called home / Tiny words / Moon lullaby / Walter / It's only obvious / Long drawn Sunday night / Blue light / Yawn / Sigh / Something for the longing / The York song / Bemused confused and bedraggled / Caveman / Underneath the window, underneath the sink / Pelican blonde / Women priests and addicts / Carole-Anne / Tropical fishbowl / The sadness of sex (part 1).
Jan 94. (lp/cd) *(SARAH 617/+CD)* **STRIVING FOR THE LAZY PERFECTION**
– Obsession No.1 / Striving for the lazy perfection / The searching / Welcome to my curious heart / Avignon / A living Ken and Barbie / Beautiful liar / A kind of Eden / Prayers to St. Jude / Lovechild / Give a little honey / I've got to wake up / The perfect reprise.

––– went to ground after above

– compilations, etc. –

1990's. (7"ep; split with BOUQUET + CRYSTAL GARDEN) *Bring On Bull; (BULL 007)* **STRIVING FOR LAZY PERFECTION**

ORIGINAL MIRRORS

Formed: Liverpool, England ... early '79 by veterans of the new wave scene, songwriters STEVE ALLEN (ex-DEAF SCHOOL) and IAN BROUDIE (ex-BIG IN JAPAN), who enlisted the help of London-based musicians, PHIL SPALDING, JONATHAN PERKINS and PETE KIRCHNER. Signing to 'Mercury' records, they debuted with the single, 'COULD THIS BE HEAVEN', previewing their 1980 eponymous debut album. A combination of uptempo, keyboard-tinkling New Wave pop and hookline choruses, the record plumbed the depths with an awful cover of Diana Ross & The Supremes' 'REFLECTIONS' (pun intended?). SPALDING was then substituted with JIMMY HUGHES prior to the release of their second collection, 'HEART, TWANGO & RAW BEAT' (1981), thankfully their last effort. However, IAN BROUDIE did go on to greater things, most notably, The LIGHTNING SEEDS, while KIRCHNER was given a call-up by none other than ageing blues rockers STATUS QUO!

Album rating: HEARTBEAT – THE BEST OF THE ORIGINAL MIRRORS compilation (*4)

STEVE ALLEN – vocals, piano, guitar (ex-DEAF SCHOOL) / **IAN BROUDIE** (b. 4 Aug'58) – guitar, keyboards, vocals (ex-BIG IN JAPAN, ex-SECRETS) / **JONATHAN PERKINS** – keyboards, guitar (ex-XTC, ex-STADIUM DOGS) / **PHIL SPALDING** – bass (ex-BERNIE TORME) / **PETE KIRCHNER** – drums

Mercury   Arista

Nov 79. (7") *(6007 245)* **COULD THIS BE HEAVEN. / NIGHT OF THE ANGELS**
Feb 80. (7") *(MER 5)* **BOYS CRY. / CHAINS OF LOVE**
Feb 80. (lp) *(9102 039)* <4264> **ORIGINAL MIRRORS**
– Sharp words / Reflections / The boys, the boys / Flying / Chains of love / Could this be Heaven / Boys cry / Night of the angels / Panic in the night / Feel like a train.

––– **JIMMY HUGHES** – bass; repl. SPALDING

Apr 81. (7") *(MER 65)* **DANCING WITH THE REBELS. / SURE YEAH**
(12"+=) *(MERX 65)* – On Broadway.
May 81. (lp) *(6359 046)* **HEART, TWANGO & RAW BEAT**
– Heart, twango and raw beat / Dancing with the rebels / Teen beat / When you're young / Things to come / Darling . . . in London / Don't cry baby / Please don't wear red / Swing together / Time has come.
Jun 81. (7") *(DREAM 1)* **20,000 DREAMERS. / TIME HAS COME**
(12"+=) *(DREAM 12)* – Dancing with the rebels.

––– after they split BROUDIE became a producer and formed The CARE (with WILD SWANS members) before he was the man behind The LIGHTNING SEEDS. KIRCHNER got a surprise call-up from STATUS QUO in later years.

– compilations, etc. –

Jun 96. (cd) *Mercury; (532594-2)* **HEARTBEAT – THE BEST OF THE ORIGINAL MIRRORS** (combination of both albums)

ORIGINAL SINS
(see under ⇒ BROTHER J.T.; 90's section)

P

PAIN TEENS

Formed: Houston, Texas, USA ... 1988 by SCOTT AYERS, his girlfriend BLISS BLOOD, along with KIRK CARR and FRANK GARYMARTIN. Fixated on twisted sexuality and and the more unsavoury impulses of the human psyche, The PAIN TEENS were a natural choice for KING COFFEY's 'Trance Syndicate' imprint, having previously debuted with 1988's eponymous set; in '89 the 'CASE HISTORIES' follow-up set was delivered. First up for the label was 1990's 'BORN IN BLOOD', a sample-hungry collection of fractured but accessible noise experimentation that set the tone for the bulk of their 90's output. Memorably described as the Marquis de Sade put to music, The PAIN TEENS' uneasy listening experience continued with 'STIMULATION FESTIVAL' (1992), 'DESTROY ME LOVER' (1993) and 'BEAST OF DREAMS' (1995), the latter recorded after the band had been reduced to a duo of BLISS and SCOTT; by this point their partnership was purely musical. Having already given up live work, the pair retired for an extended sabbatical.

Album rating: PAIN TEENS (*6) / CASE HISTORIES (*6) / BORN IN BLOOD (*6) / STIMULATION FESTIVAL (*6) / DESTROY ME, LOVER (*7) / BEAST OF DREAMS (*6)

BLISS BLOOD – vocals, percussion / **SCOTT AYERS** – guitar, samples, drums / **KIRK CARR** – bass / **FRANK GARYMARTIN** – drums

			not iss.	Anomie
1988.	(lp) <none> **PAIN TEENS**		-	

– Inside me / Unameable / Brown Jenkin / A knife / The shoemaker / Amidst the rubble / A world of destruction / Valley of the sun / Symptoms / The poor doubt blood / Where madness dwells / A continuing nightmare / Count Magnus. <cd-iss. Apr98 on 'Charnel'+=; 32> – Tapes / Innsmouth / Freezing wind / The somnambulist.

1989.	(lp) <none> **CASE HISTORIES**	-	

– Hands in fire / Bannoy / Veil of light / Puzzling diagnoses / Wot's de matter / Preppy killer / Unthinkable / Path of destruction / New woman / Bug in a can.

			not iss.	Smilin' Ear
1990.	(7"ep+red) <SE 001> **LADY OF FLAME**		-	

– Lady of flame / Prophecy / My desire / Philoop.

			Trance Syndicate	Trance Syndicate
Nov 90.	(lp/c/cd) <(TR 03/+CS/CD)> **BORN IN BLOOD**			

– The basement / Pleasures of the flesh / Shotguns / Bad in my head / The way love used to be / Secret is sickness / Lady of flame / Desu evol yaw / She shook me / Christo / My desire / Noh jam. (cd+=) – CASE HISTORIES

1991.	(7") <RAVE 024> **BONDAGE. / (other by GOD & TEXAS)**	-	

(above issued on 'Rave', below on 'Spank')

1991.	(7") <spank 01> **HANGMAN'S ROPE. / (other by The LOST)**	-	
1992.	(7") <CZ 034> **SACRIFICIAL SHACK. / SWEETHEART**	-	

(above issued on 'C/Z' records, below on 'Sub Pop')

May 92.	(7") <SP 148> **DEATH ROW EYES. / THE SMELL**	-	
Jun 92.	(lp/cd) <(TR 10/+CD)> **STIMULATION FESTIVAL**		

– Shallow hole / The dead cannot / God told me / The poured out blood / Drowning / Living hell / Indiscreet jewels / Wild world / Daughter of chaos / Evil dirt. (cd+=) – Bruised / Dog spirits / Hangman's rope / Apartment #213.

Jul 93.	(lp/cd) <(TR 17/+CD)> **DESTROY ME, LOVER**		

– Cool your power / Prowling / Tar pit / RU 486 / Dominant man / Sexual anorexia / Lisa knew / Body memory / The story of Isaac / Shock treatment.

— now pared down to the couple **BLISS + SCOTT**

Nov 95.	(lp/cd) <(TR 41/+CD)> **BEAST OF DREAMS**		Oct95

– Swimming / Manouche / Coral kiss / Accusing eyes / Swamp / Embers and ashes / Voluptus / Moonray / Frigid idol / Skids / The sweet sickness / Invitation.

			not iss.	Sub/Mission
1996.	(7") <suck! 2> **TIGRESS OF BABYLON. / (split w/ MEATHEAD)**		-	

— split up the following year

PALE FOUNTAINS (see under ⇒ SHACK)

PALOOKAS (see under ⇒ SWELL MAPS; 70's section)

PANDORAS

Formed: Los Angeles, California, USA ... 1983 by PAULA PIERCE and her all-girl crew of BAMBI CONWAY, GWYNNE KELLY and CASEY. Using sex as a musical weapon, the bunch of likely lassies made their debut with an eponymous EP in '84. Over the course of the next five years, The PANDORAS released a clutch of spunky garage-pop albums, the last of which, 'NYMPHOMANIA' (1989), sacrificed their girly charm for a shambolic sub-metal noise. Later members KIM SHATTUCK and MELANIE VAMMEN re-emerged with The MUFFS, diving into a major deal with 'Elektra' and releasing an eponymous debut album in 1993. Appropriately enough, The MUFFS were compared to the tortured grunge of HOLE, especially with regards to their second set, 'BLONDER AND BLONDER' (1995). 'HAPPY BIRTHDAY TO ME' (1997) and 'ALERT TODAY, ALIVE TOMORROW' (1999) were two of the latest sets from these pop-punkers, the latter would see SHATTUCK at her very sweetest – nah! • **Covered:** AIN'T GOT NO SOUL (Gary Fausz – James Geyer).

Album rating: IT'S ABOUT TIME (*6) / STOP PRETENDING (*6) / LIVE NYMPHOMANIA (*1) / Muffs: THE MUFFS (*5) / BLONDER AND BLONDER (*6) / HAPPY BIRTHDAY TO ME (*4) / ALERT TODAY ALIVE TOMORROW (*5) / HAMBURGER compilation (*6)

PAULA PIERCE – vocals, guitar / **GWYNNE KELLY** – organ, vocals / **BAMBI CONWAY** – bass, vocals / **CASEY** – drums

			not iss.	Moxie
Apr 84.	(7"ep) **THE PANDORAS**		-	
			Closer	Voxx
1984.	(lp) (CL 0017) <20002-1> **IT'S ABOUT TIME**		-	French

– I want him / James / He's not far / I'm here I'm gone / That's your way out / High on a cloud / It's about time / The hook / I live my life / Want, need love / It just ain't true / Why / You lie / Going is away. <re-iss. Aug88; same> (cd-iss. Jan94; VOXXCD 2021)

— **PAULA** recruited **KIM SHATTUCK** – bass, vocals / **MELANIE VAMMEN** – keyboards, vocals / **KAREN BLANKFELD** – drums, vocals

			not iss.	Rhino
May 86.	(lp) <RNLP 70857> **STOP PRETENDING**		-	

– In and out of my life (in a day) / I didn't cry / Anyone but you / You're all talk / That's your way out / You don't satisfy / Let's do right / I'm your girl / The way it's gonna be / Stop pretending / Ain't got no soul / It felt alright.

— **RITA DALBERT** – rhythm guitar, vocals; repl. KAREN

			G.W.R.	Restless
Feb 89.	(m-lp/m-c/m-cd) (GWLP 38) <72292-1/-4/-2> **ROCK HARD**			

– Run down love battery / Tryin' ain't good enough / Six times a day / He's coming / Craving / Close behind.

Jan 90.	(cd) <23362> **NYMPHOMANIA (live)**		-	

– Pacify me / Burned / Craving / Liar / Put the brakes on your heart / He's coming / Six times a day / Bad habit / Run down love battery.

— split up after above; **SUSAN HYATT** had been a later member and she subsequently joined PILLBOX

– compilations, etc. –

Nov 97.	(cd) Arf Arf; <(AA 064)> **SPACE AMAZON**		
Dec 97.	(cd) Erekta; <(60786)> **PSYCHEDELIC SLUTS**		
Feb 00.	(7") Dionysus; <(ID 745101)> **THUNDER ALLEY. / I DIDN'T CRY**		

MUFFS

— were formed by **KIM + MELANIE** with **RONNIE BARNETT** – bass / **CRISS CRASS** – drums

			not iss.	Sympathy F
Jul 91.	(7"white) <SFTRI 121> **NEW LOVE. / I DON'T LIKE YOU / YOU LIED TO ME**		-	
			not iss.	Au Go-Go
Sep 91.	(7") <ANDA 142> **GUILTY. / RIGHT IN THE EYE**		-	
			not iss.	Sub Pop
Jul 92.	(7"colrd) <SP 157> **I NEED YOU. / BEAT YOUR HEART OUT**		-	
			Elektra	Elektra
Aug 93.	(cd/c) <(9362 45251-2/-4)> **THE MUFFS**			

– Lucky guy / Saying goodbye / Everywhere I go / Better than me / From your girl / Not like me / Baby go round / North Pole / Big mouth / Every single thing / Don't waste another day / Stupid jerk / Another day / Eye to eye / I need you / All for nothing.

Oct 93.	(7") <SFTRI 238> **BIG MOUTH. / DO THE ROBOT**	-	

(above issued on 'Sympathy For The Record Industry')

— now a trio when CRISS departed

— **ROY McDONALD** – drummer (ex-REDD KROSS) repl. VAMMEN who joined LEAVING TRAINS

Apr 95.	(cd/c/lp) <(9362 45852-2/-4/-1)> **BLONDER AND BLONDER**		

– Agony / Oh Nina / On and on / Sad tomorrow / What you've done / Red eyed troll / End it all / Laying on a bed of roses / I need a face / Won't come out to play / Funny face / Ethyl my love / I'm confused / Just a game.

Jul 95.	(7"/c-s) <W 0298 X/C> **SAD TOMORROW. / GOODNIGHT NOW**		

(cd-s+=) (W 0298CD) – Become undone.

			not iss.	Sympathy..
Dec 96.	(7") **I'M A DICK. / PACER**			
			Telstar	Elektra
Jun 97.	(lp)<cd/c> (TR 027) <46523> **HAPPY BIRTHDAY TO ME**			May97

– Crush me / That awful man / Honeymoon / All blue baby / My crazy afternoon / Is it all okay? / Pennywhore / Outer space / I'm a dick / Nothing / Where only I could go / Upside down / You and your parrot / Keep holding me / Best time around.

			Honest Dons	Honest Dons
Jun 99.	(lp/cd) <(DON 24/+CD)> **ALERT TODAY ALIVE TOMORROW**			

– I wish that I could be you / Silly people / The clown / Your kiss / Numb / I'm not around / Prettier than me / Blow your mind / Another ugly face / Fast song / In / Jack Champagne. (cd+=) – The happening / Room with a view.

– compilations, etc. –

Apr 00.	(cd) Sympathy For The Record Industry; <(SFTRI 589)> **HAMBURGER**		

– Get me out of here / You can cry if you want / Brand new Chevy / New love / I don't like you / Guilty / Right in the eye / I need you / Beat your heart out / Love / Rock and roll girl / Right in the eye / Everywhere I go / You lie / Toilet paper / I'm confused / When I was down / Sick of you / No action / Become undone / Goodnight now / Nothing for me / Kids in America / I'm a dick / Pacer / My crazy afternoon / Silly people / My minds eye / The happening / Do the robot.

PANTHER BURNS (see under ⇒ FALCO, Tav)

PARACHUTE MEN

Formed: Leeds, England ... 1985 by FIONA GREGG, STEPHEN H. GREGG, ANDREW HOWES and MARK BOYCE. Another better than average indie-guitar act to sign for 'Fire' (home of BLUE AEROPLANES, etc), The PARACHUTE MEN (and woman!) made their album debut in 1988 with 'THE INNOCENTS', an enjoyably sculpted slice of melodic alt-pop. However, all was not well in the ranks, the GREGGs trimmed to a duo until the arrival of newcomers MATTHEW PARKIN and PAUL MAHER. This line-up was responsible for the second and final set, 'EARTH, DOGS AND EGGSHELLS' (1990), although the PARACHUTE MEN will always be remembered for a classy John Peel-playlisted single, 'LEEDS STATION'.

Album rating: THE INNOCENTS (*6) / EARTH, DOGS AND EGGSHELLS (*6)

FIONA GREGG (b.26 Jul'63, Norwich, England) – vocals / **STEPHEN H. GREGG** (b.29 Nov'60, Bishop Auckland, England) – guitar / **ANDREW HOWES** – bass / **MARK BOYCE** – drums

	Fire	not iss.
May 88. (12"m) (BLAZE 27T) **SOMETIMES IN VAIN. / LEEDS STATION / HEADING THE WRONG WAY (J AT 41)**	☐	-
Aug 88. (lp/cd) (FIRE LP/CD 14) **THE INNOCENTS**	☐	-

– Sometimes in vain / The innocents / No wonder / Tell everyone / Are you glad you came? / Goodbye / Past not forgotten / Maybe if she said / Quiet day / If I could wear your jacket...? / Burgess Meredith / That's too bad. (cd+=) – Leeds station / Heading the wrong way (J at 41). (re-iss. Oct91 cd/lp; 33/11 014)

—— they became an acoustic duo until a little later in 1990
—— **MATTHEW PARKIN** – bass; repl. HOWES
—— **PAUL MAHER** (b. 7 Jul'66) – drums (ex-SALVATION) repl. BOYCE

Oct 88. (7") (BLAZE 30S) **IF I COULD WEAR YOUR JACKET...? / BURGESS MEREDITH**	☐	-
(12"+=) (BLAZE 30T) – That's too bad.		
May 89. (7") (BLAZE 33S) **LEEDS STATION. / MAYBE IF I SAID**	☐	-
(12"+=/3"cd-s+=) (BLAZE 33T) – So mistaken.		
Oct 89. (7") (BLAZE 35S) **BED AND BREAKFAST. / MR. GAS**	☐	-
(12"+=) (BLAZE 35T) – Bad rain.		
Apr 90. (7") (BLAZE 40S) **EVERY OTHER THURSDAY. /**	☐	-
(12"+=) (BLAZE 40T) –		
May 90. (cd/c/lp) (FIRE CD/MC/LP 24) **EARTH, DOGS AND EGGSHELLS**	☐	-

– Mad Sadie can't levitate / Mr. Gas / Never alone / Don't cry July / Miles away / Elizabeth / Earth, dogs and eggshells / Every other Thursday / ...Yeah / Sleepless, sleepless, sleepless / Dream of kings / Fear of falling. (re-iss. Oct91 cd/c/lp; 33/22/11 024)

—— **COLLEEN BROWNE** (b.25 Aug'66, Kelowna, Canada) – bass; repl. MATTHEW
—— split after above; COLLEEN joined The PALE SAINTS

PASSIONS

Formed: Ladbroke Grove, London, England ... summer '78 out of The RIVERS OF PASSION by Dublin-born singer, BARBARA GOGAN, the ex-DERELICTS girl recruiting MITCH BARKER, CLIVE TIMPERLEY, CLAIRE BIDWELL and RICHARD WILLIAMS. They debuted early the following year with 'NEEDLES & PINS' on the small 'Soho' label, subsequently signing to Polydor's 'Fiction' outlet (home to the CURE) after the departure of BARKER. A follow-up single, 'HUNTED', preceded their first album, 'MICHAEL AND MIRANDA' (1980), before CLAIRE upped and left. With DAVID AGAR filling her shoes, the band moved upstairs to 'Polydor', the initial disappointment of a flop single, 'THE SWIMMER', soon forgotten as they eased into the Top 30 with the moodily atmospheric 'I'M IN LOVE WITH A GERMAN FILMSTAR'. However, subsequent singles failed to have the same impact, their accompanying album, 'THIRTY THOUSAND FEET OVER CHINA' (1981), only managing to scrape into the Top 100. Introducing keyboards courtesy of JEFF SMITH and also enlisting KEVIN ARMSTRONG to replace TIMPERLEY, The PASSIONS made one final plea to the alt/indie scene with another ethereal guitar offering, 'SANCTUARY' (1982). After a lengthy hiatus, BARBARA GOGAN returned via a credited appearance with European post-rock experimentalist, HECTOR ZAZOU, on the 1997 collaborative set, 'Made On Earth'.

Album rating: MICHAEL AND MIRANDA (*5) / THIRTY THOUSAND FEET OVER CHINA (*6) / SANCTUARY (*4) / PASSION PLAYS compilation (*6)

BARBARA GOGAN (b. Dublin, Ireland) – vocals, guitar / **MITCH BARKER** – vovals / **CLIVE TIMPERLEY** – guitar, vocals (ex-101'ERS) / **CLAIRE BIDWELL** – bass, vocals / **RICHARD WILLIAMS** – drums

	Soho	not iss.
Jan 79. (7") (SH 5) **NEEDLES & PINS. / BODY & SOUL**	☐	-

—— now without BARKER

	Fiction	not iss.
Nov 79. (7") (FICS 8) **HUNTED. / OH NO IT'S YOU**	☐	-
Apr 80. (lp) (FIX 3) **MICHAEL AND MIRANDA**	☐	-

– Pedal fury / Oh no it's you / Snow / Love song / Man on the tube / Miranda / Obsession / Suspicion / Palava / Absentee / Brick wall / Why me.

—— **DAVID AGAR** – bass; repl. BIDWELL who later joined The WALL

	Polydor	not iss.
Oct 80. (7") (POSP 184) **THE SWIMMER. / WAR SONG**	☐	-
Jan 81. (7") (POSP 222) **I'M IN LOVE WITH A GERMAN FILMSTAR. / (DON'T TALK TO ME) I'M SHY**	25	-
Jun 81. (7") (POSP 256) **SKIN DEEP. / I RADIATE**	☐	-
(12"+=) (POSPX 256) – Small stones.		
Sep 81. (7") (POSP 325) **THE SWIMMER. / SOME FUN**	☐	-
Sep 81. (lp/c) (POLS/+C 1041) **THIRTY THOUSAND FEET OVER CHINA**	92	-

– I'm in love with a German filmstar / Someone special / The swimmer / Strange affair / Small stones / Runaway / The square / Alice's song / Bachelor girls / Skin deep. (re-iss. Sep91 on 'Great Expectations' cd/c/lp; PIP CD/MC/LP 028)

—— **KEVIN ARMSTRONG** – guitar (ex-LOCAL HEROES SW9) + **JEFF SMITH** – keyboards (ex-LENE LOVICH) repl. TIMPERLEY

Jan 82. (7") (POSP 384) **AFRICA MINE. / I FEEL CHEAP**	☐	-
(with free 7"ep+=) (CRUSH 1) – The square / Why me / The snow / I'm in love with a German filmstar.		
May 82. (7") (POSP 435) **JUMP FOR JOY. / THE STORY**	☐	-
Sep 82. (7") (POSP 487) **SANCTUARY. / TEMPTING FATE**	☐	-
Oct 82. (lp) (POLS 1066) **SANCTUARY**	☐	-

– Jump for joy / The letter / Into night / Small talk / White lies / Sanctuary / Love is essential / Your friend / Hold on, don't go / Cars driven fast.

—— split after **STEVE WRIGHT** had already repl. ARMSTRONG

– compilations, etc. –

Feb 85. (lp) Polydor; (SPELP 85) **PASSION PLAYS**	☐	-

– I'm in love with a German filmstar / Runaway / The swimmer / Someone special / Bachelor girls / Skin deep / African mine / Jump for joy / The letter / Love is essential / Your friend / Sanctuary. (cd-iss. Jul96; 529860-2)

PASSMORE SISTERS

Formed: Bradford, West Yorkshire, England ... 1984 by males, MARTIN SADOFSKI, HOWI TAYLOR and BRIAN E. ROBERTS; ROBERT GRACE was added in 1987 by which time the group had released two EP's, 'THREE LOVE SONGS' and 'VIOLENT BLUE'. Displaying not the usual "I'm-from-Yorkshire-therefore-I'm-into-Goth" course, The PASSMORE SISTERS settled for a more restrained indie-pop route, albeit quite similar to The HOUSEMARTINS or The REDSKINS. A further two singles, 'EVERY CHILD IN HEAVEN' and 'A SAFE PLACE TO HIDE', preceded a compilation of all their jangly-pop numbers, appropriately titled 'FIRST LOVE, LAST RITES' (1988).

Album rating: FIRST LOVE, LAST RITES compilation (*5)

MARTIN SADOFSKI – vocals / **BRIAN E. ROBERTS** – guitar, vocals / **HOWI TAYLOR** – bass / **ROBERT GRACE** – drums

	Sharp	not iss.
Nov 85. (7"ep) (CAL 3) **THREE LOVE SONGS EP**	☐	-
– Dance this house down / Shatter / Goodbye to the girl.		
Jul 86. (12"ep) (CAL 4) **VIOLENT BLUE EP**	☐	-
– Violent blue / At home with the walls / Pretty but hollow / Love songs forever.		
Jun 87. (7") (CAL 6) **EVERY CHILD IN HEAVEN. / GRIM ENGLISH JOKE**	☐	-
(12") (CAL 6T) – ('A'longer) / June in the water / Difficult.		
Nov 87. (7") (CAL 7) **A SAFE PLACE TO HIDE. / ALL I NEED IS CHANGE**	☐	-
(12"+=) (CAL 7T) – Red star blue heart.		
Jul 88. (lp) (CALP 1) **FIRST LOVE, LAST RITES** (compilation)	☐	-

– Difficult / Every child in Heaven / Goodbye Billy Wild / Shatter / Sally Way / A safe place to hide / Dance the house down / June in the water / Foundry of lies / Grim English joke / Red star blue heart / All I need is change.

—— had already split in March '88, BRIAN E. + HOWI formed The HOLLOW MEN

PASTELS

Formed: Glasgow, Scotland ... 1982 by STEPHEN McROBBIE, who subsequently changed his surname to PASTEL. After a few indie outings, the band eventually settled for Alan McGee's 'Creation' records in late 1983 with a relatively stable line-up of PASTEL, guitarist BRIAN SUPERSTAR, bassist MARTIN HAYWARD and drummer BERNICE. An indie band in the truly classic sense of the term, The PASTELS' early mid-80's recordings such as 'SOMETHING GOING ON', 'MILLION TEARS' and 'I'M ALRIGHT WITH YOU' were endearingly amateurish jingle-jangle/VELVET UNDERGROUND swathes of melodic noise, the latter the band's final single for 'Creation' before they moved to the small 'Glass' label. Around this time, The PASTELS, along with fellow Scottish (then) 'shamblers' PRIMAL SCREAM and a host of others, were forever immortalised via the dubious honour of having a track included on the NME's semi-legendary C86 compilation. Perhaps inspired by this modest scrape with indie stardom (though the band remain defiantly unambitious), The PASTELS soon adopted a more coherent, harmonious sound as evidenced on their trio of 'Glass' singles and the debut album 'UP FOR A BIT WITH THE PASTELS' (1987), which included a

PASTELS (cont)

few choice moments from their earlier days. The group label-hopped yet again for the follow-up, signing with 'Chapter 22' for 1989's 'SITTING PRETTY', arguably the band's most accomplished, if not exactly consistent work. With guest appearances by ubiquitous Glasgow scenesters like EUGENE KELLY (once of the seminal VASELINES and latterly CAPTAIN AMERICA) and TEENAGE FANCLUB's NORMAN BLAKE, the album featured some of the sweetest, juiciest moments in The PASTELS' chequered career, including the fizzing 'NOTHING TO BE DONE'. The album also saw DAVID KEEGAN contributing guitar, the ex-SHOP ASSISTANT being a partner in STEPHEN's influential '53rd & 3rd' label (which signed Scots acts The SOUP DRAGONS and BMX BANDITS amongst others). At the turn of the decade, The PASTELS line-up was stabilised to a core of PASTEL, girlfriend AGGI WRIGHT and KATRINA MITCHELL, KEEGAN making occasional contributions. Signed to 'Paperhouse', the first release from the new-look PASTELS was a fine cover of American maverick DANIEL JOHNSTON's seminal 'SPEEDING MOTORCYCLE', the group subsequently teaming up with another respected US underground figure, JAD FAIR (HALF JAPANESE), on a collaborative album, 'JAD FAIR AND THE PASTELS' (1991). Working with GALAXIE 500 guru, DEAN WAREHAM (on the 1994 EP, 'OLYMPIC WORLD OF PASTELISM') further illustrated the band's cultish kudos while 'MOBILE SAFARI' (1995) was a wryly self-deprecating look at an indie band's lot. Highly influential, if never really groundbreaking, The PASTELS remain the Grandaddies (and mammies!) of the Glasgow indie music scene.
• **Songwriters:** All written by STEPHEN and group except BOARDWALKIN' (Some Velvet Sidewalk); SVS's AL LARSEN teamed up with The PASTELS on a mid-90's side project, SANDY DIRT, releasing an eponymous EP early in '96.

Album rating: UP FOR A BIT WITH THE PASTELS (*6) / SUCK ON THE PASTELS compilation (*8) / SITTIN' PRETTY (*7) / TRUCKLOAD OF TROUBLES: 1986-1993 compilation (*8) / MOBILE SAFARI (*6) / ILLUMINATION (*6) / ILLUMINATI remixes (*5)

STEPHEN PASTEL (b. STEPHEN McROBBIE) – vocals / **BRIAN SUPERSTAR** (b. BRIAN TAYLOR) – guitar / **MARTIN HAYWARD** – bass / **CHRIS GORDON** – drums

Whaam! / not iss.
Oct 82. (7") (WHAAM 005) **HEAVENS ABOVE! / TEA TIME TALES**

Creation Artefact / not iss.
Apr 83. (7"flexi) (LYN 12903) **I WONDER WHY (live) / (other track by LAUGHING APPLES)**
(above was initialy a freebie with CRE 001)

Rough Trade / not iss.
Oct 83. (7") (RT 137) **I WONDER WHY. / SUPPOSED TO UNDERSTAND**

Creation / not iss.
Mar 84. (7") (CRE 005) **SOMETHING GOING ON. / STAY WITH ME TILL MORNING**
Oct 84. (12"m) (CRE 011T) **A MILLION TEARS. / SUPRISE ME / BABY HONEY**
Nov 85. (12"m) (CRE 023T) **I'M ALRIGHT WITH YOU. / WHAT IT'S WORTH / COULDN'T CARE LESS**

Glass / Big Time
Jul 86. (7") (GLASS 048) **TRUCK TRAIN TRACTOR. / BREAKING LINES**
(12"+=) (GLASS12 048) – Truck train tractor (2).

— (in '87) they added **AGGI** – keyboards (ex-BUBA & THE SHOP ASSISTANTS) + **NORMAN BLAKE** – guitar (of The BOY HAIRDRESSERS)

Feb 87. (lp) (GLALP 022) <6032> **UP FOR A BIT WITH THE PASTELS**
– Ride / Up for a bit / Crawl babies / Address book / I'm alright with you / Hitchin' a ride / Get round town / Baby honey / Automatically yours / If I could tell you. (cd-iss. Oct88; GLACD 021) (re-iss. Sep91 on 'Paperhouse';)
Feb 87. (7") (GLASS 050) **CRAWL BABIES. / EMPTY HOUSE**
(12"+=) (GLASS12 050) – The day I got certified.
Oct 87. (7") (GLASS 053) **COMING THROUGH. / SIT ON IT MOTHER**
(12"+=) (GLASS12 053) – Lonely planet boy / Not unloved.

— guest **EUGENE KELLY** (of VASELINES) who later formed CAPTAIN AMERICA then EUGENIUS

Chapter 22 / Homestead
Apr 89. (12"m) (12CHAP 37) **BABY YOU'RE JUST YOU. / HOLY MOLY. / UGLY TOWN**
Jun 89. (lp/c/cd) (CHAP LP/MC/CD 43) <HMS 1441> **SITTIN' PRETTY**
– Nothing to be done / Anne Boleyn / Sit on it mother / Holy moly / Ugly town / Zooom / Baby you're just you / Ditch the fool / Sittin' pretty / Swerve. (also pic-lp; CHAPLP 43P) (lp re-iss. Feb95 on 'Homestead'; same as US)

— now a trio **STEPHEN, AGGI + KATRINA MITCHELL** also with **FRANCES MACDONALD** (b.11 Sep'70) – drums (ex-TEENAGE FANCLUB)

Paperhouse / Seed
Sep 91. (7") (PAPER 008) **SPEEDING MOTORCYCLE. / SPEEDWAY STAR**
(12"+=/cd-s+=) (PAPER 008 T/CD) – 4th band.
Nov 91. (7") (PAPER 011) **THRU YOUR HEART. / FIREBELL RINGING**
(12"+=/cd-s+=) (PAPER 011 T/CD) – My heart's my badge / Sign across me / Thru your heart (home recording).

— In Feb + Jun 92, they teamed up with JAD FAIR (ex-HALF JAPANESE) on his singles; THIS COULD BE THE NIGHT + HE CHOSE HIS COLOURS WELL from his 1991 album 'JAD FAIR AND THE PASTELS'. Meanwhile, KATRINA moonlighted with MELODY DOG duo alongside PAT CROOK and issued an eponymous EP for 'K' in 1991 (tracks 'Futuristic Lover', 'Tomorrow's World' and 'Sun Drenched Beach In Acapulco') and a single for 'Seminal Twang', 'CASSIE' b/w a cover of Primal Scream's 'MOVIN' ON UP' and 'LIGHT SHADE'.

Nov 92. (cd/c/lp) (PAP CD/MC/LP 008) <14239> **TRUCKLOAD OF TROUBLES: 1986-1993** (compilation)
– Thank you for being you / Thru' your heart / Kitted out / Comin' through / Over my shoulder / Truck train tractor / Crawl babies / Nothing to be done / Different

drum / Not unloved / Baby honey / Speeding motorcycle / Speedway star / What you said / Dark side of your world / Sometimes I think of you / Sign across me. (cd re-iss. Apr02 on 'Fire'; SFIRE 003)

May 93. (7") (PAPER 023) **THANK YOU FOR BEING YOU. / KITTED OUT**
(cd-s+=) (PAPER 023CD) – Sometimes I think about you.

— now w/ guests: **GERARD LOVE** (Teenage Fanclub) / **DEAN WAREHAM** (Galaxie 500).

May 94. (7"ep/cd-ep) (RUG 18/+CD) **THE PASTELS & ... OLYMPIC WORLD OF PASTELISM**
– Hot wheels / Three strip dynamite / Feedback Olympics.

— **STEPHEN, AGGI + KATRINA MITCHELL** plus various honorary PASTELS, including GERARD LOVE, NORMAN BLAKE, JONATHAN KILGOUR, DEAN WAREHAM, BILL WELLS, SARAH WARD, ISOBEL CAMPBELL, DAWN KELLY + GREGOR REID

Domino / Matador
Oct 94. (12"ep/cd-ep) (RUG 28 T/CD) <OLE 114> **YOGA / BOARDWALKIN'. / WINTER OLYMPIC GLORY / YOGA**
Domino / Domino Apr95
Feb 95. (cd/c/lp) (<WIG CD/MC/LP 17>) **MOBILE SAFARI**
– Exploration team / Mandarin / Yoga / Mobile deli / Exotic arcade / Classic line-up / Flightpaths to each other / Basement scam / Strategic gear / Token collecting / Coolport / Worlds of possibility. (lp w/free 7") **SAFARI COMPANION** – 1 / 2 / 3 / 4.
Apr 95. (12"ep/cd-ep) (RUG 36 T/CD) **WORLDS OF POSSIBILITY / PHOTOGRAM. / EVER FAR / LOVE IT'S GETTING BETTER**
Dec 95. (12"ep/cd-ep; as The PASTELS & AL LARSEN) (RUG 42/+CD) **SANDY DIRT** / Slim slow rider / Ship to shore / Matches / Moonlit lungs.
– Klein international blue / Slim slow rider / Ship to shore / Matches / Moonlit lungs.
Domino / Up
Jul 97. (12"ep/cd-ep) (RUG 55 T/CD) <UP 38> **UNFAIR KIND OF FAME / FROZEN WAVE. / CYCLE (My Bloody Valentine remix) / FROZEN WAVE (Flacco remix)** Sep97
Aug 97. (7") (RUG 52) **THE HITS HURT. / WINDY HILL**
(cd-s+=) (RUG 52CD) – G12 nights.
Oct 97. (cd/lp) (WIG CD/LP 34) <UP 41> **ILLUMINATION**
– The hits hurt / Cycle / Thomson colour / Unfair kind of fame / Fragile gang / The viaduct / Remote climbs / Rough riders / On the way / Leaving this island / G12 nights / Attic plan / Mechanised.

— in May'98, Domino offshoot label, 'Series 500', issued a collaborative effort, 'HURRICANE FIGHTER PILOT' with FUTURE PILOT AKA

Nov 98. (cd/d-lp) (WIG CD/LP 46) **ILLUMINATI**
– Magic nights (My Bloody Valentine remix) / The viaduct (Kid Loco remix) / Windy hill (Cornelius remix) / One wild moment (Stereolab remix) / Attic plan (Mouse on Mars remix) / Remote climbs (Cinema remix) / Remote climbs (John McEntire remix) / The viaduct (Ian Carmichael remix) / Thomson colour (To Rococo Rot remix) / Cycle (My Bloody Valentine remix) / On the way (Third Eye Foundation remix) / Rough riders (Future Pilot AKA remix) / Rough riders (Make Up remix) / Frozen wave (Flacco remix) / The viaduct (Bill Wells remix) / Leaving this island (Jim O'Rourke remix).
Dec 98. (12"ep) (RUG 79) **ONE WILD MOMENT (Stereolab remix). / WINDY HILL – vocal and instrumental (Cornelius remix) / THE VIADUCT – instrumental and vocal (Kid Loco remix)**

– compilations, others, etc. –

Mar 85. (7"ep) (Villa 21; VILLA 1) **HEAVENS ABOVE! / TEA TIME TALES. / I WONDER WHY (live) / TEA TIME TALES (live)**
Dec 87. (d12") Glass; (GLASS12 048) **TRUCK TRAIN TRACTOR. / BREAKING LINES / TRUCK TRAIN TRACTOR 2 // CRAWL BABIES. / EMPTY HOUSE / THE DAY I GOT CERTIFIED**
Jun 88. (lp/cd) Creation; (CRE LP/CD 031) **SUCK ON THE PASTELS**
– Baby honey / I wonder why / Something going on / Million tears / Surprise me / She always cries on Sunday / Baby honey / I'm alright with you / Couldn't care less / What's it worth. (<cd-iss. Mar94 on 'Rockville'; 6048>)
(above is to have been issued Mar'85 as 'SHE ALWAYS CRIES ON SUNDAY')
1990. (7"colrd-ep) Overground; (OVER 06) **HEAVENS ABOVE! / TEA TIME TALES. / SOMETHING GOING ON (demo) / UNTIL MORNING COMES (demo)**

PELL MELL

Formed: Portland, Oregon, USA... 1985 by Washington-born STEVE FISK, along with other instrumentally-orientated music men, BOB BEERMAN, BILL OWEN, DAVE SPALDING and GREG FREEMAN. FISK had once delivered a shared solo single in 1980, while a year later, the track 'DIGITAL ALARM', appeared on the 'Sub Pop' V/A fanzine cassette. PELL PELL opened their musical account via an eponymous, self-financed cassette in 1982. Further cassettes/LP's surfaced on either 'K' or 'S.S.T.' records, although most were a little lacking in wider audience appeal. All this changed, however, when 'Geffen' unleashed their pièce de resistance, 'INTERSTATE' (1994 – 1996 in New Zealand and UK!). Gone were the exercises in sonic minimalism, and in came reverbing ambient textures, an album the group could not improve on; witness 1997's 'Matador' effort 'STAR CITY'. STEVE FISK, of course, was already one of the greatest producers of all-time, working with the likes of NIRVANA, SOUNDGARDEN, SCREAMING TREES, grunge, more grunge, etc., while finding the time to issue numerous solo sets; check out 1991's '448 DEATHLESS DAYS' for an insight into his innovative experiments. • **PELL MELL covered:** ALL THIS AND MORE (Dead Boys).

Album rating: IT WAS A LIVE CASSETTE (*5) / RHYMING GUITARS (*4) / BUMPER CROP (*4) / FLOW (*4) / INTERSTATE (*7) / STAR CITY (*6) / Steve Fisk: 448 DEATHLESS DAYS (*6) / OVER AND THRU THE NIGHT compilation (*6) / 999 LEVELS OF UNDO (*5)

BILL OWEN – guitar / **STEVE FISK** – organ, effects / **DAVE SPALDING** – guitar / **GREG FREEMAN** – bass / **BOB BEERMAN** – drums

			not iss.	own label
1982.	(c) <*none*> **PELL MELL**		-	

– Spanner / Some things we do for fun / Dad's top drawer / Shirts and skins / Estacada / Food, clothing and shelter / Almost happy / All this and more. *<(cd+UK-iss.Feb01 as '1982: IT WAS A LIVE CASSETTE' on 'Starlight Furniture'; ST 07CD)>*

		K	K
1985.	(c) <*none*> **FOR YEARS WE STOOD CLEARLY AS ONE THING**	-	
1988.	(m-c) *<(KC 11)>* **RHYMING GUITARS**		

– New Saigon / Spy vs. spy / Par avion / Red rhythm / Week of corn. *<US re-iss. Jun90 on 'S.S.T.' lp/c/cd; SST 241/+C/CD) (UK re-iss. May93; same as SST)*

		S.S.T.	S.S.T.
1987.	(lp/c/cd) *<SST 158/+C/CD>* **BUMPER CROP**		

– Weel of fire / Dad's top drawer / All this and more / 69 or 20 / Love trek / Alligator stomp / My three sons / Estacada / Cinecitta / FTB / Pet dub / Chroma-key beach / Work, health and love. *(UK-iss.May93 'S.S.T.'; same as US)*

1991.	(7") *<SST 913>* **BRING ON THE CHINA. / SMOKE**		
Mar 92.	(lp/c/cd) *<SST 278/+C/CD>* **FLOW**		Jan91

– American eagle / Breach of promise / Bring on the China / Devil bush / Smoke / Aero / Flood / Little blue dance / Signal / Blaming the messenger / Mopping up. *(UK re-iss. May93; same as US)*

		Flying Nun	Geffen
Feb 96.	(lp/cd) *(FN/+CD 337)* *<DGC 24807>* **INTERSTATE**		Nov94

– Nothing lies still long / Revival / Anna Karina / Saucer / Pound cake / Constellation / Blacktop / Butterfly effect / Drift / Vegetable kingdom / Ether / Floating gate. *(cd re-iss. Sep98; same)*

		Matador	Matador
Jan 98.	(cd/lp) *<(OLE 288-2/-1)>* **STAR CITY**		Oct97

– Sky lobby / Salvo / Orange roughy / Interloper / Smoke house / On approach / Upstairs / In polka dots / Everything must go / Lowlight / Headset / Field of poppies / Gelatin / Coral.

STEVE FISK

		not iss.	Mr. Brown's
Jul 80.	(12"ep; various artists) *<EP 667>* **LIFE ELSEWHERE**	-	

– Woodstock / You're everything / (other artists).

		not iss.	K – A.R.P.H.
1983.	(c) <*none*> **KISS THIS DAY GOODBYE**	-	
1986.	(c) <*none*> **'TIL THE NIGHT CLOSES IN**	-	

–— with an array of session people incl. **GARY LEE CONNER, BILL OWEN, MARK LANEGAN, GREG FREEMAN, MARK PICKEREL, VAN CONNER, SAM ALBRIGHT** etc

		S.S.T.	S.S.T.
1987.	(lp/c/cd) *<(SST 159/+C/CD)>* **448 DEATHLESS DAYS**		

– Invocation / No 2nd chance / Ragged old flag / Weekend review / Diamond club / Oh little seeds / Johnny Smoke (swamp thing) / Emerging nation / Trasheap / Further demo of an assist / Break on through / Tongues / Soul of Spain / Tragedy at sea / This vacuum / Chakiri bushi / She walks / Barretta / To abide in the flesh / Priorities. *<(re-iss. May93; same)>*

		K	K
1989.	(c) *<KC 16>* **1 MORE VALLEY**	-	
1992.	(lp; by STEVE FISK, MARK HOSLER & BOB BASANICH) *<KLP 11>* **INTERNATIONAL POP UNDERGROUND**		
1993.	(cd) *<KC 20>* **OVER & THRU THE NIGHT** (compilation 1980-1987)	-	

– I wish I were dead (pt.1) / Preamble / Love x 8 / The firin' line / Government figures / One more valley / Kennedy saga (chapter VII) / The way / Taxman / Terrible weapons / You used me / Topeka hills / X mass / Doll house / Preamble / A short history of music / Filthy young people / Lying in Texas / I wish I were dead (pt.2).

–— FISK was now also part of PIGEONHED alongside BRAD frontman, SHAWN SMITH; they released a handful of sets for 'Sub Pop'

		not iss.	Astralwerks
1994.	(cd) *<ASW 6119-2>* **EXCURSIONS IN AMBIENCE**	-	
1994.	(12") *<ASW 6120>* **EXPRESS GOD REMIXES**		

		Sub Pop	Sub Pop
Mar 01.	(cd) *<(SPCD 460)>* **999 LEVELS OF UNDO**		

– My head popped / Aviation Oakie / Time, speed, language / Amateur European / Where's the fire? / L'estancia / Polymorphic light eruption / The backwards song.

PERFECT DISASTER

Formed: London, England ... early 80's as ORANGE DISASTER by PHIL PARFITT and the future rhythm section of FIELDS OF THE NEPHILIM, TONY PETTITT and NOD. This early incarnation only released one single, 'SOMETHING'S GOT TO GIVE', before changing their moniker to the ARCHITECTS OF DISASTER and issuing another one-off, 'CUCUMBER SANDWICH', in '82. Adopting the PERFECT DISASTER mantle, PHIL, along with ALISON PATES, JOHN SALTWELL and MALCOLM CATTO, crossed the English Channel to record their French-only eponymous debut (given a UK release on 'Glass' in 1987). They finally secured a domestic contract with 'Fire', the much-improved follow-up, 'ASYLUM ROAD', set free in early '88. By this time, they had undergone a sizeable personnel shift, JO WIGGS and DAN CROSS replacing SALTWELL and PATES respectively. Subterranean guitar rumblings and obsessively dark subject matter (PARFITT once worked as psychiatric nurse) were the order of the day, the band offering up another fix on 1989's 'UP' album. Yet more line-up upheavals occurred when WIGGS left to join The BREEDERS, the returning SALTWELL taking up the slack on their fourth and final set, 'HEAVEN SCENT' (1990). PARFITT would subsequently work with SPIRITUALIZED man, JASON PIERCE, before returning in his own right with OEDIPUSSY; a solitary album, 'DIVAN', appeared in '95.

Album rating: THE PERFECT DISASTER (*4) / ASYLUM ROAD (*8) / UP (*6) / HEAVEN SCENT (*6)

PHIL PARFITT – vocals, guitar / **TONY PETTITT** – bass / **NOD** (b. ALEXANDER WRIGHT) – drums

		Neuter	not iss.
1982.	(7"m; as ORANGE DISASTER) *(OD 1)* **SOMETHING'S GOT TO GIVE. / OUT OF THE ROOM / HIDING FROM FRANK**		-

		Neuter	not iss.
Nov 82.	(7"; as ARCHITECTS OF DISASTER) *(NEU 1)* **CUCUMBER SANDWICH. / FRIENDLY FIRE**		-

–— PETTITT and NOD formed the FIELDS OF THE NEPHILIM

–— PHIL PARFITT recruited **ALISON PATES** – keyboards / **JOHN SALTWELL** – bass / **MALCOLM CATTO** – drums

		Kampa	not iss.
1985.	(lp) **THE PERFECT DISASTER**	-	- France

(UK-iss.Sep87 on 'Glass'; GLALP 027)

		Glass	not iss.
Nov 87.	(12"ep) *(GLAEP 107)* **HEY HEY HEY / THE NIGHT BELONGS TO CHARLIE. / THAT'S WHAT THE DOCTOR SAYS / ELUSIVE DREAMS**		-

–— **JOSEPHINE WIGGS** (b.26 Feb'65, Letchworth, England) – bass, cello, piano; repl. SALTWELL

–— **DAN CROSS** – lead guitar, keyboards; repl. PATES

		Fire	Genius
May 88.	(12") *(BLAZE 28T)* **TV (GIRL ON FIRE). / CRACK UP F SONG TV (version)**		-
Aug 88.	(lp) *(FIRELP 11)* *<5>* **ASYLUM ROAD**		
Oct 88.	(7") *(BLAZE 31S)* **TIME TO KILL. / GARAGE**		

(12"+=) (BLAZE 31T) – ('A' version).

–— **PHIL 'Archie' OUTRAM + MARTIN LANGSHAW** – drums; repl. CATTO

Jun 89.	(lp/c/cd) *(FIRE LP/MC/CD 18)* **UP**		-

– '55 / Shout / Up / It doesn't matter / Down (here I go) / Down (falling) / Down (down) / Hey now / Go away / B-52. *(cd+=)* – Garage / Time to kill.

Oct 89.	(7") *(BLAZE 38S)* **MOOD ELEVATORS. / LISTEN (212)**		-

(12"+=) (BLAZE 38T) –

–— SALTWELL returned to repl. WIGGS who joined The BREEDERS, then ULTRA VIVID SCENE

Sep 90.	(12"ep) *(BLAZE 43T)* **RISE E.P.**		-

– Rise / Lee / Bluebell / B52.

Oct 90.	(cd/lp) *(FIRE CD/LP 27)* **HEAVEN SCENT**		-

– Rise / Father / Wires / Takin' over / Where will you go with me / Little sister (if ever days) / Shadows / Sooner or later / It's gonna come to you. *(cd+=)* – Lee / Mood elevators (original) / Bluebell live) / B-52 (live).

–— disbanded soon after, PARFITT subsequently collaborating with JASON PIERCE (of SPIRITUALIZED) prior to initiating his own outfit, OEDIPUSSY

OEDIPUSSY

–— **PARFITT** + others

		Handsome	not iss.
Apr 95.	(cd/lp) *(HAN CD/LP 001)* **DIVAN**		

Brendan PERRY (see under ⇒ DEAD CAN DANCE)

Martin PHILLIPPS (see under ⇒ CHILLS)

PHOTOS

Formed: Evesham, Midlands, England ... 1978 by former members of punk group, SATAN'S RATS, who comprised STEVE EAGLES, DAVE SPARROW and OLLY HARRISON; they released three singles namely, 'IN MY LOVE FOR YOU', 'YEAR OF THE RATS' and 'YOU MAKE ME SICK'. Having originally tried to prise JAYNE CASEY away from BIG IN JAPAN, they instead settled for WENDY WU, ex-manager of pub band CITY YOUTH. The latter was touted as Britain's dark-haired answer to DEBBIE HARRY, while the group's New-wave-ish pop-rock wasn't a million miles removed from BLONDIE. Probably on the strength of this, The PHOTOS signed to 'C.B.S.', although after only one flop single, 'I'M SO ATTRACTIVE', they moved along the corporate corridor to 'Epic'. During the following Spring of 1980, The PHOTOS developed some chart action as the single, 'IRENE', made the UK Top 60. That summer, surprisingly without a major hit to their name, WU and Co pulled off a chart coup when their eponymous debut album (complete with the purchase incentive of a free 'BLACKMAIL TAPES' lp) hit the UK Top 5. However, the exposure was to be short-lived as WENDY departed for a solo career, bailing out of a sinking ship as a series of singles had failed to chart. WU's own efforts also fell on deaf ears, while the band themselves (with new singer, CHE) took one last shot with the hopefully titled 1983 single, 'THERE'S ALWAYS WORK'. While WENDY teamed up with former VISAGE singer, STEVE STRANGE (in the pop duo, STRANGE CRUISE), EAGLES joined the more obscure BLURT and later co-founded early 90's act, BANG BANG MACHINE. • **Covered:** I SAW HER STANDING THERE (Beatles) / JE T'AIME (Serge Gainsbourg).

Album rating: THE PHOTOS (*5)

SATAN'S RATS

STEVE EAGLES (b. 1958) – guitar / **DAVE SPARROW** – bass / **OLLY HARRISON** – drums

			D.J.M.	not iss.
Oct 77.	(7") *(DJS 10819)*	**IN MY LOVE FOR YOU. / FACADE**		-

(re-iss. 1989 on 'Overground' 7"yellow/white; OVER 02)

Dec 77. (7") *(DJS 10821)* **YEAR OF THE RATS. / LOUISE**

(re-iss. 1989 on 'Overground' 7"yellow/white; OVER 01)

Mar 78. (7") *(DJS 10840)* **YOU MAKE ME SICK. / LOUISE**

(re-iss. 1991 on 'Overground' 7"clear; OVER 14)

PHOTOS

above recruited **WENDY WU** (b. WENDY CRUISE, 29 Nov'59, Winston Green) – vocals

			C.B.S.	not iss.
Nov 79.	(7") *(CBS 7984)*	**I'M SO ATTRACTIVE. / GUITAR HERO**		-
			Epic	Epic
Apr 80.	(d7") *(EPC 8517)*	**IRENE. / BARBARELLAS // SHY. / CRISSILLA**	56	-
Jun 80.	(lp) *(PHOTO 5) <NJE 36515>*	**THE PHOTOS**	4	-

– Do you have fun / Irene / Barbarellas / Now you tell me that we're through / Look at the band / Loss of contact / She's artistic / All I want / Maxine / Evelyn II / I just don't know what to do with myself. *(free-lp.w.a.)* **THE BLACKMAIL TAPES** – Last time / With honours / Sex object / Lady is a tramp / Do you wanna dance / Skateboard / Evelyn 1 / I saw her standing there. *(cd-iss. Aug98+=; 491697-2)*

Jul 80. (7";w-drawn) *(EPC 8785)* **FRIENDS. / JE T'AIME**
Sep 80. (7") *(EPC 8872)* **NOW YOU TELL ME THAT WE'RE THROUGH. / JE T'AIME**
Feb 81. (7") *(EPCA 1010)* **LIFE IN A DAY. / MORE THAN A FRIEND**
Mar 81. (lp) *(EPC 84849)* **CRYSTAL TIPS AND MIGHTY MICE**
Jul 81. (7") *(EPC 1369)* **WE'LL WIN. / YOU WON'T GET TO ME**

― split late 1981 after WENDY was replaced by CHE

WENDY WU

			Epic	not iss.
Mar 82.	(7") *(EPCA 2128)*	**FOR YOUR LOVE. / CHARLOTTE**		-
Sep 82.	(7") *(EPCA 2676)*	**RUN JILLY RUN. / NEANDERTHAL BOY**		-
Oct 83.	(7"/12") *(A/TA 3834)*	**LET ME GO. / LOVE TONIGHT**		-

PHOTOS

― had re-formed (as a trio) without WU who helped form STRANGE CRUISE

― **ANGUS HINES** – drums; repl. HARRISON

			Rialto	not iss.
Apr 83.	(7"/12") *(RIA/12RIA 16)*	**THERE'S ALWAYS WORK. / WORK PHASE**		-

― disbanded again for final time later in 1983. STEVE EAGLES joined BLURT before forming early 90's outfit, BANG BANG MACHINE

PHRANC

Born: SUSAN GOTTLIEB, 28 Aug'57, Santa Monica, California, USA. The words Jewish, folksinger and lesbian are those most commonly bandied about when discussing this uncompromising performer, or indeed when she's describing herself. Changing her name to PHRANC in the mid-70's after dropping out of high school, the budding singer subsequently fell in with the notorious early 80's L.A. punk/hardcore scene, playing guitar with the likes of CASTRATION SQUAD and CATHOLIC DISCIPLINE. The latter of these (with also CLAUD BESSY – vocals, ROBERT LOPEZ – keyboards, RICKIE JAFFE – bass & CRAIG LEE – drums) had a few tracks on various artists albums, 'San Francisco Punks' and 'Decline Of The Western Civilization'. Eventually tiring of the scene's insularity and relentless negativity, she retraced her folk roots and in 1985 released a debut album, 'FOLKSINGER' for retro specialist, 'Rhino' records. A characteristically candid and honest exploration of politics, both sexual and otherwise, the record was heartily received by more radical critics and increased her small but loyal band of fans. PHRANC then signed to 'Island' at the end of the 80's and released a belated follow-up set, 'I ENJOY BEING A GIRL' (1989). The task of bringing PHRANC to a wider audience proved too great a challenge even for a label as eclectic as 'Island' and the singer parted company with them after 1991's 'POSITIVELY PHRANC'. A pity, as she demonstrated her wide ranging appeal by supporting MORRISSEY on his UK tour the same year. Her cult indie credentials were back intact in the mid-90's, courtesy of two releases – the single, 'BULLDAGGER SWAGGER' and the 'GOOFYFOOT' EP – for the seminal "Riot Grrrl" imprint 'Kill Rock Stars', both featuring Olympia musicians headed by DONNA DRESCH. Her comeback was complete with the release of the long-awaited comeback set, 'MILKMAN' (1998), PHRANC's back-up this time stemming from L.A. woman, ANNA WARONKER, and a few seasoned auxiliaries. • **Covers:** THE LONESOME DEATH OF HATTIE CARROLL (Bob Dylan) / I ENJOY BEING A GIRL (Hammerstein-Rodgers) / MOONLIGHT BECOMES YOU (Burke-Van Heusen) / SURFER GIRL (Beach Boys) / GERTRUDE STEIN (aka PABLO PICASSO – Jonathan Richman) / MRS. BROWN YOU'VE GOT A LOVELY DAUGHTER (Hermans Hermits) / ODE TO BILLIE JOE (Bobbie Gentry) / + some traditional songs.

Album rating: FOLKSINGER (*6) / I ENJOY BEING A GIRL (*6) / POSITIVELY PHRANC (*6) / MILKMAN (*5)

PHRANC – vocals, acoustic guitar

			Stiff	Rhino
Nov 85.	(7") *(BUY 233)*	**AMAZON. / EL SALVADOR**		-

(12"+=) (BUYIT 233) – Charlotte.

Jan 86. (lp) *(SEEZ 60) <RNDA 856>* **FOLKSINGER** [ ] [Nov85]
– Noguchi / Mary Hooley / Ballad of the dumb hairdresser / Caped crusader / One o' the girls / Female mudwrestling / The lonesome death of Hattie Carroll / Amazons / Liar liar / Handicapped / Carolyn / Lifeover.

Mar 86. (7") *(BUY 247)* **THE LONESOME DEATH OF HATTIE CARROLL. / EL SALVADOR**

			Island	Island
Aug 89.	(cd/c/lp) *<(CID/ICT/ILPS 9940)>*	**I ENJOY BEING A GIRL**		

– Folksinger / I enjoy being a girl / Double decker bed / Bloodbath / Individuality / Rodeo parakeet / Take off your swastika / Toy time / Martina / Myriam and Esther / The ballad of Lucy and Ted / Moonlight becomes you.

Jul 91. (cd/c/lp) *<(CID/ICT/ILPS 9981)>* **POSITIVELY PHRANC** [ ] [Mar91]
– I like you / I'm not romantic / '64 Ford / Hitchcock / Tipton / Dress code / Why? / Gertrude Stein / Surfer girl / Outta here.

― next with **DONNA DRESCH** – bass / **TOBI VAIL** – drums / + others from TEAM DRESCH

			Kill Rock Stars	Kill Rock Stars
Aug 94.	(7") *<(KRS 230)>*	**BULLDAGGER SWAGGER. / HILARY'S EYEBROWS**		
Aug 95.	(12"ep/cd-ep) *<KRS 233 12/CD>*	**GOOFYFOOT EP**	-	

– Surferdyke pal / Mrs. Brown you've got a lovely daughter / Bulldagger swagger / Ode to Billie Joe / Goofyfoot.

― next with **STEVE McDONALD** – bass / **PHIL PARLAPIANO** – accordion / **TAL BERGMAN** – drums / **ANNA WARONKER** – b. vocals

			not iss.	Phancy
Nov 98.	(cd) *<1>*	**MILKMAN**	-	

– Twirly / The handsome cabin boy / Ozzie and Harriet / Yer the one / They lied / Where were you? / Gary / Cuffs / Lullaby / Tzena, Tzena.

Jeffrey Lee PIERCE (see under ⇒ GUN CLUB)

PIGBAG

Formed: based- Bristol, England ... 1980 by JAMES JOHNSTONE and ex-POP GROUP man, SIMON UNDERWOOD alongside OLLIE MOORE, CHRIS LEIGH, CHIP CARPENTER and ROGER FREEMAN. Managed by Linda Neville, this experimental/instrumental combo formed their own label, 'Y Records' (named after The POP GROUP's semi-legendary debut) via 'Rough Trade', issuing their seminal 'PAPA'S GOT A BRAND NEW PIGBAG' single in Spring '81. Revelling in classic brass-led soul/funk yet retaining a residue of edgy paranoia from The POP GROUP, the single climbed to the UK Top 3 over the space of a year. By this point they'd already scored two minor hits with 'SUNNY DAY' and 'GETTING UP', the latter serving as the lead track on debut set, 'DR HECKLE AND MR JIVE' (1982). A dancefloor-friendly yet consistently intriguing listen, the record limbo-danced its way from the Latin party vibes of the aforementioned 'GETTING UP' to the rolling voodoo-bones percussion of 'DOZO DON' and the bass groove/jerky jazz workouts of 'BRIAN THE SNAIL' with snake-hipped ease. Despite the record's glowing praise and Top 20 success, the band found it difficult to follow-up their massive debut single and even with the addition of a female vocalist (ANDREA JAEGAR) to spice up the sound, follow-up set, 'LEND AN EAR' (1983), didn't even chart. By early '83, the band had already split with UNDERWOOD going on to play briefly with RIP, RIG & PANIC. This wasn't the end of the story, however, 'PAPA'S GOT A BRAND NEW PIGBAG' later re-released in 1987 to tie in with a retrospective compilation; of course it was a hit all over again, and again ... in the early 90's when super-DJ PAUL OAKENFOLD and his PERFECTO ALLSTARS released a dance version.

Album rating: DR HECKLE & MR JIVE (*7) / LEND AN EAR (*4) / PIGBAG – LIVE (*4) / THE BEST OF PIGBAG compilation (*7)

JAMES JOHNSTONE – guitar, alto sax, steel drums / **OLLIE MOORE** – tenor sax, clarinet, sanza / **CHRIS LEIGH** – trumpet, percussion / **CHIP CARPENTER** – drums, percussion, tumbas / **SIMON UNDERWOOD** – bass, cello, violin (ex-POP GROUP) / **ROGER FREEMAN** – percussion, trombone, keyboards, piano

			Y Records	not iss.
May 81.	(7") *(Y 10)*	**PAPA'S GOT A BRAND NEW PIG BAG. / BACKSIDE**		-

(12"+=) (Y 10T) – Another orangutango.
(above re-dist.Mar82, hit No.3)

Oct 81. (7") *(Y 12)* **SUNNY DAY. / ELEPHANTS WISH TO BECOME NIMBLE** | 53 | - |
Jan 82. (7") *(Y 16)* **GETTING UP. / GIGGLING MUD** | 61 | - |
(12"+=) (Y 16T) – Go cat.
Mar 82. (lp/c) *(Y/YK 17)* **DR HECKLE AND MR JIVE** | 18 | - |
– Getting up / Bigbag / Dozo Don / Brian the snail / Wiggling / Brazil nuts / Orangutango / As it will be. *(cd-iss. Oct00 on 'Camden-BMG'+=; 74321 78953-2)* – Whoops goes my body / Sunny day / Another orangutango / Papa's got a brand new Pigbag.

― **BRIAN** – drums / + **OSCAR** – trombone repl. ROGER who joined DR. CALCULUS (signed to '10-Virgin', released a couple of singles and an album, 'DESIGNER BEATNIK' in '86)

Jul 82. (7"/12") *(Y/12Y 24)* **THE BIG BEAN. / SCUMDA** | 40 | - |

― **ANGELA JAEGAR** (OLIVER) – vox (ex-RIP, RIG & PANIC, ex-DROWNING CRAZE)

Feb 83. (7"/12") *(Y/YT 101)* **HIT THE 'O' DECK. / SIX OF ONE**
Feb 83. (lp/c) *(YLP/YK 501)* **LEND AN EAR**
– Weak at the knees / Hit the 'O' deck / Ubud / One way ticket to Cubesville / Jump the line / Can't see for looking / No such thing as / Listen listen (liitle man).

PIGBAG (cont)

Jun 83. (m-lp/m-c) *(YMP/YK 1001)* **PIGBAG LIVE (live)**
– Shack of scraps / Smiling faces / Sunny day / Papa's got a brand new pigbag / Jump the line / Global terrain / End of Ubud / Can't see for looking.

— they had already disbanded early '83, SIMON joined RIP, RIG & PANIC

– compilations, others, etc. –

Nov 87. (cd) *Kaz; (KAZCD 3)* **THE BEST OF PIGBAG**
– Papa's got a brand new Pigbag (extended) / Weak at the knees / Hit the 'O' deck / Getting up / Brazil nuts / Jump the line / Another orangutango (extended) / Sunny day (extended) / Big bean (extended) / Can't see for looking / Six of one / Big bag. *(re-iss cd+=)* – Listen listen little man / Papa's got a brand new Pigbag.

Sep 94. (12") *Kaz; (KAZT 94)* **PAPA'S GOT A BRAND NEW PIGBAG (mixes)**
(12") *(KAZX 94)* – ('A'mixes).

Oct 98. (cd) *Strange Fruit; (SFRSCD 72)* **THE BBC SESSIONS**
– Honk wild / Eating burgers / Vile in / Me and your shadow / Dug out / You can wiggle my toe to that / Jack Frost / En ti la terra / Ubud / Can't see for looking.

PIN GROUP (see under ⇒ MONTGOMERY, Roy)

PINK INDUSTRY (see under ⇒ PINK MILITARY)

PINK MILITARY

Formed: Liverpool, England . . . 1978 by former BIG IN JAPAN frontwoman, JAYNE CASEY. Recruiting JOHN HIGHWAY, WAYNE WADDEN, NICKY COOL and PAUL HORNBY, she initiated a career which, if not quite as high profile as her famous ex-bandmates (BILL DRUMMOND, IAN BROUDIE, HOLLY JOHNSON etc.), was held in equally high critical esteem. Released on independent local label, 'Eric's', a 1979 debut EP, 'BLOOD AND LIPSTICK', caused enough of a stir to catch the attention of 'Virgin', who subsequently handled distribution of debut album, 'DO ANIMALS BELIEVE IN GOD?' (1980). Featuring a replacement rhythm section of CHRIS JOYCE and MARTIN DEMPSEY along with pianist CHARLIE GRUFF, the record was an entrancing sequence of experimental new wave/pop boasting such enduring tracks as the needling 'BACK ON THE LONDON STAGE' and the haunting 'I CRY'. Unfortunately the album performed poorly sales wise and with the 'Virgin' deal dead in the water, CASEY took a completely different approach. Altering the name to PINK INDUSTRY, she subsequently hooked up with future FRANKIE GOES TO HOLLYWOOD member, AMBROSE REYNOLDS, for an acclaimed 1982 single, 'IS THIS THE END?' and an album, 'LOW TECHNOLOGY' (1983). Heavily electronic with snatches of samples, aberrant sax, bleeps, guitar abuse, hints of eastern promise and of course CASEY's powerful vocals, the record was a breathtakingly diverse lesson in how to apply modern technology without sounding like SPANDAU BALLET. A second set, 'WHO TOLD YOU YOU WERE NAKED' (1983), continued in a similar electro sound-collage vein later that year although it would be a further two years before the release of any new material. In the event, 1985's 'NEW BEGINNINGS' album was to be PINK INDUSTRY's death knell as CASEY decided to restructure and concentrate on a TV career.
• **Trivia:** MORRISSEY's photo was on the cover of their single, 'WHAT WOULDN'T I GIVE'.

Album rating: DO ANIMALS BELIEVE IN GOD? (*8) / LOW TECHNOLOGY (*6) / WHO TOLD YOU – YOU WERE NAKED (*6) / NEW BEGINNINGS (*5)

JAYNE CASEY – vocals (ex-BIG IN JAPAN) / **JOHN HIGHWAY** – guitar / **NICKY COOL** – keyboards, synthesizers / **WAYNE WADDEN** – bass / **PAUL HORNBY** – drums

Last Trumpet   not iss.

Feb 79. (7") *(LT 001)* **BUDDHA WALKING / DISNEY SLEEPING (live; as "PINK MILITARY STANDS ALONE")**
– Degenerated man / Sanjo Kantara / Dead lady of clowntown / Heaven / Hell.

— **STEVE TORCH** – bass repl. WADDEN

— **TIM WHITAKER** – drums (ex-DEAF SCHOOL) repl. PAUL

— **MARTIN DEMPSEY** – guitar (ex-YACHTS) repl. ROY who repl. HIGHWAY

Eric's   not iss.

Sep 79. (12"ep) *(ERIC'S 002)* **BLOOD AND LIPSTICK**
– Spellbound / Blood and lipstick / I cry / Clowntown.

— **CHRIS JOYCE** – drums (of MOTHMEN) repl. TIM (later to)

— **CHARLIE GRUFF** – keyboards + **NEIL INNES** repl. TORCH

Jun 80. (lp) *(ERIC'S 004)* **DO ANIMALS BELIEVE IN GOD?**
– Degenerated man / I cry / Did you see her / Wild west / Back on the London stage / After Hiroshima / Living in the jungle / Dreamtime / War games / Heaven – Hell / Do animals believe in God? *(re-iss. 1989 on 'Virgin'; OVED 231)*

Jul 80. (7") *(ERIC'S 005)* **DID YOU SEE HER. / EVERYDAY**

— DEMPSEY joined IT'S IMMATERIAL and later MEL-O-TONES. CHRIS JOYCE joined DURUTTI COLUMN and later SIMPLY RED. NICKY formed FACTION.

PINK INDUSTRY

JAYNE CASEY – vocals / **AMBROSE REYNOLDS** – bass, keyboards (ex-BIG IN JAPAN, ex-HOLLYCAUST (w/ HOLLY JOHNSON), ex-NIGHTMARES IN WAX (pre-DEAD OR ALIVE), ex-WALKIE TALKIES) / **JAZIO JOOLOWSKI** –

Zulu   not iss.

Feb 82. (12"ep) *(ZULU 1)* **IS THIS THE END? / 47. / DON'T LET GO / FINAL CRY**

Mar 83. (lp) *(ZULU 2)* **LOW TECHNOLOGY**
– I wish / New aims / Don't let go / Creating hours / Enjoy the pain / Savage / Send them away / Remove the stain / Heavenly / Is this the end?.

Oct 83. (lp) *(ZULU 4)* **WHO TOLD YOU – YOU WERE NAKED**
– Walk away / Not moving / Urban jazz / Fear of failure / Anyone's fashion / Situation / Two culture's / Extreme / The raft / This is the place / The only one / Time for change.

Jun 85. (7") *(ZULU 6)* **WHAT WOULDN'T I GIVE. / BOUND BY SILENCE**

Jul 85. (lp) *(ZULU 7)* **NEW BEGINNINGS**
– Stand alone / What wouldn't I give / Rain of pride / Bound by silence / The corpse / etc

Cathexis   not iss.

Nov 87. (12"ep) *(CRL 16)* **DON'T LET GO. / TICKET TO HEAVEN / EMPTY BEACH**

May 88. (lp) *(CRL 18)* **PINK INDUSTRY** (compilation)
– Enjoy the pain / Send them away / New aims / Is this the end? / Not moving / This is the place / Pain of pride / State of grace / Bound by silence / Cruel garden / What I wouldn't give / Don't let go / Ticket to Heaven / Empty beach.

— had already disbanded a year earlier

– other compilation –

Dec 95. (cd) *Audioglobe; (PINK 1CD)* **NEW NAKED TECHNOLOGY**

PIXIES

Formed: Boston, Massachusetts, USA . . . 1986 by L.A. born frontman and self-confessed UFO freak, BLACK FRANCIS (real name, deep breath . . . CHARLES MICHAEL KITRIDGE THOMPSON IV) along with guitarist JOEY SANTIAGO. Famously placing a newspaper ad requesting musicians with a penchant for PETER, PAUL AND MARY and HUSKER DU, the only taker was KIM DEAL who subsequently brought in drummer DAVID LOVERING. Originally trading under the moniker PIXIES IN PANOPLY, the band soon trimmed this down to the punchier PIXIES and began kicking up a storm on the Boston music scene with their spiky, angular noise-pop (that's two thirds noise, one third pop) and wilfully cryptic lyrics. Along with fellow Bostonians THROWING MUSES, the band were signed to '4 a.d.' by a suitably impressed Ivo Watts-Russell, the label releasing The PIXIES' debut 'COME ON PILGRIM' in late '87. Stunningly different, the record galvanised the early PIXIES sound, a bizarre hybrid of manic, strangulated vocals (often sung in Spanish), searing melodic noise and schizophrenic, neo-latin rhythms. The album drew an early core of believers but it wasn't until the release of 'SURFER ROSA' (1988) that the band were hailed as the saviours of indie rock. Taking the formula of the debut to its brain splintering conclusion, the likes of 'BONE MACHINE', the incendiary 'SOMETHING AGAINST YOU' and careering 'BROKEN FACE' were utterly compelling in their blistering intensity. The sheer unhinged abandon with which BLACK FRANCIS threw himself into these songs has to be heard to be believed. You begin to fear that the man really has lost it when he asks 'WHERE IS MY MIND' in his inimitable melancholy howl. DEAL was equally affecting on the gorgeous 'GIGANTIC', the track building from a metaphorical whisper to a scream. Truly essential, 'SURFER ROSA' remains one of the most pivotal alternative rock records of the last fifteen years. Following their first headline UK tour, the band hooked up with producer Gil Norton for the 'DOOLITTLE' (1989) album. Previewed by the haunting 'MONKEY GONE TO HEAVEN', the record showcased a cleaner, more pop-friendly sound, most notably on (then) upcoming single, 'HERE COMES YOUR MAN'. Swoonfully poptastic, this song was guaranteed to have even the most miserable SMITHS fan grinning ear to ear, putting the toss that passes for modern 'indie-pop' to eternal shame. The demented 'DEBASER' was another highlight, becoming a dependable fixture at indie discos for oh, aeons. As well as a mammoth world tour, DEAL found time for her side project, The BREEDERS. A collaboration with the delectable TANYA DONELLY (ex-THROWING MUSES), the pair released the acclaimed 'POD' album in 1990. Later that year came 'BOSSANOVA', another breathtaking collection that had the music press in rapture. Lyrically, BLACK was in his element, losing himself in science fiction fantasy while the band raged and charmed in equal measure. The album reached No.3 in the UK charts and The PIXIES could apparently do no wrong, consolidating their position as one of the biggest American acts in Europe. Yet the critics turned on them with the release of 'TROMPE LE MONDE' (1991), in keeping with the times a decidedly grungier affair. Accusations of "Heavy Metal" were way off the mark. In reality, the record was still chokka with stellar tunes, you just had to dig deeper to find them. 'PLANET OF SOUND', 'SPACE (I BELIEVE IN)' and 'MOTORWAY TO ROSWELL' were all quintessential PIXIES, FRANCIS as endearingly fascinated as ever with the mysteries of the universe. Sadly, the singer was soon to turn his obsession over to a solo venture, The PIXIES gone almost as quickly as they had arrived, leaving behind a brief but rich sonic legacy. With FRANCIS changing his name to the rather dull FRANK BLACK, he went on to release a moderately successful eponymous solo debut in 1993 and a wryly titled follow-up, 'TEENAGER OF THE YEAR' (1994), DEAL going on to make a further album with The BREEDERS. Inevitably, none of these projects approached the deranged genius of The PIXIES (Rock will never see their like again). The frontman continued to surface periodically and three albums, 'THE CULT OF RAY' (1996), 'FRANK BLACK AND THE CATHOLICS' (1998) and 'PISTOLERO' (1999), have all met with diminishing fanbase response. 'DOG IN THE SAND' followed in 2001, a more down home effort which featured some of his best songwriting for years. The fact that SANTIAGO was back on board was hardly a hindrance while occasional glimpses of FRANK's legendary lyrical genius suggested there was life in the old (black) dog yet. The man's feverish creativity

PIXIES (cont)

continued apace with the simultaneous release, in 2002, of both 'DEVIL'S WORKSHOP' and 'BLACK LETTER DAYS'. Rarely, if ever, can an artist sustain quality over such a protracted format, especially bearing in mind that the latter disc stretches to almost 20 tracks. While this, at least, might conceivably have been more focused had it been edited down to size, there's a ramshackle continuity about the record that makes for strangely addictive listening. While '...WORKSHOP' was the more sonically adrenalised of the two, both albums found BLACK's inimitable, impenetrable muse travelling America's stranger side roads. • **Songwriters:** BLACK FRANCIS penned except; WINTERLONG + I'VE BEEN WAITING FOR YOU (Neil Young) / EVIL HEARTED YOU (Yardbirds) / HEAD ON (Jesus & Mary Chain) / CECILIA ANN (Surftones) / BORN IN CHICAGO (Paul Butterfield's Blues Band) / I CAN'T FORGET (Leonard Cohen). FRANK BLACK solo:- JUST A LITTLE (Beau Brummels) / RE-MAKE, RE-MODEL (Roxy Music) / HANG ON TO YOUR EGO (Beach Boys).

Album rating: COME ON PILGRIM mini (*7) / SURFER ROSA (*10) / DOOLITTLE (*9) / BOSSANOVA (*8) / TROMPE LE MONDE (*7) / DEATH TO THE PIXIES compilation (*8) / Frank Black: FRANK BLACK (*8) / TEENAGER OF THE YEAR (*8) / THE CULT OF RAY (*5) / FRANK BLACK & THE CATHOLICS (*5) / PISTOLERO (*5) / DOG IN THE SAND (*6) / DEVIL'S WORKSHOP (*5) / BLACK LETTER DAYS (*5)

BLACK FRANCIS (b. CHARLES MICHAEL KITRIDGE THOMPSON IV, 1965, Long Beach, Calif.) – vocals, guitar / **JOEY SANTIAGO** (b.10 Jun'65, Manila, Philippines) – lead guitar / **KIM DEAL** (Mrs.JOHN MURPHY) (b.10 Jun'61, Dayton, Ohio) – bass, vocals / **DAVE LOVERING** (b. 6 Dec'61) – drums

4.a.d. Elektra

Oct 87. (m-lp) *(MAD 709) <61296>* **COME ON PILGRIM**
– Caribou / Vamos / Islade encounter / Ed is dead / The holiday song / Nimrod's son / I've been tried / Levitate me.

Mar 88. (lp/c)(cd) *(CAD/+C 803)(CAD 803CD) <61295>* **SURFER ROSA**
– Bone machine / Break my body / Something against you / Broken face / Gigantic / River Euphrates / Where is my mind? / Cactus / Tony's theme / Oh my golly! / Vamos / I'm amazed / Brick is red. *(cd+=)* – COME ON PILGRIM (m-lp)

Aug 88. (12"ep/cd-ep) *(BAD 805/+CD)* **GIGANTIC. / RIVER EUPHRATES. / VAMOS. / IN HEAVEN (LADY IN THE RADIATOR SONG)**

Mar 89. (7") *(AD 904)* **MONKEY GONE TO HEAVEN. / MANTA RAY** |60|
(12"+=/cd-s+=) *(BAD 904/+CD)* – Weird at my school / Dancing the manta ray.

Apr 89. (lp/c)(cd) *(CAD/+C 905)(CAD 905CD) <60856>* **DOOLITTLE** |8| |98|
– Debaser / Tame / Wave of mutilation / I bleed / There goes my gun / Here comes your man / Dead / Monkey gone to Heaven / La la love you / Mr. Grieves / Crackity Jones / #13 baby / Silver / Hey / Gouge away.

Jun 89. (7") *(AD 909) <66694>* **HERE COMES YOUR MAN. / INTO THE WHITE** |54|
(12"+=/cd-s+=) *(BAD 909/+CD)* – Wave of mutilation (UK surf) / Bailey's walk.

— KIM DEAL was also part of amalgamation The BREEDERS

Jul 90. (7")/c-s) *(AD/+C 0009) <66616>* **VELOURIA. / I'VE BEEN WAITING FOR YOU** |28|
(12"+=/cd-s+=) *(BAD 0009/+CD)* – Make believe / The thing.

Aug 90. (cd)(lp/c) *(CAD 0010CD)(CAD/+C 0010) <60963>* **BOSSANOVA** |3| |70|
– Cecilia Ann / Rock music / Velouria / Allison / Is she weird / Ana / All over the world / Dig for fire / Down to the wall / The happening / Blown away / Hang wire / Stormy weather / Havalina.

Oct 90. (7"/c-s) *(AD/+C 0014) <66596>* **DIG FOR FIRE. / VELVETY (instrumental)** |62|
(12"+=/cd-s+=) *(BAD 0014/+CD)* – Winterlong / Santo.

May 91. (7") *(AD 1008)* **PLANET OF SOUND. / BUILD HIGH** |27|
(c-s+=)(12"+=/cd-s+=) *(BADC 1008)(BAD 1008/+CD)* – Evil hearted you / Theme from Narc.

Sep 91. (cd)(lp/c) *(CAD 1014CD)(CAD/+C 1014) <61118>* **TROMPE LE MONDE** |7| |92|
– Trompe de Monde / Planet of sound / Alec Eiffel / The sad punk / Head on / U-mass / Palace of the brine / Letter to Memphis / Bird dream Of the Olympus mons / Space (I believe in) / Subbacultcha / Distance equals rate times time / Lovely day / Motorway to Roswell / The Navajo know.

Nov 91. (7") *(AD 1999)* **ALEC EIFFEL. / MOTORWAY TO ROSWELL** | |−|
(12"+=)(cd-s+=) *(BAD 1999)(PIX 1999CD)* – Planet of sound (live) / Tame (live).

Feb 92. (12"ep) *<66444>* **ALEC EIFFEL / LETTER TO MEMPHIS (instrumental). / BUILD LIFE / EVIL HEARTED YOU** |−|

— disbanded late in '92, with BLACK FRANCIS going solo as FRANK BLACK.

– compilations, etc. –

on '4 a.d.' / 'Elektra' unless otherwise mentioned

Sep 97. (7") *(AD 7010)* **DEBASER (demo). / #13 BABY** |23|
(cd-s) *(BAD 7010CD)* – ('A'studio) / Bone machine / Gigantic / Isla de Encanta.
(cd-s) *(BADD 7010CD)* – ('A'live) / Holiday song (live) / Cactus (live) / Nimrod's son (live).

Oct 97. (d-cd/d-c) *(DAD/+C 7011) <62118>* **DEATH TO THE PIXIES** |28|
– Cecilia Ann / Planet of sound / Tame / Here comes your man / Debaser / Wave of mutilation / Dig for fire / Caribou / Holiday song / Nimrod's son / U mass / Bone machine / Gigantic / Where is my mind / Velouria / Gouge away / Monkey gone to Heaven / Debaser / Rock music / Broken face / Isla De Encanta / Hangfire / Dead / Into the white / Monkey gone to Heaven / Gouge away / Gouge away / Here comes your man / Alidon / Hey / Gigantic / Crackity Jones / Where is my mind / Ed is dead / Vamos / Tony's theme. *(de-luxe version hit No.20 q-lp/q-cd; DADD 7011/+CD)*

Jul 98. (cd) *(GAD 8013) <62185>* **PIXIES AT THE BBC (live)** |45|
– Wild honey pie / There goes my gun / Dead / Subbacultcha / Manta Ray / Is she weird / Ana / Down to the well / Wave of mutilation / Letter to Memphis / Levitate me / Caribou / Monkey gone to Heaven / Hey / In Heaven (lady in the radiator song).

FRANK BLACK

— with **ERIC DREW FELDMAN** – bass, keyboards, synthetics (ex-CAPTAIN BEEFHEART) / **NICK VINCENT** – drums, percussion / + extra guitars **SANTIAGO, MORRIS TEPPER + DAVID SARDY**

4 a.d. Elektra

Mar 93. (lp/cd)(c) *(CAD 3004/+CD)(CADC 3004) <61467>* **FRANK BLACK** |9|
– Los Angeles / I heard Ramona sing / Hang on to your ego / Fu Manchu / Places named after numbers / Czar / Old black dawning / Ten percenter / Brackish boy / Two spaces / Tossed (instrumental version) / Parry the wind high, low / Adda Lee / Every time I go around here / Don't ya rile 'em. *(cd re-iss. Jul98; GAD 3004CD)*

Apr 93. (7") *(AD 3005) <8782-2>* **HANG ON TO YOUR EGO. / THE BALLAD OF JOHNNY HORTON**
(cd-s+=) *(BAD 3005CD)* – Surf epic.

— same trio augmented by **SANTIAGO, TEPPER + LYLE WORKMAN** – guitar

May 94. (7") *(AD 4007)* **HEADACHE. / ('A'mix)** |53| |−|
(10"/cd-s) *(BADD 4007/+CD)* – ('A'side) / Men in black / At the end of the world / Oddball.
(cd-s) *(BAD 4007CD)* – ('A'side) / Hate me / This is where I belong / Amnesia.

May 94. (d-lp/cd)(c) *(DAD 4009/+CD)(DADC 4009) <61618>* **TEENAGER OF THE YEAR** |21|
– Whatever happened to Pong? / Thalassocracy / (I want to live on an) Abstract plain / Calistan / The vanishing spies / Speedy Marie / Headache / Sir Rockaby / Freedom rock / Two reelers / Fiddle riddle / Ole Mulholland / Fazer eyes / I could stay here forever / The hostess with the mostest / Superabound / Big red / Space is gonna do me good / White noise maker / Pure denizen of the citizens band / Bad, wicked world / Pie in the sky. *(re-iss. Jul98; GAD 4009CD)*

— FRANK BLACK had earlier in the year teamed up with ex-SEX PISTOL; GLEN MATLOCK to form tribute band FRANK BLACK & THE STAX PISTOLS

Noise Annoys not iss.

Dec 95. (cd/d-lp) *(ANAN CD/V 7)* **THE BLACK SESSIONS (live in Paris)** |−|
– Two spaces / (I want to live on an) Abstact plain / Headache / Old black dawning / Superabound / Calistan / The vanishing spies / Sir Rockaby / Big red / The Jacques Tati / Oddball / Men in black / Czar / Freedom rock / (Whatever happened to) Pong / Thalasocracy / White noise maker / Los Angeles / Handyman / Modern age / Jumping beans / (I want to live on an) Abstact plain (acoustic). *(re-iss. Oct97; same)*

— now w/ **LYLE WORKMAN** – lead guitar / **DAVID McCAFFREY** – bass / **SCOTT BOUTIER** – drums

Epic Warners

Dec 95. (ltd-7") *(662 671-7)* **THE MARXIST. / BETTER THINGS** | |−|
Jan 96. (7") *(662 786-7)* **MEN IN BLACK. / JUST A LITTLE** |37|
(cd-s+=) *(662 786-2)* – Re-make, re-model.
(cd-s) *(662 786-5)* – ('A'side) / You never heard of me / Pray a little faster / Announcement.

Jan 96. (cd/c/lp) *(481 647-2/-4/-1) <43070>* **THE CULT OF RAY** |39|
– The Marxist / Men in black / Punk rock city / You ain't me / Jesus was right / I don't want to hurt you (every single time) / Mosh, don't pass the guy / Kicked in the taco / Creature crawling / Adventure and the resolution / Dance war / The cult of Ray / Last stand of Shazeb Andleeb. *(cd re-iss. Oct01 on 'Cooking Vinyl'; COOKCD 221)*

Jul 96. (7") *(663 463-7)* **I DON'T WANT TO HURT YOU (EVERY SINGLE TIME). / YOU AIN'T ME (live)** |63| |−|
(cd-s+=) *(663 463-2)* – The Marxist / Better things.
(cd-s) *(663 463-5)* – ('A'live) / Men in black (live) / Village of the sun (live) / The last stand of Shazeb Andleeb (live).

FRANK BLACK AND THE CATHOLICS

with **LYLE WORKMAN, DAVE McCAFFREY + SCOTT BOUTIER**

Play It Again Sam SpinArt

Apr 98. (7"ep/cd-ep) *(BIAS 347 7/CD)* **ALL MY GHOSTS / LIVING ON SOUL / HUMBOULDT COUNTY MASSACRE / CHANGING OF THE GUARDS** | |−|

May 98. (cd/c/lp) *(BIAS 370 CD/MC/LP) <SPART 067CD>* **FRANK BLACK AND THE CATHOLICS** |61|
– All my ghosts / Back to Rome / Do you feel bad about it / Dog gone / I gotta move / I need peace / King and Queen of Siam / Six sixty six / Solid gold / Steak 'n' sabre / Suffering / The man who was too loud. *(ltd-cd+=; BIAS 370CDX)* – All my ghosts / Living on soul / Humboudlt county massacre / Changing of the guards. *(cd re-iss. Jul00 on 'SpinArt'; same as US)*

— **RICK GILBERT** – guitar; repl. WORKMAN

Mar 99. (cd) *(CDBIAS 390CD) <SPART 070CD>* **PISTOLERO**
– Bad harmony / I switched you / Western star / Tiny heart / You're such a wire / I loved your brain / Smoke up / Billy Radcliffe / So hard to make things out / Eighty five weeks / I think I'm starting to lose it / I want to rock and roll / Skeleton man / So bay. *(lp-iss.Nov99 on 'SpinArt'; SPART 70)*

— added **ERIC DREW FELDMAN** – keyboards + **JOEY SANTIAGO** – guitar / **DAVE PHILIPS** – guitar / **MORRIS TEPPER** – guitar

Cooking Vinyl What Are?

Jan 01. (cd) *(FRYCD 098)* **ROBERT ONION / PAN AMERICAN HIGHWAY / ANGST** | |−|
Jan 01. (cd) *(COOKCD 200) <4833>* **DOG IN THE SAND**
– Blast off / I've seen your picture / St. Francis dam disaster / Robert Onion / Stupid me / Bullet / The swimmer / Hermaphroditos / I'll be blue / Llano del Rio / If it takes all night / Dog in the sand.

Feb 01. (cd-s) *(FRYCD 2)* **ST. FRANCIS DAM DISASTER / CONSTANT SORROW MAN / SLEEP** | |−|

Aug 02. (cd) *(COOKCD 243) <SPART 112>* **DEVIL'S WORKSHOP**
– Velvety / Out of state / His kingly cave / San Antonio, TX / Bartholomew / Modern age / Are you headed my way? / Heloise / The scene / Whiskey in your shoes / Fields of marigold.

PIXIES (cont)

Aug 02. (cd) *(COOKCD 240)* <SPART 113> **BLACK LETTER DAYS**
– The black rider / California bound / Chip away boy / Cold heart of stone / Black letter day / Valentine and Garuda / How you went so far / End of miles / 1826 / The farewell bend / Southbound bevy / I will run after you / True blue / Jane the queen of love / Jet black river / 21 reasons / Whispering weeds / The black rider.

– compilations, etc. –

Jul 95. (12"ep/cd-ep) *Strange Fruit; (SFPS/+CD 091)* **PEEL SESSION**
– Handyman / The man who was too loud / The Jacques Tati / Sister Isabel.
Nov 97. (cd-ep; with TEENAGE FANCLUB) *Strange Fruit; (SFRSCD 042)* **THE JOHN PEEL SESSION**
Mar 01. (cd) *4 a.d.; (GAD 2103CD)* **THE COMPLETE B-SIDES** — 53

PIZZICATO FIVE

Formed: Tokyo, Japan ... 1979 by university students and part-time sound engineers, YASUHARA KONISHI and KEITARO TAKANAMI. After recruiting fellow Western music fan, RYO KAMAMIYA, they auditioned unsuccessfully for an English speaking vocalist. Eventually locating MAMIKO SASAKI, the quartet finally debuted in the mid-80's with the single, 'AUDREY HEPBURN COMPLEX', the first in a series of kitschy releases that plundered the cheesiest bits of 60's/70's US/UK pop history in search of the perfect post-modern collage. Amid a revolving door personnel situation, the founding duo remained intact throughout the 80's and into the 90's, their sizeable Japanese success prompting US indie giant, 'Matador', to try them out on American alternative fans. However, after only one EP, 'FIVE BY FIVE', KONISHI was left to take up the reins alongside recent vocal addition, MAKI NOMIYA, after TAKANAMI finally bailed out. Suffocatingly hip and contrived or refreshingly funky according to taste, P5 were never really destined to capture the imagination of the average indie fan while their sampledelic pop deconstructions went over the head of chart audiences.

Album rating: NON-STANDARD YEARS '85-'86 compilation (*3) / COUPLES (*4) / BELISSIMA! (*5) / MADE IN USA compilation (*7) / THE SOUND OF MUSIC BY PIZZICATO FIVE (*6)

YASUHARA KONISHI + **KEITARO TAKANAMI** – electronics / **RYO KAMAMIYA** – electronics / **MAMIKO SASAKI** – vocals

                                          Teichiku not iss.

1985. (12"ep) **THE AUDREY HEPBURN COMPLEX EP** — – Japan
– 59th Street bridge song / Boy meets girl / September song / Audrey Hepburn complex.
1986. (12"ep) **PIZZICATO V IN ACTION EP** — – Japan
– From party to party / Action painting / Let's go away for awhile / What's new, Pizzicato?
1987. (cd) *(TECN 22333,223)* **NON-STANDARD YEARS** (compilation) — – Japan
(re-mixed Jun98; 15256)

                                      CBS-Sony not iss.

1987. (cd) *(32DH 637)* **COUPLES** — – Japan
– Magical connection / Summertime, summertime / They all laughed / Serial stories / Apartment / What now our love / Seven o'clock news / Odd couple and the others / My blue heaven / Party joke / Two sleepy people / Everytime we say goodbye.

— **TAJIMA TAKAO** – vocals; repl. SASAKI

1988. (cd) *(32DH 5126)* **BELISSIMA!** — – Japan
– Planets / Temptation talk / Holy triangle / World standard / Couples / Sunday impressions / Swim / Seventeen / This can't be love / Work of God.

— **MAKI NOMIYA** – vocals; repl. TAKAO who formed ORIGINAL LOVE

                                         Matador Matador

Aug 94. (m-cd/m-lp) <*OLE 096-2/-1*> **FIVE BY FIVE**
– Pizzacatomania / Twiggy, Twiggy / Baby love child / Me Japanese boy / This year's girl No.2.
Oct 94. (cd/c/lp) <*OLE 099-2/-4/-1*> **MADE IN USA** (compilation)
– I / Sweet soul revue / Magic carpet ride / Readymade FM / Baby love child / Twiggy, Twiggy / Twiggy vs James Bond / This year's girl / I wanna be like you / Go-go dancer / Catchy / Peace music.
Mar 95. (12"ep/cd-ep) <*OLE 128-1/-2*> **QUICKIE EP**
– Magic carpet ride (mixes) / Go-go dancer / I wanna be like you.
May 95. (12"ep/cd-ep) <*OLE 138-1/-2*> **QUICKIE TWO EP**
Apr 96. (7") <*OLE 167-7*> **HAPPY SAD. / IF I WERE A GROUPIE**
(cd-s+=) <*OLE 167-2*> – CDJ.

                                         Matador Atlantic

Jun 96. (cd/d-lp) *(OLE 166-2/-2)* <*92622*> **THE SOUND OF MUSIC BY PIZZICATO FIVE** — Oct95
– We love Pizzicato Five / Rock'n'roll / The night is still young / Happy sad / Groovy is my name / Sophisticated catchy / Strawberry sleighride / If I were a groupie / Sweet Thursday / CDJ / Fortune cookie. (d-lp+=) – Number five / Peace music / Airplane / Rock'n'roll.

                                         Matador Matador

Feb 97. (10"ep/cd-ep) <*OLE 223-1/-2*> **SISTER FREEDOM TAPES** — Nov96
– Airplane '96 / Domino / Snowflakes / Chicken curry / Mini Cooper / Holger and Marcus / Cornflakes / To our children's children's children / Passing by
Mar 97. (10"ep/cd-ep) <*OLE 224-1/-2*> **COMBINAISON SPACIALE**
– Baby portable rock / Ice cream meltin' mellow / Contact / Good / Tokyo mon amour / Ice cream meltin' mellow.

                                         Matador Capitol

Sep 97. (cd/lp) *(OLE 198-2/-1)* <*59181*> **HAPPY END OF THE WORLD**
– The world is spinning at 45 rpm / The Earth goes round / Trailer music / It's a beautiful day / Love's prelude / Love's theme / My baby portable player sound / Mon amour Tokyo / Collision and improvisation / Porno 3003: Music for sofa – Galaxy / Arigato we love you / Ma vie, l'ete de vie / Happy ending.

                                         Matador Matador

Oct 97. (7") *(OLE 289-7)* **MON AMOUR TOKYO. / TRAILER MUSIC**
(cd-s+=) *(OLE 289-2)* – Contact.
(cd-s+=) *(OLE 290-2)* – Happy birthday.
Oct 97. (12") <*(OLE 273-1)*> **THE WORLD IS SPINNING AT 45 RPM: P5 REMIXES VOL.1**
Oct 97. (12") <*(OLE 274-1)*> **THE WORLD IS SPINNING AT 45 RPM: P5 REMIXES VOL.2**
Nov 97. (12") <*(OLE 275-1)*> **THE WORLD IS SPINNING AT 45 RPM: P5 REMIXES VOL.3**
Nov 97. (12") <*(OLE 276-1)*> **THE WORLD IS SPINNING AT 45 RPM: P5 REMIXES VOL.4**
Dec 97. (12") <*(OLE 277-1)*> **THE WORLD IS SPINNING AT 45 RPM: P5 REMIXES VOL.5**
Dec 97. (12") <*(OLE 278-1)*> **THE WORLD IS SPINNING AT 45 RPM: P5 REMIXES VOL.6**
Jan 98. (12") <*(OLE 279-1)*> **THE WORLD IS SPINNING AT 45 RPM: P5 REMIXES VOL.7**
Jan 98. (12") <*(OLE 280-1)*> **THE WORLD IS SPINNING AT 45 RPM: P5 REMIXES VOL.8**
Apr 98. (12") *(GINA 03)* **IT'S A BEAUTIFUL DAY. / LOVE"S THEME / MON AMOUR TOKYO**
(above issued on 'Gina')
Jun 98. (cd/d-lp) <*(OLE 282-2/-1)*> **HAPPY END OF YOU** (remixes) — May98
– Love's theme (AUTOMATOR) / Trailer music (808 STATE) / Goes round (DADDY-O) / Porno 3003 (DJ DARA) / Porno 3000 (GUSGUS) / My baby portable player sound (SEAN O'HAGAN) / Happy ending (OVAL) / It's a beautiful day (JOHN OSWALD) / Love's theme (SAINT ETIENNE) / Trailer music (MOMUS) / Collision and improvisation (SHOOTER) / Contact (DIMITRI FROM PARIS) / The world is spinning at 45 rpm (DANIEL MILLER / GARETH JONES).
Aug 98. (cd/lp) <*(OLE 333-2/-1)*> **PLAYBOY AND PLAYGIRL**
– Depression / Rolls Royce / International Pizzicato 5 mansion / New song / Weekend / Magic twin candle tale / Concerto / Such a beautiful girl like you / Playboy playgirl / I hear a symphony / Drinking wine / Great invitations / Stars.

PLANET WILSON (see under ⇒ RED GUITARS)

PLASTICLAND

Formed: Milwaukee, Wisconsin, USA ... 1980 by GLENN REHSE and JOHN FRANKOVIC, who had actually played together in a mid-60's garage band. They played some live psychedelic (PINK FLOYD / CREATION-like) shows, but by the early 70's they had "progressed" into rock outfit, WILLIE THE CONQUEROR. Influenced by Britain's new-found love of "Krautrock", they became AROUSING POLARIS, although it wasn't long before another quarrel split them apart. As PLASTICLAND (with extra members DAN MULLEN and BRIAN RITCHIE), they were once again re-united, taking their first fruitful sojourn into the studio with the 1981 single, 'MINK DRESS', after which, RITCHIE joined The VIOLENT FEMMES. With punk-rock now past its sell-by date, they fashioned themselves in 60's Carnaby Street wares although this image didn't go down too well back home in Milwaukee. In 1982 they made an appearance on "Battle Of The Garages", which led to a self-issued EP, 'VIBRASONGS FROM ... POP! OP DROPS'. A debut album, 'COLOR APPRECIATION', was released for the French 'Lolita' label, its flowing dramas and sense of the absurd leading to a deal with 'Enigma' in 1985. Their first outing for the label, 'WONDER WONDERFUL WONDERLAND' (1985), was lush Lewis Carroll-style fantasy, although producer PAUL CUTLER (of DREAM SYNDICATE) might disagree. Their next groovy offering, 'SALON' (1987), showed a shift to a more "Psychedelic Shack"-style R&B/soul while the band refused to do a promotional tour, giving their label the 'old age' excuse (they were now over 40!). Despite developing musically with some awe-inspiring, occasional gigs (complete with go-go dancers), they were dropped. This led to semi-retirement, the band only surfacing to play reunion gigs, also backing veteran, TWINK, on his live album. In 1994, their 1991 recorded comeback album, 'DAPPER SNAPPINGS', was finally released by the German-based 'Repulsion' label, a UK release still pending. More releases are in the pipeline, although FRANKOVIC is now a part-time solo artist, while other offshoots, The GOTHICS and FABULON TRIPTOMETER, are also underway. • **Songwriters:** REHSE-FRANKOVIC except covers ALEXANDER (Pretty Things) / etc.

Album rating: COLOR APPRECIATION (*6) / WONDER WONDERFUL WONDERLAND (*7) / SALON (*6) / DAPPER SNAPPINGS (*6) / John Frankovic:- UNDER THE WATER LILY (*6)

GLENN REHSE – vocals, guitar, keyboards / **JOHN FRANKOVIC** – bass, vocals, percussion, bouzouki / **DAN MULLEN** – guitar, vocals / **BRIAN RITCHIE** – drums

                                         Scadillac Scadillac

Jan 81. (7") <*SC-1001*> **MINK DRESS. / OFFICE SKILLS**

— **ROB McCUEN** – drums; repl. RITCHIE who joined VIOLENT FEMMES

May 81. (12"ep) <*SC-1002*> **VIBRASONGS FROM ... POP! OP DROPS**
– Too many fingers / Standing in a room / The prince's playground / Pushy.
Mar 84. (7") <*(SC 05)*> **EUPHORIC TRAPDOOR SHOES. / RAT TAIL COMB**

                                         Lolita not iss.

1984. (lp) *(5018)* **COLOR APPRECIATION** — France
– Alexander / Disengaged from the world / Her decay / The glove / Sipping the bitterness / The garden in pain / Elongations / Driving accident prone / The mushroom hill / Euphoric trapdoor shoes / Pop! up drops / Sections / Rattail comb / Color appreciation / Magic rocking horse. <US-iss.1985 as 'PLASTICLAND'; > (UK-iss.Feb87 on 'Bam Caruso'; KIRI 034)

                                    Pink Dust- Pink Dust-
                                     Enigma Enigma

1985. (lp) <*70063-1*> **WONDER WONDERFUL WONDERLAND**
– No shine for the shoes / Gloria Knight / Transparencies, friends / Fairytale hysteria / Don't let it all pass by / The gingerbread house / Flower scene / Processes of the silverness / Non-stop kitchen / Grassland of reeds and things / Gloria Knight (reprise) / Wonder wonderful wonderland.

PLASTICLAND (cont)   THE GREAT INDIE DISCOGRAPHY   The 1980s

— **VICTOR DEMICHI** – drums; repl. McCUEN
Jun 87. (lp) <(ENIG 72179-1)> **SALON**
– Go a go-go time / What am I to say / It's a dog life / Quick commentary on wax museums / Abcessed words to climb / House / Lie of great Sedan Pinocchio / We can't / Serene it's true / Reserving the right to change my mind / Window sills / Don't antagonize me.

Repulsion   not iss.

1991. (12"ep) (EFA 15651) **LET'S PLAY POLLYANNA. / RADIANT FUZZBOX WIG. / KALEIDOSCOPIC GLANCE / ENCHANTED FORESTRY**
Feb 95. (cd) <(EFA 15660-2)> **DAPPER SNAPPINGS**
– Craved blue memorandu / High school burse / Make yourself a happening machine / The bunny bear / When you get subliminal, you really get.... / Radiant fuzzbox wig / Probing / Let's play Pollyanna / Passing over rollercoaster / House of worms / Cookies with the vaudeville glaze.

– compilations, etc. –

Jan 01. (cd) *Timothy's Brain; (TB 102)* **MINK DRESS AND OTHER CATS**
– You were such a bad time / In my black and white / I'm gonna emphasize / Pushy / The prince's playroom / Too many fingers / Standing in a room / A change in you / Mink dress / They wore sequined masks / The lady is no lady / Some ghost ship lollipop / Headlice rags and arrogance / Baby scissors / Coloe appreciation / Market place of Zesty Zeal / The mushroom hill / Office skills / Skipping down the nature trail.

PLAY DEAD

Formed: Banbury, nr. Oxford, England... Autumn 1980 by ROB HICKSON, RE VOX, PETE WADDLESTON and MARK 'WIFF' SMITH, who were soon supporting the likes of UK DECAY the following summer. Their debut single, 'POISON TAKES A HOLD', was issued around the same time while its follow-up, 'TV EYE', saw the addition of guitarist, STEVE GREEN. In 1982, they recorded their first of many John Peel sessions and signed to goth/punk orientated label, 'Jungle', releasing 'PROPAGANDA' in the process. Subsequent tours supporting SEX GANG CHILDREN and KILLING JOKE – with whom they shared a spiritual similarity – paved the way for another string of anthemic singles including the pummelling 'PROPAGANDA'. They finally unleashed their debut album, 'FROM THE PROMISED LAND', in 1984, featuring live favourite 'WALK AWAY', which believe it or not, suggested a gothic BIG COUNTRY, if that's possible! Becoming one of the many acts on the books of the 'Clay' label, PLAY DEAD featured on a December '84 edition of 'The Tube', while going on to tour Scandinavia and other parts of Europe where they were more popular. However, by March '86 (and after another album, 'COMPANY OF JUSTICE'), PLAY DEAD had finally keeled over, metamorphosing into the short-lived BEASTMASTER GENERAL.

Album rating: FROM THE PROMISED LAND (*5) / INTO THE FIRE – LIVE mini (*4) / COMPANY OF JUSTICE (*4) / THE SINGLES 82-85 compilation (*5)

ROB HICKSON – vocals / **RE VOX** – guitar / **PETE WADDLESTON** – bass / **WIFF** (b. MARK SMITH) – drums

Fresh   not iss.

Jun 81. (7") (FRESH 29) **POISON TAKES A HOLD. / INTRODUCTION**
— **STEVE GREEN** – guitar; repl. RE VOX
Oct 81. (7") (FRESH 38) **T.V. EYE. / THE FINAL EPITAPH**

Jungle   not iss.

Nov 82. (7") (JUNG 002) **PROPAGANDA. / PROPAGANDA (mix)**

Situation 2   not iss.

Sep 83. (7") (SIT 28) **SHINE. / PROMISE**
(12"+=) (SIT 28T) – Gaze.

Clay   not iss.

Apr 84. (7") (CLAY 31) **BREAK. / BLOODSTAINS**
(12"+=) (12CLAY 31) – The pleasure.
May 84. (lp) (CLAYLP 11) **FROM THE PROMISED LAND**
– Isabel / Torn on desire / Walk away / Pleasureland / Return to the east / Holy holy / No motive / Weeping blood.
Jul 84. (7"/12") (CLAY/12CLAY 35) **ISABEL. / SOLACE**
Oct 84. (7"/12") (CLAY/12CLAY 40) **CONSPIRACY. / SILENT CONSPIRACY**
Feb 85. (7") (CLAY 42) **SACROSANCT. / PALE FIRE**
(12"+=) (12CLAY 42) – Holy holy / Sacrosanct.
May 85. (m-lp) (CLAYLP 16M) **INTO THE FIRE (live)**
– Walk away / Shine / Return to the east / Break / Turn on desire / Sin of sins / The tenant / No motive.

Tanz   not iss.

Sep 85. (12"'w-drawn) (TANZ 1) **THIS SIDE OF HEAVEN. / LAST DEGREE / THIS SIDE OF HEAVEN (serious mix)**
Nov 85. (lp) (TANZLP 1) **COMPANY OF JUSTICE**
– Witnesses / Caught on the thorns / Company of justice / This side of Heaven / Judgement / Chains / Celebration / Sacrosanct / Treason / Reward. (cd-iss. Sep93 & Sep01 on 'Jungle'+=; FREUDCD 41) – Last degree / Burning down (extended).
May 86. (12") (TANZ 2) **BURNING DOWN. / STILL IN CHAINS**

— had already split in March when two members (not PETE) formed the BEASTMASTER GENERAL

– compilations, etc. –

Jul 84. (lp/c) *Jungle; (FREUD/+C 003)* **THE FIRST FLOWER**
– Shine / Sin of sins / In silence / Gaze / Propaganda / The tenant / Time / Promise / Propaganda ('84 mix) / Don't leave without me. *(cd-iss. Sep92 +=; FREUDCD 003)* – Sin of sins ('84 mix) / Poison takes a hold / Introduction / T.V. eye / The final epitaph. *(cd re-iss. Jan94 on 'Cleopatra'; CLEO 7519CD)*
Sep 84. (12") *Jungle; (JUNG 17)* **PROPAGANDA (1984 mix). / SIN OF SINS (remix)**

Feb 86. (12"ep) *Jungle; (JUNG 26T)* **IN THE BEGINNING – THE 1981 SINGLES**
Jul 86. (m-lp) *Clay; (CLAYLP 20M)* **THE SINGLES '82-'85**
Aug 86. (lp) *Dojo; (DOJOLP 34)* **CAUGHT FROM BEHIND – LIVE IN ENGLAND, FRANCE, GERMANY AND SWITZERLAND)**
– Break / Last degree / Solace / Shine / Isabel / Sin of sins / Torn on desire / This side of Heaven / Sacrosanct / The tenant.
Mar 87. (lp) *Jungle; (FREUD 015)* **THE FINAL EPITAPH – LIVE (live)**
Jun 92. (cd) *Clay; (CLAYCD 111)* **RESURRECTION** (w/ some remixes)
– Break / Isabel / Walk away / Bloodstains / Solace / No motive / Pleasureland / Pale fire / Sacrosanct / Torn on desire / Holy holy / Return to the east / Conspiracy / Sin of sins (live) / Bloodstains pleasure / Solace / Holy holy.

PLIMSOULS

Formed: Los Angeles, California, USA... late '78 as The TONE DOGS by PETER CASE (a one-time member of The NERVES), DAVE PAHOA, LOU RAMIREZ and last but not least, EDDIE MUNOZ. Having taken their new moniker from the British slang for "gym shoes", The PLIMSOULS finally debuted at the turn of the decade with the independently released classic 'ZERO HOUR' EP. Inspired by the classic Brit bands of the 1960's American invasion (especially The BEATLES), CASE and Co specialised in rootsy power-pop that influenced a generation of Stateside bands. The quartet subsequently signed to Warner Brothers subsidiary, 'Planet', releasing an eponymous full-length album in 1981, a well-produced effort that won over many post-New Wave music lovers. After becoming part of David Geffen's recently established superlabel, the trademark PLIMSOULS sound was compromised on 1983's 'EVERYTHING AT ONCE', despite having already made their mark with the Hot 100 entry, 'A MILLION MILES AWAY'. Following the band's demise, CASE would concentrate on the rootsier side of his muse, recording sporadically throughout the latter half of the 80's with non-charting albums such as the eponymous 'PETER CASE' (1986) and 'THE MAN WITH THE BLUE POST MODERN FRAGMENTED NEO-TRADITIONALIST GUITAR' (1989).

Album rating: THE PLIMSOULS (*7) / EVERYWHERE AT ONCE (*7) / ONE NIGHT IN AMERICA compilation (*6) / Peter Case: PETER CASE (*6) / THE MAN WITH THE BLUE POST MODERN FRAGMENTED NEO-TRADITIONALIST GUITAR (*6) / SIX-PACK OF LOVE (*5) / SINGS LIKE HELL (*6) / TORN AGAIN (*7) / FULL SERVICE NO WAITING (*6) / FLYING SAUCER BLUES (*6) /

PETER CASE (b. 5 Apr'54, Buffalo, New York, USA) – vocals, guitar (ex-NERVES) / **EDDIE MUNOZ** – guitar, vocals / **DAVE PAHOA** – bass, vocals / **LOU RAMIREZ** – drums, percussion

not iss.   Beat

1980. (12"ep) <BE 1001> **ZERO HOUR EP**
– Great big world / Zero hour / Hypnotized / How long will it take? / I can't turn you loose.

Planet – Warners   Planet

Mar 81. (lp) (PL 52277) <P 13> **THE PLIMSOULS**
– Lost time / Now / In this town / Zero hour / Women / Hush, hush / I want what you got / Nickels and dimes / I want you back / Mini-skirt Minnie / Everyday things.
Apr 81. (7") (K 12519) **NOW. / WHEN YOU FIND IT**

Bomp   Shaky City

May 82. (7")<12"> (BOMP 2) <BMP12 134> **A MILLION MILES AWAY. / I'LL GET LUCKY**

Geffen   Geffen   Jan82

Jul 83. (7") <29600> **A MILLION MILES AWAY. / PLAY THE BREAKS**   –   82
Sep 83. (lp) (GEF 25509) <4002> **EVERYWHERE AT ONCE**
– Shaky city / Magic touch / Oldest story in the world / Lie, beg, borrow and steal / Play the breaks / How long will it take? / A million miles away / My life ain't easy / Inch by inch / I'll get lucky / Everywhere at once.

— disbanded the following year with CASE going solo (folk-rock)

P'O (see under ⇒ WIRE; 70's section)

POGUES

Formed: North London, England... late 1983 by Tipperary-raised SHANE MacGOWAN, SPIDER STACEY and JEM FINER. MacGOWAN had earlier been part of punk outfit, The NIPPLE ERECTORS through 1978-1981; this motley crew released a solitary single, 'KING OF THE BOP' before shortening their name to The NIPS. A further few singles appeared and even an album, 'ONLY AT THE END OF THE BEGINNING', recommended for diehard POGUES fiends only. POGUE MAHONE (Gaelic for "kiss my arse") was subsequently formed by MacGOWAN and JAMES FEARNLEY (also a NIP), adding drinking buddies, ANDREW RANKEN, plus female singer/bassist CAIT O'RIORDAN. By Spring '84, they'd formed their own self-titled label, issuing a classic debut single, 'DARK STREETS OF LONDON'. Boasting all the Celtic melancholy, romance and gritted-teeth attitude which marked the best of the band's work, the track rather unfairly but predictably received an official BBC radio ban (apparently after the beeb managed to translate their name). A month later they secured a deal with 'Stiff', opting instead for The POGUES. Their Stan Brennan-produced debut album, 'RED ROSES FOR ME', broke into the UK Top 100 as they acquired growing support from live audiences the length and breadth of the country. Whether interpreting trad Irish folk songs or reeling off brilliant originals, the POGUES were apt to turn from high-spirited revelry ('STREAMS OF WHISKEY') to menacing threat ('BOYS FROM THE COUNTY HELL') in the time it took to neck a pint of guinness (in MacGOWAN's case, not very long at all). April '85 saw the release of perhaps their finest single (and first Top 20 hit), the misty-eyed, ELVIS COSTELLO-produced 'A PAIR OF BROWN EYES'. COSTELLO also oversaw the accompanying album, 'RUM, SODOMY & THE LASH' (1985), a debauched, bruisingly beautiful classic which elevated The POGUES to the position of modern day folk heroes. MacGOWAN's gift for conjuring up a feeling of time and place was never more vivid than on the likes of the aforementioned 'A PAIR..', the rousing 'SALLY MacLENNANE' and the cursing malice of 'THE SICK BED OF CUCHULAINN', while O'RIORDAN put in a spine-tingling performance as a Scottish laird on the traditional 'I'M A MAN YOU DON'T MEET EVERY DAY'. On the 16th of May '86, the latter married COSTELLO and when she subsequently left that November (after writing the Top 50 hit 'HAUNTED' for the Alex Cox film, 'Sid & Nancy'), a vital component of POGUES chemistry went with her. Around the same time, the group played 'The McMahon Gang' in Cox's movie 'Straight To Hell', meeting ex-CLASH singer JOE STRUMMER on the set: the veteran punk would subsequently deputise for the absent MacGOWAN on an early 1988 US tour. This period also saw them peak at No.3 in the album charts with 'IF I SHOULD FALL FROM GRACE WITH GOD', an album which spawned an unlikely No.2 Christmas 1987 hit in 'FAIRY TALE OF NEW YORK'. A drunken duet with KIRSTY MacCOLL, the track was certainly more subversive than the usual Yuletide fodder and for a brief period, The POGUES were bonafide pop stars, their rampant collaboration with The DUBLINERS on 'IRISH ROVER' earlier that year having already breached the Top 10. Live, the band were untouchable, MacGOWAN's errant, tin-tray wielding genius the stuff of legend, particularly for many who witnessed their storming Glasgow Barrowlands performances (needless to say, Rangers fans were mercifully thin on the ground at these celebratory Celtic shindigs). Inevitably, MacGOWAN's hard-drinking ways were beginning to affect his writing and 'PEACE AND LOVE' (1989) signalled a slow slide into mediocrity. 1990's 'HELL'S DITCH' carried on in much the same vein, although this was to be MacGOWAN's final album under The POGUES banner, his failing health incompatible with the demands of a successful major label band. While the gap-toothed frontman eventually got a solo career together, The POGUES bravely soldiered on with a surprisingly impressive hit single, 'TUESDAY MORNING', lifted from their 1993 UK Top 20 "comeback" album, 'WAITING FOR HERB'. Two years on, a nostalgically titled follow-up set, 'POGUE MAHONE', failed to rekindle their former glory, while MacGOWAN continued to dominate the limelight. In 1999, some of the POGUES (SPIDER, HUNT + RANKIN) got together as The WISEMEN, while FINER has emerged with the band LONGPLAYER. • **Songwriters**: Group compositions, except; THE BAND PLAYED WALTZING MATILDA (Eric Bogle) / DIRTY OLD TOWN (Ewan MacColl) / WILD ROVER + MADRA RUM (trad.) / MAGGIE MAY (Rod Stewart) / HONKY TONK WOMAN (Rolling Stones) / WHISKEY IN THE JAR (Thin Lizzy) / MISS OTIS REGRETS (Cole Porter) / GOT A LOT O' LIVIN' TO DO (Elvis Presley) / HOW COME (Ronnie Lane) / WHEN THE SHIP COMES IN (Bob Dylan). FINER became main writer in the mid-90's with others contributed some material. • **Trivia**: In the early '90s, they supplied the soundtrack for TV play 'A Man You Don't Meet Every Day'. The song 'Fiesta' was subsequently used on Vauxhall-Tigra TV ad after the rights were sold from their 1988 album.

Album rating: RED ROSES FOR ME (*8) / RUM, SODOMY & THE LASH (*9) / IF I SHOULD FALL FROM GRACE WITH GOD (*8) / PEACE AND LOVE (*6) / HELL'S DITCH (*6) / THE BEST OF THE POGUES compilation (*9) / THE BEST OF THE REST OF THE POGUES compilation (*7) / WAITING FOR HERB (*6) / POGUE MAHONE (*5) / THE VERY BEST OF THE POGUES compilation (*8)

NIPS

SHANE MacGOWAN (b.25 Dec'57, Kent, England) – vocals, guitar / **ADRIAN THRILLS** – guitar (NME journalist) / **SHANE 'HASLER' BRADLEY** – bass / **ARCANE** – drums / + others

		Soho	not iss.
Jun 78.	(7"; as NIPPLE ERECTORS) (SH 1/2) **KING OF THE BOP. / NERVOUS WRECK**		-
—	**LARRY HINDRICKS** – guitar; repl. THRILLS		
—	**MARK HARRIS** – drums repl. ARCANE		
Aug 79.	(7") (SH 4) **ALL THE TIME IN THE WORLD. / PRIVATE EYES**		-
—	**GAVIN DOUGLAS** – drums repl. LARRY		
—	**JAMES FEARNLEY** (b.10 Oct'54, Manchester, England) – accordion (appeared on album)		
Feb 80.	(7") (SH 9) **GABRIELLE. / VENGEANCE** (re-iss. 1980 on 'Chiswick'; CHIS 119)		-
Oct 80.	(lp) (HOHO 1) **ONLY AT THE END OF THE BEGINNING**		-
	– Love to make you cry / Vengeance / Gabrielle / King of the bop / Ghost town / Fuss 'n' bother / Venus in bovver boots / Happy song / Stupid cow / I don't want nobody to love / Infatuation / Maida Ada / Hit parade / Can't say no.		

		Test Press	not iss.
Oct 81.	(7") (TP 5) **HAPPY SONG. / NOBODY TO LOVE**		-

— split in 1982. HASLER was soon to join MEN THEY COULDN'T HANG.

– compilation –

Nov 87.	(m-lp) Big Beat; (WIKM 66) **BOPS, BABES, BOOZE & BOVVER**		-
	– King of the bop / Nervous wreck / So pissed off / Stavordale Rd. N5 / All the time in the world / Private eye / Gabrielle / Vengeance.		

POGUES

MacGOWAN + FEARNLEY plus **SPIDER STACEY** (b.PETER, 14 Dec'58, Eastbourne, England) – tin whistle (ex-NIPS) / **JEM FINER** (b.JEREMY, 29 Jul'55, Stoke, England) – banjo, guitar / **CAIT O'RIORDAN** – bass, vocals / **ANDREW RANKEN** (b.13 Nov'53, London) – drums

		Pogue Mahone	not iss.
May 84.	(7"; as POGUE MAHONE) (PM 1) **DARK STREETS OF LONDON. / THE BAND PLAYED WALTZING MATHILDA** (re-iss. Jun84 as The POGUES on 'Stiff'; BUY 207)		-

		Stiff	not iss.
Sep 84.	(lp) (SEEZ 55) **RED ROSES FOR ME**	89	-
	– Transmetropolitan / The battle of Brisbane / The auld triangle / Waxie's dargle / Boys from the county hell / Sea shanty / Dark streets of London / Streams of whiskey / Poor daddy / Dingle regatta / Greenland whale fisheries / Down in the ground where the dead men go / Kitty. (cd-iss. May87; CDSEEZ 55) (re-iss. Jan89 on 'WEA' lp/c; WX 240/+C) (cd re-iss. Jan89; 244494-2)		
Oct 84.	(7") (BUY 212) **BOYS FROM THE COUNTY HELL. / REPEALING OF THE LICENSING LAWS** (d7"+=) (BUY 212 – 207) – (see debut 45).		-
Mar 85.	(7"/7"pic-d) (BUY/DBUY 220) **A PAIR OF BROWN EYES. / WHISKEY YOU'RE THE DEVIL** (12"+=) (BUYIT 22) – Muirshin Durkin.	72	-
—	added p/t **PHIL CHEVRON** (b. RYAN, 17 Jun'57, Dublin, Ireland) – guitar, producer (ex-RADIATORS FROM SPACE)		
Jun 85.	(7",7"green/7"sha-pic-d) (BUY/PBUY 224) **SALLY MacLENNANE. / WILD ROVER** (12"+=) (BUYIT 224) – The leaving of Liverpool. (c-s++=) (BUYC 224) – Wild cats of Kilkenny.	51	-
Aug 85.	(lp/c/cd) (SEEZ/CSEEZ/CDSEEZ 58) **RUM, SODOMY & THE LASH**	13	-
	– The sick bed of Cuchulainn / The old main drag / Wild cats of Kilkenny / I'm a man you don't meet every day / A pair of brown eyes / Sally MacLennane / Dirty old town / Jesse James / Navigator / Billy's bones / The gentleman soldier / And the band played waltzing Matilda. (cd+=) – A pistol for Paddy Garcia. (re-iss. Jan89 on 'WEA' lp/c; WX 241/+C) (cd-iss. Jan89; 244495-2)		
Aug 85.	(7"/7"pic-d) (BUY/PBUY 229) **DIRTY OLD TOWN. / A PISTOL FOR PADDY GARCIA** (12"+=) (BUYIT 229) – The parting glass.	62	-
Feb 86.	(7"ep/12"ep/c-ep/7"pic-ep) (BUY/BUYIT/BUYC/PBUY 243) **POGUETRY IN MOTION** – A rainy night in Soho / The body of an American / London girl / Planxty Noel Hill.	29	-
Aug 86.	(7") (MCA 1084) **HAUNTED. / JUNK THEME** (12"+=) (MCAT 1084) – Hot dogs with everything. (above single from the motion picture, 'Sid & Nancy' on 'MCA')	42	-
—	**DARRYL HUNT** (b. 4 May'50, Bournemouth, England) – bass (ex-PRIDE O' THE CROSS) repl. CAIT		
Mar 87.	(7"; by The POGUES & THe DUBLINERS) (BUY 258) **THE IRISH ROVER. / THE RARE OLD MOUNTAIN DEW** (12"+=) (BUYIT 258) – The Dubliners fancy.	8	-
—	added **TERRY WOODS** (b. 4 Dec'47, Dublin) – banjo (now 8-piece)		

		Pogue Mahone-EMI	Island
Nov 87.	(7"; The POGUES featuring KIRSTY MacCOLL) (NY 7) **FAIRYTALE OF NEW YORK. / BATTLE MARCH MEDLEY** (12"+=)(cd-s+=) (NY 12)(CDNY 1) – Shanne Bradley.	2	
Jan 88.	(cd/c/lp) (CD/TC+/NYR 1) <90872> **IF I SHOULD FALL FROM GRACE WITH GOD**	3	88
	– If I should fall from grace with God / Turkish song of the damned / Bottle of smoke / Fairytale of New York (featuring KIRSTY MacCOLL) / Metropolis / Thousands are sailing / Fiesta / Medley:- The recruiting sergeant – The rocky road to Dublin – Galway races / Streets of Sorrow – Birmingham Six / Lullaby of London / Sit down by the fire / The broad majestic Shannon / Worms. (cd+=) – South Australia / The battle march medley. (re-iss. Jan89 on 'WEA' lp/c; WX 243/+C) (cd-iss. Jan89; 244494-2)		
Feb 88.	(7") (FG 1) **IF I SHOULD FALL FROM GRACE WITH GOD. / SALLY MacLENNANE (live)** (12"red-ep)(cd-ep+=) **ST. PATRICK'S NIGHT** (SGG 1-12)(CDFG 1) – A pair of brown eyes (live) / Dirty old town (live).	58	
Jul 88.	(7") (FG 2) **FIESTA. / SKETCHES OF SPAIN** (12"+=)(cd-s+=) (FG 2-12)(CDFG 2) – South Australia.	24	-

		WEA	Island
Dec 88.	(7") (YZ 355) **YEAH, YEAH, YEAH, YEAH, YEAH. / THE LIMERICK RAKE** (12"+=/cd-s+=) (YZ 355 T/CD) – ('A'extended) / Honky tonk woman.	43	
Jun 89.	(7"/c-s) (YZ 407/+C) **MISTY MORNING, ALBERT BRIDGE. / COTTON FIELDS** (12"+=) (YZ 407T) – Young ned of the hill. (3"cd-s++=) (YZ 407CD) – Train of love.	41	-
Jul 89.	(lp/c)(cd) (WX 247/+C)(246086-2) <91225> **PEACE AND LOVE**	5	
	– White City / Young ned of the hill / Misty morning, Albert Bridge / Cotton fields / Blue heaven / Down all the days / U.S.A. / Lorelei / Gartloney rats / Boat train / Tombstone / Night train to Lorca / London you're a lady / Gridlock.		
Aug 89.	(7"/c-s) (YZ 409/+C) **WHITE CITY. / EVERY MAN IS A KING** (12"+=) (YZ 409TX) – Maggie May (live). (cd-s+=) (YZ 409CD) – The star of the County Down.		-
May 90.	(7"/c-s; The POGUES & The DUBLINERS) (YZ 500/+C) **JACK'S HEROES. / WHISKEY IN THE JAR** (12"+=/cd-s+=) (YZ 500 T/CD) – ('B'extended).	63	-
	(theme song used by Eire in World Cup; manager Jack Charlton)		
Aug 90.	(7") (YZ 519) **SUMMER IN SIAM. / BASTARD LANDLORD** (12"+=/cd-s+=) (YZ 519 T/CD) – Hell's ditch (instrumental) / The Irish rover.	64	-
Sep 90.	(cd)(lp/c) (9031 72554-2)(WX 366/+C) <422846> **HELL'S DITCH** – The sunnyside of the street / Sayonara / The ghost of a smile / Hell's ditch / Lorca's	12	

POGUES (cont)

novena / Summer in Siam / Rain street / Rainbow man / The wake of the Medusa / House of the gods / Five green onions and Jean / Maidria Rua / Six to go.

Apr 91. (cd-s) **SAYONARA / CURSE OF LOVE / INFINITY**

Sep 91. (7") (YZ 603) **A RAINY NIGHT IN SOHO (remix). / SQUID OUT OF WATER** — 67
(12"+=) (YZ 603) – Infinity.
(cd-s+=) (YZ 603CD) – POGUETRY IN MOTION (ep).

Sep 91. (cd)(lp/c) (9031 75405-2)(WX 430/+C) **THE BEST OF THE POGUES** (compilation) <US-title 'ESSENTIAL POGUES'> — 11
– Fairytale of New York / Sally MacLennane / Dirty old town / The Irish rover / A pair of brown eyes / Streams of whiskey / A rainy night in Soho / Fiesta / Rain street / Misty morning, Albert Bridge / White City / Thousand are sailing / The broad majestic Shannon / The body of an American.

Dec 91. (7") (YZ 628) **FAIRYTALE OF NEW YORK. / FIESTA** — 36
(12"+=/cd-s+=) (YZ 628 T/CD) – A pair of brown eyes / Sick bed of Cuchulainn / Maggie May.

—— p/t JOE STRUMMER is deposed by member SPIDER who takes over vox.

May 92. (7"/c-s) (YZ 673/+C) **HONKY TONK WOMAN. / CURSE OF LOVE** — 56
(12"+=) (YZ 673T) – Infinity.
(cd-s+=) (YZ 673CD) – The parting glass.

Jun 92. (cd)(lp/c) (9031 77341-2)(WX 471/+C) **THE BEST OF THE REST OF THE POGUES** (compilation out-takes)
– If I should fall from grace with God / The sick bed of Cuchulainn / The old main drag / Boys from the County Hell / Young Ned of the hill / Dark streets of London / The auld triangle / Repeal of the licensing laws / Yeah yeah yeah yeah yeah / London girl / Honky tonk women / Summer in Siam / Turkish song of the damned / Lullaby of London / The sunnyside of the street / Hell's ditch.

—— (Sep'91) MacGOWAN left when his health deteriorated (JOE STRUMMER deputised for him on tour)

—— added 8th member & producer **MICHAEL BROOK** – infinite guitar

WEA   Chameleon

Aug 93. (7"/c-s) (YZ 758/+C) **TUESDAY MORNING. / FIRST DAY OF FOREVER** — 18
(cd-s) (YZ 758CD) – Turkish song of the damned (live).
(cd-s) (YZ 758CDX) – ('A'side) / London calling / I fought the law (both live with JOE STRUMMER).

Sep 93. (cd/c/lp) (4509 93463-2/-4/-1) <61598> **WAITING FOR HERB** — 20   Oct98
– Tuesday morning / Smell of petroleum / Haunting / Once upon a time / Sitting on top of the world / Drunken boat / Big city / Girl from the Wadi Hammamat / Modern world / Pachinko / My baby's gone / Small hours.

Jan 94. (7") (YZ 771/+C) **ONCE UPON A TIME. / TRAIN KEPT ROLLING ON** — 66
(12"+=/cd-s+=) (YZ 771 T/CD) – Tuesday morning / Paris St. Germain.

—— FEARNEY and WOODS departed, apparently due to the brief Christmas comeback of SHANE MacGOWAN

—— **SPIDER / JEM / DARRYL + RANKEN** added **JAMIE CLARKE** – banjo / **JAMES McNALLY** – accordion, uilleann pipes / **DAVID COULTER** – mandolin, tambourine

Sep 95. (7"colrd/c-s) (WEA 011 X/C) **HOW COME. / EYES OF AN ANGEL**
(cd-s+=) (WX 011CD) – Tuesday morning (live) / Big city (live).

Oct 95. (cd/c/lp) (0630 11210-2/-4/-1) **POGUE MAHONE**
– How come / Living in a world without her / When the ship comes in / Anniversary / Amadie / Love you 'till the end / Bright lights / Oretown / Pont Mirabeau / Tosspint / Four o'clock in the morning / Where that love's been gone / The sun and the moon.

—— note:- The POGUES also appeared on the flip side to KIRSTY MacCOLL's Cole Porter tribute single, 'Miss Otis Regrets' on the track 'JUST ONE OF THOSE THINGS'.

– compilations, etc. –

Mar 01. (cd/c) *Warners ESP;* (8573 87459-2/-4) **THE VERY BEST OF THE POGUES** — 18
Jan 02. (cd) *Castle;* (CMRCD 388) **STREAMS OF WHISKEY**

Robert POLLARD (see under ⇒ GUIDED BY VOICES)

POOH STICKS

Formed: Swansea, Wales ... October 1987 by HUE WILLIAMS (the son of ex-MAN and DIRE STRAITS drummer, TERRY WILLIAMS) who recruited a largely (youthful) female line-up of TRUDI, ALISON, STEPHANIE and PAUL. Setting out to satirise the po-faced boys club that represented the indie scene of the time, The POOH STICKS cut 'ON TAPE' for tiny local label, 'Fierce'. A completely inappropriate boxed set of singles followed, the humour in the semi-legendary 'I KNOW SOMEONE WHO KNOWS SOMEONE WHO KNOWS ALAN McGEE QUITE WELL' as relevant today as it was then. Music wise, the general formula was a kitsch grab-bag of classic American pop/rock, from The RASPBERRIES to CHEAP TRICK; all fine and dandy but in reality, WILLIAMS' Anglophile indie-boy vocals – and often pretty flat vocals at that – weren't exactly complementary. Nevertheless, critics were generally enamoured with their bright-eyed charm, the band collecting their early material together for 1988's eponymous mini-set. This was followed by a couple of live albums, one for Scottish label, '53rd & 3rd' and one for US alternative bastion, 'Sympathy For The Record Industry'. A debut album proper, 'THE GREAT WHITE WONDER' was released on the latter label in 1991, The POOH STICKS Stateside potential finally realised when they were signed to US-based 'BMG'-offshoot, 'Zoo'. Their major label debut, the hopefully (and no doubt ironically) titled 'MILLION SELLER' hit the shelves in 1993, the band's love of American teen-dream fantasy undimmed as they churned out another helping of three-chord guitar, cutesy harmonies and twee, occasionally humourous lyrics. That 'SUGAR BABY' was apparently inspired by a chance meeting with RANDY BACHMAN says it all really. Yet the record failed to really capture the record buying imagination – as did 1995's 'OPTIMISTIC FOOL' – The POOH STICKS remaining as curious a cult item as ever. • **Songwriters:** HUE penned except; DYING FOR IT (Vaselines).

Album rating: ALAN McGEE mini (*6) / THE POOH STICKS mini (*6) / ORGASM mini (*6) / TRADE MARK OF QUALITY mini (*4) / FORMULA ONE GENERATION (*6) / THE GREAT WHITE WONDER (*7) / MILLION SELLER (*6) / OPTIMISTIC FOOL (*6)

HUE WILLIAMS (b. 4 Mar'68) – vocals / **PAUL** – guitar / **TRUDI** – tambourine, piano / **ALISON** – bass / **STEPHANIE** – drums

Fierce   Sympathy F

Feb 88. (7"etched) (FRIGHT 011) **ON TAPE**
Aug 88. (7"etched) (FRIGHT 021) **1-2-3 RED LIGHT**
Sep 88. (5x7"etched;box) (FRIGHT 021) **1-2-3 RED LIGHT /** (FRIGHT 022) **HEROES AND VILLAINS /** (FRIGHT 023) **HEARTBREAK /** (FRIGHT 024) **I KNOW SOMEONE WHO KNOWS SOMEONE WHO KNOWS ALAN McGEE QUITE WELL /** (FRIGHT 025) **INDIE POP AIN'T NOISE POLLUTION**
Oct 88. (cd) (FRIGHT 026) **ALAN McGEE**
– How to get to Hue Pooh-Stick / Heroes and villains / Indiepop ain't noise pollution / 1-2-3 red light / Heart break / I know someone who knows someone who knows Alan McGee quite well / On tape / Please Hue, please.
Nov 88. (m-lp;etched) (FRIGHT 028) **THE POOH STICKS**
– Heroes and villains / Indiepop ain't noise pollution / 1-2-3 red light / Heartbreak / On tape.
Jan 89. (pink; m-lp) (AGAMC 005) **ORGASM (live)**
– I know someone who knows someone who knows Alan McGee quite well / Heroes and villains / Foxy boy / Force fed by love / Sex head / On tape / Indiepop ain't noise pollution / 1-2-3 red light / Heartbreak.
(above issued on '53rd & 3rd')
Jan 89. (7"; as DUMB ANGELS) (FRIGHT 033) **LOVE & MERCY. /**
(above DUMB ANGELS = HUE + TRUDI)
Mar 89. (7"one-sided) (FRIGHT 034) **DYING FOR IT**
Apr 89. (7"flexi) (F 3) **GO GO GIRL. / SIMON E**
(above issued on 'Cheree' fanzine) (below on 'Whoosh' fanzine)
Apr 89. (7"yellow-flexi) (WOOSH 007) **HARD ON LOVE**
Sep 89. (one-sided-7"ep) (ANON 2) **ENCORE EP box set**
(above was issued on 'Anonymous')
Oct 89. (7"blue-ep) <SFTRI 33> **TEENAGE HIGH**
Nov 89. (m-lp; mail-order) (FRIGHT 035) **TRADE MARK OF QUALITY**
– Young people / Foxy boy / Heroes and villains / Dare true kiss promise / Dying for it / Sex head / Heartbreak. (re-iss. Mar92 lp/cd+=; FRIGHT 048/+CD) – Heartbreak / Go go girl / Dying for it (alt. take).
Apr 90. (lp) (FRIGHT 037) <SFTRI 58> **FORMULA ONE GENERATION**
– Radio ready / Teenage high / Time to time / Susan sleepwalking / All the good that's happening / Dare true kiss promise / Teenage high 2 / Tonight / Soft beds, hard battles.
Nov 90. (7"pic-d) <SFTRI 76> **TIME TO TIME. / EMERGENCY**

Cheree   Zoo

May 91. (7") (CHEREE 17) **WHO LOVES YOU? / GOOD TIMES**
above + below featured vocals by AMELIA FLETCHER (of HEAVENLY)
Jun 91. (cd/c/lp) (CHEREE 18 CD/MC/LP) <72445-11029-2/-4> **THE GREAT WHITE WONDER**
– Young people / The rhythm of love / Who loves you / Pandora's box / Desperado / Good times / The wild one, forever / I'm in you / When sunny gets blue.
Sep 91. (one-sided-7") (CHEREE 25) **YOUNG PEOPLE**

Fierce   not iss.

Oct 92. (one-sided-7") (FRIGHT 042) **MILLION SELLER**

Zoo-RCA   not iss.

Oct 92. (7") (WALES 1) **THE WORLD IS TURNING ON. / GOODBYE DON'T MEAN I'M GONE**
(12"/cd-s) (WALES 1 T/CD) – ('A'side) / Force fed by love / True love ('A'mix).
Feb 93. (cd/c/lp) (7244 511043-2/-4/-1) **MILLION SELLER**
– Million seller / Let the good times roll / The world is turning on / Sugar baby / I saw the light / Susan sleepwalking / When the girl wants to be free / Baby wanna go round with me / Sugar mello / Rainbow rider / Goodbye don't mean I'm gone / Jelly on a plate / That was the greatest song.
Mar 93. (7") (WALES 1) **THE WORLD IS TURNING ON. / ROLL OVER EASY / WHEN THE GIRLS WANT TO BE FREE**
(12"+=/cd-s+=) (WALES 1 T/CD) – Sugar baby (acoustic) / Let the good times roll (acoustic).

Damaged Goods   not iss.

Apr 94. (7"; as HUEGENIUS) (DAMGOOD 35) **DRINK FIGHT + FUN. /**
(above was actually HUE solo)

Seed   Seed

Apr 95. (7") (<SEED 013>) **COOL IN A CRISIS. / WHEN THE NIGHT FALLS**
(cd-s+=) (<SEEDCD 013>) – Dizgo girl / She's the one.
May 95. (cd/lp) (<92513-2/-1>) **OPTIMISTIC FOOL**
– Opening night / Cool in a crisis / Starfishing / Optimistic fool / Who was it? / Bad morning girl / Miss me / Working on a beautiful thing / Up on the roof / Prayer for my demo / All things must pass / Song cycle / First of a million songs.

– compilations, etc. –

Apr 91. (m-lp) *Overground;* (OVER 018) **THE PEEL SESSIONS 88/89**
– On tape / I know someone who knows someone who knows Alan McGee quite well / Heartbreak / Indiepop ain't noise pollution / Desperado / Young people / Hard on love / Dare, truth, kiss, promise.
Mar 92. (lp/cd) *Fierce;* (FRIGHT 047/+CD) **MULTIPLE ORGASM**
– I know someone who knows someone who knows Alan McGee quite well / Heroes and villains / Foxy boy / Force fed by love / Sex head / On tape / Indiepop ain't noise pollution / 1-2-3 red light / Heartbreak / Cinnamon / When the night falls / Do something to me / Force fed by love / Tear the roof right off my head / Goody goody gumdrops / Saturday night's the big night / It's a good day for a parade / Just another minute / Do it again (a little bit slower).

POP WILL EAT ITSELF

Formed: Stourbridge, Midlands, England ... early 1985 initially as WILD AND WANDERING by vocalist/guitarist CLINT MANSELL, guitarist/keyboardist ADAM MOLE, bassist RICHARD MARCH and drummer GRAHAM CRABB. After the wittily titled '2000 LIGHT ALES FROM HOME' EP, the band adopted the POP WILL EAT ITSELF moniker in early '86. Their debut release, 'POPPIES SAY GRRR ... EP' was originally sold at a Dudley gig, although after this DIY effort was made more widely available, it subsequently became an NME single of the week and was playlisted on night time Radio One. Later that summer, the band signed to Craig Jennings' indie label, 'Chapter 22', Jennings becoming their manager after a few more singles (including a cover of SIGUE SIGUE SPUTNIK's brilliantly vacant 'LOVE MISSILE F1-11'). By the release of the impressive debut album, 'BOX FRENZY' (1987) these self-styled 'GREBO GURU's were in the process of progressing from their early guitar pop to a sample-driven hybrid of heavy punk (a la KILLING JOKE) and psyche-pop. While songs like 'BEAVER PATROL' were criticised for their schoolboy sexism, indie chart hits like the driven genius of 'THERE IS NO LOVE BETWEEN US ANYMORE' and the anthemic 'DEF CON ONE' proved they were major contenders. Fittingly then, they were duly signed up by 'R.C.A.' and scored further minor chart successes with 'CAN U DIG IT' and 'WISE UP! SUCKER', while a follow-up album, 'THIS IS THE DAY, THIS IS THE HOUR, THIS IS THIS' (1989) made the Top 30. By this point the band had long since abandoned a conventional drum kit for an electronic model and in the Spring of 1990, PWEI turned out their most dance-friendly track to date in 'TOUCHED BY THE HAND OF CICCIOLINA'. A collaboration with the infamous Italian porn star-turned MP (only in Italy!) of the same name, the record was released just in time for the World Cup, complete with crowd noises and chanting. That year's album, 'THE POP WILL EAT ITSELF CURE FOR SANITY', confirmed the trend with 'DANCE OF THE MAD BASTARDS' and 'X, Y AND ZEE'. Nevertheless, by the release of 'THE LOOKS OR THE LIFESTYLE' (1992), the band had reverted back to a living, breathing human drummer in the form of FUZZ. Although the record spawned their biggest hit to date, the Top 10 'GET THE GIRL! KILL THE BADDIES', PWEI were subsequently dropped by RCA after the live 'WEIRD'S BAR & GRILL' (1993), the band also largely dismissed by a music press that had new fish to fry. Down but not out, the grebo troopers signed a new deal with the indie label, 'Infectious', hooking up with 'FUN-DA-MENTAL' in 1994 for the anti-nazi effort, 'ICH BIN EIN AUSLANDER'. The record was a minor hit, although their fifth studio effort, the harder-edged 'DOS DEDOS MIS AMIGOS' became their highest charting album to date, almost reaching the Top 10 and proving that they could get along just fine without a major label. If any more proof was needed, the defiantly titled remix album, 'TWO FINGERS MY FRIENDS', showed that PWEI were nothing if not resilient. • **Songwriters:** Group compositions except; LIKE AN ANGEL (Mighty Lemon Drops) / ORGONE ACCUMULATOR (Hawkwind) / EVERYTHING THAT RISES (Eno) / ROCK-A-HULA BABY (Elvis Presley).

Album rating: BOX FRENZY (*8) / NOW FOR A FEAST compilation (*7) / THIS IS THE DAY, THIS IS THE HOUR, THIS IS THIS (*7) / ... CURE FOR SANITY (*5) / THE LOOKS OF THE LIFESTYLE (*6) / WEIRD'S BAR & GRILL (*4) / 16 DIFFERENT FLAVOURS OF HELL compilation (*7) / DOS DEDOS MIS AMIGOS (*5) / TWO FINGERS MY FRIENDS remixes (*5)

CLINT MANSELL (b. 7 Jan'63, Coventry, England) – vocals, guitar / **ADAM MOLE** (b. 8 Apr'62) – guitar, keyboards / **GRAHAM CRABB** (b.10 Oct'64, Sutton Coldfield, England) – drums / **RICHARD MARCH** (b. 4 Mar'65, York, England) – bass

Iguana not iss.

Feb 86. (12"ep; as WILD & WANDERING) (VYK 14) **2000 LIGHT ALES FROM HOME**
– Dust me down / Stand by me / Real cool time / Interlong / Apple tree (pt.1 & 2).

Desperate not iss.

May 86. (7"ep) (SRT 1) **THE POPPIES SAY GRRRR ... EP**
– I'm sticking with you hoo / Sick little girl / Mesmerized / There's a psychopath in my soup / Candydiosis. *(re-iss. Jun86; DAN 1)*

Chapter 22 Rough Trade

Oct 86. (7"ep) (CHAP 9) **POPPIECOCK**
– The Black country chainsaw massacreee / Monogamy / Oh Grebo I think I love you / Titanic clown / B-B-B-Breakdown.
(12"ep+=) (12CHAP 9) – THE POPPIES SAY GRRRR ... EP.

Jan 87. (12"/7") (12+/CHAP 11) **SWEET SWEET PIE. / DEVIL INSIDE / RUNAROUND**

May 87. (7") (CHAP 13) **LOVE MISSILE F1-11. / ORGONE ACCUMULATOR**
(12"ep+=) THE COVERS EP (12CHAP 13) – Everything that rises / Like an angel.
(12"ep+=) (L12CHAP 13) – ('A'-Designer Grebo mix) / Everything that rises (new version).

Sep 87. (7"pink,7"clear/7") (L+/CHAP 16) **BEAVER PATROL. / BUBBLES**
(12"ep+=) (12CHAP 16) – Oh Grebo I think I love you (new version).

Oct 87. (lp/c/cd) (CHAP LP/MC/CD 18) <ROUGHUS 33/+C/CD> **BOX FRENZY**
– Grebo guru / Beaver patrol / Let's get ugly / U.B.L.U.D. / Inside you / Evelyn / There is no love between us anymore / She's surreal / Intergalactic love mission / Love missile F1-11 / Hit the hi-tech groove / Razorblade kisses.

Jan 88. (7"pic-d/7") (L+/CHAP 20) **THERE IS NO LOVE BETWEEN US ANYMORE. / PICNIC IN THE SKY** 66 -
(12"+=) (12CHAP 20) – On the razor's edge / Kiss that girl.
(ext.12"+=) (L12CHAP 20) – ('A'extended high mix) / Hit the hi-tech groove (the M&K mix).
(12") (CLUBCHAP 20) – (above 2 tracks).

Jul 88. (7") (PWEI 001) **DEF CON ONE. / INSIDE YOU (live)** 63 -
(12"+=) (PWEI 12-001) – She's surreal (live) / Hit the hi-tech groove (live).
(12"+=) (PWEIL 12-001) – ('A'-Doomsday power mix) / She's surreal (live).

Dec 88. (lp/c/cd) (CHAP LP/MC/CD 33) **NOW FOR A FEAST** (compilation)
– The Black country chainstore massacreee / Monogamy / Oh Grebo I think I love you / Titanic clown / B-B-B-Breakdown / Sweet sweet pie / Like an angel / I'm sniffin' with you hoo / Sick little girl / Mesmerized / There's a psychopath in my soup / Candydiosis / The devil inside / Orgone accumulator.

R.C.A. R.C.A.

Feb 89. (7"/7"orange,7"green/7"s) (PB 42621/42619/42729) **CAN U DIG IT. / POISON TO THE MIND** 38 -
(cd-s+=) (PD 42620) – Radio PWEI (acapella) / ('A'-12"version).
(12"++=) (PT 42620) – The fuses have been lit.

Apr 89. (7"/7"pic-d) (PB PB 42761/42793) **WISE UP! SUCKER. / ORGYONE STIMULATOR** 41 -
(c-s+=)(12"+=/cd-s+=) (PK 42761)(PT/PD 42762) – ('A'extended) / Can u dig it (riffs mix).
(10") (PJ 42762) – ('A'side) / ('A'extended) / ('A'version).

May 89. (lp/c/cd) (PL/PK/PD 74106) <9742> **THIS IS THE DAY, THIS IS THE HOUR, THIS IS THIS** 24 -
– PWEI is a four letter word / Preaching to the perverted / Wise up! sucker / Sixteen different flavours of Hell / Inject me / Can u dig it? / The fuses have been lit / Poison to the mind / Def con one / Radio PWEI / Shortwave transmission on up to the minuteman / Satellite ecstatica / Now now James, we're busy / Wake up! time to die ... *(cd+=)* – Wise up sucker (mix). *(re-iss. cd Nov93; 74321 15792-2)*

Aug 89. (7"ep)(7"g-f-ep)(7"sha-pic-ep)(c-ep)(12"ep)(cd-ep) (PB 42883)(PB 43021)(PA 43022)(PK 43023)(PT 42884)(PD 42894) **VERY METAL NOISE POLLUTION EP** 45 -
– Very metal noise pollution / P.W.E.I.-zation / 92° F / Def con one 1989 A.D.
(12") (PT 43068) – Def con 1989 AD including:- Twilight zone / Preaching to the perverted / P.W.E.I.-zation / 92° F.

May 90. (7"/c-s) (PB/PK 44735) **TOUCHED BY THE HAND OF CICCIOLINA. / THE INCREDI-BULL MIX** 28 -
(12"+=) (PT 43736) – ('A'-Extra time mix).
(cd-s) (PD 43736) – ('A'-Extra time mix) / ('A'-Diva Futura mix) / ('A'-Renegade Soundwave mix – Smoothneck).
(12") (PT 43738) – ('A'-Diva Futura mix) / ('A'-Renegade Soundwave mix – Smoothneck).

Oct 90. (7"/c-s) (PB/PK 44023) **DANCE OF THE MAD. / PREACHING TO THE PERVERTED** 32 -
(12"ep+=/cd-ep+=) **PWEI VS. THE MORAL MAJORITY EP** (PT/PD 44023) – ('A'other mix).

Oct 90. (cd/c/lp) (PD/PK/PL 74828) **CURE FOR SANITY** 33 -
– Incredible PWEI / Dance of the Mad. The Moral Majority / Dance of the mad bastards / 88 seconds ... and still counting / X Y & Zee / City Zen radio 1990-2000 FM / Dr. Nightmares medication time / Touched by the hand of Cicciolina / 1000 x no! / Psycho sexual / Axe of man / Another man's rhubarb / Medicine man speaks with forked tongue / Nightmare at 20,000 feet / Very metal noise pollution / 92 degrees (the 3rd degree) / Lived in splendour, died in chaos / The beat that refused to die. *(re-iss. May91 pic-lp; PL 75041) (re-iss. cd Nov93; 74321 15791-2)*

Jan 91. (7"/c-s) (PB/PK 44243) **X Y & ZEE. / AXE OF MEN** 15 -
(12"box+=) (PT 44243) – Psychosexual.
(12"+=/cd-s+=) (PT/PD 44243) – ('A'-Intergalactic mix) / ('A'-Sensory amp mix).

May 91. (7"/c-s) (PB/PK 44555) **92 DEGREES. / INCREDIBLE PWEI VS. DIRTY HARRY** 23 -
(10"+=/12"+=/cd-s+=) (PX/PT/PD 44555) – Another man's rhubarb.

May 92. (7"/c-s) (PB/PK 45467) **KARMADROME. / EAT ME DRINK ME LOVE ME** 17 -
(12"+=) (PT 45467) – Dread alert in the karmadrome / ('A'version).
(cd-s) (PD 45467) – ('A'side) / PWEI-zation (original metal noise pollution).
(12"pic-d+=) (PTP 45467) – PWEI-zation (original ...) / Eat me drink me dub ...

Aug 92. (7"/c-s) (74321 11013-7/4) **BULLETPROOF! / ('A'-On-U-Sound mix)** 24 -
(12"pic-d+=) (74321 11013-6/2) – Good from far, far from good.
(12") (74321 11013-8) – ('A'-Mile high mix) / ('A'-No half measures mix).

Sep 92. (cd/c/lp) (74321 10265-2/-4/-1) **THE LOOKS OR THE LIFESTYLE** 15 -
– England's finest / Eat me drink me, love me, kill me / Get the girl, kill the baddies! / I've always been a coward baby / Spoken drug song / Karmadrome / Urban futuristic (son of South Central) / Pretty pretty / I was a teenage grandad / Harry Dean Stanton / Bulletproof!. *(re-iss. cd Nov93; 74321 15790-2)*

— added 5th member **FUZZ TOWNSHEND** (b. JOHN TOWNSHEND, 31 Jul'64, Birmingham, England) – drums

Jan 93. (7"/c-s) (74321 12880-7/-4) **GET THE GIRL! KILL THE BADDIES!. / ('A'-Adrian Sherwood mix)** 9 -
(12"+=/cd-s+=) (74321 12880-6/-2) – ('A'-Black country & western mix) or ('A'boilerhouse mix).
(cd-s) (74321 12880-5) – ('A'side) / Urban futuristic (live) / Can u dig it? (live) / Wise up! sucker! (live).

Feb 93. (cd/c/lp) (74321 13343-2/-4/-1) **WEIRD'S BAR AND GRILL** (live) 44 -
– England's finest / Eat me drink me love me kill me / Get the girl, kill the baddies!! / Wise up! sucker / 88 seconds and counting / Karmadrome / Token drug song mother / Preaching to the perverted / Axe of men / Nightmare at 20,000 feet / Always been a coward / Can U dig it / Bullet proof / Urban futuristic / There is no love between us anymore / Def con one. *(cd+=/c+=)* – Harry Dean Stanton teenage grandad.

Oct 93. (cd/c/lp) (74321 15317-2/-4/-1) **16 DIFFERENT FLAVOURS OF HELL** (compilation) 73 -
– Def con one / Wise up! sucker / Can u dig it / Touched by the hand of Cicciolina (extra time mix) / Dance of the mad / X Y & Zee (sunshine mix) / 92 degrees (Boilerhouse The Birth mix) / Karmadrome / Bullet proof / Get the girl! kill the baddies! / Another man's rhubarb / Rockahula baby / Wise up! sucker / Cicciolina (Renegade Soundwave mix). *(cd+=)* – Preaching to the perverted (remix) / Eat me drink me love me kill me / PWEi-zatin.

Infectious Nothing-Interscope

Oct 93. (c-s) (INFECT 1MC) <95887> **R.S.V.P. / FAMILUS HORRIBILUS** 27 Feb94
(cd-ep+=) (INFECT 1CD) – ('B'remixes) / ('B'live).
(12"ep+=/cd-ep+=) (INFECT 1/+CDX) – ('A'side) / ('B'-Higher later space mix agency vocal).

POP WILL EAT ITSELF (cont)

Feb 94.	(7"/7"pic-d) *(INFECT 4 G/P)* **ICH BIN EIN AUSLANDER. / CP1 #2**		28	-

(12"+=/cd-s+=) *(INFECT 4/+CD)* – ('A'-Fun-Da-Mental instrumental) / ('A'-Fun-Da-Mental extra).
(12"+=) *(INFECT 4TX)* – ('A'-Drone ranger mix) / Intense.

Sep 94.	(7"colrd) *(INFECT 9GG)* **EVERYTHING'S COOL. / LET IT FLOW**		23	-

(7"colrd) *(INFECT 9SO)* – ('A'side) / Wild west.
(cd-s) *(INFECT 9CD)* – ('A'side) / ('A'-Youth remix) / R.S.V.P. (Fluke mix).
(cd-s) *(INFECT 9CDX)* – ('A'side) / Ich bin ein Auslander (live) / Familus horribilus (live) / R.S.V.P. (live).

Sep 94.	(cd/c) *(INFECT 10 CD/MC)* <92393> **DOS DEDOS MIS AMIGOS**		11	

– Ich bin ein Auslander / Kick to kill / Familus horribilus / Underbelly / Fatman / Home / Cape connection / Menofearthereaper / Everything's cool / R.S.V.P. / Babylon. *(also d-lp/d-c/d-cd; INFECT 10 LPX/MCX/CDX)*

Mar 95.	(d-cd/d-c) *(INFECT 10 CDR/MCR)* <22> **TWO FINGERS MY FRIENDS!** (remixes)		25	

– Ich bin ein Auslander (Fun-Da-Mental) / Kick to kill (Jim Foetus seersucker mix) / Familus horribilus (mega web 2) / Underbelly (Renegade Soundwave blackout mix) / Fatman (Hoodlum Priest Fatboy mix) / Home (Orb sweet sin and salvation mix) / Cape Connection (Transglobal Underground Cossack in UFO encounter mix) / Menofearthereaper (concrete no fee, no fear mix) / Everything's cool (safe as milk mix) / R.S.V.P. (made in Japan, live at the Budokan double live Gonzo F mix) / Babylon (Loop Guru Babylon a dub fire mix) // Ich bin ein Auslander (Die Krupps mix) / Familus horribilus (Hia Nyg vocal mix) / Cape Connection (golden claw versus clock and dagger mix) / Intense / C.P.I. #2 / Cape Connection (TGV aliens, bodacious aliens mix) / Everything's cool (Dragonfly mix) / RSVP (Fluke lunch mix) / Cape Connection (Secret Knowledge transfered up mix) / Underbelly (The Drum Club bugsong mix). *(cd re-iss. Jan01; INFECT 10CDRX)*

— CRABB left to pursue own career; he formed The BUZZARD and other project The Golden Claw Music, while MARCH formed BENTLEY RHYTHM ACE

– compilations, etc. –

Jun 96.	(cd) *Camden; (74321 39339-2)* **WISE UP SUCKERS**			-
Apr 97.	(cd) *Strange Fruit; (<SFRSCD 005>)* **THE BBC RADIO 1 SESSIONS 1986-1987**			-
Oct 02.	(cd) *Castle; (CMEDD 589)* **POP WILL EAT ITSELF 1986-1994**			-

POSITIVE NOISE

Formed: Glasgow, Scotland ... 1979 by the MIDDLETON brothers ROSS (who incidentally wrote for Sounds weekly under the pseudonym of MAXWELL PARK), GRAHAM and FRASER, along with RUSSELL BLACKSTOCK and LES GAFF. Appearing on V/A compilation 'Second City Statik' with 'REFUGEES' and 'THE LONG MARCH' in 1980, POSITIVE NOISE were on the 'Statik' roster (along with MODERN ENGLISH they issued a cassette). Described by many as one of the most promising anthemic indie-dance acts, the ever-evolving PN released several singles and three albums, 'HEART OF DARKNESS' (1981), 'CHANGE OF HEART' (1982) – now without ROSS – plus 'WHEN LIGHTNING STRIKES' (1985). The latter featured newcomers JOHN TELFORD and JOHN COLETTA who superseded GAFF. They also recruited producer DAVE ALLEN (of SHRIEKBACK) to boost their now dated mid-80's sound.

Album rating: HEART OF DARKNESS (*5) / CHANGE OF HEART (*6) / WHEN LIGHTNING STRIKES (*4)

ROSS MIDDLETON – vocals, (some) piano / **GRAHAM MIDDLETON** – keyboards, vocals / **RUSSELL BLACKSTOCK** – guitar, vocals / **FRASER MIDDLETON** – bass, vocals / **LES GAFF** – drums

			Statik	not iss.
Feb 81.	(7") *(STAT 3)* **GIVE ME PASSION. / GHOSTS**			-

(12"+=) *(STAT 3-12)* – End of a dream.

May 81.	(7") *(STAT 4)* **CHARM. / ...AND YET AGAIN**			-

(12"+=) *(STAT 4-12)* – Moscow motion.

May 81.	(lp) *(STATLP 1)* **HEART OF DARKNESS**			-

– Darkness visible / Hypnosis / No more blood and soil / ...And yet again / Down there / Treachery! / Warlords / Love is a many splintered thing / Refugees / Ghosts. *(w/ free 7")* STAT 5) LOVE LIKE POVERTY

— now without ROSS; RUSSELL now frontman

Nov 81.	(7") *(STAT 8)* **POSITIVE NEGATIVE. / ENERGY**			-

(12"+=) *(STAT 8-12)* – ('A'-instrumental).

Jun 82.	(7") *(STAT 15)* **WAITING FOR THE 7th MAN. / END OF TEARS**			-
Jul 82.	(lp) *(STATLP 8)* **CHANGE OF HEART**			-

– Positive negative / Waiting for the 7th man / Out of reach / Tension / Change of heart / Feel the fear / Get up and go / Inhibitions / Obsession / Hanging on.

Sep 82.	(7"/12") *(STAT 23/+12)* **GET UP AND GO. / TENSION**			-
Sep 83.	(7") *(TAK 8)* **WHEN THE LIGHTNING STRIKES.** /			-

(12"+=) *(TAK 8-12)* –

— **JOHN TELFORD** – drums; repl. GAFF
— added **JOHN COLETTA** – guitar

Aug 84.	(7") *(TAK 22)* **MILLION MILES AWAY. / SHANTY**			-

(12"+=) *(TAK 22-12)* –

Jun 85.	(7") *(TAK 32)* **DISTANT FIRES. / SWAMP**			-

(12"+=) *(TAK 32-12)* –

Jun 85.	(lp) *(STATLP 23)* **DISTANT FIRES**			-

– When lightning strikes / I need you / Distant fires / Reckless / Embers / A million miles away / Serenade / Now is the time / Always remember / Entranced.

— disbanded after above

PRIMAL SCREAM

Formed: Glasgow, Scotland ... summer 1984 by JESUS & MARY CHAIN drummer BOBBY GILLESPIE. Signing to JAMC's label, 'Creation', in 1985, they cut two singles, GILLESPIE leaving The 'MARY CHAIN after the debut, 'ALL FALL DOWN' (1985). The first album, 'SONIC FLOWER GROOVE' (1987), was recorded by the current band line-up core of ANDREW INNES, ROBERT 'THROB' YOUNG and MARTIN DUFFY (save MANI, ex-STONE ROSES, who joined up in 1996) along with an ever-changing array of additional musicians. Released on 'Creation' boss ALAN McGEE's 'WEA' subsidiary label, 'Elevation', the album saw the band pretty much live up to their name, a primitive take on raw ROLLING STONES, STOOGES etc. with a bit of BYRDS jingle jangle thrown in. This sound served the band well through their second album, PRIMAL SCREAM (1989) until the release of 'LOADED' in early 1990. Back at 'Creation' and enamoured with the Acid House explosion, the band had enlisted the esteemed ANDREW WEATHERALL to remix 'I'M LOSING MORE THAN I'LL EVER HAVE' from the second lp. More a revolution than a remix, WEATHERALL created the stoned funk shuffle of 'LOADED', in the process bringing indie and rave kids together on the same dancefloor for the first time. PRIMAL SCREAM were now set on pushing the parameters of rock, releasing a trio of singles that defined an era, 'COME TOGETHER' (1990) was 90's style hedonist gospel that converted even the most cynical of rock bores while 'HIGHER THAN THE SUN' (1991) was perhaps the 'SCREAM's stellar moment, a narcotic lullaby beamed from another galaxy. Combining all the aforementioned tracks with a trippy 13TH FLOOR ELEVATORS cover, a heavyweight dub workout and a clutch of STONES-like beauties, 'SCREAMADELICA' (1991) was flawless. Opening with the euphoric 'MOVIN' ON UP' (the best song the 'STONES never wrote), the album effortlessly proved that dance and rock were essentially carved out of the same soulful root source, a seam that's been mined by any artist that's ever mattered. A landmark album, 'SCREAMADELICA' was awarded the Mercury Music prize in 1992 and for sheer breadth of vision the record has yet to meet its match. Inevitably, then, the GEORGE DRAKOULIAS-produced follow-up, 'GIVE OUT BUT DON'T GIVE UP' (1994) was a disappointment in comparison. Recorded in MEMPHIS, the record saw PRIMAL SCREAM trying far too hard to achieve a roughshod R&B grit. Where before they had made The STONES' sound their own, now they came across as mere plagiarists, and over-produced plagiarists at that. Granted, the likes of 'JAILBIRD' and 'ROCKS' were funkier than any of the insipid indie competition around at the time and GILLESPIE's epileptic handclap routine was always more endearing than the run-of-the-mill rock posturing. Rumours of severe drug abuse abounded at this point and few were shocked when, in January 1994, it emerged that DUFFY had survived a near fatal stabbing in America. For the next couple of years, the band kept a fairly low profile, only a contribution to the 'Trainspotting' soundtrack and an unofficial Scottish 'Euro '96' single confirmed the 'SCREAM were still in existence. But while Scotland stumbled to defeat (again!!), PRIMAL SCREAM cleaned up their act and recorded the wonderful 'VANISHING POINT' (1997). Apparently cut as an alternative soundtrack to cult 70's road movie 'Kowalski', this album was the true follow-up/comedown to the psychedelic high of 'SCREAMADELICA'. 'OUT OF THE VOID' was the band's darkest moment to date while the title track and 'STUKA' were fractured, paranoid psych-outs. Only the vintage screenshow of 'GET DUFFY' and the mellow 'STAR' offered any respite. Big on dub and low on derivation, the album was a spirited return to form for one of Scotland's most enduring and groundbreaking bands. The year of 2000 saw the 'SCREAM return with all guns blazing for the destructive release of 'EXTERMINATOR'. An aptly titled album, this was worrying music for the post Millennium tensions of anti-capitalist marches and technology protests. It shaped its own poisonous force as the listener ventured further into the set: 'KILL ALL HIPPIES' was certainly a phrase derived from the punk movement, while 'SWASTIKA EYES' had a morbid, self-asserting ring to it. GILLESPIE mixed in exuberant styles such as hip-hop ('PILLS'), trance ('ACCELERATOR') and a bit of old MY BLOODY VALENTINE tones into the devilish bru. One could only describe 'EXTERMINATOR' as a very squealing, scary disjointed affair, sort of like the soundtrack to a Jean Luc Godard horror pic, if he, er, did a horror that is. All in all, PRIMAL SCREAM were wise to return to wigged-out psychedelia – a style they were criticised for getting out of – with the self-indulgent 'VANISHING POINT'. 'EXTERMINATOR' is a valuable lesson in the art of punk: it's loud, it has balls, it's offensive, it's not all tuneful, and most importantly, it makes sense. This method was also applied to The 'SCREAM's seventh album proper, 'EVIL HEAT' (2002) which delved even deeper into GILLESPIE's obsession with dark, throbbing soundscapes. Possibly the musical equivalent to being repeatedly run over by a tank and then turned into a metal blob, the set curiously explored the avant-metal punk scene a little bit closer, with single 'MISS LUCIFER' spitting and bubbling like an unsteady jar of boiling acid. Basslines thrashed (especially on 'SKULL X'), keyboards sounding like they were being set on fire and GILLESPIE pumped up his frontman image by turning a piece of deadpan vocal into a plethora of screams. Apart from the SUICIDE connections, and the screeching, industrial electro-clash of it all, 'EVIL HEAT' (complete with sinister homemade, cut'n'paste album jacket) included some cringe-worthy moments: the lazy, drugged-up slur of nu-blues number 'THE LORD IS MY SHOTGUN', super-model KATE MOSS' dreary rendition of the NANCY SINATRA/LEE HAZELWOOD song 'SOME VELVET MORNING' and the re-working of 'RISE' (originally entitled 'BOMB THE PENTAGON', but shamelessly re-titled for fears of American

PRIMAL SCREAM (cont)

distribution). Former MY BLOODY VALENTINE casualty KEVIN SHIELDS took on the recording duty, doing his damndest to make it sound as dirty and as translucent as possible. PRIMAL SCREAM exist to be one of the globe's truest punk-rawk bands – a rare thing in these money spinning, 3-chord, pop-producing times. Like the BBC, they educate, entertain and inform ... they also make one hell'uva racket too. • **Songwriters:** GILLESPIE, YOUNG and BEATTIE, until the latter's replacement by INNES. Covered CARRY ME HOME (Dennis Wilson) / UNDERSTANDING (Small Faces) / 96 TEARS (? & The Mysterians) / KNOW YOUR RIGHTS (Clash) / MOTORHEAD (Motorhead).

Album rating: SONIC FLOWER GROOVE (*5) / PRIMAL SCREAM (*6) / SCREAMADELICA (*10) / GIVE OUT BUT DON'T GIVE UP (*7) / VANISHING POINT (*8) / ECHO DEK (*6) / EXTERMINATOR (*8) / EVIL HEAT (*6)

BOBBY GILLESPIE (b.22 Jun'64) – vocals (ex-WAKE, also drummer of JESUS & MARY CHAIN) / **JIM BEATTIE** – guitar / **ROBERT YOUNG** – bass / **TOM McGURK** – drums / **MARTIN ST. JOHN** – tambourine

Creation   not iss.

May 85. (7") (CRE 017) **ALL FALL DOWN. / IT HAPPENS**

—— added **PAUL HARTE** – rhythm guitar (GILLESPIE left JESUS & MARY)

Apr 86. (7") (CRE 026) **CRYSTAL CRESCENT. / VELOCITY GIRL**
(12"+=) (CRE 026T) – Spirea X.

STUART MAY – rhythm guitar (ex-SUBMARINES) repl. HARTE (Dec'86) / **ANDREW INNES** – rhythm guitar (of REVOLVING PAINT DREAM) repl. MAY / Guest drummers **PHIL KING** (studio) **+ DAVE MORGAN** (tour) repl. McGURK

Elevation   not iss.

Jun 87. (7") (ACID 5) **GENTLE TUESDAY. / BLACK STAR CARNIVAL**
(12"+=) (ACID 5T) – I'm gonna make you mine.

Sep 87. (7") (ACID 5) **IMPERIAL. / STAR FRUIT SURF RIDER**
(12"+=/s12"+=) (ACID 5T/+W) – So sad about us / Imperial (demo).

Oct 87. (lp/c)(cd) (ELV 2/+C)(242-182-2) **SONIC FLOWER GROOVE** 62
– Gentle Tuesday / Treasure trip / May the sun shine bright for you / Sonic sister love / Silent spring / Imperial / Love you / Leaves / Aftermath / We go down slowly. *(re-iss. Jul91; same)*

—— (Jun'87) **GAVIN SKINNER** – drums; repl. ST. JOHN

—— (Feb'88) Now a trio GILLESPIE, YOUNG + INNES augmented by **JIM NAVAJO** – guitar (BEATTIE formed SPIREA X; SKINNER also left)

—— (Feb'89) added **HENRY OLSEN** – bass (ex-NICO) / **PHILIP 'TOBY' TOMANOV** – drums (ex-NICO, ex-DURUTTI COLUMN, ex-BLUE ORCHIDS)

Creation   Mercenary

Jul 89. (7") (CRE 067) **IVY IVY IVY. / YOU'RE JUST TOO DARK TO CARE**
(12"+=)(cd-s+=) (CRE 067T)(CRESCD 067) – I got you split wide open over me.

Sep 89. (lp/c/cd) (CRE LP/C/CD 054) <2100> **PRIMAL SCREAM**
– Ivy Ivy Ivy / You're just dead skin to me / She power / You're just too dark to care / I'm losing more than I'll ever have / Gimme gimme teenage head / Lone star girl / Kill the king / Sweet pretty thing / Jesus can't save me. (free 7"ltd.) – SPLIT WIDE OPEN (demo). / LONE STAR GIRL (demo) *(cd re-iss. Jan01; same)*

—— trimmed to a trio again (GILLESPIE, YOUNG + INNES)

Creation   Sire

Feb 90. (7") (CRE 070) **LOADED. / I'M LOSING MORE THAN I'LL EVER HAVE** 16   –
(ext.12"+=/'A'Terry Farley remix-12"+=)(ext.cd-s+=) (CRE 070 T/X)(CRESCD 070) – Ramblin' Rose (live).

Jul 90. (7"/c-s)(ext.12")(ext.cd-s) (CRE/+CS 078)(CRE 078T)(CRESCD 078) <26384> **COME TOGETHER (Terry Farley mix). / COME TOGETHER (Andrew Weatherall mix)** 26   Aug90
(12") (CRE 078X) – ('A'-HypnotoneBrainMachine mix) / ('A'-BBG mix).

Jun 91. (7"/ext.12") (CRE 096/+T) **HIGHER THAN THE SUN. / ('A' American Spring mix)** 40   –
(cd-s+=) (CRESCD 096) – Higher than the Orb.

—— guest spot on above from **JAH WOBBLE** – bass

Aug 91. (7"/ext.12")(c-s) (CRE 110/+T)(CRECS 110) **DON'T FIGHT IT, FEEL IT. / ('A'scat mix featuring Denise Johnson)** 41   –
(cd-s+=) (CRESCD 110) – ('A'extended version).

Sep 91. (cd/c/d-lp) (CRE CD/C/LP 076) <26714> **SCREAMADELICA** 8
– Movin' on up / Slip inside this house / Don't fight it, feel it / Higher than the Sun / Inner flight / Come together / Loaded / Damaged / I'm comin' down / Higher than the Sun (a dub symphony in two parts) / Shine like stars. *(cd re-iss. Jan01; same) (lp-iss.Jun01 on 'Simply Vinyl'; SVLP 344)*

Jan 92. (7"ep/c-ep) (CRE/+CS 117) <40193> **DIXIE-NARCO EP** 11
– Movin' on up / Carry me home / Screamadelica.
(12"ep+=)(cd-ep+=) (CRE 117T)(CRESCD 117) – Stone my soul.

—— In Jan'94, MARTIN DUFFY was stabbed in Memphis, although he recovered soon after.

—— Line-up:- **GILLESPIE, YOUNG, INNES, DUFFY + DAVID HOOD + DENISE JOHNSON** + guest **GEORGE CLINTON** – vocals

Mar 94. (7"/c-s) (CRE/+CS 129) <18189> **ROCKS. / FUNKY JAM** 7   Apr94
(12")(cd-s) (CRE 129T)(CRESCD 129) – ('A'side) / Funky jam (hot ass mix) / Funky jam (club mix).

Apr 94. (cd/c/lp) (CRE CD/C/LP 146) <45538> **GIVE OUT, BUT DON'T GIVE UP** 2
– Jailbird / Rocks / (I'm gonna) Cry myself blind / Funky jam / Big jet plane / Free / Call on me / Struttin' / Sad and blue / Give out but don't give up / I'll be there for you. *(cd re-iss. Feb00 & Jan01; same)*

Jun 94. (7"/c-s) (CRE/+CS 145) **JAILBIRD. / ('A'-Dust Brothers mix)** 29   –
(12"+=) (CRE 145T) – ('A'-Toxic Trio stay free mix) / ('A'-Weatherall dub chapter 3 mix).
(cd-s+=) (CRESCD 145) – ('A'-Sweeney 2 mix).

Nov 94. (7"/c-s) (CRE/+CS 183) **I'M GONNA CRY MYSELF BLIND (George Drakoulias mix). / ROCKS (live)** 51   –
(cd-s+=) (CRESCD 183) – I'm losing more than I'll ever have (live) / Struttin' (back in our minds) (Brendan Lynch remix).

(10") (CRE 183X) – ('A'side) / Struttin' (back in our minds) (Brendan Lynch remix) / Give out, but don't give up (Portishead remix) / Rockers dub (Kris Needs mix).

Jun 96. (c-s/cd-s; PRIMAL SCREAM, IRVINE WELSH AND ON-U SOUND PRESENT...) (CRECS-CRESCD 194) **THE BIG MAN AND THE SCREAM TEAM MEET THE BARMY ARMY UPTOWN** (mixes:- full strength fortified dub / electric soup dub / a jake supreme) 17   –

—— In Oct'96, GILLESPIE, INNES, YOUNG & DUFFY were joined by **MANI MOUNFIELD** – bass (ex-STONE ROSES)

Creation   Reprise

May 97. (c-s) (<CRECS 245>) **KOWALSKI / 96 TEARS** 8
(cd-s+=) (<CRESCD 245>) – Know your rights / ('A'-Automator mix).

Jun 97. (c-s) CRECS 263 **STAR / JESUS** 16   –
(cd-s+=) (CRESCD 263) – Rebel dub / How does it feel to belong.
(12"+=) (CRE 263T) – ('A'mixes).

Jul 97. (cd/d-lp)(c) (CRE CD/LP 178)(CCRE 178) <46559> **VANISHING POINT** 2
– Burning wheel / Get Duffy / Kowalski / Star / If they move, kill 'em / Out of the void / Stuka / Medication / Motorhead / Trainspotting / Long life. *(cd re-iss. Jan01; same)*

Oct 97. (7") (CRE 272) **BURNING WHEEL. / HAMMOND CONNECTION** 17   –
(12"+=)(cd-s+=) (CRE 272T)(CRESCD 272) – ('A'-Chemical Brothers remix) / Higher than the sun (original).

Oct 97. (cd/7"box) (CRE CD/L7 224) **ECHO DEK** (remixes) 43   –
– Duffed up / Revolutionary / Ju-87 / First name unknown / Vanishing dub / Last train / Wise blood / Dub in vain. *(cd re-iss. Feb00 & Jan01; same)*

Feb 98. (7") (CRE 284) **IF THEY MOVE, KILL 'EM. / BADLANDS**   –
(12"+=)(cd-s+=) (CRE 284T)(CRESCD 284) – ('A'-My Bloody Valentine Arkestra mix) / ('A'-Darklands 12"disco mix).

—— added on 1998 tour **JIM HUNT** – saxophone / **DUNCAN MACKAY** – trumpet / **DARREN MOONEY** – drums

Creation   Astralwerks

Nov 99. (c-s) (CRECS 326) **SWASTIKA EYES / ('A'mix)** 22   –
(12"/cd-s) (CRE 326T)(CRESCD 326) – ('A'-Chemical Brothers mix) / ('A'-Spectre mix) / ('A'side).

Jan 00. (cd/md/c/d-lp) (CRECD/CREMD/CCRE/CRELP 239) <49260> **EXTERMINATOR** 3   May00
– Kill all hippies / Accelerator / Exterminator / Swastika eyes / Pills / Blood money / Keep your dreams / Insect royalty / MBV Arkestra (if they move kill 'em) / Swastika eyes / Shoot speed – Kill light / I'm 5 years ahead of my time. *(cd re-iss. Jan01; same)*

Mar 00. (7") (CRE 332) <8169> **KILL ALL HIPPIES. / EXTERMINATOR (Massive Attack remix)** 24   Nov00
(cd-s+=) (CRESCD 332) – The revenge of the Hammond connection.
(12"+=) (CRE 332T) – ('A'mixes).

Sep 00. (12")(cd-s) (CRE 333T)(CRESCD 333) **ACCELERATOR / I'M 5 YEARS AHEAD OF MY TIME / WHEN THE KINGDOM COMES** 34   –

Columbia   Astralwerks

Jul 02. (12"/cd-s) (672825-6/-2) **MISS LUCIFER / (mixes: panther / hip to hip / bone to bone)** 23   9

Aug 02. (cd/lp) (508923-2/-1) <87027> **EVIL HEAT**
– Deep hit of morning sun / Miss Lucifer / Autobahn 66 / Detroit / Rise / The Lord is my shotgun / City / Some velvet morning / Skull X / A scanner darkly / Space blues number 2.

Oct 02. (cd-s) (673312-2) **AUTOBAHN 66 / AUTOBAHN 66 (alter ego remix) / SUBSTANCE D** 44   –
(12") (673312-6) – (first & third tracks + alter ego instr).
(cd-s) (673312-5) – ('A'side) / ('A'live) / Shoot speed kill light.

– others, etc. –

Nov 97. (12") Creation; (PSTLS 1) **STUKA (Two Lone Swordsmen mixes)**   –

PRIMEVALS

Formed: Glasgow, Scotland ... 1983 by frontman MICHAEL "MICKY" ROONEY (no, not that one!), guitarist TOM RAFFERTY, bassist JOHN HONEYMAN, drummer RHOD BURNETT and last but not least, DON GORDON (he was later superseded by MICHAEL McDONALD). Having self-financed their own 'Raucous' debut single, 'WHERE ARE YOU?', in 1984, they were surprised to say the least when leading French independent, 'New Rose', gave them a call. Thinking that these PRIMEVALS were the NY version (i.e. The Real Kids' JOHN FELICE's combo), the Gauls invited the Scots lads to send in some material. Remarkably, the imprint thought their sound was suitable (well, JOHNNY THUNDERS, TAV FALCO and The CRAMPS were all on board at the time) and signed the band almost immediately. Described as trashy, IGGY meets THUNDERS meets NY DOLLS sounding, the PRIMEVALS embarked on their own Caledonian branch of R&B sleaze. A handful of releases for New Rose, including 'ETERNAL HOTFIRE' mini (1985) and 'SOUND HOLE' (1986), were met with very little reaction back here in 'Blighty, although on the continent they became something of a cult. When GORDON GOUDIE superseded RAFFERTY (who joined The BEAT POETS) and the label no longer needed their services, the PRIMEVALS bailed out towards the send of '87. A decade later, the members re-united for several gigs, including a great night out at the 13th Note recorded by 'Flotsam & Jetsam'. • **Covered:** DIAMOND, FURCOAT, CHAMPAGNE (Suicide) / HEYA (JJ Light) / THOUGHTS AND WORDS + TRIBAL GATHERING (Byrds) / CRAZY LITTLE THING (Captain Beefheart) / TOTAL DESTRUCTION TO YOUR MIND (Swamp Dogg).

PRIMEVALS (cont)

Album rating: ETERNAL HOTFIRE mini (*4) / SOUND HOLE (*4) / LIVE A LITTLE (*5) / NEON OVEN – LIVE (*5)

MICHAEL ROONEY – vocals, harmonica / **TOM RAFFERTY** – guitar, vocals / **DON GORDON** – lead guitar / **JOHN HONEYMAN** – bass, vocals / **RHOD 'LEFTY' BURNETT** – drums

Raucous / not iss.
Jun 84. (7") (PRIME 1) **WHERE ARE YOU? / THIS KIND OF LOVE**

New Rose / not iss.
Feb 85. (m-lp) (ROSE 47) **ETERNAL HOTFIRE**
 – My emancipation / Blues at my door / She's all mine / Have some fun / See the tears fall / Lucky I'm living.
Nov 85. (7") (NEW 55) **LIVING IN HELL. / WALK IN MY FOOTSTEPS**

–––– **MICHAEL McDONALD** – lead & slide guitars, vocals; repl. DON
Mar 86. (lp) (ROSE 80) **SOUND HOLE**
 – Eternal hotfire / Prairie chain / Primeval call / See that skin / Spiritual / Nutmeg city / Elixir of life / Fire and clay / Saint Jack / Dish of fish / Lowdown.
Jun 86. (10"m) (NEW 73) **ELIXIR OF LIFE. / SISTER / LONESOME WEEPIN' BLUES**

–––– **GORDON GOUDIE** – rhythm guitar; repl. RAFFERTY (to BEAT POETS)
Jul 87. (7") (NEW 93) **HEYA. / JUSTIFY**
 (12"+=) (NEW 92) – Down where the madness grows / Heya (pt.2).
Oct 87. (lp/c/cd) (NEW 123/+C/CD) **LIVE A LITTLE**
 – Fertile mind / Follow her down / My dying embers / All the virtues / Bleedin' black / Cottonhead / Justify / Early grave / Highway / Pink catsuit (part 1) / One sweet drink / Burden of the debt. (free 7" w/lp; Free 10) – DIAMONDS, FURCOAT, CHAMPAGNE. / (extended part 2). (cd+=) – Pink catsuit (part 2) / Diamond, furcoat, champagne / Prairie skin / Spiritual / Fire and clay / Saint Jack / Primeval call.
Apr 88. (7") (NEW 105) **FERTILE MIND. / CRAZY LITTLE THING**

–––– ROONEY, HONEYMAN + GOUDIE recruited **RICHARD MAZDA** – guitar, vocals + **PAUL BRIDGES** – drums

D.D.T. / not iss.
Feb 89. (lp) (DISPLP 21) **NEON OVEN – LIVE AT THE REX, PARIS (live 13 April, 1988)**
 – Crazy little thing / Spiritual / My dying embers / Elixir of life / Early grave / Sister / Eternal hotfire / My emancipation / Total destruction to your mind.

–––– the PRIMEVALS were briefly back in 1997

Flotsam & Jetsam – The 13th Note / not iss.
Dec 97. (7") (SHaG 13.02) **Club Beatroot Part Two**
 – I want / (other track by SWELLING MEG)

– compilations, etc. –

Jan 87. (12"ep) Strange Fruit; (SFPS 014) **THE PEEL SESSIONS (18.9.85)**
 – Saint Jack / See that skin / Spiritual / Dish of fish.
Oct 87. (lp) Greasy Pop; (GPR 127) **CHICKEN FACTORY** – / – Austra

PRIMITIVES

Formed: Coventry, England . . . September '85 by PETE TWEEDIE, STEVE DULLAHAN and PAUL COURT, who had been part of EUROPEAN SUN with male singer KEIRON. Adopting the PRIMITIVES moniker, the band recruited striking Aussie blonde, TRACY TRACY as a frontwoman, setting up their own indie label, 'Lazy' with the help of manager WAYNE MORRIS. In '86/'87, the band's first three singles, 'THRU THE FLOWERS', REALLY STUPID', and 'STOP KILLING ME' were cult indie hits, quintessential 80's distortion-pop not unlike a fantasy collaboration between The RUNAWAYS and The JESUS AND MARY CHAIN. With a new 'R.C.A.' deal in the can (the company had taken over 'Lazy', which was now essentially a subsidiary), the comparisons with BLONDIE became more than just visual, the new wave, amphetamine melodica of 'CRASH' giving The PRIMITIVES immediate Top 5 success in early '88. Their debut album, 'LOVELY', cruised into the Top 10 the following month, the highly photogenic TRACY enjoying a concentrated fifteen minutes of fame as the style press fell over themselves to have her blonde barnet on their front covers. An infectious collection of neo-psychedelic power pop, the album nevertheless failed to deliver any further major hits. Problems were compounded by personnel changes; by the time the band came to record a follow-up, DULLAHAN and TWEEDIE had both departed to join the band HATE. Though replacements had been found in ANDY HOBSON (replaced in turn, by PAUL SAMPSON on the new album) and TIG WILLIAMS respectively, 'PURE' (1989) was regarded by many reviewers as distinctly underwhelming, the album barely scraping into the Top 40. Worse, TRACY had gone ginger! The group bravely struggled on, releasing the 'GALORE' (1992) album, its commercial failure coinciding with the wise decision to call it a day in Spring '92. • **Songwriters:** Penned by COURT, except I'LL BE YOUR MIRROR (Velvet Underground) / I WANNA BE YOUR DOG (Stooges; Iggy Pop) / AS TEARS GO BY (Rolling Stones) / (YOU'RE SO SQUARE) BABY I DON'T CARE (Elvis Presley).

Album rating: LOVELY (*7) / LAZY 86-88 compilation (*8) / PURE (*5) / GALORE (*4) / BOMBSHELL: THE HITS AND MORE compilation (*7)

TRACY TRACY (b. TRACY CATTELL, 18 Aug'67, Australia) – vocals; repl. KIERON / **PAUL COURT** (b.27 Jul'65) – guitar, vocals / **STEVE DULLAHAN** (b.18 Dec'66) – bass / **PETE TWEEDIE**

Lazy / not iss.
May 86. (12"ep) (LAZY 01) **THRU THE FLOWERS / ACROSS MY SHOULDER. / SHE DON'T NEED YOU / LAZY**
Oct 86. (7") (LAZY 02) **REALLY STUPID. / WE FOUND A WAY TO THE SUN**
 (12"+=) (LAZY 02T) – Where the wind blows.
Feb 87. (7") (LAZY 03) **STOP KILLING ME. / BUZZ BUZZ BUZZ**
 (12"+=) (LAZY 03T) – Laughing up my sleeve.
May 87. (free gig-7") (LAZY 05) **OCEAN BLUE. / SHADOW**
Aug 87. (7") (LAZY 06) **THRU THE FLOWERS (new version). / EVERYTHING SHINING BRIGHT**
 (12"+=) (LAZY 06T) – Across my shoulder (original).
 (7"ltd.+=) (LAZY 06L) – ('A'original).

–––– **TIG WILLIAMS** – drums repl. TWEEDIE who joined HATE

R.C.A. / R.C.A.
Feb 88. (7") (PB 41761) **CRASH. / I'LL STICK WITH YOU** 5 / Apr88
 (10"+=) (PB 41761X) – Crash (live in studio).
 (12"+=) (PT 41762) – Things get in your way.
 (7"ep+=) (PB 41761E) – Crash (again and again) / Crash (short).
Mar 88. (lp/c/cd) (PL/PK/PD 71688) <8443> **LOVELY** 6 / Aug88
 – Crash / Spacehead / Carry me home / Shadow / Thru the flowers / Dreamwalk baby / I'll stick with you / Nothing left / Stop killing me / Out of reach / Ocean blue / Run, baby, run / Anything to change / Buzz buzz buzz. <later US copies +=> – Way behind me.
Apr 88. (7") (PB 42011) **OUT OF REACH (remix). / REALLY STUPID (live)** 25 / –
 (12"+=) (PT 42012) – Crash (live) / ('A'lp version).
 (cd-s+=) (PD 42012) – Ocean blue (lp version) / I wanna be your dog (live).
 (7"ep+=) (PB 42011E) – Crash (live) / Dreamwalk baby (live).
Aug 88. (7"/7"red,7"green,7"yellow,7"blue) (PB 42209/+E) **WAY BEHIND ME. / ALL THE WAY DOWN** 36 / –
 (12"+=/c-s+=) (PT 42210/+C) – ('A'acoustic) / ('B'-beat mix).
Sep 88. (7") **WAY BEHIND ME. / THRU THE FLOWERS (lp version)** – / –

–––– Trimmed to a trio when DULLAHAN also departed to join HATE
Jul 89. (7"/7"g-f/7"box) (PB 42947/42993/43003)(PK 42948) **SICK OF IT. / NOOSE** 24 / –
 (12"+=/cd-s+=) (PT/PD 42948) – I'll be your mirror.
 (12"blue++=) (PT 43134) – As tears go by.

–––– added **ANDY HOBSON** – bass (ex-JUNK)
Sep 89. (7"/c-s) (PB/PK 43173) **SECRETS. / I ALMOST TOUCHED YOU** 49 / –
 (7"m+=) (PB 43209) – Dizzy heights.
 (7"ep++=)(12"red-ep+=)(3"cd-ep++=) (PB 43211)(PT 43212)(PD 43174) – Secrets (demo).
 (12"m+=) (PT 43174) – Secrets (demo).

–––– **PAUL SAMPSON** – bass; repl. HOBSON (on lp)
Oct 89. (lp/c/cd) (PL/PK/PD 74252) <9934> **PURE** 33 / Dec89
 – Outside / Summer rain / Sick of it / Shine / Dizzy heights / All the way down / Secrets / Keep me in mind / Lonely streets / Can't bring me down / Way behind me / Never tell / Noose / I'll be your mirror. (cd+=) – All the way down (beat version) / I almost touched you. <US cd+=> – (4 tracks).
Jul 91. (7"/c-s) (PB/PK 44481) **YOU ARE THE WAY. / IN MY DREAM** 58 / –
 (12"+=/cd-s+=) (PT/PD 44481) – Sunpulse / Stop killing me.
Oct 91. (7") (PB 44977) **EARTH THING. / EMPHASISE**
 (12"ep+=/cd-ep+=) **THE SPELLS EP** (PT/PD 44978) – Under my spell / Haunted.
 (12"ep+=) **THE SPELLS EP** (PT 44980) – All the way down (live) / Way behind me (live).
Mar 92. (7") (PB 45345) **LEAD ME ASTRAY. / OUTSIDE (live) / YOU ARE THE WAY (live)**
 (12") (PT 45346) – ('A'side) / Slip away (live) / Earth thing (live) / Outside (live).
 (12") (PT 45360) – ('A'side) / See thru the dark (live) / Stop killing me (live).
 (cd-s) (PD 45346) – ('A'side) / Sick of it (live) / Give this world to me (live).
Apr 92. (cd/c/lp) (PD/PK/PL 75086) **GALORE**
 – You are the way / Lead me astray / Earth thing / Give this world to you / Slip away / Cold enough to kill / Hello Jesus / Empathise / See thru the dark / Kiss mine / Smile / The little black egg.

–––– disbanded around spring 1992

– compilations, others, etc. –

Aug 89. (lp/c/cd) Lazy; (LAZY/+C/CD 15) **LAZY 86-88 (early material)** 73 / –
Sep 94. (cd) R.C.A.; (74321 22635-2) **BOMBSHELL: THE HITS AND MORE**
Jun 96. (cd) Camden; (74321 39343-2) **THE BEST OF THE PRIMITIVES**
Feb 01. (cd) Burning Airlines; (PILOT 38) **BUBBLING UP (THE BBC SESSIONS)**

PRISONERS

Formed: Rochester / Medway, Kent, England . . . 1982 by GRAHAM DAY, ALLAN CROCKFORD, JAMIE TAYLOR and JOHNNY SYMONS. That year they created something of a stir when they released a self-financed debut album, 'A TASTE OF PINK!', TAYLOR's hammond organ proving the key element in an energetic sound which drew heavily on the more mod-influenced sounds of the 60's. They soon signed to Chiswick off-shoot, 'Big Beat', who unleashed the PHIL CHEVRON (future POGUES)-produced, tongue-twistingly titled but muted follow-up set, 'THE WISERMISERDEMELZA' (1983). The following year, an appearance on Channel 4's 'The Tube' afforded DAY and Co. valuable exposure and led to them contributing a track, 'REACHING MY HEAD', to their label's accompanying various artists EP, 'Four On Four: Trash On The Tube'. Subsequently striking out on their own once more, The PRISONERS released a second self-financed set, 'THE LAST FOURFATHERS', securing them an ill-fated deal with Stiff off-shoot, 'Countdown'. The resulting, TROY TATE-produced album, 'IN FROM THE COLD', was beset with problems and stretched the band's patience to breaking point. Following their 1986 demise, GRAHAM went on to join THEE MIGHTY CEASARS before forming The PRIME MOVERS (with CROCKFORD), while TAYLOR went on to greater recognition with his own JAMES TAYLOR QUARTET. Initially also comprising CROCKFORD alongside DAVID TAYLOR and SIMON 'WOLF' HOWARD, JTQ were inspired by the funky pop/theme tune interpretations of prime BOOKER T & THE MG'S, releasing a string of albums for their own 'Re-Elect The President' label. With London's rare groove/acid jazz scene beginning to move away from its inherent insularity and make an impact on the wider market, JTQ were snapped up by 'Polydor'-offshoot, 'Urban'. The group made their major label debut with 'THE THEME FROM STARSKY & HUTCH', a live favourite also featured on the accompanying album, 'WAIT A MINUTE'. Certainly, it was in a live environment that JTQ were (and still are!) best sampled, TAYLOR's mean Hammond licks guaranteed to set any dancefloor on fire. It could even be argued that TAYLOR pre-empted the current vogue for all things lounge/easy listening although his core audience of students and polo-necked groovers would undoubtedly refute any charges of cheesiness. While never actually charting, a cult following ensured that albums such as 'GET ORGANIZED' (1989) and 'DO YOUR OWN THING' (1990) were steady sellers; the uninitiated, however, are directed towards the recently released 'Music club' album, 'BLOW UP!', a fine collection featuring their legendary cover of Led Zeppelin's 'WHOLE LOTTA LOVE', eat your heart out GOLDBUG!

Album rating: A TASTE OF PINK! (*5) / THE WISERMISERDEMELZA (*7) / THE LAST FOURFATHERS (*5) / IN FROM THE COLD (*5)

GRAHAM DAY – vocals, guitar / **JAMES 'JAMIE' TAYLOR** – Hammond organ / **ALLAN CROCKFORD** – bass / **JOHNNY SYMONS** – drums

Own Up / not iss.

1982. (lp) *(OWN UP U2)* **A TASTE OF PINK!**
– Better in black / A taste of pink / Maybe I was wrong / Creepy crawlies / There can't be a place / Pretend / Coming home / Threw my heart away / Come to the / Mushroom / Till the morning light / Say your prayers / Don't call my name. *(cd-iss. Feb94; OWNPU 002CD) (re-iss. Mar85 in pink vinyl)*

Big Beat / not iss.

Nov 83. (7") *(NS 90)* **HURRICANE. / TOMORROW (SHE SAID)**
Nov 83. (lp) *(WIK 19)* **THE WISERMISERDEMELZA**
– Here come the misunderstood / A dream is gone / For now and forever / Unbeliever / Far away / Hurricane / Somewhere / Think of me / Love me lies / Tonight. *(cd-iss. May90 +=; CDWIKD 937)* – Tomorrow (she said) / Melanie / What I want / The last thing on your mind / Revenge of the Cybermen / Coming home / Reaching my head.

Ace-Chiswick / not iss.

Aug 84. (7"ep) *(SW 98)* **ELECTRIC FIT**
– Revenge of the Cybermen / Melanie / What I want / The last thing on your mind.

Own Up / not iss.

Jul 85. (lp) *(OWN UP 3)* **THE LAST FOURFATHERS**
– Nobody wants your love / Night of the Nazgul / Thinking of you (broken pieces) / I am the fisherman / Mrs. Fothergill / Take you for a ride / The drowning / F.O.P. / Whenever I'm gone / Who's sorry now / Explosion on Uranus / I drink the ocean. *(cd-iss. Feb94; OWNPU 003CD)*

Empire / not iss.

Jan 86. (lp) *(MIC 001)* **THE LAST NIGHT AT THE MIC CLUB (live)**
(shared with The MILKSHAKES)

Countdown / not iss.

Mar 86. (7") *(VAIN 4)* **WHENEVER I'M GONE. / PROMISED LAND**
(12"+=) (12VAIN 4) – Gravedigger.
May 86. (lp) *(DOWN 2)* **IN FROM THE COLD**
– All you gotta do is say / Come closer / The more I teach you / Mourn my health / I know how to please you / Deceiving eye / In from the cold / Wish the rain / Be on your way / Find and seek / Ain't no telling / The lesser evil. *(cd-iss. Sep02 on 'Big Beat'+=; CDWIKM 221)* – Whenever I'm gone / Promised land Gravedigger / Pop star party / Happiness for once.

— split in 1986 when GRAHAM joined THEE MIGHTY CAESARS (an off-shoot of MILKSHAKES). He was soon to form The PRIME MOVERS.

– compilations, etc. –

1984. (lp) *Pink Dust;* **REVENGE OF THE PRISONERS**
Apr 87. (lp) *Media Burn; (MB 17)* **THE MILKSHAKES VS. THE PRISONERS**
Dec 88. (lp) *Hangman; (HANG 23UP)* **RARE AND UNISSUED**

Bill PRITCHARD

Born: Lichfield, Midlands, England. Although virtually dismissed in good ol' Blighty, BILL found his niche around parts of Europe, mainly Belgium, Netherlands and France, where he obtained cult appeal. From 1987's eponymous debut set for 'Third Mind', "the man who could be MORRISSEY (or LLOYD COLE)", released numerous twee/electronica sets, mostly for Belgium's 'Play It Again Sam' records. A collaboration set in '88 with Frenchman, DANIEL PARC, sealed PRITCHARD's time well-spent in sunny Gaul, while a subsequent single, 'TOMMY AND CO.' (the opener for his Etienne Daho-produced masterpiece, 'THREE MONTHS, THREE WEEKS & TWO DAYS'), became a surprise US college hit the following year through MTV. With LIGHTNING SEEDS man IAN BROUDIE now at the controls, 1991's 'JOLIE' album was a pleasant enough affair and became an underground breakthrough in both Japan and Canada. However, by the mid-90's, the deadpan voice and wit of PRITCHARD found few admirers back in the UK; well, he had been staying in Belgium for some time. This was put right when the man returned in '98, courtesy of comeback set, 'HAPPINESS AND OTHER CRIMES'.

Album rating: DEATH OF BILL POSTERS collection (*6) / PARCE QUE et Daniel Darc (*5) / THREE MONTHS, THREE WEEKS AND TWO DAYS (*7) / JOLIE (*6) / HAPPINESS AND OTHER CRIMES (*5)

BILL PRITCHARD – vocals, electronics

Third Mind / not iss.

May 87. (lp) *(TMLP 19)* **BILL PRITCHARD**
– Black souls under white skies / Sheltered life / Pas de plaisanterie / White city / Arsenic & old lace / Damnosa soir / Grey parade / Greek street / Impact of the cities.
Jan 88. (lp) *(TMLP 23)* **HALF A MILLION**
– Angelique / Born blonde / Wednesday / Celia's attic / Arboreturn romance / Arena says / Cranley gardens / I wonder why? / Homelessness / Bitter green / Jerome K Jerome / Linda in drag / Helas / Fanfare / Dejeuner sur l'herbe.
Apr 88. (7"m) *(TMS 07)* **PAS DE PLAISANTERIE. / ANGELIQUE / BORN BLONDE**
Aug 88. (cd) *(TMCD 004)* **DEATH OF BILL POSTERS** (compilation of two LP's)

Play It Again Sam / I.R.S.

Aug 88. (lp/cd; split w/ DANIEL DARC) *(BIAS 100/+CD)* **PARCE QUE**
– (DD track) / Lydia (DD track) / Pigalle on a Tuesday is charming / We were lovers / (DD tracks) / Pauvre petite / (DD track) / Catherine / (DD track) / Sera-tu encore la? / (DD track).
Feb 89. (7") *(BIAS 104-7)* **TOMMY & CO. / NEW ORLEANS**
(12"+=) (BIAS 104-12) – Lying in the Bricklayer's Arms / December with a good friend.
(cd-s+=) (BIAS 104CD) – Angelique / Pas de plaisanterie.
Apr 89. (cd/lp) *(CD+/BIAS 106) <IRSD 82027>* **THREE MONTHS, THREE WEEKS AND TWO DAYS**
– Tommy and Co / Invisible state / Sometimes / Pillow talk / Cosy evenings / We were lovers / Romances sans paroles / Je n'aime que toi / Nineteen / Kenneth Baker / Better to be bitter.
Aug 89. (7") *(BIAS 132-7)* **INVISIBLE STATE. / LA VILLE**
Dec 89. (cd-ep) *<W2-6307>* **INVISIBLE STATE**
– Invisible state / Kenneth Baker / New Orleans / Angelique / Born blonde / Black souls under white skies.
Dec 89. (7") *(BIAS 146-7)* **ROMANCE SANS PAROLE. / MANDY**
Jun 91. (cd-s) *(BIAS 196CD)* **NUMBER FIVE / TOMORROW / GREEN**
Aug 91. (cd/c/lp) *(CD/MC+/BIAS 176)* **JOLIE**
– Number five / Pretty five / I'm in love forever / Anglesey / In the summer / Gustave cafe / Tears of Maxine / Violet Lee / Souvenir of summer / The lie that tells the truth.
Nov 91. (cd-s) *(BIAS 213CD)* **I'M IN LOVE FOREVER / ANGLESEY / BORN BLONDE**

Tora! / not iss.

1995. (7"m; as BEATITUDE) *(TORA! 1)* **BABY IN BRYLCREEM / 19 SUMMERS / MELODY SAID**
(above with **TIM BRADSHAW** – guitar / **TUPPY RUTTER** – bass / **PAUL BARLOW** – drums)

Ncompass / not iss.

Sep 98. (cd-ep) *(NCOMCDSIN 003)* **EVERY LOSER IN LONDON / HERBERT LOM / MEADOWHALL / GOODNIGHT (live)**
Sep 98. (cd) *(NCOMCD 004)* **HAPPINESS AND OTHER CRIMES**
– Susan's Soho parties / Every loser in London / Jimmy Mac Cay / Broadway / For the good of the people / Hippy hoorah / Atmosphere / Melody said / The Tipton slasher / Terry toy / Marie-Claire / Suddenly last summer / Cherry orchard / Le monde selon Jimmy / Live a little longer.

— PRITCHARD has since provided guests vox for CONCORDE MUSIC CLUB

PROFESSIONALS
(see under ⇒ SEX PISTOLS; 70's section)

PSYCHEDELIC FURS

Formed: London, England... 1977 by RICHARD and TIM BUTLER, JOHN ASHTON, ROGER MORRIS and DUNCAN KILBURN, who eventually completed the line-up with drummer VINCE ELY. Gaining a bit of much needed credibility via a Radio One John Peel session, the band signed to 'Epic-C.B.S.' in 1978 and released a debut single, 'WE LOVE YOU', late the following year. This was followed in early 1980 by a classic second single, 'SISTER EUROPE' and a Top 20 eponymous debut album. A vintage slice of post-punk miserabilism tracing the classic linage of VELVET UNDERGROUND, ROXY MUSIC, 'BOWIE etc., the record's discordant mesh of jagged melody, inwardly spiralling guitar and BUTLER's cracked monotone placed The PSYCHEDELIC FURS firmly at the forefront of the alternative rock scene. Subsequently relocating to New York, they worked on an even better follow-up, 'TALK TALK TALK' (1981), a record which might've made more concessions to pop/rock convention but made up for it with gloriously subversive songwriting; 'INTO YOU LIKE A TRAIN' was leeringly self explanatory, 'DUMB WAITERS' tripped out on a mangled STOOGES vibe while the lugubrious 'PRETTY IN PINK' provided the 'FURS with a near-Top 40 hit and remains their best known track. With ex-BIRTHDAY PARTY man, PHIL CALVERT, replacing ELY (who teamed up with ROBYN HITCHCOCK), the band hooked up with TODD RUNDGREN for the disappointing 'FOREVER NOW' (1982), a combination that looked interesting on paper but somehow failed to translate onto vinyl. The record nevertheless made the UK Top 20, as did 1984's 'MIRROR MOVES', by which time line-up changes had seen KEITH FORSEY and MARS WILLIAMS replace CALVERT and founding members KILBURN and MORRIS. Despite flashes of darkly melodic inspiration, a suffocatingly slick production erased any traces of mystery or danger, further testing the patience of many longtime fans. A re-released 'PRETTY IN PINK' (issued to coincide with the film of the same name, inspired by the song itself) illustrated just how lifeless the newer material was, while the terminally dull 'MIDNIGHT TO MIDNIGHT' (1987) showed no signs of an imminent return to form. With ELY back on the drum stool, a further late 80's effort, 'BOOK OF DAYS' (1989), attempted

PSYCHEDELIC FURS (cont) — THE GREAT INDIE DISCOGRAPHY — The 1980s

a more credible approach to diminishing commercial returns and minimal critical reaction. Finally, after 1991's 'WORLD OUTSIDE', the band hung up their 'FURS for good, BUTLER going on to form LOVE SPIT LOVE with RICHARD FORTUS and FRANK FERRER, releasing a one-off eponymous album for 'Imago-R.C.A.' in 1994. • **Songwriters:** RICHARD BUTLER + FURS, except MACK THE KNIFE (Bobby Darin).

Album rating: THE PSYCHEDELIC FURS (*8) / TALK TALK TALK (*7) / FOREVER NOW (*7) / MIRROR MOVES (*6) / MIDNIGHT TO MIDNIGHT (*5) / ALL OF THIS AND NOTHING compilation (*7) / BOOK OF DAYS (*4) / WORLD OUTSIDE (*4) / B-SIDES AND LOST GROOVES collection (*5) / SHOULD GOD FORGET: A RETROSPECTIVE double compilation (*8)

RICHARD BUTLER (b. 5 Jun'56, Kingston-Upon-Thames, England) – vocals / **JOHN ASHTON** (b.30 Nov'57) – lead guitar / **ROGER MORRIS** – guitar / **TIM BUTLER** (b. 7 Dec'58) – bass / **DUNCAN KILBURN** – saxophone, keyboards / **VINCE ELY** – drums (ex-UNWANTED)

			Epic	not iss.
			C.B.S.	Columbia
Oct 79.	(7")	(EPC 8005) **WE LOVE YOU. / PULSE**	-	-
Feb 80.	(7")	(CBS 8179) **SISTER EUROPE. / ******		
Mar 80.	(lp/c)	(CBS/40 84084) <36791> **THE PSYCHEDELIC FURS**	18	-

 – India / Sister Europe / Imitation of Christ / Fall / Pulse / We love you / Wedding song / Blacks / Radio / Flowers. (re-iss. Mar83) (cd-iss. Apr89 & Feb99; 493343-2) (<cd re-iss. Mar02 on 'Columbia'+=; UK-506362-2 / US-85918>) – Susan's strange / Soap commercial / Mack the knife / Flowers (demo).

Oct 80.	(7")	(CBS 9059) **MR. JONES. / SUSAN'S STRANGE**		
Apr 81.	(7")	(A 1166) **DUMB WAITERS. / DASH**	59	
May 81.	(lp/c)	(CBS/40 84892) <37339> **TALK TALK TALK**	30	89

 – Dumb waiters / Pretty in pink / I wanna sleep with you / No tears / Mr. Jones / Into you like a train / It goes on / So run down / All of this and nothing / She is mine. (re-iss. Nov84 lp/c; CBS/40 32539) (cd-iss. Apr89; CD 32539) (cd re-iss. Mar96 on 'Columbia'; 483663-2) (<cd re-iss. Mar02 on 'Columbia'+=; UK-506363-2 / US-85917>) – Mr. Jones / So run down / All this and nothing (demo).

| Jun 81. | (7"/7"pic-d) | (A/WA 1327) **PRETTY IN PINK. / MACK THE KNIFE** | 43 | |

 (12"+=) (A13 1327) – Soap commercial.

— **PHIL CALVERT** – drums (ex-BIRTHDAY PARTY) repl. ELY (to ROBYN HITCHCOCK)

| Jul 82. | (7") | (A 2549) <03197> **LOVE MY WAY. / AEROPLANE (dance mix)** | 42 | |
| Sep 82. | (lp/c) | (CBS/40 85909) <38261> **FOREVER NOW** | 20 | 61 |

 – Forever now / Love my way / Goodbye / Only you and I / Sleep comes down / President Gas / Run and run / Danger / No easy street / Yes I do (merry-go-round). (c+=) – Shadow. (re-iss. Apr86 lp/c; CBS/40 85909) (<cd re-iss. Mar02 on 'Columbia'+=; UK 506364-2 / US- 85916>) – Alice's house / Aeroplane / I don't want to be your shadow / Mary go round / President gas (live) / No easy street (live).

| Oct 82. | (7") | (A 2665) <03340> **DANGER. / (I DON'T WANT TO BE YOUR) SHADOW** | | |

 (12"+=) (TA 2665) – Goodbye (mix).

| Feb 83. | (7") | <03340> **LOVE MY WAY. / SHADOW** | - | 44 |
| May 83. | (7") | <03930> **PRESIDENT GAS. / RUN AND RUN** | - | |

— **KEITH FORSEY** – drums repl. CALVERT who joined CRIME & THE CITY SOLUTION / **MARS WILLIAMS** – saxophone (ex-WAITRESSES) repl. KILBURN + MORRIS

| Mar 84. | (7"/12") | (A/TA 4300) **HEAVEN. / HEARTBEAT (remix)** | 29 | - |
| May 84. | (lp/c/cd) | (CBS/40 25950) <39278> **MIRROR MOVES** | 15 | 43 |

 – The ghost in you / Here come cowboys / Heaven / Heartbeat / My time / Like a stranger / Alice's house / Only a game / Highwire days. (re-iss. Jan87 lp/c; 450356-1/-4) (cd-iss. May87; CD 25950) (re-iss. Jun94 on 'Columbia' cd/c; 450356-2/-4)

| May 84. | (7"/7"pic-d) | (A/WA 4470) <04416> **THE GHOST IN YOU. / CALYPSO DUB** | 68 | 59 |

 (12"+=) (TA 4470) – President Gas (live).

Jul 84.	(7")	<04577> **HERE COME COWBOYS. / ANOTHER EDGE**	-	
Sep 84.	(7")	<04627> **HEAVEN. / ALICE'S HOUSE**	-	
Oct 84.	(7"/12")	(A/TA 4654) **HEARTBEAT (Mendelssohn mix). / MY TIME**		

 (d7"+=) (DA 4654) – Here comes cowboys / Heaven.

— **PAUL GARISTO** – drums repl. DORSEY. <below 45 on 'A&M' US>

| Apr 86. | (7") | <2826> **PRETTY IN PINK. / (dub)** | - | 41 |
| Aug 86. | (7"/7"pic-d) | (A/WA 7242) **PRETTY IN PINK (film version). / LOVE MY WAY** | 18 | - |

 (12"+=) (TA 7242) – ('A'version).
 (d7"+=) (DA 7242) – Heaven / Heartbeat.

| Oct 86. | (7") | (650183-7) <06420> **HEARTBREAK BEAT. / NEW DREAM** | 26 | Mar87 |

 (12"+=) (650186-6) – ('A'version).
 (free c-s w/7"+=) (650183-0) – Sister Europe / Into you like a train / President Gas.

| Jan 87. | (7") | (FURS 3) **ANGELS DON'T CRY. / NO RELEASE** | | |

 (free c-s w/7"+=) (FURSD 3) – We love you / Pretty in pink / Love my way.

| Feb 87. | (lp/c/cd) | (450256-1/-4/-2) <40466> **MIDNIGHT TO MIDNIGHT** | 12 | 29 |

 – Heartbreak beat / Shock / Shadow in my heart / Angels don't cry / Midnight to midnight / One more word / Torture / All of the law / No release * / Petty in pink. (cd+= *) (re-iss. Feb89; 463399-1/-4/-2)

| Apr 87. | (7") | <07224> **SHOCK. / PRESIDENT GAS (live)** | - | |
| Jun 87. | (7") | **ANGEL'S DON'T CRY. / MACK THE KNIFE** | - | |

— **VINCE ELY** – drums returned to repl. GARISTO (to CURE) + WILLIAMS

| Jul 88. | (7") | (FURS 4) <07974> **ALL THAT MONEY WANTS. / BIRDLAND** | 75 | |

 (12"+=) (FURST 4) – No easy street (live).
 (d7"++=) (FURSEP 4) – Heaven (live).
 (cd-s++=) (CDFURS 4) – No tears (live).

| Aug 88. | (lp/c/cd) | (461110-1/-4/-2) <44377> **ALL OF THIS AND NOTHING** (compilation) | 67 | |

 – President Gas / All that money wants / Imitation of Christ / Sister Europe / Love my way / Highwire days / Dumb waiters / Pretty in pink / Ghost in you / Heaven / Heartbreak beat / All of this and nothing. (cd+=) – No easy street / She is mine. (re-iss. Apr91 & Oct00 cd/c; 461110-2)

| Nov 88. | (7") | <38-08499> **HEAVEN. / INDIA** | - | |
| Nov 89. | (lp/c/cd) | (465982-1/-4/-2) <45412> **BOOK OF DAYS** | 74 | |

 – Entertain me / Book of days / Should God forget / Torch / Parade / Mother-son / House / Wedding / I don't mine.

| Jan 90. | (7"/7"pic-d) | (FURS/+P 5) **HOUSE. / WATCHTOWER** | | - |

 (10") (FURSQT 5) – ('A'side) / ('A'-Flashback mix) / Badman / Totch (electric).
 (cd-s+=) – (CDFURS 5) – Badman / Torch (electric).

— **BUTLER, ASHTON + BUTLER** recruited **DON YALLITCH** – drums repl. ELY

			East West	Epic
Jun 91.	(7"/c-s)	(73855) **UNTIL SHE COMES. / MAKE IT MINE**		-

 (12"+=/cd-s+=) (73855) – Sometimes / ('A'remix).

| Jul 91. | (c-s,cd-s) | <74055> **UNTIL SHE COMES / SOMETIMES** | - | |
| Jul 91. | (cd)(lp/c) | (9031 74669-2)(WX 422/+C) <74669> **WORLD OUTSIDE** | 68 | |

 – Valentine / In my head / Until she comes / Don't be a girl / Sometimes / Tearing down / There's a world / Get a room / Better days / All about you. (re-iss. cd Feb95; same)

| Sep 91. | (7"/c-s) | **DON'T BE A GIRL. / GET A ROOM (acoustic)** | | |

 (12"+=/cd-s+=) – (2 'A'versions).

— disbanded after above

– compilations, etc. –

on 'C.B.S.' or 'Columbia' unless mentioned otherwise

| Nov 82. | (c-ep) | (A 2909) **GREATEST ORIGINAL HITS** | | |

 – Sister Europe / Pretty in pink / Dumb waiters / Love my way. (re-iss. Mar83.as 7"ep.)

| Sep 86. | (c-ep) | (450130-4) **THE 12" TAPE** | | - |

 – Pretty in pink / Love my way / Heaven / Heartbeat / Ghost in you.

| Jan 92. | (7") | **PRETTY IN PINK. / (B-side by the Only Ones)** | | |

 (cd-s+=) – (other track by Only Ones).

Oct 91.	(cd)	Castle; (CCSCD 308) **THE COLLECTION**		
May 95.	(cd)	Columbia; (480363-2) <57889> **B SIDES AND LOST GROOVES**		Oct94
Feb 97.	(cd)	Strange Fruit; (SFRSCD 003) **RADIO ONE SESSIONS**		
Oct 97.	(d-cd)	(487389-2) **SHOULD GOD FORGET: A RETROSPECTIVE**		

 – India / Sister Europe / Pulse / Mack the knife / Blacks / We love you / Imitation of Christ / Soap commercial / Pretty in pink / Blacks / I wanna sleep with you / Merry go round / President Gas / LOve my way / Sleep comes down / I don't want to be your shadow / Alice's house / The ghost in you / Here come cowboys / Heaven / Highwire days / Heartbeat / All of the law / Heartbreak beat / All that money wants / Entertain me / Should God forget / Torch / Get a room / Until she comes / All about you / There's a world outside.

| Mar 02. | (cd) | Sony; (506035-2) <86191> **BEAUTIFUL CHAOS (GREATEST HITS LIVE)** | | Nov01 |
| Oct 02. | (3xcd-box) | (509506-2) **THE PSYCHEDELIC FURS / TALK TALK TALK / FOREVER NOW** | | - |

LOVE SPIT LOVE

RICHARD BUTLER – vocals / **RICHARD FORTUS** – guitar / **TIM BUTLER** – bass / **FRANK FERRER** – drums

			Imago-RCA	Imago-RCA
Oct 94.	(cd/c)	(72787 21055-2/-4) <21030> **LOVE SPIT LOVE**		

 – Seventeen / Superman / Half a life / Jigsaw / Change in the weather / Wake up / Am I wrong / Green / Please / Codeine / St. Mary's gate / More. (<d-cd-iss. Feb01 on 'Burning Airlines'+=; PILOT 41>) – All she wants / Codeine (acoustic) / More than money (alt. take) / Song (acoustic) / Wake up (acoustic) / Wake up (live) / I am wrong (video) / Change in the weather (video).

| Oct 94. | (c-s,cd-s) | <25073> **AM I WRONG / CODEINE** | - | 83 |

PSYCHIC TV

Formed: London, England … 1982 from the ashes of THROBBING GRISTLE by NEIL MEGSON aka GENESIS P.ORRIDGE and PETER CHRISTOPHERSON. The latter soon departed to form COIL and P.ORRIDGE susbsequently steered PSYCHIC TV through its various incarnations over the course of the 80's and into the 90's. Drawing inspiration from situationist media manipulation, the cut-up technique of William Burroughs, the magick theories of Alistair Crowley and pagan/shamanistic ritual, P.ORRIDGE plotted a determinedly subversive path through what he perceived as a dysfunctional society controlled by "the managers" and organised religion. Throughout their weird and wonderful career PSYCHIC TV have been backed by the Temple Ov Psychick Youth (TOPY), a cult-style band of followers who take the P.ORRIDGE philosophy as gospel. Musically, PSYCHIC TV's early work – as heard on albums such as 'FORCE THE HAND OF CHANCE' (1982), 'DREAMS LESS SWEET' (1983) and 'THEMES' (1985) – carried on where THROBBING GRISTLE left off with an often barely listenable sonic barrage of scraping noise, jackboot rhythms and assorted disturbing samples ranging from gutteral growls to the utterances of P.ORRIDGE favourites like Charles Manson and Crowley. The mid-80's proved a turning point, however, as PTV became more immersed in psychedelic culture and unveiled their own take on the movement which they dubbed 'Hyperdelic'. 1986 also saw PTV score an unlikely minor UK hit with their most accessible (and surprisingly affecting) recording to date, 'GODSTAR', a tribute to long time gone ROLLING STONES founder BRIAN JONES (another P.ORRIDGE obsession) which rather niftily cut-up the riff from 'Brown Sugar'. The 60's/rejuvenated psychedelia theme continued with the 'MAGICKAL MYSTERY D TOUR' EP, featuring a faithful, if rather droning cover of The Beach Boys' 'GOOD VIBRATIONS'. 1986 also saw the initiation of an ambitious project to release 23 different live albums from

23 different countries on the 23rd of each month (!), 23 apparently being a magickal number. P.ORRIDGE's interest in consciousness altering substances and their ability to transform society deepened with the advent of rave culture, a visit to Chicago inspiring a series of acid-house singles subsequently collected together as 1990's 'HIGH JACK: THE POLITICS OF ECSTASY'. Much like The SHAMAN, PSYCHIC TV espoused the transformational possibilities inherent in club culture and following PSYCHIC TV's exile to California, P.ORRIDGE found a natural home in the sunshine state's consciousness altering community and a natural collaborator in veteran acid guru TIMOTHY LEARY. The forced exile came in 1992 following a police raid on The Temple Ov Psychick Youth's Hackney base, officers confiscating videos, books and magazines after a clip from a P.ORRIDGE performance was screened as part of a TV documentary on child abuse; on holiday in Nepal at the time, P.ORRIDGE and his partner were warned they could face arrest and lose custody of their daughters should they return to the UK. Unsurprisingly they decamped to the more liberal climes of Cali. Intrigued readers are pointed towards the 1995 video, 'Beauty From Thee Beast', as an entertaining introduction to PTV, the songs interspersed with clips of P.ORRIDGE dispensing his eco-shaman-evolutionary philosophy.

Album rating: FORCE THE HAND OF CHANCE (*6) / DREAMS LESS SWEET (*5) / MOUTH OF THE NIGHT (*5) / THEMES II (*5) / BEAUTY FROM THEE BEAST compilation (*6)

GENESIS P.ORRIDGE (b. Feb'49) – vocals, keyboards, violin, bass, percussion (ex-THROBBING GRISTLE) / **PETER 'SLEAZY' CHRISTOPHERSON** – organ, synthesizer, vocals (ex-THROBBING GRISTLE) / **ALEX FERGUSSON** – guitar, vocals (ex-ALTERNATIVE TV) / with guests **KENNY WELLINGTON + CLAUDE DEPPA** – brass / **ANDREW POPPY** – strings / **MARC ALMOND** – vocals

Some Bizzare / not iss.

Dec 82. (lp) (*PSY 1*) **FORCE THE HAND OF CHANCE**
– Just drifting / Terminus / Stolen kisses / Caresse / Guiltless / No go go / Ov power / Message from the temple. *(with free lp)* – THEMES:- The full pack / The mad organist / Catalan. *(<cd-iss. Jan97 on 'Cleopatra'; CLEO 9595-2>) (cd rom-iss.Nov97; SBZ 026CD)*

Dec 82. (7") (*PTV 1*) **JUST DRIFTING. / BREAKTHROUGH**
(12") (*PTV 1T*) – ('A'side) / Just drifting (midnight).

added **PAULA P.ORRIDGE** – drums, vibes / **GEOFF RUSHTON** – bass, vibes / + a cast of extra musicians & singers

C.B.S. / not iss.

Dec 83. (d-lp/c) (*CBS/40 25737*) **DREAMS LESS SWEET**
– Hymn 23 / The orchids / Botanica / Glove / Iron / Always is always / White nights / Finale / Eleusis / Medmenham / Ancient lights / Proof on / Survival / Eden 1 / Eden 2 / Eden 3 / Clouds without water / Black moon / Silver and gold / In the nursery / Circle. *(cd-iss. Aug92 on 'Some Bizzare'; SBZCD 011) <US cd-iss. 1196 on 'Thirsty Ear'; 57021>*

—— **BEE** – bass, vocals (ex-GETTING THE FEAR) repl. PETER who formed COIL / added **JORDI VALLIS** (JOHN GOSLING – ex-ZOS KIA, also a member at this time)

Sordid Sentimentale / not iss.

Jun 84. (7") (*SS3 000*) **ROMAN P. / TOPY: NEUROLOGY**

French Temple / Wax Trax

Aug 84. (12") (*TOPY 001*) **UNCLEAN. / MIRRORS**
Dec 84. (ltd-lp) (*TOPY 002*) **NEW YORK SCUM HATERS**
Dec 84. (pic-lp; deleted on next of release) (*TOPY 003*) **A PAGAN DAY - 25TH DECEMBER 1984**
– Catalogue / W kiss / Opium / Cold steel / Los Angeles / Iceland / Translucent carriages / Paris / Baby's gone away / Alice / New sexuality / Farewell. *(black-lp re-iss. Mar87; TOPY 017) (cd-iss. Jul94 on 'Cleopatra'; CLEO 9469-2)*

—— **MONTE CZAZZA** – guitar / **HILMAR ORN HILMARSSON** – keyboards / **MAX** – drums; repl. BEE & JORDI

Jul 85. (lp) (*TOPY 004*) **THEMES II**
Sep 85. (lp) (*TOPY 008*) **THEMES 3**
(*re-iss. Feb87; TOPY 019*)
Nov 85. (lp/c) (*TOPY/+C 010*) **MOUTH OF THE NIGHT**
– Dawn / Ordeal of innocence / The wedding / Rebis / Separation and undressing / Discopravity / The immune zone / Climax. *(pic-lp; TOPIC 010) (cd-iss. Nov89; TOPY 034CD) (cd re-iss. Nov93 on 'Trident'; VAULT 23)*

—— **PHILIP EBB** – keyboards / **MOUSE** – bass / **MATTHEW BEST** – drums; repl. recent three above

Mar 86. (7"; as PSYCHIC TV & The ANGELS OF LIGHT) (*TOPY 009*) **GODSTAR. / ('A'-BJ mix)** 67
(d7"+=) (*TOPYS 009*) – Discopravity (fish mix) / Yes it's the B side.
(12"/12"pic-d) (*TOPYH/TOPIC 009*) – ('A'-Hyperdelic mix) / ('A'-California mix).

—— **GENESIS, PAULA + MATTHEW** recruited **SCOTT** – guitar / **DAVE TIBET** – bass (ex-23 SKIDOO); to repl. FERGUSSON

Sep 86. (7") (*TOPY 023*) **GOOD VIBRATIONS. / ROMAN P** 65
(12"ep+=) **MAGICKAL MYSTERY D-TOUR** (*TOPYD 023*) – Interzone / Hex-sex / Godstar (ugly mix) / Je t'aime.
(12"ep) (*TOPYT 023*) – ('A'&'B'mixes) / Interzone / Hex-sex.

—— returned to anti-commercial antics by releasing a series of live albums issued on the 23rd of each month (interspersed with new recordings)

Nov 86. (lp) (*TOPY 014*) **LIVE IN PARIS**
Dec 86. (lp) (*TOPY 015*) **LIVE IN TOKYO**
Jan 87. (lp) (*TOPY 016*) **LIVE IN GLASGOW**
Mar 87. (lp) (*TOPY 018*) **LIVE IN HEAVEN**
– I hear vocals / The leg song / Paradise lost / Lies and spies / Revenge on God / Stolen lightning / Seat of broken glass / Redium.
Apr 87. (12") (*TOPY 022*) **MAGICK DEFENDS ITSELF. / PAPAL BREAKDANCE**
Jun 87. (lp) (*TOPY 026*) **LIVE IN REYKJAVIK**
Jul 87. (lp) (*TOPY 027*) **LIVE EN SUISSE**
Aug 87. (lp) (*TOPY 028*) **LIVE IN TORONTO**
Sep 87. (lp) (*TOPY 029*) **LIVE IN GOTTINGEN**
Dec 87. (m-lp) (*TOPY 030*) **TEMPORARY TEMPLE**
Feb 88. (pic-lp) (*TOPY 031*) **PSYCHIC TV**
Mar 88. (pic-lp) (*TOPY 032*) **ALBUM 10**
May 88. (lp) (*TOPY 036*) **LIVE AT MARDI GRAS**
Jun 88. (blue-lp) (*TOPY 038*) **ALLEGORY AND SELF: (THEE STARLET FIRE)**
(re-iss. Aug91 lp/cd; TOPY 038/+CD) (cd-iss. Sep94 on 'Cleopatra'; CLEO 9491-2)
Aug 88. (12"; PSYCHIC TV / JACK THE TAB) (*TOPY 037*) **TUNE IN (TURN ON TO THEE ACID TAB)**
Oct 88. (12"; by GENESIS P. ORRIDGE) (*TOPY 040*) **JOY. / THEE POLITICS OV ECSTASY**
Dec 88. (lp) (*TOPY 042*) **LIVE AT THEE CIRCUS**
Apr 89. (lp) (*TOPY 045*) **LIVE AT THEE RITZ**
May 89. (lp/c/cd) (*TOPY 46/+C/CD*) **KONDOLE / COPYCAT**
(cd re-iss. Jan94 on 'Silent'; SR 933-2)
Aug 89. (lp) (*TOPY 047*) **LIVE AT THEE PYRAMID NYC 1988**
Nov 89. (12") (*TOPY 048T*) **LOVE, WAR, RIOT. / EVE OF DESTRUCTION (vocoder mixes)**
—— TIBET had already joined DEATH IN JUNE (1989-90)
Feb 90. (12") (*TOPY 050*) **JE T'AIME (Mistress mix). / WICKED**
Mar 90. (lp/c/cd) (*TOPY 049/+CC/CD*) <*WAX 7129*> **TOWARDS THEE INFINITE BEAT**
– Infinite beat / Bliss / Drone zone / S.M.I.L.E. / I.C. water / Black rainbow / A short sharp taste OV / Mistress mix / Horror house / Jigsaw / Alien be-in / Stick insect / Money for E. *(cd re-iss. Sep94 on 'Visionary'; VICD 002)*
Jul 90. (12"ep)(cd-ep) (*TOPYT 051*)(*TOPY 051CD*) **BEYOND THEE INFINITE BEAT (Ravemaster mixes)**
(cd re-iss. Dec94 on 'Visionary'; VICD 004)
Sep 90. (cd) (*TOPY 052CD*) **LIVE AT THEE BERLIN WALL VOLUME 1**
Sep 90. (cd) (*TOPY 053CD*) **LIVE AT THEE BERLIN WALL VOLUME 2**
Nov 90. (7"etched) (*TOPY 058*) **I.C. WATER. / ALIEN BE IN**
(12"+=) (*TOPYT 058*) – ('A'versions).
Jan 91. (lp/cd) (*TOPY 020/+CD*) **LIVE IN BREGENZ**
Apr 91. (cd) (*TOPY 054CD*) **THEE CITY OV TOKYO, THEE CITY OV NEW YORK, MIDNIGHT MUSIC**
Nov 91. (cd) (*TOPY 055CD*) **CITY OV PARIS**
Nov 91. (cd) (*TOPY 062CD*) **A REAL LIVE SWEDISH SHOW**
Sep 93. (lp/cd) (*TOPY 068/+CD*) **PEAK HOUR (compilation)**
Jan 94. (12") (*TOPY 070*) **RE-MIND. / TRIBAL**
Jul 94. (12"/cd-s) (*TOPY 077/+CD*) **TRIBAL DRUM CLUB (four versions)**

Visionary / not iss.

Sep 94. (cd) (*VICD 001*) **ULTRADRUG**
– Scoring / Tempted / Swallow / Bloodstream / B-on-E / Constant high / Back to reality / Thee eagle has landed / S.U.C.K. or know / Tempter / Still B-on-E / Gone paranoid / Loose nuts.
Nov 94. (cd) (*VICD 003*) **A HOLLOW COST**
Apr 95. (cd) (*VICD 005*) **SIRENS**
– Stargods / Skreemer / Re-united (mixes 1,2,3 & 4) / Sirens.
Oct 95. (cd) (*VICD 006*) **BEAUTY FROM THEE BEAST (THEE BEAST OV GENESIS P.ORRIDGE & PSYCHIC TV)** (compilation)
– Roman P / Good vibrations / Hex sex / Godstar / Je t'aime / United '94 / Eve ov destruction / S.M.I.L.E. / I.C. water / Horror house / Back to reality / Godstar (hyperdelic mix) / Re-united (mix 4).

Etherworld / not iss.

Sep 97. (cd; by GENESIS P. ORRIDGE & THE WHITE STAINS) (*ETW 001*) **AT STOCKHOLM**

– compilations, etc. –

Apr 87. (lp; shared with Z.EV) *Dossier; (ST 3001)* **BERLIN ATONAL (live)**
– Nursery times / Skinhead moonstomp '84.
Aug 93. (cd) *Trident; (TIBCD 10)* **RARE AND ALIVE**
Sep 93. (cd) *Dossier; (EFA 08441-2)* **TEMPORARY TEMPLE / ATONAL**
Jan 94. (cd) *Semantic; (SSCDV 01)* **LISTEN TODAY**
Feb 94. (cd) *Dossier; (EFA 08454-2)* **THEE TRANSMUTION OF MERCURY**
Mar 94. (cd) *Cleopatra; (CLEO 6508-2)* **HEX SEX (THE SINGLES)**
Jun 94. (cd) *Dossier; (EFA 06446-2)* **MEIN GOTTINGEN**
Jan 95. (cd) *Dossier; (EFA 08459-2)* **ELECTRONIC NEWSPAPER**
Mar 95. (cd) *Dossier; (EFA 08467-2)* **CATHEDRAL ENGINE**
Apr 95. (cd) *Cleopatra; (CLEO 9518-2)* **GODSTAR (THE SINGLES PART II)**
Jul 95. (cd) *Dossier; (EFA 08470-2)* **ELECTRONIC NEWSPAPER ISSUE 2**
Nov 95. (cd) *Dossier; (EFA 08476-2)* **ELECTRONIC NEWSPAPER ISSUE 3**
Apr 96. (cd) *Cleopatra; (CLEO 9665CD)* **TRIP RESET**
Apr 96. (cd) *Cleopatra; (<CLEO 9711CD>)* **COLD BLUE TORCH**
May 96. (cd) *Cold Spring; (CSR 10CD)* **THOSE WHO DO NOT**
Jan 97. (cd) *Dossier; (DCD 9054)* **AL OR AL**
Feb 98. (cd) *Cold Spring;* **THEMES 2 - A PRAYER FOR DEREK JARMAN**

PUDDLE

Formed: Dunedin, New Zealand ... 1984 by GEORGE D HENDERSON alongside JENNY CROOKS, ROSS JACKSON and NORMAN DUFTY, although leader GEORGE subsequently supplanted these members with others including PETER GUTTERIDGE and LINDSAY MAITLAND; the latter was to die of an overdose in 1991. A 'Flying Nun' outfit (where else could they go?), The PUDDLE splashed out with their debut 12" EP, 'POP LIB' (1986), a noisy, experimental work with glints of psychedelia. Further low-key releases, including the ALASTAIR GALBRAITH-produced set, 'INTO THE MOON' (1992), were particularly potent down under but didn't merit a UK release.
• **Covered:** CANDY AND A CURRANT BUN (Pink Floyd).

Album rating: INTO THE MOON (*5) / LIVE AT THE TEDDY BEARS CLUB (*4)

GEORGE D HENDERSON – vocals, guitar (ex-ANDBAND) / **ROSS JACKSON** – bass / **JENNY CROOKS** – keyboards / **NORMAN DUFTY** – drums

			Flying Nun	not iss.
1986.	(12"ep) *(PUD/THIS 001)* **POP LIB** – Junk / Jealousy / Lacsydaisical / Magic words.		-	- NewZ

— **HENDERSON** recruited numerous musicians incl. **NORMA O'MALLEY** – vocals, flute / **RICHARD COTTON** – keyboards / **VIKKI WILKINSON** – bass / **LESLEY PARIS** – drums / **LINDSAY MAITLAND** – cornet / **PETER GUTTERIDGE** – guitar

1992.	(cd) *(FNCD 164)* **INTO THE MOON**		-	- NewZ

– The white birds / Psych thing / Monogamy / Into the Moon / Rat park / K3 / Everything allright / Dr. Brill / Sodom and Gomorrah / Interstellar gothic / Spaceship #9 / Billie and Franz / Candy and a currant bun.

— sadly, MAITLAND was to die of an overdose in '91

1992.	(lp) *(FN 172)* **LIVE AT THE TEDDY BEARS CLUB** (rec.1987)		-	- NewZ
1993.	(7") *(FN 278)* **THURSDAY. / TOO HOT TO BE COOL**		-	- NewZ
			Acetone	not iss.
1995.	(7") **THE POWER OF LOVE. /**		-	- French
1995.	(lp; w-drawn) **SONGS FOR EMILY VALENTINE**		-	- NewZ

— disbanded after above; HENDERSON was also part of MINK (future CLOUDBOY)

PULP

Formed: Sheffield, England ... 1981 originally as ARABACUS PULP by JARVIS COCKER while still at school. Following in the tradition of geek heart-throbs like BUDDY HOLLY, JARVIS COCKER achieved the knicker-wetting adulation he'd always aspired to through sheer hard graft and the determination of the downtrodden. His long road to stardom began in the mid-80's with the release of the 'IT' mini-lp and a prestigious JOHN PEEL session. Further releases like the 'LITTLE GIRL AND OTHER PIECES' (1985) and 'DOGS ARE EVERYWHERE' (1986) EP's saw COCKER developing as a wry and sharply observant chronicler of working class drudgery and sexual frustration, his inimitable brand of camped-up showmanship unhampered by a spell in a wheel chair (his injuries allegedly sustained after falling from a window when trying to show off to a woman!). By the release of 'FREAKS' (1987), the core of the latter day PULP was in place, violinist/guitarist RUSSELL SENIOR and keyboardist CANDIDA DOYLE beginning to move away from the band's early LEONARD COHEN/FALL hybrid to a more arty MONOCHROME SET/ULTRAVOX (John Foxx era!) type vibe. Most of the band moved to London in the late 80's, with bassist STEVE MACKAY and drummer NICHOLAS BANKS stabilising the line-up. In this incarnation, the sleek, new-look PULP recorded the 'SEPARATIONS' (1991) album, a more ambitious affair which spawned the endearingly glitter-tastic 'MY LEGENDARY GIRLFRIEND' single. The track's success encouraged PULP to set up their own label, 'Gift', through which they released a string of early 90's EP's, becoming critical darlings with some sections of the music press alongside fellow pop sculptors like SAINT ETIENNE. It wasn't long before the enigmatic JARVIS and crew were on the roster of 'Island', releasing their breakthrough 'HIS 'N' HERS' album in 1994. Previewed by the driving, tongue-in-cheek query of the 'DO YOU REMEMBER THE FIRST TIME?' single (a short film was released to tie in with the track, featuring various biz figureheads candidly talking about their "first time"), the album expertly dissected the sexual undertow of working class Britain with an incisive accuracy, mordant humour and lashings of glam posturing. The album made the UK Top 10, becoming a consistent seller and setting COCKER up as a fashion icon (Bri-Nylon, national health specs etc.). The singer was to become a star on the same scale as BRETT ANDERSON (Suede) following the success of the landmark 'COMMON PEOPLE' single. A classic pop song that almost made No.2 on the back of the Britpop zeitgeist, the single was a brilliant portrayal of the British class divide set to an almost 80's style synth-led backdrop. After the headlining act dropped out, PULP stepped in to put in one of the most acclaimed performances of their career at the 1995 Glastonbury festival, releasing the 'DIFFERENT CLASS' album in October to round off the most successful year to date in the band's career. With the social commentary as cutting as ever (the controversial 'SORTED FOR E'S AND WHIZZ') and their gift for effortlessly poignant pop intact ('DISCO 2000'), PULP consolidated their position as Britain's leading exponents of home-grown pop genius. A more downbeat COCKER returned late in '97 with the Top 10 hit, 'HELP THE AGED' (all monies going to that particular charity), while Britain awaited with much anticipation the porn-inspired 'THIS IS HARDCORE' set in '98. Another to hit the UK Top 10 (nowhere in America!), the record dabbled with the darker side of fame, set to a lounge-feel, sweaty background of a claustrophic Britain. Following up the difficult '... HARDCORE' set wasn't going to be easy, but with the aid of the legendary SCOTT WALKER as producer, PULP managed to issue a new album in the form of 'WE LOVE LIFE' (2001). Nearly three years in the making, the set reverted back to early PULP material such as songs found on 'HIS 'N' HERS' or the group's commercially brilliant 'DIFFERENT CLASS'. 'WICKERMAN' and 'THE TREES' were both fine examples of a band that had withstood the wintry climate of the music industry and still maintained an ounce of dignity and professionalism. WALKER, who had never produced before, made PULP sound as intriguing and as heart-felt as anything he has ever done. • **Songwriters:** COCKER + SIMON HINKLER collaborated on debut. COCKER, SENIOR, C. DOYLE, MANSELL penned, until 90's when COCKER was main contributor. • **Trivia:** COCKER and MACKAY directed videos for TINDERSTICKS and The APHEX TWIN. • **Note:** Not to be confused with other band fronted by ANDY BEAN + PAUL BURNELL, who released in 1979; LOW FLYING AIRCRAFT single.

Album rating: IT (*4) / FREAKS (*4) / SEPARATIONS (*5) / PULPINTRO – THE GIFT RECORDINGS compilation (*7) / HIS 'N' HERS (*9) / MASTERS OF THE UNIVERSE collecttion (*5) / DIFFERENT CLASS (*9) / THIS IS HARDCORE (*8) / WE LOVE LIFE (*7) / HITS compilation (*8)

JARVIS COCKER (b. Sep'62) – vocals, guitar, piano / **SIMON HINKLER** – keyboards, vocals repl. PETER DALTON / **PETER BOAM** – bass repl. JAMIE PINCHBECK who had repl. DAVID LOCKWOOD / **DAVID HINKLER** – keyboards, trombone / **GARY WILSON** – drums (of ARTERY) repl. WAYNE FURNISS who had repl. JIMMY SELLERS who had repl. MARK SWIFT

— plus guests **SASKIA COCKER + GILL TAYLOR** – b.vox / **TIMM ALLCARD** – keyboards

			Red Rhino	not iss.
Apr 83.	(m-lp) *(REDLP 29)* **IT**			-

– My lighthouse / Wishful thinking / Joking aside / Boats and trains / Blue girls / Love love / In many ways. *(cd-iss. Mar94 on 'Cherry Red'; CDMRED 112 w/drawn) (cd+=)* – Looking for life / Everybody's problem / There was. *(re-iss. cd Dec94 on 'Fire'; REFIRE CD15) (cd+=)* – Looking for life. *<US cd-iss. 1997 on 'Velvel'; 79750> (cd re-iss. Nov02 on 'Fire'+=; SFIRE 004CD)*

May 83.	(7") *(RED 32)* **MY LIGHTHOUSE (remix). / LOOKING FOR LIFE**			-
Sep 83.	(7") *(RED 37)* **EVERYBODY'S PROBLEM. / THERE WAS**			-

— **RUSSELL SENIOR** – guitar, violin, vocals; repl. DAVID

— **CANDIDA DOYLE** – keyboards, vocals; repl. SIMON who joined ARTERY then the MISSION)

— **MAGNUS DOYLE** – drums repl. GARY, SASKIA, GILL + TIMM

— **PETER MANSELL** – bass repl. BOAM

			Fire	not iss.
Nov 85.	(12"ep) *(FIRE 5)* **LITTLE GIRL AND OTHER PIECES** – Little girl (with blue eyes) / Simultaneous / Blue glow / The will to power. *(re-iss. Oct91)*			-
Jun 86.	(12"ep) *(BLAZE 10)* **DOGS ARE EVERYWHERE / THE MARK OF THE DEVIL. / 97 LOVERS / ABORIGINE / GOODNIGHT** *(re-iss. Oct91)*			-
Jan 87.	(7"/ext.12") *(BLAZE 17/+T)* **THEY SUFFOCATE AT NIGHT. / TUNNEL**			-
Mar 87.	(7"/12") *(BLAZE 21/+T)* **MASTER OF THE UNIVERSE (sanitised version). / MANON / SILENCE** *(re-iss. Oct91)*			-
May 87.	(lp) *(FIRE LP5)* **FREAKS**			-

– Fairground / I want you / Being followed home / Master of the universe / Life must be so wonderful / There's no emotion / Anorexic beauty / The never-ending story / Don't you know / They suffocate at night. *(cd-iss. Apr93; FIRE CD5) <US cd-iss. 1997 on 'Velvel'; 79752> (cd re-iss. Jul02; SFIRE 013CD)*

— **STEPHEN MACKAY** – bass repl. STEPHEN HAVENLAND who had repl. PETER

— **NICHOLAS BANKS** – drums, percussion repl. MAGNUS

Sep 90.	(12"ep) *(BLAZE 44T)* **MY LEGENDARY GIRLFRIEND. / IS THIS HOUSE? / THIS HOUSE IS CONDEMNED** *(re-iss. Oct91)*			-
Aug 91.	(12"ep/cd-ep) *(BLAZE 51 T/CD)* **COUNTDOWN. / DEATH GOES TO THE DISCO / COUNTDOWN (edit)** *(re-iss. Oct91)*			-
Oct 91.	(cd/c/lp) *(FIRE 33/22/11 026)* **SEPARATIONS**			-

– Love is blind / Don't you want me anymore / She's dead / Separations / Down by the river / Countdown / My legendary girlfriend / Death II / This house is condemned. *(re-iss. Jun92; same) <US cd-iss. 1995 on 'Razor & Tie'; 2090-2> (cd re-iss. Apr02; SFIRE 025CD)*

			Gift	not iss.
May 92.	(12"ep/cd-ep) *(GIF 1/+CD)* **O.U. (GONE GONE) / SPACE / O.U. (GONE GONE) (radio edit)**			-
Oct 92.	(12"ep/cd-ep) *(GIF 3/+CD)* **BABIES. / STYLOROC (NIGHTS OF SUBURBIA) / SHEFFIELD** – SEX CITY			-
Feb 93.	(7") *(7GIF 6)* **RAZZAMATAZZ. / INSIDE SUSAN (abridged; Stacks – 59 Lynhurst Grove)** (12"ep+/cd-ep+) *(GIF 6/+CD)* – (B-side; A STORY IN 3 PARTS).			-

			Island	Polygram
Oct 93.	(cd/c)(lp) *(IMCD/IMCT 159)(ILPM 2076)* <2076-518451> **PULPINTRO – THE GIFT RECORDINGS** (compilation)			

– Space / O.U. (gone gone) / Babies / Styloroc (nights of suburbia) / Razzamatazz / Sheffield – Sex city / Medley of stacks: Inside Susan (a story in 3 songs) Stacks – Inside Susan – 59 Lynthurst Grove.

Nov 93.	(7") *(IS 567)* **LIPGLOSS. / YOU'RE A NIGHTMARE**	50	
	(12"+=)(cd-s+=) *(12IS/CID 567)* – Deep fried in Kelvin. *(re-iss. Aug96) (re-iss. Oct96 on 7"red)*		
Mar 94.	(7"/c-s) *(IS/CIS 574)* **DO YOU REMEMBER THE FIRST TIME?. / STREET LITES**	33	
	(12"+=)(cd-s+=) *(12IS/CID 574)* - **The babysitter**. *(re-iss. Aug96, hit 73) (re-iss. Oct96 7"biege)*		
Apr 94.	(cd/c/lp) *(CID/ICT/ILPS 8025)* <524006> **HIS 'N' HERS**	9	Jun94
	– Joyriders / Lipgloss / Acrylic afternoons / Have you seen her lately? / She's a lady / Happy endings / Do you remember the first time? / Pink glove / Someone like the Moon / David's last summer.(cd,c+=) – Babies (remix).		
May 94.	(7"ep/c-ep/12"ep/cd-ep) *(IS/CIS/12IS/CID 595)* **THE SISTERS EP**	19	
	– Babies / Your sister's clothes / Seconds / His'n'hers. *(re-iss. Aug96) (re-iss. Oct96 on white 7"ep)*		
May 95.	(c-s) *(CIS 613)* **COMMON PEOPLE. / UNDERWEAR**	2	-
	(cd-s+=) *(CID 613)* – ('A'-Motiv8 mix) / ('A'-Vocoda mix). *(re-iss. Aug96) (re-iss. Oct96 7"yellow/12")*		
	(cd-s) *(CIDX 613)* – ('A'side) / Razzmatazz (acoustic) / Dogs are everywhere (acoustic) / Joyriders (acoustic)		

— Below second side (double A) caused controversy with tabloids and parents, due to its mis-use of drugs in JARVIS's lyrics. JARVIS was to become the hero to most and villain to the few early in 1996 at a certain awards ceremony (skinny J.C. vs. St.MICHAEL & the bouncers; who won? – you decide).

Sep 95.	(c-s) *(CIS 620)* **MIS-SHAPES / SORTED FOR E'S AND WIZZ**	2	-
	(cd-s+=) *(CID 620)* – P.T.A. (Parent Teacher Association) / Common people (live at Glastonbury). *(re-iss. Oct96 7"blue/12")*		
	(cd-s+=) *(CIDX 620)* – Common people (Motiv8 mix). *(re-iss. Aug96)*		
Oct 95.	(cd/c/lp) *(CID/ICT/ILPS 8041)* <524165> **DIFFERENT CLASS**	1	
	– Mis-shapes / Pencil skirt / Common people / I spy / Disco 2000 / Live bed show / Something changed / Sorted out for E's and wizz / F.E.E.L.I.N.G.C.A.L.L.E.D.L.O.V.E. / Underwear / Monday morning / Bar Italia.		
Nov 95.	(c-s) *(CIS 623)* **DISCO 2000 / ANSAPHONE**	7	-
	(cd-s+=) *(CID 623)* – ('A'-Motiv8 Gimp dub & Discoid mixes). *(re-iss. Aug96)* *(re-iss. Oct96 7"orange/12")*		
	(cd-s+=) *(CIDX 623)* – Live bed show (extended).		
Mar 96.	(c-s) *(CIS 632)* **SOMETHING CHANGED / MILE END**	10	-
	(cd-s+=) *(CID 632)* – F.E.E.L.I.N.G.C.A.L.L.E.D.L.O.V.E (The Moloko mix) / F.E.E.L.I.N.G.C.A.L.L.E.D.L.O.V.E. (live from Brixton Academy). *(re-iss. Aug96)* *(re-iss. Oct96 7"pink/12")*		
	now without SENIOR, who wanted to pursue new projects		
Nov 97.	(c-s/7") *(C+/IS 679)* **HELP THE AGED. / LAUGHING BOY**	8	-
	(cd-s+=) *(CID 679)* – Tomorrow never lies.		
Mar 98.	(c-s) *(CIS 695)* **THIS IS HARDCORE / LADIES MAN**	12	-
	(cd-s+=) *(CID 695)* – Professional.		
	(cd-s) *(CIDX 695)* – ('A'mixes).		
Mar 98.	(cd/c/d-lp) *(ILPSD/ICT/CID 8066)* <524492> **THIS IS HARDCORE**	1	
	– The fear / Dishes / Party hard / Help the aged / This is hardcore / TV movie / A little soul / I'm a man / Seductive Barry / Sylvia / Glory days / Day after the revolution.		
Jun 98.	(c-s) *(CIS 708)* **A LITTLE SOUL / COCAINE SOCIALISM**	22	-
	(cd-s+=) *(CID 708)* – Like a friend.		
	(cd-s) *(CIDX 708)* – ('A'alternative mix) / ('A'-Lafayette Velvet revisited mix) / That boy's evil.		
Sep 98.	(cd-s/cd-s) *(CIS/CID 719)* <572418> **PARTY HARD / WE ARE THE BOYZ / THE FEAR**	29	
	(cd-s) *(CIDX 719)* – ('A'mixes by Stretch'n'Vern & All Seeing I).		
Oct 01.	(cd-s) *(CID 786)* **SUNRISE / THE TREES / SUNRISE (fat truckers scott free mix)**	28	-
	(cd-s) *(CIDX 786)* – (first 2) / The trees (felled by I Monster).		
	(12") *(12IS 786)* – ('Aside) / The trees (felled by I Monster) / Sunrise (All Seeing I remix) / The trees (Lovejoy mix).		
Oct 01.	(cd/d-lp) *(CID/ILPSD 8109)* <586540> **WE LOVE LIFE**	6	
	– Weeds / Weeds II (the origin of the species) / The night that Minnie Temperley died / The trees / Wickerman / I love life / The birds in your garden / Bob Lind / Bad cover version / Roadkill / Sunrise.		
Apr 02.	(cd-s) *(CID 794)* **BAD COVER VERSION / YESTERDAY / FOREVER IN MY DREAMS**	27	-
	(cd-s) *(CIDX 794)* – ('A'-video mix) / Disco 2000 (by NICK CAVE) / Sorted? (by ROISON MURPHY).		
Nov 02.	(cd) *(CID 8126)* **HITS** (compilation)	71	-
	– Babies / Razzmatazz / Lipgloss / Do you remember the first time? / Common people / Underwear / Sorted for E's & wizz / Disco 2000 / Something changed / Help the aged / This is hardcore / A little soul / Party hard / The trees / Bad cover version / Sunrise / Last day of the miner's strike.		

– compilations, etc. –

Jun 94.	(cd/c/lp) *Fire; (FIRE CD/MC/LP 36)* **MASTERS OF THE UNIVERSE – PULP ON FIRE 1985-86**		
	– Little girl (with blue eyes) / Simultaneous / Blue glow / The will to power / Dogs are everywhere / The mark of the Devil / 97 lovers / Aborigine / Goodnight / They suffocate at night / Tunnel / Master of the universe (sanitised version) / Manon.		
Mar 96.	(d-cd/c/d-lp) *Nectar; (NTM CDD/C/LP 521)* **COUNTDOWN 1992-1983**	10	-
	– Countdown / Death goes to the disco / My legendary girlfriend / Don't you want me anymore / She's dead / Down by the river / I want you / Being followed home / Master of the universe / Don't you know / They suffocate at night / Dogs are everywhere / Mark of the Devil / 97 lovers / Little girl (with blue eyes) / Blue glow / My lighthouse / Wishful thinking / Blue girls / Countdown (extended).		
Jul 98.	(cd) *Connoisseur; (VSOPCD 256)* **DEATH GOES TO THE DISCO**		
Sep 98.	(cd) *E.M.I.; <79737>* **FRESHLY SQUEEZED (EARLY YEARS)**	-	-

PUSSY GALORE

Formed: Washington DC, USA ... 1985 by JON SPENCER and JULIE CAFRITZ, who first met at college in Providence, Rhode Island, the pair subsequently recruiting drummer JOHN HAMILL. The trio then invited photographer, CRISTINA MARTINEZ, to join up after she'd snapped them for the cover shot of their debut 7"ep, 'FEEL GOOD ABOUT YOUR BODY' (released on their own 'Shove' records). Featuring four tracks of primal hardcore, holocaustic industrial slime and scuzzy garage-punk, the band's nearest musical cousins were SONIC YOUTH, BIG BLACK and HUSKER DU, although PUSSY GALORE were in a noise terrorist league of their own. Adding NEIL HAGGERTY and replacing HAMMILL with former SONIC YOUTH man, BOB BERT, they took off to the more sympathetic New York, having slagged off local 'Dischord' label owner IAN McKAYE of MINOR THREAT (later FUGAZI). JON and CRISTINA set up home together, meeting up with the others to record their seriously deranged debut mini-set, 'GROOVY HATE FUCK' (1986), titles such as 'CUNT TEASE', 'TEENY PUSSY POWER' and 'YOU COOK LIKE A JEW', seeing the band court a sense of outrage that would characterise their whole career. In response to SONIC YOUTH's rumoured wholesale makeover of The BEATLES' 'White Album', SPENCER played up to the supposed rivalry by covering The ROLLING STONES' 'EXILE ON MAIN STREET' in its entirety, although only 550 cassettes were pressed. Release No.4 for the label (a joint effort with US label, 'Buy Our Records') came in the shape of 'PUSSY GALORE 5000' (1987), although by this point, CRISTINA, had opted to leave the band rather than further jeopardise her relationship with SPENCER, whom she later married. For their first full-length long-player, 'RIGHT NOW!' (1987), the band – who had now signed to 'Caroline' – were graced with the uncompromising production skills of former BIG BLACK leader, STEVE ALBINI, resulting in a marginally less shambolic, more focused slab of noise which saw the band begin to win over their critics. Later that year, NEIL was temporarily substituted with KURT WOLF, the latter's sole appearance being on the mini-set, 'SUGARSHIT SHARP' (1988). HAGGERTY returned to pick up the pieces on follow-up proper, 'DIAL M FOR MOTHERFUCKER' (1989), although shortly prior to its release, JULIE added another nail to the band's coffin by finally taking her leave. SPENCER recalled HAGGERTY and BERT into the PUSSY GALORE fold for one last ditch attempt, coming in the shape of 'LA HISTORIA DE LA MUSICA ROCK' (1990), upon which the first twisted seeds of SPENCER's subsequent BLUES EXPLOSION were sown with swaggering covers of Elvis's 'CRAWFISH' and Willie Dixon's 'RED ROOSTER' (the latter disguised as 'ERIC CLAPTON MUST DIE'). The 90's saw HAGGERTY form ROYAL TRUX, while JULIE teamed up with SONIC YOUTH's KIM GORDON in FREE KITTEN; a musically re-united JON and CRISTINA also recorded a few albums under the BOSS HOG moniker.
• **Songwriters:** JON and some with JULIE, except DAMAGED (Black Flag) / CRAWFISH (Elvis Presley) / YU GUNG (Einsturzende Neubauten) / PENETRATION IN THE CENTREFOLD (Devo) / LITTLE RED ROOSTER (Willie Dixon) / NO COUNT (Ty Wagner & The Scotchmen). BOSS HOG covered BLACK THROAT (Dark Brothers) / I IDOLIZE YOU (Ike & Tina Turner) / I'M NOT LIKE EVERYBODY ELSE (Kinks) / I2XU (Wire).

Album rating: EXILE ON MAIN STREET (*4) / RIGHT NOW! (*6) / DIAL M FOR MOTHERFUCKER (*6) / LA HISTORIA DE LA MUSICA ROCK (*5) / GROOVY HATE FUCK compilation UK (*6) / CORPSE LOVE: THE FIRST YEAR compilation (*6) / Boss Hog: DRINKIN', LECHIN' AND LYIN' mini (*3) / COLD HANDS (*3) / BOSS HOG (*5) / WHITE OUT (*6)

JON SPENCER – vocals, guitar / **JULIE 'Juicy' CAFRITZ** – guitar / **JOHN HAMMILL** – drums

		not iss.	Shove
Oct 85.	(7"ep) *<SHOV 1>* **FEEL GOOD ABOUT YOUR BODY**	-	
	– Die bitch / Car fantasy / Constant pain / HC rebellion.		
Jun 86.	(m-lp) *<SHOV 2>* **GROOVY HATE FUCK (FEEL GOOD ABOUT YOUR BODY)**	-	
	– Asshole / Cunt tease / Just wanna die / Kill yourself / Dead meat / Teeny pussy power / Spit'n'shit / You cook like a Jew / Get out / No count / Spin out.		

added **CRISTINA MARTINEZ** – guitar / **NEIL HAGGERTY** – guitar / **BOB BERT** – drums (ex-SONIC YOUTH); repl. HAMMILL who later joined ELEVATOR (he later appeared on supergroups' VELVET MONKEYS Oct90 album 'Rake'.

Dec 86.	(c;ltd) *<SHOV 3>* **EXILE ON MAIN STREET**	-	
	– Rocks off / Rip this joint / Shake your hips / Casino boogie / Tumbling dice / Sweet Virginia / Torn and frayed / Sweet black angel / Loving cup / Happy / Turd on the run / Ventilator blues / Just wanna see this face / Let it loose / All down the line / Stop breaking down / Shine a light / Soul survivor.		
Jan 87.	(m-lp) *<SHOV 4>* **PUSSY GALORE 5000**	-	
	– Pretty fuck look / Spin out / Walk / Get out / No count. <also issued on US 'Buy Our Records'; BOR 12-010>		

CRISTINA had departed in Autumn '86 and she later formed BOSS HOG

		Product Inc.	Caroline
Sep 87.	(lp) *(33PROD 19)* <CAROL 1337> **RIGHT NOW!**		
	– Pig sweat / White noise / Uptight / Biker-rock-loser / Wretch / Rope legend / Fuck you, man / White people / New breed / Alright / Knock up / NYC: 1999! / Punch out / Pussy stomp / Trash can oil drum / Fix it / Really suck / Rancid / Hell spawn. *(cd-iss. Feb88; PRODCD 19) (re-iss. Feb98 on 'Pussy Galore' cd/lp; PGCD/PGLP 1)*		

KURT WOLF – guitar; repl. NEIL

Oct 88.	(m-lp/m-c) *(MPROD/+C 15)* <PGEP 1> **SUGAR SHIT SHARP**		
	– Yu gung / Adolescent wet dream / Brick / Handshake / Sweet little hi-fi / Renegade! *(re-iss. Mar98 on 'Pussy Galore' lp/cd+=; PGEP/+CD 001)* – Penetration in the centrefold.		

NEIL returned (KURT also joined LOUDSPEAKER)

Apr 89.	(lp/c/cd) *(INC LP/MC/CD 001)* <CAROL 1369-1/-4/-2> **DIAL M FOR MOTHERFUCKER**		
	– Understand me / Kicked out / Undertaker / Dick Johnson / Eat me / Evil eye / Hang on / SM 57 / Solo = sex / D.W.D.A. / 1 hour later / Waxhead / A.D.W.D. 2. *(cd+=)* – Penetration of the centerfold / Handshake / Adolescent wet dream / Sweet little hi-fi / Brick / Renegade!. *(re-iss. Mar98 on 'Pussy Galore' cd/lp; PGCD/PGLP 002) (lp re-iss. Aug00 on 'Matador'; OLE 213-1)*		

		Sub Pop	Sub Pop
Jun 89.	(7") *<SP 37>* **DAMAGED II. / (version by TAD)**	-	
		not iss.	Supernatural
1989.	(7") *<AGN 2>* **PENETRATION IN THE CENTREFOLD. / Black Snakes: ONE SHOT WORLD**	-	- Japan

now a trio of **JON, NEIL + BOB**, when JULIE left later joining FREE KITTEN with KIM GORDON (SONIC YOUTH). She was also became part of VELVET MONKEYS.

		Rough Trade	Caroline
May 90.	(lp/c/cd) *(ROUGH/+C/CD 149)* <CAROL 1618-1/-4/-2> **LA HISTORIA DE LA MUSICA ROCK**		
	– Dedication / Revolution summer / Will you still have me / Don't Jones me / (Do) The snake / Ship comin' in / Mono! man / Crawfish / Drop dead. *(some cd's+=)* – Eric Clapton must die.		

disbanded finally just after above. JON formed JON SPENCER BLUES EXPLOSION while NEIL formed ROYAL TRUX (BOB joined ACTION SWINGERS with at first, JULIE in tow). In 1990, an alter-ego of PUSSY GALORE going by the name of BOSS HOG, featured CRISTINA and JON.

PUSSY GALORE (cont)

– compilations, etc. –

Feb 89. (lp) *Vinyl Drip; (SUK 001)* **GROOVY HATE FUCK compilation**
– Teen pussy power / You look like a Jew / Cunt tease / Just wanna die / Constant pain / Pretty fuck look / Spin out / No count / HC rebellion / Get out / Die bitch / Dead meat / Kill yourself / Asshole.

Apr 92. (cd/lp) *Hut; (HUT CD/LP 003) / Caroline; <CAROL 1706>* **CORPSE LOVE: THE FIRST YEAR** — Feb92
– Die bitch / HC rebellion / Contact pain / Car fantasy / Fuck you, man / No count solo / Why would I say it to you / Groovy phone / Shit rain / Don't give a fuck about you / Soundcheck / D.M.P. / Teen pussy power / You look like a Jew / Cunt tease / Just wanna die / Dead meat / Kill yourself / Asshole / Spit 'n shit / Turd on the run / Ventilator blues / Just wanna see his face / Let it loose / Pretty fuck look / Spin out / Walk / Get out.

Feb 98. (lp/cd) *In The Red; <(ITR 050/+CD)>* **LIVE (live 1989 last gig)**
– Nothing can bring me down / Adolescent wet dream / Sweet little hi-fi / Understand me / Pig sweat / 1 hour later / Dead meat / SM57 / DWDA / Wretch / Kicked out / Evil eye / New breed / Undertaker / Dick Johnson / Hang on / Kill yourself / Alright.

BOSS HOG

CRISTINA + JON plus **JERRY TEEL** – guitar / **KURT WOLF** – guitar / **CHARLIE ONDRAS** – drums

		Amphetam. Reptile	Amphetam. Reptile
1989.	(m-lp) *(ARR 6/68) <89176-1>* **DRINKIN', LECHIN' AND LYIN'**		

– Trigger, man / Pull out / Spanish fly / Sugar bunny / Fix me.

—— **JENS JURGENSEN** – guitar; repl. TEEL

1990. (d7"box; one maroon) *(ARR 21/167) <scale 39>* **ACTION BOX** — -
– Big fish / Bunny fly // Black throat / Not guilty.

—— **PETE SHORE** – bass (+ **TEEL** returned) to repl. JENS

Jan 91. (cd/lp) *(ARR 16/127) <89192-2/-1>* **COLD HANDS**
– Gerard / Eddy / Bug purr / Red bull / Go wrong / Pete Shore / Domestic / Duchess / Pop catastrophe.

—— SPENCER formed The BLUES EXPLOSION but returned to moonlight here as duo with his wife CRISTINA

Jun 93. (10"ep/cd-ep) *(ARR 41/278) <amrep 17>* **GIRL POSITIVE**
– Ruby / Some Sara / Cream agent / The black Betty / Hustler. <cd-iss. 1993 & Mar01 on 'Toys Factory'+=; TFCK 88743> – Big fish / Bunny fly / Black throat / Not guilty.

—— the pair added **JENS JURGENSEN** – bass (ex-SAWNS) / **HOLLIS QUEENS** – drums / **MARK BOYCE** – keyboards (ex-GOATS)

		Geffen	Geffen
Oct 95.	(cd) *<(GED 24811)>* **BOSS HOG**		

– Winn coma / Sick / Beehive / Ski bunny / Green shirt / I dig you / Try one / What the fuck / White sand / I idolize you / Punkture / Strawberry / Walk in / Texas / Sam.

Mar 96. (12"/cd-s) *(GFST/+D 22098)* **I DIG YOU. / HELL MARY / SOUL TRAP** — -

—— SPENCER concentrated on his BLUES EXPLOSION until . . .

		City Slang	In The Red
Jan 00.	(7") *(20149-7)* **WHITEOUT. / STRUCTURE**		-
	(cd-s+=) *(20149-2)* – Count me out.		
Feb 00.	(cd/lp) *(20152-2/-1) <ITR 68>* **WHITEOUT**		

– Whiteout / Chocolate / Nursery rhyme / Stereolight / Fear for you / Get it while you wait / Jaguar / Itchy & Scratchy / Trouble / Monkey.

Feb 00. (7"white) *<(ITR 067)>* **OLD SCHOOL. / COUNT ME OUT**
(above issued on 'In The Red')

Apr 00. (7") *(20156-7)* **GET IT WHILE YOU WAIT. / DRIVE ME CRAZY** — -
(cd-s+=) *(20156-2)* – Dedicated.

Oct 00. (7") *(20172-7)* **ITCHY & SCRATCHY. / ITCHY & SCRATCHY (Jim Waters remix)** — -
(cd-s+=) *(20172-2)* – ('A' video).
(cd-s) *(20173-2)* – ('A'-Scratchy remix by DJ Sweat) / ('A'-Jim Waters instrumental remix).

– others, etc. –

1996. (7") *Amphetamine Reptile; <scale 79>* **PORN #4** -
– Black throat / the COWS: The pictoral.

PYLON

Formed: Athens, Georgia, USA . . . 1980 by VANESSA BRISCOE, MICHAEL LACHOWSKI and RANDY BEWLEY, all having met at the University Of Georgia. Becoming a 4-piece with the addition of CURTIS CROWE, PYLON electrified both US and British audiences, promoting their early singles, 'COOL' and 'CRAZY', (re-promoted during a UK tour in 1982). Cool and Crazy was also an accurate description of their B-52's-esque sound, although their image was nothing out of the ordinary. After the release of debut album, 'GYRATE' (1980), they took a sabbatical, returning three years later with their long-awaited follow-up, 'CHOMP' (1983). One of their biggest fans was MICHAEL STIPE (and his band R.E.M.), their aforementioned track, 'CRAZY', later covered by the Athens legends on their 'Dead Letter Office' collection. PYLON themselves, meanwhile, went to ground for another few years, the band coaxed back in '89 for a reformation and a tour supporting both R.E.M. and The B-52's. However, only a few releases on the low-key US 'Sky' label added to their existing legacy, namely the album, 'CHAIN' (1990) and the accompanying single, 'SUGARPOP'. • **Trivia:** JENNIFER BLAIR managed PYLON and can be contacted through JIM PARKER at Sky Records, 6400 Atlantic Blvd, Suite 220, Norcross, GA 30071, U.S.A.

Album rating: GYRATE (*6) / CHOMP (*7) / HITS compilation (*7) CHAIN (*5)

VANESSA BRISCOE – vocals / **RANDY BEWLEY** – guitar / **MICHAEL LACHOWSKI** – bass / **CURTIS CROWE** – drums

		not iss.	Caution
Jan 79.	(7") *<30601>* **COOL. / DUB**	-	
		Armageddon	D.B.
Nov 80.	(lp) *(ARM 5) <DB 54>* **GYRATE**		

– Volume / Feast on my heart / Precaution / Weather radio / The human body / Read a book / Driving school *[US-only]* / Recent title *[UK-only]* / Gravity / Danger / Working is no problem / Stop it. *(UK-iss.Sep83; same)*

Feb 81. (10"ep) *(AEP 12-004)* **PYLON**
– Cool / Dub / Driving school / Danger!

1981. (7") *<DB 61>* **CRAZY. / M-TRAIN** - -
1982. (12"m) *<DB 62>* **BEEP. / ALTITUDE / FOUR MINUTES** - -
1983. (lp/c) *<DB/+C 65>* **CHOMP**
– K / Yo-yo / Beep / Italian movie theme / Crazy / M-train / Buzz / No clocks / Reptiles / Spider / Gyrate / Altitude. *(UK-iss.Jul86; same as US)*

—— disbanded 1986, although they re-formed in 1989

		not iss.	Sky
Oct 90.	(lp/cd) *<SKY 2020/+CD>* **CHAIN**	-	

– Look alive / Catch / B-complex / Sugarpop / There it is / Springtime / This – That / Go / Crunch / Very right / Metal / Outside / Sloganistic. *(UK cd-iss. Aug94; same)*

—— disbanded later in the 90's; VANESSA is now married to BOB HAY (ex-SQUALLS) and they have two children

– compilations, etc. –

1989. (cd) *D.B.; <DB 91>* **HITS** -
– Beep / Cool / Dub / Volume / Altitude / Gravity / Danger / Stop it / Feast on my heart / M-train / K / Driving school / Crazy / Yo-yo / The human body / Read a book / No clocks / Recent title / Working is no problem / Weather radio.

THE GREAT INDIE DISCOGRAPHY — The 1980s

QUEERS

Formed: North Hampton, USA . . . 1982 by the RAMONES obsessed teenagers, JOE QUEER, VAPID, B-FACE (CHRIS BARNARD) and DANNY PANIC. After the release of a 6-song EP that year they seemed to go into a 5-year hibernation, that is, until their debut album, 'GROW UP' (1990). Signed to 'Lookout!' soon afterwards, The QUEERS delivered a series of LP's, 'LOVE SONGS FOR THE RETARDED' (1993), 'BEAT OFF' (1994), 'MOVE BACK HOME' (1995) and 'DON'T BACK DOWN' (1996). In 1998, still with a penchant for sounding like clones of the RAMONES, they moved to another label, 'Hopeless', which best describes their sixth album, 'PUNK ROCK CONFIDENTIAL'. Their blend of cartoon three-chord punk'n'roll will no doubt go down well with the new wave of poppy-punk that American acts were churning out, twenty-odd years too late! • **Covered:** THAT GIRL (Livermore) / GET OVER YOU (Undertones) / HAWAII + DON'T BACK DOWN + LITTLE HONDA (Brian Wilson/Beach Boys) / END IT ALL (Muffs) / SIDEWALK SURFIN' GIRL (Curb-Hatcher) / ANOTHER GIRL (Les Hernandez) / MIRAGE (Tommy James) / MY OLD MAN'S A FATSO (Angry Samoans) / IT'S COLD OUTSIDE (Choirs) / MURDER IN THE BRADY HOUSE (Screeching Weasels) / PRETTY FLAMINGO (Manfred Mann) / I ENJOY BEING A BOY (Banana Splits) + a complete tribute to the Ramones:- ROCKET TO RUSSIA.

Album rating: GROW UP (*4) / LOVE SONGS FOR THE RETARDED (*6) / BEAT OFF (*4) / MOVE BACK HOME (*6) / DON'T BACK DOWN (*4) / PUNK ROCK CONFIDENTIAL (*3) / LATER DAYS AND BETTER DAYS demos (*4) / BEYOND THE VALLEY . . . (*5) / LIVE IN WEST HOLLYWOOD (*4) / PLEASANT SCREAMS (*6)

JOE QUEER (b. KING) – vocals, guitar / **VAPID** – guitar, vocals / **B-FACE** (b. CHRIS BARNARD) – bass, vocals / **DANNY PANIC** – drums

not iss.   Doheny
1982. (7"ep) <E 210X85> **LOVE ME EP**
– We'd have a riot doing heroin / Terminal rut / Fagtown / I want it now / Trash this place / Love me.
1984. (7"ep) <E 404Y07> **KICKED OUT OF THE WEBELOS**
– Kicked out of the webelos / Tulu is a wimp / At the mall / I spent the rent / Don't wanna work / I'm useless / This place sucks.

not iss.   Shakin' Street
1990. (lp) <Yeah Hup 010> **GROW UP**
– Squid omelet / Love love love / Boobarella / I met her at the rat / I'll be true to you / Burger king queen / Junk freak / Gay boy / Rambo rat / I don't wanna get involved / Goodbye California / Strip search. <re+UK-iss.Jul95 cd/c/lp; LOOKOUT 90 CD/MC/LP/>

not iss.   Doheny
1993. (7"ep) <U-35835M> **TOO DUMB TO QUIT**
– Nothing to do / Bonehead / I'm nowhere at all / Didn't puke / Fuck you. <re-iss. 1994 on 'Selfless'; SFLS 27>

Lookout   Lookout
1993. (cd/c/lp) <LOOKOUT 66> **LOVE SONGS FOR THE RETARDED**
– You're tripping / Ursula finally has tits / I hate everything / Teenage bonehead / Fuck this world / I can't stop farting / Feeling groovy / Debra Jean / Hi mom, it's me! / Noodlebrain / I can't stand you / Night of the livid queers / Granola head / I won't be / Monster zero / Daydreaming. (UK-iss.Jul95 cd/c; LOOKOUT 66 CD/MC)
1994. (cd/c/lp) <LOOKOUT 81> **BEAT OFF**
– Steak bomb / Drop the attitude fucker / You make me wanna puke / Teenage gluesniffer / Ben Weasel / Voodoo doll / Mirage / Grounded / Live this life / Half shitfaced / Too many twinkies / All screwed up. <UK-iss.Jul95 cd/c; LOOKOUT 81 CD/MC)>
1994. (7"ep; shared with PINK LINCOLNS) <JAW 001> **LIVE! AT SOME PRICK'S HOUSE**
– We'd have a riot doing heroin / This place sucks / Kicked out of the webelos / I want cunt / Nobody likes me / (others by PINK LINCOLNS).
(above issued on 'Just Add Water') (below on 'Ringing EAr')
1994. (7"ep) <RER 008> **LOVE AIN'T PUNK**
– Blabbermouth / Rockaway beach / (other 2 by SINKHOLE).
1994. (7"ep) <WR 06> **MY OLD MAN'S A FATSO**
– My old man's a fatso / MacArthur Park / Meatwagon / Murder in the Brady house.
(above issued on 'Wound Up')

— **HUGH O'NEILL** – drums, bass; repl. VAPID + DANNY PANIC

Feb 95. (cd-ep) <LOOKOUT 108> **SURF GODDESS EP**
– Surf goddess / Mirage (alt. take) / Get over you / Quit talkin'.
May 95. (cd/lp) <LOOKOUT 114 CD/LP> **MOVE BACK HOME**
– She's a cretin / Next stop rehab / High school psychopath II / If you only had a brain / I gotta girlfriend / Hawaii / From your body / Definitely / Everything's going my way / Cut it dude / I can't get invite to the prom / That girl / Peppermint girl.
1995. (7"ep) <CRVW 35> **LOOK MA NO FLANNEL!**
– I like young girls / Nuni in New York / Wimpy drives through Harlem / Too much flesh for Tulu / I didn't want none / Nobody likes me.
(above on 'Clearview')
Oct 96. (cd/lp) <(LOOKOUT 140 CD/LP)> **DON'T BACK DOWN**   Aug96
– No tit / Punk rock girls / I'm ok, you're fucked / Number one / Don't back down / I only drink Bud / I always new / Born to do dishes / Janelle, Janelle / Brush your teeth / Sidewalk surfin' girl / Another girl / Love, love, love / I can't get over you.
Feb 97. (7"ep) <LOOKOUT 158> **BUBBLEGUM DREAMS EP**
– Punk rock girls / Never ever ever / Little Honda / End it all.

Hopeless   Hopeless
Jun 98. (7"ep/cd-ep) <(HR 631 1/CD)> **EVERYTHING'S OK / QUEERBAIT / GET A LIFE AND LIVE IT LOSER / I ENJOY BEING A BOY**
Oct 98. (cd/lp) <(HR 636-2/-1)> **PUNK ROCK CONFIDENTIAL**
– Tamara is a punk / Everything's OK / I didn't puke / Mrs. Brown, you've got an ugly daughter / The sun always shines around you / Rancid motherfuckers / Punk rock confidential / Today I fell in love / Pretty flamingo / Motherfucker / Like a parasite / Idiot savant / I enjoy being a boy / Don't mess it up / Sayonara sucker.

— **GEOFF USELESS** – bass, vocals; repl. B-FACE/CHRIS who joined The REAL KIDS
— **RICK RESPECTABLE** – drums; repl. HUGH O'NEILL who died in 1999

May 00. (lp/cd) <(HR 643/+CD)> **BEYOND THE VALLEY . . .**
– Uncouth / Little rich working class oi-boy / Strangle the girl / I'm not a mongo anymore / Stupid fucking vegan / In with the out crowd / I wanna know / Journey to the center of your empty mind / I hate your fucking guts / Babyface (boo-hoo-hoo) / My cunt's a cunt / I just called to say fuck you / Just say cunt / Theme from beyond the valley . . .

Lookout   Lookout
Mar 01. (cd-ep) <(LK 260CD)> **TODAY**   Feb01
– Yeah, well, whatever / I don't want to go to the Moon / I've had it vwith you / I'm the boy for you / Salt Lake City.

— **MAT DRASTIC** (or) **DAN LUMLEY** – drums; repl. RICK

Apr 02. (cd/lp) <(LK 270 CD/LP)> **PLEASANT SCREAMS**
– Get a life and live it / See you later fuckface / I wanna be happy / Danny Vapid / I never got the girl / It's cold outside / Psycho over you / Generation of swine / Tic tic toc / I don't have you hanging around / Homo / You just gotta blow my mind / Debbie true / Molly Neuman.

– compilations, etc. –

1992. (d7"ep) *Doheny*; <U-33568M> **A PROUD TRADITION** (first 2 EP's)
<re-iss. 1993 on 'Selfless'; SFLS 21>
Jan 96. (cd) *Lookout!*; <LOOKOUT 130> **A DAY LATE AND A DOLLAR SHORT**
– We'd have a riot doing heroin / Terminal rut / Fagtown / I want cunt / Trash this place / Love me / Kicked out the Webelos / Tuly is a wimp / At the mall / I spent the rent / I don't wanna work / I'm useless / This place sucks / Wimpy drives through Harlem / I like young girls / Nuni in New York / Nobody likes me / Nothing to do / Nowhere at all / Mac Arthurs park / Flesh for Tulu / Fuck you / Didn't want some / Meat wagon / Don't puke / Bonehead / Wimpy drives through Harlem / Nothing to do / Gay boy / Nobody likes me / Too many twinkies / Half shitfaced / I live this life / Live broadcast WFMJ 4/11/9?
Jan 98. (cd) *Clear View*; <37> **SUCK THIS LIVE** (live)
– Squid omelet / We'd have a riot doing heroin / This place sucks / Tulu is a wimp / I want it now / Monster zero / Fuck up / Noodle brain / Granola gead / Hi mom . . . it's me!! / Teenage bonehead / Beer break / I spent the rent / Nothing to do / My old man's a fatso / Fuck you / Fuck the world / I hate everything / Ursula finally has tits / You're tripping.
Nov 98. (lp) *Selfless*; <sfls 28> **ROCKET TO RUSSIA**
– Cretin hop / Rockaway beach / Here today, gone tomorrow / Locket love / I don't care / Sheena is a punk rocker / We're a happy family / Teenage lobotomy / Do you wanna dance? / I wanna be well / I can't give you anything / Ramona / Surfin bird / Why is it always the way? (UK-iss.Mar01 on 'Liberation'; LIB 37838)
Apr 99. (cd) *Lookout*; <(LK 216CD)> **LATER DAYS AND BETTER DAYS**   Mar99
– Granola days / I hate everything / Murder in the Brady house / I won't be / Nobody likes me / I can't stop farting / Night of the livid queers / Monster zero / Too many twinkies / Teenage bonehead / Half shitfaced / Hi mom, it's me! / I live this life / Feeling groovy / Born to do dishes / Junk freak / No tit / Little Honda / End it all / I can't get over you / Never ever.
Oct 01. (cd) *Hopeless*; <(HR 658CD)> **LIVE IN WEST HOLLYWOOD** (live)
– We'd have arrived doing heroin / This place sucks / Tulu is a wimp / I want cunt / Monster zero / You're tripping / I live this life / Tamara's a punk / Mirage / No tit / Blabbermouth / Hi mom, it's me / Granola head / Noodlebrain / My old man's a fatso / Fuck you / I'm not a mongo anymore / I will be with you / Kill that girl / Kicked out of the webelos / I hate everything / Teenage bonehead / Love love love / Another girl / I only drink Bud / Punk rock girls / Ursula finally has tits / I like young girls / Nothing to do / Fuck the world.

? & THE MYSTERIANS

Formed: Saginaw, Michigan, USA . . . 1964, after abandoning the name XYZ and their Texan homeland. Early in 1966, their manager, LILY GONZALES, dispatched 750 copies of their first single, '96 TEARS'. This organ-dominated, garage classic sparked off interest from major US record company, 'Cameo', who re-issued it later in the year and it subsequently topped the US charts. They had their last chart appearance with 'I NEED SOMEBODY' before a string of flops over the course of the next few years. • **Songwriters:** RUDY MARTINEZ penned except; SHOUT (Isley Brothers) / etc. • **Trivia:** In 1967, The SEMI-COLONS featured The MYSTERIANS' on two of their instrumental tracks. ALICE COOPER later covered 'I NEED SOMEBODY',

? & THE MYSTERIANS (cont)

while STRANGLERS were one of several major artists to resurrect '96 TEARS'.
Album rating: 96 TEARS (*6)

? (aka RUDY MARTINEZ, 1945, Mexico) – vocals / **FRANK RODRIGUEZ JNR.** (b. 9 Mar'51, Crystal City, Texas) – Farfisa organ / **FRANK LUGO** (b. FRANCISCO HERNANDEZ LUGO, 15 Mar'47, Weslaco, Texas) – bass / **LARRY BORJAS** – guitar / **ROBERT MARTINEZ** – drums

	not iss.	Pa-Go-Go
Jan 66. (7"; as The MYSTERIANS) <102> **96 TEARS. / MIDNIGHT HOUR**	–	

	Cameo Parkway	Cameo
Sep 66. (7") <(C 428)> **96 TEARS. / MIDNIGHT HOUR**	37	1 Jan66

— BOBBY BALDERRAMA (b.27 Feb'50, O'Donnell, Texas) – guitar; repl. ROBERT / EDDIE SERRATO (b. 5 Dec'45, Encial, Texas) – drums; repl. LARRY (both the outgoing members were drafted into the army)

Nov 66. (lp) <C 2004> **96 TEARS**	–	66

– I need somebody / Stormy Monday / You're telling me lies / Ten o'clock / Set aside / Upside / Don't tease me / Don't break this heart of mine / Why me / Midnight hour / 96 tears. (UK-iss.Jun97 on 'Anthology'; ANT 3021)

Dec 66. (7") <(C 441)> **I NEED SOMEBODY. / '8' TEEN**		22

	Postcard	Thirsty Ear
Sep 92. (lp/c/cd) (DUBH 921/+MC/CD) **THE PHANTOMS AND THE ARCHETYPES**		–

– The phantoms and the archetypes / Born on the wrong side of town / What can you do to me now / Punk rock hotel / Superstar / Call my name / The damage is done / Darling / I can't fight / Hanging on.

Jul 93. (7") (DUBH 933) **STUPID THING. / PASSING THOUGHT**		–

(cd-s+=) (DUBH 933) – Superstar.

— HODGENS replaced by **MICK SLAVEN** – (ex-JAZZATEERS) / **SKIP REID** – (ex-ASSOCIATES) / **ANDY ALSTON** – / **JANE MARIE O'BRIEN** –

Oct 94. (lp/c/cd) (DUBH 945/+MC/CD) <57024> **WILL I EVER BE INSIDE OF YOU**		1996

– Will I ever be inside of you / You have been seen / Lover, that's all you over / Mooreefoc (misty blue) / A passing thought / Outre / Misty blue / Stupid thing / At the end of the night.

Jun 95. (cd-ep; PAUL QUINN, The NECTARINE No.9 / JOCK SCOT) (DUBH 952CD) **PREGNANT WITH POSSIBILITES EP**		–

– Tiger tiger / Will I ever be inside of you / Just another f***ed-up little druggy on the scene / Grunge girl groan.

Paul QUINN

Born: 26 Dec'51, Glasgow, Scotland. He formed BOURGIE BOURGIE in 1983 with former JAZZATEERS members (IAN BURGOYNE, KEITH BAND and KENNY McDONALD) and scraped into the Top 50 early the following year with their much lauded 'M.C.A.' debut 45, 'BREAKING POINT'. A second, 'CARELESS' flopped and the band quickly disbanded, QUINN subsequently resurfacing on a collaboration single, 'PALE BLUE EYES' (a VELVET UNDERGROUND cover) with ORANGE JUICE mainman, EDWYN COLLINS. His first solo outing, 'AIN'T THAT ALWAYS THE WAY' was another for ALAN HORNE's (the man behind 'Postcard'; Glaswegian indie home of ORANGE JUICE, AZTEC CAMERA and JOSEF K) 'Swamplands' label, pursued by yet another top indie collaboration, this time 'ONE DAY' alongside ex-YAZOO and future ERASURE man VINCE CLARKE. For the rest of the 80's, QUINN's unique and extremely fluid voice took a back seat until the early 90's heralded his return with a sort of "Postcard" supergroup, PAUL QUINN AND THE INDEPENDENT GROUP. This included hip musicians JAMES KIRK (Orange Juice), BLAIR COWAN (Lloyd Cole & The Commotions), CAMPBELL OWENS (Aztec Camera), ROBERT HODGENS (Bluebells) and ALAN HORNE!, who had revived the 'Postcard' stable for this new act. In 1992, an album 'THE PHANTOMS AND THE ARCHETYPES' took rave reviews, QUINN's crooning voice never better on songs such as, 'HANGING ON', 'PUNK ROCK HOTEL' and the excellent title track. His retro film noir style (BILLY MACKENZIE or BILLY IDOL on mood pills) was again on song, when a follow-up, 'WILL I EVER BE INSIDE OF YOU' showed remarkable beauty, a re-working of 'STUPID THING' and a cover of 'MISTY BLUE' were top notch; what happened to him after their shared EP, 'PREGNANT WITH POSSIBILITIES', is anybody's guess.

Album rating: THE PHANTOMS AND THE ARCHETYPES (*6) / WILL YOU EVER BE INSIDE OF ME (*7)

BOURGIE BOURGIE

PAUL QUINN – vocals / **IAN BURGOYNE** – guitar / **KEITH BAND** – bass (ex-JAZZATEERS) / **KENNY McDONALD** – drums

	M.C.A.	not iss.
Feb 84. (7") (BOU 1) **BREAKING POINT. / APRES SKI**	48	–
(12"+=) (BOUT 1) – ('A'extended).		
Apr 84. (7") (BOU 2) **CARELESS. / CHANGE OF ATTITUDE**		–
(12"+=) (BOUT 2) – ('A'extended).		

PAUL QUINN

— first single a collaboration with the ex-ORANGE JUICE frontman

	Swamplands	not iss.
Aug 84. (7"; PAUL QUINN & EDWYN COLLINS) (SWP 1) **PALE BLUE EYES. / BURROW**		–
Mar 85. (7") (SWP 6) **AIN'T THAT ALWAYS THE WAY. / PUNK ROCK HOTEL**		–

(12"+=) (SWX 6) – Corrina Corrina.

— In Jun'85, QUINN collaborated with VINCE CLARKE (ex-YAZOO, ex-DEPECHE MODE, now ERASURE) on 7"/12", 'ONE DAY' (Mute; TAG/12TAG 1). (this was re-issued in Apr93; same cat.no.)

PAUL QUINN AND THE INDEPENDENT GROUP

PAUL QUINN with **JAMES KIRK** – guitar (ex-ORANGE JUICE) / **ALAN HORNE** – (creator of 'Postcard' label) / **CAMPBELL OWENS** – drums (of-AZTEC CAMERA) / **BLAIR COWAN** – bass (ex-LLOYD COLE & THE COMMOTIONS) / **ROBERT HODGENS** – rhythm guitar, vocals (ex-BLUEBELLS)

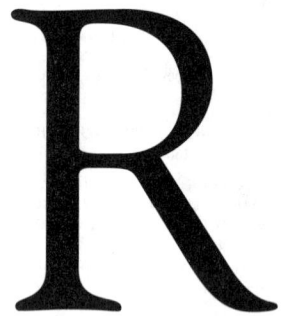

RAILWAY CHILDREN

Formed: Wigan, Lancashire, England . . . 1985 by teenagers GARY NEWBY (the band's songwriter), STEPHEN HULL, BRIAN BATEMAN and GUY KEEGAN. Signed to Manchester's 'Factory' label on the strength of a demo, the young hopefuls issued a couple of impressive singles (i.e. 'A GENTLE SOUND' and 'BRIGHTER') prior to the release of a debut album, 'REUNION WILDERNESS' (1987). Having forged a highly marketable sound lying somewhere between ECHO & THE BUNNYMEN, The SMITHS and the indie soul-strumming of Scottish acts like AZTEC CAMERA and ORANGE JUICE, The RAILWAY CHILDREN were snapped up by 'Virgin', who subsequently moulded the band into an even more commercially palatable proposition. The new improved sound was unveiled on 1988's 'RECURRENCE' album, new improved sales proving more readily available abroad than in Britain. Two years on, 'NATIVE PLACE' (1990) was well timed to fit in with the burgeoning baggy culture and the band eventually broke into the UK Top 30 with a remixed version of 'EVERY BEAT OF THE HEART'. Yet like so many jangly guitar acts who benefitted from the indie-dance craze, The RAILWAY CHILDREN found only fleeting success, a further two singles, 'SOMETHING SO GOOD' and 'MUSIC STOP' running out of chart steam. Shunted into relative obscurity once more, the band finally decided to blow the whistle on their stop-start career once and for all in the early 90's. With HULL and BATEMAN out of the way, NEWBY continued to work on a new studio set, 'DREAM ARCADE', which finally saw the light in 1999! The lead singer laid down a couple of new tracks for 'March' records, although due to some dispute over non-payment and contractual website matters the single ('SKINSHIP') was delayed until summer 2002.

Album rating: REUNION WILDERNESS mini (*7) / RECURRENCE (*4) / NATIVE PLACE (*5) / LISTEN ON (THE BEST OF THE RAILWAY CHILDREN) compilation (*7) / DREAM ARCADE (*6)

GARY NEWBY (b. 5 Jun'66, Australia) – vocals, guitar / **BRIAN BATEMAN** (b. 3 Aug'66) – guitar / **STEPHEN HULL** (b. 7 Jul'66) – bass / **GUY KEEGAN** (b.16 Jun'66) – drums

                                                Factory Virgin

Sep 86. (7") *(FAC 162)* **A GENTLE SOUND. / CONTENT**
Feb 87. (7") *(FAC 167)* **BRIGHTER. / HISTORY BURNS**
   (12"+=) *(FAC 167T)* – Careful.
Mar 87. (m-lp/m-c)(m-cd) *(FACT 185/+C)(FACD 185) <90636-1>*
   REUNION WILDERNESS   Jul87
   – Brighter / Another town / The first notebook / Big hands of freedom / Listen on / Railroad side / Careful. *(cd+=)* – A gentle sound / Content. *(cass-box-iss.Jan91; FACT 185C)* *(cd re-iss. Apr02 on 'Ether'; ETH 2CD)*

                                                Virgin   Virgin

Mar 88. (7") *(VS 1070)* **IN THE MEANTIME. / MERCILESS**
   (12"+=) *(VST 1070)* – Swallowed / Second nature.
   (cd-s+=) *(VSCD 1070)* – Second nature / Caught you.
May 88. (cd/c/lp) *(CD/TC/V 2525) <90930>* **RECURRENCE**   96
   – Somewhere south / Pleasure / Swallowed / Merciless / My word / In the meantime / Over and over / Monica's light / Chrysalis / No great objections. *(cd re-iss. Apr92; same)*
Jun 88. (7") *(VS 1084)* **SOMEWHERE SOUTH. / LISTEN ON**
   (12"+=) *(VST 1084)* – Darkness and colour.
   (10"+=) *(VSA 1084)* – You can't follow the world / Waterfall.
Aug 88. (7") *(VS 1115)* **OVER AND OVER. / A GENTLE SOUND (demo)**
   (12"+=) *(VST 1115)* – Union city blue (live).
   (cd-s+=) *(VSCD 1115)* – ('A'remix) / Big hands of freedom (live).
Mar 90. (7"/c-s) *(VS/+C 1237)* **EVERY BEAT OF THE HEART. / EVERYBODY**   68
   (10"+=/12"+=/cd-s+=) *(VS A/T/CD 1237)* – Give it away / Strange altrader. *(re-iss. Jan91 – hit No.24)*
May 90. (7"/c-s) *(VS/+C 1255)* **MUSIC STOP. / TELL ME**   66
   (d7"+=) *(VSX 1255)* – What she wants / It won't be long.
   (12"+=) *(VST 1255)* – ('A'instrumental).
   (cd-s+=) *(VSCD 1255)* – ('A'-Steve Proctor mix).
Jun 90. (cd/c/lp) *(CD TC/+V 2627) <91385>* **NATIVE PLACE**
   – Every beat of the heart / Music stop / You're young / Because / Cotton counting / It's Heaven / Something so good / Collide / Native place / Fall on / Harbour force / Blue sky. *(re-act.Mar91 – hit UK No.59)*
Oct 90. (7"/c-s) *(VS/+C 1289)* **SO RIGHT. / ('A'-Dakeyne mix)**   68
   (12"+=) *(VST 1289)* – ('A'-strawberry mix).
   (cd-s++=) *(VSCD 1289)* – Kinds of fuel.
Apr 91. (7"/c-s) *(VS/+C 1318)* **SOMETHING SO GOOD. / HOURS GO BY**   57
   (12"+=) *(VST 1318)* – After the rain / Standing too still.
   (cd-s+=) *(VSCD 1318)* – ('A'extended) / After the rain / Standing too still.
Jun 91. (7"/7"box) *(VS/+X 1255)* **MUSIC STOP. / WHAT SHE WANTS / TELL ME**
   (12") *(VST 1255)* – ('A'side) / ('A'instrumental) / ('A'-Steve Proctor mix).
   (cd-s) *(VSCDT 1255)* – ('A'side) / What she wants / ('A'-Steve Proctor mix) / ('A'extended).

—— split in 1992 when BATEMAN and HULL departed; **GARY NEWBY** soldiered on with new 'CHILDREN

                                                  Ether   not iss.

Sep 99. (cd) *(ETH 1CD)* **DREAM ARCADE**
   – Let it go / Light the fuse / What tomorrow brings / Dream arcade / Don't need / Rising closer / Wake the dreamer / Come around / Understand / These things she does. *(re-iss. Sep02; same)*

                                                 March   not iss.

Jul 02. (cd-s) *(MAR 076CD)* **SKINSHIP / THE FORGOTTEN / A PLEASURE (acoustic)**

– compilations, etc. –

Mar 93. (cd) *Nightracks; (CDNT 2) / Dutch East India; <DEI 8122>*
   RADIO 1 EVENING SHOW SESSIONS
Feb 95. (cd) *Virgin; (<CDOVD 451>)* **LISTEN ON (THE BEST OF THE RAILWAY CHILDREN)**
   – Every beat of the heart / Everybody / Give it away / Music stop / What she wants / Something so good / Hours go by / After the rain / You're young / Collide / Somewhere south / Listen on / Over and over (full remix) / A gentle sound (original demo) / Monica's light / So right (dakeyne full length remix) / In the mantime.

RAIN PARADE

Formed: Los Angeles, California, USA . . . 1981 as The SIDEWALKS by Minneapolis college mates DAVID ROBACK and MATT PIUCCI. They also numbered DAVID's younger brother STEVEN and WILL GLENN, before they opted for a name change. Their vinyl debut came with the BYRDS-like 'WHAT'S SHE DONE TO YOUR MIND' in 1982 while they found a permanent drummer in EDDIE KALWA. DAVID moonlighted with another project, RAINY DAY, but a disappointing covers album was soon forgotten when 'EMERGENCY THIRD RAIL POWER TRIP' hit the shops. Purveyors of the burgeoning "Paisley Underground" scene, the set was a throwback to the psychedelic sound of PINK FLOYD/KALEIDOSCOPE, while the guitar plucking was reminiscent of TELEVISION. The record gained a UK release on Demon's off-shoot 'Zippo' label, as did their 1984 mini-lp 'EXPLOSIONS IN THE GLASS PALACE'. The record was recorded without co-leader DAVID, however, who had left earlier in the year. 'Island' records gave them their break in '85 but surely damaged their growing reputation when they rush-released a live-set recorded in Japan, 'BEYOND THE SUNSET'. With MATT and STEVEN the sole remaining members, they recruited JOHN THOMAN and MARK MARCUM although the 1986 album, 'CRASHING DREAM', was appropriately titled, Island soon ditching them. They took a two-year hiatus before going back into the studio to finish off a double album. It never found its way to the shops, as PIUCCI joined a re-formed CRAZY HORSE, while the rest became VIVA SATURN. Relocating to San Francisco, STEVEN ROBACK and Co delivered a handful of worthy releases, none more so than 1995's 'Restless' set, 'BRIGHTSIDE'. • **Songwriters:** All written by the ROBACK's and group, except AIN'T THAT NOTHIN' (Television) / LIKE A HURRICANE (Neil Young) / WHAT GOES ON (Velvet Underground).

Album rating: EMERGENCY THIRD RAIL POWER TRIP (*7) / EXPLOSIONS IN THE GLASS PALACE mini (*6) / BEYOND THE SUNSET (*6) / CRASHING DREAM (*6) / Viva Saturn: VIVA SATURN mini (*5) / SOUNDMIND (*6) / BRIGHTSIDE (*7)

DAVID ROBACK – vocals, guitar, percussion / **MATT PIUCCI** – guitar, vocals, sitar / **WILL GLENN** – keyboards / **STEVEN ROBACK** – bass, vocals / **EDDIE KALWA** – drums

                                                 not iss.   Llama

1982. (7") *<DK 002>* **WHAT'S SHE DONE TO YOUR MIND. / KALEIDOSCOPE**
                                                 Zippo   Enigma

Aug 84. (lp) *(ZING 001) <ENIGMA 19>* **EMERGENCY THIRD RAIL POWER TRIP**   1983
   – Talking in my sleep / This can't be today / I look around / 1 hr. half ago / Carolyn's song / What she's done to your mind / Look at Merri / Saturday's asylum / Kaleidoscope / Look both ways.

—— trimmed to a quartet when DAVE left to form RAINY DAY (later OPAL). He is now part of duo MAZZY STAR

1984. (m-lp) *(ZANE 003) <71081>* **EXPLOSIONS IN THE GLASS PALACE**
   – You are my friend / Prisoners / Blue / Broken horse / No easy way down.
Feb 85. (7") *(ZIPPO 45-1)* **YOU ARE MY FRIEND. / THIS CAN'T BE TODAY**   1984

—— **MARK MARCUM** – drums repl. KALWA
—— added **JOHN THOMAN** – guitar, vocals

                                                 Island   Restless

Jun 85. (lp/c) *(IMA/IMC 17) <72086>* **BEYOND THE SUNSET** (live in Tokyo 1984)   78
   – Night shade / Prisoners / This can't be today / Blue / Eyes closed / Ain't that nothin' / Don't feel bad / 1 hr. 1/2 ago / Blue / No easy way down / Cheap wine.

                                                 Island   Island

Oct 85. (lp/c) *(ILPS/ICT 9805) <90499-1/-4>* **CRASHING DREAM**
   – Depending on you / My secret country / Don't feel bad / Mystic green / Sad eyes kill / Shoot down the railroad man / Fertile crescent / Invisible people / Gone west / Only business.

—— disbanded when PIUCCI formed GONE FISHIN' then joined CRAZY HORSE

– compilations, etc. –

Feb 92.	(cd) *Mau Mau; (MAUCD 610)* **EMERGENCY THIRD RAIL POWER TRIP / EXPLOSIONS IN THE GLASS PALACE**		□	-
Sep 02.	(cd) *Cloud; (CLOUD 6)* **PERFUME RIVER** (live)		□	-

– Kaleidoscope / This can't be today / Prisoners / Crashing dream / Blue / You are my friend / Sad eyes kill / No easy way down / Broken horse / Ain't that nothin' / What she's done to your mind / Saturday's asylum / Like a hurricane / What goes on.

VIVA SATURN

STEVEN ROBACK – guitar, piano, vocals / **JOHN THOMAN** – guitar / **MARK MARCUM**

		World Service	Heyday
Jun 89.	(m-lp) *(SERVS 003)* **VIVA SATURN**	□	□

– So glad / Brought it on yourself / Remember I'm dead / Old world / Wild town.

― **MATT PIUCCI** – guitar, vocals; repl. MARK

― added **ROSS INDEN** – bass / **CARLO NUCCIO** – drums

		Normal	Heyday	
May 94.	(cd) *(NORMAL 139CD) <ADE 009CD>* **SOUNDMIND**	□	□	1992

– Still she waits / Love the sugar / Believe / Haven't felt like / Soundmind / Suicidal lamb / Raised / Better get your nerve Paradise / Mermaid / Waiting for the train.

		Restless	Restless
Jul 95.	(cd) *<(72909-2)>* **BRIGHTSIDE**	□	□

– Send a message / Black cloud / Brightside / Here comes April / Abondoned car string me out a line / Mourn the light / Distracted / Nothing helps / Heart of you / One for my baby.

― after one shelved set, STEVEN ROBACK contemplated a solo career

RAINY DAY
(see under ⇒ MAZZY STAR; in 90's section)

RAJ QUARTET
(see under ⇒ MONOCHROME SET; 70's section)

RAM RAM KINO (see under ⇒ CRISPY AMBULANCE)

Lee RANALDO (see under ⇒ SONIC YOUTH)

Eric RANDOM

Born: Manchester, England. This one-man electronic/instrumental act first drew attention, however low-key, when his TILLER BOYS (a trio who included PETE SHELLEY of the BUZZCOCKS and FRANCIS COOKSON) released their one and only single, 'BIG NOISE FROM THE JUNGLE', in 1979. Remaining with the BUZZCOCKS' 'New Hormones' imprint (having collaborated again with SHELLEY on the FREE AGENTS lp in 1980), ERIC issued a further couple of 45's, 'THAT'S WHAT I LIKE ABOUT ME' EP and 'DOW CHEMICAL COMPANY'. During the recording of his debut solo album, 'EARTHBOUND GHOST NEED' (1982), he was also involved with two other projects, The JELL (their one and only track, 'I DARE SAY IT WILL HURT A LITTLE', featured on the 'Some Bizzare Album') and The PRESSURE COMPANY (a pseudonym for CABARET VOLTAIRE – an outfit he performed with), who issued one collaborative set, 'LIVE IN SHEFFIELD'. ERIC subsequently continued his solo career, releasing a couple of best forgotten albums that were augmented by his group, The BEDLAMITES.

Album rating: EARTHBOUND GHOST NEED (*4) / TIME SPLICE (*3) / ISHMAEL (*3)

ERIC RANDOM – vocals, keyboards, bass, guitar, saxophone / **PETE SHELLEY** – guitar, vocals / **FRANCIS COOKSON**

		New Hormones	not iss.
1979.	(7"m; by TILLER BOYS) *(ORG 3)* **BIG NOISE FROM THE JUNGLE. / SLAVES AND PYRAMIDS / WHAT ME WORRY?**	□	-

― now with **LYNN 'SEED' WALTON** – keyboards, synthesizer / + other JELL member, **LISA LISA** – clarinet (not on solo material)

Sep 80.	(12"ep) *(ORG 6)* **THAT'S WHAT I LIKE ABOUT ME**	□	-
	– Fade in / Dirty bongo / Call me / Fade out.		
May 81.	(7") *(ORG 11)* **DOW CHEMICAL COMPANY. / SKIN DEEP**	□	-
Jul 81.	(7") *(TWI 029)* **SUBLIMINAL. / 23 SKIDOO**	□	-
	(above issued for 'Les Disques Du Crepescule')		
Jan 82.	(lp) *(ORG 18)* **EARTHBOUND GHOST NEED**	□	-

ERIC RANDOM & THE BEDLAMITES

		DoubleVision	not iss.
Dec 84.	(12") *(DVR 7)* **MAD AS MANKIND. / THE FLOOD**	□	-
Feb 85.	(lp) *(DVR 11)* **TIME SPLICE**	□	-
	– Himalaya sun / Destination / Hardcore / Father can't yell.		

		Fon	not iss.
Jan 87.	(lp) *(BED 7)* **ISHMAEL**	□	-

― ERIC retired from the studio . . .

RANK & FILE (see under ⇒ DILS; 70's section)

Alan RANKINE

Born: c.1957, Bridge Of Allan, Stirlingshire, Scotland. As a guitarist, ALAN was the other half of cabaret outfit, CASPIAN, who became top Dundonian alt/dance outfit, The ASSOCIATES; the duo was completed by singer BILLY MACKENZIE. After a period that stretched from 1979 to 1983, in which the pair scored a handful of Top 20 hits (including 'Party Fears Two' and 'Club Country'), it was clear that MACKENZIE was holding all the aces. Following a stint of global travelling, RANKINE returned to London where he began producing for the likes of The COCTEAU TWINS, PAUL HAIG and Liverpool outfit, The PALE FOUNTAINS. In 1986, and having inked a deal with Belgian independent, 'Crepescule', RANKINE was ready to retake his place in the music business. His debut set, 'THE WORLD BEGINS TO LOOK HER AGE' (1986), was a mixture of instrumentals and his own LOU REED/DAVID SYLVIAN-esque vocal tracks, although most of them didn't quite hit the mark, especially with the critics. The pop-fuelled, 9-minute epic, 'THE BEST IN ME', with its NEW ORDER-style backing, failed to propel the man back to the limelight. However, 'Virgin' must've been impressed with most of the set as they let RANKINE remix four tracks from the debut (side by side with five new cuts) and release them under a follow-up title, 'SHE LOVES ME NOT' (1987). Towards the end of the decade and once again taking up with 'Crepescule', RANKINE delivered an ambient-style imaginary soundtrack score via the instrumental, 'THE BIG PICTURE SUCKS' (1989). This, and another under-par effort, 'DAYS AND DAYS' (1990), convinced RANKINE his strengths lay in other directions. In the mid-90's, ALAN began lecturing on music in Glasgow (he also contributed some songs to various pop/rock outfits) and helped students set-up their own indie imprint as part of a college course. Little did they know that the label in question, 'Electric Honey', would be the stamping ground for the now celebrated outfit, BELLE & SEBASTIAN, who debuted with 'Tigermilk' in May '96.

Album rating: THE WORLD BEGINS TO LOOK HER AGE (*5) / SHE LOVES ME NOT (*5) / BIG PICTURE SUCKS (*4) / DAYS AND DAYS (*3)

ALAN RANKINE – vocals, guitars, keyboards, etc

		Crepescule	not iss.
Sep 86.	(7"/12") *(7+/TWI 598)* **SANDMAN. / RUMOURS OF WAR**	□	-
Nov 86.	(lp) *(TWI 672)* **THE WORLD BEGINS TO LOOK HER AGE**	□	-
	– Elephant's walk in morning glory / Mission for the Don / Your very last day / The best in me / The world begins to look her age / Last bullet / Sandman / Love in adversity.		
Dec 86.	(7") *(7TWI 762)* **LAST BULLET. / YOUR VERY LAST DAY**	□	-

		Virgin	not iss.
Aug 87.	(7"/12") *(VS 971/+12)* **THE WORLD BEGINS TO LOOK HER AGE. / CAN YOU BELIEVE EVERYTHING I SAY**	□	-
Oct 87.	(lp/c/cd) *(V/TCV/CDV 2450)* **SHE LOVES ME NOT**	□	-
	– Beat fit / Days and days / Loaded / Last bullet / Your very last day / The sandman / Lose control / Break for me / The world begins to look her age.		
Nov 87.	(7"/12") *(VS/+T 1003)* **SANDMAN. / CAN YOU BELIEVE EVERYTHING I SAY**	□	-

		Crepescule	not iss.
1989.	(cd) *(TWI 8692)* **THE BIG PICTURE SUCKS**	□	-
	– Shambok / Pop off / Once in a blue one / Glory to the take and the killing / Happens every minute / Lies.		
1990.	(cd) *(TWI 8872)* **DAYS AND DAYS**	□	-

― RANKINE retired from solo work

RAPEMAN (see under ⇒ BIG BLACK)

RAZORCUTS

Formed: London, England . . . 1985 by songwriter GREGORY WEBSTER alongside TIM VASS. These 'Friends of the Earth' were part of the original C-86 anorak brigade and another pastel-hued outfit to sign for the 'Subway Organisation'. Their inaugural single, 'BIG PINK CAKE', was cut in Summer '86, prior to the arrival of Kiwi drummer, DAVID SWIFT. After a further 45, 'SORRY TO EMBARRASS YOU', the SWIFT connection led to the band releasing a one-off single, 'I HEARD YOU THE FIRST TIME', for NZ imprint, 'Flying Nun'. Another label with hip indie credibility, 'Creation', was home to the band's debut album, 'STORYTELLER' (1988), a downbeat set of melancholy indie-pop suffering at times from WEBSTER's apathetic vocals. Despite bolstering their line-up with the addition of PETE MOMTCHILOFF, STRUAN ROBERTSON and RICHARD MASON (to replace SWIFT), the band failed to sharpen their sound on the follow-up set, 'THE WORLD KEEPS TURNING' (1989). The subsequent demise of The RAZORCUTS saw WEBSTER join The CAROUSEL while VASS formed his own outfit, RED CHAIR FADE AWAY; newcomer MOMTCHILOFF joined HEAVENLY. A posthumous RAZORCUTS EP appeared the following year, while a short-lived reunion between WEBSTER and VASS took the billing of The FOREVER PEOPLE. With frequent lapses into his CAROUSEL, SATURN V and solo alter-egos during a healthy mid-90's period, WEBSTER soon took time out to plan his next venture, the indie supergroup SPORTIQUE (alongside AMELIA FLETCHER, ROB PURSEY and MARK FLUNDER). Having issued a handful of singles for various small outlets, the WEBSTER-led outfit released a couple of inspired 25-minute+ mini-sets, 'BLACK IS A VERY POPULAR COLOUR' (1999) and 'MODERN MUSEUMS' (2002). Twee-pop was alive and living in WEBSTER's head, albeit through a retro-fied WIRE-meets-AU PAIRS style.

RAZORCUTS (cont)

Album rating: STORYTELLER (*6) / THE WORLD KEEPS TURNING (*6) / Carousel: I FORGOT TO REMEMBER TO FORGET compilation (*5) / ABCDEFGHIJKLMNOPQRSTUVWXYZ (*5) / Saturn V: SKYCYCLE (*4) / Gregory Webster: MY WICKED WICKED WAYS mini (*5) / Sportique: BLACK IS A VERY POPULAR COLOUR mini (*6) / MODERN MUSEUMS mini (*7)

GREGORY WEBSTER – vocals, guitar / **TIM VASS** – bass / guest **ANGUS** – drums

Subway   not iss.
Jun 86. (7") (SUBWAY 5) **BIG PINK CAKE. / I'LL STILL BE THERE**

— **DAVID SWIFT** (b. New Zealand) – drums; repl. ANGUS
Oct 86. (7") (SUBWAY 8) **SORRY TO EMBARRASS YOU. / SUMMER IN YOUR HEART**
(12"+=) (SUBWAY 8T) – Snowbirds don't fly / Mary Day.

Flying Nun   not iss.
Jun 87. (7") (FNUK 9) **I HEARD YOU THE FIRST TIME. / FIRST DAY**
(12"+=) (FNUK 9T) – Eight times around the world / A is for alphabet.

Creation   not iss.
Feb 88. (lp) (CRELP 026) **STORYTELLER**
– Storyteler / Try a little tenderness (live) / A contract with God / Sky high / Everyday eyes / Jade / Silhouette / Brighter now / I'll still be there / The last picture show.

— **STRUAN ROBERTSON** – drums; repl. SWIFT

— added **PETE MOMTCHILOFF** – guitar / **RICHARD MASON** – backing vocals / + producer **JOHN A. RIVERS** – hammond organ
Feb 89. (lp/cd) (CRE LP/CD 045) **THE WORLD KEEPS TURNING**
– Goodnight England / Mile high towers / Change / I won't let you down / Waterfall / Flowers for Abigail / Across the meadow / Come my way / Snowbound / Steps to the sea / The world keeps turning. (cd+=) – STORYTELLER

— disbanded later in '89 when GREG joined The CAROUSEL, while the RAZORCUTS issued a further single. The same year, VASS's outfit, RED CHAIR FADEAWAY, released an eponymous lp for 'Cosmic English Music' (CTA 103). PETER subsequently joined ex-TALULAH GOSH members in HEAVENLY.

Caff   not iss.
Sep 90. (ltd-7"ep) (CAFF 10) **SOMETIMES I WORRY ABOUT YOU / FOR ALWAYS. / SORRY TO EMBARRASS YOU / MUSIC FROM BIG PINK**

— VASS subsequently re-formed RED CHAIR FADE AWAY, issuing two cd-albums for 'English Garden' in 1994 & 1997 respectively, 'MESMERIZED' (ENG 1012CD) and 'CURIOUSER AND CURIOUSER' (ENG 1013CD).

CAROUSEL

GREGORY WEBSTER – vocals, guitar + **ELIZABETH PRICE** – vocals, guitar (ex-GOSH) / with other ex-GOSH people

Cosmic English Fayre   not iss.
Oct 89. (12"ep) (CTA 102) **STRAWBERRY FAYRE EP**
– Strawberry fayre / Evergreen / Halfpennies and farthings September come again.
Apr 90. (12"ep) (CTA 104) **SORROW IS THE WAY TO LOVE**
– Sorrow is the way to love / Handmedown green / Locks and bolts / No ticket for the train.

not iss.   Summershine
Nov 91. (7"m) <SHINE 010> **WILL YOU WEAR LOVE? / YESTERDAY BOX / CERISE**

Vinyl Japan   not iss.
Apr 93. (cd/lp) (ASK CD/LP 17) **I FORGOT TO REMEMBER TO FORGET** (compilation)

FOREVER PEOPLE

— **WEBSTER + VASS** returned under another pseudonym

Sarah   not iss.
Feb 92. (7") (SARAH 054) **INVISIBLE. / SOMETIMES**

SATURN V

GREGORY WEBSTER – vocals, guitar / **KEVIN PICKERING** – guitar / **CHRIS SCOTT** – bass / **STRUAN ROBERTSON** – drums

Pop Bus   not iss.
1991. (7"flexi) (none) **SHE'S GONE** (live)

not iss.   Kokopop
1992. (7"m) <KOKO 7> **DOMINATOR. / RED STAR IN ORBIT / SKYFALL**

not iss.   Summershine
1992. (7") <SHINE 021> **HAPPY TRAILS. / ROCKET SPACESHIP**

Vinyl Japan   not iss.
Oct 92. (12"ep/cd-s) (TASK/+CD 14) **EVERYTHING TENDS TOWARDS CHAOS**
– Skyfall / Hour of pure sorrow / Machine-gun head / She's gone.
Jul 93. (lp/cd) (ASK 22) **SKYCYCLE**
– Fireball / Skyfall / Air balloon / Happy trails / Jesus stole my girlfriend / Dominator II / Machine-gun head / Stars dim slowly / Strong / Red star in orbit.

CAROUSEL

Feb 95. (m-cd) (MASKCD 50) **ABCDEFGHIJKLMNOPQRSTUVWXYZ**
– Henry please don't chop off my head / Sugarbowl / Like honey bee (honey bee) / Truelove / Sidesaddle / Baby sweetness / G.U.N. / My boy and his motorbike.

GREGORY WEBSTER

Vinyl Japan   not iss.
Apr 96. (m-cd) <MASKCD 55> **MY WICKED WICKED WAYS**
– All the greatest stories / Blue eyes crying in the rain / Clock chimes / Foolhardy / Forever England / Last night on Earth / Lonesome town / The water wide / Winter / Wonderland.

SPORTIQUE

GREGORY WEBSTER – vocals, guitar / **AMELIA FLETCHER** – keyboards, vocals (ex-HEAVENLY, ex-TALULAH GOSH) **ROB PURSEY** – bass (ex-HEAVENLY, ex-TALULAH GOSH) / **MARK FLUNDER** – drums (ex-McTELLS, ex-TELEVISION PERSONALITIES)

Where It's At…   Where It's At…
Nov 97. (7") (WIAIYWA 004) **IF YOU EVER CHANGE YOUR MIND. / ONE FOR THE ROAD**
1998. (7") (ROX 004) **THE KIDS ARE SOLID GOLD. / YOU DIDN'T HAVE TO BE SO NICE**
(above issued on 'Roxy' records)
Nov 98. (7") (WIAIYWA 008) **P58. / TINY CLUES**
Apr 99. (cd) (<WHICD 001>) **BLACK IS A VERY POPULAR COLOUR**
– Just friends / Anatomy of a fool / P58 / It couldn't last forever / The impersonator / If you ever change your mind / Tiny clues / The cover / Northern sky / A world without pity.
Jul 99. (7") (MATINEE 007) **LOVE & REMAINS. / OBSESSIVE**
(above issued on 'Matinee')
Jun 00. (7") (WIAIYWA 016) **SPORT FOR ALL. / SPORT FOR ALL (Olympic 2000 version)**

Matinee   Matinee
Oct 00. (7") (MATINEE 017) **DON'T BELIEVE A WORD I SAY. / A NATION OF SOUL**
Feb 02. (cd) (<MATCD 015>) **MODERN MUSEUMS**
– Modern museums / Cerebral vortex / Art and shopping / How many times..? / The dying fly / Suture / Definition seventy-nine / Icestorm / Obsessive. (10"lp-iss.Feb02 on 'Where It's At…'; WIALP 007)

REDD KROSS

Formed: Hawthorne, California, USA … late 1978 by schoolboy brothers JEFF McDONALD (then 15) and STEVE (only 11), initially as The TOURISTS (not UK group with ANNIE and DAVE). Completing the line-up with GREG HETSON and RON REYES, they played their first gig in 1979 as RED CROSS, opening for BLACK FLAG. Spotted by DJ and entrepreneur, Rodney Bingenheimer, they subsequently recorded an EP for 'Posh Boy' which led to the "real" International Red Cross threatening to sue them if they didn't change the group name! REDD KROSS, as they were now known, lost GREG HETSON and RON REYES in the process, both moving on to similar hardcore acts, CIRCLE JERKS and BLACK FLAG respectively. Over the course of the early to mid 80's, personnel changed like the weather and output was sparse. However, a few albums had emerged during this lean period, namely 'BORN INNOCENT' (1982) and covers mini-set, 'TEEN BABES FROM MONSANTO' (1984), REDD KROSS not exactly causing an emergency with their trashy psychedelic punk/glam, although their embryonic grunge sound was definitely ahead of its time. Just when recognition seemed to be forthcoming with 1987's 'NEUROTICA', luck ran out as their label, 'Big Time', came a cropper. The McDONALD brothers re-appeared in 1990 with their one-off covers side project, TATER TOTZ, before the pair resurfaced with a new REDD KROSS line-up and a major deal courtesy of 'Atlantic'. A comeback album, 'THIRD EYE', appeared in 1991, the band's subsequent UK output released through 'This Way Up' (home to TINDERSTICKS and IAN McNABB). Another new line-up (namely, EDDIE KURDZIEL, GERE FENNELLY and BRIAN REITZEL) was in place for 1993's 'PHASESHIFTER', which spawned three singles, 'SWITCHBLADE SISTER', 'LADY IN THE FRONT ROW' and 'VISIONARY', the latter scraping into the UK Top 75 early the following year. Later that summer, the band indulged their love of classic 70's pop with a kitschy cover of the Carpenters' 'YESTERDAY ONCE MORE', a shock UK Top 50 hit which featured SONIC YOUTH paying tribute to Karen & Richard on the B-side. A long hiatus ensued before REDD KROSS entered the fray once more in early '97 with another set of multi-coloured sonic-pop, 'SHOW WORLD', a collection that featured another minor hit single, 'GET OUT OF MYSELF'. With a long lay-off, JEFF was back in 2002 with member(s) of that dog in moonlight project, ZE MALIBU KIDS. • **Covered:** CITADEL (Rolling Stones) / HEAVEN ONLY KNOWS (Shangri-las) / DANCING QUEEN (Abba) / ANN (Stooges) / CEASE TO EXIST (Charles Manson) / etc. • **Trivia:** In 1990, REDD KROSS recorded a soundtrack for the Super-8 film, 'Desperate Teenage Lovedolls'.

Album rating: BORN INNOCENT (*4) / TEEN BABES FROM MONSANTO mini (*6) / NEUROTICA (*6) / THIRD EYE (*7) / PHASESHIFTER (*6) / SHOW WORLD (*7) / Tater Totz: ALIEN SLEESTACKS FROM BRAZIL (*5) / MONO STEREO! (*4) / TATER COMES ALIVE! (*5) / Ze Malibu Kids: SOUND IT OUT (*4)

JEFF McDONALD (b.10 Aug'63, Los Angeles) – vocals / **GREG HETSON** – guitar / **STEVE McDONALD** (b.24 May'67) – bass, vocals / **RON REYES** – drums

not iss.   Posh Boy
1981. (12"ep; as RED CROSS) <PBS 1010> **RED CROSS**
– Cover band / Annette's got the hits / I hate my school / Clorox girls / S & M party / Standing in front of a poseur. <re-iss. 1987 by REDD KROSS as 'ANNETTE'S GOT THE HITS'; same>

— now without HETSON (to CIRCLE JERKS) and REYES (to BLACK FLAG). They were repl. by a BANGLE!? (briefly) and various L.A. session people including **DEZ CADENA** (of BLACK FLAG)

not iss.   Smoke 7
1982. (lp) <smk7 103> **BORN INNOCENT**
– Linda Blair / White trash / Everyday there's someone new / Solid gold / Burn-out / Charlie / Tatum O'Tot and the fried vegetables / St. Lita Ford blues / Self

REDD KROSS (cont)

respect / Pseudo-intellectual / Kill someone you hate / Look on up at the bottom / Cellulite city / I'm alright / Cease to exist / Notes and chords mean nothing to me. *(UK-iss.Aug92 on 'Frontier' cd/lp; 4609-2L/1L)* *(re-iss. Aug00 on 'Munster'; MR 186)* *<re-iss. Jul02 on 'Frontier' lp/cd; FR 31018/+CD)>*

		not iss.	Enigma
1984.	(m-lp) <71110-1> **TEEN BABES FROM MONSANTO** (covers)	–	

– Deuce / Citadel / Heaven only knows / Ann / Saviour machine / Blow you a kiss in the wind / Linda Blair 1984.

		not iss.	Mystic
1984.	(7") **BALLAD OF A LOVE DOLL.** / White Flag: JOHNNY TREMAINE'S THEME	–	

		Big Time	Big Time
Sep 87.	(lp/cd) *(ZL/ZD 71427K)>* **NEUROTICA**		

– Neurotica / Play my song / Frosted flake / Janus, Jeanie, and George Harrison / Love is you / Peach Kelli Pop / McKenzie / Tatum O'Tot and the fried vegetables *[cd-only]* / Ballad of a love doll / What they say / Ghandii is dead (I'm the cartoon man) / Beautiful bye-byes. *<cd-iss. Nov02 on 'Five Foot Two'+=; 2003>* – Pink piece of peace / It's the little things.

		East West	Atlantic
Apr 91.	(cd/c/lp) *<(7567 82148-2/-4/-1)>* **THIRD EYE**		Nov90

– The faith healer / Annie's gone / I don't know how to be your friend / Shonen Knife / Bubblegum factory / Where I am today / Zira (call out my name) / Love is not love / 1976 / Debbie & Kim / Elephant flares.

		not iss.	Insipid
Apr 91.	(7") <WE 171> **ANNIE'S GONE.** / **SHONEN KNIFE**	–	

		Seminal Twang	not iss.
Nov 91.	(7") *IV 06>* **SUPER SUNNY CHRISTMAS.** / **HUGE WONDER**		–
Jul 92.	(7") *(Twang 14)* **TRANCE.** / **BYRDS & FLEAS**		–

(cd-s+=) *(Twang 14cd)* – Huge wonder.

— McDONALD's plus EDDIE KURDZIEL (b.25 Sep'60, Philadelphia) – guitar / GERE FENNELLY (b. 5 Aug'60, San Mateo, Calif.) – keyboards / BRIAN REITZEL (b.24 Dec'65, Ukiah, Calif.) – drums

		This Way Up	Polygram
Jun 93.	(7") *(WAY 10-11)* **SWITCHBLADE SISTER.** / **WHAT'S WRONG WITH ME?**		–

(cd-s+=) *(WAY 10-33)* – I don't know how to be your friend (live).

| Aug 93. | (7") *(WAY 15-07)* **JIMMY'S FANTASY.** / **TICO AND YOLANDA (UNDERGROUND AGAIN)** | | – |

(cd-s+=) *(WAY 15-33)* – Disco bitch.

| Sep 93. | (cd/c/lp) *<518167-2/-4/-1)>* **PHASESHIFTER** | | |

– Jimmy's fantasy / Lady in the front row / Monolith / Crazy world / Dumb angel / Huge wonder / Visionary / Pay for love / Ms. Lady Evans / Only a girl / Saragon / After school special.

| Oct 93. | (7"/10") *(WAY 20-11/88)* **LADY IN THE FRONT ROW.** / **I'LL MEET YOU HALFWAY** | | – |

(cd-s) *(WAY 20-33)* – ('A'side) / Standing in front of poseur / Oh my lover / Fancy.

| Jan 94. | (7") *(WAY 27-11)* **VISIONARY.** / **IT WON'T BE LONG** / **VISIONARY (acoustic live)** | 75 | – |

(12"+=/cd-s+=) *(WAY 27-12/33)* – ('A'side) / Any hour, every day / Oh my lover / Huge wonder (original) / Visionary (acoustic) / Disco bitch.

— In Sep'94, they shared a single 'YESTERDAY ONCE MORE' with SONIC YOUTH's 'Superstar' (both CARPENTERS covers) hit UK No.45 for 'A&M'; 580792)

| Jan 97. | (7"colrd) *(WAY 54-11)* **GET OUT OF MYSELF.** / **SO CAL V8** | 63 | – |

(cd-s+=) *(WAY 54-33)* – Teen competition (demo).
(cd-s) *(WAY 54-66)* – ('A'side) / Misery is mother / Jimmy's fantasy.

| Feb 97. | (cd/c/lp) *<524 275-2/-4/-1>* **SHOW WORLD** | | |

– Pretty please me / Stoned / You lied again / Girl god / Mess around / One chord progression / Teen competition / Follow the leader / Vanity mirror / Secret life / Ugly town / Get out of myself / Kiss the goat.

| Mar 97. | (7") *(WAY 60-11)* **MESS AROUND.** / **WHAT CHA DOIN' TO THAT GIRL** | | – |

(cd-s) *(WAY 60-33)* – ('A'side) / Crazy world / Ugly town.
(cd-s) *(WAY 60-66)* – ('A'side) / Sick love / Popular cult.

| Jun 97. | (7") *(WAY 64-11)* **SECRET LIFE.** / **DANCING QUEEN** | | – |

(cd-s+=) *(WAY 64-33)* – Follow the leader.
(cd-s) *(WAY 64-66)* – ('A'side) / Its in the sky / You lied again.

– compilations, others, etc. –

| 1990. | (7") *Posh Boy; <PBS 22>* **BURN OUT.** / **COVER BAND** | – | |

TATER TOTZ

aka McDONALD's plus DANNY BONADUCE

		not iss.	Positive
1988.	(lp) <6010> **ALIEN SLEESTACKS FROM BRAZIL**	–	

– Give peace a chance – We will rock you / Let's get together / Tomorrow never knows / I've just seen a face / Bat macumba / Don't count the waves / Bharta's boogie / Sing this all together / Bat macumba (reprise) / Don't worry Kyoko.

		not iss.	Gatanska
1990.	(cd) <6027> **MONO! STEREO: SGT. SHONEN'S PLASTIC EASTMAN BAND REQUEST**	–	

– Instant karma! / Rock on / Rain / Who has seen the wind? – Bohemian rhapsody / Telephone song / Strawberry fields forever / 1,2,3, red light / Luck of the Irish / Sisters, o sisters / Lovely Linda / Shompton in Babylon / Why? / Two virgins #9 / Tomorrow never knows (live) / Cambridge 1969 (live).

		Rockville	Rockville
Jul 93.	(m-cd/m-c) *<(ROCK 6054-2/-4)>* **TATER COMES ALIVE!**		

– Tomorrow never knows / Rain / Sisters oh sisters / Don't worry Kyoko / Flowers / Sympathy for the Devil. *(cd+=)* – Don't worry Kyoko.

ZE MALIBU KIDS

JEFF McDONALD plus people from that dog.

		Houston Party	Houston Party
Apr 02.	(cd) *<(HPR 053)>* **SOUND IT OUT**		

– Shelly Fabares / Your bed / Ze xtasy club / Outer circle / I won't forget you / Maybe it's the wrong time / Sleep therapy / Standing in the wrong line / What's wrong with Stephani? / You're so vain / Fionna Apple / Don't go / Waiting for our last time / Vacsination.

RED GUITARS

Formed: Hull, England... 1982 by JEREMY KIDD and HALLAM LEWIS, alongside JOHN ROWLEY and MATT HIGGINS. Issued on their own 'Self-Drive' label in mid '83, the chugging irony of debut single, 'GOOD TECHNOLOGY' was followed by 'FACT!', an intelligent slice of alternative pop with an ominous guitar refrain and an anti-war message. The double re-issue of 'GOOD TECHNOLOGY' early in '84 appeared prior to the moody bass reverberations of 'STEELTOWN', the latter track underlining the band's political stance. Yet it was 'MARIMBA JIVE' which gave the band most success, climbing to the top of the indie charts and forming the centrepiece of debut album, 'SLOW TO FADE' (1984). KIDD left unexpectedly shortly after the record's release, taking his label with him. Recruiting ROBERT HOLMES as a replacement, The RED GUITARS moved swiftly onwards, signing to 'Virgin'-offshoot, 'One Way' and releasing a second long player, 'TALES OF THE EXPECTED' (1985). Despite further critical acclaim, the group ultimately went their separate ways with HALLAM forming PLANET WILSON and HOLMES releasing a solo set, 'AGE OF SWING' (1989) for 'Virgin'.

Album rating: SLOW TO FADE (*7) / TALES OF THE EXPECTED (*5)

JEREMY KIDD – vocals / HALLAM LEWIS – guitar, vocals / JOHN ROWLEY – guitar, keyboards / LOU HOWARD – bass / MATT HIGGINS – drums

		Self-Drive	not iss.
Jul 83.	(7") *(SD 006)* **GOOD TECHNOLOGY.** / **HEARTBEAT GO**		–
Nov 83.	(7") *(SD 007)* **FACT.** / **DIVE (live)**		–
Jan 84.	(12") *(SD 008)* **GOOD TECHNOLOGY.** / **FACT** / **PARIS FRANCE**		–
Apr 84.	(7"/12") *(SD 009/+T)* **GOOD TECHNOLOGY.** / **HEARTBEAT GO**		–
Jun 84.	(7"/12") *(SCAR 010/T)* **STEELTOWN.** / **WITHIN FOUR WALLS**		–
Sep 84.	(7"/12") *(SCAR 014/+T)* **MARIMBA JIVE.** / **HEARTBEAT GO**		–
Nov 84.	(lp) *(SCARLP 001)* **SLOW TO FADE**		–

– Remote control / Dive / Astronomy / Cloak and dagger / Shaken not stirred / Crocodile tears / Sting in the tail / Marimba / Slow to fade. *(re-iss. Nov86 lp/c/cd+=; SCAR LP/C/CD 001)* *(cd re-iss. Oct02 on 'Cherry Red'; CDMRED 219)* – Good technology / Fact / Paris France / Steeltown / Within four walls / Heartbeat go!

— ROBERT HOLMES – vocals, guitar; repl. JEREMY KIDD who went solo

		One-Way	not iss.
Apr 85.	(12") *(OW 1)* **BE WITH ME.** /		–

— LOU HOWARD – bass; repl. BARLOW

		Virgin	not iss.
Mar 86.	(7") *(VS 832)* **NATIONAL AVENUE (SUNDAY AFTERNOON).** / **KING AND COUNTRY**		–

(12"+=) *(VS 832-12)* – Things I want.

| Mar 86. | (lp/c) *(V/TCV 2373)* **TALES OF THE EXPECTED** | | – |

– Be with me / Suspicion and fear / National Avenue (Sunday afternoon) / Love and understanding / Storyville / Marianne / Sweetwater ranch / House of love / Trains on time / Baby's got a gun. *(re-iss. Jun88 lp/c; OVED/+C 224)* *(cd-iss. 1988; CDV 2373)*

| May 86. | (7") *(VS 858)* **AMERICA AND ME.** / **MARIANNE** | | – |

(12"+=) *(VS 858-12)* – ('A' version).

| Sep 86. | (7"/12") *(VS 899/+12)* **BLUE CARAVAN.** / **SUSPICION AND FEAR** | | – |

— disbanded late 1986 and ROBERT HOLMES went solo releasing debut single, 'INTERNATIONAL SUNSHINE', in 1987. He subsequently issued one more, 'ANGEL IN THE HOUSE', from the parent set, 'AGE OF SWING' (1989)

– compilations, etc. –

| Feb 93. | (cd) *R.P.M.; (RPM 109)* **SEVEN TYPES OF AMBIGUITY** | | |

– Paris France / Fact / Dive / Marimba jive / Sting in the tale / Slow to fade / Steeltown / Heartbeat go! / Within four walls / Crocodile tears / Remote control / Shaken not stirred / Astronomy / Seven types of ambiguity / Jamaican homecoming / Be with me / Clean up / Age of swing / Train's on time / Good technology. *(re-iss. Apr00; same)*

PLANET WILSON

— were formed by HALLAM LEWIS + LOU HOWARD plus JONAH OXBURROW – drums (ex-THAT NOBLE PORPOISE)

		Virgin	not iss.
Mar 88.	(7") *(VS 1053)* **WHITE LIES.** / **VISION ON**		–

(12"+=) *(VST 1053)* – The big wheel.

| Mar 88. | (cd/c/lp) *(CD/TC+/V 2508)* **IN THE BEST OF ALL POSSIBLE WORLDS** | | – |

– Flap the bird / The big wheel / Rolling balls / Distraction / Sinister Dexter / Seven days / Love by hand / Wish it was so / White lies. *(cd+=)* – Vision on / I remain outside.

		Records Of Achievement	not iss.
Jan 89.	(12") *(12PLAN 2)* **TAKEN FOR A RIDE.** /		–
Mar 89.	(lp/cd) *(PLAN 003/+CD)* **NOT DROWNING BUT WAVING**		–

– Truth hurts / Taken for a ride / I remain outside / Golden touch / Honeymoon / Fly by night / How do I feel? / Mouth to mouth / Night swimming.

— HALLAM went on to run his own studio

RED LETTER DAY

Formed: Portsmouth, England . . . 1984 by frontman ADE OAKLEY, IAN CAMPBELL, PETE WHITE and BRIAN LEE, the latter three soon posted missing and replaced over the course of the ensuing few years by guitarist DAVIE EGAN, bassist KEITH METCALFE and drummer DARYN PRICE respectively. This line-up debuted in early '86 with the single, 'WHEREVER YOU MAY RUN', the record's post-punk stylings catching the ear of Radio One DJ, John Peel, who invited the quartet on his show for a session. Subsequently signing to 'Quiet' records (former stable of NEW MODEL ARMY), they issued two further EP's, 'RELEASED EMOTIONS' and 'TAKE ME IN YOUR ARMS', the former also the name of the label they'd sign to for a shared LP (with The SECT), 'SOFT LIGHTS AND LOUD GUITARS' (1988). Never a prolific band, RED LETTER DAY were also dogged by further personnel changes (METCALFE and EGAN were despatched around '87/'88) although they did finally emerge with their own album proper, 'MORE SONGS ABOUT LOVE AND WAR' (1991). After taking another interminable sabbatical, RLD were back with a limited-edition one-off 7", 'INSOMNIA', in '97, while the following year saw the release of only their second album in a decade and a half, 'LETHAL'; the CD 'HAPPY NEW YEAR' was appropriately delivered around the turn of the millennium. • **Note:** Not to be confused with US power-pop outfit of the late 90's.

Album rating: SOFT LIGHTS AND LOUD GUITARS (*5) / MORE SONGS ABOUT LOVE AND WAR (*5)

ADE OAKLEY – vocals, guitar / **DAVIE EGAN** – guitar; repl. IAN CAMPBELL / **KEITH METCALFE** – bass; repl. PETE WHITE / **DARYN PRICE** – drums; repl. BRIAN LEE

		Lost Generation	not iss.
Mar 86.	(7") (LG 003) **WHEREVER YOU MAY RUN. / SUSIE'S BOMBED OUT TONITE**		-
		Quiet	not iss.
Sep 86.	(12"ep) (QST 15) **RELEASED EMOTIONS EP** – Killing ground / So far away / Spark of love / Tomorrow today.		-
Jul 87.	(7"ep) (QS 018) **TAKE ME IN YOUR ARMS. / MOVING ON / THE DAY I JOINED THE HUMAN RACE**		-

—— **STEVE** – bass (ex-ORIGINAL MIRRORS) repl. METCALFE

		Released Emotions	not iss.
Jul 88.	(lp; shared with The SECT) (REM 001) **SOFT LIGHTS AND LOUD GUITARS** – It's cold outside / American dream / The war starts at midnight / Fade away / Fall apart / Barely alive / Shades / The less i see the more I think of you / The whole world gets me down / Unclean.		-
Nov 89.	(7") (TCS 001) **LAST NIGHT. / STREET HEAT**		-

—— **RAY "RAZOR"** – guitar; repl. EGAN

| 1991. | (lp) (REM 011) **MORE SONGS ABOUT LOVE AND WAR** – More songs about love and war / Chance meeting / Another day / Daze of indifference / Stranger / Unreality / Last night / Sad and happy years / Wherever you may run / Brasilia / Presence of the night. | | - |

		Incognito	not iss.
1993.	(7") (INC 036) **STOP THE WORLD. / LIMO LIFE**		-
		Ank	not iss.
1995.	(cd) (ANK 01-007-2331) **NOTHING AT THIS MOMENT IN TIME** – Never hate me alive / Hey! Anastasia / Pure / World in action / Whatever happened / Stop the world / Rain / No victims / Dealt / New heart / Outta my head / Nothing at this moment in time (parts 1 & 2).		-
		Mouthy	not iss.
Feb 97.	(ltd-7") (MOUTHY 003) **INSOMNIA. / RAIN**		-
		Holler Than Thou	not iss.
Jul 98.	(cd) (HTT 032-2) **LETHAL** – Choose noise / This is my drag / Alison / Insomnia / Lethal / Parallel suburbia / Diva / Rain / Clandestine / Worldstoomuch / Four / Insider / Drama queen / A thousand names for God.		-
		Mouthy	not iss.
Nov 99.	(cd-ep) (MOUTHY 014CD) **HAPPY NEW YEAR / DRAMA QUEEN / SUB ZERO / I DON'T NEED YOU / PARALLEL UNIVERSE (live)**		-

– compilations, etc. –

| Jun 01. | (cd) Zip; (<ZIP 005CD>) **CHANCE MEETINGS: THE BEST OF RED LETTER DAY 1985-1999** – More songs about love and war / Rain / Take me in your arms / Wherever you may run / Last night / Pure / Chance meeting / Insomnia / Dealt / Great wall of Leicester / Drama queen / It's cold outside / Killing ground / Stop the world / This is my drag / Limo life / Presence of the night / Worldstoomuch / Happy new year. | | Dec02 |

RED LORRY YELLOW LORRY

Formed: Leeds, England . . . 1982 by CHRIS REED, MARTIN FAGEN, STEVE SMITH and MICK BROWN. With FAGEN and SMITH subsequently replaced by DANE WOLFENDEN (aka WOLFIE) and PAUL SOUTHERN, RED LORRY YELLOW LORRY emerged from the fertile Leeds goth scene via a deal with the local 'Red Rhino' label. Featuring their much loved signature tune, 'HOLLOW EYES', the debut mini-album, 'TALK ABOUT THE WEATHER', arrived in 1985 and received support from John Peel amongst others. Favouring the usual prophet-of-doom vocals over noisy, discordant guitars and an almost tribal rhythm, the band built up a following parallel to contemporaries like The SISTERS OF MERCY and FIELDS OF THE NEPHILIM without really achieving the same degree of cult status and fanatical following. Nevertheless, they carved out their own niche in the market, moving to 'Beggars Banquet' offshoot, 'Situation 2', for a third set, 'NOTHING'S WRONG' (1988). By the early 90's, the line-up had undergone so many changes that REED was the only founding member left, the band forging on with 1992's 'BLASTING OFF' album. Mainman REED resurfaced in 1994 with CHRIS REEDS WOOF!, although they only managed a few German-only releases. • **Covers:** Chris Reed solo:- I FOUND OUT (John Lennon).

Album rating: TALK ABOUT THE WEATHER (*6) / PAINT YOUR WAGON (*5) / NOTHING WRONG (*5) / BLOW (*4) / BLASTING OFF (*4) / THE SINGLES 1982-1987 compilation (*7) / Chris Reeds Woof!: BIRTHDAY SKIN (*4)

CHRIS REED – vocals, guitar / **DANE WOLFENDEN** – guitar; repl. MARTIN EGAN / **PAUL SOUTHERN** – bass; repl. STEVE SMITH / **MICK BROWN** – drums

		Red Rhino	Homestead
Sep 82.	(7") (RED 20) **BEATING MY HEAD. / I'M STILL WAITING**		-
Apr 83.	(7") (RED 28) **TAKE IT ALL. / HAPPY**		-
Oct 83.	(7") (RED 39) **HE'S READ. / SET THE FIRE**		-
Mar 84.	(12"ep) (RED 48) **THIS TODAY EP** – Beating my head / He's read / Take it all / See the fire.		-
Jun 84.	(7") (RED 49) **MONKEY'S ON JUICE. / PUSH** (12"+=) (REDT 49) – Silence.		-

—— **LEON PHILLIPS** – bass; repl. PAUL

Oct 84.	(7") (RED 52) **HOLLOW EYES. / FEEL A PIECE** (12"+=) (REDT 52) – Russia.		-
Jan 85.	(lp) (REDLP 50) **TALK ABOUT THE WEATHER** – Talk about the weather / Hand on heart / Feel a piece / Hollow eyes / This today / Sometimes / Strange dream / Happy.		-
Apr 85.	(7"/ext-12") (RED/+T 55) **CHANCE. / GENERATION**		-

—— **CHRIS OLDROYD** – drums (ex-MUSIC FOR PLEASURE, ex-GIRLS AT OUR BEST) repl. BROWN who joined The MISSION

Sep 85.	(7") (RED 60) **SPINNING ROUND. / HOLD YOURSELF DOWN** (12"+=) (REDT 60) – ('A'-crash mix).		-
Feb 86.	(lp/c/cd) (RED LP/C/CD 65) **PAINT YOUR WAGON** – Last train / Head all fire / Mescal dance / Shout at the sky / Which side / Tear me up / Save my soul / Blitz. (cd+=) (REDF 65) – Hold yourself down / Generation. (free-7"w/ lp) – PAINT YOUR WAGON. / MORE JIPP (instrumental)		-
Jun 86.	(7") (RED 66) **WALKING ON YOUR HANDS. / WHICH SIDE** (12"+=) (REDT 66) – More jipp (instrumental).		-
Oct 86.	(7") (RED 73) **CUT DOWN. / RUNNING FEVER** (12"+=) (REDT 73) <HMS 074> – Pushed me.		
May 87.	(d7"/12"ep; as The LORRIES) (RED 76) **CRAWLING MANTRA. / HANGMAN // ALL THE SAME. / SHOUT AT THE SKY (live)**		

		Situation 2	Beggars Banquet
Nov 87.	(7") (SIT 49) **OPEN UP. / ANOTHER SIDE** (12"+=) (SIT 49T) – You only get what you pay for.		
Mar 88.	(7") (SIT 50) **NOTHING WRONG. / DO YOU UNDERSTAND?** (12"+=) (SIT 50T) – Calling.		
May 88.	(lp/cd)(c) (SITU 20/+CD)(SITC 20) <8480> **NOTHING WRONG** – Nothing wrong / Hands off me / Big stick / She said / Sayonara / World around / Hard-away / Only dreaming (wide awake) / Do you understand? / Never know / Time is tight [lp-only]. (cd+=) – Pushing on / You only get what you pay for / Another side / Calling / Open up. (re-iss. Jul91 lp/cd; SITL 20/+CD)		
Sep 88.	(7") (SIT 54) **ONLY DREAMING (WIDE AWAKE). / THE RISE** (12"+=) (SIT 54T) – Only dreaming (wide awake).		-
Aug 89.	(7") (SIT 60) **TEMPTATION. / DON'T KNOW WHY** (12"+=) (SIT 60T) – Blow (hard press mix).		-
Sep 89.	(lp/cd)(c) (SITU 25/+CD)(SITU 25) <9937> **BLOW** – Happy to see me / Temptation / Shine a light / Too many colours / Heaven / Gift that shines / In a world / You are everything / West wakes up / It was wrong / Blow. (cd+=) – Heaven (acoustic version). (re-iss. Jul91 lp/cd; SITL 25/+CD)		

—— disbanded after above album when new drummer CHIL broke his wrist. Reformed when REED brought in other new members **GARY WEIGHT** – lead guitar / **MARTIN SCOTT** – bass

		Sparkhead	not iss.
1991.	(12"ep) (MCD 20695) **TALKING BACK / TALKING BACK (extended). / RUNNING FEVER (live) / SAMY SOUL (live)**		-
		Deathwish	Relapse
Sep 92.	(cd/lp) (DW 2355 6CD/5LP) <RR 6109-2> **BLASTING OFF** – This is energy / It's on fire / Don't think about it / Train of hope / Talking back / Down on ice / In my mind / Sea of tears / I can see stars / Driving me.		1994

—— split for the last time early in '93

– compilations, etc. –

Feb 88.	(lp/c/cd) Red Rhino; (RED LP/C/CD 86) **SMASHED HITS** (cd-iss. May95 on 'Dojo'; DOJOCD 210)		-
Feb 94.	(cd) Cherry Red; (CDMRED 109) **THE SINGLES 1982-87** – Beating my head / I'm still waiting / Take it all away / Happy / He's read / See the fire / Monkey's on juice / Push / Silence / Hollow eyes / Feel a piece / Chance / Generation / Spinning round / Hold yourself down / Regenerate / Walking on your hands / Which side / Jipp (instrumental mix) / Cut down / Burning fever / Pushed me / Crawling mantra / Hang man / All the same / Shout at the sky. (<US+re-iss. Apr99; same>)		-
Jun 94.	(cd) Cherry Red; (CDMRED 115) **TALK ABOUT THE WEATHER / PAINT YOUR WAGON**		-
Jun 94.	(cd) Cleopatra; (cd) (<CLEO 9404>) **GENERATION: THE BEST OF RED LORRY YELLOW LORRY**		
Mar 00.	(cd) Cherry Red; (<CDNRED 167>) **THE VERY BEST OF RED LORRY YELLOW LORRY**		
Nov 01.	(cd) Anagram; (<CD<GOTH 11>) **NOTHING WRONG / BLOW**		

RED LORRY YELLOW LORRY (cont)

CHRIS REEDS WOOF!

solo with **DETLEF GERHOLD, RAINER HERZAM + STEPHAN STREUTER**

			Indigo	not iss.
1994.	(cd-ep) <1162-2>	**CHRIS REEDS WOOF!**	-	- German

– Learning to live / Living time / Big sun / I do believe.

—— next with **GEORGE SCHULZ** – drums

| 1994. | (cd) (1176-2) | **BIRTHDAY SKIN** | - | - German |

– Pulling the pieces / Birthday skin / Living time / Learning to live / I found out / I do believe / Watching the days / Honey don't you / Big sun / Run for me / Everybody (got a hold).

REDSKINS

Formed: York, England . . . 1981 as NO SWASTIKAS by NME journalist CHRIS DEAN (alias X MOORE) along with MARTIN HEWES and NICK KING. Delivering a steadfast anti-Thatcher, determinedly left-wing ideology – strongly based on the politics of the Socialist Workers Party – via a musical backdrop combining punk attitude and skinhead aggression with brassy northern soul, The REDSKINS made a brave attempt to unite youth culture under the red flag. Following a productive John Peel session, the band's independently released double A-side debut single, 'LEV BRONSTEIN' / 'PEASANT ARMY' hit the racks in summer '82, the campaign continuing the following year with another double header, 'LEAN ON ME' / 'UNIONIZE'. Championed by music journo, Gary Bushell, the band were subsequently signed to 'London' records, through whom they released the urgent call to arms of 'KEEP ON KEEPIN' ON' in 1984. With the shadow of the miners strike looming large over the mid-80's political landscape, The REDSKINS played a series of benefit gigs, pledging their solidarity and winning over new fans. The resulting interest saw them score a Top 40 hit with the highly charged 'BRING IT DOWN (THIS INSANE THING)', yet by the belated release of debut album, 'NEITHER WASHINGTON . . . NOR MOSCOW' in 1986, the miners were all but beaten and the unions were on the run from the Conservative Government. Despite its dancefloor-friendly celebration of socialist ideals and adrenaline-fuelled invective, the album received neither the critical praise nor the sales it deserved. Frozen out of the pro-Labour 'Red Wedge' movement (featuring the likes of BILLY BRAGG, PAUL WELLER, COMMUNARDS etc.) in the run-up to the 1987 election, The REDSKINS finally admitted defeat after a final single, 'IT CAN BE DONE'. Unfortunately it couldn't, even the efforts of 'Red Wedge' falling by the wayside as the Conservatives romped home again. • **Songwriters:** Group penned, except covers; 16 TONS (Tennessee Ernie Ford) / 99 AND A HALF WON'T DO (Dale Hawkins).

Album rating: NEITHER WASHINGTON . . . NOR MOSCOW (*8)

CHRIS DEAN – vocals, guitar, keyboards / **MARTIN HEWES** – bass, keyboards / **NICK KING** – drums

			C.N.T.	not iss.
Jul 82.	(7") (CNT 007)	**LEV BRONSTEIN. / PEASANT ARMY**		-
Jul 83.	(7") (CNT 016)	**LEAN ON ME. / UNIONIZE!**		-
	(12") (CNTX 016) – ('A' & 'B' different mixes)			

			Decca	not iss.
Oct 84.	(7"/12") (F/FX 1)	**KEEP ON KEEPIN' ON. / RED STRIKES THE BLUES**	43	-

—— **STEVE WHITE** – drums (of STYLE COUNCIL) repl. KING

| Jun 85. | (7") (F 2) | **(BURN IT UP) BRING IT DOWN (THIS INSANE THING). / YOU WANT IT, THEY'VE GOT IT** | 33 | - |
| | (12"+=) (FX 2) – ('A' remix). | | | |

—— **PAUL HOOKHAM** – drums (ex-WOODENTOPS) repl. WHITE (re-to STYLE COUNCIL)

Nov 85.	(7") (AD 6)	**KICK OVER THE STATUES! / YOUNG AND PROUD**		-
	(above 45 was one-off issued on 'Abstract Dance')			
Feb 86.	(7") (F 3)	**THE POWER IS YOURS . . . / 99 1/2 (WON'T DO)**	59	-
	(12"+=/d7"+=) (FX/+T 3) – Take 3 / Take your goods and bury them.			

—— brass section were **RAY CARLESS** – sax / **KEVIN ROBINSON** – trumpet, flugelhorn / **TREVOR EDWARDS** – trombone, 1/4 bottle

| Mar 86. | (lp/c) (FLP/FC 1) | **NEITHER WASHINGTON . . . NOR MOSCOW . . .** | 31 | - |

– The power is yours . . . / Kick over the statues! / Go get organized! / It can be done! / Keep on keepin' on! / (Burn it up) Bring it down! (this insane thing) / Hold on! / Turnin' loose (these furious flames) / Take no heroes! / Let's make it work! / Lean on me! / 'The return of the modern soul classic'. (cd-iss. Jan97 on 'London'; 828864-2)

| May 86. | (7") (F 4) | **IT CAN BE DONE! / A PLATEFUL OF HEAVEN** | | - |
| | (10"+=) (FXT 4) – Let's make it work. | | | |

—— disbanded again; HEWES returning to work as a despatch rider

– compilations, others, etc. –

May 87.	(12"ep) Strange Fruit; (SFPS 30)	**THE PEEL SESSIONS (9.10.82)**		-
	– Unionize! / Red strikes the blues / Kick over the statues! / The peasant army.			
Jun 94.	(cd) Dojo; (DOJOCD 188)	**LIVE (live)**		-

Lou REED

Born: LOUIS FIRBANK, 2 Mar'42, Freeport, Long Island, New York, USA. In 1958, he formed The JADES, who released two REED-penned singles, 'LEAVE HER FOR ME' / 'SO BLUE' and 'LEAVE HER FOR ME' / 'BELINDA' for 'Time' and 'Dot' respectively. Late in '64, he joined the 'Pickwick' stable of writers, achieving a local minor hit when The PRIMITIVES issued his 'The Ostrich' / 'Sneaky Pete' 45. Later in the year, he helped for the seminal VELVET UNDERGROUND. An integral part of the group's songwriting prowess, he departed in September 1970, going solo and signing to 'R.C.A.'. His eponymous 1972 debut (with Richard Robinson on production), scraped into the US Top 200, gaining nothing in renewed respect. Later that year, helped by stablemates DAVID BOWIE and MICK RONSON, he unleashed 'TRANSFORMER', gaving him his first major triumph when it reached the Top 30 on both sides of the Atlantic. It was boosted by 'WALK ON THE WILD SIDE' (a superb Top 20 single), the piano-led melancholy of 'PERFECT DAY', the raw glam of 'VICIOUS' and one-that-got-away 'SATELLITE OF LOVE'. His next album, 'BERLIN' (1973), although unfairly panned by US critics, still managed a Top 10 placing in Britain. On reflection, its subject matter of suicide and child neglect ('THE BED' and 'THE KIDS') didn't help win any new friends and it still stands as one of the most unrelentingly bleak listens in the history of rock. After the claustrophobic confessions of 'BERLIN', the live 'ROCK 'N' ROLL ANIMAL' (1974) album must have come as something of a relief to R.C.A. A technically faultless back-up band roared through a selection of old VELVETS numbers with REED hollering over the top, and while the set represented something of a concession to commercial credibility (by REED's standards anyway) it captured little of the VELVET UNDERGROUND's subtlety. It also saw REED sinking further into self-parody, hamming up his studied image of sleazy decadence to the max. 'SALLY CAN'T DANCE', released later the same year, was REED in full emotionless flight, an icy collection of biting cynicism that included the infamous 'ANIMAL LANGUAGE' track. But laughing LOU hadn't played his ace card yet, that musical two fingered salute fell to 1975's 'METAL MACHINE MUSIC', the one everyone talks about but have never had the will or mental endurance to listen to the whole way through. A double album of impenetrable feedback noise interspersed with inhuman screams, hums etc., the record successfully alienated most of REED's long suffering fans amid critical meltdown. In true contrary style, he sashayed sweetly back with the mellow 'CONEY ISLAND BABY' (1976), although the lyrics remained as brutally frank as ever. His first record for 'Arista', 'ROCK 'N' ROLL HEART' (1976) was indeed as vacantly awful as the title suggests, though the punk-inspired 'STREET HASSLE' (1978) showcased a re-energised REED, most impressively on the malicious guitar workout of 'DIRT' and the swaggering title track. After a tedious live album, REED started to show uncharacteristic signs of maturity in both his music and lyrics with 'THE BELLS' (1979) and 'GROWING UP IN PUBLIC' (1980). At the turn of the 80's, he hooked up with former Void-Oid, ROBERT QUINE, a partnership that resulted in one of the most consistent and accomplished sets in REED's solo career, 'THE BLUE MASK'. Newly married and back at his original stable, 'R.C.A.', REED proffered more domestic lyrical fare alongside darker musings. QUINE remained for one more studio album, the similarly focused 'LEGENDARY HEARTS', before breaking ranks. 1984's 'NEW SENSATIONS' was fairly low-key while 'MISTRIAL' (1986) saw REED introduce a few drum machine tracks in typical 80's style. These were competent albums but hardly essential and only the most devout REED believer could've predicted the creative, commercial and critical renaissance that would ensue with 1989's 'NEW YORK' album. A skeletal strum-athon, this was LOU REED in the raw with the sparsest of musical accompaniment. Back on familiar territory, his sardonic tales of the Big Apple's seedier side made for compelling listening. 'SONGS FOR DRELLA' (1990), a collaboration with JOHN CALE, was a heartfelt tribute to ANDY WARHOL, while 'MAGIC AND LOSS' (1992) was a sincere series of stark meditations on life and death. Despite an ill-advised VELVET UNDERGROUND reunion, REED retained critical favour, going on to release another well-received album in 1996, 'SET THE TWILIGHT REELING'. Rather than relying on the cosy reflections of an ageing iconic life, REED entered his fourth decade as a solo artist with more contrary perversity than most young bucks can muster these days. The aptly titled 'ECSTASY' (2000) found the cantankerous ex-VELVET fearlessly analysing the more uncomfortable dimensions of man's primal urges. He may be reaching pensionable age but his visceral guitar work still throbbed with the energy of misspent youth, REED aided and abetted by the rhythm section of FERNANDO SAUNDERS and TONY 'THUNDER' SMITH. • **Songwriters:** REED compositions except, SEPTEMBER SONG (Kurt Weill) / SOUL MAN (Sam & Dave). In 1979 and 1980, he co-wrote with MICHAEL FORFARA plus other group members. The single, 'CITY LIGHTS', was co-written with NILS LOFGREN. • **Trivia:** Surprisingly in 1973, WALK ON THE WILD SIDE was not banned from airplay. It contained lyrics "giving head", which had been overlooked by unstreet-wise cred. radio producers. LOU has been married twice, first to cocktail waitress, Betty on the 9th of January '73, then to Sylvia Morales on the 14th of February '80. He played guitar and composed four tracks on NICO's 'Chelsea Girl' lp in 1967. Nine years later he produced NELSON SLATER's 'Wild Angel' album, also contributing guitar, piano and vocals. In 1979 and 1981 he co-composed with NILS LOFGREN and KISS on their 'NILS' and 'THE ELDER' albums respectively. In the late 80's, he guested for RUBEN BLADES and his old friend MAUREEN TUCKER. He was also backing vocalist on SIMPLE MINDS' 'This is Your Land' / DION's 'King of The New York Streets' and TOM TOM CLUB's version of 'Femme Fatale'.

Album rating: LOU REED (*5) / TRANSFORMER (*9) / BERLIN (*7) / ROCK'N'ROLL ANIMAL (*6) / SALLY CAN'T DANCE (*5) / LOU REED LIVE (*5) / METAL MACHINE MUSIC (*1) / CONEY ISLAND BABY (*7) / ROCK AND ROLL HEART (*4) / WALK ON THE WILD SIDE – THE BEST OF LOU REED compilation (*7) / STREET HASSLE (*7) / LIVE – TAKE NO PRISONERS (*3) / THE BELLS (*5) / GROWING UP IN PUBLIC (*4) / ROCK AND ROLL DIARY 1967-1980 compilation (*6) / THE BLUE MASK (*6) / LEGENDARY HEARTS (*6) / LIVE IN ITALY (*4) / NEW SENSATIONS (*7) / MISTRIAL (*5) / NEW YORK (*8) / RETRO compilation (*7) / SONGS FOR DRELLA with John Cale (*7) / MAGIC AND LOSS (*7) / BETWEEN THOUGHT AND EXPRESSION: THE LOU REED ANTHOLOGY boxed-compilation (*7) / SET THE TWILIGHT REELING (*6) / PERFECT NIGHT LIVE IN LONDON (*6) / ECSTASY (*8)

LOU REED – vocals, guitar (ex-VELVET UNDERGROUND) / with **STEVE HOWE** – guitar / **RICK WAKEMAN** – keyboards (both of YES) / **CLEM CATTINI** – drums (ex-TORNADOES)

			R.C.A.	R.C.A.
Jun 72.	(7") <0727>	**GOING DOWN. / I CAN'T STAND IT**	-	
Jul 72.	(lp) (SF 8281) <4701>	**LOU REED**		Jun72

– I can't stand it / Going down / Walk and talk it / Lisa says / Berlin / I love you / Wild child / Love makes you feel / Ride into the Sun / Ocean. (cd-iss. Feb00 on 'RCA-Camden'; 74321 72712-2)

Aug 72. (7") (RCA 2240) <0784> **WALK AND TALK IT. / WILD CHILD**

— now with **MICK RONSON** – guitar / **HERBIE FLOWERS + KLAUS VOORMANN** – bass / **JOHN HALSEY + RITCHIE DHARMA + BARRY DE SOUZA** – drums / **RONNIE ROSS** – saxophone / **DAVID BOWIE** – backing vocals, producer

Nov 72. (lp) (LSP 4807) <4807> **TRANSFORMER** — 13 / 29
– Vicious / Andy's chest / Perfect day / Hangin' round / Walk on the wild side / Make up / Satellite of love / Wagon wheel / New York telephone conversation / I'm so free / Goodnight ladies. (re-iss. Feb81 lp/c; INT S/K 5061); hit UK No.91) (re-iss. 1984 lp/c; NL/NK 83806) (cd-iss. 1985 & Oct87 & Aug95; PD 83806) (re-iss. Sep98 d/c; 74321 60181-2/-4) (lp re-iss. Nov98 on 'Simply Vinyl'; SVLP 58) (lp re-iss. Mar99; NL 83806) (re-dist.Sep01) – hit UK No.16

Nov 72. (7") (RCA 2303) <0887> **WALK ON THE WILD SIDE. / PERFECT DAY** — 10 / 16
Feb 73. (7") <0964> **SATELLITE OF LOVE. / WALK AND TALK IT** — -
Mar 73. (7") (RCA 2318) **SATELLITE OF LOVE. / VICIOUS**
Apr 73. (7") <0054> **VICIOUS. / GOODNIGHT LADIES**

— all new band **DICK WAGNER + STEVE HUNTER** – guitar (both ex-ALICE COOPER) / **STEVE WINWOOD** – keyboards / **JACK BRUCE** – bass / **AYNSLEY DUNBAR** – drums / etc.

Oct 73. (7") <0172> **HOW DO YOU THINK IT FEELS. / LADY DAY**
Oct 73. (lp) (RS 1002) <0207> **BERLIN** — 7 / 98
– Berlin / Lady day / Men of good fortune / Caroline says I / How do you think it feels / Oh Jim / Caroline says II / The kids / The bed / Sad song. (re-iss. Oct81 lp/c; INT S/K 5150) (re-iss. 1984 lp/c; NL/NK 84388) (cd-iss. Jun86; PD 84388) (cd re-iss. Mat98; 7863 67489-2) (lp re-iss. Feb99 on 'Simply Vinyl'; SVLP 66) (lp re-iss. Mar99; 7863 67489-1)

Feb 74. (7") (APBO 0221) **CAROLINE SAYS I. / CAROLINE SAYS II** — -

— **PRAKASH JOHN** – bass (ex-ALICE COOPER) repl. TONY LEVIN / **JOSEF CHIROWSKY** – keyboards / **WHITNEY GLEN** – drums (ex-ALICE COOPER)

Feb 74. (lp/c) (APL 1/4 0472) <0472> **ROCK'N'ROLL ANIMAL** — 26 / 45
– (intro) – Sweet Jane / Heroin / White light – white heat / Lady day / Rock and roll. (re-iss. May81 lp/c; INT S/K 5086) (re-iss. 1984 lp/c; NL/NK 83664) (cd-iss. Jun86; PD 83664)

Apr 74. (7") <(APBO 0238)> **SWEET JANE (live). / LADY DAY (live)**

— **MICHAEL FORFARA** – keyboards repl. JOSEF

Aug 74. (7") <10053> **SALLY CAN'T DANCE. / VICIOUS** — -
Sep 74. (lp/c) (APL 1/4 0611) > **SALLY CAN'T DANCE** — 10
– Ride Sally ride / Animal language / Baby face / N.Y. stars / Kill your sons / Billy / Sally can't dance / Ennui. (cd-iss. Mar87; PD 80611) (re-iss. cd Feb89; ND 90308)

Oct 74. (7") (RCA 2467) <10081> **SALLY CAN'T DANCE. / ENNUI**
Mar 75. (lp) (RS 1007) <0959> **LOU REED LIVE (live)** — 62
– Walk on the wild side / I'm waiting for the man / Vicious / Oh Jim / Satellite of love / Sad song. (re-iss. Feb81 lp/c; INT S/K 5071) (cd-iss. Mar87 + Feb90; ND 83752)

— LOU now used synthesizer only.

Jul 75. (d-lp) <(CPL2 1101)> **METAL MACHINE MUSIC – (THE AMINE B RING)**
– Metal machine music A1 / A2 / A3 / A4. (re-iss. Mar91 on 'Great Expectations' cd/d-c/d-lp; PIPD C/M/L 023)

— Band now featured **MICHAEL SUCHORSKY** – percussion / **BOB KULICK** – guitar / **BRUCE YAW** – bass

Jan 76. (lp) (RS 1035) <0915> **CONEY ISLAND BABY** — 52 / 41
– Crazy feeling / Charley's girl / She's my best friend / Kicks / A gift / Oooh baby / Nobody's business / Coney island baby. (re-iss. Mar81 lp/c; INT S/K 5082) (re-iss. 1984 lp/c; NL/NK 83807) (cd-iss. Dec86 & Sep89; PD 83807)

Mar 76. (7") (RCA 2666) <10573> **CHARLEY'S GIRL. / NOWHERE AT ALL**
May 76. (7") <10648> **CRAZY FEELING. / NOWHERE AT ALL** — -

			Arista	Arista
Nov 76.	(lp/c) (ARTY/TC-ARTY 142) <4100>	**ROCK AND ROLL HEART**		64

– I believe in love / Banging on my drum / Follow the leader / You wear it so well / Ladies pay / Rock and roll heart / Temporary thing. (cd-iss. Feb93; 262271)

Nov 76. (7") <0215> **I BELIEVE IN LOVE. / SENSELESSLY CRUEL**
Apr 77. (7") (105) **ROCK AND ROLL HEART. / SENSELESSLY CRUEL**

— **STUART HEINRICH** – guitar, vocals repl. KULICK / **MARTY FOGEL** – saxophone repl. YAW

Apr 78. (lp/c) (SPART/TC-SPART 1045) <4169> **STREET HASSLE** — — / 89
– Gimme some good times / Dirt / Street hassle / I wanna be black / Real good time together / Shooting star / Leave me alone / Wait. (cd-iss. Feb93; 262270)

Apr 78. (12") **STREET HASSLE. / (same track)** — -
Jul 78. (12"ep) (ARIST12 198) **STREET HASSLE. / Waiting For The Man + Venus In Furs (by "The VELVET UNDERGROUND")** — -

— **ELLARD BOLES** – bass, guitar repl. HEINRICH. (Below released 'RCA' UK)

Mar 79. (d-lp) <red,blue-lp> (XL 03066) <8502> **LIVE – TAKE NO PRISONERS (live)** — Nov78
– Sweet Jane / I wanna be black / Satellite of love / Pale blue eyes / Berlin / I'm waiting for the man / Coney Island baby / Street hassle / Walk on the wild side / Leave me alone.

— REED now with **FORFARA, BOLES, SUCHORSKY, FOGEL** and **DON CHERRY** – trumpet

Oct 79. (lp/c) (SPART/TC-SPART 1093) <4229> **THE BELLS** — — / May 79
– Stupid man / Disco mystic / I want to boogie with you / With you / Looking for love / City lights / All through the night / Families / The bells. (cd-iss. Aug92; 262 918)

Jun 79. (7") <0431> **CITY LIGHTS. / I WANT TO BOOGIE WITH YOU**
Oct 79. (7") (ARIST 308) **CITY LIGHTS. / SENSELESSLY CRUEL** — -

— **CHUCK HAMMER** – synthesizer, guitar repl. FOGEL & CHERRY

May 80. (lp/c) (SPART/TC-SPART 1131) <9522> **GROWING UP IN PUBLIC**
– How do you speak to an angel / My old man / Keep away / Growing up in public / Standing on ceremony / So alone / Love is here to stay / The power of positive drinking / Smiles / Think it over / Teach the gifted children. (cd-iss. Aug92; 262 917)

Jun 80. (7") <0535> **THE POWER OF POSITIVE DRINKING. / GROWING UP IN PUBLIC** — -

— now with **ROBERT QUINE** – guitar / **FERNANDO SAUNDERS** – bass, vocals / **DOANE PERRY** – drums

			R.C.A.	R.C.A.
Mar 82.	(lp/c) (RCA LP/K 6028) <4221>	**THE BLUE MASK**		Feb82

– My house / Women / Underneath the bottle / The gun / The blue mask / Average guy / The heroine / Waves of fear / The day John Kennedy died / Heavenly arms. (cd-iss. Feb98; ND 84780)

Mar 83. (lp/c) (RCA LP/K 6071) <4568> **LEGENDARY HEARTS**
– Legendary hearts / Don't talk to me about work / Make up mind / Martial law / The last shot / Turn out the light / ow wow / Betrayed / Bottoming out / Home of the brave / Rooftop garden. (re-iss. Oct86 lp/c; NL/NK 89843) (re-iss. Apr91 cd/c; ND/NK 89843)

Apr 83. (7") <13558> **MARTIAL LAW. / DON'T TALK TO ME ABOUT WORK** — -
Jan 84. (d-lp/c) (PL/PK 89156) **LIVE IN ITALY (live)** — -
– Sweet Jane / I'm waiting for the man / Martial law / Satellite of love / Kill your sons / Betrayed / Sally can't dance / Waves of fear / Average guy / White light – white heat / Some kinda love / Sister Ray / Walk on the wild side / Heroin / Rock and roll.

— line-up now **SAUNDERS** plus **FRED MAHER** – drums / **PETER WOOD** – piano, synthesizer, accordion / **L. SHANKER** – electric violin

Mar 84. (7") <13841> **I LOVE YOU SUZANNE. / MY FRIEND GEORGE** — -
May 84. (12") <13849> **MY RED JOY STICK. / ('A' remix)** — -
May 84. (lp/c) (PL/PK 84998) <4998> **NEW SENSATIONS** — 92 / 56
– I love you, Suzanne / Endlessly jealous / My red joystick / Turn to me / New sensations / Doin' the things that we want to / What becomes a legend most / Fly into the Sun / High in the city / My friend George / Down at the arcade. (cd-iss. Jul86; PD 84998)

May 84. (7") (RCA 417) **I LOVE YOU, SUZANNE. / VICIOUS**
(12"+=) (RCAT 417) – Walk on the wild side.

1985. (7") <7-89468> **MY LOVE IS CHEMICAL. / PEOPLE HAVE TO MOVE**
(above issued on 'Atlantic' and taken from 'White Nights' movie)

Apr 86. (12") <14427> **THE ORIGINAL WRAPPER. / (2 'A' versions)** — -
Apr 86. (lp/c/cd) (PL/PK/PD 87190) <7190> **MISTRIAL** — 69 / 47
– Mistrial / No money down / Outside / Don't hurt a woman / Video violence / Spit it out / The original wrapper / Mama's got a lover / I remember you / Tell it to your heart. (re-iss. Oct88 lp/c/cd; NL/NK/ND 90253)

Jun 86. (7") (RCA 501) <14368> **NO MONEY DOWN. / DON'T HURT A WOMAN**
(12"+=) (RCAT 501) <14388> – ('A'dub version).

— Next from the film 'Soul Man'.

			A&M	A&M
Jan 87.	(7"; LOU REED & SAM MOORE) (AM 364)	**SOUL MAN. / Sweet Sarah (by 'Tom Scott')**	30	Nov86

<US-12"+=> <364> – My love is chemical.

— new band **MIKE RATHKE** – guitar / **ROB WASSERMAN** – bass / **FRED MAHER** – drums / **MAUREEN TUCKER** – drums on 2 (ex-VELVET UNDERGROUND)

			Sire	Sire
Jan 89.	(lp/c)(cd) (WX 246/+C)(925 829-2) <25829>	**NEW YORK**	14	40

– Romeo had Juliette / Halloween parade / Dirty Blvd. / Endless cycle / There is no time / The last great American whale / Beginning of a great adventure / Busload of faith / Sick of you / Hold on / Good evening Mr. Waldheim / Xmas in February / Strawman / Dime store mystery. (re-iss. Feb95 cd/c;)

Feb 89. (7") <9 22875-7> **ROMEO HAD JULIETTE. / BUSLOAD OF FAITH (live)** — -
Feb 89. (7") (W 7547) **DIRTY BLVD. / THE LAST GREAT AMERICAN WHALE**
(12"+=) (W 7547T) – The room.

Apr 90. (cd)(lp/c; by LOU REED / JOHN CALE) (7599 <26140-2>)(WX 345/+C) **SONGS FOR DRELLA** — 22
– Smalltown / Open house / Style it takes / Work / Trouble with classicists / Starlight / Faces and names / Images / Slip away (a warning) / It wasn't me / I believe / Nobody but you / A dream / Forever changed / Hello it's me. (re-iss. Feb91 & Jan97; same) (above re-united the two VELVET UNDERGROUND members, tributing the recently deceased ANDY WARHOL)

— MICHAEL BLAIR – percussion, drums, vocals repl. MAHER
Jan 92. (cd/lp/c) (7599 <26662-2>)(WX 435/+C) **MAGIC AND LOSS** [6] [80]
– Dorita – the spirit / What's good – the thesis / Power and glory – the situation / Magician – internally / Sword of Damocles – eternally / Goodby mass – in a chapel bodily termination / Cremation – ashes to ashes / Dreamin' – escape / No chance – regret / Warrior king – revenge / Harry's circumcision – reverie gone astray / Gassed and stoked – loss / Power and glory part II – magic transformation / Magic and loss – the summation. (cd re-iss. Jan97; same)
Mar 92. (c-s) (W 0090C) **WHAT'S GOOD. / THE ROOM** [ ] [-]
(12"+=/cd-s+=) (W 0090 T/CD) – Harry's circumcision / A dream.
— now with just **FERNANDO SAUNDERS** – basses / **TONY 'Thunder' SMITH** – drums / **MIKE RATHKE** – guitars / + guest **LAURIE ANDERSON** – backing vocals
Feb 96. (cd/c) <(9362 46159-2/-4)> **SET THE TWILIGHT REELING** Reprise Reprise [26]
– Egg cream / NYC man / Finish line / Trade in / Hang on to your emotions / Sex with your parents (motherfucker) part II (live) / Hooky wooky / The proposition / Adventurer / Riptide / Set the twilight reeling.
May 96. (c-s) (W 0351C) **HOOKY WOOKY / ON THE RUN** [ ] [ ]
(cd-s) (W 0351CD) – ('A'side) / This magic moment / You'll never know you loved.
Apr 98. (cd/c) <(9362 46917-2/-4)> **PERFECT NIGHT LIVE IN LONDON** (live) [ ] [ ]
– I'll be your mirror / Perfect day / The kids / Vicious / Busload of faith / Kicks / Talking book / Into the divine / Coney Island baby / New sensations / Why do you talk / Riptide / Original wrapper / Sex with your parents / Dirty Blvd.
Apr 00. (cd/c) <(9362 47425-2/-4)> **ECSTASY** [54]
– Paranoia key of E / Mystic child / Mad / Ecstasy / Modern dance / Tatters / Future farmers of America / Turning time around / White prism / Rock minuet / Baton rouge / Like a possum / Rouge / Big sky.

– compilations, others, etc. –

— Below releases issued on 'RCA' unless mentioned otherwise
Apr 77. (lp/c) (PL/PK 12001) <2001> **WALK ON THE WILD SIDE – THE BEST OF LOU REED** [ ] [ ]
(cd-iss. Mar87 & Oct91; PD 83753)
Jan 79. (lp/c) (NL/NK 42731) **VICIOUS** [ ] [ ]
Dec 80. (d-lp) Arista; (DARTY 8) **ROCK AND ROLL DIARY 1967-1980** [ ] [ ]
– (above featured 8 tracks by Velvet Underground)
Aug 81. (7") RCA Gold; (GOLD 523) **WALK ON THE WILD SIDE. / VICIOUS** [ ] [-]
(re-iss. Oct86 & Mar89 on 'Old Gold'; OG 9635)
Sep 82. (lp) (SF 8281) **I CAN'T STAND IT** [ ] [ ]
Oct 85. (7") A&M; (AM 283) **SEPTEMBER SONG. / Oh Heavenly Action** (by 'Mark Bingham with Johnny Adams & Aaron Neville') [ ] [ ]
May 86. (lp/c) (NK 89895) **MAGIC MOMENTS** [ ] [-]
Sep 86. (lp/c) Fame; (FA/TC-FA 3164) **NEW YORK SUPERSTAR** [ ] [-]
Feb 89. (3"cd-ep) (PD 49453) **WALK ON THE WILD SIDE / PERFECT DAY / SATELLITE OF LOVE / VICIOUS** [ ] [ ]
Sep 89. (lp/c/cd) (PL/PK/PD 90389) **RETRO** [29]
– Walk on the wild side / Satellite of love / I love you Suzanne / Wild child / How do you think it feels / Lady day / Coney Island baby / Sweet Jane (live) / Vicious / Sally can't dance / Berlin / Caroline says II / Kill your sons / White light – white heat (live). (cd+=) – I'm waiting for the man (VELVET UNDERGROUND) / Heroin (VELVET UNDERGROUND).
Mar 92. (3xcd-box/3xc-box) (PD/PK 90621) **BETWEEN THOUGHT AND EXPRESSION: THE LOU REED ANTHOLOGY** [ ] Apr92
Jan 95. (d-cd) (74321 29209-2) **STREET HASSLE / THE BELLS** [ ] [ ]
Jan 95. (d-cd) (74321 29210-2) **TRANSFORMER / BERLIN** [ ] [ ]
Oct 95. (cd/c; by LOU REED & VELVET UNDERGROUND) Global TV; (RAD CD/MC 21) **LOU REED & VELVET UNDERGROUND** [ ] [-]
Aug 96. (cd) (07863 66864-2) **DIFFERENT TIMES – LOU REED IN THE 70'S** [ ] [-]
Oct 96. (cd) Camden-RCA; (74321 43157-2) **LOU REED LIVE IN CONCERT** (live) [ ] [ ]
Sep 97. (cd/c) Camden-RCA; (74321 52375-2/-4) **PERFECT DAY** [ ] [ ]
Nov 97. (cd) Eagle; (EABCD 012) **THE MASTERS** [ ] [-]
Apr 99. (cd/c) RCA-Camden; (74321 66046-2/-4) **THE VERY BEST OF LOU REED** [ ] [-]

REEGS (see under ⇒ CHAMELEONS)

REFLECTIONS
(see under ⇒ ALTERNATIVE TV; 70's section)

R.E.M.

Formed: Athens, Georgia, USA ... spring 1980 by MICHAEL STIPE and PETER BUCK, MIKE MILLS and BILL BERRY, who soon played at a local party under the name TWISTED KITES. In 1981, through manager Jefferson Holt, they released their debut MITCH EASTER-produced 45, 'RADIO FREE EUROPE'. With its soaring melody and jangly guitar playing off STIPE's low-key vocals, the sound was unique and caught the ears of 'I.R.S.' label boss, MILES COPELAND. The latter duly signed them up and retained EASTER for the mini-lp 'CHRONIC TOWN' (1982). The five-song set was received with gushing enthusiasm and set the scene for R.E.M.'s first album proper, 'MURMUR' (1983). Co-produced by EASTER and DON DIXON, the album was a stunning debut which sharpened the hooks, honed the pealing guitar sound and generally engendered a compelling air of mystique. Much of this was down to STIPE's impenetrable lyrics and vague execution which enhanced rather than detracted from the melodic melancholy of songs like 'TALK ABOUT THE PASSION'. While this inventiveness wasn't quite consolidated with 'RECKONING' (1984), the album was slightly more accessible, leading to a Top 30 placing in the American charts. Boasting the ambling country poignancy of '(DON'T GO BACK TO) ROCKVILLE', what the record lacked in innovation it made up for in songwriting skill. Never content to tread water, the band recorded 'FABLES OF THE RECONSTRUCTION' (1985) in London with veteran folk producer JOE BOYD, an interesting pairing which made for a trippy, heavily atmospheric sound. Even the poppier 'DRIVER 8' wasn't free of the edginess which characterised the record. Dextrously combining sonic exploration and heart-melting melodies, 'LIFE'S RICH PAGEANT' (1986) was a bold step forward. Tracks like 'FALL ON ME', 'I BELIEVE' and 'CUYAHOGA' showed an assured poise which the band were undoubtedly developing through their ceaseless touring and snowballing critical acclaim. 'DOCUMENT' (1987) was even more focused, STIPE actually beginning to sound comprehensible. The sardonic, brooding 'THE ONE I LOVE' single gave R.E.M. their first US Top 10 hit, while the band's 'Warners' debut, 'GREEN' (1988), finally saw the band become a mainstream act, in terms of commercial success at least. The unashamed jaunty pop of 'STAND' (1989) gave the band their biggest hit to date while 'ORANGE CRUSH' (1989) echoed the muted moodiness of 'THE ONE I LOVE'. Elsewhere, gems like 'WORLD LEADER PRETEND' were artful examples of that rare ability to create subtle, intelligent songs that were still annoyingly hummable. After 'GREEN's release, R.E.M. undertook a mammoth world tour with the result that the next album, 'OUT OF TIME', didn't hit the shelves until 1991. For most people it was well worth the wait. Preceded by the starkly melancholy 'LOSING MY RELIGION' with its mournful mandolin refrain, 'OUT OF TIME' was a multi-million seller, hitting the top spot on both sides of the Atlantic. While 'SHINY HAPPY PEOPLE' was a mite sickly sweet after 10,000 listens, and 'RADIO' was an ill-advised foray into rap, acoustic flavoured diamonds like 'HALF A WORLD AWAY', 'COUNTRY FEEDBACK' and 'ME IN HONEY' rendered the album a classic. Equally successful but much harder going, 1992's 'AUTOMATIC FOR THE PEOPLE' was a moody masterpiece. Focusing on the more painful aspects of human existence, the album wasn't as immediate as its predecessor but the lucid beauty of tracks like 'NIGHTSWIMMING' and 'MAN ON THE MOON' (written about their tragic comic-hero, Andy Kaufman and later made into a film starring Jim Carrey, c.1999) soon slipped insidiously into your subconscious. Silencing rumours that MICHAEL STIPE was suffering from Aids, R.E.M. bounced back with the grungy 'MONSTER' (1994) album. Despite confident hits like 'WHAT'S THE FREQUENCY KENNETH' and 'CRUSH WITH EYELINER', R.E.M. were capable of more imaginative fare. The subsequent tour (the first since the late 80's) came to a premature halt when BILL BERRY suffered a brain haemorrhage. After a successful recovery, the band reconvened to record 1996's 'NEW ADVENTURES IN HI-FI' (sadly, the last with BERRY). Written mainly on the road, the album was a return to more familiar R.E.M. territory, rich in imagery and possessed of all the qualities that make R.E.M. one of rock's most respected bands. Between '...HI-FI' and 98's slightly disappointing Top 3 set 'UP', BUCK took up posts in MINUS 5 (with YOUNG FRESH FELLOWS' SCOTT McCAUGHEY) and lounge-pop/jazz supergroup, TUATARA. The aforementioned 'UP' was certainly their most pensive and melancholy record to date, UK Top 30 singles such as 'DAYSLEEPER', 'LOTUS' and 'AT MY MOST BEAUTIFUL', sitting alongside their use of LEONARD COHEN lyrics on 'HOPE'. Come the new millennium, R.E.M. were looking back as well as forward on the shiny, happy but ultimately unfulfilled 'REVEAL' (2001), attempting a marriage of their classic songcraft with the more recent experimentalism. Despite moments of lush, summery abandon, it doesn't quite come off, STIPE and Co sounding like they're still grappling with that sonic mid-life crisis. Another crisis was on hand in April 2001 when PETER BUCK allegedly got into some serious mischief while on a BA flight; his case would take until early the following year to settle. • **Songwriters:** Group compositions except 'B'side covers; THERE SHE GOES AGAIN + PALE BLUE EYES + FEMME FATALE (Velvet Underground) / TOYS IN THE ATTIC (Aerosmith) / KING OF THE ROAD (Roger Miller) / CRAZY (Pylon) / AFTER HOURS (Lou Reed) / LOVE IS ALL AROUND (Troggs) / FIRST WE TAKE MANHATTAN (Leonard Cohen) / LAST DATE (Floyd Cramer) / TIGHTEN UP (Booker T. & The MG's) / SEE NO EVIL (Television) / ACADEMY EIGHT SONG (Mission of Burma) / SUMMERTIME (Gershwin) / BABY BABY (Vibrators) / WHERE'S CAPTAIN KIRK? (Spizz) / PARADE OF WOODEN SOLDIERS (Tchaikovsky) / MOON RIVER (Henry Mancini) / THE ARMS OF YOU (Robyn Hitchcock) / THE LION SLEEPS TONIGHT (Tokens) / DARK GLOBE (Syd Barrett) / SPONGE (Vic Chesnutt). • **Trivia:** R.E.M. stands for Rapid Eye Movement.

Album rating: CHRONIC TOWN mini (*6) / MURMUR (*9) / RECKONING (*9) / FABLES OF THE RECONSTRUCTION (*8) / LIFE'S RICH PAGEANT (*8) / DEAD LETTER OFFICE compilation (*7) / DOCUMENT (*8) / EPONYMOUS compilation (*7) / GREEN (*8) / THE BEST OF R.E.M. compilation (*9) / OUT OF TIME (*9) / AUTOMATIC FOR THE PEOPLE (*10) / MONSTER (*7) / NEW ADVENTURES IN HI-FI (*8) / UP (*7) / REVEAL (*7) / Hindu Love Gods: HINDU LOVE GODS (*5)

MICHAEL STIPE (b. JOHN MICHAEL STIPE, 4 Jan'60, Decatur, Atlanta) – vocals / **PETER BUCK** (b. 6 Dec'56, Oakland, Calif.) – guitar / **MIKE MILLS** (b.17 Dec'58, Orange County, Calif.) – bass, keyboards, vocals / **BILL BERRY** (b.31 Jul'58, Duluth, Minnesota) – drums, vocals

not iss. Hib-Tone

Jul 81. (7") *(HT-0001)* **RADIO FREE EUROPE. / SITTING STILL** [-] [ ]

I.R.S. I.R.S.

Aug 82. (m-lp) *<SP 70502>* **CHRONIC TOWN** [-] [ ]
– Wolves, lower / 1,000,000 / Gardening at night / Stumble / Carnival of sorts (box cars). *(re-iss. Feb85; IRS 70502)*

Aug 83. (7") *(PFP 1017) <9916>* **RADIO FREE EUROPE. / THERE SHE GOES AGAIN** [ ] [78] Jul83

Aug 83. (lp/c) *(SP/CS 70604) <70604>* **MURMUR** [ ] [36] May83
– Radio free Europe / Pilgrimage / Laughing / Talk about the passion / Moral kiosk / Perfect circle / Catapult / Sitting still / 9-9 / Shaking through / We walk / West of the fields. *(cd-iss. 1988; CDA 7014) (cd re-iss. Mar91 ++; CDMID 129)* – There she goes again / 9-9 (live) / Gardening at night (live) / Catapult (live).

Nov 83. (7") *(PFP 1026)* **TALK ABOUT THE PASSION. / SHAKING THROUGH** [ ] [-]
(12"+=) *(PFSX 1026)* – Carnival of sorts (box cars) / 1,000,000.

Mar 84. (7") *(IRS 105) <9927>* **S). CENTRAL RAIN (I'M SORRY). / KING OF THE ROAD** [ ] [85] Jun84
(12") *(PFSX 105)* – ('A'side) / Voice of Harold / Pale blue eyes.

Apr 84. (lp/c) *(IRS A/C 7045) <70044>* **RECKONING** [91] [27]
– Harborcoat / 7 Chinese Bros. / So. central rain (I'm sorry) / Pretty persuasion / Time after time (Annelise) / Second guessing / Letter never sent / Camera / (Don't go back to) Rockville / Little America. *(cd-iss. 1988 on 'A&M'; CDA 7045) (re-iss. Oct94 on 'A&M' cd/c;)*

Jun 84. (7") *(IRS 107)* **(DON'T GO BACK TO) ROCKVILLE. / WOLVES** [ ] [-]
(12"+=) *(IRSX 107)* – 9 minus 9 (live) / Gardening at night (live).

Jun 84. (7") *<IR 9931>* **(DON'T GO BACK TO) ROCKVILLE. / CATAPULT (live)** [-] [ ]

Jul 85. (7") *(IRM 102)* **CAN'T GET THERE FROM HERE. / BANDWAGON** [ ] [-]
(12"+=) *(IRT 102)* – Burning Hell.

Jul 85. (lp/c) *(MIR F/C 1003) <5592>* **FABLES OF THE RECONSTRUCTION – RECONSTRUCTION OF THE FABLES** [35] [28] Jun85
– Feeling gravitys pull / Maps and legends / Driver 8 / Life and how to live it / Old Man Kensey / Can't get there from here / Green grow the rushes / Kokoutek / Auctioneer (another engine) / Good advices / Wendell Gee. *(cd-iss. Apr87; DMIRF 1003) (re-iss. cd Jan90; DMIRL 1503) (lp re-iss. Dec99 on 'Simply Vinyl'; SVLP 151)*

Oct 85. (7") *<52678>* **DRIVER 8. / CRAZY** [-] [ ]

Oct 85. (7") *(IRM 105)* **WENDELL GEE. / CRAZY** [ ] [-]
(d7"+=) *(IRMD 105)* – Ages of you / Burning down.
(12"+=) *(IRT 105)* – Driver 8.

Aug 86. (7") *(IRM 121) <52883>* **FALL ON ME. / ROTARY TEN** [ ] [94]
(12"+=) *(IRMT 121)* – Toys in the attic.

Aug 86. (lp/c) *(MIRG/+C 1014) <5783>* **LIFE'S RICH PAGEANT** [43] [21]
– Begin the begin / These days / Fall on me / Cuyahoga / Hyena / Underneath the bunker / The flowers of Guatemala / I believe / What if we give it away? / Just a touch / Swan swan H / Superman. *(cd-iss. Dec86; DMIRG 1014) (re-iss. cd Sep91; DMIRL 1507)*

Mar 87. (7") *(IRM 128)* **SUPERMAN. / WHITE TORNADO** [ ] [-]
(12"+=) *(IRMT 128)* – Femme fatale.

Aug 87. (7") *(IRM 145)* **IT'S THE END OF THE WORLD AS WE KNOW IT (AND I FEEL FINE). / THIS ONE GOES OUT (live)** [ ] [-]
(12"+=) *(IRMT 145)* – Maps and legends (live).

Sep 87. (7") *<53171>* **THE ONE I LOVE. / MAPS AND LEGENDS (live)** [-] [9]

Oct 87. (lp/c/cd) *(MIRG/MIRGC/DMIRG 1025) <42059>* **DOCUMENT** [28] [10] Sep87
– Finest worksong / Welcome to the occupation / Exhuming McCarthy / Disturbance at Heron House / Strange / It's the end of the world as we know it (and I feel fine) / The one I love / Fireplace / Lightnin' Hopkins / King of birds / Oddfellows local 151. *(cd re-iss. Sep91 +=; DMIRL 1508)* – Finest worksong (other mix) / Last date / The one I love (live) / Time after time etc. (live) / Disturbance at the Heron house (live) / Finest worksong (lengthy club mix). *(lp re-iss. Apr99; 499466-1)*

Nov 87. (7") *(IRM 146)* **THE ONE I LOVE. / LAST DATE** [51] [-]
(12"+=/cd-s+=) *(IRMT/DIRM 146)* – Disturbance at the Heron House (live).

Jan 88. (7") *(IRM 161)* **FINEST WORKSONG. / TIME AFTER TIME, ETC.** [50] [-]
(12"+=) *(IRMT 161) <23850>* – ('A'-lengthy club mix).
(cd-s+=) *(DIRM 161)* – It's the end of the world and we know it (and I feel fine).

Jan 88. (7") *<53220>* **IT'S THE END OF THE WORLD AS WE KNOW IT (AND I FEEL FINE). / LAST DATE** [-] [69]

Warners Warners

Nov 88. (lp/c)(cd) *(WX 234/+C)<(7599-25795-2)>* **GREEN** [27] [12]
– Pop song '89 / Get up / You are the everything / Stand / World leader pretend / The wrong child / Orange crush / Turn you inside-out / Hairshirt / I remember California / Untitled song. *(lp re-iss. Jul99; same)*

Jan 89. (7"/s7") *(W 7577/+X) <27688>* **STAND. / MEMPHIS TRAIN BLUES** [51] [6]
(12"+=/3"cd-s+=/3"s-cd-s+=) *(W 7577 T/CD/CDX)* – (The eleventh untitled song).

Mar 89. (7"/s7"/7"box/c-s) *(W 2960/+X/B/C)* **ORANGE CRUSH. / GHOST RIDERS** [28] [-]
(12"+=/3"cd-s+=) *(W 2960 T/CD)* – Dark globe.

Jun 89. (7") *<27640>* **POP SONG '89 / ('A'acoustic)** [-] [86]

Jul 89. (7"/s7") *(W 2833/+W)* **STAND. / POP SONG '89 (acoustic)** [48] [-]
(12"+=/3"cd-s+=/3"s-cd-s+=) *(W 2833 T/CD/CDX)* – Skin tight (live).

— (all above 7"singles were re-iss. in 4xbox Dec89)

Sep 89. (7") *(7-22791>* **GET UP. / FUNTIME** [-] [ ]

— R.E.M. toured early '91 as BINGO HAND JOB.

Feb 91. (7"/c-s) *(W 0015/+C) <19392>* **LOSING MY RELIGION. / ROTARY ELEVEN** [19] [4] Mar91
(12"+=/cd-s+=) *(W 0015 T/CD)* – After hours (live).
(cd-s) *(W 0015CDX)* – ('A'side) / Stand (live) / Turn you inside-out (live) / World leader pretend (live).

Mar 91. (cd/c/lp) *<(7599 26496-2/-4/-1)>* **OUT OF TIME** [1] [1]
– Radio song / Losing my religion / Low / Near wild Heaven / Endgame / Shiny happy people / Belong / Half a world away / Texarkana / Country feedback / Me in honey. *(lp re-iss. Jul99; same)*

— (the album feat. PETER HOLSAPPLE – guitar (ex-DB'S) / KRS-1 – rapper) MICHAEL STIPE released album with KRS-1 'CIVILIZATION VS.TECHNOLOGY' Oct91.

May 91. (7"/c-s) *(W 0027/+C) <19242>* **SHINY HAPPY PEOPLE. / FORTY SECOND SONG** [6] [10] Jul91
(12"+=/cd-s+=) *(W 0027 T/CD)* – Losing my religion (live acoustic).
(cd-s) *(W 0027CDX)* – ('A'side) / I remember California (live) / Get up (live) / Pop song '89 (live).
(above 'A'side feat. KATE PIERSON of The B-52'S)

Aug 91. (7"/c-s) *(W 0055/+C)* **NEAR WILD HEAVEN. / POP SONG '89** [27] [-]
(12"+=) *(W 0055T)* – Half a world away (live).
(cd-s) *(W 0055CDX)* – ('A'side) / Tom's diner (live) / Low (live) / Endgame (live).

Nov 91. (7"/c-s) *(W 0072/+C)* **RADIO SONG. / LOVE IS ALL AROUND (live)** [28] [-]
(12"+=) *(W 0072T)* – Shiny happy people (music mix).
(cd-s) *(W 0072CDX)* – ('A'side) / You are my everything (live) / Orange crush (live) / Belong (live).

Oct 92. (7"/c-s) *(W 0136/+C)* **DRIVE. / WORLD LEADER PRETEND** [11] [-]
(cd-s+=) *(W 0136CD)* – First we take Manhattan /
(cd-s) *(W 0136CDX)* – ('A'side) / It's a free world, baby / Winged mammal theme / First we take Manhattan.

Oct 92. (c-s,cd-s) *<18729>* **DRIVE / WINGED MAMMAL THEME** [-] [28]

Oct 92. (cd)(lp/c) *<(9362 45055)>(WX 488/+C)* **AUTOMATIC FOR THE PEOPLE** [1] [2]
– Drive / Try not to breathe / The sidewinder sleeps tonight / Everybody hurts / New Orleans instrumental No.1 / Sweetness follows / Monty got a raw deal / Ignoreland / Star me kitten / Man on the Moon / Nightswimming / Find the river.

Nov 92. (7"/c-s) *(W 0143/+C)* **MAN ON THE MOON. / TURN YOU INSIDE-OUT** [18] [-]
(cd-s+=) *(W 0143CD)* – Arms of love.
(cd-s) *(W 0143CDX)* – ('A'side) / Fruity organ / New Orleans instrumental /2 / Arms of love.

Jan 93. (c-s,cd-s) *<18642>* **MAN ON THE MOON / NEW ORLEANS INSTRUMENTAL #2** [-] [30]

Feb 93. (7"/c-s) *(W 0152/+C)* **THE SIDEWINDER SLEEPS TONIGHT. / GET UP** [17] [-]
(cd-s) *(W 0152CD1)* – ('A'side) / The lion sleeps tonight (live) / Fretless.
(cd-s) *(W 0152CD2)* – ('A'side) / Organ song / Star me kitten (demo).

Apr 93. (7"/c-s) *(W 0169/+C)* **EVERYBODY HURTS. / POP SONG '89** [7] [-]
(cd-s) *(W 0169CD1)* – ('A'side) / Mandolin strum / New Orleans instrumental No.1 (long version).
(cd-s) *(W 0169CD2)* – ('A'side) / Dark globe / Chance (dub).

Jul 93. (7"/c-s) *(W 0184/+C)* **NIGHTSWIMMING. / LOSING MY RELIGION (live)** [27] [-]
(one-sided-12"pic-d/cd-s) *(W 0184 TP/CD)* – ('A'side) / World leader pretend (live) / Low (live) / Belong (live).

Aug 93. (c-s) *<18638>* **EVERYBODY HURTS / MANDOLIN STRUM** [-] [29]
(12"orange+=) *<9362 40989-04>* – Belong / Orange crush (live).
(12"white or blue)(cd-ep) *<9362 40992-08>* – ('A'side) / Star me kitten (demo) / Losing my religion (live) / Organ song.

Dec 93. (7"/c-s) *(W 0211/+C)* **FIND THE RIVER. / EVERYBODY HURTS (live)** [54] [-]
(cd-s+=) *(W 0211CD1)* – World leader pretend (live).
(cd-s+=) *(W 0211CD2)* – Orange crush (instrumental).

Sep 94. (7"/c-s) *(W 0265/+C) <18050>* **WHAT'S THE FREQUENCY, KENNETH? / ('A'instrumental)** [9] [21]
(cd-s) *(W 0265CD)* – ('A'side) / Monty got a raw deal (live) / Everybody hurts (live) / Man on the Moon (live).

Oct 94. (cd/c/lp) *<(9362 45740-2/-4/-1)>* **MONSTER** [1] [1]
– What's the frequency, Kenneth? / Crush with eyeliner / King of comedy / I don't sleep I dream / Star 69 / Strange currencies / Tongue / Bang and blame / I took your name / Let me in / Circus envy / You.

Nov 94. (7"/c-s) *(W 0275/+C) <17994>* **BANG AND BLAME / ('A'instrumental)** [15] [19]
(cd-s) *(W 0275CD)* – ('A'side) / Losing my religion (live) / Country feedback (live) / Begin the begin (live).

Jan 95. (7"/c-s) *(W 0281 X/C)* **CRUSH WITH EYELINER. / ('A'instrumental)** [23] [-]
(cd-s) *(W 0281CD)* – ('A'side) / Calendar bag / Fall on me (live) / Me in honey (live) / Finest worksong (live).

— On 1st March, 1995, BILL BERRY suffered a brain haemorrhage, after collapsing during a concert in Switzerland. Thankfully, he steadily recovered during the following few months.

Apr 95. (7"/c-s) *(W 0290 X/C) <17900>* **STRANGE CURRENCIES. / ('A'instrumental)** [9] [47]
(cd-s) *(W 0290CD)* – ('A'side) / Drive (live) / Funtime (live) / Radio free Europe (live).

Jul 95. (c-s) *(W 0308 X/C)* **TONGUE / ('A'instrumental)** [13] [-]
(cd-s) *(W 0308CD)* – ('A'side) / Bang and blame (live) / What's the frequency, Kenneth? (live) / I don't sleep, I dream (live).

Aug 96. (c-s) *(W 0369C) <17529>* **E-BOW THE LETTER / TRICYCLE** [4] [49]
(cd-s+=) *(W 0369CD)* – Wall of death / Departure.

Sep 96. (cd/c/d-lp) *<(9362 46320-2/-4/-1)>* **NEW ADVENTURES IN HI-FI** [1] [2]
– How the west was won and where it got us / The wake-up bomb / New test leper / Undertow / E-bow the letter / Leave / Departure / Bittersweet me / Be mine / Binky the doormat / Zither / So fast, so numb / Low desert / Electrolite.

Oct 96. (c-s) *(W 0377C) <17490>* **BITTERSWEET ME / UNDERTOW (live)** [19] [46]
(cd-s+=) *(W 0377CD)* – Wichita lineman (live) / New test leper (acoustic).

Dec 96. (c-s) *(W 0383C) <43810>* **ELECTROLITE / THE WAKE-UP BOMB (live)** [29] [96]
(cd-s+=) *(W 0383CD)* – King of comedy (808 State mix) / Binky the doormat (live).

— now without BERRY whose place was taken up by guests

Oct 98. (c-s) *(W 0455C) <17129>* **DAYSLEEPER / EMPHYSEMA** [6] [57]
(cd-s+=) *(W 0455CD)* – Why not smile (Oxford American version).
(3"cd-s) *(W 0466CDX)* – Daysleeper / Sad professor (live in the studio).

Oct 98.	(cd/c/lp) *(9362 47151-2/-4/-1)* <47112> **UP**	**2** **3**

– Airportman / Lotus / Suspicion / Hope / At my most beautiful / The apologist / Sad professor / You're in the air / Walk unafraid / Why not smile / Daysleeper / Diminished / Parakeet / Falls to climb.

Dec 98. (c-s) *(W 466C)* **LOTUS / SURFING THE GANGES** **26** -
(cd-s+=) *(W 466CD)* – Lotus (weird mix).
(3"cd-s) *(W 466CDX)* – Lotus / Suspicion (live in the studio).

Mar 99. (cd-s) *(W 477CD)* **AT MY MOST BEAUTIFUL / THE PASSENGER (live at 'Later With Jools Holland') / COUNTRY FEEDBACK (live at 'Later With Jools Holland')** **10** -
(3"cd-s) *(W 477CDX)* – ('A'live) / So. central rain (live at 'Later With Jools Holland').

Jun 99. (cd-s) *(W 488CD)* **SUSPICION / ELECTROLITE ('Later With Jools Holland' version) / MAN ON THE MOON ('Later With Jools Holland' version)** - - tour
(3"cd-s+=) *(W 488CDX)* – ('A'live) / Perfect circle ('Later With Jools Holland' version).

Jan 00. (c-s) *(W 516C)* <*radio cut*> **THE GREAT BEYOND / MAN ON THE MOON (live)** **3** **57** Dec99
(cd-s) *(W 516CD)* – ('A'side) / Everybody hurts (live) / The one I love (live).
(above was taken from the movie/soundtrack, 'Man On The Moon', in which they contributed several other tracks)

Apr 01. (c-s) *(W 559C)* <42365> **IMITATION OF LIFE / THE LIFTING** **6** **83** May01
(cd-s+=) *(W 559CD)* – Beat a drum (Dalkey demo) / 2JN.

May 01. (cd/c/lp) <*9362 47946-2/-4/-1*> **REVEAL** **1** **6**
– Lifting / I've been high / All the way to Reno (you're gonna be a star) / She just wants to be / Disappear / Saturn return / Beat a drum / Imitation of life / Summer turns to high / The chorus and the ring / I'll take the rain / Beachball.

Jul 01. (c-s) *(W 568C)* **ALL THE WAY TO RENO (YOU'RE GONNA BE A STAR) / 165 HILLCREST (instrumental)** **24** -
(cd-s) *(W 568CDX)* – ('A'side) / Yellow river / Imitation of life (live) / Imitation of life (live – video).

Nov 01. (c-s) *(W 573C)* **I'LL TAKE THE RAIN / 32 CHORD SONG** **44** -
(cd-s+=) *(W 573CD1)* – I've been high (CD-Rom video).
(cd-s++=) *(W 573CD2)* – She just want to be (live).

– compilations, others, etc. –

—— on 'I.R.S.' unless mentioned otherwise
May 87. (lp/c/cd) <*(SP/CS/CDA 70054)*> **DEAD LETTER OFFICE** **60** **52**
(b-sides, rarities, etc.)
– Crazy / There she goes again / Burning down / Voice of Harold / Burning Hell / White tornado / Toys in the attic / Windout / Ages of you / Pale blue eyes / Rotary ten / Bandwagon / Femme fatale / Walters theme / King of the road. *(cd+=)* – CHRONIC TOWN *(re-iss. Oct94 on 'A&M' cd/c; CD/C MID 195)*

Oct 88. (lp/c/cd) *(MIRG/MIRGC/DMIRG 1038)* <6262> **EPONYMOUS** **69** **44**
– Radio free Europe / Gardening at night / Talk about the passion / So. central rain / (Don't go back to) Rockville / Can't get there from here / Driver 8 / Romance / Fall on me / The one I love / Finest worksong / It's the end of the world as we know it (and I feel fine).

Oct 88. (7") *(IRM 173)* **THE ONE I LOVE. / FALL ON ME** □ -
(12"+=/cd-s+=) *(IRMT/DIRM 173)* – So. central rain (I'm sorry).

May 90. (c) A&M; *(AMC 24109)* **MURMUR / RECKONING** □ □

Sep 91. (cd/c/lp) *(DMIRH/MIRHC/MIRH 1)* **THE BEST OF R.E.M.** **7** □
– Carnival of sorts / Radio free Europe / Perfect circle / Talk about the passion / So. central rain / (Don't go back to) Rockville / Pretty persuasion / Green grow the rushes / Can't get there from here / Driver 8 / Fall on me / I believe / Cuyahoga / The one I love / Finest worksong / It's the end of the world as we know it (and I feel fine).

Sep 91. (7"/c-s) *(IRM/+C 178)* **THE ONE I LOVE. / CRAZY** **16** □
(cd-s) *(DIRMT 178)* – ('A'side) / This one goes out (live) / Maps and legends (live).
(cd-s) *(DIRMX 178)* – ('A'side) / Driver 8 (live) / Disturbance at the Heron House (live).

Dec 91. (7") *(IRM/+C 180)* **IT'S THE END OF THE WORLD (AS WE KNOW IT). / RADIO FREE EUROPE** **39** □
(cd-s+=) *(DIRMT 180)* – Time after time, etc. (live).

—— When MICHAEL STIPE went off guesting for groups incl. GOLDEN PALOMINOS; others splintered off into . . .

HINDU LOVE GODS

not iss.   I.R.S.
Sep 85. (7") <*IRS-52867*> **NARRATOR. / GONNA HAVE A GOOD TIME TONIGHT** - □

—— with **WARREN ZEVON** – vocals (they guested on his late '89 album, 'Sentimental Hygene')

Reprise   Giant
Nov 90. (7") *(W 9502)* **RASPBERRY BERET. / WANG DANG DOODLE** □ -
(12"+=/cd-s+=) *(W 9502 T/CD)* – Mannish boy.

Nov 90. (cd/c/lp) <*(7599 24406-2/-4/-1)*> **HINDU LOVE GODS** □ □
– Walkin' blues / Travelin' riverside blues / Raspberry beret / Crosscut saw / Junco pardner / Mannish boy / Wang dang doodle / Battleship chains / I'm a one woman man / Vigilante man.

REMA REMA (see under ⇒ WOLFGANG PRESS)

RENALDO & THE LOAF

Formed: Portsmouth, England . . . 1979 by BRIAN POOLE (aka RENALDO M.) and DAVE JANSSEN (aka TED THE LOAF). Originally a tribute to the RESIDENTS, RENALDO & THE LOAF combined avant-garde humour with ludicrous instrumentation that seemed to utilise everything including the kitchen sink. After handing a homemade demo tape in to the RESIDENTS' San Franciscan HQ, the pair were signed to the associated 'Ralph' records, debuting officially in '81 with the album, 'SONGS FOR SWINGING LARVAE' (they had already distributed a cassette-only release, ' . . . PLAY STRUVE AND SNEFF'). Follow-up set, 'ARABIC YODELLING' (1983), was another impenetrably experimental effort, the insect-fixated duo saving themselves a lot of unnecessary bother by employing readymade synth sounds. Around the same time, BRIAN and DAVE actually collaborated with their long-time heroes on a video project, the results hitting the independent shops as an LP, 'TITLE IN LIMBO' (1984). Later installing a home studio with the er . . . bread they'd earned, RENALDO and Co worked on material for Some Bizzare offshoot, 'Rotcod', releasing the albums, 'OLLEH OLLEH ROTCOD' (1985) and 'THE ELBOW IS TABOO' (1987) to a less than ecstatic response.

Album rating: . . .PLAY STRUVE & SNEFF (*4) / SONGS FOR SWINGING LARVAE (*4) / ARABIC YODELLING (*6) / OLLEH OLLEH ROTCOD (*3) / THE ELBOW IS TABOO (*3)

BRIAN POOLE – guitar, percussion, piano, glockenspiel, bouzouki, vocals, harmonica, vocals / **DAVE JANSSEN** – clarinet, guitar, bouzouki, percussion

Rotcod   not iss.
Dec 79. (ltd-c) *(.rD 1)* **. . .PLAY STRUVE & SNEFF** □ -
– Meaning of W.E.I.R.D. / 16 going on 17 / Absence / 120 before zero / Of bad teeth *[cd-only]* / My favourite things *[cd-only]* / Scottish shuffle *[cd-only]* / Fluorescent showboat to Tangier *[cd-only]* / Brittle people / Dying inside / Kimbolton gnome song / The bathroom song / Untitled *[c-only]* / Letters from Lee *[c-only]*. <*cd-iss. 1994 on 'T.E.C. Tones'; 94582*> <*cd re-mast.1999 on 'E.M.G.'; ccd 102*>

—— they also issued very rare cassettes, ' . . .PLAY SONGS FROM THE SURGERY' and 'HATS OFF GENTLEMEN'

Do-It   Ralph
Apr 81. (lp) *(RIDE 6)* <*RL 8108*> **SONGS FOR SWINGING LARVAE** □ □
– Lime jelly grass / A medical man / Bali whine / Kimbolton gnome / Song / Frass / N 20 / B.P.M. / Spratt's medium / Honest Joe's Indian gets the goat on the way to the cowboy's conga / Ow! stew the red shoe / Bustle the burgoo / Is Guava a donut / A sob story / Hats off, gentlemen / Renaldo's trip to Venice / Ted's reverie. <*cd-iss. 1990 on 'T.E.C. Tones'; 90802*>

—— added guest **DAVE BAKER** – violin
May 83. (lp) <*RL 8308*> **ARABIC YODELLING** - □
– Green candle / Night / Bearded cats / The blowflies' dilemma / Dichotomy rag / A critical dance / Wilf in builth / Leery looks (from father's books) / Clean gender / Vitamin song / Lonely Rosa / J.P.W.B.C. / Like some kous-kous western / Nelda danced at daybreak / There's a cap on the lawn. <*cd-iss. 1993 on 'T.E.C. Tones'; 93082*>

—— late in '83, RENALDO & THE LOAF collaborated with the RESIDENTS on an LP, 'TITLE IN LIMBO'

Rotcod   not iss.
Nov 85. (lp) *(.rD 3)* **OLLEH, OLLEH ROTCOD** □ -
– A critical dance / Like some kous-kous western / Brittle people / The elbow is taboo / Bearded cats / She wears black / Gone to Gwondana / Fluorescent showboat to Tangier / Is Guava a donut? / Leery looks (from father's books) / Then at Iona anthem.

Nov 86. (12") *(.rD 4)* **HAMBU HODO. / HE LOVES US ALL** □ -
Sep 87. (lp) *(.rD 5)* **THE ELBOW IS TABOO** □ -
– A street called Straight / Boule / Hambu hodo / Dance for sonambulists / Here's to the oblong boys / Bread song / A critical dance / Extracting the re-re. *(cd-iss. May98 on 'Some Bizzare'; SBZ 036CD)*

above was their final release

REPLACEMENTS

Formed: Minneapolis, Minnesota, USA . . . 1980 originally as The IMPEDIMENTS by the STINSON brothers – TOMMY and BOB – along with CHRIS MARS and chief songwriter/frontman, PAUL WESTERBERG. Legendary purveyors of ramshackle three-chord punk rock, The REPLACEMENTS' early efforts were so lo-fi they were off the end of the scale. Signed to Minneapolis indie stalwart, 'Twin Tone', the band debuted with 'SORRY MA, FORGOT TO TAKE OUT THE TRASH' (1981), the record's raw-nerve attitude, cathartic melodies and twisted humour shining through the garden shed (and a particularly dilapidated one at that) production. The following year's 'STINK' stepped on the gas and upped the nihilism ('GIMME NOISE', 'FUCK SCHOOL') although 'HOOTENANNY' (1983) and 'LET IT BE' (1984) used the hormonal energy to more satisfying and constructive ends. The latter set, especially, saw WESTERBERG's breathtakingly intuitive way with a melody reach fruition; granted, the likes of 'GARY'S GOT A BONER' didn't suggest another ELVIS COSTELLO in the ascendant but the bruised beauty of 'SIXTEEN BLUE' put WESTERBERG head and shoulders above most of his contemporaries (with the honourable exception of, perhaps, HUSKER DU). The record's charms were powerful enough to attract the major label attentions of 'Sire' and in late '85, The REPLACEMENTS released the Tommy Erdelyi (formerly TOMMY RAMONE)-produced 'TIM'. Furnished with a bigger budget, the group tempered their ragged sound while retaining much of the threadbare authenticity, the hooks as razor sharp as ever. It was to be the last album to feature the departing BOB, the band's notoriously shambolic live appearances robbed of the man's more erm, eccentric tendencies (playing in a dress – radical for the time! – or indeed in the nude, was not uncommon). With ROBERT 'SLIM' DUNLAP brought in as a replacement (ha!), the band recorded what many fans and critics alike regard as their finest hour, 'PLEASED TO MEET ME' (1987). More musically adventurous in line with their growing eclecticism, the album also found WESTERBERG's songwriting prowess at its unprecedented best, 'SKYWAY' soaring heavenward while 'CAN'T HARDLY WAIT' was the killer pop song he'd been threatening to pen since the band's inception. Criminally, the rave reviews and positive momentum surrounding the album's release failed to translate into sales, The REPLACEMENTS sounding strangely muted on 1989's 'DON'T TELL A SOUL'. While the minor concessions to commerciality resulted in a Top 60 US chart entry, the band were on their last legs and 1990's 'ALL SHOOK DOWN' was a WESTERBERG solo effort in all but name. The split eventually came in 1992, TOMMY forming BASH & POP (who released an album, 'FRIDAY NIGHT IS KILLING ME' the following year), while WESTERBERG worked on his solo debut proper, '14 SONGS' (1993). Although the writing was faultless, the record lacked the unkempt charm of old, any chance of a full REPLACEMENTS reunion suffering a serious setback as BOB succumbed to a drugs overdose the following year. In the latter half of the 90's (while MARS was also delivering the odd album), WESTERBERG found acceptance – in the way of US chart fame – via two further sets, 'EVENTUALLY' (1996) and 'SUICAINE GRATIFACTION' (1999). You couldn't disguise the fact (well, you could for a while!) that his next project, GRANDPABOY, was just what WESTERBERG needed – a return to basic, anthemic rock with a twist of punk. Early in 2002, the mysterious (until now) GRANDPABOY unleashed his 'MONO' album (recorded in er, mono), most fans however opted for his simultaneous release 'STEREO', although this set was billed under his proper PAUL WESTERBERG name. While 'MONO' was obviously raw and retrofied harking back to say, The Stones' "Exile . . ." days, 'STEREO' was the complete article and returned him into the US Top 100. • **Songwriters:** Penned by WESTERBERG, except; I WILL DARE (Kiss) / ROUTE 66 (Bobby Troupe) / 20TH CENTURY BOY (T-Rex) / HEY GOOD LOOKING (Hank Williams) / CRUELLA DE VILLE (from '101 Dalmations'). • **Trivia:** Were quoted after a tour as saying 'Better hours, 9 to 5; 9 at night to 5 in the morning, that is'. Their '87 single 'ALEX CHILTON', was dedicated to legendary BOX TOPS leader.

Album rating: SORRY MA, FORGOT TO TAKE OUT THE TRASH (*6) / STINK mini (*5) / HOOTENANNY (*6) / LET IT BE (*9) / TIM (*7) / BOINK!! compilation (*8) / PLEASED TO MEET ME (*8) / DON'T TELL A SOUL (*7) / ALL SHOOK DOWN (*6) / ALL FOR NOTHING – NOTHING FOR ALL compilation (*8) / Paul Westerberg: 14 SONGS (*7) / EVENTUALLY (*6) / SUICAINE GRATIFATION (*5) / STEREO (*7) / Grandpaboy: MONO (*6) / Chris Mars: HORSESHOES AND HAND GRENADES (*6) / 75% LESS FAT (*5) / TENTERHOOKS (*6) / ANONYMOUS BOTCH (*4)

PAUL WESTERBERG (b.31 Dec'60) – vocals, rhythm guitar / **BOB STINSON** (b.17 Dec'59) – lead guitar / **TOMMY STINSON** (b. 6 Oct'66, San Diego, Calif.) – bass / **CHRIS MARS** (b.26 Apr'61) – drums

not iss.   Twin Tone

Aug 81. (7") <TTR 8120> **I'M IN TROUBLE. / IF ONLY YOU WERE LONELY**

Aug 81. (lp) <TTR 8123> **SORRY MA, FORGOT TO TAKE OUT THE TRASH**
– Takin' a ride / Careless / Customer / Hanging downtown / Kick your door down / Otto / I bought a headache / Rattlesnake / I hate music / Johnny's gonna die / Shiftless when you till Friday / Raised in the city. (UK-iss.Mar88 on 'What Goes On'; GOES ON 017) (cd-iss. Apr93 on 'Roadrunner'; RR 9089-2) (cd re-mast.Aug02 on 'Restless'; REST 7376-2)>

Jun 82. m-(lp) <TTR 8228> **STINK**
– Kids don't follow / Fuck school / Stuck in the middle / God damn job / White and lazy / Dope smokin' moron / Go / Gimme noise. (UK-iss.Mar88 on 'What Goes On'; GOES ON 020) (cd-iss. Apr93 on 'Roadrunner'; RR 9090-2) (cd re-iss. Mar95; 8228-2) <(cd re-iss. Aug02 on 'Restless', REST 73763)>

Apr 83. (lp) <TTR 8332> **HOOTENANNY**
– Hootenanny / Run it / Color me impressed / Will power / Take me down to the hospital / Mr. Whirly / Within your reach / Buck hill / Lovelines / You lose / Hayday / Treatment bound. (UK-iss.Mar88 on 'What Goes On'; GOES ON 021) (cd-iss. Apr93 on 'Roadrunner'; RR 9091-2) (cd re-iss. Feb95; TTR 8332-2) <(cd re-mast.Aug02 on 'Restless'; REST 73760)>

Aug 84. (12") <TTR 8440> **I WILL DARE. / 20TH CENTURY BOY / HEY GOOD LOOKING (live)**

Zippo   Twin Tone

Oct 84. (lp) (ZONG 002) <TTR 8441> **LET IT BE**
– I will dare / We're comin' out / Tommy gets his tonsels out / Black diamond / Androgynous / Unsatisfied / Seen your video / Gary's got a boner / Sixteen blue / Answering machine. (cd-iss. Apr93 on 'Roadrunner'; RR 9092-2) (cd-iss. Mar95 & Sep98 on 'R.C.A.'; 74321 60574-2) <(cd re-mast.Aug02 on 'Restless'; REST 73761)>

1985. (c) **THE SHIT HITS THE FAN (live bootleg)**

Sire   Sire

Nov 85. (lp/c) (K 925530-1/-4) <25330> **TIM**
– Hold my life / I'll buy / Kiss me on the bus / Dose of thunder / Waitress in the sky / Swingin' party / Bastards of young / Lay it down clown / Left of the dial / Litle mascara / Here comes a regular. (cd-iss. Jul93; 7599 25330-2)

Mar 86. (7") (W 8727) **SWINGIN' PARTY. / LEFT OF THE DIAL**
May 86. (7") (W 8679) **KISS ME ON THE BUS. / LITTLE MASCARA**

— **ROBERT 'SLIM' DUNLAP** (b.14 Aug'51, Plainview, Minnesota) – guitar; repl. BOB (he was to die on the 18th of February 1995 o.d.)

Apr 87. (lp/c/cd) (K 925557-1/-4/-2) <25557> **PLEASED TO MEET ME**
– I.O.U. / Alex Chilton / I don't know / Nightclub jitters / The ledge / Never mind / Valentine / Shooting dirty pool / Red red wine / Skyway / Can't hardly wait. (cd re-iss. Jul93; 7599 25557-2)

Jun 87. (7") (W 8297) **ALEX CHILTON. / ELECTION DAY**
(12"+=) (W 8297T) – Nightclub jitters / Route 66.

Jul 87. (7") <28151> **CAN'T HARDLY WAIT. / COOL WATER**

Jan 89. (lp/c/cd) (K 925721-1/-4/-2) <25721> **DON'T TELL A SOUL** 57
– Talent show / Back to back / We'll inherit the Earth / Achin' to be / They're blind / Anywhere's better than here / Asking me lies / I won't / Rock'n'roll ghost / Darlin' one. (cd re-iss. Jul93; 7559 25831-2)

Apr 89. (7") <22992> **I'LL BE YOU. / DATE TO CHURCH (with TOM WAITS)** 51
(below w/ guests STEVE BERLIN / MICHAEL BLAIR / BELMONT TENCH / JOHN CALE / etc.

Sep 90. (cd/c/lp) <(7599 26298-2/-4/-1)> **ALL SHOOK DOWN** 69
– Merry go round / One wink at a time / Nobody / Bent out of shape / Sadly beautiful / Someone takes the wheel / When it began / All shook down / Attitude / Happy town / Torture / My little problem / The lost. (cd re-iss. Jul93 & Feb95; same)

— (Mar'91) **STEVE FOLEY** – drums; repl. MARS who went solo
— disbanded late in 1991, TOMMY formed BASH & POP, while WESTERBERG and MARS went solo

– compilations, others, etc. –

Apr 86. (m-lp/m-c) Glass; (MGA LP/MC 016) **BOINK!!**
– Color me impressed / White and lazy / Within your reach / If only you were lonely / Kids don't follow / Nowhere is my home / Take me down to the hospital / Go.

Nov 97. (d-cd) Reprise; <(9362 46807-2)> **ALL FOR NOTHING / NOTHING FOR ALL**
– Left of the dial / Kiss me on the bus / Bastards of young / Here comes a regular / Skyway / Alex Chilton / The ledge / Can't hardly wait / I'll be you / Achin' to be / Talent show / Anywhere's better than here / Merry-go-round / Sadly beautiful / Nobody / Someone take the wheel / Can't hardly wait (the TIM version) / Birthday gal / Beer for breakfast / Till we're nude / Election day / Jungle rock / All he wants to do is fish / Date to church / Cruella De Ville / We know the night / Portland / Wake up / Satellite / Like a rolling pin / Another girl, another planet / Who knows / All shook down.

BASH & POP

TOMMY STINSON – vocals, guitar / **STEVE BRANTSEG** – guitar / **KEVIN FOLEY** – bass, vocals / **STEVE FOLEY** – drums

not iss.   Warners

Jan 93. (cd) <45133> **FRIDAY NIGHT IS KILLING ME**
– Never aim to please / Hang ups / Loose ends / One more time / Tickled to tears / Nothing / Fast & hard / Friday night (is killing me) / He means it / Tiny pieces / First steps.

PAUL WESTERBERG

Sire   Warners

Jun 93. (cd/c) <(9362 45255-2/-4)> **14 SONGS** 44
– Knockin' on mine / First glimmer / World class fad / Runaway wind / Dice behind your shades / Even here we are / Silver naked ladies / A few minutes of silence / Someone I once knew / Black eyed Susan / things / Something is me / Mannequin shop / Down love.

Jul 93. (7"/c-s) (W 0183/+C) **WORLD CLASS FAD. / SEEING HER**
(12"/cd-s) (W 0183 T/CD) – ('A'side) / Men without ties / Down love.

Oct 93. (7"/c-s) (W 0209/+C) **WORLD CLASS FAD. / CAN'T HARDLY WAIT (live)**
(cd-s+=) (W 0209CD1) – Left of the dial (live) / Another girl another planet (live).
(cd-s) (W 0209CD2) – ('A'side) / Waiting for somebody / Dyslexic heart / Answering machine (live).

Apr 96. (cd/c) (9362 46251-2/-4) <46176> **EVENTUALLY** 50
– These are the days / Century / Love untold / Ain't got me / You've had it with you / Mamadaddydid / Hide n seekin' / Once around the weekend / Trumpet clip / Angels walk / Good day / Time flies tomorrow.

Capitol   Capitol

Apr 99. (cd/c) (499145-2/-4) <59004> **SUICAINE GRATIFATION** Mar99
– It's a wonderful lie / Self defence / The best thing that ever happened / Lookin' out forever / Born for me / The final hurrah / Tears rolling up our sleeves / The fugitive kind / Sunrise always listens / Whatever makes you happy / Actor in the street / Bookmark.

GRANDPABOY

— aka **PAUL WESTERBERG**

not iss.   Monolyth

1997. (7") <7 1313> **I WANT MY MONEY BACK. / UNDONE**
1997. (cd-ep) <1315> **GRANDPABOY**
– Hot un / Ain't done much / Psychopharmacology / Lush and green / Homelessexual.

Vagrant   Vagrant

Apr 02. (cd) <(VR 368CD)> **MONO** Feb02
– High time / Anything but that / Let's not belong together / Silent film star / Knock it right out / 2 days 'til tomorrow / Eyes like sparks / Footsteps / Kickin' the stall / Between love and like / AAA.

PAUL WESTERBERG

Vagrant   Vagrant

Apr 02. (cd) <(VAG 369CD)> **STEREO** 81
– High times / I'll do anything / Let's not belong / Silent film star / Knock it right out / 2 days 'til tomorrow / Eyes like sparks / Footsteps / Kickin' the stall / Between love and like / AAA / Baby learns to crawl / Dirt to mud / Only lie worth telling / Got you down / No place for you / Boring enormous / Nothing to no one / We may be the one / Don't want never / Mr. Rabbit / Let the bad times roll / Call that gone? / (untitled). (re-iss. Jun02 on 'B-Unique'+=; BUN 025) – MONO

CHRIS MARS

plays multi-instruments + augmented by some guests

not iss.   Polygram

1992. (cd) <513198> **HORSESHOES AND HAND GRENADES**
– Reverse status / Popular creeps / Outer limits / Before it began / Get out of my life / Monkey sees / Ego maniac / Midnight carnival / I, me, we, us, them / Don't you see it / Happy disconnections / Better days / City lights on Mars / Last drop.

not iss.   Smash

1993. (cd) <8004> **75% LESS FAT**
– Stuck in rewind / No bands / Weasel / Public opinion / All figured out / Whining horse / Car camping / Skipping school / Bullshit detector / Candy liquor / Demolition / No more mud / Nightcap.

not iss.   Bar/None

1995. (cd) <52A> **TENTERHOOKS**
– White Patty rap / Forkless tree / Mary / Lizard brain / Hate it / Brother song / Water biscuits / E.I.B. negative / Haunted town / Floater.

REPLACEMENTS (cont) — THE GREAT INDIE DISCOGRAPHY — **The 1980s**

Sep 96. (cd) <*85A*> **ANONYMOUS BOTCH**
– Conquering cow farmer / Sheep spine shimmy / Narrow / Down drag / Black days / Two dreams / It's a long life / Janet's new kidney / Weather / Where and why / Funeral hymn of the small critter / I'll be gone / Cadaver dogs / New day.

Graeme REVELL (see under ⇒ S.P.K.)

REVENANTS (see under ⇒ STARS OF HEAVEN)

REVOLVING PAINT DREAM

Formed: Isle Of Dogs, London, England . . . 1983 by former LAUGHING APPLE conspirator, ANDREW INNES, a bit part guitarist with BIFF BANG POW!; both these outfits were ALAN McGEE projects, the 'Creation' boss launching RPD's debut single, 'FLOWERS ARE IN THE SKY' early '84. This retro-psychedelic gem was augmented by McGEE, plus the steadier members, NICO-esque vocalist CHRISTINE WANLESS (whom ANDREW met at Queen Mary's College) and BIFF BANG POW!'s drummer, KEN POPPLE. However, this mysterious outfit (at the time) disappeared for over three years, INNES obviously a bit more concerned with performing with another group, er . . . PRIMAL SCREAM. RPD resurfaced in the summer of 1987 with the pop-come-psyche debut mini-album, 'OFF TO HEAVEN', a directionless collection of weird indie-rock tunes. LUKE HAYES was in the fold for their 1989 follow-up, 'MOTHER WATCH ME BURN', although this turned out to be INNES' swansong.

Album rating: OFF TO HEAVEN (*5) / MOTHER WATCH ME BURN (*4)

ANDREW INNES – rhythm guitar, etc (ex-LAUGHING APPLE, of BIFF BANG POW!) / **CHRISTINE WANLESS** – vocals / **KEN POPPLE** – drums / **ALAN McGEE** – guitar, etc (also part-time)

Creation not iss.

Feb 84. (7") (*CRE 002*) **FLOWERS ARE IN THE SKY. / IN THE AFTERNOON**
– INNES became part of PRIMAL SCREAM early in '87 while WANLESS took a job as a Creation press officer while both remained with RPD.
Jun 87. (m-lp) (*CRELP 018*) **OFF TO HEAVEN**
– Flowers in the sky / Stop the world / 7 seconds.

LUKE HAYES – drums; repl. POPPLE

Jan 89. (lp) (*CRELP 039*) **MOTHER WATCH ME BURN**
– The dune buggy attack battalion / Green sea blue / Fever mountain / (Burn this house) Down to the ground / Mother wash my tears away / Garbagebrain / Electra's crying loaded in the basement / Mandra Mandra / Untitled (love song) / 300 (coda) / Reprise: Mandro Mandro / Sun, sea, sand. (cd-iss. Oct90 & May94 +=; CRECD 039) – OFF TO HEAVEN
Feb 89. (7") (*CRE 062*) **SUN, SEA, SAND. / GREEN SEA BLUE**
– INNES remained with his main job, PRIMAL SCREAM

RHYTHM SISTERS

Formed: West Riding, Yorkshire, England . . . mid-80's, not surprisingly by two sisters, DEBI and MANDI LAEK. Attired in Doc Marten boots, these ladies of indie-pop played an unusual blend of quirky tunes as heard on their debut album, 'ROAD TO ROUNDHAY PIER' (1987). The RHYTHM SISTERS added a few guys to their project, former JAM man, BRUCE FOXTON, and ex-UK SUBS drummer, STEVE STONES. Little was heard from the girls until 1990 when they worked with BILL NELSON, the great former BE-BOP DELUXE frontman signing the siblings to his 'Imaginary' imprint for what turned out to be their last outing, 'WILERBY' (1991). The latter set was originally scheduled for release as 'INFOTAINMENT' a full year previously.

Album rating: ROAD TO ROUNDHAY PIER (*4) / WILLERBY (*4)

DEBI LAEK – vocals / **MANDI LAEK** – vocals / with session people

Red Rhino not iss.

Nov 87. (lp/c/cd) (*RED LP/C/CD 87*) **ROAD TO ROUNDHAY PIER**
– Gotham / Motor / Homework / Hooked / Elderberry avenue / American boys / Wild west party.
May 88. (7"/12") (*RED/+T 92*) **AMERICAN BOYS. /**
– now augmented by other musicians (see above)

Imaginary not iss.

Feb 91. (cd/c/lp) (*ILLCD/ILLCASS/ILLUSION 027*) **WILLERBY**
– they disappeared back to the day jobs

Boyd RICE (see under ⇒ NON)

RIFF RAFF (see under ⇒ BRAGG, Billy)

RIFLE SPORT

Formed: Minneapolis, Minnesota, USA . . . early 80's by PETE "FLOUR" CONWAY, GERARD BOISSY and drummer TODD TRAINER. Inspired by the experimental hardcore antics of MISSION OF BURMA, this "third wave" DIY-punk band delivered their debut LP, 'VOICE OF REASON', in 1983. A handful of low-key sets were literally dismissed by the press and public alike and the band took off in other directions. TRAINER (with BOISSY initially) joined BRICK LAYER CAKE, BREAKING CIRCUS and SHELLAC – the latter with STEVE ALBINI, while CONWAY formed industrial punks, FLOUR; 'MACHINERY HILL' (1991) was their best contribution to rock music.

Album rating: VOICE OF REASON (*5) / WHITE (*5) / LIVE AT THE ENTRY, DEAD AT THE EXIT (*5) / PRIMO (*4) / Breaking Circus: THE VERY LONG FUSE mini (*6) / THE ICE MACHINE (*5) / Flour: FLOUR (*5) / L U V 7 1 3 (*6) / MACHINERY HILL (*6) / FOURTH AND FINAL (*4)

GERARD BOISSY – guitar / **PETE "FLOUR" CONWAY** – bass, vocals / **TODD TRAINER** – drums

not iss. Reflex

1983. (lp) **VOICE OF REASON**
1985. (12") **COMPLEX**

not iss. Ruthless

1987. (lp) <*RRRS 016*> **WHITE**
1989. (lp) **LIVE AT THE ENTRY, DEAD AT THE EXIT**

not iss. Big Money

1991. (cd) **PRIMO**
– BOISSY joined BRICK LAYER CAKE with TRAINER

BREAKING CIRCUS

STEVE BJORKLUND – vocals, guitar (ex-TERMINAL BEACH) / **PETE CONWAY** – bass / **TODD TRAINER** – drums

Homestead Homestead

Jun 85. (m-lp) <*HMS 012*> **THE VERY LONG FUSE**
– Precision / (Knife in the) Marathon / Lady in the lake / Soul of Japan / The imperial clawmaster's theme / Monster's sanctuary / Christian soldiers / Morning.
– added **PHIL HARDER** – guitar
Apr 87. (lp) <*HMS 075*> **THE ICE MACHINE**
– Song of the south / Daylight / Ancient axes / Caskets and clocks / Deadly china doll / Laid so low / Took a hammering / Waiter / Sweat blood / Where / Gun shy / Evil last night.
Nov 87. (12"ep) <*HMS 092*> **SMOKERS' PARADISE**
– BJORKLUND joined BALLOON GUY; TRAINER joined SHELLAC before forming BRICK LAYER CAKE; HARDER formed BIG TROUBLE HOUSE

FLOUR

PETE CONWAY – vocals, bass, drum programming / with others such as **CHRIS BJORKLUND** – guitar / + others

Touch & Go Touch & Go

Dec 88. (lp) <*TGLP 33*> **FLOUR**
– Intro / There's blood in my food / Love / One by one / Accordion / Coffee / Fade to grey / Red / Mirror on / The ceiling / Outro.
1990. (lp/c/cd) <*TGLP 49/+C/CD*> **L U V 7 1 3**
– Rain reign / Bodies on fire / Kick now / The face / Braindead genius / Nicky's sister / Love kills / Break away / Fish or cut bait / Midi this / Love / Red / Accordion / Grey / Coffee / Intro / 1 x 1 / Blood / Mirror / Outro / Starts a fire.
1991. (lp/c/cd) <*TGLP 63/+C/CD*> **MACHINERY HILL**
– Horseflesh / Tools / Fingerpainting / Stockings torn / Candyland / Machinery hill / Sometimes / Pig knuckled clown / Unmaculate conception / Scream for me darlin' / Beer belly polka.
Apr 94. (cd) <*TG 125CD*> **FOURTH AND FINAL**
– Sled / Rust with me / Godiva / Swept blood too / Flux deluxe / Cyannized / The cutting floor / Doorman's lament / Pretty in the parlour / Smarch.

Marc RILEY & The CREEPERS

Formed: Manchester, England . . . late 1982, by MARC RILEY after he was dismissed from The FALL by life and soul of any party, MARK E SMITH. Backed by The CREEPERS (who included PAUL FLETCHER, PETE KEOGH and EDDIE FENN), RILEY formed his own indie imprint, 'In-Tape' with Jim Khambatta. The outfit's first release, 'FAVOURITE SISTER', arrived the following summer, an unusual collision of angular FALL-esque rhythms, stripped-down VELVETS atmosphere and grim Northern vocals. A second 45, 'JUMPER CLOWN', hit the indie shops in a matter of months, a repetitive neo-rockabilly marathon complete with beat-up Wurlitzer organ and droning barbed lyrics (I wonder who about?). The equally sarcastic, chunky punkabilly of 'CURE BY CHOICE', featured on their next release, early '84's 'CREEPING AT MAIDA VALE' EP. A filler mini-compilation, 'CULL', was followed by the 'POLLYSTIFFS' single, prior to the release of their debut album proper, 'GROSS OUT' (1984). Boasting the surreal noisefest, 'EARWIG O'DOWD', alongside the crude 'GROSS' and their finest organ-grinding three minutes, 'TEACHER TRAVEL', the album nevertheless failed to generate much interest outside the independent scene. They ended quite a prolific year with a disappointing fifth single, 'SHADOW FIGURE', marking time until their second collection of goodies, 'FANCY MEETING GOD' (1985). Although again not a classic album (MARK E was making much more progress), it did however contain a couple of wee gems in 'HARRY'S CHIN' (another reference to the mysterious Harry O'Dowd!) and 'BUNKER'. Another busy year was capped by a second 'MAIDA VALE' EP (which included a snipe at PAUL WELLER in the shape of 'BARD OF WOKING') and a live album, 'WARTS 'N' ALL', the latter featuring a version of Eno's 'BABY'S ON FIRE'. Subsequently abbreviating the group's moniker to The CREEPERS, RILEY found some new recruits, namely MARK TILTON and PHIL ROBERTS, the new line-up's first album-length outing being 'MISERABLE SINNERS' (1986). Signing to 'Red Rhino', RILEY and Co released their swansong set,

Marc RILEY & The CREEPERS (cont)

'ROCK'N'ROLL LIQUORICE FLAVOUR', in 1988, sadly not a patch on their awkward but pioneering early work (The INSPIRAL CARPETS certainly took note!). After a brief spell as The LOST SOUL CRUSADERS, The CREEPERS finally split and RILEY went on to co-host a Radio One show with MARK RADCLIFFE. In 1997, the pair were the main men behind the DJ supergroup, The SHIREHORSES, who scored with a Top 30 album, 'THE WORST ALBUM IN THE WORLD EVER . . . EVER!'.

Album rating: CULL mini-compilation (*6) / GROSS OUT (*7) / FANCY MEETING GOD (*6) / WARTS 'N' ALL (*4) / MISERABLE SINNERS (*4) / ROCK'N'ROLL LICORICE FLAVOUR (*4)

MARC RILEY – vocals, keyboards (ex-FALL) / **PAUL FLETCHER** – guitar (of TOOLS YOU CAN TRUST) / **PETE KEOGH** – bass (of KISS THE BLADE) / **EDDIE FENN** – drums (of KISS THE BLADE, ex-CRAWLING CHAOS)

In-Tape not iss.

Jul 83. (7") (IT 001) **FAVOURITE SISTER. / CARRY MI CARD (DAFT HEAD)**	
Oct 83. (7") (IT 002) **JUMPER CLOWN. / VIOLIN**	
Feb 84. (7"ep) (IT 004) **CREEPING AT MAIDA VALE** – Cure by choice / Baby paints / Blow / Location Bangladesh.	
Apr 84. (m-lp) (IT 005) **CULL** (compilation of above)	
May 84. (7") (IT 006) **POLLYSTIFFS. / RAILROAD**	
Jun 84. (lp) (IT 007) **GROSS OUT** – Make Joe / Less speed / Snipe / Earwig O'Dowd / Railroad / Gross / Teacher travel / Freaky sleeper / Claptrap.	
Sep 84. (12"m) (IT 009) **SHADOW FIGURE. / HOLE 4 A SOUL / SHIRT SCENE**	
Mar 85. (lp) (IT 015) **FANCY MEETING GOD** – Breakneck 1 / We don't say / Oh! B.K. O.K.! / Judas sheep / Wanna cocktail hate tale / Breakneck 2 / Harry's chin / Poop scoop / Down in the bunker / Fly the nest.	
Oct 85. (d7"/12"ep) (IT/+T 025) **4 A's FROM MAIDA VALE** – Black dwarf / Going rates / Bard of Woking / Cold fish.	
Nov 85. (10"lp) (IT 026) **WARTS'N'ALL – LIVE IN AMSTERDAM** (live) – Breakneck 1 / Black dwarf / Pollystiffs / Jumper clown / Goin' rate / Gross / Baby's on fire / Hole 4 a soul / Bard of Woking / Shirt scene / Snipe / Make Joe / Baby paints / Cure by choice.	

CREEPERS

RILEY + FENN recruited **MARK TILTON** – guitar (ex-MEMBRANES); repl. PAUL / **PHIL ROBERTS** – bass (ex-SHRUBS); repl. PETE who remained with KISS THE BLADE (one single issued, 'YOUNG SOLDIER, late '86 and an album, STATIC WAIL' in Apr'89 on 'Soft Cushion'; KISS 223123)

May 86. (7"/12") (IT/+T 033) **BABY'S ON FIRE. / ANOTHER SONG ABOUT MOTOR BIKES**
Nov 86. (lp/c) (IT 039/+C) **MISERABLE SINNERS** – The adventures of Brian Glider / Bank of horrors / Stroke of genius / Baby's on fire / Dog on my shoulder / Chocolate box / Honest lies / Sound as a pound / Where's Walter? / Old man's treat / Another song about motorbikes.

added **SIMON TAYLOR** – guitar

Red Rhino not iss.

Jun 87. (7") (RED 079) **BRUTE. / LUCKY** ('A'-Terminally ill mix-12"+=) (REDT 079) – Rolf.
Jan 88. (lp/c/cd) (RED LP/MC/CD 082) **ROCK'N'ROLL LIQUORICE FLAVOUR** – Liquorice flavour / Sweet retreat / Cheshire life / Rosalyn / Derbyshire / Tearjerker / Fillet face / 'Cept for you / Fan club / Act your age / Bastard hat / Curl up and dye.

disbanded just after they became The LOST SOUL CRUSADERS. RILEY now works as the character, LARD.

RIP (see under ⇒ GALBRAITH, Alastair)

RIP, RIG + PANIC

Formed: Bristol, England . . . late 1980 by former POP GROUP cohorts GARETH SAGER and BRUCE SMITH, the pair taking their moniker from an album by avant-jazz man, ROLAND KIRK. SMITH's 16 year-old girlfriend, NENEH CHERRY (step-daughter of the veteran jazz trumpeter, DON CHERRY), took up the invitation to join the growing ensemble, as did MARK SPRINGER and SEAN OLIVER. Shaking up a colourful cocktail of improvised freeform jazz, African tribal sounds and schizophrenic New Wave funk/reggae, RIP, RIG + PANIC weren't exactly an easy listening experience although their dense virtuosity and skewed musical logic occasionally threw up moments of genius. Signed to 'Virgin' on the strength of their live reputation and top musical pedigree, the collective debuted in 1981 with the 'GOD' album (actually a double mini-set!). The record introduced the group's penchant for cryptically long-winded song titles, gracing tracks that suggested a meeting of The SLITS and PIGBAG and sung with scat-ish soulful aplomb by the sultry-voiced NENEH. However, the latter would take temporary maternity leave, returning to Sweden to have a baby; her replacement was ANDREA OLIVER, who would actually remain a part of the expanding ensemble when NEHEH was fit enough to resume her vocal duties. Her step-father, DON, would augment the group on their second set, 'I AM COLD' (1982), an album that featured their most accessible and well-known track, 'YOU'RE MY KIND OF CLIMATE', aired to the nation via the very first episode of cult TV sitcom, 'The Young Ones'. A final set, 'ATTITUDE' (1983), took the experimental format as far as it could go although most members bar the solo bound SPRINGER, re-grouped in the short-lived FLOAT UP CP in 1984. This metamorposised into the even more short-lived GOD, MOTHER & COUNTRY, as SAGER went off to form HEAD. NENEH, meanwhile, would go on to carve out her own highly successful solo career.

Album rating: GOD (*7) / I AM COLD (*5) / ATTITUDE (*6) / KNEE DEEP IN HITS compilation (*7) / Float Up CP: KILL ME IN THE MORNING (*4)

NENEH CHERRY (b. NENEH MARIANN KARLSSON, 10 Mar'64, Stockholm, Sweden) – vocals (ex-NAILS) / **GARETH SAGER** – guitar (ex-POP GROUP) / **SEAN OLIVER** – bass (ex-ESSENTIAL LOGIC) / **MARK SPRINGER** – piano, keyboards / **BRUCE SMITH** – drums (ex-POP GROUP) / guest **SIMON UNDERWOOD** – bass

Virgin not iss.

Aug 81. (7") (VS 445) **GO, GO, GO! THIS IS IT. / THE ULTIMATE IN FUN (IS GOING TO A DISCO WITH MY BABY)** (12"+=) (VS 445-12) – Let me move on the Gord.
Sep 81. (2xm-lp) (V 2213) **GOD** – Constant drudgery is harmful to soul, spirit and health / Wilhelm show me the diagram (function of the orgasm) / Thru' nomad eyeballs / Change your life / Knee deep in shit / Totally naked (without lock or key) / Try box out of this box / Need (de school you) / Howl! caged bird / Those Eskimo women speak frankly / The blue blue third / Shadows only there because of the sun / Beware (our leaders love the smell of napalm) / Miss Pib / It don't mean a thing if it ain't got that brod. (re-iss. Aug88; OVED 118)
Nov 81. (7"/ext-12") (VS 468/+12) **BOB HOPE TAKES RISKS. / HEY MR.E! A GRAN GRIN WITH A SHAKE OF SMILE**

ANDREA OLIVER – vocals (temp.) repl. & was added to expanding line-up (NENEH returned to Sweden to have her baby – maternity leave – she was back in line-up for subsequent releases)

STEVE NOBLE – drums (also came in) / guest **DON CHERRY** – trumpet / others on long/short-term **SARAH SARAHANDI** – viola / **DAVID DE FRIES** – tenor sax / **JEZ PARFITT** – baritone sax / **GILES LEAMAN** – percussion / **DEBBIE** – cello / **ALPH WATT** – trombone / **LOUIS MAHALO** – percussion

Jun 82. (7") (VS 507) **YOU'RE MY KIND OF CLIMATE. / SHE GETS SO HUNGRY AT NIGHT** (12"+=) (VS 507-12) – She eats her jewellery.
Jun 82. (lp) (V 2228) **I AM COLD**   *67*
– Storm the reality asylum / Warm: to the if in life / Liars shape up or ship out / Epi epi arp woosh! / Nurse increase the sedatives (the torment's no better) / Take a donkey to mystery / Tax sex / Hunger (the ocean roars it bites) / You're my kind of climate / Here gathers nameless energy (volcanos covered by snow) / Misa Luba Lone Wolf. (free 12"ep) – Another tampon up the arse of humanity / A dog's secret / Subversive wisdom / Fire eyes joyful silent tears. (re-iss. Aug88; OVED 119)
Aug 82. (7") (VS 533) **STORM THE REALITY ASYLUM. / LEAVE YOUR SPITTLE IN THE POT** (12"+=) (VS 533-12) – It's always tit for tat you foolish brats.

added **DAVID WRIGHT** – saxophone

Mar 83. (7"/ext-12") (VS 577) **BEAT THE BEAST. / IN 1619, A DUTCH VESSEL DOCKED IN THE U.S.A. WITH 20 HUMANS FOR SALE**
Apr 83. (lp) (V 2268) **ATTITUDE** – Keep the sharks from your heart / Sunken love / Rip open, But oh so long thy wounds take to heal / Do the tightrope / Intimacy, just gently shimmer / How that spark sets me aglow / Alchemy in the cemetry / Beat the beast / The birth pangs of Spring / Eros, what brings colour up the stem / Push your tiny body as high as your desire can take you / Viva x dreams. (re-iss. Aug87 lp/c; OVED/+C 63)
May 83. (7"/ext-12") (VS 582/+12) **DO THE TIGHTROPE. / BLIP THIS JIG IT'S SHANANIC**

they split later in the year, MARK SPRINGER went solo and released (in Feb'85) a solo lp, 'PIANO', for 'Illuminated' (JAMS 46)

– compilations, etc. –

Oct 90. (cd/lp) Virgin; (CDOVD/OVED 329) **KNEE DEEP IN HITS** – You're my kind of climate / Storm the reality asylum / Sunken love / Warm: to the if in life [cd-only] / Go go go (this is it) / Keep the sharks from your heart / Miss Pib [cd-only] / Thru' nomad eyeballs [cd-only] / Do the tightrope (12" version) / Beat the beast / The ultimate in fun (is going to the disco with my baby) [cd-only] / Alchemy in the cemetry / Bob Hope takes risks / Blue blue third.

FLOAT UP CP

SAGER, CHERRY, SMITH, OLIVER + SARAHANDI

Rough Trade not iss.

Jul 84. (7"/12") (RT/+T 150) **JOY'S ADDRESS. / DESERT HEART**
Oct 85. (lp) (ROUGH 77) **KILL ME IN THE MORNING** – Chemically wet / He loves me (no, no, no) / The loneliest girl / Forever party / M.A.D. / Ghost train drive / My memory / Assassins / Secret desire / Joy's address / Sexy bushes.

they had already disbanded, SAGER forming rock-orientated, HEAD

GOD, MOTHER & COUNTRY

aka **BRUCE SMITH, NENEH CHERRY + DAVID WRIGHT**

Kaz not iss.

Aug 85. (7"/12") (KAZ 60/+T) **FOOT ON THE ROCK. / ('A'dub)**

SMITH + CHERRY split up their relationship, the former joining PUBLIC IMAGE LTD. (among others), while the latter joined the short-lived KABBALA before hooking up with a new boyfriend, CAMERON McVEY, and venturing on a fruitful solo career

Brian RITCHIE (see under ⇒ VIOLENT FEMMES)

RITES OF SPRING

Formed: Washington, D.C., USA... mid 80's by GUY PICCIOTTO, EDDIE JANNEY, MICHAEL FELLOWS and BRENDAN CANTY. A seminal emo, hardcore-tinted outfit that was the stamping ground for the likes of FUGAZI (GUY and BRENDAN became part of the aforementioned legends), RITES OF SPRING signed to IAN MacKAYE's 'Dischord' set-up and released their eponymous debut LP towards the fall of '85. Heralded as a minor classic in punk/hardcore circles, the record kicked off with opener 'SPRING' and closed with 'END ON END', the latter being the title of the CD re-issue which added their only other release, the 1986 EP, 'ALL THROUGH A LIFE'. At times cathartic, other times skull-numbing, the platter was highlighted by the excellent 'HIDDEN WHEEL'. GUY and Co changed their moniker to the short-lived ONE LAST WISH, before becoming HAPPY GO LICKY; both bands released little or nothing during their brief musical tenure, although future compilations were forthcoming. With GUY and BRENDAN hitting the heights with IAN MacKAYE's FUGAZI for most of the 90's(+), MIKE FELLOWS embarked on his own solo project, MIIGHTY FLASHLIGHT (yes, that is with two I's). In early 2002, the mellower MIKE issued the folktronica and acoustic set entitled er, 'MIIGHTY FLASHLIGHT'; fuse OLDHAM/PALACE and CALLAHAN/SMOG (both of whom he used to work for) to find its lo-fi, twangy construction.

Album rating: RITES OF SPRING – END ON END compilation (*7) / One Last Wish: 1986 compilation (*5) / Happy Go Licky: WILL PLAY (*5) / Miighty Flashlight: MIIGHTY FLASHLIGHT (*7)

GUY PICCIOTTO – vocals / **EDDIE JANNEY** – guitar / **MICHAEL FELLOWS** – bass / **BRENDAN CANTY** – drums

Dischord Dischord

Nov 85. (lp) <*DIS 16*> **RITES OF SPRING**
– Spring / Deeper than inside / For want of / Hain's point / All there is / Drink deep / Other way round / Theme / By design / Remainder / Persistent vision / Nudes / End on end. <cd-iss. Nov91 as 'END OF END' +=; DIS 16CD> – ALL THROUGH A LIFE (UK-iss.Jul02 lp/cd; DIS 16CD/+CD)

Nov 86. (7"ep) <*DIS 22*> **ALL THROUGH A LIFE**
– All through a life / Hidden wheel / In silence – Words away / Patience.

—— when they split, all became ONE LAST WISH (then HAPPY GO LICKY), GUY subsequently joined FUGAZI (as did BRENDAN); FELLOWS fronted MIIGHTY FLASHLIGHT after a spell with SILVER JEWS and AIR MIAMI

– compilations, etc. –

on 'Dischord' unless mentioned otherwise

Oct 97. (cd; by HAPPY GO LICKY) <*DIS 109CD*> **WILL PLAY**
– Ansol / Peterbilt / Brigham Young / White lines / Torso butter / Casing / Twist and shout / Pastel blue eyes / Abandon me / 13 months of sunshine / Suzuki / Boca Raton / Born like steam / Battery / Don't bone me / Cutthroat answer / Pastel blue eyes / Suzuki / Ansol / Casing / D.I.Y. ansol.

Mar 00. (cd; by ONE LAST WISH) <*DIS 118*> **1986**
– Hide / Burning in the undertow / Break to broken / Friendship is far / My better half / Loss like a seed / Three unkind silences / Shadow / Sleep of the stage / One last wish / This time / Home is the place.

MIIGHTY FLASHLIGHT

MIKE FELLOWS – vocals, guitars, etc.

Jade Tree Jade Tree

Feb 02. (cd) <*JT 1066*> **MIIGHTY FLASHLIGHT**
– Several water cannons / Stop blocking / Go one. Die. Its easy / Vehicular dome / Fatherland focus / Ballet skool / Ventilating zephyrs / Forget this space / Hala hanan di halida / Lavish corduroy.

Mark ROBINSON (see under ⇒ UNREST)

Paul ROLAND

Born: c. 1959, Canterbury, England. ROLANDS' almost unique form of music led to him being named the "psych-pop guru" which ROLAND himself views as an accurate description. A truly madcap, eccentric of the 80s middle-England goth scene, PAUL ROLAND has been ploughing some of the most esoteric and barmy fields this side of the continent. Also an author on mysticism, ROLAND has respectively issued ten albums – all rare collectables – spanning over sixteen years. His songs mostly told the bizarre tales of 19th Century weirdos, set to a scathing baroque soundscape of woodwind instruments, keyboards and big-riff guitars. However, ROLAND had turned the volume down somewhat for a few acoustic fares in which he had displayed a keen and wonderful sense of balladeering folk-rock. The man's first album, 'THE WEREWOLF OF LONDON' (1980), incorporated supernatural and historical ideas fusing rock psych-pop and folk. A second set featured ROBYN HITCHCOCK of The SOFT BOYS fame, a meeting whilst working with 'Armageddon' resulted in this SYD BARRETT-esque sound. ROLAND was managed under the wing of June Bolan (widow of T.Rex's MARC), and, after a brief stint with the commercial side of the music industry, he returned to 'Armageddon' in 1985 for the excellent mini-album 'BURNT ORCHIDS'. Although ROLAND became largely unappreciated in Britain, the Americans, Europeans and Japanese couldn't get enough of his psycho-gothic warblings and his oh-so eccentric Englishness. Distribution deals were set up in the USA, France and Germany, and the albums kept on churning out; the now collectable and utterly classic 'DANSE MACABRE' (1987), 'CABINET OF CURIOSITIES' (1987) and 'HAPPY FAMILIES' (1988) – two of his best acoustic-folk albums. 'DUEL' (1989), 'MASQUE' (1990), 'ROARING BOYS' (1991) – his weakest affair – mini-covers set 'STRYCHNINE' (1992), 'SARABANDE' ('94) and his most recent offering 'GARGOYLES' (1997), continued unabated. Rumour has it that ROLAND has retired from the music industry, and this would obviously be a shame. For never has such an eccentric goth musical genius been so overlooked as ROLAND, with his massive discography and his songs about 19th century opium eating and devilish baroqueness. If there's any justice, there will be a ROLAND resurgence, but probably not. • **Songwriters:** ROLAND except covers; GARY GILMORE'S EYES (Adverts) / I CAN'T CONTROL MYSELF (Troggs) / MATHILDA MOTHER (Pink Floyd) / COME TO THE SABBAT (Black Widow) / HURDY GURDY MAN + GUINEVERE + YOUNG GIRL BLUES (Donovan) / WHO DO YOU LOVE (Bo Diddley) / STRYCHNINE (Sonics) / LADY RACHEL (Kevin Ayers) / VENUS IN FURS (Velvet Underground) / PERFUMED GARDEN OF GULLIVER SMITH + ISCARIOT + 20TH CENTURY BOY + HOT GEORGE (T. Rex) / PEGGY SUE GOT MARRIED + NOT FADE AWAY (Buddy Holly) / SLIPPIN' AND SLIDIN' (Little Richard) / GO DOWN YOU MURDERERS (Ewan MacColl) / TOO MUCH TO DREAM (Electric Prunes) / ARABIAN KNIGHTS (Siouxsie & The Banshees).
• **Trivia:** Mentor ROBYN HITCHCOCK guested on some early work.

Album rating: THE WEREWOLF OF LONDON (*5) / BURNT ORCHIDS mini (*6) / DANSE MACABRE (*7) / HOUSE OF DARK SHADOWS compilation (*6) / A CABINET OF CURIOSITIES collection (*5) / HAPPY FAMILIES (*7) / DUEL (*6) / MASQUE (*5) / ROARING BOYS (*5) / STRYCHNINE mini (*4) / SARABANDE (*4) / GARGOYLES (*4)

PAUL ROLAND – vocals, guitar (WEIRD STRINGS also featured JOHN WILLANS)

Velvet Moon / not iss.

1979. (7"w-drawn; by MIDNIGHT RAGS) (*VM 1*) **THE CARS THAT ATE NEW YORK. / OSCAR AUTOMOBILE**

1979. (7"; by WEIRD STRINGS) (*VM 1*) **OSCAR MOBILE. / ANCIENT SQUARE**

Ace / not iss.

1979. (7"; by MIDNIGHT RAGS) (*ACE 005*) **PUBLIC ENEMY. / ALCATRAZ / MAMMA SAID**

1980. (7"; by WEIRD STRINGS) (*ACE 009*) **CRIMINAL CAGE. / MILLIONAIRE**

1980. (lp) (*ACE 013*) **THE WEREWOLF OF LONDON**
– Blades of Battenburg / Brain police / Oscar automobile / Flying ace / The cares that ate New York / Public enemy / Werewolves of London / The witching hour / Lon Chaney (1883-1930) / Alcatraz / Girls [not on re-iss.]. (re-vamped.1981 on 'Armageddon'+=; ARM 9) – Angel, for the witching hour – Jack Daniels.

Moonlight / not iss.

1982. (7"; as BEAU BRUMMEL) (*MNS 004*) **HOT GEORGE. / OSCAR**

—— BEAU BRUMMEL aka **ROLAND** + **ANDY ELLISON** + **KNOX**

—— with **ANDY YOUNG** – guitar / **BRIAN GOULD** – keyboards / **CHRIS RANDALL** – keyboards / **ROGER DIAMOND** – drums

Aristocrat / not iss.

Jul 82. (7") (*ARC 1398*) **DR STRANGE. / MADELAINE**

Aftermath / not iss.

Aug 83. (12"ep) (*AEP 12-011*) **BLADES OF BATTENBURG (remix) / CAPTAIN BLOOD. / PUPPET MASTER / CAVALIER**

Aug 85. (m-lp) (*Scoop 2*) **BURNT ORCHIDS**
– Death or glory / Burnt orchids / The puppet master / Captain blood / Cairo / Green glass violins / Funhouse / Ghost ships.

Jul 86. (12"ep) (*AEP 12-012*) **DEATH OR GLORY (re-vamped version) / THE GREAT EDWARDIAN AIR RAID. / BEAU BRUMMEL / THE CURIOUS CASE OF RICHARD FIELDING**

May 87. (7"ep) (*AEP 12-013*) **GABRIELLE. / BERLIN / SWORD & SORCERY**

Imaginary / not iss.

1986. (7") (*MIRAGE 002*) **DEMON IN A GLASS CASE. / IN THE OPIUM DEN**

Bam Caruso / Revolver

Apr 87. (7") (*OPRA 081*) **MADAME GUILLOTINE. / United States Of Existence: GONE**

—— now with **GOULD / YOUNG / + BRIAN HEFFERNAN** – bass / **MATT VINYL** – drums / **PETE RIDLEY** – mandolin, violin / etc

Apr 87. (lp) (*KIRI 052*) <*SPIN 1002*> **DANSE MACABRE** — 1988
– Witchfinder General / Madame Guillotine / The great Edwardian air raid / The hanging judge / Still falls the snow / Mathilda mother / Gabrielle / Requiem / Buccaneers / In the opium den / Twilight of the gods. (cd-iss. May88; KIRI 052CD) (re-iss. Jan90 on 'Fan Club'; FC 062) (cd re-iss. May94 on 'New Rose'; 422296)

Feb 88. (7"ep) (*PABL 094*) **ALICE'S HOUSE / GO DOWN YOU MURDERERS. / HAPPY FAMILIES / JUMBEE (demo)**

—— with band **DEREK HEFFERNAN** – guitar / **CHRIS RANDALL** – keyboards / **JENNY BENWELL** – violin / **JOHN TRACEY** – bass / **SIMON JEFFREY** – drums

Constrictor / not iss.

1988. (7") (*COLL 008*) **SWORD AND SORCERY. /**

New Rose / not iss.

Dec 87. (m-lp) (*ROSE 135*) **A CABINET OF CURIOSITIES** (rare material)
– Madhouse / Wyndham Hill / Jumbee / Gary Gilmore's eyes / Burn / Walter the occultist / Stranger than strange / Demon in a glass case. (w/ free 7"+=) – Green glass violins / Berlin (live). (cd-iss. Apr88 ++=; ROSE 135CD) – Cairo / Happy families / Gabrielle / Madame Guillotine / Mad Elaine.

Feb 89. (m-lp/cd) (*ROSE 163/+CD*) **HAPPY FAMILIES**
– The curate of Cheltenham / Journey to the Pole / Nursery crimes / Cousin Emilia / Builder of follies / The best years of our lives / Aunty / Animal crackers. (lp w/ free 7") – Beau Brummel (re-recorded) / I can't control myself. (cd++=) – Go down your murders / Captain Blood.

Apr 89. (7") (*FREE 14*) **BEAU BRUMMEL. / I CAN'T CONTROL MYSELF**

Paul ROLAND (cont)

Sep 89. (lp/cd) (ROSE 178/+CD) **DUEL**
– Knights / The crimes of Dr. Cream / Reptile house / Spring heeled Jack / Nosferatu / At the edge of the world / Alice's house / Menagerie / The king must die:- Over the hills and far away – The king must die – The king is dead.

Jan 91. (lp/cd) (ROSE 231/+CD) **MASQUE**
– Dr. Syn is riding again / Pharoah / Candy says / Triumphs of a taxidermist / Grantchester fields / Meet Mr. Scratch / Masque / The mind of William Gaines / Cocoon / I dreamt I stood upon the scaffold / Matty Groves.

Nov 91. (lp/cd) (ROSE 277/+CD) **ROARING BOYS**
– Roaring boys / Resurrection Joe / Christine / The executioner's song / Thunderbird / Sad sweet smile / Tarot / The poets and the painters / Doctor Rocque / The minstrel's song (is all our love in vain?) / Come to the sabbat. (cd+=) – Hurdy gurdy man / Who do you love? / Red cadillac and a black moustache.

1992. (m-cd) (422431) **STRYCHNINE** (covers)
– Too much to dream / Arabian knights / Iscariot / Strychnine / Young girl blues / Guinevere / Lady Rachel / Venus in furs / radio sessions:- The king is dead / The great Edwardian air raid / Candy says / Ghost ships.

Gaslight   not iss.

May 94. (cd) (GASCD 501) **SARABANDE**
– The king will come / Morgan Le Fay / Beyond the realm of sleep / Sister jazz / Ophelia / Serpent's skin / A thousand and one nights / I'm not like everybody else / Waltzing the square ring again / Meadows of the sea / Me and the devil blues.

Jul 97. (cd) (GASCD 703) **GARGOYLES**
– The worlds of Jonathan Waverley / The gathering man / Alister Crowley / Culloden / Gargoyles / Atlantis / Luther / The grey cock / Last coach to the Bongo Pass / White lightning / Doctor Roque / Down to the bone.

—— ROLAND has since been conspicuous by his absence

– compilations, etc. –

1987. (cd) Pastell; (POW 6) **HOUSE OF DARK SHADOWS** — German
– Blades of Battenburg (remix) / Burnt orchids / Madelaine / Dr. Strange / The puppet master / Captain Blood / Death or glory (remix) / Cairo / Green glass violins / Lon Chaney / Ghost ships. (cd-iss. May94 on 'New Rose'; 422299)

ROLLING STONES

The Story: Apparently revealed to KEITH RICHARDS in a dream, one of the most recognisable and famous riffs in rock history formed the core of The 'STONES' breakthrough hit, '(I CAN'T GET NO) SATISFACTION'. Despite the controversial lyrics which earned a boycott from US radio and further enhanced their reputation as leering malcontents, the record hit the top of the charts on both sides of the Atlantic during the summer of '65. This opened the floodgates for a wave of No.1 singles: 'GET OFF MY CLOUD' (1965), '19TH NERVOUS BREAKDOWN' (1966) and 'PAINT IT BLACK' (1966), the latter a brooding psychedelic-tinged stampede that featured some nifty sitar playing by a cross-legged BRIAN JONES. 'AFTERMATH' (1966) was a huge step forward with JONES adding exotic touches in line with his growing admiration for the JouJouka musicians of Morocco. Meanwhile, the JAGGER/RICHARDS songwriting partnership was blossoming, tackling social issues with trenchant ease; 'MOTHER'S LITTLE HELPER' as well as the usual sexual politics; 'UNDER MY THUMB'. It was around this time that JAGGER began assuming the multitude of different masks he would use onstage and off, as one journalist aptly pointed out; "MICK JAGGER was an interesting bunch of guys". His cocky, chameleon-like affectations stood in stark contrast to KEITH RICHARDS' sullen, slightly aloof distance but it was exactly this homo-erotic chemistry that fuelled The STONES and fashioned the decadent legend of 'The Glimmer Twins' as they'd come to be known in the 70's. 'BETWEEN THE BUTTONS' (1967) contained another salacious rebel anthem in 'LET'S SPEND THE NIGHT TOGETHER' alongside the ebb and flow wistfulness of 'RUBY TUESDAY'. By this time, though, the powers that be had had just about enough of these unkempt subversives and their dubious morals. The infamous Redlands drug bust in February '67 was probably the most famous of all The 'STONES' run-in's with the law, although by no means the most serious and in the end, RICHARDS' conviction was quashed on appeal while JAGGER was given a year's probation. Yet only a few days later, MICK talked defiantly to the press about revolution and The 'STONES recorded their acerbic reply to The BEATLES' 'All You Need Is Love'. With LENNON and McCARTNEY collaborating, the band cut 'WE LOVE YOU'. Allegedly written by JAGGER in jail as a tribute to the fans who had stood by him, it came out sounding like a deliciously snide riposte to the authorities, complete with the sounds of heavy footsteps and a cell door clanging shut. While they were successful with occasional ventures into warped psychedelia, The 'STONES remained first and foremost a rock'n'roll band and their attempt at a psychedelic concept album, 'THEIR SATANIC MAJESTIES REQUEST' (1967) was always destined to sound half-baked at best. The stellar '2000 LIGHT YEARS FROM HOME' and 'SHE'S A RAINBOW' saved the album from being a complete failure although it didn't even come close to rivalling 'Sgt. Pepper'. A more honest response to The BEATLES' magnum opus, 'BEGGARS BANQUET' (1968) was the first album in a staggering burst of creativity that would see The ROLLING STONES release four of the best albums in the history of rock over a five year period. Preceded by the much needed No.1 hit, 'JUMPIN' JACK FLASH', (which marked the beginning of a fruitful partnership with JIMMY MILLER), the album saw the band realign themselves with roots music to startling effect. At this point The 'STONES were not simply imitating their heroes of the American South, they had made the music truly their own. Inspired by Mikhail Bulgakov's novel, 'The Master

And Margarita', 'SYMPATHY FOR THE DEVIL' was pure malevolent genius, MICK casting himself gleefully in the role of Beelzebub over an irresistible voodoo funk. Similarly controversial were the topical 'STREET FIGHTIN' MAN' and the leering 'STRAY CAT BLUES' which centred on a rock star and an obliging 15 year old groupie, the grinding rhythm oozing illicit sex. These subversive broadsides were alternated with threadbare country blues numbers that, save for JAGGER's barrow boy via Louisiana vocals, sounded so authentic you could almost smell the corn bread.

Album rating: OUT OF OUR HEADS (*7) / AFTERMATH (*7) / BIG HITS (HIGH TIDE AND GREEN GRASS) compilation (*8) / GOT LIVE IF YOU WANT IT (*5) / BETWEEN THE BUTTONS (*7) / THEIR SATANIC MAJESTIES REQUEST (*5) / BEGGARS BANQUET (*10)

MICK JAGGER (b.26 Jul'43, Dartford, Kent, England) – vocals, harmonica / **KEITH RICHARDS** (b.18 Dec'43, Dartford) – rhythm guitar / **BRIAN JONES** (b.28 Feb'43, Cheltenham, England) – lead guitar / **CHARLIE WATTS** (b. 2 Jun'41, Islington, London) – drums (ex-BLUES INC.) / **BILL WYMAN** (b.WILLIAM PERKS, 24 Oct'36, Lewisham, London) – bass repl. DICK TAYLOR who later joined PRETTY THINGS / **IAN STEWART** – piano (was 6th member, pushed to the background by manager)

May 65. (7") (F 12220) **(I CAN'T GET NO) SATISFACTION. / THE SPIDER AND THE FLY** — 1 —
Jun 65. (7") <9766> **(I CAN'T GET NO) SATISFACTION. / THE UNDER ASSISTANT WEST COAST MAN** — 1
Sep 65. (lp; mono/stereo) (LK/SKL 473) <429> **OUT OF OUR HEADS** 2 1 Aug 65
– She said yeah * / Mercy, mercy / Hitch hike / That's how strong my love is / Good times / Gotta get away * / Talkin' 'bout you * / Cry to me / Oh baby (we got a good thing going) * / Heart of stone / The under assistant west coast man / I'm free. <UK tracks above * were repl. by in US> – I'm alright (live) / (I can't get no) Satisfaction / Play with fire / The spider and the fly / One more try. (re-iss. Jul84 lp/c)(cd; LKD/LSLSC 5336/820 049-2) (re-iss. Jun95 on 'London' cd/c/lp; 844465-2/-4/-1)

Sep 65. (7") <9792> **GET OFF OF MY CLOUD. / I'M FREE** — 1
Oct 65. (7") (F 12263) **GET OFF MY CLOUD. / THE SINGER NOT THE SONG** 1 —
Nov 65. (lp) <451> **DECEMBER'S CHILDREN (AND EVERYBODY'S)** — 4
– She said yeah / Talkin' 'bout you / You better move on / Look what you've done / The singer not the song / Route 66 (live) / Get off of my cloud / I'm free / As tears go by / Gotta get away / Blue turns to grey / I'm movin' on (live). (UK-iss.Aug88 cd; 820 135-2) (re-iss. Jun95 on 'London' cd/c/lp; 844464-2/-4/-1)

Dec 65. (7") <9808> **AS TEARS GO BY. / GOTTA GET AWAY** — 6
Feb 66. (7") (F 12331) **19th NERVOUS BREAKDOWN. / AS TEARS GO BY** 1 —
Feb 66. (7") <9823> **19th NERVOUS BREAKDOWN. / SAD DAY** — 2
Apr 66. (lp; mono/stereo)(c) (LK/SKL 4786)(KSKC 4786) <451> **AFTERMATH** 1 2 Jul66
– Mother's little helper / Stupid girl / Lady Jane / Under my thumb / Doncha bother me / Goin' home / Flight 505 / High and dry / Out of time / It's not easy / I am waiting / Take it or leave it / Think / What to do. (US version+=) – Paint it black. (re-iss. May85 lp/c/cd; SKLD/ 4786/820 050-2) (re-iss. Jun95 on 'London' cd/c/lp; 844466-2/-4/-1)

May 66. (7") <901> **PAINT IT BLACK. / STUPID GIRL** — 1
May 66. (7") (F 12395) **PAINT IT BLACK. / LONG LONG WHILE** 1 —
Jul 66. (7") <902> **MOTHER'S LITTLE HELPER. / LADY JANE** — 8/24
Sep 66. (7") (F 12497) <903> **HAVE YOU SEEN YOUR MOTHER BABY, STANDING IN THE SHADOW?. / WHO'S DRIVING YOUR PLANE?** 5 9
Nov 66. (lp; mono/stereo)(c) (TXL/TXS 101)(KSKC 101) <1> **BIG HITS (HIGH TIDE AND GREEN GRASS)** (compilation) 4 3 Apr 66
– Have you seen your mother baby, standing in the shadows? / Paint it black / It's all over now / The last time / Heart of stone / Not fade away / Come on / (I can't get no) Satisfaction / Get off my cloud / As tears go by / 19th nervous breakdown / Lady Jane / Time is on my side / Little red rooster. (re-iss. Jun95 on 'London' cd/c/lp; 844465-2/-4/-1)

Dec 66. (lp) <493> **GOT LIVE IF YOU WANT IT (live, Royal Albert Hall)** — 6
– Under my thumb / Get off my cloud / Lady Jane / Not fade away / I've been loving you too long (to stop now) (studio) / Fortune teller (studio) / The last time / 19th nervous breakdown / Time is on my side / I'm alright / Have you seen your mother baby, standing in the shadow? / (I can't get no) Satisfaction. (UK-iss.Aug88 cd; 820 137-2) (re-iss. Jun95 on 'London' cd/c/lp; 844467-2/-4/-1)

Jan 67. (7") (F 12546) <904> **LET'S SPEND THE NIGHT TOGETHER. / RUBY TUESDAY** 3 55/1
Jan 67. (lp; mono/stereo)(c) (LK/SKL 4852)(KSKC 4852) <499> **BETWEEN THE BUTTONS** 3 2 Feb67
– Yesterday's papers / My obsession / Back street girl* / Connection / She smiled sweetly / Cool, calm and collected / All sold out / Please go home* / Who's been sleeping here? / Complicated / Miss Amanda Jones / Something happened to me yesterday. (US version*; = tracks repl. by)
– Let's spend the night together / Ruby Tuesday. (cd-iss. Jul85; 820 138-2) (re-iss. lp/cd. Dec91 on 'UFO' with free booklet) (re-iss. Jun95 on 'London' cd/c/lp; 844468-2/-4/-1)

Jul 67. (lp) <509> **FLOWERS** (compilation) — 3
(UK cd-iss. Aug88; 820 139-2) (re-iss. cd Jun95 on 'London')

Aug 67. (7") (F 12654) <905> **WE LOVE YOU. / DANDELION** 8 50/14

Nov 67. (7") <906> **SHE'S A RAINBOW. / 2,000 LIGHT YEARS FROM HOME** — 25

Dec 67. (lp; mono/stereo)(c) (TXL/TXS 103)(KTXC 103) <2> **THEIR SATANIC MAJESTIES REQUEST** 3 2
– Sing this all together / Citadel / In another land / 2,000 man / Sing this all together (see what happens) / She's a rainbow / The lantern / Gomper / 2,000 light years from home / On with the show. (re-iss. Feb86 lp/c/cd; 820 129-1/-4/-2) (re-iss. Jun95 on 'London' cd/c/lp; 844469-2/-4/-1)

Dec 67. (7"; by BILL WYMAN) <907> **IN ANOTHER LAND. / THE LANTERN** — 87

May 68. (7") (F 12782) <908> **JUMPIN' JACK FLASH. / CHILD OF THE MOON** 1 3

ROLLING STONES (cont)

Aug 68.	(7") <909> **STREET FIGHTING MAN. / NO EXPECTATIONS**	–	48
Dec 68.	(lp; mono/stereo)(c) (LK/SKL 4955)(KSKC 4955) <539> **BEGGARS BANQUET**	3	5

– Sympathy for the Devil / No expectations / Dear doctor / Parachute woman / Jigsaw puzzle / Street fighting man / Prodigal son / Stray cat blues / Factory girl / Salt of the Earth. (cd-iss. Jan83; 800 084-2) (re-iss. Jul84 lp/c; SKDL/KSKC 4955) (re-iss. Jun95 on 'London' cd/c/lp; 844471-2/-4/-1)

ROMEO VOID

Formed: Bay Area, San Francisco, California, USA ... 1979 by lyricist/singer, DEBORA IYALL (a Cowlitz Indian), along with PETER WOODS, FRANK ZINCAVAGE, BENJAMIN BOSSI and JAY DERRAH (the latter was replaced a year later by JOHN STENCH). Driven by the smouldering but streetwise sensuality of IYALL, ROMEO VOID emerged in 1981 with a debut single, 'WHITE SWEATER', on the small '415' label. The record was characterised by IYALL's disaffected musings on the vagaries of romance while the bleating sax work of BOSSI brought comparisons to the likes of X-RAY SPEX; hypnotic and minimalist, ROMEO VOID's sound had critics spellbound. A RIC OCASEK-produced follow-up EP, 'NEVER SAY NEVER' meanwhile, boasted a glossier production edge and the more commercial bent of 'BENEFACTOR' found RV aiming straight for the alternative dancefloor although the inevitable BLONDIE comparisons missed the point. Yet despite the distribution muscle of 'CBS' (who'd taken over '415'), the record failed to spawn any hit singles and ironically, it took a return to the bite of their earlier sound on third set, 'INSTINCT' (1984), to provide a minor US Top 40 hit in the shape of 'A GIRL IN TROUBLE (IS A TEMPORARY THING)'. The album itself also scraped into the Top 75 yet depite this belated success, ROMEO VOID became null and er ... void, after a final single, 'SAY NO', in early '85. IYALL went on to release a solitary solo album, 'STRANGE LANGUAGE' (1986) before concentrating on her literary aspirations. Although ROMEO VOID reunited in 1993, their activities were confined to live work.

Album rating: IT'S A CONDITION (*6) / BENEFACTOR (*6) / INSTINCTS (*6) / WARM, IN YOUR COAT compilation (*7)

DEBORA IYALL (b.1956) – vocals / **PETER WOODS** – guitar / **BENJAMIN BOSSI** – saxophone / **FRANK ZINCAVAGE** – bass / **JOHN STENCH** – drums (of PEARL HARBOR & THE EXPLOSIONS) repl. JAY DERRAH

		not iss.	415
Feb 81.	(7") <S 0012> **WHITE SWEATER. / APACHE**	–	
Mar 81.	(lp) <A 0004> **IT'S A CONDITION**	–	

– Myself to myself / Nothing for me / Talk dirty (to me) / Love is an illness / White sweater / Charred remains / Confrontation / Drop your eyes / Fear to fear / I mean it.

— **LARRY CARTER** – drums, percussion; repl. STENCH

Nov 81.	(7") <none> **NOT SAFE. / SUCCESS STORY**	–	
Feb 82.	(12"ep) <A 0007> **NEVER SAY NEVER. / IN THE DARK / PRESENT TENSE / NOT SAFE**	–	

		C.B.S.	Columbia
Sep 82.	(7") (A 2733) **NEVER SAY NEVER. / FLASHFLOOD**		
Nov 82.	(lp) (CBS 85929) <38182> **BENEFACTOR**		Aug82

– Never say never / Wrap it up / Flashflood / Undercover kept / Ventilation / Chinatown / Orange / Shake the hands of time / S.O.S.

— **AARON SMITH** – drums, percussion; repl. CARTER

Oct 84.	(7") (A 4756) <04534> **A GIRL IN TROUBLE (IS A TEMPORARY THING). / GOING TO NEON**	35	Aug84
Oct 84.	(lp) (CBS 25969) <39155> **INSTINCTS**	68	Aug84

– Out on my own / Just too easy / Billy's birthday / Going to Neon / Six days and one / A girl in trouble (is a temporary thing) / Your life is a lie / Instincts.

Jan 85.	(7") (A 5028) **SAY NO. / SIX DAYS AND ONE** (12"+=) (TA 5028) – Out on my own.		

— split in 1985 when DEBORA IYALL went solo; she released one album, 'STRANGE LANGUAGE', in '86.

– compilations, etc. –

May 92.	(cd/c) Columbia-Legacy; <CK/CT 47964> **WARM, IN YOUR COAT**	–	

– White sweater / I mean it / Charred remains / Talk dirty to me / Myself to myself / In the dark / Girl in trouble (is a temporary thing) / Out on my own / Just too easy / Wrap it up / Flashflood / Undercover kept / Chinatown / Never say never / One thousand shadows.

ROOM

Formed: Liverpool, England ... early 80's by DAVE JACKSON, ROBYN ODLUM, BECKY STRINGER and CLIVE THOMAS. A series of singles (one on cassette!) on the tiny 'Box' label led to comparisons with local heroes ECHO & THE BUNNYMEN while JACKSON's vocals were, in retrospect, something of a cross between the rich expressiveness of OMD's ANDY McCLUSKEY and the lugubrious wallowing of MORRISSEY. Subsequently signing to noted indie, 'Red Flame', the band released a debut set, 'INDOOR FIREWORKS' (1982), containing at least three semi-classics, 'IN SICKNESS AND IN HEALTH', 'CANDLE' and 'BATED BREATH'. The mini-set, 'CLEAR', followed in '83 and featured the debut of three new recruits, ALAN WILLS (from The WILD SWANS), PAUL CAVANAGH and PETER BAKER, to replace the departed ROBYN and CLIVE; PHIL LUCKING was subsequently added for around half a year. A second album proper, 'IN EVIL HOUR' (1984) was partly produced by former TELEVISION mainman, TOM VERLAINE, many of the tracks taken from sessions recorded with Radio One DJ, Janice Long. Among the delights were the infectious 'NEW DREAMS FOR OLD' (with PHIL) and the sneering 'JACKPOT JACK', while the spiky guitar of 'THE FRIENDLY ENEMY' was straight from the JOHNNY MARR school of cool. Chart success remained tantalisingly out of sight, however, and ROOM called it a day. JACKSON went on to front the similarly obscure BENNY PROFANE although echoes of his deep throated monologue style can occasionally be discerned in the efforts of PULP mainman JARVIS COCKER.

Album rating: INDOOR FIREWORKS (*7) / CLEAR! (*6) / IN EVIL HOUR (*6) / Benny Profane: DUMB LUCK CHARM (*6) / TRAPDOOR SWING (*6)

DAVE JACKSON – vocals / **ROBYN ODLUM** – guitar / **BECKY STRINGER** – bass / **CLIVE THOMAS** – drums, percussion

		Box	not iss.
1980.	(7") (BOX 001) **MOTION. / WAITING ROOM**		–
1980.	(c-s) (BOX 002) **BITTER REACTION**		–
Jul 81.	(7") (BOX 003) **IN SICKNESS AND HEALTH. / BATED BREATH**		–

		Red Flame	not iss.
May 82.	(7") (RF7 03) **THINGS HAVE LEARNT TO WALK THAT OUGHT TO CRAWL. / DREAMS OF FLYING**		–
Jul 82.	(lp) (RF 3) **INDOOR FIREWORKS**		–

– No dream / Escalator / Rewind / Chatshows / This party stinks / Heat haze / Conversation / Things have learnt to walk that ought to crawl / Candle / Bated breath / In sickness and health .

Dec 82.	(7") (RF7 15) **100 YEARS. / THE WHOLE WORLD SINGS**		–

— **ALAN WILLS** – drums (ex-WILD SWANS) repl. CLIVE / **PAUL CAVANAGH** – guitar; repl. ROBYN / added **PETER BAKER** – keyboards

Nov 83.	(m-lp) (RFB 26) **CLEAR!**		–

– Ringing / Numb / The ride / Never / Sleep tight / On the beach.

— added **PHIL LUCKING** – trumpet, trombone

Jun 84.	(7"/12") (RFB 40/+12) **NEW DREAMS FOR OLD. / ON THE BEAT**		–

— reverted to a quintet when PHIL departed

Oct 84.	(lp/c) (RFA/CRFA 42) **IN EVIL HOUR**		–

– A shirt of fire / Whirlpool / Naive / Crying red / The friendly enemy / New dreams for old / Calloused hands / Half forgotten thing / Jackpot Jack.

Mar 85.	(12"ep) (RF 12-42) **JACKPOT JACK. / FRIENDLY ENEMY / SHIRT OF FIRE / CRYING RED / NAIVE (Janice Long sessions)**		–

— disbanded late 1985

– compilations, etc. –

Feb 86.	(d-lp) Red Flame; (RF 47) **NEMESIS**		–

– (CLEAR! / IN EVIL HOUR).

Nov 88.	(12"ep) Strange Fruit; (SFPS 062) **THE PEEL SESSIONS**		–

– The storm / Here comes the floor / But when do we start to live? / Jeremiah.

BENNY PROFANE

formed by **JACKSON + STRINGER** plus **JOE McKECHNIE** – guitar, drums (ex-MODERN EON) / **ROBIN SURTEES** – guitar / **FRANK SPARKS** – drums (ex-EX POST FACTO)

		Sub'Pop UK	not iss.
May 86.	(12") (PURE 1) **WHERE IS PIG? /**		–

		Ediesta	not iss.
Jul 87.	(12"ep) (CALC 026) **DEVIL LAUGHING EP**		–

– Devil laughing / Beam me up / Stitch that / Credulous as hell.

Apr 88.	(12"ep) (CALC 048) **PARASITE / KAMIKAZE DRINKING. / HOLY COW / LITTLE GOD**		–
Sep 88.	(7") (CALC 061) **ROB A BANK. /** (12"+=) (CALC 061T) –		–

— **ROGER SINEK + DAVE BROWN**; repl. SPARKS

		Play Hard	not iss.
May 89.	(12") (DEC 24) **SKATEBOARD TO OBLIVION. / GHOST RIDERS SING RAWHIDE IN THE SKY**		–
Jun 89.	(lp) (DEC 25) **TRAPDOOR SWING**		–

– Man on the sauce / Skateboard to oblivion / Pink snow / Quickdraw McGraw meets Deadeye Dick / A handful of nothing / Rob a bank / Tear the web / Wall to wall / Stitch that / Here comes the floor.

		Imaginary	not iss.
Feb 90.	(7"one-sided) (RED ONE) **HEY WASTE OF SPACE**		–
Feb 90.	(lp) (ILLUSION 7) **DUMBLUCK CHARM**		–

– Time bomb / Maureen / Devil laughing / Walkaway / Perfect girl / Everything / Hey waste of time / Beam me up / Imaginary / Ghoul friend / She. (cd+=) – TRAPDOOR SWING lp

— disbanded after above

ROSE OF AVALANCHE

Formed: Yorkshire, England ... early 80's by PHILIP MORRIS and PAUL JAMES BERRY. Signed to 'L.I.L.' records, the band debuted in 1985 with the 'L.A. RAIN' single, following it up with the 'GODDESS' 12" and 'CASTLES IN THE SKY'. Akin to IGGY POP or even a more metallic, more accessible SISTERS OF MERCY, complete with deep-throat vocals and drumming by NICOL MACKAY (GLENN SCHULTZ on guitar and ALAN DAVIS on bass were also members at this point). They issued their debut album, 'ALWAYS THERE', the following year and with enthusiastic support from John Peel it looked as if the band were destined for more than just cult success. Following the 'FIRST AVALANCHE' (1986) album, they signed to the 'Fire' imprint, releasing a couple of singles, 'TOO MANY CASTLES IN THE SKY' and 'VELVETEEN', the latter lifted from another album that year, 'ALWAYS THERE'. After the lp, 'IN ROCK', a subsequent dispute with their label slowed down the momentum, leading to the band setting up their own label, 'Avalantic', through which they issued a string of progressively more mainstream albums beginning with 'NEVER ANOTHER SUNSET' (1989). The turn of the decade saw MORRIS and BERRY bringing in a new rhythm section of DARREN HOMER and ANDREW PARKER, this line-up completing two final sets, 'STRING 'A' BEADS' (1990) and 'I.C.E.' (1991).

Album rating: FIRST AVALANCHE (*5) / ALWAYS THERE (*6) / IN ROCK (*5) / LIVE AT THE TOWN AND COUNTRY (*5) / NEVER ANOTHER SUNSET (*5) / STRING 'A' BEADS (*4) / I.C.E. (*4)

PHILIP MORRIS – vocals / **PAUL JAMES BERRY** – guitar / **GLENN SCHULTZ** – guitar / **ALAN DAVIS** – bass / **NICOL MACKAY** – drums

                                  Leeds Independent Label   Emergo

May 85. (7") *(LIL 1)* **L.A. RAIN. / RISE TO THE GROOVE**
      (12"+=) *(12LIL 1)* – Conceal me.
Jan 86. (12"m) *(12LIL 2)* **GODDESS / A THOUSAND LANDSCAPES. / GIMME SOME LOVIN'**
— **MARK THOMPSON** – drums; repl. MACKAY
Mar 86. (lp) *(LILLP 003) <772286-1>* **FIRST AVALANCHE**
      – Stick in the works / Rise to the groove / A thousand landscapes / Conceal me / Assassin / Goddess / American girls / Gimme some lovin' / L.A. rain / Dizzy Miss Lizzy. *(re-iss. Aug89 on 'Fire'; REFIRELP 4) (re-iss. Oct91 cd/lp; FIRE 33/11 004)*

                                  Fire   Emergo

May 86. (7") *(BLAZE 9)* **TOO MANY CASTLES IN THE SKY. / ASSASSIN**
      (12"+=) *(BLAZE 9T)* – Dizzy Miss Lizzy.
Sep 86. (7") *(BLAZE 14)* **VELVETEEN. / WHO CARES**   1989
      (12"+=) *(BLAZE 14T) <EM12 5482>* – Just like yesterday.
Sep 86. (lp) *(FIRE 7) <EM 9633>* **ALWAYS THERE**   1989
      – Always there / Waiting for the sun / Majesty / Just like yesterday / Velveteen / Who cares / The mainline man / Always there. *(re-iss. Feb89 on 'Fire' lp/cd; FIRE LP/CD 7) (re-iss. Oct91 cd/lp; FIRE 33/11 007)*
Jan 87. (7") *(BLAZE 18)* **ALWAYS THERE. / WAITING FOR THE SUN**
      (12"+=) *(BLAZE 18T)* – Majesty.
      ('A'-Mainline mix-12"++=) *(BLAZE 18TR)* – The mainline man.
May 87. (d7"ep) *(BLAZE 19EP)* **TOO MANY CASTLES IN THE SKY / VELVETEEN**
      – (the mid-'86 ep's)
Apr 88. (lp) *(FIRELP 12) <772251-1>* **IN ROCK**
      – Dreamland / Not another day / Height of the clouds (part 1 & 2) / Darkorjan / Yesterday once more. *<US+=>* – ALWAYS THERE *(re-iss. Oct91 cd/lp; FIRE 33/11 012)*

                                  Contempo   not iss.

Nov 88. (lp/cd) *(CONTE/+CD 104)* **LIVE AT TOWN AND COUNTRY (live)**
      – Stick in the works / Just like yesterday / Mainline man / Velveteen / A thousand landscapes / Waiting for the sun / Always there / Dreamland / Too many castles in the sky / Gimme some lovin'.

                                  Avalantic   Rebel-SPV

Dec 88. (7") *(AVE 1)* **THE WORLD IS OURS. /**
      (12"+=) *(AVE 1T)* –
Feb 89. (7") *(AVE 2)* **NEVER ANOTHER SUNSET. / GIMME DANGER**
      (12"+=) *(AVE 2T)* – Mistakes.
Apr 89. (lp/c/cd) *(AVE LP/C/CD 001) <84091-1>* **NEVER ANOTHER SUNSET**
      – What's going down / Nowhere to run / You don't belong / The Devil's embrace / Never another sunset / Delusions / Don't fly too high / Her fatal charm / A romantic vision.
1989. (12"ep) *(AVE 4T)* **A PEACE INSIDE EP**
      – A peace inside / The Eden skies / Can you see this life / In at the deep end.
— **MORRIS + BERRY** recruited **DARREN HOMER** – bass / **ANDREW PARKER** – drums
Oct 90. (cd/lp) *(AVE CD/LP 002) <008-3096-1>* **STRING 'A' BEADS**
      – Your lights on / All we want / Make it right / If you only knew – A certain truth / String 'A' beads / If it's right for you / A different child / Be true to your love.
Nov 91. (cd/lp) *(AVE CD/LP 003) <084-3034-2>* **I.C.E.**
      – Ride the storm / Two time baby / I love the ice / Destination nowhere / The garden / Lost the chance / Wall of pain / Everything's OK / Take all the money.
— disbanded not long after above

ROTE KAPELLE
(see under ⇒ JESSE GARON & THE DESPERADOES)

ROYAL FAMILY AND THE POOR

Formed: Liverpool, England ... early 80's by multi-instrumentalist, MIKE KEANE and seasoned campaigner AMBROSE REYNOLDS. Although relatively accessible, The ROYAL FAMILY & THE POOR (who also numbered JEFF TURNER, KAREN HALEWOOD, JOHN WALSH and KIF) were one of the more obscure 'Factory' acts, releasing a one-off EP, 'ART ON 45', before vanishing completely from the music scene. They finally returned in early '86 with a single, 'WE LOVE THE MOON', followed by a belated DONALD JOHNSON (A CERTAIN RATIO)-produced debut album, 'THE PROJECT'. This was an occasionally magikal if nowhere near magical record blighted by KEANE's directionless PINK MILITARY-esque sound and sub-PETE WYLIE vocals. Changing personnel, changing labels and changing style, KEANE and his musical family recorded 'IN THE SEA OF E' (1987) against the backdrop of the emerging, ecstasy-fuelled acid-house scene; danceable but always experimental, the album improved on the debut while failing to take the group to a higher level.

Album rating: THE PROJECT (*3) / IN THE SEA OF E (*4)

MIKE KEANE – vocals, guitar, bass, drum prog, synth, piano, percussion / **AMBROSE REYNOLDS** – bass, (ex-BIG IN JAPAN) / **JEFF TURNER** – sax, clarinet, guitar, violin / **KAREN HALEWOOD** – synthesizer, vocals / **JOHN WALSH** – bass, guitar / **KIF** – drums

                                  Factory   not iss.

Feb 82. (12"ep) *(FACT 43)* **ART ON 45. / DREAM / DOMINION**
— disappeared for around four years, until ...
Jan 86. (7") *(FAC 139)* **WE LOVE THE MOON. / WHITE SATINS**
Apr 86. (lp) *(FACT 95)* **THE PROJECT**
      – I love you (restricted in a moment) / Voices / Moonfish is here / Dark and light / Radio Egypt / Discipline / The dawn song / Ritaul 1 / Power of will / Motherland.

                                  Recloose   not iss.

1986. (lp) *(LOOSE 13)* **LIVE 1983-1985 (live)**
      – Restrained in a moment / Dawn song / Visions / Transparent / Something someone / Destiny / Heartbeat.
— **MIKE** now with **SIMON CRAB** – tapes, synths, keyboards / **ANDY FRIZELL** – bass, flute / **MERLIN SHEPHERD** – sax, strings

                                  Gaia   not iss.

Jun 87. (lp) *(PHASE 003)* **IN THE SEA OF E**
      – Living light / Mr. Crow / Song for freedom / Gaia / Journey / Honesty / Creatura / No more compromise / Wounded / When the cats away / Feast of the supersensualists.
Jan 88. (12") *(PHASE 004)* **RESTRAINED IN A MOMENT. / THE PROJECT**
— KEANE abandoned this project

RUBELLA BALLET

Formed: London, England ... mid '79 by ex-FATAL MICROBES guitarist, PETE FENDER. A second division punk supergroup of sorts, the band also numbered SID ATTION (ex-FLUX OF PINK INDIANS), GEM STONE (ex-KILLJOYS) and singer(!?), ZILLAH MINX (who had replaced a number of previous singers including ANNIE ANXIETY). After a handful of mainly single releases for 'Xntrix' and 'Jungle' records, the dayglo doom-punks released their first album proper for the newly-established 'Ubiquitous', 'AT LAST IT'S PLAYTIME' (1985). Chugging mid-paced stuff, many of the tracks were dominated by ZILLAH's steamroller-flat vox which were reminiscent of the heady "Roxy" days of a young SIOUXSIE SIOUX. By this point, FENDER and STONE had been replaced by STEVE and ZILLAH's sister RACHEL, the show finally coming to a close after the release of the album, 'IF' (1986).

Album rating: BALLET BAG (*5) / AT LAST IT'S PLAYTIME (*5) / IF (*4) / BIRTHDAY BOX compilation (*5) / GREATEST TRIPS compilation (*5)

ZILLAH MINX (b.31 Mar'61, Birkenhead, England) – vocals; repl. ANNIE ANXIETY who went solo (other early singers WOMBLE, COLIN and IT) / **PETE FENDER** – guitar (of/ex-FATAL MICROBES) / **SID ATTION** (b.18 Apr'60, Sutton Coldfield, England) – drums (ex-FLUX OF PINK INDIANS) / **GEM STONE** – bass, vocals (ex-KILLJOYS, ex-FATAL MICROBES)

                                  Xntrix   not iss.

Mar 82. (C-30 cass) *(XN 2004)* **BALLET BAG**
      (re-iss. Sep85; ZN 2004) (re-iss. 1986; same)
Sep 82. (7"ep) *(XN 2005)* **THE BALLET DANCE / SOMETHING TO GIVE. / UNEMPLOYED / KRAK TRAK**

                                  Jungle   not iss.

Jan 84. (12"ep) *(JUNG 12)* **42°F. / SLANT AND SLIDE / BLIND AMBITIONS**

                                  Ubiquitous   not iss.

Feb 85. (12") *(DAYGLO 1)* **MONEY TALKS. / DEATH TRAIN**
— **RACHEL MINX** (b.12 Nov'64, Birkenhead) – bass; repl. GEM
— **STEVE** – guitar; repl. PETE who went solo
Jul 85. (lp) *(DAYGLO 2)* **AT LAST IT'S PLAYTIME**
      – Love life / Tangled web / T.V. scream / Trial thirteen / See saw / Twister / etc
Sep 86. (12") *(DAYGLO 3)* **ARCTIC FLOWERS. / FALSE FLOWERS**
Oct 86. (lp) *(DAYGLO 4)* **IF**
      – Let us out / Plastic life / 'T' / Thugs / It'll never happen to me / Animal house / Rainbow love.
— split on the 1st January 1988

– compilations, etc. –

Mar 87. (lp) *Ubiquitous; (DAYGLO 5)* **THE COCKTAIL MIX**
      – (BALLET BAG tape + THE BALLET DANCE (EP)).
1988. (d-lp) *Ubiquitous; (DAYGLO 6)* **THE RUBELLA BALLET BIRTHDAY BOX**
Feb 90. (cd/lp) *Brave – One Little Indian; (BND 2 CD/LP)* **AT THE END OF THE RAINBOW**
      – Money talks / False promise / Arctic flowers / Dreamer / Animal house / It'll never happen to me / Love potion / Rainbow love / 'T' (emotional blackmail).

RUBELLA BALLET (cont)

Feb 90. (cd) *Brave – One Little Indian; (BND 3CD)* **GREATEST TRIPS**
– The ballet dance / Something to give / Unemployed / Krak trak / 'T' (emotional blackmail) / Belfast / A dream of honey / Newz at 10 / Slant + slide / Krak trak (mk.2) / Blues (with DON BYAS) / Exit / Money talks (dub) / Love life / Tangled web / T.V. screen / Death train / See saw / Twister / Mecalito (acieed mix) / Cowboy hero (with KARA).

RUMBLEFISH

Formed: Birmingham, England . . . 1986 by mainman, JEREMY "J.P." PAIGE, along with DOMINIC CRANE, PHIL EDWARDS and RUPERT KNOWLDEN. One of the many C-86 outfits sprouting out from all areas of the UK, RUMBLEFISH (a name probably lifted from the film of the same name), released their 'Pink'-records debut, 'TUG-BOAT LINE', in 1987, having already contributed the track 'THEATRE KING' to the Merseyside label's V/A compilation, 'Beauty'. Further EP's for 'Summerhouse', 'MEDICINE' and 'DON'T LEAVE ME', preceded an unreasonable time-out until 1992 when 'East West' (in the US only), delivered their one and only long-player, 'RUMBLEFISH'. • **Note:** not to be confused with recent RUMBLE FISH on 'Velocity' records.

Album rating: RUMBLEFISH (*5)

JEREMY "J.P." PAIGE – vocals, guitar / **DOMINIC CRANE** – guitars, keyboards / **PHIL EDWARDS** – bass / **RUPERT KNOWLDEN** – drums

		Pink	not iss.
Mar 87.	(7") *(PINKY 16)* **TUG-BOAT LINE.** / (b-side)		-
	(12"+=) *(PINKY 16T)* – (3 further tracks).		
		Summerhouse	not iss.
Jan 88.	(12"ep) *(SUMS 5)* **MEDICINE**		-
	– Medicine / The lodge / Sing slim! / So lightly.		
Jun 88.	(12"ep) *(SUMS 6)* **DON'T LEAVE ME**		-
		not iss.	East West
May 92.	(cd-s) <96181> **EVERYTHING ELECTRICAL**	-	
Jun 92.	(cd/c) <92144-2/-4> **RUMBLEFISH**	-	
	– Everything electrical / Mexico / Don't leave me / Hammersmith queen / Tug-boat line / So lightly / The lodge / Need a man / What you do to me / Shimmy shammy / It's easy now.		
Aug 92.	(cd-s) **MEXICO**	-	

— split after above

SAD LOVERS AND GIANTS

Formed: Rickmansworth, England . . . 1980 by GARCE ALLARD, TRISTAN GAREL-FUNK, DAVID WOOD, CLIFF SILVER and NIGEL POLLARD. Subsequently basing themselves in Watford and releasing a couple of singles for the small indie imprint, 'Last Movement', SL&G made a brave attempt at combining trad folk influences and complex prog-rock elements with the jangly post-punk pop coming out of the US Paisley underground scene. Initiating their own 'Midnight Music' label, the quintet revealed their penchant for classically romantic lyrical wordplay with mini-set, 'EPIC GARDEN MUSIC' (1982). Their first album proper, 'FEEDING THE FLAME' (1983), found a more enthusiastic audience on the continent and while UK support came from the likes of Radio One DJ, John Peel, the band were on the verge of an imminent split. Following their demise, posthumous material surfaced in the shape of 'IN THE BREEZE' (outtakes and a Peel session) and 'TOTAL SOUND' (live on Dutch radio). ALLARD and POLLARD re-emerged early in 1987 with a new line-up (TONY McGUINNESS, JULIET SAINSBURY and IAN GIBSON) and a fresher, cleaner sound on comeback set, 'THE MIRROR TEST'. A series of 12" EP's ensued while the band set about recording a follow-up, although the collapse of their label eventually saw 'TREEHOUSE POETRY' as their final long-player in '91.

Album rating: EPIC GARDEN MUSIC mini (*5) / FEEDING THE FLAME (*6) / IN THE BREEZE collection (*5) / TOTAL SOUND mini (*5) / THE MIRROR TEST (*5) / LES ANNEES VERTES compilation (*4) / TREEHOUSE POETRY (*4) / E-MAIL FROM ETERNITY: THE BEST OF SAD LOVERS AND GIANTS compilation (*7)

GARCE ALLARD – vocals / **TRISTAN GAREL FUNK** – guitar / **DAVID WOOD** – keyboards / **CLIFF SILVER** – bass / **NIGEL POLLARD** – drums

		Last Movement	not iss.
May 81.	(7"ep) *(LM 003)* **CLE**		-
	– Imagination / Landslide / When I see you.		
Oct 81.	(7") *(LM 005)* **COLOURLESS DREAM.** / **THINGS WE NEVER DID**		-
		Midnight Music	not iss.
Sep 82.	(m-lp) *(CHIME 00.01)* **EPIC GARDEN MUSIC**		-
	– Echoplay / Clocktower lodge / Clint / Lope / Cloud 9 / Art (by me) / Alice (isn't playing) / Far from the sea. *(cd-iss. Sep88; CHIME 00.01CD)* – Imagination / Landslide / When I see you / Colourless dream / Things we never did / Lost in a moment / The tightrope touch.		
Nov 82.	(7") *(DING 1)* **LOST IN A MOMENT.** / **THE TIGHTROPE TOUCH**		-
Oct 83.	(7") *(DING 5)* **MAN OF STRAW.** / **COW BOYS (version)**		-
	(12"+=) *(DONG 5)* – Close to the sea.		
Nov 83.	(lp) *(CHIME 00.03)* **FEEDING THE FLAME**		-
	– Big tracks little tracks / On another day / Sleep (is for everyone) / Vendetta / Man of straw / Strange orchard / Burning beaches / Your skin and mine / In flux. *(cd-iss. Sep88; CHIME 00.03CD)* – Imagination / Cow boys / 3 lines / Close to the sea.		
Nov 84.	(lp) *(CHIME 00.07)* **IN THE BREEZE** (rare demos, outtakes & Peel sessions)		-
	– 50:50 / The change / Interlude / Landslide / Echoplay / Sex without gravity / There was no time / Alice (isn't playing) / 3 lines / Imagination (new recording).		
Oct 86.	(m-lp) *(CHIME 00.22)* **TOTAL SOUND** (live on Dutch radio in 1983)		-
	– Echoplay / Things we never did / Sleep (is for everyone) / Landslide / Cow boys / Man of straw / Imagination.		

— SL&G had already disbanded in 1984 although they re-formed in 1987

— **GARCE + NIGEL** recruited **TONY McGUINNESS** – guitar / **JULIET SAINSBURY** – keyboards / **IAN GIBSON** – bass

Feb 87.	(12"m) *(DONG 31)* **SEVEN KINDS OF SIN.** / **THE OUTSIDER** / **OURS TO KILL**		-
May 87.	(lp) *(CHIME 00.30)* **THE MIRROR TEST**		-
	– White Russians / Take seven / Seven kinds of sin / Wire lawn / Summer & smoke / Cuckooland / Return to Clocktower lodge / The green years / House of clouds. *(cd-iss. Mar88 +=; CHIME 0030)* – Ours to kill / A map of the world / The outsider / Life under glass.		
Jul 87.	(12"m) *(DONG 34)* **WHITE RUSSIANS.** / **A MAP OF THE WORLD** / **LIFE UNDER GLASS**		-
Mar 88.	(12"ep) *(DONG 36)* **COW BOYS (remix)** / **LOST IN A MOMENT (remix).** / **THE BEST FILM HE EVER MADE** / **THINGS WE NEVER DID (live)**		-
Nov 88.	(12"ep) *(DONG 40)* **SLEEP (IS FOR EVERYONE)** / **A REFLECTED DREAM.** / (same tracks by The Essence)		-
Nov 88.	(cd) *(CHIME 00.40CD)* **LES ANNEES VERTES** (compilation)		-
	– 50:50 / The change / Landslide / Echoplay / Sex without gravity / There was no time / Alice (isn't playing) / Clint / Things we never did / Cuckooland / Imagination / Cloud 9 / The best film he ever made / Sleep (is for everyone) / 3 lines / Seven kinds of sin / Return to Clocktower lodge / Colourless dream.		

SAD LOVERS AND GIANTS (cont)

Apr 90. (12") *(DONG 59)* **CLOCKS GO BACKWARDS (re-recorded). / COLOURLESS DREAM (re-recorded)**
Jan 01. (lp/cd) *(CHIME 01.10 S/CD)* **HEADLAND**
– Godless soul / Like thieves / One man's hell / Restless / Alaska / It's snowing / My heart's on fire / Life will kill us.
Sep 91. (lp/cd) *(CHIME 01.20 S/CD)* **TREEHOUSE POETRY**
– Toy planes in a southern sky / Lizard king / Still restless / Parachute of love / Christmas on Easter Island / Criminally sane / Jungle of lies / The sky is a glove.
—— split after above

– compilations, etc. –

Mar 96. (cd) *Cherry Red; (<CDMRED 104>)* **E-MAIL FROM ETERNITY: THE BEST OF SAD LOVERS AND GIANTS**   Sep99
– Things we never did – The best film he ever made / Clint / Alice (isn't playing) / Art (by me) / Imagination / Cowboys / On another day / Sleep (is for everyone) / In flux / The best film he ever made / White Russians / Take seven / Seven kinds of sin / Return to Clocktower Lodge / One man's hell / Alaska / The sky is a glove / Things we never did. *(re-iss. Oct00; same)*

Greg SAGE (see under ⇒ WIPERS)

Walter SALAS-HUMARA (see under ⇒ SILOS)

Kim SALMON & THE SURREALISTICS (see under ⇒ SCIENTISTS)

SALVATION

Formed: Leeds, England ... early 1983 by DANIEL MASS, CHOQUE and JAMES ELMORE. SALVATION delivered their first 12" on the 'Merciful Release' imprint later that year. 'GIRLSOUL', produced by ANDREW ELDRITCH (of SISTERS OF MERCY), also marked a distinct lack of activity for the next two years. They more than made up for this, as 1985 saw the recording (this time with The MISSION's WAYNE HUSSEY in the producer's chair) of the 'JESSICA'S CRIME' 12". The release of this single heralded the beginning of a relentless touring schedule that didn't let up for the next six months. 1986/87 saw both the 'SEEK' EP and 'DIAMONDS ARE FOREVER' mini-set unleashed nationwide, although by the latter they had become a 5-piece, originals MASS and CHOQUE enlisting PAUL MAHER, BEN FARVAK and RICHARD MIECHJE. Their maturing indie/goth-rock sound didn't just win them more and more fans (as their reasonably high indie chart placings showed), but also the interest of others in the music industry. 1988/89 were pivotal years for the group. Two 12" singles were released on the fiercely independent 'Karbon' label. The first, an acid-goth cover of Donovan's 'SUNSHINE SUPERMAN', helped the band gain major Radio One airplay, through daytime DJ's Gary Davis and Mike Read. Prestigious sold-out headline shows in London, were followed by several sell-out UK club tours. Supports with The MISSION, FIELDS OF THE NEPHILIM, The WONDER STUFF, NEW MODEL ARMY and POP WILL EAT ITSELF amongst others followed. Their position was consolidated by the release of what many consider to be their finest moments, the 'ALL AND MORE' EP. The critical acclaim afforded this release and its impressive Indie chart placing attracted the attention of major record companies; SALVATION looked to be on their way when Miles Copeland signed them to his 'I.R.S.' label late in '89. A whirlwind six months saw the release of a single, the melodic Julian Standon-produced 'DEBRIS', a support slot with new labelmates The ALARM and the criminally-ignored 'SASS' album. Success beckoned but it was not to be; infighting led to the sacking of DANNY MASS and the disintegration of the band within eighteen months. • **Trivia:** It was reported around early 1990, that JADE JAGGER once tried to get her dad (MICK) to put them on a 'STONES support slot! • **Covered:** Strange Fruit (L. Allen) / LISTEN TO HER HEART (Tom Petty).

Album rating: DIAMONDS ARE FOREVER mini (*5) / SASS (*7) / HUNGER DAYS 1985-89 compilation (*6)

DANIEL MASS – vocals / **CHOQUE HOSEIN** – guitar / **JAMES ELMORE** – bass / + a drum machine

                                                                Merciful Release   not iss.
Sep 83. (7") *(MR 025)* **GIRLSOUL. / EVELYN**
(12"+=) *(MRX 025)* – Dust up.
                                                                Batfish Inc.   not iss.
Feb 86. (7") *(BF 103)* **JESSICA'S CRIME. / THE SHINING**
(ext.12"+=) *(USS 104)* – Shattered sky.
—— added **PAUL MAHER** – drums
                                                                Ediesta   not iss.
Nov 86. (7") *(CALC 4)* **STRANGE FRUIT. / LADY FAITH**
(12"+=) *(CALCT 4)* **SEEK EP** – Angel pain / The answer.
—— **RICHARD MIECHJE** – bass; repl. ELMORE
—— added **BENOIT FARVAK** – guitar
May 87. (m-lp) *(CALCLP 022)* **DIAMONDS ARE FOREVER**
– Diamond child / Puppet master / Sea of dreams / Thunderbird / Unicorn / Listen to her heart.
                                                                Karbon   not iss.
Jul 88. (7") *(KAR 609)* **SUNSHINE SUPERMAN. / PAYOLA**
(12"+=) *(KAR 609T)* – Pearl necklace.
—— **DANIEL, RICHARD + BENOIT** recruited new members
—— **ANDREW MILLS** – guitar; repl. CHOQUE who joined the HOLLOW MEN (he later formed BLACK STAR LINER)

—— **GEORGE SCHULZ** – drums; repl. MAHER who joined PARACHUTE MEN
May 89. (12") *(KAR 612T)* **ALL AND MORE EP**
– All and more / The happening / She's an island.
                                                                I.R.S.   not iss.
Jan 90. (7") *(EIRSA 137)* **DEBRIS. / UNTITLED**
(12"+=) *(EIRST 137)* – She says.
Jun 90. (lp/cd) *(EIRSA/+CD 1033)* **SASS**
– Very go round / The innocent / To high heaven / Tumbleweed / Ravishing / (Clearing out the) Debris / Bamboo / Leave by day / Paint it rose / Johnny B. Serious.
—— disbanded late 1991 after MASS was thrown out on 1990 tour; MILLS formed LA COSTA RASA (one set for Merciful Release), while FARVAK released "white label" singles and MEICHJE became a nightclub promoter – thanks to BEN(OIT) for all this info!

– compilations, etc. –

Feb 98. (cd) *Timeslip; (TSCD 01)* **HUNGER DAYS 1985-89**
– The shining / Shattered sky / Jessica's crime / Lady faith / Angel pain / The answer / Strange fruit / Diamond child / Puppet master / Sea of dreams / Thunderbird / Unicorn / Listen to her heart / Sunshine superman / Payola / Pearl necklace / All and more / The happening / She's an island.

SAVAGE REPUBLIC

Formed: Los Angeles, California, USA ... early 80's initially as AFRICA CORPS, by UCLA students BRUCE LICHER and MARK ERSKINE. Enlisting the help of ETHAN PORT, ROBERT LOVELESS, PHIL DRUCKER and employing a startling array of industrial percussion that would make even TEST DEPT look like a school project, the duo created some of the most bleakly evocative avant-garde music of the US post-punk scene. Characterised by stark, tribal rhythms and gravel-voxed incantations, their debut album, 'TRAGIC FIGURES' (1982), favoured noise experimentalism over melody although by the time they re-emerged in 1985 (LOVELESS and DRUCKER had occupied the intervening years with side project, 17 PYGMIES), SAVAGE REPUBLIC were a relatively more accessible proposition. 1987's 'CEREMONIAL' album (their second for LICHER's 'Independent Project' label) utilised off-kilter guitar as its focus, winding hypnotic riffs round exotic world music influenced melodies. Finding a more sympathetic audience in Europe, the group (which now included BRAD LANER) subsequently recorded a mini-set for 'Play It Again Sam', 'TRUDGE' (1986), before signing a long term deal with 'Fundamental'. Two further albums, 'JAMAHIRIYA' (1988) and 'CUSTOMS' (1989), surfaced before SAVAGE REPUBLIC faded from view. LICHER continued to operate his label from the relative seclusion of the Arizona desert, having already netted a Grammy for his packaging of the debut CAMPER VAN BEETHOVEN album. Musically, he returned to the fray as SCENIC along with JAMES BRENNER and BROCK WIRTZ, exploring more widescreen celluloid territory with 'INCIDENT AT CIMA' (1995) and 'ACQUATICA' (1996), tempering his past tendency to jarring repetition with a dust-bowl/soundtrack twang. Just when you thought the SCENIC revolution was over, out comes another coup in the shape of comeback set, 'ACID GOSPEL EXPERIENCE' (2002). Okay, this was definitely a move away from past expansions, filtering now into psychedelia and wigged-out waters – you could virtually taste the desert through the magnum-opus and 18-minute+ finale of 'A JOURNEY THROUGH THE OUTER REACHES OF INNER SPACE'. Water, please. • **Covered:** VIVA LA ROCK'N'ROLL (Alternative TV) / 21st CENTURY SCHIZOID MAN (King Crimson).

Album rating: TRAGIC FIGURES (*5) / TRUDGE mini (*6) / CEREMONIAL (*6) / LIVE TREK (*5) / JAMAHIIYA (*5) / CUSTOMS (*4) / LIVE IN EUROPE 1988 (*4) / Scenic: INCIDENT AT CIMA (*6) / ACQUATICA (*7) / THE ACID GOSPEL EXPERIENCE (*6)

BRUCE LICHER – guitar / **MARK ERSKINE** – drums, percussion / **ETHAN PORT** – guitars, bass, percussion / **ROBERT LOVELESS + PHIL DRUCKER** – rhythm, etc

                                                                Sordid Sentimental   Independent Project
Mar 84. (lp) *(SSLP 001) <IP 004>* **TRAGIC FIGURES**   1982
– When all else fails ... / Attempted coup: Madagascar / Ivory Coast / Next to nothing / Exodus / On the prowl / Machinery / Zulu Zulu / Real men / Flesh that walks / Kill the fascists! / Procession / Film noir / O Adonis / Mobilization / Tragic figures. *(re-iss. Aug87 on 'Fundamental' lp/cd+=; SAVE 021/+CD)* – The empty quarter / The Ivory Coast.
—— took time off to recuperate in '83 after ROBERT LOVELESS and PHIL DRUCKER left to form the 17 PYGMIES
—— added guest **LOUISE BAILIK** – vocals
                                                                Play It Again Sam   not iss.
Jan 86. (m-lp) *(BIAS 011)* **TRUDGE**
– Trudge / Trek / Siege / Assembly.
                                                                Fundam.   Independent Project
Sep 87. (lp/cd) *(SAVE 022/+CD) <IP 018>* **CEREMONIAL**   1985
– Valetta / Andelusia / Walking backwards / 1000 days / Mediterranean / Dionysus / Ceremonial / Year of exile / Land of delusion. *<cd re-iss. Jan02 on 'Mobilization'; MOB 102>* – TRUDGE
Nov 87. (d-lp) *<(SAVE 042-043)>* **LIVE TREK 86 (live)**   1986
(c-iss.Aug88; WEBOY 002C)
—— added **BRAD LANER** – percussion
                                                                Fundam.   Fundam.
Aug 89. (lp/cd) *<(SAVE 061/+CD)>* **JAMAHIRIYA**   1988
– So it is written / Spice fields / Viva la rock'n'roll / Tabula rasa / Il papa sympatico / Pios den mila yia ti lambri / Lethal musk / Lebanon 2000 / Moujahadeen / Jamahiriya *(cd+=)* – Il papa sympatico (instrumental) / Viva la rock'n'roll (instrumental) / Moujahadeen (instrumental).

SAVAGE REPUBLIC (cont)

Dec 89. (lp/cd) <(SAVE 071/+CD)> **CUSTOMS**
– Sucker punch / Sono Cairo / Mapia / The birds of pork / Rapeman's first EP / The world (at our fingertips) / Song for Adonis / Archetype.

Oct 90. (lp/cd) <(SAVE 087/+CD)> **LIVE IN EUROPE 1988 (live)**
– Spice fields / Mobilization / Jamahiriya / Next to nothing / Kill the fascists! / Lethal musk / Viva la rock'n'roll / Siege / Year of exile / Processio / Sucker punch / O Adonis / Ivory Coast / 21st Century schizoid man / Grinch.

— had already split; LANER formed MEDICINE, LICHER relocated to Sedona in Arizona and ran his label

– compilations, etc. –

1993. (d10"lp/cd) *Independent Project;* <38/39> **RECORDINGS FROM LIVE PERFORMANCE, 1981-1983 (live)**

1994. (lp) *Independent Project;* **SAVAGE REPUBLIC** (1984-1985 plus)

Jan 02. (4xcd-box) *Mobilization;* <MOB 101-104> **SAVAGE REPUBLIC**
– (TRAGIC FIGURES / CEREMONIAL / JAMAHIRIYA / CUSTOMS)

SCENIC

— **BRUCE LICHER** – guitar, percussion, etc / **JAMES BRENNER** – bass, percussion, keyboards, etc (ex-SHIVA BURLESQUE) / **BROCK WRITZ** – drums, percussion / **ROBERT LOVELESS** – keyboards, flute, accordion, percussion, etc / **BRANDON CAPPS** – guitar, sitar

IP/World Domination – IP/World Domination

Jun 96. (cd-ep) <(IP 054)> **SAGE EP**
– Sage / Another way / Kelso run / East Mojave shuffle / Down black canyon road.

Nov 96. (cd) <(IP 050CD)> **INCIDENT AT CIMA** Nov95
– The shifting sand / The Kelso run / Incident at Cima / East Mojave shuffle / Hole in the wall / Carrying on to Cadiz / The mid hills / Down black canyon road / Chiriaco summit / Around sundown / Bossa dune / Predawn / On the dune / The road to Ivanpah / Cima dome.

Nov 97. (2x7"ep/cd-ep; split with LANTERNA) (PAR/+CD 031)<IP 058> **IN LIVE PERFORMANCE (live)**
– (2 by LANTERNA) / Angelica / Dronia.
(above issued with 'Parasol')

Apr 98. (cd) <(WD 0038-2)> <10844> **ACQUATICA** Oct96
– The tones of Peloponnesus / Ionia / Parisia / Acquatica / All fish go to Heaven / The Isle of Caldra / Deserted shores / Improvia / Angelica / Dronia / The ionic curve / Aga aludoma / Sidereal hands at the temple of Omphalos / Modula raga / Et tu, Dronius?

Hidden Agenda – Hidden Agenda

Sep 02. (cd) <(AHA 047)> **THE ACID GOSPEL EXPERIENCE** Jan03
– Year of the rat / Lightspeed / The acid gospel / Under a wing / Lunar afternoon / Skylight / Lightcord / The spheres / A journey through the outer reaches of inner space.

Sky SAXON (see under ⇒ SEEDS)

SCARS

Formed: Edinburgh, Scotland ... late '77 by ROBERT 'BOBBY' KING, PAUL RESEARCH, JOHN MACKIE and CALUMN MacKAY. This young post-punk outfit made their vinyl debut on the local 'Fast' label with the 'Adultery' single in Spring '79, 'Charisma' sufficiently impressed to sign the band to the 'Pre' offshoot. 'THEY CAME AND TOOK HER' marked the SCARS' major label debut in early 1980, while a much anticipated debut album, 'AUTHOR! AUTHOR!' arrived in Spring the following year. Ranging from the melodic new-wave guitar pop of 'ALL ABOUT YOU' to the CURE-style reverberations of 'JE T'AIME C'EST LA MORT', the record was an encouraging debut in what was a fine year for Scots artists with releases from contemporaries like JOSEF K, ORANGE JUICE etc. Unfortunately, like most of the new young Caledonian bands, the lifespan of SCARS proved surprisingly short and the band split with only one album to their name. Perhaps this was for the best as wearing tan jodphurs wrapped with garish climbing rope (!) was surely plunging New Romantic fashion to unnecessary depths.

Album rating: AUTHOR! AUTHOR! (*7)

ROBERT 'BOBBY' KING – vocals / **PAUL RESEARCH** – guitar / **JOHN MACKIE** – bass / **CALUMN MacKAY** – drums

Fast Product – not iss.

Mar 79. (7") (FAST 8) **HORRORSHOW. / ADULT-ERY**

— **STEVE 'CHICK' McLAUGHLIN** – drums; repl. CALUMN

Pre – Stiff

Feb 80. (7") (PRE 002) **THEY CAME AND TOOK HER. / ROMANCE BY MAIL**
May 80. (7") (PRE 005) **LOVE SONG. / PSYCHOMODO**
Apr 81. (7") (PRE 014) **ALL ABOUT YOU. / AUTHOR! AUTHOR!** 67
Apr 81. (lp) (PREX 5) **AUTHOR! AUTHOR!**
– Leave me in Autumn / Fear of the dark / Aquarama / David / Obsessions / Everywhere I go / The lady in the car with glasses on and a gun / Je t'aime c'est la mort / Your attention please / All about you.
Sep 81. (7") (PRKS 5) **AUTHOR! AUTHOR! / SHE'S ALIVE**
(12"+=) (PRKSX 5) – Silver dream machine.
Oct 81. (12"ep) <TEES12 04> **AUTHOR! AUTHOR! / SHE'S ALIVE. / ALL ABOUT YOU / LEAVE ME IN AUTUMN**

— split early 1982, KING subsequently went solo releasing one single, 'PAPER HEART', in 1982 (PRE 23). He later formed LIP MACHINE, who released a handful of 45's for the 'Disposable Dance' imprint.

Fran SCHOPPLER
(see under ⇒ JESSE GARON & THE DESPERADOES)

SCIENTISTS

Formed: Perth, Australia ... 1978 by KIM SALMON, JAMES BAKER, BORIS SUJDOVIC and ROD RADALJ. During the recording of their debut 1979 single 'FRANTIC ROMANTIC', RADALJ departed as did SUJDOVIC a little later. The track found its way on to UK and US shores and was subsequently licensed to Greg Shaw's US 'Bomp' label. DENIS BYRNE then became a temp bass player until IAN SHARPLES and BEN JUNIPER (guitar) were recruited for 1980's 'LAST NIGHT' EP. The SCIENTISTS stripped down to a trio soon after as JUNIPER became another personnel casualty. However, the team finally disbanded after recording an eponymous album (aka 'the PINK album'). SALMON then moved to Sydney, forming LOUIE LOUIE with drummer BRETT RIXON, although this short-lived outfit soon metamorphasised into The SCIENTISTS (Mk.2), completing the line-up with TONY THEWIS and the returning SUJDOVIC. In 1982, this more settled version of the Aussie musical boffins delivered a new single, 'THIS IS MY HAPPY HOUR'. Initially not as experimental as their moniker might suggest, The SCIENTISTS moved from a retro sonic R&B sound (once the territory of 60's outfits The TROGGS and The STOOGES) to a more gothic, bass-heavy CRAMPS meets The BIRTHDAY PARTY style. This was evident on their 1983 follow-up mini-set, 'BLOOD RED RIVER', showing SALMON at his howling best. In 1985, they relocated to London, although they soon became disillusioned when RIXON quit. He again joined for 1987's 'THE HUMAN JUKEBOX', although the drummer would later die of a heroin overdose on the 24th of December '93. KIM SALMON, meanwhile, had formed his own solo project (backed by The SURREALISTICS) at the turn of the decade, having already initiated a simultaneous and ongoing moonlighting outfit, The BEASTS OF BOURBON. A plethora of releases (by both combos) ensued, including self-explanatory SALMON solo titles such as '94's 'SIN FACTORY' and 'HELL IS WHERE MY HEART LIVES'. • **Covered:** YOU ONLY LIVE TWICE (John Barry). BEASTS OF BOURBON covered GRAVEYARD TRAIN (John Fogerty) and others.

Album rating: THE SCIENTISTS (*7) / THIS HEART DOES NOT RUN ON BLOOD mini (*4) / ATOM BOMB BABY (*6) / YOU GET WHAT YOU DESERVE (*5) / THE HUMAN JUKEBOX compilation (*6) / ABSOLUTE compilation (*7) / Beasts Of Bourbon: THE AXEMAN'S JAZZ (*5) / SOUR MASH (*5) / BLACK MILK (*4) / THE LOW ROAD (*5) / FROM THE BELLY OF THE BEASTS (*5) / GONE (*5) / BEYOND GOOD & EVIL compilation (*6) / Kim Salmon: HIT ME WITH THE SURREAL FEEL (*5) / JUST BECAUSE YOU CAN'T SEE (*5) / ESSENCE (*5) / SIN FACTORY (*5) / HELL IS WHERE MY HEART LIVES (*5) / HEY BELIEVER (*4) / KIM SALMON & THE SURREALISTS (*6) / YA GOTTA KET MAY DO MY THING (*6) / RECORD (*5)

KIM SALMON – vocals, guitar / **ROD RADALJ** – guitar / **BORIS SUJDOVIC** – bass / **JAMES BAKER** – drums

not iss. – Bomp

Mar 79. (7") <SMX 46960> **FRANTIC ROMANTIC. / SHAKE (TOGETHER TONIGHT)**

— **BEN JUNIPER** – guitar; repl. RADALJ

— **IAN SHARPLES** – bass; repl. DENIS BYRNE who repl. SUJDOVIC

not iss. – WhiRider

Mar 80. (7"ep) <WEEP 1> **LAST NIGHT**
– Last night / Bet ya lyin' / It's for real / Pissed on another planet.

— now a trio without JUNIPER

Easter – not iss.

Aug 81. (lp) <HAVE 1> **THE SCIENTISTS**
– Shadows of the night / Girl / I'm looking for you / She said she loves me / Sorry sorry sorry / That girl / High noon / Teenage dreamer / Another Sunday / Walk the plank / Larry / Making a scene / It'll never happen again.

— disbanded after recording of above; BAKER re-united with RADALJ in The HOODOO GURUS

— **SALMON** re-formed SCIENTISTS with **BRETT RIXON** – drums / **TONY THEWLIS** – guitar / **BORIS SUJDOVIC** – bass

Au Go Go – not iss.

1982. (7") (ANDA 25) **(THIS IS MY) HAPPY HOUR. / SWAMPLAND** – Austra
1983. (m-lp) (ANDA 27) **BLOOD RED RIVER** – Austra
– When fate deals it's mortal blow / The spin / Rev head / Burnout / Set it on fire / Blood red river.
Oct 83. (7") (ANDA 29) **WE HAD LOVE. / CLEAR SPOT** – Austra
Dec 83. (7"freebie) (ANDA 31) **WHEN WORLDS COLLIDE. / GHOST TRAIN** – Austra
Nov 84. (m-lp) (ANDA 32) **THIS HEART DOESN'T RUN ON BLOOD** – Austra
– Nitro / Solid gold hell / I cried no tears / Crazy heart / This life of yours.
Jun 85. (7") (ANDA 35) **ATOM BOMB BABY. / BACKWARDS MAN** – Austra
Jul 85. (m-lp) (ANDA 37) **ATOM BOMB BABY** – Austra
– Travis / Leadfoot / Bad priest / It came from out of the sky / Hell beach / Go baby go / Atom bomb baby.
Nov 85. (green-lp) (ANDA 39) **HEADING FOR A TRAUMA** – Austra
– Swampland / The wall / Fire escape / Raver / Clear spot / (This is my) Happy hour / We had love / Temple of love / Murderess in a purple dress / Psycho cook supreme / Demolition derby. (w/ free 7"; PHANDA 1) – THE OTHER PLACE. / SHE CRACKED

Karbon – Big Time

Aug 85. (lp) (KAR 101L) **YOU GET WHAT YOU DESERVE**
– Hell beach / If it's the last thing I do / Bad priest / Demolition derby / It came out of the sky / Atom bomb baby / Go baby go / Psycho supreme cook / Lead foot / Murderess in a purple dress.

SCIENTISTS (cont)

— LEANNE CHOCK – drums; repl. PHILIP HERTZE (from USA) who repl. RIXON
Nov 85. (7") *(KAR 007)* **YOU ONLY LIVE TWICE. / IF IT'S THE LAST THING I DO**
Oct 86. (lp) *(KAR 103L) <6016-1>* **WEIRD LOVE** (compilation)
– Swampland / Hell beach / Demolition derby / Murderess in a purple dress / We had love / Nitro / If it's the last thing I do / Lead foot / When fate deals its mortal blow / Atom bomb baby / Set it on fire / You only live twice.

— now trio of **SALMON, THEWLIS** + new drummer **NICK COMBE** who repl. LEANNE + BORIS (latter formed DUBROVNIKS, with BAKER + RADALJ)
Aug 87. (m-lp) *(KAR 105L)* **THE HUMAN JUKEBOX**
– Human jukebox / Shine / Distortion / Place called Bad / Hungry eyes / Brain dead / It must be nice.

— **BRETT RIXON** returned but the group soon split after tour. He was to die of a heroin overdose on 24th Dec'93.

– compilations, etc. –

Aug 85. (12"ep) *Soundwork; (SW 12-007)* **DEMOLITION DERBY** — — Belgian
– Demolition derby / Temple of love / Murderess in a purple dress / Backwards man.
May 94. (cd) *Red Eye; (REDCD 23) / Sub Pop; <SP 106>* **ABSOLUTE** 1991
– Swampland / Fire escape / We had love / Set it on fire / Blood red river / Solid gold hell / Backwards man / Murderess in a purple dress / Psycho cook supreme / Travis / Shine / Human jukebox.
Dec 00. (cd) *Citadel; (CITCD 543) / Sympathy For The Record Industry; <SFTRI 675>* **BLOOD RED RIVER**
– Set it on fire / Blood red river / Revhead / Burnout / The spin / When fate deals its mortal blow / Swampland / This is my happy hour / We had love / Clear spot / Nitro / Solid gold hell / Murderess in a purple dress / Backwards man / Demolition derby.
Nov 01. (cd) *Citadel; (CITCD 544)* **THE HUMAN JUKEBOX 1984-1986**
– Atom bomb baby / It came out of the sky / Lead foot / Hell beach / Psycho cook supreme / Go baby go / You only live twice / If it's the last thing I do / Shine / Distortion / Brain dead / It must be nice / A place called Bad / Human jukebox.

BEASTS OF BOURBON

TEX PERKINS – vocals, guitar / **KIM SALMON** – guitar, slide guitar / **SPENCER JONES** – guitar, vocals / **BORIS SUJDOVIC** – bass / **JAMES BAKER** – drums

Hybrid   Big Time

Apr 85. (lp) *(HYBLP 1) <BTA 001>* **THE AXEMAN'S JAZZ**
– Evil Ruby / Love & death / Graveyard train / Psycho / Drop out / Save me a place / Lonesome bones / The day Marty Robbins died / Ten wheels for Jesus. *(re-iss. 1988 on 'Red Eye'; RED 4) (cd-iss. May94; RED 4CD)*

Red Eye   not iss.

Nov 88. (lp/cd) *(RED LP/CD 5)* **SOUR MASH** — — Austra
– Hard work drivin' man / Hard for you / Watch your step / Playground / Door to your soul / These are the good old days / The hate inside / The big sleep / Pig / Driver man / Elvis impersonator blues / Today I started loving you again / Flathead (the fugitive) / This ol' shit / Sun gods. *(UK-iss.Mar94; same)*
Feb 89. (7"m) *(RED 17)* **HARD WORK DRIVIN' MAN. / ELVIS IMPERSONATOR BLUES / I LOVE YOU BECAUSE**
Apr 89. (d7") *(RED 18)* **THE HATE INSIDE. / THE BIG SLEEP // HARD FOR YOU. / MOANING AT MIDNIGHT**
Aug 90. (cd/lp) *(RED CD/LP 12)* **BLACK MILK** — — Austra
– Black milk / Finger lickin' / Cool fire / Bad revisited / Hope you find your way to Heaven / Words from a woman to her man / I'm so happy I could cry / You let me down / Let's get funky / A fate much worse than life / El beasto / Blue stranger / I've let you down again / Blanc garcon / Execution day / Rest in peace. *(re-iss. Mar94; same)*

— **BRIAN HENRY HOOPER** – bass, guitar; repl. BORIS
— **TONY POLA** – drums; repl. BAKER
1991. (cd) *(REDCD 26)* **THE LOW ROAD** — Austra
– Chase the dragon / The low road / Just right / There's a virus going round / Can't say no / Ride on / Straight, hard & long / Cocksucker blues / Something to lean on / Goodbye friends. *(Uk-iss.Mar94; same)*
1991. (7") *(879184-7)* **WORDS FROM A WOMAN TO HER MAN. / HOPE YOU FIND YOUR WAY TO HEAVEN (acoustic live)**
(above issued on 'Red Eye – Polydor')
1992. (m-cd) *(REDCD 20)* **JUST RIGHT** — Austra
– Just right / Getcha money ready / There's no cure / Black milk / Let's get funky. *(UK-iss.Mar94; same)*
1992. (d7") *(RED 21)* **LET'S GET FUNKY. / YOU LET ME DOWN // COOL FIRE / BLANC GARCON**
Mar 94. (cd/d-lp) *(RED CD/LP 30)* **FROM THE BELLY OF THE BEASTS (live compilation)**
– Chase the dragon / Driver man / Save me a place / Bad revisited / Black milk / Drop out / Hard for you / Straight, hard and long / Let's get funky / Cocksucker blues / Watch your step / Execution day / Good times / The world's got everything in it / No reason / Junkie girlfriends / Ramblin' man / Not gonna try no more / Kill this fire / Hope you find your way to heaven / Love and death / E.S.P. / Dead flowers / The train kept a rollin' / So agitated / Dirty water / Crawfish / Anarchy in the UK.

— **CHARLIE OWEN** – guitar (ex-DIVINYLS) repl. SALMON!
Feb 97. (cd) *(REDCD 58)* **GONE**
– Saturated / Fake / Make 'em cry / Mullett / Get on / I s'pose / What a way to live / That sinking feeling again / So long / Is that love / This day is over / Unfolded.

– compilations, etc. –

1999. (cd) *Universal; <559522-2>* **BEYOND GOOD & EVIL: THE BEST OF THE BEASTS OF BOURBON**
– Psycho / Drop out / Hard for you / Playground / Door to your soul / Let's get funky / Black milk / Finger lickin' / Cool fire / Words from a woman to her man / Execution day / Chase the dragon / JUst right / The low road / Can't say no / Saturated / Fake / Make 'em cry / Is that love / Goodbye friends / What a way to live / Hard for you / Straight, hard and long / Fake / Make 'em cry.

KIM SALMON & THE SURREALISTICS

SALMON with **BRIAN HOOPER** – bass, guitar, piano / **TONY POLA** – drums, percussion

Black Eye   Sympathy F

Nov 96. (lp) *(BLACKLP 7)* **HIT ME WITH THE SURREAL FEEL** — Austra
– The surreal feel / Bad birth / Feel / Bellyfull of slugs / The surreal feel / Black velvet / Intense / Blue velvet / The surreal feel / Torture / Devil in disguise / The surreal feel. *(<UK+US re-iss. Dec96 on 'In The Red' lp/cd; ITR 33/+CD>)*
1989. (lp/cd; as KIM SALMON) *(BLACK LP/CD 9)* **JUST BECAUSE YOU CAN'T SEE IT . . . DOESN'T MEAN IT ISN'T THERE**
– Melt (part 1) / Measure of love / Undying love / Sundown, sundown / Melt (part 2) / Weren't we bad / Sunday drive / Je t'aime / Your vicious omnipresence / You're gonna die / An articulation of the thoughts of one of society's bastards. *(cd+=)* – The surreal feel / Bad birth / Bellyfull of slugs / Black velvet / Intense / Blue velvet / Torture / The surreal feel. *(re-iss. May94; same)*
1990. (7") *(RED 879264-7) <SFTRI 178>* **LIGHTNING SCARY. / LIGHTNING SCARY II** — Austra
1991. (lp/cd) *(RED 21/+CD)* **ESSENCE** — Austra
– I'm keeping you alive / The cockroach / Self absorbtion / The butterfly effect / A pox on you / Zero blank / Lightning scary / Essence of you / Looking at the picture / Down at the soul bank / Sea anemone / 26 good works. *(UK-iss.May94 on 'Red Eye'; REDCD 21)*
1991. (7") *(867062-7)* **ZERO BLANK. / THE COCKROACH / OBVIOUS IS OBVIOUS** — Austra
1992. (cd-ep) *(863677-2)* **NON STOP ACTION GROOVE** — Austra
– Non stop action groove / I fell / You'll pay for this / Something to lean on.
1993. (cd) *(REDCD 33)* **SIN FACTORY** — Austra
– I fell / Gravity / Desensitised / Feel / Hangin' out / You'll pay for this / Come on baby / Rose coloured windscreen / Listen to your brother / In the underworld / Non stop action groove c/ Something to lean on / The 1st person. *(w/ free cd-ep; 517970-2)* **ST. VALENTINE'S DAY MASSACRE** – The cockroach / Shine / Frantic romantic / Je t'aime / I'm keeping you alive. *(UK-iss.May94; same) <US-iss.1996 on 'Deep Six'; 0654>*
May 94. (cd) *(REDCD 34)* **HELL IS WHERE MY HEART LIVES**
– Rose coloured windscreen / You'll pay for this / Something to lean on / The cockroach / Shine / Frantic romantic / Je t'aime . . . moi non plus / I'm keeping you alive.
Nov 94. (cd; as KIM SALMON WITH STM) *(REDCD 40)* **HEY BELIEVER** — Austra
– Reach out / Don't expect anything / Obvious is obvious / You know me better than that / Playground / Pass it on / Full of promise / Treachery / Ramblin' man / Hey believer. *(UK-iss.on 'Glitterhouse'; GRCD 349)*
Nov 95. (cd) *(REDCD 48)* **KIM SALMON & THE SURREALISTS**
– I wish upon you / What's inside your box? / Redemption for sale / Draggin' out the truth / Plenty more fish / Frantic romantic / I'm gonna see you compromised / Innersense / Holocaust / It's your fault. *(UK-iss.on 'Glitterhouse'; GRCD 381)*
Dec 95. (cd-s) *(851575-2)* **KIM SALMON & THE SURREALISTS** — Austra
– What's inside your box / Intense / Frantic romantic.

Half A Cow   Half A Cow

Aug 97. (cd) *(HAC 63) <111038>* **YA GOTTA LET ME DO MY THING** Jul98
– I won't tell / The zipper / You're such a freak / Undone / The connoisseur / Insurance man / Ya gotta let me do my thing / You've got layers / Alcohol / The lot / Horizontal zipper / I am a voyeur / Guilt free / Space 1999 / Medium / Put your trust in me / Caught in the zipper. *(re-iss. Jan99 on 'Citadel'+=; CITCD 541)* – **HIT ME WITH THE SURREAL FEEL**

KIM SALMON & THE BUSINESS

Half A Cow   Half A Cow

Dec 99. (cd-s) *(HAC 85)* **SAVING ME FROM ME / CAESAR'S LAMENT / LOVE ME** — Austra
Jan 00. (cd) *(HAC 86)* **RECORD**
– What's all this business? / Saving me from me / Disconnected / Share it / Don't fake it / Anticipation / Nothing can go wrong / I'll be around / Give me some notes Mike / Emperor's new clothes / New kind of angle / Behave yourself / IOU / Caesar's lament.
Feb 00. (cd-s) *(HAC 88)* **DISCONNECTED / DISCO NECK TIE (mix one) / DISCONNECTED (mix two)** — Austra
Jun 00. (cd-ep) *(HAC 95)* **I'LL BE AROUND (Escobar remix) / ANTICIPATION (Escobar remix) / I WAS A LORD OF DARKNESS / I'LL BE AROUND (album version)** — Austra

— SALMON will release a new solo set, 'E(A)RNEST' around 2002/3; he was also part of ANTENNA in the late 90's

Robert SCOTT (see under ⇒ BATS)

SCRATCH ACID (see under ⇒ JESUS LIZARD)

SCRAWL

Formed: Columbus, Ohio, USA . . . 1985 as SKULL by MARCH MAYS, SUE HARSHE and CAROLYN O'LEARY. Although the concept of an all-female rock band was hardly something new, this uncompromising trio were one of the first acts to bring seething feminist/emotional sentiments to the US indie underground. After a baptism by fire supporting the MEAT PUPPETS, the ladies cobbled together enough money to record a debut set, 'PLUS, ALSO, TOO' (1987), garnering praise from many established publications. The attendant rise in profile led to a transatlantic deal with 'Rough Trade', through whom they released a further two albums, 'HE'S DRUNK' (1989) and 'SMALLMOUTH' (1990), the former cut at PRINCE's recently built Paisley Park studio complex in Minneapolis. Although SCRAWL were already at loggerheads with their label over a proposed fourth album, the subsequent collapse of 'Rough Trade' meant that the scathing 'BLOODSUCKER' mini-album would eventually appear in 1991 on another indie imprint. In the meantime, the band were forced to bid for their own master tapes at a public auction, their back catalogue having been in limbo since Rough Trade's demise. While their all-girl exclusivity was gone following the substitution of CAROLYN by DANA MARSHALL (a male!), the music on 1993's 'VELVET HAMMER' (the first album for 'Simple Machines') was as fiercely brooding as any they had recorded to date, reflecting the trials and tribulations of the past few years. SCRAWL's fortunes finally took a turn for the better as they signed to 'Elektra' in the mid-90's, releasing two further albums, 'TRAVEL ON, RIDER' (1996) and 'NATURE FILM' (1998); the latter was a consolidation of their career to date and featured revamped versions of a few old faves alongside a handful of fresh material and a cover of PiL's 'PUBLIC IMAGE'. • **Also covered:** HIGH ROLLER (Cheap Trick) / REUTERS (Wire) / BAD SEEDS (Beat Happening).

Album rating: PLUS, ALSO, TOO mini (*6) / HE'S DRUNK (*7) / SMALLMOUTH (*6) / BLOODSUCKER (*5) / VELVET HAMMER (*5) / TRAVEL ON, RIDER (*5) / NATURE FILM (*6)

MARCH MAYS – vocals, guitar / **SUE HARSHE** – bass / **CAROLYN O'LEARY** – drums

		not iss.	No Other
May 87.	(lp) **PLUS, ALSO, TOO**	–	

– Gutterball / One word / I can't relax / Standing around / Loser / Sad / Slut / He's walkin' / Great American pastime / Afterthought. <re-iss. Nov89 on 'Rough Trade'; ROUGHUS 64>

		Rough Trade	Rough Trade
Aug 89.	(lp/c/cd) (ROUGH/+C/CD 138) <ROUGHUS 51> **HE'S DRUNK**		Mar89

– 11 / Green beer / Ready / Breaker, breaker / For your sister / Believe / I feel your pain / Let it all hang out / Small day / Rocky top / Which one are you / Major, minor. (cd+=) – PLUS, ALSO, TOO

| Apr 90. | (lp/c/cd) (ROUGH/+C/CD 150) <ROUGHUS 76> **SMALLMOUTH** | | |

– Begin / Charles / Enough / Rot / Out of mind / Absolute torture / Hymn / Tell you what / Time to come clean / I need you.

		not iss.	Feel Good All Over
1991.	(m-cd) **BLOODSUCKER**	–	

– VI plorionotos / Love's insecticide / Please have everything / Clock song / C.O.W. / High roller / Cold hearted snake. (UK-iss.May93 on 'Simple Machines' cd/c/lp; smr 17)

		Singles Only	not iss.
Jun 92.	(7") (SOL) **MISERY. / JUST PLAIN BAD**		–

— (May'92-1993) **DANA MARSHALL** (male) – drums; repl. CAROLYN

		Simple Machines	Simple Machines
Mar 93.	(7") (WHJAN) **11.59 IT'S JANUARY. / Versus: TIN FOIL STAR**		
Sep 93.	(7") <smr 21> **TELL HER EVERYTHING. / YOUR MOTHER WANTS TO KNOW**	–	
Nov 93.	(cd,c,lp) <smr 20> **VELVET HAMMER**	–	

– Your mother wants to know / Take a swing / Disappear without a trace / See / Face down / Tell me now, boy / Drunken fool / Prize / Blue green sea / Remember that day.

		not iss.	Elektra
May 95.	(7") <smr 45> **GOOD UNDER PRESSURE. / CHAOS**	–	
Aug 96.	(cd,c) <61934> **TRAVEL ON, RIDER**	–	

– Good under pressure / Garden path / I'm not stuck / From deep inside her / Story Musgrave / Easy on her mind / Hunting me down / Come back then / Louis l'amour / He cleaned up / Story Musgrave / What did he give away?

| May 98. | (cd,c) <62186> **NATURE FILM** | – | |

– Rot / You make it a crime / Charles / Don't we always get there? / Standing around / Public image / 11:59 it's January / Clock song / Everyone I saw tonight / Nature film / For your sister / 100 car pile-up / Guess I'll wait.

SCREAMING BLUE MESSIAHS

Formed: London, England . . . 1983 from the remnants of MOTOR BOYS MOTOR (who released one single and self-titled album in '82) by American singer/songwriter BILL CARTER along with CHRIS THOMPSON and KENNY HARRIS. Picked up by indie label, 'Big Beat' (subsequently home to the CRAMPS), The SCREAMING BLUE MESSIAHS made their vinyl debut in 1984 with mini-set, 'GOOD AND GONE'. The attendant interest led to a major label deal with 'WEA' the following year, the company re-issuing the debut, releasing the acclaimed 'TWIN CADILLAC VALENTINE' 12" and promoting the band via a series of hard hitting TV performances. With both media and public expectation running high, 'GUNSHY' arrived fully formed in 1986 as one of the finest debut albums of that year. Fuelled by a turbo charged rhythm section (reminiscent of DR. FEELGOOD or The WHO), itchy/scratchy guitars and CARTER's hectoring vocals, highlights included the SMITHS-go-hillbilly stomp of 'PRESIDENT KENNEDY'S MILE' alongside the discordant shuffle of preceding single, 'TWIN CADILLAC..'. A previously recorded John Peel session served as a stop-gap prior to the unveiling of a follow-up album, 'BIKINI RED' (1987). Regarded by many as a let down, the record nevertheless blessed the 'MESSIAHS with their only sniff of chart action, the demented 'I WANNA BE A FLINTSTONE' scraping into the Top 30. Yet it would be another two years – during which time the band had moved to 'Atlantic' – before any further material surfaced, 'TOTALLY RELIGIOUS' (1989) falling flat commercially and generating interest only among the most faithful of 'MESSIAHS disciples. Finally giving up on making any new converts, the group split soon after the album's release, HARRIS and THOMAS going on to form LERUE.

Album rating: GOOD & GONE (*7) / GUNSHY (*6) / Motor Boys Motor: MOTOR BOYS MOTOR (*5)

MOTOR BOYS MOTOR

BILL CARTER (b.Redcar, Teeside, England) – guitar / **CHRIS THOMPSON** – bass, guitar / **TONY MOON** – vocals, harmonica / **JOHN KINGHAM** – drums, percussion

		Silent	not iss.
1981.	(7") (SSH 4) **DRIVE FRIENDLY. / FAST 'N' BULBOUS / GROW FINS**		–
		Albion	not iss.
Mar 82.	(lp) (ALB 111) **MOTOR BOYS MOTOR**		–

– Drive friendly / Hooves / Here come the Flintstones / Yes indeedy / Clean shirt and a shave / Sacred pie / Little boy and a fat man / One down, one down / Claw boy's claw / Freeze up the truth.

SCREAMING BLUE MESSIAHS

CARTER (now) vocals, guitar / **TONY** (now) bass / **CHRIS THOMPSON** – guitar (then bass) / **KENNY HARRIS** – drums; repl. JOHN

		Big Beat	not iss.
Jul 84.	(m-lp) (NED 7) **GOOD & GONE**		–

– Someone to talk to / I want up / You're gonna change / Tracking the dog / Good and gone / Happy home. (re-iss. Apr85 on 'WEA' lp/c; WX 16/+C)

— now without TONY

		W.E.A.	Elektra
Oct 85.	(7"m) (YZ 73) **TWIN CADILLAC VALENTINE. / GOOD AND GONE / GROWING FOR GOLD**		–

(12"+=) (YZ 50T) – Happy home (live) / You're gonna change (live) / Someone to talk to (live).

| Apr 86. | (7") (YZ 69) **SMASH THE MARKET PLACE. / JUST FOR FUN** | | – |

(12"+=) (YZ 69T) – The power glide.

| May 86. | (lp/c) (WX 41/+C) <60488> **GUNSHY** | 90 | |

– Holiday head / Twin Cadillac valentine / Wild blue yonder / President Kennedy's mile / Let's go down to the woods and pray / Just for fun / Talking doll / Killer born man / Clear view.

| Jun 86. | (7") (YZ 73) **WILD BLUE YONDER. / KILLER BORN MAN** | | – |

(12"+=) (YZ 73T) – I'm mad again.

| Oct 87. | (lp/c)(cd) (WX 117/+C)(242212-2) <60755> **BIKINI RED** | | – |

– Sweet water pools / Bikini red / Lie detector / 55-the law / Jesus Chrysler drives a Dodge / I wanna be a Flintstone / Waltz / Big brother muscle / I can speak American / All shook down.

| Nov 87. | (7") (YZ 158) **BIKINI RED. / ALL SHOOK DOWN** | | – |

(12"+=) (YZ 158T) – 55-the law.

| Jan 88. | (7") (YZ 166) **I WANNA BE A FLINTSTONE. / JERRY'S ELECTRIC CHURCH** | 28 | – |

(12"pic-d+=) (YZ 166T) – ('A'version).

| Apr 88. | (7") (YZ 176) **I CAN SPEAK AMERICAN. / GOOD AND GONE** | | – |

(12"+=) (YZ 176T) – Twin Cadillac valentine.

		Atlantic	Atlantic
Oct 89.	(lp/c/cd) (<K9 60859-1/-4/-2>) **TOTALLY RELIGIOUS**		

– Four engines burning (over the USA) / Mega City one / Wall of shame / Nitro / Big big sky / Watusi's wedding / Here comes Lucky / Gunfight / Martian / All gassed up.

— disbanded soon after above release; HARRIS and THOMAS formed LERUE

– compilations, others, etc. –

| Jun 87. | (12"ep) Strange Fruit; (SFPS 003) / Dutch East India; <8315> **THE PEEL SESSIONS** (2.8.84) | | |

– Tracking the dog / Someone to talk to / Good and gone / Let's go down to the woods and pray.

| Nov 92. | (cd) Windsong; (WINCD 022) **BBC RADIO 1 LIVE IN CONCERT** (live) | | – |

SCREAMING TREES

Formed: Ellensburg, Washington, USA . . . 1985 by girthsome brothers VAN and GARY LEE CONNER along with frontman MARK LANEGAN and drummer MARK PICKEREL. Following early effort, 'CLAIRVOYANCE' (1986) for the tiny 'Velvetone' label, the group signed to respected US indie, 'S.S.T.', making their debut with the convincing 'EVEN IF AND ESPECIALLY WHEN' (1987). Fuelled by raging punk, The SCREAMING TREES were nevertheless characterised by the spectral hue of 60's psychedelia running through much of their music, LANEGAN's exotic, JIM MORRISON-esque vocals adding an air of brooding mystery on the likes of fans' favourite, 'TRANSFIGURATION'. Another couple of stirring sets, 'INVISIBLE LANTERN' (1988) and 'BUZZ FACTORY' (1989), followed before the group released a one-off EP for 'Sub Pop'. With the emerging grunge phenomenon in nearby Seattle on the cusp of world domination, The SCREAMING TREES were obviously a promising prospect for major label A&R and it came as little surprise when they signed for 'Epic'. That same year, prior to their debut for the label, the various 'TREES occupied themselves with solo projects, GARY LEE forming PURPLE OUTSIDE and releasing 'MYSTERY LANE', while brother VAN issued the eponymous 'SOLOMON GRUNDY' set the same year, both appearing on 'New Alliance'. Best of the lot, however, was LANEGAN's windswept 'WINDING SHEET', an intense, largely acoustic collection featuring a cover of Leadbelly's 'WHERE DID YOU SLEEP LAST NIGHT' (as later covered in frightening style by KURT COBAIN). Co-produced by CHRIS CORNELL, the subsequent SCREAMING TREES effort, 'UNCLE ANAESTHESIA' (1991), saw the group moving towards a more overt 70's rock sound, while 'SWEET OBLIVION' (1992) saw PICKEREL replaced with BARRETT MARTIN on a more low-key set which stood at odds with the grunge tag unwillingly forced on the band. Augmented by such Seattle "luminaries" as TAD and DAN PETERS (MUDHONEY) along with

SCREAMING TREES (cont)

DINOSAUR JR.'s J. MASCIS, LANEGAN cut an acclaimed solo follow-up, 'WHISKEY FOR THE HOLY GHOST' (1993), before beginning the long and arduous work on the material which would eventually come to make up 'DUST' (1996). Widely held up as the group's most affecting work to date, the George Drakoulias-produced album perfectly captured their threadbare grit and world-weary mysticism, the disparate elements of their sound finally fusing in harmony and exorcising the lingering spirit of grunge. During the latter part of the 90's, LANEGAN was again a solo artist, two albums for 'Sub Pop' ('Beggars Banquet' in Britain), 'SCRAPS AT MIDNIGHT' (1998) and 'I'LL TAKE CARE OF YOU' (1999), being released to mixed response and sliding out of the hard/grunge-rock circle. Meanwhile, VAN CONNOR was back in action via GARDENER, a collaborative duo that also featured Seaweed's AARON STAUFFER. In mid '99, this supergroup of sorts delivered their Lo-Fi psychedelic album for 'Sub Pop', 'NEW DAWNING TIME'. LANEGAN continued to nurse his alt-country blues on his fifth solo effort, 'FIELD SONGS' (2001), his grainy narratives given added muscle by such alt-rock notables as BEN SHEPHERD, BILL RIEFLIN, DUFF McKAGEN and MIKE JOHNSON. • Covered: SLIDE MACHINE (13th Floor Elevators). • Note: Not to be confused with the English band on 'Native' records.

Album rating: OTHER WORLDS mini (*4) / EVEN IF AND ESPECIALLY WHEN (*7) / INVISIBLE LANTERN (*5) / BUZZ FACTORY mini (*5) / UNCLE ANAESTHESIA (*6) / ANTHOLOGY – THE S.S.T. YEARS 1985-1989 compilation (*7) / SWEET OBLIVION (*7) / DUST (*9) / Mark Lanegan: THE WINDING SHEET (*6) / WHISKEY FOR THE HOLY GHOST (*7) / SCRAPS AT MIDNIGHT (*6) / I'LL TAKE CARE OF YOU (*8) / FIELD SONGS (*6)

MARK LANEGAN (b.25 Nov'64) – vocals / **GARY LEE CONNER** (b.22 Aug'62, Fort Irwin, Calif.) – guitar, vocals / **VAN CONNER** (b.17 Mar'67, Apple Valley, Calif.) – bass, vocals / **MARK PICKEREL** – drums, percussion

not iss.   Velvetone

1986. (m-lp) *<none>* **CLAIRVOYANCE**
– Orange airplane / You tell me all these things / Standing on the edge / Forever / Seeing and believing / I see stars / Lonely girl / Strange out here / The turning / Clairvoyance.

S.S.T.   S.S.T.

Feb 87. (m-lp/m-cd) *<SST/+C/CD 105>* **OTHER WORLDS**
– Like I said / Pictures in my mind / Turning / Other worlds / Barriers / Now your mind is next to mine. *(UK-iss.May93; same as US)*

Sep 87. (lp/cd) *<SST 132/+CD>* **EVEN IF AND ESPECIALLY WHEN**
– Transfiguration / Straight out to any place / World painted / Don't look down / Girl behind the mask / Flying / Cold rain / Other days and different planets / The pathway / You know where it's at / Back together / In the forest. *(cd re-iss. May93; same)*

Jul 88. (12"ep; shared w/ BEAT HAPPENING) *(AGARR 020) <110>* **POLLY PEREGUIN E.P.**
(above issued on UK '53rd & 3rd') *<US-iss.on 'Positive'>*

Sep 88. (lp/c/cd) *<(SST 188/+C/CD)>* **INVISIBLE LANTERN**
– Ivy / Walk through to the other side / Line & circles / Shadow song / Grey diamond desert / Smokerings / The second awake / Invisible lantern / Even if / Direction of the sun / Night comes creeping / She knows.

Mar 89. (m-lp/cd) *<(SST 248/+CD)>* **BUZZ FACTORY**
– Where the twain shall meet / Windows / Black sun morning / Too far away / Subtle poison / Yard trip / Flower web / Wish bringer / Revelation revolution / The looking glass cracked / End of the universe.

Glitterhouse Sub Pop

Dec 89. (d7"w /1-white) *(GR 80) <SP 48B>* **CHANGE HAS COME. / DAYS / / FLASHES. / TIME SPEAKS HER GOLDEN TONGUE**
(re-iss. Dec90 cd-ep+=; GRCD 80) – I've seen you before. *(re-iss. May93; same)*

— LEE CONNER also formed PURPLE OUTSIDE in 1990, releasing 'MYSTERY LANE'. Brother VAN with SOLOMON GRUNDY issued eponymous same year also for 'New Alliance'.

Epic   Epic

Oct 90. (12"ep) *<73539>* **UNCLE ANAESTHESIA / WHO LIES IN DARKNESS. / OCEAN OF CONFUSION / SOMETHING ABOUT TODAY (numb inversion version)**

Jun 91. (cd/c/lp) *(467 307-2/-4/-1) <EK 46800>* **UNCLE ANAESTHESIA**   Mar91
– Beyond this horizon / Bed of roses / Uncle anaesthesia / Story of her fate / Caught between / Lay your head down / Before we arise / Something about today / Alice said / Time for light / Disappearing / Ocean of confusion / Closer.

— **BARRETT MARTIN** (b.14 Apr'67, Olympia, Washington) – drums repl. PICKEREL who later joined TRULY

Oct 92. (cd/c/lp) *(471 724-2/-4/-1) <48996>* **SWEET OBLIVION**
– Shadow of the season / Nearly lost you / Dollar bill / More or less / Butterfly / For celebrations past / The secret kind / Winter song / Troubled times / No one knows / Julie Paradise.

Feb 93. (12"ep/pic-cd-ep) *(658 237-6/-2)* **NEARLY LOST YOU. / E.S.K. / SONG OF A BAKER / WINTER SONG (acoustic)**   50

Apr 93. (7"pic-d) *(659 179-7)* **DOLLAR BILL. / (THERE'LL BE) PEACE IN THE VALLEY FOR ME (acoustic)**   52
(12"colrd+=/cd-s+=) *(659 179-6/-2)* – Tomorrow's dream.

Jul 96. (cd/c/lp) *(483 980-2/-4/-1) <64178>* **DUST**   32
– Halo of ashes / All I know / Look at you / Dying days / Make my mind / Sworn and broken / Witness / Traveler / Dime western / Gospel plow.

Sep 96. (7") *(663 351-7)* **ALL I KNOW. / WASTED TIME**
(cd-s+=) *(663 351-2)* – Silver tongue.
(cd-s) *(663 351-5)* – ('A'side) / Dollar bill / Nearly lost you / Winter song (acoustic).

Nov 96. (7"white) *(663 870-7)* **SWORN AND BROKEN. / BUTTERFLY**
(cd-s+=) *(663 870-2)* – Dollar bill (U.S. radio session) / Caught between – The secret kind (U.S. radio session).

— on a long holiday from each other, maybe for ever, VAN CONNOR now moonlighting in VALIS with DAN PETERS of MUDHONEY, while BARRETT plays on tour with R.E.M., while joining PETER BUCK's supergroup, TUATARA. LANEGAN continued solo (see below)

– compilations, others, etc. –

Nov 91. (d-lp/d-cd) *<(SST 260/+CD)>* **ANTHOLOGY . . . THE S.S.T. YEARS 1985-1989**

MARK LANEGAN

— with on first **MIKE JOHNSON** – guitar / **JACK ENDINO** – bass, guitar / **KURT COBAIN** – guitar, vocals / **CHRIS NOVOSELIC** – bass / **MARK PICKEREL** – drums / **STEVE FISK** – keyboards

Glitterhouse Sub Pop

May 90. (red-lp/cd) *(GR 085/+CD) <SP 61>* **THE WINDING SHEET**
– Mockingbirds / Museum / Undertow / Ugly Sunday / Down in the dark / Wild flowers / Eyes of a child / The winding sheet / Woe / Ten feet tall / Where did you sleep last night? / Juarez / I love you little girl. *(c+cd+=)* – I love you little girl. *(re-iss. Apr94 & Oct99; same) (cd re-iss. Jun01; SP 618)*

Sep 90. (7") *(GR 0101)* **DOWN IN THE DARK. / LOVE YOU LITTLE GIRL**

— next w/ **J.MASCIS + MARK JOHNSON** (Dinosaur Jr.) / **TAD DOYLE** (Tad) / **DAN PETERS** (Mudhoney) / **KURT FEDORA** (Gobbelhoof)

Sub Pop   Sub Pop

Jan 94. (lp/cd) *<(SP/+CD 78249)>* **WHISKEY FOR THE HOLY GHOST**
– The river rise / Borracho / House a home / Kingdoms of rain / Carnival / Riding the nightingale / El Sol / Dead on you / Shooting gallery / Sunrise / Pendulum / Jesus touch / Beggar's blues. *(cd re-iss. Oct99 & Jun01; SPCD 132)*

May 94. (cd-ep) *<(SPCD 131-327)>* **HOUSE A HOME / SHOOTING GALLERY / UGLY SUNDAY / SUNRISE**

Beggars Banquet Sub Pop

Jul 98. (cd) *(BBQCD 204) <SP 419>* **SCRAPS AT MIDNIGHT**
– Hospital roll call / Hotel / Stay / Black bell ocean / Last one in the world / Wheels / Waiting on a train / Day and night / Praying ground / Because of this.

Sep 98. (7"colrd) *(BBQ 328)* **STAY. / SLIDE MACHINE**
(cd-s+=) *(BBQ 328CD)* – Death don't have no mercy.

Sep 99. (cd/lp) *(BBQ CD/LP 215) <SP 445>* **I'LL TAKE CARE OF YOU**
– Carry home / I'll take care of you / Shiloh town / Creeping coastline of lights / Ba dee da / Consider me / On Jesus program / Little Sadie / Together again / Shanty man's life / Boogie boogie.

Jun 01. (cd) *(BBQCD 224) <SP 502>* **FIELD SONGS**   May01
– One way street / No easy action / Miracle / Pill hill serenade / Don't forget me / Kimiko's dream house / Resurrection song / Field song / Love / Blues for D / She done too much / Fix.

SEA URCHINS

Formed: West Bromwich, nr.Birmingham, England . . . 1986 by JAMES ROBERTS, SIMON WOODCOCK, MARK BEVIN, ROBERT COOKSEY, PATRICK ROBERTS and BRIDGET DUFFY. Another mid-80's indie band to kickstart their career via 7" flexi fanzine freebies (namely 'CLINGFILM' and 'SUMMERSHINE'), these jingle-jangle fops were a natural first signing for soon-to-be pastoral bastion 'Sarah'. The summer of '87 also saw the release of debut single proper, 'PRISTINE CHRISTINE', by which time BEVIN had been superseded by DARREN MARTIN. Releases proved sporadic with follow-up, 'SOLACE', taking around nine months to hit the shops, the subsequent departure of DUFFY and MARTIN resulting in an even longer lay-off before a third 45, 'A MORNING ODYSSEY', eventually surfaced in 1990. Musical differences led to a final split with 'Sarah', after which the SEA URCHINS signed to 'Cheree' for a one-off 7", 'PLEASE DON'T CRY'. JAMES, PATRICK and ROBERT would go on to perform as The LOW SCENE (an old SEA URCHINS track) while a posthumous concert album (their debut!), 'LIVE IN LONDON' (1994), featured a cover of Donovan's 'SEASON OF THE WITCH'.

Album rating: LIVE IN LONDON posthumous (*5) / STARDUST compilation (*6)

JAMES ROBERTS (b. 4 Mar'70) – vocals / **SIMON WOODCOCK** (b. 2 Dec'69) – guitar / **ROBERT COOKSEY** (b.14 Nov'69) – guitar / **MARK BEVIN** (b.21 Jan'70) – bass / **BRIDGET DUFFY** (b.28 Jun'70) – tambourine, vox organ (ex-VELVET UNDERWEAR drummer) / **PATRICK ROBERTS** – drums

Kvatch   not iss.

May 87. (7"flexi) *(KVATCH 001)* **CLING FILM. / GROOVE FARM:- Baby Blue Marine**

Sha La La   not iss.

Jun 87. (7"flexi) *(Sha La La Ba Ba Ba 5)* **SUMMERSHINE. / ORCHIDS:- From This Day**

— **DARREN MARTIN** (b.25 Mar'67) – bass; repl. BEVIN

Sarah   not iss.

Aug 87. (7") *(SARAH 001)* **PRISTINE CHRISTINE. / SULLEN EYES / EVERGLADES**

Jun 88. (7") *(SARAH 006)* **SOLACE. / PLEASE RAIN FALL**

Nov 88. (7") *(FRIGHT 032)* **30.10.88 (live)**
(above issued on 'Fierce')

— now without DUFFY + MARTIN (WOODCOCK now bass + ROBERTS on guitar)

Jul 90. (7") *(SARAH 033)* **A MORNING ODYSSEY. / WILD GRASS PICTURES**

Cheree   not iss.

May 91. (7") *(CHEREE 15)* **PLEASE DON'T CRY. / TIME IS ALL I'VE SEEN**

— split + JAMES, PATRICK + ROBERT formed The LOW SCENE

– compilations, etc. –

Mar 94. (cd) *Fierce; (FRIGHT 061)* **LIVE IN LONDON** (live)
– Low scene / My ship is going down / A morning odyssey / Sullen eyes / I don't belong / Please don't cry / Season of the witch / Summershine / Open out / Rock and roll star / Slow scene / Solace / Jam / Hendrix / Pristine Christine. *(re-iss. Jun97; same)*

Mar 95. (lp/cd) *Sarah; (SARAH 609/+CD)* **STARDUST**
– Cling film / Summershine / You're so much / Pristine Christine / Sullen eyes / Everglades / Solace / Please rain fall / A morning odyssey / Wild grass pictures / Day into day.

SECOND LAYER (see under ⇒ SOUND)

SECTION 25

Formed: Blackpool, England . . . late '79 by songwriting brothers VINCENT and LARRY CASSIDY. Initially using a drum machine, the siblings soon bolstered the rhythm section with a real drummer and added guitarist PAUL WIGGIN. Signed to Manchester's 'Factory', the group made their debut in summer 1980 with the 'GIRLS DON'T COUNT' single, following it with a debut album, 'ALWAYS NOW', just over a year later. More successful in Europe than Britain, SECTION 25's minimalist sound was drawn from a similar grey area to fellow 'Factory' acts, JOY DIVISION, NEW ORDER, ACR etc, as well as the likes of KRAFTWERK and their ilk. Vocals, if there were any, echoed sinisterly as in 'ALWAYS NOW', from follow-up album, 'THE KEY OF DREAMS' (1982). Mid '83 saw a turning point, however, as the CASSIDY brothers recruited two female vocalists, ANGELA FLOWERS and JENNY ROSS (LARRY's wife), presenting a more accessible sound with the 'BACK TO THE WONDER' single and the subsequent album, 'FROM THE HIP' (1984). Yet the band seemed forever in the shadow of their more popular labelmates and after a further much delayed album, 'LOVE & HATE' (1988), they were no more having given the publishing rights to a certain JONATHAN KING. However, due to a resurgence in interest via Belgian imprint 'Les Tempes Modernes' re-issuing their backlog in the late 90's, the brothers teamed up again (with JENNY ROSS and IAN BUTTERWORTH) to release comeback set, 'ILLUMINUS ILLUMINA' (2001).

Album rating: ALWAYS NOW (*6) / THE KEY OF DREAMS (*5) / FROM THE HIP (*4) / LOVE & HATE (*4) / LIVE IN AMERICA AND EUROPE 1982 (*5) / DEUS EX MACHINA (*5) / ILLUMINUS ILLUMINA (*5) / FROM THE HIP IN THE FLESH – LIVE IN AMERICA 1985 (*5)

VINCENT CASSIDY – electronics, drum machine / **LARRY CASSIDY** – vocals, guitar / **PHIL WIGGIN** – guitar / **JOHN BRIERLEY** – drums / **JOHN HURST** – sound engineer

	Factory	not iss.
Jul 80. (12") *(fac 18t)* **GIRLS DON'T COUNT. / KNEW NOISE / UP TO YOU**		–
Jan 81. (7") *(fbn 3.006)* **CHARNEL GROUND. / HAUNTED**		–
Jun 81. (7") *(fbn 5)* **JE VEUX TON AMOUR. / OYO ACHEL ADA**		–

(above two were released on 'Factory Benelux')

Sep 81. (lp) *(fact 45)* **ALWAYS NOW**
– Friendly fires / Dirty disco / C.P. / Loose talk (costs lives) / Inside out / Melt close / Hit / Babies in the Bardo / Be brave / New horizons. *(re-iss. Jan87; same) (cd-iss. Feb92 on 'Les Tempes Modernes'+= ; LTMCD 2308)* – Girls don't count / After image / Red voice.

LEE SHALLCROSS – drums; repl. PAUL who had repl. PHIL

Jul 82. (12") *(fac 66-12)* **THE BEAST / SAKURA. / SAKURA (matrix mix) / TRIDENT**

Nov 82. (lp) *(fbn 14)* **THE KEY OF DREAMS**
– Always now / Visitation / Regions / The wheel / No abiding place / Once before / There was a time / Wretch / Sutra. *(cd-iss. Feb92 on 'Les Tempes Modernes'+= ; LTMCD 2310)* – The beast / Sakura / Je veux ton amour / Sakura (matrix mix) / Hold me.

Jun 83. (7") *(fac 68)* **BACK TO WONDER. / BEATING HEART**

added **JENNY ROSS** – vocals, keyboards / **ANGELA FLOWERS** – vocals, keyboards

May 84. (lp) *(fact 90)* **FROM THE HIP**
– The process / Looking from a hilltop / Reflection / Prepare to live / Program for light / Desert / Beneath the blade / Inspiration. *(cd-iss. Feb92 on 'Les Tempes Modernes'+= ; LTMCD 2314)* – Beating heart / Back to wonder / Crazy wisdom / Dirty disco II / Guitar waltz / Looking from a hilltop (megamix). *(cd re-iss. Oct98 ++=; same)* – Looking from a hilltop (restructure) / Dirty disco II (premix) / Beating heart (12" version).

Jun 84. (7"/12") *(fac 108/+t)* **LOOKING FROM A HILLTOP (restructure). / LOOKING FROM A HILLTOP (megamix)**

Sep 85. (12"m) *(fbn 45)* **CRAZY WISDOM. / GUITAR WALTZ / DIRTY DISCO II**

DAVID CRABTREE – guitar + **STEWART HILTON** – drums; repl. ANGELA + LEE

Dec 86. (12") *(fac 157t)* **BAD NEWS WEEK. / BAD NEWS WEEK 2 (cough mix)**

Mar 88. (lp/c) *(fact 160/+c)* **LOVE & HATE**
– Sweet forgiveness / Conquer me / Sprinkling petals into Hell / The last man in Europe / Bad news week / Tim lick my knees / Shit creek no paddle / Warhead / Cracrash.

had already disbanded in 1987; **LARRY, VIN + JENNY** recruited **IAN BUTTERWORTH** – guitar (ex-TUNNELVISION)

	Les Tempes Modernes	not iss.
May 01. (cd) *(LTMCD 2322)* **ILLUMINUS ILLUMINA**	–	– Belgian

– New horizons intro / Are you there? / Floating / There was a time / Rigi rigi / Mirror / You're on your own / Friendlt fires / One step / Opening / Virtually every / Fallen / Tape loop / Cry / Subferior / In the garden of Eden / Never mind the Sex Pistols here's the bollocks / Just to see your face.

– compilations, etc. –

on 'Les Tempes Modernes' unless stated

Sep 97. (cd) *(LTMCD 2312)* **LIVE IN AMERICA AND EUROPE 1982** (live) – Belgian
– God's playground (part 1) / Babes in the Bardo / Trident / Dirty disco / Sakura / Inside out / One true path / Floating / The beast / You leave me no choice / God's playground (part 2) / Warhead / Haunted.

Aug 99. (cd) *(LTMCD 2316)* **DEUS EX MACHINA (live and studio 1983-1985)** – Belgian
– Tchaiko (edit) / Loving no-one / Days pass by / Firefly / 4tmi / The process / Looking from a hilltop / Beneath the blade / Inspiration / Program for light / Slinky / Sweet forgiveness / Deus ex machina.

Apr 99. (cd) *(LTMCD 2318)* **LOVE & HATE (IN THE ENGLISH COUNTRYSIDE)** – Belgian
– Sweet forgiveness / Bad news week / Crazy wisdom / The guitar waltz / Sprinkling petals into Hell / Warhead / Gymnopedies / Shit creek no paddle / Conquer me / The last man in Europe / Cracrash / Bad news week (12" mix) / Crazy wisdom (demo) / The guitar waltz (demo) / The last man in Europe (demo) / Cracrash (demo) / Just to be with you.

Oct 01. (cd) *(LTMCD 2325)* **FROM THE HIP IN THE FLESH – LIVE IN AMERICA 1985** (live) – Belgian
– The process / Looking from a hilltop / Prepare to live / Program for light / Beneath the blade / Reflection / Desert / Inspiration / Dirty disco II / Inspiration / Boogie beat.

SEEDS

Formed: Los Angeles, California, USA . . . 1965 by obscure solo artist, SKY SAXON, who had released a number of low-key singles. The SEEDS signed to 'GNP Crescendo' in 1965, cracking the charts early in 1967, when a re-issue of their second 45, '(YOU'RE) PUSHIN' TOO HARD', hit the US Top 40. A wired, deceptively simple slice of garage-psych, the single remains the definitive SEEDS track and a blueprint for the punk movement of the following decade. Their next 45, 'CAN'T SEEM TO MAKE YOU MINE' (their original debut), also gave them a Top 50 hit, although they found it hard to maintain this short run of success. Previously, they had released two seminal albums (both in '66), 'THE SEEDS' and 'A WEB OF SOUND', full of weird, psychotic blues highlighting SKY's demented vocal sermonising on such reliable topics as sex, drugs and of course, rock'n'roll. Their third album, 'FUTURE', was a more exotic trip into flower-power, two tracks, 'MARCH OF THE FLOWER CHILDREN' and 'A THOUSAND SHADOWS' (their last hit) glaringly overblown on the production front. SKY subsequently sacked the rest of the band, his new formation, SKY SAXON BLUES BAND, making another album, 'A FULL SPOON OF SEEDY BLUES' in 1967. A revamped SEEDS with SKY at the helm once again, subsequently fell back into the underground scene, only managing to release a handful of 45's and a live album. In the 80's, SKY issued a number of solo albums under many guises, i.e. SKY SUNLIGHT SAXON & THE STARRY SEEDS BAND.

Album rating: THE SEEDS (*6) / A WEB OF SOUND (*6) / FUTURE (*4) / A FULL SPOON OF SEEDY BLUES (*4; by Sky Saxon Blues Band) / RAW AND ALIVE (MERLIN'S MUSIC BOX) (*5) / FALLING OFF THE EDGE collection (*6) / EVIL HOODOO collection (*7) / A FADED PICTURE collection (*6) / Sky Sunlight Saxon: IN SEARCH OF BRIGHTER COLOURS (*5) / TAKES ON GLORY (*4)

SKY SAXON

	not iss.	Ava
1961. (7"; as LITTLE RICHIE MARSH) **GOODBYE. / CRYING INSIDE MY HEART**	–	–

	not iss.	Shepherd
1962. (7"; as LITTLE RICHIE MARSH) **THEY SAY. / DARLING I SWEAR IT'S TRUE**	–	–

	not iss.	Conquest
1962. (7") **THEY SAY. / GO AHEAD AND CRY**	–	–

For the rest of 1962, SKY SAXON formed his ELECTRA FIRES. The following 2 years he founded SKY SAXON & The SOUL ROCKERS.

The SEEDS

were formed at the beginning of '65 by **SKY SAXON** – vocals, bass, saxophone / plus **JAN SAVAGE** – guitar / **DARYL HOOPER** – keyboards / **RICK ANDRIDGE** – drums

	Vocalion	GNP Crescendo
Jun 65. (7") <354> **CAN'T SEEM TO MAKE YOU MINE. / I'LL TELL MYSELF (or) DAISY MAE** *(re-iss. Apr67; same; hit No.41)*	–	
Nov 65. (7") <364> **(YOU'RE) PUSHIN' TOO HARD. / OUT OF THE QUESTION**	–	
Apr 66. (lp) <GNP 2023> **THE SEEDS**	–	

– Can't seem to make you mine / No escape / Lose your mind / Evil hoodoo / Girl I want you / Pushin' too hard / Try to understand / Nobody spoil my fun / It''s a hard life / You can't be trusted / Excuse excuse / Fallin' in love. *<US re-iss. 1988 lp/cd; GNP S/D 2023> (UK-iss.Feb84 on 'Line'; LLP 5021) (cd-iss. Sep89 on 'Line'; IMCD 900167)*

| Aug 66. (7") <370> **TRY TO UNDERSTAND. / THE OTHER PLACE** | – | |
| Oct 66. (7") (VN 9277) <372> **PUSHIN' TOO HARD. / TRY TO UNDERSTAND** | | 36 |

added **HARVEY SHARPE** – bass

| Oct 66. (lp) (VAN 8062) <GNP 2033> **A WEB OF SOUND** | | |

– Mr. Farmer / Pictures and designs / Tripmaker / I tell myself / A faded picture / Rollin' machine / Just let go / Up in her room. *<US re-iss. Oct75; same> (re-iss. Feb84 on 'Line'; OLLP 5024) <US re-iss. 1988 lp/cd; GNP S/D 2033>*

495

SEEDS (cont)

Feb 67. (7") <383> **MR. FARMER. / UP IN HER ROOM (or) NO ESCAPE**
May 67. (7") (VN 9287) **CAN'T SEEM TO MAKE YOU MINE. / DAISY MAE** — 86
Jun 67. (7") <394> **A THOUSAND SHADOWS. / MARCH OF THE FLOWER CHILDREN** — —
Aug 67. (lp; mono/stereo) (VAN/SAVN 8070) <GNP 2038> **FUTURE** — 72 / — 87
 – Introduction / March of the flower children / Travel with your mind / Out of the question / Painted doll / Flower lady & her assistant / Now a man / A thousand shadows / Two fingers pointing at you / Where is the entrance way to play / Six dreams / Fallin'. <US re-iss. 1988 lp/cd; GNP S/D 2038> (cd re-iss. Sep91 on 'Line'; IMCD 900173)
Nov 67. (7") <398> **THE WIND BLOWS YOUR HAIR. / SIX DREAMS** — —
— now without departing HARVEY
1967. (lp; as SKY SAXON BLUES BAND) <GNP 2040> **A FULL SPOON OF SEEDY BLUES** — —
 – Pretty girl / Moth and the flame / I'll help you / Cry wolf / Plain spoken / The gardener / One more time blues / Creepin' about / Buzzin' around. <re-iss. Sep76; same> <US re-iss. 1988 lp/cd; GNP S/D 2040>
— basically SKY SAXON + session people
1968. (lp) <GNP 2043> **RAW AND ALIVE (MERLIN'S MUSIC BOX)** (live) — —
 – Introduction by Humble Harv / Mr. Farmer / No escape / Satisfy you / Night time girl / Up in her room / Gypsy plays his drums / Can't seem to make you mine / Mumble and bumble / Forest outside your door / 900 million people daily all making love / Pushin' too hard. <US re-iss. 1988 lp/cd; GNP S/D 2043>
1968. (7") <408> **SATISFY YOU (live). / 900 MILLION PEOPLE DAILY MAKING LOVE** (live) — —
1969. (7") <422> **FALLIN' OFF THE EDGE OF THE WORLD. / WILD BLOOD** — —
  not iss. M.G.M.
1971. (7") <14163> **BAD PART OF TOWN. / WISH ME UP** — —
1971. (7") <14190> **LOVE IN A SUMMER BASKET. / DID HE DIE** — —
  not iss. Productions Unlimited
1972. (7") <22> **SHUCKIN' AND JIVIN'. / YOU TOOK ME BY SURPRISE** — —
— SKY SAXON folded SEEDS and formed various bands SKY SUNLIGHT / SUNLIGHT / SKY SUNLIGHT SAXON.

SKY SAXON

 New Rose not iss.
Nov 84. (lp) (ROSE 36) **MASTERS OF PSYCHEDELIA** — —
Aug 86. (lp) **A GROOVY THING** — —
Dec 88. (lp/cd; as SKY SUNLIGHT SAXON & FIRE WALL) (ROSE 155/+CD) **IN SEARCH OF BRIGHTER COLOURS** — —
 – I hear the mountains crash / Lightning lightning / Put something sweet between your lips / Barbie doll look / The big screen / Baby baby / Come on pretty girl / Kick kick / Paisley rocker / Come a here right now.

SKY SUNLIGHT SAXON

— & THE STARRY SEEDS BAND:- ELLIOTT INGBAR / MARS BONFIRE / RON BUSHY / RAINBOW STARDUST
 Psycho not iss.
Feb 85. (m-lp) (PSYCHO 29) **STARRY RIDE** (various aggregations) — —
 – Starry ride / I'm in love with life / Drums, stars & guitars / 24 hour rocker.
 Fierce not iss.
1987. (7") (FRIGHT 009) **DOG = GOD** — —
 Line not iss.
Jun 87. (lp; as SKYLIGHT SKY SAXON) (40029-1) **TAKES ON GLORY** — —
 – As much as I love you / Born to be wild / In Paradise / Swim / Aphrodite / Sodom & Gomorrah / 30 seconds over Hollywood / Love dog / Wish me up / Statue of stone / Picnic in the grass / Pushin' too far too hard / Skid row children.
— SKY + MARS now with TOM AZEVEDO – guitar / GARY STERN – bass, guitar / PAUL SCHOFIELD – drums
 not iss. Pinpoint
1989. (lp) **JUST IMAGINE** — —
 – Black & red / Focus point / Wild roses / Just imagine / Black beans / Some people / Million miles / World tribute / Thriller riff / Mr.Farmer.

– (SEEDS) compilations, etc. –

Sep 76. (lp) GNP Crescendo; (lp) **THE SEEDS IN CONCERT** (live) — —
1977. (lp) GNP Crescendo; (GNP S/S 2107) **FALLIN' OFF THE EDGE** — —
Aug 78. (lp) Sonet; (SNTF 746) **LEGENDARY MASTER RECORDINGS** — —
Apr 88. (lp/cd) Bam Caruso; (KIRI 082/+CD) **EVIL HOODOO** — —
 – March of the flower children / The wind blows your hair / Tripmaker / Try to understand / Evil hoodoo / Chocolate river / Pushing too hard / Falling off the edge / Mr. Farmer / Up in her room / Can't seem to make you mine / Pictures and designs / Flower lady and her assistant / Rollin' machine / Out of the question / Satisfy you. (pic-lp Jan89 on 'Strange Things'; STRANGEP 1) (cd re-iss. Jul91 on 'Drop Out'; DOCD 1998)
Apr 88. (7") Bam Caruso; (OPRA 091) **PUSHIN' TOO HARD. / GREENER DAY** — —
Nov 91. (cd) Drop Out; (DOCD 1992) **A FADED PICTURE** — —
 – (FIRE ESCAPE – Psychotic Reaction / SEEDS – RAW AND ALIVE – LIVE AT MERLIN'S MUSIC BOX)
Mar 94. (lp) Drop Out; (DOCD 1984) **TRAVEL WITH YOUR MIND** — —
 (re-iss. Jul95 on 'GNP Crescendo'; GNPD 2218)
May 94. (cd; SEEDS / SKY SAXON) Eva; (84210) **BAD PART OF TOWN / LIVE ALBUM BEDTIME** — —
 (re-iss. Jul00; EVAB 18)

SENATE (see under ⇒ SPEAR OF DESTINY)

SENSELESS THINGS

Formed: Twickenham, London, England ... late '86 by MARK KEDS and MORGAN NICHOLLS, who had played in a band together since their schooldays. By the release of their debut single (a 7" flexi given away free in early '88 with the fanzine, 'Shy Like You'), the line-up had solidified around BEN HARDING and CASS BROWNE, the fledgling pop punksters subsequently receiving the honour of a John Peel session. Their first release proper was the 'UP AND COMING' EP later that year, released on the self-financed 'Red' imprint. A debut mini-set, 'POSTCARD C.V.' (1989) followed on indie label, 'Way Cool', highlighting the band's continuing musical evolution. With the success of such crusty-esque fare as NED'S ATOMIC DUSTBIN and CARTER USM, along with the imminent explosion of grunge, 'Epic' deemed the SENSELESS THINGS a promising commercial possibility and, following a further couple of indie releases, the band made their major label debut in summer '91 with the 'EVERYBODY'S GONE' single. A minor Top 75 success, it was followed by the Top 50 mini-classic, 'GOT IT AT THE DELMAR', both singles featured on the album, 'THE FIRST OF TOO MANY' (1991). Displaying a quantum leap in songwriting and a newfound melodic verve, the record's promise was confirmed when the effervescent 'EASY TO SMILE' single finally took the SENSELESS THINGS into the UK Top 20 later that year. The following year's 'HOLD IT DOWN' repeated the success, although despite its admirable sentiments, the contentious 'HOMOPHOBIC ASSHOLE' single's radio-unfriendliness didn't do it any favours and it stiffed outside the Top 50. The accompanying album, 'EMPIRE OF THE SENSELESS' (1993) was another fine effort, but sank without trace after a brief appearance in the Top 40. Following 1995's 'TAKING CARE OF BUSINESS', KEDS joined The WILDHEARTS for two months before going AWOL, effectively ending The SENSELESS THINGS' long running campaign. The singer eventually resurfaced in early '96 fronting The JOLT alongside BB METS and MARTIN SHAW, an EP, 'SEX AND CHEQUES' surfacing later that year. • **Songwriters:** KEDS penned most, except; SHOPLIFTING (Slits) / BREAK IT AWAY (Perfect Daze) / APACHE (Shadows) / ANSWERING MACHINE (Replacements). • **Trivia:** BEN HARDING was once a clerk for the BBC.

Album rating: THE FIRST OF TOO MANY (*7) / EMPIRE OF THE SENSELESS (*6) / TAKING CARE OF BUSINESS (*4) / THE BEST OF THE SENSELESS THINGS compilation (*6)

MARK KEDS – vocals, guitar / **BEN HARDING** – lead guitar / **MORGAN NICHOLLS** – bass, guitar / **CASS BROWNE** – drums

 Yo Jo Jo not iss.
Feb 88. (7"flexi) (Yo Jo Jo 3) **I'M MOVING / LOW TIME / (ALL YOU'VE GOT TO DO IS) STAY TOGETHER** — —
 (above was given free with 'Shy Like You' fanzine)
 Red not iss.
Nov 88. (12"ep) (RED 001T) **UP AND COMING** — —
 – Where the secret lies / I want to go back / I don't want to talk about it / You don't want me / When you let me down. (re-iss. Feb91 12"ep+=/cd-ep+=; WC 006/+CD)
 – Girlfriend / Standing in the rain.
 Way Cool not iss.
Mar 89. (7") (WC 001) **GIRLFRIEND. / STANDING IN THE RAIN** — —
Oct 89. (7") (WC 003) **TOO MUCH KISSING. / TREVOR** — —
Nov 89. (m-lp/cd) (WC 004/+CD) **POSTCARD C.V.** — —
 – Trevor / Come together / Sneaking kisses / Laura Lamona / Shoplifting / Drunk & soppy / Back to nowhere / Teenage / Someone in you / Too much kissing / Girlfriend / Standing in the rain. (cd+) – UP AND COMING EP
 Decoy not iss.
May 90. (7") (DYS 15) **IS IT TOO LATE?. / LEO** — —
 (12"+=/cd-s+=) (DYS 15 T/CD) – Andi in a karmann / Ponyboy.
May 90. (m-lp/m-cd) (DYL 16/+CD) **IS IT TOO LATE?** — — Euro
 – Is it too late? / Leo / Andi in a karmann / Ponyboy / Celebrity / Tricia don't belong.
Jul 90. (12"ep/cd-ep) (DYS 17 T/CD) **CAN'T DO ANYTHING. / CAN'T EXPLAIN / TANGLED LINES** — —
 Epic Epic
Jun 91. (7"/c-s) (656 980-7/-4) **EVERYBODY'S GONE. / MYSTERY TRAIN** 73 —
 (12"+=/cd-s+=) (656 980-6/-2) – I'm on black and white.
Sep 91. (7") (657 449-7) **GOT IT AT THE DELMAR. / FISHING AT TESCOS** 50 —
 (c-s+=/12"+=/cd-s+=) (657 449-4/-6/-2) – Beat to Blondie / Can't remember.
Oct 91. (cd/c/lp/purple-lp) (469 157-2/-4/-1) <48988> **THE FIRST OF TOO MANY** 66 Mar92
 – Everybody's gone / Best friend / Ex teenager / It's cool to hang out with your ex / 19 blues / Should I feel it / Lip radio / In love again / Got it at the Delmar / American dad / Radio Spiteful / Chicken / Wrong number / Different tongues / Fishing at Tescos. (re-iss. Feb92 purple-lp; 469157-0)
Dec 91. (7"/c-s) (657 695-7/-4) **EASY TO SMILE. / HAZEL** 18 —
 (12"+=/cd-s+=) (657 926-6/-2) – Mollylove.
Mar 92. (7"orange/c-s) (657 926-7/-4) **HOLD IT DOWN. / CRUCIAL JUVENILIA** 19 —
 (12"+=/pic-cd-s+=) (657 926-6/-2) – Splitting hairs.
Nov 92. (7"/c-s) (658 833-7/-4) **HOMOPHONIC ASSHOLE. / BODY BAG** 52 —
 (12"+=) (658 833-6) – Just flirting.
 (cd-s++=) (658 833-2) – ('A'radio edit).
Feb 93. (7") (658 940-7) **PRIMARY INSTINCT. / RUNAWAYS** 41 —
 (12"colrd+=/cd-s+=) (658 940-6/-2) – Too much like I know you.

SENSELESS THINGS (cont) — THE GREAT INDIE DISCOGRAPHY — **The 1980s**

Mar 93. (cd/c/lp) *(473 525-2/-4/-1)* **EMPIRE OF THE SENSELESS** — 37
– Homophobic asshole / Keepsake / Tempting Kate / Hold it down / Counting friends / Just one reason / Cruel moon / Primary instinct / Rise (song for Dean & Gene) / Ice skating at the Milky Way / Say what you will / Runaways. *(re-iss. Jun93 += cd/c/lp; 474 119-2/-4/-1)* – POSTCARD CV.
Jun 93. (7"/c-s) *(659 250-7/-4)* **TOO MUCH KISSING. / KEEPSAKE / SAY WHAT YOU WILL (demo)** — 69
(cd-s) *(659 250-2)* – (1st 2 tracks) / Cruel dub / ('A'original).
Oct 94. (7") *(660 957-7)* **CHRISTINE KEELER. / HIGH ENOUGH** — 56
(12") *(660 957-6)* – ('A'side) / Jerk / The revivalist / Can't go back.
(cd-s) *(660 957-2)* – ('A'side) / Jerk / The revivalist / Driving on the right.
Jan 95. (7"colrd) *(661 116-7)* **SOMETHING TO MISS. / 16.18.21** — 57
(12"+=/cd-s+=) *(661 116-6/-2)* – Never haunted / Answering machine.
Feb 95. (cd/c/lp) *(478 368-2/-4/-1)* **TAKING CARE OF BUSINESS**
– Christine Keeler / Something to miss / Page 3 valentine / Any which way / Marlene / Role models / Watching the pictures go / Scapegoats / 16.18.21 / Touch me on the heath / Wanted / Too late / Dead sun / The way to the drugstore.

— now without KEDS who joined WILDHEARTS for a few months before going AWOL, while HARDING joined 3 COLOURS RED. KEDS re-surfaced early in 1996 with The JOLT, while it took CASS a little longer to make his return with the more pop-friendly, DELAKOTA.

– compilations, etc. –

Feb 94. (cd) *Strange Fruit; (SFRCD 127)* **THE PEEL SESSIONS**

JOLT

KEDS – vocals, guitar / **BB METS** – vocals, bass / **MARTIN SHAW** – drums

Scared Of Girls / not iss.

Oct 96. (cd-ep) *(GIRL 001CD)* **SEX AND CHEQUES EP**
– Homebreaker / Call me if you wanna / Scared of girls / Sex and cheques.
Apr 97. (one-sided-7") *(GIRL 003)* **GOODBYE TO THE 80's**

Fluffy Bunny / not iss.

Apr 98. (7"ep/cd-ep) *(FLUFF 17/+CD)* **MADE MY DAY / RUDE BOY. / WAS IT WILD? (original) / MADE MY DAY (original).**

Will SERGEANT
(see under ⇒ ECHO & THE BUNNYMEN)

SERIOUS DRINKING

Formed: Norwich, England ... early 1981 by MARTIN SIMON, LANCE, JEM, EUGENE and ANDY. With most of the members having met while studying at the University Of East Anglia, SERIOUS DRINKING set out to celebrate that most famous of student pastimes i.e. getting plastered. A kind of precursor to 90's "lad" culture, the band enjoyed a cult following throughout the 80's via albums such as 'THE REVOLUTION BEGINS AT CLOSING TIME' (1983) and 'THEY MAY BE DRINKERS ROBIN, BUT THEY'RE STILL HUMAN BEINGS' (1984), although with their staunchly socialist outlook and an offbeat sense of humour, they were a world apart from the genuine mob mentality of the 'Oi!' scene. Like their most famous fan, John Peel, the boys' other great love was football, 1990's re-issue of their debut, 'LOVE ON THE TERRACES', released to coincide with that year's World Cup. The same year saw the release of brilliantly titled compilation (complete with free beer mat!), 'STRANGER THAN TANNADICE – THE HITS, MISSES AND OWN GOALS OF SERIOUS DRINKING', 'Tannadice', for the benefit of English readers, being the home of Scottish Premier League stragglers Dundee United (although many might argue that nearby Dundee ground, 'Dens Park', is even stranger!). Said to be the inspiration for HALF MAN HALF BISCUIT and I, LUDICROUS, SERIOUS DRINKING were a little ahead of their time (time? – time gentlemen please!). In 1996 (for Euro '96), they re-formed to deliver their version of England's most famous World Cup song, 'BACK HOME'; we thought it was all over... it bloody should be.

Album rating: THE REVOLUTION STARTS AT CLOSING TIME (*5) / THEY MAY BE DRINKERS ROBIN, BUT THEY'RE STILL HUMAN BEINGS mini (*5)

MARTIN SIMON – vocals (ex-HIGSONS) / **EUGENE** – vocals / **ANDY** – guitar (ex-FARMER'S BOYS) / **JEM** – bass / **LANCE** – drums

Upright / not iss.

Sep 82. (7"ep) *(UP 4)* **LOVE ON THE TERRACES EP**
– Love on the terraces / Hypocrite / Bobby Moore was innocent / Nobody likes him.
Mar 83. (7"m) *(UP 5)* **HANGOVER. / DON'T SHOOT ME DOWN / BABY I'M DYING A DEATH**
Sep 83. (lp) *(UPLP 3)* **THE REVOLUTION STARTS AT CLOSING TIME**
– The revolution starts at closing time / Winter's over / Spirit of '66 / Love on the terraces / Bobby Moore was innocent / Hangover / Countdown to Bilko / Really good bloke / 12XU / Am I coming over to yours. *(cd-iss. Oct99 +=; PLAYCD 24)* – THEY MAY BE DRINKERS ...
Mar 84. (m-lp) *(UPLP 7)* **THEY MAY BE DRINKERS ROBIN, BUT THEY'RE ALSO HUMAN BEINGS**
May 84. (7") *(UP 8)* **COUNTRY GIRL BECAME DRUGS AND SEX PUNK. / GO FOR THE BURN!**

— **KAREN YARNELL** – drums (ex-GYMSLIPS) repl. LANCE and JEM
— **CARL KENNEDY** – also joined at some stage
— basically, they returned to the pub and the terraces, until ...

Worker's Playtime / not iss.

Jun 90. (cd/lp) *(PLAY CD/LP 14)* **STRANGER THAN TANNADICE – THE HITS, MISSES AND OWN GOALS** (part compilation)
– Love on the terraces / Don't shoot me down / Baby I'm dying a death / Hangover / Time is right / World service / Winter's over / Country girl becomes sex and drugs punk / Go for the burn / A nice piece of trout / A day at the races / He's an angry bastard but I like him / 12XU – Bobby Moore was innocent – I'm on drugs. *(cd+=)* – Love on the terraces / Spirit of '66 / Countdown to Bilko / Really good bloke / Pillars of society / Young hearts run free.

— the odd sporadic release still surfaced from the dug-out

Musical Tragedies / not iss.

Jan 93. (7") *(EFA 11366)* **RED SKIES OVER WEMBLEY. /**

Damaged Goods / not iss.

Jun 96. (7") *(DAMGOOD 101)* **BACK HOME. / CINNAMON TWIST**

SERVANTS

Formed: London, England ... 1985 by songwriter DAVID WESTLAKE, along with JOHN MOHAN, PHILIP KING and JOHN WILLS. Displaying an obvious SYD BARRETT fetish, WESTLAKE and Co made their vinyl debut with their self-financed 7", 'SHE'S ALWAYS HIDING', consolidated by an appearance on the NME's high-profile C-86 cassette. However, after a second single, 'THE SUN, A SMALL STAR', later in the year, The SERVANTS took early retirement when most of the band became involved in other projects; while WILLS joined LOOP and KING became a FELT member, the latter also moonlighted with JOHN MOHAN in 'Creation' act, APPLE BOUTIQUE, issuing a one-off 12", 'LOVE RESISTANCE', in '88. Meanwhile, WESTLAKE was already carving out his own solo career with a mini-set entitled simply 'WESTLAKE' (1987) before re-employing The SERVANTS moniker alongside newcomers LUKE HAINES, ALICE READMAN and former HOUSEMARTINS drummer, HUGH WHITAKER. A solitary single, 'IT'S MY TURN', appeared on 'Glass' records in 1989, while a long-awaited debut album for 'Paperhouse' (home of The PASTELS), 'DISINTERESTED' appeared almost a year later. Unfortunately, the title proved all too prophetic and the SERVANTS were finally laid to rest; HAINES and READMAN would achieve greater recognition with their own outfit, The AUTEURS.

Album rating: DISINTERESTED (*5) / David Westlake: WESTLAKE mini (*5)

DAVID WESTLAKE – vocals / **PHILIP KING** – bass, guitar / **JOHN MOHAN** – guitar, keyboards / **JOHN WILLS** – drums (of WISHING STONES)

Head / not iss.

Mar 86. (7") *(HEAD 1)* **SHE'S ALWAYS HIDING. / TRANSPARENT**
Oct 86. (12"ep) *(HEAD 3)* **THE SUN, A SMALL STAR / MEREDITH. / IT TAKES NO GENTLEMAN / FUNNY BUSINESS**

— split when WILLS joined LOOP and KING joined FELT (also to BIFF BANG POW!). Early in '88, KING and MOHAN got together as APPLE BOUTIQUE, releasing one-off 12", 'LOVE RESISTANCE' with b-side 'I DON'T BELIEVE IN YOU' & 'BALLAD OF JET HARRIS' on 'Creation' *(CRE 052T)*

DAVID WESTLAKE

Creation / not iss.

Nov 87. (m-lp) *(CRELP 019)* **WESTLAKE**
– The word around town / Dream come true / Rings on her fingers / Everlasting / She grew and she grew / Talk like that. *(cd-iss. Jul93; CRECD 019)*

SERVANTS

— **WESTLAKE** recruited new line-up **LUKE HAINES** (b. 7 Oct'67, Walton-On-Thames, Surrey, England) – vocals, guitar / **ALICE READMAN** (b.1967, Harrow, Middlesex, England) – bass / **HUGH WHITAKER** – drums (ex-HOUSEMARTINS)

Glass / not iss.

Sep 89. (7") *(GLASS 056)* **IT'S MY TURN. / AFTERGLOW**
(12"+=) *(GLASS12 056)* – Faithful to 3 lovers / Do or be done.

Paperhouse / not iss.

Jul 90. (cd/lp) *(PAP CD/LP 005)* **DISINTERESTED**
– Move out / Restless / Thin skinned / Hush now / Hey Mrs. John / Big future / The power of woman / Third wheel / Self destruction / They should make a statue / Look like a girl / Afterglow.

— split for the final time when HAINES and READMAN formed The AUTEURS

SEX CLARK FIVE

Formed: Huntsville, Alabama, USA ... 1984 by frontman JAMES BUTLER, RICK STOREY and TRICK McKAHA, all purveyors of Celtic-styled twee power-pop. Forming their own 'Records To Russia' imprint in '86, the SEX CLARK FIVE (DAVE was not on call with this bunch!) delivered their debut 45, 'NEITA GREW UP LAST NIGHT'. With 4th member JOY JOHNSON in tow and a subsequent deal with Bristol's 'Subway' records, the SCF unleashed the much-lauded first LP, the appropriately-titled 'STRUM & DRUM' (1988). It was hook, line and sinker for Radio One DJ John Peel, the famous one playlisting several of its catchy tunes. However, further efforts such as 'BATTLE OF THE SEX CLARK FIVE' (1989) and 'ANTEDIUM' (1993), generated little or no interest and the 'FIVE split – bits n pieces you could say (sorry folks).

Album rating: STRUM & DRUM! (*7) / BATTLE OF THE SEX CLARK FIVE (*5) / ANTEDIUM (*4)

JAMES BUTLER – vocals, guitar / **RICK STOREY** – guitar / **TRICK McKAHA** – drums

497

SEX CLARK FIVE (cont)   THE GREAT INDIE DISCOGRAPHY   The 1980s

		Subway	Records To Russia
1986.	(12"ep) NEITA GREW UP LAST NIGHT	-	

– Neita grew up last night / Red shift / Alai / I want you mine.

—— added JOY JOHNSON – bass

| Oct 88. | (lp) (SUBORG 007) STRUM AND DRUM! | | |

– The men who don't know ice / Detention girls / Valerie / A chance / Girls of Somalia / Can't shake loose / Modern fix / I love you less / While I'm here / If you see her with me (let me know) / Alai / 51-L / Faith / Kid Raja / Streamers / Sarajevo / Window to the works / She collides with me / Valerie (reprise) / Get back Yoko. <US cd-iss. 1996 on 'Beehive Rebellion'+=; > – Neita grew up last night / Red shift / I want you mine / Jeepster / The Wehrmacht's lament / Hot heart / I got use of my legs / Fool I was / When words become a kiss / Love / You left the lights on in your eyes / Have you seen her face / Accelerator / Ketchup if you can.

		not iss.	Blood Money
1989.	(cd) <59> BATTLE OF THE SEX CLARK FIVE	-	

– Afraid of bigness / Will you go steady / The Norman shuttle / Girl I like / Liberate Tibet / Accelerator / Between the zones / Satellite beach / The Norman shuttle (vocal) / Ireland / Slog song / Book / Missing / Sock hopra / I'm a fool with you / Cut up Ray / The Wehrmacht's lament / Battleline / Ballad of Sex Clark Five / Communist bloc blues.

		not iss.	Records To Russia
1991.	(12"ep) KETCHUP IF YOU CAN	-	
		not iss.	Skyclad
1993.	(cd) <131> ANTEDIUM	-	

– States rights / Love me much / World of wonder / Gothic go ahead / America under the Mongol Yoke prelude / Mongol song / She'll get mad / Feast days / Rovin dance / Fool I was / Ketchup if you can / Cold and gray / Life w/o a mind / From far away / Civil war / Knights of carumba / Strum and drum! / Because of you / That's innocence for you / I got use of my legs / Old world girl / Curley shuttle reprise / Battle of Sex Clark Five / Escaping the tube of tomorrow.

—— split after above

SEX GANG CHILDREN

Formed: London, England . . . 1982 out of PANIC BUTTON by ANDI SEX GANG and DAVE ROBERTS, who in turn recruited TERRY McLEAY and ROB STROUD. Rapidly building up a cult following, this bunch of ghoulish goth-fetish merchants (who took their offensive moniker from a line in a William Burroughs novel) released a self-financed, cassette-only live album, 'NAKED', later the same year. An appearance at Leeds' Futurama festival helped push their debut vinyl release, 'BEASTS!', an EP consisting mainly of reworked material from 'NAKED' and their first release for 'Illuminated'. A follow-up single, 'INTO THE ABYSS' rounded the year off as the band became indie chart favourites with their patented brand of scratchy guitar, shrieking, often unintelligible vocals and general musical chaos. 'SEBASTIANE', the first single from debut album, 'SONG AND LEGEND' (1983) threw grating violin into the already crowded mix courtesy of MARC & THE MAMBAS member, GINI HEWES. 1983 also saw the release of a compilation album put together by ROBERTS; entitled 'THE WHIP', it featured a duet between ANDI and MARC ALMOND, 'THE HUNGRY YEARS'. The subsequent departure of STROUD was temporarily solved by the recruitment of ex-THEATRE OF HATE man, NIGEL PRESTON; he stayed for one single, 'MAURITIA MAYER', released on 'Clay' records after The 'GANG were dropped by 'Illuminated'. Matters became even more confused as another temp sticksman, DEATH CULT's RAY MONDO, was deported as the band returned from an American tour. To add insult to injury, ROBERTS jumped ship for his new band, the catchily monikered CARCRASH INTERNATIONAL, before 1983 was out. ANDI and McLEAY soldiered on briefly with new recruits CAM CAMPBELL and KEVIN MATTHEWS before Mr SEX GANG struck out for a solo career and effectively brought the band to an end. Renewed interest following the release of a retrospective album in 1991 led to a short-lived Stateside reformation, an independently released set of new material, 'MEDEA', surfacing in 1993. • **Trivia:** Produced by NICKY GARRETT (ex-UK SUBS) early on, before TONY JAMES (ex-GENERATION X) took over.

Album rating: SONG AND LEGEND (*4) / BEASTS (*3) / ECSTASY AND VENDETTA OVER NEW YORK (*3) / THE HUNGRY YEARS: BEST OF THE SEX GANG CHILDREN compilation (*6) / Andi SexGang: BLIND! (*5) / ARCO VALLEY (*3)

ANDI SEX GANG (b. ANDREW HAYWARD) – vocals, guitar / **TERRY MacLEAY** (b. Scotland) – guitar / **DAVE ROBERTS** – bass, acoustic guitar / **ROB STROUD** – drums

		Illuminated	not iss.
Jun 82.	(12"ep) (ILL 11-12) BEASTS		-

– Cannibal queen / Times of our lives / Sense of elation. (re-iss. Feb85)

Oct 82.	(7") (ILL 15) INTO THE ABYSS. / DEICHE		-
Mar 83.	(7") (ILL 20) SONG AND LEGEND. / SEBASTIANE		-
Mar 83.	(lp) (JAMS 666) SONG AND LEGEND		-

– The crack-up / German nun / State of mind / Sebastiane / Draconian dream / Shout and scream / Killer K / Cannibal queen / Kill machine / Song and legend. (re-iss. Apr86 on 'Dojo' lp/cd; DOJO LP/CD 16)

| Jun 83. | (12"m) (ILL 22-12) SEBASTIANE / MONGOLIA. / WHO ON EARTH CAN THAT BE | | - |

—— **NIGEL PRESTON** – drummer (ex-THEATRE OF HATE) repl. STROUD who formed Huddersfield outfit AEMOTU CRII, then PINK AND BLACK

		Clay	not iss.
Sep 83.	(7"/ext.12") (CLAY/12CLAY 27) MAURITIA MAYER. / CHILDREN'S PRAYER		-

—— **RAY MONDO** – drums (ex-DEATH CULT) repl. PRESTON who was swopped into same band

—— DAVE ROBERTS left late '83 to form CAR CRASH INTERNATIONAL. Trimmed to just ANDI and TERRY with new bassist **CAM CAMPBELL** and drummer **KEVIN MATTHEWS** when RAY was deported back to home country Sierra Leone. They split in 1984, but got the 7-year itch and reformed due to support in the US. **ANDI / DAVE** (now on guitar) / **GERALD SANTANA** (b. USA) – bass / + drummer

– compilations, etc. –

| Dec 83. | (lp) Illuminated; (JAMS 34) BEASTS | | - |

– Beasts / Cannibal queen / Who on Earth can that be / Sense of elation / Into the abyss / Deiche / Salvation / Mongolia / Times of our lives. (re-iss. Aug86 on 'Dojo'; DOJOLP 30)

| Jul 84. | (12") Illuminated; (ILL 39-12) DEICHE. / DRACONIAN DREAM | | - |
| Aug 84. | (c) R.O.I.R.; (A 127) ECSTASY AND VENDETTA OVER NEW YORK (live) | | - |

(cd-iss. Aug94 on 'Cleopatra'; CLEO 3833)

Sep 85.	(12") Saderal; (SLS 12-001) DEICHE. / BEASTS		-
Apr 86.	(lp/c) Dojo; (DOJO LP/TC 13) RE-ENTER THE ABYSS		-
May 88.	(lp) Arkham House; (AHLP 1001) NIGHTLAND USA, 1983 (live)		-
May 88.	(lp) Sex; (SEX 2) LIVE IN LONDON AND GLASGOW (live)		-
Dec 91.	(cd/lp) Receiver; (RR CD/LP 149) THE HUNGRY YEARS: THE BEST OF THE SEX GANG CHILDREN		-
May 94.	(cd) Cleopatra; <(CLEO 6957)> PLAY WITH CHILDREN		
Aug 99.	(cd) Dressed To Kill; <(DRESSCD 156)> DEICHE		

– Deiche / Salvation / Mongolia / Times of our lives / Beasts / Cannibal queen / Who on earth can that be? / Sense of elation / Into the abyss / People with dirty faces.

| Aug 99. | (cd) Dressed To Kill; <(DRESSCD 157)> POP UP | | |
| Sep 99. | (cd) Dressed To Kill; <(DRESSCD 187)> MEDEA | | |

– Barbarossa / Guy wonder / Alien baby / Medea / Giaconda smile / Smile / Arms of Cicero / Boss and beauty / Shattered room / Sugar pill.

Sep 99.	(cd) Dressed To Kill; <(DRESSCD 189)> VEIL		
Sep 00.	(cd) Metrodome; (MCCD 0010) DEMONSTRATION		-
Apr 01.	(cd) Triple X; (<TX 60026CD>) EMPYRE AND FALL		

– State of mind / Killer K / Shout and scream / Sebastiane / Beats / Into the abyss (extended) / Deiche / Times of our lives / Draconian dream.

ANDI SEX GANG

		Illuminated	not iss.
Sep 84.	(7") (ILL 52) LES AMANTS D'UN JOUR. / OH HENRY		-
Jan 85.	(lp) (JAMS 48) BLIND		-

– Welcome to my world / Boss and beauty / Dead metal / Ecstasy and vendetta / Ida-ho / Last chants for the slow dance / The quick gas gang / Dying fall / Immigrant / Oh Henry / I've done it all before / Strike blind / Gas reprise. (cd-iss. Jun93 on 'Trident'; TMI 1) (<re-iss. cd Mar94 on 'Cleopatra'; CLEO 5122-2>) (cd re-iss. Aug99 on 'Dressed To Kill'; DRESS 186)

| Mar 85. | (7") (ILL 53) IDA-HO. / QUICK GAS GANG | | - |

(12"+=) (ILL 53-12) – You don't know me.

		Revolver	not iss.
Sep 86.	(12"m) (12REV 27) THE NAKED AND THE DEAD. / YOU DON'T KNOW ME / THE QUICK AND THE DEAD		-

below featured MICK RONSON – guitar

		Jungle	Jungle
Nov 88.	(7") (JUNG 42) SEVEN WAYS TO KILL A MAN. /		

(12"+=) (JUNG 42T) –

| Nov 88. | (lp) (FREUD 24) <51185> ARCO VALLEY | | Feb89 |

– 7 ways to kill a man / Queen of broken dreams / Power waits / Jesus phoned / Les amants d'un jour / Rock revo / Station 5 / Christian circus Joe / Assassin years / Belgique blue. (re-iss. Jul89 c/cd; FREUD/+C/CD 24) (cd re-iss. Aug95 on 'Triple X'; TX 511852CD) (cd re-iss. Oct99 on 'Metrodome'; METRO 241)

| Mar 89. | (7") (JUNG 48) ASSASSIN YEARS. / | | - |

(12"+=) (JUNG 48T) –

		not iss.	Cleopatra
1993.	(cd,c) <5861> GOD ON A ROPE	-	

– Bormann chain – Victor Jara / Psyche Sara / Pig of a god: Heartless Harvey – Comedy / Captain Careful / Tin house, glass . . . / Almagordo – Miriam pain / Cold hard stone / Atom dance / Patient performers / Violin valley / Egypt's ancient lovers – The last great / God dies.

—— next with **ADRIAN PORTAS** – multi / **KEVIN MATTHEWS** – drums

		Triple X	Triple X
Aug 95.	(m-cd) (<TX 51186CD>) WESTERN SONGS FOR CHILDREN		May95

– Diamond girls / Heaven shines for you / Welcome to my world / Waiting for the assassin / Beauty of lovers.

| Oct 95. | (cd; by ANDI SEX GANG & MICK ROSSI) (TX 51195CD) GABRIEL AND THE GOLDEN HORN | | |

SFERIC EXPERIMENT
(see under ⇒ KING LOSER; in 90's section)

SHACK

Formed: Liverpool, England . . . mid-80's out of semi-successful indie-pop outfit The PALE FOUNTAINS. MICK HEAD, his brother JOHN HEAD and CHRIS McCAFFREY, almost immediately recruited THOMAS 'JOCK' WHELAN and ANDY DIAGRAM (the latter from DISLOCATION DANCE and The DIAGRAM BROS) to form the seminal, tragedy struck PALE FOUNTAINS. Their debut single, '(THERE'S ALWAYS) SOMETHING ON MY MIND', set the tone for their melancholy, melodic, 60's-inspired alt-pop, like a cross between The BEATLES and LOVE. 'Virgin' were quick off the mark to sign them, their contract off to a promising start when follow-up single, 'THANK YOU', hit the Top 50 late in '82. However, sales of subsequent 45's and debut album, 'PACIFIC STREET' (1984), didn't quite meet expectations, its brassy tropical feel (with colourful image to match) a touch exotic for the average indie fan. A second album, the IAN BROUDIE-produced '...FROM ACROSS THE KITCHEN TABLE', emerged early the following year, the pleasant but hardly inspiring 'JEAN'S NOT HAPPENING' summing up PALE FOUNTAINS appeal. With their chart potential having almost completely dried up, The PALE FOUNTAINS split as the brothers HEAD re-emerged as SHACK. Along with new boys, DAVE BUTCHER, JUSTIN SMITH and MICHAEL CURTIS, they were the first act to sign for the 'Ghetto Recording Company', the first fruits of their efforts being the 1988 set, 'ZILCH'. Displaying an even stronger BEATLES influence, the album was a sterling slab of subtle, intelligent indie-pop. However, it took all of two years for the band to return, the single 'I KNOW YOU WELL' calling to mind The BEATLES' 'Taxman' with its knotty stop-start rhythms. A solitary single, 'AL'S VACATION', arrived in Spring '91 and although an album was completed, a studio fire destroyed what was thought to be the only existing master tape. Fortunately, producer Chris Allison unearthed a DAT master, although he subsequently lost it again after leaving it in a hired car. Incredibly, the fabled tape later turned up in Germany (!), the belated album finally issued in '95 (prior to that, the HEAD brothers kept themselves busy by supporting ARTHUR LEE in 1992 at Liverpool) as 'WATERPISTOL' by 'Marina' records. MICHAEL HEAD was back in a solo capacity in 1998, members of SHACK backing him up on his inaugural release, 'THE MAGICAL WORLD OF THE STRANDS'. A year later, acclaim had finally reached SHACK, with the release of the poignant 'HMS FABLE'. Described as a cross between MERCURY REV's 'Deserter's Songs' and the BEATLES' 'Abbey Road', the set documented the highs and lows in the last few years of the HEAD brothers. From heroin addiction to musical misfortune, it was all there; of course, a SHACK album wouldn't have been complete without any of these things! In turn, the music press went crazy at this stunning comeback, the result being that the album entered the British charts at No.25. Singles such as 'NATALIE'S PARTY' and 'COMEDY' furthered the band's reputation, even if the general public didn't pay much attention to this wonderful discovery. 'HMS FABLE' also topped many magazines' 'Album Of the Year' polls – a well deserved reward for a hard working but unlucky outfit.

Album rating: Pale Fountains: PACIFIC STREET (*6) / ...FROM ACROSS THE KITCHEN TABLE (*4) / LONGSHOT FOR YOUR LOVE compilation (*6) / Shack: ZILCH (*7) / WATERPISTOL (*6) / Michael Head: THE MAGICAL WORLD OF THE STRANDS (*6) / Shack: H.M.S. FABLE (*9)

PALE FOUNTAINS

MICK HEAD (b.28 Nov'61) – vocals, guitar / **JOHN HEAD** (b. 4 Oct'65) – lead guitar / **CHRIS McCAFFREY** – bass / **ANDY DIAGRAM** – trumpet (ex-DISLOCATION DANCE, ex-DIAGRAM BROS) / **THOMAS 'JOCK' WHELAN** – drums, percussion / + 6th member **M. BARRADAS** – oil drums, percussion

Operation Twilight / not iss.

Jul 82. (7") (OPT 09) **(THERE'S ALWAYS) SOMETHING ON MY MIND. / JUST A GIRL**

Virgin / –

Oct 82. (7") (VS 557) **THANK YOU. / MEADOW OF LOVE** — 48
May 83. (7"/12") (VS 568/+12) **PALM OF MY HAND. / LOVE'S A BEAUTIFUL PLACE**
Jan 84. (7"/12") (VS 614/+12) **UNLESS. / NATURAL**
Feb 84. (lp/c) (V/TCV 2274) **PACIFIC STREET**
 – Reach / Something on my mind / Unless / Southbound excursion / Natural / Faithful pillow (part 1) / (Don't let your love) Start a war / Beyond Friday's field / Abergele next time / Crazier / Faithful pillow (part 2). (re-iss. Aug87 lp/c; OVED/+C 143) (cd-iss. Nov89; CDV 2274)
Mar 84. (7"/12") (VS 668/+12) **(DON'T LET YOUR LOVE) START A WAR. / LOVE SITUATION**

— now without BARRADAS

Jan 85. (7"/12") (VS 735/+12) **JEAN'S NOT HAPPENING. / BICYCLE THIEVES**
Feb 85. (lp/c) (V/TCV 2333) **...FROM ACROSS THE KITCHEN TABLE**
 – Shelter / Stole the love / Jean's not happening / Bicycle thieves / Limit / 27 ways to get back home / Bruised arcade / These are the things / It's only hard / ...From across the kitchen table / Hey / September sting. (re-iss. Apr86 lp/c; OVED/+C 164) (cd-iss. Jul89; CDV 2333)
Jun 85. (7") (VS 750) **...FROM ACROSS THE KITCHEN TABLE. / BICYCLE THIEVES**
 (12"+=) (VS 750-12) – Thank you.
 (d7"++=) (VS 750) – Just a girl.

— disbanded when DIAGRAM returned to DISLOCATION DANCE (sadly, McCAFFREY was to die in August '89)

– compilations, etc. –

Jul 99. (cd/lp) (MA 37) **LONGSHOT FOR YOUR LOVE**
 – Just a girl / (There's always) Something on my mind / Lavinia's dream / Longshot for your love / Thank you / The Norfolk broads / Benoit's Christmas / Hey there Fred / Palm of my hand / Free / We have all the time in the world / Just a girl / Love situation.

SHACK

— **MICK HEAD + JOHN HEAD** with **DAVE BUTCHER** – keyboards / **JUSTIN SMITH** – bass / **MICHAEL KURTIS** – drums

Ghetto / not iss.

Mar 88. (7") (GTG 1) **EMERGENCY. / LIBERATION**
 (12"+=) (GTGT 1) – Faith.
 (cd-s+=) (CDGTG 1) – What's it like...
Mar 88. (lp/c/cd) (GHETT/+C/D 1) **ZILCH**
 – Emergency / Someone's knocking / John Kline / Realization / I need you / High rise, low life / Who killed Clayton Square? / Who'd believe it? / What's it like.../ The believers. (cd+=) – Liberation / Faith / High rise low life (the Bert Hardy mix).

Jun 88. (7") (GTG 2) **HIGH RISE LOW LIFE. / WHO KILLED CLAYTON SQUARE?**
 (12"+=/cd-s+=) (GTGT/CDGTG 2) – ('A'-Bert Hardy mix).
Jul 90. (7") (GTG 11) **I KNOW YOU WELL. / FEEL NO WAY**
 (ext.12") (GTG 11T) – ('A'-If you want it mix).
 (cd-s++=) (CDGTG 11) – ('A'extended).
Apr 91. (7") (GTG 14) **AL'S VACATION. / IRISH**
 (12"+=) (GTGT 14) – Feel no way.

— an album was recorded but destroyed after a studio fire (see above).

Marina / not iss.

Nov 95. (cd/lp) (MA 16 – MACD 44632) **WATERPISTOL**
 – Sgt. Major / Neighbours / Stranger / Dragonfly / Mood of the morning / Walter's song / Time machine / Mr. Appointment / Undecided / Hazy / Hey mama / London town. (re-iss. Feb98 & Jul99 cd/lp; MAR 16)

MICHAEL HEAD

— with other members of SHACK as backing

Megaphone / not iss.

Feb 98. (cd/lp) (CD/LP MEGA 01) **THE MAGICAL WORLD OF THE STRANDS**
 – Queen Matilda / Something like you / And luna / X hits the spot / The prize / Undecided (reprise) / Glynys and Jaqui / It's harvest time / Loaded man / Hocken's hey / Fontilan.
Apr 98. (7") (7MEGA 02) **SOMETHING LIKE YOU. / GREEN VELVET JACKET**
 (cd-s+=) (CDMEGA 02) – Queen Matilda (demo). (re-iss. Oct98; same)

SHACK

London / Sire

Jun 99. (c-s) (LONCS 427) **COMEDY / UNCLE DELANEY / COMEDY (No Strings)** — 44
 (cd-s) (LONCD 427) – (first two tracks) / Petroleum.
 (cd-s) (LONCDP 427) – ('A'side) / 24 hours / Solid gold.
Jun 99. (cd/c) (556113-2/-4) <31071> **H.M.S. FABLE** — 25 — Aug99
 – Natalie's party / Comedy / Pull together / Beautiful / Lend's some dough / Captain's table / Streets of Kenny / Re-instated / I want you / Cornish town / Since I met you / Daniella.
Aug 99. (c-s) (LONCS 436) **NATALIE'S PARTY / FLANNERY** — 63
 ('A'-Youth mix; cd-s+=) (LONCD 436) – Extra extra.
 (cd-s) (LONCDP 436) – ('A'side) / Too late for me now / Miss Christine.
Feb 00. (cd-s) (LONCD 445) **OSCAR / STREETS OF KENNY (acoustic) / QUEEN MATILDA (acoustic)** — 67
 (cd-s) (LOCDP 445) – ('A'side) / Captain's table (acoustic) / Daniella (acoustic).

SHANGRI-LA'S

Formed: Andrew Jackson High, Queens, New York, USA... as The BON BONS by sisters BETTY & MARY WEISS along with twins MARY-ANN and MARGIE GANSER. The girls were handed their big music biz break after being discovered by producer GEORGE 'SHADOW' MORTON who changed their name and signed them to 'Red Bird', the label owned by NY songwriters Jerry Leiber and Mike Stoller. MORTON himself penned 'REMEMBER (WALKING IN THE SAND)', an eerily melodramatic ballad with an ambitious production that cast SHADOW as an East Coast version of PHIL SPECTOR. The single hit the US Top 5 (UK Top 20) in September '64 and primed The SHANGRI-LA'S for their entrance into pop legend with 'LEADER OF THE PACK'. A half-spoken/half-sung (in MARY's trademark emotionally loaded, cheerleader-style NY accent) tale of tearful teen love, rebellion and death complete with revving motorbike/smashing glass sound effects, the track topped the US chart in late '64 and established a new benchmark in pop artistry. Further brilliantly overwrought creations followed over the next two years although only the more customary girly 'GIVE HIM A GREAT BIG KISS' and the runaway anguish of 'I CAN NEVER GO HOME ANYMORE' were significant hits. Following summer 66's unsettling spoken monologue, 'PAST, PRESENT AND FUTURE', the girls moved to 'Mercury' for a greatest hits package and a final couple of singles, 'THE SWEET SOUND OF SUMMER' and 'TAKE YOUR TIME'. The SHANGRI-LA'S split in 1967 amid legal problems with both the GANSER twins subsequently meeting unpleasant deaths (MARY ANN from encephalitis and MARGE from a drugs overdose). MORTON, meanwhile, went on to work with the likes of MOTT THE HOOPLE and The NEW YORK DOLLS.

Best CD compilation: THE BEST OF THE SHANGRI-LA'S (*8)

MARY WEISS – lead vocals / **BETTY WEISS** – vocals / **MARY-ANN GANSER** – vocals / **MARGE GANSER** – vocals

Red Bird / Red Bird

Sep 64. (7") <(RB10 008)> **REMEMBER (WALKING IN THE SAND). / IT'S EASIER TO CRY** — 14 — 5 Aug64
Dec 64. (7") <(RB10 014)> **LEADER OF THE PACK. / WHAT IS LOVE?** — 11 — 1 Oct64
Jan 65. (7") <(RB10 018)> **GIVE HIM A GREAT BIG KISS. / TWIST AND SHOUT** — — 18 Dec64
Jan 65. (7") <(RB10 025)> **MAYBE. / SHOUT** — — 91 Dec64
1965. (lp) <(RB20 101)> **THE SHANGRI-LAS – LEADER OF THE PACK** — — Mar65
 – Give him a great big kiss / Leader of the pack / Bull dog / It's easier to cry / What is love? / Remember (walking in the sand) / Twist and shout / Maybe / So much in love / Shout / Good night, my love / Pleasant dreams / You can't sit down. (re-iss. 1983 on 'Charly'; CRM 2028)

SHANGRI-LA'S (cont) — THE GREAT INDIE DISCOGRAPHY — The 1980s

1965.	(7") <(RB10 025)> **OUT IN THE STREETS. / THE BOY**	53 Mar65
1965.	(7") <(RB10 030)> **GIVE US YOUR BLESSINGS. / HEAVEN ONLY KNOWS**	29 May65
1965.	(7") <(RB10 036)> **RIGHT NOW AND NOT LATER. / TRAIN FROM KANSAS CITY**	99 Sep65
1965.	(lp) <RB20 014> **SHANGRI-LAS '65** – Right now and not later / Never again / Give us your blessings / Sophisticated boom boom / I'm blue / Heaven only knows / The train from Kansas City / Out in the streets / What's a girl supposed to do / The dum dum ditty / You cheated, you lied / The boy. (UK-iss.Mar84 on 'Charly'; CRM 2029)	
Jan 66.	(7") <(RB10 043)> **I CAN NEVER GO HOME ANYMORE. / BULLDOG**	6 Nov65
Mar 66.	(7") <(RB10 048)> **LONG LIVE OUR LOVE. / SOPHISTICATED BOOM BOOM**	33 Jan66
—	now without MARGE	
May 66.	(7") <(RB10 053)> **HE CRIED. / DRESSED IN BLACK**	65 Apr66
Aug 66.	(7") <(RB10 068)> **PAST, PRESENT AND FUTURE. / PARADISE**	59 Jun66
		Mercury / Mercury
1966.	(lp) (MCL 20096) <61099> **GOLDEN HITS** (compilation) – Leader of the pack / The train from Kansas City / Heaven only knows / Remember (walking in the sand) / I can never go home anymore / What is love? / Past, present and future / Out in the streets / Give him a great big kiss / Long live our love / Give us your blessings / Sophisticated boom boom. (re-iss. 1973 on 'Philips' lp)(c; 6336 215)(7175 031)	
1967.	(7") (MF 962) **THE SWEET SOUND OF SUMMER. / I'LL NEVER LEARN**	
1967.	(7") (MF 979) **TAKE YOUR TIME. / FOOTSTEPS ON THE ROOF**	
—	split in 1967. In 1971 MARY ANN died of encephalitis, MARGE died of a drug overdose	

– compilations, etc. –

1965.	(7"ep) Red Bird; (RB 40002) **THE SHANGRI-LAS**	
1971.	(7") Philips; (6061 027) **PAST, PRESENT AND FUTURE. / THE TRAIN FROM KANSAS CITY**	
Oct 72.	(7") Kama Sutra; (2013 024) **LEADER OF THE PACK. / REMEMBER (WALKING IN THE SAND)** (re-iss. Jul82 & Jun88 on 'Old Gold'; OG 9085)	3
1973.	(7"m) Buddah; (2011 164) **GIVE HIM A GREAT BIG KISS. / NEW YORK IS A LONELY TOWN / THE BOY FROM NEW YORK CITY**	
May 76.	(7") Charly; (CYS 1009) **LEADER OF THE PACK. / GIVE HIM A GREAT BIG KISS**	7
May 76.	(7") Contempo; (CS 9032) **LEADER OF THE PACK. / REMEMBER (WALKING IN THE SAND)**	7
1976.	(7"ep) Charly; (CEP 109) **REMEMBER (WALKING IN THE SAND) / LEADER OF THE PACK. / GIVE HIM A GREAT BIG KISS / PAST, PRESENT AND FUTURE** (cd-ep iss.Feb89; CDS 3)	
Aug 76.	(7"m) Philips; (6160 051) **PAST, PRESENT AND FUTURE. / GIVE HIM A GREAT BIG KISS / REMEMBER (WALKING IN THE SAND)**	
Sep 78.	(7") Charly; (CYS 1041) **LEADER OF THE PACK. / THE BOY FROM NEW YORK CITY**	
1978.	(lp) Charly; (CRM 2005) **TEEN ANGUISH VOL.2**	
Nov 84.	(lp/c) Topline; (TOP/KTOP 100) / Astan; <20/40 097> **LEADER OF THE PACK**	
May 87.	(cd) Topline; (TOPCD 519) **GREATEST HITS**	
Aug 87.	(cd) The Collection; (OR 0012) **SHANGRI-LAS**	
Jun 88.	(cd) Spectrum; (U 4063) **GREATEST HITS**	
Feb 89.	(cd-s) Old Gold; (OG 6114) **LEADER OF THE PACK / REMEMBER (WALKING IN THE SAND) / CHAPEL OF LOVE**	
Mar 89.	(cd) Crusader; (RMB 5633) **LEADER OF THE PACK**	
Feb 90.	(cd/c/lp) Instant; (CD/TC/INS 5021) **REMEMBER** – Leader of the pack / Give him a great big kiss / Maybe / Out in the streets / Give us your blessings / Right now and not later / Remember (walking in the sand) / I can never go home anymore / Long live our love / Past, present and future / The train from Kansas City / Shout / Twist and shout / I'm blue / You cheated, you lied / So much in love. (re-iss. Apr96 on 'Hallmark' cd/c; 30412-2/-4)	
Apr 94.	(cd) Disky; (DISK 4512) **HIT SINGLE COLLECTABLES**	
Mar 95.	(cd) The Collection; (COL 043) **THE COLLECTION**	
Apr 95.	(cd) R.P.M.; (RPM 136) **MYRMIDONS OF MELODRAMA**	

Sandie SHAW

The Story: Another 80's figure to sing SANDIE's praises was MORRISSEY, who – in his position as lead singer of up and coming indie mavericks The SMITHS – was instrumental in rejuvenating her career. In the Spring of '84, the ever youthful SHAW hit the Top 30 (and the indie charts for 'Rough Trade'!) with a cover of 'HAND IN GLOVE', MORRISSEY, MARR and Co backing her on a Top Of the Pops performance. This exposure led her to 'Polydor', for whom she released two 1986 singles, 'ARE YOU READY TO BE HEARTBROKEN' (penned by LLOYD COLE) and 'FREDERICK' (a PATTI SMITH cover). Towards the end of the decade she was back at 'Rough Trade' for a whole album, 'HELLO ANGEL' (1988), singing material by The SMITHS and even The JESUS & MARY CHAIN(!). One of the album's better tracks, 'NOTHING LESS THAN BRILLIANT' was issued as a single, although it didn't crack the charts for another six years by which time 'Virgin' had taken over the reins. In fact, her new label released a long overdue retrospective under the same title in 1994. A few years later, the cult icon of 60's pop helped set up London's Arts Clinic while regular TV appearances helped establish her as a minor celeb.

Best CD compilation: NOTHING LESS THAN BRILLIANT (*7)

		Rough Trade / not iss.
Apr 84.	(7") (RT 130) **HAND IN GLOVE. / I DON'T OWE YOU ANYTHING** (12"+=) (RTT 130) – Jeanne.	27 –
		Polydor / not iss.
May 86.	(7") (POSP 793) **ARE YOU READY TO BE HEARTBROKEN. / STEVEN (YOU DON'T EAT MEAT)** (12"+=) (POSPX 793) – Hand in glove.	68 –
Jul 86.	(7") (POSP 811) **FREDERICK. / GO JOHNNY GO** (12"+=) (POSPX 811) – Girl don't come.	
		Rough Trade / not iss.
Sep 88.	(7") (RT 220) **PLEASE HELP THE CAUSE AGAINST LONELINESS. / I WILL REMAIN (alt mix)** (12"+=/cd-s+=) (RTT 220/+CD) – Jeanne / Lover of the century.	
Oct 88.	(lp/c/cd) (ROUGH/+C/CD 110) **HELLO ANGEL** – Nothing less than brilliant / Take him / Hello angel / A girl called Johnny / Strange bedfellows / Please help the cause against loneliness / Hand in glove / Cool about you / Flesh and blood / Comrade in arms / I will remain.	
Nov 88.	(7") (RT 230) **NOTHING LESS THAN BRILLIANT. / LOVE PEACE** (12"+=/cd-s+=) (RTT 230/+CD) – I don't owe you anything / Where were you.	
		Virgin / not iss.
Nov 94.	(c-s) (VSC 1521) **NOTHING LESS THAN BRILLIANT / (THERE'S) ALWAYS SOMETHING THERE TO REMIND ME** (cd-s+=) (VSCDT 1521) – Are you ready to be heartbroken. (cd-s+=) (VSCDX 1521) – Comrade in arms.	66 –
Nov 94.	(cd/c) (VTCD 34) **NOTHING LESS THAN BRILLIANT** (compilation) – (There's) Always something there to remind me / Long live love / Girl don't come / Message understood / Nothing less than brilliant / Hand in glove / Are you ready to be heartbroken? / A girl called Johnny / I'll stop at nothing / Heaven knows I'm missing him now / You've not changed / Monsieur Dupont / I don't owe you anything / Anyone who had a heart (with B.E.F.) / Comrade in arms / Hello angel / Strange bedfellows / Words / Ev'ry time we say goodbye / Your time is gonna come / Frederick / Please help the cause against loneliness / Tomorrow / Nothing comes easy / Puppet on a string. (re-iss. Apr97 cd/c; CD/TC VIP 183)	64
—	SANDIE retired from solo work . . .	

SHELLEYAN ORPHAN

Formed: Bournemouth, England . . . 1980 by CAROLINE CRAWLEY and songwriter JEMAUR TAYLE. Sharing an enduring appreciation of the works of famous poet, Shelley, the duo took the group name from one of his works and set about conceiving a romantic musical vision of their own. Teaching themselves the rudiments of their chosen instruments, they subsequently recruited a crew of classical musicians upon their relocation to London in the early 80's. Following an unlikely support to feedback merchants The JESUS & MARY CHAIN, SHELLEYAN ORPHAN were signed up to 'Rough Trade', releasing a debut single, 'CAVALRY OF CLOUD', in '86. This was closely followed by the EVERYTHING BUT THE GIRL-esque vocal surges of 'ANATOMY OF LOVE' and a debut album, 'HELLEBORINE' (1987). Marrying the middle-England pastoral fantasy and string flourishes of NICK DRAKE to airy acoustic pop in the mould of the aforementioned EBTG, the record was an enchanting proposition utilising such classical instrumentation as oboe, cor Anglais, bassoon, cello and viola alongside lightly strummed guitars, violin etc. Two years on, 'CENTURY FLOWER' (1989) displayed a shift towards a more conventional style of songwriting while retaining the exotic flair which was their trademark. Yet despite some favourable noises from certain sections of the press and a high profile support slot to The CURE, SHELLEYAN ORPHAN never managed to rise above cult status, 'HUMROOT' (1993) being their last recording. A shame as current press darlings like The CARDIGANS and BELLE & SEBASTIAN possibly have a SHELLEYAN ORPHAN album tucked away in their collection somewhere.

Album rating: HELLEBORINE (*8) / HUMROOT (*6)

JEMAUR TAYLE – vocals, acoustic guitar / **CAROLINE CRAWLEY** – vocals, clarinet

		Rough Trade / Columbia
Sep 86.	(7") (RT 170) **CAVALRY OF CLOUD. / TANGLED PERPETUAL** (12"+=) (RTT 170) – One hundred hands (for strings).	
Apr 87.	(7") (RT 207) **ANATOMY OF LOVE. / HARMONY DRONE**	
—	duo with **DANNY THOMPSON** – double bass / **NICKY HOLLAND** – cor anglais / **STUART ELLIOT** – percussion / **PADDY BUSH** – mandolin, tambourine / **EMMA COLE** – flute / **BERNARD PARTRIDGE** – violin / **IAN JEWEL** – viola / **STEVEN ORTON** – cello / **THOMAS DAVEY** – oboe / **PRUDENCE WHITTAKER** – clarinet / **NICHOLAS HUNTER** – bassoon / **RUTH HOLDEN** – harp / **ANDREW POWELL** – harpsicord, piano / **RICHARD TOMES** – additional violin	
May 87.	(lp/c/cd) (ROUGH/+C/CD 97) <40545> **HELLEBORINE** – Helleborine / Seeking bread and Heaven / Melody of birth / Jeremiah / Anatomy of love / Midsummer pearls and plume / Epitaph ivy and woe / Blue black grape / One hundred hands / Calvary of cloud / Southern Bess – A field holler.	
—	duo with **DANNY THOMPSON** – double bass / **CHARLIE MORGAN + JIM RUSSELL** – drums / **JACKIE NORRIE** – violin / **KATIE WILKINSON + ANNETTE HALES** – viola / **MARTIN EVENS** – piano / **TONY ROBERTS** – flute / **GEOFF BLYTHE** – saxophone / **PAUL HOOKHAM** – percussion / **JACK EMBLOW** – accordion / **JEANETTE MURPHY** – French horn / **EMILY BURRIDGE + ROBERT IRVINE + ANNE-**	

Michelle SHOCKED

Born: KAREN MICHELLE JOHNSTON, 24 Feb'62, Gilmer, East Texas, USA. After a childhood spent moving around army bases with her stepfather, SHOCKED experienced a turbulent adolescence which included a spell in a psychiatric hospital (committed by her Mormon mother) and a stint as an anarcho-punk squatter in San Francisco, all grist for the songwriting mill (and inspiration for her adoption of the SHOCKED moniker) of this radical post-folk singer. Her break came in 1986 when she was talent-spotted at the Kerrville Folk Festival by 'Cooking Vinyl' bod, Pete Lawrence, the eagle eared Englishman recording an informal campfire-side set on a walkman. It was a break which SHOCKED was initially unsure about, however, the singer understandably suspicious of the machinations of the music industry. The recordings were eventually released in late '86 as 'THE TEXAS CAMPFIRE TAPES', MICHELLE no doubt, erm ... shocked (ouch!) to find herself at the top of the UK indie charts. Once again with much trepidation, the singer eventually relented to a deal with the massive 'Polygram' corporation, signing with 'London' in Britain, 'Mercury' in the States. In keeping with her fiercely held beliefs and constant striving for integrity, SHOCKED reportedly made sure that she retained some creative control, the singer vindicated by the critical and commercial success of her debut album, 'SHORT SHARP SHOCKED' (1988). As the title and cover (SHOCKED in a police stranglehold) might suggest, the record was a defiant rabble of engaging protest songs combining roots folk with rock and pop accessibility. Among the highlights were the lilting 'ANCHORAGE' and the affecting 'GRAFFITI LIMBO', an elegy for murdered street artist, Michael Stewart. While the record made the UK Top 40 and garnered a groundswell of support, a follow-up album, 'CAPTAIN SWING' (1989) was way off the mark, moving away from her lone acoustic approach in favour of more ambitious arrangements. While SHOCKED was criticised in some quarters for political preaching, her more hardcore fans thought the record wasn't radical enough. Casting these complaints aside, SHOCKED went off on a musical pilgrimage of sorts, touring America Woody Guthrie-style and recording with an array of respected roots musicians including TAJ MAHAL, POPS STAPLES, DOC WATSON and the brilliant UNCLE TUPELO. Issued as 'ARKANSAS TRAVELER' (1991), the set reclaimed some of the singer's lost critical ground although it failed to make much of an impact on the charts. Unhappy with the way she was being treated by her record label, SHOCKED subsequently sued the company and self-financed her next album, 'KIND HEARTED WOMAN' (1994), the record receiving a belated UK release two years later. With her work subsequently pressed for independent releases (i.e. 'ARTISTS MAKE LOVELY SLAVES' and 'GOOD TIMES'), it was indeed no surprise that MICHELLE went "indie" for her below par 2002 set, 'DEEP NATURAL'. • **Songwriters:** Writes all material and borrows some trad., except ZIP-A-DEE-DOO-DAH (Wrubel-Gilbert) / GOODNIGHT IRENE (Leadbelly).

Album rating: THE TEXAS CAMPFIRE TAPES (*7) / SHORT SHARP SHOCKED (*8) / CAPTAIN SWING (*5) / ARKANSAS TRAVELER (*7) / KIND HEARTED WOMAN (*5) / ARTISTS MAKES LOUSY SLAVES with Fiachnd O'Braondin (*5) / MERCURY POISE: 1988-1995 compilation (*6) / GOOD NEWS (*5) / DEEP NATURAL (*4)

MICHELLE SHOCKED – vocals, acoustic guitar

Cooking Vinyl / Mercury

Nov 86. (lp/c) (COOK/+C 002) <834581-1/-4> **THE TEXAS CAMPFIRE TAPES**
– 5 a.m. in Amsterdam / The secret admirer / The incomplete image / Who cares? / Down on St. Thomas St. / Fogtown / Steppin' out / The hepcat / Necktie / (Don't you mess around with) My little sister / The ballad of Patch eye & Meg / The secret to a long life (is knowing when it's time to go). *(cd-iss. Apr88+=' COOKCD 002)* – The chain smoker / Stranded in a limousine / Goodnight Irene. *(re-iss. Nov93 cd/c; same as US)*

Jun 87. (7") (FRY 002) **DISORIENTATED. / IF LOVE WAS A TRAIN**
(12"+=) (FRY 002T) – Chain smoker / Stranded in a limousine / Goodnight Irene.

—— now added numerous session people

London / Mercury

Aug 88. (lp/c)(cd) (CV LP/MC 1)<(834924-2)> **SHORT SHARP SHOCKED** — 33 / 73
– When I grow up / Hello Hopeville / Memories of East Texas / (Making the run to) Gladewater / Graffiti limbo / If love was a train / Anchorage / The L&N don't stop here anymore / V.F.D. / Black widow.

Sep 88. (7") (LON 193) **ANCHORAGE. / FOGTOWN** — 60 / -
(10"+=) (LONT 193) – Remodelling the Pentagon / Penny Evans (live).
(12"+=/cd-s+=) (LON X/CD 193) – Strawberry jam (live) / Penny Evans (live).

Nov 88. (7") <870611> **ANCHORAGE. / ('A'live)** — - / 66

Dec 88. (7") (LON 212) **IF LOVE WAS A TRAIN. / MEMORIES OF EAST TEXAS** — 63 / -
(12"+=) (LONX 212) – Graffiti limbo (live).
(cd-s+=) (LONCD 212) – V.F.D. / Jambouree queen.

Feb 89. (7") (LON 219) **WHEN I GROW UP. / 5 A.M. IN AMSTERDAM (live)** — 67 / -
(12"+=) (LONX 219) – Goodnight Irene.
(cd-s+=) (LONCD 219) – Camper crusade.

Nov 89. (lp/c/cd) <(838 878-1/-4/-2)> **CAPTAIN SWING** — 31 / 95
– God is a real estate developer / On the greener side / Silent ways / Sleep keeps me awake / The cement lament / (You don't mess around with) My little sister / Looks like Mona Lisa / Too little too late / Street corner ambassador / Must be luff.

Nov 89. (7"/c-s) (LON/+CS 245) **ON THE GREENER SIDE. / RUSSIAN ROULETTE**
(12"+=/cd-s+=) (LON X/CD 245) – The Titanic / Old paint.

Feb 90. (c-s) (LONCS 251) **(YOU DON'T MESS AROUND WITH) MY LITTLE SISTER / RUSSIAN ROULETTE**
(12"+=) (LONX 251) – Waters wide.

Mar 92. (7"/c-s) (LON/+CS 316) **COME A LONG WAY. / OVER THE WATERFALL (live)**
(cd-s+=) (LONCD 316) – Contest coming (cripple creek) / Jump Jim Crow.
(cd-s+=) (LOCDP 316) – Worth the weight (live) / Shaking hands (soldier's toy) (live).

Apr 92. (cd/c/lp) <(512 189-2/-4/-1)> **ARKANSAS TRAVELER** — 46 / Oct91
– 33 r.p.m. soul / Come a long way / Secret to a long life / Contest coming (Cripple Creek) / Over the waterfall / Shaking hands (soldier's joy) / Medley:-Jump Jim crow – Zip-a-dee-doo-dah / Hold me back / Strawberry jam / Prodigal daughter (Cotton-eyed Joe) / Blackberry blossom / Weaving way / Arkansas traveler / Woody's rag.

May 92. (7") (LON 321) **33 R.P.M. SOUL. / BLACKBERRY BLOSSOM (live)**
(cd-s+=) (LONCD 321) – Over the waterfall (live) / ('A'live).

Private-BMG / Private

Nov 96. (cd/c) <(01005 82145-2/-4)> **KIND HEARTED WOMAN** — Dec94
– Stillborn / Homestead / Winter wheat / Cold comfort / Eddie / Child like Grace / Fever breaks / Silver spoon / Hard way / No sign of rain.
(above was independently distributed in 1994)

not iss. / Independ.

1996. (cd; MICHELLE SHOCKED & FIACHND O'BRAONDIN) <#0001> **ARTISTS MAKE LOUSY SLAVES**
– Laundry day / Drip dry / Soul searching / New Orleans / Groove baby's lullaby / Last love / Can you see it in me / Only a prayer / Live and learn / Carrickfergus – The water is wide.

—— next with the ANOINTED EARLS

not iss. / Mood Swings

Mar 98. (cd) <162044-4WI-8049> **GOOD NEWS**
– Good news / Can't take my joy / Forgive to forget / Little Billie / What can I say? / Why do I get the feeling? / No wonder / You take the cake / Tabloid / Crying shame. *(+= hidden track)*

Mighty Sounds / Mighty Sounds

Sep 02. (cd) <(YTY 10012)> **DEEP NATURAL** — Apr02
– Joy / What can I say? / Why do I get the feeling? / Good news / Forgive to forget / That's so amazing / Peachfuzz / I know what you need / Can't take my joy / Little Billie / If not here / Moanin' dove / Hurricane burnin' down / Psalm / Go in peace.
(w/ free cd+=) **DUB NATURAL** – Go dub / I know what you dub / Match burns dub / DOD dub / House burns dub / Forget to dub / Why do I dub? / Draughts of Dublin / What dub? / Peachfuzz / Can't take my dub / Fat Brown snake dub / F2F dub.

– compilations, etc. –

Nov 96. (cd/c) *London;* <(532960-2/-4)> **MERCURY POISE: 1988-1995**
– On the greener side / Anchorage / Come along way / Quality of mercy / Street corner ambassador / Too little too late / If love was a train / When I grow up / Prodigal daughter / Over the waterfall / Holy spirit / Stillborn.

SHOCK HEADED PETERS (see under ⇒ BLAKE, Karl)

SHONEN KNIFE

Formed: Osaka, Japan ... 1981 by sisters ATSUKO and NAOKO YAMANO with fellow school student MICHIE NAKATANI. Punkette "kewpie-doll" pop heavily influenced by western culture rock and pop (like X-RAY SPEX meeting PHIL SPECTOR's RONETTES via FRANCOISE HARDY), the youthful looking trio released several albums throughout the 80's, finding their way onto many a Stateside turntable. The American interest was down to the efforts of CALVIN JOHNSON (of the BEAT HAPPENING), who had discovered them on their home turf and later distributed 1983's 'BURNING FARM' via his own 'K' label. 1986 saw the band's first bonafide US release in the shape of the album 'PRETTY LITTLE BAKA GUY', an eponymous compilation set following in 1990. KURT COBAIN, for one, was a big fan and the girls actually supported NIRVANA, subsequently moving to America around the same time. The Grunge era also saw a host of bands (including SONIC YOUTH and HOLE) paying tribute to the diminutive threesome via an album, 'Every Band Has A Shonen Knife Who Loves Them'. SHONEN KNIFE rounded off their most successful year to date with the festive frenzy, 'SPACE CHRISTMAS'. Subsequently signing to UK Creation off-shoot label, 'August' ('MCA-Victor' in the States), they issued 'LET'S KNIFE' towards

SHONEN KNIFE (cont)

the end of '92. Athough the press hype diminished, the girls kept plugging away with their trademark nursery school lyrics and day-glo buzz-pop via albums such as 'WE ARE VERY HAPPY YOU CAME' (1993), 'ROCK ANIMALS' (1994), 'BRAND NEW KNIFE' (1997) and 'HAPPY HOUR' (1998). • **Covered:** (LIVE IS LIKE A) HEAT WAVE (Martha & The Vandellas) / TOP OF THE WORLD (Carpenters) / PARADISE (Nilsson) / BOYS (Dixon-Farrell) / TILL THE END OF THE DAY (Kinks) / DON'T HURT MY LITTLE SISTER (Beach Boys) / DAYDREAM BELIEVER (hit; Monkees).

Album rating: PRETTY LITTLE BAKA GUY (*6) / SHONEN KNIFE compilation (*8) / 712 (*6) / LET'S KNIFE (*5) / WE ARE VERY HAPPY YOU CAME (*5) / ROCK ANIMALS (*4) / BRAND NEW KNIFE (*6) / HAPPY HOUR (*4)

NAOKO YAMANO (b.18 Dec'61) – vocals / **ATSUKO YAMANO** (b.22 Feb'60) – drums / **MICHIE NAKATANI** (b. 8 Oct'61) – bass

X.A.   not iss.

Aug 82. (ltd-c) **MINNA TANOSHIKU SHONEN KNIFE**   – Japan
– Banana leaf / Parrot polynesia / Man eating papaya / Saboten / Burning farm / Parallel woman / Angel's coming (live) / Spider (live) / I am a realist / Song of Crane / Tortoise brand pot cleaner / Planet X / Summertime boogie / Miracles.

Zero   K

Jul 83. (8"ep) **BURNING FARM**   – Japan
– Miracles / Parallel woman / Twist Barbie / Elephant pao pao / Tortoise brand pot scrubbing cleaner's theme / Animal song / A day at the factory / Burning farm. <cd-iss. 1995 on 'M.C.A.' Japan +=; > – Ukkari hachibei / I wanna be sedated.

May 84. (8"ep) **YAMA NO ATTCHAN**   – Jun85
– An angel has come / Cycling is fun / Elmer elevator / Banana leaf / Chinese song / Flying jelly attack / Cannibal papaya / Dali's sunflower / Insect collector / Bye bye. <cd-iss. 1995 on 'M.C.A.' Japan +=; > – Secret dance / Flying saucer attack.

Zero   Subversive

Jun 86. (8"m-lp) **PRETTY LITTLE BAKA GUY**   – Oct86
– Bear up bison / Summertime boogie / I wanna eat choco bars / Public bath / Devil house / Antonio baka guy / Ice cream day / Ah. Singapore / Riding on the rocket / Kappa ex. <US re-iss. Dec90 on 'Rockville' cd+=/c+=; 6053-2/-4> – LIVE IN JAPAN <cd-iss. 1995 on 'M.C.A.'+=; > – Fish parade / Cherry bomb.

not iss.   Gasatanka-Giant

May 90. (cd/c/lp) <6047-2/-4/-1> **SHONEN KNIFE** (compilation of BURNING FARM + YAMA NO ATTCHAN)

Seminal Twang   Rockville

Mar 91. (7") **LAZYBONE. / BLUE OYSTER CULT (Japanese version)**
Jul 91. (cd/c) <ROCK 6065-2/-4> **712**
– Shonen knife / Lazybone / Diet run / Blue Oyster Cult / Rain / The luck of the Irish / My favorite town / Faith healer / Redd Kross / White flag / Superstar / Expo '90 / Fruit loop dreams / The moon within / Baggs.
(above issued on 'Nippon Crown' in Japan)

Jul 91. (7"grey) <SP 108> **NEON ZEBRA. / BEAR UP BISON**
(above single issued for 'Sub Pop')

Nov 91. (7") (TWANG 9) **SPACE CHRISTMAS. / BEAR UP BISON**
(cd-s+=) (TWANG 9CD) – Christmas message '91.

Nov 92. (7") <6075-7> **SPACE CHRISTMAS. / CHRISTMAS MESSAGE '91**

August   Capitol

Oct 92. (cd/c/lp) (RUST 001 CD/MC/LP) <86638> **LET'S KNIFE**   Jan93
– Riding the rocket / Bear up bison / Twist Barbie / Tortoise theme 2 / Antonio baka guy / Ah Singapore / Flying jelly attack / Black bass / Cycling is fun / Watchin' girl / Tortoise theme 1 / Devil house / Insect collector / Burning farm.
(cd+=) – Space Christmas / Bear up bison / Mickey Way / Do the Bartman.

Nov 92. (7") (CAUG 001) **RIDING ON THE ROCKET. / NEON ZEBRA (English version)**
(12"/cd-s) (CAUG 001 T/CD) – ('A'side) / Milky Way / Burning farm (long version) / ('A'reprise).

Jan 93. (7") (CAUG 003) **GET THE WOW. / TWIST BARBIE**
(12"+=/cd-s+=) (CAUG 003 T/CD) – Fruit loop dreams / Don't hurt my little sister.
(cd-s) (CAUG 003CDL) – ('A'side) / Animal song / Ice cream city (John Pel session) / Neon zebra (English version).

Apr 93. (cd/lp) (RUST 004 CD/LP) **WE ARE VERY HAPPY YOU CAME** (live)
– Lazybone / Public bath / Goose steppin' mama / I wanna eat choco bars / Suzy is a headbanger / Boys / Redd Kross.

August   Virgin

Jan 94. (cd-ep) <38414> **BROWN MUSHROOMS / BUTTERFLY BOY / STRAWBERRY CREAM PUFF / TILL THE END OF THE DAY**
Jan 94. (cd/c) (RUST 009 CD/MC) <39063> **ROCK ANIMALS**
– Quavers / Concrete animals / Butterfly boy / Little tree / Catnip dream / Tomato head / Another day / Brown mushrooms / Johnny, Johnny, Johnny / Cobra versus mongoose / Music square.
May 94. (cd-s) <38433> **TOMATO HEAD** (mixes; Z-mix / Jazzy tomato head / Lemmy in there) / (Love is a) Heat wave).

M.C.A.   Big Deal

Sep 97. (d-cd) (MCD 80071) <9035> **BRAND NEW KNIFE**   Mar97
– Explosion! / Wind your spring / The perfect world / E.S.P. / Loop di loop / Wonder wine / Magic Joe / Fruit & vegetables / Tower of the sun / Keep on rockin' / Frogphobia / Buddha's face / One week. (re-iss. Mar99 on 'Big Deal'; BGD 9035) (lp-iss.Aug00; BGD 9035LP)

Big Deal   Big Deal

Nov 97. (cd-ep) <(BD 9047-2)> **EXPLOSION!**
– Explosion! / Explosion! / E.S.P. / Loop-di-loop / Wind your spring / One week. (re-iss. Mar99; same)
1998. (cd) <BD 9055> **HAPPY HOUR**
– Shonen knife planet / Konnichiwa / Cookie day / Hot chocolate / Sushi bar song / Fish eyes / Banana chips / Dolly / Jackalope / Gyoza / Catch your bus / People traps / His pet / Daydream believer.

not iss.   Orange

Aug 01. (cd-s) <70099> **ORENJI NO TAIYO / HERBS / TOP OF THE WORLD**   – Japan

– **compilations, others, etc.** –

May 94. (cd) *Tec Tones*; (19422) **KNIFE COLLECTORS**   – Japan
Mar 96. (cd) *Virgin*; <41414> **THE BIRDS AND THE B-SIDES**   – Japan
– (Love is like a) Heat wave / Gomi day / Top of the world / Ice cream city / Paradise / Little tree / Space Christmas / Fruit loop dreams / Boys / Till the end of the day / Elmer elevator / Don't hurt my little sister / Strawberry cream puff / Neon zebra / Lazybone / Public bath / I wanna eat choco bars / Redd Kross.
Apr 96. (cd) *Tec Tones*; (SHONEN) **FAN CLUB CD**   – Japan

SHOP ASSISTANTS

Formed: Edinburgh, Scotland... 1984 originally as BUBA & THE SHOP ASSISTANTS by DAVID KEEGAN, AGGI, SARAH KNEALE, ANN DONALD and LAURA McPHAIL. Following an extremely limited debut single, 'SOMETHING TO DO', on the 'Villa 21' label, the band (now without AGGI who'd been replaced by ALEX TAYLOR) released a more widely distributed follow-up, 'ALL DAY LONG' on the 'Subway Organisation' imprint. Amid increasing critical acclaim from the London-based music press, The SHOP ASSISTANTS topped the indie charts with third single, 'SAFETY NET', the first release on KEEGAN's '53rd & 3rd' label. 1986 proved to be a pivotal year as the band signed to Chrysalis offshoot 'Blue Guitar' and released their eponymous debut album, in addition contributing the delicate strum of 'IT'S UP TO YOU' to the NME's C86 tape and the noisier retro-pop of 'TRAIN FROM KANSAS CITY' to Sounds magazine's 'Showcase' sampler. Despite their ringing, girlish charm, mainstream chart success wasn't on the cards and the band fell apart the following year with TAYLOR going off to form MOTORCYCLE BOY. A subsequent reformation in 1990 was decidedly low key, the band releasing material on the capital's 'Avalanche' label. With KEEGAN later joining The PASTELS on a full-time basis, it seems like the band have finally shut up shop for good. • **Trivia:** In the early 90's, the 1986 line-up sued their management company, 'Globeshire', for being unforthcoming with a 5-figure royalty share. Due to neglect, the band had to pay over a fee of £1,000 to the taxman as they weren't registered for VAT.

Album rating: THE SHOP ASSISTANTS (*6)

AGGI – vocals (of JUNIPER BELL BER) / **DAVID KEEGAN** – guitar / **SARAH KNEALE** – bass / **LAURA MacPHAIL** – drums / plus guests **STEPHEN PASTEL** – producer, b.vocals / **ANN DONALD** – drums (later of FIZZBOMBS)

Villa 21   not iss.

Nov 84. (7"; as BUBA & THE SHOP ASSISTANTS) (002) **SOMETHING TO DO. / DREAMING BACKWARDS**

—— **ALEX(ANDRA) TAYLOR** – vocals; repl. AGGI who later joined The SUGARCUBES

Subway   not iss.

Aug 85. (7"ep) (SUBWAY 1) **ALL DAY LONG / ALL THAT EVER MATTERED. / IT'S UP TO YOU / SWITZERLAND**

53rd & 3rd   not iss.

Feb 86. (7"/12") (AGARR 001/+12) **SAFETY NET. / SOMEWHERE IN CHINA / ALMOST MADE IT**

Blue Guitar   not iss.

Sep 86. (7") (AZUR 2) **I DON'T WANNA BE FRIENDS WITH YOU. / LOOK BACK**
(12"+=) (AZURX 2) –

Nov 86. (lp/c) (AZ/AZZAZ LP 2) **THE SHOP ASSISTANTS**
– I don't wanna be friends with you / All day long / Before I wake / Caledonian road / All that ever mattered / Fixed grin / Somewhere in China / Train from Kansas City / Home again / Seems to be / All of the time / What a day to die / Nature lover. (cd-iss. Jun97 as 'WILL ANYTHING HAPPEN' on 'Overground'; OVER 62CD)

—— disbanded early 1987; ALEX joined MOTORCYCLE BOY. Re-formed late '89, McPHAIL now on bass + **MARGARITA** – drums

Avalanche   not iss.

Jan 90. (7"flexi-ep) (AGAP 001C) **HERE IT COMES / I'D RATHER BE WITH YOU / YOU TRIP ME UP / THE OTHER ONE**
(7"flexi-box-ep) (AGAP 001B) – (first 2 tracks) / Look out / Adrenalin.

May 90. (7"/c-s) (AGAP 003/+MC) **BIG 'E' POWER. / SHE SAID**
(12"+=/cd-s+=) (AGAP 003 T/CD) – One more time / ('A'version).

—— split after above and KEEGAN joined The PASTELS full-time

SHRIEKBACK

Formed: Kentish Town, London, England... 1981 by ex-GANG OF FOUR bassist, DAVE ALLEN and former XTC vocalist/keyboard player, BARRY ANDREWS. Subsequently recruiting CARL MARSH, the trio set about creating sinuous, experimental CAN/POP GROUP-esque white-boy funk, debuting with the 'TENCH' EP on indie label 'Y Records' in 1982. This was followed by 'SEXTHINKONE' and 'MY SPINE (IS THE BASS LINE)', the latter a compelling fix of reverberating, contorting rhythm alchemised from the same uncompromising, instinctive ingredients the RED HOT CHILI PEPPERS would utilise – if not with quite the same complex finesse – a few years later. A further single 'WORKING ON THE GROUND', another version of 'LINED UP' and an album, 'CARE' – picked up by 'Warners' in America – appeared over the next 18 months and 'Arista' were quick to secure their signatures. Now a quartet following the addition of MARTYN BARKER, the resulting 'JAM SCIENCE' (1984) album introduced a more synth-heavy SHRIEKBACK sound together with female backing vocals, losing a bit of the lean hunger of their earlier work but attracting a wider audience for singles 'HAND ON MY HEART' and 'MERCY DASH'. Bonafide chart success remained elusive, however, and after 'OIL AND GOLD' (1985), MARSH jumped ship while the

SHRIEKBACK (cont)

remaining members moved on to 'Island' for the piano-based 'BIG NIGHT MUSIC' (1987). On top of losing the vital MARSH/ALLEN chemistry, the band were dealt a further blow with the departure of the latter to form KING SWAMP. Although they limped on for 1988's 'GO BANG' with TACKHEAD man DOUG WIMBISH, SHRIEKBACK reached its natural conclusion at the turn of the decade, ANDREWS, ALLEN and BARKER later reuniting and resurrecting the SHRIEKBACK name for 1992's 'SACRED CITY'. Messers ANDREWS, BARKER and (ex-DAMNED man) LU EDMONDS again treated us to another SHRIEKBACK reunion of sorts courtesy of 'NAKED APES & POND LIFE' (2000), this time recordings stemming from 1995! What's "Lined Up" next lads?

Album rating: CARE (*5) / JAM SCIENCE (*5) / OIL AND GOLD (*5) / BIG NIGHT MUSIC (*5) / THE INFINITE – THE BEST OF SHRIEKBACK compilation (*7) / SACRED CITY (*4) / NAKED APES & POND LIFE (*4)

CARL MARSH – vocals (ex-OUT ON BLUE SIX) / **BARRY ANDREWS** – keyboards, vocals (ex-XTC, ex-LEAGUE OF GENTLEMEN, ex-IGGY POP, ex-RESTAURANT FOR DOGS, ex-Solo Artist) / **DAVE ALLEN** – bass (ex-GANG OF FOUR)

Y Records / Y America

Jun 82. (12"ep) (Y 21T) <YUSA 4> **TENCH EP**
– Sexthinkone / A kind of fascination / All the Greek boys (do the handwalk) / Accretions / Moth loop / Here comes my hand: clap.

Jun 82. (7") (Y 22) <YUSA 3> **SEXTHINKONE. / HERE COMES MY HAND: CLAP**

Sep 82. (7"/12") (Y 27/+T) **MY SPINE (IS THE BASS LINE). / TINY BIRDS**

Feb 83. (7") (Y 102) **LINED UP / LEPAX LEGOMENA**
(12"+=) – ('A' instrumental).

Y Records / Warners

Mar 83. (lp) (YLP 502) <23874> **CARE** Jun83
– Lined up / Clear trails / Hapax legomena / Petulant / Lines from the library / Brink of collapse / Sway / Madness into method / Evaporation / Accretions.

May 83. (7") (Y 104) **WORKING ON THE GROUND. / CLOSEWORK**
(12"+=) (YT 104) – Nightwork (dance).

Aug 83. (7") (Y 106) **LINED UP (remix). / MY SPINE (IS THE BASS LINE)**
(12"+=) (YT 106) – Madness into method (planet mix) / Accretions (monstrous dance mix).

— added **MARTYN BARKER** – drums / live only **PEDRO ORITZ** – percussion

Arista / Island

Jul 84. (7"/7"pic-d) (SHR K/PD 1) **HAND ON MY HEART. / NERVE**
(12"+=) (SHRK 12-1) – Suck.
(12"+=) (SHRK 22-1) – Cloud of nails / Mistah Linn – he's dead.

Aug 84. (lp/c) (206/406 416) **JAM SCIENCE** 85
– Hand on my heart / Newhome / Achtung / Partyline / Midnight maps / Mercy dash / Under the lights / My careful hands / Suck / Hubris.

Sep 84. (7") (SHRK 2) **MERCY DASH. / GATED JOY**
(12"+=) (SHRK 12-2) – Bricks and whistles.
(12"pic-d) (SHRK 22-2) – ('A'mix) / Hand on my heart / Jumping on the ribcage with the digital Rasta / Suck / Cloud of nails / Pump up a storm.

May 85. (7") (SHRK 3) **NEMESIS. / SUCK (live)**
(d7"+=) (FSHRK 3) – Mothloop (live) / Feelers (live).
(12"+=) (SHRK 12-3) – ('A' version).

Jun 85. (lp/c) (207/407 206) <842882-1/-4> **OIL AND GOLD**
– Malaria / Everything that rises must converge / Fish below the ice / This big hush / Faded flowers / Nemesis / Only thing that shines / Health and knowledge and wealth and power / Hammerheads / Coelacanth.

Sep 85. (7") (SHRK 4) **FISH BELOW THE ICE. / COELACANTH**
(d7"+=/12"+=) (SHRK D/12-4) – All lined up / My spine (is the bass line).

— **MIKE COZZI** – guitars; repl. MARSH who went solo (in April '92, his HAPPYHEAD issued an album, 'GIVE HAPPYHEAD', for 'Atlantic')

— guests incl. **STEVE HALLIWELL** – keyboards / **WENDY + SARAH PARTRIDGE** – backing vocals

Island / Island

Dec 86. (7") (IS 314) **GUNNING FOR THE BUDDHA. / BLUDGEONED**
(12"+=) (12IS 314) – Black light trap.

Jan 87. (lp/c/cd) (ILPS/ICT/CID 9849) <90552> **BIG NIGHT MUSIC**
– Underwaterboys / Exquisite / The reptiles and I / Sticky jazz / Cradle song / Black light trap / Gunning for the buddha / Running on the rocks / Shining path / Pretty little thing.

— when DAVE ALLEN returned to GANG OF FOUR, the line-up comprised ANDREWS, BARKER, COZZI and The PATRIDGE sisters

Jul 88. (7") (IS 343) **GET DOWN TONIGHT. / BIG FUN**
(12"+=) (12IS 343) – Big fun (acid house mix).

Nov 88. (lp/c/cd) (ILPS/ICT/CID 9910) <90949> **GO BANG!**
– Intoxication / Shark walk / Over the wire / New man / Nighttown / Go bang! / Big fun / Get down tonight / Dust and a shadow. *(cd re-iss. 1989; IMCD 27)*

— disbanded in the late 80's, ANDREWS worked on a few low-key projects before re-forming the group in 1992

World Domination / Capitol

Sep 92. (cd-ep) <15899> **THE BASTARD SONS OF ENOCH (Enochian operation) / BELOW (deep structure) / THE BASTARD SONS OF ENOCH (squeaky sons of Enoch mix)**

Feb 94. (cd) (SHRIEK 1CD) <98780> **SACRED CITY** Sep92
– Signs / Psycho drift / The bastard sons of Enoch / (Open up your) Filthy heart to me / Exquisite corpse / Below / Beatles zebra crossing / Hymn to the local gods / Every force evolves a form / 3 a.m.

— **BARRY ANDREWS + MARTYN BARKER + LU EDMONDS** plus **MARK RAUDVA + SIMON EDWARDS** (bass, percussion)

Mauve / Mushroom

Feb 00. (cd) (CDMAUVE 001) <MUSH 32173> **NAKED APES & POND LIFE**
– Stimulate the beaded hamster / Pond life / Hostage / Invisible rays / Claxon bolus / Massive custard / Jp8 / Unsong / Berlin / Baby lion / Everything's on fire / Keep-net Stevenson / String, sedatives, weaponry / Anal piss-machine.

– compilations, etc. –

Mar 84. (lp/c) Kaz; (KAZLP 1) **THE INFINITE (THE BEST OF SHRIEKBACK)**
– Lined up / Clear trails / Accretions / Sway / Into method / My spine (is the bass line) / Mothloop / Sexthinkone / Evaporation / A kind of fascination / Working on the ground. *(c-iss.Oct85; KAZMA 1) (cd-iss. Dec86; KAZCD 1)*

May 88. (lp/c/cd) Kaz; (KAZ LP/MC/CD 5) **EVOLUTION – BEST OF SHRIEKBACK VOL.2**
– Nemesis / Fish below the ice / Hand on my heart / Newhome / Despite dense weed / Midnight maps / Mercy dash / Malaria / Under the lights / My careful hands / Nerve / Lines from the library.

Apr 90. (cd/c/lp) Island; (CID/ICT/ILPS 9960) **THE BEST OF SHRIEKBACK**
– Underwaterboys / Exquisite / The reptiles and I / Sticky jazz / Cradle song / Black light trap / Gunning for the buddha / Running on the rocks / Shining path / Pretty little thing.

Jul 94. (d-cd) Essential; (ESDCD 217) **NATURAL HISTORY – THE VERY BEST OF SHRIEKBACK**
– Lined up / Clear trails / Accretions / Sway / Madness into method / My spine (is the bass line) / Mothloop / Sexthinkone / Evaporation / A kind of fascination / Working on the ground / Nemesis / Hand on my heart / Newhome / Despite dense weed / Midnight maps / Mercy dash / Malaria / Under the lights / My careful hands / Nerve / Lines from the library / Fish below the ice. *(re-mast.Jun00; ESACD 899)*

Sep 94. (cd) Arista; (07822 22636-2) **PRIESTS AND KANNIBALS: THE BEST OF SHRIEKBACK**
– Nemesis / Hammerheads / All lined up / My spine (is the bass line) / Hand on my heart / Achtung / Mercy dash / Suck / Health and knowledge and wealth and power / Nerve / Only thing that shines / Coelacanth / Nemesis (arch deviant) / Cloud of nails (pump up a storm) / Mercy dash (extended) / Fish below the ice.

Apr 01. (cd) Weatherbox; (MAUVE 002) **ABERRATIONS 1981-1984**

SHRUBS

Formed: Watford, England … mid '85 initially as the KEVIN STAPLES BAND by part-time STUMP "singer", NICK HOBBS, along with JULIAN HATTON, MICHAEL RICKETS, PHIL ROBERTS and JOHN BENTLEY. One of the noisier bands to feature on NME's C-86 V/A compilation, The SHRUBS contributed the track, 'BULLFIGHTER'S BONES', an ear-shredding clatter of loping, discordant fret abuse on the brink of sonic collapse; JOHN LYDON fronting the POP GROUP comes to mind. One of several bands to sign for the 'Ron Johnson' imprint (A WITNESS, MACKENZIES, BIG FLAME, etc), they debuted in their own right with summer '86's appropriately titled 12" EP, 'FULL STEAM INTO BRAINSTORM'. After PHIL moved on to pastures new with The CREEPERS (i.e. MARC RILEY), his position was taken by STEVE BROCKLEY who joined in time for the 'BLACKMAILER' EP and 1987's long-player, 'TAKE ME ASIDE FOR A MIDNIGHT HARANGUE'. A year later, their own label, 'Public Domain', was home to swansong set, 'VESSELS OF THE HEART'.

Album rating: TAKE ME ASIDE FOR A MIDNIGHT HARANGUE (*6) / VESSELS OF THE HEART (*4)

NICK HOBBS – vocals (also of STUMP) / **JULIAN HATTON** – guitar / **MICHAEL RICKETS** – guitar / **PHIL ROBERTS** – bass / **JOHN BENTLEY** – drums

Ron Johnson / not iss.

Jul 86. (12"ep) (ZRON 10) **FULL STEAM INTO BRAINSTORM**
– Black saloons / The dealer / Bullfighter's bones / Carbreaker / Dead teachers / Warm sea.

— **STEVE BROCKLEY** – bass; repl. PHIL who joined (MARC RILEY &) THE CREEPERS

Dec 86. (12"ep) (ZRON 17) **BLACKMAILER**
– Blackmailer / River of toads / Assassin / Animal.

— **MARK GREBBY** – bass (ex-SPLAT!) repl. STEVE

Jun 87. (lp) (ZRON 23) **TAKE ME ASIDE FOR A MIDNIGHT HARANGUE**
– Mysterious places / Luke / Fashion show / Middle men / Claykiln mouth / Blackmailer's heartache / Rivers of toads flow forever / Sinister missions / John corpse / Hail chauffeurs / Serial revelry / Farmers / Edith / Albert Ross.

Public Domain / not iss.

Sep 88. (12"ep) (DOM 001) **ANOTHER AGE (live)**

Nov 88. (lp/c/cd) (DOM 002/+CD) **VESSELS OF THE HEART**
– Papa chaperon / Cole / Resurrection chain / Ballet gorilla / Cash register brain / Mass mental (long abusive rental) / Villa burgher / Shawl blight zone / Myth night / King Urn / Sullen days are over / Mistress of the moral ground.

— split after above

SIDDLEYS

Formed: Ladbroke Grove, London, England … April 1986 by JOHNNY JOHNSON and band(wagon), ALLAN KINGDOM, ANDREW BROWN and PHIL GOODMAN, all answering an ad in a Rough Trade records store. Following a debut gig in December that year, The SIDDLEYS released a low-key one-sided/split flexi-disc, 'WHEREVER YOU GO'; all the rage during this C-86 period. The 'Medium Cool' imprint were on hand for their next showing, 'WHAT WENT WRONG THIS TIME?', a twee-pop number playlisted by

SIDDLEYS (cont)

John Peel. However, GOODMAN was now concentrating on a jazz-styled outfit and his place was taken, at first by DEAN LEGGITT, and then more permanently by DAVID CLYNCH. 'SUNSHINE THUGGERY' – released for 'Sombrero' records in October 1988 – was to be their last outing as 4th single-to-be, 'YOU GET WHAT YOU DESERVE', was shelved. A subsequent cover of Edison Lighthouse's 'LOVE GROWS (WHERE MY ROSEMARY GOES)' (from the anti-Poll Tax compilation 'Alvin Lives (In Leeds)'), did little to re-establish the band, although their own posthumous collection, 'SLUM CLEARANCE' (2001), has set the record straight.

Album rating: SLUM CLEARANCE compilation (*6)

JOHNNY JOHNSON – vocals, guitar, piano / **ALLAN KINGDOM** – guitar / **ANDREW BROWN** – bass / **PHIL GOODMAN** – drums

	Sha La La Ba Ba Ba	not iss.
May 87. (7"flexi) *(006)* **WHEREVER YOU GO** / (other by RESERVE)	□	-

	Medium Cool	not iss.
Jul 87. (7"m) *(MC 005)* **WHAT WENT WRONG THIS TIME?** / **NO NAMES . . .** / **MY FAVOURITE WET WEDNESDAY AFTERNOON**	□	-

— **DAVID CLYNCH** – drums; repl. DEAN LEGGITT who repl. GOODMAN

	Sombrero	not iss.
Aug 88. (12"ep) *(SOMBRERO 3)* **SUNSHINE THUGGERY**	□	-
– Sunshine thuggery / Are you still evil when you're sleeping? / Falling off my feet again / Bible bruising.		

— split late in '89

– **compilations, etc.** –

Jul 01. (cd) *Matinee; (matcd 005) / Clarendon; <W6 1CD>* **SLUM CLEARANCE**
– My favourite wet Wednesday afternoon / You get what you deserve / When I grow up I'll be a god / Theft / Sunshine thuggery / Are you still evil when you're sleeping? / Love with blood / What went wrong this time? / No names . . . / Bedlam on the mezzanine / Bribes and bruises / Falling off my feet again / Wherever you go / Something almost brilliant happened last night / Every day of the week / I wish I was good.

SID PRESLEY EXPERIENCE (see under ⇒ GODFATHERS)

SILOS

Formed: New York City, New York, USA . . . 1985 by WALTER SALAS-HUMARA and BOB RUPE, both veterans of the Florida alt-rock scene with outfits such as the VULGAR BOATMEN and the BOBS respectively. Adding MARY ROWELL and the first in a series of fill-in drummers, JOBS ROSS, the duo completed their self-financed debut album, 'ABOUT HER STEPS', a promising set of retro influenced alternative roots-rock. 1987 saw the band turn the corner critically with the independently released 'CUBA', a much loved collection of earthy Americana that subsequently led to The SILOS being farmed out to 'R.C.A.'. The turn of the decade witnessed their major label debut, an eponymous album that didn't quite harvest any mainstream sales. With RUPE bailing out for GUTTERBALL and CRACKER, WALTER was left to plough his own furrow, alternately recording under his own name, as The SILOS or a combination of both. With The SILOS operating on a strictly low-key basis, loyal fans were tested with two average album efforts courtesy of 'HEATER' (1998) and 'LASER BEAM NEXT DOOR' (2001). • **Covered:** I'M STRAIGHT (Jonathan Richman).

Album rating: ABOUT HER STEPS (*5) / CUBA (*7) / THE SILOS (*6) / HASTA LA VICTORIA! (*4) / SUSAN ACROSS THE OCEAN (*5) / ASK THE DUST compilation (*5) / LONG GREEN BOAT (*5) / HEATER (*5) / LASER BEAM NEXT DOOR (*4) / Walter Salas-Humara: LAGARTIJA (*5) / LEAN (*5) / RADAR (*5)

WALTER SALAS-HUMARA (b.21 Jun'61, New York City) – vocals, guitar (of VULGAR BOATMEN) / **BOB RUPE** (b.16 Sep'56. Michigan) – vocals, guitar (of the BOBS) / **MARY ROWELL** (b. 6 Sep'58, Newport, Vermont) – violin / **JOBS ROSS** – drums

	not iss.	Record Collect
Aug 85. (lp) *<RC 21>* **ABOUT HER STEPS**	-	□
– Shine it down / 4 wanted signs / Susan / Start the clock / A few hundred thank you's / Now that I've lost you / Seeing blue / Heart & soul. *(UK-iss.Dec87 on Dead Man's Curve'; DMC 020)*		
Jan 87. (cd-ep) *<RC 23>* **TENNESSEE FIRE / MAYBE EVERYTHING / GET BACK MY NAME / START THE CLOCK**	-	□

— now without ROSS

	Ediesta	Watermelon
May 87. (lp) *(CALCLP 021) <1022>* **CUBA**	□	□
– Tennessee fire / She lives up the street / For always / Margaret / Mary's getting married / Memories / Just this morning / Going round / It's alright / All falls away / Get back my name / Maybe everything / Head party / Hook in my lip / Tennessee fire #2. *(cd-iss. Jan88; CALC 021CD) (cd-iss. Jun94 & Aug99 on 'Normal'; NORMAL 123CD)*		

— now without ROWELL, although she did return occasionally after below set

	not iss.	R.C.A.
Feb 90. (cd/lp) *<2051-2R/-1R>* **THE SILOS**	-	□
– Caroline / Picture of Helen / Commodore Peter / Anyway you choose me / Maybe everything / I'm over you / Take my country back / Out of town / Don't talk that way / The only story I tell / Porque no / Here's to you.		

— now without RUPE who went on to work with GUTTERBALL and CRACKER

the band was now basically WALTER + session people. SALAS-HUMARA also moonlighted with ALEJANDRO ESCOVEDO (ex-RANK & FILE, ex-TRUE BELIEVERS) and MIKE HALL (of WILD SEEDS) in a one-off album project with The SETTERS.

	Normal	Watermelon
May 93. (cd) *(NORMAL 143CD) <1023>* **HASTA LA VICTORIA!**	□	□
– Miles away / All I know is your name / Your last life / My big car / Nobody but you / All night / Henrietta / Sometimes when I come over / Find someone / All Spring all Summer / Try tomorrow / Find a way. *(re-iss. Aug99; same)*		
May 94. (cd) *(NORMAL 163CD) <1021>* **DIABLO** <US-title 'SUSAN ACROSS THE OCEAN'>	□	Mar94
– Let's take some drugs and drive around / Upside down instead / Shaking all over the place / All she wrote / Wanna ride / Susan across the ocean / Change the locks / The sounds next door / Start to burn / Nothing's gonna last / I'm straight / Fallen angel. *(re-iss. Aug99; same)*		

	Normal	Checkered Past
Aug 98. (cd) *(NORMAL 218CD) <010>* **HEATER**	□	□
– Prison song / Northern lights / Thanks a million / Eleanora / Angels / Front porch / Arms of the sea / I like you / Stoplight / Mom out dancing / Cold hands of fate / Away. *(re-iss. Aug99; same)*		

	Blue Rose	Checkered Past
May 01. (cd/d-lp) *(BLU DP/LP 0242) <022>* **LASER BEAM NEXT DOOR**	□	Apr01
– Satisfied / Drunken moon / Sangre y lagrimas / Where ya been / I believe / The title of this song / Four on the floor / One world / Disfrute / Jean-Marie / Wooky do.		

– **compilations, etc.** –

Jun 95. (cd; The SILOS / WALTER SALAS-HUMARA) *Normal; (NORMAL 166CD) / Watermelon; <1024>* **ASK THE DUST: RECORDINGS 1980-1988**
– Shine it down / 4 wanted signs / Susan / A few hundred thank you's / Now that I've lost you / Seeing blue / Heart + soul / Carol / About her steps / Two voices / September / Cuba / Promises / Bridge / You look like Sheila / Don't go home / Nobody's business / Heartbeat / O' fat bass / Thinking about you tonight. *(re-iss. Aug99; same)*

Jun 97. (cd; WALTER SALAS-HUMARA / The SILOS) *Last Call; <301833>* **LONG GREEN BOAT**
– All falls away / Commodore Peter / Two voices / Just this morning / I'm over you / You look like Sheila / Margaret / Shine it down / Miles away / Your last life / Tennessee fire / Find a way / September / Let's take some drugs and drive around.

Sep 01. (cd) *Return To Sender; (RTS 33)* **BARCELONA (live)**
– Eleanor / Porque no / Commodore Peter / Margaret / Find a way / All spring all summer / Miles away / My big car / Get out / Stoplight / I'm over you / Susan across the ocean.

Oct 01. (cd) *Discmedia; (DM 471)* **NUESTRA VIDA**

WALTER SALAS-HUMARA

	Rough Trade	Record Collect
Apr 90. (lp/c/cd) *(ROUGH 144/+C/CD) <51>* **LAGARTIJA**	□	Nov88
– Carol / About her steps / Two voices / September / Cuba / Promises / Bridge / You look like Sheila / Don't go home / Wide open.		

	Return To Sender	Watermelon
Jul 94. (cd) *(RTS 9)* **LEAN**	□	□
– Hold on / The sounds next door / Matgaret / Caroline / All she wrote / It hurts / The only story I fell / Find a way / Upside down instead / Susan across the ocean / Going around / Tennessee fire. *(re-iss. Aug99; same)*		
Oct 95. (cd) *<1044>* **RADAR**	-	□
– Three, two, one and more / Be honest with me / Evangeline / Letter to send / Light from the box / Star / One more dance / I won, you won / Rejuvenation / Ride / Get out.		

SINK (see under ⇒ STUPIDS)

SIR HORATIO (see under ⇒ A CERTAIN RATIO)

SISTER DOUBLE HAPPINESS

Formed: San Francisco, California, USA . . . 1986 by two former members of The DICKS, namely LYNN PERKO and GARY FLOYD. This semi-legendary Texan politico-punk act debuted on a shared album, 'LIVE AT RAULS' with The BIG BOYS, before finally unleashing two further sets, 'KILL FROM THE HEART' (1983) and 'THESE PEOPLE' (1985). Having subsequently split, they teamed up with BEN COHEN and MIKEY DONALDSON, SISTER DOUBLE HAPPINESS initiating their crusade in 1988 with an eponymous album on L.A. indie label, 'S.S.T.'. Carrying on the blues/punk spirit of the DICKS, the record's rawhide intensity and bludgeoning, blistering hard rock'n'roll was convincingly carried off by the gravel-gargling vocals of GARY FLOYD, the overall effect sufficiently impressive to attract 'Warners' subsidiary, 'Reprise'. Disappointingly, the band's belated major label debut, 'HEART & MIND' (featuring guests JOHN CALE and RODDY BOTTUM), failed to capture their trademark piledriving power and by the time of the record's 1992 UK release, DONALDSON had been replaced by JEFF PALMER. FLOYD and Co were freed from the constraints of a big budget studio with 'UNCUT' (1993) – released on 'Dutch East India' – and went for broke on the blues wailing, harmonica-huffing 'HORSEY WATER' (1994), released on 'Sub Pop'. FLOYD had already issued a 'Glitterhouse' solo set, 'WORLD OF TROUBLE', a month previously and following the subsequent demise of SISTER DOUBLE HAPPINESS, would go on to release 'BROKEN ANGELS' (1995) as The GARY FLOYD BAND.

Album rating: SISTER DOUBLE HAPPINESS (*7) / HEART AND MIND (*6) / UNCUT (*6) / HORSEY WATER (*6) / Dicks: KILL FROM THE HEART (*5) / THESE PEOPLE (*5)

DICKS

GARY FLOYD – vocals / **GLEN** – guitar, bass / **BUXF** – bass, vocals, guitar / **PAT** – drums

		not iss.	Selfless
1981.	(m-lp; shared with the BIG POYS) **LIVE AT RAUL'S** (live)	–	S.S.T.

		S.S.T.	S.S.T.
Oct 83.	(lp) <(SST 017)> **KILL FROM THE HEART**		

– Anti-Klan (part 1) / Rich daddy / No Nazi's friend / Marilyn Buck / Kill from the heart / Little boys' feet / Pigs run wild / Bourgeois fascist pig / Anti-Klan (part 2) / Purple haze / Right wing – White wing / Dicks can'd swim: 1. Cock jam – 2. Razor blade dance.

— **LYNN PERKO** – drums; repl. PAT

		Alternative Tentacles	Alternative Tentacles
Jul 85.	(lp) <(VIRUS 43)> **THESE PEOPLE**		

– The police (force) / Off duty sailor / Executive dive / Sidewalk begging / Lost and divided / Dead in a motel room / Cities are burning / Doctor daddy / Decent and clean / Legacy of man / Little rock'n'roller / George Jackson.

— disbanded the following year and evolved into (see below)

– compilations, etc. –

Jun 93. (7"; shared with the BIG BOYS) Selfless; (SFLS 10-7) **LIVE AT RAUL'S**
Apr 97. (cd) Alternative Tentacles; <(VIRUS 200CD)> **DICKS 1980-1986**

SISTER DOUBLE HAPPINESS

GARY FLOYD – vocals / **BEN COHEN** (ex-POLKACIDE) – guitar / **MIKEY DONALDSON** – bass / **LYNN PERKO** – drums

		S.S.T.	S.S.T.
Jul 88.	(lp) <(SST 162)> **SISTER DOUBLE HAPPINESS**		

– Sister double happiness / Freight train / Let me in / Cry like a baby / On the beach / Poodle dog / It's our life / I tried / Sweet talker / Get drunk and die / You don't know me. (re-iss. May93 cd/c; SST 162 CD/C)

— **JEFF PALMER** – bass; repl. DONALDSON

		Reprise	Reprise
Feb 92.	(cd-s) <40356> **HEY KIDS / WHEEL'S A' SPINNING / SWEET-TALKER (acoustic) / LIGHTNING STRUCK**	–	
May 92.	(cd/c) <(7599 26657-2/-4)> **HEART AND MIND**		Apr91

– Bobby Shannon / Ain't it a shame / Exposed to you / Sweet talker / You don't know me / The sailor song / Dark heart / Heart and mind / Hey kids / I'm drowning / Don't worry / You for you.

		Sub Pop	Dutch East
Dec 92.	(7") <SP 77> **DON'T WORRY. / WHEELS A' SPINNING**		–
Jun 93.	(7") <(SP 104-276)> **DO WHAT YOU GOTTA DO. /**		
	(cd-s+=) <(SPCD 104-276)> –		
Jul 93.	(lp/cd) <(SP/+CD 105-277)> <2029> **UNCUT**		Jun93

– San Diego / Will you come / Ashes / Whipping song / Doesn't make sense / Honey don't / Keep the city clean / Do what you gotta do / Where do we run / No good for you / Lightnin' / Louise.

— **MILES MONTALBANO** – bass + **DANNY ROMAN** – guitar; repl. PALMER

		Sub Pop	Sub Pop
Nov 94.	(lp/cd) <(SP/+CD 137-337)> **HORSEY WATER**		Oct94

– Jack freak / Gurden jail / Bad line / Holly said / Waiting for anyone / A+R man / Heart of ice / Who's been fucking you / Sweet home California / Everything will be alright tomorrow.

— split after above, GARY had already recorded a solo set

– compilations, etc. –

Dec 99. (cd) Innerstate; <(INNER 7006)> **A STONE'S THROW FROM LOVE: LIVE & ACOUSTIC AT THE GREAT AMERICAN MUSIC HALL 6/17/92**
– No good for you / Here I go again / Maybe / You for you / Lightning struck / Absense / The sailor song / Running back again / Exposed to you / Hey kids / No big thang / Dark heart / Motherless children / Sweet talker / Wheels a spinning.

GARY FLOYD

		Glitterhouse	Glitterhouse
Sep 94.	(cd) <(GRCD 316)> **WORLD OF TROUBLE**		

– Maybe / A better man / World of trouble / Franklyn & Susie / Absence / Dallas / Tough / Wayfaring stranger / Lazarus / From the darkness (to the light). (re-iss. Nov97; same)

Oct 94. (7") <(THM 002)> **MORE THAN A LIFETIME. /**
(above issued on 'Tres Hombres')

— next with **DANNY ROMAN** – guitar / **JONATHAN BURNSIDE** – guitars / **KENNEY DALE JOHNSON** – drums / **ED IVEY** – bass, mandolin, etc / **DAVE ZIRBEL** – pedal steel

Jun 95. (cd; as the GARY FLOYD BAND) <(GRCD 367)> **BROKEN ANGELS**
– Won't be so sad / Spirit on the wind / More than a lifetime / One backdoor man / King bee / Laredo / Don't send me away / Loving you (is all I ever need) / Wild side of life / Baby spends my money / Angel flying too close to the ground / Can't do that.

		Innerstate	Innerstate
Nov 99.	(cd) <(INNER 7004)> **BACKDOOR PREACHER MAN**		Mar00

– Spirit on the wind / Don't send me away / Franklyn & Susie / Can't be satisfied / Won't be so sad / Spoonful / Wayfaring stranger / Bodean / A better man / More than a lifetime / The rejected ones / World of trouble / Can't do that / King Bee (kissing cousins version) / Angel flying close to the ground / Honey bee / From the darkness (to the light).

SISTERS OF MERCY

Formed: Leeds, England ... 1980 by frontman/lyricist extraordinaire, ANDREW ELDRITCH along with guitarist, GARY MARX. The original "goth" combo, ELDRITCH and Co. were among the first acts to define the genre in its lasting image of black-clad, po-faced rockers meditating on dark, impenetrable lyrics, decipherable only for those willing to substitute make-up for flour or wear pointy boots (and, more importantly, never to emerge in daylight!). For their early releases, the group employed a drum machine, christened Doktor Avalanche, issuing material on their self-financed label, 'Merciful Release'. Following the debut single, 'DAMAGE DONE', ELDRITCH and MARX recruited guitarist BENN GUNN and bassist CRAIG ADAMS, fleshing out the sound on a further series of 7 and 12 inchers, the 'ALICE' EP drawing widespread interest with its goth/alternative/dance fusion. GUNN was then replaced with ex-DEAD OR ALIVE guitarist, WAYNE HUSSEY, for the piledriving theatrics of 'TEMPLE OF LOVE'. During this time, the group had also built up a live reputation, supporting the likes of The BIRTHDAY PARTY and The PSYCHEDELIC FURS as well as appearing at the Leeds Futurama festival. Word was spreading, and in 1984, The SISTERS OF MERCY and their label were signed to a worldwide deal with 'WEA'. A debut album, 'FIRST AND LAST AND ALWAYS', appeared the following year, a worthwhile effort which saw the group almost break into the UK Top 10. Yet only a month after the record's release, the band announced they were to split, tension between ELDRITCH and MARX resulting in the latter leaving the group first. After a final concert at London's Royal Albert Hall, a bitter legal battle ensued between ELDRITCH and ADAMS/HUSSEY. At stake was the SISTERS OF MERCY moniker, ELDRITCH eventually winning out, though not before he'd hastily released a single and album, 'GIFT' (1986), under The SISTERHOOD, primarily to prevent ADAMS and HUSSEY using the title. The latter two subsequently formed The MISSION while ELDRITCH relocated to Berlin/Hamburg, retaining ex-GUN CLUB bassist, PATRICIA MORRISON (who'd played on 'GIFT') and recording 'FLOODLAND' (1987) with the help of his ever-faithful drum machine. The preceding single, 'THIS CORROSION' was suitably grandiose, all ominous vocals and OTT production courtesy of JIM STEINMAN, the single giving ELDRITCH his first UK Top 10 hit. The album achieved a similar feat, incorporating a more overtly rhythmic feel to create a kind of doom-disco sound (perfect for goths who couldn't dance anyway!). MORRISON subsequently left, ELDRITCH recruiting an array of diverse musicians including TIM BREICHENO, ANDREAS BRUHN and punk veteran, TONY JAMES (ex-SIGUE SIGUE SPUTNIK, ex-GENERATION X) to record 'VISION THING' (1990). Employing a more commercial hard rock sound, 'MORE' was one of The SISTERS' most effective singles to date while again the album was a Top 20 success. Further acclaim came in 1992 with the surprisingly consistent retrospective, 'SOME GIRLS WANDER BY MISTAKE' (1992), and its attendant single, a brilliant re-vamp of 'TEMPLE OF LOVE', Israeli warbler, OFRA HAZA, adding that extra mystical touch. After a 1991 joint tour with PUBLIC ENEMY (nice idea, but probably taking the Lollopollooza ethic a bit too far) was abandoned after poor ticket sales, not much has been heard from The SISTERS OF MERCY. ELDRITCH remains an enigmatic figure, any significant activity normally resulting in intense interest from the music press. The odds are that he'll return, though whether in the guise of The SISTERS OF MERCY remains to be seen. • **Covered:** EMMA (Hot Chocolate) / 1969 (Stooges) / GIMME SHELTER (Rolling Stones) / KNOCKIN' ON HEAVEN'S DOOR (Bob Dylan).

Album rating: FIRST AND LAST AND ALWAYS (*8) / GIFT (*7; as Sisterhood) / FLOODLAND (*8) / VISION THING (*7) / SOME GIRLS WANDER BY MISTAKE compilation (*8) / GREATEST HITS VOLUME 1 – A SLIGHT CASE OF OVERBOMBING compilation (*7)

ANDREW ELDRITCH (b. ANDREW TAYLOR, 15 May'59, East Anglia, England) – vocals / **GARRY MARX** (b. MARK PEARMAN) – guitar / + drum machine DOKTOR AVALANCHE

		Merciful Release	not iss.
1980.	(7"m) (MR 7) **THE DAMAGE DONE. / WATCH / HOME OF THE HITMAN**		–

— added **BEN GUNN** (b. BENJAMIN MATTHEWS) – guitar / **CRAIG ADAMS** (b. 4 Apr'62) – bass (ex-EXPELAIRES)

		C.N.T.	not iss.
Feb 82.	(7") (CNT 002) **BODY ELECTRIC. / ADRENOCHROME**		–

		Merciful	BrainEater
Nov 82.	(7") (MR 015) **ALICE. / FLOORSHOW**		–
Mar 83.	(7") (MR 019) **ANACONDA. / PHANTOM**		–
Apr 83.	(12"ep) (MR 021) **ALICE. / FLOORSHOW / 1969 / PHANTOM**		
May 83.	(12"ep) (MR 023) **THE REPTILE HOUSE**		

– Kiss the carpet / Lights / Valentine / Burn / Fix. (re-iss. Apr94)

— **WAYNE HUSSEY** (b. JERRY LOVELOCK, 26 May'58, Bristol, England) – guitar (ex-DEAD OR ALIVE, ex-HAMBI & THE DANCE) repl. BEN

Oct 83.	(7") (MR 027) **TEMPLE OF LOVE. / HEARTLAND**		–
	(ext.12"+=) (MRX 027) – Gimme shelter.		
Jun 84.	(7"; as The SISTERS) (MR 029) **BODY AND SOUL. / TRAIN**	46	–
	(12"+=) (MR 029T) – After hours / Body electric.		

		Merciful Release	Elektra
Oct 84.	(7") (MR 033) **WALK AWAY. / POISON DOOR**	45	–

(above w/free 7"flexi) (MR 033 – SAM 218) – Long Train.
(12"+=) (MR 033T) – On the wire.

SISTERS OF MERCY (cont)

Feb 85. (7") (MR 035) **NO TIME TO CRY. / BLOOD MONEY** — 63 / –
(12"+=) (MR 035T) – Bury me deep.
Mar 85. (lp/c) (MR 337 L/C) <60405> **FIRST AND LAST AND ALWAYS** — 14
– Black planet / Walk away / No time to cry / A rock and a hard place / Marian / First and last and always / Possession / Nine while nine / Amphetamine logic / Some kind of stranger. (cd-iss. Jul88; 240616-2) (re-iss. re-mastered.Jul92 on 'East West' lp/c; MR 571 L/C) (cd re-mast.Jun92; 9031 77379-2)

— disbanded mid-'85 . . . GARRY MARX helped form GHOST DANCE. HUSSEY and ADAMS formed The MISSION after squabbles with ANDREW over use of group name.

— ELDRITCH with ever faithful drum machine adopted

The SISTERHOOD

— recruited **PATRICIA MORRISON** (b.14 Jan'62) – bass, vocals (ex-FUR BIBLE, ex-GUN CLUB) / **JAMES RAY** – guitar / **ALAN VEGA** – synthesizers (ex-SUICIDE) / **LUCAS FOX** – drums (ELDRITCH moved to Berlin, Germany)

Merciful not iss.

Feb 86. (7") (SIS 001) **GIVING GROUND (remix). / GIVING GROUND (album version)**
Jul 86. (lp/c) (SIS 020/+C) **GIFT** — 90 / –
– Jihad / Colours / Giving ground / Finland red, Egypt white / Rain from Heaven. (cd-iss. Sep89; SIS 020CD) (re-iss. Jul94 cd/c; 1131684-2/-4)

— JAMES RAY went solo (backed with The PERFORMANCE), subsequently issuing a couple of 45's, 'MEXICO SUNDOWN BLUES' and 'TEXAS', for 'Merciful Release'. At the turn of the decade, he and his new outfit, JAMES RAY'S GANGWAR, issued a few more, 'DUSTBOAT' and 'WITHOUT CONSCIENCE', the former from a part compilation set, 'A NEW KIND OF ASSASSIN' (1989). In 1992 and '93, the band delivered two more, 'DIOS ESTA DE NUESTRO LADO' and 'THIRD GENERATION'.

The SISTERS OF MERCY

— were once again **ELDRITCH + MORRISON** obtaining rights to name

Merciful- WEA   Elektra

Sep 87. (7") (MR 39) **THIS CORROSION. / TORCH** — 7 / –
(c-s+=/12"+=/cd-s+=) (MR 39 C/T/CD) – Colours.
Nov 87. (lp/c)(cd) (MR 441 L/C)(242246-2) <60762> **FLOODLAND** — 9 / –
– Dominion / Mother Russia / Flood I / Lucretia my reflection / 1959 / This corrosion / Flood II / Driven like the snow / Neverlan. (c+=)– Torch. (cd-s++=) – Colours.
Feb 88. (7") (MR 43) **DOMINION. / SANDSTORM / UNTITLED** — 13 / –
(d12"+=) (MR 43TB) – Emma.
(c-s+=/3"cd-s+=) (MR 43 C/CD) – Ozy-Mandias.
May 88. (7"/ext.12"/ext.3"cd-s) (MR 44/+T/CD) **LUCRETIA MY REFLECTION. / LONG TRAIN** — 20 / –

— (Feb'90) ELDRITCH w/drum machine, recruited complete new line-up / **TONY JAMES** (b.1956) – bass, vocals (ex-SIGUE SIGUE SPUTNIK, ex-GENERATION X) / **ANDREAS BRUHN** (b. 5 Nov'67, Hamburg, Germany) – guitar / **TIM BRICHENO** (b. 6 Jul'63, Huddersfield, England) – guitar (ex-ALL ABOUT EVE) / guests were **MAGGIE REILLY** – b.vocals (ex-MIKE OLDFIELD) / **JOHN PERRY** – guitar (ex-ONLY ONES)

Oct 90. (7"/c-s) (MR 47/+C) <66595> **MORE. / YOU COULD BE THE ONE** — 21 / –
(cd-s+=/cd-s+=) (MR 47CD/+X) – ('A'extended).
Oct 90. (cd)(c/lp) (9031 72663-2)(MR 449 C/L) <61017> **VISION THING** — 11 / –
– Vision thing / Ribons / Destination Boulevard / Something fast / When you don't see me / Doctor Jeep / More / I was wrong. (cd re-iss. Jul00; same)
Dec 90. (7") (MR 51) **DOCTOR JEEP. / KNOCKIN' ON HEAVEN'S DOOR (live)** — 37 / –
(12"+=/cd-s+=) (MR 51 T/CD) – ('A'extended).
(ext.12") (MR 51TX) – Burn (live) / Amphetamine logic (live).

— (Oct91) **TONY JAMES** split from ELDRITCH amicably.

— Next featured vocals by **OFRA HAZA**

East West Elektra

Apr 92. (7") (MR 53) **TEMPLE OF LOVE (1992). / I WAS WRONG (American fade)** — 3 / –
(ext.12"+=) (MR 53T) – Vision thing (Canadian club mix).
(cd-s+=) (MR 53CD) – When you don't see me (German release).
Apr 92. (cd)(c/d-lp) (9031 76476-2)(MR 449 C/L) <61306> **SOME GIRLS WANDER BY MISTAKE** (1980-1983 material) — 5 / –
– Alice / Floorshow / Phantom / 1969 / Kiss the carpet / Lights / Valentine / Fix / Burn / Kiss the carpet (reprise) / Temple of love / Heartland / Gimme shelter / Damage done / Watch / Home of the hitmen / Body electric / Adrenochrome / Anaconda.

— now just **ANDREW ELDRITCH** on own with guests
Aug 93. (7"/c-s) (MR 59/+C) **UNDER THE GUN. / ALICE (1993)** — 19 / –
(12"+=/cd-s+=) (MR 59 T/CD) – ('A'-Jutland mix).
Aug 93. (cd/c/d-lp) (4509 93579-2/-4/-1) <61399-2/-4> **GREATEST HITS VOLUME 1 – A SLIGHT CASE OF OVERBOMBING** (compilation) — 14 / –
– Under the gun / Temple of love (1992) / Vision thing / Detonation boulevard / Doctor Jeep / More / Lucretia my reflection / Dominion – Mother / This corrosion / No time to cry / Walk away / Body and soul.

— ELDRITCH and his gang seem to have split from the music scene

– compilations, etc. –

Jan 94. (cd) Cleopatra; <(CLEO 6642CD)> **FIRST, LAST FOREVER**

SKELETAL FAMILY

Formed: Bingley, Yorkshire, England . . . 1982 by ANNE MARIE HURST, STAN GREENWOOD, TROTWOOD, STEVE CRANE and KARL HEINZ. Following a debut single, 'JUST A FRIEND', on the tiny 'Luggage' label in Spring '83, the band were picked up by influential local independent operation, 'Red Rhino'. A further two singles, 'THE NIGHT' and 'ALONE SHE CRIES' generated press interest prior to the debut album, 'BURNING OIL'. Bracketed with such early 80's goth merchants as BAUHAUS and SISTERS OF MERCY, The SKELETAL FAMILY were actually a more accessible proposition than their name might suggest, the female vocals (like a deeper throated SIOUXSIE SIOUX with the odd POLY STYRENE yelp) framing dark, spiralling guitars as on the impressive 'SO SURE'. The indie success of 1985's 'FUTILE COMBAT' alerted 'Chrysalis' to the band's potential yet by the release of major label debut, 'GHOSTS' (1986), ANNE-MARIE had left to join fellow pop-doomsters, GHOST DANCE. The record showcased new singer, KATRINA HUNTER (once backing vocalist for TERRY HALL's COLOURFIELD) fronting a more mainstream SKELETAL FAMILY sound, one that failed to cross over and ultimately cost them their deal as the band were subsequently dropped amid poor sales.

Album rating: BURNING OIL (*6) / FUTILE COMBAT (*7) / GHOSTS collection (*5) / THE SINGLES PLUS 1983-1985 compilation (*6) / PROMISED LAND – THE BEST OF SKELETAL FAMILY compilation (*6)

ANNE MARIE HURST – vocals / **STAN GREENWOOD** – guitar / **TROTWOOD** (b. ROGER NOWELL) – bass / **STEVE CRANE** – drums / **KARL HEINZ** – synthesizers

Luggage not iss.

Mar 83. (7") (RRP 00724) **JUST A FRIEND. / TREES**
— **HOWARD DANIELS** – drums; repl. CRANE

Red Rhino not iss.

Jul 83. (7") (RED 36) **THE NIGHT. / WAITING HERE**
— **MARTIN HENDERSON** – drums; repl. DANIELS (to MY PIERROT DOLLS)
Jan 84. (7") (RED 41) **SHE CRIES ALONE. / THE WIND BLOWS**
(12"+=) (REDT 41) – Eternal.
Apr 84. (12"ep) (REDT 42) **RECOLLECT**
– The night / Waiting here / She cries alone / The wind blows / Eternal / Lies.
Jun 84. (7") (RED 43) **SO SURE. / BATMAN**
(12"+=) (REDT 43) – Trees / Lies.
Aug 84. (lp) (REDLP 44) **BURNING OIL**
– So sure / Ritual / Burning oil / The wind blows / And I / 11:15 / Waiting here / Someone new / Black ju ju / Woman and child. (cd-iss. Feb01 on 'Anagram'+=; CDMGOTH 2) – Trees / Just a friend / The night.
— **GRAHAM PLEETH** – synthesizers; repl. KARL HEINZ
Feb 85. (7") (RED 54) **PROMISED LAND. / STAND BY ME**
(12"+=) (REDT 54) – Just a friend.
May 85. (lp) (REDLP 57) **FUTILE COMBAT**
– Hands on the clock / Move / This time / Don't be denied / Far and near / No chance / Streetlight / She cries alone / What happened / Promised land.
— **KATRINA HUNTER** – vocals (ex-COLOUR FIELD) repl. ANNE MARIE who formed GHOST DANCE
— **KEVIN PHILIPS** – drums; repl. RICHARD HAWKINS (ex-GENE LOVES JEZEBEL) who repl. MARTIN (to JUNE BRIDES) + GRAHAM

Chrysalis not iss.

Mar 86. (7") (CHS 2970) **RESTLESS. / WHAT GOES UP**
(12"+=) (CHS 12 2970) – Split him in two.
Aug 86. (7"/12") (CHS/+12 3015) **JUST A MINUTE. / BIG LOVE**
— disbanded soon after above; TROTWOOD and HUNTER formed SAY YOU

– compilations, etc. –

Oct 85. (d-c) Red Rhino; (REDC 59) **TOGETHER (BURNING OIL / FUTILE COMBAT)**
(cd-iss. 1995 on 'Dojo'; LOMACD 40)
Oct 86. (lp) Onsala International; (ONS 1) **GHOSTS**
– Puppets / Guilt / Lies / Trees / Batman / Burning oil / So sure / Stand by me / Promised land / Deception.
Mar 94. (cd) Anagram; (CDMGRAM 75) **THE SINGLES PLUS 1983-85**
(re-iss. Jun99; same)
Dec 01. (cd) Anagram; (CDMGOTH 12) **PROMISED LAND – THE BEST OF SKELETAL FAMILY**

SKEPTICS

Formed: Palmerston North, New Zealand . . . 1979 by vocalist DAVID D'ATH, guitarist ROBIN GAULD, bassist NICK ROUGHAN and drummer DON WHITE. The band originally started as a project by a group of 6th form high school students. The first SKEPTICS recording (with IAN REIDDY on bass) was in their school library at lunchtime and included such tasteful tracks as 'I AM A SPASTIC' and 'I FEEL SICK'. ROUGHAN replaced REIDDY on bass shortly after this less-than-auspicious debut. They then set about creating their own brand of dark, trip hop-anticipating industrial pop rock, to the annoyance of small-minded 70s music-loving bands in their small town. Playing support slots at local venue El Clubbo, the band secured their first tour with THE NEWMATICS. Coming second in a Battle of The Bands in Auckland (after THE GURLZ) a representative of 'Furtive' records approached them and their first recording came out in 1992, a song called 'LAST ORDERS' on a 'Furtive' compilation called 'THREE PIECE PACK'. A 5-song EP recorded at the same time as 'LAST ORDERS' entitled 'PYRONNISTS SELECTIONS' was never released as the master tape disappeared forever from the record label's office, never to be seen again. Undaunted, the band signed to 'Flying Nun' (where else!) and released the 'CHOWDER OVER WISCONSIN' (1983) EP. From 1983-1984 THE SKEPTICS ran their own Palmerston North club called Snail Clamps, named after a chalk inscription on a blackboard in the old warehouse they used for the club. This venue put on bands and SKEPTICS spin-offs like THE GO-CATS and CARLTON HESTON; 'Industrial' tapes would put out the tape 'SKEPTICS SAID' in 1984. In 1985, the band moved to Wellington and released their first real album, 'PONDS'. GAULD left the band to concentrate on university studies but was soon replaced by JOHN HALVORSEN, formerly of THE GORDONS and also playing with BAILTER SPACE. The album 'SKEPTICS III' appeared in 1988. Whilst working on the follow-up, D'ATH was diagnosed as having leukemia and died on September 4th, 1990; the album appeared a scant two months later. The band was critically feted for the bleak, dramatic complexity of the gothic arrangements on the album, and the running time would make good use of a sampler and dub-splattered rhythm alongside the sung and spoken texts used. SKEPTICS broke up after the death of D'ATH with surviving members ROUGHAN, WHITE and GAULD forming the short-lived HUB. A previously unreleased SKEPTICS single 'SENSIBLE SHOES' was released in 1991, and a 1992 box set also included a new live EP, 'IF I WILL I CAN'.

Album rating: PONDS (*5) / SKEPTICS III (*6) / AMALGM (*7) / SENSIBLE (*6)

DAVID D'ATH – vocals / **ROBIN GAULD** – guitar / **NICK ROUGHAN** – bass / **DON WHITE** – drums

Flying Nun / not iss.

1983. (12"ep) (FNCHOW 001) **CHOWDER OVER WISCONSIN** – / – NewZ
 – Boo-chang / New barking riff / Aud Balmoral / The broach / Stella / The Old Grey Whistle Test / Chowder, jelly.
1984. (c) (none) **SKEPTICS SAID** – / – NewZ
 (above issued on 'Industrial Tapes' (below licensed to 'U.L.P.')
1985. (lp) (ULP 001) **PONDS** – / – NewZ
 – Tone / Bedrock / Freely gotten gains / For Silos / Bubba clutha / Voluminous / Divine muscles flex / Ponds.

— JOHN HALVORSEN – guitar (of BAILTER SPACE, ex-GORDONS) repl. GAULD

Feb 88. (lp/cd) (FN/+CD 109) **SKEPTICS III** – / – NewZ
 – AFFCO / Feeling bad / Agitator / Turn over / La Matta / Notice / Rain / Luna / Crave.
Nov 90. (lp/cd) (FN/+CD 146) **AMALGM** – / – NewZ
 – And we bake / Felt up / Pack ice / Never tire of looking at the stars / Heathery men / Bad wiring / Threads / Spade / Sheen of gold / All sum nul.

— sadly prior to 'AMALGM', D'ATH died of leukemia on the 4th of September 1990, below were posthumous releases

1991. (10"ep) (FN 194) **SENSIBLE SHOES** – / – NewZ
 – Sensible shoes / Bub / Blue / PCH mix.
1991. (lp/cd) (FN/+CD 221) **SENSIBLE** (rec. 1985) – / – NewZ
 – You look great / Water / Pressure / Jonny come lately / Haks off / Fwoney / Blue / Men 'o' war / Splenal langwems / Bulldozer song / Baron vice / Bub / Dodunski mix / Spring / Sensible shoes.
1992. (cd-ep) (FNCD 256) **IF I WILL I CAN** – / – NewZ
 – If I will I can / Any any (live) / Two pot resin (live) / Mamouth (live). (hidden tracks+=) – And we bake (live) / Threads (live) / Sheen of gold (live).
1992. (4xcd-box) (FN 260) **BOX SET** (re-mastered) – / – Austra
 – (SKEPTICS III / AMALGM / SENSIBLE / IF I WILL I CAN)

— GAULD, ROUGHAN and WHITE resurfaced as the short-lived HUB; HALVORSEN continued with BAILTER SPACE

(WORLD OF) SKIN (see under ⇒ SWANS)

SKI PATROL (see under ⇒ LOWERY, Ian)

SLAUGHTER JOE

Formed: Hendon / Newcastle, England . . . 1984 by namesake, JOE FOSTER, a one-time member of the TELEVISION PERSONALITIES in the early 80's and subsequent to that, The MISSING SCIENTISTS. This 4-piece – who also included DAN PAN (aka TREACY), EMPIRE (also of The TVP's) and JAQUI (aka DANIEL MILLER) – only recorded one 'Rough Trade' single in 1980, a cover of Dandy Livingstone's 'BIG CITY, BRIGHT LIGHTS' backed with 'DISCOTHEQUE X', before JOE returned for spells with the TVP's. In 1984, the guitarist helped initiate ALAN McGEE's 'Creation' stable, issuing a few psychedelic 45's himself, 'I'LL FOLLOW YOU DOWN' and 'SHE'S SO OUT OF TOUCH' (the latter B-side a cover of The Byrds' rare 'I KNOW YOU RIDER'). Also in 1986, JOE guested for ex-GUN CLUB leader, JEFFREY LEE PIERCE, and married Helen Fitzgerald of The Melody Maker. The following year, JOE formed his own label, 'Kaleidoscope Sound', releasing SLAUGHTER JOE's debut album, 'ALL AROUND MY HOBBY HORSE'S HEAD' (a play on words of a STEELEYE SPAN track!) soon after. His label became the launching pad for at least one great outfit, MY BLOODY VALENTINE.

Album rating: ALL AROUND MY HOBBY HORSE'S HEAD (*5)

JOE FOSTER – vocals, guitar (ex-TELEVISION PERSONALITIES) / **RICHARD BERLIN** – electric viola / **NATHAN DETROIT** – bass / **MEMPHIS** – drums

Creation / not iss.

Jun 85. (7") (CRE 019) **I'LL FOLLOW YOU DOWN. / NAPALM GIRL** – / –
 (12"+=) (CRE 019T) – Surely some sort of Slaughter's blues / Fall apart.
Nov 86. (7") (CRE 035) **SHE'S SO OUT OF TOUCH. / I KNOW YOU RIDER** – / –
 (12"+=) (CRE 035T) – The lonesome death of Thurston Moore.

Kaleidoscope Sound / not iss.

Nov 87. (lp) (KSLP 003) **ALL AROUND MY HOBBY HORSE'S HEAD** – / –
 (cd-iss. Jun88; KSC 003)

— JOE continued with production work and Creation offshoot, 'Rev-Ola'. After many years working at Creation, JOE FOSTER returned to recording courtesy of project SELOFANE 74 (with TONY BARBER - ex-BUZZCOCKS); they released one eponymous set in 2000 for McGEE's 'Poptones'.

– compilations, etc. –

Nov 90. (cd/lp) Creation; (CRE CD/LP 084) **THE PIED PIPER OF FEEDBACK** (all his 'Creation' work) – / –

SMITHEREENS

Formed: Carteret, New Jersey, USA . . . early 1980 by JIM BABJAK and DENNIS DIKEN, who had played together in bands since the early 70's. The pair recruited MIKE MESAROS and frontman/songwriter PAT DiNIZIO, this line-up presiding over their inaugural EP in Xmas 1980, 'GIRLS ABOUT TOWN'. Save for backing up legendary writer and occasional singer, OTIS BLACKWELL (the man behind R&R classics such as 'Don't Be Cruel', 'Fever' and 'Great Balls Of Fire') on a couple of low-key recordings. The SMITHEREENS returned in their own right in '83 with another independent release, the mini-set, 'BEAUTY & SADNESS'. Described as a cross between The BEATLES, The BYRDS and AC/DC!, The SMITHEREENS were the acceptable face of alternative power-pop. Subsequently signing to 'Enigma', the band found a ready-made audience for their first album proper, 'ESPECIALLY FOR YOU' (1986) via college radio, the record's sales further boosted by a collaborative single, 'IN A LONELY PLACE', with rising folk-pop chanteuse, SUZANNE VEGA. During the late 80's, they broke into the US Top 60 a further twice with well-received albums, 'GREEN THOUGHTS' (1988) and '11' (1989). However, with the onset of Grunge in the early 90's and their ill-advised choice to contribute to the soundtrack of teen-movie, 'Class Of Nuke 'Em High', it looked as if the band's golden years had passed. 1991's 'BLOW UP' album was a miserable failure in both critical and commercial terms, the record not even managing to break the US Top 100. Subsequently signing to 'R.C.A.', the new pop-friendly SMITHEREENS suffered a similar fate with 1994's 'A DATE WITH . . .'. A five-year gap between their next release, 'GOD SAVE THE SMITHEREENS' (1999), mainman DiNIZIO had time to re-group his musical thoughts. Although not a classic by any stretch of the imagination, the album was a slight return to riff-tastic form. • **Covered:** THE SEEKER (Who) / GIRL DON'T TELL ME (Beach Boys) / DON'T BE CRUEL (Elvis Presley) / HANG TEN HIGH (. . . Frontiere) / JUST A LITTLE (Durand-Elliott) / YOU REALLY GOT ME + THE WORLD KEEPS GOING 'ROUND (Kinks) / ONE AFTER 909 (Beatles) / SOMETHING STUPID (. . . Parks) / SHAKIN' ALL OVER (Johnny Kidd) / RUDOLPH THE RED-NOSED REINDEER (Marks-Scott) / RULER OF MY HEART (Aaron Neville) / IT DON'T COME EASY (Ringo Starr) / LUST FOR LIFE (Iggy Pop). • **Note:** Not to be confused with a Dutch band of same name (c. mid-80's) who released a single, 'YOURS IS A GUARANTEE FOR LOVE'.

Album rating: BEAUTY & SADNESS mini (*5) / ESPECIALLY FOR YOU (*7) / GREEN THOUGHTS (*8) / 11 (*8) / BLOW UP (*5) / A DATE WITH THE SMITHEREENS (*4) / ATTACK OF THE SMITHEREENS (*4) / BLOWN TO SMITHEREENS compilation (*8) / GOD SAVE THE SMITHEREENS (*5) / Pat DiNizio: SONGS AND SOUNDS (*6)

PAT DiNIZIO – vocals, guitar / **JIM BABJAK** – guitar / **MIKE MESAROS** – bass / **DENNIS DIKEN** – drums

not iss. / D-Tone

Dec 80. (7"ep) <DT 150> **GIRLS ABOUT TOWN / GIRL DON'T TELL ME. / GOT ME A GIRL / GIRLS ARE LIKE THAT** – / –

not iss. / Little Ricky

1983. (m-lp) <LR 103> **BEAUTY & SADNESS** – / –
 – Beauty & sadness / Some other guy / Tracey's world / Much too much / Beauty & sadness (instrumental). (UK-iss.Jul89 on 'Enigma' lp/cd; ENVLP/CDENV 519)

Enigma / Enigma

Dec 86. (lp) <(73208-1)> **ESPECIALLY FOR YOU** – / 51 Aug86
 – Strangers when we meet / Listen to me girl / Groovy Tuesday / Cigarette / I don't want to lose you / Time and time again / Behind the wall of sleep / In a lonely place / Blood and roses / Crazy mixed-up kid / Hand of glory / Alone at midnight. (cd-iss. Mar87; CD 73208-2) (pic-lp Nov87; SEAX 73258)
Jan 87. (7"red; by The SMITHEREENS with SUZANNE VEGA) (ENIG 1) <50032> **IN A LONELY PLACE. / BEAUTY AND SADNESS** – / –
 (12"+=) (ENIGT 1) – Blood and roses / Mr. Eliminator.
Jan 87. (7"; by The SMITHEREENS with SUZANNE VEGA) <50032> **IN A LONELY PLACE. / BLOOD AND ROSES (live)** – / –
Mar 87. (7") (ENIG 2) **BEHIND THE WALL OF SLEEP. / BLOOD AND ROSES** – / Sep86
 (12"+=) (ENIGT 2) –
Jul 87. (12"m) (ENIG 3) **STRANGERS WHEN WE MEET. / THE SEEKER / HANG TEN HIGH** – / –
Dec 87. (lp/cd) <97924-1/-2> **SMITHEREENS LIVE (live)** – / –
 – Blood and roses / Behind the wall of sleep / Beauty and sadness / Alone at midnight / Strangers when we meet / The seeker.

Enigma / Capitol

Mar 88. (7") (SMIT 1) **ONLY A MEMORY. / LUST FOR LIFE** – / –
 (12"+=) (SMIT 1) – Something new.
May 88. (7") <44150> **ONLY A MEMORY. / THE SEEKER** – / 92
Apr 88. (lp/c/cd) (3375 1/4/2) <48375> **GREEN THOUGHTS** – / 60
 – Only a memory / House we used to live in / Something new / The world we knew / Especially for you / Drown in my own tears / Deep black / Elaine / Spellbound / If the Sun doesn't shine / Green thoughts.

SMITHEREENS (cont)

Jun 88.	(7") **THE HOUSE WE USED TO LIVE IN. / ONLY A MEMORY**
Oct 88.	(7") *(ENV 2)* **THE HOUSE WE USED TO LIVE IN. / RULER OF MY HEART**
	(12"+=) *(ENVT 2)* – Blood and roses (live).
	(cd-s++=) *(ENVCD 2)* – ('A'live version).
Dec 88.	(7") **DROWN IN MY OWN TEARS. / THE HOUSE WE USED TO LIVE IN**

Enigma-EMI / Capitol

| Nov 89. | (lp/c/cd) *(ENVLP/TCENV/CDENV 1000)* <91194> **11** — 41 |

– Girl like you / Blues before and after / Blue period / Baby be good / Room without a view / Yesterday girl / Cut flowers / Willian Wilson / Maria Elana / Kiss your tears away.

Nov 89.	(c-s,cd-s) <44480> **A GIRL LIKE YOU (parts I & II) / LIKE SOMEONE IN LOVE** — 38
Feb 90.	(7") *(ENV 15)* **A GIRL LIKE YOU. / CUT FLOWERS**
	(12"+=/cd-s+=) *(12/CD ENV 15)* – Like someone in love.
May 90.	(7") *(ENV 21)* **BLUE PERIOD. / MARIA ELENA (acoustic)**
	(12"+=/cd-s+=) *(12/CD ENV 21)* – Room without a view.
May 90.	(c-s,cd-s) <44516> **BLUES BEFORE AND AFTER / MARIA ELENA (acoustic)** — 94

Capitol / Capitol

| Sep 91. | (cd/c/lp) *(CD/TC/+EST 2151)* <94963> **BLOW UP** |

– Top of the pops / Too much passion / Tell me when did things go so wrong / Evening dress / Get a hold of my heart / Indigo blues / Now and then / Girl in room 12 / Anywhere you are / Over and over again / It's alright / If you want to see to shine.

| Feb 92. | (c-s,cd-s) <44784> **TOO MUCH PASSION / IF YOU WANT THE SUN TO SHINE** — 37 |

not iss. / R.C.A.

| May 94. | (cd/c) <66391-2/-4> **A DATE WITH THE SMITHEREENS** |

– War for my mind / Everything I have is blue / Miles from nowhere / Afternoon tea / Point of no return / Sleep the night away / Love is gone / Wrong way back again / Gotti / Sick of Seattle / Can't go home anymore / Life is so beautiful.

| Aug 94. | (c-s) <62942> **TIME WON'T LET ME /** |
| Jan 98. | (cd-ep; with WOOLDRIDGE BROTHERS & BILLY MANN) <58691> **DOWNBOUND TRAIN** |

– Downbound train / Fade away / Two hearts / Thunder road / No surrender.

Koch Int. / Koch Int.

| Mar 00. | (cd) <*(KOCCD 8057)*> **GOD SAVE THE SMITHEREENS** — Oct99 |

– She's got a way / House at the end of the world / Everything changes / Flowers in the blood / The long loneliness / Someday / The age of innocence / Gloomy Sunday / I believe / All revved up / Even if I never get back home / Try / The last good time.

– compilations, etc. –

| Nov 95. | (cd,c) *Capitol;* <32247> **ATTACK OF THE SMITHEREENS** (B-sides, etc) |

– Here come the Smithereens / Girl don't tell me / Girls about town / Time and time again / Don't be cruel / Hang ten high / Tracey's world / Blood and roses / Just a little / The seeker / Yesterday girl / Poor little pitiful one / Maria Elena / You really got me / One after 909 / The world keeps going 'round / Behind the wall of sleep / Something stupid / Shakin' all over / Rudolph the red-nosed reindeer / Ruler of my heart / I don't come easy / Lust for life / Like someone in love / A girl like you.

| Apr 98. | (cd,c) *Cema Special;* <19502> **THE BEST OF THE SMITHEREENS** |

– Strangers when we meet / Only a memory / A girl like you / Behind the wall of sleep / Blood and roses / Yesterday girl / In a lonely place / Too much passion / Drown in my own tears / The house we used to live in.

| Aug 98. | (cd) *Capitol;* <31481 8 31481-2/-4> **BLOWN TO SMITHEREENS - BEST OF THE SMITHEREENS** — Apr95 |

– Beauty and sadness / Strangers when we meet / Blood and roses / In a lonely place / Behind the wall of sleep / Only a memory / The house we used to live in / Drown in my own tears / A girl like you / Blue period / Blues before and after / Yesterday girl / Top of the pops / Too much passion / Miles from nowhere / Time won't let me.

PAT DiNIZIO

— with **JEAN JACQUES BURNEL** – bass, vocals (of STRANGLERS) / **THUNDER SMITH** – percussion, drums

Velvel / Velvel

| Jul 98. | (cd/c) <*(VEL 79706)*> **SONGS AND SOUNDS** — Oct97 |

– Where I am going / Nobody but me / 124 mph / Running, jumping, standing still / Everyday world / No love lost / World apart / Today it's you / Liza / Somewhere down the line / You should know / I'd rather have the blues.

SMITHS

Formed: Manchester, England ... late '82 by (STEPHEN PATRICK) MORRISSEY and JOHNNY MARR. An intellectually intense, budding pop scholar and music journalist, MORRISSEY had previously had a book, 'James Dean Isn't Dead', published by 'Babylon' and had served a stint as UK president of The NEW YORK DOLLS fan club. MARR, meanwhile, had cut his six-string teeth in a variety of Manc beat combos, the pair initially forming a songwriting partnership and subsequently bringing in drummer MIKE JOYCE and bassist ANDY ROURKE to realise their vision of The SMITHS. Kicking off at The Ritz in Manchester, the group played a series of debut gigs around the country, earning rave reviews and attracting the interest of indie label, 'Rough Trade'. Turning down a deal with the local 'Factory', The SMITHS recorded a one-off single for 'Rough Trade', 'HAND IN GLOVE', the track championed by John Peel and subsequently topping the indie charts. Wooed by the majors, MORRISSEY and Co. stuck to their principals and inked a long-term contract with 'Rough Trade'. Later that year saw the release of the Top 30 hit, 'THIS CHARMING MAN', the first real glimpse of the The SMITHS' strange allure, MARR's rhythmic exuberance buoying MORRISSEY's morose verbal complexities. This was also the first time the Great British public were treated to the legendary sight of MORRISSEY sashaying and shimmying across the Top Of The Pops stage sporting a hearing aid and a back pocketfull of gladioli.

Defiantly original, The SMITHS rapidly amassed a large, fiercely partisan fanbase with MORRISSEY as chief deity, MARR running a close second. A follow-up single, 'WHAT DIFFERENCE DOES IT MAKE', narrowly missed the Top 10 in early '84 with the breathlessly anticipated debut, 'THE SMITHS', hitting the shelves the following month. It didn't disappoint, a darkly ruminating kick in the eye for the tosspot music scene of the mid-80's and a compelling showcase for the unbounded potential of the MORRISSEY/MARR writing partnership. While the album missed the No.1 slot by a whisker, a high profile scrape with the tabloids followed soon after, the press hounds rounding on what they supposed to be ambiguous references to child abuse. The highly articulate MORRISSEY vocally put matters to right, the singer finally vindicated when a mother of one of the Moors murder victims openly supported the 'SUFFER THE LITTLE CHILDREN' track, another target of press speculation. The SMITHS were nothing if not controversial, MORRISSEY's pro-miserablist, anti-royalist and openly celibate stance making him the first real 'bedsit' non-pop star and drawing more and more attention to the group. No bad thing of course, when the music was as good as 'HEAVEN KNOWS I'M MISERABLE NOW' and 'WILLIAM, IT WAS REALLY NOTHING', another couple of fine Top 20 singles released later that summer. Both were included on the brilliant 'HATFUL OF HOLLOW' (1984) set along with a number of BBC session recordings and a few new tracks, notably the haunting 'PLEASE PLEASE PLEASE LET ME GET WHAT I WANT' and one of The SMITHS' trump cards, 'HOW SOON IS NOW' (previously released as a B-side to 'WILLIAM . . .' and subsequently as a single in its own right in early '85), a churning mantra presumably laying bare the depths of MORRISSEY's tortured soul with its bitter lyrical plea; that pop/dance outfit SOHO later managed to incorporate its ominous guitar reverb into a club hit is surely one of the great wonders of modern music. The following month saw the release of the acclaimed 'MEAT IS MURDER', MORRISSEY partly substituting the navel gazing of old for a more socially-pointed stance; slap happy headmasters, teenage thugs, child abusers and of course, those partial to a bit of steak, being the prime targets of the frontman's razor-sharp lyrical barbs. MORRISSEY wasn't hogging all the limelight, however, MARR's nimble fingered genius on the likes of 'THAT JOKE ISN'T FUNNY ANYMORE' seeing him touted as the greatest British guitarist since ERIC CLAPTON. The album gave the group their first No.1, solidifying their position as the biggest "indie" band of the decade, The SMITHS now at the peak of their powers. Next up was the irrepressible 'THE BOY WITH THE THORN IN HIS SIDE' and the scathing wit of 'BIGMOUTH STRIKES AGAIN', both featured on, and acting as preludes to 'THE QUEEN IS DEAD' (1986). Though the album was delayed due to record company hassles, with personnel difficulties (ROURKE briefly kicked out for heroin abuse, the addition of CRAIG GANNON also arising, it remains The SMITHS' magnum opus and, for many, the album of the decade. Effortlessly segueing from the darkly claustrophobic (the stinging social commentary of the title track and to a lesser extent, the lugubrious 'NEVER HAD NO ONE EVER') to the whimsically witty ('VICAR IN A TUTU') and on to the heartbreakingly poignant ('THERE IS A LIGHT THAT NEVER GOES OUT'), the album was breathtaking in its emotional sweep and musical focus. Though they would never quite reach those heights again, The SMITHS' highly prolific recording schedule continued apace with the anthemic 'PANIC' (indie kids delighting in its clarion call of 'Hang the DJ') and the breezy 'ASK', probably The SMITHS most commercial moment. The fact that, like most of their singles, it failed to break the Top 10, led to the group announcing a split with 'Rough Trade' and a new deal with 'E.M.I.'. Further controversy followed around this time as CRAIG GANNON was sacked, the guitarist duly sueing the group. Early '87 saw the release of another semi-compilation of old and new material, 'THE WORLD WON'T LISTEN', essential if only for the classic MORRISSEY angst of 'HALF A PERSON' and the sublime 'OSCILLATE WILDLY'. Though the wellspring of the MORRISSEY/MARR muse was seemingly bottomless, relations between the pair were reaching breaking point and by the release of the 'STRANGEWAYS HERE WE COME' (1987) opus, The SMITHS had already split. The album's morbid, fractured sound apparently confirmed the growing musical differences between the group's main protagonists, an inevitability perhaps, for such a consistently intense and perfectionist band. A posthumous live album, 'RANK' (1988) appeared the following year, documenting the London stop on The SMITHS' final frenzied tour of 1986. Various compilations were released in successive years, especially after 'Warners' secured the rights to The SMITHS' back catalogue in 1992, heralding a period when, ironically, most of the material was only available on US import! While MARR sessioned for the likes of The PRETENDERS and BRYAN FERRY before working with THE THE and forming ELECTRONIC with NEW ORDER's BERNARD SUMNER, MORRISSEY went on to a relatively successful, if comparitively drab solo career. As is so often the case, the sum of The SMITHS parts was always less than the whole, the group's influence on modern rock music incalculable, their unique sound echoing through the strains of countless indie success stories and untold hopefuls alike. • **Songwriters:** Lyrics – MORRISSEY / music – MARR, except HIS LATEST FLAME (Elvis Presley) / GOLDEN LIGHTS (Twinkle).

Album rating: THE SMITHS (*10) / HATFUL OF HOLLOW part compilation (*9) / MEAT IS MURDER (*10) / THE QUEEN IS DEAD (*10) / THE WORLD WON'T LISTEN part compilation (*8) / STRANGEWAYS HERE WE COME (*8) / LOUDER THAN BOMBS import (*8) / RANK (*7) / BEST . . . I compilation (*10) / BEST II compilation (*9) / THE VERY BEST OF THE SMITHS compilation (*8)

MORRISSEY (b. STEPHEN PATRICK MORRISSEY, 22 May'59) – vocals (ex-NOSEBLEEDS) / **JOHNNY MARR** (b. JOHN MAHER, 31 Oct'63) – guitar, harmonica, mandolins, piano / **ANDY ROURKE** (b.1963) – bass / **MIKE JOYCE** (b. 1 Jun'63) – drums

Rough Trade / Sire

May 83. (7") *(RT 131)* **HAND IN GLOVE. / HANDSOME DEVIL** [ ] [-]
Nov 83. (7") *(RT 136)* **THIS CHARMING MAN. / JEANE** [25] [-]
(12") *(RTT 136)* – ('A'side) / Accept yourself / Wonderful woman.
Jan 84. (7") *(RT 146)* **WHAT DIFFERENCE DOES IT MAKE?. / BACK TO THE OLD HOUSE** [12] [-]
(12"+=) *(RTT 146)* – These things take time.
Feb 84. (lp/c) *(ROUGH/+C 61) <25065>* **THE SMITHS** [2] [ ]
– Reel around the fountain / You've got everything now / Miserable lie / Pretty girls make graves / The hand that rocks the cradle / Still ill / Hand in glove / What difference does it make? / I don't owe you anything / Suffer little children. *(cd-iss. May87; ROUGHCD 61) (cd re-iss. 1989 on 'Line'; LICD 9.00308) (re-iss. cd/c)(ltd-10"lp Nov93 on 'WEA'; 4509 91892-2/-4)(SMITHS 1)*
May 84. (7") *(RT 156)* **HEAVEN KNOWS I'M MISERABLE NOW. / SUFFER LITTLE CHILDREN** [10] [ ]
(12"+=) *(RTT 156)* – Girl afraid.
Aug 84. (7") *(RT 166)* **WILLIAM, IT WAS REALLY NOTHING. / PLEASE PLEASE PLEASE LET ME GET WHAT I WANT** [17] [ ]
(12"+=) *(RTT 166)* – How soon is now?
Nov 84. (lp/c) *(ROUGH/+C 76)* **HATFUL OF HOLLOW** (with BBC sessions *) [7] [-]
– William, it was really nothing / What difference does it make? * / These things take time * / This charming man * / How soon is now? / Handsome devil * / Hand in glove / Still ill * / Heaven knows I'm miserable now / This night has opened my eyes * / You've got everything now * / Accept yourself * / Girl afraid / Back to the old house * / Reel around the fountain * / Please please please let me get what I want. *(cd-iss. May87; ROUGHCD 76) (re-iss. cd/c)(ltd-d10"lp Nov93 on 'WEA'; 4509 91893-2/-4)(SMITHS 2)*
Jan 85. (7") *(RT 176)* **HOW SOON IS NOW?. / WELL I WONDER** [24] [-]
(12"+=) *(RTT 176)* – Oscillate wildly.
Feb 85. (7") **HOW SOON IS NOW?. / THE HEADMASTER RITUAL** [-] [ ]
Feb 85. (lp/c) *(ROUGH/+C 81) <25269>* **MEAT IS MURDER** [1] [ ]
– The headmaster ritual / Barbarism begins at home / Rusholme ruffians / I want the one I can't have / What she said / How soon is now? / That joke isn't funny anymore / Nowhere fast / Well I wonder / Meat is murder. *(cd-iss. May87; ROUGHCD 81) (re-iss. cd/c)(ltd-d10"lp Nov93 on 'WEA'; 4509 91895-2/-4)(SMITHS 3)*
Mar 85. (7") *(RT 181)* **SHAKESPEARE'S SISTER. / WHAT SHE SAID** [26] [ ]
(12"+=) *(RTT 181)* – Stretch out and wait.
Jul 85. (7") *(RT 186)* **THAT JOKE ISN'T FUNNY ANYMORE. / MEAT IS MURDER (live)** [49] [ ]
(12"+=) *(RTT 186)* – Nowhere fast / Shakespeare's siste / Stretch out and wait (all live).
Sep 85. (7") *(RT 191)* **THE BOY WITH THE THORN IN HIS SIDE. / ASLEEP** [23] [ ]
(12"+=) *(RTT 191)* – Rubber ring.

—— added **CRAIG GANNON** – guitar, bass (ex-AZTEC CAMERA, ex-BLUEBELLS)

May 86. (7") *(RT 192)* **BIGMOUTH STRIKES AGAIN. / MONEY CHANGES EVERYTHING** [26] [ ]
(12"+=) *(RTT 192)* – Unloveable.
Jun 86. (lp/c) *(ROUGH/+C 96) <25426>* **THE QUEEN IS DEAD** [2] [70]
– Frankly Mr. Shankly / I know it's over / Never had no one ever / Cemetery gates / Big mouth strikes again / Vicar in a tutu / There is a light that never goes out / Some girls are bigger than others / The queen is dead / The boy with the thorn in his side. *(cd-iss. May87; ROUGHCD 96) (re-iss. cd/c)(ltd-d10"lp Nov93 on 'WEA'; 4509 91896-2/-4)(SMITHS 4)*
Jul 86. (7") *(RT 193)* **PANIC. / VICAR IN A TUTU** [11] [ ]
(12"+=) *(RTT 193)* – The draize train.
Oct 86. (7") *(RT 194)* **ASK. / CEMETRY GATES** [14] [ ]
(12"+=/c-s+=) *(RTT 194/+C)* – Golden lights.

—— Reverted to a quartet, when GANNON left to join The CRADLE.

Feb 87. (7") *(RT 195)* **SHOPLIFTERS OF THE WORLD UNITE. / HALF A PERSON** [12] [ ]
(12"+=) *(RTT 195)* – London.
Feb 87. (lp/c/cd) *(ROUGH/+C/CD 101)* **THE WORLD WON'T LISTEN** (part compilation) [7] [-]
– Panic / Ask / London / Big mouth strikes again / Shakespeare's sister / There is a light that never goes out / Shoplifters of the world unite / The boy with the thorn in his side / Asleep / Unloveable / Half a person / Stretch out and wait / That joke isn't funny anymore / Oscillate wildly / You just haven't earned it yet baby / Rubber ring. *(c+=)* – Money changes everything. *(re-iss. cd/c)(ltd-d10"lp Nov93 on 'WEA'; 4509 91898-2/-4)(SMITHS 5)*
Apr 87. (7") *(RT 196)* **SHEILA TAKE A BOW. / IS IT REALLY SO STRANGE?** [10] [ ]
(12"+=) *(RTT 196)* – Sweet and tender hooligan.
Jun 87. (d-lp/d-c/d-cd) *(ROUGH/+C/CD 255) <25569>* **LOUDER THAN BOMBS** (compilation) [38] [62] Apr87
– Is it really so strange? / Sheila take a bow / Sweet and tender hooligan / Shoplifters of the world unite / Half a person / London / Panic / Girl afraid / Shakespeare's sister / William, it was really nothing / You just haven't earned it yet, baby / Golden lights / Ask / Heaven knows I'm miserable now / Unloveable / Asleep / Oscillate wildly / These things take time / Rubber ring / Back to the old house / Hand in glove / Stretch out and wait / This night has opened my eyes / Please, please, please, let me get what I want. *(cd re-iss. Feb95 on 'WEA'; 4509 93833-2)*
Aug 87. (7") *(RT 197)* **GIRLFRIEND IN A COMA. / WORK IS A FOUR-LETTER WORD** [13] [ ]
(12"+=/c-s+=) *(RTT 197/+C)* – I keep mine hidden.
Sep 87. (lp/c/cd) *(ROUGH/+C/CDR 106) <25649>* **STRANGEWAYS HERE WE COME** [2] [55]
– A rush and a push and the land is ours / I started something I couldn't finish / Death of a disco dancer / Girlfriend in a coma / Stop me if you think you've heard this one before / Last night I dreamt that somebody loved me / Unhappy birthday / Paint a vulgar picture / Death at one's elbow / I won't share you. *(re-iss. cd/c)(ltd-d10"lp Nov93 on 'WEA'; 4509 91899-2/-4)(SMITHS 6)*
Oct 87. (7") **STOP ME IF YOU THINK YOU'VE HEARD THIS ONE BEFORE. / I KEEP MINE HIDDEN** [-] [ ]
Nov 87. (7") *(RT 198)* **I STARTED SOMETHING I COULDN'T FINISH. / PRETTY GIRLS MAKE GRAVES** [23] [ ]
(12"+=) *(RTT 198)* – Some girls are bigger than others (live).
(c-s++=) *(RTT 198C)* – What's the world (live).
Dec 87. (7") *(RT 200)* **LAST NIGHT I DREAMT THAT SOMEBODY LOVED ME. / NOWHERE FAST (BBC version)** [30] [ ]
(12"+=) *(RTT 200)* – Rusholme Russians (BBC version).
(cd-s++=) *(RTT 200CD)* – William, it was really nothing (BBC version).

—— they broke-up in August '87, ROURKE and JOYCE splintered with ADULT NET before joining MORRISSEY when he went solo.

– compilations, etc. –

Note; on 'Rough Trade' UK / 'Sire' US, unless otherwise mentioned.

Aug 88. (lp/c/cd/dat) *(ROUGH/+C/CD 126) <25786>* **RANK (live October '86)** [2] [77]
– The queen is dead / Panic / Vicar in a tutu / Ask / Rusholme ruffians / The boy with the thorn in his side / What she said / Is it really so strange? / Cemetry gates / London / I know it's over / The draize train / Still ill / Bigmouth strikes again / (Marie's the name) His latest flame – Take me back to dear old blighty. *(re-iss. cd/c)(ltd-d10"lp Nov93 on 'WEA'; 450991900-2/-4)(SMITHS 7)*
Nov 88. (3"cd-ep) *(RTT 215CD)* **THE HEADMASTER RITUAL / NOWHERE FAST (live) / MEAT IS MURDER (live) / STRETCH OUT AND WAIT (live)** [ ] [-]
Nov 88. (3"cd-ep) *(RTT 171CD)* **BARBARISM BEGINS AT HOME / SHAKESPEARE'S SISTER / STRETCH OUT AND WAIT** [ ] [-]

—— (Note:- 12"singles from Jan84 / May84 / Sep85 / Jul86 / Oct86 were issued on 3"cd-ep Nov88 – add suffix of CD to cat no.).

Oct 88. (12"ep/cd-ep) *Strange Fruit; (SFPS/+CD 055)* **THE PEEL SESSIONS** (18.5.83) [ ] [-]
– What difference does it make? / Reel around the fountain / Miserable lie / Handsome devil.

—— Note; Below on 'WEA' UK/ 'Sire' US unless otherwise mentioned.

Jul 92. (7"/c-s) *(YZ 0001/+C)* **THIS CHARMING MAN. / WONDERFUL WOMAN / ACCEPT YOURSELF** [8] [-]
(cd-s+=) *(YZ 0001CD)* – Jeane.
Aug 92. (cd)(lp/c) *(4509 90044-2)(SMITHS 8/+C) <45042>* **BEST . . . 1** [1] [ ]
– This charming man / William, it was really nothing / What difference does it make / Stop me if you think you've heard it before / Girlfriend in a coma / Half a person / Rubber ring / How soon is now? / Hand in glove / Shoplifters of the world unite / Sheila take a bow / Some girls are bigger than others / Panic / Please please please let me get what I want.
Sep 92. (7"/c-s) *(YZ 0002/+C)* **HOW SOON IS NOW. / HAND IN GLOVE** [16] [-]
(cd-s+=) *(YZ 0002CD1)* – The queen is dead / Handsome devil / I started something I couldn't finish.
(cd-s+=) *(YZ 0002CD2)* – I know it's over / Suffer little children / Back to the old house.
Oct 92. (7"/c-s) *(YZ 0003/+C)* **THERE IS A LIGHT THAT NEVER GOES OUT. / HANDSOME DEVIL (live)** [25] [ ]
(cd-s+=) *(YZ 0003CD1)* – I don't owe you anything / Hand in glove / Jeane.
(cd-s+=) *(YZ 0003CD2)* – Money changes everything (live) / Some girls are bigger than others (live) / Hand in glove (live).
Nov 92. (cd)(lp/c) *(4509 90406-2)(SMITHS 9/+C)* **BEST II** [29] [ ]
– The boy with a thorn in his side / The headmaster ritual / Heaven knows I'm miserable now / Ask / Osciliate wildly / Nowhere fast / Still ill / That joke isn't funny anymore / Shakespeare's sister / Girl afraid / Reel around the fountain / Last night I dreamt somebody loved me / There is a light that never goes out.
Feb 95. (7"/c-s) *(YZ 0004/+C)* **ASK. / CEMETARY GATES** [62] [-]
(cd-s+=) *(YZ 0004CD)* – Golden lights.
Mar 95. (cd/c) *(4509 99090-2/-4)* **"SINGLES"** [5] [ ]
– Hand in glove / This charming man / What difference does it make? / Heaven knows I'm miserable now / William, it was really nothing / How soon is now? / Shakespeare's sister / That joke isn't funny anymore / The boy with the thorn in his side / Bigmouth strikes again / Panic / Ask / Shoplifters of the world unite / Sheila take a bow / Girlfriend in a coma / I started something I couldn't finish / Last night I dreamt that somebody loved me / There is a light that never goes out.
Jun 01. (cd) *(8573 88948-2)* **THE VERY BEST OF THE SMITHS** [30] [-]

SNAKES OF SHAKE

Formed: Glasgow, Scotland . . . 1984 by SEORI BURNETTE, SANDY BROWN, ROBERT RENFREW, TZEN VERMILLION and RHOD BURNETT. Country-tinged indie-rockers in the trademark West Of Scotland mould, the SNAKES OF SHAKE issued a mini-set, 'SOUTHERN CROSS', its title track simultaneously released in Spring '85. It wouldn't be the first time the song would surface, although by the time it revamped a year later, both VERMILLION and BURNETT had been substituted by (WILSON) NEIL SCOTT and IAIN SHEDDON respectively. Their one and only full-length set, 'GRACELANDS AND THE NATURAL WOOD' (1987), would again feature what had now become their theme tune although the collapse of their label, 'Making Waves', put paid to any chances they might have had. Getting a foothold once more on the music business ladder, three former SNAKES (SEORI, WILSON and IAIN, together with KEITH GILES and session man extrordinaire, BJ COLE) re-emerged in 1988 as SUMMERHILL. Following a few West Coast/BYRDS-influenced releases including the mini-set, 'LOWDOWN', the line-up was slightly amended when SHEDDON was replaced with MICHAEL STURGIS. Finally rewarded for their years of struggle, SUMMERHILL were snapped up by 'Polydor', the resulting 'WEST OF HERE' set hitting the shops early in 1990. Described (probably unfairly) as a countrified, poor man's DEACON BLUE, the band received a smattering of positive reviews but failed to make their mark on the ever fickle and evolving pop-rock scene. • **Covered:** DO RIGHT WOMAN, DO RIGHT MAN (Dan Penn – Spooner Oldham) / WILD HORSES (Rolling Stones).

Album rating: SOUTHERN CROSS mini (*4) / GRACELANDS AND THE NATURAL WOOD (*6) / Summerhill: LOWDOWN (*5) / WEST OF HERE (*5)

SNAKES OF SHAKE (cont)

SEORI BURNETTE – vocals, guitar, harmonica / TZEN VERMILLION – guitar / SANDY BROWN – piano, accordion, vocals / ROBERT RENFREW – bass, slide guitar, vocals / RHOD BURNETT – drums

			Tense But Confident	not iss.
Mar 85.	(m-lp)	(TBC 1) SOUTHERN CROSS	□	–
Mar 85.	(12"m)	(GOBS12-1) SOUTHERN CROSS. / LIFE'S TOO STRONG / INDISPENSIBLE	□	–

— (WILSON) NEIL SCOTT – guitar; repl. VERMILLION

— IAIN SHEDDON – drums (ex-JOLT) repl. RHOD BURNETT

			Making Waves	not iss.
Aug 86.	(7")	(SURF 116) SOUTHERN CROSS. / YOU WALK (12"+=) (SURFT 116) – ('A'-part 2).	□	–
Jul 87.	(cd/c/lp)	(CD/C+/SPRAY 106) GRACELANDS AND THE NATURAL WOOD	□	–

– Southern cross / Make it shine / Gracelands / No reason / Strange affair / Man the man / Sender down / Last resort / Like no ther / Get me out of here.

SUMMERHILL

— were formed by SEORI, (WILSON) NEIL, IAIN / + KEITH GILES – bass, vocals / guest B.J. COLE – steel guitar (session man extraordinaire)

			Rocket 5	not iss.
Jun 88.	(7")	(HUCS 102) I WANT YOU. /	□	–
			Diabolo	not iss.
Oct 88.	(m-lp)	(SORCM 4) LOWDOWN	□	–

– Rosebud / I'll keep you in mind / Lately / Knew I would return / Hold back the heartache / It's gonna be alright / I can't stay / Say goodbye.

— MICHAEL STURGIS – drums; repl. IAIN

			Polydor	not iss.
Oct 89.	(7"/7"g-f)	(TTRC/+G 1) HERE I AM. / (12"+=) (TTRCX 1) –	□	–
Mar 90.	(7"/c-s)	(TTRC/+S 2) DON'T LET IT DIE. / KEEP YOU IN MIND (10"+=/12"+=/cd-s+=) (TTRC T/X/D 2) – Do right woman, do right man / It's gonna be alright.	□	–
Mar 90.	(cd/c/lp)	(843130-2/-4/-1) WEST OF HERE	□	–

– Don't let it die / Here I am / If you hold a gun / The ballad of Summerhill / I've found a friend / If I knew you better / Somehow, somewhere / Lately / I have a reason / Last to find out. (cd+=/c+=) – Wild horses (live in the studio).

| Apr 90. | (7") | (TTRC 3) WILD HORSES. / RIVER BLUE (12"+=/cd-s+=) (TTRC X/D 3) – Please don't go away. | □ | – |

— later that year, two ex-SUMMERHILL members (they had now split) teamed up with singer, SUMISHTA BRAHM, on a one-off 13 FRIGHTENED GIRLS single, 'Lost At Sea'. The following year, WILSON SCOTT joined HORSE LATITUDES, who released a mini-set, 'SEPTEMBER SONGS'. SUMMERHILL re-formed in the mid 90's

			Tupelo	not iss.
Jan 95.	(cd-s)	(TTRCD 4) NO MATTER WHAT YOU DO	□	–

SNEAKY FEELINGS

Formed: Dunedin, New Zealand ... 1980 by MATTHEW BANNISTER, DAVID PINE, KATHRYN TYRIE and MARTIN DURRANT. Named after an ELVIS COSTELLO track, each of the quartet shared the singing and songwriting duties. A first appearance by the band on seminal 1981 compilation 'Dunedin Double' was followed up by jangly single 'BE MY FRIEND'. DURRANT then spent time overseas, which meant the band had to take a hiatus, replacing TYRIE with new bassboy JOHN KELCHER. 1984 would bring the critically feted debut 'FEELINGS LP, 'SEND YOU' (also on 'Flying Nun'). The following year saw the release of the excellent "new man" single 'HOUSE HUSBAND', whilst 1986 brought the appearance of another single, 'BETTER THAN BEFORE'. The band's easy critical ride would be slowed by the release of 'SENTIMENTAL EDUCATION' (1987). 'HARD LOVE STORIES' (1988) was DURRANT's final release with the band, who replaced him on drums with ROSS BURGE; KELCHER's departure in 1989 saw the end of SNEAKY FEELINGS. Plucky axeman BANNISTER went on to form folk-pop outfit DRIBBLING DARTS, and would later recruit DURRANT briefly to drum for this band.

Album rating: SEND YOU (*6) / WAITING FOR TOUCHDOWN (*5) / SENTIMENTAL EDUCATION (*5) / HARD LOVE STORIES (*5) / Dribbling Darts Of Love: FLORID DABBLERS VOTING (*5) / PRESENT PERFECT (*5)

MATTHEW BANNISTER – vocals, guitar, keyboards, synthesizer / **DAVID PINE** – vocals, guitars / **KATHRYN TYRIE** – bass / **MARTIN DURRANT** – drums

			Flying Nun	Flying Nun
Jan 82.	(d12"ep; with Various Artists)	(FNDUN 1/2) DUNEDIN DOUBLE EP	–	– NewZ

– Pity's sake / There's a chance / Backroom / (others by The CHILLS, The VERLAINES + The STONES).

| May 83. | (7") | (FN 015) BE MY FRIEND. / AMNESIA | – | – NewZ |
| 1984. | (lp) | (FNFEEL 1) SEND YOU | – | – NewZ |

– Waiting for touchdown / Throwing stones / Strangers again / Someone else's eyes / Not to take sides / P.I.T. song / Won't change / Everything I want – Not to take sides (reprise). (cd-iss. 1990 +=; FN 205CD) – Ready or not / Cry you out of my eyes / Maybe you need to come back.

— JOHN KELCHER – bass, keyboards; repl. TYRIE who injured her arm

1985.	(12")	(FNFEEL 2) HUSBAND HOUSE. / STRANGE AND CONFLICTING FEELINGS	–	– NewZ
1986.	(7")	(FNFEEL 3) BETTER THAN BEFORE. / WOULDN'T CRY, HERE'S TO THE OTHER SIX	–	– NewZ
Apr 87.	(lp)	(FNUK 2) WAITING FOR TOUCHDOWN	□	–

– Better than before / Waiting for touchdown / Someone else's eyes / Strangers again / Wouldn't cry / Not to take sides / Throwing stones / Major Barbara / The strange and conflicting feelings of separation and betrayal / Husband house / Won't change.

| Nov 87. | (lp/cd) | (FNE 14/+CD) SENTIMENTAL EDUCATION | □ | – |

– All you've done / Coming true / Wasted time / Backroom / Walk to the square / A leeter to you / Trouble with Kay / It's so easy / Now / I'm not going to let her bring me down / Wouldn't cry / Major Barbara / Broken man / Husband house / The strange and conflicting feelings of separation and betrayal / Strangers again / Better than before / Amnesia.

| Dec 87. | (7") | (FNFEEL 5) COMING TRUE. / WASTED TIME | – | – NewZ |
| Nov 88. | (lp/cd) | (FNE 26/+CD) HARD LOVE STORIES | □ | – |

– In the shape of a heart / Your secret's safe with me / Dad + the family dog / Further + further away from you / Parked / This be the verse / Hard love / Leuin dream / Discipline / Take me there / Long time gone.

| 1989. | (7") | (FN 119) LONG TIME GONE. / (free 7") (FN 12) – | – | – NewZ |

— ROSS BURGE – drums; repl. DURRANT

— split mid-'89 when KELCHER also departed, forming CREELEY while PINE joined DEATH RAY CAFE. A SNEAKY FEELINGS reunion in 1990 heralded three further live songs for Radio One; subsequently added to CD re-issue of 'SEND YOU'. ROSS BURGE subsequently joined The MUTTON BIRDS

DRIBBLING DARTS (OF LOVE)

MATTHEW BANNISTER – vocals, guitar / **ALAN GREGG** – bass (ex-REMARKABLES) / **ALICE BULMER** – violin

			Flying Nun	not iss.
Feb 91.	(12"ep)	(FN 161) SHOOT EP	–	– NewZ

– You have improved me / Forget it / If you're looking for good / No sooner here (than it's gone).

— added **RICHARD FOULKES JR.** – drums; who at times was repl. by MARTIN DURRANT

| 1992. | (cd-ep) | (FN 197) FLORID DABBLERS VOTING | □ | – |

– Let me be mean / Digging for worms / Love and friendship / Only my shadow / Depending on you. (cd-iss. 1993 +=; FN 213) – SHOOT

| Jul 94. | (cd) | (FNCD 247) PRESENT PERFECT | □ | – |

– Hey Judith / How to waterski / Stuck inside the birth canal / Question and the answer / Life's a mistake (worth repeating) / The Big Bopper / Present perfect / Try not to explain / Whatever she does / Hole in my head / Remember.

| Sep 94. | (cd-s) | (FN 273) HEY JUDITH / HOW TO WATERSKI / IT'S NOT UNNATURAL / LET ME BE MEAN (original) | – | – NewZ |

— BANNISTER retired from the music biz

SNEETCHES

Formed: San Francisco, California, USA ... 1985 by MIKE LEVY, MATT CARGES and Englishman, DANIEL SWAN. A bright indie power-pop trio, they initially inked a deal with UK-based imprint, 'Kaleidoscope Sound', releasing debut single, 'ONLY FOR A MOMENT' (in the summer of '88), a month prior to its parent mini-set, 'LIGHTS OUT! WITH THE SNEETCHES'. This in turn, took them on to 'Creation' records ('Alias' in the US) and a first full-set, 'SOMETIMES THAT'S ALL WE HAVE' (1989), a darker but positively feel-good array of tunes that was somewhat out of place in this prepubescent shoegazing period. With the addition of former STINGRAYS bassist, ALEJANDRO "ALEC" PALAO (also from Britain), The SNEETCHES continued into the next decade, unruffled by the advent of grunge and rave. 'SLOW' (1990) and a lengthy singles-only time with US indie stalwarts, 'Bus Stop', kept their heads above water, although it was a meeting – and a subsequent 1993 album collaboration – with CHRIS WILSON (of The FLAMIN' GROOVIES), that set them apart from their contemporaries. Their final effort, 'BLOW OUT THE SUN' (1994), had its moments of BEATLES-esque, retro-pop, but all was lost on a care-less public. • **Covered:** SHE MAY CALL YOU UP TONIGHT (Brown – Martin) / HE'S FRANK (Monochrome Set) / I WANNA BE WITH YOU (Raspberries) / PRETTY GIRL (Easybeats).

Album rating: LIGHTS OUT! WITH THE SNEETCHES (*5) / SOMETIMES THAT'S ALL WE HAVE (*7) / SLOW (*5) / CHRIS WILSON & THE SNEETCHES mini (*5) / BLOW OUT THE SUN (*4) / STARFUCKER (*5)

MIKE LEVY – vocals, bass / **MATT CARGES** – guitar / **DANIEL SWAN** – drums

			Kaleidoscope Sound	not iss.
Jun 88.	(12"m)	(KS 106) ONLY FOR A MOMENT. / 54 HOURS / WELL ... ALRIGHT	□	–
Jul 88.	(m-lp)	(KSLP 007) LIGHTS OUT! WITH THE SNEETCHES	□	–

– I need someone / In my car / Lorelei / 54 hours / I don't expect her for you / Home again / No one knows / Only for a moment. (cd-iss. Apr91 on 'Creation'; CRECD 077)

			Creation	Alias
Apr 89.	(lp/cd)	(CRELP 43/+CD) <A 002/+D> SOMETIMES THAT'S ALL WE HAVE	□	□

– Unusual sounds / Don't turn back / In a perfect place / Empty sea / Sometimes that's all we have / Run in the sun / Mrs Markle / Nowhere at all / Take my hand / Another shitty day / You're gonna need her / It's looking like me.

| Jun 89. | (12"m) | <A 004> PLEASE DON'T BREAK MY HEART / HE'S FRANK / LOVE COMES MY WAY | – | □ |

— added **ALEJANDRO 'ALEC' PALAO** – bass (ex-STINGRAYS) / LEVY now vocals/guitar

| Nov 90. | (lp/c/cd) | <A 008/+C/D> SLOW | – | □ |

– Things we'll never see / Over 'round each other / Heloise / Broke up in my hands / Crystal ball / What's in your mind / Voice in my head / Wish you would / How does it feel / Let us go / She may call you up tonight.

			not iss.	Bus Stop
1991.	(7")	<BUS 010> SHE DOES EVERYTHING FOR ME. / FLYING ON THE GROUND IS WRONG	–	□

SNEETCHES (cont)

1992.	(7") <BUS 025> **...AND I'M THINKING. / I THINK IT'S ALRIGHT**	-	-
1993.	(7") <BUS 033> **A GOOD THING. / JULIANNA WHY**	not iss.	Jelly Bean
1993.	(7") <Mayu-02> **SHE MAY CALL YOU UP TONIGHT. / PRETTY GIRL**	Elefant	not iss.
1993.	(7") (ER 119) **SUNNYSIDE DOWN** – ...And I'm thinking / Try and make it all work.	-	- Spain

—— next a collaboration with **CHRIS WILSON** (ex-FLAMIN' GROOVIES)

Marilyn   Marilyn

Oct 93. (m-cd/m-lp; by CHRIS WILSON & THE SNEETCHES) <(USM CD/LP 1023)> **CHRIS WILSON & THE SNEETCHES**
 – If wishes were horses / Never love again / He who waits / Goin' back / Between the lines / I'll cry alone / Slow death.

SpinArt   SpinArt

Sep 94. (lp/cd) <(SPART 20/+CD)> **BLOW OUT THE SUN**
 – Weather scene / Saving it for me / Good thing / Light on above / Behind the shadow / ...And I'm thinking / What I know / Little things / All of everything / Try to make it all work.

—— disbanded after above album

– compilations, etc. –

Nov 91. (lp/c/cd) *Alias;* <A 016/+C/D> **1985-1991**   -   -
Jul 93. (m-cd) *Bus Stop;* (BUS 1003-2) **THINK AGAIN**   -   -
Nov 94. (cd) *Creation – Rev-Ola;* (CREV 031CD) **OBSCUREYEARS**   -
 – (THINK AGAIN / plus several others).
May 95. (10"lp/m-cd) *Bus Stop;* <(BUS 1006/+2)> **STARFUCKER**   Apr95
 – Watch me burn / Caroline goodbye / The fool for you / Come along with me / This thime / They keep me running / The dog in you.

SNUFF

Formed: Hendon, London, England ... 1986 by DUNCAN REDMONDS, SIMON CRIGHTON and ANDY WELLS. Leavening the "straight edge" seriousness of much hardcore from across the pond, SNUFF set out their agenda with 'NOT LISTENING ANYMORE', a debut single that struck a chord with Radio One DJ John Peel. Released on the 'Workers Playtime' label in the spring of '89, it was to feature in the man's final Festive 50 of the 80's. By that time, it had also appeared on first album, 'SNUFF SAID ...', the comic book funsters introducing their penchant for mind-bogglingly unpronounceable titles, raucous, good-time melodic hardcore/punk and amphetamine party-piece cover trashings of pop hits such as Tiffany's 'I THINK WE'RE ALONE NOW'. Famed for their manic live shows and diehard following, it came as a bit of a surprise when they split in summer '91 after a final gig at Kilburn National Ballroom. With healthy patronage from American practitioners such as GREEN DAY and NOFX, however, the lads were persuaded to re-group in 1994 along with new members, trombonist DAVE and hammond player LEE M. Subsequently signing to 'Deceptive', the trio returned in characteristic style at Xmas '95 with a version of the theme from vintage Brit TV sitcom, 'WHATEVER HAPPENED TO THE LIKELY LADS'. A comeback album, 'DEMMAMUSSABEBONK' (1996), meanwhile, saw LOZ replacing SIMON but demonstrated the trio had lost none of their roughneck charm or sense of humour. On the contrary, the trio entered the most prolific period of their career, releasing a mini-covers set, 'POTATOES AND MELONS AT WHOLESALE PRICES (DIRECT TO YOU THE PUBLIC)' in '97 and a further long player, 'TWEET TWEET MY LOVELY', the following year. In April '99, members of SNUFF and LEATHERFACE united in Honest Dons outfit, DOGPISS, releasing one album 'EINE KLEINE PUNKMUSIK'. 'NUMB NUTS' (2000) took the SNUFF campaign into the new millennium with a whopping 16 tracks, all reliably under the 3 minute mark. 'BLUE GRAVY: PHASE 9', meanwhile, was a mini-set by comparison although its willingness to experiment with everything from 60's R&B, ska and soul to neo-psychedelia was a shot in the eye to anyone who'd written them off as a one-trick novelty act. • **Covers:** CAN'T EXPLAIN (Who) / DO NOTHING + YOU'RE WONDERING NOW (Specials) / REACH OUT I'LL BE THERE (Four Tops) / I CAN SEE CLEARLY NOW (Johnny Nash) / I THINK WE'RE ALONE NOW (Rubinoos) / PURPLE HAZE (Jimi Hendrix) / IN SICKNESS & IN HEALTH (Chas & Dave) / MAGIC MOMENTS (hit. Perry Como) / RIVERS OF BABYLON (hit. Boney M) / SHADOWS OF LOVE (Dozier-Holland-Holland) / SOUL LIMBO (Booker T.) / etc. • **Trivia:** SNUFF also did versions of themes for TV commercials (Bran Flakes + Shake'n'vac + Cadbury's Flake) and more recently 'ANY OLD IRON'.

Album rating: SNUFF SAID ... (*6) / REACH (*5) / DEMMAMUSSABEBONK (*7) / POTATOES AND MELONS AT WHOLESALE PRICES (*6) / TWEET TWEET MY LOVELY (*5) / NUMB NUTS (*5) / BLUE GRAVY PHASE 9 (*7)

SIMON CRIGHTON (b.11 Dec'66) – guitar, vocals / **DUNCAN REDMONDS** (b.22 Aug'64) – drums, vocals / **ANDY WELLS** (b. 4 Jul'63) – bass

Workers Playtime   Aftertan

Apr 89. (7"ep/cd-ep) (PLAY 008) **NOT LISTENING ANYMORE EP**   -
 – Not listening / Dead and buried / That's enough / For both sides – No one home.(re-iss. Jul96; same)
Nov 89. (lp/c/cd) (PLAY-LP/MC/CD 010) **SNUFF SAID: GORBLIMEYGUVSTONEMEIFHEDIDN'TTHROWA WOBBLERCHACHACHACHACHACHACHACHACHA YOU' REGOINGHOMEINACOSMICAMBULANCE**
 – Words of wisdom / Some how / Now you don't remember / Not listening / I see – H.M. Trout / Too late / Another girl / Win some lose some /

Pass me by / Keep the best / Night of the Li's / Purple haze / Little git / What kind of love. (re-iss. Apr95; same) <US cd-iss. 1996 on 'Fat Wreck Chords'+=; 543> – NOT LISTENING EP
Apr 90. (12"ep/cd-ep) (PLAY 011-T/CD) **FLIBBEDDEDYDIBBIRDDYDOB**
 – Rods and mockers / Do nothing / Shake'n'black / Can't explain / Ecstasy / Reach out / Hazy shade of winter / Do it quick / City attacked by rats / Bran flakes / In sickness & in health. (12"ep re-iss. Mar95; same) <US cd-iss. Aug96 on 'Fat Wreck Chords'; 544>

—— split August '91 after mail-order final gig lp 'KILBURN NATIONAL BALLROOM 17/11/90'. ANDY joined LEATHERFACE for a few years.

10 Past 12   K

Jun 91. (7"m) (IPU 027) **THAT'S FINE. / DEN DEN / WHAT KIND OF LOVE?**   -   -
Jul 91. (12"ep) **THAT'S FINE. / I CAN SEE CLEARLY NOW / YOU'RE WONDERING NOW**
Apr 92. (lp/cd) (PARKA 003/+CD) **REACH**
 – I know what you want / Teabag / The damage is done / Spend, spend, spend / If I tried / Hellbound / Smile (that's fine) / It's you / Bingo / Ichola buddha / Porro / Sweet dreams. (re-iss. Jun97 on 'K'; KLP 012)

—— **DUNCAN, ANDY + SIMON** re-formed in 1994, although the latter was replaced a year later by **LOZ** – guitar, vocals. Other 2 members were **DAVE** – trombone / **LEE M** – hammond organ, vocals (late bass)

Deceptive   Fat Wreck Chords

Dec 95. (7"one-sided) (BLUFF 019) **THEME FROM 'WHATEVER HAPPENED TO THE LIKELY LADS'**
Feb 96. (cd/c/lp) (BLUFF 023 CD/MC/LP) <533> **DEMMAMUSSABEBONK**
 – Vikings / Defeat / Dick trois / Martin / Nick Northern / Batten down the hatches / G to D / Sunny places / Horse and cart / Squirrels / Cricklewood / B / Punchline / Who.
Mar 96. (7"ep/cd-ep) (BLUFF 026/+CD) **LONG BALL TO NO-ONE (EP)**
 – Caught in session / Nick Northern / Walk / Dow dow boof boof.
Aug 96. (7"ep/cd-ep) (BLUFF 033/+CD) **DO DO DO (EP)**
 – Standing in the shadows of love / I will survive / Soul limbo / It must be boring being in Snuff.
Jun 97. (10"m-lp/m-cd) (BLUFF 042 TN/CD) <556> **POTATOES AND MELONS AT WHOLESALE PRICES (DIRECT TO YOU THE PUBLIC)**
 – Rivers of Babylon / Whatever happened to the Likely Lads / Shadows of love / Soul limbo / Come and gone / It must be boring being Snuff / Ye olde folke twatte / Magic moments / Russian fields / Time dub / Pink purple.
Apr 98. (7"ep/cd-ep) (BLUFF 061/+CD) <563> **SCHMINKIE MINKIE PINKIE EP**   May98
 – Nick Motown / Spicy / Medaka no gakoh / Bit cosy.
May 98. (cd/lp) (BLUFF 056 CD/LP) <562> **TWEET TWEET MY LOVELY**
 – No reason / Ticket / Timebomb / Lyehf taidu leikh / Nick Motown / Brickwall / Arsehole / Bob / All you need / Etc. / The thief / Verdidn't / Bit cosy / Take me home (piss off).
Nov 98. (7") (BLUFF 065) **YUKI. / ROMEO & JULIET**
 (cd-s+=) (BLUFF 065CD) – Rockafeller skank.
Oct 99. (7"ep/cd-ep) (BLUFF 072/+CD) **DOWN BY YURR EP**
 – Pixies / Chalk me down for more / 2 winds / Sweet dreams.
Mar 00. (cd/lp) (BLUFF 074 CD/LP) <601> **NUMB NUTS**
 – Pixies / It's a long way down / SQ11 / Marbles / Numb nuts / Reach / Another wet weekend / EFL vs concrete / Fuck off / Yuki / Hilda Ogden and thick plottens / Soup of the day / Cake / Bottom of the river / Chalk me down for more / Romeo & Juliet / Rockafeller skank.
May 00. (7"ep/cd-ep) (BLUFF 076/+CD) **SWEET DAYS EP**
 – Sweet days / Inmate / Combination mullet / Bacharach.

12:10   Fat Wreck Chords

May 01. (m-cd/10"m-lp) (1210 01 CD/V) <FAT 627> **BLUE GRAVY PHASE 9**   Jun01
 – Split / Prisoner abroad / Blue gravy / Emperor / Damaged / Ichola buddha / Night of the Li's / Caught in session (live) / Ecstasy (live).

– compilations, etc. –

Jan 95. (cd) *Vinyl Japan;* (ASKCD 048) **KILBURN NATIONAL 27.11.90 (live)**
 (re-iss. Jan97; same)
Sep 97. (cd/lp) *Vinyl Japan;* (MASKCD/ASKLP 073) **CAUGHT IN SESSION**
Oct 98. (cd) *Konkurrel;* (FISH 4CD) **IN THE FISHTANK**
Oct 99. (7"ep/cd-ep) *V8;* (004/005) **AUSTRALIAN TOUR EP**

SOFT CELL (see under ⇒ ALMOND, Marc)

SONIC YOUTH

Formed: New York City, New York, USA ... early 1981 by THURSTON MOORE and KIM GORDON. They replaced an early embryonic rhythm section with LEE RANALDO and RICHARD EDSON. After numerous releases on various US indie labels (notably Glenn Branca's 'Neutral' records), they signed to 'Blast First' in the U.K. First up for the label was 'BAD MOON RISING' in 1985, showing them at their most menacing and disturbing, especially on the glorious 'DEATH VALLEY 69' (a macabre reference to killer Charles Manson) with LYDIA LUNCH providing dual vox. They subsequently secured a US deal with 'S.S.T.', heralding yet another socially passionate thrash effort with 'EVOL'. A sideline project, CICCONE YOUTH, saw KIM and the lads plus MIKE WATT (of fIREHOSE), take off MADONNA's 'INTO THE GROOVE(Y)', which became a surprise dancefloor fave. Two more classic pieces, 'SISTER' (1987) & 'DAYDREAM NATION' (1988), finally secured them a major deal with 'D.G.C.' (David Geffen Company). In the early 90's, they smashed into the UK Top 40 with the album 'GOO', featuring a cameo by CHUCK D (of PUBLIC ENEMY) on the track/single 'KOOL THING'. The album, which sweetened their garage-punk/art-noise collages with melodic hooks, also included their deeply haunting tribute to KAREN CARPENTER, 'TUNIC (SONG FOR KAREN)'. They supported PUBLIC ENEMY that year, also stepping out with NEIL YOUNG on his 'Ragged Glory' tour in '91 (much to the distaste of YOUNG's more conservative fans!). In 1992, many thought 'DIRTY' to be a disappointment, the record being overproduced and overtaken by their new rivals and labelmates NIRVANA. By the mid-late 90's, they had returned to ground roots with acoustic psychedelia and the albums, 'EXPERIMENTAL JET SET' (1994), 'WASHING MACHINE' (1995) and 'A THOUSAND LEAVES' (1998) were again lauded by the alternative music press. All members had also taken on side solo projects, KIM featuring in all-star punk-grunge affair, FREE KITTEN. SONIC YOUTH returned towards the end of the decade with an appropriately-titled set, 'GOODBYE 20th CENTURY' (1999), a record in which they took on the works of avant-garde composers CHRISTIAN WOLFF, JOHN CAGE and CORNELIUS CARDEW. 'NYC GHOSTS & FLOWERS' (2000) was also a tribute of sorts, inspired by the beat poets who once upon a time fed their wayward muse on the Big Apple's mean streets. Featuring an Allen Ginsberg-derived title and William Burroughs cover art, the album was only partly successful in capturing the wild-eyed passion of the era. Their first straight up rock'n'roll album (if SONIC YOUTH could ever be described as dealing in straight up rock'n'roll) in almost five years, 'MURRAY STREET' (2002) found RENALDO and Co (with JIM O'ROURKE now a fully paid up member) reining in much of their tendency to free-form noise experimentation with a refreshingly prudent approach to their too often wearingly familiar craft. • **Songwriters:** MOORE / RANALDO / GORDON compositions, except I WANNA BE YOUR DOG (Stooges) / TICKET TO RIDE + WITHIN YOU WITHOUT YOU (Beatles) / BEAT ON THE BRAT + others (Ramones) / TOUCH ME, I'M SICK (Mudhoney) / ELECTRICITY (Captain Beefheart) / COMPUTER AGE (Neil Young). Their off-shoot CICCONE YOUTH covered INTO THE GROOVE (Madonna) / ADDICTED TO LOVE (Robert Palmer) / IS IT MY BODY (Alice Cooper) / PERSONALITY CRISIS (New York Dolls) / CA PLANE POUR MOI (Plastic Bertrand) / MOIST VAGINA = (MV) (Nirvana). FREE KITTEN covered: OH BONDAGE UP YOURS (X-Ray Spexs). • **Trivia:** Early in 1989, they were featured on hour-long special TV documentary for Melvyn Bragg's 'The South Bank Show'.

Album rating: CONFUSION IS SEX (*6) / KILL YR IDOLS (*4) / BAD MOON RISING (*8) / EVOL (*8) / SISTER (*9) / DAYDREAM NATION (*9) / GOO (*9) / DIRTY (*7) / EXPERIMENTAL JET SET, TRASH AND NO STAR (*6) / WASHING MACHINE (*8) / A THOUSAND LEAVES (*6) / GOODBYE 20th CENTURY (*7) / NYC GHOSTS & FLOWERS (*4) / MURRAY STREET (*6) / Lee Ranaldo: FROM HERE TO INFINITY (*4) / EAST JESUS (*7) / Thurston Moore: PSYCHIC HEARTS (*8) / ROOT (*7)

THURSTON MOORE (b.25 Jul'58, Coral Gables, Florida) – vocals, guitar / **KIM GORDON** (b.28 Apr'53, Rochester, N.Y.) – vocals, bass / **LEE RANALDO** (b. 3 Feb'56, Glen Cove, N.Y.) – vocals, guitar repl. ANN DEMARIS / **RICHARD EDSON** – drums repl. DAVE KEAY

Feb 84. (m-lp) *(ND 01)* **SONIC YOUTH (live)** — Neutral / not iss. German
– The burning spear / I dreamt I dreamed / She's not alone / I don't want to push it / The good and the bad. *(re-iss. cd Oct87 on 'S.S.T.'; SSTCD 097)*

— **JIM SCLAVUNOS** – drums repl. EDSON

Feb 84. (lp) *(ND 02)* **CONFUSION IS SEX** — / — German
– Inhuman / The world looks red / Confusion is next / Making the nature scene / Lee is free / (She's in a) Bad mood / Protect me you / Freezer burn / I wanna be your dog / Shaking Hell. *(re-iss. cd Oct87 on 'S.S.T.'; SSTCD 096)*

— **BOB BERT** – drums repl. SCLAVUNOS (still featured on 2 tracks)

Oct 83. (m-lp) *(ZENSOR 10)* **KILL YR. IDOLS** — Zensor / not iss. German
– Protect me you / Shaking Hell / Kill yr. idols / Brother James / Early American.

1984. (c) *<none>* **SONIC DEATH (SONIC YOUTH LIVE)** — not iss. / Ecstatic Peace
– Sonic Death (side 1) / Sonic Death (side 2). *(UK cd-iss. Jul88 on 'Blast First'; BFFP 32CD)*

Dec 84. (12"; by SONIC YOUTH & LYDIA LUNCH) *<1-12>* **DEATH VALLEY '69. / BRAVE MEN (RUN IN MY FAMILY)** — not iss. / Iridescence

Mar 85. (lp) *(BFFP 1)* *<HMS 016>* **BAD MOON RISING** — Blast First / Homestead
– Intro / Brave men rule / Society is a hole / I love her all the time / Ghost bitch / I'm insane / Justice is might / Death valley '69. *(cd-iss. Nov86+=; BFFP 1CD)* – Satan is boring / Flower / Halloween. *<US cd re-iss. 1995 on 'Geffen'; 24512>*

Jun 85. (12"ep; by SONIC YOUTH & LYDIA LUNCH) *(BFFP 2)* *<HMS 012>* **DEATH VALLEY '69. / I DREAMT I DREAMED / INHUMAN / BROTHER JAMES / SATAN IS BORING**

Jan 86. (12",12"yellow) *(BFFP 3)* **HALLOWEEN. / FLOWER**
Jan 86. (7") *(BFFP 3)* **FLOWER. / REWOLF (censored)**
(12"+=) – ('A'side) / Satan is boring (live).
Mar 86. (etched-12") *(BFFP 3-B)* **HALLOWEEN II**

— **STEVE SHELLEY** (b.23 Jun'62, Midland, Michigan) – drums repl. BOB BERT who joined PUSSY GALORE

May 86. (lp/c) *(BFFP 4/+C)* *<SST/+C/CD 059>* **EVOL** — Blast First / S.S.T.
– Green light / Star power / Secret girl / Tom Violence / Death to our friends / Shadow of a doubt / Marilyn Moore / In the kingdom / Madonna, Sean and me.

(cd-iss. Nov86+=; BFFP 4CD) – Bubblegum. *<US cd re-iss. 1995 on 'Geffen'; 24513>*

Jul 86. (7") *(BFFP 7)* *<SST 80>* **STAR POWER. / BUBBLEGUM**
(12"+=) *(BFFP 7T)* *<SST 80-12>* – Expressway.

— added guest **MIKE WATT** – bass (of fIREHOSE)

Nov 86. (12"; as CICCONE YOUTH) *(BFFP 8)* **INTO THE GROOVE(Y). / TUFF TITTY RAP / BURNIN' UP**

Jun 87. (lp/c/cd) *(BFFP 20/+C/CD)* *<SST/+C/CD 134>* **SISTER**
– White cross / (I got a) Catholic block / Hot wire my heart / Tuff gnarl / Kotton crown / Schizophrenia / Beauty lies in the eye / Stereo sanctity / Pipeline – killtime / PCH. *(cd+=)* – Master-Dik (original). *<US cd re-iss. 1995 on 'Geffen'; 24514>*

Jan 88. (m-lp) *(BFFP 26T)* *<SST 155>* **MASTER-DIK**
– Master-Dik / Beat on the brat / Under the influence of the Jesus & Mary Chain: Ticket to ride / Ringo – He's on fire / Florida oil / Chines jam / Vibrato – Guitar lick – Funky fresh / Our backyard / Traffik.

Jan 88. (lp/c/cd; as CICCONE YOUTH) *(BFFP 28/+C/CD)* *<C1/C4/C2 75402>* **THE WHITEY ALBUM** — Blast First / Capitol — 63
– Needle-gun (silence) / G-force / Platoon II / Macbeth / Me & Jill / Hendrix Cosby / Burnin' up / Hi! everybody / Children of Satan / Third fig / Two cool rock chicks / Listening to Neu! / Addicted to love / Moby-Dik / March of the Ciccone robots / Making the nature scene / Tuff titty rap / Into the groovey. *<US cd re-iss. 1995 on 'Geffen'; 24516>*

Feb 88. (d-one-sided-7" on 'Fierce') *(FRIGHT 015-016)* **STICK ME DONNA MAGICK MOMMA / MAKING THE NATURE SCENE (live)**
(also soon issued as normal-7")

Oct 88. (d-lp/c/cd) *(BFFP 34/+C/CD)* *<2602339>* **DAYDREAM NATION** — Blast First / Torso — 99
– Teenage riot / Silver rocket / The sprawl / 'Cross the breeze / Eric's trip / Total trash / Hey Joni / Providence / Candle? / Rain king / Kissability / Trilogy: The wonder – Hyperstation – Eliminator Jr.

— Late in '88, KIM teamed up with LYDIA LUNCH and SADIE MAE to form one-off project HARRY CREWS. Their live appearances were issued in Apr 90 as 'NAKED IN GARDEN HILLS' for 'Big Cat' UK + 'Widowspeak' US.

Feb 89. (12") *(BFFP 46)* **TOUCH ME, I'M SICK. / (Halloween; by MUDHONEY)**

Jun 90. (cd/c/lp) *<(7599 24297-2/-4/-1)>* **GOO** — W.E.A. / D.G.C. — 32 / 96
– Dirty boots / Tunic (song for Karen) / Mary-Christ / Kool thing / Mote / My friend Goo / Disappearer / Mildred Pierce / Cinderella's big score / Scooter + Jinx / Titanium expose. *(re-iss. cd Oct95 on 'Geffen'; GFLD 19297)*

Sep 90. (7") *(GEF 81)* **KOOL THING. / THAT'S ALL I KNOW (RIGHT NOW)** — Geffen / Geffen
(12"+=) *(GEF 81T)* – ('A'demo version).
(cd-s++=) *(GEF 81CD)* – Dirty boots (rock & roll Heaven version).

— In Autumn '90, THURSTON was part of 'Rough Trade' supergroup VELVET MONKEYS.

Apr 91. (m-lp/m-c/m-cd) *(DGC/+C/D 21634)* **DIRTY BOOTS** (all live, except the title track) — D.G.C. / D.G.C. — 69
– Dirty boots / The bedroom / Cinderella's big score / Eric's trip / White kross. *(re-iss. cd Apr92; DGLD 19060)*

— Early in '92, THURSTON and STEVE also teamed up with RICHARD HELL's off-shoot group The DIM STARS.

Jun 92. (7") *(DGCS 11)* **100%. / CREME BRULEE** — 28
(10"orange+=/12"+=) *(DGC V/T 11)* – Hendrix necro.
(cd-s++=) *(DGCTD 11)* – Genetic.

Jul 92. (d-lp/c/cd) *<(DGC/+C/D 24485)>* **DIRTY** — 6 / 83
– 100% / Swimsuit issue / Theresa's sound-world / Drunken butterfly / Shoot / Wish fulfillment / Sugar Kane / Orange rolls, angel's spit / Youth against fascism / Nic fit / On the strip / Chapel Hill / JC / Purr / Creme brulee. *(d-lp+=)* – Stalker. *(re-iss. cd Oct95; GFLD 19296)*

Oct 92. (7") *(GFS 26)* **YOUTH AGAINST FASCISM. / PURR** — Geffen / D.G.C. — 52
(10"colrd+=) *(GFSV 26)* – ('A'version).
(12"++=/cd-s++=) *(GFST/+D 26)* – The destroyed room (radio version)

Apr 93. (7"/c-s) *(GFS/+C 37)* **SUGAR KANE. / THE END OF THE END OF THE UGLY** — 26
(10"blue+=/cd-s+=) *(GFS V/TD 37)* – Is it my body / Personality crisis.

Apr 94. (10"silver/c-s/cd-s) *(GFS V/C/TD 72)* **BULL IN THE HEATHER. / RAZORBLADE** — 24

May 94. (cd/c/blue-lp) *<(GED/GEC/GEF 24632)>* **EXPERIMENTAL JET SET, TRASH AND NO STAR** — 10 / 34
– Winner's blues / Bull in the heather / Starfield road / Skink / Self-obsessed and sexxee / Bone / Androgynous mind / Quest for the cup / Waist / Doctor's orders / Tokyo eye / In the mind of the bourgeois reader / Sweet shine.

— In Sep 94; 'A&M' released CARPENTERS tribute album, which contained their single 'SUPERSTAR'. It was combined with also another cover from REDD KROSS, and reached UK No.45.

Oct 95. (cd/c/d-lp) *<(GED/GEC/GEF 24925)>* **WASHING MACHINE** — 39 / 58
– Becuz / Junkie's promise / Saucer-like / Washing machine / Unwind / Little trouble girl / No queen blues / Panty lies / Becuz coda * / Skip tracer / The diamond sea. *(cd+= *)*

Apr 96. (12"/cd-s) *(GRS T/D 22132)* **LITTLE TROUBLE GIRL / MY ARENA / THE DIAMOND SEA (edit)**

Feb 98. (12"ep/cd-ep; SONIC YOUTH & JIM O'ROURKE) *<(SYR 003/+CD)>* **INVITO AL CIELO EP**
– Invito al cielo / Hungara vivo / Radio-Amatoroj.
(above issued on own 'Sonic Youth Records')

May 98. (d-cd/d-lp) *<(GED/GEF 25203)>* **A THOUSAND LEAVES** — 38 / 85
– Contre le sexisme / Sunday / Female mechanic now on duty / Wildflower soul / Hoarfrost / French tickler / Hits of sunshine (for Allen Ginsberg) / Karen Koltrane / The ineffable me / Snare / Girl / Heather angel.

Jun 98. (7") *(GFS 22332)* **SUNDAY. / MOIST VAGINA** — 72
(cd-s+=) *(GFSTD 22332)* – Silver panties ('A'edit).

SONIC YOUTH (cont)

— THURSTON collaborated with DON FLEMING and JIM DUNBAR on the freeform/experimental project, FOOT, releasing 'S/T' for 'God Bless'

		Smells Like	Smells Like
Nov 99.	(d-lp/d-cd) <(SYR 04/+CD)> **GOODBYE 20th CENTURY**		

– Edges / Six / Six for new time for Sonic Youth / + – / Voice piece for soprano / Pendulum music // Having never written a note for percussion / Six / Burdocks / Four / Piano piece #3 / Enfantine / Treatise.

		Geffen	Geffen
May 00.	(cd/lp) <(490665-2/-1)> **NYC GHOSTS AND FLOWERS**		

– Free city rhymes / Renegade princess / Nevermind (what was it anyway) / Small flowers crack concrete / Side 2 side / Streamsonik subway / NYC ghosts and flowers / Lightnin'.

Jun 02. (cd) <(493319-2)> **MURRAY STREET**
– The empty page / Disconnection notice / Rain on tin / Karen revisited / Radical adults lick godhead style / Plastic sun / Sympathy for the strawberry.

– compilations, others, etc. –

Feb 92.	(cd) Sonic Death; <(SD 13001)> **GOO DEMOS LIVE AT THE CONTINENTAL CLUB (live)**		Nov89
Mar 95.	(cd/c) Blast First; (BFFP 113 CD/C) **CONFUSION IS SEX / KILL YR IDOLS**		–
Mar 95.	(cd) Warners-Rhino; (8122 71591-2) **MADE IN THE U.S.A.** (1986 soundtrack)		
Apr 95.	(cd) Blast First; (BFFP 119CD) **SCREAMING FIELDS OF SONIC LOVE**		–
May 97.	(pic-lp) Sonic Death; (SYLB 1) **LIVE IN BREMEN (live)**		–
Jun 97.	(12"ep/cd-ep) Sonic Youth; (SYR 1/+CD) **SYR VOL.1**		

– Anagrama / Improvisation ajout'e / Tremens / Mieux: de corrosion.

Jul 98. (cd) S.Y.R.; (SYR 1) **SILVER SESSION FOR JASON KNUTH**
Aug 98. (cd) Goofin' (GOO 2CD) **HOLD THAT TIGER (live 1987)**
Jul 00. (cd; by SONIC YOUTH & YAMATSUKA EYE) Ecstatic Peace; <(E 38CD)> **TV SHIT**

LEE RANALDO

		Blast First	S.S.T.
Jul 87.	(m-lp/c) (BFFP 9/+C) <SST 113> **FROM HERE ⇒ ETERNITY**		

– Time stands still / Destruction site / Ouroboron / Slodrown / New groove loop / Florida flower / Hard left / Fuzz-locusts / To Mary / Lathe speaks / The resolution / King's egg. (re-iss. May93 on 'S.S.T.' lp/c/cd; same as US)

		not iss.	Blast First
Oct 95.	(cd) <BFFPCD 103> **EAST JESUS**	–	

– Bridge / Time stands still / Destruction site / Oroboron / Slo drone / Some distortion / Live #1 / New groove loop / Some hammering . . . / Walker grooves / Fuxx – Locusts / To Mary (x2) / Lathe speaks / Deva, Spain / Resolution – King's Ogg.

— GORDON+ MOORE were involved in a one-off 7" by MIRROR/DASH, 'ELECTRIC PEN. / GUM <E #12>

FREE KITTEN

KIM GORDON – vocals, bass, guitar / **JULIE CAFRITZ** – vocals, guitar (ex-PUSSY GALORE)

		not iss.	Ecstatic Peace
1992.	(m-cd) <E#22> **CALL NOW**	–	

– Platinumb / Smack / Falling backwards / Oneness / Dick / Skinny butt.

		not iss.	SP Radiation
1992.	(7") <015> **BLUE CIRCLE**	–	

— added **MARK IBOLD** – bass (of PAVEMENT) + **YOSHIMI** – drums, trumpet

		not iss.	Sympathy..
1993.	(7") <SFTRI 256> **OH BONDAGE UP YOURS. / 1,2,3**	–	
		not iss.	S.O.S.
1993.	(7") <01> **CLEOPATRA. / LOOPSE LIPS**	–	
			In The Red
1993.	(7") <(TR 015)> **JOHN STARKS BLUES. / GUILTY PLEASURES**	–	
		not iss.	Radiation
1994.	(7") <RARE 015> **SEXY BOY. / DARBY SPEAK**	–	
		Wiiija	Kill Rock Stars
Jun 94.	(cd) (WIJ 036CD) **UNBOXED** (compilation)		

– Skinny butt / Platinumb / Smack / Falling backwards / Oneness / Dick / Yoshimi Vs. Mascis / Oh bondage up yours / 1-2-3 / Party with me punker / John Stark blues / Guilty pleasures / Sexy boy / Cleopatra / Loose lips / Oh baby.

— there were other singles collected on their compilation, see above

Jan 95. (7"one-sided) (LTD 002) **HARVEST SPOON**
Feb 95. (cd/lp) (WIJ 041 CD/V) <KRS 240> **NICE ASS**
– Harvest sppon / Rock of ages / Proper band / What's fair / Kissing well / Call back / Blindfold test / Greener pastures / Revlon liberation orchestra / The boaster / Scratch the D.J. / Secret sex friend / Royal flush / Feelin' / Alan Licked has ruined music for an entire generation.

Feb 96. (7"ep) (WIJ 047V) **PUNKS SUING PUNKS EP** | | – |
– Kitten bossa nova / Punk v. punk / Coco's theme.

Oct 97. (12"ep) (WIJ 074) **CHINATOWN EXPRESS. / NEVER GONNA SLEEP / GAA** | | – |
Oct 97. (cd/lp) (WIJ CD/LP 1076) <KRS 285> **SENTIMENTAL EDUCATION**
– Teenie weenie boppie / Top 40 / Never gonna sleep / Strawberry milk / Played yrself / Dr. Spooky's spatialized Chinatown express / Bouwerie's boys / Records sleep / Picabo who / Sentimental education / One forty five / Eat cake / Gaa / Daddy long legs / Noise doll.

— KIM would surface again with IKUE MORI + DJ OLIVE on the cd/d-lp 'SYR5' in 2000

THURSTON MOORE

		Geffen	D.G.C.
May 95.	(cd/c/d-lp;colrd 3-sides) <(GEF/GEC/GED 24810)> **PSYCHIC HEARTS**		

– Queen bee and her pals / Ono soul / Psychic hearts / Pretty bad / Patti Smith math scratch / Blues from beyond the grave / See-through play-mate / Hang out / Feathers / Tranquilizor / Staring statues / Cindy (rotten tanx) / Cherry's blues / Female cop / Elergy for all dead rock stars.

		Forced Exposure	Forced Exposure
Dec 96.	(cd; by JIM SAUTER, DON DIETRICH & THURSTON MOORE) <(FE 015)> **BAREFOOT IN THE HEAD** (rec. 1988)		

– All doors look alike / Tanned moon / On the phrase "ass-backwards" / The date-reduced loaf / Concerning the sun as a cool solid.

— next with TOM SURGAL + WILLIAM WINANT

		Victo	Victo
Mar 97.	(cd) <(VICTOCD 045)> **PIECE FOR JETSUN DOLMA**		
		Corpus Hermeticum	Corpus Herme
Apr 97.	(cd) (HERMES 011) **KLANGFARBENMELODIE**		
		Father Yod	Father Yod
May 97.	(cd; by THURSTON MOORE & PHIL MILSTEIN) (HOTYOD 1) **SONGS WE TAUGHT THE LORD VOL.2**		
		Little Brother	Little Brother
Jul 97.	(cd; by THURSTON MOORE & NELS CLINE) <(LB 011CD)> **PILLOW WAND** (re-iss. Feb99 on 'Skycap'; RTD 3012002-2)		
		Xeric	Xeric
Aug 98.	(cd/lp; by LOREN MAZZACANE CONNORS, JEAN-MARC MONTERA, THURSTON MOORE & LEE RANALDO) <(X 99 0/5)> **mmmr**		

– (untitled) / (untitled) / (untitled).

		Lo Record.	Lo Record.
Oct 98.	(cd/lp) <(LCD/LLP 011)> **ROOT** (V/A remixes)		
		Fourth Dimension	Fourth Dimension
Feb 99.	(10"lp) <(FDCD 57)> **NOT ME. / LYDIA's MOTH**		
		Materiali Sonori	Materiali Sonori
Mar 99.	(cd; by THURSTON MOORE, EVAN PARKER & WALTER PRATI) <(MASDO 90106)> **THE PROMISE**		

– The promise / Is / Our future / Our promise / Are / Children / All children. (lp-iss.Apr99 on 'Get Back'; FT 803)

SOUL ASYLUM

Formed: Minneapolis, Minnesota, USA . . . 1981 as LOUD FAST RULES, by ex-AT LAST guitarist DAN MURPHY and ex-SHITS frontman DAVE PIRNER, who were subsequently joined by KARL MUELLER then PAT MORLEY. Very much in the mould of HUSKER DU and The REPLACEMENTS, SOUL ASYLUM joined the latter at 'Twin Tone' records, while the former's BOB MOULD produced their 1984 debut album, 'SAY WHAT YOU WILL'. Later that year, MORLEY departed while the rest of the band took a break, SOUL ASYLUM subsequently returning in 1986 with GRANT YOUNG on their follow-up, 'MADE TO BE BROKEN'. A fusion of 60's pop and 70's punk, the album (also produced by MOULD) showed PIRNER blossoming into a cuttingly perceptive lyricist. Later that year, the band delivered another fine set, 'WHILE YOU WERE OUT', the record attracting major label attention in the form of 'A&M'. Fulfilling their contract with 'Twin Tone', SOUL ASYLUM cut a covers set, 'CLAM DIP AND OTHER DELIGHTS', displaying their wide range of tastes from Barry Manilow's 'MANDY' to Foreigner's 'JUKEBOX HERO'. In 1988, A&M issued the LENNY KAYE and ED STASIUM produced album, 'HANG TIME', an endearing collection of gleaming power-pop nuggets that occasionally veered off the beaten track into country. Their second and final release for A&M, 'SOUL ASYLUM AND THE HORSE THEY RODE IN ON' (1990), saw PIRNER spiral into despair despite the album's critical acclaim. Disillusioned with the major label inertia, the frontman took a break from amplified noise while his colleagues resumed their day jobs. Staking their chances on yet another major label, SOUL ASYLUM subsequently signed to 'Columbia' and achieved almost instant success with the album 'GRAVE DANCERS UNION' in 1992. This was mainly due to the massive interest in the TOM PETTY-esque 'RUNAWAY TRAIN', a single that hit the American Top 5 in the summer of '93. The track's radio-friendly success paved the way for more typically abrasive numbers such as 'SOMEBODY TO SHOVE' and 'BLACK GOLD', PIRNER landing on his feet as he wooed sultry actress, Winona Ryder (he appeared with her in the film, 'Generation X'). SOUL ASYLUM subsequently became MTV darlings and friends of the stars, such luminaries as BOB DYLAN, PETER BUCK and GUNS N' ROSES professing to fan status. In 1995, they returned with a new drummer, STERLING CAMPBELL, and a new album, 'LET YOUR DIM LIGHT SHINE', another worldwide seller which spawned the melancholy Top 30 gem, 'MISERY'. MURPHY and PIRNER (latter part-time) had also moonlighted in the countrified GOLDEN SMOG with among others the JAYHAWKS' GARY LOURIS and MARC PERLMAN. An EP of covers in '92 was finally followed up by an album in '96, 'DOWN BY THE OLD MAINSTREAM'. A few years later y'all supergroup added BIG STAR's JODY STEPHENS to replace the drumming PIRNER, a second set, 'WEIRD TALES', gaining many plaudits. • **Covers:** MOVE OVER (Janis Joplin) / RHINESTONE COWBOY (Glen Campbell) / BARSTOOL BLUES (Neil Young) / SEXUAL HEALING (Marvin Gaye) / ARE FRIENDS ELECTRIC (Tubeway Army) / SUMMER OF DRUGS (Victoria Williams) / WHEN I RAN OFF AND LEFT HER (Vic Chesnutt).

SOUL ASYLUM (cont)

Album rating: SAY WHAT YOU WILL (*6) / MADE TO BE BROKEN (*6) / WHILE YOU WERE OUT (*6) / HANG TIME (*6) / CLAM DIP AND OTHER DELIGHTS (*5) / SOUL ASYLUM AND THE HORSE THEY RODE IN ON (*8) / GRAVE DANCERS UNION (*7) / LET YOUR DIM LIGHTS SHINE (*6) / CANDY FROM A STRANGER (*5) / BLACK GOLD: THE BEST OF SOUL ASYLUM compilation (*8)

DAVE PIRNER (b.16 Apr'64, Green Bay, Wisconsin) – vocals, guitar / **DAN MURPHY** (b.12 Jul'62, Duluth, Minnesota) – guitar, vocals / **KARL MUELLER** (b.27 Jul'63) – bass / **PAT MORLEY** – drums, percussion

Rough Trade / Twin Tone

Aug 84. (m-lp) *<TT 8439>* **SAY WHAT YOU WILL**
– Long day / Voodoo doll / Money talks / Stranger / Sick of that song / Walking / Happy / Black and blue / Religiavision. *<US re-iss. May89+=; same>* – Dragging me down / Do you know / Spacehead / Broken glass / Masquerade. (UK cd-iss. Mar93 as 'SAY WHAT YOU WILL CLARENCE . . . KARL SOLD THE TRUCK' on 'Roadrunner'; RR 9093-2) (cd re-iss. Mar95 on 'Twin Tone'; TTR 8439-2)

–––– **GRANT YOUNG** (b. 5 Jan'64, Iowa City, Iowa) – drums, percussion; repl. MORLEY

Sep 86. (lp) *(ROUGH 102).<TT 8666>* **MADE TO BE BROKEN**
– Tied to the tracks / Ship of fools / Can't go back / Another world another day / Made to be broken / Never really been / Whoa! / New feelings / Growing pain / Lone rider / Ain't that tough / Don't it (make your troubles seem small). (cd re-iss. Mar93 on 'Roadrunner'+=; RR 9094-2) – Long way home. (cd re-iss. Sep98 on 'R.C.A.'; 74321 60573-20)

Sep 86. (7") **TIED TO THE TRACKS.** /

What Goes On / Twin Tone

Mar 88. (lp) *(GOES ON 16) <TT 8691>* **WHILE YOU WERE OUT** — 1987
– Freaks / Carry on / No man's land / Crashing down / The judge / Sun don't shine / Closer to the stars / Never too soon / Miracles mile / Lap of luxury / Passing sad daydream. (cd-iss. Mar93 on 'Roadrunner'; RR 9096-2) (cd re-iss. Feb95 on 'Twin Tone'; TTR 8691-2)

May 88. (m-lp) *(GOES ON 22) <TT 8814>* **CLAM DIP AND OTHER DELIGHTS** — 1987
– Just plain evil / Chains / Secret no more / Artificial heart / P-9 / Take it to root / Jukebox hero / Move over / Mandy / Rhinestone cowboy. (cd-iss. Mar93 on 'Roadrunner'; RR 9097-2) (cd re-iss. Feb95 on 'Twin Tone'; TTR 8814-2)

–––– split but re-formed adding guest **CADD** – sax, piano

A&M / A&M

Jun 88. (7"/12") *(AM/+Y 447)* **SOMETIME TO RETURN. / PUT THE BOOT IN**
(12"-iss.Jun91 +=; same) – Marionette.

Jun 88. (lp/c/cd) *(AMA/AMC/CDA 5197) <395197-1/-4/-2>* **HANG TIME**
– Down on up to me / Little too clean / Sometime to return / Cartoon / Beggars and choosers / Endless farewell / Standing in the doorway / Marionette / Ode / Jack of all trades / Twiddly dee / Heavy rotation. (re-iss. Sep93 cd/c; CD/C MID 189)

Aug 88. (7") *(AM 463)* **CARTOON. / TWIDDLY DEE**
(12"+=) *(AMY 463)* – Standing in the doorway.

Sep 90. (cd/c/lp) *(5318-2/-4/-1) <75021 5318-2/-4/-1>* **SOUL ASYLUM & THE HORSE THEY RODE IN ON**
– Spinnin' / Bitter pill / Veil of tears / Nice guys (don't get paid) / Something out of nothing / Gullible's travels / Brand new shine / Grounded / Don't be on your way / We / All the king's friends. (re-iss. Sep93 cd/c; CD/C MID 190)

Jan 91. (7") **EASY STREET. / SPINNING**
(12"+=) – All the king's friends / Gullible's travels.

Columbia / Columbia

Oct 92. (cd/c/lp) *(472253-2/-4/-1) <48896>* **GRAVE DANCERS UNION** — 11
– Somebody to shove / Black gold / Runaway train / Keep it up / Homesick / Get out on / New world / April fool / Without a trace / Growing into you / 99% / The Sun maid. *(re-dist.Jul93; hit UK No.52)* (UK No.27 early '94)

Mar 93. (10"ep/cd-ep) *(659 088-0/-2)* **BLACK GOLD. BLACK GOLD (live) / THE BREAK / 99%**

May 93. (c-s,cd-s) *<74966>* **RUNAWAY TRAIN / NEVER REALLY BEEN (live)** — 5

Jun 93. (7"/c-s) *(659 390-7/-4)* **RUNAWAY TRAIN. / BLACK GOLD (live)** 37 —
(12"+=) *(659 390-6)* – By the way / Never really been (live).
(cd-s++=) *(659 390-2)* – Everybody loves a winner. (- Black Gold).
(above single returned into UK chart Nov'93 to hit No.7)

Aug 93. (12"ep/cd-ep) *(659 649-6/-2)* **SOMEBODY TO SHOVE / SOMEBODY TO SHOVE (live). / RUNAWAY TRAIN (live) / BY THE WAY (demo)** 34 —
(c-ep) *(659 649-4)* – ('A'side) / Black gold (live) / Runaway train (live).

Jan 94. (7"/c-s) *(659 844-7/-4)* **BLACK GOLD. / SOMEBODY TO SHOVE** 26 —
(cd-s+=) *(659 844-2)* – Closer to the stairs / Square root.
(cd-s+=) *(659 844-5)* – Runaway train (live).

Mar 94. (7"/c-s) *(660 224-7/-4)* **SOMEBODY TO SHOVE. / BY THE WAY** 32 —
(cd-s+=) *(660 224-2)* – Stranger (unplugged) / Without a trace (live).
(cd-s++=) *(660 224-5)* – ('A'mix).

–––– **STERLING CAMPBELL** – drums; repl. YOUNG

Jun 95. (cd/c) *(480 320-2/-4) <57616>* **LET YOUR DIM LIGHT SHINE** 22 6
– Misery / Shut down / To my own devices / Hopes up / Promises broken / Bittersweetheart / String of pearls / Crawl / Caged rat / Eyes of a child / Just like anyone / Tell me when / Nothing to write home about / I did my best.

Jun 95. (c-s,cd-s) *<77959>* **MISERY / HOPE** — 20

Jul 95. (7"white/c-s) *(662 109-7/-4)* **MISERY. / STRING OF PEARLS** 30 —
(cd-s+=) *(662 109-2)* – Hope (demo) / I did my best.

Nov 95. (c-s) *(662 478-4)* **JUST LIKE ANYONE / DO ANYTHING YOU WANNA DO (live)** 52 —
(cd-s+=) *(662 478-2)* – Get on out (live).
(cd-s) *(662 478-5)* – ('A'side) / You'll live forever (demo) / Fearless leader (demo).

Feb 96. (c-s,cd-s) *<78215>* **PROMISES BROKEN / CAN'T EVEN TELL** — 63

–––– now a trio of PIRNER, MURPHY + MUELLER

May 98. (cd/c) *(487265-2/-4) <67618>* **CANDY FROM A STRANGER**
– Creatures of habit / I will still be laughing / Close / See you later / No time for waiting / Blood into wine / Lies of hate / Draggin' out the lake / Blackout / The game / Cradle chain.

– compilations, etc. –

Sep 00. (cd) *Columbia; (499874-2)* **GRAVE DANCERS UNION / LET YOUR DIM LIGHT SHINE**

Sep 00. (cd) *Columbia; (498656-2) <63669>* **BLACK GOLD: THE BEST OF SOUL ASYLUM**
– Just like anyone / Cartoon / Closer to the stars (live) / Somebody to shove / Close / String of pearls / Tied to the tracks / Runaway train / Sometime to return / Misery / We 3 / Without a trace / I will still be laughing / Black gold / Summer of drugs / Candy from a stranger / Stranger (live) / Can't even tell / Only for you.

Jul 01. (cd) *Sony Special; <52163>* **RUNAWAY TRAIN**

SOULED AMERICAN

Formed: Chicago, Illinois, USA . . . 1988 by frontman, CHRIS GRIGIROFF, a plaintive off-key vocalist likened to a hybrid of NEIL YOUNG, WOODY GUTHRIE, COWBOY JUNKIES and The BAND. Along with fellow songsmith JOE ADDUCCI, guitarist SCOTT TUMA and drummer JAMEY BARNARD, SOULED AMERICAN signed on the dotted line for seminal indie imprint, 'Rough Trade', releasing in quick succession two sets, 'FE' (1988) and 'FLUBBER' (1989). Influenced by a pot-pourri of sound ranging from roots/country to R&B/dub, the quartet were finally finding their musical feet courtesy of 1990's classy third set, 'AROUND THE HORN'. Featuring gems such as 'SECOND OF ALL', 'I KEEP HOLDING BACK THE TEARS' and a cover of Little Feat's 'SIX FEET OF SNOW', the set was an investment to all Lo-Fi stars (i.e. UNCLE TUPELO, WILL OLDHAM, SMOG, SILVER JEWS, etc) – or should have been. 'SONNY' in 1992, rounded off their heyday with 'Rough Trade', although this set was primarily a covers album featuring timeless numbers such as John Prine's 'IF YOU DON'T WANT MY LOVE', The Louvin Brothers' 'CHANGIN' THE WORDS' and a Hank Williams fave 'PLEASE DON'T LET ME LOVE YOU'. Subsequent albums, 'FROZEN' (1994) and 'NOTES CAMPFIRE' (1996) – released on the German-based 'Moll' label – showed more of that good ol' country twang GRIGIROFF, TUMA, ADDUCCI (now without BARNARD) and their loyal fanbase had settled into. Youth took over.

Album rating: FE (*6) / FLUBBER (*6) / AROUND THE HORN (*7) / SONNY (*6) / FROZEN (*5) / NOTES CAMPFIRE (*5)

CHRIS GRIGIROFF – vocals, guitar / **SCOTT TUMA** – vocals, guitar / **JOE ADDUCCI** – vocals, bass / **JAMEY BARNARD** – drums

Rough Trade / Rough Trade

Jan 89. (lp/c/cd) *(ROUGH/+CCD 131) <RUS/CRUS/CDRUS 48>* **FE** — 1988
– Notes campfire / Field and stream / Soldier's joy / Full picture / Make me laugh make me cry / Fisher's hornpipe / Tall boy blues / Magic bullets / Lottery Brazil / Goin' home / She broke my heart / True swamp too / Feel better.

Apr 89. (lp/c/cd) *(ROUGH/+CCD 141)* **FLUBBER**
– All good things / Mar'boro man / Wind to dry / Drop in the basket / Heywire / The torch singer / True swamp / Marleyphine Hank / You and you alone / Cupa cowfee / Over the hill / Zillion / Why, are you.

Feb 90. (lp/c/cd) *(ROUGH/+CCD 151)* **AROUND THE HORN**
– Around the horn / Second of all / Old old house / Durante's hornpipe / Rise about it / Six feet of snow / Willdawg / I keep holding back the tears / You / Luggy Di / In the mud.

Apr 92. (cd/c/lp) *(R 280-2/-4/-1)* **SONNY**
– Sonny / Dark as a dungeon / Please don't let me love you / Buck dancer's choice / If you don't want my love / Changin' the words / Little Bessie / Blue eyes cryin' in the rain / Rock that cradle Lucy / Not over.

–––– now without BARNARD

Moll / Moll

Dec 94. (cd/lp) *<(EFA 12107-2/-1)>* **FROZEN**
– Frozen / Sitdown / Two of you / Rain delay / Downblossom / Heyman / Better who / Lucky / Heyday. *(cd re-iss. Jul98 on 'Checkered Past'; CPR 008)*

Feb 97. (cd/lp) *<(EFA 12119-2/-1)>* **NOTES CAMPFIRE**
– Before tonight / Set in / Flat / Born (free) / Waterdown / All my friends / Deal / Suitors bridge. *(cd re-iss. Apr99 on 'Catamount'; CCR 001)*

–––– disbanded after above

– compilations, etc. –

May 99. (d-cd) *Tumult; (TM 11)* **FRAMED VOL.1: FE / FLUBBER**

May 99. (d-cd) *Tumult; (TM 12)* **FRAMED VOL.2: AROUND THE HORN / SONNY**

SOUND

Formed: Wimbledon, London, England . . . 1978 out of punk act The OUTSIDERS by mainman ADRIAN BORLAND along with GRAHAM GREEN, MICHAEL DUDLEY and initially JAN. After making their vinyl debut in 1979 with the 'PHYSICAL WORLD' EP, the band signed to the 'Korova' label and released a debut album, 'JEOPARDY' (1980). Gloomy, paranoid alternative pop/rock distinguished by its edgy bass and washes of synth, the band's approach generally met with good reviews even if the likes of 'MISSILES' and 'JEOPARDY' sound overly earnest and naive in hindsight. As a darker sideline, BORLAND and GREEN recorded as SECOND LAYER, the album 'WORLD OF RUBBER' surfacing in '82. 'FROM THE LION'S MOUTH' (1982) appeared the same year, The SOUND subsequently securing a major label deal with 'WEA' and releasing 'ALL FALL DOWN' (1982). Despite a glossier production and more commercial material like 'CALLING THE NEW TUNE', sales didn't meet the label's expectations and The SOUND were back on more familiar indie territory – with 'Statik' – for 1984's mini-set, 'SHOCK OF DAYLIGHT'. Its lead track (and accompanying single),

'COUNTING THE DAYS', was one of BORLAND's most accessible and surprisingly affecting compositions to date, akin to a fusion of The COMSAT ANGELS and The PSYCHEDELIC FURS. The rest of the material was equally impressive, especially the shimmering guitar atmospherics of 'LONGEST DAYS'. The following year's full-length 'HEADS AND HEARTS' album was even more refined and embellished the sound with sax, yet the band was reaching the end of its lifespan and BORLAND split for a solo career after 1987's 'THUNDER'. The man later went into production work with Dublin band, INTO PARADISE, while around the same time he (& His Citizens) released their first album, 'ALEXANDRIA' (1989). The 90's produced a handful of other sets for ADRIAN, 'BRITTLE HEAVEN' (1992), 'CINEMATIC' (1996) and '5:00 A.M.' (1997). Sadly, ADRIAN was to die on the 26th of April, 1999.

Album rating: JEOPARDY (*6) / FROM THE LION'S MOUTH (*5) / ALL FALL DOWN (*4) / HEADS AND HEARTS (*6) / IN THE HOTHOUSE (*6) / THUNDER UP (*5) / Adrian Borland & The Citizens: ALEXANDRIA (*5) / BRITTLE HEAVEN (*5) / 5:00 A.M. (*5)

OUTSIDERS

ADRIAN BORLAND (b. 6 Dec'57) – vocals, guitar / **BOB LAWRENCE** – bass / **ADRIAN JAMES** – drums

Raw Edge / not iss.

Oct 77. (lp) (RER 001) **CALLING ON YOUTH**
– Calling on youth / Break free / On the edge / Hit and run / Start over / Weird / I'm screwed up / Walking through a storm / Terminal case.
Nov 77. (7"ep) (RER 002) **ONE TO INFINITY**
– One to infinity / New uniform / Freeway / Consequences.
Apr 78. (lp) (RER 003) **CLOSE UP**
– Vital hours / Observations / Fixed up / Touch and go / White debt / Count for something / Out of place / Keep the pain inside / Face to face / Semi-detached life / Conspiracy of war.

Xciting Plastic / not iss.

May 78. (7"; w-drawn) (none) **VITAL HOURS. / TAKE UP**

—— late '78, **GRAHAM GREEN** – bass; repl. BOB

—— **MICHAEL DUDLEY** – drums, percussion; repl. JAMES

—— with also initially **JAN** – percussion, they changed name to . . .

SOUND

Tortch / not iss.

Dec 79. (7"ep) (TOR 003) **PHYSICAL WORLD EP**
– Cold beat / Physical world / Unwritten law.
May 80. (lp; shelved) (TOR 008) **THE SOUND**

—— added **BI MARSHALL** (b. BENITA) – keyboards

Korova / not iss.

Sep 80. (7") (KOW 10) **HEYDAY. / BRUTE FORCE**
Oct 80. (lp) (KODE 2) **JEOPARDY**
– I can't escape myself / Heartland / Hour of need / Words fail me / Missiles / Heyday / Jeopardy / Night versus day / Resistance / Unwritten law / Desire. (cd-iss. Mar02 on 'Renacent'+=; RENCD 4) – Heartland (live) / Brute force (live) / Jeopardy (live) / Coldbeat (live).

—— **MAX MAYERS** (b. COLVIN) – keyboards; repl. BI

Sep 81. (7") (KOW 21) **SENSE OF PURPOSE. / POINT OF NO RETURN**
(12"+=) (KOW 21T) – Cold beat.
Nov 81. (lp) (KODE 5) **FROM THE LION'S MOUTH**
– Winning / Sense of purpose / Contact the fact / Skeletons / Judgement / Fatal flaw / Possession / The fire / Silent air / New dark age. (cd-iss. Mar02 on 'Renascent'; RENCD 5)
Mar 82. (7") (KOW 23) **HOT HOUSE. / NEW DARK AGE**

WEA / WEA

Nov 82. (lp) (240019-1) **ALL FALL DOWN**
– All fall down / Party of the mind / Monument / In suspense / Where the love is / Song and dance / Calling the new tune / Red paint / Glass and smoke / We could go far. (cd-iss. Mar02 on 'Renascent'+=; RENCD 6) – One and a half minute song / Sorry / As feeling dies.

—— **GRAHAM BAILEY** – bass; repl. GREEN

Statik / not iss.

Mar 84. (m-lp/m-c) (STAB/+C 1) **SHOCK OF DAYLIGHT**
– Golden soldiers / Longest days / Counting the days / Winter / New way of life / Dreams then plans.
May 84. (7") (TAK 16) **COUNTING THE DAYS. / NEW WAY OF LIFE**
(12"+=) (TAK 16-12) – Dreams then plans.
Nov 84. (7") (TAK 28) **ONE THOUSAND REASONS. / BLOOD AND POISON**
(12"+=) (TAK 28-12) – Steal your air.
Mar 85. (lp/c) (STAT LP/C 24) **HEADS AND HEARTS**
– Whirlpool / Total recall / Under you / Burning part of me / Love is not a ghost / Wildest dreams / One thousand reasons / Restless time / Mining for heart / World as it is / Temperature drop. (cd-iss. Dec86 as 'COUNTING THE DAYS'+=; CDST 24) – SHOCK OF DAYLIGHT (cd-iss. Mar02 as 'SHOCK OF DAYLIGHT' + 'HEADS AND HEARTS' on 'Renascent'+=; RENCD 1X) – Counting the days / Blood and poison / Steel your air.
Jun 85. (7") (TAK 34) **TEMPERATURE DROP. / OILED**
Nov 85. (d-lp) (STATDLP 1) **IN THE HOTHOUSE** (live)
– Winning / Under you / Total recall / Skeletons / Prove me wrong / Wildest dreams / Burning part of me / Heartland / Hothouse / Judgement / Counting the days / Red paint / Silent air / Sense of purpose / Missiles. (cd-iss. Mar02 on 'Renascent'+=; RENCD 2X) – Monument / Fire.

Play It Again Sam / not iss.

May 87. (7") (BIAS 063) **HAND OF LOVE. /**
(12"+=) (BIAS 063T) –
May 87. (cd/lp) (CD+/BIAS 053) **THUNDER UP**
– Acceleration group / Hand of love / Barria Alta / Kinetic / Iron years / Prove me wrong / Shot up and shut down / Web of wicked ways / I give you pain / You've got a way.
Oct 87. (7") (BIAS 049) **IRON YEARS. /**
(12"+=) (BIAS 049T) –

—— they split at the turn of the year

– compilations, etc. –

Mar 02. (cd) *Renascent*; (RENCD 3) **PROPAGANDA**
– No salvation / Deep breath / Cost of living / Quarter past two / Night versus day / Physical world / Statik / Music business / Propaganda / Words fail me / One more escape / Missiles.

ADRIAN BORLAND

—— went solo, augmented by The CITIZENS (on first two sets & single)

Sep 89. (lp/cd) (BIAS 125/+CD) **ALEXANDRIA**
– Light the sky / Rogue beauty / Crystalline / Shadow of your grace / Weight if stuff / She's my heroine / Beneath the big wheel / Community call / Other side of the world / Deep deep blue / No ethereal.
Mar 90. (7") (BIAS 155) **BENEATH THE BIG WHEEL. /**
Mar 92. (cd) (BIAS 215CD) **BRITTLE HEAVEN**
– Brittle heaven / Flight 23 / Universe of you / Faithful / Prisoners of the sun / European streets in the rain / Nowhere to fall / All the words in the world / Lowlands / Truth that lights the way / Healing kiss / Box of happy memories / Ashes / Tidal wave goodbye.
Apr 92. (7") **ALL THE WORLDS. /**

Resolve / not iss.

Mar 96. (cd) (RES 002) **CINEMATIC**
– Dreamfuel / Bright white light / When can I be me / Cinematic / Night cascade / Neon and stone / Long dark train / Antartica / Western veil / We are the night / Dreamfuel 2 / I can't stop the world / Heading emotional / The south / Spanish hotel / March.

Earth / not iss.

Sep 97. (cd) (EAR 001CD) **5:00 A.M.**
– Stray bullets / Dangerous stars / Vampiric / Baby moon / City speed / Kissing in the dark / I'm your freedom / The spinning room / Redemption's knees / Between buildings / Over the under / Before the day begins.
Sep 97. (c-ep) (EAR 002CD) **OVER THE UNDER**

SECOND LAYER

—— was a sideline for **BORLAND + GREEN** (augmented by drum machine)

Tortch / not iss.

1979. (7"ep) (TOR 001) **FLESH AS PROPERTY**
– Courts or wars / Metal sheet / Germany. (re-iss. 1981 on 'Fresh'; FRESH 5) (shelved re-iss. 1980 on 'Cherry Red'; CHERRY 21)
1980. (7"ep) (TOR 006) **STATE OF EMERGENCY. / I NEED NOISE / THE CUTTING MOTION**

Cherry Red / not iss.

Feb 82. (lp) (BRED 14) **WORLD OF RUBBER**
– Underneath the gloss / Fixation / In bits / Save our souls / Distortion / Zero / Definition of honour / Japanese headset / Black flowers.

Licensed / not iss.

Aug 88. (d-lp) (LD 8711) **SECOND LAYER**

SOUP DRAGONS

Formed: Bellshill, Lanarkshire, Scotland . . . 1985 by SEAN DICKSON, JIM McCULLOCH, ROSS SINCLAIR and SUSHIL K DADE. Taking their name from cult kids TV show, 'The Clangers', The SOUP DRAGONS were initially signed to the 'Subway' label for whom they released the 'SUN IN THE SKY' EP and a follow-up, 'WHOLE WIDE WORLD'. The band's BUZZCOCKS/UNDERTONES three-chord flurry gained valuable exposure later that summer when the latter single's B-side, 'PLEASANTLY SURPRISED', was featured on the NME's C86 compilation. One unlikely fan was ex-WHAM! manager, Jazz Summers, who masterminded the next phase of their career via the 'Raw TV' label and oversaw the release of a string of singles including their first Top 75 chart entry, 1987's 'CAN'T TAKE NO MORE'. Further singles, 'SOFT AS YOUR FACE' and 'THE MAJESTIC HEAD' found them dabbling with a 60's retro sound, 'Sire' trying and failing to break the band into the mainstream with a long awaited debut album, 'THIS IS OUR ART' (1988). Moving back to 'Raw TV' and re-evaluating their approach, DICKSON & Co. emerged in the second half of 1989 with two singles, 'BACKWARDS DOG' and 'CROTCH DEEP TRASH', critics only too ready to mention the similarities with the latest STOOGES-fixated offering from fellow Glaswegians, PRIMAL SCREAM. Following the replacement of ROSS with PAUL QUINN, detractors were furnished with further ammunition amid accusations of bandwagoneering as the 'DRAGONS released the singalong indie/dance crossover, 'MOTHER UNIVERSE', in 1990. The accompanying album, 'LOVEGOD' (1990), confirmed the transformation and The SOUP DRAGONS finally broke big time a few months later with a cover of the Rolling Stones' 'I'M FREE'. Transforming an R&B jangle into a stoned, fringe-shaking anthem for the baggy generation – complete with reggae toasting courtesy of JUNIOR REID – really didn't do the band much good in retrospect. Despite being a massive worldwide hit and an MTV stalwart, the track's success couldn't prevent The SOUP DRAGONS dying a swift commercial death when the scene came to an abrupt end in the early 90's. Granted, they spun it out with a re-issued 'MOTHER UNIVERSE' but yet another change in direction on 'HOTWIRED' (1992) made no headway with a music buying public who'd simply moved on, the band's chequered career

SOUP DRAGONS (cont)

eventually coming to a close after their short-lived tenure with 'Big Life'. After a very disappointing US-only set in '95 bombed for DICKSON's new SOUP DRAGONS, SUSHIL – who'd moonlighted with The TELSTAR PONIES – returned a few years later with his own FUTURE PILOT A.K.A. project. Meanwhile, DICKSON made his comeback under the guise of The HIGH FIDELITY, a personal experiment into the field of psychedelic rock. After debuting on a friends' compilation CD, DICKSON managed to release the warped punk/pop single 'ADDICTED TO TV' (issued on Japanese imprint 'Plastique' due to popular demand). Since his explorations with 'THE HIGH FIDELITY' (which began as a bit of a laugh apparently), he issued a handful of delicious but disturbing singles, among them 'LOVE DUP' and '2-UP, 2-DOWN'. These borrowed heavily from the ilk of The JESUS & MARY CHAIN. DICKSON subsequently released 'DEMONSTRATION' (1999), a full length album which boasted his craft for writing catchy but experimental pop. Songs such as 'THE NATIONAL ANTHEM' and 'LAZY B' would act as hard evidence if DICKSON was ever to be accused of dull indie imitation. However, subsequent single 'UNSORRY' seemed to lack the flair and substance seen in some of his earlier work. • **Songwriters:** DICKSON compositions, except PURPLE HAZE (Jimi Hendrix) / OUR LIPS ARE SEALED (Go-Go's) / I'M NOT YOUR STEPPING STONE (Monkees).

Album rating: THIS IS OUR ART (*6) / LOVEGOD (*7) / HOTWIRED (*5) / HYDROPHONIC (*3) / High Fidelity: DEMONSTRATION (*7) / THE OMNICHORD ALBUM (*6)

SEAN DICKSON (b.21 Mar'67) – vocals, guitar / **JIM McCULLOCH** (b.19 May'66) – guitar, vocals / **ROSS SINCLAIR** – drums / **SUSHIL K. DADE** (b.15 Jul'66) – bass (ex-WAKE)

Subway / not iss.

Feb 86. (ltd.7"ep) *(SUBWAY 2)* **THE SUN IN THE SKY**
– Quite content / Swirling round the garden with you / Fair's fair / Not for Humbert.
May 86. (7") *(SUBWAY 4)* **WHOLE WIDE WORLD. / I KNOW EVERYTHING**
(12"+=) *(SUBWAY 4T)* – Pleasantly surprised.

– May 86, SEAN (bass) & JIM (guitar) were part-time auxiliaries of BMX BANDITS who were fronted by DUGLAS and released 'SAD'. / 'E102' on '53rd & 3rd' label. JIM played on their Jan'87 follow-up 'WHAT A WONDERFUL WORLD'. / 'THE DAY BEFORE TOMORROW'.

Raw TV Products / not iss.

Sep 86. (7",7"red,7"blue) *(RTV 1)* **HANG TEN!. / SLOW THINGS DOWN**
(12"+=) *(RTV 12-1)* – Just mind your step girl / Man about town with chairs.
Jan 87. (7") *(RTV 2)* **HEAD GONE ASTRAY. / GIRL IN THE WORLD**
(12"+=/12"w-poster+=) *(RTV/+P 12-2)* – So sad I feel.
Jun 87. (7") *(RTV 3)* **CAN'T TAKE NO MORE. / WHITEWASH** — 65
(12"+=) *(RTV 12-3)* – A-Ha! experience.
(12"ep) *(RTVL 12-3)* – ('A'&'B'live) / Hang ten! (live) / Purple haze (live).
Aug 87. (7") *(RTV 4)* **SOFT AS YOUR FACE. / IT'S ALWAYS AUTUMN** — 66
(12"+=) *(RTV 12-4)* – Our lips are sealed / Soft as your face – arrangement.
(double-groove 12"+=) *(RTV 12-4D)* – Can't take no more (vocal squad version) / Whole wide world (live).
Mar 88. (7") *(RTV 5)* **THE MAJESTIC HEAD. / 4-WAY BRAIN**
(12"+=) *(RTV 12-5)* – Them.
(12"pic-d+=) *(RTV 12-5P)* – Corporation headlock.

Sire / Sire

Apr 88. (lp/c)(cd) *(WX 169/+C)(K 925702-2)* <25702> **THIS IS OUR ART** — 60
– Kingdom chairs / Great empty space / The majestic head / Turning stone / Vacate my space / On overhead walkways / Passion protein / King of the castle / Another dream ticket / Soft as your face / Family ways. *(cd re-iss. Jul91; K 925702-2)*
Jun 88. (7") *(W 7820)* **KINGDOM CHAIRS. / WHITE CRUISING**
(12") *(W 7820T)* – ('A'side) / I'm not your stepping stone / All because of you.
(10") *(W 7820TE)* – ('A'&'B'live) / Family way (live) / King of the castle (live).

Raw TV / Big Life

Jul 89. (7") *(RTV 6)* **BACKWARDS DOG. / BURN OUT**
(12"+=) *(RTV 6T)* – Superchery / Kill kill kill me.
Oct 89. (7") *(RTV 7)* **CROTCH DEEP TRASH. / YOU CAN FLY**
(ext.12"+=) *(RTV 7T)* – Superangel / ('A'dub version).

– PAUL QUINN – drums repl. ROSS. / added guest ALEX McLAREN – guitar

Mar 90. (7") *(RTV 8)* **MOTHER UNIVERSE. / ('A'-Solar mix)**
(12"+=) *(RTV 8T)* – ('A'-Love dub mix).
(cd-s++=) *(RTV 8CD)* – 4-way brain.
May 90. (cd/c/lp) *(SOUP CD/MC/LP 2)* <842985> **LOVEGOD** — 60 / 88 Oct90
– Mother Universe / Backwards dog / Softly / Drive the pain / Lovegod / Dream E-forever / Sweetmeat / Kiss the gun / Love you to death / Beauty freak / Lovedog (dub) / Crotch deep trash. *(cd+=)* – (2 extra mixes) *(re-iss. Aug90 on 'Big Life'+= cd/c/lp; SOUP CD/MC/LP 2)* (hit UK No.7)
Jul 90. (7"/c-s/ext.12") *(RTV 9/+MC/T)* <877568> **I'M FREE (featuring JUNIOR REID). / LOVEGOD (dub)** — 5 / 79 Sep90
(cd-s+=) *(RTV 9CD)* – ('A'-12"version).
(12") *(RTV 9R)* – ('A'-Terry Farley Boys Own mix) / Backwards dog (remix).

Big Life / Big Life

Oct 90. (7"/c-s) *(BLR/+C 30)* **MOTHER UNIVERSE. / BACKWARDS DOG** — 26
(12"+=/cd-s+=) *(BLR T/CD 30)* – ('A'dub remix) / ('A'-'89 remix).
Aug 91. (7"/c-s) *(BLR 56)* **ELECTRIC BLUES. / UNEARTHED**
(12"+=/cd-s+=) *(BLRT/BLC 56)* – Solar rise / ('A'dub version).
Apr 92. (7"/c-s) *(BLR/+C 68)* <865764> **DIVINE THING. / DRIVING** — 53 / 35
(12"+=/cd-s+=) *(BLR T/CD 68)* – ('A'revisited) / American sweetmeat.
May 92. (cd/c/lp) *(BLR CD/MC/LP 15)* <13178> **HOTWIRED** — 74 / 97
– Pleasure / Divine thing / Running milk / Getting down / Forever yesterday / No more / Understanding / Dream on (Solid gone) / Everlasting / Absolute heaven / Everything / Sweet layabout / Mindless.
Sep 92. (12"ep/c-ep/cd-ep) *(867416)* **PLEASURE / PLEASURE (revisited). / WHAT YOU WANT / DIVE-BOMBER** — 69
(cd-ep) – ('A'revisited) ... repl. by 'Man'.
(cd-s+=) – ('A'revisited) / I'm free (original) / Mother universe / Electric blues.

– SUSHIL joined The TELSTAR PONIES
– DICKSON virtually solo + a plethora of session people and special guests incl. TINA WEYMOUTH, NEVILLE STAPLES, BOOTSY COLLINS

not iss. / Polygram

Jan 95. (cd,c,lp) <522732> **HYDROPHONIC**
– One way street / Don't get down (get down) / Do you care? / May the force be with you / Contact high / All messed up / The time is now / Freeway / Rest in peace / J.F. junkie / Automatic speed queen / Out of here / Motherfunker / Black and blues / Hypersonic re-entry.

– DICKSON would later surface with outfit ...

HIGH FIDELITY

SEAN DICKSON – vocals, guitar / with **PAUL DALLAWAY** – guitars / **ADRIAN BARRY** – bass / **ROSS McFARLANE** – drums, percussion

Vinyl Japan / not iss.

Nov 96. (7") *(PAD 033)* **ADDICTED TO A TV. / PELVIC ROCK**

Plastique / not iss.

Jun 97. (7") *(FAKE 01)* **ITHANKU. / BERRY BERRY BONG BONG**
(cd-s+=) *(FAKE 01CDS)* – ('A'-mission central mix).
(cd-s) *(FAKE 01CDX)* – ('A'mixes; incl. corporate instrumental).
Apr 98. (7") *(FAKE 02)* **COME AGAIN. / PLASTIQUE – TRONICA**
(cd-s+=) *(FAKE 02CDS)* – (part 3) / (part 4) / (part 5).
(12") *(FAKE 02TX)* – ('A'mixes).
Jul 98. (c-s) *(FAKE 03MC)* **LUV DUP / LAZY B**
(cd-s+=) *(FAKE 03CDS)* – ('A'version).
Sep 99. (7") *(FAKE 101)* **2 UP – 2 DOWN. / SUGAR FREE**
(cd-s+=) *(FAKE 101CD)* – Nothing left to fight.
Mar 00. (cd) *(FAKE 103CD)* **DEMONSTRATION**
– Omnichord intro / Luv dup / Ithanku / Odyssey of a psychonaut / Unsorry / Lazy. B / The national anthem / A change is gonna come? / Bollywood bubblegum experiment / 2 up – 2 down / Greeneye monster / Cola-coca / Patch Granville / Never bollocks the mind. *<US-iss.Apr02 on 'Freedom In Exile'; 12>*
Jul 00. (7") *(FAKE 104)* **UNSORRY. / UNSORRY (version 2)**
(cd-s+=) *(FAKE 104CDS)* – Sometimes the kids are not alright.
(cd-s) *(FAKE 104CDX)* – ('A'side) / Smokin cheeba cheeba / Sugar dub / Sick of it all.
Nov 00. (cd-s; w-drawn) *(FAKE 105CDS)* **A CHANGE IS GONNA COME?**
Mar 01. (cd-s) *(FAKE 106CD1)* **SCREAM IF YOU WANT TO GO FASTER / BASED ON A TRUE STORY / THE PLANXTY CANNON TRILOGY**
(12") *(FAKE 106X)* – ('A'-Terminalhead mix) / ('A'-Mission Control mix original by Arthur Baker).
(cd-s+=) *(FAKE 106CD2)* – ('A'side).
Apr 01. (cd) *(FAKE 107CD)* **THE OMNICHORD ALBUM**
– Scream if you want to go faster / Electromale / Omnichord 4am / Plastiquetronica / Pig might fly / Ice cream / Commercial suicide / Paradise syndrome / Hi-fi / Nothing left to fight.

– the HIGH FIDELITY (12" 'NO GOOD (TO ME)' was not the same outfit)

SOUTHERN CULTURE ON THE SKIDS

Formed: Chapel Hill, North Carolina, USA ... 1982 by songwriter RICK MILLER, who after a few personnel hitches finally found MARY HUFF and DAVE HARTMAN. S.C.O.T.S.' first track recorded, 'LOVE IN 4D', appeared on a V/A compilation, 'More Mondo', although these Southern-fried rockabilly hillbillies set out their stall courtesy of some finely-tuned LP's. The eponymous, 'SOUTHERN CULTURE ON THE SKIDS', got the (12") ball rolling in 1985, and eventually led (after several LP's on various imprints) to a deal with 'Geffen' and two further albums, 'DIRT TRACK DATE' (1996) and 'PLASTIC SEAT SWEAT' (1997). In 2000, the addition of CRISPY BESS and a fresh contract with 'TVT', resulted in yet another retro-fried hoedown, 'LIQUORED UP AND LACQUERED DOWN'. They'd been now on the go (quite literally!) for nearly 20 years and if you could imagine KATE PIERSON (of The B-52's) mixing it up with hells-a-poppin' BIG BOPPER in the musical sequel of a new 'Flintstones' movie, you'd have just about got it in one. • **Covered:** numerous.

Album rating: SOUTHERN CULTURE ON THE SKIDS mini (*5) / TOO MUCH PORK FOR JUST ONE FORK (*6) / FOR LOVERS ONLY (*5) / PECKIN' PARTY (*6) / DITCH DIGGIN' (*5) / DIRT TRACK DATE (*7) / GIRLFIGHT mini (*5) / PLASTIC SEAT SWEAT (*5) / LIQUORED UP AND LACQUERED DOWN (*6)

RICK MILLER – vocals, guitar / **MARY HUFF** – bass, organ, fiddle, vocals / **DAVE HARTMAN** – drums, percussion

not iss. / Spool

1984. (7"ep) <SO 17584> **VOODOO BEACH PARTY EP**
– Rock-a-hula rock / Swamp / Voodoo beach party / I knew a girl ((who never said no).

not iss. / Lloyd Street

1985. (m-lp) <SP 002> **SOUTHERN CULTURE ON THE SKIDS**
– Bop bop bop / Primitive guy / I dig tunnels / Psycho surfing / Cocktail song / Rockabilly mud / Atom age trucker / Demon death / Nothing song.

not iss. / Moist

1990. (7") <MR 102> **CLYDE'S LAMENT. / C.W. JAMES, 0-0 SPY**
1991. (cd) <MR 104> **TOO MUCH PORK FOR ONE FORK**
– Eight piece box / Roadside wreck / Come and get it / Cicada rock / Back in the woods / Big pine tree / Voodoo cadillac / Firefly / She bought a dog / Dick's theme / Chitt'lin strut / Stone in my pocket / Suede pussycat / CW James, 00-spy / Chicken fist / Five dollar shoes.

SOUTHERN CULTURE ON THE SKIDS (cont)

			not iss.	Giant Claw
1991.	(7") <GCS 007> **COME AND GET IT. / CICADA ROCK**		-	-
			not iss.	Zontar
1992.	(7"ep) <ZR 003> **SANTO! SINGS**		-	
	– Viva del Santo / Camel walk / Mexy melt / Wall-eyed.			
			not iss.	Safe House
1992.	(cd) <SH 2108> **FOR LOVERS ONLY**		-	
	– For lovers only / Biscuit eater / Barnyard ballbuster / Nashville toupee / Fatman's twist / Skunk / Sheik's walk / Wish I was in love / Daddy was a preacher but mama was a go-go girl / King of the mountain / The man that wrestles the bear / Link's lung / Clyde's lament / For lovers only (reprise). *(UK-iss.Nov96; same)*			
1993.	(7"; with DON HOWLAND as "LOS FALANAS") <SFTRI 217> **NAKEMA. / JOHNNY B. BADD**		-	
1993.	(7"; with DON HOWLAND as "LOS FALANAS") <SFTRI 270> **COCKROACH BLUES. / BIRDNEST BLUES**		-	
	(above 2 issued on 'Sympathy For The Record Industry')			
1993.	(10"m-lp/m-cd) <(FED 3-1/-2)> **PECKIN' PARTY (live)**			
	– Run chicken run / Eight piece box / Kudzu limbo / Cicada rock / Walleyed / Daddy was a preacher but mama was a go-go girl.			
	(above issued on 'Feedbag' + re-iss. Sep98; *same*)			
1994.	(cd/pic-lp) <SH 2114> **DITCH DIGGIN'**			
	– Too much pork for just one fork / Put your teeth up on the window sill / Tunafish every day / My house has wheels / The great atomic power / The little things / Jack the ripper (parts 1 & 2) / Chicken shit farmer / The fly that rode from Buffalo / Lordy, lordy / Mudbuggy / Ditch diggin' / New cooter boogie / Wig-out / Rumors of surf. *(UK-iss.Nov96; same)*			
			not iss.	Baylor
1994.	(7") <Bay 10> **GOSSIP AND RUMORS**		-	
	– Rumors of surf / (track by the A-BONES).			
			not iss.	Demolition Derby
1994.	(7") <DD 009> **WHITE TRASH. / I'M BRANDED**		-	
			not iss.	Hi-Fi Todd
1995.	(7"; split w/ COCTAILS) <45 9/24/94> **THE WEDDING BELLS TWIST**		-	
			not iss.	Sympathy F
1995.	(7"; with DON HOWLAND as "LOS FALANAS") <SFTRI 328> **TANTRUM. / TANTRUM (the blue witch mix)**		-	
1995.	(7"; with DON HOWLAND as "LOS FALANAS") <SFTRI 360> **HELL BLUES. / TAXMAN BLUES**		-	
			Louder	not iss.
Jun 96.	(7"m) *(LOUD 14)* **WHITE TRASH. / BSA 441 / TWO PIGS IN A BLANKET**			-
			not iss.	Estrus
Sep 96.	(d7"ep/cd-ep) <ES/+D 796-7> **SANTO SWINGS EP**		-	
	– Viva del Santo! / Walleyed / Mexi melt / Camel walk / Double shot / Scratch my back.			
Dec 96.	(10"ep) <(SFTRI 286)> **GIRLFIGHT**			
	– Girlfight / Whole lotta things / El mysterioso / Twistin' (on a red hot spike) / Hey Chuck Berry / Wheels.			
			Telstar	Geffen
1996.	(cd-ep) <GED 22111> **SOUL CITY**		-	
	– Soul city / Red beans n' reverb / Two pigs in a blanket / BSA 441.			
Dec 96.	(cd/c/lp) *(TR 20)* <DGCD 24821> **DIRT TRACK DATE**			Sep96
	– Voodoo cadillac / Soul city / Greenback fly / Skullbucket / Camel walk / White trash / Firefly / Make Mayan a Hawaiian / Fried chicken and gasoline / Nitty gritty / 8 piece box / Galley slave / Whole lotta things / Dirt track date.			
Oct 97.	(cd/c/lp) *(TR 030)* <DGCD 25154> **PLASTIC SEAT SWEAT**			Sep97
	– Shotgun / Earthmover / Dance for me / Banana puddin' / 40 miles to Vegas / Love-a-rama / Deja varoom / Country funk / Strangest ways / Theme from "The Cheaters" / House of bamboo / Carve that possum.			
Jan 98.	(cd-s) <1151> **HOUSE OF BAMBOO**		-	
	– House of bamboo / Country girl / The sweeper.			
			not iss.	Monkey Dog Music
Nov 98.	(m-cd) <120084> **ZOMBIEFIED (AUSTRALIAN TOUR)**		-	
	– Intro / Zombiefied / Undertaker / Swamp thing / She's my witch / Bloodsucker / Sinister purpose / Torture / Devil's stomping ground.			
——	added **CHRIS "CRISPY" BESS** – keyboards, rhythm guitar			
			not iss.	T.V.T.
Oct 00.	(cd) <TVT 2170> **LIQUORED UP AND LAQUERED DOWN**		-	
	– Liquored up and laquered down / Hittin' on nothing / Pass the hatchet / Corn liquor / Drunk and lonesome (again) / Cheap motels / Just how lonely / I learned to dance in Mississippi / King of the mountain / The corn rocket / Damaged goods / Over it / Haw river stomp.			
——	the band also featured on a plethora of Various Artists sets			

SPACEMEN 3

Formed: Rugby, Warwickshire, England . . . 1983 by SONIC BOOM (PETE KEMBER) and JASON PIERCE. They enlisted PETE BAINES and ROSCO as a rhythm section and through their manager, Gerald Palmer, they signed to indie label, 'Glass'. In 1986, they debuted with 'SOUND OF CONFUSION', a primal embryo for "shoegazers" to come. Their follow-up, 'THE PERFECT PRESCRIPTION', set the world alight (well! the indie world anyway), with some clever pulsating, psychedelic garage-noise intertwined with melancholy bursts of beauty and experimentation, i.e 'WALKIN WITH JESUS' (again!), 'TRANSPARENT RADIATION' and 'TAKE ME TO THE OTHER SIDE'. In 1989, they were back again with a third set, 'PLAYING WITH FIRE', featuring the 10-minute squall of 'SUICIDE', and 'REVOLUTION' (later covered by MUDHONEY). SONIC BOOM's heroin addiction was taking its toll during the early 90's and with JASON having founded SPIRITUALIZED, the group were heading for their own proverbial rocketship to oblivion. Their final outing, 'RECURRING' (1991), recorded amid escalating tension, was a slight disappointment. By this time, SONIC had gone solo, subsequently going under the guise of SPECTRUM. His debut was followed by two albums of patchy, yet somewhat appealing albums, 'SOUL KISS (GLIDE DIVINE)' (1992) and 'HIGH LOWS AND HEAVENLY BLOWS' (1994). The ever prolific KEMBER went on play with mid 90's outfit, JESSAMINE, who to date have released a string of albums including 1997's 'ANOTHER FICTIONALIZED HISTORY'. Around the same time, KEMBER/SONIC simultaneously resurfaced with a SPECTRUM set, 'FOREVER ALIEN', released on the '3rd Stone' imprint. The SPECTRUM posse subsequently indulged their passion for prehistoric analog synth by hooking up with legendary early electronic experimentalists SILVER APPLES. The resulting 'LAKE OF TEARDROPS' (1998) was pretty much what you'd expect from such a collaboration with the respective parties' dedication to retroactivity precluding any startling intergalactic innovation. During the 90's, SONIC BOOM was also part of indie noisesters, EXPERIMENTAL AUDIO RESEARCH alongside (initially) KEVIN SHIELDS (of MY BLOODY VALENTINE) and EDDIE PREVOST (of AMM). EAR – as they were known for short – were primarily concerned with exploring the boundaries where stark ambience meets uncompromising guitar manipulation/noise, making their first lunar mission via a US-only debut CD-album, 'MESMERISED' (1994). Reflecting his love of collectable vinyl, SONIC BOOM decided to release a 5" single, 'POCKET SYMPHONY' a few months later. Subsequently securing a UK deal with 'Big Cat', EAR finally got round to issuing their first studio venture (actually recorded during their formative year), 'BEYOND THE PALE', in 1996. Over the course of the ensuing two years or so, the group were surprisingly prolific, completing a trio of long-players, 'PHENOMENA 256' (1996), 'THE KONER EXPERIMENT' (1997) and 'MILLENNIUM MUSIC' (1998) for three separate labels. Of late, the avant-garde troupe (who had now lost SHIELDS and MARTIN) introduced a revolutionary technique called "circuit bending" on their sixth album, 'DATA RAPE' (1998). 'VIBRATIONS' (2000) continued to tweak the listener into submission, EAR opening their musical account on this occasion with the spaced-out 'KALIMBELL'. • **Songwriters:** KEMBER or PIERCE material until the 90's when KEMBER penned all. Covered; IT'S ALRIGHT (Bo Diddley) / CHE + ROCK'N'ROLL IS KILLING MY LIFE (Suicide) / WHEN TOMORROW HITS (Mudhoney) / COME TOGETHER + STARSHIP (MC5) / MARY-ANNE (. . .Campbell) / ROLLER COASTER (13th Floor Elevators).

Album rating: SOUND OF CONFUSION (*7) / THE PERFECT PRESCRIPTION (*8) / PLAYING WITH FIRE (*8) / RECURRING (*8) / PERFORMANCE posthumous (*7) / DREAM WEAPON – ECSTASY IN SLOW MOTION posthumous: (*7) / TAKING DRUGS TO MAKE MUSIC TO TAKE DRUGS TO posthumous (*5) / SPACEMEN ARE GO! posthumous (*3) / FOR ALL THE FUCKED UP CHILDREN IN THE WORLD posthumous (*4) / TRANSLUCENT FLASHBACKS collection (*6) / Sonic Boom: SPECTRUM (*5) / Spectrum: SOUL KISS (GLIDE DIVINE) (*6) / HIGH LOWS AND HEAVENLY BLOWS (*6) / FOREVER ALIEN (*6) / Experimental Audio Research: MESMERISED (*6) / BEYOND THE PALE (*6) / PHENOMENA 256 (*7) / THE KONER EXPERIMENT (*5) / MILLENNIUM MUSIC (*7) / DATA RAPE (*6) / LIVE AT THE DREAM PALACE (*6) / PESTREPELLER (*5) / VIBRATIONS mini (*5) / CONTINUUM (*6)

SONIC BOOM (b. PETE KEMBER, 19 Nov'65) – vocals / **JASON PIERCE** (b.19 Nov'65) – guitar / **STEWART (ROSCO) ROSSWELL** – keyboards / **PETE (BASSMAN) BAINES** – bass

		Glass	not iss.
Jun 86.	(lp) *(GLA 018)* **SOUND OF CONFUSION**		-
	– Losing touch with my mind / Hey man / Roller coaster / Mary Anne / Little doll / 2:35 / O.D. catastrophe. *(re-iss. Sep89 on 'Fire' lp/c/cd; REFIRE CD/MC/LP 5)* <US cd-iss. 1994 on 'Taang!'; 93>		
Dec 86.	(12"m) *(GLAEP 105)* **WALKIN' WITH JESUS (SOUND OF CONFUSION). / ROLLERCOASTER / FEEL SO GOOD**		-
Jul 87.	(12"m) *(GLAEP 108)* **TRANSPARENT RADIATION / ECSTASY SYMPHONY / TRANSPARENT RADIATION (FLASHBACK). / THINGS'LL NEVER BE THE SAME / STARSHIP**		-
Aug 87.	(lp/c) *(GLA LP/MC 026)* **THE PERFECT PRESCRIPTION**		-
	– Take me to the other side / Walking with Jesus / Ode to street hassle / Ecstasy – Symphony / Feel so good / Things'll never be the same / Come down easy / Call the doctor / Soul 1 / That's just fine. *(re-iss. Dec89 on 'Fire' lp/c/cd; REFIRE LP/MC/CD 6)* <US cd-iss. 1994 on 'Taang!'; 94>		
Mar 88.	(12") *(GLASS 12-054)* **TAKE ME TO THE OTHER SIDE. / SOUL 1 / THAT'S JUST FINE**		-
Jul 88.	(lp/cd) *(GLA LP/CD 030)* **PERFORMANCE** (live 1988 Holland)		-
	– Mary-Anne / Come together / Things'll never be the same / Take me to the other side / Roller coaster / Starship / Walkin' with Jesus. *(re-iss. May91 & Apr02 on 'Fire' cd/c/lp; REFIRE CD/MC/LP 11)*		

—— **WILLIE B. CARRUTHERS** – bass / **JON MATLOCK** – drums repl. ROSCO + BAINES who formed The DARKSIDE

		Fire	not iss.
Nov 88.	(7") *(BLAZE 29S)* **REVOLUTION. / CHE**		-
	(12"+=/cd-s+=) *(BLAZE 29 T/CD)* – May the circle be unbroken.		
Feb 89.	(lp/c/cd) *(FIRE LP/MC/CD 16)* **PLAYING WITH FIRE**		-
	– Honey / Come down softly to my soul / How does it feel? / I believe it / Revolution / Let me down gently / So hot (wash away all my tears) / Suicide / Lord can you hear me. *(free-12"ep/cd-ep+=)* – Starship / Revolution / Suicide (live) / Repeater / Live intro theme (xtacy). <US cd-iss. 1994 on 'Taang'; 97> <d-lp-iss.Sep99 on 'Space Age'; ORBIT 011LP>		
Jul 89.	(7") *(BLAZE 36S)* **HYPNOTIZED. / JUST TO SEE YOU SMILE HONEY** (part 2)		-
	(12"+=/3"cd-s+=) *(BLAZE 36 T/CD)* – The world is dying.		
	(free 7"flexi w.a) *(CHEREE 5)* – EXTRACTS FROM A CONTEMPORARY SITAR EVENING (with other artists).		
Jan 91.	(7") *(BLAZE 41)* **BIG CITY. / DRIVE**		-
	(12"+=/cd-s+=) *(BLAZE 41 T/CD)* – Big City (everybody I know can be found here).		
	(12"w-drawn) *(BLAZE 41TR)* – ('A' remix) / I love you (remix).		
Feb 91.	(cd/lp)(s-lp) *(FIRE CD/LP 23)(FIRELP 23S)* **RECURRING**	46	-
	– Big city (everybody I know can be found here) / Just to see you smile (orchestral) / I love you / Set me free – I've got the key / Set me free (reprise) / Feel so bad (reprise) /		

517

SPACEMEN 3 (cont)   THE GREAT INDIE DISCOGRAPHY   **The 1980s**

Hypnotized / Sometimes / Feelin' just fine (head full of shit) / Billy Whizz – blue 1. *(cd+=)* – When tomorrow hits / Why couldn't I see / Just to see you smile (instrumental) / Feel so sad (demo) / Drive.

—— they had already folded June '90.

– compilations, etc. –

Dec 90. (cd/d-lp) *Fierce; (FRIGHT 042/+CD)* **DREAM WEAPON / ECSTASY IN SLOW MOTION**
 (re-iss. Nov95 on 'Space Age' cd/d-lp; ORBIT 001 CD/LP) (cd re-iss. May02 on 'Sympathy For The Record Industry'; SFTRI 211)
Jun 94. (cd/lp) *Taang!; <TAANG 96 CD/LP>* **THE SINGLES**
Nov 94. (cd) *Bomp; (<BCD 4047>)* **TAKING DRUGS TO MAKE MUSIC TO TAKE DRUGS TO** *(demos of 1986)*
 (re-iss. Mar00 on 'Space Age'; ORBIT 023CD)
May 95. (cd/lp) *Sympathy For The Record Industry; (<SFTRI 136 CD/B>)* **FOR ALL FUCKED UP CHILDREN OF THE WORLD WE GIVE YOU . . .** (debut recording session)
 (cd re-iss. Jun00 & May02; SFTRI 368CD)
May 95. (cd) *Bomp; (<BCD 4044>)* **SPACEMEN ARE GO!**
 (re-iss. Jun00; same)
Jun 95. (cd/d-lp) *Fire; (FLIP CD/DLP 003)* **TRANSLUCENT FLASHBACKS (THE GLASS SINGLES)**
 (cd re-iss. Aug01; same)
Sep 95. (cd) *Taang; <TAANG 95CD>* **LIVE AT THE MILKWEG 6/2/88** (live)
 – Mary Ann / Come together / Things'll never be / Take me to the other side / Rollercoaster / Walking with Jesus / Repeater / Starship / Revolution / Suicide.
Oct 95. (cd) *Fierce; (FRIGHT 063)* **THE CHOICE IS REVOLUTIONORHERION**
Nov 95. (cd/d-lp) *Space Age; (ORBIT 002 CD/LP)* **LIVE IN EUROPE 1989** (live)
Mar 97. (d-cd) *Nectar; (NTMCDD 534)* **1 + 1 = 3**

SONIC BOOM

(PETE KEMBER solo with **WILLIE B. CARRUTHERS** and also **PHIL PARFITT + JO WIGGS** of PERFECT DISASTER)

                                                        Silvertone   Sympathy

Oct 89. (12"ep/cd-ep) *(ORE T/CD 11)* **ANGEL. / ANGEL** (version) / **HELP ME PLEASE**
Feb 90. (cd/c/lp) *(ORE CD/MC/LP 506)* **SPECTRUM**   65
 – Pretty baby / If I should die / Lonely avenue / Help me please / Angel / Rock'n'roll is killing my life / You're the one. *(free 10" w-lp) (SONIC 1)* – **DRONE DREAM EP:** OCTAVES. / TREMELOS *<US-iss.Oct97 as 'WHEN CAME BEFORE AFTER' on 'Sympathy For The Record Industry'; SFTRI 493>*
Apr 91. (7"colrd) *<SFTRI 75>* **TREMELOS. / ECSTACY (IN SLOW MOTION)**
Apr 91. (7"; gig freebie) *(SONIC 2)* **(I LOVE YOU) TO THE MOON AND BACK. / CAPO WALTZ** (live)

—— SONIC BOOM has now featured in E.A.R. (EXPERIMENTAL AUDIO RESEARCH), who after first low-key album 'MESMERISED' in 1994 on 'Sympathy For The Record Industry), released for 'Big Cat' the 1996 lp/cd 'BEYOND THE PALE' *(ABB 96/+CD)*. It featured KEVIN SHIELDS (of; we still think; MY BLOODY VALENTINE), KEVIN MARTIN (of GOD) and EDDIE PREVOST. SONIC BOOM and E.A.R. released a split 7" in Jul'98 on 'Earworm' (WORM 22)

—— In Mar 92, HONEY TONGUE (aka MATTOCK + WIGGS) released lp 'NUDE NUDES' on 'Playtime'; *AMUSE 012CD*.

SPECTRUM

KEMBER, CARRUTHERS, etc

                                                Silvertone   Warners

Jun 92. (7") *(ORE 41)* **HOW YOU SATISFY ME. / DON'T GO** (instrumental 2)
 (12"clear+=/cd-s+=) (ORE 41 T/CD) – My life spins around your every smile / Don't go (instrumental 1).
Jun 92. (cd/c/lp) *(ORE CD/C/LP 518) <41501>* **SOUL KISS (GLIDE DIVINE)**
 – How you satisfy me / Lord I don't even know my name / The drunk suite (overture) / Neon sigh / Waves wash over me / (I love you) To the Moon and back / My love for you never died away but my soul gave out and wit / Sweet running water / Touch the stars / Quicksilver glide divine / The drunk suite / Phase me out (gently). *(re-iss. Apr95; same)*
Sep 92. (7") *(ORE 44)* **TRUE LOVE WILL FIND YOU IN THE END. / MY LIFE SPINS AROUND YOUR EVERY SMILE**   70
 (12"/cd-s) (ORE T/CD 44) – ('A'side) / To the moon and back / Waves wash over me.

—— now w/ **KEVIN COWAN** – guitar (ex-DARKSIDE) repl. FORMBY

Sep 92. (d7") *<SFTRI 188>* **TRUE LOVE WILL FIND YOU IN THE SUN. / TASTE THE OZONE // DON'T GO (PLEASE STAY). / DRUNK SUITE – QUICKSILVER GLIDE DIVINE**
Nov 92. (7") *<SFTRI 209>* **SANTA CLAUS (as the Sonics). / CHRISTMAS MESSAGE FROM SONIC BOOM**
Aug 93. (7") *(ORE 56)* **INDIAN SUMMER. / BABY DON'T YOU WORRY (California lullabye)**
 (12"+=/cd-s+=) (ORE T/CD 56) – It's alright / True love will find you in the end.
Oct 94. (12"ep/cd-ep) *(ORE T/CD 65)* **UNDO THE TABOO / IN THE FULLNESS OF TIME. / TURN THE TIDE (SUB AQUA) / GO TO SLEEP**
Nov 94. (cd/lp) *(ORE CD/LP 532)* **HIGHS, LOWS AND HEAVENLY BLOWS**
 – Undo the taboo / Feedback / Then I just drifted away / Take your time / Soothe me / All night long / Don't pass me by / I know they say / Take me away.

Oct 96. (10"ep) *<SFTRI 278>* **SPECTRUM 10**   not iss.   Sympathy F
 – California lullabye / It's alright / Indian summer / True love . . . (alt. version) / Through the rhythm.

—— SONIC BOOM also became part of JESSAMINE, an outfit who released a few albums including 'Another Fictionalized History' in '97.

—— now with **ALF HARDY** – synthesizers

                                                3rd Stone   Reprise

Oct 96. (cd-ep) *<46303>* **SONGS FOR OWSLEY**
 – Owsley / Liquid intentions / Feels like I'm slipping away / Sine study #1 / The new Atlantis.
Aug 97. (d-lp/cd) *(ORBIT 008/+CD) <46715>* **FOREVER ALIEN**
 – Feels like I'm slipping away / The stars are so far (how does it feel?) / Close your eyes and you'll see / Delia Derbyshire / Owsley / Forever alien / Matrix / Like . . . / The new Atlantis / The end. *(UK+=)* – Sounds for a thunderstorm (for Peter Zinovieff) / Liquid intentions / Sine study.
Sep 97. (cd-ep) *(ORBIT 010CD)* **FEELS LIKE I'M SLIPPING AWAY**
 – Feels like I'm slipping away / Forever alien / Dream time / What comes before after? *<US-iss.Jun00; same>*
Oct 98. (cd/lp; as SPECTRUM & SILVER APPLES) *(ORBIT 016 CD/LP)* **A LAKE OF TEARDROPS**
 – Streams of sorrow / Sixth sense / The edge / Second sight / Whirlwind / (I don't care if you) Never come back.
Jun 99. (cd; split w/ IMAJINARY FRIENDS) *(ORBIT 017CD)* **INTERFACE / COME OUT TO PLAY**
 – Against the grain / Taste the night / (5 by other group).

EXPERIMENTAL AUDIO RESEARCH

SONIC BOOM – effects, etc (of SPECTRUM) / **KEVIN SHIELDS** – guitar (of MY BLOODY VALENTINE) / **EDDIE PREVOST** – percussion (of A.M.M.) / **KEVIN MARTIN** – sax, effects (of GOD)

                                                not iss.   Sympathy F

Jun 94. (cd) *<SFTRI 279>* **MESMERISED**
 – D.M.T. symphony (overture to an inhabited zone) / Mesmerise 4901 / California nocturne / Guitar feedback manipulation.
Oct 94. (5") **POCKET SYMPHONY**
                                                 Big Cat   Big Cat
Jun 96. (lp/cd) *<(ABB 96/+CD)>* **BEYOND THE PALE** (rec.1992)   Feb96
 – Beyond the pale / The calm before / In the cold light of day / The calm beyond / Dusk / The circle is blue.
                                                 not iss.   Man's Ruin
Sep 96. (10"; as EAR) *<MR 001>* **DELTA 6 (HYDROPHONIC)**

—— now without SHIELDS; he was repl. by **TOM PRENTICE** – electric viola / **PETE BAIN** – lap steel / **SCOTT RILEY** – hammer guitar

                                               Space Age   Sympathy F

Sep 96. (d-lp/cd) *(ORBIT 005/+CD) <SFTRI 459>* **PHENOMENA 256**
 – Delta 6 (hydrophonic) / Space themes part 1 & 2 (tribute to John Cage in C, A, G, E) / Sub aqua (left channel) – Tidal (centre channel) – Lunar (right channel) / Ring modulator / As the night starts closing in / Phenomena 256 (3 piece suite) / Spacestation / Mood for a summer sundown. *(re-iss. Apr98; same)*

—— the usual quartet added **THOMAS KONER + ANDY MELLWIG** – rhythms

                                               Mille Plateau   Mille Plateau

Mar 97. (cd/lp) *(<CDMILLEPLATEAU 36>)* **THE KONER EXPERIMENT**
 – (track 1-10).
                                                 Via Satellite   Via Satellite
May 97. (7"split) *(<VSAT 006>)* **SPUTNIK. / Thurston Moore & Don Fleming: TELSTAR**

—— now **SONIC BOOM, EDDIE PREVOST, PETE BASSMAN (BAIN) + TOM PRENTICE**
                                                Atavistic   Atavistic

Jan 98. (d-lp; 3-sided/cd) *(<ALP 72/+CD>)* **MILLENIUM MUSIC**
 – Delysid / Digitana / The enigma coda.
                                                Space Age   Space Age
Jul 98. (cd/d-lp) *<(ORBIT 013 CD/LP)>* **DATA RAPE**
 – Track 1-8.
                                                Earworm   not iss.
Aug 98. (7",7"clear) *(WORM 22)* **INTERLUDE. / TRANSISTOR MUSIC**
                                                Ochre   Ochre
Sep 98. (10"ep) *<(OCH 025)>* **DEATH OF A ROBOT**
Nov 98. (7"one-sided) *(WORM 35)* **DATA RAPE (part 9)**
 (above iss. on 'Earworm') (below on 'Histrionic')

—— now just down to **SONIC BOOM**

Apr 99. (cd; as E.A.R. and JESSAMINE) *<(HIST 02)>* **LIVING SOUND** (live)
 – Track 1-7.
 above with **ANDY BROWN, DAWN SMITHSON, MICHAEL FAETH + REX RITTER**
Jul 99. (cd/lp; as E.A.R.) *<(OCH 009 CD/LV)>* **PESTREPELLER**
 – Beyond the point of no return (part one) / Beyond the point of no return (part two) / Automatic music (for oscillator, ring modulator & filter cluster).
Apr 00. (cd) *<(OCH 015LCD)>* **LIVE AT THE DREAM PALACE, NEW ORLEANS RECORDED 27.11.98** (live)
 – Modulo 2 / Song for a seraphim.
                                                Rocket Girl   Rocket Girl
Nov 00. (m-lp/m-cd) *(RGIRL 18/+CD)* **VIBRATIONS**
 – Kalimbell / Ring / Synchrondipity / Wired waves / Tripple.
                                                Space Age   Space Age
Oct 01. (cd; as E.A.R.) *<(ORBIT 26CD)>* **CONTINUUM**
 – Submarine / Buzz / Shimmer / Swing / Ebb / Echo gull / Whisper incantor / See-saw.

SPACE NEGROS

Formed: Boston, Massachusetts, USA ... 1975 (yes, probably this early) by multi-talented ERIK LINDGREN, a man devoted to synth-pop and the progressive of New Wave through his largely independent recording output – this man took "indie" music/musak to a new extreme. With various and numerous personnel (including MARTIN SWOPE and ROGER MILLER, one-half of MISSION OF BURMA and future BIRDSONGS OF THE MESOZOIC leaders), The SPACE NEGROS surfaced from the recording studio with some extremely weird and wonderful pop-song arrangements, mainly on EP's at first. From 1979's 'MAXIMUM CONTRAST...', to their un-newsworthy split in 1985 (or thereabouts!), the cosmic ones created unusual sounds – check their numerous 'DIG ARCHAEOLOGY...' volumes from the 90's and you'll see this was no straightforward band. LINDGREN, of course, settled down (a little) with 'BURMA offshoot, BIRDSONGS ...

Album rating: DIG ARCHAEOLOGY II: 1975-1986 collection (*7)

ERIK LINDGREN – multi, etc / with **CLINT CONLEY** – bass (of MISSION OF BURMA) / **ROGER "THE BEAD" MILLER** – guitar (of MISSION OF BURMA) / **BOBY BEAR** – drums

		not iss.	Sounds Interested
1979.	(7"ep) <SIEP 001> **MAXIMUM CONTRAST FROM MOMENT TO MOMENT** – Demolition zone / 1984 / Man to man / What should we do / Wrong conclusions / Untitled.	-	

— added at various times:- **MICHAEL COHEN** – percussion / **STEVE ADAMS** – wind / **JOE SCHEER** – violin / **LINDA BROWN** – vocals / **DEB ROTH** – vocals / **BRYN CARLSON** – drums / **CARL BIANCUCCI** – bass / **G. ANDREW MANESS** – guitars / **ERIC ROSE** – guitar / **ARAM HELLER** – guitar / **GENE ROMA** – bass, etc.

		not iss.	Arf! Arf!
1980.	(7"ep) <AA 001> **GO COMMERCIAL EP** – One bad imitation / Itinerary / Puppy love / Publis service announcement / Halitosis / Four o'clock / Megabuck / I wanna be invaded / Happenings ten years time ago.	-	
1981.	(7") <AA 003> **BACK IN THE USSR. / GO TO HELL**	- not iss.	own label
1981.	(9"flexi) <none> **TELL WHITE LIES EP** – Concentration / Talk talk / Let's go to the moon / MDMDM / What should we do / Martians have landed / Seedy blooze / Let's go to the ice (cream parlour).		
		not iss.	Eat
1981.	(12"ep; as FAMILY FUN) <none> **RECORD**	- not iss.	Jingle Jungle
Dec 81.	(7"ep) <001> **HAVE A LOUSY CHRISTMAS** – Jingle hell / We wish you a lousy Christmas / We wish you a lousy Xmas / Deck the halls (with POISON SUMAC) / Silent fright.		

— MILLER and SWOPE joined BIRDSONGS OF THE MESOZOIC

		Glass	not iss.
Sep 85.	(12"ep) (GLALP 013) **PINK NOISE** – Innards / Mini-mammoths / Pop tops.		-

— they split in 1985, LINDGREN also joined BIRDSONGS ...

– compilations, etc. –

all on 'Arf! Arf!' records unless mentioned otherwise

1987.	(lp) <AA 038> **...DO GENERIC ETHNIC MUSAK VERSIONS OF ALL YOUR FAVOURITE PUNK/PSYCHEDELIC SONGS FROM THE SIXTIES** <(UK cd+re-iss. Dec97 +=; same)> – (extra tracks).	-	
1992.	(cd) <AA 035> **DIG ARCHAEOLOGY: 1980-1990** (UK-iss.Dec97; same as US)	-	
1992.	(cd) <AA 040> **DIG ARCHAEOLOGY II: 1975-1986** – Concentration / Talk talk / What should we do / Martians have landed / All punked out / Music for safety Ed glass / Seedy blooze / I can't talk now / Happenings ten years time ago / Gymnopedie No.3 / Demolition zone / Out to launch / By the winding river / Iron man / Pink noise: Innards – Mini-mammoths – Pop tops / Flames in trains / Untitled / Anti-gravity / And many, many more II / Murder on Mass Ave. (UK-iss.Dec97; same as US)	-	
Apr 96.	(cd) <AA 055> **DIG ARCHAEOLOGY VOLUME 2 1981-1983** (UK-iss.Dec97; same as US)	-	
Jul 00.	(cd) <AA 064> **SPACE AMAZON**	-	

SPEAR OF DESTINY

Formed: Westminster, London, England ... late 1982 by ex-THEATRE OF HATE mainmen, KIRK BRANDON and STAN STAMMERS. The latter outfit initially traded under the name, The PACK, releasing a couple of singles on manager Terry Razor's 'SS' label, before evolving into THEATRE OF HATE in early 1980. By this point, the line-up numbered BRANDON, SIMON WERNER, JONATHAN WERNER and LUKE RANDALL, the group releasing a promising double A-side debut, 'ORIGINAL SIN' / 'LEGION' towards the end of the year. With JAMIE STUART and STEVE GUTHRIE replacing the WERNER brothers, the group released a live set, 'HE WHO DARES WINS' in Spring of the following year. Following a change of name from the controversially monikered 'SS' to the slightly less controversial 'Burning Rome', the band's label issued a further two singles, 'REBEL WITHOUT A BRAIN' and 'NERO'. Although the group were beginning to develop their pulverising rhythmic assault, BRANDON brought in a whole new line-up (BILLY DUFFY, the aforementioned STAMMERS, NIGEL PRESTON and JOHN BOY LENNARD) prior to the recording of debut album 'WESTWORLD'. Produced by CLASH guitarist MICK JONES and released in early '82, the record was characterised by BRANDON's punk-choirboy vocal bombast and PRESTON's rolling thunder drums, LENNARD's twilight sax lines adding an air of desolation. Although Top 20 success led to intense major label interest, the group chose to remain independent, at least for the final few months of their career. With the implosion of THEATRE OF HATE later that summer, BRANDON and STAMMERS formed SPEAR OF DESTINY with CHRIS BELL and LASCELLES AMES, their 'Burning Rome' label taken on by 'Epic'. Preceded by the 'FLYING SCOTSMAN' single, the keenly anticipated 'GRAPES OF WRATH' (1983) was met with a muted critical reception upon its release in Spring '83, barely scraping into the Top 75. More personnel changes ensued with LENNARD back on sax, DOLPHIN TAYLOR replacing BELL and NEIL PYZER added on keyboards. After a one-off single in early '84, 'PRISONER OF LOVE', MICKEY DONNELLY replaced the departing LENNARD while ALAN ST. CLAIRE was added as a second guitarist. With a fuller sound, the resulting 'ONE-EYED JACKS' (1984) more accurately realised BRANDON's alternative power-rock vision, almost making the Top 20 and ushering in the most creative and commercially fruitful period of the singer's career. 'WORLD SERVICE' (1985) was released amid a hectic bout of touring, the group building up a sizeable fanbase who helped take the album to a near-Top 10 placing. Ironically, however, no Top 40 singles were forthcoming and SPEAR OF DESTINY split with their label, the existing line-up falling apart. Going back to the drawing board, BRANDON surfaced a year later with new recruits, STEVIE BLANCHARD, VOLKER JANSSON and the BARNACLE brothers, PETE and STEVE. Newly signed to '10-Virgin', SPEAR OF DESTINY at last scored the elusive Top 20 hit with 'NEVER TAKE ME ALIVE', while the accompanying album, 'OUTLAND' (1987) became their biggest selling effort to date. Just when it looked as if the group might move up to first division status, BRANDON was incapacitated by illness and the group were forced to lie low for almost a year. By the release of 'THE PRICE YOU PAY' (1988), the momentum seemed to have been irrevocably lost, BRANDON putting the lid on his band for what was conceivably the last time. The early 90's, however, saw BRANDON touring alongside fellow veteran STAMMERS and newcomers MARK THWAITE / BOBBY RAE MAYHEM under both the THEATRE OF HATE and SPEAR OF DESTINY monikers. This regrouping susbequently resulted in a one-off album, 'SOD'S LAW' (1992), for the resurrected 'Burning Rome' label; largely ignored by press and public alike, the record's failure led to BRANDON burying the name for good. The new decade brought further bad luck for the singer (now partly based in Denmark), as he lost a court battle with BOY GEORGE (whom he once played alongside in an early incarnation of CULTURE CLUB) following the latter's claim that he'd had a homosexual relationship with BRANDON. Beleaguered but clearly not beaten, he re-emerged in 1995 with KIRK BRANDON's 10:51, releasing an album, 'STONE IN THE RAIN'. Whether or not we needed a second coming of SPEAR OF DESTINY mattered little, unless of course you had followed KIRK in all his trials and tribulations. A Celtic-styled SOD unleashed the anthemic, 'RELIGION', in 1998, and a follow-up 'VOLUNTEERS' (2000) showed he/they weren't quite finished with the music world. Watch out for a THEATRE OF HATE comeback. Surely not!?

Album rating: Theatre Of Hate: HE WHO DARES WINS – LIVE AT THE WAREHOUSE, LEEDS (*5) / WESTWORLD (*8) / REVOLUTION compilation (*9) / Spear Of Destiny: GRAPES OF WRATH (*6) / ONE-EYED JACKS (*5) / WORLD SERVICE (*6) / OUTLAND (*7) / S.O.D. – THE EPIC YEARS compilation (*8) / THE PRICE YOU PAY (*5) / SOD'S LAW (*4) / Kirk Brandon's 10.51: STONE IN THE RAIN (*4) / Spear Of Destiny: RELIGION (*5) / VOLUNTEERS (*4)

PACK

KIRK BRANDON (b. 3 Aug'56) – vocals, guitar / **SIMON WERNER** – guitar / **JONATHAN WERNER** – bass / **JIM WALKER** – drums (ex-PUBLIC IMAGE LTD.)

		S.S.	not iss.
1979.	(7") (PAK 1) **BRAVE NEW SOLDIERS. / HEATHEN**		-
		Rough Trade	not iss.
Nov 79.	(7") (RT 025) **KING OF KINGS. / NUMBER 12** (re-iss. 1980 as 7"ep; all 4 above on 'S.S.'; SS 1N2- SS 2N1)		

— Early 1980, they had evolved into ...

THEATRE OF HATE

LUKE RANDALL – drums repl. WALKER

		S.S.	not iss.
Nov 80.	(7") (SS 3) **ORIGINAL SIN. / LEGION**		-

— **JAMIE STUART** – bass + **STEVE GUTHRIE** – guitar repl. both WERNERS

Mar 81.	(lp) (SSSSS 1P) **HE WHO DARES WINS – LIVE AT THE WAREHOUSE, LEEDS** (live) – The original sin / Do you believe in the westworld / The klan / Conquistador / Poppies / Incinarator / Judgement hymn / 63 / Rebel without a brain / Legion.		-
		Burning Rome	not iss.
Apr 81.	(12") (BRR 1) **REBEL WITHOUT A BRAIN. / MY OWN INVENTION**		-
Jul 81.	(12") (BRR 1931) **NERO. / INCINERATOR**		-

— **KIRK BRANDON** brought in entire new line-up **BILLY DUFFY** – guitar / **STAN STAMMERS** – bass (ex-STRAPS) repl. JAMIE who joined RITUAL then DEATH CULT / **NIGEL PRESTON** – drums / **JOHN BOY LENNARD** – saxophone

Jan 82.	(7") (BRR 2) **DO YOU BELIEVE IN THE WESTWORLD?. / PROPAGANDA** (12"+=) (BRR T2-2T) – Original sin (version) / Ministry of broadcast.	40	-
Feb 82.	(lp) (TOH 1) **WESTWORLD** – Do you believe in the westworld? / Judgement hymn / 63 / Love is a ghost / The wake / Conquistador / The new trail of tears / Freaks / Anniversary / The klan / Poppies. (re-iss. May91; BRR 010LP) (with free 7"ep) **ORIGINAL SIN / LEGION.// HEATHEN (The PACK) / BRAVE NEW SOLDIERS (The PACK)** (cd+=) – Incinerator / Rebel without a brain / Propaganda / Legion / Nero. (cd re-iss. Jan96 on 'Dojo'; DOJOCD 220) (cd-iss. Sep97 on 'Snapper'+=; SMMCD 511)	17	-

SPEAR OF DESTINY (cont)

May 82. (7") *(BRR 3)* **THE HOP. / CONQUISTADOR** — 70 / -

— reverted to a quartet, when DUFFY also joined The (DEATH) CULT.

Nov 82. (7") *(BRR 4)* **EASTWORLD. / ASSEGAI** — □ / -
(12"+=) *(BBR 4T)* – Poppies.

— Had already disbanded Autumn '82. LENNARD moved to Canada to form DIODES. PRESTON joined The SEX GANG CHILDREN, and was later another to join The CULT

– compilations, etc. –

Jun 81. (c) *Straight Music; (TOH 1)* **LIVE AT THE LYCEUM (live)**
Feb 82. (lp) *S.S.; (SSSSS 1P)* **HE WHO DARES WINS – LIVE IN BERLIN (live)**
(cd-iss. Jun96 on 'Loma'; LOMACD 35)
Aug 84. (lp/d-c) *Burning Rome; (TOH 2)* **REVOLUTION** (The Best Of . . .)
– Legion / The original sin / Rebel without a brain / My own invention / Nero / Do you believe in the westworld? / Propaganda / The hop / Incinerator / Eastworld / Americanos. *(d-c+=)* – HE WHO DARES WINS *(cd-iss. Feb93 on 'Line')*
Mar 85. (live-7"ep) *Bliss; (TOH 1EP)* **THE WAKE / LOVE IS A GHOST. / POPPIES / LEGION**
Nov 85. (12"ep) *Burning Rome; (BRRT 1985)* **THE HOP / CONQUISTADOR. / ORIGINAL SIN / WESTWORLD?**
Apr 86. (lp) *Dojo; (DOJOLP 19)* **ORIGINAL SIN LIVE (live)**
Jul 93. (cd) *Mau Mau; (MAUCD 637)* **TEN YEARS AFTER**
(re-iss. Jun98 on 'Diablo'; DIAB 860)
Jun 95. (cd) *Anagram; (CDGRAM 93)* **THE COMPLETE SINGLES COLLECTION**
Aug 96. (cd) *Receiver; (RRCD 229)* **RETRIBUTION OVER THE WESTWORLD 1996**
Mar 98. (d-cd) *Eastworld; (TOH 001DCD) / Amsterdamned; <70017>* **THEATRE OF HATE ACT 1** — Mar99
– (REVOLUTION / LIVE IN SWEDEN)
Mar 98. (d-cd) *Eastworld; (TOH 002DCD) / Amsterdamned; <70020>* **THEATRE OF HATE ACT 2** — Mar99
– (TEN YEARS AFTER / HE WHO DARES WINS)
Mar 98. (cd) *Snapper; (SMMCD 527)* **ARIA OF THE DEVIL**
Jul 98. (d-cd) *Eastworld; (TOH 003DCD) / Amsterdamned; <70021>* **THEATRE OF HATE ACT 3** — Mar99
– (RETRIBUTION / BINGLEY HALL)
Sep 98. (d-cd) *Eastworld; (TOH 004DCD)* **THEATRE OF HATE ACT 4**
– (THE SESSIONS / LIVE AT THE ASTORIA)
Sep 98. (d-cd) *Eastworld; (TOH 005DCD)* **THEATRE OF HATE ACT 5**
– (THE SINGLES / WHO DARES WINS)
Sep 99. (cd) *Cherry Red; (<CDMGRAM 93>)* **THE COMPLETE SINGLES COLLECTION**
Oct 99. (cd) *Yeaah; (YEAAH 2)* **THE SINGLES COLLECTION** — Oct99
(re-iss. Sep01 on 'Music Club'; MCCD 472)
May 00. (cd) *Receiver; (RRCD 273)* **LOVE IS A GHOST (live 14/6/1981)**
May 00. (cd) *Snapper; (<SMCD 206>)* **THE BEST OF THEATRE OF HATE**

– (The PACK) compilations, etc. –

Apr 82. (7"ep) *Cyclops; (CLCLOPS 1)* **LONG LIVE THE PAST (demos from Aug'78)**
– Thalidomide / King of kings / St.Teresa / Abattoir.
1982. (c) *Donut; (DONUT 2)* **THE PACK LIVE 1979 (live)**

SPEAR OF DESTINY

— were almost immediately formed by **KIRK + STAN** with **CHRIS BELL** – drums (ex-KING TRIGGER, ex-THOMPSON TWINS) / **LASCELLES AMES** – saxophone (ex-MIGHTY DIAMONDS) ('Burning Rome' was taken over by 'Epic')

Epic C.B.S.

Feb 83. (7") *(SPEAR 1)* **FLYING SCOTSMAN. / THE MAN WHO TUNES THE DRUMS** — □ / -
(12"+=) *(SPEAR13 1)* – Africa.
Apr 83. (lp/c) *(EPC/40 25318)* **GRAPES OF WRATH** — 62 / -
– The wheel / Flying Scotsman / Roof of the world / Aria / Solution / Murder of love / The preacher / Omen of the times / The man who tunes the drums / Grapes of wrath. *(re-iss. Apr86 lp/c; EPC/40 32779)*
May 83. (7"/7"pic-d) *(A/WA 3372)* **THE WHEEL. / THE HOP** — 59 / -
(d7"+=) *(DA 3372)* – The preacher (live) / Grapes of wrath (live).
(12"+=) *(TA 3372)* – Solution (live) / Roof of the world (live) / Love is a ghost (live).

— **JOHN LENNARD** – saxophone returned to the fold repl. LASCELLES / **DOLPHIN TAYLOR** – drums (ex-STIFF LITTLE FINGERS, ex-TOM ROBINSON BAND) repl. BELL who joined The SPECIMEN then GENE LOVES JEZEBEL / added **NEIL PYZER** – keyboards, saxophone (ex-HOWARD DEVOTO, ex-The CASE)

Jan 84. (7") *(A 4068)* **PRISONER OF LOVE. / ROSIE** — 59 / -
(12"+=) *(TA 4068)* – Grapes of wrath (1984).
(d7"+=) *(DA 4068)* – Rainmaker (live) / Don't turn away (live).

— **BRANDON, STAMMERS, PYZER + TAYLOR** added **ALAN St.CLAIRE** – guitar / **MICKEY DONNELLY** – saxophone (ex-The CASE) repl. LENNARD

Apr 84. (7") *(A 4310)* **LIBERATOR. / FORBIDDEN PLANET** — 67 / -
(12"+=) *(TA 4310)* – ('A'dub version) / ('A'extended).
Apr 84. (lp/c) *(EPC/40 25836)* **ONE-EYED JACKS** — 22 / -
– Rainmaker / Young men / Everything you ever wanted / Don't turn away / Liberator / Prisoner of love / Playground of the rich / Forbidden planet / Attica / These days are gone. *(re-iss. Feb88 lp/c450886-1/-4;)*
May 85. (7") *(A 6333)* **ALL MY LOVE (ASK NOTHING). / LAST CARD** — 61 / -
(12"+=) *(TA 6333)* – Walk in the shadow.
(12"+=) *(QTA 6333)* – The wheel (live) / Prisoner of love (live) / Liberator (live).

Jul 85. (7") *(A 6445)* **COME BACK. / COLE YOUNGER** — 55 / -
(12"+=) *(TA 6445)* – Young men (the return of).
Aug 85. (lp/c) *(EPC/40 26514)* **WORLD SERVICE** — 11 / -
– Rocket ship / Up all night / Come back / World service / I can see / All my love (ask nothing) / Mickey / Somewhere in the east / Once in her lifetime / Harlan County.

— **BRANDON** recruited entire new band when STAMMERS + PYZER formed CRAZY PINK REVOLVERS. Newcomers:- **STEVIE BLANCHARD** – guitar (ex-TOM ROBINSON BAND) / **VOLKER JANSSON** – keyboards (ex-BERLIN) / **STEVE BARNACLE** – bass, keyboards / **PETE BARNACLE** – drums

10-Virgin Virgin

Jan 87. (7") *(TEN 148)* **STRANGERS IN OUR TOWN. / SOMEWHERE OUT THERE** — 49 / -
(12"+=) *(TENX 148)* – Time of our lives / ('A'&'B' versions).
(d12"++=) *(TENZ 148)* – ('A'&'B'dub versions).

— **MIKE PROCTOR** – guitar repl. STEVIE B.

Mar 87. (7") *(TEN 162)* **NEVER TAKE ME ALIVE. / LAND OF SHAME** — 14 / -
(ext.12"+=) *(TENX 162)* – Pumpkin man / Embassy song.
(3"cd-s+=) *(TENZ 162)* – Jack Straw / The man that never was.

— **MARCO PIRRONI** – guitar (ex-ADAM & THE ANTS, ex-MODELS) repl. PROCTOR

Apr 87. (lp/c/cd) *(DIX/CDIX/DIXCD 59) <90579>* **OUTLAND** — 16 / Oct87
– Outlands / Land of shame / The traveller / Was that you? / Strangers in our town / The whole world's waiting / Tonight / Miami vice / Never take me alive. *(c-ep+=)* – Time of our lives / Pumpkin man / Embassy song / Jack straw / The man that never was. *(re-iss. Mar91)*
Jul 87. (7") *(TEN 173)* **WAS THAT YOU?. / WAS THAT YOU? (live)** — 55 / -
(12"+=/12"pic-d+=) *(TENT/+P 173)* – Miami vice / Outlands.
(live-12"+=) *(TENR 173)* – Land of shame / Jack Straw. <US-iss. 5 track cd-ep>
Sep 87. (7") *(TEN 189)* **THE TRAVELLER. / LATE NIGHT PSYCHO** — 44 / -
(12"+=) *(TENR 189)* – Strangers in our town (live) / Mickey (live).

— **ALAN St.CLAIRE** – guitar returned to repl. PIRRONI / **CHRIS BOSTOCK** – bass (ex-JO BOXERS) repl. STEVE

Virgin Virgin

Sep 88. (7") *(VS 1123)* **SO IN LOVE WITH YOU. / MARCH OR DIE** — 36 / -
(12"+=) *(VST 1123)* – ('A'extended).
(cd-s+=) *(VSCD 1123)* – Junkman.
(10"+=) *(VSA 1123)* – Jungle.
Oct 88. (cd/c/lp) *(CD/TC+/V 2549)* **THE PRICE YOU PAY** — 37 / -
– So in love with you / Tinseltown / The price / I remember / Dreamtime / Radio radio / If the guns / View from a tree / Junkman. *(cd+=)* – Soldier soldier / Brave new world. *(re-iss. Mar91)*
Nov 88. (7"/7"g-f) *(VS/+G 1144)* **RADIO RADIO. / LIFE GOES ON** — □ / -
(10"+=) *(VSA 1144)* – Made in London.
(cd-s++=) *(VSCD 1144)* – ('A'extended).
(12"+=) *(VST 1144)* – ('A'extended) / Spirits.

— In the 90's, **KIRK** brought back **STAN STAMMERS** – bass / + newcomers **MARK THWAITE** – guitar / **BOBBY RAE MAYHEM** – drums. Toured as TOH & SOD

Burning Rome not iss.

Sep 92. (12"/cd-s) *(BRR 47 T/CD)* **BLACK COUNTRY GIRL. / BABYLON TALKING**
Oct 92. (lp/c/cd) *(BRR/+MC/CD 011)* **SOD'S LAW**
– Goldmine / Into the rising Sun / Black country girl / When the bull comes down / Slow me down / T.C.B. / In the city / Babylon talking / Crystalize / Killing ground. *(c+=)* – Rave on Albion. *(cd++=)* – Captain America. *(cd re-iss. Sep97 on 'Snapper'++=; SMMCD 512)* – Chemical head / Paradise / Burn out.

KIRK BRANDON'S 10:51

Anagram not iss.

Mar 95. (7") *(ANA 55)* **CHILDREN OF THE DAMNED. / SATELLITE**
(cd-s+=) *(CDANA 55)* – At her majesties request.
Apr 95. (cd) *(CDGRAM 92)* **STONE IN THE RAIN**
– Stone in the rain / Communication ends / How long? / Satellite / Children of the damned / Europa / Psycho woman / Revolver / Propaganda / Heroes / Future world / Spirit tribe.

SPEAR OF DESTINY

— returned to the fold in 1997:- **KIRK BRANDON** with **JOHN McNUTT** – guitar / **ART SMITH** – drums

Eastworld Amsterdamned

Nov 97. (cd) *(SOD 001CD) <70018>* **RELIGION** — □ / Oct98
– Rainy day / Iona / Prison planet / Magic eye / Mile in my shoes / X / Female hero (7 letters) / Werewolves / Slayride / Total kontrol.

Do-little not iss.

Dec 99. (cd-s) *(LITTLE 009CD)* **UPHILL BACKWARDS**
May 00. (cd) *(DO 010CD)* **VOLUNTEERS**
– Some kind of normal / Nothing under the sun / Silver forest / Volunteers / Paranoia / Judas / Never take me alive / Uphill backwards / Penny black / Iceman / End of days.

– compilations, etc. –

Feb 86. (12"ep) *Old Gold; (OG 4007)* **FLYING SCOTSMAN / THE WHEEL. / PRISONER OF LOVE / LIBERATOR**
May 87. (lp/c/cd) *Epic; (450872-1/-4/-2)* **S.O.D. – THE EPIC YEARS** — 53 / -
– The wheel / Rainmaker / Prisoner of love / Playground of the rich / Young men / Up all night / Come back / All my love (ask nothing) / Mickey / Liberator.
Nov 91. (cd/c) *Old Gold; (OG 3/2 303)* **SPEAR OF DESTINY**
Jul 93. (cd) *Mau Mau; (MAUCD 638)* **LIVE AT THE LYCEUM 22.12.85 (live)**
(re-iss. Jun99 on 'Diablo'; DIAB 9002)
Apr 94. (cd) *Windsong; (WINCD 055)* **THE BBC RADIO ONE LIVE IN CONCERT (live)**

SPEAR OF DESTINY (cont)

Mar 95.	(cd) Virgin; (CDOVD 049) **TIME OF OUR LIVES – THE BEST OF SPEAR OF DESTINY**		–

– Never take me alive / Outlands / Traveller / Strangers in our town / Miami vice / Time of our lives / Man that never was / So in love with you / March or die / I remember / Radio radio / Life goes on / If the guns / Was that you.

Mar 98.	(d-cd) Eastworld; (SOD 002DCD) / Amsterdamned; <70016> **SPEAR OF DESTINY PSALM 1** – (ELEPHANT DAZE / LIVE AT THE FORUM)		Mar99
Mar 98.	(d-cd) Eastworld; (SOD 003DCD) / Amsterdamned; <70022> **SPEAR OF DESTINY PSALM 2** – (OUTLANDS – THE DEMOS / LIVE AT THE NATIONAL)		Mar99
Jun 98.	(d-cd) Eastworld; (SOD 004DCD) / Amsterdamned; <70023> **SPEAR OF DESTINY PSALM 3** – (MANOR MOBILE IN SESSION / BARROWLANDS LIVE 1985)		Mar99
Sep 98.	(d-cd) Eastworld; (SOD 005DCD) **SPEAR OF DESTINY PSALM 4** – (S.O.D. THE SESSIONS / LIVE AT THE LYCEUM)		–
Sep 98.	(d-cd) Eastworld; (SOD 006DCD) **SPEAR OF DESTINY PSALM 5** – THE BOYS BRIGADE / LIVE AT THE ACE)		–
Sep 98.	(cd) Recall; <146> **THE BEST OF SPEAR OF DESTINY**	–	
May 00.	(cd) Receiver; (<RRCD 285>) **THE PREACHER (live 1983)**		–
Nov 02.	(cd; by KIRK BRANDON) Eastertone; (<ESRC 001>) **ANTHOLOGY**		–
Dec 02.	(4xcd-box; by KIRK BRANDON) Eastertone; (ESRC 002) **ANTHOLOGY**		–

The SENATE

(**KIRK BRANDON** + **RUSTY EGAN** ex-SKIDS, ex-VISAGE)

Jul 84.	(7") Burning Rome; (BRR 7) **THE ORIGINAL SIN. / DO YOU BELIEVE IN THE WESTWORLD?**		–
Jul 84.	(7") W.A.R.; (WAR 1) **THE ORIGINAL SIN. / DO YOU BELIEVE IN THE WESTWORLD?** (live) (12"+=) (12WAR 1) – ('A'extended).		–

SPEED THE PLOUGH

Formed: Haledon, New Jersey, USA . . . 1982 as The TRYPES, by JOHN BAUMGARTNER who had been school friends of new wave/psychedelic outfit The FEELIES. When The FEELIES, (BILL MILLION & GLEN MERCER) decided to take a hiatus in 1983/84, they guested on the EP, 'THE EXPLORER'S HOLD. They also played together on Sunday nights at the local Peanut Gallery bar, a series dubbed, "Music For Neighbors". In 1986 when The FEELIES sorted out their problems, the TRYPES became SPEED THE PLOUGH. Many gigs later, their first album was issued in 1989, a set of avant-garde psychedelia, drawing inspiration from RAVI SHANKAR, BRIAN ENO and PHILIP GLASS. Three more appeared in the first half of the 90's, the best of which was 1995's 'MARINA'.

Album rating: SPEED THE PLOUGH (*6) / WONDER WHEEL (*7) / MASON'S BOX (*4) / MARINA (*5)

JOHN BAUMGARTNER – vocals, keyboards, etc / with **GLEN MERCER** + **BILL MILLION** (of The FEELIES)

		not iss.	Coyote
1984.	(12"ep; as TRYPES) <COYEP 006> **THE EXPLORERS HOLD**	–	

– (From the) Morning glories / Love you to / Music for neighbors / The undertow.

— now without part-time FEELIES who re-joined said outfit

— JOHN enlisted **MILLION** + **MARC FRANCIA** – guitars, drums / **FRANK O'TOOLE** – guitar / **PETE PEDULLA** – bass, trumpet / **TONI PARUTA** – wind / **JIM DeROGATIS** – percussion, drums

		not iss.	Twin/Tone
1989.	(cd) <88136> **SPEED THE PLOUGH**	–	

– River street / Veszprem / Big bus / Tommy's house / Ella's way / Cardinal rules / No one's alone / Blue bicycle / Fathers and sons / Everyday needs. <re-iss. 1991 on 'East Side Digital'; ESD 8066-2>

— now with **MILLION, FRANCIA, O'TOOLE** + **BRENDA SAUTER** – bass (ex-FEELIES) / **MICHAEL LIPTON** – guitars

		East Side Digital	East Side Digital
1991.	(cd/c) <ESD 8053-2/-4> **WONDER WHEEL**	–	

– Aeroplane / The tide won't tire / The story of the moon / Coal and courage / Hemlock tree / Cutting branches for a temporary . . . / Final day / Trains / Centerville / One of your friends / The Plough and the stars.

— added **RICHARD BARNES** – guitars

Jan 94.	(cd) <ESD 8087-2> **MASON'S BOX**	–	

– Lock and key / Deepest brown / The roof is off (the stars are there and . . .) / Napoleon / Follow your visions / Oh, the paradise / Wide awake / Book of reasons / Seven stairs / Song / Morrow bay / Screen door.

Jul 96.	(cd) <(ESD 8110-2)> **MARINA**		Nov95

– Just a little / Written each day / Said and done / Once in a while / Late birds / A saint restored / High wine / Love song / Bayswater lane / A hard friend to keep / Hourglass / In the atmosphere / Marina.

— SAUTER was also part of WILD CARNATION (with husband RICHARD BARNES), who issued one US album 'TRICYCLE' for 'Delmore' in 1995.

S.P.K.

Formed: Sydney, Australia . . . 1978 as SURGICAL PENIS KLINIK, by mental hospice carer, DEREK THOMPSON (aka OBLIVION), with one of his patients, NE/H/IL (er.. NEIL) along with DOMINIK PINKER. Early singles, 'GERMANIK', 'SLOGAN' and 'MEAT PROCESSING SECTION' were Australian-only affairs, as was debut album, 'INFORMATION OVERLOAD UNIT' (1981). Britain was treated to its first taste of the band's uncompromising industrial noise via 1982's 'LEICHENSCHREI', released under the less squeamish moniker of SOZIALISTISCHES PATIENTEN KOLLEKTIV (a German organisation committed to lobbying for the rights of mental patients). A cassette only release, 'FROM SCIENCE TO RITUAL' (1984) – with GRAEME REVELL now replacing NE/H/IL and PINKER – followed in early '84, the same month as a German release, 'AUTO-DA-FE'. As contrary with regards to their moniker as the music itself, SPK subsequently announced that their initials now stood for SYSTEMS PLANNING KORPORATION. They'd also recruited a Chinese female "singer", SINAN LEONG, replacing THOMPSON, the last remaining founder member. Having incredibly secured a deal with 'Warners', the band made their break for the big time with the 'MACHINE AGE VOODOO' (1984) album. Bracketed with contemporaries TEST DEPT. and EINSTURZENDE NEUBAUTEN, SPK had a similar penchant for ear-crippling live displays of metal-bashing and general sonic mayhem, the memorable screening of the 'METAL DANCE' single on Channel 4's 'The Tube', about as close to mainstream indie fame as SPK came. 'ZAMIA LEHMANNI' (1986) saw them back on indie label, 'Side Effekts', the record a complete departure towards the classical sounds of ancient Greece. A final two albums, 'OCEANIA' (1988) and 'DIGITALES AMBIGUA, GOLD & POISON', followed in 1988 before the band split for good. GRAEME REVELL also released a couple of simultaneous solo sets, 'THE INSECT MUSICIANS' (1987) and 'NECROPOLIS AMPHIBIAN REPTILES' (1988), employing the "music" of insects!

Album rating: INFORMATION OVERLOAD UNIT (*4) / LEICHENSCHREI (*3) / AUT DA FE (*5) / MACHINE AGE VOODOO (*6) / GOLD AND POISON (*5) / OCEANIA (*6) / ZAMA LEHMANNI (*4)

SURGICAL PENIS KLINIK

OBLIVION (b. DEREK THOMPSON) – synthesizer, tapes, metal percussion, vocals / **NE/H/IL** (b. NEIL LUSTMORE) – synthesizer, tapes, vocals / **PINKER** – drums, metal percussion, vocals

		P.R.S.	not iss.
Apr 79.	(7") (2617) **GERMANIK. / NO MORE / CONTACT**	–	– Austra
Nov 79.	(7"m) (2655) **SLOGAN. / MEKANO / CONTACT**	–	– Austra
		Industrial	not iss.
Jun 80.	(7") (IR 0011) **MEAT PROCESSING SECTION**		–

– Slogan / Mekano. (different titles on label)

		Side Effekts	not iss.
Feb 81.	(lp) (SER 01) **INFORMATION OVERLOAD UNIT**		–

– Emanation machine R. Gie 1916 / Suture / obsession / Macht schrecken / Berufsverbot / Ground zero: infinity zone / Stammheim torturkammer / Retard / Epilept: convulse / Kaltbruchig acideath. (re-iss. May85 on 'Normal'; NORMAL 09) (cd-iss. Sep92 on 'Grey Area-Mute'; SPK 1CD)

		M Squared	not iss.
Jul 81.	(7") (M 2009) **SEE SAW. / CHAMBERMUSIK**	–	– Austra
		Sterile	not iss.
Nov 81.	(c) (SRC 4) **LIVE AT THE CRYPT** (live) (UK-iss.Apr85; same)	–	– Austra
		Side Effekts	Thermidor
1982.	(lp; as SOZIALISTISCHES PATIENTEN KOLLEKTIV) (SER 002) <T-9> **LEICHENSCHREI**		

– Genetic transmission / Postmortem / Desolation / Napalm (terminal patient) / Cry from the sanitorium / Baby blue eyes / Israel / Internal bleeding / Chamber music / Despair / The agony of the plasma / Day of pigs / War of Islam / Maladia Europa (the European sickness). (cd-iss. Sep92 on 'Grey Area-Mute'; SPK 2CD)

May 83.	(12"; as SEPPUKU) (SER 003) **DEKOMPOSITIONES**		–

– Another dark age / Twilight of the idols / Culturecide.

— **GRAEME REVELL** – synthesizer, electronics, metal bashing; repl. NE/H/IL + PINKER

		Plasma	not iss.
Jan 84.	(c) (PLASMA 004) **FROM SCIENCE TO RITUAL**		–
		Walter Ulbright	not iss.
Jan 84.	(lp) (WULP 002) **AUTO-DA-FE**	–	– German

– Contakt / Germanik / Mekano / Retard / Slogun / Metal field / Walking on dead steps / A heart that breaks (in no time or place). (cd-iss. Jan93 on 'Grey Area-Mute'+=; SPK 4CD) – Another dark age / Twilight of the idols / Culturecide.

S.P.K.

— they claimed it now stood for SYSTEMS PLANNING KORPORATION

— **SINAN (LEONG)** – voice (& many guests); repl. last original DEREK

		WEA	Elektra
Sep 84.	(7"/12") (YZ 24/+T) **JUNK FUNK. / HIGH TENSION**		
Nov 84.	(lp) (WX 10) <60386-1> **MACHINE AGE VOODOO**		

– Junk funk / With love from China / High tension / One world / Flesh and steel / Metropol / Metal dance / Thin ice / Crime of passion.

		Desire	not iss.
Apr 85.	(7"/12") (WANT/+X 1) **METAL DANCE. / WILL TO POWER**		–
		Side Effekts	not iss.
May 86.	(12") (SFX 01) **IN FRAGRANTE DELICTO. / INVOCATION (TO SECULAR HERESIES)**		–
Oct 86.	(lp) (SER 09) **ZAMIA LEHMANNI**		–

– Invocation (to secular heresies) / Palms crossed in sorrow / Romanz in moll (romance in a minor key) / In the dying moments / In fragrante delicto (intro) / In fragrante delicto / Alocasia metallica / Necropolis / The garden of earthy delights. (re-iss. Nov92 on 'Grey Area-Mute' lp/cd+=; SPK 3/+CD) – The doctrine of eternal ice.

Jan 88.	(lp) (SER 011) **OCEANIA**		–

– Oceania / The doctrine of eternal ice / Breathless / Mouth to mouth / Kambuja / Crack! / Seduction / Dies Irae. (cd-iss. Jun88 +=; DFX 01) – In fragrante delicto / Necropolis / In the dying moments.

Sep 87. (12") (NT12 3008) **OFF THE DEEP END. /**
Feb 88. (12") (NT12 3016) **BREATHLESS** (remix). /
(re-iss. May88; NET 002)
Feb 88. (lp/c)(cd) (NTL/+C 30017)(<NTCD 035>) **DIGITALES AMBIGUA, GOLD & POISON**
– Breathless / Mouth to mouth / Sheer naked aggression / Crack! / The doctrine eternal ice / Invocation (to secular heresies) / White island / Palms crossed in sorrow / Alocasia metallica / The garden of earthly delight.

—— disbanded later in the year

– compilations, etc. –

Aug 92. (cd-box) *Grey Area-Mute; (CDSPKBOX 1)* **S.P.K. CD-BOX SET**

GRAEME REVELL

—— also combined a solo career

Jul 87. (lp) (BRU 001) **THE INSECT MUSICIANS**
(cd-iss. Jul94 +=; BRUT 1CD) – NECROPOLIS AMPHIBIAN REPTILES
Jan 88. (lp) (BRU 002) **NECROPOLIS AMPHIBIAN REPTILES**
– Necropolis amphibians & reptiles / Countless saladine / Chimpnas-apes of the union Canada / Allegebrah / Ebony tower in the Orient water / The Balli / St. Adolf's comet / Natural form of the holy light / Rhama margarine / Lea tantaaria / Great God father nieces.

—— wrote many film scores from 1993's 'HARD TARGET' onwards

SPRINGFIELDS
(see under ⇒ VELVET CRUSH; in 90's section)

Tobin SPROUT (see under ⇒ GUIDED BY VOICES)

SQUIRREL BAIT

Formed: Louisville, Kentucky, USA ... 1985 by DAVID GRUBBS, PETER SEARCY, BRIAN McMAHAN, BRITT WALFORD and ETHAN BUCKLER (the latter two subsequently made way for BEN DAUGHTREY and CLARK JOHNSON respectively during debut session cuts). A seminal indie hardcore act with a neat line in adolescent humour, SQUIRREL BAIT set their first musical trap in early '86 with an eponymous HUSKER DU-esque album for Steven Joerg's 'Homestead' imprint. Their lifespan was brief however, the band effectively extinct as college captured them following the release of the excellent 'SKAG HEAVEN' (1987). While most of the posse were buried in their books, SEARCY formed The BIG WHEEL and GRUBBS (with JOHNSON) worked on a trio of thrash-metal/noise sets as BASTRO, the latter two surprisingly featuring drummer, JOHN McENTIRE, before he crawled off to form TORTOISE. The most famous by-product of SQUIRREL BAIT, however, was SLINT, an influential indie outfit formed from the ashes of the former band's final line-up (i.e. McMAHAN, WALFORD, DAVID PAJO and ETHAN BUCKLER). In 1991, GRUBBS initiated GASTR DEL SOL, a more intelligent, musically complex proposition which originally saw him working with BUNDY K BROWN and the ubiquitous McENTIRE (in a guest capacity) on the 1993 mini-set, 'THE SERPENTINE SIMILAR'. The latter sticksman also featured on the following single, '20 SONGS LESS', a collaboration with GRUBBS and JIM O'ROURKE (BUNDY had already joined TORTOISE). Having been part of the 'TeenBeat' operation, GASTR DEL SOL signed with 'Drag City' for 1994's acclaimed long-player, 'CROOKT, CRACKT, OR FLY', a subtle, spellbinding record that made genuine innovations in the use of dense acoustic guitar textures and traversed the boundaries of standard indie-rock structures. Never one to shirk a challenge, GRUBBS (and some local friends/musicians) took it upon himself to create a mini-orchestral suite scored to the usual freeform rules, the resulting 17-minute long 'HARP FACTORY ON LAKE STREET' (1995), taking the post-rock ethos into uncharted territory. The following year, GASTR DEL SOL returned to a more song-based approach on 'UPGRADE & AFTERLIFE', a slightly disappointing set which featured a cover of John Fahey's 'DRY BONES IN THE VALLEY'. The partnership of GRUBBS and O'ROURKE was tied up with the 'CAMOUFLEUR' (1998) album, an impressive swansong that found the pair in a more reflective mood, dabbling in a cinematic mix of folk and avant-jazz influences. Around the same time, GRUBBS was carving out his own "new age" solo career, releasing three albums, 'BANANA CABBAGE ...' (1997), 'THE THICKET' (1998) and with MATS GUSTAFSSON, 'APERTURA' (1999), before the turn of the century. GRUBBS returned in 2000 with an entourage of post-rock candidates in the form of JOHN McENTIRE, DANIEL CARTER and MATS GUSTAFSSON, who all contributed to the album 'THE SPECTRUM BETWEEN' (2000). Where JIM O'ROURKE had strayed from the GASTR DEL SOL experimentations in favour of traditional folk-songwriting, GRUBBS stayed grounded in the company of his fellow comrades, delivering a very fine avant-experimental album indeed. One which was to be matched two-times over; first with 'THIRTY MINUTE RAVEN' (2001, featuring French guitarist NOEL AKCHOTE, organist, CHARLIE O and QUENTIN ROLLET) and then secondly, the advent of GRUBB's debut acoustic, melancholy set 'RICKETS & SCURVY' (2002), lyrics co-written by cult author Rick Moody.

Album rating: SQUIRREL BAIT (*6) / SKAG HEAVEN (*7) / Bastro: RODE HARD AND PUT UP WET (*4) / DIABLO GUAPO (*4) / SING THE TROUBLED BEAST (*5) / Gastr Del Sol: THE SERPENTINE SIMILAR mini (*6) / CROOKT, CRACKT, OR FLY (*7) / UPGRADE & AFTERLIFE (*7) / CAMOUFLEUR (*7) / David Grubbs: BANANA CABBAGE POTATO LETTUCE ONION ORANGE (*3) / THE THICKET (*5) / THE COXCOMB (*5) / APERTURA with Mats Gustafson (*5) / THE SPECTRUM BETWEEN (*6) / RICKETS AND SCURVY (*6)

PETER SEARCY – vocals / **BRIAN McMAHAN** – guitar, vocals / **DAVID GRUBBS** – guitar / **CLARK JOHNSON** – bass; repl. ETHAN BUCKLER / **BEN DAUGHTREY** – drums; repl. BRITT WALFORD (played on two debut tracks)

Jan 86. (lp) <(HMS 028-1)> **SQUIRREL BAIT**
– Hammering so hard / Thursday / Sun god / When I fall / The final chapter / Mixed blessing / Disguise. <cd/lp-iss.Feb97 on 'Drag City'; DEX 10/DC 102)>
Nov 86. (7") <(HMS 061)> **KID DYNAMITE. / SLAKE TRAIN COMING**
Mar 87. (lp/cd) <(HMS 072-1/-2)> **SKAG HEAVEN**
– Kid Dynamite / Vigil's return / Black light poster child / Choose your poison / Short straw wins / Too close to the fire / Slake train coming / Rose Island road / Tape to California. <cd/lp-iss.Feb97 on 'Drag City'; DEX 11/DC 103)>

—— split in 1988, singer SEARCY forming BIG WHEEL with guitarist and co-songwriter, GLENN TAYLOR, along with the rhythm section of MIKE BRADEN and SCOTT LANKFORD. The quartet released hard-rock/metal album, 'EAST END' for 'Giant' records in 1989, while two further albums, 'HOLIDAY MANOR' (1992) and 'SLOWTOWN' (1993) surfaced for 'Mammoth'.

BASTRO

—— meanwhile, GRUBBS + JOHNSON formed this outfit

Sep 88. (m-lp/m-c) <(HMS 111/+C)> **RODE HARD AND PUT UP WET**
– (I've) Been brown / Three eggs in a sock / Counterrey: bhutan / Gold fillings / Loam / Extract.

—— added **JOHN McENTIRE** – drums

Apr 89. (7") <(HMS 131-7)> **SHOOT ME A DEAR. / GOITER BLAZES**
Jul 89. (lp/c/cd) <(HMS 132-1/-4/-2)> **DIABLO GUAPO**
– Tallow waters / Filthy five filthy ten / Guapo / Flesh-coloured house / Short-haired robot / Can of whoopass / Decent skin / Engaging the reverend / Wurlitzer / Pretty smart on my part / Hoosier logic / Shoot me a deer.
1990. (cd/c/lp) <HMS 164-2/-4/-1> **SING THE TROUBLED BEAST**
– Demons begone / Krakow, Illinois / I come from a long line of ship-builders / Tobacco in the sink / Recidivist / Floating home / Jefferson-in-drag / The sifter / Noise – Star / Recidivist.
1990. (7") **NOTHING SPECIAL. / (other by MY DAD IS DEAD)**
Nov 91. (7"ep) (GR 0171) **A L'OMBRE DE NOUS (IN OUR SHADOW) / PRODUKT. / (others by CODEINE)**

—— disbanded after above, McENTIRE later formed TORTOISE

GASTR DEL SOL

DAVID GRUBBS – vocals, guitar, piano / **BUNDY K. BROWN** – bass (of TORTOISE) / with **JOHN McENTIRE** – percussion (of TORTOISE)

Jun 93. (m-cd/m-lp) <TB 95> **THE SERPENTINE SIMILAR**
– Watery Kentucky / Easy company / Jar of fat / Ursus arctos wonderfilis / Eye street / For Soren Mueller / The serpentine orbit / Even the odd orbit. <re-iss. 1997 on 'Drag City'; DC 106> (UK-iss.Jun97 on 'Dexter's Cigar' cd/lp; DEX 13 CD/LP)

—— GRUBBS now with **JIM O'ROURKE** – guitar / guests were McENTIRE + STEVE BUTTERS – percussion

Jan 94. (7") <TB 125> **20 SONGS LESS. /**
Nov 94. (cd/c) <DC 43 CD/C> **CROOKT, CRACKT, OR FLY**
– Wedding in the park / Work from smoke / Parenthetically / Every five miles / Thos. Dudley ah old must dye / Is that a rifle when it rains? / C in cake / Wrong soundings. (UK-iss.Dec96; same as US)
Jan 95. (12"ep/cd-ep) <DC 54/+CD> **MIRROR REPAIR**
– Photographed yawning / Eight corners / Dictionary of handwriting / Why sleep / Mirror repair.
below with help from **McENTIRE, JEB BISHOP + BOB WESTON**
Aug 95. (cd-s) <19> **HARP FACTORY ON LAKE STREET**

—— <above issued on 'Table Of Elements'>

—— now the pair had guests **TONY CONRAD + KEVIN DRUMM**

Dec 96. (d-lp/cd) <(DC 90/+CD)> **UPGRADE AND AFTERLIFE**
– Our exquisite replica of "eternity" / Rebecca Sylvester / Sea incertain / Hello spiral / Relay / Crappie tactics / Dry bones in the valley.

—— the duo with past musicians

Feb 98. (cd/lp) (WIG CD/LP 44) <DG 133> **CAMOUFLEUR**
– Seasons reverse / Blues subtitled no sense of wonder / Black horse / Each dream is an example / Mouth canyon / Puff dew / Bauchredner.

DAVID GRUBBS

—— with various people incl. **JOHN McENTIRE, TONY CONRAD, BUNDY K BROWN, MARY ANN STEWART, JOSHUA ABRAMS + JED BISHOP**

Mar 97. (cd) <(ZINC 30)> **BANANA CABBAGE POTATO LETTUCE ONION ORANGE**
Sep 98. (lp/cd) <(DC 160/+CD)> **THE THICKET**
– The thicket / Two shades of blue / Fool summons train / Orange disaster / Amleth's gambit / 40 words on worship / Swami vivekananda way / Buried in the wall / On worship.

SQUIRREL BAIT (cont)

	Rectangle	not iss.
Feb 99. (12"ep) *(RECAA 1)* **THE COXCOMB** (above issued on 'Rectangle' below on 'Blue Chopsticks')		
Jul 99. (cd; by DAVID GRUBBS & MATS GUSTAFSSON) *(BC 2CD)* **APERTURA** – Apertura (part 1) / Apertura (part 2).		
Jul 00. (lp/cd) <*(DC 186/+CD)*> **THE SPECTRUM BETWEEN** – Seagull and eagull / Whirlweek / Stanwell perpetual / Gloriette / A siver in the timber / Show me who to love / Pink rambler / Preface / Two shades of green.		

	Rectangle	not iss.
Jun 01. (cd) *(RECAC 2)* **THIRTY MINUTE RAVEN**		
Jul 01. (cd) *(RECAAA 1)* **AUX NOCTAMBULES** – Aux noctambules.		

	Blue Chopsticks	Blue Chopsticks
Feb 02. (cd) <*(BC 9CD)*> **ACT ONE, SCENE FIVE** – (parts 1-4).		

	Fat Cat	Fat Cat
May 02. (cd/lp) <*(FAT CD/LP 21)*> **RICKETS AND SCURVY** – Transom / Don't think / A dream to help me sleep / The nearer by and by / I did no such roaming / Pinned to the spot / Aloft / Precipice / Crevasse / Kentucky karaoke.		

– compilations, etc. –

Dec 00. (cd) *Blue Chopsticks;* <*(BC 5CD)*> **THE COXCOMB / AVACADO ORANGE**

Jan 02. (pic-lp) *Rectangle;* *(RECAA 1)* **THE COXCOMB / AUX NOCTAMBULES**

STARS OF HEAVEN

Formed: Dublin, Ireland ... 1985 by STEPHEN RYAN, STAN ERRAUGHT, PETER O'SULLIVAN and BERNARD WALSH. Although only around for a couple of years, The STARS OF HEAVEN made their mark via two albums, 'SACRED HEART HOTEL' (1986) and 'SPEAK SLOWLY' (1988). Bolstered by a debut single, 'CLOTHES OF WIRE' (for 'Hotwire' in '85), their signing came down to that man John Peel, who playlisted the countrified/C-86 track on his night time Radio One show. Influenced by GRAM PARSONS/BYRDS, their aforementioned debut LP showcased a band in transition, although they never really got a chance to progress further. In 1988, after the heavily-delayed 'SPEAK SLOWLY' album finally reached the shops, the band disintegrated – there was just too much competition for every "indie" band to succeed (and 'Rough Trade' had signed most of them!). STEPHEN RYAN would subsequently find a host of (mainly) other Irish musicians to form The REVENANTS, although only one set, 'HORSE OF A DIFFERENT COLOUR' (1993), was released.

Album rating: SACRED HEART HOTEL mini (*6) / SPEAK SLOWLY (*5) / Revenants: HORSE OF A DIFFERENT COLOUR (*5)

STEPHEN RYAN – vocals, guitar / **STAN ERRAUGHT** – guitar (ex-PERIDOTS) / **PETER O'SULLIVAN** – bass, vocals / **BERNARD WALSH** – drums

	Hotwire	not iss.
Dec 85. (7") *(HWS 853)* **CLOTHES OF PRIDE. / ALL ABOUT YOU**		

	Rough Trade	not iss.
Sep 86. (m-lp) *(RTM 73)* **SACRED HEART HOTEL** – Sacred heart hotel / Talk about it now / Moonstruck / So you know / You could only say what anyone could say / Folksong / Man without a shadow. *(re-iss. May87 on lp as 'RAIN ON THE SEA' +=; ROUGH 113)* – Never saw you / Before Holyhead / Widow's walk / Someone's getting tired of you.		
Mar 87. (7") *(RT 203)* **NEVER SAW YOU. / WIDOW'S WALK** (12"+=) **THE HOLYHEAD EP** *(RTT 203)* – Before Holyhead / Someone's getting tired of you.		
Jun 88. (lp/c/cd) *(ROUGH 131/+C/CD)* **SPEAK SLOWLY** – Unfinished dreaming / Little England / What else could you do / Paradise of lies / 2 o'clock waltz / 28 lights of Tetouan / Leave as you came / Every other day / Three kings day / Ghost cars. *(cd+=)* – Clothes of pride.		

— disbanded later in 1988

REVENANTS

— were formed by **STEPHEN RYAN** – vocals, guitar / **DOUG STEEN** – guitar / **DON RYAN** – keyboards / **JEREMY IRVIN** – bass / **CHRIS HEANEY** – drums / plus **EILEEN GOGAN** – vocals (ex-WOULD BE'S) / **RAY HARMON** – bass (ex-SOMETHING HAPPENS) / **EAMONN RYAN** – drums (ex-SOMETHING HAPPENS)

	Hunter-London	not iss.
Sep 93. (cd/c) *(LON CD/MC 931)* **HORSE OF A DIFFERENT COLOUR** – Let's go getting down / Marry money / Ted's time / You for whom silence / Sympathy / William Byrd / The drinking side of me / Capercailye / Xmas card / Speak slowly / Doctor said / Forbidden mourning. *(cd re-iss. Aug99 on 'Independent'; INDCD 008)*		

— the band split after above; The REVENANTS of the late 90's were in fact from Arizona (ex-SUICIDE KINGS)

STATE OF PLAY
(see under ⇒ CURVE; in 90's section)

STAYRCASE (see under ⇒ THANES)

ST. CHRISTOPHER

Formed: York, England ... 1984 by GLEN MELIA, a singer/songwriter with a fondness for everything twee. From 1984 to the early 90's, ST. CHRISTOPHER (MELIA and chums including TERRY BANKS) delivered a plethora of 7" singles and two mini-type-sets, 'BACHARACH' (1990) and 'MAN, I COULD SCREAM' (1992). All fitted in neatly to the post-C-86 scene of twee-pop aethetics and believe it or not, it got more fashionable with each release; especially in the US. Records for 'Vinyl Japan' (mainly albums this time around), kept interest in ST. CHRISTOPHER ticking over. His/their last album to-date, 'GOLDEN BLUE' (2000), was however, an album too far.

Album rating: BACHARACH mini (*6) / MAN, I COULD SCREAM (*5) / LOVE YOU TO PIECES (*5) / DIG DEEP BROTHER compilation (*7) / LIONESS (*5) / GOLDEN BLUE (*3)

GLEN MELIA – vocals, guitar / at various times:- **TERRY BANKS** – guitar (future TREE FORT ANGST leader)

	Groove & Move	not iss.
Mar 84. (7") *(GM 001)* **CRYSTAL CLEAR. / MY FOND FAREWELL**		
Nov 86. (7") *(GM 003)* **GO AHEAD, CRY. / CHARMELLE**		

	Veston	not iss.
1987. (7"flexi) *(VOD 001)* **FOREVERMORE STARTS HERE. / REMEMBER ME TO HER / SINKING SHIPS**		

	Clarity	not iss.
1988. (7"flexi) *(CLARITY 1)* **JOSEPHINE WHY. / I WISH I HADN'T HURT HER / TELL THE WORLD**		

	Sarah	Bus Stop
Feb 89. (7"m) *(SARAH 015)* **YOU DESERVE MORE THAN A MAYBE. / THE KIND OF A GIRL / THE SUMMER YOU LOVE**		
Jul 89. (7"m) *(SARAH 020)* **ALL OF A TREMBLE. / MY FORTUNE / THE HUMMINGBIRD**		
Feb 90. (7"m) <*BUS 3*> **ALL OF A TREMBLE. / OUR SECRET / EVEN THE SKY SEEMS BLUE**		
Apr 90. (10"m-lp) *(SARAH 403)* **BACHARACH** – A prayer for the sun / The thrill of the new / And I wonder / Almost December / She can wait forever / Who's next on Cupid's hit-list / The love of a sister / Gabriel.		
Jun 90. (7") *(SARAH 034)* **ANTOINETTE. / SALVATION**		
May 91. (7") *(SARAH 046)* **SAY YES TO EVERYTHING. / IT'S SNOWING ON THE MOON**		

	Vinyl Japan	not iss.
Feb 92. (lp/cd) *(ASK/+CD 06)* **MAN, I COULD SCREAM** – This fear of losing / Cathedrak high / The last laugh / Alpine village / Dark / Don't make a stranger of yourself / Here comes the past / A man bewitched / Tranquility / Natasha, I know / If you have to dream / Stab.		
Jun 93. (cd) *(ASKCD 026)* **DIG DEEP BROTHER 1984-1990** (compilation) – Forevermore starts here / To the mountain / Charmelle / Who's next on Cupid's hit-list / Climb on forever / If I could capture / My fond farewell / Even the sky seems blue / Rivers run dry / Awe / I wish I hadn't seen her / Remember me to her / Tell the world / Our secret / Crystal clear / Rollercoaster / Where in the world / Josephine why / All of a tremble / On the death of my son / Sinking ships / For one so weak / My fortune / How can you tell / Wanda.		
Nov 93. (7"ep) *(DRYL 19)* **FRENCH RADIO SESSIONS EP** (above issued on 'Slumberland')		
Feb 94. (cd) *(ASKCD 27)* **LOVE YOU TO PIECES** – Away / Ladder / Crush / Baptise me baby / Wildest dreams / Everything now / Magic spell / Liberty / For the world to see / Dive / Stars belong to me / Pieces.		
1994. (7") *(ER 122)* **YOUNG NUN. / WITH HER IN MIND**	–	Spain
1995. (7") *(ER 142)* **SHE LOOKS LIKE YOU. / ECSTASY, PASSION AND PAIN** (above 2 issued on 'Elefant')		
Oct 96. (cd) *(ASKCD 53)* **LIONESS** – Loneliness is a friend of mine / Tangled up in blue / Jewels in your hair / Utopian / Hell / She looks like you / With her in mind / Where you are everything is / As good as married / Flirtation / Loneliness is a friend of mine (reprise).		

	Parasol	Parasol
Dec 00. (cd) (<*PARCD 043*>) **GOLDEN BLUE** – North wind / Riverbank / Majestic / The devil from nowhere / Old and in the way / Chemical king / The first or the last / Black girl / Low / Weird things / Tell me there's a God.		

STEPHEN (see under ⇒ CLEAN)

Martin STEPHENSON

Born: 1965, Durham, England. STEPHENSON began his musical career in 1983 with busking outfit, The DAINTEES. Signed to the local 'Kitchenware' label by boss Keith Armstrong, the band – who at this point were a trio completed by JOHN STEEL and ANTHONY DUNN – made their vinyl debut at Christmas '83 with the sublime (and hopefully titled!) 'ROLL ON SUMMERTIME'. This was followed with the 'TROUBLE TOWN' single and the 'INFERNO' EP before the band recruited a drummer, PAUL SMITH, to anchor the sound and embarked upon recording a debut album, 'BOAT TO BOLIVIA' (1986). Rootsy pop wearing its heart on its sleeve and infused with folk, country and blues, the record saw STEPHENSON draw comparisons with such vintage acoustic balladeers as LEONARD COHEN and AL STEWART. Glowing reviews and a swelling grassroots following – due in no small part to the man's sterling live performances – saw the album graze the lower end of the UK chart. Embellished with violin, flute, dobro etc. courtesy of a sizeable cast of musicians, 1988's 'GLADSOME, HUMOUR & BLUE' was again acclaimed and gave STEPHENSON his first Top 40 hit. As might be expected for a folk singer from the North East, his work had always been at least partly concerned with the plight of the downtrodden and dispossessed and 'SALUTATION ROAD' (1990) contained some of his most openly political statements to date including 'LEFT US TO BURN' (an anti-Thatcher broadside) and 'MIGRANTS'. While not exactly crossing over to a mainstream audience, the album (part of a licensing deal with 'London') proved his most successful to date. The 90's have seen his profile dip somewhat, STEPHENSON roping in punk stalwart, PAULINE MURRAY and FATIMA MANSIONS man, CATHAL COUGHLAN, for 'THE BOY'S HEART' (1992). A best of compilation and previously recorded set, 'HIGH BELLS RING THIN' (1993) wrapped things up with 'Kitchenware' and the man moved to re-issue specialist, 'Demon', for 1995's 'YOGI IN MY HOUSE'. After the slightly introspective 'BEYOND THE LEAP, BEYOND THE LAW' (1997), the acoustic folk-rocker delivered four varying CD-sets, the eponymous 'MARTIN STEPHENSON' (1999), 'LILAC TREE' (2000), 'LIVE IN THE 21st CENTURY' – as MARTIN STEPHENSON & THE DAINTEES (2001) and 'DOWN TO THE WOOD' – with JIM HORNSBY (2002). • **Covered:** HIGH COIN (Van Dyke Parks) / LET'S CALL THE WHOLE THING OFF (Ira & George Gershwin) / etc.

Album rating: BOAT TO BOLIVIA (*8) / GLADSOME, HUMOUR AND BLUE (*7) / SALUTATION ROAD (*5) / THIS BOY'S HEART (*5) / THERE COMES A TIME – THE BEST OF MARTIN STEPHENSON & THE DAINTEES compilation (*6) / HIGH BELLS RING THIN (*5) / SWEET MISDEMEANOUR (*6) / YOGI IN MY HOUSE (*6) / BEYOND THE LEAP, BEYOND THE LAW (*7) / MARTIN STEPHENSON (*5) / LILAC TREE (*6) / LIVE IN THE 21st CENTURY (*5) / COLLECTIVE FORCE (*6) / DOWN TO THE WOOD (OR MARTIN & JIM GO BINAURAL) (*5)

DAINTEES

MARTIN STEPHENSON – vocals, acoustic guitar / **JOHN STEEL** – piano, organ / **ANTHONY DUNN** – bass

Kitchenware not iss.

Dec 83. (7") *(SK 3)* **ROLL ON SUMMERTIME. / INVOLVED WITH LOVE**
Sep 84. (7") *(SK 13)* **TROUBLE TOWN. / BETTER PLAN**
(12"+=) *(SKX 13)* – Jealous mind.
(above re-iss. Jan87 with free ltd.c-s 'DAINTEES LIVE' hit No.58) – Running waters / Crocodile cryer / Boat to Bolivia / Tremelo man.
May 86. (7"ep) *(SKEP 1)* **INFERNO EP**
– Running water / Look down, look down (live) / Synergy.

MARTIN STEPHENSON & THE DAINTEES

—— added guest **PAUL SMITH** – drums, percussion

Kitchenware Capitol

May 86. (lp/c) *(KWLP/KWC 5)* **BOAT TO BOLIVIA** 85
– Crocodile cryer / Coleen / Little red bottle / Tribute to the late Reverand Gary Davis / Running water / Candle in the middle / Piece of the cake / Look down, look down / Slow lovin' / Caroline / Rain. *(re-iss. Mar87; same c+=)* – Boat to Bolivia. *(cd+=; 828045-2)* – Slaughterman / Wholly humble heart.
Jun 86. (7") *(SK 25)* **CROCODILE CRYER. / LOUIS (acoustic version)**
(12") *(SKX 25)* – ('A'full version) / ('B'live version).
Aug 86. (7") *(SK 26)* **SLOW LOVIN'. / TRIBUTE TO THE LATE REVEREND GARY DAVIS**
(12"+=) *(SKX 26)* – Smile on the summertime / Look down, look down (live).
Oct 86. (7") *(SK 27)* **BOAT TO BOLIVIA. / SLAUGHTERMAN** 70
(12"+=) *(SKX 27)* – Wholly humble heart.
(d12"+=) *(SKXD 27)* – Crocodile cryer (full version) / Louis (live).

—— **MICK WATSON** – keyboards, percussion, sax, string arr. repl. STEEL / added **GYPSY DAVE SMITH** – dobro guitar / **GARY DUNN** – lead + rhythm guitars Guests inc. **VIRGINIA ASTLEY** – flute / **ANNE STEPHENSON** – violin / **CAROLINE LAVELLE** – cello / **CAROLINE BARNES** – violin / **FAY EVANS** – viola / **D.BREWIS** – guitar, keyboards / **SHEILA & SHERYL PARKER** – backing vocals

Apr 88. (lp/c)(cd) *(KWLP/KWC 8)(828091-2) <91751>* **GLADSOME, HUMOUR AND BLUE** 39
– There comes a time / Slaughterman / The wait / I can see / The old church is still standing / Even the night / Wholly humble heart / Me and Matthew / Nancy / Goodbye John / I pray.
Jun 88. (7") *(SK 36)* **WHOLLY HUMBLE HEART. / GET GET GONE**
(12"+=) *(SKX 36)* – Come back to me.
(12"+=/cd-s+=) *(SK XR/CD 36)* – I can see (live) / Slow lovin' (live).
Oct 88. (7") *(SK 34)* **THERE COMES A TIME. / RUNNING WATER**
(12"+=) *(SKX 34)* – Little red bottle (live) / Coleen (live).
(12"+=) *(SKXR 34)* – Crocodile cryer (live) / Coleen (live).

—— **MARTIN** retains **ANTHONY, GARY + MICK** (now bass), plus guests **ANDREA MACKIE** – vocals / **PETE ANDERSON** – producer, guitar, sitar / **JEFF DONOVAN** - **SKIP EDWARDS** – keyboards, organ / **LARRY KNIGHT** – guitar / **LENNY CASTRO** – perc. / **DUSTY WAKEMAN** – bass / **DON REED** – viola / **LEE THORNBERG** – trumpet / **LEN PRICE** – sax / **GREG SMITH** – baritone sax / **BEVERLEY DAHLEE SMITH** – flute / **STEVE GROVE** – tenor sax / **FREEBO** – tuba / **DONNIE GERRARD, SHAUN MURPHY, LAURA CREAMER** – backing vocals

Apr 90. (7"/c-s) *(SK/+TC 44)* **LEFT US TO BURN. / BIG NORTH LIGHTS**
(12"+=/cd-s+=) *(SK X/CD 44)* – Eyot / Kathy (live).
May 90. (cd/c/lp) *(828198-2/-4/-1) <94638>* **SALUTATION ROAD** 35
– Left us to burn / Endurance / In the heat of the night / Big north lights / Long hard road / Spoke in the weel / Heart of the city / Too much in love / We are storm / Migrants / Morning time / Salutation road.
Jun 90. (7"/c-s) *(SK 46/+TC)* **ENDURANCE. / MEN CAN BE FLUNG**
(12"+=/cd-s+=) *(12SK/SKCD 46)* – Release the first.

—— **PAUL SMITH** – drums returned adding also to The **DUNN's; BRENDAN HEALEY** – piano / **FRANKIE GIBBON** – organ, b.vocals / **PAULINE MURRAY, FRED PURSER** (both ex-PENETRATION) and **CATHAL COUGHAN** (of FATIMA MANSIONS) – backing vocals

Jun 92. (7"/c-s) *(SK/+TC 57)* **BIG SKY NEW LIGHT. / SONG ABOUT THE MEMBER / WAKE ME IN THE MORNING** 71
(cd-s) *(SKCD1 57)* – ('A'side) / You really had a heart / Peace of mind / Let's call the whole thing off.
(cd-s) *(SKCD2 57)* – ('A'side) / Far away meadows / Should my friends be gone / Every night.
Jul 92. (cd/c/lp) *(828324-2/-4/-1)* **THE BOY'S HEART** 68
– Big sky new light / The boy's heart / We can roll / Ballad of the English rose / Neon skies / Hollywood fields / Sentimental journey / Sunday halo / 8.30 Mowbray morning / (Least we're) Map in the world / Him, her and the Moon / Cab attack.
Mar 93. (cd/c) *(828398-2/-4)* **THERE COMES A TIME – THE BEST OF MARTIN STEPHENSON & THE DAINTEES** (compilation)
– Little red bottle / Crocodile cryer / Wholly humble heart / Spoke in my wheel / Big sky new light / Me & matthew / Running waters / There comes a time / Left us to burn / Nancy / You really had a heart / Rain / We are storm / Hollywood fields / Salutation road / Look down, look down / Candle in the middle / Don't be afraid of the night.
Apr 93. (cd/c) *(KWCD/KWC 23)* **HIGH BELLS RING THIN** (rec.1990)
– You really had a heart / Looking for some peace of mind / Song about the member / Should my friends be gone / Don't be afraid of the night / Far away meadows / Synergy / Wake me in the morning / I like in the east / Him, her and the Moon / Every night / Music and life / Let's call the whole thing off.

MARTIN STEPHENSON

Demon Demon

Feb 95. (cd) *(<FIENDCD 762>)* **YOGI IN MY HOUSE** Oct95
– Solomon / In fire / Taker on the globe / Think only of the child / New wave / Spirit child / Bridge of nae hope / Fair company / Gone the gipsy Davey / Always us / Dance the last goodbye.
below featured **JOE GUILLEN** – guitar
Oct 95. (cd) *(<FIENDCD 770>)* **SWEET MISDEMEANOUR**
– Maverick waltz / Can't find the door-knob / Sweet misdemeanour / Candyman / I could never be happy / Rag time groove / Dream of you / South wind / Tremolo man / Talking to the child / Keep this time / Ball of fire / Hold me, love me / Smokey mokes.
Nov 97. (cd) *(<FIENDCD 938>)* **BEYOND THE LEAP, BEYOND THE LAW**
– Losing all part of the team / Testing time / Great star of fraternity / Wholly humble heart (Irish version) / Carry my friend / The crying / Song of love and desertion / Great spirit / Out of communion / The waves / Hollow days / Indian summer.

*Floating Floating
World World*

Jun 99. (cd) *(FW 002)* **MARTIN STEPHENSON**
– Look down, look down / Slaughterman / Better plan / All ways us / Songs of love and desperation / Sweet misdemeanor / Little red bottle / Coleen / Bridge of nae hope / Running water / Taker on the globe / New wave / Wait.
May 00. (cd) *<(FW 003)>* **LILAC TREE**
– Rainbow / Orange / Posey Rorer (for Dolph) / Lilac / 2 sorrows / Folk singer / Bluebottle theory (light step travel) / Kathy / All men condemned (for Ray Stubbs) / Nu found light / O so far removed / Rowen berries (for Karen). *(re-iss. Oct01 on 'Blueprint'; BARBCD 001)*

Fresh Ear not iss.

Aug 01. (cd; by MARTIN STEPHENSON & THE DAINTEES) *(FRESHCD 101)* **LIVE IN THE 21st CENTURY (live)**
– Wholly humble heart / Left us to burn / Orange (is the colour of joy) / All ways us / Little red bottle / Soloman / Bye bye bluebell / You are the one / We are storm / Goodbye John / Me and Matthew / Involved with love / Running water / I pray.

Force Force

Aug 02. (cd) *(<FORCD 001>)* **COLLECTIVE FORCE** Oct01
– Orange is the colour of joy / The sun's coming out / All ways us / Highland bossanova / Home / Walking in the dark / Summer's gone / Orange is the colour of joy (Bachini remix) / Blind man's blues / Time for Jesus / Robert Smith Wright in person / Toodle oodle oohi / Every step of the way / Collective force / Long forgotten / Sounds of the garden / Baba num sana / Spirit song / Rowan berries / Henry Fosebrook and the Woodland Orchestra.

*Barbaraville United
 States*

Nov 02. (cd; by MARTIN STEPHENSON & JIM HORNSBY) *(BVCD 002) <161>* **DOWN TO THE WOOD (OR MARTIN AND JIM GO BINAURAL)** Feb03
– The south wind / Testing time / Great spirit / Flop eared mule / Black mountain rag / Cromarty rag / All men condemned / Jim's mellow blue / Home / And we danced / Home (version 2) / Maverick waltz / Cannonball rag / Hungry hash house.

Duglas T. STEWART (see under ⇒ BMX BANDITS)

STOCKHOLM MONSTERS

Formed: New York, USA … early 80's by brothers TONY and KARL FRANCE, the other half of the indie/dance act comprising JOHN RHODES and SHAN HIRA. Discovered by 'Factory' boss, Anthony Wilson, the band packed their suitcases for Manchester, England and debuted in 1981 with the 12" 'FAIRY TALES'. Akin to a more tribal, airy, pastel-hued NEW ORDER, The STOCKHOLM MONSTERS were readily identifiable as a "Factory" band, the proof of the pudding being further singles, 'HAPPY EVER AFTER' and 'MISS MOONLIGHT'. In 1984, the quartet finally got round to issuing a full-set, 'ALMA MATER', although its lack of sparkle or indeed anything approaching a hookline alienated prospective fans. Although they carried on for another couple of years, they gave up the ghost after a final PETER HOOK-produced single, 'PARTYLINE' b/w 'MILITIA', failed to raise their profile.

Album rating: ALMA MATER (*4) / THE LAST ONE BACK (ARCHIVE 1980-1987) (*4) / ALL AT ONCE compilation (*6)

TONY FRANCE – vocals / **KARL FRANCE** – bass / **JOHN RHODES** – keyboards / **SHAN HIRA** – drums

STOCKHOLM MONSTERS (cont)   THE GREAT INDIE DISCOGRAPHY   The 1980s

		Factory	not iss.
Sep 81.	(12") *(FACT 41)* **FAIRY TALES. / DEATH IS SLOWLY COMING**		-
	(re-iss. 7".Jan82; FAC 41)		
Aug 82.	(7") *(FAC 58)* **HAPPY EVER AFTER. / SOFT BABIES**		-
Mar 83.	(12"m) Factory Benelux; *(FBN 19)* **MISS MOONLIGHT. / THE LONGING / LAFAYETTE**	-	- Belgian
Mar 84.	(lp) *(FACT 80)* **ALMA MATER**	-	-
	– Terror / Where I belong / Decalogue / Winter / Five o'clock / Life's two faces / Your uniform / E.W. / To look at her / Something's got to give. *(cd-iss. Apr01 on 'Les Tempes Modernes'+=; LTM 2330)* – All at once / National pastime / Militia / How corrupt is Rough Trade? / Kan kill! / Stupid (1987 demo) / Your uniform / Life's two faces.		
Jun 84.	(7") *(FAC 107)* **ALL AT ONCE. / NATIONAL PASTIME**		-
Aug 85.	(12") Factory Benelux; *(FBN 46)* **HOW CORRUPT IS ROUGH TRADE? / KAN KILL!**	-	- Belgian
Mar 87.	(12"ep) Materiali Sonori; *(MASO 70002)* **GREETINGS TWO** – Party line / Militia / Dumbstruck.	-	- Italy
Apr 87.	(12"m) *(FAC 146)* **PARTYLINE. / MILITIA / PARTYLIVE**		-

— disbanded after above

– compilations, etc. –

on 'Les Tempes Modernes' unless mentioned otherwise

Apr 01.	(cd) *(LTM 2335)* **THE LAST ONE BACK (ARCHIVE 1980-1987)** (demos)	-	- Belgian
	– No more / Dear / Before your eyes / Stupid / House is not a home / When I smile (live) / Where I belong (live) / Hand over fist (live) / Partyline (live) / How corrupt is Rough Trade? / Kan kill! / Systems failing (live) / M/C (live) / Endless you (live) / Future / Copulation / Fairy tales / Catch me in confusion / We are nation / Love is a dose.		
Apr 01.	(cd) *(LTM 2337)* **ALL AT ONCE (SINGLES 1981-1987)**	-	- Belgian
	– Fairy tales / Death is slowly coming / Happy ever after / Soft babies / Miss Moonlight (1984 remix) / The longing / Lafayette / All at once / National pastime / How corrupt is Rough Trade? / Kan kill! / Partyline / Militia / Dumbstruck / Partylive / Miss Moonlight / Shake it to the bank.		

STONE ROSES

Formed: Sale & Chorley, Gtr. Manchester, England ... 1984 by IAN BROWN, JOHN SQUIRE, RENI, ANDY COUZENS and PETER GARNER who took their name from a group called ENGLISH ROSE and The ROLLING STONES. After a MARTIN HANNETT produced 45, they signed a one-off deal with 'Black' records and in 1988, were snapped up by ANDREW LAUDER's 'Jive' subsidiary, 'Silvertone'. They soon became darlings of the music press after the indie success of the single, 'ELEPHANT STONE' (1988), a gloriously uplifting piece of pristine pop. Propelled by RENI's consummate drumming and featuring SQUIRE's dizzy, spiralling guitar, the track was a blueprint for the group's eponymous debut album, released the following year. Surely a contender for album of the decade, the record was flawless, from the ominous opening bass rumble of 'I WANNA BE ADORED' to the orgasmic finale of 'I AM THE RESURRECTION'. This life-affirming hybrid of BYRDS-style psychedelia and shuffling rhythmic flurries remains the definitive indie album, its all-pervading influence more pronounced with each successive crop of guitar bands. Incredibly, the band topped the magic of their debut with the 'FOOL'S GOLD' single, which exploded into the Top 10 later that year. A seminal guitar-funk workout, it was the crowning glory of the 'Baggy' movement with which The STONE ROSES had become so closely affiliated, and marked a creative highpoint in their career. After a few one-off shows (that have since achieved almost mythical status) and a solitary single, 'ONE LOVE', the following year, the band went to ground. In the five years that followed, the band fought a protracted court battle with 'Silvertone', eventually signing with 'Geffen' for a reported record sum of $4,000,000. After much speculation and intrigue into when or if a follow-up would finally appear, the appropriately titled 'SECOND COMING' was eventually released in 1994. A month previously, they had enjoyed a return to the singles chart with the ZEPPELIN-esque 'LOVE SPREADS'. On the album, the effervescent pop of old took second place to riff-heavy guitar workouts, alienating many of their original fans. Nevertheless, the blistering funk-rock of 'BEGGING YOU' partly made up for any excess noodling by SQUIRE. As the STONES ROSES faithful dusted down their flares and beany hats in readiness for the band's headlining spot at the 1995 Glastonbury festival, they were again bitterly disappointed. At the last minute the band pulled out, apparently due to SQUIRE breaking his collarbone, young pretenders OASIS stealing the show in their absence. They had failed to seize the moment and from here on in, it was all downhill. Despite an ecstatically received Winter tour, SQUIRE shocked the music world by departing the following Spring (RENI had already quit a year earlier). BROWN and MANI bravely soldiered on for a headlining appearance at the 1996 Reading Festival but were given a critical mauling (particularly by the NME), finally splitting later that year. It was a sorry, messy end for a band that had seemed, at one point, to be on the brink of world domination and it remains a bitter irony that their duller Manchester progeny, OASIS, seem to have inherited the success that tragically eluded the 'ROSES. While SQUIRE has gone on to relative success with The SEAHORSES, their sound pales next to the magic of The STONE ROSES, a band that remain as fondly remembered as any in the history of rock. • **Songwriters:** Mainly SQUIRE but with other members also collaborating. The SEAHORSES was mainly SQUIRE, except a few by HELME. one with FLETCHER. NOEL GALLAGHER (Oasis) co-wrote 'LOVE ME AND LEAVE ME'. • **Trivia:** Their debut album artwork was a pastiche of a Jackson Pollock splatter job painted by the multi-talented SQUIRE.

Album rating: THE STONE ROSES (*10) / TURNS INTO STONE collection (*6) / SECOND COMING (*7) / THE COMPLETE STONE ROSES compilation (*8) / GARAGE FLOWER exploitation (*5) / THE VERY BEST OF THE STONE ROSES compilation (*9)

IAN BROWN (b.20 Feb'63, Ancoats, Manchester) – vocals / **JOHN SQUIRE** (b.24 Nov'62, Broadheath, Manchester) – guitar, vocals / **PETER GARNER** – rhythm guitar / **ANDY COUZENS** – bass / **RENI** (b. ALAN WREN, 10 Apr'64) – drums

		Thin Line	not iss.
Sep 85.	(12") *(THIN 001)* **SO YOUNG. / TELL ME**		-

— now a quartet when PETER departed

		Revolver	not iss.
May 87.	(12"m) *(12REV 36)* **SALLY CINNAMON. / HERE IT COMES / ALL ACROSS THE SANDS**		-
	(re-iss. Feb89; same) (re-iss. Dec89 cd-ep+=; CDREV 36) – ('A'demo). (hit No.46) *(re-iss. Nov00; REVXD 36)*		

— (1987) **GARY 'MANI' MOUNFIELD** (b.16 Nov'62, Crumpsall, Manchester) – bass, vocals repl. COUZENS who later joined The HIGH.

		Silvertone	Silvertone
Oct 88.	(7") *(ORE 1)* **ELEPHANT STONE. / THE HARDEST THING IN THE WORLD**		-
	(12"+=) *(ORE 1T)* – Full fathoms five. *(re-iss. Feb90 c-s/cd-s; ORE 1 C/CD)*; hit No.8. *(cd-s re-iss. Oct96; same)*		
Mar 89.	(7") *(ORE 2)* **MADE OF STONE. / GOING DOWN**		-
	(12"+=) *(ORE 2T)* – Guernica. *(re-iss. Mar90 c-s/cd-s; ORE 2 C/CD)*; hit No.20. *(cd-s re-iss. Oct96; same)*		
Apr 89.	(lp/c/cd) *(ORE LP/MC/CD 502)* <1184-1/-4/-2> **THE STONE ROSES**	19	86
	– I wanna be adored / She bangs the drum / Waterfall / Don't stop / Bye bye badman / Elizabeth my dear / (Song for my) Sugar spun sister / Made of stone / Shoot you down / This is the one / I am the resurrection. *(re-iss. Aug91 as 2x12"+=; OREZLP 502)* – Elephant stone / Fool's gold. *(cd re-iss. Mar97; same) (d-cd re-iss. as 10th ANNIVERSARY EDITION; 059124-2)* – (w/ extra tracks). – (hit UK No.26)		
Jul 89.	(7"/7"s) *(ORE/+X 6)* **SHE BANGS THE DRUM. / STANDING HERE**	36	-
	(12"+=/12"s+=) *(ORE T/Z 6)* – Mersey Paradise. (c-s++=/cd-s++=) *(ORE C/CD 6)* – Simone. *(re-entered chart Mar90; hit No.34) (cd-s re-iss. Oct96; same)*		

		Silvertone	Jive
Nov 89.	(7"/ext.12") *(ORE/+T 13)* <1315-1> **FOOL'S GOLD. / WHAT THE WORLD IS WAITING FOR**	8	Mar90
	(c-s+=/cd-s+=) *(ORE C/CD 13)* – ('A'extended). *(flipped over re-entered chart Sep90; hit No.22) (re-iss. remix May92; hit No.73) (cd-s re-iss. Oct96; same)* (12") *(ORET 13)* – ('A'-The Top Won mix) / ('A'-The Bottom Won mix).		
Nov 89.	(12"ep) <1301> **I WANNA BE ADORED / (long version) / GOING DOWN / SIMONE**	-	
Jul 90.	(7"/c-s/12"/cd-s) *(ORE/+C/T/CD 17)* <1399-1/-2> **ONE LOVE. / SOMETHING'S BURNING**	4	
	(cd-s re-iss. Oct96; same)		
Sep 91.	(7"/c-s) *(ORE/+C 31)* **I WANNA BE ADORED. / WHERE ANGELS PLAY**	20	-
	(12"+=/cd-s+=) *(ORE T/CD 31)* – Sally Cinnamon (live). *(cd-s re-iss. Oct96; same)*		
Jan 92.	(7"/c-s) *(ORE/+C 35)* **WATERFALL (remix). / ONE LOVE (remix)**	27	
	(12"+=/cd-s+=) *(ORE T/CD 35)* – ('A'&'B'extended versions). *(cd-s re-iss. Oct96; same)*		
Apr 92.	(7"/c-s) *(ORE/+C 40)* **I AM THE RESURRECTION. / ('A'-Pan & scan radio version)**	33	
	(12"+=) *(ORET 40)* – Fool's gold (The Bottom Won mix). (cd-s++=) *(ORECD 40)* – ('A'-5:3 Stoned Out club mix). *(cd-s re-iss. Oct96; same)*		
Jul 92.	(cd/c/lp) *(ORE CD/C/LP 521)* **TURNS INTO STONE** (demos & rare)	32	-
	– Elephant stone / The hardest thing in the world / Going down / Mersey Paradise / Standing here Where angels play / Simone / Fools gold / What the world is waiting for / One love / Something's burning. *(cd re-iss. Mar97 & Mar99; same)*		

		Geffen	Geffen
Nov 94.	(7"/c-s) *(GFS/+C 84)* **LOVE SPREADS. / YOUR STAR WILL SHINE**	2	
	(cd-s+=) *(GFST 84)* – Breakout. (12"++=) *(GFSTD 84)* – Groove harder.		
Dec 94.	(cd/c/lp) <(GED/GEC/GEF 24503)> **SECOND COMING**	4	47 Jan95
	– Breaking into Heaven / Driving south / Ten storey love song / Daybreak / Your star will shine / Straight to the man / Begging you / Tightrope / Good times / Tears / How do you sleep? / Love spreads. (cd+=) – (untitled hidden track No.90). *(lp re-iss. Aug99 on 'Simply Vinyl'; SVLP 111)*		
Feb 95.	(7"/c-s) *(GFS/+C 87)* **TEN STOREY LOVE SONG. / RIDE ON**	11	
	(12"+=/cd-s+=) *(GFST/+D 87)* – Moses.		

— In Apr'95, RENI quit and was replaced by **ROBERT MADDIX** (ex-GINA GINA).

Oct 95.	(c-s) *(GFSC 22060)* **BEGGING YOU / ('A'-Chic mix)**	15	
	(cd-s++=) *(GFSTD 22060)* – ('A'-Stone Corporation mix) / ('A'-Lakota mix) / ('A'-Young American primitive remix). (12") *(GFST 22060)* – ('A'-Carl Cox mix) / ('A'-Development Corporation mix).		

— Late in March '96, SQUIRE left to pursue new venture, The SEAHORSES. The STONE ROSES continued and in Aug'96, they recruited **AZIZ IBRAHIM** (ex-SIMPLY RED) / **NIGEL IPPINSON** – keyboards

— They officially split in Nov'96, after MANI joined PRIMAL SCREAM. IBRAHIM would join IAN BROWN and eventually issue his solo album in 1999, thoughtfully titled 'AZIZ'.

– compilations, etc. –

on 'Silvertone' unless mentioned; who else?

Jan 92.	(8xcd-s-box-set) *(SRBX 1)* **SINGLES BOX**		-
Nov 92.	(10x12"box-set) *(SRBX 2)* **SINGLES BOX**		-

STONE ROSES (cont)

Apr 95.	(c-s) (OREC 71) **FOOL'S GOLD '95** / ('A'extended mix) (12"+=/cd-s+=) (ORE T/CD 71) – ('A'-Tall Paul remix) / ('A'-Cricklewood Ballroom mix).	23
May 95.	(cd/c/lp) (ORE CD/C/ZLP) **THE COMPLETE STONE ROSES**	4
Nov 96.	(cd/c/lp) (GARAGE CD/C/LP 1) **GARAGE FLOWER** (early demos) (cd re-iss. Aug g99; same)	58
Jun 97.	(7"ep) Fierce; (FRIGHT 044) **SPIKE ISLAND EP** (interviews, etc.)	
Feb 99.	(c-s/cd-s) Jive Electro; (052309-4/-2) **FOOL'S GOLD / FOOL'S GOLD** (Grooverider mix) / **RABBIT IN THE MOON**	25
Oct 00.	(cd/d-lp) (926015-2/-1) **THE REMIXES**	41
Nov 02.	(cd/d-lp) (926037-2/-1) **THE VERY BEST OF THE STONE ROSES** – I wanna be adored / She bangs the drums / Ten storey love song / Waterfall / Made of stone / Love spreads / What the world is waiting for / Sally Cinnamon / Fools gold / Begging you / Elephant stone / Breaking into heaven / One love / This is the one / I am the resurrection.	19

STRAITJACKET FITS

Formed: Brockville, Auckland, New Zealand ... 1986 by songwriters SHAYNE CARTER alongside a rhythm section of DAVID WOOD and JOHN COLLIE; ANDREW BROUGH as added in '87. Both SHAYNE (ex-BORED GAMES) and JOHN had been part of the legendary DOUBLE HAPPYS, who for some time had been the darlings of Auckland having issued some quintessential releases including 1985's 'CUT IT OUT' EP. Signed to 'Flying Nun', the STRAITJACKET FITS followed in the established Kiwi tradition of The CHILLS, The CLEAN etc., although they preferred their music with a bit more of a punch then many bands on the NZ scene. Although they debuted in 1987 with the 'LIFE IN ONE CHORD' EP, it would be another two years before the release of their first album, 'HAIL', licensed for UK release by 'Rough Trade'. Despite featuring many songs previously released on the EP, the album also boasted a version of Leonard Cohen's 'SO LONG MARIANNE', a surprising but effective cover sitting comfortably with the band's darkly atmospheric garage drone. Subsequently securing a deal with 'Arista', the band released follow-up set, 'MELT', in 1991, although like the bulk of their musical countrymen, they failed to attract a wider crossover audience. Back on 'Flying Nun', for third set, 'BLOW', the band finally gave up the ghost after a final single, 'IF I WERE YOU', in late '93. SHAYNE CARTER had already teamed up with PETER JEFFERIES (ex-THIS KIND OF PUNISHMENT) on a collaborative single for 'Flying Nun'; he is now leader of DIMMER.

Album rating: Double Happys: NERVES compilation (*7) / Straitjacket Fits: HAIL (*6) / HAIL compilation (*7) / MELT (*5) / BLOW (*4) / STRAITJACKET FITS compilation (*7) / Dimmer: I BELIEVE YOU ARE A STAR (*5)

BORED GAMES

SHAYNE CARTER – vocals, guitar / **FRASER BATTS** + **JEFF HARFORD** + **JONATHAN MOORE** + **TERRY MOORE**

Flying Nun   not iss.

1982. (12"ep) (FNLUDO 001) **WHO KILLED COLONEL MUSTARD EP** – Happy endings / I don't get it / Joe 90 / Bridesmaid.

— added **WAYNE ELSEY** (ex-STONES; who appeared on V/A compilation 'Dunedin Double' 2x12"ep + 1-ep, 'Another Disc Another Dollar')

DOUBLE HAPPYS

SHAYNE CARTER + **WAYNE ELSEY** plus **JOHN COLLIE** – drums

Flying Nun   not iss.

1984. (7") (FN 026) **THE OTHER'S WAY. / ANYONE ELSE WOULD**
1985. (12"ep) (FNDH 002) **CUT IT OUT EP** – Needles and plastic / Some fantasy / Moss monster / Nerves.

— tragedy struck when ELSEY died later in 1985

– compilations, etc. –

Jun 91. (m-lp) Avalanche; (ONLYMLP 012) **HOW MUCH TIME LEFT, PLEASE** – Big fat Elvis / Beer cans on the ground / Guilt / Anyone else would / I don't wanna see you again.

Jan 93. (cd) Flying Nun; (FNCD 196) **NERVES** – The other's way / Big fat Elvis / Moss monster / Wrapped up in myself again / Anyone else would / Needles and plastic / Some fantasy / I don't wanna see you again / I can't say / Nerves.

WEEDS

SHAYNE CARTER + **JEFF HARFORD** + **JOHN COLLIE** + **ROBERT SCOTT** + **CHRIS HEALEY** + **MICHAEL MORLEY**

E.S.T.   not iss.

1984. (c-s) (EST 18) **SOUNDTRACK TO THE STORY**
1985. (c-s) (EST 22) **PAY IT ALL BACK**

Flying Nun   not iss.

1985. (7") (FNEED 001) **WHEATFIELDS. / TROUBLE**

ORANGE

ANDREW BROUGH + **JONATHAN MOORE** + **PETER BRAGAN**

Flying Nun   not iss.

1986. (12"ep) (FN 047) **FRUIT SALAD LIVES** – Fruit salad lives / Walk out on your on / No reason to hide / What's in a name / Fly.

STRAITJACKET FITS

SHAYNE CARTER – vocals, guitar / **ANDREW BROUGH** – vocals, guitar, keyboards / **DAVID WOOD** – bass (ex-WORKING WITH WAIT; released 2 singles in 1984/5) / **JOHN COLLIE** – drums

Flying Nun   not iss.

1987. (12"ep) (FN 80 – FNE 25) **LIFE IN ONE CHORD** – Dialling a prayer / All that that brings / Sparkle that shines / She speeds.
1988. (lp) (FN 105) **HAIL** – Telling tales / Dead heat / Hail / Only you knew / Take from the years / So long Marianne / Grate / Fabulous things / Life in one chord / This taste delight.
1988. (12") (FN 108) **HAIL. / SO LONG MARIANNE** (re-iss. 1988; FN 114)

Rough Trade   Rough Trade

Nov 89. (cd/c/lp) (CDR/ROUGHC/R 147) <ROUGHUS 73> **HAIL** (compilation) – Dialing a prayer / All that that brings / Hail / Sparkle that shines / She speeds / So long Marianne / Grate / Fabulous things / Life in one chord / This taste delight.

Flying Nun   not iss.

1990. (cd) (FNCD 142) **HAIL** (compilation) – Dialing a prayer / Telling tales / Dead heat / Hail / Only you knew / She speeds / Sparkle that shines / Take from the years / So long Marianne / Grate / Fabulous things / All that that brings / Life in one chord / This taste delight.
1990. (7") (FN 151) **SPARKLE THAT SHINES. / GRATE**
1990. (7") (FN 175) **BAD NOTE FOR A HEART. / IN SPITE OF IT ALL** (cd-s+=) (FN 176) – Skin to wear (remix) / Hail (live).

— **MARK PETERSEN** – guitar (ex-CABBAGE BOMBER) repl. BROUGH who formed BIKE

1991. (d7") (FN 180) **DOWN IN SPLENDOUR. / SEEING U FLED (live) // CAVE IN. / MISSING PRESUMED DROWNED (George Martin knew my father mix)**

Arista   Arista

Oct 91. (cd/c) (261/411 908) <ARCD 8645> **MELT** – Bad note for a heart / Missing presumed drowned / Melt against yourself / Head wind / Down in splendour / A.P.S. / Quiet come / Such a daze / Skin to wear / Hand in mine / Roller ride / Cast stone. (NZ-iss.on 'Flying Nun'; FN 174) Jun91
Oct 91. (cd-ep) <ASCD 2244> **MISSING FROM MELT EP** – Missing presumed drowned / Bad note for a heart / Skin to wear (stripped mix) / In spite of it all / Cave in.
Dec 91. (cd-s) <ASCD 2356> **ROLLER RIDE / DOWN IN SPLENDOUR (live) / BAD NOTE FOR A HEART (live) / A.P.S. (live)**
1992. (cd-ep) (FN 242) **DONE EP** – Done / Spacing / Solid / Whiteout.
1993. (c-s/cd-s) (FNUN 265) **CAT INNA CAN / SYCAMORE / SATELLITE**
Sep 93. (cd/c) (FNCD/FNMC 251) <18697> **BLOW** May93 – Done / Falling / Joyride / Cat inna can / Sycamore / Brother's keeper / Train / Let it blow / If I were you / Turn / Way / Burn it up / Spacing.
Nov 93. (c-s/cd-s) (FNUN 285) **IF I WERE YOU (remix) / BROTHER'S KEEPER (demo) / BURN IT UP (demo)**

— disbanded after above; SHAYNE CARTER worked with PETER JEFFERIES and later formed DIMMER; PETERSEN formed SHAFT

– compilations, etc. –

Jan 00. (cd) Flying Nun; (DFN 406) **STRAITJACKET FITS** – Dialling a prayer / Burn it up / Headwind / She speeds / Down in splendour / Let it blow / If I were you / Missing presumed drowned / Rollerride / Sparkle that shines / Bad note for a heart / Done / A.P.S. / Cat inna can / Life in one chord / Cast stone. (ltd-bonus+=) – A.P.S. (live session) / Such a daze (live session) / Brittle / Sycamore / Skin to wear (stripped back mix).

DIMMER

SHAYNE CARTER with **GARY SULLIVAN** – drums (ex-GOBLIN MIX, CHUG, ex-JEAN-PAUL SARTRE EXPERIENCE, ex-SOLID GOLD HELL) / **ANDREW SPRAGGON** + **NED NGATAE**

Flying Nun   Sub Pop

Nov 95. (7") (FN 310) <SP 326> **CRYSTALATOR. / DAWN'S COMING IN**
Nov 96. (7"/c-s) (FN/+TC 399) **DON'T MAKE ME BUY OUT YOUR SILENCE. / PACER (extended)**

Sony Columbia   not iss.

Nov 99. (cd-s) (668560-2) **EVOLUTION / SAD GUY / EVOLUTION (tryhard remix)**
Jul 01. (cd) (50242-22000) **I BELIEVE YOU ARE A STAR** – Drop you off / All the way to her / Seed / Evolution / Smoke / Drift / I believe you are a star / Pendulum / Powercord / Under the light / Sad guy.

STRAWBERRY SWITCHBLADE

Formed: Glasgow, Scotland ... early 80's by JILL BRYSON and ROSE McDOWALL. This new wave female duo made their debut in 1983 with the introspective 'TREES AND FLOWERS' single, such indie scene notables as KATE ST. JOHN and RODDY FRAME lending their musical expertise. Cult acclaim turned into bonafide Top 5 success the following year when the bewitching pop atmospherics of 'SINCE YESTERDAY' gave the girls a brief period of fame. With no further major hits to support it, an eponymous debut album made a similarly brief appearance in the Top 30, the girls following in Glasgow's long C&W tradition and making a last ditch attempt to breathe some life into their career with a cover of the Dolly Parton classic, 'JOLENE'. Despite a Top 60 placing, the duo subsequently called it a day with McDOWALL going on to perform with INTO A CIRCLE and various other experimental projects like DEATH IN JUNE and PSYCHIC TV; she also delivered a solo version of Blue Oyster Cult's 'DON'T FEAR THE REAPER'.

Album rating: STRAWBERRY SWITCHBLADE (*6)

ROSE McDOWALL – vocals, guitar / **JILL BRYSON** (b.11 Feb'61) – vocals, guitar / with guests **KATE ST. JOHN** – oboe (ex-RAVISHING BEAUTIES) / **RODDY FRAME** – acoustic guitar (of AZTEC CAMERA) / **MARK 'BEDDERS' BEDFORD** – bass (of MADNESS)

		92HappyC.	not iss.
Jul 83.	(7") (HAP 001) **TREES AND FLOWERS. / GO AWAY**		-
	(12"+=) (HAPT 001) – Trees and flowers (just music).		

—— now with **GARY HITCHINS** + **ALAN PARK** – keyboards / **BORIS WILLIAMS** – drums / **DAVE MORRIS** – percussion / **BRUCE NOCKLES** – trumpet

		Korova	not iss.
Oct 84.	(7") (KOW 38) **SINCE YESTERDAY. / BY THE SEA**	5	-
	(12"+=) (KOW 38T) – Sunday morning.		
Mar 85.	(7") (KOW 39) **LET HER GO. / BEAUTIFUL END**	59	-
	(12"+=) (KOWT 59) – Michael walks by night.		
Apr 85.	(lp/c) (KODE/CODE 11) **STRAWBERRY SWITCHBLADE**	25	-
	– Since yesterday / Deep water / Another day / Little river / 10 James Orr Street / Let her go / Who knows what love is / Go away / Secrets / Being cold.		
May 85.	(7") (KOW 41) **WHO KNOWS WHAT LOVE IS. / POOR HEART**		-
	(12"+=) (KOW 41T) – Let her go (mix).		
Sep 85.	(7") (KOW 42) **JOLENE. / BEING COLD**	53	-
	(12"+=) (KOW 42T) – Black taxi.		

—— split late '85; ROSE subsequently joined UK act, INTO A CIRCLE

ROSE McDOWALL

		Rio Digital	not iss.
Sep 88.	(7"/12") (7/12 RDS 3) **DON'T FEAR THE REAPER. / CRYSTAL DAYS**		-

—— ROSE subsequently joined CURRENT 93, NURSE WITH WOUND and DEATH IN JUNE; she became part of metallic, SORROW, with ROBERT LEE

Dan STUART (see under ⇒ GREEN ON RED)

STUMP

Formed: based- London, England ... 1983 by former MICRODISNEY members MICK LYNCH (who actually replaced SHRUBS-bound original singer NICK HOBBS) and ROB McKAHEY, alongside KEV HOPPER and CHRIS SALMON. The inimitable STUMP made their debut on the ubiquitous 'Ron Johnson' label in early '86 with the acclaimed 'MUD ON A COLON' EP, featuring the madcap indulgence of 'GRAB HANDS'. Championed by Radio 1's John Peel, the band's clanking rhythms, atonal, wobbling guitars and demented vocals/lyrics were brought to an even wider audience via the inclusion of the seminal 'BUFFALO' on the NME C86 compilation. Witnessing LYNCH barking out the "How Much Is The Fish? ... Does The Fish Have Chips?" refrain on Channel 4's 'The Tube' was surely one of the musical highlights of the 80's, certainly one of the most talked about. For anyone who missed it first time round, the track was duly featured on debut mini-set, 'QUIRK OUT' (1986), released on the 'Stuff' label following the financial collapse of 'Ron Johnson'. A period of furious studio beavering ensued, eventually resulting in a full length debut proper, 'A FIERCE PANCAKE' (1988). The first release of their new major label deal with 'Ensign', the record pleased hardcore fans with such SPLODGE/BEEFHEART-esque behaviour as 'CHARLTON HESTON' (apparently "keeps his vest on!") but received a cold shoulder from a music press keen to distance themselves from anything remotely C86. Criminally ignored, the band took one last shot at success with a re-issued 'BUFFALO' later that year; its failure and the band's subsequent split remain one of indie music's more vexing injustices.

Album rating: QUIRK OUT (*7) / A FIERCE PANCAKE (*8)

MICK LYNCH – vocals (ex-MICRODISNEY) repl. NICK HOBBS who joined SHRUBS / **CHRIS SALMON** – guitar / **KEV HOOPER** – bass / **ROB MacKAHEY** – drums (ex-MICRODISNEY)

		Ron Johnson	not iss.
Feb 86.	(12"ep) (ZRON 6) **MUD ON A COLON**		-
	– Orgasm way / Grab hands / Ice the leviant / 55-0-55.		

		Stuff	not iss.
Oct 86.	(m-lp) (STUFF 2) **QUIRK OUT**		-
	– Tupperware stripper / Our fathers / Kitchen table / Buffalo / Everything in its place / Bit part actor. (c-iss.May87; STUFFCU 2)		

		Ensign	not iss.
Feb 88.	(7") (ENY 612) **CHAOS. / ICE THE LEVIANT**		-
	(12"+=) (ENYX 612) – Safe sex.		
Mar 88.	(cd)(c/lp) (CCD 1641)(Z+/CHEN 9) **A FIERCE PANCAKE**		-
	– Lying it down / In the green / Roll the bodies over / Bone / Eager bereaver / Chaos / Alcohol / Charlton Heston / A fierce pancake / (A visit to the) Doctor / Heartache.		

—— (the track, 'CHARLTON HESTON', featured The IRRESISTABLE FORCE)

Jun 88.	(7") (ENY 614) **CHARLTON HESTON. / THE RATS**	72	-
	(12"+=) (ENYX 614) – Angst forecast.		
Nov 88.	(7") (ENY 619) **BUFFALO. / THE SONG REMAINS THE SAME**		-
	(12"+=) (ENYX 619) – Thelma.		

—— disbanded early 1989 and KEV HOOPER went solo. In May '90, he issued the single, 'THE SOUND OF GYROSCOPES', and album (Jul'90), 'STOLEN JEWELS' for the 'Getty' label. MICK and ROB re-formed STUMP in Sep '91.

– compilation, others, etc. –

Feb 87.	(12"ep) Strange Fruit; (SFPS 019) **THE PEEL SESSIONS** (5/2/86)		-
	– Down on the kitchen table / Orgasm way / Grab hands / Buffalo.		

STUPIDS

Formed: Ipswich, Suffolk, England ... December '83 by a loose, pseudonymous crew with a core of TOMMY STUPID, MARTY TUFF, ED WENN and STEVIE SNAX. Inspired by US hardcore icons such as The CIRCLE JERKS and SUICIDAL TENDENCIES, The STUPIDS took their own irreverent approach to slamdiving and skateboarding via a series of albums on their own 'Children Of The Revolution Records'. A precursor to bands like SNUFF and The SENSELESS THINGS, The STUPIDS quickly acquired cult status, a deal with 'Vinyl Solution' ensuring a wider audience for the 'VAN STUPID' (1987) and 'JESUS MEETS THE STUPIDS' (1987) albums (by the release of which MARTY had been substituted with PAULY PIZZA) while the continuing support of John Peel made sure they were heard by a varied cross section of the indie community. Comparisons were often drawn between The STUPIDS and Aussie hardcore pranksters The HARD-ONS, both bands sharing a juvenile sense of humour and a dedication to anarchic live sets. Never the most stable of bands, it came as little surprise when they finally fell apart in 1989. The various band members were also simultaneously involved with their own bands (BAD DRESS SENSE, SCHNOZZER and FRANKFURTER II), ED and PAULY subsequently forming SINK at the turn of the decade. For the remainder of the 90's, WENN split his duties between work and projects, BIG RAY and K-LINE. • **Note:** It was an American SINK that issued '100 TONS' single for 'X-Mist' in 1992.

Album rating: PERUVIAN VACATION (*6) / RETARD PICNIC (*6) / VAN STUPID (*6) / JESUS MEETS THE STUPIDS (*6) / THE STUPIDS COLLECTION (*6) / Sink: MAMA SINK compilation (*6)

TOMMY STUPID (b. WITHERS) – vocals, guitar, drums / **ED SHRED** (b. WENN) – guitar, bass, vocals / **STEVIE SNAX** – bass / **MARTY TUFF** – guitar

		Children Of The Revolution	not iss.
Mar 85.	(7"ep) (COR 3) **VIOLENT NUN EP**		-
	– Elephant man / What happens next / So much fun / It's gotta be love / Who do you think you are? / Skid row / Taken too many / You die / Waste away / I'm ill / I don't like nobody / Waltz of the new wavers.		
May 86.	(lp) (GURT 9) **PERUVIAN VACATION**		-
	– It's fun to you / Wipe out / You shoulda listened / Always never fun / I scream inside / You die / Peruvian vacation / This is the norm? / So much fun / Born to built to grind / In bed at night / I don't wanna get involved with you / The pit / Life's a drag. (cd-iss. Sep93 on 'Clay'+=; CLAYCD 116) – VIOLENT NUN EP / Leave your ears behind / (11 rare tracks).		
Oct 86.	(lp) (GURT 15) **RETARD PICNIC**		-
	– The memory burns / Sleeping troubles / Terrordome / Heard it all before / Jesus, do what you have to do / Yah dude!! / Something's got to give / Hawaiian vacation / Shaded eyes / Frankfurter / Slumber party massacre / Waltz of the new wavers / Your little world / Killed by a cripple / We suck / Peoiple in your neighbourhood / I'm so lazy / Wipe out. (cd-iss. Nov93 on 'Clay'+=; CLAYCD 117) – (Stupids flexi / Feedback sessions / Retard Picnic out-takes).		

—— **PAULY PIZZA** – bass; repl. MARTY

		Vinyl Solution	not iss.
May 87.	(m-lp) (SOL 2) **VAN STUPID**		-
	– Texan vacation / Layback session / Rootbeer death / Sorry it blew my head / I don't like nobody (porno mix) / Vampire / Stoopie boys (commando mix).		
Jul 87.	(lp; as BAD DRESS SENSE) (SOL 4) **GOODBYE . . . IT WAS FUN**		-
	– G.C.B. / Could I ever / Truth / Cynical smile / Life's demand / Never mine / Always away / Need to love.		

—— no ED or TOMMY on above

below with **TOMMY + ED** plus **BOBBY JONES**

Aug 87.	(12"ep) (FART 1) meet (FRANKFURTER) ep		-
	– Hot babes / Mega-zombie / Pasta boy / Raise the breadknife / Freak E. Frank & the get Frank crew / Gimme donuts / Inbred zombies / More of the same.		
Dec 87.	(lp) (SOL 7) **JESUS MEETS THE STUPIDS**		-
	– You'll never know / Skid row / Stupid Monday / Bug blood / Fridge / Pig man / Brat's bite / Dog log / Bowl of cheerios / Slit your wrist / Animal crackers / Do you really have to? (w/ free 7"ep)		

—— disbanded the following year

– compilations, etc. –

Sep 88.	(12"ep) Strange Fruit; (SFPS 054) **PEEL SESSIONS** (12.5.87)		-
	– Life's a drug / Heard it all before / Shaded eyes / Dog bog / Stupid Monday.		

SINK

ED SHRED – vocals, guitar / **PAULY DUNCAN** – bass

		Poontang	not iss.
Jan 89.	(7"ep) (POON 1) **TAKE THE HOSSES WITH THE LOSSES**		-
	– Diamonds / I hate yourself / Some lilac evening / Mama sink / Birthday song / For what it's worth (acoustic).		
Jun 89.	(7"ep) (POON 2) **ON THE TRACKS, FEELING BLUE**		-
	– Blue noodles / Slippin' thru my hands / Blues man / Fire and brimstone / If only you were lonely.		

		Decoy	not iss.
Jan 90.	(lp) (DYL 6) **ANOTHER LOVE TRIANGLE**		-
	– On the tracks / Jigsaw catch / Squirrels / Backwater / Return to the previous angel / Big red car / This time . . . / Cut the mustard / Diamonds / Talking at the evening / Hard as hate / For what it's worth / Baby / Perspective / Eternal man.		
Feb 90.	(7"ep) (DYS 4) **DON'T BURN THE HOOK**		-
	– At the circus / Y.D. blues / Kick / Chocolate love.		

STUPIDS (cont)

— new drummer **JAMES KERMACK** (ex-PERFECT DAZE)

Jun 90. (m-lp) *(DYL 12)* **OLD MAN SNAKE AND THE FAT, BLACK PIG**
– Seams / Keep on living blues / Angel turns blue / Won't sell my guitar / Mr Passion / Sometime somewhere (bad blood) / Bad van blues. *(cd-iss. Aug90 +=; DYL 12CD)* – ANOTHER LOVE TRIANGLE + 'DON'T BURN THE HOOK' ep

Nov 90. (m-lp/m-cd) *(DYL 21/+CD)* **MAMA SINK THE FIRST 18 YEARS (1963-1989)** (compilation of first 2 EP's)

Full Circle / not iss.

1991. (7"m) *(VEG 1)* **DRAIN PIPE JANE. / GRANDMA'S KITCHEN / TICKET OFFICE BLUES**

City Slang / not iss.

Jan 92. (lp/cd) *(EFA 04072/+CD)* **VEGA-TABLES**
– Digging / Buddha #1 / One final kick in the head / Bloodshot / Pepper / Shivers / Vega-tables / Buddha #2 *[cd-only]* / Drainpipe Jane / Echo / Buddha #3 / Misery town / Revenge / What do you think? / Buddha #4.

— split after above

BIG RAY

ED WENN – vocals, guitar / **JOHN RUSCOE** – guitar, vocals / **STEVE COX** – keyboards / **PAUL DUNCAN** – bass / **JAMES KERMACK** – drums

City Slang / not iss.

1992. (cd/lp) *(SLANG 020 CD/LP)* **NAKED**
– Windfall / Treat you right / Free range flesh / Missing a train / Evergreen / Open house / Spaces inbetween / Watch me / Richer in body & soul / Feeling tired & useless / Carousel / Squirrels.

— added **CLIVE WATLING** – percussion

Dirter / not iss.

Apr 93. (7"m) *(7DROMS 8)* **FREE RANGE FLESH. / BUZZING / SLAUGHTERHOUSE OF DECENCY**

CHOCOLATE

ED WENN – vocals, guitar / **WOLFIE RETARD** – bass / **WJ RUSCOE** – drums, vocals

Dirter / not iss.

Aug 93. (m-cd) *(DPROMCD 15)* **SUBSTITUTE FOR SEX**
– Kittredge / S.O.F.T. / Painless / Evening star / Bobby told me / Walking appetites / Bang juice.

— added **SIMON FINBOW** – vocals / **JASON WHITTAKER** – samples

Out Of Step / not iss.

Jul 95. (7"m) *(WOOS 1S)* **DEAD SKIN. / PEANUT JAR / STUPID MOTHERFUCKER**

Oct 95. (7"m/cd-s) *(WOOS 4 S/CDS)* **BLUE STREAK. / ITEMS OF INTEREST / FAT HAVANA**

— now without JASON (was back in place for album)

Mar 96. (7"ep) *(WOOS 11S)* **SLOW & LOW**
– Sugar free promise / Mr Pepper / Bully bars / Missile attack / How & when / Ain't no feeble bastard / Serious loss of down / 46 / Do I fit? / You're too punk / Negligible / Coughing up blood.

Apr 96. (cd/lp) *(CD/LP WOOS 1)* **HUNG, GIFTED AND SLACK**
– Junior F / Working for an idiot / Open season / Blue streak / Break the mould / Don't need you / Butt hickey / Operation Mongoose / Dead skin / Tyndale / Bragging and gagging / Stupid jerk / Dumb fuck / One for the bear / Fake sense of calm / The man with the plan.

— **CLIVE WATLING** – vocals, guitar; repl. FINBOW
— **ANDREW RUSCOE** – bass; repl. WOLFIE + JASON

Nov 96. (7"ep) *(WOOS 15S)* **SALE COPY ONLY, NOT FOR REVIEW**
– Community / Lost your way / Ego-central / J. Edna / I wish I smoked.

— CHOCOLATE are no longer; expect a compilation in 2003

BIG RAY

ED, JOHN, PAUL + STEVE plus **PAUL READ** – drums, vocals / **RUPERT COULSON** – percussion, vocals

Recovery / not iss.

1999. (cd) *(none)* **YOU GET WHAT YOU DESERVE**
– Starlight / Driven / Ticking over / Alone at closing / Moontown / Paperback / Dance class / Slaughterhouse of decency / Heavy metal boy / Screaming sun / Trying to tell you / Help me find me.

Boss Tuneage / not iss.

Mar 02. (cd) *(BOSTAGE 566)* **BUSINESS CLASS**
– Car / Duckpin / You me and EBT / House at Wilson / I envy you / Chocolate / Beautiful ghosts / So unfair / Funny bloke / Buzzing / Mefloquine dreams / Be lucky / Iron days / Selfish.

K-LINE

ED WENN – guitar, vocals / **ZAC LEEKS** – vocals / **PAUL DUNCAN** – bass / **JAMES SHERRY** – drums (ex-DONE LYING DOWN)

Boss Tuneage / not iss.

Apr 02. (7"ep/cd-ep) *(BOSTAGE 710/578)* **IN THE RED**
– Broken Holmes / Stay poor / Future primitives.

— added **RICH MATTHEWS** – guitar

STYLE COUNCIL (see under ⇒ WELLER, Paul)

SUBHUMANS

Formed: Melksham, Wiltshire, England ... 1981 by main writer DICK LUCAS, BRUCE, GRANT and TROTSKY. Inspired by the uncompromising ideology of CRASS, anarcho-punks The SUBHUMANS concerned themselves with human rights, vegetarianism and a hankering for the downfall of the Tories. This much was evident from a series of EP's in the early 80's, namely, 'DEMOLITION WAR', 'REASONS FOR EXISTENCE' and 'RELIGIOUS WARS'. The self-explanatory 'THE DAY THE COUNTRY DIED', was the title of their late 1982 debut album, although this was the last recording to feature GRANT who was replaced by PHIL. The following year, the band set up their own label, 'Bluurg', to release both their own recordings and those of other acts with a similarly militant outlook. Moving towards a more heavyweight punk sound, LUCAS and Co continued to release the odd album or two before they metamorphosed into ska/reggae/punk fusion act, CULTURE SHOCK, in 1987. Towards the end of the decade, by which time they had delivered three albums, DICK broke away to spearhead his own outfit, CITIZEN FISH. Driving home his 90's free spirit message more successfully than ever before, LUCAS continued to command the festival/crusty crowd with a conscientious but ebullient mixture of politico skank-punk beginning with the 'FREE SOULS IN A TRAPPED ENVIRONMENT' set. CITIZEN FISH are still going strong (if that's the right term), their most recent piece of work being the album, 'LIFE SIZE' (2001).

Album rating: THE DAY THE COUNTRY DIED (*6) / TIME FLIES ... BUT AEROPLANES CRASH (*5) / FROM THE CRADLE TO THE GRAVE (*5) / WORLDS APART (*5) / EP-LP (*5) / 29:29 SPLIT VISION (*5) / Culture Shock: GO WILD! (*5) / ONWARDS AND UPWARDS (*5) / ALL THE TIME (*5) / Citizen Fish: FREE SOULS IN A TRAPPED ENVIRONMENT (*6) / WIDER THAN A POSTCARD (*5) / MILLENNIA MADNESS (*5) / THIRST (*4) / ACTIVE INGREDIENTS (*5) / LIFE SIZE (*4)

DICK (b. RICHARD LUCAS) – vocals / **BRUCE** – guitar / **GRANT** – bass / **TROTSKY** – drums

Spiderleg / not iss.

Nov 81. (7"ep) *(SOB 1)* **DEMOLITION WAR**
– Parasites / Drugs of youth / Animal / Who's gonna fight in the third world war / Society / Human error. *(re-iss. 1988 on 'Bluurg'; XEP 1)*

Apr 82. (7"ep) *(SDL 5)* **REASONS FOR EXISTANCE**
– Big city / Reason for existance / Cancer / Peroxide. *(re-iss. 1988 on 'Bluurg'; XEP 2)*

Aug 82. (7"ep) *(SDL 7)* **RELIGIOUS WARS**
– Religious wars / Love is . . . / Work experience / It's gonna get worse. *(re-iss. 1988 on 'Bluurg'; XEP 3)*

Dec 82. (lp) *(SDL 9)* **THE DAY THE COUNTRY DIED**
– All gone dead / Ashtray dirt / Killing / Minority / Nothing I can do / Mickey Mouse is dead / Dying world / Subvert city / Big brother / No / New age / I don't wanna die / Zyklon B-movie / No more gigs / Black and white / 'Til the pigs come round. *(re-iss. 1988 on 'Bluurg' lp/c; XLP 1/+C) (cd-iss. Jun91 lp/c/cd; XLP 1/+/CD)*

— **PHIL** – bass; repl. GRANT

Bluurg / not iss.

Jun 83. (7"ep) *(FISH 2)* **EVOLUTION / SO MUCH MONEY. / GERM / NOT ME**

Nov 83. (12"ep) *(FISH 5)* **TIME FLIES . . . BUT AEROPLANES CRASH**
– Get out of my way / First aid / Word factory / People are scared / Susan / I don't wanna die / Everyday life / Work-rest-play-die.

Jun 84. (lp/c) *(FISH 8/+C)* **FROM THE CRADLE TO THE GRAVE**
– Forget / Waste of breath / Where's the freedom? / Adversity / Reality is waiting for a bus / Wake up screaming / Rain / From the cradle to the grave. *(cd-iss. Mar92; FISH 8CD)*

Dec 84. (7"ep) *(FISH 10)* **RATS EP**
– Joe Public / Labels / When the bomb drops / Rats.

Jan 86. (lp/c) *(FISH 12/+C)* **WORLDS APART**
– 33322 / British disease / Heads of state / Apathy / Fade away / Businessmen / Someone is lying / Pigman / Can't hear the words / Get to work on time / Carry on laughing / Straightline thinking / Ex teenage rebel / Power games / 33322. *(cd-iss. Nov91; FISH 12CD)*

Oct 86. (lp/c) *(FISH 14/+C)* **EP-LP**
– Parasites / Drugs of youth / Animal / Society / Who's gonna fight in the third world war? / Human error / Big city / Peroxide / Reason for existence / Cancer / Religious wars / Love is . . . / It's gonna get worse / Work experience / Evolution / So much money / Germ / Not me. *(cd-iss. Nov91; FISH 14CD)*

Oct 87. (lp/c) *(FISH 16/+C)* **29:29 SPLIT VISION**
– Somebody's mother / Think for yourself / Walls of silence / Heroes / Dehumanisation / Worlds apart / New boy / Time flies. *(cd-iss. Mar92; FISH 16CD)*

— had already split early '87, and above was posthumous

– compilations, others –

Jun 91. (lp/c/cd) *Bluurgh; (FISH 12/+C/CD)* **TIME FLIES . . . BUT AEROPLANES EP / RATS EP**

CULTURE SHOCK

DICK, BRUCE, PHIL + TROTSKY

Bluurg / not iss.

May 87. (lp) *(FISH 18)* **GO WILD**
– Punks on postcards / Go wild (my son) / Messed up / Six foot rooms / Ten per cent off / Circles / Mother's on the phone / All (messed up) together. *(<re-iss. Feb93; same>)*

Apr 88. (lp/c) *(FISH 20/+C)* **ONWARDS & UPWARDS**
– Pressure / Colour T.V. / Fast forward / You are not alone / Joyless / If you don't like it / Civilization street / United / Catching flies / When the fighting's over / Open mind surgery / Don't worry about it / I.S.D. *(<cd-iss. Feb93; FISH 20CD>)*

Nov 89. (lp/c) *(FISH 23/+C)* **ALL THE TIME!**
– Countdowns / Twenty questions / Upside down / The time it takes / Four minutes / Northern Ireland / Northern Ireland (dub) / Onwards. *(<re-iss. Feb93; same>)*

– compilations, etc. –

Aug 95. (cd) *Bluurg;* **GO WILD / ALL THE TIME!**

CITIZEN FISH

DICK, PHIL + TROTSKY with **JASPER** – bass

Bluurg / Bluurg

Oct 90. (lp/c/cd) (<FISH 24/+C/CD>) **FREE SOULS IN A TRAPPED ENVIRONMENT**
– Supermarket song / Break into a run / Rainbows / Possession / Small scale wars / Home economics / Paint / Talk is cheap / Face off / Youth / Flesh and blood / Get off the phone / Experiment Earth / How to write ultimate protest songs / Charity. (cd-iss. Apr94; FISH 24CD)

Jan 92. (7") <LK 60> **DISPOSABLE DREAM. / FLESH AND BLOOD II**
(above issued on 'Lookout!')

Mar 92. (lp/c/cd) (<FISH 26/+C/CD>) **WIDER THAN A POSTCARD**
– Sink or swim / Language barrier / Same old starving millions / Conditional silence / Big big house / Mind bomb / Chili pain / Give me Beethoven / Talk it over / Offended / Central nervous system / Traffic lights / Smells like home.

Nov 93. (lp/cd) (FISH 28/+CD) **LIVE FISH (live)**

Jan 94. (lp/c/cd) (<FISH 31/+C/CD>) **FLINCH**
– TV dinner / Naked / Small talk / Time control / Dividing lines / Media men / Bag lady / First impressions / Wet cement / Circular vision / Social insecurity / Invisible people / Flinch.

Bluurg / Lookout!

Sep 95. (lp/cd) (FISH 34/+CD) <LK 123> **MILLENNIA MADNESS** Oct95
– P.C. musical chairs / Next big thing / Can't be bothered / 2000 and one / Panic in the supermarket / Can't complain / Faster / Phone in sick / Refugees go west / Backlash / Friends / Skin.

Lookout / Lookout

Sep 96. (cd/lp) (<LK 152>) **THIRST**
– Feeding / Pop songs / City on a river / Used to work / Plasticash / Scene 496: Care in a Melksham / Words on overtime / Talk about the weather / Catholic sex confession / Criminal / What Charlie said / Fill me up.

Nov 98. (7"ep) (<LK 209>) **HABIT – 4 SONG EP**
– Habit / Phone in sick (live) / Overheard / I had to guess.

Jun 99. (cd) <LK 212> **ACTIVE INGREDIENTS**
– Active ingredients / The Bob song / Oslo / Bitter and twisted / Digging a hole / Sacred cows / Pills / Habit / Isolated incidents / Barking / Heard it all before / Deep neurotic / Not for sale.

Honest Don's / Honest Don's

Jun 01. (lp/cd) (<DON 036/+CD>) **LIFE SIZE**
– Over the fence / Revolution / Out of control / Picture this / Internal release / Autographs / Back to zero / Choice of viewing / Lose the instructions / Somewhere to go / Shrink the distance / Will swap.

SUBURBAN NIGHTMARE (see under ⇒ DWARVES)

SUDDEN SWAY

Formed: Peterborough, England ... 1980 by MIKE McGUIRE and PETE JOSTIN, who were augmented by various personnel during the formative years of their career. Over this period a couple of self-financed singles had the music press raving, the second of which, the 'TO YOU, WITH REGARD' EP, sold well enough to gain a respectable placing in the indie charts. With the addition of SIMON CHILDS, the SUDDEN SWAY set-up became more stable, the band almost inking a deal with majors 'C.B.S.' and 'Virgin'. Following a further single on their own label ('Chant') however, the ACR/SHRIEKBACK-influenced trio moved on to Warners subsidiary 'Blanco Y Negro', pre-dating the modern craze for remixing by gleefully churning out eight(!) different versions of 'SING SONG', their skewed interpretation of the label's request for a pop song. Confusing if not alienating their small but loyal fanbase, it was followed by another wilfully unconventional attempt to subvert their status as a major label backed "pop" outfit in the shape of 1986's double-12" EP, 'SPACEMATE'. In the wake of the inevitable parting of the ways, 'Rough Trade' would bail the band out and release a 7" EP, 'AUTUMN CUT BACK JOB LOT OFFER', featuring eight 1-minute variations on a single theme. In 1988, they finally delivered their first "normal" LP, '76 KIDS FOREVER', a quasi-concept affair that formed the basis for a pioneering series of shows bordering on interactive performance art. SIMON, quite wisely perhaps, departed soon after, leaving McGUIRE and JOSTINS to go a league beyond with 1990's swansong, 'KO-OPERA'. The pair subsequently channeled their creative powers into 'Klub Londonium', another mischievous adventure which sent its devotees/members on the equivalent of a post-modern orienteering course around the capital!

Album rating: SPACEMATE (*6) / '76 KIDS FOREVER (*5) / KO-OPERA (*6)

MICHAEL McGUIRE – vocals / **PETE JOSTINS** – instruments

Chant / not iss.

1980. (7",c-s) (CHANT 1) **JANE'S THIRD PARTY. / DON'T GO**

Aug 81. (12"ep) (CHANT 2-EJSP 9692) **TO YOU, WITH REGARD EP**
– Alleluia! / The psychic sons / Pretty people again / Dance of joy / Tales of talking town.

— added **SIMON CHILDS** – guitar

Feb 84. (12"m) (CHANT 3) **THE TRAFFIC TAX SCHEME. / SIR SAVOIR HER VALOUR / HE SAYS CONSCIENCE**

Blanco Y Negro / not iss.

Mar 86. (7"ep/12"ep) (NEG 18 V1/V5) **SING SONG**
– A Finepro demonstration (8 different versions).

Sep 86. (2x12"ep) (BYN 8) **SPACEMATE**

Rough Trade / not iss.

Jan 87. (7"ep) (RT 183) **AUTUMN CUT BACK JOB LOT OFFER**
– (8 versions).

Dec 87. (12") (RTT 213) **SAT'DAY MORNIN' EPISODE. / THE BARMY ARMY**

May 88. (lp) (ROUGH 133) **'76 KIDS FOREVER**
– Phoenix family protection plan / Sol (store detective man) / The barmy army / So you're alright then / I've got a Tinitron amusement centre / Only a grebo / Reverend Peter bio teacher / Once in every weekend / Trisha listen / The ballad of Brancaster / Never in Netherton / '76 kids forever / Hush puppy yummy.

— now without SIMON

Mar 90. (lp)(c) (CD+/R 142)(ROUGHC 142) **KO-OPERA**
– League of the unfashioned / League of the incomplete / League of the violated / League of the uniformed / League of the delirious / League of the nouveau poore / League of the postal modernists / League of the disappointed.

— disappeared after above

– compilations, etc. –

Nov 86. (12"ep/c-ep) Strange Fruit; (SFPS/+C 005) / Dutch East India; <DEI 8316> **PEEL SESSION (16.11.83)** Apr95
– Let's evolve / Relationships.

SUGARCUBES (see under ⇒ BJORK)

SUMMERHILL (see under ⇒ SNAKES OF SHAKE)

SUN AND THE MOON (see under ⇒ CHAMELEONS)

SURGICAL PENIS KLINIK (see under ⇒ S.P.K.)

SWALLOW

Formed: Seattle, Washington, USA ... 1987 by ROD MOODY, ANDY SCHEEN, CHRIS PUGH and SCOTT SCHICKLER. The former had served time with future grunge messers, JEFF AMENT (PEARL JAM) and BRUCE FAIRWEATHER (MOTHER LOVE BONE) in rehearsal band, DERANGED DICTION. Part of the massive and incestuous Seattle hardcore scene of the late 80s and early 90s, SWALLOW released their debut single 'TRAPPED' / 'GUTS' in '88. Although the A-side was a moody pop song it was the thrashy B-side which was a better indicator of what to expect from the band. The music was typical of that coming out of Seattle at the time, however, MOODY'S shrieking vocals sounded like a tone deaf ROBERT PLANT. The self-titled debut album came and went in 1989 without stirring too much interest. It soon became apparent that the group would never have earned a record deal had it not been for PUGH'S long-standing friendship with 'Sub Pop' co-owner BRUCE PAVITT. A second album was recorded with BUTCH VIG at the helm was shelved in the 'Sub Pop' vaults under the "never mix business with pleasure" section. The band split soon afterwards.

Album rating: SWALLOW (*5)

ROD MOODY – vocals, guitar (ex-DERANGED DICTION) / **CHRIS PUGH** – guitar (ex-YOUNG PIONEERS) / **ANDY SCHEEN** (aka ANDY SPRINGSHEEN) – bass / **SCOTT SCHICKLER** – drums (ex-LIMP RECHERDS)

Tupelo / Sub Pop

Jun 88. (7",7"yellow) <SP 14> **GUTS. / TRAPPED**

May 89. (lp/cd) (TUP LP/CD 001) <SP 24> **SWALLOW**
– Zoo / Foetus / Coffin / Guts / Hard / Cold / B.S.A. / Trim / Home.

— **CRAIG BRADFORD** – drums; repl. SCOTT

— the group split in 1992 after recording a shelved set; MOODY joined SPIKE and PUGH formed CREEP (the pair would re-unite in CRIME FAMILY)

SWAMP CHILDREN (see under ⇒ A CERTAIN RATIO)

SWANS

Formed: New York, USA ... 1982 as a vehicle for the musical experimentation of MICHAEL GIRA. With an initial line-up of GIRA, ROLI MOSSIMAN, NORMAN WESTBURG, HARRY CROSBY and JONATHAN KANE, SWANS made their less than graceful debut with an EP in 1982, following it up with debut album, 'FILTH' (1983), both releases appearing – in Europe at least – on the German 'Zensor' label. Subsequently signing to British indie imprint, 'K.422', and replacing KANE with IVAN NAHEM, the band unleashed the pulverising 'COP' (1984) album. A harsh lesson in rock deconstruction, the record found GIRA and Co taking a metamorphic pneumatic drill to the form and pounding it till it barely even resembled music. Lyrically, GIRA was also scraping the margins, focusing on the blackest, most violent, paranoid and disturbing elements of life's dark side; 'RAPING A SLAVE' for instance, this controversial track also appearing as the lead track to a subsequent EP. Not music to play to your grandchildren then, but a brutally honest response to what GIRA perceived as the rotten core of human (and certainly American) society. Previewed by the memorably titled 'TIME IS MONEY (BASTARD)', 'GREED' (1986) was the next instalment in SWANS' dismantling of the capitalist rock beast, taking horror-industrial minimalism to new depths via a skeletal soundtrack of stark piano and percussion. Introducing the haunting vocals of JARBOE (MOSSIMAN had decamped to form WISEBLOOD), the 'HOLY MONEY' album continued along the same (production) lines later that year. 1987 proved a turning point as GIRA and JARBOE created SKIN as an outlet for their more fragile, acoustic creations, albums such as 'BLOOD, WOMEN, ROSES' (1987) and 'SHAME, HUMILITY, REVENGE' (1988) representing a more endearing flipside to the brutality of SWANS. Both albums appeared on 'Product Inc.', as did SWANS' 'CHILDREN OF GOD' (1988), a double set which introduced a new rhythm section (TED PARSONS and ALGYS 'AL' KIZYS) and found the band showing definite signs of mellowing. The shift was underlined with a surprise acoustic reading of Joy Division's 'LOVE WILL TEAR US APART', issued as a single in summer '88. Incredibly, perhaps, the band signed to corporate giant, 'M.C.A.', in 1989, releasing 'THE BURNING WORLD' as their major label debut. The partnership didn't last long, however, GIRA and JARBOE subsequently forming their own 'Young God' label for the release of '10 SONGS FOR ANOTHER WORLD', a third SKIN project issued under the revamped moniker WORLD OF SKIN (after Brit cock-rockers SKIN claimed the name). 1991's 'WHITE LIGHT FROM THE MOUTH OF INFINITY' moved even further away from the rampant nihilism of GIRA's earlier work, the man sounding uncannily like NICK CAVE (ironically another former prophet of doom who now seems to have found at least a measure of spiritual redemption) in places; while the brilliantly morose 'FAILURE' was the GIRA we all know and love, 'SONG FOR THE SUN' was positively joyous, suggesting there was indeed some light filtering through to the man's formerly opaque world view. Subsequent 90's albums, 'LOVE OF LIFE' (1992), 'OMNISCENCE' (1992), 'THE GREAT ANNIHILATOR' (1995) and 'SOUNDTRACKS FOR THE BLIND' (1996) continued in a similarly (relatively) accessible vein although the latter marked their ahem, SWAN(S)-song as GIRA and JARBOE decided the project had reached its natural conclusion. Nevertheless, 1995 had proved a fruitful year for SWANS-related material as GIRA launched a book, 'The Consumer And Other Stories', through HENRY ROLLINS' publishing operation, '21/3/61' as well as his debut solo set, 'DRAINLAND'. JARBOE, meanwhile, also released a debut solo set the same year, 'SACRIFICIAL CAKE'. MICHAEL GIRA resurfaced in 1998 with his BODYLOVERS project (including other SWANS as well as MINISTRY and ULTRA VIVID SCENE members) and issued the 'NUMBER ONE OF THREE' set. In 1999 with his ANGELS OF LIGHT project (featuring KURT RALSKE, BILL RIEFLIN, LARRY MULLINS, PHIL PULEO, etc.). They have since delivered a string of acoustic-biased but powerful sets, 'NEW MOTHER' (1999), 'HOW I LOVED YOU' (2001) and 'WE WERE ALIVE!' (2002).

Album rating: FILTH (*6) / COP (*7) / GREED (*6) / HOLY MONEY (*6) / CHILDREN OF THE GOD (*7) / FEEL GOOD NOW (*6) / THE BURNING WORLD (*6) / WHITE LIGHT FROM THE MOUTH OF INFINITY (*7) / THE GREAT ANNIHILATOR (*6) / SOUNDTRACKS FOR THE BLIND (*5) Angels Of Light: NEW MOTHER (*6) / HOW I LOVED YOU (*7) / WE WERE ALIVE! (*5)

MICHAEL GIRA – vocals (ex-LITTLE CRIPPLES) / **ROLI MOSSIMAN** – piano, percussion / **NORMAN WESTBURG** – guitar / **HARRY CROSBY** – bass / **JONATHAN KANE** – drums, percussion

Zensor   Labour
1982.   (7"ep) **EP #1**
– Speak / Laugh / Sensitive skin / Take advantage. *(UK-iss.Sep90 on 'Young God'; YGEP 001)*

Zensor   Neutral
1983.   (lp) *<ND 02>* **FILTH**
– Stay here / Big strong boss / Blackout / Power for power / Freak / Right wrong / Thank you / Weakling / Gang. *(UK-iss.Sep90 on 'Young God' cd+=/c/lp; YGCD/YGMC/YGLP 1) – Speak / Laugh / Sensitive skin / Take advantage. (re-iss. Sep90 on 'Young God' lp/c; YG LP/CD 001) (cd re-iss. Aug94 on 'Sky'; SKY 75061CD)*

K.422   P.V.C.
— **IVAN NAHEM** – drums; repl. JONATHAN who joined The HOOD
Nov 84.   (lp) *(KCC 001)* **COP**
– Half life / Job / Why hide / Clayman / I crawled / Raping a slave / Your property / Cop / Butcher / Thug / Young god / This is mine. *(cd-iss. Jan89 ; KCCCD 001)*
Feb 85.   (12"ep) *(KDE 12-1)* **I CRAWLED / RAPING A SLAVE. / YOUNG GOD / THIS IS MINE**
Jan 86.   (12") *(KDE 12-2)* **TIME IS MONEY (BASTARD). / SEALED IN SKIN / TIME IS MONEY (mix)**
Mar 86.   (lp) *(KCC 2)* **GREED**
– Time is money (bastard) / Money is flesh / Another you / Greed.

— **JARBOE** – keyboards, vox; repl. MOSSIMAN who formed WISEBLOOD
Sep 86.   (lp) *(KCC 3)* **HOLY MONEY**
– A hanging / You need me / Fool / A screw (holy money) / Another you / Money is flesh / Coward / A screw (mix) / Black mail / A screw. *(cd-iss. Feb88 +=; KCCCD 3) – GREED*
Sep 86.   (12") *(KDE 3-12)* **A SCREW (HOLY MONEY). / BLACKMAIL / A SCREW**
Nov 86.   (d-lp) **PUBLIC CASTRATION IS A GOOD IDEA (live)**
– Money is flesh / Fool / A screw / Anything for you / Coward / A hanging / Stupid child / Another you. *<cd-iss. Jul99 on 'Thirsty Ear'; 57071>*

— **TED PARSONS** – drums + **ALGYS 'AL' KIZYS** – bass; repl. NAHEM + CROSBY who both formed OF CABBAGES AND KINGS (they issued a few releases, mainly an eponymous set plus the 'FACE' album in '88.

Product Inc   Caroline
Aug 87.   (7") *(PROD 16)* **NEW MIND. / I'LL SWALLOW YOU**
(12"+=) *(12PROD 16)* – Damn you to hell.
Oct 87.   (d-lp/c)(cd) *(33/C PROD 17)(PRODCD 17) <CAROL 1346-1/-4/-2>* **CHILDREN OF GOD**
– New mind / In my garden / Sex god sex / Blood and honey / Like a drug / You're not real, girl / Beautiful child / Trust me / Blackmail / Real love. *(cd+=)* – Our love lies.
Jun 88.   (7"red) *(PROD 23)* **LOVE WILL TEAR US APART. / TRUST ME**
(12"+=/cd-s+=) *(PROD 23 T/C)* – ('A'-Black version) / New mind (purple version).
(12"red+=) *(PROD 23B)* – Our love lies.

Love One   not iss.
Aug 88.   (d-lp) *(LOVE ONE)* **FEEL GOOD NOW**
– Intro / New mind / Blood and honey / Trust me / Willy in Ravensburg / Sex god sex / Various audience tricks / Like a drug / Beautiful child / Blackmail / Children of God / Beautiful reprise – The town and country backstab cowardice / Thank you / Various audience members / Hello to our friends / Blind love / Thank you, goodbye, good luck.

— guests incl. **STEVEN** – bass + **VINNY** – drums repl. ALGYS + TED

M.C.A.   not iss.
Apr 89.   (7") *(MCA 1322)* **SAVED. / NO CRUEL ANGEL**
(12"+=/cd-s+=) *(MCAT/DMCAT 1332)* – See you more.
May 89.   (lp/c/cd) *(MCG/MCGC/DMCG 6047)* **THE BURNING WORLD**
– The river that runs with love won't run dry / Can't find my way home / Mona Lisa, Mother Earth / (She's a) Universal emptiness / Saved / I remember who you are / Jane Mary, cry one tear / See no more / God damn the sun.
Aug 89.   (7") *(MCA 1347)* **CAN'T FIND MY WAY HOME. / UNIVERSAL EMPTINESS**
(12"+=/12"g-f+=)(cd-s+=) *(MCAT/+G 1347)(DMCAT 1347)* – Was he ever alive?
Nov 89.   (12"/cd-s) **SAVED. / SEE NO MORE (acoustic) / NO CRUEL ANGEL**

— w/ guests **ANTON FIER** (GOLDEN PALOMINOS) / **CLINTON STEELE** (MARY MY HOPE) / **HAHN ROWE** (HUGO LARGO)

Young God   not iss.
Apr 91.   (cd/c/d-lp) *(YG CD/MC/LP 003)* **WHITE LIGHT FROM THE MOUTH OF INFINITY**
– Better than you / Power and sacrifice / You know nothing / Song for dead time / Will we survive / Love will save you / Failure / Song for the sun / Miracle of love / When she breathes / Why are we alive? / The most unfortunate lie. *(cd re-iss. Aug94 on 'Sky'; SKY 75060CD)*
Nov 91.   (cd/c/lp) *(YG CD/MC/LP 004)* **BODY TO BODY, JOB TO JOB**
(compilation of live & out takes from 1982-85)
– I'll cry for you / Red sheet / Loop 33 / Your game / Seal it over / Whore / We'll hang out for that / Half life / Loop 21 / Get out / Job / Loop 1 / Mother, my body disgusts me / Cop / Only I can hear, only I can touch / Thug. *(cd re-iss. Aug94 on 'Sky'; SKY 75063CD)*
Feb 92.   (cd/c/lp) *(YG CD/MC/LP 005)* **LOVE OF LIFE**
– Love of life / The golden boy that was swallowed by the sea / The other side of the world / Her / The sound of freedom / Amnesia / Identity / In the eyes of nature / She crys / God loves America / No cure for the lonely. *(cd re-iss. Aug94 on 'Sky'; SKY 75064CD)*
Apr 92.   (12") **LOVE OF LIFE (M. Gira remix). / AMNESIA (Martin Bisi re mix)**
(cd-s+=) – Picture of Maryanne.

Young God   Dog Gone
Oct 92.   (cd/c/lp) *(YG CD/MC/LP 007) <5160>* **OMNISCENCE**   Jan93
– Mother's milk / Pow r sac / Will serve / Her / Black eyed dog / Amnesia / Love of life / (----) / The other side of the world / Rutting / God loves America / Omnipotent. *(cd re-iss. Aug94 on 'Sky'; SKY 75160CD)*

Young God   Invisible
Jan 95.   (cd/d-lp) *(YG CD/LP 009) <INV 35CD>* **THE GREAT ANNIHILATOR**
– In / I am the sun / She lives! / Celebrity lifestyle / Mother, father / Blood promise / Mind / Body / Light / Sound / My buried child / Warm / Alcohol the seed / Killing for company / Mother's milk / Where does a body end / Telepathy / The great annihilator / Out. *(cd re-iss. Jan02; YG 18CD)*
Aug 96.   (10") *(ART 01)* **ANIMUS. / FAILURE**
(above issued on 'Arts & Commerce')

Young God   Atavistic
Oct 96.   (d-cd) *(YGCD 010) <61959>* **SOUNDTRACKS FOR THE BLIND**
– Red velvet corridor / I was a prisoner in your skull / Helpless child / Live through me / Yumyab killers / Beautiful days / Volcano / Mellothumb / All lined up / Surrogate 2 / How they suffer / Animus / Red velvet wound / Sound / Her mouth is filled with honey / Bloodsection / Jypogirl / Minus something / Empathy / I love you this much / YRP / Fans lament / Secret friends / Final sac / YRP 2 / Surrogate drone. *(re-iss. Feb99 on 'Atavistic'; ALP 59CD) (re-iss. Oct01; same)*

— disbanded in '97

– compilations, etc. –

Nov 92.   (cd) *K.422; (KCC 001CD)* **COP / YOUNG GOD**
(re-iss. Aug94 on 'Sky'; SKY 75068CD)
Nov 92.   (cd) *K.422; (KCC 002CD)* **GREED / HOLY MONEY**
(re-iss. Aug94 on 'Sky'; SKY 75069CD)
Jun 96.   (cd) *World Service; (RTD 1573140-2)* **DIE TUR IST ZU**
– Liget's breath / Hilfios kind / Ich sehe die alle in einer reihe / Y.R.P. / You know everything / M-F / Sound section.
Jan 97.   (cd) *Atavistic; <(ALP 57CD)>* **KILL THE CHILD (live)**   Mar96
Jan 97.   (cd) *Atavistic; <(ALP 58CD)>* **REAL LOVE**   Mar96
Feb 98.   (d-cd) *Relapse; <(RR 6996-2)>* **SWANS ARE DEAD (live '95-'97)**
Feb 99.   (d-cd) *Atavistic; <(ALP 76CD)>* **CHILDREN OF GOD / WORLD OF SKIN**
Apr 99.   (d-cd) *Young God; <(FR 002)>* **SWANS AND VARIOUS FAILURES 1988-1992**
Jun 99.   (d-cd) *Thirsty Ear; <(THI 57059-2)>* **COP / YOUNG GOD / GREED / HOLY MONEY**
Mar 00.   (d-cd) *Young God; <(YG 11CD)>* **FILTH / BODY TO BODY, JOB TO JOB**

SKIN

— an off-shoot duo of **MICHAEL GIRA + JARBOE + NORMAN WESTBERG, HARRY CROSBY, RONALDO GONZALES**

Product Inc.   not iss.
Mar 87.   (7") *(7PROD 3)* **1000 YEARS. / MY OWN HANDS**
(12"+=) *(12PROD 3)* –

Mar 87. (lp/cd) *(33/CD PROD 4)* **BLOOD, WOMEN, ROSES**
– 1000 years / Cry me a river / We'll fall apart / Still a child / The man I loved (with LESTER YOUNG) / Red rose / Blood on your hands. *(re-iss. Jun89 d-lp; PROD 33-025)* – SHAME, HUMILITY, REVENGE *(cd+=)* – My own hands / 1000 years (remix) / Girl: come out (remix).
Jun 87. (7") *(PROD 6)* **GIRL: COME OUT. / ('A'dub version)**
May 88. (lp/cd) *(33/CD PROD 11)* **SHAME, HUMILITY, REVENGE**
– Nothing without you / Everything at once / Breathing water / The center of your heart / Cold bed / 24 hours / Turned to stone / One small sacrifice. *(cd+=)* – I wanna be your dog.
— now w/ **ROLI MOSSIMANN / CLINTON STEELE / TONY MAIMONE**

Young God / not iss.

Oct 90. (cd/lp; as WORLD OF SKIN) *(YG CD/MC/LP 002)* **10 SONGS FOR ANOTHER WORLD**
– Please remember me / Drink to me only with thine eyes / The child's right / Everything for Maria / I'll go there, take me home / Black eyed dog / A parasite and other memories / Dream dream / You'll never forget / Mystery of faith. *(cd re-iss. Aug94 on 'Sky'; SKY 75062CD)*

JARBOE

Hyperium / not iss.

Sep 92. (cd/lp) *(3910002-2/-1)* **THIRTEEN MASKS**
(cd re-iss. Aug94 on 'Sky'; SKY 75065CD)

Young God / not iss.

Jul 95. (cd) *(YGCD 008)* **SACRIFICIAL CAKE**
– Lavender girl / Ode to V / Shimmer 1 / My buried child / Not logical / Spiral staircase / Yum yab / Surgical savior / Cache toi / Tragic seed / Troll lullaby / Deflowered / The body lover / Shimmer 2 / Act 3 / Troll.

Cold Spring / not iss.

Jun 96. (7") *(CSR 11P)* **CACHE TOI. /**

MICHAEL GIRA

Sub Rosa / not iss.

Jun 95. (cd) *(SR 086)* **DRAINLAND**
– You see through me / Where does your body begin? / I see them all lined up / Unreal / Fan letter / Your naked body / Low life form / If you . . . / Why I ate my wife / Blind.

ANGELS OF LIGHT

MICHAEL GIRA + a plethora of musicians (see biog for some)

Young God / Atavistic

Apr 98. (d-cd; as The BODY LOVERS) *(FR 001) <ATA 103>* **NUMBER ONE OF THREE**
– (untitled tracks)
Apr 99. (cd) *(FR 003) <YG 08CD>* **NEW MOTHER**
– Fragment / Praise your name / New mother / Angels of light / Inner female / This is mine / Shame / Intermission / The man with the silver tongue / Real person / Forever yours / How we end / The garden hides the jewel / Not alone / Song for my father / His entropic highness / Fear of death.

Young God / Young God

Mar 01. (cd) *<(YG 16CD)>* **HOW I LOVED YOU**
– Evangeline / Untitled love song / My true body / Jennifer's sorry / Song for Nico / New city in the future / My suicide / New York girls / Public embarrassment blues / Two women.
2002. (ltd-cd) **WE WERE ALIVE! (live)**

SWIMMING POOL Q'S

Formed: Athens, Georgia, USA . . . 1978 by songwriter JEFF CALDER, guitarist BOB ELSEY, bassist PETE JARKINAS and drummer ROBERT SCHMID, although things really got underway when co-vocalist to-be, ANNE RICHMOND BOSTON, joined (as a joke initially!). Yet another bunch of college friendly folk-jangle pop/rockers to be thrown up by the fertile Athens music scene, the embarrassingly badly named SWIMMING POOL Q'S saw out the 70's with a US-only debut 45, 'RAT BAIT'. Subsequently signing to 'D.B.' (also home to PYLON), the quintet surfaced in summer '81 with a punningly-titled debut long-player, 'THE DEEP END'. After three years in the Southern wilderness, the SPQ's returned with a new rhythm section (J.E. GARNETT and BILLY BURTON) and a major label deal with 'A&M'. The resulting eponymous set was a more polished affair, CALDER's harmonies coming across like a presumably unintentional hybrid of LINDSAY BUCKINGHAM and A-HA backed by a less countrified GUADALCANAL DIARY. A further set, 'BLUE TOMORROW' (1986), met with a less than enthusiastic response, the group immediately dropped as a result. CALDER and Co then altered their gameplan with a 12" EP, 'FIRING SQUAD FOR GOD', before signing off in fine style with a swansong album for 'Capitol', 'WORLD WAR TWO POINT FIVE' (1989). CALDER would re-emerge with his band the SUPREME COURT, while ANNE settled down with her husband, ROB GAL (of The COOLIES).

Album rating: THE DEEP END (*4) / THE SWIMMING POOL Q'S (*7) / BLUE TOMORROW (*5) / WORLD WAR TWO POINT FIVE (*6)

JEFF CALDER – vocals, guitar / **ANNE RICHMOND BOSTON** – vocals, keyboards / **BOB ELSEY** – guitar / **PETE JARKINAS** – bass / **ROBERT SCHMID** – drums

not iss. / Clorinated

1979. (7") *<SPQR 079V>* **RAT BAIT. / THE A-BOMB WOKE ME UP**

Armageddon / D.B.

Jun 81. (lp) *(ARM 12) <DB 55>* **THE DEEP END**
– Little misfit / Big fat tractor / Stick in my hand / The A-bomb woke me up / Rat bait / Restless youth / Stock car sin / Walk like a chicken / Black bus / Overheated / I like to take orders from you. *<cd-iss. 2001 +=; DB 55CD>* – Model trains (are better than rock and roll) / Tussle (I wear glasses) / Stingray / White collar drifter / Home-in / Working in the nut plant / Walk like a chicken / Going through the motions / Short stuff / 1789 / Building with a clock on top / I'm a Q.

— **J.E. GARNETT** – bass; repl. PETE
— **BILLY BURTON** – drums; repl. ROBERT

A&M / A&M

Jul 85. (7") *(AM 263)* **THE BELLS RING. / PURPLE RIVERS**
(12"+=) *(AMY 263)* – Celestion.
Jul 85. (lp/c) *(AMA/AMC 5012)* **THE SWIMMING POOL Q'S**   Nov84
– The bells ring / Pull back my spring / Purple rivers / The knave / Some new highway / Just property / Silver slipper / She's bringing down the poison / Celestion / Sacrificial altar.
Feb 86. (7") *(AM 300)* **PRETTY ON THE INSIDE. / BLUE TOMORROW**
(w/ free 7") – PURPLE RIVERS. / THE BELLS RING
1986. (lp/cd) *<395107-1/-2>* **BLUE TOMORROW**
– Now I'm looking about now / She's lookin' real good (when she's lookin') / Pretty on the inside / Laredo radio / Wreck around / More than one Heaven / Corruption / Blue tomorrow / A dream in gray / Big fat tractor.
1987. (12"ep) *<DB 87>* **THE FIRING SQUAD FOR GOD**

not iss. / Capitol

1989. (lp/c/cd) *<C1/C4/C2 91068>* **WORLD WAR TWO POINT FIVE**
– 1943 A.D. / I'd rather feel this pain (than be nowhere) / You don't wanna grow up to be like that / In the place of milk and honey / The lord of wiggling / The common years / Broken pieces / Sweet reward / More often that never / Good money gone bad / The firing squad for God.

— disbanded later in '89; ANNE concentrated on her family life with hubby, ROB GAL (of The COOLIES). She returned to recording in the 90's (aged 36), releasing an album, 'THE BIG HOUSE OF TIME', co-written with CALDER and her husband. It also contained a handful of cover versions:- LEARNING HOW TO LOVE YOU (John Hiatt) / WHEN YOU DANCE I CAN REALLY LOVE (Neil Young) / DARLING BE HOME SOON (Lovin' Spoonful) / BANKS OF THE OHIO (Welsh-Farmer).

TALL DWARFS

Formed: Dunedin, New Zealand . . . early 80's by CHRIS KNOX, who had previously initiated what was possibly the first ever NZ punk act, The ENEMY. The latter outfit quickly earned a reputation but never actually released any records, subsequently evolving into TOY LOVE with a line-up of KNOX, ALEC BATHGATE, JANE WALKER, MIKE DOOLEY and PAUL KEAN. A more commercially viable New Wave-biased unit, TOY LOVE were signed to the New Zealand arm of 'WEA' and made their debut with the critically acclaimed 'REBEL' single in summer '79. While generally acknowledged as being a pivotal influence on the coming decade's proliferation of NZ bands, KNOX and Co failed to make much headway outside of their homeland; a further single, 'DON'T ASK ME', and a solitary eponymous album were generally regarded as being disappointing and unrepresentative of the band's infamous live show (wherein KNOX had taken to slashing himself in true masochistic rock'n'roll style). Following a final independently released single, 'BRIDE OF FRANKENSTEIN', TOY LOVE were finally divorced, buckling under the weight of a punishing touring schedule. It didn't take KNOX and BATHGATE long to surface with a new outfit, TALL DWARFS, regularly cited as the grandaddy of all the 'Flying Nun' bands. The latter label became home to the band in 1982, prior to which the duo had released the 'THREE SONGS' EP. While DOOLEY had also initially been part of the set-up, KNOX and BATHGATE soon pared the group down to a two-man operation, working from the most basic of home studios to complete a string of DIY EP's: 'LOUIS LOVES HIS DAILY DIP' (1982), 'CANNED MUSIC' (1983) and the Australian-only 'SLUGBUCKET HAIRY BREATH MONSTER' (1984). These releases established the trademark TALL DWARFS sound, a melange of retro garage, psychedelia and melodic punk buried in droning fuzz guitar with occasional forays into acoustic pop. It served the band well over the course of the 80's although they didn't actually release a full length album until the turn of the decade. 1985 had seen the release of mini-set, 'THAT'S THE SHORT AND LONG OF IT', while two years later, 'HELLO CRUEL WORLD' served as a career retrospective for UK fans. The band's bonafide debut album, 'WEEVILLE' finally arrived in 1990, by which time KNOX's songwriting had begun to take on a less confrontational hue. A true bedroom warrior, KNOX had already completed a string of domestic solo releases including 'SONGS FOR CLEANING GUPPIES' (1983) and 'SEIZURE' (1989). He maintained his prolific release schedule into the 90's with the likes of 'CROAKER' (1991) and 'POLYFOTO, DUCK SHAPED PAIN & GUM' (1994), the latter album one of the few to gain a full UK release. While showcasing his consistently thought-provoking lyrics and sly humour, KNOX's solo material tended, if anything, to be more self-indulgent than TALL DWARFS although the likes of 'FORK SONGS' (1992) and the more recent 'STUMPY: THE ALBUM' (1997) were hardly easy listening.

Album rating: Toy Love: TOY LOVE (*4) / Tall Dwarfs: HELLO CRUEL WORLD compilation (*6) / WEEVILLE (*6) / FORK SONGS (*4) / THE SHORT & SICK OF IT compilation (*6) / 3 E.P.'s compilation (*6) / STUMPY: THE ALBUM (*5) / 50 FLAVOURS OF GLUE (*5) / Chris Knox: SONGS FOR CLEANING GUPPIES mini (*5) / MONK III-AD 1987 (*4) / NOT GIVEN LIGHTLY (*5) / SEIZURE (*6) / CROAKER (*6) / POLYFOTO, DUCK SHAPED PAIN & GUM (*6) / SONGS OF YOU & ME (*7) / YES!! (*5) / ALMOST mini collection (*4) / BEAT (*4) / Alec Bathgate: GOLD LAME (*5)

TOY LOVE

CHRIS KNOX (b. 2 Sep'52, Invercargill, NZ) – vocals, guitar (ex-ENEMY) / **ALEC BATHGATE** – guitar (ex-ENEMY) / **JANE WALKER** – keyboards / **MIKE DOOLEY** – drums (ex-ENEMY) / **PAUL KEAN** – bass

		Elektra	not iss.
Jul 79.	(7") **REBEL. / SQUEEZE**	–	– NewZ
		Deluxe	not iss.
Jan 80.	(7") **DON'T ASK ME. / SHEEP**	–	– Austra
Jun 80.	(lp) **TOY LOVE**	–	– Austra

– I don't mind / Swimming pool / Death rehearsal / Bride of Frankenstein / Toy Love song / Photographs of naked ladies / Bedroom / The crunch / Ain't it nice / Cold meat / Don't catch fire / Green walls / Pull down the shades / Frogs / Fast ostrich.

| 1980. | (7") **BRIDE OF FRANKENSTEIN. / AMPUTEE SONG / GOOD OLD JOE** | – | – Austra |

— two live CD collections, 'LIVE AT THE COOK' – VOLUMES 1 & 2 were issued in NZ in 2000

TALL DWARFS

CHRIS KNOX – vocals, guitar, keyboards, bass, percussion, etc / **ALEC BATHGATE** – guitar, vocals / **MIKE DOOLEY** (soon repl. by drum loops – he joined SNAPPER much later

		Furtive	not iss.
Jul 81.	(12"ep) (FUR 1) **THREE SONGS EP**	–	– NewZ

– Nothing's gonna happen / Luck or loveliness / All my hollowness to you. (re-iss. 1984 on 'Flying Nun'; FNOTI)

		Flying Nun	not iss.
1982.	(12"ep) (FNWEE 1) **LOUIS LIKES HIS DAILY DIP**	–	– NewZ

– Louis the first / Maybe / Pictures on the floor / Paul's place / Clover / Song of the silents / Louis the second.

| 1983. | (12"ep) (FNTIN 1) **CANNED MUSIC** | – | – NewZ |

– Canopener / Beauty / This room is wrong / Walking home / Turning brown & torn on two / Woman / Shade for today.

| 1984. | (12"ep) (FNSLUG 001) **SLUGBUCKET HAIRYBREATH MONSTER** | – | Austra |

– The brain that wouldn't die / I've left memories behind / Phil disease (day 1) / Phil's disease (day 4) / Crush.

— added musicians on various strings, etc

| 1985. | (12"ep) (FNLONG 1) **THAT'S THE SHORT AND LONG OF IT** | – | – NewZ |

– Nothing's going to happen / Nothing's going to stop it / The hills are alive / Clover / Pretty poison / Sleet / Burning blue / Carpetorabber / Gone to the worms / Woman / Get outta the grange / Scrapbook.

| 1986. | (12"ep) (FNSICK 001) **THROW A SICKIE** | – | – NewZ |

– Underhand / Road & hedgehog / Attack of the munchies / Come inside / The universality of neighbourliness / The big dive / No place / And other kinds / Farewell. (cd-iss. 1992 as 'THE SHORT AND SICK OF IT' +=; FNCD 199)

		Flying Nun	Homestead
Dec 87.	(lp) (FNE 15) <HMS 113> **HELLO CRUEL WORLD** (compilation 1981-1984 EP's)		

(NZ-iss.1990; FN 113) <US cd-iss. 1995; same>

| 1989. | (12"ep) (FNE 27 – FN 098) **DOGMA** | | |

– Lurlene Bayliss / Waltz of the good husband / The slide / Cant / Dog / Missed again.

| 1990. | (lp/c/cd) (FN/+C/CD 166) <HMS 143> **WEEVILLE** | | |

– Lag / What more / Breath / Skin of my teeth / Pirovette / Licky / Bodies / Mr. Brocolli / Lie / Winer / Rorschach / Tip of my tongue / Ozone / Hallelujah boy.

| Jan 92. | (cd) (FN 218) **FORK SONGS** | – | – NewZ |

– Dare to tread / We bleed love / Wings / Skirt / Thought disorder / Small talk / Lowlands / Life is strange / Daddy / All is fine / Two humans / Oatmeal / Boys / Think small.

| Apr 94. | (3x12"lp/cd) (FN/+CD 296) **3 E.P.'S** (compilation) | | |

– For all the waiters in the world / Entropy / What goes up / High rise / Starry eyed and wholly brained / Folding / Neusyland / Two dozen lousy hours / Bob's yer uncle / More 54 / Archaeuptery / Ain't it funny / Senile dementia / Bee to honey / Post modern deconstructivist blues / Kid stuff / Selfdeluded dreamboy (in a mess) / Our advice to you.

— added **IVAN MUNJAK** – drum loop

		Flying Nun	Flying Nun
Feb 97.	(cd) <(FNCD 384)> **STUMPY: THE ALBUM**		

– Swan song / They like you undone / Green green grass of someone else's home / Severed head of Julio / Crocodile / Macrame / Song of the jealous lover / Honey, I'm home / Jesus the beast / Cruising with Cochran / Things / Mojave / Box of aroma / Ghost town / Deep-fried / Disorientated boogie / And that's not all!! / Pull the thread (and unravel me) / Dessicated / Albumen / Two minds / Up.

| Jan 00. | (cd-ep) **GLUEY GLUEY & 'THE EAR-FRIEND'** | – | – NewZ |

– Gluey gluey / Ice breaker / Fragile / The ear friend (trailer) / Foolish hearts / The ear friend.

| Jan 00. | (cd) (DFN 412) **50 FLAVOURS OF GLUE** | – | – NewZ |

– Gluey gluey / The communion / If I were a piece of shit / Like someone else / Baby / The fatal flaw of the new / The ugly mire of deep held feelings / Endure / The future see / Just do it! / Mistaken (once again) / Fatty fowl in gravy stew / Round these walls / Fragile / Totalitarian chant of freedom / Smacked / Over the hill.

CHRIS KNOX

		Flying Nun	not iss.
1983.	(m-lp) (FNME 1) **SONGS FOR CLEANING GUPPIES**	–	– NewZ

– A shadow's tale / The room is going around in circles / Nostalgia's no excuse / Inside / The man with the cardboard guitar / Jane and John / Photographs / Row, row, row, row, row, row your boat / Oh!! happiness!! / Over and out. (cd-iss. 2000 +=;) – More or less (lethargy) / Jesus loves you / Me and the insects / Use at your leisure / Sandfly / Everybody wishes they were someone else / Backing away / Song of the silents / 1954 / Justification song.

| 1987. | (c) **MONK III-AD 1987** | – | – NewZ |

(above issued on 'Walking Monk')

| 1989. | (lp) (FN 125 – FNE 30) **SEIZURE** | – | – German |

– The face of fashion / The woman inside of me / Statement of intent / Filling me / Not given lightly / Break! / Uncle Tom's cabin / Wanna! / And I will cry / Rapist / Grand mal / Voyeur / Honesty's not enough / My dumb luck / Ache. (cd-iss. Jan00; DFN 125)

| 1989. | (m-lp) (FN 127) **NOT GIVEN LIGHTLY / GUPPIPLUS** | – | – NewZ |

– Not given lightly / SONGS FOR CLEANING GUPPIES (8 out 10 tracks). (UK-iss.Nov98 of 'NOT GIVEN LIGHTLY' on 'Curveball' 12"/cd-s; CURVE 3/+CD)

1990.	(7"/12") (FN 152/153) **NOT GIVEN LIGHTLY. /**	–	– NewZ
1990.	(10") (FN 155) **SONG FOR 1990**	–	– NewZ
1991.	(lp/c/cd) (FN/+C/CD 165) **CROAKER**	–	– NewZ

– Dunno much about life . . . but I know how to breathe / Liberal backlash angst (the excuse) / Lapse / Citric acid / Growth spurt / A song of the only child / Meat / Once when alone / Plenty / Hp5 / Coloured / Song of the good wife / Panic!

		Flying Nun	Communion
Apr 93.	(cd) <COMM 28> **MEAT** (compilation)	–	

– (SEIZURE + CROAKER albums; omits some tracks)

| Mar 94. | (cd) (FNCD 249) <COMM 34> **POLYFOTO, DUCK-SHAPED PAIN & "GUM"** | | Dec93 |

– Polyfoto / Split / Inside story / Replace me / (And you think it all started with) Trim / Glide / Under the influence / Not a victim / Psmosis / Get a life / Heart

TALL DWARFS (cont)

failure / Letter from L.A. / God sez "No!" to cosmetic surgery / Blameless / Outer skin / Intensive care / Honey stung paws / Mum's the word / View from the bridge / Space / Self pity's just a name for feeling low.

Jul 94. (7") *(FN 266)* **UNDER THE INFLUENCE. / STASIS** *Flying Nun / Caroline*

Feb 95. (7"ep/cd-ep) *(FN/+CD 316)* **ONE FELL SWOOP**
– One fell swoop / Giving her away / S.O.S. / Shapnel / Mother.

Apr 95. (cd/c) *(FNCD/FNMC 313) <CAROL 1788>* **SONGS OF YOU & ME** May95
– Vol au vent / Lamini ol the craslie pool / Song to welcome the onset of maturity / Belly up and grinning / Half man – half mole / Brave / Sympathy for the cripple / Limited liabilty / Giving her away / Chemicals are our friends / Young female caucasian / Rust / Instant mashed potato 2 / Mirror mirror / Open / Hubba-hubba has been hoot / One fell swoop / Nothing comes clear / Dixie / Instant mashed potato.

Sep 97. (cd) *(FN 400)* **YES!!**
– Joy of sex / Sweaty hide of circumstance / Pibroch / Backstab boogie / Ballad of a victim of the economic... / Gold / Tantamount to treasury / Uncoupled / Engaged / Uncertainty people / Penultimatum / Almost tempted / Flaky pastry / Ndidi.

not iss.   Thirsty Ear

Aug 00. (cd) *<57090>* **BEAT**
– It's love / The man in the crowd / My only friend / The hell of it / When I have left this mortal coil / Everyone's cool / The pulse below the ear / What do we do for love? / I wanna look like Darcy Clay / Denial song / Becoming something other / Ghost / Laughter.

– compilations, etc. –

Jun 99. (m-cd) *Dark Beloved Cloud; <DBC 220>* **ALMOST** (out-takes 1989-1995)
– Don't worry, B major / Pesticide / The song of the would-be Messiah / Tina / Conspicuous consumption / The emperor's new status / Maxillofacial homograft / The counsellor's song / Goodbye to Greg / The grip.

ALEC BATHGATE

Flying Nun   not iss.

1995.   (7") *(FN 333)* **PET HATES. / HAPPY HOUND** NewZ

Oct 96. (lp/cd) *(FN/+CD 353)* **GOLD LAME**
– Win your love / Ain't it strange (our aching hearts) / Carl's arrows / Happy head / Pet hates / Slow parade (won't fly) / Your heavy dream (won't fly) / Run / Gold lame / Love, love, love / No taxi to Hoboken / Happy hound / Friday in the ground / Train to Skaville / Life ain't easy (when you're dead) / Monkey puzzle.

TALULAH GOSH

Formed: Oxford, England ... early '86 by PETER MOMTCHILOFF, PEBBLES (aka ELIZABETH PRICE), MARIGOLD (aka AMELIA FLETCHER), her brother MATHEW FLETCHER and ROBERT PURSEY, the latter being replaced by CHRIS SCOTT. Named after the headline from a CLARE GROGAN interview in the NME, TALULAH GOSH hit upon the novel idea of simultaneously releasing two singles as their debut. The songs in question, 'BEATNIK BOY' and 'STEAMING TRAIN', appeared in late '86 on Edinburgh label, '53rd & 3rd', both climbing high in the indie charts. Latterly easy pickings for the music press, this asexual looking boy-girl outfit were part of a wider indie anorak brigade reminiscent of a pastel VELVET UNDERGROUND or a moody SHANGRI-LA'S. With PEBBLES forming The CAROUSEL and EITHNE FARRY joining soon after, TG released an eponymous single in Spring '87 as a primer for their ironically titled debut album, 'ROCK LEGENDS VOL.69'. Early the following year, the English version of The PASTELS delivered another two 45's hot on the heels of each other, namely 'BRINGING UP BABY' (from the EP 'WHERE'S THE COUGAR MATEY?') and 'TESTCARD GIRL', although they disbanded soon after. AMELIA re-emerged with a solo single, 'CAN YOU KEEP A SECRET?', subsequently guesting for The WEDDING PRESENT and The POOH STICKS. In the early 90's, the band were to resurface under a different moniker, HEAVENLY, with more or less the same line-up including original TG member, PURSEY. Signed to home of twee, 'Sarah' records, the band released a series of singles which suggested the band had come of age at last. A mini-set, 'HEAVENLY VS. SATAN', appeared in '91, while a debut album proper 'LE JARDIN DE HEAVENLY' arrived in the summer of '92. Not exactly the most ambitious of bands, these perennial underachievers nevertheless warmed the hearts of their fans with further releases throughout the early to mid 90's. Tragically, in 1997, MATHEW FLETCHER committed suicide and the band decided HEAVENLY would change their name. In 1998, AMELIA and Co (CATHY ROGERS, PETER MOMTCHILOFF, ROB PURSEY and DJ DOWNFALL) were back with a new outfit, MARINE RESEARCH, guaranteeing twee-pop never left the indie scene. Released on the iconic 'K' records, 'SOUNDS FROM THE GULF STREAM' (1999), was their only long-player. Once again a personnel change prompted a moniker alteration. TENDER TRAP was chosen as AMELIA (who'd moonlighted with SPORTIQUE), ROB and DOWNFALL carried on the twee-pop tradition via excellent comeback set, 'FILM MOLECULES' (2002). • **HEAVENLY covered:** NOUS NE SOMMES PAS DES ANGES (Serge Gainsbourg) / YOU TORE ME DOWN (Flamin' Groovies) / ART SCHOOL (Jam).

Album rating: ROCK LEGENDS VOL.69 (*5) / THEY'VE SCOFFED THE LOT compilation (*7) / Heavenly: HEAVENLY VS. SATAN mini (*6) / LE JARDIN DE HEAVENLY (*6) / OPERATION HEAVENLY (*6) / Marine Research: SOUNDS FROM THE GULF STREAM (*6) / Sportique: / Tender Trap: FILM MOLECULES (*7)

PEBBLES (b. ELIZABETH PRICE, 6 Nov'66, Bradford, England) – vocals / **MARIGOLD** (b. AMELIA FLETCHER, 1 Jan'66, London, England) – vocals, guitar / **PETER MOMTCHILOFF** – guitar / **CHRIS SCOTT** (b.31 Oct'61, Hemel Hempstead, England) – bass / **MATHEW FLETCHER** (b. 5 Nov'70, London) – drums

53rd & 3rd   not iss.

Nov 86. (7") *(AGARR 004)* **BEATNIK BOY. / MY BEST FRIEND**
Nov 86. (7") *(AGARR 005)* **STEAMING TRAIN. / JUST A DREAM**
(12"+=) *(AGARR 004-005 T)* – Beatnik boy / My best friend.

— **EITHNE FARRY** (b.21 May'65, London) – vocals; repl. PEBBLES who later formed The CAROUSEL

May 87. (7") *(AGARR 008)* **TALULAH GOSH. / DON'T GO AWAY**
(12"+=) *(AGARR 008T)* – Escalator over the hill.

Jan 88. (7") *(AGARR 014)* **BRINGING UP BABY. / THE GIRL WITH STRAWBERRY HAIR**
(12"+=) *(AGARR 014T)* **WHERE'S THE COUGAR MATEY? EP** – I can't get no satisfaction, thank God / Do you remember? / Sunny inside.

Feb 88. (7") *(AGARR 016)* **TESTCARD GIRL. / WAY OF THE WORLD**
Oct 88. (lp) *(AGAS 004)* **ROCK LEGENDS VOL.69**
– Beatnik boy / My best friend / Just a dream / Steaming train / Talulah gosh / Don't go away / Escalator over the hill / My boy says / Way of the world / Testcard girl / Bringing up baby / I can't get no satisfaction, thank God / The girl with strawberry hair. *(cd-iss. Jun91 on 'Avalanche'; ONLYCD 011)*

— split later in 1988. CHRIS and EITHNE formed SATURN 5, while PETER joined The RAZORCUTS. TG later released compilation below.

Mar 91. (lp) *Sarah; (SARAH 604)* **THEY'VE SCOFFED THE LOT** (radio sessions)

AMELIA

Fierce   not iss.

1988.   (7") **CAN YOU KEEP A SECRET? / WRAP MY ARMS AROUND HIM**

HEAVENLY

AMELIA, MATHEW, PETER + ROBERT PURSEY (b.27 May'64, Chipping Sodbury, England) – bass

Sarah   K

Feb 90. (7") *(SARAH 030)* **I FELL IN LOVE LAST NIGHT. / OVER AND OVER**
Nov 90. (7") *(SARAH 041)* **OUR LOVE IS HEAVENLY. / WRAP MY ARMS AROUND HIM**
Feb 91. (m-lp) *(SARAH 603)* **HEAVENLY VS. SATAN**
– Cool guitar boy / Boyfriend stays the same / Lemonhead boy / Shallow / Wish me gone / Don't be fooled / It's you / Stop before you say it.

— added **CATHY ROGERS** (b.29 May'68, Tatsfield, England) – keyboards, vocals

Jul 91. (7") *(SARAH 051)* **SO LITTLE DESERVE. / I'M NOT SCARED OF YOU**
Feb 92. (7") *()* **SHE SAYS. / ESCORT CRASH ON MARSTON STREET**
(above issued on 'K')

Jun 92. (lp/cd) *(SARAH 610/+CD)* **LE JARDIN DE HEAVENLY**
– Starshy / Tool / Orange corduroy dress / Different day / C is the Heavenly option / Smile / And the birds aren't singing / Sort of mine. *<US+=>* – So little deserve / I'm not scared of you.

Jul 93. (7") *(SARAH 081)* **P.U.N.K. GIRL. / HEARTS AND CROSSES**
Aug 93. (7") *(SARAH 082)* **ATTA GIRL. / DIG YOUR OWN GRAVE / SO?**
(cd-s+=) *(SARAH 082CD)* – P.U.N.K. girl / Hearts and crosses.

Jul 94. (cd-ep) *<025>* **P.U.N.K. GIRL EP**
– P.U.N.K. girl / Hearts and crosses / Atta girl / Dig your own grave / So?

Sep 94. (clear-lp) *(AGAS 623/+CD) <033>* **THE DECLINE AND FALL OF THE HEAVENLY**
– Me and my madness / Modestic / Skipjack / Itchy chin / Sacramento / Three star compartment / Sperm meets egg, so what? / She and me.

Wiiija   K

Sep 96. (7"pink) *(WIJ 58) <073>* **SPACE MANATEE. / YOU TORE ME DOWN / ART SCHOOL**
Oct 96. (cd/lp) *(WIJ CD/LP 1053) <059>* **OPERATION HEAVENLY**
– Trophy girlfriend / K-klass kisschase / Space manitee / Ben Sherman / By the way / Cut off / Nous ne sommes pas des anges / Mark angel / Fat Lenny / Snail trail / Pet monkey.

– compilations, etc. –

May 96. (d-lp/d-cd; by TALULAH GOSH) *K; (<KLP 44/+CD>)* **BACKWASH** (all material)

Elefant   not iss.

Jul 97. (cd) *(ER 1017)* **THIS IS HEAVENLY** (compilation)

MARINE RESEARCH

AMELIA FLETCHER – vocals / **PETER MOMTCHILOFF** – guitar / **CATHY ROGERS** – vocals, keyboards / **ROB PURSEY** – bass / **DJ DOWNFALL** (b. JOHN STANLEY) – drums

Where It's At Is Where You Are   not iss.

Oct 98. (7") *(WIAIWYA 7)* **QUEEN B. / Y.Y.U.B.** K   K

Feb 99. (7") **SICK & WRONG. / (other by BUILT TO SPILL)**
Jul 99. (7"/cd-s) *(KLP 104)* **PARALLEL HORIZONTAL. / ANGEL IN THE SNOW / I CONFESS**
Aug 99. (cd) *(<KLP 100>)* **SOUNDS FROM THE GULF STREAM**
– Parallel horizontal / You and a girl / Hopefulness to hopelessness / Queen B / Chucking out time / Glamour gap / At the lost and found / Venn diagram / End of the affair / Y.Y.U.B.

— the group split after above; PETE joined WOULD-BE GOODS, while AMELIA + ROB joined SPORTIQUE (alongside GREGORY WEBSTER, ex-RAZORCUTS)

TENDER TRAP

AMELIA + ROB + DJ

	Fortuna Pop	not iss.
May 02. (7"m) *(FPOP 38)* **OH KATRINA. / BADGE OF LOVE / DYSPRAXIC**	□	-
Jul 02. (7") *(<IPU 102>)* **FACE OF '73. / FIN (Downfall mix)**	□	-
Jul 02. (lp/cd) *(<KLP 126/+CD>)* **FILM MOLECULES**	□	-

– Fin / Oh Katrina / You and me / Face of '73 / That girl / Talk in song / Chemical reaction / Son of Dorian Gray / Emma / Dyspraxic / Love is red/green / Brown eyes / You are gone (so you should go). *(cd-iss.Jul02 on 'Fortuna Pop'; FPOP 40)*

TAPPI TiKARRASS (see under ⇒ BJORK)

Troy TATE

Born: Liverpool, England. His formative punk days were spent fronting CLASH-esque, Cheltenham-based outfit, INDEX, who finally got round to issuing their debut single, 'JET LAG' (although only 500 of them hit the small independent shops) in 1978. TROY left RUSSELL ELLIOTT (bass) and DAVE HOUGH (drums) to carry on without him having taken the opportunity to join ex-REZILLOS members in the outfit, SHAKE. He stayed for two 45's, 'INVASION OF THE GAMMA MEN' and 'WOAH YEAH!', the last of which was released around the same time as his summer '81 solo debut, 'THOMAS'. It was for his time with The TEARDROP EXPLODES, however, that TROY TATE would become best known, although his tenure was cut short even before their untimely break-up in 1983. FASHION was the next port of call for this musical mercenary, but that too lasted under a year, the man opting for a more secure solo career. Having signed to 'Rough Trade', a single, 'I DON'T KNOW WHAT LOVE IS', appeared in July '83 while the remixed version of 'THOMAS' that surfaced a year later was his first for 'Sire'. Now seven years in the business, TROY finally delivered his debut album, 'TICKET TO THE DARK', in 1984, a safe mixture of alternative pop that did little in the sales department. A follow-up, 'LIBERTY', in 1985, was, I suppose, appropriately titled as his record company set him free soon after.

Album rating: TICKET TO THE DARK (*5) / LIBERTY (*4)

TROY TATE – vocals, guitar (ex-INDEX, ex-SHAKE) / with various personnel

	Whi-Fi	not iss.
Jun 81. (7") *(WHY 3)* **THOMAS. / LONDON'S SWINGING**	□	-

—— he also joined The TEARDROP EXPLODES at this point

| Jan 82. (10"ep) *(WHY 6)* **LIFELINE (HOLD ONTO THAT). / KAMIKAZE / THOMAS** | □ | - |

—— after above, he left COPE and Co. to join FASHION, although he subsequently left them to continue his solo career

	Rough Trade	not iss.
Jul 83. (7") *(RT 134)* **I DON'T KNOW WHAT LOVE IS ANYMORE. / I'M MAD**	□	-

(12"+=) *(RTT 134)* – Lifeline.

—— his band consisted of **JON HURST** – keyboards / **PETE RIZZO** – bass / **ALI PATERSON** – drums

	Sire	not iss.
Jul 84. (7") *(W 9222)* **THOMAS. / E 209**	□	-
(12"+=) *(W 9222T)* – What cha gonna do next?		
Sep 84. (lp) *(925160-1)* **TICKET TO THE DARK**	□	-

– Party / Thomas / Love is . . . / Winning team / All the way up / Whip crack away / Safety net / House of the new breed / Lifeline / I'm not your toy.

| Jun 85. (7"/12") *(U 9043/+T)* **SORROW. / HIGH ALTITUDE** | □ | - |
| Jul 85. (lp) *(925312-1)* **LIBERTY** | □ | - |

– Sorrow / Girl on a ferry / Merry go round / High altitude / Liberty / All in a row / Tomorrow I'll be gone / Round and round / God's puppet / Airport of silence.

—— TROY retired from the music biz

TATER TOTZ (see under ⇒ REDD KROSS)

TEARDROP EXPLODES (see under ⇒ COPE, Julian)

TEENAGE FILMSTARS (see under ⇒ BALL, Edward; 70's section)

TELESCOPES

Formed: Burton-Upon-Trent, Staffordshire, England . . . 1987 by STEPHEN LAWRIE, JOANNA DORAN, DAVE FITZGERALD, ROBERT BROOKS and DOMINIC DILLON. Their first release in '88 was actually a track on a shared flexidisc with LOOP, 'FOREVER CLOSE YOUR EYES'. The following year, 'Cheree' also issued a further couple, 'KICK THE WALL' and '7th DISASTER', before US label, 'What Goes On' took over the reins. A debut album, 'TASTE' (1989), carried on in their trademark JESUS & MARY CHAIN/RIDE guitar fusion, although their label subsequently went belly up. Left in debt to the tune of a 5-figure sum, ALAN McGEE of 'Creation' duly bailing them out by buying out the rights for their songs. A clutch of singles – including minor hit 'FLYING' – previewed a long-awaited bonafide follow-up album in 1992, 'UNTITLED'; EDWARD BALL (ex-TELEVISION PERSONALITIES) guested on the set which showed them mellowing towards a more harmonious, archetypally 'Creation' outfit. With a new moniker in place (UNISEX), LAWRIE and DORAN – picking up film soundtrack man, NICK HEMMING, ANDREW FOSTER and DAN THOMPSON – were underway once more. The 1996 single, 'THEY DO FEEL STRANGE', was released for 'Heaven' and duly became a minor hit in France. Subsequent releases, including NME Single Of The Week, 'CRITICAL CONDITION', paved the way for a deal with 'Double Agent' records and finally the release of their long-awaited (but obviously dated) debut set, 'STRATOSPHERE' (2001).

Album rating: TASTE (*7) / UNTITLED (*6) / STRATOSFEAR as Unisex (*4) / THIRD WAVE (*5) / Unisex: STRATOSHERE (*4)

STEPHEN LAWRIE (b.28 Mar'69, East Hartford, England) – vocals / **JOANNA DORAN** (b. West Midlands, England) – guitar, vocals / **DAVID FITZGERALD** (b.30 Aug'66, Wellingborough, England) – guitar / **ROBERT BROOKS** (b.11 Apr'69, Burton-Upon-Trent) – bass / **DOMINIC DILLON** (b.26 Sep'64, Bolton, England) – drums

	Cheree	not iss.
1988. (7"flexi) *(CHEREE 1)* **FOREVER CLOSE YOUR EYES. / (Loop: Soundhead)**	□	-
Jan 89. (7") *(CHEREE 2)* **KICK THE WALL. / THIS IS THE LAST OF WHAT'S COMING NOW**	□	-
Apr 89. (12"ep) *(CHEREET 4)* **7th # DISASTER / NOTHING. / THIS PLANET / COLD**	□	-

	What Goes On	not iss.
Sep 89. (12"ep) *(WHAT 15T)* **THE PERFECT NEEDLE / SADNESS PALE. / S.H.C. BURN / YOU CANNOT BE SURE**	□	-
Oct 89. (lp/cd) *(GOES ON 32/+CD)* **TASTE**	□	-

– And let me drift away / I fall, she screams / Oil seed rape / Violence / Threadbare / The perfect needle / There is no floor / Anticipating nowhere / Please, before you go / Sufferscation / Silent water / Suicide. *(re-iss. cd Jul90 on 'Cheree'; CHEREE 9 CD)*

	Fierce	not iss.
Jan 90. (12"ep/cd-ep) *(GOES ON 18 T/CD)* **TO KILL A SLOW GIRL WALKING EP**	□	-

– To kill a slow girl walking / Treasure / Forever now / Pure sweetest ocean.

| 1990. (lp/cd) *(FRIGHT/+CD 039)* **TRADE MARK OF QUALITY** (compilation) | | - |

– There is no floor / Sadness pale / Perfect needle / 7th disaster / Threadbare / Violence / Anticipating nowhere / Please before you go / Suicide.

	Creation	Tristar
Jun 90. (7") *(CRE 081)* **PRECIOUS LITTLE. / NEVER HURT YOU**	□	-
(12"+=)(cd-s+=) *(CRE 81T/CRESCD 81)* – Deep hole / Sense.		
Nov 90. (7") *(CRE 092)* **EVERSO. / NEVER LEARN NOT TO LOVE**	□	-
(12"+=)(cd-s+=) *(CRE 092T/CRESCD 092)* – Wish of you.		
Feb 91. (7") *(CRE 103)* **CELESTE. / ALL A DREAMS**	□	-
(12"+=)(cd-s+=) *(CRE 103T/CRESCD 103)* – Celestial.		
Jul 91. (12"ep)(cd-ep) *(CRE 108T)(CRESCD 108)* **FLYING / SOUL FULL OF TEARS. / HIGH ON FIRE / THE SLEEPWALK**	79	-
Jun 92. (cd/lp)(c) *(CRE CD/LP 079)(CCRE 079)* <57564> **UNTITLED**	□	Mar94

– Splashdown / High on fire / You set my soul / Spaceships / The presence of your grace / And / Flying / Yeah / Ocean drive / Please tell mother / To the shore.

—— split after above

UNISEX

STEPHEN LAWRIE – vocals, guitar / **JOANNE DORAN** – vocals / **NICK HEMMING** – percussion, keyboards, multi / **ANDREW FOSTER** – bass / **DAN THOMPSON** – drums

	Heaven	Double Agent
1996. (7") <DA 010> **DO THEY FEEL STRANGE. / MAN ABOUT TOWN**	□	□

	not iss.	Kooky Disc
Oct 97. (7") <003> **TV COWBOY. / (other by GOOD MORNING CANADA)**	-	□

	Double Agent	Double Agent
Apr 00. (cd-ep) <DA 012CD> **DEADLOCK**	□	□

– Deadlock / TV cowboy / Smash it in, kick it on / Airtight / Deadlock reprise.
(12"ep) <DA 012LP> – ('A'side) / ('A-Agent 15 mix)' / ('A'-Charlie don't surf's cooking on gas mix)' / ('A'-reprise).

| Jul 00. (7") <DA 013> **CRITICAL CONDITION. / (other by CLASS)** | - | □ |
| Aug 01. (cd) *(<DA 016CD>)* **STRATOSFEAR** | □ | □ |

– The fuller force of the sun / Calmer song / Departure lounge / The anti gravity league / A second swell / Sidekick and Emo / Midnight in the stratosfear / Let the night roar / Autopilot / In among the breakers.

TELESCOPES

re-formed in 2001 with **STEPHEN + JO**

	Double Agent	Double Agent
Jul 02. (cd) *(<DA 017CD>)* **THIRD WAVE**	□	□

– A cabin in the sky / 3D Jesus ashtray / Tesla death ray / My name is Zardak (drop your weaponz) / A good place to hide / When Nemo sank the Nautilus / Winter #2 / Moog destroys / The atoms of the sea / You and I are the foxboy noises. *(<lp-iss.Oct02 on 'Isota'; SODY 007>)*

10,000 MANIACS

Formed: Jamestown, New York, USA . . . 1981 by NATALIE MERCHANT and J.C. LOMBARDO, who had been part of the band, STILL LIFE. Initially a new wave covers outfit, the group (which was completed by ROBERT BUCK, STEVEN GUSTAFSON, DENNIS DREW and JERRY AUGUSTYNAK) debuted on the obscure 'Christian Burial' label in 1982 with the mini-album, 'HUMAN CONFLICT NUMBER FIVE'. After a further full-length set, 'THE SECRETS OF THE I-CHING' (1984), which scaled the UK indie chart and won praise from Radio 1 guru John Peel, the group secured an international

10,000 MANIACS (cont)

deal with 'Elektra'. Produced by veteran folk man, Joe Boyd, 'THE WISHING CHAIR' (1985) saw the band develop their eclectic, rootsy sound, although it wasn't until the release of 'IN MY TRIBE' (1987) that 10,000 MANIACS began to reap some commercial rewards to match their growing critical acclaim. By this point LOMBARDO had departed after the previous year's heavy touring alongside R.E.M., the group further changing their strategy by enlisting the services of another seasoned producer, Pete Asher. The result was a sparer sound and sharpened songwriting which emphasised MERCHANT's hypnotically plangent vocals, the group scoring minor US hits with 'LIKE THE WEATHER' and 'WHAT'S THE MATTER HERE?'. A cover of Cat Stevens' 'PEACE TRAIN' failed to chart, the band later withdrawing the track from subsequent pressings following hardline Islamic comments made by the former singer/songwriter. Perhaps as a result, the follow-up set, 'BLIND MAN'S ZOO' (1989), took a more political stance, though the enigmatic MERCHANT stopped short of preaching, the album becoming a transatlantic Top 20 hit. Following the accompanying tour, the band took a brief sabbatical, eventually returning in September '92 with another successful set, 'OUR TIME IN EDEN'. The minor hit, 'CANDY EVERYBODY WANTS', was backed with a suitably lugubrious reading of Morrissey's 'EVERYDAY IS LIKE SUNDAY' while CD formats included a MERCHANT/MICHAEL STIPE duet on a version of R.E.M.'s country-tinged classic, 'DON'T GO BACK TO ROCKVILLE'. By the release of the languorous 'UNPLUGGED' (1993) set, however, MERCHANT was disillusioned with the group's attitude and left soon after for a solo career. While 10,000 MANIACS replaced MERCHANT with ex-member, JOHN LOMBARDO and new frontwoman MARY RAMSEY, the group's former focal point almost made the US Top 20 in summer '95 with her debut solo set, 'Tigerlily'. Minus MERCHANT, 10,000 MANIACS carried on regardless, releasing the sorry folk-rock set, 'LOVE AMONG THE RUINS', in 1997. It looked like their next outing, 'EARTH PRESSED FLAT' (1999), would be their last, as ROBERT BUCK sadly died of liver failure in 2000. • **Songwriters:** lyrics – NATALIE / music – JC LOMBARDO until his departure. MERCHANT was then the main writer with DREW or BUCK. Covered: I HOPE THAT I DON'T FALL IN LOVE WITH YOU (Tom Waits) / STARMAN – MOONAGE DAYDREAM (David Bowie) / THESE DAYS (Jackson Browne) / BECAUSE THE NIGHT (Patti Smith Group) / MORE THAN THIS (Bryan Ferry).

Album rating: HUMAN CONFLICT NUMBER FIVE mini (*4) / SECRETS OF THE I-CHING (*5) / THE WISHING CHAIR (*6) / IN MY TRIBE (*8) / BLIND MAN'S ZOO (*7) / HOPE CHEST: THE FREDONIA RECORDINGS 1982-1983 collection (*5) / OUR TIME IN EDEN (*7) / MTV UNPLUGGED (*5) / LOVE AMONG THE RUINS (*5) / THE EARTH PRESSED FLAT (*4) / John And Mary: VICTORY GARDENS (*6) / THE WEEDKILLER'S DAUGHTER (*5)

NATALIE MERCHANT (b.26 Oct'63) – vocals / **ROBERT BUCK** (b. 1 Aug'58) – guitar, synthesizers / **J.C. LOMBARDO** (b. JOHN, 30 Sep'52) – rhythm guitar, bass / **STEVEN GUSTAFSON** (b.10 Apr'57, Madrid, Spain) – bass, guitar / **DENNIS DREW** (b. 8 Aug'57, Buffalo, N.Y.) – organ / **JERRY AUGUSTYNAK** (b. 2 Sep'58, Lackawanna, N.Y.) – drums

		not iss.	Christian Burial
1982.	(m-lp) **HUMAN CONFLICT NUMBER FIVE**	-	

– Orange / Planed obsolescence / Anthem for doomed youth / Groove dub / Tension. (UK-iss.Jun84 on 'Press'; P 2010)

Jan 84.	(lp) **SECRETS OF THE I-CHING**	-	

– Grey victory / Pour de Chirico / Death of Manolette / Tension / Daktari / Pit viper / Katrina's fair / The Latin one / My mother the war. (UK-iss.Aug84 on 'Press'; P 3001)

		Reflex	Reflex
Mar 84.	(12"m) (RE 1) **MY MOTHER THE WAR (remix). / PLANNED OBSOLESCENCE / NATIONAL EDUCATION WEEK**		
		Elektra	Elektra
Jun 85.	(7") (EKR 11) **CAN'T IGNORE THE TRAIN. / DAKTARI**		

(12"+=) (EKR 11T) – Grey victory / The colonial wing.

Nov 85.	(lp/c) (EKT 14/+C) **THE WISHING CHAIR**		

– Can't ignore the train / Just as the tide was a-flowing / Scorpio rising / Lilydale / Maddox table / Everyone a puzzle lover / Arbor day / Back o' the Moon / Tension takes a tangle / Among the Americans / Grey victory / Cotton alley / My mother the war. (cd-iss. 1989; 960 428-2)

Nov 85.	(7"w/drawn) (EKR 19) **JUST AS THE TIDE WAS A-FLOWING. / AMONG THE AMERICANS**	-	
Jan 86.	(7") (EKR 28) **SCORPIO RISING. / ARBOR DAY**		

—— trimmed to a quintet when LOMBARDO departed to form JOHN AND MARY

Aug 87.	(7") (EKR 61) **PEACE TRAIN. / THE PAINTED DESERT**		
Aug 87.	(lp/c)(cd) (EKT 41/+C)(960 738-2) <60738> **IN MY TRIBE**		37

– What's the matter here? / Hey Jack Kerouac / Like the weather / Cherry tree / Painted desert / Don't talk / Peace train / Gun shy / Sister Rose / A campfire song / City of angels / Verdi cries. (initial copies cont. Elektra sampler with X / The CALL; SAM 390)

Nov 87.	(7") (EKR 64) **DON'T TALK. / CITY OF ANGELS**		

(12"+=) (EKR 64T) – Goodbye (Tribal outtake).

Mar 88.	(7") (EKR 71) **WHAT'S THE MATTER HERE?. / VERDI CRIES**		-

(12"+=/cd-s+=) (EKR 71T) – Like the weather (live) / Gun shy (live).

Jul 88.	(7") (EKR 77) <69418> **LIKE THE WEATHER. / A CAMPFIRE SONG**		68 May88

(12"+=/12"w-poster) (EKR 77T/+W) – Poison in the well (live) / Verdi cries (live).

Jul 88.	(7") <69388> **WHAT'S THE MATTER HERE? / CHERRY TREE**	-	80
May 89.	(lp/c)(cd) (EKT 57/+C)(960 815-2) <60815> **BLIND MAN'S ZOO**	18	13

– Eat for two / Please forgive us / The big parade / Trouble me / You happy puppet / Headstrong / Poison in the well / Dust bowl / The lion's share / Hateful hate / Jubilee.

Jun 89.	(7"/c-s) (EKR 93) <69298> **TROUBLE ME. / THE LION'S SHARE**		44

(12"+=/3"cd-s+=/3"s-cd-s+=) (EKR 93 T/CD/CDX) – Party of God.

Sep 89.	(7") <69253> **YOU HAPPY PUPPET. / GUNSHY**	-	

Nov 89.	(7"ep) (EKR 100) **EAT FOR TWO / WILDWOOD FLOWER. / DON'T CALL US / FROM THE TIME YOU SAY GOODBYE**		-

(12"/12"w/poster/3"cd-s) (EKR 100 T/TW/CD) – (1st & 2nd track) / Gun shy (acoustic) / Hello in there.
(10") (EKR 100TE) – (1st & 4th track) / What's the matter here? (acoustic) / Eat for two (acoustic).

Sep 92.	(7"/c-s) (EKR 156/+C) <64700> **THESE ARE DAYS. / CIRCLE DREAM**	58	66

(cd-s) (EKR 156CD) – I hope that I don't fall in love with you.
(cd-s) (EKR 156CDX) – ('A'side) / Medley:- Starman – Moonage daydream / These days.

Sep 92.	(cd/c/lp) <(7559 61385-2/-4/-1)> **OUR TIME IN EDEN**	33	28

– Noah's dove / These are days / Few and far between / Stockton gala days / Gold rush brides / Jezebel / How you've grown / Candy everybody wants / Circle dream / If you intend / I'm not the man. (cd+=) – Tolerance.

Feb 93.	(c-s,cd-s) <64665> **CANDY EVERYBODY WANTS / I HOPE THAT I DON'T FALL IN LOVE WITH YOU**	-	67
Mar 93.	(7"/c-s) (EKR 160/+C) **CANDY EVERYBODY WANTS. / EVERYDAY IS LIKE SUNDAY**	47	-

(cd-s+=) (EKR 160CD1) – Don't go back to Rockville (with MICHAEL STIPE co-vocals) / Sally Ann.
(cd-s+=) (EKR 160CD2) – Don't go back to Rockville (with MICHAEL STIPE) / ('A' MTV version).
(cd-s) (EKR 160CD3) – ('A'side) / Eat for two (live) / My sister Rose (live) / Hey Jack Kerouac (live).

Aug 93.	(cd-ep) <66296> **FEW AND FAR BETWEEN / CANDY EVERYBODY WANTS / TO SIR WITH LOVE / LET THE MYSTERY BE**	-	95
Oct 93.	(7"/c-s) (EKR 175/+C) **BECAUSE THE NIGHT. / STOCKTON GALA DAYS**	65	-

(cd-s+=) (EKR 175CD) – Let the mystery be / Sally Ann.

Oct 93.	(c-s,cd-s) <64595> **BECAUSE THE NIGHT / EAT FOR TWO**		11
Oct 93.	(cd/c) <(7559 61569-2/-4)> **MTV UNPLUGGED (live)**	40	13

– These are days / Eat for two / Candy everybody wants (MTV version) / I'm not the man / Don't talk / Hey Jack Kerouac / What's the matter here / Gold rush brides / Like the weather / Trouble me / Jezebel / Because the night / Stockton gala days / Noah's dove.

—— 10,000 MANIACS split when NATALIE went solo. The rest re-formed in 1995 and added ex-original JOHN LOMBARDO and his (JOHN AND MARY) partner MARY RAMSEY on vocals and violin.

		Geffen	Geffen
Sep 97.	(c-s) (GFSC 22284) <19411> **MORE THAN THIS / BEYOND THE BLUE**		25 Jul97

(12"+=/cd-s+=) (GFST/+D 22284) – ('A'-Tee's radio mix).

Oct 97.	(cd) <(GED 25009)> **LOVE AMONG THE RUINS**		Jun97

– Rainy day / Love among the ruins / Even with my eyes closed / Girl on a train / Green children / A room for everything / More than this / Big star / You won't find me there / All that never happens / Shining light / Across the fields.

		Bar/None	Bar/None
May 99.	(cd/c) <(BARNONE 106)> **THE EARTH PRESSED FLAT**		Apr99

– The Earth pressed flat / Ellen / Once a vity / Glow / On & on (mercy song) / Somebody's Heaven / Cabaret / Beyond the blue / Smallest step / In the quiet morning / Time turns / Hidden in my heart / Who knows where the times goes? (cd+=) – Rainbows.

—— ROBERT BUCK died of liver failure in 2000

– compilations, others, etc. –

Oct 90.	(lp/c)(cd) Elektra; (EKT 79/+C)<(7599 60962-2)> **HOPE CHEST**		

– (HUMAN CONFLICT NUMBER FIVE / THE SECRETS OF I-CHING)

JOHN AND MARY

JOHN LOMBARDO – vocals, bass, guitars / **MARY RAMSEY** – vocals, keyboards, violin, viola / with **ROBERT BUCK, JEROME AUGUSTYNIAK** – drums / etc.

		Rykodisc	Rykodisc
Jul 91.	(cd) <(RCD 10203)> **VICTORY GARDENS**		

– Red wooden beads / Azalea festival / Piles of dead leaves / We have nothing / Rags of flowers / I became alone / Open window / July 6th / Pram / Canadien errant.

—— guests:- **ALEX CHILTON, MARY MARGARET O'HARA, ANDREW CASE, BOB WISEMAN, SCOTT MILLER, DAVID KANE, JOANNE RAMSEY + BUCK**

Mar 93.	(cd) <(RCD 10259)> **THE WEEDKILLER'S DAUGHTER**		

– Two worlds parted / Angels of stone / Your return / Clare's scarf / Cemetery ridge / Nightfall / I wanted you / One step backward / Fly me to the north / Clouds of reason / Maid of mist / Poor murdered woman.

TESTCARD-F (see under ⇒ GEE MR. TRACY)

THANES

Formed: Edinburgh-based, Scotland ... mid-80's as The GREEN TELESCOPE by LENNY HELSING, who had more than a slight penchant for garage/R&B of the mid-60's (i.e. PRETTY THINGS, STANDELLS and REMAINS). Along with BRUCE LYALL, DENIS BOYLE and IAN BINNS, the GT became the first act to record for the psychedelic-biased 'Imaginary' label (later home to the MOCK TURTLES and the BACHELOR PAD). Their debut single, 'TWO BY TWO', was duly followed by 'FACE IN THE CROWD' (for the obscure 'Wump' imprint), although LENNY and his motley crew decided to change their moniker to The THANES. These noble lords of the psychedelic indie frontier opened up their vinyl account in September '87, via a Jamie Watson-produced cracker, 'HEY GIRL (LOOK WHAT YOU'VE DONE)'. Fast Forward and 'D.D.T.' records were also behind their acclaimed Retro-fied first full-set, 'THANES OF CAWDOR' (1988), while the same partnership released a further handful of singles. Moving across the corridor to 'Nightshift' (run by Grangemouth man, BRIAN GUTHRIE, brother of Sir Robin of the COCTEAU TWINS), they showcased one last set, 'BETTER LOOK BEHIND YOU'. The multi-talented LENNY (a vocalist, guitarist, drummer, etc) had already moonlighted with other projects such as The STAYRCASE and The OFFHOOKS, both of which released a bit of vinyl in 1988. The barren years of the 90's were put aside when The THANES re-formed in July 2000 for a prestigious US concert at the Las Vegas Grind alongside their Beat-en heroes, The STANDELLS and The REMAINS. The THANES even had time to conjure up a comeback single, 'IT'S JUST A FEAR', for Stateside-based 'Sundazed'. • Covered: I CAN'T STOP THINKING ABOUT HER (Chapters) / L.S.D. (GOT A MILLION $) (Tom McGuinness) / I WANNA HEAR YOU SAY YEAH (Gray-Munroe) / etc.

Album rating: THANES OF CAWDOR (*5) / BETTER LOOK BEHIND YOU (*5)

GREEN TELESCOPE

BRUCE LYALL – vocals, guitar / **LENNY HELSING** – lead guitar, vocals, harmonica / **DENIS BOYLE** – bass / **IAN BINNS** – drums

		Imaginary	not iss.
Dec 85.	(7"ep) (MIRAGE 001) **TWO BY TWO / A GLIMPSE. / MAKE ME STAY / THINKIN' ABOUT TODAY**		-
		Wump	not iss.
Aug 86.	(7") (BIF 4811) **FACE IN THE CROWD. / THOUGHTS OF A MADMAN**		-

— changed their group moniker to . . .

THANES

		D.D.T.	not iss.
Sep 87.	(7"ep) (DISP 008) **HEY GIRL EP**		-
	– Hey girl (look what you've done) / What can I do / Wish you'd stayed away / Touch.		
	(12"ep+=) (DISP 008T) –		
Jan 88.	(lp) (DISPLP 011) **THANES OF CAWDOR**		-
	– Keep you out / You'll be blue / Days go slowly by / She was mine / Buzz buzz yeh yeh / Where have all the good times gone / All gone now / Kicks and chicks / Won't you c'mon girl / When I love you / Girls / Cold as ice / Before I go / Some kinda fun.		
Aug 88.	(12"ep) (DDTEP 001) **HUBBLE BUBBLE**		-
Jan 89.	(7") (DISP 020) **I'LL REST. / BABY COME BACK**		-
Jul 89.	(10"ep) (DDTEP 004) **BETTER LOOK BEHIND YOU**		-
		Nightshift	not iss.
Feb 90.	(lp) (NISHI 211) **BETTER LOOK BEHIND YOU**		-
	– Can't stop thinking about her / Wonder if / Baby come back / L.S.D. (got a million $) / I'll rest / I wanna hear you say yeah / Lost or found / Don't let her dark your door.		

— disbanded in the early 90's; HELSING continued with offshoots the OFFHOOKS, the NATURALS and the STAYRCASE

OFFHOOKS

LENNY HELSING with also **CALVIN BURT** – vocals, drums / **CLIVE** – guitar, harmonica, tambourine / + **ANDY** – bass

		D.D.T.	not iss.
Jun 88.	(m-lp) (DISPLP 018) **OFF THE HOOK**		-
	– Greed / I'm a nothing / Heartbreaking girl / No more tears / Got no lovin' / I can take it.		

— CALVIN was later the drummer for POLICECAT

STAYRCASE

IAN – vocals / **ALAN** – guitar, vocals / **DAVE** – bass, vocals / **LENNY HELSING** – drums, vocals

		Mumblin'	not iss.
Aug 88.	(m-lp) (MR 451) **THE STAYRCASE**		-
	– I know you lied / Who dat? / I want you / Disgust / Down around me / 1906 / Irritation / I wanna come back.		

THANES

re-formed with the same line-up

		Sundazed	Sundazed
Nov 00.	(7") (<S 156>) **IT'S JUST A FEAR. / SUN DIDN'T COME OUT TODAY**		

THAT PETROL EMOTION

Formed: Derry, N.Ireland . . . 1984 by the O'NEILL brothers, SEAN and DAMIAN (both ex-UNDERTONES) along with CIARAN McLAUGHLIN, REAMANN O'GORMAN and US-born frontman, STEVE MACK. Basing themselves in London from the mid-80's onwards, the band made their vinyl debut in summer '85 with the independently released 'KEEN'. A further indie single, 'V2' followed a few months later before 'Demon' took them on for a critically acclaimed ROLI MOSSIMAN-produced debut album, 'MANIC POP THRILL' (1986). Strikingly different from The UNDERTONES' three-chord rush, THAT PETROL EMOTION dealt in a more caustic, politicised brand of alternative pop/rock which embraced elements of 60's garage and psychedelia, their potential subsequently recognised by 'Polydor'. The major label backing paid almost immediate dividends as the band narrowly missed the UK Top 40 with their next single, 'BIG DECISION'. A follow-up album, 'BABBLE' (1987) appeared a couple of months later and landed the band their first and only Top 30 success; despite vocal support from the likes of John Peel and the NME, THAT PETROL EMOTION seemed unable to convert their potential into sales. Moving on to 'Virgin', they came up with the more experimental 'END OF THE MILLENNIUM PSYCHOSIS BLUES' (1988), featuring O'NEILL's political coup de grace, 'CELLOPHANE'. Yet he was unhappy with the life of a professional musician and subsequently moved back to Derry. A potentially fatal blow was overcome with the recruitment of JOHN MARCHINI and the songwriting development of McLAUGHLIN, the group attempting a final shot at pop glory with the 'SENSITIZE' and 'HEY VENUS' singles. Both were culled from 1990's 'CHEMICRAZY' album and both fell cruelly short of the Top 40 to the exasperation of the band, their label and their many advocates in the media. Dropped by 'Virgin', the band stuck it out for one final set, 'FIREPROOF' (1993) on their own 'Koogat' label before finally throwing in the towel. • Songwriters: Most written by O'NEILL's except covers; ME AND BABY BROTHER (War) / FOR WHAT IT'S WORTH (Buffalo Springfield) / NON-ALIGNMENT PACT (Pere Ubu) / ZIGZAG WANDERER (Captain Beefheart) / HEY BULLDOG (Beatles) / CINNAMON GIRL (Neil Young) / FUNTIME (Iggy Pop).

Album rating: MANIC POP THRILL (*7) / BABBLE (*8) / END OF THE MILLENNIUM PSYCHOSIS BLUES (*6) / CHEMICRAZY (*5) / FIREPROOF (*6)

STEVE MACK (b.19 May'63, New York City, USA) – vocals (ex-EAGER SIN BABIES) / **SEAN O'NEILL** (b. JOHN, 26 Aug'57) – guitar (ex-UNDERTONES) / **DAMIAN O'NEILL** (b.15 Jan'61) – bass, keyboards (ex-UNDERTONES) / **REAMANN O'GORMAIN** (b. 7 Jun'61) – guitar / **CIARAN McLAUGHLIN** (b.18 Nov'62) – drums

		Pink	not iss.
Jun 85.	(7") (PINKY 004) **KEEN. / A GREAT DEPRESSION ON SLUM NIGHT**		-
	(re-iss. Oct86; PINKY 13T)		
		Noise A Noise	not iss.
Oct 85.	(7") (NAN 1) **V2. / THE GONEST THING**		-
	(12"+=) (NAN 1T) – Happiness drives me round the bend.		
		Demon	Demon
Apr 86.	(7") (D 1042) **IT'S A GOOD THING. / THE DEADBEAT**		-
	(12"+=) (D 1042T) – Mine.		
May 86.	(lp/c/cd)<US-orange-lp> (<FIEND/+CASS/+CD 70>) **MANIC POP THRILL**	84	
	– Fleshprint / Can't stop / Lifeblood / Natural kind of joy / It's a good thing / Circusville / Mouth crazy / Tight lipped / A million miles away / Lettuce / Cheepskate / Blind spot. (cd+=) – V2 / Jesus said / The deadbeat. (cd re-iss. Mar97 on Diabolo'; DIAB 823)		
Jul 86.	(7") (D 1043) **NATURAL KIND OF JOY. / CAN'T STOP**		
	(12"+=) (D 1043T) – Non-alignment pact / Jesus said.		
		Polydor	Polydor
Mar 87.	(7"/12") (TPE/+X 1) **BIG DECISION. / SOUL DEEP**	43	-
	(ext.10"+=) (TPE/+T 1) – Split!		
May 87.	(lp/c/cd) (TPELP/+MC/+CD 1) <833132-1/-4/-2> **BABBLE**	30	
	– Swamp / Spin cycle / For what it's worth / Big decision / Static / Split! / Belly bugs / In the playpen / Inside / Chester Burnette / Creeping to the cross. (cd re-mast.Feb01 +=; 549565-2) – Big decision (12" mix) / Swamp (12" mix) / Creeping to the cross (7" mix) / Soul deep / Dance your ass off.		
Jun 87.	(7") (TPE 2) **SWAMP. / DANCE YOUR ASS OFF**	64	-
	(12"+=) (TPEX 2) – Creeping to the cross (live).		
	(7"ep++=) (TPEE 2) – Me and baby brother (live).		
		Virgin	Virgin
Oct 87.	(7") (VS 1022) **GENIUS MOVE. / PARTY GAMES**	65	-
	(12"+=) (VST 1022) – Mouthcrazy.		
Sep 88.	(lp/c/cd) (V/TCV/CDV 2550) <91019-1/-4/-2> **END OF THE MILLENNIUM PSYCHOSIS BLUES**	53	
	– Sooner or later / Every little bit / Cellophane / Candy love satellite / Here it is . . . take it! / The price of my soul / Groove check / The bottom line / Tension / Tired shattered man / Goggle box / Under the sky.		
Oct 88.	(7") (VS 1116) **CELLOPHANE. / THINK OF A WOMAN**		
	(12"+=/cd-s+=) (VST/VSCD 1116) – Hot head / Fast 'n' bullbous.		

— **JOHN MARCHINI** – bass; repl. SEAN O'NEILL (only temporary until 1989 then full-time)

Feb 89.	(10"ep/3"cd-ep) (VSA/VSCD 1159) **GROOVE CHECK / CHEMICRAZY. / TENSION (live) / UNDER THE SKY (live)**		
Mar 90.	(7") (VS 1242) **ABANDON. / FAT MOUTH CREED**	73	-
	(12"+=) (VST 1242) – Jewel.		
	(cd-s+=) (VSCD 1242) – ('A'-Boys own mix) / Headstaggered.		
Apr 90.	(cd/c/lp) (CD/TC+/V 2618) <91354-2/-4/-1> **CHEMICRAZY**	62	
	– Hey Venus / Blue to black / Mess of words / Sensitize / Another day / Gnaw mark / Scum surfin' / Compulsion / Tingle / Head staggered / Abandon / Sweet shiver burn.		
May 90.	(7") (VS 1261) **SENSITIZE. / CHEMICRAZY (revitalized)**		-
	(10"+=/12"+=/cd-s+=) (VSAX/VST/VSCDT 1261) – Abandon (Boys Own mix) / Groove check this groove.		
Aug 90.	(7") (VS 1290) **HEY VENUS. / ('A'-Mad Thatcher mix)**	49	-
	(12"+=/cd-s+=) (VST/VSCD 1290) – (2-'A'mixes).		

— **FRANK TREISCHLER** – bass (ex-YOUNG GODS) repl. MARCHINI

Jan 91.	(7") (VS 1312) **TINGLE. / ('A'-Hard bop edit)**	49	-
	(12"+=) (VST 1312) – ('A')mix.		
	(cd-s+=) (VSCD 1312) – Light and shade / Hey Bulldog.		
	(12") (VSTX 1312) – ('A'-Christmas mix) / 'A'-Jazz tup mix).		
Apr 91.	(7"ep/12"ep) (VS/+T 1261) **SENSITIZE. / ABANDON (mix) / GROOVE CHECK**	55	-
	(10"ep+=/c-ep+=/cd-ep+=) (VS X/C/CD 1261) – Cinnamon girl.		

— **MARCHINI** now returned to substitute TREICHE who went back to the YOUNG GODS

		Koogat	Rykodisc
Mar 93.	(12"ep/cd-ep) *(GAT 1 T/CDS)* **DETONATE MY DREAMS. / BLUE TO BLACK (extended) / BIG HUMAN THING**		-
Apr 93.	(cd/c/lp) *(GAT 1 CD/MC/LP)* <*RCD/RAC+/10289*> **FIREPROOF**		Feb94

– Detonate my dreams / Catch a fire / Last of the true believers / Too late blues / 7th wave / Infinite thrill / Speed of light / Shangri-la / Heartbeat mosaic / Metal mystery. *(cd re-mast.Aug00 on 'Essential'; ESMCD 903)*

| Jul 93. | (12"ep/cd-ep) *(GAT 2 T/CDS)* **CATCH A FIRE (re-mix). / FUN TIME / LITTLE BIKINI / CHROME** | | - |

— disbanded at the end of April 1994; the O'NEILL brothers formed RARE

– compilations, others, etc. –

| Oct 87. | (12"ep) *Strange Fruit; (SFPS 038)* **THE PEEL SESSIONS** | | - |

– Blind spot / Lettuce / V2 / Can't stop.

| Dec 89. | (m-lp/m-cd) *Strange Fruit; (SFPMA/+CD 205) / Dutch East India; <DEI 8401>* **DOUBLE PEEL SESSIONS II** | | - |
| Aug 00. | (cd) *Essential; (ESMCD 902)* **LIVE** (live) | | - |

THEATRE OF HATE (see under ⇒ SPEAR OF DESTINY)

THEE MIGHTY CAESARS (see under ⇒ CHILDISH, Wild Billy; 70's section)

THEE MILKSHAKES (see under ⇒ CHILDISH, Wild Billy; 70's section)

THELONIOUS MONSTER

Formed: Los Angeles, California, USA … 1986 by BOB FORREST, along with K.K., PETE WEISS, JOHN HUCK, BILL STOBAUGH, DIX DENNEY and CHRIS HANDSOME. A freewheeling collective of assorted Cali alternative types, THELONIOUS MONSTER made their vinyl debut on hardcore-punk label, 'Epitaph' with the self explanatory 'BABY … YOU'RE BUMMIN' MY LIFE OUT IN A SUPREME FASHION' (1986). The shambolic stylings of this free-for-all ragbag translated to the band's stage show which had already earned a formidable reputation for inspired sloppiness, the whole shebang saved from self-indlulgence by FORREST's emotive lyrics/vocalising. A further couple of albums, 'NEXT SATURDAY AFTERNOON' (1987) and 'STORMY WEATHER' (1989) for metal label, 'Combat', found the 'MONSTER refining their ramshackle brand of blues/country roots and punk, even convincing 'Capitol' to take them on for 1992's 'BEAUTIFUL MESS'. Boasting an array of hip names such as DAN PIRNER, TOM WAITS and BENMONT TENCH, the album benefitted from the major label recording budget, allowing FORREST to exorcise his demons in a more cohesive, polished setting. After several years in the proverbial wilderness, BOB was back in the studio with a new outfit, The BICYCLE THIEF. The group's excellent debut set, 'YOU COME AND GO LIKE A POP SONG' (1999) included youthful guitarist JOSH KLINGHOFFER, producer/bassist JOSH BLUM, drummer KEVIN FITZGERALD and appearances from seasoned campaigners ANNA WARONKER and JOHN FRUSCANTE. Curiously enough, the album was given another release by 'Artemis' in 2001, this time with a couple of fresh songs and a restructured track listing – MARK HUTNER (who had been a co-songwriter on the original version) turned up as FORREST's new guitarist. • **Covered:** LISTEN TO THE MUSIC (Doobie Brothers) / SEE THAT MY GRAVE IS KEPT CLEAN (Blind Lemon Jefferson) / FOR MY LOVER (Tracy Chapman) / WEAKNESS IN ME (Joan Armatrading).

Album rating: BABY … YOU'RE BUMMIN' MY LIFE OUT IN A SUPREME FASHION (*5) / NEXT SATURDAY AFTERNOON (*7) / STORMY WEATHER (*8) / BEAUTIFUL MESS (*7) / Bicycle Thief: YOU COME AND GO LIKE A POP SONG (*8; re-issue *7)

BOB FORREST – vocals / with guitarists **CHRIS HANDSOME, BILL STOBAUGH, DIX DENNEY, K.K.** / bassist **JON HUCK** / drums **PETE WEISS**

		not iss.	Epitaph
1986.	(lp/c)(cd) <*EPI/EPC-TM 1*><*86427-2*> **BABY … YOU'RE BUMMIN' MY LIFE OUT IN A SUPREME FASHION**	-	

– Psychofuckindelic / Yes yes no / Positive train / Let me in the house / Thelonious monster / Joke song / Huck's jam / Union street / Try / …And the rest of the band / Life's a groove / Twenty-four hours / Happy #12c #35.

		Relativity	Relativity
Jul 87.	(12"ep) <*88561-8154-1*> **THE BOLDNESS OF STYLE**	-	

– Walk on water / If I / Listen to the music (live).

| Aug 87. | (lp) <*(88561-8174-1)*> **NEXT SATURDAY AFTERNOON** | | |

– Swan song / Lookin' to the west / Hang tough / Michael Jordan / Low boy (butterflies are free) / Key to life … tonite / Walk on water / Anymore / Saturday afternoon / Zelda / Pop star / Tree 'n' Sven orbit the planet.

— **MIKE MARTT** – guitar; repl. STOBAUGH

— **ROB GRAVES** – bass; repl. HUCK

| 1989. | (cd) <*88561-1002-2*> **STORMY WEATHER** | - | |

– So what if I did / Oh (no sense at all) / Lena Horne still sings stormy weather / For my lover / My boy / Colorblind / Real kinda hatred / Nuthin's perfect / Sammy Hagar weekend / You better run / See that my grave is kept clean. <*d-cd-iss. 1989 on 'Combat'+=; >* – NEXT SATURDAY AFTERNOON

— **FORREST** with various guests **TOM WAITS, DAVE PIRNER, DAN MURPHY, BENMONT TENCH, MICHAEL PENN** etc

		not iss.	Capitol
Oct 92.	(cd/c) <*C2/C4 80227*> **BEAUTIFUL MESS**	-	

– I live in a nice house / Blood is thicker than water / Body and soul? / Adios lounge (with TOM WAITS) / I get so scared / Song for a politically correct girl from the valley / Ain't never been nuthin' for me in this world / Bus with no driver / Vegas weekend / Weakness in me / The beginning and the end #12 N35.

above was their last album before breaking up – after several years away **FORREST** returned …

BICYCLE THIEF

BOB with **JOSH KLINGHOFFER** – guitars, keyboards / **JOSH BLUM** – bass / **KEVIN FITZGERALD** – drums / **ANNA WARONKER** – vocals

		not iss.	Goldenvoice
1999.	(cd) <*none*> **YOU COME AND GO LIKE A POP SONG**	-	

– Hurt / Tennis shoes / Rainin' (4 am) / Aspirations / Max, Jill called / Off street parking / L.A. country hometown blues / MacArthur Park revisited / Everyone asks / It's alright / Rhonda meets the birdman / Cereal song / Boy at a bus stop.

— **MARK HUTNER** – (new) guitar

		not iss.	Artemis
2001.	(cd) <*751-070-2*> **YOU COME AND GO LIKE A POP SONG**	-	

– Song for a Kevin Spacey movie / Stoned / Max, Jill called / Tennis shoes / Off street parking / L.A. country (hometown blues) / Hurt / It's rainin' (4 am) / Everyone asks / Trust fund girl / MacArthur Park revisited / Cereal song / Boy at a bus stop.

THESE IMMORTAL SOULS

Formed: Europe … late 1986 by breakaway members of Australian outfit, CRIME & THE CITY SOLUTION: ROWLAND S. HOWARD (also a former sidekick of NICK CAVE in The BIRTHDAY PARTY), his brother HARRY HOWARD and EPIC SOUNDTRACKS (a Brit and one-time member of experimental punks, SWELL MAPS). Expanding the line-up to a quartet with the addition of GENEVIEVE McGUCKIN, THESE IMMORTAL SOULS remained with 'Mute' ('S.S.T.' in America), home to their aforementioned musical progenitors. Stylistically, the group carried on in the same vein as these past masters, recounting tales of damned romanticism through the trademark American gothic lens to a brooding, bluesy musical backing. The single, 'MARRY ME (LIE, LIE)', also opened up their debut long-player, 'GET LOST (DON'T LIE)' (1987), a record that received glowing reviews but appealed to the usual post-goth crowd without crossing over. ROWLAND and Co took their time over a prophetically titled follow-up, 'I'M NEVER GONNA DIE AGAIN' (1992), the band enjoying a critical resurrection after their spell in the musical wilderness. With a third album now seven years in the waiting, it seems THESE IMMORTAL SOULS have finally been laid to rest.

Album rating: GET LOST (DON'T LIE) (*7) / I'M NEVER GONNA DIE AGAIN (*6)

ROWLAND S. HOWARD – guitar (ex-CRIME & THE CITY SOLUTION, ex-BIRTHDAY PARTY) / **GENEVIEVE McGUCKIN** – keyboards / **HARRY HOWARD** – bass (ex-CRIME & THE CITY SOLUTION) / **EPIC SOUNDTRACKS** – drums (ex-CRIME & THE CITY SOLUTION, ex-RED CRAYOLA, ex-SWELL MAPS)

		Mute	S.S.T.
Sep 87.	(12"ep) *(12MUTE 63)* <*SST 183*> **MARRY ME (LIE, LIE) / OPEN UP AND BLEED. / BLOOD AND SAND, SHE SAID**		
Oct 87.	(lp/cd) *(STUMM/CDSTUMM 48)* <*SST 164*> **GET LOST (DON'T LIE)**		

– Marry me (lie, lie) / Hide / Hey! little child / These immortal souls / I ate the knife / Blood and sand, she said / One in shadow, one in sun. *(cd+= alternative versions of)* – Open up and bleed / Blood and sand, she said / I ate the knife / These immortal souls.

		Mute	Elektra
Oct 92.	(12"ep/cd-ep) *(12/CD MUTE 90)* **KING OF KALIFORNIA E.P.**		

– The king of Kalifornia / Bad / My one eyed daughter (live in Las Vegas) / Up on the roof.

| Oct 92. | (cd) *(CDSTUMM 98)* <*61396*> **I'M NEVER GONNA DIE AGAIN** | | |

– The king of Kalifornia / Shamed / Black milk / Hyperspace / So the story goes / Insomnicide / All the money's gone / Crowned / Bad / My one eyed daughter / Up on the roof.

— disbanded soon after above set

THE THE

Formed: Swadlincote, Derbyshire, England … 1979 as a studio project by MATT JOHNSON who was part of post-punk outfit The GADGETS, at the same time. JOHNSON signed to indic label, '4 a.d.' in 1980, unleashing the poignant single, 'CONTROVERSIAL SUBJECT'. JOHNSON released a further debut album for the label in summer '81, 'BURNING BLUE SOUL', although in effect it was a THE THE recording in all but name, JOHNSON being the sole permanent member of the group. Signing briefly to 'Some Bizzare', THE THE released another three singles, 'COLD SPELL AHEAD', 'PERFECT' and the brilliant 'UNCERTAIN SMILE', before securing a deal with 'Epic'. The long awaited and much anticipated 'SOUL MINING' was eventually released in late '83, JOHNSON's critical favour and cult standing seeing the album reach the UK Top 30. An entrancing, ambitious pop record with a brooding undertow, the keening 'THIS IS THE DAY' stands among the best of JOHNSON's work, the album's claustrophobic lyrics marking out JOHNSON as a bedsit commentator par excellence. For live work, JOHNSON recruited the likes of ex-ORANGE JUICE man, ZEKE MANYIKA, JIM THIRLWELL and JOOLS HOLLAND, the latter actually having guested on the album. Three years in the making, 'INFECTED' (1986) was JOHNSON's tour de force, a scathing attack on the industrial, economic and moral wasteland that was Thatcher's Britain. Nowhere was this better articulated than the malignant power of the album's centrepiece, 'HEARTLAND', JOHNSON berating 80's material gain and America's all-pervasive influence through gritted teeth. The pumping electro-soul of the title track, meanwhile, dealt with sexual obsession and the AIDS crisis, the attendant devil-masturbating video causing a storm of controversy. Other highlights included the tortured 'OUT OF THE BLUE (INTO THE FIRE)' and the breathy duet with NENEH CHERRY, 'SLOW TRAIN TO DAWN', JOHNSON's mastery of mood and atmosphere, together with a crack troupe of guest musicians making this one of the most realised albums of the decade. Accompanied by a full-length video/film (which was aired on Channel 4), the record also gave JOHNSON some belated Top 20 success. Spurred on, the restless maverick subsequently recruited a permanent band to turn THE THE into a group proposition, namely DAVID PALMER, JAMES ELLER and ex-SMITHS guitarist JOHNNY MARR. Though the resulting album, 'MIND BOMB' (1989) was THE THE's most successful to date (Top 5), its caustic barrage of political ranting lacked the twisted pop subtlety of its predecessor and left some critics unimpressed (a guest spot from SINEAD O'CONNOR on 'KINGDOM OF RAIN' made up for the pop tones of 'THE BEAT(EN) GENERATION'). Retaining the same core of musicians while adding keyboard player, D.C. COLLARD, THE THE eventually resurfaced with a full length album in the form of 'DUSK' (1993). Previewed by the harmonica howl of 'DOGS OF LUST', the album saw JOHNSON once again wrestling with his inner demons in his disturbingly insinuating way. A mid-life dark-night-of-the-soul, JOHNSON has rarely bared his soul or expressed his despair as affectingly as on the very SMITHS-esque 'SLOW EMOTION REPLAY', MARR literally wringing the pathos from his chiming guitar. This cathartic collection of urban blues nevertheless ended on something of a more hopeful note with 'LONELY PLANET', JOHNSON coming to some kind of peace with himself and the world. The record deservedly reached No.2, becoming the most successful THE THE release to date and making up the critical and commercial ground lost with 'MIND BOMB'. Of course, the ever restless JOHNSON turned his hand to something completely different, so to speak, for his next full-length release; 'HANKY PANKY' (1995) was a tribute album to his hero, country star HANK WILLIAMS, although only the track 'I SAW THE LIGHT' was of much note. Given short shrift by critics (the same ones probably), the record saw JOHNSON going out on a limb, no doubt alienating many of his long-time fans, although he was distant from them after relocating to Sherman Oaks in California. Then again, anyone familiar with the work of this elusive genius knows to expect the unexpected. Not the most prolific of artists these days, JOHNSON emerged blinking into the harsh electronic light of the new millennium with 'NAKEDSELF' (2000). The record (released on Interscope's 'Nothing' records – home to NINE INCH NAILS) only just scraped into the UK Top 50 and featured flop single, 'SHRUNKEN MAN'.

Album rating: Matt Johnson: BURNING BLUE SOUL (*7) / The The: SOUL MINING (*7) / INFECTED (*8) / MIND BOMB (*8) / DUSK (*7) / HANKY PANKY (*4) / NAKEDSELF (*5) / 45 RPM – THE SINGLES OF . . . compilation (*8)

GADGETS

MATT JOHNSON – guitars / **COLIN TUCKER** – synthesizers / **JOHN HYDE** – synthesizers (both ex-PLAIN CHARACTERS)

Final Solution / not iss.

Dec 79. (lp) *(FSLP 001)* **GADGETREE**
– Kyleaking / Making cars / Narpath / UFO import No.1 / Slippery / Singing in the rain / Only one me / Shouting 'Nispers' / There over there / Termite mound / Sleep / Devil's dyke / Six mile bottom / UFO import No.2 / Autumn 80 / Duplicate / Bog track / Thin line. *(re-iss. Jun89 on 'Plastic Head' lp/cd; PLAS LP/CD 013)*

—— They continued as a studio set-up with MATT's help.

Dec 80. (lp) *(FSLP 002)* **LOVE, CURIOSITY, FRECKLES & DOUBT**
– Bodorgan / Gadget speak / Checking to make sure / Aeron / Leave it to Charlie / Prayers / Happy endido / Quatt / Pictures of you / Aaft / Railway line through blubber houses / She's queen of toyland / Sex / It wasn't that way at all / The death and resurrection of Jennifer Gloom / Bill posters will be prosecuted. *(re-iss. Jun89 on 'Plastic Head' lp/cd; PLAS LP/CD 016)*

—— next featured **PETER ASHWORTH** dubbed in instead of MATT

Glass / not iss.

Jan 83. (lp/c) *(GLA LP/C 006)* **THE BLUE ALBUM**
– We had no way of knowing / Space in my heart / Bodies without heads / The boyfriend / Uneasy listening / Juice of love / Discuss the sofa / Long empty train / Bite the sawdust / Broken fall. *(re-iss. Jun89 on 'Plastic Head' lp/cd; PLAS LP/CD 016)*

Jun 83. (7"/12"; unissued) *(GLASS/+12 026)* **WE HAD NO WAY OF KNOWING. / ACID BATH**

THE THE

MATT JOHNSON (b.15 Aug'61, Essex, England . . . raised London) – vocals, guitar, etc. (also of The GADGETS) / **KEITH LAWS** – synthesizers, drum machine / **PETER 'Triash' ASHWORTH** – drums / **TOM JOHNSTON** – bass

4 a.d. / not iss.

Jul 80. (7") *(AD 10)* **CONTROVERSIAL SUBJECT. / BLACK AND WHITE**

—— next with guests **GILBERT & LEWIS** (of WIRE) on 2nd last track

Aug 81. (lp; as MATT JOHNSON) *(CAD 113)* **BURNING BLUE SOUL**
– Red cinders in the sand / Song without an ending / Time again for the golden sunset / Icing up / Like a Sun risin' thru my garden / Out of control / Bugle boy / Delirious / The river flows east in Spring / Another boy drowning. *(re-iss. Sep83; same) (re-iss. credited to THE THE, Jun93 cd)(c; HAD 113CD)(HADC 113); hit UK No.65 <us cd-iss. 1993 on 'Warners'; 45266>*

Some Bizzare / not iss.

Sep 81. (7") *(BZ 4)* **COLD SPELL AHEAD. / HOT ICE**
(re-iss. Aug92, 12"pic-d/cd-s;)

—— **MATT JOHNSON** was now virtually **THE THE**, although he was augmented by others on tour.

Epic / Epic

Oct 82. (7") *(EPCA 2787)* **UNCERTAIN SMILE. / THREE ORANGE KISSES FROM KAZAN** | 68 | - |
(12"+=,12"yellow+=) (EPC13 2787) – Waiting for the upturn.

Dec 82. (7") **UNCERTAIN SMILE. / WAITING FOR THE UPTURN** | - | - |

Feb 83. (7") *(EPCA 3119)* **PERFECT. / THE NATURE OF VIRTUE** | - | - |
(12"+=) (EPCA13 3119) – The nature of virtue II.

Sep 83. (7") *(A 3710)* **THIS IS THE DAY. / MENTAL HEALING PROCESS** | 71 | |
(w/ free-7") *(same)* – Leap into the wind / Absolute liberation.
(12") *(TA 3710)* – ('A'side) / I've been waiting for tomorrow (all of my life).

—— added live **ZEKE MANYIKA** – drums (of ORANGE JUICE) / **JIM THIRLWELL** / **JOOLS HOLLAND** – piano (ex-SQUEEZE) / **THOMAS LEER** – synthesizers, keyboards

Oct 83. (lp/c) *(EPC/40 25525)* <EK 39266> **SOUL MINING** | 27 | |
– I've been waiting for tomorrow (all of my life) / This is the day / The sinking feeling / Uncertain smile / The twilight hour / Soul mining / Giant. (free-12"ep.w.a.) **PERFECT. / SOUP OF MIXED EMOTIONS / FRUIT OF THE HEART** *(c+=)* – Perfect / Three orange kisses from Kazan / Nature of virtue / Fruit of the heart / Soup of mixed emotions / Waiting for the upturn. *(cd-iss. Jun87+=; CD 25525)* – Perfect. *(re-iss. Mar90 cd/c/lp; 466337-2/-4/-1) (cd re-iss. Apr02 +=; 504465-2)*

Nov 83. (7") *(A 3588)* **UNCERTAIN SMILE. / DUMB AS DEATH'S HEAD** | | - |
(12") *(TA 3588)* – ('A'side) / Soul mining.

—— guests for next album **ROLI MOSSIMAN** / **NENEH CHERRY** / **DAVID PALMER** / **STEVE HOGARTH** / **ANNA DOMINO** / **JAMIE TALBOT** / **WAYNE LIVESEY** / **ZEKE MANYIKA** / etc.

May 86. (12"m) *(TRUTH 1)* **SWEET BIRD OF TRUTH. / HARBOUR LIGHTS / SLEEPING JUICE** | | - |

Jul 86. (7") *(TRUTH 2)* **HEARTLAND. / BORN IN THE NEW S.A.** | 29 | - |
(12"+=) *(TRUTH T2)* – Flesh and bones.
(d12"++=) *(TRUTH D2)* – Perfect / Fruit of the heart.
(12"+=) *(TRUTH Q2)* – Sweet bird of truth.
(c-s++=) *(TRUTH C2)* – Harbour lights.

Oct 86. (7") *(TRUTH 3)* **INFECTED. / DISTURBED** | 48 | |
(12"+=/12"uncensored+=) *(TRUTH T/Q 3)* – ('A'-energy mix).
(d12"++=) *(TRUTH D3)* – Soul mining (remix) / Sinking feeling.
(c-s+=) *(TRUTH C3)* – ('A'-Skull crusher mix) / Soul mining / Sinking feeling.

Nov 86. (lp/c/cd) *(EPC/40/CD 26770)* <40471> **INFECTED** | 14 | 89 |
– Infected / Out of the blue (into the fire) / Heartland / Angels of deception / Sweet bird of truth / Slow train to dawn / Twilight of a champion / The mercy beat. *(cd+=)* – ('A'-INFECTED singles remixed) *(TA 3588) (cd re-iss. Apr02; 504466-2)*

Jan 87. (7") *(TENSE 1)* **SLOW TRAIN TO DAWN. / HARBOUR LIGHTS** | 64 | |
(12"+=/12"w-stencil+=) *(TENSE T/D 3)* – The nature of virtue.

May 87. (7") *(TENSE 2)* **SWEET BIRD OF TRUTH. / SLEEPING JUICE** | 55 | |
(12"+=) *(TENSE T2)* – Harbour lights.
(c-s++=)(cd-s++=) *(TENSE C2)(CDTHE 2)* – Soul mining (12"mix).

—— THE THE were again a group when **MATT** with past session man **DAVID PALMER** – drums (ex-ABC) / recruited **JOHNNY MARR** – guitar (ex-SMITHS) / **JAMES ELLER** – bass (ex-JULIAN COPE)

Feb 89. (7") *(EMU 8)* **THE BEAT(EN) GENERATION. / ANGEL** | 18 | |
(12"box+=/cd-s+=/3"cd-s+=) *(EMUB/EMUCD/CBEMU 8)* – Soul mining (mix).
(12"+=/pic-cd+=) *(EMUT/CPEMU 8)* – ('A'-Palmer mix) / ('A'-campfire mix).

May 89. (lp/c/cd) *(463319-1/-4/-2)* <45241> **MIND BOMB** | 4 | |
– Good morning beautiful / Armageddon days are here (again) / The violence of truth / Kingdom of rain / The beat(en) generation / August & September / Gravitate to me / Beyond love. *(cd re-iss. Apr02; 504467-2)*

Jul 89. (7"/c-s) *(EMU/+C 9)* **GRAVITATE TO ME. / THE VIOLENCE OF TRUTH** | 63 | |
(12"+=/cd-s+=) *(EMUT/CDEMU 9)* – I've been waiting for tomorrow (all of my life).
(etched-12") *(EMUE 9)* – ('A'dub) / I've been waiting for tomorrow.

Sep 89. (7"/c-s) *(EMU/+C 10)* **ARMAGEDDON DAYS ARE HERE (AGAIN). / ('A'orchestral)** | 70 | |
(12"+=) *(EMUT 10)* – The nature of virtue / Perfect.
(cd-s+=) *(CDEMU 10)* – Perfect / Mental healing process.
(10"ep) *(EMUQT 10)* **THE THE V. WORLD EP** – ('A'side) / The nature of virtue / Perfect / Mental healing process.
(etched-12") *(EMUE 10)* – ('A'edit) / Perfect.

Feb 91. (12"/c-s) *(655 798-6/-4)* **JEALOUS OF YOUTH. / ANOTHER BOY DROWNING (live)** | 54 | |
(cd-s+=) **SHADES OF YOUTH EP** *(655 796-8)* – Solitude / Dolphins.

—— added **D.C. COLLARD** – instruments

Jan 93. (7"marble) *(658 457-7)* **DOGS OF LUST. / THE VIOLENCE OF TRUTH** | 25 | |
(12"pic-d+=/cd-s+=) *(658 457-6/-2)* – Infected (live).
(cd-s) *(658 457-5)* – ('A'side) / Jealous of youth (live) / Beyond love (live) / Armageddon days are here (again) (D.N.A. remix).

Jan 93. (cd/c/lp) *(472468-2/-4/-1)* <53164> **DUSK** | 2 | |
– True happiness this way lies / Love is stronger than death / Dogs of lust / This is the night / Slow emotion replay / Helpline operator / Sodium light baby / Lung shadows / Bluer than midnight / Lonely planet. *(cd re-iss. Apr02; 504468-2)*

THE THE (cont) — THE GREAT INDIE DISCOGRAPHY — **The 1980s**

Apr 93. (12"red-ep/cd-ep) *(659 077-6/-9)* **SLOW MOTION REPLAY. / DOGS OF LUST (3 mixes by Jim Thirlwell)** [35]
(cd-ep) *(659077-0)* – ('A'side) / Scenes from Active Twilight (parts I-V).

Jun 93. (12"/cd-ep/cd-ep) *(659 371-6/-2)* **LOVE IS STRONGER THAN DEATH. / THE SINKING FEELING (live) / THE MERCY BEAT (live) / ARMAGEDDON DAYS ARE HERE (AGAIN) (live)** [39]
(cd-ep) *(659 371-5)* – ('A'side) / Infected / Soul mining / Armageddon days are . . .

Jan 94. (c-ep/12"cd/cd-ep) *(659811-4/-6/-2)* **DIS-INFECTED EP** [17]
– This was the day / Dis-infected / Helpline operator (sick boy mix) / Dogs of lust (germicide mix).

Jan 95. (c-ep/10"/cd-ep) *(661091-0/-6/-9)* <*61119*> **I SAW THE LIGHT / I'M FREE AT LAST. / SOMEDAY YOU'LL CALL MY NAME / THERE'S NO ROOM IN MY HEART FOR THE BLUES** [31] Aug95

Feb 95. (cd/c/10"lp) *(478139-2/-4/-0)* <*66908*> **HANKY PANKY** [28]
– Honky tonkin' / Six more miles / My heart would know / If you'll be a baby to me / I'm a long gone daddy / Weary blues from waitin' / I saw the light / Your cheatin' heart / I can't get you off of my mind / There's a tear in my beer / I can't escape from you.

Nothing–Interscope Nothing–Interscope

Feb 00. (cd) (<*490510-2*>) **NAKEDSELF** [45]
– Boiling point / Shrunken man / The whisperers / Soul catcher / Global eyes / December sunlight / Swine fever / Diesel breeze / Weather belle / Voidy numbness / Phantom walls / Salt water.

Apr 00. (cd-ep) *(497273-2)* **THE SHRUNKENMAN EP** [-]
– Shrunken man / (mixes by DAAU / JOHN PARISH / FOETUS).

Jun 02. (cd-s) *(672855-2)* **PILLARBOX RED** [-]

– compilations, others, etc. –

Dec 88. (d-cd) *Epic; (CDTT 241)* **SOUL MINING / INFECTED** [-]
May 02. (d-cd) *Epic; (504469-2) / Sony; <86611>* **45 RPM – THE SINGLES OF . . .** [60]
Jul 02. (4xcd-box) *Epic; (507902-2)* **LONDON TOWN 1983-1993** [-]

THEY MIGHT BE GIANTS

Formed: Brooklyn, New York, USA . . . 1985 by former Bostonians, JOHN FLANSBURGH and JOHN LINNELL, who poached the group name from an early 70's movie starring George C. Scott. In true DIY fashion, this enterprising duo set up a "Dial-A-Song" service to preview their work, gathering up the cream of the material on offer for an eponymous debut album via NY indie, 'Bar None'. Licensed for the UK by 'Rough Trade', the record introduced British listeners to their quirky folk/punk hybrid and geek-appeal, drawing critical comparisons with everyone from R.E.M. to DEVO and even The RESIDENTS. Rising from relative obscurity to become college radio heroes in the space of a few years, THEY MIGHT BE GIANTS found alternative fame with follow-up set, 'LINCOLN' (1989), the band's offbeat combination of surreal/subversive lyrics and sherbet-laced melodies making them the toast of America's alternative scene. A subsequent transatlantic deal with 'Elektra' saw the duo score an unlikely UK Top 10 hit single with 'BIRDHOUSE IN YOUR SOUL', while the accompanying album, 'FLOOD', made the Top 20 despite its wilful experimentation. Mainstream success was fleeting, however, further singles failing to make the grade and a third album, 'APOLLO 18' (1992), proving too challenging even for many hardened fans. Things improved with the addition of four new band members in time for 'JOHN HENRY' (1994), the album pushing them to new heights back home and even securing them a soundtrack appearance on 1995 kids movie, 'Mighty Morphin Power Rangers'. Of late, the group has released two albums, 'FACTORY SHOWROOM' (1997) and 'SEVERE THE DAMAGE' (1998), the latter a live set which included a new track, 'DOCTOR WORM' and seven untitled songs written on the night! THEY MIGHT BE GIANTS have since released two more quirky sets, 'MINK CAR' (2001) and 'NO!' (2002), and have provided the theme tune to the successful "kids?" TV sit-com, 'Malcolm In The Middle'; all together now: "you're not the boss of me now". • **Covered:** ONE HERE PARADE (Phil Ochs) / 25 O'CLOCK (Dukes Of Stratosphear) / LADY IS A TRAMP (Hart-Rodgers) / JESSICA (Allman Brothers Band) / WHIRLPOOL (Meat Puppets) / .

Album rating: THEY MIGHT BE GIANTS (*7) / LINCOLN (*6) / DON'T LET'S START compilation (*6) / FLOOD (*4) / APOLLO 18 (*4) / JOHN HENRY (*6) / FACTORY SHOWROOM (*5) / SEVERE TIRE DAMAGE (*5) / MINK CAR (*6) / NO! (*5) / DIAL-A-SONG: 20 YEARS OF . . . double compilation (*8)

JOHN FLANSBURGH (b. 6 May'60, Boston) – vocals, guitar, bass drum / **JOHN LINNELL** (b.12 Jun'59, New York City) – vocals, accordion, keyboards

Rough Trade Restless

Oct 87. (lp/c) *(ROUGH/+C 15)* <*REST 72603*> **THEY MIGHT BE GIANTS**
– Everything right is wrong again / Put your hand inside the puppet head / Number three / Don't let's start / Hide away folk family / 32 footsteps / Toddler hiway / Rabid child / Nothing's gonna change my clothes / (She was a) Hotel detective / She's an angel / Youth culture killed my dog / Boat of car / Chess piece face / Absolutely Bill's mood / I hope that I get old before I die / Alienation's for the rich / The day / Rhythm section want ad. *(cd-iss. Mar89; RTDCD 57) (cd re-iss. Nov90 on 'Elektra'; EKT 80CD) (cd re-iss. Sep02 on 'Restless'; REST 72603)*

Jun 88. (7") <*72605*> **DON'T LET'S START. / WE'RE THE REPLACEMENTS**
(12"+=) – When it rains it snows / The famous polka.

One Little Indian / Bar None

Jan 89. (12"ep) *(12TP 22)* **THEY'LL NEED A CRANE / I'VE GOT A MATCH. / KISS ME, SON OF GOD / I'LL SINK MANHATTAN**

Feb 89. (lp/c/cd) *(TP LP/C/CD 12)* <*REST 72600*> **LINCOLN** [89] Dec88
– The world's address / I've got a match / Santa's beard / You'll miss me / They'll need a crane / Shoehorn with teeth / Stand on your head / Snowball in Hell / Kiss me, son of God / Ana Ng / Cowtown / Lie still, little bottle / Purple toupee / Cage & aquarium / Where your eyes don't go / Piece of dirt / Pencil rain. *(re-iss. Jun91 on 'Elektra' cd; 7559 61145-2)(EKT 89C) (cd re-iss. Sep02 on 'Restless'; same as US)*

Mar 89. (12"ep) *(12TP 24)* **ANA NG / NIGHTGOWN OF THE SULLEN MOON. / IT'S NOT MY BIRTHDAY / LIE STILL, LITTLE BOTTLE**

Elektra Elektra

Feb 90. (7") *(EKR 104)* **BIRDHOUSE IN YOUR SOUL. / HOT CHA** [6]
(12"+=/cd-s+=) *(EKR 104 T/CD)* – Hearing aid / Ant.

Mar 90. (cd)(lp/c) <*(7559 60907-2/-4)*> **FLOOD** [14] [75] Feb90
– Theme from Flood / Birdhouse in your soul / Lucky ball and chain / Istanbul (not Constantinople) / Dead / Your racist friend / Particle man / Twisting / We want a rock / Someone keeps moving my chair / Hearing aid / Minimum wage / Letterbox / Whistling in the dark / Hot cha / Women & men / Sapphire bullets of pure love / They might be giants / Road movie to Berlin.

May 90. (7"/c-s) *(EKR 110/+C)* **ISTANBUL (NOT CONSTANTINOPLE). / JAMES K. POLK** [61] [-]
(12"+=) *(EKR 110T)* – Stormy pinkness.
(cd-s++=) *(EKR 110CD)* – ('A'-Brownsville mix).

Sep 90. (7"/c-s) **DON'T LET'S START (remix). / LETTERBOX**
(12"+=/cd-s+=) – Your racist friend (remix).

May 91. (7"/c-s) **ANA NG. / THEY'LL NEED A CRANE**
(12"+=/cd-s+=) – (She was a) Hotel detective / Don't let's start.

Jan 92. (7"/c-s) **THE STATUE GOT ME HIGH. / SHE'S ACTUAL SIZE**
(12"/cd-s) – ('A'side / I'm def / Which describes how you're feeling (1985 demos).

Mar 92. (cd)(lp/c) *(7559 61257-2)(EKT 104/+C)* **APOLLO 18** [99]
– Dig my grave / I palindrome I / She's actual size / My evil twin / Mammal / The statue got me high / Spider / The guitar (the lion sleeps tonight) / Dinner bell / Narrow your eyes / Hall of heads / Which desribes how you're feeling / See the constellation / If I wasn't shy / Turn around / Hypnotist of ladies / Fingertips / Space suit.

Apr 92. (7"/c-s) <*66394*> **THE GUITAR (THE LION SLEEPS TONIGHT). / ('A'extended)**
(12"+=) – Larger than life (Joshua Fried's remake of 'She's Actual Size') / ('A'outer planet mix) / ('A'other outer planet mix).
(cd-s+=) – Cabbage town / Siftin'.

— The 2 JOHNS added; **TONY MAIMONE** (b.27 Sep'52, Cleveland, Ohio) – bass / **BRIAN DOHERTY** (b. 2 Jul'62, Brooklyn) – drums

Sep 94. (cd/c) <*(7559 61654-2/-4)*> **JOHN HENRY** [59]
– Subliminal / Snail shell / Sleeping in the flowers / Unrelated thing / AKA driver / I should be allowed to think / Extra saviour faire / Why must I be sad? / Spy / O do not forsake me / No one knows my plan / Dirt bike / Destination Moon / A self called nowhere / Meet James Ensor / Thermostat / Window / Out of jail / Stomp box / The end of the tour.

Oct 94. (7"ep/c-ep/12"ep/cd-ep) *(EKR 194/+C/T/CD)* <*66198*> **BACK TO SKULL EP**
– Snail shell / She was a hotel detective (1994 version) / Mrs. Train / Snail dust (the Dust Brothers remix of Snail shell).

Dec 94. (cd-ep) <*66272*> **WHY DOES THE SUN SHINE? (THE SUN IS A MASS OF INCANDESCANT GAS) / JESSICA / WHIRLPOOL / SPY** [-]

— now with a plethora of backing musicians

Nov 96. (cd-s) <*63995*> **S-E-X-X-Y. / SENSURROUND / UNFORGOTTEN / WE'VE GOT A WORLD THAT SWINGS / S-E-X-X-Y. (extended)** [-]

Feb 97. (cd/c) <*(7559 61862-2/-4)*> **FACTORY SHOWROOM** [89]
– S-E-X-X-Y / Till my head falls off / How can I sing like a girl? / Exquisite dead guy / Metal detector / New York City / Your own worst enemy / XTC vs. Adam Ant / Spiraling shape / James K. Polk / Pet name / I can hear you / The bells are ringing.

Cooking Vinyl / Restless

Aug 98. (cd) *(COOKCD 156)* <*REST 72965*> **SEVERE TIRE DAMAGE (live)**
– Doctor Worm / Severe tire damage / They got lost / Why does the sun shine? / Birdhouse in your soul / She's an angel / XTC vs. Adam Ant / Istanbul (not Constantinople) / Anang / First kiss / Spider / Particle man / She's actual size / S-E-X-X-Y / Meet James Esnor / Till my head falls off / About me.

Jan 99. (cd-s) *(FRYCD 078)* **DOCTOR WORM / BIRDHOUSE IN YOUR SOUL / ISTANBUL (NOT CONSTANTINOPLE) / XTC VS. ADAM ANT**

not iss. / Good Noise

Feb 99. (d-cd) <*18*> **MIGHTATHON** [-] [-] net

— **GRAHAM MABY** – bass; repl. MAIMONE

May 00. (cd-ep) <*17940*> **WORKING UNDERCOVER FOR THE MAN**
– Rest awhile / Working undercover for the man / I am a human head / Empty bottle collector / On the drag / (excerpts) / Robot parade.

Play It Again Sam / Restless

Jul 01. (c-s) *(PIASREST 001MC)* **BOSS OF ME / REPREHENSIBLE** [21]
(cd-s+=) *(PIASREST 001CD)* – Xcitement.

Nov 01. (cd) *(PIASREST 004CD)* <*73744*> **MINK CAR**
– Bangs / Cyclops rock / Man, it's so loud in here / Mr. Xcitement / Another first kiss / I've gotta fang / Hovering sombrero / Yeh yeh / Hopeless bleak despair / Drink! / My man / Older / Mink car / Wicked little critta / Finished with lies / She thinks she's Edith Head / Working undercover for the man.

Nov 01. (cd-ep) <*REST 73756*> **HOLIDAYLAND (festive)** [-]
– Santa Claus / Santa's beard / Feast of lights / Careless Santa / O Tannenbaum.

Dec 01. (cd-s) *(PIASREST 006CD)* **MAN, IT'S SO LOUD IN HERE (mixes by radio / album / Hot 2002)** [-]

Rounder Rounder

Jun 02. (cd) <*(ROUCD 8113)*> **NO!**
– Fibber island / Four of two / Robot parade / No! / Where do they make balloons? / In the middle, in the middle, in the middle / Violin / John Lee supertaster / The Edison museum / The house at the top of the tree / Clap your hands / I am not a grovery bag / Wake up call / Lazyhead and sleepybones / Bed bed bed / Sleepwalkers.

THEY MIGHT BE GIANTS (cont)

– compilations, etc. –

Nov 89. (lp/c/cd) *Rough Trade; (TP LP/C/CD 14)* **DON'T LET'S START**
Jul 91. (cd/c) *Restless; <REST 72646-2/-4>* **MISCELLANEOUS T**
(B-sides, etc)
(UK cd-iss. Sep02; same as US)
Mar 97. (d-cd) *Restless; <REST 72931>* **THEN: THE EARLIER YEARS**
– (THEY MIGHT BE GIANTS + LINCOLN + MISCELLANEOUS T) *(UK-iss.Sep02; same as US)*
Sep 02. (d-cd) *Rhino; <(8122 78139-2)>* **DIAL-A-SONG: 20 YEASRS OF THEY MIGHT BE GIANTS**
– Birdhouse in your soul / Ana Ng / Don't let's start / Boss of me / Older / Istanbul (not Constantinople) / Doctor Worm / The guitar / Dr. Evil / New York City / Particle man / Cyclops rock / Minimum wage / Man, it's so loud in here / We're the REplacements / Why does the sun shine (the sun is a mass of incandescent gas) (live) / Your racist friend / Bangs / Snail shell / Twisting / Another first kiss / They'll need a crane / The statue got me high / (She was a) Hotel detective / Put your hand inside the puppet head / I palindrome I / She's an angel / How can I sing like a girl? / James K. Polk / Meet James Ensor / Mammal / Pet name / No! / I can hear you / Spider / I should be allowed to think / Fingertips / She's actual size / Spy / Stormy pinkness / Exquisite dead guy / Robot parade / Boat of car / S-E-X-X-Y / Number three / The end of the tour / The might be giants / Hey Mr. DJ, I thought you said we had a deal / Nightgown of the sullen moon / Snowball in Hell / Purple toupee / Cowtown.
Nov 02. (cd) *Idlewild; <(IDLE 102)>* **THEY GOT LOST**

THINKING FELLERS UNION LOCAL 282

Formed: San Francisco, California, USA ... 1987 by HUGH SWARTS, plus BRIAN HAGEMAN, MARK DAVIES and ANNE EICKELBERG. Arty, experimental indie/noise merchants to a man (and woman!), THINKING FELLERS UNION LOCAL 282 liked nothing better than to create stubbornly off-kilter musi-forms by doing strange things with such un-rock'n'roll instruments as banjo, trombone and mandolin. The quirky quartet made their debut in 1988 with the extremely rare cassette-only release, 'WORMED, BY LEONARD' (a tribute to Leonard Nimoy); this, like its follow-up, 'TANGLE', was issued on the 'Thwart' imprint, a label run by the band's own HUGH SWARTS. Moving on to 'Matador' at the turn of the decade, they made at least some concessions to musical convention with 'LOVELYVILLE', flickering melodies clearly discernible through the avant-garde fog. The uninitiated are directed towards 1992's 'MOTHER OF ALL SAINTS', a twenty-plus collection of bonafide "songs" interspersed with snippets of wilful weirdness. SWARTS and Co moved even further towards relative songwriting "normality" with 1994's low-key 'STRANGERS FROM THE UNIVERSE', their final effort for 'Matador'. A further couple of independently released albums, 'PORCELAIN ENTERTAINMENTS' and 'I HOPE IT LANDS', appeared in the mid-90's although it took over 5 years to return with 'BOB DINNERS AND LARRY NOODLES PRESENT . . .' (2001).

Album rating: WORMED, BY LEONARD (*4) / LOVELYVILLE (*5) / TANGLE (*5) / MOTHER OF ALL SAINTS (*6) / STRANGERS FROM THE UNIVERSE (*4) / THE FUNERAL PUDDING (*5) / I HOPE IT LANDS (*6) / PORCELAIN ENTERTAINMENTS (*4) / BOB DINNERS AND LARRY NOODLES PRESENT . . . (*4)

HUGH SWARTS – vocals, guitar / **MARK DAVIES** – guitar, banjo, trombone / **BRIAN HAGEMAN** – guitar, mandolin, viola / **ANNE EICKELBERG** – bass, vocals / **PAUL BERGMANN** – drums, accordion, vocals

not iss.   Thwart

1988. (c) *<THW 002>* **WORMED, BY LEONARD**
– It's seven / Hell rules / Leaky bag / I don't know / Milva spectre / Nipper / Oregon trail / Misfits park / Coming and going / Mr. Tuna's big old place / Narlus spectre / K.L.T.X. / Truck driving man / Out in the kitchen / Serious matter / Mile wide / Motorin' flarey Henderson / Indigestion. *(UK-iss.Oct95 & Dec96 on 'Thwart' d-lp/cd+=; THW 002-1/-2)* – Get off my house / Scraping skin off my shoulder / Trevor / Superstar / If I were in a shoe / Squidder boy / Fat Christmas / Not in the popply dimension.
1989. (lp) *<THW 012>* **TANGLE**
– Sister hell / Prelmnlrl / It wasn't me / Keeps repeating / Sports car / Burning up / What time is it / Change your mind / Cold cold cold ground / Choke. *<cd-iss. 1995; THW 012CD>*

—— added **JAY PAGET** – guitar, drums, keyboards; repl. BERGMANN

Matador   Matador

Dec 91. (cd/c/lp) *<OLE 031>* **LOVELYVILLE**
– Four o'clocker 2 / Not this world / Nail in the head / Green-eyed lady / Mother uncle delicious tasty / Sweet vibrated with the traffic and . . . . / Mark my words / Push / More glee / Big hands / The marshall / Sinking boats / Motorin' Flarey Jenkins / 2x4s / Nothing solid / Maverick / Wonderbread display / The meat display / Strife is good / The marshall's boots / The world is changing for good / The demise of Craig.
Nov 92. (cd/c/d-lp) *<OLE 043>* **MOTHER OF ALL SAINTS**
– Untitled / Gentlemen's lament / Catcher / Hornet's heart / Star Trek / Tell me / Heaven for addled imbeciles / Hive / Hummingbird in a cube of ice / None too fancy / Wide forehead / Infection / Pleasure circle / Tight little thing / Hosanna loud Hosanna / Tuning notes / Shuddering big butter / 1" tall / Raymond H. / Untitled / Cistern / El cerrito / Fishbowl.
1993. (cd-ep) **WHERE'S OFFICER TUBA?**
– Wide forehead / A gentleman's lament / Outhouse of the Pryeeeee / I am beautiful, I am good / Hive / Heaven for real idiots / Strolling big butter / 282 years.
(above issued on 'Hemiola')
Feb 94. (10"ep/cd-ep) *<OLE 068-1/-2)>* **ADMONISHING THE BISHOPS**
– Hurricane / Undertaker / Million dollars / Father.   Oct93

Oct 94. (cd/lp) *<(OLE 109-2/-1)>* **STRANGERS FROM THE UNIVERSE**   Sep94
– My pal the tortoise / Socket / Bomber pilot WWII / Hundreds of years / Guillotine / Uranium / February / Pull my pants up tight / Cup of dreams / The oxenmaster / The operation / The piston and the shaft / Communication / Noble experiment.

not iss.   Amarillo

1995. (12") **EVERYDAY. / SELECTIONS FROM A FISTFUL OF DOLLARS**

Communion   Communion

Dec 96. (lp/cd) *<(COMM 43/+CD)>* **I HOPE IT LANDS**
– The poem / A lamb's lullaby / Empty cup / I hope it lands / Lizard's dream / Comad adrift toward Mars / Elgin Miller / Hudson bottom dance / Jagged ambush bug / Brains / Rampaging fuckers of anything on the crazy planet / Cuckoo at the world / Inspector fat ass / The arbeiter / Triple X / Booth delirium / Hills.
Apr 01. (lp/cd) *<(COMM 53/+CD)>* **BOB DINNERS AND LARRY NOODLES PRESENT TUBBY TURDNER'S CELEBRITY AVALANCHE**
– Another clip / Sno cone / You will be eliminated / Holy ghost / Everything's impossible / Birth of a rock song / You in a movie / Boob feeder / In the stars I can sizzle like a battery / El cerrito / '91 Dodge van / Reminder / The barker / He keeps himself fed.

– others, etc. –

Mar 94. (cd)/(lp) *Brinkman; (BR 21CD) / Ajax; (AJAX 038-1)* **THE FUNERAL PUDDING**   Jan95
– Waited too long / Flames up / Firing squad / 23 Kings crossing / Heavy head / Give me back my golden arm / Sidewinder / The invitation / (untitled).
Jan 96. (cd) *Return To Sender; <(RTS 21)>* **PORCELAIN ENTERTAINMENTS**
– The piston and the shaft (live) / Undertaker (live) / Green eyed lady (live) / Egg danger (live) / Quacky (live) / Selections from "A Fisftfull Of Dollars" (live) / Paul Borge / Chickens' escape plan / Chicken keeper / 52 girlfriends / White box / Tunnel tube / Release / The soilie smutchy / Mission's eve. *(re-iss. Aug99; same) (lp-iss.Oct00 on 'Fruit Tree'; FT 809)*

THIN WHITE ROPE

Formed: Davis, Sacramento, California, USA ... 1984 by mainman GUY KYSER. Despite being initially lumped in with the retro psyche/country movement peopled by the likes of RAIN PARADE and The LONG RYDERS, THIN WHITE ROPE's debut album, 'EXPLORING THE AXIS', suggested more in common, spiritually at least, with the parched desert-rock of HOWIE GELB and his GIANT SAND project. The album found its way into the hands of Demon off-shoot label, 'Zippo', who gave it a UK release in late '85 although it wasn't until the release of 1987's acclaimed 'MOONHEAD' that THIN WHITE ROPE (named after William Burroughs' memorable description of the male ejaculation) began attracting the recognition they so richly deserved. The twin guitar assault of messrs. KYSER and KUNKEL brought frequent comparisons with NEIL YOUNG/CRAZY HORSE's trademark sonic alchemy while the frontman's twisted lyrics did indeed suggest a love of Burroughs' dark surrealism. 'IN THE SPANISH CAVE' followed a year later as their critical standing soared, the band subsequently signing to 'R.C.A.' in 1989. The resulting 'SACK FULL OF SILVER' (1990) was received with slightly less enthusiasm and with diminishing critical and creative returns, the band was amicably wound up in summer '92. A farewell gig was recorded and released the following year as 'THE ONE THAT GOT AWAY'. All the members continued with other projects while KYSER combined songwriting with studying for a degree. • **Covered:** ROADRUNNER (Bo Diddley) / AIN'T THAT LOVIN' YOU BABY (Jimmy Reed) / TOWN WITHOUT PITY (hit; Gene Pitney) / SOME VELVET MORNING (Lee Hazlewood) / MAY THIS BE LOVE (Jimi Hendrix) / YOO DOO RIGHT (Can) / THE MAN WITH THE GOLDEN GUN (John Barry) / BORN TO FLAMES (13th Floor Elevators) / OUTLAW BLUES (Bob Dylan) / EYE (Foster Children) / THEY'RE HANGING ME TONIGHT (Love – Wolpert) / HERE SHE COMES NOW (Velvet Underground) / etc.

Album rating: EXPLORING THE AXIS (*6) / MOONHEAD (*8) / IN THE SPANISH CAVE (*7) / SACK FULL OF SILVER (*7) / THE RUBY SEA (*5) / THE ONE THAT GOT AWAY (*5) / WHEN WORLDS COLLIDE (*5) / SPOOR compilation (*4)

GUY KYSER – vocals, guitar / **ROGER KUNKEL** – guitar / **STEPHEN TESLUK** – bass; who repl. KEVIN STAYHODOR / **JOZEF BECKER** – drums; repl. FRANK FRENCH (ex-TRUE WEST)

Zippo   Frontier

Sep 85. (lp/c) *(ZONG/+CASS 006) <FRO 1015>* **EXPLORING THE AXIS**
– Down in the desert / Disney girl / Soundtrack / Lithium / Dead grammas on a train / The three song / Eleven / Roger's tongue / The real west / Exploring the axis. *(cd-iss. Jul90; ZONGCD 006) (cd re-iss. Apr97 on 'Diablo'+=; DIAB 824)* – BOTTOM FEEDERS
Jan 87. (lp) *(ZONG 017) <FRO 1020>* **MOONHEAD**
– Not your fault / Wire animals / Take it home / Thing / Moonhead / Wet heart / Mother / Come around / If those tears / Crawl piss freeze. *(w/free-flexi-7"; FRT 104)* – WIRE ANIMALS. / WET HEART *(cd-iss. Jul90 +=; ZONGCD 017)* – Waking up / Valley of the bones / Atomic imagery / Ain't that lovin' you baby. *(cd re-iss. Apr97 on 'Diablo'+=; DIAB 825)*
Sep 87. (m-lp) *(ZANE 005)* **BOTTOM FEEDERS** (rare, etc.)
– Ain't that loving you baby / Macy's window / Waking up / Valley of the bones / Atomic imagery / Rocket U.S.A. (live).

—— added **JOHN VON FELDT** – bass

Demon   Frontier

Mar 88. (lp/cd) *(FIEND/+CD 114) <46151-2>* **IN THE SPANISH CAVE**
– Mr. Limpet / Ring / It's o.k. / Ahr-Skidar / Red sun / Elsie crashed the party / Timing / Astronomy / Wand / July. *(cd+=)* – BOTTOM FEEDERS (m-lp) *<US-c++=>* – Munich Eunich.

—— now without JOZEF who joined GAME THEORY (now full-time)

THIN WHITE ROPE (cont)

Oct 88. (m-lp) (VEX 8) **RED SUN**
 – Red sun / Town without pity / The man with the golden gun / They're hanging me tonight / Some velvet morning / Red sun (original). (cd-iss. May92;)

—— added **MATTHEW ABOUREZK** – drums

May 90. (cd/c/lp) (PD/PK/PL 90469) <9994-2/-4/-1> **SACK FULL OF SILVER** R.C.A. R.C.A. Feb90
 – Hidden lands / Sack full of silver / Yoo do right (can) / The napkin song / Americana – The ghost / Whirling Dervish / The tiggle song / Diesel man / On the floe. (re-iss. Jul92 on 'Frontier' clear-lp; 34638-1)

Apr 91. (7") <(SP 94)> **ANTS ARE CAVEMEN. / LITTLE DOLL** (live) Sub Pop Sub Pop Frontier Frontier

May 91. (m-cd/m-lp) <(FCD/FLP 1035)> **SQUATTERS RIGHTS**
 – Caravan / Roadrunner / Film theme / May this be love / Everybody's been burned / I knew I'd want you.

Aug 91. (cd/c/lp) <(34632-2/-4/-1)> **THE RUBY SEA**
 – The ruby sea / Tina and Glen / Puppet dog / Bartender's rag / Midwest flower / Dinosaur / The lady vanishes / Up to midnight / Hunter's moon / Christmas skies / The fish song / The clown song. (cd re-iss. Jul98 on 'Diablo'+=; DIAB 828) – SQUATTER'S RIGHTS

—— disbanded on 28th June 1992 after their last concert below

– compilations, others, etc. –

on 'Frontier-RCA' unless mentioned otherwise

Mar 93. (d-cd/d-c/d-lp) <(34642-2/-4/-1)> **THE ONE THAT GOT AWAY (live)**
 – Down in the desert / Disney girl / Eleven / Not your fault / Wire animals / Take it home / Mr. Limpet / Elsie crashed the party / Red sun / Some velvet morning / Triangle song / Yoo doo right / Tina & Glen / Napkin song / Ants are cavemen / Fish song / Bartender's rag / Hunter's moon / Astronomy / Outlaw blues / It's o.k. / Wreck of the ol' 97 / Roadrunner / Take it home / Munich Eunich / Silver machine / The clown song. (d-cd re-iss. Jul98 on 'Diablo'; DIAB 829)

Dec 93. (ltd-7") (4678-7) **MOONHEAD. / THE RUBY SEA**

May 94. (cd/lp) Munster; (MR 047 CD/LP) / Bird Cage; <11778> **WHEN WORLDS COLLIDE** (demos, etc.) Mar94
 – Down in the desert / Valley of the bones / Moonhead / Elsie crashed the party / Red sun / Eleven / The ruby sea / Roadrunner / Take it home / Tina and Glen / Macy's window / (untitled) / Wire animals / Diesel man / Some velvet morning / Napkin song / Ants are cavemen / Burn the flames / Fish song.

Feb 95. (cd/lp) <(31064-2/-1)> **SPOOR**
 – Radio afternoon / Town without pity / Red sun / The man with the golden gun / They're hanging me tonight / Some velvet morning / Ants are caveman / Little doll / Outlaw blues / Born to flames / Eye / Skinhead / Tina and Glen / Munich Eunich / God rest ye merry gentlemen / Here she comes now.

THIRST (see under ⇒ BLUE ORCHIDS)

13th FLOOR ELEVATORS

Formed: Austin, Texas, USA . . . 1965 by ROKY ERICKSON and TOMMY HALL, together with STACY SUTHERLAND, BENNY THURMAN and JOHN IKE WALTON. ERICKSON had originally written and recorded 'YOU'RE GONNA MISS ME' with his first band, The SPADES, the single being released on the small 'Zero' label. A local hit, the record gained national notoriety in early '66 after being picked up by the 'International Artists' label. Around this time, self-styled psychedelic explorer, TOMMY HALL, had introduced ERICKSON to the aforementioned musicians (all three were ex-LINGSMEN) and The 13th FLOOR ELEVATORS were launched into orbit. The frenzied garage thrash of 'YOU'RE GONNA MISS ME' stood out from the pack by dint of ERICKSON's apocalyptic vocal threats and HALL's bizarre amplified jug playing. In addition to his idiosyncratic musical accompaniment, HALL penned most of the lyrics, setting out his agenda according to the chemically-enhanced evolution-of-man ethos espoused by the likes of acid guru, TIM LEARY. Debuting with 'THE PSYCHEDELIC SOUNDS OF THE 13TH FLOOR ELEVATORS' in 1966, the band had unleashed nothing less than a musical manifesto for mind expansion. But if the idea was to promote the use of halucinogenics, then the sirens on the DMT-tribute, 'FIRE ENGINE', surely encouraged any sane person never to go near the stuff, sounding more like the tortured wailing of lost, limbo-locked souls. Likewise 'MONKEY ISLAND', with ERICKSON howling like a man possessed. Elsewhere on the album, tracks like 'ROLLERCOASTER' and 'REVERBERATION (DOUBT)' made for thrilling, if uneasy listening, and it was obvious that a trip to the 13th floor with ROCKY and Co. was somewhat different from the rosy hue that the psychedelic experience had taken on in popular mythology. The follow-up, 'EASTER EVERYWHERE' (1967), was a slightly more contemplative affair, opening with the hypnotic brilliance of 'SLIP INSIDE THIS HOUSE' (the subject of an equally essential 90's interpretation by PRIMAL SCREAM) through the trippy 'SHE LIVES (IN A TIME OF HER OWN)' and on to the frantic 'LEVITATION'. Inevitably, the Texan police were none too amused with the band's flagrant advocacy of drugs and after escalating harassment, ERICKSON found himself in court shortly after the album's release. Charged with possession of a small amount of hashish, he was faced with a choice of jail or mental hospital and rather illadvisedly chose the latter. This effectively signalled the end for the band, although a disappointing live album was released the following year and a final studio album appeared in 1969. 'BULL OF THE WOODS' was made up largely of SUTHERLAND-penned tunes although it contained the sublime 'MAY THE CIRCLE REMAIN UNBROKEN', ERICKSON's vocal all the more haunting in light of his tragic incarceration. Subjected to years of mind-numbing drugs and electro shock therapy, ROCKY was finally released in 1972 after a judge declared him sane. Ironically no doubt somewhat less sane after this experience, ERICKSON started making music again, forming a band, BLIWB ALIEN, and immersing himself in B-movie horror nonsense. After a stint in the studio with fellow Texan, DOUG SAHM, of SIR DOUGLAS QUINTET fame, ERICKSON released the inspired psychosis of the 'RED TEMPLE PRAYER (TWO HEADED DOG)' single in 1975. An album, 'ROCKY ERICKSON AND THE ALIENS' surfaced in 1980 and included such wholesome fare as 'DON'T SHAKE ME LUCIFER', 'CREATURE WITH THE ATOM BRAIN' and 'STAND FOR THE FIRE DEMON'. Yet this was no po-faced heavy-metal posturing, ERICKSON actually believed what he was singing about, lending the record a certain level of intensity, despite the cliched hard rock backing. A series of singles and compilations appeared sporadically throughout the 80's, and after ERICKSON was hospitalised again for a short period, 'Warner Bros.' executive and longtime ELEVATORS fan, BILL BENTLEY, masterminded a tribute album, 'Where The Pyramid Meets The Eye', featuring the likes of The JESUS AND MARY CHAIN and JULIAN COPE. Although a collection of early material, 'ALL THAT MAY DO MY RHYME', appeared in 1975 on The BUTTHOLE SURFERS' 'Trance Syndicate' label, ERICKSON appears to have no interest in writing new material. Music biz legend paints the man as an acid casualty, and while he definitely appears to live in a world of his own making, his wayward genius continues to win the respect and admiration of fans the world over. • **Songwriters:** ERICKSON penned except; I'M GONNA LOVE YOU TOO (Buddy Holly) / HEROIN (Velvet Underground) / BLOWIN' IN THE WIND (Bob Dylan) / etc.

Album rating: THE PSYCHEDELIC SOUNDS OF (*7) / EASTER EVERYWHERE (*6) / LIVE exploitation (*4) / BULL OF THE WOODS exploitation (*5) / THE BEST OF THE 13th FLOOR ELEVATORS compilation (*7) / HIS EYE IS ON THE PYRAMID compilation (*8) / Roky Erickson: ROCKY ERICKSON & THE ALIENS (*8) / THE EVIL ONE (*5) / CLEAR NIGHT FOR LOVE mini (*4) / GREMLINS HAVE PICTURES (*4) / DON'T SLANDER ME (*5) / CASTING THE RUNES collection (*4) / THE HOLIDAY INN TAPES fan-club (*4) / OPENERS exploitation (*4) / LIVE AT THE RITZ (*4) / YOU'RE GONNA MISS ME: THE BEST OF ROKY ERICKSON compilation (*7) / MAD DOG compilation (*4) / ALL THAT MAY DO MY RHYME (*6) / NEVER SAY GOODBYE (*7)

The SPADES

—— (had already recorded a single 'I NEED A GIRL', before ROKY joined)

—— **ROKY ERICKSON** (b. ROGER KYNARD ERICKSON, 15 Jul'47, Dallas, Texas) – vocals, harmonica / **JOHN KERNEY** – guitar, vocals

1965. (7") <10002> **YOU'RE GONNA MISS ME. / WE SELL SOUL** not iss. Zero

13th FLOOR ELEVATORS

—— were formed by **ROKY** and **STACEY SUTHERLAND** – lead guitar (ex-LINGSMEN) / **BENNY THURMAN** – bass, electric violin (ex-LINGSMEN) / **JOHN IKE WALTON** – drums (ex-LINGMEN) / **TOMMY HALL** – blow jug, lyrics

Jan 66. (7") <5269> **YOU'RE GONNA MISS ME. / TRIED TO HIDE** not iss. Contact
 <re-iss. Apr66 on 'Hanna Barbara'; HBR 492> <re-iss. Jun66 on 'International Artists'; 107>; hit No.55> (UK-iss.Nov78 on 'Radar' 7"green; ADA 13)

—— **RONNIE LEATHERMAN** – bass repl. BENNY who formed PLUM NELLY

Aug 66. (lp) <IALP 1> **THE PSYCHEDELIC SOUNDS OF** not iss. Int.Artists
 – You're gonna miss me / Roller coaster / Splash 1 / Don't fall down / Reverberation (doubt) / Fire engine / Thru the rhythm / You don't know / Kingdom of Heaven / Monkey island / Tried to hide. <re-iss. 1977; same> (UK-iss.Nov78 on 'Radar'; RAD 13) (re-iss. Feb88 on 'Decal'; LIK 19) (cd-iss. 1990's on 'Decal-Charly'; CDGR 110) (cd re-iss. Jan99 on 'Spalax'; 14819) (lp re-iss. Nov99; same as US)

Oct 66. (7") <111> **REVERBERATION (DOUBT). / FIRE ENGINE**

—— **DAN GALINDO** – bass + **DANNY THOMAS** – drums repl. RONNIE + JOHN IKE

Feb 67. (7") <113> **I'VE GOT LEVITATION. / BEFORE YOU ACCUSE ME**

Apr 67. (lp) <IALP 5> **EASTER EVERYWHERE**
 – Slip inside the house / Slide machine / She lives in a time of her own / Nobody to love / It's all over now, baby blue / Earthquake / Dust / I've got levitation / I had to tell you / Postures (leave your body behind). <re-iss. 1977; same> (UK-iss.May79 on 'Radar'; RAD 15) (re-iss. Apr88 on 'Decal'; LIK 28) (cd-iss. Jan99 on 'Spalax'; 14888) (lp re-iss. May99; same as US)

Oct 67. (7") <121> **SHE LIVES (IN A TIME OF HER OWN). / BABY BLUE**

Dec 67. (7") <122> **SLIP INSIDE THIS HOUSE. / SPLASH 1**

—— Disbanded early '68, due to ROKY being imprisoned for possession of a miniscule amount of hash. He once escaped but was then kept there for another 3 years, and suffered thorazine plus electric shock treatment. **DUKE DAVIS** – bass had briefly repl. GALINDO. DANNY THOMAS and DUKE were to become The GOLDEN DAWN. The original 13th FLOOR ELEVATORS reformed in 1972. In 1984, they gigged again with line-up (ERICKSON, WALTON, LEATHERMAN and GREG 'Catfish' FORREST-guitar). In Autumn 1978, STACEY was shot dead by his wife.

– others, compilations, etc. –

on 'International Artists' unless otherwise mentioned

1968. (lp) <IALP 8> **LIVE** (studio out-takes, b-sides, demos; with false applause)
 – Before you accuse me / She lives in a time of her own / Tried to hide / You gotta take that girl / I'm gonna love you too / Everybody needs somebody to love / I've got levitation / You can't hurt me anymore / Roller coaster / You're gonna miss me. (UK-iss.May88 on 'Decal'; LIK 30)

13th FLOOR ELEVATORS (cont)

Date	Format	Details
1968.	(7") <126>	**MAY THE CIRCLE BE UNBROKEN. / I'M GONNA LOVE YOU TOO**
1969.	(lp) <IALP 9>	**BULL OF THE WOODS** (rec. early '68)
		– Livin' on / Barnyard blues / Till then / Never another / Rose and the thorn / Down by the river / Scarlet and gold / Street song / Doctor Boom / With you / May the circle remain unbroken. (UK-iss.Jul88 on 'Decal'; LIK 40) (cd-iss. Jan99 on 'Spalax'; 14886) (lp re-iss. Aug99; same as US)
1969.	(7") <130>	**LIVIN' ON. / SCARLET AND GOLD**
Oct 78.	(7"ep) Austin; <RE 1>	**YOU REALLY GOT ME. / WORD / ROLL OVER BEETHOVEN**
1985.	(lp) Texas Archives; <TAR LP-4>	**FIRE IN MY BONES**
1987.	(lp) Texas Archives; <TAR LP-7>	**ELEVATOR TRACKS** (some live 1966)
1988.	(lp) Big Beat; (WIK 82)	**I'VE SEEN YOUR FACE BEFORE** (live bootleg '66) (cd-iss. Jun89; CDWIK 82)
1988.	(lp) 13th Hour; <(13-LP-1)>	**DEMOS EVERYWHERE** (US-title 'THE ORIGINAL SOUND OF . . .')
Nov 88.	(cd) Charly; (CDCHARLY 150)	**EASTER EVERYWHERE / BULL OF THE WOODS**
Jun 89.	(cd) Charly; (CDCHARLY 159)	**THE PSYCHEDELIC SOUNDS OF / LIVE**
Aug 91.	(4xcd-box) Decal; (LIKBOX 2)	**THE COLLECTION** – (all 1960's albums) <In 1979, these appeared on a 12-lp box of 'International Artists'>
Jul 93.	(cd) Thunderbolt; (CDTB 124)	**OUT OF ORDER (LIVE AT THE AVALON BALLROOM)**
Jun 94.	(cd) Thunderbolt; (CDTB 147)	**LEVITATION – IN CONCERT** (live)
Apr 95.	(cd) Thunderbolt; (CDTB 153)	**THE REUNION CONCERT**
Dec 95.	(cd) Nectar; (NTMCD 516)	**THE BEST OF THE 13th FLOOR ELEVATORS** – You're gonna miss me / Levitation / I had to tell you / She lives (in a time of her own) / Never another / I'm gonna love you too (live) / Thry the rhythm / The kingdom of Heaven / Slip inside this house / Mpnkey island / Splash 1 / Fire engine / Dr. Doom / Roller coaster / Earthquake / Reverberation (doubt) / May the circle remain unbroken / You're gonna miss me (live). (re-iss. Jul99 on 'Eva'; 642370)
Sep 96.	(cd) Thunderbolt; (CDTB 508)	**THE INTERPRETER** (re-iss. Jun99; CDTB 198)
Nov 97.	(cd) Music Club; (MCCD 324)	**ALL TIME HIGHS**
Nov 97.	(cd) Eagle; (EAGCD 069)	**THE MASTERS**
Oct 99.	(cd) Thunderbolt; (CDTB 199)	**THE INTERPRETER VOL.2**
Nov 99.	(d-cd) Recall; (SMDCD 190)	**HIS EYE IS ON THE PYRAMID**

ROKY ERICKSON

Date	Format	Details
1975.	(7"; with BLIEB ALIEN) <1000>	**RED TEMPLE PRAYER (TWO HEADED DOG). / STARRY EYES** (not iss. Mars)
Sep 77.	(7") (VS 180) <003>	**BERMUDA. / INTERPRETER** (Virgin / Rhino)
Dec 77.	(7"ep) (101)	**TWO HEADED DOG / I HAVE ALWAYS BEEN HERE BEFORE. / MINE, MINE, MIND / CLICK YOUR FINGERS APPLAUDING THE PLAY** (Sponge / not iss. France)

ROKY ERICKSON AND THE ALIENS

with DUANE ASLAKSEN – guitar / STEVE BURGESS – bass / ANDRE LEWIS – keyboards / FUZZY FURIOSO – drums / BILL MILLER – autoharp

Date	Format	Details
Aug 80.	(7") (CBS 8888)	**CREATURE WITH THE ATOM BRAIN. / THE WIND AND MORE** (C.B.S. / not iss.)
Aug 80.	(lp) (CBS 84463)	**ROKY ERICKSON & THE ALIENS** – Two headed dog / I think of demons / Don't shake me Lucifer / I walked with a zombie / Night of the vampire / Cold night for alligators / White faces / Creatures with the atom brain / Mine, mine, mind / Stand for the fire demon. (re-iss. Jan87 as 'I THINK OF DEMONS' on 'Edsel'+=; ED 222) – (2 tracks). (cd-iss. Jun97; EDCD 528)
Oct 80.	(7") (CBS 9055)	**MINE MINE MIND. / BLOODY HAMMER (long version)**

ROKY ERICKSON

Date	Format	Details
1981.	(lp; as ROKY ERICKSON AND THE ALIENS) <0005>	**THE EVIL ONE** (not iss. / 415 Records) – Two-headed dog (red temple prayer) / I think of demons / Creature with the atom brain / Wind and more / Don't shake me Lucifer / Bloody hammer / Stand for the the fire demon / Click your fingers applauding the play / If you have ghosts / I walked with a zombie / Night of the vampire / It's a cold night for alligators / Mine mine mind / Sputnik / White faces. <cd-iss. 1987 was a compilation on 'Enigma-Pink Dust'; 72212-2>
1984.	(7") <DY 002>	**DON'T SLANDER ME. / STARRY EYES** (not iss. / Dynamite)
1985.	(m-lp) (ROSE 69)	**CLEAR NIGHT FOR LOVE** (New Rose / not iss. France) – You don't love me yet / Clear night for love / The haunt / Starry eyes / Don't slander me.
Apr 86.	(12") (OBG 004T) <LW 5>	**THE BEAST. / HEROIN (live)** (One Big Guitar / Live Wire)
Jan 87.	(lp) (FIEND 66) <72109-1>	**GREMLINS HAVE PICTURES (live 1975-1982 with his bands)** (Demon / Enigma Nov85/Nov86) – Night of the interpreter / Song to Abe Lincoln / John Lawman / Anthem / Warning / Sweet honey pie / Cold night for alligators / I am / Heroin / I have always been here before / Before the beginning / Click your fingers applauding the play / If you have ghosts / Damn thing / Sputnik. (cd-iss. Oct90 with extra tracks; FIENDCD 66)
Jun 87.	(lp) (FIEND 86)	**DON'T SLANDER ME** – (contains some of 'THE EVIL ONE' lp)
Sep 87.	(lp) (FC 030)	**THE HOLIDAY INN TAPES** (Fan Club / not iss.)

next with WILL SEXTON + CHRIS HOLYHAUS – guitar / FREDDIE KRC – drums

Date	Format	Details
1988.	(lp) (FC 046)	**LIVE AT THE RITZ** (live Feb'87) – You're gonna miss me / Don't shake me / Don't shake me Lucifer / Night of the vampire / Two headed dog / Splash 1 / Take a good look at yourself / Clear night for love / Bloody hammer.

next with ET (aka EVILHOOK WILDLIFE) BRIAN S.CURLEY / KERRY GRAFTON / TIM GAGAN + DAVE CAMERON

Date	Format	Details
Feb 88.	(12") (PRAY 007)	**CLEAR NIGHT FOR LOVE. / YOU DON'T LOVE ME YET** (Fundam. / not iss.)
Dec 88.	(7"ep) (ROK 88)	**ACOUSTIC EP** (field recordings) (Rok / not iss.) – Right track now / Mr. Tambourine man / (interview excerpt 1980) / Creature with the atom brain / For you.
1990.	(7"colrd) <SFTRI 152>	**YOU DON'T LOVE ME YET. / I AM HER HERO, SHE IS MY HEROIN** (Sympathy.. / Sympathy..)
1992.	(7") <SFTRI 201>	**HASN'T ANYONE TOLD YOU (live). / THE INTERPRETER (live)**
Nov 94.	(7"ltd.) (TR 28)	**WE ARE NEVER TALKING. / PLEASE JUDGE (acoustic version)** (Trance Syndicate / Trance Syndicate)
Feb 95.	(lp/cd) <(TR 33/+CD)>	**ALL THAT MAY DO MY RHYME** – I'm gonna free her / Starry eyes / You don't love me yet / Please judge / Don't slander me / We are never talking / For you (I'd do anything) / For you / Clear night for love / Haunt / Starry eyes.

– compilations, others, etc. –

Date	Format	Details
Aug 87.	(lp/pic-lp) 5 Hours Back; (TOCK 007/+P)	**CASTING THE RUNES** (cd-iss. Jan99 on 'R.E.'; RE 1) (above live Nov79 with The EXPLOSIVES; aka CAM KING – lead guitar / WILLIE COLLIE – bass / FREDDIE KRC – drums)
1987.	(7"colrd) Scatterbrainchild; <SR 07>	**THE HAUNT OF ROKY ERICKSON** – Cold night for alligators / Can't be brought down.
Mar 88.	(lp) 5 Hours Back; (TOCK 010)	**OPENERS**
Jun 88.	(red-lp) 5 Hours Back; (TICK 001)	**TWO TWISTED TALES** (interview)
1988.	(cd) Fan Club; (ROKY 1)	**CLICK YOUR FINGERS APPLAUDING THE PLAY**
Sep 91.	(cd/c) Restless; <72532-2/-4>	**YOU'RE GONNA MISS ME: THE BEST OF ROKY ERICKSON** – Don't shake me Lucifer / Bermuda / Nothing in return / Click your fingers applauding the play / I am / I have always been here before / White faces / Night of the vampire / Don't slander me / Starry eyes / If you have ghosts / Can't be brought down / Creature with the atom brain / I walked with a zombie / Interpreter / Two-headed dog (red temple prayer) / You're gonna miss me / Wake up to rock'n'roll / Gonna die more / I'm a demon / Leave my kitten alone.
May 92.	(cd/c) Swordfish; (SFMD CD/+D 001)	**MAD DOG** (1976-83)
Oct 92.	(cd/lp) New Rose; (422404)	**LIVE DALLAS 1979 (live with The NERVEBREAKERS)**
Feb 93.	(cd) Swordfish; (SFMCD 2)	**LOVE TO SEE YOU BLEED** – Bloody hammer / Every time I look at you / Miss Elude / Haunt / Laughing things / You don't love me yet / Creature with the atom brain / I think of demons / Two headed dog / Red temple prayer / Bumblebee zombie / Click your fingers applauding / The play / Mine mine mind / Things that go bump in the night / Here today . . . gone tomorrow / Realise your my sweet brown angel eyes / I love to see you bleed / Please don't kill my baby.
Feb 99.	(cd) Emperor Jones; <(EJ 26)>	**NEVER SAY GOODBYE** (rare material) – Unforced peace / I love the living you / I pledge allegiance / Pushing and pulling / Save me / Think of as one / Birds'd crash / Be and bring me home / I've never known this 'til now / "2 gone and number / I lovbe the blind man / Something extra / You're an unidentified flying object.
Apr 99.	(cd) Triple X; <(TX 70024CD)>	**DEMON ANGEL**

THIS KIND OF PUNISHMENT

Formed: New Plymouth, New Zealand ... 1981 out of NOCTURNAL PROJECTIONS by brothers GRAEME and PETER JEFFERIES, both multi-instrumentalists who would be major figures in the NZ music scene over the next two decades. After the collapse of their short-lived early 80s combo NOCTURNAL PROJECTIONS, the brothers founded an outfit to move away from the then current back-to-basics punk sound to more artistic and experimental modes of musical expression. And, over the course of three albums and an EP, they succeeded admirably. 'THIS KIND OF PUNISHMENT' LP was an aggressive, harsh, primitive, uneasy-listening platter of skin-crawling vocals, out-of-kilter organ drones, minimal guitars and an idiosyncratic percussion sound that veered between completely excising drums from the mix or having booming, brain-bashing, overpowering beats. The second LP, 1984's 'A BEARD OF BEES', took 18 months to record as the duo were obsessive about the sound of their records; upon completion of the record they released the platter as a private pressing rather than through their label, 'Flying Nun', because they preferred the sound of the vinyl released from another pressing plant. This long-awaited and in-production album garnered favourable comparisons to JOY DIVISION. A frightening, gloomy, lo-fi 4-track existential horrorshow, '. . .BEES' used everything from

THIS KIND OF PUNISHMENT (cont)   THE GREAT INDIE DISCOGRAPHY   The 1980s

piano to mandolin to electric viola – not to mention smashed beer crates – to render the listener uncomfortable and haunted and claustrophobic, with occasional band member CHRIS MATTHEWS putting in vocal duties upon occasion. The '5 BY 4' EP (1985) found the band taking a sonic road away from their darkest hours, with the title referencing the fact that the EP had 5 songs played, by, well, 4 people. It was no less idiosyncratic or jolly than the rest of PUNISHMENT's releases, with its ration of lathe-grinding guitars and underwater piano, but it was just, well, a different kind of esoteric aural punishment. The 'IN THE SAME ROOM' EP (1987) was the band's final release, apart from an 'Ajax' records compilation box set in 1993. Helped out by notable musicians like ALASTAIR GALBRAITH, MICHAEL MORLEY and SHANE CARTER, the PUNISHMENT set about delivering a final farewell somewhat gentler and easier-to-take than most of the rest of their output, but still no walk-in-the-musical-park. A prolific PETER JEFFRIES went on to produce several albums including 'AT SWIM 2 BIRDS' (1987, named after the cult surrealistic novel by Irish author Flann O'Brien); 'THE LAST GREAT CHALLENGE IN A DULL WORLD' (1990), 'ELECTRICITY' (1995); 'CHORUS OF INTERLUDES' (1996); 'ELEVATOR MADNESS' (1996); 'SUBSTATIC' (1998) and 'CLOSED CIRCUIT' (2001). These albums all featured his trademark idiosyncratic musical virtuosity and interest in strange, dissonant sounds, and he collaborated with a number of artists including BRUCE RUSSELL, ROBBIE MUIR, MICHAEL HILL, ANITA GALATIS-ANKER, MECCA NORMAL/JEAN SMITH, STEPHEN KILROY, KATHY BULL and SHAYNE CARTER. Brother GRAEME, meanwhile, founded CAKEKITCHEN (taking its name from a 1988 solo album of GRAEME's, 'MESSAGES FOR THE CAKEKITCHEN'. As prolific as his sonic sibling, he spent the next decade or so after the project's late 80s inception putting out the albums 'TIME FLOWING BACKWARDS' (1991); 'FAR FROM THE SUN' (1993); 'STOMPIN' THROUGH THE BONEYARD' (1995); 'THE DEVIL AND THE DEEP BLUE SEA' (1996) and 'EVERYTHING'S GOING TO WORK OUT JUST FINE' (1997). Cult icon JEFFRIES (singing and playing guitar, piano and viola) consolidated his iconoclastic stature by churning out gloomy VELVET UNDERGROUND-style post-punk art rock, collaborating with a slew of other artists on his productions: ALASTAIR GALBRAITH, ROBERT KEY, RACHAEL KING, JEAN-YVES DOUET, KITH MCLEAN, HUW DAINOW and, yes, brother PETER. Seems like those two have music in their veins instead of blood, and the New Zealand music scene would have been a lot poorer without their efforts.

Album rating: THIS KIND OF PUNISHMENT (*4) / BEARD OF BEES (*7) / IN THE SAME ROOM (*6) / Peter Jefferies: AT SWIM 2 BIRDS with Jono Lonie (*7) / THE LAST GREAT CHALLENGE IN A DULL WORLD (*7) / ELECTRICITY (*5) / A CHORUS OF INTERLUDES compilation (*6) / ELEVATOR MADNESS (*5) / SUBSTATIC (*7) / CLOSED CIRCUIT (*5) / Graeme Jefferies: MESSAGES FOR THE CAKEKITCHEN (*6) / Cakekitchen: TIME FLOWING BACKWARDS (*6) / ORLD OF SAND (*6) / FAR FROM THE SUN (*6) / STOMPIN' THRU THE BONEYARD (*6) / THE DEVIL AND THE DEEP BLUE SEA (*7) / EVERYTHING'S GOING TO WORK OUT JUST FINE (*5)

NOCTURNAL PROJECTIONS

GRAEME JEFFRIES – multi / **PETER JEFFRIES** – multi, vocals

own label / not iss.

1981. (c) *(NOC 001)* **THINGS THAT GO BUNT IN THE NIGHT** – / – NewZ
1981. (c) *(NOC 002)* **NOVEMBER 1981** – / – NewZ
1982. (7") *(NOC 003)* **IN PURGATORY. / NERVE ENDS IN POWER LINES** – / – NewZ

Hit Singles / not iss.

1982. (7"ep) *(HIT 001)* **ANOTHER YEAR** – / – NewZ
– You'll never know / Isn't that strange / Could it be increased / Difficult days / Out of my hands.
1983. (7"ep) *(HIT 003)* **NOCTURNAL PROJECTIONS** – / – NewZ
– Understanding / Another year / In darkness.

– compilations, etc. –

1995. (cd) *Raffmond; (RAFF 015-2)* **NERVE ENDS IN POWER LINES** – / – NewZ
– In purgatory / People told me / Another year / Difficult days / Walk in a straight line / You'll never know / No problem here / Moving forward / Could it be increased / Nerve ends in power lines / Restoration.

THIS KIND OF PUNISHMENT

—— same line-up

Flying Nun / not iss.

1983. (lp) *(FNTKP 001)* **THIS KIND OF PUNISHMENT** – / – NewZ
– After the fact / Instrumental / Don't take those / In view of the circumstances / Two minutes drowning / If an axe is an arm / Another funeral / Some more than others / Ahead of their time. <US cd-iss. 1990's on 'RoofBolt'; 001>

—— added **CHRIS MATTHEWS** – (some) vocals

1984. (lp) *(FNTKP 002)* **BEARD OF BEES** – / – NewZ
– Prelude / From the diary of Hermann Doubt / The horrible tango / Trepidation / East meets west / Turning to stone / Although they appear / The sleepwalker / An open denial. *(NZ c-iss.1990 on 'Xpressway'; M/WAY 15)* <US cd-iss. 1990's on 'Ajax'; AJAX 26>
1985. (12"ep) *(FNTKP 003)* **5 BY 4 EP** – / – NewZ
– Mr. Tic Toc / What can I say? / Flipper go home / North head / Out of my hands.

—— next w/ guests **MICHAEL MORLEY** (of DEAD C) / **ALASTAIR GALBRAITH** (ex-RIP) / **SHAYNE CARTER** (of DOUBLE HAPPYS)

1987. (lp) *(FNTKP 004)* **IN THE SAME ROOM** – / – NewZ
– Immigration song / Overground in China / Holding / Left turns right / On various days / Don't go / The men by the pool / Ivan Fyodorvitch / Worlds fail me. *<US cd-iss. 1990's on 'Ajax'+=; AJAX 30>* – 5 By 4 EP

Xpressway / not iss.

1988. (c) *(X/WAY 2)* **TKP LIVE 1985 (live)** – / – NewZ

—— PETER JEFFERIES joined up with The RIP

PETER JEFFERIES

Flying Nun / not iss.

1987. (m-lp; as PETER JEFFERIES & JONO LONIE) *(FN 070)* **2 BIRDS AT SWIM** – / – NewZ
– Introduction / Thief with the silver / Piano (one) / Interalia / At swim 2 birds / Tarantella / Where the flies sleep / The standing stone / Aerial / Short was fast / Piano (two). <(UK/US cd-iss. Apr97 on 'Drunken Fish'; DFR31)>

Xpressway / Ajax

1990. (7"; as PETER JEFFERIES & ROBBIE MUIR) *(X/WAY 11)* <AJAX 016> **CATAPULT. / FATE OF THE HUMAN CARBINE** – / – NewZ

—— next with **BRUCE RUSSELL, MICHAEL MORLEY, ROBBIE YEATS, ALASTAIR GALBRAITH + KATHY BULL**

1990. (lp/cd) *(X/WAY 16)* <AJAX 017/+CD> **THE LAST GREAT CHALLENGE IN A DULL WORLD** – / – NewZ
– Chain or reaction / On an unknown beach / Guided tour of an unknown street / The house of weariness / Cold view / Likewise / The fate of the human carbine / Catapult / The last great challenge in a dull world / While I've been waiting / Neither do I / The other side of reason / Listening in. (UK-iss.Sep92; same)
1991. (2x7"ep; as PETER JEFFERIES & ROBBIE MUIR) <AJAZ 020> **SWERVE** – / – NewZ
– Swerve / Image of a single thought / Don't call me, I'll call you / A chorus of interludes.
1993. (7"; as PETER JEFFERIES & STEPHEN KILROY) <AJAX 027> **CROSSOVER. / WINED UP** – / – NewZ

Flying Nun / Ajax

1990's. (7'; as SHAYNE CARTER & PETER JEFFERIES) *(FNCJ 001)* **RANDOLF'S GOING HOME EP** – / – NewZ
1990's. (7"/c-s; as SHAYNE CARTER & PETER JEFFERIES) *(FN 236)* **SPARK OFF A WIRE. / KNOCKED OUT OR THEREABOUTS** – / – NewZ

—— next with **SHAYNE CARTER, ROBBIE MUIR + BRUCE RUSSELL**

Jan 95. (cd) <AJAX 039> **ELECTRICITY** – / – NewZ
– Wined up / Quality / Clear by morning / Dear boss / Scattered logic / Electricity / By small degrees / Next / Snare / Don't look down / Couldn't write a book / Every once in a while / Just nothing / Crossover / White prole / Brighten or bleed / Scissors.
Jun 96. (cd) <AJAX 052> **A CHORUS OF INTERLUDES** (collection of rare singles) –
– Crossover / Image of a single thought / Lassitude / Don't call me, I'll call you / Guided tour / Swerve / Wined up / Knocked out or thereabouts / A chorus of interludes / Spark off a wire / Reaching for an end.

—— at this point, PETER joined supergroup 2 FOOT FLAME; the latter's **JEAN SMITH** also joined PETER below

Emperor Jones / Emperor Jones

Oct 96. (cd/lp) <(EJ 09 CD/LP)> **ELEVATOR MADNESS**
– Elevator madness / The strange case of Stuart Townsend / World in a blanket / Loop / Echoes / 28 years / Satellites and sparks / Shut out / Sunset.

—— now augmented by **MICHAEL HILL** – guitars, etc. + **ANITA-GALATIS-ANKER** – instruments

Nov 98. (cd) <(EJ 20CD)> **SUBSTATIC** Sep98
– Index / Signal / Damage / Kitty loop / Three movements.

—— added **CHRIS FRAZER SMITH + MARK CASS STEVENS**

Oct 01. (cd) <(EJ 40CD)> **CLOSED CIRCUIT**
– Time and the singular man / Crocodile / hatever you ant / Closed circuit / Line in tail out / Age for the innocent / Dryest month in 100 years / Coming home with you / Red sky / King in the clown's new clothes / State of the nation / Talkin' bout nuthin' / Ghostwriter.

CAKEKITCHEN

GRAEME JEFFERIES – vocals, guitar, viola, piano / with **MAXINE FLEMING** – (some) vocals

Flying Nun / not iss.

1988. (m-lp; as GRAEME JEFFERIES) *(FNGRJ 1)* **MESSAGES FOR THE CAKEKITCHEN** – / NewZ
– All the colours run dry / Reason to keep swimming / Prisoner of a single passion / Nothing that's new / The simple tapestry of fate / If the Moon dies / The cardhouse / The greenkeepers / Is the timing wrong? <US cd-iss. 1992 on 'Ajax'; AJAX 024>
1990. (12"ep) *(FN 126)* **THE CAKEKITCHEN** – / – NewZ
1990. (lp) *(FN 137)* **CAKEKITCHEN** – / – NewZ

—— **JEFFERIES** now with **RACHEL KING** – bass / **ROBERT KEYS** – drums, percussion

Homestead / Homestead

1991. (cd/c) <HMS 156> **TIME FLOWING BACKWARDS** –
– Dave the pimp / Witness to your secrets / Silence of the sirens / Machines / File under filed / Airships / Walked over Texas / One plus one equals one / Is it only Monday? / Boat to the ceiling.
1992. (cd/c) <HMS 176> **WORLD OF SAND** –
– Ordeal by water / World of sand / Walking on glass / Don't be fooled by the label / Tomorrow came today / This perfect day / Dogs and cats / McCarthy / Isle of Pittsburg / Crimson to gunmetal.

—— **JEFFERIES** with newcomers **KEITH McLEAN** – bass / **HUW DAINOW** – drums

Jul 93. (cd) <(HMS 198-2)> **FAR FROM THE SUN**
– Stranger than paradise / Overexcited / Fahrenheit 451 / Big fat mouth / Greater windmill street blues / Man in the mirror / Far from the sun / Troubled in the underworld / Buried it in the yard.

—— **JEFFERIES** now with **JEAN-YVES DOUET** – drums (with help from **DAINOW + ALASTAIR GALBRAITH**)

not iss. / Merge

Mar 95. (cd) <MRG 079> **STOMPIN' THRU THE BONEYARD**
– Tell me why you lie / Even as we sleep / Bad bodied girl / Hole in my shoe / Mr. Adrian's lost in his last panic attack / The mad clarinet / This questionaire / Harriett row / Another sad story.

543

THIS KIND OF PUNISHMENT (cont)

— guest HAMISH KILGOUR repl. DAINOW

Oct 96. (cd) <MRG 113> **THE DEVIL AND THE DEEP BLUE SEA**
– Old grey coast / Bald old bear / Prophet of the underground / I know you know / You make a god of money / Baby I luv you / Ballad of Oxford Circus / Everything turned orange / Take it easy with me / Escape to Fire Island.

not iss. Raffmond

1996. (7") <RAFF 016-7> **BALD OLD BEAR. / DOWN AT THE COOLER**

— now totally solo bar **MARCUS ARCHER** – drums

Freek Freek

Jun 98. (cd/lp) <(FRR 025 CD/LP)> **EVERYTHING'S GOING TO WORK OUT JUST FINE**   Aug97
– Everything's going to work out just fine / Hot sex overdrive / You never run out of luck / Jessica's secret pt.2 / The cellar of fun / Overground rail catastrophe / All the tea in China / The great fire.

Gotcha not iss.

1990's. (7") (001) **WILDGEESES. / LITTLE FOXES**   German

THIS MORTAL COIL

Formed: Wadsworth, London, England . . . 1983 by IVO WATTS-RUSSELL, aided by producer JOHN FRYER. The brainchild of '4 a.d.' mainman, IVO, THIS MORTAL COIL was basically a loose collective of mainly 4ad artists gathered together with the intention of creating atmospheric and inspiring gothic-esque sounds, most effectively through their startling cover versions (see further below). With the COCTEAU TWINS (ELIZABETH FRASER and ROBIN GUTHRIE) initially taking a lead role, THIS MORTAL COIL made their mark with a haunting cover of Tim Buckley's 'SONG TO THE SIREN', wherein LIZ FRASER's lyrical mystical mantra was actually coherent to the unfamiliar ear. Originally intended as a B-side to a version of MODERN ENGLISH's '16 DAYS' (with the latter act's ROBBIE GREY on vocals), the track secured a minor chart place and has since become a cult classic (even providing inspiration for The CHEMICAL BROTHERS, or The DUST BROTHERS as they were known at the time!). Encouraged by the response, IVO took the opportunity to provide a wider platform for the emerging talent on his label, roping in selected personnel from DEAD CAN DANCE, COLOURBOX, WOLFGANG PRESS and X-MAL DEUTSCHLAND alongside vocalists HOWARD DEVOTO (ex-MAGAZINE) and GORDON SHARPE (of CINdYTALK – a non '4 a.d.' act) to record a full-length THIS MORTAL COIL album, 'IT'LL END IN TEARS'. Preceded by the 'KANGAROO' single (from the pen of Alex Chilton), the 1984 set cracked the UK Top 40, its combination of low-key covers (featuring another Chilton number, 'HOLOCAUST') and moody instrumentals receiving lavish praise from the critics. IVO continued to expand his record company with new US acts (i.e. The PIXIES, THROWING MUSES, etc), lending a different flavour to the 1986 follow-up, 'FILIGREE & SHADOW'. Featuring new singer/writer DOMINIC APPLETON (from another non '4ad' act, BREATHLESS), this double-set contained a number of more well-known but just as inventive interpretations including Van Morrison's 'COME HERE MY LOVE', Tim Buckley's 'I MUST HAVE BEEN BLIND' and Talking Heads' 'DRUGS'. It was five years before TMC's third and final album, the UK Top 30 double-set, 'BLOOD' (1991), starring a stripped down cast of musicians including stalwart, APPLETON, alongside KIM DEAL, TANYA DONELLY, CAROLINE CRAWLEY (from SHELLEYAN ORPHAN) and HEIDI BERRY. More accessible than its two predecessors, the record was nevertheless a graceful swansong, featuring as it did engaging renditions of CHRIS BELL classics, 'YOU AND YOUR SISTER' and 'I AM THE COSMOS'. The proverbial 7-year itch came to an end when IVO resurfaced with a new outfit, The HOPE BLISTER. Similar in some respects to TMC, it gathered together friends such as LOUISE RUTKOWSKI, AUDREY RILEY and LAURENCE O'KEEFE on "comeback" dreamy-pop album, 'SMILE'S OK' (1998). • **Songwriters:** IVO and some 4 a.d. musicians, except; GATHERING DUST (Modern English) / ANOTHER DAY (Roy Harper) / NOT ME (Colin Newman) / THE JEWELLER (Tom Rapp) / HELP ME LIFT YOU UP (Mary Margaret O'Hara) / NATURE'S WAY (Spirit) / STRENGTH OF STRINGS + WITH TOMORROW (Gene Clark) / MY FATHER (. . . Collins) / I WANT TO LIVE (. . . Ogan) / FIRE BROTHERS (. . . Duncan) / MR. SOMEWHERE (. . . Walsh) / SEVERAL TIMES (. . . Nooten) / CAROLYN'S SONG (. . . Roback) / LATE NIGHT + TARANTULA (Syd Barrett) / TILL I GAIN CONTROL AGAIN (. . . Crowell) / I COME AND STAND AT EVERY DOOR (Byrds). The HOPE BLISTER covered DAGGER (Neil Halstead) / ONLY HUMAN (Heidi Berry) / SWEET UNKNOWN (Cranes) / LET THE HAPPINESS IN (David Sylvian) / IS JESUS YOUR PAL (Slow Blow) / THE SPIDER AND I (Eno) / HANKY PANKY NO HOW (John Cale).

Album rating: IT'LL END IN TEARS (*8) / FILIGREE & SHADOW (*7) / BLOOD (*7) / Hope Blister: SMILE'S OK (*6) / UNDERARMS (*3)

IVO WATTS-RUSSELL (b.1955) – tapes, loops, etc. / **JOHN FRYER** – instruments, producer with **COCTEAU TWINS:- ELIZABETH FRAZER** – vox / **ROBIN GUTHRIE** – guitar

4 a.d. 4ad-Reprise

Sep 83. (7") (AD 310) **SONG TO THE SIREN. / 16 DAYS (reprise)**   66
(12"+=) (BAD 310) – Gathering dust.
(above 'B'sides featured **ROBBIE GREY** – vocals (of MODERN ENGLISH) (below 'A'side featured **MARTIN McCARRICK** – cello, strings (of WILLING SINNERS; MARC ALMOND) / **GORDON SHARPE** – vocals (of CINDYTALK) / **SIMON RAYMONDE** – guitar, tapes (of COCTEAU TWINS)

Aug 84. (7") (AD 410) **KANGAROO. / IT'LL END IN TEARS**
below album featured above musicians, plus **GINI BALL** – violin (of WILLING SINNERS) / DEAD CAN DANCE: **LIZA GERRARD** – accordion, vocals / **BRENDAN PERRY** – bass drone, drum / **PETER ULRICH** – percussion / COLOURBOX: **STEVEN YOUNG** – piano / **MARTYN YOUNG** – sitar, guitar, bass / X-MAL DEUTSCHLAND: **MANUELA RICKERS** – guitar / WOLFGANG PRESS: **MARK COX** – organ / **HOWARD DEVOTO** – vocals (ex-MAGAZINE)

Oct 84. (lp/c) (CAD/+C 411) <96269> **IT'LL END IN TEARS**   38
– Kangaroo / Song to the siren / Holocaust / FYT / Fond affections / The last ray / Waves become wings / Another day / Barramundi / Dreams made flesh / Not me / A single wish. (cd-iss. 1986; CAD 411CD) <US cd-iss. 1993 on 'Warners'; 45454>

— Retained guests **SIMON RAYMONDE** / **PETER ULRICH** / **MARK COX** / **STEVEN YOUNG** plus new BREATHLESS: **DOMINIC APPLETON** – vocals / **RICHENEL** – vocals / DIF JUZ: **DAVID CURTIS** – guitar / **ALAN CURTIS** – guitar / **RICHARD THOMAS** – saxophone / MODERN ENGLISH: **ANDREW GRAY** – guitar / / **JEAN** – vocals / **ALISON LIMERICK** – vocals / **CAROLINE SEAMAN** – vocals / **KEITH MITCHELL** – guitar / **DIERDRE RUTOWSKI** – backing vocals / **LOUISE RUTOWSKI** – backing vocals / **KEITH MITCHELL** – guitar / **NIGEL K.HINE** – guitar / **CHRIS PYE** – guitar / **JOHN TURNER** – organ, keyboards / **TONY WAEREA** – didgeridoo / **ANNE TURNER + LES McKUEN** – choir

Sep 86. (d-lp/c)(cd) (DAD/+C 609)(DAD 609CD) **FILIGREE & SHADOW**   53
– Velvet belly / The jeweller / Ivy and neet / Meniscus / Tears / Tarantula / My father / Come here my love / At first, and then / Strength of strings / Morning glory / Inch-blue / I want to live / Mama K I / Filigree & shadow / Firebrothers / Thais I / I must have been blind / A heart of glass / Alone / Mama K II / The horizon bleeds and sucks its thumb / Drugs / Red rain / Thais II. <US cd-iss. 1993 on 'Warners'; 45453>

Sep 86. (ltd-10") (BAD 608) **COME HERE MY LOVE. / DRUGS**

— They used past musicians, plus **CAROLINE CRAWLEY, KIM DEAL + TANYA DONELLY, DOMINIC APPLETON, HEIDI BERRY +** The **RUTOWSKI's**, etc.

Apr 91. (d-lp/c/cd) (DAD/+C/CD 609) **BLOOD**   28
– The lacemaker / Mr. Somewhere / Ardialu / With tomorrow / Loose joints / You and your sister / Nature's way / I come and steal at every door / Bitter / Baby Ray baby / Several times / The lacemaker II / Late night / Ruddy and wretched / Help me lift you up / Carolyn's song / DD and E / Til I gain control again / Dreams are like water / I am the cosmos / (Nothing but) Blood. <US cd-iss. 1993 on 'Warners'; 45452>

above was their final release

– compilations, etc. –

Dec 89. (cd) Alex; <1426> **THIS MORTAL COIL**
Mar 93. (cd) Warners; <45135> **1983-1991**

HOPE BLISTER

IVO – producer / with **LOUISE RUTOWSKI** – vocals / **AUDREY RILEY** – strings / **LAURENCE O'KEEFE** – bass (ex-LEVITATION) / **SUE DENCH** – viola / **LEO PAYNE + CHRIS TOMBLING** – violin / **RITCHIE THOMAS** – drums, percussion, sax

4 a.d. Mammoth

Jul 98. (cd) (CAD 8008) <980197> **SMILE'S OK**
– Dagger / Only human / Outer skin / Sweet unknown / Let the happiness in / In Jesus your pal / The spider and I / Hanky panky no how.

Apr 99. (cd) <M2> **UNDERARMS** (remixes)

Tracey THORN
(see under ⇒ EVERYTHING BUT THE GIRL)

THREE JOHNS

Formed: Leeds, England . . . 1981 by art-college buddies JOHN HYATT, JON LANGFORD (also of Leeds stalwarts The MEKONS) and JOHN BRENNAN. Socialists to a man (or even a John!), the trio formed against a background of rampant Thatcherism and fervent Rock Against Racism activity, their debut single, 'ENGLISH WHITE BOY ENGINEER' (a MEKONS cover) a damning indictment of South Africa's apartheid system. As much renowned for their manic sense of humour and boozing as for their benefit gigging and community activities, the THREE JOHNS proceeded to infiltrate the indie charts with a string of offbeat singles including 'MEN LIKE MONKEYS' and 'PINK HEADED BUG'. A debut album, 'ATOM DRUM BOP' (1984) found the band casting around for a focus to their drum machine-driven sound, while a subsequent tour of the States inspired 1986's more impressive follow-up, 'THE WORLD BY STORM'. Driving, pulsing indie-rock fuelled by HYATT's strident vocal proclamations, the record featured such singalong anti-US diatribes as 'DEATH OF THE EUROPEAN' and 'TORCHES OF LIBERTY'. Never more than a part-time concern, the band drifted apart following a disastrous American tour and final, patchy album, 'THE DEATH OF EVERYTHING' (1988). While LANGFORD balanced his MEKON activities with record production, HYATT concentrated on his career as a college lecturer.

Album rating: ATOM DROP BOP (*6) / THE WORLD BY STORM (*7) / THE DEATH OF EVERYTHING (*5) / EAT YOUR SONS (*5) / CRIME PAYS compilation (*6)

JON LANGFORD – vocals, guitar (also of MEKONS) / **JOHN HYATT** – vocals, drums (ex-SHEENY AND THE GOYS, ex-ANOTHER COLOUR) / **JOHN BRENNAN** (b. PHIL) – bass (ex-25 RIFLES)

C.N.T. not iss.

May 82. (7") (CNT 003) **ENGLISH WHITE BOY ENGINEER. / SECRET AGENT**

Jan 83. (7") (CNT 011) **PINK HEADED BUG. / LUCY IN THE RAIN**
(above 2 re-iss. Jan84 as 12"ep 'SOME HISTORY' on 'Abstract'; 12ABS 022)

May 83. (12"ep) (CNT 013) **MEN LIKE MONKEYS / TWO MINUTE APE? / WINDOLENE / MARX'S WIFE / PARIS 1941**

Abstract / *not iss.*

Sep 83. (7") (ABS 019) **A.W.O.L. / ROOSTER BLUES**
(12"+=) (12ABS 019) – Image or animal / Kick the dog right out.
Mar 84. (7") (ABS 023) **DO THE SQUARE THING. / ZOWEE**
(12"+=) (12ABS 023) – World of the workers / Kinky beat.
Aug 84. (m-lp/c) (ABT/+C 010) **ATOM DROP BOP**
– Teenage nightingales to wax / 3 junk / Sun of mud / Missing / Do not cross the line / The Devil's music / Dr. Freedom / No place / Class war (!). *(c/ repl.(!) track, w/ +=)* – World of the workers / A.W.O.L. / Do the square thing.
May 85. (7") (ABS 034) **DEATH OF THE EUROPEAN. / HEADS LIKE CONVICTS**
(12"+=) (12ABS 034) – Rabies / 20th century boy.
Nov 85. (7") (ABS 036) **BRAINBOX (HE'S SO BRAINBOX). / WATCH IT GO**
(12"+=) (12ABS 036) – Men without bones.
Apr 86. (7") (ABS 040) **SOLD DOWN THE RIVER. / ROSE OF YORKSHIRE**
(12"+=) (12ABS 040) – Fruitflies.
May 86. (lp/c) (ABT/+C 012) **THE WORLD BY STORM**
– King car / Sold down the river / The ship that died of shame / Demon drink / Torches of liberty / Death of the European / World by storm / Atom drum bop / The crunge / Johnny was a good man / Coals to Newcastle. *(c+=)* – Watch it go / Brainbox (he's so brainbox). *(free live 7"w/ lp)* – ENGLISH WHITE BOY ENGINEER / DEVIL'S MUSIC. / A.W.O.L. / INDUSTRY
Nov 86. (lp) (ABT 015) **CRIME PAYS – ROCK'N'ROLL IN THE . . . DEMONOCRACY (1982-86)** (compilation)
– English white boy engineer / Pink headed bug / Men like monkeys / Windolene / Rooster blue / A.W.O.L. / Do the square thing / Zowee / Death of the European / Brainbox (he's so brainbox) / Sold down the river.
Aug 87. (7") (ABS 043) **NEVER AND ALWAYS. / TURN UP THOSE DOWN HEARTED BLUES**
(12"+=) (12ABS 043) – ('A'-Adrian Sherwood remix).
Mar 88. (7") (ABS 049) **TORCHES OF LIBERTY. / BIG WHALES (NEVER LIVE)**

T.I.M. / *Caroline*

Oct 88. (lp/cd) (MOT LP/CD 20) <CAROL 1363-1/-2> **THE DEATH OF EVERYTHING**
– The king is dead / Bullshitaco / Moonlight in Vermont / Go ahead bikini / Spin me around / Nonsense spew from my song machine / Humbug / Fast fish / Downhearted blues / Never and always.

Tupelo / *not iss.*

Oct 90. (cd/c/lp) (TUP CD/MC/LP 018) **EAT YOUR SONS**

— split after above, LANGFORD continued with the MEKONS and later released a solo album

– compilations, etc. –

May 87. (lp) *Last Time Around*; (LAST 001/+C) **LIVE IN CHICAGO** (live)
1992. (c) *ROIR*; <A 160> **DEATHROCKER SCRAPBOOK** (out-takes)
– Incredible Wendy Frith / Nightmare / Snitch / Burn while you learn / Hello Dickie / Conversation with Freud / Is your brain your own? / Mouths to feed / You're not like Manson, are you? / Mountain man / Buzz be goode / Machinery seeds / Cheap computer / We won't wobble / Peter's advertising agency / One fine day / High standards / Press is a toad / Ballad of Colin Buggers / Compensation / Fill me up / Spider spaceship.
Jun 96. (cd) *Dojo*; (DOJOCD 225) **THE BEST OF THE THREE JOHNS**

THREE O'CLOCK

Formed: Sun Valley, California, USA . . . early 80's by MICHAEL QUERCIO, LOUIS GUTIERREZ, MIKE MARIANO and DANNY BENAIR, who were formerly known as The SALVATION ARMY. Their debut, 'BAROQUE HOEDOWN', was released late in 1982 on France's 'Lolita' records, basically a fairly reverential stab at classic psych/bubblegum pop. Gaining exposure via the emerging Paisley Underground movement (RAIN PARADE, DREAM SYNDICATE, etc), The THREE O'CLOCK followed-up with the slightly improved 'SIXTEEN TAMBOURINES', subsequently gaining a contract with Miles Copeland's 'I.R.S.' (now with PATRICK WANINGHAM replacing GUTIERREZ for one album only – STEVEN ALTENBERG deputising thereafter). In 1988, after a further two patchy sets, 'ARRIVE WITHOUT TRAVELING' (1985) and 'EVER AFTER' (1987), the band – now with future JELLYFISH frontman, JASON FALKNER replacing short-lived member STEVEN ALTENBERG – hooked up with PRINCE's 'Paisley Park' label for their swansong set, 'VERMILLION'. QUERCIO would join GAME THEORY only to form his own band PERMANENT GREEN LIGHT in the early 90's; he subsequently formed underground superband, JUPITER AFFECT. • **Songwriters:** QUERCIO and GUTIERREZ, some with MARIANO; except covers SORRY (Easybeats) / IN MY OWN TIME (Bee Gees) / FEEL A WHOLE LOT BETTER (Byrds) / LUCIFER SAM (Pink Floyd) / etc. • **Trivia:** WILL GLENN (Rain Parade) played viola/violin on first two albums and WENDY & LISA guested on their final outing.

Album rating: BAROQUE HOEDOWN mini (*6) / SIXTEEN TAMBOURINES (*7) / ARRIVE WITHOUT TRAVELING (*6) / EVER AFTER (*5) / VERMILLION (*4) / Permanent Green Light: PERMANENT GREEN LIGHT mini (*6) / AGAINST NATURE (*7) / Jupiter Affect: JUPITER AFFECT mini (*6) / INSTRUCTIONS FOR THE TWO WAYS OF BECOMING ALICE (*7)

MICHAEL QUERCIO – vocals, bass, percussion / **LOUIS GUTIERREZ** – guitar, vocals, percussion / **MIKE MARIANO** – keyboards, vocals, percussion / **DANNY BENAIR** – drums, vocals, percussion (ex-QUICK)

Lolita / *not iss.*

Dec 82. (m-lp) (5003) **BAROQUE HOEDOWN** — France
– With Cantaloupe girlfriend / I go wild / Marjorie tells me / Sorry / As real as real. *(some copies +=)* – Feel a whole lot better / In love in too / Lucifer Sam.
Dec 83. (lp) (5008) **SIXTEEN TAMBOURINES** — France
– Jetfighter / Stupid Einstein / And so we run / Fall to the ground / A day in Erotica / Tomorrow / In my own time / On my own / When lightning starts / Seeing is believing. *(cd-iss. May86 +=(LOLITA 1101-2)* – BAROQUE HOEDOWN *(re-iss. 1991 on 'Frontier' +=; 4605-2-L)* – BAROQUE HOEDOWN / Around the world. *(cd re-iss. Jul02 on 'Frontier'; FRP 3101-2)*

— PATRICK WANINGHAM – guitar, vocals; repl. LOUIS who helped to form MARY'S DANISH

I.R.S. / *I.R.S.*

Sep 85. (7") (IRM 101) **HAND IN HAND. / WATCHING PICTURES**
(12"+=) (IRT 101) – I go wild.
Oct 85. (lp/c) (MIRF/+C 1002) <5591> **ARRIVE WITHOUT TRAVELLING**
– Her head's revolving / Each and every lonely heart / Underwater / Mrs. Green / Hand in hand / Knowing when you smile / Half the way there / Simon in the park / Another world / The girl with the guitar / Spun gold.

— STEVEN ALTENBERG – guitar, vocals; repl. WANINGHAM

Feb 87. (lp/c) (MIRF 1016) <5833> **EVER AFTER**
– Suzie's on the ball now / Look into your eyes / When we can / The penny girls / Follow him around / Warm aspirations / Step out of line / We are one / If you could see my way / Songs and gentle hands.
Apr 87. (7") (IRM 127) **WARM ASPIRATIONS. / REGINA CAELI**
(12"+=) (IRMT 127) – Suzie's on the ball.

— JASON FALKNER – guitar, vocals; repl. ALTENBERG

Paisley Park / *Paisley Park*

Jun 88. (lp/c/cd) <(925717-1/-4/-2)> **VERMILLION**
– Vermillion / To be where you are / When she becomes my girl / World on fire / Neon telephone / On paper / Ways of magic / Time is going slower / Love has no heart / Through the creepy town.

— split in '89 FALKNER later turning up in JELLYFISH and subsequently went solo; QUERCIO joined the last days of GAME THEORY

– compilations, etc. –

1985. (lp; as The SALVATION ARMY) *Frontier*; <FLP 1008> **BEFOUR THREE O'CLOCK**
1992. (cd/c; as BEFOUR THREE O'CLOCK) *Frontier*; <34639-2/-4> **HAPPEN HAPPENED**
– Happen happened / For hours / Fight songs / Mind gardens / She turns to flowers / Grimly forming / Seventeen forever / Going home / Cellophane nirvana / She turns to flowers / Upside down / Seventeen forever / Mind gardens / Grimly forming / While we were in your room talking to / Minuet / Happen happened / I am your guru / Going home. *(UK lp/cd-iss. Jul02 on 'Frontier'; FRO 31008/31049CD)*
Jul 02. (cd) *Collectors Choice*; (CCM 0292-2) **ARRIVE WITHOUT TRAVELING / EVER AFTER**

PERMANENT GREEN LIGHT

MICHAEL QUERCIO – vocals, bass / **MATT DEVINE** – guitar, vocals / **CHRIS BRUCKNER** – drums

not iss. / *Gasatanka*

Nov 92. (7") **WE COULD JUST DIE. / THE TRUTH THIS TIME**
Feb 93. (m-cd) <6093-2> **PERMANENT GREEN LIGHT**
– We could just die / The truth this time / Ballad of Paul K / Bright light / The sky is falling / Your name on everything / Chris drops in (originally titled "Against nature").
Oct 93. (7") **SUMMERTIME. / STREET LOVE**
Nov 93. (cd) <6127-2/-4> **AGAINST NATURE**
– Honestly / Street love / Wintertime's a-comin', Martha Raye / Portmanteau / All this and Alistair Cooke / Something on me / (You and I are the) Summertime / Marianne gave up her hand / Fireman / All for you / Sleepyhead.

— DEVINE joined POSSUM DIXON and MEDICINE; repl. by **BERNARD YIN**

1995. (7") **YOU ARE THE QUEEN OF MARKET STREET. / TOGETHER**
1996. (7") **HITLER WITH MASCARA. / ANGELA DAVIS HAIR**

— YIN departed and QUERCIO changed their moniker to . . .

JUPITER AFFECT

QUERCIO + BRUCKNER added **JASON SHAPIRO** – guitar (ex-CELEBRITY SKIN) / **DAN EPSTEIN** – guitar (ex-LAVA SUTRA)

Aerial Flip / *Aerial Flip*

Aug 98. (m-cd) <(AF 008CD)> **JUPITER AFFECT**
– Big monster chains / Angela Davis hair / #17 dream / Velocity / Throwing in the towel.

Eggbert / *Eggbert*

Nov 00. (cd) <(ER 80028)> **INSTRUCTIONS FOR THE TWO WAYS OF BECOMING ALICE** — Jun00
– White knuckle sound / Loved one's lies / Goodbye Arthur (le morte d'Arthur) / Inside (Isis rising) / I see the sun / Michael and Mary / Druscilla I dig your scene / The chemical wedding of Christian Rosencreutz / Together / Bring back the wonderful girl / Good time / Ice cream lolly / We don't believe you.

THROWING MUSES

Formed: Boston, Massachusetts, USA . . . 1983 by KRISTIN HERSH and her half-sister, TANYA DONELLY, who duly recruited a rhythm section of ELAINE ADAMEDES and BECCA BLUMEN; DAVID NARCIZO replaced the latter in '84. After an independently released US-only EP, the group were signed up (alongside fellow Bostonians, The PIXIES) to British indie label, '4 a.d.', the first American band to be bestowed such an honour. Produced by Gil Norton, the band's eponymous debut album (featuring new bassist LESLIE LANGSTON) centred around the emotional anguish of chief writer HERSH; her tortured, BUFFY SAINTE-MARIE-like wailing and oblique

THROWING MUSES (cont)

lyrics conjured up an air of ill-defined unease on the likes of 'RABBIT'S DYING' and 'SOUL SOLDIER' while the twisting, folk-noir minimalism of the music lent proceedings an uncomfortable unpredictability. Raved over in Britain (John Peel was a particularly vocal fan) but largely ignored at home, the 'MUSES consolidated their cult appeal with a further couple of EP's the following year before 1988's slightly disappointing follow-up proper, 'HOUSE TORNADO'. The record signalled a move towards the more accessible territory staked out in 'HUNKPAPA' (1989), US college radio's increasing influence seeing their native fanbase mushrooming. Feeling creatively stifled by HERSH's lion's share of the songwriting, DONELLY subsequently formed her own outfit, The BREEDERS while simultaneously working on her final 'MUSES album, 'THE REAL RAMONA' (1991). A breakthrough set which contained some of the group's most immediate compositions ('COUNTING BACKWARDS' was perhaps the nearest HERSH has come to writing a pop song), DONELLY's contributions a blueprint for the more straightforward alternative pop she would perfect in BELLY. Taking then 'MUSES bassist, ABONG with her, DONELLY finally left the band in 1992, leaving a core of HERSH and NARCIZO. Welcoming LANGSTON back into the fold, HERSH proved THROWING MUSES was still a going concern with the soft grunge-friendly distortion of 'RED HEAVEN' (1992), the band's highest (UK) charting album to date. Nevertheless, the 'MUSES' muse took time out in 1994 to complete a solo debut, 'HIPS AND MAKERS'. Produced by LENNY KAYE and featuring a guest appearance from MICHAEL STIPE, the album found HERSH probing her troubled psyche through a skewed, childlike lens, distorting the sparse acoustic backing and making for compelling listening. Hailed by critics, the record made the UK Top 10 and saw the singer gaining belated recognition from an often reluctant music press. 1995 saw the release of the sixth THROWING MUSES album, 'UNIVERSITY', another fine set which maintained the hi-octane approach of its predecessor. The following years' 'LIMBO' was exactly that, the group becoming a little directionless and stale, although its highlights were the minor hit, 'SHARK'. During the last two years of the decade, KRISTIN delivered a couple of fine long-players, 'STRANGE ANGELS' (1998) and 'SKY MOTEL' (1999), the latter her best work to date; it also was a truly "solo" affair. HERSH's fourth solo set was concentrated on the folky side of her muse, the veteran singer/songwriter once again handling all the instrumental and arranging duties. While this lent the album a singular grace and a feeling of continuity, there was little of the sonic juxtaposition so effectively employed by the 'MUSES. Highlights included a cover of Cat Stevens' 'TROUBLE' and the tense '37 HOURS'. • **Songwriters:** KRISTIN lyrics / group compositions except; AMAZING GRACE (trad. hit Judy Collins) / CRY BABY CRY (Beatles) / RIDE INTO THE SUN (Velvet Underground) / MANIC DEPRESSION (Jimi Hendrix) / WHEN THE LEVEE BREAKS (Led Zeppelin) / CRAYON SUN + IF (Latin Playboys) / JAK (Mission Of Burma). HERSH solo:- PANIC PURE (Vic Chesnutt) / JESUS CHRIST (Alex Chilton) / CAN THE CIRCLE BE UNBROKEN (. . . Carter) / PENNYROYAL TEA (Nirvana) / EVERYBODY'S GOT SOMETHING TO HIDE EXCEPT ME AND MY MONKEY (Beatles).
Album rating: THROWING MUSES (*8) / THE FAT SKIER mini (*6) / HOUSE TORNADO (*6) / HUNKPAPA (*5) / THE REAL RAMONA (*8) / RED HEAVEN (*7) / THE CURSE (*5) / UNIVERSITY (*7) / LIMBO (*6) / Kristin Hersh: HIPS AND MAKERS (*6) / STRANGE ANGELS (*6) / SKY MOTEL (*8) / SUNNY BORDER BLUE (*6)

KRISTIN HERSH (b. 7 Aug'66, Atlanta, Georgia) – vocals, lead guitar, piano / **ELAINE ADAMEDES** – bass / **TANYA DONELLY** (b.14 Jul'66) – rhythm guitar, vocals / **DAVID NARCIZO** (b. 6 May'66) – drums, percussion, vocals; repl. BECCA BLUMEN

not iss. *Throwing Muses*

Nov 85. (7"ep) <NONTM 1> **STAND UP / DIRT IS ON THE FLOOR. / THE PARTY / SANTA CLAUS**

–––– **LESLIE LANGSTON** (b. 1 Apr'64) – bass, vocals; repl. ELAINE

4 a.d. *4ad-Sire*

Sep 86. (lp/c)(cd) (CAD/+C 607)(CAD 607CD) **THROWING MUSES**
– Call me / Green / Hate my way / Vicky's box / Rabbit's dying / America (she can't say no) / Fear / Stand up / Soul soldier / Delicious cutters.

Mar 87. (12"ep/c-ep) (BAD 701/+C) **CHAINS CHANGED**
– Cry baby cry / Finished / Reel / Snail head.

Aug 87. (m-lp/c) (CAD/+C 706) <25640> **THE FAT SKIER**
– Soul soldier / Garoux des larmes / Pool in eyes / A feeling / You cage / Soap and water / And a she-wolf after the war.

Mar 88. (lp/c)(cd) (CAD/+C 802)(CAD 802CD) <25710> **HOUSE TORNADO**
– Colder / Mexican woman / The river / Juno / Marriage tree / Run letter / Saving grace / Drive / Downtown / Giant / Walking in the dark. (cd+=) – THE FAT SKIER

Jan 89. (lp/c)(cd) (CAD/+C 901)(CAD 901CD) <25855> **HUNKPAPA** 59
– Devil's roof / Bea / Dizzy / No parachutes (say goodbye) / Dragonhead / Fall down / I'm alive / Angel / Mania / The burrow. (c+=) – Take. (cd++=) – Santa Claus.

Feb 89. (7") (AD 903) **DIZZY. / SANTA CLAUS**
(12"+=/10"+=)(cd-s+=) (BAD/+D 903)(BAD 903CD) – Mania (live) / Downtown (live).

–––– TANYA with DAVID (only in '89) formed off-shoot The BREEDERS. She stayed with the MUSES until next album's completion. **FRED ABONG** – bass repl. her

Jan 91. (7") (AD 7001) <21833> **COUNTING BACKWARDS. / AMAZING GRACE** 70
(12"+=/cd-s+=) (BAD/+CD 1001) – Some sun / Cotton mouth.

Feb 91. (cd)(lp/c) (CAD 1002CD)(CAD/+C 1002) <26489> **THE REAL RAMONA** 26
– Counting backwards / Him dancing / Red shoes / Graffiti / Golden thing / Ellen West / Dylan / Hook in her head / Not too soon / Honey chain / Say goodbye / Two step.

Nov 91. (7") (AD 1015) <40135> **NOT TOO SOON. / CRY BABY CRY**
(12"+=/cd-s+=) (BAD 1015/+CD) – Dizzy (remix) / Him dancing (remix).

–––– (Sep'91) DONELLY and ABONG had now quit to form BELLY in 1992

–––– **KRISTIN + NARCIZO** recruited newcomer **BERNARD GEORGES** (b.29 Mar'65, Gonaive, Haiti) – bass

Jul 92. (12"ep/cd-ep) (BAD 2012/+CD) **FIREPILE / MANIC DEPRESSION. / SNAILHEAD / CITY OF THE DEAD** 46
(12"ep/cd-ep) (BADR 2012)(BAD 2012CDR) – ('A'remix) / Jack / Ride into the Sun / Handsome woman.

Aug 92. (cd)(lp/c) (CAD 2013CD)(CAD/+C 2013) <26897> **RED HEAVEN** 13
– Furious / Firepile / Die / Dirty water / Stroll / Pearl / Summer Street / Vic / Backroad / The visit / Dovey / Rosetta stone / Carnival wig. *(free-lp w.a.)* **LIVE (live)** – Juno / Marriage tree / Pearl / Stand up / Dovey – Mexican woman / Run letter / Soap and water / Rabbit dying / Cry baby cry / Counting backwards – Handsome woman / Take / Soul soldier / Bea / Delicate cutters.

Nov 92. (cd) (TAD 2019CD) **THE CURSE (live)** 74
– Manic depression / Counting backwards / Fish / Hate my way / Furious / Devil's roof / Snailhead / Firepile / Finished / Take / Say goodbye / Mania / Two step / Delicate cutters / Cottonmouth / Pearl / Vic / Bea.

Dec 94. (7") (AD 4018) **BRIGHT YELLOW GUN. / LIKE A DOG** 51
(12"+=/cd-s+=) (BAD 4018/+CD) – Red eyes / Crayon sun.

Jan 95. (cd)(lp/c) (CAD 5002CD)(CAD/+C 5002) <45796> **UNIVERSITY** 10
– Bright yellow gun / Start / Hazing / Shimmer / Calm down, come down / Crabtown / No way in Hell / Surf cowboy / That's all you wanted / Teller / University / Snake face / Fever few.

Jul 96. (7") (AD 6016) **SHARK. / TAR MOOCHERS** 53
(7") (ADD 6016) – ('A'side) / Limbobo.
(cd-s++=) (BAD 6016CD) – Serene swing.

4 a.d. *Rykodisc*

Aug 96. (cd)(lp/c) (CAD 6014CD)(CAD/+C 6014) <10354> **LIMBO** 36
– Buzz / Ruthie's knocking / Freeloader / The field / Limbo / Tar kisser / Tango / Serene / Mr. Bones / Night driving / Cowbirds / Shark.

Sep 96. (7"etched) (TAD 6017) <51052> **RUTHIE'S KNOCKING**

Jan 97. (cd-s) (NONTM 12) <51055> **FREELOADER / IF / TAKE HEEL TOE**

–––– disbanded later in '97

– compilations, etc. –

Jul 98. (d-cd) *4 a.d.;* (DAD 8014CD) / *Rykodisc;* <8017> **IN A DOGHOUSE**
– (THROWING MUSES album tracks) / (CHAINS CHAINED ep tracks) / Call me / Sinkhole / Green / Hate my way / Vicky's box / America (she can't say no) / Fear / Raise the roses / And a she wolf after the war / Fish / Catch / Lizzie Sage / Clear and great / Doghouse / People.

KRISTIN HERSH

first below featured **MICHAEL STIPE** (R.E.M.) / **JANE SCARPANTONI** – cello

4 a.d. *Sire*

Jan 94. (12"ep/cd-ep) (BAD 4001/+CD) **YOUR GHOST / THE KEY. / UNCLE JUNE AND AUNT KIYOTI / WHEN THE LEVEE BREAKS** 45

Feb 94. (cd)(lp/c) (CAD 4002CD)(CAD/+C 4002) <45413> **HIPS AND MAKERS** 7
– Your ghost / Beestung / Teeth / Sundrops / sparky / Houdini blues / A loon / Velvet days / Close your eyes / Me and my charms / Tuesday night / The letter / Lurch / The cuckoo / Hips and makers. (cd re-iss. Jul98; same)

Apr 94. (7"/c-s) (AD 4006) <45667> **A LOON. / VELVET DAYS** 60 Jun94
(12"ep+=/cd-ep+=) (BAD 4006/+CD) – Sundrops / Me and my charms.

4 a.d. *Rykodisc*

Dec 95. (cd-ep) (TAD 5017CD) <1049> **THE HOLY SINGLE**
– Jesus Christ / Amazing grace / Sinkhole / Can the circle be unbroken.

Feb 98. (cd) (CAD 8003CD) <10429> **STRANGE ANGELS** 64
– Home / Like you / Aching for you / Cold water coming / Some catch flies / Stained / Shake / Hope / Pale / Baseball field / Heaven / Gazebo tree / Gut pageant / Rock candy brains / Cartoons.

Mar 98. (cd-ep) (TAD 8005CD) **LIKE YOU / SHAKE (live to tape) / YOUR GHOST (live to tape)**

Jun 99. (7") (AD 9007) **ECHO. / PENNYROYAL TEA**
(cd-s+=) (BAD 9007CD) – Everybody's got something to hide except for me and my monkey.

Jun 99. (cd) (CAD 9008CD) <79010> **SKY MOTEL**
– Echo / White trash moon / Fog / Costa Rica / A cleaner light / San Francisco / Cathedral heat / Husk / Caffeine / Spring / Clay feet / Faith.

Nov 99. (cd-s; promo) <01> **A CLEANER LIGHT / HATE MY WAY (acoustic) / GAROUX DES LARMES (acoustic) / A CRY BABY CRY (acoustic)**

4 a.d. *4 a.d.*

Mar 01. (cd) <(CAD 2102CD)> **SUNNY BORDER BLUE**
– Your dirty answer / Spain / 37 hours / Silica / William's cut / Summer salt / Trouble / Candyland / Measure / White suckers / Ruby / Flipside / Listerine.

THROWN UPS (see under ⇒ MUDHONEY)

TIMES (see under ⇒ BALL, Edward; 70's section)

TIN TIN (see under ⇒ DUFFY, Stephen)

TOILING MIDGETS (see under ⇒ AMERICAN MUSIC CLUB)

Russ TOLMAN (see under ⇒ TRUE WEST)

TONES ON TAIL (see under ⇒ BAUHAUS)
Winston TONG (see under ⇒ TUXEDOMOON)
Frank TOVEY (see under ⇒ FAD GADGET)
TOY LOVE (see under ⇒ TALL DWARFS)

TRANSLATOR

Formed: Los Angeles, California, USA ... 1979 by singer-songwriters STEVE BARTON and ROBERT DARLINGTON, who recruited LARRY DEKKER and DAVE SCHEFF. Moving up the coast to San Francisco, the quartet signed to the 'Columbia'-backed independent label, '415', releasing their debut album, 'HEARTBEATS AND TRIGGERS', in 1982. Opening with their much loved JOHN LENNON tribute, 'EVERYWHERE THAT I'M NOT', the record betrayed BARTON and DARLINGTON's BEATLES fixation while filtering it through a glinting New Wave lens. Sophomore effort, 'NO TIME LIKE NOW' (1983), stands as a transitional affair before 1985's more accomplished eponymous set; the latter would actually prove to be the band's final studio set, a creative peak of sorts that was matched by the more intricate displays of musical dexterity heard on 1986's swansong live set, 'EVENING OF THE HARVEST'. • **Covered:** TODAY (Jefferson Airplane) / CRY ME A SHADOW (Beatles).

Album rating: HEARTBEATS AND TRIGGERS (*6) / NO TIME LIKE NOW (*5) / TRANSLATOR (*6) / EVENING OF THE HARVEST (*7) / TRANSLATION compilation (*6) / EVERYWHERE THAT WE WERE: THE BEST OF TRANSLATOR compilation (*7)

STEVE BARTON – vocals, guitar / **ROBERT DARLINGTON** – vocals, guitar, harmonica / **LARRY DEKKER** – bass / **DAVID SCHEFF** – drums, percussion

		C.B.S.	415-Columbia
Nov 82.	(lp) <(CBS 85953)> **HEARTBEATS AND TRIGGERS**		

– Everywhere that I'm not / Necessary spinning / My heart / Everything you see / When I am with you / Nothing is saving me / Dark region / Sleeping snakes / Favourite drug / Everywhere / Your heart.

| Oct 83. | (lp/c) (CBS/40 25674) <38927> **NO TIME LIKE NOW** | | |

– Un-Alone / Beyond today / I hear you follow / Break down barriers / L.A., L.A. / I love you / No time like now / Everything is falling / Simple things / The end of their love / About the truth / Circumstance laughing.

| Nov 83. | (7") (A 3715) **UN-ALONE. / L.A., L.A.** | | |
| Jun 85. | (lp/c) (CBS/40 26460) <39984> **TRANSLATOR** | | |

– Gravity / Fall forever / Come with me / Friends of the future / New song / Another American night / O Lazarus / Inside my mind / Heaven by a string / Breathless agony.

| Jul 85. | (7") (A 6377) **COME WITH ME. / DIZZY MISS LIZZY** | | |
| 1986. | (lp) **EVENING OF THE HARVEST** (live) | – | |

– Standing in line / These old days / Crazier everyday / I need you to love / Is there a Heaven singing / Winter crying / Stony gates of time / Complications / Point of no return / Toiling of the bells / Evening of the harvest.

—— disbanded after above

– compilations, etc. –

| Dec 86. | (lp) Columbia; <40529> **EVERYWHERE THAT I'M NOT: A RETROSPECTIVE** | – | |

– Everywhere that I'm not / Sleeping snakes / O Lazarus / Alone / Gravity / Today / I need you to love / Everywhere / Standing in line / When I am with you / These old days / I hear you follow.

| Aug 95. | (cd) Oglio; <81580> **TRANSLATION** | – | |

– Everywhere that I'm not / Un-alone / Everywhere / I hear you follow / Standing in line / Today / Gravity / Necessary spinning / These old days / O Lazarus / No time like now.

| Mar 96. | (cd) Legacy-Columbia; <64778> **EVERYWHERE THAT WE WERE: THE BEST OF TRANSLATOR** | – | |

– Everywhere that I'm not / O Lazarus / Un-alone / Come with me / Everywhere / No time like now / Gravity / Sleeping snakes / Stony gates of time / Everything is falling / Cry for a shadow / When I am with you / I love you / Favorite drug / Necessary spinning / Circumstance laughing.

TREACHEROUS JAYWALKERS (see under ⇒ SPAIN; 90's section)

T. REX (see under ⇒ BOLAN, Marc)

TRIFFIDS

Formed: Perth, Australia ... 1978 by New Zealand-born DAVID McCOMB, his brother ROBERT and ALSY McDONALD were soon added. Following a string of domestic singles releases on obscure labels and several personnel changes, The TRIFFIDS were signed to appropriately named Aussie independent imprint, 'Hot', making their vinyl debut in 1983 with the eerie, sun-parched sounds of the 'TREELESS PLAIN' album. Screeching violins circled over McCOMB's gloomy intonations like vultures, the atmospheric likes of 'RED PONY' echoed years later in the work of The TINDERSTICKS amongst others. Follow-up set, 'RAINING PLEASURE', surfaced the following year but it was 1986's acclaimed 'BORN SANDY DEVOTIONAL' which saw The TRIFFIDS make their mark on European territory. With the subtle nuances of pedal steel/slide guitar player, 'EVIL' GRAHAM LEE, lending the sound a new depth, the full extent of the band's transatlantic influences were apparent on the awesome 'WIDE OPEN ROAD', while the melancholy sparseness of BIRT's vocal lent proceedings a ghostly hue. Getting er . . ., back to nature, they recorded the hastily released follow-up, 'IN THE PINES' in a sheep-shearing shed in the Australian outback (!), thankfully minus any live bleating. With the subsequent addition of extra guitarist ADAM PETERS and a major label deal courtesy of 'Island', at last The TRIFFIDS looked to be set for major alternative success. The resulting 'CALENTURE' (1987) album didn't disappoint, McCOMB's stark portraits thrown into sharp relief by Gil Norton's superior production. Yet despite a UK Top 75 hit with 'A TRICK OF THE LIGHT', success proved as elusive as ever, the band roping in MORRISSEY producer, Stephen Street, for 1989's 'BLACK SWAN'. The album scraped the lower regions of the chart but failed to score with such potential hit singles as 'GOODBYE LITTLE BOY' and 'BURY ME DEEP IN LOVE'. With recognition seemingly as far off as ever, The TRIFFIDS split at the turn of the decade, the posthumously released live album, 'STOCKHOLM' (1990) serving as a fair epitaph. While DAVID McCOMB went on to work with The BLACKEYED SUSANS and record a solo album, 'LOVE OF WILL' (1994), for 'Mushroom', the brooding spirit of The TRIFFIDS has infused the work of such gothic country luminaries as The WALKABOUTS, WILLARD GRANT CONSPIRACY and The HANDSOME FAMILY. DAVID would subsequently give up the music world to concentrate on family life, although this was cut short on the 1st of February, 1999, when he died following a car crash. • **Songwriters:** DAVID McCOMB penned except covers; / INTO THE GROOVE (Madonna) / BRIGHT LIGHTS BIG CITY (Jimmy Reed) / GOOD MORNING, GOOD MORNING (Beatles).

Album rating: TREELESS PLAIN (*7) / RAINING PLEASURE mini (*8) / BORN SANDY DEVOTIONAL (*7) / IN THE PINES (*6) / CALENTURE (*8) / THE BLACK SWAN (*7) / STOCKHOLM (*5) / AUSTRALIAN MELODRAMA compilation (*8) / David McComb: LOVE OF WILL (*6)

DAVID McCOMB (b.17 Feb'62) – vocals, guitar, piano, etc. / **ROBERT McCOMB** – violin, guitar, keyboards, vocals / **MARGARET GILLARD** – keyboards; repl. PHIL KAKULAS / **WILL AKERS** – bass; repl. BYRON SINCLAIR + ANDREW McGOWAN / **ALSY McDONALD** – drums, percussion, vocals

		ShakeSome Action	not iss.
Jul 81.	(7") (SG-MX 57828) **STAND UP. / FARMERS NEVER VISIT NIGHT CLUBS**	– not iss.	– Austra Resonant
Dec 81.	(7"ep) (REZ011-13198) **REVERIE**	–	– Austra

– Reverie / Place in the sun / Joan of Arc / This boy.

—— **JILL YATES** – keyboards; repl. GILLARD
—— **BYRON SINCLAIR** – bass; returned to repl. WILL

		not iss.	No Records
Aug 82.	(7") (K 8889) **SPANISH BLUE. / TWISTED BRAIN**	–	– Austra

—— **MARTYN CASEY** – bass, vocals; repl. SINCLAIR
—— **SIMON CROMACK** – percussion; repl. YATES

| Dec 82. | (7"ep) (K 9003) **BAD TIMING AND OTHER STORIES** | – | – Austra |

– Bad timing / Left to rot / Being driven / Snake pit.

—— **JILL BIRT** – keyboards, (some vocals) repl. SIMON

		Hot UK	not iss.
Nov 83.	(lp) (HOT 1003) **TREELESS PLAIN**		–

– Red pony / Branded / My baby thinks she's a train / Roseval / I am a lonesome hobo / Place in the sun / Play thing / Old ghostrider / Hanging shed / Hell of a summer / Madeline / Nothing can take your place. (cd-iss. Nov91; HOTCD 1003)

| Dec 83. | (7") (HOT 707) **BEAUTIFUL WASTE. / PROPERTY IS CONDEMNED** | – | – Austra |
| Dec 84. | (m-lp) (MINIHOT 1) **RAINING PLEASURE** | | |

– Jesus calling / Embedded / St. James Infirmary / Everybody has to eat / Ballad of Jack Frost / Property is condemned / Raining pleasure. (re-iss. Jun94; same)

| Apr 85. | (12"m) (HOT12 007) **FIELD OF GLASS / BRIGHT LIGHTS BIG CITY / MONKEY ON MY BACK** | | |

—— added **'Evil' GRAHAM LEE** – steel guitar (of The APARTMENTS)

| Aug 85. | (7") (HOT7 26) **YOU DON'T MISS YOUR WATER (TILL YOUR WELL RUNS DRY). / CONVENT WALLS** | | – |

(12"+=) (HOT12 26) – Beautiful water / ('A'instrumental). (re-iss. 7"ep Oct94; HEP7 26)

| May 86. | (7") (HOT 30) **WIDE OPEN ROAD. / TIME OF WEAKNESS** | | – |

(12"+=) (HOT12 30) – Dear Miss Lonely Hearts / Native bride.

| Jun 86. | (lp) (HOTLP 1023) **BORN SANDY DEVOTIONAL** | | – |

– The seabirds / Estuary bed / Chicken killer / Tarrilup Bridge / Lonely stretch / Wide open road / Life of crime / Personal things / Stolen property / Tender is the night (the long fidelity). (cd-iss. Mar95 on 'Mushroom'; D 19457)

| Nov 86. | (lp) (HOTLP 1028) **IN THE PINES** | | – |

– Suntrapper / In the pines / Kathy knows / 25 to 5 / Do you want me near you? / Once a day / Just might fade away / Better off this way / Only one life / Keep your eyes on the hole / One soul less on your fiery list / Born Sandy Devotional / Love and affection. (re-iss. Jun94; same) (cd-iss. Mar95 on 'Mushroom'; D 19480)

—— added **ADAM PETERS** – guitar (ex-FLOWERPOT MEN)

		Island	not iss.
Oct 87.	(7") (IS 337) **BURY ME DEEP IN LOVE. / BABY CAN I WALK YOU HOME**		–

(12"+=) (12IS 337) – Region unknown.
(cd-s++=) (CID 337) – Vagabond holes.

| Nov 87. | (lp/c/cd) (ILPS/ICT/CID 9885) **CALENTURE** | | – |

– Bury me deep in love / Kelly's blues / A trick of the light / Hometown farewell kiss / Unmade love / Open for you / Holy water / Blinded by the hour / Vagabond holes / Jerducuttup man / Calenture / Save what you can. (cd re-iss. Dec89; IMCD 46) (cd-iss. Mar95 on 'Mushroom'; D 19458)

TRIFFIDS (cont) THE GREAT INDIE DISCOGRAPHY The 1980s

Jan 88. (7") *(IS 350)* **A TRICK OF THE LIGHT. / LOVE DECEIVER** | 73 | - |
(10"+=) *(10IS 350)* – Bad news always reminds me of you.
(12"+=/cd-s+=) *(12IS/CID 350)* – Everything you touch turns to time.
Aug 88. (7") *(IS 367)* **HOLY WATER. / GOOD MORNING, GOOD MORNING**
(12"+=/cd-s+=) *(12IS/CID 367)* – Raining pleasure / Red pony.

—— added guests **PHIL KAKULAS** (who returned) + **RITA MENENDEZ**

Mar 89. (7"; by DAVE McCOMB * ADAM PETERS) *(IS 410)* **I DON'T NEED YOU. / WILLIE THE TORCH**
(12"+=) *(12IS 410)* – Liberty and a thousand fares.
Apr 89. (lp/c/cd) *(ILPS/ICT/CID 9928)* **THE BLACK SWAN** | 63 | - |
– Too hot to move, too hot to think / American sailors / Falling over you / Goodbye little boy / Bottle of love / The spinning top song / Butterflies into worms / The clown prince / Good fortune Rose / New Year's greetings / Blackeyed Susan Brown / Fairytale love. *(re-iss. cd Mar95 on 'Mushroom')*
Apr 89. (7") *(IS 413)* **FALLING OVER YOU. / GO HOME EDDIE**
(12"+=/cd-s+=) *(12IS/CID 413)* – Shell of a man / You minus me.
May 89. (7") *(IS 420)* **GOODBYE LITTLE BOY. / GO HOME EDDIE**
(12"+=) *(12IS 420)* – Shell of a man.
(10"++=/cd-s++=) *(10IS/CID 420)* – You minus me.
Aug 89. (7") *(IS 424)* **BURY ME DEEP IN LOVE. / RENT**
(12"+=/cd-s+=) *(12IS/CID 424)* – Into the groove.

M.N.W. not iss.

Jul 90. (lp/c/cd) *(MNW X/MCX/MCXD 9)* **STOCKHOLM** (live on Swedish radio late 1989)
– Property is condemned / Hell of a summer / Personal things / Raining pleasure / Lonely stretch / Sure the girl I love / Wide open road / Keep your eyes on the hole / In the pines / Billy / I am a lonesome hobo / How could I help but love you. *(cd-iss. Mar95 on 'Mushroom'; D 30231)*

—— disbanded late in 1989

– compilations, etc. –

Oct 87. (12"ep) *Strange Fruit; (SFPS 036) / Dutch East India; <8340>* **THE PEEL SESSIONS** (5/5/85)
– Life of crime / Chicken killer / Lonely stretch.
Dec 94. (cd) *Mushroom; (D 31182)* **AUSTRALIAN MELODRAMA (THE BEST OF THE TRIFFIDS)**
– Red pony / Hell of a summer / Beautiful waste / Raining pleasure / Bright lights, big city / The seabirds / Wide open road / Lonely stretch / Tender is the night / Bury me deep in love / trick of the light / Hometown farewell kiss / Unmade love / Jerdacuttup man / Save what you can / Falling over you / Goodbye little boy / New Year's greetings / In the pines.

DAVID McCOMB

Foundation not iss.

Sep 91. (12") **THE MESSAGE. / SONG OF NO RETURN / ('A'club version)**
(cd-s+=) – I've heard things turn out this way.

Mushroom not iss.

Mar 94. (c-ep/cd-ep) *(C/D 11589)* **SETTING YOU FREE / HOME FOR FALLEN ANGELS / YOU'VE GOT A FUNNY WAY OF SHOWING YOU LOVED ME / MY FRIEND SLEEP**
Mar 94. (cd/c) *(D/C 31071)* **LOVE OF WILL**
– Clear out my mind / Setting you free / Day of the ascension / Deep in a dream / Nothing good / The Lord burns every clue / Lifelike / Lover sister number one / Heard you had a bed / Inside of me / Leaning / I want to conquer you / Pack up your troubles.

—— DAVID died on 1st February 1999

TROTSKY ICEPICK (see under ⇒ URINALS; 70's section)

TRUE BELIEVERS

Formed: Austin, Texas, USA ... 1984 by the ESCOVEDO brothers ALEJANDRO and JAVIER. Both veterans of the local punk/roots scene (ALEJANDRO had previously helped form the influential RANK & FILE), the siblings completed their line-up with DANNY DeGORGIO and JOHN DEE GRAHAM. Signed to the then 'E.M.I.'-backed 'Roots' label, 'Rounder', the group made their debut with an eponymous album in 1986 having already built up a grassroots following through local live work. Impressed by its balls-out, raggedy-assed rock'n'roll pedigree, critics deemed the record a success and the TRUE BELIEVERS subsequently began work on a follow-up. In the event, a breakdown in communications between the band and their label led to the album being shelved; the TRUE BELIEVERS subsequently called it a day with ALEJANDRO going on to a solo career. Nearly a decade on, the long lost recordings were finally made available by 'Rykodisc' as a 2 on 1 package, 'HARD ROAD' (1994), together with the band's debut. • **Note:** Not to be confused with early 80's US indie band, plus a religious outfit who issued 'Time Ain't Long', in 1990.

Album rating: TRUE BELIEVERS (*6) / HARD ROAD compilation (*6)

ALEJANDRO ESCOVEDO – guitar, vocals (ex-NUNS) / **JAVIER ESCOVEDO** – guitar, vocals / **DANNY DeGORGIO** – bass / added **JON DEE GRAHAM** – guitars / + various drummers

EMI America | EMI America

1986. (lp/c) *(AML/TC-AML 3107) <46960>* **TRUE BELIEVERS**
– Tell her / Ring the bell / So blue about you / Rebel kind / Train around the bend / Lucky moon / We're wrong / I get excited / Sleep enough to dream / Rain won't help you when it's over.

—— new drummer **KEVIN FOLEY** – drums

—— after recording an album (see tracks below) they were dropped by their label. They split after **HECTOR MUNOZ** – drums; repl. KEVIN
—— **J.D. FOSTER** – bass, vocals (ex-DWIGHT YOAKAM) repl. DANNY

– compilations, etc. –

Mar 94. (cd) *Rykodisc; <(RCD 40287)>* **HARD ROAD**
– (TRUE BELIEVERS lp tracks) / She's got / All mixed up / One moment to another / Who calls my name / Outside your door / Wild eyed and wound up / Nobody's home / Only a dream / Please don't fade away.

TRUE WEST

Formed: Los Angeles, California, USA ... 1980 by former SUSPECTS members (with STEVE WYNN), RUSS TOLMAN and GAVIN BLAIR, plus KEN LACEWELL (later replaced by KEVIN STAYDOHAR), FRANK FRENCH and last incoming member RICHARD McGRATH. Loosely affiliated with L.A.'s Paisley Underground scene, TRUE WEST made their vinyl debut in early '83 with an eponymous EP on their own 'Bring Out Your Dead' label. French label, 'New Rose', picked them up for mini-set, 'HOLLYWOOD HOLIDAY' a few months later, a record that featured their debut EP in its entirety alongside a handful of new tracks. Among these was a cover of Pink Floyd's 'LUCIFER SAM', an appropriate choice for a band that often sounded like a cross between FLOYD and mid-period BYRDS. Following JOSEF BECKER's (who himself had replaced FRENCH) exit to THIN WHITE ROPE, the band recruited STEVE PACKENHAM and signed to the 'P.V.C.' label (Clapham's 'Zippo' in the UK) for 'THE DRIFTERS'; darkly ruminating, downward spiralling laments such as 'AND THEN THE RAIN' ensured the record ranked as one of the band's finest, TOLMAN's hypnotic guitar work reminiscent of TOM VERLAINE or BOB DYLAN. When he himself departed for a solo career soon after the record's release, the group brought in scene stalwarts, MATT PUICCI and CHUCK PROPHET for 1986's 'HAND OF FATE' album. Tragically, the latter proved to be the band's swansong as STAYDOHAR suffered a fatal brain tumour the following year.
• **Covered:** HAPPENINGS TEN YEARS TIME AGO (Yardbirds) / LUST FOR LIFE (Iggy Pop) / SUSPICIOUS MINDS (hit; Elvis Presley).

Album rating: HOLLYWOOD HOLIDAY (*5) / DRIFTERS (*5) / HAND OF FATE (*5) / Russ Tolman: TOTEM POLES & GLORY HOLES (*7) / DOWN IN EARTHQUAKE TOWN (*6) / GOODBYE JOE (*5) / ROAD MOVIE (*4) / SWEET SPOT (*4) / CITY LIGHTS (*5) / NEW QUADRAPHONIC HIGHWAY (*5)

GAVIN BLAIR – vocals / **RUSS TOLMAN** (b.15 Aug'56) – guitar / **RICHARD McGRATH** – guitar / **KEVIN STAYDOHAR** – bass; repl. KEN LACEWELL / **JOSEF BECKER** – drums; repl. FRANK FRENCH

not iss. True West

1982. (7") *<TW 666>* **LUCIFER SAM. / MAS REFICUL**

not iss. Bring Out Your Dead

Jan 83. (12"ep) *<BOYD-1001>* **TRUE WEST**
– (5 tracks from below mini-set)

New Rose not iss.

Apr 83. (m-lp) *(ROSE 23)* **HOLLYWOOD HOLIDAY**
– Steps to the door / I'm not there / And then the rain / Hollywood holiday / Lucifer Sam / It's about time / Throw away the key / You.

—— **STEVE PACKENHAM** – drums; repl. BECKER who joined THIN WHITE ROPE

Zippo P.V.C.

Dec 84. (lp) *(ZONG 004) <PVC 8921>* **DRIFTERS**
– Look around / At night they speak / Speak easy / Shot you down / What about you / Hold on / And then the rain / Backroad bridge song (what could I say) / Ain't no hangman / Morning light. *<US+=>* – HOLLYWOOD HOLIDAY. *(also on 'New Rose' lp/c; ROSE 45/+C) (cd-iss. Sep90; ROSE 23CD)*
Jun 85. (7") *(45-3)* **SHOT YOU DOWN. / 1969**

—— TOLMAN departed for a solo career in 1985 (see below). The remaining members carried on with guest help from MATT PUICCI + CHUCK PROPHET

not iss. CD Presents

1986. (cd) *<041>* **HAND OF FATE**
– Falling away / Gunner / Just one chance / Mark time / Trim the fat / Hand of fate / Waved me by / Lost at daybreak / Happening ten years time ago / No comebacks.

—— sadly STAYDOHAR died of a brain tumour in '87 and the band split

– compilations, etc. –

1990. (m-cd) *Skyclad; <62>* **TV WESTERN + BEST WESTERN**
1992. (cd) *Skyclad; <127>* **TWO TRUE**
– Steps to the door / I'm not here / And then the rain / Hollywood holiday / Lucifer Sam / It's about time / Throw away the key / You / Look around / At night they speak / Speak easy / Shot you down / What about you / Hold on / And then the rain / Backroad bridge song (what could I say) / Ain't no hangman / Morning light / Throw away the key.
May 98. (cd) *BOYD; <(1003-2)>* **BIG BOOT: LIVE** (live 22 November, 1984)
– Backroad bridge song / Waved me by / Happenings ten years time ago / And then the rain / Hold on / It's about time / Hollywood holiday / Look around / You / Lust for life / Lucifer Sam / Suspicious minds.

RUSS TOLMAN

Zippo Down There

Sep 86. (lp) *(ZONG 012) <72210>* **TOTEM POLES AND GLORY HOLES**
– Lookin' for an angel / Talking Hoover Dam blues / Four winds / Everything you need and everything you want / Galveston mud / Better than before / I am not afraid / Nothin' slowin' me down / Play hard to forget / Waitin' for rain. *(cd-iss. Oct93 on 'Diablo'; DIAB 802)*

TRUE WEST (cont)

Oct 86. (7") (ZONG 45-3) **TALKING HOOVER DAM BLUES. / SOLITARY MAN**
    Demon / Skyclad

Aug 88. (lp) (FIEND 125) <TRUE 54> **DOWN IN EARTHQUAKE TOWN**
– Vegas / Domino / Down in earthquake town / Palm tree land / Midnight / Planes, trains, automobiles / Baby / Face you wear / Jump into the fire / You don't have to say goodbye.

— next with **JON KLAGES** – guitar / **DAVE PROVOST** – bass / **DAVE DREWRY** – drums / + others on session
    New Rose / Skyclad

Nov 90. (lp/cd; as RUSS TOLMAN & THE TOTEM POLEMEN) <WEST 65> **GOODBYE JOE**
– Marla Jane / Portrait of blue / The Devil and the sea / Ragged but righteous / Blame it on the girl / Hollywood holiday / Soul murder / Murphy's barn / God only knows / Bob's house of failure.

1992. (cd-ep) (NEW 164) **SLEEPING ALL ALONE**

May 94. (cd) (ROSE 280) **ROAD MOVIE** (rec.1992)
– Pride and shame / Sleeping all alone / The one who got away / Mr. Submarine / Something about a rowboat / I don't wanna talk about the weather / For a smile / That's my story and I'm sticking to it / Lonesome fugitive / Gila bend / Letters they flatter / Pride and shame (reprise).
    not iss. / Brilliant

1994. (cd) **SWEET SPOT**
– Are you the one? / I'm alive / Your constant confusion / Stuck like glue / Thank you / Tonight (is all we have) / She's got big plans / I'm gonna miss you / The best is yet to come / I can see clearly now / Dry your pretty eyes / Sweet spot.
    not iss. / Blue Rose

1998. (cd) <BLUCD 0047> **CITY LIGHTS**
– Monterey / You oughta see her drive / I want out / Two drinks from genius / Loser's club / King city / She's my alibi / Your sister / Perfume on a faded rose / Salinas / Building a decent human being / Big ol' wedding party.
    Blue Rose / Weed

Jun 00. (cd) (BLUCD 0121) <7901> **NEW QUADRAPHONIC HIGHWAY** — Sep00
– There I am / That's not the way / Quadraphonic highway / Respect and consideration / How to do everything right / I've had a few / Tolman comes alive / Thanks a lot / Don't rain on me today / Empty bottle / Kohoutek calling / (untitled).

– compilations, etc. –

Nov 93. (cd) *Diablo;* (DIAB 802) **TOTEM POLES AND GLORY HOLES / DOWN IN EARTHQUAKE TOWN**

TRYPES
(see under ⇒ FEELIES + SPEED THE PLOUGH)

TUMOUR CIRCUS
(see under ⇒ DEAD KENNEDYS; 70's section)

TURBINES

Formed: Roxbury, Massachusetts, USA ... mid 80's by JOHN HOVORKA, JACK HICKEY, DAVID SHIBLER and FRED NAZZARO. Signed to 'Big Time', the band made their debut in 1986 with the 'LAST DANCE BEFORE THE HIGHWAY' album, a raucous blast of brooding, bluesy twisted Americana that saw them loosely associated with the insurgent cowpunk scene. French label, 'New Rose' were to release follow-up, 'MAGIC FINGERS AND HOURLY RATES' (1987), although the TURBINES quickly ran out of steam.

Album rating: LAST DANCE BEFORE THE HIGHWAY (*5) / MAGIC FINGERS AND HOURLY RATES (*5)

JOHN HOVORKA – vocals, guitar / **JACK HICKEY** – guitar / **FRED NAZZARO** – drums / **DAVID SHIBLER** – bass
    Big Time / Big Time

May 86. (lp) <(BTA 007)> **LAST DANCE BEFORE THE HIGHWAY**
– Skull & crossbones / That's the way / Highway 51 / Slop / Wah-hey / Throw it down / Rock in my pocket / Hangin' tough.
    New Rose / not iss.

Jun 87. (lp) (ROSE 118) **MAGIC FINGERS AND HOURLY RATES**
– Rules of the road / Roy's hotel / Eye for an eye / Big motor man / Stray dog / Nowhere fast / Last ride / She's my witch / 1969 / Little pig.

— never quite got into gear and disbanded soon after

TWANG

Formed: Manchester/Preston, England ... 1985 by JOHN TWANG, ANDY LADD, DAVE HINDMARSH and LEN. Fusing dancefloor elements of A CERTAIN RATIO and The FIRE ENGINES, TWANG's first record, 'WHAT'S THE RUB', was available on a 'Lyntone' flexidisc towards the end of '85. They subsequently signed to the 'Ron Johnson' imprint the following year, releasing a small handful of 45's, 'SHARP', the EP 'KICK & COMPLAIN' and 'SNAPBACK', before breaking up.

Album rating: never released any

ANDY LADD – vocals / **DAVE HINDMARSH** – guitar / **JOHN TWANG** – bass / **LEN** – drums
    Ron Johnson / not iss.

Oct 86. (7") (ZRON 14) **SHARP. / EIGHT AT A TIME**

Mar 87. (12"ep) (ZRON 22) **KICK & COMPLAIN EP**
– Cut candidate / Cold tongue bulletin / Sharp / Every home should have one.

Nov 87. (12") (ZRON 29) **SNAPBACK. / SNAPBACK (defence mix)**

— all returned to their day jobs

28th DAY (see under ⇒ MANNING, Barbara)

23 SKIDOO

Formed: London, England ... 1979 by FRITZ HAAMAN, J.C.M. and A. LIM, taking their name from Aleister Crowley's 'Book Of Lies'. They subsequently issued a debut 45, 'ETHICS', with further sporadic vinyl appearances reaching the shops in the early 80's. These featured artwork by future ('The Face') designer, Neville Brody, the man applying his trade on 'LAST WORDS' and 'THE GOSPEL ACCORDING TO NEW GUINEA'. 1982's 'SEVEN SONGS' mini-set showed more diversity especially on opening tracks, 'KUNDALINI' and 'VEGAS EL BANDITO'. Drawing comparisons with CABARET VOLTAIRE and THROBBING GRISTLE, this percussive/industrial dub unit's originality lay in the use of ethnic African/Indonesian styles (samples/dialogue stemming from Kung Fu movies). During the following two years, they delivered another two studio sets, 'THE CULLING IS COMING' (1983) and the more stripped-down funk of 'URBAN GAMELAN' (1984). The latter featured ANDREW WEATHERALL (later of SABRES OF PARADISE), in one of his earliest vinyl appearances; however, barring a few further EP's (including 1986's 'ASSASSINS OF SOUL'), it was sadly to be their last work. With the whole of the 90's in the wilderness, 23 SKIDOO reunited in 2000 for an eponymous comeback set.

Album rating: SEVEN SONGS mini (*5) / THE CULLING IS COMING (*5) / URBAN GAMELAN (*7) / JUST LIKE EVERYBODY collection (*6) / 23 SKIDOO (*5) / JUST LIKE EVERYBODY PART TWO collection (*5)

J.C.M. (JOHNNY) TURNBULL – guitar, congas, percussion / **A. LIM (ALEX TURNBULL)** – bass, percussion / **FRITZ HAAMAN** (b. FRITZ CATLIN) – drums, percussion / early members **SAM + TOM**
    Pineapple / not iss.

Jul 81. (7") (PULP 23) **ETHICS. / ANOTHER BABY'S FACE**
    Fetish / not iss.

Sep 81. (7"promo) (FE 10) **LAST WORDS. / VERSION**

Oct 81. (12"m) (FE 11) **THE GOSPEL COMES TO NEW GUINEA. / LAST WORDS**
(re-iss. Oct01 on 'Ronin'; RDP 16) (re-iss. May02 cd/lp; RDCD/RDLP 6)

Feb 82. (m-lp) (FM 2008) **SEVEN SONGS**
– Kundalini / Vegas el bandito / Mary's operation / Lock groove / New testament IV / Porno base / Quiet pillage. (re-iss. Feb85 on 'Illuminated'; JAMS 47) (re-iss. Nov00 on 'Ronin' cd/lp; RDCD/RDLP 003)

May 82. (12"m) (FP 20) **TEARING UP THE PLANS. / JUST LIKE EVERYBODY / GREGOUKA**

— added **DAVID TIBET** – instruments (of PSYCHIC TV)
    Operation Twilight / not iss.

Feb 83. (lp) (OPT 23) **THE CULLING IS COMING**
– Banishing / Invocation / Flashing / Stifling / Healing / 9-2 contemplation / S-matrix / 9-3 insemination / Shrine / Mahakala. (re-iss. Nov88 on 'Laylah'; LAY 23) (cd-iss. Apr90; LAY 23CD) (re-iss. Sep00 on 'Skidoo' cd/lp; SKCD/SKLP 03)

— added **MR. SKETCH** – bass, samples
    Illuminated / not iss.

Nov 83. (12") (ILL 28-12) **COUP. / VERSION (IN THE PALACE)**

May 84. (12") (ILL 38-12) **LANGUAGE. / ('A'version)**

Jul 84. (lp) (JAMS 40) **URBAN GAMELAN**
– Fuck you G.I. (23 F.P.M.) / Fire / Misr wakening / Jalan Jalan / Urban gamelan / Sirens / Helicopters / Kongo-do / Language dub / Drunkards reprisal / Coup de grace. (re-iss. Nov00 on 'Ronin' cd/lp; RDP CD/LP 004)

Mar 85. (12") (ILL 58-12) **OOZE. / ('A'version)**

— early '86, 'GI (AMERICAN EPILOGUE)' was on b-side of 400 BLOWS single

Aug 86. (12"ep) (12LEV 72) **ASSASSINS OF SOUL**
– T.O.Y. (Thoughts Of You) / Assassin / Ooze.

— disbanded after above. TIBET was already part of PSYCHIC TV and he soon joined DEATH IN JUNE and others NURSE WITH WOUND, etc. Some members became BAHALA-NA GANG, who released in 1990 a version of ISLEY BROTHERS' 'Summer Breeze' for 'Ronin' label. FRITZ and SAM were also part of LAST FEW DAYS. 23 SKIDOO (**TURNBULL, TURNBULL, CATLIN + MARTIN**) were back again towards the new millennium.
    Virgin / E.M.I.

Jul 00. (cd/d-lp) (CD+/V 2912) <849412> **23 SKIDOO**
– Freeze frame / Dirty Lo / Interzonal / Hendang / Catch 23 / Crossfire / Where you at / Atmosfear / Dawning / Meltdown / Dusk to dawn / Ayu.

– compilations, etc. –

Apr 87. (lp) *Bleeding Chin;* (BC 1) **JUST LIKE EVERYBODY**
– Kundalini / Vegas el bandito / I.Y. / Just like everybody / Assassin / Coup / Urban gamelan act 1 / Congo do / Language dub / Drunkards reprise / Shrine / Porno base. (re-iss. Sep00 on 'Skidoo' cd/lp; SKCD/SKLP 05)

Nov 02. (cd) *Ronin;* (RDCD 8) **JUST LIKE EVERYBODY PART TWO** (1986-2000)
– Roninstep / Meltdown / What y'all gon' do / Eye spy / 23 break / 100 dark / Lightening beats / Cushite / The best / Suspense / Mr. Lee, are you ready? / Clan break / Elephants / Reachin' break / Liquid noise / Return of the dragon / Recoup.

TWO NICE GIRLS

Formed: Austin, Texas, USA ... 1989 by er, actually "three" nice girls, GRETCHEN PHILLIPS, KATHY KORNILOFF and LAURIE FREELOVE. Signed to 'Rough Trade', this rootsy singing/songwriting-based outfit impressed many critics with their 1989 eponymous debut album, the girls taking a democratic approach to both scripting their songs and performing them; a nod towards their guiding influences, the track 'SWEET JANE (WITH AFFECTION)' was a clever coupling of The Velvet Underground classic and Joan Armatrading's 'Love And Affection'. The turn of the decade saw FREELOVE depart for a solo career (she released the 'SMELLS LIKE TRUTH' album on 'Ensign' in 1991), replacements MEG HENTGES and PAM BARGER making for a fuller, if more cluttered sound on 1991's swansong, 'CHLOE LIKED OLIVIA' (1991).

Album rating: TWO NICE GIRLS (*5) / LIKE A VERSION mini (*4) / CHLOE LIKED OLIVIA (*4)

LAURIE FREELOVE – vocals, guitar / **GRETCHEN PHILLIPS** – vocals, mandolin, bass, guitar / **KATHY KORNILOFF** – vocals, guitar, synthesizer / with a plethora of session people

		Rough Trade	Rough Trade
Jun 89.	(lp/c/cd) (ROUGH/+C/CD 135) <ROUGHUS 59> **TWO NICE GIRLS**		

– The sweet postcard / Follow me / Goons / Money / I spent my last $10.00 (on birth control and beer) / Sweet Jane (with affection) / My heart crawls off / Looking out / Heaven on Earth / Kick.

— **MEG HENTGES** – vocals, bass, guitar, piano + **PAM BARGER** – drums, vocals, percussion; repl. FREELOVE who issueed her own solo album, 'SMELLS LIKE TRUTH', for 'Ensign' in 1991

Apr 90. (m-lp/m-cd) (RTM 235/+CD) **LIKE A VERSION**
– I feel (like makin') love / Bang bang / Top of the world / Speed racer / Cotton crown / I spent my last $10.00 (on birth control and beer)

1991. (cd) (RTR 262-2) **CHLOE LIKED OLIVIA**
– Let's go bonding / Eleven / For the inauguration / Princess of power / Throw it all away / Rational heart / The queer song / Only today / Noona's revenge / Swimming in circles.

— they split after above

TYRANNOSAURUS REX
(see under ⇒ BOLAN, Marc)

UK DECAY

Formed: Luton, Bedfordshire, England ... 1978 out of The RESISTORS by JOHN ABBOT aka ABBO, MARTYN SMITH aka SEGOVIA and STEVE HARLE. Adopting the UK DECAY moniker at the turn of the decade, the band's first release under the new name came via a limited edition split EP with fellow Luton band, PNEU-MANIA. Further changes came with the recruitment of the latter's guitarist, STEVE SPON, bolstering the sound on early 1980's 'THE BLACK CAT' EP. By this point the group had become one of the prime movers in the fermenting goth scene, the serrated punk, vaguely P.I.L. feel of the music making up for the horsemen-of-the-apocalypse vocals and cod-occult lyrics of tracks like 'SHATTERED' and 'LAST IN THE HOUSE OF FLAMES'. The latter two were featured on the long awaited debut album, 'FOR MADMEN ONLY' (1981), followed up by the 'RISING FROM THE DREAD' EP a year later. Yet even as the band were enjoying indie chart success and the loyal attentions of flour-faced fans, they played their last gig in late '82 – released the following year as 'A NIGHT FOR CELEBRATION' – with SPON going on to form goth outfit IN EXCELSIS and the remaining members carrying on as FURYO.

Album rating: FOR MADMEN ONLY (*6)

ABBO (b. JOHN ABBOTT) – vocals, guitar / **SEGOVIA** (b. MARTYN SMITH) – bass / **STEVE HARLE** – drums

		Plastic	not iss.
1979.	(7"ep) (PLAS 001) **UK DECAY / CARCRASH. / (PNEU-MANIA:- Exhibition / Coming Attack)**		-

— added **STEVE SPON** – guitar, piano (ex-PNEU-MANIA)

Feb 80. (7"ep) (PLAS 002) **THE BLACK CAT EP**
– Black cat / Middle of the road man / Message distortion / Disco romance. (re-iss. Oct81; same)

		Fresh	not iss.
Sep 80.	(7") (FRESH 12) **FOR MY COUNTRY. / UNWIND TONIGHT** (re-iss. 1982 on 'UK Decay')		-
Feb 81.	(7") (FRESH 26) **UNEXPECTED GUEST. / DRESDEN** (re-iss. 1982 on 'UK Decay')		-
Oct 81.	(7") (FRESH 33) **SEXUAL. / TWIST IN THE TALE**		-
Oct 81.	(lp) (FRESHLP 5) **FOR MADMEN ONLY**		-

– Duel / Battle of the elements / Shattered / Stage struck / Last in the house of flames / Unexpected guest / Sexual / Dorian / Decadence / Mayday malady / For madmen only.

— **TWIGGY** – bass; repl. SEGOVIA

— **EDDIE BRANCH** – bass; repl. TWIGGY

		Corpus Christi	not iss.
Aug 82.	(12"ep) (CHRIST ITS 1) **RISING FROM THE (D)READ / TESTAMENT. / WEREWOLF / JERUSALEM OVER (THE WHITE CLIFFS OF DOVER)**		-

— split but left behind below cassette

		UK Decay	not iss.
Aug 83.	(c) (DK 6) **A NIGHT FOR CELEBRATION** (last gig)		-

– Unwind / Werewolf / Dresden / Barbarian / Barbarians / Sexual / Stage struck / Rising from the dead / Twist in the tale / Unexpected guest / Testament / Black cat / UK Decay / For my country / Unwind.

— SPON joined IN EXCELSIS with ex-RITUAL members

FURYO

— stemmed from MEAT OF YOUTH who appeared on 'The BATCAVE' various artists album.

ABBO / STEVE HARLE / EDDIE BRANCH + ALBIE DE LUCA – guitar

		Anagram	not iss.
Apr 84.	(m-lp) (MGRAM 12) **FURYO**		-

– The gold of our lives / Vultures / In the arena / Monster of a thousand heads / The opera in the air.

Oct 84. (12") (12ANA 24) **LEGACY (ANDANTE). / KING OF HEARTS / CAVALCADE**

— ABBO later found and aided EMF

ULTRAMARINE

Formed: Chelmsford, Essex, England ... 1984 as A PRIMARY INDUSTRY, an avant-garde noise-merchant troupe formed by IAN COOPER and PAUL HAMMOND, alongside other musicians, JEMMA, GUY and SIMON. In the early 90's, IAN and PAUL became ULTRAMARINE after basing themselves in Leamington Spa. The duo were showered with praise during 1992 after the release of their album, 'EVERY MAN AND WOMAN IS A STAR', a trip into left field Balearic territory complete with distinctive fairground organ and samples. Just prior to this, they had taken a canoe trip with AMERICA's (the band, that is) organist, DEWEY BUNNELL. In the Autumn of '93, they managed to scrape into the UK Top 50 with the SOFT MACHINE/KEVIN AYERS-influenced 'UNITED KINGDOMS' album, which featured veteran Canterbury legend, ROBERT WYATT. They took another about turn in 1995, with the release of the uninspiring US West Coast type album, 'BEL AIR'. • **Songwriters:** Group except HEART OF GLASS (Blondie) / HYMN (Kevin Ayers). • **Trivia:** Another group (probably Eastern European) named ULTRAMARINE issued two albums 'DE' and 'E SI MALA', (1990-1993).

Album rating: A Primary Industry: ULTRAMARINE (*6) / Ultramarine: WYNDHAM LEWIS (*6) / FOLK (*6) / EVERY MAN AND WOMAN IS A STAR (*8) / UNITED KINGDOMS (*8) / BEL AIR (*6) / A USER'S GUIDE (*5)

A PRIMARY INDUSTRY

IAN COOPER – acoustic guitar, keyboards, prog. / **PAUL HAMMOND** – bass, keyboards, programming / **JEMMA MELLERIO** – vocals / **GUY** – keyboards / **SIMON HAMMOND** – drums

Les Tempes Modernes / not iss.

Nov 84. (7") (CSBTV:V) **AT GUNPOINT. / PERVERSION**
- (re-iss. Feb86 on 'N.I.S.S.' 12"; C88TV)

Sweatbox / not iss.

Nov 85. (12"ep) (SOX 007) **7 HERTZ**
- Cicatrice / Obeah / Biting back / Bled dry.
Oct 86. (lp) (SAX 015) **ULTRAMARINE**
- Body blow / Beacon Hill / Shear / Sans orange / Cicatrice / Watchword weal / Gush / Raw umber / Silesia / Rose madder.
Jul 87. (7") (OX 22) **HEART OF GLASS. / WHERE IS YOUR VORTEX**
(12") (BOX 25) – ('A'extended) / ('A'extended).
Mar 88. (m-lp) (BOX 26) **WYNDHAM LEWIS**
- The liquid brown detestable Earth / Fokker Bomb-shit / The song of the militant romance / If so the man you are / End of enemy interlude / Merde alors!

— changed group name to ...

ULTRAMARINE

— GUY replaced by **RICHARD HASLAM** – keyboards / **FRANK MICHIELS** – percussion / **STAF VERBEEK** – accordion

Sweatbox / not iss.

Jun 89. (m-lp) (BOX 28) **WYNDHAM LEWIS**
- (the re-issue of A PRIMARY INDUSTRY m-lp)

Crepuscule / not iss.

Mar 90. (lp/cd) (TWI 894/+CD) **FOLK**
- Lobster / Antiseptic / Bronze eye / Bastard folk / Bullprong / Softspot / Vulgar streak / The golden target. (re-iss. cd Nov94 & Oct02 on 'Offshore'+=; OSHCD 1) – Stella / Interstellar.

Dancyclopaedia / not iss.

Sep 90. (12"ep) (DAN 002) **STELLA. / INTERSTELLAR / ULTRABASS (Eddy De Cierca mix)**

— basically now duo of IAN + PAUL

Brainiak / Dali – Chameleon

May 91. (12") (BAUBJ 11) **STELLA CONNECTS. / STELLA BREATHS**
Oct 91. (12"ep) (BRAINK 019) **WEIRD GEAR. / WEIRD GEAR (version) / BRITISH SUMMERTIME**
Dec 91. (cd/m-lp) (BRAIN KCD/MKLP 21) <61443> **EVERY MAN AND WOMAN IS A STAR**
- Discovery / Weird gear / Pansy / Money / Stella / Geezer / Panther / British summertime / Lights in my brain / Canoe trip / Skyclad / Gravity. (re-iss. & re-mixed Jul92 on 'Rough Trade' cd)(lp+=; R 292)(RT 896) – Nova Scotia / Saratoga. (cd re-mast.Jul02 on 'Les Tempes Modernes'; LTMCD 2345) (cd re-iss. Nov02 on 'Darla'; DRL 131CD)

Rough Trade / Dali – Chameleon

May 92. (7"ltd.) (45REV 7) **SARATOGA. / NOVA SCOTIA**
Nov 92. (12"ep/cd-ep) (R 294-0/-3) <66324> **NIGHTFALL IN SWEETLEAF** 1993
- Panther (Coco Steel remix) / Lights in my brain (Spooky mix) / Geezer (Sweet Exorcist mix). <US+=> – Weird gear.
Mar 93. (12"ep)(cd-ep) (066324)(PRCD 8737) **WEIRD GEAR (remix) / LIGHTS IN MY BRAIN (Spooky mix) / GEEZER (Sweet Exorcist mix) / PANTHER (Coco Steel & Lovebomb mix) / OUTRO**

— now with **ROBERT WYATT** – vocals ('A'above) / **SIMON KAY** – Hammond organ / **JIMMY HASTINGS** – clarinet, flute, piccolo, sax / **JIM RATTIGAN** – accordion / **ROBERT ATCHISON** – violin / **PHIL JAMES** – trumpet, harmonica / **PAUL JOHNSON** – percussion

Blanco Y Negro / Unitary

Jul 93. (7"/c-s) (NEG 65/+C) **KINGDOM. / GOLDCREST** 46
(12"/cd-s) (NEG 65 T/CD) – ('A'side) / ('B'extended) / ('A'extended mix).
Aug 93. (cd/c/lp) (4509 93425-2/-4/-1) **UNITED KINGDOMS** 49
- Source / Kingdom / Queen of the Moon / Prince Rock / Happy land / Urf / English heritage / Instant kitten / The badger / Hooter / Dizzy fox / No time. (cd re-iss. Jan97; same)

Jan 94. (c-ep/12"ep/cd-ep) (NEG 67 C/T/CD) **THE BAREFOOT EP** 61
- Happy land (remixed by DRUMMIE ZEB) / Hooter (remixed by CARL CRAIG) / The badger (remixed by RICHARD H. KIRK) / Urf (remixed by FILA BRAZILLIA).
Jan 95. (12"/c-s) (NEG 76 T/C) **HYMN. / HYMN (mix)**
(cd-s+=) (NEG 76CD1) – Base element.
(cd-s+=) (NEG 76CD2) – ('A'mix).
Aug 95. (cd/c/clear-d-lp) (0603 11206-2/-4/-1) **BEL AIR**
- Welcome / Buena vista / Maxine / Pioneer spirit / Mutant / Fantasy filter / 78 / I got sane / Schnaltz / Citizen / Alter ego / Free radical / Harmony Street / K-V / Escape velocity / Rainbow brew / Everyone in Brazil. (cd re-iss. Jan97; same)
Apr 96. (c-s; ULTRAMARINE featuring DAVID McALMONT) (NEG 87C) <76> **HYMN (David McAlmont mix) / HYMN (Kevin Ayers mix) / BASE ELEMENT** 65
(cd-s+=) (NEG 87CD1) – (first & last track) / Our love / Love life.
(12") (NEG 87T) – Hymn (U-ziq mix) / Hymn (Luke Slater mix) / Our love / Love life.
(cd-s) (NEG 87CD2) – Hymn (U-ziq mix) / Hymn (Luke Slater mix) / Hymn (Paul Sampson's lullabye mix) / Hymn (Sugar J mix) / Hymn (Mouse On Mars: a sleep mix) / Hymn (Ultramarine & Kevin Ayers version).

New Electronica / not iss.

Jan 98. (12") (ELEC 34T) **ON THE BRINK. / SURFACING / 4U (mix)**
Feb 98. (cd/d-lp) (ELEC 36 CD/LP) **A USER'S GUIDE**
- All of a sudden / Surfacing / Sucker 4 U / On the brink / Zombie / By turns / Ambush / 4 U version / Ghost routine / What machines want.

— the group have since split

UNDERNEATH (see under ⇒ BLAKE, Karl)

UNREST

Formed: Washington DC, USA ... early 80's by school friends MARK ROBINSON, PHIL KRAUTH and TIM MORAN. Inspired by their home city's fertile scene, this melodic hardcore trio issued a couple of early singles and a debut album, 'TINK OF S.E.' (1987) through their own 'Teen Beat' label. Harnessing the energy of punk while still celebrating the diversity of their influences and steering clear of hardcore's inherent singularity, the band indulged in covers of The Troggs' 'WILD THING' and King Crimson's '21st CENTURY SCHIZOID MAN'. Following a further two well received albums, 'MALCOLM X PARK' (1988) and 'KUSTOM KARNAL BLACKXPLOITATION' (1990), PARK was replaced by BRIDGET CROSS, who made her debut on 1992's 'IMPERIAL F.F.R.R.'. A rather unlikely link-up with '4 a.d.' resulted in the 'PERFECT TEETH' (1993) album, an enjoyable set of Amerindie-rock punctuated by the X-files experimentation of 'FOOD & DRINK SYNTHESIZER' and encased in a Robert Mapplethorpe cover shot of 80's goddess, CATH CARROLL. In the event, it proved to be the band's epitaph save for compilation set, 'FUCK PUSSY GALORE (& ALL HER FRIENDS)' (1993), KRAUTH going on to release solo set, 'SILVER EYES' (1995) while ROBINSON concentrated on his 30's retro project, GRENADINE. A trio consisting of ROBINSON, JENNY TOOMEY and ROB CHRISTIANSEN, the latter outfit attempted to pay tribute to the halcyon days of swing and lounge jazz in their own inimitable fashion. Following a debut single, 'TRILOGY', the group released the 'GOYA' (1993) album on 'Shimmy Disc', following it up with '94's 'NOPALITOS' (featuring a cover of Burt Bacharach's 'THIS GIRL'S IN LOVE WITH YOU'). Amid a muted critical reception, ROBINSON increasingly concentrated on AIR MIAMI, along with CROSS and new recruits LAUREN and MIKE. Remaining with '4 a.d.', the band contributed a track to a label sampler before releasing a debut single, 'AIRPLANE RIDER', in Autumn '95. With a new rhythm section of FONTAINE TOUPS and BEN CURRIER in place, the band subsequently recorded an acclaimed debut album, 'ME, ME, ME' (1995). MARK ROBINSON subsequently formed OLYMPIC DEATH SQUAD, issuing the angular rock album 'BLUE' (1996) before moving onto create the wig-out rock'n'roll group FLIN FLON, alongside TRUE LOVE ALWAYS' MATT DATESMAN and COLD COLD HEARTS' bassist NATTLES. The group issued three albums, 'A-OK' (1998), 'BOO-BOO' (1999) and 2002's 'CHICOTIMI', before ROBINSON ventured into the world of solo experimental music via a handful of 'TeenBeat' albums; 2000's 'TASTE' and 'TIGER BANANA' were worthy ambient classics, whereas 2001's 'CANADA'S GREEN HIGHWAYS' displayed ROBINSON's remarkable songwriting skills. • **Covered:** DEAF (Crispy Ambulance) / UFO (ESG) / SEX MACHINE (Crawling Chaos) / WHEN IT ALL COMES DOWN (Miaow) / LOVE TO KNOW (Tracy Thorn).

Album rating: IMPERIAL F.F.R.R. (*6) / PERFECT TEETH (*6) / FUCK PUSSY GALORE compilation (*6) / Air Miami: ME, ME, ME (*6) / Grenadine: GOYA (*6) / NOPALITOS (*6) / Olympic Death Squad: BLUE (*5) / Flin Flon: A-OK (*4) / BOO-BOO (*5) / CHICOUTIMI compilation (*5) / Mark Robinson: TASTE mini (*6) / TIGER BANANA (*6) / CANADA'S GREEN HIGHWAYS (*5)

MARK ROBINSON – vocals, guitar / **TIM MORAN** – bass / **PHIL KRAUTH** – drums

not iss. / Teenbeat

May 85. (c-s) <TEENBEAT 2> **UNREST**
Aug 85. (c-s) <TEENBEAT 6> **LISA CAROL FREEMONT**
Nov 85. (7"ep) <TEENBEAT 7> **SO YOU WANNA BE A RNR STAR**

— **CHRIS THOMSON** – bass; repl. MORAN
Oct 87. (m-lp) <TEENBEAT 14> **TINK OF S.E.**
- 91st century schizoid man / Wild thang / etc.
(UK-iss.1989 on 'Hageland'; HR 015)
Sep 88. (c) <TEENBEAT 23> **TWISTER**

UNREST (cont)

— **DAVE PARK** – bass; repl. THOMSON
Mar 89. (7") <TEENBEAT 28> **CATCHPELLET. /** *not iss. Caroline*
Apr 89. (lp/c) <CAROL 1366-1/-4> **MALCOLM X PARK**
 – Malcolm X park / Can't sit still / Strutter / Dago red / Ben's chili bowl / Lucifer rising / The gas chair / Ragged (clthd hsbnd) / Oils / Dalmations / Stranger in my own home town / Oh yeah c'mon / Disko magic / Christ in a Castro '59 / The hill. <cd-iss. Nov99 on 'Teenbeat'; TEENBEAT 231> (cd-iss. Jan00 on 'No.6'; KAR 047-2)
Apr 90. (cd) <CAROL 1399-1/-4 – TEENBEAT 35> **KUSTOM KARNAL BLACKXPLOITATION**
 – Invoking the godhead / Shag / Click click / Teenage suicide / Coming hot and proud / The foxey playground / Chick Chelsea delux / She makes me shake like a soul machine / Butch Willis is a psychopath / Konfusion / Kill Whitey / Lord Shiva / Black power dynamo / Eyeball from the socket . . . <cd re-iss. Nov99 on 'Teenbeat'; TEENBEAT 238> (UK cd-iss. Jan00 on 'No.6'; KAR 046-2)

 K   Teenbeat
Mar 91. (7") <IPU 17 – TEENBEAT 42> **YES SHE IS MY SKINHEAD GIRL. / HYDROPLANE / FEELING GOOD FIXATION**
Mar 91. (7") <TEENBEAT 49> **CHERRY CHERRY. /** *not iss. Sub Pop – Teenbeat*
Apr 91. (7"ep) <SP 103 – TEENBEAT 63> **A FACTORY RECORD**
 – Deaf / UFO / Sex machine / When it all comes down.

— **BRIDGET CROSS** – bass (ex-VELOCITY GIRL) repl. DAVE
 not iss. Teenbeat
Jan 92. (7") <TEENBEAT 84> **BAVARIAN MODS AND OTHER HITS**
Jul 92. (7"ep) <TEENBEAT 70> **ISABEL BISHOP**
 – Isabel / Love to know / Wharton hockey club.
 Guernica No.6 – Teenbeat
Aug 92. (cd/c/lp) <GU 1 CD/C/LP> <KAR 018 – TEENBEAT 77> **IMPERIAL F.F.R.R.** Jul92
 – Volume reference tone / Suki / Imperial / I do believe you are blushing / Champion nines / Sugar shack / Isabel / Cherry cream on / Firecracker / June / Loyola. (lp with free-7") – Yes, she is my skinhead giel / Hydrofoil No.3 / Full frequency range recording. (cd++=) – Wednesday & proud. (the free 7" was finally issued May97 on 'K'; IPU 17)
 4 a.d.   Warners
May 93. (m-lp/m-cd) (BAD 3007/+CD) <45271> **ISABEL BISHOP EP**
 – Isabel / Teenage suicide / Love to know / Nation writer / Yes she is my skinhead girl / Wednesday & proud / Wharton hockey club.
Jul 93. (cd)(lp/c) (CAD 3012CD)(CAD/+C 3012) <45401> **PERFECT TEETH**
 – Angel I'll walk you home / Cath Carroll / So sick / Light command / Food & drink synthesizer / Soon it is going to rain / Make out club / Breather X.O.X.O. / West Coast love affair / Six layer cake / Stylized ampersand. (cd re-iss. Jul98; GAD 3012CD)
Oct 93. (12"/cd-s) (BAD 3015/+CD) **CATH CARROLL (remix). / HYDRO**
 Teenbeat   Teenbeat
Jun 93. (7"colrd) <TEENBEAT 105> **CATH CARROLL. / SO SO SICK / CAPEZIO BOWLER**
Jun 93. (m-cd) <TEENBEAT 105> **CCEP**
 – Cath Carroll (10cc mix) / Vibe out! / Goodbye / Hydroplane (33 min)
Aug 93. (7") <TEENBEAT 98> **SO SICK**
Dec 93. (7") **WHERE ARE ALL THOSE PUERTO RICAN BOYS? / (other by STEREOLAB)**
Apr 94. (7"ep) <(TEENBEAT 133)> **ANIMAL PARK EP**
 – Afternoon train / Hey hey Halifax / Light command.

— split in 1994, PHIL KRAUTH releasing one 'Teenbeat' solo set (cd/lp), 'SILVER EYES' in May '96 (TB 205-2/-1)

 – compilations, etc. –

Jan 94. (cd/lp) Matador; (OLE 024-2/-1) / Teenbeat; <67> **FUCK PUSSY GALORE (& ALL HER FRIENDS)** (1983-1987) Dec93
 – Can't sit still / Cats / Die grunen / Holiday in Berlin / 91st century schizoid man / The hill (part 2) / A picnic at Hanging Rock / Live on a hot August night / Chastity ballad / Judy says (part 2) / The tundra / Wild thang / Laughter / The 'S' street shuffle (with a beat) / Over the life / Hope / So you want to be a RNR star / Scott & Zelda / The hill / Happy song / Rigormortis / Communist part / She makes me free to be me / Sammy's mean mustard / Greg Hershey where are you? / Egg cheer.
Aug 95. (cd/lp) Teen Beat; <(TB 175-2/-1)> **B.P.M.** (a collection 1991-1994)
 – June / Cath Carroll (re-mix) / When it all comes down / So so sick / Hydrofoil No.4 / Winona (XY) / Winona (XX) / Folklore / Imperial (re-mix) / Cherry cherry / Hey London / Bavarian mods / Vibe out / Hi-tec theme / Wednesday & proud.

MARK ROBINSON

 Teenbeat   Teenbeat
Dec 87. (c) <TEENBEAT 17> **BLACK CHRISTMAS**
Dec 88. (c) <TEENBEAT 27> **KINGXMAS**
Dec 89. (7"; as MARK E SUPERSTAR) <TEENBEAT 37> **SAMMY SUPREME MY MAN!**

GRENADINE

MARK ROBINSON – vocals, guitar / **JENNY TOOMEY** – guitar, vocals (ex-TSUNAMI, etc) / **ROB CHRISTIANSEN** – guitar, trombone (ex-EGGS)
 not iss.   Teenbeat
1992. (7") **TRILOGY. /** *Shimmy Disc   Teenbeat*
Nov 92. (lp/c/cd) (SHIMMY 059/+MC/CD) <TEENBEAT 99> **GOYA**
 – Goya / Philco / Decca / I only have eyes for you / In a world without heroes / Pinky tuscadero / Cherishino / Gillen (excerpt sometimes) / Ticket / Demarest / Fillings / Decca reprise.
 Simple Machines   Simple Machines
1994. (7") **DON'T FORGET THE HALO. /**
 Simple Machines   Teenbeat
Aug 94. (7"ep) (SMR 031) <TEENBEAT 166> **CHRISTIANSEN EP**
 – Christiansen / Snuck (re-mix) / Screw (re-mix).

Oct 94. (cd/lp) (SMR 23 CD/V) <TEENBEAT 155> **NOPALITOS**
 – Mexico big sky / Steely Daniel / Puddle / What on earth has happened to today's / Note in his pocket / Hell over Hickory dew / Speeding / Roundabout on a Tuesday / Drama club / The barnacle / Snik / This girl's in love with you.

AIR MIAMI

MARK ROBINSON – vocals, guitar / **BRIDGET CROSS** – guitar, vocals / with **LAUREN FELDSHER** – bass / **MIKE FELLOWS** – drums
 not iss.   Teenbeat
Sep 94. (7") <TEENBEAT 147> **AIRPLANE RIDER. / STOP SIGN**
 4 a.d.   Warners
Sep 95. (7"ep)(cd-ep) (AD 5014)(BAD 5014CD) **FUCK YOU, TIGER EP**
 – I hate milk (remix) / Warm Miami May / Afternoon train (remix) / See-through plastic.

— **FONTAINE TOUPS** – bass (ex-VERSUS) repl. LAUREN
— **BEN CURRIER** – drums (ex-EGGS) repl. MIKE
— both repl. by **GABRIEL STOUT** – drums (now a trio)
Nov 95. (lp/cd) (CAD 5011/+CD) <46000> **ME, ME, ME** Sep95
 – I hate milk / World Cup fever / Seabird / Special angel / Afternoon train / Dolphin expressway / Sweet as a candy bar / You sweet little heartbreaker / Neely / Bubble shield / The event horizon / Definitely beachy / Reprise. (cd re-iss. Jul98; GAD 5011CD)

 – others, etc. –

Jul 98. (cd-ep) <TEENBEAT 257> **WORLD CUP FEVER (remixes)**

OLYMPIC DEATH SQUAD

MARK ROBINSON (solo project)
May 96. (lp/cd) <(TEENBEAT 200-2/-1)> **BLUE**
 – This is riot gear / Maple leaf / Show your age / Newfoundland / Sometimes I can breathe / Ski jump / Wakefield Street / Shortsleeve / The anti-kidnapping song / Yeah, uh-huh.

PROJECT

MARK ROBINSON with VERSUS members **MELISSA FARRIS + PHIL SATLOF**
Aug 97. (7") <TEENBEAT 226> **THE CELLULOID DREAMS OF SUPERMAN. / IN THE DRINK**

FLIN FLON

MARK ROBINSON with **NATTLES** – bass (ex-COLD COLD HEARTS) / **MATT DATESMAN** – drums (of TRUE LOVE ALWAYS)
Jan 98. (7") <TEENBEAT 241> **SWIFT CURRENT. /**
Sep 98. (cd/lp) <TEENBEAT 252-2/-1> **A-OK**
 – Kamloops / Red deer / Ukraina / Buffal narrows / Yellowknife / Moose jaw / Odessa / Medicine hat / Whitehorse / Colgate.
Aug 99. (cd) <TEENBEAT 274> **BOO-BOO**
 – Upper ferry / Shuffle board / Mistaken point / Jumpers / Floods / Trinity / Virgin arm / Leading tickets / Happy adventure / St. Patrick's.

 – compilations, etc. –

Jul 02. (cd) <(TEENBEAT 285)> **CHICOUTIMI** Apr02
 – Rimouski / Mistassini / Chicoutimi / Happy adventure / Flatbush (Samantha) / Jumpers / Floods / Leading tickles / Virgin arms / Kamloops.

MARK ROBINSON

— added **FONTAINE TOUPS + RICHARD BALUYUT** (of VERSUS)
Sep 00. (m-cd) <(TEENBEAT 302)> **TASTE** Jul00
 – Taste / Proposal / Presentation / Performance.
Oct 00. (cd) <(TEENBEAT 307)> **TIGER BANANA**
 – French good looks / Volunteers conquering fires / Catalog and classify / Difficult situations / Water crashing in / I am the King of Prussia / Starflighter / Full-length taffeta gown / The time of our lives / Putting up good numbers / To the ocean.
Jun 01. (cd) <(TEENBEAT 297)> **CANADA'S GREEN HIGHWAYS** May01
 – Aluminium / 100% guaranteed / Angels in waiting / Wonderful / Dilated pupils / Peanuts and Cracker Jack / Misplaced on the kitchen floor / I'm still breathing / Sylvian Cote / Arlington station.

URGE OVERKILL

Formed: Chicago, Illinois, USA . . . 1986 by NATIONAL 'NASH' KATO, EDDIE 'KING' ROESSER and BLACKIE 'BLACK CAESAR' ONASSIS. Naming themselves after a FUNKADELIC track and setting out on a mission to resurrect the cream of 70's kitsch in a post-modern punk style, URGE OVERKILL made their debut in 1987 with the self-financed 'STRANGE, I . . .' EP. Chicago's hip 'Touch & Go' label were alert to the possibilities, snatching them up for a debut album, 'JESUS URGE SUPERSTAR' (1989). AC/DC and CHEAP TRICK were the most common reference points, though all in the best possible taste of course, the lads even indulging in a cover of Jimmy Webb's 'WICHITA LINEMAN' to make sure people got the message. The main criticism was the ropey production, BUTCH VIG making sure that 'AMERICRUISER' (1990) didn't head the same way. Another alternative figurehead, STEVE ALBINI, oversaw the graft on the acclaimed 'SUPERSONIC STORYBOOK' (1991), their partnership subsequently turning sour when the former BIG BLACK man publicly chastised them for their defiant decadence (well, that's if you can call touring Chicago in a horse-drawn carriage sipping aperatifs decadence) and concrete commitment to all things kitsch. A stop-gap mini-set, 'STULL', preceded their signing to 'Geffen', a record that featured their peerless take on Neil Diamond's 'GIRL YOU'LL BE A WOMAN SOON'. Later featured as a key inclusion on the soundtrack to Quentin Tarantino's masterful 'Pulp Fiction', the song was also a UK Top 40 hit in its own right without actually drawing in many moviegoers to the weird and wonderful universe of URGE OVERKILL itself, no doubt the name putting them off! Their first major label release, 'SATURATION' (1993) further distanced them from the harsh extremism of their hometown punk scene, the band benefitting from residual interest in the insurgent grunge movement and scoring two minor UK hit singles. Amid the wave of mid-90's publicity following the 'Pulp Fiction' success, URGE OVERKILL were inspired to release their most lovable album to date, 'EXIT THE DRAGON' (1995). In '96, arguments between NATO and ROESER resulted in the latter departing but new band recordings for '550 Music' were abandoned; NASH went solo post-millennium and covered Steely Dan's 'DIRTY WORK' on his solo set, 'DEBUTANTE' (2000).

Album rating: JESUS URGE SUPERSTAR (*4) / AMERICRUISER (*4) / THE SUPERSONIC STORYBOOK (*6) / STULL mini (*6) / SATURATION (*7) / EXIT THE DRAGON (*8) / Nash Kato: DEBUTANTE (*5)

NATIONAL 'Nash' KATO (b.31 Dec'65, Grand Forks, North Dakota) – vocals, guitar / **EDDIE 'King' ROESSER** (b.17 Jun'69, Litchfield, Minnesota) – bass / **BLACKIE 'Black Caesar' ONASSIS** (b. JOHNNY ROWAN, 27 Aug'67, Chicago) – vocals, drums

		not iss.	Ruthless
1986.	(12"ep) <RRU 013> **STRANGE, I . . .**	-	

– All worked out / Art of man / My new church / Snakemobile / Systems.

		Touch & Go	Touch & Go
1989.	(7") <TG 27> **WICHITA LINEMAN. / HEAD ON**	-	
May 89.	(lp) <(TGLP 37)> **JESUS URGE SUPERSTAR**		

– God Flintstone / Very sad trousers / Your friend is insane / Dump dump dump / Last train to Heaven / The Polaroid doll / Head on / Crown of laffs / Dubbledead / Easter '88 / Wichita lineman / Eggs.

Jun 90.	(cd/c/lp) <(TG CD/MC/LP 52)> **AMERICRUISER**		

– Ticket to L.A. / Blow chopper / 76 ball / Empire builder / Faroutski / Viceroyce / Out on the airstrip / Smokehouse. (cd+=) – JESUS URGE SUPERSTAR

| Jul 90. | (7") <TG 55> **TICKET TO L.A. / (I'M ON A) DRUNK** | - | |
| Mar 91. | (cd/c/lp) <(TG CD/MC/LP 70)> **THE SUPERSONIC STORYBOOK** | | |

– The kids are insane / The candidate / (Today is) Blackie's birthday / Emmaline / Bionic revolution / What is artane? / Vacation in Tokyo / Henhough: The greatest story ever told / Theme from Navajo.

		not iss.	Sub Pop
1991.	(7"yellow) <SP 109> **NOW THAT'S THE BARCLOUDS. / WHAT'S THIS GENERATION COMING TO?**	-	

		Roughneck	Touch & Go
Jun 92.	(m-cd/m-lp) (NECKM CD/MC 009) <TG CD/LP 86> **STULL**		

– Girl you'll be a woman soon / Stull (part 1) / Stitches / What's this generation coming to / (Now that's) The barclouds / Goodbye to Guyville. (cd re-iss. Aug96 on 'Nectar'; NTMCD 522)

		Geffen	Geffen
Jun 93.	(cd/c/lp) <(GED/GEC/GEF 24529)> **SATURATION**		

– Sister Havana / Tequilla sundae / Positive bleeding / Back on me / Woman 2 woman / Bottle of fur / Crackbabies / The stalker / Dropout / Erica Kane / Nite and grey / Heaven 90210. (cd+=) – Operation: Kissinger.

Aug 93.	(7"/c-s) (GFS/+C 51) **SISTER HAVANA. / WOMAN 2 WOMAN**	67	

(12"+=/cd-s+=) (GFST/+D 51) – Operation: Kissinger.

| Oct 93. | (7"red/c-s) (GFS/+C 57) **POSITIVE BLEEDING. / NITE AND GREY** | 61 | |

(12"+=/cd-s+=) (GFST/+D 57) – Quality love (Hong Kong demo).

| Nov 94. | (c-s) (MCSC 2024) <54935> **GIRL YOU'LL BE A WOMAN SOON / (track by The Tornadoes)** | 37 | 59 |

(cd-s+=) (MCSTD 2024) – (tracks by other artists).
above from the cult Tarantino film, 'Pulp Fiction', on 'M.C.A.'

| Aug 95. | (cd/c/lp) <(GED/GEC/GEF 24818)> **EXIT THE DRAGON** | | |

– Jay walkin' / The break / Need some air / Somebody else's body / Honesty files / This is no place / The mistake / Take me / View of the rain / Last night – Tomorrow / Tin foil / Monopoly / And you'll say / Digital black – epilogue. (cd re-iss. Feb98; same)

— disbanded soon after above

– compilations, etc. –

| Jul 95. | (d-cd/t-lp) Edel; (6613 2/1 RAD) **10 YEARS OF WRECKING** | | - |

NASH KATO

with **ONASSIS** + others

		not iss.	Loose Groove
Apr 00.	(cd) <33668> **DEBUTANTE**	-	

– Zooey suicide / Queen of the gangsters / Octoroon / Cradle robbers / Blow / Debutante / Dirty work / Rani (don't waste it) / Los Angelena / Black satin jacket / Pillow talk / Born in the eighties / Blue wallpaper.

UT

Formed: New York, USA . . . 1978 by NINA CANAL, JACQUI HAM and SALLY YOUNG. Following the demise of their 'Lust-Unlust' imprint in 1980, the girls took flight to London, surfacing a year later with the cassette-only release, 'UT LIVE'. Little was heard from them (bar a few singles) until 1986's 'CONVICTION' album, a more focused affair developing their early experimental "No Wave" sound. Nevertheless, they were still known to indulge in a spot of instrument swopping on stage (basically guitar, bass and drums). Increasingly drifting into SONIC YOUTH-esque territory, they signed to 'Blast First', releasing three albums in the space of three years: an early live set, 'IN GUT'S HOUSE' (1988) and the STEVE ALBINI-produced swansong, 'GRILLER' (1989).

Album rating: UT LIVE (*5) / CONVICTION (*6) / EARLY LIVE LIFE (*5) / IN GUT'S HOUSE (*6) / GRILLER (*6)

SALLY YOUNG – vocals, guitar, bass, violin / **JACQUI HAM** – vocals, bass, guitar / **NINA CANAL** – drums, guitar, bass (ex-DARK DAY)

		not iss.	Outtapes
Dec 81.	(c) <C-52> **UT LIVE (live)**	-	

– Mere animal in a pre-fact clamour / Ambule H.C.B. / Not any more / Swamp / Glue.

		not iss.	Infidelity
1982.	(7") **WHILE I WAIT. / AMPHETA SPEAK**	-	
		Outro	Outro
Feb 84.	(12"ep) <OUTRO 1> **UT EP**	-	

– Sham shack / This bliss / New colour / Exile goes out.

| Jun 85. | (12"ep) <(OUTRO 2)> **CONFIDENTIAL. / BEDOUIN / TELL IT** | | |
| May 86. | (lp) (OUTRO 3) **CONVICTION** | | |

– Confidential / Sick / Phoenix hotel / Absent farmer / Stain / Prehistory / Bedouin / Kcahsmahs (spare coconut) / Mouse sleep.

		Blast First	Blast First
May 87.	(lp) <(BFFP 12)> **EARLY LIVE LIFE (live)**		

– Fire in Philadelphia / Brink over chicken / Surgery / Ampheta speak / While I wait / Mouse sleep / Sharp's loose / This bliss / No manifesto / Feed / Limbo.

| Jan 88. | (2x12"ep/cd) <(BFFP 17/+CD)> **IN GUT'S HOUSE** | | |

– Evangelist / I.D. / Swallow / Big wing / Hotel / Homebled / Shut fog / Mosquito botticelli / Dirty net / Landscape. (cd re-iss. Nov93; same)

— added **CHARLIE D** – drums

| Feb 89. | (lp/cd) <(BFFP 36/+CD)> **GRILLER** | | |

– Safe burning / How it goes / Canker / Rummy / Posse necks / Fuel / Wailhouse / Scrape / Spore / Griller / Doctor No.

— split soon after above; HAM formed DIAL (alongside R. SMITH plus D. WEEKS) and released one set, 'INFRACTION' (1996).

THE GREAT INDIE DISCOGRAPHY — The 1980s

VASELINES

Formed: Bellshill, Lanarkshire, Scotland . . . 1986 by EUGENE KELLY and FRANCES McKEE. A seminal Scottish band which would've earned their place in indie folklore even without the patronage of one KURT COBAIN, The VASELINES released two influential singles in '87/'88 on the small '53rd & 3rd' label, 'SON OF A GUN' (with B-side cover of Divine's 'YOU THINK YOU'RE A MAN') and 'DYING FOR IT'. Lo-fi before lo-fi was even invented, the records sounded as if they'd been recorded in a shed; wonderful bursts of noisy guitar scree and bubblegum melody with McDONALD and McKEE harmonising over sordid, tongue-in-cheek proclamations of lust. Enlisting a rhythm section of JAMES SHEENAN and CHARLIE KELLY, the group finally got round to recording a debut album, 'DUM-DUM' (1989). Opening with the blasphemous rock'n'roll cacophony of 'SEX SUX (AMEN)', the record boasted such tasteful vignettes as 'MONSTER PUSSY' and 'TEENAGE SUPERSTAR'. Perhaps they finally ran out of vaseline, but the group seemed to disappear almost as quickly as they'd burst onto Scotland's insular scene, splitting in 1990. They would no doubt have faded into the annals of Bellshill musical history hadn't NIRVANA released a cover of 'MOLLY'S LIPS' in early '91 (they also covered 'SON OF A GUN' and performed a beautiful version of 'JESUS DOESN'T WANT ME FOR A SUNBEAM' on their 'MTV UNPLUGGED' set), 'Seminal Twang' subsequently re-issuing an EP compilation later that year (interested parties should seek it out, if only for the peerless 'RORY RIDES ME RAW'!). At the Reading festival later that year, EUGENE KELLY joined NIRVANA onstage for 'MOLLY'S LIPS', his new band CAPTAIN AMERICA supporting NIRVANA on their subsequent world tour. With a line-up numbering KELLY, GORDON KEEN, RAYMOND BOYLE and ANDY ROY, CAPTAIN AMERICA released their eponymous debut EP in late '91. KELLY's trademark laconic drawl was still in evidence although, surprise, surprise, their sound was markedly more 'grunge', on lead track 'WOW!' at least. The remaining songs, meanwhile, sounded spookily close to musical cousins TEENAGE FANCLUB, only the driving 'GOD BLESS LES PAUL' retaining the wicked spirit of The VASELINES. After another EP the following Spring (featuring a cover of the Beat Happening's 'INDIAN SUMMER'), the group changed their name to EUGENIUS following legal threats from Marvel comics. An album, 'OOMALAMA' was released later that year, yet despite the interest surrounding KELLY, the record failed to rise above cult status. A similar fate befell 'MARY QUEEN OF SCOTS' (1994), the group now residing at their natural home, 'Creation', alongside fellow under-achievers 18 WHEELER, BMX BANDITS, etc. A freak motorcycle accident later in '94, led to the disappearance of KELLY, although he was apparently sighted in Lower Manhattan having a 2-week bender with a Lemonhead (er, EVAN DANDO, to be exact!). Crawling back from the wreckage in 1996, EUGENIUS recorded a one-off 45 for Jamie Watson's 'Human Condition'. 'WOMB BOY RETURNS', was as slick and sublime as any VASELINES recording a decade earlier, its B-sides could have been attributed to the aforementioned binge. EUGENE subsequently teamed up with the TEENAGE FANCLUB's GERRY LOVE and RAY McGINLEY to form the short-lived ASTROCHIMP, releasing one single 'DRAGGIN'' for the local 'Shoeshine' imprint (also home to the RADIO SWEETHEARTS).

Album rating: DUM DUM (*7) / ALL THE STUFF AND MORE . . . compilation (*8) / Eugenius: OOMALAMA (*6) / MARY QUEEN OF SCOTS (*7)

EUGENE KELLY – vocals, guitars / **FRANCES McKEE** – vocals, guitar / with hired musicians

	53rd & 3rd	not iss.
Sep 87. (12"ep) (AGARR 010) **SON OF A GUN. / RORY RIDES AWAY / YOU THINK YOU'RE A MAN**	☐	-
Mar 88. (7") (AGARR 017) **DYING FOR IT. / MOLLY'S LIPS**	☐	-
(12"+=/cd-s+=) (AGARR 017 12/CD) – Teenage superstars / Jesus wants me for a sunbeam. (7" re-iss. Aug91 on 'Seminal Twang'; TWANG 4)		

— added **JAMES SEENAN** – bass / **CHARLIE KELLY** (EUGENE's brother) – drums

Jan 90. (lp) (AGAS 007) **DUM DUM**	☐	-
– Sex sux / Sloshy / Monster pussy / Teenage superstar / No hope / Oliver twisted / The day I was a horse / Dum-dum / Hairy / Lovecraft. (cd-iss. + remastered Mar91 on 'Avalanche'; ONLYCD 009)		

— disbanded in 1990 and KELLY briefly joined The PASTELS; much later, McKEE would form his own SUCKLE outfit

– compilations, etc. –

Jun 92. (cd/lp) *Avalanche;* (ONLY CD/LP 013) **ALL THE STUFF AND MORE . . .**
– Son of a gun / Rory rides me raw / You think you're a man / Dying for it / Molly's lips / Teenage superstars / Jesus wants me for a sunbeam / Sex sux (amen) / Slushy / Monsterpussy / Bitch / No hope / Oliver twisted / Day I was a horse / Dum-dum / Hairy / Lovecraft / Dying for it (the blues) / Let's get ugly. (re-iss. Oct95; same)

Feb 94. (lp/cd) *Sub Pop;* (<SP/+CD 145>) **THE WAY OF THE VASELINES – A COMPLETE HISTORY** (as above) ☐ Jul92

CAPTAIN AMERICA

EUGENE KELLY – vocals, guitar / **GORDON KEEN** – lead guitar (of BMX BANDITS) / **JAMES SEENAN** – bass / **ANDY BOLLEN** – drums; repl. live guest **BRENDAN O'HARE** – drums (of TEENAGE FANCLUB)

	Paperhouse	Atlantic
Nov 91. (12"ep) (PAPER 014) **WOW / BED-IN. / WANNA BEE / GOD BLESS LES PAUL**	☐	-
Apr 92. (12"ep) (PAPER 016) **FLAME ON. / BUTTERMILK / INDIAN SUMMER**	☐	-

— had to change their moniker after legal threats by Marvel comics

EUGENIUS

— **KELLY + KEEN + RAYMOND BOYLE** – bass; repl. SEENAN who formed the PAINKILLERS with FRANCES McKEE

— **ROY LAWRENCE** – drums; repl. BOLLEN + part-time O'HARE

Sep 92. (cd/c/lp) (PAP CD/MC/LP 011) <82426> **OOMALAMA**
– Oomalama / Breakfast / One's too many / Bed-in / Hot dog / Down on me / Flame on / Here I go / I'm the Sun / Buttermilk / Aye aye. (cd+=) – Wow! / Wannabee / Indian summer.

	Creation-August	Atlantic
Jul 93. (7") (caug 005) **CAESAR'S VEIN. / GREEN BED**	☐	-
(12"+=/cd-s+=) (caug 005 t/cd) – Mary Queen Of Scots.		
Nov 93. (12"ep/cd-ep) (caug 008 t/cd) **EASTER BUNNY / HOMESICK. / CAESAR'S VEIN / SEX SUX**	☐	-
Jan 94. (cd) (RUST 008CD) <82562> **MARY QUEEN OF SCOTS**	☐	-
– Pebble-shoe / On the breeze / Blue above the rooftops / The Moon's a balloon / Mary Queen of Scots / Easter bunny / Let's hibernate / Friendly high / River Clyde song / Tongue rock / Fake digit / Love, bread and beers.		

— KELLY moonlighted on an album by Celtic outfit DE DANNAN

	Human Condition	not iss.
Sep 96. (7") (HC 0013) **WOMB BOY RETURNS. / SEVEN OUT**	☐	-
(cd-s+=) (HCCD 0013) – Bridge / Sixty-nine minus twelve.		

ASTRO CHIMP

— **EUGENE** plus **GERRY LOVE + RAY McGINLEY** (of TEENAGE FANCLUB)

	Shoeshine	not iss.
Nov 96. (7") (SHOE 006) **DRAGGIN'. / SHE'S MY SUMMER GIRL**	☐	-

VELVET MONKEYS (see under ⇒ B.A.L.L.)

VELVET UNDERGROUND

Formed: New York City, New York, USA . . . early 1965, by LOU REED and JOHN CALE, who nearly hit as The PRIMITIVES with the single, 'The Ostrich'. They met modern pop artist, ANDY WARHOL, who invited German chanteuse NICO to join the set-up alongside STERLING MORRISON and MO TUCKER. Early in 1966, they signed to 'MGM-Verve', and soon began work on what was to be their debut album, 'THE VELVET UNDERGROUND AND NICO'. The album was a revelation, strikingly different from the love and peace psychedelia of the day, The VELVETS vision was decidedly darker and more disturbing. Combining sublime melodies and nihilistic noise, it featured eleven superb ahead-of-their-time classics, notably the brutally frank and frenetic 'HEROIN', the S&M 'VENUS IN FURS' and the garage raunch of 'WAITING FOR THE MAN'. It also contained three NICO sung beauties, 'FEMME FATALE', 'ALL TOMORROW'S PARTIES' and 'I'LL BE YOUR MIRROR'. The record only managed a brief stay in the US Top 200, as did the 1967 follow-up, 'WHITE LIGHT, WHITE HEAT', which included the 17-minute white noise freak-out of 'SISTER RAY'. With CALE now out of the picture, the focus fell on REED's songwriting for the self-titled third album. An altogether mellower set of more traditionally structured songs, the highlight was undoubtedly REED's beautiful lullaby, 'PALE BLUE EYES'. The band's last studio album, 'LOADED', was the closest The VELVET UNDERGROUND ever came to mainstream rock and an indicator of the direction REED would take in his solo career. 'SWEET JANE' and 'ROCK 'N' ROLL' marked his creative peak, a final glorious burst of guitar noise before the group disbanded and the myth started to crystallise. And that was that. Except it wasn't, not come 1992 anyway, when many a precious, pasty faced obsessive went even whiter with horror as The VELVET UNDERGROUND reformed. Many more fans, however, eagerly shelled out their hard earned cash for a reunion tour and album as CALE and REED became buddies once more. The live shows were apparently rather joyous and the accompanying vinyl document, 'LIVE MCMXCIII' (1993), was an enjoyable romp through all the favourites. After the death of STERLING MORRISON in 1995, however,

VELVET UNDERGROUND (cont)

the prospect of further VELVETS activity looked doubtful. Yet despite the reunion, despite LOU REED's dodgy hairdo, despite everything, The VELVET UNDERGROUND of the 60's remain perennially cool and insidiously influential. Basically, alternative music begins and ends with VU and they have been cited as the inspiration for punk rock. A decade after that, a generation of indie groups (i.e. JESUS & MARY CHAIN, early PRIMAL SCREAM, MY BLOODY VALENTINE, etc.) paid barely disguised homage to their heroes.
• **Songwriters:** REED compositions, except some by group. Many rock acts have covered their material, but so far not surprisingly, none have managed to score a major chart hit yet. • **Miscellaneous:** In 1990, REED and CALE re-united on a tribute album to the deceased ANDY WARHOL. NICO had earlier died on the 18th of July '88 after suffering a brain haemorrhage due to a fall from her bike while on holiday in Ibiza. • **Trivia:** Their debut LP sleeve featured a gimmick peeling-banana-skin sticker. They reformed for a gig in Paris, 15 June 1990. UK's Channel 4 featured a night-long session of all their previous work.

Album rating: THE VELVET UNDERGROUND AND NICO (*10) / WHITE LIGHT – WHITE HEAT (*9) / THE VELVET UNDERGROUND (*8) / LOADED (*8) / ANDY WARHOL'S VELVET UNDERGROUND FEATURING NICO compilation (*7) / LIVE AT MAX'S KANSAS CITY exploitation (*2) / SQUEEZE (*3) / THE VELVET UNDERGROUND AND LOU REED compilation (*6) / 1969 – THE VELVET UNDERGROUND LIVE exploitation (*7) / GREATEST HITS compilation (*6) / V.U. unreleased set (*7) / ANOTHER VIEW exploitation (*4) / THE BEST OF THE VELVET UNDERGROUND (THE WORDS AND MUSIC OF LOU REED) compilation (*7) / LIVE MCMXCIII reunion (*5)

LOU REED (b. LOUIS FIRBANK, 2 Mar'44, Long Island, N.Y.) – vocals, guitar (ex-JADES, ex-PRIMITIVES) / **JOHN CALE** (b. 9 Dec'42, Garnant, Wales) – bass, viola, vocals, etc. / **STERLING MORRISON** – guitar / **MAUREEN TUCKER** – drums / plus **NICO** (b. CHRISTA PAFFGEN, 16 Oct'38, Cologne, Germany) – vocals (also – Solo artist)

Verve   Verve

Oct 66. (7") <10427> **ALL TOMORROW'S PARTIES. / I'LL BE YOUR MIRROR**

Dec 66. (7") <10466> **SUNDAY MORNING / FEMME FATALE**

Oct 67. (lp; stereo/mono) (S+/VLP 9184) <5008> **THE VELVET UNDERGROUND AND NICO**   Dec66
– Sunday morning / I'm waiting for the man / Femme fatale / Venus in furs / Run run run / All tomorrow's parties / Heroin / There she goes again / I'll be your mirror / Black angel's death song / European son to Delmore Schwartz. *(re-iss. Oct71 on 'M.G.M.'; 2315 056) (re-iss. Aug83 on 'Polydor' lp/c; SPE LP/MC 20) (cd-iss. 1986 on 'Polydor'; 823 290-2) (cd re-iss. May96 on 'Polydor'; 531 250-2) (lp re-iss. Jun99 on 'Simply Vinyl'; SVLP 90) <(d-cd-iss. Apr02 on 'Polydor'+=; MLST 756)>* – (NICO tracks) / (mono versions) / (various versions). *(hit UK No.59)*

——— trimmed to a quartet when NICO preferred the solo life

Jan 68. (7") <10543> **WHITE LIGHT – WHITE HEAT. / HERE SHE COMES NOW**

Mar 68. (7") <10560> **I HEARD HER CALL MY NAME. / HERE SHE COMES NOW**

Jun 68. (lp; stereo/mono) (S+/VLP 9201) <5046> **WHITE LIGHT / WHITE HEAT**   Dec67
– White light – white heat / The gift / Lady Godiva's operation / Here she comes now / I heard her call my name / Sister Ray. *(re-iss. Oct71 on 'MGM Select'; 2353 024) (re-iss. Apr84 on 'Polydor' lp/c; SPE LP/MC 73) (cd-iss. 1986 on 'Polydor'; 825 119-2) (cd re-iss. May96 on 'Polydor'; 531 251-2) (lp re-iss. Apr00 on 'Simply Vinyl'; SVLP 200)*

——— **DOUG YULE** – bass, vocals, keyboards, guitar; repl. CALE who went solo

M.G.M.   M.G.M.

Apr 69. (lp) (CS 8108) <4617> **THE VELVET UNDERGROUND**   Mar 69
– Candy says ... / What goes on / Some kinda love / Pale blue eyes / Jesus / Beginning to see the light / I'm set free / That's the story of my life / The murder mystery / Afterhours. *(re-iss. Nov71 on 'MGM Select'; 2353 022) (re-iss. Mar76;) (re-iss. Sep83 on 'Polydor'; SPE LP/MC 39) <US re-iss. Apr85; 815454> (cd-iss. May96 on 'Polydor'; 531 252-2)*

May 69. (7") <14057> **JESUS. / WHAT GOES ON**

——— **BILLY YULE** – drums repl. TUCKER who had a baby. **MO TUCKER** returned in 1970 and BILLY only appeared on MAX's live album (see compilations)

Atlantic   Cotillion

Jan 71. (7") <44107> **WHO LOVES THE SUN? / OH! SWEET NUTHIN'**

Apr 71. (lp) (2400 111) <9034> **LOADED**   Aug70
– Who loves the sun? / Sweet Jane / Rock and roll / Cool it down / New age / Head held high / Lonesome cowboy Bill / I found a reason / Train around the bend / Oh! sweet nuthin'. *(re-iss. 1972 lp/c; K/K4 40113) (cd-iss. Jun88 & Feb93 on 'Warners'; 7567 90367-2) (d-cd-iss. May97 as 'LOADED (THE FULLY LOADED EDITION)' on 'Rhino'+=; 8122 72563-2) – (diff.mixes & demos, etc.) (lp re-iss. Oct97 on 'Simply Vinyl'; SVLP 22)*

Apr 71. (7") (2091 008) **WHO LOVES THE SUN. / SWEET JANE**

——— (Aug70) now with no originals The YULE's brought in newcomers **WALTER POWERS** – bass repl. LOU REED who went solo in 1971. (1971) **WILLIE ALEXANDER** – guitar repl. MORRISON who took a doctorate in English. MO TUCKER finally departed to raise her new family and eventually had five children in total, before going solo in 1980.

Polydor   not iss.

Feb 73. (lp) (2383 180) **SQUEEZE**
– Little Jack / Mean old man / She'll make you cry / Wordless / Dopey Joe / Crash / Friends / Jack and Jane / Send no letter / Louise.

——— Folded soon after above, DOUG sessioned for ELLIOTT MURPHY and later joined AMERICAN FLYER.

they re-formed early in 1993; **REED, CALE, MORRISON + TUCKER**

Sire   Sire

Oct 93. (d-cd/d-c) <(9362 45464-2/-4)> **LIVE MCMXCIII (live 1993)**   70
– We're gonna have a good time together / Venus in furs / Guess I'm falling in love / After hours / All tomorrow's parties / Some kinda love / I'll be your mirror / Beginning to see the light / The gift / I heard her call my name / Femme fatale / Hey Mr. Rain / Sweet Jane / Velvet nursery rhyme / White light – white heat / I'm sticking with you / Black angel's death song / Rock'n'roll / I can't stand it / I'm waiting for the man / Heroin / Pale blue eyes / Coyote.

Feb 94. (7"/c-s) (W 0224/+C) **VENUS IN FURS (live). / I'M WAITING FOR THE MAN (live)**   71
(cd-s+=) (W 0224CD) – Heroin (live) / Sweet Jane (live).

——— On the 30th August 1995, STERLING MORRISON died of lymphoma.

——— Group inducted into the Rock'n'roll Hall Of Fame, and performed 'LAST NIGHT I SAID GOODBYE TO A FRIEND', REED's tribute to recently deceased STERLING.

– compilations, others, etc. –

Dec 71. (d-lp) *M.G.M.;* (2683 006) **ANDY WARHOL'S VELVET UNDERGROUND FEATURING NICO**
– I'm waiting for the man / Candy says / Run, run, run / White light – white heat / All tomorrow's parties / Sunday morning / I heard her call my name / Femme fatale / Heroin / Here she comes now / There she goes again / Sister Ray / Venus in furs / European son / Pale blue eyes / Black angel's death song / Beginning to see the light.

Aug 72. (lp) *Atlantic;* (K 30022) / *Cotillion;* <9500> **LIVE AT MAX'S KANSAS CITY (live 22 Aug'70)**   May72
– I'm waiting for the man / Sweet Jane / Lonesome Cowboy Bill / Beginning to see the light / I'll be your mirror / Pale blue eyes / Sunday morning / New age / Femme fatale / After hours. *(cd-iss. Jun93 on 'Warners'; 7567 90370-2)*

Jun 73. (7"m; as LOU REED & VELVET UNDERGROUND) *M.G.M.;* (2006 283) **CANDY SAYS. / I'M WAITING FOR THE MAN / RUN RUN RUN**

Aug 73. (7") *Atlantic;* (K 10339) **SWEET JANE (live). / ROCK AND ROLL (live)**

Oct 73. (lp) *Verve;* (2315 258) / *Pride;* <0022> **THE VELVET UNDERGROUND AND LOU REED**

1974. (lp) *M.G.M.;* <4950> **ARCHETYPES**

1976. (ltd-7"m) *A.E.B.;* **FOGGY NOTION – INSIDE YOUR HEART. / I'M STICKING WITH YOU / FERRYBOAT BILL**

Feb 79. (d-lp) *Mercury;* (6643 900) <SRM2 7504> **1969 – THE VELVET UNDERGROUND LIVE (live)**   Apr74
– I'm waiting for the man / Lisa says / What goes on / Sweet Jane / We're gonna have a real good time together / Femme fatale / New age / Rock and roll / Beginning to see the light / Ocean / Pale blue eyes / Heroin / Some kinda love / Over you / Sweet Bonnie Brown – It's just too much / I'll be your mirror / White light – white heat. *(re-iss. Nov84; PRID 7) (re-iss. 1987; 834 823-1) (re-iss. 1988 as 'VOL.1' & 'VOL.2' cd/c; 834823-2/-4 & 834824-2/-4)*

Nov 80. (d-lp)(d-c) *Polydor;* (2664 438)(3578 485) **GREATEST HITS**

Oct 82. (12"ep) *Polydor;* (POSPX 603) **HEROIN / VENUS IN FURS. / I'M WAITING FOR THE MAN / RUN RUN RUN**

Feb 85. (lp/c) *Polydor;* (POLD/+C 5167) <823721> **V.U. (rare rec.68-69)**   47   85
– I can't stand it / Stephanie says / She's my best friend / Lisa says / Ocean / Foggy notion / Temptation inside your heart / One of these days / Andy's chest / I'm sticking with you. *(cd-iss. Jun87; 825 092-2)*

May 86. (5xlp-box)(5xcd-box) *Polydor;* (VUBOX 1)(815 454-2) **BOXED SET**
– (first 3 albums, plus V.U. & ANOTHER VIEW)

Aug 86. (lp/c/cd) *Polydor;* (829 405-1/-4/-2) **ANOTHER VIEW**
– We're gonna have a good time together / I'm gonna move right in / Hey Mr. Rain (version 1) / Ride into the Sun / Coney Island steeplechase / Guess I'm falling in love / Hey Mr. Rain (version 2) / Ferryboat Bill / Rock and roll (original).

Feb 88. (12") *Old Gold;* (OG 4049) **I'M WAITING FOR THE MAN. / HEROIN**

Mar 88. (12") *Old Gold;* (OG 4051) **VENUS IN FURS. / ALL TOMORROW'S PARTIES**

Sep 88. (lp) *Plastic Inevitable;* <FIRST 1> **THE VELVET UNDERGROUND ETC.**
– The ostrich / Cycle Annie / Sneaky Pete / Noise.

Sep 88. (lp) *Plastic Inevitable;* <SECOND 1> **THE VELVET UNDERGROUND AND SO ON**
– It's alright (the way you live) / I'm not too sorry / Stephanie says.

Oct 89. (lp/c/cd) *Verve;* <(841 164-1/-4/-2)> **THE BEST OF THE VELVET UNDERGROUND (THE WORDS AND MUSIC OF LOU REED)**
– I'm waiting for the man / Femme fatale / Run run run / Heroin / All tomorrow's parties / I'll be your mirror / White light – white heat / Stephanie says / What goes on / Beginning to see the light / Pale blue eyes / I can't stand it / Lisa says / Sweet Jane / Rock and roll.

Oct 95. (cd/c) *Global;* (RAD CD/MC 21) **THE BEST OF LOU REED & VELVET UNDERGROUND**   56

Oct 95. (4xcd-box) *Polydor;* <(527887-2)> **PEEL SLOWLY AND SEE**   Sep95

Oct 00. (cd) *Universal;* <(AA314 549133-2)> **THE MILLENNIUM COLLECTION: THE BEST OF...**

Jul 01. (cd) *Polydor;* (549690-2) **ROCK AND ROLL: AN INTRODUCTION TO THE VELVET UNDERGROUND**

Aug 01. (4xcd-box) *Captain Trip;* (CTCD 35053) **FINAL VU 1971-1973 (live)**
– (LIVE IN LONDON 1971 / LIVE IN THE NETHERLANDS 1971 / LIVE IN WALES 1972 / MASSACHUSETTS 1973)

Oct 01. (3xcd-box) *Polydor;* <(557665-2)> **BOOTLEG SERIES VOL.1: THE QUINE TAPES**

——— (see also LOU REED discography for other tracks on comps & B's)

——— Also tribute albums 'HEAVEN AND HELL' 1, 2 & 3 were issued Oct'90-Feb'92, all on 'Imaginary' records, as was another '15 MINUTES'.

THE GREAT INDIE DISCOGRAPHY | The 1980s

VENUS FLY TRAP

Formed: Northampton, England ... late 80's by ALEX NOVAK (ex-ATTRITION and TEMPEST) and DAVE FREAK who were soon joined by CURTIS, NIGEL and JOHN. Their eclectic style of alternative rock, blended the post-punk JOY DIVISION-esque sound with mid-eigthties goth rock structures alongside dance-inspired sampling plus use of drum machine to create a unique, almost psychedelic hybrid. Originaly ignored on their home turf the band's demo of the track, 'MORPHINE', reached the attention of French label 'Danceteria', via linked imprint 'Tuesday' records, who set about putting out their debut mini-album 'MARS' (1989) which collected together a number of their early singles including 'RUBY RED', 'DESOLATION RAILWAY' and the aforementioned 'MORPHINE'. Amazingly in the light of British apathy, the set managed a top 30 placing in the French charts; their success in mainland Europe being something that would continue throughout their career. This was especially due to – by the band's own admission – the fact that they were not content to follow the music fashion of the time, leaving them hard to pigeonhole for the UK music press. Another well received 12" followed in the form of the Suicide cover 'ROCKET U.S.A.' (1990). This was produced by KEVIN HASKINS, formerly of their inspirational Northampton brethren BAUHAUS, with their debut album proper, 'TOTEM', following the same year. PAT FISH of JAZZ BUTCHER fame, produced their next single, 'ACHILLES HEEL', succeeded by their next full-length offering 'PANDORA'S BOX' (1992). This set excelled from its forebears and saw the band's subject matter move into more political territory. The band also did the unconventional move of releasing their 'JEWEL: LIVE IN PRAGUE' (1991) record in Czechoslavakia, where it had been recorded at a gig in the capital's Futurum Festival in the spring of 1991. The ensuing year saw their last record for 'Danceteria', which came in the form of singles compilation 'SHEDDING ANOTHER SKIN' (1993). Moving on to the 'Spectre' label the band issued their third LP proper 'LUNA TIDE' (1994) which showcased VFT moving into a more lucid sounding rock format. The next three years saw the band doing a heavy rotation of European gigs and NOVAK also took time to focus on his music journal 'Bizarre' which championed the left of centre music such as the gothic and industrial rock movements. After a brief studio hiatus, the group came back strongly in 1997 with the 'Soundbuster' released 'DARK AMOUR', a set assisted by the production of NOVAK's one time ATTRITION band mate MARTIN BOWES. This full-length offering witnessed the group again turning towards the more alternative fringes with splurges of industrial and psychedelic stylings. VFT subsequently hit out with another compilation piece 'ANTHOLOGY OF THE FOOD', which included hits and rarities. The busy NOVAK could also be heard via his side-project, the electronically underpinned outfit NOVA GALAXIE ROBOTNIK (originally monikered NOVAK STATE CONSPIRACY).

Album rating: MARS mini (*5) / TOTEM (*6) / PANDORA'S BOX (*6) / JEWEL – LIVE IN PRAGUE (*5) / SHEDDING ANOTHER SKIN compilation (*6) / LUNA TIDE (*7) / DARK AMOUR (*5) / ANTHOLOGY OF THE FOOD compilation (*7)

ALEX NOVAK – vocals / **DAVE FREAK** – acoustic guitar / **NIGEL** – bass

Tuesday not iss.

Mar 88. (12"m) *(TUE 872)* **MORPHINE. / CATALYST / I GET FLOWERS**
Aug 88. (12"m) *(TUE 881)* **DESOLATION RAILWAY. / VIOLINS & VIOLENCE / UP THERE**

Danceteria not iss.

Apr 89. (m-lp/m-cd) *(DAN MLP/CD 011)* **MARS** (compilation)
– Shadows whisper Mecca / Flowers / Morphine / Ruby red / Desolation railway / Hazy future / How the mighty / Catalyst / Violins and violence / Up there.

—— added **CURTIS** – guitar / **JOHN** – percussion

Jan 90. (12"/cd-s) *(12DAN/DANCD 021)* **ROCKET U.S.A. / CLOUD 9 LIPS / OPIUM WAR**
Jan 90. (lp/c/cd) *(DAN LP/C/CD 024)* **TOTEM**
– Out of your depth / Smash heroes / Eternity rising / Cloud 9 lips / Rainy Latvian wedding / Folie a famile / Rose coloured spectacle / Recrimination revival / Europa your my totem.
May 90. (12"ep/cd-ep) *(12DAN/DANCD 035)* **EUROPA**
– Europa / Morphine (live) / Shadowplay (live) / World turned upside down (live) / Rocket U.S.A. (live).
Mar 91. (12"/cd-s) *(12DAN/DANCD 049)* **ACHILLES HEEL. / WEEP HOTEL / TV FALLS FROM A WINDOW**
Jan 92. (cd/lp) *(DAN CD/LP 058)* **PANDORA'S BOX**
– Shadow ministry / World turned upside down / Jewel encrusted hands / Monument to the sublime / Ruby revisited / Sidewinder / Deathwatch a beatle / Achilles heel / Shedding another skin.
Dec 91. (cd) *(AZ 0001)* **JEWEL – LIVE IN PRAGUE (live)** – Czech
– Morphine / Tribute to smash heroes / Jewel encrusted hands / Weep hotel / Sidewinder / Shadow ministry / Cloud 9 lips / Achilles heel / Rocket U.S.A. / Shadowplay.
(above issued on 'A.Z.Y.L.')
May 92. (cd) *(DANCD 104)* **SHEDDING ANOTHER SKIN** (compilation)
– Morphine / Catalyst desolation railway / Up there / Rocket U.S.A. / Cloud 9 lips / Europa / Achilles heel / Weep hotel.

—— **NOVAK** now with **GARY LENNON** – guitar / **NEIL RIDLEY** – bass / **ANDY DENTON** – drums

Spectre not iss.

Feb 95. (cd) *(SPV 084-25272)* **LUNA TIDE** – Europe
– 19th incident / Crocodile / Moscow menagerie / Urban sprawl I / My ships coming in / Jupiter collision / Storm clouds are gathering / Seed sown starword / Urban sprawl II / Heretic.

Soundbuster not iss.

Mar 97. (cd) *(SB 006)* **DARK AMOUR** – Europe
– Passport to dark amour (requiem) / Pulp sister / I am a camera / 28th March / Lifeforces / Indian good luck symbol / Vendetta / Decaying orbit part 1 & 2 (redemption).
—— ALEX moonlighted with NOVAK STATE CONSPIRACY (featuring SIMON COLEBY) and released the 'Dion Fortune' set, 'ZEITGEIST' in '94

– compilations, etc. –

2001. (cd) *Spiral Archive;* **ANTHOLOGY OF THE FOOD** – Poland
– I get flowers / Ruby red / Hazy future / Rocket U.S.A. / Cloud 9 lips / Opium war / Smash heroes / Rose coloured spectacle / Europa / Achilles heel / Weep hotel / TV falls from a hotel window / World turned upside down / 19th incident / Pulp sister / 28th March / 13 o'clock.

VERLAINES

Formed: Dunedin, New Zealand ... 1981 by songwriter GRAEME DOWNES, GREG KERR, CRAIG EASTON, ANITA PILLAI and PHILIP HIGHAM; the latter three making way for JANE DODD after their first recordings. One of many cult Kiwi acts to sign to NZ's 'Flying Nun' label along with The CHILLS etc. (with whom they recorded the fabled 'DUNEDIN' EP), The VERLAINES' choppy guitar-pop/rock sound was more contemporary and complex than the retro-fixated approach of the latter act, DOWNES' classical training lending an interesting twist to his material. Debuting with the domestic EP, '10 O'CLOCK IN THE AFTERNOON' in 1984, the band (drummer ALAN HAIG had been replaced by ROBBIE YEATS) issued their debut album, 'HALLELUJAH ALL THE WAY HOME', the following year. Increased American/European interest subsequently led to a deal with 'Homestead', the label releasing 1988's follow-up set, 'BIRD-DOG' and the wittily titled 'SOME DISENCHANTED EVENING' (1990). Having relocated to the States, The VERLAINES were subsequently picked up by established alternative bastion, 'Slash' and following an extended break from the spotlight, the band finally surfaced in 1994 with 'WAY OUT WHERE'. By this point, DOWNES was the only remaining founder member, a line-up of DARREN STEADMAN, MIKE STOODLEY and PAUL WINDERS recording an enjoyable set of frantic indie-rock which stated its point without ever threatening to worry the genre's leading lights. DOWNES was most affecting when he took his foot off the gas, achieving an almost GRANT LEE BUFFALO-style atmosphere on 'BLACK WINGS'. After the disappointing 'OVER THE MOON' set in '97, DOWNES – now a lecturer at the University of Otago in NZ – returned for a stripped-down solo set, 'HAMMERS AND ANVILS' (2001).

Album rating: HALLELUJAH ALL THE WAY HOME (*6) / JUVENILIA compilation (*6) / BIRD-DOG (*6) / SOME DISENCHANTED EVENING (*5) / READY TO FLY (*4) / WAY OUT WHERE (*5) / OVER THE MOON (*4) / Graeme Downes: HAMMERS AND ANVILS (*5)

GRAHAM DOWNES – vocals, guitar, piano, oboe / **GREG KERR** – drums / **JANE DODD** – bass, vocals; latter repl. bassist PHILIP HIGHAM, guitarist CRAIG EASTON and keyboard player ANITA PILLAI

Flying Nun Homestead

Jan 82. (d12"ep) *(FNDUN 1/2)* **DUNEDIN DOUBLE EP** – NewZ
– Angela / Crisis after crisis / You cheat yourself of everything that moves / (others by The CHILLS, The STONES and The SNEAKY FEELINGS).
—— **ALAN HAIG** – drums; repl. KERR
1983. (7") *(FN 014)* **DEATH AND THE MAIDEN. / C.D. JIMMY JAZZ AND ME** – NewZ
—— **ROBBIE YEATS** – drums, xylophone; repl. HAIG
1984. (12"ep) *(FN 022)* **10 O'CLOCK IN THE AFTERNOON** – NewZ
– Baud to tears / Pyromaniac / Joed out / Burlesque / Wind song / You say you.
Sep 86. (lp/c) *(FN 040/+C)* **HALLELUJAH ALL THE WAY HOME**
– It was raining / All laid on / The lady and the lizard / Don't send me away / Lying in state / Phil too? / For the love of Ash Grey / The ballad of Harry Noryb. (cd-iss. Jul96; FNCD 40) <cd-iss. 1990's; HMS 138>
Oct 86. (12") *(FN 053)* **DOOMSDAY. / NEW KINDA HERO**
Sep 87. (lp) *(FNUK 10)* <HMS 88> **JUVENILIA** (compilation)
– Death and the maiden / Angela / Baud to tears / Crisis after crisis / Burlesque / Joed out / Pyromaniac / You say you / Wind song / You cheat yourself of everything that moves. (NZ-iss.1992; FNCD 195) (cd-iss. Jul96; FNCD 195)
Nov 88. (lp)<cd> *(FNE 21)* <HMS 095-2> **BIRD-DOG**
– Makes no difference / You forget love / Take good care of it / Just mum / Slow sad love song / Only dream left / Dippy's last trip / Bird-dog / Icarus missed / C.D. Jimmy Jazz and me.
—— **MIKE STOODLEY** – bass; repl. DODDS
1990. (lp/c/cd) *(FN/+C/CD 129)* <HMS 162> **SOME DISENCHANTED EVENING**
– Jesus what a jerk / The funniest thing / Whatever you run into / Faithfully yours / Damn shame / This train / Down the road / We're all gonna die / Anniversary / Come Sunday / It was. (re-iss. Jul96; same)
1991. (7") *(FN 159)* **THE FUNNIEST THING. / YOU FORGET LOVE**
—— **GREGG CAIRNS** – drums; repl. YEATS who continued with The DEAD C

Slash Slash

Jul 91. (cd/c) <2-/4-26771> **READY TO FLY**
– Gloom junky / Overdrawn / Tremble / Such as I / Hurricane / War in my head / Inside out / See you tomorrow / Hole in the ground / Ready to fly / Moonlight on snow / Hold on.
—— **DOWNES** now with **STOODLEY** plus **PAUL WINDERS** – guitars, vocals / **DARREN STEADMAN** – drums
Dec 93. (cd/c) *(828 388-2/-4)* <45321> **WAY OUT WHERE** – Sep93
– Mission of love / I stare out . . . / This valentine / Blanket over the sky / Cathedrals under the sea / Aches in whisper / Way out where / Lucky in my dreams / Black wings / Stay gone / Incarceration / Dirge.

VERLAINES (cont)

— now without STOODLEY

Flying Nun / not iss.

Jan 00. (cd) *(486880-2)* **OVER THE MOON** (rec. 1996)
– Hanging by strands / Bonfire / Sky-blue window / Jailhouse 4:00 am / Feather fell / Perfect day / When I fall / Uncle Big Jaw's late night farewell / Dunderhead / Dawdling on the bridge / Writing on the wall / Reasons for living / Coming back to you.

— disbanded in '97; WINDERS formed VALVE

GRAEME DOWNES

Matador / Flying Nun

Aug 01. (cd) *(OLE 506-2) <FNCD 454>* **HAMMERS AND ANVILS**
– Hammers and anvils / Cole Porter / Alright by me / January song / Cattle, cars and chainsaws / Day of the dead / Shoreleave / Song for a Hollywood road movie / Gucci / Getting out of it / Sunday kickaround / Rock'n'roll hero / Mastercontrol.

VERY THINGS (see under ⇒ CRAVATS; 70's section)

VICTIMS OF PLEASURE (see under ⇒ ASTLEY, Virginia)

Holly Beth VINCENT (see under ⇒ HOLLY & THE ITALIANS)

VIOLENT FEMMES

Formed: Milwaukee, Wisconsin, USA ... 1982 by GORDON GANO, BRIAN RITCHIE and VICTOR DE LORENZO. Discovered by JAMES HONEYMAN-SCOTT (of The PRETENDERS) and signed to 'Slash' in the States, the group delivered their much-loved eponymous debut in September '83 (licensed to 'Rough Trade' in the UK). With their acoustic cowpunk assault and sarcastic, angst-ridden lyrics, the VIOLENT FEMMES were taken to heart as flagbearers for indie geek-rock; the likes of 'GONE DADDY GONE', 'UGLY' and 'ADD IT UP' were classic slices of adolescent alienation, the album going on to sell more than a million copies with the barest of promotion and no hit singles. Follow-up, 'HALLOWED GROUND' (1984), was met with a more muted response; save the definitive 'COUNTRY DEATH SONG', the record lacked the downtrodden impetus of the debut and disappointed many who had raved over the debut. The 'FEMMES redeemed themselves somewhat with the JERRY HARRISON-produced 'THE BLIND LEADING THE NAKED' (1986), an exhilarating cover of T.Rex's 'CHILDREN OF THE REVOLUTION' illustrating what they were capable of when they managed to focus some of their schizophrenic zeal. Yet it was too little too late and the band chose to lick their wounds – separately. RITCHIE had recorded a solo album for 'S.S.T.' the previous year, while GANO and DE LORENZO worked on separate projects. The trio eventually returned with '3' (1989), another directionless set which failed to add much to the band's legend, likewise 'WHY DO BIRDS SING' (1991). The release of compilation album, 'ADD IT UP' (1993) marked the premature end of their tenure with 'Slash' and the band subsequently signed to 'Elektra' for 1994's 'NEW TIMES'. Neither this or the following year's 'ROCK!!!!!' (1995) added much to the VIOLENT FEMMES legacy and the band remain victims of the classic first album syndrome. GANO and Co celebrated their birthplace by releasing an album entitled, 'VIVA WISCONSIN' (1999), a cracking set that was spoiled by the punky, rush-released 'FREAK MAGNET' (2000). • **Songwriters:** All written by GANO-RITCHIE, except CHINESE ROCKS (Heartbreakers) / DO YOU REALLY WANT TO HURT ME (Culture Club).

Album rating: VIOLENT FEMMES (*8) / HALLOWED GROUND (*6) / THE BLIND LEADING THE NAKED (*6) / 3 (*5) / WHY DO BIRDS SING? (*6) / ADD IT UP (1981-1993) compilation (*8) / NEW TIMES (*5) / VIVA WISCONSIN (*6) / FREAK MAGNET (*5) / ROCK!!!!! (*3)

GORDON GANO (b. 7 Jun'63, New York, USA) – vocals, guitar / **BRIAN RITCHIE** (b.21 Nov'60) – bass / **VICTOR DE LORENZO** (b.25 Oct'54, Raccine, Wisconsin) – drums

Rough Trade / Slash

Sep 83. (lp) *(ROUGH 55) <23845>* **VIOLENT FEMMES**
– Blister in the Sun / Kiss off / Please do not go / Add it up / Confessions / Prove my love / Promise / To the kill / Gone daddy gone / Good feeling. *(re-iss. Mar87 on 'Slash'+=; SLMP 15)* – Ugly / Gimme the car. *(re-iss. Sep99 on 'Slash'; 3942 28259-2)* *<d-cd-iss. Jul02 on 'Rhino'+=; 8122 78242-2>* – (a CD of rare material).
Dec 83. (7") *(RT 147)* **UGLY. / GIMME THE CAR**
(12"+=) *(RTT 147)* – Good feeling / Gone daddy gone.

Slash – London / Slash – Reprise

Jun 84. (7") *(LASH 1)* **GONE DADDY GONE. / ADD IT UP**
(12"+=) *(LASHX 1)* – Jesus walking on the water.
Jul 84. (lp/c) *(SLAP/SMAC 1) <25094>* **HALLOWED GROUND**
– Country death song / I hear the rain / Never tell / Jesus walking on the water / I know it's true but I'm sorry to say / Hallowed ground / Sweet misery blues / Black girls / It's gonna rain.
Sep 84. (7") *(LASH 3)* **IT'S GONNA RAIN. / JESUS WALKING ON THE WATER**
(12"+=) *(LASHX 3)* – Prove my love.
Feb 86. (7") *(LASH 7)* **CHILDREN OF THE REVOLUTION. / HEARTACHE**
(12"+=) *(LASHX 7)* – Good feeling.

Feb 86. (lp/c)(cd) *(SLAP/SMAC 10)(828-130-2) <25340>* **THE BLIND LEADING THE NAKED** [81] [84]
– Old Mother Reagan / No killing / Breakin' hearts / Special / Love and me make three / Candlelight song / I held her in my arms / Children of the revolution / Good friend / Heartache / Cold canyon / Two people. *(cd+=)* – Country death song / Black girls / World without mercy.
Apr 86. (7") *(LASH 7)* **CHILDREN OF THE REVOLUTION. / WORLD WITHOUT MERCY**
(12"+=) *(LASHX 7)* – Good feeling.

— Disbanded in 1988. GORDON and VICTOR joined EUGENE CHADBOURNE (of SHOCKABILLY). BRIAN RITCHIE went solo (see below).

Jan 89. (lp/c/cd) *(828130-2/-4/-1) <25819>* **3** [93]
– Nightmares / Just like my father / Dating days / Fat / Fool in the full Moon / Nothing worth living for / World we're living in / Outside the palace / Telephone book / Mother of a girl / See my ships. *(cd re-iss. Mar00; 8573 81958-2)*

— added **MICHAEL BEINHORN** – keyboards, producer

May 91. (7"/c-s) *(LASH/LASCS 29)* **AMERICAN MUSIC. / PROMISE (live)**
(ext.12"+=) *(LASHX 29)* – Kiss off (live).
(cd-s++=) *(LASCD 29)* – (all 4 tracks).
May 91. (cd/c/lp) *(828239-2/-4/-1) <26476>* **WHY DO BIRDS SING?**
– American music / Out the window / Do you really want to hurt me? / Hey nonny nonny / Polygran used to be / Girl trouble / He likes me / Life is a scream / Flamingo baby / Lack of knowledge / More money tonight / I'm free. *(cd re-iss. Mar00; 8573 81959-2)*
Sep 91. (12"ep/cd-ep) *(LASH/LASCD 31)* **DO YOU REALLY WANT TO HURT ME? / DANCE, MOTHERFUCKER, DANCE / TO THE KILL**
Oct 93. (cd/c) *<(45403-2/-4)>* **ADD IT UP (1981-1993)** (compilation)
– Intro / Waiting for the bus / Blister in the Sun / Gone daddy gone / Gordon's message / Gimme the car / Country death song / Black girls / Jesus walking on the water / 36-24-36 / I held her in my arms / I hate the T.V. / American is / Old Mother Reagan / Degradation / Dance, motherfucker, dance / Lies / American / Out the window / Kiss off / Add it up / Vancouver / Johnny. *<cd re-iss. Sep99; 3984 28258-2>*

— **GUY HOFFMAN** – drums (ex-BODEANS) repl. VICTOR + MICHAEL

Elektra / Elektra

May 94. (cd-s) *<66186>* **MACHINE / MACHINE (version) / BALKAN FALCON / CHINESE ROCKS / COLOR ME ONCE**
May 94. (cd/c/lp) *<(7559 61553-2/-4/-1)>* **NEW TIMES** [90]
– Don't start me on the liquor / New times / Breakin' up / Key of Z / 4 seasons / Machine / I'm nothing / When everybody's happy / Agememnon / This island life / I saw you in the crowd / Mirror mirror (I see a damsel) / Jesus of Rio.

Cooking Vinyl / Beyond

Oct 99. (cd) *(COOKCD 189) <6385 78024-2>* **VIVA WISCONSIN (live October 1998)** [Nov99]
– Prove my love / I'm nothing / Country death song / Blister in the sun / Gimme the car / Don't talk about my music / Confessions / Hallowed ground / Life is an adventure / Old Mother Reagan / Ugly / Good feeling / Dahmer is dead / American music / Special / Sweet words of angels / Black girls / Gone daddy gone / Add it up / Kiss off.
Feb 00. (cd) *(COOKCD 187) <6385 78058-2>* **FREAK MAGNET**
– Hollywood is high / Freak magnet / Sleepwalkin' / All I want / New generation / In the dark / Rejoice and be happy / Mosh pit / Forbidden / When you died / At your feet / I danced / I'm bad / Happiness is / A story.

Cooking Vinyl / Cold Front

Oct 00. (cd) *(COOKCD 203) <4409>* **ROCK!!!!!**
– Living a lie / Tonight / Bad dream / I danced / Thanksgiving (no way out) / Dahmer is dead / Life is an adventure / She went to Germany / I wanna see you again / Didgeriblues / Death drugs / Sweet worlds of angels.
(above was actually issued in Australia mid-1995)

– others, etc. –

Jun 92. (cd-ep) *Alex; <2742>* **AUSTRALIAN TOUR (live)**

BRIAN RITCHIE

had gone solo in-between breaks

S.S.T. / S.S.T.

Oct 87. (lp/cd) *<(SST/+CD 141)>* **THE BLEND**
– Alphabet / Arab song / Austrian anthill / Days of the blend / Doin' the best we can / Feast of fools / John the revelator / Nuclear war / Song of the highest tower / The toad / Two fat dogs.
1988. (12"ep) *<SST 186>* **NUCLEAR WAR (Deutsch). / ('A'-English version) / ALPHABET**
1988. (12"ep) *<SST 187>* **ATOMKRIEG. /**
Feb 89. (lp/cd) *<(SST/+CD 202)>* **SONIC TEMPLE AND THE COURT OF BABYLON**
– Bells / Sonic temple and the court of Babylon / Why did you lie to me? / Sun Ra from Outer Space / Dance*? / Christian for one day / A.D. / Mayerling (let's drink some wine) / No resistin' a Christian / So it goes / Hasan I sabbah / Reach out.
Feb 89. (12"ep/cd-ep) *<(SST/+CD 227)>* **SUN RA MAN FROM OUTER SPACE. /**

not iss. / Dali

1990. (cd/c) *<DD/DC 89023>* **I SEE A NOISE**
– Eva / 2 tongues, 2 minds / Please don't cry for me / Why is that baby's head so big? / Song without any end / Quo Vadis / Animals / The man with the cigarette in his nose / Religion ruined my life / Song of the cricket / I see a noise.

VIRGIN PRUNES

Formed: Dublin, Ireland ... 1977 by FIONAN HANVEY aka GAVIN FRIDAY, GUGGI, DAVE-ID BUSARAS SCOTT, DIK EVANS (brother of U2's THE EDGE), STRONGMAN and POD. As musical ambassadors of the secretive artistic community known as Lypton Village – PAUL HEWSON aka BONO was also part of the close-knit group which had been inspired by the punk explosion across the water in England – The VIRGIN PRUNES courted controversy with the calculated outrage of their performance-art style gigs.

Likely to feature everything from transvestitism to homo-erotic simulation, the band's live reputation continually overshadowed their recorded output. This didn't prevent them signing to 'Rough Trade', though, following on from a split single with The HIGSONS and a self-financed EP, 'TWENTY TENS'. The resulting 'IN THE GREYLIGHT' EP brought further critical acclaim while the band lent new meaning to interactive art by releasing their debut "album", 'NEW FORM OF BEAUTY' in three separate parts and in three different formats. Appropriately enough, The VIRGIN PRUNES' music was as abrasive, schizophrenic and fragmented as their approach to performing with a distinct gothic overtone to proceedings. '(WHAT SHOULD WE DO WHEN) BABY TURNS BLUE' and 'PAGAN LOVE SONG' previewed 1982's COLIN NEWMAN (WIRE)-produced 'IF I DIE, I DIE' album, FRIDAY's vocal contortions as demanding as ever in a set which strayed closer to conventional songwriting territory. Inevitably, the band struggled to keep the shock factor intact, the subsequent departure of GUGGI and DIK in 1984 proving a major setback. Produced by SOFT CELL's DAVE BALL, 'THE MOON LOOKED DOWN AND LAUGHED' (1986) failed to halt the decline and FRIDAY struck out on a solo career in 1987 with a cover of The Rolling Stones' 'YOU CAN'T ALWAYS GET WHAT YOU WANT'. Following the release of live set, 'THE HIDDEN LIE – LIVE IN PARIS' (1987), the remains of the band carried on fruitlessly as The PRUNES while FRIDAY pursued his own warped muse via a deal with 'Island'. Having met collaborator, MAURICE ROYCROFT aka THE MAN SEEZER at his recently opened Dublin club, FRIDAY proceeded to indulge his interest in vintage European cabaret-noir with 'EACH MAN KILLS THE THING HE LOVES' (1989). Featuring musicians in the employ of both LOU REED and TOM WAITS, the record found FRIDAY wrestling the usual demons of sex, death, madness etc., in the spirit of KURT WEILL, BERTOLD BRECHT and the like. While some critics hailed it as the best work of his career, they weren't quite so enthusiastic about the more rock-centric 'ADAM 'N' EVE' (1992) upon which FRIDAY forced his 70's glam fantasies. Despite valuable mainstream exposure with contributions to the award-winning 1993 film, 'In The Name Of The Father', FRIDAY remains a cult figure, '95's 'SHAG TOBACCO' album making few concessions to fashion. • **Songwriters:** GAVIN FRIDAY, who also launched solo career in 1989 and covered NEXT (Jacques Brel) / DEATH IS NOT THE END (Bob Dylan) / THE SLIDER (T.Rex). • **Trivia:** GAVIN wrote three songs for model NAOMI CAMPBELL's 'Babywoman' album.

Album rating: IF I DIE, I DIE (*8) / HERESIE (*5) / THE MOON LOOKED DOWN AND LAUGHED (*6) / THE HIDDEN LIE (*6) / Gavin Friday: EACH MAN KILLS THE THING HE LOVES (*6) / ADAM AND EVE (*5) / SHAG TOBACCO (*6)

GAVIN FRIDAY (b. FIONAN HANVEY) – vocals / **GUGGI** (b. DEREK ROWEN) – vocals / **DAVE-ID BUSARAS SCOTT** (b. DAVID WATSON) – narrator / **DIK EVANS** – guitar / **STRONGMAN** (b. TREVOR ROWAN) – bass / **POD** (b. ANTHONY MURPHY) – drums

Baby / not iss.

Jan 81. (7"ep) *(BABY 001)* **TWENTY TENS**
– I've been smoking all night / Revenge / The children are crying.
— **HAA LACKI BINTTII** – percussion, electronics repl. POD

Rough Trade / not iss.

Jul 81. (7"ep) *(RT 072)* **IN THE GREYLIGHT. / WAR / MOMENTS AND MINE (DESPITE STRAIGHT LINES)**
Oct 81. (7"ep) *(RT 089)* **NEW FORM OF BEAUTY PART ONE**
– Sandpaper lullaby / Sleep / Fantasy dreams.
Nov 81. (10"ep) *(RT 090)* **NEW FORM OF BEAUTY PART TWO**
– Come to daddy / Sweet home under white clouds / Sad world.
Dec 81. (12"ep) *(RT 091T)* **NEW FORM OF BEAUTY PART THREE**
– The beast (seven bastard suck) / The slow children (Abbagal) / Brain damage / No birds to fly.
Dec 81. (7"/10"/12"; box) *(RT 089-91)* **A NEW FORM OF BEAUTY** (compilation)
(cd-iss. Jan94 on 'New Rose'; NR 452042)
Apr 82. (7") *(RT 106)* **PAGAN LOVE SONG. / DAVE-ID IS DEAD**
(12"+=) *(RT 106-12)* – Pagan lovesong (vibe akimbo).
— male **MARY O'NELLON** – drums; repl. HAA LACKI BINTTII who became PRINCESS TINYMEAT and issued three singles for 'Rough Trade' between '85-'87; 'SLOBLANDS', 'BUN IN THE OVEN' and 'DEVILCOCK'.
Oct 82. (7") *(RT 119)* **(WHAT SHOULD WE DO WHEN) BABY TURNS BLUE. / YEO**
(12"+=) *(RT 119T)* – Chance of a lifetime.
Nov 82. (lp) *(ROUGH 49)* **IF I DIE, I DIE**
– Ulakennalmloy / Decline and fall / Sweet home under white clouds / Bau-Dachong / Pagan love song / Baby turns blue / Ballad of the man / Walls of Jericho / Caucasian walk / Theme for thought. *(cd-iss. Jun90; LCD 49)* *(cd re-iss. Jan94 on 'New Rose'; NR 452043)*
— GUGGI and DIK departed

Baby / Touch & Go

Apr 85. (lp/c) *(BABY/+T 002)* **OVER THE RAINBOW (RARITIES 1981-83)**
– Down the memory lane / Red nettle / Mad bird in the wood / Jigsawmentallama / The king of junk / Just a love song / The happy head / Third secret / Heresie / We love Deirdre / Rhetoric / Man on the corner / Nisam lo / Loved one / Go 'T' away Deirdre. *(cd-iss. Feb88 +=; BABY 002CD)* – HERESIE
— GAVIN FRIDAY made guest appearances for The FALL on 1984's 'CALL FOR ESCAPE ROUTE' 12", and 'WONDERFUL AND FRIGHTENING WORLD OF . . . ' album.
— In 1986, The VIRGIN PRUNES were back with **GAVIN, MARY** (now guitar), **DAVE-ID, STRONGMAN** and the returning **POD** – drums
Jan 86. (lp/c/cd) *(BABY 005/+C/+CD)* <TG 9> **THE MOON LOOKED DOWN AND LAUGHED**
– Heaven / Love lasts forever / Sons find devils / Alone / The Moon looked down and laughed / Uncle Arthur's lonely world / Don't look back / Betrayal / Deadly sins. *(cd-iss. Jan94 on 'New Rose'; NR 422474)*

Jun 86. (7") *(BABY 003)* <TG 15> **LOVE LASTS FOREVER. / LOVE LORNALIMBO**
(12") *(BABY 004)* – ('A'side) / I like the way you're frightened.
Nov 86. (7") *(BABY 006)* <TG 16> **DON'T LOOK BACK. / WHITE HISTORY BOOK**
(12"+=) *(BABY 007)* – Day of ages.
May 87. (lp/c/cd) *(BABY/+C/+CD 008)* **THE HIDDEN LIE – LIVE IN PARIS** (live June '86)
– Sweet home (under white clouds) / Lady day / God bless the child (with RAY CHARLES) / Never ending story / Pagan love song / Love is danger / The Moon looked down and laughed / Caucasian walk / The blues song. *(cd re-iss. Jan94 on 'New Rose'; NR 422473)*
Jan 88. (2x10"lp) *(BABY 011)* **HERESIE**
– We love Dierdre / Rhetoric / Down the memory lane / Man on the corner / Nisam Lo / Loved one / Got away Dierdre / LIVE IN PARIS (parts 1 & 2). *(cd-iss. Jan94 on 'New Rose'; NR 422475)*
— they altered their moniker slightly to The PRUNES and issued two late 80's albums, 'LITE FANTASTIC' (BABYCD 012) and 'NADA' (BABYCD 013)

– compilations, etc. –

Jan 94. (cd) *New Rose; (NR 453041)* **PAGAN LOVESONG**
Jan 94. (cd) *New Rose; (NR 422476)* **ARTFUCK**
Mar 97. (cd) *Burning Airlines; (PILOT 007)* **GREATEST HITS**
Jan 98. (cd) *Cleopatra; (<CLP 0179>)* **SONS FIND DEVILS (THE BEST OF THE VIRGIN PRUNES)**
– Ulakanakulot / Decline and fall / Pagan love song / New form of beauty / Walls of Jericho / Caucasian walk / Bernie and Attricia sing / Rhetoric / Sweet home under white clouds / Pig children / Come to daddy / Under Arthur's lonely world / Down the memory lane.

GAVIN FRIDAY

went solo augmented by **SIMON CARMODY**

Baby / not iss.

Aug 87. (7"colrd) *(BABY 009)* **YOU CAN'T ALWAYS GET WHAT YOU WANT. / BLESSINGS**

GAVIN FRIDAY & THE MAN SEEZER

with **MAN SEEZER** – keyboards / **MARC RIBOT** – guitar, banjo + **MICHAEL BLAIR** – drums, percussion (both of TOM WAITS' band) / **BILL FRISELL** – guitar / **FERNANDO SAUNDERS** – bass, guitar + **HANK ROBERTS** – cello (both of LOU REED's band)

Island / Island

May 89. (7") *(IS 408)* **EACH MAN KILLS THE THINGS HE LOVES. / EXTRACT FROM THE BALLAD OF READING GAOL**
(12"+=) *(12IS 408)* – ('A'instrumental).
May 89. (lp/c/cd) *(ILPS/ICT/CID 9925)* <842586> **EACH MAN KILLS THE THING HE LOVES**   Aug89
– Each man kills the thing he loves / He got what he wanted / Tell tale heart / Man of misfortune / Apologia / Dazzle and delight / Rags to riches / The next thing to murder / Love is just a word / You take away the Sun / Another blow on the bruise / Death is not the end.
Aug 89. (7") *(IS 430)* **YOU TAKE AWAY THE SUN. / THE NEXT THING TO MURDER**
(12"+=) *(12IS 430)* – Love is just a word.
(cd-s++=) *(CID 430)* – ('A'version).
Mar 90. (7") *(IS 455)* **MAN OF MISFORTUNE. / EACH MAN KILLS THE THING HE LOVES**
(cd-s+=) *(CID 455)* – You take away the sun.

GAVIN FRIDAY

— (solo) with The BIG NO NO: **MAURICE SEEZER** / **DANNY BLUME** – guitar (ex-KID CREOLE) / **ERIK SANTO** (ex-LOUNGE LIZARDS)
Feb 92. (7") *(IS 506)* **I WANT TO LIVE. / LAUGH, CLOWN, LAUGH**
(c-s+=/cd-s+=) *(12IS/CID 506)* – He got what he wanted.
Mar 92. (cd/c/lp) *(CID/ICT/ILPS 9984)* <512090> **ADAM 'N' EVE**
– I want to live / Falling off the edge of the world / King of trash / Why say goodbye? / Saint Divine / Melancholy baby / Fun & experience / The big no no / Where in the world? / Wind and rain / Eden.
Apr 92. (c-s/7") *(C+/IS 522)* **KING OF TRASH. / REX MORTUS EST**
(12"+=/cd-s+=) *(12IS/CID 522)* – Geek love.
Sep 92. (c-s/7") *(C+/IS 533)* **FALLING OFF THE EDGE OF THE WORLD. / SIBYL VANE'S SUICIDE**
(12"+=/cd-s+=) *(12IS/CID 533)* – Wake up screaming.
above A-side featurued a duet with MARIA McKEE
Mar 94. (c-s/7"; by BONO & GAVIN FRIDAY) *(C+/IS 593)* **IN THE NAME OF THE FATHER. / EDEN**   46
(12"+=/cd-s+=) *(12IS/CID 593)* – (2-'A'mixes).
above from the film of the same name
Aug 95. (cd/c) *(CID/ICT 8036)* <524126> **SHAG TOBACCO**   Jan96
– Shag tobacco / Caruso / Angel / Little black dress / The slider / Dolls / Mr. Pussy / You me and World War Three / Kitchen sink drama / My twentieth century / The last song I'll ever sing / Le roi d'amour. *(cd re-iss. Sep96; IMCD 227)*
Oct 95. (c-s) *(CIS 615)* **ANGEL ('A'-Space hop mix) / A THOUSAND YEARS / MACUSHLA**
(12") *(12IS 615)* – (first 2 tracks) / ('A'-Space Hop dub) / ('A'-Fallen mix).
(cd-s) *(CID 615)* – ('A'side) / ('A'-Tim Simenon mix) / ('A'-Howie B mix) / ('A'-Danny Gee mix).
Jan 96. (12"ep/c-ep/cd-ep) *(12IS/CIS/CID 621)* **YOU ME AND WORLD WAR THREE (The Grid – Armageddon & Orbiting Planet mixes). / YOU ME AND WORLD WAR THREE (Tim Simenon movie mix) / BILLY BOOLA**

VIRGIN PRUNES (cont)

— GAVIN retained co-writer **MAURICE SEEZER** – instruments / **ANDREW PHILPOTT** – instruments / **BARNES GOULDING** – drums

M.C.A. M.C.A.
Feb 98. (cd) *(<11751>)* **THE BOXER** (original soundtrack)
– In the shadow of a gun / Holy family 1 / To the peace line / The boxer / Twelve noon / You broke my heart / Semtex / Night band / Peace / The fight's over / Angus dei / The funeral / Holy family II / End of story, peacemaker / The boxer / Everything's gonna be alright.

— **MALCOLM TRAVIS** – drums (ex-SUGAR) repl. DAVIS
Mar 96. (cd/lp) *<(OLE 187-2/-1)>* **AT THE VANISHING POINT** ☐ ☐ Feb96
– Handcuffs / Fingertips / Permission / Bored to death / The one that got away / Hound / Amy arrow / Camp climax / Yacky do / You make me feel weird / Film / Harlem nocturne.

— PRESCOTT and his team went off to various other projects

VOLCANO SUNS

Formed: Boston, Massachusetts, USA ... 1983 by former MISSION OF BURMA drummer, PETER PRESCOTT (now a songwriter), along with GARY WALEIK and STEVE MICHENER; the latter two were respectively superseded by JON WILLIAMS and JEFF WEIGAND before any recordings. Fusing punk and folked-up power-pop, VOLCANO SUNS were one of the most adventurous of the 'Homestead' records outfits. Albums such as 1985's 'THE BRIGHT ORANGE YEARS' and '86's 'ALL NIGHT LOTUS PARTY', set out their musical stall, although further personnel changes (BOB WESTON for bassist WEIGAND and CHUCK HAHN for guitarist WILLIAMS) created their own problems; 1988's 'BUMPER CROP' was a little average by comparison. A shift to the equally-influential indie imprint, 'S.S.T.', resulted in albums No.4 and 5, 'FARCED' (1988) and double-set 'THING OF BEAUTY' (1989), the latter featuring a guest guitar slot for DAVID KLEILER. A second label move, this time to 'Quarter Stick', found the band a little obvious in direction and resulted in their break-up in '94. Almost immediately, PRESCOTT re-grouped with some old mates (EDD YAZIJIAN, BOB MOSES and BULLET LaVOLTA's KURT DAVIS) to form indie noiseniks, KUSTOMIZED. Three records for seminal label, 'Matador'; 'MYSTERY OF ...' – a mini-set – (1994), 'THE BATTLE FOR SPACE' (1995) and 'AT THE VANISHING POINT' (1996) – the latter with former BOB MOULD cohort, MALCOLM TRAVIS – have since graced our airwaves. Talking of vanishing, where is PRESCOTT? • **Covered:** NEEDLE'S IN THE CAMEL'S EYE (Brian Eno + Phil Manzanera) / KICK OUT THE JAMS (MC5) / RED EYE EXPRESS (Devo) / KUSTOMIZED covered DEAD SOULS (Joy Division) / SURGEON'S GIRL (Wire) / I'M STRANDED (Saints) / BORED TO DEATH (Government Issue) / YACKY DO (Fireballs).
Album rating: THE BRIGHT ORANGE YEARS (*6) / ALL NIGHT LOTUS PARTY (*7) / BUMPER CROP (*5) / FARCED (*3) / THING OF BEAUTY (*6) / CAREER IN ROCK (*5) / THE BATTLE FOR SPACE (*6) / AT THE VANISHING POINT (*6)

PETER PRESCOTT – drums, vocals (ex-MISSION OF BURMA) / **JEFF WEIGAND** – bass; repl. STEVE MICHENER / **JON WILLIAMS** – guitar; repl. GARY WALEIK

Homestead Homestead
Aug 85. (lp) *<(HMS 020)>* **THE BRIGHT ORANGE YEARS**
– Jak / Descent into Hell / Truth is stranger than fishing / Balancing act / Promise me / (I'm gonna) Make you mine / Cover / The mouth that roared / Cornfield / Animals / It's stewtime / Silvertone.
Oct 86. (lp) *<(HMS 070)>* **ALL NIGHT LOTUS PARTY**
– White elephant / Cans / Room with a view / Blown stack / Engines / Walk around / Sounds like bucks / Four letters / Dot on the map / Village idiot / Ride the cog.
Nov 86. (7") *<(HMS 057)>* **SEA CRUISE. / GREASY SPINE**

— PRESCOTT recruited **BOB WESTON** – bass, trumpet / **CHUCK HAHN** – guitar
Aug 87. (lp/c/cd) *<HMS 087/+C/CD>* **BUMPER CROP**
– Magic sky / Offsprings / The central / Local wise men / Time off / Wellness / Bumper crop / Curse of the name / Lummox / Peal out / Testify / Color my world. *(cd+=)* – Tree stomp.

— **GARY WALEIK** – guitar (a past member) repl. HAHN (on some)
S.S.T. S.S.T.
Sep 88. (lp/c/cd) *<(SST 210/+C/CD)>* **FARCED**
– Can I have the key / Brother Superior / Belly full of lead / Meat potatoes / Definite maybe / Where the wrecks go / Nature and me / Laff riot / Slopen hood / Commune / What's happening to me? / Shriney / Neck of rubber.

— added **DAVID KLEILER** – guitar (guest on last lp) to repl. WILLIAMS
Nov 89. (d-lp/c/cd) *<(SST 257/+C/CD)>* **THING OF BEAUTY**
– Barricade / It's a conspiracy / Man outstanding / Courageous stunts / No place / Noodle on the couch / Ask the pundits / Arm and a leg / How to breathe / Rite of way / Soft hits / Malamondo / Deeply moved / Now file / Fill the void / Nightmare country / Needle's in the camel's eye / Kick out the jams / Redeye express / Mud / Veteran / Hang up.

Quarterstick Quarterstick
May 91. (7") *<QS 03>* **BLUE RIB. / OPENINGS**
Jun 91. (lp/c/cd) *<(QS 04/+C/CD)>* **CAREER IN ROCK** ☐ May91
– Blue rib / Binds that tie / Mystery date / Silly misunderstanding / Total eclipse / Horrorscope / Punching bag / Show / Sensitacho / Hey monarch.

— disbanded after above ...

KUSTOMIZED

PETER PRESCOTT – vocals, guitar / **EDD YAZIJIAN** – guitar, violin, organ / **BOB MOSES** – bass / **KURT DAVIS** – drums (ex-BULLET LAVOLTA)

Matador Matador
Aug 94. (m-lp/m-cd) *<OLE 90-1/-2>* **THE MYSTERY OF**
– Big trick / Full / Overnight namedrop / It lives! / Nothing, not no one / Dead souls.
Jan 95. (7"m) *(OLE 120-7)* **THE DAY I HAD SOME FUN. / SURGEON'S GIRL / I'M STRANDED**
Feb 95. (cd/lp) *<(OLE 113-2/-1)>* **THE BATTLE FOR SPACE**
– The day I had some fun / Throw your voice / Puff piece / The 5th / Gorgeous / 33 1/3 / The place where people meet / Phantasmagoria, now / La geune / Air freshener.

THE GREAT INDIE DISCOGRAPHY — The 1980s

WAH!

Formed: Liverpool, England... early '79 as WAH! HEAT by ex-CRUCIAL THREE member (alongside JULIAN COPE and IAN McCULLOCH), PETE WYLIE. Roping in ROB JONES and PETE YOUNGER, WYLIE cut a debut single, 'BETTER SCREAM', for the 'Inevitable' label, subsequently recruiting a whole new line-up – the interestingly named KING BLUFF, CARL WASHINGTON, JOE MUSKER – for a follow-up, 'SEVEN MINUTES TO MIDNIGHT' (absolutely no relation to the similarly titled IRON MAIDEN screecher!). The latter track caught the attention of 'WEA' subsidiary, 'Eternal', WYLIE signing up, abbreviating the name to WAH! and replacing MUSKER with ex-IT'S IMMATERIAL man, PAUL BARLOW. Summer '81 saw the release of a flop single, 'FORGET THE DOWN!' and a long awaited debut album, 'NAH! POO! THE ART OF BLUFF' (1981), the sound of the band becoming more focused with the arrival of another ex-IT'S IMMATERIAL musician, HENRY PRIESTMAN. Issued under the moniker of SHAMBEKO! SAY WAH!, Spring '82's 'REMEMBER' indicated a change in direction and by the release of the SPECTOR-esque pop/soul classic, 'THE STORY OF THE BLUES', the transformation was complete. It was also extremely successful, a new line-up centering around the core of WYLIE and a recalled WASHINGTON – PRIESTMAN going on to form white soulboys, The CHRISTIANS – seeing the track make the UK Top 3. At last it seemed as if WYLIE's wayward muse was beginning to pay dividends yet a follow-up, 'HOPE (I WISH YOU'D BELIEVE ME)' barely scraped the Top 40 and ensuing record company problems delayed any further releases for more than a year. WYLIE & Co. eventually returned in summer '84, going Top 20 with the appropriately named 'COME BACK (THE STORY OF THE REDS)' and adopting a harder hitting, more politically abrasive approach. The accompanying album, 'A WORD TO THE WISE GUY' (1984), made the Top 30 although yet again a further single, 'WEEKENDS', stiffed. Compilation set, 'THE WAY WE WAH!' (1984) signalled the end of the line for WAH! in all its multifarious guises, WYLIE later resurfacing in a solo capacity (backing help courtesy of The OEDIPUS WRECKS) with the commercial yet soulful pop favourite, 'SINFUL'. It was a sizeable Top 20 hit yet what was really sinful was the predictable floundering of follow-up single, 'DIAMOND GIRL' and the 'SINFUL' (1987) album. Disappearing for the remainder of the 80's, Liverpool's most dogged pop veteran returned in the early 90's with a remixed 'SINFUL' after his profile had been raised by a guest spot on The FARM's massive 'ALL TOGETHER NOW' single. Despite critical plaudits as ever, both a single, 'DON'T LOSE YOUR DREAMS' and album, 'INFAMY! OR I DIDN'T GET WHERE I AM...' (1991), sank without trace. Tragically, it seems that despite WYLIE's continuing penchant for exclamation marks, the man never really got his point across fully to the average pop fan!!! Having done his back in, WYLIE didn't make his long awaited return to the studio for nigh on a decade, eventually surfacing with 'SONGS OF STRENGTH & HEARTBREAK' (2000). The record was hardly a radical departure for the scouse veteran, harking back to his pop heyday but unlikely to win many new converts.

Album rating: NAH! POO! THE ART OF BLUFF (*5) / A WORD TO THE WISE GUY (*5; as The Mighty Wah!) / THE WAY WE WAH! compilation (*7) / Pete Wylie: SINFUL (*6) / INFAMY! – OR I DIDN'T GET WHERE I AM TODAY (*4) / SONGS OF STRENGTH & HEARTBREAK (*6; The Mighty Wah!)

WAH! HEAT

PETE WYLIE (b.22 Mar'58) – vocals, guitar (ex-CRUCIAL THREE) / **ROB 'Jonie' JONES** – drums (ex-CRASH COURSE, w/Pete Wylie) / **PETE YOUNGER** – bass (ex-THOSE NAUGHTY LUMPS) repl. COLIN WILLIAMS + J.CULT

			Inevitable	not iss.
Jan 80.	(7")	(INEV 001) **BETTER SCREAM. / (HEY DISCO) JOE**	☐	-

— WYLIE recruited **KING BLUFF** – keyboards, synthesizer / **CARL WASHINGTON** – bass; repl. YOUNGER / **JOE MUSKER** – drums (ex-DEAD OR ALIVE) repl. JONES to The HIGH FIVE / + on tour **COLIN REDMOND** – guitar

| Nov 80. | (7") | (INEV 004) **SEVEN MINUTES TO MIDNIGHT. / DON'T STEP ON THE CRACKS** | ☐ | - |

WAH!

— **PAUL BARLOW** – drums (of IT'S IMMATERIAL) repl. MUSKER

			Eternal	not iss.
Jun 81.	(7")	(SLATE 1) **FORGET THE DOWN! / THE CHECKMATE SYNDROME**	☐	☐
Jul 81.	(lp)	(CLASSIC 1) **NAH! POO! THE ART OF BLUFF**	33	-

– The wind-up / Other boys / Why'd you imitate the cut-out / Mission impossible / Somesay / The seven thousand names of Wah! / Sleeep (a lullaby for Josie) / Seven minutes to midnight / The death of Wah!. (<cd-iss. Apr01 on 'Castle'+=; CMRCD 010>) – Forget the down / Checkmate syndrome / Other boys (Wah! Heat version) / Seven thousand names of Wah! (NME tape version) / Seven minutes to midnight (joo) / Forget the down (Ian Broudie mix) / Someday (Ian Broudie mix).

— **HENRY PRIESTMAN** – keyboards (of IT'S IMMATERIAL) repl. BLUFF

Oct 81.	(7"/12")	(SIMEY 1/+T) **SOMESAY. / FORGET THE DOWN**	☐	-
Apr 82.	(7"; as SHAMBEKO! SAY WAH!)	(ZAZU 1) **REMEMBER. / CATWALK BLUES**	☐	-
	(12"+=)	(ZAZU 1T) – A crack is a crack.		

— WYLIE + WASHINGTON enlisted **CHARLIE GRIFFITHS** – synthesizer / **JAY NAUGHTON** – piano / **CHRIS JOYCE** – drums (ex-DURUTTI COLUMN, etc.) / **The SAPPHIRES** – backing vox

| Nov 82. | (7") | (JF 1) **THE STORY OF THE BLUES. / TALKIN' BLUES** | 3 | ☐ |
| | (12"+=) | (JF 1T) – Seven minutes to midnight (live). | | |

			WEA	not iss.
Mar 83.	(7")	(X 9880) **HOPE (I WISH YOU'D BELIEVE ME). / SLEEEP**	37	-
	(12"+=)	(X 9880T) – You can't put your arms around a memory / Year of decision / Le spwah.		

The MIGHTY WAH!

			Beggars Banquet	not iss.
Jul 84.	(7")	(BEG 111) **COME BACK (THE STORY OF THE REDS). / THE DEVIL IN MISS JONES**	20	-
	(12"+=)	(BEG 111T) – ('A'-holiday romance version).		
Jul 84.	(lp)	(BEGA 54) **A WORD TO THE WISE GUY**	28	-

– Yuh learn I / Weekends / Everwanna / The lost generation / Yuh learn II / I know there was something / Yuh learn III / In the bleak – (Body and soul) – Midwinter / Papa crack – God's lonely man / What's happening here / Yuh learn IV / Come back (the story of the reds). (re-iss. Jan89 on 'Beggars Banquet-Lowdown' lp/c)(cd; BBL/+C 54)(BBL 54CD) (<cd re-iss. Apr01 on 'Castle'+=; CMRCD 036>) – Talkin' blues (story of the blues – part 2) / Don't step on the cracks / Yuh learn (version) / Comeback (holiday romance version) / Devil in Miss Jones / Remember.

| Sep 84. | (7") | (BEG 117) **WEEKENDS. / SHAMBEKO (THE LOST GENERATION)** | ☐ | ☐ |
| | (12"+=) | (BEG 117T) – Body and soul (acoustic) / Something wrong with Eddie / Weekend (original). | | |

— had already split in 1984, CHRIS JOYCE joined SIMPLY RED

PETE WYLIE

— (solo, with **The OEDIPUS WRECKS**)

			M.D.M.	not iss.
Apr 86.	(7")	(MDM 7) **SINFUL. / I WANT THE MOON, MOTHER**	13	-
	(d7"+=)	(MDMD 7) – Sophie's sinful (for Maurice and Kabelle) / Joy of being booed.		
	(12"+=)(3"cd-s+=)	(MDM 7-12)(CDT 28) – Fourelevenfortyfour / ('A'mix) / If I love you.		
Sep 86.	(7"/12")	(MDM 12/+12) **DIAMOND GIRL. / SPARE A THOUGHT**	57	-

			Siren	not iss.
Jul 87.	(7"/12")	(SRN 54/+12) **IF I LOVE YOU. / NEVER FALL FOR A WHORE**	☐	-
Aug 87.	(lp/c/cd)	(SRNLP/SRNC/CDSRN 10) **SINFUL**	☐	-

– Sinful / Shoulder to shoulder / Break out the banners / Fourelevenfortyfour / If I love you / Train to Piranhaville / We can rule the world / All the love. (re-iss. Apr90 on 'Virgin' lp/c; OVED/+C 290)

| Oct 87. | (7") | (SRN 59) **FOURELEVENFORTYFOUR. / THE MARKSMAN** | ☐ | - |
| | (12"+=)(cd-s+=) | (SRN 59-12)(SRNCD 59) – Sinful (song of the sinful angel). | | |

— late 1990, WYLIE guested for The FARM on their hit single, 'All Together Now'

PETE WYLIE & WAH... THE MONGREL

— with The FARM

			Siren	not iss.
Apr 91.	(7"/c-s)	(SRN 138/+C) **SINFUL! / FOURELEVENFORTYFOUR**	28	-
	(12")	(SRN 138-12) – ('A'side) / ('A'-Tribal mix).		
	(cd-s+=)	(SRNCD 138) – (all 3 tracks).		
Jun 91.	(7")	(SRN 141) **DON'T LOSE YOUR DREAMS (excerpt from A Teenage Opera part 154). / IMPERFECT**	☐	-
	(12"+=/cd-s+=)	(SRN T/CD 141) – Seamless.		
Aug 91.	(cd/c/lp)	(CDSRN/SRNMC/SRNLP 33) **INFAMY! OR I DIDN'T GET WHERE I AM TODAY**	☐	-

– Don't lose your dreams (excerpt from a teenage opera part 15) / Never gonna stop: no heshmesh / I didn't get where I am today / Circle of salt / John 3:16 – The one tonight / Everything! (a song for Dennis Wilson) / From carpenter to king / Long tall Scally (the ballad thereof) / Getting out of it... / Sinful! (tribal mix).

| Sep 91. | (7") | (SRN 143) **LONG TALL SCALLY. /... AND THE GOOD GUYS DON'T DIE** | ☐ | - |
| | (12"+=/cd-s+=) | (SRN T/CD 143) – Everything (but The Wah!) for Dennis Wilson acapella everything includes orchestrals ultimately. | | |

The MIGHTY WAH!

— re-formed with **WYLIE** and Co.

			Columbia	Columbia
Nov 98.	(c-s/cd-s)	(666720/4/-2) **HEART AS BIG AS LIVERPOOL / I STILL LOVE YOU / JE T'AIME, JE T'AIME / THE RETURN OF ROCK AND ROLL**	☐	-

WAH! (cont)

Apr 00. (cd) (<WENCD 209>) **SONGS OF STRENGTH & HEARTBREAK** — *When! When!*
– Never loved as a child / Sing all the saddest songs / Disneyland forever / I still love you / Hope you fall (in love) / Hey! Mona Lisa / Loverboy / Alone / Heart as big as Liverpool / Je t'aime, je t'aime / The return of rock and roll / The country epic (can't stop cryin').

– (WAH!) compilations, etc. –

Nov 83. (lp) *Wonderful World of Wah; (WW 1)* **THE MAVERICK YEARS 80-81 (the official bootleg)**
– Remember / Somesay / The truth about Eddie / The checkmate syndrome / I know there was something . . . / Shambeko / Sleeep / What's happening here? / Seven minutes to midnight / The bible or maths. (<cd-iss. Apr01 on 'Castle'+=; CMRCD 011>) – (extra tracks).

Nov 84. (lp/c) *WEA; (WX 11/+C)* **THE WAY WE WAH!** (compilation)
– Other boys / Somesay / The seven thousand names of Wah! / Seven minutes to midnight / The death of Wah! / The story of the blues parts 1 & 2 / Sleeep (a lullaby for Josie) / You can't put your arms around a memory / Hope (remix) / Remember.

Sep 87. (12"ep) *Strange Fruit; (SFPS 035)* **THE PEEL SESSIONS** (22.8.84)
– Basement blues / The story of the blues / Better scream / Weekends / Yuh learn.

Oct 00. (d-cd) *Essential; (<ESDCD 892>)* **THE HANDY WAH! HOLE** (1979-2000)

WAKE

Formed: Glasgow, Scotland . . . April 1981 by former ALTERED IMAGES original CAESAR, JOE DONNELLY and STEVEN ALLEN. After a one-off self-financed 7", 'ON OUR HONEYMOON', the band – with newcomers CAROLYN ALLEN BOBBY GILLESPIE on the B-side – joined the black-clad ranks of Tony Wilson's 'Factory' stable, where their brooding blend of NEW ORDER and The CURE fitted in perfectly. A debut LP, 'HARMONY' (1982), showcased their derivative but effective sound, although barring a few sporadic singles, it would be all of three years before a follow-up, 'HERE COMES EVERYBODY' (1985). Of these aforementioned 45's, only 'TALK ABOUT THE PAST' was of any note, featuring as it did DURUTTI COLUMN's VINI REILLY on piano; note that by late 1983, GILLESPIE opted out for PRIMAL SCREAM and The JESUS & MARY CHAIN. Subsequently dropped by Factory, The WAKE were resurrected by the infamously fey 'Sarah' label, CAESAR, STEVEN and CAROLYN even managing to borrow a couple of ORCHIDS (MATTHEW DRUMMOND and JAMES MOODY) for their 1990 comeback album, 'MAKE IT LOUD'. A tad brighter, if not quite opening the proverbial curtains just yet, the record was an interesting combination of effete vocals, hard-edged jangling, tinkling electric piano and of course that cheap electro drumbeat. Like fellow Glaswegians, the BLUE NILE, The WAKE took their time between albums, 1994's ironically titled 'TIDAL WAVE OF HYPE' their only other release of the decade. • **Covered:** LIVING FOR THE CITY (Stevie Wonder).

Album rating: HARMONY (*7) / HERE COMES EVERYBODY (*4) / MAKE IT LOUD (*5) / TIDAL WAVE OF HYPE (*4)

CAESAR – vocals, guitar (ex-ALTERED IMAGES) / **JOE DONNELLY** – bass / **STEVEN ALLEN** – drums

Scan / not iss.

Jan 82. (7") *(SCN 01)* **ON OUR HONEYMOON. / GIVE UP**

—— (guest on last B-side) **BOBBY GILLESPIE** – bass; repl. JOE

—— added **CAROLYN ALLEN** – keyboards

Factory / not iss.

Oct 82. (lp) *(FACT 60)* **HARMONY**
– Judas / Testament / Patrol / The old men / Favour / Heartburn / An immaculate conception.

Aug 83. (video; Various Artists) *(FACT 71)* **A Factory Outing**
– Uniform / (other 'Factory' bands)

Oct 83. (12") *Factory Benelux; (FBN 24)* **SOMETHING OUTSIDE. / HOIST**

—— **ALEX 'MAC' MacPHERSON** – bass; repl. GILLESPIE who formed PRIMAL SCREAM and joined The JESUS & MARY CHAIN (as a drummer!)

Mar 84. (7"/ext-12") *(FAC 88/+12)* **TALK ABOUT THE PAST. / EVERYBODY WORKS SO HARD**

—— MacPHERSON departed leaving a trio CAESAR, CAROLYN + STEVEN

Mar 85. (7") *(FAC 113)* **OF THE MATTER. / OF THE MATTER (version)**

Dec 85. (lp) *(FACT 130)* **HERE COMES EVERYBODY**
– Oh Pamela / Send them away / Sail through / Melancholy man / World of her own / Torn calendar / All I asked you to do / Here comes everybody.

—— next added temp. bassist **JOHN RAHIM**

May 87. (12"ep) *(FAC 177T)* **SOMETHING THAT NO ONE ELSE COULD BRING EP**
– Gruesome castle / Pale spectre / Furious seas / Plastic flowers.

—— **MATTHEW DRUMMOND** – guitar + **JAMES MOODY** – bass (both of the ORCHIDS) repl. RAHIM

Sarah / Widely Distributed

Dec 89. (7") *(SARAH 021)* **CRUSH THE FLOWERS. / CARBRAIN**

Nov 90. (m-lp/m-cd) *(SARAH 602/+CD)* **MAKE IT LOUD**
– English rain / Glider / Firestone tyres / American grotto / Joke shop / Holy head / Henry's work / Cheer up Ferdinand.

Aug 91. (7") *(SARAH 048)* **MAJOR JOHN. / LOUSY POP GROUP**

—— now without STEVEN

—— added guests **DUNCAN CAMERON** – bass + **DAVID McLEAN** – keys

May 94. (lp/cd) *(SARAH 618/+CD) <WDRU 028>* **TIDAL WAVE OF HYPE**
– Shallow end / Obnoxious Kevin / Crasher / Selfish / Provincial disco / I told you so / Britain / Back of beyond / Solo project / Down on your knees (Brit mix) / Big noise, big deal. <US cd+=> – Major John / Lousy pop group.

—— split after above; CAESAR joined The ORCHIDS for a short while

– compilations, etc. –

May 02. (cd) *Les Tempes Modernes; (LTMCD 2323)* **HARMONY AND SINGLES** (remastered)

May 02. (cd) *Les Tempes Modernes; (LTMCD 2332)* **HERE COMES EVERYBODY PLUS SINGLES** (remastered)

Jul 02. (cd) *Les Tempes Modernes; (LTMCD 2336)* **HOLYHEADS**
– (MAKE IT LOUD / TIDAL WAVE OF HYPE).

WAKE OOLOO (see under ⇒ FEELIES)

WALKABOUTS

Formed: Seattle, Washington, USA . . . 1984 by CHRIS ECKMAN and CARLA TORGERSON, the line-up completed by the former's brothers, GRANT and CURT, although MICHAEL WELLS replaced CURT before any recording. After an EP on the 'Necessity' label in '85, the group released a debut album, 'SEE BEAUTIFUL RATTLESNAKE GARDENS' (1987), for the obscure 'Pop Llama'. Adding GLENN SLATER on keyboards, the group signed to 'Sub Pop', issuing the acclaimed 'CATARACT' (1989). In comparison to the bulk of the grunge acts on the label, the group's rugged folk-rock sound was more reminiscent of the wild scenery of the American North West (Appalachian Mountains to be exact!) than the grimy clubs of Seattle. In that sense, the band were never really part of the 'Sub Pop' phenomenon although they continued to release fine, but generally ignored albums at a prolific pace. Garnering further cult acclaim for the 'SCAVENGER' (1991) and 'NEW WEST MOTEL' (1993) sets (the latter seeing TERRI MOELLER replace GRANT), the group subsequently indulged themselves with a covers album, 'SATISFIED MIND' (1993). Interpreting material by the likes of GENE CLARK, JOHN CALE, NICK CAVE and CHARLIE RICH, the group wore their influences proudly, their subsequent album, 'SETTING THE WOODS ON FIRE' (1994), leaning more towards the rootsy side of things. Strangely, The WALKABOUTS were always more popular in Europe than the States, the group subsequently signing to 'Virgin', for whom they recorded the masterful 'DEVIL'S ROAD' (1996). Among their transatlantic cousins, The WALKABOUTS had most in common with the likes of GALLON DRUNK and TINDERSTICKS, the latter group's DICKON HINCHCLIFFE adding violin flourishes on 'THE LEAVING KIND'. Also, in common with TINDERSTICKS, the group employed the services of an orchestra, more specifically The Warsaw Philharmonic. Their swooning strings were used to stunning effect alongside gorgeous melody and shimmering guitar vibrato on the album's epic lead track, 'THE LIGHT WILL STAY ON'. Ranking as one of the best songs they've ever recorded, the track was partly dedicated to CHARLIE RICH, who passed away the previous year. The mid to late 90's also saw the core writing partnership of CHRIS ECKMAN and CARLA TORGERSON find another outlet for their seemingly inexhaustible creativity. Under the CHRIS and CARLA tag, they released the pared down live set, 'SHELTER FOR AN EVENING' (1993) although this was eclipsed by 'LIFE FULL OF HOLES' (1995), featuring musical compadres such as R.E.M.'s PETER BUCK and TINDERSTICKS' STUART STAPLES. The band once again utilised strings on 1997's 'NIGHTTOWN', another consummate exploration of America's decaying fringes which didn't even see the light of day in that country. Having been so roundly ignored in their backyard, it was perhaps inevitable that so much time spent gigging in Europe would result in the internalisation of their immediate musical environment: while CHRIS and CARLA's third album, 'SWINGER 500' (1998) was markedly more influenced by the duo's continental cousins (TINDERSTICKS et al), both 'TRAIL OF STARS' (2000) and 'TRAIN LEAVES AT EIGHT' (2000) interpreted these influences in different ways, the former leaning heavily on the neo-gothic tone of its string textured ambience while the latter was a brilliantly conceived musical, geographical and spiritual journey through Europe, interpreting everyone from JACQUES BREL to NEU!. With 'ENDED UP A STRANGER' (2002), The WALKABOUTS reached some kind of shadowy pinnacle on their own, near two decades-long musical journey to the end of the night, deliciously drunk on their own disillusionment and revelling in the near religious fervour of their bleakly elegant symphonies. • **Covered:** ON THE BEACH + LIKE A HURRICANE + ALBUQUERQUE (Neil Young) / BIG BLACK CAR (Big Star) / FREE MONEY (Patti Smith) / FEEL LIKE GOING HOME (Charlie Rich) / LOOM OF THE LAND (Nick Cave) / PEOPLE SUCH AS THESE (Jacques Brel) / SHOT BAYOU (22 Pistepirkko) / HOW MANY TIMES (MUST THE PIPER BE PAID FOR HIS SONG) (Mickey Newbury) / SORRY ANGEL (Serge Gainsbourg) / CORCOVADO (QUIET NIGHTS OF QUIET STARS) (Antonio Carlos Jobim) / SANITORIUM BLUES (Townes Van Zandt) / COWBELLS SHAKIN' (Scott Walker) / GLORY ROAD (Neil Diamond) / DE ANDRE + DISAMISTADE (Fabrizio De Andre) / DEAR DARLING (Mary Margaret O'Hara) / AND SHE CLOSED HER EYES (Stina Nordenstam) / BLUE & GREY SHIRT (American Music Club) / BUFFALO BALLET (John Cale) / CAN YOU FLY (Freedy Johnson) / DEATH'S

THRESHOLD STEP #2 (Midnight Choir) / CELLO SONG (Nick Drake) / DOWN WHERE THE DRUNKARD'S ROLL (Richard Thompson) / LEB WOHL! (Neu!) / YESTERDAY IS HERE (Tom Waits) / THE RIVER PEOPLE (Go-Betweens) / SATISFIED MIND (Porter Wagoner) / POOR SIDE OF TOWN (Johnny Rivers) / POLLY (Gene Clark) / MAGGIE'S FARM (Bob Dylan) / LOVER'S CRIME (Pewee Maddux) / LET'S BURN DOWN THE CORNFIELD (Randy Newman) / LOSWERDEN (Tilman Rossmy) / THE TRAIN LEAVES AT EIGHT (Mikis Theodorakis) / WAKE ME UP BEFORE I SLEEP (Deus) / THE STORM ARE ON THE OCEAN (Carter Family) / IN A SLIPSHOD STYLE (Solex) / THAT'S HOW I LIVE (Blumfeld) / CHRIS & CARLA also covered other artists.

Album rating: SEE BEAUTIFUL RATTLESNAKE GARDENS (*4) / CATARACT (*7) / RAG & BONE mini (*6) / SCAVENGER (*6) / NEW WEST MOTEL (*6) / SATISFIED MIND (*6) / SETTING THE WOODS ON FIRE (*6) / DEVIL'S ROAD (*5) / DEATH VALLEY DAYS... compilation (*5) / NIGHTTOWN (*6) / TRAIL OF STARS (*4) / TRAIN LEAVES AT EIGHT (*6) / ENDED UP A STRANGER (*7) / DRUNKEN SOUNDTRACKS... collection (*6) / WATERMARKS collection (*5) / Chris & Carla: SHELTER FOR AN EVENING (*7) / LIFE FULL OF HOLES (*6) / NIGHT BETWEEN STATIONS... (*5) / SWINGER 500 (*6) / LJUBLJANA (*6)

CHRIS ECKMAN – vocals, guitar / **CARLA TORGERSON** – vocals, guitar / **CURT ECKMAN** – bass / **GRANT ECKMAN** – drums

not iss.   Necessity
Mar 85. (12"ep) <001> **22 DISASTERS**
– Ask me another / Trouble time / Tools of the trade / 22 disasters / Hope in anchor.
1987. (7") <S 001> **LINDA EVANS. / CYCLONE**

—— **MICHAEL WELLS** – bass; repl. CURT ECKMAN

—— added part-time 5th member **LARRY BARRETT** – banjo, mandolin

not iss.   Pop Llama
1987. (lp/c/cd) <PL+/C/CD 4129> **SEE BEAUTIFUL RATTLESNAKE GARDENS**
– Jumping off / Breakneck speed / The wellspring / John Reilly / Robert McFarlane blues / This rotten tree / Laughingstock / Glass palace / Feast or famine / Ballad of Moss Head / Who-knows-what / Rattlesnake theme / Weights and rivers. *(UK-iss.Jan90 on 'Still Sane'; 089204) (cd-iss. Jun97 & Mar00 on 'Glitterhouse'+=; GRCD 335)* – Linda Evans / Mai Tai time / Cyclone / Gather round / Certain gift.

—— added **GLENN SLATER** – keyboards

Sub Pop   Sub Pop
Mar 89. (lp) <SP 31> **CATARACT**
– Whiskey XXX / Hell's soup kitchen / Whereabouts unknown / End in tow / Bones of contention / Home as found / Smokestack / The wicked skipper.
Feb 90. (orange;m-lp/m-c/m-cd) <SP 56/+A/B> **RAG AND BONE**
– The anvil song / Ahead of the storm / Medicine hut / Wreck of the old #9 / Mr.Clancy / Last ditch. *(m-cd/m-c+=) – CATARACT (UK cd-iss. Nov96 & Mar00 on 'Glitterhouse'; GRCD 85)*
Sep 91. (lp/c/cd) <SP 124/+A/B> **SCAVENGER**
– Dead man rise / Stir the ashes / The night watch / Hang man / Where the deep water goes / Blown away / Nothing is stranger / Let's burn down the cornfield / River blood / Train to mercy. *(UK cd-iss. Nov96 & Mar00 on 'Glitterhouse'; GRCD 161)*
Oct 91. (cd-ep) <SP 117> **WHERE THE DEEP WATER GOES / STIR THE ASHES / BIG BLACK CAR / ON THE BEACH**

—— **TERRI MOELLER** – drums; repl. GRANT

—— added part-time **BRUCE WIRTH** – pedal steel guitar, mandolin
Jul 92. (12"ep/cd-ep) (SP/+CD 39-197) <SP 150> **DEAD MAN RISE**   Apr92
– Dead man rise / The anvil rise / Long black veil (live) / Hangman (live) Train to mercy (gospel remix).
Feb 93. (12"ep/cd-ep) (SP/+CD 81/251) **JACK CANDY**
– Jack candy / Yesterday is here / Like a hurricane / Prisoner of Texas.
Mar 93. (lp/cd) (SP/+CD 81-252) <CM 28> **NEW WEST MOTEL**
– Jack Candy / Sundowner / Grand theft auto / Break it down gently / Your hope shines / Murdering stone / Sweet revenge / Glad nation's death song / Long time here / Wondertown (part 1) / Drag this river / Snake mountain blues / Findlay's motel / Unholy dreams. *(cd re-iss. Nov96 & Mar00 on 'Glitterhouse'; GRCD 70081)*
May 93. (d7"ep/cd-ep) (SP/+CD 89-270) **YOUR HOPE SHINES**
– Your hope shines / Wondertown (part two) / Shine a light / Inauguration day.

Sub Pop   Creative Man
Nov 93. (lp/cd) (SP/+CD 116-294) <83048> **SATISFIED MIND**
– Satisfied mind / Loom of the land / River people / Polly / Buffalo ballet / Lovers crime / Shelter for an evening / Dear darling / Poor side of town / Free money / Storms are on the ocean / Feel like going home / Will you miss me when I'm gone? *(cd re-iss. Nov96 & Mar00 on 'Glitterhouse'; GRCD 294)*
Mar 94. (cd-ep) (SPCD 129-321) **GOOD LUCK MORNING**
– Good morning luck / Night drive (truck stop version) / Findlay's motel (live) / Nothing is a stranger (live).
May 94. (lp/c/cd) (SP/+MC/CD 128-319) <30> **SETTING THE WOODS ON FIRE**
– Good luck morning / Firetrap / Bordertown / Feeling no pain / Old crow / Almost wisdom / Sand and gravel / Night drive (truck stop version) / Hole in the mountain / Pass me over / Up in the graveyard / Promised. *(cd re-iss. Nov96 & Mar00 on 'Glitterhouse'; GRCD 319)*

Dindisc   not iss.
Mar 96. (c-s) (DINSC 152) **THE LIGHT WILL STAY ON / DEVIL'S ROAD**
(cd-s+=) (DINSD 152) – Incognito / Winded.

Virgin   Virgin Schallplatter
Apr 96. (cd/c) (CD/MC VIR 46) <841349> **DEVIL'S ROAD**
– The light will stay on / Rebecca wild / Stopping off place / Cold eye / Christmas valley / Blue head flame / When fortune smiles / For all this / Fairground blues / Leaving kind / Forgiveness song.
Jun 97. (cd) (CDVIR 57) <844280> **NIGHTTOWN**
– Follow me an angel / These proud streets / Tremble (goes the night) / Unwind / Lift your burdens up / Prayer for you / Immaculate / Nocturno / Heartless / Nightbirds / Forever gone / Harbour lights / Slow red dawn.

—— **BAKER SAUNDERS** – bass; repl. WELLS who formed PLUTO BOY

Glitterhouse   Glitterhouse
Sep 99. (cd) <(GRCD 450)> **TRAIL OF STARS**   Apr00
– Desert skies / Straight to the stars / Gold / Last tears / Crime story / Hightimes / Harvey's quote to me / On the day / Till I reach you / Drown / No one the wiser. *(d-lp iss.Mar00; GR 450-1)*
Mar 00. (cd-s) (GRCD 461) **DROWN / BONNIE AND CLYDE / LOST IN THE SCRAPS**
May 00. (cd) <(GRCD 490)> **TRAIN LEAVES AT EIGHT**   Aug00
– The train leaves at eight / Man from Reno / That black guitar / Disamistade / Silenci / Hard winds blowin' / Everyone kisses a stranger / People such as these / Wake me up before I sleep / Solex in a slipshod style / That's how I live / And she closed her eyes / Death's threshold step #2 / 'Leb' wohl.

Glitterhouse   Innerstate
Oct 01. (cd) (GRCD 538) <7012> **ENDED UP A STRANGER**   Apr02
– Lazarus heart / Radiant / Life: the movie / More heat than light / Fallen down moon / See it in the dark / Mary Edwards / Lest we forget / Winslow Place / Cul-de-sac / Incidento / Climb / Ended up a stranger.

– compilations, etc. –

Nov 96. (cd) *Glitterhouse;* <(GRCD 404)> **DEATH VALLEY DAYS: LOST SONGS AND RARITIES 1985-1995**
– Drunk (on a civilized rule) / 1 + 1 / Barnstorming / Chain gang / On the beach / Big black car / Cello song / Maggie's farm / Break it down gently / Train to mercy (Italia version) / Yesterday is here / Prisoner of Texas / Inauguration day / Pass me on over / Like a hurricane / House of the rising sun / Losweden / Sand & gravel strings.
Aug 02. (d-cd) *Glitterhouse;* <(GRCD 561)> **DRUNKEN SOUNDTRACKS: LOST SONGS & RARITIES 1995-2000**
– Drunken soundtracks / Unbreakable / People such as these / Shot bayou / How many times (must the piper be paid for his song) / Sorry angel / Undermine / Call me back again / On the day / Desert skies / Albuquerque / The getaway / Bonnie and Clyde (live with Nighttown Orchestra) / Rage on / Death's black train / Thieves like us / Corcovado (quiet nights of quiet stars) / Cover of darkness / Silver city / Sanitorium blues / Cowbells shakin' / Come along / The light will stay on / Desierto / Glory road / Winded / Incognito / Master of none / Theme from where the air is cool and dark.
Nov 02. (cd) *Innerstate;* <(7016)> **WATERMARKS: SELECTED SONGS 1991-2002**
– Till I reach you / Rebecca wild / The light will stay on / Winslow Place / Drown / Follow me an angel / Lift your burdens up / Christmas valley / Prayer for you / Disamistade / Bordertown / Grand theft auto / Long time here / Loom of the land / Train to mercy.

CHRIS & CARLA

CHRIS ECKMAN + CARLA TORGERSON with various guests

Sub Pop   Sub Pop
Jul 93. (cd) <(SPCD 92/264)> **SHELTER FOR AN EVENING (live)**
– River blood / Long time here / Jack candy / Wichita lineman / Down where the drunkards roll / Stir the ashes / Hangman / Sweet revenge / Glad nation's death song / Train to mercy / On the beach / Maggie's farm.

Global Warming   Glitterhouse
Feb 95. (cd) <GRCD 360> **LIFE FULL OF HOLES**
– Precursor / Storm crazy / Death at low water / The tower / Nights between stations / Take me / Sleep will pass us by / Sandy river moon / The silent crossing / Comfort of a stranger / Life full of holes / Velvet fog / Never gonna fall / The cool and the dark. *(UK-iss.Mar00; same as US)*
Nov 95. (cd) <GRCD 383> **NIGHTS BETWEEN STATIONS: LIVE IN THESSALONIKI 1995 (live with MYLOS ALL-STARS)**
– Where the air is cool and dark / Nights between stations / Prisoner of Texas / The silent crossing / Storm crazy / Sleep will pass us by / Sweet revenge / Storms are on the ocean / Lungs / Velvet fog / Inauguration day / Sand & gravel.
1997. (7"red) <DHL 0020> **RUNAROUND. / (other by WILLARD GRANT CONSPIRACY)**
(above issued on 'Dahlia')
Mar 98. (cd/lp) (GLOB CD/LP 2) <GRCD 432> **SWINGER 500**   May98
– The good news first / Electric wire / New love ends / Black rope tied / Fear / Swinger 500 / Funny how time slips away / Bingo catastrophe / Blue winter snow / Mercury rising / Famous last words.

– compilations, etc. –

1999. (cd) *Wingnut;* <53> **LJUBLJANA (live official bootleg from 1995)**
– Nights between stations / The silent crossing / Sleep will pass us by / On the beach / Grand theft auto / Storm crazy / Loom of the land / Velvet fog / Take me / Snake mountain blues / The tower / Feel like going home / Will you miss me when I'm gone?

CHRIS ECKMAN

with various personnel

Glitterhouse   not iss.
2000. (cd) (GRCD 476) **A JANELA**   German
– Fireworks / Intrusions / The drag / Rua Augusta / Ghostface / Deadwood / Fadista / A Janela / May you have strength / The other side of night / 20 minutes on a train / Sonhos e smobras.

Scott WALKER

The Story Later in '67, SCOTT WALKER left JOHN MAUS and GARY LEEDS (after some arguments with JOHN) and went solo, hitting the heights until the 70's (his melancholy ballads later influencing the likes of JULIAN COPE). SCOTT scored late 60's solo hits with the controversial 'JACKIE', 'JOANNA' and 'LIGHTS OF CINCINATTI' as well as the albums, 'SCOTT' (1967), 'SCOTT 2' (1968; a UK No.1) and 'SCOTT 3' (1969). He also contributed backing vocals to The BEATLES' 'All You Need Is Love' world broadcast in 1967, by this point even hosting his own TV show on BBC1. With the release of cult classic, 'SCOTT 4' (1969), however, he faded from popular stardom and languished in MOR hell for much of the early 70's. The man briefly re-emerged mid-decade as part of a reformed WALKER BROTHERS, enjoying a UK Top 10 with a cover of Tom Rush's 'NO REGRETS'. SCOTT eschewed the lure of the beckoning nostalgia circuit, however, leading the band in a radically different direction for 1978's 'NITE FLIGHTS' (the brothers' final album together). WALKER eventually resurfaced in solo mode with the tortured 'CLIMATE OF HUNTER' in 1984, hardly a record to kickstart his career. 'Virgin' were suitably unimpressed with the commercial returns and he subsequently signed to 'Fontana' in 1985. Although he recorded with BRIAN ENO, the project was never completed; similarly, SCOTT's collaborative work with former JAPAN warbler, DAVID SYLVIAN produced no concrete results. It would be a further eleven years before he came out with new work in the form of 95's 'TILT'. As out-there as WALKER has yet ventured, fans and critics alike agreed that while he mightn't be the most prolific artist, his darkly compelling experiments are worth waiting for.

Album rating: SCOTT (*7) / SCOTT 2 (*8) / SCOTT (*7) / ...SINGS SONGS FROM HIS TV SERIES special (*4) / SCOTT 4 (*8) / 'TIL THE BAND COMES IN (*6) / THE MOVIEGOER (*4) / ANY DAY NOW (*4) / STRETCH (*4) / WE HAD IT ALL (*4) / FIRE ESCAPE IN THE SKY: THE GODLIKE GENIUS OF SCOTT WALKER compilation (*7) / SCOTT WALKER SINGS JACQUES BREL collection (*6) / CLIMATE OF HUNTER (*7) / BOY CHILD; THE BEST OF SCOTT WALKER 1967-1970 compilation (*8) / TILT (*5) / POLA X soundtrack (*6)

SCOTT WALKER

re-issued old recordings

Liberty / Liberty
1966. (7"ep; as SCOTT ENGEL) (LEP 2261) **SCOTT ENGEL**
– I broke my own heart / What do you say / Are these really mine / Crazy in love with you.

Capitol / Capitol
May 66. (7"; with JOHN STEWART) (CL 15440) **I ONLY CAME TO DANCE WITH YOU. / GREENS**

Philips / not iss.
Dec 66. (7"ep; 1-side by JOHN MAUS) (BE 12597) **SOLO SCOTT – SOLO JOHN**
– (SCOTT WALKER:- The gentle rain / Mrs. Murphy.

—— solo after the WALKER BROTHERS split

Philips / Smash
Aug 67. (lp; stereo/mono) (S+/BL 7816) **SCOTT** — 3 / —
– Mathilde / Montague Terrace (in blue) / Angelica / Lady came from Baltimore / When Joanna loved me / My death / Through a long and sleepless night / The big hurt / Such a small love / You're gonna hear from me / Always coming back to me / Amsterdam. (re-iss. Mar92 & Jun00 on 'Fontana' cd/c; 510 879-2/-4)
Nov 67. (7") (BF 1628) <2156> **JACKIE. / THE PLAGUE** — 22 / 1
Mar 68. (lp; stereo/mono) (S+/BL 7840) **SCOTT 2** — 1 / —
– Jackie / Best of both worlds / The amorous Humphrey Plugg / Black sheep boy / Next / The girls from the street / Plastic palace people / Wait until dark / The girls and the dogs / Windows of the world / The bridge / Come next Spring. (re-iss. Aug92 & Jun00 on 'Fontana' cd/c; 510 880-2/-4)
Apr 68. (7") (BF 1662) <2168> **JOANNA. / ALWAYS COMING BACK TO YOU** — 7 / —
Mar 69. (lp) (SBL 7882) **SCOTT 3** — 3 / —
– It's raining today / Copenhagen / Rosemary / Big Louise / We came through / Butterfly / Two ragged soldiers / 30th century man / Winter night / Two weeks since you've gone / Sons of / Funeral tango / If you go away. (re-iss. Aug92 & Jun00 on 'Fontana' cd/c; 510 881-2/-4)
Jun 69. (7") (BF 1793) <2228> **LIGHTS OF CINCINNATI. / TWO WEEKS SINCE YOU'VE GONE** — 13 / —
Jun 69. (lp) (SBL 7900) **... SINGS SONGS FROM HIS TV SERIES** — 7 / —
– I have dreamed / The impossible dream / Will you still be mine / When the world was young / Who (will take my place) / If she walked into my life / The song is you / The look of love / Country girl / Someone to light up my life / Only the young / Lost in the stars.
Nov 69. (lp; as NOEL SCOTT ENGEL) (SBL 7913) **SCOTT 4**
– The seventh seal / On your own again / World's strongest man / Angels of ashes / Boy child / The old man's back again / Hero of the war / Duchess / Get behind me / Rhymes of goodbye. (re-iss. Aug92 & Jun00 on 'Fontana' cd/c; 510 882-2/-4)
Dec 70. (lp) (6308 035) **'TIL THE BAND COMES IN**
– Prologue / Little things (that keep us together) / Jean the machine / Joe / Thanks for Chicago, Mr. James / Long about now / Time operator / Cowbells shakin' / 'Til the band comes in / The war is over / Stormy / The hills of yesterday / What are you doing the rest of your life / Rueben James / It's over. (cd-iss. Aug96 on 'Beat Goes On'; BGOCD 320)
Oct 71. (7") (6006 168) **I STILL SEE YOU. / MY WAY HOME**
Oct 72. (lp) (6308 127) **THE MOVIEGOER**
– This way Mary / Speak softly love / Glory road / That night / The summer of '42 / Easy come easy go / The ballad of Sacco and Vanzetti (here's to you) / Face in the crowd / Joe Hill / All his children / Come Saturday morning / The look of love. (re-iss. on 'Contour'; 6870 633)
May 73. (7") (6006 311) **THE ME I NEVER KNEW. / THIS WAY MARY**
May 73. (lp) (6308 148) **ANY DAY NOW**
– Any day now / All my love's laughter / Do I love you / Ain't no sunshine / Maria Bethania / Cowboy / When you get right down to it / The me I never knew / If ships were made to sail / We could be flying.

C.B.S. / Columbia
Oct 73. (7") (1795) **A WOMAN LEFT LONELY. / WHERE LOVE HAS DIED**
Nov 73. (lp) (65725) **STRETCH**
– Sunshine / Just one smile / A woman left lonely / No easy way down / That's how I got to Memphis / Use me / Frisco depot / Someone who cared / Where does brown begin / Where love has died / I'll be home.
Jul 74. (7") (2521) **DELTA DAWN. / WE HAD IT ALL**
Aug 74. (lp) (80254) **WE HAD IT ALL**
– Low down freedom / We had it all / Black rose / Ride me down easy / You're young and you'll forget / The house song / Old five and dimers like me / Whatever happened to Saturday night / Sundown / Delta dawn.

—— SCOTT shelved solo career when the WALKERS re-formed in 1975
—— went solo again in '84

Virgin / Virgin
Mar 84. (7") (VS 666) **TRACK 3. / BLANKET ROLL BLUES**
Mar 84. (lp/c) (T/TCV 2303) **CLIMATE OF HUNTER** — 60 / —
– Rawhide / Dealer / Track 3 / Sleepwalker's woman / Track 5 / Track 6 / Track 7 / Blanket roll blues. (re-iss. Aug88 lp/c; OVED/+C 149) (cd-iss. Nov89; CDV 2303)

—— retired from music until ...

Fontana / Drag City
May 95. (cd/lp) (526 859-2/-1) <DC 134CD> **TILT** — 27 / Nov97
– Farmer in the city / The cockfighter / Bouncer see bouncer... / Manhattan / Face on breast / Bolivia '95 / Patriot (a single) / Tilt / Rosary.

Barclay / not iss.
Jun 00. (cd) (547608-2) **POLA X** (soundtrack) — — French
– The time is out of joint / Light / Meadow / The darkest forest / Extra blues (by SMOG) / Never again / Iza kana zanbi (by FAIRUZ) / Trang mo ben suo / Zai na yao yuan de di fang / The church of the apostles / Bombupper / River of blood / Blink (by SONIC YOUTH) / Running / Closing / Isabel.

– (SCOTT WALKER) compilations, etc. –

on 'Philips' unless otherwise stated
Dec 67. (c-ep) (MCP 1006) **GREAT SCOTT!**
– Jackie / When Joanna loved me / The plague / Mathilde.
Dec 67. (lp) Ember; (EMB 3393) **LOOKING BACK WITH SCOTT WALKER**
(cd-iss. Nov00 & Jul02 on 'Repertoire'; REP 4604)
Jan 70. (lp) (SBL 7910) **THE BEST OF SCOTT WALKER**
(re-iss. Nov71 as 'THIS IS SCOTT WALKER'; 6382 007) (re-iss. Jun82; 6381 073) (re-iss. Oct83; PRICE 43)
Oct 72. (lp) (6382 052) **THIS IS SCOTT WALKER – VOL.2**
Jan 76. (lp) Contour; (6870 679) **THE BEST OF SCOTT WALKER**
Mar 76. (d-lp) (6625 017) **SPOTLIGHT ON SCOTT WALKER**
Nov 81. (lp) (6359 090) **SINGS JAQUES BREL**
(cd-iss. Sep92 on 'Fontana' cd/c; 838212-2/-4)
Sep 81. (lp) Zoo; (ZOO 2) **FIRE ESCAPE IN THE SKY – THE GODLIKE GENIUS OF SCOTT WALKER**
Aug 82. (7") Old Gold; (OG 9244) **JOANNA. / LIGHTS OF CINCINNATI**
Jun 90. (cd/c/lp) Fontana; <(842832-2/-4/-1)> **BOY CHILD: 67-70** — / 1992
– Montague Terrace (in blue) / Such a small love / The amorous Humphrey Plugg / The girl from the streets / Plastic palace people / The bridge / It's raining today / Copenhagen / Big Louise / We came through / The seventh seal / On your own again / Boy child / The old man's back again (dedicated to the neo-Stalinist regime) / Angels of ashes / Prologue / Little things (that keep us together) / Time operator / Epilogue, the war is over (sleepers). (re-iss. Jun00; 542705-2)
Dec 96. (cd) Razor & Tie; (RE 2120-2) **IT'S RAINING TODAY: THE SCOTT WALKER STORY 1967-1970**
May 97. (cd) Beat Goes On; <(BGOCD 358)> **STRETCH / WE HAD IT ALL**
Dec 97. (cd) Spalax; (14566) **EARLY TEN YEARS**
Mar 99. (cd) Fontana; (538605-2) **SCOTT ON SCREEN**
Mar 01. (cd/c) Castle Pulse; (PLS CD/MC 367) **IN THE BEGINNING**
Jul 01. (cd) Platinum; (PLATCD 672) **14 ORIGINAL RECORDINGS**

WALKINGSEEDS

Formed: Liverpool, England ... 1986 out of the ashes of mid 80's gothabilly noise outfit The MEL-O-TONES (like a serious HALF MAN HALF BISCUIT) by FRANK MARTIN, BOB PARKER and JOHN NEESAM. A three-month spell as CORINTHIANS was put aside with the release of The WALKINGSEEDS' debut EP, 'KNOW TOO MUCH' in summer '86. JOHN subsequently dropped out prior to a debut album, 'SKULLFUCK', its title inspired by a GRATEFUL DEAD sleeve. In 1988, the psych/grunge terrorists employed the services of KRAMER, the BONGWATER man producing their follow-up album 'UPWIND OF DISASTER, DOWNWIND OF ATONEMENT'. The band continued to label-hop when the 'Glass' imprint dissolved, the 90's beginning with their version of BEVIS FROND's 'REFLECTIONS IN A TALL MIRROR' (available as a mail-order single on 'Clawfist'). Following '91's swansong 'EARTH IS HELL', BOB and TONY went on to form The DEL-BLOODS, who in turn became WHITE BITCH. • **Covered:** SUNSHINE OF YOUR LOVE (Cream) / ASTRONOMY DOMINE (Pink Floyd) / etc. • **Trivia:** Their song MARK CHAPMAN was about the killer of JOHN LENNON, if you didn't know already.

MEL-O-TONES

FRANK MARTIN – vocals / **BOB PARKER** – bass, guitar / **JOHN NEESAM** – drums / were MARTIN DEMPSEY + BOB BELLIS (ex-YACHTS the founders of this lot)

Probe Plus / not iss.

Mar 85. (m-lp) *(PROBE 3)* **MEL-O-TONES**
– Bomb sutra / Burton buzz / Lice age / I walked with a Bugs Bunny bendy toy.

Sep 85. (12"ep) *(PP 13)* **MELONHEADED**
– Mad Jesus / Seedy lotion / Happy hour // Happy hour / Melonhead.

WALKINGSEEDS

FRANK, BOB + JOHN

Probe Plus / not iss.

Jun 86. (12"ep) *(PP 19T)* **KNOW TOO MUCH**
– Tantric wipeout /

—— **BAZ SUTTON** – guitar (ex-MARSHMALLOW OVERCOAT) / **TONY MOGAN** – drums (ex-MARSHMALLOW OVERCOAT) repl. NEESAM

Mar 87. (12") *(CEDE 2)* **MARK CHAPMAN. / BLATHERING OUT**
(above single released on own 'Moral Burro' label)

Nov 87. (lp) *(PROBE 13)* **SKULLFUCK**
– Iron man / Doom patrol / 666 squadron / When girls the world / Life vs. filth / Blue cheer / Kill kill for inner peace / Obeying the law / St. Alban's / Blathering out. *(cd-iss. Apr00 on 'God Bless'; NOIR 012CD)*

Glass / Communion

Mar 89. (lp/cd) *(GLA LP/CD 034)* <9> **UPWIND OF DISASTER, DOWNWIND OF ATONEMENT**
– 281 f / We rise / Sexorcist / Wreck of the white star / Imperious, vain, selfish and wilful / Louie, Louie, Louie / Help me, mummy's gone / Slow dance of golden lights / Mad river blues.

—— **ANDY ROWAN** – guitar; repl. SUTTON who joined The LA'S

1989. (12"ep) *(GLAEP 110)* **SHAVED BEATNIK**

—— guest **NICK SALOMAN** (BEVIS FROND) – guitar

1989. (m-lp) *(MGLALP 037)* **SENSORY DEPRIVATION CHAMBER QUARTET DWARF**

—— **LEE WEBSTER** – bass; repl. ROWAN

Clawfist / not iss.

Feb 90. (7"mail-o) *(PIS 1)* **REFLECTION IN A TALL MIRROR. / (Bevis Frond: SEXORCIST)**

Paperhouse / Shimmy Disc

May 90. (7") *(PAPER 001)* **GATES OF FREEDOM. / ASTRONOMY DOMINE**

May 90. (cd/c/lp) *(PAP CD/MC/LP 001)* <SHIMMY 36> **BAD ORB, WHIRLING BALL**
– Gates of freedom / Weight of the years / Mortal blues / Broken cup / She said she said / Peter's trip / Caged beatnik / World's ok / Skullfuck.

Snakeskin / not iss.

1991. (cd/lp) **EARTH IS HELL** (live)

not iss. / Fist Puppet

1990's. (7") <011> **ROLLIN' MACHINE. / PLAYBOY STOMP**

—— **PARKER, MARTIN, MOGAN / + KYME + MIDDLETON**

Butcher's Hook / not iss.

1993. (m-cd) *(HOOK 2CD)* **MIRRORSHADES** — Austra
– Mirrorshades / Krellmetal / Mescalito / Bleak generation / G-spot.

Dental / not iss.

Feb 94. (ltd-7") *(DENT 1)* **BEAT THEM ALL TO DEATH. /**

—— took a hike when BOB and TONY formed DEL-BLOODS who issued 'BLACK RABBIT'. They went on to become WHITE BITCH who released 'ANIMAL WOMAN'. FRANK and the two were part of BATLOAF's 'Meat Out Of Hell' (a parody of MEAT LOAF), while BAZ and LEE joined FROTH.

WALL

Formed: Sunderland, England ... late '77 by IAN LOWERY, ANDZY GRIFFITHS, JOHN HAMMOND and BRUCE ARCHIBALD. Signed to the local 'Small Wonder' label, this straightahead punk outfit released 'NEW WAY' as their debut single in Spring '79. By the release of their follow-up, 'EXCHANGE', both HAMMOND and ARCHIBALD had been replaced by NICK WARD and RAB FAE BEITH. Following the replacement of LOWERY with KEELY and the addition of new member ANDY HEED FORBES, the band released the 'GHETTO' EP at the turn of the decade, closely followed by a debut album, 'PERSONAL TROUBLES AND PUBLIC ISSUES' (1981) – WARD and KELLY were now absent. Released on indie label, 'Fresh', the album was enough to impress 'Polydor', who – possibly finding a replacement for the recently departed SHAM 69 – issued a new single, 'REMEMBRANCE'. By this point the band had slimmed down to a trio of ANDZY, RAB and HEED, plus former PASSIONS girl CLAIRE BIDWELL, a tour support to STIFF LITTLE FINGERS helping to raise their profile. Yet by the release of 'DIRGES AND ANTHEMS' (1982), the band had fallen out with their major label backers over the usual stumbling block of musical direction. Sticking to their guns, The WALL signed to indie label, 'No Future' and released an EP with The Beatles' 'DAY TRIPPER' as the lead track.

Album rating: PERSONAL TROUBLES & PUBLIC ISSUES (*5) / DIRGES AND ANTHEMS (*5) / THE PUNK COLLECTION compilation (*6)

IAN LOWERY – vocals / **ANDYZ GRIFFITHS** – bass, vocals / **JOHN HAMMOND** – lead guitar, vocals / **BRUCE ARCHIBALD** – drums

Small Wonder / not iss.

Apr 79. (7"m) *(SMALL 13)* **NEW WAY. / SUCKERS / UNIFORMS**

—— **NICK WARD** – guitar; repl. HAMMOND
—— **RAB FAE BEITH** – drums (ex-PATRIK FITZGERALD) repl. ARCHIBALD

Sep 79. (7") *(SMALL 21)* **EXCHANGE. / KISS THE MIRROR**

—— **KELLY** – vocals; repl. LOWERY who formed SKI PATROL, etc.
—— added **ANDY HEED FORBES** – keyboards, guitar (ex-STRAPS)

Fresh / not iss.

Apr 80. (7"m) *(FRESH 17)* **GHETTO. / ANOTHER NEW DAY / MERCURY**

—— **PETE WILSON** – keyboards, guitar; repl. KELLY + WARD

Sep 80. (7"m) *(FRESH 27)* **HOBBY FOR A DAY. / REDEEMER / 8334**

—— now without PETE

Nov 80. (lp) *(FRESHLP 2)* **PERSONAL TROUBLES AND PUBLIC ISSUES**
– Fight the fright / In nature / Storm / Syndicate / Windows / Delay / Ghetto / Unanswered prayers / Mercury / Cancer / Career mover / One born every day. *(with a free 7"ep)*

Polydor / not iss.

Apr 81. (7"m) *(POSP 260)* **REMEMBRANCE. / ILLSI NAO / HOOLIGAN NIGHTS**

—— **GRIFFITHS, FORBES + BEITH** added **CLAIRE BIDWELL** – sax, vocals (ex-PASSIONS)

Nov 81. (7"m) *(POSP 365)* **EPITAPH. / REWIND / NEW REBEL**

—— added **BAZ** – guitar

Apr 82. (lp) *(POLS 1048)* **DIRGES AND ANTHEMS**
– Who are you / Nice to see you / Wunderkind / Epitaph / Money whores / Barriers / Walpurgis night / Only dreaming / Footsteps / Chinese whispers / Anthem / Pete's song / Tyburn / Everybody's ugly / English history.

—— now without BAZ + CLAIRE, the latter forming JU-KAN-JU

No Future / not iss.

Nov 82. (7"ep) *(OI 21-7)* **DAY TRIPPER / ANIMAL GRIP. / WHEN I'M DANCING / CASTLES**
(12"ep+=) *(OI 21-12)* – Ceremony / Industrial nightmare / Hall of miracles / Spirit dance / Funhouse.

—— broke-up after above

– compilations, etc. –

Nov 98. (cd) *Captain Oi; (AHOYCD 095)* **THE PUNK COLLECTION**
– New way / Suckers / Uniforms / Exchange / Kiss the mirror / Ghetto / Another new day / Mercury / Hobby for a day / Fight the fright / In nature / Syndicate / Windows / Career mother / One born every day / Day tripper / Growing up / When I'm dancing / Spirit dance / Fun house.

WALL OF VOODOO

Formed: Los Angeles, California, USA ... 1977 by STAN RIDGWAY and the MORELAND brothers, MARC and BRUCE, the line-up completed by JOE NANINI and CHAS T. GRAY. Spotted by Miles Copeland and signed to his 'I.R.S.' label in 1980, they released an eponymous EP later the same year. Filtering a country/folk twang through new wave synths, WALL OF VOODOO had come up with one of the most bizarre takes on American roots music to date. The nearest comparison was DEVO, while RIDGWAY's distinctive, heavily-accented vocal was pitched somewhere between IGGY POP and The B-52's FRED SCHNEIDER. All in all an interesting, often er... challenging and occasionally humourous listen – check out the jackboot cover of Johnny Cash's 'RING OF FIRE'. Following on from 1981's debut album, 'DARK CONTINENT', the tongue-in-cheek but patronising dumbness of 'MEXICAN RADIO' gave the band their only hit single (transatlantic Top 75!) and pushed the 'CALL OF THE WEST' (1982) set into the US Top 50. Other highlights included the harmonica-enhanced poke at the 9 to 5 lifestyle of 'FACTORY' and the instrumental piano and theramin travelogue of former single, 'ON INTERSTATE 15'. But the band were subsequently dealt a body blow with the departure of RIDGWAY (readers may recall, or prefer to forget rather, the man's moose-voiced solo yarn, 'CAMOUFLAGE' – a UK Top 5 hit in 1986), recruiting ANDY PRIEBOY in his place and soldiering on with the 'SEVEN DAYS IN SAMMYSTOWN' (1986) album. While they retained a cult following, the new-look WALL OF VOODOO failed to build on the pioneering spirit of their early work and finally split after 1988's live set, 'UGLY AMERICANS IN AUSTRALIA AND BULLSHIT CITY'. • **Songwriters:** RIDGWAY words / group compositions. From the mid-80's, PRIEBOY and group (bar LUEKHARDT) wrote material. They also covered MONA (Bo Diddley) / DO IT AGAIN (Beach Boys) / DARK AS A DUNGEON (M.Travis) / PRETTY BOY FLOYD (Woody Guthrie) / THE GOOD, THE BAD AND THE UGLY (Ennio Morricone).

Album rating: DARK CONTINENT (*7) / CALL OF THE WEST (*8) / GRANMA'S HOUSE compilation (*8) / SEVEN DAYS IN SAMMYSTOWN (*4) / HAPPY PLANET (*3) / UGLY AMERICANS IN AUSTRALIA ... (*5) / THE INDEX MASTERS compilation (*6)

STAN RIDGWAY (b. 5 Apr'54) – vocals, harmonica, keyboards / **MARC MORELAND** – guitar / **BRUCE MORELAND** – bass, keyboards / **JOE NANINI** – drums, percussion / **CHAS T. GRAY** – bass, keyboards, synthesizers

WALL OF VOODOO (cont)

Sep 80. (12"ep) <SP 70401> **WALL OF VOODOO** — Illegal / I.R.S.
 – Long arm / The passenger / Can't make love / Struggle / Ring of fire / Granma's house. <remix re-iss. Nov81 on 'Index'; EPC 01>
Oct 81. (lp) <(SP 70022)> **DARK CONTINENT**
 – Red light / Tow minutes till lunch / Animal day / Full of tension / Me and my dad / Back in the flesh / Tsetse fly / Call box (1-2-3) / This way out / Good times / Crack the bell.
— now a quartet when BRUCE departed
Oct 82. (7") (ILS 0031) **ON INTERSTATE 15. / THERE'S NOTHING ON THIS SIDE**
Oct 82. (lp) (ILP 010) <70026> **CALL OF THE WEST** — / 45
 – Tomorrow / Lost weekend / Factory / Look at their way / Hands of love / Mexican radio / Spy world / They don't want me / On Interstate 15 / Call of the west. (cd-iss. 1986 on 'I.R.S.'; CD 70026)
Jan 83. (7"/12") (ILS/ILS12 0036) <9912> **MEXICAN RADIO. / CALL OF THE WEST** — 64 / 58
— MARC + CHAS recruited new members NED LEUKHARDT – drums repl. NANINI / ANDY PRIEBOY – vocals repl. STAN RIDGWAY who went solo
Nov 84. (7") (IRS 116) **BIG CITY. / ROOM WITH A VIEW** — I.R.S. / I.R.S.
— added the returning BRUCE MORELAND – keyboards, bass
Mar 86. (7"/12") (IRM/IRMT 111) **FAR SIDE OF CRAZY. / THE WRONG WAY TO HOLLYWOOD**
May 86. (lp/c) (MIRF/+C 1006) <5662> **SEVEN DAYS IN SAMMYSTOWN**
 – Far side of crazy / Business of love / Faded love / Mona / Room with a view / Blackboard sky / Big city / Dark as the dungeon / Museums / Tragic vaudeville / (Don't spill my) Courage.
May 87. (7") (IRM 135) **DO IT AGAIN. / BACK IN THE LAUNDROMAT**
 (12"+=) (IRMT 135) – Far side of crazy.
Jun 87. (lp/c) (MIRF/+C 1022) <5997> **HAPPY PLANET**
 – Do it again / Hollywood the second time / Empty room / Chains of luck / When the lights go out / Love is a happy thing / Country of man / Joanne / Elvis bought Dora a Cadillac / The grass is greener / Ain't my day.
— guest ROGER MASON – keyboards; repl. BRUCE who left again
Jun 88. (lp) (ILP 022) <42140> **UGLY AMERICANS IN AUSTRALIA AND BULLSHIT CITY (live)** — Illegal / I.R.S.
 – Red light / Crazy, crazy Melbourne / Wrong way to Hollywood / Living in the red / Blackboard sky / Pretty Boy Floyd / The heart never can tell / Far side of crazy / Ring of fire / Mexican radio. (cd+=) – The grass is greener.

– compilations, etc. –

Jul 84. (lp) I.R.S.; (IRSA 7048) **GRANMA'S HOUSE**
 – Ring of fire / Long arm / The passenger / Can't make love / On interstate 15 / Lost weekend / Mexican radio / Call box / Red light / Tomorrow / Crack the bell / Call of the west / Granma's house.
Jul 92. (cd) Mau Mau; (MAUCD 619) / Restless; <70111> **THE INDEX MASTERS** (most live)
 – Longarm / Passenger / Can't make love / Struggle / Ring of fire / Granma's house / End of an era / Tomorrow / Animal day / Invisible man / Red light / The good, the bad and the ugly / Hang 'em high / Back in flesh / Call box (1-2-3).

— WALL OF VOODOO tracks appeared on 1992 the STAN RIDGWAY compilation, 'SONGS THAT MADE THIS COUNTRY GREAT, THE BEST OF STAN RIDGWAY'

WALTONES

Formed: Manchester, England ... 1986 by JAMES KNOX, MARK COLLINS, MANNY LEE and ALEX FYANS. A C-86 outfit, after their time instead of ahead of it, The WALTONES debuted their uptempo jingle jangle sound on a spring '87 single, 'DOWNHILL', for 'Medium Cool'. A follow-up, 'SHE LOOKS RIGHT THROUGH ME', again used The BYRDS via 'Postcard'-era as a starting point while revealing a talent for absorbing the trendy sounds of the day (i.e. HOUSEMARTINS, WEDDING PRESENT, The SMITHS, etc). In the summer of '88, they delivered a third platter, 'SPELL IT OUT', followed by a single and album of the same name, 'THE DEEPEST' (1988), which featured CLINT BOON (future INSPIRAL CARPETS guy). In 1990, the quartet returned as CANDLESTICK PARK (a venue in the US where The BEATLES once performed!) but after only one single and a shelved set they split; COLLINS would subsequently join The CHARLATANS.

Album rating: THE DEEPEST (*5)

JAMES KNOX – vocals, harmonica / **MARK COLLINS** – guitar / **MANNY LEE** – bass / **ALEX FYANS** – drums

Medium Cool / not iss.

Apr 87. (7") (MC 004) **DOWNHILL. / CLOSEST TO**
Oct 87. (12"m) (MC 007) **SHE LOOKS RIGHT THROUGH ME. / SPECIAL 20 / BURNING CONSCIENCE**
Jul 88. (7") (MC 011) **SPELL IT OUT. / (I'VE GOT) NOTHING**
 (12"+=) (MC 011T) – Thanks a million.
Oct 88. (7") (MC 016) **THE DEEPEST. / FALLING IN LOVE**
 (12"+=) (MC 016T) – (Black & blue) Rainfall.
 (cd-s++=) (CALC 066) – (CORN DOLLIES tracks on 'Ediesta').
Nov 88. (lp) (MC 018) **THE DEEPEST**
 – Everything's just fine / The deepest / Don't understand / When it all turns sour / She's everywhere but here / Smile / A million different ways / Rainfall / What's gone wrong? / I've got nothing.
Feb 89. (12"; w-drawn) (MC 022T) **LISTEN TO YOUR HEART** — - / -
— changed their name to CANDLESTICK PARK

Nov 90. (12"; as CANDLESTICK PARK) (DING 67) **ALL THE TIME IN THE WORLD. / PROMISED LAND / SAFE** — Midnight Music / not iss.
— ADRIAN DONAHUE – drums; repl. FYAN
— CANDLESTICK PARK were scheduled for an album release, 'REINVENT THE WHEEL' in August 1991 (CHIME 01.11/+CD)
— COLLINS would subsequently join The CHARLATANS

WANDERERS (see under ⇒ SHAM 69; 70's section)

Ben WATT (see under ⇒ EVERYTHING BUT THE GIRL)

Mike WATT (see under ⇒ MINUTEMEN)

WE ARE GOING TO EAT YOU (see under ⇒ HAGAR THE WOMB)

WEATHER PROPHETS

Formed: London, England ... 1980 as THE LOFT by PETER ASTOR, BILL PRINCE and ANDY STRICKLAND. Recruiting sticksman, DAVE MORGAN, the band became one of the first acts to record for 'Creation', releasing the 'WHY DOES THE RAIN' single in Autumn '84. It would be a full year before the appearance of a follow-up, 'UP THE HILL AND DOWN THE SLOPE', by which time the band were on the verge of a split. While BILL went off to form The WISHING STONES and ANDY founded The CARETAKER RACE, ASTOR and MORGAN initiated The WEATHER PROPHETS with OISIN LITTLE and GREENWOOD GOULDING. Remaining with 'Creation', MORGAN & Co. released the 'DIESEL RIVER' (1986) album, benefitting from the cult acclaim that the enigma of The LOFT had generated. ASTOR was still following his BYRDS/VELVET UNDERGROUND fixation, the subsequent near-hit, 'SHE COMES FROM THE RAIN', sounding like a proto-STONE ROSES. Like the accompanying LENNY KAYE-produced album, 'MAYFLOWER' (1987), the track appeared on 'Elevation', Alan McGee's short-lived dalliance with 'Warners'. When the project fell through, the band shifted back to 'Creation', crossover success still tantalisingly out of sight. Giving up the ghost after a final album, 'JUDGES, JURIES AND HORSEMEN' (1988), ASTOR remained with 'Creation' for a solo career, cutting two obscure albums, 'SUBMARINE' (1990) and 'ZOO' (1991). MORGAN, meanwhile, went on to play briefly with fashionable Camden country-rockers, The ROCKINGBIRDS. ASTOR returned in 1997 with his new outfit, The WISDOM OF HARRY, an altogether different kettle of fish to what The LOFT and The WEATHER PROPHETS were all about. With its journey into indie-electronica, ASTOR's WOH debut set, 'STARS OF SUPER 8' (a 1999 compilation of singles) took off into ambient territory and this was not a one-off. WISDOM OF HARRY returned with another batch, 'HOUSE OF BINARY' (2000), while ASTOR now plotted a commercial comeback with ELLIS ISLAND SOUND, (c.2002). • **Songwriters:** ASTOR main penmrith, except WHO BY FIRE (Leonard Cohen).

Album rating: Loft: ONCE AROUND THE FAIR compilation (*8) / Weather Prophets: DIESEL RIVER (*5) / MAYFLOWER (*7) / JUDGES, JURIES & HORSEMEN (*5) / TEMPERANCE HOTEL (*5) / Pete Astor: SUBMARINE (*6) / ZOO (*5) / PARADISE (*5) / GOD AND OTHER STORIES (*6) / Wisdom Of Harry: STARS OF SUPER 8 (*6) / HOUSE OF BINARY (*6) / Ellis Island Sound: ELLIS ISLAND SOUND (*4)

LOFT

PETE ASTOR (b. ABE SMITH, 1959, Colchester, England) – vocals, guitar / **ANDY STRICKLAND** (b.16 Jul'59, Isle Of Wight) – guitar / **BILL PRINCE** (b.19 Jul'62, Devon, England) – bass / **DAVE MORGAN** – drums

Creation / not iss.

Sep 84. (7") (CRE 009) **WHY DOES THE RAIN. / LIKE**
Apr 85. (12"ep) (CRE 015T) **UP THE HILL AND DOWN THE SLOPE / YOUR DOOR SHINES LIKE GOLD. / LONELY STREET / TIME**
Jul 85. (7") (CRE 015) **UP THE HILL AND DOWN THE SLOPE. / TUESDAY TIME**

— disbanded in '85 when BILL formed The WISHING STONES and ANDY formed The CARETAKER RACE

– compilations, etc. –

Sep 89. (lp/cd) (CRE LP/CD 047) **ONCE AROUND THE FAIR**
 – Why does the rain / Skeleton staircase / Lonely street / Your door shines like gold / Time / Winter / Like / On a Tuesday / The canal and the big red town / Up the hill and down the slope.

WEATHER PROPHETS

— ASTOR + MORGAN plus OISIN LITTLE – guitar / GREENWOOD GOULDING – bass

Creation / not iss.

May 86. (7") (CRE 029) **ALMOST PRAYED. / YOUR HEARTBEAT BREATHES THE LIFE INTO ME**
 (12"+=) (CRE 029T) – Like Frankie Lymon / Wide open arms. (d7"+=) (CRE 029D) – Downbound train / Stone in my path way.

WEATHER PROPHETS (cont) — THE GREAT INDIE DISCOGRAPHY — The 1980s

Oct 86. (7") (CRE 031) **NAKED AS THE DAY YOU WERE BORN. / IN MY ROOM**
  (12"+=) (CRE 031T) – Wrst friend I ever had.

Rough Trade / not iss.
Nov 86. (lp/cd) (RT D/CD 2-40) **DIESEL RIVER**
  – Almost prayed / Worm in my brain / Your heartbeat breathes the life into me / Stones in my passway / Like Frankie Lymon / Wide open arms / Downbound train / Head over heels. (cd+=) – In my room / Worst friend I ever had. (US cd-iss. Apr94 on 'Tristar'; 57785>

Elevation / not iss.
Mar 87. (12") (ACID 1T) **SHE COMES FROM THE RAIN. / WIDE OPEN ARMS / HAPPY** — 62
  (12") (ACID 1TX) – (first 2 tracks) / You upset the grade of living when you die / Who by fire.
Apr 87. (lp/c) (ELV 1/+C) **MAYFLOWER** — 67
  – Why does the rain / The key to my love is green / Can't keep my mind off you / Mayflower / Head over heels / She comes from the rain / Almost prayed / Faithful / Swimming pool blue / Walking under a spell / Naked as the day you were born / Sleep.
Jul 87. (7") (ACID 2) **WHY DOES THE RAIN. / MIDNIGHT MILE**
  (12"+=) (ACID 2T) – Mayflower / Annalea.

—— (Apr'88) now a trio when OISIN departed

Creation / Combat
Apr 88. (7") (CRE 054) **HOLLOW HEART. / JOE SCHMO THE ESKIMO**
  (12"+=) (CRE 054T) – Sleeping when the sun comes up / Chinese Cadillac.
Jun 88. (cd/lp) (CRE CD/LP 033) <8244> **JUDGES, JURIES AND HORSEMEN**
  – Always the light / Hollow heart / Poisons mind / Well done Sonny / Born inbetween / Thursday seems a year ago / Bury them deep / You bring the miracles / Never been as good / Ostrich bed. (free 7" w/lp) (CREFRE 2) **ODDS AND ENDS:- Sin bin - Get fishy - 1000 hangover's later. / SLEEPING LIGHTLY ON THE ANCIENT PATH** (cd+=) – Stepping lightly on the ancient path / Sleeping when the sun comes up / Joe Shimo & the eskimo. (re-iss. May94 +=; same)
Aug 88. (7") (CRE 056) **ALWAYS THE LIGHT. / BLUE ROOFTOP**
  (12"+=) (CRE 056T) – Hill house / Somersaults.

— compilations, etc. —
on 'Creation' unless mentioned otherwise
Nov 89. (lp/cd) (CRE LP/CD 050) (RT D/CD 2-40; Positive; <6046>) **TEMPERANCE HOTEL** (sessions, etc.)
  – The key to my love is green / You're my ambulance / Mayflower / Midnight mile / Why does the rain / Can't keep my mind off you / In my room / Odds and ends / Sleep / Chinese Cadillac / Blue rooftop / I saw the light / Stepping lightly on the ancuient path / Joe Shcmo and the Eskimo / Hollow heart (live) / Chinese Cadillac (live).
Jun 91. (cd/c/lp) (CRECD/C-CRE/CRELP 085) **'87 LIVE (live)**
  – Why does the rain / Head over heels / Poison mind / Like Frankie Lymon / Worm in my brain / She comes from the rain / Mayflower / Your heartbeat breathes the life into me / The key to my love is green / Hollow heart / Almost prayed.

PETER ASTOR

Creation / not iss.
Aug 90. (cd/c/lp) (CRECD/C-CRELP 065) **SUBMARINE**
  – Beware / Walk into the wind / Firesong / Your Sun leaves the sky / Holy road / I wish I was somewhere else / Emblem / On top above the driver / Submarine / Chevron. (free 7" w/lp) – **AFTERNOON. / INTERLUDE**
Nov 90. (12"ep)(cd-ep) (CRE 094T)(CRESCD 094) **WALK INTO THE WIND (version) / YOUR SUN LEAVES THE SKY. / SUBMARINE / FIRESONG**
Mar 91. (12"ep)(cd-ep) (CRE 099T)(CRESCD 099) **CHEVRON. / BEWARE (acoustic) / ON TOP ABOVE THE DRIVER (acoustic) / EMBLEM (acoustic)**
May 91. (cd/c/lp) (CRECD/C-CRE/CRELP 090) **ZOO**
  – Six-day weekend / Harvest moon / We move in an arc whose grace we never see / What was and what could never be / Street of lights / Heart-shaped swimming pool / Ghost sister / Seaplane / Letter to nowhere / The emperor, the dealer and the birthday boy / Blue walking days / Thirteen and seven centuries.
Nov 91. (7") (CRE 114) **DER KAISER, DER DEALER UND DAS GEBURTSTAGSKIND. / Times: LINDY BLEU**

PETER ASTOR & THE HOLY ROAD

Danceteria / not iss.
Apr 92. (cd/c/lp) (DAN CD/C/LP 105) **PARADISE**
  – Almost falling in love / She took the TV / Love, full-on / Secret life / Guy Fawkes' night / Donnelly / Hotel at the end of the world / Sideways and the golden egg / Lost soul / Paradise.
Jun 92. (cd-ep) (DANCD 110) **ALMOST FALLING IN LOVE / LEAVING TRAIN / NEVER BEEN AS GOOD AS THIS / JOE'S REVENGE**

PETER ASTOR

Apr 93. (cd-s) (DAN 9302CD) **DISCO LIGHTS / DANCING LATE AT NIGHT / YOU WERE PERFECT THEN**
May 93. (cd) (DAN 9304CD) **GOD & OTHER STORIES**
  – Big dumb song / The monkey / God / Disco lights / Miss A / Still Wednesday / The lost weekend starts here / St. Paul's mambo / On Saturday night / Another Sunday / Underground / No food is blue / Ha ha ha / Big dumb song again. (re-iss. Feb95; same)

WISDOM OF HARRY

—— PETE ASTOR – vocals, multi

Wurlitzer Jukebox / not iss.
Mar 98. (7") (WJ 33) **PURE GOLD HENRY. / SPORTS POD**

Lissy's / not iss.
Apr 98. (10"ep/cd-ep) (LISS 28/+CD) **STAYING IN WITH THE WISDOM OF HARRY**

Static Caravan / not iss.
Sep 98. (7") (VAN 2.0) **ALMOND ORANGE. /**

Motorway / not iss.
Feb 99. (7") (MOTOR 031) **FRAGMENTS OF HARRIS. / X SCREEN**

Faux Lux / Matador
Aug 99. (lp/cd) (FLUX 003/+CD) <OLE 383-2> **STARS OF SUPER 8**
  – C.C.'s dark days / Shotgun / Pure gold Henry / Disney queen / Hansa toy corporation / Samovaar / Fragments of Harris / 23 sky / Sports pod / X screen / Marsh blues / Valley boys / Loved.

Matador / Matador
Aug 00. (7") (OLE 421-7) **CONEY ISLAND OF YOUR MOUTH. / HAL CHOC**
  (cd-s) (OLE 421-2) – ('A'side) / Vent Aziz / Angelhound / Schtumm.
Aug 00. (cd/lp) (<OLE 414-2/-1>) **HOUSE OF BINARY**
  – Hello / Unit one / Coney Island of your mind / Caesar boots / March of the Otaku / Theme from Eggboy / Boxed / Disco C / Woke up buzzing / Sleepwalking / The year without speaking / I'm going to make my life right / Palefinger / The wisdom.
May 01. (7") (OLE 488-7) **CAESAR BOOTS. / SHINY SHINY PIMPMOBILE**
  (cd-s) (OLE 488-2) – ('A'side) / Rebellious jukebox (Peel session) / Primo Tory / Dub delux.

ELLIS ISLAND SOUND

PETER ASTOR + DAVE SHEPPARD

Heavenly / E.M.I.
Jul 02. (cd/d10"-lp) (HVN CD/LP 34) <538809> **ELLIS ISLAND SOUND**
  – Republica evescarra / Olympic 2020 / Cyanide / Your twisted sister / / Vis charm / Ranch stuff / Six shooter annex / Data centre / Half nelson / Theme from Milos / Ocean spray.

Gregory WEBSTER (see under ⇒ RAZORCUTS)

WEDDING PRESENT

Formed: Leeds, England . . . 1984 by ex-teachers DAVID GEDGE and PETE SOLOWKA (father Ukrainian) along with KEITH GREGORY and SHAUN CHARMAN. They gained a deal with local indie label, 'Reception', in 1985 and, with appearances on John Peel's radio 1 show, quickly grew into a cult act. Debut album, 'GEORGE BEST' (1987) was one of the key 80's indie releases, GEDGE's tunefully challenged monotone combining with the fast and furious punk-jangle racket to somehow create something more than the sum of its parts. Towards the end of the decade, they were finally signed to a major record company, 'R.C.A.', their first release on the label, 'UKRAINSKI . . .', surprising many with its marriage of Ukranian folk styles and indie-rock. GEDGE reverted to his trademark lovelorn lyrical fashion for follow-up proper, 'BIZARRO', a record that disappointed many longtime fans. Nevertheless, The WEDDING PRESENT were nothing if not prolific, even achieving the accolade of a Guinness Book Of Records entry in 1992 when every one of their monthly single (7"only) releases hit the UK Top 30 (The 12 hits also contained an unusual cover version on the B-side, see below). Despite the departure of all founding members save GEDGE (SALOWKA left in the early 90's to form The UKRAINIANS), 1994's 'WATUSI' again found the band in favour with the critics if not commanding the fanbase they once had. In 1998, GEDGE re-invented himself as a SERGE GAINSBOURG or BURT BACHARACH-type crooner in the project/duo, CINERAMA, alongside SALLY MURRELL, his sort of JANE BIRKIN, you could say. An album, 'VA VA VOOM', was a marked change of direction from the WEDDOES bust-a-gut blasts, into EDWYN COLLINS glutty vocals. CINERAMA completed their second batch, 'DISCO VOLANTE' (2000), while the romantic GEDGE and MURRELL returned all 'STARRY EYED' (one of the tracks incidentally) on 2002's 'TORINO'. • **Songwriters:** GEDGE compositions, except GETTING NOWHERE FAST (Girls At Our Best) / WHAT BECOME OF THE BROKEN HEARTED (Jimmy Ruffin) / I FOUND THAT ESSENCE RARE (Gang Of Four) / IT'S NOT UNUSUAL (Tom Jones) / FELICITY (Orange Juice) / MAKE ME SMILE (COME UP AND SEE ME) (Steve Harley & Cockney Rebel) / BOX ELDER (Pavement) / SHE'S MY BEST FRIEND (Velvet Underground) / MOTHERS (Jean Michel Satre) / CUMBERLAND GAP (Leadbelly) / CATTLE AND CANE (Go-Betweens) / DON'T CRY NO TEARS (Neil Young) / THINK THAT IT MIGHT (Altered Images) / FALLING (Julee Cruise) / PLEASANT VALLEY SUNDAY (Monkees) / LET'S MAKE SOME PLANS (Close Lobsters) / ROCKET (Mud) / THEME FROM SHAFT (Isaac Hayes) / CHANT OF THE EVER CIRCLING SKELETAL FAMILY (Bowie) / GO WILD IN THE COUNTRY (Bow Wow Wow) / U.F.O. (Barry Gray) / STEP INTO CHRISTMAS (Elton John) / JUMPER CLOWN (Marc Riley). CINERAMA covered: LONDON (Smiths) / ELENORE (Turtles) / YESTERDAY ONCE MORE (Carpenters) / DIAMONDS ARE FOREVER (John Barry). • **Trivia:** STEVE ALBINI (ex-BIG BLACK) produced their early 90s material.

Album rating: GEORGE BEST (*9) / TOMMY collection (*8) / UKRAINSKI VISTUPU V JOHNA PEELA (*5) / BIZARRO (*7) / SEAMONSTERS (*7) / THE HIT PARADE 1 compilation (*7) / THE HIT PARADE 2 compilation (*6) / WATUSI (*5) / MINI (*4) / SATURNALIA (*5) / Cinerama: VA VA VOOM (*6) / DISCO VOLANTE (*5) / THIS IS CINERAMA collection (*6) / JOHN PEEL SESSIONS collection (*5) / TORINO (*5) / CINERAMA HOLIDAY collection (*5)

WEDDING PRESENT (cont)

DAVID GEDGE (b.23 Apr'60) – vocals, guitar / **PETE SOLOWKA** (b. Manchester) – guitar / **KEITH GREGORY** (b. 2 Jan'63, County Durham) – bass / **SHAUN CHARMAN** (b.Brighton) – drums

		Reception	not iss.
May 85.	(7") (REC 001) **GO OUT AND GET 'EM BOY. / (THE MOMENT BEFORE) EVERYTHING'S SPOILED AGAIN** (re-iss. Sep85 on 'City Slang'; CSL 001)	☐	-
Feb 86.	(7") (REC 002) **ONCE MORE. / AT THE EDGE OF THE SEA**	☐	-
Apr 86.	(12"ep) (REC 002-12) **DON'T TRY AND STOP ME MOTHER** – Go out and get 'em boy / (The moment before) Everything's spoiled again / Once more / At the edge of the sea.	☐	-
Jul 86.	(7") (REC 003) **THIS BOY CAN'T WAIT. / YOU SHOULD ALWAYS KEEP IN TOUCH WITH YOUR FRIENDS** (ext.12"+=) (REC 003-12) – Living and learning.	☐	-
Feb 87.	(7",7"white/12") REC 005(/+12) **MY FAVOURITE DRESS. / EVERY MOTHER'S SON / NEVER SAID** (2,000 copies of above single were also given free with debut lp)	☐	-
Sep 87.	(7") (REC 006) **ANYONE CAN MAKE A MISTAKE. / ALL ABOUT EVE** (c-s+=/12"+=) (REC 006 C/12) – Getting nowhere fast.	☐	-
Oct 87.	(lp/c/cd) (LEEDS 001/+C/CD) **GEORGE BEST** – Everyone thinks he looks daft / What did your last servant die of? / Don't be so hard / A million miles / All this and more / Getting nowhere fast * / My favourite dress / Shatner / Something and nothing / It's what you want that matters / Give my love to Kevin / Anyone can make a mistake / You can't moan can you / All about Eve *. (c+=/cd+= * tracks) (<cd re-iss. Oct97 on 'Cooking Vinyl' 4x10"lp-box++/cd+=; COOK/+CD 134>) – Nobody's twisting your arm / Nothing comes easy / Don't laugh / I'm not always so stupid / Why are you being so reasonable now? / Not from where I'm standing / Give my love to Kevin / Getting better / Pourquoi es tu devenue si raisonnable?	47	-

— **SIMON SMITH** (b. 3 May'65, Lincolnshire) – drums repl. SHAUN to POPGUNS

Feb 88.	(7") (REC 009) **NOBODY'S TWISTING YOUR ARM. / I'M NOT ALWAYS SO STUPID** (12"+=/cd-s+=) (REC 009 12/CD) – Nothing comes easy / Don't laugh.	46	-
Jul 88.	(lp/c/cd) (LEEDS 002/+C/CD) **TOMMY** (compilation 4 singles + Peel sessions) – Go out and get 'em boy / (The moment before) Everything's spoiled again / Once more / At the edge of the sea / Living and learning / This boy can't wait / You should always keep in touch with your friends / Felicity / What becomes of the broken hearted? / Never said / Every mother's son / My favourite dress. (<cd-iss. Oct97 on 'Cooking Vinyl'; COOKCD 135>)	42	-
Sep 88.	(7") (REC 011) **WHY ARE YOU BEING SO REASONABLE NOW?. / NOT FROM WHERE I'M STANDING** (12"+=) (REC 011-12) – Give my love to Kevin (acoustic) / Getting better. (c-s++=/cd-s++=) (REC 011 C/CD) – Pourquoi es tu devenue si raisonable?. (s7") (REC 011F) – Pourquoi es tu devenue si raisonable?. / Give my love to Kevin (acoustic).	42	-

— added guest **LEN LIGGINS** – vocals, violin (ex-SINISTER CLEANERS, Solo artist) others played assortment of instruments in Ukrainian style.

		R.C.A.	R.C.A.
Apr 89.	(lp/c/cd) (PL/PK/PD 74104) **UKRAINSKI VISTUPI V JOHNA PEELA** (Ukrainian style John Peel sessions) – Davny chasy / Yikhav kozak za dunai / Tiutiunyk / Zadmav didochok svitit misyats / Katrusyai Vasya vasyl'ok / Hude dn ipro hude Verkhovyno. (was to have been issued as 10"m-lp, Nov88 on 'Reception'; REC 010) (cd re-iss. Sep00 as 'UKRAINIAN JOHN PEEL SESSIONS' on 'Fresh Air'; FRESHCD 100)	22	-

— reverted to usual 4-piece & style

Sep 89.	(7"/c-s) (PB/PK 43117) **KENNEDY. / UNFAITHFUL** (c-s+=/12"+=/cd-s+=) (PT/PK/PD 43118) – One day all this will all be yours / It's not unusual.	33	-
Oct 89.	(lp/c/cd) (PL/PK/PD 74302) <2173> **BIZARRO** – Brassneck / Crushed / No / Thanks / Kennedy / What have I said now / Granadaland / Bewitched / Take me / Be honest. (cd+=) – Brassneck (extended) / Box elder / Don't talk, just kiss / Gone. (cd re-mast.Aug01 on 'Camden'++=; 74321 86965-2) – One day this will all be yours / Unfaithful / It's not unusual.	22	☐
Feb 90.	(7"/c-s) (PB/PK 43403) **BRASSNECK. / DON'T TALK, JUST KISS** (c-s+=/12"+=/cd-s+=) (PK/PT/PD 43404) – Gone / Box elder.	24	-
Sep 90.	(7"ep/c-ep)(12"ep/cd-ep) (PB/PK 44021)(PT/PD 44022) **THE 3 SONGS EP** – Corduroy / Make me smile (come up and see me) / Crawl. (10"+=) (PJ 44022) – Take me (live).	25	-

		R.C.A.	First Warning
Apr 91.	(7") (PB 44495) **DALLIANCE. / NIAGARA** (c-s+=)(12"+=/cd-s+=) (PK 44495)(PT/PD 44496) – She's my best friend. (10"++=) (PJ 44495) – What have I said now? (live).	29	-
May 91.	(lp/c/cd) (PD/PK/PL 75012) <75708> **SEAMONSTERS** – Dalliance / Dare / Suck / Blonde / Rotterdam / Lovenest / Corduroy / Carolyn / Heather / Octopussy. (cd+=) – Niagara / Dan Dare / Fleshworld. (cd re-mast.Aug01 on 'Camden'++=; 74321 86966-2) – Make me smile (come up and see me) / She's my best friend.	13	☐
Jul 91.	(12"ep/cd-ep) (PT/PD 44750) **LOVENEST (edit) / MOTHERS. / DAN DARE / FLESHWORLD**	58	-

— **PAUL DORRINGTON** – guitar (ex-TSE TSE FLY, ex-AC TEMPLE) repl. SOLOWKA to UKRAINIANS

Jan 92.	(7") (PB 45185) **BLUE EYES. / CATTLE AND CANE**	26	-
Feb 92.	(7") (PB 45183) **GO-GO DANCER. / DON'T CRY NO TEARS**	20	-
Mar 92.	(7") (PB 45181) **THREE. / THINK THAT IT MIGHT**	14	-
Apr 92.	(7") (PB 45311) **SILVER SHORTS. / FALLING**	14	-
May 92.	(7") (PB 45313) **COME PLAY WITH ME. / PLEASANT VALLEY SUNDAY**	10	-
Jun 92.	(7") (PB 45313) **CALIFORNIA. / LET'S MAKE SOME PLANS**	16	-
Jun 92.	(cd/c/lp) (PD/PK/PL 75343) <75711> **THE HIT PARADE 1** (compilation of last 6 singles) (cd re-iss. Sep96 on 'Camden'; 74321 40073-2)	22	☐
Jul 92.	(7") (PB 10115) **FLYING SAUCER. / ROCKET**	22	-
Aug 92.	(7") (PB 10117) **BOING!. / THEME FROM SHAFT**	19	-
Sep 92.	(7") (PB 10116) **LOVESLAVE. / CHANT OF THE EVER CIRCLING SKELETAL FAMILY**	17	-
Oct 92.	(7") (PB 11691) **STICKY. / GO WILD IN THE COUNTRY**	17	-
Nov 92.	(7") (PB 11692) **THE QUEEN OF OUTER SPACE. / U.F.O.**	23	-
Dec 92.	(7"red) (PB 11693) **NO CHRISTMAS. / STEP INTO CHRISTMAS**	25	-

— The above 12 singles, were limited to 15,000 copies, and hit peak chart position on its first week of issue.

| Jan 93. | (cd/c/lp) (PD/PK/PL 74321) <75711> **THE HIT PARADE 2** – (all last 6 'A'&'B' singles above) (free lp w/lp+=) **BBC SESSIONS** – (all 12 of the years' A-sides). | 19 | - |

— **DARREN BELK** – guitar, bass; repl. GREGORY who later formed CHA CHA COHEN

		Island	Polygram
Sep 94.	(c-ep/12"ep/cd-ep) (CIS/12IS/CID 585) **YEAH YEAH YEAH YEAH YEAH / THE BIKINI / FLAME ON / HIM OR HER (WHAT'S IT GONNA BE)** (cd-ep) (CIDX 585) – ('A'side) / Gazebo / So long baby / Spangle.	51	-
Sep 94.	(cd/c/lp) (CID/ICT/ILPS 8014) <524044> **WATUSI** – So long, baby / Click click / Yeah yeah yeah yeah yeah / Let him have it / Gazebo / Shake it / Spangle / It's a gas / Swimming pools, movie stars / Big rat / Catwoman / Hot pants.	47	☐
Nov 94.	(c-s/7") (C+/IS 591) **IT'S A GAS. / BUBBLES** (12"purple+=/cd-s+=) (12IS/CID 591) – ('A'acoustic) / Jumper clown.	☐	-

— SMITH was another turn up in CHA CHA COHEN

		Cooking Vinyl	Cooking Vinyl
Jan 96.	(10"m-lp/m-cd) (<COOK/+CD 094>) **MINI** – Drive / Love machine / Go, man, go / Mercury / Convertible / Sports car. (cd+=) – Sucker / Waiting on the guns / Jet girl.	☐	☐

— line-up now **DAVID GEDGE** + **SIMON SMITH** plus newcomers **SIMON CLEAVE** – guitar (ex-TSE TSE FLY) / + guest on last mini-cd **JAYNE LOCKEY** – bass, vocals (ex-TSE TSE FLY)

Aug 96.	(7") (FRY 048) **2, 3, GO. / UP** (cd-s+=) (FRYCD 048) – Jet girl / Real thing.	67	-
Sep 96.	(2x10"lp/c/cd) (<COOK/+CD 099>) **SATURNALIA** – Venus / Real thing / Dreamworld / 2, 3, go / Snake eyes / Hula doll / Big boots / Montreal / Skin diving / Jet girl / Kansas / 50s.	36	☐
Jan 97.	(7") (FRY 063) <5053> **MONTREAL. / PROJECT CENZO** (7") (FRY 053X) – ('A'side) / Where everybody knows your name. (cd-s) (FRYCD 053) – ('A'side) / Sports car / My favourite dress (live) / Brassneck (live).	40	☐

— they officially split after above

– compilations, etc. –

Oct 86.	(12"ep) Strange Fruit; (SFPS 009) **THE PEEL SESSIONS** (26.2.86) – What becomes of the broken hearted / This boy can't wait / Felicity / You should always keep in touch with your friends. (c-ep iss.Jun87; SFPSC 009) (cd-ep iss.Aug88; SFPSC 009)	☐	-
Nov 88.	(12"ep/cd-ep) Nighttracks; (SFNT/+CD 016) **THE EVENING SHOW SESSIONS** (20.4.86) – Everyone thinks he looks daft / I found that essence rare / Shatner / My favourite dress.	☐	-
Oct 93.	(lp/cd) Strange Fruit; (SFR LP/CD 122) **JOHN PEEL SESSIONS 1987-1990** – Give my regards to Kevin / Getting nowhere fast / A million miles / Something and nothing / Take me I'm yours / Unfaithful / Why are you being so reasonable now? / Happy birthday / Dalliance / Heather Blonde / Niagara.	☐	-
Jun 97.	(cd) Strange Fruit; (<SFRSCD 029>) **THE EVENING SESSIONS 1986-1994**	☐	☐
Apr 98.	(cd) Cooking Vinyl; (<COOKCD 146>) **JOHN PEEL SESSIONS 1992-1995**	☐	☐
Sep 99.	(cd) Cooking Vinyl; (COOKCD 184) / SpinArt; <SPIN 78> **SINGLES 1995-1997**	☐	Oct99
Nov 99.	(4xcd-box) Cooking Vinyl; (COOKCD 117) / SpinArt; <SPIN 75> **REGISTRY** – (GEORGE BEST / TOMMY / MINI / SATURNALIA)	☐	☐

CINERAMA

DAVID LEWIS GEDGE – vocals, guitar / **SALLY MURRELL** – vocals, programming / with **DARE MASON** – guitar, theremin / **MARTY WILLSON-PIPER** – guitar (of The CHURCH) / **ANTHONY COOTE** – bass (of ANIMALS CAN SWIM) / **DAVEY RAY MOORE** – keyboards (of PUSHA) / **RICHARD MARKANGELO** + **CHE ALBRIGHTON** – drums, percussion / **JULIA PALMER** + **ABIGAIL TRUNDLE** – cello / **RACHEL DAVIES** – violin / **DUNCAN BRIDGEMAN** – flute / **THIBAULT DE MONTFORT** – oboe / **DEREK CRABTREE** – trumpet / **EMMA POLLOCK** – vocals (of DELGADOS)

		Cooking Vinyl	SpinArt
Jul 98.	(7") (FRY 072) **KERRY KERRY. / 7X** (7") (FRY 072X) – ('A'side) / Mr Kiss Kiss Bang Bang. (cd-s) (FRYCD 072) – ('A'side) / Love / Au pair.	71	-
Aug 98.	(lp/cd) (COOK/+CD 150) <68> **VA VA VOOM** – Maniac / Comedienne / Hate / Kerry Kerry / Barefoot in the park / You turn me on / Ears / Me next / Hard, fast and beautiful / Dance, girl, dance / Honey rider.	☐	Oct98
Oct 98.	(7") (FRY 077) **DANCE, GIRL, DANCE. / EARS (acoustic version)** (cd-s) (FRYCD 077) – ('A'side) / Crusoe / Model spy. (cd-s) (FRYCD 077X) – Pacific / King's Cross.	☐	-

		Elefant	not iss.
Aug 99.	(ltd-7") (ER 210) **PACIFIC. / KING'S CROSS**	☐	-

— **SIMON CLEAVE** – guitar (ex-TSE TSE FLY) was added to duo

— + added **TERRY DE CASTRO** – bass (ex-GOYA DRESS) / **SIMON PEARSON** – drums (ex-GOYA DRESS)

Feb 00. (cd-s) *(TONECD 001)* **MANHATTAN / LONDON / FILM**
Jun 00. (cd-s) *(TONECD 002)* **WOW / 10 DENIER / GIGOLO**
Aug 00. (cd-s) *(TONECD 003)* **LOLLOBRIGIDA / SEE THRU / SLY CURL**
Sep 00. (cd/lp) *(TONE CD/LP 004)* <42401> **DISCO VOLANTE** Oct00
– 146 degrees / Lollobrigida / Your charms / Heels / Unzip / Apres ski / Superman / Because I'm beautiful / Let's pretend / Wow (extended) / Your time startys here.
Nov 00. (cd-s) *(TONECD 005)* **YOUR CHARMS / REEL 2 DIALOGUE / GIRL ON A MOTORCYCLE**
Apr 01. (cd) *(TONECD 006)* <42402> **JOHN PEEL SESSIONS** (1998-2000)
– Comedienne / Maniac / You turn me on / Honey rider / Pacific / Dance, girl, dance (acoustic) / 146 degrees / Reel 2 dialogue 2 / Film / Elenore / Kerry Kerry (live) / Hard fast and beautiful (live).
Apr 01. (7"m) *(TONE 007)* **SUPERMAN. / SUPERMAN (Spanish version) / HARD FAST AND BEAUTIFUL (Spanish version)**
(cd-s) *(TONECD 007)* – ('A'side) / Starry eyed / Yesterday once more.

— session strings repl. PEARSON

Oct 01. (7"m) *(TONE 008)* **HEALTH AND EFFICIENCY. / HEALTH AND EFFICIENCY (French version) / LOLLOBRIGIDA (French version)**
(cd-s) *(TONECD 008)* – ('A'side) / Swim / Diamonds are forever.
Jun 02. (cd-s) *(TONECD 010)* **QUICK BEFORE IT MELTS / EARS (acoustic) / AS IF**
Jul 02. (cd) *(TONECD 011)* <42404> **TORINO**
– And when was she bad / Two girls / Estrella / Cat girl tights / Airborne / Quick, before it melts (extended) / Tie me up / Careless / Close up / Starry eyed / Get up and go / Get smart / Health and efficiency.
Aug 02. (cd-s) *(TONECD 012)* **CARELESS / THIS ISN'T WHAT IT LOOKS LIKE / SPARKLE LIPSTICK**
Sep 02. (cd) *(TONECD 013)* **CINERAMA HOLIDAY** (compilation)
– Wow / 10 denier / Gigolo / Lollobrigida / See thru / Sly curls / Your charms / Reel 2 dialogue 2 / Girl on a motorcycle / Superman / Starry eyed / Yesterday one more / Superman (Spanish version) / Dura rapida y hermosa.

– compilations, etc. –

Oct 00. (cd) *Cooking Vinyl; (COOKCD 180) / SpinArt; <SPIN 82>* **THIS IS CINERAMA**
– Kerry Kerry / Love / Au pair / 7x / Mr. kiss kiss bang bang / Dance, girl, dance / Model spy / Crusoe / Pacific / King's Cross / Manhattan / Film / London / Ears.

WEEDS (see under ⇒ STRAITJACKET FITS)

WEEKEND (see under ⇒ YOUNG MARBLE GIANTS)

Paul WELLER

Born: 25 May '58, Woking, Surrey, England. (see The JAM for further details). Formed STYLE COUNCIL in early '83 with former MERTON PARKAS keys player, MICK TALBOT, and talented young sticksman, STEVE WHITE. Though it was merely a matter of months since WELLER had folded The JAM, The STYLE COUNCIL followed a radical new direction, taking the agit-soul of CURTIS MAYFIELD as their inspiration and fashioning a very 80's hybrid of cocktail jazz, breezy pop and white funk. Scoring immediately with the Top 5 'SPEAK LIKE A CHILD', the group went Top 3 later that year with the 'LONG HOT SUMMER' EP, its sultry lead track arguably the best the group ever penned and the creative pinnacle of what they were trying to achieve. Previewing The STYLE COUNCIL's debut album, 'CAFE BLEU' (1984), the mellow atmospherics of 'MY EVER CHANGING MOODS' gave the group another huge hit in early '84. The album itself was a lush fusion of summery jazz and easy soul, the keening strum of 'YOU'RE THE BEST THING' making the Top 5. WELLER became increasingly political as the decade wore on, the rousing soul/funk of 'SHOUT TO THE TOP' and 'WALLS COME TUMBLING DOWN' an indication of the direction The JAM may have taken had they still been in existence. With the miners strike in full effect, politics were very much still an issue in rock/pop and WELLER and Co. released a benefit single, 'SOUL DEEP', at Christmas '84 under the COUNCIL COLLECTIVE banner. With production handled by HEAVEN 17's MARTYN WARE, the project included the likes of JIMMY RUFFIN, JUNIOR (GISCOMBE), VAUGHN TOULOUSE, DIZZY HEIGHTS and DEE C. LEE. The latter became not only WELLER's other half but a full-time backing singer for The STYLE COUNCIL, her sweet soul tones helping make 'OUR FAVOURITE SHOP' (1985) a mid-80's classic. The overall sound was more satisfying and the writing was sharper; 'COME TO MILTON KEYNES' was WELLER's most cutting slice of social commentary since The JAM heyday. Come 1986, The STYLE COUNCIL became heavily involved in the 'Red Wedge' movement alongside the likes of The COMMUNARDS and BILLY BRAGG, attempting to educate music fans into voting for the right party in the upcoming elections i.e. Labour. Such an openly party political stance was probably doomed to failure from the start, the attendant tour floundering and the Tories of course, predictably romping home. It was the last time WELLER would lay his beliefs on the line and the failure of the project seemed to lie at the heart of the lugubrious meanderings of the double set, 'THE COST OF LOVING' (1987). The following year's 'CONFESSIONS OF A POP GROUP' (1988) was similarly lacking in focus, its string arrangements and classical pretensions seeing The STYLE COUNCIL sinking in a mire of self-indulgence. The record failed to spawn any major hits and didn't even make the Top 10; when 'Polydor' refused to release a proposed fifth set, WELLER finally adjourned the 'COUNCIL and retired to re-evaluate his career. Now without a band or a recording deal, WELLER eventually regained his thirst for music via the low-key PAUL WELLER MOVEMENT, a band comprising STEVE WHITE, JACKO PEAKE, PAUL FRANCIS, MAX BEESLEY, DAMON BROWN, CHRIS LAWRENCE and DJ PAULO HEWITT along with backing singers DEE C.LEE, DR. ROBERT and CAMELLE HINDS. The subsequent early late 1990/early 1991 shows saw the singer once again armed with a guitar and suggested that he'd been reacquainting himself with his record collection, more specifically late 60's R&B and psychedelia. The 'MOVEMENT released a sole single, 'INTO TOMORROW' on the DIY 'Freedom High' label. It squeezed into the Top 40 nonetheless and WELLER eventually whittled down the bulk of the group for a more basic sound, signing with 'Go! Discs' and debuting with 'UH HUH OH YEH' in late summer '92. Hailed as the best thing he'd done in years, the single went into the Top 20 and the PAUL WELLER revival was up and running. The music press had given the singer a wide berth since the heyday of The STYLE COUNCIL and as the plaudits began to roll in for his eponymous debut album, were eventually forced to admit that, yes, WELLER was undergoing something of a creative rebirth. Matching the visceral, emotional punch of the music, the lyrics were of a decidedly more personal nature, eschewing politics for matters of the soul and the heart. With the ebullient 'SUNFLOWER' single and the attendant 'WILD WOOD' (1993) album, WELLER's star was most definately in the ascendant. Characterised by a crisp, uncluttered Brendan Lynch production, the record saw WELLER distill his influences into vintage singer/songwriter maturity. With his voice now sufficiently rough around the edges to complement such material, the likes of the resonating, meditative folkiness of the title track assumed a greater depth. The album reached No.2, featuring in many end of year polls (Mercury Prize), the chino wearing ghost of The STYLE COUNCIL now finally laid to rest. While the UK music press were still largely fixated on US grunge, WELLER was nothing if not instrumental in the upcoming Brit-pop debacle. Cited by the likes of OASIS as a guiding influence, the Modfather, as WELLER came to be known, was everything that the hordes of mop-topped chancers aspired to. It was a role that WELLER fitted into naturally, OCEAN COLOUR SCENE's STEVE CRADDOCK was already a regular musical collaborator, while NOEL GALLAGHER would guest on WELLER's forthcoming No.1 album, 'STANLEY ROAD'. Released in Spring '95 as Brit-pop was reaching its zenith, the album was earthier than anything WELLER had recorded in his career to date. Again produced by LYNCH, the record was previewed by the blistering single, 'THE CHANGINGMAN', its lyrics signalling an even more personal bent to WELLER's writing as the looking-good-for-30-something star even began appearing in the British style press. Elsewhere on the album, WELLER covered Dr. John's 'I WALK ON GILDED SPLINTERS' although it was the spirit of ERIC CLAPTON or NEIL YOUNG that most often came to mind. WELLER was at his most affecting on the ballads, the deeply felt 'YOU DO SOMETHING TO ME', the beautiful gospel-soul of album closer 'WINGS OF SPEED' and the brilliantly evocative hammond/wurlitzer musings of 'BROKEN STONES'. Of course, a backlash was inevitable, and certain sections of the music press derided WELLER's new material as tired 'Dad-rock', an incestuous Brit-pop conspiracy which continually looked to the past instead of breaking new ground. While this may have been true to a certain degree, and WELLER was partly responsible for the vexing success of the terminally workmanlike OCEAN COLOUR SCENE, the man was simply integrating retro influences into his muse as he'd done all the way through his career; it's the fact that these influences changed which seems to annoy some writers. Keeping his profile high with various festival appearances (as well as a predictable guest spot at OASIS' Knebworth show), WELLER (now signed to 'Island' following the demise of 'Go! Discs') eventually returned to the fray in summer '97 with the storming 'BRUSHED' single. Arguably standing among the best of WELLER's work to date, the track was propelled by a stone solid/funky as hell rhythmic thrust (courtesy of WHITE), combining mod, psychedelia and rock in a fashion that he's only previously hinted at. 'Raw' is probably the best word to describe it and the best word to describe the accompanying album, 'HEAVY SOUL' (1997), WELLER's voice as impressive as ever on a set which nevertheless too often relies on 'authentic' sound over songwriting. 1998, saw the release of two Top 30 singles, 'BRAND NEW DAY' and the 'WILD WOOD' remixes EP, mainly to complement the delivery of his best of package, 'MODERN CLASSICS – THE GREATEST HITS'. Come the new millennium the doggedly determined WELLER underwent yet another creative renaissance with the acclaimed 'HELIOCENTRIC' (2000). The record mightn't have struck a zeitgeist-style chord like 'STANLEY ROAD' but it confirmed his ever changing muse was still as fertile as ever. It was also one of the most PAUL WELLER-sounding albums he'd ever done, a rich, life affirming blend of soulful, occasionally psychedelic retro influences. That very richness was the key ingredient of 'DAYS OF SPEED' (2001), a document of WELLER's recent solo tour which – in its pared down acoustica (and included old JAM numbers!) – served to underline the sheer breadth and consistency of the man's songwriting. Just to note, PAUL was cleared of all rape charges in October 2000 (from four years previous) and stated at the time the unfairness of the anonymity law not protecting the innocently accused. On the music front once again, WELLER released his umpteenth solo set, 'ILLUMINATION' (No.1 in September 2002), a soulful and back to basics album that featured the Top 10 single, 'IT'S WRITTEN IN THE STARS'. • **Songwriters:** WELLER penned except for TALBOT's STYLE COUNCIL instrumentals. They also covered MOVE ON UP (Curtis Mayfield) / PROMISED LAND (Joe Smooth) / OHIO (Neil Young). WELLER solo:- FEELIN' ALRIGHT (Traffic) / SEXY SADIE

Paul WELLER (cont)

(Beatles) / I'M ONLY DREAMING (Small Faces) / I SHALL BE RELEASED (Bob Dylan).
Album rating: Style Council: CAFE BLEU (*5) / OUR FAVOURITE SHOP (*6) / HOME AND ABROAD – LIVE (*4) / THE COST OF LOVING (*5) / CONFESSIONS OF A POP GROUP (*3) / THE SINGULAR ADVENTURES OF THE STYLE COUNCIL compilation (*7) / HERE'S SOME THAT GOT AWAY collection (*4) / Paul Weller: PAUL WELLER (*6) / WILD WOOD (*9) / LIVE WOOD (*6) / STANLEY ROAD (*8) / HEAVY SOUL (*7) / MODERN CLASSICS – THE GREATEST HITS compilation (*8) / HELIOCENTRIC (*7) / DAYS OF SPEED (*6) / ILLUMINATION (*6)

STYLE COUNCIL

PAUL WELLER (b.25 May'58, Woking, Surrey, England) – vocals, guitar (ex-JAM) / **MICK TALBOT** (b.11 Sep'58) – keyboards (ex-MERTON PARKAS) / **STEVE WHITE** – drums / plus various guests.

		Polydor	Polydor
Mar 83.	(7") (TSC 1) **SPEAK LIKE A CHILD. / PARTY CHAMBERS**	4	
May 83.	(7") (TSC 2) **MONEY GO ROUND. / (part 2)**	11	
	(12") (TSCX 2) – ('A'side) / Headstart for happiness / Mick's up.		
Aug 83.	(7"ep/12"ep) (TSC/+X 3) **LONG HOT SUMMER / PARTY CHAMBERS. / PARIS MATCH / LE DEPART**	3	
Nov 83.	(7") (TSC 4) **SOLID BOND IN YOUR HEART. / IT JUST CAME TO PIECES IN MY HAND** / ('A'instrumental)	11	
Oct 83.	(m-lp) <815277> **INTRODUCING THE STYLE COUNCIL** – (above songs)	–	

		Polydor	Geffen
Feb 84.	(7") (TSC 5) <29359> **MY EVER CHANGING MOODS. / MICK'S COMPANY**	5	29
	(12"+=) (TSCX 5) – Spring, Summer, Autumn.		
Mar 84.	(lp/c/cd) (TSC LP/MC 1)(817535-2) <4029> **CAFE BLEU** <US-title 'MY EVER CHANGING MOODS'>	2	56
	– Mick's blessings / My ship came in / Blue cafe / The Paris match / My ever changing moods / Dropping bombs on the Whitehouse / A gospel / Strength of your nature / You're the best thing / Here's the one that got away / Headstart for happiness / Council meetin'. (cd+=) – The whole point of no return. (re-iss. cd Sep95; same)		
May 84.	(7") (TSC 6) <29248> **YOU'RE THE BEST THING. / BIG BOSS GROOVE**	5	76
	(12") (TSCX 6) – ('A'dub version).		
Oct 84.	(7") (TSC 7) **SHOUT TO THE TOP. / GHOSTS OF DACHAU**	7	–
	(12"+=) (TSCX 7) – Piccadilly trail / ('A'instrumental).		
Dec 84.	(7"; as COUNCIL COLLECTIVE) (MINE 1) **SOUL DEEP. / (part 2)**	24	–
	(12"+=) (MINEX 1) – ('A'version) / (striking miner's interview).		

(above single gave proceeds to miner's strike & the deceased miner David Wilkie's widow) The COLLECTIVE featured guests JIMMY RUFFIN, JUNIOR GISCOMBE, VAUGHN TOULOUSE, DEE C.LEE and DIZZY HEIGHTS. Production handled by MARTYN WARE (Heaven 17).

May 85.	(7"ep/12"ep) (TSC/+X 8) **WALLS COME TUMBLING DOWN. / THE WHOLE POINT II / BLOODSPORTS**	6	–
Jun 85.	(lp/c/cd) (TSC LP/MC 2)(825700-2) <24061> **OUR FAVOURITE SHOP** <US title 'INTERNATIONALISTS'>	1	
	– Homebreakers / All gone away / Come to Milton Keynes / Internationalists / A stone's throw away / The stand up comic's instructions / Boy who cried wolf / A man of great promise / Down in the Seine / The lodgers / Luck / With everything to lose / Our favourite shop / Walls come tumbling down. (cd+=) – Shout to the top. (c+=) – (interview). (cd re-iss. Aug90; same)		
Jun 85.	(7") (TSC 9) **COME TO MILTON KEYNES. / WHEN YOU CALL ME**	23	–
	(12"+=) (TSCG 9) – Our favourite shop / ('A'club) / The lodgers (club mix).		
Aug 85.	(7") <28941> **OUR FAVOURITE SHOP. / BOY WHO CRIED WOLF**	–	
Sep 85.	(7") (TSC 10) **THE LODGERS (remix). / YOU'RE THE BEST THING (live)**	13	–
	(d7"+=) (TSCDP 10) – Big boss groove (live) / Long hot summer (live).		
	(12"+=) (TSC?? 10) – Big boss groove (live) / Move on up (live).		
	(12"+=) (TSCX 10) – Medley: Money go round – Soul deep – Strength of your nature.		
Mar 86.	(7"ep/12"ep) (CINEX 1/12) **HAVE YOU EVER HAD IT BLUE. / MR. COOL'S DREAM**	14	
May 86.	(lp/c/cd) (TCS LP/MC 3)(829143-2) **HOME AND ABROAD – LIVE (live)**	8	–
	– The big boss groove * / My ever changing moods / The lodgers / Headstart for happiness / (When you) Call me / The whole point of no return / Our favourite shop * / With everything to lose / Homebreakers / Shout to the top / Walls come tumbling down / Internationalists. (cd+= *) (cd re-iss. Aug90; same)		
Jun 86.	(7") <28674> **INTERNATIONALISTS. / (WHEN YOU) CALL ME**	–	

		Polydor	Polydor
Jan 87.	(7"/12") (TSC/+X 12) **IT DIDN'T MATTER. / ALL YEAR ROUND**	9	
Feb 87.	(2x12"lp/c)(cd) (TSC LP/MC 4)(<831433-2>) **THE COST OF LOVING**	2	
	– It didn't matter / Right to go / Waiting / Walking the night / The cost of loving / Heaven's above / Fairy tales / Angel / A woman's song. (re-iss. Oct90)		
Mar 87.	(7") (TSC 13) **WAITING. / FRANCOISE**	52	
	(12"+=) (TSCX 13) – Theme from 'Jerusalem'.		
Oct 87.	(7") (TSC 14) **WANTED (FOR WAITER). / THE COST OF LOVING**	20	
	(12"+=/c-s+=) (TSC X/CS 14) – There's soup in my flies.		
	(cd-s++=) – The cost.		
May 88.	(7") (TSC 15) **LIFE AT A TOP PEOPLE'S HEALTH FARM. / SWEET LOVING WAYS**	28	
	(12"+=/cd-s+=) (TSC X/CD 15) – Spark (live) / ('A'version).		
Jun 88.	(lp/c/cd) (TSC LP/MC)(<835785-2>) **CONFESSIONS OF A POP GROUP**	15	
	– It's a very deep sea / The story of someone's shoe / Changing of the guard / The little boy in a castle / A dove flew down from the elephant / The gardener of Eden (a three piece suite):- In the beginning – The gardener of Eden – Mourning the passing of time / Life at a top people's health farm / Why I went missing / How she threw		

Jul 88.	(7"ep/12"ep) (TSC 16) **HOW SHE THREW IT ALL AWAY / IN LOVE FOR THE FIRST TIME. / LONG HOT SUMER / I DO LIKE TO BE B-SIDE THE A-SIDE**	41	
Feb 89.	(7") (TSC 17) **PROMISED LAND. / CAN YOU STILL LOVE ME**	27	
	(12") (TSCXS 17) – ('A'-Joe Smooth's alternate club) / ('B'club) / ('B'dub).		
	(cd-s) (TSCCD 17) – ('A'-Juan Atkins mix) / ('A'-Pianopella mix) / ('B'-dub).		
	(cd-s) (TSCD 17) – ('A'side) / ('A'extended) / ('B' vocal) / ('B'dub).		
	(7"box) (TSCB 17) – ('A'-Juan Atkins mix) / ('B'side).		
Mar 89.	(lp/c)(cd) (TSC TV/TC 1)(837896-2) **THE SINGULAR ADVENTURES OF THE STYLE COUNCIL** (compilation)	3	–
	– You're the best thing / Have you ever had it blue (extended) / Money go round (parts 1 & 2) / My ever changing moods (extended) / Long hot summer (extended) / The lodgers / Walls come tumbling down / Shout to the top / Wanted / It didn't matter / Speak like a child / A solid bond in your heart / Life at a top people's health farm / Promised land. (c+=/cd+=) – How she threw it all away / Waiting.		
May 89.	(7") (LHS 1) **LONG HOT SUMMER ('89 mix). / EVERYBODY'S ON THE RUN**	48	–
	(12"+=/cd-s+=) (LHS X/CD 1) – ('A'&'B' different mixes).		

—— Disbanded Mar'90. WELLER went solo, see below.

– compilations, etc. –

on 'Polydor' unless mentioned otherwise

Nov 87.	(cd-ep) (TSCCD 101) **CAFE BLEU**		–
	– Headstart for happiness / Here's one that got away / Blue cafe / Strength of your nature.		
Nov 87.	(cd-ep) (TSCCD 102) **BIRDS AND BEES**		–
	– Piccadilly trail / It just came to pieces in my hands / Spin drifting / Spring, Summer, Autumn.		
Nov 87.	(cd-ep) (TSCCD 103) **MICK TALBOT IS AGENT '88**		–
	– Mick's company / Mick's blessing / Mick's company.		
Jan 90.	(7") Old Gold; (OG 9924) **LONG HOT SUMMER. / SPEAK LIKE A CHILD**		
Jan 90.	(7") Old Gold; (OG 9929) **YOU'RE THE BEST THING. / MY EVER CHANGING MOODS**		
Jul 93.	(cd/c) (519 372-2/-4) **HERE'S SOME THAT GOT AWAY**	39	
Feb 96.	(cd/c) (529 483-2/-4) **THE STYLE COUNCIL COLLECTION**	60	
Aug 00.	(cd)(d-lp) (557900-2)(549134-1) **GREATEST HITS**	28	

PAUL WELLER

with **STEVE WHITE** – drums, percussion / **JACKO PEAKE** – sax, flute, b.vox / **DEE C.LEE, DR.ROBERT + CAMELLE HINDS** – b.vox

		Freedom High	London
May 91.	(7"/c-s; as PAUL WELLER MOVEMENT) (FHP/+C 1) **INTO TOMORROW. / HERE'S A NEW THING**	36	1992
	(12"+=/cd-s+=) (FHP T/CD 1) – That spiritual feeling / ('A'demo).		

		Go! Discs	London
Aug 92.	(7"/c-s) (GOD/+MC 86) **UH HUH OH YEH. / FLY ON THE WALL**	18	
	(12"+=/cd-s+=) (GOD X/CD 86) – Arrival time / Always there to fool you.		
Sep 92.	(cd/c/lp) (<828 343-2/-4/-1>) **PAUL WELLER**	8	Oct92
	– Uh huh oh yeh / I didn't mean to hurt you / Bull-rush / Round and round / Remember how we started / Above the clouds / Clues / Into tomorrow / Amongst butterflies / The strange museum / Bitterness rising / Kosmos. (re-iss. Apr94; same)		
Oct 92.	(7"/c-s) (GOD/+MC 91) **ABOVE THE CLOUDS. / EVERYTHING HAS A PRICE TO PAY**	47	
	(12"+=/cd-s+=) (GOD X/CD 91) – All year round (live) / Feelin' alright.		

—— now with **STEVE WHITE** – drums, percussion / **MARCO NELSON** – bass

		Go! Discs	Go! Discs
Jul 93.	(7"/c-s) (GOD/+MC 102) **SUNFLOWER. / BULL-RUSH – MAGIC BUS (live)**	16	
	(12"+=/cd-s+=) (GOD X/CD 102) – Kosmo's sxdub 2000 / That spiritual feeling (new mix).		
Aug 93.	(7"/c-s/10"/cd-s) (<GOD/+MC/T/CD 104>) **WILD WOOD. / ENDS OF THE EARTH**	14	
Sep 93.	(cd/c/lp) (<828 435-2/-4/-1>) **WILD WOOD**	2	Oct93
	– Sunflower / Can you heal us (holy man) / Wild wood – instrumental (pt.1) / All the pictures on the wall / Has my fire really gone out? / Country / 5th season / The weaver – instrumental (pt.2) / Foot of the mountain / Shadow of the Sun – Holy man (reprise) / Moon on your pyjamas. (re-iss. Apr94 +=; same) – Hung up.		
Nov 93.	(7"ep/c-ep/10"ep/cd-ep) (GOD/+MC/T/CD 107) **THE WEAVER EP**	18	–
	– The weaver / This is no time / Another new day / Ohio (live).		
Mar 94.	(7"ep/c-ep/12"ep/cd-ep) (GOD/+MC/X/CD 111) **HOME OF THE CLASSIC EP**	11	–
	– Hung up / Foot of the mountain (live from Albert Hall) / The loved / Kosmos (Lynch Mob bonus beats).		
Sep 94.	(cd/c/lp) (828 561-2/-4/-1) <00601> **LIVE WOOD (live)**	13	
	– Bull rush – Magic bus / This is no time / All the pictures on the wall / Remember how we started? / Dominoes / Above the clouds / Wild wood / Shadow of the Sun / (Can you hear us) Holy man – War / 5th season / Into tomorrow / Foot of the mountains / Sunflower / Has the fire really gone out?.		
Oct 94.	(7"ep/c-ep/12"ep/cd-ep) (GOD/+MC/X/CD 121) **OUT OF THE SINKING. / SUNFLOWER (Lynch Mob dub) / SEXY SADIE**	20	–

—— with **STEVE WHITE** – drums / **DR.ROBERT** – bass, vocals (ex-BLOW MONKEYS) / **STEVE CRADDOCK** – guitar / **MARK NELSON** – bass / **HELEN TURNER** – strings, organ / **BRENDAN LYNCH** – organ, co-producer / + guests **MICK TALBOT / CARLEEN ANDERSON / STEVE WINWOOD / NOEL GALLAGHER / YOLANDA CHARLES / CONSTANTINE WEIR**

Apr 95.	(12"ep/c-ep/cd-ep) (GOD X/MC/CD 127) **THE CHANGINGMAN / I'D RATHER GO BLIND / IT'S A NEW DAY, BABY / I DIDNT MEAN TO HURT YOU (live)**	7	

May 95. (cd/c/lp)(6x7"pack) (<828 619-2/-4/-1>)(850070-7) **STANLEY ROAD** | **1** | |
- The changingman / Porcelain gods / I walk on gilded splinters / You do something to me / Woodcutter's son / Time passes / Stanley Road / Broken stones / Out of the sinking / Pink on white walls / Whirlpool's end / Wings of speed.
Jul 95. (7"ep/c-ep/cd-ep) (GOD/+MC/CD 130) **YOU DO SOMETHING TO ME / A YEAR LATE. / MY WHOLE WORLD IS FALLING DOWN / WOODCUTTER'S SON** | **9** | - |
Sep 95. (7"/c-s) (GOD/+MC 132) **BROKEN STONES. / STEAM** | **20** | - |
(cd-s+=) (GODCD 132) – Whirlpool's end / Porcelain gods.

— WELLER was also part of one-off supergroup The SMOKIN' MOJO FILTERS alongside PAUL McCARTNEY and NOEL GALLAGHER. They had a Top 20 hit late '95 with 'COME TOGETHER'.

Feb 96. (7"ep/cd-ep) (GOD/+CD 143) **OUT OF THE SINKING EP** | **16** | - |
- Out of the sinking / I shall be released / Porcelain gods / Broken stones.
Aug 96. (7"/c-s/cd-s) (GOD/+MC/CD 149) **PEACOCK SUIT. / EYE OF THE STORM** | **5** | - |
                                            Island   Polygram
Jun 97. (cd/c/lp) (CID/ICT/ILPS 8058) <524277> **HEAVY SOUL** | **2** | Aug97 |
- Heavy soul / Peacock suit / Up in Suzie's room / Brushed / Driving nowhere / I should have been there to inspire you / Heavy soul (part 2) / Friday Street / Science / Golden sands / As you lean into the light / Mermaids.
Aug 97. (7"ep-cp/cd-ep) (CIS/CIS/CID 666) **BRUSHED EP** | **14** | - |
- Brushed / Ain't no love in the heart of the city / Shoot the dove / As you lean into the light.
Oct 97. (7"ep/c-ep/cd-ep) (CIS/IS/CID 676) **FRIDAY STREET EP** | **21** | - |
- Friday street / Sunflower (live) / Brushed (live) / Mermaids (live).
Nov 97. (c-s/cd-s/7") (CIS/CID/IS 683) **MERMAIDS. / EVERYTHING HAS A PRICE TO PAY ('97 version) / SO YOU WANT TO BE A DANCER** | **30** | - |
Nov 98. (c-s/7") (C+/IS 711) **BRAND NEW START. / RIGHT UNDERNEATH IT** | **16** | - |
(cd-s+=) (CID 711) – The riverbank (new version).
Nov 98. (cd/c/d-lp) (CID/ICT/ILPSD 8080) <524558> **MODERN CLASSICS – THE GREATEST HITS** (compilation) | **7** | - |
- Out of the sinking / Peacock suit / Sunflower / The weaver / Wild wood / Above the clouds / Uh huh oh yeh / Brushed / The changingman / Friday Street / You do something to me / Brand new start / Hung up / Mermaids / Broken stones / Into tomorrow. (lp-box; IBX 8080) (d-cd; CIDD 8080)
Dec 98. (7"ep/12"ep/cd-ep) (IS/12IS/CID 734) **WILD WOOD EP** | **22** | - |
- Wild wood (mixes; original / Portishead / Sience (Psychonauts).
Apr 00. (cd/c/lp) (CID/ICT/ILPS 8093) <542394> **HELIOCENTRIC** | **2** | May00 |
- He's the keeper / Frightened / Sweet pea, my sweet pea / A whale's tale / Back in the fire / Dust and rocks / There is no drinking after you're dead / With time and temperance / Picking up sticks / Love-less.
May 00. (12"/cd-s) (12IS/CID 760) **HE'S THE KEEPER. / HELIOCENTRIC / BANG-BANG** | | - |
Aug 00. (12"/cd-s) (12IS/CID 764) **SWEET PEA, MY SWEET PEA. / BACK IN THE FIRE (BBC session) / THERE IS NO DRINKING AFTER YOU'RE DEAD (noonday underground mix)** | **44** | - |
                            Independiente   Epic
Oct 01. (cd/d-lp) (ISOM 26 CD/LP) <80703> **DAYS OF SPEED** (live) | **3** | - |
- Brand new start / Loved / Out of the sinking / Clues / English rose / Above the clouds / You do something to me / Amongst butterflies / Science / Back in the fire / Down in the Seine / That's entertainment / Love-less / There's no drinking after you're dead / Everything has a price to pay / Wild wood / Headstart for happiness / A town called Malice. (cd re-iss. Aug02; same)

— in summer 2002, WELLER featured on NOONDAY UNDERGROUND's single, 'I'll Walk Right In'.

Sep 02. (10"m/cd-s) (ISOM 63 TE/MS) **IT'S WRITTEN IN THE STARS. / HORSESHOE DRAMA / PUSH BUTTON AUTOMATIC** | **7** | - |
(cd-s+=) (ISOM 63SMS) – ('A'side) / The butterfly collector / Carnation.
Sep 02. (cd/lp) (ISOM 33 CD/LP) <892000> **ILLUMINATION** | **1** | - |
- Going places / A bullet for everyone / Leafy mysteries / It's written in the stars / Who brings joy / Now the night is here / Spring (at last) / One x one / Bag man / All good books / Call me No.5 / Standing out in the universe / Illumination.
Nov 02. (cd-s) (ISOM 65S) **LEAFY MYSTERIES / TALISMAN / WILD WOOD** (live) | **23** | - |
(cd-s) (ISOM SMS) – ('A'side) / Broken stones (live) / Peacock suit (live).

Paul WESTERBERG (see under ⇒ REPLACEMENTS)

David WESTLAKE (see under ⇒ SERVANTS)

WE'VE GOT A FUZZBOX AND WE'RE GONNA USE IT

Formed: Balsall Heath, Birmingham, England ... 1985 by MAGGIE and JO DUNNE, TINA O'NEILL and VICKIE PERKS. A series of singles on the 'Vindaloo' label helped stamp the trademark FUZZBOX sound (although inspired by KLEENEX and DELTA 5) on the indie nation's consciousness; distorted guitars, frantic drums and girly chants made mini-classics of tracks such as 'XX SEX' and 'RULES AND REGULATIONS', occasional attacks of TONY BASIL-style vocal hiccuping thrown in for good measure. Following the Top 75 success of the 'ROCKIN' WITH RITA (HEAD TO TOE)' Various Artists VINDALOO SUMMER SPECIAL EP, the girls were launched into the heady world of major labeldom courtesy of 'WEA'. The fun-tastic 'LOVE IS THE SLUG' saw the band have a further brush with the charts while a debut album proper, 'BOSTIN' STEVE AUSTIN' (1987) was testament to girl power a full decade before The SPICE GIRLS were foisted upon an unsuspecting nation. By 1989 the group had cracked the Top 20 with the 'INTERNATIONAL RESCUE' single although the dayglo amateurism of old had given way to a cleaner sound and a more consumer-friendly image (they had taken to wearing 'Thunderbirds' clobber!). With their name now abbreviated to FUZZBOX, the gang released what was to be their final Top 5 album, 'BIG BANG!' (1989), many longtime fans lamenting the compromised sound on further hit singles such as 'PINK SUNSHINE' and 'SELF'. It came as little surprise, then, when, in summer 1990, PERKS departed for a solo career and the remaining trio elected to call it a day. • **Songwriters:** Group compositions except; SPIRIT IN THE SKY (Norman Greenbaum) / BOHEMIAN RHAPSODY (Queen) / WALKING ON THIN ICE (Yoko Ono) / TROUBLE (Elvis Presley).

Album rating: BOSTIN' STEVE AUSTIN (*6) / BIG BANG! (*5) / THE FUZZBOX STORY... compilation (*6)

VICKY PERKS (b.9 Oct'68) – vocals / **JO DUNNE** (b.11 Nov'68) – bass, guitar, drums / **MAGS DUNNE** (b. 5 Jun'64) – vocals, percussion / **TINA O'NEILL** (b.20 Jan'69) – sax, drums

                             Vindaloo   not iss.
Mar 86. (7"ep) (UGH 11) **...FUZZBOX... EP** | **41** | - |
- X x sex / Do I want to? / Rules and regulations / She.
(12"ep blue or lilac+=) (UGH 11T) – Aaarrrggghhh!!!.
Oct 86. (7"/7"pic-d) (UGH 14/+N) **LOVE IS THE SLUG. / JUSTINE / SPIRIT IN THE SKY** | **31** | - |
(12"+=/12"pic-d+=/c-s+=) (UGH 14 T/TN/C) – Radio fuzz / Console me.
                            Vindaloo-WEA   Geffen
Dec 86. (lp/c) (FBOX/+C 1) <24149> **BOSTIN' STEVE AUSTIN** | | |
- Love is the slug / Wait and see / Jackie / Spirit in the sky / XX sex / Alive / What's the point / You got me / Hollow girl / Console me / Rules and regulations / Pre-conceptions.
Jan 87. (7") (YZ 101) **WHAT'S THE POINT. / FUZZY RAMBLINGS FEVER** | **51** | - |
(12"+=) (YZ 101T) – Bohemian rhapsody.
Feb 87. (7") (YZ 347) **LOVE IS THE SLUG. / JUSTINE / CONSOLE ME** | | |
                            WEA   Geffen
Feb 89. (7") (YZ 347) **INTERNATIONAL RESCUE. / RAINING CHAMPAGNE** | **11** | - |
(12"+=) (YZ 347T) – Barbarella.
(cd-s++=) (YZ 347CD) – Love is the slug.
May 89. (7"/7"box/c-s) (YZ 401/+B/C) **PINK SUNSHINE. / WHAT'S THE POINT** | **14** | - |
(12"+=/cd-s+=) (YZ 401 T/CD) – ('A'extended) / Spirits in the sky.
Jul 89. (7"/c-s) (YZ 408/+C) <21327> **SELF! / WAIT AND SEE** | **24** | |
(12"+=/cd-s+=) (YZ 408 T/CD) – Bohemian rhapsody.
Aug 89. (lp/c)(cd) (WX 282/+C)(248066-2) <24185> **BIG BANG** | **5** | |
- Pink sunshine / Fast forward futurama / Jamaican sunrise / Walking on thin ice / Versatile for discos and parties / Do you know? / International rescue / Self! / Irish bride / Beauty.
Oct 89. (7"/c-s) (YZ 435/+C) **WALKING ON THIN ICE. / RULES AND REGULATIONS** | | - |
(12"+=/cd-s+=) (YZ 435 T/CD) – ('A'-Fuzz dub mix).
May 90. (7"/c-s) (YZ 486/+C) **YOUR LOSS MY GAIN. / PINK SUNSHINE** (acoustic) | | - |
(12"+=/cd-s+=) (YZ 486 T/CD) – ('A'version).

— disbanded in August '90. VICKY went solo and others were going to form another group, although this failed to materialise; MAGGIE DUNNE would join BABES IN TOYLAND post-millennium

FUZZBOX

— re-formed in late in 2001; **MAGGIE + JO**

                            Almafame   not iss.
Jan 02. (cd) Almafame; (ALMACD 14) **360 DEGREES** | | - |
(above release was probably shelved)

– compilations, etc. –

Nov 00. (cd) Yeaah; (YEAAH 34) **FUZZ AND NONSENSE** (demos, etc)
Feb 01. (d-cd) Cherry Red; (<CDMRED 179>) **THE FUZZBOX STORY: RULES AND REGULATIONS TO PINK SUNSHINE**
May 02. (cd) Cherry Red; (<CDMRED 213>) **THE BBC SESSIONS**

WILD ANGELS (see under ⇒ JAZZATEERS)

WILD FLOWERS

Formed: Wolverhampton, Midlands, England ... 1983 out of the ashes of ANOTHER DREAM by DAVE NEWTON, NEAL COOK and DAVE FISHER (DAVE ATHERTON and PETE WALDRON were also part of the band's first incarnation before MARK ALEXANDER replaced them). After a few early singles and an album, 'THE JOY OF IT ALL' (1984), their frontman NEWTON left to form The MIGHTY LEMON DROPS. With former member ATHERTON returning to the fold, the group signed through owners Craig Jennings and Jem Kemp to the Warwick based indie, 'Chapter 22' in 1985. With their US influenced trad rock sound, they found little favour in the UK indie scene, instead preferring to concentrate on breaking into the lucrative American market. A series of flop singles ensued before the release of a long awaited second set proper (1987's 'DUST' was a compilation), 'SOMEWHERE SOON' (1988). In the late 80's, they upped sticks and left for San Rafael and Burbank, California, the group being the first British act to sign for 'Slash', releasing 'TALES LIKE THESE' at the turn of the decade. However, although they had found a new drummer in SIMON ATKINS by this time, the WILD FLOWERS' recording career was clearly failing to blossom.

Opting for a more sympathethic American audience and evolving into a heavy-metal act, The WILD FLOWERS re-surfaced in '97 with a new US-only album, 'BACKWOODS', a 17-track affair that included a cover of ELO's 'Livin' Thing'.

Album rating: THE JOY OF IT ALL (*5) / DUST mini compilation (*5) / SOMETIME SOON (*6) / TALES LIKE THESE (*5) / BACKWOODS (*4)

NEAL COOK – vocals, guitar / **DAVE NEWTON** – guitar, vocals (ex-ACTIVE RESTRAINT) / **MARK ALEXANDER** – bass; repl. PETE WALDRON / **DAVE FISHER** – drums

		No Future	not iss.
Jan 84.	(7") *(FS 11)* **MELT LIKE ICE. /** Reflex		-
		Chapter 22	not iss.
Mar 84.	(7") *(RE 2)* **THINGS HAVE CHANGED (WHICH SHOULD HAVE STAYED THE SAME). / SECOND THOUGHT**		
Jun 84.	(lp) *(LEX 2)* **THE JOY OF IT ALL**		

—— **DAVE ATHERTON** – guitar, keyboards returned to repl. NEWTON who formed MIGHTY LEMON DROPS

		Chapter 22	not iss.
Apr 86.	(7"m) *(CHAP 5)* **IT AIN'T SO EASY. / JOSEPH SAID / AT THE CAVE OF MY HEART**		-
Sep 86.	(7") *(CHAP 8)* **A KIND OF KINGDOM. / WHERE MY HEART LIES** (12"+=) *(12CHAP 8)* – Lonesome road.		
Jun 87.	(7"promo) **NO SURPRISE. / DUST**	-	-
Aug 87.	(lp) *(CHAPLP 15)* **DUST** (compilation)		
Feb 88.	(7") *(CHAP 24)* **BROKEN CHAINS. / KEEP ON RUNNING** (12"+=) *(12CHAP 24)* – Something to mention / Glory.		
Apr 88.	(12"ep) *(12CHAP 29)* **TAKE ME FOR A RIDE / NO SURPRISE.** / ('A'version) / DAWN PARADE		
May 88.	(lp) *(CHAPLP 25)* **SOMETIME SOON**		

—— **SIMON ATKINS** – drums; repl. FISHER

		London	Slash
Apr 90.	(cd/c/lp) *(828 192-2/-4/-1) <26133-2/-4/-1>* **TALES LIKE THESE** – Shakedown / This feeling's gone / Put the blame on me / No holy spirits / Tales like these / Green hotel / Someone's stolen (my dreams) / Love like fire / Fever tree / Hopes crash down. *(cd+=)* – Can't get enough / Await.		

—— COOK, ATHERTON, ATKINS + bass player **BILL MORRIS**

—— relocated to the West Coast and still toured until …

		not iss.	Surf
Jul 97.	(cd) *<2401>* **BACKWOODS** – Sideshow / Silently told / Nowhere / Midnight / Good reason / Road to ruin / One step / What happens now / Tattoo / Fall down easy / Livin' thing / Mescalin / Count ten / Getting away / Kings of nowhere / Your barricades / Cheap perfume.	-	

WILD SWANS

Formed: Liverpool, England … 1981 by two former TEARDROP EXPLODES members PAUL SIMPSON and GERARD QUINN, alongside JEREMY KELLY (drummer ALAN WILLIS was soon added). Being the last act to sign for Bill Drummond's soon-to-be-wound-up 'Zoo' records, The WILD SWANS only managed to release one 12" single, 'A REVOLUTIONARY SPIRIT', although they managed to assume minor cult status in the process. Obviously influenced by the fresh noises emanating from across the Northern border (i.e. the 'Postcard' label), The WILD SWANS attempted to initiate a parallel "Sound Of Young Mersey" movement. However, by mid '82, the band's dream had fragmented into two separate entities; KELLY and QUINN formed The LOTUS EATERS along with singer PETER COYLE, while SIMPSON found The CARE with the help of local veteran IAN BROUDIE and crew. In the summer of '83, the former outfit scored a soaraway, sunkissed Top 20 hit with 'FIRST PICTURE OF YOU', although SIMPSON and Co. struggled with their debut, 'MY BOYISH DAYS (DRINK TO ME)'. While ironically, The CARE had a Top 50 entry ('FLAMING SWORD') with a follow-up, The LOTUS EATERS failed to build on their early success, a series of singles and even an album, 'NO SENSE OF SIN' (1984), falling wide of the chart mark. The belated release of a (May '82) WILD SWANS John Peel session was sufficient to swing public opinion in favour of a bonafide reformation. The WILD SWANS Mk.II consisted of SIMPSON, KELLY and new bass player, JOSEPH FEARON, the trio signing a prestigious deal with Seymour Stein's 'Sire' label. For most fans, 'BRINGING HOME THE ASHES' (1988) was worth the wait, an impressive set of songs regrettably rendered outdated by dint of their once heralded trademark sound. Now without KELLY but with a feast of Merseyside talent, including IAN BROUDIE, IAN McNABB and CHRIS SHARROCK, the duo of SIMPSON and FEARON completed a WILD SWAN-song in the shape of 1990's 'SPACE FLOWER' set. FEARON later re-emerged with an original WILD SWAN, ALAN WILLIS under the banner of TOP, a pop-tastic baggy combo who managed to deliver a handful of singles and an album, 'EMOTIONAL LOTION' (1991). The LOTUS EATERS (COYLE and KELLY) were back due to popular demand in 2001, the album 'SILENTSPACE', worth the lengthy wait.

Album rating: BRINGING HOME THE ASHES (*7) / SPACE FLOWER (*6) / Lotus Eaters: NO SENSE OF SIN (*6) / SILENTSPACE (*6) / THE FIRST PICTURE OF YOU collection (*6) / Care: DIAMONDS AND EMERALDS compilation (*6)

PAUL SIMPSON – vocals, keyboards (ex-TEARDROP EXPLODES) / **GERARD QUINN** – keyboards (ex-TEARDROP EXPLODES) / **JEREMY KELLY** – guitar (ex-SYSTEMS) / **ALAN WILLIS** – drums; guest **ALAN** – bass

		Zoo	not iss.
Jan 82.	(12") *(CAGE 009)* **A REVOLUTIONARY SPIRIT. / GOD FORBID**		-

—— guest **BAZ HUGHES** – bass; repl. ALAN (before they disbanded mid '82). ALAN WILLIS joined The ROOM and later PALE FOUNTAINS (then SHACK).

– compilation, etc. –

Nov 86.	(12"ep/c-ep) *Strange Fruit; (SFPS/+C 006)* **THE PEEL SESSIONS** (1.5.82) – No bleeding / Enchanted / Thirst.		-

LOTUS EATERS

GERARD QUINN – keyboards / **JEREMY KELLY** – guitar / **PETER COYLE** – vocals

		Sylvan-Arista	Arista
Jun 83.	(7",7"pic-d/12") *(SYL/+12 1)* **THE FIRST PICTURE OF YOU. / THE LOTUS EATER**	15	
Sep 83.	(7",7"pic-d/12") *(SYL/+12 2)* **YOU DON'T NEED SOMEONE NEW. / TWO VIRGINS TENDER**	53	
Mar 84.	(7",7"pic-d/12") *(SYL/+12 3)* **SET ME APART. / MY HAPPY DREAM**		
May 84.	(lp/c) *(206/406 263)* **NO SENSE OF SIN** – German girl / Love still flows / Can you keep a secret / Out on your own / Put your torch on love / Set me apart / You fill me with need / The first picture of you / Alone of all her sex / It hurts / You need someone new. *(cd-iss. Jul01 on 'Vinyl Japan'+=; ASKCD 131)* – Two virgins tender / My happy dream / Evidence / Endless / Soul in sparks / Church at Llanbadrig / The lotus eater / Out on your own (12" version).		
Jun 84.	(7") *(SYL 4)* **OUT ON YOUR OWN. / ENDLESS** (ext.12"+=) *(SYL12 4)* – Endless (instrumental).		
Feb 85.	(7") *(SYL 5)* **IT HURTS. / THE EVIDENCE** (12"+=) *(SYL12 5)* – It hurts – Prestissimo.		

—— disbanded in 1985, after record company dropped them. COYLE went solo. In Jan'89, their hit was re-issued by 'Old Gold' (OG 9853); b-side other artist.

CARE

PAUL SIMPSON – vocals, keyboards / **IAN BROUDIE** – vocals, guitar (ex-BIG IN JAPAN, ex-SECRETS) / augmented by **PAUL SANGSTER** – bass / **TONY WHELAN** – drums

		Arista	Arista
Jul 83.	(7") *(KBIRD 1)* **MY BOYISH DAYS (DRINK TO ME). / AN EVENING IN THE RAIN** (12"+=) *(KBIRD12 1)* – Sad day for England.		
Oct 83.	(7",7"pic-d) *(KBIRD 2)* **FLAMING SWORD. / MISERICORDE** (12"+=) *(KBIRD12 2)* – On the white cloud.	48	
Mar 84.	(7") *(KBIRD 3)* **WHATEVER POSSESSED YOU. / BESIDES** (12"+=) *(KBIRD12 3)* – Besides 2.		

—— disbanded later in '84, BROUDIE went into production and later formed The LIGHTNING SEEDS

– compilations, etc. –

Jun 97.	(cd) *Camden; (74321 50023-2)* **DIAMONDS & EMERALDS** – Diamonds and emeralds / An evening in the ray / Chandeliers / Flaming sword / Cymophane / Love crowns and crucifies / Temper temper / White cloud / Caretaking / My boyish days / Sad day for England / Soldiers and sailors / Whatever possessed you / Such is life / What kind of world / Nature prayed upon / Flaming sword / Misericorde / Besides 1 and 2.		-

WILD SWANS

—— were reformed by **SIMPSON + KELLY** plus **JOSEPH FEARON** – bass

		Sire	Sire
Mar 88.	(7") *(W 7973)* **YOUNG MANHOOD. / HOLY HOLY** (12"+=) *(W 7973T)* – The world of milk and blood.		
Apr 88.	(lp/c/cd) *(925 697-1/-4/-2)* **BRINGING HOME THE ASHES** – Young manhood / Bible dreams / Bitterness / Northern England / Arcangels / Whirlpool heart / Bringing home the ashes / The worst year of my life / Mythical beast / Nomad forever. *(re-dist.Sep88)*		
Aug 88.	(7") *(W 7765)* **BIBLE DREAMS. / 1982** (12"+=) *(W 7765T)* – Pure evil.		

—— **SIMPSON + FEARON** added **CHRIS SHARROCK** – guitars, organ (ex-ICICLE WORKS) / **IAN BROUDIE** – guitars, organ, producer (of LIGHTNING SEEDS) / **IAN McNABB** – guitars, vocals (ex-ICICLE WORKS)

Nov 90.	(cd/c/lp) *(26154-2-4/-1)* **SPACE FLOWER** – Melting blue delicious / Butterfly girl / Tangerine temple / Immaculate / Space flower / Chocolate bubblegum / I'm a lighthouse / Magic hotel / Vanilla melange / Sea of tranquility.		

—— disbanded again soon after above

LOTUS EATERS

were re-formed by **COYLE + KELLY**

		Vinyl Japan	Vinyl Japan
Aug 01.	(7"ep/cd-ep) *(PAD/TASK 072)* **STAY FREE EP** – Stay free / It hurts (acoustic) / Face of the century (acoustic) / Bodywave (acoustic).		-
Oct 01.	(cd/lp) *<ASK CD/LP 122>* **SILENTSPACE** – Bodywave / Feel it / Stay free / Can your kisses fly / Lost in flow / Sara / Face of the century / Minimal emotion / Stereo vision / Come together / State of mind.		
		Neurot	not iss.
Nov 02.	(cd) *(NEUROT 023CD)* **MIND CONTROL FOR INFANTS**		-

– compilations, etc. –

Mar 98.	(cd) *Vinyl Japan; (ASKCD 077)* **THE FIRST PICTURE OF YOU** – The first picture of you / German girl / Alone of all her sex / When you look at boys / Out on our own / Love still flows / You fill me with need / Stranger so far / Two virgins tender / Put your touch on love / Can you keep a secret / Start of the search / Signature tune.		-

Harvey WILLIAMS (see under ⇒ ANOTHER SUNNY DAY)

Marty WILLSON-PIPER (see under ⇒ CHURCH)

Phil WILSON (see under ⇒ JUNE BRIDES)

WIN (see under ⇒ FIRE ENGINES)

WINDBREAKERS

Formed: Mississippi, USA . . . 1981 by the songwriting duo of TIM LEE and BOBBY SUTLIFF. Another bunch of rootsy Power-poppers to ride out from the American deep south, the unfortunately monikered WINDBREAKERS released a couple of self-financed EP's before becoming one of the first indie acts to release an album for 'Homestead'. The record in question was 'TERMINAL'; issued in the summer of '85, one of its highlights was a collaborative cover of Television's 'GLORY' performed with Paisley underground posse, The RAIN PARADE. After a French-only LP for 'Closer', 1987 saw two albums of impressively varied melodic pop-rock, 'RUN' and 'A DIFFERENT SORT', the latter of which was recorded solely by TIM together with session players. However, the pair were back on song in 1989, releasing 'AT HOME WITH BOBBY & TIM', before finding drummer/producer MITCH EASTER for a final fling with the 'ELECTRIC LANDLADY' (1991).
• **Covered:** WALTZING MATILDA (Barber-Barber) / DON'T TAKE HER OUT OF MY WORLD (Katrina & The Waves) / THINGS WE NEVER SAY (Howard Wuefling) / SO YOU WANT TO BE A ROCK'N'ROLL STAR (Byrds) / HEY LITTLE CHILD (Alex Chilton).
Album rating: TERMINAL (*5) / RUN (*6) / A DIFFERENT SORT (*7) / AT HOME WITH BOBBY & TIM (*6) / ELECTRIC LANDLADY (*6)

BOBBY SUTLIFF – vocals, guitar / **TIM LEE** – vocals, guitar

			not iss.	Big Monkey
1983.	(7"ep)	**MEET THE WINDBREAKERS EP**	–	–
1983.	(7"ep)	**ANY MONKEY WITH A TYPEWRITER EP**	–	–

			Homestead	Homestead
Jun 85.	(lp) <(HMS 005)>	**TERMINAL**		

– On and on / Changeless / Stupid idea / A girl and her bible / Can't go on this way / All that stuff / New red shoes / Again / Glory / From a distance / Running out of time.

			Closer	not iss.
1985.	(lp) (CL 0029)	**DISCIPLES OF AGRICULTURE**	– French	–

– Rerun / Make a fool out of me / You never give up / I never thought / Ya gotta go away / I'll be there / New red shoes / That stupid idea / Again / All that stuff / Lonely beach.

			Zippo	D.B.
Jan 87.	(lp) (ZONG 015) <DB 79>	**RUN**		

– Don't wanna know / This time – She said / Visa cards and antique mirrors / Run / You don't know / Ghost town / I'll be back / Voices in my head / Braver on the telephone / Don't say no / Nation of two.

— next was virtually LEE on his own

Nov 87.	(lp) (ZONG 022) <DB 85>	**A DIFFERENT SORT**		

– Knowing me / Fit in / You closed your eyes / Better left unsaid / So far away / A different sort / So much / We never understand / Forget again / Any longer.

— re-united once more **BOBBY** + **RAPHAEL SEMMES** – bass / **MARK WYATT** – keyboards / **BRUCE GOLDEN** – percussion / etc

1989.	(d-lp,c,cd) <DB 95>	**AT HOME WITH BOBBY & TIM**	–	

– Just fine / I thought you knew / On the wire / Down to it / Ill at ease / Cold, cold rain / Our little war / Portrait of blue / Saw you again / Give me a reason / Closer to home / Off & on / Changeless / That stupid idea / A girl & her bible / Can't go on this way / All that stuff / New red shoes / Again / Glory / From a distance / Running out of time.

— **MITCH EASTER** – (now on) drums

1991.	(cd,c,lp) <DB 152>	**ELECTRIC LANDLADY**	–	

– Colorblind / Big ideas / Keep it on your mind / Elayne lies looking at the sky / Since I last saw you / Girl from Washington / The Devil and the sea / Wall / Do not be afraid / Tell me something / Forever ago / Waltzing Matilda / Rerun / Make a fool out of me / You never give up / I never thought / You gotta go away / I'll be there.

1991.	(12"ep)	**I'LL BE BACK EP**	–	

– I'll be back / Don't take her out of my world / Things we never say.

— disbanded after above

– compilations, etc. –

2002.	(cd) *Paisley Pop*; <080766>	**BOXING DAY (live)**	–	

– Changeless / New red shoes / I'll be back / I never thought / Glory / Stupid idea / What goes on / Bad sermonette / Hey little child / You never give up / Blue and gray / So you want to be a rock'n'star.

WISHING STONES

Formed: London, England . . . mid 80's by ex-LOFT conspirator, BILL PRINCE, who recruited SETH HODDER, KAREN O'KEEF and SERVANTS drummer, JOHN WILLS. Described as a fusion of EDWYN COLLINS and JULIAN COPE, The WISHING STONES began their vinyl career with a couple of 45's for 'Head', 'BEAT GIRL' and 'NEW WAYS', the latter produced by ex-RED CRAYOLA man, MAYO THOMPSON. For a third single, 'THE OLD ROAD OUT OF TOWN', BILL introduced Glaswegians, JOHN F. NIVEN, STUART 'THE BULL' GARDEN and ANDREW KERR, the record issued on the new indie 'Sub Aqua' imprint. A final single followed later in '88, the scheduled album, 'WILDWOOD', not actually appearing until late '91. Following on from The WISHING STONES sporadic career, BILL moved on to take up the post of production editor for 'Q' magazine.
Album rating: WILDWOOD (*5)

BILL PRINCE (b.19 Jul'62, Devon, England) – vocals, guitar (ex-LOFT) / **SETH HODDER** – guitar / **KAREN O'KEEF** – bass / **JOHN WILLS** – drums (of SERVANTS)

			Head	not iss.
Oct 86.	(7") (HEAD 2)	**BEAT GIRL. / TWO STEPS TAKE ME BACK**		–
Apr 87.	(7") (HEAD 6)	**NEW WAYS. / A HOME IS NOT A HOME**		–

(12"+=) (HEAD 6-12) – Wildwood / Holed up.

— **BILL** recruited **JOHN F. NIVEN** – guitar / **STUART 'THE BULL' GARDEN** – bass / **ANDREW KERR** – drums (WILLS joined LOOP)

			Sub Aqua	not iss.
Jun 88.	(7") (AQUA 001)	**THE OLD ROAD OUT OF TOWN. / OVER MY HEAD**		–

(12"+=) (AQUA 001-12) – Holler in the swamp / ('A'version).

Nov 88.	(12"m) (AQUA 005-12)	**DEAD MAN'S LOOK. / (I FEEL LIKE) NO ONE I'VE MET / THERE SHE GOES**		–

— an lp failed to materialise around this time, although it did later

			Heavenly	not iss.
Dec 91.	(lp) (HVNLP 004)	**WILDWOOD**		–

– Lost in the well / Wildwood / Long time coming / Spitchwick / Big black sky / Hanging tree / Too many mansions / Slow wheel's turn / Dying on the vine / The long road out of town / Dead man's look.

— BILL had already returned to music journalism (see above); KERR joined SPIREA X while NIVEN runs 'Southpaw' records (home to MOGWAI, etc); THE BULL works for 'Duty Free' records

WOLFGANG PRESS

Formed: London, England . . . 1980 as REMA REMA by MICK ALLEN, MARC COX, GARY ASQUITH and MARCO PIRRONI. Signing to Ivo's '4 a.d.' imprint, they issued a solitary EP before changing their name to MASS and releasing a further single, 'YOU AND I' and album, 'LABOUR OF LOVE' (1981). Subsequently opting for the more complex moniker, WOLFGANG PRESS, COX was by this time the sole survivor, injecting new blood in the shape of ANDREW GRAY and MICHAEL ALLEN. While the name The WOLFGANG PRESS may mean zero to many indie fans, no one could accuse the band of not paying their dues; boasting the longest track record of any '4 a.d.' outfit, this oddball trio have served more than a decade and a half with the label. During that time they've experimented with the whole gamut of popular music styles, beginning life as an angst-ridden avant-garde terrorist proposition with 'THE BURDEN OF MULES' (1983) album before going on to record a series of more adventurous EP's over the next two years, namely 'SCARECROW', 'WATER' and 'SWEATBOX'. A long awaited follow-up album, 'STANDING UP STRAIGHT', finally appeared in 1986, signalling to their growing fanbase that musical compromise wasn't on the agenda. Yet following tentative steps towards a more soulful, CAN meets ROXY MUSIC sound on 'BIRD WOOD CAGE' (1988) – which contained their classic homage to Kennedy & Onassis, 'KANSAS' – The WOLFGANG PRESS embraced the possibilities of the dance scene with 1991's acclaimed 'QUEER' album. Released at the height of indie-dance crossover mania, the album (which featured a cover of Randy Newman's 'MAMA TOLD ME NOT TO COME') nevertheless remained aloof from the pack, ALLEN's semi-detached vocals lending an almost PET SHOP BOYS feel to tracks like 'DARK SIDE OF THE MOON'-sampling 'TIME'. Apparently inspired by hearing DE LA SOUL's classic 'Three Feet High And Rising', the band's move towards a more groovy sound was confirmed with 1995's 'FUNKY LITTLE DEMONS'.
• **Trivia:** ELIZABETH FRASER of The COCTEAU TWINS and MARTIN McCARRICK of MARC ALMOND's WILLING SINNERS guested on the album 'STANDING UP STRAIGHT'.
Album rating: THE LEGENDARY WOLFGANG PRESS . . . (*6) / BIRD WOOD CAGE (*7) / QUEER (*6) / FUNKY LITTLE DEMONS (*6) / EVERYTHING IS BEAUTIFUL compilation (*6)

REMA REMA

MICK ALLEN – vocals, bass (ex-MODELS) / **MARK COX** – keyboards / **GARY ASQUITH** – guitar, vocals / **MARCO PIRRONI** – guitar, vocals (ex-MODELS) / **MAX** (aka DOROTHY) – drums (ex-B-SIDES)

			4 a.d.	not iss.
Apr 80.	(12"ep) (BAD 5)	**WHEEL IN THE ROSES**		–

– Feedback song / Rema Rema / Fond affections / Instrumental.

— Had already disbanded Autumn 1979. MARCO joined ADAM & THE ANTS, etc. MAX reverted to real name DOROTHY, and became a solo artist.

MASS

were formed by **MICK, MARK + GARY** / + **DANNY BRIOTTET** – drums

			4 a.d.	not iss.
Nov 80.	(7") (AD 14)	**YOU AND I. / CABBAGE**		–
May 81.	(lp) (CAD 107)	**LABOUR OF LOVE**		–

— broke-up after GARY and DANNY left to later become RENEGADE SOUNDWAVE

WOLFGANG PRESS

were formed by **MICK + MARK / ANDREW GRAY** – guitar

		4 a.d.	not iss.
Jul 83.	(lp) *(CAD 308)* **THE BURDEN OF MULES**	☐	-

– Lisa (the passion) / Prostitute I / The burden of mules / Complete and utter / Prostitute II / Slow as a child / Journalists / Give it back / On the hill.

Aug 84.	(12"ep) *(BAD 409)* **SCARECROW**	☐	-

– Ecstasy / Deserve / Respect.

Mar 85.	(12"ep) *(BAD 502)* **WATER**	☐	-

– Tremble (my girl doesn't) / My way / The deep Briny / Fire eater.

Aug 85.	(12"ep) *(BAD 506)* **SWEATBOX/ MUTED./ HEART OF STONE/ I'M COMING HOME (MAMA)**	☐	-
Nov 85.	(lp) *(CAD 514)* **THE LEGENDARY WOLFGANG PRESS AND OTHER TALL STORIES**	☐	-

– Ecstasy / Deserve / Tremble (my girl doesn't) / My way / Fire eater / Sweatbox / Heart of stone / I'm coming home (mama). *(cd-iss. Feb87 +=; CAD 514CD)* – THE BURDEN OF MULES (tracks +) / The deep Briny / Muted. *(cd re-iss. Jul98; GAD 514CD)*

added guests **MARTIN McCARRICK** – cello / **ELIZABETH FRASER** – vocals

Jul 86.	(lp) *(CAD 606)* **STANDING UP STRAIGHT**	☐	-

– My life / Hammer the halo / I am the crime / Rotten fodder / Dig a hole / Bless my brother / Fire-fly / Forty days, thirty nights. *(cd-iss. Feb87; CAD 606CD) (cd re-iss. Jul98; GAD 606CD)*

Apr 87.	(7"ep/c-ep) *(BAD/+C 702)* **BIG SEX / THE WEDDING. / THE GREAT LEVELLER / THAT HEAT / GOD'S NUMBER**	☐	-
Aug 88.	(12"ep/cd-ep) *(BAD 804/+CD)* **KING OF SOUL (crowded mix). / KOS (version) / KOS (7"mix)**	☐	-
Nov 88.	(lp/c)(cd) *(CAD/+C 810)(CAD 810CD)* **BIRD WOOD CAGE**	☐	-

– King of soul / Raintime / Bottom drawer / Kansas / Swing like a baby / See my wife / The holy man / Hang on me / Shut that door. *(cd+=)* – BIG SEX EP. *(cd re-iss. Jul98; GAD 810CD)*

Jan 89.	(7"ep/12"ep) *(BAD/+12 902)* **ASSASSINATION K – KANSEROUS / KANSAS. / SCRATCH / TWISTER**	☐	-
May 89.	(12"ep) *(BAD 907)* **RAINTIME (remix). / BOTTOM DRAWER (remix)/ SLOWTIME**	☐	-

(cd-ep+=) (BAD 907CD) – Longtime ('A'version) / Assassination K – Kanserous.

Apr 91.	(12"ep/cd-ep) *(BAD 1003/+CD)* **TIME. / TIMELESS / DARK TIME**	☐	-
May 91.	(7") *(AD 1007)* **MAMA TOLD ME NOT TO COME. / ('A'version)**	☐	-

(12"/cd-s) (BAD 1007/+CD) – ('A'club mixes; Bad Boy / Inside Out).

Aug 91.	(cd)(lp/c) *(CAD 1011CD)(CAD/+C 1011)* **QUEER**	☐	-

– Birmingham / Mama told me not to come / Heaven's gate / Riders on the heart / Question of time / Louis XIV / Fakes and liars / Honey tree / The birdy song / Dreams and light / Sucker – Mother Valentine – Sucker / Mamen. *(cd re-iss. Jul98; GAD 1011CD)*

May 92.	(7") *(AD 2006)* **A GIRL LIKE YOU. / ANGEL**	☐	-

(12"+=/cd-s+=) (BAD 2006/+CD) – ('A'-1000 times mix) / ('A'-Born to be kissed mix).

Jan 95.	(7") *(AD 5001)* **GOING SOUTH. / GOING SOUTH (country style)**	☐	-

(cd-s+=) (BAD 5001CD) – Going south (440 mix) / Chains (Wobble mix). *(12") (BAD 5001)* – Going south (440 mix) / 11 years (Sabres main mix 2) / Christianity (Sherwood mix).

Jan 95.	(cd)(lp/c) *(CAD 4016CD)(CAD/+C 4016)* **FUNKY LITTLE DEMONS**	75	-

– Going south / 11 years / Blood satisfaction / Chains / Christianity / Derek the confessor / So long dead / Executioner / She's so soft / New glass / Fallen not broken / People say. *(cd w/ free cd)* – (remixes by BARRY ADAMSON, ADRIAN SHERWOOD, MICHAEL BROOK & SABRES OF PARADISE). *(cd re-iss. Jul98; GAD 4016CD)*

disbanded in 1995

– compilations, etc. –

Oct 01.	(cd) *4 a.d.; (GAD 2104CD) <72104>* **EVERYTHING IS BEAUTIFUL**	☐	☐

– Birdie song / Dreams and light / Going south / Sweatbox / Chains / Heavens gate / Kansas (Flood mix) / Honey tree / Sucker / Executioner (Adamson mix) / Slowtime / A girl like you / Respect / Mama told me not to come / Shut that door / I am the crime / People say (live).

WOLFHOUNDS

Formed: Romford, Essex, England ... 1985 out of The CHANGELINGS by DAVID CALLAHAN, PAUL CLARK, ANDY GOLDING, ANDY BOLTON and FRANK STEBBING. Initially signed to the 'Pink' label, The WOLFHOUNDS made an immediate impact with the 'CUT THE CAKE' EP in 1986. It's impressive diversity was enough to secure the band a slot on the famed NME C86 compilation which they filled with the infectious, upbeat archetypal guitar-pop of 'FEELING SO STRANGE AGAIN'. A series of singles, 'THE ANTI-MIDAS TOUCH', 'CRUELTY' and 'ME', ushered in a mediocre debut album, 'UNSEEN RIPPLES FROM A PEBBLE' (1987), while the subsequent replacement of BOLTON and CLARK – with DAVID OLIVER and MATTHEW DEIGHTON respectively – coincided with a move to a denser sound. Previewed on the singles, 'SON OF NOTHING', 'RENT ACT' and anti-consumerist diatribe, 'HAPPY SHOPPER', the new approach was fleshed out on 'BRIGHT AND GUILTY' (1989), a well received album at times vaguely akin to a more listenable WEDDING PRESENT. Later that year, with their melodic instincts still intact, the band went for broke on mini-set, 'BLOWN AWAY', turning up the distortion and giving vent to their noisier impulses. Not exactly in step with the mood of the times, the trio (DAVE, ANDY and FRANK) bowed out on a low point with 'ATTITUDE' (1990), CALLAHAN relocating to New York where he formed MOONSHAKE (with MARGARET FIEDLER) while GOLDING and STEBBING worked together in CRAWL. MOONSHAKE signed to 'Creation' in 1991 before surfacing on 'Too Pure' records, where they eventually debuted with an album, 'EVA LUNA', a free-form avant-garde jazz odyssey akin to a wailing GALLON DRUNK fused with The POP GROUP or The FALL.

Album rating: UNSEEN RIPPLES FROM A PEBBLE (*6) / THE ESSENTIAL WOLFHOUNDS (*6) / BRIGHT & GUILTY (*8) / BLOWN AWAY mini (*7) / LOST BUT HAPPY compilation (*7) / Moonshake: EVA LUNA (*6) / BIG GOOD ANGEL mini (*6) / THE SOUND YOUR EYES SHOULD FOLLOW (*5) / DIRTY AND DIVINE (*7)

DAVE CALLAHAN – vocals / **PAUL CLARK** – guitar / **ANDY GOLDING** – guitar / **ANDY BOLTON** – bass / **FRANK STEBBING** – drums

		Pink	not iss.
Mar 86.	(12"ep) *(PINKY 8)* **CUT THE CAKE / L.A. JUICE. / DEADTHINK / ANOTHER LAZY DAY ON THE LAZY 'A'**	☐	-
Sep 86.	(7") *(PINKY 14)* **THE ANTI-MIDAS TOUCH. / RESTLESS SPELL**	☐	-

(12"+=) (PINKY 14T) – Midget horror / One foot wrong / Slow lokis.

Apr 87.	(7") *(PINKY 18)* **CRUELTY. / I SEE YOU**	☐	-

(12"+=) (PINKY 18T) – Whale on the beach.

May 87.	(lp) *(PINKY 19)* **UNSEEN RIPPLES FROM A PEBBLE**	☐	-

– Me / Sandy / Rain stops play / Goodbye laughter / Lost but happy / The anti-midas touch / In transit / Cruelty / Rule of thumb / Progress caff / Public footpath blues / Handy Howard.

		Idea	not iss.
Nov 87.	(7")/c-s) *(IDEA/ISEAC/ 10)* **ME. / DISGUSTED**	☐	-

(12"+=) (IDEAT 10) – Hand in the till / Cold shoulder.

now without BOLTON

		September	not iss.
May 88.	(12"ep) *(SEPT 07T)* **SON OF NOTHING / COTTONMOUTH. / SECOND SON / TORTURE**	☐	-
		Midnight	not iss.
Nov 88.	(lp)(cd) *(CHIME 0032S)(COLIN 1CD)* **THE ESSENTIAL WOLFHOUNDS** (compilation)	☐	-

– L.A. juice / Rain stops play / The anti-midas touch / Stars in the tarmac / Rule of thumb / Slow Loris / Another hazy day on the lazy "A" / Me / Cruelty / Cut the cake / Sandy / Restless spell. *(cd-iss. 1990 +=; CHIME 00.38CD)* – In transit / Goodbye laughter / Handy Howard.

DAVID OLIVER – bass; repl. CLARK

Nov 88.	(12"ep) *(DONG 043)* **RENT ACT. / EVERYBODY / DIED THE SMALL DEATH / RECYCLE**	☐	-

added **MATTHEW DEIGHTON** – guitar

Feb 89.	(lp/c/cd) *(CHIME 048/+C/CD)* **BRIGHT & GUILTY**	☐	-

– Non-specific song / Charterhouse / Happy shopper / Useless second cousin / Ex-cable street / Tomorrow attacking / Son of nothing / Ropeswing / Rent act / Invisible people / A mess of paradise. *(cd+=)* – Cottonmouth / Second son / Torture / No soap in a dirty war / Red tape, red light / Natural disasters.

Mar 89.	(one-sided-7") *(DING 046)* **HAPPY SHOPPER**	☐	-

(12"+=) (DONG 046) – No soap in a dirty war / REd tape red light / Natural disasters.

now without DEIGHTON

Oct 89.	(m-lp/m-c/m-cd) *(CHIME 057 F/C/CD)* **BLOWN AWAY**	☐	-

– Rite of passage / Tropic of Cancer / Living fossil / Dead sea burning / Blown away / Skyscrapers / Personal.

now without OLIVER

May 90.	(lp/c/cd) *(CHIME 1.07/+CC/CD)* **ATTITUDE**	☐	-

– Gutter charity / Vertical grave / Blue nowhere / Side effects / Celeste / Magic triggers / Feeding frenzy / Abstract hopeful / Hall of mirrors / Disinformation. *(cd+=)* – Guitarchitecture / Everybody's traveling / Free speech impediment.

split at the start of '90. A year later GOLDING and STEBBING formed CRAWL, while CALLAHAN formed MOONSHAKE

– (WOLFHOUNDS) compilations, etc

Apr 96.	(cd) *Cherry Red; (CDMRED 126)* **LOST BUT HAPPY** (1986-1990)	☐	-

– Lost but happy / L.A. juice / Another hazy day on the lazy "A" / Anti-midas touch / Restless spell / Son of nothing / Torture / Happy shopper / Rent act / Non-specific song / Rite of passage / Tropic of Cancer / Dead sea burning / Blown away / Gutter charity / Vertical grave / Magic triggers.

MOONSHAKE

DAVE CALLAHAN – vocals, guitar / **MARGARET FIEDLER** (b. New York) – vocals, guitar (ex-ULTRA VIVID SCENE) / **JOHN FRENNETT** – bass / **MIG** – drums

		Creation	not iss.
May 91.	(12"ep)(cd-ep) *(CRE 101T)(CRESCD 101)* **FIRST EP**	☐	-

– Gravity / Coward / Coming / Hanging / Coward.

		Too Pure	Matador – Atlantic
Apr 92.	(12"ep/cd-ep) *(PURE 9 T/CD)* **SECOND HAND CLOTHES. / BLISTER / DROP IN THE OCEAN**	☐	-
Oct 92.	(12"ep/cd-ep) *(PURE 13 T/CD)* **BEAUTIFUL PIGEON. / BEESIDE / HOME SURVIVAL KIT**	☐	-
Oct 92.	(lp/cd) *(PURE 16/+CD) <OLE 056 – 92274>* **EVA LUNA**	☐	Jul93

– City poison / Sweetheart / Spaceship earth / Beautiful pigeon / Mugshot heroine / Wanderlust / Tar baby / Seen and not heard / Bleach and salt water / Little thing / Secondhand clothes / Blister / Drop in the ocean.

May 93.	(m-cd) *(PURE 22CD) <OLE 092>* **BIG GOOD ANGEL**	☐	Jun94

– Two trains / Capital letters / Girly loop / Seance / Flow / Helping hands.

now without MARGARET + JOHN who formed LAIKA

she was replaced by **RAYMOND M. DICKATY** – saxophones, clarinet, flute / guests; **JOHNNY DAWE** – bass (of COLLAPSED LUNG) / **KATHARINE DIFFORD** – vocals (of DUOPHONIC ULTRA HIGH FREQUENCY DISCS) / **POLLY HARVEY** – vocals / **ANDREW BLICK** – trumpet

WOLFHOUNDS (cont)

May 94. (lp/cd) (*PURE/+CD 33*) <*43014*> **THE SOUND YOUR EYES CAN FOLLOW** [Too Pure] [American]
– Joker John / Your last friend in this town / Just a working girl / The sound your eyes can follow / Ghosts of good intention / We're making war / Shadows of tall buildings / Right to fly / The grind / Into deep neutral.

—— **CALLAHAN + DICKATY** hired **MARY HANSEN + KATHERINE GIFFORD** – vocals (of & ex-STEREOLAB) / guest **MICHAEL ROTHER** – drums (ex-NEU!)

Aug 96. (cd-ep) <*CZ 083*> **CRANES / GAMBLER'S BLUES / NIGHTTRIPPER II** [World Domination] [C/Z]
Oct 96. (cd) (*WDOM 028CD*) <*C/Z 085*> **DIRTY AND DIVINE** May96
– Exotic siren song / Cranes / Up for anything / Gambler's blues / Nothing but time / Aqualisa / Hard candy / House on fire / Taboo.

—— disbanded in 1997; DAVE worked with STEREOLAB ... 2000 ...

WONDER STUFF

Formed: Stourbridge, Midlands, England ... early 1986 by ex-EDEN drummer turned frontman, MILES HUNT, together with MALCOLM TREECE, THE BASS THING and MARTIN GILKS. After a couple of EP's on their own 'Farout' label, the group signed to 'Polydor' in late '87, initially lumped in with contemporaries like POP WILL EAT ITSELF and CRAZYHEAD under the music press-created 'grebo' banner. It soon became clear, however, that The WONDER STUFF were a unique proposition in their own right, as evidenced on the debut album, 'THE EIGHT LEGGED GROOVE MACHINE' (1988), a diverse collection of sparkling, hard-edged indie pop. HUNT was as bitingly uncompromising in his lyrics as he was in his relations with the media, the sardonic singer ever reliable for a controversial comment. While 'A WISH AWAY' narrowly missed the Top 40, another single, the wry 'IT'S YER MONEY I'M AFTER BABY', just nosed its way into the chart, the track backed by the self-explanatory 'ASTLEY IN THE NOOSE'. 'WHO WANTS TO BE THE DISCO KING?' asked HUNT in his inimitable bad attitude style, taking the WONDER STUFF into the Top 30 for the first time in early '89. A comparatively sensitive side was glimpsed on the jaunty 'DON'T LET ME DOWN' later that year, a Top 20 hit and a taster for the follow-up album, 'HUP' (1989). With the addition of JAMES TAYLOR on organ and MARTIN BELL on banjo/mandolin (no, not THAT JAMES TAYLOR and not THAT MARTIN BELL!), the record combined their high-octane pop/rock with a loose folky feel. It also marked their first major success, reaching the Top 5 and establishing the group as a headlining act. The success brought internal tensions to a head, however, with THE BASS THING (aka ROB JONES) departing for New York where he later formed 8-piece outfit The BRIDGE AND THE TUNNEL CREW (JONES subsequently died from heart problems in 1993). With PAUL CLIFFORD coming in as a replacement, the group entered the most high profile period of their career. Following on from the Top 20 success of the groovy 'CIRCLESQUARE' single, The WONDER STUFF scored a massive hit with the insanely catchy and ultimately annoying 'SIZE OF A COW'. A third set, 'NEVER LOVED ELVIS' (1991), made the Top 3 later that summer, a more mature set which nevertheless lacked the raw charm of old. A marriage made in heaven/hell (delete according to taste), The WONDER STUFF teamed up with comedic loonies VIC REEVES & BOB MORTIMER for a cover of TOMMY ROE's 'DIZZY', giving the group their one and only No.1 single later that year. With the help of rootsy chanteuse KIRSTY MacCOLL, the 'WELCOME TO THE CHEAP SEATS' EP (1992) contined the band's folk/indie hybrid, as did the group's final album, 'CONSTRUCTION FOR THE MODERN IDIOT' (1993). Increasingly disillusioned by their failure to break the American market and the direction of the British music scene, The WONDER STUFF finally signed off with the surprisingly ebullient 'HOT LOVE NOW! EP' (1994) and a farewell performance at the 1994 Phoenix festival. While HUNT went on to work as a presenter for MTV before forming VENT 414, the other members subsequently founded the group WEKNOWWHEREYOULIVE. Towards the end of the millennium, MILES HUNT was back in solo form, releasing 'COMMON THREADS' and 'HAIRY ON THE INSIDE' during this spell. • **Songwriters:** Group music / HUNT lyrics except; GIMME SOME TRUTH (John Lennon) / THAT'S ENTERTAINMENT (Jam) / INSIDE YOU (Pop Will Eat Itself) / COZ I LUV YOU (Slade).

Album rating: THE EIGHT LEGGED GROOVE MACHINE (*6) / HUP (*6) / NEVER LOVED ELVIS (*7) / CONSTRUCTION FOR THE MODERN IDIOT (*5) / IF THE BEATLES HAD READ HUNTER ... THE SINGLES compilation (*8) / CURSED WITH INSINCERITY (*6)

MILES HUNT – vocals, guitar / **MALCOLM TREECE** – guitar, vocals / **THE BASS THING** (b.ROB JONES) – bass / **MARTIN GILKS** – drums, percussion (ex-MIGHTY LEMON DROPS)

[Farout] [not iss.]

Feb 87. (7"ep) (*GONE ONE*) **IT'S NOT TRUE ... / A WONDERFUL DAY. / LIKE A MERRY GO ROUND / DOWN HERE**
Sep 87. (7") (*GONE 002*) **UNBEARABLE. / TEN TRENCHES DEEP**
(12"+=) (*GOBIG 002*) – I am a monster / Frank.

[Polydor] [Polygram]

Apr 88. (7") (*GONE 3*) **GIVE GIVE GIVE ME MORE MORE MORE. / A SONG WITHOUT AN END** 72 -
(12"+=/cd-s+=) (*GONE X/CD 3*) – Meaner than mean / See the free world.
Jul 88. (7") (*GONE 4*) **A WISH AWAY. / JEALOUSY** 43 -
(12"+=/cd-s+=) (*GONE X/CD 4*) – Happy-sad / Goodbye fatman.

Aug 88. (lp/c)(cd) (*GON LP/MC 1*)(*837135-2*) <*837802*> **THE EIGHT LEGGED GROOVE MACHINE** 18
– Redbury joy town / No for the 13th time / It's yer money I'm after baby / Rue the day / Give give give me more more more / Like a merry go round / The animals and me / A wish away / Grin / Mother and I / Some sad someone / Ruby horse / Unbearable / Poison. (cd-iss. Apr95; same) (cd re-mast.Oct00; 549263-2)
Sep 88. (7"ep/12"ep/cd-ep) (*GONE/+X/CD 5*) **IT'S YER MONEY I'M AFTER BABY / ASTLEY IN THE NOOSE. / OOH, SHE SAID / RAVE FROM THE GRAVE** 40 -
Feb 89. (7") (*GONE 6*) **WHO WANTS TO BE THE DISCO KING?. / UNBEARABLE (live)** 28 -
(12"+=/cd-s+=) (*GONEX/GONCD 6*) – Ten trenches deep (live) / No for the 13th time (live).

—— added guests **JAMES TAYLOR** – organ (ex-PRISONERS) / **MARTIN BELL** – banjo

Sep 89. (7"/c-s) (*GONE/GONCS 7*) **DON'T LET ME DOWN, GENTLY. / IT WAS ME** 19 -
(12"+=/cd-s+=) (*GONEX/GONCD 7*) – ('A'extended).
Oct 89. (lp/c/cd) (*841 187-1/-4/-2*) **HUP** 5 -
– 30 years in the bathroom / Radio ass kiss / Golden green / Let's be other people / Piece of sky / Can't shape up / Good night though / Don't let me down, gently / Cartoon boyfriend / Unfaithful / Them, big oak trees / Room 410. (re-iss. cd Apr95; same) (cd re-mast.Oct00; 549264-2)
Nov 89. (7"/c-s) (*GONE/GONCS 8*) **GOLDEN GREEN. / GET TOGETHER** 33 -
(12"+=/cd-s+=) (*GONEX/GONCD 8*) – Gimme some truth.

—— (Mar'90) **PAUL CLIFFORD** – bass; finally repl. The BASS THING (left '89); he later formed 8-piece The BRIDGE AND THE TUNNEL CREW.

May 90. (7"/c-s) (*GONE/GONCS 10*) **CIRCLESQUARE. / OUR NEW SONG** 20 -
(12"+=/cd-s+=) (*GONEX/GONCD 10*) – ('A'-Paranoia mix).
Mar 91. (7"/c-s) (*GONE/GONCD 11*) **THE SIZE OF A COW. / RADIO ASS KISS (live)** 5 -
(12"+=/cd-s+=) (*GONEX/GONCD 11*) – Give give give me more more more (live).
May 91. (7"/c-s) (*GONE/GONCS 12*) **CAUGHT IN MY SHADOW. / GIMME SOME TRUTH (live)** 18 -
(12"+=/cd-s+=) (*GONEX/GONCD 12*) – ('A'extended).
Jun 91. (cd/c/lp) (*847 252-2/-4/-1*) **NEVER LOVED ELVIS** 3 -
– Mission drive / Play / False start / Welcome to the cheap seats / The size of a cow / Sleep alone / Reaction / Inertia / Maybe / Grotesque / Here come everyone / Caught in my shadow / Line poem. (re-iss. cd Apr95; same) (cd re-iss. Oct00; 549265-2)
Aug 91. (7"/c-s) (*GONE/GONCS 13*) **SLEEP ALONE. / EL HERMANO DE FRANK** 43 -
(12"+=/cd-s+=) (*GONEX/GONCD 13*) – The takin' is easy.

—— In Oct'91, they teamed up with comedian VIC REEVES (& BOB MORTIMER) on No.1 hit cover of Tommy Roe's 'DIZZY'. Next single with guest, KIRSTY MacCOLL

Jan 92. (7"ep/c-ep) (*GONE/GONCS 14*) **WELCOME TO THE CHEAP SEATS** 8 -
– Welcome to the cheap seats / Me, my mum, my dad and my brother / Will the circle be unbroken / That's entertainment.
(cd-ep+=) (*GONECD 14*) – ('A'naked mix) / Caught in my shadw (bare mix) / Circlesque (butt naked mix) / Can't shape up again.

—— added **MARTIN BELL** – fiddle, accordion, mandolin, guitar, sitar, keyboards and 6th member **PETE WHITTAKER** – keyboards

Sep 93. (7"ep/c-ep/12"ep/cd-ep) (*GONE/GONCS/GONEX/GONCD 15*) **ON THE ROPES EP** 10 -
– On the ropes / Professional disturber of the peace / Hank and John / Whites.
Oct 93. (cd/c/lp) (*519 894-2/-4/-1*) **CONSTRUCTION FOR THE MODERN IDIOT** 4 -
– Change every light bulb / I wish them all dead / Cabin fever / Hot love now / Full of life (happy now) / Storm drain / On the ropes / Your big assed mother / Swell / A great drinker / Hush / Sing the absurd. (cd re-mast.Oct00; 549266-2)
Nov 93. (7") (*GONE 16*) **FULL OF LIFE (HAPPY NOW). / CLOSER TO FINE** 28 -
(cd-s+=) (*GONCD 16*) – Burger standing / A curious weird and ugly scene.
(cd-s) (*GONCDX 16*) – ('A'-Dignity mix) / Change every light bulb (dub mix) / I wish them all dead (dub mix).

—— Note: Ex-member ROB JONES (THE BASS THING) died mysteriously on 30 Jul'93 in his New York apartment.

Mar 94. (7"ep/c-ep/cd-ep) (*GONE/GONEX/GONCD 17*) **HOT LOVE NOW! EP** 19 -
– Hot love now! / Just helicopters / I must've had something really useful to say / Room 512, all the news that's fit to print.
(cd-ep) (*GONCDX 17*) – ('A'cardinal error mix) / Unrest song / Flour babies / The Tipperary triangle.

—— disbanded after July Phoenix Festival; MILES went on to work for MTV and form VENT 414 and go solo

WE KNOW WHERE YOU LIVE

—— **TREECE / CLIFFORD / GILKS / + ANGE** – vocals (ex-EAT)

[H.M.D.] [not iss.]

Nov 95. (7"ep/cd-ep) (*HMD 0016/0012*) **DON'T BE TOO HONEST. / CONFESSIONS OF A THUG / EXCUSE ME?**

[Noise Factory] [not iss.]

Jun 96. (7") (*NFRS 002*) **DRAPED. / MENTAL HYGIENE (demo version)**
(cd-s+=) (*NFRCD 002*) – Crude manipulator (crude version).

VENT 414

—— **MILES HUNT** – vocals, guitar / **MORGAN NICHOLLS** – bass (ex-SENSELESS THINGS) / **PETE HOWARD** – drums (ex-EAT)

[Polydor] [not iss.]

Sep 96. (7"/c-s) (*575328-7/-4*) **FIXER. / KISSING THE MIRROR** 71 -
(cd-s+=) (*575328-2*) – Give it whole / Dimki pense.
(12"+=) (*575326-6*) – Shimmy.

WONDER STUFF (cont)

Oct 96. (cd/c/lp) *(533048-2/-4/-1)* **VENT 414**
– Fixer / Fits and starts / At the base of the fire / The last episode / Laying down with / life before you / Correctional / Easy to talk / Night out with a foreign fella / Kissing the mirror / At one / 2113 / Guess my god.

Nov 96. (7"/c-s) *(575534-7/-4)* **LIFE BEFORE YOU. / THE LAST EPISODE**
(cd-s+=) *(575535-2)* – Your latest innuendo / Manifold 36 boro.

MILES HUNT

—— w/ **MALCOLM TREECE** – guitar, vocals + **MARTIN BELL** – violin

Gig   Orchard

Mar 99. (cd) *(GIG 1002-2)* **COMMON THREADS (live)**
– Don't let me down gently / Give, give, give, me more, more, more / It's your money I'm after, baby / (blah, blah one) / Manna from Heaven / (blah, blah two) / Your latest innuendo / Fixer / Circle square / Caught in my shadow / Mission drive / (blah, blah three) / A wish away. *(re-iss. Dec00 as 'BY THE TIME I GOT TO JERSEY'; GIG 1007-2)* <US-iss.Mar00 on 'Orchard' with new title; 689>

May 99. (cd) *(GIG 1012-2)* <868> **HAIRY ON THE INSIDE**   Mar00
– Manna from Heaven / Everything is not okay / Immortalising chase / Getting over you / Let's hope I get it right this time / The slow drowning / Four to the floor / Someone like the kingbird / Amongst the old reliables / Not in my plans. *(hidden track)*

Mar 00. (cd-ep) <5008> **LIFE'S GREAT!**
– The truth at last / A quick fix / The feeling I've been waiting for / Smoked / Yes and a no.

Gig   Gig

Dec 00. (cd-ep) <7707> **5 SONGS**
– How many saints / The terrible / Straight lines / Line 'em up / Muzzle.

WONDER STUFF

HUNT, GILKS, JONES + TREECE re-formed for a reunion gig

Eagle   not iss.

Jun 01. (d-cd) *(EDGCD 179)* **CURSED WITH INSINCERITY (live 2000)**
– Can't shape up / A wish away / Unbearable / Full of life (happy now) / Caught in my shadow / Cartoon boyfriend / Here comes everyone / Circle Square / Golden green / Welcome to the cheap seats / The size of a cow / Red berry joy town / Ruby horse / Sleep alone / Donation / Room 512, any chance that's fit to print / On the ropes / Who wants to be the disco king? / Ten trenches deep / Mission drive / Give, give, give, me more, more, more / It's your money I'm after, baby / No, not for the 13th time / Don't let me down gently / A song without an end / Good night though.

– compilations, etc. –

Sep 94. (7"/c-s/cd-s) *Polydor; (GONE/GONCS/GONCD 18)* **UNBEARABLE. / INSIDE YOU / HIT BY A CAR**   16
(cd-s) *(GONCDX 18)* – ('A' original) / Ten trenches deep / I am a monster / Frank.

Sep 94. (cd/c) *Polydor; (521 397-2/-4/-1)* **IF THE BEATLES HAD READ HUNTER . . . THE SINGLES**   8
– Welcome to the cheap seats / A wish away / Caught in my shadow / Don't let me gently / Size of a cow / Hot love now! / Dizzy / Unbearable / Circlesquare / Who wants to be the disco king? / Golden green / Give give give me more more more / Sleep alone / Coz I luv you / Full of life / On the ropes / It's yer money I'm after baby / It's not true.

Jul 95. (cd) *Windsong; (WINCD 074)* **LIVE IN MANCHESTER (live)**   74

Nov 00. (d-cd) *Polydor; (549454-2)* **LOVE BITES AND BRUISES: THE WONDER STUFF ANTHOLOGY**

MILES HUNT CLUB

HUNT with **MICHAEL FERENTINO** – bass, guitars, keyboards, vocals + **ANDRES KARU** – drums, percussion, keyboards

Eagle   Red Ink

Mar 02. (cd-s) *(EAGXS 217)* **EVERYTHING IS NOT OKAY / THE TERRIBLE SELVES / MUZZLE**

Apr 02. (cd) *(EAGCD 197)* <19351> **THE MILES HUNT CLUB**   Aug02
– Everything is not okay / Traces / Not in my plans / Diluted / Straight lines / Amongst the old reliables / Smoked / The truth at last / The feeling I've been waiting for / Line 'em up / Love can make you sorry / Flapping on the pier (pt.2).

WOODENTOPS

Formed: Northampton, England . . . 1983 by ROLO McGINTY, SIMON MAWBY, FRANK DE FREITAS, BENNY STAPLES and ALICE THOMPSON. After a one-off debut single, 'PLENTY', for Dave Balfe's 'Food' label, this innovative indie act signed to 'Rough Trade' and released a string of acclaimed singles including 'MOVE ME' and 'IT WILL COME'. A much anticipated debut album, 'GIANT' (1986) brought almost universal praise from the press and The WOODENTOPS' quirky blend of manic drumming, twanging guitar and acoustic punkabilly skiffle attracted a cult fanbase (the skinny bare-chested ROLO proving the object of their affections). The following year's 'LIVE HYPNOBEAT LIVE' (1987) placed the tracks in a more confrontational context and by the release of their swansong, 'WOODEN FOOT COPS ON THE HIGHWAY' (1988), the band had developed into one of the most visionary indie bands of the era. On the back of their adoption by the Balearic dance scene, ROLO and Co returned in 1991 with a house single, 'THE WOODENTOPS VS. BANG THE PARTY' on the 'Hyperactive' label. The rest of the 90's were spent touring Asia and Japan where they had become more popular.

Album rating: GIANT (*7) / LIVE HYPNOBEAT LIVE (*6) / WOODEN FOOT COPS ON THE HIGHWAY (*6)

ROLO McGINTY – vocals, acoustic guitar (ex-INNOCENTS, ex-JAZZ BUTCHER) / **SIMON MAWBY** – guitar / **ALICE THOMPSON** – keyboards / **FRANK DeFREITAS** – bass / **PAUL HOOKHAM** – drums

Food   not iss.

Jul 84. (7") *(FOOD 2)* **PLENTY. / HAVE YOU SEEN THE LIGHTS**
(12"+=) *(SNAK 2)* – Everybody.

Rough Trade   Columbia

Apr 85. (7") *(RT 165)* **MOVE ME. / DO IT ANYWAY**
(12"+=) *(RTT 165)* – Steady steady.

—— **BENNY STAPLES** (b.New Zealand) – drums; repl. HOOKHAM (to REDSKINS)

Aug 85. (7") *(RT 167)* **WELL WELL WELL. / GET IT ON (John Peel session)**
(12"+=) *(RTT 167)* – Cold inside.

Nov 85. (7") *(RT 169)* **IT WILL COME. / SPECIAL FRIEND**
(12"+=) *(RTT 169)* – Plutonium rock.

May 86. (7"/12") *(RT/+T 177)* **GOOD THING. / TRAVELLING MAN**

Jun 86. (lp/c) *(ROUGH/+C/CD 87)* <40468> **GIANT**   35
– Get it on / Good thing / Give it time / Love train / Hear me James / (Love affair with) Everyday living / So good today / Shout / History / Travelling man / Last time / Everything breaks. *(cd-iss. May87 +=; ROUGHCD 87)* – Well well well. *(<cd re-iss. Jul01 on 'Cherry Red'++=; CDMRED 190)* – It will come / Special friend / Plutonium rock.

Sep 86. (7") *(RT 178)* **(LOVE AFFAIR WITH) EVERYDAY LIVING. / SO GOOD TODAY**   72
(d7"+=) *(RTD 178)* – Move me / Well well well.

Rough Trade   Epic

Apr 87. (7") **GIVE IT TIME. / WHY**

Apr 87. (lp/c/cd) *(ROUGH/+C/CD 117)* <40861> **LIVE HYPNOBEAT LIVE (live in Los Angeles)**
– Well well well / Love train / Travelling man / Get it on / Plenty / Why / (Love affair with) Everyday living / Good thing / Everything breaks / Move me. *(cd+=)* – Do it anyway / Steady steady / Cold inside / Stop this car. *(<cd re-iss. Oct01 on 'Cherry Red'+=; CDMRED 195>)*

—— **ANNE STEPHENSON** – keyboards, violin (ex-COMMUNARDS) repl. ALICE

Jan 88. (7") *(RT 179)* **YOU MAKE ME FEEL. / STOP THIS CAR**
(12"+=) *(RTT 179)* – ('A' & 'B' mixes).

Feb 88. (lp/c/cd) *(ROUGH/+C/CD 127)* <40861> **WOODEN FOOT COPS ON THE HIGHWAY**   48
– Maybe it won't last / They can say what they want / You make me feel / Wheels turning / Stop this car / Heaven / What you give out / Tuesday Wednesday / In a dream. *(<cd re-iss. Apr02 on 'Cherry Red'+=; CDMRED 208>)* – You make me feel / I want your love / Keep a knockin' / Hallelujah / Why.

—— After splitting in 1988, **ROLO, BENNY + SIMON** returned with . . .

—— BANG PARTY:- **KID BATCHELOR + FRANKIE FONCETT**

Hyperactive   not iss.

May 91. (7"ep) *(HYPER 1)* **WOODENTOPS VS. BANG THE PARTY**
– Tainted world / (+2 other mixes by BANG THE PARTY).

Oct 91. (7") *(HYPER 2)* **STAY OUT OF THE LIGHT**

—— ROLO McGINTY subsequently joined GARY LUCAS

WOULD-BE-GOODS

Formed: London, England . . . 1987 by JESSICA GRIFFIN, a one-time songwriter/employee of 'El' man, MIKE ALWAY. With The MONOCHROME SET on backing, Singapore-raised JESSICA was thrust into the limelight via her debut 'El' debut single, 'FRUIT PARADISE'. The WOULD-BE-GOODS delivered their second 45, 'THE CAMERA LOVES ME', which simultaneously hit the shops in August '88, the exact same time as the parent LP, also entitled 'THE CAMERA LOVES ME'. Taking her cue from the heady post-C-86 days of a few years previously, the would-be JESSICA delivered a sort of sophisticated and mature twee-pop. However, lack of promotion through her unwillingness to perform live, led to sparse future recordings, 'MONDO' (1993) for a Japanese imprint, her only output for some time to come. The record was put straight with the release of The WOULD-BE-GOODS' comeback single, 'EMMANUELLE BEART', in 2001, her entourage of support this time stemming from one-time HEAVENLY guitarist and twee stalwart, PETER MOMTCHILOFF. The following year, 'Matinee' ('Fortuna Pop!' in the UK) released her long-awaited third LP, 'BRIEF LIVES' (2002), a truly sweet set. Viva la indie. Power to twee.

Album rating: THE CAMERA LOVES ME (*5) / MONDO (*5) / BRIEF LIVES (*7)

JESSICA GRIFFIN – vocals / with The MONOCHROME SET, etc.

El   not iss.

Oct 87. (7") *(GPO 28)* **FRUIT PARADISE. / HANGING GARDENS OF REIGATE**

Aug 88. (7") *(GPO 39)* **THE CAMERA LOVES ME. / CECIL BEATON'S SCRAPBOOK**

Aug 88. (lp) *(ACME 14)* **THE CAMERA LOVES ME**
– The camera loves me / Velazquez and I / Cecil Beaton's scrapbook / Pinstriped rebel / Rose du Barry / Marvellous boy / Young man from Caracas / Amaretto / Motorbike girl / Death a la carte / Perfect dear. *(<cd+US-iss.Mar98 on 'Richmond'+=; MONDE 13CD>)* – Wrong way around / End of the world / Bayswater blues / By the light of the cynical moon. *(cd re-iss. Aug02 +=; ACME 14CD)* – Fruit paradise / Hanging gardens of Reigate.

not iss.   Trattoria

Apr 93. (cd) *<menu 12>* **MONDO**   Japan
– Ecuador days / Casanova '92 / Black pearls of Polynesia / Lisbon beat / Gigi geographic / Trinidad affair / Angel square / Exotica / Dream lover / La Fonda de sol / Christmas in Haiti / Run for your life. *(<UK/US-iss.Apr99 on 'Richmond'; MONDE 22CD>)*

—— **GRIFFIN** added **PETER MOMTCHILOFF** – guitar (ex-HEAVENLY) / **ORSON PRESENCE** – keyboards / **STRUAN ROBERTSON + JIM KIMBERLEY** – drums

WOULD-BE-GOODS (cont)

			Matinee	Matinee
Sep 01.	(cd-ep) (<MATINEE 30>) **EMMANUELLE BEART**		□	□
	– Emmanuelle Beart / Je leche les vitrines / Everybody wants my baby / Words.			

			Fortuna Pop!	Matinee
Feb 02.	(7"m) (FPOP 30) **SUGAR MUMMY. / SPANISH TRAGEDY / PERFECT DEAR (2001)**		□	–
Apr 02.	(cd) (FPOP 33) <MATINEE 17> **BRIEF LIVES**		□	Mar02
	– Mystery Jones / Bad Lord Byron / Vivre sa vie / Flashman / Esperanza / Richard III / A season in hell / Fancy man / Dilettante / Butterfly kiss / Diminuendo / Rich and strange / Whitsun bride / Trying to be bad / Elegant rascal / 1999.			
—	**JESSICA + PETER** added **LUPE NUNEZ-FERNANDEZ** – bass, vocals + **DEBBIE GREEN** – drums, vocals			

WRECK SMALL SPEAKERS ON EXPENSIVE STEREOS (see under ⇒ DEAD C)

Mr. WRIGHT (Kevin) (see under ⇒ ALWAYS)

Robert WYATT

Born: ROBERT ELLIDGE, 28 Jan'45, Bristol, England. While at school he formed The WILDE FLOWERS with the HOPPER brothers, which soon spliced into two groups, CARAVAN and SOFT MACHINE. The latter was the band WYATT joined in 1966, but after four albums ('THE SOFT MACHINE', 'VOLUME 2', 'THIRD' & 'FOURTH'), he estranged himself from the group in '71, forming his own MATCHING MOLE. The previous year, his record label 'C.B.S.', had issued his first solo album, 'THE END OF THE EAR', which was assisted by fellow SOFT MACHINE members supplying the jazz-rock feel. In the summer of '73, WYATT was paralysed from the waist down after falling from a window, convalescing for several months at Stoke Mandeville hospital. He returned the following year (now confined to a wheelchair), his single, a version of The MONKEES' 'I'M A BELIEVER' hitting the Top 30. Richard Branson had given him a break on 'Virgin' records earlier in the year, WYATT subsequently critically heralded for his NICK MASON-produced album, 'ROCK BOTTOM' (1974). The set featured such gems as 'SEA SONG' and 'LITTLE RED RIDING HOOD HITS THE ROAD' (in two parts). His second for the label, 'RUTH IS STRANGER THAN RICHARD' (1975), showed an even deeper side, WYATT covering CHARLIE HAYDEN's jazz track, 'SONG FOR CHE'. In 1977, he had another stab at the pop charts, a dire cover version of CHRIS ANDREWS' 'YESTERDAY MAN' being his final recording for some time. He signed to indie, 'Rough Trade' in 1980, releasing a number of singles prior to his comeback album, 'NOTHING CAN STOP US NOW' (1982). This featured his classy re-working of ELVIS COSTELLO and CLIVE LANGER's 'SHIPBUILDING'. In 1983, through constant airplay by Radio 1 DJ John Peel, the anti-Falklands war song gained a Top 40 placing. He continued to spread his political messages through his music, although he has never been one to preach, his songs retaining an intensely personal quality. • **Songwriters:** WYATT penned except: GRASS (Ivor Cutler) / STRANGE FRUIT (Billie Holiday) / AT LAST I AM FREE (Chic) / STALIN WASN'T STALLIN' (Golden Gate Quartet) / BIKO (Peter Gabriel). • **Trivia:** WYATT also provided session drums for SYD BARRETT (1969) / KEVIN AYERS (early 70's) / HENRY COW (1975) / NICK MASON (1981) / RAINCOATS (1981 and '83).
Album rating: THE END OF AN EAR (*6) / Matching Mole: MATCHING MOLE (*6) / MATCHING MOLE'S LITTLE RED RECORD (*6) / Robert Wyatt: ROCK BOTTOM (*7) / RUTH IS STRANGER THAN RICHARD (*7) / NOTHING CAN STOP US (*8) / ANIMALS mini (*4) / OLD ROTTENHAT (*6) / DONDESTAN (*6) / A SHORT BREAK mini (*5) / FLOTSAM JETSAM (*5) / GOING BACK A BIT: A LITTLE HISTORY OF ROBERT WYATT compilation (*8) / SHLEEP (*7)

ROBERT WYATT (solo) – vocals, drums (ex-SOFT MACHINE) w / **DAVID SINCLAIR** – oboe (of CARAVAN) / **MARK CHARIG** – cornet (of SOFT MACHINE) / **ELTON DEAN** – sax / plus **NEVILLE WHITEHEAD** – bass / **CYRIL AYERS** – percussion

			C.B.S.	Columbia
Oct 70.	(lp) (64189) <31846> **THE END OF AN EAR**		□	□
	– Las Vegas tango (part 1) / To Mark everywhere / To saintly Bridget / To Oz alien Daevyd and Gilly / To Nick everyone / To caravan and Brother Jim / To the old world (thank you for the use of your body) / To Carla, Marsha and Caroline (for making everything beautifuller) / Las Vegas tango (part 2). (re-iss. Aug80 on 'Embassy' lp/c; CBS/40 31846) (cd-iss. Apr93 on 'Sony Europe')			

MATCHING MOLE

WYATT with retained guest **D.SINCLAIR** and band **DAVE McRAE** – keyboards / **BILL McCORMICK** – bass (ex-QUIET SUN) / **PHIL MILLER** – guitar (ex-DYBLE, COXHILL & THE MB's) (same label)

Apr 72.	(lp) (64850) <32148> **MATCHING MOLE**	□	□
	– O Caroline / Instant pussy / Signed curtain / Part of the dance / Instant kitten / Dedicated to Hugh, but you weren't listening / Beer as in braindeer / Immediate curtain. (re-iss. Mar82; CBS 32105) (cd-iss. Mar93 on 'Beat Goes On'; BGOCD 175)		
Apr 72.	(7") (8101) **O CAROLINE. / SIGNED CURTAIN**	□	–
Oct 72.	(lp) (65260) **MATCHING MOLE'S LITTLE RED RECORD**	□	□
	– Gloria gloom / God song / Flora fidgit / Smoke signal / Starting in the middle of the day we can drink all our politics away / Marchides / Nan's true hole / Righteous rumba / Brandy as in Benji. (cd-iss. Jul93 on 'Beat Goes On'; BGOCD 174) (cd re-iss. Mar97 on 'Columbia Rewind'; 471488-2)		
—	In the summer of '73, WYATT was paralysed from the waist down after falling from a window. After a year convalescing, but still in a wheelchair;		

ROBERT WYATT

returned as solo vocalist. He was augmented by guests/friends **FRED FRITH** – percussion / **HUGH HOPPER** – bass / **GARY WINDO** – wind / **LAURIE ALLEN** – drums / **MIKE OLDFIELD** – guitar / **RICHARD SINCLAIR** – bass / **IVOR CUTLER** – vox, keyboards / **ALFREDA BENGE** – vocals

			Virgin	Virgin
Jul 74.	(lp/c) (V/TCV 2017) <13112> **ROCK BOTTOM**		□	□
	– Sea song / A last straw / Little Red Riding Hood hits the road (part 1) / Alifib / Alife / Little Red Riding Hood hit the road (part 2). (cd-iss. Feb89; CDV 2017)			
Sep 74.	(7") (VS 114) **I'M A BELIEVER. / MEMORIES**		29	
—	WYATT retained FRITH, ALLEN & WINDO and contributions from **PHIL MANZANERA** – guitar / **BILL McCORMICK** – bass / **BRIAN ENO** – synthesizers / **JOHN GREAVES** – bass / **MONEZI FEZI** – trumpet / **GEORGE KHAN** – saxophone			
May 75.	(lp/c) (V/TCV 2034) **RUTH IS STRANGER THAN RICHARD**		□	□
	– Muddy house: (a) Solar flames – (b) Five black notes and one white tone – (c) Muddy mouth / Soup song / Sonia / Team spirit 1 & 2 / Soup for Che. (cd-iss. Feb89; CDV 2034)			
Apr 77.	(7") (VS 115) **YESTERDAY MAN. / SONJA**		□	–
—	accompanied only by **McCORMICK** – bass / **HARRY BECKETT** – flugelhorn (B-side)			

			Rough Trade	not iss.
Mar 80.	(7") (RT 037) **ARAUCO. / CAIMENERA**		□	–
—	now used only **MOGOTSI MOTHLE** – double bass / **FRANK ROBERTS** – keyboards			
Nov 80.	(7") (RT 052) **AT LAST I AM FREE. / STRANGE FRUIT**		□	–
Feb 81.	(7") (RT 046) **STALIN WASN'T STALLIN'. / STALINGRAD** (P. Blackman)		□	–
—	now with **ESMAIL SHEK** – tabla / **KADIR DURUESH** – shenzi			
Aug 81.	(7") (RT 81) **GRASS. / TRADE UNION** (Dishari featuring Abdus Salique)		□	–
Apr 82.	(lp) (ROUGH 35) **NOTHING CAN STOP US**		□	–
	– Born again cretin / At last I am free / Quantanera / Grass / Stalin wasn't stalling / The red flag / Strange fruit / Arauco / Strange fruit / Trade union / Stalingrad. (re-iss. Apr83 lp+=/c+=; ROUGH/+C 35) – Shipbuilding. (cd-iss. May87; ROUGHCD 35)			
—	Above album featured musicians as 1980-82.			
—	In Apr'82, WYATT was credited on BEN WATT ep 'SUMMER INTO WINTER'.			
—	guests **STEVE NIEVE** – piano / **MARK BEDDERS** – double bass / **MARTIN HUGHES** – drums / **CLIVE LANGER** – organ / **ELVIS COSTELLO** – b.vox			
Aug 82.	(7") (RT 115) **SHIPBUILDING. / MEMORIES OF YOU** (12"-iss.Nov82+=; RTT 115) – Round midnight. (re-iss. Apr83; same); hit No.35)		□	–
—	now with ? plus **HUGH HOPPER**, etc.			
May 84.	(m-lp) (ROUGH 40) **THE ANIMAL FILM (Soundtrack)**		□	–
	– (no tracks listed) (cd-iss. Jul94)			
Aug 84.	(12"ep) (RTT 149) **WORK IN PROGRESS**		□	–
	– Biko / Amber and the amberines / Yolanda / Te rescuerdo Amanda.			
Oct 85.	(7"/12"; ROBERT WYATT with The SWAPO SINGERS) (RT/+T 168) **THE WIND OF CHANGE. / NAMIBIA**		□	–

			Rough Trade	Gramavision
Dec 85.	(lp/c) (ROUGH/+C 69) <18 8604-1/-4> **OLD ROTTENHAT**		□	□
	– Alliance / The United States of amnesia / East Timor / Speechless / The age of self / Vandalusia / The British road / Mass medium / Gharbzadegi / P.I.A. (cd-iss. Nov86; ROUGHCD 69)			
Sep 91.	(cd/c/lp; one-side with BENGE) (R 274-2/-4/-1) **DONDESTAN**		□	□
	– Costa / The sight of the wind / Worship / Catholic architecture / Shrink rap / Left on man / Lisp service / CP jeebies / Dondestan.			

			Blueprint	not iss.
Nov 92.	(cd+book) (BP 108CD) **A SHORT BREAK**		□	–
	– A short break / Tubab / Kutcha / Ventilatir / Unmasked. (re-iss. Apr96; same)			

			Hannibal	unknown
Sep 97.	(cd) (HNCD 1418) **SHLEEP**		□	□
	– Heaps of sheeps / Duchess / Maryan / Was a friend / Free will and testament / September the ninth / Alien / Out of season / Sunday in Madrid / Blues in Bob minor / Whole point of no return.			
—	the next A-side featured **PAUL WELLER** – guitars, vocals			

			Trade 2	not iss.
Sep 97.	(7") (TRDSC 010) **FREE WILL AND TESTAMENT. / THE SIGHT OF THE WIND**		□	–

– compilations, others, etc. –

Mar 81.	(d-lp) Virgin; (VGD 3505) **ROCK BOTTOM / RUTH IS STRANGER THAN RICHARD**	□	□
Apr 82.	(7"ep; ROBERT WYATT & MEMBERS OF CAST) Virgin; (VS 499) **FROM MAN TO WOMAN**	□	–
Dec 84.	(lp) Rough Trade; (RTSP 25) **1982-1984**	□	–
Feb 85.	(12") Recommended; (RE 1984) **THE LAST NIGHTINGALE. / ON THE BEACH AT CAMBRIDGE**	□	□
—	next 'B'side by "The GRIMETHORPE COLLIERY BAND".		
Sep 85.	(7") T.U.C.; **THE AGE OF SELF. / RAISE YOUR BANNERS HIGH**	□	–
Sep 87.	(12"ep) Strange Fruit; (SFPS 037) **THE PEEL SESSIONS** (10.9.74)	□	–
	– Soup song / Sea song / Alife / I'm a believer.		
Jan 93.	(cd) Rough Trade; (R 2952) **MID EIGHTIES**	□	–
Jul 94.	(cd; by MATCHING MOLE) Windsong; (WINCD 063) **BBC RADIO 1 LIVE IN CONCERT** (live)	□	–
Jul 94.	(d-cd) Virgin; (CDVM 9031) **GOING BACK A BIT: A LITTLE HISTORY OF...**	□	–
Aug 94.	(cd) Rough Trade; (R 3112) **FLOTSAM AND JETSAM**	□	–

Pete WYLIE (see under ⇒ WAH!)

Steve WYNN (see under ⇒ DREAM SYNDICATE)

THE GREAT INDIE DISCOGRAPHY   The 1980s

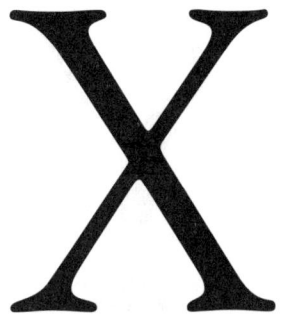

X-MAL DEUTSCHLAND

Formed: Hamburg, Germany ... 1980 by ANJA HUWE, MANUELA RICKERS, FIONA SANGSTER, RITA SIMON and CARO MAY (the latter two were subsequently replaced by MANUELA ZWINGMAN and lone male, WOLFGANG ELLERBROCK). Having issued a couple of 12" singles in their homeland (including the first version of 'INCUBBUS SUCCUBUS'), they were a surprise signing to '4 a.d.' in 1982 after a support slot to the COCTEAU TWINS. Despite refusing to compromise with regards to singing in English, HUWE's vocals were used to startling effect on the band's debut album, 'FETISCH' (1983). Broodingly different in common with all the acts on the label, X-MAL DEUTSCHLAND's gothic post-punk displayed some definite SIOUXSIE-like overtones. However, the departure of ZWINGMANN (for PETER BELLENDIR) seemed to upset the delicate balance of their sound and, although their follow-up set, 'TOCSIN' (1984) briefly entered the Top 75 their dark charm seemed to have deserted them. Discarded by '4 a.d.', X-MAL took refuge at a Phonogram offshoot 'X-Ile' and delivered (after a couple of singles) an album, 'VIVA', in 1987. This failed to halt the decline, ANJA and WOLFGANG overhauling the band and introducing new blood for the unashamedly poppy set, 'DEVILS' (1989).

Album rating: FETISCH (*7) / TOCSIN (*5) / VIVA (*3) / DEVILS (*2)

ANJA HUWE – vocals / **MANUELA RICKERS** – guitar / **FIONA SANGSTER** – keyboards / **WOLFGANG ELLERBROCK** – bass; repl. RITA SIMON / **MANUELA ZWINGMAN** – drums; repl. CARO MAY

		Zick Zack	not iss.
Dec 81.	(12") **SCHWARZE WELT. / DIE WOLKEN / GROBSTADTINDIANER**	–	– German
Jan 83.	(12") *(6060)* **INCUBBUS SUCCUBUS. / BLUT IST LEIBE / ZU JUNG ZU WAN**	–	– German
		4 a.d.	not iss.
Mar 83.	(lp) *(CAD 302)* **FETISCH**		
	– Qual / Geheimnis / Young man / In der nacht / Orient / Hand in hand / Kaempfen / Danghem / Boomerang / Stummes kind. *(cd-iss. Jun87 +=; CAD 302CD)* – Qual (remix) / Zeit / Sehnsucht. *(cd re-iss. Jul98; GAD 302CD)*		
May 83.	(12") *(BAD 305)* **QUAL (remix). / ZEIT / SEHNSUCHT**		–
Sep 83.	(7"/12") *(AD/BAD 311)* **INCUBBUS SUCCUBUS II. / VITO**		

– **PETER BELLENDIR** – drums; repl. ZWINGMAN

Jun 84.	(lp) *(CAD 407)* **TOCSIN**	66	–
	– Mondlicht / Eiland / Reigen / Tag fur tag / Augen-Blick / Begrab mein herz / Nachtschatten / Xmas's in Australia / Derwisch. *(cd-iss. Jun87 +=; CAD 407CD)* – Incubbus succubus II / Vito. *(cd re-iss. Jul98; GAD 407CD)*		
		Red Rhino Europe	not iss.
Oct 85.	(12"ep) *(RRET 1)* **SEQUENZ / JAHR UM JAHR. / AUTUMN / POLARLICHT**		–
		X-Ile – Phonogram	not iss.
Sep 86.	(7"/12") *(XMAL 1/+12)* **MATADOR. / PAHO**		–
	(12") *(XMALR 1-12)* –		
Feb 87.	(7") *(XMAL 2)* **SICKLE MOON. / ILLUSION**		–
	(ext.12"+=) *(XMAL 2-12)* – In onyx.		
Mar 87.	(lp/c)(cd) *(XMA LP/MC 1)(830862-2)* **VIVA**		–
	– Matador / Eisengrau / Sickle moon / If only / Feuerwerk / Illusion / Morning (will there really be) / Manchmal / Polarlicht / Ozean / Dogma 1. *(cd+=/c+=)* – Illusion four.		

– **ANJA + WOLFGANG** recruited new members **FRANK Z + WESLEY PLASS** – guitars / **CURT CRESS** – drums / + producer **HENRY STAROSTE** – keyboards

		Metrognome	not iss.
Feb 89.	(lp/cd; as X-MAL) *(837940-1/-2)* **DEVILS**		– German
	– I'll be near you / Searchlights / You broke my heart / Sleepwalker / When devils come / Heavens and seas / Dreamhouse / I push it harder / I should have known / All in my hands.		

– disbanded after the disaster that was above

– compilations, etc. –

Nov 86.	(12"ep) *Strange Fruit; (SFPS 017)* **THE PEEL SESSIONS** (13.5.85)		–
	– Polarlicht / Der wind / Jahr um jahr / Autumn.		

XYMOX

Formed: Amsterdam, Netherlands ... 1981 as CLAN OF XYMOX by RONNY MOORINGS, PIETER NOOTEN, FRANK WEYZIG and ANKE WOLBERT. Following the domestic release of debut mini-album, 'SUBSEQUENT PLEASURES', the band were signed to prominent UK indie label, '4 a.d.', releasing an eponymous follow-up set in 1985. Trading in arty electro-rock, the group sat rather uneasily alongside the more COCTEAU-esque experimentation of the label's roster as a whole. This was particularly pronounced when the likes of The PIXIES and The THROWING MUSES began to give the label more of an American slant, 1987's 'MEDUSA' album their parting shot as XYMOX – their newly abbreviated moniker – moved on to 'Polydor'. Although the band had moved toward a more accessible sound by this point, the electro-pop of 1989's 'TWIST OF SHADOWS' album (complete with trademark Vaughan Oliver artwork and string arrangements courtesy of Tony Visconti) sounded decidedly dated. By turns reminiscent of ULTRAVOX, DEPECHE MODE and even NEW ORDER (especially 'IMAGINATION'), the record – which strangely made the US charts! – seemed stuck in a mid-80's groove while all the aforementioned artists (well, maybe not ULTRAVOX!) had moved on. And despite moving to England, the band failed to build a sufficient fanbase, leaving 'Polydor' after 'PHOENIX' (1991) and striking out on their own for 'METAMORPHOSIS' (1992) and 'HEADCLOUDS' (1993). Well into the millennium, CLAN OF XYMOX (reverting to their original moniker) are still treading the boards and have issued their umpteenth set, 'NOTES FROM THE UNDERGROUND', in 2001. • **Songwriters:** MOORINGS except WILD IS THE WIND (Tompkins – Washington). • **Trivia:** MICHAEL BROOK and GAVIN WRIGHT guested on the 1991 album.

Album rating: SUBSEQUENT PLEASURES (*4) / CLAN OF XYMOX (*7) / MEDUSA (*6) / TWIST OF SHADOWS (*5) / PHOENIX (*4) / METAMORPHOSIS (*3) / HEADCLOUDS (*4) / HIDDEN FACES (*4) / CREATURES (*4) / LIVE (*4) / NOTES FROM THE UNDERGROUND (*4)

CLAN OF XYMOX

RONNY MOORINGS – vocals, guitar, keyboards / **PIETER NOOTEN** – vocals, keyboards / **FRANK** – guitar, keyboards / **ANKE WOLBERT** – bass, keyboards, vocals

		own label	not iss.
1983.	(ltd-lp) *(NONCOL 7)* **SUBSEQUENT PLEASURES**	–	– Dutch
	– A day (where are you) / Stumble and fall / No words / Stranger / Equal ways / 7th time / Going round / Muscoviet musquito / Strange 9 to 9 / Call it weird / Abysmal thoughts. *<US cd-iss. May94 on 'Alex'; 4419> (cd-iss. Jun97 on 'Pseudonym'; CDP 1013DD) (cd re-iss. Jun01 on 'Pandemonium'; efa 15278-2)*		
		4 a.d.	4 a.d.
May 85.	(lp) *(CAD 503)* **CLAN OF XYMOX**		–
	– A day / No words / Stumble and fall / Cry in the wind / Stranger / Equal ways / Seventh time / No human can drown. *(cd-iss. 1988 +=; CAD 503CD)* – (2- 12"remixes). *(cd re-iss. Jul98; GAD 503CD)*		
May 85.	(12") *(BAD 504)* **A DAY. / STRANGER**		–
Nov 86.	(lp/cd) *(CAD 603/+CD) <941>* **MEDUSA**		
	– Theme I + II / Medusa / Michelle / Louise / Lorrentine / Agonised by love / Masquerade / After the call / Back door. *(cd re-iss. Jul98; GAD 613CD)*		

– **BURT BARTON** – keyboards repl. PIETER / **WILL ANVERS** – drums repl. FRANK / guest **ELISA RICHARDS** – backing vocals

Nov 87.	(12"m) *(BAD 711)* **BLIND HEARTS. / A MILLION THINGS / SCUM**		–

XYMOX

MOORINGS + WOLBERT

		Wing-Polydor	Atlantic
May 89.	(7") *(WING 5)* **OBSESSION. / IN A CITY**		
	(12")(cd-s) *(WINGX 5)(871707-2)* – ('A'side) / ('A'club) / Hitchhiker's dance guide.		
May 89.	(lp/c/cd) *(839 233-1/-4/-2) <871707-1/-4/-2>* **TWIST OF SHADOWS**		
	– Evelyn / Obsession / Craving / Blind hearts / The river / A million things / Tonight / Imagination / In a city / Clementina.		
Feb 90.	(12",cd-s) *<873000>* **IMAGINATION. / SENSES COALESCE**	–	85

– **RONNY + ANKE** brought back **PIETER**

May 91.	(12"/cd-s) *(PZ 146/+CD)* **PHOENIX OF MY HEART. / ('A'-Wild Thing intro-outro mix)**		
Jun 91.	(cd/c/lp) *(848516-2/-4/-1)* **PHOENIX**		
	– Phoenix of my heart / Wild thing outro / At the end of the day / The shore down under / Mar the days / Believe me sometimes / Wonderland / Written in the stars / Dancing barefoot / Smile like Heaven / Crossing the waters.		
		X-Ult	Freestyle
Jul 92.	(12"/cd-s) *(12/CD XYM 101)* **DREAM ON. / ('A'instrumental) / SOUL FREE**		
		Zok	J.R.S.
Oct 92.	(cd) *(XYCD 1001) <35826>* **METAMORPHOSIS**		
	– Tightrope walker / Dream on / B who U wanna B / Sedated / XDD / Revolve / High and low / Love me / Real / Awakening. *(re-iss. Oct94; ZCDXY 005)*		
Mar 93.	(12"/cd-s) *(ZCDXY 002)* **REACHING OUT (remix). / THE BEGINNING**		–
May 93.	(7") *(XY 003)* **SPIRITUAL HIGH. / WILD IS THE WIND**		–
	(12"/cd-s) *(ZVIXYCM/ZCDXY 003)* – (3 'A'mixes).		
		Zok	Off Beat
May 93.	(cd/c/lp) *(ZCDXY/ZCSXY/ZVIXY 004) <25004>* **HEADCLOUDS**		Jan94
	– Spiritual high / It's your life / Prophecy / Wild is the wind / A single day / Love thrills / The beginning / Reaching out / Headclouds / January. *(cd re-iss. Apr94; same)*		

577

XYMOX (cont)

Dec 94. (cd) *(34037-2)* **REMIX** (Koch Int. / Koch Int.)
  – Spiritual high / eaching out / Dream on / Sedated / Awakening / A single day / Soul free / B who U wanna B / Reel / Headclouds / Revolve / January / Tightrope walker / Prophecy / Help your life / Love thrills / XDD / The beginning / High and low / Love me.

Clan Of XYMOX

RONNY MOORINGS + NINA (keyboards) / **MOJCA** (guitar, vocals) / **RUI** (drums)
(Lava / Tess)

Jun 97. (12"; as CLAN OF XYMOX) *(EFA 064922)* <16> **OUT OF THE RAIN / GOING ROUND '97 / FLATLANDS**
Oct 97. (cd) *(EFA 06493-2)* <15> **HIDDEN FACES**
  – Out of the rain / This world / Going round '97 / The child in me / Wailing wall / It's all a lie / Sing a song / Troubled soul / Special friends / Piano piece / Your vice / November / The story ends.
Nov 97. (cd-s) *(EFA 06492-2)* **A DREAM OF BLUE**
(Pandemonium / Metropolis)
May 99. (cd) *(efa 15265-2)* <MET 128> **CREATURES** – Apr99
  – Jasmine and Rose / Crucified / Taste of medicine / Undermined / Consolation / Waterfront / Creature / All I have / Falling down / Without a name / Doubts.
Oct 99. (cd-ep) <MET 155> **CONSOLATION (radio) / JASMINE AND ROSE / REASON / CONSOLATION**
Oct 00. (d-cd) *(efa 15275-2)* <MET 176> **LIVE (live)**
  – Stranger / Cry in the wind / This world / Jasmine and Rose / A day / Louise / Creature / Back door / Out of the rain / Taste of medicine / Going round '97 / Obsession / Muscoviet mosquito / Michelle / Craving / Consolation / Agonized by love / Hypocrite / The story ends / Jasmine and Rose / Stranger.
Oct 00. (cd-ep) <MET 191> **LIBERTY / NUMBER 1 / AT YOUR MERCY / LIBERTY**
Oct 01. (cd) *(efa 15277-2)* <MET 222> **NOTES FROM THE UNDERGROUND** – Sep01
  – Innocent / I want you now / Internal darkness / At your mercy / Anguis / Number one / Into Ber Weh / The bitter sweet / Liberty / Something wrong / Mysterium / The same dream.

– compilations, etc. –

Nov 01. (cd) *Strange Fruit; (SFRSCD 102)* **THE JOHN PEEL SESSIONS**
  – Stranger / Muscoviet mosquito / Seventh time / After the call / Agonised by love / Mesmerised.

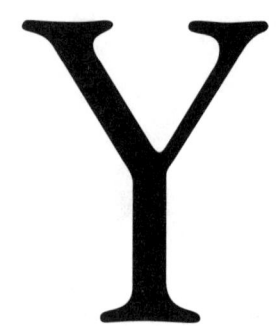

YEAH JAZZ

Formed: Uttoxeter, Staffordshire, England ... 1983 by KEVIN HEAD and MARK 'CHATS' CHATFIELD, who completed the line-up with STU BALLANTYNE and IAN HITCHINS. Debuting unusually with a cassette EP, 'JULIE AND THE SEA LIONS', YEAH JAZZ progressed towards an increasingly folk-orientated sound with the addition of violinist FRANK SWEENEY, a man more used to helping out indie popsters, The JUNE BRIDES. A belated follow-up EP, 'THIS IS NOT LOVE', secured them a minor indie chart hit, although they found this small feat hard to repeat. Ex-HIGSONS man, TERRY EDWARDS joined after a further single, augmenting the sound with his distinctive sax playing on the band's first release for 'Cherry Red', 'SHARON'. The man also had a hand in the production of YEAH JAZZ's debut set, 'SIX LANE ENDS' (1988), the mysterious CHIEF replacing IAN prior to the album's release. Contractual problems dogged the band for the next few years, with a second indie-player, 'APRIL', finally given a release date in 1993. HEAD and CHATS resurfaced in '96 with a new moniker, a new line-up and a new label, 'Scout', releasing the 'SHORT STORIES' album as BIG RED KITE.

Album rating: SIX LANE ENDS (*6) / APRIL (*5) / Big Red Kite: SHORT STORIES (*5)

KEVIN HEAD (b.11 Apr'64) – vocals / **CHATS** (b. MARK CHATFIELD, 1 Apr'62) – guitar / **STU BALLANTYNE** – bass / **IAN HITCHINS** – drums
(Distinctive / not iss.)

Jun 84. (c-ep) **JULIE AND THE SEA LIONS / AMERICAN PLANES. / JULIE AND THE SEA LIONS / ANOTHER SHATTERED DREAM / TOGETHER WE BLEED**

—— with guest **FRANK SWEENEY** – violin (ex-JUNE BRIDES, ex-RINGING)
(Upright / not iss.)

Jun 86. (12"ep) *(UPT 14)* **THIS IS NOT LOVE. / ANY DAY / CHILDISH GAMES / BOB'S SONG**
Oct 86. (7") *(UP 18)* **SHE SAID. / RAIN**
  (12"+=) *(UPT 18)* – Travel scrabble.

—— added **TERRY EDWARDS** – saxophone, guitar, producer (ex-HIGSONS)
(Cherry Red / not iss.)

Nov 87. (7") *(CHERRY 100)* **SHARON. / THE GIRL THE YEARS WERE KIND TO**
  (12"+=) *(CHERRY 100T)* – This is not love.

—— **CHIEF** – drums; repl. IAN
Apr 88. (lp) *(BRED 82)* **SIX LANE ENDS**
  – Sharon / Stones / Lee Marvin / All of my days / Freeland / Step into the light / Heaven / The girl the years were kind to / Dirty windows / Make a flat / Stranger than fiction / All the stars.
Oct 88. (12"m) *(CHERRY 101T)* **MORNING O'GRADY. / STEP INTO THE LIGHT**

—— split the following year only to return to the live circuit in '91
(Native / not iss.)

May 93. (cd) *(NTVCD 76)* **APRIL**

—— **HEAD + CHATS** recruited **DAVE BLANT** – bass, keyboards, accordion / **LEE BEDDOW** – keyboards, guitar / **FREDDY HOPWOOD** – percussion
(Scout / not iss.)

May 96. (cd; as BIG RED KITE) *(SR 1010)* **SHORT STORIES**

YEAH YEAH NOH

Formed: Leicester, England ... early 1984 by former music journalist DEREK HAMMOND on vocals, JOHN GRAYLAND, ADRIAN CROSSAN and MARC DOREY. Signing to MARC RILEY's 'In-Tape' imprint, they released a plethora of singles/EP's over the course of the next few years, including 'COTTAGE INDUSTRY', 'BEWARE THE WEAKLING LINES' and 'PRICK UP YOUR EARS' (collected together as the 'WHEN I AM A BIG GIRL' album). With a vocalist sounding like MORRISSEY on mogadon and a penchant for classic 60's jingle-jangle pop, YEAH YEAH NOH were enjoyable if hardly innovative. Their relatively brief lifespan came to an end in late '85 following the release of the first album proper, 'CUTTING THE HEAVENLY LAWN OF GREATNESS ... LAST RITES FOR THE GOD OF LOVE'. The record featured another version of the accompanying single, 'ANOTHER SIDE TO MRS.QUILL', under the dubiously cryptic title of 'HOME-OWNERSEXUAL'. Slated by critics, YEAH YEAH NOH were perhaps too clever for their own good, the ever evolving indie scene leaving them by the wayside.

Album rating: WHEN I AM A BIG GIRL compilation (*5) / CUTTING THE HEAVENLY LAWN OF GREATNESS . . . (5) / LEICESTER SQUARE: THE BEST OF YEAH YEAH NOH compilation (*7)

DEREK HAMMOND – vocals, acoustic guitar / **JOHN GRAYLAND** – guitars / **ADRIAN CROSSAN** – bass / **SUE DOREY** – drums, vocals

In-Tape not iss.

Jun 84. (7"m) *(IT 008)* **COTTAGE INDUSTRY. / BIAS BINDING / TOMMY OPPOSITE**
Oct 84. (7") *(IT 010)* **BEWARE THE WEAKLING LINES. / STARLING PILLOW CASE AND WHY?**
Jan 85. (book) *(IT 011)* **BUMPER ANNUAL** – special
Jan 85. (7"m) *(IT 012)* **PRICK UP YOUR EARS. / BROWN SHIRT /** Terry And Gerry: BIAS BINDING
May 85. (m-lp) *(IT 016)* **WHEN I AM A BIG GIRL** (compilation)
– Cottage industry / Brown shirt / 1901 / Starling pillowcase and why? / Prick up your ears / Beware the weakling lines / Tommy opposite / Bias binding.

—— added **TOM SLATER** – guitar

Sep 85. (7") *(IT 020)* **(ANOTHER SIDE TO) MRS. QUILL. / WENDY IN THE WOODS**
(12"+=) *(ITT 020)* – Penetration.
Oct 85. (lp) *(IT 021)* **CUTTING THE HEAVENLY LAWNS OF GREATNESS . . . LAST RITES FOR THE GOD OF LOVE**
– Temple of convenience / Prick up your ears / Married Miss New Jersey / Starling pillowcase and why? / Houdini / Susie's party / Panacea's pictures / She said she said / Syealing in the name of the Lord / Home-ownersexual / The short cut way to Saturday / Crimplene seed lifestyle / See through nature / Zoological gardens / Blood soup.
Nov 85. (7") *(IT 023)* **TEMPLE OF CONVENIENCE. / THE TIME BEINGS**
(12"+=) *(ITT 023)* – Mr. Hammond is out to lunch.

—— split some time '86. HAMMOND formed two groups, The NEW NEW SEEKERS and The TIME BEINGS.

– compilations, etc. –

May 86. (lp) *Buggum; (BAAD 2)* **FUN ON THE LAWN LAWN LAWN**
Apr 87. (12"ep) *Strange Fruit; (SFPS 026)* **THE PEEL SESSIONS (19.1.86)**
– The superimposed man / Stealing in the name of the Lord / (It's) Easier to suck than to sing.
May 01. (cd) *Cherry Red; (<CDMRED 183>)* **LEICESTER SQUARE (THE BEST OF YEAH YEAH NOH)**
– The superimposed man / Another side to Mrs. Quill / Prick up your ears / Pink green / Temple of convenience / Beware the weakling lines / Starling pillowcase and why / See through nature / Zoological gardens / Cottage industry / Penetration / Hands up for happiness / The short-cut way to Saturday / Stealing in the name of the Lord / Married Miss Jersey / Mr. Hammond is out to lunch / Crimplene seed lifestyle / Chocolate river / Bias binding / Blood soup.

YO LA TENGO

Formed: Hoboken, New Jersey, USA . . . 1984 by IRA KAPLAN and GEORGIA HUBLEY, who advertised for musicians. Finally, through much time and varied personnel, they stabilised their line-up with DAVE SCHRAMM and MIKE LEWIS. This configuration recorded the 1986 debut album, 'RIDE THE TIGER', introducing the band's countrified acoustic-rock which drew on the likes of VELVET UNDERGROUND, LOVE and RAIN PARADE. Following the departure of SCHRAMM and LEWIS, KAPLAN assumed writing duties for 'NEW WAVE HOT DOGS', providing the band with their first of many credible and critically acclaimed albums. 1989's 'PRESIDENT YO LA TENGO' was more experimental while 'FAKEBOOK' (1990) was a beguiling album of rootsy covers (see below). Throughout the 90's, the band have released a string of albums for 'City Slang', taking an increasingly left-field direction. Of late, the band have released their best record for some time in 'AND THEN NOTHING TURNED ITSELF INSIDE-OUT' (2000), while offshoot DUMP (aka JAMES McNEW, etc) issued their 6th-ish set, 'THAT SKINNY MOTHERFUCKER WITH THE HIGH VOICE?' (2001). • **Songwriters:** SCHRAMM on debut / taken over by KAPLAN. Covered; KICK ME HARD (NBRQ) / YELLOW SARONG (Scene Is Now) / THE ONE TO CRY (Escorts) / HERE COMES MY BABY (Cat Stevens) / EMULSIFIED (Rex Garvin & The Mighty Carvers) / GRISELDA (Peter Stampfel) / SPEEDING MOTORCYCLE (Daniel Johnston) / ANDALUCIA (John Cale) / OKLAHOMA, U.S.A. (Kinks) / TRIED SO HARD (Flying Burrito Brothers) / YOU TORE ME DOWN (Flamin' Groovies) / A HOUSE IS NOT A MOTEL (Love) / I THREW IT ALL AWAY (Bob Dylan) / IT'S ALRIGHT (Velvet Underground) / THE WHOLE OF THE LAW (Only Ones) / DREAMING (Blondie) / etc. DUMP covered: JUST FOR YOU (Wreckless Eric) / THROW OUT THE LIFELINE (. . . Adams) / OUTERSPACEWAYS, INC. (Sun Ra) / OWN THING (Shaggs) / MOON RIVER (Henry Mancini) / WANTED MAN (Bob Dylan) / MORNING MORNING (Fugs) / LETTER (Fish & Roses) / ET MOI, ET MOI, ET MOI (Dutronc-Lanzmann) / EVERLASTING LOVE (Cason-Gayden) / ON THE RIGHT TRACK NOW (13th Floor Elevators) + an album of Prince songs. • **Trivia:** YO LA TENGO duetted with TARA KEY for the film 'I Shot Andy Warhol'. Hip film director, Hal Hartley is a big fan, often using the band's music in his movies.

Album rating: NEW WAVE HOT DOGS (*6) / FAKEBOOK (*7) / PRESIDENT YO LA TENGO (*6) / THAT IS YO LA TENGO (*7) / PAINFUL (*7) / ELECTR-O-PURA (*6) / GENIUS + LOVE = YO LA TENGO compilation (*5) / I CAN HEAR THE HEART BEATING AS ONE (*7) / AND THEN NOTHING TURNED ITSELF INSIDE-OUT (*6) / Dump: SUPERPOWERLESS (*5) / I CAN HEAR MUSIC (*6) / A PLEA FOR TENDERNESS (*5) / WOMEN IN ROCK mini (*5) / THAT SKINNY MOTHERFUCKER WITH THE HIGH VOICE? (*5)

IRA KAPLAN – guitar, vocals / **GEORGIA HUBLEY** – drums, vocals / +2 (guitarist + bassist)

not iss. Egon

Nov 85. (7") **THE RIVER OF WATER. / A HOUSE IS NOT A MOTEL**

—— **DAVE SHRAMM** – vocals, guitar; repl. unknown
—— **MIKE LEWIS** – bass; repl. unknown

Shigaku Coyote

Feb 87. (lp) *(SHIGLP 2) <8676>* **RIDE THE TIGER** 1986
– The cone of silence / The evil that men do / The forest green / The pain of pain / The way some people die / The empty pool / Alrok's bells / Five years / Screaming dead balloons / Living in the country. *(cd-iss. Aug94 on 'City Slang'; EFA 0491827) <US cd-iss. Jun96 on 'Matador'; OLE 205> (cd re-iss. Jun00 on 'City Slang'; 840892-2)*

—— **STEPHEN WICHNEWSKI** – bass; repl. LEWIS + SCHRAMM

What Goes On Coyote

Nov 87. (lp) *(GOESON 13) <87125>* **NEW WAVE HOT DOGS**
– Clunk / Did I tell you / House fall down / Lewis / Lost in Bessemer / It's alright / The way that you live / 3 blocks from Groove Street / Let's compromise / Serpentine / A shy dog / No water / The story of jazz.
May 89. (lp) *(GOESON 28) <88142>* **PRESIDENT YO LA TENGO**
– Barnaby, hardly working / Drug test / The evil that men do / Orange song / Alyda / The evil that men do / I threw it all away. *(cd-iss. Aug94 on 'City Slang' +=; EFA 049252-2)* – NEW WAVE NEW DOGS *<(re-iss. Jun96 on 'Matador' cd/d-lp; OLE 206-1)>*

—— **AL GRELLER** – double bass; repl. WICHNEWSKI

Enigma Bar/None

1990. (lp/cd) *(72641) <20>* **FAKEBOOK**
– Can't forget / Griselda / Here comes my baby / Barnaby, hardly working / Yellow sarong / You tore me down / Emulsified / Speeding motorcycle / Tried so hard / The summer / Oklahoma, U.S.A. / What comes next / The one to cry / Andalucia / Did I tell you / What can I say. *(UK-iss.1994 on 'City Slang'; EFA 04062-26) (UK cd-iss. JUn00 on 'City Slang'; 848766-2)*

—— **GENE HOLDER** – producer (also last one), bass repl. STEPHEN

City Slang City Slang

Jul 91. (lp/cd) *(EFA 04068/+CD) <SLANG 009>* **WHAT IS YO LA TENGO**
– Detouring America with horns / Upside down / Mushroom cloud of hiss / Swing for life / Five cornered drone (crispy duck) / Some kinda fatigue / Always something / 86 second blowout / Out the window / Sleeping pill / Satellite.

—— added **JAMES McNEW** – bass (of DUMP, ex-CHRISTMAS)

Alias City Slang

May 92. (cd-ep) *(A 026CD) <SLANG 021>* **UPSIDE DOWN / (THE) FARMER'S DAUGHTER / OUT OF CONTROL / UPSIDE DOWN (ONE MORE TIME) / SUNSQUASHED**
Jun 92. (lp/cd) *(A 021/+CD) <SLANG 26>* **MAY I SING WITH YOU**
– Out the window / Swing for life / Walking away from you / Five cornered drone (crispy duck) / Fog over Frisco.

City Slang Matador-Atlantic

Oct 93. (cd/c/lp) *(EFA 04927-2/-4/-1) <OLE 069 – 92298>* **PAINFUL**
– Big day coming / From a motel 6 / Double dare / Superstar – Watcher / Nowhere near / Sudden organ / A worrying thing / I was the fool beside you far too long / The whole of the law / Big day coming / I heard you looking.

Matador Matador

Nov 93. (7") *<(OLE 060-7)>* **SHAKER. / FOR SHAME OF DOING WRONG** (demo) Aug93
(cd-s+=) *<(OLE 060-2)>* – What she wants.
Nov 93. (7") *<(OLE 071)>* **BIG DAY COMING. /**
Apr 94. (cd-s) *<(OLE 080-2)>* **FROM A MOTEL 6 / ASHES ON THE GROUND / NUTRICIA** Jan94

City Slang Matador-Atlantic

Apr 95. (7") *(EFA 04954-7) <OLE 139>* **TOM COURTNEY. / THE BIOSEXUAL BOOGIE**
(cd-s+=) *(EFA 04954-2)* – Treading water / Bad politics / My hearts reflection.
May 95. (cd/lp) *(EFA 04955-2/-1) <OLE 132 – 92550>* **ELECTR-O-PURA**
– Decora / Flying lesson / The way grows late / Tom Courtenay / False ending / Pablo and Andrea / Paul is dead / False alarm / The ballad of red buckets / Don't say a word / (Straight down to the) Bitter end / My heart's reflection / Attack on love / Blue line swinger.

Matador Matador

Sep 95. (7"ep/cd-ep) *<OLE 171>* **CAMP YO LA TENGO**
Dec 96. (d-lp/cd) *<(OLE 194-2)>* **GENIUS + LOVE = YO LA TENGO** (compilation) Sep96
– Evanescent psychic pez drop / Demons / Fog over Frisco / Too late / Hanky panky nohow / Ultra-powerful short wave radio picks up music from Venus / Up to you / Somebody's baby / Walking away from you / Artificial heart / Cast a shadow / I'm set free / Barnaby, hardly working / Some kinda fatigue / Speeding motorcycle / Her grandmother's gift / From a motel 6 / Gooseneck problem / Surfin' with the Shah / Ecstacy blues / Too much (part 1) / Blitzkreig bop / One self: Fish girl / Enough / Drum solo / From a motel 6 / Too much (part 2) / Sunsquashed.
Feb 97. (7") *(WORM 4)* **BLUE-GREEN ARROW. / WATCHING THE SUN RISE (or) JOHNNY CARSON**
(above on 'Earworm' / below 45 on 'Planet')
Mar 97. (7"ltd) *(PUNK 016)* **ROCKET NO.9. /** ('A'mix)
Apr 97. (12"/cd-s) *<OLE 250-1/-2>* **AUTUMN SWEATER (4 remixes)**
Apr 97. (cd/lp) *<(OLE 222 2/1)>* **I CAN HEAR THE HEAR BEATING AS ONE**
– Return to hot chicken / Moby octopad / Sugarcube / Damage / Deeper into movies / Shadows / Stockholm syndrome / Autumn sweater / Little Honda / Green arrow / One PM again / Lie and how we told it / Center of gravity / Spec bebop / We're an American band / My little corner of the world.

YO LA TENGO (cont) — THE GREAT INDIE DISCOGRAPHY — The 1980s

Aug 97. (7") <(OLE 272-7)> **SUGARCUBE. / BUSY WITH MY THOUGHTS**
(cd-s+=) <(OLE 272-2)> – Summer / Loony tunes.
Nov 97. (7") <(OLE 291-7)> **LITTLE HONDA. / LITTLE HONDA (live)**
(cd-s+=) <(OLE 291-2)> – ('A'side) / No return / By the time it gets dark / Black hole.
Feb 98. (cd-ep) <(OLE 295-2)> **LITTLE HONDA / NO RETURN / HOW MUCH I LIED / BE THANKFUL / BLACK HOLE / BY THE TIME IT'S GETTING DARK**
Feb 00. (cd/d-lp) <(OLE 371-2/-l)> **AND THEN NOTHING TURNED ITSELF INSIDE-OUT**
– Everyday / Our way to fall / Saturday / Let's save Tony Orlando's house / Last days of disco / The crying of lot G / You can have it all / Tears are in your eyes / Cherry chapstick / From black to blue / Madeline / Tired hippo / Night falls on Hoboken.
Oct 00. (12"/cd-s) <(OLE 484-1/-2)> **DANELECTRO (remixes by Q-UNIQUE, KIT CLAYTON & NOBUKAZU TAKEMURA)**
Nov 02. (12"/cd-s) <(OLE 568-1/-2)> **NUCLEAR WAR (version 1) / NUCLEAR WAR (version 2). / NUCLEAR WAR (version 3) / NUCLEAR WAR (version 4)**

DUMP

JAMES McNEW – vocals, multi / **IRA KAPLAN** – keyboards, guitar / **GEORGIA HUBLEY** – guitars, vocals

Brinkman / Brinkman

Sep 93. (cd) <(BRCD 13)> **SUPERPOWERLESS**
– Hands of fear / So sedimentary / Secret blood / Good medicine / Formerly one-eye / Dark road / Just for you / Outerspaceways, Inc. / Sea wall / Broken conscience / Throw out the lifeline / Quality of hurt / 19 1/2 / Moon river / Superpowerless / Ode to Shaggs' own thing / Love theme from "Providence" / Knox's lament / How many bells?
1994. (7") <001> **EASTER DRESS. / ALMOST HOME**
<above issued on 'Favorite Thing'> <below on 'Smells Like . . .'>
Feb 95. (10"ep) <016> **INTERNATIONAL AIRPORT EP**
May 95. (cd) <BRCD 29> **I CAN HEAR MUSIC**
– Slow down / Jury duty / Hope, Joe / Into fall / Flap my arms / Letter / Relocation program / Invisible / Morning morning / Don't let on / Wanted man / Curl / Zusann says / Liberty spikes / Burning / It's not alright / Beyond the door / Never comes. *(UK-iss.May98; same as US)*
Feb 97. (7") <(HBEP 029-7)> **PHANTOM PERSPECTIVE. / THE LIE**
(above issued on 'Hi-Ball')
Jun 98. (cd) <(BRCD 70)> **A PLEA FOR TENDERNESS**
– Big bands / So long / Clarity / My head in your hands / Again / Deep in your heart / Et moi, et moi, et moi / Little hat / Woo-woo / White worms / Positively Jeff Eliphant / Knicks win / Everlasting love / Made for it / Return to Dump / On the right track now.

Shrimper / Shrimper

Jan 99. (m-cd) <(SHR 103)> **WOMEN IN ROCK**
– Horrible / Words get stuck in my throat / Lucy Grealy / Loved / Plea for Dump.
Mar 01. (cd) <(SHR 106CD)> **THAT SKINNY MOTHERFUCKER WITH THE HIGH VOICE?**
– 1999 / Raspberry beret / Erotic city / The beautiful ones / When U were mine / How come U don't call me anymore? / Pop life / A love bizarre / Girls + boys / Dirty mind / An honest man / Another lonely Christmas.

Neil YOUNG

Born: 12 Nov'45, Toronto, Canada. He was raised in Winnipeg until 1966, when he drove to America in his Pontiac hearse. NEIL had cut his teeth in local instrumental outfit, The SQUIRES, who released one '45 'THE SULTAN'. / 'AURORA' for 'V' records in September '63. The following year, NEIL formed The MYNHA BIRDS and joined forces with RICKY JAMES MATTHEWS (later to become RICK JAMES). Although many songs were recorded, only one saw the light of day; 'MYNHA BIRD HOP' for 'Columbia' Canada. They signed to 'Motown' (first white people to do so) but were soon dropped when they found out that RICKY had dodged the draft. He subsequently met up with past acquaintance, STEPHEN STILLS, and formed BUFFALO SPRINGFIELD. Constant rivalry led to YOUNG departing for a solo venture after signing for new label, 'Reprise', in Spring '68. His eponymous debut with arranger/producer JACK NITZSCHE, then DAVID BRIGGS, was finally issued in early 1969. A fragile, acoustic affair, the album was a tentative start to YOUNG's mercurial solo career, songs like 'THE OLD LAUGHING LADY' and 'THE LONER' hinting at the genius to come. The album was also a guinea pig for 'Warners' (then) new 'CSG' recording process, YOUNG later complaining bitterly about the resulting sound quality. 'EVERYBODY KNOWS THIS IS NOWHERE' (1969), however, was the sound of YOUNG in full control. Hooking up with a bunch of hard-bitten rockers going by the name of CRAZY HORSE, the record marked the beginning of a long and fruitful partnership that's still going strong almost thirty years on. With 'CINNAMON GIRL', DOWN BY THE RIVER' and 'COWGIRL IN THE SAND', this bruising musical synergy saw YOUNG scaling cathartic new heights and the guitar interplay would become a template for the primal improvisation of YOUNG's live work. Although 'AFTER THE GOLDRUSH' (1970) was partly recorded with CRAZY HORSE and featured the blistering 'SOUTHERN MAN', most of the album was by turns melancholy, bittersweet and charming in the style of the gorgeous ballad, 'HELPLESS', he'd contributed some months earlier to the CSN&Y album, 'DEJA VU'. 'BIRDS' and 'I BELIEVE IN YOU' stand as two of the most poignant love songs of YOUNG's career while the title track was a compelling lament of surreal poetry, based on a script written by actor DEAN STOCKWELL. The album gave YOUNG his breakthrough, going Top 10 in Britain and America but it was the 1972 single, 'HEART OF GOLD' and subsequent album, 'HARVEST', which made YOUNG a household name. Most of the tracks were recorded in Nashville with a band called The STRAY GATORS, piano and production duties falling to JACK NITZSCHE. His biggest selling album to date, the finely crafted country crooning of 'OUT ON THE WEEKEND' and 'HEART OF GOLD' was the closest YOUNG ever came to MOR and true to his contrary style, the next few years saw him trawling the depths of his psyche for some of the most uncompromising and uncommercial material of his career. After the fierce sonic assault of the live 'TIME FADES AWAY' (1973) album, YOUNG went back into the studio with CRAZY HORSE to record a tribute to DANNY WHITTEN, their sad-voiced singer who'd overdosed on heroin the previous year. Just as YOUNG was due to begin recording, another of his friends, BRUCE BERRY (STEPHEN STILLS' guitar roadie), succumbed to smack the morose, drunken confessionals that resulted from those sessions eventually appeared a couple of years later as the 'TONIGHT'S THE NIGHT' (1975) album. Arguably YOUNG's most essential release, this darkly personal chronicle of drug oblivion veered from the resigned melancholy of 'ALBUQUERQUE' to the detached, twisted country of 'TIRED EYES', while the visceral catharsis of 'COME ON, BABY, LET'S GO DOWNTOWN' (an earlier live recording with a WHITTEN vocal) cranked up the guitars to match the unrelenting intensity level. Following 'Warners' reluctance to release the album, YOUNG set about writing yet another batch of hazy confessionals upon his return from touring the 'TONIGHT'S THE NIGHT' material. Deeply troubled by his increasing estrangement from actress CARRIE SNODGRASS (with whom he'd had a son, ZEKE), he shacked himself up in his new Malibu pad and penned 'ON THE BEACH' (1974). When every other rock star in L.A. was desperately trying to forget they'd ever hung out with CHARLES MANSON, YOUNG wrote 'REVOLUTION BLUES' in response to the Manson Family killings. 'AMBULANCE BLUES' was just as darkly compelling and the album remains an obscure classic. After a brief, ill-starred reunion with CROSBY, STILLS & NASH, YOUNG came up with a set entitled 'HOMEGROWN', which 'Warners' deemed too downbeat to release. Instead, they relented to the belated issue of 'TONIGHT'S THE NIGHT'.

Album rating: NEIL YOUNG (*7) / EVERYBODY KNOWS THIS IS NOWHERE (*8; with Crazy Horse) / AFTER THE GOLD RUSH (*10) / HARVEST (*9) / JOURNEY THROUGH THE PAST soundtrack (*3) / TIME FADES AWAY (*6) / ON THE BEACH (*9) / TONIGHT'S THE NIGHT (*8)

NEIL YOUNG – vocals, guitar (ex-BUFFALO SPRINGFIELD) with **JIM MESSINA** – bass / session men, etc.

Reprise / Reprise

Jan 69. (lp) <(RSLP 6317)> **NEIL YOUNG**
– The Emperor of Wyoming / The loner / If I could have her tonight / I've been waiting for you / The old laughing lady / String quartet from Whiskey Boot Hill / Here we are in the years / What did I do to my life / I've loved her so long / The last trip to Tulsa. *(re-iss. 1971 lp/c; K/K4 44059) (cd-iss. 1987; K2 44059)*
Mar 69. (7") <0785> **THE LONER. / SUGAR MOUNTAIN**
Sep 69. (7") (RS 23405) **THE LONER. / EVERYBODY KNOWS THIS IS NOWHERE**

NEIL YOUNG with CRAZY HORSE

with **DANNY WHITTEN** – guitar / **BILLY TALBOT** – bass / **RALPH MOLINA** – drums / **BOBBY NOTKOFF** – violin

Jul 69. (lp) <(RSLP 6349)> **EVERYBODY KNOWS THIS IS NOWHERE** — 24 May69
– Cinnamon girl / Everybody knows this is nowhere / Round and round (it won't be long) / Down by the river / The losing end (when you're on) / Running dry (requiem for the rockets) / Cowgirl in the sand. *(re-iss. 1971 lp/c; K/K4 44073) (cd-iss. 1988; K2 44059)*
Jul 69. (7") <0836> **DOWN BY THE RIVER (edit). / THE LOSING END (WHEN YOU'RE ON)**

Late 1969, NEIL YOUNG was also added to CROSBY, STILLS, NASH (& YOUNG).

Aug 70. (7") (RS 23462) **DOWN BY THE RIVER (edit). / CINNAMON GIRL (alt.take)**

NEIL YOUNG

with **NILS LOFGREN** – guitar (of GRIN) repl. NOTKOFF
Aug 70. (7") <0898> **OH LONESOME ME (extended). / I'VE BEEN WAITING FOR YOU (alt.mix)**
Sep 70. (lp) <(RSLP 6383)> **AFTER THE GOLD RUSH** — 7 8
– Tell me why / After the gold rush / Only love can break your heart / Southern man / Till the morning comes / Oh lonesome me / Don't let it bring you down / Birds / When you dance I can really love / I believe in you / After the goldrush / Cripple Creek ferry. *(re-iss. 1971 lp/c; K/K4 44088) (cd-iss. Jul87; K2 44088)*
Sep 70. (7") <20861> **OH LONESOME ME (extended). / SUGAR MOUNTAIN**
Jun 70. (7") <0911> **CINNAMON GIRL (alt.mix). / SUGAR MOUNTAIN** — 55
Oct 70. (7") (RS 20958) <0958> **ONLY LOVE CAN BREAK YOUR HEART. / BIRDS** — 33
Jan 71. (7") <0992> **WHEN YOU DANCE I CAN REALLY LOVE. / SUGAR MOUNTAIN** — 93
Feb 71. (7") (RS 23488) **WHEN YOU DANCE I CAN REALLY LOVE. / AFTER THE GOLDRUSH**

Neil YOUNG (cont)

solo with The STRAY GATORS. (CRAZY HORSE now recorded on their own). NEIL's musicians: **JACK NITZSCHE** – piano / **BEN KEITH** – steel guitar / **TIM DRUMMOND** – bass / **KENNY BUTTREY** – drums. guests included **CROSBY, STILLS & NASH, LINDA RONSTADT, JAMES TAYLOR** plus The **LONDON SYMPHONY ORCHESTRA**

Feb 72. (7") (K 14140) <1065> **HEART OF GOLD. / SUGAR MOUNTAIN** — 10 / 1

Mar 72. (lp/c) (K/K4 54005) <MS 2032> **HARVEST** — 1 / 1
 – Out on the weekend / Harvest / A man needs a maid / Heart of gold / Are you ready for the country? / Old man / There's a world / Alabama / The needle and the damage done / Words (between the lines of age). (cd-iss. May83; K 244131)

Apr 72. (7") (K 14167) <1084> **OLD MAN. / THE NEEDLE AND THE DAMAGE DONE** — / 31

Jun 72. (7"; by NEIL YOUNG & GRAHAM NASH) <1099> **WAR SONG. / THE NEEDLE AND THE DAMAGE DONE** — - / 61

— **JOHNNY BARBATA** – drums (ex-CROSBY, STILLS & NASH) repl. BUTTREY

Sep 73. (lp/c) (K/K4 54010) <MS 2151> **TIME FADES AWAY (live)** — 20 / 22
 – Time fades away / Journey through the past / Yonder stands the sinner / L.A. / Love in mind / Don't be denied / The bridge / Last dance.

Oct 73. (7") <1184> **TIME FADES AWAY (live). / LAST TRIP TO TULSA (live)** — - / —

— now used session people including **CRAZY HORSE** members **BEN KEITH** – steel guitar had now repl. WHITTEN who o.d.'d August 1972.

Jul 74. (7") (K/K4 54014) <R 2180> **ON THE BEACH** — 42 / 16
 – Walk on / See the sky about to rain / Revolution blues / For the turnstiles / Vampire blues / On the beach / Motion pictures / Ambulance blues.

Jul 74. (7") (K 14360) <1209> **WALK ON. / FOR THE TURNSTILES** — / 69

— Had just earlier in 1974, re-united with CROSBY, STILLS & NASH

— recorded solo lp in '73. Musicians: **NILS LOFGREN** / **BEN KEITH** / **BILLY TALBOT** / **RALPH MOLINA**

Jun 75. (lp/c) (K/K4 54040) <MS 2221> **TONIGHT'S THE NIGHT** — 48 / 25
 – Tonight's the night (part I) / Speakin' out / World on a string / Borrowed tune / Come on baby let's go downtown / Mellow my mind / Roll another number (for the road) / Albuquerque / New mama / Lookout Joe / Tired eyes / Tonight's the night (part II). (cd-iss. Jul93; 7599 27221-2)

YOUNG FRESH FELLOWS

Formed: Seattle, Washington, USA ... 1982 by SCOTT McCAUGHEY, CHUCK CARROLL and TAD HUTCHINSON. Coming straight outta the American Northwest a full decade before the area became grunge central, The YOUNG FRESH FELLOWS made a minor stir in 1984 with their debut album, 'THE FABULOUS SOUNDS OF THE PACIFIC NORTHWEST'. Released on indie label, 'PopLlama Products', the record's awkwardly charming guitar pop allure was summed up on 60's girl-group pastiche, 'A HUMBLE GUY', The FELLOWS' student geek appeal setting a precedent for a celebrated lineage of college radio favourites throughout the 80's and into the 90's. Sorting out the self-confessed dodgy bass sound with the addition of JIM SANGSTER, the band conceived a worthwhile follow-up in the acclaimed (at least in Rolling Stone) 'TOPSY TURVY' (1985). From the self-mocking humour and roots flourishes of 'SEARCHIN USA' onwards, the album displayed a fuller, more confident sound without sacrificing the teen-crisis appeal (BEN FOLDS might just have copped an earful of 'THE NEW JOHN AGAR'), eclecticism still the name of the game with the garage-blues hoedown of 'YOU'VE GOT YOUR HEAD ON BACKWARDS' proving an undisputed highlight. The something-for-everyone musical policy and attendant critical praise continued with 'THE MEN WHO LOVED MUSIC' (1987) and the subsequent string of albums for new label, 'Frontier': 'TOTALLY LOST' (1988), 'THIS ONE'S FOR THE LADIES' (1989), 'ELECTRIC BIRD DIGEST' (1991) and 'IT'S LOW BEAT TIME' (1992). The turn-of-the-decade replacement of CARROLL with FASTBACKS man, KURT BLOCH, lent a further dimension to the band's sound and the country roots stylings first introduced on 'TOPSY . . .' became progressively more prominent. While anything more than cult recognition remains unlikely, a mark of the band's peer group admiration was the recruitment of McCAUGHEY for touring services with spiritual compadres R.E.M., the frontman having released his solo debut, 'MY CHARTREUSE OPINION', in 1989. This album was given a fresh coat of paint several years later, so to speak, when it was remixed by SCOTT's new rough-edged jangle-pop outfit, The MINUS 5. Also featuring R.E.M.'s PETER BUCK, The POSIES' KEN STRINGFELLOW and JON AUER, the alt-rock supergroup had already unleashed two sets, 'OLD LIQUIDATOR' (1994) and 'THE LONESOME DEATH OF BUCK McCOY' (1997). Meanwhile, McCAUGHEY et all were part of ROB MORGAN's makeshift outfit, The SQUIRRELS, who issued a few albums from the early 90's. • **Songwriters:** McCAUGHEY except WHERE IS GROOVY TOWN? (. . . Chesterman) / YOU'VE GOT YOUR HEAD ON BACKWARDS (. . . Roslie) / Scott McCaughey/Minus 5: YOU'LL NEVER SEE MY FACE AGAIN (Bee Gees) / PEOPLE SAY (Barry-Greenwich) / BASING STREET (Nick Lowe) / and a few with JIMMY SILVA.

Album rating: THE FABULOUS SOUNDS OF THE PACIFIC NORTHWEST (*7) / TOPSY TURVY (*7) / THIS ONE'S FOR THE LADIES (*7) / THE MEN WHO LOVED MUSIC (*8) / TOTALLY LOST (*7) / ELECTRIC BIRD DIGEST (*8) / INCLUDES A HELMET (*8) / Scott McCaughey: MY CHARTREUSE OPINION (*5) / Minus 5: OLD LIQUIDATOR (*5) / THE LONESOME DEATH OF BUCK McCOY (*6)

SCOTT McCAUGHEY – vocals, bass / **CHUCK CARROLL** – guitar / **TAD HUTCHINSON** – drums

 not iss. Walkthrufyre

Apr 84. (lp) <493> **THE FABULOUS SOUNDS OF THE PACIFIC NORTHWEST**
 – Rock'n'roll pest control / All messed up / Gus theme / Think better of me / Power mowers theme / Empty set takes a vacation / View from above / Big house / This little mystery / A humble guy / Down by the pharmacy / Teenage dogs in trouble / You call that lonely? / That letter / Young Fresh Fellows theme. <cd-iss. May95 on 'Pop Llama'+=; PLCD 101)> – TOPSY TURVY

— added **JIM SANGSTER** – bass (SCOTT switched to guitar)

 not iss. Pop Llama

Jun 85. (7") **YFF UPDATE THEME. / THREE SIDES TO THIS STORY**

 not iss. East Side Digital

Nov 85. (lp) <ESD 8023> **TOPSY TURVY**
 – Searchin' U.S.A. / How much about last night do you remember? / Where is groovy town? / The new John Agar / Sharing patrol theme / You've got your head on backwards / Two lives / Mr. Salamander's review / Trek to stupidity / Topsy turvy theme / Hang out right / Agar's revenge / Good things go. <cd-iss. 1993 on 'Pop Llama'; 20>

 not iss. Pop Llama

Dec 86. (7") **BEER MONEY. / FILLET OF SOUL / CRUSTERS THEME**

 Frontier Frontier

Aug 87. (lp) <(FLP 1021)> **THE MEN WHO LOVED MUSIC** — / Mar87
 – Just sit / TV dream / Get outta my cave / Why I oughta / Unimaginable zero summer / When the girls get here / Amy Grant / Hank, Karen and Elvis / My friend Ringo / Two brothers / I got my mojo working (I thought) / I don't let the little things get me down / Ant farm / Where the hell did they go? / Happy death theme / Beer money / Aurora bridge / Broken basket / Three sides to this story / Young Fresh Fellows update theme / Back room of the bar. <(re-iss. Jul91 cd+=/c+=; 4611-2/-4)> – REFRESHMENTS

Sep 87. (m-lp) <FRT 105> **REFRESHMENTS**

Apr 88. (lp/c/cd) <4616-1/-4/-2> **TOTALLY LOST**
 – Everything's gonna turn out great / Failure / The universal trendsetter / Don't look at my face you might see what I mean / I'd say that you were upset / No help at all / No one really knows / Little softy / I blew my stack / Take my brain away / Celebration / Picky piggy / Totally lost (complete version) / You're not supposed to laugh / World tour '88. <cd-iss. Jul91; FCD 1028)>

Jan 89. (lp) **BEANS AND INTOLERANCE** (the bootleg album)

— **KURT BLOCH** – guitar (ex-FASTBACKS) repl. CARROLL who went into numerous session work

Sep 89. (lp/c/cd) <4622-1/-4/-2> **THIS ONE'S FOR THE LADIES**
 – This one's for the ladies / Still there's hope / Carrot head / Middle man of time / Wishing ring / New old song / Family gun / Rotation / Taco wagon / Picture book / Lost track of time / Miss lonely hearts / Deep, down and inbetween / When I'm lonely again – One day you die / Don't you wonder how it ends?

Oct 89. (7") **MY BOYFRIEND'S IN KILLDOZER. / (other by SCRUFFY THE CAT)**
 (above issued on 'Cruddy', below on 'Pop Lllama')

1990. (7") **DIVORCE #9. / HALLOWEEN**

Sep 90. (7") **TWO GUITARS BASS AND DRUMS. / SOMEONE I CARE ABOUT**
 (above on 'Pravda', below 2 on 'CRuddy')

Oct 90. (7") **DANCIN' IN THE MOONLIGHT. / DO YOU CARE THEME** (as "Gunsharpners")

Nov 90. (7") **MOTOR BROKE. / EQUATOR BLUES**

Jan 91. (7") **DON'T BLAME IT ON YOKO. / WITH A BIG BOOK**

Mar 91. (7"m) **SICK AND TIRED OF ME. / THEY RAIDED THE JOINT / BOOZE PARTY**
 (above on 'Skullduggery', below on 'Lance Rock')

Apr 91. (7"ep) **PURPLE SWEATER / 2 GUITARS. / ROTATION / SESAME STREET**

May 91. (cd/c/lp) <4631-2/-4/-1> **ELECTRIC BIRD DIGEST**
 – Telephone tree / Sittin' on a pitchfork / Looking around / Hillbilly drummer girl / Whirlpool / Once in a while / Teen thing / Thirsty / Fear, bitterness and hatred / Hard to mention / Tomorrow's gone (and so are you) / Evening / There's a love / Swiftly but gently.

May 91. (7"box-set) **HITS FROM THE BREAKUP ALBUM**
 (above issued on 'ESC Brand', below on 'Electrobird')

May 91. (7"m) **ZIP-A-DEE-DOO-DA. / SKYSCRAPER OF FACTS / TEEN THING**

Sep 91. (7"m) <none> **I HATE EVERYTHING. / FETID / I'M NOT BITTER**
 (above issued on no label, below on 'Pop Llama')

Dec 91. (7") **MATHISIZATION. / NEW YFF THEME (w/ Richard Peterson)**

 Munster Frontier

Mar 92. (7") (3467-7) **DARK CORNER OF THE WORLD. / (other by DHARMA BUMS)**

Apr 92. (cd) (MR 015CD) **SOMOS LOS MEJORES**

Jan 93. (cd/c) <(34643-2/-4)> **IT'S LOW BEAT TIME!** — / Oct92
 – Low beat jingle / Right here / Snow white / Mr. Anthony's last / Whatever you are / Two headed fight / Minor bird / Faultless / Crafty clerk / Low beat / Love is a beautiful thing / She sees color / Monkey say / 99 girls / She won't budge.

— split in '93, TAD went into alt-rock session work, as did SCOTT

– compilations, etc. –

Jun 90. (lp/cd) Utility; (UTIL 010/+CD) **INCLUDES A HELMET**
 – Why I oughta / My friend Ringo / Two lives / Gorilla / Amy Grant / A thing like that / No one realy knows / Young Fresh Fellows theme.

Dec 93. (10"m-lp) Munster; **TEMPTATION ON SATURDAY**
 – Supersnazz (pt.1) / Dear red / Everybody said was wrong / City of joy – Carla Togerson / Rabbit run – Terry Adams / Roller coaster by the sea / Teengenerate. <m-cd-iss. Apr95 on 'Pop Llama'; 9117>

May 94. (7"ep; as BOATRAMPMEN) Cruddy; **RAMPAGE EP**

Oct 94. (7") Telstar; **GORILLA TIME. / NO! GORILLA**

YOUNG FRESH FELLOWS (cont) **THE GREAT INDIE DISCOGRAPHY** The 1980s

SCOTT McCAUGHEY

with **TAD HUTCHISON, BEN VAUGHN, CHUCK CARROLL, DENNIS DIKEN, JIMMY SILVA, CONRAD UNO, ERIC SCOTT, EMILY BISHTON, ALDO JONES** etc

                   not iss. Pop Llama

1989. (lp) *<PL 0733>* **MY CHARTREUSE OPINION**
– Losing battle / Happy for the box / The big dead end / A sobering thought / Real true tragedy incident / You'll never see my face again / I might have listened / Evolution / Shut them out / Big deal / The real prime directive / People say / Sittin' round doin' nothin' / Roller coaster blues. *<re-iss. 1993; PL 183> <re-iss. 1994 on 'East Side Digital' cd+=/c+=; ESD 8038-2/-4>* – Far exchange / Waking up / Party town U.S. / Lathe. *<cd re-iss. Aug97 by the MINUS 5 of SCOTT McCAUGHEY on 'Hollywood'; 162127>*

MINUS 5

SCOTT McCAUGHEY – vocals, multi / **PETER BUCK** – bass, etc (of R.E.M.) / **KEN STRINGFELLOW** – rhythm guitar, vocals (of POSIES) / **JON AUER** – guitars, etc (of POSIES) / with **JIM SANGSTER** – bass / etc

                 Glitterhouse East Side Digital

Dec 94. (cd) *(GRCD 350) <ESD 8080-2>* **OLD LIQUIDATOR**
– Winter goes away / Worse / All the time / Find a finger / Emperor of the bathroom / Vulture / Algerian hook / Story / How many bones / Basing Street / No more glory / When it comes my way / House of four doors (theme) / Brotherhood of pain / Heartache for sale / Drunkard's lullaby / House of four doors (end theme). *<re-iss. Nov97 on 'Hollywood'; 162126>*

Sep 95. (cd-ep) *<ESD 8086-2>* **EMPEROR OF THE BATHROOM**
– Emperor of the bathroom / Heartache for sale / Story / Vulture (take 2) / This little woody.

               not iss. Hollywood

May 97. (cd) *<162115>* **THE LONESOME DEATH OF BUCK McCOY**
– The rest of the world / Cross every line / Empty room / Wasted bandage / Boeing spacearium / My mummy's dead / Moonshine girl / Popsycle shoppe / Wouldn't want to care / Spidery moon / Bullfight / Hate me more.

             Houston Party not iss.

Oct 00. (7") *(HPRV 020)* **A THOUSAND YEARS AWAY. /**

YOUNG MARBLE GIANTS

Formed: Cardiff, Wales … 1978 by the MOXHAM brothers, STUART and PHILIP along with frontwoman, ALISON STATTON. The combination of STUART's highly original songwriting talent, PHILIP's "singing" bass and STATTON's spectral vocals has long been held up as one of the post-punk era's most unique and enchanting musical propositions. 'Rough Trade' supremo, Geoff Travis, for one, was quick to spot their talent, promptly signing the trio and issuing a debut maxi-single in 1980. Minimalist in execution and featuring the sparsest of electronic percussion with occasional primitive organ accompaniment, there really were no musical reference points save for JAYNE CASEY/PINK MILITARY at a pinch. The band's one and only album, 'COLOSSAL YOUTH' (1980) received almost universal acclaim, featuring as it did such quietly considered YMG mini-masterpieces as 'SEARCHING FOR MR RIGHT', 'WURLITZER JUKEBOX' and 'CHOCI LONI'. Following it up with an equally engrossing EP, 'TESTCARD' (1981), the band looked set for major cult success as the record climbed into the upper reaches of the indie chart. Yet The YOUNG MARBLE GIANTS dissolved almost as quickly and mysteriously as they'd formed, STATTON going on to form the lite jazz-influenced WEEKEND with SPIKE, SIMON BOOTH and seasoned jazzmen, HARRY BECKETT and LARRY STABBINS. Sticking with 'Rough Trade', STATTON & Co. released a debut WEEKEND single, 'THE VIEW FROM HER ROOM', in 1982, its bossa-nova swing nevertheless retaining the restraint of her earlier work. Another two singles followed, the jazzier 'PAST MEETS PRESENT' and 'DRUMBEAT FOR BABY', prior to a debut album, 'LA VARIETE' (1982). An eclectic collection ranging from the string-led atmospherics of 'SLEEPY THEORY' to the almost pre-SAINT ETIENNE-esque 'THE END OF THE AFFAIR', the record was the first of only two albums before the outfit again split down the middle. BOOTH and STABBINS subsequently formed WORKING WEEK to indulge their passion for soul-jazz while STATTON moved back to Cardiff. STUART MOXHAM, meanwhile, had founded The GIST upon the break-up of his former band, releasing a debut single, 'YANKS', in late '81. This was followed by the acclaimed 'LOVE AT FIRST SIGHT' in summer '82, a decidedly more conventional slice of atmospheric guitar pop subsequently echoed by The BLUE NILE. Despite the release of a fine accompanying album, 'EMBRACE THE HERD' (1983), the project was once again short-lived and no more was heard from any of the former 'GIANTS until 1987 when Belgian label, 'Crepuscule', persuaded the original trio to reform for a one-off single. MOXHAM continued to work in both a solo capacity and alongside other artists, balancing his musical endeavours with a career as an animator.

Album rating: COLOSSAL YOUTH (*9) / SALAD DAYS compilation (*7) / Weekend: LA VARIETE (*7) / LIVE AT RONNIE SCOTT'S mini (*5) / Gist: EMBRACE THE HERD (*6) / Various: NIPPED IN THE BUD (*7) / Stuart Moxham: SIGNAL PATH (*5) / CARS IN THE GRASS (*6) / FINE TUNING (*6)

ALISON STATTON (b. Mar'58) – vocals / **STUART MOXHAM** – guitar, organ, vocals / **PHILIP MOXHAM** – bass

               Rough Trade not iss.

Feb 80. (lp) *(ROUGH 8)* **COLOSSAL YOUTH**
– Searching for Mr. Right / Include me out / The taxi / Eating noddemix / Constantly changing / N.I.T.A. / Colossal youth / Music for evening / The man amplifier / Choci Loni / Wurlitzer jukebox / Salad days / Credit in the straight world / Brand-new-life / Wind in the rigging. *(cd-iss. Jun90; ROUGH CD 8) (cd re-iss. Apr94 on 'Crespuscule'; TWI 984-2)*

May 80. (7"m/12"m) *(RT/+T 043)* **RADIO SILENTS. / FINAL DAYS / CAKE WALKING**
Mar 81. (7"ep/12"ep) *(RT/+T 059)* **TESTCARD EP**
– Click talk / Zebra trucks / Posed by models / Sporting life / The clock / This way.

– split two ways; STATTON formed WEEKEND, while the MOXHAM's re-united as The GIST

The GIST

STUART MOXHAM – vocals, instruments / **PHIL MOXHAM** – bass / **LEWIS MOTTRAM** – bass (with on lp) **PHILIP LEGG** – bass, guitar, percussion (ex-ESSENTIAL LOGIC + LORA LOGIC) / **DAVE DEARNALEY** – drums (of The LION, THE WITCH & THE WARDROBE) / with guests **EPIC SOUNDTRACKS** – drums / **ALISON STATTON + WENDY SMITH + VIV GOLDMAN + DEBBIE PRITCHARD + NIXON** – vocals / **CHARLES BULLEN + JAKE BOWIE** – percussion

               Rough Trade not iss.

Nov 80. (7"/12") *(RT/+T 053)* **THIS IS LOVE. / YANKS**
Jun 82. (7") *(RT 085)* **LOVE AT FIRST SIGHT. / LIGHT AIRCRAFT**
Feb 83. (7") *(RT 125)* **FOOL FOR A VALENTINE. / FOOL FOR A DUB**
Mar 83. (lp) *(ROUGH 25)* **EMBRACE THE HERD**
– Far concern / Love at first sight / Fretting away / Public girls / Clean bridges / Simian / Embrace the herd / Lambic pentameter / Carnival headache / Concrete slopes / The long run / Dark shots. *(<cd-iss. May99 on 'Rykodisc' +=; RCD 10465>)*
– Four minute warning / Problem attics / Light aircraft / Love at first sight (demo).

WEEKEND

ALISON STATTON – vocals, bass / **SIMON BOOTH** (b.12 Mar'56) – guitar, drum machine / **SPIKE** – guitar, viola / + guests **PHIL MOXHAM** – bass / **LARRY STABBINS** (b. 9 Sep'49) – saxes / **ROY DODDS** – drums / **DAVE HARWOOD** – violin, bass / **HARRY BECKETT** – trumpet, flugelhorn / **ANNIE WHITEHEAD** – trombone / **DAWSON MILLER** – percussion

               Rough Trade not iss.

May 82. (7"/12") *(RT/+T 097)* **THE VIEW FROM HER ROOM. / LEAVES OF SPRING**
Jul 82. (7"/12") *(RT/+T 107)* **MIDNIGHT SLOWS. / PAST MEETS PRESENT**
Oct 82. (7") *(RT 116)* **DRUM BEAT FOR BABY. / SLEEPY THEORY** (12"+=) *(RTT 116)* – Weekend off.
Nov 82. (lp) *(ROUGH 39)* **LA VARIETE**
– The end of the affair / Weekend stroll / Summerdays / Drum beat for baby / A life in the day of . . . – part 1 / A life in the day of . . . – part 2 / Sleepy theory / Woman's eyes / Weekend off / Red planes / Nostalgia. *(cd-iss. Jun90; ROUGHCD 39) (<re-iss. Sep00 on 'Vinyl Japan' cd+=/lp; ASK CD/LP 118>)* – Drumbeat / Red planes / Nostalgia / Summerdays (instrumental).

– **ALISON + SIMON** were joined by **KEITH TIPPETT** – piano

Aug 83. (m-lp) *(RTM 139)* **LIVE AT RONNIE SCOTT'S (live)**
– Where flamingos fly / Winter Moon / Nostalgia / Weekend off / A day in the life of . . .

– disbanded; SIMON formed WORKING WEEK with SPIKE + recruited ex-WEEKEND sessioners. They were also part of VIC GODARD's group. ALISON teamed up with (IAN) DEVINE of LUDUS to form DEVINE & STATTON. In Oct'94, ALISON STATTON & SPIKE released a one-off set, 'TIDAL BLUES' for 'Vinyl Japan' (ASKCD 1037).

– (YOUNG MARBLE GIANTS) compilations, etc. –

1984. (lp) *Rough Trade; (ROUGH 57)* **NIPPED IN THE BUD**
– YOUNG MARBLE GIANTS: Final days / Radio silents / Cakewalking / This way / Posed by models / The clock / Clicktalk / Zebra trucks / Sporting life / The GIST: Yanks / This is love / Love at first sight / WEEKEND: The view from her room / Leaves of spring / Midnight slows / Past meets present / Drum beat for baby / Sleep theory.
Apr 95. (cd-ep) *Vinyl Japan; (TASKCD 047)* **THE '81 DEMOS**
– Drumbeat / Red planes / Nostalgia / Summerdays (instrumental).
May 00. (cd) *Vinyl Japan; (<ASKCD 113>)* **SALAD DAYS**   Jun00
– Have your toupee ready / N.I.T.A. / Brand-new-life / Zebra trucks / Choco Loni / Wind in the rigging / The man shares his meal with his beast / The taxi / Constantly changing / Music for evenings / Credit in the straight world / Eating noddemix / Radio silents / Hayman / Loop the loop.

STUART MOXHAM

– **STUART** with **ALISON + ANDREW** plus others (on first)

             Feel Good All Over Feel Good All Over

Mar 93. (cd; as STUART MOXHAM & THE ORIGINAL ARTISTS) *(<FGAO 015>)* **SIGNAL PATH**
– Over the sea / Between edits / Her shoes (are right) / Knives (always fail) / Broken heart blues / It says here / No one road / That's my love / I wonder why / Remember / It took you / Mutual gaze / Yeah x3 / Unit of desire.

               Vinyl Japan not iss.

Mar 95. (cd) *(ASKCD 035)* **CARS IN THE GRASS**
– My criteria / Hello world / Return to work / The tug of love / Night by night / Soft eject / Against creating war / God knows / The appropriate response / Cars in the grass / Drifting west.

             not iss. Feel Good All Over

Feb 96. (cd) *<FGAL 7003>* **FINE TUNING**
– God knows / Broken heart blues / When I dream / Credit in the straight world / Hanging on / Mutual gaze / Oh boy / N.I.T.A. / Night ny night / This is love / I wish / Final day / One of these days.

YUNG WU (see under ⇒ FEELIES)

ZODIAC MOTEL
(see under ⇒ BIRDLAND; see 90's section)

The 1990s+

✸ ✸ ✸

ABBC (see under ⇒ CALEXICO)

ABERDEEN

Formed: Palm Desert, North Hollywood, Los Angeles, California, USA... early 1994 by JOHN GIRGUS, BETH ARZY and JENNI JOYNER. Naming themselves after the birthplace of NIRVANA (or quite possibly the northern city of Scotland!?), ABERDEEN set out their musical stall via a few single releases for seminal twee Brit-pop indie institution, 'Sarah'. 'BYRON' in '94 and 'FIREWORKS' in '95, harked back to the days of C-86 bands, US groups now catching on by the droves. Typical of this ilk was the lovelorn, minimalistic and beat-friendly ABERDEEN, whose third 45, 'SNAPDRAGON' (for 'Sunday' records) looked to have been their swansong; BETH joined The CASINO ASHTRAYS (and later The TREMBLING BLUE STARS). However, the original trio + two newcomers were back together seven years later, aided by one-time MIGHTY LEMON DROPS stalwart DAVID NEWTON at the controls. The fruits of their labour bore out the long-awaited debut long-player, 'HOMESICK AND HAPPY TO BE HERE' (2002), their love of Scottish indie bands (i.e. TRASH CAN SINATRAS, The ORCHIDS) was evident on gems such as 'THOUSAND STEPS' and 'HANDSOME DRINK'. • **Covered:** HOW DEEP IS YOUR LOVE (Bee Gees).

Album rating: HOMESICK AND HAPPY TO BE HERE (*5)

BETH ARZY – vocals, bass / **JOHN GIRGUS** – guitar, drum programming / **JENNI JOYNER** – guitar, keyboards, vocals

	Sarah	not iss.
Oct 94. (7"m/cd-s) (SARAH 093/+CD) **BYRON. / TOY TAMBOURINE / FRAN**	□	-
Mar 95. (7"m/cd-s) (SARAH 097/+CD) **FIREWORKS. / WHEN IT DOESN'T MATTER / SUPER SUNNY SUMMER**	□	-

—— now without JENNI

	Sunday	not iss.
Aug 95. (7") (SUNDAY 035) **SNAPDRAGON. / I THINK I'M FALLING**	□	-

—— after the split BETH joined CASINO ASHTRAYS; she also guested for The TREMBLING BLUE STARS (c. 2001)

—— the original trio re-formed; added **BRIAN GIRGUS** – drums / **KELLY** – keyboards

	Tremelo Arm Users Club	Better Looking
May 02. (7") (TRM 001) **SINK OR FLOAT. / DRIVE**	□	-
Jun 02. (cd) (TRMC 002) <902> **HOMESICK AND HAPPY TO BE HERE**	□	□

– Cities & buses / Clouds like these / Drive / Handsome drunk / Homesick / In my sleep / Sink or float / Sunny in California / That cave ... that Moon / Thousand steps.

aBLe

Formed: Uppsala, Sweden... 1993 by songwriters BO LARSES and LOTTA NYBLAD, along with JOHAN GILLE, ERIK HELLSTROM and JAKE FRODELL. A main ingredient of the band's early work and its formation was the romantic coupling of GILLE and NYBLAD who had met and fallen in love while studying at Uppsala University. The two began to pen songs together and soon put the rest of the group on board for their debut album, 'PRESTIGELESS LOVESOUNDS' (1996). A competent first effort, it was however sadly followed the succeeding year by the break-up of GILLE and NYBLAD as lovers. To make matters worse their label ('Harry Lime') also went into freefall as did their subsequent imprint 'North Of No South'. Fortunately, the band did continue to write material during this uneasy period and album material was issued by 'Blackbean & Placenta Tape Club' under the aptly named title 'LOST LOVE SONGS' (1999). This set showcased the group's blend of lucid indie pop, a la fellow Swedes the CARDIGANS and alt country under the influence of the ground-breaking GRAM PARSONS and TOWNES VAN ZANDT. A well-placed use of staple country instrumentation, i.e. the banjo and lap steel guitar, made this an interesting and poignant effort all round with such standout tracks as 'SAIL ON A MILL' and 'FOR A PURPOSE'.

Album rating: PRESTIGELESS LOVESOUNDS (*5) / LOST LOVE SONGS (*5)

JOHAN GILLE – vocals, guitar, banjo, percussion / **LOTTA NYBLAD** – vocals, harmonica / **ERIK HELLSTROM** – guitars, vocals, clarinet / **BO LARSES** – bass / **JAKE FRODELL** – drums / plus **ANDERS NILSSON** + **RICKARD LUNDBERG**

	Harry Lime	not iss.
Aug 96. (cd) (HLR 963-2) **PRESTIGELESS LOVESOUNDS**	-	- Sweden

– I was so in love (and now I don't know why) / Her place is my place / Ugly glasses / Split / What's the use? / It's getting late / Plain life / It might hurt but it won't get me down / Brian, no / Grampa / April sky / And a way to end this life.

—— had already disbandeded towards the end of '97

	Blackbean & Placenta	Blackbean & Placenta
Nov 99. (cd) <(BBTPC 160)> **LOST LOVE SONGS**	□	□

– Trouble among the horses / For a purpose / Thrill / As long as these eyes can see / Sail on a mill / The end of it / We might never meet again / Screw you around / Push your luck / You're my only one / Can't share you / Anniversary.

ABUNAI!

Formed: Boston, Massachusetts, USA ... mid 1990's by DAN PARMENTER, BRENDAN QUINN and JOE TURNER. The group were united by a passion for SYD BARRETT and soon became a quartet with the inclusion of like-minded KRIS THOMPSON. ABUNAI! made their SYD BARRETT fascination apparent with the release of their debut album, 'UNIVERSAL MIND DECODER', in 1997. The songs were laden with trippy sound effects, swirling distorted guitars and breathless phased vocals. The band appeared undaunted by the grandiose sound they were aiming for and were rewarded with an accomplished sounding set. During the recording of the album THOMPSON was also working on a side project, The LOTHARS. This outfit were an experimental group he had formed along with JOHN BERNHARDT after having seen the film 'Theremin: An Electric Odyssey'. This celluloid was a biographical account of the development of the theremin and the instrument's subsequent importance in the evolution of electronic music. The duo recruited RAMONA HERBOLDSHEIMER and ABUNIA! member BRENDAN QUINN for the recording of their debut album. 'MEET THE LOTHARS' (1998). Unsurprisingly, the music on the album was chiefly played on theremins and although it was at times interesting, it catered for an extremely niche market. THOMPSON and QUINN returned to the fold for the recording of the second ABUNIA! album, 'THE MYSTIC RIVER SOUND', in 1999. This was a concept album of sorts with the group pretending to be different bands on each of the songs, with the album meant to be a snapshot of the Boston music scene. The group avoided this becoming messy by not venturing too far from their preferred neo-psychedelic, space rock. Although the album fell short of what it had hoped to be, the group's ambition was again admirable. The 2000 follow up, 'ROUND WOOD', was a selection of music from three years worth of jamming sections and consequently it sounded sketchy and incomplete.

Album rating: UNIVERSAL MIND DECODER (*6) / THE MYSTIC RIVER SOUND (*6) / ROUND-WOUND (*5) / Lothars: MEET THE LOTHARS (*6)

DAN PARMENTER – vocals, bass / **BRENDAN QUINN** – guitar, vocals, violin / **KRIS THOMPSON** – organ, synthesizer, theremin (ex-PREFAB MESSIAHS) / **JOE TURNER** – percussion, drums

	Camera Obscura	Camera Obscura
Oct 97. (cd) <CAM 006CD> **UNIVERSAL MIND DECODER**	-	□

– Cosmo gun / Inspiration / 77 Gaza Strip / Suspension bridge / Gypsy Davy / Chromatic moire / Calvary Cross / Quiet storm / Dreaming of light / Cosmo gun (silencer). (UK-iss.Apr00; same as US)

| Jun 99. (cd) <CAM 021CD> **THE MYSTIC RIVER SOUND** | - | □ |

– Tomorrow / Barbara Allen / Learning to ask / To think that you knew / Song of Roland / Vanishing point / Sweet William / Can't always see / Mechanical kingdom / Rock song / Toast. (UK-iss.Apr00; same as US)

| Nov 00. (10"ep) <003> **DEEP MU FLUX + 2** | - | □ |

– Deep Mu flux / Lockjam (pt.2) / Organic kingdom.

| Dec 00. (cd) <(CAM 039CD)> **ROUND-WOUND** | - | □ Nov00 |

– The sound museum / Time of the funk-lords / 740XL / Herb-skirt / Do that thing / Soul motiv / 'Bwow winds!' / The fearsome bat-man / Drowning in light / Anti-twilight arch / Wound 'round / L.T. TOP.HVY.BTM / Altairian excavation site / Motorcycle boots / Rolling of the stones / 2CT-7 / Electric Reynolds / Overscan / Genetic epidemic / Barsoom / Buzz bombb.

—— disbanded in 2002; THOMPSON continued with The LOTHARS

LOTHARS

KRIS THOMPSON – theremin, percussion / **JON BERNHARDT** – theremin (of PEE WEE FIST) / **BRENDAN QUINN** – violin, theremin / **RAMONA HERBOLDSHEIMER** – bass, guitar, theremin

	Camera Obscura	Camera Obscura
Mar 99. (cd) <(CAM 018)> **MEET THE LOTHARS**	□	□ Oct98

– Dust mah space broom / Cowboys lament / Term, also / Sad song / Charo UK / Cat and the mean old man / The coronation of King Lothar / Beat hive. (hidden track+=) – (untitled).

—— added **DEAN STIGLITZ** – theremin

	not iss.	Wobbly Music
Aug 99. (cd) <TOTTER 002> **G.C. 3 AND OTHER SONGS (live)**	-	□

– G.C. 3 / The prodigy / The marriage of Queen Lothera / Bleep-bloop / Scary boat ride / I'll never hear 'D' in quite the same way...

| Sep 00. (cd) <TOTTER 004> **OSCILLATE MY METALLIC SONATAS (live)** | - | □ |

– Gypsy song / Metallic sonata No.1 / Banjolin / Bleep bloop / The marriage of Queen Lothera / Metallic sonata No.2 / The trot / Metallic sonata No.3 / Hooray for Dane / Gypsy song (reprise) / The feudal resistance.

| Nov 00. (cd-ep) <TOTTER 005> **HAPPY HOLIDAYS** | - | □ |

– Om slaw / Auld lang syne.

| Oct 02. (cd) <TOTTER 006> **CONNECTED (live)** | - | □ |

– Fall like stars / Inside / With my eyes closed / Of the inner light.

A.C. ACOUSTICS

Formed: Glasgow, Scotland ... 1992 by Kenmore-raised songwriter, PAUL CAMPION. Supporting the likes of MAZZY STAR and PJ HARVEY at Glasgow's Barrowlands, the band's initial line-up was completed by ROGER WARD, CAZ RILEY and DAVE GORMLEY. After an infamous gig at Glasgow's Garage supporting hard-core act NO MEANS NO, the boys were snapped up by respected indie label, 'Elemental'. Their early indie-rock sound was crystallised on a handful of inspired, sporadic releases reminiscent of PAVEMENT or MERCURY REV, fuelling expectations for an album of skewed sonic brilliance. The band went to ground for a couple of years, resurfacing late in '96 with a new guitarist MARK RAINE and a single 'STUNT GIRL'. During their hiatus they recorded an album in Wales, which was deemed unacceptable for release. Their debut album proper, 'VICTORY PARTS' finally saw light of day in the summer of '97. In their absence, MOGWAI, URUSEI YATSURA, etc, had already found minor success after taking the lead from AC's early work. Much of this was evident come the release of 2000's epic 'UNDERSTANDING MUSIC', which took the atmospheric, chamber-rock format into new uncharted soundscapes. 'O' was issued two years later and enhanced this formula with CAMPION's vocals whispering away in a darkened corner to the rest of the group's sparse compositions. Tracks such as 'HOLD' and 'CLONE OF AL CAPONE' could've easily be credited to LEONARD COHEN, although the A.C. ACOUSTICS certainly managed to do justice to themselves by creating such a deep and offbeat album.

Album rating: ABLE TREASURY mini (*5) / VICTORY PARTS (*6) / UNDERSTANDING MUSIC (*8) / O (*7)

PAUL CAMPION – vocals / **ROGER WARD** – guitar / **CAZ RILEY** – bass / **DAVE GORMLEY** – drums

		El'e'mental	Trance
Nov 93.	(7"blue) (ELM 16S) **SWEATLODGE. / MV**		-
Apr 94.	(m-lp/m-cd) (ELM 21 MLP/MCD) <31> **ABLE TREASURY**		Jan95
	– Mother head sander / King Dick / Three / Leather buyer / Fat Abbey / Sister grab operator / Oregon pine washback / MV / Sweatlodge.		
Nov 94.	(12"ep/cd-ep) (ELM 25 T/CD) **HAND PASSES PLENTY EP**		-
	– Hand passes plenty / Love lies broken pieces / Love lies (Equamnemo mix) / Emily.		

— **MARK RAINE** – guitar; repl. WARD

Nov 96.	(7") (ELM 30S) **STUNT GIRL. / SHOKA**		-
	(cd-s+=) (ELM 30CDS) – Skeptic wrist eye / Sidenova.		
Mar 97.	(7") (ELM 29S) **I MESSIAH AM JAILER. / HIGH DIVERS**		-
	(7") (ELM 29SX) – ('A'side) / Violent peep.		
	(cd-s) (ELM 29CDS) – (all 3 tracks).		
Jun 97.	(cd/lp) (ELM 31 CD/LP) **VICTORY PARTS**		-
	– Hand passes empty / Stunt girl / Ex-quartermaster / Admirals all / Hammerhead / Kill Zane / Fast / Continuity freak / High divers / Absent luck liner / I messiah am jailer / Can't see anything / (Red not yellow).		

		Yoyo	not iss.
Nov 98.	(7"ep/cd-ep) (YO/+CD 3) **LIKE RIBBONS EP**		-
	– Like ribbons / Lemon / Lunar page.		
Feb 99.	(7"ep) (YO 4) **SHE'S WITH STARS EP**		-
	– She's with stars / Dirty Paris / Lilo Lilo.		
	(cd-ep+=) (YOCD 4) – Stunt girl (the PmFf remix).		

		Cooking Vinyl	not iss.
Sep 00.	(7") (FRY 096) **CRUSH. / LUKE ONE**		-
	(cd-s) (FRYCD 096) – ('A'side) / Ridley rider (MC Sleazy remix) / Ridley rider (MC Sleazy remix).		
Sep 00.	(cd) (COOKCD 201) **UNDERSTANDING MUSIC**		-
	– Luke one / Chinese summer / Crush / Ridley rider / She kills for kicks / Dry salvage / Knot of knots / Super cup / B2 / Arcane action man / Flies / Parrot pine / Walter strains.		
Feb 02.	(cd) (COOKCD 219) **O**		-
	– Intro / Hold / A bell (of love rings out for you) / Clone of Al Capone / 16 4 2010 / Bright anchor (anchor me) / Interlude / Killed by fuck / Suck on silence / Conspicuously leaving (without saying goodbye) / Victoria / Poem / Outro.		

A CAMP (see under ⇒ CARDIGANS)

ACETONE

Formed: based- Los Angeles, California, USA ... 1992 originally as the quartet, SPINOUT, by RICHIE LEE, MARK LIGHTCAP and STEVE HADLEY (the other member, SCOOTER HENRY, departed before they became ACETONE). Having met at the remote Cal Arts establishment, the trio pooled their skills to create a unique desert hybrid of post-grunge'n'funk. Coupled with their well-documented fondness for narcotics and a penchant for hot-rod/surf stylings, the ACETONE sound attracted the attention of Virgin offshoot imprint, 'Hut'. Their 1993 debut, 'CINDY', displayed their kaleidoscopic retro sound in a mainly instrumental setting, although RICHIE's throaty vocals were put to good use on the follow-up. Recorded in Nashville, the mini-set of country covers, 'I GUESS I WOULD' (1995), found them chewing on a more commercially-oriented fix. A tour of America, however, first with Brit-rock brats, THE VERVE, and then with manic Mancunians, OASIS, set them back on rock's doomed highway. A year later, ACETONE delivered their second full set, 'IF YOU ONLY KNEW' (1996), although their tenure with 'Hut' was soon to come to an end. Emerging from their twilight world of drugs and booze, the trio released the eponymous 'ACETONE', their first for 'Vapour' and their most high profile outing to date. Onwards and upwards, ACETONE pitched their final assault on the indie-rock world by unleashing their 5th set, 'YORK BLVD.' (2000). Narcolepsy had been at times overridden courtesy of numbers such as 'LIKE I TOLD YOU', although their trademark countrified Lo-Fi was still intact on the majority of tracks. Probably haunted by the failure to break into the mainstream (i.e. RICHARD ASHCROFT / THE VERVE), RICHIE LEE sadly took his own life on the 25th of July 2001. • **Covers:** I'M BRANDED (Link Wray) / ALL FOR THE LOVE OF A GIRL (Johnny Horton) / JUANITA (Flying Burrito Brothers) / BORDER LORD (Kris Kristofferson) / THE LATE JOHN GARFIELD BLUES (John Prine) / SOMETIMES YOU JUST CAN'T WIN (Smokey Stover) / I GUESS I WOULD (Jerry Cole) / HOW SWEET I ROAMED (Blake-Sanders) / DON'T TALK (Beach Boys) / THEME FROM A SUMMER PLACE (Discant-Steiner) / DIAMONDHEAD (Phil Manzanera).

Album rating: CINDY (*7) / I GUESS I WOULD mini (*5) / IF YOU ONLY KNEW (*5) / ACETONE (*6) / YORK BLVD. (*6)

RICHIE LEE – vocals, bass / **MARK LIGHTCAP** – guitar, vocals / **STEVE HADLEY** – drums, vocals

		Hut	Vernon Yard
Jun 93.	(12"ep/cd-ep) (HUT T/CD 30) <2> **ACETONE EP**		Apr95
	– I'm gone / For a few dollars more / D.F.B. / Cindy.		
Sep 93.	(7") (HUT 38) **PINCH. / I'M BRANDED**		-
	(12"+=/cd-s+=) (HUT T/DG 38) – Don't talk.		
Oct 93.	(cd/c/lp) (CDHUT/HUTMC/HUTLP 13) <V2/V4 39068> **CINDY**		
	– Come on / Pinch / Sundown / Chills / Endless summer / Intermission / Louise / Don't cry / No need swim / Barefoot on Sunday.		
Jan 94.	(ltd-7"minty) (HUT 47) **COME ON. / PINCH (demo) / THEME FROM A SUMMER PLACE**		-
Jan 95.	(m-cd/m-lp) (HUTM CD/LP 21) **I GUESS I WOULD**		-
	– Juanita / The late John Garfield blues / I guess I would / Sometimes you just can't win / All for the love of a girl / How sweet I roamed / Border Lord.		
Oct 95.	(7") (HUT 62) **THE FINAL SAY. / O.I.E.**		-
	(cd-s+=) (HUTCD 62) – Diamondhead.		
Mar 96.	(cd) (CDHUT 31) <12> **IF YOU ONLY KNEW**		
	– If you only knew / I don't really care / In the light / I've enjoyed as much of this as I can stand / The final say / When you're gone / Hound dog / 99 / What I see / Nothing at all / Always late.		

		Vapour	Vapor
Mar 98.	(cd) <(9362 46818-2)> **ACETONE**		Oct97
	– Every kiss / All the time / Germs / Might as well / Shobud / All you know / Good life / Dee / Waltz / Another minute / So slow / Chew.		

— added **GREG LEISZ** – pedal steel + **JASON YATES** – organ

Oct 00.	(cd/lp) <47900-2/-1> **YORK BLVD.**	-	
	– Things are gonna be alright / Wonderful world / 19 / Vibrato / Like I told you / It's a lie / Bonds / One drop / Vaccination / Stray.		

— sadly, LEE was to commit suicide on the 25th of July, 2001

ACID HOUSE KINGS

Formed: Stockholm, Sweden ... 1991 by brothers JOHAN and NIKLAS ANGERGARD with JOAKIM ODLUND. Inspired by the likes of shoegazing luminaries The SMITHS and the early pop sound of PET SHOP BOYS, these Swedish twee-indie boys debuted in 1992 with their aptly-titled EP 'PLAY POP!', and wasted no time in following it up with their first set, 'POP, LOOK & LISTEN' (1992). Unfortunately these releases and an ensuing EP, 'MONACO GP' (1994), did not get the attention that they deserved and the band duly took a three-year sabbatical to follow their other musical paths. Reconvening in '97 for the 7", 'YES! YOU LOVE ME', and the succeeding sophomore full-length set, 'ADVANTAGE ACID HOUSE KINGS', the brothers ANGERGARD were back. This set showcased the trio's patent pop writing ability and skill at finding that catchy hook, while their next album, 'MONDAYS ARE LIKE TUESDAYS AND TUESDAYS ARE LIKE WEDNESDAYS' (2002), was another career highlight. This latter set was preceded by the departure of ODLUND, replaced by JULIA LANNERHEIM whose added vocal impact gave rise to many a comparison to the indie pop of BELLE & SEBASTIAN. AHK managed to achieve the hard balance of naive sounding pop although underpinned with intelligent melody with strong instrumental skills. The brothers ANGERGARD were never ones to laze; both also ran other similarly veined groups while proping up AHK. Even before this outfit NIKLAS had formed RED SLEEPING BEAUTY back in 1989 with the assistance of KRISTINA BORG, MIKAEL MATSSON and CARL JOHAN NASSTROM. Originally coming out in '93 with the EP, 'POP SOUNDS', the group followed this up with a handful of other 7"s and other mini-efforts, while two well received LPs, 'BEDROOM' (1995) and 'SOUNDTRACK' (1997), before they split up in early 1998. JOHAN on the other hand had teamed up with KAROLINA KOMSTEDT in 1994 to form the group CLUB 8; the two also having an on/off relationship over the next eight years. They came out strongly with the 1995 single 'ME TOO' and debuted long-playing-wise the following year with 'NOUVELLE'. Over the course of their next three LPs, 'FRIEND I ONCE HAD' (1998), 'CLUB 8' (2001) and 'SPRING CAME' (2002) the pair moved from local notoriety to larger international fame. Their sound stemming from the twee pop regions of AHK and evolving through their four albums into a SAINT ETIENNE-esque dance-beat laden with alternative pop styling. ODLUND, too, also found fame outside of AHK's hold, via the SMITHS-inspired outfit STARLET, who with the aid of fellow members JONAS FARM, HENRIK MARTENSSON, ANDERS BAECK and LUDVIG ENGELBERT,

ACID HOUSE KINGS (cont)

arrived with their debut LP, 'FROM THE ONE YOU LEFT BEHIND' (1997). This was brilliantly succeeded by their career highlight offering, 'STAY ON MY SIDE' (2000), an album they did not manage to emulate when the mediocre third full-length set 'WHEN SUN FALLS ON MY FEET' (2002) hit the shops. • **Covered:** I DIDN'T MEAN TO HURT YOU (Felt) / ALMOST (Orchestral Manoeuvres In The Dark).

Album rating: POP, LOOK & LISTEN (*5) / ADVANTAGE ACID HOUSE KINGS (*6) / MONDAYS ARE LIKE TUESDAYS AND TUESDAYS ARE LIKE WEDNESDAYS (*6) / Red Sleeping Beauty: SOUNDTRACK (*6) / SINGLES compilation (*6) / Club 8: NOUVELLE (*5) / FRIEND I ONCE HAD (*7) / MISSING YOU: THE REMIXES mini (*5) / CLUB 8 (*6) / SPRING CAME, RAIN FELL (*7) / Starlet: FROM THE ONE YOU LEFT BEHIND (*5) / STAY ON MY SIDE (*7) / WHEN SUN FALLS ON MY FEET (*5)

NIKLAS ANGERGARD – vocals, guitar / **JOAKIM ODLUND** – guitar / **JOHAN ANGERGARD** – bass, etc.

		Marsh Marigold	not iss.
Jan 92.	(cd-ep) *(GOLD 10)* **PLAY POP!**	-	- German

– She fakes apples / Hey what's up? / Hopefully / Anorak days.

Nov 92. (cd) *(MARI 04)* **POP, LOOK & LISTEN** – – German
– Thirteen again / I'll still be there / Your favourite flower / Say yes / Please be / Christmas / Song of the colour red / Mrs. Green / Times / Autumn afternoon / Adorable / Sadly, I've never loved.

Jun 93. (7") *(EPSILON)* **COOP WITH CORNFLAKES ZOO** – – Sweden
– Tea and coffee / Their lives are as sad as mine / (others by ALIENOR).
(above issued on 'Alienor' records)

Jun 94. (m-cd) *(GOLD 17)* **MONACO G.P.** – – German
– The boy still dreams / Wonder / Can you tell me it's over? / I didn't think your kiss would affect me / Summer days / The boy still dances.

                                         Harmony   not iss.
1997. (7"ep) *(h* 002)* **YES! YOU LOVE ME** – – German
– Yes! you love me / First time / The boy still dreams (acoustic) / Wonder (acoustic).

                                         not iss. Shelflife
1998. (cd) *<LIFE 5>* **ADVANTAGE ACID HOUSE KINGS**
– This and that / Yes! you love me / Family friend / Heaven's just a kiss away / ...But I was wrong / First time / Paris / From the notes I've made so far / Wake up! / I can't let go / A lover's weekend / Brighter.

                                         Labrador not iss.
1999. (7") *(LAB 11)* **WE ARE THE ACID HOUSE KINGS. / SUMMER LOVING** – – Sweden

---- **JULIA LANNERHEIM** – guitar; repl. ODLUND

                                         not iss. Hidden Agenda
Feb 02. (cd) *<AHA! 038>* **MONDAYS ARE LIKE TUESDAYS AND TUESDAYS ARE LIKE WEDNESDAYS** –
– Sunday morning / Start anew / She keeps hoping / Brown and beige are my favourite colours / This love is all we need / Summer's on it's way / Swedish hearts / You're a beautiful loser / A new day, a new career / Say yes if you love me / Mondays are like Tuesdays / One two three four.

                                         Labrador not iss.
Sep 02. (cd-ep) *(LAB 32)* **SAY YES IF YOU LOVE ME** – – Sweden
– Almost / Crying / Save it for the weekend / Say yes if you love me / We're the Acid House Kings.

RED SLEEPING BEAUTY

NIKLAS ANGERGARD – vocals, guitar / **KRISTINA BORG** – vocals / **MIKAEL MATSSON** – guitar / **CARL-JOHAN NASSTROM** – bass

                                         Marsh Marigold not iss.
Nov 92. (3"cd-ep) *(GOLD 12)* **POP SOUNDS** – – German
– Summer tells stories / The trumpet song / Make me smile / Cinema / Christmas.

                                         not iss. Somersault
1994. (7"m) *<2 Somers>* **SEASONS CHANGE. / TRY / SUGARBOWL** –
                                         not iss. Motorway
1994. (7"ep) *<MOTOR 3>* **TOP OF THE POPS** – – Japan
– Promise me / For fun / Can you say love will last? / Rules.
                                         not iss. Sunday
Aug 95. (7"ep) *<SUNDAY 038>* **SMILE EP** –
– Don't say you love me / You & me / Happy birthday.
                                         Siesta   not iss.
Nov 95. (cd-s) *(SIESTA 29)* **SICK AND TIRED / WEALTH OF IMAGINATION / THE CHIME SONG** – – Spain
1997. (cd) *(SIESTA 54CD)* **SOUNDTRACK** – – Spain
– The young pretenders / Soul provider / The things I'd say / Nervous / Summer at its best / Enough / Casino classic / Certainly / How do you kill your food? / It happens / Your opinion / The light that guides you / You're all there is.

---- split after above; MIKAEK formed The SHERMANS

– compilations, etc. –

Dec 95. (cD) *Marsh Marigold; (MARI 07)* **BEDROOM** – – German
– For once / Pop song / Down by the sea / Selfish / You're the kind / Yesterday's lies / Cold hearts / Bicycling.

Jan 00. (cd-ep) *Siesta; (SIESTA 75)* **SINGLE EP** – – Spain
– Stupid boy / Two hearts / Rocketship / Florida / Instant replay.

Mar 00. (cd/lp) *Siesta; (SIESTA 76 CD/LP)* **SINGLES** –
– Sick and tired / Wealth of imagination / The chime song / Her favourite cliche / You're the kind / Summer tells stories / The trumpet song / Make me smile / Cinema / Christmas / Seasons change / Try / Sugarbowl / Don't say you love me / You & me / Happy birthday / Promise me / For fun / Can you say love will last / Rules / Stay.

CLUB 8

JOHAN ANGERGARD – mult / **KAROLINA KOMSTEDT** – vocals

                                         Siesta   not iss.
Nov 95. (7"ep) *(SIESTA 25)* **EP** – – Spain
– Me too / Before I came / Girlfriend.

Jul 96. (m-cd) *(SIESTA 42)* **NOUVELLE** – – Spain
– Blue skies / Don't be gone / Breakdown / She never calls me / Loveaffair / Sunday afternoon / Those charming men / All dressed up and shy / I guess I was wrong / Look out! / (UK-iss.Jul02 +=; same) – Mee too / Before I came / Girlfriend.
                                         March   March
Sep 98. (cd/lp) *<MAR 35 CD/LP>* **THE FRIEND I ONCE HAD** –
– Everlasting love / All I can do / Someday / I wish you'd stay / Holiday / The end of the affair / Summer rain / Calcutta / Tomorrow never comes / Better days / Karen / Missing you.

Nov 98. (cd-s) *(LAB 3)* **MISSING YOU / THE FRIEND I ONCE HAD / MISSING YOU (remix)** – – Sweden
(above issued on 'Labrador')

Nov 99. (m-cd/m-lp) *<(MAR 43 CD/LP)>* **MISSING YOU: THE REMIXES** – Jun99
– Missing you (Eurodisco remix) / My heart won't break / The best of seasons / Missing you (making love to a machine mix) / My heart won't break (minty cut mix) / The friend I once had.
                                         Labrador Hidden Agenda
Aug 01. (cd) *(LAB 18)* *<AHA! 024>* **CLUB 8** – Sweden
– Love in December / Boyfriends stay / She lives by the water / The sands and the sea / Falling from grace / Hope for winter / London / Say a prayer / A place in my heart / I don't need anyone / Keeping track of time.

Feb 02. (cd) *(LAB 22)* *<AHA! 036>* **SPRING CAME, RAIN FELL** – Sweden
– We're simple minds / Spring came, rain fell / Spring song / Close to me / Baby, I'm not sure if this is love / The chance I deserve / I give up too / Friends and lovers / Teenage life / Karen song / The girl with the Northern Soul collection / We set ourselves free.
                                         Labrador Labrador
Apr 02. (cd-ep) *(<LAB 28>)* **SUMMER SONGS** – Sweden
– Things we share / Mornings / You and me / Don't stop the night / Sounds from the gulf stream.

STARLET

JOAKIM ODLUND – guitar / **JONAS FARM** – vocals, guitar / **ANDERS BAECK** – keyboards / **HENRIK MARTENSEN** – bass / **LUDVIG ENGELBERT** – drums

                                         Parasol   Parasol
Aug 97. (cd) *<(PARCD 027)>* **FROM THE ONE YOU LEFT BEHIND** –
– Pin-up / Love-story of the year / Wendy / Au-pair / Afraid / Girlfriend / It could happen / As you leave / Boom boom love! / Astrid.

May 00. (cd) *<PARCD 054>* **STAY ON MY SIDE** –
– I'm home / Homewater / At least in my heart / In the disco / Internal affairs / Scent of you / Diary and herself / Silver sportscar / Moving on / Friends.

Feb 02. (cd) *<PARCD 073>* **WHEN SUN FALLS ON MY FEET** –
– Malmo / With sand in my eyes / When sun falls on my feet / Make that stone beat like a heart again / Not alone / Sunshine / To sleep this evil day away / And how it breaks / Christine / Stop and let it go.

ACTION FIGURES

Formed: Fairfax, Virginia, USA ... early 90's by JEFF SMITH, CHRIS PILLER and JIM WATERS. Pinching from melody providers R.E.M and adding their own darkly comic effect, The ACTION FIGURES debuted in 1992 with the sparklingly new 'BIG WONDERFUL', a tribune of sketchy melancholia disguised as four-fingered power chord rock. After this impressive debut the band seemed to have disappeared off the face of the earth until the release of 'LITTLE CITIZENS', a deeper, more developed record issued through the 'Eggbert' label in 1995, a good three years later. The 'LAURAVILLE' (which was a song title from the latter) EP kept the band busy during 1995. It included three new tracks and three from the band's previously released set. The band have since been inconspicous by their absence.
• **Covered:** SHE'S GOT A RIGHT (... Easdale) / DANDELION (Rolling Stones) / WHISPER, WHISPER (Bee Gees).

Album rating: BIG WONDERFUL (*6) / LITTLE CITIZENS (*7)

CHRIS PILLER – vocals, bass, keyboards / **JIM WATERS** – guitar, vocals / **JEFF SMITH** – guitar, bass / **JOSH ROWLEY** – drums

                                         not iss. Eggbert
1992. (cd) *<80008>* **BIG WONDERFUL** –
– American crawl / Birdhouse / Having fun with my gun / New Christy minstrel / Big wonderful blue / Nine o'clock / One time two times three times / She screams Elvis is king / Second class believer / When Patty talks / Sense to me / Come on down / Flag girl.

1995. (cd) *<80016>* **LITTLE CITIZENS** –
– Lauraville / Caroline / Idoline / She's got a right / Super heroine / Reckless Miranda / Tough with love / Perfect hole / U.S. supreme boy / Animal pictures / Tree / Dandelion.

Sep 95. (cd-ep) *<80021>* **LAURAVILLE EP** –
– Lauraville / See-saw park / Guilty Gene / Whisper, whisper / Nine o'clock / Lauraville.

---- disbanded after above

ACTION SWINGERS

Formed: New York City, New York, USA ... early 90's by mainman, NED HAYDEN, along with former PUSSY GALORE member JULIA CAFRITZ and SONIC YOUTH drummer BOB BERT; the fourth devotee was bassman HOWIE PYRO. Not the greatest rock band in the world by any means, the ACTION SWINGERS were nevertheless rifftasticly melodious although poorly produced. Grungy and Lo-Fi – like WEEN meeting SONIC YOUTH on a bad day out – the 'SWINGERS produced three full sets, the last of which was the appropriately titled 'QUIT WHILE YOU'RE AHEAD' (1994).

Album rating: ACTION SWINGERS (*4) / MORE FAST NUMBERS mini (*4) / DECIMATION BLVD. (*4) / QUIT WHILE YOU'RE AHEAD (*5)

NED HAYDEN – vocals, guitar / **JULIA CAFRITZ** – guitar, vocals (ex-PUSSY GALORE) / **HOWIE PYRO** – bass / **BOB BERT** – drums (ex-SONIC YOUTH)

		not iss.	Primo Scree
Sep 91.	(cd,c) *<SCREE 6>* **ACTION SWINGERS**	-	

– Song / Cuban bush / Nacho / Watch out / Funky Manc / Fire / Hot rock action / I'm dead / UFO / Fully loaded / Instrumental / Skicap! *(hidden track+=)* – Untitled instrumental.

— CAFRITZ left

		Wiiija	not iss.
Jul 92.	(m-cd) *(WIJ 14CD)* **MORE FAST NUMBERS**		-

– Knocked out cold / You want my action / Incinerated / I'm sick / Courtney Love.

— on tour (c. 1993) **TIM CEDAR** – drums (ex-LOVEBLOBS) repl. BERT

		Newt	Caroline
Jun 94.	(lp/cd) *(TOAD 6/+CD) <CARL 1738>* **DECIMATION BLVD.**		May93

– I don't wanna be this way / Anyway that you want / Glad to be gone / Searching for kicks / No heart and soul / Whow do you work this thing / I can't get no action / You only know my name / Nothing to me now / Fooled again / Too far gone / Waiting for my chance / You better keep your big mouth shut / Defective.

Oct 94.	(cd) *(TOAD 7CD) <CAROL 1750>* **QUIT WHILE YOU'RE AHEAD**		Sep94

– Kicked in the head / Bum my trip / Miserable life / Dear of a fucked up planet / Blow job / Bent / I got the blues / Nembutal sunset / In the hole / Losing my cool.

— disbanded later in '94, BERT joined The CHROME CRANKS

– compilations, etc. –

Aug 99.	(cd) *Reptilian; (REP 034CD)* **THE COMPLETE LONDON TOE RAG**		

ADD N TO (X)

Formed: South London, England ... 1994 by former Radio Prague DJ, BARRY SMITH, alongside ANN SHENTON and STEVEN CLAYDON, taking their puzzling moniker from a mathematical formula. Moog and theremin dole-meisters of the Nth degree, ADD N TO X debuted early in 1996 with 'VERO ELECTRONICS', a strangely strange set of mind-blowing knob twiddling. The following year, after inking a deal with 'Satellite', the eardrum-bashing futurists had two NME Singles Of The Week, 'THE BLACK REGENT' and 'KING WASP'. Early in 1998, they established themselves with an innovative electro A-Bomb of sound in their second long-player, 'ON THE WIRES OF OUR NERVES'. Extreme and trailblazing, like STEREOLAB/SUICIDE with a rocket shoved up their rectum, the album's lengthy, disorientated tracks were a prime feature of DJ, Mary Ann Hobbs' Radio One "Breeze Block" show. After turning down the majors, ADD N TO X subsequently signed to semi-seminal indie, 'Mute', their first outing being the wonderful 'LITTLE BLACK ROCKS IN THE SUN'. In September that year, they were probably the first band ever to play underground at a nuclear shelter, the bunker in question being in the rural backwaters of north east Fife near Anstruther. ADD N TO (X) caused a little rumpus the following Spring with the single 'METAL FINGERS IN MY BODY', due to the accompanying animated porn clip. This track, alongside classic electro-gems such as 'ROBOT NEW YORK' and 'REVENGE OF THE BLACK REGENT', made their third set 'AVANT HARD' (1999), the most pioneering cyberpunk since DEVO donned their boiler-suits. SHENTON, CLAYDON, SMITH and HIGH LLAMAS drummer ROB ALLUM returned with more 'tronic frolics of sorts, 'ADD INSULT TO INJURY' (2000), created an eclectic barrage of synth-punk that ear-bashed its way (at times) through the black holes of your mind. 'LOUD LIKE NATURE' in 2002, saw the group expand their electronica-meets-punk brand of sexy post-punk and it even saw the inclusion of rock icon KIM FOWLEY singing on two numbers.

Album rating: VERO ELECTRONICS (*5) / ON THE WIRES OF OUR NERVES (*8) / AVANT HARD (*9) / ADD INSULT TO INJURY (*7) / LOUD LIKE NATURE (*7)

BARRY SMITH – synthesizer / **ANN SHENTON** – programming/ **STEVEN CLAYDON** – synthesizer

		Blow Up	not iss.
Jan 96.	(cd/lp) *(BLOW UP 004 CD/LP)* **VERO ELECTRONICS**		-

– Inevitable fast access / A silhouette of a man and a wasp / Meetings in compact boxes / A very uncomfortable status (wet disco) / Inevitable fast access (sleeze) / A very uncomfortable status (mathematical) / Aphine repetition. *(cd re-iss. Aug97 & Nov99; same)*

		Satellite	Mute
Jun 97.	(12") *(STL 003)* **THE BLACK REGENT. / MURMUR ONE**		-
Oct 97.	(12") *(STL 007)* **KING WASP./ HIT ME**		-
Nov 97.	(ltd-12") *(PIAO 10)* **DEMON SEED. / (a track by FRIDGE)**		-

(above single issued on 'Piao!')

— added **ROB HALLUM** (of the HIGH LLAMAS)

Feb 98.	(cd/d-lp) *(STL 010 CD/LP) <69053>* **ON THE WIRES OF OUR NERVES**		May98

– We are Add N To X / Murmur one / Sound of accelerating concrete / Gentle Germans / The black regent / Planet Munich / Nevermind / King Wasp / Orgy of Bubastus / Grey body, green gun / On the wires of our nerves / Hit me / Sir Ape.

— all above as **ADD N TO X**

		Mute	Mute
Jul 98.	(10"ep/cd-ep) *(10/CD MUTE 219)* **LITTLE BLACK ROCKS IN THE SUN. / VOICES 1-3**		-
Mar 99.	(12"/cd-s) *(12/CD MUTE 224)* **METAL FINGERS IN MY BODY. / THIS IS THE FLEX (Hi-Fi & Lo-Fi mixes)**		-
Apr 99.	(cd/d-lp) *(CD+/STUMM 170) <9091>* **AVANT HARD**		

– Barry 7's contraption / Robot New York / Skills / Steve's going to teach himself who's boss / FYUZ / Buckminster fuller / Revenge of the black regent / Metal fingers in my body / Ann's eveready equestrian / Oh yeah, oh no / Machine is bored with love.

Aug 99.	(7") *(7MUTE 231)* **REVENGE OF THE BLACK REGENT. / IRON MAN**		-

(12"+=) *(12MUTE 213)* – ('A'side) / Old lady Ealing does man experiments / Is that alright FYUZ / March of the pure mathematical genius that ends (and results in war).
(cd-ep+=) *(CDMUTE 231)* – Metal fingers in my body (CD-Rom).

Oct 99.	(7") *(SMALL 008)* **LIVE 1940 (Rommel & Raisin mix). / Canter: VOTEL, ANDY**		-

(above issued on 'Slut Smalls')

— now with **ROB ALLUM** – drums (of HIGH LLAMAS)

Oct 00.	(7") *(MUTE 254)* **PLUG ME IN. / VIC HALLAM SYSTEM**		

(12"/cd-s) *(12/CD MUTE 254)* – ('A'side) / Murray's space shoes (Plug Me In disco remix) / Hey double double.

Oct 00.	(cd/lp) *(CD+/STUMM 187) <9137>* **ADD INSULT TO INJURY**		

– Adding N to X / Brothel charge / You must create / Kingdom of shades / Mister Bobby / The poke 'er 'ole / Plug me in / Hit for cheese / MDMH / BP Perine / Incenerator No.1 / Regent is dead.

Mar 01.	(12"/cd-s) *(12/CD MUTE 258)* **THE POKE 'ER 'OLE. / WHITE SCRAPIE / PLUG ME IN**		-

(cd-s) *(LCDMUTE 258)* – ('A'mixes).

May 01.	(cd-s; as ADD N TO FU(X)A) *(RGIRL 22) <69822>* **AND ANOTHER THING!**		Jun02

– (2 untitled tracks).
(above issued on 'Rocket Girl')

Oct 02.	(12"/cd-s) *(12/CD MUTE 278)* **TAKE ME TO YOUR LEADER. / THE TREES ARE DREAMLESS LEAFLESS GENIUS / THE MONKEY SKIRT MARTYRS**		
Oct 02.	(cd/lp) *(CD+/STUMM 204) <9194>* **LOUD LIKE NATURE**		

– Total all out water / Electric village / Sheez mine / Invasion of the polaroid people / Party bag / Quantum leap / Pink light / Up the punks / Take me to your leader (make me really happy) / Lick a battery (tongues across the terminals) / U baby / Large number / All night lazy.

– compilations, etc. –

Oct 01.	(cd/d-lp; Various Artists) *Lo; (LCD/LLP 25)* **BARRY 7'S CONNECTORS** (mixes)		-

ADEN

Formed: Washington, D.C., USA ... 1995 by JEFF GRAMM, FRED KOVEY and JOSH KLEIN, the trio having met at the University of Chicago. Originally billed under the moniker, DINGLE, they soon changed this for the release of their debut 7", 'SCOOBY DOO', on which they elicited the production skills of CHRIS HOLMES of SABALON GLITZ fame. Moving on from here, the group issued their eponymously-titled debut full-length outing, 'ADEN' (1997), a record featuring such standout tracks as 'PLUNKY' and 'SNOWY SIDEWALKS'. After this offering, the band took on the further assistance of KEVIN BARKER on guitar. There followed a little hiatus as KOVEY and GRAMM moved to Washington DC (not unfamiliar territory for the latter as his father Phil was a Texan senator). KLEIN, meanwhile, stayed put working as a music writer; BARKER continued his academic pursuits. The end of the decade saw the indie popsters come back together, albeit without KLEIN, to record their sophomore LP 'BLACK COW' (1999). This was quickly succeeded by their third album 'HEY 19' a year later; both of their last two albums named after STEELY DAN tracks. ADEN's sound was more akin to the early work of BELLE & SEBASTIAN, tending towards the lighter end of the indie pop margin. On their fourth full-length project, 'TOPSIDERS' (2002), the group were again back to the quartet format with the addition of MATT DATESMAN on drums. This album was easily their best so far, displaying a far more competent and at ease ADEN with the added guest work of LADYBUG TRANSISTOR's SASHA BELL.

Album rating: ADEN (*4) / BLACK COW (*5) / HEY 19 (*4) / TOPSIDERS (*5)

JEFF GRAMM – vocals, guitar / **FRED KOVEY** – bass / **JOSH KLEIN** – drums

		Fortune 4	Fortune 4
Jun 97.	(cd) *<(FOR4-2)>* **ADEN**		

– Snowy sidewalks / Cause you tears / Would you have stayed / When you left / Scooby Doo / Still cross my mind / Don't act sad / Reverie / Plunky / City lights / Walking in circles / What makes you sad? / DC song.

— added **KEVIN BARKER** – guitar / + now without KLEIN

		Teenbeat	Teenbeat
Jul 99.	(cd) *<TEENBEAT 266>* **BLACK COW**	-	

– New fast / I knew you would go / Sadness / Haunt me / Green / New 3/4 / Counting the days / Part of a losing team / (Swords and) Falconry / Collapsing / Why can't I make you happy / Left off here.

ADEN (cont)   THE GREAT INDIE DISCOGRAPHY   The 1990s

Jul 00. (cd) <(TEENBEAT 286)> **HEY 19** — Jun00
- Matinee idol / Gulf Coast league / Country bar in the city / Home repair / House of Klein (everything's fine at the) / 10 hour day / Pimlico / Rockulator (rock me now) / Dull reactor / Dear John / Some odd relief / Brief summer rains.

—— added **MATT DATESMAN** – drums

Jun 02. (cd) <(TEENBEAT 326)> **TOPSIDERS**
- Intro / Racking up mistakes / Mango tree / Pop song / River's rising / The chase / Rapt attention / Boggle champs / Smiles and frowns / Readenator / Intertwining hands. *(re-iss. Sep02 on 'Trust Me'; TMR 012)*

ADORABLE

Formed: Coventry, England... 1991 out of the CANDY THIEVES by Polish-born frontman, PIOTR FIJALKOWSKI, plus ROBERT DILLAN, KEVIN GRITTON and WILL. Signing to 'Creation' records, these ALAN McGEE proteges issued their official debut EP, 'SUNSHINE SMILE', in the spring of '92. Taking up where ECHO & THE BUNNYMEN and PSYCHEDELIC FURS left off, ADORABLE fitted nicely into the void previously filled by the "baggy" and "shoegazing" scenes. Although never quite breaking out of the indie chart ghetto, the band followed up a further clutch of singles with a debut album, 'AGAINST PERFECTION' (1993), which scraped into the Top 75. However, after only three years in the indie limelight (and a second album, 'FAKE' – 1994), they disbanded, going out with a damp squib rather than a bang with a gig in Brussels. PIOTR, meanwhile, dreamed of a comeback that would propel him to stardom, although his time leading a synth duo with a female vocalist came to nothing. Late in '96, PIOTR (now PETE), together with his guitar-playing sibling, KRYZ, slowly evolved into a band after finding new recruits, SIMON DUNFORD, BOB BROWN and CHRIS PARSONS. Naming themselves, POLAK, a derogatory term used for a Polish person, PETE and Co bounced back in 1998 with a cracking pop single, appropriately titled, '2 MINUTES 45'. Additional singles 'I'M SICK' and 'IMPOSSIBLE', preceded – and were featured on – their debut album, '3x3' (1999), a record mightily influenced by The BUNNYMEN. With the replacement of journalist DUNFORD with MATTHEW SIGLEY, the group signed a deal with 'One Little Indian', for whom they delivered two further sets, 'SWANSONGS' (2000) and 'RUBBERNECKING' (2002).

Album rating: AGAINST PERFECTION (*6) / FAKE (*5) / Polak: 3x3 (*6) / SWANSONGS (*6) / RUBBERNECKING (*6)

PIOTR FIJALKOWSKI – vocals, guitar / **ROBERT DILLAN** – guitar / **WILL** – bass / **KEVIN GRITTON** – drums

	Money To Waste	not iss.
Dec 91. (ltd-12") *(none)* **SUNSHINE SMILE. / I'LL BE YOUR SAINT / BREATHLESS**		–
	Creation	SBK-Capitol
Apr 92. (7") *(CRE 127)* <19780> **SUNSHINE SMILE. / A TO FADE IN** (12"+=/cd-s+=) *(CRE 127T)(CRESCD 127)* – Sunburnt.		–
Jul 92. (7") *(CRE 133)* **I'LL BE YOUR SAINT. / SUMMERSIDE** (12"+=/cd-s+=) *(CRE 133T)(CRESCD 133)* – Self-imperfectionist.		–
Oct 92. (7") *(CRE 140)* **HOMEBOY. / CONTENTED EYE** (12"+=/cd-s+=) *(CRE 140T)(CRESCD 140)* – Pilot.		–
Jan 93. (12"ep)(cd-ep) *(CRE 153T)(CRESCD 153)* **SISTINE CHAPEL CEILING / EVERYTHING'S FINE. / SEASICK MARTYR / OBSESSIVELY YOURS**		–
Mar 93. (cd/lp)(c) *(CRE CD/LP 138)(C-CRE 138)* <81416> **AGAINST PERFECTION**	70	May93
– Glorious / Favourite fallen idol / A to fade in / I know you too well / Homeboy / Sistine chapel ceiling / Cut #2 / Crash sight / Still life / Breathless. <US+=> – Sunshine smile / I'll be your saint.		
Apr 93. (12"ep)(cd-ep) *(CRE 159T)(CRESCD 159)* **FAVOURITE FALLEN IDOL. / MIRROR-LOVE / COOL FRONT 23-6**		–
May 94. (12"ep)(cd-ep) *(CRE 172T)(CRESCD 172)* **KANGAROO COURT. / DINOSAUR #3 / BALLROOM**		–
Aug 94. (7") *(CRE 177)* **VENDETTA. / SENSE AND NONSENSE** (cd-s) *(CRESCD 177)* – ('A'side) / The floating game / The house is rotten.		–
Sep 94. (cd/lp)(c) *(CRE CD/LP 165)(C-CRRE 165)* **FAKE**		–
– Feed me / Vendetta / Man in a suitcase / Submarine / Lettergo / Kangaroo court / Radio days / Go easy on her / Road movie / Have you seen the light. *(w/7")* – VENDETTA (World Cup karaoke mix). / MAN IN A SUITCASE (Mr. Gritton has left the building mix)		

POLAK

PETE FIJALKOWSKI – vocals, guitar / **KRYZ FIJALKOWSKI** – guitar (ex-BARDOTS) / **SIMON 'SPIKE' DUNFORD** – keyboards (ex-BARDOTS) / **BOB BROWN** – bass / **CHRIS PARSONS** – drums

	Generic	not iss.
Jun 98. (cd-s) *(GEN 0245)* **2 MINUTES 45 / NOT LISTENING / LAST ORDERS / 2 MINUTES 45 (John Cage mix)**		–
Oct 98. (cd-s) *(GEN 0244)* **I'M SICK / I'LL LIE TO YOU / PRIVATE GOD**		–
Apr 99. (7"/cd-s) *(GEN 0247/0243)* **IMPOSSIBLE. / SELL MY GUITAR / GOODBYE JOE**		–
Jun 99. (cd) *(GEN 0242)* **3x3**		–
– 2 minutes 45 / Not listening / Last orders / I'm sick / I'll lie to you / Private god / Impossible / Sell my guitar / Goodbye Joe.		

—— **MATTHEW SIGLEY** – keyboards (ex-EARTHMEN) repl. DUNFORD who became a journalist

	One Little Indian	not iss.
Apr 00. (cd) *(TPLP 307CD)* **SWANSONGS**		–
– Last thing / Tracer / Nobody's cowboy song / Gutter song / Storm coming / (untitled) / Impossible / Love in reverse / Shipwrecked / Hang up.		
Jul 02. (cd-s) *(324 TP7CD)* **JOYRIDER / TWO SEPARATE STATES / BURN ON**		–
Aug 02. (cd) *(TPLP 334CD)* **RUBBERNECKING**		–
– Don't wake me / Love lies / Joyrider / Sign / Bar angel / Dumbstruck / Something wrong / Payback / Untitled / Rubbernecking / Come down.		

ADVENTURES IN STEREO (see under ⇒ SPIREA X)

AERIAL-M (see under ⇒ SLINT)

AEREOGRAMME (see under ⇒ FUKUYAMA)

AFGHAN WHIGS

Formed: Denver, Colorado, USA ... Autumn '86, by GREG DULLI and RICK McCOLLUM who met in a prison. The pair moved to Cincinatti, Ohio, after signing for Seattle based indie label 'Sub Pop' in 1989, their independently released debut set, 'BIG TOP HALLOWEEN' (1988), having caused something of a stir with its proto-grunge exhortations. Produced by Seattle maestro, Jack Endino, the album, 'UP IN IT', worked around the same formula, hinting at their wider country and soul influences. After a further set for 'Sub Pop', 'CONGREGATION' (1992), and an EP of soul covers, 'UPTOWN AVONDALE', the group were plucked from the mire of grunge cultdom by 'Elektra' in the major label stampede following NIRVANA's success. A former film student, DULLI cannily negotiated the right to creative control over the band's videos, his acting ambitions duly realised in 1994 when he scored the part of JOHN LENNON in Stuart Sutcliffe's story, 'Backbeat'. The 'WHIGS major label debut, 'GENTLEMEN', pushed all the right critical buttons, fleshing out their grungy noir-soul sound against a typically hard-bitten lyrical background. Although the record surprisingly failed to make the US charts, it scored a Top 60 placing in the UK. DULLI's rendition of Barry White's 'CAN'T GET ENOUGH OF YOUR LOVE', was an indication of where AFGHAN WHIGS were headed with 'BLACK LOVE'. An even more soul-centric offering, the album almost scraped into the British Top 40, the band now signed to 'Mute' (still on 'Elektra' US). 'Columbia' took up the reins for er ... 1998's '1965', a celebration of rock music's debt to the power of sex. Recorded in New Orleans, the record was hailed as their long promised masterpiece, a writhing, sweaty slab of post-grunge voodoo soul. DULLI matched this aggression later in the year, after a brawl with a steward earned him a few days in intensive care and a fractured skull ... er to boot. Subsequently the singer threatened action on the Texas nightclub even though it was alleged that he was the main instigator. Early in 2001, DULLI and Co disbanded. • **Covered:** MY WORLD IS EMPTY WITHOUT YOU + I HEAR A SYMPHONY + COME SEE ABOUT ME (Diana Ross & The Supremes) / CHALK OUTLINE (Paul K & The Weathermen) / BEWARE (Al Green) / TRUE LOVE TRAVELS ON A GRAVEL ROAD (Percy Sledge) / BAND OF GOLD (Freda Payne) / THE DARK END OF THE STREET (Dan Penn) / READY (Scrawl) / LITTLE GIRL BLUE (Rodgers-Hart) / I KEEP COMING BACK (Austell-Graham) / IF I ONLY HAD A HEART (from 'The Wizard Of Oz') / CREEP (Radiohead) / LITTLE GIRL BLUE (Hart-Rodgers) / CREEP (TLC) / MR. SUPERLOVE (Ass Ponys) / REVENGE (Patti Smith) / EASILY PERSUADED (Martha Reeves & The Vandellas) / YOU'VE CHANGED (Carey-Fisher) / I WANT TO GO TO SLEEP (Harold Chichester) / MOON RIVER (Henry Mancini) / IF THERE'S A HELL BELOW (WE'RE ALL GOING TO GO) (Curtis Mayfield) / SUPERSTITION (Stevie Wonder) / MISS WORLD (Hole) / PAPA WAS A RASCAL (James Booker) / LOST IN THE SUPERMARKET (Clash).

Album rating: BIG TOP HALLOWEEN (*4) / UP IN IT (*6) / CONGREGATION (*8) / GENTLEMEN (*8) / BLACK LOVE (*6) / 1965 (*8)

GREG DULLI – vocals, guitar / **RICK McCOLLUM** – guitar / **JOHN CURLEY** – bass / **STEVE EARLE** – drums

	not iss.	Ultrasuede
Oct 88. (lp) *<001>* **BIG TOP HALLOWEEN**	–	
– Here comes Jesus / In my town / Priscilla's wedding day / Push / Scream / But listen / Big top Halloween / Life in a day / Sammy / Doughball / Back o' the line / Greek is extra.		
	Sub Pop	Sub Pop
Apr 89. (7") *<SP 32>* **I AM THE STICKS. / WHITE TRASH PARTY**	–	
Apr 90. (cd/c/lp/orange-lp) *<SP 60>* **UP IN IT**		
– Retarded / White trash party / Hated / Southpaw / Amphetamines and coffee / Now can we begin / You my flower / Son of the south / I know your secret. *(cd/c+=)* – I am the sticks. *(UK-iss.Aug90 on 'Glitterhouse'; GR 0092) (cd re-iss. Sep98; SPCD 60)*		
Oct 90. (7",7"red) *<SP 84>* **SISTER BROTHER. / HEY CUZ**	–	
Dec 90. (12"ep) *(SP 4-115)* **THE RETARD EP**	–	–
– Retarded / Sister brother / Hey cuz / Turning in two. *(cd-ep May93; SPCD 4-115)*		
Jan 92. (cd-s) *<SP 133>* **TURN ON THE WATER / CHALK OUTLINE / MILES IZ DED**	–	
Jan 92. (lp/cd) *<(SP 183/+CD)>* **CONGREGATION**		
– Her against me / I'm her slave / Turn on the water / Conjure me / Kiss the floor / Congregation / This is my confession / Dedicate it / The temple / Let me lie to you / Tonight. *(cd re-iss. Sep98; same)*		
Jan 92. (7") *<(SP32,5/187)>* **TURN ON THE WATER. / MILES IZ DED**		
(12"+=/cd-s+=) *(SP/+CD 187)* – Delta kong / Chalk outline.		

AFGHAN WHIGS (cont)

May 92. (7"white,7"lavender) <SP 142> **CONJURE ME. / MY WORLD IS EMPTY WITHOUT YOU**
Aug 92. (12"/cd-s) (SP42/+CD 203) **MY WORLD IS EMPTY WITHOUT YOU. / CONJURE ME / YOU MY FLOWER**
Oct 92. (7"ep) <SP54 216> **UPTOWN AVONDALE EP: BAND OF GOLD. / COME SEE ABOUT ME**
  (12"+=/cd-s+=) <(SP53/+CD 215)> – True love travels on a gravel road / Beware.
  (cd-s++=) <(SP 175b)> – Rebirth of the cool.

                                                                 Blast First   Elektra

Sep 93. (7") (BFFP 89) **GENTLEMEN. / MR. SUPERLOVE**
  (12"+=/cd-s+=) (BFFP 89 T/CD) – The dark end of the street.
Oct 93. (lp/cd) (BFFP 90/+CD) <7559 61501-2> **GENTLEMEN**   58
  – If I were going / Gentlemen / Be sweet / Debonair / When we two parted / Fountain and fairfax / What jail is like / My curse / Now you know / I keep coming back / Brother Woodrow – Closing prayer. (lp w /free 7"ep) – ROT. / TONIGHT

— guests on the album: **HAROLD CHICHESTER** – keyboards / **BARB HUNTER** – cello / **JODY STEPHENS** – vocals / **MARCY MAYS** – vocals

Feb 94. (7"ep/12"ep/cd-ep) (BFFP 95/+T/CD) **BROKEN PROMISES EP**
  – Debonair / My curse / Little girl blue / Ready.
  (cd-ep) (BFFP 95CDL) – ('A'side) / Rot / I keep coming back / Tonight.

— In Mar'94, 'MR. SUPERLOVE' was issued on B-side of ASS PONY's single on 'Monocat'.

Aug 94. (7"ep/cd-ep) (BFFP 96/+CD) **WHAT JAIL IS LIKE EP**
  – What jail is like / Revenge / Easily persuaded / My curse.
  (10"ep) (BFFP 96T) – ('A'side) / Now you know (live) / Gentlemen (live) / My world is empty without you / I hear a symphony (live).
  (12"ep/cd-ep) <61708-1/-2> – What jail is like / Mr. Superlove / The dark end of the street / Little girl blue / What jail is like (live) / Now you know (live) / My world is empty without you / I hear a symphony (live).

— **PAUL BUCHIGNANI** – drums; repl. EARLE

                                                           Mute   Elektra

Feb 96. (10"ep/cd-ep) (10/CD MUTE 128) **HONKY'S LADDER E.P.**
  – Honky's ladder / Blame, etc. / If I only had a heart / Creep.
Mar 96. (cd/c/lp) (CD/C+/STUMM 143) <61896> **BLACK LOVE**   41   79
  – Crime scene part one / My enemy / Double day / Blame, etc. / Step into the light / Going to town / Honky's ladder / Night by candlelight / Bulletproof / Summer's kiss / Faded.
Aug 96. (cd-ep) (CDMUTE 199) **GOING TO TOWN / GOING TO TOWN (live at Modern Rock) / YOU'VE CHANGED / I WANT TO GO TO SLEEP / MOON RIVER**

— **MICHAEL HORRIGAN** – drums; repl. PAUL

                                                   Columbia   Columbia

Oct 98. (cd-s) (COL 666576-2) **SOMETHIN' HOT (album version) / SOMETHIN' HOT (12" remix) / MISS WORLD / PAPA WAS A RASCAL**
Oct 98. (cd/c) (491486-2/-4) <69450> **1965**
  – Somethin' hot / Crazy / Uptown again / Sweet son of a bitch / 66 / City soleil / John the baptist / The slide song / Neglekted / Omerta / The vampire Lanois.

— added **JOSH PAXTON** – keyboards / **SUSAN MARSHALL + DOUG FALSETTI** – backing vocals

— disbanded in February 2001

A HANDFUL OF DUST
(see under ⇒ DEAD C.; 80's section)

AINTS!
(see under ⇒ LAUGHING CLOWNS; 80's section)

AIRHEAD

Formed: Maidstone, Kent, England . . . 1987 by songwriter MIKE WALLIS and STEVE MARSHALL, who became The APPLES after being joined by the KESTEVEN brothers, BEN and SAM. At the turn of the decade the alternative popsters signed to 'Korova', almost immediately (due to the existence of another similarly monikered outfit) opting for JEFFERSON AIRHEAD. After one LEIGH GORMAN-produced single, 'CONGRATULATIONS' in early '91 and its follow-up, 'SCRAP HAPPY', they inevitably perhaps received objections from the management of 60's stalwarts, JEFFERSON AIRPLANE. They soon put paid to this idea and resumed life simply as AIRHEAD. With this minor controversy over, the lads floated into the lower regions of the UK singles charts with their third attempt, 'FUNNY HOW'. They started 1992 on a high as the single, 'COUNTING SHEEP' and the much delayed accompanying debut album, 'BOING!', both hit the Top 40 (the latter was originally scheduled for release the previous Spring under the shelved 'JEFFERSON AIRHEAD' banner!). This BYRDS meets WONDER STUFF set also contained what turned out to be their final chart entry, 'RIGHT NOW', the band taking off for a last ditch effort, 'THAT'S ENOUGH', on the much smaller 'Mother Tongue' label.

Album rating: BOING! (*5)

MIKE WALLIS – vocals / **STEVE MARSHALL** – keyboards / **BEN KESTEVEN** – bass / **SAM KESTEVEN** – drums

                                              Korova-WEA   not iss.

Mar 91. (7"; as JEFFERSON AIRHEAD) (KOW 45) **CONGRATULATIONS. / SOMETHING BLUE**
  (12"+=/'A'-society mix-12"+=) (KOW 45T/+X) – ('A'demo).
Jun 91. (7"; as JEFFERSON AIRHEAD) (KOW 46) **SCRAP HAPPY. / TAKE MY TRAIN**
  (12"+=) (KOW 46T) – ('A'-12"mix).

Sep 91. (7") (KOW 47) **FUNNY HOW. / KEEP THE APPLE**   57
  (12"+=/cd-s+=) (KOW T/CD 47) – ('A'extended).
Dec 91. (7") (KOW 48) **COUNTING SHEEP. / TAKE MY TRAIN**   35
  (12"+=) (KOWT 48) – ('A'demo).
  (cd-s++=) (KOWCD 48) – Keep the apple.
Jan 92. (cd)(c/lp) (9031 74679-2)(CODE/KODE 17) **BOING!**   29
  – Scrap happy / I might fall / Right now / Funny how / Easy / I don't mind / Congratulations / Wish you were here / Isn't it rich? / Everybody needs.
Feb 92. (7"/c-s) (KOW/+C 49) **RIGHT NOW. / THE ENEMY**   50
  (12"+=) (KOWT 49) – ('A'demo).
  (cd-s++=) (KOWCD 49) – Through my window.

— BEN also became a member of the POPINJAYS in 1992

                                             Mother Tongue   not iss.

May 93. (10"ep/12"ep/cd-ep) **THAT'S ENOUGH. / THEY DON'T KNOW / SOMEONE SHOULD HAVE TOLD ME**

— split after above

AIR MIAMI
(see under ⇒ UNREST; 80's section)

AIRPORT 5
(see under ⇒ GUIDED BY VOICES; 80's section)

AISLERS SET (see under ⇒ HENRY'S DRESS)

ALCOHOL FUNNYCAR

Formed: Seattle, Washington, USA . . . 1991 by Ohio resident (Antioch College) and songsmith BEN LONDON, former LOVE BATTERY bassist TOMMY SIMPSON and percussionist BUZZ CROCKER. The energetic 3-piece issued the harmonic punk EP 'BURN' (1993), establishing themselves as a tune-strong rock outfit, joining the hordes of underground new-American punk bands of that time. Their debut album, 'TIME TO MAKE DONUTS' (1993), seemed like an extended version of the aforemetioned EP, with only two new tracks and a couple of fillers, which had been included into the mix. Still, it was a prime chance, for all those who had not heard the skilful and melodic pop of ALCOHOL FUNNYCAR first time round, to hear it again on this ten track LP reminiscent of early HUSKER DU or, more recently, EVERCLEAR. After a hectic touring schedule, CROCKER abruptly left the band during the planning and rehearsal for the group's follow-up set 'WEASELS' (1995). New drummer JOEL TRUEBLOOD was subsequently recruited for the band's finest album to date. 'WEASELS' may have been highly unoriginal but it beautifully captured the thrashy Minneapolis punk scene with a jaded flash. Tracks may have occasionally been overexposed, but it was hard not to fall for LONDON's aching lyrics about relationships, whilst he was singing with a completely genuine voice.

Album rating: BURN mini (*5) / TIME TO MAKE THE DONUTS (*6) / WEASELS (*7)

BEN LONDON – vocals, guitar / **TOMMY 'BONEHEAD' SIMPSON** – bass (ex-LOVE BATTERY) / **BUZZ CROCKER** – drums

                                           not iss.   C/Z-Volcano

Feb 93. (m-cd) <36058> **BURN**
  – Time / Burn / Aggravation / Pawn / Snapping the straw.
Dec 93. (cd) <36069> **TIME TO MAKE THE DONUTS**
  – Shapes / Get it right / Try to understand / All about it / Marble head / Time / Tumble down / Last night / Aggravation / AFC theme song.

— **JOEL TRUEBLOOD** – drums; repl. BUZZ

Oct 95. (cd) <36081> **WEASELS**
  – Objects / Red wine / Chicken wings / Overtaken / Kindling / Weasels / Napoleon / Abandoned / Shoot you down / Closed / Sun spots / Lay down.

— the next year, the band split and drove back to their proverbial pub

ALFIE

Formed: Manchester, England . . . 1998 by LEE GORTON, IAN SMITH, MATT McGEEVER, SAM MORRIS and percussionist SEAN KELLY. This folksy/indie quintet apparently started making music as a reaction against the millions of floppy-haired, guitar strumming NOEL GALLAGHER lookalikes drifting around the Manchester scene. After a brief article in the NME, the group became friends with DAMON GOUGH (aka BADLY DRAWN BOY) who signed them to his 'Twisted Nerve' venture. Three EP's followed; 'BOOKENDS', 'THE ALFIE' and, perhaps the best, 'MONTEVIDEO'. The sound was like much of the current Manchester scene in the sense that it was more focused and sublime than a handful of HAPPY MONDAYS or OASIS records. Wispy and acoustic songs with fading cello and melodic vocals was the direction for the band's debut album, 'IF YOU HAPPY WITH YOU NEED DO NOTHING' (2001), which reflected the floating calmness of BELLE & SEBASTIAN, while still possessing the rockier and emotionally quaint edge of The DOVES, or fellow Mancunians ELBOW. After a critically and commercialy successful tour of the UK, ALFIE managed to find time to record their sophomore effort 'A WORD IN YOUR EAR' (2002), a more simplistic but accomplished record.

ALFIE (cont)

Album rating: IF YOU HAPPY WITH YOU NEED GO NOTHING (*7) / A WORD IN YOUR EAR (*6)

LEE GORTON – vocals / **IAN SMITH** – guitar / **MATT McGEEVER** – cello / **SAM MORRIS** – bass / **SEAN KELLY** – percussion, drums

			Twisted Nerve	Beggars Banquet
Feb 00.	(7"ep)	*(TN 011)* **ALFIE EP**		-
	– Sure and simple time / Ooze a lullaby / Check the weight.			
Aug 00.	(7"ep)	*(TN 016)* **BOOKENDS EP**		-
	– James's dream / Bookends / Talking song / James's dream 2.			
Nov 00.	(10"ep)	*(TN 019)* **MONTEVIDEO EP**		-
	– Montevideo / It's just about the weather / You make no bones / Montevideo (reprise) / Manor House farm.			
Apr 01.	(lp/cd)	*(TN 026/+CD)* <40145> **IF YOU HAPPY WITH YOU NEED DO NOTHING**	62	
	– Bookends / It's just about the weather / James's dream / 2 up 2 down / You make no bones / Umlaut / Sure and simple time / Check the weight / Talking song / Manor house farm / Montevideo.			
Aug 01.	(7")	*(TN 033)* **YOU MAKE NO BONES. / DON'T MAKE ME BLUE**	61	-
	(cd-s) *(TN 033CD)* – ('A'side) / Reverse midas touch / Wormwood.			
	(7") *(TN 033R)* – ('A'-Any Votel remix) / Ooze a lullaby (lost children's desk remix).			
Mar 02.	(7")	*(TN 037)* **A WORD IN YOUR EAR. / CLOUDY LEMON**		-
	(cd-s+=) *(TN 037CD)* – ('A'-J-Walk remix).			
Mar 02.	(lp/cd)	*(TN 038/+CD)* <40157> **A WORD IN YOUR EAR**		
	– A word in your ear / Cloudy lemonade / Bends for 72 miles / Halfway home / Not half / The reverse midas touch / Summer lanes / Me and mine / Rain, heaven, hail / The lighthouse keeper.			

ALIEN CRIME SYNDICATE (see under ⇒ MEICES)

ALISON'S HALO

Formed: Tempe, Phoenix, Arizona, USA ... late 1992 by CATHERINE COOPER, ADAM COOPER, DAVID ROGERS and ROGER BROGAN. Part of the musical arena dubbed "beautiful noise:, the group's brand of heavy space-rock was much akin to the early work of THE VERVE and like them owed much to earlier British shoegaze bands in the shape MY BLOODY VALENTINE and The CURE, especially riding high on the latter's pop-goth styling. The HALO's early career saw them touring with the likes of the aforementioned VERVE and the BOO RADLEYS, giving them a vantage point when they debuted with the superb 7", 'DOZEN', in 1995. This early single with 'CALENDAR' B-side, showcased the band's brilliant musicianship and ability to create loud yet contemplative trippy rock. Their debut album, 'EYEDAZZLER 1992-1996' (1998), only appeared some years later and was more of a compilation of the band's material; collecting together demos, outtakes and live music. However it did serve as a competent reading of the outfit's sonic development, from their more naive loud and rocky beginnings to the numbed down and sonorous territory that the band began to move in. It was more the pity that their output was never more than these few fine releases.

Album rating: EYEDAZZLER 1992-1996 compilation (*7)

CATHERINE COOPER – vocals, guitar / **ADAM COOPER** – guitar / **DAVID ROGERS** – bass / **ROGER BROGAN** – drums

			not iss.	own label
1993.	(c-ep)	<none> **SLUG EP**	-	
	– Leech / Slowbleed / Tom / Race bannon (instrumental).			

			not iss.	club demo
1994.	(c-ep)	<none> **HALO EP**	-	
	– Tom / Wishes.			

			not iss.	Independent Project
1995.	(7")	<IPR 49> **DOZEN. / CALENDAR**	-	

— split late in 1996

– compilations, etc. –

Jun 98.	(cd) *Burnt Hair; (SINGE 018) / Orchard; <4776>* **EYEDAZZLER 1992-1996**		2000
	– Raindrop / Wishes / Melt / Chime / Always April / Slowbleed / Torn / Leech / Sunshy / Chalkboard James. (+ 2 hidden live tracks)		
2002.	(cd-ep) *<net>* **8 BIT EP**	-	-
	– Cobra . Race bannon / Chula / 8 bit / Jaguar / Alpha fuzz.		

ALL NATURAL LEMON & LIME FLAVORS

Formed: Ringwood, New Jersey, USA ... 1995 by JOSHUA BOOTH, the brothers BRIAN and STEVEN DOHERTY, MARC SORRILLO and JEREMY WINTER. The latter had been writing songs from his Oakland bedroom since 1989 at the tender age of 14. A few years later, he joined SENEPEDE, a teen glam rock band who auditioned for 'Interscope' records. The change came when WINTER got hold of some MY BLOODY VALENTINE albums and virtually disregarded eveything else. In time (spring '94, to be exact), SENEPEDE evolved into ALL NATURAL LEMON & LIME FLAVORS, although WINTER himself was lounging out as JETT BRANDO; a few cassettes exist with producer PETE MURPHY at the helm. Spacy, trippy and at times twee, ALL NATURAL ... created their sonic sculptures (fuse MY BLOODY VALENTINE, The BOO RADLEYS and The PALE SAINTS) on their overlooked, but classy eponymous mini-set of 1996; re-released five years later in full extended form by 'Gern Blandsten'. The same label were to deliver a single, 'I AM WHERE YOU ARE' and their full-length follow-up, 'TURNING INTO SMALL' (1998), a slightly disappointing attempt which might've done well several shoegazing years previously. With ANL&LF taking a sabbatical, JEREMY WINTER (with the help of other 'NATURAL musicians) arrived back on the scene post-millennium as JETT BRANDO; the charming but intense 'THE MOVEMENT TOWARD YOU' (2000) showed space-pop was still in vogue.

Album rating: ALL NATURAL LEMON & LIME FLAVORS (*7) / TURNING INTO SMALL (*5) / STRAIGHT BLUE LINE compilation (*6) / Jett Brando: MOVEMENT TOWARD YOU (*6)

JOSHUA BOOTH – vocals, guitar, keyboards / **STEVEN DOHERTY** – vocals, guitar, keyboards, violin / **JEREMY WINTER** – vocals, bass, AM radio frequencies / **MARC SORRILLO** – guitar, accordion, autoharp / **BRIAN DOHERTY** – drums

			not iss.	Rocket Science
1996.	(7")	<003> **CATCHER. / SPAUN**	-	
	(UK-iss.Mar98; same)			

			not iss.	Koombia
1996.	(m-cd)	<koom 001> **ALL NATURAL LEMON & LIME FLAVORS**	-	
	– Muffin 57 / Saturn jig / Salad forest / All the time / How come? / Jayne baby / Blue balloons / Wondered why. (cd-iss. Mar98 on 'Gern Blandsten'; GERN 036CD) (lp-iss.Aug00; GERN 036) <US re-iss. Jan01 on 'Gern Blandsten'+=; GERN 051> – String of stars / How come? / Tea with honey / Nice soup / Yellow.			

			Gern Blandsten	Gern Blandsten
Oct 97.	(7")	<(GERN 027)> **I AM WHERE YOU WERE. / REPETITIVE MONOTONOUS**		1996
Mar 98.	(lp/cd)	<(GERN/+CD 36V)> **TURNING INTO SMALL**		
	– You can never tell / Your imagination / Puzzled into pieces / Lattershed / When things come falling / In between and after / False from above / Snowflake eye / Emergency turn off / Paradigm somehow.			

			Hidden Agenda	not iss.
Jul 98.	(7")	*(AHA 005)* **THAT FAMILIAR LOOK TO YOU. / EXPLODED VIEW**		1996

– compilations, etc. –

Aug 00.	(cd) *Gern Blandsten; <(GERN 044)>* **STRAIGHT BLUE LINE** (singles)		Jun00
	– Repetitive monotonous / Catcher / Spaun / Exploded view / Linear force / Purple puddles / The number knows its names / That familiar look to you / I am where you were / Spin cycle.		

JETT BRANDO

JEREMY WINTER with other ANL&LF members (**BRIAN DOHERTY**) plus **PETE MURPHY** – bass, keyboards / **DAVID LETO** – drums

			Gern Blandsten	Gern Blandsten
Jun 00.	(lp/cd)	<(GERN 046/+CD)> **THE MOVEMENT TOWARD YOU**		
	– The center of gravity (sink right down) / Waiting . . . / Well, well / Athuna / Love you blues / Won't you treat it like a storm? / All your tongues / More than becoming / Nobody wants to know / In the dead hot sun / Who is to decide.			

			not iss.	Go Kart
Nov 02.	(m-cd)	<96> **JAGGED JUNCTION**	-	
	– Heavy rotation / Be so kind / Until you fall / Way side blues / Systems fall / Sass.			

ALPHA STONE (see under ⇒ DARKSIDE)

ALUMINUM GROUP

Formed: Chicago, Illinois, USA ... 1994 by brothers JOHN and FRANK NAVIN, who named their act after a line of furniture designed by Charles and Ray Eames. Associated with the Wicker Park music scene, they first appeared as members of the hardcore WOMEN IN LOVE, around 1983. Longtime fans of chamber-pop like the CARPENTERS and SERGIO MENDES, they eventually decided to move in this direction themselves, little knowing that easy-listening orchestrated pop would become fashionable again around the mid-1990s. Self-released debut 'WONDER BOY' (1995) was a mixed-bag of gentle chamber-pop compositions, owing as much to modern indie-pop like MAGNETIC FIELDS and EVERYTHING BUT THE GIRL, as to their easy idols like BACHARACH and MANCINI. There is a playful sensibility to the album, evident with their bold interpretations of Guns n' Roses' 'SWEET CHILD O' MINE' and Lerner & Loewe's 'LOVERLY'. It was another three years until their follow-up LP, 'PLANO' was released, and by now the ALUMINUM GROUP included guitarist JOHN RIDENOUR, drummer JOHN BLAHA, bassist EDDIE CARLSON and keyboardist LIZ CONANT. Again, finely composed chamber-pop, although at times remarkably reminiscent of MAGNETIC FIELDS, highlights included the plaintive opener 'CHOCOLATES' and the flawless refinery of 'STAR WISH'. 1998's 'PEDALS' saw the ALUMINUM GROUP take a positive step forwards, abandoning the derivative elements of their sound, and moving towards more sophisticated, darkly atmospheric arrangements. 'ROSE SELAVY'S VALISE' typified their new sound and direction; a brooding epic of sweeping synths, horns and guitars. 'PELO' (2000) represented a further musical progression, and a greater emphasis on electronics and layering of sounds and effects. The

ALUMINUM GROUP (cont)

'GROUP's 2002 release 'HAPPYNESS' – possibly their finest – contained elements of their previous three albums, and denoted contemporary indie-pop at its most elegant and inspired.

Album rating: WONDER BOY (*5) / PLANO (*6) / PEDALS (*7) / PELO (*5) / HAPPYNESS (*6)

JOHN NAVIN – guitars, etc / **FRANK NAVIN** – guitars, etc

not iss.   Aluminium Group

1995. (cd) <70074> **WONDER BOY**
– Chocolates / Pretty mouth and green my eyes / Beatrice / Baby / Sweet child o' mine / That fossil that you call your lover / In the age of fable / Lovely / Tripping over boxes / Girl's bike / Greenstreet. <re-iss. May99 on 'Monty Fresh'+=; MF 33CD>
– Salut au monde / Kalypso and Odysseus / The laughing pool / Come back Miss Battle / Searching for my Omeo / They're not losing a daughter / Byzantium / Pink Chanel / Tell me where you are / The smallest man in the world.

── added **JOHN RIDENOUR** – guitar / **LIZ CONANT** – keyboards / **EDDIE CARLSON** – bass / **JOHN BLAHA** – drums

Minty Fresh   Minty Fresh

Aug 98. (cd) <MF 29CD> **PLANO**
– Chocolates / Angel on a trampoline / A boy in love / Sugar & promises / The mattachine society / Sunday morning / 9 months later / Sad gay life / Steam / Star wish / Photograph / Storytime.

── the NAVIN's added various guests

Dec 99. (cd) <(MF 34CD)> **PEDALS**   Aug99
– Rose Selavy's valise / Lie detector test / Paperback / Easy on your eyes / Miss Tate / Two-bit faux construction / A blur in your vision / Jinxed / Impress me / $35.

Hefty   Hefty

Nov 00. (cd) <(HEFTY 025)> **PELO**   Oct00
– Pussycat / If you've got a lover, you've got a life / Good-bye goldfish, hi piranha / Worrying kind / Satellite / Cannot make you out / Tom of Finland / Pussy reports / Geraldine / Sermon to the frogs.

── the NAVIN's were augmented by **JOHN RIDENOUR, DOUG McCOMBS, JOHN HERNDON, JOHN McENTIRE, LIZ CONANT, REBECCA GATES, SUSAN VOELZ, ROB MAZUREK, LARRY BEERS, GRAEME GIBSON + KENNY SLUITER**

Wishing Tree   Wishing Tree

Sep 02. (cd) <(WTR 105)> **HAPPYNESS**
– Tiny decision / I blow you kisses / Pop / Two lights / We're both hiding / Kid / Speed dial / Oxygen / Be killed / Stroke.

AMERICAN ANALOG SET

Formed: Austin, Texas, USA . . . 1994 out of Dallas' ELECTRIC COMPANY (no connection to MEDICINE) by songwriter ANDREW KENNY, LISA ROSCHMANN and MARK SMITH, adding LEE GILLESPIE to form a quartet. After the group had re-formed under the new title, AMERICAN ANALOG SET, they were signed by 'Emperor Jones', a side label set up by KING COFFEY's (of BUTTHOLE SURFERS fame) 'Trance Syndicate', releasing the single 'DIANA SLOWBURNER 2' (which was taken from the '96 slo-core debut 'THE FUN OF WATCHING FIREWORKS'). The beautiful 'FROM OUR LIVING ROOM TO YOURS' was issued one year later along with the two-track EP 'LATE ONE SUNDAY & THE FOLLOWING MORNING'. It's sparse lo-fi edge nicely with KENNY's whispering vocals, an audience might have been convinced that they had tears in your ears! Unfortunately, AAS, returned in 1999 with the disappointing 'THE GOLDEN BAND', which was, in no way whatsoever, a chip off the old block. Two subsequent releases, the long-player 'KNOW BY HEART' (2001) and the mini 'UPDATES' (2002) – both for 'Tiger Style' – revealed KENNY and Co to be as cerebral and Lo-Fi as ever; the latter remixed batch saw them cover Her Space Holiday's 'THESE DAYS' and well as opening with the newly recorded 'DESERT EAGLE'.

Album rating: THE FUN OF WATCHING FIREWORKS (*7) / FROM OUR LIVING ROOM TO YOURS (*7) / THE GOLDEN BAND (*5) / THROUGH THE 90's . . . collection (*6) / KNOW BY HEART (*7) / UPDATES mini (*5)

ANDREW KENNY – vocals, guitar / **LISA ROSCHMANN** – keyboards / **LEE GILLESPIE** – bass / **MARK SMITH** – drums

Emperor Jones   Emperor Jones

Apr 96. (7") <EJ 03-7> **DIANA SLOWBURNER. / HIGH FIDELITY VS. GUY FIDELITY**

May 96. (cd/lp) <EJ 04 CD/LP> **THE FUN OF WATCHING FIREWORKS**
– Diana slowburner II / On the run's where I'm from / On my way / Dim stars (the boy in my arms) / Gone to earth / Trespassers in the stereo field / Too tired to shine II / It's alright.

Oct 97. (12"ep/cd-ep) <(DRL 048/+CD)> **LATE ONE SUNDAY & THE FOLLOWING MORNING**
– Late one Sunday / The following morning.
(above issued on 'Darla')

Jul 97. (7") <EJ 013> **MAGNIFICENT SEVENTIES. / WAKING UP IS HARD TO DO**

Nov 97. (cd/lp) <EJ 14 CD/LP> **FROM OUR LIVING ROOM TO YOURS**   Jul97
– Magnificent seventies / Using the hope diamond as a doorstop / Blue chaise / Where have all the good boys gone / White house / Two way diamond I / Two way diamond II / Don't wake me. (re-iss. Jan01; same)

Jul 99. (7") <EJ 25> **THE ONLY LIVING BOY AROUND. / IT'S ALL ABOUT US**

Jul 99. (cd) <EJ 28CD> **THE GOLDEN BAND**
– Weather report / A good friend is always around / It's all about us / A schoolboy's charm / The wait / New drifters / II / III / IV / The golden band / I must soon quit the scene / Will the real Danny Radnor please stand? (lp-iss.Aug00; EJ 28LP)

2000. (7"; split w/ ADVENTURES IN STEREO) <issue #2> **TRESPASSERS IN THE STEREO**
– Living room incidental #2 / The corduroy kid / (others by AIS).
(above issued on 'After Hours' fanzine)

May 01. (cd) <EJCD 42> **THROUGH THE 90's: SINGLES AND UNRELEASED** (compilation)
– The only living boy around / Waking up is hard to do / On my way / High fidelity vs. Guy fidelity / Thin fingers / Living room incidental #2 – The corduroy kid / Don't wake me / Dr. Pepper / Where did you come from (reprise) / Magnificent seventies / It's all about us / Diana slowburner II / Mellow fellow – Gone to earth (live) / Tow way diamond I – II – Don't wake me (live).

Tiger Style   Tiger Style

Sep 01. (cd/lp) <(TS 018 CD/LP)> **KNOW BY HEART**
– Punk as fuck / The only one / Little foxes through fences / The postman / Choir vandals / Gone to earth / Million young / The kindness of strangers / Know by heart / Slow company / Aaron and Maria / We're computerizing and we just don't need.

Oct 01. (7") <TS 019> **NEW EQUATION. / ALL I WANT**

Jul 02. (m-lp/m-cd) <(TS 026/+CD)> **UPDATES**
– Desert eagle / These days / Aaron and Maria / Know by heart / The postman / We're computerizing and we just don't need.

AMERICAN FOOTBALL (see under ⇒ JOAN OF ARC)

AM/FM

Formed: Philadelphia, Pennsylvania, USA . . . 1999 by BRIAN SOKEL and MICHAEL PARSELL; originally started as a side-project away from the former's main group occupation FRANKLIN. PARSELL, meanwhile, had cut his musical teeth via FRAIL and GOODBYE BLUE MONDAY, the pair now fleshing out these fledgling tunes with a variety of instrumentation and studio effects. 1999 saw the duo debut with the EP, 'AUDIOT', a record which also included help from SOKEL's FRANKLIN bandmates, JOSHUA MILLS and GREG GIULIANO. Following this up with the full-length outing 'MUTILATE US' (2001), SOKEL and PARSELL showed they had musical room to move in, combining country rock, indie PAVEMENT-esque pop, seventies-style riffing and much besides into a well worked lo-fi whole. They issued their sophomore album 'GETTING INTO SINKING' that same year, augmented this time by INK AND DAGGER's TERRY YERVES at the production controls. With hardly a pause for breath the group emerged again the following year with the quietly uplifting EP, 'THE SKY IS THE NEW GROUND'.
• **Covered:** DISNEY GIRLS (Beach Boys) / HEY, THAT'S NO WAY TO SAY GOODBYE (Leonard Cohen).

Album rating: MUTILATE US (*6) / GETTING INTO SINKING (*7)

BRIAN SOKEL – vocals, multi (ex-FRANKLIN) / **MICHAEL PARSELL** – drums, guitar (ex-SCIENCE OF, ex-FRAIL) / plus **JOSHUA MILS** – bass (of FRANKLIN) / **GREG GIULIANO** – drums (of FRANKLIN)

not iss.   Skylab

1999. (cd-ep) <SKY 10> **AUDIOT**
– The death they claim / We will study your life / A poor sense of timing / Say what? / Neverever / Straight around / Those long arms.

Polyvinyl   Polyvinyl

Mar 01. (lp/cd) <(PRC 041/+CD)> **MUTILATE US**
– (Mutilate us) / Secretly odds in knowing normal worlds / A best man (Put my girlfriend on fire) / You and me at 53 / Those long arms / Yours recklessly / Leanne, the seasons persist / When I died in Sebastopol / Time flows much more slowly this way / When Larry and Gary get married / Disney girls (1957) / Success rides a shiny white line / Mutilate us. (cd re-iss. Aug01 on 'Cooking Vinyl'; COOKCD 210)

Jul 01. (cd-s) <FRYCD 103> **A BEST MAN (PUT MY GIRLFRIEND ON FIRE) / COME SUCK DOWN A CLOUD**
(above issued on 'Cooking Vinyl')

Dec 01. (lp/cd) <(PRC 044/+CD)> **GETTING INTO SINKING**   Oct01
– Virgins! virgins! / If we burned all the assholes the Earth would look like the sun / All your dreams come true / The death they claim / And then I got to thinking about the animals / Call me up / I was never here two seconds ago / Head gone vertical / It fell out of my head / Hey, that's no way to say goodbye / Come suck down a cloud / Getting into sinking.

Oct 02. (cd-ep) <PRC 053CD> **THE SKY IS THE NEW GROUND**
– Every start / Gone in three / Mrs. Astronaut / All to remember.

A MINOR FOREST

Formed: San Francisco, California, USA . . . 1993 by ERIK HOVERSTEN and ANDEE CONNORS. The pair debuted with 'FLEMISH ALTRUISM' (1996), an album characterised by the production work of third and fourth members, STEVE ALBINI and BOB WESTON who also contributed in the songwriting department. Described as beefy-rock with a lo-fi melodic ambience thrown in for good measure (i.e. SLINT, LOW, SHELLAC), the record (released on 'Thrill Jockey' in the US) certainly had a few choice titles. BRIAN PAULSON took over the controls for 1998's 'ININDEPENDENCE', JOHN TREVOR BENSON filling the shoes of the ever in-demand ALBINI and WESTON. • **Covered:** FATAL WOUND (Uncle Tupelo) / LADY (Little River Band) / MASTER OF PUPPETS (Metallica).

Album rating: FLEMISH ALTRUISM (CONSTITUENT PARTS 1993-1996) (*6) / ININDEPENDENCE (*6) / SO, WERE THEY IN SOME SORT OF FIGHT? collection (*6)

ERIK HOVERSTEN – vocals, guitar, bass / **ANDEE CONNORS** – drums, vocals / with **STEVE ALBINI + BOB WESTON** augmenting & writing

A MINOR FOREST (cont)   THE GREAT INDIE DISCOGRAPHY   The 1990s

				not iss.	own label
1994.	(12"mauve) **A MINOR FOREST**			Divot	Divot

				not iss.	1995 Chrysanthemum
Nov 96.	(7") <(DVT 004)> **TALKING TO THE MAN FROM LUSK. / Gainer: BASTION**				

				Runt	Thrill Jockey
Feb 97.	(7") **NO ONE LIKES AN OLD BABY. / Three Mile Pilot: THE APPROACH**			-	

				Thrill Jockey	Thrill Jockey
Mar 97.	(d-lp/cd) (RUNT 27) <THRILL 34/+CD> **FLEMISH ALTRUISM (CONSTITUENT PARTS 1993-1996)**				Oct96

– But the pants stay on / Bill's mom likes to fuck / Ed is 50 / So Jesus was at the last supper / Jacking off George Lucas / Speed for Gavin / Perform the critical straw transfer / Dainty Jack and his amazing technicolor / Beef rigger / The loneliest enuretic. (re-iss. Jul97 on 'Thrill Jockey'; same as US)

──── **JOHN TREVOR BENSON** – bass, tapes, guitar; repl. ALBINI + WESTON

				Thrill Jockey	Thrill Jockey
Aug 98.	(d-lp/cd) <(THRILL 56/+CD)> **ININDEPENDENCE**				

– Dutch fist / Erik's budding romance / Look at that car, it's full of ... / ... It's salmon! / Smell of hot / Michael Anthony / Discoler.

				not iss.	Tree
Sep 98.	(7") **split with SWEEP THE LEG JOHNNY**			-	

──── disbanded on November 1st, 1998; LOVERSTEN continued with avant-jazz outfit, THRENODY ENSEMBLE who issued 'Timbre Hollow' early 2000 – BENSON and CONNORS formed TICWAR.

– compilations, etc. –

May 00. (d-cd) *My Pal God*; <(MPG 018)> **SO, WERE THEY IN SOME SORT OF FIGHT?** Oct99
– No one likes an old baby / Fatal wound / Cocktail party / So were they in some sort of fight? / Three long piles / Putting the gay back in reggae / Five bucks on pump number seven / Wussy / Inter-continental stalker (and so does the) / Disco party / The ball window (excerpt) // John gets leftovers again / Well swayed / (Talking to the) Man from Lusk / Fuck the hours / Fatal E's / Water song / Armigh is a hovercraft / Speed for Gavin (the lesser version) / Lady / The convent / Shaggy parasol.

AMNESIA (see under ⇒ MEDICINE)

AMP

Formed: Wales ... around 1995 by driving force RICHARD WALKER, previously a collaborator with The SECRET GARDEN and the DISTANCE project. WALKER teamed up with French singer, KARINE CHARFF, after impressing her with a cassette/short story recording from 1992. Also recruiting MATT ELLIOT (now THIRD EYE FOUNDATION) and MATT JONES (of CRESCENT), these self-proclaimed "Trans European Esoterrorists" began recording, and in 1996 released singles 'GET THERE' and 'LE PETIT CHAT', alongside debut album 'SIRENES'. Occupying musical territory somewhere between shoegazing and the Bristol 'Trip Hop' sound, AMP had created a work of sweeping soundscapes, echoing ambience and waves of feedback. Guitars, drums and vocals are layered and distorted, often rendered almost incomprehensible. Through these waves of sound come occasional moments of clarity and rhythm, like on 'MATILDA'S SHORTS WAVE' and 'NOVEMBER'. 1997 saw the line-up altering, with JONES and ELLIOT leaving, and WALKER and CHARFF developing a closer working relationship side by side with GARETH MITCHELL and GUY COOPER, whom WALKER had known from his SECRET GARDEN days. The product of this new collaboration was 'ASTRALMOONBEAMPROJECTIONS', their first release for the 'Kranky' label. The panoramic scope of 'SIRENES' remained, but they delved deeper (and louder) into shoegaze sonic experimentation, although CHARFF's vocals seemed a little less imperceptible, like on 'STELLATA' – a highlight of the album. The same year, and recorded in a one-day session by WALKER and MITCHELL (and subsequently re-mixed), AMP released the eighty-seven minute, four-track ambient masterpiece, 'PERCEPTION'. A drifting, majestic, melting pot of sounds, drones and feedback, extra touches include 'RECEIVE's Gregorian chanting, used to haunting effect. With MITCHELL leaving to form PHILOSOPHER'S STONE, WALKER and CHARFF followed-up 'PERCEPTION' with a collection of singles, rarities and B-sides – 'PASSE-PRESENT' (1998). An extremely varied collection of compositions, it even includes an AMP version of 'SCARBOROUGH FAIR', with WALKER on harmonium and accordion. The same year they created 'STENORETTE', this time assisted by programmer OLIVIER GAUTHIER and producer RICHARD HAMPSON. In 1999, WALKER worked alone on the LP 'SYZYGY: MUSIC FOR MISFITS & MALCONTENTS', as A.M.P. STUDIO. Effectively an AMP album, but with a few slight variations – like a looping piano and drum on 'VORTEX DANSE' – and no vocal input from CHARFF. A.M.P. STUDIO's second release, 'UNCONSCIOUS COUNTRY', with COOPER recruited to provide bass and rhythm, had a meditative feel, characterized by rolling echoes of sound. AMP returned with 2001's 'SAINT CECILIA SINSEMILLA', a collection of tracks from a European radio session and live date; the live context allows CHARFF's vocals full opportunity to impress.

Album rating: SIRENES (*6) / ASTRALMOONBEAMPROJECTIONS (*5) / PERCEPTION (*7) / PASSE-PRESENT collection (*6) / STENORETTE (*7) / SYZYGY: MUSIC FOR MISFITS AND MALCONTENTS (*6) / UNCONSCIOUS COUNTRY (*5) / SAINT CECILIA SINSEMILLA (*6) / L'AMOUR INVISIBLE (*6)

KARINE CHARFF – vocals / **RICHARD WALKER** – instruments / **GARETH MITCHELL** – instruments / with also part-timers early on **GUY COOPER + MATT ELLIOT** (of SECRET GARDEN)

				Linda's Strange Vacation	not iss.
Oct 96.	(7") (LSD 01) **GET THERE. / REMEMBER**			L.S.D.	-
Oct 96.	(lp) (LSD 02) **SIRENES**				-

– Souvenir / Rave mantra / Frieze / So be it / Merry go down / November / Matilda's shorts wave / etc. (cd-iss. Jun97 on 'Wurlitzer Jukebox'; WJ 9)

				Wurlitzer Jukebox	not iss.
Nov 96.	(7") (WJ 7) **FRISE. / LE PETIT CHAT**				-

				Kranky	Kranky
May 97.	(d-lp/cd) <(KRANK 017/+CD)> **ASTRALMOONBEAMPROJECTIONS**				

– Onehopesinuncertainty / Shadowfall [d-lp-only] / Lightdripglow / Transmigration / Interlude / Stellata / Shiftime / Polemic / Allghtfarout [d-lp-only] / Celestialreturn.

				Darla	not iss.
1997.	(d-cd) (DRL 36) **PERCEPTION**				-

– Perception / Receive / Perception returns / Perceive.

1997. (12"clear; as A.M.P.) (DRL 38) **HEART AND SOUL DISSOLVES. / HEART AND SOUL RESOLVES / (UNTITLED)** -

──── now without GARETH who formed PHILOSOPHER'S STONE

				Earworm	not iss.
Sep 97.	(one-sided-7"clear; as AMP STUDIO) (WORM 8) **MISSTYPE DOLITTLE**				-

				Wurlitzer Jukebox	not iss.
1998.	(7") (WJ 15) **BEYOND. / LUTIN**				-

				Ochre	not iss.
Oct 98.	(cd-ep) (OCH 031CD) **SUNFLOWER EP**				-

				Kranky	Kranky
Oct 98.	(lp/cd) <(KRANK 031/+CD)> **STENORETTE**				Nov98

– Intwo / Tomorrow / When / You are here / Songs / Zoe / Two / Tango non / Sunflower / Just-ice / Bilboquet / Outlier.

A.M.P. STUDIO

──── now down to just **RICHARD**

				Amberly	not iss.
1998.	(7") (AMY 001) **WISH EP**				-

– Slip / Tiller.

				A.A.R.	not iss.
Aug 99.	(cd) (AAR 001CD) **SYZYGY: MUSIC FOR MISFITS AND MALCONTENTS**				-

– In side out / Vortex danse / Spaced ship sleep / Syzygy /

──── added **GUY COOPER** – bass, etc.

				Fourth Dimension	not iss.
Feb 00.	(cd) (FDCD 61) **UNCONSCIOUS COUNTRY**				-

– Lost (parts 1-3) / Found (parts 1-4).

				Ochre	not iss.
May 00.	(cd/d-lp) (OCH 017 L/+CD) **ALIEN REGISTRATION OFFICE**				-

– Blow up / 32 paths virtually / 231 gates around / Some kind of ... / Bird blues / Morning song / Love is all ... / Blow up (instrumental).

AMP

──── **RICHARD + KARINE** plus **OLIVIER GAUTHIER** – programmer / **JAN ZERT** – electronics

				Space Age Recordings	not iss.
Apr 01.	(cd) (ORBIT 27CD) **SAINT CECILIA SENSEMILLA** (radio session 1998 / live 1999)				-

– Get there / Tango non / Hum field modulator / Icu / Oh Jesus / Outlier / Stellata / Intersun / Sunflower.

Jun 02. (cd) (ORBIT 29CD) **L'AMOUR INVISIBLE** -
– Crazyhead / L'amour invisible / Curious smile / How can we be sure / Where was when / Glasshouse jam / It ain't easy / Love flies by / Junkyard blues / Go.

– compilations, etc. –

Apr 98. (blue-lp/cd) *Enraptured*; (<RAPT CD/LP 16>) **PASSE-PRESENT**
– Remember / Ombres / Scarborough fair / Get there / Le petit chat / Noir et noir / Lutin. 2 / Frise / Yonder (instrumental).

AMPHETAMEANIES

Formed: Glasgow, Scotland ... 1998 by 10-piece fronted by blonde JANE CHALMERS and skinhead STAN MILLAR, along with her musician chums HELEN LLOYD, JENNY (aka MISS DIVERSE) and LINDSEY WATSON, plus his pals RAT, ALEX HUNTLEY, MICK COOKE, GORDON DAVIDSON and JOEL GRAY (some of whom moonlighted with BELLE & SEBASTIAN, LUNGLEG and THE KARELIA). Ska-rawkers (in every sense of the paraphrase!), this cartoon-esque girl/boy outfit/ensemble released a handful of singles, the best of which was 'LAST NIGHT' and 'WHISKY'; the latter was delightfully influenced by The REZILLOS and SPLODGENESSABOUNDS. Live outings included a trip to Paris early in '99, while a riotous 'T In The Park' slot brought them a tidy earner. The following year, decade, century, whatever, saw the entourage deliver their schizoid debut set, 'RIGHT LINE IN NYLONS'.

Album rating: RIGHT LINE IN NYLONS (*7)

JANE CHALMERS – vocals (of LUNGLEG) / **STAN MILLAR** – vocals / **HELEN LLOYD** – hammond organ, backing vocals / **RAT** – guitars / **ALEX HUNTLEY** – guitars, backing vocals, keyboards (of THE KARELIA) / **MISS DIVERSE** (b. JENNY) – saxophone, backing vocals, percussion / **LINDSEY WATSON** – trombone, backing vocals, big drum / **MICK COOKE** – trumpet, glockenspiel, backing vocals, big drum / **GORDON DAVIDSON** – bass, percussion, backing vocals / **JOEL GRAY** – drums, percussion, very big drum

AMPHETAMEANIES (cont)

Jul 98. (7") *(SHaG 13.09)* **Club Beatroot Part Nine**
– Speed fever / VERA CRUISE: Wasted sounds.
(above was released in conjunction with 'The 13th Note')   [Flotsam & Jetsam / not iss.]

Dec 98. (7") *(SHaG 021)* **AROUND THE WORLD IN 5 1/2 MINUTES**
– Mo'ska / Tales of the Arizona highway patrol.

Apr 99. (7"/cd-s) *(SHaG/+CD 024)* **LAST NIGHT. / SUSIETHEMUPPET**

Oct 99. (7") *(SHaG 026)* **TREATY AT HARTHILL**
– Whisky / NEWTOWN GRUNTS: Everywhere she goes.

Jul 00. (cd) *(SHaG 027)* **RIGHT LINE IN NYLONS**
– Last night / Bedroom holiday / Ghost bus / Speed fever / Prince Albert / Fiend or foe / Point blank / Whisky / The sun shines down / Theme from Radio Spytime / Driving home / Life without you / Susiethemuppet / 60 hours in Albuquerque.

AMPS (see under ⇒ BREEDERS)

ANASTASIA SCREAMED

Formed: Boston, Massachusetts, USA … 1987 by CHRIS BURDETT and CHRISTOPHER CUGINI, who subsequently added SCOTT LERNER and vocalist ANDY JAGOLINZER. After a few well-received local indie 45's, the band relocated to Nashville after replacing relative newcomers with CHICK GRANING and CHARLIE BOCK. These free-flowing hardcore singles found their way into Europe on import, the band subsequently winning a contract in 1990 with 'Fire' subsidiary outlet, 'Roughneck'. Touring the college circuit with THROWING MUSES (GRANING was to become the beau of TANYA DONELLY), ANASTASIA SCREAMED finally unveiled their debut set, 'LAUGHING DOWN THE LIMEHOUSE', a collection of unclassifiable alternative rock. A second album, 'MOONTIME' (1991), was met with similar press enthusiasm, although ANASTASIA SCREAMED for the last time early the following year. GRANING formed SCARCE in Rhode Island a few years later, although he was subsequently to suffer a brain aneurysm on the 12th June '95 which stopped him recording for some time. Against all the odds however, GRANING recovered sufficiently to re-record and promote the band's debut long-player, 'DEADSEXY', which saw a release through 'A&M' a month later. However, GRANING's career was er, again scarce as his musical career took a backseat. In the autumn of 2001, the man delivered a solo set entitled 'M.T.' via the internet. • **Covered:** BUICK MACKANE (T. Rex).

Album rating: LAUGHING DOWN THE LIMEHOUSE (*6) / MOONTIME (*5) / Scarce: RED mini (*5) / DEADSEXY (*6) / Chick Graning: M.T. (*5)

ANDY JAGOLINZER (b.11 Jun'69, Framingham, Mass.) – vocals / **CHRISTOPHER CUGINI** (b.23 Nov'66, Malden, Mass.) – guitar / **SCOTT LERNER** (b. 3 Mar'66) – bass / **CHRIS BURDETT** (b. 8 Mar'68) – drums

not iss. / Killing Floor

1987. (7") **WHAT KIND OF TRUTH IS THIS? / GRAVITY**

— **CHICK GRANING** (b.28 Oct'66, Vancouver, Canada) – vocals; repl. ANDY
— **MICHAEL LORD** – bass; repl. LERNER

Dec 88. (12") **ELECTRIC LIZ. /**

— **CHARLIE BOCK** (b.26 Jan'65, Nashville, USA) – bass; repl. SCOTT

Roughneck / Fire

Aug 90. (7") *(HYPE 2)* **SAMANTHA BLACK. / SUN CELEBRATION**
(12"+=) *(HYPE 2T)* – What kind of truth is this?

Sep 90. (cd/lp) *(NECK CD/LP 002)* <FIREUS 7 2/1> **LAUGHING DOWN THE LIMEHOUSE**
– Beautiful / Lime / Disintegrations, yesterday / The skidder – ? violet / Searcher No.9 (song 16) / Tide / Parts of us / Tricked into feel / Shade / Samantha Black / Notown.

Mar 91. (12"ep/cd-ep) *(HYPE 008 T/CD)* <FIREUS 9> **15 SECONDS OR 5 DAYS**
– 15 seconds or 5 days / Buick Mackane / (When I don't think) I can hang on / Samantha Black / Tide.

Oct 91. (12"ep/cd-ep) *(HYPE 012 T/CD)* **TORNADO**
– Tornado / The pick up / Dig a pony / Roadside trash.

Oct 91. (cd/lp) *(NECK CD/LP 007)* **MOONTIME**
– Tornado / Out of the light / Stand by / One deep breath / She must / Dead in the grass / Get a load of that machine / 15 seconds or 5 days / Fall to ceiling / Blues (featuring DON BYAS) / Dead ants.

— split in 1992; GRANING later formed SCARCE

SCARCE

CHICK GRANING – vocals, guitar / **JOYCE RASKIN** – vocals, bass / **JUD EHRBAR** – drums

not iss. / Delmore

Oct 93. (7") <DE7 01> **DAYS LIKE THIS. / SCORPION TRAY**

not iss. / All The Money

Feb 94. (7") **HOPE. / SOMETHING**

Domino / Rockamundo

Jun 94. (7") *(RUG 13)* **ALL SIDEWAYS. / DOZEN**

Big Cat / Tumble Gear

Aug 94. (m-lp/m-cd) *(ABB 75X/+CD)* <1> **RED**
– All sideways / Dozen / Days like this / Scorpion tray / Hope / Something.

Oct 94. (12"ep/cd-ep) *(ABB 76/+CD)* **ALL SIDEWAYS EP**
– All sideways / What are you thinking about? / It was dry / Honey simple.

— session man **MIKE LEVESQUE** – drums; repl. JUD who formed The SPACE NEEDLE

Paradox / not iss.

Apr 95. (7") *(PDOX 003)* **FREAKSHADOW. / THIS TOWN**
(cd-s+=) *(PDOXD 003)* – Salvador Sammy / Bottomfeeder.

Jun 95. (7") *(PDOX 005)* **GLAMOURIZING CIGARETTES. / SUDDEN DOWNTOWN POLO CLUB**
(cd-s+=) *(PDOXD 005)* – Angels from Montgomery / Ashes to ashes.

Jul 95. (cd/c/lp) *(PDOX CD/MC/LP 001)* **DEADSEXY**
– Honeysimple / Freakshadow / Days like this / Sing me Stella / Glamourizing cigarettes / Girl through me / Karona khrome / All sideways / So, thrill me / Sense of quickness / Given / Obviously midnight.

— **JOSEPH PROPATIER** – drums; repl. MIKE

A&M / A&M

Jul 96. (cd/c/lp) <(31454 0561-2/-4/-1)> **DEADSEXY** (re-recorded)
– Honeysimple / All sideways / Rains of Kansas / Summertime / Glamourizing cigarettes / Crimea river / Days like this / Stella / Freakshadow / Salvador Sammy / Sense of quickness / Obviously midnight.

— disbanded in September '96 due to GRANING's poor health

CHICK GRANING

not iss. / Chick Graning

Oct 01. (cd) <none> **M.T.**   [- / - net]
– All is lost in Hollywood (I still feel good) / Desperation code / M.T. / Blues for cello / If you didn't know it / I, soul possession / Tomorrow is a good day for dying / Merci / No yesterdays / Superfine.

….AND YOU WILL KNOW US BY THE TRAIL OF DEAD

Formed: Olympia, Washington, USA … 1994 by CONRAD KEELY and former MUKILTEO FAIRIES singer/percussionist JASON REECE. The duo of noisy songsmiths – who had been friends since childhood – detached themselves from the indie circuit in Olympia, subsequently flitting to Austin, Texas. They began performing loud, riotous concerts, which often escalated into violence and/or the destruction of musical equipment. New recruits KEVIN ALLEN and NEIL BUCSH regularly contributed to the mayhem, earning themselves full-time positions in the increasingly popular group. AYWKUBTTOD (probably one of the best named bands in ages) could've been pitched somewhere between The WHO and MOGWAI due to their sharp-edged sonic anarchism. Their intense blasts of instumentation were matched with complex quiet/loud sections, fumbling pianos and screeching guitars … like SLINT, but without the boring bits. In 1997, the group issued a limited edition live cassette which ultimately led to their signing to 'Trance Syndicate' in early 1998. It was with 'Trance Syndicate' that the troupe released their eponymous debut album to much critical acclaim. The set also met unexpected success, thanks to thousands of dedicated fans who had already recognised the talent before …AND YOU WILL KNOW… were even signed. 'MADONNA' followed in 1999 on 'Merge', and boasted the single 'MISTAKES AND REGRETS', plus a much feted performance at 'All Tomorrow's Parties' where the group produced an unhealthy wall of feedback after their 30-minute onslaught. The single wasn't too bad either; crashing drums, demonic bass lines, Mach-speed guitars and the lines "If I had to make a list/of my mistakes and regrets/I'd put your name on top/and every line after that", all mixed to complete perfection.

Album rating: … AND YOU WILL KNOW US BY THE TRAIL OF DEAD (*7) / MADONNA (*8) / SOURCE TAGS & CODES (*7)

CONRAD KEELY (b. Plano, Texas) – vocals, drums, harpsicord, trumpet, sax / **JASON REECE** – vocals, accordion, violin, harp (ex-MUKILTEO FAIRIES) / **KEVIN ALLEN** (b.23 May'72, Norman, Oklahoma) – guitar, trumpet, ukelele / **NEIL BUSCH** – bass, samples

Trance Syndicate / Trance Syndicate

Jan 98. (lp/cd) <(TR/+CD 66)> **…AND YOU WILL KNOW US BY THE TRAIL OF DEAD**
– Richter scale madness / Novena without faith / Fake fake eyes / Half of what / Gargoyle waiting / Prince with a thousand enemies / Ounce of prevention / When we begin to steal … *(cd re-iss. Nov00 on 'Domino'; REWIG 10)*

Merge / Merge

Oct 99. (lp/cd) <(MRG 171/+CD)> **MADONNA**
– And you will know them… / Mistakes & regrets / Totally natural / Blight takes all / Clair de Lune / Flood of red / Children of the hydra's teeth / Mark David Chapman / Up from redemption / Aged dolls / The day the air turned blue / A perfect teenhood / Sigh your children. *(UK re-iss. May00 on 'Domino' cd/d-lp; WIG CD/LP 84)*

Domino / not iss.

Nov 00. (cd-ep) *(RUG 114CD)* **MISTAKES AND REGRETS EP**   [69]
– Mistakes and regrets / Half of what (new vocal) / Electronic bird mating ritual.

Interscope / Interscope

Mar 02. (cd/lp) <(493249-2/-4)> **SOURCE TAGS & CODES**   [73 / Feb02]
– It was there that I saw you / Another morning stoner / Baudelaire / Homage / How near how far / Heart in the hand of the matter / Monsoon / Days of being wild / Relative ways / After the laughter / Source tags and codes.

Apr 02. (7") *(497715-7)* **ANOTHER MORNING STONER. / HOMAGE (session)**   [54]
(cd-s) *(497716-2)* – ('A'side) / Baudelaire (Peel session) / Richter scale madness (Peel session) / ('A'-video).

Sep 02. (7") *(497777-7)* <497639> **RELATIVE WAYS. / HOMAGE**   [Nov01]
(cd-s+=) *(497777-2)* – Blood rites / The blade runner.

AN EMOTIONAL FISH

Formed: Dublin, Ireland … 1988 by GERARD WHELAN, DAVE FREW who teamed up with ENDA WYATT and MARTIN MURPHY after moving back to their native city from London. The 'FISH soon had a healthy buzz surrounding them after early gigs and were one of the lucky bands to be given a break via U2's new 'Mother' label. Following on from the domestic

AN EMOTIONAL FISH (cont)

success of debut single, 'CELEBRATE', the chest beating Irish Top 10 anthem was given a full UK release for 'East West'. Radio One (on the strength of a session) subsequently sponsored a UK tour and the group seemed set for the same success as fellow Celts like HOTHOUSE FLOWERS. Things went awry however, as the music press turned on the band amid criticisms of the sponsorship deal and the 1990 eponymous debut album met with some scathing reviews. Basically it was the same critical treatment meted out to patrons U2 i.e. overblown, earnest, pompous etc; in reality, the band's sound was unlikely to accrue as much interest in Britain as it had in their native Ireland. America was kinder to the group but only just; while they failed to reach the stadium rock heights they might've, they did find an audience on the college-rock circuit. 'JUNKPUPPETS' (1993) carried on in much the same vein and attracted much the same criticism, while by the release of 1995's independently issued 'SLOPER', most pundits had lost interest.

Album rating: AN EMOTIONAL FISH (*5) / JUNKPUPPETS (*4) / SLOPER (*4)

GERARD WHELAND (b.14 Jul'64) – vocals / **DAVE FREW** (b.30 Apr'62) – guitar / **ENDA WYATT** (b.13 Jun'60) – bass / **MARTIN MURPHY** (b/. 9 Nov'67) – drums; with guest vox of **JIL TURNER**

		East West	Atlantic
Jun 90.	(7"/c-s) (YZ 489/C) **CELEBRATE. / ANYWAY**	46	-
	(ext.12"+=) (YZ 489T) – Jonathan and Doodle pip.		
	(cd-s++=) (YZ 489CD) – Brick it up (live).		
Aug 90.	(lp/c/cd) (WX 359/+C/CD) **AN EMOTIONAL FISH**	40	-
	– Celebrate / Grey mother / Blue / Lace Virginia / Julian / All I am / Change / Colours / That demon jive / Brick it up.		
Aug 90.	(7"/c-s) (YZ 502) **LACE VIRGINIA. / MOVE ON**		-
	(12"+=) (YZ 502T) – Man's world / The last time.		
	(cd-s+=) (YZ 502CD) – Talk.		
Nov 90.	(7"/c-s) (YZ 745/+C) **BLUE (new version). / AN OBVIOUS SONG**		-
	(12"+=/cd-s+=) – The island.		
Aug 91.	(10"ep/cd-ep) (YZ 613 TE/CD) **THE CELEBRATION EP (live)**		-
	– The island / Mother / Lace Virginia / Celebrate.		
Dec 91.	(cd-ep) <PRCD 3828-2> **LIVE BAIT**	-	
	– Celebrate / Grey matter / Jonathan and doodle pip / All I am (live on KCRW) / Rock and roll / Change.		
May 93.	(7"/c-s) (YZ 745/+C) **RAIN. / CARELESS**		-
	(10"+=/cd-s+=) (YZ 745 TE/CD) – Higher ground.		
Jun 93.	(cd/c/lp) (4509 92357-2/-4/-1) <82473> **JUNKPUPPETS**		-
	– Rain / Harmony central / Sister change / If God was a girl / Careless child / Star / Hole in my heaven / Innocence / Half moon / Digging this hole / Yeh yeh yeh.		

		Blue Music	Z.Y.X.
Oct 94.	(c-ep/cd-ep) (WMC/WCD 22) **TIME IS ON THE WALL EP**		-
	– Time is on the wall / Mistake factory / Time is on the wall (acoustic) / Analyse me (demo).		
Nov 94.	(cd) (298149-2) <20345> **SLOPER**		1995
	– Time is on the wall / Summertime / Aeroplanes / Clowns / Other planet girl / Happy families / Mistake factory / Disco Vera / Superman / Dirt / [UK-only] Leoncavallo / Air / [UK-only] It belongs to the world / [US-only] Strange things. (re-iss. Feb96 on 'Pure'; 2260)		
Dec 94.	(c-ep/cd-ep) (WMC/WCD 24) **AEROPLANES EP**		-
	– Aeroplanes (rainbow mix) / Clowns / Aeroplanes (Chinatown mix) / Strange things.		
Mar 95.	(c-ep/cd-ep) (WMC/WCD 27) **SUPERMAN EP**		-
	– Superman / Happy families / Digging this hole / France Carroll (acoustic) / Dublin (acoustic).		

— disbanded after above

ANGELFISH
(see under ⇒ GOODBYE MR MACKENZIE; 80's section)

ANGELICA

Formed: Lancaster, England ... 1994 by schoolgirls HOLLY, CLAIRE, BRIGIT and RACHEL, their musical initiation test came via a performance at a working men's club in Morecambe. However, it would take three years and the end of their schooling to finally get around to producing their debut 45, appropriately titled 'TEENAGE GIRL CRUSH' – No.4 in John Peel's end of the year Festive 50 (in 1997). Drawing a line through 60's girl groups such as The SHANGRI-LA'S to 90's riot grrrl acts such as BIKINI KILL, the young foursome signed to 'Fantastic Plastic', delivering the twee-friendly 'WHY DID YOU LET MY KITTEN DIE?' – Alternative Single of 1999 as voted by Radio One listeners. Towards the end of that year, ANGELICA shot up the indie charts with their third single, 'BRING BACK HER HEAD', and rounded off the millennium by touring alongside ASH and MUSE. A mini-set, 'THE END OF A BEAUTIFUL CAREER' (2000), followed that spring, while not long after, another single, 'TAKE ME IN YOUR DISEASE', topped the indie charts. Conspicuous by the absence, the girls finally got around to delivering their first full-length set, 'THE SEVEN YEAR ITCH' (2002). • **Note:** not to be confused with 'Warner Bros.' outfit of the late 90's.

Album rating: THE END OF A BEAUTIFUL CAREER mini (*6) / THE SEVEN YEAR ITCH (*5)

HOLLY ROSS – vocals, guitar / **CLAIRE WINDSOR** – guitar / **BRIGIT COLTON** – bass / **RACHEL PARSONS** – drums

		Deceptive	not iss.
Jul 97.	(ltd-7") (BLUFF 046) **TEENAGE GIRL CRUSH. /**		-

		Fantastic Plastic	not iss.
Mar 99.	(cd-s) (FPS 015) **WHY DID YOU LET MY KITTEN DIE? / LIPSTICK KISS / YELLOW PINK & BLUE**		-
Nov 99.	(7"/m/cd-s) (FP7 017) **BRING BACK HER HEAD. / NOTHING SPECIAL / KING FOR A DAY**		-
Apr 00.	(m-cd/10"m-lp) (FPCD/FPLP 002) **THE END OF A BEAUTIFUL CAREER**		-
	– All I can see / Bring back her head / Concubine blues / Sea shanty / You fake you make it / Why did you let my kitten die? / Fireflies.		
Aug 00.	(7"/cd-s) (FP7/FPS 021) **TAKE ME I'M YOUR DISEASE. / ACHING / CORN RIGGS**		-

		Almafame	not iss.
Apr 02.	(cd) (VICTORY 02) **THE SEVEN YEAR ITCH**		-
	– I want a piece of the action / Misdemeanor / Liberation is wasted on me / Evergreen / Reynard the fox / Golden lillies / The apple, the book / Guilty as sin / Your religion is me / Rosemary call the goddess.		

ANGELS OF LIGHT
(see under ⇒ SWANS; 80's section)

ANGORA
(see under ⇒ HEART THROBS; 80's section)

ANIMALS THAT SWIM

Formed: London, England ... January 1989 by self-proclaimed genius/poet, HANK STARRS, alongside his brothers, HUGH and AL BARKER. Releasing two self-financed 45's on 'Beachheads In Space' during the next year ('KING BEER' and 'ROY'), ATS earned column inches in the music press as critics marvelled at their prodigious talent. 'Che' records also took note and issued their third single, the excellent and now very rare '50 DRESSES'. In 1994, they were ensconced in the studio over a six-month period, piecing together the material for their debut album, 'WORKSHY'. 'Alternative Tentacles' subsidiary 'El-e-mental' obviously thought they were industrious enough to make it and released the album later that Autumn. Previewed by the single, 'MADAME YEVONDE', the album was hailed by reviewers who raved over STARRS' melancholy wanderings, his voice reminiscent of CATHAL COUGHLAN (of FATIMA MANSIONS), MARK GOLDTHORPE (ex-ARTERY) or even JACQUES BREL; CRABTREE's vaguely mariachiesque trumpet playing also set them apart. Highlights of the album included most of the aforementioned singles, the forthcoming one-that-got-away, 'PINK CARNATIONS' and a tribute to the cult US singer/songwriter, 'VIC' (CHESNUTT). Upon their overdue return in 1996, things seemed to turn pear-shaped as a follow-up set, 'I WAS THE KING, I REALLY WAS THE KING', failed to keep up the impossibly high standards they'd set themselves. Nearly five years in the musical wilderness, BARKER, STARRS, CRABTREE et al were back in circulation via third set, 'HAPPINESS FROM A DISTANT STAR' (2001), another visceral but polished and glossy example of a band that really should have made it big time. • **Songwriters:** STARRS – HUGH BARKER and some with CRABTREE. • **Trivia:** DEL also moonlights for BARK PSYCHOSIS while ANTHONY does the same for MAMBO TAXI.

Album rating: WORKSHY (*9) / I WAS THE KING, I REALLY WAS THE KING (*7) / HAPPINESS FROM A DISTANT STAR (*7)

HANK STARRS – vocals, drums / **HUGH BARKER** – guitar / **AL BARKER** – guitar, keyboards, vocals / **DEL CRABTREE** – trumpet / **ANTHONY COOTE** – bass

		Beach Heads In Space	not iss.
May 92.	(7") (BIS 001) **KING BEER. /**		-
Feb 93.	(7") (BIS 002) **ROY. / WEARY MIND**		-

		Che	Big Bop
Aug 93.	(10"ep) (che 5) **50 DRESSES / CHAPEL MARKET. / HOLLOWAY AVIATOR / OREGON STATE FAIR**		-

		El-e-mental	not iss.
Sep 94.	(7"m/cd-s) (ELM 23 S/CD) **MADAME YEVONDE. / ME AND CAPTAIN AMERICA / MAY**		-
Sep 94.	(cd/lp) (ELM 24 CD/LP) <510> **WORKSHY**		1996
	– How to make a chandelier / Smooth steps / Roy / Pink carnations / St. Francis / Action at Tescos / King Beer / Barney / Susie's friends / Madame Yevonde / Vic / Silent film / Stay with me.		

— (spring '95) they now have a new drummer **KARL**

Mar 95.	(7"ep/cd-ep) (ELM 26 S/CD) **PINK CARNATIONS / KANDY KARS. / NEW BOOTS / HARRY DEAN / DEL FRESCO**		-
Feb 96.	(7"/cd-s) (ELM 35 S/CD) **THE GREENHOUSE. / LOG CITY ROAD / THEY ALL SAILED AWAY**		-
May 96.	(7"/cd-s) (ELM 36 S/CD) **FADED GLAMOUR**		-
Jun 96.	(cd/c/lp) (ELM 37 CD/MC/LP) **I WAS THE KING, I REALLY WAS THE KING**		-
	– Faded glamour / A good Xmas / The longest road / East St. O'Neill / The greenhouse / Shipley / Kilkats and vinegar / London Bridge / Bed island / Near the Moon / Despatches from Lulu / The good old way.		

— split in January 1997 – re-formed after the millennium

		Snowstorm	not iss.
Jun 01.	(7"/cd-s) (SNOWS 014/+CD) **THE MOON AND THE MOTHERSHIP. / THEME FROM DRIVING HOME / GIUSEPPE MESSINA**		-
Jun 01.	(cd/lp) (STORM 010 CD/LP) **HAPPINESS FROM A DISTANT STAR**		-
	– All your stars are out / Sixteen letters / Dirt / Homunculus / The Moon and the mothership / The last thing you said to me / The bathtube / Sing and rejoice, fortune is smiling on you / Mackie's wake / Happiness from a distant star / Seven days / A good day for everyone / Voices from beyond the grave.		

ANNIE CHRISTIAN

Formed: Leith, Edinburgh, Scotland ... spring '97 by main songwriter, LARRY LEAN, CHRIS ADAMS, DAVID HUNTER and ANDREW HASTINGS (another member does the floating job!), all possessing a penchant for PRINCE and the late political comedian, BILL HICKS. Managed by Bruce Findlay (Radio DJ, famous for overseeing SIMPLE MINDS' rise to fame), the quartet delivered their debut, 'LOVE THIS LIFE', early the following year. They fitted neatly into the MANICS / STEREOPHONICS brand of rifferama rock, their gothic lyrics overpowering enough to set them apart. ANNIE CHRISTIAN continued to rock on, releasing several other singles and a debut album, 'TWILIGHT' (1999), issued in the States a year later as 'SOFTCORE'.
• **Covered:** TRANSMISSION (Joy Division).

Album rating: TWILIGHT (*6)

LARRY LEAN – vocals, guitar / **CHRIS ADAMS** – guitar / **DAVID HUNTER** – bass / **ANDREW HASTINGS** – drums

Equipe Ecosse – V2 / Orchard

Mar 98. (7") *(EQE 500139-7)* **LOVE THIS LIFE. / THE SHATTERED BURLESQUE**
(cd-s+=) *(EQE 500139-3)* – Satellites spin.
May 98. (7") *(EQE 500190-7)* **SOMEDAY MY PRINCE WILL COME AGAIN. / WHILE YOU SLEEP**
(cd-s+=) *(EQE 500190-3)* – This world has no time for lovers.
Sep 98. (7") *(EQE 500253-7)* **THE OTHER WAY. / TRANSMISSION**
(cd-s+=) *(EQE 500253-3)* – Drugs work.
Feb 99. (7") *(EQE 500516-7)* **KISS THE DAY GOODBYE. / GET IT ON**
(cd-s+=) *(EQE 500516-3)* – 500 miles low.
Mar 99. (cd/lp) *(EQE 100214-2/-1) <6435>* **TWILIGHT** <US title 'SOFTCORE'> Jul00
– Love this life / Kiss the day goodbye / The other way / Secret and lies / Here is the news / Clearwater goldmine / Nothing is real / Ode to an Indian summer / The boy with the golden arm / Hicks (1961-1994) / Someday my prince will come again / Stupid thoughts / Twilight. *(CD-ROM tracks+=)* – The other way (video) / Kiss the day goodbye (video). *(cd re-iss. Dec00 as 'SOFTCORE' on 'Filthy Mouth'; FM 1)*

V2 / not iss.

Apr 99. (7") *(VVR 500674-7)* **LOVE THIS LIFE. / THE BOY WITH THE GOLDEN ARM (live)**
(cd-s+=) *(VVR 500674-3)* – Clearwater goldmine (live).

Filthy Mouth / not iss.

Dec 00. (cd) *(FM 2)* **SATURDAY NIGHT SUNDAY MORNING**

ANNIVERSARY

Formed: Kansas, USA ... 1996 by JAMES DAVID, ADRIANNE VERHOVEN, JOSH BERWANGER, CHRISTIAN JANKOWSKI and JUSTIN ROELOFS. The ANNIVERSARY celebrated the release of their debut album 'DESIGNING A NERVOUS BREAKDOWN' in 2000, a set which displayed a willingness to experiment which elevated their sound above the standard jangly indie pop being produced by a plethora of bands at the time. Their DAVE TRUMFIO-produced follow-up, 'YOUR MAJESTY' (2002), was a significant progression and showed the band were confident and capable enough to fully realise their early experimentations. Prog-rock influenced numbers such as 'HUSAM, HUSAM' and 'FOLLOW THE SUN' are fully rounded homages to their musical peers and, impressively, the group (complete with boy-girl vocals) manage this without ever succumbing to the genre's endemic pretensions. The album also succeeded in balancing the artier songs with more straight-forward rockers without sounding inconsistent.

Album rating: DESIGNING A NERVOUS BREAKDOWN (*6) / YOUR MAJESTY (*7)

JUSTIN ROELOFS – vocals, guitar / **JOSH BERWANGER** – vocals, guitar / **ANDRIENNE VERHOEVEN** – vocals, keyboards / **JAMES DAVID** – bass / **CHRISTIAN JANKOWSKI** – drums

not iss. / Paper Brigade

May 98. (7") **ALL RIGHT FOR NOW. / (other by PROUDENTALL)**

Heroes & Villains / Heroes & Villains

Oct 99. *<(HV 002)>* **split w/ GET UP KIDS**
– (GET UP KIDS tracks) / Vasil / Bluey. *<(re-iss. Feb00 on 'Vagrant'; VR 341)>*

Vagrant / Vagrant

Jan 00. (lp/cd) *<(VR 342/+CD)>* **DESIGNING A NERVOUS BREAKDOWN**
– The heart is a lonely hunter / All things ordinary / Perfectly / The D in Detroit / Emma discovery / Shu Shubat / Till we earned a holiday / Without Panasos / Hart crane / Outro in no minor.
Sep 00. (7"ep) **THE ANNIVERSARY (TOUR) EP**
– All right for now / Hold me tonight / Low tide and hospital bed.
(above issued on 'Good Guys and Bad Buddies' records)
Nov 00. (7") *<(VR 350)>* **TO NEVER DIE YOUNG. / (other by HOT ROD CIRCUIT)** Oct00
Jan 01. (7") *<SP 538>* **WHAT'S MY NAME? MY NAME IS ... WHAT!! WHAT!? / TU-WHIT TO-WHOO**
(above issued on 'Sub Pop')
Dec 01. (cd-ep) *(VR 358CD)* **split w/ SUPERDRAG** Nov01
– O' lady butterfly / Anais / Up in the sky / (other 3 by SUPERDRAG).

B-Unique / Vagrant

Jul 02. (cd) *(BUN 024) <VR 359CD>* **YOUR MAJESTY** Jan02
– Sweet Marie / Crooked crown / Peace, pride and regret / Husam Husam / The siren sings / Never die young / Tu-whit tu-whoo / The ghost of the river / Devil on my side / The death of the king / Follow the sun.
Sep 02. (7"/cd-s) *(BUN 035 7/CDS)* **SWEET MARIE. / TU-WHIT TO-WHOO**

ANT (see under ⇒ HEFNER)

ANTENNA

Formed: Bloomington, Indiana, USA ... early 90's by former BLAKE BABIES, JOHN P. STROHM and FREDA BONER/LOVE; reason being that JULIANA HATFIELD had ventured solo. Along with VESS RUHTENBERG, JACOB SMITH and occassional member ED ACKERMAN, ANTENNA released their first album 'SWAY' within a year of forming. Their sound was typical of the time with groups such as the LEMONHEADS playing countrified indie pop. Soon after the release of their debut both RUHTENBERG and LOVE departed and PATRICK STURGEON took over on the drums. 1992 saw the band progress with their more complete sounding EP, 'SLEEP', a record quickly followed in 1993 with the album 'HIDEOUT'. By this time, the group's line up featured ED ACKERMAN (of POLARA) full-time who's virtuoso guitar playing offered the band a new dimension. Much to the dismay of their fans, the group was to release only one more EP before calling it a day. It was all the more frustrating as 'FOR NOW' (1993) was heralded as their strongest collection of songs to date. Leader STROHM was quickly back in the studio with new outfit VELO-DELUXE. This time STROHM was producing darker and heavier music, their first album 'SUPERELASTIC' (1994) was critically well received, however, its commercial failure led to the band being dropped by their label. Unperturbed, STROHM then formed JOHN P. STROHM AND THE HELLO STRANGERS and in 1996 released the album 'CALEDONIA'. This was another commercial failure leading STROHM to earn a living as a touring guitarist with bands including the LEMONHEADS. • **Covered:** OUTDOOR MINER (Wire). • **Note:** Not to be confused with the 'Les Disques Du Crepescule' outfit (from Belgium) who issued 'Camino Del Sol' in '83, or another outfit who released the 'Brazil' 12" in '98. There was also an Australian act of the late 90's named ANTENNA – they released the album 'Installation'.

Album rating: SWAY (*6) / HIDEOUT (*4) / INSTALLATION (*) / Velo-Deluxe: SUPERELASTIC (*6) / John P. Strohm: CALEDONIA (*6) / VESTAVIA (*6)

JOHN P. STROHM – vocals, guitar (ex-BLAKE BABIES) / **FREDA LOVE/BONER** – drums (ex-BLAKE BABIES) / **VESS RUHTENBERG** – guitar, vocals / **JAKE SMITH** – bass, vocals / + guests

Mammoth / Mammoth

Jun 92. (cd/c/lp) *<(MR 0030-2/-4/-1)>* **SWAY** Nov91
– Delta 88 / Snakes / All I need / 2-3 / Girl who fell to Earth / Eyes of a stranger / Spinning dreams / Sleep / Say a prayer / 7 times / Weight of the world / Cast away demons / Blood red.
Nov 92. (cd-ep) *(MR 0038-2)* **SLEEP EP**
– Sleep / All I need / Wallpaper (demo) / Outdoor miner.

— **PATRICK SPURGEON** – drums; repl. FREDA

Apr 93. (cd/c/lp) *<(MR 0046-2/-4/-1)>* **HIDEOUT**
– Shine / Wallpaper / Stilllife / Rust / Dreamy / Don't be late / Fade / Easy listening / Danger buggy / Second skin / Hallelujah / Grey St.
Oct 93. (7") *<(MR 0054-7)>* **FOR NOW. / WALLPAPER** Sep93
(cd-s+=) *<(MR 0054-2)>* – Swoon / Given way.

— disbanded the following Spring when JAKE and FREDA had a baby then got married

---

VELO-DELUXE

STROHM recruited **KENNY CHILDERS** – bass (of GO MAN GO) / **MITCH HARRIS** – drums (ex-MARMALADE)

Mammoth / Mammoth

Oct 94. (cd/lp) *<(MR 0089-2/-1)>* **SUPERELASTIC**
– Superelastic / Velo-deluxe / Simple / Dirtass / Alibi / Desiree / Angels / Skin and bones / Saturday / Eleven / Said / Miracle. *(re-iss. Feb95 on 'Dedicated' cd/lp; DED CD/LP 020)*

Dedicated / not iss.

Feb 95. (7"ep) *(VELO 1)* **E.P.**

— STROHM was briefly a part of The LEMONHEADS before going solo

---

JOHN P. STROHM

— with basically past friends, etc

Flat Earth / Flat Earth

Dec 96. (cd; as JOHN P. STROHM AND THE HELLO STRANGERS) *<(FLT 106)>* **CALEDONIA** Oct96
– Slip away / Tangelo / Jennifer and Jean / Someone besides me / Geronimo's Cadillac / Fool / Backseat driver / Kill the lights / Freightliner / Powderkeg / Love theme / Thelma / See you around. *(re-iss. Aug97 on 'Demon'; FIENDCD 932)*

Easy Tiger / not iss.

Apr 98. (7") *(MUSE 002)* **WOULDN'T WANT TO BE ME. / DRIVE THRU**

— now with **ED ACKERSON, PETER ANDERSON + KENNY CHILDERS**

Blue Rose / Flat Earth

Nov 99. (cd) *(BLUCD 0090) <FLT 113>* **VESTAVIA** Feb99
– Wouldn't want to be me / Home / Better than nothing / Drive-thru / Jesus let me in / The ballad of lobster boy / Eva Braun / For awhile / Sylvia / In your dreams / Mission Dolores / Edison medicine.

APPENDIX OUT

Formed: Glasgow, Scotland ... summer '94 by ALI ROBERTS and DAVE E. WHITE, inspired by a gig from country Lo-Fi'ers, PALACE. In fact it would be their leader, WILL OLDHAM, who released the first vinyl outing by APPENDIX OUT, entitled 'ICE AGE'. Subsequently, the group of acoustic No-Fi troubadours enlisted the help of cellist LOUISE D and percussionist EVA PECK, the latter bringing sparse rhythm to the combo's folky weep-core. With the APPENDIX OUT line-up almost finalised, they donated material to the Up Records compilation CD '4x4' while split single 'WELL-LIT TONIGHT' was much sought after in some music quarters. This immediately caught the attention of eager-beaver labels planning to take folk/country screaming into the the 21st Century. But it was astonishingly US imprint 'Drag City' who came up trumphs when they signed the band in 1997 – adding them to a list of brilliant new generation songsmiths. This prompted the release of the outfit's debut set, 'THE RYE BEARS A POISON' – a groundbreaking achievement for a "wee" band in '97 – most definitely a Sunday morning record, with its calming guitars, emotional vocals and splendid tranquillity reminiscent of NICK DRAKE's 'Pink Moon' era. Things could only get better for APPENDIX OUT. ROBERTS added guitarist-cum-percussionist GARETH EGGIE and flautist/keyboard-player EVA PECK to the cauldron of country karma who debuted on the band's second and most realised work, 'DAYLIGHT SAVING' (1999). Sticking with the WILL OLDHAM vs SMOG formula, the set was unique in its own right with songs such as opener 'FOUNDLING', leading the way to what should have blasted BELLE & SEBASTIAN out of the proverbial water. Of course, the troupe's style was very much American, but that's not to say APPENDIX OUT should not have been an asset to new Scottish music. Their softly spoken harmonies, mandolin breaks and acoustic set-ups were/are very much rooted in traditional folk (they even covered Anne Briggs 'LOWLANDS'), giving them the opportunity to shine where other bands would only sparkle. 'LIEDER FUR KASPER HAUSER', a 7" EP, was to be the group's next release late in '99. It featured the tracks 'EIN GRAUERSTAR IN DER KAVALLERIE' and the sombre instrumental 'AN DER NACHTIMMEL GEWOHNT', both of which helped inspire ROBERTS in his own traditional solo venture 'THE CROOK OF MY ARMS' (2001), which was recorded over a one-day period in Glasgow. He subsequently regrouped APPENDIX OUT to issue their fantastic folksy cover-pleaser EP 'A WARM AND YEASTY CORNER' (2002), which included a rendition of the Incredible String Band's 'A VERY CELLULAR SONG' and Ewan MacColl's 'THE FIRST TIME EVER I SAW YOUR FACE', to name two. Other tracks such as 'SALLY FREE AND EASY' and 'JOSEPHINE' were given the APPENDIX spin, with hushed flutes, pianos and a whole host of acoustic instruments adding to the outfit's sparse effect.

Album rating: THE RYE BEARS A POISON (*6) / DAYLIGHT SAVING (*6) / THE NIGHT IS ADVANCING (*8) / Alasdair Roberts: THE CROOK OF MY ARM (*6)

ALI ROBERTS (b. ALASDAIR, Callander) – vocals, guitar / **DAVE E. WHITE** – bass, violin, keyboards

		Palace	Palace
Dec 96.	(ltd-7") <PR 10> **ICE AGE. / PISSED WITH YOU**		Jan96

— added **EVA PECK** – drums / **LOUISE D** – cello

		Creeping Bent	not iss.
Sep 97.	(7") (bent 027) **WELL LIT TONIGHT. / (other track by the Leopards)**		-

		Drag City	Drag City
Oct 97.	(lp/cd) <DC 126/CD> **THE RYE BEARS A POISON** – Our sea / Brazil / East Coast wedding / Many-legged boatmen / Frozen blight / Wild I lived in Flanders / Seagulls, belts / Lassie, lie near me / The harp key / Autumn.		
Jun 98.	(7") (bent 034) **LASSIE, LIE NEAR ME. / (other track by Policecat)** (above issued on 'Creeping Bent', below on 'Liquefaction'/'Bad Jazz'>		
Jul 98.	(7"ep) <Bebop 3> **SECOND PERTHSHIRE HOUSE SONG / ROUND REEL OF EIGHT / TWELVE OF THEM / HAY BALE BLUES. / (others by Songs: Ohia)** (UK-iss.2000 on 'Bad Jazz'; same)		
Jan 99.	(7"ep) (MILK 001) **BOYHOOD / WILD LIVING. / (others by the MONGERS)** (above issued on 'Galvani')		-

— **ALI ROBERTS** recruited **TOM CROSSLEY** – drums (of INTERNATIONAL AIRPORT) / **GARETH EGGIE** – guitar, percussion / **DAVE ELCOCK + KATE WRIGHT**

Jul 99.	(lp/cd) (<DC 152/+CD>) **DAYLIGHT SAVING**		Apr99
	– Foundling / The grey havens / Tangled hair / The scything / Little owl / Row upstream / Merchant city / Exile / Arcan lore. (lp re-iss. Aug00; same)		
Nov 99.	(7") <WEST 007> **LIEDER FUR KASPAR HAUSER**	-	
	– Ein grauerstar in der kavallerie / An den nachtnimmel gewohnt. (above on 'Western Vinyl')		

— added **MARK** (of DEN ALMA; with GARETH)

Mar 01.	(cd) (<DC 189CD>) **THE NIGHT IS ADVANCING**		Apr01
	– A path to our beds / The seven widows (the springs of night) / The groves of Lebanon / Golden tablets of the sun / Year waxing, year waning / Fortified jackdaw grove / The night is advancing / Cyclone's vernal retreat / (Bringing the yearlings) Home / Hexen in the anticyclone / Campfire's burning (round) / Organise a march.		

		Shingle Street	not iss.
Apr 02.	(cd-ep) (SHING 001) **A WARM AND YEASTY CORNER** – Window over the bay / Sally free and easy / The first time ever I saw your face / Josephine / A very cellular song.		-

ALASDAIR ROBERTS

		not iss.	Secretly Canadian
Apr 01.	(cd,lp) <SC 48CD> **THE CROOK OF MY ARM** – Lord Gregory / As I came in by Huntly town / Bonnie lass among the heather / The magpie's nest / Ploughboy lads / Lowlands / Master Kilby / Standing in yon flowe'ry garden / Ye banks and braes o' bonny Doon / The flase bride / The month of January / The wife of Ushers Well.	-	

APPLESEED CAST

Formed: Lawrence, Kansas, USA ... 1997 by CHRISTOPHER CRISCI, AARON PILLAR, JASON WICKERSHEIM and LOUIE RUIZ. Taking their cue from various indie/emo bands from across the US, The APPLESEED CAST signed to the 'Deep Elm' imprint and after issuing a few label samplers, the band delivered their debut LP, 'END OF THE RING WARS' (1998), a fluid fusion of straight-edged hardcore, blustering melodies and complex rhythms reminiscent of SLINT. After a split EP with labelmates RACE CAR RIOT and PLANES MISTAKEN FOR STARS, The 'CAST issued the progessively more ambitious sophomore set, 'MARE VITALIS', in 2000. Its strange experimental flurries and heavy-handed guitar effects paved the way for the group's new adventures into the obscure, as the once no-bull emo collective dabbled in a bit of electro madness for companion sets 'LOW LEVEL OWL' – VOLUMES 1 and 2 (2001). This marked the demise of bassist WICKERSHEIM – who was replaced by MARCIA YOUNG – and the beginning of a whimsical and complex musical direction for the band as they beeped, whizzed, thrashed and droned through two sets of great Prog-rock craziness.

Album rating: THE END OF THE RING WARS (*6) / MARE VITALIS (*5) / LOW LEVEL, VOL.1 (*5) / LOW LEVEL, VOL.2 (*6) / LOST SONGS collection (*5)

CHRISTOPHER CRISCI – vocals, guitar / **AARON PILLAR** – guitar / **JASON WICKERSHEIM** – bass / **LOUIS RUIZ** – drums

		Deep Elm	Deep Elm
Aug 98.	(cd) <DER 370CD> **THE END OF THE RING WARS** – Marigold & patchwork / Anthero / On sidewalks / Moment #72 / Stars / December 27, 1990 / The last ring / 16 days / Dreamland / Portrait / Untitled 1. (UK-iss.Oct99; same as US)		

— **JOSH BARUTH** – drums; repl. RUIZ

1999.	(7") **SKATTER IK IGNITO.**		-
Aug 99.	(cd-ep) <DER 378CD> **PLANES MISTAKEN FOR STARS / RACE CAR RIOT / APPLESEED CAST** – (tracks by PLANES MISTAKEN FOR STARS + RACE CAR RIOT) / Tale of the aftermath / Remedios the beautiful.		
Mar 00.	(cd) <(DER 386)> **MARE VITALES** – The immortal soul of Mundo Cani / Fishing the sky / Forever longing the golden sunsets / Mare mortis / Santa Maria / Secret / ...And nothing less / Poseidon / Kilgore trout / Storms / (untitled). (lp-iss.Apr01; DER 386LP)		

— **MARCIA YOUNG** – bass; repl. WICKERSHEIM

Sep 01.	(cd) <(DER 396)> **LOW LEVEL, VOL.1**		Aug01
	– The walking of Pertelotte / On reflection / Blind man's arrow / Flowers falling from dying hands / Messenger / Doors lead to questions / Steps and numbers / Sentence / Bird of paradise / Mile marker / Convict / A tree for trails / Signal / View of a burning city.		
Nov 01.	(cd) <(DER 397)> **LOW LEVEL, VOL.2**		Oct01
	– View of a burning city (reprise) / Strings / A place in line / Shaking hands / Rooms and gardens / Ring out the warning bell / Sunset drama king / The last in a line / Decline / The argument / Reaction / Confession.		

– compilations, etc. –

Nov 02.	(cd) Deep Elm; <(DER 420)> **LOST SONGS**		Oct02
	– E to W / Peril, parts 1-3 / Novice / Facing north / Take / State N w/K / House on a hill / Beach gray / Novice ambient cannibalization.		

APPLES (IN STEREO)

Formed: Denver, Colorado, USA ... 1993 initially as The APPLES by singer-songwriter, ROBERT SCHNEIDER who, along with producer JEFF MANGUM enlisted the help of JIM McINTYRE, HILARIE SIDNEY (a friend of his from his MARBLES days) and ROBERT PARFITT. Part of the 'Elephant 6' musicians collective that also included NEUTRAL MILK HOTEL and OLIVIA TREMOR CONTROL, the APPLES covered poppier territory than their counterparts, debuting with an eponymous EP in '93. What with the surge in popularity for the name APPLES, SCHNEIDER and Co tacked on (IN STEREO) to the end of their moniker to prevent any confusion, showcasing their new name on 1995's 'FUN TRICK NOISEMAKER'. Breezy, bright, wide-eyed and charming, the record was feted by Lo-Fi connoisseurs on both sides of the Atlantic for its melodic BEACH BOYS-esque simplicity and unpretentious references to US kids TV nostalgia. With MANGUM already uprooting to another part of the country to regroup his NEUTRAL MILK HOTEL, SCHNEIDER took up the reins for a second album proper, 'TONE SOUL EVOLUTION' (1997); the previous year, a compilation set of obscure early material, 'SCIENCE FAIRE', had been heartily received by critics and collectors alike, while The MARBLES collection (from '92/'93), 'PYRAMID LANDING', was also unearthed. Following on from, and indeed inspired by OLIVIA TREMOR CONTROL's 'Black Foliage' (and of course, The BEATLES), APPLES (IN STEREO) brewed up a heady series of sets from 1999's 'HER WALLPAPER REVERIE' (1999), 'THE DISCOVERY OF A WORLD INSIDE THE MOONE' (2000) and 'VELOCITY OF SOUND'

(2002). SCHNEIDER was indeed in touch with his retro inner psyche, crafting carefree "melan-delic" candy-coated songs at will. • **Covered:** HEROES AND VILLAINS (Beach Boys).

Album rating: FUN TRICK NOISEMAKER (*7) / SCIENCE FAIRE compilation (*7) / TONE SOUL EVOLUTION (*6) / HER WALLPAPER REVERIE (*8) / THE DISCOVERY OF A WORLD INSIDE THE MOONE (*6) / SOUND EFFECTS 1992-2000 compilation (*7) / VELOCITY OF SOUND (*5) / Marbles: PYRAMID LANDING (*6) / Secret Square: SECRET SQUARE (*5)

ROBERT SCHNEIDER – vocals (ex-MARBLES) / **ROBERT PARFITT** – guitar / **JIM McINTYRE** – bass / **HILARIE SIDNEY** – drums (of-MARBLES)

Jun 93. (7"ep; as the APPLES) <E 6001> **TIDAL WAVE EP**
– Tidal wave / Motorcar / Turncoat Indian / Haley / Not the same / Stop along the way / Running in circles.

—— now without PARFITT who formed VINCE MOLE & HIS CALCIUM ORCHESTRA

—— added **JOHN HILL** – guitar, vocals (ex-DRESSY BESSY)

1994. (7"ep; as the APPLES) <BUS 044> **HYPNOTIC SUGGESTION EP**
– Hypnotic suggestion / Touch the water / Glowworm / To love the vibration of the bulb.

1994. (7"; as the APPLES) <small-fi 4> **TIME FOR BED – I KNOW YOU'D DO WELL.** / (other 2 by OLIVIA TREMOR CONTROL)

1994. (7"; as The APPLES) <100GM 017> **split w/ SPORTSGUITAR**

1995. (7"flexi; as The APPLES) (WJ 2) **ROCKET PAD.** / (w/ **HEARTWORMS**)

—— now without McINTYRE who was repl. by guest KURT HEASLEY – guitar

May 95. (lp/cd) <SPART 42/+CD> **FUN TRICK NOISEMAKER**
– Narrator / Tidal wave / High tide / Green machine / Winter must be cold / She's just like me – Taking time / Glowworm / Dots 1-2-3 / Lucky charm / Innerspace / Show the world / Love you Alice – D / Pine away. (UK-iss.Dec96 & re-iss. Jun00; same as US)

Nov 96. (lp/cd) <(SPART 48/+CD)> **SCIENCE FAIRE** (compilation)
– Tidal wave / Motorcar / Turncoat Indian / Haley / Not the same / Stop along the way / Running in circles / Hypnotic suggestion / Touch the water / Glowworm / To love the vibration of the bulb / Time for bed – I know you'd do well / Rocket pad. (re-iss. Jun00; same)

—— added **ERIC ALLEN** – bass, vocals

Nov 97. (lp/cd) <(SPART 57/+CD)> **TONE SOUL EVOLUTION**
– Seems so / What's the number? / About your fame / Shine a light / Get there fine / Silvery light of a dream / We'll come to be / Tin pan alley / You said that last night / Try to remember / Find our way / Coda.

—— added **CHRIS McDUFFIE** – keyboards, percussion

Jun 99. (m-lp/m-cd) (WORM 45/+CD) <SPART 72> **HER WALLPAPER REVERIE**
– Her room is a rainy garden (Wallpaper Reverie theme) / Morning breaks (and roosters complain) / The shiney sea / The significance of a floral print / Strawberryfire / From outside, in floats a music box / Ruby / She looks through empty windows / Questions and answers / Drifting patterns / Y2k / Les amants / Benefits of lying (with your friend) / Ruby, tell me / Together they dream into the evening. (re-iss. Jun00 on 'SpinArt' m-lp/m-cd; SRT 80072/+CD)

Apr 00. (7") (WORM 64) **EVERYBODY LET UP.** /

Jun 00. (cd-ep) (<SRT 80080CD>) **LOOK AWAY**
– Look away / Behind the waterfall / Everybody let up / Her pretty face / The friar's lament.

Jul 00. (7") <RHINO 74489> **split w/ BIS**

Jul 00. (cd) (COOKCD 195) <SRT 83CD> **THE DISCOVERY OF A WORLD INSIDE THE MOONE**
– Go / The rainbow / Stream running over / 20 cases suggestive of . . . / Look away / What happened then / I can't believe / Submarine dream / Allright – Not quite / The bird that you can't see / Stay gold / The afternoon. (lp-iss.Jul00; SPART 83)

Sep 00. (7") (FRY 101) **THE BIRD THAT YOU CAN'T SEE.** / **HER PRETTY FACE**
(cd-s) (FRYCD 101) – ('A'side) / Everybody let up / The friar's lament.

Sep 01. (cd-ep) (<SPART 95CD>) **LET'S GO!**
– Signal in the sky (let's go!) / If you want to wear a hat (let's go!) / Heroes and villains / Stream running over (acoustic) / Signal in the sky (let's go!) (acoustic).
(above issued on 'SpinArt')

Oct 02. (cd) (COOKCD 227) <SPART 100> **VELOCITY OF SOUND**
– Please / Rainfall / That's something I do / Do you understand? / Where we meet / Yore days / Better days / I want / Mystery / Baroque / She's telling lies.

– compilations, etc. –

2000. (mp3) EMusic **LIVE IN CHICAGO** (live)
– I can't believe / Ruby / Go! / Seems so / What's the # / Heroes and villains / Get there fine / Show the world / Dots 1,2,3.

Aug 01. (cd) Cooking Vinyl; (COOKCD 218) **SOUND EFFECTS 1992-2000**
– Motorcar / Touch the water / Time for bed – I know you'll do well / Tidal wave (radio mix) / Lucky charm (radio mix) / Winter must be cold / Seems so / Tin Pan Alley / Ruby / Strawberryfire / 20 cases of suggestive of . . . / The bird that you can't see / Not the same (acoustic) / She's just like me (acoustic).

MARBLES

ROBERT SCHNEIDER, HILARIE SIDNEY + SEARS SILVERTONE – multi

1995. (7") <BUS 041> **GO MARILEE.** / **GRANT ME THE DAY**

Feb 97. (lp/cd) <(SPART 53/+CD)> **PYRAMID LANDING (AND OTHER FAVORITES)** (rec.1992-1993)
– Top of the morning / Swimming / Sun to shine / Death of my bride / Get together / Pyramid landing / Rather be a scarecrow / Laughing / Bottom of the sea / Kite / Hidden curtain / Play – Fair / Go Marilee / Grant me the day.

Feb 98. (7") <(E6 009)> **I LOVE SUMMER DAYS.** / **OUR SONG (FOR EIRENE)**

SECRET SQUARE

HILARIE SIDNEY – vocals, drums, etc / **LISA JANSSEN** – bass, etc (ex-NEUTRAL MILK HOTEL)

1995. (7") **SECRET SQUARE.** /
Feb 97. (lp/cd) <(E6 005/+CD)> **SECRET SQUARE**
– I love J.S. / I've been watching / Plunky / We know / Sparkly green couch / Sad endings / Means of escape / Candy says / Relative / Light of the sun / Aerodynamic.

VON HEMMLING

—— aka **JIM McINTYRE** – instruments

1998. (7") <E6 011> **MY COUNTRY TIS OF THESE.** / **A FINE APPLESEED**

Feb 99. (one-sided; lp) <(SHRAT 8801)> **J.W. KELLOGG**

APPLIANCE

Formed: Exeter, Devon, England ... 1995 by JAMES BROOKS, DAVID IRELAND and STUART CHRISTIE; the latter was replaced by MICHAEL PARKER after an appearance ('WEIGHTLESS CONDITIONS') on a compilation album, 'Elitism For All'. Influenced by STEREOLAB, NEU! and MY BLOODY VALENTINE, the trio issued their post-rock, 'Star Wars'-type trilogy of 10"ers over the course of the next year; the appliance of indie science, you could say! Signed to 'Mute' in 1999, the multi-talented (they play numerous instruments) trio delivered their debut long-player, 'MANUAL', an excursion into indie electronica that was both futuristic and retro-fied. Soft-spoken BROOKS and his sonic backers pieced together a few more teutonic EP's for their new millennium fanbase, while a follow-up LP, 'IMPERIAL METRIC', hit the shops in summer 2001. The latter combined an eclectic range of melodic and spaced-out synth-rock anthems which gradually percolated with every listen – crash out on 'H2o'.

Album rating: MANUAL (*7) / SIX MODULAR PIECES mini (*5) / IMPERIAL METRIC (*6) / ARE YOU EARTHED? (*5)

JAMES BROOKS – vocals, guitar / **MICHAEL PARKER** – bass; repl. STUART CHRISTIE who formed HARMONY 400 / **DAVID IRELAND** – drums

Jul 97. (10"ep) (none) **ORGANISED SOUND EP**
– IKB / Pleasure driving / Open / Concentration to brightness / Smoother.

Oct 97. (10"ep) (PLASTIC 001) **INTO YOUR HOME EP**
– For tonight / Mach one / Slow drive / We are not stationary / This is the place.

Mar 98. (7",7"blue) (WORM 12) **OUTER.** / **REV A**

Jul 98. (10"colrd-ep/cd-ep) (RAPT 20/+CD) **TIME AND SPACE EP**
– Number three channel is clear / King of the flight simulator / In the event of just looking / Ursa Major.

Apr 99. (7") (MUTE 227) **FOOD MUSIC.** / **SPIES OF ROTA**
(cd-s+=) (CDMUTE 227) – Rev A.

Sep 99. (cd-ep) (CDMUTE 229) **PACIFICA**
– Pacifica / We are not built to last / Lalo.

Sep 99. (cd/lp) (CD+/MUTE 177) <9101> **MANUAL**
– Soft landing / Food music / Throwing a curve ball / Aquaplane / Heroes of Telemark / Hot pursuit / Enjoy your nutrition / Pre-rocket science / Soyuz / Pacifica.

Apr 00. (cd-ep) <888047> **D4 (MANUAL REMIXES)**
– Soft landing (TO ROCOCO ROT) / Throwing a curve ball (TARWATER) / Hot pursuit (KREIDLER) / Heroes of Telemark (POLE).

Jun 00. (m-cd/m-lp) (CD+/STUMM 186) <9134> **SIX MUDULAR PIECES**
– Ex4 / Personal stereo / Derailleur, king of the mountain / 20 minutes from the east / Kinski in Helsinki / Slow roller.

Jun 01. (cd/lp) (CD+/STUMM 189) <9157> **IMPERIAL METRIC**
– Separate animals / Map of the territory / FLF / Land, sea and air / Comrades (in a Moscow hotel) / H2O / Skylight / AM/PM / A little more information / Navigating the nursery slopes / A gentle cycle revolution / Where has the space race gone?

Jul 01. (7") (MUTE 245) **A GENTLE CYCLE REVOLUTION.** / **NOCTURNAL WALKER**
(cd-s) (CDMUTE 245) – ('A'side) / FLF (precious bodily fluids) / Homing devices.

Oct 01. (7") (MUTE 266) **LAND, SEA AND AIR.** / **AM/PM (Simian remix)**
(cd-s+=) (CDMUTE 266) – ('A'-Bridge & Tunnel tough mix) / A gentle revolution (video).

APPLIANCE (cont)

Jan 03. (cd) <9192> **ARE YOU EARTHED?** – – Aug02
– Tuesday is nearly over / Go native / Fruits of the sea / Mountains I / As far as I can see / Violins / The blue rider / 88 / Bring out the boats / Mountains II / Are you earthed?

ARABESQUE / BEAUMONT (see under ⇒ BLUEBOY)

ARAB STRAP

Formed: Falkirk, Scotland ... 1995 by AIDAN MOFFAT and MALCOLM MIDDLETON. The former had already given up his day job at the local Sleeves record shop to team up with songwriter, JASON "JT" TAYLOR, in his outfit, BAY. This low-key band with drummer! AIDAN (augmented on their second release by RONNIE YOUNG, WILL HEGGIE – ex-COCTEAU TWINS – and ROSS BALLANY), released a couple of RED HOUSE PAINTERS-esque CD's, namely 'HAPPY BEING DIFFERENT' (1994) and 'ALISON RAE' (1995), the latter including a Lo-Fi cover of Roxy Music's 'IN EVERY DREAM HOME A HEARTACHE' and also coming free with an acoustic CD featuring a version of Nick Drake's 'WHICH WILL'. AIDAN, meanwhile, was plotting his own breakaway group, ARAB STRAP (named after a device used for horse-breeding and better known for something bought from a sex shop), re-establishing a friendship with MALCOLM while writing songs together in the latter's bedroom. A debut ARAB STRAP single, 'THE FIRST BIG WEEKEND', was warmly received by the music press in September '96, critics describing it as "trainspotting for the music world". AIDAN's drug/drink-fuelled life was portrayed in painful detail in a couple of the narrative songs from debut album, 'THE WEEK NEVER STARTS ROUND HERE' (incidentally the rhythm section was completed by GARY MILLER and DAVID GOW). His bittersweet, off-the-cuff, Scots-accented sagas of broken romance were squeezed between Lo-Fi mumblings of occasional pure genius – several of these provided by their equally wasted pal, JOHN MAUCHLINE. MALCOLM's guitar-plucking, meanwhile, came from the laid back school of cool, often played while literally lying on his back. The album was heralded by many (including John Peel) as the next big thing in exotic sound. It included seminal classics, 'THE CLEARING', 'COMING DOWN', 'I WORK IN A SALOON', 'WASTING' and 'DEEPER'. Their live set (including an early afternoon spot at Scotland's 'T In The Park' that added a host of singalong friends), was a mixture of apathy-in-concrete attitude with most people shouting for their favourite, 'THE FIRST BIG WEEKEND'; the track was subsequently used as the backing (with a new coherent talker!) on the Guinness ad (yes, that one that says about 38 per cent of all strippers were educated in a convent!). A year on, with word of mouth cult status ensured, ARAB STRAP finally achieved minor chart glory when 'THE GIRLS OF SUMMER' EP dented the Top 75. Following on from a double header tour with drinking buddies, MOGWAI, the now bearded AIDAN and Co delivered a surprise Top 50 hit, 'HERE WE GO' (a double A-side with 'TRIPPY'), one of the many low-rent, X-rated classics on their Top 40 Spring 1998 follow-up, 'PHILOPHOBIA'. Having signed up with 'Go Beat' early in '99, ARAB STRAP proceeded to deliver a disappointing stop-gap limited-edition live set, 'MAD FOR SADNESS'. Four months later, the 'CHERUBS' EP made amends and was one of the highlights of their rush-released third studio album, the over commercialised 'ELEPHANT SHOE'. However, after a two year vacation from the music scene, The 'STRAP returned in 2001 with their deeply poetic fourth outing 'THE RED THREAD'. Theme'd, as ever, around sex and love and drinking in the central belt of Scotland, the duo refused to change their style of song structure. But with single 'LOVE DETECTIVE' harking back to ARAB STRAP's earlier moments (thumping house beats, accompanied by MIDDLETON's sparse guitar playing) and closing track 'TURBULENCE' delivering a fine closure – if not conclusion – it's a wonder why this pair of talented musicians even strayed from their nest in the first place. Of late, AIDAN and a plethora of other, mainly Scottish musicians/singers, have got together for one set, 'Y'ALL GET SCARED NOW, YA HEAR' (2001) under the REINDEER SECTION banner. September 2002 was certainly an eventful month for MOFFAT and MIDDLETON with the release of both solo projects: the former with LUCKY PIERRE minimalist instrumental set, 'HYPNOGOGIA', the latter with his solo effort, '5.14 FLUOXYTINE SEAGULL ALCOHOL JOHN NICOTINE' – the jury was certainly out on MOFFAT's noodlings.

Album rating: THE WEEK NEVER STARTS ROUND HERE (*8) / PHILOPHOBIA (*8) / MAD FOR SADNESS (*6) / ELEPHANT SHOE (*7) / THE RED THREAD (*8) / Lucky Pierre: HYPNOGOGIA (*4) / Malcolm Middleton: 5.14 FLUOXYTINE SEAGULL ALCOHOL JOHN NICOTINE (*6)

AIDAN MOFFAT – vocals, keyboards / **MALCOLM MIDDLETON** – guitar / **GARY MILLER** – bass / **DAVID GOW** – drums

Chemikal Underground / Chemikal Underground

Sep 96. (7") (CHEM 007) **THE FIRST BIG WEEKEND. / GILDED** – –
—— interruptions/tape narrative by **JOHN MAUCHLINE**
Nov 96. (lp/cd) (<CHEM 010/+CD>) **THE WEEK NEVER STARTS ROUND HERE** – 1997
– Coming down / The clearing / Driving / Gourmet / I work in a saloon / Wasting / General plea to a girlfriend / The first big weekend / Kate Moss / Little girls / Phone me tonight / Blood / Deeper.
Mar 97. (12"/cd-s) (CHEM 013/+CD) **THE CLEARING (guest starring Isobel Campbell & Chris Geddes). / (remixed by Hungry Lions) (remixed by Iain Hanlon & Jonathan Hilditch)** – –
Sep 97. (12"ep/cd-ep) (CHEM 017/+CD) **THE GIRLS OF SUMMER E.P.** 74 –
– Hey! fever / Girls of summer / The beautiful barmaids of Dundee / One day, after school.
Nov 97. (7"m) (LISS 22) **THE SMELL OF OUTDOOR COOKING. / THEME TUNE / BLACKSTAR** – –
(above issued on 'Lissy's', below on 'Too Many Cooks')
1998. (7") (BROTH 001) **LIVE: PACKS OF THREE. / BLOOD** – –

Chemikal Underground / Matador

Mar 98. (10"/cd-s) (CHEM 20 T/CD) **HERE WE GO. / TRIPPY** 48 –
Apr 98. (cd) (CHEM 21CD) <OLE 315> **PHILOPHOBIA** 37 May98
– Packs of three / Soaps / Here we go / New birds / One day, after school / Islands / The night before the funeral / Not quite a yes / Piglet / Afterwards / My favourite muse / I would've liked me a lot last night / The first time you're unfaithful.
Sep 98. (7") (CHEM 27) **(AFTERNOON) SOAPS. / PHONE ME TOMORROW** 74 –
(12"+=/cd-s+=) (CHEM 27 T/CD) – ('A'side) / Toy fights / Forest hills.

Go Beat / not iss.

May 99. (cd/lp) (547387-2/-1) **MAD FOR SADNESS (live)** – –
– Intro – My favourite muse / Packs of three / New birds / Toy fights / Here we go / Phone me tomorrow / Girls of summer / Piglet / Blood / Afterwards. <US cd-iss. Jul00 on 'Jetset'; 029>
Aug 99. (12"ep/cd-ep) (GOB X/CD 21 – 561263-1/-2) **CHERUBS E.P.** – –
– Cherubs / Motown answers / An eventful day / Pulled.
—— next with guests, **CORA BISSETT, BARRY BURNS + ALAN WYLIE**
Sep 99. (cd/lp) (547805-2/-1) **ELEPHANT SHOE** – –
– Cherubs / One four seven one / Pyjamas / Autumnal / Lay the day free / Direction of strong man / Tanned / Aries the ram / The drinking eye / Pro-(your) life / Hello daylight. <US cd-iss. Jun00 on 'Jetset'; 028>

Chemikal Underground / Matador

Nov 00. (12"/cd-s) (CHEM 048/+CD) **FUKD ID VOL.2 EP** – –
– Rocket, take your turn / Blackness.
Jan 01. (12"/cd-s) (CHEM 049/+CD) **LOVE DETECTIVE. / BULLSEYE / WE KNOW WHERE YOU LIVE** 66 –
Feb 01. (lp/cd) (CHEM 050/+CD) <OLE 503> **THE RED THREAD** – –
– Amor veneris / Last orders / Scenery / The Devil-tips / The long sea / Love detective / Infrared / Screaming in the trees / Haunt me / Turbulence.
May 01. (12"/cd-s) (CHEM 051/+CD) **TURBULENCE (mixes by BIS, ARAB STRAP & JASON FAMOUS)** – –

LUCKY PIERRE

—— aka (French DJ) **AIDAN MOFFAT** with the **FORCE**

Lucky / not iss.

Feb 99. (7") (LUCKY 001) **PIERRE'S FINAL THOUGHT. / SOMETIMES I FEEL LIKE A MOTHERLESS CHILD** – –
Jul 99. (12") (LUCKY 02) **BLANK FOR YOUR OWN MESSAGE** – –

Melodic / not iss.

May 02. (12") **ANGELS ON YOUR BODY. / BOGEY ON MY SIX** – –
Sep 02. (lp/cd) (MELO 013/+CD) **HYPNOGOGIA** – –
– Angels of your body / Nurse flamingo / Shatterproof / Ghost two / The heart of all that is / The bit in the woods / Sometimes I feel like a motherless child / White Heaven in Hell / Ghost one / Bedwomb.

MALCOLM MIDDLETON

Chemikal Underground / not iss.

Sep 02. (cd) (chem 062cd) **5.14 FLUOXYTINE SEAGULL ALCOHOL JOHN NICOTINE** – –
– Crappo the clown / Wake up / The loneliest night of my life come calling / Best in me / Cold winter / Bring down (preprise) / Rotten heart / Speed on the M9 / 1, 2, 3, 4 / Birdwatcher / The king of bring / Devil and the angel.

BAY

JASON "JR" TAYLOR – vocals, guitar, bass / with **AIDAN MOFFAT** – drums!

Noise Annoys / Cargo

Nov 94. (m-cd) (ANANCD 2) **HAPPY BEING DIFFERENT** – –
– Four miles / Spleen / Embossed and embellished / A shock in store for Piggsy / Kate / Your day out.
—— **JR** now with **AIDAN / + WILL HEGGIE** – bass (of LOWLIFE, ex-COCTEAU TWINS) / **ROSS BALLANY** – drums / **RONNIE YOUNG** – guitar
Oct 95. (cd) (ANANCD 6) **ALISON RAE** – –
– Washington / Pure / Home / Dutch / Siamese / In every dream home a heartache / In Lisa's living room / Ruptured / Are you alone? / A great red shark / Surely someone somewhere. (w/ free cd) **ACOUSTIC** – Washington / Pure / Surely someone somewhere / Concrete lions / Spleen / Obligatory / Kate / Four years / Spaniard / Which will.

ARCHERS OF LOAF

Formed: Chapel Hill, North Carolina, USA ... 1991 by university students ERIC BACHMANN and ERIC JOHNSON (both Asheville born lads) who recruited MATT GENTLING and CLAY BOYER; the latter was replaced by MARK PRICE early in '92. Following an offer from a local fanzine to record a one-off single, mainman BACHMAN diverted his attention from Chapel Hill punks, SMALL (with whom he was playing at the time) and concentrated on ARCHERS OF LOAF's first recording session. The fruits of their labour emerged in the shape of 'WRONG', a heartfelt blast of grungy, melodic hardcore/punk reeking of adolescent frustration, pent-up emotion and a hip record collection. San Franciscan label, 'Alias', were suitably impressed to offer the band a deal, their first single, 'WEB IN FRONT', appearing in early '93. With its neo lo-fi, angular sound, the ARCHERS were initially compared with PAVEMENT although subsequent releases revealed a band with a wide ranging array of influences inconsistent with an art-rock tag. The

ARCHERS OF LOAF (cont)

much anticipated debut album, 'ICKY METTLE', appeared later that year, confirming the band's credentials and putting the fertile musical breeding ground of Chapel Hill firmly on the map. A John Peel session and a critically acclaimed EP ('ARCHERS OF LOAF VS. THE GREATEST OF ALL TIME') later, the ARCHERS were being pestered by a string of major labels including MADONNA's 'Maverick'. Choosing to remain resolutely independent, the band stuck with 'Alias' and concentrated on writing material for a follow-up album, 'VEE VEE'. Released in 1995 amid much critical praise, the record displayed a marked leap in songwriting ability and a more considered stylistic approach, further enhancing the band's desirability amongst the record industry big boys. Following the release of a B-sides collection, 'THE SPEED OF CATTLE' (1996), ARCHERS OF LOAF remained with 'Alias' for a third album proper, 'ALL THE NATION'S AIRPORTS' (1996). In 1998, to mark the end of a somewhat topsy-turvy career, AOL delivered their swansong set, 'WHITE TRASH HEROES', an album that harked back to their heady days of yore while progressing with that unmistakable "indie" sound; a live set, 'SECONDS BEFORE THE ACCIDENT' (recorded at the Cat's Cradle in Chapel Hill '98), took the final bow in 2000. The croaking BACHMANN resurfaced a little earlier courtesy of CROOKED FINGERS, a collaboration with MAN OR ASTROMAN?'s BRIAN CAUSEY that took elements of Lo-Fi and electro-folk. An eponymous debut was followed by 'BRING ON THE SNAKES' (2001), two sets soaked in tales of booze and blues; 'NEW DRINK FOR AN OLD DRUNK' a track from the debut close to most of our sad lives. ERIC was another indie icon to move into the world of film scores, 'SHORT CAREERS' (2002), was by all accounts worthy of a man with er... a long career – so far. • Covers: FUNNELHEAD (Treepeople) / Crooked Fingers: SUNDAY MORNING COMING DOWN (Kris Kristofferson) / SOLITARY MAN (Neil Diamond) / WHEN U WERE MINE / THE RIVER (Bruce Springsteen) / UNDER PRESSURE (David Bowie / Queen).

Album rating: ICKY METTLE (*7) / VEE VEE (*6) / THE SPEED OF CATTLE compilation (*7) / ALL THE NATION'S AIRPORTS (*6) / WHITE TRASH HEROES (*5) / SECONDS BEFORE THE ACCIDENT (*5) / Barry Black: BARRY BLACK (*6) / TRAGICAL ANIMAL STORIES (*6) / Crooked Fingers: CROOKED FINGERS (*5) / BRING ON THE SNAKES (*4) / Eric Bachmann: SHORT CAREERS (*5)

ERIC BACHMANN – vocals, guitar (ex-SMALL) / **ERIC JOHNSON** – guitar / **MATT GENTLING** – bass / **MARK PRICE** – drums; repl. CLAY BOYER

			not iss.	Stay Free
1992.	(7") <none>	WRONG. / SOUTH CAROLINA	-	
			Alias	Alias
Jul 93.	(7") (A-041S)	WEB IN FRONT. / BATHROOM		
	(cd-s+=) (A-041CD) – Tatyana.			
Sep 93.	(lp/c/cd) (A-049/+C/D)	ICKY METTLE		
– Web in front / Last word / Wrong / You and me / Might / Hate paste / Fat / Plumb line / Learo, you're a hole / Sick file / Toast / Backwash / Slow worm.
Sep 93.	(7") (A-053S)	WRONG. / (other track by SMALL)		
Feb 94.	(7")	FUNNELHEAD. / (other by The Treepeople)	-	
	(above on 'Sonic Bubblegum')			
Mar 94.	(7") (A-066S)	WHAT DID YOU EXPECT? / ETHEL MERMAN		
Sep 94.	(12"ep/cd-ep) (A-070/+D)	ARCHERS OF LOAF VS. THE GREATEST OF ALL TIME		
– Audiowhore / Lowest part is free / Freezing point / Revenge / All hail the black market.
Feb 95.	(7") (A-072S)	HARNESSED IN SLUMS. / DON'T BELIEVE THE GOOD NEWS		
	(cd-s+=) (A-072CD) – Telepathic traffic.			
Mar 95.	(lp/cd) (A-064/+D) <60064>	VEE VEE		
– Step into the light / Harnessed in slums / Nevermind the enemy / Greatest of all time / Underdogs if Nipomo / Floating friends / 1985 / Fabricoh / Nostalgia / Let the loser melt / Death in the park / Worst has yet to come / Underachievers march and fight song.
Mar 96.	(lp/cd) (A-094/+D) <60094>	THE SPEED OF CATTLE (compilation)		
– Wrong / South Carolina / Web in front / Bathroom / Tatyana / What did you expect? / Ethel Merman / Funnelhead / Quinn beast / Telepathic traffic / Don't believe the good news / Smokin pot in the hot city / In the hot city / Mutes in the steeple / Revenge / Bacteria / Freezing point / Powerwalker / Backwash.
Sep 96.	(lp/cd) (A-100/+CD) <60100>	ALL THE NATION'S AIRPORTS		
– Strangled by the stereo wire / All the nation's airports / Scenic pastures / Worst defence / Attack of the killer bees / Rental sting / Assassination on Xmas eve / Chumming the ocean / Vocal shrapnel / Bones of her hands / Bumpo / Form & file / Acromegaly / Distance comes in droves / Bombs away.
Sep 96.	(7") (A-103)	VOCAL SHRAPNEL. / DESTINY		
Feb 97.	(10"lp)<m-cd> (A-115) <60115>	VITUS TINNITUS		
– Harnessed in slums / Underdogs of Nipomo / Greatest of all time / Form and file / Audio whore / Nostalgia / Vocal shrapnel (remix) / Scenic pastures (remix).
Nov 98.	(cd) (A 128D) <60128>	WHITE TRASH HEROES		Sep98
– Fashion bleeds / Dead red eyes / INS / Perfect time / Slick tricks and bright lights / One slight wrong move / Banging on a dead drum / Smokers in love / After thge last laugh / White trash heroes.

––– disbanded after above

– compilations, etc. –

Jul 00.	(cd) Alias; <(A 143)>	SECONDS BEFORE THE ACCIDENT (live 1998)		
– Dead red eyes / Fabricoh / Vocal shrapnel / Web in front / Let the loser melt / Strangled by the stereo wire / Fashion bleeds / You and me / Might / Revenge / South Carolina / Lowest part is free / Plumbline / Wrong / White trash heroes / Chumming the oceans.

BARRY BLACK

––– aka **ERIC BACHMANN** – multi / + session instrumentals

			Alias	Alias
Oct 95.	(lp/cd) (A 085/+D) <60085>	BARRY BLACK		
– Train of pain / Mighty fields of tobacco / The broad majestic haw / Sandviken stomp / Fisherman thugs / Cockroaches / Vampire lounge / Golden throat / Rabid dog / Animals are for eating / Boo bary blip / Cowboys and thieves / I can't breathe / Staticus von carrborrus.
Aug 97.	(lp/cd) (A 122/+D) <60122>	TRAGIC ANIMAL STORIES		Jul97
– The horrible truth about plankton / When sharks smell blood / Duelling elephants / Derelict vultures / Iditorod sled dogs / Chimps / Slow Loris' lament / Drowning spider / Tropical fish revival / Snail trail of tears.

CROOKED FINGERS

ERIC BACHMANN + BRIAN CAUSEY (of MAN OR ASTROMAN?)

			not iss.	Sub Pop
Sep 99.	(cd-s) <SP 472>	ATCHAFALAYAN DEATH WALTZ / JULIETTE	-	
			not iss.	Red Pig
Dec 99.	(cd-s) <1>	BROKEN MAN / RED DEVIL DAWN	-	
			Warm	Warm
Jan 00.	(cd) <WARM 100CD>	CROOKED FINGERS	-	
– Crowned in chrome / New drink for the old drunk / Pigeon kicker / Man who died of nothing at all / Broken man / Black black ocean / Juliette / She spread her legs and flew away / Under sad stars / A little bleeding.
Feb 01.	(cd) <(WARM 103CD)>	BRING ON THE SNAKES		
– The rotting strip / Devils train / Surrender is treason / Sad love / Doctors of deliverance / Every dull moment / Here come the snakes / There's a blue light.
			Merge	Touch & Go
May 02.	(cd-ep) (MRG 208) <T&G 508>	RESERVOIR SONGS		
– Sunday morning coming down / Solitary man / When U were mine / The river / Under pressure.

ERIC BACHMANN

––– w/ **ANDREJ CURTY + WADE RITTENBERRY + EVAN THOMAS + EUNICE KANG**

			not iss.	Merge
2002.	(cd) <MRG 212>	SHORT CAREERS	-	
– Good morning sleepyhead / Forks and knives / A diamond is the Devil's eye / Finding the holes filling the gaps / Jimmy the enforcer / Aspirin vs. arsenic / Short careers / The mysterious death death of Robert Tower / Nosebleed / Vision and execution / Reach out and touch someone / Ty Cobb.

ARCWELDER

Formed: Minneapolis, Minnesota, USA ... 1988 as TILT-A-WHIRL by brothers ROB and BILL GRABER, along with SCOTT McDONALD. Under this moniker, they recorded their debut single in 1988 under their own steam. This effort paid off getting them signed to local label, 'Big Money Inc.', who released their first full-set, 'THIS' (1990). Unfortunately the creators of the amusement park ride, Tilt-a-whirl, were none too amused with the association and set up legal proceedings against the band, forcing them to, within a fortnight, change their name. The boys rapidly accepted choosing the new name ARCWELDER, which was an instrumental track from 'THIS'. They also had to put up with the added indignity – although fairly humourous action – of placing a disclaimer tag on the original release. Their second album, 'JACKET MADE IN CANADA' (1991), a comical title referring to the origin of the sleeve production of many American indie releases of this period, was emitted a year later. This album validated these boys as an original force in alternative rock scene; they combined their punk and hardcore influences from bands like their local legends, HUSKER DU, with newer more grunge-style patterning. It would not be facetious to say that there was definitely a two-way relationship of influence going on between ARCWELDER and the now rocketing skyward Seattle alt-rock scene. 1992 saw 'WELDER tour with Minnesotan's FLOUR who were contracted to 'Touch and Go' and, after a gig in Chicago attended by the head of this label, Corey Rusk, signed on the dotted line. In quick succession the group's new masters put out their third and fourth LP's, 'PULL' (1993) and 'XERXES' (1994). The latter of these sets really showed the band brilliantly binding together all of their origins and combining this with new found inspiration to create a sound that could be truly called their own. This development continued into their fifth piece, 'ENTROPY' (1996), but unfortunately for the these self-deprecating rockers their other commitments called them away, only to resurface three years later with the album, 'EVEREST' (1999). This outing showed the same high-level of integrity to their music that ARCWELDER's fans have come to expect and showed no lacking in vigour or evolution due to their long absence. • **Covered:** I AM THE WALRUS (Beatles) / SIGN OF THE TIMES (Prince).

Album rating: THIS (*5) / JACKET MADE IN CANADA (*5) / PULL (*5) / XERVES (*6) / EVEREST (*6)

BILL GRABER – guitar, bass, vocals / **ROB GRABER** – bass, guitar / **SCOTT McDONALD** – drums, vocals

			not iss.	Sonic Boom
1988.	(ltd-7"; as TILT-A-WHIRL) <none>	PINT OF BLOOD. / DEFINE MY LIFE	-	
			not iss.	Big Money
1990.	(lp)	THIS	-	
– This / Such a very long time / Blue / What am I supposed to do / Living legend / What have I done to me / Arc welder / Pint of blood / Moment of passion / It won't change / Understanding.
1991.	(lp)	JACKET MADE IN CANADA	-	
– Harmonic instrumental / Daydream / Missing / Hint taken / Left / Plastic / Favor / When you're gone / Everything / Staback / I hates to lose / Bon sez. <US re-iss. Jul95; 13>
1992.	(7")	I AM THE WALRUS. / SIGN OF THE TIMES	-	

ARCWELDER (cont)

	Duophonic Super	not iss.
Sep 92. (7") **FAVOR. / PLASTIC**		-
	Touch & Go	Touch & Go
Oct 92. (7") <(TG 105)> **RALEIGH. / WALLS / ROSA**		
Feb 93. (lp/cd) <(TG 108/+CD)> **PULL**		

– Truth / What did you call it that for / And then again / It's a wonderful lie / Raleigh / Cranberry sauce / Criminal / Will when you won't / Remember to forget / Lahabim / Just not moving / Finish my song / You.

Apr 94. (lp/cd) <(TG 126/+CD)> **XERXES**

– Smile / All my want for need / All mixed together / Passing thought / Free bird / Let down / Down to the wire / Change / Attic / Pound / Carpal tunnel song / I hear and obey.

Oct 95. (7") <(TG 153)> **CAPITAL ALLEN. / WHITE ELEPHANT**
May 96. (lp/cd) <(TG 158/+CD)> **ENTROPY**   Apr96

– Doubt / Free me / Unknown / Snake oil / Blowin' smoke / Ad infinitum / Captain Allen / I promise not to be an asshole / And now / Know / Vengeance / Turn to / Andrew's hymn / Ash.

Oct 99. (cd) <(TG 204CD)> **EVEREST**

– Never the same / Do something right / I know how you are / Treasured island / All in good time / Chicken / Paying respect / Why did I care / Will you stay? / Head / Witness / You will A ghostly bishop / Never counted / I gave this up for you.

A.R.E. WEAPONS

Formed: New York City, New York, USA ... 1998 by bassist MATTHEW McAULEY, synth-man TOM and vocalist BRIAN F. McPECK. A.R.E. (Atomic Revenge Extreme) WEAPONS were the thumping, pounding, no-bullshitters of American avant-electro music, or the fresh New York underground, which boasted The MOLDY PEACHES, BLACK DICE, INTERPOL and, of course, the charming STROKES. It could be fair to say that WEAPONS were a template for the heaving, aggressive, claustrophobic atmosphere of NYC – or as Dostoevsky put it; "cultivating anger underground". The members of said group were hard-toking, hard-drinking, hard-fighting ex-street punks, two thirds homeless and all the better for it. Apparently, they began playing by getting drunk for a week and just coming up with songs. Their battered SUICIDE and GARY NUMAN-like music was taken out of the bedroom and into the streets c. early 2000, with the band playing a handful of regular shows around the East-Village art galleries (many of them accumulating in violence, debauchery or just sheer drug-induced madness). By this time, the group were beginning to build up quite a reputation as the New York underground scene was drifting from the sewers up into the houses, radios and music papers. 'Rough Trade', who signed both The STROKES and The MOLDY PEACHES were convinced by Jarvis Cocker (of all people!) to enlist A.R.E. WEAPONS. By July 2001, the group had issued 'STREET GANG', a 'Warriors'-esque tale of a street-fighting hide-and-seek on the edgy streets of the Big Apple, with razor-sharp beats, hardcore basslines et al. The second track on the single, 'BLACK MERCEDES', had singer BRIAN mumble, "nobody ever follow me into a fight ... 'cause I'm too unstable". And unstable it was, too. Another single, 'NEW YORK MUSCLE' was issued towards the end of the year and the group were also featured on a compilation 'Electroclash'. In 2002, TOM bailed out and was subsequently replaced by manager, PAUL SEVIGNY.

Album rating: debut album issued early 2003

BRIAN F. McPECK – vocals / **MATTHEW McAULEY** – bass / **TOM** – synthesizer

	Rough Trade	Rough Trade
Jul 01. (7") (RTRADES 022) **STREET GANG. / BLACK MERCEDES**	72	-
(cd-s+=) (RTRADESCD 022) – Saigon.		
Nov 01. (12") (RTRADES 027) **NEW YORK MUSCLE / NEW YORK (instrumental). / CHAMPION CHAINS / BE NICE**		-
(cd-s) (RTRADESCD 027) – (first & third) / Champion chains (be nice).		

—— **PAUL SEVIGNY** – instruments; repl. TOM

ARNOLD

Formed: London, England ... early 1996 as PATIO by ROB, PHIL MORRIS (aka CAINEY), MARK SAXBY and PHIL PAYNE. Following the death of vocalist ROB, the remaining members renamed themselves ARNOLD, abandoning their indie guitar pop of old for a darker, more introspective direction. Creation's ALAN McGEE was suitably impressed enough to sign them up, the first fruits of their new deal surfacing as the mini-album, 'THE BARN TAPES', in spring '97. Always in a scrape or a boxing match of some sort – with the "Blond Fox" MORRIS in the thick of it – ARNOLD were attempting to be the next FACES or BIG STAR. 1998's rustic 'HILLSIDE' album finally saw ARNOLD's sound come together, mainstream success still eluding them despite unanimous critical acclaim from the music press. With 'Creation' out of the way and now in the hands of a top major, the band's career looked to have taken a nosedive. However, it would be that man McGEE again who helped bail out the band. Inking a deal with his new 'Poptones' imprint, ARNOLD feted out a new long-player, 'BAHAMA' (2001), heady visions of summer, BRIAN WILSON and PHIL SPECTOR were awash straight from the opening number 'CLIMB'. 2002's self-titled EP for 'Lucky Pierre', set in multi-coloured concrete what the "Arnie" lads were all about; taste 'SWEET SWEET SWEET NOTHING'.

Album rating: THE BARN TAPES (*6) / HILLSIDE (*7) / BAHAMA (*6)

PHIL MORRIS (aka CAINEY) – vocals, drums / **MARK SAXBY** – guitar / **PHIL PAYNE** – bass

	Creation	Sony
May 97. (m-cd/10"m-lp) (CRE CD/LP 218) **THE BARN TAPES**		-

– Float my boat / Calling Ira Jones / Face / Dog on the stairs / Windsor park / Sun / 2 chairs / Medication time.

Aug 97. (7") (CRE 257) **TWIST. / HILLSIDE**		-
(cd-s+=) (CRESCD 257) – Holly lodge.		
Apr 98. (7") (CRE 287) **FLEAS DON'T FLY. / BIG BLACK CLOUD**		-
(cd-s+=) (CRESCD 287) – On the bus.		
Jun 98. (7") (CRE 293) **FISHSOUNDS. / JOHNNY WAS A DABBLER**		-
(cd-s+=) (CRESCD 293) – Two chairs.		
Jul 98. (cd/lp) (CRE CD/LP 231/+L) <69333> **HILLSIDE**		

– Fleas don't fly / Ira Jones goes to the country / Hillside / Fishsounds / Country biscuit / Windsor park / Curio / Rabbit / Goodbye grey / Face / Rubber duck (parts 1, 2 & 3) / Mickey's mother / Moroccan roll (part 2) / Catherine day. (cd re-iss. Jan01; same)

Sep 98. (7") (CRE 300) **WINDSOR PARK. / FLIGHTLESS BIRD**		-
(cd-s+=) (CRESCD 300) – Pocket rocket.		

	Poptones	not iss.
Aug 01. (7"ep) (MC 50215) **OH MY**		-
Oct 01. (cd) (MC 5021CD) **BAHAMA**		-

– Climb / Tiny car / Hangman's waltz / Jus de lune / Oh my / Easy / Boo you / Other son / Pavey ark.

	Lucky Pierre	not iss.
Jul 02. (cd-ep) (LUPR 01) **THE ARNOLD EP**		-

– You're a star / God knows / South / Wild colonial girl / Sweet sweet sweet nothing.

ASH

Formed: N. Ireland ... 1989 by TIM WHEELER (then 12 years of age) and MARK HAMILTON, relocating to Downpatrick, County Down a few years later where they officially formed the trio with RICK McMURRAY. ASH's precocious talents were quickly spotted by American record moguls eager for more punk-centric guitar music which would also cross over to the pop market. Though they eventually opted to sign with 'Reprise', the trio had already released their debut set, 'TRAILER' on 'Infectious'. Their starry-eyed, bushy-tailed but ultimately derivative blend of indie punk finally became a part of the pop vocabulary when the catchy 'GIRL FROM MARS' skyrocketed into the UK Top 20 in summer '95. This was pursued by another Top 20 hit later that year in 'ANGEL INTERCEPTOR'. With the hype machine going into overload, the group hit the UK Top 5 in Spring of the following year with 'GOLDFINGER', the single trailing a No.1 album, '1977' (1996). Apparently a reference to the year 'Star Wars' was released rather than any reference to safety-pins and saliva, the record included all their hit singles to date and confirmed their increasingly melodic approach. Keeping their profile high with festival appearances, the band later added another guitarist, CHARLOTTE HATHERLEY in summer '97. She made her debut on ASH's theme for the much lauded Ewan McGregor/Cameron Diaz film, 'A LIFE LESS ORDINARY', another Top 10 in late '97. While the indie scene continues to cry out for something innovative, it remains difficult to envisage any figureheads less ordinary than ASH (songs!). Surprisingly 'Kerrang!-friendly, the quartet lost a little of their indie cred with the release of their third album proper, 'NU-CLEAR SOUNDS' (1998), a record that quickly vacated the Top 10 with the accompanying single, 'JESUS SAYS', only managing to make a Top 20 placing. With sex (group, that is), drugs (abuse) and rock'n'roll (Tim Wheeler in the buff!) all the ingredients were in the latest promo instalment for ASH's single 'NUMBSKULL'. Unfortunately the viewing public, and for that matter the buying public, didn't get much of a look-in, as the EP (like many others at the turn of the century) was ineligible for the charts via a new ruling by those pesky compilers. Older and wiser, the ASH posse returned in 2001 with their first material of the new millennium, 'FREE ALL ANGELS'. Previewed by the hit singles, 'SHINING LIGHT' and 'BURN BABY BURN', the record recaptured some of their mid-period spunk and used it to temper the aural hangover of its predecessor. • **Songwriters:** WHEELER or w/ HAMILTON except covers; PUNKBOY (Helen Love) / GET READY (Temptations) / DOES YOUR MOTHER KNOW (Abba) / LOSE CONTROL (Backwater) / BLEW (Nirvana) / WHO YOU DRIVIN' NOW? (Mudhoney). • **Trivia:** The cover sleeve of their single, 'KUNG FU', had a photo of French former Man U star footballer, ERIC CANTONA, giving his famous throat and neck tackle on an abusive Crystal Palace supporter in 1995.

Album rating: TRAILER mini (*7) / 1977 (*9) / LIVE AT THE WIRELESS live official bootleg (*5) / NU-CLEAR SOUNDS (*7) / FREE ALL ANGELS (*6) / INTERGALACTIC SONIC SEVENS compilation (*8)

TIM WHEELER – vocals, guitar / **MARK HAMILTON** – bass / **RICK McMURRAY** – drums

	La La Land	not iss.
Feb 94. (7") (LA LA 001) **JACK NAMES THE PLANETS. / DON'T KNOW**		-

	Infectious	Reprise
Aug 94. (7"ep) (INFECT 13S) **PETROL. / THE LITTLE POND / A MESSAGE FROM OSCAR WILDE AND PATRICK THE BREWER**		-
(cd-s+=) (INFEVT 13CD) – Things. (re-iss. Nov96; same)		
Oct 94. (cd/c/lp) (INFECT 14 CD/MC/LP) <45985> **TRAILER**		Oct95

– Season / Message from Oscar Wilde and Patrick the brewer / Jack names the planets / Intense thing / Uncle Pat / Message from Mr. Waterman / Get out / Petrol / Obscure thing. (lp w/ free 7"yellow) (INFECT 14S) SILVER SURFER. / JAZZ '59 <diff.tracks US> (re-iss. Jan01 cd/c/lp; INFECT 14 CD/MC/LPX)

Oct 94. (7") (INFECT 16S) **UNCLE PAT. / DIFFERENT TODAY**		-
(cd-s+=) (INFECT 16CD) – Hulk Hogan bubble bath. (re-iss. Nov96; same)		
Mar 95. (7") (INFECT 21J) <17706> **KUNG FU. / DAY OF THE TRIFFIDS**	57	Nov95
(cd-s+=) (INFECT 21CD) – Luther Ingo's star cruiser. (re-iss. Nov96 & Jan01; same)		

ASH (cont)

Jul 95.	(7"/c-s) *(INFECT 24S/24MC)* **GIRL FROM MARS. / CANTINA BAND** — 11

(cd-s+=) *(INFECT 24CD)* – Astral conversations with Toulouse Lautrec. *(re-iss. Nov96 & Jan01; same)*

Sep 95. (7"cold-various) <*G26*> **PETROL. / PUNKBOY** — –
Oct 95. (7"/c-s/cd-s) *(INFECT 27S/27MC/27CD)* **ANGEL INTERCEPTOR. / 5 A.M. ETERNAL / GIVE ME SOME TRUTH** — 14
(re-iss. cd-s Nov96 & Jan01; same)

Dec 95. (7"red) *(FP 004)* **GET READY. / ZERO ZERO ZERO**
(above 45 issued on 'Fantastic Plastic')

Apr 96. (7"/c-s) *(INFECT 39 S/MC)* **GOLDFINGER. / I NEED SOMEBODY / SNEAKER** — 5
(cd-s+=) *(INFECT 39CD)* – Get ready. *(re-iss. Nov96 & Jan01; same)*

May 96. (cd/c/lp) *(INFECT 40 CD/MC/LP)* <*46191*> **1977** — 1
– Lose control / Goldfinger / Girl from Mars / I'd give you anything / Gone the dream / Kung Fu / Oh yeah / Let it flow / Innocent smile / Angel interceptor / Lost in you / Darkside lightside. *(cd+=hidden track)* – Sick of vomiting. *(lp re-iss. Jan01; same)*

Jun 96. (7"yellow/c-s) *(INFECT 41 S/MC)* **OH YEAH / T. REX / EVERYWHERE IS ALL AROUND / OH YEAH (quartet version)** — 6
(cd-s) *(INFECT 41CD)* – (first 3 tracks) / Does your mother know. *(re-iss. Nov96 & Jan01; same)*

— added **CHARLOTTE HATHERLEY** – guitar (ex-NIGHTNURSE)

Infectious — Dreamworks

Oct 97. (7"blue/c-s) *(INFECT 50 S/MC)* **A LIFE LESS ORDINARY. / WHERE IS LOVE GOING / WHAT DEANER WAS TALKING ABOUT** — 10
(cd-s+=) *(INFECT 50CD)* – Halloween. *(re-iss. Jan01; same)*

Sep 98. (7") *(INFECT 059S)* **JESUS SAYS. / TAKEN OUT** — 15
(c-s+=/cd-s+=) *(INFECT 059 MCS/CDS)* – Heroin, vodka, white noise.
(cd-s) *(INFECT 059CDSX)* – ('A'side) / Radiation / Dancing on the Moon. *(re-iss. Jan01; same)*

Oct 98. (cd/c/lp) *(INFECT 060 CD/MC/LP)* <*50121*> **NU-CLEAR SOUNDS** — 7 Sep99
– Projects / Low ebb / Jesus says / Wild surf / Death trip 21 / Folk song / Numbskull / Burn out / Aphrodite / Fortune teller / I'm gonna fall. *(re-iss. Jan01; same)*

Nov 98. (7") *(INFECT 061S)* **WILD SURF. / STORMY WATERS** — 31
(c-s+=/cd-s+=) *(INFECT 061 MCS/CDS)* – When I'm tired.
(cd-s) *(INFECT 061CDSX)* – ('A'side) / Lose control / Gonna do it soon. *(re-iss. Jan01; same)*

— added on tour **DJ DICK KURTAINE** – turntables

Apr 99. (d7"red-ep) *(INFECT 62)* **NUMBSKULL EP**
– Numbskull / Blew / Who you drivin' now? / Jesus says (live).
(cd-ep+=) *(INFECT 62EP)* – Girl from Mars (live) / Fortune teller (live). *(re-iss. Jan01; same)*

Jan 01. (7"/c-s) *(INFECT 98 S/MCS)* **SHINING LIGHT. / WARMER THAN FIRE** — 8
(cd-s+=) *(INFECT 98CDS)* – Gabriel.
(cd-s) *(INFECT 98CDSX)* – ('A'side) / Feel no pain / Jesus says (headrock valley beats lightyear 12"mix) / ('A'-CD-ROM video).

Apr 01. (7") *(INFECT 99S)* **BURN BABY BURN. / THINKING ABOUT YOU** — 13
(cd-s+=) *(INFECT 99CDSX)* – Submission (Arthur Baker remix).
(cd-s) *(INFECT 99CDS)* – ('A'side) / 13th floor (session) / Only in dreams (session).

Apr 01. (cd/c/lp) *(INFECT 100 CD/MC/LP)* **FREE ALL ANGELS** — 1
– Walking barefoot / Shining light / Burn baby burn / Candy / Submission / Someday / Pacific palisades / Shark / Sometimes / Nicole / There's a star / World domination.

Jul 01. (d7") *(INFEC 101S)* **SOMETIMES, / SKULLFULL OF SULPHUR / SO THE STORY GOES. / TEENAGE KICKS** — 21
(cd-s) *(INFEC 101CDS)* – (first 3 tracks) / ('A'-video).
(cd-s) *(INFEC 101CDSX)* – (first & fourth tracks) / Melon farmer (live) / (video mixer update).

Oct 01. (d7") *(INFEC 106S)* **CANDY. / WATERFALL // NOCTURNE. / STAY IN LOVE FOREVER** — 20
(cd-s) *(INFEC 106CDS)* – (first 3 tracks) / ('A'-video).
(cd-s) *(INFEC 106CDSX)* – (first & fourth tracks) / Sweetness of death by the obsidian knife.

Jan 02. (cd-s) *(INFEC 112CDS)* **THERE'S A STAR / NO PLACE TO HIDE / COASTING / THERE'S A STAR (video)** — 13
(cd-s) *(INFEC 112CDSX)* – ('A'side) / Here comes the music / Grey will fade / (video excerpts).

Aug 02. (cd-s) *(INFEC 119CDS)* **ENVY / TONIGHT YOU BELONG TO ME / I SHALL NOT DIE** — 21
(cd-s) *(INFEC 119CDSX)* – ('A'side) / Bad karma blues / I don't mind.
(d7"+=) *(INFEC 119S)* – I shall not die.

Sep 02. (cd/d-lp) *(INFEC 120 CD/LP)* **INTERGALACTIC SONIC SEVENS** (compilation) — 3
– Burn baby burn / Envy / Girl from Mars / Shining light / A life less ordinary / Goldfinger / Jesus says / Oh yeah / Jack names the planets / Sometimes / Kung Fu / Candy / Angel interceptor / Uncle Pat / Wildsurf / Walking barefoot / Petrol / There's a star / Numbskull. *(2xcd+=/4xlp+=; INFEC 120CDB)* – No place to hide / Warmer than fire / Where is our love going / Taken out / 13th floor / Stormy waters / Message from Oscar Wilde / Who you drivin' now / Stay in love forever / Sweetness of death by the obsidian knife / Melon farmer / Nocturne / Gabriel / Coasting / Lose control / I need somebody / Sneaker / Cantina band / Astral conversations with Toulouse Lautrec / Day of the triffids / Hallowe'en / Thinking about you.

– compilations, etc. –

Feb 97. (cd) *Death Star; (DEATH 3)* **LIVE AT THE WIRELESS** (live)
– Darkside lightside / Girl from Mars / Oh yeah / T.Rex / I'd give you anything / Kung Fu / What Deaner was talking about / Goldfinger / Petrol / A clear invitation to party. *(lp-iss.Jan01; DEATH 3LP)*

Dec 02. (cd-s) *Double Dragon; (DD 2007)* **JACK NAMES THE PLANETS**

ASHA VIDA

Formed: Detroit, Michigan, USA ... 1993 by JESSE RAFFERTY, CRAIG BADYNEE, ERIC PIETI and RYAN ANDERSON. The band's sound ranged from their beginnings as an etheral space-rock outfit in the vein of peers such as ALISON'S HALO and luminaries of the genre, SPIRITUALIZED. Over the course of time, they waded into more unconventional Prog-rock territory, although with a less structured approach that was associated with this genre in the seventies. AV had providence behind them as the alternative press were looking for a style outside grunge to next promote, and on this wave the band managed to get their debut 45, 'ESKIMO SUMMER', issued following the handing over of a demo to their like-minded brethren WINDY AND CARL. The quality of their ensuing weird and wonderful live spectacles meant that they received even greater critical attention, their 7" 'PINION' also going down a storm with the alternative muso hacks. In the succeeding period between this release and their debut album, 'AS ONE OF ONE' (1997), the band saw the departure of ANDERSON who teamed up with WINDY AND CARL's RANDALL NIEMAN to form the similarly veined FUXA. 'VIDA's premier set already witnessed them moving into more experimental pastures, while still packing a breathtaking sonic punch. This was continued and furthered on their sophomore LP, 'NATURE'S CLUMSY HAND' (1998), a record which included the near 20-minute aural deluge of 'DIEM PARDIDI'. This venture saw the band truly jump head first into the improvised progressive space-rock arena.

Album rating: AS ONE OF ONE mini (*6) / NATURE'S CLUMSY HAND (*7)

CRAIG BADYNEE – vocals, guitar, bass, keyboards / **ERIC PIETI** – guitar, keyboards / **JESSE RAFFERTY** – percussion, drums / RYAN ANDERSON (left early on to join FUXA)

not iss. — Audrey's Diary

1993. (7") <*003.93*> **ESKIMO SUMMER. / STELLAR VOICES** — –

not iss. — Binausic

1995. (7") **PINION. / (other by GODZUKI)** — –

Icon — not iss.

Jul 97. (m-cd) *(IC 128CD)* **AS ONE OF ONE**
– Lacedaemon / (+4).

Burnt Hair — Orchard

Apr 98. (cd) *(BUR 16)* <*4775*> **NATURE'S CLUMSY HAND**
– If buon tempo verra! / Per aspera ad astra / Poena sensus / Sic itur ad astra / Diem pardidi / Vocat aestus in Umbrum.

— the group have since split

ASHBY

Formed: Boston, Massachusetts, USA ... some time in 2000 by multi-talented – i.e. songwriter, singer, instrumentalist – EVELYN POPE, alongside producer and electronics man, WILLIAM COWIE. Taking inspiration from TORTOISE, SEA AND CAKE and MOUSE ON MARS, while loosely mixing a concoction with SAINT ETIENNE, The CARDIGANS and BURT BACHARACH, ASHBY delivered their classy pop-meets-electronica set, 'POWER BALLADS', in 2001.

Album rating: POWER BALLADS (*7)

EVELYN POPE – vocals, multi / **WILLIAM COWIE** – producer / + **AMY GEDDES** – strings

Marina — EFA

Nov 01. (cd) *(MA 54)* <*6764*> **POWER BALLADS**
– West Coast town / Trip 66 / Old gold / Horizon / Escapade / Serene smile / Continuity / Last another day / Likeminded / Space bossa nova / Favorite son / Slip away.

Richard ASHCROFT (see under ⇒ VERVE)

ASHLEY PARK

Formed: Vancouver, Canada ... 1998 by TERRY MILES by musical journeyman, TERRY MILES, who had first began recording with the group CINNAMON which also comprised TOM WILLIAMS, KEVIN COOPER and MARK DESOUZA. The group released one cassette 'WEIRD PLANET' (1994) and an album 'CREAM SODA' in 1996, before MILES and COOPER formed the KELLY AFFAIR. This outfit completed one album of kitsch pop, 'WELCOME TO THE KELLY AFFAIR', before MILES became sidetracked by ASHLEY PARK. Originally MILES had joined forces with a group of friends (CHRISTOPHER HARRIS and MICHAEL WHITE) with the intention of making a documentary depicting the beauty of America's landscapes. Inexplicably, the end product of this venture was an album, 'TOWN AND COUNTRY', released in 2000, a massive leap forward for MILES in terms of craftsmanship. The album was notable for its warm sonic landscapes and uplifting, BEACH BOYS/BACHARACH-esque, harmonies. The 2001 follow up, 'AMERICAN SCENE', was another scenic musical road trip, with MILES making no attempt to hide his influences.

Album rating: Cinnamon: CREAM SODA (*5) / Kelly Affair: WELCOME TO . . . THE KELLY AFFAIR (*6) / Ashley Park: TOWN AND COUNTRY (*6) / THE AMERICAN SCENE (*6)

CINNAMON

TERRY MILES – vocals, guitar / **TOM WILLIAMS** – lead guitar / **KEVIN COOPER** – bass / **MARQ DeSOUZA** – drums

			not iss.	own label
1994.	(c)	**WEIRD PLANET**	-	
1996.	(cd)	**CREAM SODA**	-	

– Cream soda / Jusgement day (in the sun) / Super hi-fi love song / Crazy / 1970 / Valerie & Kim / I'll never know / Raygun / Swim or shine / Veronica / America / Jenny falls apart.

			Not Lame	Not Lame
Jun 98.	(cd)	<(NL 043)> **WELCOME TO . . . THE KELLY AFFAIR**		

– Photographs of four / That school / We're okay / Other girls / Another edit / It falls away / On the phone / Suburban salute / Last summer / In your room. *(bonus+=)* – Supersweet – Under the stove (demo) / Under the stove (demo).

―― COOPER + DeSOUZA formed SATURNHEAD who released a few albums

ASHLEY PARK

TERRY MILES – vocals, guitar, bass, piano / **CHRISTOPHER HARRIS** – banjo, marimba, cello, keyboards / **MICHAEL WHITE** – drums / + other session people

			Kindercore	Kindercore
Mar 01.	(cd)	<(KC 055)> **TOWN AND COUNTRY**		Oct00

– Town and country / Everyone under the sun / Lucy and the bourgeousie / Moles / By the stereo / Just a song / Town and country LL and LLL / Take your shoes off / It's not too late / In the country / N.Y. / Summer end / Bonnie and Clyde / The university scene.

―― **KELLY HAIGH** – vocals; repl. WHITE + HARRIS

			not iss.	Darling
Nov 01.	(cd)	<8> **THE AMERICAN SCENE**	-	

– The old masquerade / The last day in the life of Grand / Around the world / The last train home v/ Return to me / The American scene / Tell me why / Paris / Clear the corners / The great divide / Arkansas, until the sun / Re-entry day / Little dogs / Rocket on the highway / I know I love you.

ASHTRAY BOY

Formed: Chicago, Illinois, USA . . . 1993 by RANDALL LEE, recruiting the assistance of DAVE TRUMFIO and JUSTIN NIIMI. Antipodean indie popster, LEE had previously worked with CANNANES and was also at the helm of NICE. The latter of these bands, had been a short-lived, two LP affair, 'NICE' (1992), and 'APPLE PIE' (1993), although both had nonetheless showcased LEE's songwriting prowess and his melodious indie pop credentials. Following the end of NICE, LEE – who would routinely travel to and from Sydney, Australia and the US – put together the Stateside-based ASHTRAY BOY, releasing the debut album, 'HONEYMOON SUITE' (1993) to widespread alternative press acclaim in late 1993; worthy of note was the guest vocals, of soon to be massive, indie diva, LIZ PHAIR. Following this release, LEE formed an Australian branch of ASHTRAY BOY with the aid of THOMAS TALLIS and NEIL JOHNSTON. The 'BOY subsequently delivered their sophomore full-length set, 'MACHO CHAMPIONS' (1995), which was split between the two outfits, as all future outings were. Interestingly on this second set the Australian AB do a cover of the American ASHTRAY BOY's 'LITTLE NATURE CHILD' from the debut outing. LEE took his unique indie pop sound and concept forward with the release of the third LP, 'CANDYPANTS BEACH', which was highlighted by a cover of Neil Young's 'HEART OF GOLD', a great reinterpretation by the downunder strand of AB. With fourth set, 'EVERYMAN'S FOURTH DIMENSION', LEE's writing was noticeably maturing, and he again demonstrated good use of guest vocalisation, this time in the shapes of MARY DYER and CATH CARROLL.

Album rating: Nice: NICE (*7) / APPLE PIE (*6) / Ashtray Boy: HONEYMOON SUITE (*6) / MACHO CHAMPIONS (*5) / CANDYPANTS BEACH (*5) / THE EVERYMAN'S 4th DIMENSION (*6)

NICE

RANDALL LEE – vocals, guitar (ex-CANNANES) / **SUSANNAH STUART-LINDSAY** – vocals, etc.

			not iss.	Feel Good All Over
Jan 92.	(cd)	<FGAO 11> **NICE**	-	

– Dear John / Head in the hay / All for you / Caress me / Anthem / Theme from Nice / Circuit diagram / Oversized hen / No drinkin' buddies / Christiana amore / Pastoral disaster / Return to Nice.

| Oct 93. | (cd) | <FGAO 19> **APPLE PIE** | - | |

– Cassandra Nova / Mr. Lee / Cup of coffee / On my back in the madhouse / Total moon / My perfect fire / Hi tension / Curse of the Lees / Seven daze / Doledrums / Cunning and sly / Fucked around / Now.

ASHTRAY BOY

LEE with **DAVE TRUMFIO** – sitar, double bass / **JUSTIN NIIMI** – drums

			Feel Good All Over	Feel Good All Over
Jan 94.	(cd)	<(FGAO 20)> **THE HONEYMOON SUITE**		Nov93

– Ananda Marga / Shirley MacLaine / Observatory hill / There is a fountain / Time for a baby / How Charles destroyed the inland sea / Infidel / Little nature child / Hit / Love in a bakery / The honeymoon suite. <re-iss. Jan96 on 'Scout'; SR 1003)>

―― LEE introduced **THOMAS TALLIS** – bass / **NEIL JOHNSTON** – drums

			Ajax	Ajax
Nov 94.	(cd)	<AJAX 033CD> **MACHO CHAMPIONS**	-	

– I am sponge / Amy Grant super number / Val and Gina / Walrus / Song for Rupert / Eddie / Let's raise our glasses / Roy / Maureen / Paunch / Little nature child / Woman alone.

| Jul 95. | (cd) | <AJAX 044CD> **CANDYPANTS BEACH** | - | |

– Dead body in the surf / Chicken / She's taken up snoring / Salmon in your eyes / Road kill / Cows on the roof / Heart of gold / Toothpaste / Dentist from Dulwich hill / The smallest Christmas tree / Candypants beach / One leg / Day job.

| Dec 96. | (lp/cd) | <(AJAX 057/+CD)> **THE EVERYMAN'S 4TH DIMENSION** | | Oct96 |

– Vacuum cleaner salesman / Little boy / Corn jack / Neighbours from hell / (Onto the) Goat / Saying "no" to romper room / The everyman's 4th dimension / Sapphire island / A universal occult / Tour vehicle / Dromedary camel / The tourist living in a world of pain.

―― disbanded after above

ASIAN DUB FOUNDATION

Formed: Farringdon, London, England . . . 1993 by DR. DAS, PANDIT G and MASTER D, a tutor, an assistant and a student respectively at an inner city community music programme designed for young aspiring Asian musicians/DJ's/MC's/etc. Initially trading as a sound system, ADF began making their own records the following year. Signed to 'Nation' (home of TRANSGLOBAL UNDERGROUND), the trio issued the 'CONSCIOUS' EP prior to adding unorthodox sitar-influenced guitarist, CHANDRASONIC, synth man SUN-J and stage dancer, BUBBLE-E. Taking up the agit-prop, slash'n'burn politico-musical baton from the ailing SENSER, ADF fought off the neo-Nazis with an inflammatory combination of Bengali folk, drum'n'bass and punk that strangely and uniquely recalled the spirit of ALTERNATIVE TV's MARK PERRY. In 1995, this radical troupe unleashed their debut long player, 'FACTS AND FICTIONS', a surprising cohesive set given the amount of disparate musical strands running through each track. Amassing a cult following drawn from both the indie and dance communities (much in the same way that The PRODIGY rose to such giddy heights a few years earlier), ADF soon found themselves under the wing of 'London' offshoot, 'FFRR' in 1997. Gaining more column inches and higher chart placings with each successive release via the incendiary singles, 'NAXALITE', 'BUZZIN', 'FREE SATPAL RAM' and 'BLACK WHITE', the long awaited follow-up set, 'RAFI'S REVENGE' (1998; 1997 in France!) blazed a trail into the UK Top 20. Nominated for a 'Mercury Award', the album didn't win but received some free televised publicity/criticism courtesy of Fantasy Football thingy/ 3 Lions/"comedian", David Baddiel, who obviously prefers the fluffier sounds of the LIGHTNING SEEDS. While working on their follow-up set (scheduled for 2000), ADF were trying to convince the Home Office to "Free SATPAL RAM", the Asian man still in prison after 13 years.

Album rating: FACTS AND FICTIONS (*7) / RAFI'S REVENGE (*9) / COMMUNITY MUSIC (*7)

MASTER D (DEEDER SAIDULLAH ZAMAN) – rapping / **PANDIT G** (JOHN ASHOK PANDIT) – turntables, voice / **DR. DAS** (ANIRUDDHA DAS) – bass, programming, voice

			Nation	not iss.
Aug 94.	(12"ep/cd-ep)	(NR 42 T/CD) **CONSCIOUS EP.**		-

– Debris / Tu meri / Jericho / Witness.

―― added **CHANDRASONIC (STEVE CHANDRA SAVALE)** – guitar, programming, vocals (ex-HEADSPACE, ex-The HIGHER INTELLIGENCE AGENCY)

―― added **SUN-J** (SANJAY GULABHAI TAILOR) – synths / + dancer **BUBBLE-E**

| Apr 95. | (12"ep/cd-ep) | (NR 51 T/CD) **REBEL WARRIOR** | | - |

– Rebel warrior / Nazrul dub / Strong culture / Rivers of dub.

| Oct 95. | (cd/lp) | (NAT CD/LP 58) **FACTS AND FICTIONS** | | - |

– Witness / PKNB / Jericho / Rebel warrior / Journey / Strong culture / Th9 / Tu meri / Debris box / Thacid 9 (dub version) / Return to Jericho (dub version). *(cd re-iss. Aug98; NATCDM 058)*

| May 96. | (12"ep/cd-ep) | (NR 61 T/CD) **CHANGE A GONNA COME** | | - |

– Change a gonna come / Operation eagle eye / C.A.G.C. (via pirate satellite) / Jerico (CAPA D dub).

			Damaged Goods	not iss.
Jul 97.	(7"; split with ATARI TEENAGE RIOT)	(DAMGOOD 132) **split**		

			Sub Rosa	not iss.
Jul 97.	(12"; split with EUPHONIC)	(QUANTUM 605) **TRIBUTE: . . . SOUND SYSTEM / WAY OF THE EXPLODING FIST**		-

―― now as ASIANDUBFOUNDATION

			FFRR	Polygram
Oct 97.	(7")	(F 320) **NAXALITE. / CHARGE**		-

(12"+=/cd-s+=) (FX/FCD 320) – ('A'+'B'mixes)

| Feb 98. | (7") | (F 326) **FREE SATPAL RAM. / TRIBUTE TO JOHN STEPHENS** | 56 | - |

(12"+=/cd-s+=) (FX/FCD 326) – ('A'-Primal Scream & Brendan Lynch mix) / ('A'-ADF Sound System mix).

| Apr 98. | (12"ep/cd-ep) | (FX/FCD 335) **BUZZIN'** (mixes) / **DIGITAL UNDERCLASS** | 31 | |

(cd-ep) (FCDP 335) – ('A'extended) / Free Satpal Ram (live) / Charge (live) / Naxalite (live).

| May 98. | (cd/c/d-lp) | (556 006-2/-4/-1) <556 053> **RAFI'S REVENGE** | 20 | |

– Naxalite / Buzzin' / Black white / Assassin / Hypocrite / Charge / Free Satpal Ram / Operation eagle lie / Change / Tribute to John Stevens. *(cd re-iss. Sep99; 3984 28193-2)*

| Jun 98. | (12"/cd-s) | (FX/FCDP 337) **BLACK WHITE / BLACK WHITE (maximum roach mix). / NAXALITE (Underdog mix) / NAXALITE (Underdog instrumental)** | 52 | - |

(cd-s) (FCD 337) – ('A'side / Rafi / Assassin (live) / Buzzin' (live).

| Sep 98. | (12"ep/cd-ep) | (FX/FCD 348) <570289> **NAXALITE / CULTURE MOVE EP** | | Nov98 |

– Naxalite (main mix) / Culture move (pusher sound mix) / Free Satpal Ram (Russell Simmons mix) / Culture move (urban decay mix) / Culture move (silver haze mix).

ASIAN DUB FOUNDATION (cont)

		FFRR	E.M.I.
Mar 00. (12"/cd-s) (FX/FCD 376) **REAL GREAT BRITAIN. / ('A'-Freqnasty acid monsta mix & dub)**		41	-
(cd-s) (FCDP 376) – ('A'side) / Officer XX (ADF jump up version) / ('A'-Jazzwad real Jamaica mix).			
Mar 00. (cd) (8573 82042-2) <38204-2> **COMMUNITY MUSIC**		20	May00
– Real Great Britain / Memory war / Officer XX / New way, new life / Riddim I like / Collective mode / Crash / Colour line / Taa deem / The judgement / Truth hides / Rebel warrior / Committed to life / Scaling new heights.			
May 00. (12"/cd-s) (FX/FCD 378) **NEW WAY, NEW LIFE. / ('A'-Dry & Heavy vocal & dub mixes)**		49	-
(cd-s) (cd-s) (FCDP 378) – ('A'side) / Real Great Britain (live) / Crash (live).			

—— the group issued a new album early in 2003

ASPERA AD ASTRA

Formed: Philadelphia, Pennsylvania, USA ... summer 1996 by MATT WERTH, MIKE ROBINSON, JUSTIN TRIPP and DREW MILLS. After WERTH made the trip from Bill Clinton's native Little Rock, Arkansas to join the rest of the band, they quickly set about recording and promoting themselves via some inspired gigs which gleaned them the ear of 'Tree' records, who allocated them to a split single with HALEAH. With providence in their favour, MARC BIANCHI (of HALEAH) went ahead and issued their debut full-length set, 'PEACE' (1998), on his imprint 'Audio Information Phenomena'. This inaugural piece showcased the band's blend of psychedelic revival, a la the 'Elephant 6' collective, which also borrowed from eighties shoegazing sensibility bringing a more open and rock sound to their feedback trickery. Following on from this came the departure of frontman WERTH who moved on to running his own label 'File 13' in his newly-adopted city. In order to replace the loss, drummer MILLS stepped up to the mic handing his sticks over to new member CHRIS POWELL. With the new line-up in place, the neo-psychedelists were teamed up with fellow trip-head Philadelphians the LILYS for a self-titled split LP issued in 2000. This release kept the fans happy, while the band meanwhile set about putting down tracks for their sophomore album proper, 'SUGAR AND FEATHERED' (2001), This platter used the experienced hand of I AMONG's MICHAEL DEMING at the production controls, providing the discerning record buying public with their most accomplished piece so far; it also came under their abbrieviated moniker, ASPERA.

Album rating: PEACE (*5) / SUGAR & FEATHERED (*6)

MATT WERTH – bass / **MIKE ROBINSON** – vocals, keyboards / **JUSTIN TRIPP** – guitar, keyboards / **DREW MILLS** – drums

		not iss.	Tree
1997. (7") **Postmarked Stamped Series split w/ HALEAH**		-	
		not iss.	Audio Information Phenomena
1998. (cd) <AIP 03> **PEACE**			-
– Talking to walking / Sick n' sad / Step into me / This whim breathes / Fat in the eye / Scannin' lights / The yellowed skin / Take it easy / (untitled).			

—— **CHRIS POWELL** – drums; temp / **MILLS** now vocals

		not iss.	Insound
1999. (cd-ep) <4> **WINGED WITH RHYMES**		-	
– Godspeed / Twenty minutes of the day / After all.			
		Tiger Style	Tiger Style
Jun 00. (cd/lp) (<TS 002 CD/LP>) **ASPERA AD ASTRA / THE LILYS split**			
– (4 tracks by THE LILYS) / Good beat down / Bring back the walls / Feed the fantasy / Tin pan miracles.			

ASPERA

		Big Wheel	Big Wheel
May 01. (lp/cd) <(BWR 0242/+CD)> **SUGAR AND FEATHERED**			
– Great leaps / Say say good bye bye / Sugar walls / Pearl and brine / Hummingbird / Another blue frisbee / Come and get it / Don't look down (at everyone) / Goodnight / Twenty minutes of the day / Tiptoe breaker / Sun to sun. <cd re-iss. Sep02 on 'Jagjaguwar'; JAG 52CD)>			
		not iss.	Suicide Squeez
Mar 02. (cd-ep) <SS 19> **BIRDS FLY EP**		-	
– Birds fly / Heaven's on your right side / Mean dog's grin / The ground and sky look dry / Sometimes I'm not around.			

ASPHALT RIBBONS (see under ⇒ TINDERSTICKS)

ASS PONYS

Formed: Cincinnati, Ohio, USA ... 1988 by CHUCK CLEAVER, DAN KLEINGERS (both out of LUNCHBUDDIES and a band called GOMEZ), plus JOHN ERHARDT and former LIBERTINES' bassman RANDY CHEEK. After delivering a debut album, 'MR. SUPERLOVE' for the small 'Okra' label at the turn of the decade, the band suffered some setbacks when distributor 'Rough Trade' went under. With a new drummer DAVE MORRISON in tow, the band began work on a follow-up set although this too was subject to delay as the 'PONYS' run of bad form continued. Belated released on Germany's 'Normal' label, the JOHN CURLEY (of AFGHAN WHIGS)-produced 'GRIM' (1992) was a more focused affair than their raw, spasmodic and undisciplined previous effort. Although subsequently signed to 'A&M' (alongside the likes of MONSTER MAGNET), the careworn ASS PONYS have yet to enjoy the privilege of a UK release for their last two albums, 'ELECTRIC ROCK MUSIC' (1994) and 'THE KNOWN UNIVERSE' (1996); these would be their last efforts for a major as they were given the bum's rush. For the rest of the 90's, The ASS PONYS resorted to the quiet underground life, although they did get kicked back into gear via a 5th set, 'SOME STUPID WITH A FLARE GUN' (2000). CLEAVER's unmistakable rootsy nasal-nauseating vox over-shadowed the gutsy "indie" cowpunk lyrics, but all was at least going upwardly mobile for the band. 2001's 'LOHIO' (a perfect title) kicked in with 'LAST NIGHT IT SNOWED', another promising effort of a set that also attributed the acting giant, 'DONALD SUTHERLAND' on track 3.

Album rating: MR. SUPERLOVE (*6) / GRIM (*6) / ELECTRIC ROCK MUSIC (*6) / THE KNOWN UNIVERSE (*6) / SOME STUPID WITH A FLARE GUN (*5) / LOHIO (*6)

CHUCK CLEAVER – vocals, guitar (ex-LUNCHBUDDIES, ex-GOMEZ) / **JOHN ERHARDT** – guitar, pedal steel, bass, vocals / **RANDY CHEEK** – bass, guitar, vocals (ex-LIBERTINES) / **DAN KLEINGERS** – percussion, drums (ex-LUNCHBUDDIES, ex-GOMEZ)

		not iss.	Okra
Jun 90. (cd) <9> **MR. SUPERLOVE**		-	
– Hey Swifty / Ford Madox Ford / Eleven: eleven / (We all love) Peanut butter / Laughing at the ghosts / Mr. Superlove / Thank you for the roses / Ride Ramona / Fingers fall / Bible house.			

—— **DAVE MORRISON** – drums, percussion; repl. KLEINGERS (on most)

		not iss.	Safe House
Aug 93. (cd) <SH-2104-2> **GRIM**		-	
– Big rock ending / Azalea / It's not happening / No dope no cigarettes / Ballpeen / Not since Superman died / I love Bob / Stupid / Dirty backseat car thing / High Heaven / Julia Pastrana / Disappointed / Her father was a sailor / The big E / Good with guns / California bingo.			
		A&M	A&M
Nov 94. (cd) <540270-2> **ELECTRIC ROCK MUSIC**		-	
– Grim / Little bastard / Ape hanger / Place out there / Lake Brenda / Wall eyed girl / Live until I die / Peanut '93 / Banlon girl / Gypped / Blushing bride / Earth to grandma / Otter side. (UK-iss.1997; same as US)			
Mar 95. (7") **LITTLE BASTARD. / YOU, MY FLOWER**		-	

—— **BILL ALLETZHAUSER** – guitars, banjo, vocals; repl. ERHARDT

Apr 96. (cd) <540478> **THE KNOWN UNIVERSE**		-	
– Shoe money / Under cedars and stars / God tells me to / Blow Oskar / Cancer show / Dead fly the birds / And she drowned / Redway / French muscleman / It's summer here / John boat / Hagged / Some kind of fun.			
		Checkered Past	Checkered Past
Jun 00. (cd) <(CPR 018)> **SOME STUPID WITH A FLARE GUN**			Apr00
– Pretty as you please / Astronaut / Fighter pilot / Love tractor / Your amazing life / Sidewinder / Swallow you down / X-tra nipple / Magnus / Casper's coming home / Kitten / Between the trees.			
Jan 02. (cd) <(CPR 024)> **LOHIO**			Jun01
– Snowed / Kung Fu reference / Donald Sutherland / Black dot / Dried / Only / Fire in the hole / (Baby) I love you (baby) / Calendar days / Baby in a jar / Dollar a day / Butterfly / Nothing stars today.			

ASTRID

Formed: Stornoway, Isle Of Lewis, Scotland ... 1996 initially as KITE MONSTER by CHARLES CLARK, WILLIAM CAMPBELL and GARETH RUSSELL, the lads from the breezy Western Isles finding drummer, GARY THOM, while playing sporadic gigs in the city of Glasgow. After fate shone down on this luscious pop sensation, the group were asked to support BELLE AND SEBASTIAN at a one-day festival in the aforementioned city. Scottish wannabe rock/indie-pop sensation EDWYN COLLINS was fortunate to hear their single on Sean Hughes' GLR show and almost immediately invited the band to record with him in his home studio. The result was the cutesy/sweet single 'IT'S TRUE', a hybrid collection of The BYRDS, TEENAGE FANCLUB and SUPERGRASS in their heyday. Following the single, was album 'STRANGE WEATHER LATELY' (1999), which was, again, produced and recorded by COLLINS. Its slight fault lay with the band's easy-flowing songs and styles evident on such tracks/singles as 'HIGH IN THE MORNING', 'REDGROUND' and 'BOY OR GIRL'; all flops. Chords jangled like nothing on earth and the set was awash with CLARK's cheerful and unintentionally menacing vocals; incidentally, three tracks were played on Jamie Oliver's BBC2's 'Naked Chef' cookery programme having already won an award at the Austin, Texas South By Southwest festival. After issuing the summery pop single, 'IT NEVER HAPPENED' and playing an eagerly awaited performance at T In The Park, the group issued their sophomore set, 'PLAY DEAD' (2000), a sparkling indie pop record. This was followed by a feted session for John Peel and the release of the single 'TICK TOCK', which featured the fantastic B-side 'GLASTONBURY SONG'. A limited edition single (500 copies distributed) 'CHERRY CHERRY' was subsequently issued, although only on a first-come, first served basis for fans/record collectors et al. Lately, ASTRID members have moonlighted with Scottish/Irish collective, The REINDEER SECTION.

Album rating: STRANGE WEATHER LATELY (*6) / PLAY DEAD (*6)

CHARLES CLARK – vocals, acoustic guitar / **WILLIAM CAMPBELL** – vocals, guitar / **GARETH RUSSELL** – bass / **GARY THOM** – drums

ASTRID (cont) — THE GREAT INDIE DISCOGRAPHY — The 1990s

			Fantastic Plastic	not iss.
Jun 97.	(7"; as KITEMONSTER) *(FP 007)* **RUBBER DOLL. /**		☐	-
Apr 98.	(ltd-cd-ep) *(FP 008)* **NO REASON / STANDING IN LINE / SEE THE SUN**		☐	-
Jul 98.	(ltd-7"one-sided) *(FP7 011)* **WHAT TO SAY**		☐	-
Nov 98.	(7"ep/cd-ep) *(FP/+7 012)* **HI-FI LO-FI EP** – Distance / I can see you / Can you feel it / 5 o'clock. *(cd-ep re-iss. Sep00; same)*		☐	-
Mar 99.	(ltd;cd-ep/7"ep) *(FP/+7 013)* **IT'S TRUE. / FOR YOUR GIRLFRIEND / BOSTON** *(re-iss. Sep00; same)*		☐	-
Jul 99.	(7") *(FP7 014)* **HIGH IN THE MORNING. / THE WAY I FEEL** (cd-s+=) *(FPS 014)* – God song.		☐	-
Jul 99.	(cd/lp) *(FP CD/LP 001)* **STRANGE WEATHER LATELY** – Kitchen T.V. / Plastic skull / High in the morning / Zoo / Standing in line / Bottle / Redground / Like a baby / Stop / Dusty / Boat song / Boy or girl / W.O.P.R.M. *(lp w/ free 7") (cd re-iss. Sep00; same)*		☐	-
Oct 99.	(cd-ep/7"ep) *(FPS/FP7 016)* **REDGROUND. / COMPLAIN / WEIRD CLOUDS**		☐	-
Dec 99.	(7"white) *(FP7 018)* **BOY OR GIRL. / SLEIGHRIDE**		☐	-
——	NEIL PAYNE – drums (ex-SMILES) repl. THOM			
Aug 00.	(7"ep/cd-ep) *(FP7/FPS 020)* **MODES OF TRANSPORT EP** – Modes of transport / Tangle & tussle / Make heat / Starting to show.		☐	-
Dec 00.	(cd-s) *(FPS 024)* **CHERRY CHERRY / LONELY GIANT**		-	- mail-o
Feb 01.	(7"ep/cd-ep) *(FP7/FPS 023)* **TICK TOCK EP** – Tick tock / Just yet / Glastonbury song.		☐	-
Mar 01.	(cd/purple-lp) *(FP CD/LP 003)* **PLAY DEAD** – It never happened / Tick tock / Wrong for you / Crying boy / Alas / Play dead / Fat girl / Just one name / Hard to be a person / Paper / Modes of transport / What you're thinking / Taken for granted / Horror movies.		☐	-
May 01.	(7") *(FP7 025)* **IT NEVER HAPPENED. / JIMMY** (cd-s+=) *(FPS 025)* – Turnaround.		☐	-

ASTRID (see under ⇒ WILLIAMSON, Astrid)

ASTRO CHIMP
(see under ⇒ VASELINES; 80's section)

AT THE DRIVE-IN

Formed: El Paso, Texas, USA ... 1994 by frontman CEDRIC BIXLER and twin guitarists OMAR RODRIGUEZ and JIM WARD. Recorded between bouts of hard-bitten touring, the band's first two 7" singles, 'HELL PASO' and 'ALFARO VIVE, CARAJO' served notice of a hardcore storm brewing in the Texas badlands. Night after night spent playing to dismal crowds was rewarded when 'Flipside' caught them at an empty L.A. bar and signed them up for a debut album, 'ACROBATIC TENEMENT'. Released in early '97, the record's blistering emotional outpourings and precocious mastery of punk dynamics won over critics across the board while another stint of touring – with new recruits TONY and PALL – cultivated a grassroots fanbase. A subsequent mini-set, 'EL GRAN ORGO' was issued on the 'Offtime' imprint later that year, after which followed a period of insecurity as the band searched in vain for a label willing to take on their sophomore album. 'IN CASINO OUT' (1998) was finally sponsored by the independent 'Fearless' operation, a label more often associated with pop/punk fare. Nevertheless, the album – recorded almost entirely live with only a few overdubs – represented the closest ATDI had yet come to capturing the passionate drive of their live work. Yet more touring ensued as the band played with the likes of FUGAZI and ARCHERS OF LOAF before undertaking their first European jaunt in Spring '99. Later that summer the 'VAYA' EP showed that their relentless road schedule was paying handsome dividends in terms of musical sharpness and songwriting depth, 'Virgin' records signing up the Texas troopers for their third and most highly acclaimed album to date, 'RELATIONSHIP OF COMMAND' (2000). Released on the BEASTIE BOYS' 'Grand Royal' (with whom 'DEN' had merged), produced by Ross 'SLIPKNOT' Robinson and mixed by Andy Wallace, the record had critics reaching for the superlatives in an attempt to describe their unflinchingly honest and unrelentingly intense sound. After disclaiming "indefinite hiatus", ATD had literally split into two camps, The MARS VOLTA, which featured members BIXLER and RODRIGUEZ, and SPARTA, set up by WARD, HINOJOS and HAJJAR. The former, who issued the brilliant 'TREMULANT' EP in 2002, had strayed away from their restrictive "emo" tag and began performing rambunctious live shows which often leaned towards the experimental. IKEY OWENS of The Long Beach Dub All-Stars lended a hand, as did MICHAEL WARD (both flirted with prog-dub outfit DE FACTO). While The MARS VOLTA recreated the same volatile intensity as SCRATCH ACID and MELT BANANA, SPARTA would ultimately stick with the hard-edged punk formula of early BLACK FLAG and FUGAZI (circa 'Repeater'). After issuing the heavily criticised 'AUSTERE' EP on Spielberg/Geffen's 'Dreamworks' imprint, the group issued the overtly angst and typically difficult 'WIRETAP SCARS' (2002), a mixed bag of guitar-fuelled disdain and post-punk noise that had a distinct aftertaste of regret, worry and self-doubt.

Album rating: ACROBATIC TENEMENT (*7) / IN/CASINO/OUT (*7) / RELATIONSHIP OF COMMAND (*7) / Sparta: WIRETAP SCARS (*7)

CEDRIC BIXLER – vocals / **OMAR RODRIGUEZ** – guitar / **JIM WARD** – guitar, vocals

		not iss.	Western Breed – Offtime
Dec 94.	(7"m) **HELL PASO. / EMPTINESS IS A MULE / RED PLANET**	-	☐
Jun 95.	(7"ep) **ALFARO VIVE, CARAJO!. / BRADLEY SMITH / INSTIGATE THE ROLE** <*re-iss. 1990's on 'Headquarter'*>	-	☐

		not iss.	Flipside
Feb 97.	(cd) <*FLIP 94CD*> **ACROBATIC TENEMENT** – Star flight / Schaffino / Ebroglio / Initiation / Communication drive-in / Skips on the record / Paid vacation time / Ticklish / Blue tag / Coating of arms / Porfirio Diaz. *(UK-iss.Jan00; same as US)*	-	☐

—— added **PALL HINOJOS** – bass / **TONY HAJJAR** – drums

		not iss.	One Foot – Offtime
Sep 97.	(cd-ep) <*62*> **EL GRAN ORGO** – Give it a name / Honest to a fault / Winter month novelty / Fahrenheit / Picket fence cartel / Speechless.	-	☐

		Fearless	Fearless
Jul 98.	(cd) <*F 034CD*> **IN/CASINO/OUT** – Alpha Centauri / Chanbara / Hulahoop wounds / Napoleon Solo / Pickpocket / For now ... we toast / A devil among tailors / Shaking hand incision / Lopsided / Hourglass / Transatlantic foe. *(UK-iss.Aug00; same as US)*	-	☐
Nov 98.	(7") **DOORMAN'S PLACEBO. / (other track by AASSEE LAKE)**	-	☐

—— <above iss. on 'Nerd' records>

Oct 99.	(12"ep) *(F 040-1)* **VAYA** – Rascuache / Proxima centauri / Ursa minor / Heliotrope / Metrognome arthritis / 300 MHz / 198d. *(UK-iss.Oct99; same as US) (cd-ep iss.Aug00; FO 40CD)*	-	☐

		Thick	Thick
Mar 00.	(7"pic-d) <*(THK 066)*> **CATACOMBS. / (other by Burning Airlines)** *(UK re-iss. Oct00; same)*	☐	☐

		Big Wheel	Big Wheel
May 00.	(12"ep/cd-ep) <*(BWR 0223/+CD)*> **BIG WHEEL RECREATION** – Extracurricular / Autorelocator / (two others by Sunshine).	☐	☐

		Grand Royal	Grand Royal
Aug 00.	(7") <*(GR 91)*> **ONE ARMED SCISSOR. / PATTERN AGAINST USER** (cd-s+=) <*(GR 91CD)*> – Incetardis.	64	☐

		Virgin	Virgin
Sep 00.	(cd/lp) <*CDVUS/VUSLP 184*> <*49999*> **RELATIONSHIP OF COMMAND** – Arcarsenal / Pattern against user / One armed scissor / Sleepwalk capsules / Invalid litter dept. / Mannequin republic / Enfilade / Rolodex propaganda / Quarantined / Cosmonaut / Non-zero possibility / Catacombs.	33	☐
Oct 00.	(7"colrd) **BUDDYHEAD. / (other by Murder City Devils)**	-	☐
Dec 00.	(7") *(VUS 189)* **ROLODEX PROPAGANDA. / EXTRACURRICULAR** (cd-s+=) *(VUSCD 189)* – One armed scissor (Lamacq version).	54	-
Mar 01.	(7") *(VUS 193)* **INVALID LITTER DEPT. / INITIATION (Lamacq version)** (cd-s+=) *(VUSCD 193)* – Quarantined (Lamacq version). (cd-s) *(VUSDX 193)* – ('A'side) / Take up thy stethoscope and walk (Lamacq version) / Metrognome arthritis.	50	-

—— split later in 2001

MARS VOLTA

CEDRIC BIXLER + OMAR RODRIGUEZ

		Gold Standard	Gold Standard
Mar 02.	(12"ep/cd-ep) <*(GSL 54/+CD)*> **TREMULANT EP** – Cut that city / Concertina / Eunuch provocateur.	☐	☐

SPARTA

JIM WARD – vocals, guitar / **PAUL HINOJOS** – guitar / **TONY HAJJAR** – drums / **MATT MILLER** – bass (ex-BELKNAP)

		Dreamworks	Dreamworks
Apr 02.	(cd-s) *(450844-2)* **AUSTERE EP** – Mye / Cataract / Vacant skies / Echodyne harmonic (de-mix).	☐	-
Aug 02.	(cd) *(450393-2)* <*450366*> **WIRETAP SCARS** – Cut your ribbon / Air / Mye / Collapse / Sans cosm / Light burns clear / Cataract / Red alibi / Rx coup / Glasshouse tarot / Echodyne harmonic / Assemble the empire.	☐	☐

AUBURN LULL

Formed: Lansing, Michigan, USA ... 1994 by SEAN HEENAN, JASON KOLB, ELI WEKENMEN and JASON WEISINGER. Instantly recognisable – alongside WINDY & CARL and ASHA VIDA – on the Michigan-based space-rock scene, AUBURN LULL, "krafted" their ambient-pop initially on their heady debut 12" single, 'THE DUAL GROUP', in '97. With KOLB performing live for like-minded MAHOGANY, the 'LULL and their next release, 'ALONE I ADMIRE', was slightly put on hold. Finally unleashed in 1999 and produced by MAHOGANY's ANDREW PRINZ, the set was a magical debut, registering tracks such as 'THE LAST BEAT' and 'OLD MISSION', in the hearts and minds of the ever-evolving neo-psychedelic community.

Album rating: ALONE I ADMIRE (*7)

SEAN HEENAN – vocals, guitars / **JASON KOLB** – guitars / **ELI WEKENMEN** – guitars / **JASON WEISINGER** – drums

		Burnt Hair	Orchard
1997.	(12"ep) <singe 009> **THE DUAL GROUP**	-	-
Mar 99.	(cd) (singe 020) <4759> **ALONE I ADMIRE**		2000

– Stockard drive / Desert / Old mission / Blur my thoughts again / Early evening reverie / The last beat / Tidal / Between trains / Finland station. *(+ untitled hidden track) (re-iss. Dec01 on 'Darla'; DRL 122)*

―― JASON KOLB had already joined MAHOGANY (a few releases in 2000)

		Zeal	not iss.
May 02.	(7") *(ZEAL 003)* **NORTH TERRITORIAL.** /	-	- Swiss

AUDIO LEARNING CENTER (see under ⇒ POND)

AUTEURS

Formed: Southgate, London, England ... early 1992 by LUKE HAINES (ex-SERVANTS) and girlfriend ALICE READMAN. They quickly signed to 'Fire', soon moving to Virgin off-shoot label, 'Hut', and indie chart surfing with their debut single, 'SOWGIRL' later in the year. Glossy garage indie/punk merchants, fronted by the flamboyant but cynical HAINES, The AUTEURS sound was characterised by the singer's brooding lyrical complexities. The addition of cellist, JAMES BANBURY produced an extra dimension to their standard guitar, bass, drums approach and the debut album's encouragingly critical reception was matched by a UK Top 40 placing for 'NEW WAVE' (1993) and a nomination for the Mercury Music Award. Their third single, 'LENNY VALENTINO', almost scraped into the UK Top 40, the track relating to the debut album sleeve, which depicted Lenny Bruce dressed as Rudolph Valentino. HAINES preoccupations both, another favoured subject of the controversial frontman was the British Class System, 'THE UPPER CLASS' appearing on the follow-up set, 'NOW I'M A COWBOY' (1994). The record secured a Top 30 placing, although the group's critical acclaim continued to outweigh their commercial appeal. A remix set, 'THE AUTEURS VS U-ZIQ' appeared, although it wasn't until 1996 that a long-awaited third album materialised. Produced by STEVE ALBINI, this atmospheric offering combined HAINES' downbeat tales of intrigue with grinding organs, discordant guitars and mournful strings to often hypnotic effect. Despite garnering further plaudits, the record sold poorly and after a clutch of final gigs, HAINES wound the band up, subsequently releasing an album under the moniker of BAADER-MEINHOF (first mentioned on the bleak 'TOMBSTONE' track). In 1998, HAINES teamed up with two former members of BALLOON, JOHN MOORE (ex-EXPRESSWAY) and singer, SARAH NIXEY, in the more melodic, BLACK BOX RECORDER. Signing a major deal with 'Chrysalis', it didn't look likely that either their singles, 'CHILD PSYCHOLOGY' and 'ENGLAND MADE ME' or the latterly-titled accompanying album, would return the moody HAINES to earlier heights. 1999 saw the man discarding previous projects to reincarnate The AUTEURS. Comeback set, 'HOW I LEARNED TO LOVE THE BOOTBOYS', included their nostalgic look back to 70's glam-rock in the shape of minor hit single, 'THE RUBETTES'. The turn of the millennium saw the turn of BLACK BOX RECORDER again, 'THE FACTS OF LIFE' (2000) hitting the Top 40 after its title track made it all the way into the Top 20. A well-received comeback shimmered with SAINT ETIENNE-esque riffs along with jazzy piano trills that would be more at home in a fifties noir film. The ever prolific LUKE HAINES set about creating his own solo sojourn, two albums, 'CHRISTIE MALRY'S OWN DOUBLE ENTRY' soundtrack and 'THE OLIVER TWIST MANIFESTO' (both 2001). The former was based on a novel by B.S. Johnson and featuring his rendition of Nick Lowe's 'I LOVE THE SOUND OF BREAKING GLASS', while the latter veered towards a slightly more electronic sound with HAINES' predictable angst directed at wrong- do'ers all over the world. Surely not! • **Covers:** Black Box Recorder: SEASONS IN THE SUN (Jacques Brel) / ROCK'N'ROLL SUICIDE (David Bowie) / UPTOWN TOP RANKING (hit; Althea & Donna) / LORD LUCAN IS MISSING (Potter-Zuban).

Album rating: NEW WAVE (*7) / NOW I'M A COWBOY (*8) / AFTER MURDER PARK (*7) / HOW I LEARNED TO LOVE THE BOOT BOYS (*6) / Baader-Meinhof: BAADER-MEINHOF (*5) / Black Box Recorder: ENGLAND MADE ME (*6) / THE FACTS OF LIFE (*7) / THE WORST OF ... compilation (*6) / Luke Haines: CHRISTIE MALRY'S OWN DOUBLE ENTRY soundtrack (*6) / THE OLIVER TWIST MANIFESTO (*7)

LUKE HAINES (b. 7 Oct'67, Walton-On-Thames, Surrey, England) – vocals, guitar (ex-SERVANTS) / **ALICE READMAN** (b. 1967, Harrow, England) – bass (ex-SERVANTS) / **GLENN COLLINS** (b. 7 Feb'68, Cheltenham, England) – drums (ex-DOG UNIT, ex-VORT PYLON)

		Hut	Caroline
Dec 92.	(12"ep/cd-ep) *(HUT T/CD 24)* **SHOWGIRL. / GLAD TO BE GONE / STAYING POWER**		-

―― added **JAMES BANBURY** – cello

Mar 93.	(cd/c/lp) *(CDHUT/HUTMC/HUTLP 7)* <1735> **NEW WAVE**	35	

– Showgirl / Bailed out / American guitars / Junk shop clothes / Don't trust the stars / Starstruck / How could I be wrong / Housebreaker / Valet parking / Idiot brother / Early years / Home again. *(free 7"w/lp on cd+c+=)* – Untitled.

May 93.	(10"ep/12"cd-ep) *(HUT EN/T/CD 28)* **HOW COULD I BE WRONG. / HIGH DIVING HORSES / WEDDING DAY**		-

―― **BARNEY CROCKFORD** – drums; repl. COLLINS

		Hut	Vernon Yard
Nov 93.	(7") *(HUT 36)* **LENNY VALENTINO. / DISNEY WORLD**	41	-

(12"/cd-s) *(HUT T/CD 36)* – ('A'side) / Car crazy / Vacant lot / ('A'original mix).

Apr 94.	(7") *(HUTG 41)* **CHINESE BAKERY. / ('A'acoustic)**	42	-

(7"/cd-s) *(HUT/+CD 41)* – ('A'side) / Government bookstore / Everything you say will destroy you.
(12") *(HUTDX 41)* – ('A'side) / ('A'acoustic) / Modern history.

May 94.	(cd/c/lp) *(CDHUT/HUTMC/HUTLP 16)* <39597> **NOW I'M A COWBOY**	27	

– Lenny Valentino / Brainchild / I'm a rich man's toy / New French girlfriend / The upper classes / Chinese bakery / A sister like you / Underground movies / Life classes – Life model / Modern history / Daughter of a child. *(lp w /free 1-sided 7") (HUTLPX 16)* – MODERN HISTORY (acoustic).

Nov 94.	(m-cd/m-lp) *(DGHUT/HUTMLP 20)* **THE AUTEURS VS U-ZIQ** (remixes)		-

– Lenny Valentino No.3 / Daughter of a child / Chinese bakery / Lenny Valentino No.1 / Lenny Valentino No.2 / Underground movies.

		Hut	Hut
Dec 95.	(7"ep/c-ep/cd-ep) *(HUT/+C/CD 65)* **BACK WITH THE KILLER E.P.**	45	-

– Unsolved child murder / Back with the killer again / Former fan / Kenneth Anger's bad dream.

Feb 96.	(10"ep/cd-ep) *(<HUT EN/CD 66>)* **LIGHT AIRCRAFT ON FIRE / BUDDHA (demo). / CAR CRASH / X – BOOGIE MAN**	58	-
Mar 96.	(cd/c/lp) *(<DGHUT/HUTMC/HUTLP 33>)* **AFTER MURDER PARK**	53	

– Light aircraft on fire / The child brides / Land lovers / New brat in town / Everything you say will destroy you / Unsolved child murder / Married to a lazy lover / Buddha / Tombstone / Fear of flying / Dead Sea navagators / After Murder Park.

May 96.	(10"ep/cd-ep) *(<HUT EN/CD 68>)* **"KID'S ISSUE" EP**		-

– Buddha / A new life a new family / After murder park.

BAADER-MEINHOF

―― **HAINES** with others **JAMES BANBURY + ANDY NICE** – cello / **JUSTIN ARMITAGE** – violin / **GARY STRASBOURG** – drums / **KULJIT BHAMRA** – percussion, tabla

		Hi-Rise	not iss.
Nov 95.	(7") *(FLAT 24)* **BAADER-MEINHOFF. / MEET ME AT THE AIRPORT**		-

		Hut	Hut
Oct 96.	(cd/lp) *(<CDHUT/HUTLP 36>)* **BAADER-MEINHOF**		Feb97

– Baader Meinhof / Meet me at the airport / There's gonna be an accident / Mogadishu / Theme from Burn Warehouse Burn / GSG-29 / ...It's a moral issue / Back on the farm / Kill Ramirez / Baader Meinhof.

BLACK BOX RECORDER

―― **HAINES** with **JOHN MOORE** – guitar (ex-JESUS & MARY CHAIN, ex-EXPRESSWAY, ex-REVOLUTION 9, ex-BALLOON) / **SARAH NIXEY** – vocals (ex-BALLOON)

		Chrysalis	Jetset
May 98.	(7") *(CHS 5082)* **CHILD PSYCHOLOGY. / GIRL SINGING IN THE WRECKAGE**		-

(cd-s+=) *(CDCHS 5082)* – Seasons in the sun.

Jul 98.	(7") *(CHS 5091)* **ENGLAND MADE ME. / LORD LUCAN IS MISSING**		-

(cd-s) *(CDCHS 5091)* – ('A'side) / Factory radio / Child psychology (audio) / Child psychology (video).

Jul 98.	(cd/d-lp) *(493907-2/1)* <TWA 21CD> **ENGLAND MADE ME**		1999

– Girl singing in the wreckage / England made me / New baby boom / It's only the end of the world / Ideal home / Child psychology / I C one female / Uptown top ranking / Swinging / Kidnapping an heiress / Hated Sunday.

―― JOHN MOORE would soon form ABSINTHE EXPORTER

AUTEURS

―― **HAINES** with old line-up

		Hut	not iss.
May 99.	(cd/c) *(HUT CD/MC 53)* **HOW I LEARNED TO LOVE THE BOOTBOYS**		-

– The Rubettes / 1967 / How I learned to love the bootboys / Your gang, our gang / Some changes / School / Johnny and the Hurricanes / The south will rise again / Asti Spumante / Sick of Hare Krishna / Lights out / Future generation.

Jun 99.	(7"/c-s) *(HUT/+MC 113)* **THE RUBETTES. / GET WRECKED AT HOME**	66	-

(cd-s+=) *(HUTCD 113)* – Breaking up.

BLACK BOX RECORDER

―― with the main/same line-up/trio

		Nude	Jetset
Apr 00.	(7") *NUD 48S)* **THE FACTS OF LIFE. / SOUL BOY**	20	-

(cd-s+=) *(NUD 48CD1)* – Start as you mean to go on.
(cd-s) *(NUD 48CD2)* – ('A'side) / Brutality / Watch the angel, not the wine.

May 00.	(cd) *(NUDE 16CD)* <TWA 36CD> **THE FACTS OF LIFE**	37	

– The art of driving / Weekend / The English motorway system / May queen / Sex life / French rock'n'roll / The facts of life / Straight rock / Gift horse / The Deverall twins / Goodnight kiss. <US+=> – Start as you mean to go / Brutality.

Jul 00.	(7") *(NUD 51S)* **THE ART OF DRIVING. / THE FACTS OF LIFE (remixed by the Chocolate Layers)**	53	-

(cd-s) *(NUD 51CD1)* – Rock'n'roll suicide.
(cd-s) *(NUD 51CD2)* – ('A'side) / Uptown top ranking (remix) / The facts of life (radio) / The facts of life (video).

		Jetset	Jetset
Aug 01.	(cd) *(<TWA 40CD>)* **THE WORST OF BLACK BOX RECORDER** (compilation B-sides, etc)		

– Seasons in the sun / Watch the angel not the wire / Jackie sixty / Start as you mean to go on / The facts of life (Pulp remix) / Lord Lucan is missing / Wonderful life / Uptown top ranking (BBR remix) / Brutality / Factory radio / Soul boy / Rock'n'roll suicide / The facts of life (video) / Child psychology (video) / The art of driving (video) / England made me (video).

LUKE HAINES

— with **JAMES BANBURY** – cello, drums, programming

	Hut	not iss.

Jun 01. (cd) *(CDHUT 65)* **CHRISTIE MALRY'S OWN DOUBLE ENTRY**
(soundtrack)
– Discomania / In the bleak midwinter / How to hate the working classes / The ledger / Bernie's funeral – Auto asphixiation / Discomaniax / Alchemy / Art will save the world / I love the sound of breaking glass / England, Scotland and Wales / Celestial discomania / Essexmania.

Jul 01. (cd) *(CDHUT 66)* **THE OLIVER TWIST MANIFESTO**
– Rock'n'roll communique No.1 / Oliver Twist / Death of Satah Lucas / Never work / Discomania / Mr. and Mrs. Solanas / What happens when we die / Christ / The spook manifesto / England vs. America / The Oliver Twist manifesto.

AUTOCLAVE (see under ⇒ HELIUM)

AUTOCOLLANTS (see under ⇒ WATLING, Laura)

AVOCADO BABY (see under ⇒ MILKY WIMPSHAKE)

AZURE RAY

Formed: Athens, Georgia, USA … 2000 by ORENDA FINK and MARIA TAYLOR (both ex-BRIGHT EYES), initial assistance stemming from ERIC BACHMANN (of CROOKED FINGERS). The female duo had originally met at art college in Birmingham, Alabama, in the mid-90's and quickly found musical kinship that led to an acoustic partnership under the moniker LITTLE RED ROCKET. With the added help of LOUIS SCHEFANO and GREG NOBLES, the band issued their debut LP, 'WHO DID YOU PAY' (1997), soon after signing to 'Tim/Kerr' records. Their sound on this nascent album was much compared to similarly female-led indie rock outfits (BELLY and LUSH), and to a degree furrowed the same ground although with enough success to see them ink a deal with major label 'Geffen'. Unfortunately for the band they were never to see the fruits of this work, as their mother label got taken over by 'Universal' and they got lost in the melee. Unfortunately, consequent disappointment led to the departure of the rhythm section, with FINK and TAYLOR meanwhile retaining the name and relocating to Athens, Georgia. Here they came under the tutelage of CAROL and HUGH BURNHAM of GANG OF FOUR fame, who managed and helped them eventually – with the new backing section of JACQUE FERGUSON and SCOTT SOSEBEE – put out their sophomore album 'IT'S IN THE SOUND' (2000). A genial slice of mid-sixties, Fab Four-esque rock, it was lauded much more than their initial offering. Following this piece, the girls dropped the LRR title and became AZURE RAY. It was not only a name change that happened; AR's sound was a more pared-down and melancholic affair. They debuted with the eponymously-titled full-length outing 'AZURE RAY' (2001), a quiet dream pop affair that heralded their more wintry but nonetheless inspiring new musical direction. Their balladeering star was defiantly in the ascendancy with the issue of EP, 'NOVEMBER', early the following year and this was quickly followed up by the summer issue of their second set, 'BURN AND SHIVER', a record which showed the emotional and sonorous quality of the group's work. With praise flowing in from the musical press, the pair were also being paid homage by their musical peers; they contributed a guest slot (on the track 'The Great Escape') for MOBY's '18' set. While ORENDA and MARIA were also part of MAYDAY in the early 00's, they also combined with Athens musicians, ANDY LeMASTER and CLAY LEVERETT on the moody pop outfit/album, 'NOW IT'S OVERHEAD' (2001).

Album rating: Little Red Rocket: WHO DID YOU PAY (*4) / IT'S IN THE SOUND (*5) / Azure Ray: AZURE RAY (*5) / BURN AND SHIVER (*6) / November mini (*6) / Now It's Overhead: NOW IT'S OVERHEAD (*5)

LITTLE RED ROCKET

ORENDA FINK – vocals, acoustic guitar / **MARIA TAYLOR** – vocals, acoustic guitar, keyboards / **GREG NOBLES** – bass / **LOUIS SCHEFANO** – drums

	not iss.	Tim/Kerr

1997. (cd) *<TK 171>* **WHO DID YOU PAY**
– Sick of pretty / Silver girl / Wheels and weather / I'm a fake / Light is everywhere / Maybe / New country / Same old feeling / Back to where I started / Goodbye / What I don't know.

— **JACQUE FERGUSON** – bass (of BIG ATOMIC) repl. NOBLES

— **SCOTT SOSEBEE** – drums (of JAPANCAKES) repl. SCHEFANO

	not iss.	Monolyth

Jun 00. (cd) *<1329>* **IT'S IN THE SOUND**
– I believe in what you do / California / Wandering eye / Star / Love / Ocean in the sky / Italian song / Spell / Lies / It's in the sound / Sunday driving / (Lost souls) Low tones.

AZURE RAY

ORENDA + MARIA and various top producers, etc

	Warm	Warm

Jan 01. (cd) *<(WRM 102CD)>* **AZURE RAY**
– Sleep / Displaced / Don't make a sound / Untitled / Another week / Rise 4th of July / Safe and sound / Fever / For no one / How will you survive.

Apr 02. (cd) *<WRM 106CD>* **BURN AND SHIVER**
– Favorite cities / The new year / Seven days / Home / How you remember / Trees keep growing / A thousand years / While I'm still young / Your weak hands / We exchanged words / Raining in Athens / Rest your eyes.

	Saddle Creek	Saddle Creek

Nov 02. (m-cd) *<(LBJ 41)>* **NOVEMBER**
– November / For the sake of the song / No signs of pain / Just a faint line / I will do these things / Other than this world.

NOW IT'S OVERHEAD

ANDY LeMASTER – vocals, multi (of BRIGHT EYES) / **MARIA TAYLOR** – keyboards, vocals / **ORENDA FINK** – bass, vocals / **CLAY LEVERETT** – drums, vocals

	not iss.	Saddle Creek

Sep 01. (cd) *<LBJ 38>* **NOW IT'S OVERHEAD**
– Blackout curtain / Who's Jon / Hi / Hold your spin / 6th grade roller / Wonderful scar / With a subtle look / Goodbye highway / A skeleton on display.

AZUSA PLANE

Formed: Clifton Heights, nr. Philadelphia, Pennsylvania, USA … mid-90's by JASON DiEMILIO and QUENTIN STOLZFUS when they provided the backbeat to new independent psychedelia in Philadelphia along with collegues BARDO POND. The band issued their debut album, 'TYCHO MAGNETIC ANOMALY AND THE FULL CONSCIOUSNESS OF HIDDEN HARMONY' in April 1997, just after the VELVET UNDERGROUND tribute single 'LOU, NICO, STERLING, JOHN AND MAUREEN'. The group's sound, similar to their peers, comprised of rusting harmonies with jangling guitars and heavy, scattered Gonzo induced melodies. If the listener imagined the demon son of JEFFERSON AIRPLANE engaged in a round of midnight golf with the Devil, they would still not come close to the unsalvagable noise AZUSA PLANE were capable of making. Totally instrumental (one track almost reached the 28-minute mark), the duo released two more albums of exactly the same calibre, 'AMERICA IS DREAMING OF UNIVERSAL STRING THEORY' (1998) and 'RESULT DIES WITH THE WORKER' (1999) (although the former may be a bit more weird than the latter), before STOLTZFUS embarked on his own misadventures in the world of radio-friendly warped pop. MAZARIN began in early 1999, when BRIAN McTEAR joined the former drummer to escape the freaky underground of psychedelia. They issued the respected and well-received single, 'WHEAT', which may have sounded similar to the MONKEES if they had been maliciously assaulted by DONOVAN and a gang of psychedelic Morris-dancers (eh!). The 20-something pair now work closely together and an album (under the working title of 'WATCH IT HAPPEN') was scheduled for released in the first months of the new century. However, only the odd 7" release came about every few months, until that is … 2001 heralded a new long-player. 'THE HIGHWAY'S JAMMED WITH BROKEN GUITAR HEROES' marked AZUSA's swansong set with two lengthy abstract pieces, the longest 'NO FUTURE', intertwining strumming guitars and tapelooping under one big heavenly 28-minute assault.

Album rating: TYCHO MAGNETIC ANOMALY AND THE FULL CONSCIOUSNESS OF HIDDEN HARMONY (*5) / AMERICA IS DREAMING OF UNIVERSAL STRING THEORY (*8) / RESULT DIES WITH THE WORKER (*7) / THE HIGHWAY'S JAMMED WITH BROKEN GUITAR HEROES (*5)

JASON DiEMILIO – guitar / with live **QUENTIN STOLTZFUS** – drums / **JASON KNIGHT** – guitar (ex-MARINERNINE, ex-CHINA THE BEAUTIFUL) / plus **ERNEST-MICHAEL KRANICH + ELSIE VON CYON**

	not iss.	Colorful Clouds For Acoustics

Dec 95. (ltd-7") *<001>* **FALL. / MEANDER**

1996. (ltd-7") *<002>* **BEYOND INFINITE. / (other by FUXA)**
(UK-iss.Jan98 on 'Doorstep Vinyl'; DV 002)

1996. (ltd-7") *<003>* **EVERY WAVE HAS ITS OWN INTEGRITY. / (other by LOREN MAZZACANE CONNORS)**

1996. (ltd-7"blue) *<004>* **SHE WAS INTO S&M AND BIBLE STUDIES. NOT EVERYONE'S CUP OF TEA SHE WOULD ADMIT TO ME. HER CUP OF TEA SHE WOULD ADMIT TO NO ONE. / (other by ROY MONTGOMERY)**

1996. (7") *<ROCO 15>* **HAL. / (other by LAB RAT)**
(UK-iss.Jan98 on 'Road Cone')

	Enraptured	not iss.

Nov 96. (7") *(RAPT45 06)* **MINIMALIST PLOT TO DESTROY MODERN ROCKISM. / Grimble Grumble: SECOND MIND**

	Black Bean & Placenta Tape Club	not iss.

Mar 97. (7") *(BBPTC 59)* **"FENDER" & "MOOG": A STUDY OF TWO DISTINCT QUALIFIERS**
– Fender: six strings of tonal and atonal vibrations / Moog: 32 keys of polar and bipolar oscilations.

	Burnt Hair	not iss.

Apr 97. (7") *(SINGE 11)* **LOU, NICO, STERLING, JOHN AND MAUREEN. / THIS IS NOT SPACEROCK**

	Camera Obscura	not iss.

Apr 97. (cd) *(CAM 002CD)* **TYCHO MAGNETIC ANOMALY AND THE FULL CONSCIOUSNESS OF HIDDEN HARMONY**
– Temporal continuum / Implications of holomovement / The miracle of the octave / Armonia apmanes phaneros kreisson. *(re-iss. Apr00; same)*

	Amish	not iss.

Mar 98. (12"ep) *(AMI 010)* **JACQUES OFFENBACH'S OPERA EFFORTS**
– 1863 / 1872 / 1875 / 1875.

AZUSA PLANE (cont)

—— DiEMILIO added **PETER JEFFERIES** – guitar

	Colorful Clouds Of Acoustics	Colorful Clouds Of Acoustics
Apr 98. (d-cd) <(DBC 016-017)> **AMERICA IS DREAMING OF UUNIVERSAL STRING THEORY** – Strings 1-9.	□	□

—— now without KNIGHT

	Rocket Girl	not iss.
1998. (7") (RGIRL 5) **UNITED STATES INVESTMENT IN OTHER COUNTRIES.** / Loopdrop: SIEMPRE AZUL	□	–

	Motorway	not iss.
Aug 98. (7") (MOTOR 023) **THE LAST OF THE FAMOUS ELECTRONIC PLAYBOYS A.** / **THE LAST OF THE FAMOUS ELECTRONIC PLAYBOYS B**	□	–

	Ochre	not iss.
Sep 98. (10") (OCH 024) **CHELTENHAM (part 1).** / **CHELTENHAM (part 2)**	□	–

	Lissy's	not iss.
Feb 99. (7") (LISS 16) **CALVIN JOHNSON HAS SAVED ROCK FOR AN ENTIRE GENERATION.** / Juicy Eureka: AIR BEDLAM	□	–

	Colorful Clouds For Acoustics	Colorful Clouds For Acoustics
Mar 99. (cd) <(CLOUD 18)> **RESULT DIES WITH THE WORKER (live)** – Intro / Phi Lam Fraternity, Philadelphia, PA / Pontiac Grille, Philadelphia, PA / Khyber Pass pub, Philadelphia, PA / Mellatronic Festival, Washington, DC / Transmissions Festival, Chapel Hill, NC / The Garage, London, UK / Terrastock 1, Providence, RI / Terrastock 2, San Francisco, CA / Outro.	□	□

	not iss.	Little Mafia
1999. (7") **MECHANICAL SOUND RECONSTRUCTIONS.** / (other by the AHIMSA OBSERVATORY)	–	□

	not iss.	Monster Truck
1999. (7") **PHILADELPHIA 1999.** / (other by ARIEL M)	–	□

	not iss.	Earworm
1999. (ltd-7") **SONG FOR CLAUDIA CARDINALE.** / (other by Octal)	–	□

	K-raa-n	not iss.
Jun 99. (7") (K 001-7) **AN UNRECOGNISABLE PARADIGM SHIFT.** / Tin Foil Star: FOLLOW ME HOME	□	–

—— now without QUENTIN who formed MAZARIN

Feb 01. (cd) (K 024) **THE HIGHWAY'S JAMMED WITH BROKEN HEROES** – No future / No fun.	□	–

– compilations, etc. –

2000. (12"ep) Blackbean & Placenta; **THE AZUSA PLANE** – Lou, Nico, Sterling, John and Maureen / Hi how are you / Autumn lament / Pop world.	□	–

—— there were also a number of cassettes (some split)

SPIRES OF OXFORD

JASON DiEMILIO

	Colorful Clouds	Colorful Clouds
Jul 97. (cd) <(LOUD 013CD)> **SPIRES OF OXFORD** – Graves of two English soldiers on Concord battleground / By the statue of King Charles at Charing Cross.	□	□

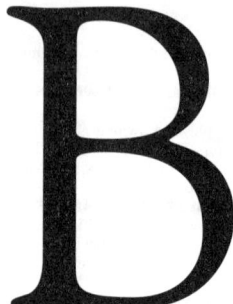

BAADER-MEINHOF (see under ⇒ AUTEURS)

BABES IN TOYLAND

Formed: Minneapolis, Minnesota, USA ... 1987 by KAT BJELLAND, MICHELLE LEON and LORI BARBELO. Signing to influential local label, 'Twintone', the all-girl group released an early proto-grunge classic in the Jack Endino-produced 'SPANKING MACHINE' (1990). Featuring such white hot blasts of feminine subversiveness as 'HE'S MY THING' and 'PAIN IN MY HEART', the album opened the floodgates for a slew of similar angry young women (i.e. L7 and HOLE, whose JENNIFER FINCH and COURTNEY LOVE respectively, LYDIA LUNCH soundalike BJELLAND had previously played with in SUGAR BABY DOLL). Over the course of the next year, they released a mini-album, 'TO MOTHER', replaced MICHELLE with MAUREEN HERMAN and signed to 'Warner Bros', releasing a second album proper, 'FONTANELLE' in the Spring of '92. Produced by LEE RANALDO of SONIC YOUTH, the record breached the UK Top 30 on the back of rave reviews from both the inkies and the metal press. Following a stop-gap part live set, 'PAINKILLERS', the BABES took a sabbatical, BJELLAND turning up in STUART GRAY's (her husband) outfit, LUBRICATED GOAT, while moonlighting with CRUNT. BABES IN TOYLAND returned in 1995 with 'NEMESISTERS', which disappointed many of their more hardcore following by including covers of 'WE ARE FAMILY' (Sister Sledge), 'DEEP SONG' (Billie Holiday) and 'ALL BY MYSELF' (Eric Carmen). In 2001, KAT resurfaced once again with KATASTROPHY WIFE – album 'AMUSIA' – featuring her new husband GLEN/RICH MATTSON. • **Other BIT covers:** WATCHING GIRL (Shonen Knife) / THE GIRL CAN'T HELP IT (Little Richard) / CALLING OCCUPANTS OF INTERPLANETARY CRAFT (Klaatu) / HUBBLE BUBBLE TOIL AND TROUBLE (Manfred Mann).

Album rating: SPANKING MACHINE (*7) / TO MOTHER (*7) / FONTANELLE (*8) / PAINKILLERS (*5) / NEMESISTERS (*6) / LIVED collection (*5) / VILED collection (*5) / Katastrophy Wife: AMUSIA (*5)

KAT BJELLAND (b. KATHERINE, 9 Dec'63, Woodburn, Oregon) – vocals, guitar / **MICHELLE LEON** – bass / **LORI BARBERO** (b.27 Nov'60) – drums, vocals

	not iss.	Treehouse
Jul 89. (7",7"green) <TR 017> **DUST CAKE BOY.** / **SPIT TO SEE THE SHINE**	–	□

	not iss.	Sub Pop
Apr 90. (7",7"gold) <SP 66> **HOUSE.** / **ARRIBA**	–	□

	Twin Tone	Twin Tone
Jul 90. (cd/lp/mauve-lp) <TTR 89183-2/-4/-1> **SPANKING MACHINE** – Swamp pussy / He's my thing / Vomit heart / Never / Boto (w)rap / Dogg / Pain in my heart / Lashes / You're right / Dust cake boy / Fork down throat. (re-iss. +c Dec91 on purple-lp)	–	□
Jun 91. (m-cd/m-c/m-lp) <(TTR 89208-2/-4/-1)> **TO MOTHER** – Catatonic / Mad pilot / Primus / Laugh my head off / Spit to see the shine / Pipe / The quiet room.	□	□

—— (Mar'92) **MAUREEN HERMAN** (b.25 Jul'66, Philadelphia, Pennsylvania) – bass (ex-M+M STIGMATA drummer) repl. MICHELLE whose roadie boyfriend John Cole was killed by a burglar

	Strange Fruit	Dutch East India
Mar 92. (cd/10"m-lp) (SFPMCD/SFPMA 211) <8413> **THE PEEL SESSIONS (live on John Peel show)** – Catatonic / Ripe / Primus / Spit to see the shine / Pearl / Dogg / Laugh my head off / Mad pilot.	□	□

	Southern	Warners
Aug 92. (cd/c/red-lp) (18501-2/-4/-1) <2-/4-26998> **FONTANELLE** – Bruise violet / Right now / Blue bell / Handsome & Gretel / Blood / Magick flute / Won't tell / The quiet room / Spun / Short song / Jungle train / Pearl / Real eyes / Mother / Gone.	24	□
Nov 92. (7"purple) (18503-7) **BRUISE VIOLET.** / **GONE** (12"+=/cd-s+=) (18503-6/-2) – Magick flute.	□	□
Jun 93. (cd/c/lp) (18512-2/-4/-1) <45339> **PAINKILLERS (part live)** – He's my thing / Laredo / Istigkeit / Ragweed / Angel hair / Fontanellette (live at CBGB's): Bruise violet – Bluebell – Angel hair – Pearl – Blood – Magick flute – Won't tell – Real eyes – Spun – Mother – Handsome & Gretel.	53	□

—— KAT married STUART GRAY and sidelined with bands, CRUNT and KATSTU

CRUNT

— **KAT BJELLAND / STUART GRAY** (of LUBRICATED GOAT) + **RUSSELL SIMINIS** (of JON SPENCER BLUES EXPLOSION)

		Insipid Trance Syndicate	Insipid Trance Syndicate
1993.	(7") *(IV-31)* **SWINE. / SEXY**		
Mar 94.	(lp,blue-lp/cd) <*(TR 19/+CD)*> **CRUNT**		Feb94

– Theme from Crunt / Swine / Black heart / Unglued / Changing my mind / Snap out of it / Sexy / Punishment / Spam / Elephant.

BABES IN TOYLAND

— re-formed (see last line-up)

		Reprise	Reprise
Apr 95.	(cd/c/lp) <*(9362 45868-2/-4/-1)*> **NEMESISTERS**		

– Hello / Oh yeah! / Drivin' / Sweet '69 / Surd / 22 / Ariel / Kiler on the road / Middle man / Memory / S.F.W. / All by myself / Deep song / We are family.

May 95.	(12"ep/c-ep/cd-ep) *(W 0291 TEX/C/CD)* **SWEET '69 / S.F.W. (live) / SWAMP PUSSY (live)**		-
Sep 95.	(c-s/cd-s) *(W 0313 C/CD)* **WE ARE FAMILY (Arthur Baker remix) / ('A'-Ben Grosse remix)**		-

(12"+=) *(W 0313T)* – (2 other Baker & Grosse mixes).

— In 1998, KAT's alternative/metal supergroup rock opera, Songs Of The Witchblade: A Soundtrack To The Comic Books, was released on CD (Dreamworks; DRMD 50102) featuring her alongside PETER STEELE (Type O Negative), BUZZ OSBORNE (Melvins), JIM THIRLWELL (Foetus), among others.

– compilations, etc. –

Mar 00.	(cd) *Almafame; (ALMACD 11)* **LIVED (live)**		-

– Dr. Timothy Leary (intro) / He's my thing / Handsome and Gretel / Blue bell / Sweet 69 / Ripe / Mad pilot / Right now / Dogg / Fork down throat / Ya' know that guy / Hubble bubble toil and trouble / Fair is foul and foul is fair / Big top astroanquility (video) / Bruised violet (video) / Memory (video).

May 00.	(d-cd) *Snapper; (SMDCD 299)* **NATURAL BABE KILLERS**		-

– Bruised violet / Won't tell / Jungle train / We are family / Big top / Magic flute / Memory / Dogg / Fork down throat / Mad pilot / Ripe / Ya know that guy / Spun / Primus / Sweet 69 / Hubble bubble toil and trouble / Fair is foul and foul is fair / Flesh crawl.

Aug 00.	(cd) *Almafame; (ALMACD 12)* **DEVIL**		-

– Oh yeah! / Spun / Bruised violet / Primus / Fake fur condo / Won't tell / Magick flute / Ya so fucking what / Jungle train / Knife song / Flesh crawl / Intermentstral / We are family / More, more, more (demo) / Calling occupants of interplanetary craft (demo) / Babes In Toyland photo album.

Apr 01.	(cd) *Cherry Red;* <*(CDMRED 181)*> **MINNEAPOLISM: LIVE – THE LAST TOUR**		Apr01
Apr 01.	(cd) *Almafame; (ALMACD 15)* **VILED**		-
Jun 01.	(cd) *Fuel 2000;* <*061125*> **THE FURTHER ADVENTURES OF . . .**	-	
Nov 01.	(cd) *Cherry Red; (CDMRED 199)* **THE BBC JOHN PEEL SESSIONS 1990-92**		-
Nov 01.	(3xcd-box) *Dressed To Kill; (MIDRO 783)* **INTERMENSTRAL**		-
Jan 02.	(cd) *Brilliant; (BT 33084)* **COLLECTOR'S ITEM**		-

KATASTROPHY WIFE

BJELLAND + RICH MATTSON – guitar / **MARK MALLMAN** – organ / **KEITH ST. LOUIS** – bass

		Almaflame	Yeaah
Aug 01.	(cd-s) *(KATWIF 01)* **GONE AWAY / HAPPY PICK-UP TRUCK / GONE AWAY (Fierce Elvis' suicide wedding mix)**		-
Mar 02.	(cd) <*19*> **AMUSIA**	-	

– Gone away / Bommerang doll / Git go / Rosacea / Pretty car / Anathema / Knife fight / Haunted / Window / Widdershins.

BABYBIRD

Formed: Sheffield, England . . . 1988 by Telford born singer STEPHEN JONES. He had been a prolific writer in his bedroom, composing over 400 songs, some of which appeared on five well-received albums between mid-'95 and mid-'96. Each album came with a voting section on which the buyer was asked to write in with their "best of" lists. The top 12 appeared on BABYBIRD's "GREATEST HITS" later in '96, JONES finally coming to prominence that summer as he signed to 'Echo', roped in a full band (JOHN PEDDER, ROBERT GREGORY, LUKE SCOTT and HUW CHADBOURN) and had his first bonafide Top 30 hit with the 'GOODNIGHT' single. BABYBIRD only really took flight with 'YOU'RE GORGEOUS', however, a massive Top 3 hit and a masterstroke of pop genius which managed to weld JONES' wonderfully subversive lyrics to a twinkling, soaring melody and chorus. A simultaneous album, 'UGLY BEAUTIFUL' (1996) made the Top 10, although critics who'd praised his more endearing amateurish early recordings were unsure about this leap into semi-accessible chartbound territory. Nevertheless, a growing army of fans who'd never even heard the other albums (mainly because they were so rare it was impossible to get hold of them!) put a third single, 'CANDY GIRL' into the Top 10. A series of much talked about live appearances emphasized JONES performance-arty background, the singer drawing comparisons with PULP's JARVIS COCKER. Of late, STEPHEN and Co have been back in the public eye, 1998 seeing them hovering around the fringes of the UK Top 30 with a couple of singles and an album, 'THERE'S SOMETHING GOING ON'. Forgetting about all commercial interferences, mainman STEPHEN JONES put his head down to create some of the best work of his career and issued it as 'BUGGED' (2000), a collection of ten dark pop songs ranging from the sinister (and brief charting single) 'THE F-WORD' to the calm and lyrical 'OUT OF SIGHT'. JONES, taking a nod from artists such as MERCURY REV and The FLAMING LIPS, created something that was life-like, abstract and poignant all at once; ballad 'ALL I WANT IS LOVE' fitted this criteria, while 'THE WAY YOU ARE' was a fine example of dedicated songwriting. Something of a diversion, and under his own name, JONES issued his ambient masterpiece, '1985-2001' the following year. Obviously taking a wink at The APHEX TWIN's 'Selected Ambient Works 85-92', the set was such a departure from JONES' normal indie fare, that many critics and fans could not believe it was his own work. The album consisted of three CD's, all featuring breakbeats, clicks, beeps, samples and a whole host of weird sounds – some even went to the lengths of comparing it to AUTECHRE and MATMOS. Further 'TWIN comparisons were made in conjuction with the minimalist piano segues on the album and vocal samples/hooks. All in all, a fantastic break from the norm for somebody who had unfairly been dubbed a 'one hit wonder' in the past. Perhaps it was true in the pop sense, but ultimately STEPHEN JONES had a lot more to offer.

Album rating: I WAS BORN A MAN (*8) / BAD SHAVE (*7) / FATHERHOOD (*6) / THE HAPPIEST MAN ALIVE (*8) / UGLY BEAUTIFUL (*6) / THERE'S SOMETHING GOING ON (*7) / BUGGED (*7) / Stephen Jones: 1985-2001 collection (*8) / ALMOST CURED OF SADNESS (*5)

STEPHEN JONES (b.16 Sep'62) – vocals, guitar – with band; **LUKE SCOTT** (b.25 Aug'69) – guitar / **HUW CHADBOURN** (b. 7 Dec'63) – keyboards / **JOHN PEDDER** (b.29 May'62) – bass / **ROBERT GREGORY** (b. 2 Jan'67) – drums

		Baby Bird	not iss.
Jul 95.	(cd) *(BABYBIRD 001)* **I WAS BORN A MAN**		-

– Blow it to the Moon / Man's tight vest / Lemonade baby / C.F.C. / Cornershop / Kiss your country / Hong Kong blues / Dead bird sings / Baby bird / Farmer / Invisible tune / Alison / Love love love.

Oct 95.	(cd/d-lp) *(BABYBIRD CD/LP 002)* **BAD SHAVE**		-

– KW Jesus TV roof appeal / Bad jazz / Too handsome to be homeless / Steam train / Bad shave / Oh my God, you're a king / The restaurant is guilty / Valerie / Shop girl / W.B.T. / Hate song / 45 & fat / Sha na na / Bug in a breeze / It's okay / Happy bus / Swinging from tree to tree.

Dec 95.	(cd/d-lp) *(BABYBIRD CD/LP 003)* **FATHERHOOD**		-

– No children / Cooling towers / Cool and crazy things to do / Bad blood / Neil Armstrong / I was never here / Saturday / Goodnight / I don't want to wake up with you / Iceberg / Aluminium beach / Goddamn it, you're a kid / Daisies / Failed old singer / Fatherhood / Dustbin liner / Not about a girl / Good weather / But love / May me.

Apr 96.	(cd/lp) *(BABYBIRD CD/LP 004)* **THE HAPPIEST MAN ALIVE**		-

– Razorblade shower / Sundial in a tunnel / Little white man / Halfway up the hill / Horsesugar / Please don't be famous / Louse / Copper feel / Seagullably / Dead in love / Candy girl / Gunfingers / Married / In the country / Planecrash Xmas / This beautiful disease / You'll get a slap / In the morning.

		Echo	Atlantic
Jul 96.	(7") *(ECS 024)* **GOODNIGHT. / JULY**	28	-

(cd-s+=) *(ECSCD 024)* – Harry and Ida swop teeth.
(cd-s) *(ECSCX 024)* – ('A'side / Shellfish / Girl with money.

Oct 96.	(c-s) *(ECSMC 026)* **YOU'RE GORGEOUS / BEBE LIMONADE**	3	-

(cd-s+=) *(ECSCX 026)* – Ooh yeah / Car crash.
(cd-s) *(ECSCD 026)* – ('A'side) / You're gorgeous too / Honk Kong blues / KW Jesus TV roof appeal.

Oct 96.	(cd/c/d-lp) *(ECH CD/MC/LP 011)* <*83049*> **UGLY BEAUTIFUL**	9	1997

– Goodnight / Candy girl / Jesus is my girlfriend / I didn't want to wake you up / Dead bird sings / Atomic soda / You're gorgeous / Bad shave 2 / Cornershop / King Bing / You & me / 45 & fat / Too handsome to be homeless / July / Baby bird. *(cd re-iss. Mar99; same)*

Jan 97.	(c-s) *(ECSMC 031)* **CANDY GIRL / FARMER**	14	-

(cd-s+=) *(ECSCD 031)* – You're gorgeous (BBC session) / Oh what a beautiful day.
(cd-s) *(ECSCX 031)* – ('A'side) / Bad shave (BBC session) / Cooling towers (BBC session) / Amtrack.

Apr 97.	(ltd-7"pic-d) *(ECSPD 033)* **CORNERSHOP. / ALUMINIUM**		-
May 97.	(c-s) *(ECSMC 033)* **CORNERSHOP / HAPPIEST MAN ALIVE**	37	-

(cd-s) *(ECSCD 033)* – ('A'side) / Death of the neighbourhood II / Shop girl / You're gorgeous (original demo – 1991).
(cd-s) *(ECSCX 033)* – ('A'side) / Death of the neighbourhood I / Pretty little graves / Cornershop (original demo – 1987).

— now without HUW who left left early in '98

		Echo	Imprint
Apr 98.	(7"pic-d) *(ECS 060)* **BAD OLD MAN. / FUCKLOVE**	31	-

(cd-s+=) *(ECSCD 060)* – Hospital bed.
(cd-s) *(ECSCX 060)* – ('A'side) / All I know / Comeback scumbag.

Aug 98.	(7"pic-d) *(ECS 065)* **IF YOU'LL BE MINE. / POOLSIDE**	28	-

(c-s+=/cd-s+=) *(ECS MC/CD 065)* – Worn.
(cd-s) *(ECSCX 065)* – ('A'side) / Memorise / I want nothing.

Aug 98.	(cd/c/lp) *(ECH CD/MC/LP 024)* <*111059*> **THERE'S SOMETHING GOING ON**	28	-

– Bad old man / If you'll be mine / Back together / I was never here / First man on the sun / You will always love me / The life / All men are evil / Take me back / It's not funny anymore / There's something going on.

Feb 99.	(7"clear) *(ECS 073)* **BACK TOGETHER. / IF YOU'LL BE MINE (acoustic)**	22	-

(cd-s) *(ECSCD 073)* – ('A'side) / Like before / C.F.C.
(cd-s) *(ECSCX 073)* – ('A'side) / Sunshine / Hate song.

Jul 99.	(7") *(MUSE 006)* **DRUNK CAR. / East River Pipe: CYBERCAR**		-

(above issued on 'Easy Tiger')

Mar 00.	(7") *(ECS 92)* **THE F-WORD. / JUST A LITTLE**	35	-

(cd-s+=) *(ECSCD 92)* – ('A'-Steve Osborne mix).
(cd-s) *(ECSCX 92)* – ('A'side) / Beat the boys up / Bad old man (video).

May 00.	(7") *(ECS 97)* **OUT OF SIGHT. / IN THE COUNTRY**	58	-

(cd-s+=) *(ECSCD 97)* – Love love love.
(cd-s) *(ECSCX 97)* – ('A'side) / I 4 U / The F-word (video).

Jun 00. (cd/c/lp) (ECH CD/MC/LP 32) **BUGGED**
– The F-word / Getaway / Out of sight / Fireflies / Eyes in the back of my head / Till you die / Wave your hands / All I want / The way you are / One dead groove. *(cd hidden+=)* – The Xmas god of New York.

STEPHEN JONES

Santuary / not iss.

Aug 02. (cd) (SANCD 121) **ALMOST CURED OF SADNESS**
– Key to the brain / Under the rainbow / Radio's been thinking again / Good day in a bad world / Friend / Pretty fucking happy / Your time / Little thug / Sitting in my graveyard / Jesus freaks and candy asses / Someplace far away / Quaaludes / Almost cured of sadness. *(hidden track+=)* – I can sing a rainbow.

– compilations, etc. –

Aug 97. (cd) *Baby Bird;* <60804> **GREATEST HITS**
– Goddamn it, you're a kid / Man's tight vest / KW Jesus TV roof appeal / Bad blood / Kiss your country / Hong Kong blues / Razor blade shower / Sha na na / Aluminium beach / Alison / Grandma begs to be 18 again / I was never here / Petrol cigarette / Losing my hair / Saturday / Invisible tune / Failed old singer / Swinging from tree to tree / Anot about a girl / In the morning.
Dec 97. (cd) *Babybird;* (BABYBIRD 005) **DYING HAPPY** – mail-o
– Metal waterpistol / Cheap astronaut / Lead cloud / It's alright dad, isn't it / Grandma begs to be 18 again / The unemployable rub oil on her coffin / TV / Homesick satellites / When everyone speaks English, the world will explode / Petrol cigarette / Tomorrow's gone / Losing my hair.
Sep 00. (cd-ep) *Animal House;* (ANICD 110) **DOUBLE A EP**
Oct 01. (d-cd; as STEPHEN JONES) *Easy Tiger;* (ETA 002CD)
1985-2001
– Nevercoming home / The rice trail / 0-1-800 Jesus / Sawcuts / Nervous ice in cheap cola / Do you think he was singing it? / The broken 88 / Squeeze the trigger gently / Arthritis kid / Jokeshop bullethole / Tolls on the freeway / Gang cult No.5: the black reindeers / Here we attack / 17 Blue Sun Road, Yellow Hill / 25 watt halo / Baby's coming / Hai / The restaurant is guilty II / Baby Jesus opens his presents / Tealeaves on the rooftiles / Waking up in the coffin / Always bright / Loveable thug / Commercial suicide.
Nov 02. (6xcd-box) *Castle;* CMYBOX 560) **THE LO-FI ALBUMS REMASTERED/BOXED**
– (I WAS BORN A MAN / BAD SHAVE / FATHERHOOD / THE HAPPIEST MAN ALIVE / GREATEST HITS / UNTITLED)

Burt BACHARACH

Born: 12 May'28, Kansas City, Missouri, USA. Classically trained and apprenticed as a conductor for Marlene Dietrich, BURT BACHARACH's career as a composer of exquisitely crafted MOR got off the ground as far back as 1957 when country troubadour Marty Robbins topped the British chart with 'THE STORY OF MY LIFE'. While it also made the Top 20 in his home country and initiated major Stateside success, the UK would henceforth be a lucrative market for the American and one where his light-handed style was to impact upon the music scene for decades to come. Crooners such as Perry Como and Gene Pitney were also the recipients of BACHARACH material during this era although it wasn't until the early 60's that the composer, together with his longtime lyricist/partner HAL DAVID, began a hugely successful working relationship with DIONNE WARWICK. Through the early to late 60's, the singer scored an incredible run of US hits supplied by the BACHARACH/DAVID duo including 'I SAY A LITTLE PRAYER' (of which ARETHA FRANKLIN later cut a definitive version), 'WALK ON BY' and 'DO YOU KNOW THE WAY TO SAN JOSE'. In Britain meanwhile, the likes of SANDIE SHAW, DUSTY SPRINGFIELD, FRANKIE VAUGHAN, TOM JONES and CILLA BLACK were saturating the chart with breezy songs buoyed up on that unmistakable combination of jazz/bossa sophistication, impeccable craft, innovative arrangements and pop insouciance. Yet for all its unashamedly commercial clout, it was a highly intelligent formula ripe for subversion. Psychedelic popsters LOVE were perhaps the best example of a band who absorbed the BACHARACH ethic and translated it into a rock idiom, unleashing an exposive version of 'MY LITTLE RED BOOK' on their debut album and taking twisted orchestral pop to its ultimate conclusion on the landmark 'Forever Changes'. The latter track had originally featured on the 1965 soundtrack, 'What's New Pussycat?', one of a handful of films scored by BACHARACH and DAVID in the fertile mid to late 60's period. In 1969, BURT cut the classic 'MAKE IT EASY ON YOURSELF', only his second release as a recording artist but one which effectively captured his essential genius. Produced by Phil Ramone and released on A&M (Herb Alpert had also previously hit with BACHARACH material), the album found a reticent performer rising to the challenge of singing (which, to be fair, was never his strongest point) his own songs already definitively cut by other artists. Predictably perhaps, the composer reclaimed songs such as 'I'LL NEVER FALL IN LOVE AGAIN' and 'MAKE IT EASY ON YOURSELF' by retuning the arrangements in such a way that they still have a distinct, separate identity today. While The CARPENTERS scored their first major hit with the BACHARACH/DAVID-penned 'CLOSE TO YOU' and undoubtedly looked to the duo as inspiration for their seminal MOR sound, the 70's were lean years for BURT as he split with HAL DAVID and went through a marriage break-up. The 1980's were brighter as he began writing again and scored two successive number one's with 'THAT'S WHAT FRIENDS ARE FOR' and 'ON MY OWN'. Having already influenced the alternative Hollywood scene in the 1960's, BACHARACH again proved an unlikely 90's icon for a whole generation of British indie acts. While his sugary confections weren't too hard to discern as an influence on such twee rosters as 'Sarah' records and pop magpies such as SAINT ETIENNE, meat and potatoes rockers like OASIS confirmed BACHARACH as a major touchstone. In 1998, one of the founding fathers of alternative music, ELVIS COSTELLO, teamed up with BACHARACH on the acclaimed 'PAINTED FROM MEMORY' album while the man himself sealed his indie/dad rock credentials by performing on Jools Holland's 'Later' TV show.

Best CD compilation: THE LOOK OF LOVE: THE BURT BACHARACH COLLECTION (*9)

Eric BACHMANN / Barry BLACK
(see under ⇒ ARCHERS OF LOAF)

BACK TO THE PLANET

Formed: In a ex-dole office squat(!) . . . Peckham, London, England . . . 1989 by FIL (the girl) WALTERS and four self-confessed unwashed and proud-of-it male musicians!; FRAGGLE, GUY McAFFER, CARL HENDRICKSE and HENRY CULLEN. Spaced-out, skanking mainstays of the thriving crusty scene, the group built up a grass roots following through extensive festival touring and gigs in the capital. Following a series of self-financed tapes and a one-off single, 'REVOLUTION OF THOUGHT', the group were picked up by 'London' records subsidiary, 'Parallel'. The 'TEENAGE TURTLES' single followed amid general acclaim and an NME Single Of The Week award, the group's engaging mash-up of pop, metal, phat beats and wigged-out dub seeing them bracketed alongside fellow agitators like SENSER and DUB WAR. A further couple of fine singles, 'PLEASE DON'T FIGHT' and 'DAYDREAM', surprisingly failed to dent the charts and despite a Top 40 placing for debut album, 'MIND AND SOUL COLLABORATORS' later that year, the collective soon found themselves out in the commercial cold. No doubt more comfortable with the DIY ethos of the scene which spawned them, BACK TO THE PLANET resumed their rounds of the festival circuit, finding time to release a follow-up set, 'MESSAGES AFTER THE BLEEP' (1995), on their own 'Arthur Mix' label.

Album rating: MIND AND SOUL COLLABORATORS (*7) / MESSAGES AFTER THE BLEEP (*6)

FIL 'the girl' WALTERS (b.31 Jan'70, Dartford, Kent, England) – vocals / **FRAGGLE** (b. DAVID FLETCHER, 5 Aug'68, Kent) – guitar / **GUY McAFFER** (b.27 May'69) – keyboards / **CARL HENDRICKSE** (b.28 Jan'70, London) – bass / **HENRY CULLEN** (b.10 Oct'69, Lewisham, London) – drums

Arthur Mix / not iss.

1991. (c) (BTTP 1) **WARNING THE PUBLIC** – mail-o
– Teenage turtles / London City / You're the judge / Starved by ignorance / Misunderstood / Human error / Daydream.
Feb 92. (12") (12BTTP 2) **THE REVOLUTION OF THOUGHT. /**
Aug 92. (c) (BTTP 3) **EARZONE FRIENDLY** – mail-o
Aug 92. (c) (BTTP 4) **LIVE VOL.1** (live) – mail-o

Parallel / not iss.

Apr 93. (c-s) (LLLCS 3) **TEENAGE TURTLES / REPRISE**
(12"+=/cd-s+=) (LLL X/CD 3) – ('A'extended).
Jun 93. (c-s/12"/cd-s) (LLL CS/X/CD 6) **PLEASE DON'T FIGHT. / MANWOMAN 2000 /** ('A'mix)
Aug 93. (7"/c-s) (LLL/+CS 8) **DAYDREAM. / (2-'A'mixes)**
(12"/cd-s) (LLL X/CD 8) – ('A'side) / Breakin' roots / Takin' time / ('A'mix).

London / not iss.

Sep 93. (cd/c/lp) (828437-2/-4/-1) **MIND AND SOUL COLLABORATORS** 32
– Please don't fight / Crossed lines / Daydream / Mother / Misunderstood / Starved by ignorance / London City / Teenage turtles / Hard edge few / Sleepless nights.

— dropped by 'London' records for no apparent reason?!

Arthur Mix / not iss.

Mar 95. (12"ep/cd-ep) (BTTP 006 V/CD) **A SMALL NUCLEAR DEVICE**
– Flexing muscle / Immanent deities / Meditational thoughts / Colour sex.
Mar 95. (cd/c/lp) (BTTP 007 CD/C/V) **MESSAGES AFTER THE BLEEP!**
– Tidal motion / Electro rays / Flexing muscles / Immanent deities / Elemental bliss / Never let them / Meditational thoughts / Colour sex / Criminal / Super powers / Under your skin.

— seemed to have ceased from recording duties.

– compilations, etc. –

Jan 95. (c) *Arthur Mix;* (BTTP 5) **A POTTED HISTORY** – mail-o
– (1992 cassette tracks +) / The revolution of thought / Go go lemmings / Thoughts in a day / Let our roots breathe / Rub in the cream / Sunshine / Betty Boop / The revolution of thought (dub).

BACKWATER

Formed: Downpatrick, County Down, Northern Ireland . . . 1990 by schoolmates, BARRY PEAK and BOYD LOWE, who gigged sporadically with a conveyer belt of rhythm musicians. Around the mid-90's the line-up finally cemented around RYAN McAULEY and RICHARD BASSETT, the band enjoying inclusion on three various artists EP collections for 'Noisebox'

BACKWATER (cont)

before sharing a single, 'DIDACTIC NO' with fellow indie cohorts, BEAR. Now part of the growing 'Che' indie stable, BACKWATER emerged from relative obscurity early in '96 with their "own" single, 'SUPERCOOL'. The band kept up a heavy touring and recording schedule throughout the year, a debut set, 'ANGELS ARE COOL', finally seeing the light of day towards the end of the year; differentiating between the writing styles of PEAK and LOWE, the album veered from the former's drifting muse to the latter's manic freakouts. However, the loss of BASSETT and subsequently LOWE inevitably slowed down their progress, the releases reduced to a trickle of low-key 7"ers.

Album rating: ANGELS ARE COOL (*6)

BARRY PEAK (b. 7 Jun'74) – vocals, guitar / **BOYD LOWE** (b.1974) – guitar, vocals / **RYAN McAULEY** (b. 4 Oct'72) – bass / **RICHARD BASSETT** – drums

—— Jun94-Mar95, they appeared on three various artists cd-ep's (VOL.2, 3 & 4) on 'Noisebox'; *NBX 004 / 006 / 009*

		Delete X-Ten	Che not iss.
Nov 95.	(7") (X10 03) **DIDACTIC NO.** / (other track by Bear)	-	-
		Che	not iss.
Jan 96.	(7") (che 48) **SUPERCOOL.** /	-	-
Apr 96.	(7") (che 50) **SHADY.** / WORLD FLY PAST	-	-
	(cd-s) (che 50cd) – ('A'side) / Single and celibate / My mouth's a devil / Real happy if it wasn't so damned sad.		
Sep 96.	(7") (che 56) **MEMORY.** / SILVER SURFER	-	-
	(cd-s+=) (che 56cd) – Explosions / Purgatory (I think I've just seen the light).		
Oct 96.	(cd/lp) (che 57 cd/lp) **ANGELS ARE COOL**	-	-
	– Supercool / Didactic no / Start / Vehicle / Magic place / You gave me life and I messed it up / Memory / I was bad / Shady / Angels are cool / She's sonic / Christmas song.		

—— **SEAN ROBINSON** (b. 8 Apr'74) – drums; repl. BASSETT

—— now without LOWE who retired to his hobbie

Jan 97.	(cd-s) <62025> **PURE SONIC RAIN**	-	-
Feb 97.	(7"; tour freebie) (che 64) **THINGS LOOK BETTER . . .**	-	-

		Gorgonzola	not iss.
1997.	(7") (GORGON 2) **IN THESE LAST DAYS.** / HOT RHYTHM	-	-

		Fantastic Plastic	not iss.
May 98.	(cd-ep) (FP 009) **EARTHLY FACES IN ALIEN PLACES**	-	-

—— split after above

BADLY DRAWN BOY

Formed: Early 1997, as a one-man vehicle for the highly charged but eccentric DAMON GOUGH. The Bolton-born – or at least in a village outside it – first initiated his weird brand of gnome-ish psychedelia when he self-financed (with graphic designer ANDY VOTEL) an EP on his own 'Twisted Nerve' label. 'EP1' (released in September '97) was quickly pursued by the following year's 'EP2', a contract with 'XL Recordings' (home of The PRODIGY) just around the corner. In the Autumn of '98, his third set, the imaginatively titled 'EP3' hit the shops, this BECK-esque trio of tracks finally making the more discerning music punter sit up and listen. Prior to this, GOUGH had contributed the track, 'Nursery Rhyme', to the acclaimed UNKLE album, 'Psyence Fiction'. Minor hits 'ONCE AROUND THE BLOCK' and 'ANOTHER PEARL' preceded a long-awaited debut set, 'THE HOUR OF THE BEWILDERBEAST' (2000), the UK Top 20 entry a mixture of NICK DRAKE's quiet, cello-driven folk and SPRINGSTEEN's poor-man's blues. Three Top 30 singles followed the Mercury Prize-winning album; 'DISILLUSION', 'ONCE AROUND THE BLOCK' and 'PISSING IN THE WIND', with the latter video starring Joan Collins.

Album rating: THE HOUR OF THE BEWILDERBEAST (*8) / ABOUT A BOY soundtrack (*7) / HAVE YOU FED THE FISH? (*5)

DAMON GOUGH – vocals, instruments & things / with various session people

		Twisted Nerve	not iss.
Sep 97.	(7"ep) (TN 001) **EP1**	-	-
	– Riding with Gabriel Greenburg / Shake the rollercoaster / No point in living / Sugarstealer / No point in living (reprise).		
Apr 98.	(7"ep) (TN 002) **EP2**	-	-
	– I love you all / The treeclimber / I love you all (I loop you all Andy Votel mix) / Thinking of you.		

		Twisted Nerve – X.L.	Toy
Oct 98.	(7") (TNXL 001R) **ROAD MOVIE.** / MY FRIEND CUBILAS	-	-
	(10"ep) (TNXL 001T) – ('A'side) / Spooky driver / I need a sign / Meet me on the horizon.		
	(cd-ep) (TNXL 001CD) – ('B'side) / Interlude / Kerplunk by candlelight / Meet me on the horizon.		
Mar 99.	(10"ep) (TNXL 002T) **IT CAME FROM THE GROUND** / WALKMAN (demo 1) / OUTSIDE A LIGHT (1 & 2) / WALKMAN (demo 2)	-	-
	(cd-ep+=) (TNXL 002CD) – ('A'-Andy Votel remix).		
	(7") (TNXL 002R) – (above remix) / Whirlpool.		
Aug 99.	(7") (TNXL 003) **ONCE AROUND THE BLOCK.** / SOUL ATTITUDE	46	-
	(cd-s+=) (TNXL 003CD) – ('A'-Radio Luxembourg mix).		
	(7") (TNXL 003R) – ('A'-Andy Votel mix) / Another pearl.		
Dec 99.	(cd) <1> **HOW DID I GET HERE?**	-	-
	– My friend Cubilas / I need a sign / Interlude / Meet on the horizon / Road movie / Kerplunk by candlelight / It came from the ground / Outside is a light (one) / Soul attitude / Whirlpool / It came from the ground (Andy Votel mix).		

		Twisted Nerve – X.L.	Twisted Nerve – X.L.
Jun 00.	(10"/cd-s) (TNXL 004 T/CD) **ANOTHER PEARL.** / DISTANT TOWN / CHAOS THEORY	41	-
	(cd-s) (TNXL 004CD2) – ('A'mixes).		
Jun 00.	(cd/c/lp) (TNXL CD/MC/LP 133) <87211> **THE HOUR OF THE BEWILDERBEAST**	13	-
	– The shining / Everybody's stalking / Bewilder / Fall in a river / Camping next to water / Stone on the water / Another pearl / Body rap / Once around the block / This song / Bewilderbeast / Magic in the air / Cause a rockslide / Pissing in the wind / Blistered heart / Disillusion / Say it again / Epitaph.		
Sep 00.	(10") (TNXL 005T) **DISILLUSION.** / WERECKING THE STAGE / DISILLUSION (Mr Scruff mix)	26	-
	(cd-s) (TNXL 005CD) – (first 2) / Bottle of tears.		
	(cd-s) (TNXL 005CD2) – ('A'side) / ('A'-Blue States mix) / ('A'-Black lodge mix).		
Nov 00.	(ltd-10") (TNXL 008T) **THE SHINING**	-	- wdrawn
Nov 00.	(7") (TNXL 009) **ONCE AROUND THE BLOCK.** / TUMBLEWEED / THE SHINING (Avalanches good for the weekend mix)	27	-
	(cd-s+=) (TNXL 009CD) – (first & third tracks) / The shining (Capitol K mix).		
	(cd-s) (TNXL 009CD2) – ('A'side) / ('A'-Andy Votel mix) / ('A'-Nick Faber mix).		
May 01.	(10"/cd-s) (TNXL 010 T/CD) **PISSING IN THE WIND.** / SPITTING IN THE WIND / THE SHINING (minotaur shock mix)	22	-
	(cd-s) (TNXL 010CD2) – ('A'side) / Magic in the air (WDET Detroit mix) / Everybody's stalking (WDET Detroit mix).		

		Twisted Nerve	Artist Direct
Mar 02.	(7") (TNXL 012) **SILENT SIGH.** / DONNA AND BLITZEN (KCRW acoustic session) / PIANO MEDLEY (KCRW acoustic session)	16	-
	(cd-s) (TNXL 012CD) – ('A'side) / ('A'-acoustic) / Better way / ('A'-version).		
	(cd-s) (TNXL 012CD2) – ('A'side) / ('A'-Broadway project mix) / ('A'-Zongamin remix).		
Apr 02.	(cd/lp) (TNXL CD/LP 152) <1019> **ABOUT A BOY** (soundtrack)	6	-
	– Exit stage right / A peak you reach / Something to talk about / Dead duck / Above you, below me / I love N.Y.E. / Silent sigh / Wet, wet, wet / River, sea, ocean / S.P.A.T. / Rachel's flat / Walking out of stride / File me away / A minor incident / Delta (little boy blues) / Donna and Blitzen.		
Jun 02.	(7") (TNXL 014) **SOMETHING TO TALK ABOUT.** / WALK IN THE PARK WITH ANGIE / HAMSTER COUNTDOWN	28	-
	(cd-s) (TNXL 014CD) – ('A'-side) / ('A'-Four Tet convention mix) / ('A'-Misty Dixon mix).		
	(cd-s) (TNXL 014CD2) – ('A'side) / Above you below me (electric bedroom version) / My name's not down.		
Oct 02.	(7") (TNXL 015) **YOU WERE RIGHT.** / LAST FRUIT	9	-
	(cd-s+=) (TNXL 015CD) – You were right (live at Glastonbury).		
Nov 02.	(cd/lp) (TNXL CD/LP 156) <1066> **HAVE YOU FED THE FISH?**	10	-
	– Coming in to land / Have you fed the fish? / Born again / 40 days, 40 nights / All possibilities / I was wrong / You were right / Centrepeace / How? / The further I slide / Imaginary lines / Using our feet / Tickets to what you need / What is it now? / Bedside story.		

BALLBOY

Formed: Edinburgh, Scotland ... late 90's by songwriter/guitarist and primary school teacher GORDON McINTYRE, a man more than a little influenced by the narrative doodlings of BELLE & SEBASTIAN. Backed by student KATIE GRIFFITHS, nursery nurse NICK REYNOLDS and sound technician GARY MORGAN (who replaced an earlier line-up – see below), he unveiled his jangly, reflective muse on 1999's debut EP, 'SILVER SUITS FOR ASTRONAUTS'. With his slightly fey vocals, bittersweet twenty/thirty-something musings and pithy character sketches, comparisons with B&S's STUART DAVID were unavoidable. No bad thing though as McINTYRE carried it all off with more charm and grace than most indie hopefuls can muster, his voice imparting a rare authenticity. Summer 2000 follow-up, 'I HATE SCOTLAND.. EP', proved he wasn't scared of a bit of controversy, its scathing title track (dedicated to 'Keep Clause 28' "campaigner", Brian Souter) a flipside to Saltire-waving Caledonian romance while hidden track, 'THE SASH MY FATHER WORE', ironically exposed Scotland's "dirty secret" of religious bigotry. Although more musically adventurous than its predecessor, the record maintained acoustic strumming as BALLBOY's preferred field of play. With a third EP in the can, the group sensibly issued a compilation album (a kind of "3 EPS" type thing) to an eager set of fans. 'CLUB ANTHEMS' (2002) was more social club than dance club, with the aforementioned 'I HATE SCOTLAND' making a brave appearance as the opening track. Other tracks (and the titles are great!) included 'SEX IS BORING', 'I'VE GOT PICTURES OF YOU IN YOUR UNDERWEAR' and, wait for it, 'ALL THE RECORDS ON THE RADIO ARE SHITE', which received an unfair lambasting by an NME hack (stick to The VINES, man, eh!).

Album rating: CLUB ANTHEMS compilation (*7)

GORDON McINTYRE – guitars, narration / **KATIE GRIFFITHS** – keyboards / **NICK REYNOLDS** – bass / **GARY MORGAN** – drums, percussion; repl. ALEXIS BEATTIE, CHRIS LOWRIE, JOHN McLEAN + ELIZABETH McLEAN

		sl	Manifesto
Nov 99.	(cd-ep) (lone 06) **SILVER SUITS FOR ASTRONAUTS – 4 SONGS**	-	-
	– Donald in the bushes with a bag of glue / A day in space / Dumper truck racing / Public park a.k.a dogs not kids.		

BALLBOY (cont)

Jul 00. (cd-ep) *(lone 08)* **I HATE SCOTLAND.. EP**
– Essential wear for future trips to space / I hate Scotland.. / One sailor was waving / Olympic cyclist (acoustic version). *(hidden track+=)* – Donald Jr.; The sash my father wore.

Mar 01. (cd-ep) *(lone 10)* **GIRLS ARE BETTER THAN BOYS EP**
– Leave the earth behind you and take a walk into the sunshine / I've got pictures of you in your underwear / Swim for health / They'll hang flags from cranes upon my wedding day.

Feb 02. (cd) *(lone 11) <43301>* **CLUB ANTHEMS** (compilation)
– Donald in the bushes with a bag of glue (new version) / A day in space (new version) / Dumper truck racing / Public park a.k.a. dogs not kids / Essential wear for future trips to space / I hate Scotland.. / One sailor was waving / Olympic cyclist (acoustic version) / Leave the earth behind you and take a walk into the sunshine / I've got pictures of you in your underwear / Swim for health / They'll hang flags from cranes upon my wedding day / Postcards from the beach / Sex is boring (acoustic version). *<US tracks in different order>*

Apr 02. (cd-ep/7"ep) *(lone 15/+5)* **ALL THE RECORDS ON THE RADIO ARE SHITE EP**
– All the records on the radio are shite / Building for the future / Stars and stripes / Welcome to the New Year.

BAMBULE
(see under ⇒ CINdYTALK; 80's section)

BANDIT QUEEN

Formed: Manchester, England . . . 1992 by one-time PJ HARVEY-influenced music journo, TRACY GOLDING, along with JANET WOLSTENHOLME and DAVID GALLEY, the trio taking their moniker from a true story (made into a movie) about an Indian woman who becomes an outlaw leader after surviving violence and torture at the hands of her kidnappers. Defiantly feminist, these feisty indie chicks sweetened their bitter rants with a fair dose of pop acumen on their one and only 'Playtime' album, 'HORMONE HOTEL' (1995).

Album rating: HORMONE HOTEL (*6)

Playtime   Mammoth

Apr 93. (10"ep/cd-ep) *(AMUSE 17 T/CD)* **DIRT + SOUL EP**
– Cross dressed blues / Dirt + soul / Big hearts bleed / Full tank of petrol. *(re-iss. Oct93; same)*

Feb 94. (cd-ep) *(AMUSE 22CD)* **SCORCH / FRIDA KAHLO / HIGH HEELS AND PEARLS**

Jun 94. (7") *(AMUSE 024)* **QUEEN BEE. / BIG SUGAR EMOTIONAL THING**

Nov 94. (12"/cd-s) *(AMUSE 25 T/CD)* **MISS DANDYS. / DIRT & SOUL (speed mix) / HOLLYWOOD FAIR**
(re-iss. May95; same)

Feb 95. (cd/c/lp) *(AMUSE 26 CD/MC/LP) <130>* **HORMONE HOTEL**
– Scorch / Back in the belljar / Miss Dandys / Nailbiter / Give it to the dog / Petals and razorblades / Overture for beginners / Big sugar emotional thing / Essence vanilla / Oestrogen / Frida Kahlo / Hormone hotel. *(cd+=)* – Blue black.

Feb 95. (7") *(AMUSE 27)* **GIVE IT TO THE DOG. / FACELIFT**
(cd-s+=) *(AMUSE 27CD)* – Touchstone.

—— subsequently disbanded

BARCELONA

Formed: Washington, D.C., USA . . . summer 1998 by JENNIFER CARR, JASON KORZEN, IVAN RAMISCAL and CHRISTIAN SCANNIELLO (drums). Computer (and soccer) fanatics, they teamed up with HOLLAND and SEA-SAW producer TREVOR KAMPMANN, and began the computer-based recording of their debut album. Signed to 'March' records, and with artwork by 'Teenbeat's MARK ROBINSON, 'simon BASIC' was released in the US in July 1999. Playful, quirky offerings like 'C-64' and 'THE DOWNSIDE OF COMPUTER CAMP', ensured the popularity and subsequent impact of their debut. After touring with ' . . . BASIC', and releasing the 'ROBOT TROUBLE' EP (which included an excellent cover of Men Without Hats' classic 'POP GOES THE WORLD') and single/EP 'STUDIO HAIR GEL', out came second LP, 'ZeRo-oNe-INFINITY'. 'BUGS' and 'KASEY KELLER' continued BARCELONA's winning '80s style synth-pop formula, although 2001's follow-up 'TRANSHUMAN REVOLUTION' seemed to lack the ideas and vision of their previous two sets.

Album rating: simon BASIC (*7) / ZeRo-oNe-INFINITY (*5) / TRANSHUMAN REVOLUTION (*4)

JASON KORZEN – vocals, guitar / **IVAN RAMISCAL** – moog/keyboards, guitars / **JENNIFER CARR** – bass / **CHRISTIAN SCANNIELLO** – drums

March   March

Jul 99. (cd) *<(MAR 049)>* **simon BASIC**   Jun99
– Why do you have so much fun without me? / Sunshine delay / Indian names / C-64 / Fabled age / Space guy blues / I know what you think of me / 1-2 / Unreal / Summer songs / The downside of computer camp.

May 00. (cd-ep) *<MAR 058>* **ROBOT TROUBLE**
– Robot trouble / Robot trouble (Autumn Teen Sound bug free mix) / Social engineering / Sunshine delay / Pop goes the world.

Aug 00. (cd-ep) *<MAR 062>* **STUDIO HAIRGEL**
– Studio hairgel / Studio hairgel (James Figurine mix) / Studio hairgel (the follicular control freakz' wunderkind labcoats-of-the-gods mis-formulated and controlled by Laboratoires Baxendale) / You're not far off / Buying records won't make me feel better.

Jan 01. (cd) *<(MAR 066)>* **ZeRo-oNe-INFINITY**   Oct00
– Studio hair gel / Bugs / Paging system operator / Electronic company / I have the password to your Shell account / Bass and drums (for modern users) / Replicant / Obsoletion / Robot trouble / Have you forgotten the bomb? / 1980-1990 / Haunted by the ghost of Patt / My mom's new boyfriend / Kasey Keller.

Pulcec   Pulcec

Oct 01. (cd) *<(PUL 005)>* **TRANSHUMAN REVOLUTION**   Sep01
– Everything makes me think about sex / West coast radio / Watching you watching us / Human simulation / Teenage pop star / Fleeting fame / April 1978 / I get the message / Beautiful / Planet jerk / The power of Jen.

BARDO POND

Formed: Philadelphia, Pennsylvania, USA . . . mid 90's by ISOBEL SOLLENBERGER, brothers MICHAEL and JOHN GIBBONS, CLINT TAKEDA and JOE CULVER. Being spat straight out of the noise/psychedelia scene, the band – after issuing a handful of 45's on the 'Compulsive' label – delivered their deviant debut, 'BUFO ALVARIUS, AMEN 29:15' for 'Drunken Fish' in 1995. The album, supposedly named after the Colorador river-area that was notorious for its hallucinogenic divisions, read like a pile of trashy noise, recorded in warped conditions (see MERCURY REV's 'Yer Self Is Steam' and 'Boces') that sounded like confused random acts of sheer pointlessness. 'BIG LAUGHING JYM', a collection of home recordings and out-takes proved that the 'POND were once again content with making noise for the sake of er . . . making noise. This was followed up by 1996's 'AMANITA' and a freshly signed contract with 'Matador'. One year later 'LAPSED' appeared and rekindled hope in the band's sound. Instead of being completely lost in BARDO POND's music, the album led you into deep and strange crazy activities making you feel like you were bogged down in a brilliant insane battle with your head. In 1997, the band also augmented ROY MONTGOMERY in the project, HASH JAR TEMPO, the collaborative issuing 'WELL OILED' and two years later, 'UNDER GLASS'. Their latest release was the fiesty 9-tracker, 'SET AND SETTING', a combination of grunge psychedelia and minimalist rock unleashed in 1999. 'Lull' was a beautiful reminder of what this band were actually capable of, while 'THIS TIME (SO FUCKED)' exemplified rock assault and raw power house distortion which, in the long run, is what BARDO POND were all about. 2001's 'DILATE' expanded their spaced-out musical constructions, SOLLENBERGER's double-tracked er . . . emotional dilations mushrooming the band onto the edges of indie superstardom.

Album rating: BUFO ALVARIUS, AMEN 29:15 (*7) / BIG LAUGHING JYM mini (*6) / AMANITA (*6) / LAPSED (*6) / SET AND SETTING (*8) / DILATE (*7)

ISOBEL SOLLENBERGER – vocals, flute / **MICHAEL GIBBONS** – guitar, vocals / **JOHN GIBBONS** – guitar, vocals / **CLINT TAKEDA** – bass, vocals / **JOE CULVER** – drums, vocals

not iss.   Compulsiv

Jan 94. (7") *<014>* **DIE EASY. / APPLE EYE**

Mar 94. (7") *<009>* **TRIP FUCK. / HUMMINGBIRD MOUNTAIN**
(above issued on 'Drunken Fish')

Nov 94. (7") *<025>* **DRAGONFLY. / BLUES TUNE**

Che   Drunken Fish

Jul 95. (7") *(che 34)* **NEW DRUNKS. / (other track by Bear)**

Sep 95. (lp/cd) *(che 33cd) <DFR 15 LP/CD>* **BUFO ALVARIUS, AMEN 29:15**   Jan95
– Adhesive / Back porch / On a side street / Capillary river / No time to waste / Absence / Vent. *(cd+=)* – Amen.

Matador   Drunken Fish

Apr 96. (cd/d-lp) *(OLE 180-2/-1) <DRF 23CD/DBL 12>* **AMANITA**
(UK-title 'HIGH FREQUENCIES')
– Limerick / Sentence / Tantric porno / Wank / The high frequency / Sometimes words / Clean sweep *[d-lp only]* / Yellow turban / Rumination / Be a fish / Tapir song / Brambles *[d-lp only]* / RM.

Siltbreeze   Siltbreeze

Nov 96. (ltd-7") *<(SB 62)>* **TESTS FOR NEW SWORDS. / GOOD FRIDAY**

Matador   Matador

Nov 97. (cd/lp) *<(OLE 210-2/-1)>* **LAPSED**   Oct97
– Tommy gun angel / Pick my brain / Flux / Anandamide / Green man / Straw dog / Aldrin.

Aug 99. (cd/lp) *<(OLE 364-2/-1)>* **SET AND SETTING**
– Walking stick man / This time (so fucked) / Datura / Again / Lull / Cross current / Crawl away / #3.

Aug 00. (ltd-10"ep) *<none>* **SLAB**
– Off the precipice / Hit / The deak.

Apr 01. (cd/d-lp) *<(OLE 459-2/-1)>* **DILATE**
– Two planes / Sunrise / Inside / Aphasia / Favorite uncle / Swig / Despite the roar / lb. / Hum / Ganges. *(d-lp+=)* – Summerflux.

May 01. (12"ep) *<OLE 522-1>* **DESPITE THE ROAR (IN SPITE OF THEMSELVES) / HIGHLANDS. / (other 2 by Mogwai)**
not iss.   Three Lobed — tour

Mar 02. (cd-ep) *<TLR 005>* **PURPOSEFUL AVAILMENT**
– Orange horse / Thalay sagar (tortures torture).

not iss.   Camera Obscura

Sep 02. (m-lp; split w/ SubArachnoid Space) *<CAM 054LP>* **EUPHRATES / Tigris**

not iss.   Time-Lag

Oct 02. (ltd-7") *<010>* **TERRASTOCK 5**
– Button / Water sinks into fire.

– compilations, etc. –

Oct 95. (m-lp/m-cd) *Compulsiv; <036 LP/CD>* **BIG LAUGHING JYM**
(compilation of out-takes, etc)
– Dispersion / Respite / Clearhead / Champ / Soaked. *(cd+=)* – Hummingbird mountain II (a return trip) / Dragonfly.

BARDOTS

Formed: Norwich, England ... 1989 by brothers STEVE and NEIL COX, ANDY MURPHY and SIMON DUNFORD, all of whom were studying at the University of East Anglia at the time. Their first release, 'SOFAELAINE' (1990), was indeed a flexidisc issued by local promoters, 'Wilde Club'. The BARDOTS even had the honour of becoming the Wilde Club's first signing and they duly released debut single proper, 'SAD ANNE'. The ensuing year saw the band move to the more established imprint, 'Cheree', a transaction that also saw them introduce KRZYSZTOF FIJALKOWSKI for their 1992 follow-up single, 'PRETTY O'. This release began to give the BARDOTS some music press attention, their style of brooding alternative rocky pop placed at the right time for the new Brit-rock scene dubbed "new glam" and led by the emerging SUEDE. The group's intellectual, self-obsessed themes, fitted in well with this barrage of new shoegazers; their latest addition, the cross-dressing and sexually ambivalent, FIJALKOWSKI, ploughed the same furrow of youth confusion and exploration as the aforementioned band's frontman, BRETT ANDERSON. Capitalising on their new found fame, the group released a further two 7"ers, 'SHALLOW' and 'CRUELTY BLONDE', following these up with the debut set, 'EYE-BABY' (1993). Unfortunately this year would see 'Cheree' out of the picture, leaving the band in the unsigned wastelands again, a fate inspiring them to do a DIY release single, 'WE ARE FIASCO', on their newly created 'Pygmy' records. The superseding year saw the departure of MURPHY, whose duties were taken up by YVES ALTANA, of WONKY ALICE fame. New member, ALTANA, as well as providing guitar, also controlled the knobs in the studio for the band's sophomore full-length set, 'V-NECK', which unfortunately due to various difficulties, only saw the light of day in 1996, by which time the changeable music hacks had lost interest in the group and their sound. Thus the BARDOTS conceded to commercial failure, and they disbanded that same year.

Album rating: EYE-BABY (*5) / V-NECK (*7)

SIMON DUNFORD – vocals, guitar / **ANDY MURPHY** – guitar / **STEVE COX** – bass / **NEIL COX** – drums

			Wilde Club	not iss.
Nov 90.	(12")	(WILDE 001) **SAD ANNE. / SUMMERHOUSE**	☐	–

— added **KRYZS FIJALKOWSKI** – guitar

			Cheree	not iss.
Jan 92.	(12"ep/cd-ep)	(Cheree 25) **PRETTY O / MISS ANOTHER. / +2**	☐	–
Jun 92.	(12"m)	(Cheree 29) **SHALLOW / ASHAMED / TWO HUNDRED SIX**	☐	–
Aug 92.	(12"m)	(Cheree 30T) **CRUELTY BLONDE. / DON'T LET ME DOWN / SKIN DIVING**	☐	–
Sep 92.	(cd/c/lp)	(Cheree 31 CD/MC/LP) **EYE-BABY** – Pretty O / Chained up / Cruelty blonde / Sister Richard / Slow asleep / Sunsetted / My cute thought / Obscenity thing / Gloriole / Caterina / A / Shallow.	☐	–

			Pygmy	not iss.
1993.	(12"ep)	(Pygmy 1) **WE ARE FIASCO. / +3**	☐	–

			not iss.	Blissed-Out
1993.	(cd)	**SAD ANNE** (compilation)	–	☐ Canada

			Che	not iss.
Apr 96.	(7"white)	(che 43) **CARRION. / MAKING MONEY**	☐	–
May 96.	(cd)	(che 44cd) **V-NECK** – Carrion / Annabel / Irene / Bad feeling / English lovers / Skin-diving / Berlitz / How could I hurt you? / Violent love / Somebody could die across my throne and I . . . / The colony room / Feeling juvenile.	☐	–

— after they disbanded, SIMON joined POLAK (ex-ADORABLE)

BAREFOOT CONTESSA

Formed: Cambridgeshire, England ... 1994 by GRAHAM GARGIULO and HELENE DINEEN, who met at a PJ HARVEY gig in the capital and decided to put together a band, naming it after a fifties film starring Humphrey Bogart; they subsequently recruited DINESH 'DES' BHATT and ANDY KINGSTON (of THRILLED SKINNY fame). GARGIULO had also tasted a little bit of musical fame with the CHARLOTTES, while DINEEN had in her teen years a deal with 'Creation' records. Due probably to the fact that the lead duo in BC had had some experience with the fickle record industry, they went for the unorthodox but very independent move of recording their eponymous debut album, 'BAREFOOT CONTESSA' (1995), before even doing a live show. Releasing this on their own 'Indie 500' imprint, in as you might have guessed, a limited pressing of 500. These sold out fairly quickly, especially with the backing of Radio One DJ, Mark Radcliffe, who enjoyed the band's blend of noir-ish country blues and folk rock, which led to comparisons with the likes of MAZZY STAR. Later the same year the BAREFOOT ones released their first single, 'TO BE CONTINUED'. With their star in the ascendancy, the band were near signing a deal with '4 a.d.', but this unfortunately fell through. However, it did not dampen their ambitions as a great gig in the summer of 1996 at the high-profile Phoenix music festival and the delivery of their sophomore full-length set, 'YOU CAN'T GO HOME AGAIN', was released under their own steam. Providence was at hand for the band, as their sound gleaned the attention of producer Clive Martin, who not only wanted to record them, but also was setting up his own imprint, 'Global Warming'. During the initial sessions though, BHATT and KINGSTON dropped out and were soon to be replaced by ex-BACK TO THE PLANET sticksman, JAMES CORNER. Perhaps due to this slight alteration and their musical style getting decidedly heavier, they chose to go under the name of CODACHROME. Simultaneously though BC continued to record tracks for their third full-length set, 'BLUES FOR A HONEY', released by the fledgling imprint in 1999. To drum up interest in the new record, the band took on more members for their promotional gigs, with PAOLO DEGREGORIO and ANN MARIE becoming the most full-time new members out of the invited stand-in muscians. The newly bolstered group took the millennium by storm courtesy of their fourth full-set, 'OH, THE SWEET POWER', a record which appeased the public and critics alike.

Album rating: BAREFOOT CONTESSA (*6) / YOU CAN'T GO HOME AGAIN (*5) / BLUES FOR A HONEY (*6) / OH, THE SWEET POWER (*7)

HELENE DINEEN – vocals / **GRAHAM GARGIULO** – guitar (ex-CHARLOTTES) / **DINESH 'DES' BHATT** – bass / **ANDY KINGSTON** – drums (ex-THRILLED SKINNY)

			Indie 500	not iss.
Jun 95.	(cd)	(LOLA 1CD) **BAREFOOT CONTESSA** – Eve / Saved / Such sweet sorrow / Gone too soon for my time / Carnal knowledge / To be continued / How can you say you really feel / The big lie / No means yes.	☐	–
Nov 95.	(7")	(LOLA 2) **TO BE CONTINUED. / HILL 66**	☐	–
Apr 97.	(cd)	(LOLA 3CD) **YOU CAN'T GO HOME AGAIN** – What's done is done / Three years / Miss peaches / Someone over me / To know and not care / Shoulder / Liddle friendship song / Switched off / Candy's by and by / Jumped heart first and still reeling / Bring me summer.	☐	–
1997.	(cd-ep)	(LOLA 4CD) **HAPPY TOGETHER** – Happy together / Ice / Rider / Honeymaker.	☐	–

— **JAMES CORNER** – drums (ex-BACK TO THE PLANET) repl. DINESH + ANDY

			Global Warming	not iss.
Mar 99.	(cd)	(GLOBCD 4) **BLUES FOR A HONEY** – My worldly goods / He's gone to town / Lullaby N.Y. / On a high / Superanything / Gracie / Your star / We are each other / Happy together / Treasure / The best of times, the worst of times.	☐	–

— for live gigs added another 3 incl. **PAOLO DeGREGORIO** – keyboards (ex-NEW RADICALS) + **ANN MARIE** – bass

			Indie 500	not iss.
Jun 00.	(cd)	(LOLA 5CD) **OH, THE SWEET POWER** – Chair love / Sweet and strong / Found new treasure / Not satisfied / Silver dagger / In exile / Poppies / Last chance girl / O help me Jesus / Weekends.	☐	–

BARE JR.

Formed: Nashville, Tennessee, USA ... 1997 by singer/songwriter BOBBY BARE JR., son of the 50's/60's country star who had a major US hit in '58 with 'The All American Boy'. BOBBY BARE, MIKE 'GRIMEY' GRIMES, DEAN TOMASEK, KEITH BROGDON and TRACEY HACKNEY arrived with their 1998 debut EP 'CUSTOM GAUGE', a heart-on-their-sleeves fusion of country and dirty rock and roll and sounded like the upstart younger brother of STEVE EARLE & THE DUKES. The EP was followed that same year with the band's debut single, 'YOU BLEW ME OFF', with their first album 'BOO-TAY' not far behind. Whilst recording the album the band made use of their country connections enlisting BOBBY BARE SR. and CARRIE AKRE of the group GODDESS on backing vocals. The album's stand out track 'I HATE MYSELF' was co-written with SHEL SILVERSTEIN, already famous for having penned the JOHNNY CASH track 'A Boy Named Sue' (among others). A second album 'BRAINWASHER' followed in 2000; lyrically this was a slightly more personal affair, although the self-effacing humour was lost in the mix.

Album rating: BOO-TAY (*5) / BRAINWASHER (*4)

BOBBY BARE JR. – vocals / **MICHAEL GRIMES** – guitar / **TRACY HACKNEY** – electric dulcimer, samples, vocals / **DEAN TOMASEK** – bass / **KEITH BROGDON** – drums

			not iss.	Immortal-Epic
Sep 98.	(cd)	<69353> **BOO-TAY** – Boo-Tay / Nothin' better to do / The most / You blew me off / Tobacco spit / Faker / Patty McBride / Give nothing away / Soggy Daisy / Love-less / I hate myself / Naked albino / I wanna live / Why won't you love me.	–	☐
Oct 98.	(cd-ep)	<41701> **CUSTOM GAUGE EP** – Why won't you love me / You blew me off / The most / Guitar playin' woman.	–	☐

			Virgin America	Virgin
Apr 01.	(cd-s)	(VUSCD 195) **YOU BLEW ME OFF (Hager mix) / YOU'RE RUINING MY LIFE / WHY DO I NEED A JOB (live)**	☐	☐
Apr 01.	(cd)	(CDVUS 188) <50135> **BRAINWASHER** – Overture (love theme from Brainwasher) / Brainwasher / If you choose me / Why do I need a job / You never knew (I lied) / Shine / God / Miss you the most / Kiss me / Dog / Limpin' / Devil doll / Gasoline listerine.	☐	☐ Oct00

BARK PSYCHOSIS

Formed: Woodford, East London, England ... 1988 by former schoolmates GRAHAM SUTTON, JOHN LING and MARK SIMNOTT, whose ambitions to be the next NAPALM DEATH shocked classmates and teachers alike at an end of term free day two years previously. In fact, BARK PSYCHOSIS performed their first gig two supporting the aforementioned group's rivals, EXTREME NOISE TERROR. The subsequent exposure led to a deal with indie imprint, 'Cheree', three 45's, 'CLAW HAMMER, 'ALL DIFFERENT THINGS' and 'NOTHING FEELS' being released at the turn of the decade. Taking avant-garde pop extremism to its outer limits, BARK PSYCHOSIS combined elements of shoegazing while drawing inspiration from such leftfield luminaries as SPACEMEN 3, SWANS, JOY DIVISION and latter period TALK TALK! Following the addition of DANIEL GISH (on keyboards) in 1991, the band's next two singles appeared via '3rd Stone', the second of which, 'SCUM' received music press plaudits for its 20 minute-plus sonic textures and hypnotic noise. Moving on up to Virgin subsidiary 'Circa', the band began the arduous task of completing a debut album during which time GISH walked out as inter band tensions reached an all-time high. Early in 1994, preceded by an accompanying single, 'A STREET SCENE', the album, 'HEX' finally hit the shops, although by the time of its release LING had bailed out. GRAHAM SUTTON branched out into the electronic world via, BOYMERANG. • **Covered:** THREE GIRL RHUMBA (Wire).

Album rating: HEX (*8) / INDEPENDENCY collection (*7) / GAME OVER collection (*6)

GRAHAM SUTTON – vocals, samples, etc / **JOHN LING** – bass, samples, etc / **MARK SIMNOTT** – drums

		Cheree	not iss.
Aug 89.	(7"flexi) *(Cheree 5)* **CLAW HAMMER. / (other side by The FURY THINGS)**		
Apr 90.	(12") *(Cheree 6T)* **ALL DIFFERENT THINGS. / BY-BLOW**		
Nov 90.	(12") *(Cheree 10T)* **NOTHING FEELS. / I KNOW**		
	(cd-s+=) *(Cheree 10CD)* – All different things / By-blow.		

— added **DANIEL GISH** – keyboards

		3rd Stone	not iss.
Apr 92.	(12"ep) **MAN MAN. / BLOOD RUSH / TOOLED UP**		
Sep 92.	(12"/cd-s; 22 minutes) **SCUM**		

— now without GISH

		Circa	Plan 9-Caroline
Jan 94.	(10"/cd-s) *(YR A/CD 109)* **A STREET SCENE. / RESERVE SHOT-GUNMAN**		
Feb 94.	(cd/c/lp) *(CIR CD/C/CA 29)* <*CAROL 1753*> **HEX**		
	– The loom / A street scene / Absent friend / Big shot / Fingerspit / Eyes and smiles / Pendulum man.		
May 94.	(12"white/cd-s) *(YR T/CD 117)* **BLUE. / HEX / BIG SHOT**		

— split with LING while the above album was in process of being released, their swansong gig coming in April '94. GRAHAM SUTTON formed electronia act, BOYMERANG (one set, 'Balance Of The Force' 1997)

– compilations, etc. –

Jul 94.	(cd) *3rd Stone;* (<*STONE 010CD*>) **INDEPENDENCY** (early 90's singles)		
Mar 97.	(cd) *3rd Stone;* (<*STONE 031CD*>) **GAME OVER**		
	– Blue / Three girl rhumba / I know / All different things / Man man / Bloodrush / A street scene / Murder city / Scum / Pendulum man (live).		

BASH & POP
(see under ⇒ REPLACEMENTS; 80's section)

BASINGER
(see under ⇒ CHESTERFIELDS; 80's section)

BATTERSHELL

Formed: New York City, New York, USA ... mid 90's by guitar-playing frontwoman TAMMY LYNN, along with JAMIE R BAKER and CHARLIE LAUTH. Led by native Californian LYNN's skilled guitar playing, the bands brand of alternative pop punk soon established them in the Big Apple. A record deal ensued with 'Ng' in 1995, and they wasted no time in releasing their debut EP, 'BEAUTIFUL PRINCESS OF SPIT'. Much touring followed and the band was oft compared to other female-led alternative rock bands such as Chicago's VERUCA SALT. Following their nationwide exposure the group unleashed their debut LP, 'SUNSHINE IN POPOPIA' (1997), a set that showcased their talent for penning a good melody, although still having the punk credentials to give it balls. BAKER subsequently departed the outfit and was superseded on bass duties by the talented HANNAH HEAD. This new line-up continued to entertain the festival circuit, exemplified at 'Lilith Fair' in 1999, where there performance was deemed good enough to feature on the documentary film made about the festival. The same year saw the issue of their second album, 'LUV PUNKS' (named after what fans had dubbed their musical style) and showed that BATTERSHELL had been honing and improving; noteworthy tracks include a sparky cover of Billy Idol's semi-classic, 'WHITE WEDDING'.

Album rating: SUNSHINE IN POPOPIA (*4) / LUV PUNKS (*5)

TAMMY LYNN – vocals, guitar / **JAMIE R. BAKER** – bass, vocals / **CHARLIE LAUTH** – drums

		not iss.	Ng
Nov 95.	(cd-ep) **BEAUTIFUL PRINCESS OF SPIT EP**		
	– Spray / Say goodnight to the cat named after Mozart / Weed (dirty magazine) / Prick.		
Jan 97.	(cd) <*20008*> **SUNSHINE IN POPOPIA**		
	– 4 leaf clover / Lavender Moses / Bee song / Say goodnight to the cat named after Mozart / Po's valentine / Mess / Shower song / Weed (dirty magazine) / Motorcycle marmalade / Marysville.		
Sep 99.	(cd) <*30004-2*> **LUV PUNKS**		
	– Enter freak museum / Circus tragedy / Electric chair / Better now / Luv punks / Radio Romeo / Holy roller / Arizona / White wedding / Japan / Porno star / 2 chords / Dizzy the tattooed dog / Inbred picnic / Exit freak museum.		

BAWL

Formed: Dublin, Ireland ... mid 90's by brothers MARK, DARREN and JASON CULLEN, plus STEPHEN McBRIDE. Surfacing on their own label, 'Dependent', BAWL's first two singles, 'BATHROOM' (STICKY ROCK) and 'GIRLS NIGHT OUT', were released either side of Xmas '95. Ireland's answer to Brit-pop or yet another would-be SMITHS or HOUSEMARTINS successor, the band delivered two further lyrically tongue-in-cheek singles, 'GLEN CAMPBELL NIGHTS' and 'BEYOND SAFE WAYS', the latter of which featured on their debut album, 'YEAR ZERO' (1996).

Album rating: YEAR ZERO (*6)

MARK CULLEN – vocals, guitar / **DARREN CULLEN** – guitar / **STEPHEN McBRIDE** – bass / **JASON CULLEN** – drums

		Dependent	not iss.
Nov 95.	(7") *(BAWL 001)* **BATHROOM. / KITSH**		
Jan 96.	(7"/cd-s) *(DEPE 002/+CD)* **GIRLS NIGHT OUT. / HOW CAN I UPSET YOU / FAT BOY**		
May 96.	(7"/cd-s) *(DEPE 003/+CD)* **GLEN CAMPBELL NIGHTS. / BEST DRESSED GIRL / JUST BECAUSE**		
Aug 96.	(7") *(DEPE 004)* **BEYOND SAFE WAYS. / PARALLEL**		
	(cd-s+=) *(DEPE 004CD)* – Perfect hairstyle / Some people need others (demo).		
Sep 96.	(cd/c/lp) *(DEPA D/M/V 005)* **YEAR ZERO**		
	– Approaching zero / Older and older / My spine hurts / Beyond safe ways / Mistake / Shallow / Sticky rock / Fake it / Ex-boyfriend / Mechanic from Rhyll / Girls = songs / Unfinished / Some people need others / He's all that great about pop.		
Dec 96.	(7"/c-s) *(DEPS S/M 005)* **STICKY ROCK. / LEVER**		
	(cd-s+=) *(DEPSD 005)* – I go wild.		
Feb 97.	(7"/c-s) *(DEPS S/M 006)* **HE'S ALL THAT'S GREAT ABOUT POP. / CROCODILES**		
	(cd-s+=) *(DEPSD 006)* – Bones / Some people need others (acoustic).		

— disbanded after above

BAY (see under ⇒ ARAB STRAP)

BEACH BOYS

The Continuing Story... BRIAN WILSON had become obsessed with outdoing The BEATLES who he saw as a threat, a paranoia that grew stronger after his first forays into the world of LSD. He first took the drug in the summer of '65 and it changed his approach to music, to his whole life in fact, with BRIAN later stating that his mind was opened and it scared the shit out of him. BRIAN then enlisted the unlikely help of erstwhile ad sloganeer Tony Asher to express the lyrical mood of these new pieces, and the result was 'PET SOUNDS'. Released in May '66, it still holds the coveted "best album of all-time" position among many critics, with fragile highlights being 'GOD ONLY KNOWS', 'WOULDN'T IT BE NICE' and 'CAROLINE NO', which perfectly evoked BRIAN's turbulent emotional state. Reportedly devastated at the album's lack of success in his home country (yes, it did hit Top 10) and feeling outdone by The BEATLES' 'Revolver' and DYLAN's 'Blonde On Blonde', he upped his drug use and vowed to go one better, dreaming of the ultimate studio masterpiece. Initially pencilled in for inclusion on 'PET SOUNDS' in its earliest incarnation, 'GOOD VIBRATIONS' was released in October that year and soon became their biggest ever selling single. With its pioneering use of the theramin and complex vocal arrangements, its success vindicated BRIAN's vision of grand sonic tapestries over the formulaic pop that other members (most notably MIKE LOVE and his father) wanted to churn out. Around this time, BRIAN began working on his masterpiece (with self-styled L.A. boho scenester/songwriter VAN DYKE PARKS), which had a working title of 'DUMB ANGEL', later changing to 'SMILE'. The sessions that resulted are the stuff of legend, with BRIAN's mental condition deteriorating rapidly under the weight of his own expectation. Among BRIAN's more whimsical foibles were having a box filled with sand so he could play piano barefoot "like on the beach, man" (Surf's Up, indeed). More worrying was the pathological superstition which saw him attempt to destroy tapes of the abandoned 'SMILE' album, although these did surface later on albums 'SMILEY SMILE', 'HEROES AND VILLAINS' and 'SURF'S UP'. From this point on, BRIAN retreated even further from the world at large and spent much of the following decade in bed. A string of average, occasionally good albums followed with DENNIS emerging as a fairly talented songwriter. Recorded after the band's acrimonious split with 'Capitol', 1971's 'SURF'S UP' was the highlight of this period with its 'SMILE'-era title track and spirited contributions from other band members. DENNIS WILSON's association with the infamous Charles Manson, albeit before he went on his killing spree in 1969, probably brought more attention than any music the band released at this time.

Album rating: PET SOUNDS (*10) / SMILEY SMILE (*7) / WILD HONEY (*6) / FRIENDS (*5) / 20/20 (*6) / SUNFLOWER (*7) / SURF'S UP (*7)

BRIAN WILSON (b.20 Jun'42, Inglewood, California) – vocals, percussion / **CARL WILSON** (b.21 Dec'46) – guitar, vocals / **DENNIS WILSON** (b. 4 Dec'44) – vocals, drums / **MIKE LOVE** (b.15 Mar'44, Baldwin Hills, California) – vocals / **AL JARDINE** (b. 3 Sep'42, Lima, Ohio) – vocals, guitar

Apr 66.	(7"; by BRIAN WILSON *(CL 15438)* <*5610*> **CAROLINE, NO. / SUMMER MEANS NEW LOVE**		32 Mar66

BEACH BOYS (cont)

Apr 66.	(7") (CL 15441) <5602> **SLOOP JOHN B. / YOU'RE SO GOOD TO ME**		2	3 Mar66
	(re-iss. Jun79; CL 16052)			
May 66.	(lp; stereo/mono) <(S+/T 2458)> **PET SOUNDS**		2	10
	– Wouldn't it be nice / You still believe in me / That's not me / Don't talk (put your head on my shoulder) / I'm waiting for the day / Let's go away for awhile / Sloop John B. / God only knows / I know there's no answer / Here today / I just wasn't made for these times / Pet sounds / Caroline, no. (re-iss. Jun81 on 'Greenlight'; GO 2002) (re-iss. May82 on 'Fame'; FA 3018) (re-iss. Aug86 lp/c; EMS/TC-EMS 1179) <(cd-iss. Jun90; 7-48421)> – Hang on to your ego / Trombone Dixie. (re-iss. Nov93 on 'Fame' cd/c; CD/TC FA 3298) (lp re-iss. Dec99 on 'Simply Vinyl'; SVLP 149)			
Jul 66.	(7") (CL 15459) <5706> **GOD ONLY KNOWS. / WOULDN'T IT BE NICE**		2	39 / 8
	(re-iss. Jun79; CL 16053)			
Oct 66.	(7") <5676> **GOOD VIBRATIONS. / LET'S GO AWAY FOR AWHILE**		–	1
Oct 66.	(7") (CL 15475) **GOOD VIBRATIONS. / WENDY**		1	–
	(re-iss. Jun79; CL 16054)			
Apr 67.	(7") (CL 15502) **THEN I KISSED HER. / MOUNTAIN OF LOVE**		4	–
	(re-iss. Jun79; CL 16055)			

Capitol / Brother

Aug 67.	(7") (CL 15510) <1001> **HEROES AND VILLAINS. / YOU'RE WELCOME**		8	12 Jul67
	(re-iss. Jun79; CL 16056)			
Sep 67.	(7"; BRIAN WILSON & MIKE LOVE) (CL 15513) <1002> **GETTIN' HUNGRY. / DEVOTED TO YOU**		–	–
Nov 67.	(lp; stereo/mono) <(S+/T 9001)> **SMILEY SMILE**		9	41 Sep67
	– Heroes and villains / Vegetables / Fall breaks and back to winter / She's goin' bald / Little pad / Good vibrations / With me tonight / Wind chimes / Gettin' hungry / Wonderful / Whistle in. (cd-iss. Nov98 on 'Magic'; 497576-2)			

Capitol / Capitol

Nov 67.	(7") (CL 15521) <2028> **WILD HONEY. / WIND CHIMES**		29	31
	(re-iss. Jun79; CL 16057)			
Dec 67.	(7") <2068> **DARLIN'. / HERE TODAY**		–	19
Jan 68.	(7") (CL 15527) **DARLIN'. / COUNTRY AIR**		11	–
	(re-iss. Jun79; CL 16058)			
Mar 68.	(lp; stereo/mono) <(S+/T 2859)> **WILD HONEY**		7	24 Dec67
	– Wild honey / Aren't you glad / I was made to love her / Country air / A thing or two / Darlin' / I'd love just once to see you / Here comes the night / Let the wind blow / How she boogalooed it / Mama says.			
May 68.	(7") (CL 15545) <2160> **FRIENDS. / LITTLE BIRD**		25	47
	(re-iss. Jun79; CL 16059)			
Jul 68.	(7") (CL 15554) <2239> **DO IT AGAIN. / WAKE THE WORLD**		1	20
	(re-iss. Jun79; CL 16060)			
Sep 68.	(lp; stereo/mono) <(S+/T 2895)> **FRIENDS**		13	Jun68
	– Meant for you / Friends / Wake the world / Be here in the mornin' / When a man needs a woman / Passing by / Anna Lee, the healer / Little bird / Be still / Busy doing nothin' / Diamond head / Transcendental meditation.			
Dec 68.	(7") (CL 15572) <2360> **BLUEBIRDS OVER THE MOUNTAIN. / NEVER LEARN NOT TO LOVE**		33	61
	(re-iss. Jun79; CL 16061)			
Feb 69.	(7") (CL 15584) <2432> **I CAN HEAR MUSIC. / ALL I WANT TO DO**		10	24
	(re-iss. Jun79; CL 16062)			
Feb 69.	(lp) <(EST 133)> **20/20**		3	68
	– Do it again / I can hear music / Bluebirds over the mountain / Be with me / All I want to do / The nearest faraway place / Cottonfields / I went to sleep / Time to get alone / Never learn not to love / Our prayer / Cabinessence.			
Jun 69.	(7") (CL 15598) <2530> **BREAK AWAY. / CELEBRATE THE NEWS**		6	63
	(re-iss. Jun79; CL 16063)			

Stateside / Reprise

Feb 70.	(7") <0894> **ADD SOME MUSIC TO YOUR DAY. / SUSIE CINCINNATTI**		–	64
Sep 70.	(7") <0929> **SLIP ON THROUGH. / THIS WHOLE WORLD**		–	–
Nov 70.	(7") (SS 2181) <0957> **TEARS IN THE MORNING. / IT'S ABOUT TIME**		–	–
Nov 70.	(lp) (SSL 8251) <6382> **SUNFLOWER**		29	Sep70
	– Slip on through / This whole world / Add some music to your day / Got to know the woman / Deirdre / It's about time / Tears in the morning / All I wanna do / Forever / Our sweet love / At my window / Cool, cool water. (re-iss. Nov80 on 'Caribou'; 31773) – Cottonfields. (re-iss. Jul91 on 'Epic' cd/c; 467836-2/-4)			
Dec 70.	(7"; by DENNIS WILSON & RUMBO) (SS 2184) **SOUND OF FREE. / LADY**		–	–
Feb 71.	(7") <0998> **COOL, COOL WATER. / FOREVER**		–	–
Jun 71.	(7") (SS 2190) <1015> **LONG PROMISED ROAD. / DEIRDRE**		–	–
Oct 71.	(7") <1047> **LONG PROMISED ROAD. / TILL I DIE**		–	89
Nov 71.	(7") (SS 2194) **DON'T GO NEAR THE WATER. / STUDENT DEMONSTRATION TIME**		–	–
Nov 71.	(lp) (SSL 10313) <6453> **SURF'S UP**		15	29 Aug71
	– Don't go near the water / Long promised road / Take a load off your feet / Disney girls (1957) / Student demonstration time / Feel flows / Lookin' at tomorrow / A day in the life of a tree / 'Til I die / Surf's up. <re-iss. Nov80 on 'Caribou'; 31774> (re-iss. Jul91 on 'Epic' cd/c; 467835-2/-4)			

BEACHBUGGY

Formed: Doncaster, England ... 1997 by JACK STRAKER, AL B. KIRKEY and the eccentirc double drumming duo of DANNY SICKS and A.D. After several DIY-produced singles on their own imprint, 'Ostrich GT', and some fairly wild gigs, the Yorkshire quartet got their DIY dabblings firmly off the ground with the release of their debut LP, 'UNSAFE ... AT ANY SPEED' (1998), on indie imprint 'Sympathy For The Record Industry'. A competent effort showcasing their garage punk credentials and surfer rock stance, although unfortunately not to the tastes of their native music critics, prompting the band to relocate stateside to Chicago. Here they honed their sound further, and with the help of veteran indie knob-twiddler, STEVE ALBINI, they self-financed the studio time for their second full-length outing, 'SPORT FURY' (2001). A more satisfying listen than its predecessor, it displayed that the group had more miles in the musical tank, and more ideas to boot.

Album rating: UNSAFE.. AT ANY SPEED! (*5) / SPORT FURY (*5)

JACK STRAKER – vocals, guitar / **AL B. KIRKEY** – bass / **DANNY SICKS** – drums / **A.D.** – drums

Ostrich G.T. / not iss.

1997.	(7"amber) (GT 0) **CAN'T GET ENOUGH. / THERE'S A PLACE (IN MY HEART) / G.T.O.**		–
1997.	(7"red) (GT 2) **CHRYSLER 440. / FUEL INJECTION (IT'S BETTER) / DE TOMASO**		–
1997.	(7"colrd) (GT 4) **GENERAL ELECTRIC PILOT. / BONNEVILLE / (WE DON'T HAVE) A MACHINE**		–

Sympathy F / Sympathy F

May 98.	(7") <(SFTRI 499)> **FIREBIRD SPECIAL. / MIDWEST**		
Sep 98.	(cd/lp) <(SFTRI 539 CD/LP)> **UNSAFE.. AT ANY SPEED**		
	– Radio ad / Kill Straker! / Heavy hitter / General electric pilot / San Francisco / Hey! Jack / Firebird special / Aluminium / Four four O / Quarter mile machine / The driver.		

555 / not iss.

Jun 99.	(7") (555/18) **YA JUST A LITTLE PUNK. / THE CHAUFFEUR**		–

Poptones / Poptones

May 01.	(7") (MC 5039S) **KICKIN' BACK. / I GOT ROOT BEER**		–
May 01.	(cd) (<MC 5039CD>) **SPORT FURY**		Apr02
	– Kickin' back / Bad guys wear black / Touch my stuff (you can die) / From the south / Science fiction / Godspeed my friend / It might be the jets / The fastest time / Just a little punk / Cuba / Tom's dead / Radio ad (Italia).		
Oct 01.	(7") (MC 5056S) **FROM THE SOUTH. / INFOMATION**		–
May 02.	(cd-ep) (MC 5072SCD) **KICKIN' BACK EP**		–
	– Kickin' back / Ha! ha! / Take a ride / I got root beer / Infomation.		

BEACHWOOD SPARKS

Formed: Los Angeles, California, USA ... June 1998 by CHRIS GUNST, DAVE SCHER, BRENT RADEMAKER, PETER KINNE, JOSH SCHWARTZ and AARON SPERSKE. The band's first release 'DESERT SKIES', came from the stable of 'Bomp!', while follow-up, 'MIDSUMMER DAYDREAM', was their inauguration for 'Sub Pop'. The 45 was stunning in places, however, its lack of cohesion made it ultimately unsatisfying. Inspired by the American west coast sound of the 60's, BEACHWOOD SPARKS' self-titled debut album, released in 2000, was a refreshing departure from the usual hardcore grunge being produced by 'Sup Pop'. The music on 'BEACHWOOD SPARKS' was gentle and laid back reminiscent of the psychedelic country rock of BUFFALO SPRINGFIELD, both rootsy and uplifting. 2001 saw the release of 'ONCE WE WERE TREES' on which the band retained the same formula and applied it to more polished and masterly songs further enhancing their reputation as the leaders of this growing sub-genre. The 2002 EP, 'MAKE THE COWBOY ROBOTS CRY', saw a slight tweaking of the sound that had served the band so well on their previous two efforts. Like the debut, the band tried to encompass many different sounds resulting in a confusing collection of songs.

Album rating: BEACHWOOD SPARKS (*6) / ONCE WE WERE TREES (*7)

CHRIS GUNST – vocals, guitar (ex-STRICTLY BALLROOM) / **JOSH SCHWARTZ** – vocals, guitar / **DAVE SCHER** – slide guitar, keyboards / **BRENT RADEMAKER** – bass (ex-FURTHER) / **PETE "SLEIGHER" KINNE** – percussion / **AARON SPERSKE** – drums (of LILYS) repl. TOM SANFORD

not iss. / Bomp!

Oct 98.	(7") <BMP 148> **DESERT SKIES. / MAKE IT TOGETHER**	–	
	(UK-iss.May00; same as US)		

Sub Pop / Sub Pop

May 99.	(7") <SP 458A> **MIDSUMMER DAYDREAM. / WINDOWS '65**	–	–
—	KINNE + SCHWARTZ departed (the latter formed NORTHERN LIGHTS)		
Mar 00.	(cd) <(SPCD 503)> **BEACHWOOD SPARKS**		
	– Desert skies / Ballad of never rider / Silver morning after / Singing butterfly / Sister Rose / This is what it feels like / Canyon ride / The reminder / The calming seas / New county / Something I don't recognize / Old sea miner / See, oh three / Sleeping butterfly. <(lp-iss.Jul00 on 'Bomp!'; BLP 4077)>		

Houston Party / not iss.

Mar 01.	(7") (HPRV 027) **ONCE WE WERE TREES. / WAKE UP LITTLE SUSUE**		–

Rough Trade / Sub Pop

Oct 01.	(cd-ep) (RTRADESCD 035) **BY YOUR SIDE / THE SUN SURROUNDS ME / QUIETLY BE / CLOSE THE DOOR LIGHTLY WHEN YOU GO**		–
Oct 01.	(cd/d-lp) (RTRADE CD/LP 036) <SPCD 545> **ONCE WE WERE TREES**		
	– Germination / Confusion is nothing new / The sun surrounds me / You take the gold / Hearts mend / Let it run / Old manatee / The hustler / Yer selfish ways / By your side / Close your eyes / Banjo press conference / Jugglers' revenge / The good night whistle / Once we were trees. (cd re-iss. May02; same)		
Jun 02.	(m-cd) (RTRADESCD 057) <SPCD 593> **MAKE THE COWBOYS ROBOTS CRY**		May02
	– Drinkswater / Hibernation / Ponce de Leon blues / Sing your thoughts / Galapagos / Ghost dance 1492.		

BEAR

Formed: Sheffield, England . . . summer 1994 by CHRIS TROUT, a veteran of "real" indie outfits including mid-80's starter, KILGORE TROUT (two KT 12"ep's surfaced:- 1986's 'STICK IT IN THE BANK MAN' and 1989's 'BAD PUDDINGS'). AC TEMPLE would request his services (as bass player) between '86 and '91, while the man enjoyed spells with SPOONFED HYBRID (with former PALE SAINTS mainman, IAN MASTERS), COPING SAW and more recently, LAZERBOY. TROUT established his own lo-fi psychedelia in the form of BEAR debut 'DISNEYTIME' (1996). The set ranged from FLAMING LIPS-esque noisiness to dried out post-rock psyche, with subliminal, drug-induced sounds floating, as if they had not yet found sanctuary at the bottom of TROUT's open-ended ocean. He surfaced again in 1998 with 'SCHADENFREUDE' and in 1999 with the stranger than strange single 30-minute track CD album, 'THE SHORTEST DAY'. • **Note:** Not to be confused with 70's 'Verve' act from Boston (w/ ERIC KAZ) who issued 'Greetings, Children Of Paradise'.

Album rating: DISNEYTIME (*5) / SCHADENFREUDE (*5) / THE SHORTEST DAY mini (*6)

CHRIS TROUT – vocals, guitar / **SALLY CREWE** (b. New York, USA) – bass, vocals / **MARK LOOSE PARSONS** – drums (ex-KILGORE TROUT)

		own label	not iss.
Feb 95.	(cd-s) **TRACKS** – Counting / Never die / Not even people.	☐	-

		Mook	not iss.
Jul 95.	(7"; by COPING SAW) (MKO1-1) **SLAMINA. / ROCK OF ANGELS**	☐	-

		Che	not iss.
Jul 95.	(7") (che 34) **IF THERE'S SUCH A THING AS ANGELS. /** (other track by Bardo Pond)	☐	-

—— TROUT recruited **DUNCAN WHEAT** – bass / **ROSS ORTON** – drums – SALLY CREWE (now a UK resident) subsequently formed OSCAR and released 7":- 'STARTING LINE'

Nov 95.	(7") (X10 03) **DISPOSABLE. /** (other by Backwater) (above issued on 'Delete X-Ten')	☐	-
Jan 96.	(7"ep) (che 45) **BUGS** – Bugs / Backbone / Sandcastle.	☐	-
May 96.	(cd) (che 58) **DISNEYTIME** – Mess of my wires / Exing boxes / Unlucky penny / Dogs in Heaven / Bugs / A cure for everyday life / Strongest arms / Disposable / Backbone / Disneytime.	☐	-

—— TROUT enlisted to tour/promote **JAMIE WOOD** – bass / **JIM TAYLOR** – drums, trumpet; repl. ANDY PYNE (ex-UNION WIRELESS)

		Vespertine	not iss.
Apr 98.	(7"m) (VES 005) **ZERO ONE TO CONTROL. / SONG-U-LIKE / BUCKLEY**	☐	-
May 98.	(cd) (VES 006) **SCHADENFREUDE** – Binary / Zero one to control / Taxi for Lester Bangs / Roses are blue / Sign of the dog / Sally-James / Day return to nowhere / Arse biscuit / Counting chickens / Everything is fine / Already there / Let our best intentions shine / Reichswagen.	☐	-

—— added live **ANNA HAWKINS** – keyboards (+ studio) + **ZAC NELLIST** – guitar

		Bear	not iss.
Feb 99.	(m-cd) **THE SHORTEST DAY** – The shortest day.	☐	-

—— new live keyboard-player **MICHAEL ASH**

BEATLES

The Continuing Story... 'RUBBER SOUL' (1965), written and recorded in just over a month, was the sound of The BEATLES in flux, shedding their clean cut image and interpreting the influence of BOB DYLAN's pioneering folk-rock experiments. Despite the transformation taking place, the sound was more fluid and assured, the songwriting more mature. LENNON's 'IN MY LIFE' was beautifully bittersweet while McCARTNEY almost equalled 'YESTERDAY' with 'MICHELLE' and the lilting 'NORWEGIAN WOOD' saw HARRISON's first forays into sitar work. The album was sandwiched between pioneering double A-sided singles 'DAY TRIPPER' / 'WE CAN WORK IT OUT' (1965) and 'PAPERBACK WRITER' / 'RAIN' (1966). 'RAIN' was the first overtly psychedelic BEATLES record, innovative in its use of rhythm and featuring an undulating LENNON vocal (a style much mimicked by many of todays crop of young bands). Its potential was fully realised on 'REVOLVER' (1966), oft cited as The BEATLES' pinnacle achievement and as one of the best albums ever made. McCARTNEY excelled himself with the string-cloaked melancholy of 'ELEANOR RIGBY', while HARRISON's biting 'TAXMAN' kicked off the album in strident style. But it was the psychedelic numbers which made most impact. 'SHE SAID SHE SAID' was a swirling piece of trip-pop, while 'TOMORROW NEVER KNOWS' remains one of the most bizarre and enigmatic songs in The BEATLES' canon. With a working title of 'THE VOID', the song was based on one of LENNON's first profound acid trips and was partly inspired by the ancient religious text beloved of hippies at the time, 'The Tibetan Book Of The Dead'. With a hypnotic drum sound that many have since tried and failed to recreate, backwards guitar that sounded like a flock of screeching pterodactyls and LENNON's mantra-like vocals, the record set a precedent in psychedelic rock. At this stage The BEATLES were already preoccupied with the possibilities of the recording studio and significantly, the band played their last gig in San Francisco's Candlestick Park the same month 'REVOLVER' was released. Ensconced in Abbey Road Studios, the band came up with the double A-side, 'PENNY LANE' / 'STRAWBERRY FIELDS FOREVER'. Released in February '67, the single's effects-laden innovation was a taster for The BEATLES' much heralded psychedelic concept album 'SGT. PEPPER'S LONELY HEARTS CLUB BAND'. Its release coinciding perfectly with the fabled 1967 'Summer Of Love', the record was a landmark in new studio technique. Utilising the (then) pioneering four-track recording process, the band painstakingly pieced together ornate pieces of sonic intricacy that set new standards. It contained many classics such as 'LUCY IN THE SKY WITH DIAMONDS' (wrongly thought by many to be about L.S.D.), 'SHE'S LEAVING HOME' and the never-ending 'A DAY IN THE LIFE', complete with prolonged intentionally stuck-in-the-groove outro. Fans and critics alike made it "their greatest album of all time", although many others thought it too overblown as well as over-produced. A month later, the anthemic 'ALL YOU NEED IS LOVE' gave them another No.1, helped no doubt by its simultaneous worldwide TV broadcast. The death of BRIAN EPSTEIN cast a shadow over the celebrations but the band moved on, filming/recording 'MAGICAL MYTERY TOUR' (1967). A trippy film and soundtrack inspired by KEN KESEY and his bunch of technicolour minstrels, it contained the infamous LENNON-penned surrealism of 'I AM THE WALRUS'. Screened on British TV on Boxing Day 1967, the film was almost universally panned. Unbowed, The BEATLES decamped to India for spiritual retreat with the Maharishi Mahesh Yogi, during which time they accumulated much of the material that would form the 'WHITE ALBUM'. Upon their return to English shores, they set about forming the 'Apple Corporation', which would handle all the business dealings of the band as well as functioning as a label for The BEATLES and likeminded talent. The first release was 'HEY JUDE' / 'REVOLUTION' (1968), the former a rousing torch song, the latter a stinging attack by LENNON on would-be radicals. Eventually released in November '68, 'THE BEATLES (White Album)' was a sprawling double set recorded in an environment of tension and breakdown of inter-band communications. Yet it contained some of The BEATLES finest songs, 'HARRISON's solemn 'WHILE MY GUITAR GENTLY WEEPS', LENNON's gorgeous 'DEAR PRUDENCE' and 'JULIA', a moving tribute to his mother. The album also included the cryptic genius of LENNON's 'HAPPINESS IS A WARM GUN' while 'REVOLUTION No.9' was The BEATLES at their most defiantly experimental.

Album rating: RUBBER SOUL (*9) / REVOLVER (*10) / SGT. PEPPER'S LONELY HEARTS CLUB BAND (*10) / MAGICAL MYSTERY TOUR (*8) / THE BEATLES 'White Album' (*10)

Dec 65.	(7") (R 5389) <5555> **DAY TRIPPER. / WE CAN WORK IT OUT**	1	5 1

(re-iss. Dec85; same) (re-iss. cd-s.1989)

Dec 65.	(lp; mono)(lp; stereo) (PMC 1267)(PCS 3075) <2442> **RUBBER SOUL** – Drive my car / Norwegian wood (this bird has flown) / You won't see me / Nowhere man / Think for yourself / The word / Michelle / What goes on / Girl / I'm looking through you / In my life / Wait / If I needed someone / Run for your life. (c-iss.1970's) (cd-iss. Apr87; CDP 746440-2); hit UK No.60) (re-iss. Nov88 lp/c; PMC/TC-PMC 1267)	1	1
Feb 66.	(7") <5587> **NOWHERE MAN. / WHAT GOES ON**	-	3 81
Jun 66.	(7") (R 5452) <5651> **PAPERBACK WRITER. / RAIN**	1	1 23

(re-iss. Mar76; same); hit No.23) (re-iss. Jun86; same) (re-iss. cd-s.1989)

Aug 66.	(7") (R 5493) <5715> **YELLOW SUBMARINE. / ELEANOR RIGBY**	1	2 11

(re-iss. Aug86; same); hit No.63) (re-iss. cd-s.1989)

Aug 66.	(lp; mono/stereo) (PMC/PCS 7009) <2576> **REVOLVER** – Taxman / Love you to / I want to tell you / Eleanor Rigby / Here, there and everywhere / Good day sunshine / For no one / Got to get you into my life / I'm only sleeping / She said she said / And your bird can sing / Doctor Robert / Tomorrow never knows / Yellow submarine. (c-iss.1970's) (cd-iss. Apr87; CDP 746441-2); hit UK No.55) (re-iss. Nov88 lp/c; PMC/TC-PMC 7009)	1	1
Feb 67.	(7") (R 5570) <5810> **PENNY LANE. / STRAWBERRY FIELDS FOREVER**	2	1 8

(re-iss. Mar76; same); hit No.32) (re-iss. Feb87; same); hit No.65) (re-iss. cd-s.1989)

Jun 67.	(lp; mono/stereo) (PMC/PCS 7027) <2653> **SGT. PEPPER'S LONELY HEARTS CLUB BAND** – Sgt.Pepper's lonely hearts club band / With a little help from my friends / Lucy in the sky with diamonds / Getting better / Fixing a hole / She's leaving home / Being for the benefit of Mr.Kite / Within you without you / When I'm sixty-four / Lovely Rita / Good morning, good morning / Sgt. Pepper's lonely hearts club band (reprise) / A day in the life. (c-iss.1970's) (cd-iss. Jun87; CDP 746442-2); hit UK No.3) (re-iss. Nov88 lp/c; PMC/TC-PMC 7027) (re-iss. Jun92; same); hit UK No.6)	1	1
Jul 67.	(7") (R 5620) <5964> **ALL YOU NEED IS LOVE. / BABY YOU'RE A RICH MAN**	1	1 34

(re-iss. Jul87; same); hit No.47) (re-iss. cd-s.1989)

Nov 67.	(7") (R 5655) <2056> **HELLO GOODBYE. / I AM THE WALRUS**	1	1 56

(re-iss. Nov87; same); hit No.63) (re-iss. cd-s.1989)

Dec 67.	(d7"ep; stereo/mono) (S+/MMT 1) **MAGICAL MYSTERY TOUR** – Magical mystery tour / Your mother should know / Flying / Fool on the hill / Blue Jay way / I am the walrus.	2	-
Dec 67.	(lp) (imported) <2835> **MAGICAL MYSTERY TOUR (Soundtrack)** – (above UK-ep, plus 1967 singles) (UK-iss.Oct76, cd-iss. Sep87; CDP 748 062-2); hit UK 52)	31	1

BEATLES (cont)

Mar 68. (7") (R 5675) <2138> **LADY MADONNA. / THE INNER LIGHT** | 1 | 4 |
| | | 96 |

(re-iss. Mar88; same); hit No.67) (re-iss. cd-s.1989)

Aug 68. (7") (R 5722) <2276> **HEY JUDE. / REVOLUTION** | Apple 1 | Apple 1 |
| | | 12 |

(re-iss. Mar76; same); hit No.12) (re-iss. Aug88; same); hit No.52) (re-iss. cd-s.1989)

Nov 68. (d-lp; mono/stereo) (PMC/PCS 7067-8) <101> **THE BEATLES (White Album)** | 1 | 1 |

– Back in the U.S.S.R / Dear Prudence / Glass onion / Ob-la-di-ob-la-da / Wild honey pie / The continuing story of Bungalow Bill / While my guitar gently weeps / Happiness is a warm gun / Martha my dear / I'm so tired / Blackbird / Piggies / Rocky raccoon / Don't pass me by / Why don't we do it in the road / I will / Julia / Birthday / Yer blues / Mother nature's son / Everybody's got something to hide except me and my monkey / Sexy Sadie / Helter skelter / Long long long / Revolution 1 / Honey pie / Savoy truffle / Cry baby cry / Revolution 9 / Good night. (re-iss. Sep78 white-lp; same) (cd-iss. Aug87; CDP CDS 746443-2); hit UK No.18) (re-iss. Nov88 lp/c; PCS/TCPCS 7067) (d-cd re-iss. Nov98; 496895-2)

BEATNIK FILMSTARS

Formed: Bristol, England... late 1990 by ANDREW JARRETT, JON KENT, ANDY HENDERSON and IAN ROUGHLY – who subsequently became a reassembled 5-piece with the addition of co-writer JEZ FRANCIS – having all moved to the city from other parts of the country. However, JARRETT and KENT had originally cut their teeth with The GROOVE FARM who delivered a plethora of garage-type surf-pop singles from 1986. Subsequently inspired by the likes of the PALE SAINTS, TEENAGE FANCLUB and GALAXIE 500, the BEATNIK FILMSTARS made a concerted effort to musically distance themselves from the prevailing "baggy" and "shoegazing" scenes, setting up their own 'Big Sky' label after intitially being courted by 'Rough Trade'. Low-key rather than Lo-Fi at this stage in their career, the band garnered an initial buzz of acclaim with the guitar soundscapes of vinyl debut, 'MAHARISHI' (1991). After a further couple of 45's, the BEATNIK posse – JARRETT, FRANCIS, ROUGHLY, JOHN AUSTIN and TIM RIPPINGTON – signed a long-term deal with 'La-Di-Da', the indie label finally issuing their first album proper (although it was a singles compilation!), 'LAID BACK AND ENGLISH', in the summer of '94. As the aforementioned FRANCIS began to redirect the band through the increasing influence of his songwriting, The BEATNIK FILMSTARS (TOM ADAMS having replaced ROUGHLY) made more of an impact with a fresh collection, 'ASTRONAUT HOUSE', which included the memorably titled single, 'APATHETIC ENGLISH SWINE'. The latter three releases were licensed to 'Caroline' in the States, the band (whose eclectic style was now more akin to GUIDED BY VOICES) subsequently concentrating on the larger American market; 1997 saw the US-only release (on 'Merge') of 'IN HOSPITABLE'. In 1999, JARRETT, AUSTIN and ADAMS resurfaced as KYOKO, a slow-fi, very laid back, mellow pop band – in fact, according to JARRETT himself "they were so quiet, it was almost impossible to hear them!". The man himself went on to front another "Mobstar" outfit (his own label), The BLUEBEAR, a experimental country-tinged lo-fi pop act lying somewhere between BADLY DRAWN BOY, The SMITHS and LAMBCHOP. • **Covers:** Groove Farm: NO FRIEND OF MINE (Sparkles) / RED DRESS (Alvin Stardust) / EPISTLE TO DIPPY (Donovan) / DANNY SAYS (Ramones) / STEP INSIDE LOVE (Cilla Black) / VALLERI (Monkees) / Beatnik Filmstars: WHEN PEOPLE ARE DEAD (Go-Betweens) / TUGBOAT (Galaxie 500) / GOOD THINGS, PROUD MAN (Sebadoh) / Kyoko: HE DISPENSES WITH TIMID AFTERTHOUGHTS (Steward) / LAST CHRISTMAS (Wham!) / PROTECTION (Massive Attack) / TORCH (Soft Cell) / Bluebear: I WANT A DOG (Pet Shop Boys).

Album rating: Groove Farm: ALVIN IS KING (*5) / PLUG (THE STORY OF POP SO FAR) (*5) / TOTALLY TOTAL (*6) / THE BEST PARTS VOLUME ONE compilation (*7) / Beatnik Filmstars: MAHARISHI mini (*7) / LAID BACK AND ENGLISH compilation (*5) / ASTRONAUT HOUSE (*7) / BEEZER compilation (*5) / ALL POPSTARS ARE TALENTLESS SLAGS mini (*6) / PHASE 3 (*5) / IN HOSPITABLE (*6) / BOSS DISQUE (*6) / Kyoko: CO-INCIDENTAL MUSIC (*6) / PURE UNDISCO (*6) / Bluebear: FOOD FIGHT AT THE LAST CHANCE SALOON (*6)

GROOVE FARM

ANDREW JARRETT – vocals, guitar / **JON KENT** – guitars / **CHAD** – bass / **DARREN PRICE** – drums

Raving Pop Blast / not iss.

Mar 87. (7"ep) (RPBGF 001) **SORE HEADS AND HAPPY HEARTS**
– Heaven is blue / It always rains on Sunday / God's tears / My feet keep slipping.

— **RUPERT TAYLOR** – organ, bass; repl. CHAD

Nov 87. (7"ep) (RPBGF 002) **ONLY THE MOST IGNORANT GUTLESS SHEEP-BRAINED POLTROON CAN DENY THEM NOW**
– In the summertime / Captain Fantastic / Couldn't get to sleep / Surfin' impossible.

— (see the SEA URCHINS for a 7"flexi 'BABY BLUE MARINE' on 'Kavatch')

Subway / not iss.

Nov 87. (7") (SUBWAY 15) **SURFIN' INTO YOUR HEART. / ME! ME! ME!**
(12"ep+=) (SUBWAY 15T) – **GOING BANANAS WITH THE GROOVE FARM** – Turning me upside down / Hawaii 5 seconds / What better way to be / No friend of mine.

— **JEZ BUTLER** – drums; repl. DARREN

May 88. (12"ep) (SUBWAY 19T) **THE BIG PLASTIC EXPLOSION!**
– The big black explosion (it's alright, it's alright) / Nancy Sinatra / Riot on Sunset Strip / Baby blue marine / Red dress.

Oct 88. (10"ep) (SUBWAY 22N) **DRIVING IN YOUR NEW CAR**
– Driving in your car (mini mix) / Expanding reindeer / I can't dance with you / Epistle to dippy.

Nov 88. (lp) (SUBORG 9) **ALVIN IS KING**
– (Out of my mind) Over you / An average day in the life / What better way to be / Empty heart / Back of my mind / Timebomb! / Sad for you / Driving in your new car / The time is now / (I can't stand) Another sunny day.

— ('HEAVEN IS BLUE' red 7"flexi was given free with Woosh fanzine 006 – other track by ESMERELDA'S KITE – 'Vampire Girl')

Raving Pop Blast / not iss.

Apr 89. (12"ep) (RAVE 1T) **HATE US AND WE'LL LOVE YOU TO DEATH**
– Cloud 8 / Strum / She is so / Shine / Out of my mind over you (live).

Sep 89. (lp) (RAVE 005LP) **PLUG (THE STORY OF POP SO FAR)**
– I'm never going to fall in love again / I don't blame you / Please don't make me unhappy / World would die for you / Number one / It's not that I can't it's just that I don't want to / No one like you / It might not mean that much to you but it means a lot to me / Corrupt / Drag me under / Discotheque / I don't like you (but I can't get used to it) / Forever is a long time / Plug.

1990. (ltd-7"ep) (RAVE 20) **BAGISM EP**
– The best part of being with you (live) / Captain Fantastic (live) / Surfin' into your heart (live) / Danny says (radio session).

– compilations, etc. –

Feb 01. (cd) Mobstar; (MOBSTAR 015) **TOTALLY TOTAL! (LIVE 86-90)**
– live:- Cloud 8 / Captain Fantastic / Surfin' into your heart / Baby blue marine / Don't you try that old routine on me / Couldn't get to sleep / Back of my mind / Crazy day sunshine girl / Nancy Sinatra / Heaven is blue / Timebomb! / Stop / The big black plastic explosion (it's alright it's alright) / Surfin' into your heart / Surfin' impossible / The best part of being with you / It always rains on Sunday / demos:- Valleri / Get out of my life / Turning me upside down / Captain Fantastic / Heaven is blue / Oh gosh! / Surfin' impossible! / Step inside love / You can't deny it, can you? / Basil / Something's strange about the rain.

Apr 01. (cd) Mobstar; (MOBSTAR 018) **THE BEST PARTS VOLUME 1**
– Heaven is blue / Just a silly phase I'm going through / Baby blue marine (session) / Baby please don't make me happy / The best part of being with you / Sad for you (alt.) / What better way to be (4-track demo) / It always rains on Sunday / Strum / Captain Fantastic (session) / Baby blue marine (flexi disc version) / Surfin' into your heart (live) / The big black plastic explosion (alt.) / God's tears / Couldn't get to sleep / Basil / Crazy day sunshine girl / It might not mean that much to you / Nancy Sinatra (alt.) / Turning me upside down (session) / In the summertime / No one like you.

BEATNIK FILMSTARS

ANDREW JARRETT – vocals, guitar, etc. / **JON KENT** – guitar / **ANDY HENDERSON** – bass / **IAN ROUGHLY** – drums

Big Sky / not iss.

May 91. (m-lp) (BS 001) **MAHARISHI**
– Jazz / More / Down / Brighter / Ian Day / Pop girl / Hurt / Long way to go / Breakable. (cd-iss. 1999 on 'Mobstar' +=; MOBSTAR 014) – Pop girl (live) / Tugboat (live) / Diseaser 2 / Just flowers / Institutionalised / You're so beautiful / Higherplane.

Summershine / not iss.

Jan 92. (7") (SHINE 016) **CLOTHES. / WHEN PEOPLE ARE DEAD**

Vinyl Japan / not iss.

Sep 92. (12"ep) (TASK 12) **THEMES FROM FOREVERDRONE**
– Missed / Snowdrifter / 9 or 7 / Moreover.

— **JOHN AUSTIN** – guitar, etc; repl. KENT

— **JERRY 'JEZ' FRANCIS** – bass; repl. HENDERSON

— added **TIM RIPPINGTON** – guitar

La-Di-Da / Caroline

Jul 93. (7"orange-ep) (LADIDA 026) **REVOLT INTO STYLE**
– Revolt into style / Ruminants' diseases / Sing Elvis / Coup de soleil.

Nov 93. (7"purple-ep) (LADIDA 029) **LAP DOG KISS**
– Charlie Batman / Totally lost control completely / 8 sq. ft. six / Ill book No.3.

Dec 93. (7"clear-flexi) (TRAN 004) **SUMMER PARTY II BOMB**
– Killing cowboys / Gane's space nitemare / Diseaser 3.
(above issued on 'Tranquil')

Jun 94. (lp/cd) (LADIDA 027/+CD) <CAROL 9400-2> **LAID BACK AND ENGLISH** (compilation of singles)
– Ciao America / You can't fake sadness / Clean / Kick in the head / Sick / Tearing apart my world / Haircut / Skill / Revolt into style / Follow cats / Missed / Ambulance / Swillyagro / Orange / Band A / Diseaser 399. (10"m-lp-iss.1998 on 'Mobstar'; MOBSTAR 009)

Jul 94. (7") (LADIDA 036) **APATHETIC ENGLISH SWINE. / GUM / CLOTHES** (new version)

Sep 94. (cd) (LADIDA 037) <9403> **ASTRONAUT HOUSE** Apr95
– La fruitmousse / Slag dogs / Disco dogs / Wreck my style / Astronaut house / Kefpler's first law / Apathetic english swine / We don't want to / Protein + / What goes around comes around / New improved formula / Best idea probably / (Beat) Clear (beat) clear (beat) clear.

— **TOM ADAMS** – drums; repl. ROUGHLY

Lo-Fi / not iss.

1995. (7"ep) (LOW 5) **BRIDEGROOMS** French
– Albert Trumans last xxxmas / Pop scum (French version) / The party / My alter ego.

not iss. / Slumberland

May 95. (7"ep; some pink) <SLR 43> **PINK NOIZE EP**
– 50/50 split / White relief / Flake / National pool drama / Raw

BEATNIK FILMSTARS (cont)

		Mobstar	No-Life
1995.	(7"white/blue-ep) *(MOBSTAR 001)* **BIGOT SPONGER HAIRCUT POLICY. / DOGSTAR / POP SCUM (no-fi version)**	☐	-
1995.	(7"red-ep) *(MOBSTAR 003)* **NEW BOYFRIEND AND BLACK SUIT. / VICIOUS BOOKSELLER / ZETLAND HARDWARE / LIFE WITH THE LIONS**	☐	-
1996.	(7"white-ep) *(MOBSTAR 006)* **SUPREMER QUEENER. / I AM A PIONEER / SEVENTIES FLICK / A CRAZE EXPLODING**	☐	-
1996.	(7"ep) *(HAPPY 09)* **BLUE NOIZE EP**	☐	-

– Pilot Jack Vanderbelt / Chips / Always meet in a light grey place / Blue noize / Chocolate mouth.
(above issued on 'Happy-Go-Lucky')

Jan 97. (m-cd) *(MOBSTAR 008CD)* <NLCD 14> **PHASE 3**
– Milk / The family that plays together / Favourite stuff / A guide for a lonely gunman / Climbing mountains / New jam shoes / While bloke with skin / Rumpus throw / Three down / Disco-tech / Wing off a plane / New boyfriend and black suit / Seventies flick / I won't wait / Undermining. *(m-lp-iss.May97 on 'No-Life'; NLLP 3)*

Mobstar Scratch

Jun 97. (m-cd) *(MOBSTAR 009)* <SCRATCH 27> **ALL POPSTARS ARE TALENTLESS SLAGS**
– Wasted / Pilot Jack Harrison / Faze down face down / 13th annual showdown / Eight dollar haircut / Hopeless will do battle / Tense / I am a pioneer.

Noise-o-lution Merge

Jun 97. (7"ep) <MRG 122> **OFF-WHITE NOIZE EP**
– Star in descent / Shepherds' breath / Off-white noize / Our celestial pilot / Free expression protest song / (interlude)(reprise) / Trust me, I'm a doctor / Wrong-piano.

Sep 97. (cd) <MRG 125> **IN HOSPITABLE**
– Phone kids (edit) / Hep boys (into krautrock) / Artist v star / Ransack the misfits / Look up and be amazed / Wrong / Footstands / Buffalo Bill haircut / Atlas / Now I'm a millionaire / 0, minus 16 minus 3-0 / My incident free life / Geiger water deep / Skiving in mono / Everything is relative – This is a take / Mess / Is this is rad? / Lifestyles of the rich and famous / Fracture / Phone kids (complete).

––– now without RIPPINGTON

Sep 98. (cd) *(NOLCD 45)* <MRG 145> **BOSS DISQUE**
– Nature of things (sick leave scamps) / Hairstyle of a smug bastard / Less than one in ten / Our eyes have rays / Tenancy "hustle" blues / Steve A / Life amongst the cowboys / Let's get entertainment / Pop drama (camp it up) / Chicago road repairs / Try some to see / Squeamish / Better in space / Extreme relatives / Romance's final image / I can tame lions / Leisure / Free hearing aids for the blind / Not now and not never / Consolation to a bar room socialist / His part in the death of a lottery winner / Goodbye Miss Barcelona. *(hidden track+=)* – Fickle pop fans.

––– the band evolved into KYOKO

– compilations, etc. –

Feb 96. (cd) *Mobstar; (MOBSTAR 005) / Slumberland; <SLR 58>* **BEEZER (A COLLECTION OF EP'S SESSIONS & OUT-TAKES)**
– Bigot Sponger haircut policy / Tearing apart my world / 8 sq. ft. six acoustic / Revolt into style / Flake / Vicious bookseller / 50/50 split / Charlie Batman / White relief / Skill / My alter ego / Totally lost control completely / Albert Trumans last Xmas / Sing Elvis / Blind painter injured / Raw / The party / Gane's space nightmare / Diseaser / Gum / Dog star / Killing cowboys / National pool drama.

1999. (ltd; m-cd) *Mobstar; (MOBSTAR 012)* **CHICAGO NOISE (live)**
– Now I'm a millionaire / Steve A / Ransack the misfits / Artist v star / Mess / New jam shoes / Hep boys (into krautrock) / Pop dramas (camp it up).

KYOKO

ANDREW JARRETT – vocals, guitar / **JOHN AUSTIN** – piano, guitar / **TOM ADAMS** – drums

Mobstar not iss.

Jun 99. (m-cd) *(MOBSTAR 013)* **ONE: MINI**
– Yellow / 1.1.53 / Magic hands / Trip up a number / Stars / Facing up reality / H.bond / Treat you better.

Nov 99. (7"m) *(MOBSTAR 016)* **17 STITCHES. / LAY ON YOUR BACK / POSTCARDS**

555 Music not iss.

Jan 01. (cd) *(555CD 22)* **CO-INCIDENTAL MUSIC**
– Track one / Boats / Reality dawns on a second rate sit-com actor / He dispenses with timid afterthoughts / Milk is harmless / A mile to save your neck / P.E.T.S. / Yellow (Grangeer's lonespaceranger mix) / Better days! coming now / Track ten / Ex-filmstar.

Pet Sounds not iss.

Mar 01. (cd) *(PETO 024CD)* **UNPURE DISCO**
– Southville to the sun / The stars are full of lies / Queens (an unusual burst of optimism) / Drunk / Fireman / Keep it to yourself / Slow handshake / Boy cowboy / Break every bone / Saturday night outfit / Melt.

BLUEBEAR

ANDREW JARRETT and various guest personnel

Mobstar not iss.

Feb 02. (cd-ep) *(MOBSTAR 026)* **BRAIN DEAD A&R MAN BLUES**
– Brain dead A&R man blues / Food fight at the last chance saloon / 4 track mind (Christmas mix) / Soundtrack to the summer (live).

Apr 02. (cd) *(MOBSTAR 025)* **FOOD FIGHT AT THE LAST CHANCE SALOON**
– Soundtrack to the summer / Food fight at the last chance saloon / This job don't get easier / Brain dead A&R man blues / Too many funerals / My weakness / Wisdom of the truck driving man / Wild romance / Rigor mortis blues / Beautiful crazy / Filling in holes / Post vs. chic / Blue / Kitty kitty / Postcards to the Moon. *(hidden track+=)* – I want a dog.

Aug 02. (cd-ep) *(MOBSTAR 030)* **LO-FIDELITY RADIO FRIENDLY SUMMER HIT**
– Lo-fidelity radio friendly summer hit / Bittersweet / Lazy daydreaming Bluebear / The future's not orange, it's blues.

BEAUMONT (see under ⇒ BLUEBOY)

BECAUSE (see under ⇒ FURNITURE; 80's section)

BECK

Born: BECK HANSEN, 8 Jul'70, Los Angeles, California, USA. After absorbing the strains of primitive country blues artists like LEADBELLY and MISSISSIPPI JOHN HURT, along with the aural terrorism of hardcore noise, the 17-year old BECK relocated to New York in 1989 to try his hand on the post-punk East Village folk scene. Broke, he retired to L.A., setting himself up in the (now) trendy Silverlake district, playing low key gigs in local coffeehouses. Spotted by 'Bongload' owner TOM ROTHROCK, he was offered some studio time and the resulting sessions produced the 'LOSER' (1993) single. Caned by L.A.'s alternative radio stations, its popularity led to BECK signing with 'Geffen'. 'LOSER' (1994) in its re-issued, major label form went top 20 in both Britain and America, its slow burning hip hop blues turning the rosy cheeked BECK into an overnight slacker anti-hero. The 'MELLOW GOLD' (1994) album went some way towards crystallising BECK's skewed vision of a modern folk music that encapsulated roots blues, hip hop, country, noise-core and psychedelia. While the record went on to sell half a million copies, BECK's unique contract allowed him the option of recording for other labels. 'STEREOPATHIC SOUL MANURE' (1994) was a U.S. only release of rough early material on the small 'Flipside' label, while 'ONE FOOT IN THE GRAVE' (1995) was a mainly acoustic set released on CALVIN JOHNSON's 'K' records, its stark harmonica-driven title track remaining a highlight of the BECK live experience. Any dubious whispers of "one-hit wonder" were cast aside with the release of 1996's 'ODELAY', a record that topped many end of year polls and turned BECK into the music world's coolest hep cat. Garnering gushing praise from the dance, rock and hip hop communities alike, the album's effortless fusion of disparate styles was breathtaking. The cut'n'paste surrealism of the lyrics flourished imagery of a lucidness to match BOB DYLAN's 60's work and indeed, the gorgeously bittersweet 'JACKASS' used Dylan's 'IT'S ALL OVER NOW BABY BLUE' as a shimmering harmonic backdrop. The album segued smoothly from distortion and dissonance into downhome steel guitar hoedown, all the while retaining an irresistibly funky backbeat. For now, this pop auteur/wunderkid can do no wrong, his live experience is a dayglo potted history of American music and any readers who were lucky enough to catch his glorious set at the Chelmsford V97 festival, will know that BECK doesn't take too kindly to bottle throwing eunuchs! Towards the end of 1998, BECK found himself in the midst of another legal wrangle with label 'Geffen' when a dispute over who was to release his new 14-day recorded 'MUTATIONS' resulted in the label taking full control. The latter was subsequently released to critical acclaim due to Nigel Godrich's production of BECK's live direction. With less label fuss but with more media frenzy, the Lo-Fi loner issued his 4th 'Geffen' set, 'MIDNITE VULTURES' (1999), which proved to be a dark contrast between that and the aforementioned 'MUTATIONS'. After the strange kitsch-adelic sound of 'MIDNITE VULTURES', BECK reverted back to folksy troubadour mode once again complemented by producer Nigel Godrich. A wistful seventh album from the ever eclectic, robot-dancing HANSEN, 'SEA CHANGE' (2002) saw him revisiting the days of 'ONE FOOT IN THE GRAVE' and the Godrich produced no-fi album 'MUTATIONS'. With its gentle melodies and sombre, quasi-romantic overtones, BECK, as always, spiced up the mix by adding harpsicord, trombone, violins and pedal steel to give the set a swift breezy sound – like a psychedelic GRAM PARSONS. Well, he always has been really. • **Songwriters:** BECK writes most of his material, some with KARL STEPHENSON. 'LOSER' used a sample of DR.JOHN's 'I Walk On Guilded Splinters'. Covered: I'M SO GREEN (Can) / HALO OF GOLD (Moby Grape). • **Trivia:** The 'Geffen Rarities Vol.1' album of various artists, featured the BECK track, 'Bogusflow'.

Album rating: A WESTERN HARVEST FIELD BY MOONLIGHT (*4) / GOLDEN FEELINGS mini (*3) / MELLOW GOLD (*7) / STEREOPATHETIC SOULMANURE (*4) / ONE FOOT IN THE GRAVE (*6) / ODELAY (*9) / MUTATIONS (*7) / MIDNITE VULTURES (*8) / SEA CHANGE (*7)

BECK (HANSEN) – vocals, acoustic guitar with guests **RACHEL HADEN** – drums, vocals / **ANNA WARONKER** – bass, vocals / **PETRA HADEN** – violin, vocals / **MIKE BOITO** – organ / **DAVID HARTE** – drums / **ROB ZABRECKY** – bass

not iss. Flipside

1992. (ltd-7"blue-ep) <FLIP 46> **TO SEE THAT WOMAN OF MINE / MTV MAKES ME WANNA SMOKE CRACK. / (other side 2 tracks by BEAN)**

not iss. Sonic Enemy

Jan 93. (c) <none> **GOLDEN FEELINGS**
– The fucked up blues / Special people / Magic stationwagon / No money no honey / Trouble all my days / Bad energy / Schmoozer / Heartland feeling / Super golden black sunchild / Soul sucked dry / Feelings / Gettin home / Will I be ignored by the Lord / Bogus soul / Totally confused / Muthafukka / People gettin busy.

not iss. Bongload

1993. (ltd-12") <BL 5> **LOSER. / STEAL MY BODY HOME**
1994. (ltd-7") <BL 11> **STEVE THREW UP. / MUTHERFUCKER / (CUPCAKE)**
(both above UK-iss.Jan95; same) *(cd-s iss.Dec97 & Oct00; BL 11CDS)*

BECK (cont)

		not iss.	Fingerpaint
1994.	(10"m-lp) <FP 02> **A WESTERN HARVEST FIELD BY MOONLIGHT**	-	

– Totally confused / Mayonaisse salad / Gettin' home / Blackfire choked our death / Feel like a piece of shit (mind control) / She is all (gimme something to eat) / Pinefresh / Lampshade / Feel like a piece of shit (crossover potential) / Mango (Vader rocks!) / Feel like a piece of shit (cheetoes time) / Styrofoam chicken (quality time). <re-iss.Sep95; same> (UK cd-iss. Oct97 & May98; same)

		Geffen	D.G.C.
Mar 94.	(7"/c-s) <DGC S7-19/CS-12 270> **LOSER. / ALCOHOL**	-	10

(cd-s+=) <DGCDM-21930> – Corvette bumper / Soul suckin' jerk (reject) / Fume.

Mar 94.	(7"/c-s) (GFS/+C 67) **LOSER. / ALCOHOL / FUME**	15	-

(cd-s) (GFSTD 67) – ('A'side) / Totally confused / Corvette bumper / MTV makes me want to smoke crack.

Mar 94.	(cd/c/lp) (GED/GEC/GEF 24634) <DGCD/DGC 24634> **MELLOW GOLD**	41	13

– Loser / Pay no mind (snoozer) / Fuckin with my head (mountain dew rock) / Whiskeyclone, Hotel City 1997 / Soul suckin jerk / Truckdrivin neighbors downstairs (yellow sweat) / Sweet sunshine / Beercan / Steal my body home / Nitemare hippy girl / Motherfuker / Blackhole. <lp-iss. on 'Bongload' (hidden track cd+=) – Analog odyssey. (lp re-iss. Apr97 & Sep99 & Jan01 on 'Bongload'; BL 12> (lp re-iss. Nov98 on 'Simply Vinyl'; SVLP 44)

May 94.	(cd-ep) <DM-22000> **BEERCAN / GOT NO MIND / ASSKIZZ POWERGRUDGE (PAYBACK '94) / TOTALLY CONFUSED / SPANKING ROOM / BONUS NOISE**	-	
May 94.	(7"/c-s; w-drawn) (GFS/+ 73) **PAY NO MIND (SNOOZER). / SPECIAL PEOPLE**	-	

(12"+=/cd-s+=)<US cd-ep> (GFST/+D 73)<GED 21911> – Trouble all my days / Supergolden (sunchild).

— BECK featured on Various Artists 'Mammoth' EP 'JABBERJAW: GOOD TO THE LAST DROP'. In the same year, with CHRIS BALLEW of The PRESIDENTS . . . and under the moniker of CASPAR AND MOLLUSK, they issued the single, 'TWIG'. He was also featured on below alongside CALVIN JOHNSON – vocals (ex-BEAT HAPPENING), SCOTT PLOUFF – drums / JAMES BERTRAM – bass / +2

		not iss.	K
Aug 94.	(cd/c) <(KLP 28 CD/C)> **ONE FOOT IN THE GRAVE**	-	

– He's a mighty good leader / Sleeping bag / I get lonesome / Burnt orange peel / Cyanide breath mint / See water / Ziplock bag / Hollow log / Forcefield / Fourteen rivers fourteen floods / Asshole / I've seen the land beyond / Outcome / Girl dreams / Painted eyelids / Atmospheric conditions. (UK-iss.Nov95; lp-iss.Jun97; KLP 28) (re-iss. Oct98; same)

Nov 94.	(7",7"brown) <iPU 45> **IT'S ALL IN YOUR MIND. / FEATHER IN YOUR CAP / WHISKEY CAN CAN**	-	

(UK-iss.Jan02; same as US)

		D.G.C.	D.G.C.
Jun 96.	(c-s) (GFSC 22156) **WHERE IT'S AT / WHERE IT'S AT (Mario C & Mickey P remix)**	35	61

(cd-s+=)<US cd-ep> (GFSTD 22156)<DGC CD-22214> – Bonus beats.
(12"++=)<US 12"ep> (GFST 22156)<DGC 12-22214> – ('A'-U.N.K.L.E. remix).

Jun 96.	(cd/c; as BECK!) (GED/GEC 24908) <DGCD/DGC 24823> **ODELAY**	18	16

– Devils haircut / Hotwax / Lord only knows / The new pollution / Derelict / Novacane / Jack-ass / Where it's at / Minus / Sissyneck / Readymade / High 5 (rock the catskills) / Ramshackle / Diskobox. <lp-iss.Apr97 & Sep99 on 'Bongload'; BL 030LP> (lp-iss.Nov98 on 'Simply Vinyl'; SVLP 51)

Nov 96.	(7") (GFSC 22183) **DEVILS HAIRCUT. / LLOYD PRICE EXPRESS**	22	94

(cd-s)<US cd-ep> (GFSTD 22183)<GED 22175> – ('A'side) / Dark and lovely (Dust Brothers remix) / American wasteland (Mickey P remix).
<US 12"ep++=> <DGC 12-22222> – Lloyd Price express / Clock.
(cd-s) (GFSXD 22183) – ('A'side) / ('A'-Noel Gallagher remix) / Groovy Sunday (Mike Simpson remix) / Trouble all my days.

Mar 97.	(7") (GFS 22205) **THE NEW POLLUTION. / ELECTRIC MUSIC AND SUMMER PEOPLE**	14	78

(c-s) (GFSC 22205) – ('A'side) / Richard's hairpiece (Aphex Twin remix).
(cd-s)<US cd-ep> (GFSTD 22205) <GED 22204> – (all 3 tracks).
(cd-s)<US 12"ep> (GFSTXD 22205) <DGC12 22300> – ('A'side) / 'A'-Mario C & Mickey P remix) / Lemonade.
(rel.Europe 12" May97 on 'Play It Again Sam'; 22300)

May 97.	(7") (GFS 22253) **SISSYNECK. / FEATHER IN YOUR CAP**	30	

(c-s) (GFSC 22253) – ('A'side) / The new pollution (remix by Mickey P).
(cd-s) (GFSTD 22253) – (all 3 tracks).

Aug 97.	(d7"/cd-ep) (GFS/+D 22276) <22303> **JACK-ASS (Butch Vig mix). / STRANGE INVITATION (orchestral version) / DEVIL GOT MY WOMAN // JACK-ASS (Lowrider mix). / BURRO / BROTHER**		-
Aug 97.	(12"ep) <DGC12 22303> **JACK-ASS / BURRO. / STRANGE INVITATION / BROTHER**	-	97
Oct 97.	(7"/c-s) (GFS/+C 22293) **DEADWEIGHT / ERASE THE SUN**	23	

(cd-s+=) (GFSTD 22293) – SA-5.

— BECK with **SMOKEY HORMEL** – guitar / **ROGER MANNING** – keyboards, percussion / **JUSTIN MELDAL JOHNSON** – bass / **JOEY WARONKER** – drums

Nov 98.	(cd/c) (GED/GEC 25184) <25309> **MUTATIONS**	24	13

– Cold brains / Nobody's fault but my own / Lazy flies / Cancelled check / We live again / Tropicalia / Dead melodies / Bottle of blues / O Maria / Sing it again / Static / Diamond bollocks / Runners dial zero. (lp/7"box-iss. on 'Bongload'; BL 39)

Dec 98.	(7"/c-s) (GFS/+C 22365) **TROPICALIA. / HALO OF GOLD**	39	

(cd-s+=) (GFSTD 22365) – Black balloon.

Oct 99.	(7"pic-d/c-s) (497181-7/-4) **SEXX LAWS. / SALT IN THE WOUND**	27	

(cd-s+=) (497181-2) – ('A'-Wizeguyz mix).
(cd-s) (497182-2) – ('A'side) / This is my crew / ('A'-Malibu mix).

Nov 99.	(cd/c) (490485-2/-4) **MIDNITE VULTURES**	19	34

– Sexx laws / Nicotine & gravy / Mixed bizness / Get real paid / Hollywood freaks / Peaches & cream / Broken train / Milk & honey / Beautiful way / Pressure zone / Debra. (lp-iss.Mar00 on 'Bongload'; BL 46)

Mar 00.	(7") (497312-7) **MIXED BIZNESS. / DIRTY DIRTY**	34	-

(cd-s+=) (497300-2) – ('A'video).
(cd-s) (497301-2) – ('A'side) / Sexx laws (video).

Sep 02.	(cd) <(493393-2)> **SEA CHANGE**	20	8

– The golden age / Paper tiger / Guess I'm doing fine / Lonesome tears / Lost cause / End of the day / It's all in your mind / Round the bend / Already dead / Sunday sun / Little one / Side of the road.

– compilations, etc. –

Apr 94.	(cd) *Flipside*; <FLIP 60> **STEREOPATHETIC SOULMANURE** (home recordings '88-'93)	-	

– Pink noise (rock me Amadeus) / Rowboat / Thunder peel / Waitin' for a train / The spirit moves me / Crystal clear (beer) / No money no honey / 8.6.82 / Total soul future (eat it) / One foot in the grave / Aphid manure heist / Today has been a fucked up day / Rollins power sauce / Puttin it down / 11.6.45 / Cut 1/2 blues / Jagermeister pie / Ozzy / Dead wildcat / Satan gave me a taco / 8.4.82 / Tasergun / Modesto. (UK-iss.Dec95 & Nov97 & Sep00 d-lp/cd; FLIP 660/+CD)

BEDHEAD

Formed: Dallas, Texas, USA . . . 1991 by songwriters BUBBA KADANE and his brother MATT, the quintet being completed by TENCH COXE, KRIS WHEAT and TRINI MARTINEZ. In 1994, they finally released their debut, 'WHAT FUN LIFE WAS', for The BUTTHOLE SURFERS' label, 'Trance Syndicate'. Slo-core, melancholy psychedelia-influenced rock, similar to LOW and even sleepier than The RED HOUSE PAINTERS, the mysterious BEDHEAD kept such a low profile at this particular time that they were virtually unknown outside America. Two years went by before their 'Rough Trade' follow-up, 'BEHEADED' (1996), gained some belated press recognition having been cited as an inspiration by such alternative luminaries as STEREOLAB. BEDHEAD awakened once more in early '98, the album 'TRANSACTION DE NOVO' seeing them back with 'Trance Syndicate'. Although they split in August 1998, the BEDHEAD brothers resurfaced on a joint effort, 'MACHA LOVED BEDHEAD' (2000), with experimental indie group, MACHA. • **Covered:** DISORDER (Joy Division) / GOLDEN BROWN (Stranglers).

Album rating: WHAT FUN LIFE WAS (*6) / BEHEADED (*7) / TRANSACTION DE NOVO (*6)

BUBBA KADANE – vocals / **MATT KADANE** – guitar / **TENCH COXE** – guitar / **KRIS WHEAT** – bass / **TRINI MARTINEZ** – drums

		Trance Syndicate	Trance Syndicate
Apr 94.	(lp/cd) <(TRANCE 21/+CD)> **WHAT FUN LIFE WAS**		

– Liferaft / Haywire / Bedside table / The unpredictable landlord / Crushing / Unfinished / Powder / Foaming love / To the ground / Living well / Wind down.

Nov 94.	(cd-ep) <(TR 28CD)> **4 SONG E.P. 19:10**		

– Heiszahobit / Dead language / What I'm here for / Disorder. (12"ep-iss.Nov97; TR 29LP)

Mar 96.	(10"ep/cd-ep) <(TR 42/+CD)> **THE DARK AGES. / INHUME / ANY LIFE**		

		Rough Trade	Mayking
Sep 96.	(cd/lp) <(R 405-2/-1)> **BEHEADED**		

– Beheaded / The rest of the day / Left behind / What's missing / Smoke / Burned out / Roman candle / Withdrew / Felo de sen / Lares and Penatia / Lost me works.

		Trance Syndicate	Trance Syndicate
Feb 98.	(lp/cd) <(TR 67/+CD)> **TRANSACTION DE NOVO**		

– Exhume / More than ever / Parade / Half thought / Extramundane / Forgetting / Lepidoptera / Psychodomatica / Present.

Oct 98.	(10") <TR 69> **LEPIDOPTERA. / LEPER**	-	

— had already disbanded in August 1998; the KADANE brothers went on to work with MACHA

BEEZUS

Formed: Champaign-Urbana, Illinois, USA . . . 1995 by LORETTA GAFFNEY, ELIZABETH MAJERUS and JOY GADRINAB. Their 1995 debut album, 'BREAKFAST WAS WEIRD' took on a burst of aggressive, 3 minute, indie pop tunes that failed to offer anything that had not been done before. Their second album 'LIVES OF SAINTS' released in 1997 was heralded as a massive progression. This was an altogether more focused album with stronger melodies and lyrics, unfortunately by this time the public had lost interest in the riot grrrl scene and so the album failed to make any great impact. In 1998 the band expanded into a four-piece with the addition of BRIAN RUNK as a second guitarist. With this formation the group released the single 'I'LL CALL YOU BLUE' in 1998 before disbanding the following year. 1999 did see the release of a posthumous EP 'DASHBOARD' which again provided evidence of what might've been had the band begun recording eight or nine years earlier.

Album rating: BREAKFAST WAS WEIRD (*5) / LIVES OF THE SAINTS (*6)

LORETTA GAFFNEY – vocals, guitar / **ELIZABETH MAJERUS** – vocals, bass / **JOY GADRINAB** – drums

		Parasol-Mud	Parasol-Mud
1995.	(cd) <(MUD 010)> **BREAKFAST WAS WEIRD**		

– One time too many / Repulsion / Wombat / 60 hours / Sylvie / Kangaroo / Road ouuta normal / Slip / Hell's half acre / Ghostfuck / Jesus boys / Too bad / S.U.A.F.M. / Carol Thomas Neely / In your jeans / Sleepwalk. <re-iss. Sep99; same>

Nov 96.	(7") <(MUD 021)> **split with BRAID**		
Feb 97.	(7") <(MUD 024)> **I'LL CALL YOU BLUE. / SLACK MOTHERFUCKER**		

Sep 97. (cd) <(MUD 027)> **LIVES OF THE SAINTS**
– Keeper / I'll call you blue / Rebel girl / Contender / Shy / Buttercup / Triple catastrophe / Note you'll never see / One who pays / Accident prone / Ring around.
1998. (cd-ep) <4939> **DASHBOARD EP**
– Dashboard saints / Twist in the wind / Complicated life / What do you know.

—— disbanded early in 1999

BELLATRIX

Formed: Keflavik, Iceland ... 1992 by ELIZA MARIA GEIRSDOTTIR, ANNA MARGRET HRAUNDAL, SIGRUN EIRIKSDOTTIR, ESTER "BIBI" ASGEIRSDOTTIR and their male drummer KARL AGUST GUDMUNDSSON. After releasing a full length album in Iceland (it never quite reached the shores of any other country) the group abandoned their native Icelandic tongue, setting off for England where they were warmly accepted into the 'In the City' new music competition. Signed to indie label 'Global Warming', the ensemble issued their debut mini-album, 'G' (1999), which showed comparisons to BJORK and KENICKIE, although unfavourable comments were thrown at them like rotten fruit. Mixing a warm brand of pop with a spicy European flavour, the frontwoman ELIZA (a trained violinist and opera singer) provided the unique vocals, that, quite frankly, didn't sound anything like BJORK. What remained was the "we just wanna have fun" pop sensibility that was exemplified on the follow up single, 'SILVERLIGHT', in early '99.

Album rating: STRANGER TALES (*5) / G mini (*6) / IT'S ALL TRUE (*6)

ELIZA MARIA GEIRSDOTTIR – vocals, violin / **ANNA MARGRET HRAUNDAL** – guitar / **SIGRUN EIRIKSDOTTIR** – guitar, keyboards / **ESTER ASGEIRSDOTTIR** – bass / **KARL AGUST GUDMUNDSON** – drums

	Feel Good All Over	not iss.
Feb 96. (cd) (1002) **STRANGER TALES**	-	Sweden

– (You die) Today / My friend the cow (beljan min) / Sleeping beauty (saetasta pyrnirosin) / The frogprince / Pluck of a feather / Fear / Darkness (myrkriae) / Icarus / Anna / Who wants to suffer? (hver vill pJast?) / Wild way / O, eh er svo svong!

	Global Warming	not iss.
Feb 99. (cd) (GLOBCD 3) **G**	-	

– Silverlight / Another dimension / A string / Once more / Crash / Sleeping beauty / Great expectations / Ikarus.

	Fierce Panda	not iss.
Oct 99. (7") (NING 085) **JEDI WANNABE. / GREAT EXPECTATIONS (live)**		-

(cd-s+=) (NING 085CD) – Crash.

Feb 00. (7") (NING 090) **THE GIRL WITH THE SPARKLING EYES. / STING**
(cd-s+=) (NING 090CD) – ('A'demo).
May 00. (7") (NING 096) **SWEET SURRENDER. / BYE FOR NOW**
(cd-s+=) (NING 096CD) – I love ya.
May 00. (cd) (NING 014CD) **IT'S ALL TRUE**
– Sweet surrender / The girl with the sparkling eyes / Jediwannabe / Daredevil / Strange encounter / If I fall / This boy will be mine / Tamed tiger / Always / Madness / Lullabye.

Sep 00. (7") (NING 101) **JEDIWANNABE. / HAPPY GO LUCKY**	65	-

(cd-s+=) (NING 101CD) – ('A'-Helen Love mix).
(12"++=) (NING 101T) – ('A'-Hedrock Valley beats).

BELLE AND SEBASTIAN

Formed: Glasgow, Scotland ... early '96 by ex-choirboy/boxer!, STUART MURDOCH (the main songwriter) and ISOBEL CAMPBELL, who met and recruited additional members STUART DAVID, RICHARD COLBURN, STEVIE JACKSON and CHRIS GEDDES in a local cafe. They borrowed the group name from a popular 70's children's TV series (from France) about a young boy and his Pyrenees mountain dog. Two months into their career, the expanded outfit released a very limited (1000 copies) college financed album, 'TIGERMILK', which gained sufficient airplay on national radio to ensure encroaching cult status. By the end of the year (and now with 7th member, SARAH MARTIN) they had unleashed their second set, 'IF YOU'RE FEELING SINISTER', which went on to sell in excess of 15,000 copies and gained much respect from end of the year critic polls. Since then, BELLE AND SEBASTIAN have hit the singles chart three times with a series of highly desirable EP's, 'DOGS ON WHEELS', 'LAZY LINE PAINTER JANE' (with former THRUM larynx-basher MONICA QUEEN on excellent form) and culminating with their critically acclaimed Top 40 entry, '3.. 6.. 9 SECONDS OF LIGHT'. The fact that they've scaled such giddy heights of indie stardom with only a minimum of promotion and a handful of gigs speaks volumes for the quality of their vintage twee C-86-esque sound. By late summer '98, expectations for a new album had reached fever pitch, critics unanimously hailing 'THE BOY WITH THE ARAB STRAP' as one of the year's finest (sadly, too late for esteemed Mercury Prize) and helped ease it into the Top 20. Their by now trademark combination of fey vocals, killer hooklines and avant-pop experimentalism resulted in some of B&S's most infectious tracks to date. With the spirit of NICK DRAKE ghosting in and out of focus (especially on 'SLEEP THE CLOCK AROUND' and 'A SUMMER WASTING'), this troupe of Glaswegian revivalists succeeded in putting the 60's and 70's through an 80's filter, incredibly coming up with something quintessentially 90's! The uninitiated should head straight for the holy trinity of tracks opening side two wherein BELLE & SEBASTIAN do an "ARAB STRAP" so to speak, the "Bairn"-like narrative of 'A SPACE BOY DREAM' complementing the BOLAN-esque stomp of the title track and sandwiching the brassy, BOO RADLEYS (but don't let that put you off!) style 'DIRTY DREAM NUMBER TWO'. Fans eager to get a glimpse of these elusive Scots shysters in the flesh should keep their eyes peeled, actual gigs are woefully few and far between. Extra-curricular activities, meanwhile, included a US 'Sub Pop' 7" from STUART DAVID's spoken word/electro outfit, LOOPER (with also his wife, Wee KARN and his brother, RONNIE BLACK). They would continue as a unit early in 1999, releasing a debut album for 'Jeepster', while ISOBEL's side project, The GENTLE WAVES, also released a long-player on the same label. In July that year and due to demand from everybody bar possibly PETE WATERMAN and his STEPS (who were somewhat peeved about losing the recent Brit Newcomers award due to internet voting), BELLE & SEBASTIAN re-distributed their semi-quasi debut 'TIGERMILK'; this time it hit the UK Top 20. After a two-year recording gap, B&S confidently returned with their fourth studio outing, the sublime, if not translucent 'FOLD YOUR HANDS CHILD, YOU WALK LIKE A PEASANT'. From its flaky opener, 'I FOUGHT IN THE WAR', listeners could detect that this album would be pale in comparison to the aforementioned 'BOY WITH THE ...'. It seemed that, since the band had apparently broken into the mainstream of America, that their sound was becoming more MOR, more tweaked, more ... STUART MURDOCH. With that in mind, however, MURDOCH did allow other band members to take the artistic reins: JACKSON and CAMPBELL sang on more songs than usual, slightly thwarting the ever-impending NICK DRAKE references. It could be just that B&S, like many other artists, followed a pivotal record with one that was weaker. Or maybe the group had simply lost their edge. On the eve of the release for this album they started doing press interviews – something that was frowned upon during their earlier years. The band also covered uncharted territory by issuing the album 'STORYTELLING' (2002), the soundtrack to the Todd Solondz film of the same name. A bleak look into American suburbia, the movie was a follow-up to the highly controversial (and highly uncomfortable) work 'Happiness'. It eventually got edited so much by the producers that Solondz vowed never to make another movie again. Unfortunately, so was the B&S score, which didn't make the final cuts. And it's a shame really, because the group almost redeemed themselves by attempting to create proper film music. 'FREAK', 'FUCK THIS SHIT' and the humourously entitled 'BLACK AND WHITE UNITE' (believe it, you have to see the film to get the joke) all made for good soundtrack material. The only let down being the inclusion of 'sound-bites' from the film which were inter-spliced with the music. Unnecessary, and ultimately tiring, dialogue such as "Nigger, fuck me ..." was hardly worthy of 'Pulp Fiction' proportions. Still, an interesting enough album to accompany an interesting enough film. ISOBEL, meanwhile, collaborated with celebrated Falkirk-born avant-jazz man, BILL WELLS, on the album 'GHOST OF YESTERDAY' (a take on the legendary BILLIE HOLIDAY).

Album rating: TIGERMILK (*8) / IF YOU'RE FEELING SINISTER (*8) / THE BOY WITH THE ARAB STRAP (*9) / FOLD YOUR HANDS CHILD, YOU WALK LIKE A PEASANT (*7) / STORYTELLING (*7) / Gentle Waves: THE GREEN FIELDS OF FOREVERLAND (*6) / SWANSONG FOR YOU (*6)

STUART MURDOCH (b. 1967) – vocals, acoustic guitar / **ISOBEL CAMPBELL** – cello, vocals / **STEVIE JACKSON** – guitars, vocals / **STUART DAVID** – bass / **RICHARD COLBURN** – drums / **CHRIS GEDDES** – piano

	Electric Honey	not iss.
May 96. (lp) (EHRLP 5) **TIGERMILK**		-

– The state I am in / Expectations / She's losing it / You're just a baby / Electronic renaissance / I could be dreaming / We rule the school / My wandering days are over / I don't love anyone / Mary Jo. *(re-iss. Jul99 on 'Jeepster' cd/c/lp; JPR CD/MC/LP 007)* – hit No.13

—— added **SARAH MARTIN** – violin, saxophone / and also extra member **MICK COOKE** – trumpet

	Jeepster	Enclave-Capitol
Nov 96. (cd/c/lp) (JPR CD/MC/LP 001) <56713> **IF YOU'RE FEELING SINISTER**		Feb97

– Stars of track and field / Seeing other people / Me and the Major / Like Dylan in the movies / The fox in the snow / Get me away from here, I'm dying / If you're feeling sinister / Mayfly / The boy done wrong again / Judy and the dream of horses.

May 97. (7") (JPR7 001) **DOG ON WHEELS. / THE STATE I AM IN (demo)**	59	-

(12"+=/cd-s+=) (JPR 12/CDS 001) – String bean Jean / Belle & Sebastian.

—— guest on below, **MONICA QUEEN** – vocals (of THRUM)

Aug 97. (7") (JPR7 002) **LAZY LINE PAINTER JANE. / YOU MADE ME FORGET MY DREAMS**	41	-

(12"+=/cd-s+=) (JPR 12/CDS 002) – Photo Jenny / A century of Elvis.

Oct 97. (7"ep) (JPR7 003) **3.. 6.. 9 SECONDS OF LIGHT EP**	32	-

– A century of fakers / Le pastie de la bourgeoisie.
(12"ep+=/cd-ep+=) (JPR 12/CDS 003) – Beautiful / Put the book back on the shelf / *(hidden track-)* Songs for children.

—— added guest **NEIL ROBERTSON** – bass

	Jeepster	Matador
Sep 98. (cd/c) (JPR CD/MC 003) <OLE 311> **THE BOY WITH THE ARAB STRAP**		12

– It could have been a brilliant career / Sleep the clock around / Is it wicked not to care? / Ease your feet in the sea / A summer wasting / Seymour Stein / A space boy dream / Dirty dream number two / The boy with the arab strap / Chickfactor / Simple things / The rollercoaster ride.

Dec 98. (12"ep/cd-ep) (JPR 12/CDS 009) **THIS IS JUST A MODERN ROCK SONG / I KNOW WHERE THE SUMMER GOES. / THE GATE / SLOW GRAFFITI** - - -chart

below featured the MAISONETTES

BELLE AND SEBASTIAN (cont)

May 00.	(7") *(JPR7 018)* **LEGAL MAN. / WINTER WOOSKIE**	15	-
	(cd-s+=) *(JPRCDS 018)* <OLE 448> – Judy is a dick slap.		
	(12") *(JPR12 018)* – ('A'side) / Judy is a dick slap (extended).		
Jun 00.	(cd/md/lp) *(JPR CD/MD/LP 010)* <OLE 429> **FOLD YOUR HANDS CHILD, YOU WALK LIKE A PEASANT**	10	80
	– I fought in a war / The model / Beyond the sunrise / Waiting for the moon to rise / Don't leave the light on baby / The wrong girl / The chalet lines / Nice day for a sulk / Woman's realm / Family tree / There's too much love.		

— STUART DAVID left after the recording of above

Jun 01.	(7") *(JPR7 022)* **JONATHAN DAVID. / THE LONELINESS OF A MIDDLE DISTANCE RUNNER**	31	-
	(12"+=/cd-s+=) *(JPR 12/CD 022)* – Take your carriage clock and shove it.		
Nov 01.	(7") *(JPR7 023)* **I'M WAKING UP TO US. / I LOVE MY CAR**	39	-
	(12"+=/cd-s+=) *(JPRCDS 023)* – Marx and Engels.		
Jun 02.	(cd/lp) *(JPR CD/LP 014)* <OLE 512> **STORYTELLING**	26	
	– Fiction / Freak / Dialogue: Conan, early Letterman / Fuck this shit / Night walk / Dialogue: Jersey's where it's at / Black and white unite / Consuelo / Dialogue: Toby / Storytelling / Dialogue: Class rank / I don't want to play football / Consuelo leaving / Wandering alone / Dialogue: Mandingo cliche / Scooby driver / Fiction (reprise) / Big John Shaft.		

– compilations, etc. –

Mar 00.	(cd) *Jeepster; (JPRBOX 001) / Matador; <OLE 313>* **LAZY LINE PAINTER JANE** (the first 3 EP's)		Oct00

the GENTLE WAVES

ISOBEL CAMPBELL with **RICHARD COLBURN, STUART MURDOCH, CHRIS GEDDES + STEVIE JACKSON**

		Jeepster	Jeepster
Mar 99.	(7") *(JPR7 011)* **WEATHERSHOW. / EVENSONG**		-
Apr 99.	(cd/lp) *(JPR CD/LP 006)* <4026> **THE GREEN FIELDS OF FOREVERLAND . . .**		
	– Hangman in the shadow / Evensong / Renew & restore / Emmanuelle, skating on thin ice / Rose I love you / Enchanted place / Tree lullaby / Dirty snow for the burnt ground / Weathershow / Chapter in the life of Matthew / To salt a scar.		
Oct 00.	(12"ep/cd-ep) *(JPR 12/CDS 019)* **FALLING FROM GRACE. /**		-
	– Falling from grace / Going home / October's sky / Hold back a thousand hours.		
Nov 00.	(cd/lp) *(JPR CD/LP 011)* <4051> **SWANSONG FOR YOU**		
	– Let the good times begin / Partner in crime / Falling from grace / Loretta Young / Sister woman / Solace for pain / Flood / Pretty things / There is no greater gold / There was magic, then.		

BELLINI (see under ⇒ DON CABALLERO)

BELLRAYS

Formed: Riverside, California, USA . . . 1990 by LISA KEKAULA and guitarist BOB VENNUM (who were later to marry), alongside drummer RAY CHIN and ex-GREY SPIKES guitarist TONY FATE, prompting VENNUM's transition to bass. The BELLRAYS spent years building a following on the L.A. gig scene, and in 1994 formed their own label, 'Vital Gestures', releasing two albums, 'LET IT BLAST' and 'GRAND FURY'. Formerly a jazz singer with BOB IN THE ROSE THORNS, KEKAULA provided the BELLRAYS' STOOGES-influenced driven rock-punk with a soulful edge. A turning point for the band came in 1999 at the Texas South By Southwest Festival, where they impressed ALAN McGEE, and subsequently signed with his 'Poptones' imprint; the subsequent 'MEET THE BELLRAYS' set, featured material from their previous albums. The BELLRAYS have since landed supporting slots with NASHVILLE PUSSY, ROCKET FROM THE CRYPT, and labelmates The HIVES. • **Covered:** NIGHTS IN VENICE (Saints).

Album rating: IN THE LIGHT OF THE SUN (*5) / LET IT BLAST (*7) / GRAND FURY (*7) / MEET THE BELLRAYS (*7) / THE RAW COLLECTION compilation (*6)

LISA KEKAULA – vocals / **BOB VENNUM** (b. VINCENT) – bass, guitar / **TONY FATE** – guitar (ex-SINS, ex-REACTORS, ex-GREY SPKIES) / **RAY CHIN** – drums

		not iss.	Vital Gesture
1992.	(c) <VGR 001> **THE BELLRAYS**	-	
1993.	(c) <VGR 004> **IN THE LIGHT OF THE SUN**	-	
	– Crazy water / Wandering spirits / Footprints on water / Same ground / Can I make you want me? / Tell me what the sun said / He's gone wrong / Blue, blue, blue / You'd better find a way / In the light of the sun / The ghost I'm after / Tell me what you've been working on. <cd-iss. May02 on 'In Music We Trust'; IMWT 005CD>		
1995.	(7"m) <VGR 006> **YOU'RE SORRY NOW. / ONE FOR THE HEART / TRAIN TRAIN TRAIN**	-	
1998.	(7") <#004> **GOOD THING. / HALF A MIND**	-	
	(above issued on 'Revenge', below on 'Fandango')		
1998.	(7") <FR 013> **NIGHTS IN VENICE. / (other by ADAM WEST)**	-	
Apr 99.	(cd) <VGRCD 010> **LET IT BLAST**	-	
	– Future now / Changing colors / Cold man night / Today was / Kill the messenger / Blue cirque / Good behavior / Testify / Dark horse pigeon / Hole in the world / Dead / Killer man / Fuzzhead / King of the world / Black honey / Blues for Godzilla / Get on thru. *(UK-iss.Jul02; same as US)*		

		not iss.	Extra Ball
1999.	(7") <XTR 003> **PINBALL CITY. / (other by FIREBALLS OF FREEDOM)**	-	-

		not iss.	Safety Pin
1999.	(7"ep) <SP 014> **FUCK X-MAS!!**	-	-
	– Merry Xmas baby / Rocket ship Santa / (other 2 by STREET WALKIN' CHEETAHS).		

		No Tomorrow	Uppercut
Nov 00.	(7") *(NTC 707)* **SUICIDE BABY. / CHEMICAL**	-	-
Jan 01.	(cd/lp) <UC 001 CD/LP> **GRAND FURY**	-	
	– Noise fragment / Too many houses in here / Fire on the moon / Snake city / Ska driver / Screwdriver / Heat cage / Evil morning / Zero P.M. / Do you speak English / Stupid fuckin' people / Have a little faith in me / Monkey house / Little funky jam / Warhead / Under the mountain / They glued your head on upside down / Hello hello. *(UK-iss.Apr02; same as US)*		

		not iss.	Flapping Jet
2001.	(8"ep) <FLAP 014> **SMASH THE HITS!**	-	
	– Mind's eye / Swastika / Gather darkness (live on KXLU). *(UK-iss.Jun02; same as US)*		

		Poptones	not iss.
Apr 02.	(7") *(MC 5069S)* **FIRE ON THE MOON. / STUPID FUCKING PEOPLE**		-
	(cd-s) *(MC 5069SCD)* – ('A'side) / Destroy all everything / I'm a lover.		
May 02.	(cd) *(MC 5069CD)* **MEET THE BELLRAYS**	73	-
	– Too many houses in here / Fire on the moon / Hero cage / Zero P.M. / Under the mountain / They glued your head on upside down / Changing colors / Dark horse pigeon / Hole in the world / Dead / Killer man / Blue cirque / Testify / Blues Godzilla.		
Jul 02.	(7") *(MC 5073S)* **THEY GLUED YOUR HEAD ON UPSIDE DOWN. / THE SAME WAY**	75	-
	(cd-s+=) *(MC 5073SCD)* – The dream police.		
Oct 02.	(7") *(MC 5075S)* **FIRE ON THE MOON. / DESTROY ALL EVERYTHING**		-
	(cd-s+=) *(MC 5075SCD)* – I'm a lover.		

– compilations, etc. –

Nov 02.	(cd/lp) *Uppercut; <UCCD/UCLP 004>* **THE RAW COLLECTION** (singles)	-	

BELLTOWER

Formed: New York City, New York, USA . . . early 90's by singer/bassist/occasional movie-and-television star BRITTA PHILLIPS and guitarist JODY PORTER; MARK BROWNING was the third part of the group equasion. Before constructing this alternative pop outfit with PORTER, PHILLIPS had quite a small but noteworthy career in acting, appearing in the film, 'Satisfaction' with Julia Roberts and Liam Neeson and as the voice of the title-character, 'Jem', in the US cartoon series. Acting work aside the newly-formed duo moved the band to London in 1990, and with the assistance of TERRY BICKERS behind the production desk, they released their debut EP, 'EXPLORATION DAY', which was an NME single of the week. Two more critically acclaimed singles, 'IN HOLLOW' and 'FLIGHT' followed before 1992's TERRY BICKERS-produced 'POPDROPPER', the band's only full-length album. Loosely affiliated with the maudlin shoegazing scene of that period, albeit with more confident and clearcut vocals, the LP was a wistfully trippy mix of drugsmeared cuts where gargantuan reverberating guitars mixed with acoustic strings and quiet, thoughtful piano. Both women would take turns on vocals, with the strength of PHILLIPS' singing contrasting nicely with her partner's more laid-back crooning. The band hopped continents once again back to the States and recruited bassist ADAM SCHLESINGER, who would later appear in with IVY and FOUNTAINS OF WAYNE. A 1995 single, 'UNDERWATERTOWN' on 'Scratchie' followed before the band called it quits in 1996. PHILLIPS went on to join ULTRABABYFAT and LUNA, as well as playing with BEN LEE; PORTER followed SCHLESINGER into FOUNTAINS OF WAYNE as well as founding ASTROJET.

Album rating: POPDROPPER (*5)

BRITTA PHILLIPS – vocals / **JODY PORTER** – guitar, vocals / **MARK BROWNING** – bass

		Ultimate	East West
May 91.	(12"ep/cd-ep) *(TOPP 004 T/CDS)* **EXPLORATION DAY EP**		
	– Outshine the sun / Beatnixon blues / Solstice / Never going home. *(re-iss. Oct92; same)*		
Oct 91.	(7") *(TOPP 006)* **IN HOLLOW. / ONE WAY LINE**		-
	(12"ep/cd-ep) *(TOPP 006 T/CDS)* – ('A'side) / Plasticman / Mercurial / Elements of place.		
May 92.	(7"colrd) *(TOPP 009)* **FLIGHT. / MY CHURCH**		-
	(12"+=/cd-s+=) *(TOPP 009 T/CDS)* – Digital kettle.		
Aug 92.	(cd/c/lp) *(TOPP CD/MC/LP 002)* <92183-2/-4> **POPDROPPER**		
	– Grounded / In hollow / One dimensional / Slipstream / Too late / Outshine the sun / Solstice / Flight / Eyes on the time / Plastic man / Everytime. *(lp w/free 7"; FREE 001)* – OVERSEER. / SEA OF SMILES		

— **ADAM SCHLESINGER** – bass; repl. MARK

		not iss.	Scratchie
1995.	(7") **UNDERWATERTOWN. / ORBITAL**	-	

— split in '96; PORTER augmented FOUNTAINS OF WAYNE (with SCHLESINGER) before forming ASTROJET; PHILLIPS joined ULTRABABYFAT, BEN LEE and LUNA

BELLY

Formed: Providence, Rhode Island, USA . . . late '91 by ex-THROWING MUSES and BREEDERS co-leader TANYA DONELLY. Recruiting brothers, THOMAS and CHRIS GORMAN along with FRED ABONG, DONELLY set her pet project in motion with the 'SLOWDUST' EP in summer '92, BELLY remaining with '4 a.d.' (the label that had been home to both DONELLY's previous outfits). Produced by The PIXIES maestro, Gil Norton, the record introduced BELLY's hypnotic blend of provocative musings and strident, infectious indie-rock, a style which flowered on the follow-up EP, 'GEPETTO' (featuring a cover of The Flying Burrito Brothers' classic 'HOT BURRITO #2') and the hit single 'FEED THE TREE'. The debut album, 'STAR' narrowly missed the UK No.1 spot, DONELLY's little-girl-lost sweetness occasionally transforming into a fearsome howl. Similarly, DONELLY's lyrics were by turns twisted and twee, this delicate balance undoubtedly part of the band's appeal. Despite this incredible start, a second set, the Glyn Johns-produced, 'KING', took off in a rockier direction, losing some of the BELLY mystique in the process. Though the record made the UK Top 10, its relative critical and commercial failure eventually led to DONELLY splitting the group up and heading for a solo career. In 1997, her debut, 'LOVESONGS FOR UNDERDOGS', was released to minimal impact, although it did contain two minor hits, 'PRETTY DEEP' and 'THE BRIGHT LIGHT'. • **Covered:** TRUST IN ME (Sherman – Sherman; for 'Jungle Book') / ARE YOU EXPERIENCED (Jimi Hendrix).

Album rating: STAR (*8) / KING (*7) / SWEET RIDE – THE BEST OF BELLY compilation (*7) / Tanya Donelly: LOVESONGS FOR UNDERDOGS (*5) / BEAUTYSLEEP (*6)

TANYA DONELLY (b.16 Jul'66, Newport, Rhode Island) – vocals, guitar / **THOMAS GORMAN** (b.20 May'66, Buffalo, N.Y.) – guitar **FRED ABONG** – bass / **CHRIS GORMAN** (b.29 Jul'67, Buffalo) – drums

	4 a.d.	Sire
Jun 92. (12"ep/cd-ep) *(BAD 2009/+CD)* **SLOWDUST**		
– Dusted / Slow dog / Dancing gold / Low red moon.		
——— **GAIL GREENWOOD** (b.10 Mar'60) – bass repl. FRED		
Nov 92. (7") *(AD 2018)* **GEPETTO. / SEXY S**		
(12"+=/cd-s+=) *(BAD 2018/+CD)* – Hot burrito #1 / Sweet ride.		
Jan 93. (7"/c-s) *(AD/+C 3001)* **FEED THE TREE. / DREAM ON ME**	32	-
(12"+=/cd-s+=) *(BAD 3001/+CD)* – Trust in me / Star.		
Jan 93. (cd)(lp/c) *(CAD 3002CD)(CAD/+C 3002) <45187>* **STAR**	2	59
– Someone to die for / Angel / Dusted / Every word / Gepetto / Witch / Slow dog / Low red moon / Feed the tree / Full Moon, empty heart / White belly / Untogether / Star / Sad dress / Stay. *(cd re-iss. Jul98; GAD 3002CD)*		
Mar 93. (c-ep)(cd-ep) *(BADC 2018)(BADD 2018CD)* **GEPETTO (remix) / IT'S NOT UNUSUAL / STAR (demo)**	49	
(12"ep/cd-ep) *(BADR 2018)(BAD 2018CD)* – ('A'side / Hot burrito #1 / Sexy S / Sweet ride.		
Feb 93. (cd-ep) *<941 547-2>* **LOW RED MOON / ARE YOU EXPERIENCED? / IT'S NOT UNUSUAL (3 mixes) / FULL MOON, EMPTY HEART (3 mixes)**	-	
Apr 93. (c-s) *<18570>* **FEED THE TREE / STAR**	-	95
Jan 95. (7"/c-s) *(AD/+C 5003)* **NOW THEY'LL SLEEP. / THIEF**	28	
(12"+=/cd-s+=) *(BAD 5003/+CD)* – Baby's arm / John Dark.		
Feb 95. (cd)(lp/c) *(CAD 5004CD)(CAD/+C 5004) <45833>* **KING**	6	57
– Puberty / Seal my fate / Red / Silverfish / Super-connected / The bees / King / Now they'll sleep / Untitled and unsung / Lil' Ennio / Judas my heart. *(cd re-iss. Jul98; GAD 5004CD)*		
Jul 95. (7"clear) *(AD 5007)* **SEAL MY FATE. / BROKEN / JUDAS MY HEART (live)**	35	
(cd-s) *(BAD 5007CD)* – ('A'-U.S. radio mix) / Spaceman / Diamond rib cage / Think about your troubles.		
(cd-s) *(BADD 5007CD)* – ('A'live) / White belly (live) / Untitled and unsung (live) / The bees (live).		
——— disbanded in July '96		

– compilations, etc. –

Jul 02. (cd) *4 a.d.; (GAD 2211CD) / Rhino; <78246>* **SWEET RIDE – THE BEST OF BELLY**		Jun02
– Spaceman / Gepetto / Super-connected / Broken / Hot burrito #1 / Trust in me / Feed the tree / Dusted (live) / Seal my fate / Judas mon coeur / Are you experienced? / Thief / Full moon, empty heart / Now they'll sleep / Lilith / Slow dog / Dream on me / Sweet ride.		

TANYA DONELLY

——— with **DEAN FISHER + WALLY GAGEL** – bass / **RICH GILBERT** – guitars / **STACY JONES** – guitar / + others

	4 a.d.	Warners
Nov 96. (d7"ep)(cd-ep) *(ADD 6018)(BAD 6018CD)* **SLIDING & DRIVING**		
– Bum / Restless / Human / Swoon.		
Aug 97. (7") *(AD 7007)* **PRETTY DEEP. / VANILLA (Wally's mix)**	55	
(cd-s) *(BAD 7007CD)* – ('A'side) / Spaghetti / Morna.		
(cd-s) *(BADD 7007CD)* – ('A'side) / These days / Influenza.		
Sep 97. (cd)(lp/c) *(CAD 7008CD)(CAD/+C 7008) <46495>* **LOVESONGS FOR UNDERDOGS**		
– Pretty deep / The bright light / Landspeed song / Mysteries of the unexplained / Lantern / Acrobat / Breathe around you / Bum / Clipped / Goat girl / Manna / Swoon.		
Nov 97. (7") *(AD 7012)* **THE BRIGHT LIGHT. / THE BRIGHT LIGHT (live)**	64	-
(cd-s) *(BAD 7012)* – ('A'side) / Bury my heart / How can you sleep.		
(cd-s) *(BADD 7012)* – ('A'side) / Life on Sirius / Moon over Boston.		
Nov 01. (cd) *(BAD 2108CD)* **SLEEPWALK**		-
– The storm / After your party (with BILL JANOVITZ) / Days of grace / Last rain.		
Feb 02. (cd) *(CAD 2201CD) <72201>* **BEAUTYSLEEP**		
– Life is but a dream / The storm / The night you saved my life / Keeping you / Moonbeam monkey / Wrap-around skirt / Another moment / Darkside / So much song / The wave / The shadow.		

Brendan BENSON

Born: 1970, Michigan, Detroit, USA. In his early twenties, BENSON moved from the dreary streets of Motor City's suburbs and flitted to Berkeley in sunny California. There he met up with songwriter JASON FALKNER, a man famous in the 90's for fronting indie outfit JELLYFISH. FALKNER co-wrote and produced the songs on BENSON's debut 'ONE MISSISSIPPI' (1996), although the album was at first rejected by 'Virgin' records. The LP, a scorching meld of jangly guitar and BIG STAR-esque riffs, along with BENSON's tender harmonic vocals was revamped by JANE'S ADDICTION producer Ethan James, who added a cleaner, polished sound that satisfied 'Virgin' (the FALKNER cuts were issued later on vinyl-only "Lo-Fi-Cool" promos as 'WELL-FED BOY'). The disruption of Virgin's major label, radio-friendly demands put off BENSON and FALKNER, with the two moonlighting on other albums – namely by DAN CASTELLANETA, WHIRLWIND HEAT and THE MOOD ELEVATOR. Five years down the line and BENSON (with FALKNER still in tow) delivered the sparkling 'LAPALCO' (2002), a shimmering summer record that ended up on most "best of year" lists.

Album rating: ONE MISSISSIPPI (*8) / LAPALCO (*9)

BRENDAN BENSON – vocals, guitars / with **JASON FAULKNER**

	Virgin America	Virgin
May 97. (cd) *(CDVUS 117) <41853>* **ONE MISSISSIPPI**		Sep96
– Tea / Bird's eye view / Sittin' pretty / I'm blessed / Crosseyed / Me just purely / Got no secrets / How 'bout you / Emma J / Insects rule / Maginary girl / House in Virginia / Cherries / Strawberry rhubarb pie.		
1997. (cd-ep) **WELL FED BOY**	-	
	V2	Star Time
Apr 02. (7"ep/cd-ep) *(VVR 501970-7/-3)* **FOLK SINGER EP**		-
– Folk singer / Son of a welder / Unfortunate guy / Feel like myself.		
Jul 02. (7") *(VVR 501979-7)* **TINY SPARK. / MEANING TO WRITE**		-
(cd-s+=) *(VVR 501979-3)* – No dial tone.		
Oct 02. (7") *(VVR 502051-7)* **GOOD TO ME. / OLD FASHIONED**		-
(cd-s+=) *(VVR 502051-3)* – Pleasure seeker (live).		
Oct 02. (cd) *(VVR 101991-2) <ST 6>* **LAPALCO**		Feb02
– Tiny spark / Metarie / Folk singer / Life in the D / Good to me / You're quiet / What / Eventually / I'm easy / Pleasure seeker / Just like me / Jetlag.		

BETA BAND

Formed: London, England ... 1994 by ex-patriate Scotsman, STEVE MASON, the St. Andrews-born singer meeting up with Edinburgh University students, decksman JOHN MacLEAN, drummer ROBIN JONES and GORDON ANDERSON on a train down to the capital. There they worked at various day jobs while sharing a flat in Shepherd's Bush, although ill-health forced ANDERSON to return home in August '96. Portsmouth-born RICHARD GREENTREE, formerly bassist of SINISTER FOOTWEAR would become part of the zany quartet in early '97 after being introduced through mutual friends, PUSHERMAN. Discovered and subsequently produced by THE VERVE's NICK McCABE (who saw some potential in their psychedelic transcendental dub malarky), they were signed to 'Regal' records. A pot-pourri of sound right enough (STONE ROSES or The MOONFLOWERS – remember them? – on a mantric mission!), the lads issued three EP's in the space of a year, 'CHAMPION VERSIONS', 'THE PATTY PATTY SOUND' and the excellent 'LOS AMIGOS DEL BETA BANDIDOS'. By popular demand (the vinyl was changing hands for upwards of £40 a time!) these were soon collected together on one shiny cd/album, simply titled 'THE THREE E.P.'S'. Lauded by the more discerning factions of the music press (the NME for one!), the bumbling art-rockers (by-passing the fashion stakes completely; safari suits, judo gear and horror of horrors, STEVE's "smart-arse" shell-suit being the disorder of the day) found themselves in the Top 40 by Autumn '98 with a long player that hung together surprisingly well. The sound of "baggy" ten years on, filtered through a kingsized bong, BETA standards such as 'DRY THE RAIN' ("It Will Be Alright"), 'INNER MEET ME', 'SHE'S THE ONE', 'DR. BAKER' and 'NEEDLES IN MY EYES' will surely come to be regarded as underground classics. To end the year, MASON moonlighted as KING BISCUIT TIME, releasing (to coincide with the latest edition of the band's zany in-house comic!) a bizarre EP of spaced-out drum'n'bass, '"SINGS" NELLY FOGGIT'S BLUES IN "ME AND THE PHARAOHS"'. With expectation and hype rife about the recording schedules and rumoured double-disc set of their debut set proper, the band were finally ready to promote 'THE BETA BAND' long-player in June '99. However, delays due to an objection from JIM STEINMAN (for the sample/use of his BONNIE TYLER – 'Total Eclipse Of The Heart' collaboration) and the band's post-release qualms that it was "fucking awful" contributed to complete bewilderment within the press and its readers. At the end of June, the album shot into the Top 20 despite poor reviews stating over-production was its downfall (or was it just plain arsing about?). Opening with the self-explanatory 'THE BETA BAND RAP' (which might've been handled better by the BONZO's in the 60's!) and finishing with the baffling 'THE COW'S WRONG', the album shocked fans who thought the quartet were perhaps a tad over-indulgent. On reflection though, The BETA BAND's original stage interpretations of the tracks could not be faulted. It's just a pity that critical cohorts like the MANICS were beginning to be proved right. As unfazed as ever, The BETA BAND shambled back into the fray with 'HOT SHOTS II' (2001; and a Top 20 hit!), the irony of the self-mocking title belying a half decent, occasionally brilliant set which certainly came closer to realising the

BETA BAND (cont)

promise of their early EP's. There was more focus, less sonic soup for the sake of it and more determined attempts at discernible songs. Which isn't to say they no longer walked that tightrope between endearingly wayward invention and rampant self-indulgence, the guiding hand of R&B producer C-Swing lending a contemporary edge to their urban meta-folk. • **Covered:** ONE (Nilsson). • **Trivia:** They guested on SPIRITUALIZED's 'Abbey Road' EP early '98.

Album rating: THE THREE E.P.'S (*9) / THE BETA BAND (*7) / HOT SHOTS 2 (*7)

STEVE MASON – vocals, percussion, drums, etc / **JOHN MacLEAN** – turntable, sampling / **RICHARD GREENTREE** – bass (ex-SINISTER FOOTWEAR) / **ROBIN JONES** – drums, percussion / GORDON ANDERSON departed before any recordings

		Regal	Astralwerks
Jul 97.	(12"ep) *(REG 16)* **CHAMPION VERSIONS** – Dry the rain / I know / B + A / Dogs got a bone.		-
Mar 98.	(2x12"ep/cd-ep) *(REG 18/+CD)* **THE PATTY PATTY SOUND** – Inner meet me / The house song / The monolith / She's the one.		-
Jul 98.	(cd-ep) *(REG 20CD)* **LOS AMIGOS DEL BETA BANDIDOS** – Push it out / It's over / Dr. Baker / Needles in my eyes.		-
Sep 98.	(cd) *(7243 4 97385 2 2)* <6252> **THE THREE E.P.'S** (compilation)	35	18
Jun 99.	(cd/d-lp) *(REG 30 CD/LP)* <6268> **THE BETA BAND** – The Beta Band rap / It's not too beautiful / Simple boy / Round the bend / Dance o'er the border / Brokenupadingdong / Number 15 / Smiling / The hard one / The cow's wrong.	18	
Jan 00.	(12"/cd-s) *(REG 40/+CD)* **TO YOU ALONE. / SEQUINSIZER**		-
Jul 01.	(12"/cd-s) *(REG 60/+CD)* **BROKE. / WON / DANCE O'ER THE BORDER**	30	-
Jul 01.	(d-lp/cd) *(REG 59/+CD)* <10446> **HOT SHOTS 2** – Squares / Al Sharp / Humanbeing / Gone / Dragon / Broke / Quiet / Alleged / Life / Eclipse. *(bonus cd+=; REG 59CDL)* – Won.	13	
Oct 01.	(12"/cd-s) *(REG 65/+CD)* **HUMAN BEING. / UNKNOWN / THE HARD ONE**	57	-
Jan 02.	(12"/cd-s) *(REG 69/+CD)* **SQUARES. / SQUARES (Bloah mix) / QUIET (acoustic – from 99X Atlanta session)**	42	-

KING BISCUIT TIME

aka **STEVE MASON** – vocals, etc

		Regal	Astralwerks
Dec 98.	(12"ep/cd-ep) *(REG 025/+CD)* **"SINGS" NELLY FOGGIT'S BLUES IN "ME AND THE PHARAOHS"** – Fatherriver / Niggling discrepancy / Little white / Eye o' the dug.		-
Jun 00.	(12"ep/cd-ep) *(REG 049/+CD)* <49657> **NO STYLE EP** – I walk the earth / Untitled / I love you / Time to get up.		Jul00

BETTIE SERVEERT

Formed: Amsterdam, Netherlands . . . 1990 by CAROL VAN DIJK, PETER VISSER, HERMAN BUNSKOEKE and BEREND DUBBE. Naming themselves, bizarrely enough, after a caption underneath a photo of Dutch/US tennis player, Bettie Stove (the literal translation is Bettie serves!), BETTIE SERVEERT got their break when US indie 'Matador' copped an earful of the band's demo tape. The label almost immediately issued their debut single, 'TOMBOY', a long-player, 'PALOMINE' (1992), hot on its heels the following month. Licensed in Britain to 4ad's 'Guernica' offshoot, the album's infectious, vaguely 60's indie-rock with a continental flavour was the toast of critics, even featuring a cover of a Sebadoh number, 'HEALTHY SICK'. Switching to 'Beggars Banquet', the band marked time while in the studio recording their more downbeat follow-up set, 'LAMPREY' (1995), by releasing the title track of their debut early in '94. A few years later, BETTIE SERVEERT failed to resurrect their fading star with third set, 'DUST BUNNIES' (1997), initial interest in the band receding. Of late, the Dutch also-rans were sighted on the fans-only 'Brinkman' imprint with the release of ' . . .PLAYS VENUS IN FURS' (1998) – a Velvet Underground tribute. VAN DYJK and VISSER were back for a fourth set proper in 2000, 'PRIVATE SUIT' – produced by JOHN PARISH – harking back to their melancholy days of yore and laying bare (oooh, that cover!) all that was cool about the band.

Album rating: PALOMINE (*8) / LAMPREY (*7) / DUST BUNNIES (*6) / . . .PLAYS VENUS IN FURS (*4) / PRIVATE SUIT (*6)

CAROL VAN DIJK – vocals, guitar / **PETER VISSER** – guitar / **HERMAN BUNSKOEKE** – bass / **BEREND DUBBE** – drums

		Guernica	Matador
Nov 92.	(cd/c/lp) *(GU 3 CD/C/LP)* <OLE 046> **PALOMINE** – Leg / Palomine / Kid's alright / Brain-tag / Tom boy / Under the surface / Balentine / This thing nowhere / Healthy sick / Sundazed to the core / Palomine (small). *(cd re-iss. Jul98; same)*		Jan93
Dec 92.	(7"ep/cd-ep) <OLE 032> **TOM BOY EP** – Tom boy / Smile / Balentine / Maggot.	-	
Sep 93.	(cd-s) <OLE 061> **KID'S ALRIGHT / GET THE BIRD / TOTALLY FREAKED OUT**	-	

		Beggars Banquet	Matador
Feb 94.	(12"/cd-s) *(BBQ 28 T/CD)* <OLE 075> **PALOMINE. / SILENT SPRING / SMALL**		Nov94
Jan 95.	(cd/c/lp) *(BBQ CD/MC/LP 169)* <OLE 121> **LAMPREY** – Keepsake / Ray ray rain / D. Feathers / Re-feel-it / 21 days / Cybor*D / Tell me, sad / Crutches / Something so wild / Totally freaked out / Silent spring. *(lp w/free ltd 7")*		
Jan 95.	(10"ep/cd-ep) *(BBQ 46 TT/CD)* <OLE 122> **CRUTCHES. / SHADES / ENTIRE RACES**		
Mar 95.	(7"/c-s) *(BBQ 50/+C)* **RAY, RAY RAIN. / LOOK BACK IN ANGER** *(cd-s+=) (BBQ 50CD)* – What friends?		-
Jul 95.	(cd-ep) *(BBQ 58CD)* <OLE 150> **SOMETHING SO WILD / TRIGGER CUT / CRUTCHES (BBC session) / STANLEY PARK**		
Feb 97.	(7") *(BBQ 308)* **WHAT FRIENDS. / SPINE** *(cd-s+=) (BBQ 308CD)* – Genuine life form.		-
Mar 97.	(cd/c/lp) *(BBQ CD/MC/LP 189)* <OLE 196> **DUST BUNNIES** – Geek / The link / Musher / Dust bunny / What friends? / Misery galore / Story in a nutshell / Sugar the pill / Rudder / Pork and beans / Fallen foster / Co-coward / Heaven.		
May 97.	(cd-s) *(BBQ 314CD)* **CO-COWARD / ALMOST MONKEYS**		- not iss. / Brinkman
Apr 97.	(7") <BRTS 65> **ALL THE OTHER FISH. /**	-	fans
Aug 98.	(cd) <BKMN 74> **. . .PLAYS VENUS IN FURS (live)** – Beginning to see the light / Stephanie says / What goes on / Venus in furs / Sunday morning / Black angel's death song / I can't stand it / European son / Rock & roll / Afterhours.	-	fans

		not iss.	Hidden Agenda
Sep 00.	(cd) <17> **PRIVATE SUIT** – Unsound / Satisfied / Private suit / Mariachi souls / ReCall / Auf wiedersehen / Sower & seeds / White tales / John Darmy / My fallen words / Healer.	-	

BEULAH

Formed: San Francisco, California, USA . . . mid 90's by songwriter MILES KUROSKY and BILL SWAN. Contributers to the 'Elephant 6' label, the duo issued their debut EP, 'SMALL CATTLE IN A SNOWSTORM' in 1997, later recruiting ANNE MELLINGER to record the first full-length album, 'HANDSOME WESTERN STATES', the same year. Two years down the line, the distant but superb second set, 'WHEN YOUR HEARTSTRINGS BREAK', was released, the recording comprising now of the two original founders plus STEVE LaFOLLETTE, PAT NOEL, STEVE ST CIN and BILL EVANS. The album reeked of the desolate isolation of love, and heavily relied on a contribution of style and quality due to its dreamy love songs and luscious strings. The long-player set them apart from any other band on the 'Elephant 6' imprint proving BEULAH had no peers. 'THE COAST IS NEVER CLEAR' (2001) saw BEULAH take a wry, twisted turn away from the pop-rock they had once been associated with, instead moving into melodic territory whilst still keeping a tac-sharp sense of humour. With more developed songs and sweeping musicianship, the group were up there with contemporaries SWEARING AT MOTORISTS and RED HOUSE PAINTERS (without the gloom).

Album rating: HANDSOME WESTERN STATES (*5) / WHEN YOUR HEARTSTRINGS BREAK (*8) / THE COAST IS NEVER CLEAR (*7)

MILES KUROSKY – vocals, guitar / **BILL SWAN** – trumpet, guitar

		Elephant 6	Elephant 6
Oct 97.	(7"ep) <E6 012> **A SMALL CATTLE DRIVE IN A SNOWSTORM EP** – ((love) John, she (love)s Paul / Slo-mo for the masses / Dig the subatomic holdout #1 / S.O.S.		
—	added **ANNE MELLINGER / ANA PITCHON** – various		
Oct 97.	(cd) <E6 014CD> **HANDSOME WESTERN STATES** – Maroon bible / Lay low for the letdown / Disco: the secretaries blues / The rise and fall of our hero's reward / ((love) John, she (love)s Paul / Slo-mo for the masses / I've been broken (I've been fixed) / Queen of the populists / Shotgun dedication / Rust with me / Delta / Dig the subatomic holdout #2. *(re-iss. Mar00; same)*		
—	ANNE repl. by **STEVE LaFOLLETTE** – bass / **BILL EVANS** – Moog synthesizer / **PAT NOEL** – keyboards / **STEVE ST CIN** – drums		

		Shifty Disco	Shifty Disco
Jan 99.	(7") *(DISCO 9901)* **SUNDAY UNDER GLASS. / I (LOVE) JOHN, SHE (LOVE)S PAUL**		

		Sugar Free	Sugar Free
Apr 99.	(cd) <(SF 012CD)> **WHEN YOUR HEARTSTRINGS BREAK** – Score from Augusta / Sunday under glass / Matter vs. space / Emma Blowgun's last stand / Calm go the wild seas / Ballad for the lonely Argonaut / Comrade's twenty sixth / The aristocratic swells / Silverado days / Warmer / If we can land on the Moon, surely I can win your heart. *(re-iss. Jul99 & Jan02 on 'Shifty Disco'; SHIFTY 9905)*		Mar99

		Shifty Disco	Velocette
Oct 99.	(cd-s) *(DISCOQUICK 3)* **SCORE FROM AUGUSTA / MAROON BIBLE / ALL POINTS NORTH**		-
Apr 00.	(cd-s) *(DISCOQUICK 4)* **EMMA BLOWGUN'S LAST STAND / DISCO: THE SECRETARIES BLUES / DIG THE SUBATOMIC HOLDOUT #2**		-
Aug 01.	(cd-s) *(DISCOQUICK 13)* **POPULAR MECHANICS FOR LOVERS / THE BATTLE CRY OF THE WEST / WEIGHT OF MY TEARS**		-
Sep 01.	(cd) *(SHIFTY 0103)* <943000> **THE COAST IS NEVER CLEAR** – Hello resolven / A good man is easy to kill / What will you do when your suntan fades? / Gene Autry / Silver lining / Popular mechanics for lovers / Gravity's bringing us down / Hey brother / I'll be your lampshade / Cruel minor change / Burned by the sun / Night is the day turned inside out. *(re-iss. Jan02; same)*		
Dec 02.	(7") *(DISCOQUICK 16)* **GENE AUTRY. /**		-

BICYCLE THIEF
(see under ⇒ THELONIOUS MONSTER; 80's section)

BIFFY CLYRO

Formed: Glasgow, Scotland . . . 1999 by the trio of SIMON NEIL, JAMES JOHNSTON and BEN JOHNSTON. Fusing an aggro-pop cocktail sound of NIRVANA and SOUNDGARDEN, they honed their youthful expertise with tours supporting the likes of the LLAMA FARMERS and SUNNA.

The group began doing the toilet circuit before issuing a few independently produced singles, 'INAME' (for AEREOGRAMME's 'Babi Yaga' imprint) and 'THEKIDS ...'. Their own brand of punk/emo rock was taken a step further early in 2001 when they were signed by 'Beggars Banquet', almost immediately issuing their impressive '27' single (a Kerrang! SOTW). 'JUSTBOY' and '57' (a Top 75 hit) followed hot on its heels, while their debut set, 'BLACKENED SKY' (2002) set out their stall to an already devoted fanbase. More MINOR THREAT than GREEN DAY, BIFFY CLYRO still managed to keep the whole fare melodic yet enduring with their tales of broken relationships, a million miles more meaningful than any current sports-clad punk, wrapped up in a clean, tight production sheen.

Album rating: BLACKENED SKY (*6)

SIMON NEIL – vocals, guitar / **JAMES JOHNSTON** – bass, vocals / **BEN JOHNSTON** – drums, vocals

		Babi Yaga	not iss.
2000.	(cd-s) (1cd) **INAME / ALL THE WAY DOWN CHAPTER 2 / TRAVIS PERKINS**	–	-
		Electric Honey	not iss.
Oct 00.	(cd-ep) **THEKIDSWHOPOPTODAYWILLROCKTOMORROW ep** – 27 / Hope for an angel / Justboy / Less the product.	–	-
		Beggars Banquet	not iss.
Apr 01.	(7"/cd-s) (BBQ 352/+CD) **27. / INSTRUCTIO4 / BREATHEHER**	–	-
Oct 01.	(7"/cd-s) (BBQ 355/+CD) **JUSTBOY. / BEING GABRIEL / UNSUBTLE**	–	-
Feb 02.	(7") (BBQ 358) **57. / KILL THE OLD TORTURE THEIR YOUNG (evening session)** (cd-s) (BBQ 358CD) – ('A'side) / Hope for an angel (evening session) / Time is an imploding unit / Waiting for green.	61	-
Mar 02.	(cd/lp) (BBQ CD/LP 226) **BLACKENED SKY** – Joy. discovery. invention / 27 / Justboy / Kill the old torture their young / Go slow / Christopher's river / Convex concave / 57 / Hero management / Solution devices / Stress on the sky / Scary Mary.	–	-
Jul 02.	(7") (BBQ 361) **JOY. DISCOVERY. INVENTION. / ALL THE WAY DOWN** (cd-s) (BBQ 361CD) – ('A'side) / Toys toys toys choke toys toys toys / Houses of roofs.	–	-

BIF NAKED

Born: 1971, New Delhi, India. BIF's early years read like a rock and roll version of a Mills and Boon heroine. She was the love child of young private school travellers and was then adopted, brought back from India by missionaries to America and raised in Canada. While at the University of Winnipeg, BIF joined a local group named JUNGLE MILK, moving on from there to become lead vocalist for GORILLA GORILLA, at which point she took on the name, BIF NAKED. She moved on from this band to join CHROME DOG, as she felt she would be able to assert her antagonistic leanings better with this hardcore punk mob. Unfortunately though the masculine orientated group would not allow BIF to expand on more feminine subject matter. Thus she moved on to join Canadian punk band, DYING TO BE VIOLENT, but unfortunately the same problems arose as with her former group, leading her to stay on only briefly with DTBV. BIF took the truest route to personal artistic integrity; going solo and releasing an EP, 'FOUR SONGS AND A POEM' in 1994, with the ensuing full-length set, 'BIF NAKED' (1995) – co-written with producer JOHN R DEXTER – following the same year (this album was also re-issued that year on BIF's own label, 'Her Royal Majestys'). This outing gained BIF many new admirers, making her a bit of a feminist icon, with her no-messing punk attitude. 1995 was also a crucial year for BIF as she decided to put an end to years of alcohol and drug abuse, and instead concentrate on her chosen musical path. Following this, BIF spent several years touring and promoting herself, her big break coming in 1998 with a contract for the Atlantic-run 'Lava' imprint, who released her second full-length album, 'I BIFICUS' (1998). The record was a good blend of pop and punk styles, although never selling-out as many so-called punk bands have.

Album rating: BIF NAKED (*6) / I BIFICUS (*5)

BIF NAKED – vocals / with various session people

		not iss.	Plum
1994.	(cd-ep) **FOUR SONGS AND A POEM** – Make like a tree / Tell on you / Never along / Succulent / My Satan poem.	–	
		Concrete – Edel	Aquarius
Nov 95.	(cd) (CD 008624-2) <6661> **BIF NAKED** – Everything / Make like a tree / Daddy's getting married / Tell on you / Never alone / Over you / Succulent / My whole life / The letter / My bike / The gross, gross man.		
Nov 95.	(cd-s) (0086265RAD) **DADDY'S GETTING MARRIED / TELL ON YOU / SUCCULENT**		-
1997.	(cd-ep) **OKENSPAY ORDWAY I. (aka THINGS I FORGOT TO TELL MOMMY)** (spoken word) – Test / Intro / Infected tattoo / Rock star man / You got the job / Alphabet poem / Dress / We're arseholes / Half a day a week / Alcohol is the root / Zoinks! / Calling all / T.V. baby / Interruption / Metal queen / Alcohol or comedy / Isabelle / Insomnia / Obsessed w/ childhood / No me drink / Canadians / Porno brainwash / 32 fuetes / Ahhhh / I'm yer peer / Factory hot rod / Goodbye / All you ever do / Singin' / Stumpy the mouse / Snowboarding / Poem #357651 / Gig tits / My Satan poem.	–	Canada
Feb 98.	(cd) **I BIFICUS** – I died / Any day now / Spaceman / Moment of weakness / Lucky / Sophia / Chotee / Violence / The peacock song / Anything / Only the girl / Twitch. <US re-iss. 1999 on 'Lava-Atlantic'; >	–	

1998.	(cd-s) **SPACEMAN** (mixes; Boomtang Boys / radio / I Bificus)		
		not iss.	Atlantic
2000.	(cd-ep) **ANOTHER 5 SONGS AND A POEM** – I died / Twitch / Vampire / Lucky (guitar mix) / We're not gonna take it / Eine tasse tee (a poem).	–	Canada

BIG LEAVES

Formed: Waunfawr, nr. Caernarfon, Wales ... 1996 by OSIAN GWYNEDD, his brother MEILIR GWYNEDD, KEVIN TAME and vocalist RHODRI SION, initially naming themselves BEGANIFS (when all four were only 11!). After being quite literally laughed at by their entire hometown for selling home made recordings of themselves, the little tykes grew up. Mistaken as 'BIG LEAVES' (a name which the group said they found "beautiful") by a venue promoter who couldn't pronounce the original Welsh title at an early gig, the band were subsequently signed to 'Crai' records. Releasing two EP's 'TRWNGWSG' and 'BELINDA' in 1998, they also made a guest appearance on CATATONIA's second set (OSIAN shared a flat with their guitarist). Influenced from the MONKEES, QUEEN and GEORGE HARRISON, the 4-piece were compared to their good friends The SUPER FURRY ANIMALS, the weird pop combo producing their next 12"-only single, 'SLY ALIBI' (issued on 'Whipcord' records). An extensive tour with CATATONIA and the 'FURRYs followed, BIG LEAVES branching out for an album, 'PWY SY'N GALW?', in 2000. With the addition of drummer MATT HOBBS (OSIAN now on keyboards), The BIG LEAVES signed to Cardiff-based 'Boobytrap' records, their debut being single, 'ELECTRO MAGNETIC POLLUTION'. Later in 2001, the band featured in a Channel 4 Wales TV documentary, 'Dydd ar ol Dydd', while they pushed out some more singles of various labels. They are currently smarting a deal with Cardiff-based 'Townhill' records (a subsidiary of 'Sony') after they received heavy plaudits for a concert at Southwest x South West in Austin, Texas.

Album rating: PWY SY'N GALW? (*6)

RHODRI SION – vocals / **MEILIR GWYNEDD** – guitar / **KEVIN TAME** – bass / **OISAN GWYNEDD** – drums, keyboards

		own label	not iss.
1997.	(7"; as BEGANIFS) **LLYGAID GWYDER**	–	Welsh
		Ankst	not iss.
1997.	(7"ep; as BEGANIFS) **FFRAETH EP**		
		Crai	not iss.
Feb 98.	(cd-ep) (CRAICD 062) **TRWNGWSG EP** – Dal fy llaw / Trwngwsg / Bier / Un o'r pla / Henffych. (re-iss. Sep99; same)		–
Feb 99.	(cd-ep) (CRAICD 066) **BELINDA EP** – Seithenyn / Hanasamianast / Dydd ar oi dydd / Hodges blues / Tourettes. (re-iss. Sep99; same)		–
		Whipcord	not iss.
Jun 99.	(7") (WCRACK 002) **SLY ALIBI. / DOUBLE TROUBLE**		–
Nov 99.	(7") (WCRACK 003) **RACING BIRDS. / GETAWAY DAY** (cd-s+=) (WCRACK 003CD) – Meillionen.		–
Mar 00.	(cd) **PWY SY'N GALW?** – Dilyn dy drwyn / Pryderus wedd / Meillionen / Whistling sands / Bler / PhD / Synfyfyrio / Byw fel ci / Pwy sy'n galw? / Barod I wario / Seithenyn.		
		Metropolis	not iss.
Jun 00.	(7"ep/cd-ep) (MET/+CD 1) **FINE. / SHOT IN THE DARK / FINGERTIP WORLD**		–
—	added **MATT HOBBS** – drums (OSIAN moved to keyboards)		
		Dell'Orso	not iss.
Jun 01.	(10"ep/cd-ep) (EDDA 02/+CD) **ANIMAL INSTINCT EP** – Animal instinct / Hang on to your halo / Automatic / Nicole.		–
		Boobytrap	not iss.
Aug 01.	(cd-s) (BOOB 009CD) **ELECTRO MAGNETIC POLLUTION. / PALADINO'S PILLS (HAND OF GOD)**		–
		Crai	not iss.
Feb 02.	(7"ep) **SIGLO EP**		
		Dell'Orso	not iss.
Nov 02.	(cd-s) (EDDA 06CD) **SPEAKEASY /**		

BIG'N

Formed: Joliet, Illinois, USA ... 1990 by BRIAN A. WNUKOWSKI, TODD JOHNSON, his brother CHRIS and WILLIAM AKINS. Recording melodic rock in WNUKOWSKI's basement, the tight-knit group issued a handful of singles in the early '90's for various labels that were small enough to collapse under the weight of a few 7"s. CHRIS parted with the band just before the release of their debut album, 'CUTTHROAT' (1992), issued on the German label 'Gasoline Boost', to minor acclaim. MIKE CHARTRAND stepped in as bassist in time for a European tour and a distribution deal with Chicago-based record label 'Skin Graft'. The outfit delivered the sophomore set, 'DISCIPLINE THROUGH SOUND' (1995), an album that applauded the band on its technical and musical abilities, but not much else. Singer AKINS grunted through the entire set. It was no surprise that the group collapsed in 1997, after a brief split recording with post-rockers OXES (check out the EP on 'Box Factory' records), with WNUKOWSKI gliding into various projects including EMPEROR PENGUIN and CHECK ENGINE. However, there may still be a glint in the eye of the BIG'N, as the former members reunited at TODD JOHNSON's wedding in 2001, where there was talk of a reformation ...
• **Covered:** T.N.T. (Ac-Dc).

Album rating: CUTTHROAT (*5) / DISCIPLINE THROUGH SOUND (*4)

WILLIAM AKINS – vocals / **TODD JOHNSON** – guitar / **CHRIS JOHNSON** – bass / **BRIAN A. WNUKOWSKI** – drums

			not iss.	Headstagger
1990.	(7"ep)	**BIG'N. /**	-	

			not iss.	Ratfish
1991.	(7"ep)	**HOSS. /**	-	

			not iss.	Spontaneous Combustion
1993.	(7",7"blue) <SCR 001>	**MUSKET. / TIGHT ONE**	-	

— **MIKE CHARTRAND** – bass; repl. CHRIS

			not iss.	Gasoline Boost
1993.	(7")	**RAZORBACK. / MITE**	-	
1994.	(cd) <9>	**CUTTHROAT**	-	

– Chinese jet pilot / Dirt farmer / Loco / Razorback / Musket / Age old trick / Jackalope / King hot pants / Mite / Bait.

			not iss.	Skin Graft
Jul 96.	(cd) <GR 23.5 – GB 10>	**DISCIPLINE THROUGH SOUND**	-	

– Tropy / Final song / Moonshine / Bird of prey / Dying breed / El Diablo III / Dry / Lucky 57 / White Russian. *(hidden bonus track)*

— split in 1997; WNUKOWSKI joined CHECK ENGINE

BIG RAY (see under ⇒ STUPIDS)

BIKERIDE

Formed: California, USA ... 1997 under mainman TONY CARBONE. Debuting in 1997 with the mini-album, 'HERE COMES THE SUMMER' (1997), the title gave away the happy-go-lucky indie pop sound CARBONE was trying to produce. A blend of classic BEACH BOYS-stylings and the melodies of the great BURT BACHARACH, their sound seemed to enhance the lo-fi pseudo sixties teen pop sound. The band's first full-length set proper, 'THIRTY-SEVEN SECRETS I ONLY TOLD AMERICA', arrived two years later and accept for being fairly aurally pleasing, which was run-of-the-mill for the genre, it was a rather vacuous outing. The group took a step closer to a more musically competent sound courtesy of their second offering 'SUMMER WINNERS, SUMMER LOSERS' (2000), a record still not really achieving the warm seasonal sound that it seems they intended. A subsequent journey to Brazil for CARBONE seemed to be the catalyst for the band's (bolstered by SEAN HOW?, CHARLES GRAY, ADAM DIEBERT and CHRIS PETROZZI) quality upgrade for their masterwork, 'MORNING MACUMBA' (2002). This record displayed a brilliant marriage between the rhythms of carnival country and the songwriting deities of sixties pop sounds; producing a work most indie lo-fi bands, who were not suffering from sunlight deficiency, would've been proud of.

Album rating: HERE COMES THE SUMMER! mini (*5) / THIRTY-SEVEN SECRETS I ONLY TOLD AMERICA (*6) / SUMMER WINNERS, SUMMER LOSERS (*6) / MORNING MACUMBA (*7)

TONY CARBONE – vocals, multi

			not iss.	Choclaty
1997.	(m-cd) <001>	**HERE COMES THE SUMMER!**	-	

– Iron feather / On my bike / Stupid 44 / Tonight you belong to me / Catching raindrops in Rome / Everyday / The 4th of July / God's kids / Josephine / Summer friends. *(hidden tracks+=)* – Bikeride #9 / Junebug / Fourth of July / August brought you back.

— added **NEAL KUZEE** + **ERICK HAUSER** + **JEFF DUBE** + **MIKE HAMADA**

			Hidden Agenda	Hidden Agenda
Nov 98.	(7"ep) <AHA 007>	**AMERICA'S FAVORITE OMELETTES EP**		

– America's favorite omelettes / Our lips are sealed / God's kids / The four of us in June.

Sep 99. (cd) <AHA 010> **THIRTY-SEVEN SECRETS I ONLY TOLD AMERICA**
– Erik and Angie / That's math! / America's favorite omelettes / Jennifer / Peeling an orange / Blue jeans / A wet and watery blue / The letter dropper / Do you like ping-pong? / Samarah / Parasol / Clean sports, clean living / Can you hear?

— added **GREG ROBERTS** – drums + **CHRIS FAHEY** – theremin

Aug 00. (10"ep) (AHA 012) **DOGS EP**
– Jennifer / Continental divide / Estate d'amore / Carl Wilson suite / You stepped on my guitar / Shawna / Endless PCH / Handlebars.

Oct 00. (7"ep) <AHA 016> **RASPET EP**
– New Year's girl / A summer long / Grady Moseley / Fine and dandy / Country driving / El Roy / Being and nothingness / You're coming with me.

Dec 00. (cd) <(AHA 020)> **SUMMER WINNERS, SUMMER LOSERS**
– Here comes the summer / Meghan / New years girl / Carl Wilson suite / You stepped on my guitar / Shawna / El Roy / Continental divide / Grady Moseley / Fine and dandy / Leah and Nikki / A summer song / Handlebars / Country driving / Bean and nothing else / The four of us in June / Estate d'Amore / Endless PCH / Our lips are sealed. <re-iss. Sep01 on 'Houston Party'; HPR 039CD)>

— **CARBONE** with **SEAN HOW?** – guitar / **CHARLES GRAY** – keys / **ADAM DIEBERT** – bass / **CHRIS PETROZZI** – drums

Sep 02. (cd) <AHA 046> **MORNING MACUMBA**
– Radio Ougadougou / Fakin' amnesia / Knees on top / Norwegia / Catch that spark / Whispering winds / The Americans in Rome / Moonracing / Small faces / Sleepyhead / Lemonade.

BIKESHED (see under ⇒ MAGNETIC NORTH POLE)

BIKINI KILL

Formed: Olympia, Washington, USA ... late 1990 by former stripper KATHLEEN HANNA, TOBI VAIL and KATHI WILCOX, who all met at their local Evergreen College and named themselves after their feminist fanzine. The band released a few low-key albums for the 'Kill Rock Stars' label (one produced by IAN MacKAYE of FUGAZI), adamantly resisting the temptation to sign for a major. Self-styled "Riot-Grrl" spokeswomen and figureheads for a new generation of fearless female punkettes, BIKINI KILL obviously took at least some of their cues from original femme-punks, The SLITS and The RAINCOATS, although musically they combined fragments of SONIC YOUTH and X-RAY SPEX. HANNA was undoubtedly the band's controversial focal point, allegedly appearing T-shirtless on stage in one incident having scrawled "Kill Me" on her chest in lipstick! The feisty frontwoman was also said to have spray-painted "Smells Like Teen Spirit" on KURT COBAIN's house, an action which inspired him to write the legendary song of the same name. In 1993, BIKINI KILL toured and recorded together with UK counterparts, HUGGY BEAR, releasing a split album, 'YEAH YEAH YEAH' (issued by 'Wiiija' in the UK). JOAN JETT produced the subsequent single, 'REBEL GIRL', released around the same time as their first official long-player, appropriately-titled 'PUSSYWHIPPED'. Following the demise of the "Riot Grrl" movement, it was to be two long years before BIKINI KILL re-emerged with what was to be their final statement, 'REJECT ALL AMERICAN' (1996).

Album rating: BIKINI KILL (*6) / PUSSYWHIPPED (*7) REJECT ALL AMERICAN (*6) / Julie Ruin: JULIE RUIN (*6) / Le Tigre: LE TIGRE (*7) / FEMINIST SWEEPSTAKES (*5) / FROM THE DESK OF MR. LADY mini (*5)

KATHLEEN HANNA(-DANDO) (b. 9 Jun'69, Portland, Oregon) – vocals, bass, drums / **KATHI WILCOX** (b.19 Nov'69, Vancouver, Washington) – bass, vocals, drums / **TOBI VAIL** (b.20 Jul'69, Auburn, Washington) – drums, vocals, bass (ex-SOME VELVET SIDEWALK, ex-GO TEAM) / **BILLY BOREDOM** (b. WILLIAM F. KARREN, 10 Mar'65, Memphis, Tenn.) – guitar, vocals

			not iss.	K
1991.	(7") <)	**BOY/GIRL. / (split w/ Slim Moon)**	-	
1991.	(c) <demo>	**REVOLUTION GIRL STYLE NOW**		

– Candy / Daddy's l'il girl / Feels blind / Suck my left one / Carnival / This is not a test / Double dare ya / Liar.

			Kill Rock Stars	Kill Rock Stars
Nov 92.	(m-lp) <(KRS 204)>	**BIKINI KILL**		

– Double dare ya / Liar / Carnival / Suck my left one / Feels blind / Thurston hearts the who. <cd-iss. Mar94 +=; KRS 204CD)> – YEAH YEAH YEAH

			Catcall	Kill Rock Stars
Mar 93.	(lp; shared with HUGGY BEAR) (PUSS 001)	**YEAH YEAH YEAH**		

– White boy / This is not a test / Don't need you / Jigsaw youth / Resist psychic death / Rebel girl / Outta me.

			Wiiija	Kill Rock Stars
Oct 93.	(cd/lp) (WIJ 028 CD/V) <KRS 218>	**PUSSYWHIPPED**		

– Blood one / Alien she / Magnet / Speed heart / Lil red / Tell me so / Sugar / Star bellied boy / Hamster baby / Rebel girl / Star fish / For Tammy Rae.

1994. (7"m) <KRS 212> **NEW RADIO. / REBEL GIRL / DEMIREP**
May 95. (7"ep) <KRS 250> **THE ANTI-PLEASURE DISSERTATION**
– In accordance to natural law / Strawberry Julius / Anti-pleasure dissertation / Rah! rah! replica.
Sep 95. (7") <KRS 253> **I LIKE FUCKING. / I HATE DANGER**

			Kill Rock Stars	Kill Rock Stars
Apr 96.	(cd/lp) <KRS 260 CD/LP)>	**REJECT ALL AMERICAN**		

– Statement of vindication / Capri pants / Jet ski / Distinct complicity / False start / R.I.P. / No backrub / Bloody ice cream / For only / Tony Randall / Reject all American / Finale.

— disbanded around Spring '98, VAIL joined FRUMPIES having already guested on PHRANC's 1995 solo EP, 'Goofyfoot'.

– compilations, etc. –

Jun 98. (cd) *Kill Rock Stars;* <(KRS 298CD)> **THE SINGLES** — May98
– New radio / Rebel girl / DemiRep / In accordance to natural law / Strawberry Julius / Anti-pleasure dissertation / Rah! rah! replica / I like fucking / I hate danger.

JULIE RUIN

KATHLEEN HANNA with **PAUL SCHUSTER** – mixer

			Kill Rock Stars	Kill Rock Stars
Oct 98.	(lp/cd) <(KRS 297/+CD)>	**JULIE RUIN**		Aug98

– Radical or pro-parental / U.G.I. / A place called won't be there / Tania / Aerobicide / Apt. #5 / My morning is summer / I wanna know what love is / The punk singer / On language / Crochet / Interlude / Stay monkey / Breakout a town / Love letter.

LE TIGRE

KATHLEEN HANNA plus **SADIE BENNING** + **JOHANNA FATEMAN**

			Wiiija	Mr. Lady
Nov 99.	(cd/lp) (WIJ CD/LP 1108) <MRLR 07 CD/LP>	**LE TIGRE**		Oct99

– Deceptacon / Hot topic / What's ya take on Cassavettes / The empty / Phanta / Eau d'bedroom dancing / Phanta / Let's run / My my metrocard / Friendship station / Dude yr so crazy!! / Les and Ray. *(UK lp re-iss. Feb02; same as US)*

Nov 99. (7"ep/cd-ep) (WIJ 107) **HOT TOPIC / HOT TOPIC. / YR CRITIQUE / THEY WANT US TO MAKE A SYMPHONY**

— **MELISSA YORK** – drums; repl. J.D. SAMSON; repl. BENNING

			Chicks On Speed	Mr. Lady
Oct 01.	(cd/lp)	(efa 29905-2/-1) <MRLR 19CD> **FEMINIST SWEEPSTAKES**	□	□

– LT tour theme / Shred A / Fake French / FYR / On guard / Much finer / Dyke march 2001 / Tres bien / Well well well / TGIF / My art / Cry for everything bad that's ever happened / Keep on livin'. *(cd re-iss. Feb02 on 'Mr Lady'; same as US)*

			Mr. Lady	Mr. Lady
Jan 02.	(m-cd)	<(MRLR 14)> **FROM THE DESK OF MR. LADY**	□	□

– Get off the internet / Bang! bang! / They want us to make a symphony / Yr critique / Gone B4 yr home / Mediocrity rules.

Feb 02.	(m-lp)	<(MRLR 24LP)> **REMIX** (remixes)	□	□

– Tres bien / On guard / Mediocrity rules / Dyke march 2001 / Deceptacon / Much finer. *(re-iss. May02 on 'Chicks On Speed' m-cd/m-lp; efa 29907-2/-1)*

BILLY MAHONIE

Formed: Hackney, London, England ... late 1997, although both guitarist GAVIN BAKER and drummer HOWARD MONK had rehearsed in a boy band in 1994(!). During this year BAKER and MONK had apparently lost touch musically and emotionally, with all creative procession lost in the realms of obscure pop. The pair took on the influence of jazz, i.e. MILES DAVIS, BUDDY RICH or recent post-rockers TORTOISE, it seemed BAKER and MONK had discovered a musical form which ignored binary rules in order to achieve full creative liberation. Hence the birth of BILLY MAHONIE and the recruitment of two bassists KEVIN PENNEY and HYWELL DINSDALE, who contributed nicely towards the group's unusual blast of sonic strain (which impressed many a dull student at the MAHONIE's first gig in December '97). In early 1998 the ensemble hibernated in a cramped basement in Chiswick, laying down eight tracks (despite suffering from a number of illnesses including broken bones, migraines, retina infection, mental health, etc) of quiet/loud dynamic revelry. Unike MOGWAI and TORTOISE before them, MAHONIE concentrated on a more rock'n'roll standpoint, blending terrifying riffs with BAKER'S sullen guitar melodies, using them to scene-heightening effect. This was apparent on 1998's two 7" singles, 'HOON AND WHISTLING SAM' and 'ON THE BRINCK', although this grew a little too thin come their debut album, 'THE BIG DIG' (1999). Nevertheless, the album still had its strong points which overshadowed weakness. Tracks such as 'FLAGIOLETTES' and 'WILLIAM DERBYSHIRE', displayed passion as well as devotion, exampled by the fiery dramatics of PETE TOWNSHEND meets er, ...AND YOU WILL KNOW US BY THE TRAIL OF DEAD in a seedy strip joint ... this is zeitgeist! – or is it?

Album rating: THE BIG DIG (*7) / WHAT BECOMES BEFORE (*5)

GAVIN BAKER – guitar / **HYWELL DINSDALE** – bass / **KEVIN PENNEY** – bass / **HOWARD MONK** – drums (of CLIENTELE)

			Fierce Panda	not iss.
Jul 98.	(7")	(NING 57) **HOON.** / (other by Rothko)	□	□
Nov 98.	(cd-ep)	(NING 65) **HOON** / (others by Seafood & Tiny Too)	□	□

			Livid Meerkat	not iss.
Sep 98.	(7")	(NUNG 002) **WHISTLING SAM.** / **ON THE BRINCK**	□	□

			Gold Hole	not iss.
Jan 99.	(7"ep)	(GOLE 003) **LITTLE FEET.** / **MAN WITH THE WOMAN HEAD** / **ARE WE ROLLING**	□	□

			Stupid Cat	not iss.
May 99.	(7"ep)	(SCAT 04) **WORLD INACTION** / **LET THE EAT SHIT.** / (other 2 by Jullander)	□	□

			Too Pure	Too Pure
Jul 99.	(cd/lp)	(<pure 94 cd/lp>) **THE BIG DIG**	□	□

– Watching people speaking when you can't hear what they're saying / We accept American dollars / Flagiolettes / Manywhere M1 / Drago / Glenda / William Derbyshire / Manywhere M5 / Yeah, yeah, yeah, yeah, yeah.

Jun 99.	(3xcd-ep's; at gigs)	(pure 96cd 1/2/3) **COME ON BILLY MAHONIE GIVE IT YOUR BEST SHOT**	□	□

– Manywhere M2 / Dollars / On the brinck (8-track) / Manywhere M4 / The evil door / Drago (8-track) / No no no no no / Harmonics / Man with the woman head (8-track).

Oct 99.	(d12"ep/cd-ep; freebie/gig)	(pure 100) **ONE THOUSAND YEARS OF BILLY MAHONIE / LESS FLAGIOLETTES.** / **WE ACCEPT AMERICAN DOLLARS** (Bows remix) / **MANYWHERE M25** (Hefner remix)	□	□

			Norman	not iss.
Nov 99.	(ltd-7")	**JONATHAN WHISKEY.** / (other BILLY MAHONIE track covered by Seafood)	□	□

			Speakerphone	not iss.
Nov 00.	(7")	(DIAL 011) **FLUME.** / **AU LAC CONTRAIRE**	□	□

			Southern	Southern
Oct 01.	(cd/d-lp)	(<18587-2/-1>) **WHAT BECOMES BEFORE**	□	□

– Fishing with a man for a shark / Nacho steals from work / Dusseldorf / Hey Mr. Jukes / Keeper's drive / Simple solutions seldom are / False calm / Lothe / The day without end / I, Heston / Paysted way / A warning to the curious / Terylene / Bres lore.

BIRDDOG

Born: Portland, Oregon, USA ... mid 90's originally as the solo project of Lexington, Kentucky native and singer/songwriter, BILL SANTEN. Departing from his home state, SANTEN travelled around the Western seaboard before laying his anchor in Portland. Here, he made a fortunate connection with alternative folk-rock songwriter ELLIOTT SMITH, who got behind the mixing controls for BIRDDOG's debut 7", 'KILLER'. SMITH stayed on board to produce several more tracks for the mini-album 'THE TRACKHOUSE, THE VALLEY, THE LIQUOR STORE DRIVE-THRU' (1998). This was a competent bluesy folk effort, although the music papers pigeonholed it with SMITH's similar solo work. The ensuing album proper 'GHOST OF THE SEASON' (1998) saw BIRDDOG's sound bolstered with the introduction of a five-piece band. Again a reasonable set, although without any real substance to lift it out of being a little too obscure sounding. With the sophomore LP, 'A SWEET AND BITTER FANCY' (2001), the group began to hit its stride, offering a set that could easily sit among its country/folk-inspired peers; on that point, great guest work included stints from ELLIOTT SMITH and JULIAN WIESENECK on the song 'THIRD AND SOUTH' and EDITH FROST on the track 'RATTLESNAKES'.

Album rating: THE TRACKHOUSE, THE VALLEY, THE LIQUOR STORE DRIVE-THRU (*4) / GHOST OF THE SEASON (*4) / A SWEET AND BITTER FANCY (*7)

BILL SANTEN – vocals, guitar / with **BRUCE SALTMARSCH**

			not iss.	Anonymous
1995.	(7")	**TEN LATER.** / **BROKEN LADY BLUES**	–	□

— SANTEN now with **NEIL GILPIN** + **CHARLIE CAMPBELL**

			not iss.	Undercover
1996.	(7")	**KILLER.** / **PARKED CAR HOMESTEAD**	–	□

— SANTEN added **GLEN KOTCHE** – drums / **CHRIS TESLUK** – cello, guitar, vocals

			Sugar Free	Sugar Free
Apr 98.	(m-cd)	<SF 003> **THE TRACKHOUSE, THE VALLEY, THE LIQUOR STORE DRIVE-THRU**	–	□

– Uptown / Killer / Lights of Amarillo / This came along / Last song / Parked car homestead / Saturday night. *(UK-iss.Mar99; same as US)*

— added **STEVE POULTON** – bass, piano, guitar, vocals / **MORGAN PICKEREL** – vocals, piano

Sep 98.	(cd)	<SF 008> **GHOST OF THE SEASON**	–	□

– Deadlights / Thunderbirds & motorcycles / Blue steel / Ghost of the season / Great escape / Trigger / Halloween / Rats / Fruita / Johnson dozer.

— now without POULTON + PICKEREL

			Alice In Wonderland	Happy Birthday To Me
Nov 01.	(cd)	<(AW 072068)> <1826> **A SWWET AND BITTER FANCY**	□	□ Oct01

– Singapore creek seduction / Third and south / Circling low / Rattlesnakes / Betty / Banyon highway / Baseball / Summer again / Ten later / Midnight hours.

BIRDIE

(see under ⇒ EAST VILLAGE; 80's section)

BIRDLAND

Formed: near Coventry, Midlands, England ... 1988 by the VINCENT brothers, ROBERT and LEE, who had formerly played with ZODIAC MOTEL. The latter outfit only managed a solitary album, 'THE STORY OF ROLAND FLAGG' and a couple of singles before evolving into BIRDLAND. Late in '88, the bleach-blonde retro rockers – now also numbering GENE KALE and SID ROGERS – signed to 'Lazy' (once home to The PRIMITIVES), scoring a handful of minor hits, namely 'HOLLOW HEART', 'PARADISE' and 'SLEEP WITH ME'. Late in 1990, they were snapped up by MCA-backed 'Radioactive' (US-only) and 'Toshiba' (Japan-only), although this leap to major status failed to live up to the hype. Despite a further couple of hits with 'ROCK'N'ROLL NIGGER' and 'EVERYBODY NEEDS SOMEBODY', they pulled the plug after the relative failure of their eponymous debut album in '91. • **Covers:** ROCK'N'ROLL NIGGER (Patti Smith) / SEE NO EVIL (Television).

Album rating: BIRDLAND (*5) / Zodiac Motel: THE STORY OF ROLAND FLAGG (*4)

ZODIAC MOTEL

ROBERT VINCENT – vocals / **LEE VINCENT** – guitar / **GENE KALE** – drums

			Swordfish	not iss.
Feb 87.	(lp)	(SWFLP 001) **THE STORY OF ROLAND FLAGG**	□	□
Apr 87.	(7")	(SWF 004) **SUNSHINE MINER.** / **CRESCENDO**	□	□

(12"+=) (ZOMO 1) – Inside my mind / Sugarblood.

Aug 87.	(12"ep)	(ZOMO 2) **CRYSTAL INJECTION** / (**I CAN ONLY GIVE YOU) EVERYTHING.** / **DESTINY RANCH** / **STEPHANIE BLUE**	□	□

BIRDLAND

— added **SID ROGERS** – bass

			Lazy	Radioactive
Mar 89.	(7")	(LAZY 13) **HOLLOW HEART.** / **SUGARBLOOD**	70	–

(7"ep+=/12"ep+=) **THE BIRDLAND EP** (LAZY 13 D/T) – Crystal / Got to get away.

Jun 89.	(7")	(LAZY 14) **PARADISE.** / **WHITE**	70	–

(12"ep+=) **EP 2** (LAZY 14T) – Rage. *(some with 'Stay')*

Jan 90.	(7"ep/12"ep/cd-ep)	(LAZY 17/+T/CD) **SLEEP WITH ME** / **WANTED.** / **HOLLOW HEART** (acoustic) / **SLEEP WITH ME** (acoustic)	32	–
Sep 90.	(7"ep/12"ep/cd-ep)	(LAZY 20/+T/CD) **ROCK'N'ROLL NIGGER** / **FUN FUN FUN.** / **ROLLER COASTER** / **PROTECTION**	47	–
Jan 91.	(7")	(LAZY 24) **EVERYBODY NEEDS SOMEBODY.** / **DON'T HANG ON**	44	–

(12"+=) (LAZY 24T) – Shoot you down (acoustic) / Untitled.
(cd-s+=) (LAZY 24CD) – Shoot you down (acoustic) / Twin sons.
(7"ep+=) (LAZY 24D) – Twin sons / Exit (acoustic).

Feb 91. (cd/c/lp) (LAZY 25 CD/MC/LP) <RAR 10214> **BIRDLAND** 44
– Shoot you down / Sleep with me / Don't look back / Wake up dreaming / Letter you know / Rock'n'roll nigger / Everybody needs somebody / Beat me like a star / She belongs to me / Exit. (cd+=) – Hollow heart / Crystal / Got to get away.
Jun 91. (m-cd) <RARDS 54181> **BIRDLAND**
– Sleep with me / Don't hang on / Wanted / White / Protection / Sleep with me (acoustic).
—— disbanded soon after being dropped by their record label

BIS

Formed: Glasgow, Scotland ... late 1994 by teenagers MANDA RIN and brothers SCI-FI STEVEN (who also became part of Kraut-rockers, GANGER) and JOHN DISKO. Initially gaining exposure through the tight-knit fanzine network, BIS were the first outfit to appear on The DELGADOS' now influential D.I.Y. label, 'Chemikal Underground', the release in question being the 7" maxi, 'DISCO NATION'. In March '96, BIS also became the first bonafide indie band to play live on Top Of The Pops with a track, 'KANDY POP', from their Top 30 EP, 'THE SECRET VAMPIRE SOUNDTRACK'. Their blend of cutesy brat-pop – like ALTERED IMAGES meeting The SLITS – was developed over a further couple of low-key 45's before they finally signed on the dotted line for The BEASTIE BOYS' trendy 'Grand Royal' label (remaining independent in the UK through 'Wiiija') after turning down 50 major imprints. The trio subsequently forsook unappreciative Britain (where the press was increasingly turning against them after all the hype) to try Japan, where they soon became a top act, shifting 100,000 units of their 1997 debut album, 'THE NEW TRANSISTOR HEROES', in the space of only a few weeks. During this spell, BIS' imprint 'teen-c! recordingz' were still in operation, delivering releases by mates, LUGWORM, DICK JOHNSON and PINK KROSS, before winding up operations. Returning to UK shores in 1998, they eventually hit the Top 40 again with 'EURODISCO', a taster from the accompanying second album proper 'SOCIAL DANCING' (1999). Produced by left-wing GANG OF FOUR member ANDY GILL, the album didn't do much to raise BIS' profile on the songwriting front. After second track 'I'M A SLUT', the cheesy chorus-lines and the shouty bubblegum pop lyrics made you want to cringe like you'd just witnessed a family member embarrassing themselves at karaoke. GILL's production became tiresome too; for a militant underground punk-rocker he spent too much time tweaking the album's production, so by the end it almost sounded as sugar-coated as a BRITNEY SPEARS record. Not good, not bad, just mindless shallow pop ... there's nothing worse. Things didn't get much better, with the release of the maturing 'MUSIC FOR A STRANGE WORLD' EP in 2000 and the Euro pop-tinged 'RETURN TO CENTRAL' (2001), which saw them add influences as diverse and as uncanny as NEW ORDER and CAN. Granted, this was a million miles away from the tooth-rotting 'KANDY POP', but the production still remained the same; staid, dull and polished to such a high sheen that even hard core fans of the band had forgotten their lo-fi indie roots. A collaboration with Detroit's electro-clash heroes ADULT was soon to be delivered in the form of mini-album 'PLASTIQUE NOUVEAU' (2002), with the underground group providing a new spin on the BIS method, which by this time was beginning to sound like ERASURE and KRAFTWERK meeting in a Glaswegian indie disco. Big in Japan, apparently. • **Songwriters:** SCI-FI or group, except THE BOY WITH THE THORN IN HIS SIDE (Smiths) / GERM FREE ADOLESCENTS (X-Ray Spex) / LOVE WILL TEAR US APART (Joy Division) / HURT (New Order) / SHACK UP (A Certain Ratio) / A VIEW FROM A HILL (Section 25) – 4 of the latter from the 'Factory' EP.
Album rating: THE NEW TRANSISTOR HEROES (*6) / INTENDO mini of demos & B-sides (*5) / SOCIAL DANCING (*6) / RETURN TO CENTRAL (*6)

MANDA RIN (b. AMANDA MacKINNON, 22 Mar'77) – vocals, keyboards, recorder / **SCI-FI STEVEN** (b. STEVEN CLARK, 20 Mar'76) – vocals, synthesizers / **JOHN DISKO** (b. JOHN CLARK, 21 Aug'78) – guitar

Chemikal Underground not iss.

Aug 95. (7"m) (Chem 002) **DISCO NATION. / PLASTIK PEOPLE / CONSPIRACY A GO-GO**
Dec 95. (7"ep; various artists) (che 47) **ICKY-POO AIR-RAID**
(above issued on 'Che')
Mar 96. (7"ep/cd-ep) (Chem 003/+cd) **THE SECRET VAMPIRE SOUNDTRACK** 25
– Kandy pop / Secret vampires / Teen-c power! / Diska.

teen-c! not iss.

Jun 96. (7"ep/c-ep/cd-ep) (SKETCH 001/+CS/CD) **BIS VS. THE D.I.Y. CORPS** 45
– This is fake d.i.y. / Burn the suit / Dance to the disco beat.

Southern K

Jun 96. (7") (IPU 66) **KEROLEEN. / ("Heavenly":- Trophy Girlfriend)**

Wiiija Capitol

Oct 96. (7"ep/c-ep/cd-ep) (WIJ 55/+MC/CD) **ATOM POWERED ACTION! EP** 54
– Starbright boy / Wee love / Team theme / Cliquesuck.
Mar 97. (7") (WIJ 67) **SWEET SHOP AVENGERZ. / I'LL GET YOU BACK** 46
(7") (WIJ 67X) – ('A'side) / Rollerblade zero.
(cd-s+=) (WIJ 67CD) – Ninja hi skool.
Apr 97. (cd/c/lp) (WIJ CD/MC/LP 1064) <56007> **THE NEW TRANSISTOR HEROES** 55
– Tell it to the kids / Sweet shop avengerz / Starbright boy / Popstar kill / Mr. Important / Antiseptic poetry / Popyura / Skinny tie sensurround / Poster parent / Monstarr / Everybody thinks that they're going to get theirs / Rebel soul / Photo shop / X-defect / Lie detector test / Dinosaur germs. <US lp on 'Grand Royal'; GR 45>
Apr 97. (7"ep; split w/ PINK KROSS VS LUGWORM) (GUIDE 11) **POP SONG / ROCCO NEGRO / (other two by LUGWORM)**
(above issued on 'Guided Missile')
May 97. (7") (WIJ 69) **EVERYBODY THINKS THAT THEY'RE GOING TO GET THEIRS. / STATEMENT OF INTENT** 64
(7") (WIJ 69X) – ('A'side) / Girl star.
(cd-s+=) (WIJ 69CD) – Cookie cutter kid.
Nov 98. (c-s) (WIJ 086C) **EURODISCO / LIKE ROBOTS** 37
(cd-s+=) (WIJ 086CD) – Cinema says.
(7") (WIJ 086) – ('A'side) / Stray cat blues.
(12") (WIJ 086TR) – ('A'mixes; Les Rhythmes Digitales / DJ Scissorkicks / Klute / original).
Feb 99. (7") (WIJ 095) **ACTION AND DRAMA. / GERM FREE ADOLESCENTS** 50
(cd-s) (WIJ 095CD) – ('A'side) / Not even close / 17 hours.
(cd-s) (WIJ 095CDX) – ('A'side) / Eurodisco (Les Rhythmes Digitales mix) / Eurodisco (DJ Scissorkicks mix).
Mar 99. (cd/c/lp) (WIJ CD/MC/LP 1088) <96439> **SOCIAL DANCING** Aug99
– Making people normal / I'm a slut / Eurodisco / Action and drama / Theme from Tokyo / The hit girl / Am I loud enough / Shopaholic / Young alien types / Detour / Sale or return / It's all new / Listen up.
Jul 99. (7") (WIJ 101) **DETOUR. / KISS AND TELL**
(cd-s+=) (WIJ 101CD) – Why don't we go home.

Wiiija V2

Jun 00. (12"ep/cd-ep) (WIJEP 116 T/CD) <81> **MUSIC FOR A STRANGER WORLD**
– Dead wrestlers / Are you ready / How can we be strange / I want it all / Beats at the office / Punk rock points. <US re-iss. 2001 on 'Lookout'; LK 263>
Jul 00. (7") (74489) **POWERPUFF GIRLS. / (other track by APPLES IN STEREO)**
(above issued on 'Rhino')

Chemikal Underground not iss.

Oct 01. (12"ep/cd-ep) (chem 058/+cd) **FUKD ID VOL.5**
– Brainclouds / European / Mamelodi sundown / Situation.

Artful SpinArt

Jan 02. (cd) (ARTFULCD 42) <SPART 98> **RETURN TO CENTRAL** Sep01
– What you're afraid of / Silver spoon / Black pepper / The end starts today / Protection / Two million / Chicago / Metal box / We're complicated / Robotic / A portrait from space.

Oscarr not iss.

May 02. (12"ep) (OSC 004) **FACT 2002 EP**
– Love will tear us apart / Hurt / Shack up / A view from a hill.

SpinArt SpinArt

Jul 02. (m-lp) (<SPART 110>) **PLASTIQUE 33**
– Protection / Robotic / Sound of sleet / Don't let the rain come down / The end starts today / Make it through / Brainclouds / Protection / The end starts today.

– compilations, etc. –

Dec 96. (cd-ep) teen-c; <SKETCH 001> **THIS IS TEEN-C POWER**
– Kill yr boyfriend / School disco / Kandy pop / This is fake D.I.Y. / Burn the suit / Teen-c power.
Aug 98. (m-cd) Grand Royal; (7581 480060-2) <GR 60> **INTENDO** (demos & B-sides)
– Grand Royal with cheese / Girl star / Clockwork punk / Famous / Ninja hi skool / Kid cut / Automatic freestyle / I'll get you back / Cookie cutter kid / Grand Royal with cheese.

KITCHEN

AMANDA plus **RYAN SEAGRIST** (b. Vero Beach, Florida) – guitar, vocals, etc (ex-DISCOUNT)

Damaged Goods not iss.

Apr 01. (7"/cd-s) (DAMGOOD 195/+CD) **BETTER ON THE FLOOR. / AND HE LOVES IT / WE'RE JUST THE YOUTH**

BIVOUAC

Formed: Derby, England ... early 90's by songwriter PAUL YEADON, along with GRANVILLE MARSDEN and ANTHONY HODKINSON. Straight outta Derby as the US grunge scene exploded in the UK, BIVOUAC may have seemed unlikely candidates for beating the Americans at their own game. Yet by the mid-90's, the band had been signed to 'Geffen', home to NIRVANA amongst others and a far cry from the band's early days co-headlining with JACOB'S MOUSE. Initially securing a deal with Workers Playtime offshoot, 'Elemental', the band issued a debut single/EP, 'A.B.C.', closely following it up with 'SLACK' and 'GOOD DAY SONG'. Whether by accident or design, BIVOUAC sounded like they'd lived in Seattle all their lives, right down to the choppy, buzz-saw guitar riffs and Americanised vocal style. No bad thing at the time of course, as the band secured themselves support slots with such US alt-rock aristocrats as FUGAZI and The JESUS LIZARD. 1993 also saw the release of their debut album, 'TUBER', a major label bidding war ensuing as the big boys vied for the lads' signatures. Going the whole hog and signing for 'Geffen', the band concentrated their efforts on cracking the American market, KEITH YORK replacing the departing HODKINSON. By the release of 1995's follow-up album, 'FULL SIZE BOY', however, the grunge scene had splintered and BIVOUAC's moment seemed to have passed.
Album rating: TUBER (*7) / FULL SIZE BOY (*7)

PAUL YEADON – vocals, guitar / **GRANVILLE MARSDEN** – bass / **ANTHONY HODKINSON** – drums

		El-e-mental	Engine
May 92.	(12"ep) (ELM 002T) **A.B.C. / FISHES. / STICK STUCK / ME, TED AND CHARLES**	☐	-
Oct 92.	(12"ep/cd-ep) (ELM 004 T/CD) **SLACK. / TOWLD / TWO STICKS**	☐	-
Jun 93.	(c-ep) <3> **DERBY & JOAN** (compilation) – ABC / Fishes / Stick stick / Me, Ted & Charles / Slack / Towld Two sticks.	-	☐
Jun 93.	(7") (ELM 10S) **GOOD DAY SONG. / SQUEAKER, BESS, BREAD, BEANS AND CASH** (cd-s+=) (ELM 10CD) – Trepanning.	☐	-
Jun 93.	(cd/c/lp) (ELM 11 CDX/LP) **TUBER** – Good day song / Big question mark / Dragging your weight around / Rue / Deadend friend / Drank / Steel strung / The need / The bell foundry / Bad day song.	☐	Mar94
Aug 93.	(7") (ELM 12S) **THE BELL FOUNDRY. / LEAD** (cd-s+=) (ELM 12CD) – Saltwater heal.	☐	-
May 94.	(10"ep/7"ep/cd-ep) (ELM 20/+S/CD) **MARKED AND TAGGED E.P.** – And then she ate / Spine / Art, science and making things.	☐	-
—	**KEITH YORK** – drums (ex-DOCTOR PHIBES & THE HOUSE OF WAX EQUATIONS) repl. HODKINSON		

		Geffen	D.G.C.
May 95.	(7") (GFS 89) **THINKING. / FAMILIAR** (cd-s+=) (GFSTD 89) – In the arse end of nothing.	☐	-
Jul 95.	(7"/c-s) (GFS/+C 90) **MONKEY SANCTUARY (CYNIC). / 45 SEATED STANDING NIL** (cd-s+=) (GFSTD 90) – Deadend friend.	☐	-
Jul 95.	(cd/c/lp) (GED/GEC/GEF 24561) <DGCD 24803> **FULL SIZE BOY** – Not going back there again / Thinking / Trepanning / Gecko or skink / Monkey sanctuary (cynic) / My only safe bet / Familiar / Mattress / Mainbrake / Bing bong / Lounge lizard / The ray is related to the shark.	☐	☐
—	split after the failure of above		

BLACK BOX RECORDER (see under ⇒ AUTEURS)

BLACK DICE

Formed: Brooklyn, New York, USA . . . 1997. BLACK DICE are hard to really file under any one particular genre. If pushed for a categorization, then they probably lived in the experimental regions beyond punk and hardcore, with a room mate in the form of electronica who visited regularly. BD explored feedback, differing time signatures, and pretty much 'noise' to the full. Their sonic investigations were conducted, it seemed, in much the same vein as LOU REED's influential and experimental double-LP 'METAL MACHINE MUSIC' (1975). This is not to say that their output was similar to this record, but rather it was testing in the same water; distancing the listener with the alienation, but at the same time, waking them up to think about and feel the 'noise'. BD's debut single appeared on 'Gravity' records in 1998, followed soon after by the release of the beautifully titled 'SEMEN OF THE SUN' single on 'Tapes' records. They reached the attention of the 'Troubleman Unlimited' label, who released their debut LP in the millennium, 'NUMBER 3'. The album was a hard listen, sometimes at points becoming accessible, but never staying there long, although avoiding the pretension that sometimes came with this experimental ground. They followed this up the next year with the EP 'COLD HANDS', which delved even further into the dark regions of hardcore noise. Although, it is probably safe to say that this will never appear in the mainstream, it was a great accolade to the band that they chose to take the music and sound to places they believe it should, and had not, travelled.

Album rating: BLACK DICE mini (*6) / COLD HANDS mini (*7) / LOST VALLEY (*7)

unknown members

		not iss.	Gravity
Feb 98.	(7") **BLACK DICE**	-	☐
		not iss.	Vermin Scum
1999.	(7") **BLACK DICE**	-	☐
		Three One G	Troubleman
May 00.	(10"m-lp/m-cd) <042> **NUMBER 3** – (15 untitled tracks).	-	☐
Apr 01.	(m-cd) <074> **COLD HANDS** – Cold hands / Smile friends / The raven / Birthstone.	-	☐
2001.	(7") <084> **SEMEN OF THE SUN**	-	☐
Jul 01.	(7";w/book) (31G 17) **BLACK DICE**	☐	-
—	split an album with ERASE ERRATA		
		Tigerbeat 6	not iss.
Nov 02.	(3"cd-s) (MEOW 063) **LOST VALLEY**	☐	-
—	about to release, 'BEACHES & CANYONS' early in 2003		

BLACK GRAPE
(see under ⇒ HAPPY MONDAYS; 80's section)

BLACK HEART PROCESSION

Formed: San Diego, California, USA . . . 1996 by PALL JENKINS, TOBIAS NATHANIEL (ex industrial metaller with THREE MILE PILOT) and MARIO RUBALCABA. Bursting onto the slo-core indie scene in late '96, THE BLACK HEART PROCESSION were not your average goth miserabilists. With songs of eerie quietness, heart-breaking tenderness and crashing crescendos, you might've forgiven PALL and Co for being just screwed-up romantics. After touring the US, 'Headhunter' records issued the debut album '1' (1998), and as you may have guessed '2' (1999) followed subsequently, as did the best of the bunch, the horribly underrated 'THREE' (2000). The latter displayed ten songs, all equally meriting MERCURY REV's 'Deserters Songs', or 'Mutiny' by The BIRTHDAY PARTY. Sprawling pianos, hollow guitars, scary shrieks and PALL's baritone/falsetto vocals and bitterly pessimistic lyrics all equated to the release of one of the most romantically gothic records of the new millennium. From the ROWLAND S. HOWARD-esque drone of 'ONCE SAID AT THE FIRES', to the tender and devastating 'TILL WE HAVE TO SAY GOODBYE' (accompanied by a gut-wrenching bow-saw solo) the set allowed the listener to roam about a thick foggy landscape, while never actually leaving the house. Two years later, and THE BLACK HEART PROCESSION had a sudden change of direction. Firstly, PALL JENKINS, for some reason, had changed his name to PAULO ZAPPOLI, MARIO RUBALCABA was replaced with DIMITRI DZIENSUWSKI, percussionist JOE PLUMMER was recruited as a full-time member and the band now played a melodramatic form of calypso goth (if that genre actually exists!). This was apparent on 2002's well-received 'AMORE DEL TROPICO', an album that was much greater in ambition and scope than any of the band's previous releases. Gone were the humming gothic anthems (well, sort of), as they were replaced with temperamental, hot-blooded latin rhythms, trumpets, maracas et al. 'TROPICS OF LOVE', a swinging ballad with staccato piano was a highlight, as was the beautiful lament 'THE INVITATION'. But there was ultimately something missing from the set of grandeur songs. Were The HEART's just getting too cocky? Were they playing down to their critics by releasing an uptempo album? Who knows? But one thing was certain; The BLACK HEART PROCESSION laughed in the shadows, while other bands enjoyed sulking in the sunlight.

Album rating: 1 (*6) / 2 (*6) / THREE (*8) / AMORE DEL TROPICO (*7)

PALL A JENKINS – vocals, guitar, organ, synths, bass, etc / **TOBIAS NATHANIEL** – keyboards, drums, guitar, etc (ex-THREE MILE PILOT) / **MARIO RUBALCABA** – drums (ex-CLIKITAT IKATOWI)

		not iss.	Headhunter
May 98.	(cd/lp) <080> **1** – The waiter / The old kind of summer / Release my heart / Even thieves couldn't lie / Blue water – Black heart / Heart without a home / The winter my heart froze / Stitched to my heart / Square heart / In a tin flask / A heart the size of a horse.	-	☐
May 99.	(cd) <20894> **2** – The waiter No.2 / Blue tears / A light so dim / Your church is red / When we reach the hill / Outside the glass / Gently off the edge / It's a crime I never told you about the diamonds in your eyes / My heart might stop / Beneath the ground / The waiter No.3.	-	☐
—	added **JASON CRANE** – trumpet (of ROCKET FROM THE CRYPT)		
		Up	Up
Feb 00.	(12"ep/cd-ep) <(UP 077/+CD)> **A 3 SONG RECORDING** – A truth quietly told / Destroying the city of hearts / Song about a . . .	☐	Dec99
		not iss.	Galaxia
2000.	(cd-ep) <006> **FISH THE HOLES ON FROZEN LAKES** – Innocence / Descent / Remembrance.	-	☐
—	now without MARIO who remained as a guest		
		Touch & Go	Touch & Go
Aug 00.	(lp/cd) <(TG 210/+CD)> **THREE** – We always know / Guess I'll forget you / Once said at the fires / Waterfront (the sinking road) / Till we have to say goodbye / I know your ways / Never from this heart / A heart like mine / The war is over / On ships of gold.	☐	☐
May 01.	(7") **BETWEEN THE MACHINES. / AFTER THE LADDER** (above issued on 'Suicide Squeeze', below issued on 'Speakerphone')	-	☐
Nov 01.	(7") (DIAL 016) **LOVE SINGS A SUNRISE** – LSSR / The hideaway.	☐	-
Oct 02.	(d-lp/cd) <(TG 232/+CD)> **AMORE DEL TROPICO** – The end of love / Tropics of love / Broken world / Why I stay / The invitation / Did you wonder / A sign on the road / Sympathy crime / The visitor / The waiter #4 / A cry for love / Before the people / Only one way / Fingerprints / The one who has disappeared.	☐	☐

BLACK REBEL MOTORCYCLE CLUB

Formed: San Francisco, California, USA . . . early 1999 by high school musicians ROBERT TURNER and PETER HAYES, eventually recruiting drummer NICK JAGO from the garage club scene around the city's Bay Area. If the film 'The Wild One' – from which BLACK REBEL MOTORCYCLE CLUB had grabbed their name – had been soundtracked by this particular group, all proverbial hell would have ensued. After extensively touring between San Francisco and L.A., the trio of leather-clad, brooding dirty rock'n'rollers decided to issue a self-produced demo of thirteen tracks, which finally wormed its way onto the A&R desk of 'Virgin' records. The group were signed in late 2000, and headed off on a tour with The DANDY WARHOLS across America, pulling in much praise and fanbase from the college circuit. They arrived on the shores of Britain just in time to feel the hype of the new garage revival (STROKES et al), and were thoroughly lauded by the NME and rock stars such as NOEL GALLAGHER and JIM REID. This was even before the debut album, 'B.R.M.C.' (2001) was released, so one can imagine the commotion when it turned out to be one of the finest rock'n'roll albums of the last decade. Fuzzy guitar, jiving chrouses, big hairy sweaty percussion – it had it all. The LP entered the Top 20 and they sold out an entire tour before going on the road with OASIS. Here's hoping BRMC aren't just a sparkle in the passing fads of popular music, but a continuous fiery flare . . .

BLACK REBEL MOTORCYCLE CLUB (cont)

Album rating: B.R.M.C. (*7)

PETER HAYES – vocals, guitar, bass, harmonica, keyboards / **ROBERT TURNER** – vocals, bass, guitar, keyboards / **NICK JAGO** – drums, percussion

		Virgin	Virgin
Feb 01.	(7"ep) **RED EYES AND TEARS / SCREAMING GUN. / AS SURE AS THE SUN / WHITE PALMS**	-	
Mar 01.	(7") **RIFLES.** /	-	
May 01.	(7") **LOVE BURNS.** /	-	
Oct 01.	(7") (VUS 224) **WHATEVER HAPPENED TO MY ROCK'N'ROLL (PUNK SONG). / RED EYES AND TEARS** (cd-s+=) (VUSCD 224) – U.S. government / Fail-safe.		Nov01
Jan 02.	(cd) (CDVUS 207) <10045> **BLACK REBEL MOTORCYCLE CLUB** – Love burns / Red eyes and tears / Whatever happened to my rock'n'roll (punk song) / Awake / White palms / As sure as the sun / Rifles / Too real / Spread your love / Head up high / Salvation. (lp-iss.Jan02; VUSLP 207)	25	Apr01
Jan 02.	(7") (VUS 234) **LOVE BURNS. / AT MY DOOR** (cd-s) (VUSCD 234) – ('A'side) / Screaming gun / Rifles.	37	-
Jan 02.	(cd-ep) **SCREAMING GUN EP** – Fail-safe / Down here / At my door / TV loop (down deep) / Screaming gun.	-	
May 02.	(7") (VUS 245) **SPREAD YOUR LOVE. / TONIGHT'S WITH YOU** (cd-s+=) (VUSDX 245) – Simple words. (cd-s) (VUSCD 245) – ('A'side) / The weight is more / Loaded gun.	27	-
Sep 02.	(7") (VUS 257) **WHATEVER HAPPENED TO MY ROVK'N'ROLL (PUNK SONG). / RIFLES (live)** (cd-s) (VUSCD 257) – ('A'side) / Shuffle your feet (XFM session) / ('A'-video).	46	-

BLACK SWAN NETWORK (see under ⇒ OLIVIA TREMOR CONTROL)

BLACK TAMBOURINE

Formed: Washington, D.C., USA ... 1989 by PAM BERRY, ARCHIE MOORE, BRIAN NELSON and MIKE SCHULMAN. Although BT's recorded output was anything but expansive, they were regarded as groundbreaking in the US indie scene of the early 90s and beyond added to this the later work of all members involved was also highly inspirational for their contempoaries. Ignoring their city of conception's famous hardcore scene pioneered by the likes of FUGAZI, the band instead turned towards the alternative pop meanderings and shoegazing stylistics of British bands like the PASTELS and The JESUS & MARY CHAIN. Following several compilation appearances and guest work, their debut 7" proper, 'THROW AGGI OFF THE BRIDGE' (a comedy nod to the PASTELS' frontman STEPHEN and his girlfriend AGGI WRIGHT) was released in 1990 by 'Audrey's Diary'. A handful of further singles saw light, including 'BY TOMORROW' (issued on SCHULMAN's own imprint, 'Slumberland'). Yet after only two years on the go, and without an LP, 1991 saw BLACK TAMBOURINE split, leaving 'Slumberland' to subsequently collect all their recorded work together on the posthumously released, 'COMPLETE RECORDINGS' (1999) album. Yet for the band's line-up the story did not end there. SCHULMAN devoted more of his time to running and signing bands for his nascent label, and in so doing created, by the end of the decade, one of the most highly regarded indie imprints, with a roster enviable by most. NELSON and MOORE, likewise, put more time into their other musical project, VELOCITY GIRL. BERRY went through a succession of groups, including the twee pop trio, GLO-WORM, whom she formed with the aide of indie veterans TERRY BANKS and DAN SEARING. This outfit was to be about as long-lasting as BT, breaking up after only a year and with only several EP releases under their belt. Yet, as with BERRY's former band, they, and the music-buying public, benefitted from 'K' records' later releasing the album 'GLIMMER' (1996), which collected together G-W's work, including a lovely cover of the Cure hit, 'FRIDAY I'M IN LOVE'. From the remanants of this experiment, BERRY moved on to the SHAPIROS, which were put together with the help of BART (of HYDROPLANE fame), TRISH (of the HEARTWORMS) and SKOOTER (from VERONICA LAKE). Although they too, were not to last long in this format, they released the competent indie pop EP, 'MONTH OF DAYS / DO YOU KNOW' (1995), which included BERRY's old colleague MOORE on production. BERRY subsequently formed CASTAWAY STONES, which featured former conspirators of both BLACK TAMBOURINE and the SHAPIROS, its tweaked late 60s rock/pop sound was a refreshing change, best showcased on the debut LP, 'MAKE LOVE TO YOU' (2000). Also noteworthy, was BERRY's part played in the foundation and running of the influential alternative press magazine, 'Chickfactor'. • **Covers:** CAN'T EXPLAIN (Love) / GLO-WORM covered: FRIDAY I'M IN LOVE (Cure) / CRAZY TOWN (Velocity Girl).

Album rating: COMPLETE RECORDINGS compilation (*7) / Glo-Worm: GLIMMER (*7) / Shapiros: COMPILATION (*5) / Castaway Stones: MAKE LOVE TO YOU (*5)

PAM BARRY – vocals / **ARCHIE MOORE** – bass, guitar, vocals (of VELOCITY GIRL) / **BRIAN NELSON** – guitar, bass, drums (of VELOCITY GIRL) / **MIKE SCHULMAN** – drums, guitar (of WHORL)

		not iss.	Slumberland
1990.	(7"; Various Artists) <SLR 1> **What Kind Of Heaven Do You Want** – Pam's tan / (other artists).	-	
1991.	(7"red-ep) <SLR 9> **BY TOMORROW / PACK YOU UP. / BLACK CAR / (+1)**	-	

		not iss.	Audrey's Diary
Jan 92.	(7") <001.92> **THROW AGGI OFF THE BRIDGE.** /		-

— after they split early in 1992, MOORE and NELSON continued with VELOCITY GIRL, SCHULMAN continued with Slumberland records

– compilations, etc. –

| Apr 99. | (cd) Slumberland; <(SLR 37)> **COMPLETE RECORDINGS** – For ex-lovers only / Black car / Pack you up / Can't explain / I was wrong / Throw Aggi off the bridge / Drown / We can't be friends / By tomorrow / Pam's tan. <10"lp-iss.1999 on 'Fantastic'; FAN 011> | | |

GLO-WORM

PAM – vocals, guitar / **TERRY BANKS** – drums (ex-TREE FORT ANGST, ex-ST. CHRISTOPHER) / **DAN SEARING** – bass

		not iss.	Somersault
1994.	(7") <4 Somers> **HOLIDAY.** /	-	

		not iss.	Slumberland
May 95.	(7"m) <SLR 045> **WISHING WELL. / BEYOND THE SEA / CHANGE OF HEART**	-	

— had already split below before set

		K	K
1996.	(7"m) **TRAVELOGUE.** /		
May 96.	(cd) <(KLP 54CD)> **GLIMMER** – Travelogue / Useless / Change of heart / One million rainy days / Wishing well / April street / Beyond the sea / Friday I'm in love / Holiday / Downtown / Tilt-a-whirl / Stars above / Crazy town / I will remember you (live).		Apr96

— TERRY and DAN later joined The SATURDAY PEOPLE (aka ARCHIE MOORE, etc) but with different instruments

SHAPIROS

PAM with **BART** (of CAT'S MIAOW!) / **SKOOTER** (of VERONICA LAKE) + **TRISH** (of HEARTWORMS)

		not iss.	Fantastic
1995.	(7") <FAN 001> **MONTH OF DAYS. / DO YOU KNOW**	-	

		not iss.	Pop Factory
1995.	(7") <PROOF 7> **CROSS YOUR MIND.** /	-	

		not iss.	Drive-In
Apr 96.	(7"; Various Artists) <DRIVE 1> **Drive-In Season EP** – Paris Kiss / (others by CAT'S MIAOW! + SINGING BUSH + MADISON ELECTRIC).	-	

		not iss.	Library
Jun 98.	(7") <SHHH 2> **split w/ PENCIL TIN** – Gone by fall / He said, she said / (other 2 by PENCIL TIN).	-	

– compilations, etc. –

| Apr 02. | (cd) Library; <(SHHH 19)> **COMPILATION** – Paris kiss / Cry for a shadow / Month of days / Gone by fall / Makes me smile / Cut / Do you know / Hundred times / He said, she said / Cross your mind / Will you still love me tomorrow / When I was Howard Hughes. | | |

CASTAWAY STONES

PAM with **GREG PAVLOVCAK** – guitar, vocals

		not iss.	Shelflife
Mar 99.	(7") <LIFE 8> **LEAVE NO STONE UNTURNED.** /	-	
Apr 99.	(cd) <LIFE 11> **MAKE LOVE TO YOU** – Up all day / Lost and found / Night time is the city's only star / Rose in the Devil's garden / The revolution creaks on a bed / Under London skies / Pinball, 1973 / Brazil / Autumn II / Everybody's having a good time.	-	

		not iss.	Boa
1999.	(7") <HISS 15> **IN THE DEVIL'S GARDEN.** /	-	

— afterwards, GREG joined The SATURDAY PEOPLE

BLACKTOP (see under ⇒ DIRTBOMBS)

BLAGGERS I.T.A.

Formed: London, England ... summer 1988 initially as PEASANT ARMY by frontman MATTY 'BLAG' alongside a cast of equally militant musical comrades. Founded on a staunch anti-fascist platform, The BLAGGERS communicated their firmly held beliefs through a frantic musical barrage of punk, ska, hip-hop and reggae. By their own admittance not the greatest of musicians, the band – in the time honoured punk style – made up in attitude what they lacked in ability. After a series of seriously angry releases on their own 'Words Of Warning' label (they'd previously released an album in '89 under the BLAGGERS moniker), the band finally issued their debut album proper, 'UNITED COLOURS OF BLAGGERS I.T.A.', in early '93. With a snowballing reputation earned largely via their blistering live work, the band subsequently found themselves the subject of a major label bidding war. 'Parlophone' eventually secured the band's signatures, a Top 40 hit later that summer with 'STRESSS' suggesting a bright future. Things turned pear-shaped, however, after MATTY was involved in a fight with Melody Maker journalist, Dave Simpson, the altercation a result of revelations regarding the frontman's previous Nazi sympathies. The band were subsequently dropped as the appropriately titled 'BAD KARMA' (1994) album sank without trace. Although they carried on with a series of releases on their own

BLAGGERS I.T.A. (cont)

'Disinformation' label, the posse suffered an irreparable split following the sacking of MATTY in summer '95. Sadly, at the age of 36, MATTY (or MATTHEW ROBERTS) died of a suspected drug overdose on the 22nd of February, 2000. • **Covered:** GUNS OF BRIXTON (Clash) / MURDER OF LIDDLE TOWERS (Angelic Upstarts). • **Trivia:** 'HERE'S JOHNNY' was a dig at Prime Minister of the time John Major.

Album rating: ON YER TOES (*5) / BLAGGERMUFFIN' mini (*5) / FUCK FASCISM ... (*4) / UNITED COLOURS OF BLAGGERS (*6) / BAD KARMA (*5)

MATTY 'BLAG' (b. MATTHEW ROBERTS, 1964) – vocals / **BILKO** – vocals / **SERIOUS STEVE** – guitar / **MATT VINYL** – bass / **JEZZ THE JESTER** – drums

Oi! / *not iss.*

May 89. (lp; as BLAGGERS) *(OIR 014)* **ON YER TOEZ**
– On yer toes / Young blaggers / Crazy / Skateboard bop / Weekend warning / Bronco bullfrog / Shaw tailor / Nufting (blagged again) / Jailhouse doors / Freedom fighters / Britains dream / Ireland / Greetings from Ireland / Save your hate / House of the fascist scum / Nice on Blaggers. *(cd-iss. Jun98 on 'Mad Butcher'; MBC 001CD)*

— **JASON 'Wrist Action Jackson' COOK** – drums; repl. CAB who repl. JEZZ / **GARY THE SQUATTER** – rhythm guitar (of UNDER THE GUN) repl. BILKO

Network 90 / *not iss.*

Nov 90. (7"m; as BLAGGERS) *(WWFC 1)* **IT'S UP TO YOU. / GET OUTTA HERE / MEAT**

— **PAUL THE PIG** – guitar (of TRENCH FEVER) repl. GARY
— **CHRISTIE** – vocals, rants, etc; repl. PAUL
— others included **CARLOS** – keyboards / **BRENDAN** – trumpet / **OLAF** (b. Germany) – saxophone

Words Of Warning / *not iss.*

Nov 91. (m-lp) *(WOW 019)* **BLAGGERMUFFIN**
– Pitbull mentality / Guns of Brixton / etc *(re-iss. Jun93; same)*
Apr 92. (7") *(WOW 22)* **HERE'S JOHNNY. / BEFORE I HANG** *(re-iss. May93; same)*
1992. (one-sided-lp) *(WOWLTD 23)* **GOD SAVE THE COCKROACH**
1992. (7"ep) *(KON 001)* **BEIRUT / WHAT FOR. / REAL WORLD / WONDERFUL WORLD** — *German*
1992. (gig-lp) *(920071)* **FUCK FASCISM, FUCK CAPITALISM; SOCIETY'S FUCKED** — *German*
– It's up to you (live) / I don't know (live) / Get outta here (live) / Meat (live) / 10 years on (live) / Emergency (live) / Naples (live) / No choice (live) / It's up to you / Get outta here / Meat / Mutha fukka / I don't know / Naples / No choice / Victory to the A.N.C. / Beirut / Real world / What for / Wonderful world. *(cd-iss. Mar97 on 'Knock Out'; KONCD 002)*
(above 2 issued on 'Nightmare')
Nov 92. (7") *(LAPD 187)* **THE WAY WE OPERATE. / THATCHER CHILLIN'**
(above released on 'Fluffy Bunny' records)

— now w/out OLAF who returned to his homeland after a racist fracas at a COCK SPARRER gig in December '92

Jan 93. (cd/lp) *(WOW CD/LP 027)* **UNITED COLOURS OF BLAGGERS I.T.A.**
– When the gun is cocked / It's up to you / Part II – Battle of Waterloo / Search and destroy / Wild side (ram-ravers mix) / That's where it ends / The way we operate (x-tatic mix) / Here's Johnny (post election mix) / Before I hang (double deckers mix) / The way to die / United States of devastation / Young blaggers / Pitbull mentality / Ten men dead / Bastard chillin'.

Parlophone / *Parlophone*

Jun 93. (7") *(ITA 1)* **STRESSS. / THE WAY TO DIE / WILD SIDE / STRESSS** — 56
(12"+=/cd-s+=) *(12/CD ITA 1)* – The way to die (extended).
Sep 93. (7"yellow) *(ITAY 2)* **OXYGEN. / U.S.D.** — 51
(7"green) *(ITAG 2)* – ('A'side) / TEN MEN DEAD
(12") *(12ITA 2)* – ('A'side) / The way we operate in 1993.
(cd-s+=) *(CDITA 2)* – (all 4 tracks)
Dec 93. (7"orange) *(ITAO 3)* **ABANDON SHIP. / HERE'S JOHNNY (live)** — 48
(7"turquoise) *(ITAT 3)* – ('A'side) / JOSEPHINE BAKER
(cd-s+=) *(CDITA 3)* – Stresss.
(12") *(12ITA 3)* – ('A'side) / Bastard chillin' I (live) / Oxygen (mix) / Abandon ship (mix).
Oct 94. (12") *(12ITA 4)* **MANTRAP. / GUNS OF BRIXTON / ROAD TO BASRA**
(cd-s) *(CDITA 4)* – (1st 2 tracks) / Pirate shutdown / Shutdown.
Oct 94. (cd/c/lp) *(CD/TC+/PCSD 156)* **BAD KARMA**
– The hits / 1994 / Mantrap / Bad karma / Famine queen / Stresss / Abandon ship / Nation / Garden of love / Slam / Hate generator / Oxygen.

Damaged Goods / *not iss.*

Jan 95. (7"colrd) *(DAMGOOD 58)* **THRILL HER WITH A GUN. / DIARY THIEF**

Disinformation / *not iss.*

May 95. (7"/cd-s; as BLAGGERS IN THE AREA) *(BITA 1/+CD)* **RUMBLEFISH. / DEATH BY COOL / DxC (eastern mix) / RUMBLEFISH (demo)**
Sep 95. (7"ep/cd-ep) *(BITA 2/+CD)* **GUNS OF BRIXTON / JOYRIDER ON THE ROAD TO BASRA. / THRILL HER WITH A GUN / DAIRY THIEF**
Sep 95. (cd-ep) *(BITA 3CD)* **I.T.A. SESSIONS**

— had already split when MATTY was sacked from the band; JASON formed C&W outfit, RENO. MATTY died from a suspected drug overdose 22/02/2000

BLAMELESS

Formed: Sheffield, England ... early 1994 when JASON, MATT and JON bumped into each other after spilling out of the pub at closing time. Almost immediately, the trio became a quartet with the addition of gruff EDDIE VEDDER-esque vocalist, JARED DALEY. While a debut song, 'TOWN CLOWNS' for the 'Rough Trade Singles Club' sparked an A&R stampede for their signatures, the lads honed their craft before opting for 'China' records. After releasing their first single for the label, 'DON'T SAY YOU'RE SORRY', BLAMELESS were spirited away to the States (Boston, exactly!) to cut an album's worth of material. Compared with everyone from The POLICE to PEARL JAM, the quartet previewed their debut long-player with a further couple of singles, both 'MORE THAN I' and a re-issue of 'TOWN CLOWNS' failing to live up to the hype. 'THE SIGNS ARE ALL THERE' (1995), meanwhile, wasn't exactly the career launching pad the band had banked on; although it was re-issued on the back of a belated Top 30 hit, 'BREATHE (A LITTLE DEEPER)', in the spring of '96, sales figures didn't meet expectations. As usual, long-term development was sacrificed as a young band failed to meet impossibly high standards and of course, the record company was blameless.

Album rating: THE SIGNS ARE ALL THERE (*6)

JARED DALEY – vocals / **MATT** – guitar / **JASON** – bass **JON** – drums

Rough Trade Sing. Club / *not iss.*

Jan 95. (ltd-7") *(45REV 27)* **THE SIGNS WERE ALL THERE. / TOWN CLOWNS**

China / *Atlantic*

Mar 95. (7"/c-s/etched-10") *(WOK/+MC/T 2053)* **DON'T SAY YOU'RE SORRY. / SIGNS ...**
(cd-s+=) *(WOKCD 2053)* – Made up my mind / Poor disguise.
Jul 95. (7"/c-s) *(WOK/+MC 2060)* **MORE THAN I. / ALL THE WHILE**
(cd-s+=) *(WOKCD 2060)* – Jaded superstar / Rusty gold.
Oct 95. (7"red) *(WOKMC 2046)* **TOWN CLOWNS. / NEVER BELIEVER** — 56
(cd-s) *(WOKCD 2046)* – ('A'side) / Sympathy / Second hand prima donna / Swing.
(cd-s) *(WOKCDR 2046)* – ('A'side) / Long gone / Are you worried? / Nan.
Oct 95. (cd/c) *(WOL CD/MC 1059)* <82770> **THE SIGNS WERE ALL THERE**
– Town clowns / Don't say you're sorry / Signs ... / More than I / Digger / Sympathy / What if? / So debonair / Blueprint / News / Made up my mind / Worthless / In leather. *(re-iss. Apr96; same)*
Mar 96. (7") *(WOK 2070)* **BREATHE (A LITTLE DEEPER). / TOWN CLOWNS (acoustic)** — 27
(cd-s+=) *(WOKCD 2070)* – What if? / Tomorrow you might be dead.
(cd-s) *(WOKCDR 2070)* – ('A'side) / Her with the starlight eyes / Platform / Dear God.
May 96. (7"blue/c-s) *(WOK/+MC 2077)* **SIGNS ... / BREATHE (A LITTLE DEEPER) – acoustic** — 49
(cd-s+=) *(WOKCD 2077)* – Never believer / Maybe tomorrow.

— disbanded after above

BLAST OFF COUNTRY STYLE

Formed: Harrisonburg, Virginia, USA ... 1993 by one-time SEXUAL MILKSHAKE drummer, CHRIS CALLAHAN, along with bassist PHIL SWEENEY (ex-DON'T PANIC, ex-TWO FACED JUDY), guitarist MARY McCUE and vocalist EVELYN HURLEY. The former's oufit, SEXUAL MILKSHAKE, delivered only one FALL/SONIC YOUTH-esque album for 'Teenbeat' in 1992, 'SING ALONG IN HEBREW' (featuring a cover of Ultimate Spinach's 'BALLAD OF THE HIP DEATH GODDESS') and were known for their leader/guitarists invention "the Gregtar" (two separate guitars transfixed into one guitar neck although plugged into two amps!). When other main member, TODD/RUSTY MASSE (4th member/bassists were AME DREAD then JILL MURPHY) founded a new outfit, The GOLLYPOPS, CALLAHAN, meanwhile, initiated his own "indie"-style group, BLAST OFF COUNTRY STYLE. Crafting their down-to-earth indie-pop scented with a little B-52's-esque bubblegum, BOCS unveiled their debut LP, the singles compilation 'C'MON AND ...', in 1994. Towards the end of the year, and after a joyous appearance at the Lollapalooza festival, the girls and boys were out again with first album (mini-set) proper, 'RAINBOW MAYONNAISE DELUXE' (1994) – more novelty than country. EVELYN (girlfriend of UNREST's MARK ROBINSON) would resurface in 'Teenbeat' outfit, HOT PURSUIT.

Album rating: C'MON AND BLAST OFF COUNTRY STYLE compilation (*7) / RAINBOW MAYONNAISE DELUXE mini (*4) / Sexual Milkshake: SING-A-LONG IN HEBREW (*7)

SEXUAL MILKSHAKE

TODD/RUSTY MASSIE – vocals / **GREG ALLEN** – guitar! / **JILL MURPHY** – bass; repl. AME DREAD / **CHRIS CALLAHAN** – drums

not iss. / *Teenbeat*

Nov 90. (7") <TEENBEAT 55> **SPACE GNOME. /**
<re-iss. Apr94; TEENBEAT 135>
Feb 92. (lp/cd) <TEENBEAT 75/+CD> **SING-A-LONG IN HEBREW**
– Love bubbles are gummy / White angst octane / Ballad of hip death goddess / Cave bacon, volume 3 / Ghostgod / etc

— split when TODD/RUSTY formed The GOLLYPOPPS; SM release below

BLAST OFF COUNTRY STYLE

EVELYN HURLEY – vocals / **MARY MacCUE** – guitar / **PHIL SWEENEY** – bass (also of The GOLLYPOPPS) / **CHRIS CALLAHAN** – drums

		Teenbeat	Teenbeat
Jan 93.	(7"ep) <*TEENBEAT 94*> **I LOVE ENTERTAINMENT EP** – Social firefly / Hey hey I love you bitch! / Ding dong / Teenage unicorn.	–	☐
Aug 93.	(7"ep) <*TEENBEAT 104*> **PRETTY SNEAKY SIS' EP** – Lonesome Johnson / Weiner dude attitude / Nun in a frigid cell / The boy whose head exploded / Far out law / Why, I oughta!	–	☐
Oct 93.	(7"ep) <*TEENBEAT 114*> **GIGGLES 'N GLOOM EP** – Giggles 'n gloom / Barf city U.S.A. / Comet song / Lake Eerie / G'n'G (reprise).	–	☐
Jan 94.	(7"ep) <*TEENBEAT 124*> **WHAT GIVES? EP** – All she wants to do is ride her bike / The Devil and Emmanuel Lewis / (+1).	–	☐
Mar 94.	(m-lp/m-cd) <(*TEENBEAT 131/+CD*)> **C'MON AND BLAST OFF COUNTRY STYLE** (singles compilation) – Social firefly / Hey hey I love you bitch! / Ding dong / Teenage unicorn / Lonesome Johnson / Weiner dude attitude / Nun in a frigid cell / The boy whose head exploded / Far out law / Why, I oughta! / Giggles 'n gloom / Barf city U.S.A. / Comet song / Lake Eerie / G'n'G (reprise) / All she wants to do is ride her bike / The Devil and Emmanuel Lewis.	☐	Feb94 ☐
Nov 94.	(lp/cd) <*TEENBEAT 144/+CD*> **RAINBOW MAYONNAISE DELUXE** – Cutie pie / Buttercup / Come out and play / Where the geeks are / Tough luck, Trashcan! / Sunburn / Standard green / Mayonnaise rainbow / Demon school dropout / Monkey wrench.	–	☐
Nov 95.	(10"ep/cd-ep) <(*TB 184-1/-2*)> **IN MY ARMS EP** – Bedtime bandit / You're mine / Rock it man / Burnt by the sun / Boy in the bubble / He's my kind of guy.	☐	☐

— **ALLISON RIGO** – guitar; repl. MacCUE

		not iss.	White Devil
Jan 96.	(7") <*001*> **WILD WEST SHOWDOWN. / GAFNEY**	–	☐

— split later in 1996; EVELYN teamed up with TUSCADERO members to form HOT PURSUIT

BLEACH

Formed: Ipswich, England . . . 1989 by songwriting brothers NEIL and NICK SINGLETON together with STEVE SCOTT and frontwoman SALLI CARSON (a former Anglian TV researcher). Released on the 'Way Cool' label in 1990, the 'ECLIPSE' EP (allegedly recorded during an eclipse of the sun!) introduced the BLEACH blueprint of distorted guitars, scattershot drumming and female vocals. Equally at home on the workaday nihilism of 'WIPE IT ALL AWAY' as the moody soundscapes of 'CRIMSON O', CARSON switched easily from in-your-face grrrl to ethereal songstress as conditions demanded. The record won praise from the indie press and BLEACH followed it up with the 'SNAG' EP, another critical favourite that heightened anticipation for a debut album proper. By the release of 'KILLING TIME' in 1992, however, the shoegazing scene – a sound that BLEACH had helped pioneer – was at its peak and BLEACH were ironically overlooked in favour of RIDE, SLOWDIVE, CURVE etc. Now signed to 'Musidisc', the band (complete with the newly shaven-headed CARSON) pushed on with a mini-album, 'HARD', and a second long player, 'FAST', both released in 1993. With US grunge all the rage, even the shoegazing bands had fallen by the wayside and it came as no surprise when BLEACH finally split up later that year. • **Note:** not to be confused with late 90's hardcore/punk act.

Album rating: BLEACH SINGLES compilation (*6) / KILLING TIME (*7) / HARD mini (*4) / FAST mini (*5)

NEIL SINGLETON (b.14 Sep'65) – guitar / **NICK SINGLETON** (b. 2 Feb'68) – bass / **SALLI CARSON** (b. 6 Oct'66, Yorkshire) – vocals / **STEVE SCOTT** (b.29 Nov'63, Norwich) – drums

		Way Cool	Artlos
Oct 90.	(12"ep/cd-ep) (*WAY 8 T/CD*) **ECLIPSE E.P.** – Decadence / Wipe it away / Crimson 'O'.	☐	–
Feb 91.	(12"ep/cd-ep) (*WAY 10 T/CD*) **SNAG E.P.** – Bethesda / Seeing / Dipping / Burn.	☐	–

		Artlos	Artlos
1991.	(lp/cd) (*EFA 01826/+CD*) **BLEACH SINGLES** (compilation)	☐	–

		Musidisc	Dali-Chameleon
Feb 92.	(7") (*MU 111*) **SHOTGUN. / BONE** (12"+=/cd-s+=) (*MU 111 T/CD*) – First and last.	☐	☐
Mar 92.	(cd/c/lp) (*10901-2/-4/-1*) <*61356*> **KILLING TIME** – First / Headless / Push / Paint my face / Friends / Fall / Trip and slide / Shotgun / Surround / Tangle. *(re-iss. Feb93)*	☐	☐
Sep 92.	(m-cd/m-lp) (*10964-2/-1*) **HARD** – Fuse / Can / Dead eyes / Hit on me / Baby toes / Fragment.	☐	
Jul 93.	(m-cd/m-lp) (*11032-2/-1*) **FAST** – Teenage monk / Hate song / Cosy / If we are dead / Action time / Relax.	☐	–

— split some time in '93

BLEED

Formed: London, England . . . 1994 by siblings RITA and NOEL FARRAGHER along with GRAHAM HANKS and ANDREW PARESI (the latter had formerly sessioned for The BLACK VELVET BAND). Forming their own label, the band issued a series of EP's and 7" singles prior to the release of debut album, 'THE GOOD TIMES ARE KILLING ME' (1995). One such single, 'IT MAKES MONEY', was the subject of some controversy as the band promoted its anti-porn message by sending an anonymous fax to top shelf magazine, 'Forum'. Despite an unrelentingly grim lyrical slant taking in depression, low self esteem, male violence etc., the album itself was at least partially redeemed by a relatively airy semi-acoustic musical backing and sympathetic PJ HARVEY/KATE BUSH-esque vocals. A sceptical indie press gave the band short shrift, however and a follow-up set, 'ACTION MAN' (1997) surfaced to little interest.

Album rating: THE GOOD TIMES ARE KILLING ME (*5) / ACTION MAN (*5)

RITA FARRAGHER – vocals / **NOEL FARRAGHER** – guitar / **GRAHAM HANKS** – bass / **ANDREW PARESI** – drums

		Bleed	not iss.
1992.	(12"ep) (*BLEED 1*) **unknown**	☐	–
Feb 93.	(12"ep) (*BLEED 2*) **LADYKILLER LAUREATE. / SPIT IT OUT / IF I WERE A RICH MAN**	☐	–
May 93.	(12"ep) (*BLEED 3*) **A TUNE WITH A VIEW. / TAKE BACK THE NIGHT / DON'T YOU JUST LOVE IT?**	☐	–
Dec 93.	(ltd-7") (*BLEED 4LTD*) **MAD COW DISEASE. /**	☐	–
Apr 94.	(7") (*BLEED 5*) **IT MAKES MONEY. / THE LOONY LEFT** (cd-s+=) (*BLEED 5CD*) – A tune with a view.	☐	–
Jul 95.	(lp/cd) (*BLEED 6/+CD*) **THE GOOD TIMES ARE KILLING ME** – No means no / Good times, bad times, mummy and me / Bloodbath / Kiss of death / The art of contradiction / Slaughter / It makes money / God's little angel / Misogynistic baby / Addicted / Cradle.	☐	–
Jun 97.	(cd) (*BLEED 7CD*) **ACTION MAN**	☐	–

BLESSED ETHEL

Formed: Malvern, England . . . early '92 by frontwoman SARA DORAN and her partner in crime, guitarist/vocalist DAN BARNES. The pair concocted the idea of forming a band after writing songs together on their second hand Bontempi organ before recruiting the rhythm section of MIKE HARRIS and RICK HUNUBAN. Fired by the suffocating, Tory-infested rural environment of their hometown, BLESSED ETHEL first kicked against the pricks in the summer of '93 with a rabid JOHN ROBB (ex-MEMBRANES)-produced single, 'DOG'. Barking mad but brilliant, the record was backed by a commentary on the infamous Castlemorton rave held in the nearby locale, 'SOMETHING WEIRD', and, like most of their material, sparked on the sexually loaded lyrical jousting between co-wordsmiths, SARA and DAN. Second and third 45's for '2 Damn Loud', 'RAT' and 'TWO MINUTE MIND' (both unleashed in the first half of '94), lived up to their demented bumpkin punk expectations; if you can imagine the REZILLOS picking a fight with PIXIES then you're probably not halfway there. However, just as things looked bright for the band – and ear-shattering for their audience – an 18-month vinyl absence prior to release of a single, 'VERONICA' and accompanying album, 'WELCOME TO THE RODEO' (1995), saw them lose momentum.

Album rating: WELCOME TO THE RODEO (*5)

SARA DORAN – vocals / **DAN BARNES** – vocals, guitar / **MIKE HARRIS** – bass / **RICK HUNUBAN** – drums

		2 Damn Loud	not iss.
Aug 93.	(7"colrd) (*2DM 03*) **DOG. / SOMETHING WEIRD / CRYSTAL TIPS**	☐	–
Jan 94.	(7") (*2DM 04*) **RAT. /** (cd-s+=) (*2DMCD 04*) –	☐	–
May 94.	(7") (*2DM 05*) **TWO MINUTE MIND. /** (12"+=/cd-s+=) (*2DMM T/CD 05*) –	☐	–
Oct 95.	(7") (*2DM 10*) **VERONICA. / FAT STAR** (cd-s+=) (*2DMCD 10*) –	☐	–
Nov 95.	(cd/lp) (*2DM CD/LP 12*) **WELCOME TO THE RODEO** – Pullman car to Venus / Calico B / Confidential / Another world / Hangin' in the sun / That man / Shooting cowboys / Fat star / Veronica / Rope / Blue movie / Into the sun / Two minute mind.	☐	–

— disbanded after above

BLIND MR. JONES

Formed: Hackney & Marlow, East London, England . . . 1991 by RICHARD MOORE, WILL TEVERSHAM, JAMES FRANKLIN and JON WHITE. After a string of highly successful rehearsals, the group took their shoegazing styled rock to live audiences, generating enough respect from minor indie celebrities. An EP, 'EYES WIDE' was released by 'Cherry Red' under the guidance of SLOWDIVE's NEIL HALSTEAD early in 1992, their debut album, 'STEREO MUSICALE' followed the same year. Relying on indie and progessive pop, the album was lifted by newcomer JON TEGNER's willowed flute but let down by its space pop paralysis. The band continued to play live in a host of unextravagant living rooms (!), before delivering their second set, the strangly peculiar 'TATOOINE' in 1994. • **Covered:** LONESOME BOATMAN (. . . Furey).

Album rating: STEREO MUSICALE (*6) / TATOOINE (*5)

RICHARD MOORE – vocals, guitar / **JAMES FRANKLIN** – guitar / **WILL TEVERSHAM** – vocals, bass / **JON WHITE** – drums

		Cherry Red	not iss.
Feb 92.	(cd-ep) **EYES WIDE EP** – Over my head / Eyes wide / Going on cold / Henna and swayed.	☐	–

— added **JON TEGNER** – flute

BLIND MR. JONES (cont)

Sep 92. (cd-ep) *(CHERRY 125)* **CRAZY JAZZ**
– Fading fast / Dolores / Featherweight.
Oct 92. (cd/lp) *(CD+/BRED 100)* **STEREO MUSICALE**
– Sisters / Spooky vibes * / Regular disease / Small caravan / Flying with Lux / Henna and swayed / Lonesome boatman / Unforgettable waltz * / Going on cold * / Spook easy / One watt above darkness / Dolores / Against the glass. *(cd+= *)* <US cd-iss. Aug95 on 'Planet 3'; 40201>
Feb 94. (7") *(CHERRY 130)* **SPOOKY VIBES. / CALIBAN**
May 94. (cd) *(CDBRED 113)* **TATOOINE**
– Hey / Disneyworld / Viva / Fisher / See you again / Big plane / Drop for days / Surfer baby / Please me / What's going on / Mesa.

――― disbanded some time in '94

BLINK

Formed: Dublin, Ireland . . . early 90's by DERMOT, ROBBIE, BRIAN and BARRY. Post-baggy musical chameleons, BLINK operate in the DIY spirit of punk with the added help of modern day dance technology. Signed to 'Parlophone', the band debuted with the 'GOING TO NEPAL' in late '93, following it up with 'IT'S NOT MY FAULT' in Spring '94. Produced by indie guru, Gil Norton, and ambient veteran STEVE HILLAGE, 'A MAP OF THE UNIVERSE' (1994) was a debut album which managed to push beyond the realms of bog standard indie-dance fare, pitting DERMOT's JAMES ATKIN (EMF)-style vocals and quirky lyrics against an alternately hypnotic, funky and propulsive musical backdrop. Strangely, even the dramatic synth-string flourish of 'CELLO' failed to crack the charts and BLINK duly called it a day in the mid-90's.

DERMOT – vocals / **ROBBIE** – keyboards / **BRIAN** – bass / **BARRY** – drums

E.M.I. / not iss.

Oct 93. (7") *(EM 292)* **GOING TO NEPAL. / IS GOD REALLY GROOVY**
(12"+=/cd-s+=) *(12/CD EM 292)* – ('A' extended mix).

Parlophone / Parlophone

Apr 94. (c-s/7") *(TC+/R 6376)* **IT'S NOT MY FAULT. / ED'S GOT A NEW CAR / SHINY JIM**
(12"+=/cd-s+=) *(12R/CDR 6376)* – Five new friends.
Jul 94. (c-s/7") *(TC+/R 6385)* **HAPPY DAY. / ('A'mix)**
(cd-s+=) *(CDR 6385)* – Everything comes, everything goes / Hank.
Aug 94. (cd/c) *(<CD/TC PCS 7369>)* **A MAP OF THE UNIVERSE**
– It's not my fault / Cello / Happy day / Everything comes everything goes / Show (be precious) / Fundamentally loveable creature / Love me / The greatest trick / Going to Nepal / There's something wrong with Norman's mom / Christmas 22 / Is God really groovy? / Separation.
Oct 94. (c-s) *(TCR 6393)* **CELLO / WONDERFUL SCENE**
(cd-s+=) *(CDRS 6393)* – ('A'ambient mix) / ('A'-Millwall brick mix).
(cd-s) *(CDR 6393)* – ('A'side) / Fundamentally loveable creature (live) / Love me (live) / ('A'live).

BLINK-182

Formed: Poway, nr. San Diego, California, USA . . . 1992 by vocalist/guitarist TOM DELONGE, bassist MARK HOPPUS and drummer SCOTT RAYNOR. This post new cartoon punk outfit began when DELONGE and BARKER met in college. Soon, they were distributing their collection of demos (all which would later appear on 'BUDDHA' debut set) to A&R upstarts. Unfortunately their quest did not succeed, forcing our mangled, spiky-haired heroes to issue their second, self-financed set 'CHESHIRE CAT' (1995), whilst still under the name of BLINK. However, with pressures from an Irish group of the same name, the band re-emerged as BLINK-182 – the 182 in question, being the number of times Al Pacino said "fuck" in the movie, 'Scarface' – and issued the more successful 'DUDE RANCH' (1997). The album boasted college anthem 'DICK LIPS' which sent the boys quite literally on the road to semi-stardom via a little help from supportive peers GREEN DAY and NOFX. Major labels began to show interest, BLINK-182 (with new drummer TRAVIS BARKER) finally signing on the dotted line with 'M.C.A.' at the beginning of 1999. 'ENEMA OF THE STATE' (which featured porn actress Janine scantily clad in a nurse's uniform) surfaced in that summer and went on to achieve double platinum sales throughout America and Europe. Memorable single, 'WHAT'S MY AGE AGAIN?' (a catchy two minute punk/pop rant), saw the trio run naked through L.A. (in the video at least!) and earned them a cameo performance in "ironic" teen sex movie, 'American Pie'. No underlying message, it seemed like BLINK-182 were just out to drink, party and get nekid! Indeed, their next offering hinted as much. Forgetting the decidedly dismal 'THE MARK, TOM & TRAVIS SHOW' a year earlier, 'TAKE OFF YOUR PANTS AND JACKET' (2001), smashed in at No.1 in the US album charts and also broke into the UK Top 5, thanks to the hit single, 'THE ROCK SHOW'. In 2002, and with spare studio time in hand, TOM and TRAVIS (and producer JERRY FINN) formed side-project, BOXCAR RACER. Recruiting new kids on the block, guitarist DAVID KENNEDY and bassist ANTHONY CELESTINO, they declared their love for emocore and post-punk hardcore through a well-received self-titled album.

Album rating: BUDDHA (*5) / CHESHIRE CAT (*6) / DUDE RANCH (*7) / ENEMA OF THE STATE (*6) / THE MARK, TOM & TRAVIS SHOW (*4) / TAKE OFF YOUR PANTS AND JACKET (*6) / Boxcar Racer: BOXCAR RACER (*6)

TOM DELONGE (b.13 Dec'75) – vocals, guitar / **MARK HOPPUS** (b.15 Mar'72) – bass / **SCOTT RAYNOR** – drums

not iss. / unknown

1993. (7"ep; as BLINK) **FLY SWATTER EP**

not iss. / Kung Fu

1994. (cd/lp) <78765-2/-1> **BUDDHA**
– Carousel / T.V. / Strings / Fentoozler / Time / Romeo & Rebecca / 21 days / Sometimes / Degenerate / Point of view / My pet Sally / Reebok commercial / Toast and bananas / The girls next door / Don't. *(re-iss. Jan99 & Jul99; same)*

not iss. / Rapido

Jun 96. (cd-ep) <RAP 14> **WASTING TIME – 1996 AUSTRALIAN TOUR EP**
– Wasting time / Wrecked him / Lemmings / Enthused. *(UK-iss.Apr98; RAP 30)*

Grilled Cheese / Grilled Cheese

Nov 96. (cd) <(GRL 001)> **CHESHIRE CAT**   May95
– Carousel / M + M's / Fentoozler / Touchdown boy / Strings / Peggy Sue / Sometimes / Does my breath smell? / Cacophony / T.V. / Toast and bananas / Wasting time / Romeo and Rebecca / Ben wah balls / Just about done / Depends. *(re-iss. Nov00 on 'M.C.A.'; 488136-2)*
Nov 96. (cd-s) <(GRL 701)> **THEY CAME TO CONQUER . . . URANUS**   Dec95
– Waggy / Wrecked him / Zulu.
May 97. (cd-ep) <(CSGRL 004)> **DICK LIPS EP**
– Dick lips / Apple shampoo / Wrecked him / Zulu.
Jul 97. (cd/lp) <(CRGD/LPGRL 4)> **DUDE RANCH**   67
– Pathetic / Voyeur / Dammit / Boring / Dick lips / Waggy / Enthused / Untitled / Apple shampoo / Emo / Josie / A new hope / Degenerate / Lemmings / I'm sorry. <cd re-iss. Nov97 on 'M.C.A.'; MCD 11624>
Dec 97. (7") **DAMMIT. / DAMMIT (Growing Up edit)**

――― **TRAVIS BARKER** (b.14 Nov'75) – drums (ex-AQUABATS, ex-PSYCHO BUTTERFLY) repl. SCOTT

Nov 98. (cd-ep) <55513> **JOSIE / WASTING TIME / CAROUSEL / I WON'T BE HOME FOR CHRISTMAS**
Dec 98. (7") **I WON'T BE HOME FOR CHRISTMAS**

M.C.A. / M.C.A.

Sep 99. (c-s) *(MCSC 40219)* <radio cut> **WHAT'S MY AGE AGAIN? / PATHETIC (live)**   38   59 Jul99
(cd-s+=) <(MCSTD 40219)> – Untitled (live).
(cd-s) <(MCSXD 40219)> – ('A'side) / Josie (live) / Aliens exist (live).
Oct 99. (cd) *(MCD 11950)* <111950> **ENEMA OF THE STATE**   15   9 Jun99
– Don't leave me / Adam's song / The party song / Wendy clear / Going away to college / Dysentery Gary / Aliens exist / All the small things / Mutt / Anthem / What's my age again? / Dumpweed.
Mar 00. (c-s) *(MCSC 40223)* <155606> **ALL THE SMALL THINGS / DAMMIT (live)**   2   6 Nov99
(cd-s+=) *(MCSXD 40223)* – ('A'live) / ('A'-CD-Rom video).
(cd-s) *(MCSTD 40223)* – ('A'side) / Dumpweed (live) / What's my age again? (live).
Jun 00. (c-s) *(MCSC 40219)* **WHAT'S MY AGE AGAIN? / PATHETIC (live)**   17   –
(cd-s+=) *(MCSZD 40219)* – Untitled (live) / ('A'-CD-Rom).
(cd-s) *(MCSYD 40219)* – ('A'side) / Josie (live) / (interview on CD-Rom).
Nov 00. (cd) <(112379-2)> **THE MARK, TOM AND TRAVIS SHOW – THE ENEMA STRIKES BACK! (live)**   69   8
– Dumpweed / Don't leave me / Alines exist / Family reunion / Going away to college / What's my age again? / Dick lips / Blow job / Untitled / Voyeur / Pathetic / Adam's song / Peggy Sue / Wendy clear / Carousel / All the small things / Mutt / The country song / Dammit / Man overboard / (plus a whole bunch of funny shit in between).
Jun 01. (cd) <(112627-2)> **TAKE OFF YOUR PANTS AND JACKET**   4   1
– Anthem (part 2) / Online songs / First date / Happy holidays you bastard / Story of a lonely guy / The rock show / Stay together for the kids / Roller coaster / Reckless abandon / Everytime I look for you / Give me one good reason / Shut up / Please take me home / What went wrong / Time to break up / Fuck a dog / Man overboard (video).
Jul 01. (cd-s) *(MCSTD 40259)* <radio cut> **THE ROCK SHOW / TIME TO BREAK UP / MAN OVERBOARD**   14   71
Sep 01. (7") *(MCS 40264)* **FIRST DATE. / DON'T TELL ME IT'S OVER**   31   –
(cd-s+=) *(MCSTD 40264)* – Mother's day.

BOXCAR RACER

TOM DELONGE + TRAVIS BARKER plus **DAVID KENNEDY** – guitar / **ANTHONY CELESTINO** – bass

M.C.A. / M.C.A.

May 02. (cd) *(112947-2)* <112894-2> **BOX CAR RACER**   27   12
– I feel so / All systems go / Watch the world / Tiny voices / Cat like thief / And I / Letters to God / My first punk song / Sorrow / There is / The end with you / Elevator / Instrumental.
Jun 02. (7") *(MCS 40290)* **I FEEL SO. / CAT LIKE THIEF**   41   –
(cd-s+=) *(MCSTD 40290)* – ('A'-guitar intro) / ('A'-video).

BLISTERS (see under ⇒ KARELIA)

BLONDE REDHEAD

Formed: based – New York, USA . . . 1993 by Japanese-born KAZU MAKINO, who met Italian, jazz-loving, twin brothers AMEDEO and SIMONE PACE. Described as the re-birth of no-wave, they were snapped up by SONIC YOUTH's STEVE SHELLEY for his 'Smells Like' imprint. An eponymous set was subsequently followed up by 1995's 'LA MIA VITA VIOLENTA', the latter taking the sound of SONIC YOUTH and lyrical themes of Catholic/Communist guilt influencd by the homosexual novelist/filmmaker, Pier Paolo Pasolini. A few years later, BLONDE REDHEAD made a shift to 'Touch & Go', the results being the third DIY-sounding set, 'FAKE CAN BE JUST AS GOOD' (1997). The 1998 album, 'IN AN EXPRESSION OF THE INEXPRESSIBLE' (co-produced by FUGAZI's GUY PICCIOTTO with

BLONDE REDHEAD (cont) — THE GREAT INDIE DISCOGRAPHY — The 1990s

JOHN GOODMANSON), was the odd trio's coming of age, a noisy, art-core masterpiece seemingly custom built for a companion piece movie. • **Covered:** SLOGAN (Serge Gainsbourg).
Album rating: BLONDE REDHEAD (*6) / FAKE CAN BE JUST AS GOOD (*6) / IN AN EXPRESSION OF THE INEXPRESSIBLE (*7) / MELODY OF CERTAIN DAMAGED LEMONS (*6)

KAZU MAKINO – vocals, guitar / **AMEDEO PACE** – vocals, guitars / **SIMONE PACE** – drums, keyboards, programming / **TADA HIRANO** – bass

			not iss.	Oxo
1993.	(7") <OXO 009>	**BIG SONG. / AMESCREAM**	–	☐
			not iss.	Smells Like
Dec 94.	(7") <slr 007>	**VAGUE. / JET STAR** (UK-iss.Apr97; same as US)	–	☐

— now without TADA; repl. by **MAKI TAKAHASHI** – bass

Jan 95.	(cd) <slr 011>	**BLONDE REDHEAD**	☐	☐
		– I don't want U / Sciura sciura / Astro boy / Without feathers / Snippet / Mama Etta / Swing pool / Girl boy. (UK-iss.Sep95; same as US)		
Feb 95.	(7") (45REV 36)	**FLYING DOUGLAS. / HARMONY** (above issued for 'Rough Trade Singles Club')	☐	–
Jun 95.	(7") <slr 014>	**10 FEET HIGH. / VALENTINE** (UK-iss.Apr97; same as US)	☐	☐
Sep 95.	(cd) <slr 018>	**LA MIA VITA VIOLENTA**	–	☐
		– (I am taking out my Eurotrash) I still get rocks off / Violent life / U.F.O. / I am there while you choke on me / Harmony / Down under / Bean / Young Neil / 10 feet high / Jewel.		

— added guest **VERN** – bass (of UNWOUND)

			Touch & Go	Touch & Go
Mar 97.	(7") <(TG 168)>	**SYMPHONY OF TREBLE. / KASUALITY**	☐	☐
Apr 97.	(lp/cd) <(TG 169/+CD)>	**FAKE CAN BE JUST AS GOOD**	☐	☐
		– Kazuality / Symphony of treble / Water / Ego maniac kid / Bipolar / Pier Paolo / Oh James / Futurism vs. passeism.		
Mar 98.	(7") <(TG 188)>	**SLOGAN. / LIMITED CONVERSATION**	☐	☐
Sep 98.	(lp/cd) <(TG 196/+CD)>	**IN AN EXPRESSION OF THE INEXPRESSIBLE**	☐	☐
		– Luv machine / 10 / Distilled / Missile / Futurism vs. passeism pt.2 / Speed x distance = time / In an expression of the inexpressible / Suimasen / Led Zep / This is for me and I know everyone knows / Justin joyous.		
May 00.	(cd/lp) <(TG 216 CD/LP)>	**MELODY OF CERTAIN DAMAGED LEMONS**	☐	☐
		– Equally damaged / In particular / Melody of certain three / Hated because of great qualities / Loved despite of great faults / Ballad of lemons / This is not / A cure / For damaged / Mother.		
Sep 00.	(m-lp/m-cd) <(TG 219/+CD)>	**MELODIE CITRONIQUE**	☐	☐
		– En particular (French) / Odiata per le sue virtu (Italian) / Chi e e non e / Slogan / Four damaged lemons (for the damaged remix – Third Eye Foundation).		

– compilations, etc. –

Aug 99.	(d-lp) Smells Like; <(slr 032)>	**BLONDE REDHEAD / LA MIA VITA VIOLENTA**	☐	☐

BLOOMSDAY (see under ⇒ BATHERS)

BLUEBEAR (see under ⇒ BEATNIK FILMSTARS)

BLUEBOY

Formed: Reading, England ... around 1989 by KEITH GIRDLER and PAUL STEWART, who had met in 1983 and had already fronted a small, but unsuccessful indie pop outfit, FEVERFEW. The twosome decided to give music another shot and reputedly recorded their first single, 'CLEARER' in a friend's shed. They duly sent the finished product to 'Sarah' records, who issued it in 1991. With this small victory under their belts, the band went from duo to sextet with the recruitment of GEMMA TOWNLET, HARVEY WILLIAMS (from ANOTHER SUNNY DAY), MARK and LLOYD. The 'POPKISS' EP followed a year later, and hot on its heels was the debut LP, 'IF WISHES WERE HORSES' (1992). This showcased the band's twee indie pop foundations, with TOWNLET's cello work and extra vocal help, opening up the group's sound to more intelligent melodic structures. The ensuing year saw the delivery of several more singles, 'MEET JOHNNY RAVE' and 'SOME GORGEOUS ACCIDENT', keeping the band's toe in until the follow-up full-set, 'UNISEX' arrived in early 1995. This piece further broadened the group's range showing the wholesome maturity of their songwriting, which now stretched into the genres of light jazz and string arrangements. This was also to be the last BLUEBOY recording for LLOYD and MARK, who departed the band, MARTIN ROSE stepped into the drum duties and the ever-talented TOWNLET took over the bass parts. Unfortunately, 'Sarah' ceased to be, although boss MATT HAYNES began a similar project, 'Shinkansen', which he signed the band to. Their first release on the fledgling imprint was the 7", 'LOVE YOURSELF' (1996), but soon after its release GIRDLER and STEWART's musical crew departed them, forcing them to recruit a whole new line-up consisting of CATH CLOSE, JAMES NEVILLE and IAN GARDNER for their third album, 'THE BANK OF ENGLAND' (1998). Whether it was due to the new group dynamics or a change of heart, the sound on this set was distinctly different, displaying a tendency towards a weightier sound, where the band seems a little lost. This offering was also to be their last as BLUEBOY, GIRDLER and STEWART continuing on as ARABESQUE. For the millennium, they assumed the moniker BEAUMONT, with old colleagues ROSE, CLOSE and new acquaintances, LORRAINE CARROL, LEIGH SAUNDERS and RICHARD PREECE. Here the duo returned to what they were good at, putting out twee indie-pop, but heading even more down the road of classic sixties icons such as BURT BACHARACH and SERGE GAINSBOURG. The turn of the century saw the release of their pleasant first offering, 'THIS IS BEAUMONT', followed two years later by 'DISCOTHEQUE A LA CARTE' (2002). It seemed with these two offerings the band were at their most comfortable, the lynch-pin members GIRDLER and STEWART obviously finding their musical strengths. A sideline of GIRDLER, LOVEJOY (led incidentally by PREECE) saw this outfit issue two sets, 'SONGS IN THE KEY OF LOVEJOY' (2000) and 'WHO WANT TO BE A MILLIONAIRE' (2002); they also covered two Biff Bang Pow! tracks, 'HUG ME HONEY' and 'BEAT HOTEL'.

Album rating: IF WISHES WERE HORSES mini (*6) / UNISEX (*5) / THE BANK OF ENGLAND (*4) / Beaumont: THIS IS ... (*5) / DISCOTHEQUE A LA CARTE mini (*5) / Lovejoy: SONGS IN THE KEY OF LOVEJOY (*5) / WHO WANTS TO BE A MILLIONAIRE? (*6)

KEITH GIRDLER – vocals / **PAUL STEWART** – guitar

			Sarah	Widely Distributed
Aug 91.	(7") (SARAH 055)	**CLEARER. / ALISON**	☐	☐

— added **HARVEY WILLIAMS** – guitar (of ANOTHER SUNNY DAY, of FIELD MICE) / **GEMMA TOWNLET** – vocals, cello / **MARK** – bass / **LLOYD** – drums

Jul 92.	(m-lp/m-cd) (SARAH 612/+CD)	**IF WISHES WERE HORSES**	☐	–
		– Candy bracelet / Cloud babies / Too good to be true / Fondette / Sea horses / Clear skies / Happiness and smiles / Amoroso.		
Aug 92.	(7"m) (SARAH 065)	**POPKISS. / CHELSEA GUITAR / FEARON**	☐	–
Jan 93.	(6"clear flexi) (SARAH 070)	**CLOUD BABIES (live)**	☐	–
Apr 93.	(7"m) (SARAH 074)	**MEET JOHNNY RAVE. / ELLE / AIR FRANCE** (cd-s+=) (SARAH 074CD) – Popkiss.	☐	–
Jul 93.	(7"ep/cd-ep) (SARAH 080/+CD)	**SOME GORGEOUS ACCIDENT EP**	☐	–
		– Try happiness / A gentle sigh / Stephanie.		
Apr 94.	(7"m/cd-s) (SARAH 088/+CD)	**RIVER. / NIMBUS / HIT**	☐	–
Apr 94.	(lp/cd) (SARAH 620/+CD)	**UNISEX**	☐	–
		– So catch him / Cosmopolitan / Marble Arch / The joy of living / Fleetway / Also ran / Boys don't matter / Self portrait / Lazy thunderstorms / Finistere / Always there / Imipramine.		

— now without MARK + LLOYD (**TOWNLET** now on bass)

— added **MARTIN ROSE** – drums

May 95.	(7"ep) (AQUA 1)	**BIKINI (live at Le Bikini)**	☐	–
		– Chelsea guitar / Air France / Sea horses. (above on 'Aquavinyle')		
Jul 95.	(7"/cd-s) (SARAH 099/+CD)	**DIRTY MAGS. / LOONY TUNES / TOULOUSE**	☐	–

— trimmed down to **GIRDLER + STEWART**

			Shinkansen	not iss.
Oct 96.	(7") (SHINKANSEN 4)	**LOVE YOURSELF. / MELANCHOLIA**	☐	–

— added **CATH CLOSE** – vocals / **JAMES NEVILLE** – bass / **IAN GARDNER** – drums

Jun 98.	(7") (SHINKANSEN 9)	**1.6.98 EP**	☐	–
		– Marco Polo / What do people do all day. (cd-ep+=) (SHINKANSEN 9CD) – Love yourself / Melancholia.		
Jul 98.	(cd) (SHINK 12CD)	**THE BANK OF ENGLAND**	☐	–
		– Joined-up writing / Miss U.K. / Love yourself / By appointment / Marco Polo / Jennifer yeah! / Disco bunny / Chadwick / Ask the family / Bradford, Texas / Angel at my table.		

ARABESQUE

GIRDLER + STEWART

			Siesta	not iss.
May 95.	(7") (SIESTA 19)	**INTRODUCING THE SUMMER SOUNDS OF ... EP**	☐	–
		– Roma / Do nothing / Brazil 94.		
Oct 97.	(7"ep) (SIESTA 59)	**THE GROOMING GAMBIT EP**	☐	–
		– Love is ... / Pink champagne / The rogue.		

— added **RICHARD PREECE** – guitar (ex-SPINNING WHEEL)

LOVEJOY

RICHARD PREECE – vocals, guitar / **ALLY BOARD** – backing vocals / **KEITH GIRDLER** – vocals, etc.

			Matinee	not iss.
Mar 00.	(7") <MATINEE 012>	**A TASTE OF THE HIGH LIFE EP**	☐	–
		– Getting away with it all / Merry go round / Winter L.D.		
Oct 00.	(cd) (MATCD 008)	**SONGS IN THE KEY OF LOVEJOY**	☐	–
		– A taste of the high life / Penelope London / Thank your lucky stars / Radio / Sunset sky / Live alone forever / Fantasy island / The girl from headquarters / Butter wouldn't melt / Tomorrow's world.		
Dec 00.	(7"ep) (MATINEE 025)	**A CHRISTMAS WISH EP**	☐	–
		– I dream of angels / Snow falling softly / Snow falling softly (bent fabric mix).		
Aug 01.	(7") (MATINEE 028)	**PLAYS BIFF BANG POW!**	–	☐
		– Hug me honey / The beat hotel.		
Oct 02.	(cd) (MATCD 018)	**WHO WANTS TO BE A MILLIONAIRE?**	☐	–
		– Who wants to be a millionaire? / You fell from grace / Plastic flowers / Nothing happens here / Snow falling softly (bent fabric mix) / The beat hotel / Night on earth / Millionaire ... maybe / Don't you (wish you'd never met me)?		

BEAUMONT

— **GIRDLER + STEWART**

Mar 00.	(lp/cd) (SIESTA 112)	**THIS IS ...**	☐	–
		– Introduction / Bacharach / Hey Barbara / Theme from Beaumont / Girlie /		

Oncampus / Girl and maths / Love is 1998 / Aftershave / His London / City pretty / Cross country.

Jul 01. (10"m-lp/m-cd) (*SIESTA 95 LP/CD*) **DISCOTHEQUE A LA CARTE**
– Discotheque a la carte / The look of love / In conversation with . . . / A discotheque a la carte (le salon mix).

BLUETIP

Formed: Washington DC, USA . . . mid-90's out of SWIZ by JASON FARRELL and DAVE STERN. Recruiting JAKE KLUMP and ZAC ELLER, the band began gigging around the local hardcore scene while FARRELL's graphic art skills eventually brought BLUETIP to the attention of FUGAZI hardcore guru IAN MacKAYE. Signing them to his legendary 'Dischord' label and guiding them through the stresses of writing and recording, MacKAYE also handled production duties on debut album, 'DISCHORD No.101' (1996). While this was firmly in the bile-filled, noisy DC post-punk tradition, 'JOIN US' (1998) took its cue from a wider sonic palate, its rhythmic attack driven by new sticksman DAVE BRYSON. The shock departure of founding member STERN spurred on FARRELL to hone his songwriting skills for the 'HOT(-)FAST(+)UNION' EP and 'POLYMER' (2000) album, the JAMES DEAN-alike taking a leaner, more direct approach.

Album rating: DISCHORD No.101 (*6) / JOIN US (*5) / POLYMER (*7)

JASON FARRELL – vocals, guitar / **DAVE STERN** – guitar / **JAKE KUMP** – bass / **ZAC ELLER** – drums

Dischord   Dischord

Jun 96. (cd/lp) <(*DIS 101 CD/V*)> **DISCHORD No.101**
– Nickelback / Past tense / Precious / If I ever sleep again / 3x2 slow / Sacred heart of the highway / Texas to west / Sweet superior / L.M.N.O.P. / Mapped out / Gainer / Tangle.

DAVE BRYSON – drums; repl. ZAC + other temps

Nov 98. (cd/lp) <(*DIS 116 CD/V*)> **JOIN US**
– Yellow light / Cheap rip / Join us / Castanet / Carbon copy / Salinas / F- / I even drive like a jerk / Bad flat / Jersey blessed / Cold start / Slovakian.

Jul 00. (cd-ep) <(*SLOWDIME 29*)> **HOT(-)FAST(+)UNION**
– Hot fast union / Split up kid / Persistent / Compliment the negative / Anti-Pope. (above issued on 'Slowdime')

now without STERN

Oct 00. (cd/lp) <(*DIS 121 CD/V*)> **POLYMER**   Sep00
– Polymer / New young residents / New shoe premonition / Stereo tinnitus / Getting in / Magnetified / Astigmatic / Don't punch your friend (for being slow) / Anti-bloom / Broke the lease / (untitled).

BLUETONES

Formed: Hounslow, London, England . . . 1994 by brothers MARK and SCOTT MORRISS, along with ADAM DEVLIN and ED CHESTERS. An indie band in the classic sense of the term, The BLUETONES stood somewhat apart and aloof from the Brit-pop class of '95. The previous year, they'd contributed the track, 'No.11', (later retitled 'BLUETONIC') to a 'Fierce Panda' compilation EP, 'Return To Splendour', before attracting attention from A&M's 'Superior Quality' label early in 1995. A struttingly assured live proposition, the initial buzz surrounding the band was almost tangible. It came as little surprise when a debut single, 'ARE YOU BLUE OR ARE YOU BLIND?' crashed into the charts at No.31, followed later in the long, hot summer of '95 by Top 20 hit, 'BLUETONIC'. A further series of gigs followed before the band narrowly missed the UK No.1 spot in early '96 with the 'SLIGHT RETURN' single. A classic slice of jangle-pop following the time-honoured lineage of The BYRDS, The SMITHS, The LA's and The STONE ROSES, MORRIS even donned a duffel coat(!) for the video, his nimble footed shuffle and boyish good looks generating talk of another IAN BROWN in the ascendant. The long awaited album, 'EXPECTING TO FLY' was released almost simultaneously, reaching the UK No.1 spot and eventually going platinum. Listeners expecting a series of breezy strumalongs were disappointed; the album's dense, evershifting sound rewarded repeated listening, classic rock references slipping in and out of focus but never revealing themselves fully. The catchy 'CUT SOME RUG' was the next single, making the Top 10 ahead of a new track, 'MARBLEHEAD JOHNSON' later that year. 1998's sophomore effort, 'RETURN TO THE LAST CHANCE SALOON' found the Londoners flirting with a bit of rootsy Americana, a sound that blended pleasantly if not spectacularly with their trademark indie rock. 'SOLOMON BITES THE WORM' and 'IF . . . .' both made the Top 20, the latter's title might well have got fans asking themselves questions such as what if . . . the BLUETONES finally made that classic album they've been promising for years. Unfortunately, 'SCIENCE & NATURE' (2000) wasn't to be that record. Instead, it was another set of fine if ultimately unremarkable trad-indie from a band who undoubtedly have the talent to do better.

Album rating: EXPECTING TO FLY (*8) / RETURN TO THE LAST CHANCE SALOON (*6) / SCIENCE & NATURE (*6) / THE SINGLES collection (*7)

MARK MORRISS – vocals / **ADAM DEVLIN** – guitars / **SCOTT MORRISS** – bass, vocals / **ED CHESTERS** – drums, percussion

Superior   Polydor

Feb 95. (7"blue; mail-o) (*TONE 001*) **SLIGHT RETURN. / FOUNTAINHEAD**   -   -

Jun 95. (7") (*BLUE 001X*) **ARE YOU BLUE OR ARE YOU BLIND?. / STRING ALONG**   31
(12"+=/cd-s+=) (*BLUE 001 T/CD*) – Driftwood.

Oct 95. (7"/c-s) (*BLUE 002 X/MC*) **BLUETONIC. / GLAD TO SEE Y'BACK AGAIN?**   19
(12"+=/cd-s+=) (*BLUE 002 T/CD*) – Colorado beetle.

Dec 95. (cd-ep) <*1142*> **BLUETONES COMPANION**   -
– Are you blue or are you blind? / String along / Driftwood / Bluetonic / Colorado beetle / Glad to see y' back again.

Superior   A&M

Jan 96. (7"/c-s) (*BLUE 003 X/MC*) **SLIGHT RETURN. / DON'T STAND ME DOWN**   2
(cd-s+=) (*BLUE 003CD*) – Nae hair on't.

Feb 96. (cd/c/lp/s-lp) (*BLUECD/BLUEMC/BLUELP/BLUELPX 004*) <*540475*> **EXPECTING TO FLY**   1
– Talking to Clarry / Bluetonic / Cut some rug / Things change / he fountainhead / Carnt be trusted / Slight return / Putting out fires / Vampire / A parting gesture / Time & again.

Apr 96. (7"/c-s) (*BLUE 005 X/MC*) **CUT SOME RUG. / CASTLE ROCK**   7
(cd-s+=) (*BLUE 005CD*) – The devil behind my smile.

Sep 96. (7"/c-s) (*BLUE 006 X/MC*) **MARBLEHEAD JOHNSON. / THE SIMPLE THINGS / NIFKIN'S BRIDGE**   7
(cd-s+=) (*BLUE 006CD*) – Are you blue or are you blind?

Feb 98. (7"/c-s) (*BLUE X/M 007*) **SOLOMON BITES THE WORM. / I WAS A TEENAGE JESUS**   10
(cd-s+=) (*BLUED 007*) – I walked all night.

Mar 98. (cd/c/lp) (*BLUE D/M/V 008*) <*LC 0485*> **RETURN TO THE LAST CHANCE SALOON**   10
– Tone blooze / Unpainted Arizona / Solomon bites the worm / U.T.A. / 4-day weekend / Sleazy bed track / If . . . / The jub-jub bird / Sky will fall / Ames / Down at the reservoir / Heard you were dead / Broken starr. *(hidden track on cd+=)* – Woman done gone left me.

Apr 98. (7"/c-s) (*BLUE X/M 009*) **IF . . . / BLUE SHADOWS**   13
(cd-s+=) (*BLUED 009*) – The watchman.

Jul 98. (7"/c-s) (*BLUE X/M 010*) **SLEAZY BED TRACK. / THE BALLAD OF MULDOON**   35
(cd-s+=) (*BLUED 010*) – Blue.

Superior   Mercury

Feb 00. (c-s) (*BLUEM 012*) **KEEP THE HOME FIRES BURNING / PLEASE STOP TALKING**   13   -
(cd-s+=) (*BLUEDD 012*) – Be careful what you dream / ('A'video).
(cd-s) (*BLUED 012*) – ('A'side) / Armageddon (outta here) / Favourite son.

May 00. (c-s) (*BLUEM 013*) **AUTOPHILIA / IT'S A BOY**   18   -
(cd-s+=) (*BLUED 013*) – Thought you'd be taller.
(cd-s) (*BLUEDD 013*) – ('A'side) / Soup du jour / Vostok of love.

May 00. (cd/c/lp) (*BLUE CD/MC/LP 014*) <*7474*> **SCIENCE & NATURE**   7
– Zorro / The last of the great navigators / Tiger Lily / Mudslide / One speed gearbox / Blood bubble / Autophilia / Keep the home fires burning / The basement song / Slack jaw / Emily's pine. *(cd+=)* – Keep the home fires burning (video) / Autophilia (video).

Mar 02. (7") (*BLUE 016*) **AFTER HOURS. / INGIMARSSON**   26   -
(cd-s) (*BLUED 016*) – ('A'side) / Groovy Roussos / Sail on sailor.
(cd-s) (*BLUEDD 016*) – ('A'side) / Reverse cowgirl / Woman in love.

Apr 02. (cd) (*BLUECD 017*) **THE SINGLES** (compilation)   14   -
– Are you blue or are you blind? / Bluetonic / Slight return / Cut some drug / Marblehead Johnson / Solomon bites the worm / If . . . / Sleazy bed track / 4 day weekend / Keep the home fires burning / Autophilia / How I learned to stop worrying and love my car / Mudslide / After hours / Freeze dried pop (dumb it up) / Persuasion / Bluetones big score. *(d-cd+=; BLUEDD 017)* – After hours / Pretty ballerina / Blue / Blue shadows / That's life.

BLUMFELD

Formed: Hamburg, Germany . . . 1992 by JOCHEN DISTELMEYER, EIKE BOHLKEN and ANDRE RATTAY. One of the few German guitar-based bands to break through the enduringly untrendy preconceptions held by many UK music journos, BLUMFELD surprisingly sang in their native tongue although their music was inspired by the angular noise of American acts like SONIC YOUTH, BIG BLACK and early PAVEMENT. Distributed in the UK by 'Cargo', 'ICH-MASCHINE' (1994), introduced their heavily politicised, determinedly anti-fascist agenda although obviously German-language night classes were essential for us mono-lingual English speakers. Subsequently signing to 'Big Cat', BLUMFELD confusingly enough released a French titled follow-up set, 'L'ETAT ET MOI' (1995), their overtly intellectual art-rock not exactly going down a storm with the Brit-pop boys of the mid-90's.

Album rating: ICH-MASCHINE (*5) / L'ETAT ET MOI (*5)

JOCHEN DISTELMEYER – vocals, guitar, piano / **EIKE BOHLKEN** – bass, guitar, harmonica / **ANDRE RATTAY** – drums, percussion

What's So Funny . . .   not iss.

1992. (cd) **ICH-MASCHINE**   -   - German
– Ghettowelt / Von der unmoglichkeit "nein" zu sagen, ohne sich umzubringen / Viel zu fruh und immer wieder; liebeslieder / Dosis / Zeitoetslager / Lab uns nicht von sex reden / Aus den kriegstagebuchern / Sex.bomben / Pickleface ist back in town / Nichtschwimmer – NachGeburt / Penismomolog / Ich-maschine. *(UK-iss.Oct94 on 'Cargo'; 2915-2)*

Big Cat   Big Cat

Feb 95. (7") (*ABB 82S*) **DRAUSSEN AUF KAUTION. / JET SET**   -   -

Mar 95. (lp/cd) (<*ABB 73/+CD*>) **L'ETAT ET MOI**
– Draussen auf kaution / Jet set / 2 oder 3 dinge, die ich von dir weiss / Walkie, talkie / Eine eigene geschichte / Verstarker / Ich – Wie es wirklich war / L'etat et moi (Mein vorgehen in 4, 5 satzen) / Sing sing / Evergreen / Superstarfighter / You make me.

Aug 95. (cd-ep) (*ABB 95*) **VERSTARKER / ANDERES ICH / DER ANGRIFF DER GEGENWART AUF MEINE UBRIGE ZEIT / LANGSAM**

Jun 99. (cd) *(ABB 100740-2)* **OLD NOBODY**
– Eines tages / Tausend tranen tief / Mein system kennt keine Grenzen / Status: Quo Vadis / The lord of song / Kommst du mit in den Alltag / Ein lied von zwei menschen / Pro familia / So lebe ich / Old nobody / So lang es liebe gibt.

BLUR

Formed: Colchester, Essex, England ... 1989 by DAMON ALBARN, GRAHAM COXON, ALEX JAMES and DAVE ROWNTREE. Initially they went under the moniker of SEYMOUR before opting for The GREAT WHITE HOPES. Finally settling with BLUR, they soon were on the books of David Balfe's 'Food' label, a subsidiary of Parlophone. There, they secured their first UK Top 50 entry with 'SHE'S SO HIGH', an early PINK FLOYD-influenced tune, that rode the coat-tails of the baggy brigade. With the ghost of SYD BARRETT even more pronounced, they created one of the more psychedelic singles of the era in 'THERE'S NO OTHER WAY', the record hitting Top 10 in '91. Another single, 'BANG', preceded their debut album, 'LEISURE', a record that received mixed reviews at the time. Still mainly a singles orientated outfit, they progressed dramatically with the much-improved, 'MODERN LIFE IS RUBBISH' (1993) album, which featured some classy tracks including the hits, 'FOR TOMORROW', 'CHEMICAL WORLD' and 'SUNDAY SUNDAY'. Although they had come on leaps and bounds creatively, this wasn't translated into sales. With the release of 'GIRLS AND BOYS', however, they embarked upon a commercial renaissance that saw the record become their biggest hit to date. It was the opening track on the critically approved 'PARKLIFE' album, which also spawned further hits, 'TO THE END' and the title track (co-sung with actor PHIL DANIELS). By this point they had evolved into a mod-ish indie-pop combo, ALBARN supplying the cockney barra-boy delivery over a musical backdrop that drew from the rich English pop heritage, once the domain of such luminaries as The SMALL FACES and The KINKS. The following year, 1995, saw them win the battle to the coveted No.1 spot with 'COUNTRY HOUSE', beating rivals OASIS who were sharpening their tongues for an onslaught of media slagging. However, BLUR lost ground in the credibility stakes, when their 'GREAT ESCAPE' album failed to impress the critics. OASIS, on the other hand, were scaling new heights with their 2nd album. 1997 marked a slight return to favour, both the single, 'BEETLEBUM', and their eponymous 5th album hitting pole position. With BLUR taking a slight sabbatical from the recording studio, GRAHAM COXON took the opportunity to release a respectable solo effort, 'THE SKY IS TOO HIGH', the BLUR factor and a few good reviews nearly carrying it into the Top 30. Having involved themselves with various remixers (including WILLIAM ORBIT, MOBY, THURSTON MOORE, ADRIAN SHERWOOD and JOHN McENTIRE on the once Japanese-only 'BUSTIN' & DRONIN') over the course of the last year or so, BLUR were seeing clearly once again. In March '99, the gospel-led 'TENDER' went straight to No.2 while the accompanying album, '13' (DAMON had recently split with ELASTICA's JUSTINE FRISCHMANN) topped the chart. Further singles, 'COFFEE & TV' (with COXON taking the lead) and 'NO DISTANCE LEFT TO RUN', only managed to reach the Top 20, it would seem BLUR (like possibly OASIS to come?) were beginning to falter slightly. A good time to release a greatest hits set then, 'BEST OF BLUR' (2000) – only a UK Top 3 – coming exactly a decade after the release of their debut single. The album charted Colchester's own pop idols through the various incarnations of their career with the conspicuous underrepresentation of 'MODERN LIFE ...', their transitional but commercially flat 1993 effort. GRAHAM COXON also released his second solo effort, 'GOLDEN D', the same year, a spiky, DIY follow-up to his debut which found him revisiting Mission Of Burma's 'FAME AND FORTUNE' and 'THAT'S WHEN I REACH FOR MY REVOLVER'. The most pertinent millennial development in the BLUR camp, however, arguably came with the inception of GORILLAZ, the pop world's very first "virtual" dub/hip hop outfit. The brainchild of ALBARN and cartoonist JAMIE HEWLETT (creator of cult comic heroine 'Tank Girl', herself the inspiration for Lara Croft and a forerunner of the "girlpower" shenanigans), this cutting edge project also benefitted from the talents of CIBO MATTO's MIHO MATORI, hip hop beats merchant DAN 'THE AUTOMATOR' NAKAMURA, reggae bassist DAN JUNIOR and white funk veterans TINA WEYMOUTH and CHRIS FRANTZ (ex-TALKING HEADS, TOM TOM CLUB). As for the band "members", they were cute but dim lead singer 2-D (NOT based on DAMON as everyone thought), sinister, scowling guitarist MURDOC, b-boy RUSSEL and the mysterious, oriental NOODLE. GORILLAZ' debut EP, 'TOMORROW COMES TODAY' arrived in late 2000 while the seminal 'CLINT EASTWOOD' single was released the following year. A lurching slice of feelgood dub-hop which made the UK Top 5 and even the Italian Top 10, the track was a definite contender for single of the year. More importantly for a virtual band, the brilliantly inventive video brought the characters to life in a way that the eponymous 'GORILLAZ' (2001) album did not. Still, there were plenty of sterling pop thrills to be had amidst the occasionally unfocused dubscapes while ironically, perhaps, ALBARN's cockney leer sounded better in this environment than in the confines of BLUR. While the live shows may not quite have lived up to the hype, hits to the band's web site (www.gorillaz.com) dominate the EMI server's traffic. The future of rock'n'roll may be upon us .... • **Covered:** MAGGIE MAY (Rod Stewart) / LAZY SUNDAY (Small Faces). • **Trivia:** DAMON's father, KEITH ALBARN, used to be the manager of 60's rock outfit, The SOFT MACHINE.

Album rating: LEISURE (*6) / MODERN LIFE IS RUBBISH (*8) / PARKLIFE (*9) / THE GREAT ESCAPE (*7) / BLUR (*8) / 13 (*6) / THE BEST OF BLUR compilation

(*9) / Graham Coxon: THE SKY IS TOO HIGH (*6) / THE GOLDEN D (*5) / CROW SIT ON BLOOD TREE (*5) / THE KISS OF MORNING (*8) / Gorillaz: GORILLAZ (*9) / G SIDES collection (*7)

DAMON ALBARN (b.23 Mar'68, Whitechapel, London) – vocals / **GRAHAM COXON** (b.12 Mar'69, Germany) – guitars / **ALEX JAMES** (b.21 Nov'68, Dorset, England) – bass, vocals / **DAVE ROWNTREE** (b. 8 Apr'63) – drums

			Food-EMI	S.B.K.
Oct 90.	(c-s/7") *(TC+/FOOD 26)* **SHE'S SO HIGH. / I KNOW**		48	-
	(12") *(12FOOD 26)* – ('A'-Definitive) / Sing / I know (extended).			
	(cd-s) *(CDFOOD 26)* – ('A'side) / I know (extended) / Down.			
Apr 91.	(c-s/7") *(TC+/FOOD 29)* **THERE'S NO OTHER WAY. / INERTIA**		8	-
	(ext.12"+=/cd-s+=) *(12/CD FOOD 29)* – Mr.Briggs / I'm all over.			
	(12") *(12FOODX 20)* – ('A'remix). / Won't do it / Day upon day (live).			
Jul 91.	(c-s/7") *(TC+/FOOD 31)* **BANG. / LUMINOUS**		24	
	(ext.12"+=) *(12FOOD 31)* – Explain / Uncle Love.			
	(cd-s+=) *(CDFOOD 31)* – Explain / Beserk.			
Aug 91.	(cd/c/lp) *(FOOD CD/TC/LP 6)* <97880> **LEISURE**		7	
	– She's so high / Bang / Slow down / Repetition / Bad day / Sing / There's no other way / Fool / Come together / High cool / Birthday / Wear me down.			
Dec 91.	(c-s,cd-s) <07374> **THERE'S NO OTHER WAY / EXPLAIN**		-	82
Mar 92.	(c-s/7") *(TC+/FOOD 37)* **POPSCENE. / MACE**		32	
	(12"+=) *(12FOOD 37)* – I'm fine / Garden central.			
	(cd-s+=) *(CDFOOD 37)* – Badgeman Brown.			
Apr 93.	(c-s) *(TCFOOD 40)* **FOR TOMORROW. / INTO ANOTHER / HANGING OVER**		28	
	(12"+=) *(12FOOD 40)* – Peach.			
	(cd-s) *(CDFOOD 40)* – ('A'extended) / Peach / Bone bag.			
	(cd-s) *(CDSFOOD 40)* – ('A'side) / When the cows come home / Beachcoma / For tomorrow (acoustic).			
May 93.	(cd/c/lp) *(FOOD CD/TC/LP 9)* <89442> **MODERN LIFE IS RUBBISH**		15	
	– For tomorrow / Advert / Colin Zeal / Pressure on Julian / Star shaped / Blue jeans / Chemical world / Sunday Sunday / Oily water / Miss America / Villa Rosie / Coping / Turn it up / Resigned.			
Jun 93.	(7"red) *(FOOD 45)* **CHEMICAL WORLD. / MAGGIE MAY**		28	
	(12"/cd-s) *(12/CD FOOD 45)* – ('A'side) / Es Schmecht / Young and lovely / My ark.			
	(cd-s) *(CDFOODS 45)* – ('A'side) / Never clever (live) / Pressure on Julian (live) / Come together (live).			
Oct 93.	(7"yellow) *(FOODS 46)* **SUNDAY SUNDAY. / TELL ME, TELL ME**		26	
	(12") *(12FOODS 46)* – ('A'side) / Long legged / Mixed up.			
	(cd-s) *(CDFOODS 46)* – ('A'side) / Dizzy / Fried / Shimmer.			
	(cd-s) *(CDFOODX 46)* – ('A'side) / Daisy bell / Let's all go The Strand.			
Mar 94.	(7"/c-s) *(FOODS/TCFOOD 47)* **GIRLS AND BOYS. / MAGPIE / PEOPLE IN EUROPE**		5	-
	(cd-s) *(CDFOOD 47)* – ('A'side) / People in Europe / Peter Panic.			
	(cd-s) *(CDFOODS 47)* – ('A'side) / Magpie / Anniversary waltz.			
Apr 94.	(cd/c/lp) *(FOOD CD/TC/LP 10)* <29194> **PARKLIFE**		1	Jun94
	– Girls and boys / Tracy Jacks / End of a century / Park life / Bank holiday / Bad head / The debt collector / Far out / To the end / London loves / Trouble in the message centre / Clover over Dover / Magic America / Jubilee / This is a low / Lot 105.			
May 94.	(c-s) *(TCFOOD 50)* **TO THE END / GIRLS AND BOYS (Pet Shop Boys remix) / THREADNEEDLE STREET**		16	
	(12"/cd-s) *(12/CD FOOD 50)* – (1st 2 tracks; 2 versions of 2nd).			
	(cd-s) *(CDFOODS 50)* – ('A'side) / Threadneedle Street / Got yer.			
	(above featured LETITIA of STEREOLAB. Next with actor PHIL DANIELS.			
Jun 94.	(c-s,cd-s) <58155> **GIRLS AND BOYS / GIRLS AND BOYS (Pet Shop Boys radio mix) / MAGGIE MAY**		-	59
Aug 94.	(c-s/cd-s) *(TC/CDS FOOD 53)* **PARKLIFE. / SUPA SHOPPA / THEME FROM AN IMAGINARY FILM**		10	
	(12") *(12FOOD 53)* – (1st 2 tracks) / To the end (French version).			
	(cd-s) *(CDFOOD 53)* – (1st track) / Beard / To the end (French version).			
Nov 94.	(c-s/7") *(TCFOOD/FOODS 56)* **END OF A CENTURY. / RED NECKS**		19	
	(cd-s+=) *(CDFOOD 56)* – Alex's song.			
			Food	Virgin
Aug 95.	(c-s/7") *(TC+/FOOD 63)* **COUNTRY HOUSE. / ONE BORN EVERY MINUTE**		1	
	(cd-s+=) *(CDFOOD 63)* – To the end (with FRANCOISE HARDY).			
	(cd-ep) *(CDFOODS 63)* – ('A'live) / Girls and boys (live) / Parklife (live) / For tomorrow (live).			
Sep 95.	(cd/c/lp) *(FOOD CD/MC/LP 14)* <40855> **THE GREAT ESCAPE**		1	
	– Stereotypes / Country house / Best days / Charmless man / Fade away / Top man / The universal / Mr. Robinson's quango / He thought of cars / It could be you / Ernold Same / Globe alone / Dan Abnormal / Entertain me / Yuko and Hiro.			
Nov 95.	(c-s) *(TCFOOD 69)* **THE UNIVERSAL / ENTERTAIN ME (the live it! remix)**		5	
	(cd-s+=) *(CDFOODS 69)* – Ultranol / No monsters in me.			
	(cd-ep) *(CDFOOD 69)* – ('A'live) / Mr. Robinson's quango (live) / It could be you (live) / Stereotypes (live).			
Feb 96.	(c-s/7") *(TC+/FOOD 73)* **STEREOTYPES. / THE MAN WHO LEFT HIMSELF / TAME**		7	
	(cd-s+=) *(CDFOOD 73)* – Ludwig.			
Apr 96.	(c-s/7") *(TC+/FOOD 77)* **CHARMLESS MAN. / THE HORRORS**		5	
	(cd-s+=) *(CDFOOD 77)* – A song / St. Louis.			

— BLUR were joint winners (with rivals OASIS; NOEL) of the Ivor Novello Award for songwriter of the year.

May 96.	(d-cd; ltd on 'EMI Japan') *(TOCP 8400)* **LIVE AT THE BUDOKAN (live)**		-	-

— ALEX JAMES helped to form one-off indie supergroup ME ME ME alongside JUSTIN WELCH (Elastica –), STEPHEN DUFFY and CHARLIE BLOOR. Had a UK Top 20 hit in Aug'96 with 'HANGING AROUND'.

BLUR (cont)

		Food	Virgin
Jan 97.	(7"red) *(FOOD 89)* **BEETLEBUM. / WOODPIGEON SONG**	1	
	(cd-s+=) *(CDFOODS 89)* – ('A'-Mario Caldato Jr mix) / Dancehall.		
	(cd-s) *(CDFOOD 89)* – ('A'side) / All your life / A spell for money.		
Feb 97.	(cd/c/lp) *(FOOD CD/TC/LP 19)* <42876> **BLUR**	1	61
	– Beetlebum / Song 2 / Country sad ballad man / M.O.R. / On your own / Theme from retro / You're so great / Death of a party / Chinese bombs / I'm just a killer for your love / Look inside America / Strange news from another star / Movin' on / Essex dogs.		
Apr 97.	(7"purple) *(FOOD 93)* **SONG 2 / GET OUT OF THE CITIES**	2	
	(cd-s+=) *(CDFOODS 93)* – Polished stone.		
	(cd-s) *(CDFOOD 93)* – ('A'side) / Bustin' & dronin' / Country sad ballad man (live acoustic).		
Jun 97.	(7"white) *(FOOD 98)* **ON YOUR OWN. / POP SCENE (live) / SONG 2 (live)**	5	
	(cd-s+=) *(CDFOOD 98)* – On your own (live).		
	(cd-s) *(CDFOODS 98)* – ('A'side) / Chinese bombs (live) / Moving on (live) / M.O.R. (live).		
Sep 97.	(c-s/7"orange) *(TC+/FOOD 107)* **M.O.R. (Alan Moulder road version). / SWALLOWS IN THE HEATWAVE**	15	-
	(cd-s+=) *(CDFOOD 107)* – Movin' on (William Orbit mix) / Beetlebum (Moby's minimal house mix).		
Mar 98.	(d-cd) *(TOCP 504445)* **BUSTIN' AND DRONIN'**		
Mar 99.	(c-s/7"blue) *(TC+/FOOD 117)* **TENDER. / ALL WE WANT**	2	
	(cd-s+=) *(CDFOOD 117)* – Mellow jam (short version).		
	(cd-s) *(CDFOODS 117)* – ('A'side) / French song (full version) / Song 2 (video).		
Mar 99.	(cd/c/d-lp) *(FOOD CD/MC/LP 29)* <99129> **13**	1	80
	– Tender / Bugman / Coffee & TV / Swamp song / 1992 / B.L.U.R.E.M.I. / Battle / Mellow song / Trailerpark / Caramel / No distance left to run / Trimm trabb / Optigan 1.		
Jun 99.	(c-s) *(TCFOOD 122)* **COFFEE & TV / X-OFFENDER (Damon – Controls freaks bugman remix)**	11	-
	(cd-s+=) *(CDFOOD 122)* – Coyote (Dave's bugman remix).		
	(12"++=) *(12FOOD 122)* – Trade stylee (Alex's bugman remix) / Metal hip slop (Graham's bugman remix).		
	(cd-s) *(CDFOODS 122)* – ('A'side) / (above 2).		
Nov 99.	(c-s) *(TCFOOD 123)* **NO DISTANCE LEFT TO RUN / BEAGLE 2 / SO YOU**	14	-
	(cd-s) *(CDFOODS 123)* – ('A'side) / Battle (U.N.K.L.E. remix).		
	(cd-s) *(CDFOODS 123)* – ('A'side) / Tender (Cornelius mix).		
Oct 00.	(12") *(12FOOD 135)* **MUSIC IS MY RADAR. / BLACK BOOK**	10	
	(cd-s+=) *(CDFOOD 135)* – Headist / Into another (live).		
	(c-s+=) *(TCFOOD 135)* – She's so high.		
	(cd-s) *(CDFOODS 135)* – ('A'side) / She's so high / Seven days (live).		
Oct 00.	(cd/c/d-lp) *(FOOD CD/TC/LPD 33)* <50457> **BLUR: THE BEST OF** (compilation)	3	Nov00
	– Beetlebum / Song 2 / There's no other way / The universal / Coffee & TV / Parklife / End of a century / No distance left to run / Tender / Girls and boys / Charmless man / She's so high / Country house / To the end / On your own / This is a low / For tomorrow (visit to Primrose Hill extended) / Music is my radar. *(d-cd+=; FOODCDS 33)* – LIVE: She's so high / Girls and boys / To the end / End of a century / Charmless man / Beetlebum / MOR / Tender / No distance left to run.		

– compilations, etc. –

Sep 99.	(cd-ep-box) Food; *(BLURBOX 10)* **10th ANNIVERSARY BOX SET**		-
	– (all 22 hit singles)		

GRAHAM COXON

		Transcopic	Caroline
Aug 98.	(cd/lp) *(TRAN 005 CD/LP)* <7560> **THE SKY IS TOO HIGH**	31	
	– That's all I wanna do / Where'd you go? / In a salty sea / Day is far too long / R U lonely? / I wish / Hard and slow / Me you, we two / Waiting / Who the fuck? / Morning blues. *(cd re-iss. Dec01 & Oct02; same)*		
Jun 00.	(cd/lp) *(<527024-2/-1>)* **THE GOLDEN D**		
	– Jamie Thomas / The fear / Satan I gratan / Fame and fortune / My idea of hell / Lake / Fags and failure / Leave me alone / Keep hope alive / Oochy woochy / That's when I reach for my revolver / Don't think about always. *(cd re-iss. Oct02; same)*		
Jul 01.	(7"/cd-s) *(TRAN 011/+CD)* **THANK GOD FOR THE RAIN. / YOU WILL NEVER BE**		-
Aug 01.	(cd/d-lp) *(TRAN 010 CD/LP)* **CROW SIT ON BLOOD TREE**		-
	– Empty word / I'm goin' away / All has gone / Burn it down / Too uptight / Big bird / Tired / Hurt prone / Bonfires / Thank God for the rain / You never will be / A place for grief. *(re-iss. Oct02; same)*		
Oct 02.	(7") *(TRAN 020)* **ESCAPE SONG. / MOUNTAIN OF REGRET**		-
Oct 02.	(cd/d-lp) *(TRAN CD/LP 018)* **THE KISS OF MORNING**		-
	– Bitter tears / Escape song / Locked doors / Baby, you're out of your mind / It ain't no lie / Live line / Just be mine / Do what you're told to / Mountain of regret / Latte / Walking down the highway / Song for the sick / Good times.		

GORILLAZ

DAMON ALBARN – vocals (of DELTRON 3030) / **DAN "THE AUTOMATOR" NAKAMURA** – producer / **MIHO HATORI** – vocals (of CIBO MATTO) / **JAMIE HEWLETT** – visuals / plus **KID KOALA + DEL THA FUNKEE HOMOSAPIEN** – vocals / **2-D** – keyboards / **MURDOC** – bass / **RUSSEL** – drums / **NOODLE** – guitar / + **TINA WEYMOUTH** – vocals (ex-TALKING HEADS)

		Parlophone	Virgin
Nov 00.	(12") *(12R 6545)* **TOMORROW COMES TODAY. / ROCK THE HOUSE / LATIN SIMONE**		-
	(cd-s+=) *(CDR 6545)* – ('A'-video).		
Mar 01.	(c-s) *(TCR 6552)* <radio cut> **CLINT EASTWOOD / CLINT EASTWOOD (Ed Case refix) / DRACULA**	4	57 Aug01
	(cd-s+=) *(CDR 6552)* – ('A'CD-Rom).		
	(12") *(12R 6552)* – ('A'side) / ('A'-Ed Case refix full) / ('A'-Phil Life cypher version).		
Mar 01.	(cd/d-lp) *(531138-2/-1)* <33748> **GORILLAZ**	3	14 Jun00
	– Re-hash / 5-4 / Tomorrow comes today / New genius (brother) / Clint Eastwood / Man research (clapper) / Punk / Sound check (gravity) / Double bass / Rock the house / 19-2000 / Latin Simone / Starshine / Slow country / M1 A1 / Clint Eastwood (Ed Case refix full version) / 19-2000 (soul child mix). *(cd+=)* – Dracula / Left hand Suzuki method.		
—	in May'01, DAMON ALBARN & EINAR ORN BENEDIKTSSON released the soundtrack to '101 REYKJAVIK' for 'E.M.I.'; *(532989-2)*		
Jun 01.	(c-s) *(TCR 6559)* **19-2000 / HIP ALBATROSS**	6	-
	(cd-s) *(CDR 6559)* – ('A'side) / ('A'-Soulchild remix) / Left hand Suzuki method.		
	(12"++=) *(12R 6559)* – ('A'-Wiseguys house of wisdom remix).		
Oct 01.	(c-s) *(TCR 6565)* **ROCK THE HOUSE / GHOST TRAIN**	18	-
	(cd-s+=) *(CDR 6565)* – 19-2000 (video).		
	(cd-s) *(CDRS 6565)* – ('A'side) / Sounder / Faust / (making of the 'Rock The House' video).		
Feb 02.	(12") *(12R 6573)* **TOMORROW COMES TODAY. / TOMORROW (dub) / FILM MUSIC (mode remix)**	33	-
	(cd-s) *(CDR 6573)* – ('A'side) / Film music / Tomorrow dub (Spacemonkeys mix) / ('A'-video).		
Mar 02.	(cd) *(536942-0)* <11967> **G SIDES** (compilation)	65	84
	– 19/2000 (Soulchild mix) / Dracula / Rock the house / Sounder / Faust / Clint Eastwood (Phi life cypher version) / Ghost train / Hip albatross / Left hand Suzuki method / 12D3 / Clint Eastwood (video) / Rock the house (video).		

BOARDS OF CANADA

Formed: Pentland Hills, nr. Edinburgh, Scotland ... 1995 by MICHAEL SANDISON and MARCUS EOIN. The group earned their acclaim after recording a ridiculous amount of tracks which became available on the now legendary 'TWOISM' mini-LP – limited to 100 copies and ever so collectable. Next up was for experimental electronica label 'Skam' who signed the pair in 1996. Hailed as Skam's greatest release to date, the 'HI SCORES' EP set the ball rolling for the team in 1996 (now worth over £500). Audiences couldn't get enough of its catchy but simple, A-B-C (or L.F.O.) synth formats and melodies. References were, of course, made to The APHEX TWIN and JEGA, however 'HI SCORES' had a better twisted back-beat to it than, say, RICHARD D. JAMES' cult 'ANALOGUE BUBBLEBATH VOL.1'. It fooled listeners into thinking the band were American by its sheer 1992 hip-hop nostalgia and chilled out beach party vibes. This impressive debut was quickly followed up in late 1996 by a series of tracks for 'UMV' and 'Slam/Musik Aus Strom' side project label 'Mask', with 1998 witnessing the unfettering of the excellent "difficult" third release, 'MUSIC HAS THE RIGHT TO CHILDREN'. Cool as well as deeply serene, the album (distributed by 'Warp' and 'Matador') intensified that early 90's Miami trip-hop identity and added in a little scratching and sampling for good measure. A prime example of this was the single out-take, and the most famous track you'll hear from the album, 'ROYGBIV', which sounded like the Terminator doing slow motion break dancing in a crowded Beverly Hills house party. 1999 saw the latest from BOC, a PEEL SESSIONS EP, another triumph from the Peel acres and an entry into the 'Matador' 10th anniversary collection, 'Everything Is Nice'. The duo finally returned with a two track EP, 'A BEAUTIFUL PLACE IN THE COUNTRY', towards the end of 2000. The single was an unexpected trip into the psychedelic shenanigans that were about to be, once again, explored by The BOARDS OF CANADA. In February 2002, their long-awaited sophomore album, 'GEOGADDI', was released to huge critical acclaim, which resulted in their first interview with the NME. For this they described the open Scottish wilderness as an inspiration for their hallucinogenic, spaced-out synth doodlings. They also declared that the meaning of their moniker was indeed (as older readers may recall!) lifted from an educational company whose films on science and nature had been shown while the pair had attended school. This reflected a lot of the new album; one track in question 'DANDELION' had a backwards moog drone accompanied by a man (actor Leslie Nielsen from 'Naked Gun' fame!) narrating a TV documentary about a diving team; this segued into the six and a half minute epic 'SUNSHINE RECORDER'. Track 16, 'THE DEVIL IN THE DETAILS', had a simple keyboard riff on a loop which played the insane shrills of a child and the voice of a distorted, disjointed telephone operator. 'GEODADDI' (a near Top 20 entry) was much darker and yet much more layered in terms of themes, music and ambience. For two guys living in the countryside this was quite a feat, a real slice of math-electronica that was both gentle and eerily sublime.

Album rating: TWOISM mini (*7) / HI SCORES mini (*7) / MUSIC HAS THE RIGHT TO CHILDREN (*9) / PEEL SESSIONS (*7) / GEOGADDI (*9)

MICHAEL SANDISON (b. 14 Jul'71) – electronics / **MARCUS EOIN** (b.27 May'73) – electronics

		Music 70	not iss.
Aug 95.	(ltd; m-lp) *(BOARD 1)* **TWOISM**		-
	– Sixtyniner / Directline / Iced cooly / Basefree / Twoism / Seeya later / Melissa juice / Smokes quantity. *(re-iss. Nov02 on 'Warp' m-lp/m-cd+=; WARP LP/CD 70)* – 1986 summer fire.		

		Skam	not iss.
Dec 96.	(m-lp) *(SKA 8)* **HIGH SCORES**		-
	– Hi scores / Turquoise hexagon sun / Nlogax / June 9th / Seeya later / Everything you do is a balloon. *(m-cd-iss. Nov02; SKA 8CD)*		
Jan 98.	(7") *(KMAS 1)* **AQUARIUS. / CHINOOK**		-

		Warp – Skam	Matador
Mar 98.	(10") *(WAP10 55)* **ROYGBIV. / TELEPHASIC WORKSHOP**		-
Apr 98.	(cd/d-lp) *(WARP CD/LP 55 – SKALD 1)* <OLE 299-2/-1> **MUSIC HAS THE RIGHT TO CHILDREN**		
	– Wildlife analysis / An eagle in your mind / The color of the fire / Telephasic		

BOARDS OF CANADA (cont)

workshop / Triangles & rhombuses / Sixtyten / Turquoise hexagon sun / Kaini industries / Bocuma / Roygbiv / Rue the whirl / Aquarius / Olson / Pete standing alone / Smokes quantity / Open the light / One very important thought. *(d-lp+=)* – Happy cycling.

			Warp	Warp
Jan 99.	(cd-ep)	*(<WAP 114CD>)* **PEEL SESSIONS**		Mar99

– Aquarius (version 3) / Happy cycling / Olson (version 3).

Nov 00. (12"/cd-s) *(<WAP 144/+CD>)* **IN A BEAUTIFUL PLACE OUT IN THE COUNTRY EP**
– Kid for today / Amo bishop Roden / In a beautiful place out in the country / Zoetrope.

Feb 02. (cd/t-lp) *(<WARP CD/LP 101>)* **GEOGADDI** [21]
– Ready let's go / Music is math / Beware the friendly stranger / Gyroscope / Dandelion / Sunshine recorder / In the annexe / Julie and Candy / The smallest weird number / 1969 / Energy warning / The beach at Redpoint / Opening the mouth / Alpha and Omega / I saw drones / The devil in the details / A is to B as B is to C / Over the horizon radar / Dawn chorus / Diving station / You could feel the sky / Corsair / Magic window.

BONE-BOX

Formed: Manchester, England . . . late 90's by JAY TAYLOR, a former stalwart of GOLDBLADE (fronted by ex-MEMBRANES man JOHN ROBB). Along with five other recruits, including GOLDBLADE drummer ROB HAYNES, these bluesy punk rockers (fuse The FALL or The BIRTHDAY PARTY with TOM WAITS!) kicked off with the single 'CANCION' in 2000. Subsequently signing to 'Ugly Man' the following year, the poorly-monikered BONE-BOX delivered their EP, 'BRIDGE OF BROTHERHOOD AND UNITY'. However, it would be 2002's debut set, 'WORKING THE RIBALD RATIO', that made people take note; rock'n'roll was back for the 21st Century.

Album rating: WORKING THE RIBALD RATIO (*7)

JAY TAYLOR – vocals, guitar (ex-GOLDBLADE) / **ROB HAYNES** – drums (of GOLDBLADE) / + 4

			Butcher's Wig	not iss.
Apr 00.	(7")	*(SYRUP 007)* **CANCION. / TRUSTY HOUND**		–
			Ugly Man	not iss.
Aug 01.	(cd-ep)	*(ugly 24)* **BRIDGE OF BROTHERHOOD AND UNITY**		–

– Bridge of brotherhood and unity / My week = your year / Don't be 10 / The chief / Tenterhooks.

Jun 02. (cd) *(man 6)* **WORKING THE RIBALD RATIO**   [ ] –
– Low / Trusty hound / Base tastes / Bridge of brotherhood and unity / Shake my frame / The incumbent noise / My week = your year / Charivari / One track heart / Bite radius / Sweatlacedblues / Ennui / Bail bail bail.

BONFIRE MADIGAN (see under ⇒ **TATTLE TALE**)

Tracy BONHAM

Born: 1969, Boston, Massachusetts, USA, although her large family relocated to Eugene, Oregon, where she took up violin at an early age. After dropping out of music school, TRACY found herself part of the tight-knit Boston alt-rock scene as she left behind her classical training and took up the guitar. While her live sets got people talking, she cut a debut EP, 'THE LIVERPOOL SESSIONS', for local indie label, 'Cherrydisc'. 'Island' were also sufficiently impressed with the budding singer/songwriter's talent to release the record on the 'Island Red' imprint in late summer '95. The company also signed her up for an album, the resulting 'THE BURDENS OF BEING UPRIGHT' issued in summer '96. While the record made the Top 60 in America, TRACY couldn't quite follow ALANIS MORRISETTE into the UK market, her approach perhaps just a little too abrasive for the Top 40. Favouring the softly softly build-up then all-out screaming assault of grunge, BONHAM nevertheless leavened her autobiographical broadsides with a dose of tongue-in-cheek humour. While comparisons with Boston compadres such as THROWING MUSES, BREEDERS, etc., were predictable, BONHAM showed off her English influences with a cover of PJ Harvey's '50 FT. QUEENIE' on subsequent single, 'MOTHER MOTHER'. • **Covered:** LUST FOR LIFE (Iggy Pop).

Album rating: THE BURDENS OF BEING UPRIGHT (*6) / DOWN HERE (*6)

TRACY BONHAM – vocals, guitar / with session band

			Island Red	Cherrydisc
Sep 95.	(10"ep/cd-ep)	*(10IR/CIRD 109) <22810>* **THE LIVERPOOL SESSIONS E.P.**		

– Sunshine / Dandelion / 18 heads will roll by / The real / Talk too much / I'm not a waif / Big foot.

			Island	Island
Jun 96.	(cd/c)	*<524 187-2/-4>* **THE BURDENS OF BEING UPRIGHT**		54

– Mother mother / Navy bean / Tell it to the sky / Kisses / Brain crack / One / One hit wonder / Sharks can't sleep / Bulldog / Every breath / 30 seconds / Real.

Sep 96. (7") *(IS 644)* **MOTHER MOTHER. / 50ft QUEENIE (live)**   [ ] –
(cd-s+=) *(CID 644)* – Navy bean (live).
(cd-s) *(CIDX 644)* – ('A'side) / Dandelion / 18 heads will roll by.

Nov 96. (7"white) *(IS 651)* **SHARKS CAN'T SLEEP. / I'M NOT A WAIF**
(cd-s+=) *(CID 651)* – Bulldog.
(cd-s) *(CIDX 651)* – ('A'side) / Lust for life / 50ft Queenie (live).

—— In Sep'98, her 2nd album, 'TRAIL OF A DUST DEVIL' was shelved in UK

Mar 00. (cd-s) *<562 618-2>* **BEHIND EVERY GOOD WOMAN (Fuji pop mix) / BEHIND EVERY GOOD WOMAN (AC radio) / FREED / MEATHOOK**   – [ ]

Apr 00. (cd) *<524 564-2>* **DOWN HERE**   – [ ]
– Freed / Behind every good woman / You don't know me / Fake it / Cold day in hell / Jumping bean / Oasis hotel / Second wind / Thumbelina / Meathook / You can't always not get what you don't want / Give us something.

BONNIE 'PRINCE' BILLY (see under ⇒ **OLDHAM, Will**)

Clint BOON EXPERIENCE! (see under ⇒ **INSPIRAL CARPETS**)

BOO RADLEYS

Formed: Liverpool, England . . . 1988, by schoolmates SICE and MARTIN CARR. Another friend, TIM BROWN, was invited to join after teaching MARTIN how to play guitar. They took the group name from a weird character in the film, 'To Kill A Mockingbird'. The quartet was complete when they found drummer STEVE HEWITT. They worked hard on the Mersey gig circuit but no major deal was forthcoming. Come 1990, they finally found a home with small indie label, 'Action', who released their debut lp 'ICHABOD AND I'. On its merit, they were invited by the illustrious DJ John Peel to session for Radio 1. This led to a signing for 'Rough Trade', who issued 3 popular EP's between late 1990 & 91. They then moved to 'Creation', their psychedelic, BYRDS-influenced jangle-pop soon making them favourites of the music press (Singles Of The Week, etc). The release of 1992's 'EVERYTHING'S ALRIGHT FOREVER' and the following years' masterful 'GIANT STEPS' album infused their sugary pop with screeching guitars and jagged brass accompaniment. The latter secured them their first Top 20 placing, the tracks 'I HANG SUSPENDED', 'BARNEY (. . . AND ME)' and 'LAZARUS' being effervescent highlights. Early to rise in '95, they scored their first Top 10 hit with 'WAKE UP BOO!', taken from their similarly titled No.1 album. The single was subsequently spoiled after it was played to death as the theme tune for ITV's Breakfast TV. In 1996, SICE (aka EGGMAN) released a patchy solo album, while The BOO's returned with another slice (or SICE!) of nostalgic pop, 'C'MON KIDS'. After the album 'KINGSIZE' was released to some mixed reviews (towards the end of '98), the unhappy BOO's were quite literally treading water(beds) until their demise early the following year.
• **Songwriters:** CARR lyrics / group music, except TRUE FAITH (New Order) / ALONE AGAIN OR (Love) / ONE OF US MUST KNOW (Bob Dylan) / THE QUEEN IS DEAD (Smiths). • **Trivia:** MERIEL BARHAM of The PALE SAINTS provided vocals on 2 tracks for GIANT STEPS album. ED BALL (ex-TV PERSONALITIES) often made guest appearances.

Album rating: ICHABOD AND I (*5) / EVERYTHING'S ALRIGHT FOREVER (*7) / GIANT STEPS (*9) / WAKE UP! (*8) / C'MON KIDS (*6) / KINGSIZE (*6) / Eggman: FIRST FRUITS (*5)

SICE (b. SIMON ROWBOTTOM, 18 Jun'69, Wallasey, England) – vocals, guitar / **MARTIN CARR** (b.29 Nov'68, Thurso, Scotland) – guitar / **TIM BROWN** (b.26 Feb'69, Wallasey) – bass / **STEVE DREWITT** (b. Northwich, England) – drums

			Action	not iss.
Jul 90.	(lp)	*(TAKE 4)* **ICHABOD AND I**		–

– Eleanor everything / Bodenheim Jr. / Cweatzle / Sweet salad birth / Hip clown rag / Walking 5th carnival / Kaleidoscope / Happens to us all.

—— **ROB CIEKA** (b. 4 Aug'68, Birmingham, England) – drums repl. DREWITT to BREED

			Rough Trade	not iss.
Oct 90.	(12"ep/cd-ep)	*(RTT 241/+CD)* **KALEIDOSCOPE EP**		–

– Kaleidoscope / How I feel / Aldous / Swansong.

Apr 91. (12"ep/cd-ep) *(R 201127-10/-13)* **EVERY HEAVEN EP**   [ ] –
– The finest kiss / Tortoiseshell / Bluebird / Naomi.

Sep 91. (12"ep/cd-ep) *(R 275-0/-3)* **BOO UP! EP** (Peel sessions)   [ ] –
– Everybody / Sometime soon she said / Foster's van / Song for up!

Dec 91. (cd) *(R 3012)* **LEARNING TO WALK** (compilation of above 3 EP's)   [ ] –

			Creation	Columbia
Feb 92.	(12"ep)(cd-ep)	*(CRE 128T)(CRESCD 124)* **ADRENALIN EP**		–

– Lazy day / Vegas / Feels like tomorrow / Whiplashed.

Mar 92. (cd/c/lp) *(CRE CD/MC/LP 120) <52912>* **EVERYTHING'S ALRIGHT FOREVER**   [55]   Aug92
– Spaniard / Towards the light / Losing it (song for Abigail) / Memory babe / Skyscraper / I feel nothing / Room at the top / Does this hurt / Sparrow / Smile fades fast / Firesky / Song for the morning to sing / Lazy day / Paradise.

Jun 92. (7") *(CRE 128)* **BOO! FOREVER. / DOES THIS HURT**   [67]   –
(12"+=)(cd-s+=) *(CRE 128T)(CRESCD 128)* – Buffalo Bill / Sunfly II: Walking with the kings.

Nov 92. (7") *(CRE 137)* **LAZARUS. / LET ME BE YOUR FAITH**   [76]   –
(12"+=)(cd-s+=) *(CRE 137T)(CRESCD 137)* – At the sound of speed / Petroleum.

—— added **STEVE KITCHEN** – trumpet, flugel horn / **JACKIE ROY** – clarinet / **LINDSAY JOHNSTON** – cello

Jul 93. (7") *(CRE 147)* **I HANG SUSPENDED. / RODNEY KING (St. Etienne mix)**   [77]   –
(12"+=)(cd-s+=) *(CRE 147T)(CRESCD 147)* – As bound a stomorrow / I will always ask where you have been though I know the answer.

Jul 93. (cd/c/d-lp) *(CRE CD/MC/LP 149) <53794>* **GIANT STEPS**   [17]   Aug93
– I hang suspended / Upon 9th and Fairchild / Wish I was skinny / Leaves and sand / Butterfly McQueen / Rodney King (song for Lenny Bruce) / Thinking of ways / Barney (. . . and me) / Spun around / If you want it, take it / Best lose the fear / Take the time around / Lazarus / One is for / Run my way runway / I've lost the reason / The white noise revisited. (lp re-iss. Aug98; same)

Oct 93. (7"/c-s) *(CRE/+CD 169)* **WISH I WAS SKINNY. / PEACHY KEEN**   [75]   –
(12"+=)(cd-s+=) *(CRE 169T)(CRESCD 169)* – Furthur / Crow eye.

BOO RADLEYS (cont)

THE GREAT INDIE DISCOGRAPHY

The 1990s

Feb 94. (7"/c-s) (CRE/+CS 178) **BARNEY (. . .AND ME). / ZOOM** 48 -
(12"+=)(cd-s+=) (CRE 178T)(CRESCD 178) – Tortoiseshell / Cracked lips, homesick.

May 94. (7") (CRE 187) **LAZARUS. / (I WANNA BE) TOUCHDOWN JESUS** 50 -
(12"+=) (CRE 187T) – ('A'-Secret Knowledge mix) / ('A'-Ultramarine radio mix).
(cd-s+=) (CRESCD 187) – ('A'acoustic) / ('A'-St. Etienne mix).
(cd-s) (CRESCD 187X) – ('A'-Secret Knowledge mix) / ('A'-Ultramarine mix) / ('A'-Augustus Pablo mix) / ('A'-12"mix).

Feb 95. (c-s) (CRECS 191) **WAKE UP BOO! / JANUS** 9 -
(cd-s+=) (CRESCD 191) – Blues for George Michael / Friendship song.
(12") (CRE 191T) – Wake up Boo!: Music for astronauts / Janus / Blues for George Michael.
(cd-s) (CRESCD 191X) – Wake up Boo!: Music for astronauts / . . .And tomorrow the world / The history of Creation parts 17 & 36.

Mar 95. (cd/c/lp) (CRE CD/MC/LP 179) <67249> **WAKE UP!** 1
– Wake up Boo! / Fairfax scene / It's Lulu / Joel / Find the answer within / Reaching out from here / Martin, Doom! it's 7 o'clock / Stuck on amber / Charles Bukowski is dead / 4am conversation / Twinside / Wilder. (cd re-iss. Aug98; same)

May 95. (c-s) (CRECS 202) **FIND THE ANSWER WITHIN / DON'T TAKE YOUR GUN TO TOWN** 37 -
(cd-s+=) (CRESCD 202) – Wallpaper.
(12"++=) (CRE 202T) – The only word I can find / Very together.
(cd-s) (CRESCD 202X) – ('A'-High Llamas mix) / The only word I can find / Very together.

Jul 95. (c-s) (CRECS 211) **IT'S LULU / THIS IS NOT ABOUT ME** 25 -
(cd-s+=) (CRESCD 211) – Reaching out from here (the High Llamas mix / Martin, doom! it's seven o'clock (Stereolab mix).
(cd-s) (CRESCD 211X) – ('A'side) / Joel (Justin Warfield mix) / Tambo / Donkey.

Sep 95. (c-s/7") (C+/CRE 214) **FROM THE BENCH AT BELVIDERE. / HI FALUTIN'** 24 -
(cd-s+=) (CRESCD 214) – Crushed / Nearly almost time.

Creation Mercury

Aug 96. (7") (CRE 220) **WHAT'S IN THE BOX? (SEE WHATCHA GOT). / BLOKE IN A DRESS** 25 -
(cd-s+=) (CRESCD CRESCD 220) – Flakes / ('A'-Kris Needs mix).
(cd-s) (CRESCD 220X) – ('A'side) / Atlantic / The absent boy / Annie and Marnie.

Sep 96. (cd/c)(d-lp) (CRECD/CCRE 194)(CRELP 194L) <534256> **C'MON KIDS** 20
– C'mon kids / Meltin's worm / Melodies for the deaf / Get on the bus / Everything is sorrow / Bullfrog green / What's in the box? (see whatcha got) / Four saints / New Brighton promenade / Fortunate sons / Shelter / Ride the tiger / One last hurrah. (lp w/ free 7") SKYWALKER. / FRENCH CANADIAN BEAN SOUP

Oct 96. (7") (CRE 236) **C'MON KIDS. / SPION COP** 18 -
(cd-s+=) (CRESCD 236) – Too beautiful / Bullfrog green (ultra living mix).
• (cd-s) (CRESCD 236X) – ('A'side) / Nothing to do but scare myself / From the bench at Belvidere (Ultramarine mix) / Fortunate sons (Greg Hunter remix).

Jan 97. (7") (CRE 248) **RIDE THE TIGER. / VOTE YOU** 38 -
(cd-s+=) (CRESCD 248) – A part I know so well / Everything is sorrow (Grantby remix).
(cd-s) (CRESCD 248X) – ('A'side) / Roadie / Safe at home / C'mon kids (Mekon remix).

Creation Creation

Oct 98. (10") (CRE 299X) **FREE HUEY. / SPANISH LIZARDS** 54 -
(cd-s+=) (CRESCD 299) – ('A'-environmental science remix).
(cd-s) (CRESCD 299X) – ('A'side) / ('A'mixes).

Oct 98. (cd/d-lp)(c) (CRE CD/LP 228)(CCRE 228) **KINGSIZE** 62
– Blueroom in archway / The old newsstand at Hamilton Square / Free Huey / Monuments for a dead century / Heaven's at the bottom of this glass / Kingsize / High as monkeys / Eurostar / Adieu clo clo / Jimmy Webb is God / She is everywhere / Comb your hair / Song for the blueroom / The future is now.

——— the band split early '99; CARR formed BRAVE CAPTAIN

EGGMAN

——— i.e. **SICE** with **ROB CIEKA** – drums / **ED BALL** – bass (ex-TIMES) / **SEAN JACKSON** – lead guitar (of 18 WHEELER) / **TIM BROWN** – piano, etc / etc

Creation Tristar

May 96. (7"/c-s) (CRE/+CS 225) **NOT BAD ENOUGH. / IDENTIKIT**
(cd-s+=) (CRESCD 225) – We won the war.

May 96. (cd/lp)(c) (CRE CD/LP 201)(CCRE 201) <36910> **FIRST FRUITS**
– Purple patches / Tomas / That's that then (for now) / Not bad enough / The funeral song / Replace all your lies with truth / Out of my window / Look up / I'll watch your back / First fruits fall.

BOOTH AND THE BAD ANGEL
(see under ⇒ JAMES; 80's section)

BOSS HOG
(see under ⇒ PUSSY GALORE; 80's section)

BOUQUET

Formed: Hunters Bar, Sheffield, England . . . 1991 by NEIL SHUMSKY and his friend RACHEL. Carrying on from the twee-pop/C-86 days of a few years previously, BOUQUET released a number of singles/EP's, etc, prior to the departure of RACHEL in '93. Taking a 3-year rest from the business, SHUMSKY returned to the studio with two other, er chumsky's in the shape of rhythm lads CHRIS MABBS and SHAUN ALCOCK. 1997's comeback single, 'BEFORE I DIE I'D LIKE TO SEE A FLYING SAUCER', paved the way finally for a long-time-coming debut set, 'CORAL KINGDOM' (1998); a second guitarist would be added for the Japan-only 45, 'MY FAVOURITE FLOWERS', in 2001.

Album rating: CORAL KINGDOM (*5)

NEIL SHUMSKY – vocals, 12-string guitar / **RACHEL** – vocals, guitar

Caramel not iss.

Apr 92. (7"m) (Caramel one) **ELDERBERRY PLACE. / SHINE SO BRIGHTLY / SNOWING**

Waaaah!! not iss.

Jul 92. (7"m) (BULL 7-0) **WARMEST GLOW. / (other 2 by The ORCHIDS + The CRYSTAL GARDEN)**

Nov 92. (7"flexi) (POST 4) **MAGIC TRAIN. / (other artist)**
(above issued on 'Pillarbox Red')

Jan 93. (7"ep) (BULL 11-0) **THE PINK BLOSSOM IN OUTER SPACE EP**
– Dream all the way / Summer swirl / Apple orchard / Forever.

——— RACHEL departed in 1993; in 1996 SHUMSKY recruited **CHRIS MABBS** – bass / **SHAUN ALCOCK** – drums

Aquavinyle not iss.

Jan 97. (7"m) (AQUA 03) **BEFORE I DIE I'D LIKE TO SEE A FLYING SAUCER. / CARAMEL GIRL / BUTTERFLIES** - - French

Jan 98. (7"m) (AQUA 05) **MINIMINOU. / SAD TO SAY / THE BOTTOM OF THE GARDEN** - - French
(UK-iss.May98 on 'Popstar'; POP 02)

Popstar not iss.

Apr 98. (cd) (POPCD 1) **CORAL KINGDOM**
– In the golden eternity / Travelling companion / Bouquet of angels / Citrus grove lullaby / Train magique / The land beyond the sky / Uluru's charl / Electric fluff / Ramblin' gamblin' man / Wine and romance / Chie Kato's dream / Deep sea gallery / You are what you eat.

——— added **DARREN O'CONNOR** – guitar

Clover not iss.

Apr 01. (7") **MY FAVOURITE FLOWERS. / PLAIN SAILING** - - Japan

BOWERY ELECTRIC

Formed: Manhattan, New York, USA . . . 1992 by vocalist/guitarist LAWRENCE CHANDLER and vocalist bassist MARTHA SCHWENDENER. Arriving in 1994 with the 'BOWERY ELECTRIC' EP, their music was deliberately uncomfortable sounding with hushed vocals and stifling, atmospheric electronics. Their debut album, also titled 'BOWERY ELECTRIC' (1995), was all fuzzy guitars and gentle drums building an eerie and relentless mood throughout. BOWERY's second set, 'BEAT' (1996), was another ethereal drone, however the inclusion of hip-hop and techno rhythms led to wider critical acclaim. The experimental remix album, 'VERTIGO' (1997), saw the band further immerse themselves in electronica. 'LUSHLIFE' (2000) was a return to their familiar sheogazing head music sound, although it did display a more traditional sensibility with regards to song structure.

Album rating: BOWERY ELECTRIC (*7) / BEAT (*7) / VERTIGO (*6) / LUSHLIFE (*5)

LAWRENCE CHANDLER – vocals, guitar / **MARTHA SCHWENDENER** – vocals, bass / **MICHAEL JOHNGREN** – drums

not iss. High Fidelity

1994. (d7"ep) <none> **BOWERY ELECTRIC** -
– Drop / Let me down / Head on fire / Only sometimes.

Kranky Kranky

Aug 95. (blue-lp/cd) <KRANK 007/+CD> **BOWERY ELECTRIC** -
– Sounds in motion / Next to nothing / Long way down / Another road / Over and over / Deep sky objects / Slow thrills / Out of phase / Drift away. (UK-iss.Mar97; same as US)

——— **WAYNE MAGRUDER** – drums; repl. JOHNGREN

Nov 96. (cd) <KRANK 014CD> **BEAT** -
– Beat / Empty words / Without stopping / Under the sun / Fear of flying / Looped / Black light / Inside out / Coming down / Postscript. (UK-iss.Aug97 on 'Beggars Banquet'+=; BBL 188CD) – Low density.

not iss. Happy Go Lucky

1997. (12") <013> **ELECTRIC SLEEP. / BLOW UP** -

Beggars Banquet Beggars Banquet

Aug 97. (d-cd) (BBQ 315CDD) <81315> **VERTIGO**
– Fear of flying / Fear of flying (Chasm mix) / Black light (Osymyso mix) // Without stopping (Witchman mix) / Coming down (Immersion mix) / Black light (Dunderhead mix) / Empty words (Twisted Science mix) / Fear of flying (Third Eye Foundation mix) / Elementary particles (Main mix).

——— now without a permanent drummer

Jan 00. (12"/cd-s) (BBQ 341 T/CD) **FREEDOM FIGHTER / FREEDOM FIGHTER (vocal remix). / FREEDOM FIGHTER (instrumental remix) / SOUL CITY**

Feb 00. (cd/lp) (BBQ CD/LP 213) <80213> **LUSHLIFE**
– Floating world / Lushlife / Shook ones / Psalms of survival / Soul city / Freedom fighter / Saved / Deep blue / After landing / Passages.

David BOWIE

The Continuing Story . . . BOWIE then made yet another about face; dallying briefly with themes of fascism and dictatorship, he recorded the stark 'STATION TO STATION' (1976) album, before relocating to Berlin with BRIAN ENO and continuing his move towards experimental/avant-garde rock. The resulting albums, 'LOW' and 'HEROES', both released in 1977, were fairly successful in the UK despite containing some of BOWIE's most uncommercial work to date. After a final album with ENO, BOWIE returned

David BOWIE (cont)

to more conventional rock, gaining another No.1 hit with his resurrection of Major Tom on 'ASHES TO ASHES' (1980).

Album rating: LOW (*10) / HEROES (*9)

— now collaborated with **BRIAN ENO** – synthesizers
RICKY GARDINER – guitar repl. SLICK

Jan 77.	(lp/c) (PL/PK 12030) <2030> **LOW**		2	11

– Speed of life / Breaking glass / What in the world / Sound and vision / Always crashing in the same car / Be my wife / A new career in a new town / Warszawa / Art decade / Weeping wall / Subterraneans. *(re-iss. Dec80 on 'RCA Int.' lp/c; INTS/INTK 5065) ;hit UK 85 in Jun83) (re-iss. Mar84 on 'RCA Int.' lp/c/cd; NL/NK/PD 83856) (re-iss. Aug91 on 'E.M.I.' cd/c/lp; CD/TC+/EMD 1027) (+=)* – (bonus tracks). *(hit UK No.64)*

Feb 77.	(7") (PB 0905) <10905> **SOUND AND VISION. / A NEW CAREER IN A NEW TOWN**		3	69
Jun 77.	(7") (PB 1017) <11017> **BE MY WIFE. / SPEED OF LIFE**			

— next guest **ROBERT FRIPP** – guitar who repl. RICKY GARDINER.

Oct 77.	(7") (PB 1121) <11121> **HEROES. / V2-SCHNEIDER**		24	
Oct 77.	(lp/c) (PL/PK 12522) <2522> **HEROES**		3	35

– Beauty and the beast / Joe the lion / Heroes / Sons of the silent age / Blackout / V-2 Schneider / Sense of doubt / Moss garden / Neukoln / Black out / The secret life of Arabia. *(re-iss. Dec80 lp/c; INTS/INTK 5066) (hit UK 75 in Jun83) (re-iss. Nov84 lp/c/cd; NL/NK/PD 83857) (re-iss. Apr91 on 'E.M.I.' cd/c/lp; CD/TC+/EMD 1025) (+=)* – Joe the Lion (1991 remix) / Abolumajor.

Jan 78.	(7") (PB 1190) <11190> **THE BEAUTY AND THE BEAST. / SENSE OF DOUBT**		39	

BOWLFISH

Formed: Harrow, England ... 1992 by main songwriter STEVE LOWE, plus STEVE GENT and PHIL MARTIN. A mix'n'match power trio featuring a bearded hippy, a babyfaced indie-kid and a bequiffed STRAY CATS fan, BOWLFISH made their vinyl debut in summer '92 with the 'DOGBERRY' single. Released on indie label, 'Roughneck', the track's amphetamine punk-pop was followed up by the denser, more adventurous guitar textures of 'MRS FRANK' in early '93. A third single, 'TWISTED HIPS', previewed debut album, 'THE BISCUIT' (1993), although a subsequent one-off single (the intriguingly titled 'FACEACHE', which came backed with a cover of Pulp's 'LIPGLOSS') on US indie label, 'Domino', proved to be the BOWLFISH epitaph. Presumably the two STEVE's have returned to their favourite pastime, birdwatching!

Album rating: THE BISCUIT (*4)

STEVE LOWE – vocals, guitar, percussion / **STEVE GENT** – bass, percussion / **PHIL MARTIN** – drums, percussion, vocals

			not iss.	Twenty
			Roughneck	not iss.
1992.	(cd-s) <3> **DOGBERRY. / BANG BANG BANG**		-	
Jan 93.	(10"/cd-s) (HYPER 020 T/CD) **MRS. FRANK. /**			-
Jun 93.	(7") (HYPE 25) **TWISTED HIPS. /**			
	(cd-s+=) (HYPE 25CD) –			
Oct 93.	(cd/lp) (NECK CD/LP 13) **THE BISCUIT**			-

– Bubba / Bufflehead / Brigh 'n' sigh / Sultana / Twisted hips / Reggie / Dirty Darren / Brutus.

			Domino	not iss.
Jun 94.	(12"/cd-s) (RUG 20 T/CD) **FACEACHE. / JIM DEMON / LIPGLOSS**			-

— disbanded later in '94

BOWS

Formed: Coupar Angus, Perthshire, Scotland ... 1998 by (black British singer) LUKE SUTHERLAND after the break-up of his indie-experimental band, LONG FIN KILLIE who had formed in the late 80's. Strange as it may seem, LFK began practising in his mother's – Lady Duncan of Jordanstone's – mansion. He made regular visits to her laundry room, where they spent their first three years pulling together enough material for debut set 'HOUDINI' (1995). The quartet became a critically acclaimed folk/jazz group who mixed primitive BETA BAND techniques with fiddle riffs and kazoo solos! After 1996's 'VALENTINO', the Scottish four were involved in a near fatal car accident which, arguably split the group (although it was said that they had nothing in common by that time), leaving enough space for recovery and a third release, 'AMELIA'; SUTHERLAND would, in turn go his own way. The troubled frontman began writing a book, 'Jelly Roll', inspired by his touring days with LFK, about the descent of a Scottish jazz band on the road. When released, the novel became an instant success, winning over critics and nominations for the Whitbread Book Of The Year. SUTHERLAND established BOWS in '98 when he went into partnership with singer/songwriter SIGNE HOIRUP WILLE-JORGENSEN and ex-PhD student RUTH EDMOND. 'BLUSH' was issued the following year, becoming the catalyst for SUTHERLAND's second novel 'Sweet Meat'. His honest lyrics and MASSIVE ATTACK-like cool enabled him to pull off such gems as 'BIG WINGS' and 'IT'LL BE HALF TIME IN ENGLAND SOON', sending them into the darkest crevice of the human mind. Creepy backing tunes and orchestrated malevolence made this particular set float just above average.

Album rating: Long Fin Killie: HOUDINI (*7) / VALENTINO (*6) / AMELIA (*5) / Bows: BLUSH (*6) / CASSIDY (*6)

LONG FIN KILLIE

LUKE SUTHERLAND – vocals / **PHIL** – guitar / **COLIN** – bass / **DAVEY** – drums

		Too Pure	Warners
Oct 94.	(12"yellow-ep/cd-ep) (PURE 12/CD 39) **BUTTERGUT EP**		-

– The Lamberton lamplighter / Boy racer / Butterbelly.

— next featured **MARK E. SMITH** – vocals (of The FALL)

May 95.	(7") (PURE 44) **HOLLYWOOD GEM. / THE HEADS OF DEAD SURFERS**		-
	(cd-s+=) (PURECD 044) – Flaccid tabloid / Stacked.		
Jun 95.	(cd) (PURECD 47) <43036> **HOUDINI**		Jul95

– Man Ray / How I blew it with Houdini / Homo erectus / The heads of dead surfers / Montgomery / Love smothers allergy / Hollywood gem / The Lamberton lamplighter / Corngold / Idiot hormone / Rockethead on mandatory surveillance / Flower carrier / Unconscious gangs of men.

Apr 96.	(cd-ep) (PURECD 58) **HANDS AND LIPS EP**		-

– Hands and lips / Angel / Nation / Clinch.

May 96.	(lp/cd) (PURE/+CD 54) <43076> **VALENTINO**		Jul96

– Godiva / Pele / Kitten heels / A thousand wounded astronauts / Hands and lips / Valentino / Coward / Girlfriend / Matador / Cop / Cupid / Fresher.

		Too Pure	Too Pure
Oct 97.	(7") (PURE 75) **LIPSTICK. / CZ**		-
	(cd-s+=) (PURE 75CDS) – Love life.		
Nov 97.	(lp/cd) (<PURE/+CD 74>) **AMELIA**		Apr98

– British summertime / Lipstick / Kismet / Resin / Sugar helping / Ringer / Chrysler / Bigger than England / Headlines / Gold swinger / Deep house / Yawning at comets.

— disbanded; DAVEY had already joined Dutch/English band, DONKEY

BOWS

LUKE SUTHERLAND – vocals, multi / **SIGNE HOIRUP WILLE-JORGENSEN** – vocals / **RUTH EDMOND** – vocals

Mar 99.	(cd-s) (PURE 82CDS) **BIG WINGS / SPEED MARINA / KING DELUXE / BIG WINGS (version)**		-
May 99.	(cd/lp) (<PURE 90 CD/LP>) **BLUSH**		Aug99

– Big wings / Troy Polenta's big break / Blush / Overfor Kommer / King Deluxe / Speed marina / No.4 / Britannica / Aquavella / It'll be half time in England soon / Girls lips glitter / Sleepyhead / Rockets.

Jun 99.	(7") (PURE 97S) **BLUSH. / ('A'-Ellis Island mix)**		-
	(cd-s+=) (PURE 97CDS) – Heart and two stars.		
Oct 99.	(7") (PURE 88S) **BRITANNICA. / TOTAL FUCKING MASSACRE**		-
	(cd-s+=) (PURE 88CDS) – ('A'-Scissorkicks mix) / ('A'-CD-Rom).		
Mar 01.	(cd-s) (PURE 102CDS) **PINK PUPPET (mixes; Mike Paradinas / Gonzales / Papa November / full reading of story)**		-
Apr 01.	(cd) (PURE 104CD) **CASSIDY**		-

– Luftsang / Cuban welterweight rumbles hidden hitmen / Man fat / All 4 Onassis / Uniroyal / B boy blunt / Wonderland / DJ / Blue steeples / Hey Vegas / Sun electric / Ton ten all the way home.

BOXCAR RACER (see under ⇒ BLINK 182)

BOXHEAD ENSEMBLE

Formed: Chicago, Illinois, USA ... 1996 by MICHAEL KRASSNER who would employ a revolving cast of friends and musicians such as WILL OLDHAM and KEN VANDERMARK to assist with his recording. The first release by BOXHEAD ENSEMBLE was the soundtrack to the documentary film 'DUTCH HARBOR'. Following the lives of Alaskan fisherman and shot in black and white, the stark imagery in the film is perfectly supported by the expansive and intelligent music provided by the group. The next venture for the 'ENSEMBLE was to tour the film and improvise the accompanying music each night. The highlights of this tour were captured on the album 'THE LAST PLACE TO GO' (1998), which further displayed the group's ability to create evocative and impressive music. KRASSNER and Co's talents were again on show with the release of 'TWO BROTHERS' (2001). This time around the collective involved diverse contributors such as Argentinian composer and reedist GUILLERMO GREGORIO, WILCO stalwart JEFF TWEEDY and violist and trumpeter DAVID CURRY amongst others. The music was mysterious and orchestral, a truly original and inspiring set of songs which defied the conventions of any musical genre. Additionally KRASSNER was also involved in the group the LOFTY PILLARS. The first album by this trio, which also consisted of FRED LONBERG-HOLM and WILL HENDRICKS, featured far more traditional songwriting than the BOXHEAD ENSEMBLE records. Although the masterful talent was still evident, 'WHEN WE WERE HERE' (2000) was an album of piano based American folk ballads. The second album, 'AMSTERDAM' (2001), was another timeless collection of lush heartbreaking songs capable of competing with any of the seemingly endless flow of quality Americana albums appearing around this time.

Album rating: DUTCH HARBOR: WHERE THE SEA BREAKS ITS BACK soundtrack (*7) / THE LAST PLACE TO GO (*6) / TWO BROTHERS (*7) / Lofty Pillars: WHEN WE WERE LOST (*6) / AMSTERDAM (*7)

MICHAEL KRASSNER – vocals, guitar / with guest musicians

		Atavistic	Atavistic
Apr 97.	(cd) <(ALP 85CD)> **DUTCH HARBOR: WHERE THE SEA BREAKS ITS BACK**		

– Introduction / Unalaska island / For the glory of the wind and the water / Ship supply / Telegraph hill / The ravens / Mother Gromoff / Captain's bay road / At sea / The valley / Ebb's folly / In closing.

BOXHEAD ENSEMBLE (cont)

Oct 98. (cd) <(ALP 96CD)> **THE LAST PLACE TO GO** (live)
– Introduction / Coastal boarder / Nobody / Dust and rain / Fading cold / Two ravens / Carolyn's theme / The last place to go / Choices made / Deep sea / Far gone – Big sky. (d-cd+=) – Black dissimulation / Solo / Send in the clowns / Who / Big sky. <(lp-iss.Dec99 on 'Secretly Canadian'; SC 022LP)>

Nov 99. (cd-ep) <(ALP 105CD)> **NIAGARA FALLS EP**
– New York one / New York seven / New York ten / Boston encore two / Boston nine / New York twelve / (untitled).

Aug 01. (cd) <(ALP 126CD)> **TWO BROTHERS**
– Still / From this point onward / When Johnny comes marching home / Two brothers / The half-light / Requiem / Sba? / Come again no more / Epilogue.

LOFTY PILLARS

MICHAEL KRASSNER – vocals, guitar / **WIL HENDRICKS** – acoustic guitar, piano, accordion, vocals / with various session people

Atavistic   Atavistic

Jul 00. (cd) <(ALP 315CD)> **WHEN WE WERE LOST**
– Lost / At the station / Anna Lee / Prodigal son / Still life / Snow / Response / Someone / I have become you / Snow / Victim.

— now a trio when they added **FRED LONBERG-HOLM** – arranger

Sep 01. (cd) <(ALP 323CD)> **AMSTERDAM**
– Amsterdam / Roll down / Guest of dishonour / Fade away / Sons of solemn men / Eulogy / Field of honour / Mothers of arms / Three men / Wasted / Down the river / Farewell song / Longing / Underworld.

BOYFRIEND

Formed: Glasgow, Scotland ... 1992 by STEPHEN JOLLIE, MARK McAVOY, DEREK McKEE and GEORGE WATSON. If you can imagine indie kings the TEENAGE FANCLUB in the same studio as ORANGE JUICE, the monotone and oft out-of-tune BOYFRIEND would be the love-child. Having said that, the quartet were a good band if not outstanding, probably the reason why ALAN McGEE's 'Creation' (home to friends TFC) thought it wise to sub-let the quartet to subsidiary 'August'. BOYFRIEND's debut single, 'HEY BIG STAR', was a promising start to their indie-rock campaign, its driving seventies, NEIL YOUNG-esque guitars brooding side by side with more 'FANCLUB-styled vox. Parent album, 'HAIRY BANJO' (1993), set the band's stall out right from the start, although why they thought we needed another TFC was anybody's guess. However, 1993 was a prolific year for BOYFRIEND, a further single/EP 'LEATHERED' and a much-overlooked(!) mini-set 'RUBBER EAR', all hitting the indie shops; the latter's fitting finale was a squeaky, ill-advised cover of Paul McCartney & Wings' 'JET'. They took off to that great gig in the sky soon afterwards.

Album rating: HAIRY BANJO (*6) / RUBBER EAR mini (*5)

STEPHEN JOLLIE / **MARK McAVOY** / **GEORGE WATSON** / **DEREK McKEE**

August – Creation   not iss.

Feb 93. (12"ep/cd-ep) (caug 002 t/cd) **HEY BIG STAR / JAHLOPPEE. / GUITARIST NIPPLE / FLEW OUT**

Mar 93. (cd/lp) (caug 003 cd/lp) **HAIRY BANJO**
– Hey big star / Summerthing / Kojak / Guitarist nipple / Rockwieller / Searching / Leathered / Two / Don't even try / Girl on my mind / Why should I pretend? / Air you breathe / Sunburnt.

Apr 93. (12"ep/cd-ep) (caug 004 t/cd) **LEATHERED EP**

Oct 93. (m-cd) (rust 006cd) **RUBBER EAR**
– The ripple / Got a notion / The apple / Going out / Jet.

— disbanded in 1994

BOYRACER

Formed: Wetherby, nr. Leeds, England ... 1990 by guitarist/vocalist STEWART ANDERSON, guitarist/keyboardist RICHARD ADAMS, bassist SIMON (yep, no surname, in best indie style) and drummer JAMES. Named after local town circuit car driver assholes, their debut single-to-be, 'PATRIC WALKER' was canned. The noisy indiepoppers played their first gig with BEATNIK FILMSTARS in 1991 and recorded their first single 'RAILWAY' and half a split 7" with Louisville, KY group HULA HOOP that year. ADAMS left the band to pursue his first love, dream project The HOOD just before the release of the 'NAKED' 7" in '92. Signed to 'Sarah' records in 1993 they released the quickly-recorded (a constant theme with the band) 'B IS FOR BOYRACER' EP and played many gigs with Australian label stablemates EVEN AS WE SPEAK. ANDERSON walked out after being told by the band's publisher that he couldn't sing, just as he was recording his vocal tracks. JAMES and SIMON went off to sell t-shirts for INSPIRAL CARPETS while the latest incarnation of BOYRACER came together with MATTY GREEN on guitar, (ex-HOOD) NICOLA HODGKINSON on bass and KEVIN on drums, as well as STEWART back on vocals. Within weeks they recorded the band's first full-length set 'MORE SONGS ABOUT FRUSTRATION AND SELF-HATE'. The album's self-effacing lo-fi post-punk pop-primitivism was greeted with wry acceptance of a band that can barely play, although it made an acceptably entertaining racket at the same time. The 'BEST FLIPSTAR' EP in 1994 was recorded on a tour in France in a bar as the band drank the same watering hole dry. KEVIN quit that June (the band seeming to go through more members than 'Spinal Tap' does drummers!) and BOYRACER was briefly whittled down to a three-piece again before GED MEGURN could take over on the old skins-pounding for the recording of their third 'Sarah' single, 'PURE HATRED 96'. The band played a session for much-respected-and-loved Radio One DJ JOHN PEEL and did some shows supporting The WEDDING PRESENT before setting off on a US tour with The ROPERS, as well as HENRY'S DRESS and The SOFTIES. This was followed in short order by the 'WE ARE MADE OF THE SAME WOOD' LP (1995) Mixing equal parts noise and careful pop melody along with experimentation and occasional synthesizer squelches, this album by the ever-changing band was well received critically. Never one to rest on their laurels, however, the irrepressible BOYRACER burnt rubber to New York City at the expense of 'Zero Hour' records (who had put out an odd 5" record in 1996, 'WEST RIDING HOUSE') for mastering of their third full-length album, 'BOYRACER IN FULL COLOUR'. This album, panned by critics, sold poorly and caused the band to split up ... but yes ... you've guessed it ... not forever, as December 2000 saw them rising from their never-peaceful sonic grave with members STEWART, bassist JEN (from RABBIT IN RED) and drummer FRANK (from BRIGHT LIGHTS) to play at the Knitting Factory, NYC, with an all-star line-up including The AISLERS SET, GIRLFRENDO, COMET GAIN and SPORTIQUE. FRANK would break his drumkit and his thumb at this gig ... but still stay in the band. The extended (over half of North England) family of the group continued with the help of various people like ARA, KELLY SLUSHER, MATT HARTMAN, MIKE SCHULMAN and GERARD MCGURN. At the rate they go through members, don't be surprised if you too – yes you – get a call-up to hit the stage with them soon ... • **Covered:** ELECTRICITY (Orchestral Manoeuvres In The Dark) / JET BOY JET GIRL (Elton Motello).

Album rating: MORE SONGS ABOUT FRUSTRATION AND SELF-HATE (*5) / WE ARE MADE OF THE SAME WOOD mini (*6) / IN FULL COLOUR (*5) / BOYFUCKINGRACER compilation (*7) / TO GET A BETTER HOLD YOU'VE GOT TO LOOSEN YR GRIP (*6) / BSIDES AND BESIDES demo collection (*5) / Steward: GET ME A SEAT NEXT TO SOMEONE NICE (*5) / AS TIGHT AS AN OWL as Hula Boy (*5) / GOOD BYE TO EVERY THING YOU LOVE (*5) / I WAS THE ONLY BOY ON THE NETBALL TEAM (*5) / HORSELAUGH ON MY EX (*5) / BANG THERE GOES MY YOUTH (*5)

STEWART ANDERSON – vocals, guitar / **RICHARD ADAMS** – guitar, keyboards / **SIMON CHADWICK** – bass / **JAMES GUILD** – drums

Fluff   not iss.

Apr 92. (7") (none) **RAILWAY. / REVERSE**

Jul 92. (7"ep) (none) **ONE FOR SORROW / NEW ZEALAND 2. / (other 2 by HULA HOOP)**

Pure Hatred   not iss.

Feb 93. (d7"flexi-ep) (PH 1) **GO FLEXI CRAZY**
– Tested / Bitter / I love you shut up / Speedtrap / Kittin with a whip.

A Turntable Friend   not iss.

Mar 93. (7"m) (TURN 14) **NAKED. / NO FUEL / NEW ZEALAND SONG**

— now without ADAMS who had already formed The HOOD

Sarah   not iss.

May 93. (7"ep/cd-ep) (SARAH 076/+CD) **B IS FOR BOYRACER**
– I've got it and it's not worth having / Jesus Suzanne Christ / Black fantastic splitting / Beautiful lines.

Jul 93. (10"m-lp; by BOYRACER and HULA HOOP) (TURN 18) **LOUISVILLE – LEEDS – T.K.O.!**
– Sanguine / She comes alone / My town / Trying too hard / This has gone on too long / (others by HULA HOOP). (above issued on 'A Turntable Friend')

Oct 93. (7"ep/cd-ep) (SARAH 085/+CD) **FROM PURITY TO PURGATORY**
– Cog / David Byrne / Distraction / Doorframe / Close.

not iss.   Hedonist

Nov 93. (7"flexi) (none) **REVERSE (new version)**

not iss.   Slumberland

Feb 94. (7"ep) (SLR 35) **AUL 36X EP**
– Short changed / Sex / Spiteful punk rock song #2 / Sunshine and violence / Stabbed / Short changed revisited.

Wurlitzer Jukebox   not iss.

Feb 94. (7"flexi) (none) **BOYRACER. / Sabine: PAINTING PORTRAITS**

— (Feb'94) ANDERSON recruited newcomers **MATTY GREEN** – guitar / **NICOLA HODGKINSON** – bass (ex-HOOD) / **KEVIN** – drums

A Turntable Friend   Slumberland

May 94. (lp)<cd> (TURN 20) <SLR 028> **MORE SONGS ABOUT FRUSTRATION AND SELF-HATE**
– A friend for life / Passion flower / That's progress / Chanteuse / Skill / Fifteen / My new shoes / Why bother asking me now? / Is it me or is it cold? / New Zealand jazz / Define beauty / Hatemail / Jazz B. / Giving way / The useless romantic / Second is always second. (cd+=) – Short changed / Sex / Spiteful punk rock song #2 / Sunshine and violence / Stabbed / Short changed revisited / Tested / Railway (new version).

Jun 94. (7") <WISH 5> **ONE STEP FORWARD. / (other by The ROPERS)**

Jul 94. (7"ep) (LOW 003) **BEST FLIPSTAR EP**
– Meadowhall / Feathers / Hairdryer song / Spindle / New Jimmy bar rock. (above issued on 'Lo-Fi Recordings') (below issued on 'Sarah')

Sep 94. (7"ep/cd-ep) (SARAH 096/+CD) **PURE HATRED 96 EP**
– He gets me so hard / Wanting for all the wrong reasons / Denatured / E.J.K. / Don't just don't.

— now without KEVIN; ANDERSON took over drums

— added **GED MEGRUN** – drums

BOYRACER (cont)

Mar 95. (10"m-lp/m-cd) (TURN 24/+CD) <SLR 048> **WE ARE MADE OF THE SAME WOOD** / Jan96
– Twisted love / Superhip / You're breaking his heart / Area 51 revisited / Finger pie / ?ost modernist retro bullshit / Bring me the hair of Phil Oakey / Vitamin B / Michael / In love with these times / Your dark secrets / Serious teeth. (10"lp w/ free 7"flexi; TURN 23F) – ELECTRICITY. / SEX (live) (re-iss. Dec96 on 'Slumberland'; same as US)

Oct 95. (5") <none> **WEST RIDING HOUSE. / BOYFRIENDS**
(above issued on 'Zero Hour', below on 'Happy Go Lucky')

Dec 95. (10"lp) **PAIN, PLUNDER AND PERSONAL LOSS** (home recordings 1994-1995)
– You're breaking his heart / Everything I touch is diseased / Dog me / Miserable drama queen / Pink sunset / Implications / Denatured / Meadowhall (version one) / Passionflower / Intentions are redefined / Casual / Foam.

Jan 96. (1-sided 7") <SLR 049> **ONE SIDE OF BOYRACER**
– Turquoise mood / I am looking for somewhere else.

                                                            A Turntable Friend / *Zero Hour*
Jan 96. (7"ep,1-sided 12"ep) (TURN 26) **THE RACER 100 EP** (live)
– Your unspoken desires / Boxing Day / Untouched by conversation / Baleen / Re-run / Baleen (instrumental).

Apr 96. (7") (TURN 28) **FALSE ECONOMY. / (other track by MY FAVORITE)**

Apr 96. (cd/c/lp) <ZHD 1140-2/-4/-1> **IN FULL COLOUR**
– Buffalo / Small consolation / Two / We were wrong / New punk song / Talk of aching / Goblin / Deeper still / D.F. (F.B. mix) / W.R.H. (disco version) / Her fame fades quickly / Foam / Aluminium heart / Too good to ignore / Ask too much / This is part of me / Deviant / Blazing fruit / A.T.M. (version) / Loosening all your fears / Doorframe (ambient version).

                                                            not iss. / *Jigsaw*
Apr 96. (7") <003> **THE RHYTHM OF THE CHICKEN SHAKE**
– Doorframe / Your unspoken desires.

                                                            not iss. / *Honey Bear*
1996. (7"ep) **A MISTAKE THAT COST YOU DEARLY EP**
– Snowly / A sense of purpose / I can walk from here / G/A minor.

                                                            not iss. / *Rocket Racer*
1996. (7"ep) <RR 001> **LIVE ON W.A.H.M.** (live)
– Baleen / West Riding house / Small consolation / Foam.

                                                            not iss. / *Happy Go Lucky*
Feb 97. (7") <011> **PRESENT TENSE. / DOUBTFUL**

                                                            Black Bean & Placenta / not iss.
Jul 97. (m-lp) (BBPTC 75LP) **LIVE AT STACHES** (live 10 May, 1996)
– West Riding house / Deeper still / New punk song / Post modernist retro bullshit / Feathers / Baleen / Your unspoken desires / Doorframe.

―― disbanded in 1997

HULA BOY

aka **STEWART ANDERSON**

                                                            Meller Welle / not iss.
May 94. (7"ep) (MEL 13) **MERMAID SISTER EP**

                                                            Sticky / not iss.
Aug 94. (ltd-7") (STICKY 5) **SLIP IT INSIDE. /**

                                                            Harriet / *Harriet*
Jul 95. (7") <Harr 33> **JANUARY 17, 1912. /**

Sep 98. (cd) <(SPY 08)> **AS TIGHT AS AN OWL WITH THE HULA BOY** / Sep97
– School closings 2010 / Comfort eating / My lowdown / Croissants and coffee / River of honey and mud / Time travel / You never used to be this tough / Our secret knowledge / Garden / Shape / Take these wings / Kisses like punches / Let's spend some money (we don't have) / What's the point? / The unwritten rule (electro version) / Cupid shrugged / Do I really have to go on? / (untitled).

STEWARD

aka **STEWART ANDERSON**

                                                            555 Record / not iss.
Sep 97. (lp) (555/8) **GET ME A SEAT NEXT TO SOMEONE NICE**
– Waste / Feed my scars tonite / Paint the windows shut / £3.99 / Hamfisted, chromatic / Choking on cold air / Counterfeit astonishment / A new technique / Denied by circumstance / Compassion is found in the strangest of places / Despite everything / Greenstick fractures / Blvd 4 / Pinsharp focus / A real natural / Sweet (fridge) / Towpath legacy (part 2) / Such thoughts of you / Blvd 3 – Missing you / CD EP pts 1 and 2.

                                                            Rocket Racer / not iss.
Nov 97. (7"ep) (RR 003) **ADAM, MARCO, ME EP**
– Conserve, consider, create / You are too generous with your time / Alphabetically yours.

                                                            Orgasm / *Blackbean + Placenta*
1998. (7") (SPASM 18) **THE LAST WASPS OF SUMMER. / DOWNPOUR REMIX**

1998. (12"ep) <ACME 55> **THERE IS NO MONEY IN ROCK AND ROLL**
– My eye teeth / Indecision / Transpennine / Arcadia 64 / Concentration – Break / M.E.T. 2 / Sing for yr supper / Jet boy jet girl / Matty-lectro / Can we see the framework?

                                                            555 Record / *Darla*
Apr 99. (lp)<cd> (555LP 5) <DRL 087> **GOOD BYE TO EVERY THING YOU LOVE** <US diff. tracks> / Jul99
– Can't force the hand / Loverboy / There is good when we try / Backpedal / I would see you right / Bit part actor come good / XXX / Who is in yr corner? / An unpaid debt / XXX / The days run thru our fingers / XXX / Low blood sugar / I spent my money too quickly / Cindy two / Where are our ambitions? / Options / I stir with good intentions / Conserve, consider, create! / Fly guy / XXX / Aperture / Downfall.

1999. (7"ep) <Steward 06> **YOU'LL NEVER BE THAT YOUNG AGAIN**
– You'll never be that young again / Putnam, Potter, Goodwin, Dunphy circa 88 / Worst fears confirmed / Theme revisited: the sell out expectant.

1999. (7"ep) <Steward 07> **THE MAN WITH THE TINY HANDS**
– The man with the tiny hands / Ice cream for breakfast / I feel glove / He dispenses with timid afterthoughts / Party parting.

2000. (cd) <Steward 08> **I WAS THE ONLY BOY ON THE NETBALL TEAM** (various remixes by others, etc.)

―― <above also issued on 'Blackbean + Placenta'; BBPTC 191>
(below issued on 'Jonathon Whisky')

2000. (7"ep) <Whiskey 4> **split w/ HOOD**
– SilverSodaPop (ONESTAR) – Steward remix / I'm a woman, not just a toy / Flatter me without concern for prejudice.

Oct 00. (cd) (555CD/20) **HORSELAUGH ON MY EX**
– You can't fuck with nature / Something to crave / My true friends are golden / Poised for great things / Rupert Pumpkin king of my heart / He is a genius with his hands / Take me home and make use of me / He dispenses with timid afterthought / Waiting for our pasts to catch up with us / You have too much time on your hands / Don't be square (be there) / Hey leopard / Our love was tragic / Pissing out the poison / Goodbye Leeds 4 / Digital boogie / Golden years squandered / Happy new years / You took the words right out of my mouth / Heaven.

―― ANDERSON's work as STEWARD continued as collaborative with The CANNANES; after the 'FELICITY' EP, 'COMMUNICATING AT AN UNKNOWN RATE' was issued in Oct'00

Jan 02. (cd) (555BANG 1) **BANG! THERE GOES MY YOUTH**
– Bad / He is a genius with his hands / You live yr life in ffwd / You say you don't love me / Dial tone collective / 8-30 yr looking great / I am the magnificent / Happy new years (version) / etc. etc. etc . . .

BOYRACER

―― ANDERSON re-formed the band late in 2000 with **MATTY GREEN + JEN** – bass (ex-RABBITS IN RED) + **FRANK** – drums (ex-BRIGHT LIGHTS) / **ARA** – guitar / plus others **GERARD McGURN, KELLY SLUSHER, MATT HARTMAN + MIKE SCHULMAN**

                                                            555 / *555*
May 02. (cd) (<555CD 40>) **TO GET A BETTER HOLD YOU'VE GOT TO LOOSEN YR GRIP**
– Sarah and Sarah / Temper / They're making money off you / Nothing left / Stars and car parks / Tell me where my hands should go / Glitter / Eyes shining with determination / In love / Jon Al Dente, impressive one stop customer relations / Matty's song / Grand rapids / Yr arrogance is not lost / Razor / Nostalgia for a time I hardly remember / Come out 2nite / Heaven is not broken / Kachina doll / Priorities / Everyday is Christmas with you / Temper (version) / Sarah and Sarah (version).

– compilations, etc. –

Jul 01. (cd) *555*; (<555CD 30>) **BOYFUCKINGRACER**
– He gets me so hard / Black fantastic / A friend for life / Yr unspoken desire / Razor / Tested / Small consolation / Stabbed / Foam / Passionflower / Yr breaking his heart / Baleen / False economy / I've got it / Buffalo / My town / We were wrong / Cog / Her frame fades quickly / I am looking for somewhere else / Short change / Is it me, or is it cold / Feathers / Friend / Meadowball / Vitamin B / New punk song / One step forward / West Riding house / Superhip / The useless romantic / Spindle / In love with these times.

Oct 02. (cd) *555*; <555CD 45> **BSIDES AND BESIDES**
– Patric Walker / Room / This is all I know / My new shoes / I love you, shut up / Open your heart / Your lack of interest does not interest me / If I wdere more truthful / David Byrne / Boxing Day / Broken limb / Untitled / Chanteuse / Electricity / Untitled #2 / Bitter (live) / This is easy / Smooth / My town (non-acoustic) / This is all I know / New Zealand song (original) / Only such a smile / New punk song (live) / I stole everything / Re-run / Roper one (original) / Smells like (original) / Surround.

BOY SETS FIRE

Formed: Delaware, USA . . . 1994 by NATHAN GRAY, JOSH LATSHAW, CHAD ISTVAN, DARRELL HYDE and MATT KRUPANSKI. Playing militant yet emotionally fraught agit-prop hardcore in the traditional sense of the term, BOY SETS FIRE first blazed a trail across the scene in 1995 with a self financed debut single, 'Consider'. This was followed by a split single and finally, on the 'Initial' label, a debut album, 'THE DAY THE SUN WENT OUT' (1997). A second split was in turn followed by a sophomore album, 'IN CHRYSALIS' (1999), after which HYDE was replaced by ROB AVERY. Despite the reservations of some fans, a move to the larger 'Victory' label for 'AFTER THE EULOGY' (2000) found them as politically uncompromising as ever. The mini-set, 'THIS CRYING, THIS SCREAMING, MY VOICE IS BEING BORN' was released later the same year. • **Covered:** LIVE WIRE (Motley Crue).

Album rating: THE DAY THE SUN WENT OUT (*6) / AFTER THE EULOGY (*6)

NATHAN GRAY – vocals / **CHAD ISTVAN** – guitar / **JOSH LATSHAW** – guitar / **DARRELL HYDE** – bass / **MATT KRUPANSKI** – drums

                                                            not iss. / own label
1995. (7"; split w/ JAZZ MAN'S NEEDLE) **CONSIDER. /**
                                                            Initial / *Initial*
Oct 97. (lp/cd) <(IR 19/+CD)> **THE DAY THE SUN WENT OUT**
– Pure / Cringe / The fine art of falling / Another badge of courage / Swingset / The power remains the same / In hope / Toy gun anthem / Cadence / 65 factory outlets / Hometown report card / Live wire.

                                                            not iss. / *Equal Vision*
Jan 99. (m-cd) **IN CHRYSALIS**

                                                            EQV 51
Aug 99. (cd-ep; shared with SNAPCASE) <EQV 51> **SNAPCASE vs BOY SETS FIRE**
– (two by SNAPCASE) / Unspoken request / Channel.

―― BOY SETS FIRE also split an EP with COALESCE around the late 90's

―― **ROB AVERY** – bass; repl. HYDE

BOY SETS FIRE (cont)

Apr 00. (lp/cd) <(VR 119/+CD)> **AFTER THE EULOGY** — Victory / Victory
 – After the eulogy / Rookie / Pariah under glass / When rhetoric dies / Still waiting for the punchline / The abominations of those virtuous / Our time honorer tradition of cannibalism / (Compassion) As skull fragments on the wall / My life in the knife trade / Across five years / Twelve step hammer program / Unspoken request / The force majeure.

Nov 00. (m-cd) **THIS CRYING, THIS SCREAMING, MY VOICE IS BEING BORN** — not iss. / Magic Bullet
 – Vehicle / In the wilderness . . . no one can hear you scream / Endorsement / Blame (live at eleven) / My own restraints / Resection.

BRAID

Formed: Champaign-Urbana, Illinois, USA . . . 1993 by ex-FRICTION drummer/singer BOB NANNA and ROY EWING, who were joined by PETE HAVRANEK and JAY RYAN after the former placed an ad in mag Maximum Rock'n'Roll. Another to get on the emo-core bandwagon, BRAID initially suffered a series of personnel changes when RYAN broke off to join HUBCAP; he was subsequently deputised by KATE REUSS, although after only one gig she too departed. Fully committed and underway when singer CHRIS BROACH joined (he took over guitar duties when PETE left in summer '94), BRAID finally released their debut single, 'RAINSNOWMATCH', later that year. An LP, 'FRANKIEWELFAREBOYAGEFIVE' (1995), showcased their FUGAZI-meets-JAWBOX sound, while further 45's 'NIAGARA' and 'I'M AFRAID OF EVERYTHING', marked time before they released their sophomore effort, 'THE AGE OF OCTEEN' (1996). A new drummer, DAMON ATKINSON (who replaced ROY), was in place for a further batch of releases including 1998's 'FRAME & CANVAS' long-player. Energy-fuelled math-rock pop, the album is unrelenting from the word go and especially the opener 'THE NEW NATHAN DETROITS'. However, the band split the following year leaving behind a handful of posthumous releases including the disappointing concert set, 'LUCKY TO BE ALIVE' (2000). • **Covered:** MY LIFE (Billy Joel) / BABY, NOW THAT I'VE FOUND YOU (Foundations) / THIS CHARMING MAN + THERE IS A LIGHT THAT NEVER GOES OUT (Smiths) / ALWAYS SOMETHING THERE TO REMIND ME (Bacharach-David) / TROMPHE LE MONDE (Pixies).

Album rating: FRANKIEWELFAREBOYAGEFIVE (*5) / THE AGE OF OCTEEN (*5) / FRAME & CANVAS (*6) / LUCKY TO BE ALIVE (*4) / MOVIE MUSIC VOL.ONE (*6) / MOVIE MUSIC VOL.TWO (*5)

BOB NANNA – vocals, drums (of FRICTION) / **ROY EWING** – drums / **PETE HAVRANEK** – guitar (of 42 LOADS, of INKADINK) / **TODD BELL** – bass; repl. JAY RYAN who joined HUBCAP and DIANOGAH / short-term member KATE REUSS also left

 —— brought in **CHRIS BROACH** – guitar, vocals; when PETE left

Oct 94. (7"ep) <PRC 004> **RAINSNOWMATCH EP** — not iss. / Polyvinyl
 – Sounds like violence / Motion light / Perfect pitch. (UK-iss.Nov96 on 'Enclave'; same)

Jun 95. (cd) <2> **FRANKIEWELFAREBOYAGEFIVE** — not iss. / Divot
 – Angel falls / Capricorn / Minuet / New dollar building / Lining Lake Michigan / Wax wings / Garner hall music room / Hugs from boys / Three point turn / Eeyore and easel / Red dye company / Summer salt / X marks the hope box / Brass knuckle sandwich / Dolores / Under the influence of tricycle mechanics / Featherweight / Ornamental / Kissy windmill print / Jane describes John / Quarters / I-57 / Yawn London / Vest of interest / Pipsqueak / Zero Frisco.

Jun 95. (7") <003> **NIAGRA. / THAT CAR CAME OUT OF NOWHERE** — not iss. / Grand Theft Auto

Jun 96. (7"m) <PRC 008> **I'M AFRAID OF EVERYTHING. / NOW I'M EXHAUSTED / RADISH WHITE ICICLE** — not iss. / Polyvinyl

Nov 96. (7") <(MUD 021)> **split w/ BEEZUS** — Mud / Mud

Jan 97. (lp/cd) <(MUD LP/CD 018)> **THE AGE OF OCTEEN** — / Nov96
 – My baby smokes / Nineteen 75 / Divers / Jimmy go summer / Movie clock star / Eulalia, Eulalia / Grace car part one / Harrison Ford / American typewriter / The chandelier swing / Autobiography.

 —— **DAMON ATKINSON** – drums (of FIGUREHEAD) repl. ROY

Oct 97. (7") <PRC 17> **FIRST DAY BACK. / HUGS FROM BOYS** — Polyvinyl / Polyvinyl
Feb 98. (7") **FOREVER GET SHORTER. / (other by The Get Up Kids)**
 (above issued on 'Tree' records)
Apr 98. (cd/lp) <(PRC 18 CD/V)> **FRAME & CANVAS**
 – The new Nathan Detroits / Killing a camera / Never will come for us / First day back / Collect from Clark Kent / Milwaukee sky rocket / A dozen roses / Urbana's too dark / Consolation prizefighter / Ariel / Breathe in / I keep a diary.
Nov 98. (cd-s) (DESOTOBB 27) <PRC 022> **ALWAYS SOMETHING THERE TO REMIND ME. / (other track by BURNING AIRLINES)**
 (above issued on 'DeSoto' UK)
Aug 99. (7") <PRC 26> **PLEASE DRIVE FASTER. / CIRCUS OF THE STARS**

 —— had already split in the Autumn of '99

Apr 00. (cd) <(PRC 30CD)> **MOVIE MUSIC VOL.ONE** (compilation) — / Mar00
 – Sounds like violence / Motion light / Perfect pitch / I'm afraid of everything / Radish white icicle / Now I'm exhausted / Fire makes the house grow / Niagara / That car came out of nowhere / (Strawberry Ann) Switzerland / What a wonderful puddle / First day back / Hugs from boys / Forever got shorter / Please drive faster / Circus of the stars / You're lucky to be alive.

Apr 00. (cd) <(PRC 31CD)> **MOVIE MUSIC VOL.TWO** (compilation) — / Mar00
 – Elephant / Jimmy go swimmer – Eulalia, Eulalia / Catykat / Grand theft Autumn / To kiss a trumpet player / I'm glowing and you're the reason / Do you love coffee? / The consolation prizefighter / Bridge to Canada / Painting Nebraska / Collect from Clark Kent / Roses in the car / My life / Baby, now that I've found you / This charming man / There is a light that never goes out / Always something there to remind me / Trompe le monde.

Apr 00. (q-lp) <(PRC 32)> **MOVIE MUSIC VOL.1 & 2** — Big Wheel / Glue Factory

Jul 00. (cd) <(BWR 0229)> <7> **LUCKY TO BE ALIVE** — / Mar00
 – Autobiography / The new Nathan Detroits / Killing a camera / Please drive faster / Forever got shorter / What a wonderful puddle / Never come for us / You're lucky to be alive / Grace car / A dozen roses / Breathe in / Milwaukee sky rocket / Divers / First day back / I'm afraid of everything / The chandelier swing / Capricorn. (re-iss. Jul00 on 'Oglio'; 7007-2)

BRAIN DONOR
(see under ⇒ COPE, Julian; 80's section)

BRAINIAC

Formed: Dayton, Ohio, USA . . . early '92 by TIM TAYLOR and JUAN MONASTERIO as an experimental bedroom project. Fleshing out the line-up with TYLER TRENT and MICHELLE BODINE, the pair began building a fearsome reputation via a serious local gigging schedule. Following the release of a US-only debut single, 'SUPER DUPER SEVEN' on the 'Limited Potential' label and a split 7" with riot-grrrls, BRATMOBILE, the quartet signed to indie label, 'Grass', for a debut album, 'SMACK BUNNY BABY' (1993). Produced by GIRLS AGAINST BOYS bassist, ELI JANNEY, the record was lauded in the underground press for its uncompromising attitude and noisy dissonance, resulting in big money offers which BRAINIAC unceremoniously rejected. Replacing BODINE with JOHN SCHMERSAL, the band remained with 'Grass' for a second album, 'BONSAI SUPERSTAR' (1995), before hitching their wagon to Chicago-based house of noise, 'Touch & Go'. First up for the label was the interestingly titled 'HISSING PRIGS IN STATIC COUTURE', a more experimental outing that once again brought attention from industry big guns; JOHN SCHMERSAL had superseded MICHELLE. Tragedy struck, however, as TAYLOR was killed in a freak car accident shortly after the completion of Spring '97's 'ELECTRO-SHOCK FOR PRESIDENT' mini-set.

Album rating: SMACK BUNNY BABY (*6) / BONSAI SUPERSTAR (*5) / HISSING PRIGS IN STATIC COUTURE (*7) / ELECTRO-SHOCK FOR PRESIDENT mini (*5)

TIM TAYLOR (b. 1969) – vocals / **MICHELLE BODINE** – guitar / **JUAN MONASTERIO** – bass / **TYLER TRENT** – drums

Sep 92. (7"ep) <Limp 015> **SUPERDUPERSEVEN** — not iss. / Limited Potential
 – Ride / Supersupersonic / Simon says.

Dec 92. (7"; split w/ BRATMOBILE) **I COULD OWN YOU** — not iss. / 12 x 12 Grass

Oct 93. (lp/cd) <(GROW 004-1/-2)> **SMACK BUNNY BABY** — Grass / Grass
 – I, fuzzbot / Ride / Smack bunny baby / Martian dance invasion / Cultural zero / Brat girl / Hurting me / I could own you / Anesthetize / Draag / Get away. (re-iss. Mar95 & Dec95; same)

May 94. (7"; split w/ LAZY) **DEXATRIUM. /**
 (above issued on 'Simple Solutions')

Feb 95. (lp/cd) <(GROW 45-1/-2)> **BONSAI SUPERSTAR** — / Nov94
 – Hot metal dobermans / Hands of the genius / Fucking with the altimiter / Radio Apeshot / Transmissions after zero / Juicy (on a Cadillac) / Flypaper / Sexual frustration / To the baby-counter / You wrecked my hair / Meathook manicure / Status: Choke / Collide.

 —— **JON SCHMERSAL** – guitar; repl. MICHELLE

Oct 95. (7"ep/cd-ep) <(TG 148/+CD)> **INTERNATIONALE** — Touch & Go / Touch & Go
 – Go freaks go / Silver iodine / Simon says.

Mar 96. (lp/cd) <(TG 155/+CD)> **HISSING PRIGS IN STATIC COUTURE**
 – Indian poker (part 3) / Pussyfootin' / Vincent come on down / This little piggy / Strung / Hot seat can't sit down / Vulgar trade / Beekeepers maxim / Kiss me u jacked up jerk / 70 kg man / Indian poker (part 2) / Nothing ever changes / I am a cracked machine.

Apr 97. (12"ep/cd-ep) <(TG 174/+CD)> **ELECTRO-SHOCK FOR PRESIDENT**
 – Fresh new eyes / Flash ram / Fashion 500 / The turnover / For my beloved / Mr. Fingers.

 —— tragically, on the 23rd of May '97, TAYLOR died in a car smash; the group decided to disband – SCHMERSAL was to form ENON after a spell with MORELLA'S FOREST

BRANDTSON

Formed: Cleveland, Ohio, USA . . . 1996 by MYK PORTER, MATT TRAXLER, JOHN SAYRE and percussionist JARED JOLLEY. This emo-tinged quartet began life on the 1997 release 'RADIOWAVES AND GIBBERISH', before signing with 'Deep Elm' and issuing the bleeding-edged 'LETTERBOX' LP in 1998. Thrash guitar and emotive vocal harmonies were BRANDTSON's bag, and they soon earned comparisons with early FUGAZI and The AFGHAN WHIGS. BRANDTSON delivered 'THE FALLEN STAR COLLECTION' in 1999, a roaming rock epic full of songs so mature, they might well have been mulled wine. It was quickly followed by the mini LP, 'TRYING TO FIGURE EACH OTHER OUT' (1999), which contained a hidden remix of the ensemble's most popular song, 'AS YOU WISH' (from the '...STAR COLLECTION', and revamped by Ohio electronica duo FURNACE ST.) plus six other crackers. 'DIAL IN SOUNDS', delivered in 2002, was the band's most ambitious work, however, stretching the emo tag to infinity, plus cranking up the noise for over 40 minutes of pure American angst rock, with standout tracks 'MARK IT A ZERO' and the indispensible shakedown 'ANYTHING AND EVERYTHING'.

Album rating: LETTERBOX (*5) / FALLEN STAR COLLECTION (*7) / ...TRYING TO FIGURE EACH OTHER OUT (*5) / DIAL IN SOUNDS (*5)

MYK PORTER – vocals, guitar / **MATT TRAXLER** – guitar / **JOHN SAYRE** – bass / **JARED JOLLEY** – vocals, drums

			Deep Elm	Deep Elm
Jul 98.	(cd) <(DER 366CD)>	**LETTERBOX**		Mar98

– Round 13 / Blindspot / Words for you / Still life / Day's end / Ninovoh / Strand / Cloudless / January / Glutton for tragedy / (untitled).

Oct 99.	(cd) <(DER 380CD)>	**FALLEN STAR COLLECTION**		Aug99

– As you wish / Breaking ground / Potential getaway driver / Things look brighter / Summer in St. Claire / Shannon said / Fighting gravity / Waking up to yellow / Long walk home / Probably nothing / New favorite pastime.

Aug 00.	(cd) <(DER 392CD)>	**...TRYING TO FIGURE OUT EACH OTHER**		

– Sic transit Gloria (glory fades) / 12th and middle / Leaving Ohio / Boys lie / Grace thinks I'm a failure / Bricks and windows.

Mar 02.	(cd) <(DER 408)>	**DIAL IN SOUNDS**		

– Mark it a zero / The rookie year / With friends like you / Some kind of jet pilot / Cherokee red / Command Q, command Z / Guest list / Anything and everything / Little rounder / Fireworks and phonecalls.

BRASSY

Formed: Manchester, England ... early 1994 by US-born singer, MUFFIN SPENCER (her big brother is none other than JON SPENCER of the BLUES EXPLOSION; MUFFIN arrived in England late 80's). On a mission to recreate the sound of her Brit-rock idols The SMITHS (especially MORRISSEY), she enlisted the help of KAREN FROST, STEFAN GORDON and JONNY BARRINGTON and after many rehearsals the band were ready to play live. It was the 'Costermonger' label (home of fellow SMITHS-esque fans, GENE) who took the plunge, although their sound was now more akin to that of ELASTICA. A debut 7", 'BOSS', finally hit the shops in early '96, although by the release of a third single, 'SURE THING' (their second was 'STRAIGHTEN OUT'), MUFFIN and Co were possibly too brassic to carry on.

Album rating: GOT IT MADE (*6)

MUFFIN SPENCER (b. New Hampshire, USA) – vocals, guitar / **STEFAN GORDON** – guitar / **KAREN FROST** – bass, vocals / **JONNY BARRINGTON** (aka DJ SWETT) – drums, decks

			Costermonger	not iss.
Mar 96.	(7") (COST 007)	**BOSS. / ROUTE OUT**		–
Jul 96.	(7") (COST 008)	**STRAIGHTEN OUT. / RIGHT BACK**		–
	(cd-s+=) (COST 008CD) – Boss (remix).			
Jul 97.	(7") (COST 010)	**SURE THING. / BOOT DANCING**		–
	(cd-s+=) (COST 010CD) – Sure thing (shake it loose).			

			Wiiija	Wiiija
May 99.	(d7"ep/cd-ep) (WIJ 098/+CD)	**BONUS BEATS**		–

– Good times / Secrets / Back in business / Bonus beats.

Aug 99.	(7") (WIJ 098)	**I CAN'T WAIT. / I GOTTA BEEF**		–
	(cd-s+=) (WIJ 098CD) – So hot it hurts.			
Feb 00.	(7") (WIJ 109)	**WORK IT OUT. / LET DOWN**		–
	(cd-s+=) (WIJ 109CD) – Move.			
May 00.	(cd/lp) (<WIJ CD/LP 1111>)	**GOT IT MADE**		Jul00

– In / No competition / Parkside / Work it out / That's the way / L Vs. S / I can't wait / You got it / Whole stole the show / Play some D / Nervous / Good times / Put you right / Micstyle / I gotta beef / B'cos we rock. (cd+=) – B.R.A.S.S.Y.

Oct 00.	(cd-ep) (WIJ 123CD)	**PLAY SOME D**		

– B'cos we rock (Nextmen remix) / I can't wait (Rob Swift remix) / Work it out (DJ Assault remix) / Play some D (DJ Swett remix) / All-new.

BRATMOBILE

Formed: Olympia, Washington, USA ... 1991 by ERIN SMITH, ALLISON WOLFE and MOLLY NEUMAN. Having already helped set the Riot Grrrl ball rolling with the 'Girl Germs' fanzine, the trio decided to relay their message through the male-dominated medium of alternative rock. Following an appearance on a 1991 compilation, 'Kill Rock Stars', put together by the 'K' label and a debut live set at Olympia's International Pop Underground convention (run by the ever industrious CALVIN JOHNSON, supremo of aforesaid 'K'), BRATMOBILE released their debut single proper, 'KISS AND RIDE', on 'Homestead' in Summer '93. An inaugural album, 'POTTYMOUTH' (1993) followed on 'Kill Rock Stars'; sassy pop/hardcore/punk with severe attitude in the vein of BIKINI KILL and HUGGY BEAR, the record even featured a tongue-in-cheek cover of the Runaways' CHERRY BOMB. Although a few guest drummers subsequently replaced NEUMAN (who joined The FRUMPIES and The PEECHEES), the band cut only one further recording, 1994's mini-set, 'THE REAL JANELLE'. While a PEEL SESSIONS EP served as a postscript to the band's short-lived career, ERIN and ALLISON went on to play together in the short-lived, one-set outfit COLD COLD HEARTS. The BRATMOBILE originals re-formed in May 1999, released two further surf-rock efforts for 'Lookout!', 'LADIES, WOMEN AND GIRLS' (2000) and 'GIRLS GET BUSY' (2002).

Album rating: POTTYMOUTH (*6) / THE REAL JANELLE mini (*6) / LADIES, WOMEN AND GIRLS (*5) / GIRLS GET BUSY (*4) / Cold Cold Hearts: COLD COLD HEARTS (*4)

ALLISON WOLFE – vocals / **ERIN SMITH** – guitar, vocals / **MOLLY NEUMAN** – drums, vocals

			not iss.	K
1992.	(7") <PUNK 1>	**COOL SCHMOOL. / (other by HEAVENS TO BETSY)**	–	

			not iss.	12 x 12
Dec 92.	(7") split w/ BRAINIAC		–	4 Letter Words

			not iss.	Simple Machines – Working Holidays
Dec 92.	(7") **THROWAWAY. / (other by Tiger Trap)**		–	

			Homestead	Homestead
May 93.	(7") <smwh 05> split w/ VERONICA LAKE			

			Kill Rock Stars	Kill Rock Stars
Jun 93.	(7"m) <(HMS 178-7)>	**KISS AND RIDE. / NO YOU DON'T / QUEENIE**		
Jun 93.	(lp/cd) <KRS 208/+CD>	**POTTYMOUTH**		

– Love thing / Stab / Cherry bomb / Throwaway / P.R.D.C.T. / Some special / Fuck yr fans / Polaroid baby / Panik / Bitch theme / Richard / Cool schmool / Juswanna / (untitled). (cd+=) – Kiss & ride / No you don't / Queenie. (UK cd-iss. Apr00; same as US)

— guest drummer repl. MOLLY NEUMAN who joined The FRUMPIES before forming The PEECHEES

Aug 94.	(m-cd/m-lp) <(KRS 219 CD/EP)>	**THE REAL JANELLE**		

– The real Janelle / Brat girl / Yeah, huh? / Die / ...And I live in a town where the boys amputate their hearts / Where eagles dare (with SLIM MOON).

— when they split – **WOLFE + SMITH** reunited as ...

COLD COLD HEARTS

Apr 97.	(lp/cd) <KRS 278/+CD>	**COLD COLD HEARTS**	–	

– V.R. / Any resemblance... / 5 signs: Scorpio / Cute boy discount / Broken teeth / Lady! reversible! (alleged.) / Maybe scabies / 1-2-3... many! / Sorry yer band band sux / (You're so sweet) Baby donut / State trooper in the left lane, Nattles!

BRATMOBILE

WOLFE, SMITH + NEUMAN

			Lookout	Lookout
Nov 00.	(cd/lp) <(LK 252 CD/LP)>	**LADIES, WOMEN AND GIRLS**		Oct00

– Eating toothpaste / Gimme brains / It's common (but we don't talk about it) / Not in dog years / In love years / Cheap trick record / In love with all my lovers / 90's nomad / Well you wanna know what? / Flavor of the month club / Affection training / Do you like me like that? / Come hitcher / Girlfriends don't keep.

Jun 02.	(cd/lp) <(LK 280 CD/LP)>	**GIRLS GET BUSY**		May02

– I'm in the band / Shop for America / Shut your face / Don't ask don't tell / That's happening / Cryin' tryin' lyin' / What's wrong with you? / Idiot lover / Are you a lady? / Pagan baby / Chicken or the egg / United we don't / Take the pain and use it.

– compilations, etc. –

May 94.	(cd-ep) Strange Fruit; (SFPSCD 089) / Dutch East India; <8357> **THE PEEL SESSION** (live 7/25/93)			

– There's no other way – No you don't / Bitch theme / Make me Miss America (aka "...and I live in a town where the boys amputate their hearts") / Panik.

BRAVE CAPTAIN

Born: MARTIN CARR, 29 Nov'68, Thurso, Scotland. Former guitarist with Liverpool outfit, The BOO RADLEYS, CARR quit after a soured relationship in 1996; he formed the enigmatic BRAVE CAPTAIN a few years later. For anyone who'd heard the experimental indie-pop tinglings of CARR's original group, 'THE FINGERTIP SAINT SESSIONS VOL.1' was no let down for those expecting shimmering guitars, reminscent of late BEATLES or BRIAN WILSON (just before he lost his marbles – so to speak). Suffice to say that CARR had maintained his credibility as a songwriter throughout this mini-album, which was packed full of punches and surprises. For one, high-pitched SICE was pale in comparison to CARR's formal, if not experimental baritone musings which accompanied his fragile and graceful collection of modern pop songs. Examples of this could be found in the opening three minutes of 'RAINING STONES', and again on the epic closing track 'LITTLE BUDDAH', which clocked in at around 22 minutes. Subsequently, the brave one issued his debut album proper on the post-Creation (DICK GREEN and MARK BOWEN) 'Wichita' imprint in 2000. Entitled 'GO WITH YOURSELF', this sophomore set acted as a sequel to CARR's aforementioned mini-set; a sort of 'FINGERTIP SAINT SESSIONS VOL 2', if it must be told. Along with the usual array of neo-melodies, CARR bravely employed the distant whispers of sadcore to his ever impending gleam. 'ASSEMBLY OF THE UNREPRESENTED' sounded like the sort of thing you would hear at a BOO RADLEY's reunion, while CARR's guitars and multi-instrumental accompaniment laid the solid foundations for one of indie's unsung protagonists. So, with everything good and well, BRAVE CAPTAIN ventured further into his musical field of unknown with the EP, 'BETTER LIVING THROUGH RECKLESS EXPERIMENTATION' (2001). Sporting a 'Rock-on' salute on the cover, the set generated column inches from hacks who had before ignored CARR and his ingenious incarnations. Cardiff's same, independently run 'Boobytrap' imprint issued BRAVE CAPTAIN's brilliant

BRAVE CAPTAIN (cont) — THE GREAT INDIE DISCOGRAPHY — The 1990s

single 'CORPORATION MAN' in 2001, on a limited run. Those who were lucky enough to get their mits on the single knew that CARR had finally surpassed himself musically, with the title track employing the jumpy, guitar driven indie/punk that launched The SUPER FURRY ANIMALS into indie stardom. If perhaps, the single was given a bigger release the same might've just happened to the increasingly brilliant BRAVE CAPTAIN.

Album rating: THE FINGERTIP SAINT SESSIONS VOL.1 mini (*7) / GO WITH YOURSELF (*7) / ADVERTISEMENTS FOR MYSELF (*8)

MARTIN CARR – vocals, guitar, bass, organ (ex-BOO RADLEYS) / with **GORWEL OWEN** – hammond, glockenspiel, minimoog, etc / **TONY ROBINSON + GARY ALESBROOK** – trumpet / **DAFYDD IEUAN** – drums / **MATT SIBLEY** – saxophone / etc

			Wichita	Thirsty Ear
Aug 00.	(m-cd/10"m-lp) (WEBB 003/+LP)	**THE FINGERTIP SAINT SESSIONS VOL.1**		-
	– Raining stones / Big red control machine / Starfish / Third unattended bag on the right / The tragic story / Little buddah.
Oct 00.	(cd/lp) (WEBB 004/+LP)	**GO WITH YOURSELF**		-
	– The monk jumps over the wall / Assembly of the unrepresented / Tell her you want her / Where is my head? / Ein Hoff Le / Hermit versus the world / Running off the ground / Reuben / Go with yourself.
Mar 01.	(7"ep/cd-ep) (WEBB 009S/+CD)	**BETTER LIVING THROUGH RECKLESS EXPERIMENTATION EP**		-
	– Better living through reckless experimentation / Canton hotel (these questions are very easy) / Me and you glue / Stronger.
Mar 01.	(cd) <57098>	**NOTHING LASTS HE SANG ONLY THE EARTH AND THE MOUNTAINS**	-	
	– The monk jumps over the wall / The tragic story / Tell her you want her / Big red control machine / Where is my head / Raining stones / Assembly of the unrepresented / Reuben / Ein Hoff le / Hermit versus the world / Third unattended bag on the right / Go with yourself.
Jun 01.	(cd-s) (BOOB 007CD)	**CORPORATION MAN / CORPORATION MAN WAS BROUGHT TO YOU BY THE MAKER OF MONKEY BEER**		-
	(above issued on 'Boobytrap')
Oct 02.	(cd/lp; as BRAVECAPTAIN) (WEBB 030/+LP)	**ADVERTISEMENTS FOR MYSELF**		-
	– The sound of Wichita / Birth of the project / Stand up and fight / The Blair Bush project live @ the old skool / Rod's got one / I was a teenage death squad / Bee's of the Left Banque / Dive / This weight that you have found / Kissinger / Betsi's beads / Fucking Sunday / Wreckers off message / Mobilise / Down between / My mind pictures / Zrifle / Release / Love will see us through.

BREEDERS

Formed: Boston, Massachusetts, USA . . . 1989 by TANYA DONELLY (of THROWING MUSES) and KIM DEAL (of The PIXIES) as a side project to their respective musical careers, an opportunity to exercise their frustrated songwriting talent. Recruiting JOSEPHINE WIGGS (of PERFECT DISASTER) on bass and SHANNON DOUGHTY (of the late, great SLINT) on drums, the BREEDERS cut their debut outing, 'POD', in a matter of weeks. Released in May 1990, the album rapidly achieved cult status, even enjoying a hearty endorsement from one KURT COBAIN. Inevitably, the record was compared with The PIXIES by critics although in reality there was little in common between the two bands. Where The PIXIES were enigmatic and frenetic, The BREEDERS were deliberate, dark and intense. While the pace picked up with 'HELLBOUND', tracks like the opener, 'GLORIOUS' and 'IRIS' were more representative of the record as a whole and if their cover of LENNON's 'HAPPINESS IS A WARM GUN' didn't add much to the original, it sounded so BREEDERS-like within the context of the album that they could've conceivably penned it themselves. The group recorded a further EP, 'SAFARI' (1992), with the original line-up before DONELLY went off to work full-time with her own outfit, BELLY. Following The PIXIES' demise later that year, DEAL devoted all her energies to a BREEDERS follow-up album. Enlisting her sister KELLEY in place of the departed DONELLY, the band released the 'CANNONBALL' single in Autumn '93. With its undulating guitar riff and pneumatic rhythm section, the track became an alternative classic, tearing up indie dancefloors across the country. The subsequent album, 'LAST SPLASH', powered into the UK Top 5 upon its release the following month. While much of the set sounded less focused than the debut, it nevertheless contained another stellar guitar pop moment in 'DIVINE HAMMER', also released as a single. Although the album's sales topped the million mark, things went quiet on The BREEDERS front, save for a lone 10" EP in 1994. The following year, (KIM) DEAL did surface in the guise of The AMPS, releasing an album, 'PACER', on '4 a.d.'. • **Songwriters:** KIM DEAL wrote bulk from 1992 onwards. • **Covered:** HAPPINESS IS A WARM GUN (Beatles / George Harrison) / LORD OF THE THIGHS (Aerosmith) / SO SAD ABOUT US (Who). The AMPS covered JUST LIKE A BRIAR (Tasties).

Album rating: POD (*7) / LAST SPLASH (*9) / TYLER TK (*7) / Amps: PACER (*6)

TANYA DONELLY (b.14 Jul'66, Newport, Rhode Island) – rhythm guitar, vocals (of THROWING MUSES) / **KIM DEAL** (b.10 Jun'61, Dayton, Ohio, USA) – guitar, vocals (of The PIXIES) / **JOSEPHINE WIGGS** (b.26 Feb'65, Letchworth, England) – bass, cello, vocals (of PERFECT DISASTER) / **SHANNON DOUGHTY** (aka MIKE HUNT) (b. BRITT WALFORD, Louisville, Kentucky) – drums (of SLINT) repl. NARCIZO and another from HUMAN SEXUAL RESPONSE

			4 a.d.	Elektra
May 90.	(cd)(lp/c) (CAD 0006CD)(CAD/+C 0006) <61331>	**POD**	22	
	– Glorious / Doe / Happiness is a warm gun / Oh! / Hellbound / When I was a painter / Fortunately gone / Iris / Opened / Only in 3's / Limehouse / Metal man.

— **DONELLY, KIM DEAL, JO WIGGS + JON MATLOCK** (of SPIRITUALIZED)

Apr 92.	(12"ep/cd-ep) (BAD 2003/+CD)	**SAFARI**	69	
	– Safari / So sad about us / Do you love me now? / Don't call home.

— now **KIM** her sister **KELLEY DEAL** (b.10 Jun'61, Dayton) – guitar, vocals / **JO WIGGS** – bass, vox / **JIM MacPHERSON** (b.23 Jun'66, Dayton) – drums, vocals (ex-RAGING MANTRAS) / (DONELLY formed BELLY)

Aug 93.	(12"ep/cd-ep) (BAD 3011/+CD) <64566>	**CANNONBALL. / CRO-ALOHA / LORD OF THE THIGHS / 900**	40	44 Nov93
Sep 93.	(cd)(lp/c) (CAD 3014CD)(CAD/+C 3014) <61508>	**LAST SPLASH**	5	33
	– New Year / Cannonball / Invisible man / No aloha / Roi / Do you love me now? / Flipside / I just wanna get along / Mad Lucas / Divine hammer / S.O.S. / Hag / Saints / Drivin' on 9 / Roi (reprise).
Oct 93.	(7"clear/c-s) (AD/+C 3017) <66260>	**DIVINE HAMMER. / HOVERIN'**		59
	(10"ep+=)(cd-ep+=) (BADD 3017)(BAD 3017CD) – I can't help it (if I'm still in love with you) / Do you love me now Jr (J. Mascis remix).
Jul 94.	(10"ep) (BADD 4012)	**HEAD TO TOE. / SHOCKER IN GLOOMTOWN / FREED PIG**	68	-
	(cd-ep+=) (BAD 4014CD) – Saints.

AMPS

KIM DEAL / JIM MacPHERSON / NATHAN FARLEY + LUIS LERMA

			4 a.d.	4 a.d.
Oct 95.	(12"ep/cd-ep) (BAD 5015/+CD)	**TIPP CITY / JUST LIKE A BRIAR. / EMPTY GLASSES** (Kim's basement 4 track version)	61	
Oct 95.	(cd)(lp/c) (CAD 5016CD)(CAD/+C 5016) <61623>	**PACER**	60	
	– Pacer / Tipp city / I am decided / Mom's drunk / Bragging party / Hoverin' / First revival / Full on idle / Breaking the split screen barrier / Empty glasses / She's a girl / Dedicated. (cd re-iss. Jul98; GAD 5016CD)

BREEDERS

— new 1997 line-up, included **KIM DEAL + JIM MacPHERSON** plus **MICHAEL O'DEAN** – guitar / **NATE FARLEY** – guitar / **LOUIS NERMA** – bass / **CARRIE BRADLEY** – violin

— **TYLER TRENT** – drums; repl. MacPHERSON who later joined GUIDED BY VOICES

— 2001/2 line-up **KIM + KELLEY** with **RICHARD PRESLEY** – guitar (ex-FEAR) / **MANDO LOPEZ** – bass / **JOSE MEDELES** – drums

			4 a.d.	Elektra
Mar 02.	(10"ep) (TAD 2203)	**OFF YOU. / LITTLE FURY / THE SHE**		-
	(cd-s iss.May02; TAD 2203CDP)
May 02.	(lp/cd) (CAD 2205/+CD) <62766>	**TITLE TK**	51	
	– Little fury / London song / Off you / The she / Too alive / Son of three / Put on a side / Full on idle / Sinister Foxx / Forced to drive / T and T / Huffer.
Sep 02.	(7") (AD 2213)	**SON OF THREE. / BUFFY THEME**	72	
	(cd-s+=) (BAD 2213CD) – Safari (live).

BRIAN JONESTOWN MASSACRE

Formed: San Francisco, California, USA . . . 1991 by ANTON NEWCOMBE, MATT HOLLYWOOD, DEAN TAYLOR, MARA REGAL, DAWN THOMAS, BRIAN GLAZE and shamanic leader JOEL GION, although throughout their career they employed more than 40 different musicians. Named after, both, the ex- ROLLING STONES guitarist and a mass cult suicide in America in the 1960's, the band clearly hoped to be perceived as darkly debaucherous. Their 1995 debut 'METHODRONE' was a muddy cross between MY BLOODY VALENTINE and The JESUS & MARY CHAIN, with distorted guitars and fuzzy psychedelic atmospherics. Their next effort 'THEIR SATANIC MAJESTIES' SECOND REQUEST' (1996) borrowed more than just its name from The 'STONES. A knowing pastiche of late 60's psychedelic experiments, the album did well to carve out an identity of its own. The group released two more albums that year 'TAKE IT FROM THE MAN' and 'THANK GOD FOR MENTAL ILLNESS'; however they were now lifting from MICK and KEEF's sixties rock and roll sound. Their next three releases, 'GIVE IT BACK' (1997) 'STRUNG OUT IN HEAVEN' (1998) and 'BRINGING IT ALL BACK HOME AGAIN' (2000), continued along the same lines, although the latter borrowed from GRAM PARSONS'-influenced 70's sound. The 2001 release, 'ZERO: SONGS FROM THE ALBUM BRAVERY, REPETITION AND NOISE' (featuring The WARLOCKS' BOBBY HECKSHER), was a sudden departure for the band who were now paying homage to the British post-punk groups of the 1980's. Once again the band managed to wear their influences fully on their sleeves whilst enforcing a sense of originality.

Album rating: METHODRONE (*5) / THEIR SATANIC MAJESTIES' SECOND REQUEST (*7) / THAKE IT FROM THE MAN! (*7) / THANK GOD FOR MENTAL ILLNESS (*6) / GIVE IT BACK! (*6) / STRUNG OUT IN HEAVEN (*6) / BRINGING IT ALL BACK HOME AGAIN mini (*6) / ZERO: SONGS FROM THE ALBUM BRAVERY, REPITITION AND NOISE mini (*5) / BRAVERY REPETITION AND NOISE (*6)

ANTON NEWCOMBE – vocals, guitar / **DEAN TAYLOR** – guitar / **MARA REGAL** – organ / **MATT HOLLYWOOD** – bass / **DAWN THOMAS** – accordion / **BRIAN GLAZE** – drums

			Bomp!	Bomp!
1992.	(7") <BOMP 140>	**SHE MADE ME. / EVERGREEN**	-	
1993.	(7") <BOMP 143>	**CONVERTIBLE. / THEIR MAJESTIES' SECOND REQUEST (ENRIQUE'S DREAM)**	-	
Aug 95.	(cd) <(BCD 4050)>	**METHODRONE**		
	– Evergreen / Wisdom / Crushed / That girl suicide / Wasted / Everyone says / Short wave / She made me / Hyperventilation / Records / I love you / End of the day / Outback / She's gone / (untitled).

BRIAN JONESTOWN MASSACRE (cont)

Date	Format	Cat#	Title / Tracks
Jun 96.	(cd)	<1026>	**THEIR SATANIC MAJESTIES' SECOND REQUEST** (live in the studio)

– All around you (intro) / Donovan said / In India you / No come down / (Around you) Everywhere / Jesus / Before you / Miss June '75 / Anemone / Baby (prepraise) / Feelers / Bad baby / Cause I love her / (Baby) Love of my life / Here it comes / All around you (outro).
(above & below issued on 'Tangible')

Jun 96. (7") **NEVER EVER. / FEELERS**

—— **JEFF DAVIS** – guitar; repl. MARA

Jul 96. (cd) <BCD 4055> **TAKE IT FROM THE MAN!**
– Vacuum boots / Who? / Oh Lord / Caress / (David Bowie I love you) Since I was six / Straight up and down / Monster / Take it from the man / B.S.A. / Mary, please / Monkey puzzle / Fucker / Dawn / Cabin fever / In my life / The be song / My man Syd / Straight up and down. (UK-iss.Nov96; same)

Nov 96. (cd) <BCD 4061> **THANK GOD FOR MENTAL ILLNESS**   Oct96
– Spanish bee / It girl / 13 / Ballad of Jim Jones / Those memories / Stars / Free and easy (take 2) / Down / 'Cause I love her / Too crazy to care / Talk – action = shit / True love / Sound of confusion. (re-iss. Sep00; same)

—— **PETER HAYES** – guitar; repl. THOMAS
—— added **MIRANDA RICHARDS** – guitar, vocals
—— **ADAM HAMILTON** – drums; repl. GLAZE

Sep 97. (cd) <BCD 4068> **GIVE IT BACK!**   Aug97
– Super-sonic / This is why you love me / Satellite / Malela / Salaam / Whoever you are / Sue / (You better love me) Before I am gone / Not if you were the last dandy on Earth / #1 hit jam / Servo / The Devil may care (mom & dad don't) / Their satanic second request.

not iss.   Committee To Keep Things Evil

1997. (12"ep) <EVIL 1> **NOT IF YOU WERE THE LAST DANDY ON EARTH. / (a 30 min. speech by A.A. Newcombe)**

1997. (12"ep) <EVIL 2> **THIS IS WHY YOU LOVE ME**
– This is why you love me / Satellite / Servo / Courtney Taylor. (UK-iss.Aug00 on 'Tangible'; TAN 0776)

1997. (12"ep) <EVIL 3> **BRIAN JONESTOWN MASSACRE**
– Not if you were the last dandy on Earth / Love / Nothing to lose / Summer / I've been waiting / The Devil may care (mom & dad don't) / I've been waiting (demo).

T.V.T.   T.V.T.

May 98. (cd-s) **LOVE / WASTING AWAY (demo) / THIS IS WHY YOU LOVE ME**

Aug 98. (cd/lp) <TVT 5780-2/-1> **STRUNG OUT IN HEAVEN**   Jun98
– Going to hell / Let's pretend it's summer / Wasting away / Jennifer / Got my eye on you / Nothing to lose / Love / Maybe tomorrow / Spun / I've been waiting / Dawn / Lantern / Wisdom.

Which   Which

Jun 99. (m-cd) <WHI 2767CD> **BRINGING IT ALL BACK HOME AGAIN**   May99
– The way it was / Mansion in the sky / Reign on / The godspell according to Newcombe / All things great and small / Arkansas revisited. <lp-iss.Jun00; WHI 2767)>

—— added **BOBBY HECKSHER** – guitar (of WARLOCKS)

Bomp   Bomp

Nov 00. (m-cd) <EVIL 4> **ZERO: SONGS FROM THE ALBUM BRAVERY, REPETITION AND NOISE**
– Let me stand next to your flower / Sailor / Open heart surgery / Whatever hippie bitch / If love is the drug, then I want to O.D. / New kind of sick.

Nov 01. (cd) <EVIL 5> **BRAVERY, REPETITION AND NOISE**   Oct01
– Just for today / Telegram / Stolen / Open heart surgery / Nevertheless / Sailor / You have been disconnected / Leave nothing for Sancho / Let me stand next to your flower / If I love you? / (I love you) Always / If I love you?

Nov 01. (12"ep) <EVIL 6> **IF I LOVE YOU? EP**
– If I love you? / (I love you) Always / If I love you? (extended).

– compilations, etc. –

1995. (ltd-lp) *own label*; <none> **SPACEGIRL AND OTHER FAVORITES**
– Crushed / That girl suicide / Deep in the Devil's eye & you / Kid's garden / When I was yesterday / Spacegirl / Spacegirl (revisted).

BRICK LAYER CAKE

Formed: Chicago, Illinois, USA . . . early 90's by STEVE ALBINI cohort and SHELLAC drummer, TODD TRAINER, initially as a diversion from his main occupation. Roping in GERARD BOISSY from RIFLE SPORT and producer BRIAN 'EXPENSIVE' PAULSON, TRAINER signed to 'Touch & Go' and released a debut mini album, 'CALL IT A DAY' (1991) – containing their first EP release 'EYE FOR AN EYE, TOOTH FOR A TOOTH'. Hypnotic, noisy and occasionally dreamy, the record's guitar swirls brought to mind the likes of J&MC and LOOP. A full three years passed before their follow-up, 'TRAGEDY – TRAGEDY' hit the shops, an equally intense offering that would serve as a swansong.

Album rating: CALL IT A DAY mini (*5) / TRAGEDY – TRAGEDY (*6) / WHATCHAMACALLIT (*5)

TODD TRAINER – drums (of SHELLAC, ex-RIFLE SPORT) / **GERARD BOISSY** (ex-RIFLE SPORT) / **BRIAN 'EXPENSIVE' PAULSON** – producer, etc

not iss.   Ruthless

1990. (12"ep) **EYE FOR AN EYE, TOOTH FOR A TOOTH**
– Eye for an eye / Going to go / Winter park.

Touch & Go   Touch & Go

Nov 91. (m-lp/m-cd; BRICK LAYER CAKE featuring TODD TRAINER) <TG 75/+CD> **CALL IT A DAY**   Oct91
– Night / Sitting pretty / Call it a day / Show stopper / Kiss of death / Killer / Execution / Boissy flour Paulson trainer / Happy hour / Curtains / Clockwork. <(cd+=)> – EYE FOR AN EYE, TOOTH FOR A TOOTH

Oct 94. (lp/cd) <TG 127/+CD> **TRAGEDY – TRAGEDY**
– Christ / Gone today / Thin ice / Precious / Thirteenth drink / Cold day in Hell / Reach me now / Doomsday / Cakewalkmusic / Elevenovens / Boissy Paulson / Trainer / Icing Inc.

—— TODD's remained with SHELLAC until . . . (now a solo act)

Apr 02. (cd) <TG 222CD> **WHATCHAMACALLIT**   Mar02
– Stars / Whats her face / Softie / Once upon a skin / Whatchamacallit / The wedding / Icing on the cake / Heaven to the oven / Cakewalkmusic / Electrical audio / Eleven ovens / Icing Inc.

BRIDESHEAD

Formed: Wiesbaden & Frankfurt, Germany . . . spring 1993 by MARTIN NELTE, ZWEN KELLER, HANNS-CHRISTIAN MAHLER, PAUL ENGLING and DANIEL KUBSCH. BRIDESHEAD released their first EP, 'THIS IS MALL MUSIC', for the 'Apricot' imprint in '95, their blend of relaxed, summery indie-pop brilliantly delivered on opener, 'SAME STORY DIFFERENT DAY'. A few years in the making, their debut album 'SOME PEOPLE HAVE ALL THE FUN' (1998) was another German-only affair, as were the majority of their efforts until their US/UK-issued retrospective set, 'IN AND OUT OF LOVE', hit the indie shops in 2002; by this time RAHOUL ANDERS and KAI REINHART had superseded KUBSCH. • **Covered:** IF YOU COULD LOVE ME (Orange Juice).

Album rating: SOME PEOPLE HAVE ALL THE FUN (*6) / IN AND OUT OF LOVE compilation (*6)

MARTIN NELTE – vocals / **ZWEN KELLER** – guitar / **HANNS-CHRISTIAN MAHLER** – guitar / **PAUL ENGLING** – bass / **DANIEL KUBSCH** – drums

Apricot   not iss.

1995. (cd-ep) (APRICD 001) **THIS IS MALL MUSIC!**   German
– Same story different day / The lie that tells the truth / Swinging love.

Marsh Marigold   not iss.

Jul 98. (cd) (MARI 15) **SOME PEOPLE HAVE ALL THE FUN**   German
– Real art / The leaf-h / Decartes / Arrogance or elegance / It's been time / In the movies / The elastic / Shampoo bubble / Life without a thrill / The man I was / In embrace / It's not a poem / Shortsightedness / Hidden talents / Don't wait.

Sep 99. (7"ep) (GOLD 21) **SPENDING WARM SUMMER DAYS OUTDOORS**   German
– On your trail / Books & TV / Sysiphos / Books'n'bossa.

not iss.   Shelflife

1999. (7") <LIFE 16> **SINCERELY YOURS / WHEN I'M IN LOVE. / (others by other artist)**

Apricot   not iss.

Oct 00. (7") (APRIVIN 013) **PRESENT TIME. / (other by DEN BARON)**   German

—— now without MAHLER; + two extra drummers **KAI REINHARDT + RAHOUL ANDERS** – disbanded in 2001

– compilations, etc. –

Jul 02. (cd/lp) Apricot; (efa 27374-2/-1) / Shelflife; <LIFE 43> **IN AND OUT OF LOVE**   Oct02
– Same story different day / The lie that tells the truth / Books & TV / Sincerely yours / Swinging love / Books'n'bossa / Present time / If you could love me / On your trail / Sysiphos / When I'm in love / Life is scheduled / No answer / Morning.

BRIDEWELL TAXIS

Formed: Leeds, England . . . 1983 by Leeds United fans and local record shop (Crash & Jumbo) workers, MICK ROBERTS, GLENN SCULLION, CHRIS WALTON, SIMON SCOTT, GARY WILSON and SEAN McELHONE. They turned semi-pro in the 80's having being helped by Al Neville, who set up his own 'Grateful Dead'-like label. Supporting the likes of INSPIRAL CARPETS and sounding a little reminiscent of The HAPPY MONDAYS, the group – armed with some xylophones, etc – released a flexi-disc, 'LIES', before issuing two proper singles at the turn of the decade, 'JUST GOOD FRIENDS' and 'GIVE IN'. 1990 saw two more, 'HONESTY' and 'SPIRIT', although the band suffered a major setback early the following year when frontman ROBERTS was scarred attempting to stop a pub brawl. Back into action, The 'TAXIS released their Chris Nagle-produced version of Blue Oyster Cult's 'DON'T FEAR THE REAPER'. However, with a sharp change of direction (DEACON BLUE were cited), The BRIDEWELLS delivered their debut album proper (a compilation, 'INVISIBLE TO YOU' appeared a year previously), 'CAGE' (1992).

Album rating: INVISIBLE TO YOU compilation (*5) / CAGE (*4)

MICK ROBERTS – vocals / **SEAN McELHONE** – guitar / **GARY WILSON** – keyboards / **CHRIS WALTON** – trombone / **SIMON SCOTT** – bass / **GLENN SCULLION** – drums

Stolen   not iss.

1989. (12"ep) (BLAG 1) **JUST GOOD FRIENDS / TOO LONG. / WILD BOAR / HOLD ON**

Mar 90. (12"ep) (BLAG 2) **GIVE IN / WHOLE DAMN NATION. / WHOLE DANCE NATION**

Aug 90. (12") (BLAG 3) **HONESTY / AEGIS**
(cd-s+=) (BLAG 3CD) – Aegis (live) / Just good friends (live).

Nov 90. (12"ep) (BLAG 4) **SPIRIT. / IN GOD WE TRUST / INVISIBLE**

May 91. (7"/c-s) (BLAG 6) **DON'T FEAR THE REAPER. / FACE IN THE CROWD**
(12"+=/cd-s+=) (BLAG 6 T/CD) – ('A'-What Noise remix).

Jul 91. (lp/c/cd) (BLAG 7/+C/CD) **INVISIBLE TO YOU '89-'91**
(compilation of above singles)

BRIDEWELLS

Expression / not iss.

Jul 92. (12"ep/cd-ep) (EXPEP/+D 1) **SMILE EP**
– Smile I still care / World of lies / Missing link / Return.
Oct 92. (lp/c/cd) (EXPAL/+MC/CD 14) **CAGE**
– Cage / Devil inside / Way of the world / Girl / Juggler / Smile I still care / Snake eyes / Clear as the day / Paris / Inner city blues / Rachel / Sail the wind.

— split early the following year

BRIDGET STORM (see under ⇒ THRUSH PUPPIES)

BRIGHT

Formed: Boston, Massachusetts, USA . . . 1994 by space-rock afficionados MARK DWINELL and JOE LaBRECQUE. Following the cassette release of some rehearsal-time sessions, the independent 'Ba-Da-Bing!' imprint (run by Ben Goldberg), signed up the duo for an eponymous CD-set in 1996. 'Darla' (home to many blissed-out frontrunners), took the option to let the band loose on two further albums, 'ALBATROSS GUEST HOUSE' (1997 recordings of the aforementioned cassette) and 'BLUE CHRISTIAN' (1998), the latter complemented by new space cadets, PAUL LaBRECQUE (JOE's brother) and JAY DUBOIS. Returning to the roster of 'Ba-Da-Bing!', BRIGHT delivered their 4th set proper, 'FULL NEGATIVE (OR) BREAKS', in 2000.

Album rating: BRIGHT (*7) / ALBATROSS GUEST HOUSE (*7) / BLUE CHRISTIAN (*6) / FULL NEGATIVE (OR) BREAKS (*5)

MARK DWINELL – vocals, guitar, bass, accordion, saxophone / **JOE LaBRECQUE** – drums

not iss. / Ba-Da-Bing!

Aug 96. (cd) <BING 006> **BRIGHT**
– Canal / The res / Enthusiasm / Off / Merrimac / Point / Lake Killala / Elting 1901 / Switch / Mugged / Redefine / All the wheels go / Pannonica / Perennials / Bohm and Pribahm. (UK-iss.Nov98; same as US)
1997. (7"m) <BING 012> **PLYMOUTH ROCK. / SUPERSTRINGS / NOVA**

Darla / Darla

Sep 97. (cd) <(DRL 044)> **ALBATROSS GUEST HOUSE**
– You need some sleep / Tonal / Titan / On life after death / The glowing pickpocket / Forever more or less / Quaker / Takoma / Teo / I've stopped breathing / O! / Last great patron / Transmissions / Stringing up lights / Language of the house / From tree to tree / Seventy-four / Somewhere away from the city / Albatross / Attractor.

— added **PAUL LaBRECQUE** – guitar + **JAY DUBOIS** – bass

Aug 98. (lp/cd) <(DRL 066/+CD)> **BLUE CHRISTIAN: BLISS OUT VOLUME 12**
– Fuller / Trip to the sound-alike finals / Tapping / Blue christian / Grand Mal / Europa / Not this not that.

not iss. / Orchard

Mar 00. (m-cd) <3846> **MY LIFE AND STYLE**

Ba-Da-Bing! / Ba-Da-Bing!

Oct 00. (cd/lp) <(BING 24/+LP)> **FULL NEGATIVE (OR) BREAKS**
– Heart of the park / Yeah! holy stones / Full negative / The fall / Parable of the bicycle / I'm colliding / Blue lines / The spire will be your landmark / Must I be furious? (lp w/free lp+=) – THE MILLER FANTASIES

BRIGHTER

Formed: based- Brighton, England by KERIS HOWARD, his girlfriend ALISON and third member ALEX SHARKEY although their roots were in Worthing. An indie-pop combo with leanings to the pastel side of The JESUS & MARY CHAIN, the group signed to the seminal imprint, 'Sarah'. From 1989, they issued a handful of mediocre pop tunes starting with the EP, 'AROUND THE WORLD IN 80 DAYS'. 'NOAH'S ARK' splashed out the following year, although over a full ten months went by before the mini-set, 'LAUREL'. 'DISNEY' (their swansong in 1992), showcased enough promise but missed that vital sparkle that other groups in their stable maintained. While ALISON returned to school as a sixth-form teacher in nearby Hove, KERIS and SHARKEY formed the short-lived HAL. Towards the end of the millennium, KERIS teamed up with multi-talented LAURA BRIDGE (ex-HOOD and of KICKER) to form HARPER LEE, taking the mame from the American author who wrote 'To Kill A Mockingbird'. Signing to 'Matinee' records, the twee/indie duo delivered two full-length sets, 'GO BACK TO BED . . .' (2000) and 'EVERYTHING'S GOING TO BE OK' (2002). Squeezed in between these two LP's, KERIS was part of another 'Sarah'-linked act, The TREMBLING BLUE STARS. Ah! nice.

Album rating: LAUREL mini (*4) / Harper Lee: GO BACK TO BED . . . (*5) / EVERYTHING'S GOING TO BE OK (*4)

KERIS HOWARD – vocals, guitar / **ALISON** – keyboards / **ALEX SHARKEY** – bass

Sarah / not iss.

Jul 89. (7"m) (SARAH 019) **AROUND THE WORLD IN 80 DAYS. / INSIDE OUT / TINSEL HEART**
Mar 90. (7") (SARAH 027) **NOAH'S ARK. / I DON'T THINK IT MATTERS / DOES LOVE LAST FOREVER?**
Jan 91. (10"m-lp/m-c/m-cd) (SARAH 404/+C/CD) **LAUREL**
– Christmas / Frostbite / Summer becomes winter / Something to call my own / Ocean sky / Out to sea / Maybe / Journey's end.

Sep 91. (7"ep) (SARAH 56) **HALF-HEARTED EP**
– Poppy day / Half-hearted / So you said.
Oct 92. (10"ep/cd-ep) (SARAH 069/+CD) **DISNEY EP**
– Killjoy / British summertime / Hope springs eternal / Never ever / End.

— split in 1992/3

HAL

— **KERIS HOWARD + ALEX SHARKEY**

Vinyl Japan / not iss.

Aug 94. (cd-ep) (TASK 30) **ELECTION DAY**
– Election day / Clear about this / I wish I'd never said that / Somedays.

— SHARKEY went on to form FOSCA and PINKIE (the latter released the mini-album, 'MY LITTLE EXPERIMENT' on 'Planting Seeds' c. 2001)

HARPER LEE

— **KERIS HOWARD** – vocals, guitar, keyboards (also of TREMBLING BLUE STARS) + **LAURA BRIDGE** – guitar, drums, keyboards (of KICKER, ex-HOOD)

Matinee / Matinee

Jan 00. (7") (Matinee 14) **DRY LAND. / NO HAPPY ENDING**
Oct 00. (7") (Matinee 19) **BUG. /**
Mar 01. (cd) (MATCD 9) **GO BACK TO BED . . .**   Feb01
– Seem so right / Doing nothing / Dry land / Only connect / Deep dark ocean / Brooklyn Bridge / Bug / Clifton Street passage / Your life / (untitled).
Oct 01. (cd-s) (Matinee 32) **TRAIN NOT STOPPING. / I COULD BE THERE FOR YOU / THE SEA GENTLY LIFTING**
Oct 02. (cd) (MATCD 20) **EVERYTHING'S GOING TO BE OK**   Aug02
– Miserable town / Unreciprocated / Train not stopping / The thought of you and him / The forest alone / City station / Fine bones / I can bear this no longer / This better life.

BRIGHT EYES

Formed: Nebraska, USA . . . by 15 year-old singer/guitarist CONNOR OBERST and a rotating cast of musicians. Incredibly OBERST already had two albums under his belt as frontman with slacker band COMMANDER VENUS. Formed in 1994 and comprising OBERST, BEN ARMSTRONG, ROBB NANSEL and TOM BAECHLE, COMMANDER VENUS released their debut 'DO YOU FEEL AT HOME?' on their own 'Saddle Creek' label in 1995. The next two years saw the departure of ARMSTRONG and BAECHLE, who were replaced by TIM KASHER and MATT BOWEN, before the release of their second and final album 'UNEVENTFUL VACATION'. OBERST had clearly been thinking about a long term career in the music industry and not only had he invested in the 'Saddle Creek' record label he had been holding back a number of songs for future release. These songs, which were recorded between 1995-1997, became the first BRIGHT EYES album. Informatively called 'A COLLECTION OF SONGS: RECORDED 1995-1997', it was released in 1998 and further cemented OBERST's reputation as a prodigious talent worth watching out for. Another equally impressive album 'LETTING OFF HAPPINESS' was released the same year. OBERST's work rate was as astonishing as his songwriting ability. He released the album, which really saw him coming of age, 'FEVERS AND MIRRORS' in 2000, before contributing to a split album, 'OH HOLY FOOL: THE MUSIC OF SON, AMBULANCE & BRIGHT EYES' and then a further solo album, 'LIFTED OR THE STORY IS IN THE SOIL, KEEP YOUR EAR TO THE GROUND' (2002). With his side-project, DESAPARECIDOS, OBERST – alongside LANDON HEDGES, DENVER DALLEY, IAN McELROY and MATT BAUM – released their take-on acoustic-based indie rock in the shape of emo-spiked set, 'RED MUSIC / SPEAK SPANISH' (2002).

Album rating: Commander Venus: THE UNEVENTFUL VACATION (*5) / Bright Eyes: A COLLECTION OF SONGS (*5) / LETTING OFF THE HAPPINESS (*7) / FEVERS AND MIRRORS (*7) / LIFTED OR THE STORY IS IN THE SOIL, KEEP YOUR EAR TO THE GROUND (*7) / Desaparecidos: READ MUSIC – SPEAK SPANISH (*7)

COMMANDER VENUS

CONOR OBERST – vocals, guitar / **ROBB NANSEL** – guitar / **TODD BAECHLE** – bass / **BEN ARMSTRONG** – drums

not iss. / Saddle Creek

1995. (cd) **DO YOU FEEL AT HOME?**
– Peppermints / Showcase showdown / My other car is a spaceship / Judy Blume / Radio announcer / It is fun to grow ornamental peppers / Calling Sooyoung / When two vowels go walking; the first one does the talking / Sunny slope / Pennsylvania made you sick / Do you feel at home?

— **CONOR + ROBB** added **MATT BOWEN + TIM KASHER**

not iss. / Thick

Jul 97. (cd) <THK 49> **THE UNEVENTFUL VACATION**
– Jean's T.V. / Refused by light / We'll always have Paris / Uneventful vacation (pt.1) / Lock n' chase / Life as expected / The way things had to be / Dress to please / The walk-around problem / My collapsing frame / Raining holiday (part 2) / The role of the hero in antiquity.

BRIGHT EYES

CONOR OBEREST – vocals, guitar, keyboards / with **ANDY LeMASTER** – bass, guitar / **MIKE MOGIS** – multi / **KEVIN BARNES** – keyboards / **TED STEVENS + JEREMY BARNES** – drums, percussion

BRIGHT EYES (cont)

		Saddle Creek	Saddle Creek

Mar 98. (cd) <LBJ 19> **A COLLECTION OF SONGS**
– The invisible gardener / Patient hope in new show / Saturday as usual / Falling out of love at this volume / Exaltation on a cool, kitchen floor / The awful sweetness of escaping sweet / Puella quam amo est pulchra / Driving fast through a big city at night / How many lights do you see? / I watched you taking off / A celebration upon completion / Emily, sing something sweet / All of the truth / One straw (please) / Lila / A few minutes on Friday / Supriya / Solid Jackson / Feb. 15th / The 'feel good' revolution. <re-iss. Jun00; same>

Mar 99. (cd) <LBJ 23> **LETTING OFF THE HAPPINESS**   Nov98
– If winter ends / Padraic my prince / Contrast and compare / The city has sex / The difference in the shades / Touch / June on the West Coast / Pull my hair / A poetic retelling of an unfortunate seduction / Tereza and Thomas. <re-iss. Apr01 on 'Wichita'; WEBB 011>

— **JOE KNAPP** – percussion (of SON, AMBULANCE) repl. TED + JEREMY

	Wichita	Saddle Creek

Jun 00. (cd-ep) <LBJ 30> **EVERY DAY AND EVERY NIGHT**
– A line allows progress, a circle does not / A perfect sonnet / On my way to work / A new arrangement / Neely O'Hara. (UK-iss.Nov02; same as US)

Jul 00. (cd) (WEBB 001) <LBJ 32> **FEVERS AND MIRRORS**   Jan00
– A spindle, a darkness, a fever, and a necklace / A scale, a mirror, and these indifferent clocks / The calendar hung itself / Something vague / The movement of a hand / Arienette / When the curious girl realizes she is under glass / Haligh, haligh, a lie, Haligh / The center of the world / Sunrise, sunset / An attempt to tip the scales / A song to pass the time.

Sep 00. (7") (WEBB 005S) **THE CALENDAR HUNG ITSELF. / (other by HER SPACE HOLIDAY)**
(cd-s+=) (WEBB 005SCD) – (2 by HER SPACE HOLIDAY).

Jan 01. (cd/lp; split w/ SON, AMBULANCE) <LBJ 34> **OH HOLY FOOLS**
– (S,A track) / Going for the gold / (S,A track) / Oh, you are the roots that sleep beneath my feet ... (...and hold the earth in place) / (S,A track) / No lies, just love / (S, A track) / Kathy's with a K's song. (UK-iss.Nov02; same as US)

Mar 01. (7") <SP 528> **I WILL BE GRATEFUL FOR THIS DAY. / WHEN THE CURIOUS GIRL REALIZES SHE IS UNDER GLASS AGAIN**
(above issued on 'Sub Pop')

May 01. (7") (WEBB 012S) **DRUNK KID CATHOLIC. / FEBRUARY 15th**
(cd-s+=) (WEBB 012SCD) – I have been eating for you.

— **MIKE SWEENEY** – drums; repl. KNAPP

Jul 02. (cd-ep) (WEBB 031SCD) **THERE IS NO BEGINNING TO THE STORY EP**
– From a balance beam / The messenger bird's song / We are free men / Loose leaves.

Aug 02. (cd) (WEBB 034) <LBJ 46> **LIFTED OR THE STORY IS IN THE SOIL, KEEP YOUR EAR TO THE GROUND**
– Big picture / Method acting / False advertising / You will, you will, you will / Lover I don't have to love / Bowl of oranges / Don't know when but a day is gonna come / Nothing gets crossed out / Make war / Waste of paint / From a balance beam / Laura Laurent / Let's not shit ourselves (to love and to be loved).

Nov 02. (7") (WEBB 037S) **LOVER I DON'T HAVE TO LOVE. / AMY IN THE WHITE COAT**
(cd-s+=) (WEBB 037SCD) – Out on the weekend.

DESAPARECIDOS

CONOR OBERST – vocals, guitar / with **DENVER DALLEY** – vocals, guitar / **LANDON HEDGES** – bass / **MATT BAUM** – drums / **IAN McELROY** – keyboards

	Wichita	Saddle Creek

Feb 02. (7") (WEBB 027S) <LBJ 40> **WHAT'S NEW FOR FALL. / THE HAPPIEST PLACE ON EARTH**   Dec01
(cd-s+=) (WEBB 027SCD) – Give me the pen.

Apr 02. (cd) (WEBB 028) <LBJ 42> **READ MUSIC – SPEAK SPANISH**   Feb02
– What's new for fall / Man and wife, the former (financial planning) / Manana / Greater Omaha / Man and wife, the latter (damaged goods) / Mall of America / The happiest place on earth / Survival of the fittest – It's a jungle out there / $$$$ / Hole in one.

BRILLIANTINE (see under ⇒ DAMBUILDERS)

BRITISH SEA POWER

Formed: Brighton, England ... late 2000 by YAN (guitar/vocals), NOBLE (guitar), WOOD (drums) and HAMILTON (bass/vocals). This eccentric quartet created ripples of interest with their JOY DIVISION-inspired indie-rock gigs and unusual stage aesthetics (large stuffed birds and matching military uniforms!). Releasing first single, 'FEAR OF DROWNING' on their own 'Golden Chariot' label in spring 2001, BSP also continued to run their own monthly club night, Club Sea Power, at Brighton venues The Lift and The Freebutt. After witnessing BRITISH SEA POWER in their natural environment, an impressed Geoff Travis of 'Rough Trade' promptly signed them up. Subsequently releasing two singles, 'REMEMBER ME' and 'THE SPIRIT OF ST. LOUIS', the lads continue to pay rock homage to British marine wildlife.

Album rating: expecting debut mid 2003

YAN – vocals, guitar / **NOBLE** – guitar / **HAMILTON** – bass, vocals / **WOOD** – drums

	Golden Chariot	not iss.

Aug 01. (7") (none) **FEAR OF DROWNING. / A WOODEN HORSE**

	Rough Trade	not iss.

Dec 01. (7") (RTRADES 032) **REMEMBER ME. / A LOVELY DAY TOMORROW**
(cd-s+=) (RTRADESCD 032) – Birdy.

Apr 02. (7") (RTRADES 048) **THE SPIRIT OF ST. LOUIS. / THE LONELY**
(cd-s+=) (RTRADESCD 048) – No Red Indian.

Nov 02. (7") (RTRADES 069) **CHILDHOOD MEMORIES. / STRANGE COMMUNICATION**
(cd-s+=) (RTRADESCD 069) – Beetroot fields.

BROADCAST

Formed: Birmingham, England ... mid-1995 by TRISH KEENAN, ROJ STEVENS, TIM KELTON, JAMES CARGILL and STEVE PERKINS (the latter played drums for COOLER THAN JESUS, a band that included MENSWEAR's SIMON). Openly admitting the heavy influence of Stateside psychedelic 60's outfit, the UNITED STATES OF AMERICA, BROADCAST specialise in retro-futuristic avant-pop constructed from soundtrack samples, slo-mo beats and synth experimentation. Early the following year, the neatly-pressed quintet delivered their first 45, 'ACCIDENTALS', for the tiny limited edition-only label, 'Wurlitzer Jukebox'; today the single is fetching upwards of £50. Subsequently finding a natural home at STEREOLAB's 'Duophonic', BROADCAST released two further rare singles, 'LIVING ROOM' and 'THE BOOK LOVERS' EP, both written unconventionally in waltz-time. Having also contributed the track, 'LIGHTS OUT', to the V/A NME C-96 compilation, the band had their entire recorded output to date collected together on the 'Warp' album, 'WORK AND NON WORK' (1997). • **Trivia:** KEENAN and Co also remixed SAINT ETIENNE's 'Angel' for their recent 'Casino Classics' album.

Album rating: WORK AND NON WORK compilation (*7) / THE NOISE MADE BY PEOPLE (*8)

TRISH KEENAN – vocals / **ROJ STEVENS** – keyboards / **TIM KELTON** – guitar / **JAMES CARGILL** – bass / **STEVE PERKINS** – drums (ex-COOLER THAN JESUS)

	Wurlitzer Jukebox	not iss.

Jan 96. (7") (WJ 6) **ACCIDENTALS. / WE'VE GOT TIME**

	Duophonic Super 45's	not iss.

May 96. (ltd-7") (DS45 14) **LIVING ROOM. / PHANTOM**

Nov 96. (12"ep/cd-ep) (DS45/+CD 16) **THE BOOK LOVERS / MESSAGE FROM HOME. / ACCORDING TO NO PLAN / THE WORLD BACKWARDS**

	Warp	Warp

Jun 97. (cd/c/lp) (<WARP CD/MC/LP 52>) **WORK AND NON WORK** (compilation)
– The accidentals / The book lovers / Message from home / Phantom / We've got time / Living room / According to no plan / The world backwards / Lights out.

	Warp	Tommy Boy

Nov 99. (7"/cd-s) (WAP 125/+CD) **ECHO'S ANSWER. / TEST AREA**

Feb 00. (12"ep/cd-ep) (WAP 129/+CD) **EXTENDED PLAY**
– Papercuts / Bellydance / Where youth and laughter go / Dave's dream.

Apr 00. (cd/lp) (WARP CD/LP 65) <TB 1413> **THE NOISE MADE BY PEOPLE**
– Long was the year / Unchanging window / Minus one / Come on let's go / Echo's answer / Tower of our timing / Paper cuts / You can fall / Until then / City in progress / Dead the long day.

May 00. (7") (7WAP 132) **COME ON LET'S GO. / DISTANT CALL**
(cd-s+=) (WAP 132CD) – ('A'side) / Locusts / Chord simple.

Oct 00. (12"ep/cd-ep) (WAP 141/+CDS) <TB 1439> **EXTENDED PLAY TWO**   Sep00
– Illumination / Unchanging window – Chord simple / A man for Atlantis / Poem of dead song / Drums on fire.

BROCCOLI

Formed: Dundee, Scotland ... early '92 by singer/guitarist GRANT MILES (apparently a former nude model at an art college!), bassist BENNI ESPOSITO and drummer GRAEME GILMOUR – hardy vegetables indeed. Trash-punk/pop and strongly inspired by The DAMNED and LEATHERFACE, BROCCOLI sprung into action in '94 via a split EP with fellow Dundonians, MUPPET MULE (an off-shoot of SPARE SNARE). 1995 was indeed a prolific year for the perky trio, three further indie singles for as many labels shooting out, while tours with Americans J CHURCH proved tasty. The 'BROCCOLI' mini-set for 'Rugger Bugger' the following year, was however their last outing with Art College kid BENNI, who was superseded by former APPLEORCHARD guy SCOTT STEWART. Having been a fan of 70's/80's Mod band, The LAMBRETTAS, GRANT and the lads chose a cover of their 'DA-A-A-ANCE' for their next 45. While promoting their first full-set, 'HOME' (1998), BROCCOLI ("home" now in London's Gypsy Hill) toured alongside likeminded SNUFF, JUNE OF 44, LEATHERFACE and HOOTON 3 CAR, although basically these musical meatpackers were an out and out singles combo.

Album rating: BROCCOLI mini (*5) / HOME (*6) / THE SINGLES 1993-1998 compilation (*7)

GRANT MILES – vocals, guitar / **BENNI ESPOSITI** – bass / **GRAEME GILMOUR** – drums

	Chute	not iss.

1994. (ltd-7"ep) (CHUTE 002) **NEGLECT IT / WELTSCHMERTZ / (other tracks by Muppet Mule)**

	Rooster	not iss.

Jan 95. (7"m) (RSTR 002) **BROKEN. / 10 JOURNEY TROUSERS / FIDO**

	Rumblestrip	not iss.

Jun 95. (7") **ALL SMILES. / PONDLIFE**

BROCCOLI (cont)

		Rugger Bugger	Snuffy Smile
Nov 95.	(7") *(DUMP 030)* **RELENT. / 100 DAYS AND COUNTING**	□	–
1996.	(7"m) **LEAN. / SIDLEDOWN / PR EXORCISE**	□	–
Aug 96.	(m-lp/m-cd) *(SEEP 19/+CD)* **BROCCOLI**	□	–

—— **SCOTT STEWART** – bass, vocals (ex-APPLEORCHARD) repl. BENNI

| 1997. | (7"ep) **DA-A-A-ANCE / SHORT STRAW FATE. /** (other 2 by International Jet Set) (above issued on 'Snuffy Smile') | □ | – |
| May 98. | (lp/cd) *(SEEP 23/+CD)* **HOME**
 – Constance / Chestnut road / I am a robot / R.S.V.P. / Sleep tight / Home / The tens / Tongue tied / Short straw fate / Well wishing. | □ | – |

		Speedwax	not iss.
Jul 98.	(7"ep) *(ATOM 006)* **LODGED / THE TENS. /** (others by Pinto)	□	–

		Solent	not iss.
Sep 98.	(7"tour) *(SNT 01)* **DEFENCE. /** Starfish: **NEW EDITOR**	□	–

		Crackle	not iss.
Nov 98.	(7"ep) *(VYM 021)* **CHESTNUT ROAD EP** – Chestnut Road / Television / Crackle song / Split up.	□	–

		Speedwax	not iss.
Aug 99.	(7",7"green) *(ATOM 012)* **LAST ONE. /**	□	–

– compilations, etc. –

| May 99. | (cd) *Rugger Bugger;* *(SEEP 28CD)* **THE SINGLES 1993-1998**
 – Neglect it / Weltschmertz / Broken / 10 journey trousers / Fido / All smiles / Pondlife / Relent / 100 days and counting / Lean / Sidledown / PR exorcise / Da-a-a-ance / Short straw fate / Jamaica Street / Untitled / Neglect it / Lodged / The tens / Defence / Chestnut road / Television / Crackle song / Split up. | □ | – |

BROKEN SPINDLES (see under ⇒ FAINT)

BROTHER JT

Born: JOHN TERLESKY, Philadelphia, Pennsylvania, USA. He and DAN McKINNEY formed The ORIGINAL SINS around a decade earlier, a basic garage-rock revivalists with more than a hint of crazed-up grunge; PETER BUCK (R.E.M.) produced their 'EAT THIS' mini set. As a solo artist under the moniker BROTHER JT, mad-monk TERLESKY had toned down the rock and pumped up the alternative psych-out stylings with a lyrical content and approach that gleaned many comparisons to SYD BARRETT's solo efforts. Debuting in 1996 with the mini-album, 'MUSIC FOR THE OTHER HEAD', a record that showcased the reason why he was highly placed in the local scene dubbed "Psychedelphia". The set included the acid-influenced twenty-minute rock doodlings of 'COMET' and the out-there psych-punk of 'BLUR (TWAS)'. BJT's full-length album proper, 'RAINY DAY FUN', appeared later that same year. Sophomore set, 'COME ON DOWN', was a high-point for this musical project and showed TERLESKY's refreshing staunch stance on doing things his weird and wonderful way. Following these albums came the equally bizarre efforts of 'HOLY GHOST STORIES' (1998) and 'WAY TO GO' (1999), his left-field live shows being captured on the following year's release 'DOSED AND CONFUSED: LIVE '94-'97'. Superseding this came the studio LP, 'MAYBE WE SHOULD TAKE SOME MORE' (2002), which witnessed BJT's eclectic use of the spectrum of rock music, although all mashed and blended into his own unique vision. 'SPIRITUALS', the other full-length set of the same year was, by TERLESKY's own admission, his most approachable offering to date and featured some more sing-along chilled acoustic numbers in the shape of 'MELLOW'. Also of small note was that this album was issued under the slightly expanded moniker of BROTHER JT3. The workaholic TERLESKY could also be heard throughout the BJT period in the similarly veined but heavier big band approach of the outfit VIBROLUX, which also included fellow Pennslyvania acid revivalist the PHOTON BAND's ART DIFURIO; BJT did a split LP, 'DOOMSDAY ROCK' (1998), with his VIBROLUX. • **Covered:** ROUTE 66 (Barry-Kim) / LOVE TUNNEL (. . . Roberts) / DIZZY (Tommy Roe).

Album rating: Original Sins: SIN WILL FIND YOU OUT (*5) / BIG SOUL (*7) / THE HARDEST WAY (*7) / SELF DESTRUCT mini (*5) / PARTY'S OVER (*5) / MOVE (*3) / OUT THERE (*3) / ACIDBUBBLEPUNK (*3) / BETHLEHEM (*3) / SUBURBAN PRIMITIVE (*5) / Brother JT: "MUSIC FOR THE OTHER HEAD" mini (*6) / RAINY DAY FUN (*5) / COME ON DOWN (*6) / WAY TO GO (*5) / MAYBE WE SHOULD TAKE SOME MORE? (*5) / SPIRITUALS (*5)

JT (b. JOHN TERLESKY) – vocals, guitar / **DAN McKINNEY** – organ / **KEN BUSSIERE** – bass, vocals / **DAVE FERRARA** – drums

		Roadrunner	Grudge
Oct 86.	(lp) *(RR 9679)* <*GR 0956*> **SIN WILL FIND YOU OUT** – Conjuration of the watcher / Curse / To the Devil a daughter / Slice of finger / Bitches from Hell / Succubus / Pandora's box / Thunder war / Ecchantress of death / Disease bombs.	□	□

		not iss.	Bar/None
1987.	(7") <*AHAON 45-01*> **JUST 14. / SUGAR SUGAR**	–	□
1987.	(lp) <*AHAON 003*> **BIG SOUL** – Just 14 / Not gonna be all right / Can't feel a thing / Posession / All in my head / Your way / My mother's mirror / Road to Emmaus / Party's over now / Help yourself / Read your mind / Why don't you smile, Joan? / Inside-out / Big soul. *<cd-iss. 1996 on 'Bar/None-Capitol'+=; AHAON 041>* – I want to live / Sugar sugar / Route 66 / Timekeeper.	–	□

		Music Maniac	Skyclad
1989.	(cd) <*17-001-2*> **THE HARDEST WAY** – Heard it all before / Now's the time / Tearing me in 2 / Why you love me so / Can't get over you / The hardest way / Out of my mind / You can't touch me / Don't fit in / Rather be sad / I can't say / She understands / Ain't no tellin' / End of the world / Party's over / Can't stop dancing / Beast in me / Lacerations / Just 14 (and a half).	–	□

Dec 90.	(m-cd/m-lp) *(MMCD/MMLP 035)* <*PSONIK 88-2/-1*> **SELF DESTRUCT** – Do it / Looking at the sun / Feel / Nowhere to go (from here but down) / Alice D. / Higher / Rise / Black hole.	□	□
Jan 91.	(7") <*PSONIK 89*> **ALICE D. / DIZZY**	–	□
1991.	(7") <*GH 134*> **COCA COLA. / JUICY FRUIT** (above issued on 'Get Hip', below on 'Dog Meat')	–	□
1991.	(12"ep) <*Dog 020*> **PARTY'S OVER**	–	□
Feb 92.	(cd/lp) <*PSONIK 98-2/-1*> **MOVE** – She's on my side / Wake up / Watch you dance / I surrender / Talking to you / Like an animal / Move / Saturday / All good things / Feel so fine / Getting the feeling / Forest for the trees / I'll be around / Waiting / Between the lines / If I knew / Closing my eyes / I never dreamed / Break the chains / Hit or miss / Nothing's everything / It's a good life / Not today / Devil's music.	–	□
Apr 92.	(12"ep) <*PSONIK 108*> **EAT THIS EP** – She's on my side / Watch you dance / Like an animal / Donut shop song / Looking in my mirror / Drivin' home.	–	□
Jun 92.	(7") <*PSONIK 118*> **WATCH YOU DANCE. / GOIN' DOWN**	–	□
Nov 92.	(cd) <*PSONIK 138*> **OUT THERE** – Get off / One good reason / C'mon / Wipe out / Get into it / Killing time / Dead gone train / Sally Kirkland / Love tunnel / Goin' down / Dizzy.	–	□
Apr 93.	(12"ep) <*PSONIK 148*> **SALLY KIRKLAND**	–	□

—— now with session drummers when FERRARA departed

		not iss.	Bedlam
May 94.	(cd) <*70-007*> **ACIDBUBBLEPUNK** – Almost everything / Wheel / Beautiful seconds / April / Drop out / Surfin' worm / Drivin' round / Sunshine games / Lay in the sun / (It's really not so) Groovy (anymore) / She'll be / Track twelve.	–	□
1995.	(lp) <*none*> **TURN YOU ON**	–	□

		not iss.	Radioactive
1995.	(7") <*RARE 010*> **AFTERNOON JAM SESSION**	–	□

		not iss.	Chaos
1995.	(7") <*Chaos 69*> **GET YOU THERE. / COME ON UP**	–	□

—— guests = **RAY KETCHUM** – percussion / **CHRIS MARX** – guitar

		not iss.	Bar/None
Oct 96.	(cd) <*AHAON 084*> **BETHLEHEM** – Bethlehem / Wish I was here / Shopping trip to Mercury / Let's do it slow / My struggles / Souls on ice / One way out / Beautiful day / Happy birthday, Jesus / Hang me / Cold cold world / Sunday nights.	–	□

		Blood Red	Nail
1997.	(7"ep) **AMERICAN CHEESE PRODUCT**	□	□
Dec 97.	(m-cd) *(BR 5005)* <*1080*> **SUBURBAN PRIMITIVE** *(10"m-lp-iss.Mar98; BRLP10 005)*	□	□

– compilations, etc. –

| 1999. | (cd) *Bedlam;* <*be 008*> **RADIO FRIENDLY / TURN YOU ON** | – | □ |

BROTHER J.T.

JOHN TERLESKY – vocals, guitar / with **DIFURIA** (of VIBROLUX)

		not iss.	Twisted Village
1991.	(lp) <*TWI 005*> **DESCENT**	–	□
1992.	(lp) <*TWI 020*> **MESHES OF THE AFTERNOON**	–	□

		not iss.	Dog Meat
1992.	(lp; as FUZZ FACE) <*dog 042*> **BAD THOUGHTS**	–	□

		not iss.	Mind Cure
1993.	(7"; as CRUSH NOVA) <*MC 2702*> **ICE CREAM CONE. / MOON PIE**	–	□

		not iss.	Bedlam
1994.	(lp) <*6812*> **HOLY GHOST STORIES**	–	□

		Siltbreeze	Siltbreeze
Apr 96.	(m-lp/m-cd) <*(SB 041-1/-2)*> **"MUSIC FOR THE OTHER HEAD"** – Comet / Music for / Blur (twas) / Mind (I don't . . . if you . . . or rot).	□	Feb96

		Drunken Fish	Drunken Fish
Dec 96.	(cd) <*(DFR 30)*> **RAINY DAY FUN** – Is it soup yet? / This is the life / Beginning to smile / Intangible mack truck / Hi / Rider rider / When it rains / Oh mother / Slowly / Rainy day fun / Lights on, nobody's home / Live better electrically / (untitled).	□	Aug96
May 97.	(cd; by BROTHER JT & VIBROLUX) *(SB 65CD)* <*6868*> **DOOMSDAY ROCK** (above issued on 'Siltbreeze' UK / 'Bedlam' US)	□	□
Oct 97.	(cd) <*(DFR 35)*> **COME ON DOWN** – Message to the listener / Try not to try / Do less, be more / Lazy / Thank you St. Jude / It keeps raining / Red cathedral / A little more nothing / Come on down / Had to be / Little man.	□	□

		not iss.	Apartment
1999.	(10"ep) <*aparec 011*> **TAKE OFF ZEBRA BABY**	–	□

—— **JOHN** added **DAVE FERRARA** – drums + **BILL MELCHER** – bass (ex-CRACK BABY)

		Drag City	Drag City
Sep 99.	(lp/cd; as BROTHER JT3) <*(DC 176/+CD)*> **WAY TO GO** – Ur / Come around / Way to go / Naked / Little did I know / Throwaway / Floating / Cloud ten.	□	□
Nov 01.	(7"ep) *(TONG 002)* **HERE THE WAVES** (above issued on 'Tongue')	□	–

—— added **JAMIE KNERR** – guitar

| Mar 02. | (lp/cd; as BROTHER JT3) <*(DC 219/+CD)*> **SPIRITUALS**
 – Poor wayfaring stranger / Be with us / Summer / Praise be / Mellow / Lord you are the wine / Right there / Mole in the ground / Say no more. | □ | □ |

– compilations, others, etc. –

| 1998. | (cd) *Bedlam;* <*be 006*> **DOSED AND CONFUSED: LIVE '94-'97** | – | □ |
| Feb 02. | (cd) *Birdman;* <*(BMR 035)*> **MAYBE WE SHOULD TAKE SOME MORE?**
 – Jesus guitar – First thoughts / Twain / Ring that bell / Juice / S.O.S. / Watcha gonna do? / Layin low / Turnpike / Ragamuff / Child of the sun / Muff, VA. / Lay it on / Moon chant / Cheap motel / Honeysuckle / Lassitude / Dave's thing / Lullaby. | □ | Jan02 |

Ian BROWN

Born: 20 Feb'63, Ancoats, Manchester, England. Having hit the heights with the iconic STONE ROSES for nearly a decade, IAN was ready to hit out on his own. In early '98, the man launched his solo career (via a new deal with 'Polydor') by releasing the single, 'MY STAR', a taster from his debut album, 'UNFINISHED MONKEY BUSINESS', which also reached the Top 5. However, BROWN subsequently landed himself in deep water when he was charged with threatening behaviour on a flight between Paris and Manchester. Astonishingly sentenced to four months in prison at the end of October, the singer was released a couple of months early that Christmas eve. Back in circulation the following year, BROWN guested for 'Mo Wax' duo U.N.K.L.E. on the track, 'BE THERE'. Album No.2, 'GOLDEN GREATS', was completed and in the Top 20 towards the end of 1999. Previewed by the hit single, 'LOVE LIKE A FOUNTAIN', the set showed IAN (and co-writer DAVE McCRACKEN) venturing away from the staid and into every funkin' Rock genre under the sun. BROWN surfaced almost two years later with the brilliant orchestral driven single 'F.E.A.R.', in which he turned the letters of the word into a poetic acronym which resulted in a Top 20 hit. His third album proper, 'MUSIC OF THE SPHERES' was issued in October 2001 to almost unanimous critical acclaim and reinforced his self-confidence as an artist when it climbed into the Top 3. • **Covered:** BILLIE JEAN + THRILLER (Michael Jackson).

Album rating: UNFINISHED MONKEY BUSINESS (*6) / GOLDEN GREATS (*7) / MUSIC OF THE SPHERES (*7)

on mostly all vocals/instruments except co-writers **AZIZ IBRAHIM** – guitars, etc / **SIMON MOORE** – drums / **NIGEL IPPINSON** – keyboards, bass / guests **MANI MOUNFIELD** + **NOEL GALLAGHER** + **DENISE JOHNSON** + co-writer/mixer **ROBBIE MADDIX**

			Polydor	Polydor
Jan 98.	(7") *(571 987-7)*	**MY STAR. / SEE THE DAWN**	5	-
	(cd-s+=) *(571 987-2)* – Fourteen.			
Feb 98.	(cd/c/lp) *(539 565-2/-4/-1)*	**UNFINISHED MONKEY BUSINESS**	4	-
	– Intro under the paving stones / The beach / My star / Can't see me / Ice cold cube / Sunshine / Lions / Corpses in their mouths / What happened to ya part 1 / What happened to ya part 2 / Nah nah / Deep pile dreams / Unfinished monkey business.			
Mar 98.	(7") *(569 654-7)*	**CORPSES. / JESUS ON THE MOVE / COME AGAIN (part one)**	14	-
	(cd-s) *(569 657-2)* – (first 2 tracks) / Lions (with Denise).			
Jun 98.	(7") *(569 092-7)*	**CAN'T SEE ME (Bacon & Quarmby remix). / CAN'T SEE ME (Bacon & Quarmby vocal dub)**	21	-
	(cd-s+=) *(044 045-2)* – Under the paving stones: The beach (Gabriel's 13th dream remix) / ('A'video).			
	(cds) *(044 047-2)* – ('A'side) / ('A'-Harvey's invisible mix) / Come again part 2 / My star (CD-ROM video).			
	(12"++=) *(044 047-6)* – ('A'-Harvey's instrumental).			
Oct 99.	(7") *(561 516-7)*	**LOVE LIKE A FOUNTAIN. / THE FISHERMAN**	23	-
	(cd-s+=) *(561 516-2)* – ('A'-CD-Rom mix).			
	(cd-s) *(561 517-2)* – ('A'side) / ('A'-Stereo MC's mix) / ('A'-Aim mix).			
Nov 99.	(cd/c/lp) *(543 141-2/-4/-1)* <543720> **GOLDEN GREATS**		14	Feb00
	– Gettin' high / Love like a fountain / Free my way / Set my baby free / So many sisters / Golden gaze / Dolphins were monkeys / Neptune / First world / Babasonicos.			
Feb 00.	(7") *(561 637-7)*	**DOLPHINS WERE MONKEYS. / CORPSES (live radio session)**	5	-
	(cd-s) *(561 637-2)* – ('A'side) / Billie Jean / ('A'-Goldfinger mix) / ('A'-CD-Rom).			
	(cd-s) *(561 638-2)* – ('A'side) / ('A'-Unkle vs. South mix) / Love like a fountain (Andy Votel's remix).			
Jun 00.	(7") *(561 844-7)*	**GOLDEN GAZE. / SUNSHINE (live radio session)**	29	-
	(cd-s) *(561 844-2)* – ('A'side) / ('A'-Andy Gray remix) / Love like a fountain (Laj & Quakerman remix) / ('A'-CD-Rom).			
	(cd-s) *(561 845-2)* – ('A'side) / Thriller / ('A'-Sharktank's dirt it up remix).			
Sep 01.	(7") *(587 284-7)*	**F.E.A.R. / (instrumental)**	13	-
	(c-s) *(587 284-4)* – ('A'side) / ('A'-side with DANN).			
	(cd-s+=) *(587 284-2)* – Hear no see no speak no (extended) / ('A'video).			
Oct 01.	(cd/c) *<(589 126-2/-4>)* **MUSIC OF THE SPHERES**		3	-
	– F.E.A.R. / Stardust / The gravy train / Bubbles / Hear no see no / Northern lights / Whispers / El mundo pequeno / Forever and a day / Shadow of a saint.			
Feb 02.	(7") *(570538-7)*	**WHISPERS. / EL MUNDO PEQUENO**	33	-
	(cd-s) *(570538-2)* – ('A'side) / ('A'video) / Superstar / My star (remix).			
Nov 02.	(cd/d-lp) *(065927-2/-1)* **REMIXES OF THE SPHERES** (remixes)			-

Franklin BRUNO
(see under ⇒ NOTHING PAINTED BLUE)

Peter BRUNTNELL

Born: 26 Jan'64, Auckland, New Zealand. The son of a Welsh father who worked for the foreign office, BRUNTNELL was used to moving around during his childhood, living in England and finally Vancouver, Canada where he began his singer-songwriter career. The start of the 90's saw BRUNTNELL leave North America and return to English soil where he formed the short-lived MILKWOOD. Now in his thirties, PETER was subsequently taken under the wing of Pete Smith (who had previously worked in the studio with The POLICE and STING), who secured him a contract with HERB ALPERT and JERRY MOSS's 'Almo Sounds' label (Stateside home of GARBAGE). 1995 saw the release of his debut album, 'CANNIBAL', a country-tinged affair that won praise from the likes of Mojo magazine. Two years on, BRUNTNELL was hailed as one of the best unsung alternative singer-songwriters in Britain with the release of follow-up set, 'CAMELOT IN SMITHEREENS' (1997). If TEENAGE FANCLUB's later work or SON VOLT's earlier stuff was your bag, then BRUNTNELL provided the listener with an Anglo-sized/Americana view of his own homelands, witnessed fully on his third set, 'NORMAL FOR BRIDGWATER' (1999). BRUNTNELL repeated the formula three years later with the splendid 'ENDS OF THE EARTH' (2002), a record both compelling and retro-fied; WILCO, EITZEL and WHISKEYTOWN rolled into one Southern Hemisphere combination.

Album rating: CANNIBAL (*6) / CAMELOT IN SMITHEREENS (*7) / NORMAL FOR BRIDGWATER (*6) / ENDS OF THE EARTH (*8)

PETER BRUNTNELL COMBINATION

PETER BRUNTNELL – vocals, guitar / **MATT BACKER** – guitar / **FELIX HARPER** – bass

			Almo Sounds	not iss.
Jul 95.	(c-s/cd-s) *(MC/CD ALMOS 002)*	**I WILL, I WON'T / VOODOO SUPERMAN / BENT OUT OF SHAPE / DIANNE (acoustic)** *(re-iss. May96; same)*		-
Jan 96.	(cd-ep) *(CDALMOS 0204F)*	**ASTRONAUT / BROADWAY / FOOD FOR THE MOON / SHAKE (live)**		-
Apr 96.	(cd) *(ALMOCD 002)* **CANNIBAL**			-
	– I want you / I will, I won't / Astronaut / Heron speaks / Bent out of shape / Dianne / Let me out / Cannibal / Trip to commercial / Blue mouse / My little girl.			

PETER BRUNTNELL

May 97.	(7") *(7ALM 33)* **HAVE YOU SEEN THAT GIRL AGAIN. / ALREADY DEAD**		-
	(cd-s+=) *(CDALM 33)* – Calling cards.		
Aug 97.	(7"/c-s) *(7/MC ALM 34)* **CAMELOT IN SMITHEREENS. / BLACK EYED DOG**		-
	(cd-s+=) *(CDALM 34)* – If your house is on fire.		
Sep 97.	(cd/c/lp) *(ALM CD/MC/LP 14)* **CAMELOT IN SMITHEREENS**		-
	– Panelbeater / Camelot in smithereens / Have you seen that girl again / I'm after you / Bewitched / 25 reasons / Saturday Sam / Vera / Shake / Panelbeater (reprise) / Ellison.		
Dec 97.	(cd-s) *(CDALM 42 7F)* **SATURDAY SAM / PINHEAD / FLY (featuring Melissa Jo Heathcote)**		-

		Slow River	Slow River
May 99.	(cd) *(cd)* <(SRRCD 043)> **NORMAL FOR BRIDGWATER**		
	– Handful of stars / You won't find me / N.F.B. / Forgiven / By the time my head gets to Phoenix / Played out / Cosmea / Lay down the curse / Shot from a spring / Jurassic parking lot / Flow you are / Outlaw (may the sun always shine).		
Jun 99.	(cd-ep) *<SCDS 227411>* **BY THE TIME MY HEAD GETS TO PHOENIX / HANDFUL OF STARS / YOU WON'T FIND ME (acoustic) / DO ANYTHING YOU WANNA DO**	not iss.	Black Porch
Aug 02.	(cd; as the PETER BRUNTNELL COMBINATION) **ENDS OF THE EARTH**	-	
	– Here comes the swells / One drink away / City stars / Tabloid reporter / Downtown / (intermission) / Rio Tinto / Laredo Kent / Ends of the earth / Black aces / Murder in the afternoon / Lonesome Charlie.		

BUBONIQUE
(see under ⇒ COUGHLAN, Cathal; 80's section)

Jeff BUCKLEY

Born: 17 Nov'66, Orange County, California, USA. The offspring of the late, great TIM BUCKLEY, JEFF's chosen career as a musician, singer and songwriter was always destined to bear the heavy burden of his father's unique legacy (note: in this instance JEFF appears out of alphabetical sequence). To his credit, BUCKLEY Jnr. persevered at carving out a distinctive niche in the musical landscape of the early 90's, plugging away on the once legendary Greenwich Village scene of New York. Torch rather than tortured, JEFF utilised his inherited multi-octave vocal chords in ever more impressive and innovative fashion, both in tackling an eclectic variety of cover material (see below) and lavishly dramatic originals. Given his first British break in 1994, via 'LIVE AT THE SIN-E' EP (1992 in America) on the 'Big Cat' label, BUCKLEY was a surprise success at the grunge overload of Reading 1994. Coinciding with his appearance was the release of his major label ('Columbia') debut, 'GRACE', an emotionally raw and occasionally claustrophobic listen that gained almost unanimous praise from UK critics and enjoyed a brief residence in the Top 50. Tracks such as 'SO REAL', 'LAST GOODBYE' and 'DREAM LOVER', suggested a mercurial talent in the ascendant, although the lad had possibly listened to too much LED ZEPPELIN as a youth. Eventually resuming his recording career early in 1997 with TOM VERLAINE (ex-TELEVISION) at the controls, JEFF looked like making a severe dent in the rock mainstream with a follow-up to 'GRACE', although subsequent sessions proved problematic. Fate was to deal a cruel hand when, on the 29th of May '98, JEFF, like his father before him, was cut down in his prime; hardly a typical rock'n'roll death, the young singer was swept away by a powerful current while swimming in Memphis harbor. Exactly a year later, the half-finished project BUCKLEY had been working on at the time of his death was posthumously released as 'SKETCHES FOR MY SWEETHEART THE DRUNK'. A double CD partly curated by his mother, the UK Top 10 set gave an indication as to where JEFF was headed as well as serving as a convincing last word on the career of a man many considered a genius. Well, it wasn't quite the last word, that honour falling to 'MYSTERY WHITE BOY: LIVE '95-'96

(2000), a collection of live performances culled from the DAT recordings of his 'Grace' tour. Like the posthumous live recordings of his father, this record will no doubt be cherished by hardcore fans although its interest to the wider music buying public (outside the UK where it hit the Top 10) might well be more limited. • **Covers:** JE N'EN CONNAIS PAS LA FIN (Edith Piaf) / THE WAY YOUNG LOVERS DO (Van Morrison) / LILAC WINE (Elkie Brooks) / HALLELUJAH (Leonard Cohen) / KANGA ROO (Big Star) / KICK OUT THE JAMS (MC5) / YARD OF BLONDE GIRLS (Audrey Clark) / BACK IN N.Y.C. (Genesis) / SATISFIED MIND (J.Hayes & J.Rhodes).

Album rating: LIVE AT SIN-E mini (*6) / GRACE (*8) / SKETCHES FOR MY SWEETHEART THE DRUNK (*8) / MYSTERY WHITE BOY (*6) / LIVE A L'OLYMPIA (*5)

JEFF BUCKLEY – vocals, guitars, harmonium, organ, dulcimer / with **MICK GRONDAHL** – bass / **MATT JOHNSON** – drums, percussion / plus MICHAEL TIGHE – guitar / **GARLY LUCAS** – magicalguitarness

		Big Cat	Columbia
Apr 94.	(m-lp/m-cd) (ABB 61/+CD) <77296> **LIVE AT SIN-E (live)**		

– Mojo pin / Eternal life / Je n'en connais pas la fin / The way young lovers do.

		Columbia	Columbia
Aug 94.	(cd/c/lp) (475928-2/-4/-1) <57528> **GRACE**		50

– Mojo pin / Grace / Last goodbye / Lilac wine / So real / Hallelujah / Lover, you should've come over / Corpus christi Carol / Eternal life / Dream brother. *(lp re-iss. Jun99 on 'Simply Vinyl'; SVLP 77)*

May 95.	(cd-s) <475928> **LAST GOODBYE / LAST GOODBYE (edit) / KANGA-ROO**		-
May 95.	(10"ep/cd-ep) (662042-0/-2) **LAST GOODBYE. / LOVER, YOU SHOULD'VE COME OVER (live) / TONGUE (live)**	54	-

(cd-ep) (662042-5) – ('A'side) / Dream brother (live) / So real (live).

1996.	(m-cd) <662155> **LIVE FROM THE BATACLAN (live)**	-	-

– Dream brother / The way young lovers do / Je n'en connais pas la fin / Hallelujah.

—— sadly, JEFF was to die in a drowning accident on the 29th of May '97

– posthumous releases, etc. –

May 98.	(d-cd/d-c/d-lp) (488661-2/-4/-1) <67228> **SKETCHES FOR MY SWEETHEART THE DRUNK**	7	64

– The sky is a landfill / Everybody here wants you / Opened once / Nightmares by the sea / Yard of blonde girls / Witches' rave / Morning theft / Vancouver / You & I / Nightmares by the sea (alt) / New Year's prayer / Haven't you heard / I know we could be so happy baby (if we wanted to be) / Murder suicide meteor slave / Back in N.Y.C. / Gunshot glitter *[cd-only]* / Demon John / Your flesh is so nice / Jewel box / Satisfied mind.

May 98.	(cd-ep) (665791-2) **EVERYBODY HERE WANTS YOU / THOUSAND FOLD / ETERNAL LIFE (road version) / HALLELUJAH (live)**	43	-

(cd-ep) (665791-5) – ('A'side) / Lover, you should've come over (live and acoustic) / Tongue (live).

May 00.	(cd/c/lp) (497972-2/-4/-1) <69592> **MYSTERY WHITE BOY – LIVE '95-'96**	8	-

– Dream brother / I woke up in a strange place / Mojo pin / Lilac wine / What will you say / Last goodbye / Eternal life / Grace / Moodswing whiskey / The man that got away / Kanga-roo / Hallelujah - I know it's over. *(d-cd+=; 497972-9)* – That's all I ask / Lover, you should've come over / So real. *(cd re-iss. Apr02; same)*

Oct 01.	(cd) (503204-9) **LIVE A L'OLYMPIA (live)**	-	-

– Lover, you should have come over / Dream brother / Eternal life / Kick out the jams / Lilac wine / Grace / That's all I ask / Kashmir / Je n'en connais pas la fin / Hallelujah / What will you say (with ALIM QASIMOV).

Oct 02.	(cd) (501178-2) **THE GRACE EP'S**		-

– others, etc. –

Oct 02.	(cd) Circus; (FYL 014) **SONGS TO NO ONE 1991-1992**		-

BUDDHA ON THE MOON

Formed: Houston, Texas, USA ... early 1990's. Essentially a solo project, BUDDHA ON THE MOON was the moniker adopted by H.K. KAHNG when he released the EP, 'ALLES IST GUT', in 1993. Over the next few years, KAHNG issued a number of other singles and leant his hand to remixing for other acts such as the ELECTROSONICS. In 1997, WARREN DEFEVER (of HIS NAME IS ALIVE) produced the BUDDHA ON THE MOON EP, 'CREPE PAPER AIRPLANE'. DEFEVER'S production afforded the music more focus than there had been on KAHNG's previous lo-fi efforts. The album 'STRATOSPHERIC' was released later the same year and received warm critical acclaim for its engaging blissed-out tone and KAHNG's passionate delivery. Another album, 'THE LAST AUTUMN DAY', followed in 1998, and showed KAHNG was influenced by genres other than just shoegazing. The album featured the BEATLES-esque song 'GLIDER' and an astonishing cover version of the Nick Drake track 'WHICH WILL'. KAHNG then took a sabbatical from BUDDHA to concentrate on his side-project, IMAGINARY FRIEND, a group he had formed with his wife NANCY. The band had already released the forgettable 'WHIMSY' single in 1997, while in 1998 they released the much-improved EP, 'LETTERS HOME'.

Album rating: STRATOSPHERIC (*6) / THE LAST AUTUMN DAY (*6)

H.K. KAHNG – vocals, instruments

		not iss.	Farrago
1993.	(7"ep; Various Artists) <frg-01> **ALLES IST GUT!**	-	
Feb 94.	(7") <frg-03> **BROKE. /**	-	
1994.	(10"ep) <frg-06> **TRANSLUCENCE**	-	
		not iss.	Entangled
1995.	(7") <001> **YARDSALE. / A DEEP SLEEP FOR STEPHEN**	-	

1996.	(7"ep) <QUID 006> **ON HOLIDAY. /**		not iss.	Quiddity
1996.	(7"ep) **CREPE PAPER EP**		-	-

		Drive-In – Farrago	Drive-In – Farrago
Jan 97.	(7") <drive 02> **HOW NEAR OR HOW FAR. / (other by The STEINBECKS)**	-	
Jun 97.	(cd) <(drive 12 – frg-010)> **STRATOSPHERIC**		

– As you said / Summershines / Now that you're a star / Judas Iscariot / Coastal hwys / Norfolk windmills / Of the clouds / My own private undoing.

1998.	(cd) <(drive 20 – frg-011)> **THE LAST AUTUMN DAY**		

– Stratospheric / Crepe paper airplane / Providence / Butterfly collector / Glider / Ordinary sky / The esplanade / Which will / ...Like a cold white light...

IMAGINARY FRIEND

H.K. + NANCY KAHNG

		not iss.	Drive-In
Mar 97.	(7"ep) <drive 06> **WHIMSY EP**	-	

– Marigold /

Nov 97.	(7"ep) <drive 17> **LETTERS HOME EP**		-
		Bad Jazz	not iss.
Jun 99.	(7") (BEBOP 6) **THE LEAVES. /**		-

BUFFALO DAUGHTER

Formed: Japan ... 1993 by SuGAR YOSHINAGA and YUMIKO OHNO alongside DJ, MOOG YAMAMOTO. Playing a hybrid of indie pop, trip hop and funky rock, the trio spliced their instrumental recordings with samples and electronica in a similar vein to MARK NISHITA (aka MONEY MARK) and legendary Brooklyn sound experimentalists, the BEASTIE BOYS. Debuting in 1994 with the album, 'SHAGGY HEADDRESSERS', and superseding this a year later with their sophomore set, 'AMOEBA SOUNDSYSTEM' (1995), the band unleashed their sound on their native country and began to gain notoriety further afield courtesy of their music being featured on various computer games and adverts. Quick to pick up on their unique sound was the BEASTIE BOYS' label, 'Grand Royal', who signed them up the ensuing year and released the single, 'LEGEND OF THE YELLOW BUFFALO' in 1996; their third full-length set, 'CAPTAIN VAPOUR ATHELETES', was hot its heels. To further push their sound and associate BUFF DAUGH with other luminaries working in the same aural field, the BEASTIES' subsequently issued the 'SOCKS, DRUGS AND ROCK & ROLL' EP, which featured remixes of their 'CAPTAIN ...' album, by MONEY MARK, JAMES LAVELLE's UNKLE, and ALEC EMPIRE. Capitalising on their new Stateside and European fanbase, the band from the land of the rising sun, ploughed on with their fourth set proper, 'NEW ROCK' (1998), a platter that showed a maturity in their songwriting and a new found balance between their own recorded material and adroit sample choices, producing something which stood between the likes of more dance orientated indie pop and DJ SHADOW's work on 'Psyence Fiction'. This was again followed by 'WXBD', a remix collaboration issued the following year alongside their fifth album, 'GREAT FIVE LAKES' (1999), another experimental slice of sonic mastery, but without the novel impact of the erstwhile release, 'NEW ROCK'.

Album rating: CAPTAIN VAPOUR ATHLETES (*5) / NEW ROCK (*6) / GREAT FIVE LAKES (*4)

SuGAR YOSHINAGA – vocals, multi / **YUMIKO OHNO** – vocals, multi / **MOOG YAMAMOTO** – turntables

		unknown	not iss.
1994.	(m-lp) **SHAGGY HEADDRESSERS**	-	- Japan
1995.	(m-lp) **AMOEBA SOUNDSYSTEM**	-	- Japan

<above two – US cd-iss. 1999 on 'Cardinal'; >

		Grand Royal	Grand Royal
Apr 97.	(7") <(GR 027)> **THE LEGEND OF THE YELLOW BUFFALO**		Jul96

– Cold summer / Daisy.

Apr 97.	(lp/cd) <(GR 030)> **CAPTAIN VAPOUR ATHLETES**		Aug96

– Counter parrot / Cold summer / Vampeeee / Silver turkey / California blues / Dr. Mooooog / Brush your teeth / Kelly / Big Wednesday / Baby amoeba goes south / LI303VE / Vapour action forever.

Jun 97.	(12"ep/cd-ep) <(GR 043/+CD)> **SOCKS, DRUGS AND ROCK AND ROLL**		

– Dr. Moog / Daisy pushed up / Big Wednesday / untitled / Daisy / Silver turkey.

Mar 98.	(12"ep/cd-ep) <(GR 056/+CD)> **NEW ROCK (Cornelius remix). / GREAT FIVE LAKES (mixes incl. by Kut Masta Kurt) / R&B (RHYTHM AND BASEMENT) (Elite Force remix)**		
Apr 98.	(d-lp/cd) <(GR 052/+CD)> **NEW ROCK**		Mar98

– New rock / R&B (Rhythm & Basement) / Great five lakes / What's the trouble with my silver.... / Autobacs / Socks, drugs and rock'n'roll / Airport rock / Super blooper / Sad guitar / No Tokyo / No new rock / Sky high / Down sea / Jellyfish blues.

Sep 99.	(m-cd) <(GR 078CD)> **WXBD (remixes)**		

– Great five lakes / Super blooper / Great five lakes / Sky high + down sea / Socks, drugs and rock'n'roll / R&B (Rhythm & Basement) / Jellyfish blues / Super blooper.

BUFFALO SPRINGFIELD

Formed: Los Angeles, California, USA ... March '66. In a well-documented incident, STEPHEN STILLS and guitarist RICHIE FUREY were caught in a traffic jam on Sunset Strip, when by pure chance, STILLS recognised the driver of a black hearse, NEIL YOUNG. Along with bass player and fellow Canadian BRUCE PALMER, YOUNG had travelled down to Hollywood to try his luck in the fabled City of Angels. This fated get-together also led to another member being recruited, drummer DEWEY MARTIN. STILLS and YOUNG clashed right from the off, but it was essentially this tension that fuelled the band's creative spark in a JAGGERS/RICHARDS kind of fashion. Taking their name from a type of steamroller, and with the help of the SONNY & CHER management team of CHARLIE GREENE and BRIAN STONE, the band were signed to Atlantic offshoot 'Atco' in a matter of months. With the combined talent of STILLS and YOUNG's soaring harmonies and driving rhythm, the band often came on like a country-fied BEATLES, although their albums are notable for their striking stylistic diversity. The ambitiously eccentric, YOUNG-penned debut single, 'NOWADAYS CLANCY CAN'T EVEN SING', did nothing, while 'BURNED', the 2-minute pop thrill of a follow-up, fared equally badly. But then STILLS struck gold with the famous protest anthem 'FOR WHAT IT'S WORTH', released in the same month as the band's fine eponymous debut album. The song concerned itself with the previous summer's riots whereby a coterie of businessmen had threatened Sunset Strip's nightlife by proposing the building of a business district. Of course the students were none too happy, especially when 300 protesters were arrested. The song was duly adopted by rebels everywhere as a general mascot for fighting the good fight, and its vaguely psychedelic, menacing tone perfectly evoked the feelings of persecution felt by the emerging flower children. Throughout 1967, the band was rocked by internal squabbling with various members coming and going. An album, 'STAMPEDE', was recorded but never quite completed. It later surfaced as a bootleg and one track from it, 'DOWN TO THE WIRE', featuring an impassioned YOUNG vocal, was included on his, 'DECADE' (1976) compilation. YOUNG also missed the bands slot at the Monterey Pop Festival, DAVID CROSBY taking his place. Despite all this, the band completed a follow-up, 'BUFFALO SPRINGFIELD AGAIN', which was issued in late '67. Opinions on the album are mixed with some critics deeming it a classic of its time, others criticising its watered down production. The best moments are YOUNG's JACK NITZSCHE-arranged numbers, 'BROKEN ARROW' and 'EXPECTING TO FLY', the latter possessed a haunting, lysergic quality. STILL's compositions, 'BLUEBIRD' and 'ROCK AND ROLL WOMAN', lack the sophistication of YOUNG's surreal epics but are enjoyable none the less. The tension between YOUNG and STILLS eventually finished the band (DAVID CROSBY once commenting that they used their guitars as weapons, on stage and off!) with a final album, 'LAST TIME AROUND', released after the split. YOUNG contributed the fragile 'I AM A CHILD' and one other song before leaving the band early on during the sessions. YOUNG went on to an erratic, often mercurial career, while STILLS went off to help form CROSBY, STILLS and NASH (re-united with YOUNG in 1970). FURAY meanwhile, went off to join country rockers POCO. Along with The BYRDS and LOVE, BUFFALO SPRINGFIELD were one of the most influential, if somewhat short-lived bands to come out of L.A.

Album rating: BUFFALO SPRINGFIELD (*7) / BUFFALO SPRINGFIELD AGAIN (*9) / LAST TIME AROUND (*6) / THE BEST OF BUFFALO SPRINGFIELD ... RETROSPECTIVE compilation (*8) / EXPECTING TO FLY compilation (*7)

STEPHEN STILLS (b. 3 Jan'45, Dallas, Texas) – lead guitar, vocals / **NEIL YOUNG** (b.12 Nov'45, Toronto, Canada) – lead guitar, vocals / **RICHIE FURAY** (b. 9 May'44, Dayton, Ohio) – vocals, guitar / **BRUCE PALMER** (b. 1944, Liverpool, Canada) – bass; repl. KEN KOBLUN / **DEWEY MARTIN** (b.30 Sep'42, Chesterfield, Canada) – drums (ex-DILLARDS)

		Atlantic	Atco
Oct 66.	(7") <6428> **NOWADAYS CLANCY CAN'T EVEN SING. / GO AND SAY GOODBYE**	-	-
Dec 66.	(7"w-drawn) <6452> **BURNED. / EVERYBODY'S WRONG**	-	-
Jan 67.	(lp; stereo/mono) (588/587 070) <SD+/33-200> **BUFFALO SPRINGFIELD** – Don't scold me (*) / Go and say goodbye / Sit down I think I love you / Nowadays Clancy can't even sing / Everybody's wrong / Hot dusty roads / Flying on the ground / Burned / Do I have to come right out and say it? / Leave / Pay the price / Out of my mind. <re-iss. Feb67 stereo/mono; SD+/33-200-A> – For what it's worth (repl.track (*); hit US No.80> (re-iss. 1971; K 30028) (cd-iss. Feb93; 7567 90389-2)		Dec66
Jan 67.	(7") (584 077) <6459> **FOR WHAT IT'S WORTH. / DO I HAVE TO COME RIGHT OUT AND SAY IT?**		7

on stage KEN KOBLUN and **JIM FIELDER**, latter of The MOTHERS, repl. PALMER, although PALMER did return occasionally. / **DOUG HASTINGS** – guitar repl. YOUNG (also DAVID CROSBY guested at Monterey)

BOB WEST – bass & **CHARLIE CHIN** – banjo deputise for above reshuffles

| Jul 67. | (7") <6499> **BLUEBIRD. / MR. SOUL** | - | 58 |

STILLS, FURAY, MARTIN and the returning YOUNG recruit **JIM MESSINA** (b. 5 Dec'47, Maywood, Calif.) – bass repl. FIELDER who joined BLOOD SWEAT & TEARS

Oct 67.	(7") (584 145) <6519> **ROCK'N'ROLL WOMAN. / A CHILD'S CLAIM TO FAME**		44 Sep67
Jan 68.	(lp; stereo/mono) (588/587 091) <SD+/33-226> **BUFFALO SPRINGFIELD AGAIN** – Mr. Soul / A child's claim to fame / Everydays / Expecting to fly / Bluebird / Hung upside down / Sad memory / Good time boy / Rock'n'roll woman / Broken arrow. (re-iss. 1971; K 40014) (cd-iss. Jul88; 790 391-2)		44 Nov67
Feb 68.	(7") (584 165) <6545> **EXPECTING TO FLY. / EVERYDAYS**		98 Jan68
Jun 68.	(7") (584 189) <6572> **UNO MUNDO. / MERRY-GO-ROUND**		-
Aug 68.	(7") <6602> **KIND WOMAN. / SPECIAL CARE**	-	

with original line-up they recorded another album, but they had split by May'68. MESSINA who had always been their sound recordist posthumously assembled line-up

| Oct 68. | (7") <6615> **ON THE WAY HOME. / FOUR DAYS GONE** | - | 82 |
| Dec 68. | (lp) (228 024) <SD33-256> **LAST TIME AROUND**
– On the way home / It's so hard to wait / Pretty girl why / Four days gone / Carefree | 42 | Aug68 |

country day / Special care / The hour of not quite rain / Questions / I am a child / Merry-go-round / Uno mundo / Kind woman. (re-iss. 1971; K 40077) (cd-iss. Mar94 on 'Atco'; 7567 90393-2)

— After their split, NEIL YOUNG went solo and joined STEPHEN STILLS in CROSBY, STILLS NASH & YOUNG. FURAY formed POCO adding later MESSINA. DEWEY MARTIN tried in vain to use BUFFALO SPRINGFIELD name.

– compilations, etc. –

on 'Atlantic' UK / 'Atco' US; unless otherwise mentioned

Mar 69.	(lp) (228 012) <SD33-283> **RETROSPECTIVE – THE BEST OF BUFFALO SPRINGFIELD** – For what it's worth / Mr. Soul / Sit down I think I love you / Kind woman / Bluebird / On the way home / Nowadays Clancy can't even sing / Broken arrow / Rock'n'roll woman / I am a child / Go and say goodbye / Expecting to fly. (re-iss. 1971; K 40071) (cd-iss. Jul88; 790 417-2)	42	Feb69
Oct 69.	(7") Atco; (226 006) **PRETTY GIRL WHY / QUESTIONS**	-	-
Oct 70.	(lp) (K 2462 012) **EXPECTING TO FLY**	-	-
Oct 72.	(7"ep) (K 10237) **BLUEBIRD / MR. SOUL. / ROCK'N'ROLL WOMAN / EXPECTING TO FLY**	-	-
Dec 73.	(d-lp) (K 70001) <SD2 806> **BUFFALO SPRINGFIELD**	-	-
Jul 01.	(4xcd-box) Rhino; <(8122 74324-2)> **BOX SET**	-	-

— some BUFFALO SPRINGFIELD live tracks appeared on NEIL YOUNG's compilation lp 'JOURNEY THROUGH THE PAST', and two on his 'DECADE' triple in '77.

BUFFALO TOM

Formed: Boston, Massachusetts, USA . . . 1986 by BILL JANOVITZ, CHRIS COLBOURN and TOM MAGINNIS. Signed to 'S.S.T.', the band debuted in summer '89 with an eponymous album of high octane melodic hardcore. Though drawing countless comparisons with DINOSAUR JR. (J. MASCIS produced them), the group ploughed on, developing their own unique sound and garnering critical praise for the impressive writing talents of JANOVITZ and COLBOURN. Somewhat akin to a grunge hybrid of HUSKER DU and VAN MORRISON, these soulful indie rockers signed to 'Beggars Banquet' subsidiary, 'Situation 2', for their follow-up set, 'BIRDBRAIN'. However, it was with the acclaimed 'LET ME COME OVER' (1992), that BUFFALO TOM's bruised beauty really began to resonate, the classic 'TAILLIGHTS FADE' warranting gushing but deserved praise from the music press. By taking their collective foot off the noise accelerator, the group had given the songs time to catch their breath and enjoy the scenery. This didn't translate into major sales, however, the record stalling just inside the UK Top 50. 'BIG RED LETTER DAY' (1993) went for a slicker sound, this approach paying off as the album became the first BUFFALO TOM record to make the Top 20. Released just prior to the band's 1995 Reading Festival appearance, 'SLEEPY EYED' proved that JANOVITZ and co. had the talent and ability to last the course, their sound noticeably more confident and mature. In fact, JANOVITZ was sufficiently sure of his talents to attempt a solo set in 1996, the rootsy 'LONESOME BILLY'. 'SMITTEN' (1998) was basically more of the same from the Boston crew, if a little more adventurous in the way of arrangements. JANOVITZ shone on the likes of the string-enhanced 'SCOTTISH WINDOWS' while fans of the BUFFALO mainman lapped up the stripped-bare beauty of his post-millennial solo set, 'UP HERE' (2001).
• **Covers:** SHE BELONGS TO ME (Bob Dylan) / HEAVEN (Psychedelic Furs) / THE SPIDER AND THE FLY (Rolling Stones) / ALL TOMORROW'S PARTIES (Velvet Underground) / BLUE (Rain Parade) / WAH WAH (George Harrison) / CUPID COME (My Bloody Valentine) / HAWAIIAN BABY (Spinnanes) / GUIDING STAR (Teenage Fanclub).

Album rating: BUFFALO TOM (*6) / BIRDBRAIN (*6) / LET ME COME OVER (*9) / (BIG RED LETTER DAY) (*8) / SLEEPY EYED (*8) / SMITTEN (*7) / ASIDES FROM BUFFALO TOM compilation (*9) / BESIDES: A COLLECTION OF B-SIDES AND RARITIES compilation (*5) / Bill Janovitz: LONESOME BILLY (*5) / UP HERE (*6)

BILL JANOVITZ – vocals, guitar / **CHRIS COLBOURN** – bass / **TOM MAGINNIS** – drums

		S.S.T.	S.S.T.
Oct 89.	(lp/c/cd) <(SST/+C/CD 250)> **BUFFALO TOM** – Sunflower suit / The plank / Impossible / 500,000 warnings / The bus / Racine / In the attic / Flushing stars / Walk away / Reason why. (cd re-iss. Apr92 on 'Megadisc'; MDC 7896) (re-iss. Oct92 on 'Beggars Banquet' lp/c/cd+=; BBQ LP/MC/CD 126) – Blue / Deep in the ground.		Jul89
		Caff Corp	not iss.
Feb 90.	(7"ltd) (CAFF 006) **ENEMY (live). / DEEP IN THE GROUND**		-
		Megadisc	Megadisc
Feb 90.	(7") (MD 5266) **SUNFLOWER SUIT. / BLUE**	-	- Dutch
Jun 90.	(12"/cd-s) <(MD 12/C 5276)> **CRAWL. / BLEEDING HEART / BLUE**		
		Situation 2	Beggars Banquet
Oct 90.	(12"ep) (SIT 71T) **BIRDBRAIN. / REASON WHY (live acoustic) / HEAVEN (acoustic)**		
Oct 90.	(cd)(c/lp) (SITU 31CD)(SIT C/U 31) <2434-2/-4> **BIRDBRAIN** – Birdbrain / Skeleton key / Caress / Guy who is me / Enemy / Crawl / Fortune teller / Baby / Directive / Bleeding heart. (cd+=) – Heaven (acoustic) / Reason why (live acoustic). (cd re-iss. Sep95 & Nov97 on 'Beggars Banquet'; BBL 31CD)		
May 91.	(12"ep/cd-ep) (SIT 77 T/CD) **FORTUNE TELLER. / STYMIED (acoustic) / WAH WAH (live) / BUMBLE BEE**		
		Situation 2	R.C.A.
Feb 92.	(12"ep/cd-ep) (SIT 86 T/CD) **VELVET ROOF. / CRUTCH / SALLY BROWN / SHE BELONGS TO ME**		

BUFFALO TOM (cont)

Mar 92. (cd)(c/lp) (SITU 36CD)(SIT C/U 36) <61105> **LET ME COME OVER** [49]
– Staples / Taillights fade / Mountains of your head / Mineral / Darl / Larry / Velvet roof / I'm not there / Stymied / Porchlight / Frozen lake / Saving grace. (cd+=/c=) – Crutch. (cd re-iss. Nov97 on 'Beggars Banquet'; BBL 36CD)

May 92. (10"ep/12"ep/cd-ep) (SIT 96 TT/T/CD) **TAILLIGHTS FADE / BIRDBRAIN (live). / LARRY (live) / SKELETON KEY (live)**
Beggars Banquet / Beggars Banquet

Oct 92. (7",7"green) (BBQ 6) **MINERAL. / SUNFLOWER SUIT**
(cd-s+=) (BBQ 6CD) – Crawl / The bus.

Sep 93. (cd/c/lp) (BBQ CD/MC/LP 142) <92292> **(BIG RED LETTER DAY)** [17]
– Sodajerk / I'm allowed / Tree house / Would not be denied / Latest monkey / My responsibility / Dry land / Torch singer / Late at night / Suppose / Anything that way. (cd re-iss. Nov97; BBL 142CD)

Sep 93. (12"ep/cd-ep) (BBQ 20 T/CD) **SODAJERK. / WOULD NOT BE DENIED. / WITCHES / THE WAY BACK**

Sep 93. (7") <98366> **SODAJERK. / WITCHES**

Nov 93. (7") (BBQ 25) **TREE HOUSE. / LATE AT NIGHT (live acoustic)**
(12"+=/cd-s+=) (BBQ 25 T/CD) – Let's make anything that way (live acoustic).
Beggars Banquet / Atlantic

Apr 94. (12"ep/cd-ep) (BBQ 30 T/CD) **I'M ALLOWED. / FOR ALL TO SEE / BUTTERSCOTCH**

Apr 94. (cd-ep) <95942> **I'M ALLOWED / BUTTERSCOTCH / ANYTHING THAT WAY (live acoustic) / LATE AT NIGHT (live acoustic)**
Beggars Banquet / East West

Jun 95. (10"ep/cd-ep) (BBQ 49 TT/CD) **SUMMER. / CLOUDS / DOES THIS MEAN YOU'RE NOT MY FRIEND?**

Jul 95. (cd/c/lp) (BBQ CD/MC/LP 177) <61782> **SLEEPY EYED** [31]
– Tangerine / Summer / Kitchen door / Rules / It's you / When you discover / Sunday night / Your stripes / Sparklers / Clobbered / Sundress / Twenty-points (the ballad of sexual dependency) / Souvenir / Crueler. (cd re-iss. Nov97; BBL 177CD)

Nov 95. (7"orange) (BBQ 64) **TANGERINE. / BREATHE**
(cd-s+=) (BBQ 64CD) – The spider and the fly.
Beggars Banquet / Polydor

Sep 98. (7") (BBQ 329) **WISER (edit). / CUPID COME**
(cd-s+=) (BBQ 329CD) – Hawaiian baby.

Sep 98. (cd/lp) (BBQ CD/LP 205) <557867> **SMITTEN**
– Rachael / Postcard / Knot it in / The bible / Scottish windows / White paint morning / Wiser / See to me / Register side / Do you in / Under milkwood / Walking wounded.

Feb 99. (cd-s) (BT 2000CD) **KNOT IN IT / RACHEL / POSTCARD (radio session)**
(above issued on 'Megadisc', below issued on 'Ignition')

Oct 99. (7"/c-s/cd-s) (IGN/+SMC/SCD 16) **GOING UNDERGROUND. / Liam Gallagher & Steve Craddock: CARNATION** [6]

Sep 00. (cd) (BEGA 2028CD) <82028> **ASIDES FROM BUFFALO TOM – THE BEST OF 1988-1999** (compilation) Aug00
– Summer / Sodajerk / Taillights fade / Mineral / Kitchen door / Enemy / Sunflower suit / Tree house / Larry / Postcard / Tangerine / Rachael / I'm allowed / Birdbrain / Velvet roof / Going underground / Late at night / Wiser (single edit).

May 02. (cd) (BBL 2033CD) <82033> **BESIDES: A COLLECTION OF B-SIDES AND RARITIES** (compilation)
– Witches / For all to see / She belongs to me / Bumble bee / Never noticed / The way back / Sally Brown / Hawaiian baby / Butterscotch / Wah-wah / Anchors aweigh / Breathe / The spider and the fly / Clouds / Cupid come / Does this mean you're not my friend? / Guiding star / All tomorrow's parties.

BILL JANOVITZ

with **JOEY BURNS** – upright bass, vocals / **JOHN CONVERTINO** – drums / and guests CRAIG SCHUMACHER, HOWE GELB + NEIL HARRY
Beggars Banquet / Beggars Banquet

Dec 96. (cd/lp) (BBQ CD/LP 186) <80186> **LONESOME BILLY** Jan97
– Girl's club / Think of all / Shoulder / Gaslight / Ghost in my piano / Strangers / My funny valentine / Peninsula / Talking to the Queen / Red balloon.

— now with **PHIL AIKEN** – keyboards + **CHRIS TOPPIN** – vocals
not iss. / Spin Art

Aug 01. (cd) <SPIN 93> **UP HERE**
– Atlantic / Best kept secret / Up here / Half a heart / Goodnight, whereever you are / Minneapolis / Like you do / Like shadows / Light in December / Long island.

BUFF MEDWAYS
(see under ⇒ CHILDISH, Wild Billy; 70's section)

BUILT TO SPILL

Formed: Boise, Idaho, USA . . . early 90's by songwriter and chief, DOUGH MARTSCH, who had just left TREEPEOPLE. Basically a one-man operation (with bassist BRETT NELSON and drummer RALF in tow), BUILT TO SPILL first emerged in 1993 with the 'ULTIMATE ALTERNATIVE WAVERS' album on 'C/Z' records, MARTSCH subsequently securing a deal with Seattle's Up!' label ('City Slang' in the UK and Europe) and releasing the acclaimed 'THERE'S NOTHING WRONG WITH LOVE' in late '94; RALF had now been replaced by ANDY CAPPS. The album's beguiling blend of strident, largely acoustic guitar and strings engendered enough underground support to see BTS secure a series of dates on the following year's Lollapalooza tour (by which point the band's ever varying line-up consisted of MARTSCH, a rhythm section of JAMES BERTRAM and DAVE SCHNEIDER plus cellist JOHN McMAHON, the latter becoming a permanent fixture) as well as a prestigious support slot to the FOO FIGHTERS. In the ensuing A&R melee, 'Warners' won their signatures and bundled them off to the studio to what turned out to be a jinxed third album. Although SCOTT PLOUFF had replaced SCHNEIDER as a permanent sticksman, the sessions didn't exactly go smoothly and after some material was eventually laid down, damage to the tapes forced the trio to begin from scratch. 'Warners' bailed out at this point, the album eventually surfacing in the form of the appropriately titled 'PERFECT FROM NOW ON' (1997) via 'Up!/City Slang'. Embellished by the cello of McMAHON and mellotron of ROBERT ROTH, the album was met with glowing praise from the press, MARTSCH no doubt breathing a sigh of relief to see his work in the shops at last. BUILT TO SPILL did however appear on the 'Warner Bros' roster in early 1999, through their classiest effort yet, 'KEEP IT LIKE A SECRET', a record that gained a well-deserved high spot of No.120 in the Billboard charts. MARTSCH and Co released two further post-millennium sets, the customary 'LIVE' (2000) and the US Top 100 breaker, 'ANCIENT MELODIES OF THE FUTURE' (2001), the latter another swaggering move forwards. • Covered: BY THE WAY (Heavenly) / SOME THINGS LAST A LONG TIME (Jad Fair & Daniel Johnston) / CORTEZ THE KILLER (Neil Young) / SINGING SORES MAKE PERFECT SWORDS (Love As Laughter) / VIRGINIA REEL AROUND THE FOUNTAIN (Halo Benders). • Note: For MARTSCH's other work with The HALO BENDERS, see under BEAT HAPPENING (his sidekick being the outfit's leader, CALVIN JOHNSON).

Album rating: ULTIMATE ALTERNATIVE WAVERS (*6) / THERE'S NOTHING WRONG WITH LOVE (*6) / PERFECT FROM NOW ON (*8) / KEEP IT LIKE A SECRET (*8) / LIVE (*5) / ANCIENT MELODIES OF THE FUTURE (*6)

DOUGH MARTSCH (ex-TREEPEOPLE, of-HALO BENDERS) – vocals, guitar / **BRETT NELSON** – bass, etc (ex-BUTTERFLY TRAIN) / **RALF** – drums
not iss. / C/Z

Oct 93. (cd) **ULTIMATE ALTERNATIVE WAVERS**
– The first song / Three years ago today / Revolution / Shameful dread / Nowhere nothin' fuckup / Get a life / Built to spill / Lie for a lie / Hazy / Built too long (pts.1, 2 & 3). (UK-iss.Jan96 on 'Fire'; FIRECD 51)

— **ANDY CAPPS** – drums (ex-BUTTERFLY TRAIN) repl. RALF
City Slang / Up!

Sep 95. (7") (EFA 04962-7) **CAR. / SCARIN**
(cd-s+=) (EFA 04962-2) – Some things last a long time.

Oct 95. (cd/lp) (EFA 04963/2-1) <UP 006> **THERE'S NOTHING WRONG WITH LOVE** Sep94
– In the morning / Reasons / Big dipper / Car / Fling / Cleo / The source / Twin falls / Somer / Distopian dream girl / Israel's song / Stab. (cd+=) – (hidden track).

Oct 95. (cd-ep; shared with CAISTIC RESIN) <018> **EP**
– When not being stupid is not enough / One thing / (other two by CAUSTIC RESIN).

Dec 95. (7") (EFA 04970-7) **IN THE MORNING. / SO AND SO SO AND SO FROM WHEREVER WHEREVER**
(cd-s+=) (EFA 04970-2) – Terrible perfect.

— **SCOTT PLOUF** – drums (ex-SPINANES) repl. JAMES DILLON
— added guests **ROBERT ROTH** – mellotron / **JOHN McMAHON** – cello
— abandoned by 'Warners' when master tapes were damaged

Feb 97. (cd/lp) (EFA 04992-26/08) <UP 033> **PERFECT FROM NOW ON**
– Randy described eternity / I would hurt a fly / Stop the show / Made up dreams / Velvet waltz / Out of site / Kicked in the sun / Untrustable (part 2).
City Slang / Warners

Feb 99. (cd) (847171-2) <46952> **KEEP IT LIKE A SECRET** Jan97
– The plan / Center of the universe / Carry the zero / Sidewalk / Bad light / Time trap / Else / You were right / Temporarily blind / Broken chairs.

Feb 99. (7") <(IPU 89)> **BY THE WAY. / Marine Research: SICK & WRONG**
(above issued on 'K')

Jun 99. (7") (08723-7) **CENTER OF THE UNIVERSE. / FORGET REMEMBER WHEN**
(cd-s) (08723-2) – ('A'side) / Now and then / Big dipper (live acoustic) / Kicked it in the sun (live acoustic).

Aug 99. (cd-ep) (URA 008) **CARRY THE ZERO EP**
– Carry the zero / Sidewalk / Forget remember when / Now and then / Kicked it in the sun (live) / Big dipper (live).
(above issued on 'Spunk')

May 00. (cd) (20161-2) **LIVE (live)**
– The plan / Randy described eternity / Stop the show / Virginia reel around the fountain / Cortez the killer / Car / Singing sores make perfect swords / I would hurt a fly / Broken chairs.

Jul 01. (cd) <47954> **ANCIENT MELODIES OF THE FUTURE** [94]
– Strange / The host / In your mind / Alarmed / Trimmed and burning / Happiness / Don't try / You are / Fly around my pretty little miss / The weather.

– compilations, etc. –

May 96. (cd) K; <(KLP 52CD)> **THE NORMAL YEARS** Apr96
– So and so so and so wherever / Shortcut / Car / Some things last a long time / Girl / Joyride / Some / Sick and wrong / Still flat / Terrible – Perfect.

BUNNYGRUNT

Formed: Webster Grove / St. Louis, Missouri, USA . . . 1993 by MATT HAMISH, RENEE DULLUM and KAREN REED. After debuting on the 'Silly Moo' label in 1993 (with 'CRIMINAL BOY'), the pretty twee-pop trio issued a collection of 7" singles and EP's (notably the strange 'STANDING HAMPTON' and 'THE BUNNYGRUNT FAMILY NOTE BOOK') before a shift to 'No life' in 1995. The debut album, 'ACTION PANTS!', followed, the record proving to be a complete mess due to the band's personnel upheavals.

Rumour had it that when bassist DULLUM departed during the sessions for the album, she wouldn't grant the band any of her material, resulting in a shambolic and short release. Recruiting new bassist JEN WOLFE, the band returned on top form with deliberately uptempo 'JEN-FI', a corker of a record spawning crazy pop tunes and equally crazy titles, eg. 'I HAVE JUST HAD BROKEN-HEART SURGERY, LOVE WON'T BYPASS ME AGAIN'.

Album rating: ACTION PANTS! mini (*4) / JEN-FI (*6)

MATT HAMISH – guitar / **RENEE DULLUM** – bass / **KAREN REED** – drums

			not iss.	Silly Moo
1993.	(7")	**CRIMINAL BOY. /**	-	No Life
			not iss.	
1994.	(7"ep)	**STANDING HAMPTON EP**	-	
1995.	(m-cd)	**ACTION PANTS!**	-	

– Superstar 666 / Transportation pants / I am curious partridge / Just like suppertime / G.I.2k / Criminal boy / Tadpole / Open up and say Oblina.

—— RENEE departed prior to above taking several songs with her

—— **JEN WOLFE** – bass; repl. RENEE

1996.	(7") <MAR 015> **THE BUNNYGRUNT FAMILY NOTEBOOK**	-	

– Inanimate objects / Fish of life.
(above issued on 'March') (below on 'Aeptophilia')

Nov 96.	(7") **BLUE CHRISTMAS. /**	-	
1996.	(7") <001> **JOHNNY ANGEL. /**	-	
1997.	(7"; as the APRICOTS) <002> **EVERYDAY. /**	-	

(above 2 issued on 'Septophilia') (below on 'Kitty-Boo')

| 1997. | (7"ep) <BOO!-002> **TEAM BUNNYGRUNT vs. TEAM TULLYCRAFT** | - | |

– No name slob / The ballad of Floppy and the charmers / (two by TULLYCRAFT).

| 1998. | (cd) <NL 017> **JEN-FI** | - | |

– Big fake out / Wild summer, wow! / AM is for talkin', FM is for rockin' / Names of trees / Downbeat for danger / Jenny not any dots / Here come the vampires / We suspect he was trying to spell monkey / Constantly fighting / Last train to regretsville / Good tiger, bad tiger / Truly Vermont / Tommy can dance the rerun / Future home of planet reptile / I just had broken-heart surgery, love won't bypass me again.

BURNING AIRLINES (see under ⇒ JAWBOX)

BURNING BRIDES

Formed: Philadelphia, Pennsylvania, USA ... March 1999 by guitarist/vocalist DIMITRI COATS and bassist/girlfriend MELANIE CAMPBELL. They apparently dropped out of art school and spent two years travelling the States "in search of an environment responsive to their rock needs". After spells in Portland, San Francisco, and Boston, they finally settled in South Philadelphia, and soon hooked up with drummer MIKE AMBS. Their aggressive, heavy rock sets soon gained them an ardent following and after record label interest, the BB's finally signed with locally based 'File 13'; a US tour with acts such as ZEN GUERILLA and the GREENHORNES, also helped to a growing fanbase. Recorded in 2000, and released in 2001, debut LP 'FALL OF THE PLASTIC EMPIRE' achieved widespread acclaim, and led to comparisons with The PIXIES and er, AC/DC, amongst others. An album with a distinctly 'live' feel – probably due to the cavernous recording room – 'IF I'M A MAN' was brazen contemporary rock at its best.

Album rating: FALL OF THE PLASTIC EMPIRE (*8)

DIMITRI COATS – vocals, guitar / **MELANIE CAMPBELL** – bass / **MIKE AMBS** – drums

			File 13	File 13
Apr 01.	(cd) <FT 35> **FALL OF THE PLASTIC EMPIRE**		-	-

– Plank of fire / Glass slipper / If I'm a man / Arctic snow / At the levity ball / Stabbed in the back of the heart / Rainy days / Elevator / Blood on the highway / Plastic empire. (UK-iss.Feb02; same as US)

—— **JASON KOURKOUNIS** – drums (ex-MULE, ex-DELTA 72) repl. MIKE

			V2	not iss.
Nov 02.	(cd-ep) (VVR 502169-3) **GLASS SLIPPER EP**			-

– Glass slipper / Blood on the highway / Overhead metal erection.

BUSY SIGNALS

Formed: Minneapolis, Minnesota, USA ... 1999 as the musical moniker of solo artist HOWARD W. HAMILTON III. The erstwhile BABES IN TOYLAND road crew member sold off his car and bought himself a sampler and an eight-track in order to put down his odd brand of uptempo lo-fi indie pop. Debuting around late 1999 with the 7", 'HEADPHONEWORLD', HAMILTON followed it up with BUSY SIGNAL's full-length outing 'BABY'S FIRST BEATS' (2000). Comparisons to his work include BECK's 'Odelay' period and the type of trip-hop inspired pop of MONEY MARK. His ensuing sophomore LP, 'PRETEND HITS' (2001) was, by his own admission, "a party record for people who never go to parties". It held together some gems such as 'BUCKLE DOWN', a track featuring the rapping of PHONTE and the assistance of fellow Minnesotan HAR MAR SUPERSTAR. The succeeding year saw the double delivery of his third and fourth albums, 'PURE ENERGY' and 'BUSY BEATS', both sets marking his improved technical prowess and displaying his underlying keen sense of pop melody; meanwhile, HAMILTON also joined the outfit SAUCER.

Album rating: BABY'S FIRST BEATS (*6) / PRETEND HITS (*5) / PURE ENERGY (*5)

HOWARD W. HAMILTON III – electronics, etc

			Sugar Free	Sugar Free
Mar 00.	(cd) <(SF 017CD)> **BABY'S FIRST BEATS**			Jul00

– Headphoneworld / I'm so slippery / Birds on high / Clogged airways / Futon hopper / 88's and 73's / Low on the foodchain / Taxidermy / Stormy stormy stormy / Long funnel / Constantly awesome / Show me your gems / Ladies and germs. (lp-iss.Feb00 on 'Earworm'; WORM 61)

| May 00. | (7") <SUGARFREE 016-7> **HEADPHONEWORLD. / TOO MUCH TOGETHERNESS** | - | |
| Jul 00. | (7"m) (BEBOP 20) **ALL THE YOUNG DESIGNERS. / EXPLORIN' / WHALEWATCH** | | - |

(above issued on 'Bad Jazz')

| Jul 01. | (cd) <SF 022CD> **PRETEND HITS** | - | |

– The new you / Buckle down / The freeway / All the young designers / Attention please / She's got soul / Hyper reality check / We still give a fuck / Fresh like a clear gel / Keep busy / Busy busy busy / Tomorrow's ways today.

| Mar 02. | (cd) <SF 023CD> **PURE ENERGY** | - | |

– Pure energy / Friend of a friend / The freeway / Autopilot / Explorin' / Cans / Better books / Go lite / Whalewatch / All the young designers / Too much togetherness / Autopilot.

– compilations, etc. –

| Apr 02. | (cd) Sidewinder; <(SDWR 2)> **BUSY BEATS** | | |

– Headphoneworld / The new you / Freeway / Long funnel / Birds on nigh / Constantly awesome / All the young designers / Clogged airways / Low on the foodchain / We still give a fuck / She's got soul / Keep busy / I'm so slippery / Tomorrow's ways today. (re-iss. Sep02; same)

BUSYTOBY (see under ⇒ WOLFIE)

Bernard BUTLER

Born: 1 May'70, Stamford Hill, London, England. Temporarily putting aside his violin and piano, BUTLER took up guitar as a young teenager, idolizing JOHNNY MARR (of The SMITHS) in the mid-80's. In 1989, after an unsuccessful year at London's Queen Mary College, he answered an ad in the NME; it was to join SUEDE. His creative and imaginative songwriting helped the band and their chief wordsmith, BRETT ANDERSON reach the heady heights in the first half of the 90's, although a personality clash with the SUEDE mainman led BUTLER to seek out pastures new in the summer of '94. After a brief spell working with ALL ABOUT EVE singer JULIANNE REGAN, he began putting pen to paper once more in his new London abode (shared with wife, Elisa). He provided the song, 'YES', for the up and coming, flashily extravagant soul singer, DAVID McALMONT, thus the partnership McALMONT & BUTLER duly signed to Virgin offshoot, 'Hut'. A terrific follow-up single, 'YOU DO', gave the pair another UK Top 20 hit, while the accompanying album, 'THE SOUND OF...' became their swansong in late 1995; unfortunately they just couldn't stop backstabbing each other in the press. BERNARD subsequently worked with BRYAN FERRY, AIMEE MANN, EDWYN COLLINS, EDDI READER, NENEH CHERRY and made a substantial contribution to the BOOTH & THE BAD ANGEL project (aka TIM BOOTH of JAMES and ANGELO "Twin Peaks" BADALAMENTI). The following year (1997), BUTLER signed to 'Creation' and worked on his debut solo album, 'PEOPLE MOVE ON'. Released in the Spring of '98 and containing two Top 30 hits, 'STAY' and 'NOT ALONE', it knocked on the door of the Top 10 after receiving rave reviews. A largely acoustic affair the record saw BUTLER re-invent himself as a tortured balladeer, although the OTT production and ghosts of his more elaborate recent past seemed to haunt him. The esteemed guitarist went on to play the festival circuit, his axework outshining even the great MARR, especially his electric set at 'T In The Park'. Although it barely nudged the Top 50, 'FRIENDS AND LOVERS' (1999) offered further proof that BUTLER was a meticulous rock classicist. While there was nary a trace of the ruminating acoustica he'd so lovingly crafted on his debut, the album reflected BUTLER's genuine and convincing dedication to decadent 70's Brit-rock.

Album rating: PEOPLE MOVE ON (*6) / FRIENDS AND LOVERS (*5)

BERNARD BUTLER – vocals, guitar (ex-SUEDE, ex-McALMONT & BUTLER) / with **MAKOTO SAKAMOTO** – drums / and guests **DENISE JOHNSON** – backing vocals / **NICK WOLLAGE** – sax / **EDWYN COLLINS** – vocals / **GEORGE SHILLING** – cello / **RICHARD BISSILL** – French horn / & The Brilliant Strings conducted by BILLY McGEE: GINI BALL, JACKIE NORRIE, MARGARET ROSEBERRY, ANNE WOOD, ANNA HEMERY, SALLY HERBERT + ANNE STEPHENSON – violins / CHRIS PITISILLIDES + ELLEN BLAIR – viola / DINAH BEAMISH + SIAN BELL – cello

			Creation	Columbia
Jan 98.	(7"/c-s) (CRE/+CS 281) **STAY. / HOTEL SPLENDIDE**		12	-
	(cd-s+=) (CRESCD 281) – Sea.			
Mar 98.	(7"/c-s) (CRE/+CS 289) **NOT ALONE. / BYE BYE**		27	-
	(cd-s+=) (CRESCD 289) – It's alright.			
Apr 98.	(cd/lp)(c) (CRE CD/LP 221)(CCRE 221) <69332> **PEOPLE MOVE ON**		11	

– Woman I know / You just know / People move on / A change of heart / Autograph / You light the fire / Not alone / When you grow / You've got what it takes / Stay / In vain / I'm tired. (cd re-iss. Jan01; same)

Jun 98.	(7"/c-s) (CRE/+CS 297) **A CHANGE OF HEART. / MY DOMAIN**		45	-
	(cd-s+=) (CRESCD 297) – More than I thought.			
Oct 99.	(7"/c-s/cd-s) (CRE/+CS/SCD 324) **YOU MUST GO ON. / (version)**		44	-

Oct 99. (cd/c/lp) *(CRECD/C-CRE/CRELP 248)* <63651> **FRIENDS AND LOVERS** □43 □Feb00
– Friends & lovers / I'd do it again if I could / Cocoon / Smile / You must go on / No easy way out / Everyone I know is falling apart / What happened to me / Let's go away / Precious / Has your mind got away? / You'll feel it when you're mine. *(cd re-iss. Jan01; same)*

Setanta Setanta

Jun 01. (cd-s; as BERNARD BUTLER & EDWYN COLLINS) *(SETCD 084)* <1084> **MESSAGE FOR JOJO / CAN'T DO THAT (THE HOOVER) / CLEAN** □ □Jul02
(12") *(SET 084T)* – ('A'-Trevor Jackson remix) / Can't do that (the hoover) (the Victorian Spaceman remix) / ('A'-radio edit).

BUTTERFLY CHILD

Formed: Belfast, N. Ireland ... 1991 by JOE CASSIDY who was the only permanent member. The band made their welcomed appearance in 1991 with two EP's on the 'H.ark' label (run by AR KANE) followed by a signing to 'Rough Trade' two years later and the release of the 'GHETTO SPEAK' EP. The debut album 'ONOMATAPOEIA' (1993) saw the group being categorised into the Brit pop and indie scene, when, actually, BUTTERFLY CHILD had a unique sound of their own, mixing JOHN CALE aesthetics with BRIAN WILSON-esque madness. Critically acclaimed, but providing low sales, the outfit issued 'HONEYMOON SUITE' in 1995 after signing with 'Dedicated' records. A shift to Chicago's 'Hit It!' records proved perfect timing for CASSIDY (and his revolving door of musicians) as he recorded and released what is known as the group's finest set to date, 'SOFT EXPLOSIVES' – an indie classic lost in an ignorant world of mainstream pop.

Album rating: ONOMATOPEIA (*6) / THE HONEYMOON SUITE (*6) / SOFT EXPLOSIVES (*7)

JOE CASSIDY – vocals, guitar / with **PACE** – bass / **WILLIAM SHARPE** – guitar / drum machine + **RICHARD THOMAS** – drums (ex-DIF JUZ) was also a p/t member

H.ark! not iss.

Nov 91. (cd-ep) **TOOTHFAIRY EP** □ □
1992. (ep) **EUCALIPTUS EP** □ □

Rough Trade not iss.

Jul 93. (12"ep/cd-ep) *(R 299-0/-3)* **GHETTO SPEAK EP** □ □
– Nymphs sing the blues / Kissed / Your lover, my harbour / Entertain these thoughts.
Aug 93. (cd/d-lp) *(R 308-2/-6)* **ONOMATAPOEIA** □ □
– Ave / Our lady Mississippi / Lunar eclipse / Who said what to whom? / Young virgins call for mutiny / X:celcius / Cancer killed Capricorn / Triumphant / Verte ecole / Stars light up Orleans / Queen glass / Eva. <*US cd-iss. Apr97 on 'Hit It!'; 4>*

Dedicated Hit It!

1994. (7") **JUICE. / MAN AND WOMAN** □ □
1994. (10"ep/cd-ep) *(CHILD 1 T/CD)* **BEAUJOLAIS ep** □ □
– Passion is the only fruit / Half a crown / Curtain call / One more pull on the hearts strings.
1995. (10"ep/cd-ep) *(CHILD 3 T/CD)* **FLAMING BURLESQUE ep** □ □
– Flaming burlesque (Odysseus mix) / Flaming burlesque (Icarus mix) / Charms me to sleep / Threadbare.
Feb 96. (cd/c/lp) *(DED CD/MC/LP 019)* <14> **THE HONEYMOON SUITE** □ □Oct97
– Mother have mercy / Passion is the only fruit / Ghost on your shoulder / Flaming burlesque / Unwashed, uncool / Carolina and the be bop review / Deep south / Louis as Anna / Six urchins / Botany Bay / Towns come tumblin' / I shall hear in Heaven.

— CASSIDY now with **GREG SURAN** – multi / **DAVID SUYCOTT** – drums / **JOHN HERNDON** – percussion, drums / **ELLIOT GOLUB** – violin / **EVERETT ZIATOFF-MIRSKY** – viola

Hit It! Hit It!

Aug 98. (cd) *(<HIT 24>)* **SOFT EXPLOSIVES** □ □Apr98
– Big soft mouth / Drunk on beauty / Holy hymn / Number one / When you return / Mad bird / Beautiful girls / 1929 / Someone's sister / Zeppelin catches fire at speed / Don't talk to me / Reprise / Gringo / Life without the compass / Sound of love breaking apart.

BUTTERGLORY

Formed: Visalia, California, USA ... early 1990's by MATT SUGGS and DEBBY VANDER WALL. Having relocated to Lawrence, Kansas, the group released their debut album 'CRUMBLE' in 1994. Although the record was let down by poor production, the group's obvious ability for crafting superb, jagged melodies was still evident. This was followed by a collection of singles and EP's that pre-dated the 'CRUMBLE' recordings. Although 'DOWNED' (1995) was a compilation, it sounded cohesive and, in fact, was better received than their aforementioned first trial. The BUTTERGLORY's next collection of original material 'ARE YOU BUILDING A TEMPLE IN HEAVEN?' was released in 1996. Unfortunately for the group their lo-fi, skewed guitar sound was seen as too similar to PAVEMENT, who, by this time, had cornered that section of the market. The group's final album 'RAT TAT TAT' (1997) saw them trying to escape the PAVEMENT comparisons by sacrificing the music's rawness in favour of a cleaner more consumer-friendly sound. The results were largely positive with the duo concentrating more on structure and melody and no longer hiding behind fuzz and noise. There was an even more subdued sound to MATT SUGGS' debut solo album 'GOLDEN DAYS BEFORE THEY END' (2000), his lazy, laconic vocals and straight forward guitar hooks echoed the KINKS circa 1970 or even BELLE AND SEBASTIAN. However, sinister lyrics depicting nightmarish characters afforded the album its own identity.

Album rating: CRUMBLE (*6) / DOWNED: A SINGLES COLLECTION compilation (*7) / ARE YOU BUILDING A TEMPLE IN HEAVEN? (*6) / RAT TAT TAT (*5) / Matt Suggs: GOLDEN DAYS BEFORE THEY END (*7)

MATT SUGGS – vocals, guitar / **DEBBY VANDER WALL** – vocals, drums / with guest **CRAIG COMSTOCK** – organ

Konkurrent Merge

1992. (7"ep) <*MRG 029*> **ALEXANDER BENDS EP** □ □
– Alexander bends / Luna / Bike / Two kings, one queen.
1993. (7"ep) <*MRG 046*> **OUR HEADS EP** □ □
– Pocket of scabs / Better gardens, better homes / Yeoman / Sad moustache men / Back of my hand / You are the drum.
Jul 94. (7"ep) <*lb 004*> **CURSIVE EP** □ □
– It took the first / Holding back / She can't hide from radios / Your nose, my head. (above issued on 'Little Brother')
Nov 94. (cd) <*MRG 071CD*> **CRUMBLE** □ □
– Waiting for the guns / Forty-four / Cactus / Jinxed / Peasants, kings / Trapped / Summer's Tom / Thimble / The skills of the star pilot / He left us nothing / Those Mooney stars / When we sleep / Ring finger / Our (proud) mascot / The drums were lost.
Jun 95. (d7"ep) <*MRG 084*> **WAIT FOR ME EP** □ □
– Stuck / A toast to the Queen / Demons and avalanches / Chump or champ?
Jul 95. (cd) <*MRG 087CD*> **DOWNED: A SINGLES COLLECTION** (compilation) □ □
– Stuck / A toast to the Queen / Demons and avalanches / Chump or champ? / Alexander bends / Luna / Bike / Two kings, one queen / Pocket of scabs / Better gardens, better homes / Yeoman / Sad moustache men / Back of my hand / You are the drum / It took the first / Holding back / She can't hide from radios / Your nose, my head.

— added **STEPHEN NARON** – bass / + guests **DAVID TRUMFIO** + **MIKE HAGLER** + **DEANNA VARAGONA** + **JONATHAN MARX**

Jan 96. (7"m) <*MRG 104*> **SHE'S GOT THE AKSHUN! / HAVEN'T YOU ALREADY HEARD? / PLACES IN THE MIND** □ □
May 96. (cd) <*(K 167) <MRG 098CD>* **ARE YOU BUILDING A TEMPLE IN HEAVEN?** □ □Feb96
– She clicks the sticks / The halo over your head / Sit in the car / You'll never be (as good as that) / Boy burning down / On button on / The captain stood sturdy / Edward Brown / She's got the akshun! / When her brow curls / Rivers / It's still raing / Handsome / The lion weeps tonight.

— now down to original duo again

Dec 97. (cd) <*(K 179) <MRG 133CD>* **RAT TAT TAT** □ □Oct97
– On a horse / Tundra / Novelty in two / Oh goodness / Come on! / Her comedy's a bore / Fight fight fight / Serpentine / Carmen cross / Widows smirk / Hexed / You said a mouthful / No beads or rosaries / Happy 1234.

MATT SUGGS

MATT – vocals, guitars (+ slide) / with **STEPHEN NARON** – bass / **JOHN ANDERSON** – percussion / **ED ROSE** – recorder

Merge Merge

Jun 00. (cd) <*(MRG 177CD)*> **GOLDEN DAYS BEFORE THEY END** □ □
– Skeleton blues (in B flat minor) / Soon the moon will glow / Eloise / Where's your patience, dear? / The rambler vs. the vulture – Devils dance / Harold had a hunch / Where's your patience, dear? / Farewell to a tightrope queen / Western zephyr / Rambler's ride / Walk with him / Kisses.

BUTTER 08 (see under ⇒ CIBO MATTO)

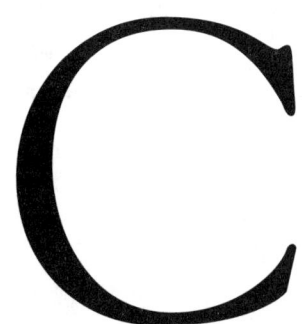

CADALLACA (see under ⇒ SLEATER-KINNEY)
CAGNEY & LACEE (see under ⇒ GALAXIE 500)

CAKE

Formed: Sacramento, California, USA ... 1994 by JOHN McCREA, GREG BROWN, VICTOR DAMIANI, VINCENT DI FIORE and TODD ROPER. Along with fellow mavericks, 311, the success of CAKE has helped resurrect that long-forgotten bastion of southern rock, 'Capricorn' records (once home to the legendary ALLMAN BROTHERS BAND). Don't expect mutton chops and slide guitar though, as CAKE were raised on more eclectic influences, CRACKER and THEY MIGHT BE GIANTS among them. McCREA and BROWN's complex guitar numbers were matched by countrified covers:- MULTIPLY THE HEARTACHES (Kathy Dee) / I WILL SURVIVE (hit; Gloria Gaynor) / PERHAPS, PERHAPS, PERHAPS (Davis-Farres) / SAD SONGS AND WALTZES (Willie Nelson). After a US-only album, 'MOTORCADE OF GENEROSITY' failed to gain much attention in '94/'95, they returned two years later, playing with much fervor on the million seller, 'FASHION NUGGET'. Two semi-classics were subsequently lifted from the record, both 'THE DISTANCE' and 'IT'S COMING DOWN' distinguished from the alternative rock pack by the hazily melancholy trumpet flurries of VINCENT DI FIORE. 1998 saw them break the US Top 40 once again with a further slice of post-ironic US indie, 'PROLONGING THE MAGIC', although their attempts to woo the mainstream were hit and miss. After changing labels from independent ('Capricorn') to Major ('Columbia'), the combo issued 'COMFORT EAGLE' (2001), a definite sequel to 1998's 'PROLONGING ...', with much the same CAKE mix. Acid Jazz, mariachi horns and catchy choruses all added to the experience, which although it was all fine and well, didn't exactly break the mould for the band or turn them into RADIOHEAD (CAKE doing RADIOHEAD? Now that would be interesting!). The single 'SHORT SKIRT – LONG TROUSERS' was fantastic and surprisingly didn't become a global smash as it featured McCREA's catchiest lyrics to date.

Album rating: MOTORCADE OF GENEROSITY (*4) / FASHION NUGGET (*6) / PROLONGING THE MAGIC (*6) / COMFORT EAGLE (*7)

JOHN McCREA – vocals, acoustic guitar, organ / **GREG BROWN** – electric guitar, organ / **VICTOR DAMIANI** – bass / **VINCENT DI FIORE** – trumpet, percussion / **TODD ROPER** – drums, percussion

			Capricorn	Capricorn
Nov 94.	(cd) <532 506-2> **MOTORCADE OF GENEROSITY**		-	-

– Commanche / Ruby sees all / Up so close / Pentagram / Jolene / Haze of love / You part the waters / Is this love? / Jesus wrote a blank cheque / Rock and roll lifestyle / I bombed Korea / Mr. Mastodon farm / Ain't no good. (UK-iss.Jul97; same)

Mar 97.	(7"/c-s) <574 220-7/-4> **THE DISTANCE. / STICK SHIFTS AND SAFETY NETS**	22	-

(cd-s) (574 220-2) – ('A'side) / Multiply the heartaches / Jolene (live) / It's coming down.

Mar 97.	(cd/c) <(532 857-2/-4)> **FASHION NUGGET**	53	36 Sep96

– Frank Sinatra / The distance / Friend is a four letter word / Open book / Daria / Race car ya-yas / I will survive / Stickshifts and safetybelts / Perhaps, perhaps, perhaps / It's coming down / Nugget / She'll come back to me / Italian leather sofa / Sad songs and waltzes. <clean version Sep97; 534228>

May 97.	(7"/c-s) <574 470-7/-4> **I WILL SURVIVE. / RUBY SEES ALL**	29	-

(cd-s+=) (574 470-2) – Rock'n'roll lifestyle.

Aug 97.	(7") (574 716-7) **FRANK SINATRA. / MR. MASTODON FARM**		-

(cd-s+=) (574 717-2) – ('A'live).

Oct 98.	(cd) <(538092-2)> **PROLONGING THE MAGIC**		33

– Satan is my motor / Mexico / Never there / Guitar / You turn the screws / Walk on by / Sheep go to Heaven / When you sleep / Hem of your garment / Alpha beta parking lot / Let me go / Cool blue reason / Where would I be?

Apr 99.	(c-s) (870810-7) <radio play> **NEVER THERE / I WILL SURVIVE**	66	78 Nov98

(cd-s) (870811-2) – ('A'side) / Cool blue reason / Is this love (live) / Never there (video).
(cd-s) (870813-2) – ('A'side) / The distance / You part the waters (live) / The distance (video).

Oct 01.	(c-s) (672040-4) **SHORT SKIRT – LONG JACKET / ARCO ARENA (vocal)**	63	

(cd-s+=) (672040-2) – Meanwhile, Rick James ... / ('A'-video).

Nov 01.	(cd) (501540-2) <62132> **COMFORT EAGLE**		13 Jul01

– Opera singer / Meanwhile Rick James / Shadow stabbing / Short skirt – Long jacket / Commissioning a symphony in 'C' / Arco arena (instrumental) / Comfort eagle / Long line of cars / Love you madly / Pretty pink ribbon / World of two.

CAKE LIKE

Formed: New York, USA ... late 1992 by actress turned amateur guitarist, NINA HELLMAN, together with her equally inexperienced comedienne turned bassist, KERRI KENNEY; she had featured in cable shows, 'Viva Variety' and 'The State'. After a few false starts, the group was completed by mutual acquaintance and drummer JODY SEIFERT, the trio spotted by jazz experimentalist, JOHN ZORN, who, in turn, invited the girls to record on his 'Avant' imprint. The results were released late '94 in the shape of 'DELICIOUS', a spontaneous and cathartic blast of (BREEDERS-meets-BABES IN TOYLAND) alternative-rock firmly in the NY tradition. Subsequently signing to 'Warners' offshoot, 'Vapor', CAKE LIKE rose to the occasion with follow-up, 'BRUISER QUEEN' (1997).

CABLE

Formed: Derby, England ... 1994 by art-school lads, MATT BAGGULEY, DARIUS HINKS, PETER DARRINGTON and NEIL COOPER. After honing their skills at small venues around the nearby Nottingham locale, they released a couple of early limited edition 7"ers for 'Krunch!', namely 'SALE OF THE CENTURY' and 'SEVENTY'. Taking their "wired", discordant indie-rock down south to the capital, CABLE were picked up by 'Infectious', who almost immediately delivered their first widely distributed effort, 'BLINDMAN'. With former MEMBRANES man JOHN ROBB at the production helm, they powered their way into '96 with the re-release of 'SEVENTY', their fourth single and a highlight of the accompanying debut mini-set, 'DOWN-LIFT THE UP-TRODDEN'. Despite being packaged in BLUESBREAKERS pastiche artwork with sleevenotes depicting the band as modern day blues saviours, the actual sound was closer to a relentless, hard-driving PAVEMENT. Over the course of the next year (by which time COOPER had been replaced by RICHIE MILLS – apparently recruited from an Exchange & Mart ad!), they laid the ground work for their first long-player, 'WHEN ANIMALS ATTACK' (1997), with two singles, 'WHISPER FIRING LINE' and 'BLUEBIRDS ARE BLUE'. The album also installed CABLE in the UK Top 50 for the first time via the single, 'FREEZE THE ATLANTIC', although a further track, 'GOD GAVE ME GRAVITY', failed to spark the same interest. After an electrifying EP, 'LIVE AT THE BRIXTON PRISON', in the tradition of JOHNNY CASH (whose 'RING OF FIRE' they actually covered), CABLE began working with ex-BUGGLES, YES & ASIA man, GEOFF DOWNES. A new single, 'ARTHUR WALKER', appeared in late 1998, a taster from the following year's second full-set, 'SUB-LINGUAL'.

Album rating: DOWN-LIFT THE UP-TRODDEN (*6) / WHEN ANIMALS ATTACK (*6) / SUB-LINGUAL (*7)

MATT BAGGULEY – vocals, guitar / **DARIUS HINKS** – guitar / **PETE DARRINGTON** – bass / **NEIL COOPER** – drums

		Krunch!	not iss.
Jan 95.	(ltd-7") (KRUNCH 2) **SALE OF THE CENTURY. / HYDRA**		-
Jun 95.	(ltd-7") (KRUNCH 3) **SEVENTY. / OUBLIETTE**		-

		Infectious	not iss.
Sep 95.	(7") (INFECT 25S) **BLINDMAN. / GIVE 'EM WHAT THEY WANT**		-

(cd-s+=) (INFECT 25CD) – Hydra.

Feb 96.	(7") (INFECT 29W) **SEVENTY. / SPORTS CARS AND DEVIL WORSHIP**		-

(cd-s+=) (INFECT 29CD) – Dead wood for green.

Mar 96.	(m-cd/m-lp) (INFECT 32 CD/LP) **DOWN-LIFT THE UP-TRODDEN**		-

– New set of bruises / Choice / Blindman / Hydra / Seventy / Murdering spree / Sale of the century / Oubliette.

— (after above recording) **RICHIE MILLS** – drums; repl. NEIL

Sep 96.	(7") (INFECT 33S) **WHISPER FIRING LINE. / CAN'T FIND MY WAY HOME**		-

(cd-s+=) (INFECT 33CD) – Murdering spree (elevated).

Apr 97.	(7"m) (INFECT 36S) **BLUEBIRDS ARE BLUE. / APPARANTLY / ACTION REPLAY REPLAY**		-

(cd-s) (INFECT 36CD) – (first & third tracks) / Horse drawn and quartered / The clairvoyant.

May 97.	(cd/lp) (INFECT 35 CD/LP) **WHEN ANIMALS ATTACK**		-

– Souvenir / Bluebirds are blue / Signature tune / Freeze the Atlantic / Ultra violet / I'm always right / The colder climate / Whisper firing line / God gave me gravity / From here you can see yourself / Do the tube.

Jun 97.	(7") (INFECT 38S) **FREEZE THE ATLANTIC. / THE (WE DID THE MUSIC FOR THE SPRITE AD) BLUES**	44	-

(7"clear) (INFECT 38SX) – ('A'side) / Ring of fire.
(cd-s) (INFECT 38CD) – (all 3 tracks).

Aug 97.	(7"m) (INFECT 45S) **GOD GAVE ME GRAVITY. / DINKY / ELECTRO GAZELLE**		-

(cd-s+=) (INFECT 45CD) – Let's marengue.

Sep 97.	(cd-ep) (INFECT 48CD) **LIVE AT THE BRIXTON PRISON EP**		-

– Ultraviolet / Bluebirds are blue / Ring of fire / Seventy / San Quentin / Oubliette.

Oct 98.	(7") (INFECT 066S) **ARTHUR WALKER. / VERTIGO**		-

(cd-s) (INFECT 066CDS) – ('A'side) / Tick tock alarm clock / ('A'-CD-rom video).

May 99.	(cd) (INFECT 058CD) **SUB-LINGUAL**		

– Song 1 / Arthur Walker / Pocket promise / Hexagon eye / Honolulu / Brothers and sisters / Widower / Land speed record / Yesterday on the horizon / Autobahn head / Commprendez.

— CABLE looked to have split

CAKE LIKE (cont)

Album rating: DELICIOUS (*7) / BRUISER QUEEN (*5) / GOODBYE, SO WHAT? (*6)

NINA HELLMAN – vocals, guitar / **KERRI KENNEY** – vocals, bass / **JODY SEIFERT** – drums

Avant / Avant

Nov 94. (cd) <(AVANT 029)> **DELICIOUS**
– Billy boy / Burn leg / Sweet 15 / Fruitcake / Suck / Homewrecker / Fall down / Lovely ladies / Abraham Lincoln / Jane / Spaceguy.

Vapor- / Vapor-
Warners / Warners

Jun 97. (cd) <(9362 46601-2)> **BRUISER QUEEN**
– The new girl / Wendy / Mr. Fireman / Groovy / Latin lover / Pretty new / Lorraine's car / Franchise / Cancer / The American woman / Truck stop hussy / Destroyed.

Jul 97. (cd-s) (W 0409CD) **LORRAINE'S CAR / COME AND PLAY**
Jul 99. (cd) <(9362 47320-2)> **GOODBYE, SO WHAT?**
– Lucky one / My guy / Don't tell / Ashley / Dead to me / Getaway / Superstore / Swell / Blacked out and blue / God's alright / Frequent flyer / Miss you.

CALEXICO

Formed: California, USA ... 1990 by JOEY BURNS and JOHN CONVERTINO. CALEXICO had always been known as the obscure offshoot band to HOWE GELB's masters of alt country, GIANT SAND. True, both BURNS and CONVERTINO have enjoyed success in GELB's weird, tumbling desert band, but CALEXICO had moved from "backing band" with their third album proper, 'HOT RAIL'. It all began when BURNS met session musician CONVERTINO in L.A. At that point, he was touring with GIANT SAND and invited CONVERTINO to accompany the band on their European tour. After the tour had ended, the duo moved to Tucson, Arizona and began playing and collecting weird instruments from a down-town store Chicago Music. A group was formed, FRIENDS OF DEAN MARTINEZ and the strange musical instruments were put to good use: harps, accordions, marimba and vibraphone were all added to the mix of jazzy lounge music, which, in turn, was so bad it was sheer brilliant. But the band were to split after a disagreement with founder BILL ELM. Session work followed, and BURNS and CONVERTINO were beginning to build a strong musical prowess. They finally put plan into action in 1996, recording and issuing the lo-fi porch soundtrack 'SPOKE' (issued on the German label 'Haus Musik'), which caught the attention of 'Touch & Go' records. 'THE BLACK LIGHT', arguably their best work, was unfettered in 1998 to widespread critical acclaim. It was hard to categorise CALEXICO's music: a strange amalgamation of blues, post-rock, surf music, Portuguese/Mexican Mariachi fused with MORRICONE's sweeping soundtracks. Basically, it sounded like CALEXICO's (a small railway town on the Californian/Mexican border) national anthem, if it were to have one. The same energy could be heard on the follow-up, 'HOT RAIL' (2000). Much the same record (almost like a Part 2), but slightly inferior, the set again treated us to the Desert experience with singles 'BALLAD OF CABLE HOGUE' and 'SERVICE AND REPAIR' to boot. The group were still faithful to GELB, however, appearing on albums 'Chore Of Enchantment' (in 2000) and 'Confluence' (in 2001). Meanwhile, CONVERTINO and BURNS moonlighted with yet another outfit, ABBC, along with Parisians GABRIEL NAIM AMOR and THOMAS BELHOM. Their collaborative work, 'TETE A TETE', was released towards the end of 2000 – think eerie western and experimental textured jazz. • **Covered:** CHANEL #5 (Mark Eitzel).

Album rating: "SPOKE" (*7) / THE BLACK LIGHT (*8) / HOT RAIL (*8) / ABBC: TETE A TETE (*6)

JOEY BURNS – vocals, guitar, bass, cello, accordion, organ (of GIANT SAND) / **JOHN COVERTINO** – drums, vibes, organ, marimba, percussion, accordion (of GIANT SAND) / **TASHA BUNDY** – drums

not iss. / All City

1996. (7") <ALLCITY 2> **LAQUER. / DRAPE**
(UK-iss.Oct97 on 'All City'; same)

not iss. / Wabana

1996. (7") <ORE 004> **SPARK. / THE RIDE**

— guests **BRIDGET KEATING** – violin / **DAVID COFFMAN** – guitar

Quarter / Quarter
Stick / Stick

Sep 97. (cd) <(QS 51CD)> **"SPOKE"** — Aug97
– Low expectations / Mind the gap / Mazurka / Sanchez / Haul / Slag / Paper route / Glimpse / Navy cut / Spokes / Scout / Point Vicente / Wash / Ice cream jeep / Windjammer / Mazurka / Removed / Hitch / Stinging nettle. (re-iss. May00; same)

— **NICK LUCA** – Spanish guitar; repl. COFFMAN

— + guests **HOWE GELB** + **NEIL HARRY** + **GABRIEL LANDIN**

City Slang / Quarter
Stick

Oct 98. (cd/d-lp) (efa 08707-2/-1) <QS 54CD> **THE BLACK LIGHT** — May98
– Gypsy's curse / Fake fur / Ride (part II) / Where water flows / The black light / Sideshow / Chach / Missing / Minas de cobre (for better metal) / Over your shoulder / Vinegaroon / Trigger / Sprawl / Stray / Old man waltz / Bloodflow / Frontera.
Oct 98. (cd-s) (08713-2) **STRAY / LAQUER / DRAPE**
Apr 99. (7"/cd-s) (08719-7/-2) **THE RIDE (PART II). / MINAS DE COBRE** (mixes; extend-o-mix / Spatial / acoustic)

— they also issued a few concert/gig ltd-CD's 'ROAD MAP' (1999) and 'TRAVELALL' (2000); 'AEROCALEXICO' (2001) and 'SCRAPING' (2000) followed

— **JOHN + JOEY** with **NICK LUCA** – guitar / **RUBEN MORENO + MARTIN WENK** – trumpets / **MADELEINE SOSIN** – violin / etc

Apr 00. (7") (20154-7) **BALLAD OF CABLE HOGUE. / CRYSTAL FRONTIER**
(cd-s+=) (20154-2) – Hard hat.

May 00. (cd/lp) (20153-2/-1) <2006-2> **HOT RAIL** 57
– El picador / Ballad of Cable Hogue / Ritual road map / Fade / Untitled III / Sonic wind / Muleta / Mid-town / Service and repair / Untitled II / Drenched / 16 track scratch / Tree avisos / Hot rail.
Sep 00. (cd-s) (20167-2) **SERVICE AND REPAIR / CROOKED ROAD AND THE BRIAR / BANDERILLA**
Mar 01. (d7"ep) (20173-7) **CRYSTAL FRONTIER / CHANEL #5. / CROOKED ROAD AND THE BRIAR / BANDERILLA**
(cd-s) (20173-2) – (first 2 tracks) / ('A'-widescreen mix) / ('A'-acoustic).
(12") (20173-6) – ('A'-widescreen mix) / ('A'-buscemi remix) / Untitled 3 (virus style mix).

— in 2001, they were out with 'EVEN MY SURE THINGS FALL THROUGH' a low-key CD-ep for 'City Slang' in the US

ABBC

CONVERTINO + BURNS with **GABRIEL NAIM AMOR** – guitar, violin + **THOMAS BELHOM** – percussion, etc.

Wabana / Wabana

Nov 00. (cd/lp) <(ORE 24/+CD)> **TETE A TETE**
– La valse des 24 heures / Elevator baby / En route to the blanchisserie / Mobile home / Orange trees in the yard / Gilbert / Pluie sans nuages / The wrestler's masque / Je voudrais me rappeller / Le savon se dissout dans la rigole. (re-iss. Jul01 on 'Cargo' cd/lp; CAR 031 CD/LP)

Easy Tiger! / not iss.

Apr 01. (7") (MUSE 009) **GILBERT. / BUTTERFLY MOUTH**

CALIFONE (see under ⇒ RED RED MEAT)

CALL AND RESPONSE

Formed: Bay Area, San Francisco, California, USA ... late 1990's by CARRIE CLOUGH, SIMONE RUBI, DAN JUDD, TERRI LOWENTHAL and JORDAN DALRYMPLE. The group released their breezy, sunkissed debut single 'ROLLERSKATE' in early 2001, which displayed the band's keen sense of harmony and love for 1960's West Coast music (BEACH BOYS, FREE DESIGN, etc). The pleasantly infectious, self-titled debut followed the same year. The syrupy, kaleidoscopic groove they created was saved from becoming tiresome by the inclusion of dual male/female vocals and light-hearted lyrics.

Album rating: CALL AND RESPONSE (*6)

CARRIE CLOUGH – vocals, electone organ / **DAN RUDD** – vocals, guitar, synths / **SIMONE RUBI** – wurlitzer, moog, farfisa, synths, vocals / **TERRI LOEWENTHAL** – bass, vocals / **JORDAN DALRYMPLE** – drums, percussion, organ vocals

not iss. / Shelflife

Mar 00. (7") <LIFE 19> **ROLLERSKATE. / SUN**

Kindercore / Kindercore

Mar 01. (cd/lp) <KC 059 CD/LP> **CALL AND RESPONSE**
– Blowin' bubbles / Rollerskate / Nightflight / California floating in space / Colors / Map / The fool / I know you want me / Lightbulb / Stars have eyes. <cd remixed.Sep01 on 'Emperor Norton'; 7044> – All night long / When the lights are out.

CALVIN KRIME (see under ⇒ SEAN NA-NA)

CAMBER

Formed: New York City, New York, USA ... 1995 by BARRY LOTT, CORBY CALDWELL, JOEY DELLACROCE and drummer CHRIS CHIN. Infusing SLINT's bold rock-out vision with SSHELLAC's fiery bursts of sonic noise, this surprisingly melodic quartet from the Big Apple were unfairly shunted by NYC's typically wank-art scene and the uber-coverage it received post-millennium. Akin to fellow natives, THUNDERBOLT and hardcore enthusiasts BLACK DICE, CAMBER signed with emo label 'Deep Elm' and issued their debut set 'BEAUTIFUL CHARADE' (1997), a soaring post-punk mess with a soulful spirit at its core. Their John Agnello-produced follow-up 'ANYWAY, I'VE BEEN THERE' (1999) took a less aggressive stance, and displayed the group's new-found love for melodies, as well as solidly constructed songs. However, 2002's sombre 'WAKE UP AND BE HAPPY' (surely an in-joke) reflected the dampening mood of a city after the 9/11 attacks. Recorded in a basement, in mostly single-takes (you could hear the creaking of the floor as members tip-toed about), songs such as 'EXPAT' and 'A TRICK I LEARNED IN THE ARMY' resurrected whatever emo traits the ensemble had hidden in their earlier, more refined days.

Album rating: BEAUTIFUL CHARADE (*5) / ANYWAY, I'VE BEEN THERE (*6) / WAKE UP AND BE HAPPY (*5)

BARRY LOTT – vocals, guitar / **CORBY CALDWELL** – guitar / **JOEY DELLACROCE** – bass / **CHRIS CHIN** – drums

Deep Elm / Deep Elm

Jul 98. (cd) <(DER 359)> **BEAUTIFUL CHARADE** — Mar97
– Hollowed-out / First / Beautiful charade / Marking the days / Odds & ends / Clean / 206 / Question makrs / Sever.
Jun 99. (cd) <(DER 375)> **ANYWHERE, I'VE BEEN THERE**
– P / Temporary / Spirit gum / Punching out / Wait / 38th & eighth / Sad one / Broken glass / Improbable upside / Home movies.

— **ROGER COLETTI** – drums; repl. CHIN

Apr 02. (cd) <(DER 405)> **WAKE UP AND BE HAPPY**
– Devil you know / Short sleeve / West village idiot / Wake up and be happy / Darling daughter / Expat / Make yourself comfortable / Lenny / Plissken / A trick I learned in the army / What do you want this to be?

THE GREAT INDIE DISCOGRAPHY — The 1990s

CAMERA OBSCURA

Formed: Glasgow, Scotland ... Spring '96 by TRACYANNE and fellow student JOHN, GAVIN and DAVID were found around various venues and shops although they still hadn't found a drummer. Radio station 'Beat Patrol' was the first to take note of this SIMON & GARFUNKEL-esque folk trio, 'PARK AND RIDE' and 'PORCELAIN' were played ensuring interest from local indie imprint, 'Andmoresound'. In March '98, 'PARK AND RIDE' became their debut single, airplay this time via Steve Lamacq and John Peel. However, due to nerves and the lack of a drummer, CAMERA OBSCURA still hadn't played a worthy gig; RICHARD COLBURN of BELLE & SEBASTIAN had helped them out during an earlier outing. Towards the end of the year, a support slot to ASTRID remedied their tentative teething problems and a second single, 'YOUR SOUND', was released to healthy response. Subsequently opening for SNOW PATROL and LUNA, they duly initiated their own 'Park & Ride' monthly club at the 13th Note cafe. However, little was seen in the way of new releases (bar a part-compilation, 'RARE UK BIRD' on Japanese import!), until that is, US-based label 'Troubleman Unlimited' delivered their debut LP proper, 'TO CHANGE THE SHAPE OF AN ENVELOPE' (2000); they had now found drummer LEE THOMPSON, while DAVID went off to pursue his own dream.

Album rating: TO CHANGE THE SHAPE OF AN ENVELOPE (*6)

TRACYANNE – vocals / **JOHN** – vocals, guitar / **GAVIN** – vocals, guitar / **DAVID** – bass

Andmoresound iss.

Mar 98. (7") (AND 09 45) **PARK AND RIDE. / SWIMMING POOL**

Dec 98. (7"ep/cd-s) (AND 11 45/CDS) **YOUR SOUND. / AUTUMN TIDES / ANNAWALTZERPOSE**

Quattro / not iss.

Dec 99. (m-cd) (quattro-014) **RARE UK BIRD** — Japan
– Park and ride / Swimming pool / Your sound / Autumn tides / Annawaltzerpose / Eastwood / Railway station / Eighties fan.

— **LEE THOMPSON** – drums; repl. DAVID

Troubleman / Troubleman Unlimited Unlimited

Jul 00. (lp) (<TMU 047>) **TO CHANGE THE SHAPE OF AN ENVELOPE** — May00
– Trigger system / Cinematheque / Theory on sex as an art form / Sarasota / Twenty five diamonds / Aeronautical / Sound / Song de la luna.

Andmoresound iss.

Jun 01. (7"/cd-s) (and 16 45/cds) **EIGHTIES FAN. / SHINE LIKE A NEW PIN / LET'S GO BOWLING**

Nov 01. (lp/cd) (and 17 33/cd) **BIGGEST BLUEST HI FI**
– Happy new year / Eighties fan / Houseboat / Pen and notebook / Swimming pool / Anti western / I don't do crowds / The sun on his back / Double feature / Arrangements of shapes and space.

CAMPAG VELOCET

Formed: London, England ... early '93 by Portsmouth-born schoolfriends ARGE (IAN CATER) and PETE VOSS, the latter deemed a misfit, who actually found out later in life that he had an indentation to the brain (apparently due to a boyhood accident in which he fell out of a loft). Having acquired a home at bassist BARNEY SLATER's Kentish Town (London) pad, the trio began marathon rehearsal sessions, only stopping for the occasional bag of mushrooms (magic they weren't!). Having gone through a plethora of drummers, CAMPAG VELOCET finally recruited LASCELLES LASCELLE GORDON (ex-guitarist with the BRAND NEW HEAVIES, wow!) and supported other local lads, LO FIDELITY ALLSTARS. CV released a couple of singles at the turn of '97, a split affair with the REGULAR FRIES and a highly-rated EP, 'DRENCROM VELOCET SYNTHEMESC'. Akin to HAWKWIND, STEVE HILLAGE and CRISPY AMBULANCE, their harsh musical soundscapes of repetitive "Laandaan beat" rhythms were on full course for the 'SAUNTRY SLY CHIC' single in April '98. A whole year later, the CAMPAG's were back in town (so to speak) with a new single, 'TO LOSE LA TREK', although it would be another six months before its parent album would appear. The S&M-obsessed 'BON CHIC BON GENRE' (1999), hit all the right buttons on nearly every track. From the short-sharp-shock of the opening title track to arguably the record's finest modern-day prog-punk piece, 'PIKE IN MY LIFE', the album was a seminal work worthy of the heaps of praise it received.

Album rating: BON CHIC BON GENRE (*8)

PETE VOSS – vocals, percussion / **IAN CATER (aka ARGE)** – guitars, keyboards, programming / **BARNEY SLATER** – bass / **LASCELLES LASCELLE (GORDON)** – drums, percussion, samples (ex-BRAND NEW HEAVIES)

Fierce Panda / not iss.

Nov 97. (7") (Ning 41) **DRENCROM (VELOCET SYNTHEMESC). / (other side by Regular Fries)**

Rabid Badger / not iss.

Nov 97. (12"ep) (Nang 1) **IT'S THE TEENAGE ARGOT... EP**
– Drencrom (Velocet synthemesc) / Drencrom (Litso mix) / Out on the plinth / Out on the plinth (NYDX mix).

Apr 98. (12"ep/cd-ep) (Nang 3/+CD) **SAUNTRY SLY CHIC / GAKSTACKERS / TV EYE**

Play It Again Sam / not iss.

Mar 99. (7") (PIASX 001) **TO LOSE LA TREK. / POSTPONED NATIVE PLEASURES (part 1)**
(12"+=/cd-s+=) (PIASX 001 T/CD) – I forget.

Sep 99. (cd/d-lp) (PIASX CD/LP 003) **BON CHIC BON GENRE**
– Bon chic bon genre / Only answers delay our time / Cacophonous bubblegum / To lose la trek / Vito Satan / Sauntry sly chic / Drencrom velocet synthemesc / Skin so soft / Pike in my life – Schiaparelli cat / Caught unawares / Harsh shark.

Feb 00. (12") (PIASX 101T) **VITO SATAN. / DRENCROM VELOCET SYNTHEMESC (Mao mix) / BON CHIC BON GENRE (Underdog mix)** 75
(cd-s) (PIASX 101CD) – ('A'single mix) / Sauntry slight return / Bon chic bon genre (hard skin mix).

CAN

Formed: Cologne, Germany ... 1968 initially as INNER SPACE by HOLGER CZUKAY and IRMIN SCHMIDT. MICHAEL KAROLI and JAKI LIEBEZEIT were soon recruited along with DAVID JOHNSON and black American vocalist MALCOLM MOONEY. Later that year, JOHNSON bailed out prior to their debut album, 'MONSTER MOVIE' (1970). Having studied under KARL-HEINZ STOCKHAUSEN, CZUKAY and SCHMIDT (who were also influenced by JOHN CAGE, TERRY RILEY and The VELVET UNDERGROUND) pioneered their own take on avant-garde minimalism, creating a hypnotic, free-form sound, relentless in its intensity. The album included a 20-minute piece, 'YOU DOO RIGHT', extracted from a marathon improv-session and highlighting the very real dementia of MOONEY's ravings. He suffered a nervous breakdown soon after and was subsequently replaced by the Japanese 'vocalist' DAMO SUZUKI prior to recording 'SOUNDTRACKS'. More improvised beauty was evidenced on their next set, the German Top 40 classic, 'TAGO MAGO' (1971), a sprawling double-set that featured two of their more hypnotic tracks, 'HALLELUWAH' and 'MUSHROOM'. On their next two releases, 'EGE BAMYASI' and 'FUTURE DAYS', CAN explored even more ritualistic textures alongside SUZUKI's partly-spoken tri-lingual ramblings. SUZUKI subsequently returned to Japan to become a Jehovah's Witness, after a final gig at the 1973 Edinburgh Festival. Vocal duties were now shared by KAROLI and SCHMIDT on the more percussive 'SOON OVER BABALUMA' album (1974). They signed to Richard Branson's innovative 'Virgin' label the following year, 'LANDED' being a prime example of British-influenced avant-garde rock. In 1976, they surprised many by having a Top 30 hit, 'I WANT MORE', penned by PINK FLOYD's DAVID GILMOUR. With the addition of ROSKO GEE and sessionman REEBOP KWAKU BAAH, they moved in a more African/reggae influenced direction; CZUKAY having already withdrawn from most of the proceedings. Their final efforts were of little significance, the 1979 album interesting only for its re-hash of Offenbach's 'CAN-CAN', which had previously been released as a single. KAROLI, SCHMIDT and CZUKAY all continued in the 80's as solo artists, the latter teaming up once again with LIEBEZEIT (and JAH WOBBLE) on the 1982 album 'FULL CIRCLE'. The original line-up reformed in 1986 for an album, 'RITE TIME', but the record lacked the inspiration and originality that characterised CAN's earlier work. The band remain highly regarded, cited as a major influence by artists as diverse as CARL CRAIG and PRIMAL SCREAM. Even The FALL paid homage to them by crediting a song as 'I AM DAMO SUZUKI'. A plethora of post-CAN work (mainly from CZUKAY) appeared from time to time, although their legacy was always from the experimental 70's. More recently (on the 17th of November, 2001), the death of MICHAEL KAROLI filtered through to the media. He would be sadly missed by his great friend CZUKAY.

Album rating: MONSTER MOVIE (*7) / SOUNDTRACKS (*6) / TAGO MAGO (*7) / EGE BAMYASI (*7) / FUTURE DAYS (*7) / LIMITED EDITION collection (*6) / SOON OVER BABALUMA (*6) / LANDED (*5) / FLOW MOTION (*5) / UNLIMITED EDITION collection (*5) / SAW DELIGHT (*6) / CANNIBALISM compilation (*7) / OUT OF REACH (*3) / CAN (*4) / DELAY 1968 exploitation (*5) / RITE TIME (*5) / CANNIBALISM II compilation (*6) / CANNIBALISM III compilation (*5) / ANTHOLOGY 1968-1993 compilation (*8) / Holger Czukay: CANAXIS 5 with Rolf Dammers (*7) / MOVIES (*7) / ON THE WAY TO THE PEAK OF NORMAL (*5) / FULL CIRCLE (*5) / DER OSTEN IST ROT (*5) / ROME REMAINS ROME (*7) / RADIO WAVE SURFER (*4) / MOVING PICTURES (*5) / GOOD MORNING STORY (*5) / LA LUNA (*5) / Michael Karoli with Polly Estes; DELUGE (*7) / Jaki Liebezeit: PHANTOM BAND (*5) / FREEDOM OF SPEECH (*5) / NOWHERE (*5) / Irmin Schmidt: FILM MUSIK (*5) / TOY PLANET (*5) / FILM MUSIK VOL.2 (*5) / FILM MUSIK VOL.3 & 4 (*5) / MUSIC AT DUSK (*5) / IMPOSSIBLE HOLIDAYS (*5)

IRMIN SCHMIDT (b.29 May'37, Berlin, Germany) – keyboards / **HOLGER CZUKAY** (b.24 Mar'38, Danzig, Germany) – bass, electronics / **DAVID JOHNSON** – flute / **MICHAEL KAROLI** (b.29 Apr'48, Straubing, Germany) – guitar, violin / **JAKI LIEBEZEIT** (b.26 May'38, nr.Dresden, Germany) – drums / **MALCOLM MOONEY** – vocals

Music Factory / not iss.

Nov 68. (7"; by IRMIN SCHMIDT) **KAMA SUTRA. /** — German

— Now a quintet when JOHNSON departed (below issued Germany Aug'69)

U.A. / U.A.

May 70. (lp) (UAS 29094) **MONSTER MOVIE**
– Father cannot yell / Mary, Mary so contrary / You doo right / Outside my door.
(cd-iss. Jun89 on 'Spoon-Mute'; SPOONCD 004)

— **KENJI 'DAMO' SUZUKI** (b.16 Jan'50, Japan) – vocals repl.MOONEY who suffered a nervous breakdown

Sep 70. (7") Liberty; **SOUL DESERT. / SHE BRINGS THE RAIN** — German

Sep 71. (lp) (UAS 29283) **SOUNDTRACKS**
– Deadlock / Tango whiskyman / Deadlock (instrumental) / Don't turn the light on, leave me alone / Soul desert / Mother sky / She brings the rain. (cd-iss. Jun89 on 'Spoon-Mute'; SPOONCD 005)

Date	Format / Catalog / Title		
1971.	(7") **TURTLES HAVE SHORT LEGS. / HALLELUWAH** (edit)	-	- German
1971.	(7") **SPOON. / SHIKAKO MARU TEN**	-	- German
Feb 72.	(d-lp) (UAD 60009-10) **TAGO MAGO**		
	– Paperhouse / Mushroom / Oh yeah / Halleluwah / Aumgn / Peking O / Bring me coffee or tea. (cd-iss. Jul89 on 'Spoon-Mute'; SPOONCD 006-007)		
Nov 72.	(lp) (UAS 29414) <063> **EGE BAMYASI**		
	– Pinch / Sing swan song / One more night / Vitamin C / Soup / I'm so green / Spoon. (cd-iss. Jun89 on 'Spoon-Mute'; SPOONCD 008)		
Feb 73.	(7") (UP 35506) **SPOON. / I'M SO GREEN**		
Jun 73.	(lp) (UAS 29505) <213> **FUTURE DAYS**		
	– Future days / Spray / Moonshake / Bel Air. (cd-iss. Jun89 on 'Spoon-Mute'; SPOONCD 009)		
Oct 73.	(7") (UP 35596) <446> **MOONSHAKE. / FUTURE DAYS** (edit)		

— trimmed to a quartet when DAMO SUZUKI left to become a Jehovah's Witness. Now **SCHMIDT / KAROLI** (shared vocals) **CZUKAY + LIEBEZEIT**

Nov 74.	(lp) (UAG 29673) <343> **SOON OVER BABALUMA**		
	– Dizzy dizzy / Come sta, la luna / Splash / Chain reaction / Quantum physics. (cd-iss. Jun89 on 'Spoon-Mute'; SPOONCD 010)		
Dec 74.	(7") (UP 35749) **DIZZY DIZZY. / SPLASH**		

		Virgin	Polydor
Sep 75.	(lp) (V 2041) **LANDED**		
	– Full moon on the highway / Half past one / Hunters and collectors / Vernal equinox / Red hot Indians / Unfinished. (cd-iss. Jun87; CDV 2041) (re-iss. Aug88; OVED 194)		

— approx Mar76, tried two vocalists one a Malayan, the other **MICHAEL COUSINS** (English). added **DAVID GILMOUR** – guest/composer (3) b.vocals of PINK FLOYD

Jul 76.	(7") (VS 153) **I WANT MORE. / . . . AND MORE**	26	
Oct 76.	(lp) (V 2071) **FLOW MOTION**		
	– I want more / Cascade waltz / Laugh till you cry . . . live till you die / . . . And more / Babylonian pearl / Smoke (E.F.S. No.59) / Flow motion. (cd-iss. Jun87; CDV 2071) (re-iss. Aug88; OVED 88)		
Nov 76.	(7") (VS 166) **SILENT NIGHT. / CASCADE WALTZ**		-

— added **ROSKO GEE** – bass + **REEBOP KWAKU BAAH** (b. Konongo, Ghana) – percussion (both ex-TRAFFIC) (HOLGER now synths., samplers)

Mar 77.	(lp) (V 2079) **SAW DELIGHT**		
	– Don't say no / Sunshine day and night / Call me / Animal waves / Fly by night. (cd-iss. Jun87; CDV 2079) (re-iss. Aug88; OVED 195)		
Apr 77.	(7") (VS 172) **DON'T SAY NO. / RETURN**		-

— HOLGER went on a few holidays (& solo). The rest of the band below (**SCHMIDT, KAROLI, LIEBEZEIT, BAAH & GEE**) recorded album.

		Lightning	Peters Int.
Jun 78.	(7") (LIG 545) **CAN-CAN. / CAN BE**		
Jul 78.	(lp) (LIP 4) <9024> **OUT OF REACH**		
	– Serpentine / Pauper's daughter and I / November / Seven days awake / Give me no roses / Like Inobe God / One more day. (re-iss. Jun86 on 'Thunderbolt'; THBL 025) (cd-iss. Nov88; CDTB 025) (cd re-iss. May99 on 'MagMid'; MM 030)		

		Laser	not iss.
Jul 79.	(lp) (LASL 2) **CAN**		
	– All gates open / Safe / Sunday jam / Sodom / Aspectacle / E.F.S.No.99: "can can" / Ping pong / Can be. (re-iss. Feb85 as 'INNER SPACE' on 'Thunderbolt'; THBL 020) (cd-iss. Jun87; THBL 020)		

— had already split late '78. JAKI formed PHANTOM BAND and collaborated with HOLGER. IRMIN went solo and formed BRUNO SPOERRI. MICHAEL in '84 went solo. All their releases were mainly German only. **CAN** re-formed 1969 line-up 20 years on.

		Mercury	not iss.
Oct 89.	(lp/c/cd) (838 883-1/-4/-2) **RITE TIME**		-
	-On the beautiful side of a romance / The without law man / Below this level (patient's song) / Movin' right along / Like a new world / Hoolah hoolah / Give the drummer some / In the distance lies the future. (cd-iss. Oct94 on 'Spoon-Mute'; SPOONCD 029)		

		White Label	not iss.
Sep 90.	(cd)(c)(lp) **FISHERMAN'S FRIEND REMIXES**		-

– compilations, others, etc. –

on 'United Artists' unless otherwise mentioned

Aug 74.	(lp) (USP 103) **LIMITED EDITION**		-
May 76.	(d-lp) Caroline; (CAD 3001) **UNLIMITED EDITION**		-
Nov 76.	(lp) Sunset; (SLS 50400) **OPENER** (71-74 material)		-
Oct 78.	(d-lp) (UDM 105-6) **CANNIBALISM**		-
May 81.	(7") Virgin; (VS 422) / Polydor; **I WANT MORE. / . . . AND MORE**		
	(12"+=) (VS 422-12) – Silent night.		
1981.	(lp) (SPOON 011) **DELAY 1968**	-	- German
	– Butterfly / Pnoom / 19th century man / Thief / Man named Joe / Uphill / Little star of Bethlehem. (cd-iss. Jun89 on 'Spoon-Mute'; SPOONCD 012)		
Oct 81.	(lp) Virgin; (OVED 3) **INCANDESCENCE**		
1982.	(c) Pure Freude; (PF 23) **ONLYOU**		- German
Mar 83.	(12"ep) Cherry Red; (12CHERRY 57) **MOONSHAKE. / TURTLES HAVE SHORT LEGS / ONE MORE NIGHT**		
Jan 85.	(c) Tago Mago; (TM 4755) **PREHISTORIC FUTURE**	-	- France
Jun 91.	(cd) Spoon-Mute; (SPOONCD 23-24) **UNLIMITED EDITION** (new collection)		
Nov 92.	(cd) Spoon-Mute; (SPOONCD 021) **CANNIBALISM II**		
	– Uphill / Pnoom / Connection / Mother Upduff / Little star / T.V. spot / Doko E. / Turtles have short legs / Shikaku maru ten / Gomorrha / Blue bag / Red hot Indians / Half past one / Flow motion / Smoke / I want more . . .and more / Laugh till you cry / Aspectacle animal waves / Sunshine day and night / E.F.S. No.7 / Melting away.		
Oct 94.	(cd) Spoon-Mute; (SPOONCD 3031) **ANTHOLOGY 1968-1993**		
Feb 95.	(cd) Spoon-Mute; (SPOONCD 022) **CANNIBALISM III**		
	– (solo work 1979-1991 from CZUKAY, SCHMIDT, LIEBEZEIT & KAROLI)		
Oct 95.	(cd) Strange Fruit; (SFRCD 135) **LIVE AT THE BBC** (Peel sessions)		
May 97.	(t-lp/d-cd) Grey Area; (SPOON/+CD 39-40) **SACRILEGE**		
Mar 99.	(d-cd+video+book) Spoon-Mute; (SPOON 041) **CAN BOX**		
Sep 99.	(d-cd) Spoon-Mute; (SPOON 042/043) **CAN LIVE** (live)		

HOLGER CZUKAY

		Music Factory	not iss.
1968.	(lp; by HOLGER CZUKAY with ROLF DAMMERS) (SRS 002) **CANAXIS 5**	-	- German
	– Boat woman song / Canaxis. (re-iss. 1981 on 'Spoon'; SPOON 015) (cd-iss. Feb95 on 'Spoon-Mute'; SPOONCD 015)		

— CZUKAY with other CAN members augmenting

		E.M.I.	not iss.
Nov 79.	(7") (EMI 5005) **COOL IN THE POOL. / OH LORD GIVE US MORE MONEY** (re-iss. Jul83; same)		-
Jan 80.	(lp) (EMC 3319) **MOVIES**		-
	– Cool in the pool / Oh Lord give us some money / Persian love / Hollywood symphony. (cd-iss. Jan98 on 'Spoon'; SPOONCD 35)		

— 1980, CZUKAY released 12"ep 'LES VAMPYRETTES' in Germany with CONRAD PLANK & AXEL GROS on 'Electrola'; (F 667.226)

— mid'81, CZUKAY teamed up with JAH WOBBLE and JAKI LIEBEZEIT to releases 12"ep 'HOW MUCH ARE THEY?' for 'Island'; (12WIP 6701)

— most of the tracks appeared on below 'Virgin' German album.

Feb 82.	(lp/c) (EMC/TC-EMC 3394) **ON THE WAY TO THE PEAK OF NORMAL**		
	– Ode to perfume / On the way to the peak of normal / Witches multiplication table / Two bass shuffle / Hiss'n'listen. (cd-iss. Jan98 on 'Spoon'; SPOONCD 36)		
Mar 82.	(7") (EMI 5280) **ODE TO PERFUME. / PERSIAN LOVE**		

		Virgin	not iss.
1982.	(lp; by HOLGER CZUKAY, JAH WOBBLE & JAKI LIEBEZEIT) (205 866-320) **FULL CIRCLE**	-	- German
	– How much are they? / Where's the money? / Full circle R.P.S. (No.7) / Mystery R.P.S. (No.8) / Trench warfare / Twilight world. (cd-iss. May92 on 'Virgin'; CDOVD 437)		

— In Oct'83, he teamed up with JAH WOBBLE (again) & The EDGE (U2), to release mini-album 'SNAKE CHARMER' for 'Island'; (IMA 1)

May 84.	(lp/c) (V/TCV 2307) **DER OSTEN IST ROT**		
	– The photo song / Bankel rap '82 / Michy / Rhonrad / Collage / Esperanto socialiste / Der osten ist rot / Das massenmedium / Schaue vertrauensvoll in die zukunft / Traum mal wieder. (re-iss. Apr86 lp/c; OVED/+C 161)		
May 84.	(7") (VS 671) **THE PHOTO SONG. / DAS MASSENMEDIUM** (12"+=) (VS 671-12) – Biomutanten.		-
Jan 87.	(lp/c) (V/TCV 2408) **ROME REMAINS ROME**		
	– Hey ba ba re bob / Blessed Easter / Sudentenland / Hit hit flop flop / Perfect world / Music in the air. (cd-iss. Jan88+=; CDV 2408) – DER OSTEN IST ROT (lp)		

— (Mar'88) collaborated next with DAVID SYLVIAN on album 'PLIGHT AND PREMONITION' for 'Venture' cd/c/lp; (CD/TC+/VE 11)

— next with **SHELDON ANCEL** – vocals / **M.KAROLI** – guitar / **J.LIEBEZEIT** – drums

Jan 91.	(cd/c/lp) (CD/TC+/V 2651) **RADIO WAVE SURFER**		
	– Rhine water / It ain't no crime / I get weird dreams / Saturday night movie / Dr. Oblivion / We can fight all night / Get it sweet / Ride a radio wave / Atmosphere tuning / Voice of Bulgaria / Late night radio / Through the freezing snow / Encore.		

		Mute	not iss.
May 93.	(cd) (CDSTUMM 125) **MOVING PICTURES**		-
	– Longing for daydreams / All night long / Radio in an hourglass / Dark moon / Floatspace / Rhythms of a secret life.		

		Sideburn	not iss.
Mar 98.	(d-cd; by HOLGER CZUKAY & DR. WALKER) (efa 12339-2) **CLASH**		-
	below with SCHMIDT, LEBEZEIT, KAROLI, WOBBLE, etc		

		Tone Casualties	Tone Casualties
Nov 99.	(cd) (TCCD 9944) **GOOD MORNING STORY**		
	– Invisible man / Good morning story / Dancing in wide ciecles / World of the universe / Atlantis / Mirage.		
Jun 00.	(cd) (TCCD 9945) **LA LUNA**		
	– La luna (on electronic night ceremony).		

CANDIDATE

Formed: London, England . . . 1998 by childhood friends CHRIS WHITE and IAN PAINTER, plus brothers ALEX and JOEL MORRIS. Inspired by '90s American lo-fi, they self-released demos and were eventually picked up by indie label 'Snowstorm' in 1999. Three EPs were released this same year – 'GOOD WORKS', 'TAKE OVER TOKYO' and 'LEADER', their talent and promise boosted when self-financed and produced debut LP, 'TAKING ON THE ENEMY'S SOUND' – released in August 2000 – was critically acclaimed by the NME. Their atmospheric, melancholic compositions – featuring gentle guitars, keyboards and percussion – drew comparisons with GRANDADDY and BADLY DRAWN BOY. 'TIGER FILES' (2002) marked a subtle progression of the CANDIDATE sound, while 'NUADA' – following in October – featured compositions inspired by PAUL GIOVANNI's 'The Wicker Man' music from 1974.

Album rating: TAKING ON THE ENEMY'S SOUND (*5) / TIGER FLIES (*5) / NUADA: MUSIC INSPIRED BY THE FILM THE WICKER MAN (*7)

CANDIDATE (cont)

JOEL MORRIS – vocals / **ALEX MORRIS** – guitar / **IAN PAINTER** – bass / **CHRIS WHITE** – drums

Snowstorm / not iss.

May 99. (7"ep) *(SNOWS 001)* **GOOD WORKS EP**
– Sleep on, tiger / Dada / Swim home.
Aug 99. (7") *(SNOWS 003)* **TAKE OVER TOKYO. / THE SEA IS FOR FISH**
(cd-s+=) *(SNOWS 003CD)* – Rocket science.
Dec 99. (7"ep/cd-ep) *(STORM 004/+CD)* **LEADER EP**
– If you want your daughter / Ten principles of statecraft.
Apr 00. (cd/lp) *(STORM 002 CD/LP)* **TAKING ON THE ENEMY'S SOUND**
– The great American starving band / Load it all on me / Stay outside / Play something / Silver boats / Swim home / Caboose / Somerset / Son of Kong / Bird machine.
Nov 01. (cd-ep) *(SNOWS 017CD)* **TALK ABOUT TROUBLES**
– Talk about troubles / Colder than summer / Carousel / I am the walker / Don't forget me / The hole (demo).
Jan 02. (cd) *(STORM 012CD)* **TIGER FLIES**
– Avalanche / Talk about troubles / Light through stones / Hawaiian police / Honey / Cactus Jack / Burn low / Hangman's waltz / Head to toe in white / The hole / The wreck of the breeze / Medicine ball / This is the way / Last days of the war.
Jun 02. (7"ep) *(SNOWS 021)* **HAWAIIAN DAYS EP**
– Hawaiian police / Divorce song / Something you don't know.
(cd-s+=) *(SNOWS 021CD)* – The old fashioned rules.
Oct 02. (cd) *(STORM 017CD)* **NUADA: MUSIC INSPIRED BY THE FILM THE WICKER MAN**
– Barrel of fear / Sowing song / Tomorrow's tomorrow / Beautiful birds / Song of the Oss / Save us / Circle of ash / Burrowhead / Rain on the roof / Island 34 / Modern parlance.

CANDYLAND

Formed: South London, England ... 1990 by vocalist FELIX TOD and guitarist DAVID WESLEY AYERS JR. This interracial band – including members from Somalia, Jamaica and the UK – would eventually add bass player KENEDIID OSMAN, drummer DERRICK McKENZIE and keyboardist COLIN PAYNE to complete their lineup. The band's first demo was produced by legendary producer Gil Norton, of PIXIES and ECHO & THE BUNNYMEN fame and they were invited to play the Great British Music Weekend at Wembley even before the release of their first single, 'FOUNTAIN O' YOUTH' (1991). A prolific year for CANDYLAND, 1991 would also see the release of their 'BITTER MOON' single and first and only album, 'SUCK IT AND SEE'. The latter had a cover sporting a banana and suggesting oral sex, a nod to the famous VELVET UNDERGOUND cover. The long player was received enthusiastically by an initially supportive music press, who would eventually turn on the band because of PAYNE'S previous occupation as a failed stockbroker. The LP was as musically eclectic as the countries the members came from, interspersing druggie dance beats with terse, laid back guitar cuts and 60's swirling psychedelic pop. TOD'S lyrics and vocals ooze fey romanticism and twee asexuality in equal measures, but the strength of the effort still wasn't enough to keep the band from going down. TOD became a producer in 1993, producing four albums for HEATHER NOVA and one for her brother, reggae dub-boy MISHKA.

Album rating: SUCK IT AND SEE (*5)

FELIX TOD – vocals / **DAVID WESLEY AYERS JNR** – guitar / **KENEDIID OSMAN** (b. Somalia) – bass

Non Fiction / East West

Feb 91. (7") *(YES 4) <096306>* **FOUNTAIN O' YOUTH. / FOUNTAIN O' YOUTH (demo)** [72]
(12"+=/cd-s+=) *(YES XR/CD 4)* – ('A'-hands on mix).

— added **COLIN PAYNE** (b. Southend, England) – keyboards / **DERRICK McKENZIE** (b. Jamaica) – drums

Nov 91. (7") *(YES 7)* **BITTER MOON. / I'M A GOOD GIRL**
(12") *(YESX 7)* – ('A'-Voodoo mix).
Apr 92. (cd/c/lp) *(511989-2/-4/-1) <91765-2/-4/-1>* **SUCK IT AND SEE**
– Precious / Fountain o' youth / Bitter moon / Something to somebody / Reternity / Rainbow / Ivy to oak / Kingdom / The body is the book / Behold the motherlode / We will not leave.
Nov 92. (7") *(YES 9)* **KINGDOM** / **('A'mix)**
(12"+=/cd-s+=) *(YES X/CD 9)* – ('A'-Chapman & Verse mix).

Fiction / not iss.

Feb 93. (7") *(FICS 37)* **RAINBOW. / SUN ON SKIN**
(cd-s+=) *(FICCD 37)* – ('A'-mixes).

— split early in 1993

CANDYSKINS

Formed: Oxford, England ... 1989 by NICK COPE, his brother MARK, NICK BURTON, KARL SHALE and JOHN HALLIDAY; the moniker stemming from a FIRE ENGINES song. Towards the end of 1990, this seminal Brit-pop act (pre-dating neighbours RADIOHEAD and SUPERGRASS) surfaced with their debut single, 'SUBMARINE SONG'. A sophomore 45, 'SHE BLEW ME AWAY' was followed by a self-financed long-player 'SPACE I'M IN' (1991), which was picked up by 'Geffen' records in the States. This wasn't without its problems after the people that be objected to their sampling of the Stones' 'Sympathy For The Devil'; they immediately substituted it with a full-on cover of Stephen Stills' 'FOR WHAT IT'S WORTH'. 'Geffen' spun out a second album, 'FUN' (1993), leaving the band a little perturbed – in February '97, the COPE brothers were charged with criminal damage after spray-painting "No Fun" on their former employer's wall. Finally finding a worthy new home at 'Ultimate' records in '96, The BEATLES-fixated CANDYSKINS even cracked the UK singles charts – at a time when OASIS were numero uno – courtesy of 'MRS. HOOVER', 'MONDAY MORNING' (Top 40!) and 'HANG MYSELF ON YOU'. With a fanbase that probably shifted good money for everything OASIS, and the critics dismissing them as a quitessential Brit-pop joke, it was no surprise when The CANDYSKINS popped out for good, leaving behind yet another patchy album, 'DEATH OF A MINOR TV CELEBRITY' (1998). Fame ... what's her name? • **Covered:** I'VE GOTTA GET A MESSAGE TO YOU (Bee Gees) / THE DAY THE WORLD TURNED DAYGLO (X-Ray Spex) / SHE DON'T USE JELLY (Flaming Lips).

Album rating: SPACE I'M IN (*6) / FUN (*4) / SUNDAY MORNING FEVER (*5) / DEATH OF A MINOR TV CELEBRITY (*5)

MARK COPE – vocals / **NICK COPE** – guitars / **NICK BURTON** – lead guitar / **KARL SHALE** – bass / **JOHN HALLIDAY** – drums

Long Beach / not iss.

Nov 90. (12"m) *(Beach 5T)* **SUBMARINE SONG. / JUST LIKE RAIN / FREEDOM BUS**
Apr 91. (12"m) *(Beach 6T)* **SHE BLEW ME AWAY. / ALL OVER NOW / WITHOUT LOVE**

Stuff / not iss.

May 91. (lp) *(STUFFU/U 4)* **SPACE I'M IN**
– So easy / Submarine song / Black and blue / Get together / Freedom bus / 10 feet high / She blew me away / Third World blues / Not sad to see you go / For what it's worth / Never will forget you / Space I'm in / Without love. *(re-iss. Oct91 on 'Geffen' cd/c/lp; GED/GEC/GEF 24370)*
Jul 91. (12"ep) *(STUFFU/U 3)* **YOU ARE HERE EP**
– Freedom bus / So easy / To be here now / Love me.

Geffen / Geffen

Sep 91. (7") *<DGCS 3>* **SUBMARINE SONG. / NOT SAD TO SEE YOU GO**
(12"+=) *<DGCT 3>* – Love me / Just like rain.
Feb 93. (cd/c/lp) *(<GED/GEC/GEF 24494>)* **FUN**
– Wembley / Fun / House at the top of the hill / Tired of being happy / Land of love / Everybody loves you / Everything just falls apart on me / You are here / Grass / Dig it deep / Let's take over the world / All over now. *(cd re-iss. Nov96; same)*
Feb 93. (7") *(GFS 30)* **WEMBLEY. / ALL OVER NOW**
(12"+=/cd-s+=) *(GFST/+D 30)* – Elevate me.
Jul 93. (12"/cd-s) *(GFST/+D 44)* **LAND OF LOVE. / YOU ARE HERE / I'D LOVE TO TAKE YOU HOME**

Rotator / not iss.

Nov 95. (7") *(RRSV 102)* **MRS. HOOVER. / DISCO HELL**
(cd-s+=) *(RRSVD 102)* – Head of a pin.

Ultimate / not iss.

Jun 96. (7") *(TOPP 043)* **GET ON. / DON'T WANT TO BE A MAN**
(cd-s) *(TOPP 043CD)* – ('A'side / Don't give it up / Kidney scan.
Aug 96. (7") *(TOPP 048)* **CIRCLES. / CAMEL HAIR SUIT**
(cd-s) *(TOPP 048CD)* – ('A'side) / Bad hair day / Turn it off.
Oct 96. (7") *(TOPP 051)* **MRS. HOOVER. / I'VE GOTTA GET A MESSAGE TO YOU** [65]
(cd-s) *(TOPP 051CD)* – ('A'side) / Disco hell / Head of a pin.
(cd-s) *(TOPP 051CDX)* – ('A'side) / Hard to say / The day the world turned dayglo.
Jan 97. (7") *(TOPP 055)* **MONDAY MORNING. / COMMUNIST FREAK** [34]
(cd-s) *(TOPP 055CD)* – ('A'side) / Godhead / Whatever it takes.
(cd-s) *(TOPP 055CDX)* – ('A'side) / Joke of the week / Just keeps happening.
Mar 97. (cd/c/yellow-lp) *(TOPP CD/MC/LP 054)* **SUNDAY MORNING FEVER**
– Mrs. Hoover / 24 hours (u.s.e.d) / Car crash / Monday morning / Get on / Europe and Japan / Hang myself on you / Disco hell / Circles / Face the day / D.R.U.N.K. / No no no / Help me / In my hair.
Apr 97. (7") *(TOPP 059)* **HANG MYSELF ON YOU. / DOWNTOWN** [65]
(cd-s) *(TOPP 059CD)* – ('A'side) / In my hair (demo) / Aeroplane.
(cd-s) *(TOPP 059CDX)* – ('A'side) / Boomerang / Cracked up.

— **BRETT GORDON** – bass; repl. SHALE

Nov 97. (7") *(TOPP 063)* **FEED IT. / CAR CRASH (acoustic)**
(cd-s) *(TOPP 063CD)* – ('A'side) / Dogs deluxe / Help me (JB oceanhead mix).
(cd-s) *(TOPP 063CDX)* – ('A'side) / Circles (live) / Get on (live).
Mar 98. (7") *(TOPP 065)* **YOU BETTER STOP. / MAKE YOUR OWN KIND OF MUSIC**
(cd-s) *(TOPP 065CD)* – ('A'side) / Just another day / She don't use jelly.
(cd-s) *(TOPP 065CDX)* – ('A'side) / Ball and chain / Kerosene.
Sep 98. (7") *(TOPP 070)* **SOMEWHERE UNDER LONDON. / MOBILE PHONE**
(cd-s) *(TOPP 070CD)* – ('A'side) / Destiny / L.A.D.C.
(cd-s) *(TOPP 070CDX)* – ('A'side) / Earthquake / What you go.

Velvel / Velvel

Sep 98. (c-ep) *<VELDJ 78712-4>* **NUTRITION FACTS**
– Feed it / Swimming pool / Loser friendly.
Oct 98. (cd) *(<VELDJ 79738>)* **DEATH OF A MINOR TV CELEBRITY**
– Feed it / It's a sign / Death of a minor TV celebrity / Loser friendly / Swimming pool / Somewhere under London / Song / Songbird / Teenage suicide / Friday night, Saturday morning / Going nowhere.
Dec 98. (m-cd) *<VELDJ 78718-2>* **A BRIEF HISTORY** (compilation)
– For what it's worth / Submarine / Wembley / Monday morning / Loser friendly / Feed it.

— disbanded after above

… THE GREAT INDIE DISCOGRAPHY … The 1990s

CANE 141

Formed: Galway, Ireland … 1995 by singer/songwriter MICHAEL SMALLE, GERARD CONNOLLY, with SHANE BURKE and a whole host of others – COLM HOGAN, RONAN BURKE, PAUL BRENNAN – joining in late 1998. After issuing a handful of largely ignored singles, this soft, folky Irish version of GORKY'S ZYGOTIC MYNCI issued the whispy debut album 'SCENE FROM 6AM' in late '98 to quiet critical acclaim and homecoming praise. Two years later, and a label switch to 'Setanta', the group delivered the more country-tinged, 'GARDEN TIGER MOUTH', a record with much admiration from the British and (especially) the Irish music press. AMERICAN MUSIC CLUB's troubled songwriter MARK EITZEL was so impressed with the band's striking musical abilities, he offered his vocals for 2002's EP 'NEW DAY PARADE' (on the track 'HORROR').

Album rating: SCENE FROM 6AM (*5) / GARDEN TIGER MOTH (*6)

MICHAEL SMALLE – vocals, guitar, synths, percussion / **GERARD CONNOLLY** – vocals, acoustic guitar, organ, bass / **SHANE BURKE** – bass, organ / **PAUL MAYE** – drums

 Secret   not iss.

Jul 98. (cd) *(SECCD 22)* **SCENE FROM 6AM**
 – Summerlong / The set-up / Easter in west / Down Angel road / Whither I roam / Carnival song / When you ride away / We should get together / Super 8.

— **COLM HOGAN** – drums, percussion; repl. MAYE

— added **RONAN BURKE** – organ / **PAUL BRENNAN** – synths
Nov 99. (cd-s) *(SEC 004)* **MORE NEW FRIENDS**

 Decor – Setanta Setanta

Nov 00. (7") *(DECOR 001)* **THE GRAND LUNAR.** /
Mar 01. (cd) *(<DECOR 002CD>)* **GARDEN TIGER MOTH** Jul02
 – Eager boy comics / The grand lunar / In the sky, the lucky stars / Real spacemen never walk anywhere / Photocredit one / New day parade / The party / Photocredit two / Scene from 6am / Me and Michael / The look-out kid.
Jul 01. (cd-s) *(DECOR 003CD)* **NEW DAY PARADE / HORROR**
 (with MARK EITZEL) / THE LOOK-OUT KID (landing rehearsal mix by Sean O'Hagan)

 Track & Field not iss.

Mar 02. (7") *(LANE 13)* **CYCLE VARIATION / IT GREW IN THE FIRE**
 (split w/ STEPHEN HERO)

— **SANDRA FRIEL** – vocals, concertina, accordion, keyboards, synths; repl. RONAN who became a p/t member

CAPITOL CITY DUSTERS

Formed: Washington D.C., USA … early 90's as The DUSTERS by main songwriter ALEC BOURGEOIS, BILL COLGROVE and BEN AZZARA. Treading a similar path to their DC-punk forebearers, FUGAZI, etc., The DUSTERS came up with their debut set, 'THIS AIN'T NO JUKEBOX …' (1991). All veterans of the flourishing local emocore scene, these musical journeymen took other musical trips while The DUSTERS settled for another moniker. Around the mid-90's, The CAPITOL CITY DUSTERS re-united and even found themselves on the legendary 'Dischord' imprint (run by FUGAZI's IAN MacKAYE) for comeback single 'FOREST FIRE'. With MARC LACASSE taken on board – COLGROVE had set up a web business with JAWBOX mainman, BILL BARDOT – for their next release, the album 'SIMPLICITY' (1998), the band were now touring all over the US and Europe. Post-millennium, and after another quite lengthy musical exile (which involved MARC being substituted for JESSE QUITSLAND), the CCD's got together for another rough batch of songs, 'ROCK CREEK' (2001).

Album rating: THIS AIN'T NO JUKEBOX … WE'RE A ROCK'N'ROLL BAND (*5) / SIMPLICITY (*5) / ROCK CREEK (*4)

ALEC BOURGEOIS – vocals, guitar / **BILL COLGROVE** – bass (ex-FOUNDATION) / **BEN AZZARA** – drums (of JUNCTION)

 not iss. Amphetam. Reptile

1991. (cd; as The DUSTERS) <4050> **THIS AIN'T NO JUKEBOX … WE'RE A ROCK'N'ROLL BAND**
 – This ain't no jukebox … we're a rock'n'roll band / Take a chance on love / The truck won't start / Phantom of the Strip / How could you / Hellbound train / Street legal / What can I say / Blues highway / Look what the cat drug in.

— disbanded for a while until they altered group moniker

— … **HAGGERTY** – bass, vocals; repl. COLGROVE

 not iss. Dischord

Oct 96. (7") <DIS 110> **FOREST FIRE. / SEVENTEEN**

 Dischord Super Bad

1997. (10"ep; split) <6> **FOREST FIRE / SEVENTEEN / (2 other tracks by The MOST SECRET METHOD)**

— **MARC LACASSE** – bass, guitar, vocals; repl. HAGGERTY

Nov 98. (lp/cd) <(DIS 1215/+CD)> **SIMPLICITY**
 – Minutemen song / Day away / Second to run / Forest fire / Breather / Falling down stairs / Treason / Not me now / Killing ground / Seventeen / Letter "E".

— **JESSE QUITSLUND** – bass, vocals (ex-VILE CHERUBS) repl. MARC
Jan 01. (7") *(BC 068)* **REASON.** / **(other by AINA)**
 (above issued on 'B-core')
Mar 02. (cd/lp) <(DIS 127 CD/V)> **ROCK CREEK**
 – Superimposed / Signal sound (E2) / Reason / (This is the story of) Revolution / Cancer / Rock creek park / They saved Reagan's brain / Versus / Sound fountain / Freedom.

CAP'N JAZZ (see under ⇒ JOAN OF ARC)

CAPTAIN AMERICA
(see under ⇒ VASELINES; 80's section)

CAPTAIN SOUL

Formed: London, England … 1997 under the moniker HOOVERDAM by singer/songwriter ADAM HOWORTH, NEIL BARROW, JOHN GARNER and MARTIN WELSH. Issuing only one single in 2000 on 'Sire' ('SOMETHING TO BELIVE IN'), HOOVERDAM was practically held ransom by giants 'Sire', until the group's contract expired and they were reborn as CAPTAIN SOUL. The quartet issued the summery, uptempo indie pop jam that was 'T-SHIRT 69', on ALAN McGEE's 'Poptones' record, before embarking on a European tour and recording their BYRDS-esque debut album 'BEAT YOUR CRAZY HEAD AGAINST THE SKY'. Full of jangling surf guitars, soaring keyboard melodies and a head full of good acid, The BEACH BOYS' BRUCE JOHNSON and TERRY MELCHER offered the CAPTAIN SOUL free production credits come the recording of their eagerly awaited sophomore set.

Album rating: BEAT YOUR CRAZY HEAD AGAINST THE SKY (*6)

ADAM HOWORTH – vocals, guitar / **NEIL BARROW** – vocals, bass / **JOHN GARNER** – vocals, drums / **MARTIN WELSH** – guitar

 3rd Stone not iss.

Apr 00. (cd-s; as HOOVERDAM) *(STONE 039CD)* **SOMETHING TO BELIEVE IN / FRAGILE AS A BUTTERFLY**

 Poptones not iss.

Jan 01. (7") *(MC 5016S)* **T-SHIRT 69. / T-SHIRT (alternate recording)**
Mar 01. (cd) *(MC 5016CD)* **BEAT YOUR CRAZY HEAD AGAINST THE SKY**
 – T-shirt 69 / Coming up for air / Your time / Headlights / What's it all about / Fragile as a butterfly / There goes my life / Something to believe in / Last chance saloon / When the orchestra plays.
Apr 01. (7") *(MC 5043S)* **YOUR TIME. / MANKILLER (acoustic)**

 – compilations, etc. –

Jun 02. (cd-s) *Rayman*; (RAY 003CD) **T-SHIRT 69 / YOUR TIME / SOMETHING TO BELIEVE IN (demo) / FRAGILE AS A BUTTERFLY (demo)**

CARDIGANS

Formed: Jonkoping, Sweden … October 1992 by songwriters PETER SVENSSON and MAGNUS SVENINGSSON, along with LARS-OLAF JOHANSSON, BENGT LAGERBERG and cutesy bombshell, NINA PERSSON. Despite the fact the band's founding members came from a heavy-metal background, The CARDIGANS' sound leaned more towards fragile, angelic indie-pop drawing on the melodic traditions of fellow Swedes, ABBA and UK pop ironists BEAUTIFUL SOUTH as well as French 60's pop (especially FRANCOISE HARDY's Burt Bacharach period). They initially released an album in Sweden before signing to Polydor UK and in 1995/96, scored minor successes with 'CARNIVAL', 'SICK & TIRED' and 'RISE & SHINE', all stemming from their UK debut album, 'LIFE' (1995). In the late summer of '96, they peaked critically with the starry-eyed 'LOVEFOOL', a near Top 20 hit first time around and an even bigger success upon its re-issue in conjunction with the 'Romeo & Juliet' soundtrack in 1997. The song was a standout track on their acclaimed follow-up set, 'THE FIRST BAND ON THE MOON', although the band no doubt came to regard it as something of an albatross round their necks. Presumably a reaction to being filed under Scando-pop, the more deliberately experimental 'GRAN TURISMO' (1998) saw the band sacrifice some of their charm for instant "alternative" appeal. PERSSON's subsequent activities included fruitful collaborations with TOM JONES and DAVID ARNOLD, while in 2001 she resurfaced with a new outfit, A CAMP. Together with SHUDDER TO THINK's NATHAN LARSON and augmented and produced by MARK LINKOUS (of SPARKLEHORSE fame), their eponymous set was an alt-countrified pot-pourri of pleasant cuts including a cover of Paul Westerberg's 'ROCK'N'ROLL GHOST'. • Covered: SABBATH BLOODY SABBATH + IRON MAN (Black Sabbath) / MR. CROWLEY (Ozzy Osbourne) / BOYS ARE BACK IN TOWN (Thin Lizzy).

Album rating: EMMERDALE (*6) / LIFE (*8) / FIRST BAND ON THE MOON (*7) / GRAN TURISMO (*6) / A Camp: A CAMP (*7)

NINA PERSSON (b. Karlskoga, Sweden) – vocals / **PETER SVENSSON** – guitar / **MAGNUS SVENINGSSON** – bass / **LARS-OLAF JOHANSSON** – keyboards / **BENGT LAGERBERG** – drums, flute

 Trampolene not iss.

Feb 94. (cd) *(TRACD 1501)* **EMMERDALE** – Sweden
 – Sick & tired / Black letter day / In the afternoon / Over the water / After all … / Cloudy sky / Our space / Rise and shine / Celia inside / Sabbath bloody sabbath / Seems hard / The last song. *(UK-iss.Jan97 on 'Stockholm' cd/c; 523215-2/-4)* (re-iss. May99; same)
May 94. (cd-s) *(TRACDS 501)* **RISE & SHINE / AFTER ALL** – Sweden
Aug 94. (cd-s) *(TRACDS 502)* **BLACK LETTER DAY / I FIGURED OUT** – Sweden
Sep 94. (cd-s) *(TRACDS 503)* **SICK & TIRED / PLAIN PARADE / LAIKA / POOH SONG** – Sweden

CARDIGANS (cont)

		Stockholm-Polydor	Minty Fresh
Nov 94.	(7"/c-s) (PO/+CS 336) **SICK & TIRED. / PLAIN PARADE** (cd-s) (PZCD 336) – ('A'side) / Pooh song / The boys are back in town / Carnival (Puck version).		-
May 95.	(7"/c-s) (PO/+CS 345) **CARNIVAL. / MR. CROWLEY** (live) (cd-s+=) (PZCD 345) – Emmerdale. (re-iss. Nov95, hit No.35; same)	72	-
Jun 95.	(cd/c/lp) (523556-2/-4/-1) <MF 15> **LIFE** – Carnival / Gordon's garden party / Daddy's car / Sick & tired / Tomorrow / Rise & shine / Beautiful one / Travelling with Charley / Fine / Celia inside / Hey! get out of my way / After all. (cd re-iss. May99; same) (lp re-iss. Sep99 on 'Simply Vinyl'; SVLP 114)	58	
Sep 95.	(c-s) (577311-4) **SICK & TIRED / PLAIN PARADE** (cd-s+=) (577311-2) – Laika / Pooh song.	34	
Feb 96.	(7"/c-s) (577824-7/-4) **RISE & SHINE. / PIKE BUBBLES** (cd-s+=) (577825-2) – Cocktail party bloody cocktail party.	29	

		Stockholm-Polydor	Mercury
Sep 96.	(7"white/c-s) (575528-7/-4) **LOVEFOOL. / NASTY SUNNY BEAM** (cd-s+=) (575295-2) – Iron man (first try).	21	
Sep 96.	(cd/c/lp) (<533117-2/-4/-1>) **FIRST BAND ON THE MOON** – Your new cuckoo / Been it / Heartbreaker / Happy meal II / Never recover / Step on me / Lovefool / Loser / Iron man / The great divide / Choke. (cd re-iss. May99; same)	18	35
Nov 96.	(7"brown/c-s) (575966-7/-4) **BEEN IT. / BEEN IT (radio)** (cd-s+=) (575966-2) – Blah blah blah / Losers (first try). below was featured on the film 'Romeo & Juliet'	56	
Apr 97.	(c-s) (571050-4) **LOVEFOOL / ('A'-Todd Terry remix)** (cd-s+=) (571050-2) – ('A'-Todd Terry's frozen sun mix). (cd-s) (571051-2) – ('A'side / Sick & tired (live) / Carnival (live) / Rise & shine (live).	2	-
Aug 97.	(7"/c-s) (571633-7/-4) **YOUR NEW CUCKOO. / LOVEFOOL (radio)** (cd-s+=) (571633-2) – I figured out (demo '93) / After all (demo '93). (cd-s) (571661-2) – ('A'radio) / ('A'-Hyper disco mix) / ('A'-Super stereo mix).	35	
Oct 98.	(c-s) (567988-4) **MY FAVOURITE GAME / LOVEFOOL (live)** (cd-s+=) (567991-2) – ('A'-Wubbledub mix). (cd-s) (567989-2) – ('A'side) / War / Sick and tired (live).	14	
Oct 98.	(cd/c) (<559081-2/-4>) **GRAN TURISMO** – Paralyzed / Erase – Rewind / Explode / Starter / Hanging around / Higher / Marvel hill / My favourite game / Do you believe / Junk of the hearts / Nil.	8	
Feb 99.	(c-s) (563535-4) **ERASE – REWIND / MY FAVOURITE GAME** (cd-s+=) (563533-2) – Explode (remixed) / ('B'-CD-Rom). (cd-s) (563535-2) – ('A'side) / ('A'mixes; Cut La Roc vocal mix & Naid remix).	7	
Jul 99.	(c-s) (561268-4) **HANGING AROUND / MY FAVOURITE GAME (acoustic radio session)** (cd-s) (561268-2) – ('A'side) / Erase – Rewind (CD-Rom video; banned directors cut). (cd-s) (561269-2) – ('A'side) / My favourite game (Rollo from Faithless remix) / ('A'-CD-Rom video).	17	-
—	The CARDIGANS backed TOM JONES on a collaborative single, 'Burning Down The House'. In April 2000, NINA PERSSON & DAVID ARNOLD hit UK No.49 with the single 'THEME FROM RANDALL & HOPKIRK (DECEASED)'.		

– compilations, etc. –

May 97.	(10xcd-ep-box) Border; (CARDSIN 1) **THE COMPLETE SINGLES COLLECTION**		-
—	there is also a Various Artists tribute album (TR 012CD)		

A CAMP

NINA PERSSON / + **NATHAN LARSON** – instruments (of SHUDDER TO THINK) / with **MARK LINKOUS** + guests, etc.

		Polydor	Universal
Aug 01.	(7"/cd-s) (15216-7/-2) **I CAN BUY YOU. / ANGEL OF SADNESS / CHARLIE CHARLIE**	46	-
Sep 01.	(cd) (014851-2) <415594> **A CAMP** – Frequent flyer / I can buy you / Angel of sadness / Such a bad comedown / Song for the leftovers / Walking the cow / Hard as a stone / Algebra / Silent night / The same old song / The oddness of the Lord / Rock'n'roll ghost / The bluest eyes in Texas / Elephant.		

CARDINAL (see under ⇒ Davies, Richard)

CAROUSEL (see under ⇒ RAZORCUTS)

CARTER THE UNSTOPPABLE SEX MACHINE

Formed: Streatham, South London, England ... 1988 by FRUITBAT (LES CARTER) and JIM BOB (JIM MORRISON). They had both been in early 80's outfit The BALLPOINTS, and after a lengthy period with real jobs, they formed the group JAMIE WEDNESDAY in 1984; signing to 'Rough Trade' subsidiary label 'Pink', they released two singles before disbanding in early '87. The following year they became CARTER THE UNSTOPPABLE SEX MACHINE, debuting that summer with 'SHELTERED LIFE', railing against shady landlords. It was the first in a memorable, if occasionally grating series of DIY agit-pop/punk singles which characterised an era of British indie music; "baggy" had died a lingering death and "grunge" was lumbering over the horizon, a time when all kinds of sub-standard ephemera made the cover of the NME. CARTER were at least entertaining, an undulatingly melodic follow-up single, 'SHERIFF FATMAN', unlucky not to chart (it later became their first Top 30 hit when re-released in the summer of '91). By this point, CARTER mania had firmly gripped the student nation and you couldn't go to any gig without seeing the ubiquitous '30 SOMETHING' baseball shirt. The 1991 album of the same name followed on from the sample-happy drum-machine-driven crusty pop of the debut, '101 DAMNATIONS' (1990), and provided a further controversial hit in the anti-army brutality rant, 'BLOODSPORTS FOR ALL'. The chirpy cockney duo (now signed to 'Chrysalis') topped off their annus glorious with a riotous headlining slot at the Reading Festival. There was some grief, however, as the ever vigilant ROLLING STONES legal team made explicit their concern over 'AFTER THE WATERSHED's none too subtle lift from JAGGER and Co.'s 'RUBY TUESDAY'. Following a Christmas re-issue of 'RUBBISH' (featuring one of their inimitable cover versions on the b-side, The Pet Shop Boys' 'RENT' coming in for the CARTER treatment this time around), the group returned in Spring '92 with one of their finest singles, 'THE ONLY LIVING BOY IN NEW CROSS'. A third set, ironically titled '1992 – THE LOVE ALBUM' topped the UK chart, another round of witty punning and HALF MAN HALF BISCUIT style humour. With the advent of American underground domination however, CARTER sounded increasingly tame, subsequent albums 'POST HISTORIC MONSTERS' and 'WORRY BOMB' entering the Top 10 but not hanging around. After a mid-90's split, the band, now signed to indie label, 'Cooking Vinyl', returned in 1997 and 1998 with the largely ignored 'A WORLD WITHOUT DAVE' and 'I BLAME THE GOVERNMENT'. JIM MORRISON virtually went solo in '99 resurfacing with his own JIM'S SUPER STEREOWORLD and signing to 'Fierce Panda'. After two DIY singles, 'BONKERS IN THE NUT' and 'COULD U B THE 1 I WAITED 4', he finally issued a debut. Pomp-punk and the kitchen sink also best described a follow-up mini-set in 2002, 'IN A BIG FLASH CAR ON A SATURDAY NIGHT'; it was a marked improvement on JIM and FRUITBAT's alter-ego collaboration, WHO'S THE DADDY NOW?, which resulted in a one-off single in 2001, 'THE BEEPER SONG'. • **Covered**: RANDY SCOUSE GIT (Monkees) / EVERYBODY'S HAPPY NOWADAYS (Buzzcocks) / BEDSITTER (Soft Cell) / THIS IS HOW IT FEELS (Inspiral Carpets) / PANIC (Smiths) / MANNEQUIN (Wire) / KING ROCKER (Generation X) / DOWN IN THE TUBE STATION AT MIDNIGHT (Jam) / ANOTHER BRICK IN THE WALL (Pink Floyd) / THE IMPOSSIBLE DREAM (Mitch Leigh – Joe Darion) / HIT (Sugarcubes) / SPEEED KING (These Animal Men) / SILVER DREAM MACHINE (David Essex). • **Trivia**: Surprisingly it was JONATHAN KING who gave them tabloid exposure in his 'Sun' column.

Album rating: 101 DAMNATIONS (*9) / 30 SOMETHING (*8) / 1992 – THE LOVE ALBUM (*7) / POST-HISTORIC MONSTERS (*8) / STARRY EYED AND BOLLOCK NAKED (A COLLECTION OF B-SIDES) (*6) / WORRY BOMB (*5) / STRAW DONKEYS – THE SINGLES compilation (*6) / A WORLD WITHOUT DAVE mini (*5) / I BLAME THE GOVERNMENT (*4) / LIVE! (*5) / SESSIONS collection (*5) / Jim's Super Stereoworld: JIM'S SUPER STEREOWORLD (*6) / IN A BIG FLASH CAR ON A SATURDAY NIGHT mini (*5)

JAMIE WEDNESDAY

JIM 'Jim Bob' MORRISON (b.22 Nov'60) – vocals, acoustic guitar / **LES 'Fruitbat' CARTER** (b.12 Feb'58) – bass / **LINDSEY HENRY** – trumpet / **SIMON LOWE** – brass / **DEAS LEGGETT** – drums

		Pink	not iss.
Nov 85.	(12"ep) (PINKY 6) **VOTE FOR LOVE / THE WALL. / WHITE HORSES / BUTTONS AND BOWS**		-
May 86.	(12"ep) (PINKY 10) **WE THREE KINGS OF ORIENT AREN'T. / LAST NIGHT I HAD THE STRANGEST DREAM / I THINK I'LL THROW A PARTY FOR MYSELF**		-
—	disbanded Feb'87		

CARTER THE UNSTOPPABLE SEX MACHINE

— was duo formed by **JIM BOB & FRUITBAT** who now both played guitar with back-up of tape machines & **JIM BOB** – vocals

		Big Cat	Chrysalis
Aug 88.	(12"m) (BBA 03) **SHELTERED LIFE. / IS THIS THE ONLY WAY THROUGH TO YOU? / GRANNY FARMING IN THE U.K.** (re-iss. Jun94 on 'Southern' cd-ep; 18620-2)		-
Nov 89.	(12"ep) (ABB 100T) **SHERIFF FATMAN / R.S.P.C.E. / TWIN-TUB WITH GUITAR / EVERYBODY'S HAPPY NOWADAYS**		-
Jan 90.	(lp/c/cd) (ABB/+C/CD 101) <21881> **101 DAMNATIONS** – A perfect day to drop the bomb / Midnight on the murder mile / The road to Domestos / An all-American sport / 24 minutes to Tulsa Hill / Good grief / Charlie Brown / Everytime a churchbell rings / Good grief / Sheriff Fatman / G.I. blues. (re-dist.Sep91; same; hit No.29)		
May 90.	(12"/cd-s) (ABB 102 T/CD) **RUBBISH. / RENT / ALTERNATIVE ALF GARNET**		
Oct 90.	(export; m-lp/m-cd) (ABB 103X/+CD) **HANDBUILT FOR PERVERTS**	-	-

		Rough Trade	not iss.
Oct 90.	(7") (RT 242) **ANYTIME, ANYPLACE, ANYWHERE. / RE-EDUCATING RITA** (12"+=/cd-s+=) (RTT 242/+CD) – Alternative title / Randy sarf git.		-
Jan 91.	(7"/c-s) (R 2011 268-7/-6) **BLOODSPORTS FOR ALL. / 2001: A CLOCKWORK ORANGE** (12"+=/cd-s+=) (R 2011 268-0/-3) – Bedsitter.	48	-
Feb 91.	(cd/c/lp) (RT 2011 270-2/-4/-1) <21884> **30 SOMETHING** – Surfin' USM / My second to last will and testament / Anytime anyplace anywhere / Prince in a pauper's grave / Shopper's paradise / Billy's smart circus / Bloodsport	8	

CARTER THE UNSTOPPABLE SEX MACHINE (cont)

for all / Sealed with a Glasgow kiss / Say it with flowers / Falling on a bruise / The final comedown. <US-iss.Aug91 on 'Chrysalis'; same as US> (re-iss. Jan92 on 'Chrysalis' cd/c/lp; CCD/ZCHR/CHR 1897); hit UK 21) (re-iss. Feb95; same as US)

		Chrysalis	Chrysalis
Jun 91.	(7") (USM 1) **SHERIFF FATMAN. / R.S.P.C.E.**	23	

(c-s+=/12"+=/cd-s+=) (USM X/XMS/CD 1) – Twin-tub with guitar / Everybody's happy nowadays.

| Oct 91. | (7"/c-s) (USM/+XMC 2) **AFTER THE WATERSHED. / THE 90's REVIVAL / A NATION OF SHOPLIFTERS** | 11 | - |

(12"+=/cd-s+=) (USM X/CD 2) – This is how it feels.

| Dec 91. | (7"/c-s) (USM/+XMC 3) **RUBBISH. / ALTERNATIVE ALF GARNET** | 14 | - |

(12"+=/cd-s+=) (USM X/CD 3) – Rent.

| Apr 92. | (7"/c-s/12"/cd-s) (USM/+XMC/X/CD 4) **THE ONLY LIVING BOY IN NEW CROSS. / WATCHING THE BIG APPLE TURN / PANIC** | 7 | - |

| May 92. | (cd/c/lp) (CCD/ZCHR/CHR 1946) <21946> **1992 – THE LOVE ALBUM** | 1 | |

– 1993 / Is wrestling fixed? / The only living boy in New Cross / Suppose you gave a funeral and nobody came / England / Do re mi, so far so good / Look mum, no hands / While you were out / Skywest and crooked / The impossible dream. (re-iss. Mar94 & Feb95 cd/c;)

| Jun 92. | (7"/c-s/12"/cd-s) (USM/+XMC/X/CD 5) **DO RE MI, SO FAR SO GOOD / MANNEQUIN. / KING ROCKER / DOWN IN THE TUBE-STATION AT MIDNIGHT** | 22 | - |

| Nov 92. | (7"/c-s/12"/cd-s) (USM/+XMC/X/CD 6) **THE IMPOSSIBLE DREAM / TURN ON, TUNE IN AND SWITCH OFF / WHEN THESAURUSES RULED THE WORLD / BRING ON THE GIRLS** | 21 | - |

| Aug 93. | (7"/c-s) (USM/+XMC 7) **LEAN ON ME I WON'T FALL OVER. / HIT** | 16 | - |

(12"+=/cd-s+=) (12/CD USM 7) – Always the bridesmaid never the bride.

| Sep 93. | (cd/c/lp) (CD/TC+/CHR 7090) **POST HISTORIC MONSTERS** | 5 | - |

– 2 million years B.C. / The music that nobody likes / Mid day crisis / Cheer up, it might never happen / Stuff the jubilee! / A bachelor for Baden Powell / Spoilsports personality of the year / Suicide isn't painless / Being here / Evil / Sing fat lady sing / Travis / Lean on me I won't fall over / Lenny and Terence / Under the thumb and over the Moon. (re-iss. Feb95; same)

| Oct 93. | (7"/c-s) (USM/+XMC 8) **LENNY AND TERENCE. / HER SONG** | 40 | - |

(12"+=/cd-s+=) (12/CD USM 8) – Commercial fucking suicide (part 1) / Stuff the jubilee (1977).

| Mar 94. | (c-s/7") (TC-/USM 10) **GLAM ROCK COPS. / LEAN ON ME (I WON'T FALL OVER) (by The FAMILY CAT)** | 24 | - |

(12"+=/cd-s+=) (12USM/CDUSMS 10) – ('A'-GRID mixes).
(cd-s) (CDUSM 10) – ('A'side) / Bloodsports for all (by SULTANS OF PING F.C.) / Lenny and Terence (by BLADE) / Falling on a bruise (by PUBLIC WORKS).

| Mar 94. | (cd/c/lp) (CD/TC+/CHR 6069) **STARRY EYED AND BOLLOCK NAKED (A COLLECTION OF B-SIDES)** (compilation) | 22 | - |

– Is this the only way to get through to you? / Granny farming in the UK / R.S.P.C.E. / Twin tub with guitar / Alternative Alf Garnett / Re educating Rita / 2001: A clockwork orange / The 90's revival / A nation of shoplifters / Watching the big apple turn over / Turn on, tune in and switch off / When Thesauruses ruled the Earth / Bring on the girls! / Always the bridesmaid never the bride / Her song / Commercial f**king suicide / Stuff the jubilee (1977) / Glam rock cops. (re-iss. Feb95 & Sep98; same)

—— added **WEZ BOYNTON** – drums (ex-RESQUE)

| Nov 94. | (c-s/7") (TC+/USM 11) **LET'S GET TATTOOS. / ESPECIALLY 4 U** | 30 | - |

(cd-s+=) (CDUSMS 11) – Speed king / Silver dream machine.
(cd-s) (CDUSM 11) – ('A'side) / Turbulence / King for a day.

| Jan 95. | (c-s/7"colrd) (TC+/USM 12) **THE YOUNG OFFENDER'S MUM. / TROUBLE** | 34 | - |

(cd-s+=) (CDUSMS 12) – This one's for me.
(cd-s) (CDUSM 12) – ('A'side) / Rubbish (live) / Suicide isn't painless (live) / Falling on a bruise (live).

| Feb 95. | (cd/c/d-lp) (CD/TC+/CHR 6096) **WORRY BOMB** | 9 | - |

– Cheap'n'cheesy / Airplane food – airplane fest food / The young offender's mum / Gas (man) / The life and soul of the party dies / My defeatest attitude / Worry bomb / Senile delinquent / Me and Mr.Jones / Let's get tattoos / Going straight / God, Saint Peter and the guardian angel / The only looney left in town / Ceasefire. (d-cd+=) (CDCHRX 6096) **DOMA SPORTOVA . . . LIVE IN ZAGREB, 20/5/94** – Alternative Alf Garnett / Do re mi so far so good / A bachelor pad for Baden Powell / Re-educating Rita / The only living boy in New Cross / Lean on me I won't fall over / Granny farming in the U.K. / Travis / Sing fat lady sing / Lenny and Terence / Commercial fucking suicide part 1.

| Sep 95. | (c-s/7"red) (TC+/USM 13) **BORN ON THE 5th OF NOVEMBER. / D.I.V.O.R.C.E.F.G.** | 35 | - |

(cd-s) (CDUSM 13) – ('A'side) / Tomorrow when you die / The aftertaste of Paradise / Airplane food.

| Oct 95. | (cd/c/lp) (CD/TC+/CHR 6110) **STRAW DONKEY . . . THE SINGLES** (compilation) | 37 | - |

– A sheltered life / Sheriff Fatman / Rubbish / Antime anyplace anywhere / Bloodsport for all / After the watershed (early learning the hard way) / The only living boy in New Cross / Do re mi, so far so good / The impossible dream / Lean on me (I won't fall over) / Lenny and Terence / Glam rock cops / Let's get tattoos / The young offender's mum / Born on the 5th of November. (cd re-iss. Sep97; same)

—— CARTER split for around a year after above

		Cooking Vinyl	Cooking Vinyl
Mar 97.	(m-lp/m-cd) (<COOK/+CD 120>) **A WORLD WITHOUT DAVE**	73	Apr97

– Broken down in broken town / A world without Dave / Before the war / Nowhere fast / Johnny Cash / And God created Brixton. (cd+=) – Stand up and be counted / Negative equity / Road rage.

		Cooking Vinyl	True North
Jan 98.	(cd) (COOKCD 136) <TN 163> **I BLAME THE GOVERNMENT**		Sep98

– The wrong place at the wrong time / 23:59 end of the world / Sunshine / The undertaker and the hippy protest singer / Sweetheart sugar baby / Growing old disgracefully / The man who bought the world winning the war / I blame the government / Citizen's band radio / Psycho Bill / Closedown / Girls can keep a secret.

| Feb 99. | (cd) (COOKCD 149) **LIVE! (live)** | | |

– 24 minutes from Tulse Hill / Rubbish / Do re mi (so far so good) / Anytime anyplace anywhere / A prince in a pauper's grave / A perfect day to drop the bomb / Say it with flowers / Rent / Cheer up it might never happen / The taking of Peckham 123 / Lenny and Terence (with JAMES ATKIN) / Suicide isn't painless / Growing old disgracefully / Elvis lives and Carterbreakamerica / Airplane food / Let's get tattoos / The model.

– compilations, etc. –

| Oct 98. | (cd) Cooking Vinyl; (COOKCD 165) **SESSIONS** (BBC 1991, 1994, 1997) | | - |

– Sheriff Fatman / A prince in pauper's grave / Sealed with a Glasgow kiss / A sheltered life / Alternative Alf Garnett / Re-educating Rita / Commercial flippin' suicide / Granny farming in the UK / Johnny Cash / Nowhere fast / Girls can keep a secret.

JIM'S SUPER STEREOWORLD

—— yes, JIM MORRISON (the – only – living one in New Cross!) all alone

		Fierce Panda	Music Blitz
Jul 99.	(7") (NING 076) **BONKERS IN THE NUT. / YOU'RE MY MATE (AND I LIKE YOU)**		-

(cd-s+=) (NING 076CD) – Rock'n'roll relay race.

| Nov 99. | (7") (NING 086) **COULD U BE THE 1 I WAITED 4. / JIM'S SUPER STEREOWORLD SIGN TO FIERCE PANDA** | | - |

(cd-s) (NING 086CD) – ('A'side) / Put your lips together and blow / World of disco.

| Mar 01. | (cd) <30006> **JIM'S SUPER STEREOWORLD** | - | |

– Bonkers in the nut / Greetings earthlings (we come in peace) / Pear shaped world / Superslob / Thw happiest man alive / Could U B the 1 I waited 4 / 1000 feet above the earth / A bad day / The king is dead / My name is John (and I want you back) / When you're gone (pts.1-2) / Touchy feely.

		Tenforty Sound	not iss.
Feb 02.	(m-cd) (BMW/JSSW 1042) **IN A BIG FLASH CAR ON A SATURDAY NIGHT**		-

– Heads will rock / Young dumb (and full of fun) / Big flash car / Jim's mobile disco / Hey Kenny / Mission control / Candy floss / Tight pants / Happier times.

| Jul 02. | (cd-ep) (JIMCITY 1043) **BUBBLEGUM E.P.** | | - |

– Bubblegum / Hair metal / Young & dumb & full of fun / 1st time caller (long time listener).

CARTWHEEL (see under ⇒ WATLING, Laura)

CASH AUDIO

Formed: Chicago, Illinois, USA . . . 1994 as CASHMONEY by JOHN HUMPHREY (who had been part of the outfit, GOD AND TEXAS) and SCOTT GIAMPINO; they had originally started out as jazz-rockers The LATE GREAT DANES, although no records were released. A low-key debut 45 for 'Tug-O-War' in 1996, 'OIL CAN', led to a deal with 'Touch & Go' and the unfettering of debut LP, 'BLACK HEARTS & BROKEN WILLS' (1997), a record produced by BRIAN DECK (RED RED MEAT). The latter also worked and guested on their follow-up, 'HALOS OF SMOKE AND FIRE' (1998), a record that branded them unfairly as the poor man's JON SPENCER BLUES EXPLOSION. However, the duo became really unstuck when the 'Cash Money' rap label threatened to sue them, leaving the guys with no qualms about altering their name to CASH AUDIO; an album 'THE ORANGE SESSIONS' was recorded during this troubled period. In 2000, CASH AUDIO delivered their take on contemporary blues and cowpunk, 'GREEN BULLET', virtually TOM WAITS on rockabilly pills. • **Covered:** HIDE AWAY (Freddie King) / MY HOME IS A PRISON (Lonesome Sundown) / RUMBLE (Link Wray). • **Note:** Not to be confused rap artist, CASH MONEY, who recorded with partner, MARVELOUS in the late 80's.

Album rating: Cashmoney: BLACK HEARTS AND BROKEN WILLS (*5) / HALOS OF SMOKE AND FIRE (*6) / Cash Audio: GREEN BULLET (*5) / THE ORANGE SESSIONS (*4)

CASHMONEY

JOHN HUMPHREY – vocals, guitar (ex-GOD AND TEXAS) / **SCOTT GIAMPINO** – drums (ex-ROSEHIPS)

		not iss.	Tug-O-War
1996.	(7") <002> **OIL CAN. / HELICOPTER RIDE**	-	

		Touch & Go	Touch & Go
Apr 97.	(cd) <(TG 177CD)> **BLACK HEARTS AND BROKEN WILLS**		

– Short change / Oil can / Lazy / Lonesome stranger / Train to ruin / Lightning fire / River / Death note / Damn damn damn / Good as gold / True blue / Afternoon shade / Totem / Nightwind.

—— added guests **BRIAN DECK** – keyboards, producer (of RED RED MEAT) / **COREY RUSK, JEFF HAMILTON, WARREN ELLIS + KEVIN JUNIOR**

| Mar 98. | (cd) <(TG 187CD)> **HALOS OF SMOKE AND FIRE** | | |

– Pie and gas / Bad case of bitter pills / El Toro / Do it again / Ashes to the wind / Midnight shakes / Drowning boat / Hey blackbird / Mask of Amontiago / Run like hell / Flight of the greyhound ghost / Evangeline.

		Orange	not iss.
May 99.	(d7"ep) (ORANGE 001) **LETTER TO STAX. / HIDE AWAY // SPACE IS THE PLACE. / RUMBLE**		-

(re-iss. Oct00; same)

CASH AUDIO

— changed their moniker slightly (same line-up)

                                              Touch & Go / Touch & Go

May 00. (cd) <(TG B213CD)> **GREEN BULLET** — / Apr00
 — Who killed the blues? / Miles to coast / The power of tequila / Capitol city blues / Gold dust majesty / Shifty-eyed devil / Wrong again / 44 blues / Black and sweet / Got to hurry.

                                              Orange / Orange

Mar 01. (10"m-lp/cd) <(OR/+A 007)> **THE ORANGE SESSIONS** (rec. 1999) — / Feb01
 — Don't put me on front street / Chicken heart / Fast forward / Here comes the wrecking ball / The way to El Dorado / My home is prison / Pork chop / Hey you / Letter to Stax / Hide away / Space is the place / Rumble. (cd+=) – (20 minute interview).

CASINO ASHTRAYS (see under ⇒ WATLING, Laura)

CAST

Formed: Liverpool, England . . . 1994 by ex-LA'S guitarist JOHN POWER, alongside KEITH O'NEIL, LIAM TYSON and PETER WILKINSON. Bassist POWER had become increasingly disillusioned with The LA'S interminable absence from the music scene, taking his future into his own hands and developing his 60's influenced songwriting within a more solid framework. Fortuitously, POWERS' strident, melodic sound was perfectly in tune with the emerging retro fixated Brit-pop sound and, with the influential backing of OASIS, CAST crashed into the Top 20 in the summer of '95 with 'FINETIME'. Surfing on a wave of frothy powerchords and an irrepressibly buoyant melody, 'ALRIGHT' followed soon after, the track becoming something of a theme tune and a definitive highlight of their debut set, 'ALL CHANGE'. Released later that Autumn, the album divided the critics, some raving over its immaculate melodic appeal, some deriding its workmanlike adherence to "classic songwriting". Whatever, there was no doubting POWER's ear for a tune, and the sublime 'SANDSTORM' gave the band a further Top 10 hit in early '96. CAST's solid style inevitably translated well to the live arena and they built up a rabid following of beany-topped fans, the same constituency of check-shirted "lads" who frequented OASIS and OCEAN COLOUR SCENE gigs. In Autumn '96, the group scored their first Top 5 with 'FLYING', a lilting new track which further showcased their mastery of BEATLES-esque pop dynamics. However, the critics were just dying to sink their claws into this resolutely untrendy outfit, with the fine 'MOTHER NATURE CALLS' (1997) unfairly receiving mixed reviews. Detractors rounded on POWER's spiritually-enhanced muse and mystical leanings but there was no arguing with the life-affirming power inherent in songs like 'GLIDING STAR', another Top 10 smash in summer '97. Influenced by the WHO on a 'Magic Bus'-type thing (with production from GIL NORTON and string accompaniment courtesy of DAVID ARNOLD) POWER and Co retro-fied their way back into the charts with 'BEAT MAMA'. A hook-line festival-friendly tune, it previewed their third Top 10 album, 'MAGIC HOUR' (1999), yet another to gain the support from both the Indie and Modern Rock factions. Unfortunately, when they arrived back with a fourth set, 'BEETROOT' (2001), CAST were no longer in vogue – or for that matter in the album charts.

Album rating: ALL CHANGE (*7) / MOTHER NATURE CALLS (*6) / MAGIC HOUR (*5) / BEETROOT (*4)

JOHN POWER (b.14 Sep'67) – vocals, guitar (ex-LA'S) / **LIAM TYSON** (b. 7 Feb'69) – guitar / **PETER WILKINSON** (b. 9 May'69) – bass (ex-SHACK) / **KEITH O'NEIL** (b.18 Feb'69) – drums

                                  Polydor / Polydor

Jul 95. (7"green/c-s/cd-s) (579 506-7/-4/-2) **FINETIME. / BETTER MAN / SATELLITES**   17 / –

Sep 95. (7"blue/c-s/cd-s) (579 926-7/-4/-2) **ALRIGHT. / FOLLOW ME DOWN / MEET ME**   13 / –

Oct 95. (cd/c/d-lp) (529 312-2/-4/-1) **ALL CHANGE**   7 / –
 — Alright / Promised land / Sandstorm / Mankind / Tell it like it is / Four walls / Finetime / Back of my mind / Walkaway / Reflections / History / Two of a kind.

Jan 96. (7"orange/c-s) (577 872-7/-4) **SANDSTORM. / HOURGLASS / BACK OF MY MIND**   8 / –
 (cd-s+=/tin-cd-s+=) (577 873/903-2) – Alright (live).

Mar 96. (7"clear/c-s) (576 284-7/-4) **WALKAWAY. / FULFILL / FINETIME (acoustic)**   9 / –
 (cd-s) (576 285-2) – (first 2 tracks) / Mother.

Oct 96. (7"/c-s) (575 476-7/-4) **FLYING. / BETWEEN THE EYES / FOR SO LONG**   4 / –
 (pic-cd-s+=) (575 477-2) – Walkaway.

Mar 97. (7"/c-s) (573 648-7/-4) **FREE ME. / COME ON EVERYBODY / CANTER**   7 / –
 (cd-s+=) (573 649-2) – ('A'acoustic).
 (cd-s) (573 651-2) – ('A'side) / Release my soul / Dancing on the flames.

Apr 97. (cd/c/lp) (537 567-2/-4/-1) **MOTHER NATURE CALLS**   3 / –
 — Free me / On the run / Live the dream / Soul tied / She sun shines / I'm so lonely / The mad hatter / Mirror me / Guiding star / Never gonna tell you what to do (revolution) / Dance of the stars. (special edition d-cd Nov97; 539681-2)

Jun 97. (7") (571 172-7) **GUIDING STAR. / OUT OF THE BLUE**   9 / –
 (c-s+=) (571 172-4) – Keep it alive.
 (cd-s+=) (571 173-2) – Free me (live) / Mirror me (live).
 (cd-s) (571 295-2) – ('A'side) / Keep it alive / Redemption song (live) / ('A'acoustic).

Sep 97. (c-s) (571 500-4) <6025> **LIVE THE DREAM / HOLD ON / FLOW**   7 / Apr98
 (cd-s) (571 501-2) – (first 2 tracks) / Effectomatic who / ('A'acoustic).
 (cd-s) (571 685-2) – (first & third tracks) / On the run.

Nov 97. (c-s) (569 256-4) **I'M SO LONELY / THINGS YOU MAKE ME DO / THEME FROM**   14 / –
 (cd-s) (569 057-2) – (first 2 tracks) / Never gonna tell you / History.
 (cd-s) (569 059-2) – (tracks 1 & 3) / History.

Apr 99. (c-s) (563592-4) **BEAT MAMA / GET ON YOU / HOEDOWN**   9 / –
 (cd-s) (563593-2) – (first 2 tracks) / 3 nines are 28.
 (cd-s) (563595-2) – (first & third tracks) / Whiskey song.

May 99. (cd/c/d-lp) (547176-2/-4/-1) **MAGIC HOUR**   6 / –
 — Beat mama / Compared to you / She falls / Dreamer / Magic hour / Company man / Alien / Higher / Chasing the day / The feeling remains / Burn the light / Hideaway.

Jul 99. (c-s) (561227-4) **MAGIC HOUR / ALLBRIGHT**   28 / –
 (cd-s) (561227-2) – ('A'side) / Gypsy song / I never wanna lose you.
 (cd-s) (561228-2) – ('A'side) / Beat mama / What you gonna do.

Jul 01. (c-s) (587175-4) **DESERT DROUGHT / COBWEBS**   45 / –
 (cd-s+=) (587175-2) – ('A'-Deserts dry mouth mix) / ('A'video).
 (cd-s) (587176-2) – ('A'side) / Curtains (purple curtains mix) / ('A'-Solomon remix).

Jul 01. (cd/lp) (589096-2/-1) **BEETROOT**   – / –
 — Desert drought / Heal me / Curtains / Kingdoms and crowns / Giving it all away / Lose myself / I never can say / High wire / Meditations / Jetstream / U-turn / Universal grinding wheel / Engaged.

CASTAWAY STONES (see under ⇒ BLACK TAMBOURINE)

CASTOR

Formed: Champaign-Urbana, Illinois, USA . . . 1995 by singer/guitarist JEFF GARBER and bassist DEREK NIEDRINGHAUS. This emo combo managed, on their 'Mud' label albums 'CASTOR' (1995) and 'TRACKING SOUNDS ALONE' (1999 – released after the band split in 1998) and the 'CARNIVAL' EP to create work that was critically lauded as being experimental and original but actually tuneful at the same time, which is no mean feat. Coming from a soundwave that included other Champaign-Urbana acts like HUM and HONCHO OVERLOAD, CASTOR shared identifiable sonic traits with these art rockers, but still managed to distinguish themselves from their hometown peers with songs about indie staples like depression, angst, and angry broody introspection. GARBER and NIEDRINGHAUS joined NATIONAL SKYLINE after CASTOR's demise, with GARBER also putting in an appearance in MORNING BECOMES ELECTRIC alongside vocalist BILL JOHNSON, previously of BAD FLANNEL and HONCHO OVERLOAD. Two MORNING BECOMES ELECTRIC songs appeared on the 'Cover The Earth: A Mud Records Compilation'.

Album rating: CASTOR mini (*5) / TRACKING SOUNDS ALONE (*6)

JEFF GARBER – vocals, guitar / **DEREK NIEDRINGHAUS** – bass

                                  Mud / Mud

1996. (m-cd) <MUD 011> **CASTOR EP**   – / –
 — Anecdotes / Pontiac / Grind in motion / Deremal frame / Dust gun / Trans / The package / Baroque.

Mar 97. (7") <MUD 020> **CARNIVAL. / MISS ATLANTIC**   – / –

— disbanded in January 1998; an EP was shelved

Sep 99. (cd) <MUD 021> **TRACKING SOUNDS ALONE**   – / –
 — Stay lo / Moving backwards / Trackstar / Five hours later / Carnival / The halo befriends me / 1000 miles from nowhere / Above water / Tracking sounds alone.

— both GARBER + NIEDRINGHAUS joined NATIONAL SKYLINE; the project of JEFF DIMPSEY of HUM

CATATONIA

Formed: Cardiff, Wales . . . 1991 by songwriters MARK ROBERTS and PAUL JONES, who had both been part of 'Ankst' label outfit, Y CRYFF. Having found OWEN POWELL from The CRUMB BLOWERS and sultry blonde singer, CERYS MATTHEWS, they set about taking their style of Welsh accented hooks to the alternative indie scene. However, things did not get off to a flying start, when the group offended the label's strict Welsh-only language policy and were moved on to another leek-biased label, 'Crai', where they released two singles in 1993/94. In the summer of '94, Geoff Travis's 'Rough Trade Singles Club' label issued 'WHALE', Travis subsequently grabbing them for his 'Blanco Y Negro'. 1996 became a shining year for them with four hit singles and a well-received album, the Stephen Street-produced 'WAY BEYOUND BLUE' denting the Top 40. Much was anticipated for a glorious 1998 after they hit the Top 40 in late '97 with 'I AM THE MOB'. All predictions came true as CERYS and Co stormed the Top 3 as early as January that year with the X-Files inspired 'MULDER AND SCULLY'. This was only one of the many successes (others being 'ROAD RAGE', 'STRANGE GLUE' and 'GAME ON') taken from their acclaimed chart-topping album, 'INTERNATIONAL VELVET', although indie sex symbol CERYS would also team up with SPACE for the tongue-in-cheek romantic duet, 'The Ballad Of Tom Jones'. Never far away from the limelight and with the help of producer TOMMY D., CATATONIA returned in Spring '99 via Top 10 smash, 'DEAD FROM THE WAIST DOWN'. The highest of three hits (the other two being 'LONDINIUM' and 'KARAOKE QUEEN') taken from their follow-up No.1 album, 'EQUALLY CURSED AND BLESSED', the 5-piece indie-pop outfit were going into the 21st Century on a high note. With an incredible amount of hits under their belts, a hectic touring schedule, press and PR hounding the group constantly, it seemed like things were beginning

CATATONIA (cont)

to erode within CATATONIA. Singer and indie 'babe' MATTHEWS admitted to the press that she had had a breakdown during the group's pandemonious year. The result was the very disappointing 'PAPER SCISSORS STONE' (2001), a cynical, alter-ego version of the album that set their names in stone, 'INTERNATIONAL . . .'. Missing was the sweet pop charm and charisma of MATTHEWS' throaty vocals and in its place was the rancid leftovers of a band gone awry. The album was treated nonchalantly by the press, however fans of the group re-emerged to show their support as the album sauntered its way into the Top 20 (as well as single 'STONE BY STONE'). It was to be a sad departure from the music scene, as CATATONIA officially called it a day in September 2001.

Album rating: THE SUBLIME MAGIC OF CATATONIA European compilation or THE CRAI EP'S (*7) / WAY BEYOND BLUE (*7) / INTERNATIONAL VELVET (*8) / EQUALLY CURSED AND BLESSED (*6) / PAPER SCISSORS STONE (*5) / GREATEST CATATONIA HITS compilation (*8)

CERYS MATTHEWS (b.11 Apr'69) – vocals / **MARK ROBERTS** (b. 3 Nov'69, Colwyn Bay, Wales) – guitar (ex-Y CYRFF) / **OWEN POWELL** (b. 9 Jul'67, Cambridge, England) – guitar (ex-CRUMB BLOWERS) / **PAUL JONES** (b. 5 Apr'60, Colwyn Bay) – bass (ex-Y CYRFF) / **ALED RICHARDS** (b. 5 Jul'69, Llanelli, Carmarthen, Wales) – drums

		Crai	not iss.
Sep 93.	(c-ep)(cd-ep) *(C 039L)(CD 039B)* **FOR TINKERBELL EP**		-
	– For Tinkerbell / New mercurial heights / Dimbran / Sweet Catatonia / Gyda Gwen – New mercurial heights (Welsh mix).		
Jun 94.	(c-s)(cd-s) *(C 042L)(CD 042B)* **HOOKED. / FALL BESIDE HER / DIFRYCHEULYD (SNAIL AMBITION)**		-
	(above 2 re-iss. together Dec98; CRAI 064)		

		Rough Trade Sing. Club	not iss.
Aug 94.	(7") *(45rev 33)* **WHALE. / YOU CAN**		-

		Nursery	not iss.
Feb 95.	(7"red) *(NYS 12L)* **BLEED. / THIS BOY CAN'T SWIM**		-
	(cd-s+=) *(NYSCD 12)* – Painful.		
Nov 95.	(cd) *(NYSCD 12X)* **THE SUBLIME MAGIC OF CATATONIA** (compilation)	-	- Europe
	– Bleed / This boy can't swim / Painful / Dream on / Whale / You can / Hooked / Fall beside her / Difrycheulyd (Snail ambition). *(hidden track +=)* – Cariadon ffol.		

		Blanco Y Negro	Atlantic
Dec 95.	(7"white; mail-o) *(SAM 1746)* **BLOW THE MILLENNIUM BLOW. / BEAUTIFUL SAILOR**		-
Jan 96.	(7"/c-s) *(NEG 85/+C)* **SWEET CATATONIA. / TOURIST**	61	-
	(cd-s) *(NEG 85CD)* – ('A'side) / Acapulco gold / Cut you inside (demo).		
Apr 96.	(7"yellow) *(NEGAT 88X)* **LOST CAT. / TO AND FRO**	41	-
	(c-s/cd-s) *(NEGAT 88 CAS/CD1)* – ('A'side) / All girls are fly / Indigo blind.		
	(cd-s) *(NEG 88CD2)* – ('A'side) / Sweet Catatonia (live – Mark Radcliffe 1FM session) / Whale (live – Mark Radcliffe 1FM session).		
Sep 96.	(7") *(NEG 93)* **YOU'VE GOT A LOT TO ANSWER FOR. / DO YOU BELIEVE IN ME?**	35	-
	(cd-s+=) *(NEG 93CD1)* – Dimbran.		
	(cd-s) *(NEG 93CD2)* – You can / All girls are fly.		
	(c-s) *(NEG 93CAS)* – ('A'side) / Blow the millennium blow (Splott remix).		
Sep 96.	(cd/c/lp) *(0630 16305-2/-4/-1)* **WAY BEYOND BLUE**	40	-
	– Lost cat / Sweet Catatonia / Some half baked / Ideal called wonderful / You've got a lot to answer for / Infantile / Dream on. *(lp w/free 7"/cd w/hidden track)* – Gyda Gwen. *(lp re-iss. Jun99; same)*		
Nov 96.	(7"red) *(NEG 97)* **BLEED. / DO YOU BELIEVE IN ME? (live – Reading Festival 1FM)**	46	-
	(cd-s) *(NEG 97CD2)* – Bleed (live evening session 1FM).		
	(cd-s) *(NEG 97CD1)* – ('A'side) / Way beyond blue (live – Mark Radcliffe 1FM session) / Painful (live – Reading Festival 1FM).		
	(c-s) *(NEG 97CASS)* – ('A'side) / Way beyond blue (live – Mark Radkiffe 1FM session) / Bleed (live – evening session 1FM).		
Oct 97.	(7"orange/c-s) *(NEG 107/+CASS)* **I AM THE MOB. / JUMP OR BE SANE**	40	-
	(cd-s+=) *(NEG 107CD)* – My selfish Gene / ('A'-Luca Brasi mix).		
Jan 98.	(7"blue/c-s) *(NEG 109/+CASS)* **MULDER AND SCULLY. / NO STONE UNTURNED**	3	-
	(cd-s+=) *(NEG 109CD)* – Mantra for the lost / ('A'-The Ex-files).		
Feb 98.	(cd/c/lp) *(<3984 20834-2/-4/-1>)* **INTERNATIONAL VELVET**	1	-
	– Mulder and Scully / Game on / I am the mob / Road rage / Johnny come lately / Goldfish and paracetamol / International velvet / Why I can't stand one night stands / Part of the furniture / Don't need the sunshine / Strange glue / My selfish gene. *(lp w/ free 12"/radio sessions)* – International velvet / No stone unturned / Murder & Scully / Strange glue.		
—	Feb'98:- CERYS featured on a SPACE hit, 'The Ballad Of Tom Jones'		
Apr 98.	(7"yellow/c-s) *(NEG 112/+CASS)* **ROAD RAGE. / I'M CURED**	5	-
	(cd-s+=) *(NEG 112CD)* – Blow the millennium (pt.2) / ('A'-Ghia).		

		Blanco Y Negro	Imprint
Jul 98.	(7"red/c-s) *(NEG 113/+CASS)* **STRANGE GLUE. / THAT'S ALL FOLKS**	11	-
	(cd-s+=) *(NEG 113CD)* – Road rage (live).		
Oct 98.	(7"green/c-s) *(NEG 114/+CASS)* **GAME ON. / STRANGE GLUE (live acoustic)**	33	-
	(cd-s+=) *(NEG 114CD)* – Mulder and Scully (live in Newport).		
Mar 99.	(7"orange) *(NEG 115/+C)* **DEAD FROM THE WAIST DOWN. / BRANDING A MOUNTAIN**	7	-
	(cd-s+=) *(NEG 115CD)* – Bad baby boy.		
Apr 99.	(cd/lp) *(3984 27094-2/-4/-1) <83294>* **EQUALLY CURSED & BLESSED**	1	Mar00
	– Dead from the waist down / Londinium / She's a millionaire / Storm the palace / Karaoke queen / Bulimic beats / Shoot the messenger / Postscript / Valarian unwanted / Nothing hurts / Dazed beautiful and bruised.		
Jul 99.	(7"/c-s) *(NEG 117/+C)* **LONDINIUM. / INTERCONTINENTAL**	20	-
	(cd-s+=) *(NEG 117CD)* – Apathy revolution.		
Nov 99.	(7"/c-s) *(NEG 119/+C)* **KARAOKE QUEEN. / DON'T WANNA TALK ABOUT IT**	36	-
	(cd-s+=) *(NEG 119CD)* – All girls are fly (da-be).		
Jul 01.	(7"/c-s) *(NEG 134/+C)* **STONE BY STONE. / LONG TIME LONELY**	19	-
	(cd-s+=) *(NEG 134CD)* – Apple core (full extended mix).		
Aug 01.	(cd/c/lp) *(8573 88848-2/-4/-1)* **PAPER SCISSORS STONE**	6	-
	– Godspeed / Immediate circle / Fuel / What it is / Stone by stone / Mother of misogyny / Is everybody here on drugs / Imaginary friends / Shore leave / Apple core / Beautiful loser / Blues song / Village idiot / Arabian derby.		
—	the band split a month later		

– compilations, etc. –

Sep 02.	(cd) *Blanco Y Negro; (0927 49193-2)* **GREATEST CATATONIA HITS**	24
	– Mulder & Scully / The ballad of Tom Jones / Strange glue / Road rage / Stone by stone / Londinium / Game on / Dead from the waste down / You've got a lot to answer for / Baby, it's cold outside / Karaoke queen / Lost cat / I am the mob / Sweet Catatonia / Bleed. *(d-cd+=; 0927 49194-2)* – Do you believe in me / The mother of misogyny / Indigo blind / Godspeed / Imaginary friend / Way beyond blue / Dream on / Whale / Branding a mountain / Acapulco gold. *(hidden track+=)* – All girls are fly / Blues song.	

CATHERINE WHEEL

Formed: Great Yarmouth, England . . . April 1990 by ROB DICKINSON and BRIAN FUTTER, completing the line-up with DAVE HAWES and NEIL SIMS and taking their moniker from a type of firework. The quartet recorded a demo on their own 8-track bedroom studio, the results released early the following year by independent imprint, 'Wilde Club', as debut single/EP, 'SHE'S MY FRIEND'. A second rough sounding EP, 'PAINFUL THING', also found its way into the indie charts resulting in them securing a contract with recently re-activated major label, 'Fontana' (recently home to a TEARDROP EXPLODES compilation, who incidentally, CATHERINE WHEEL bear more than a musical passing resemblance to). Becoming an integral part of the early 90's "shoegazing" scene, the CATHERINE WHEEL steadily built up a fanbase through committed gigging and a couple of minor UK hit singles, namely the 7-minute epic, 'BLACK METALLIC' and 'BALLOON'. Both featured on their TIME FRIESE-GREENE (TALK TALK)-produced debut set, 'FERMENT' (early '92), a Top 40 entrant with enough guitar bashing to hint at their future incarnation as a fully-fledged Rock band. In the meantime, ROB and Co finally cracked the Top 40 with 'I WANT TO TOUCH YOU' and subsequently revealed their eclectic musical tastes with a covers EP, running through versions of Scott Walker's '30th CENTURY MAN', Husker Du's 'DON'T WANT TO KNOW IF YOU ARE LONELY' and Mission Of Burma's 'THAT'S WHEN I REACH FOR MY REVOLVER' (they also did a version of Pink Floyd's 'WISH YOU WERE HERE'). 1993 hardly went off with a bang, however, as the GIL NORTON-produced follow-up set, 'CHROME', suffered at the hands of fickle critics, although steadfast fans did push it into the Top 60. Turning their attention to the States, CATHERINE WHEEL began to ferment a heavier, more rhythmic rock sound, finally laying to rest the "shoegazing" soundscapes of old on, er . . . "comeback" album, 'HAPPY DAYS' (1995). Despite featuring a duet, 'JUDY STARING AT THE SUN', with the BREEDERS' leading lady, TANYA DONELLY, the record went down like a damp squib in Britain. Nevertheless, burgeoning Stateside interest led to a deal with 'Chrysalis' and in 1998, they returned with an ever more Kerrang!-friendly sound on their fourth set, ADAM & EVE', a surprise success in the States after a gruelling coast to coast BUSH-like tour. Longtime bassist HAWES was subsequently given his marching orders prior to the recording of fifth album, 'WISHVILLE'. This may in part explain the poor reviews afforded the record upon its 2000 release, although the blame also seems to lie in the halfhearted songwriting, certainly well below the standard set by DICKINSON on previous outings.

Album rating: FERMENT (*7) / CHROME (*7) / HAPPY DAYS (*5) / LIKE CATS AND DOGS collection (*5) / ADAM AND EVE (*6) / WISHVILLE (*5)

ROB DICKINSON (b.23 Jul'65, Norwich, England) – vocals, guitar / **BRIAN FUTTER** (b. 7 Dec'65, London) – guitar, vocals / **DAVE HAWES** (b.10 Nov'65) – bass / **NEIL SIMS** (b. 4 Oct'65, Norwich) – percussion, drums

		Wilde Club	not iss.
Jan 91.	(12"ep) *(WILDE 4)* **SHE'S MY FRIEND / UPSIDE DOWN. / WISH / SALT**		-
May 91.	(12"ep/cd-ep) *(WILDE 5)* **PAINFUL THING / SHALLOW / SPIN / I WANT TO TOUCH YOU**		-

		Fontana	Fontana
Nov 91.	(7") *(CW 1)* **BLACK METALLIC. / LET ME DOWN AGAIN**	68	-
	(12"+=/cd-s+=) *(CW X/CD 1)* – Crawling over me / Saccharin.		
Jan 92.	(7") *(CW 2)* **BALLOON. / INTRAVENOUS**	59	-
	(12"+=/cd-s+=) *(CW X/CD 2)* – Painful thing (live) / Let me down again (live).		
Feb 92.	(cd/c/lp) *(510903-2/-4/-1) <512510>* **FERMENT**	36	Jun92
	– Texture / I want to touch you / Black metallic / Indigo is blue / She's my friend / Shallow / Ferment / Flower to hide / Tumbledown / Bill and Ben / Salt. *(incl. free 7"ep)*		
Apr 92.	(d7"/12"ep/cd-ep) *(CW/+X/CD 3)* **I WANT TO TOUCH YOU. / URSA MAJOR SPACE STATION/ / OUR FRIEND JOEY. / COLLIDEOSCOPE**	35	-
	(12") *(CWT 3)* – (first 7") / Half life.		
	(cd-s) *(CWCDX 3)* – (first 7") / Wish / Black metallic.		
Nov 92.	(12"ep/cd-ep) *(CW X/CD 4)* **30th CENTURY MAN. / DON'T WANT TO KNOW IF YOU ARE LONELY / THAT'S WHEN I REACH FOR MY REVOLVER**	47	-

664

CATHERINE WHEEL (cont)

Jul 93. (7"/c-s) *(CW/+MC 5)* **CRANK. / COME BACK AGAIN** — 66 / —
(12") *(CWT 5)* – ('A'side) / Black metallic / Painful ting.
(cd-s) *(CWCD 5)* – ('A'side) / La la la-la-la / Something strange.
(cd-s) *(CWCDX 5)* – ('A'side) / Pleasure / Tongue twisted.
Sep 93. (7") *(CW 6)* **SHOW ME MARY. / FLOWER TO HIDE (live)** — 62 / —
(cd-s+=) *(CWCDA 6)* – Car / Girl stand still.
(cd-s) *(CWCDB 6)* – ('A'side) / These four wheels / Smother.
(12") *(CWT 6)* – ('A'side) / High heels / Mouth full of air.
Sep 93. (cd/c/lp) *(<518039-2/-4/-1>)* **CHROME** — 58 / Jun93
– Kill rhythm / I confess / Crank / Broken head / Pain / Strange fruit / Chrome / The nude / Ursa Major space station / Fripp / Half life / Show me Mary.
── guests on above album:- TIM FRIESE-GREENE and AUDREY RILEY.
Jul 95. (10") *(CW 7)* **WAYDOWN. / CRANK / WISH YOU WERE HERE (XFM session)** — 67 / —
(cd-s) *(CWCD 7)* – ('A'side) / Show me Mary (XFM session) / Kill rhythm.
(cd-s) *(CWDD 7)* – ('A'side) / Chrome / Broken head (XFM sessions).
Sep 95. (10"ep) *(CW 8)* **JUDY STARING AT THE SUN / GOD INSIDE MY HEAD. / CRANK (live) / WAYDOWN (live)**
(cd-ep) *(CWCD 8)* – (first 2 tracks) / Glitter.
(cd-ep) *(CWDD 8)* – (first 2 tracks) / Backwards guitar / Angelo Nero.
(above 'A'side featured TANYA DONELLY of BREEDERS)
Nov 95. (cd/c)(d-lp) *(<514717-2/-4>)(526850-1)* **HAPPY DAYS** — / May95
– God inside my head / Waydown / Little muscle / Heal / Empty head / Receive / My exhibition / Eat my dust you insensitive fuck / Shocking / Love tips up / Judy staring at the sun / Hole / Fizzy love / Glitter / Kill my soul.

Chrysalis   Polygram

Dec 97. (10"ep) *(10CHS 5071)* **THE DELICIOUS EP** — 53 / —
– Delicious / Eat my dust you insensitive f**k / Crank (live) / Texture (live).
(cd-ep) *(CDCHS 5071)* – ('A'side) / Future boy / Judy staring at the sun (with TANYA DONELLY) / Heal.
Feb 98. (7"colrd) *(CHS 5077)* **MA SOLITUDA. / KILL RHYTHM (live)** — 53 / —
(cd-s) *(CDCHSS 5077)* – ('A'side) / Delicious / Descending babe / Paranoia.
(cd-s) *(CDCHSS 5077)* – ('A'-Tim Friese-Greene mix) / Delicious (live) / Willing to wait / Lucifer.
Apr 98. (7") *(CHS 5086)* **BROKEN NOSE. / LITTLE MUSCLE (live)** — 48 / —
(cd-s) *(CDCHS 5086)* – ('A'side) / Crank (live) / Texture (live) / Black metallic (live).
(cd-s) *(CDCHSS 5086)* – ('A'side) / Flower to hide (live) / Heal (live) / I want to touch you (live).
May 98. (cd/c/d-lp) *(493099-2/-4/-1) <534864>* **ADAM AND EVE** — 53 / Jul98
– Future boy / Delicious / Broken nose / Phantom of the American mother / Ma solituda / Satellite / Thunderbird / Here comes the fat controller / Goodbye / For dreaming.

Chrysalis   Columbia

Sep 00. (cd/lp) *(526664-2/-1) <69515>* **WISHVILLE**
– Sparks are gonna fly / Gasoline / Lifeline / What we want to believe in / All of that / Idle life / Mad dog / Ballad of a running man / Creme caramel. *(special d-cd+=; 528664-2)* – live:- Lifeline / Crank / Fripp / Ma solituda / Heal / Future boy / Intravenus / Little muscle.

– compilations, etc. –

Sep 96. (cd) *Polygram; (<532456-2>)* **LIKE CATS AND DOGS** (B-sides, rarities, etc)
– Heal 2 / Wish you were here / Mouthful of air / Car / Girl stand still / Saccharine / Backwards guitar / Tongue twisted / These four walls / High heels / Harder than I am / La-la-la.

CATHETERS

Formed: Seattle, Washington, USA … 1998 by BRIAN STANDEFORD, DEREK MASON, DAVE BROZOWSKI, PAUL and LARS. The band debuted in 1999 with the eponymously titled set, 'THE CATHETERS', a record showcasing their brand of high-octane punk revival (think oldies, DEAD BOYS and The SAINTS). A great first effort, although it did not alter from the derivative style of bad-to-the-bone rock 'n' roll. Following this, PAUL and LARS departed the group with LEO GEBHART stepping in to take up bass duties. On the vital strength of their inaugural long-player, the punksters were given a deal with influential indie label 'Sub Pop'. The CATHETERS also found themselves touring alongside vintage grungers MUDHONEY, which expanded their following and gave them greater airtime for their sophomore effort 'STATIC DELUSIONS AND STONE-STILL DAYS' (2002). This second set ploughed pretty much the same field as its predecessor. But for some energetic lucid PAGANS-style punk rock, it still did well and was recorded in a mammoth 36-hour studio session. • Covered: HANG UP (Wailers).

Album rating: THE CATHETERS (*5) / STATIC DELUSIONS AND STONE-STILL DAYS (*7)

BRIAN STANDEFORD – vocals, guitar / **DEREK MASON** – guitar / **LARS** – guitar / **PAUL** – bass / **DAVEY BROZOWSKI** – drums

not iss.   eMpTy

Sep 99. (7"m) *<MTR 375>* **THE KIDS KNOW HOW TO ROCK. / NO PLACE TO GO / ROCKET FUEL** — / —
Oct 99. (lp/cd) *<MTR 380/+CD>* **THE CATHETERS** — / —
– Never look back / Back in the game / Those nights are gone / Treat me like you should / Do what I want / Teenage trash / Restless eyes / Got no reason / Ain't so bad / The kids know how to rock. *(UK-iss.Aug02; same as US)*

Sub Pop   Sub Pop

2000. (7") *<SP 474>* **PUT IT TOGETHER. / DAYS GONE BY** — / —
── **LEO GEBHART** – bass; repl. PAUL + LARS
2001. (7") *<SPC-KP 005>* **IT CAN'T STAY THIS WAY (FOREVER). / MEANS TO AN END** — / —
May 02. (lp/cd) *<(SP/+CD 568)>* **STATIC DELUSIONS AND STONE-STILL DAYS** — / Mar02

– Been there before / I fall easy / 3000 ways / Nothing / The door shuts quickly / Bleary haze / Build a home / Endless avenues / Disguise myself / Clock on the wall / What have they done to you?
May 02. (cd-s) *(SPCD 596)* **3000 WAYS / NOTHING** — / —
Sep 02. (7"orange) *(SP 578)* **BUILD A HOME. / HANG UP** — / —
Oct 02. (7"m) *(SP 604)* **I FALL EASY. / PALE HORSE / LOOKS GOOD ON ME** — / —

CAT POWER

Formed: by CHAN MARSHALL (pronounced 'Shan'), a Southern States-born 20-something singer/songwriter trading in gothic-folk music. In 1996, after releasing her demos on two low-key indie label albums, she virtually gave up the ghost, until that is, she was spotted backing LIZ PHAIR at a New York gig by 'Matador' label boss Gerard Cosley and SONIC YOUTH's STEVE SHELLEY. The former subsequently signed her up, the latter, with the addition of guitarist TIM FOLJAHN, became her backing band. The results were soon featured on that year's "comeback" set, 'WHAT WOULD THE COMMUNITY THINK', her recording life back in full swing with a support slot to stablemate, LIZ PHAIR. However, again reluctant to gain any recognition for this fine work, she jumped ship to Australia with SMOG's BILL CALLAHAN. There she was introduced to JIM WHITE and MICK TURNER (both of DIRTY THREE), who helped out on her fourth attempt to break through, 'MOONPIX' (1998); the self-explanatory 'THE COVERS RECORD' followed a few years later. • **Covered:** Y IS HERE (Tom Waits) / S. WALKER (TKO Punishment) / (I CAN'T GET NO) SATISFACTION (Rolling Stones) / KINSPORT TOWN (trad) / TROUBLED WATERS (Coslow-Johnston) / NAKED IF I WANT TO (Moby Grape) / SWEE DEE DEE (Michael Hurley) / I FOUND A REASON (Velvet Underground) / WILD IS THE WIND (Tiomkin-Washington) / RED APPLES (Smog) / PATHS OF VICTORY (Bob Dylan) / SALTY DOG (trad.) / SEA OF LOVE (Phil Phillips).

Album rating: DEAR SIR mini (*5) / MYRA LEE (*6) / WHAT WOULD THE COMMUNITY THINK (*8) / MOONPIX (*8) / THE COVERS ALBUM (*6)

CHAN MARSHALL (b.1972) – vocals, guitar, piano

not iss.   Making Of Americans

1994. (7") *<none>* **HEADLIGHTS. / DARLING SAID SIR** — / —

not iss.   Runt

Oct 95. (10"m-lp/m-cd) *<RUNT 6>* **DEAR SIR** — / —
– 3 times / Rockets / Itchyhead / Y is here / S. Walker / Mr. Gallo / (untitled) / No matter / Headlights. *(UK-iss.May00 on 'Plain'; PLAIN 102CD) (lp-iss.May01; PLAIN 102)*

not iss.   Smells Like

Mar 96. (cd) *<SLR-019>* **MYRA LEE** — / —
– Enough / We all die / Great expectations / Top expert / Ice water / Still in love / Rockets / Faces / Fiance / Wealthy man / Not what you want.
── with **TIM FOLJAHN** – guitar (of TWO DOLLAR GUITAR) / **STEVE SHELLEY** – drums (of SONIC YOUTH)

not iss.   Undercover

Sep 96. (7") *<UNCV 003>* **PSYCHIC HEARTS. / WE DANCE / JOHNNY'S GOT A GUN** — / —

Matador   Matador

Sep 96. (cd/lp) *<(OLE 202-2/-1)>* **WHAT WOULD THE COMMUNITY THINK**
– In this hole / Good clean fun / What would the community think / Nude as the news / They tell me / Taking people / Fate of the human carbine / King rides by / Bathysphere / Water & air / Enough / The coat is always on.
Dec 96. (7"split) **CAT POWER GOES TO GUV'NERVILLE**
– Clear the room / GUV'NER: Great expectations.
(above issued on 'Wiiija')
Jan 97. (7"/cd-s) *<(OLE 240-1/-2)>* **NUDE AS THE NEWS. / SCHIZOPHRENIA'S WEIGHTED ME DOWN**
── now with **JIM WHITE** – drums / **MICK TURNER** – guitar
Sep 98. (cd/lp) *<(OLE 286-2/-1)>* **MOONPIX**
– American flag / He turns down / No sense / Say / Metal heart / Back of your head / Moonshiner / You may know him / Colors and the kids / Cross bones style / Peking saint. *(special cd+=)* – Sea of love / Schizophrenia weighted me down / Kinsport town.
Mar 00. (cd/lp) *<(OLE 426-2/-1)>* **THE COVERS RECORD**
– (I can't get no) Satisfaction / Kinsport town / Devil's daughter / Naked if I want to / Swee dee dee / In this hole / I found a reason / Wild is the wind / Red apples / Paths of victory / Salty dog / Sea of love.

CAT'S MIAOW!

Formed: Brunswick, Australia … May '92 by seasoned indie-poppers, KERRIE BOLTON, ANDREW WITHYCOMBE, BART and CAMERON, the latter two were part of early 90's twee Melbourne-based outfit, GIRL OF THE WORLD; BART also became a member of The SHAPIROS (with ex-BLACK TAMBOURINE vocalist PAM BERRY). Strongly influenced by The PASTELS, The TELEVISION PERSONALITIES and all things nice and C-86, GOTW released a handful of 45's in 1992/93 and the posthumous, 'WONDERBOY'. The CAT'S MIAOW! quartet were also around in these halcyon (twee) days of the early to mid 90's, issuing a plethora of songs via cassettes, split singles and various artists compilations; their own collection, 'A KISS AND A CUDDLE' (1996), were lifted from these recordings. In 1997, the quartet chose to branch out into other fields, taking the new moniker HYDROPLANE in the process. Two albums (1999's 'HOPE AGAINST HOPE' and 2001's 'THE SOUND OF CHANGING PLACES') and several 45's into their career, HYDROPLANE have proved to be dark, dreamy and enlightening indie-pop all at the same time; think The PALE SAINTS and The CRANES. • **Covered:** I FALL TO PIECES (Patsy Cline) / BABY I LOVE YOU (Ronettes) / RIGHT BACK WHERE WE STARTED (Maxine Nightingale) / Hydroplane: WE CROSSED THE ATLANTIC (Pip Proud) / NOT TO BOTHER ME (Missing Links) / WHEN I WAS HOWARD HUGHES (Shapiros) / IF YOU SPOKE TO ME I WOULDN'T KNOW WHAT TO SAY (Veronica Lake) / NEVER SAY DIE (Black Sabbath).

Album rating: A KISS AND A CUDDLE compilation (*6) / SONGS FOR GIRLS TO SING compilation (*6) / THE LONG GOODBYE: BLISS OUT, VOL.14 compilation (*5) / Hydroplane: HYDROPLANE (*5) / HOPE AGAINST HOPE (*6) / THE SOUND OF CHANGING PLACES (*5) / Girl Of The World: WONDERBOY mini compilation (*5)

GIRL OF THE WORLD

TIM BEST – vocals, guitar / **BART** – guitar, bass (ex-BLAIRMAILER) / **CAMERON** – drums

                                                  Parasol   not iss.

1992. (7"ep) *(PAR 013)* **TRAVEL EP** – / – Austra
 – Travel / Not ever / Why don't we? / All those days.
1992. (7"ep) *(PAR 018)* **LE CIRQUE. / GREEN SONG** – / – Austra

— their 'TINSEL SURF DARLINGS' featured on 'Parasol' V/A EP, 'Happy Holidays'

                                                  Heaven   not iss.

Dec 93. (7") *(HV 11)* **5 YEARS OLD. / 3000 FT.** – / –

– compilations, etc. –

1995. (m-cd) *Parasol; (<MUD 010>)* **WONDERBOY** – / Sep99
 – Wonderboy / Circus / Before she goes / 3000' / Sarah / Five years old / Last of a dying breed / Road movie theme.

CAT'S MIAOW!

KERRIE BOLTON – vocals (ex-BEAT POETS, ex-TRA LA LA) / **BART** – guitar / **ANDREW WITHYCOMBE** – bass (of BLAIRMAILER, of AMPERSANDS) / **CAMERON** – drums

                                             Toytown   not iss.

1992. (c) *(Toy 19)* **LITTLE BABY SOURPUSS** – / – Austra
 – Nothing new / Climb my stairs / I really don't know / You trip me up / Georgie / Memphis '54 / Autumn / Sunday / Cheek / Walk on by / Wimp out.
1992. (c) *(Toy 20)* **PET SOUNDS** – / – Austra
 – Third floor fire escape view / You left a note on the table / I hate myself more than you do / Icecream / Saviour for the hurrying man / Shortsighted / Indian summer / Talking to trees.
1993. (c-ep) *(Toy 25)* **FROM MY WINDOW** – / – Austra
 – Aurora / A day in the life / It might never happen / Nothing's ever quite that simple / Brighter star / The Phoebe I know / Little and small / From my window / Get over it / Tangle my toes / Sleepyhead / A 50's ballad / Dust from a memory / Neu monotonic fm / The street where you live / A few words.

                                               Golf   not iss.

1993. (c) *(hole-in 1)* **HOW DID EVERYTHING GET SO FUCKED UP** – / – Austra
 – Make a wish / Hollow inside / Coffee / Faded / Not like I was doing anything / I can't sleep thinking you hate me / Disappointed / I wanted none of this / Halo / Fire damage / Leather beards / Tundra / Bulb.

                                              Contrast   Sunday

1993. (7") *(CT 002)* **I REALLY DON'T KNOW. / (split w/ other artists)** – / – Belgium
1994. (7"ep) *<SUNDAY 032>* **THIRD FLOOR FIRE ESCAPE VIEW / SHORT SIGHTED. / NOTHING NEW / AUTUMN** – / –

                                        Wurlitzer Jukebox Quiddity

1995. (7") *(WJ 3)* **SHOOT THE MOON. / (other by STEREOLAB)** – / –
1995. (7"ep) *<Quid 001>* **I KEPT ALL YOUR LETTERS EP** – / –
 – You know it's true / Seventeen / What time is it there? / I can't sleep thinking you hate me.
1995. (7"ep) *<Quid 004>* **THIS IS ALL I EVER WANTED EP** – / –
 – I fall to pieces / Let me brush the hair from your face / Portland, Oregon / One of us is in the wrong place.
1996. (7"ep) *<Quid 010>* **I CAN'T HELP BUT LOVE YOU EP** – / –
 – If things had been different / Crying / Dont worry this isn't about you / Nothing can stop us.

                                              not iss. Spit and a Half

1996. (7") *<Spit 031>* **split w/ STINKY FIRE ENGINE** – / –
 – Smitten / Right back where we started from / (other by above).

                                              Drive-in Drive-in

1996. (7"ep; Various Artists) *<Drive 001>* **Drive-In / Seasons** – / –
 – Stay / (other artists; SHAPIROS, SINGING BUSH + MADISON ELECTRIC).
1996. (7"ep) *<Drive 08>* **J'EN AI MARRE EP** – / –
 – Peut-etre que rien jamais / Laisses-moi froler cheveux de ton visage / Revant de toi / Troisieme etage.
Nov 97. (cd) *<(Drive 14)>* **SONGS FOR GIRLS TO SING** – / –
 – Hollow inside / Make a wish / Light the beacon / Not like I was doing anything / You left a note on the table / Baby I love you / You know it's true / Seventeen / What time is it there? / I can't sleep thinking you hate me / I fall to pieces / Let me brush the hair from your face / Portland, Oregon / One of us is in the wrong place / Stay / Smitten / Right back where we started / Do you think it will snow tonight? / The others way / Shoot the Moon / Firefly / Barney and me / Millions of tiny lights / L.A. international airport / If things had been different / Crying / Don't worry this isn't about you / Nothing can stop us / Peut-etre froler les cheveux de ton visage / Revant de toi / TRoisieme etage / Nothing can stop us now (live) / Crying (live) / Third floor fire escape view (live) / Let it flow (live).

                                              not iss. Clover

1998. (7"ep; Various Artists) *<703>* **Melbourne Holiday** – / – Japan
 – I hate myself more than you do / (other artists).

— in 1998, as HOVERCRAFT, they released the 'STEREO SPECIFIC POLYMERIZATION' in Australia

— had already split to form other outfit below

– compilations, etc. –

Mar 97. (cd) *Bus Stop; <(BUS 1015-2)>* **A KISS AND A CUDDLE** (from the early tapes) – / Nov96
 – Aurora / A day in the life / It might never happen / Nothing's ever quite that simple / Brighter star / The Phoebe I know / Little and small / From my window / Get over it / Tangle my shoes / Sleepyhead / A 50's ballad / A few words / Ferry No.6 / Short sighted / You left a note on the table / Autumn / Nothing new / Climb my stairs / Third floor fire escape view / Faded / Hollow inside / I wanted none of this / Disappointed / version 2:- Third floor fire escape view / Short sighted / Nothing new / Autumn / Climb my stairs.
1998. (cd; as BART & FRIENDS) *<Drive 24>* **BART AND FRIENDS** – / –
May 99. (10"ep/cd-ep) *Darla; <(DRL 84-1/-2)>* **THE LONG GOODBYE: BLISS OUT, VOL.14** – / Jul99
 – Phoebe / Firefly / Faded / Third floor / If things had been different.

HYDROPLANE

— same line-up as CAT'S MIAOW!

                                              Drive-In Drive-In

1996. (one-sided-7") *<Drive 05>* **EXCERPTS FROM FORTHCOMING LP** – / –
Jun 97. (cd) *<(Drive 09)>* **HYDROPLANE** – / –
 – Wurlitzer jukebox / Piano movement with percussion / Song for the meek / I hear a new world / New monotonic FM / House warming / 14th July / Reprise / Beloved invader / Interlude / New monotonic FM (acoustic) / LDR / Send in the clowns.
Jul 97. (7"m) *(WJ 030)* **WE CROSSED THE ATLANTIC. / PLEASE DON'T SAY GOODBYE / HEY JOE** – / –
 (above issued on 'Wurlitzer Jukebox')
May 98. (12"ep) *<(Drive 22)>* **THE LOVE YOU BRING** – / –
 – The love you bring / Oregon snow / Can't you hear the beat of a broken heart / Questions I can't answer.

                                              Bad Jazz Drive-In

Aug 98. (7") *(Bebop 5)* **WHEN I WAS HOWARD HUGHES. / IF YOU SPOKE TO ME, I WOULDN'T KNOW WHAT TO SAY** – / –
Dec 98. (7"white) *(ER-197)* **FAILED ADVENTURE. / NOW YOU KNOW EVERYTHING THERE IS TO KNOW** – / –
 (above issued on 'Elefant' singles club)
Oct 99. (lp/cd) *(Bebop 11/+CD)* *<Drive 33>* **HOPE AGAINST HOPE** – / –
 – Stars / Grand Central / Summer without sun / How can you tell me / With someone like you / Station to station / Don't you know / Follow / Too far out / Something I've got to tell you.
Feb 00. (7"m) *(Duske 16)* **INTERNATIONAL EXILES. / BIKE WHEEL ON A CHAIR / BLACKOUT** – / –
 (above issued on 'Liquefaction Empire', below on 'Little Prints')
Jun 00. (7"m) *<none>* **RADIOS APPEAR. / EMBASSY CAFE / CHERRY LAKE** – / –

                                              Drive-In Drive-In

Sep 01. (cd) *<(Drive 51)>* **THE SOUND OF CHANGING PLACES** – / –
 – Merry-go-round / Farmer's Boys flexi disc / Bouncing ball / Closing in / International exiles / Kangaroo map / Tap dance routine / Shy quiet type / Mauve xylophone / Embassy cafe / Cry my heart / World without you. *(lp-iss.on 'Bad Jazz'; Bebop 40)*

CECIL

Formed: Liverpool, England . . . 1993 by ageing teenagers, STE WILLIAMS, ANTONY HUGHES, PATRICK HARRISON, JAY BENNETT and ALLY LAMBERT. After taking part in a 'Battle Of The Bands', competition they found themselves on the roster of EMI's 'Parlophone' imprint. Subsequent tours supporting SKUNK ANANSIE, BLAMELESS and The LEVELLERS, helped raise their profile, although critics found it difficult to pigeonhole the band in either the hard-rock or alternative categories. Fusing crunching, hard-driving riffs with WILLIAMS' emotive vocals, CECIL released a trio of competent if hardly groundbreaking singles prior to their first full set, 'BOMBAR DIDDLAH' (1996). Late the following year, with support from the likes of Kerrang!, the 5-piece scored their first of two minor hits with 'HOSTAGE IN A FROCK', the singer a bit overdressed in the accompanying video. The second of these, 'THE MOST TIRING DAY', previewed the follow-up album, 'SUBTITLES' (1998), although a bonafide breakthrough seemed as distant as ever.

Album rating: BOMBAR DIDDLAH (*5) / SUBTITLES (*5)

STE WILLIAMS – vocals / **ANTONY HUGHES** – guitar / **PATRICK HARRISON** – guitar / **JAY BENNETT** – bass / **ALLY LAMBERT** – drums

                                        Parlophone Parlophone

Oct 95. (7") *(R 6418)* **NO EXCUSES. / UPSIDE DOWN SMILE** – / –
 (cd-s+=) *(CDR 6418)* – Friend (demo).
Mar 96. (7") *(R 6427)* **MY NECK. / WALLOW IN FUSION** – / –
 (cd-s+=) *(CDR 6427)* – Revealing symptom / My piano neck.
Jun 96. (7") *(R 6435)* **MEASURED. / SPIRIT LEVEL** – / –
 (cd-s+=) *(CDR 6435)* – The plastics keep coming.
Nov 96. (cd/c/lp) *(CD/TC+/PCS 7384)* *<854162>* **BOMBAR DIDDLAH** – / Mar97
 – Dream awake / Plastics keep coming / Spirit level / Upside down smile / Fishes / My neck / No excuses / Poshinalagweedy.
May 97. (7") *(R 6467)* **RED WINE AT DEAD TIME. / BOMBAR DIDDLAH** – / –
 (cd-s+=) *(CDR 6467)* – So Long Marianne.
 (cd-s) *(CDRS 6467)* – ('A'side) / Look out for my love / Friend.
Oct 97. (7"green) *(R 6471)* **HOSTAGE IN A FROCK. / STUBBORN FEATHER** 68 / –
 (Dave Bascombe mix; cd-s+=) *(CDRS 6471)* – Upside down smile (live).
 (cd-s) *(CDR 6471)* – ('A'-Tim Palmer mix) / Antique / Dream awake (live).

CECIL (cont)

Mar 98. (7"colrd) (R 6490) **THE MOST TIRING DAY. / SLIPHILLCLIMB** 69 -
(cd-s+=) (CDRS 6490) – On the inside.
(cd-s) (CDR 6490) – ('A'side) / Tinsel scar / When you're in love with a beautiful woman.
Mar 98. (cd/c/lp) (859821-2/-4/-1) **SUBTITLES**
– Larger than a mountain to the ant / Zips for lips / The most tiring day / Red wine at dead time / Fullstop / Acres / Hostage in a frock / Measured / Lovetooth 14 / Charm wrestling / In the day and aged.

— split after above

CELL

Formed: Hoboken, New Jersey, USA ... early 90's by New York underground veterans, JERRY DIRIENZO (ex-VIA), IAN JAMES (ex-FLOWER), DAVID MOTAMED (ex-DAS DAMEN) and KEITH NEALY (ex-SWINEDIVE). Mates with SONIC YOUTH (KEITH had been a technician for STEVE SHELLEY), CELL used their contacts to secure an initial deal with THURSTON MOORE's 'Ecstatic Peace' label, releasing their debut single, 'NEVER TOO HIGH', in 1991. The SONIC YOUTH connection also helped them net a Stateside deal with the David Geffen Company (DGC), a debut album, 'SLO*BLO', surfacing the following year. Scraping the mutoid sludge from the Grunge barrel, CELL specialised in layers of mesmerising monster riffing with occasional forays into noise abandon, naming their album after a slow action fuse. Following a solitary single in '93, 'CROSS THE RIVER', CELL broke out for one more stab at cult fame, unlocking the door to more mind-numbing guitar abuse via the album, 'LIVING ROOM' (1994).

Album rating: SLO*BLO (*5) / LIVING ROOM (*5)

JERRY DIRIENZO – vocals, guitar (of VIA; w/ THALIA of COME) / **IAN JAMES** – guitar, vocals (of FLOWER) / **DAVID MOTAMED** – bass (of DAS DAMEN) / **KEITH NEALY** – drums (of SWINEDIVE)

not iss.   Ecstatic Peace

1991. (12") <E# 14> **NEVER TOO HIGH. / STRATOSPHERE**

City Slang   D.G.C.

Sep 92. (7"blue) (EFA 04905-03) **FALL. / CIRCLES**
Oct 92. (lp/c/cd) (E 04909/+C/CD) <DGCD 24506> **SLO*BLO** Feb93
– Fall / Wild / Cross the river / Dig deep / Stratosphere / Two / Everything turns / Tundra / Bad day / Hills.
Nov 92. (7") <E# 23> **WILD. / AUF WIEDERSEHEN**
(above issued on 'Ecstatic Peace/ D.G.C.')
Apr 93. (7"blue) (EFA 04921-45) **CROSS THE RIVER. / CHINA LATINA**
(cd-s+=) (EFA 04921-03) – So cool / Free money.
Jan 94. (7") (EFA 04928-7) **MILKY. / TWO WEEKS**
(cd-s+=) (EFA 04928-2) – Deranged.
Feb 94. (cd/lp) (EFA 04933-2/-1) <DGCD 24633> **LIVING ROOM**
– Milky / China Latina / Sad & beautiful / Goodbye / Chained / Come around / Living room / Fly / Halo / Soft ground / Camera / Blue star.

— disbanded after above

CENTRO-MATIC

Formed: Denton, Texas, USA ... 1995 by renaissance man, WILL JOHNSON, a prolific songwriter who recruited MATT PENCE, MARK HEDMAN and cellosist/violinist SCOTT DANBOM. Coming from the North Texas region where "winters are unidentifiable and small town high school football is king", CENTRO-MATIC issued their blistering lo-fi indie-pop debut, 'REDO THE STACKS' in 1997 – a twenty-three song classic of the genre that perfectly showcased JOHNSON's raw but bittersweet musical outlook. By 1998 (and mirroring the informal lo-fi/indie explosion of GRANDADDY, MERCURY REV and The FLAMING LIPS) the tightly assembled group issued a cassette-only release, 'LINE. CONNECTION. AIM', full of clumsily recorded gems, displaying their love for one-take-wonders, background clattering, distorted guitars and, of course, JOHNSON's pained lyrics sung with a pressing tongue. Over the coming years, CENTRO-MATIC delivered a handful of disjointed releases, beginning with 'NAVIGATIONAL' (1999) and the compendium 'STATIC VS. THE STRINGS VOL.1' (1999), a collection of outtakes, B-sides and songs that were generally thought of as discarded. One may have assumed that CENTRO ... had run out of ideas, or were just playing funny buggers, although this notion was dispelled come 2000 and the delivery of yet another two fine albums; 'ALL THE FALSEST HEARTS CAN TRY' and SOUTH SAN GABRIEL's (JOHNSON's hushed CENTRO side-project) 'SONGS/MUSIC'. Whilst not only establishing the latter, and recording a beautiful stripped-down country lo-fi album, akin to LOW or HAYDEN, JOHNSON and PENCE managed to moonlight (and take a considerable back-seat stance) with the free rockers The FOXYMORONS. Since then, JOHNSON and his team have been fruitfully busy, jumping between CENTRO-MATIC and solo billing courtesy of two of his best works so far, 'DISTANCE AND CLIME' (2001) by CENTRO-MATIC and 'MURDER OF TIDES' (2002) by JOHNSON himself.

Album rating: REDO THE STACKS (*5) / LINE. CONNECTION. AIM (*5) / NAVIGATIONAL (*5) / THE STATIC VS. THE STRINGS VOL.1 collection (*6) / ALL THE FALSEST HEARTS CAN TRY (*8) / SONGS-MUSIC by South San Gabriel (*7) / DISTANCE AND CLIME (*5) / Will Johnson: MURDER OF TIDES (*6)

WILL JOHNSON – vocals, guitar / with **SCOTT DANBOM** – violin / + **MATT PENCE** – drums, etc.

not iss.   own label

1995. (c) <none> **NON-DIRECTIONAL JETPACK RACE**
1996. (7"ep) <none> **THE TRANSISTOR EP**
1996. (7") <none> **FORGET THE SIXTH STEP**
1997. (7") <none> **TYMPANUM**

not iss.   Steve

Mar 97. (cd) <9717> **REDO THE STACKS**
– The pilot's on the wall / Parade of choosers / Terrified anyway / Post-it notes from the state hospital / Fidgeting wildly / The cannon-ball shot / Part of this accident / Am I the manager or am I not? / Cannot complete / Are you ready for the shutdown? / Don't smash the qualifying man / Hoist up the popular ones / Starfighter, No.1479 / Bitter (did you notice that?) / Rock and roll eyes / If I had a dartgun / Tied to the trailer / My supermodel girlfriend gone AWOL / You're like everyone / Take the original frame / Capture the aimless boy / Mandatory on the attack / (untitled).

not iss.   Headwound

1998. (c) <001> **LINE. CONNECTION. AIM**
– The injury specialist / Nothing could be better / Huge in every city / Sure grip maximum / The massacre went well / Most everyone will find / If we had our say / They tell us that they're loaded out / The little guitars / Line connection aim / Say something – 95 frowns.

— added **MARK HEDMAN** – bass

not iss.   Idol

Apr 99. (cd) <17> **NAVIGATIONAL**
– Nevermind the sounds / All hail the label scouts / Ruin this with style / With respect to alcohol / Ordinary days / This vicious crime / Cross you that way / Ballad of private rifle sound / Not forever now / Numbers one and three / Lasted 'til today / Hazlitt takes to shore / Line. Connection. Aim / The Panacea tonight / The massacre went well / The beautiful ones.

not iss.   Good

1999. (cd-s) <GR 002> **LOVE HAS FOUND ME SOMEHOW. / (other by TRIPPING DAISY)**

Munich   Quality Park

Aug 99. (cd) <2> **THE STATIC VS. THE STRINGS VOL.1** (compilation)
– Calling up the bastards / Who's telling you now? / The execution of some sixty odd drummers / Neighbors habits downtown / Recaptured the silent way / Repellant feed / Turning your decisions / Wrecking this show / D. Boon-free (a ninth grade crime) / Say something – 95 frowns / Curb your turbulence (rock show is coming) / Now that you have blown away the cards / You might need this now – Most peaceful yeough / Keep the Phoenix in slow motion.

Feb 01. (cd) (MRCD 208) <5> **ALL THE FASTEST HEARTS CAN TRY** May00
– Cool that you showed us how / The blisters may come / Call the legion in tonight / Strategy room / Huge in every city / Saving a free seat / Save us, Tothero / Most everyone will find / Gas blowin' out of our eyes / Magic cyclops / Would go over / Hercules now! / Members of the show 'em how it's done / Aerial spins – Nautical wilderness.
Feb 01. (cd-ep) <6> **CENTRO-MATIC + VERMONT**
– Old blue / Strong sentences / Celebrated departure / (other 3 by VERMONT).
Mar 01. (cd; as SOUTH SAN GABRIEL) (MRCD 210) <22> **SONGS/MUSIC** Sep00
– Ninety secretaries / down / Proud son of Gaffney / To accompany / The fireworks treatment / With broken hands / The ensuing light of day / One-hundred thousand bridesmaids / Glacial slurs / Innocence kindly waits / Destroyer.

not iss.   Idol

Aug 01. (cd) <30> **DISTANCE AND CLIME**
– The connection's not so civilized / Fountains of fire / Scrap the new rails / To unleash the horses now / Tundra (pt.7) / The given geography / Truth flies out / Janitorial on channel fail / On the Sagtikos / Actuator's great / Tonight is not it / Decorated equals / Patiently standing / Upton to Riverhead to Mastic / Call down the system and the ranks.

WILL JOHNSON

— with **SCOTT DANBOM**

not iss.   Undertow

Mar 02. (cd) <CD 006> **MURDER OF TIDES**
– Murder of tides (westerlies) / Commonly linked / The riot jack / Philo Manitoba / Karcher's contacts / Re-run pills / River Koltolwash / In a motionless way / Tent of total mystery / The yellow signals.

CERBERUS SHOAL

Formed: Portland, Maine, USA ... 1994 by CALEB MULKERIN, CHRISS SUTHERLAND, TOM ROGERS and JOSH OGDEN, who flitted to Boston where they quickly became intergrated with the local music scene. After issuing a handful of 7" singles, this quartet of punk-infused psych-garage rockers delivered a self-titled mini-CD just before OGDEN was permanently replaced by KRISTEN HEDGES; keyboardist DAVID MULDER was also added. The group toured the US in 1995 and issued two EP's the following year: 'LIGHTHOUSE IN ATHENS' – PARTS 1 & 2 – plus 'AND FAREWELL TO HIGHTIDE' (1997). By this point, they had long since forgotten about their punkier incarnation (although the occasional blast of a power-chord could be heard somewhere in there), while the ensemble decided to develop and explore the further reaches of Prog-rock, or, in their case, soundtrack-rock. They issued the 'ELEMENTS OF STRUCTURE / PERMANENCE' album, initially intended for the soundtrack to a short film, the set clocked in at fifty minutes and featured only two slow-building tracks – the band, taking notes from sludgy psych-rockers BARDO POND. THOMAS KOVACEIC and TIM HARBESON from the small indie group TARPIGH joined the line-up and CERBERUS SHOAL for the release of their next full-set, 'HOMB' (1999), a far cry from their rockier past, the set included swirling effects, trumpets and wave-like melodies that could wash the listener into unconsciousness. 'CRASH MY MOON YACHT' appeared the following year, and employed a more abrasive, minimalistic tone with strenuous attention to instrumental detail, as did 'MR. BOY DOG' (2002), arguably the band's finest hour; a double CD of eerie instrumentals set to dense Eastern atmospherics.

CERBERUS SHOAL (cont)

Album rating: CERBERUS SHOAL mini (*5) / AND FAREWELL TO HIGHTIDE (*5) / ELEMENTS OF STRUCTURE – PERMANENCE (*6) / HOMB (*6) / CRASH MY MOON YACHT (*4) / MY BOY DOG (*7)

CHRISS SUTHERLAND – vocals, bass / **CALEB MULKERIN** – guitar / **JOSH OGDEN** – guitar / **TOM ROGERS** – drums / **ERIC LaPERNA** – drums, percussion

				not iss.	Stella White
1995.	(m-cd)	<004>	**CERBERUS SHOAL**	-	

– Omphalos / Breathing machines (live).

— **KRISTEN HEDGES** – guitar, vocals; repl. OGDEN

— added **DAVID MULDER** – keyboards

				Tree Roots	Tree Roots
1996.	(cd-ep)	<TREE 01CD>	**LIGHTHOUSE IN ATHENS PART ONE**	-	
1996.	(cd-ep)	<TREE 02CD>	**LIGHTHOUSE IN ATHENS PART TWO**	-	
Mar 98.	(cd)	<(TREE 03CD)>	**AND FAREWELL TO HIGHTIDE**		Jul97

– Falling to pieces (pt.1) / Broken springs spring forth from broken clocks / J.B.O. vs. Blin / Make winter a driving song / Falling to pieces (pt.2). *(re-iss. Oct99 on 'Rosewood Union'; UNION 019) <(re+UK-iss.Oct02 on 'Temporary Residence'+=; TTR 41)>* – LIGHTHOUSE IN ATHENS PART ONE / LIGHTHOUSE IN ATHENS PART TWO

— now without HEDGES

				not iss.	A.I.P.
1998.	(cd)	<001>	**ELEMENTS OF STRUCTURE / PERMANENCE**	-	

<(re+UK-iss.Oct02 on 'Temporary Residence'; TTR 45)>

— **THOMAS KOVACEIC** – guitar, vocals + **TIM HARBESON** – keyboards, trumpet (ex-TARPIGH) repl. MULDER

				not iss.	Temporary Residence
1999.	(cd)	<TTR 24CD>	**HOMB**	-	

– Harvest / Omphalos / Myrrh (waft) / Myrrh (loop) / Myrrh (reprise).

				not iss.	Pandemonium
Jul 00.	(cd)	<PAN 40>	**CRASH MY MOON YACHT**	-	

– Changabang I / Breathing machines / Elle besh / Changabang II / Long winded / Changabang III / Yes sir, no sir / Asphodel.

— **MULKERIN, SUTHERLAND + ROGERS** with **COLLEEN KINSELLA, KARL GREENWALD + ERIN DAVIDSON**

				not iss.	North East India
2001.	(cd-s)		**GARDEN FLY, DRIP EYE**	-	

				Temporary Residence	Temporary Residence
2001.	(cd-ep)		**TRAVELS IN CONSTANTS**	-	

– My machines / Christopher's winded.

| Mar 02. | (d-cd) | <TTR 39CD)> | **MY BOY DOG** | | |

– Round valley / Nataraja / Camel bell / Stumblin' block / Tongue drongue / Vuka / Unmarked boxes / Telikos II / (untitled) / Nod / (untitled) / An Egypt that does not exist.

CHA CHA COHEN

Formed: Austin, Texas ... 1994 when expatriot Australian singer, JAQI DULANY, met up with two former members of The WEDDING PRESENT, KEITH GREGORY and SIMON SMITH, who actually still reside in Leeds! JAQI, who had been an integral part of arty-farty rock outfit, The DUSTDEVILS, moved to New York where she gained employment working as a casino croupier at a nearby Native American reservation. Writing and posting songs to each other by airmail or E-mail, this unusual band released their debut 7", 'SPARKY'S NOTE', before putting pen to paper for Glasgow's seminal imprint, 'Chemikal Underground'. Three further singles of BLONDIE-esque guitar-pop were delivered between 1996 and late 1998, an eponymous album and UK tour in early '99 saw GREGORY and his girl receive plaudits from the likes of the NME and Uncut. If you can imagine CICCONE YOUTH (aka SONIC YOUTH) being backed by a BECK staccato then you have the picture. With DULANY flitting to Leeds (she also married KEITH) and the group taking on newcomer TANYA MELLOTT, CHA CHA COHEN finally released their long-awaited sophomore set, 'ALL ARTISTS ARE CRIMINALS', in late summer 2002; it had been due the previous year. The record explored JAQI's cynicism of life in corpulent America; she had spent time in the Big Apple as hotel casino croupier.

Album rating: CHA CHA COHEN (*7) / ALL ARTISTS ARE CRIMINALS (*6)

JAQI DULANY (b. Sydney, Australia) – vocals, guitar (ex-DUSTDEVILS) / **KEITH GREGORY** (b. 2 Jan'63, County Durham) – guitar (ex-WEDDING PRESENT) / **SIMON SMITH** (b. 3 May'65, Lincolnshire) – drums (ex-WEDDING PRESENT) / **ALAN THOMAS** – keyboards, guitar

				Hemiola	not iss.
Oct 95.	(7")	(HEM 008)	**SPARKY'S NOTE. / SNARES OF URGOIL URMA**		-

				Chemikal Underground	not iss.
Jul 96.	(7"ep)	(chem 005)	**538 EP**		-

– Seed / Post trailer / Fairy Stan / Six years.

| May 97. | (12"ep/cd-ep) | (chem 014/+cd) | **SPOOK ON THE HIGH LAWN (mixes; album / Sasha Frere-Jones remix / Hood remix) / R.O.C. Development** | | |
| Oct 98. | (7") | (chem 031) | **FREON SHORTWAVE. / STREET SOUP** | | - |

(cd-s+=) *(chem 031cd)* – Non-sequitur.

| Jan 99. | (lp/cd) | (chem 032/+cd) | **CHA CHA COHEN** | | - |

– He's jet / Serpentine slip / The words I hate / The joke / Freon shortwave / Cool slate / Spook on the high lawn / Nothing to do / Snares of Urgoil Urma / Song for Guyda / Trick or treat / Street soup.

— added **TANYA MELLOTT** – guitar

| Sep 02. | (cd) | (chem 055cd) | **ALL ARTISTS ARE CRIMINALS** | | - |

– A=A / August / Taxi, taxi / Kodiak / Century life / Wavemaker / Last minute girl / To the letter / Heck Singhi / Trigger raft.

CHA CHA 2000 (see under ⇒ PROLAPSE)

CHAINSAW KITTENS

Formed: Bartlesville, Oklahoma, USA ... late 80's by main writer, TYSON MEADE, along with conspirators TRENT BELL, MARK METZGER, KEVIN McELHANEY and TOM LEADER. The 'KITTENS are frequently spoken of as the most overlooked American alternative rock band of their era. They certainly have the talent and a catalogue of sound material to boot, so it seems a mystery to many why prodigious record sales and fame have not come their way. The group were signed up, fairly quickly after their formation, by 'Mammoth', who put out the band's first full-length set, 'VIOLENT RELIGION' (1990). This album unfortunately did not bring the band immediate notice, although it was an above par debut with some truly worthwhile tracks such as 'SHE'S GONE MAD'. However through a combination of touring, and the massively increased interest in the American alternative rock scene, the boys started to get some deserved acknowledgement. Their subsequent album, 'FLIPPED OUT IN SINGAPORE' (1992) had all the makings of a near-classic; primarily they had BUTCH VIG behind the production desk, who had recently been showered with adulation for his work on NIRVANA's 'Nevermind' (1991). CK had also added guitarist TRENT BELL and swapped their rhythm section; replacing LEADER for AARON PRESTON and MCELHANEY for CLINT McBAY. Following this piece the McBAY and PRESTON pairing took their leave, to be replaced by MATT JOHNSON and ERIC HARMON respectively. The release of the EP 'ANGEL ON THE RANGE' (1993), further proved the band's technical ability, the eponymously titled track being one of the stand-outs of KITTEN's output as a whole. The boys moved on swiftly sending off another full-length set, 'POP HEIRESS' (1994), which in subject matter and style has been compared much to DAVID BOWIE's 'Ziggy Stardust' era and IGGY POP, both artists that CK frontman, MEADE confesses to being a huge fan of. The sound of this set is also enhanced by the work of experienced British producer, JOHN AGNELLO. SMASHING PUMPKINS who had gigged with CK in the early years of the decade decided shortly after this release to sign the boys to their label, 'Scratchie', releasing their next album, the self-titled, 'CHAINSAW KITTENS', two years later in '96. This set which is also known as 'Oklahoma Speedway', was another highly accomplished work with some high-energy pop-rock tunes combined with some inspired string arrangements. For anyone who looked at the sleevenotes and thought that the drummer had again changed, it is in fact still HARMON, but trading under the new title ERIC EDWARD BONES. A long break was had by CK after this set, only resurfacing at the turn of the century with 'THE ALL AMERICAN' (2000); a full-set that equalled any of their former output, and ending on a double cover; a rather dark interpretation of the Go-Go's 'WE GOT THE BEAT' segued onto Iggy Pop's 'NIGHTCLUBBING'. • **Trivia:** CK's promo video for the single from EP 'HIGH IN HIGHSCHOOL' was made by a young Spike Jonze, who was later to become famed for his work on the promo videos for the BEASTIE BOYS ('Sabotage) and FATBOY SLIM ('Praise You') which he also starred in as the head of the dance troupe.

Album rating: VIOLENT RELIGION (*4) / FLIPPED OUT IN SINGAPORE (*4) / ANGEL ON THE RANGE (*3) / POP HEIRESS (*6) / CHAINSAW KITTENS (*5) / THE ALL AMERICAN (*7)

TYSON MEADE – vocals, guitar / **TRENT BELL** – guitar / **MARK METZGER** – guitar / **KEVIN McELHANEY** – bass / **TOM LEADER** – drums

				Mammoth	Mammoth
Jan 92.	(cd/c/lp)	<(MR 0021-2/-4/-1)>	**VIOLENT RELIGION**		Nov90

– Bloodstorm / Skinned knees (kitten theme) / Boyfriend song / Mother (of the ancient birth) / I'm waiting (Leanne's song) / Here at the end / Bliss (we're small) / Feel like a drugstore / Savior boyfriend collides / Violent religion / Death-out at party central / She's gone mad.

— **CLINT McBAY** – bass; repl. KEVIN

— **AARON PRESTON** – drums; repl. TOM

| May 92. | (cd/c) | <(MR 0034-2/-4)> | **FLIPPED OUT IN SINGAPORE** | | |

– Connie I've found the door / High in high school / 2nd theme / Flipped out in Singapore / My friend delirium / She gets / Never to be found / Shannon's Fellini movie / When you shoot / Hold / Ezekial walks through Sodom & Gomorrah / Angels self destruct.

| Dec 92. | (cd-ep) | <(MR 0042-2)> | **HIGH IN HIGH SCHOOL EP** | | |

– High in high school / Connie I've found the door / Couple No.23 / Stuck / One / Walk softly (for D.M.).

| Nov 93. | (cd/c/lp) | <(MR 0062-2/-4/-1)> | **ANGEL ON THE RANGE** | | Oct93 |

– Kick kid / Angel on the range / John Wayne dream / Mary's belated wedding present / Lazy little dove / Sgt. Whore / Little fishes.

— **MATTHEW JOHNSON** – bass; repl. CLINT

— **ERIC EDWARD BONES** – drums; repl. AARON

— **MIKE HOSTY** – lap steel guitar; repl. METZGER

				Atlantic	Atlantic
Feb 95.	(cd/c)	<(7567 92318-2/-4)>	**POP HEIRESS**		Nov94

– Sore on the floor / Loneliest China place / Pop heiress dies / Closet song / Dive into the sea / Burn you down / I ride free / Silver millionaire / Media star hymn / Soldier on my shoulder / Justine find Heaven / We're like ...

CHAINSAW KITTENS (cont) THE GREAT INDIE DISCOGRAPHY The 1990s

                                            not iss. Polygram
Oct 96. (cd/c) <534002> **CHAINSAW KITTENS**   [-]   [   ]
   – Dorothy's last fling / Heart catch thump / Tongue trick / King monkey smoke / Bones in my teeth / Waltz across debris / Ballad of newsman 5 / Mouthful of glass / Leash / Bicycle head / All (no surprise) / Sounder / Madhatter's blues / Speedway Oklahoma.
                                            Four   Four
                                            Alarm   Alarm
Oct 00. (cd) <(FAR 450CD)> **THE ALL AMERICAN**   [   ]   [   ]
   – Light / All American wiggle wiggle / International me / Calling from space / How many light bulbs / Shutdown / Hedonist / John Wayne / Wedding / Gleaming soft white teens / The treasure is love / We got the beat – Nightclubbing.

CHAPPAQUIDDICK SKYLINE
(see under ⇒ PERNICE BROTHERS)

CHAPTERHOUSE

Formed: Reading, England . . . late '87 by ANDREW SHERRIFF, STEPHEN PATMAN, SIMON ROWE, JON CURTIS and ASHLEY BATES. After thoroughly polishing their skills in the studio they toured as a support to SPACEMEN 3, their dense, effects-driven sound subsequently casting them as leading lights of the early 90's "shoegazing" scene. So called due to the scenester's tendency to favour distortion pedals over showmanship, CHAPTERHOUSE (along with LUSH, BLEACH, MOOSE, RIDE etc.) became sitting targets for music press criticism. Moving to London in 1990, they signed to the newly formed 'Dedicated' label and were initially heralded as indie music's great white hopes following an impressive couple of EP's, 'FREE FALL' and 'SUNBURST', along with the sublime 'PEARL'. With a steadily growing reputation, 1991's debut album, 'WHIRLPOOL', narrowly missed the Top 20 and the band looked set for great things. It all went pear-shaped following an ill-fated attempt to make some headway in the US and with the shoegazing backlash at full strength, a follow-up album, 'BLOOD MUSIC' (1993), was to be the final, ahem . . . chapter in the band's relatively brief career. While the likes of MY BLOODY VALENTINE and RIDE continued to evolve and amass critical aclaim, CHAPTERHOUSE lasted only as long as the scene itself. • **Songwriters:** All SHERRIFF or PATMAN or combined. Covered; RAIN (Beatles) / LADY GODIVA'S OPERATION (Velvet Underground) / LOSING TOUCH WITH MY MIND (Spacemen 3).

Album rating: WHIRLPOOL (*6) / BLOOD MUSIC (*5) / ROWNDERBOWT compilation (*7)

STEPHEN PATMAN (b. 8 Nov'68, Windsor, England) – vocals, guitar / **ANDREW SHERRIFF** (b. 5 May'69, Wokingham, England) – vocals, guitar / **SIMON ROWE** (b.23 Jun'69) – guitar / **ASHLEY BATES** (b. 2 Nov'71) – drums / **RUSSELL BARRETT** (b. 7 Nov'68, Vermont, USA) – bass (ex-BIKINIS) repl. JON CURTIS

                                            Dedicated Arista
Aug 90. (12"ep/cd-ep) (STONE 001 T/CD) **FREE FALL**   [   ]   [-]
   – Falling down / Need (somebody) / Inside of me / Sixteen years.
Nov 90. (7") (STONE 002) **SOMETHING MORE. / RAIN**   [   ]   [-]
   (12"ep+=/cd-ep+=) **SUNBURST EP** (STONE 002 T/CD) – Satin safe / Feel the same.
Mar 91. (7") (STONE 003) **PEARL. / COME HEAVEN**   [67] [-]
   (12"+=) (STONE 003T) – In my arms.
   (cd-s++=) (STONE 003CD) – Pearl (edit).
Apr 91. (cd/c/lp) (DED CD/MC/LP 001) **WHIRLPOOL**   [23] [-]
   – Brother / Pearl / Autosleeper / Treasure / Falling down / April / Guilt / If you want me / Something more. (free-ltd.one-sided-12"w-lp) – DIE DIE DIE
Oct 91. (12"ep/cd-ep) (HOUSE 001/+CD) **MESMERISE. / PRECIOUS ONE / SUMMER CHILL / THEN WE'LL RISE**   [60]   [-]
Jul 93. (7"purple) (HOUSE 003) **SHE'S A VISION. / DON'T LOOK NOW**   [   ]   [-]
   (12"+=) (HOUSE 003T) – ('B'-sitar trance mix) / For what it's worth (demo).
   (cd-s+=) (HOUSE 003CD) – ('B'-sitar trance mix) / Deli (dark jester mix).
Aug 93. (7") (HOUSE 004) **WE ARE THE BEAUTIFUL. / AGE**   [   ]   [-]
   (12"colrd+=/cd-s+=) (HOUSE 004 T/CD) – Frost.
Sep 93. (cd/c/lp) (DED CD/MC/LP 11) **BLOOD MUSIC**   [   ]   [-]
   – Don't look now / There's still life / We are the beautiful / Summer's gone / Everytime / Deli / On the way to fly / She's a vision / Greater power / Confusion trip / Love forever.
Oct 93. (cd-s) <2640> **WE ARE THE BEAUTIFUL / WE ARE (extended)**   [-]   [   ]

─── sank without trace after lukewarm reviews of above album

─── ASHLEY resurfaced in the breakbeat electronic duo, CUBA (one set in '99, 'LEAP OF FAITH'), alongside Canadian CHRISTOPHER ANDREWS. Meanwhile, RUSSELL was doing his bit with London 4-piece INNER SLEEVE and the BIKINIS.

– compilations, etc. –

Nov 96. (d-cd) (DEDCD 025) **ROWNDERBOWT**   [   ]   [-]
   – Falling down / Sixteen years / Something more / Satin safe / Rain / Pearl / Mesmerise / She's a vision / We are the beautiful / Frost / For what it's worth / Breather / Don't look now / There's still life / Then we'll rise / In my arms / Losing touch with my mind / Ecstasy II / Dream on (demo) / Until you try (demo) / Kane (demo) / More than I can take (demo) / Brighter (demo) / Feel (demo) / Don't look now / We are the beautiful / Picnic / Die, die, die.

CHARLATANS (UK)

Formed: Northwich, Cheshire, England . . . late 1989 by MARTIN BLUNT, ROB COLLINS, JON BROOKES and JON BAKER. They soon found a frontman in singer TIM BURGESS and after a few attempts at getting a record deal, they set up their own 'Dead Dead Good' label. Early in 1990, they scored a massive indie hit with the 'INDIAN ROPE' single. Following the explosion of the "Madchester" scene, the label was taken over by the Beggars Banquet subsidiary, 'Situation 2', for whom they recorded their first Top 10 hit, 'THE ONLY ONE I KNOW'. Another hammond-driven classic, 'THEN', preceded a late summer chart topping debut album, 'SOME FRIENDLY'. A relatively quiet year followed, during which MARTIN BLUNT nearly retired due to severe depression. However, it was actually BAKER who departed after playing at London's Royal Albert Hall. Come 1992, MARK COLLINS (ex-WALTONES) was drafted in and things looked brighter when the single, 'WEIRDO', gave them another Top 20 hit. Their second album, however, ('BETWEEN 10TH AND 11TH'), was given the thumbs down by the music press, hence its failure to secure a respectable chart placing. This was not the only setback that year, as ROB COLLINS was charged with aiding and abetting an armed robbery. A year later, although maintaining his innocence, he was sentenced to several months in jail, later being released in early 1994 on good behaviour. 'CAN'T GET OUT OF BED', saw them return in fine style, and was lifted from the Top 10 album 'UP TO OUR HIPS'. TIM then moonlighted on singles by SAINT ETIENNE and The CHEMICAL BROTHERS, before the group were back to their best on the eponymous 1995 album. From its retro cover art, to the 'Sympathy For The Devil'-style single, 'JUST WHEN YOU'RE THINKIN' THINGS OVER', the album was an obvious homage to The ROLLING STONES. Tragically, on 23rd of July '96, ROB COLLINS was killed when his car spun off a road in Wales. The coroners report concluded that he was the driver and also that he had twice the legal amount of alcohol in his blood. They had just recorded their fifth album, 'TELLIN' STORIES', preceded by their biggest hit singles to date, 'ONE TO ANOTHER' and 'NORTH COUNTRY BOY'. With The CHARLATANS momentum seemingly unstoppable while every other 'baggy' band fell by the wayside, BURGESS and Co celebrated their longevity with a career retrospective, 'MELTING POT' (1998). With newboy TONY ROGERS finally getting his chance to perform in the place of COLLINS and with the group signing a major deal via 'M.C.A.', The CHARLATANS were ready to take their place back in indie-rock – albeit minus a few hundred thousand admittedly stolen by their accountant, Trevor Williams. Their sixth album, 'US AND US ONLY' (1999), was a test of sorts, its subsequent No.2 peak position in the UK charts an indication that they were still wanted by their ageing fanbase; the STONE ROSES, THE VERVE and OASIS, where were they now? Seven albums and still going strong, The CHARLATANS set out their stall for the 21st century with Top 3 set, 'WONDERLAND' (2001). This time around BURGESS was wielding a bit of soulpower, reaching for the skies with a hitherto unheard falsetto on hit singles such as 'LOVE IS THE KEY' and 'A MAN NEEDS TO BE TOLD'. The grooves were also slicker and sexier, hints of CURTIS MAYFIELD's funkier moments revealing themselves on the latter especially. • **Songwriters:** Group compositions except; I FEEL MUCH BETTER ROLLING OVER (Small Faces). On their eponymous 1995 album, the track 'HERE COMES A SOUL SAVER' featured a guitar riff remarkably similar to that of PINK FLOYD's 'Fearless' (from 'Meddle' 1971).

Album rating: SOME FRIENDLY (*8) / BETWEEN 10th & 11th (*5) / UP TO OUR HIPS (*7) / THE CHARLATANS (*8) / TELLIN' STORIES (*8) / MELTING POT compilation (*8) / US AND US ONLY (*7) / WONDERLAND (*5) / LIVE IT LIKE YOU LOVE IT – THE BEST OF THE CHARLATANS LIVE collection (*6)

TIM BURGESS (b.30 May'68) – vocals (ex-ELECTRIC CRAYONS) repl. BAZ KETTLEY / **ROB COLLINS** (b.23 Feb'63) – organ / **JON BAKER** (b.1969) – guitar / **JON BROOKS** (b.1969) – drums / **MARTIN BLUNT** (b.1965) – bass (ex-MAKIN' TIME, ex-TOO MUCH TEXAS w / TIM)

                                            Dead Dead
                                            Good   not iss.
Feb 90. (7") (GOOD ONE SEVEN) **INDIAN ROPE. / WHO WANTS TO KNOW**   [89]   [-]
   (12"+=) (GOOD ONE TWELVE) – You can talk to me. (re-iss. Jul91 12"/cd-s; GOOD 1 T/CD, hit No.57) (re-iss. cd-s Oct96)

                                            Situation 2 Beggars Banquet
May 90. (7") (SIT 70) **THE ONLY ONE I KNOW. / EVERYTHING CHANGED**   [9]   [   ]
   (12"+=) (SIT 70T) – Imperial 109.
   (cd-s++=) (SIT 70CD) – You can talk to me.
Sep 90. (7"/c-s) (SIT 74/+C) **THEN. / TAURUS MOANER**   [12]   [   ]
   (12"+=/cd-s+=) (SIT 74 T/CD) – ('A'-alternate take) / ('B'instrumental).
Oct 90. (lp/c/cd/s-lp) (SITU 30/+MC/CD/R) <2411> **SOME FRIENDLY**   [1]   [73]
   – You're not very well / White shirt / Opportunity / Then / 109 pt.2 / Polar bear / Believe you me / Flower / Sonic / Sproston Green. (cd+=) – The only one I know. (cd re-iss. Sep95 on 'Beggars Banquet'; BBL 30CD)
Feb 91. (7"/c-s) (SIT 76/+CS) **OVER RISING. / WAY UP THERE**   [15]   [   ]
   (12"/c-s+/cd-s+=) (SIT 76 T/TC/CD) – Happen to die / Opportunity Three (re-work).

─── **MARK COLLINS** – guitar (ex-WALTONES, ex-CANDLESTICK PARK) repl. BAKER

Oct 91. (7"/c-s) (SIT 84/+C) **ME IN TIME. / OCCUPATION H. MONSTER**   [28]   [   ]
   (12"+=/cd-s+=) (SIT 84 T/CD) – Subtitle.
Feb 92. (7"/c-s) (SIT 88/+C) **WEIRDO. / THEME FROM 'THE WISH'**   [19]   [-]
   (12"+=/cd-s+=) (SIT 88 T/CD) – Sproston Green (U.S. remix) / ('A'-alternate take).

CHARLATANS (UK) (cont)

		Beggars Banquet	Beggars Banquet
Mar 92.	(lp/c/cd) (SITU 37/+MC/CD) <61108> **BETWEEN 10th AND 11th**	21	–

– I don't want to see the lights / Ignition / Page one / Tremelo song / The end of everything etc / Subtitle / Can't even be bothered / Weirdo / Chewing gum weekend / (No one) Not even the rain. *(re-iss. cd Sep95 on 'Beggars Banquet'; BBL 37CD)*

| Jun 92. | (c-s) (SIT 97C) **TREMELO SONG (alternate take) / THEN (live) / CHEWING GUM WEEKEND (live) / TREMELO SONG** | 44 | – |

(12") *(SIT 97T)* – Happen to die (unedited) repl. last version.
(cd-s) *(SIT 97CD1)* – ('A'side) / Happen to die (unedited) / Normality swing (demo).
(cd-s) *(SIT 97CD2)* – ('A'live April '92) / Then (live) / Chewing gum weekend (live).

— ROB COLLINS was imprisoned in Sep'93 for taking part in a robbery. (see above) He had already recorded below while awaiting trial, and was free just in time to feature on Top Of The Pops.

		Beggars Banquet	Beggars Banquet
Jan 94.	(7"/c-s) (BBQ 27/+C) **CAN'T GET OUT OF BED. / WITHDRAWN**	24	–

(12"+=/cd-s+=) *(BBQ 27 T/CD)* – Out.

| Mar 94. | (cd-ep) (BBQ 31CD) **I NEVER WANT AN EASY LIFE IF ME AND HE WERE EVER TO GET THERE / ONLY A BOHO / SUBTERRAINEAN / CAN'T GET OUT OF BED (demo)** | 38 | – |
| Mar 94. | (cd/c/lp) (BBQ CD/MC/LP 147) <92352> **UP TO OUR HIPS** | 8 | |

– Come in number 21 / I never want an easy life / If me and he were ever to get there / Can't get out of bed / Feel flows / Autograph / Jesus hairdo / Up to our hips / Patrol / Another rider up in flames / Inside – looking out. *(re-iss. cd Sep95; BBL 147CD)*

| Jun 94. | (c-s) (BBQ 32C) **JESUS HAIRDO / PATROL (Dust Brothers mix)** | 48 | – |

(12"+=) *(BBQ 32T)* – Feel flows (the carpet kiss mix).
(cd-s+=) *(BBQ 32CD1)* – Stir it up / Feel flows (Van Basten mix).
(cd-s) *(BBQ 32CD2)* – ('A'side) / I never want an easy life / Another rider up in flames / Up to our hips (BBC Radio 1 live sessions).

| Dec 94. | (7"/c-s) (BBQ 44/+C) **CRASHIN' IN. / BACK ROOM WINDOW** | 31 | – |

(12"+=/cd-s+=) *(BBQ 44 T/CD)* – Green flashing eyes.

| May 95. | (7"/c-s) (BBQ 55/+C) **JUST LOOKIN'. / BULLET COMES** | 32 | – |

(cd-s+=) *(BBQ 55CD)* – Floor nine.

| Aug 95. | (c-s) (BBQ 60C) **JUST WHEN YOU'RE THINKIN' THINGS OVER / FRINCK / YOUR SKIES ARE MINE** | 12 | – |

(cd-s+=) *(BBQ 60CD)* – Chemical risk (toothache remix).
(12") *(BBQ 60T)* – (first 2 tracks) / Chemical risk dub (toothache remix) / Nine acre dust (Dust Brothers mix).

| Aug 95. | (cd/c/d-lp) (BBQ CD/MC/LP 174) <92602> **THE CHARLATANS** | 1 | |

– Nine acre court / Feeling holy / Just lookin' / Crashin' in / Bullet comes / Here comes a soul saver / Just when you're thinkin' things over / Tell everyone / Toothache / No fiction / See it through / Thank you. *(d-lp+=)* – Chemical risk (toothache remix).

— On 23rd July '96, ROB COLLINS was killed in a car crash (see above).

| Aug 96. | (7"/c-s/cd-s) (BBQ 301/+C/CD) **ONE TO ANOTHER. / TWO OF US / REPUTATION** | 3 | – |

— MARTIN DUFFY – keyboards (of PRIMAL SCREAM) augmented

		Beggars Banquet	M.C.A.
Mar 97.	(7"/c-s/cd-s) (BBQ 309/+C/CD) **NORTH COUNTRY BOY. / AREA 51 / DON'T NEED A GUN**	4	–
Apr 97.	(cd/c/lp) (BBQ CD/MC/LP 190) <11622> **TELLIN' STORIES**	1	

– With no shoes / North country boy / Tellin' stories / One to another / You're a big girl now / How can you leave us / Area 51 / How high / Only teethin' / Get on it / Rob's theme / Two of us / Reputation.

| Jun 97. | (7"/c-s) (BBQ 312/+C) **HOW HIGH. / DOWN WITH THE MOOK** | 6 | – |

(cd-s+=) *(BBQ 312CD)* – Title fight.

| Oct 97. | (7") (BBQ 318) **TELLIN' STORIES. / KEEP IT TO YOURSELF** | 16 | – |

(c-s+=) *(BBQ 318C)* – Thank you (live).
(cd-s++=) *(BBQ 318CD)* – Clean up kid.

		Beggars Banquet	Beggars Banquet
Feb 98.	(cd/c/lp) (BBQ CD/MC/LP 198) <80198> **MELTING POT** (compilation)	4	

– The only one I know / Then / Opportunity three / Over rising / Sproston Green (U.S. version) / Weirdo / Theme from the wish / Patrol (The Chemical Brothers mix) / Can't get out of bed / I never want an easy life if me & he were ever to get there / Jesus hairdo / Crashin' in / Just lookin' / Here comes a soul saver / Just when you're thinkin' things over / One to another / North country boy. *(cd re-iss. May02; same)*

— (1997) TONY RODGERS was now the replacement for ROB

		M.C.A.	Universal
Oct 99.	(7") (MCS 40220) **FOREVER. / WHEN YOUR SHIP COMES IN**	12	–

(c-s/cd-s+=) *(MCS C/TD 40220)* – Great place to leave.
(cd-s) *(MCSXD 40220)* – ('A'side) / Sleepy little sunshine boy / ('A'-CD enhanced).

| Oct 99. | (cd/c/lp) (MCD/MCC/MCA 60069) <112058> **US AND US ONLY** | 2 | |

– Forever / Good witch, bad witch / Impossible / The blonde waltz / A house is not a home / Senses / My beautiful friend / I don't care where you live / The blind stagger / Good witch, bad witch / Watching you.

| Dec 99. | (7") (MCS 40225) **MY BEAUTIFUL FRIEND. / SCORCHED** | 31 | – |

(c-s/cd-s+=) *(MCS C/TD 40225)* – Your precious love.
(cd-s) *(MCSXD 40225)* – ('A'mixes + CD-enhanced).

| May 00. | (7"/cd-s) (MCS/+XD 40231) **IMPOSSIBLE. / YOU GOT IT I WANT IT** | 15 | – |

(c-s/cd-s) *(MCS C/TD 40231)* – ('A'side) / Don't go giving it up / ('A'-video).

| Aug 01. | (7") (7") (MCS 40262) **LOVE IS THE KEY. / VIVA LA SOCIALE** | 16 | – |

(cd-s+=) *(MCSTD 40262)* – It's about time.

| Sep 01. | (cd/d-lp) (MCD/MCA 60076) <014910> **WONDERLAND** | 2 | – |

– You're so pretty – we're so pretty / Judas / Love is the key / A man needs to be told / I can't get over losing you / The bell and the butterfly / And if I fall / Wake up / Is it in you? / Ballad of the band. *(d-lp+=)* – Right on / Love to you.

| Nov 01. | (7") (MCS 40271) **A MAN NEEDS TO BE TOLD. / SHOTGUN** | 31 | – |

(cd-s+=) *(MCSTD 40271)* – Ballad of the band (Ianocce remix).
(cd-s) *(MCSXD 40271)* – ('A'side) / All I desire / Love is the key (live) / ('A'-video).

| Apr 02. | (12") (MCST 40283) **YOU'RE SO PRETTY – WE'RE SO PRETTY. / ('A'-Lo Fidelity Allstars) / SILLY THING** | | |

(cd-s) *(MCSTD 40283)* – ('A'side) / ('A'-Lo Fidelity Allstars) / Room 118.

| Jul 02. | (cd) (MCD 60080) <64169-2> **LIVE IT LIKE YOU LOVE IT – THE BEST OF THE CHARLATANS LIVE** (live) | 40 | Oct02 |

– Love is the key / Judas / Tellin' stories / The man needs to be told / One to another / The only one I know / Impossible / North country boy / You're so pretty – we're so pretty / Weirdo (with JOHNNY MARR) / How high / Forever / And if I fall / Sproston green.

– compilations, etc. –

| May 02. | (cd) *Beggars Banquet; (BEGL 2032CD)* **SONGS FROM THE OTHER SIDE** (B-sides) | 55 | – |

CHARMING

Formed: New Jersey, USA ... late 1994 by university students RAVI KRISHNASWAMI and DAVE SHERWIN (fellow engineering students at the University of Virginia); they later added singer SHANA LIE-NELSON, guitarist JAMIE PEREZ and bassist CHRIS GARVEY. Beginning to gain a local following, CHARMING recorded the 'RITUAL' EP on KRISHNASWAMI's four-track, although LIE-NELSON and PEREZ soon bailed out, while singer NICOLE STOOPS was added to the line-up. After a long break, they eventually re-surfaced in 1997 with debut album 'GIANT' – a charming collection of gentle indie-pop tunes (released on the 'Twee Kitten' label). Now with a new bassist, JOHN CICCONE, 2001's follow-up, 'CHAMPAGNE AND MAGAZINES', was a split release between the 'Twee Kitten' and 'Shelflife' imprints. Adding organs, piano, trombone and trumpet for a more sophisticated sound, the album had an airy, soothing feel, and tracks such as the jaunty 'GUILTY BY ASSOCIATION' and the demure title-track, were amongst their best work.

Album rating: GIANT (*5) / CHAMPAGNE AND MAGAZINES (*6)

SHANA LIE-NELSON – vocals / **RAVI KRISHNASWAMI** – guitars, keyboards / **JAMIE PEREZ** – guitar / **CHRIS GARVEY** – bass / **DAVE SHERWIN** – drums

		not iss.	own label
1995.	(7"ep) **RITUAL EP**	–	

— NICOLE STOOPS – vocals; repl. SHANA + JAMIE

		not iss.	Twee Kitten
1997.	(cd) <TK 004> **GIANT**	–	

– Social / Mississippi / Nobody's perfect / Ritual / Doll Starr / Waltz / December / What's in her? / Radio / Paralyzed / Free advice / Nothing to say.

— JAY B FLATT – bass; repl. JOHN CICCONE who repl. GARVEY
— CHRIS REITZ – drums; repl. SHERWIN

		not iss.	Shelflife
Nov 01.	(cd) <LIFE 41> **CHAMPAGNE AND MAGAZINES**	–	

– Let me take you out / A year and four months / Downtown / Where have I been / April / Guilty by association / You were not meant for me / Charlottesville, 1997 / How unkind / The interview / Champagne and magazines.

CHAVEZ

Formed: Lower Manhattan, New York, USA ... 1993 out of the short-lived WIDER by MATT SWEENEY, who enlisted CLAY TARVER (ex-BULLET LAVOLTA), JAMES LO (ex-LIVE SKULL) and DAVEY HOSKINS; the latter was replaced by SCOTT MASCIARELLI after the completion of rough demos. One of the many alt-rock acts to put pen to paper for 'Matador', CHAVEZ's long-playing introduction came with 1995's highly praised 'GONE GLIMMERING', an experimental Lo-Fi effort taking its cue from 70's Krautrock pioneers as well as modern day practitioners such as TORTOISE and SLINT. This was, surprisingly, critically and musically surpassed the following year with 'RIDE THE FADER', although of late, CHAVEZ have been conspicuous by their absence from the recording scene.

Album rating: GONE GLIMMERING (*7) / RIDE THE FADER (*8)

MATT SWEENEY – vocals, lead guitar (ex-SKUNK, ex-WIDER) / **CLAY TARVER** – guitar (ex-BULLET LAVOLTA) / **JAMES LO** – drums (ex-LIVE SKULL) / **SCOTT MASCIARELLI** – bass; repl. DAVEY HOSKINS

		City Slang	Matador
Sep 94.	(7") (EFA 04944-7) **REPEAT THE ENDING. / HACK THE SIDES AWAY**		

		Matador	Matador
Jul 95.	(cd/lp) <(OLE 133-2/-1)> **GONE GLIMMERING**		May95

– Nailed to the blank / Spot / Break up your band / Laugh track / Ghost by the sea / Pentagram ring / In our pools / The flaming gong / Wakeman's air / Relaxed fit.

| Oct 95. | (cd-ep) <(OLE 146-2)> **PENTAGRAM RING / THE NERVE / YOU FADED / HACK THE SIDES AWAY / REPEAT THE ENDING** | | |
| Nov 96. | (cd/lp) <(OLE 200-2/-1)> **RIDE THE FADER** | | |

– Top pocket man / Guard attacks / Unreal is here / New room / Tight around the jaws / Lions / Our boys will shine tonight / Memorize this face / Cold joys / Flight '96 / Ever overpsyched / You must be stopped.

— folded after above

CHECK ENGINE
(see under ⇒ SWEEP THE LEG JOHNNY)

CHEEKY MONKEY

Formed: Glasgow, Scotland ... 1997 by FRANCIS MACDONALD, a seasoned campaigner via BMX BANDITS, The PASTELS, TEENAGE FANCLUB, EUGENIUS and more recently the RADIO SWEETHEARTS and SPEEDBOAT. However, one part of this unusual outfit was from across the Atlantic, New York to be exact. MICHAEL SHELLEY had just issued his POPular solo set, 'Half Empty' (1997) and was corresponding through the internet with FRANCIS. Unique – well at least for stony broke indie merchants! – the pair wrote several songs over the phone and when that got too pricy a tape was sent by MICHAEL. Making a hectic recording schedule by the skin of their teeth, but with MICHAEL still in America for the time being, FRANCIS finally delivered their efforts via his own 'Shoeshine' records. A single, 'THAT KIND OF GIRL', was almost immediately pursued by their hastily-recorded warts-n-all pop set, 'FOUR ARMS TO HOLD YOU' (1998); if you're missing BIG STAR, The BEACH BOYS and The HOLLIES, this might be for you. • **Covered:** GERRY CHEEVERS (Chixdiggit) / MONKEY MAN (Bo Diddley).

Album rating: FOUR ARMS TO HOLD YOU (*5)

FRANCIS MACDONALD – drums, instruments, vocals (ex-see above) / **MICHAEL SHELLEY** – vocals, instruments

                                       Shoeshine Big Deal

Feb 98. (7") *(SHOE 010)* **THAT KIND OF GIRL. / FREE AGAIN**
Mar 98. (cd) *(SHOECD 002)* <9049> **FOUR ARMS TO HOLD YOU**   Jan98
 – That kind of girl / Monkey man / Big dumb boy / Robert Lloyd / Down / Uddingston church gun terror / I wanna live with you / Gerry Cheevers / Chasin' each other around the room / All I can do is cry / Let it flow / You don't want me anymore. *(lp-iss.Jul98; SHOELP 002)*

— FRANCIS re-joined TEENAGE FANCLUB late in 2000

CHEMICAL PILOT
(see under ⇒ McGEE, Alan; 80's section)

Vic CHESNUTT

Born: 1965, Georgia, Atlanta, USA. Confined to a wheelchair since 1983 after a car crash left him paraplegic, CHESNUTT developed a distinctive singing/songwriting style so popular among fellow musicians that 'Columbia' recently released a tribute album, 'Sweet Relief – Gravity Of The Situation: The Songs Of Vic Chesnutt' (1996). Among the contributors were such luminaries as MADONNA, SMASHING PUMPKINS and R.E.M.; the latter connection had already proved pivotal in the direction of the man's career with MICHAEL STIPE having produced his first two albums, 'LITTLE' (1989) and 'WEST OF ROME' (1991). Critics centred on the bitterness and vivid despair of the lyrics, CHESNUTT trawling the depths of his psyche for 1994's 'DRUNK'. A characteristically semi-detached, ironic delivery leavened the weight of CHESNUTT's burden while by this point, he'd also begun to flesh out the rootsy, acoustic sparseness of his sound, adhering to a more disciplined approach to song structure. The following year's 'IS THE ACTOR HAPPY', meanwhile, found VIC indulging his eccentricity in a concept affair based on the notion of playing live. While 1996 saw his peers paying their dues to his alcohol-sodden muse on the aforementioned tribute album, CHESNUTT himself hooked up with local band WIDESPREAD PANIC for an album, 'NINE HIGH A PALLET', released on the recently revamped 'Capricorn' under the moniker, BRUTE. The rise of the alt-country scene has certainly done CHESNUTT little harm, 'THE SALESMAN & BERNADETTE' (1998) seeing the man working with Nashville revivalists LAMBCHOP and elder stateswoman of country-rock, EMMYLOU HARRIS. Employing a multi-instrumental tapestry including clarinet, euphonium and trumpet, the record offered up positively zestful efforts – lyrics aside of course – like 'UNTIL THE LED' alongside the trademark lugubriousness. • **Covered:** SNOWBLIND FRIEND (Hoyt Axton).

Album rating: LITTLE (*6) / WEST OF ROME (*7) / DRUNK (*8) / IS THE ACTOR HAPPY? (*7) / NINE HIGH A PALLET as Brute (*7) / ABOUT TO CHOKE (*7) / THE SALESMAN & BERNADETTE (*7) / MERRIMENT with Mr. And Mrs. Keneipp (*7) / LEFT TO HIS OWN DEVICES demos (*6)

VIC CHESNUTT – vocals, guitar

                                  Texas Hotel Texas Hotel

1989. (lp) <*TXH 020*> **LITTLE**
 – Isadora Duncan / Danny Carlisle / Giupetto / Bakersfield / Mr. Riley / Rabbit fox / Speed racer / Soft Picasso / Independence day / Stevie Smith. *(UK cd-iss. Feb95 & Jul96; TXH 020-2)*
Jan 92. (cd) <*TXH 021-2*> **WEST OF ROME**
 – Latent blatant / Withering away / Sponge / Where were you / Lucinda Williams / Florida / Stupid preoccupation / Panic / Miss Mary / Steve Willoughby / West of Rome / Big huge valley / Soggy tongues / Fuge. *(UK-iss.Jul94 & Jul96; same)*
Mar 94. (cd/lp) <*(TXH 022-2/-1)*> **DRUNK**
 – Sleeping man / Bourgeois and biblical / One of many / When I ran off and left her / Dodge / Gluefoot / Drunk / Naughty fatalist / Super Tuesday / Kick my ass. *(re-iss. Jul96; same)*

— now backed by his wife TINA, plus the SCARED SKIFFLE BAND: ALEX McMANUS + JIMMY DAVIDSON and various session people

Apr 95. (cd) <*(TXH 023-2)*> **IS THE ACTOR HAPPY?**
 – Gravity of the situation / Sad Peter Pan / Strange language / Onion soup / Doubting woman / Wrong piano / Free of hope / Betty lonely / Thumbtack / Thailand / Guilty by association. *(re-iss. Jul96; same)*

— next was a collaboration between VIC and the band WIDESPREAD PANIC

                                      not iss. Capricorn

Jan 96. (cd; as BRUTE) <*42030*> **NINE HIGH ON A PALLET**
 – Westport ferry / Blight / Good morning Mr. Hard on / I ain't crazy enough / Protein drink – Sewing machine / Let's get down to business / George Wallace / PC / Snowblind / Miserable / Bastards in bubbles / Cataclysm.

— now with a session people

                                      P.L.R. Capitol

Nov 96. (cd) *(PLR 005-2)* <*37556*> **ABOUT TO CHOKE**
 – Myrtle / New town / Ladle / Tarragon / Swelters / (It's no secret) Satisfaction / Little vacation / Degenerate / Hot seat / Giant sands / Threads / See you around

— augmented by the group **LAMBCHOP** and others inc. guest **EMMYLOU HARRIS**

                                    P.L.R. Polygram

Sep 98. (cd/lp) *(PLR CD/LP 011)* <*538239*> **THE SALESMAN & BERNADETTE**   Nov98
 – Duty free / Bernadette & her crowd / Replenished / Maiden / Until the led / Scratch, scratch, scratch / Mysterious tunnel / Arthur Murray / Prick / Woodrow Wilson / Parade / Blanket over the head / Square room / Old hotel.

— next with **KELLY & NIKKI KENEIPP** – instruments / etc

                                    Backburner Backburner

Aug 00. (cd; as VIC CHESNUTT AND MR. AND MRS. KENEIPP) <*(BB 008CD)*> **MERRIMENT**   May00
 – Merriment / Fissle / Feather / Sunny pasture / Haiku / Mighty monkey / D.N.A. / Deeper currents / Merriment (reprise) / You may not be interested.

– compilations, etc. –

Jul 94. (cd) *Texas Hotel*; <*(TXH 0213)*> **SAMPLER**
Jun 01. (cd) *SpinArt*; <*(SPART 092CD)*> **LEFT TO HIS OWN DEVICES**   Apr01
 – Deadline / Very friendly lighthouse / Fish / Twelve Johnnies / Wounded prince / We should be so brave / Cash / In amongst the millions / Hermitage / Caper / Thought you were my friend / My last act / Distortion / Squeak / Look at me.

— a various artists tribute album, 'SWEET RELIEF – GRAVITY OF THE SITUATION: THE SONGS OF VIC CHESNUTT' was released in Aug'96 on 'Columbia'; (484137-2/-4)

CHESTNUT STATION

Formed: Chicago, Illinois, USA ... 1997 by a collective of Windy City musicians led by 'Drag City' veteran, RIAN MURPHY (who performed with PALACE/OLDHAM and APPENDIX/ROBERTS teams), along with younger brother BRENDAN MURPHY, RICK RIZZO (of ELEVENTH DREAM DAY and EDITH FROST), MARK GREENBERG (ex-COCTAILS), plus JOHN WHITNEY and PAUL CAPORINO. Taking a cheery and bright side of the pop spectrum, CHESTNUT STATION delivered their eponymous debut in spring the following year. However, aforementioned commitments elsewhere were to curtail the sextet for a few years until their next batch of songs, 2001's full-length covers LP, 'IN YOUR LIVING ROOM'. Opening with Mitch Ryder's 'BREAKOUT!' and closing with Allen Toussaint's 'WHAT DO YOU WANT THE GIRL TO DO?', this album was a worthy attempt at reincarnating 60's pop-pastiche and giving it a new modern groove.

Album rating: IN YOUR LIVING ROOM (*6)

RIAN MURPHY – vocals, tambourine / **MARK GREENBERG** – organ (ex-COCTAILS, of EDITH FROST) / **RICK RIZZO** – guitar, vocals (of ELEVENTH DREAM DAY, of EDITH FROST) / **JOHN WHITNEY** – guitar, vocals / **PAUL CAPORINO** – bass / **BRENDAN MURPHY** – drums

                                    not iss. Drag City

Mar 98. (cd-ep) <*DC 121*> **CHESTNUT STATION**
 – Born on the fourth of July / True identity / Double impact / Pure luck / 101 dalmations.
Jan 01. (cd) <*DC 199*> **IN YOUR LIVING ROOM (live)**
 – Breakout! / Right on / The boomerang / Everything is gonna be everything / Pinch me (baby convince me) / Snowblind friend / Fat man / Sitting on my sofa / Elephant candy / What do you want the girl to do?

CHICKS ON SPEED

Formed: Munich, Germany ... 1997 by MELISSA LOGAN, ALEX MURRAY-LESLIE and KIKI MOORSE. This prolific and slightly daunting electro-trash trio ran three record companies, a clothing line and were established avant-garde film makers and artists as well as performing scuzz-art punk noise to the tune of early KRAFTWERK and SUICIDE. They formed after meeting in an art cafe in 1997 and issued the limited edition 7" single 'SMASH METAL', as well as performing gimmicky shows in abandoned mental hospitals. Their self-released debut album, 'WILL SAVE US' (2000), proved poular on the minimilistic art scene front, and the group joined the new breed of electro ponces (LADYTRON, A.R.E. WEAPONS, etc.) with pretenious heed. An unnecessary "rarities" compilation appeared the same year entitled 'THE RE-RELEASES OF THE UN-RELEASES', as did the rather strenuous sophomore delivery 'MONSTERS RULE THE WORLD', which saw the ladies move into a more rockier criteria. Bitchin'.

Album rating: ...WILL SAVE US ALL (*7)

MELISSA LOGAN – vocals, programming / **ALEX MURRAY-LESLIE** – vocals, programming / **KIKI MOORSE** – vocals, programming

		Go	not iss.
May 98.	(7"; by DJ HELL with CHICKS ON SPEED) (Go 10 – efa 29560-7) **WARM LEATHERETTE. / DJ Hell: WARM LEATHERETTE**	-	- German
Oct 98.	(7"; by MAUSE with CHICKS ON SPEED) (Go 9 – efa 29559-7) **EURO TRASH GIRL. / EURO TRASH GIRL (version)**	-	- German
Mar 99.	(d7"ep; by DMAX CREW / CHICKS ON SPEED / The BOOB MONSTER) (Go 08 – 29558-7) **SMASH METAL EP** – For all the boys in the world / All over the world / Procrastinator / Seppi welt / Stop ad / Ohhh / Lush life / Lovely girls.	-	- German
Oct 99.	(7"; by CHICKS ON SPEED vs PULSINGER, GAIER/REENTS) (Go 7 – 29557-7) **MIND YOUR OWN BUSINESS (original). / MIND YOUR OWN BUSINESS (Patrick Pulsinger remix)**	-	- German
Nov 99.	(12"ep; as CHICKS ON SPEED with CHRISTOPHER JUST) (Go 7 – 29556-6) **GLAMOUR GIRL EP** – Special intro / Glamour girl / Turn of the century.	-	- German

		Go – Monika	not iss.
Feb 00.	(10") (go 5.5 – Monika 11 – efa 07707-6) **KALTES KLARES WASSER (CoS version). / KALTES KLARES WASSER (Morgenstern version)**	-	- German

		Arthur Whiskey	not iss.
Apr 00.	(7") (5) **POST POLICE RAZZIA IN THE LECORBUSIER LOUNGE MARSEILLE. / (other track by V/VM)**	-	- German

		Chicks On Speed	Chicks On Speed
Apr 00.	(cd/lp) (<efa 29901-2/-1>) **...WILL SAVE US ALL** – Stop records advert / Give me back my man / For all the boys in the world / Glamour girl / Pedstang (re)issue / Little star / Warm leatherette / Kaltes klares wasser / Yes I do! / Procratinator / Mind your own business / The floating pyramid over Frankfurt that the taxi driver saw when he was landing / Euro-trash girl.		
Sep 00.	(12"ep/cd-ep) (COS 002/+CD – 29902-6/-2) **CHIX 52** – Strobe light / Give me back my man / Song for a future generation / The chixmachine.	-	- German
Nov 00.	(12"ep/cd-ep) (efa 29903-6/-2) **MONSTERS RULE THIS WORLD**	-	- German
2001.	(12"; as MALARIA! vs. CHICKS ON SPEED) (superdj 2013) **KALTES KLARES WASSER. / ('A'-Lazerboy remix by Electrochemie LK)**	-	- German
	(12") (superdj 2013r) – ('A'-remix by DJ Koze & the Tease) / ('A'-Barbara Morgenstern mix) / ('A'-Rudeboy mix by Thomas Schumacher). (above issued on 'Superstar')		
Jan 02.	(12"ep/cd-ep) (efa 29904-6/-2) **CHICKS ON SPEED VS. KREIDLER** – Polar love / Sliding down your ribcage / Frequent flyer lounge song / Where the wild roses grow.	-	-
Jun 02.	(12") (efa 29908-6) **FASHION RULES! (original). / FASHION RULES! (alter ego remix)**	-	-

– compilations, etc. –

Oct 00.	(cd) K; <KLP 120> **RE-RELEASES OF THE UN-RELEASES**	-	
Jan 01.	(12") K; <KLP 124> **EURO TRASH GIRL. / ANGEL IN BLACK (DJ MAUSE remix)**	-	- German

CHIMERA

Formed: Belfast, N.Ireland ... summer '91 by songwriters TED LAVERTY and EILEEN HENRY, along with STEVEN EMERSON and WILLIE VINCENT. Catapulting onto the Belfast rock scene in 1991, the haunting 4-piece debuted alongside THROWING MUSES and the FRANK BLACK combo The PIXIES. After a brief Mark Goodier session for Radio One in late 1991, the fragile ensemble released the brilliant set 'LUGHNASA' in 1993. The album, full of loss and intergrity boasted EILEEN's rising vocals and slammed them in the same column as The COCTEAU TWINS, although with a more schizoid punkier edge. The group went on to deliver a final effort, 'EARTH LOOP' (1996), before calling it a day.

Album rating: LUGHNASA (*4) / EARTH LOOP (*5)

EILEEN HENRY – vocals / **TED LAVERTY** – guitar / **STEVEN EMERSON** – bass / **WILLIE VINCENT** – drums, percussion

		Beechwood	not iss.
Nov 92.	(one-side-7") (7EXP 001) **HEALS ME**	-	

		Flute	not iss.
Mar 93.	(12"/cd-s) (FLUTE 3 T/CD) **ELLIS BLEEDS. / PUSH / SLOW BURN (reprise)**		-
May 93.	(cd/c/lp) (FLUTE 4 CD/MC/LP) **LUGHNASA** – Slow burn / Ellis bleeds / Cyan daze / Heals me (feels so strange) / I let go / Fade away / Dreams going under / Innocence / Push.		
Jun 93.	(one-sided-7") (FLUTE 5) **CYAN DAZE** (12"+=/cd-s+=) (FLUTE 5 T/CD) – Heals me (feels so strange).		-

		Grass	not iss.
Apr 95.	(m-cd) (56) **THE DAY STAR ep** – 2 sunny / Let me be around / Closer / (untitled).		-
Jul 96.	(cd) (13035) **EARTH LOOP** – Liquid star / Blown away / Catch me / Tiago / Night song / All I need / God heart / Let me be around / Lately / 2 sunny / Bass mover / Don't feel the same / Lost in space.		-
1996.	(cd-s) **CATCH ME (new mixes; San Francisco / San Francisco instrumental / MX vs. BMX / Potbelly dub)**		-

—— split after above

CHINA DRUM

Formed: Ovingham-upon-Tyne, Northumbria, England ... 1989 by singing drummer ADAM LEE, bassist DAVE McQUEEN and his guitar-playing brother BILL McQUEEN; drummer JAN ALKELMA was subsequently added. Paying their dues by gigging hard around the toilet circuit of Northern England, the trio finally got round to self-financing a debut single, 'SIMPLE', in 1993. In addition to their full-on power-punk flurry, the record showcased their "sensitive" side with an acoustic track, 'MEANING'. They also pared things down with 'BISCUIT BARREL', a newly softened-up version of a stompalong live favourite that sat alongside 'GREAT FIRE' on their summer '94 GREEN DAY/THERAPY?-esque EP, the first of two releases for 'Fluffy Bunny'. The following year's 'BARRIER' EP was also released in the States, although most of the material had been previously issued in the UK. A one-off cover of Kate Bush's 'WUTHERING HEIGHTS' (a split 7" with the FLYING MEDALLIONS on 'Fierce Panda') preceded a major record deal with Beggars Banquet off-shoot, 'Mantra', through whom they issued a series of singles: 'FALL INTO PLACE', 'PICTURES', 'CAN'T STOP THESE THINGS' and 'LAST CHANCE'. The latter two scored minor chart placings while their long-awaited debut set, 'GOOSEFAIR' (1996), nearly hit the UK Top 50. Around the same time, the trio toured Bosnia to raise money for charities working in the war-torn region while their aforementioned album elbowed for chart position in America with Stateside competitors like OFFSPRING and GREEN DAY (again!). The challenge from across the water eventually proved too much and despite a further couple of minor hits, CHINA DRUM's second album, 'SELF MADE MANIAC' (1997), failed to impress the public.

Album rating: GOOSEFAIR (*6) / SELF MADE MANIAC (*6)

ADAM LEE – vocals (+ some drums) / **DAVE McQUEEN** – vocals, bass / **BILL McQUEEN** – vocals, guitar

		China Drum	Bitzcore
Apr 93.	(cd-s) (CC 193) <1696> **SIMPLE / ON MY WAY / MEANING (acoustic)**		

		Fluffy Bunny	510
Jul 94.	(10"ep/cd-ep) (FLUFF 6/+CD) **GREAT FIRE / BISCUIT BARREL (acoustic). / MEANING / DOWN BY THE RIVER (live)**		-
Mar 95.	(10"ep/cd-ep) (FLUFF 8/+CD) <FTD 11293> **BARRIER EP** – Barrier / Simple / Biscuit barrel / One way down / Great fire / Meaning.		Jun95

		Fierce Panda	not iss.
Jul 95.	(7") (NING 06) **WUTHERING HEIGHTS. / (B-side by The Flying Medallions)**		-

—— added **JAN ALKELMA** – drums

		Mantra	M.C.A.
Sep 95.	(10"ep/cd-ep) (MNT 2 TT/CD) **FALL INTO PLACE / SIMPLE (original version). / ON MY WAY / BARRIER (live)**		-
Dec 95.	(7"green) (MNT 4) **PICTURES. / LAST CHANCE (acoustic)**	-	-
Jan 96.	(cd-ep) (MNT 4CD) **ROLLING HILLS AND SOAKING GILLS** – Fall into place / Simple / Barrier / Biscuit barrel / One way down / Great fire / Meaning.		
Feb 96.	(7"/c-s) (MNT 8/+C) **CAN'T STOP THESE THINGS. / WUTHERING HEIGHTS** (cd-s+=) (MNT 8CD) – Drown it.	65	-
Apr 96.	(7"/c-s) (MNT 10/+C) **LAST CHANCE. / WALK** (cd-s+=) (MNT 10CD) – Cut them out / Careful with that chieftain, Adam.	60	-
Apr 96.	(cd/c/lp) (MNT CD/MC/LP 1002) <11438> **GOOSEFAIR** – Can't stop these things / Cloud 9 / Fall into place / Situation / Simple / Biscuit barrel F.M.R. / God bets / Pictures / (Had a good idea on) Monday / Last chance / Take it back / The meaning / Better than me.	53	
Jul 96.	(7") (MNT 12) **WIPEOUT. / BASEBALL IN THE DARK** (cd-s+=) (MNT 12CD) – Biscuit barrel / Sleazeball (Empirion mix).		-
Aug 97.	(7") (MNT 21) **FICTION OF LIFE. / PULL** (cd-s+=) (MNT 21CD) – Bubblegum buzz / Baseball in the dark (acoustic). (cd-s+=) (MNT 21CD2) – ('A'side) / Fall at your feet / Jack / Down by the river (acoustic).	65	-
Sep 97.	(7") (MNT 22) **SOMEWHERE ELSE. / LOSER** (cd-s+=) (MNT 22CD) – Wrong again / Bothered (acoustic). (cd-s+=) (MNT 22CD2) – ('A'side) / Sleazeball / Don't throw it / ('A'acoustic).	74	-
Oct 97.	(cd/c/lp) (MNT CD/MC/LP 1009) <81009> **SELF MADE MANIAC** – One thing / Guilty deafness / Somewhere else / Fiction of life / All I wanna be / Down by the river / Another toy / 60 seconds / Foxhole / Control / Stop it all adding up / Bothered.		Feb98
Apr 98.	(7") (MNT 30) **STOP IT ALL ADDING UP. / GUILTY DEAFNESS (live)** (cd-s+=) (MNT 30CD) – Wipe out (live) / Baseball in the dark (live).		-
Jun 00.	(7"; as The DRUM) (MNT 57) **HORNS FRONT. / WATER** (cd-s+=) (MNT 57CD) – Bullbar.		-

CHISEL

Formed: Washington D.C., USA ... 1990 by TED LEO, JOHN DUGAN and CHRIS NORBORG. LEO, who had cut his teeth in the East Coast hardcore scene, came to the capital and experimented with his newly formed trio, a hybrid sound of late seventies punk, with British sixties mod flavours, all under a DIY garage sonicscape. The band's reputation and influence, in the indie rock sphere, went much further than its lifespan and recorded output. For the first few years the band CHISEL bolstered their support with much touring, with the likes of such indie luminaries as FUGAZI, and the release of a handful of singles, which were collected together by 'Gern Blandsten' on

'NOTHING NEW' in 1995; their debut album proper, '8 A.M. ALL DAY', came out a year later. This was quickly followed by another full-set gem, 'SET YOU FREE', late that same year. The trio's time as CHISEL was to be short-lived, 1997 seeing them disband. Although NORBORG secured a small stint in the HEARTWORMS, it was LEO who rose like a phoenix from the ashes. Filling in musical time, LEO formed punk rock outfit, SIN-EATERS, with his brother DANNY (formerly of NATIVE NOD) and VAN PELT's bassist SEAN GREENE making a name for themselves touring the East Coast. They disbanded after only a year and with no recorded output. DANNY went on to form The HOLY CHILDHOOD, which TED, now groupless, began touring and supplying some production work until he formed TED YEO AND THE PHARMACISTS in 1999. The same year he released his first LP, 'RX/PHARMACISTS' – with his new cohorts – which, although experimental, was fairly panned by the critics. Unperturbed, the band issued a shared album with ONE AM RADIO, in joint aid of their respective labels; 'Gern Blandsten', and 'Garbage Czar'. A mini-album, 'TROUBLE IN TREBLE' followed several years later, before a real return to form was seen – by LEO and the band – with the release of the second album, 'THE TYRANNY OF DISTANCE'.

Album rating: NOTHING NEW mini (*6) / 8 A.M. ALL DAY (*7) / SET YOU FREE (*7) / Ted Leo & The Pharmacists: RX – PHARMACISTS (*5) / TREBLE IN TROUBLE mini (*6) / THE TYRANNY OF DISTANCE (*7)

TED LEO – vocals, guitar, organ / **CHRIS NORBORG** – bass, vocals / **JOHN DUGAN** – drums, organ

Sep 91. (7") **SWAMP FOX – SPIKE. / LISTEN** — not iss. / Assembly

Aug 93. (7") **SPECTACLES. / (other by Brian, Colin, Vince)** — Gern Blandsten / Gern Blandsten

Aug 94. (7"ep) <GERN 012> **SUNBURN EP**
 – Little gidding / 3 o'clock high / Sunburn.

Apr 95. (m-lp/m-cd) <GERN 019/+CD> **NOTHING NEW** (compilation)
 – Innocents abroad / Waffle house / Your star is killing me / Bliss / Nothing new / Beta ray Bill / Dream bar / 1 in 10. (cd+=) – Little gidding / 3 o'clock high / Sunburn.

Jan 96. (lp/cd) <GERN 021/+CD> **8 A.M. ALL DAY**
 – Hip straights / The dog in me / What about Blighty? / Je m'appelle zero / Your star is killing me / Looking down at the Great Wall of China / Theme for a pharmicist / 8 a.m. all day / Red haired Mary / Out for kicks / Citizen of Venus / Breaking up with myself.

Feb 97. (7") <GERN 031> **IT'S ALRIGHT, YOU'RE O.K. / THE GUNS OF MERIDIAN HILL**

Sep 97. (lp/cd) <GERN 033/+CD> **SET YOU FREE** — Apr97
 – On warmer music / All my kin / It's alright, you're o.k. / The muteable mercury / The town crusher / The unthinkable is true / River high / Every is a good trip / Do go on / Privileged and impotent / Oh dear friends / Am amateur thief / In our time / Morley Timmons / The O.T.S. / Rip off the gift / The last good time.

— CHISEL disbanded in 1997; TED formed the short-lived SIN-EATERS with his brother DANNY (ex-NATIVE NOD) and SEAN GREENE (ex-VAN PELT)

TED LEO / PHARMACISTS

TED + **JODI BUONANNO** (of SECRET STARS) / **JIMMY CANTY** – guitar / **AMY FARINA** – drums, vocals

Sep 99. (lp/cd) <(GERN 041/+CD)> **RX / PHARMACISTS** — Gern Blandsten / Gern Blandsten
 – Call off the invasion – Flydocious invasion / The pharmacist v. The Secret Stars / Walking through / The "nice people" argument / Mr. Annoyatron Brown / The king of time / Version: to decline to make some tea / Soon dubward / Set you free / The northeast corridor / Lui prima mobile / Friends and bands / Head in the freezer / Version: to decline to take a shower / Congressional decision / Version: whisper: courage / SM 11: 11 – The trumpet of the martians / "(None)" / Out of step '88!

Sep 00. (m-cd) <9> **TREBLE IN TROUBLE** — not iss. / Ace Fu
 – Abner Louima v. Gov. Pete Wilson / Come baby come / The 11th / Treble in trouble / Little girl in bloom.

— brought in brother **DANNY** – drums

Aug 01. (cd/lp) <(LK 268 CD/LP)> **THE TYRANNY OF DISTANCE** — Lookout / Lookout Jun01
 – Biomusicology / Parallel or together? / Under the hedge / Dial up / Timorous me / Stove by a whale / The great communicator / Squeaky fingers / My vein llin / The gold finch and the red oak tree / St. John the divine / You could die (or this might end).

CHIXDIGGIT!

Formed: Calgary, Canada ... early 90's by school mates MIKE, MARK and KJ (in '93 they added bass player turned drummer, JASON HIRSCH). Initially a ruse to sell T-shirts with the CHIXDIGGIT! moniker, the idea turned into a real band as the lads decided to actually learn to play their instruments. An unusual signing for 'Sub Pop', CHIXDIGGIT! were compared to the RAMONES and modern day pop-punks, GREEN DAY, summer 96's eponymous debut album fitting right in with the prevailing mood of the US alternative scene. The following year, having amicably split from Sub Pop over musical differences, the comic strip punks found a new home at 'Honest Don's' where they unleashed 'BORN ON THE FIRST OF JULY', another happy-go-lucky collection of hook-laden toons. Dismissing a BOOMTOWN RATS covers EP, 'CHRONIC FOR THE TROOPS' (shared with The GROOVIE GHOULIES) and a collection 'BEST HUNG CARROT IN THE FRIDGE' in 1998 and 1999 respectively, CHIXDIGGIT! finally delivered their difficult third set, 'FROM SCENE TO SHINING SCENE' (2000). • **Covered:** FAITH (George Michael).

Album rating: CHIXDIGGIT! (*5) / BORN ON THE FIRST OF JULY (*6) / BEST HUNG CARROT IN THE FRIDGE collection (*5) / FROM SCENE TO SHINING SCENE (*5)

K.J. JANSEN – vocals, guitar / **MARK O'FLAHERTY** – guitar / **MIKE EGGERMONT** – bass / **JASON HIRSCH** – drums

1993. (c) <demo> **HUMPED** — not iss. / own label Canada / Van Horne
 – I should have played football in high school / Where's your mom? / Van Horne / I wanna hump you.

1995. (7") <LLR 017> **BEST HUNG CARROT IN THE FRIDGE. / GRUNGEBABY / FAITH** — not iss. / Lance Rock Canada

May 96. (7") <SP 336> **SHADOWY BANGERS FROM A SHADOWY DUPLEX. / SONG FOR "R"** — Sub Pop / Sub Pop

Jun 96. (lp/cd) <(SP/+CD 355)> **CHIXDIGGIT!** — May96
 – Dolphins love kids / Great legs / Where's your mom? / Henry Rollins is no fun / I wanna hump you [cd-only] / Song for "R" / Stacked like that / Hemp hemp hooray / 323 / Angriest young men (we're the) / Toilet seat's coming down / Shadow bangers from a shadowy duplex / Van Horne / I drove the coquihalla / (I feel like) Gerry Cheevers (stitch marks on my heart).

Nov 97. (7") (DON 012-7) **CHUPA CABRAS. / 20 TIMES** — Honest Don's / Honest Don's

May 98. (lp/cd) <(DON 016/+CD)> **BORN ON THE FIRST OF JULY** — Apr98
 – Gettin' air / Quit your job / Sikome beach / Chupacabras / My girl's retro / My restaurant / Julianne / 20 times / O-H-I-O / Haven't got time for / 2000 flushes / Brunette summer.

— **DAVE ALCOCK** – drums; repl. HIRSCH

Nov 98. (cd-ep; shared w/ Groovie Ghoulies) <delm 01> **CHRONIC FOR THE TROOPS**
 – Don't believe what you read / A tonic for the troops / She gets all the girls. // others by Groovie Ghoulies

Nov 99. (cd) <delm 02> **BEST HUNG CARROT IN THE FRIDGE** (early collection)
 – CD-ROM track / Best hung carrot in the fridge / Grungebaby / Faith / I should have played football in high school / Mila, Caroline and me / King of Kensington / Church / My debutante.
 (above two issued on 'Delmonico')

Aug 00. (cd) <DON 28CD> **FROM SCENE TO SHINING SCENE**
 – My dad vs. P.M. / Spanish fever / Thursday night / Melissa Louise / Aromatherapy / Folks are gone / Moro foxe / Sweaty and hairless / Going to the peelers? / Summer please / Born to Toulouse.

CHOCOLATE (see under ⇒ STUPIDS)

CHOCOLATE USA

Formed: Tampa Bay, Florida, USA ... 1989 by JULIAN KOSTER, along with ALAN EDWARDS, LIZA WAKEMAN, PAUL WELLS and KEITH BLOCK. Originally plying their trade under the moniker MISS AMERICA, they were forced to change it due to legal wrangles around 1992. CHOCOLATE CITY USA were extremely influential for their psychedelic revival sound which reached its zenith with the 'Elephant 6' musical collective, alongside such luminaries as NEUTRAL MILK HOTEL, APPLES IN STEREO and OLIVIA TREMOR CONTROL (KOSTER was a lynch-pin member of the former of these), peaking in the mid to late 90s. The band's sonic experimentalism worked on the basis of multi-instrumentalism and genre transversing hooked around solid and well-written pop melodies. They were also, in true indie fashion, more orientated towards their fanbase, notably setting up 'Chocolaty Good Smash Hit of the Month Club' for their card-carrying members, which included every month, a run-down on current events in the band's life and a new track. As well as running a regular spot on radio and an annual music festival, CCUSA still found time to record their debut LP, 'ALL JETS ARE GONNA FALL TODAY', which was issued under their own steam, although later put back in the shops by 'Bar/None' records in 1992. The indie imprint also released their sophomore full-length effort, 'SMOKE MACHINE', which followed two years later. This was a sprawling set of aural investigations, although well anchored in pop-song structure, making it quite a definitive recording for the lo-fi avant-garde rock scene that was to continue to expand throughout the decade. It also marked the end of the group. Although as mentioned above, KOSTER, went on to work with NEUTRAL MILK HOTEL, pushing his alternative star further into the leftfield ascendancy. As well as his commitments to NMH, KOSTER dabbled with the side-project, MUSIC TAPES, along with his fellow band member, JEREMY BARNES. Again the music of MT mirrored his other styles, with KOSTER firmly at the controls as mad scientist in his musical laboratory. MT debuted in 1998 with the 7", 'PLEASE HEAR MR. FLIGHT CONTROL', showcasing that they were to take their musical wanderings further via the use of an array of musical instruments seldom found in the pop sphere. Their musical life culminated in the inaugural album, '1st IMAGINARY SYMPHONY FOR NOMAD' (1999), which was recorded on a wax cylinder, a wire recorder and tape machines, as well as being accompanied on release by a comic book. • **Note:** Not to be confused with dance outfit, CHOCOLATE CITY.

Album rating: ALL JETS ARE GONNA FALL TODAY (*5) / SMOKE MACHINE (*6) / Music Tapes: 1st IMAGINARY SYMPHONY FOR NOMAD (*5)

CHOCOLATE USA (cont)

JULIAN KOSTER – vocals, guitar, accordion / **LIZA WAKEMAN** – violin / **ALAN EDWARDS** – guitars / **PAUL WELLS** – bass / **KEITH BLOCK** – drums / + others who stayed for a while (WELLS + EDWARDS were repl. by **GEORGE HARRIS, GERRY HAMMILL + CHRIS IRVIN**)

not iss.   Bar/None

1992. (cd) <26> **ALL JETS ARE GONNA FALL TODAY**
– Test / All jets are gonna fall today / Doogie love theme – Wysotsky's tea / My little two eyes / 100 feet tall / Feelies show / Skyphilis – Air raid / Shower song / Wash my face / Two dogs / Vocal exercise No.1 / Crashing song / Luniks furniture / Kriss Ford / Kathy / Nervous aged catalunian / Loud / Smile.

— **KOSTER, WAKEMAN + BLOCK** recruited **BILL CULLEN HART + ERIC HARRIS** – multi / + drummer **JESSE ROGERS**

Sep 94. (cd) <48> **SMOKE MACHINE**
– The molk part / USA: Milkiest theme / Bookbag / My cherry bomb / Another lego in the cross / The boy who stuck his head in the dryer / The milkier part / Playing in the mud / Ugly girl / Milk (theme) / Isn't a lie . . . – Glow worm / We stole the cow.

— KOSTER split the band after above

MUSIC TAPES

JULIAN KOSTER with various 'Elephant 6' project (orchestra) members incl. **JEREMY BARNES** (of NEUTRAL MILK HOTEL)

Elephant 6 Elephant 6
Earworm   not iss.

Oct 97. (7"ep) <(E6 010)> **1st IMAGINARY SYMPHONY EP**

Merge   Europe
Merge

Nov 98. (7") (WORM 32) **THE TELEVISION TELLS US. / FREEING SONG BY REINDEER**

Jun 99. (cd) (MRG 158/+CD) <29458> **1st IMAGINARY SYMPHONY FOR NOMAD**
– Song for soon to be sailor / 1st imaginary symphony by vaccume cleaner / Song of the nomad lost / "Pulled out to sea . . ." / March of the father fists / Nomad tell us / Aliens / Song of Leo Castles / What the single made the needle sing / The clapping hands / Sea's song for sailor / The television tells us / An orchestration's overture / Song for the death of parents / Warning! / Fanfare for speeding bullet / Wishing well at caper's end.

CHROME CRANKS

Formed: Ohio, USA . . . 1988 by PETER ARON (the songwriter), WILLIAM WEBER (the guitarist), BRIAN DRISCOLL (the bassist) and KENDALL DAVIS (the drummer). With four years getting nowhere fast, The CHROME CRANKS crossed several borders to New York where they found a new rhythm section (JERRY TEEL and DAN WILLIS on bass and drums respectively). Signed to 'P.C.P.' records, this sleazy garage rock outfit (like a twist between The STOOGES and The JESUS & MARY CHAIN), the band issued a handful of 45's and subsequently an eponymous debut set in 1994 with drummer CHARLIE HANSEN in tow. By the following year, they had struck gold by inviting former SONIC YOUTH and PUSSY GALORE sticksman, BOB BERT, into the fold; TEEL had stemmed from The HONEYMOON KILLERS. BERT brought the band experience, although sophomore set, 'DEAD COOL' (1995), didn't give them the break they needed, many thought they lacked the raw edge and gutsy swagger they portrayed on their debut. For the next few years, the 'CRANKS carried on in their own inimitable fashion, walking the walk and talking the talk. Undisputably a great live act. • **Covered:** LOST WOMAN (Yardbirds) / LITTLE JOHNNY JEWEL (Television) / AUTOMODOWN (Devo) / COOL AS ICE (Suicide) / THE SLIDER (T. Rex) / THE PUSHER (Hoyt Axton) / FIRE ESCAPE (Scientists).

Album rating: THE CHROME CRANKS (*7) / DEAD COOL (*5) / LOVE IN EXILE (*5) / OILY CRANKS compilation (*4) / LIVE IN EXILE (*4)

PETER AARON – vocals, guitar / **WILLIAM WEBER** – guitar / **BRIAN DRISCOLL** – bass / **KENDALL DAVIS** – drums

P.C.P.   P.C.P.

1992. (7") <PCP 006> **DARKROOM. / BURN, BABY BURN**
1992. (7") <PCP 008> **EIGHT-TRACK MIND. / COLLISION BLUES**

— **DAN WILLIS** – drums; repl. DAVIS
— **JERRY TEEL** – bass (ex-HONEYMOON KILLERS) repl. DRSCOLL

1992. (7") <SFTRI 135> **WAY-OUT LOVER. / SOME KINDA CRIME**
(above on 'Sympathy For The Record Industry', below on 'Insipid')

1992. (7") <IV-17> **COME IN AND COME ON. / STUCK IN A CAVE**

1993. (7") <HS 93732> **MAKIN' OUT WITH SATAN (with BEWITCHED). / (other by METAHEAD)**
(above issued on 'Helter Skelter')

— **CHARLIE HANSEN** – drums; repl. PHIL RUST who repl. WILLIS

Jul 94. (7") <PCP 011> **VICE SQUAD DICK. / (other by FOETUS)**
(cd-s+=) <PCP 011CD> – Little Johnny Jewel / (other by FOETUS).

Jan 95. (cd/lp) <(PCP 016-2/-1)> **THE CHROME CRANKS**
– Dark room / Subway man / Drag house / Driving bad / Eight track mind / No.1 girl / Doll in a dress / Backdoor maniac / Stuck in a cave / Lo-end buzz / Outta my heart.

— **BOB BERT** – drums (ex-SONIC YOUTH, ex-PUSSY GALORE) repl. HANSEN

May 95. (m-cd/m-lp) (efa 11590-2/-1) <CRYPT 56> **DEAD COOL**
– Dead cool / Desperate friend / Way-out lover / Down so low / Blood shot eye / Nightmare in pink / Shine it on / Burn baby burn [UK] / Lost woman [US].
(above issued on 'Crypt', below on 'World Domination')

1996. (7") <WDOM 25S> **LOST WOMAN (live). / (other by PSYCLONE RANGERS)**

Oct 95. (7") <(PCP 031-7)> **LOST TIME BLUES. / JULIE, DO YA LOVE ME?**
(cd-s+=) <(PCP 031-2)> – Electric heart / Heaven (take me now).

Insipid   not iss.
Vinyl
Konkurrent P.C.P.

Oct 96. (7") (IV 34) **AUTOMODOWN. / (other by Coctails)**

Dec 96. (lp/cd) (K 172/+CD) <PCP 026> **LOVE IN EXILE**   Sep96
– Movie star / Hot blonde cocktail / Wrong number / Hit the sand / Lost time blues / Receiver / See that my grave is kept clean / Down for the hit / We're going down / Movie star 2 / Dirty son (lie down – Fade out) / Curtains for my baby.

Echotastic   not iss.

Jul 97. (7") (ECH 003/4) **split w/ Kim Salmon & The SURREALISTS**
– Wrapped up in red / Draghouse (live) / (other 2 by KIM SALMON).

Konkurrent Au-Go-Go

Nov 97. (cd) (K 181CD) <224> **LIVE IN EXILE (live)**
– See that my grave is kept clean / Dirty son (Lie down – Fade out) / Lost time blues / Down for the hit / Hot blonde cocktail / Wrong number / Hit the sand / Nightmare in pink / Dead man's suit / Way-out lover / Draghouse / We're going down / Darkroom / Fire escape / The pusher / Stuck in a cave / Dead cool / The slider / Burn baby burn.

– compilations, etc. –

Apr 97. (lp/cd) Atavistic; <(ALP/ACD 11)> **OILY CRANKS**   Feb97
– Come in and come on / Fool on ice / Way-out lover / Doll in a dress / Comeback / Cool as ice / Foul stench of love / She's got a brain / (I was) Sleeping.

CHUBBIES

Formed: South California, USA . . . 1994 by (half-Greek/half-French) JEANNETTE KANTZALIS. Maximising from the efforts of riot grrrl punk, JEANNETTE and her sparse team of cohorts (i.e. drummer CHRISTENE KINGS) signed to 'Sympathy For The Record Industry'; the singer had issued a few self-financed cassingles. Summer 1995 saw the release of The CHUBBIES first proper disc, 'I'M THE KING', an LP that whisked the adolescent listener into delights such 'BOYS DON'T MATTER' and 'PUNK BOYS DON'T RAPE'. Now a threesome with the addition of bassist KELLY, the chubby ones delivered the girl-meets-Freud 7", 'CAN I CALL YOU DADDY (WHEN WE MAKE LOVE)'. After a handful of singles and LP's (including 1997's 'TRES FLORES'), KANTZALIS revised The CHUBBIES as a one-woman band. Subsequent releases such as 2001's 'DIRTY DAYS AND DIRTY NIGHTS' and 2002's 'NEW WAVE BOYFRIENDS', kept the lass in high profile, well at least with the young-minded twee/indie fanbase. • **Covered:** GOOD GIRLS DON'T (BUT I DO) (Feigler) / KID (Pretenders) / SAILOR MOON (trad.) / FOX ON THE RUN (Sweet).

Album rating: I'M THE KING (*6) / TRES FLORES (*6) / AMERICAN SWAGGER (*5) / DIRTY DAYS AND DIRTY NIGHTS (*5) / NEW WAVE BOYFRIENDS (*5)

JEANNETTE KANTZALIS – vocals, guitar

not iss.   Kantzalis

1994. (c-s) **CHUBBIES / PHUZZ split**
1994. (c-s) **SHE'S YOUR DAUGHTER EP**
1994. (c-s) **KANTZALIS DANCE PARTY**

— added **CHRISTENE KINGS** – drums

Sympathy F Sympathy F

Jul 95. (lp/cd) <SFTRI 382> **I'M THE KING**
– Matty loyal / Girl noise / No ego / Boys don't matter / When I do wrong I do it so right / Save me / Young idea / Punk boys don't rape / Jean's dry / Just like a man.

— added **KELLY** – bass, vocals

1996. (7") <SFTRI 415> **CAN I CALL YOU DADDY (WHEN WE MAKE LOVE). / GEETAR SLUT**

Aug 96. (cd-ep) <SFTRI 440> **PLAY ME**
– Play me / Good girls don't (but I do) / Geetar slut / Sailor moon / I am sex / Can I call you daddy (when we make love) / Kid.

May 97. (lp/cd) <(SFTRI 472/+CD)> **TRES FLORES**   Apr97
– Heather dances by herself / Play me / Coin in the fountain / Vegas song (I'm still here) / Blasted / I don't want you / Didjahaftasaythat? / Me without a gun / Tenille / I'm not that girl.

— now without KELLY; repl. by **MARK "DWAG" AKIN** – guitar / **NIKO LYRAS** – bass

Feb 99. (10"ep/cd-ep) <(SFTRI 563/+CD)> **YOUR FAVORITE EVERYTHING**
– Shut up now / When I was your girlfriend / Living in Hell / Your favorite everything / Suburban rock dolls / Darkest one of all / Tightrope.

1999. (7") **WHEN I WAS YOUR GIRLFRIEND. / FOX ON THE RUN**
(above issued on 'Remedial')

— now down to **KANTZALIS** solo

May 00. (cd) <(SFTRI 606CD)> **AMERICAN SWAGGER**
– Pseudochrist / She wanted more / Do you know how this feels? / Dirty days, dirty nights / Don't say / Multi-millionaire / Working class girls / I wanna go home / My rules / You should go down (it gets me higher).

2001. (cd) <1> **DIRTY DAYS AND DIRTY NIGHTS**
(above issued on 'Uncontrolled Pussy')

May 02. (cd) <SFTRI 692> **NEW WAVE BOYFRIENDS**
– Johnny breathe / Brian / Davey, I'm a shooting star / Ricky you shouldn't be spying on me / C'mon Christopher / Randy (have a bitchen summer) / I adore Theodore / Kevin's heaven / Joey's hero.

– compilations, etc. –

1999. (cd) Mutant; <35> **SHE WANTED MORE**

CHUG
(see under ⇒ **LOOK BLUE GO PURPLE**; 80's section)

CHUNK (see under ⇒ SUPERCHUNK)

CIAO BELLA

Formed: Alameda, California, USA ... early 90's by singer/songwriters MARIO HERNANDEZ and JAMIE McCORMICK, two durable friends into twee indie pop. Under the banner of TEENY HI-FI, the studio duo released their debut 7" single, 'WEEKEND GO', in 1992. With little in the way of concerts and gigs, CIAO BELLA took a sort of hiatus until 1997's 'IN EP' and their long-awaited eponymous set for 'March' records. A longer sabbatical ensued as McCORMICK went off to produce for The AISLERS SET and The FAIRWAYS, with HERNANDEZ instigating his own brief solo sojourn under the banner of FROM BUBBLEGUM TO SKY for the album, 'ME AND MY TWO FRENCH BOYS' (2000).

Album rating: CIAO BELLA (*5) / From Bubblegum To Sky: ME AND AMY AND THE TWO FRENCH BOYS (*6)

MARIO HERNANDEZ (b. 1967, San Antonio, Texas) – vocals, guitar / **JAMIE McCORMICK** – vocals, guitar

		not iss.	Teeny
1992.	(7"; as TEENY HI-FI) <001> **WEEKEND GO.** /	-	
		not iss.	Endearing
1997.	(7"ep) **IN EP**	-	
		not iss.	March
1997.	(cd) <032> **CIAO BELLA**	-	

– In / How low / Old school digital watch / Dropped once / Meet the great life / Another pill / Astronauts in love / Details from the deep end / We were always too young / Sink / I've should I? / Brown make-up / Party song / Feeling low.

— McCORMICK left to concentrate on production work; The FAIRWAYS, etc.

FROM BUBBLEGUM TO SKY

MARIO HERNANDEZ solo

		not iss.	Eenie Meenie
Nov 99.	(7") <MARS 001> **MY 1000 YEARS WITH ROBOTS**	-	
Feb 00.	(cd) <MARS 002> **ME AND AMY AND THE TWO FRENCH BOYS**	-	

– Hello, hello, hi / Shaboom they said / Don't let the day go mistreating you / She floats / You of summer / Ask the space invader / Major J / I wanna be an American boy / Me and Amy and the two French boys / My 1000 years with robots / Beat to beat.

CIBO MATTO

Formed: New York City, New York, USA ... 1994 out of LEITOH LYCHEE (aka "Frozen Lychee Nut") by Japanese-born females, MIHO HATORI and YUKA HONDA, the latter an ex-member of the BROOKLYN FUNK ESSENTIALS, the former from Tokyo rap act, KIMIDORI. Translated from the Italian as "food madness", CIBO MATTO became the toast of NY trendies as they gigged around the city, the hype generated seeing the duo sign to 'Warners' after a couple of independent singles. Early in '96, the girls unleashed their debut album, 'VIVA! LA WOMAN', wherein music was truly the food of love as HATORI and HONDA paid tribute to culinary delights in cryptic franglais against a colourful, often surreal trip-hop/indie collage of beats and samples. Meanwhile, the pair (including part-time CM member, RUSSELL SIMINS from JON SPENCER BLUES EXPLOSION), along with RICK LEE and MIKE MILLS (not of R.E.M.!) spent time in the studio as BUTTER 08. The resulting sessions/tapes were sent to MIKE D of The BEASTIE BOYS who released an eponymous set in 1996 for his 'Grand Royal' imprint. With HONDA and HATORI recruiting SEAN LENNON and various guests (ARTO LINDSAY, JOHN and BILLY from MEDESKI plus SEBASTIAN STEINBERG of SOUL COUGHING), CIBO MATTO came out to play for sophomore set, 'STEREO TYPE A' (1999), a fusion of trip-hop, funk and jazz with an overall indie feel. • **Covered:** BLACK HOLE SUN (Soundgarden) / AGUAS DE MARCO (Antonio Carlos Jobim) / SING THIS ALL TOGETHER (Rolling Stones).

Album rating: VIVA! LA WOMAN (*7) / SUPER RELAX mini (*6) / STEREO TYPE A (*5) / Butter 08: BUTTER 08 (*7)

MIHO HATORI – vocals / **YUKA HONDA** – keyboards, programmer (ex-BROOKLYN FUNK ESSENTIALS) / **RUSSELL SIMINS** – drums (of JON SPENCER BLUES EXPLOSION) guests

		not iss.	El Diablo
1995.	(7") **BIRTHDAY CAKE.** / **BEEF JERKY**	-	
1995.	(7") **KNOW YOUR CHICKEN.** / **BLACK HOLE SUN**	-	
		Error	not iss.
1995.	(cd-ep) **CIBO MATTO EP**	-	- Japan

– Beef jerky / Birthday cake / Know your chicken / Black hole sun / Crumbs.

		Warners	Warners
Mar 96.	(cd/c/lp) <(9362 45989-2/-4/-1)> **VIVA! LA WOMAN**		Jan96

– Apple / Beef jerky / Sugar water / White pepper ice cream / Birthday cake / Know your chicken / Theme / The candy man / Le pain perdu / Artichoke.

Jul 96.	(c-s) (W 0356C) **KNOW YOUR CHICKEN.** / ('A'mix)		-
	(cd-s+=) (W 0356CD) – ('A'mixes)		
Jan 97.	(12"ep/cd-ep) <(1-/2-46478)> **SUPER RELAX EP**		

– Sugar water (Morricone mix) / Sugar water (Morricone version) / Spoon / BBQ / Aguas de Marco / Sing this all together / Sugar water / Crumbs / Sugar water (Morricone extended).

— SIMINS was repl. by **TIMO ELLIS** – drums / **DUMA LOVE** – percussion / **SEAN LENNON** – bass (solo artist)

Jul 99.	(cd) <(9362 47345-2)> **STEREO TYPE A**		Jun99

– Working for vacation / Spoon / Flowers / Lint of love / Moonchild / Sci-fi Wasabi / Clouds / Speechless / King of silence / Blue train / Sunday part I / Sunday part II / Stone / Mortming.

Jul 99.	(cd-s) **WORKING FOR VACATION** / **EVERYONE LOVES THE SUNSHINE** / **VAMOS A LA PLAYA**	- not iss.	Japan FIII
May 00.	(12") <44854> **MOONCHILD (D's funky space reincarnation).** / **MOONCHILD (jazzy dub #1)**	-	

BUTTER 08

HATORI, HONDA, SIMINS (latter on vocals!) plus **RICK LEE** – bass, guitar, sampling (of SKELETON KEY) / **MIKE MILLS** – bass, guitar / with also **SEAN LENNON** – keyboards

		Grand Royal	Grand Royal
Apr 97.	(lp/cd) <(GR 029/+CD)> **BUTTER**		Sep96

– 9 mm / Shut up / Butter of 69 / Dick serious / How do I relax / It's the rage / Mono Lisa / What are you wearing / Sex symbol / Degobrah / Hard to hold / Butterfucker.

CINEMA

Formed: Glasgow, Scotland ... mid-90's by the initially mysterious DJ duo of GREGOR REID and CRAWFORD TAIT who met while working at the Acme Recorded Music for Film and Television. Experimenting with tape loops, synths and the proverbial kitchen sink, they pieced together (quite literally!) their debut 'Domino' Series 500 platter, 'MOMENTO MORI'; rhythmic and eerie beyond description (former workmate JOHN CARPENTER would be close!), the pair went on to complete further examples of industrial waste via further singles, 'RECORDED MUSIC LIBRARY' and the extended 7" EP! film soundtrack 'THEY NICKNAMED ME EVIL'; this was rumoured to have been unearthed in a skip outside their workplace. Following a mini-set, 'YOUR INTRODUCTORY RECORD' in 2000, CINEMA finally resurfaced in August 2002 with their debut album proper, 'BEFORE THE DARK'. Atmospheric and moody with jazzy hip-hop breakbeats in the shape of DJ SHADOW, this was like a discarded 70's soundtrack given the remix treatment – nice.

Album rating: YOUR INTRODUCTORY RECORD mini (*6) / BEFORE THE DARK (*6)

GREGOR REID + CRAWFORD TAIT – electronics, etc

		Series 500 Domino	not iss.
Aug 97.	(12") (SER 505) **MOMENTO MORI.** / **THE MAKER (REMADE)**		- not iss.
		Domino	
Aug 98.	(12"/cd-s) (Rug 72 t/cd) **CINEMA RECORDED MUSIC LIBRARY**		-

– P. Beretta (parts 1 and 2) / Astro.

Apr 99.	(7"ep) (Rug 86) **THEY NICKNAMED ME EVIL EP**		-

– They nicknamed me evil / The beating / Pursuit of evil / Stalk the discotheque / Electro killer / Anything with a pulse / Music box / Tone death / Dialogue.

Oct 00.	(m-cd/m-lp) (Wig cd/lp 85) **YOUR INTRODUCTORY RECORD**		-

– Drive by / Getting away with it / Breaks / Russian roulette / Ichiban assassin / Scimitar.

— now credited as **CINEMA RECORDED MUSIC LIBRARY** on the sleeve

Aug 02.	(cd/lp) (Wig cd/lp 113) **BEFORE THE DARK**		-

– Before the dark / Pendulum / Reflections / Almost there / After dark / Lost / Coming up for air / Undercurrent / Headspin / Crash and burn / The dawn.

Sep 02.	(7") (Rug 146) **BEFORE THE DARK.** / **LOST**		-

CINERAMA (see under ⇒ WEDDING PRESENT; 80's section)

CINNAMON (see under ⇒ ASHLEY PARK)

CINNAMON

Formed: Sweden ... 1994 by lynch-pin members, JIRI NOVAK and FRIDA DIESEN, with the ensuing help of SAMUEL LAXBERG and CHRISTIAN EKWALL. Inevitably compared to fellow Swedish indie popsters, The CARDIGANS, the band both benefitted and suffered from the comparison, their sound being in a similar acoustic pop vein although without the twee stylistics of the bigger luminaries. The group debuted with the EP, 'VOX' (1995), and followed this up with the LP, 'SUMMER MEDITATION', which, due to the attention The CARDIGANS were now receiving, meant that the majors had stepped in for their sophomore album, 'THE COURIER' (1997). Although this was a competent piece of songwriting, and felt by many critics to be sadly unheard, CINNAMON were dropped by their label. Undeterred, the band went back to their indie roots, the millennium seeing them issue their third full-length outing, 'VERTIGO' (on 'March' records). A decidedly heavier and more energetic piece, similar in vein to their Swedish brethren's 'Gran Tourismo' set, they found it difficult to escape the "Scando-pop" pigeonhole they had been placed into.

Album rating: SUMMER MEDITATION (*5) / THE COURIER (*7) / THE MANY MOODS OF CINNAMON mini (*5) / VERTIGO (*6)

FRIDA DIESEN – vocals, synthesizers, guitar / **JIRI NOVAK** – guitar, keyboards / **SAMUEL LAXBERG** – bass / **CHRISTIAN EKWALL** – drums

		Polygram	Polygram
1995.	(cd-ep) **VOX**	-	- Sweden

CINNAMON (cont)

1996. (cd) **SUMMER MEDITATION** — Sweden
 – Vox revisited / I wanted it, but now I'm not sure anymore / Backwards / London town / Seaweed / Me as Helen of Troy / Moments / Secret lover / Promenade / I can't recall / Hopeless case / Take me (out tonight).

May 97. (cd) <524248> **THE COURIER**
 – Girl on the boat / Hopeless case / Me as Helen of Troy / Missing persons file / And suddenly clarity / The promenade / A northwest passage / Backwards / I wanted it, but now I'm not so sure anymore / Baby shining bright / Heavenly option / Secret lover.

Jul 99. (m-cd/m-lp) (<MAR 044-2/-1>) **THE MANY MOODS OF CINNAMON** March / Jun99
 – Maybe in the next life / Did you think I would ever let you go? / Nothing / Springtime of my life / Scorpio rising / You and me against the world / Space park (live).

Jun 00. (cd/lp) (<MAR 053 CD/LP>) **VERTIGO**
 – I used to be your loneliness / Nothing / Did you ever think I would ever let you go? / Take your time / Stars collide / World of crime / A few grains of sand for working your whole life / Averon / Maybe in your next life / March of the Cinnamons / More than you bargained for / Angel eyes.

CIRCULATORY SYSTEM
(see under ⇒ OLIVIA TREMOR CONTROL)

CIRCUS LUPUS

Formed: Washington DC, USA ... early 90's by CHRIS THOMPSON, CHRIS HAMELY, SETH LORINCZI and ARIKA CASEBOLT. Not typical of the standard 'Dischord' fare, to whom they were signed, CIRCUS LUPUS first made their mark in Spring '92 with the 'SUPER GENIUS' set. Produced by ELI JANNEY (of GIRLS AGAINST BOYS fame), the record found favour with the US college circuit, although it would be the JOAN JETT-produced single, 'POPMAN', that defined their musical independence. The following year, they roped in producer, Don Zientara, who worked on the band's second and final long-player, 'SOLID BRASS'.

Album rating: SUPER GENIUS (*5) / SOLID BRASS (*5)

CHRIS THOMPSON – vocals / **CHRIS HAMELY** – guitar / **SETH LORINCZI** – bass, guitar / **ARIKA CASEBOLT** – drums

Dischord Dischord

May 92. (cd/c/lp) <(DIS 63 CD/C/V)> **SUPER GENIUS**
 – Unrequited / Cyclone Billy / Pacifier / Breaking point / Straight through the heart / Marbles / Mean hot & blessed / Cat kicking jerk / Blue baby / Amish blessing / Pulp.
Sep 92. (7") <(DIS 73V)> **POPMAN. / PRESSURE POINT**
Mar 93. (7"; shared with CRAIN) (CPS 3) **CIRCUS LUPUS & CRAIN E.P.**
 (above issued on 'Compulsive')
Jul 93. (cd/c/lp) <(DIS 79 CD/C/V)> **SOLID BRASS**
 – Turn right circle / 7 x 4 x 1 / I always thought you were an asshole / And you won / New cop car / Texas minute / Deviant gesture catalog / Takes about an hour: Epilepsy / Pop man / Heather / Pressure point. (cd+/c+=) – Popman (version).

—— disbanded after above

CITIZEN FISH
(see under ⇒ SUBHUMANS; 80's section)

Allen CLAPP (see under ⇒ ORANGE PEELS)

CLASS

Formed: Boston, Massachusetts, USA ... mid 90's out of ZAIUS by PETER GREEN (no, not that one!), founder of indie label 'Double Agent' and the man behind fanzine, 'Splashdown'. Along with vocalist/violinist LEIGH TSAI, they created their own quite unique ambient-driven lo-fi pop, evident on a handful of singles and debut long-player, 'FIRST CLASS' (1998). Not quite as prolific as they were from 1997-98, the CLASS system still managed to deliver another album, the mini 'A QUIET LIFE' in 2001.

Album rating: FIRST CLASS (*6) / A QUIET LIFE mini (*5)

PETER GREEN – vocals, guitar / **LEIGH TSAI** – vocals, violin

not iss. Double Agent

Jan 97. (7"ep) <DA 004> **CLASS**
 – Always all alone / Greys / I'm not always so stupid / Yuko and Hiro.
1997. (7") <DA 005> **FEELING FINE. / Metronome: IT'S WHAT WE'RE IN**
1998. (lp) <DA 008> **FIRST CLASS**
 – Greys / Abstraction / Electron / Could you ever love me? / Feeling fine / Reprise / N. / This love is not wrong / Overdose / Learned helplessness. <cd-iss. 2000 on 'Orchard'; 3897>
1998. (7") <DA 011> **HOLDING HANDS. / STROBE LIGHTS**
1999. (12") <DA 013> **CRITICAL CONDITION. / (other by UNISEX)**
Aug 01. (m-cd) <(DA 014CD)> **A QUIET LIFE**
 – Strobe light / Sierra (chasing my dream) / Strobe light (like that mix) / Holding hands / Strobe light (smooth operator remix) / Japanese technology / Strobe light (Brave Captain remix) / Number one.

CLAW HAMMER

Formed: Long Beach, California, USA ... mid 80's by former PONTIAC BROTHERS frontman, JON WAHL, along with ROB WALTHER and RICK SORTWELL. Strangely enough, CLAW HAMMER debuted on vinyl in Australia, the 'POOR ROBERT' EP hitting the shops at the turn of the decade. Pounding out a deal with the incredibly prolific US imprint, 'Sympathy For The Record Industry', the trio delivered their eponymous debut set in 1990, featuring weird and wonderful versions of Gordon Lightfoot's 'SUNDOWN', Pere Ubu's 'FINAL SOLUTION' and Hampton-Kelling's 'HEY OLD LADY AND BERT'S SONG'. A creative, punk-like update of QUICKSILVER MESSENGER SERVICE, WAHL, WALTHER and newcomers CHRIS BAGAROZZI and BOB LEE armed themselves with the CLAW HAMMER sound and set about deconstructing DEVO's 'Q: ARE WE NOT MEN, A: WE ARE DEVO' in its entirety. Around the same time they issued a covers EP, 'DOUBLE PACK WHACK ATTACK'; artists chosen this time were Patti Smith, Eno, Pere Ubu and Devo again(!), while original material surfaced on the early '92 album, 'RAMWHALE'. At this junction of the band's career, WAHL also moonlighted with the RED AUNTS as BAGAROZZI augmented DOWN BY LAW. Picked up by BRETT GUREWITZ's 'Epitaph' label, CLAW HAMMER released the acclaimed 'PABLUM' (1993), in turn attracting the attentions of big wigs 'Interscope'. A couple of years in the making, 1995's major label debut, 'THANK THE HOLDER UPPERS', was as uncompromising as ever, while 1997's JIM DICKINSON-produced, 'HOLD YOUR TONGUE (AND SAY APPLE)', revelled in its hard-nosed Memphis sleaze/punk.

Album rating: CLAW HAMMER (*5) / Q: ARE WE NOT MEN? – A: WE ARE DEVO (*4) / RAMWHALE (*5) / PABLUM (*6) / THANK THE HOLDER UPPERS (*6) / HOLD YOUR TONGUE (AND SAY APPLE) (*5)

JON WAHL – vocals, guitar (ex-PONTIAC BROTHERS) / **ROB WALTHER** – bass / **RICK SORTWELL** – drums

Grown Up Wrong / not iss.

1989. (12"ep) **POOR ROBERT EP** — Austra
 Sympathy F Sympathy F
Oct 89. (7"ep) <SFTRI 37> **F.U.B.A.R.**
Mar 90. (cd/lp) <SFTRI 57> **CLAW HAMMER**
 – Shell shocked / Warm Spring night / Brother Brick says / Drop II / Sundown / Hey old lady and Bert's song / Papa's got us all tied in knots / Mr. Pizzazz / Petri dish / Poor Robert / Three fifteen / Final solution / Candle opera / Drop. (UK-iss.1993; same as US)

—— **CHRIS BAGAROZZI** – guitar + **BOB LEE** – drums; repl. SORTWELL
1991. (cd-ep) **DOUBLE PACK WHACK ATTACK**
Oct 91. (lp) <SFTRI 119> **Q: ARE WE NOT MEN? A: WE ARE DEVO (the DEVO album live in studio)**
Jan 92. (cd) <SFTRI 120> **RAMWHALE**
 – Naked / Succotash / Maheney bus ride / Beat rice / Sticky thing / Crave / People in my peephole / Three fifteen / Don't walk away / Stough.
1993. (7") <SFTRI 229> **MALTHUSIAN BLUES. / THE DAY OF THE TRIFFIDS**

Epitaph Epitaph

Apr 93. (cd/c/lp) <(86425 CD/MC/LP)> **PABLUM**
 – Vigil smile / William Tell / Montezuma's hands / Speak softly / Nick / Nut powder / Shitting gold bricks / Malthusian blues / Pablum of my mind.

Interscope Interscope

May 95. (cd/c) <92515> **THANK THE HOLDER UPPERS**
 – Superthings / When Dan's in town / Sweaty palms / Five filths dead / Bums on the flow / Hollow legs / Bedside coffee table roses / Blind pig / Each hit / Lazy brains / Ol' factory blues – Nose hair.
Apr 97. (cd) <90105> **HOLD YOUR TONGUE (AND SAY APPLE)**
 – The day it rained pigeon shit / Valley so high / Black eyed blues / Queen's lead helmet / Sugar breath / Gnashville / Hind sight / Ass kisser's union / Water / Air plant / Formaldehyde / Caravan.

Medfly Medfly

Jun 97. (12") <(MEDFLY 001)> **KILOWATT. / FLYSPRAY**
Feb 98. (12") <(12MED 003)> **PEOPLE LOVE. /**

– compilations, etc. –

Aug 96. (m-cd) Sympathy For The Record Industry; <(SFTRI 447CD)> **'SCUSE THE EXCURSION**
 – Caravan / Nightmare / All blues / Sick fish belly up.

CLEARLAKE

Formed: Rottingdean, Brighton, England ... 1998 out of The FISH BROTHERS by songwriter JASON PEGG along with fellow art students SAM HEWITT, DAVID WOODWARD and JAMES BUTCHER. Hailed as one to watch by the NME in early 2000, CLEARLAKE unveiled their debut 45, 'WINTERLIGHT', for the 'Domino' offshoot imprint, 'Dusty Company'. Inspired by SYD BARRETT, VAN DER GRAAF and The CARDIGANS, the quintessentially eclectic 4-piece showed promise at such an embryonic stage in their musical career. Further singles, 'DON'T LET THE COLD IN' and 'SOMETHING TO LOOK FORWARD TO', heralded the coming of CLEARLAKE and marked time before the release of their first set, 'LIDO' (2001). This record was, however, a little parochial for a group who were one of Britain's leading indie hopefuls. Critics either loved or hated it. PEGG's nasal-straining whining guaranteeing a rising fanbase to quite possibly turn to COLDPLAY for relief. • **Covered:** CINNAMON GIRL (Neil Young).

Album rating: LIDO (*6)

JASON PEGG – vocals, guitar, harmonica / **SAM HEWITT** – keyboards, oboe, vocals / **DAVID WOODWARD** – bass, omnichord / **JAMES BUTCHER** – drums, chordette

Dusty Company / not iss.

Feb 00. (7"/cd-s) (*MOTE 100/+CD*) **WINTERLIGHT. / JUMBLE SAILING**
May 00. (7"/cd-s) (*MOTE 101/+CD*) **DON'T LET THE COLD IN. / I HANG ON EVERY WORD YOU SAY**
Oct 00. (7") (*MOTE 102*) **SOMETHING TO LOOK FORWARD TO. / DAYBREAK**
(cd-s+=) (*MOTE 102CD*) – Let's get out of here.
Apr 01. (cd/lp) (*MOOX 103 CD/LP*) **LIDO**
– Clearlake lido / Sunday evening / Don't let the cold in / Something to look forward to / These things are sent to try us / I hang on every word you say / Let go / Daybreaking / Jumble sailing / Life can be so cruel / I want to live in a dream / Winterlight.
May 01. (7") (*MOTE 104*) **LET GO. / DON'T LIE TO YOURSELF**
(cd-s+=) (*MOTE 104CD*) – Cinnamon girl.

CLIENTELE

Formed: London, England ... summer 1997 by ALASDAIR MACLEAN, INNES PHILLIPS, HOWARD MONK and JAMES HORNSEY. Self-professed lovers of the sound of psychedelic revisionists like GALAXIE 500 and FELT, CLIENTELE like them take on their influences from the VELVET UNDERGROUND and LOVE to the more pastoral folk of DONOVAN. Appearing originally on the 'Fierce Panda' V/A compilation, 'Cry Me A Liver' (1997) – with the track 'WE COULD WALK TOGETHER' – the band continued on the up and up, with several more single releases, notably 'ALL THE DUST AND GLASS' (1998), which gained them a top ten slot in 'Time Out New York's best record of the year chart, exemplifying that it was not just their native critics who were raving about them. By the following year, PHILLIPS decided to depart to follow different musical grounds with RELICT, although on seemingly amiable terms, as his first few efforts garnered the help of his ex-band members. CLIENTELE continued to produce musical gems into the early millennium. One of them, the 7" 'I HAD TO SAY THIS', became a single of the month in the influential Record Collector publication. Unfortunately the turn of the century also saw the departure of MONK – due to academic commitments – being replaced by MARK KEEN. Meanwhile the band toured the American East Coast, while the indie imprints, 'March' and 'Pointy', unfettered the EP, 'A FADING SUMMER' and the full-length set 'SUBURBAN LIGHT' respectively. Both of these platters were compilations of sorts, collecting together the group's early singles and other outtakes. New material was not far off with the release of the split single, 'I CAN'T SEEM TO MAKE YOU MINE', with RELICT. CLIENTELE's side featured a lovely duet with PAM BERRY (once of BLACK TAMBOURINE and SHAPIROS fame). In the same vein followed the 10" EP, 'LOST WEEKEND', released in 2002.

Album rating: SUBURBAN LIGHT compilation (*6)

ALASDAIR MacLEAN – vocals, guitar / **INNES PHILLIPS** – guitar, vocals / **JAMES HORNSEY** – bass / **HOWARD MONK** – drums (of BILLY MAHONIE)

Pointy / Merge

Jun 98. (7") (*POINT 001*) **WHAT GOES UP. / FIVE DAY MORNING**
Mar 99. (7") (*KANE 002*) **ALL THE DUST AND GLASS**
– Reflections after Jane / An hour before the light.
(above issued on 'Johnny Kane', below issued on 'Motorway')
Jul 99. (7") (*MOTOR 034*) **LACEWINGS. / SATURDAY**

—— PHILLIPS left to form The RELICT (see further below)
Dec 99. (7") (*POINT 002*) **I HAD TO SAY THIS. / MONDAY'S RAIN**

—— **MARK KEEN** – drums; repl. HOWARD
Jan 00. (ltd-7"yellow) (*ER 217*) **(I WANT YOU) MORE THAN EVER. / 6 A.M. MORNINGSIDE**
(above issued on 'Elefant', below issued on 'March')
Jun 00. (10"ep/cd-ep) (*MAR 060/+CD*) **A FADING SUMMER**
– An hour before the light / Driving south / Bicycles / Saturday.
Nov 00. (cd) (*POINT 003CD*) <*MRG 487*> **SUBURBAN LIGHT** (compilation)
– I had to say this / Rain / Reflections after Jane / We could walk together / Monday's rain / Joseph Cornell / An hour before the light / (I want you) More than ever / Saturday / Five day morning / Bicycles / As night is falling / Lacewings.
Feb 01. (7") (*KANE 004*) **I CAN'T SEEM TO MAKE YOU MINE. / The Relict: HELD IN GLASS**

Drive-in / Drive-in

Jan 02. (7") <(*DRIVE 39*)> **SIX FOOT DROP. / (other track by CLOCK STRIKES THIRTEEN)**

Earworm / Acuarela

Feb 02. (10"ep)<cd-ep> **WORM 78 <20> LOST WEEKEND EP**
– North school drive / Boring postcard / Emptily through Holloway / Kelvin parade / Last orders.

—— the debut album proper, 'THE VIOLET HOUR' is expected in July 2003

the RELICT

INNES PHILLIPS with the CLIENTELE

Johnny Kane / not iss.

Oct 99. (ltd-7") (*KANE 003*) **SOUTHERN WAY. / THE NIGHT THAT CHANGED OUR MINDS**

Smashing Time! / not iss.

Aug 00. (ltd-7") (*00-01*) **ALONG THE AVENUE. / SWEETEN YOUR EYES**

CLINIC

Formed: Crosby, Liverpool, England ... 1997 initially as mid-90's indie act, PURE MORNING, by the surgical crew of ADE BLACKWELL and HARTLEY. PM released a couple of singles in 1994, before being snapped up by 'Radarscope'. However, after only three more 7"ers and an album, '2 INCH HELIUM BUDDHA', the outfit ground to a halt in '96. Subsequently opening new doors for themselves as CLINIC (now with BRIAN CAMPBELL and CARL TURNEY), they delivered three singles on their own imprint, 'Aladdin's Cave Of Golf', starting with that Autumn's quirky and weirdly-titled, 'IPC SUBEDITORS DICTATE OUR YOUTH' (an NME SOTW!). 1998's 'MONKEY ON YOUR BACK', was a second attempt at experimentation, their landscape soundings the toast of Glastonbury; they were actually voted the festival's Best New Band. A third effort, 'CEMENT MIXER', showed CLINIC at their eclectic best, breaking free from the usual indie-rock tags. The debut album 'CLINIC' in 1999 was actually a compilation of everything they had done up to now, 'Domino' records realising a good thing when they also churned out subsequent singles, 'THE SECOND LINE' (a minor UK hit) and the brooding, punked up 'THE RETURN OF EVIL BILL'. The latter was a pre-taster for their debut album proper, 'INTERNAL WRANGLER' (2000), a fusion of mod-punk and eerie nocturnal ballads. 2002's 'WALKING WITH THEE' (featuring a classic title track!) set out CLINIC's stall of sound once again, although after two years away these men in white coats certainly needed an examination.

Album rating: Pure Morning: 2 INCH HELIUM BUDDHA (*5) / Clinic: CLINIC mini compilation (*8) / INTERNAL WRANGLER (*7) / WALKING WITH THEE (*6)

PURE MORNING

ADE BLACKBURN – vocals, guitars, keyboards / **HARTLEY** – keyboards, guitar / (+2)

Kool Tone / not iss.

Mar 94. (7") (*KT 002*) **I DON'T WANT YOU AROUND. /**

Amulet / not iss.

Oct 94. (7") (*AMULET 01*) **SICK PROFIT. /**

Radarscope / not iss.

Apr 95. (7") (*SCAN 01*) **ALL THE GUESTS SMILE SO SWEETLY. /**
(cd-s+=) (*SCANCS 01*) –
Feb 96. (7") (*SCAN 12*) **SCUM. /**
(cd-s+=) (*SCANCS 12*) –
Apr 96. (7") (*SCAN 16*) **DINKY. / FAKE LADY**
(cd-s+=) (*SCANCS 16*) – Police car atrocity / Containers.
Jun 96. (cd/lp) (*SCAN CD/LP*) **2 INCH HELIUM BUDDHA**
– Scum / All the guests smile so sweetly / Stunted boy / Funky hospital / Slow ambulance / Dirge / I don't want you around / Foxhole / Game over / Fun / Dinky / Harrison.
Jul 96. (7") (*SCAN 22*) **FOXHOLE. / IPC**
(cd-s+=) (*SCANCS 22*) – The gardener.

CLINIC

—— added **BRIAN CAMPBELL** – bass / **CARL TURNEY** – drums

Aladdin's Cave Of Golf / not iss.

Sep 97. (7"m) (*GOLF 001*) **I.P.C. SUBEDITORS DICTATE OUR YOUTH. / PORNO / D.P.**
Mar 98. (7") (*GOLF 002*) **MONKEY ON YOUR BACK. / D.T.**
(cd-s+=) (*GOLFCD 002*) – Evil Bill.
Aug 98. (7") (*GOLF 003-7*) **CEMENT MIXER. / KIMBERLEY**
(cd-s+=) (*GOLFCD 003*) – Voot.

Domino / not iss.

Apr 99. (m-cd/m-lp) (*WIG 65 CD/LP*) **CLINIC** (compilation)
– I.P.C. subeditors dictate our youth / Porno / D.P. / Monkey on your back / D.T. / Evil bill / Cement mixer / Kimberley / Voot. <US cd-iss. Mar02 as '3 EPs' on 'Domino'; 6>
Jun 99. (7") (*RUG 91*) **THE SECOND LINE. / MAGIC BOOTS**
(cd-s+=) (*RUG 91CD*) – Dr. G.
Apr 00. (7") (*RUG 93*) **THE RETURN OF EVIL BILL. / THE MAJESTIC** 70
(cd-s+=) (*RUG 93CD*) – The castle.
May 00. (lp/cd) (*WIG 78/+CD*) **INTERNAL WRANGLER**
– Voodoo wop / The return of evil bill / Internal wrangler / DJ shangri-la / The second line / C.Q. / T.K. / Earth angel / Distortions / Hippy death suite / 2nd foot stomp / 2-4 / Goodnight Georgie
Jul 00. (7"m) (*RUG 108*) **DISTORTIONS. / JO / LOVE IS A TOOL**
(cd-s+=) (*RUG 108CD*) – Cutting grass.
Oct 00. (7") (*RUG 116*) **THE SECOND LINE. / MAGIC BOOTS** 56
(cd-s+=) (*RUG 116CD*) – Dr. G.
(cd-s) (*RUG 116CDX*) – ('A'side) / Porno / Internal wrangler.

Domino / Universal

Feb 02. (7") (*RUG 134*) **WALKING WITH THEE. / SPHINX**
(cd-s+=) (*RUG 134CD*) – Mechanical madrigal.
Feb 02. (cd/lp) (*WIG CD/LP 100*) <*064101*> **WALKING WITH THEE** 65 Mar02
– Harmony / The equaliser / Welcome / Walking with thee / Pet eunuch / Mr. Moonlight / Come into our room / The vulture / The bridge / Sunlight bathes our home / For the wars.
May 02. (7") (*RUG 137*) **COME INTO OUR ROOM. / CHRISTMAS**
(cd-s+=) (*RUG 137CD*) – Circle I.

CLINTON (see under ⇒ CORNERSHOP)

CLOUDBERRY JAM

Formed: Linkoping, Sweden ... 1991 by JENNIE MEDIN, JORGEN WARNSTROM, PER VALSINGER, HENRIK SUNDQVIST and PER BYSTROM. Debuting in 1992 with the EP, 'LA LA LA', the band made little ground outside their home country. Yet within two years the group were beginning to find their own musical feet, showcased on the more unique sounding EP, 'THE ART OF BEING COOL'. Here CJ displayed an interesting mix of soul and jazzy influences, placing them more within the lounge pop groove. Their work continued to mature and diversify over the ensuing years, and the release of their debut album, 'BLANK PAYCHECK' (1995), showed a band in pretty much full control of its faculties, especially shown by the strong and lovely vocal input of MEDIN. With the pedal to the metal, the band came out with another great full-length piece, 'PROVIDING THE ATMOSPHERE', a year later. This set effectively helped them to shed the depreciating 'Scando-pop' dubbings and saw them move into more space-rock – a la STEREOLAB, territory. Noteworthy were the massive sales the album received over in Japan. Working at full pace now, the band put out their third LP proper, 'IMPOSSIBLE SHUFFLE' (1997), which concreted their individual sound to the record buying public. The same year also saw the release of 'GOING FURTHER', which sought to collect the band's previous singles. Unfortunately as the band sat at the top of their game, frontwoman MEDIN chose to return to her college course, and without her pivotal singing the band split-up in the succeeding year.

Album rating: THE ART OF BEING COOL mini (*4) / BLANK PAYCHECK (*4) / PROVIDING THE ATMOSPHERE (*7) / THE IMPOSSIBLE SHUFFLE (*5)

JENNIE MEDIN – vocals / **HENRIK SUNDQVIST** – multi / **JORGEN WARNSTROM** – guitar / **PER VALSINGER** – bass / **PER BYSTROM** – drums

		North Of No South	not iss.	
1992.	(7"flexi) (Nonsfl 1) **DITION STILL UNKNOWN II**	-	-	Sweden
1992.	(cd-ep) (Nons 2-2) **LA LA LA EP**	-	-	Sweden

– False friend / Are you happy? / Lovesong / Safer place / Seems like (demo).

1994.	(m-cd) (Nons 7-2) **THE ART OF BEING COOL**	-	-	Sweden

– Elevator / Hey baby / Spleen / Kingfisher – Intermission / Before time / C-song.

1995.	(cd) (Nons 14-2) **BLANK PAYCHECK**	-	-	Sweden

– Walking in my sleep / Yeah! / This and that / Couching / Twice as cool / By your side / Intermission: Lost in syncopation / Hold on / Waiting for another day / Someday soon / Please don't / Monday's back in town.

1996.	(cd-s) (Nons 30-2) **ANOTHER MOMENT FOLLOWS / SCORCH**	-	-	Sweden
1996.	(cd) (Nons 32-2) **PROVIDING THE ATMOSPHERE**	-	-	Sweden

– Cliches / Going further / Nothing to declare / Another moment follows / Direction still unknown / Peace and quiet / LIfe in this way / Roll the dice / Some things are better left to be / Come back and stay / Connected / Wandering, wondering / Whatever happens / Could it be?

1997.	(cd-s) (Nonscd 50) **COME BACK AND STAY / ELEVATOR**	-	-	Sweden
May 98.	(cd) (Nonscd 61) **THE IMPOSSIBLE SHUFFLE**	-	-	Sweden

– Intro / Song that keeps us sane / Day after day / Keep on wishing / I think you should know / Out of control / That's alright / Water / Do what I wanna do / One minute of foolishness / Wide awake / Let me know why / Everything you are.

Jul 98.	(cd-ep) **TIME TO MOVE ON**	-	-	Sweden

— the group have now disbanded

– compilations, etc. –

1997.	(cd) Stockholm; (533 493) **GOING FURTHER**	-	-	Sweden

– Going further / Nothing to declare / Another moment follows / Roll the dice / Peace and quiet / Cliches / Lost in syncopation / This and that / Monday's back in town / Directions still unknown / Twice as cool / Come back and stay.

CLUB 8 (see under ⇒ ACID HOUSE KINGS)

COAL PORTERS
(see under ⇒ LONG RYDERS; 80's section)

COAST

Formed: Aberdeen, Scotland ... early 90's by young upstarts DANNY YOUNG, PAUL FYFE, MARK LAWRENCE and JOHN RUSSELL. With all the usual mid-90's traits (jangly-pop with folkie harmonies with touches of KINGMAKER and THOUSAND YARD STARE), COAST found a deal with relatively fresh label, 'Sugar', a debut single 'POLLY'S DOMAIN' hitting the shops the following summer. By this time, COAST had er, moved somewhat inland and to the over-populated city that was London; STONE ROSES/VERVE producer Paul Schroeder was on hand for their third 45, 'NOW THAT YOU KNOW ME'. Always on the verge of something big, the quartet delivered a handful of singles before bowing out with their one and only full-set, 'BIG JET RISING' (1997). • **Note:** Don't get confused with the 12" dance act of early '97 who issued 'Tales From the Hard Side' on 'Sliced'.

Album rating: BIG JET RISING (*5)

DANNY YOUNG – vocals, guitar / **PAUL FYFE** – guitar / **MARK LAWRENCE** – bass / **JOHN RUSSELL** – drums

		Fluxus	not iss.
1991.	(7"m) (FL 001) **HEADLIGHT. / SOUNDHOLE / BLUE GREEN**		-
		Sugar	not iss.
Jun 95.	(7") (SUGA 3V) **POLLY'S DOMAIN. / YOU CAN LOOK**		-
	(cd-s+=) (SUGA 3CD) – Sleepy.		
Oct 95.	(7") (SUGA 5V) **SLUGS. / PRETEND**		-
	(cd-s+=) (SUGA 5CD) – Shag wild.		
Mar 96.	(7") (SUGA 8V) **NOW THAT YOU KNOW ME. / TENDER CAGE**		-
	(cd-s+=) (SUGA 8CD) – She wears a frown.		
Aug 96.	(7") (SUGA 12V) **HEADLINES IN THE SUN. / PAINTED IN BLUE**		-
	(cd-s+=) (SUGA 12CD) – Wouldn't you like to?		
Mar 97.	(7") (SUGA 15V) **DO IT NOW. / IT'S NOT TOO LATE**		-
	(cd-s+=) (SUGA 15CD1) – Bullseye.		
	(cd-s) (SUGA 15CD2) – ('A'mixes).		
Apr 97.	(cd/lp) (SUGA 13 CD/LP) **BIG JET RISING**		-

– Britannia / Now that you know me / Headlines in the sun / Entertain me / Sister we sung / Slugs / Do it now / Shag wild / You'll feel mysterious tomorrow / Eating / Oh no, something's wrong / Weekend's over.

— disbanded after above

COAX (see under ⇒ DENTISTS; 80's section)

COBRA VERDE

Formed: Cleveland, Ohio, USA ... 1992 by former DEATH OF SAMANTHA members JOHN PETKOVIC and DOUG GILLARD along with DAVE SWANSON and DON DEPEW. Indie rockers DEATH OF SAMANTHA (along with drummer STEVE-O) enjoyed limited success in the latter half of the 1980's, releasing three albums and an EP. The albums 'STRUNGOUT ON JARGON' (1986), 'WHERE THE WOMAN WEAR THE GLORY' (1988) and 'COME ALL YE FAITHLESS' (1989) were competent enough and, their second album in particular, occasionally showed real promise, however they were to disband in 1989. This early apprenticeship served them well, as when COBRA VERDE arrived with their debut 'VIVA LA MUERTE' (1994), it was an assured album of dirty, blues rock made all the more raw sounding with their seedy lyrics detailing unsavoury subjects such as sex and death. The group delivered more of same on the swaggering 1995 EP, 'VINTAGE CRIME'. 1997 saw the release of 'EGOMANIA' a compilation of rarities and new songs including 'STILL BREAKING DOWN' featuring harmonies by ROBERT POLLARD of GUIDED BY VOICES. POLLARD had recently dismissed his fellow band mates and COBRA VERDE had volunteered themselves as replacements. Under the banner of GUIDED BY VOICES, they recorded the album 'Mag Earwhig!' in '97. This served to raise their profile prior to the release of 'NIGHTLIFE' (1999), another rollicking collection of IGGY POP-influenced songs.

Album rating: STRUNGOUT ON JARGON (*7) / WHERE THE WOMEN WEAR THE GLORY (*7) / COME ALL YE FAITHLESS (*6) / Cobra Verde: VIVA LA MUERTE (*7) / EGOMANIA (LOVE SONGS) (*6) / NIGHTLIFE (*6)

DEATH OF SAMANTHA

JOHN PETKOVIC – vocals, guitar, clarinet / **DOUG GILLARD** – guitar, keyboards, vocals / **DAVE SWANSON** – bass, guitar, drums / **STEVE-O** – drums

		not iss.	St. Valentine
1985.	(7") **AMPHETAMINE. / SIMPLE AS THAT**	-	
1985.	(7") <SVR 005> **COCA COLA & LICORICE. / LISTEN TO THE MOCKINGBIRD**	-	
		Homestead	Homestead
Mar 86.	(lp) <HMS 039> **STRUNGOUT ON JARGON**	-	

– Coca cola & licorice / Simple as that / Bed of fire / Ham & eggs 99c / Conviction / Grapeland (I'm getting sick) / Sexual dreaming / Turquoise hand / Couldn't forget 'bout that (one item).

Dec 86.	(m-lp) <(HMS 071)> **LAUGHING IN THE FACE OF A DEAD MAN**		Sep86

– Blood & shaving cream / Werewolves of London / The set up (of Madame Sosostris) / Yellow fever / American horoscopes & the bad prescription.

Nov 88.	(lp/c/cd) <(HMS 121/+C/CD)> **WHERE THE WOMEN WEAR THE GLORY AND THE MEN WEAR THE PANTS**		

– Harlequin tragedy / Good Friday / Sylvia Plath / Lucky dog (lost my pride) / Monkey face / Savoir city / Staring through it now / That's all that matters / Blood creek.

| Dec 89. | (7") <HMS 149> **ROSENBERG SUMMER. / HEROES** | - | |
| Dec 89. | (lp/c/cd) <(HMS 150/+C/CD)> **COME ALL YE FAITHLESS** | - | |

– Announcement / Roses rejoice / Rosenberg summer / Geisha girl / Now it's your turn (to be a martyr) / Looking for a face / Machine language / Oh, laughter / New soldier, new sailor / Nostalgicaly yours / Come to me / Amnesia.

— disbanded after above

COBRA VERDE

PETKOVIC, GILLARD + SWANSON recruited **DON DEPEW** – bass, guitar, piano

		Scat	Scat
Oct 94.	(cd) <(SCT 036-2)> **VIVA LA MUERTA**		

– Was it good / Gimme your heart / Montenegro / Despair / Debt / Already dead / Until the killing time / I thought you knew (what pleasure was) / Cease to exist.

| 1995. | (7") <SCAT 44> **LEATHER. /** | - | |
| Sep 95. | (7") <(SP 310)> **ONE STEP AWAY FROM MYSELF. / EVERYTHING TO YOU** | | |

(above issued on 'Sub Pop', below on 'Wabana')

| 1995. | (7"m) <ORE 2> **BLOOD ON THE MOON. / (other 3 by MOVIOLA)** | | |
| Dec 95. | (12"ep/cd-ep) <(SCT 052-1/-2)> **VINTAGE CRIME** | | Nov95 |

– Catalogue / World doesn't end / Media whore / Wish I was here / Every god for himself / Fire of love.

| Jan 97. | (7") <(GH 190)> **FOR MY WOMAN. / (other by LEAVING TRAINS)** | | |

(above issued on 'Get Hip', below on 'Simple Solution')

COBRA VERDE (cont) — THE GREAT INDIE DISCOGRAPHY — The 1990s

Feb 97. (7") <ss 013> **STRIPED WHITE JETS. / (other by LOTION)**
Mar 97. (7"m) <ORE 10> **TERRORIST. / (other 2 by GUIDED BY VOICES)**
(above on 'Wabana', below on 'Carcrashh')
Mar 97. (7") *(CRASHH 08)* **split w/ ETHER NET**

—— **ROBERT POLLARD** (of GUIDED BY VOICES) guested on below

Jun 97. (cd) <*(SCAT 67)*> **EGOMANIA (LOVE SONGS)** (part compilation)
– Everything to you / A story I can sell / Still breaking down / Leather / Underpants / Blood on the moon / Until it's gone / For my woman / Chinese radiation / Never my love.

—— the whole band also teamed up with POLLARD in GUIDED BY VOICES

                                                                      Motel   Motel
Jun 00. (cd) <ROOM 4CD> **NIGHTLIFE**   Oct99
– One step away from myself / Conflict / Crashing in a plane / Every god for himself / Casino / What makes a man a man / Between the seasons / Heaven in the gutter / Don't let me love you / Tourist / Back to Venus / Don't burden me with dreams / $2 souvenir / Pontius Pilate.

COCKEYED GHOST

Formed: New York, USA … mid 90's by ADAM MARSLAND (the main writer), ROB CASSELL and JAMES HAZLEY. A popular indie power-pop outfit, COCKEYED GHOST were heralded by music critics, although this was not turned into the proverbial pop of gold the band might've deserved. After the release of their well-received 'KEEP YOURSELF ALIVE' debut in 1996, they were included on the bill for SHONEN KNIFE's Stateside tour. 'NEVEREST' (1997) was a surprise nomination for a BAM award, although this did not stop the band going through a series of personnel changes. Left with the band name, MARSLAND continued with a new, er, COCKEYED GHOST, featuring substitutes ROBBIE REIS, KURT MEDLIN and ROBERT RAMOS. The group's third full-set, 'THE SCAPEGOAT FACTORY' (1999), was an inspired comeback set, MARSLAND had finally found his BEACH BOYS-meets-mod niche. 2001's 'LUDLOW 6:18' – following the demise of 'Big Deal' records – was a tad disappointing to say the least, a sort of bookends turned concept piece that found little favour among new fans.

Album rating: KEEP YOURSELF AMUSED (*6) / NEVEREST (*5) / THE SCAPEGOAT FACTORY (*7) / LUDLOW 6:18 (*5)

ADAM MARSLAND – vocals, guitar / **ROB CASSELL** – bass / **JAMES HAZLEY** – drums
                                                                    Big Deal Big Deal
1996.   (cd) <BGD 9031> **KEEP YOURSELF AMUSED**
– About Jill / Disappear / At the bookstore / Dirty bastard / Keep the sun / Call me Charley / Married yet / Using you / Dogs that say no / Banished / Lonely ball. *(UK-iss.Mar99; same as US)*

Sep 97. (cd) <BGD 9046> **NEVEREST**
– Buzz / Binghamton / Halo boy / Walking in winter / I'm ok you're not ok / Special / Koreatown / Third wheel / F/U / Asian hero worship / End groove. *(UK-iss.Mar99; same as US)*

—— **ROBBIE RIS** – bass; repl. CASSELL
—— **KURT MEDLIN** – drums, percussion; repl. HAZLEY
—— added **ROBERT RAMOS** – backing vocals

Mar 99. (cd) <*(BGD 9060)*> **THE SCAPEGOAT FACTORY**   Feb99
– I hate rock'n'roll / I wish I was a girl / Where's my best friend / Big big yeah / Falling down the hill / Fates cry foul / Crap / Imagine you're dead / Something to prove / Then I'll be happy / Coda for Carl / I hate rock'n'roll / Wonderland.
                                                                    not iss. Karma Frog
2001.   (cd) <618> **LUDLOW 6:18**   -
– Ground 0:00 / Ludlow 6:18 / Ginna Ling / Karma frog / December / How can you stand it / Burning me out (of the record store) / The foghorn / Tears of joy / Theme from Ludlow 6:18 / Old trails.

COCTAILS

Formed: Kansas City, Missouri, USA … 1989 by vocalists and multi-instrumentalists MARK GREENBERG, BARRY PHIPPS, JOHN UPCHURCH and ARCHER PREWITT. The COCTAILS employed a varied assortment of instruments such as organs, clarinets, vibraphones and banjos to achieve their 1960's frenzied, kitsch, lounge music. Debuting in 1990 with their self-financed EP 'HIP HIP HOORAY' the group displayed their talent for effectively fusing jazz and pop; think MARTIN DENNY or MILES DAVIS. The band's willingness to experiment was shown on their 1991 full-length debut 'HERE NOW TODAY' which, although impressive in places, had the feel of a work in progress. The group benefitted from a move to Chicago where they immersed themselves in the city's jazz scene. Their first release after relocating was the 'SONGS FOR CHILDREN' EP, a record which saw the group move away from the pop influences evident in their earlier cuts. Two more jazz EP's, '3/4 TIME' and 'WINTER WONDERLAND' followed in 1993 before the band made a surprising U-turn the following year with the guitar pop album 'PEEL'. The group kept their fans guessing with the release of jazz album 'LONG SOUND' in 1995 and then a self-titled guitar album the following year. Their reputation for being an incredible live act was showcased on their final album, 'LIVE AT LOUNGE AX, CHICAGO' (1996), recorded on New Year's Eve, 1995, this concert was always intended to be the group's swansong and proved to be a fitting tribute. PREWITT is now content to be part of SEA AND CAKE and a solo artist, while GREENBERG took up a position with CHESTNUT STATION.

Album rating: HERE NOW YODAY (*5) / PEEL (*7) / LONG SOUND (*6) / LIVE AT LOUNGE AX, CHICAGO (*6) / THE COCTAILS (*3)

ARCHER PREWITT – vocals, guitar, drums / **MARK GREENBERG** – organ, bass, drums, vocals / **JOHN UPCHURCH** – organ, banjo / **BARRY PHIPPS** – bass, saxophone
                                                                    not iss. Hi Ball
1990.   (12"ep) **HIP HIP HOORAY!**   -
1991.   (lp) **HERE NOW TODAY**   -
1991.   (7"ep) **SONGS FOR CHILDREN EP**   -
                                                                    Moll   Carrot Top
Nov 92. (cd) <SAKI001CD> **THE EARLY HI BALL YEARS** (compilation)   -
– Whoopsy daisy / Road hog / Wet suit / Intermission / Talkin' about my baby / Clown's coffee / Walkin' down the street / Mr. E. Claffin / Martin Denny's sake rock / Bold rat / West couch place / It's all right / Since October / Don't got time / City gone / In a tub / Dom casual / Jobless / Old grey mare / Cakewalk / China song / Florence / Prisoner of the highway / Waiting for Godot. *(UK-iss.Jan00; same as US)*
1993.   (cd-ep) **3/4 TIME EP**   -
Nov 93. (cd-ep) **WINTER WONDERLAND**   -
May 95. (cd) <SAKI 002CD> **LONG SOUND** (rec. August 1992)   -
– Steam / China song / Monkeys and seals / Stray horn / Tenement / Twilight for Henry / Waterlogged / Clown's coffee / Far east / Gripper bite. *(UK-iss.Jun00; same as US)*
Aug 95. (cd) (efa 12114-2) <SAKI 003CD> **PEEL**   1994
– Miss Maple / Peel / And you could / Postcard / Daylight / Wicked ways / Weather king / 2000 / Moment of the day / Cottonbelt / Even time.
Mar 96. (cd) (efa 12118-2) <SAKI 010CD> **THE COCTAILS**
– When I come around / Circles / City sun / Cadali / So low / Grace / Starling / Never knew / Low road / Hey / Sun is down / Cast stones / Last organ.

—— had already disbanded 31st of December, 1995; PREWITT continued with SEA AND CAKE and went solo while GREENBERG joined CHESTNUT STATION

– compilations, etc. –

Sep 96. (cd) *Carrot Top*; <SAKI 013CD> **LIVE AT THE LOUNGE AX, CHICAGO** (live)
– Skeleton bones / Wood bee / First snowfall / Whoopsy daisy / Don't got time / Even time / Miss Maple / Cast stones / Low road / Cadali / New organ / The tingler / The penguin – Powerhouse / Florence / And you could / Wheels / Walkin' down the street / Talkin' 'bout my baby / Why. *(UK-iss.Jan00; same as US)*

ARCHER PREWITT

with various session people
                                                                    Hi-Ball   Hi-Ball
Jun 97. (d-lp) <(HBLP 0497)> **IN THE SUN**   Apr97
– Leave it gone / Good man / Rush hour / You walk by / I'm all you know / In the midst / Work / Best is yet to come / Moore country run / City ride / Let me fade away / In the sun. <cd-iss. Mar98 on 'Carrot Top'; SAKI 015CD>
                                                                    Carrot Top Carrot Top
Oct 99. (cd) <(SAKI 022CD)> **WHITE SKY**
– Raise on high / Shake / White sky (instrumental) / Summer's end / Last summer days / Walking on the farm / Motorcycles / Final season / I'll be waiting. <(lp-iss.Nov99 on 'Hi-Ball'; HBLP 1099)>
Dec 00. (m-cd) <(SAKI 026CD)> **GERROA SONGS**   Nov00
– Gerroa / The bay / Meant to be / Along the coast / Another peace of mind / Waves waltz / Tell me now / Her magic.
                                                                    Thrill   Thrill
                                                                    Jockey   Jockey
Jun 02. (cd/lp) <(THRILL 108/+LP)> **THREE**
– Over the line / Tear me all away / When I'm with you / Two can play / I'm coming over / Gifts of love / Second time trader / Atmosphere / Behind your sun / No defense / Another day / Sister ice / The race / The day to day.

CODEINE

Formed: based- New York, USA … early 90's by STEVE IMMERWAHR, JOHN ENGLE and CHRIS BROKAW, the latter subsequently joining COME and replaced by MATTHEW McGUIGAN. Named after a brand of painkiller, CODEINE (who'd recorded a scuzzy near 10-minute version of Harry Nillson's 'WITHOUT YOU') specialise in painfully slow, lingering songs which make the shoegazing bands of the early 90's seem positively animated. Signed to 'Sub Pop', the trio debuted in 1991 with 'FRIGID STARS', its slo-mo textures, languid vocals and general air of solemnity ranging through mogodon riffing, semi-acoustic strumming with 'W.' (even the song titles were minimalist!) even stark piano, to strangely hypnotic effect. The following year saw the release of a full length debut album, 'THE WHITE BIRCH', prompting more superlatives from the critics and ensuring a cult following. Not music to play before a night out! • **Covered:** PROMISE OF LOVE (MX-80 Sound).

Album rating: FRIGID STARS (*7) / BARELY REAL mini (*5) / THE WHITE BIRCH (*6)

STEPHEN IMMERWAHR – vocals, bass / **JOHN ENGLE** – guitar / **DOUGLAS SCHARIN** – drums; repl. JOSH MADELL who had briefly depped for CHRIS BROKAW (who joined COME as a guitarist)
                                                                    Sub Pop   Sub Pop
Apr 91. (lp/c/cd) <sp 107/+A/B> **FRIGID STARS**   -
– D / Gravel bed / Pickup song / New year's / Second chance / Cave-in / Cigarette machine / Old things / 3 angels / Pea.
Jul 92. (7"clear) <#45 – sp 155> **REALIZE. / BROKEN-HEARTED WINE**   -
Nov 92. (m-lp/m-cd) <(sp/+cd 51-213)> **BARELY REAL**
– Realize / Jr / Barely real / Hard to find / W. / Promise of love.
May 93. (7") *(WH-MARCH)* **IDES. / Cocktails: Working Holiday**
(above issued on 'Simple Machines')

—— added guest guitarist **DAVID GRUBBS** (on below)
Nov 93. (7") <(sp 117-295)> **TOM. / SOMETHING NEW**

May 94. (lp/cd) (sp/+cd 118-299) **THE WHITE BIRCH**
- Sea / Loss leader / Vacancy / Kitchen light / Washed up / Tom / Ides / Wird / Smoking room.
— **MATTHEWS McGUIGAN** – drums; repl. SCHARIN
— split later in '94; STEPHEN formed the group RAYMOND in '98 and released the 7", 'SWELLING VIOLINS' for 'First Love'; <001>

CODY

Formed: Oxford, England . . . August 1996 by JOE BOULTER, CHRIS FISH, STEVE JEFFERIS and JOHN JOHNSON; the original line-up also included a keyboard player and a violinist, although they departed fairly swiftly. Of the lasting members, JEFFERIS had proved himself worthy with 'Sarah'-records-signed band, ORLANDO. In 1997, they debuted with the 7", 'SIMPLE', a record displaying the band's mixture of 80s-styled experimental pop with space-rock flavours. This initial single and further gigs garnered the band some attention, notably on Radio One's 'Sound City'. Unfortunately the group were not happy with the praise and inevitable pigeonholing and took time out to recuperate and get a better handle on the sound they wished to be linked with. Thus the following year saw CODY with some more up-to-date technology, and with it a change in their sound towards a more 90s dance-rock orientated sound, with beats provided by their new purchase, the legendary 303 sampler. Their new style was showcased on the 1998 sophomore single, 'DARK BLUE' (1998) and the debut EP, 'ANTICYCLONE' (the latter on 'Shinkansen', the imprint that had risen from the ashes of 'Sarah'). Happier with their more distinctive and less derivative sound, the group went on to release the EP, 'ROUNDER' (1999), following this up in the ensuing year with their initial full-length set, 'STILLPOINT PRIMER'.

Album rating: STILLPOINT PRIMER (*6) / DISTANCE LEARNER (*6)

JOE BOULTER – vocals, keyboards, programming / **CHRIS FISH** – keyboards / **STEVE JEFFERIS** – guitars, visuals (ex-SHELLEY – aka ORLANDO) / **JOHN JOHNSON** – guitars, vocals

		Shifty Disco	not iss.
Oct 97.	(cd-s) (Disco 9709) **SIMPLE / ABSENTMINDED**		-
		Kooky	not iss.
Jul 98.	(7") (Kookydisc 006) **DARK BLUE. / WRONGFOOTED**		-
		Shinkansen	not iss.
Oct 98.	(7") (SHINKANSEN 13) **ANTICYCLONE. / PHOTOGENIC**		-
	(cd-s+=) (SHINKANSEN 13CD) – Dovetails / Holding pattern.		
Aug 99.	(cd-ep) (SHINKANSEN 17CD) **ROUNDER EP**		-
	– Rounder / Cuts and grazes / Ordinance / Pipistrelle.		
Nov 00.	(cd) (SHINKANSEN 29CD) **STILLPOINT PRIMER**		-
	– Never expect any more / August song / Ideas are allies / Sleepy park royal / From the edge of maps / Headlights rush forever / Ghost shakers / Stickleback / Chromophone / Black wings in a blue sky.		
Apr 02.	(cd-s) (SHINKANSEN 34) **UPLIFT / FLEXIBILITY / AQUAPLANER**		-
Jun 02.	(cd) (SHINKANSEN 37) **DISTANCE LEARNING**		-
	– Uplift / Share and enjoy / Bolero and cipher / Cooperativa / Dorian / Evening falls / Oscillator / A single thread / In our own time / Ripples run forever / Sentinels.		

COLD COLD HEARTS (see under ⇒ BRATMOBILE)

COLDPLAY

Formed: London, England . . . early 1998 by CHRIS MARTIN and PHIL HARVEY, the latter would become their manager/financer/5th member after CHRIS found new pals/musicians – JON BUCKLAND, Edinburgh-born GUY BERRYMAN and WILL CHAMPION – while at university. These VERVE inspired mellow-ites issued a limited pressing of 500 copies of their self-financed debut, 'THE SAFETY' EP. After interest from 'Fierce Panda' (who released their single 'BROTHERS AND SISTERS'), the group looked set to conquer the indie charts with their new style of JEFF BUCKLEY-esque melancholia. 'BLUE ROOM' EP (1999) – and their first for 'Parlophone' – featured the classy Chris Alison-produced track 'HIGH SPEED', a dreamy "psychefeelia" song; touching, moody and soft, oh so soft! Supporting tortured HEAD brothers SHACK, enabled the band to delve further into the twisted world of moving rock and reach deeper into the minds of fans who had not yet overcome the departure of Brit pop. Come in Mr. ASHCROFT . . . your time is up! A second single, 'SHIVER', was their first to break into the UK Top 40, however, this would be well surpassed when summer 2000 follow-up, 'YELLOW', slid into the Top 5. The album, 'PARACHUTES' (2000), received rave reviews from all and sundry and shot into the UK charts at No.1 – it would subsequently touch American hearts and souls not long after. Warm, melancholy and passionate were a few select words to describe this Mercury Prize nomination which also featured a further Top 10 hit and Virgin playlist fave, 'TROUBLE'. The boys were back on top form (and No.1) in 2002, come the release of their second full-length album, 'A RUSH OF BLOOD TO THE HEAD'. It displayed all of the same qualities of the first, although the songs seemed to sit with the listener longer. An example of this was the single 'IN MY PLACE', a poignant but uplifting track that showed-off MARTIN's voice well, not to mention the rest of the group's excellent musicianship. The album glided from one song to the next, like a paper aeroplane in the breeze. At times, sounding almost identical to old ECHO AND THE BUNNYMEN, MARTIN must've taken notes from the old post-New Wave romantics, as at the end of 2002 he began dating a certain actress named Gwyneth Paltrow. Turn on the TV and you will probably hear some commercial or cult programme use 'THE SCIENTIST' as a theme – the world was indeed progressing and COLDPLAY were winning Grammys.

Album rating: PARACHUTES (*9) / A RUSH OF BLOOD TO THE HEAD (*9)

CHRIS MARTIN – vocals, piano / **JON BUCKLAND** – guitar / **GUY BERRYMAN** (b. Scotland) – bass / **WILL CHAMPION** – drums

		own label	not iss.
Apr 98.	(7"ep) (none) **THE SAFETY ep**		-
	– Bigger stronger / No more keeping my feet on the ground / Such a rush.		
		Fierce Panda	not iss.
Apr 99.	(7") (NING 068) **BROTHERS AND SISTERS. / EASY TO PIECES**		-
	(cd-s+=) (NING 068CD) – Only superstition.		
		Parlophone	Capitol
Oct 99.	(12"ep/cd-ep) (12R/CDR 6528) **BLUE ROOM EP**		-
	– Bigger stronger / Don't panic / See you soon / High speed / Such a rush.		
Mar 00.	(7") (R 6536) **SHIVER. / FOR YOU**	35	-
	(cd-s+=) (CDR 6536) – Careful where you stand.		
Jun 00.	(c-s/7") (TC+/R 6538) <radio cut> **YELLOW. / HELP IS ROUND THE CORNER**	4	48 Feb01
	(cd-s+=) (CDR 6538) – No more keeping my feet on the ground.		
Jul 00.	(cd/c/lp) (527783-2/-4/-1) <30162> **PARACHUTES**	1	51 Dec00
	– Don't panic / Shiver / Spies / Sparks / Yellow / Trouble / Parachutes / High speed / We never change / Everything's not lost.		
Oct 00.	(c-s/cd-s/7") (TC/CD+/R 6549) **TROUBLE. / BROTHERS AND SISTERS / SHIVER (Jo Whiley lunchtime social)**	10	-
Aug 02.	(c-ep/12"ep/cd-ep) (TCR/12R/CDR 6579) **IN MY PLACE / ONE I LOVE / I BLOOM BLAUM**	2	-
Aug 02.	(cd/c/lp) (5405-4-2/-4/-1) <40504> **A RUSH OF BLOOD TO THE HEAD**	1	5
	– Politik / In my place / God put a smile upon your face / The scientist / Clocks / Daylight / Green eyes / Warning sign / A whisper / A rush of blood to the head / Amsterdam.		
Nov 02.	(7") (R 6588) **THE SCIENTIST. / 1.36 (featuring Tim Wheeler & Simon Pegg)**	10	-
	(cd-s+=) (CDR 6588) – I ran away.		

COLD WATER FLAT

Formed: Amherst, Massachusetts, USA . . . 1990 by PAUL JANOWITZ, TED SILVA and PAUL HARDING. Following in the grand tradition of Boston guitar acts, COLD WATER FLAT combined noise, melody, experimentation and hooklines in equal measure. While they also boasted the talents of BILL JANOWITZ's brother, PAUL, most commentators agreed that debut album, 'LISTEN' (1993), was impressive enough to withstand the inevitable BUFFALO TOM comparisons. Released in the UK on the tiny 'Bittersweet' label, the record was accompanied by a split single with SLEEPYHEAD, 'LOST AND LAZY'. Having accrued a fair number of respectable support slots and a growing press reputation, the band signed to Boston's influential 'Fort Apache' label, handled by 'M.C.A.' First up was 'MAGNETIC NORTH POLE', a rolling, soaring, bruising epic akin to a Stateside MANIC STREET PREACHERS with the obligatory grunge factor intact. Confusingly enough, the lads decided to release their follow-up set as an eponymous affair, hitting the shops a month after the single in Spring '95.

Album rating: LISTEN (*6) / COLD WATER FLAT (*6)

PAUL JANOWITZ – vocals, guitar / **TED SILVA** – bass / **PAUL HARDING** – drums

		Bittersweet	Sonic Bubblegum
Aug 93.	(cd) (BITTERSWEET 002) <SB 9> **LISTEN**		
	– Swollen sonnet / Count out your space / Lost & lazy / Listerine / Instrumental / Dig / Roll me over / Blue clowns / Permanent scars of color / Everything you are.		
Aug 93.	(7") (BITTERSWEET 003) **LOST AND LONELY. / Sleepyhead: Gingerbread House**		-
		Fort Apache – MCA	Fort Apache – MCA
Feb 95.	(7"/c-s) (FAS/+C 1) **MAGNETIC NORTH POLE. / SO TIRED**		-
	(cd-s+=) (FASTD 1) – What a day it was.		
Mar 95.	(cd/c) <(MCAD/MCC 11210)> **COLD WATER FLAT**		
	– Virus road / King of the underground / Numb / Magnetic North Pole / Mistaken / Beautiful / Rescue lights / It's over / All I had / She is / Hold my head.		
Apr 95.	(cd-s) **KING OF THE UNDERGROUND / COUNTRY SONG / MISTAKEN (acoustic) / BEAUTIFUL (live)**	-	

— disbanded soon after above

COLOSSAMITE (see under ⇒ DAZZLING KILLMEN)

COMBUSTIBLE EDISON

Formed: Providence, Rhode Island, USA . . . 1992 out of 80's alt-rock group, CHRISTMAS, by LIZ COX (who subsequently adopted the name of MISS LILY BANQUETTE) and MICHAEL CUDAHY (aka THE MILLIONAIRE). Although they'd been around the indie block a few times, it was 1986 then '89 before CHRISTMAS released a few albums, 'IN EXCELSIOR DAYGLO' and 'ULTRAPROPHETS OF THEE PSYKICK REVOLUTION'. THE MILLIONAIRE then took off for Las Vegas, forming the TIKI WONDER HOUR soon after, a sizeable lounge act ensemble that toured the small cabaret circuit and became skint in the process (thus his ironic name). Inspired by the experience nevertheless, THE MILLIONAIRE returned to team up with LIZ as COMBUSTIBLE EDISON, the line-up completed by his brother, NICK CUDAHY, PETER DIXON and AARON OPPENHEIMER. Taking their cue from Mexican lounge muso, JUAN GURELA ESQUIBEL, they served their music with a jazzy swing and a cool alternative twist, eccentrically kitted out 40's/50's movie style in tuxedos. One of Sub Pop's less predictable signings, COMBUSTIBLE EDISON laid down their new style on debut album, 'I, SWINGER' (1994), their own compositions lounging easily with their cover of Julie London's 'CRY ME A RIVER'. A couple of years went by before the release of their follow-up, 'SCHIZOPHONIC!' (1996), during which time the easy listening revival was at its peak.

Album rating: I, SWINGER (*7) / SCHIZOPHONIC! (*5) / THE IMPOSSIBLE WORLD (*6)

CHRISTMAS

LIZ COX + MICHAEL CUDAHY + DAVE RICK (of PHANTOM TOLBOOTH)

		not iss.	Big Time
1986.	(lp) **IN EXCELSIOR DAYGLO**	-	

– Big plans / Loved ones / Boys' town work song / True soldier of love / Tommy the true / Girl police / Dig we must / Peewee / Everything you know is wrong / Pumpkinhead / A pig amongst men / The hottest sun / Fish eye sandwich / Junk.

		I.R.S.	I.R.S.
Jun 89.	(lp/c/cd) <(EIRSA/+C/CD 1012)> **ULTRAPROPHETS OF THEE PSYKICK REVOLUTION**		

– Stupid kids / This is not a test / Richard Nixon / Hot dog / Punch and Judy / Great Wall of China / Human chain / War hog / He loves them all too much / Royal klutch tattoo / My operator / Hymn.

— **JAMES McNEW** – bass (of YO LA TENGO) repl.
1990. (7") **STUPID KIDS. /** | - | |

— disbanded in '91; McNEW joined YO LA TENGO and DUMP

COMBUSTIBLE EDISON

MISS LILY BANQUETTE (b. LIZ COX) – vocals / **THE MILLIONAIRE** (b. MICHAEL CUDAHY) – vocals / **PETER DIXON** – hi-fi organ / **NICK CADAHY** – double bass / **AARON OPPENHEIMER** – vibraphone

		Domino	Sub Pop
Sep 93.	(7") **CRY ME A RIVER. / SATAN SAYS**	-	
Feb 94.	(7") (RUG 10) **BLUE LIGHT. / SUMMER SAMBA**		-

(cd-s+=) (RUG 10CD) – Satan says / Metropolitan.

		City Slang	Sub Pop
Mar 94.	(cd/lp) (EFA 04934-2/-1) <SP 244CD> **I, SWINGER**		

– Cadillac / The Millionaire's holiday / Breakfast at Denny's / Intermission / Cry me a river / Impact! / Guadaloupe / Carnival of souls / The veldt / Surabaya Johnny / Spy vs. spy / Theme from "The Tiki Wonder Hour".

— in 1995, COMBUSTIBLE EDISON scored most of the soundtrack for the movie, 'Four Rooms'.

Feb 96.	(cd/lp) (RTD 3460002-2/-1) <SP 313> **SCHIZOPHONIC!**		

– Alright, already / Bluebeard / Checkered flag / One eyed monkey / Solid state / Yeux sans visage / "52" / Short double latte / Mudhead / Morticia / Objet d'amour / Corner table / Lonelyville. (cd re-iss. Feb00 on 'Bungalow'; EFA 61502-2)

Mar 96.	(7") (RTD 3460001-7) **SHORT DOUBLE LATTE. / HELLRAISER**		-

(cd-s+=) (RTD 3460001-3) – Satan says.

Jun 96. (12"/cd-s) (RTD 3460003-0/-3) **BLUEBEARD (mixes; album / space patrol 2000 / F.P.M. old fashioned / Buddy mikro / space patrol 2000 dub)**

		Bungalow	Sub Pop
Oct 98.	(cd) (EFA 61546-2) <SP 431> **THE IMPOSSIBLE WORLD**		-

– Utopia / Call of the space siren / Laura's aura / 20th century / Cat o' nine tails / Pink victim / Dior / Hot and bothered / Mr. Pushin came to shore / Seduction / Tickled to death / The garden of earthly delights / Utopia (Scanner's reprise). (re-iss. Feb00; same)

— have been inactive since above

COME

Formed: (based) Boston, Massachusetts, USA ... 1989 by former DANGEROUS BIRDS, LIVE SKULL and UZI mainwoman, THALIA ZEDEK, along with former CODEINE man, CHRIS BROKAW and a rhythm section of ARTHUR JOHNSON and SEAN O'BRIEN. Quite possibly the most convincing exponent of brooding feminine intensity since PATTI SMITH (an obvious influence alongside HOLE's COURTNEY LOVE), ZEDEK first stamped her tortured personality over the emerging grunge scene in summer '91 with the 'CAR' single. Hailed by the critics, the track introduced the trademark COME sound, crushing fragments of SONIC YOUTH, NIRVANA and even BLACK SABBATH into painful emotional wounds. A follow-up single, 'FAST PISS BLUES', further raised expectations for debut album, 'ELEVEN: ELEVEN' (1992) and cemented COME's growing reputation as true guardians of the blues' dark flame. The album itself was met with almost universal acclaim, from the broken-down desolation of 'SUBMERGE' onwards a seriously heavy going trip through COME's often despairing world. Switching from 'Matador' to 'Beggars Banquet', they previewed follow-up set, 'DON'T ASK, DON'T TELL' (1994), with the slo-mo frustration of 'WRONG SIDE', a flavour of the album's mogadon-pace vegetation. Some fresh blood was injected with 1996's 'NEAR LIFE EXPERIENCE' album, however, O'BRIEN and JOHNSON replaced initially by BUNDY K BROWN and MAC McNEILLY and then TARA JANE O'NEILL and KEVIN COULTAS. Guests BETH HEINBERG and ED YAZIJIAN's piano and violin flourishes also added a bit of melancholy colour and subtlety to proceedings. Around the same time the band also backed STEVE WYNN on his solo set, 'Melting In The Dark', while BUNDY and BROKAW hooked up with each other once more as part of the acclaimed PULLMAN project. COME returned in 1998 with another new rhythm section, WINSTON BRAMEN and DANIEL COUGHLIN taking the band back to basics on 'GENTLY DOWN THE STREAM'. THALIA, meanwhile, was setting out her own stall via a Suffragette Sessions Tour with The INDIGO GIRLS, her repertoire now dramatically going through a sort of menopausal state and floating into folk, blues and torch ballads. This was evident on her solo debut for 'Matador', 'BEEN HERE AND GONE' (2001), a record that saw her cover Leonard Cohen's 'DANCE ME TO THE END OF LOVE'. A few more classic reinterpretations could be found on THALIA's follow-up mini-set, 'YOU'RE A BIG GIRL NOW' (2002): these were the Bob Dylan-penned title track and 'CANDY SAYS' (Velvet Underground). • **COME Covered:** I GOT THE BLUES (Rolling Stones).

Album rating: ELEVEN: ELEVEN (*6) / DON'T ASK, DON'T TELL (*7) / NEAR LIFE EXPERIENCE (*7) / GENTLY DOWN THE STREAM (*6) / Thalia Zedek: BEEN HERE AND GONE (*7) / YOU'RE A BIG GIRL NOW mini (*6)

THALIA ZEDEK – vocals, guitar, harmonica (ex-LIVE SKULL, ex-UZI) / **CHRIS BROKAW** – guitar, vocals, keyboards (ex-CODEINE) / **ARTHUR JOHNSON** – drums (ex-BAR B Q KILLERS) / **SEAN O'BRIEN** – bass (ex-KILKENNY CATS)

		not iss.	Sub Pop
Aug 91.	(7"white) <#34> **CAR. / LAST MISTAKE**	-	

		Placebo	Matador
Apr 92.	(12"ep/cd-ep) <SP 115> **CAR. / LAST MISTAKE / SUBMERGE**	-	

Dec 92.	(lp/cd) (PILL A/CD 1) <OLE 045> **ELEVEN: ELEVEN**		

– Submerge / Dead Molly / Brand new vein / Off to one side / Bell / William / Sad eyes / Power failure / Orbit. (cd+=) – Car / Last mistake.

		Beggars Banquet	Nov92 Matador
Jan 93.	(10"m) (PILL 3) <OLE 027> **FAST PISS BLUES. / I GOT THE BLUES / BRAND NEW VEIN**		
Apr 94.	(7"/12"/cd-s) (BBQ 34/+T/CD) <OLE 086> **WRONG SIDE. / LOIN OF THE SURF / SVK**		Mar94
Oct 94.	(cd/c/lp) (BBQ CD/MC/LP 160) <OLE 108> **DON'T ASK, DON'T TELL**		

– Finish line / Mercury falls / Yr reign / Poison / Let's get lost / String / German song / In/Out / Wrong side / Arrive.

Feb 95.	(10"ep/cd-ep) (BBQ 48 TT/CD) **STRING / WHO JUMPED ON MY GRAVE. / GERMAN SONG / ANGELHEAD**		-

— **THALIA + CHRIS** were joined by **BUNDY K BROWN** – bass (ex-ELEVENTH DREAM DAY) / **MAC McNEILLY** – drums (then) **TARA JANE O'NEIL** – bass (of RODAN) / **KEVIN COULTAS** – drums (of RODAN) / guests **BETH HEINBERG** – piano / **ED YAZIJIAN** – violin

		Domino	Matador
Apr 96.	(cd-s) (RUG 43CD) **SECRET NUMBER / PRIZE / HURRICANE II**		-
May 96.	(m-cd/m-lp) (WIG CD/LP 25) <OLE 192> **NEAR LIFE EXPERIENCE**		

– Hurricane / Weak as the moon / Secret number / Bitten / Shoot me first / Walk on's / Half life / Slow-eyed.

— around this period, they worked with STEVE WYNN (ex-DREAM SYNDICATE) on his 1996 set, 'Melting In The Dark'.

— BUNDY became part of DIRECTIONS IN MUSIC and side-project, PULLMAN, the latter also featuring BROKAW

— **ZEDEK + BROKAW** recruited **WINSTON BRAMEN** – bass / **DANIEL COUGHLIN** – drums, percussion

Feb 98.	(cd/d-lp) (WIG CD/LP 43) <OLE 254> **GENTLY DOWN THE STREAM**		

– One piece / Recidivist / Stomp / Sorry too late / Saints around my neck / Silk city / Middle of nowhere / The fade-outs / A jam blues / New coat / The former model / March.

– compilations, etc. –

1990's.	(lp) Come: <88203> **RAMPTON**	-	

– Submerge / Dead Molly / Brand new vein / Off to one side / Bell / William / Sad eyes / Power failure / Orbit / Fast piss blues / I got the blues.

THALIA ZEDEK

with **CHRIS BROKAW** – bass, slide guitar, guitars

		Matador	Matador
Jul 01.	(cd) <(OLE 519-2)> **BEEN HERE AND GONE**		

– Excommunications (everybody knows) / Back to school / Strong / Temporary guest / Treacherous thing / Dance me to the end of love / 1926 / Desanctified (full circle) / Something else / 10th lament / Manha de carnaval.

— now with **MEL LEDERMAN** – piano (of VICTORY AT SEA) + **DAVID MICHAEL CURRY** – viola (of WILLARD GRANT CONSPIRACY)

		Acuarela	Kimchee
Nov 02.	(m-cd) (NOIS 32) <022> **YOU'RE A BIG GIRL NOW**		

– Everything unkind / Candy says / No substitutions / JJ85 / You're a big girl now / No fire.

COME ONS

Formed: Detroit, Michigan, USA ... 1999 by a roost of the scene's Garage Rock revivalists, led by DEANNE IOVAN of GORE GORE GIRLS, including DIRTBOMBS drummer PATRICK PANTANO, JIM JOHNSON on guitar and keyboardist KO MELINA ZYDECO. The group issued their scuzz-ball racket 'THE COME ONS' in 2000; produced by Jim Diamond for 'Sympathy For The Record Industry'. In 2001 they delivered another Diamond-produced set, although the group's musical direction had changed somewhat; in amongst

the mix were instrumentals, atmospheric experimentations and a wad of floor-fillers for those hot Detroit niteclubs (sic). Organist NATE CAVALIERI was also on board, but was subsequently nicked by other Detroit hipsters, The SIGHTS. • **Covered:** NEEDLE IN A HAYSTACK (Marvelettes) / I GET SO EXCITED (Grant Gordon) / I FEEL GOOD ALL OVER (Scott Blackwell) / I WANNA BE LOVED (Thomas) / RIP HER TO SHEDS (Blondie).
Album rating: THE COME ONS (*6) / HIP CHECK! (*7)

DEANNE IOVAN – vocals, bass (ex-GORE GORE GIRLS) / **JIM JOHNSON** – guitar / **KO MELINA ZYDECO** – keyboards / **PATRICK PANTANO** – drums (of DIRTBOMBS)

not iss. — own label

1999. (c-s) <none> **WHATCHA' GOT?**
– Whatcha' got? / Knee jerk / Red lips & fingertips / Operation: get down.

Sympathy F — Sympathy F

Jun 00. (lp/cd) <(SFTRI 608/+CD)> **THE COME ONS**
– Whatcha got? / Oooh / When I woke up this morning / At the bus stop (pt.1) / I get so excited / Operation get down / Nice and easy / What's a girl got to do? / Knee jerk / Red lips & fingertips / Sugar fortified / At the bus stop (part 2) / I feel good all over / Loaded heart / He's a man / I wanna be loved / At the bus stop (part 3).

— now without KO who was repl. by temps SCOTT CRAIG then ABBEY TAYLOR before they too departed

Sep 01. (7") (SFTRI 617) **WHATCHA GOT? / NEEDLE IN A HAYSTACK**
Oct 01. (lp/cd) <(SFTRI 670/+CD)> **HIP CHECK!**
– It's alright / Mesmerizer / Something fool / Keep the change / Bello amore / Strangelove / Hip check! / Sunday drive / Heavy / Get it / I'll show you why / Dollar in my pocket.

— added **EDDIE BARANEK** – guitar (of SIGHTS)
— **NATE CAVALIERI** – organ (of SIGHTS) repl. BARANEK

Sweet Nothing — not iss.

Apr 02. (7"m) (7SN 011) **DON'T TELL ME. / GROUNDED / TWINE TIME**

— now a trio of IOVAN, PANTANO + JOHNSON

COMET

Formed: Mesquite, Texas, USA ... early '94 by JIM STONE, his brother NEIL, DANIEL HUFFMAN and JOSH. Bored with the drastic heat and cactus ridden scenery, COMET noticed that fate was on their side and took full advantage when unsung hero (and one time MERCURY REV vocalist) DAVE BAKER offered to produce their complicated, film inspired EP 'PORTRAIT' (1995). It was not surprising then that the same cult denominator rode the faders for the band's debut set 'CHANDELIAR MUSINGS' which surfaced in 1997, just one year out on missing the trip-rock revolution that the REV and FLAMING LIPS would finally sucumb to. Part SLINT and part TANGERINE DREAM, the album took the listener on a space holiday to, er Button Moon (depending on what kind of chemicals you were indulging in), mixing soft ambient rock with PINK FLOYD-esque harmonics and a gift for uplifting melodies that the term "new adventures in hi-fi" was most definitely invented for.

Album rating: CHANDELIAR MUSINGS (*5)

JIM STONE – vocals, guitar / **DANIEL HUFFMAN** – guitar / **NEIL STONE** – bass, vocals / **JOSH** – percussion

not iss. — Last Beat

Nov 95. (cd-s) <9> **THIS IS FREEDOM**
– Portrait / Rocket flare.

Dedicated — Dedicated

Apr 97. (cd) (DEDCD 30) <44000> **CHANDELIAR MUSINGS** — Oct96
– Rocket flare / Day at the races / She's a mastermind / Soundtrack to the short film: Lifelines / Shogun girl / Birds are little dinosaurs / Formula one driver blues / American flyer.

— disappeared after above

COMET GAIN

Formed: London, England ... 1993 by songwriter DAVID FECK and singer SARAH BLEACH, along with SAM PLUCK, JAX COOMBES (a female) and PHIL SUTTON. Starting out as the 'Riot Grrrl' movement was in full swing, COMET GAIN released a series of amateurish but promising singles before signing to 'Wiiija' in late '94. The following spring, the shamholic, twee but charming punksters released their debut album, 'CASINO CLASSICS', surprisingly finding favour with the American underground elite (i.e. JON SPENCER, THURSTON MOORE of SONIC YOUTH, etc). A string of EP's/singles (including an appearance on NME's C-96 cassette) kept their profile fairly high before the release of a much anticipated 1997 follow-up set, 'SNEAKY'; a shortened version 'MAGNETIC POETRY' was issued in the UK. All bar DAVID moved on to form their own group, VELOCETTE, while the man in question recruited a new band (including KAY ISHIKAWA on bass) to augment on comeback set, 'TIGERTOWN PICTURES' (1999). As much lo-fi as it was soulful punk, the set started nicely enough with 'RECORD COLLECTION' and 'SKINNY WOLVES', although by the end the formula was wearing a bit thin. However, after a few years in the proverbial wilderness, FECK turned up the volume once more via a set made in heaven, 'REALISTES' (2002). Cult US imprint 'Kill Rock Stars' payed COMET GAIN a compliment by releasing the set and advancing KATHLEEN HANNA (of LE TIGRE) to augment their rolicking, helter skelter sound.

Album rating: CASINO CLASSICS (*6) / SNEAKY or MAGNETIC POETRY (*6) / TIGERTOWN PICTURES (*5) / REALISTES (*7)

SARAH BLEACH – vocals / **DAVID FECK** – guitar / **SAM PLUCK** – guitar / **JAX COOMBES** – keyboards, bass / **PHIL SUTTON** – drums

Soul Static Sound — not iss.

Sep 94. (7"ep) (SOUL 5) **HOLLOWAY SWEETHEARTS EP**
– Another weekend / Icpress file / Kids at the club / Goodbye part one.

Wiiija — Beggars Banquet

Mar 95. (7"one-sided) (LTD 003) **A MILLION AND NINE**
Apr 95. (cd/lp) (WIJ 42 CD/V) **CASINO CLASSICS**
– Footstompers / A million and nine / Turnpike county blue / Last night / Original arrogance / Another girl / Music upstairs / Villain / Stay with me / Charlie / Just seventeen / Ghost of the Roman Empire / Intergalactic starved / Chevron action flash.
Oct 95. (7"ep/cd-ep) (WIJ 46 V/CD) **THE "GETTIN' READY" EP**
– Baby's alright / The shining path / Charlie / White noise.
Apr 96. (7"ep/cd-ep) (WIJ 50 V/CD) **SAY YES TO INTERNATIONAL SOCIALISM EP**
– Hideaway / Say yes / California / Sunsets at her window.
Feb 97. (7") (WIJ 66) **STRENGTH. / A FILM BY KENNETH ANGER**
(cd-s+=) (WIJ 66CD) – Letting go.
Sep 97. (cd) <85009> **SNEAKY**
– Strength / Raspberries / Language of the spy / Steps to the sea / (These are the dreams of the) Working girl / Pier Angeli / Pussycat / Tighten up / Say yes / A film by Kenneth Anger / Sunsets at her window / Shining path.
Oct 97. (cd/lp) (WIJ CD/LP 1054) **MAGNETIC POETRY**
– Strength / Raspberries / Language of the spy / Steps to the sea / (These are the dreams of the) Working girl / Pier Angeli / Final horses / Tighten up.

— BLEACH, COOMBES + PLUCK left to form VELOCETTE
— **DAVID FECK** recruited **KAY ISHIKAWA** – bass / **DARREN, RACHEL + BLAIR**

Mei Mei — not iss.

Jun 98. (7") (MEI 001) **JACK NANCE HAIR. / WE ARE ALL ROTTEN**

Kill Rock Stars — Kill Rock Stars

Dec 98. (7"m) <(KRS 323)> **IF I HAD A SOUL. / HE WALKED BY NIGHT / THE BROTHERS OF THE BLOCK**

Piao! — not iss.

Aug 99. (7"ep) (PIAO 17) **RED MENACE – 3 SONGS EP**
– Orwell liberty dance / Young lions devour / Hands fit.

Where It's At... — Kill Rock Stars

Mar 00. (cd) (WIACD 002) <KRS 346> **TIGERTOWN PICTURES** — Sep99
– Record collection / Skinny wolves / Jack Nance rising / Deficient love / Germ of youth – Ghosts of sulphate / Radar / Transmission lost / Hate soul / When you come back I'll feel like Jesus coming off the cross / Dreaming of Tigertown / Saturday night facts of life / The ballad of Cable Hogue / Jasper Johns / The final anesthetic. (lp-iss.Jul00 on 'Fortuna Pop'+=; FPOP 17) (free 7") – HATE SOUL. / WHEN YOU COME BACK I'LL FEEL LIKE JESUS ON A CROSS

Fortuna Pop — not iss.

Apr 01. (7") (FPOP 26) **YOU CAN HIDE YOUR LOVE FOREVER. / BEATNIK**

— **DAVID, KAY, JON SLADE** + newcomer **M.J. "WOODY" TAYLOR** – drums recruited guests **KATHLEEN HANNA** – vocals (of LE TIGRE, ex-BIKINI KILL) / **PETER MOMTCHILOFF** – lap steel / **CHRISTOPHER APPLEGREN** – drums (of PEECHEES, of PATTERN)

Milou Studies — Kill Rock Stars

Apr 02. (lp/cd) (2 MIL/+CD) <KRS 378> **REALISTES** — Mar02
– The kids at the club / Why I try to look so bad / I close my eyes to think of God / My defiance / Carry on living / Moments in the snow / Ripped-up suit! / She never understood / Movies / Labour / Don't fall in love if you want to die in peace / Realistes.

COMMANDER VENUS (see under ⇒ BRIGHT EYES)

COMPOUND RED

Formed: Milwaukee, Wisconsin, USA ... 1987 by ANDY REIS, MIKE ALLEN, JOHN LYMAN and DAVE HENDERLEITER. Taking their cue from fellow emocore outfits such as The PROMISE RING, COMPOUND RED delivered a plethora of demo cassette releases during a prolific time in the late 80's and early 90's. This eventually led to full-set proper, 'MR. MICROCOSM' (1993). However, after split EP with SANDBOX, vocalist LYMAN moved to Minneapolis. This was only a temporary glitch as they subsequently teamed up once more to record for 'DeSoto' records who delivered their comeback set, 'ALWAYS A PLEASURE' (1998). After a tour alongside The PROMISE RING, things looked bleak when LYMAN picked up sticks again; this time replacement GREG STEFFKE only managed a year in the job before COMPOUND RED cracked. • **Covered:** ONE (Three Dog Night).

Album rating: MR. MICROCOSM (*5) / ALWAYS A PLEASURE (*6) / PRESS PLAY AND RECORD collection (*5)

JOHN LYMAN – vocals / **MIKE ALLEN** (b.10 Feb'69) – guitar / **ANDY REIS** (b. 2 Oct'69) – bass / **DAVE HENDERLEITER** (b.25 Jun'69) – drums

not iss. — own label

1987. (ltd-c) <none> **HARD LEFT**
1987. (ltd-c) <none> **AT THE ALTAR**
– Slipknot / Tickled / Mudsling / Left side / Recall / At the altar / Things we fear / Lottery / Meet Betty / Spikoly / Wild thing.
1989. (ltd-c) <none> **COMPOUND RED**
– At the altar / Tickled / Control / Infectious / Every time / California / You don't like the life / Recall / Fireplace (live).
1990. (ltd-c) <none> **THE CENTER NEVER MOVES**
– Time of your life / Not me / Run away / Loosing it / My eye.
1991. (ltd-c) <none> **DAIRY MEAT AND HORSEPOWER**
– Time of your life / Candyland / Man with two toes / Black whole / Dispenser.

COMPOUND RED (cont) — THE GREAT INDIE DISCOGRAPHY — The 1990s

				not iss.	Hardspun
1992.	(ltd-7")	<01>	**ETHER NET. / ONE**	-	
1993.	(ltd-cd)	<02>	**MR. MICROCOSM**	-	

– She moves / Door to door / Dispenser / Suck / Mr. fix-it head / Song / Black hole / Carbondale / Time of your life / Ether net.

1995. (7"ep) **split w/ SANDBOX**

—— added JIM MINOR (b.23 Jan'74) – guitar

			not iss.	Lombardo
1996.	(ltd-7")	**ANGEL DANCED AWAY. / NOW I AM AN ANCHOR**	-	

			not iss.	Clique
1996.	(ltd-7")	**TOP RANK ASTRONAUT.** / Sidekick Kato: AUGUST 5th	-	

			DeSoto	DeSoto
1997.	(ltd-7")	**PETER PAN'S SHADOW. / TWENTY MILES UP (THERE IS NO AIR)**	-	
Aug 98.	(cd) <(DESOTO 25)> **ALWAYS A PLEASURE**			May98

– Versus the ocean / Return / Goodbye to Paris / Volcano kisses / Sway / Color of contrast / Cancel the sound / Sky / Speed so slow / The learning curve / Art of building. (re-iss. Apr00; same)

—— GREG STEFFKE (b.27 Dec'71) – vocals; repl. LYMAN

			not iss.	Tree
1999.	(ltd-7")	**BUILDING (version 2). / Very Secretary: NAGARKOT**	-	

—— disbanded late 1999; they became The CONDITION and issued a CD-EP; MINOR later joined NATIONAL SKYLINE

– compilations, etc. –

Dec 99. (d-cd) *Compound Red; <023370>* **PRESS PLAY AND RECORD** (1987-1999)   -

COMPULSION

Formed: King's Cross, North London … early 1992 by Irish exiles JOSEPHMARY, GARRET LEE, SID RAINEY and JAN-WILLEM ALKEMA, all veterans of the alternative music scene. JOSEPHMARY and LEE, as members of THEE AMAZING COLOSSAL MEN, had even been signed to 'Virgin' at one point although the deal fell through and the band split halfway through the recording of their second album. COMPULSION had no such headaches, forming their own label, 'Fabulon', after a year of twiddling their thumbs and fruitlessly seeking out pub gigs. An eponymous debut EP arrived in early '93, taking no prisoners with a razorwire guitar attack and vicious, strangulated vocals. The lyrical themes were equally uncompromising, the NIRVANA-esque 'RAPEJACKET' putting forward the idea that everyone is raped by life's hardships in one way or another. 'NINE FOURTH', meanwhile, recalled with disgust yet another Conservative electoral victory. With airplay from Radio One DJ, Mark Goodier, and support from the music press, COMPULSION already had a healthy buzz going by the release of follow-up EP, 'CASSEROLE'. Tours with CREDIT TO THE NATION and SHED SEVEN as well as an appearance at that year's Phoenix festival prompted interest from 'One Little Indian', through whom they released mini-set, 'SAFETY' and full-length debut album, 'COMFORTER' (1994). Drawing praise from both the indie and rock communities, the album carried on where the EP's left off, mixing sonic guitar barrages with more melancholy reflections and combining bitter realism with flights of surreal fancy and black humour. The record even nudged into the Top 60 although spin-off single, 'BASKETCASE', failed to chart. After a prolonged absence, COMPULSION returned in 1996 with follow-up album, 'THE FUTURE IS MEDIUM', apparently recorded in one session. After the split soon afterwards, GARRET LEE moved away to another pulsebeat via the big beat/electronica that was 'JACKNIFE LEE'. Signed to HOWIE B's 'Pussyfoot' records, he ventured out with a few EP's 'A DOG NAMED SNUGGLES' and 'COOKIES', which preceded debut set, 'MUY RICO!' (1999); BENTLEY RHYTHM ACE or The PROPELLERHEADS it was not!

Album rating: SAFETY mini (*5) / COMFORTER (*6) / THE FUTURE IS MEDIUM (*6) / I LIKE COMPULSION compilation (*7) / Jacknife Lee: MUY RICO! (*6) / PUNK ROCK HIGH ROLLER (*5)

JOSEPHMARY – vocals / **GARRET LEE** (b. Dublin, Ireland) – guitar / **SID RAINEY** – bass / **JAN-WILLEM ALKEMA** (b. Holland) – drums

			Fabulon	not iss.
Feb 93.	(12"ep) (FLON 12-01) **COMPULSION EP**			-

– Find time / Rapejacket / Easterman / Ninefourth / Purring not laughing / Accident ahead.

Apr 93. (12"ep) (FLON 12-02) **CASSEROLE EP**   -
– Yabba yabba yes yes yes / Crying / How do I breathe? / Here comes Ambrose Beasley / Security.

			One Little Indian	Elektra
Oct 93.	(m-lp/m-c/m-cd) (TPLP 49M/+C/CD) **SAFETY**			

– Why do we care / Plan / Joseph Engelheart / Pink and forty nine / Little Miss Whirlwind / Little marks.

Feb 94. (12"ep/cd-ep) (85 TP12/TP7CD) **MALL MONARCHY**   -
– Mall monarchy / A little mistake / Galvanised / F. Byron Farnsworth.

Mar 94. (cd-ep) <66228-2> **BOOGIE WOOGIE**   -
– Accident ahead / Ninefourth / Yabba yabba yes yes yes / Why do we care? / Find time.

			One Little Indian	Interscope
Mar 94.	(lp/c/cd) (TPLP 59/+C/CD) <92456> **COMFORTER**			59	Jun94

– Rapejacket / Delivery / Mall monarchy / Ariadne / Late again / Air-raid for the neighbours / Why do we care? / Yancy Dangerfield's delusions / Lovers / I am John's brain / Eating / Bad cooking / Dick, Dale, Rick and Ricky / Domestique / Oh my fool life / Jean could be wrong. (cd+=) – COMPULSION + CASSEROLE (ep tracks) (cd re-iss. Jan99; same)

Jun 94. (c-s) (95 TP7C) **BASKETCASE / LATE NIGHT TV**   -
(12"+=/cd-s+=) (95 TP12/TP7CD) – Bagelflask / Children of Ausburg.

Feb 96. (7") (105 TP7) **QUESTION TIME FOR THE PROLES. / SPOTLIGHT INTO SPACE**   -
(cd-s) (105 TP7CD) – ('A'side) / Millions / Drop / Burst.

May 96. (lp/c/cd) (TPLP 79/+C/CD) **THE FUTURE IS MEDIUM**   -
– All we heard was a dull thud / Question time for the proles / Juvenile scene detective / It's great / They're breeding the grey things again / Fast songs / Western culture collector / Happy monsters / Belly laugh / Is this efficient living? / Down the edifice / Happy ending / Burst / Lost on Abbey Road / Spotlight into space / Me. (cd re-iss. Jan99; same)

Jun 96. (7"/c-s) (115 TP7/+C) **JUVENILE SCENE DETECTIVE. / TOP OF THE WORLD**   -
(cd-s+=) (115 TP7CD) – Uniformity is go / After you with that pistol.
(12") (115 TP12ST) – ('A'mixes; Howie B / Graham Massey / Scanner / Static).
(cd-s+=) (115 TP7CDL) – ('A'-Howie B's Flesh Wound).

—— disbanded after above

– compilation, etc. –

Jun 02. (cd) *One Little Indian; (TPLP 850CD)* **I LIKE COMPULSION**
– Mall monarchy / Belly laugh / Accident ahead / Eating / Juvenile scene detective / Yabba yabba yes yes yes / Domestique / How do I breathe? / Rapejacket / All we heard was a dull thud / Why do we care? / Basketcase / Question time for the proles / Western culture collector / Fast songs / Easterman / Jean could be wrong.

JACKNIFE LEE

GARRET LEE – vocals, electronics

		Pussyfoot	not iss.
Oct 98.	(cd-ep) (PUSSY 030CD) **JACKNIFE PROUDLY ANNOUNCE THE RETURN OF THE GOLDEN AGE OF THE SHOWBAND**		-

– A dog named Snuggles / Kati Rocky / Sweet potato / Toot sweet boogie woogie.

Apr 99. (12"ep/cd-ep) (PUSSY/+CD 033) **KITTY LITTER EP**   -
– Cookies / Here kitty kitty / Brown glitter. (re-iss. Jul99; same)

May 99. (d-lp/cd) (PUSSYLP/+CD 017) **MUY RICO!**   -
– Here kitty kitty / Cookies / Miss Whopper / Brown glitter / A dog named Snuggles / Spermy daydream / Toot sweet boogie woogie / Sweet potato / Kati Rocky.

		Palm Pictures	Palm Pictures
Mar 00.	(12"ep)(cd-ep) (12PP 7016-1)(PPCD 7016-2) **BURSTIN' OFF THE BACKBEAT. / 1972 SQUAREDANCE DOCUMENTARY IN SOUND / BURSTIN' OFF THE BACKBEAT (Jacknife Lee mix)**		-
May 00.	(12"ep)(cd-ep) (12PP 7031-1)(PPCD 7031-2) **ALOHA SATELLITE SPECIAL (mixes)**		-
Jun 00.	(cd/d-lp) (<PALM CD/LP 2024>) **PUNK ROCK HIGH ROLLER**		Jan01

– 1970's dictator chic / Aloha satellite special / Do your thing cornball / I love your sauce / I think about you / Easy / Cookies / Juice machine / Shush dafty / My baby got the beat / Burstin' off the backbeat / Jacknife is your friend, let me in.

Oct 00. (7") (PP7 7039-1) **EASY. / IT TAKES POUND COIN LOVE**   -
(cd-s+=) (PPCD 7039-2) – Punk rock high roller.

CONDITION BLUE (see under ⇒ SPARE SNARE)

CONFETTI (see under ⇒ FAT TULIPS)

Bobby CONN

Born: Chicago, Illinois, USA. CONN originally broke through with local outfit CONDUCENT. The weird, wonderful and at times fairly disturbing CONN began playing with the prog-rockers in 1989 and remained there until their break-up in 1994 when he decided to go it alone. He rapidly made a name for himself in the city's alternative scene with his gloriously mad live sets which would veer from strange modes of dress and make-up to some fairly unconventional interplay with the audience. With the assistance of ex-CONDUCENT member DJ LE DEUCE on turntables (electric violin supplied by MONICA BOU BOU), CONN cut several EPs over the next two years and made a proper full-length debut in 1997 with the eponymously titled 'BOBBY CONN'. This set showcased his alternative rock credentials although this labelling did not really pin down the kind of sonic craziness he and his cohorts unleashed. The tracks came in all sorts of colours from disco-tinged rock to tracks like 'WHO'S THE PAUL #16' which supplied the listener with slowed down samples from PAUL McCARTNEY's back catalogue. Although at times the set seems a little vacuous, CONN's own musical skill managed to make it an interesting listen. He was also lucky to have the support of his hometown's own Wicker Park avant garde music scene which had rallied round and boosted the careers of such luminaries as grrrl rioter LIZ PHAIR and helped catapult him into the bigger musical arena with his follow-up album 'RISE UP!' (1998). The ensuing year saw the issue of the unhinged but great EP 'LLOVESSONNGS' which included a weird version of Badfinger's massively covered track 'WITHOUT YOU'. Moving into the next century saw CONN still with the support of BOU BOU – plus JONNY RIDE, NICK SULA, JONATHAN JOHN and COLBY STARCK – for his third LP proper 'THE GOLDEN AGE' (2001), a record which displayed his now fairly appealing ability to mix genres and play proverbial magpie with riffs and melody lifted from the pantheon of rock and pop.

Album rating: BOBBY CONN (*5) / RISE-UP! (*7) / THE GOLDEN AGE (*5)

BOBBY CONN – vocals, guitars, piano, drums / with various session people incl. DYLAN POSA, WEASEL WALTER, THYMME JONES, MONICA BOUBOU + JEFF DAY

	not iss.	CDC Inter..
1995. (7") WHO'S THE PAUL? / THE SPORTSMAN	-	

	Atavistic	Truckstop
May 97. (7") <672> NEVER GET AHEAD. / ME, MOST OF ALL	-	
May 97. (cd) (ALP 302CD) <2> **BOBBY CONN**		

– Overture / Axis '67 (part 1) / No kids, no money / Never get ahead / Who's the Paul? #16 / Who's the Paul? #33 / Payback / The sportsman / Axis '67 (part 3). *(re-iss. Mar02; same)*

	Atavistic	Thrill Jockey
Sep 98. (lp/cd) (ALP 306CD) <THRILL 59/+CD> **RISE-UP!**		

– The twilight of the empire / Rise up! / Axis '67 (part 2) / United nations / California / Passover *[not on lp]* / A conversation / Baby man / White bread / Lullaby / Ominous drone / Rise up, now!. *(UK lp-iss.on 'Thrill Jockey'; THRILL 59) (re-iss. Mar02; same)*

Dec 99. (12"ep/cd-ep) <(THRILL 75/+CD)> **LLOVESSONNGS**
– Free love / Virginia / Without you / Maria B.

— his next line-up **MONICA BOU BOU** – electric violin / **COLBY STARCK** – drums / **JONATHAN JOHN** – bass, keyboards / **NICK SULA** – keyboards

Oct 01. (lp/cd) <(THRILL 84/+CD)> **THE GOLDEN AGE**
– A taste of luxury / Angels / You've come a long way / The best years of our lives / Winners / The golden age / No revolution / Pumper / Whores. *(re-iss. May02; same)*

CONTAINE (see under ⇒ VERSUS)

COOPER TEMPLE CLAUSE

Formed: Reading, England ... 1999 by vocalist BEN GAUTREY, TOM BELLAMY, DAN FISHER, DIDZ, KIERAN MAHON and JOHN HARPER. Like a mad hybrid between KULA SHAKER and GAY DAD, The COOPER TEMPLE CLAUSE were rocking out in a bad/good way, while slyly winking at their newly composed fanbase. We can imagine it: six geezers (with deliberately 'ironic' mullet hair-cuts) from Reading, playing trash glam Britrock and being crowned as NME darlings. Yet for a band that were supposed to be christening a new type of Brit-rock, The COOPER TEMPLE CLAUSE's debut EP 'THE HARDWARE' (in March 2001) recycled the old GAY DAD, WARM JETS, DANDY WARHOLS vibe that simply made them look like stringent copycats. However, after the guitar strumming pop-rock double-A single 'FILM-MAKER' / 'BEEN TRAINING DOGS' (a Top 20 hit early 2002), CTC came of age through their debut UK Top 30 album 'SEE THIS THROUGH AND LEAVE'. Featuring hit-to-be, 'WHO NEEDS ENEMIES?', the album was relentless to the end; if you were sick of OASIS and the Brit-rock crew, this was for you.

Album rating: SEE THIS THROUGH AND LEAVE (*7)

BEN GAUTREY – vocals / **DAN FISHER** – guitar / **TOM BELLAMY** – guitar, effects / **KIERAN MAHON** – keyboards / **DIDZ HAMMOND** – bass / **JON HARPER** – drums

	Morning-BMG	BMG Inter..
Mar 01. (d7"ep; 1 white) (MORNING 2) **THE HARDWARE EP**		-
– The Devil walks in the sand / Solitude / Way out west / Sister soul.		
May 01. (cd-ep) (MORNING 5) **THE WARFARE EP**		
– Panzer attack / I'll still write / Mansell.		
(d7"ep; 1 white+=) (MORNING 6) – Panzer attack (acoustic).		
Sep 01. (7") (MORNING 11) **LET'S KILL MUSIC. / GIRL INK AGE**	41	-
(cd-s) (MORNING 9) – ('A'side) / Panzer attack (Dirty Sanchez remix) / ('A'-video).		
(cd-s) (MORNING 10) – ('A'side) / My darling (nasty angel) / ('A'-Dirty Sanchez remix).		
Dec 01. (cd-ep) <29903> **THE HARDWARE EP + THE WARFARE EP**	-	
Jan 02. (7"/cd-s) (MORNING 17/15) **FILM-MAKER. / BEEN TRAINING DOGS**	20	-
(cd-s+=) (MORNING 16) – Safe enough distance away.		
Feb 02. (cd/d-lp) (MORNING 18/20) <92034> **SEE THIS THROUGH AND LEAVE**	27	
– Did you miss me? / Film-maker / Panzer attack / Who needs enemies? / Amber / Digital observations / Let's kill music / 555-4823 / Been training dogs / The lake / Murder song. *(d-cd-iss. +=; MORNING 19)* – The Devil walks in the sand / Way out west / I'll still write / Panzer attack (live) / Let's kill music (live) / Film-maker (video) / Let's kill music (video) / Been training dogs (live).		
May 02. (cd-s) (MORNING 23) **WHO NEEDS ENEMIES? / BEFORE THE MOOR / ONE QUICK FIX**	22	-
(cd-s) (MORNING 24) – ('A'side) / Lapitu (bedtime story) / Not quite enough.		
(cd-s) (MORNING 25) – ('A'side) / Jesus, you smoke too / ('A'-enhanced video).		

COP SHOOT COP

Formed: Brooklyn, New York, USA ... summer '88 by singer/bassist TOD A (ASHLEY), DAVE QUIMET, PHIL PULEO and sampler JAMES COLEMAN; second bassist (JACK) NATZ was added in '89. Operating from the same seething well of unrelenting negativity as NY "No Wave" pioneers like DNA and MARS, COP SHOOT COP set out to create hateful R&R noise in the most uncompromising, unlistener-friendly style they could muster. Utilising a rhythmic, guitarless sound driven by two bass players, the band made their debut in 1988 with the mini-set, 'HEADKICK FACSIMILE'. Also released on the 'Supernatural Organization' imprint was their 1990 follow-up, 'CONSUMER REVOLT', subsequently unveiled in the UK a few years later on 'Big Cat'. By this time, CSC had already showcased their anti-pop racket on 'WHITE*NOISE' (1991), although surprisingly, given their militant opposition to corporate culture, the band signed a major label deal with 'Interscope'. First up was an EP, 'SUCK CITY', followed by by the slightly more consumer friendly 'ASK QUESTIONS LATER' (1993), an album that found the noisemeisters allowing their claustrophobic sound more room to breathe. Similarly, 1994's 'RELEASE' was easier on the ear with repeated listening, although as far as NY underground kudos is concerned, COP SHOOT COP were still taking no prisoners. However, shortly afterwards the group disbanded (see below).

Album rating: HEADKICK FACSIMILE mini (*4) / CONSUMER REVOLT (*4) / WHITE-NOISE (*5) / ASK QUESTIONS LATER (*7) / RELEASE (*6)

TOD A. (b. ASHLEY) – bass, vocals / **DAVE QUIMET** – samples / **PHIL PULEO** – drums, metal

	not iss.	Supernatural Organization
1988. (m-lp) **HEADKICK FACSIMILE**	-	

– Shine on Elizabeth / Mistake / Smash retro / Triumphal theme / Lie / Fire in the hole. *(re-iss. 1994 +=; > – Robert Tilton handjob.*

— added **JACK NATZ** – bass + **JIM COLEMAN** (aka FILER – samples – samples

1989. (12"ep) **PIECEMAN** — -
– Robert Tilton handjob / Disconnected 666 / Eggs for rib (speedway).

— now without QUIMET

Feb 90. (lp) **CONSUMER REVOLT** — -
– Lo. Com. denom / She's like a shot / Waiting for the punchline / Disconnected 666 / Smash retro / Burn your bridges / Consume / Fire in the hole / Pity the bastard / Down come the Mickey / Hurt me baby / System test / Eggs for rib. *(UK + re-iss. Apr92 on 'Big Cat' lp/cd/cd; ABB 33/+C/CD)*

	Big Cat	Big Cat
Oct 91. (lp/c/cd) <(ABB 29/+C/CD)> **WHITE*NOISE**		

– Discount rebellion / Traitor – Martyr / Coldest day of the year / Feel good / Relief / Empires collapse / Corporate protopop / Heads I win, tails you lose / Chameleon man / Where's the money? / If tomorrow ever comes / Hung again.

	Big Cat	Interscope
Aug 92. (12"ep/cd-ep) (ABB 39 T/SCD) <96116> **SUCK CITY EP**		Nov92
– Nowhere / Days will pass / We shall be changed / Suck city (here we come).		
Apr 93. (d-lp/d-cd) (ABB 45/+CD) <92250> **ASK QUESTIONS LATER**		Mar93
– Surprise, surprise / Room 429 / Nowhere / Migration / Cut to the chase / $10 bill / Seattle / Furnace / Israeli dig / Cause and effect / Got no soul / Everybody loves you (when you're dead) / All the clocks are broken.		
Jun 93. (12"green-ep/cd-ep) (ABB 53 T/SCD) **$10 BILL. / CAUSE AND EFFECT / SEATTLE**		-
Dec 93. (12"ep/cd-ep) (ABB 54 T/SCD) **ROOM 429 E.P.**		-
– Room 429 / Ambulance song / Fragment / Shine on Elizabeth (live).		

— added **STEVE McMILLEN** – guitar, trumpet

Aug 94. (12"/cd-s) (ABB 68 T/SCD) **TWO AT A TIME**	-	w-drawn
Sep 94. (lp/cd) (ABB 69/+CD) <92424> **RELEASE**		

– Interference / It only hurts when I breathe / Last legs / Two at a time / Slackjaw / Lullaby / Any day now / Swimming in circles / Turning inside out / Ambulance song / Suckerpunch / The divorce / Money-drunk.

Jan 95. (12"ep/cd-ep) (ABB 78 T/SCD) **ANY DAY NOW / NEW GOD. / THE QUEEN OF SHINBONE ALLEY / TRANSMISSION**

	Submission	not iss.
Jul 96. (7"/cd-s; with MEATHEAD) (SUCK 3/+CD) **KILL A COP FOR CHRIST AND BRING US HIS HEAD**		-

— split later in '96 with TOD A forming veteran alt-rock supergroup, FIREWATER – QUIMET followed him in '97 after a spell with MOTHERHEAD BUG

CORAL

Formed: Hoylake, Liverpool, England ... 1996 by neighbourhood friends JAMES SKELLY, IAN SKELLY, PAUL DUFFY, LEE SOUTHALL, BILL RYDER-JONES and finally NICK POWER on organ. Picking up were The LA'S left off, fellow scousers, The CORAL unleashed their Mersey-flavoured debut single 'SHADOWS FALL' in 2001 and were, instantly, hailed by NME as the best new band in England. 'THE OLDEST PATH' EP was released in the same year, as hype surrounding the band began to reach fever pitch. The momentum was carried into 2002 which saw the release of the 'SKELETON KEY' EP and also their self-titled UK Top 5 debut album. A joyous, neo-psychedelic record, the eponymous 'THE CORAL', established the group as natural successors to the long line of great Liverpudlian bands and, no, that does not include SPACE.

Album rating: THE CORAL (*8)

JAMES SKELLY – vocals, guitar / **LEE SOUTHALL** – guitar, vocals / **NICK POWER** – organ / **BILL RYDER-JONES** – guitar, trumpet / **PAUL DUFFY** – bass, saxophone / **IAN SKELLY** – drums

	Deltasonic	not iss.
Jul 01. (cd-s) (DLTCD 1) **SHADOWS FALL / SIMON DIAMOND / A SPARROW'S SONG**		-
Dec 01. (cd-ep) (DLTCD 3) **THE OLDEST PATH EP**		-
– The oldest path / God knows / Short ballad / Flies.		

	Sony	Sony
Apr 02. (cd-ep) (672522-2) <87023> **SKELETON KEY EP**		

– Skeleton key / Dressed like a cow / Darkness / Sheriff John Brown / Skeleton key (video). <US-only+=> – The oldest path.

	Deltasonic	Sony
Jul 02. (7") (DLT 005) **GOODBYE. / GOOD FORTUNE**	21	
(cd-s+=) (DLTCD 005) – Travelling circus / ('A-CD rom).		
(cd-s) (DLTCD2 005) – ('A'side) / Dressed like a cow (live) / Goodbye (live) / The Coral mini movie (video).		
Jul 02. (cd/lp) (DLT CD/LP 006) <508478> **THE CORAL**	5	Feb03

– Spanish man / I remember when / Shadows fall / Dreaming of you / Simon Diamond / Goodbye / Waiting for the heartaches / Skeleton key / Wildfire / Badman / Calenders and clocks. *(lp+=)* – Simian technology. *(hidden cd track+=)* – Time travel.

CORNDOLLY

Formed: Champaign-Urbana, Illinois, USA . . . 1992 by AMY GOSSOW and ANGIE HEATON. Signed to the 'Mud' label, these post-feminist rockers debuted with 'COME OUT / SEX KITTEN', and followed up with the 'HUMAN CANNONBALL' EP in 1993. CORNDOLLY proved a short-lived set-up though, and HEATON soon formed a new band, LIQUORETTE, releasing the album 'WHILE YOU WORK, I SLEEP'. HEATON finally went solo in 1996, and recorded 'CALAMITIES AND RESTITUTION'. Reminiscent of SCRAWL and the GO-GO's, her solo debut contained soulful ('TRANS AM') and tender ('I CAN'T REMEMBER') moments. Further enhancing her solo career and reputation, 1998's 'SPARKLE' was even more confident and assured than her debut. The ebullient 'FLYING' is just one of several highlights from this excellent release. • **Covered:** LIQUORETTE covered Hole's 'ASKING FOR IT'.

Album rating: CORNDOLLY (*6) / Liquorette: WHEN YOU WORK I SLEEP (*5) / Angie Heaton: CALAMITIES AND RESTITUTION (*5) / SPARKLE (*6)

AMY GOSSOW – vocals, bass / **WENDY O'NEAL** – guitar, vocals / **ANGIE HEATON** – drums, vocals

			Mud	Mud
1992.	(7") **COME OUT. / SEX KITTEN**		-	-
1993.	(cd) <*MUDCD 008*> **CORNDOLLY**		-	

– Waterbed / Car crash / Sex kitten / Come out / Human cannonball / Squirting banana dildo / No song / Afterschool special / The difference / Angie / Mudfucker.

1993.	(7"m) <*MUD 012*> **HUMAN CANNONBALL. / SQUIRTING BANANA DILDO / NO SONG**			
			not iss.	Dalmatian
1994.	(7") <*002*> **AFTERSCHOOL SPECIAL. / THE DIFFERENCE**		-	

— ANGIE HEATON went solo after a time with LIQUORETTE, WENDY O'NEAL went on to release the single, 'A SIMPLE OPERATION'

LIQUORETTE

— aka **ANGIE HEATON** with a few others

1995. (cd) <*MUDCD 014*> **WHEN YOU WORK I SLEEP**
– Don't quit your job Joan / I work in a mall / Once mommy would buy me new shirts / Video game / Oh Sheila / Asking for it / No no no / Seventy-two hours / Trinket land / When you work I sleep / Little girl street / Gum sharers / Look around / Molly McGarvey / Cindianapolis / Margaret Los / Vic Frith / Light bulb / Santa Claus / Prancer and dancer / What is purchased is what is pure and chaste. *(UK-iss.Feb98; same as US)*

ANGIE HEATON

- vocals, guitar, keyboards / with **HENRY FRAYNE** – bass, guitar

1996. (cd) <*MUDCD 015*> **CALAMITIES AND RESTITUTION**
– Polly do you wanna? / See how you are / I can't remember / Fall / Trans am / So shy / Where's Ed / Pretty as pretty does / Johnette Napolitano / The pleiades / Supperstar / Savior / Easy chair / Gold comes from broken hearts.

— next with **NICK RUDD, CHARLIE DODD + ADAM SCHMITT**

Feb 98. (cd) <*(MUDCD 029)*> **SPARKLE**
– Let go / Flying / Rollerskate / Hydroplane / Umbrella Sarah / Super falling star / You've got time / Sparkle / Walk away Renee / Blacksmith / If you ever change your mind.

CORNELIUS

Born: KEIGO OYAMADA, 27 Jan'69, Setagaya-ku, Tokyo, Japan. After beginning his career in a Japanese teen band, FLIPPER'S GUITAR, CORNELIUS (who took his nom de plume from a character in the cult film, 'The Planet Of The Apes') branched out into the world of production/remix work (his credits include PIZZICATO 5 and MONEY MARK) while running his own label, 'Trattoria'. Inevitably, this jack of all trades also released his own solo work augmented by his ever-faithful sidekick, BRYAN, who functions as his personal translator as well as being a DJ and lyricist. Having achieved near superstar status in Japan, CORNELIUS turned his attention to Western shores signing to 'Matador'. Early in '98, the first fruits of his labour emerged in the shape of the 'FREE FALL' single, while the follow-up single, 'CHAPTER 8 . . .' was another to be taken from his debut set, 'FANTASMA'. Pilfering from various eras of pop culture, the "monkey" man from the East created a vertible cornucopia of bleeps, tunes and samples; the duo themselves describe their sound as akin to a hard/loungecore MICHAEL JACKSON. Nearly four years on from 'FANTASMA', KEIGO reconvened his trippy CORNELIUS project. 'POINT' (2002) was another exotic pot-pourri of playful sounds from neo-psychedelia to bossa nova and retro-New Wave; it was hard to see how the man could fail.

Album rating: THE FIRST QUESTION AWARD (*6) / 69/96 (*8) / FANTASMA (*8) / POINT (*7)

KEIGO OYAMADA – vocals, guitar, bass, drums / **BRYAN** – lyrics

			not iss.	Trattoria
Sep 93.	(cd-ep) <*PSCR 5045*> **HOLIDAYS IN THE SUN ep**		-	- Japan

– Raise your hand together (Cornelius mix) / Raise your hand together (320 light years mix) / Diamond bossa / The sun is my enemy (long) / The sun is my enemy (sunset boo-goo-loo mix).

Sep 93.	(cd-s) <*PSDR 5012*> **THE SUN IS MY ENEMY / DIAMOND BOSSA / THE SUN IS MY ENEMY (instrumental)**	-	- Japan
Nov 93.	(cd-s) <*PSDR 5036*> **PERFECT RAINBOW / PELE / PERFECT RAINBOW (instrumental)**	-	- Japan
Jan 94.	(cd-s) <*PSCR 5050*> **(YOU CAN'T ALWAYS GET) WHAT YOU WANT / THE FIRST QUESTION AWARD – PREVIEW / (YOU CAN'T ALWAYS GET) WHAT YOU WANT (instrumental)**	-	- Japan
Feb 94.	(cd) <*PSCR 5080*> **THE FIRST QUESTION AWARD**	-	- Japan

– The sun is my enemy / (You can't always get) What you want / Silent snow stream / Perfect rainbow / Bad moon rising / Cannabis / Raise your hand together (Cornelius mix) / The back door to Heaven / Theme from First Question Award / The love parade / Moon light story.

Jun 95.	(cd-s) <*PSDR 5070*> **MOON LIGHT STORY / INTO SOMETHING (live) / MOON LIGHT STORY (instrumental)**	-	- Japan
Nov 95.	(cd) <*PSCR 5420*> **69/96**	-	- Japan

– 69/96 a space odyssey prelude (in Atami) / Moon walk / Brand new season / Volunteer ape man (disco) / 1969 (case of Monsieur Kamayatsu) / How do you feel? / 1969 / Last night in Africa / 1996 / Blow my mind / 69/96 girl meets cassette / Concerto No.3 from The Four Seasons (pink bloody sabbath) / Heavy metal thunder / Rock-96 / World's end humming (reprise in Hawaii) / A68.SE.

		Matador	Matador
Jun 96.	(cd) <*PSCR 5480*> **96/69** (remixes)		- Japan
Mar 98.	(7") *(OLE 308-7)* **FREE FALL. / CLASH**		-

(cd-s+=) *(OLE 308-2)* – Brand new season / Typewriter lesson.

May 98. (7") *(OLE 319-7)* **CHAPTER 8 – SEASHORE AND HORIZON. / COUNT FIVE OR SIX**
(cd-s+=) *(OLE 319-2)* – The micro Disneycal world tour / Fantasma spot.

Jun 98. (cd/lp) *(OLE 300-1/-1>)* **FANTASMA**
– Mic check / Micro Disneycal world tour / New music machine / Clash / Count five or six / Magoo opening / Star fruits surf rider / Chapter 8 – Seashore and horizon / Free fall / 2010 / God only knows / Thank you for the music / Fantasma.

Oct 98. (12"/cd-s) *(OLE 320-1/-2)* **STAR FRUITS SURF RIDER / STAR FRUITS BLUE (Damon Albarn mix)**
(cd-s) *(OLE 320-4)* – ('A'side) / Ball in kick off / Star fruits green.

Mar 99. (cd) *(OLE 349-2)* **FM (FANTASMA REMIXES)**
Mar 99. (cd; Various Artists) *(OLE 350-2)* **CM**
Feb 02. (12"/cd-s) *(OLE 544-1/-2)* **DROP. / DROP (Kings Of Convenience mix) / DROP (Herbert mix)**
Feb 02. (cd/lp) *(OLE 332-2/-1)* **POINT (FROM NAKEMEGURO TO EVERYWHERE)** Jan02
– Bug (electric last minute) / Point of view point / Smoke / DRop / Another view point / Tone twilight zone / Bird watching at inner forest / I hate hate / Brazil / Fly / Nowhere.

Aug 02. (12") *(OLE 555-1)* **POINT OF VIEW POINT. / POINT OF VIEW POINT (Yann Tomita mix) / ANOTHER VIEW POINT**
(cd-s+=) *(OLE 555-2)* – ('A'video).

CORNERSHOP

Formed: Preston, England . . . 1987, evolving from GENERAL HAVOC by Asian songwriting brothers, TJINDER and AVTAR SINGH. They first came to attention of the music press late in 1992, when they publicly derided MORRISSEY for his alleged racist leanings. Already signed to the up and coming 'Wiiija' label, they delivered their debut EP, 'IN THE DAYS OF FORD CORTINA', in a blaze of publicity. Described as JESUS & MARY CHAIN with sitars, the unconventional Sikh/white thrash fusion was entertaining if hardly professional. Inevitably the initial press hype soon backfired on them, although they struggled on through a clutch of patchy albums including 'HOLD ON IT HURTS' (1994) and 'WOMAN'S GOTTA HAVE IT' (1995). Major alterations were subsequently carried out on the 'SHOP, after which TJINDER re-opened for business in 1997 with the sonic nirvana of 'WHEN I WAS BORN FOR THE 7th TIME'. A surprise Top 40 success, well worthy of merit with its consummate blend of hip hop, Indian folk, country and indie funk, the album spawned the classic 'BRIMFUL OF ASHA' (a ltd-edition original release, it went on to hit the top of the charts in early '98). The record also featured a suitably exotic version of the Beatles' 'NORWEGIAN WOOD (THIS BIRD HAS FLOWN)', while 'CANDYMAN' took elements from LARRY CORYELL's 'The Opening'. CORNERSHOP subsequently toured the States and Europe for almost a year after the album's release. Mentally and physically exhausted, the irate TJINDER SINGH and his equally worn associate BEN AYRES hibernated in a South London studio, preparing their off-shoot band CLINTON's debut album (following a back-catalogue of three 12" singles over four years). Released on their own 'Meccico' imprint (through 'Hut'), 'DISCO AND THE HALFWAY TO DISCONTENT' (1999), didn't exactly sound like the kind of record that was made by two men who were on the verge of musical breakdown. Opening track, 'PEOPLE POWER IN THE DISCO HOUR', made the speakers pound like a nomadic tribesman beating from the inside. Other tracks dabbled in sitar techniques, that for once, didn't sound like some mystical KULA SHAKER thing! The theme of disco ran throughout the set, occasionally taking inspiration from their dub reggae peers, proving that CLINTON had, most definitely, danced those blues away! CORNERSHOP returned in glorious style in 2002, courtesy of album 'HANDCREAM FOR A GENERATION'. The set featured the single 'LESSONS LEARNED FROM ROCKY 1 TO ROCKY 3', a brilliantly funky, fuzz disco tune which reinstated the band's status and had the fans all dancing at the same time. Although the set wasn't just a loose collection of modern disco-rock, it also delved deeply into psychedelia and even, sometimes, Brit pop (OASIS bassist PAUL McGUIGAN made a feted appearance). While managing to meld styles from Eastern and Western music, CORNERSHOP also played with the formula which made 'BRIMFUL . . .' so special in the first place; catchy choruses and even catchier instrumental hooks.

Album rating: HOLD ON IT HURTS (*5) / WOMAN'S GOTTA HAVE IT (*5) / WHEN I WAS BORN FOR THE 7th TIME (*9) / HANDCREAM FOR A GENERATION (*7) / Clinton: DISCO AND THE HALFWAY TO DISCONTENT (*8)

TJINDER SINGH (b. 8 Feb'68, New Cross, Wolverhampton, England) – guitar / **AVTAR SINGH** (b.11 May'65, Punjab, India) – bass, vocals / **DAVID CHAMBERS** (b.1969, Lincoln, England) – drums / **ANTHONY SAFFERY** – sitar / **NEIL MILNER** – tapes

	Chapati Heat	not iss.

Dec 91. (7"ep; as the GENERAL HAVOC) *(BIRD 1)* **FAST JASPAL EP**
– Moonshine / Vacuum cleaner / Another cup of tea, Arch Deacon?

—— **BEN AYRES** (b. BENEDICT, 30 Apr'68, St John's, Canada) – guitar, vocals; repl. ANTHONY + NEIL

	Wiiija	Merge

Jan 93. (7"ep; some colrd) *(WIJ 019V)* **IN THE DAYS OF FORD CORTINA EP**
– Waterlogged / Moonshine / Kawasaki (more heat than chapati) / Hanif Kureishi scene.
Apr 93. (10"ep) *(WIJ 22V)* **LOCK STOCK & DOUBLE-BARREL**
– England's dreaming / Trip easy / Summer fun in a beat up Datsun / Breaking every rule language English.
(cd-ep+=) *(WIJ 22CD)* – (hidden track).
Jul 93. (m-cd) *(WAKEUP 001)* **ELVIS SEX-CHANGE**
– (above 2 EP's)
Jan 94. (7"ep/cd-ep) *(WIJ 29 V/CD)* **READERS' WIVES EP**
– Readers' wives / Inside Rani (short version) / Tandoori chicken.
Jan 94. (cd/c/lp) *(WIJ 030 CD/C/V)* <MRG 74> **HOLD ON IT HURTS** Jan95
– Jason Donovan – Tessa Sanderson / Kalluri's radio / Readers' wives / Change / Inside Rani (long version) / Born disco; died heavy metal / Counteraction / Where d'u get your information / Tera mera pyar / You always said my language would get me into trouble. *(lp w/ free 7")* – BORN DISCO; DIED HEAVY METAL (disco mix). / ENGLAND'S DREAMING
Mar 94. (7"ep/cd-ep) *(WIJ 033 V/CD)* **BORN DISCO; DIED HEAVY METAL. / THE SAFETY OF OBJECTS / REHOUSED**
Apr 94. (7") *(XPI 24)* **SEETAR MAN. / (track by Blood Sausage)**
(above issued on 'Clawfist')
—— CHAMBERS departed before below album

	Wiiija	Luaka Bop – Warners

Apr 95. (7"etched) *(LTD 004)* **6 A.M. JULLANDAR SHERE**
May 95. (cd/lp) *(WIJ 045 CD/V)* <46018> **WOMAN'S GOTTA HAVE IT**
– 6 a.m. Jullandar shere / Hong Kong book of Kung Fu / Roof rack / My dancing days are done / Call all destroyer / Camp orange / Never leave yourself (vocal overload mix) / Jamsimran king / Wog / Looking for a way in / 7.20 a.m. Jullander shere.
Aug 95. (7") *(CIP 101)* **MY DANCING DAYS ARE DONE. / Prohibition: I AM NOT A FISH** – – French
(above issued on French label, 'Bruit Distordu')
Feb 96. (12"ep/cd-ep) *(WIJ 048 V/CD)* **6 A.M. JULLANDAR SHERE: The Grid & Star Liner mixes**
– (Jeh Jeh mix) / (All Fetters Loose mix) / (original).
—— AVTAR departed around 1995/96, leaving **TJINDER + BEN** to recruit **PETER BENGRY** – percussion / **ANTHONY SAFFREY** – sitar, harmonium, keyboards (returned) / **NICK SIMMS** – drums, tambourene
Jun 96. (12"ep) *(WIJ 049V)* <43648> **W.O.G. – THE U.S. WESTERN ORIENTAL MIXES**
– (original) / (Freaky's) / (Witchman's Assimilation) / Freaky's Acid DJ) / (Witchman's extended beats).
Dec 96. (12"etched) *(ROOT 011)* **BUTTER THE SOUL**
(above released on 'Art Bus')
Jun 97. (7") *(WIJ 70)* **GOOD SHIPS. / FUNKY DAYS ARE BACK AGAIN**
(12"+=/cd-s+=) *(WIJ 70 T/CD)* – ('A'-Intro – instrumental / 'B' extended beats mix)
Aug 97. (7") *(WIJ 75)* **BRIMFUL OF ASHA. / EASY WINNERS (part 1)** 60 –
(cd-s+=) *(WIJ 75CD)* – Rehoused / ('A'-Sofa Surfers mix).
(cd-s) *(WIJ 75CDX)* – ('A'side) / Easy winners (part 2) / Counteraction / ('A'-Mucho Macho mix).
(12") *(WIJ 75T)* – ('A'side) / It's Indian tobacco my friend.
Sep 97. (cd/c/d-lp) *(WIJ CD/MC/LP 1065)* <46576> **WHEN I WAS BORN FOR THE 7th TIME** 17 –
– Sleep on the left side / Brimful of Asha / Butter the soul / Chocolat / We're in yr corner / Funky days are back again / What is happening? / When the light appears boy / Coming up / Good shit / Good to be on the road back home again / It's Indian tobacco my friend / Candyman / State troopers / Norwegian wood (this bird has flown).
Nov 97. (12"etched) *(ROOT 014T)* **BRIMFUL OF ASHA (Norman Cook remix)**
Feb 98. (7"/c-s) *(WIJ 81/+MC)* **BRIMFUL OF ASHA. / ('A'-Norman Cook remix)** 1 –
(12"+=) *(ROOT 014T)* – ('A'-Norman Cook extended).
(cd-s++=) *(WIJ 81CD)* – U47S.
May 98. (c-s) *(WIJ 80C)* <44524> **SLEEP ON THE LEFT SIDE / ('A'-Les Rhythms Digitales mix)** 23 –
(12"+=/cd-s+=) *(WIJ 80 T/CD)* – ('A'-Ashley Beadle mix) / ('A'-Ashley Beadle extended).
Nov 98. (12"ltd) *(WIJ 093T)* **CANDYMAN (mixes; Rob Swift vocal & instrumental / Schizoid Man / Uptight Vienna)**
—— added **PAUL McGUIGAN** – bass (ex-OASIS)

	Wiiija	V2

Feb 02. (12") *(ROOT 22)* **LESSONS LEARNED FROM ROCKY I TO ROCKY III**
(12") *(ROOT 23)* – ('A'mixes).
Mar 02. (7") *(WIJ 129)* <27741> **LESSONS LEARNED FROM ROCKY I TO ROCKY III. / RETURNING FROM THE WRECKAGE** 37 May02
(cd-s+=) *(WIJ 129CD)* – ('A'-Osymyso mix).
(cd-s) *(WIJ 129CD2)* – ('A'-mixes; Cowcube / Midfield General instrumental / DEtroit Grand Pubahs).
Apr 02. (cd/lp) *(WIJ CD/LP 1115)* <27126> **HANDCREAM FOR A GENERATION** 30
– Heavy soup (with OTIS CLAY) / Staging the plaguing of the raised platform / Music plus 1 / Lessons learned from Rocky I to Rocky III / Wogs will walk / Motion the 11 / People power / Sounds super recordings / The London radar / Spectral mornings (with NOEL GALLAGHER) / Slip the drummer one / Heavy soup (outro).
Aug 02. (7") *(WIJ 130)* **STAGING. / GREEN P'S** –
(cd-s+=) *(WIJ 130CD)* – Lessons learned from Rocky I to Rocky III (video).
(cd-s) *(WIJ 130CD2)* – ('A'-Super Jaws mix) / Straight aces / Motion the 11 (Guigsy's mix).

CLINTON

—— alter-ego of **TJINDER + BEN**

	Wiiija	not iss.

Dec 94. (etched-12") *(JJAR 001)* **JAM JAR (Marv Johnson mix) / EVERYBODY KNOWS THAT THE MOST IMPORTANT PEOPLE SPEAK FIRST**
Sep 95. (etched-12") *(ROOT 010)* **SUPERLOOSE! (Bobby Austin mix) / FINANCIAL HEADACHE**
Apr 97. (12") *(ROOT 012)* **SUPERLOOSE! (Automator Hot Vox mix). / SUPERLOOSE! (Automator instrumental)**
Mar 99. (7") *(ROOT 013)* **DAVID D. CHAMBERS. / INSTRUMENTAL / VOCAL**

	Hut	Astralwerks

Aug 99. (12"/cd-s) *(HUT T/CD 116)* **BUTTONED DOWN DISCO. / ('A'-Scratch perverts boil in the bag mix) / ('A'-Fila Brazillia disco frisco mix)**
Sep 99. (cd/c/lp) *(CDHUT/HUTMC/HUTLP 56)* <ASW 48792-2> **DISCO AND THE HALFWAY TO DISCONTENT** Feb00
– People power in the disco hour / Saturday night and dancing / Buttoned down disco / Hip-hop bricks / Electric ice cream (Miami jammies) / G.T. road / Hot for May sound / Sing hosana / Mr. President / Giddian di rani / Before the fizz is gone / Welcome to Tokyo Otis Clay. <US+=> – David D. Chambers / Fila Brazillia disco Frisco mix.
Apr 00. (12"/cd-s) *(HUT T/CD 125)* <38700> **PEOPLE POWER IN THE DISCO (mixes; Wiseguys / Los Amigos Invisibles / Romanthony)** Feb00

CORPORATION OF NOISE
(see under ⇒ BALL, Edward; 70's section)

COSMIC ROUGH RIDERS

Formed: Castlemilk, Glasgow, Scotland . . . 1998 by one-time THIEVES vocalist DANIEL WYLIE and his guitar-playing buddy STEPHEN FLEMING. They began by recording a skeleton bones demo of tracks in a community centre-cum-studio (on a Glasgow Council grant) and through the forthcoming months, the pair found new members, GARY CUTHBERT, MARK BROWN and JAMES CLIFFORD. CRR also developed an important and equally compelling sound, borrowing styles from The BYRDS, NEIL YOUNG, GRAM PARSONS and even, at times, BRIAN WILSON. This was evident on their self-financed debut set, 'DELIVERANCE' (1999), which could be described as a mixed bag of neo-country TEENAGE FANCLUB fused with a Lo-Fi BEACH BOYS whispering away somewhere at the back of a spiritual surf club. 'UNGRATEFUL' was perhaps the sharpest opener on an album for some time, its steel-stringed guitar taking no prisoners; WYLIE's softly sung vocal was equal to the breezy accompaniment of his band. The COSMIC ROUGH RIDERS released their sophomore set, 'PANORAMA' (2000), to much critical acclaim, here and across the Atlantic(!). The record might well have been a soundtrack to a great Scottish western, if, erm, Westerns were, er, shot here. Again drawing references from such luminaries as the JAYHAWKS and current alt-country meisters KNIFE IN WATER, the album was more varied via musical scope, not to mention musical talent. Neatly structured songs, awash with violin, acoustic guitar and a crisp backing melody, suggested that even if the band failed at moments (e.g. 'BROTHER GATHER ROUND') began with a tremendous pop'n'rock riff but then faded to almost nothing), their passion and country spirit finally led them to the musical promised land. ALAN McGEE, ex-honcho at 'Creation' records, seemed more than impressed with the band's development and signed the group to his 'Poptones' imprint where they issued the single 'LOSER' and its parent long-player, 'ENJOY THE MELODIC SUNSHINE' (2000). Early the following year, they paid homage to the late, great ALEX HARVEY, by covering his 'ACTION STRASSE'; it was showcased on a BBCTV tribute. In July 2001, the CRR had their first UK Top 40 hit via 'REVOLUTION (IN THE SUMMERTIME?)', it looked like the band were heading for the big time. However, by the following March, WYLIE had opted for a solo venture leaving the rest to ponder their futures.

Album rating: DELIVERANCE (*8) / PANORAMA (*8) / ENJOY THE MELODIC SUNSHINE (*8)

DANIEL WYLIE (b. 2 Jan'72) – vocals (ex-THIEVES) / **STEPHEN FLEMING** – electric guitar / **GARY CUTHBERT** – acoustic guitar / **JAMES CLIFFORD** – bass / **MARK BROWN** – drums

Jun 99. (cd) (<RAFT 001>) **DELIVERANCE** — Raft / Raft
 – Ungrateful / Rape seed children / Patience / What's your sign / Country life / Still a mother's son / Baby, you're so free / Emily darling / Brand new car / Here comes my train / Lady in the lake / Glastonbury revisited / Garden of Eden / New day dawning. *(re-iss. Jul00; same)*

Mar 00. (cd) (<RAFT 002>) **PANORAMA**
 – Revolution (in the summertime) / Have you heard the news today / Brother gather round / The gun isn't loaded / Value of life / You've got me / Afterglow / The pain inside / The charm / I call her name / The loser / Can't get any closer / To be someone / Back home again.

 Poptones / not iss.
Oct 00. (7") *(MC 5015 S7)* **THE LOSER. / PAIN INSIDE**
Nov 00. (cd/lp) *(MC 5015 CD/LP)* **ENJOY THE MELODIC SUNSHINE**
 – Brother gather round / The gun isn't loaded / Glastonbury revisited / Baby, you're so free / Value of life / Revolution (in the summertime?) / Have you heard the news today / Sometime / Melanie / Pain inside / Charm / The loser / You've got me / Emily darling / Morning sun.

Feb 01. (7") *(MC 5033S)* **MELANIE. / UNIVERSAL THING**
 (cd-s+=) *(MC 5033SCD)* – Annie.
Apr 01. (7") *(MC 5042S)* **BABY, YOU'RE SO FREE. / NOTHING TO LOSE**
 (cd-s+=) *(MC 5042SCD)* – The sound of windchimes.
 (cd-s) *(MC 5042SCX)* – ('A'side) / Alright / Your eyes.
Jul 01. (7") *(MC 5047S)* **REVOLUTION (IN THE SUMMERTIME?). / MOVE ALONG** 35
 (cd-s+=) *(MC 5047SCD)* – The gun isn't loaded (live).
 (cd-s) *(MC 5047SCX)* – ('A'side) / River runs dry / ('A'-live).
Sep 01. (7") *(MC 5052S)* **PAIN INSIDE. / I GOT OVER YOU** 36
 (cd-s+=) *(MC 5052SCD)* – Camera shy.
 (cd-s) *(MC 5052SCX)* – ('A'side) / Laura Nyro / Melanic acoustic.

 — in Mar'02, WYLIE decided to leave; FLEMING took over vocal duties
Sep 02. (cd) *(MC 5060CD)* **PURE ESCAPISM** (compilation of B-sides)
 – Pain inside (remix) / Annie / Laura Nyro / I got over you / Camera shy / Universal thing / Nothing to lose / River runs dry / Sound of windchimes / Alright / Move along / Your eyes / Melanie (acoustic) / *(CD-Rom tracks)* – Melanie / Baby you're free / Revolution (in the summertime?) / Pain inside (remix).
 (above was issued in Japan in December 2001)

COTTON MATHER

Formed: Austin, Texas, USA ... 1991 by ROBERT HARRISON, WHIT WILLIAMS, MATT HOVIS and GREG THIBEAUX. Apparently NOEL GALLAGHER's favourite American indie outfit, COTTON MATHER have been playing simple, stripped-down independent rock'n'roll since they issued an ultra-rare demo/mini entitled 'CRAFTY FLOWER ARRANGER' in 1992. Egged-on by a small legion of fans and with record companies queing around the corner to sign them, they issued the clean-sheen of 'COTTON IS KING' (1994), a moderate debut, filled with what would become their signature British 60's sound. The sophomore 'KONTIKI' (1997) was a much more musically established set, with the band branching out on pianos, keyboards and tape hiss. This time, COTTON MATHER had ditched the polish-and-shine production of their debut and settled for a much more spontaneous sound. The band were very quiet for almost three years before issuing the disappointing 'HOTEL BALTIMORE' EP (2000, and featuring the tour band of JOSH GRAVELIN and DANA MIZER). They later teamed up with DAVE FRIDMANN (of MERCURY REV) to record their third-album proper, 'THE BIG PICTURE' (2002). The first single to be taken from the album '40 WATT SOLUTION', was a keyboard driven psychedelic guitar pop song reminiscent of the BEACH BOYS and The BEATLES alike.

Album rating: COTTON IS KING (*5) / KONTIKI (*7) / HOTEL BALTIMORE mini (*5) / THE BIG PICTURE (*7)

ROBERT HARRISON – vocals, guitar / **WHIT WILLIAMS** – guitar / **MATT HOVIS** – bass / **GREG THIBEAUX** – drums, guitar

 not iss. / Elm
1994. (cd) <921-2> **COTTON IS KING**
 – Lost my motto / Mr. Should / Cross the rubicon / Payday / Miss information / Ivanhoe / April's fool / The world's boutique / Saving myself / The new king of trash / The words of shamen Roger / The end of the line.

 — **DANA MIZER** – drums; repl. HOVIS + THIBEAUX
 Copper / Copper
Mar 98. (cd) <(CPR 2240)> **KONTIKI** Nov97
 – Camp hill rail operator / Homefront cameo / Spin my wheels / My before and after / Private Ruth / Vegetable row / Aurora Bori Alice / Church of Wilson / Lily dreams on / Password / Animal show drinking song / Prophecy for the golden age / She's only cool / Autumn's birds. <*re-iss. Mar99 on 'Rainbow Quartz'; RQTZ 021*)>

 — now without MIZER – but he returned; added **JOSH GRAVELIN** – bass
 Rainbow Quartz / Rainbow Quartz
Nov 99. (m-cd) <(RQTZ 028)> **HOTEL BALTIMORE**
 – Lost my motto / El matador / Baby freeze queen II / Missing the boat / John Wayne jung (music for short film theme) / Dream girl / Alter boy (Jimbo's theme).
Oct 01. (cd-s) <(RQTZ 063)> **40 WATT SOLUTION / MONTEREY HONEY (acoustic) / HEAVEN'S HELPING**
Nov 01. (cd) <(RQTZ 061)> **THE BIG PICTURE** Oct01
 – Last of the Mohicans / Marathon man / Baby freeze queen / 40 watt solution / Glory eyes / Monterey honey / AMPs of sugarland / Panama slides / Pine box builder / Story of Anna / Ramon finds waterfalls / Waterfalls / Running coyote advances.

COUNTRY TEASERS

Formed: Edinburgh, Scotland ... 1992 by singing guitarist BENEDICT R. WALLERS (the archetypal barbed bard of sorts), along with the rhythm section of SIMON STEPHENS and GEORGE MILLER. With guitarist ALAN CRICHTON borrowed from sister group THE MALE NURSE – which also featured BEN – the 4-piece CT's cut a couple of garage/punkabilly numbers including 'ONLY WHITTLIN' (which later featured on Guided Missile's 'Hits & Missiles' V/A set in 1999). Inspired by the sounds of BILLY CHILDISH, The FALL and CAPTAIN BEEFHEART – 'BITCHES' FUCK-OFF' being a prime example, the COUNTRY TEASERS rumbled on to deliver their 'PASTORAL ...' debut album in Spring '95. Sticksman ECK KING would subsequently supersede MARK CARR, a short-termer brought in to take the place of MILLER, who was more interested in other Beatles-esque band, The KAISERS. Towards the end of the year, just after a one-off EP was recorded (released by BEN and the group's alter-ego, ALAN COUNTRY DAVIDSON, a third guitarist RICHARD GREENAN was in place. A second album, 'SATAN IS REAL AGAIN', was issued in 1996, while their "SCOTTISH SINGLE" was another to be released by 'Guided Missile'. Keeping personnel was becoming quite a problem when STEPHENS bailed out of a second European tour late '96. ALASDAIR MacKINVEN (from THE MALE NURSE) was duly drafted in on bass, although he remained as guitarist when GREENAN departed. Early in 1998, CRICHTON was no longer a member and sadly he was to die (misadventure) the following February. Meanwhile, WALLERS, STEPHENS, MacKINVEN had recruited yet another MALE NURSE refugee, LAWRENCE WORTHINGTON, and this was the new line-up to sign for US-based 'Epitaph' records. The long-awaited third album proper, 'DESTROY ALL HUMAN LIFE' (there had been a Guided Missile compilation, 'BACK 2 THE FUTURE', in '98), finally hit the indie shops in Spring 1999 and contained fine covers of Sherill-Sutton's 'ALMOST PERSUADED' and the traditional 'GO AWAY FROM MY WINDOW'. ROBERT McNEILL was subsequently added to boost the numbers up to five again and for US tours, although STEPHENS would make them four and a half! (a quarintet, quite possibly because he became part-time) after the 'IDIOTS V SPASTICS' EP in 2000. The group subsequently issued what was to be their oddest album ever, the sinisterly-titled 'SCIENCE HAT, ARTISTIC CUBE, MORAL NOSEBLEED EMPIRE' in 2002. Released as a 'rarities' pack, the album fused the band's jet-black humour with some interesting biblical references and a few good instumentals to boot. Amongst the highlights were the covers of Euro techno group 2 UNLIMITED's early 90's smash 'NO LIMITS' (no, I'm not kidding) and ICE CUBE's 'WE HAD TO TEAR THIS MOTHERFUCKER UP'. 'I'M A NEW PERSON, MA'AM' was a genuine heartfelt country song, whereas 'COMPRESSOR' and 'CAN'T SING' ventured into obscure territory. Great if you're a fan of The COUNTRY TEASERS, but if not, try some of their earlier stuff first.

Album rating: THE PASTORAL-NOTRUSTIC WORLD OF THEIR GREATEST HITS (*5) / SATAN IS REAL AGAIN (*5) / DESTROY ALL HUMAN LIFE (*7) / SCIENCE HAT, ARTISTIC CUBE, MORAL NOSEBLEED EMPIRE rarities (*7)

BENEDICT R. WALLERS – vocals, guitar, keyboards / **SIMON STEPHENS** – bass / **GEORGE MILLER** – drums (also of KAISERS) / (1994) added **ALAN CRICHTON** (b.1970) – guitar
 Crypt / Crypt
Nov 94. (7") *(efa 11588-7)* **NUMBER 1 MAN. / ANYTIME, COWBOY**
 <*US + re-iss. Nov96; CRYPT 69*)>
Apr 95. (cd/10"lp) *(efa 11594-2/-1)* <CRYPT 60> **THE PASTORAL-NOTRUSTIC WORLD OF THEIR GREATEST HITS** Jan96
 – How I found Black-Brodie / Only my saviour / Bitches' fuck-off / O, nurse! / Anytime, cowboy 2 / Mosquito / Drove a truck / Been too long / Black cloud wandering / Stand by your man / Anytime, cowboy / Number 1 man.

 — **ECK KING** – drums; repl. short-stay member MARK CARR who'd repl. MILLER who continued with KAISERS
 — added **RICHARD GREENAN** – guitar
Jul 96. (cd/lp) *(efa 012877-2/-1)* <CRYPT 66> **SATAN IS REAL AGAIN** Oct96
 – Wide-open beaver of Nashville / Black change / Panty shots / It is my duty / Devil on my back / Little black clouds / Lies / Thank you God for making me an angel / Cripples / Some hole / Don't like people / Country fag / Satan is real again / These things shall pass.
 Guided Missile / not iss.
Sep 96. (7") *(GUIDE 09)* **THE SCOTTISH SINGLE**
 – The last bridge of Spencer Smith / Prettiest slave on the barge.

 — (late '96) **ALASDAIR MacKINVEN** – bass; repl. STEPHENS for a tour
 — (1997) **STEPHENS** returned to repl. GREENAN (MacKINVEN now on guitar)
 Nana / not iss.
Mar 97. (7") *(NANA 03)* **SECRETS IN WELSH. / TOUGH LUCK ON JOCK** welsh

 — in Jun'97, the COUNTRY TEASERS were part of the 'Guided Missile' single as ALAN COUNTRY DAVIDSON; unreleased BEN stuff incl. 'Trendy Mick Fleetwood' on the 'AGAINST COUNTRY TEASERS' *(GUIDE 18)*
 – After one thing / Bryson's the baker / Small shark in the tiny pool / Adam wakes up / Kenny Malcolm on smack / Henry Krinkle's theme.

 — (1998) **BEN, SIMON + ALASDAIR** were joined by **LAWRENCE WORTHINGTON** – drums; repl. KING (CRICHTON also departed in 1998; he died in February '99)
 Epitaph / Epitaph
Apr 99. (cd/lp) <(8325-2/-1)> **DESTROY ALL HUMAN LIFE** Feb99
 – Reynard the fox / Golden apples / David I hope you don't mind / Hairy wine / Deliverance from misrule / Almost persuaded / Go away from my window / Broken Jews etc. / Women and children first / Come back Maggy / Song of the white feather club secretary.

COUNTRY TEASERS (cont)

May 99. (ltd-7"ep) *(GUIDE 35)* **GUIDED MISSILE SPLIT SINGLE BY COUNTRY TEASERS and AMNESIAC GODZ**
– (2 by AMNESIAC GODZ) / Hairy wine / Reynard the fox.

— added **ROBERT McNEILL** – bass, guitar

Mar 00. (7"ep) *(GUIDE 40)* **THE REBEL: IDIOTS V SPASTICS EP**
– The idiot / Julie's resolution / The spastic / Un Canadien errant.

— (late 2000) – STEPHENS was now only part-time (**WESLEY WILLIS**) replaced him

— **WALLERS + MILLER** recruited **KANAAN TUPPER** – bass

– compilations, etc. –

Apr 98. (cd) *Guided Missile; (GUIDE 27CD)* **BACK 2 THE FUTURE**
(compilation 1992-97)
– Let's have a shambles! / Good pair of hands / Kill / No limits / I get hard / Tights / Go down, mighty Devil / "The risk" / Get your hole / Milkman / I know my name is there / Women & children 1st (live) / Lies (live) / Tainted love (live) / "Axe" Greenan (live) / Drove a truck (live) / Prettiest slave on the barge (live) / Country roads (live).

Apr 02. (d-lp/cd) *In The Red; (<ITR 032/+CD>)* **SCIENCE HAT, ARTISTIC CUBE, MORAL NOSEBLEED EMPIRE**
– Compressor / Getaway / Some hole / I'm a new person, ma'am / $4.99 / Mollusc in country / Happy feet / No limits / Hat on the red / Secrets in Welsh / Adam wakes up / Loose tongues get into tight places / After one thing / Treble life No.2 / The last bridge of Spencer Smith / Can't sing / We had to tear this motherfucker up / Only whittlin' / Postman Pak and his lazy black & white cunts / Tough luck on Jock. *(d-lp+= – (20 more!).*

COURTNEY LOVE (see under ⇒ LOIS)

COUSTEAU

Formed: London, England ... 1998 by frontman LIAM McKAHEY, along with DAVEY RAY MOOR, CRAIG VEAR, JOE PEET and ROBIN BROWN. Taking Brit-pop towards (and past) the new millennium via debut single, 'THE LAST GOOD DAY OF THE YEAR' – from parent eponymous album released in November '99, COUSTEAU were hotly tipped by many music journos as the next big thing. Fusing SCOTT WALKER vocals and BURT BACHARACH bittersweet melodies, the quintet delivered a handful of heartworn singles in 2000/2001 after they signed a worldwide deal with 'Palm Pictures'. Their long-awaited sophomore album, 'SIRENA' (2002), was another decent enough record that somehow lacked that extra ingredient to push them above the surface of a music audience looking for something fresh in the indie market.

Album rating: COUSTEAU (*6) / SIRENA (*7)

LIAM McKAHEY – vocals / **ROBIN BROWN** – guitar, vocals / **DAVEY RAY MOOR** – piano, vocals / **JOE PEET** – bass, violin, vocals / **CRAIG VEAR** – drums, percussion

Oct 99. (cd-ep) *(WARMCD 6)* **THE LAST GOOD DAY OF THE YEAR / CAPTAIN SWING / LOVE IN THE MEANTIME / THE LAST GOOD DAY OF THE YEAR (album)** *(Global Warming / Palm Pictures)*

Nov 99. (cd) *(GLOBCD 5) <PALM 2058-2>* **COUSTEAU** — Oct00
– Your day will come / The last good day of the year / Mesmer / Jump in the river / How will I know / (Shades of) Ruinous blue / You my lunar queen / She don't hear your prayer / One good reason / Wish you were her / Of this goodbye. *(lp-iss.Mar01 on 'Palm Pictures'; PALMLP 2058)*

Jun 00. (7") *(PP7 20321)* **SHE DON'T HEAR YOUR PRAYER. / LOVERS IN A LOVELESS PLACE**
(cd-s+=) (PPCD 20332) – Late September rain.

Oct 00. (7") *(PP7 70431)* **THE LAST GOOD DAY OF THE YEAR. / CAPTAIN SWING**
(cd-s+=) (PPCD 70432) – Rachel lately.

Apr 01. (7") *(PP7 70491)* **WISH YOU WERE HER. / TO KNOW HER**
(cd-s+=) (PPCD 70492) – The cuttlefish walks the cuttlefish waltz.

Jun 02. (7") *(PP7 074)* **TALKING TO MYSELF. / SHORT SIGHTED, BEAUTIFUL & SHY**
(cd-s+=) (PPCD 70742) – Last secret of the sea.

Jun 02. (cd) *(<PALMCD 2083-2>)* **SIRENA**
– Nothing so bad / Damn these hungry times / Talking to myself / Peculiarly you / Salome / Please don't cry / No medication / After the fall / Last secret of the sea / Heavy weather / She bruise easy / Have you seen her.

COWS

Formed: Minneapolis, Minnesota, USA ... mid-80's by SHANNON SELBERG, along with NORM ROGERS, THOR EISENTRAGER and KEVIN RUTMANIS. Like fellow native Minnesotans, and hardcore legends, HUSKER DU, the COWS went for the noisy approach to music making. A sound for the initiated, the band began gigging with their inimitable style of the bare bones of rock, with barely recognisable song structures and even less detectable lyrics. Yet this was their point, creating a wall of primal sound, that binned the normal pleasantries of even the more outlandish alternative rock acts. Frontman SELBERG not only provided their screaming presence, but also played trumpet, which led some critics to place the band's output into the more experimental reaches of the jazzcore movement. Debuting in 1987, with their full-length set, 'TAINT PLURIBUS TAINT UNUM', the band unleashed their noise-rock on the record buying public and proceeded with the backing of indie imprint, 'Amphetamine Reptile' to issue more than a creditable careers worth of LPs and compilations. Although as their rock offerings went on, their sound did in many respects begin to resemble a slightly more perceptable hard rock sound, it never strayed too far from their cacophonous beginnings, but on the other hand always exemplified a willingness to experiment. The early 90s saw the highpoint of their musical time, via the releases of their stand-out full-length offerings, 'CUNNING STUNTS', and 'SEXY PEE STORY', records that also showcased the COWS' great sense of humour. Always respected amongst their hardcore peers, their ninth and latest to date, 'SORRY IN PIG MINOR' (1998), was produced by the MELVINS' BUZZ OSBORNE (aka KING BUZZO), giving this release a wholesome and deep sound, treating their music with the respect its longevity and boundary-pushing ways deserved.
• **Covered:** 39 LASHES (Tim Rice – Andrew Lloyd Webber) / MEMORIAL (Tucumcari Rattlers).

Album rating: TAINT PLURIBUS, TAINT UNUM (*6) / DADDY HAS A TAIL! (*4) / EFFETE AND IMPUDENT SNOBS (*4) / PEACETIKA (*5) / CUNNING STUNTS (*7) / SEXY PEE STORY (*6) / ORPHAN'S TRAGEDY (*5) / OLD GOLD 1989-1991 compilation (*6) / WHORN (*4) / SORRY IN PIG MINOR (*5)

SHANNON SELBERG – vocals, trumpet / **THOR EISENSTRAGER** – guitar / **KEVIN RUTMANIS** – bass / **SANDRIS RUTMANIS** – drums

1987. (lp) *<TR 007>* **TAINT PLURIBUS, TAINT UNUM** *(not iss. – Treehouse)*
– Koyaanisqatsi / Cow jazz / Carchase / Sieve / On plasma pond / Yellowbelly / Redhouse / Carnival ride / The pictorial / Tourist / Summertime bone / Mother (I love that bitch) / Weird kitchen.

1988. (7"m) *<TR 013>* **CHOW. / I REMEMBER YOU / PORKY PIG FACTORY**

— **TONY OLIVERI** – drums; repl. SANDRIS

Jul 89. (lp) *<ARR 89-163>* **DADDY HAS A TAIL!** *(Amphetam. Reptile)*
– Shaking / Camouflage monkey / Part my konk / Burn in the alley / Chow / By the throat / I miss her beer / Sugar / Chasin' Darla / Sticky and sweet.

Mar 90. (lp/cd) *(ARR 8-86) <89817-2/-2>* **EFFETE AND IMPUDENT SNOBS**
– Memorial / Dirty leg / Bi Mickey / Preyed on / The immigrant song / Whitney in the woodpile / Nancy boy cocaine whore blues / Cartoon corral / Little bit / Put me down / Sittin' around.

Apr 90. (7") *<scale 30>* **SLAP BACK. / ONE O'CLOCK HIGH**

— **NORM ROGERS** – drums (ex-JAYHAWKS) repl. TONY

Mar 91. (lp/cd) *(ARR/+CD 18/145) <89216-1/-2>* **PEACETIKA**
– Hitting the wall / John Henry / The man / I'm missing / Can't die / 3-way Lisa / Good cop / Peacetika. *(UK cd+=)* – DADDY HAS A TAIL

Dec 91. (7") *<IV-7>* **WOMAN INSIDE. / THEME FROM MIDNIGHT COWBOY**

— <above issued on 'Insipid Vinyl'>

1992. (cd) *(ARR 28/182) <amrep 007>* **CUNNING STUNTS**
– Heave ho / Walks alone / Contamination / Mr. Cancelled / Mine / Theme from Midnight cowboy / Everybody / Two little pigs / The woman inside / Terrifique / Down below / Ort.

Dec 92. (7"yellow) *<(scale 50)>* **PLOWED. / IN THE MOUTH**
(cd-s+=) (ARR 224CD) – Joan Baez / I love you.

1993. (cd) *(ARR 40/261) <amrep 015>* **SEXY PEE STORY**
– Blown / Shitbeard / Doing the obvious / Ch / 39 lashes / Uptown suckers / Sexy pee story / The ouch cube / Mrs. Cancelled / You owe me / Sugar torch.

Apr 94. (7"purple) *<scale 65>* **COW ISLAND. / CHICKEN RHYTHM** — tour

Sep 94. (lp/cd) *(ARR/+CD 55/335) <amrep 028>* **ORPHAN'S TRAGEDY** — Aug94
– Cow island / Pussy is a monarchy / Orphan's tragedy / Allergic to myself / Unrefixed / The bucket / Pickled garbage soup / I'm both / Witch hunt / Taxi / Baby love / My Bob / Shot down / Smell shelf.

Jan 96. (cd) *(ARRCD 68011) <ARR 47>* **OLD GOLD 1989-1991** (compilation)
– Shaking / Camouflage monkey / Part my konk / Bum in the alley / By the throat / I miss her beer / Sugar / Chasin' Darla / Sticky and sweet / Memorial / Dirty leg / Big Mickey / Preyed on / Whitey in the woodpile / Cartoon corral / Little bit / Hitting the wall / I'm missing / Can't die / 3-way Lisa / Good cop / Peacetika / One o'clock high.

1996. (7") *<scale 79>* **PICTORAL. / (other by BOSS HOG)**

— **FREDDY VOTEL** – drums; repl. NORM

Mar 96. (lp/cd) *(ARR 70013/+CD) <amrep 050>* **WHORN**
– Divorcee more / A oven / The warden / Mas – no mas / Four things / Tropic of cancelled / The new girl / Organized meat / Massa peel / A gift called life / Jikan.

Jun 97. (7") *(PAN 007)* **Erase yer Head**
– Four things / HEADCLEANER: Bill.
(above issued on 'Pandemonium') (below on 'Thick')

Nov 97. (10"pic-d) *(THK 053)* **THE MISSING LETTER IS YOU**

Mar 98. (cd/lp) *<amrep 066>* **SORRY IN PIG MINOR**
– Cabin man / Finished again / No I'm not coming out / Dear dad / Eureka fun day / Death in the tall weeds / El Shiksa / Life after Beth / Saliva of the fittest / Felon of Troy / Say uncle.

Graham COXON (see under ⇒ BLUR)

CRABS

Formed: Portland, Oregon, USA ... mid 90's by the singer/songwriter duo, JONN LUNSFORD and LISA JACKSON. Having released a handful of 45's for JONN's brother BRET's 'Knw-yr-own' imprint, The CRABS finally inked a deal with nonether than 'K' records. Now unleashed to a wider audience, 1995's 'JACKPOT' album saw them characterise their pot-pourri of indie pop sounds. After issuing their sophomore 'BRAINWASHED' set a year later, they

added keyboard-player SARAH DOUGHER for 'WHAT WERE FLAMES NOW SMOULDER' (1997); 1999's 'SAND AND SEA' disappointed that much they split not long afterwards.
Album rating: JACKPOT (*5) / BRAINWASHED (*5) / WHAT WERE ONCE FLAMES NOW SMOULDER (*6) / SAND AND SEA (*4)

JONN LUNSFORD – vocals, guitar / **LISA JACKSON** – vocals, drums

			not iss.	Knw-yr-own
1993.	(c-s)	**X-MAS WITH THE CRABS**	-	
1993.	(7"ep) <KNW 08> **DREAMBOAT**		-	
1994.	(7"ep) <KNW 09> **SORE**		-	
			not iss.	Soda Girl
1995.	(7"ep) **ALIEN GIRL**		-	K
			K	
Jul 95.	(lp/cd) <KLP/KCD 42> **JACKPOT**			

– She is a titan / Iron curtain / Angeline / Golden boy / Tsunami / Swallow the sea / Alien girl / Something in my life / Sharkbite / Maxamillion / Landmine.

Sep 96. (lp/cd) <(KLP/KCD 56)> **BRAINWASHED**   Aug96
– Promise land / Sad song / Brainwashed / Anything + everything / Prom night / Unforgivable / Meltdown / Speechless / Spilt milk / Jean Paul Satre / Quicksand.
Dec 96. (7"m) <IPU 62> **ANYTHING & EVERYTHING. / PROM NIGHT / SUGAR TOWN**

—— added **SARAH DOUGHER** – keyboards
Sep 97. (cd) <(KCD 74)> **WHAT WERE ONCE FLAMES NOW SMOULDER**
– Confess / Love & hate / February 15th / New fool / Mission impossible / Slip / Debutante / Temper temper / Holiday / Private eye / 1863 / Time has come and gone.
Apr 99. (lp/cd) <(KLP/KCD 95)> **SAND AND SEA**
– Tumbling away / Market size / Ladies' choice reprise / Bricks of gold / Sand and sea / End of the world / Snow in summertime / Bends / Classic crabs / I surrender.

CRACKER

Formed: Redlands, California, USA ... 1990 by DAVID LOWERY and DAVE LOVERING (former members of top cult US acts). While LOVERING had been a sidekick for FRANK BLACK in The PIXIES, LOWERY had been in CAMPER VAN BEETHOVEN, who were known for releasing a string of albums for 'Rough Trade' in the 80's and the classic track 'TAKE THE SKINHEADS BOWLING'. Alternately acoustic laid-back/hard rockin' grunge cowpunks fusing TOM PETTY or IAN HUNTER like songs with twanging country rock, CRACKER emerged in 1992 with the tongue in cheek, 'TEEN ANGST (WHAT THE WORLD NEEDS NOW)'. This was swiftly followed up with an impressive eponymous debut set. Though not a straight grunge act by any means, the band nevertheless appealed to a similar grunge crowd and a follow-up set, 'KEROSENE HAT' (1994) spawned a grunge mini-anthem in 'LOW'. The album itself sold close to a half million copies, a more experimental outing that saw them cover The Grateful Dead's 'LOSER'. A third set, 'THE GOLDEN AGE' (1996) meanwhile, saw LOVERING getting back to his roots in line with the burgeoning "No Depression" alternative country scene. Another US-only release, 'GENTLEMEN'S BLUES', was released in September '98 to a lukewarm critical reception. CRACKER's touring schedule continued unabated as LOWERY and Co even called up old CVB mates JONATHAN SEGEL, VICTOR KRUMMENACHER, CHRIS PEDERSEN and GREG LISHER to augment selected live shows; an album, 'THE CRACKER TRAVELING APOTHECARY SHOW' was their next release. Early in 2002, CRACKER finally delivered their long-awaited 5th studio long-player, 'FOREVER', a record that re-established LOWERY's long-lost lyrical wit; another live set, 'HELLO, CLEVELAND!' (2002), was too much too soon. • **Covered:** WITHERING AWAY (Vic Chesnutt) / FUCKING UP (Neil Young) / GOOD TIMES, BAD TIMES (Led Zeppelin) / BLUE ROSEBUDS (Residents) / YOU AIN'T GOING NOWHERE (Bob Dylan) / RAINY DAYS AND MONDAYS (Carpenters) / SHAKE SOME ACTION (Flamin' Groovies) / VICTORIA (Kinks) / WHITE RIOT (Clash).
Album rating: CRACKER (*7) / KEROSENE HAT (*8) / THE GOLDEN AGE (*5) / GENTLEMEN'S BLUES (*5) / GARAGE D'OR double compilation (*7) / THE CRACKER TRAVELING APOTHECARY SHOW live (*6) / FOREVER (*6) / HELLO, CLEVELAND! LIVE FROM THE METRO (*5)

DAVID LOWERY (b.10 Sep'60, San Antonio, Texas) – vocals, guitars (ex-CAMPER VAN BEETHOVEN) / **JOHNNY HICKMAN** – guitar, vocals / **BOB RUPE** (b.16 Sep'56, Michigan) – bass (ex-SILOS) / **DAVE LOVERING** (b. 6 Dec'61, Boston, Mass.) – drums (ex-PIXIES)

		Virgin America	Virgin
Mar 92.	(c-s) <98551> **TEEN ANGST (WHAT THE WORLD NEEDS NOW). / CAN I TAKE MY GUN TO HEAVEN**		Jun92

(12"+=) <98551> – China.
(cd-s++=) <98551> – ('A'version).
Apr 92. (cd/c/lp) (CDVUS/VUSMC/VUSLP 48) <91816-2/-4> **CRACKER**   Feb92
– Teen angst (what the world needs now) / Happy birthday to me / This is Cracker soul / I see the light / St. Cajetan / Mr. Wrong / Someday / Can I take my gun to Heaven / Satify you / Another song about the rain / Don't f*** me up (with peace and love) / Dr. Bernice.
Aug 92. (c-s) <12592> **HAPPY BIRTHDAY TO ME / JAMES RIVER**   -
(cd-s+=) <12592> – ('A'side) / ('A'remix).
Sep 92. (cd-ep) <12627> **TUCSON**   -
– River Euphrates / I ride my bike / Euro-trash girl / Bad vibes everybody.

—— **DAVEY FARAGHER** – bass, vocals; repl. RUPE
—— **MICHAEL URBANO** – drums; repl. LOVERING
Mar 94. (c-s) <38427> **LOW / NOSTALGIA**   -   64

May 94. (7"/c-s) (VUS/+C 80) **LOW. / TEEN ANGST (WHAT THE WORLD NEEDS NOW)**   43   -
(cd-s) (VUSDG 80) – ('A'side) / I ride my bike / Sunday train / Whole lotta trouble.
(10"colrd) (VUSA 80) – ('A'side) / River Euphrates / Euro-trash girl / Bad vibes everybody.
(re-iss. Nov94; same) – (hit UK No.54)
Jun 94. (cd/c) (CDVUS/VUSMC 67) <39012> **KEROSENE HAT**   44   59 Sep93
– Low / Movie star / Get off this / Kerosene hat / Take me down to the infirmary / Nostalgia / Sweet potato / Sick of goodbyes / I want everything / Lonesome Johnny blues / Let's go for a ride / Loser. (cd+=) – No songs: Eurotrash girl + I ride my bike / Hi-desert biker math lab. (c+=) – No songs; Euro-trash girl + I ride my bike / Kerosene hat (acoustic).
Jul 94. (c-ep/cd-ep) (VUSC/+D 83) <38443> **GET OFF THIS / HAPPY BIRTHDAY TO ME / CHINA / DR. BERNICE**   41
(cd-ep) (VUSDG 83) – ('A'side) / Fucking up (live) / Blue Danube / Don't fuck me up (with peace and love).
(10"ep) (VUSA 83) – ('A'side) / Steve's hornpipe / Mr. Wrong / I want everything (acoustic).
Sep 94. (c-s/cd-s) <38449> **EURO-TRASH GIRL / RIVER EUPHRATES / BAD VIBES EVERYBODY / BLUE DANUBE BLUES / WHY DO I KEEP FUCKING UP**
Apr 96. (cd/c) <41498> **THE GOLDEN AGE**   -   83
– I hate my generation / I'm a little rocket ship / Big dipper / Nothing to believe in / The golden age / 1000 flower power maximum / Dixie Babylon / I can't forget you / Sweet thistle pie / Useless stuff / How can I live without you / Bicycle Spaniard.

—— **LOWERY, HICKMAN + RUPE** recruited **FRANK FUNARO** – drums + **KENNY MARGOLIS** – keyboards, accordion
Sep 98. (cd/c) <46263> **GENTLEMAN'S BLUES**   -
– Good life / Seven days / Star / James river / My life is totally boring without you / Been around the world / World is mine / Lullabye / Waiting for you girl / Trails and tribulations / Wild one / Gentlemen's blues / I want out of the circus / Wedding day / Hallelujah.

—— LOWERY played live with ex-CAMPER VAN BEETHOVEN members **VICTOR KRUMMENACHER + GREG LISHER, JONATHAN SEGAL + CHRIS PEDERSEN**

		not iss.	own label
Aug 01.	(cd) **THE CRACKER TRAVELING APOTHECARY SHOW (live)**	-	

– Be my love / Dr. Bernice / Tania / Cracker sells out (audience baiting) / 100 flower power maximum / I ride my bike / Mao / Payed vacation: Greece / Cruel (audience participation) / I'm a little rocketship / Eye of Fatima pt.I and II / Wedding day / Dixie Babylon / Sinner song / White BMW 928 (post game interview).

—— added **BRANDY WOOD** – bass

		Cooking Vinyl	Black Porch
Jan 02.	(cd) (COOKCD 231) <11341> **FOREVER**		

– Brides of Neptune / Shine / Don't bring us down / Guarded by monkeys / Ain't that strange / Miss Santa Cruz county / Superfan / Sweet Magdalena of my misfortune / Merry Christmas Emily / Forever / Shameless / One fine day / What you're missing. <US w/fee cd+=> – HELLO, CLEVELAND!
Jul 02. (cd) (COOKCD 241) **HELLO, CLEVELAND! LIVE FROM THE METRO (live)**   -
– Seven days / The good life / Lonesome Johnny blues / Big dipper / Around the world / Teen angst / Crackersoul / Sweet thistle pie / The world is mine / Low / Pictures of matchstick men / videos: Guarded by monkeys / Forever / Merry Christmas Emily / Shine.

– compilations, etc. –

Mar 00. (d-cd) Virgin; <49005> **GARAGE D'OR**
– Teen angst (what the world needs now) / This is Cracker soul / I see the light / Low / Get off this / Sweet potato / Euro-trash girl / Shake some action / Sweet thistle pie / I'm a little rocket ship / Big dipper / Seven days / Been around the world / Be my love / Heaven knows I'm lonely now / The eyes of Mary // Surfbilly (BBC session) / The golden age (live featuring ADAM DURITZ & JOAN OSBORNE) / You ain't going nowhere (live) / Hollywood cemetary / Whole lotta trouble / I want out of the circus (live) / Steve's hornpipe / Mr. Wrong (live) / Sunday train / Lonesome Johnny blues (live) / Rainy days and Mondays / China.

Sarah CRACKNELL (see under ⇒ SAINT ETIENNE)

CRANBERRIES

Formed: Limerick, Ireland ... 1990 initially as covers band The CRANBERRY SAW US (corny, or what!) by brothers NOEL and MIKE HOGAN, plus FERGAL LAWLER. The inclusion of singer DOLORES O'RIORDAN, saw the release the following year of an independent single, 'UNCERTAIN'. The quartet returned to the studio late in '91, subsequently resurfacing on the 'Island' label with 'DREAMS', 'LINGER' and 'PUT ME DOWN'. These tracks were featured on 1993's glorious debut album, 'EVERYBODY ELSE IS DOING IT, SO WHY CAN'T WE', which went on to sell a million in America (a year later it went platinum in Britain). An indie style major outfit, initially described as The Irish SUNDAYS, The CRANBERRIES were distinguished by DOLORES' heavily accented vocals, endearing naive and girlish one minute, howling banshee-style the next. An acquired taste, definitely, but one which millions seemingly, erm, acquired, drawn in no doubt by their canny way with a romantic Celtic melody. After their slow beginnings, The CRANBERRIES were now hot property, the UK music press finally recognised their unique talent. Confusingly for newly acquainted fans, a follow-up album, 'NO NEED TO ARGUE' hit the shops the same year ('94), previewed by the grunge like 'ZOMBIE', a 'loud' single (in every sense of the word), which made the UK Top 20. Incredibly, the track became a massive international hit for rave outfit, AMY, who took it back into the UK Top 20 in 1995. A third set, 'TO THE FAITHFUL DEPARTED' (1996) saw the band enlisting gloss-rock producer, Bruce Fairbairn, in what was

CRANBERRIES (cont)

surely a move to further dominate the American market. Songs about Bosnia, John Lennon etc, didn't prevent it from cleaning up commercially once more, although most critics were unimpressed. If the CRANBERRIES thought they were harshly treated by the press on this occasion, they hadn't dreamt of the stick they would endure for next record, 'BURY THE HATCHET' (1999). Although its initial sales were once again promising both in the UK and US, the album quickly tailed off into the proverbial oblivion (six feet under it would seem); surely babe DOLORES and her melancholy muckers couldn't get away with this sort of thing again. The appropriately titled 'WAKE UP AND SMELL THE COFFEE' (2001) tried hard to recover lost ground, even to the extent of renewing their production partnership with Stephen Street. Yet despite valiant attempts at trimming the musical flab, the album weighed in at a gross Top 50 in the US and an even more disheartening No.61 placing in the UK. • **Songwriters:** DOLORES and NOEL, except (THEY LONG TO BE) CLOSE TO YOU (Carpenters) / GO YOUR OWN WAY (Fleetwood Mac). • **Trivia:** They supported MOOSE in the summer of '91, DOLORES guesting on their 1992 album, 'XYZ'.

Album rating: EVERYBODY ELSE IS DOING IT, SO WHY CAN'T WE (*8) / NO NEED TO ARGUE (*7) / TO THE FAITHFUL DEPARTED (*4) / BURY THE HATCHET (*4) / WAKE UP AND SMELL THE COFFEE (*4) / STARS: THE BEST OF 1992-2002 compilation (*7)

DOLORES O'RIORDAN (b. 6 Sep'71) – vocals, acoustic guitar / **NOEL HOGAN** (b.25 Dec'71) – guitar / **MIKE HOGAN** (b.29 Apr'73) – bass / **FERGAL LAWLER** (b. 4 Mar'71) – drums

		Xerica	not iss.
Oct 91.	(12"ep) (XER 14T) **UNCERTAIN / NOTHING LEFT AT ALL. / PATHETIC SENSES / THEM**		

		Island	Island
Sep 92.	(7") (IS 548) **DREAMS. / WHAT YOU WERE** (12"+=/cd-s+=) (12IS/CID 548) – Liar.	–	–
Feb 93.	(7") (C+/IS 556) **LINGER. / REASON** (12"/cd-s) (12IS/CID 556) – ('A'side) / How (radical mix).	74	–
Mar 93.	(cd/c/lp) (CID/ICT/ILPS 8003) <514156> **EVERYBODY ELSE IS DOING IT, SO WHY CAN'T WE?** – I still do / Dreams / Sunday / Pretty / Waltzing back / Not sorry / Linger / Wanted / Still can't . . . / I will always / How / Put me down. (re-dist.Nov93; same) (re-iss. Mar94; hit UK No.1)	64	18
Oct 93.	(c-s) <862800> **LINGER / HOW**	–	8
Jan 94.	(c-s/7") (C+/IS 559) **LINGER. / PRETTY (live)** (10"+=/cd-s+=) (10IS/CID 559) – Waltzing black (live) / I still do (live).	14	–
Apr 94.	(c-s/7") (C+/IS 594) <864436> **DREAMS. / WHAT YOU WERE** (cd-s+=) (CID 594) – Liar. (cd-s) (CIDX 594) – ('A'live) / Liar (live) / Not sorry (live) / Wanted (live).	27	42 Mar94

Jun'94; DOLORES featured on JAH WOBBLE's hit 'The Sun Does Rise'.

Sep 94.	(c-s/7") (C+/IS 600) **ZOMBIE. / AWAY** (cd-s+=) (CID 600) – I don't need. (cd-s) (CIDX 600) – ('A'extended) / Waltzing black (live) / Linger (live).	14	–
Oct 94.	(cd/c/lp) (CIS/ICT/ILPS 8029) <524050> **NO NEED TO ARGUE** – Ode to my family / I can't be with you / 21 / Zombie / Empty / Everything I said / The icicle melts / Disappointment / Ridiculous thoughts / Dreaming my dreams / Yeats' grave / Daffodil lament / No need to argue.	2	6
Nov 94.	(c-s/7") (C+/IS 601) **ODE TO MY FAMILY. / SO COLD IN IRELAND** (cd-s+=) (CID 601) – No need to argue / Dreaming my dreams. (cd-s) (CIDX 601) – ('A'live) / Dreams (live) / Ridiculous thoughts (live) / Zombie (live).	29	–
Feb 95.	(c-s/7") (C+/IS 605) **I CAN'T BE WITH YOU. / (THEY LONG TO BE) CLOSE TO YOU** (cd-s+=) (CID 605) – Empty (BBC session). (cd-s) (CIDX 605) – ('A'-BBC session) / Zombie (acoustic) / Daffodil lament (live).	23	–
Jul 95.	(c-s/7") (C+/IS 616) **RIDICULOUS THOUGHTS. / LINGER** (cd-s+=) (CID 616) – Twenty one (live) / Ridiculous thoughts (live).	20	–
Apr 96.	(c-s) (CIS 633) **SALVATION / I'M STILL REMEMBERING** (cd-s+=) (CID 633) – I just shot John Lennon.	13	–
May 96.	(cd/c/colrd-lp) (CID/ICT/ILPS 8048) <524234> **TO THE FAITHFUL DEPARTED** – Hollywood / Salvation / When you're gone / Free to decide / War child / Forever yellow skies / The rebels / I just shot John Lennon / Electric blue / I'm still remembering / Will you remember? / Joe / Bosnia.	2	4
Jul 96.	(c-s) (CIS 637) **FREE TO DECIDE / CORDELL** (cd-s+=) (CID 637) – The picture I view. (cd-s) (CIDX 637) – ('A'side) / Salvation (live) / Bosnia.	33	–
Nov 96.	(c-s) <854802> **FREE TO DECIDE / WHEN YOU'RE GONE**	–	22
Apr 99.	(c-s) (572568-4) **PROMISES / SWEETEST THING** (cd-s+=) (572591-2) – Linger (live). (cd-s) (572593-2) – ('A'side) / Dreams (live) / Promises (live).	13	–
Apr 99.	(cd/c/d-lp) (524644-2/-4/-1) <524611> **BURY THE HATCHET** – Animal instinct / Loud and clear / Promises / You and me / Just my imagination / Shattered / Desperate Andy / Saving grace / Copycat / What's on my mind / Delilah / Fee fi fo / Dying in the sun. (d-cd iss.Apr00 +=; 542507-2) – Sorry son / Baby blues / The sweetest thing / Woman without pride / Such a shame / Papparazzi on mopeds // Promises (live) / Animal instinct (live) / Loud and clear (live) / You and me (live) / Shattered (live) / Desperate Andy (live) / Delilah (live)	7	13
Jul 99.	(c-s/cd-s) (56219 1-4/7-2) **ANIMAL INSTINCT / PAPARAZZI ON MOPEDS** (cd-s+=) (562198-2) – ('A'side) / Ode to my family (live) / Baby blues / Salvation (live).	54	
Oct 99.	(c-s) (562412-4) **JUST MY IMAGINATION / GOD TO BE WITH YOU** (cd-s+=) (562414-2) – Zombie (live). (cd-s) (562415-2) – ('A'side) / Such a shame / Promises (live).		

		M.C.A.	M.C.A.
Oct 01.	(cd-s) (MCSTD 42070) **ANALYSE / ANALYSE (oceanic) / I CAN'T BE WITH YOU (live)**		–
Oct 01.	(cd) (112706-2) <112739> **WAKE UP AND SMELL THE COFFEE** – Never grow old / Analyse / Time is ticking out / Dying inside / This is the day / The concept / Wake up and smell the coffee / Pretty eyes / I really hope / Every morning / Do you know / Carry on / Chocolate Brown. (UK+=) – In the ghetto / Dreams (live) / Promises (live).	61	46
Sep 02.	(cd) (063386-2) <063277> **STARS: THE BEST OF 1992-2002** (compilation) – Dreams / Linger / Zombie / Ode to my family / I can't be with you / Ridiculous thoughts / Salvation / Free to decide / When you're gone / Hollywood / Promises / Animal instinct / Just my imagination / You and me / Analyse / Time is ticking out / This is the day / Daffodil lament / New New York / Stars. (d-cd+=; 063354-2) – Zombie (live) / Ode to my family (live) / Animal instinct (live) / Salvation (live) / Daffodil lament (live) / Zombie (video).	20	

– compilations, etc. –

Nov 95.	(d-cd) **EVERYBODY ELSE IS DOING IT, SO WHY CAN'T WE? / NO NEED TO ARGUE**		
Apr 02.	(4xcd-box) Island; (<586707-2>) **TREASURE BOX**		

CRANES

Formed: Portsmouth, England . . . 1986 by the sister and brother team of ALISON and JIM SHAW. Their first foray into the music business was the self-financed and distributed cassette, 'FUSE', a primitive blueprint of the distinctive gothic minimalism which formed the bulk of their early EP's. In addition to contributing tracks to various compilation albums, the group issued a debut mini-set, 'SELF NON SELF', on the small 'Bite Back!' label in 1989 before signing with the 'BMG' subsidiary, 'Dedicated', in the early 90's. Briefly lumped in with the shoegazing scene of the time, in reality The CRANES were a far more complex and disturbing listen; over the course of four EP's, 'INESCAPABLE', 'ESPERO', 'ADORATION' and 'TOMORROW'S TEARS', the group (now augmented by MARK FRANCOME and MATT HOPE) developed an alternately bleakly beautiful/menacingly claustrophobic sound highlighting ALISON's vocal fusion of LYDIA LUNCH and CLARE GROGAN and feeding off the same celestial energy supply as The COCTEAU TWINS. A debut album proper, 'WINGS OF JOY', appeared in 1991 to general critical acclaim; the band did have their detractors of course, such extreme music drawing extreme opinions. Goth-pop stalwarts, The CURE, were impressed enough to invite the band on tour, the influence of ROBERT SMITH and Co apparent on Top 40 follow-up album, 'FOREVER' (1993). Inevitably, subsequent set 'LOVED' (1994) followed in an increasingly easier-on-the-ear vein, yet despite continuing cult appeal, The CRANES failed to make any inroads to chart success with the likes of 'LA TRAGEDIE D'ORESTES' (1996) and 'POPULATION FOUR' (1997). The ALISON and JIM combination enrolled two new CRANES (PAUL SMITH and JON CALLENDER) to the fold for 2001's comeback set, 'FUTURE SONGS'. Released on their own 'Dadaphonic' imprint, the album – and ALISON in general – more coherent than ever before, as witnessed on tracks such as 'LILLIES' and 'FLUTE SONG'.

Album rating: SELF NON SELF mini (*4) / WINGS OF JOY (*7) / FOREVER (*8) / LOVED (*6) / LA TRAGEDIE D'ORESTES ET ELECTRA (*5) / POPULATION 4 (*4) / FUTURE SONGS (*6)

ALISON SHAW – vocals / **MARK FRANCOME** – guitar / **MATT COPE** – guitar / **JIM SHAW** – drums

		Bite Back	not iss.
May 89.	(m-lp) (BB 017) **SELF NON SELF** – One from the slum / Beach mover / Joy lies within / Focus breathe / Heaven or bliss / Fuse / Reach / Nothing in the middle nothing at the end. (m-cd-iss. Nov92 on 'Dedicated'+=; DEDCD 006) – (2 extra). <US cd-iss. Nov97 on 'Dedicated'; 44016>		–

		Dedicated	Dedicated-R.C.A.
Aug 90.	(12"ep) (CRANE 001T) **INESCAPABLE EP** – Inescapable / Give / Dada 331 / Inescapable II.		–
Nov 90.	(12"ep/cd-ep) (CRANE 002 T/CD) **ESPERO EP** – I hope / EG shining / Cha cha esqueta.		–
May 91.	(12"/cd-s) (CRANE 003 T/CD) **BRIGHTER. / ADORATION**		–
Sep 91.	(12"ep/cd-ep) (CRANE 004 T/CD) **TOMORROW'S TEARS / CASA BLANCA. / SIXTH OF MAY / DREAMLESS**		–
Sep 91.	(cd/c/lp) (DED CD/MC/LP 003) <3007> **WINGS OF JOY** – Watersong / Thursday / Living and breathing / Leaves of summer / Starblood / Wish / Tomorrow's tears / Beautiful sadness / Hopes are high / Adoration. (cd+=) – Sixth of May. (re-iss. Nov92; same) – (w/ free 5"cd-s) (CRANE 005CD)	52	Nov91
Mar 93.	(12"ep/cd-ep) (CRANE 006 T/CD) **ADRIFT. / EVERYWHERE / UNDERWATER**		
May 93.	(cd/c/lp) (DED CD/MC/LP 009) <66212> **FOREVER** – Everywhere / Cloudless / Jewel / Far away / Adrift / Clear / Sun and sky / And ever / Golden / Rainbows.	40	
Sep 93.	(7") (CRANE 007) **JEWEL (remix). / CLEAR (scalpicin mix)** (7") (CRANE 007-2) – ('A'side) / Cloudless (Thai mix). (7") (CRANE 007-3) – ('A'side) / Love her to Heaven (II). (cd-ep) (CRANE 007CD) – (all 4 tracks).	29	

		Dedicated	Arista
Aug 94.	(7"m) (CRANE 008) **SHINING ROAD. / LILIES / SEPTEMBER** (cd-s+=) (CRANE 008CD) – Green song 7. (7"m) (CRANE 008-2) – ('A'-Braver mix) / Lilies (Flood mix) / Don't close your eyes.	57	–
Sep 94.	(cd/c/lp) (DED CD/MC/LP 016) <18769> **LOVED** – Shining road / Pale blue sky / Reverie / Lillies / Are you gone? / Loved / Beautiful friend / Bewildered / Gone this far / Paris and Rome.		Oct94
May 96.	(ltd-cd) (DEDCD 024) <44003> **LA TRAGEDIE D'ORESTES ET ELECTRA**		Oct96

| Feb 97. | (cd/c) (DED CD/MC 026) <44005> **POPULATION 4**
– Tangled up / Fourteen / Breeze / Can't get free / Stalk / Sweet unknown / Angel bell / On top of the world / Brazil / Let go / To be / Lemon tree. |
| May 97. | (cd-ep) (CRANE 10CD) **CAN'T GET FREE / PERFECT WORLD / LEMON TREE / TRUMPET SONG** (pier scene from 'Scarborough Ahoy!') |

— JIM + ALISON recruited PAUL SMITH – bass + JON CALLENDER – drums

Dadaphonic   Instinct

| Jun 01. | (cd/lp) (DADA 001 CD/LP) <592> **FUTURE SONGS**
– Future song / Submarine / Flute song / Sunrise / Don't wake me up / Driving in the sun / Fragile / Eight / Even when / Everything for / The making of heavenly trousers / Fragile / Don't wake me up / In the reeds. |

Elefant   not iss.

| Nov 02. | (7"clear) (ER 242) **THE MOON CITY. /** |

– compilations, etc. –

| Sep 97. | (d-cd) Dedicated; (DEDCD 035) <44019> **THE EP COLLECTION VOL.1 & 2** |

Ian CRAUSE (see under ⇒ DISCO INFERNO)

CRAYON (see under ⇒ TULLYCRAFT)

CREAMS
(see under ⇒ DEEP FREEZE MICE; 80's section)

CREATION

Formed: Middlesex, England ... 1961 as (5-piece!) MARK FOUR by KENNY PICKETT, JACK JONES and EDDIE PHILLIPS. Under the guidance of manager ROBERT STIGWOOD they released a couple of flop singles for 'Mercury'. Following a further two stiffs for 'Decca' and 'Fontana' respectively, they changed their line-up in mid-66 and became The CREATION. They also employed new manager TONY STRATTON-SMITH who found American producer SHEL TALMY and a new label, 'Planet'. Things started looking up when the group unleashed 2 superb 45's in 1966, 'MAKING TIME' and 'PAINTER MAN', both hitting the UK Top 50 (aided by alleged chart hyping from TONY). The former marked their finest moment, a blistering combination of searing R&B and psychedelia while the latter hit No.1 in Germany. When they moved to 'Polydor' in 1967, however, they ran out of steam and split the year after. Unfortunately their only LP release had been in Germany, where they had found some degree of success. In 1996, The CREATION were back on song with a fresh set, 'POWER SURGE', released for who else, 'Creation' records. • **Trivia:** PHILLIPS was the first person to play guitar with a violin bow, a feat later achieved by JIMMY PAGE of LED ZEPPELIN. • **Songwriters:** PICKETT or PHILLIPS plus covers:- ROCK AROUND THE CLOCK (Bill Haley) / TRY IT BABY (Marvin Gaye) / LIKE A ROLLING STONE (Bob Dylan) / BONY MORONIE (Larry Williams) / HEY JOE (hit; Jimi Hendrix) • **Trivia:** In 1970, PICKETT co-wrote UK No.1 hit 'Grandad' for CLIVE DUNN (Dad's Army) with HERBIE FLOWERS. PICKETT was later to write 'TEACHER TEACHER' for DAVE EDMUNDS, before he co-wrote some more songs with BILLY BREMNER. **Legacy:** PAINTER MAN was a 1979 UK Top 10 hit for BONEY M, while much later The GODFATHERS (in 1990) and RIDE (in 1994) covered HOW DOES IT FEEL TO FEEL. Many have been inspired by them including TELEVISION PERSONALITIES / TIMES / BIFF BANG POW and the label 'Creation'.

Album rating: HOW DOES IT FEEL TO FEEL compilation (*8) / POWER SURGE (*7)

MARK FOUR

KENNY PICKETT (b. 3 Sep'47, Ware, England) – vocals / **EDDIE PHILLIPS** (b.EDWIN, 15 Aug'45, Leytonstone, England) – lead guitar / **MICK THOMPSON** – rhythm guitar / **JOHN DALTON** – bass / **JACK JONES** (b. 8 Nov'44, Northampton, England) – drums

Mercury   not iss.

| May 64. | (7") (MF 815) **ROCK AROUND THE CLOCK. / SLOW DOWN** |
| Aug 64. | (7") (MF 825) **TRY IT BABY. / CRAZY COUNTRY HOP** |

Decca   not iss.

| Aug 65. | (7") (F 12204) **HURT ME IF YOU WILL. / I'M LEAVING** |

Fontana   not iss.

| Feb 66. | (7") (TF 664) **WORK ALL DAY (SLEEP ALL NIGHT). / GOING DOWN FAST** |

— Split after final gig on 6th June 1966. DALTON joined The KINKS.

CREATION

BOB GARNER – bass (ex-TONY SHERIDAN BAND) repl. THOMPSON

Planet   Planet

| Jun 66. | (7") (<PLF 116>) **MAKING TIME. / TRY AND STOP ME** | 49 | |
| Oct 66. | (7") (<PLF 119>) **PAINTER MAN. / BIFF BANG POW** | 36 | |

KIM GARDNER – bass (ex-BIRDS) repl. GARNER

Polydor   Decca

Jun 67.	(7") (56177) **IF I STAY TOO LONG. / NIGHTMARES**
Oct 67.	(7") (56207) **LIFE IS JUST BEGINNING. / THROUGH MY EYES**
Nov 67.	(7") <32227> **HOW DOES IT FEEL TO FEEL. / LIFE IS JUST BEGINNING**

| Jan 68. | (7") (56230) **HOW DOES IT FEEL TO FEEL. / TOM TOM** |

RON WOOD – guitar (ex-BIRDS) repl. DIGGER who had briefly repl. PICKETT. PICKETT returned to repl. PHILLIPS + GARDNER

| May 68. | (7") (56246) **MIDWAY DOWN. / THE GIRLS ARE NAKED** |

— Disbanded soon after above. PICKETT continued to write for SHEL TALMY and he also became road manager for LED ZEPPELIN in America. RON WOOD joined The FACES and later became a member of The ROLLING STONES. GARDNER co-formed ASHTON, GARDNER & DYKE who had a 1970 Top 3 hit with 'RESURRECTION SHUFFLE'. He later formed BADGER. JACK JONES drifted into cabaret session work.

— CREATION re-formed in the mid-80's with PHILLIPS, PICKETT, NOBBY DALTON – bass (ex-KINKS) + MICK AVORY – drums (ex-KINKS)

Jet   not iss.

| Apr 87. | (7") (JET 7-047) **A SPIRIT CALLED LOVE. / MAKING TIME**
(12"+=) (JET 12-047) – Mumbo jumbo. |

— PHILLIPS, etc, without PICKETT formed pub band CUCKOOS NEST. In 1994, The CREATION re-formed with PICKETT, JONES + PHILLIPS

Creation   Rykodisc

| Jul 94. | (7") (CRE 200) **CREATION. / SHOCK HORROR**
(cd-s+=) (CRECD 200) – Power surge. |
| Mar 96. | (cd/lp) (CRE CD/LP 176) **POWER SURGE**
– Creation / Power surge / Someone's gonna bleed / Shock horror / That's how I found love / Killing song / Nobody wants to know / City life / English language / Free men live forever / Ghost division / O+N. |

— on the 10th Jan'97, KENNY PICKETT died of a heart attack at his home

– compilations, etc. –

| Sep 73. | (lp) Charisma; (CS 8) **CREATION '66-67** |
| Oct 73. | (7") Charisma; (CB 213) **MAKING TIME. / PAINTER MAN**
(re-iss. Nov77 on 'Raw'; RAW 4) |
| Sep 82. | (lp) Edsel; (ED 106) **HOW DOES IT FEEL TO FEEL**
– How does it feel to feel / Life is just beginning / Through my eyes / Ostrich man / I am the walker / Tom Tom / The girls are naked / Painter man / Try and stop me / Biff bang pow / Making time / Cool jerk / For all that I am / Nightmares / Midway down / Can I join your band?. (cd-iss. Aug90; EDCD 106) – Uncle Bert / Like a rolling stone / If I stay too long / Hey Joe. (lp re-iss. Feb00 on 'Get Back'; GET 519) |
| 1983. | (lp) Eva; (12005) **THE MARK FOUR / THE CREATION**
(cd-iss. 1992 & Jul99; EVAB 16) |
| May 84. | (7") Edsel; (E 5006) **MAKING TIME. / UNCLE BERT** |
| 1985. | (7"ep; by MARK FOUR) Bam Caruso; (OPRA 037) **LIVE AT THE BEAT SCENE CLUB**
– Hurt me if you will / Got my mojo working / That's how strong my love is. |
Apr 93.	(m-lp) Edsel; (NESTCD 904) **PAINTER MAN**
Oct 93.	(cd/lp) Cohesion; (COCRD/COCRL 1) **LAY THE GHOST (live)**
Apr 98.	(cd) Diablo; (DIAB 857) **OUR MUSIC IS RED WITH PURPLE FLASHES**
Oct 98.	(cd) Retroactive; (RECD 9002) **MAKING TIME – CREATION VOL.1**
(re-iss. Jun00; SD 8937)
Oct 98.	(cd) Retroactive; (RECD 9003) **BIFF BANG POW – CREATION VOL.2**
(re-iss. Jun00; SD 8936)
Mar 99.	(cd) Repertoire; (REP 4735) **WE ARE THE PAINTERMEN**
Feb 00.	(lp) Get Back; (GET 518) **THE SINGLES COLLECTION**

CREEPER LAGOON

Formed: San Francisco, California, USA ... 1997 by a multi-instrumentalist going under the unlikely name of SHARKY LAGUANA. After virtually giving up looking for work all over the States, the singer/guitarist turned busker spent some months fasting in a Santa Cruz monastery. He thought his luck had changed when an eccentric Bostonian person wanted to become his manager. However, this was curtailed when his condo was burnt to the ground by fire-raising squatters below him; he was subsequently awarded a surprise 5-figure sum due to landlord negligence – no fire alarm! Enjoying his newfound wealth while also buying up recording equipment, SHARKY made friends with his new lodger/squatter, IAN SEFCHICK, and together they formed CREEPER LAGOON. Recruiting the rhythm section of GEOFFREY CHISHOLM and DAVID KOSTINER, they gained support from production giants, The DUST BROTHERS, the pair helping create their well-received debut set (musically akin to a more upbeat PAVEMENT), 'I BECOME SMALL AND GO' (1998). CREEPER LAGOON re-appeared on 'Spin Art', 'DreamWorks' and 'Arena Rock' records during a hectic time post-millennium. Sophomore outing, 'TAKE BACK THE UNIVERSE AND GIVE ME YESTERDAY' (2001), was obviously better produced and more subdued than its predecessor, although sonic anthems such as 'WRECKING BALL', maintained their stance in the indie-rock scene.

Album rating: I BECOME SMALL AND GO (*7) / TAKE BACK THE UNIVERSE AND GIVE ME YESTERDAY (*6)

SHARKY LAGUANA – vocals, multi-instruments

not iss.   Slabco Enterprises

| 1994. | (c) <none> **CREEPER LAGOON** |

not iss.   Shrimper

| 1994. | (c) **SHASTA COMPLEX**
– Over the rainbow / Upland fiesta / Back down / Atom smasher / Treason blue sunrise / Distress traffic / Colorado / You let me down / Secrecy of communication / Half as strong / That's your decision. |

		not iss.	Cactus Rum
1995.	(c) <none> **DEATH SENTENCE**	-	

– This portion will check / What the hell do you want / Eyes of Hazel / The Stalin epigram / Twelve / Yellow black sheets of rain / 20 miles south – Small town in Michigan / X kiss the unknown / Goodbye Tuesday.

		not iss.	Ratfish
1995.	(7"lp) <none> **CREEPER LAGOON VS. THE DEAD C**	-	

– Tonight was fun / The girl who fell to Earth / August Pascal / Fucking snob.

—— added **IAN SEFCHICK** – guitar, vocals / **GEOFFREY CHISHOLM** – bass; repl. BUSH BRINGLEMAN / **PATRICK MAGNAN** – drums

		Shifty Disco	Dogday
Dec 97.	(cd-ep) <3500> **CREEPER LAGOON**	-	

– Dear deadly / Sylvia / Drop your head / Empty ships / Second chance.

Oct 98. (7") (DISCO 9809) **DEAR DEADLY. / MOLLY** | | - |

—— **DAVID KOSTINER** – drums; repl. PATRICK

		Polydor	Nicklebag
Oct 98.	(cd-s) **WONDERFUL LOVE / THE FOUNTAIN**		-
Nov 98.	(cd) (559323-2) <6> **I BECOME SMALL AND GO**		May98

– Wonderful love / Tracy / Empty ships / Dreaming again / Prison mix / Sylvia / Dear deadly / Black hole / Drink and drive / Second chance / He made us all blind / Claustrophobia.

—— **DAN CARR** – bass; repl. CHISHOLM

		not iss.	SpinArt
Oct 00.	(cd-ep) <SPIN 87> **WATERING GHOST GARDEN**	-	

– Centipede eyes / Roman hearts / Big money struggle / Chain smoker / My friends adore you / God will understand.

		Dreamworks	Dreamworks
Jun 01.	(cd) <(DRD 50043)> **TAKE BACK THE UNIVERSE AND GIVE ME YESTERDAY**		

– Chance of a lifetime / Wrecking ball / Sunfair / She loves me not / Up all night / Naked days / Under the tracks / Dead man saloon / Hey sister / Cellophane / Keep from moving / Lover's leap / Here we are.

—— **SHARKY** recruited **JASON BASSLER** – drums / **MILES TUFFLI** – guitar / **RACHEL LASTIMOSA** – keyboards, backing vocals

		not iss.	Arena Rock
Dec 02.	(cd-ep) <28> **REMEMBER THE FUTURE**	-	

– So little to give / The way it goes / There's a new girl / Kisses and pills / Crisis.

CREEPERS (see under ⇒ RILEY, Marc)

CRESCENT

Formed: Huyton, Liverpool, England … 1995 by bassist SEAN LONGWORTH and drummer JOEY HARRISON, initially for a school talent show, when they were only fourteen. Later joined by guitarist KARL ROWLANDS, The CRESCENT began an association with the LA'S former frontman LEE MAVERS, whom they backed at gigs. Inspired by the music of the LA'S and OASIS, The CRESCENT endured a period of instability, and eventually decided to end their association with the increasingly erratic MAVERS. The recruitment of vocalist WAYNE WHITFIELD completed the line-up, and with interest from several UK record labels, they signed on with 'Hut'. May 2002 saw the release of debut single 'ON THE RUN, an impressive slice of STONES-influenced indie-rock which scraped into the Top 50. With subsequent gigs around the UK, The CRESCENT delivered two more minor chart hits, 'TEST OF TIME' and 'SPINNIN' WHEELS', both lifted from their promising eponymous debut set released that autumn. • **Note:** Not to be confused with punk act of mid 90's or the lo-fi/ambient project on the late 90's.

Album rating: THE CRESCENT (*7)

WAYNE WHITFIELD – vocals / **KARL ROWLANDS** – guitar / **SEAN LONGWORTH** – bass / **JOEY HARRISON** – drums

		Hut	E.M.I.
May 02.	(7") (HUT 153) <546398> **ON THE RUN. / ONE WAY TICKET**	49	Jun02
	(cd-s+=) (HUTCD 153) – Mayday.		
Jul 02.	(7") (HUT 157) **TEST OF TIME. / OPEN QUESTION**	60	-
	(cd-s+=) (HUTCD 157) – Sun too long.		
Sep 02.	(7") (HUT 160) **SPINNIN' WHEELS. / JUMPING JACK FLASH**	61	-
	(cd-s) (HUTCD 160) – ('A'side) / Freedom, peace and liberty / High tide.		
	(cd-s) (HUTDX 160) – ('A'side) / ('A'-Evening session) / Highly likely / One to another.		
Sep 02.	(cd/lp) (CDHUT/HUTLP 78) **THE CRESCENT**		-

– On the run / Streets of tide / Parallel / Wake up / Test of time / Another day / Spinnin' wheels / Not good enough / Told U so / Stay on.

CRINGER (see under ⇒ J CHURCH)

CROCKETTS

Formed: Aberystwyth, Ceredigion, Wales … early 1996 by local college/uni teenagers, OWEN CASH, Irish-born DAVEY MacMANUS, DAN BOONE and RICH TURPIN. A mischievous Celtic-punk outfit lying somewhere between RAMONES or The CLASH, The CROCKETTS unleashed their own self-financed mini-set, 'FROG ON A STICK' (1996), before they were snapped up by Virgin V2 offshoot, 'Blue Dog', after being spotted at Dublin's In The City festival. First up for the label was the EP, 'HELLO AND GOOD MORNING'; released in September '97, it was pure unadulterated punk-pop that even GREEN DAY would have been proud of. A series of singles preceded their debut album, 'WE MAY BE SKINNY & WIREY' (1998), an appropriate title as the lads had about as much meat on them as a vegetarian barbeque.
• **Covered:** RHINESTONE COWBOY (Glen Campbell).

Album rating: WE MAY BE SKINNY & WIREY (*7) / THE GREAT BRAIN ROBBERY (*6)

DAVEY MacMANUS – vocals, guitar / **DAN BOONE** – guitar / **RICH TURPIN** – bass / **OWEN CASH** – drums

		Crocketts	not iss.
1996.	(c; as MR CROCKETT) (none) **STUFF YOUR CHERRY PIE**		-

– Bacon butties / Peace talks in a cafe / Billy and the dragon / Wake me in the morning / Your face is dripping / Stunner / Palisade / Blue dog.

| Nov 96. | (m-cd; as The CROCKETTS – 20th CENTURY VIKINGS) (none) **FROG ON A STICK** | | - |

– Piggy eyes / Rasta Vega / Banana striped T-shirt / The last note / Stunner / The stone age gypsy / Billy and the dragon.

—— In 1997, The CROCKETTS (as GEORGEOUS FAME & THE 3 DEGREES) split a single, 'GREEN GREEN GRASS OF HOME' / 'PEDRO' with MURRY THE HUMP on 'Blue Dog Singles Club' (No.5)

		Blue Dog – V2	Imprint
Sep 97.	(10"ep/cd-ep) (BDG 500035-8/-3) **HELLO AND GOOD MORNING EP**		-

– Will you still care / Stunner / Cars and football / Wednesdays in my bed.

Mar 98.	(7") (BDG 500156-7) **LOVED YA ONCE. / CASH KITTY**		-
	(cd-s+=) (BDG 500156-3) – 21st birthday party (live) / Frog on a stick (demo).		
May 98.	(7") (BDG 500159-7) **FLOWER GIRL / MRS DONNELLY**		-
	(cd-s+=) (BDG 500159-3) – Banana breath baby (live) / Three lie ins (demo).		
Sep 98.	(cd/lp) (BDG 100241-2/-1) <120290> **WE MAY BE SKINNY & WIREY**		Nov98

– Flower girl / Love ya once / Explain / Blust boy / Girl next door / Tennessee / Will you still care / Six soon to be seven / Bucket and spade / Autumn afternoon / Strony guy / Blue dog / (untitled).

Oct 98.	(7"blue/cd-s) (BDG 500252-7/-3) **EXPLAIN. / RHINESTONE COWBOY / INSIDE HEAD ON**		-
May 99.	(7") (BDG 500775-7) **JAMES DEAN-ESQUE. / BILLY THE BUNT**		-
	(cd-s+=) (BDG 500775-3) – Rapid pulsing breaths.		
Oct 99.	(cd-ep) (BDG 501082-3) **NINTENDO FALLACY**		-

– Mrs playing dead / Son of the Devil / Sit back sucker and say / Smoulder / Beauty and the beast / Dont curse in front of my kids.

Apr 00.	(cd-s) (BDG 501133-3) **HOST / YOU DON'T KNOW NOTHING (live) / BEAST WITH TWO BACKS (live)**		-
	(cd-s) (BDG 501133-8) – ('A'live) / Will you still care? (live) / Strong guy (live).		
Apr 00.	(cd/lp) (BDG 101181-2/-1) **THE GREAT BRAIN ROBBERY**		-

– 1939 returning / Mrs Playing dead / Host / Chicken vs macho / On something / Lucifer / Survival of the prettiest / Pity youth doesn't last / One shake / Million things / Ella Luciana / Ladykiller.

Jul 00.	(cd-s) (BDG 501320-8) **ON SOMETHING / HOST (featuring MARY HOPKIN) / OPPOSITE ENDS**		-
	(cd-s) (BDG 501320-3) – ('A'live) / Beauty and the beast (acoustic) / Ella Luciana (live).		
Oct 00.	(7") (BDG 501502-7) **1939 RETURNING. / CHICKEN VS MACHO (featuring MARY HOPKIN)**		-

('A'-August 2000; cd-s+=) (BDG 501502-3) – Happy as a bastard.
('A'-BBC live; cd-s+=) (BDG 501502-8) – That's for sure.

Brian CROOK (see under ⇒ RENDERERS)

CROOKED FINGERS (see under ⇒ ARCHERS OF LOAF)

CROWNHATE RUIN (see under ⇒ HOOVER)

CROWSDELL

Formed: Jacksonville, Florida, USA … 1990 by bassist, PAUL CROWSDELL and singer/guitarist SHANNON WRIGHT, the pair adding drummer, LAURIE WALL shortly afterwards. This two-girl/one-guy PAVEMENT-esque outfit chose the name of the former, although embarrassment led to the man adopting the new surname of HOWELL. Out of the savings from a recent bereavement, PAUL sent a number of demo tapes to various labels around the States, although it would be North Carolina's 'Jettison' imprint (run by Todd Goss) who would take CROWSDELL under their wing. In 1993, two singles, 'LICKETY SPLIT' and 'MEANY', appeared, although it was a third for 'Figurehead', 'DARREN', that would get the attention of UK label, 'Big Cat'. Radio One DJ, John Peel, was an early admirer of their work, while PAVEMENT's STEVE MALKMUS (who else!) took up the chance to produce their debut album, 'DREAMETTE'. Released during a well-received Lollapalooza tour in Spring '95, its melodic alt-country-esque guitar-rock saddled with SHANNON's tales of heartfelt woe endeared them to fans from all walks of life. It took two long years before the release of a follow-up, 'WITHIN THE CURVE OF AN ARM' (1997), another charming slice of indie rock/pop that improved with every listen. With the band having separated, the delightful SHANNON moved to the backwoods (so to speak) of North Carolina, where she carved out a solo career. 'FLIGHTSAFETY' in 1999, saw her emerging in her own right as the female equivalent of say, ELLIOTT SMITH, the singles 'CAPTAIN OF QUARANTINE' and 'YOU'RE THE CUP' both featured here. The following year's 'MAPS OF TACIT', took even bolder steps into conceptual leanings and arty minimalisation, her character vignettes might well have come from the pen of NICO rather than her own inner self. 'DYED IN THE WOOL' (2001), comprised a more solemn SHANNON than her previous work portrayed, chamber pop made way at times for gothic earthiness resulting in a NICO-meets-SIOUXSIE SIOUX deepness and scream rolled into one. Augmented by members of the RACHEL'S, the LOFTY PILLARS and EDITH FROST, this album veered indie poetry into deconstructed rock courtesy of tracks such as 'LESS THAN A MOMENT' and 'VESSEL FOR A MINOR MALADY'. • Covers: SHANNON WRIGHT:- ASLEEP (Smiths) / I STARTED A JOKE (Bee Gees).

Album rating: DREAMETTE (*7) / WITHIN THE CURVE OF AN ARM (*6) / Shannon Wright: FLIGHTSAFETY (*6) / MAPS OF TACIT (*6) / DYED IN THE WOOL (*7)

SHANNON WRIGHT (b. 8 Nov'74, Baltimore, Maryland, USA) – vocals, guitar / **PAUL HOWELL** (b. PAUL VAN CROWSDELL) – bass / **LAURIE WALL** – drums

		not iss.	Jettison
1992.	(7") <JET 020> **LICKETY SPLIT. / FRACTIONS**	-	
1992.	(d7") <JET 027> **MEANY. / SAD EYES / NEW // KUSTOM. / SKYSCRAPERS**	-	
		not iss.	Figurehead
1992.	(7") <012> **DOWN. / BUBBLES**	-	
		Big Cat	not iss.
Feb 95.	(7"pink) (ABB 80S) **SUGAR-COATED. / TRUNK**		-
Apr 95.	(lp/cd) (ABB 83/+CD) **DREAMETTE** – Down / Sugar coated / Tease / Sad eyes / Dee-lovely / Weak / Spillin / Weight less / Waltz / Handbook / Grace / Waiting.		-
Sep 95.	(12"ep/cd-ep) (ABB 94 T/CD) **THE END OF ANOTHER SUMMER EP** – Tease / Middle / Friv / Spy 56 / Mama.		
Apr 97.	(7") (ABB 124S) **POPSICK. / SPY 56** (cd-s+=) (ABB 124CD) – Mama.		
Jun 97.	(lp/cd) (ABB 125/+CD) **WITHIN THE CURVE OF AN ARM** – Popsick / Five stars / Mooncalf / Lurking in sagas / You want me dead / Floridian lamb / W.C. Haley / Pharmaceutical fingers / Patches / Sunny sparkle / Cut and paste / Wake the lass / Foul.		-
Aug 97.	(cd-s) (ABB 127SCD) **LURKING IN SAGAS / KUSTOM MADE / PLASTIC GIRL**		-

SHANNON WRIGHT

- vocals, guitar, etc

		All City	All City
Mar 99.	(7") <AC 10> **A TIN CROWN FOR THE SOCIAL BASH. / YOU'RE THE CUP**		

—— next with **JOEY BURNS** – bass + **ERIC BACHMANN** – piano

		Quarter Stick	Quarter Stick
May 99.	(lp/cd) <(QS 56/+CD)> **FLIGHTSAFETY** – Floor pile / All these things / Rich hum of air / You're the cup / Twilight hall / Captain of quarantine / Holland / Hobos on parade / William's Alabama / Yard grass / Heavy crown.		Apr99
1999.	(7") **CAPTAIN OF QUARANTINE. / WISH YOU WELL** (above issued on 'Put It On A Cracker')	-	

—— next with **ANDY BAKER** – bass + **BRIAN TEASLEY** – drums

May 00.	(cd) <(QS 68CD)> **MAPS OF TACIT** – Absentee / Within the quilt of demand / Fences of pales / Ribbons of you / Flask welder / Dirty facade / Heavy crown / Noise / The hover is ajar / Regulation scorrer / Ember days / Pay no mind.		
Apr 01.	(ltd-cd-ep) <QS 70CD> **PERISHABLE GOODS EP** – Hinterland / Foul / I started a joke / Azalea / Familiar settings / Capsule of you / The path of least persistence.	-	
Aug 01.	(cd) <QS 72CD> **DYED IN THE WOOL** – Less than a moment / The hem around us / Hinterland / Vessel for a minor malady / You hurry wonder / Dyed in the wool / Method of sleeping / Surly demise / Colossal hours / The path of least persistence (figure II) / The sable / Bells.	-	
		not iss.	Grey Flat
Oct 02.	(7") <07 WRIGHJUNI> **A JUNIOR HYMN. / ASLEEP**	-	

CRUNT (see under ⇒ BABES IN TOYLAND)

CUB

Formed: Vancouver, Canada ... 1992 by all-girl trio, LISA MARR, ROBYNN IWATA and VALERIA FELLINI, who met at the University of British Columbia. Although having not much musical prowess amongst them, the fledgling group nevertheless began performing live fairly quickly, gaining skill and confidence along the way. Their sound ranged somewhere in the catchy, melodious world of punk-pop, or as some critics dub it "cuddlecore", and was showcased on the debut '92 EP, 'PEP', issued by local label, 'Mint', run by IWATA's sibling, RANDY. Hot on its heels was their initial full-length set, 'BETTI-COLA' (1993), which included the tracks from the erstwhile EP and more new songs, while also featuring a cover by Dan DeCarlo (of 'Archie' comics fame). Following this set, FELLINI parted ways with CUB, and her position was filled by LISA G, who had got in contact with the band using the fanzine, 'Self-Esteem Queen'. The group went from strength to strength with their next full-length offering, 'COME OUT, COME OUT' (1994), which due to the added dissemination of their material by Stateside imprint, 'Lookout', meant they were now getting wider attention across the border. This piece, turned its face on the critics who had derided the band as merely puerile, as it displayed a maturity in both subject-matter and song structure, placing the group more within the context of the riot grrrl scene. This position was furthered by the release of their third LP, 'BOX OF HAIR', which superseded it two years later. The ensuing twelve months saw the issue of what was to be their final outing, the compilation 'MAULER' (1997), as by early summer of that year, the band officially handed in their resignations which were published on RANDY's imprint's official website. • **Songwriters:** MARR except CAST A SHADOW (Beat Happening) / SURFER GIRL (Beach Boys) / etc.

Album rating: BETTI-COLA (*8) / COME OUT, COME OUT (*7) / BOX OF HAIR (*6) / MAULER compilation (*5)

LISA MARR – vocals, bass / **ROBYNN IWATA** – guitar / **VALERIA FELLINI** – drums

		Lookout	Mint
Sep 92.	(7"gold-ep) <MRS 002> **PEP** – Go fish / What the water gave me / Motel 6 / Party / Flying carpet.	-	
May 93.	(7"clear-ep) <MRS 004> **HOT DOG DAY** – My chinchilla / Electrick chair / Nicolas Bragg / Pretty pictures / They don't / Picnic.	-	
1993.	(7") **THE MINT IS A TERRIBLE THING TO TASTE (split w/ Coal)**	-	
Nov 93.	(d7"blue) <MRS 005> **BETTI-COLA. / HELLO KITTY / +2**	-	
Nov 93.	(cd) <MRD 002> **BETTI-COLA** (compilation of 2 EP's and sessions) – PEP / HOT DOG DAY / + It's true / Someday / Cast a shadow / The day we met / Surfer girl / Little star / My assassin / Tell me now / Lucky 7 / Through my hoop / Leapfrog / Backwoods / What the water gave me.	-	
May 94.	(7"clear) <MRS 009> **VOLCANO** – Your bed / Cast a shadow (live).	-	- gig

—— **LISA G** – drums, guitar; repl. FELLINI

Jan 95.	(cd) <MRD 005> **COME OUT, COME OUT** – Ticket to Spain / Everything's geometry / My flaming red bobsled / Isabelle / Your bed / Tomorrow go away / Life of crime / I'm your angel / Por favor / New York City / Voracious / So far apart / Vacation.	-	
Aug 95.	(7"ep/cd-ep) (LOOKOUT 124/+CD) <MRS-013/MRD-008> **THE DAY I SAID GOODBYE** – The day I said goodbye / Exit / (other 2 by the POTATOMEN).		
Aug 96.	(cd/lp) (LOOKOUT 143 CD/LP) <MRD/MRL 021> **BOX OF HAIR** – Freaky / Pillow queen / Magic 8 ball / Loaded / Main and Broadway / Box of hair / One last kiss / Way to go / Mom and dad / S.G. / Riverside / Not what you think.		Jul96
		Au-Go-Go	Au-Go-Go
Feb 97.	(cd) <(ANDA 214)> **MAULER – A COLLECTION OF SINGLES** (compilation) – You know he did / Nicolas Bragg / The day I said goodbye / She's like a rainbow / Exit / Pregnant / My flaming red bobsled / Pillow queen / Green eyes / Freaky / FB song / Secret nothing / Go fish / New York City / Runaway / My chinchilla.		

—— disbanded on the 10th June, 1997

CUB COUNTRY (see under ⇒ JETS TO BRAZIL)

CUCKOO (see under ⇒ JETPLANE LANDING)

CUL DE SAC

Formed: Chicago, Illinois, USA ... 1990 by GLENN JONES (not the gospel/R&B solo artist), ROBIN AMOS and CHRIS GUTTMACHER. Located squarely at the avant-garde end of the alternative rock avenue, CUL DE SAC made their vinyl debut in 1992 with a limited edition UK-only 7" single, 'SAKHALIN', followed closely by a debut album, 'ECIM' (1992). Throwing together disparate strands of world music, 60's/70's psychedelic experimentalism and rootsy folk, the band were augmented in their ambitious endeavours by bass player, CHRIS FUJIWARA, steel guitarist/violinist, ED YAZIJIAN, effects man, PHIL MILSTEIN and guest vocalist, DREDD FOOLE. A series of singles on various obscure indie labels appeared over the next few years while a belated follow-up album, 'I DON'T WANT TO GO TO BED', surfaced in summer '95; a double set released on 'Flying Nun', the record was a ramshackle collection of largely instrumental workouts that steadfastly defied pigeonholing. Following the replacement of GUTTMACHER with JOHN PROUDMAN, the quartet released their second album proper, 'CHINA GATE' (1996) opening with the HAROLD ADAMSON and VICTOR YOUNG mid-century written title track. CUL DE SAC subsequently worked with veteran folk/roots man, JOHN FAHEY, on third album, 'THE EPIPHANY OF GLENN JONES' (1997). With a slightly revised line-up (with newcomers MICHAEL BLOOM and JON PROUDMAN), CUL DE SAC completed their 5th set, 'CRASHES TO LIGHT, MINUTES TO ITS FALL' in 1999, a math-rock extravaganza of melodic but yet experimental delights. AMOS and his keyboard synthesizer rolled off surfadelic Middle Eastern rhythms, like meeting ASH RA TEMPEL with CAN. A posthumous set, 'IMMORTALITY LESSONS' (2002), were actually recordings taken from a disastrous radio station gig at Brandeis University that turned out to be okay; they briefly re-united (May 2002) to augment CAN idol DAMO SUZUKI.

Album rating: ECIM (*5) / I DON'T WANT TO GO TO BED compilation (*7) / CHINA GATE (*6) / CRASHES TO LIGHT, MINUTES TO ITS FALL (*6) / IMMORTALITY LESSONS (*5)

GLENN JONES – guitar / **ROBIN AMOS** – multi (ex-GIRLS) / **CHRIS GUTTMACHER** – drums (of BULLET LAVOLTA) / added 4th member **CHRIS FUJIWARA** – bass / plus **ED YAZIJIAN** – steel guitar, violin / **PHIL MILSTEIN** – sampler / guest **DREDD FOOLE** – vocals

		Shock	not iss.
1992.	(7"ltd) (SX 017) **SAKHALIN. / CANT**		
		Pell	Northeastern
Oct 92.	(lp/cd) (PELL 11/12) <5503> **ECIM** – Death kit train / The moon scolds the morning star / Stranger at Coney Island / Homunculus / The Portland cement factory at Monolith, California / Nico's dream / The invisible worm / Song to the siren / Electar / Lauren's blues.		Nov91

CUL DE SAC (cont)

— now without ED who joined KUSTOMIZED

		not iss.	Nuf Sed
Jan 93.	(7") **DOLDRUMS. / …HIS TEETH GOT LOST IN THE MATTRESS …**	–	

		not iss.	Lunar Rotation
1993.	(7") **FRANKIE MACHINE. / K**	–	

		not iss.	New World Of Sound
1993.	(7") **MILK DEVIL. / RAIN MOTHS**	–	

		Flying Nun	Thirsty Ear
Jun 95.	(d-lp/cd) *(FN/+CD 330)* <57029> **I DON'T WANT TO GO TO BED** (compilation)		1997

– Abandoned hospital / Doldrums / Graveyard for robots / The fraud of satisfaction / Roses in the wallpaper / This is the metal that do not born / Lover Hat, Massachusetts / The Kim Parker report / Count Donut / For seasickness / Lully's gangrene. *(cd re-iss. Sep98; same)*

— **JOHN PROUDMAN** – drums; repl. GUTTMACHER

Jun 96.	(cd) *(FNCD 376)* <57023> **CHINA GATE**		May96

– China gate / Sakhalin / Nepenthe / Doldrums / Virgin among cannibals / …His teeth got lost in the mattress… / Hemispheric events command / The fourth eye / The colomber / China gate (reprise) / Utopia Pkwy. *(re-iss. Sep98; same)*

Sep 97.	(cd; JOHN FAHEY & CUL DE SAC) <57037> **THE EPIPHANY OF GLENN JONES**	–	

– Tuff / Gamelan collage / The new red pony / Maggie Campbell blues / Our puppet selves / Gamelan guitar / Come on in my kitchen / Magic mountain / More nothing / Nothing.

— **MICHAEL BLOOM** – bass; repl. FUJIWARA
— **MICHAEL KNOBLACH** – drums; repl. PROUDMAN

		Earworm	Thirsty Ear
Dec 98.	(7") *(WORM 39)* **THE PORTLAND CEMENT FACTORY AT MONOLITH, CALIFORNIA. / HAGSTROM**		–

— **JON PROUDMAN** returned to repl. KNOBLACH

May 99.	(cd) <57064> **CRASHES TO LIGHT, MINUTES TO ITS FALL**	–	

– Etaoin shrdlu / K / A voice through a cloud / Into the cone of cold / Far off, the fabulous iron serpent whistles / Father silence / Hagstrom / Sands of Iwo Jima / Auf der Maur / On the roof of the world.

— played their last gig in summer 1999; re-formed to back DAMO SUZUKI (ex-CAN) in May 2002

– compilations, etc. –

May 02.	(cd) *Strange Attractors Audio House;* <7> **IMMORTALITY LESSONS** (live)	–	

– Etaoin without shrdlu / Enhoft remain / Immortality lessons / Tartarugas / Frozen in fury on the roof of the world / The dragonfly's bright eye / Liturgy / Flying music from Faust / Blue in E.

John CUNNINGHAM

Born: 1969, Liverpool, England; not to be confused with Scottish multi-instrumentalist formerly of trad-folk outfit, Silly Wizard. A throw-back from the late 70's arty scene in Brighton (where he was raised), and a casualty of a string of musical disappointments, CUNNINGHAM wore his heart on his sleeve come the singer/songwriter's debut outing, the mini-LP 'BACKWARDS STEPS' (1989) – produced by "Housemartians" (sic) guitarist, STAN CULLIMORE. However, it wasn't until 1992's beautifully raw 'SHANKLY GATES' that the soft-voiced folk troubadour really came into his own. Then living in France, CUNNINGHAM received more than a few column inches, but no sales to match, coming across as a modern day NICK DRAKE. This comparison was even more defined come the sophomore effort 'BRINGING IN THE BLUE' (1994), a quiet, hazy and sometimes sombre set which echoed DONOVAN's mid-60's and DRAKE's 'Bryter Layter' period, if not borrowing snippets from CAT STEVENS. After its release, CUNNINGHAM hardly toured and spent five years writing and recording his largely ignored swansong, 'HOMELESS HOUSE' (1998), which showcased his incredible songwriting talents, as well as a stripped-down, almost demo-like production – again, straining comparisons to DRAKE's final album 'Pink Moon'. But, lucky for the rest of the world, this was not to be CUNNINGHAM's final release; 2002's 'HAPPY-GO-UNLUCKY' was a collaborative effort with FUGU's MEHDI ZANNAD, who arranged the entire string section in a return favour for CUNNINGHAM's mixing work on FUGU's debut, 'Fugul'. The title of his most recent album summed up the mood of the set; happy songs based around situations depicting sheer bad luck. Unfortunately, like poor NICK DRAKE and the best of the rest, CUNNINGHAM will only be truly appreciated by audiences when he's not around anymore. Hopefully not for some time to come.

Album rating: BACKWARDS STEPS mini (*5) / SHANKLY GATES (*5) / BRINGING IN THE BLUE (*6) / HOMELESS HOUSE (*7) / HAPPY-GO-UNLUCKY (*7)

JOHN CUNNINGHAM – vocals, guitar

		La-Di-Da	not iss.
Dec 89.	(m-lp) *(LADIDA 006)* **BACKWARDS STEPS**		–

– Backwards steps / Another photograph / Mean old heart / Castles & graves / You'll never know / In wait.

1992.	(cd) *(LADIDA 020)* **SHANKLY GATES**		–

– Punch drunk / Hollow truce / Shankly gates / Spit and polish / Dim crusade / Red stone / Fold down graciously / Comic book notions / Five minutes too late / Marysport / I'm coming home / Master grin.

Oct 94.	(cd) *(LADIDA 033)* **BRINGING IN THE BLUE**		–

– Paradise chosen / Release / Bringing in the blue / Unarmed / Paris green / High falling / Remembrance day / Oblivious to change / Talktown / Improve the shining hour.

		Les Disques	not iss.
1999.	(cd) *(1405)* **HOMELESS HOUSE**	–	– Belgian

– Public information song / Imitation time / Homeless house / Quiet and slow time / Nothing will change my mind / Taming the family / What about now? / Infinity is ending.

		Parasol	Parasol
Oct 02.	(cd) *(<PARCD 083>)* **HAPPY-GO-UNLUCKY**		

– Losing myself too / Here it is / Way to go / Can't get used to this / It isn't easy / You shine / Invisible lines / Welcome to the world / Take your time / It goes on.

CURSIVE

Formed: Omaha, Nebraska, USA … 1995 by TIM KASHER, CLINT SCHNASE, MATT MAGINN and STEVE PEDERSON. With a couple of singles ('THE DISRUPTION' and 'SUCKER AND DRY') already under their belt the group released their debut album 'SUCH BLINDING STARS FOR STARVING EYES' in 1997. The music was powerful and stark, perfectly complimented by KASHER's shrill, desperate vocals and heartfelt lyrics. The following year the group issued their second album, 'THE STORMS OF EARLY SUMMER: SEMANTICS OF SONG', before disbanding soon afterwards. CURSIVE did not remain dormant for long and they returned in 2000 with a new guitarist, TED STEVENS, premiered on fresh album, 'DOMESTICA'. The set was centered around KASHER's recent divorce which, coupled with STEVENS' guitar playing, afforded the songs a greater intensity. The follow up, 'BURST AND BLOOM' (2001), saw very little progress and the addition of cellist GRETTA COHN seemed like a shallow attempt to make their music more sophisticated. An eight-song split disc, 'EIGHT TEETH TO EAT YOU', shared with Japanese group EASTERN YOUTH, hit the shops in 2002. Again the songs were fierce and emotive and, by now, the cello sounded more like an integral part of the music and less like a lazy afterthought. KASHER had by now, explored another avenue in his side-project, The GOOD LIFE. With producers A.J. and MIKE MOGIS performing alongside the likes of TODD BAECHLE (of The FAINT) and CURSIVE's CLINT SCHNASE, KASHER had found his niche on two retro-fied sets, 'NOVENA ON A NOCTURN' (2000) and 'BLACK OUT' (2002). Trawling the sounds (but nothing else) of early 80's pre-Brit-pop acts such as The CURE, OMD, The SMITHS and MARC & The MAMBAS, The GOOD LIFE were taking on a darker, melancholic approach to their electronic peers across the water.

Album rating: SUCH BLINDING STARS FOR STARVING EYES (*5) / THE STORMS OF EARLY SUMMER: SEMANTICS OF SONG (*5) / DOMESTICA (*7) / 8 TEETH TO EAT YOU split (*5) / Good Life: NOVENA ON A NOCTURN (*7) / BLACK OUT (*6)

TIM KASHER – vocals, guitar / **STEPHEN PEDERSON** – guitar, vocals / **MATT MAGINN** – bass, vocals / **CLINT SCHNASE** – drums

		not iss.	Saddle Creek
1996.	(7"ep) **THE DISRUPTION EP**	–	

		not iss.	Zero Hour
1996.	(7") **SUCKER AND DRY. /**	–	

		not iss.	Crank!
Sep 97.	(lp) <crc 014> **SUCH BLINDING STARS FOR STARVING EYES**	–	

– After the movies / Downhill racers / Ceilings crack / The dirt of the vineyard / Target group / Eight light minutes / Vermont / Dedication to desertion / Warped the wood floors / Retirement / The farewell party. <cd-iss. on 'Interplanetary Truckers Union'; 80207>

May 98.	(10"ep) <crc 018> **split w/ SILVER SCOOTER**		

– (4 tracks by SILVER SCOOTER) / Returns and exchanges / Pulse / Tides rush in. <cd-ep iss.May99; crc 027>

		not iss.	Saddle Creek
Nov 98.	(cd) <LBJ 22> **THE STORMS OF EARLY SUMMER: SEMANTICS OF SONG**	–	

– The rhyme scheme / A career in transcendence / Road to financial stability / Tempest / Break in the new year / Proposals / Semantics of sermon / A little song and dance / When summer's over will we dream of spring / Northern winds / Absence makes the day go longer.

— **KASHER + MOGIS + PEDERSON** recruited **TED STEVENS** – guitar, vocals (of LULLABY FOR THE WORKING CLASS) – PEDERSON formed WHITE OCTAVE

Jun 00.	(cd) <LBJ 31> **DOMESTICA**	–	

– The casualty / The martyr / Shallow means, deep ends / Making friends and acquaintances / A red so deep / The lament of pretty baby / The game of who needs who the worst / The radiator hums / The night I lost the will to live.

— added **GRETTA COHN** – cello

Jul 01.	(cd-ep) <LBJ 35> **BURST AND BLOOM**	–	

– Sink to the beat / The great decay / Tall tales, tell tales / Mothership, mothership, do you read me? / Fairytales tell tales.

		Five One	Better Looking
Aug 02.	(m-cd; split w/ EASTERN YOUTH) *(FIVE 003)* <12> **8 TEETH TO EAT YOU**		Jun02

– Excerpts from various notes strewn around the bedroom / Am I not yours? / Escape artists / May flowers / (4 tracks by EASTERN YOUTH).

GOOD LIFE

TIM KASHER – vocals, guitar / **CLINT SCHNASE** – drums / **TODD BAECHLE** – keyboards (of FAINT) / **MIKE MOGIS** – bass, keyboards (ex-LULLABY FOR THE WORKING CLASS) / **A.J. MOGIS** – bass (ex-LULLABY FOR THE WORKING CLASS)

CURSIVE (cont)

Dec 00. (cd) <(BLR 004)> **NOVENA ON A NOCTURN**   Better Looking / Better Looking Oct00
- A dim entrance / The Moon red handed / Your birthday present / An acquaintance strikes a chord / Twenty two / What we fall for when we're already down / Waiting on wild horses / The competition / A golden exit. *(re-iss. Oct02; same)*

— **KASHER** with **MIKE MOGIS** plus **JIHA LEE** – Flute, keyboards, synthesizer (of BRIGHT EYES) / **LANDON HEDGES** – bass, guitar (of DESAPARECIDIOS) / **MIKE HEIM** – keyboards / **RYAN FOX** – organ, piano, synths

Nov 02. (cd) <(LBJ 43)> **BLACK OUT**   Saddle Creek / Saddle Creek May02
- Black out / The beaten path / Some bullshit escape / O'Rourke's, 1:20 a.m. / Early out the gate / The new denial / Black out / I am an island / Drinking with the girls / After O'Rourke's, 2:10 a.m. / Empty bed / Don't make love so hard / Off the beaten track / Black out.

CURVE

Formed: London, England ... 1991 by TONI HALLIDAY and her songwriting partner DEAN GARCIA. They had previously been part of the group STATE OF PLAY (one album 'BALANCING THE SCALES' in '86), before TONI ventured solo and released her sole 1989 album, 'HEARTS AND HANDSHAKES'. As CURVE, the pair broke through commercially, DAVE STEWART helping them delelop a much more modern approach on his 'Anxious' label (GARCIA was a friend of DAVE's since playing on EURYTHMICS' albums 'Touch' and 'Be Yourself Tonight'). A pseudo-punk gothic rock act, the sultry dark identity and distinctive vox of TONI combined ideally with the dreamy guitar-playing of DEAN, CURVE's line-up being completed by guitarist CHRIS SHEEHAN and drummer MONTI. The band debuted with 'THE BLINDFOLD EP' in March '91, just as the "shoegazing" scene was reaching its zenith. A kind of palefaced, quasi-industrial cousin to MY BLOODY VALENTINE, the band initially had many critics eating out of their hand. A further two EP's, 'FROZEN' and 'CHERRY' made the Top 40, while in early '92, CURVE cracked the Top 30 with the dark, sexy, 'FAIT ACCOMPLI' single, their finest three minutes. The following month saw the release of a debut set, 'DOPPELGANGER', which met with mixed reviews and suggested that the CURVE sound wore thin over the course of a whole album. A further EP, 'BLACKERTHREETRACKER', and a follow-up album, 'CUCKOO' (1993) saw CURVE lose their creative and commercial momentum, eventually splitting amicably in 1994 when GARCIA decided to devote more time to his family. HALLIDAY's profile remained fairly high with a guest vocal on the hauntingly brilliant LEFTFIELD track, 'ORIGINAL', before CURVE finally made a comeback on 'Universal' records in 1997 courtesy of the 'CHINESE BURN' single. Parent album, 'COME CLEAN' (1998), saw the duo still combining electronic stylings with groovy alternative rock, the critics in the US especially loving the accessiblity of tracks such as 'SOMETHING FAMILIAR' and 'KILLER BABY'. With more major label legal wrangles ensuing, HALLIDAY and GARCIA took the opportunity to provide some new recordings on a website, an album ' . . . HATE FEST' was issued via www.curve.co.uk. A long-awaited (and shelved) follow-up, 'GIFT' finally hit the shops in 2002 through 'Artful' and 'Hip-O' records respectively UK/US. CURVE were back on track here, all menacing, eerie and downright dirty on electro-ballads such as 'CHAINMAIL', 'POLAROID' and 'PERISH', filling time before fans could buy the next GARBAGE set. • **Covered:** I FEEL LOVE (Donna Summer). • **Trivia:** TONI sang backing vox on ROBERT PLANT'S 'Shaken Not Stirred' and RECOIL's 'Bloodline' albums.

Album rating: DOPPELGANGER (*7) / CUCKOO (*6) / COME CLEAN (*4) / GIFT (*6) / State Of Play: BALANCING THE SCALES (*4) / Toni Halliday: HEARTS AND HANDSHAKES (*4)

STATE OF PLAY

TONI HALLIDAY (b.1965, Sunderland, England) – vocals (ex-UNCLES) / **DEAN GARCIA** (half Hawaiian, lives Kentish Town) – bass / **ROMO** / **BAVIN**

Apr 86. (7") *(VS 850)* **NATURAL COLOURS. / LOST SOULS**   Virgin / not iss.
(12"+=) *(VS 850-12)* – ('A'extended).
Jun 86. (7") *(VS 873)* **ROCKABYE BABY. / METROPOLIS**
(12"+=) *(VS 873-12)* – ('A'extended).
Jul 86. (cd/c/lp) *(CD/TC+V 2382)* **BALANCING THE SCALES**
- Naked as the day you were born / Natural colour (remix) / Rockabye baby / Workman / Human kind / Winds of change / We go under / Take me to the king / Lost souls. *(c+=)* – The trout / Strange air. *(cd++=)* – Rescue.

TONI HALLIDAY

Apr 88. (7") *(ANX 003)* **WEEKDAY. / TOP OF THE TREE**   Anxious / W.T.G.
(12"+=) *(ANXT 003)* – ('A'extended).
(cd-s++=) *(ANXCD 003)* – Get out of the rain.
Jul 88. (7") *(ANX 005)* **LOVE ATTRACTION. / CHILD**
(12"+=) *(ANXT 005)* – ('A'-Sub culture mix).
(cd-s++=) *(ANXCD 005)* – ('A'instrumental).
Mar 89. (7") *(ANX 010)* **TIME TURNS AROUND. / DULL MAN**
(12"+=/cd-s+=) *(ANX T/CD 010)* – ('A'-Euro Tech mix).
Jul 89. (lp/c/cd) *(ZL/ZK/ZD 71680)* <45251> **HEARTS AND HANDSHAKES**
- Time turns around / Cut up / Love attraction / Make a wish / Welcome to Heaven / Ode to Anna / Woman in mind / Weekday / I want more / Tales of tomorrow / The price you have to pay / Hearts and handshakes. *(cd+=)* – Dull man / Child.

Jul 89. (7") *(ANX 013)* **WOMAN IN MIND. / CHEMICAL COMEDOWN**
(Thicker versions; 12"+=/cd-s+=) *(ANX T/CD 013)* – ('A'live).

CURVE

(HALLIDAY & GARCIA) with **CHRIS SHEEHAN** – guitar / **MONTI** – drums

Mar 91. (7"ep/12"ep/cd-ep) *(ANX/+T/CD 27)* **THE BLINDFOLD EP**   Anxious 68 / Charisma -
- Ten little girls / I speak your every word / Blindfold / No escape from Heaven.
May 91. (7"/c-s) *(ANX/+C 30)* **COAST IS CLEAR. / FROZEN**   34 / -
(12"+=/cd-s+=) **THE FROZEN EP** *(ANX T/CD 30)* – The colour hours / Zoo.
Oct 91. (7"/c-s) *(ANX/+C 35)* **CLIPPED. / DIE LIKE A DOG**   36 / -
(12"+=/cd-s+=) **THE CHERRY EP** *(ANX T/CD 35)* – Galaxy / Cherry.
Feb 92. (7"/c-s) *(ANX/+C 36)* **FAIT ACCOMPLI. / ARMS OUT**   22 / -
(12"+=/cd-s+=) *(ANX T/CD 36)* – Sigh.
(12") *(ANXTX 36)* – ('A'extended) / Coast is clear (live) / Die like a dog (live).
Mar 92. (cd/c/lp) *(ANX CD/MC/LP 77)* <92108> **DOPPELGANGER**   11 / -
- Already yours / Horror head / Wish you dead / Doppelganger / Lillies dying / Ice that melts the tips / Split into fractions / Think & act / Fait accompli / Sandpit.

— **DEBBIE SMITH + ALEX** – guitar; repl. CHRIS

Jul 92. (7"/c-s) *(ANX/+C 38)* **HORROR HEAD. / MISSION FROM GOD**   31 / -
(12"+=/cd-s+=) *(ANX T/CD 38)* – Today is not the day / Falling free.
Jun 93. (cd/c/lp) *(ANX CD/MC/LP 80)* **RADIO SESSIONS**   72 / -
- Ten little girls / No escape from Heaven / The colour hurts / The coast is clear / Die like a dog / Horror head / Arms out / Split into fractions.

— with **MONTI** – ever faithful drummer / and guest **SALLY HERBERT** – violin

Aug 93. (12"ep/c-ep/cd-ep) *(ANX T/C/CD 42)* **BLACKERTHREETRACKER EP**   39 / -
- Missing link / On the wheel / Triumph.
(cd-ep) *(ANXCDX 42)* – Missing link (screaming bird mix) / Rising (mix) / Half the time (mix).
Sep 93. (cd/c/lp) *(ANX CD/MC/LP 81)* <39061> **CUCKOO**   29 / -
- Missing link / Crystal / Men are from Mars woman from Venus / All of one / Unreadable communication / Turkey crossing / Super blaster / Left of mother / Sweetest pie / Cuckoo.

— split in July '94 although they re-formed in '96.

Sep 96. (7") *(LIP 001)* **PINK GIRL WITH THE BLUES. / RECOVERY**   FatLip / not iss. -
(cd-s+=) *(LIPCD 001)* – Black Delilah.

— In Nov'97, TONI HALLIDAY featured on PAUL VAN DYK's minor UK hit single 'Words'.

Dec 97. (12"/cd-s) *(UMT/UMD 80423)* **CHINESE BURN** (mixes; Steve Osborne / Paul Van Dyk / Lunatic Calm / Witchman's Eye Of The Storm / Headcase Medipac / **ROBBING CHARITY / COME CLEAN**   Universal / Universal
May 98. (12"/cd-s) *(UMT/UMD 80489)* **COMING UP ROSES. /**   51
(cd-s) *(UMDX 80489)* –
May 98. (cd) *(UMD 80475)* <53121> **COME CLEAN**
- Chinese burn / Coming up roses / Something familiar / Dog bone / Alligators getting up / Dirty high / Killer baby / Sweetback / Forgotten sanity / Cotton candy / Beyond reach / Come clean / Recovery.

Jun 02. (cd) *(ARTFULCD 48)* <159819> **GIFT**   Artful / Hip-O Sep01
- Hell above water / Gift / Want more need less / Perish / Hung up / Chainmail / Fly with the high / My tiled white floor / Polaroid / Bleeding heart.

– compilations, others, etc. –

2001. (mp3) *Curve; (none)* **OPEN DAY AT THE HATE FEST (live)**   - / -
- Nowhere / The birds they do fly / Che / Turnaround / You don't know / Backwards glance / Speedcrash / Storm / Caught in the alleyway / Open day at the hate fest.
May 02. (mp3) *Curve; (none)* **THE NEW ADVENTURES OF CURVE**   - / -
- Answers / Till the cows come home / Every good girl / Cold comfort / Star / Nice and easy / Signals and alibis / Sinner / Joy.

Holger CZUKAY (see under ⇒ CAN)

THE GREAT INDIE DISCOGRAPHY — The 1990s

DADAMAH
(see under ⇒ MONTGOMERY, Roy; 80's section)

DAISIES (see under ⇒ MEDAL)

DAISY CHAINSAW

Formed: London, England . . . early 90's by KATIE JANE GARSIDE, main songwriter CRISPIN GREY, RICHARD ADAMS and VINCE JOHNSON. A one-hit indie wonder if there ever was one, DAISY CHAINSAW were famous for about five minutes in 1992 after hitting the UK Top 30 with grunge-pop ditty, 'LOVE YOUR MONEY'. The lead track of their independently released 'LOVESICKPLEASURE' EP, the song centred around GARSIDE's kooky delivery; dressed like a Dickensian beggar girl, her combination of wide-eyed innocence and ragged rebellion stirred up controversy in much the same way as BOW WOW WOW had done a decade earlier. Unfortunately, unlike Malcolm McLaren's former proteges, they only had the one gimmick as 'One Little Indian' (the band subsequently snubbed MADONNA's 'Maverick' label) found out when debut album, 'ELEVENTEEN' (1992), didn't exactly set the charts alight. Any hopes of further success were extinguished with GARSIDE's subsequent departure, due to press furore surrounding alleged revelations of childhood sexual abuse. The remaining trio re-emerging to a predictably hostile reception with 1994's ' . . .FOR THEY KNOW NOT WHAT THEY DO'.
• **Trivia:** A single, 'PIPACHI' (CRISPIN's dogs name), was withdrawn from sale in March 1992.

Album rating: ELEVENTEEN (*5) / . . .FOR THEY KNOW NOT WHAT THEY DO (*3)

KATIE JANE GARSIDE – vocals / **CRISPIN GRAY** (b. JOHN ORION) – guitar / **RICHARD ADAMS** – bass / **VINCE JOHNSON** (b. Toronto, Canada) – drums

		Deva	A&M
Jan 92.	(7"/c-s) (DEVA 001/+C) **LOVE YOUR MONEY. / GET REAL PLEASURE**	26	-
	('LOVE SICK PLEASURE EP' 12"+=/cd-s+=) (DEVA 001 T/CD) – Sick of sex.		
	(above originally issued on 'Deva' only Nov91; same)		

		One Little Indian	A&M
Mar 92.	(7"/c-s) (82 TP7/+C) **PINK FLOWER. / ROOM 11**	65	-
	(12"+=/cd-s+=) (82 TP12/TP7CD) – All the kids agree.		
Mar 92.	(cd-ep) <75021-2403-2> **LOVE SICK PLEASURE**	-	
	– Love your money / Pink flower / Sick of sex / All the kids agree / Room 11.		
Sep 92.	(cd/c) (TPLP 100 CD/C) <314-540031-2/-4> **ELEVENTEEN**	62	Oct92
	– I feel insane / You may be my friend / Dog with sharper teeth / Hope your dreams come true / Natural man / Love your money / Lovely ugly brutal world / Use me use you / The future free / Pink-flower / Waiting for the wolves / Everything is weird.		
Nov 92.	(12"ep/cd-ep) (92 TP12/TP7CD) **HOPE YOUR DREAMS COME TRUE. / PROPELLER PUNCH / QUEUE FOR TRANSATLANTIC ALIEN**		-
——	now without GARSIDE, She was repl. by **BELINDA LEITH** – vocals		
Mar 94.	(7") (100 TP7) **LOVE ME FOREVER. / DIAMOND OF THE DESERT**		
Apr 94.	(7") (110 TP7) **THE FUTURE TREE. / ZEBRA HEAD**		
Jun 94.	(cd/c) (TPLP 111 CD/C) **. . .FOR THEY KNOW NOT WHAT THEY DO**		-
	– The future tree / Belittled and beaten down / Sleeping with Heaven / Love me forever / Candyfloss / Life tomorrow / Zebra head / Unit shifter / Diamond of the desert / Mosquito / Greatest God's divine / Voice of a generation / Looking for an angel.		

		Fluffy Bunny	not iss.
Jun 95.	(cd-s) (SPLIT 1CD) **YOU'RE GRUESOME / SIR WILLIAM POWERS / LOVE ME FOREVER**		-
——	never reunited for any other recordings; in 1999 CRISPIN was back with KATIE in the band QUEEN ADREENA		

Cynthia DALL

Born: Sacramento, California, USA. Relocating to San Francisco, CINDY DALL (as she then known) hooked up with arch miserablilist BILL CALLAHAN as a collaborator in his otherwise solo venture, SMOG. Inking a deal with 'Drag City' ('Domino' – also current home of SMOG), DALL released a mysterious solo album in 1996. Scaling new heights in underground anonymity/modesty, the album came without any artist credits, nor was it graced with a title. Nevertheless, this particular toy story had a happy endng as critics generally gave DALL's obscurely minimalist creations the thumbs up. After a very long wait, CYNTHIA – as she was now credited – returned to the fore via a new set, 'SOUND RESTORES YOUNG MEN' (2002), her somber, icy vox embracing such songs as 'GOD MADE YOU', 'NEST OF DEAD CHILDREN' and the cover of Bryan Ferry's 'BOYS AND GIRLS'.

Album rating: UNTITLED (*7) / SOUND RESTORES YOUNG MEN (*7)

CINDY DALL – vocals, guitars / with **JIM O'ROURKE** – piano, guitar, etc (of TORTOISE) / **RIAN MURPHY + TOM MALLON** – drums

		Domino	Drag City
Mar 96.	(cd/lp; as CINDY DALL) (WIG CD/LP 23) <DR 73> **UNTITLED**		
	– Christmas (California) / Berlin, 1945 / Lion becomes dragon / Holland / Bright night / For Tiara / Grey and castles / Aaron Matthew.		

		Drag City	Drag City
Sep 02.	(lp/cd) <(DC 132/+CD)> **SOUND RESTORES YOUNG MEN**		
	– Be safe with me / God made you / Extreme cold / Zero / I played with boys / The party / Not one / Wastebasket kid II / Nest of dead children / Boys and girls / I'm not tempted / Snakeblood and vodka.		

DAMBUILDERS

Formed: Honolulu, Hawaii, USA . . . 1989 out of The EXACTONES by DAVE DERBY and ERIC MASUNAGA; The EXACTONES' notable releases were LPs 'WHERE ARE THE EXACTONES' (1986), 'CRASH HARMONY' (1987) and 'SWING THE CAT' (1988). Soon after forming under their new moniker the twosome recorded the lo-fi album 'A YOUNG PERSON'S GUIDE' (1990). This was meant to be a demo recording but after the 'Cuacha' imprint got hold of it they issued it untouched. Their ensuing sophomore album, 'GEEK LUST' (1991), showcased their alternative pop sound akin to the likes of R.E.M. while taking its more melodic influences from early BOWIE and ENO. This set also signalled the beginning of their '50 songs for 50 states project' in which they planned to write a song for every state over the course of their musical career exemplified here by the tracks 'ARKANSAS' and 'NO RAUM FOR YOU / DAKOTA NORTH'. Soon after this record, the band recruited the help of JOAN WASSAR and KEVIN MARCH to bolster their alt-pop sound. The quartet's third LP, 'ISLINGTON PORN TAPES' (1992), furthered their US appeal and included tracks from their EP, 'TOUGH GUY PROBLEM'. Now reaching the top of their form the band attracted the attention of major label 'East West' who put out their 'ENCENDEDOR' (1994) full-length set which aptly displayed the enormous talent of violinist WASSER adding both melody and rhythmic elements with her dramatic style. 'RUBY RED' released the succeeding year continued on this sojourn, the band moving down a somewhat grungier rock road from their earlier more CROWDED HOUSE-esque beginnings. This continued through onto the full-length set 'GOD DAMBUILDERS BLESS AMERICA' (1996), but was stopped short by the technological sophistication of LP 'AGAINST THE STARS' (1997), the band opting for all the trappings of the modern studio plus the mixing prowess of Robbie Adams, whose clients had included the likes of U2. DAVE DERBY, KEVIN MARCH (recently of LLOYD COLE's band) and IVY's DOMINIQUE DURAND subsequently took on a new billing as BRILLIANTINE. Having toured on many continents, the sprightly and melodic indie-pop act opened their account with 'VAINGLORY' (1997). Together with a new set of session friends (plus DURAND), DERBY and Co delivered a second outing, 'MY LIFE AND THE BEAUTIFUL GAME' (2000).

Album rating: A YOUNG PERSON'S GUIDE (*6) / GEEK LUST (*7) / ISLINGTON PORN TAPES (*5) / ENCENDEDOR (*7) / RUBY RED (*4) / GOD DAMBUILDERS BLESS AMERICA (*5) / AGAINST THE STARS (*5) / Brilliantine: VAINGLORY (*4) / MY LIFE AND THE BEAUTIFUL GAME (*5)

DAVE DERBY – vocals, bass / **ERIC MASUNAGA** – guitar / **DEBBIE FOX** – violin, vocals / **TYRAN GEORGE** – acoustic guitar / **DANIEL GLASS** – drums

		Cuacha	not iss.
1990.	(lp) (LOCO 1) **A YOUNG PERSON'S GUIDE**	-	- German
	– God wears glasses / Kevin Keegan / Four eyes / Love is all around you / Radio is king / Rose Vitta / I'm a bum / Joan / I hate weekends / She's coming down / The night I fell / Hibachi in the rain / Splash / Swing the cat / Letter / Approach the horse, sexually / Teenage bum. (<UK cd-iss. Oct94 + US cd-iss. Jan98; same as German>)		
——	**STUART WRIGHT** – percussion, drums; repl. DANIEL		
1991.	(7") **POP SONG = FOOD. / YO MAMAFISH**	-	
	(above issued on 'Puppethead')		
1991.	(lp) (LOCO 5) **GEEK LUST**	-	- German
	– Yo mamafish / Myron's girlfriend / Mr. Insomnia / P.P. man / Fur / Leather / The lesser poet / The wellwishers / Pop song = food / St 100/6. <US cd-iss. Jan98 +=; same as German> – No raum for you – Dakota, north / Arkansas.		
——	**JOAN WASSAR** – violin, vocals; repl. DEBBIE		
——	**KEVIN MARCH** – drums; repl. STUART		
1992.	(lp) (LOCO 7) **ISLINGTON PORN TAPES**	-	- German
	– Copsucker / Louisiana / Heather / Idaho / Colin's heroes / Smell / Shrine / Candyguts / Dose / Montana / Pennsylvania. <US cd-iss. Jan98; same as German>		

		not iss.	Rockville
1992.	(7"m) **NEW JERSEY. / OREGON / WYOMING**	-	

		not iss.	SpinArt
1992.	(7") <spart 006> **SHRINE. / CANDYGUTS**		
Dec 93.	(12"ep/cd-ep) <spart 010> **TOUGH GUY PROBLEM**	-	
	– Louisiana / Idaho / Heather / Candyguts / Dose.		

DAMBUILDERS (cont)

		not iss.	Pop Narcotic
1992.	(7") <narc 002> **SMELL. / COLLIN'S HEROES**	-	

		not iss.	Atlantic
Apr 94.	(cd/c) <92356> **ENCENDEDOR**	-	

– Copsucker / Smell / Kill Haole day / Slo-mo Kikaida / Idaho / Colin's heroes / Collective / Shrine / Delaware / Fur.

		not iss.	Elektra
Aug 95.	(cd/c) <61831> **RUBY RED**	-	

– Smooth control / Special Ed / Teenage loser anthem / Drive by kiss / Lazy eye / Bending machine / Velocidad / Rocket to the Moon / Cosmonaut / St. Tamarindo / Down / I forget myself.

1996.	(7"m) <007> **COLORADO. / MISSISSIPPI / MICHIGAN**	-	

(above issued on 'Hepcat')

Jul 97.	(cd/c) <62034> **AGAINST THE STARS**	-	

– Digitize / Break up with your boyfriend / Burn this bridge / Herstory / You might want me around / You'll never know / Itch it / Discopolis / Luster / I was wrong / On the slide / Seek and destroy / Wished on the wrong star.

— disbanded when JOAN and KEVIN joined GRIFTERS offshoot outfit, THOSE BASTARD SOULS; DERBY formed BRILLIANTINE

– compilations, etc. –

Feb 97.	(cd) Cortex; (CTX 066CD) <5647> **GOD DAMBUILDERS BLESS AMERICA**		Nov96

– New Jersey / Wyoming / Louisiana / Idaho / Maryland / Colorado / Montana / Peensylvania / Oregon / Delaware / North Dakota / Arkansas / Oklahoma / Mississippi / Michigan.

BRILLIANTINE

DAVE DERBY – vocals, guitar / with guests **DOMINIQUE DURAND** – bass, vocals (of IVY) / **KEVIN MARCH** – drums

		not iss.	Hep-Cat
Feb 97.	(cd) <10011> **VAINGLORY**	-	

– Goodbye to St. Bishop's park / At least that's the way / Credit card effigy / Your star might fade / When the curtian / Crash / Weakling / Mistaken / Vainglory / Indefinitely / Digame! / Moving forward / Destiny / Lying around / Motel 5th / Ulrike / Control le freak.

— now with guests DURAND + **PHOEBE SUMMERSQUASH** (of SMALL FACTORY) + **CLAUDIA GONSON** (MAGNETIC FIELDS) + **DAVE SPALDING** (PELL MELL) + **MICHAEL KOTCH** (of RUTH RUTH)

		Deep Reverb	Deep Reverb
Sep 00.	(cd) <(DEEPREV 015)> **MY LIFE AND THE BEAUTIFUL GAME**		

– Underwater camera / Better life / Saddest day / U-bahn girl / Madeline / It would be so nice to really care / Experimental lifestyle / We gonna live forever / Another Munich / Trans sister / Back on her Meds / (untitled).

DAME FATE (see under ⇒ TUSCADERO)

DAMON & NAOMI (see under ⇒ GALAXIE 500)

DANDY WARHOLS

Formed: Portland, Oregon, USA ... mid 90's by buzzed-up guys, COURTNEY TAYLOR and PETER HOLMSTROM, who, with rhythm section, ERIC HEDFORD and feisty babe, ZIA McCABE, emerged from their recording basement in 1996. After a one-off double mini-CD, the harmony-fuelled psychedelia of 'DANDYS RULE OK', they inked a deal with 'Capitol', although they riled their bosses by failing to deliver on a promised set of songs; exposure in the Rolling Stone was subsequently mis-timed. Unsurprisingly the band gave themselves a proverbial kick up the ass and rose from their drug ashes with a fine set of songs, two of which ('EVERYDAY SHOULD BE A HOLIDAY' and 'NOT IF YOU WERE THE LAST JUNKIE ON EARTH') were UK Top 30 singles and preceded their Top 20 album, '...THE DANDY WARHOLS COME DOWN' (1998). Spending just over a year in the studio, The DANDY WARHOLS emerged with the most accomplished set to date, 'THIRTEEN TALES FROM URBAN BOHEMIA' (2000). It took a little while for audiences to catch on to its excellent pop sensibilities, as the album didn't really become a hit for the band until their notoriously catchy single 'BOHEMIAN LIKE YOU' (virtually ignored on its initial release) was used to great effect in a mobile phone ad. Surprisingly, on its second outing, the song crashed into the UK Top 5 and suddenly people had forgotten that The DANDY WARHOLS were perhaps the coolest band around. The final outcome of the set was more focused on creating an atmosphere, or a feeling instead of ten drugged-up love songs and three great singles (as was the case on 'COME DOWN'). Hippy cowboy anthem 'GET OFF' served as proverbial candy for the ear, while 'COUNTRY LEVER' and the strange musings on 'HORSE PILLS' really set the tone for one of the fullest and freshest albums of the year. It's going to be a hard one to follow ... • **Covers:** THE WRECK OF THE EDMUND FITZGERALD (Gordon Lightfoot) / etc.

Album rating: DANDYS RULE OK (*6) / ...THE DANDY WARHOLS COME DOWN (*7) / THIRTEEN TALES FROM URBAN BOHEMIA (*8)

COURTNEY TAYLOR – vocals, guitar / **PETER HOLMSTROM** – guitar / **ERIC HEDFORD** – drums / **ZIA McCABE** – bass

		Tim/Kerr	Tim/Kerr
Sep 95.	(cd-s) <TK 0088> **THE LITTLE DRUMMER BOY / DICK / (IT DOESN'T TAKE A GENIUS)**	-	-
Dec 95.	(2xm-cd) <(TK95CD 0091)> **DANDYS RULE OK**		

– Introduction by young Tom / Dandy Warhol's T.V. theme song / Ride / Best friend / Not your bottle / (Tony, this song is called) Lou Weed / Nothin' to do / Coffee and tea wrecks / Genius / Dick / Just try / Nothing (lifestyle of a tortured artist for sale) / Grunge Betty / Prelude – It's a fast-driving rave-up with the Dandy Warhols sixteen minutes – Finale // Little drummer boy / Dick / (It doesn't take a) Genius / Untitled. *(re-iss. Sep98 on 'Capitol'; 496409-2) (re-iss. Sep00 on 'Dandy'; DR 001)*

		Capitol	Capitol
Jan 96.	(pic-d-cd) <(TK 95PD 104)> **RIDE / WE LOVE YOU DICK**		
Feb 98.	(c-s/7"purple) (TC+/CL 797) **EVERYDAY SHOULD BE A HOLIDAY. / ONE (ULTRA LAM WHITE BOY)**	29	

(cd-s+=) (CDCL 797) – Head.

Apr 98.	(7") (CL 800) **NOT IF YOU WERE THE LAST JUNKIE ON EARTH. / GENIUS (live)**	13	

(cd-s+=) (CDCLS 800) – Ride (live).
(cd-s) (CDCL 800) – ('A'side) / ('A'live) / It's a fast drivin' rave up with the Dandy Warhols sixteen minutes (live).

May 98.	(cd/c) <(8 36505-2/-4)> **...THE DANDY WARHOLS COME DOWN**	16	

– Be-in / Boys better / Minnesoter / Orange / I love you / Not if you were the last junkie on earth / Every day should be a holiday / Good morning / Whipping tree / Green / Cool as Kim Deal / Hard on for Jesus / Pete International airport / The creep out. *(d-lp iss.Mar98 on 'Tim/Kerr'; TK 1671)*

Jul 98.	(7") (CL 805) **BOYS BETTER. / NOTHIN' TO DO**	36	-

(cd-s+=) (CDCL 805) – Grunge Betty.
(cd-s) (CDCLS 805) – ('A'side) / The wreck of the Edmund Fitzgerald / Free for all.

May 00.	(7") (CL 821) **GET OFF. / PHONE CALL**	38	-

(cd-s+=) (CDCLS 821) – White gold.
(cd-s) (CDCL 821) – ('A'side) / Not if you were the last junkie on earth (live) / I love you (live).

Jun 00.	(cd) (857787-2) **THIRTEEN TALES FROM URBAN BOHEMIA**	51	-

– Godless / Mohammed / Nietzsche / Country leaver / Solid / Horse pills / Get off / Sleep / Cool scene / Bohemian like you / Retarded / Shakin' / Big Indian / The gospel. *(d-lp iss.Oct00; SCZ 787) (re-iss. Nov01; same)* – hit UK No.32

Aug 00.	(7") (CL 823) **BOHEMIAN LIKE YOU. / HELLS BELLS**	42	-

(cd-s+=) (CDCLS 823) – Lance.
(cd-s) (CDCL 823) – ('A'side) / Retarded / Dub song.

Jul 01.	(12"/cd-s) (12CL/CDCL 829) **GODLESS / ('A'-Massive Attack remix / dub / instrumental)**	66	-
Oct 01.	(c-s) (TCCL 829) **BOHEMIAN LIKE YOU / HELLS BELLS / LANCE**	5	-

(cd-s) (CDCL 829) – ('A'side) / Retarded / Dub song.

Mar 02.	(c-s) (TCCL 835) **GET OFF / STARS (acoustic)**	34	-

(CDCL 835) – Eight days a week (acoustic) / ('A'-video).

– compilations, etc. –

Oct 02.	(d-cd) E.M.I.; (541130-2) **DANDY'S RULE OK / THIRTEEN TALES FROM URBAN BOHEMIA**		-

DANIELSON FAMILE

Formed: Clarksboro, New Jersey, USA ... 1993. A real family affair, the group was comprised of DANIEL SMITH and his spouse ELIN, both his sisters MEGAN and RACHEL, brother DAVID on the drum stool and extended family members CHRIS and MELISSA PALLADINO. This bunch of God-rockers released their debut 'A PRAYER FOR EVERY HOUR' in 1995, a confusing cacophony of sound made all the more unlistenable with DANIEL's bleating falsetto-preaching christianity, a tad over the top. The 1997 follow up, 'TELL ANOTHER JOKE AT THE OL' CHOPPIN BLOCK', was further proof that rock and roll should remain the Devil's domain. The 'FAMILE's next three albums 'TRI-DANIELSON, VOL.1' (1998), 'TRI-DANIELSON, VOL.2' (1999) and 'FETCH THE COMPASS KIDS' (2001), displayed a steady improvement in the group as a whole, however, DANIEL's shrieking God-bothering continued throughout. If The BYRDS and STEVIE WONDER failed to make christianity cool with the kids, this bunch of weirdos – "like BEEFHEART fronting The PARTRIDGE FAMILY" – would have had to have sold their souls to Beelzebub to stand any chance.

Album rating: A PRAYER FOR EVERY HOUR (*6) / TELL ANOTHER JOKE AT THE OL' CHOPPIN' BLOCK (*7) / TRI-DANIELSON!!! (ALPHA) (*7) / TRI-DANIELSON!!! (OMEGA) (*6) / FETCH THE COMPASS KIDS (*6)

DANIEL SMITH – vocals, acoustic guitar / **RACHEL SMITH** (RACHEL GALLOWAY) – organ, vocals / **MEGAN SMITH** – vocals, bells / **ANDREW SMITH** – percussion / **ELIN K. SMITH** – / **CHRIS X. SMITH** (CHRIS PALLADINO) – keyboards / **DAVID SMITH** – drums / plus others **TEDDY SMITH** (TED VALEKIS) – banjo, bass / **MELISSA PALLADINO + BECKY TAIT** – bassoon, sax

		Tooth & Nail	Tooth & Nail
Jun 95.	(cd) <TNR 1037CD> **A PRAYER FOR EVERY HOUR**	-	

– Nice of me / Feeling tank / Ugly tree / Like a vacuum / Need a beard / Pepcid 20 mg. / Birds / 1,000 push-ups / God bless / Guilt scout / What to wear / Do a good turn daily / Burn in Hart / Hot air / Be your wild man / Pray 1,995 prayers / Headz in the cloudz / Soul / Heimlich remover / Naive child / Tell me oh you / In the malls not for them / No foundation / Pretty. <re-iss. Feb01 on 'Secretly Canadian'; SC 41CD>

Feb 97.	(d10"brown-lp/cd) <TNR 1072/+CD> **TELL ANOTHER JOKE AT THE OL' CHOPPIN' BLOCK**	-	

– A no no / Ye olde battle axe / Me to datee / The lord's rest / Flesh thang / Jersey loverboy / I am beloved's / Big baby / Deviled egg / Quest for thrills / Smooth death / Jokin' at the block. <UK+re-iss. Feb01 on 'Secretly Canadian'; SC 42CD>

May 98.	(cd) <TNR 1104CD> **TRI-DANIELSON!!! (ALPHA)**	-	

– Southern paws – intro / Southern paws / Rubbernecker / Body English / Runnin' to brother / Between the lines of the scout signs / A meeting with your maker / Gorgeous / Pottymouth / The elderly / Holy kisser's block party / Flesh / Lord did you hear Harrison? <UK+re-iss. Feb01 on 'Secretly Canadian'; SC 43CD>

DARKSIDE

Formed: Rugby, England . . . late '89 by ex-SPACEMEN 3 members, PETE (BASSMAN) BAINES and STEWART (ROSCO) ROSSWELL; other original DARKSIDE personnel were NICK HADYN and KEVIN COWAN. Signing to 'Situation 2', they debuted the following spring with a single, 'HIGHRISE LOVE'. Later that year, an album 'ALL THAT NOISE' hit the indie charts, its heavily 60's influenced sound a grab-bag of references taking in everything from The BYRDS and CREEDENCE CLEARWATER REVIVAL to DOORS-style ambience. Unsurprisingly, the spectre of SPACEMEN 3 also hung heavy in the air although BAINES' droning, SUICIDE-influenced vocals tended to grate over the course of a whole album. A mail order-only long player, 'PSYCHEDELICISE SUBURBIA', was made available through the band's own 'Acid Ray' records in 1991 while a follow-up debut album proper, 'MELOMANIA', followed in early '92. Again, The DARKSIDE explored the 60's in enjoyably enough garage fashion without managing to nail down a memorable sound of their own. Faced with critical and commercial indifference, the band finally called it a day after a final single, 'LUNAR SURF EXPERIMENT', in summer '93. PETE BAIN, best known as the quiet member of SPACEMAN 3, established ALPHA STONE in early 1995 and issued the gentle 'STEREOPHONIC POP ART MUSIC' a year later. Pretty much just BAIN, he drifted through the warm musical landscapes of early PINK FLOYD, ENO and TANGERINE DREAM like a tumbleweed made out of, well, weed! Of course, the listener would be dimly impressed if they had not ingested some sort of psychedelic narcotic, but BAIN's lush transcient overtones had to be applauded. He issued the aptly titled 'SOULWEED' in 1997, a spacy translucent effort which combined the best of psychedelia and subtle noisecore followed by the highlight of his career, 2001's 'LIFES A MOTORWAY', which proved to be a sublime eulogy to BAIN's troubled musical lifespan. SPACEMAN 3's unsung genius. • **Covers:** BRIGHT LIGHTS BIG CITY (Jimmy Reed) / S.O.S. (Terry Randall) / WHEN FATE DEALS ITS MORTAL BLOW (Scientists) / FRANKIE TEARDROP (Suicide).

Album rating: ALL THAT NOISE (*6) / MELOMANIA (*6) / Alpha Stone: STEREOPHONIC POP ART MUSIC (*5) / SOULWEED (*4) / ELASTICATED WAVEBAND (*4) / LIFE'S A MOTORWAY (*4)

PETE (BASSMAN) BAINES – bass (ex-SPACEMEN 3) / **STEWART (ROSCO) ROSSWELL** – drums (ex-SPACEMEN 3) / **KEVIN COWAN** – guitar / **NICK HADYN** – guitar, vocals

Situation 2 / Beggars Banquet – RCA

Apr 90. (12"m) *(SIT 068T)* **HIGHRISE LOVE. / THE KILLING TIME / CAN'T THINK STRAIGHT**

—— now without HADYN (PETE now added vocals / COWAN organ, bass)

Aug 90. (12") *(SIT 72T)* **WAITING FOR THE ANGELS. / SWEET VIBRATIONS**
(cd-s+=) *(SIT 72CD)* – ('A'edit) / Highrise love.

Nov 90. (lp/c)(cd/pic-lp) *(SIT U/C 29)(SITU 29 CD/P) <3029>* **ALL THAT NOISE**
– Guitar voodoo / Found love / She don't come / Good for me / Love in a burning universe / All that noise / Spend some time / Don't stop the rain / Soul deep / Waiting for the angels.

—— added **CRAIG WAGSTAFF** – drums (ROSCO added organ, guitar)

Jun 91. (lp; mail-order) *(DARK 2)* **PSYCHEDELICISE SUBURBIA (live)**
– Guitar voodoo / She don't come / Are you for real / Spend some time / Love in a burning universe / Highrise love / Good for me / Sweet vibration / Soul deep / Theme '91.
(above on 'Acid Ray' records) (below on 'Munster')

Nov 91. (2x7"ep) *(DARK 3)* **LOADED ON BLISS**
– Always pleasure / This mystic morning / Guitar voodoo / Sweet vibration. (10"ep+=) *(DARK 3)* – Highrise love and Theme '91.

Jan 92. (lp/c)(cd/pic-lp) *(SIT U/C 34)(SITU 34 CD/P) <61121-2>* **MELOMANIA**
– Always pleasure / Feeling flow / Tornado / This mystic morning / Someday / Are you for real / 24 hours / Cry for me / Rise.

Jun 92. (12"ep/cd-ep) *(SIT 95 T/CD)* **MAYHEM TO MEDIATE**
– Straightest shot / This time is mine / Heart of the sun / This mystic morning (remix) / This mystic morning (dub) / Cry for me (remix).

Bomp / Bomp

Feb 93. (7"ep) *<(BMP 141)>* **LUNAR SURF EP**
– Retroglide / S.O.S. / Spacewalk.

Munster / Munster

Jul 93. (7") **WHEN FATE DEALS ITS MORTAL BLOW. / FRANKIE TEARDROP**

—— split after above

ALPHA STONE

PETE BAINES – vocals, guitars, synths / **ANDY SMITH** – bass / **DANNIE PAYNE** – drums

Bomp! / Bomp!

Sep 96. (cd/lp) *<(BCD/BLP 4054)>* **STEREOPHONIC POP ART MUSIC** – Apr96
– Special one / Destiny angel / Transfixed / Farmer C / Astro / Fall on me / A hard day's fun / Martian interlude.

Feb 97. (cd) *<BCD 4062>* **SOULWEED**
– Vesuvio one / Soulless zone / You're not foolin' me / Swamp gas / Ghost house / Soulweed / Slow motion mind / Vesuvio two. *(hidden track +=)* – You're not foolin' me (version).

Enraptured / not iss.

Aug 98. (cd/lp) *(RAPT CD/LP 18)* **ELASTICATED WAVEBAND**
– Intro / Lose your mind / Sazman / Space blues / Dans de Jardin avec Alphastone / Theme to "The Leafblower" / Soon the moon / Outro.

Nov 00. (cd-ep) *(RAPTCDEP 32)* **LIFE'S A MOTORWAY**
– Life's a motorway / Motorway (doinky mix by Flowchart) / Motorway (changing lane mix by Accelera Deck) / Motorway (bliss mix by Pacifica) / Motorway (HGV mix by Steve Janes).

Mar 01. (cd/d-lp) *(RAPT CD/LP 33)* **LIFE'S A MOTORWAY**
– Life's a motorway / Here it comes / Retroglide / Electro blues / Losing touch with you / Getting close to nowhere / Feel the rain / Cool earth sensation / Last exit / Motorway reprise. *(hidden track+=)* – (untitled).

DARK STAR (see under ⇒ LEVITATION)

DARYLL-ANN

Formed: Ermelo, Netherlands . . . 1991 by male guitarist and co-songwriter ANNE SOLDAAT, bassist JEROEN VOS and singer COEM PAULUSMA. The latter (who subsequently became a biologist!) was actually replaced by his twin brother and soon-to-be co-writer, JELLE PAULUSMA, while their original drummer was given the boot in favour of JEROEN KLEIJN; although this was after two limited Dutch releases, the 'DECIBEL' EP and 'RENKO' (1992) album. Allegedly taking their name from a character in US police show, 'Hill Street Blues', this bunch of retro indie-rockers began to achieve some recognition after moving to Dutch capital, Amsterdam, in 1993. Subsequently signed to 'Virgin' subsidiary, 'Hut', on the strength of a cassette demo tape, the band released a riff-tastic debut EP, 'I COULD NEVER LOVE YOU' in early '94. It seemed the improbably named DARYLL-ANN were as keen on American music culture as they were on the country's infamous TV programming, a definite TELEVISON (as in the band) influence at work, at least in PAULUSMA's guitar playing. As for his vocals, they came across like a Euro/US version of BRETT ANDERSON's inimitable nasal affectations. A mini-album, 'SEABORNE WEST' finally surfaced in 1995, among its varied delights a tongue-in-cheek version of Carly Simon's 'YOU'RE SO VAIN' (also released as a single). Having toured alongside labelmate giants, The SMASHING PUMPKINS and THE VERVE, they petered out somewhat, becoming one of the many forgotten "retro-rock" alternative acts. However, they were still active in the homeland releasing the odd folksy, jingle-jangle rock album, the best of which being 1999's 'HAPPY TRAUM' (named after a folk guitarist). • **More covers:** THIRTEEN (Big Star) / HOT SMOKE IN SASAFRASS (Prince – Cox).

Album rating: RENKO (*5) / SEABORNE WEST (*6) / WEEPS (*4) / HAPPY TRAUM (*5) / D.A. LIVE (*4) / TRAILER TALES (*4)

COEM PAULUSMA – vocals, tambourine / **ANNE SOLDAAT** – guitar, vocals / **JEROEN VOS** – bass / **FRANK VAN DER BIJ** – drums

Kelt / not iss.

1991. (cd-ep) **DECIBEL** – Dutch

Solid / not iss.

1992. (cd) *(527-9019-21)* **RENKO** – Dutch
– Decibel / Pretty in everything / Ocean girl / Into the open / Blind / Never say never / Times to come / Mailman's eyes / Mirror mind / Showbizz / (unknown).

—— **JELLE PAULUSMA** – vocals, guitar; repl. COEM
JEROEN KLEIJN – drums; repl. FRANK

Hut / Vernon Yard

Feb 94. (7") *(HUT 40)* **I COULD NEVER LOVE YOU. / MY LAST CALL**
(12"+=/cd-s+=) *(HUT T/DG 40)* – Friends / She is, I'm not.

May 94. (12"ep/c-ep/cd-ep) *(HUT TM/CM/DM 44)* **COME AROUND EP**
– Come around / Doll / Shamrock / Good thing / Mirror mind / Ocean girl.

Jul 94. (cd-ep) *<HUSCD 5>* **DARYLL-ANN**
– I could never love you / Come around / Shamrock / Doll / Friends / My last call.

Mar 95. (7") *(HUT 52)* **STAY. / THIRTEEN**
(12"+=/cd-s+=) *(HUT T/DG 52)* – Hot smoke in sasafrass.

Mar 95. (cd/c/lp) *(CDHUT/HUTMC/HUTLP 26) <VY 8>* **SEABORNE WEST**
– Stay / Low light / The doctor & I / Sheila / All right / Holida why / You're so vain / Birthmark / Boy you were / Liquid / H.P. confirm.

Jun 95. (7") *(HUT 58)* **YOU'RE SO VAIN. / FRIENDS**
(cd-s+=) *(HUTDG 58)* – The doctor & I.

Excelsior / not iss.

1997. (cd) **WEEPS** – Dutch
– Tools R us / Always share / A proper line / Mean love / Sheeszalitch / Springfever / Scott and Lesley / Tremble forte / Safe beef / Elegy / April / Summerdaze / Rollercoaster / My only world / Ocean drive / Dustyfied.

1999. (cd) *(0101)* **HAPPY TRAUM** – Dutch
– Surely justice / Everybody's cool / All by myself / Ask anyone / Desmond don't go / The miracle legion / When you cry / Money or love / Riverside / Freedom is a gift / Feelings / Trip the stairs / The leaves / Hope, love and happiness. <US-iss.Sep01; same>

| 2000. | (cd) **D.A. LIVE** (live) | - | - | Dutch |

- Tools R us / The doctor & I / Mirror mind / Allright / Stay / H.P. confirm / I could never love you / Always share / Everybody's cool / Riverside / All by myself / Surely justice / Desmond don't go / Trip the stairs.

—— next was virtually **JELLE** solo

| 2002. | (cd) **TRAILER TALES** | - | - | Dutch |

- A piece of work (I'm trying her) / It's only love / Serenades for the lonely / Equally sympathy / Pines and grenadine / Marching / Swords and words / Old school / Borderland / Rosemary girl / Her manic frame / Trailer tales.

DASHBOARD CONFESSIONAL

Formed: Boca Raton, Florida, USA ... 2000 by singer, songwriter, and driving force CHRISTOPHER CARRABA. CARRABA had fronted bands like the VACANT ANDIES and FURTHER SEEMS FOREVER, but found the solo process to be more receptive and gainful to the material he was writing. As DASHBOARD CONFESSIONAL he released debut LP, 'THE SWISS ARMY ROMANCE', in late 2000 on 'Drive-Thru' records. A solid first effort, it contained finely composed indie acoustic songs like 'LIVING IN YOUR LETTERS', although there wasn't much to distinguish it from similar indie releases. In 2001, now on 'Vagrant' records, he released the 'DROWNING' EP, and second full-set, 'THE PLACES YOU HAVE COME TO FEAR THE MOST'. CARRABA's heartfelt musings occasionally weighed heavy with naivety, but then they did appear to target the teen market. 'SCREAMING INFIDELITIES' became a Modern Rock hit, adopted by many US indie/pop kids. In a busy (and successful) year for DASHBOARD CONFESSIONAL, CARRABA also hit the road, firstly a joint tour with the WEAKERTHANS, then as part of the 'Vagrant Across America' tour with labelmates including HOT ROD CIRCUIT. Maintaining the momentum, the melancholic 'SO IMPOSSIBLE' EP was released in late 2001, and DASHBOARD CONFESSIONAL became a duo with the recruitment of SUNNY DAY REAL ESTATE's DAN HOERNER.

Album rating: THE SWISS ARMY ROMANCE (*5) / THE PLACES YOU HAVE COME TO FEAR THE MOST (*6)

CHRISTOPHER CARRABA – vocals, guitars, etc. (ex-FURTHER SEEMS FOREVER)

| | | not iss. | Drive-Thru |

| Nov 00. | (cd) <*DRIVETHRU 22CD*> **THE SWISS ARMY ROMANCE** | - | |

- Screaming infidelities / The sharp hint of new tears / Living in your letters / The Swiss Army romance / Turpentine chaser / A plain morning / Age six racer / Again I go unnoticed / Ender will save us all / Shirts and gloves / (untitled). *(UK-iss.Jul01; same as US)*

| | | not iss. | Fiddler |

| Mar 01. | (cd-ep) <*12*> **THE DROWNING EP** | - | |

- Drowning / Anyone anyone? / For Justin.

| | | Vagrant | Vagrant |

| Mar 01. | (cd) <(*VR 354CD*)> **THE PLACES YOU HAVE COME TO FEAR THE MOST** | | |

- The brilliant dance / Screaming infidelities / The best deceptions / This ruined puzzle / Saints and sailors / The good fight / Standard lines / Again I go unnoticed / The places you have come to fear the most / This bitter pill. *(re-iss. Mar02 on 'B-Unique'; BUN 018) (re-iss. Aug02 on 'Universal'; 910354-2)*

—— added **DAVE HOERNER** – guitar (of SUNNY DAY REAL ESTATE)

| Dec 01. | (cd-ep) <*VR 362*> **SO IMPOSSIBLE** | | |

- For you to notice ... / So impossible / Remember to breathe / Hands down.

| | | not iss. | Eulogy |

| Apr 02. | (cd-ep) <*36*> **SUMMER KISSES EP** | - | |

- Living in your letters / The sharp hint of new tears / Turpentine chaser / Ender will save us all.

DATSUNS

Formed: Cambridge, New Zealand ... 1997 by FOLD DE DATSUN, CHRISTIAN LIVINGSTONE, PHIL SOMERVELL and MATT OSMENT, calling themselves The TRINKETS and dominating the college rock scene until their mighty rise in 2002. Winning battle of the bands competitions in and around Cambridge, the four-piece garage rock collective issued minor singles on their own 'Hell Squad' imprint, before embarking on a whirlwind tour of Australia, which ultimately gave them the confidence to venture into the cut-throat world of the British music scene. They were in luck, however, thanks to the garage rock revival of The WHITE STRIPES et al, and were hailed by many a music rag as "the best new band since the last best new band" (joke). 'Virgin' offshoot label 'V2' stepped in and offered The DATSUNS – whose live performances got almost as messy as ... TRAIL OF DEAD's – a record contract, thrusting the floppy-haired foursome into the limelight. A single 'I'M IN LOVE' was issued in 2002 and made John Peel's revolving playlist, not to mention an addition on his 'Live At Fabric' compilation. The group successfully lived up to the hype by releasing their self-titled debut at the close of the year.

Album rating: THE DATSUNS (*8)

DOLF DE DATSUN – vocals, bass / **CHRISTIAN LIVINGSTONE** – guitar, vocals / **PHIL SOMERVELL** – guitar, vocals / **MATT OSMENT** – drums

		Hellsquad	not iss.
2000.	(ltd-7") (*HS 002*) **SUPER GYRATION! / HOOTCHIE MAMA**		-
2001.	(7"purple) (*HS 003*) **FINK FOR THE MAN. / TRANSISTOR**		-
May 02.	(7") (*HS 005*) **LADY. / MF FROM HELL**		-
Sep 02.	(ltd-7") (*HS 007*) **IN LOVE / LITTLE BRUISE**	-	- tour
Sep 02.	(ltd-7") (*HS 008*) **SITTIN' PRETTY. / THE TERRIBLE POWER**	-	- tour

		V2	not iss.
Sep 02.	(cd-s) (*VVR 502095-3*) **IN LOVE / SUPERGYRATION**	25	-
Oct 02.	(cd) (*VVR 102096-2*) **THE DATSUNS**	17	-

- Sittin' pretty / MF from Hell / Lady / Harmonic generator / What would I know / At your touch / Fink for the man / In love / You build me up / Freeze sucker. *(lp-iss. on 'Sweet Nothing'; SNLP 019)*

| Nov 02. | (cd-s) (*VVR 502122-3*) **HARMONIC GENERATOR** | | - |
| | (cd-s) (*VVR 502122-8*) – | | |

DAVID DEVANT & HIS SPIRIT WIFE

Formed: London, England ... mid-90's by frontman VESSEL (Mr. GEORGESON to his bank manager!), plus his entertaining live crew, PROFESSOR RIMSCHOTT, THE COLONEL, ICE MAN, COCKY YOUNG 'UN and ex-MONOCHROME SET guitarist, FOZ. Two independently released singles appeared in 1995, namely 'PIMLICO' and the carrot-top baiting 'GINGER', the latter an audience participating highlight of the group's outrageous live set. Having signed to 'Rhythm King', the band went through a lean 1996 as three singles in a row failed to chart, although it would be the aforementioned 'GINGER' that would finally see him haunt the Top 60. A follow-up, 'THIS IS FOR REAL' and an accompanying debut album, 'WORK, LOVELIFE, MISCELLANEOUS' (1997), also made the charts, an only partially successful attempt to translate the VESSEL's BOWIE-esque theatrics and performance art onto vinyl. Highlights included 'GINGER', 'LIE DETECTOR', 'MISCELLANEOUS' and 'THE LAST EVER POP SONG', all enjoyably comical glammed-up cabaret pastiches which no doubt had the real DAVID DEVANT (a Victorian-era magician apparently!) turning in his grave. After being delayed for around a year and a half, the group were back on song courtesy of a sophomore set, 'SHINEY ON THE INSIDE' (released October 2000), by which time the group had since disolved. This set was never going to re-establish them as cult artists, although it did have its glamorous highlights, namely opener 'RADAR' 'and 'SPACE DADDY'.

Album rating: WORK, LOVELIFE, MISCELLANEOUS (*6) / SHINEY ON THE INSIDE (*5)

VESSEL (b. DAVID GEORGESON) – vocals / **FOZ** (b. JAMES FOSTER) – guitar (ex-MONOCHROME SET) / **THE COLONEL** (b. CARLOW) – bass / **BRYN** – keyboards / **PROFESSOR RIMSCHOTT** (b. EGERTON) – drums

		Humbug	not iss.
Aug 95.	(7"ep/cd-ep) (*HUM/+CD 4*) **PIMLICO**		-

- Pimlico / This is for real / My magic life / David's coming back.

| Nov 95. | (cd-s; as DAVID DEVANT) (*HUM 10*) **GINGER** | | - |

		Rhythm King	not iss.
Aug 96.	(7"/cd-s) (*KIND 1 V/CD*) **COOKIE. / ONE HAND / TROUBLE**		-
Nov 96.	(7") (*KIND 2VL*) **LIE DETECTOR. / SOUNDTRACK TO THE FILM "LIGHT ON THE SURFACE"**		-
Nov 96.	(7") (*KIND 3VL*) **MISCELLANEOUS. / BALLROOM**		-
Mar 97.	(7"/c-s) (*KIND 4 VLE/C*) **GINGER. / SLIP IT TO ME** (live)	54	-
	(cd-s+=) (*KIND 4CD*) – Life on a crescent (session) / Parallel universe part 2.		
Jun 97.	(7") (*KIND 5V*) **THIS IS FOR REAL. / EVERYTHING FITS INTO PLACE**	61	-
	(cd-s+=) (*KIND 5CD*) – ('A'side) / Why can't someone else.		
	(cd-s) (*KIND 5CDX*) – ('A'side) / Ghost in my house (live) / Pimlico (live).		
Jun 97.	(cd/c/lp) (*KIND CD/MC/LP 1*) **WORK, LOVELIFE, MISCELLANEOUS**	70	-

- Ginger / Miscellaneous / Lie detector / The lasty ever love song / I think about you / Parallel universe / Re-invent the wheel / This is for real / I'm not even going to try / Light on the surface / Goodnight. *(lp w/ free 7")* –

Oct 97.	(7") (*KIND 6VLE*) **LIE DETECTOR (Dave Eringa mix). / WHO WE ARE (alternative vocal)**		-
	(cd-s+=) (*KIND 6CD*) – This is for real (mix).		
	(cd-s) (*KIND 6CDX*) – ('A'side) / Black & white (mix) / This is for real (mix).		

		Kindness	not iss.
2000.	(cd-s) **RADAR / DOLPHIN SQUARE / INCURABLE**		-
Aug 00.	(cd-s) (*KIND 8CD*) **SPACE DADDY / BORN YESTERDAY / IMPOSTERS** (mixed up)		-
Oct 00.	(cd) (*KINDCD 2*) **SHINEY ON THE INSIDE**		-

- Radar / One track mind / Dangerous dilettante / 21 / Sex maniacs / One thing after another / Space daddy / Groover / Shiney on the inside / Here come the imposters / Take a deep breath.

Richard DAVIES

Born: 1964, Sydney, Australia. DAVIES took up songwriting while at university, forming his first professional band, The MOLES, in the late 80's with fellow disaffected law students. Despite claiming not to even like each other, the band managed to release two EP's and a debut album, 'UNTUNE THE SKY' (1992), before upping sticks and moving to London together in 1993 in the hope that they'd find a more appreciative audience for their wildly experimental, off-kilter garage retro-pop. While the UK indie press were sympathetic, however, The MOLES split soon after and although a final album, 'INSTINCT' appeared on US label, 'Flydaddy' ('Fire' in the UK) in 1994, it was a DAVIES solo effort in all but name. A move to the US (more specifically Boston, Massachusetts) saw DAVIES hooking up with San Franciscan music student, ERIC MATTHEWS, after the pair had listened to each other's recent demo tapes. In 1993, The CARDINAL released their 'TOY BELL' EP although it was 1995's eponymous debut album that had the critics raving. With MATTHEWS' sublime brass and string arrangements complementing DAVIES' songwriting verve, they had fashioned a work of baroque pop glory that harked back to the late 60's without sounding derivative. Yet despite the acclaim, internal tension led to an early split with both MATTHEWS and DAVIES going on to release solo material. Despite being so short-lived, the influence of The CARDINAL was writ large over DAVIES' solo debut, 'THERE'S NEVER BEEN A CROWD LIKE THIS', released on 'Flydaddy' in 1996. Two years later, DAVIES was back with another work of flawed genius, 'TELEGRAPH', having toured with spiritual compadres, The FLAMING LIPS, as his backing band. 'BARBARIANS' (2000) – complete with "Uncle Sam" stars'n'stripes stovepipe hat on the sleeve – disregarded all things orchestral and took on a back to basics guitar-infused garage-pop sound side by side with cerebral ballads. Yes, DAVIES was now Americanised.

• **Covered:** CARDINAL covered SINGING TO THE SUNSHINE (US 60's-band; Mortimer).

Album rating: Moles: UNTUNE THE SKY (*6) / INSTINCT mini (*6) / Cardinal: CARDINAL (*7) / Richard Davies: THERE'S NEVER BEEN A CROWD LIKE THIS (*7) / TELEGRAPH (*7) / BARBARIANS (*6)

The MOLES

RICHARD DAVIS – vocals, flute, guitar / with **ARTHUR BEECHCROFT** – keyboards / **OLIVER STRAUCH** – bass / **HAMISH KILGOUR** – drums (of CLEAN) / **DAVID NEWGARDEN** – horns

		Seaside	not iss.
Dec 90.	(12"ep) **UNTUNE THE SKY**	-	- Austra
	– Accidental saint / Rich man (original mix) / Surf's up.		
Dec 91.	(12"ep) **TENDRILS AND PARACETAMOL**	- R.T.P.	- Austra not iss.
Jan 92.	(cd) (10) **UNTUNE THE SKY**	-	- Austra

– Bury me happy / Tendrils and paracetamol / This is a hapy garden / Breathe me in / Lonely hearts get what they deserve / Crown souls / Rebecca / Europe by car / Curdle / Wires / Nailing Jesus to the cross. <(UK/US cd-iss. Apr00 on 'Flydaddy'+=; FLY 037)> – Accidental saint / Rich man (original) / Surf's up / What's the new Mary Jane? / Going down / Saint Jack / Let's hook up and get some.

		Seaside	Ringers Lactate
1992.	(d7"ep) **WHAT'S THE NEW MARY JANE? / GOING DOWN. // SAINT JACK / LET'S HOOK UP AND GET SOME**		
		Fire	Austra Flydaddy
Oct 94.	(m-cd) (FIRECD 42) <FLY 003CD> **INSTINCT**		

– Minor royal march / Eros lunch (1963) / Already in black / Instinct / Cars for Kings Cross / Cassie peek / Raymond, did you see the red queen? / Treble metal / The crasher. (re-iss. Dec99 on 'Flydaddy'; same as US) (re-iss. Jul01 on 'Gern Blandsten'; GERN 055CD)

—— split when DAVIES formed The CARDINAL with ERIC MATTHEWS

CARDINAL

RICHARD DAVIES – guitar, vocals / **ERIC MATTHEWS** (b.12 Jan'69, Oregon) – vocals, guitars, trumpet, bass, piano / **TONY LASH** – percussion, drums, production / **BOB FAY** was on debut; he lsater joined SEBADOH

		Flydaddy	Flydaddy
Jan 95.	(7"ep) <(FLY 001-7)> **THE TOY BELL EP**		
	– Big mink / It turns on in a circle on a pedestal / Poolside '75 / Swearshirt gown.		
		Dedicated	Flydaddy
Feb 95.	(cd) (DED CD/LP 018) <FLY 004> **CARDINAL**		

– If you believe in Christmas trees / Last poems / Bog mine / You've lost me there / Public melody #1 / Dream figure / Tough guy tactics / Angel darling / Singing to the sunshine / Silver machines. (re-iss. Dec99 on 'Flydaddy'; same as US) (re-iss. Jul01 on 'Gern Blandstein'; GERN 056CD)

| Jun 95. | (cd-s) **DREAM FIGURE. / SILVER MACHINES / SINGING TO THE SUNSHINE** | - | |

RICHARD DAVIES

		Flydaddy	Flydaddy
Mar 96.	(cd/lp) <(FLY 016-2/-1)> **THERE'S NEVER BEEN A CROWD LIKE THIS**		

– Transcontinental / Sign up maybe for being / 6/4 on / Chips Rafferty / Why not bomb the movies? / Jubilee / In between moods / Hard river / Topple into my fantasy / Showtime.

		Blue Rose	Flydaddy
Apr 96.	(cd-ep) (BRRC 1004-2) **CHIPS RAFFERTY / 6/4 ON (demo) / IN BETWEEN MOODS (demo) / CARS FOR KINGS CROSS (live) / ALREADY IN BLACK (live)**		-
Jun 96.	(cd-ep) <FLY 056CD> **SIGN UP MAYBE FOR BEING / 6/4 ON (demo) / IN BETWEEN MOODS (demo) / CARS FOR KINGS CROSS (live) / ALREADY IN BLACK (live)**	-	

—— with **RONALD JONES** – guitars, etc (of FLAMING LIPS)

| Mar 98. | (cd/lp) (BRRC 100115-2/-1) <FLY 025> **TELEGRAPH** | | |

– Cantina / Surface of the sun / Confederate cheerio call / Papillon / Crystal clear / Eye camera / Close to the storyline / Main street electrical parade / Evergreen / Days to remember.

| Apr 98. | (7") (BRRC 500144-7) **CANTINA. / IN BETWEEN MOODS (demo)** | | - |
| | (cd-s+=) (BRRC 500144-3) – Cars for Kings Cross (live) / Already in black (live). | | |

—— next with **JEFF BERLIN** – drums

		not iss.	Kindercore
Jun 00.	(cd) <kc 043> **BARBARIANS**	-	

– Coldest day / Palo Alto / Stars / Great republic / The kiss off / May / Amsterdam / Kissinger's banjo / F.O.G. / Formulas.

John DAVIS
(see under ⇒ SEBADOH; the FOLK IMPLOSION)

DAWN OF THE REPLICANTS

Formed: Galashiels, Scotland . . . 1996 by Teesside-raised singer-songwriter, PAUL VICKERS along with guitarist, ROGER SIMIAN, the latter spending the bulk of his student loan on a mail-order debut EP, 'SO FAR SO SPITFIRE' (recorded as The REPLICANTS). Available from early '97, the record's R.E.M.-esque lead track, 'COCAINE ON THE CATWALK', was given airplay by both John Peel and Mark Radcliffe, selling out its initial 500 copies almost immediately. Expanding the line-up with addition of former schoolmates, DONALD KYLE, MIKE SMALL and GRANT PRINGLE, The DAWN OF THE REPLICANTS released a second single, 'HOGWASH FARM' on their 'dumbSULK trigg-er' imprint and after interest from the likes of 'Che', 'Too Pure' and 'Chemikal Underground', they opted to sign on the dotted line for Warner Brothers subsidiary 'eastwest'. Their major label tenure got off to a prolific start with the release of three EP's (namely 'VIOLENT SUNDAYS', 'ALL THAT CHEYENNE CABOODLE' and 'RHINO DAYS') in the latter half of '97, the lead tracks being re-recorded versions of 'COCAINE ON THE CATWALK', 'LISA BOX' and the brand new 'RADARS' respectively. With music press acclaim steadily growing, the Borders lads notched up their first chart entry with the morbidly infectious 'CANDLEFIRE', a song that invoked the ghosts of early 80's Liverpool (i.e. IAN McCULLOCH, JULIAN COPE and The ROOM's DAVE JACKSON). The heavy release schedule continued unabated with the much anticipated Top 75 debut set, 'ONE HEAD, TWO ARMS, TWO LEGS' (1998), a pot-pourri of wilful experimentation and contrasting styles that collected together all of the aforementioned tracks side by side with fresh material such as 'WINDY MILLER' (Trumpton revisited REPLICANTS style), the U2 goes Lo-Fi 'SO SLEEPY' and the lyrically enigmatic (not for the first time) 'SGT GROWLEY'. The following April, a second set 'WRONG TOWN, WRONG PLANET, THREE HOURS LATE' (1999) was issued, although its disappointing sales returns were to lead to 'eastwest' letting them go. The group subsequently went into a sort of hibernation with only VICKERS resurfacing as spokesman for indie offshoot duo, PLUTO MONKEY. They released a couple of 45's and an album, 'LITTLE BRENDA: BLUEGRASS MISSION' (2000) for 'Shifty Disco', but what had happened to the DOTR. An answer was unveiled in September 2002, when John Peel sessions heralded new songs from their long-awaited third set, 'TOUCHING THE PROPELLER'. Released on 'Flying Sparks' records (home of GORDON HASKELL and THEA GILMORE), the record was a raw and dusty batch of rough-hewn songs, one of them 'SMOKE WITHOUT FIRE' featuring SUSI O'NIELL on theremin and other assorted instruments.

• **Covered:** BALLAD OF A THIN MAN (Bob Dylan).

Album rating: DAWN OF THE REPLICANTS (*8*) / WRONG TOWN, WRONG PLANET, THREE HOURS LATE. (*7) / TOUCHING THE PROPELLER (*6) / Pluto Monkey: LITTLE BRENDA: BLUEGRASS MISSION (*6)

PAUL VICKERS – vocals, synthesizer / **ROGER SIMIAN** – guitar, keyboards, vocals

		dumbSULK trigg-er	not iss.
Jan 97.	(7"ep; as The REPLICANTS) (DST 7-1) **SO FAR SO SPITFIRE EP**	-	- mail-o

– Cocaine on the catwalk / Digging bear / Lisa box / Bizarre concoction.

—— added **DONALD KYLE** – bass, guitar / **MIKE SMALL** – guitar, keyboards, vocals / **GRANT PRINGLE** – drums, keyboards, vocals

Jun 97.	(10") (SAM 2063) **HOGWASH FARM. / CHAOS IN AN INKWELL**	-	
		eastwest	not iss.
Aug 97.	(d7"ep/cd-ep) (EW 115/+CD) **VIOLENT SUNDAYS E.P.**		-

– Cocaine on the catwalk (re-recording) / Non capisco / Only small birds do / Beyond the nest.

| Sep 97. | (d7"ep/cd-ep) (EW 125/+CD) **ALL THAT CHEYENNE CABOODLE E.P.** | | - |

– Lisa box (re-recording) / Diggin' bear (re-recording) / Will you ever phone? / Skullcrusher.

| Nov 97. | (d7"ep/cd-ep) (EW 134/+CD) **RHINO RAYS E.P.** | | - |

– Radars / Bionic stardust / The wrong turnstile / Seasick odyssey.

Jan 98.	(10") (EW 147 TE/CD1) **CANDLE FIRE. / SKULLCRUSHER (David Holmes & Tim Goldsworthy remix)**	52	-
	(cd-s+=) (EW 147CD1) – Leaving so soon?		
	(cd-s) (EW 147CD2) – ('A'side) / Leaving iota / Chesty Morgan.		
Feb 98.	(cd/c/lp) (0630 19600-2/-4/-1) **ONE HEAD, TWO ARMS, TWO LEGS**	62	-

– Cocaine on the catwalk / Candle fire / Ten sea birds / Lisa box / Return of the board game / Windy Miller / Radars / So sleepy / Let them eat coal / Sgt Growley / Hogwash farm / Sleepy spiders / Float on a raft / Mary Louise / Fatal firework.

| Mar 98. | (7"ep/cd-ep) (EW 157/+CD) **HOGWASH FARM (THE DIESEL HANDS E.P.)** | 65 | - |

– Hogwash farm (re-built) / Night train to Lichtenstein / The duchess of Surin / Crow valley.

| Jun 98. | (12"ep/cd-ep) (EW 166 T/CD) **I SMELL VOODOO E.P.** | | - |

– Mary Louise / Ballad of a thin man / Myrhh tingle / Dual converter.

| Aug 98. | (7"/cd-s) (NING 59/+CD) **BORN IN BASKETS. / Inner Sleeve: Come Alive** | | - |

(above 'GOING DOWN THE TUBES WITH . . . single was on 'Fierce Panda')

| Apr 99. | (cd/c/lp) (3984 26474-2/-4/-1) **WRONG TOWN, WRONG PLANET, THREE HOURS LATE.** | | - |

– Gasoline vine / Love is a curse / Rule the roost / Sub erotic fields / Zulu kites / Wheelie bin drive / Cabin fever / Jack Fanny's gym / Science fiction freak / Big hefty hounds / The soil idea / Tear dog eyes / Get a bright flame / Howlin' in the dark / Hand relief / Fearless vampire hunters.

DAWN OF THE REPLICANTS (cont)

Apr 99. (12"ep/cd-ep) *(EW 197 T/CD1)* **RULE THE ROOST. / ON THE RADIO / RUNNING INTO TROUBLE**
(cd-s) *(EW 197CD2)* – ('A'side) / Chaos in an inkwell (original dumb-SULK version) / Sgt Growley (Peel session version).
Jul 99. (7") *(EW 204)* **SCIENCE FICTION FREAK. / YELLOW BEATLE**
(cd-s+=) *(EW 204CD)* – Buffalo ballet.

Flying Sparks / not iss.

Sep 02. (cd-s) *(TDBCDS 12)* **LEAVING TOWN / SMOKE WITHOUT FIRE / COCAINE ON THE CATWALK (original dumb/SULK trigg-er version)**
Sep 02. (cd) *(TDBCD 067)* **TOUCHING THE PROPELLER**
– Hollywood hills / Leaving town / Smoke without fire / Black and white rainbows / Sweet little nowhere blue / Rockefeller Center, 1932 / Trout fishing / No room at the inn / Falling down / Afraid of the ground.

PLUTO MONKEY

PAUL VICKERS + one other

Shifty Disco / not iss.

Feb 00. (7") *(DISCO 0002)* **JETSTREAM. / GYMNASTICS**
Sep 00. (cd) *(SHIFTY 0004)* **LITTLE BRENDA: BLUEGRASS MISSION**
– Wild wild potion / Joe Meek / Double Dutch / Thirsty dragons / Jetstream / Ping pong sass / Forty reels / Rice cake rabbit soul / Dangerous beak / Who holds the monkey / Don't stack them with apes / Quiet life.
Oct 00. (7"m) *(DISCOQUICK 10)* **JOE MEEK. / MEEKSVILLE SOUND IS DEAD / DUEL AT THE RODEO**

DAZZLING KILLMEN

Formed: St. Louis, Missouri, USA . . . 1990 by frontman NICK SAKES, along with learned but young jazz musicians DARIN GRAY and BLAKE FLEMING; TIM GARRIGAN was added after a long series of 7" singles and their 'DIG OUT THE SWITCH' (1993) for a small French imprint. The DAZZLING KILLMEN (what a really dumb name for a band!), subsequently released the odd record or two before the break-up of the band took them to pastures new; GARY and GARRIGAN into one-album's-worth YOU FANTASTIC! and SAKES to the equally er, "dazzling" COLOSSAMITE; SAKES is now with SICBAY. • **Covered:** POPTONES (Public Image Ltd).

Album rating: DIG OUT THE SWITCH (*7) / FACE OF COLLAPSE (*7) / RECUERDA compilation (*7) / You Fantastic!: YOU FANTASTIC! (*5) / Colossamite: ECONOMY OF MOTION (*5) / Sicbay: THE FIRELIT S'COUGHS (*5)

NICK SAKES – vocals, guitar / **DARIN GRAY** – bass / **BLAKE FLEMING** – drums

not iss. / Sawtooth

1990. (7") <*SWTH 002*> **NUMB. / BOTTOM FEEDER**

not iss. / Crime Life

1991. (7") <*CL 001*> **TORTURE. / GHOST LIMB**

not iss. / Skin Graft – Sluggo

1992. (7") <*GR 01*> **KILLING FEVER. / (2 other tracks by MOTHER'S DAY)**
1992. (7") <*GR 03*> **MEDICINE ME. / POPTONES**

Intellectual Convulsion / not iss.

Apr 93. (lp/cd) <*(SPASM 006/+CD)*> **DIG OUT THE SWITCH** — French
– Serpentarium / Dig the hole / Captain is dead / Bottom feeder / Here comes Mr. Big Face / Spiral mirror / Reactor / No / Premonition / Torture / Ghost limb / Numb / Code blue.

— added **TIM GARRIGAN** – guitar

Skin Graft / Skin Graft

1993. (c) <*GR 08*> **LOUNGE AX: LIVE (live)**
– Bottom feeder (reprise) / Serpentarium / Dig the hole / Big face / Spiral mirror / No / Premonition / My lacerations / Medicine me / Torture / Numb / Code blue.
Apr 94. (cd) <*(GR 12CD)*> **FACE OF COLLAPSE** — Feb94
– Staring contest / Bone fragments / My lacerations / Blown (face down) / Windshear / Painless one / In the face of collapse / Agitator.

— disbanded after above; FLEMING joined jazz act, LADDIO BOLOCKO, who issued one set, 'Life & Times'

– compilations, etc. –

Jul 96. (cd) *Skin Graft*; <*(GR 36CD)*> **RECUERDA**
– Medicine me / My lacerations / Poptones / Bottom feeder / Serpentarium / Dig out the hole / Here comes Mr. big face / Spiral mirror / No / Premonition / Torture / Numb / Code blue / ****** / Ghost limb / Torture (live) / Killing fever (live) / Numb (live) / Bottom feeder (live).

YOU FANTASTIC!

GRAY + GARRIGAN

Skin Graft / Skin Graft

Oct 96. (cd-ep) <*(GR 38CD)*> **RIDDLER EP** — Sep96
– (10 untitled tracks).
Jun 97. (cd-s) <*(GR 42CD)*> **PALS**
Nov 98. (cd) <*(GR 56CD)*> **YOU FANTASTIC!**
– Friendless / Songless / Mono / Subtraction / Start / Slowly / Muted / Phoneless / Cicero's July / Retraction / Speaken / Memphis / Chronic / Start / Aachen / Sickless / January / March / Louisville / Homeless / Slowly.

— GARRIGAN joined PHUT

COLOSSAMITE

NICK SAKES with **ED RODRIGUEZ** – guitar

Skin Graft / Skin Graft

Mar 97. (cd-ep) <*(GR 34CDEP)*> **ALL LINGO'S CLAMOUR**
– Bewilderbeast / My driving hand / No entran moscas / The down sound / For the sake of structure / It to isn't.

1998. (cd-ep) <*GR 48CD*> **FRISBEE**
Mar 99. (cd) <*(GR 55CD)*> **ECONOMY OF MOTION** — Oct98
– The hot house / Mr. Somebody does somthing / The eagle and the sea / Heat vs. temperature / Pee dio / Busy little hands / Tooth of Davinci / Arkansas halo / An open-minded taxidermist / Neither sniff nor crictor / Doom + doom = doom / Dark, sliding shapes.
1999. (cd-ep) **CAMERA WITHIN**
– Camera within / Boorman 6 girl / Imagine among / The light.

— they also split a 7" single w/ WHITE TORNADO

SICBAY

SAKES + RODRIGUEZ recruited **DAVE ERB** – guitar / **JONATHON WARNBERG** – drums

not iss. / Obtuse Mule

2001. (cd) **THE FIRELIT S'COUGHS**
– Listening to sound / 3 hours / Matamoros / Who wrote the night? / Right eye, left eye / The sighting / Felsenmeer / Unanimal / Sink the town / Berthode / Offshore / Candlelight lipstick.

not iss. / Learning Curve

2001. (7") **split w/ VAZ**

Kelley DEAL 6000

Formed: Minneapolis, Minnesota, USA . . . April '95 by floating member of The BREEDERS and twin-sister of the more famous KIM, KELLEY DEAL. A one-time computer systems analyst, KELLEY subsequently threw herself head first into the rock'n'roll lifestyle with The BREEDERS. Things came to a head in late '94 after that year's Lollapolooza tour when she was arrested for possession of heroin in her hometown of Dayton, Ohio. Recovering from her addiction via a court enforced period in a rehab unit in St.Paul's, Minnesota, she returned to the studio. Originally working under the moniker of SOLID STATE, the vocalist/guitarist initiated a writing partnership with JESSE COLIN ROSS and DAVE SHOUSE (of The GRIFTERS), the results surfacing as the debut KELLEY DEAL 6000 album, 'GO TO THE SUGAR ALTAR'. By the time of its release in late '95 on her own 'Nice Record Label', the trio had become a quintet with the addition of MARTY NEDICH and NICK HOOK, although ROSS would subsequently be replaced by STEVE SALETT. Life affirming alt-rock epistles from the mind of an ex-junkie were the order of the day, European-based label, 'Play It Again Sam', sufficiently impressed to offer a new deal for '97's 'BOOM! BOOM! BOOM!'. In the meantime, her label was working on a scheduled album by The FROGS.

Album rating: GO TO THE SUGAR ALTAR (*6) / BOOM! BOOM! BOOM! (*5)

KELLEY DEAL (b.10 Jun'61, Dayton, Ohio, USA) – vocals, guitar (ex-BREEDERS) / **MARTY NEDICH** – bass / **NICK HOOK** – drums / also with **JESSE COLIN ROSS + DAVE SHOUSE** (of The GRIFTERS)

Shangri-la / Shangri-la

1996. (7") **TRIXIE DELICIOUS. / MIXIE DELICIOUS**

Bittersweet / Nice Record Label

Jul 96. (cd) *(BIT 007CD)* <*6001*> **GO TO THE SUGAR ALTAR** — Dec95
– Canyon / How about hero / Dammit / Sugar / Hundred tires / Head of the cult / Nice / Trixie delicious / Marooned / Tick tock / Mr. Goodnight. <*re-iss. 1997 on 'New West'; 36856*>
Nov 96. (cd-s) *(BIT 008)* **CANYON / GET THE WRITING**

— **STEVE SALETT** – drums; repl. ROSS who suffered drug problems

Play It Again Sam / Nice Record Label

Oct 97. (cd-s) *(BIAS 354CD)* **BRILLO HUNT. / MY BOYFRIEND DIED**
Nov 97. (cd) *(BIAS 361CD)* <*6002*> **BOOM! BOOM! BOOM!** — Aug97
– Brillo hunt / Shag / My boyfriend died / Baby I'm king / When he calls me kitten / Box / Stripper / Where did the home team go / Total war / Scary / Future boy / Drum solo / Skylark / Confidence girl / Get the writing off my back.

— towards the end of the 90's KELLEY rejoined The BREEDERS

DEAR NORA

Formed: Portland, Oregon, USA . . . 1999 by vocalist/guitarist KATY DAVIDSON, bassist RYAN WISE and drummer MARIANNA RITCHEY. DEAR NORA were named after a music professor whom the band found inspiring while attending Portland's Lewis & Clark College. The trio had all gone to this college and played in various bands including JUNCTION CITY and NAVINS; along with JAKE LONGSTRETH, WISE and RITCHEY were members of WOLF COLONEL. Motivated by a love of 60s music, forging guitars and sugary bubblegum-girl-group sounds, the combo self-released several cassettes before issuing an eponymous 7" EP on the local 'Magic Marker' indie imprint. This was followed up with an eight-song all-acoustic EP, 'DREAMING OUT LOUD', featuring songs written and performed by DAVIDSON during a mere 24 hours. 2001 would bring the debut long-player, 'WE'LL HAVE A TIME', which would hit the aural Grafenberg spot of many music critics for its versatile two-part happy harmonies and hummable hook-laden cuts. DAVE LONGSTRETH (brother of JAKE) would put in guest guitar appearances and paint the album's cover. After relocating to San Francisco and playing solo shows, DAVIDSON reformed the group, with drummer MARCI MARTINEZ (formerly TEAM DRESCH) and flute player CHLOE SCOTT putting in appearances on 'THE NEW YEAR' EP (2002). This release explored a mellower, more melancholic direction than the updated wall-of-sound-type album that preceded it, finding DAVIDSON in much more philosophical and tersely emotional mode, with her heart-core-exploring vocals adding a brilliant dimension to the songs. RITCHEY founded The BADGER KING and put out 'THE LIGHTHOUSE, THE GIANT' LP (2002), the title of which gave away the portentous, somewhat pretentious angle the album would take. RITCHEY's untypical, wide-ranging, interesting vocals help carry the songs through moments of willful obscurity and condescension to the listener during the lo-fi stew of traditional rock instrumentation, computers and glockenspiel.

Album rating: WE'LL HAVE A TIME (*6) / THE NEW YEAR E.P. (*5)

KATY DAVIDSON – vocals, guitar / **RYAN WISE** – bass (of WOLF COLONEL) / **MARIANNA RITCHEY** – drums

not iss. Magic Marker

2000. (7"ep) <MMR 8> **YOU MAKE ME SMILE. / (+3)**
2000. (7"ep) **DREAMING OUT LOUD**
  – Just one more thing / One two three four / Dreaming out loud / Out to dry / My autobiography / In my room / Slow and strong / My guitar.

— added guest guitarist **DAVE LONGSTRETH**

Feb 01. (cd) <MMR 12> **WE'LL HAVE A TIME**
  – Rollercoaster / 'Round and 'round / Since you went away / You looked like a portrait / When the wind blows / Springtime fall / I'm turned inside out / Everyone's the same / Early to bed / Number twelve / From my bedroom window / A lullaby.

Jun 02. (m-cd) <MMR 21> **THE NEW YEAR E.P.**
  – The new year / Coda to dreaming out loud / Holding on / Unscene (but heard) / Coda to lullaby / A polar bear / On to SEptember / How it changed the town / As vast as you / If I were a boy / Coda to the new year.

— they also split a single with MATES OF STATE

DEATH CAB FOR CUTIE

Formed: Bellingham, Washington, USA ... late 1996 by frontman, singer/songwriter and all around innovator BEN GIBBARD, who began his career in the strange world of Lo-Fi casio pop – The ALL-TIME QUARTERBACK!. After writing a handful of songs he recruited guitarist CHRISTOPHER WALLA, NICK HARMER and drummer NATHAN GOOD, to form the devilishly-titled DEATH CAB FOR CUTIE. An amalgamation of MODEST MOUSE's tripped-out guitar hooks and BUILT TO SPILL's solid indie rock sensibility, their debut album 'SOMETHING ABOUT AEROPLANES' (1999), caught the ears of the indie sect and left them crying out for more. Well, in between re-issuing the aforementioned ALL-TIME QUARTERBACK! eponymous set (1999), GIBBARD and Co started work on what was to become 'WE HAVE THE FACTS AND WE'RE VOTING YES' (2000), possibly the outfit's greatest achievement to date. GIBBARD's voice soared in songs such as 'SCIENTIST STUDIES' and the title track, but seems fractured and poignant on the romantic 'THE EMPLOYMENT PAGES'. DCFC delivered a modest EP, 'FORBIDDEN LOVE' in the same year, which contained three new cuts and two altenative arrangements of '405' and 'COMPANY CALLS EPILOGUE' (both on 'WE HAVE THE FACTS . . .'). They followed this with 'THE PHOTO ALBUM' (2001), which seemed to be taking the group in a new direction, namely that of BELLE & SEBASTIAN, NICK DRAKE and often the reflectiveness of DONOVAN. 'YOU CAN PLAY THESE SONGS WITH CHORDS' (2002) was orginally intended as a demo-only cassette, but was released including the collective's earlier singles 'PROVE MY HYPOTHESIS' and 'SONG FOR HUCKABLY'. • **Covered:** THIS CHARMING MAN (Smiths) / WAIT (Secret Stars) / WHY I CRY (Magnetic Fields).

Album rating: SOMETHING ABOUT AIRPLANES (*7) / ALL-TIME QUARTERBACK! by All-Time Quarterback! (*6) / WE HAVE THE FACTS AND WE'RE VOTING YES (*7) / THE PHOTO ALBUM (*8) / YOU CAN PLAY THESE SONGS WITH CHORDS early collection (*5)

BEN GIBBARD – vocals, guitars, organ / + guest vocalists **CHRISTOPHER WALLA** + **ABIGAIL HALL**

Elsinor Elsinor

Nov 97. (c) <els 012> **YOU CAN PLAY THESE SONGS WITH CHORDS**
  – President of what? / Champagne from a paper cup / Pictures in an exhibition / Hindsight / That's incentive / Amputations / Two cars / Line of best fit. <cd-iss. Oct02 on 'Barsuk'+=; BARK 28> – This charming man / TV trays / New candles / Tomorrow / Flustered – Hey tomcat! / State street residential / Wait / Prove my hypothesis / Song for Kelly Huckaby / Army corps of architects.

— added **CHRISTOPHER WALLA** – guitar, organ, guitar, etc / **NICK HARMER** – bass, keyboards / **NATHAN GOOD** – drums

Oct 98. (7"ep) <els 014> **YOUR BRUISE. / Revolutionary Hydra: LINEAR TIME / ANACORTES TYPE WRITER / CRUEL OCEANOGRAPHY**

— BEN plays bass for REVOLUTIONARY HYDRA

Jun 99. (cd) <els 017cd> **SOMETHING ABOUT AIRPLANES** Mar99
  – Bend to squares / President of what? / Champagne from a paper cup / Your bruise / Pictures in an exhibition / Sleep spent / The face that launched 1000 ships / Amputations / Fake frowns / Line of best fit.
  <blue-lp iss.2002 on 'Sonic Boom'; SBR 002>

Sep 99. (cd; as ALL-TIME QUARTERBACK!) <els 025cd> **ALL-TIME QUARTERBACK!**
  – Plans get complex / Dinner at eight in the suburbs / Cleveland (live) / Empire state (live) / Rules broken / Untitled / Factory direct (live) / Why I cry / Underwater (live) / Sock hop (live) / Send packing. (UK-iss.Jul02 on 'Barsuk'+=; BARK 26) – Plans get complex (video).
  above record was down to GIBBARD on his own

not iss. Sonic Boom

Sep 99. (7"clear) <SBR 003> **PROVE MY HYPOTHESIS. / WAIT**
  (UK-iss.Aug00; same)

not iss. Sub Pop

Mar 00. (7") <SP 496> **UNDERWATER! / THE ARMY CORPS OF ARCHITECTS**

Barsuk Barsuk

Mar 00. (cd) <BARK 11> **WE HAVE THE FACTS AND WE'RE VOTING YES**
  – We have all the facts and we're voting yes / The employment pages / For what reason / Lowell, MA / Little fury bugs / 405 / Company calls / Company calls (epilogue) / No joy in mudville / Scientist studies. (UK-iss.Aug00 on 'Fierce Panda'+=; NONG 26CD) – Song for Kelly Huckaby / Prove my hypothesis / Wait.

— **MICHAEL SCHORR** – drums; repl. GOOD

Nov 00. (cd-ep) <(BARK 15)> **THE FORBIDDEN LOVE** Oct00
  – Photobooth / Technicolor girls / Song for Kelly Huckaby / 405 (acoustic) / Company calls epilogue (alternate take).

Fierce Panda Barsuk

Feb 02. (cd-s) (NING 115CD) **A MOVIE SCRIPT ENDING / PHOTO BOOTH / TECHNICOLOR GIRLS**
Feb 02. (cd) (NONG 24CD) <BARK 21> **THE PHOTO ALBUM** Oct01
  – Steadier footing / A movie script ending / We laugh indoors / Information travels faster / Why you'd want to live here / Blacking out the friction / I was a kaleidoscope / Styrofoam plates / Coney Island / Debate exposes doubt. (UK+=) – Gridlock caravans / 20th century towers / All is full of love. (lp-iss.Apr02 on 'Barsuk'+=; BARK 21LP) – Gridlock caravans.
May 02. (7") (NING 116) **I WAS A KALEIDOSCOPE. / 405 (acoustic)**
  (cd-s) (NING 116CD) – ('A'side) / We laugh indoors (dub) / Stability.
Aug 02. (7") (NING 126) **WE LAUGH INDOORS. / DEBATE EXPOSES DOUBT (acoustic session)**
  (cd-s) (NING 126CD) – ('A'side) / For what reason (alternate) / I was a kaleidoscope (live).

— BEN GIBBARD is now with indie supergroup, POSTAL SERVICE, alongside JIMMY TAMBORELLO of FIGURINE

DELAKOTA

Formed: London, England ... early 1998 by former SENSELESS THINGS drummer, CASS BROWNE, and his pal, DES MURPHY. The duo promptly undertook an eclectic mission to rekindle the spirit of the ROLLING STONES, SLY STONE, STONE ROSES or in fact anything "stoned". The lads were lucky enough to be premiered live on Newsnight to an estimated TV audience of a couple of million! Yes that's right, BBC2's late-night programme hosted by the man politicians fear the most, Jeremy Paxman, invited the duo/band to play a few tracks while "The Pax" grilled Radio One DJ, STEVE LAMACQ and Creation boss, ALAN McGEE on the merits of modern pop/rock music. On the strength of this and a white-label demo of 'CINCINNATI', they signed to the 'Go! Beat!' imprint. The pair issued their first official single, 'BROTHERS', a riffing punk/rap tune that crashed into the proverbial eardrums of the indie fraternity. The follow-up, 'THE ROCK', changed direction and vibe, something DELAKOTA would attempt with each successive single. A Top 60 breakthrough, the song was similarly followed by a new version of 'C'MON CINCINNATI', taken from that September's most promising album release, 'ONE LOVE' (1998).

Album rating: ONE LOVE (*8)

CASS BROWNE – vocals, guitar (ex-SENSELESS THINGS) / **DES MURPHY** – samples, turntable

Go! Beat Go! Beat

Jul 98. (12"/cd-s) (GOB X/CD 10) **THE ROCK (mixes)** 60
Sep 98. (7"; DELAKOTA featuring ROSE SMITH) (GOB 11) **C'MON CINCINNATI. / C'MON CINCINNATI (organs village mix)** 55
  (12"+=/cd-s+=) (GOB X/CD 11) – The spectre.
  (above was originally released as a/their white-label 12")
Sep 98. (cd/c/lp) (557861-2/-4/-1) <11> **ONE LOVE** 58 Nov98
  – C'mon Cincinnati / I thought I caught / Too tough / 555 / Rock / Stealy / Brothers / On the trail / Metallic blue / Hook, line and sinker / End of line / Show me the door.
Feb 99. (7") (GOB 14) **555. / I WILL KRUSH YOU** 42
  (cd-s) (GOBCD 14) – ('A'side) / All over the world / Show me the door (Adam & Eve remix).
  (cd-s) (GOLCD 14) – ('A'side) / I thought I caught (David Holmes remix) / ('A'-Sound 5 remix).

London not iss.

Aug 00. (cd-s) (LONCD 450) **GOT IT LIKE THAT / THE FOX / DOWN IN THE BASEMENT**

DELGADOS

Formed: Glasgow, Scotland ... late 1994 by ex-university graduates, ALUN WOODWARD, EMMA POLLOCK, STEWART HENDERSON and PAUL SAVAGE. Not only did they kickstart Scotland's flagging (nae, virtually dead) indie scene, they did it by initiating their own imprint, 'Chemikal Underground'. The label's debut, 'MONICA WEBSTER', was greatly received by the music press and of course, who else? DJ John Peel, their angular guitar reminiscent of PAVEMENT, although ALUN and EMMA's twee vocal touches called to mind BELLE & SEBASTIAN. Single after single continued to impress until the excellent debut album, 'DOMESTIQUES', surfaced in late '96. Their "difficult" second album, 'PELOTON' (1998), managed to crack the

DELGADOS (cont)

UK Top 60, spurred on by indie hits, 'PULL THE WIRES FROM THE WALL' and 'THE WEAKER ARGUMENT DEFEATS THE STRONGER'. But perhaps it was their third and most accomplished set, 'The GREAT EASTERN' (named after a shelter in Glasgow's East end) which secured the group's ever growing reputation. For one, the album itself had not one weak point among the ten-or-so tracks, which segued like needle into thread. The DELGADOS owe much of this feat to the whistling flutes, assortment of horns and ambiguous use of orchestration which popped up throughout the set's dizzying array of songs. Stand out tracks (and, boy, did they really stand out!) included 'AMERICAN TRILOGY', 'AYE TODAY' and the frail accompaniment of closing number, 'MAKE YOUR MOVE'. Although the album failed to crack the mainstream, it did reach the minor regions of the charts, as did aforementioned single 'AMERICAN TRILOGY'. So, God bless the much dismissed DELGADOS – where would ARAB STRAP, MOGWAI and now majors-tempted BIS be without them and their seminal label?! • **Covers:** THE DIRGE (New Bad Things) / SACRE CHARLEMAGNE (France Gall) / A VERY CELLULAR SONG (Incredible String Band) / HOW CAN WE HANG ON TO A DREAM? (Tim Hardin).

Album rating: DOMESTIQUES (*9) / PELOTON (*8) / THE GREAT EASTERN (*8) / HATE (*8)

ALUN WOODWARD – vocals, guitar / **EMMA POLLOCK** – vocals, guitar / **STEWART HENDERSON** – bass / **PAUL SAVAGE** – drums

		Chemikal Underground	March
Jul 95.	(7") *(chem 001)* **MONICA WEBSTER. / BRAND NEW CAR**	☐	-
Aug 95.	(7"ep/cd-ep) *(SCAN/+CS 07)* **THE LAZARWALKER EP**	☐	-
	– Primary alternative / Lazarwalker / Buttonhole / Blackwell.		
	(above iss. on 'Radarscope') (below iss. on 'Boa'; B-side alter-ego)		
Dec 95.	(ltd-7") *(HISS 4)* **LIQUIDATION GIRL. / Van Impe: unknown**	☐	-
Dec 95.	(7"; various artists) *<che 47>* **I've Only Just Started To Breathe**	☐	-
Mar 96.	(7"ep/cd-ep) *(chem 004/+cd)* **CINECENTRE. / THIRTEEN GLIDING PRINCIPLES / M. EMULATOR**	☐	-
Aug 96.	(7"ep/cd-ep) *(chem 006/+cd)* **UNDER CANVAS / EEN TELF. / BEAR CLUB / STRATHCONA**	☐	-
Oct 96.	(7") *(100gm 18)* **BOOKER T JONES. / (other track by URUSEI YATSURA)**	-	- Japan
	– Booker T Jones / (other track by URUSEI YATSURA).		
	(above on Japanese '100 Guitar Mania' via 'Stolen Ecstasy' series)		
Oct 96.	(7"ep/cd-ep) *(chem 008/+cd)* **SUCROSE / CHALK. / EUROSPRINT / THE DIRGE**	☐	-
Nov 96.	(lp/cd) *(chem 009/+CD)* *<MAR 027>* **DOMESTIQUES**	☐	☐
	– Under canvas under wraps / Leaning on a cane / Strathcona slung / Tempered; not tamed / One more question / Big business in Europe / Falling & landing / Akumulator / Sucrose / Pinky / Friendly conventions / Smaller mammals / 4th channel / d'Estus morte.		
Jun 97.	(7") *(LISS 20)* **SACRE CHARLEMAGNE. / (other by The NEW BAD THINGS)**	☐	-
	(above release on 'Lissys')		
Mar 98.	(d7"/cd-s) *(chem 022/+cd)* **EVERYTHING GOES AROUND THE WATER. / BLACKPOOL / THE DROWNED AND THE SAVED**	☐	-
May 98.	(7") *(chem 023)* **PULL THE WIRES FROM THE WALL. / MAURON CHANSON**	69	-
	(cd-s+=) (chem 023cd) – Mark the day.		
Jun 98.	(cd) *(chem 024cd)* **PELOTON**	56	-
	– Everything goes around the water / The arcane model / The actress / Clarinet / Pull the wires from the wall / Repeat failure / And so the talking stopped / Don't stop / Blackpool / Russian orthodox / The weaker argument defeats the stronger.		
Sep 98.	(7") *(chem 029)* **THE WEAKER ARGUMENT DEFEATS THE STRONGER. / A VERY CELLULAR SONG**	☐	-
	(cd-s+=) (chem 029cd) – The actress – Irian Jaya remix.		

		Chemikal Underground	Beggars Banquet
Apr 00.	(lp/cd) *(chem 040/+cd)* *<81021>* **THE GREAT EASTERN**	72	May00
	– The past that suits you best / Accused of stealing / American trilogy / Reasons for silence / Thirteen gliding principles / No danger / Aye today / Witness / Knowing when to run / Make your move.		
May 00.	(7") *(chem 039)* **AMERICAN TRILOGY. / EUPHORIA HEIGHTS**	61	-
	(cd-s+=) (chem 039cd) – How can we hang on to a dream?		
	(cd-s+=) (chem 039cdx) – ('A'-CD rom) / Make your move.		
Sep 00.	(7") *(chem 044)* **NO DANGER. / THE CHOICES YOU'VE MADE**	☐	-
	(cd-s+=) (chem 044cd) – Don't sleep.		

		Mantra	not iss.
Sep 02.	(7") *(MNT 75)* **COMING IN FROM THE COLD. / COALMAN**	☐	-
	(cd-s+=) (MNT 75CD) – Crutches.		
Oct 02.	(cd/lp) *(MNT CD/LP 1031)* **HATE**	57	-
	– The light before we land / All you need is hate / Woke from dreaming / The drowning years / Coming in from the cold / Child killers / Favours / All rise / Never look at the sun / If this is a plan.		

– compilations, etc. –

Sep 97.	(cd) *Strange Fruit; (SFRSCD 037)* **BBC SESSIONS**	☐	-
	– Primary alternative / I've only just started to breathe / Lazarwalker / Indian fables / Under canvas under wraps / Sucrose / Teen elf / Thirteen gliding principles / Friendly conventions / Tempered; not tamed / Falling and landing. *(re-iss. May00; same)*		

DELICATESSEN

Formed: Leicester, England ... early 90's by mainman NEIL CARLILL, plus CRAIG BROWN, WILL FOSTER and STUART DAYMEN. Named after the infamous French film of the same name, this bunch of innovative indie guitar merchants made their debut on 'Big Life'-offshoot, 'Starfish', with the 'INVITING BOTH SISTERS OUT TO DINNER' single in autumn '94. The impressive 'C.F. KANE' followed in early '95, a nod to their cinematic influences against a suprisingly effective musical backdrop of blackboard-scraping guitar crescendos and aching melody. With a soundtrack to a BBC short film, 'George And Ramona', already under their belts, the band issued their debut album, 'SKIN TOUCHING WATER', later in '95. Unfortunately, DELICATESSEN's wilful experimentalism didn't really figure on the more musically conservative Brit-pop agenda of the day, 1996's follow-up set, 'HUSTLE INTO BED', meeting a similarly overlooked fate. A change of label (to 'Viper') and a return to form in '98 with the sublime, 'THERE'S NO CONFUSING SOME PEOPLE' (1998), ensured all was not lost. Tracks like 'LIGHTBULBS AND MOTHS', 'VARIOUS PETS', 'A PRIEST IN HALF' and 'SWEET' were obvious gems (the latter two ended the set in classic style), although NEIL and WILL thought better and moved on to indie supergroup, LODGER.

Album rating: SKIN TOUCHING WATER (*6) / HUSTLE INTO BED (*6) / THERE'S NO CONFUSING SOME PEOPLE (*8)

NEIL CARLILL (b. 1966) – vocals / **CRAIG BROWN** (b. 1973) – guitar, flute / **WILL FOSTER** (b. 1973) – bass, keyboards, acoustic guitar / **STUART DAYMEN** (b. 1972) – drums, percussion

		Starfish	not iss.
Oct 94.	(7") *(STF 1)* **INVITING BOTH SISTERS OUT TO DINNER. / A TENTH**	☐	-
	(cd-s+=) (STFC 1) – Zebra – Monkey – Liar.		
Apr 95.	(10"/cd-s) *(STF T/D 2)* **C.F. KANE. / MICE HAIR / EMBALMING THE DEAD ENTERTAINER**	☐	-
May 95.	(cd/lp) *(STF CD/LP 001)* **SKIN TOUCHING WATER**	☐	-
	– I'm just alive / C.F. Kane / Zebra – Monkey – Liar / Red, blue and green / Watercress / Classic adventure / Appeased / Chomsky / You cut my throat, I'll cut yours / Sick of flying saucers / Smiling you're stupid / Inviting both sisters out to dinner / Advice / Love's liquid / Froth / If she was anybody else.		
Jul 95.	(7") *(STF 3)* **I'M JUST ALIVE. / YES/NO IN ANY LANGUAGE**	☐	-
	(cd-s+=) (STFD 3) – Revelations of a domestic.		
Aug 96.	(7") *(STF 4)* **MONKEY SUIT. / THIS SLEEP THING**	☐	-
	(cd-s+=; w/free video) (STFD 4) – Make some mad tea.		
Aug 96.	(cd/c/lp) *(STF CD/MC/LP 2)* **HUSTLE INTO BED**	☐	-
	– Dear boss letter / Extra / Hustle into bed / Monkey suit / Buy a chance to breathe / Full-tilt in Paris / I'd love to shut up / My lungs into / Vanilla folders / Doc Prof / 8 pills / Bentine / Bad dog.		
—	added 5th member **JON WOOD** – violin		

		Viper	not iss.
Feb 98.	(cd) *(VIP 002CD)* **THERE'S NO CONFUSING SOME PEOPLE**	☐	-
	– Another meal turns up / Lightbulbs and moths / Various pets / Psycho / He killed himself in 1980 / Boy dough / Cruel country / A priest in half / Sweet.		

— NEIL and WILL jointly formed indie supergroup, LODGER, with a member of POWDER and SUPERGRASS!

DELICIOUS MONSTER

Formed: Birmingham, England ... 1991 by a very sexually liberated RACHEL MAYFIELD. The group debuted on their own label in 1992 by releasing the bizarre and psychedelic nine-and-a-half minute 'BLOOD'. Music journos and stunned fans had great expectations for these fresh debutantes who could only rival the likes of BARDO POND, SONIC YOUTH and Frank Black sidekick, KIM DEAL. 'POWER MISSY', a screaming anthemic power-ridden single was released to much glory three months later, witnessing the femme fatale fronted DELICIOUS MONSTER tour Europe, playing their inside-out rock to dozens of frightened crowds. Masturbation being their favourite subject (MAYFIELD was once quoted saying: "Masturbation is great ... that's what our next single is going to be about ..."), the ball-wrenching 4-piece caught the attention of indie label 'Beechwood'. They signed them to their side project imprint, 'Flute' in late '92 where they issued the full-length long player 'JOIE DE VIVRE' (1993). After that things seemed to disintegrate as the band drifted away into the endless world of lost hopefuls, providing inspiration for up-and-coming girl-fronted combos such as ELASTICA, LUSH and CAY. RACHEL subsequently worked with GALLON DRUNK while carving out her own solo career.

Album rating: JOIE DE VIVRE (*6)

RACHEL MAYFIELD – vocals / + 3 guys

		Pure Savage	not iss.
1992.	(12"ep) *(EYE 01)* **DULL DULL DULL**	☐	-

		Flute – Beechwood	not iss.
Aug 92.	(cd-ep) *(FLUTE 1CD)* **POWER MISSY / BEST BABE / BIGGEST HIGH / BLOOD**	☐	-
Nov 92.	(7") *(FLUTE 2)* **SNUGGLE. / SIMULATE**	☐	-
	(cd-s+=) (FLUTE 2CD) – Double double.		
Oct 93.	(7") *(FLUTE 6)* **RIPPED. / I.O.U.**	☐	-
	(cd-s+=) (FLUTE 6CD) – Peace.		

Nov 93. (cd/c/lp) *(FLUTE 7 CD/MC/LP)* **JOIE DE VIVRE**
– Power missy / Ripped / Secret place / Warm / Big love / In you in me / Snuggle / Some relief / Talk to me / For her.
Dec 93. (7") *(FLUTE 8)* **BIG LOVE.** /
(cd-s+=) *(FLUTE 8CD)* –

—— split after above

DELTA 72

Formed: Philadelphia, Pennsylvania, USA ... summer 1994 by GREGG FOREMAN, SARAH STOLFA and BENJAMIN AZZARA, with the soon to be added attraction of KIM THOMPSON (of CUPID CAR CLUB fame). Their sound blended sixties style British invasion R&B with punk rock sensibilities to create a frenetic honest indie rock style. They debuted in the mid-90s with their 7", 'ON THE ROCKS', and followed it up with their debut LP, 'THE R&B MEMBERSHIP' (1996). A blistering opening set, which rarely gave their audience time to think let alone get bored, featured the work of their sticksman, JASON KOURKOUNIS (ex-MULE), who moved in to replace AZZARA. During the period between this record and their sophomore full-length set, 'THE SOUL OF A NEW MACHINE' (1997), THOMPSON bailed out and his position was ably filled by that of BRUCE RECKAHN (formerly of the GOATS). This second piece clearly did not suffer from the changes, with the players having a seemingly more confident approach, leading to a more interesting listen, although with no apparent displacement of energy. From a whirlwind start D72 slowed down in their production rate with their third album, '000', not appearing in the shops until three years later. Although some fans may have disliked the slower pace of this release, for the majority it was appreciated for its mature songwriting and its soulful leanings, showcasing STOLFA's organ work to the full. • **Covered:** CINDERELLA (Sonics).

Album rating: THE R&B OF MEMBERSHIP (*7) / THE SOUL OF A NEW MACHINE (*5) / 000 (*6)

GREGG FOREMAN – vocals, guitar / **SARAH STOLFA** – organ / **KIM THOMPSON** – bass (of CUPID CAR CLUB) / **BENJAMIN AZZARA** – drums

	not iss.	Kill Rock Stars – Dischord
Jun 95. (7"m) *<KRS 247 – DIS 98.5>* **ON THE ROCKS. / GOT A TRAIN TO CATCH / HIP COAT**	–	

—— **JASON KOURKOUNIS** – drums (ex-MULE) repl. AZZARA

	Touch & Go	Touch & Go
Jun 96. (7") *<TG 161>* **TRIPLE CROWN**		
– Rich girls like to steal / Cinderella/		
Jul 96. (m-lp/m-cd) *<TG 172/+CD>* **THE R&B OF MEMBERSHIP**		
– Introduction / On the lam / Rich girls like to steal / Satellite / Get down / It's all over / Frigid / One the rocks / 7 & 7 / Capitol contingency / Trick baby / Hustler.		

—— **BRUCE RECKAHN** – bass (of GOATS) repl. THOMPSON

Jun 98. (lp/cd) *<TG 182/+CD>* **THE SOUL OF A NEW MACHINE**		Aug97
– Introduction part 2 / Monopoly of your mouth / Mainline (part 1) Floorboard shake / The cut / Wiretapping / I've dreamt of leaving . . . ever since you told me / Mainline (part 2) / It's alright / Scratch / Up in the high numbers / The takedown / Blow out / The scope / Go go Kitty / In to the a.m. / We hate the blues		

—— **MARK BOYCE** – organ; repl. SARAH

Jul 99. (cd-ep) *<TG 202CD>* **SOREGA DOUSHITA**
– Pleased and honored (parts 1 & 2) / Green eyes / Mainline (pt.2) / Wiretapping / Take down.
Mar 00. (cd) *<TG 212>* **000**
– Are you ready? / The doctor is in / Just another let down / 3 day packet plan / Incident @ 23rd / I feel fine / Ten lbs. / Hip coat / Great paper chase No.1 / Sun the secret prince.
Apr 00. (7") *<TG 217>* **THE DOCTOR IS IN. / THE CHAMP** –

DEMOLITION DOLL RODS

Formed: Detroit, Michigan, USA ... mid 90's by MARGARET DOLL ROD, her sister CHRISTINE DOLL ROD and guitarist DANNY DOLL ROD (actually GORIES guitarist DANNY KROHA). The group of trashy, cross-dressing, drag queen, speed-garage rockers issued the shambolic lo-fi scuzz album 'TASTY' (1997) before being snapped up by 'Matador' in 1998. Like label-mates GUITAR WOLF, the troupe of G-string wearing thrash punks literally hacked at their instruments until they broke under the immense pressure of feedback induced noise. 'Matador' issued 'T.L.A' in 1999, and The DEMOLITION DOLL RODS embarked on a brief tour with both IGGY POP and, unsurprisingly, The CRAMPS. • **Covered:** WILD CHILD (. . . Bray) / SPOONFUL (Willie Dixon).

Album rating: TASTY (*5) / T.L.A. (*7)

MARGARET DOLL ROD – vocals, rhythm guitar / **DANNY DOLL ROD** (b. DAN KROHA) – guitar, vocals (ex-GORIES) / **CHRISTINE DOLL ROD** – drums

	In The Red	In The Red
Jun 97. (lp/cd) *<ITR 048/+CD>* **TASTY**		Mar97
– Motor city dragway / If you can't hang / Wild child / Doo walka-walka / Maverick girl / Come out of the rain / Queen bee drag racin' / Psycho Kitty / Raw / Lil darlin' / This little monkey / Spoonful.		

	Matador	Matador
Jul 99. (cd) *<OLE 366-2>* **T.L.A.**		
– Secret place / Fast one / Got a little lovin' / Fooling around / Married for the weekend / Velvet surprise / Sex machine / U look good / Rock it up / Feast / Move to the music / Good love / Hey love / Best friends / Carry me away.		

DENIM (see under ⇒ FELT; 80's section)

DENISON / KIMBALL TRIO (see under ⇒ JESUS LIZARD; 80's section)

DEPARTURE LOUNGE

Formed: London, England . . . 1998 by former ROBIN HITCHCOCK & THE EGYPTIANS guitarist, TIM KEEGAN, along with percussionist LINDSAY JAMIESON, guitarist CHRIS ANDERSON and bass player JAKE KYLE. DEPARTURE LOUNGE's debut album, 'OUT OF HERE' (supplemented by the previously released 'OUT OF THERE' EP), was produced by SIMON RAYMONDE of the COCTEAU TWINS and issued in 2000. The album was an easy-going collection of songs afforded a level of class by the group's multi-instrumentalist capabilities. In 2001, the group took up a six-month residency in Nashville's slow bar and honed their talents by playing alongside the likes of JOSH ROUSE and LAMBCHOP. 2001 also saw the release of another album, 'JETLAG DREAMS', followed by the 2002 release 'TOO LATE TO DIE YOUNG'. Each of the albums had their merits, however the band's refusal to settle on one sound caused confusion and inconsistency. • **Note:** the DEPARTURE LOUNGE release in 1999 'Deplounge 2' was indeed by an outfit fronted by JASON MOORE.

Album rating: OUT OF HERE/THERE (*7) / JETLAG DREAMS (*6) / TOO LATE TO DIE YOUNG (*6)

TIM KEEGAN – vocals, guitars, harmonica (ex-ROBYN HITCHCOCK & THE EGYPTIANS) / **CHRIS ANDERSON** – guitar, keyboards, oboe, stylophone, saxophone, vocals / **JAKE KYLE** – bass, double bass, trumpet, vocals / **LINDSAY JAMIESON** – percussion, drums, flute, keyboards, harmonica

	Meek Giant	Flydaddy
Apr 00. (cd-ep) *(MEEK 004CD)* **OUT OF THERE e.p.**		
– El intro / The new you / Starport / Disconnected / Late night drive / Johnny A / Los exitos.		
Apr 00. (cd) *<FLY 39>* **OUT OF HERE**	–	
– Music for pleasure / The new you / Slow news day / Disconnected (remix by Lindsay Jamieson) / Win them back / Save me from happiness / Postcard from a friend / Johnny A. / Stay on the line / (We've got) Everything we need / (untitled).		
Oct 00. (12"ep) *(MEEK 005V)* **GOLDFIELD EP**		–
– Be good to yourself / Straight line to the kerb / Tubular Belgians in my goldfield.		

	not iss.	Grimsey
2001. (7") *<GR 017>* **JOHNNY A. / FORTUNADO**		

	Bella Union	Bella Union
Sep 01. (cd) *(<BELLACD 704>)* **JETLAG DREAMS**		
– Equestrian skydiving / Runway doubts / Too late to die young / A strange descent / Purple fluffy haze / Beyond the beltway / Charles de Gaulle to Belleville.		

	Bella Union	Nettwerk
Feb 02. (cd-s) *(BELLACD 31)* **KING KONG FROWN / EQUESTRIAN SKYDIVING (Venus hum satellite city mix) / GROW YOUR OWN**		
Mar 02. (cd) *(BELLACD 32) <30250>* **TOO LATE TO DIE YOUNG**		–
– Straight line to the kerb / What you have is good / King Kong frown / I love you / Alone again, and . . . / Tubular Belgians in my goldfield / Be good to yourself / Over the side / Coke & flakes / Silverline / Animals on my mind. (re-iss. Nov02; same)		

DESAPARECIDOS (see under ⇒ BRIGHT EYES)

DESC (see under ⇒ KHAYA)

dEUS

Formed: Antwerp, Belgium . . . 1991 by TOM BARMAN alongside RUDY TROUVE, KLAUS JANZOONS, JULLE DE BORGHER and STEF CARLENS. Beginning life as a VIOLENT FEMMES / VELVET UNDERGROUND covers outfit, this experimental art-rock collective were picked up by 'Island' in 1994, initially making an impact via their appearance at that year's Glastonbury festival. A UK debut single, 'SUDS & SODA' (they had issued 'ZEA' in Belgium), was closely followed by 'VIA', TOM WAITS and CAPTAIN BEEFHEART being the most commonly cited reference points – in fact the latter's right hand man, ERIC DREW FELDMAN produced them. Open-ended in the established tradition of late 60's/early 70's Euro-rock yet pregnant with the potential to be as abrasive as early BIG BLACK or even BLACK FLAG, dEUS' avant-garde pop polarised opinion; you either loved it or hated it. Certainly more challenging than many of the identikit grunge albums doing the rounds at the time, 'WORST CASE SCENARIO' (1994) focused the band's wayward muse into a listenable whole; it also proved that there was more to Belgian music than plastic Europap passed off as "techno". dEUS released a follow-up set, 'IN A BAR, UNDER THE SEA' (1996), an album that contained their only Top 50 single to date, 'LITTLE ARITHMETICS'. Following the epic 'ROSES' single, dEUS returned in 1999 with the David Bottrill-produced 'THE IDEAL CRASH', an album of subdued intensity which underscored their ability to experiment without sounding gratingly self indulgent. dEUS have been a little inactive of late, although RUDY TROUVE resurfaced in 2000 when co-credited on an album, 'SUBSONIC 6', with LOU BARLOW (of Sebadoh). • **Songwriters:** Group (BARMAN (words) / CARLENS some with SERGEY) or (TROUVE + JANZOONS with VERMEERSCH + VERVLOESEM) except a sample of

dEUS (cont)

FRANK ZAPPA on their 1994 album. In 1996, BARMAN, CARLENS and WARD became the writers.

Album rating: MY SISTER IS MY CLOCK (*6) / WORST CASE SCENARIO (*8) / IN A BAR, UNDER THE SEA (*7) / THE IDEAL CRASH (*8) / NO MORE LOUD MUSIC: THE SINGLES compilation (*7)

TOM BARMAN – vocals / **KLAUS JANZOONS** – violin / **RUDY TROUVE** – guitar / **JULLE DE BORGHER** – drums / **STEF KAMIL CARLENS** – bass

			own label	not iss.
1993.	(cd-ep) *(none)* **ZEA EP**		-	- Belgian

– Zea intro replica / Zea / Right as rain / Great American nude.

			Island	Polygram
Jul 94.	(7") *(IS 598)* **SUDS & SODA. / SECRET HELL**			

(12"+=/cd-s+=) *(12IS/CID 598)* – Texan coffee / It. furniture in the far west.

Sep 94. (7") *(IS 599)* **VIA. / VIOLINS AND HAPPY ENDINGS**
(12"+=/cd-s+=) *(12IS/CID 599)* – Great American nude (strip mix) / Niche.

Oct 94. (cd/c/lp) *(CID/ICT/ILPS 8028) <524045>* **WORST CASE SCENARIO** — Feb95
– Intro / Suds & soda / W.C.S. (first draft) / Jigsaw you / Morticiahair / Via / Right as rain / Mute / Lets get lost / Hotellounge (be the death of me) / Shake your hip / Great American nude / Secret hell / Divebomb djingle.

Jan 95. (c-s/7") *(C+/IS 603)* **HOTELLOUNGE (BE THE DEATH OF ME). / JIGSAW YOU (live)** 55 -
(cd-s+=/cd-s+=) *(CID/+X 603)* – Whose Vegas (is it anyway).

Jan 95. (cd) *(IMCD 8031)* **MY SISTER IS MY CLOCK** - - mail-o
– Middlewave / Almost white / Health insurance / Little ghost / How to row a cat / Only a colour to her / Sick sugar / Sweetness / Horror party jokes / Void / Sans titre pour sira / Glovesong / Lorre in the forest.

— **CRAIG WARD** (b. Scotland) – guitar; repl. TROUVE who formed KISS MY JAZZ (with CRAIG also in tow)

Jul 96. (7"/10") *(IS/10IS 630)* **THEME FROM TURNPIKE. / OVERFLOW / MY LITTLE CONTESSA** 68
(cd-s+=) *(CID 630)* – Worried about Satan.

Oct 96. (c-s/7"pic-d) *(C+/IS 643)* **LITTLE ARITHMETICS. / MY WIFE JAN** 44 -
(cd-s+=) *(CID 643-854 719-2)* – The tugboat / Everything is the same (except no one believes me).

Nov 96. (cd/c/lp) *(CID/ICT/ILPS 8052) <524296>* **IN A BAR, UNDER THE SEA** Mar97
– I don't mind what ever happens / Fell off the floor, man / Opening night / Theme from Turnpike / Little arithmetics / Gimme the heat / Serpentine / A shocking lack thereof / Supermarketsong / Memory of a festival / Guilty pleasures / Nine threads / Disappointed in the sun / For the roses / Wake me up before I sleep.

Mar 97. (7"pic-d) *(IS 645)* **ROSES. / I SUFFER ROCK** 56 -
(cd-s+=) *(CID 645)* – Nine threads (demo) / Difficult day.
(cd-s) *(CIDX 645)* – ('A'-Vermeersch version) / Via (live) / Hotel lounge (be the death of me) (live) / Jigsaw you (live).

Sep 97. (c-s/7"pic-d) *(C+/IS 663)* **LITTLE ARITHMETICS. / FELL OFF THE FLOOR, MAN** (Dust Brothers edit)
(cd-s+=) *(CID 663)* – Me & your mother / Disappointed in the sun.

Mar 99. (cd/c/lp) *(CID/ICT/ILPS 8082)* **THE IDEAL CRASH** 64
– Put the freaks up front / Silver dew / One advice space / Magic hour / The ideal crash / Instant Street / Magdalena / Everybody's weird / Let's see who goes down first / Dream sequence #1.

Apr 99. (7") *(IS 742)* **INSTANT STREET. / DREAM SEQUENCE** 49 -
(cd-s) *(CID 742)* – ('A'side) / Sam Peckinpah's daughter / You can't deny what you liked as a child.
(cd-s) *(CIDX 742)* – ('A'side) / There / Everybody's weird (demo).

Jun 99. (7") *(IS 750)* **SISTER DEW. / 13 (live)** 62 -
(cd-s+=) *(CID 750)* – A shocking lack thereof (session).
(cd-s) *(CIDX 750)* – ('A'side) / Sister dew (enhanced) / Gimme the heat (live) / Little arithmetics (live).

Oct 99. (7") *(IS 760)* **THE IDEAL CRASH. / EVERYBODY'S WEIRD** - -
(cd-s+=) *(CID 760)* – Put the freaks up front (session) / Instant street (session) / ('A'CD-Rom).
(cd-s) *(CIDX 760)* – ('A'side) / One advice space / You can't deny what you liked as a child / Magdalena (live) / Gimme the heat (live).

— compilations, etc. —

Nov 01. (cd) *Universal; (586637-2)* **NO MORE LOUD MUSIC – THE SINGLES** -
– Suds & soda / Via / Hotellounge (be the death of me) / Theme from Turnpike / Little arithmetics / Roses / Fell off the floor man / Instant street / Sister dew / Ideal crash / Nothing really ends.

DEVILS
(see under ⇒ DUFFY, Stephen; 80's section)

D4

Formed: Auckland, New Zealand ... 1998 by JIMMY CHRISTMAS and DION PALMER after having met at a party and subsequently discovering a mutual fondness for garage rock. The duo then recruited bassist VAUGHAN and drummer BEAVER before releasing their self-titled, self-financed debut EP in 1999. The record captured the balls-out spirit of their Antipodean counterparts AC/DC and the uncompromising rawness of The STOOGES. 2001 saw the Australian-release of the group's first full length album, '6TWENTY', an unrelenting, juggernaut of an album that served to remind the listener of rock'n'roll's live fast, die young ethos. • **Covered:** JOHN ROCK (Dogs) / SANTA CLAUS + DON'T BELIEVE IN CHRISTMAS (Sonics) / PIRATE LOVE (Johnny Thunders) / INVADER ACE (Guitar Wolf) / MYSTEREX (Scavengers).

Album rating: 6TWENTY (*6)

DION PALMER – vocals, guitar (ex-RAINY DAYS) / **JIMMY CHRISTMAS** – vocals, guitar / **VAUGHAN** – bass / **BEAVER** – drums

			Flying Nun	not iss.
1999.	(cd-ep) *(FNCD 439)* **THE D4**		-	- NewZ

– Girl / Come on! / Outta blues / What U want.

2000. (7") *(none)* **LADIES MAN. / NORTH SHORE BITCH** - - NewZ
(above issued on own label)

2000. (cd-s) *(FNCD 446)* **LADIES MAN / NORTH SHORE BITCH / PARTY (live)** - - NewZ

			S.D.Z.	not iss.
Feb 02.	(7") *(SDZ 003)* **ROCK'N'ROLL MOTHERFUCKER. / RUNNING ON EMPTY**		-	- NewZ

			Infectious	Hollywood
Jul 02.	(7") *(INFEC 116S)* **PARTY. / GIRL**			-

(cd-s+=) *(INFEC 116CDSX)* – ('A'side) / Outta blues / North shore beach.

Sep 02. (7") *(INFEC 117S)* **GET LOOSE. / JOHN ROCK** 64
(cd-s+=) *(INFEC 117CDS)* – Joe Orton's wedding / ('A'-Peel session).

Sep 02. (cd/lp) *(INFEC 115 CDX/LPX) <162388>* **6TWENTY** Mar03
– Rock'n'roll motherfucker / Party / Come on! / Pirate love / Running on empty / Ladies man / Invader ace / Little baby / Rebekah / Mysterex / Exit to the city / Heartbreaker / Get loose.
(above initially issued in 2001 NZ on 'Flying Nun'; *FNCD 449*)

Nov 02. (7") *(INFEC 121S)* **COME ON! / SANTA CLAUS** 50 -
(cd-s+=) *(INFEC 121CDS)* – Don't believe in Christmas.

DHARMA BUMS

Formed: Portland, Oregon, USA ... 1987 out of The WATCHMEN and PERFECT CIRCLE by JEREMY WILSON, ERIC LOVRE, JIM TALSTRA and JOHN MOEN. Yet another band to have been influenced by the colourful Paisley underground scene of the early 80's (RAIN PARADE, DREAM SYNDICATE, etc), The DHARMA BUMS (named after a Jack Kerouac book) signed to established US indie retro label, 'Frontier', releasing debut album 'HAYWIRE' around the start of '89. A follow-up set, 'BLISS' (1991), fared better critically although that didn't prevent them from splitting after a final LP offering, 'WELCOME' (1992). In April 1993, JEREMY returned from a long break in Costa Rica to ignite a new outfit, PILOT, complete with past friends from the group PERFECT CIRCLE, RIC JOHNSTON and PATRICK GUNDRUN. Releases for 'Tim/Kerr', 'Elektra' and 'Mercury' from 1995 onwards (including the celebrated 'STRANGERS WALTZ' in 1998) showed promise but nothing earth-shattering as the band fizzled out. Probably their most disappointing event was the shelving of 1995's 'HISS' long-player by the corporate people at 'Elektra'. • **Note:** Watch out for a similarly named dance band who released EP's for 'B.M.G.'.

Album rating: HAYWIRE (*4) / BLISS (*6) / WELCOME (*4) / Pilot: WHEN THE DAY HAS BROKEN (*4) / STRANGERS WALTZ (*6)

JEREMY WILSON (b. 1969) – vocals / **ERIC LOVRE** – guitar, vocals / **JOHN MOEN** – drums, vocals / **JIM TALSTRA** – bass

			not iss.	Pop Llama
Feb 89.	(7") **HAYWIRE. / SHAKE**		-	

			Diablo	Frontier
Mar 89.	(lp) *(SORC 5) <4620>* **HAYWIRE**			

– Timeyard / Boots of leather / Cruel acres / Over – Under / Walking stick / Mutiny / Hope of the hour / Jet pilot / Dropping out / Farmyard / Flowers / Haywire.

			Frontier	Frontier
May 91.	(cd/c/lp) *<(4625 2L/4L/1L)>* **BLISS**			Nov90

– Pumpkinhead / Higher / Plunger / Far gone from / 20,000 tears / Stayed up late / Time together / Pigweeds / B-sting / You've seen fire / This horse is / Gold / A place to be.

Apr 92. (cd/c/lp) *<(34636-2/-4/-1)>* **WELCOME** Dec91
– The light in you / First time – Last time / Good advice / Incestuous / Porch song / A push me pull me / Favor / Wreck around town / Bright orange spot / Words / Aces.

May 92. (7") *<(34676-7)>* **GIVIN' IN. / SHAKE SOME ACTION**

— split some time in 1992

PILOT

JEREMY WILSON plus **PATRICK GUNDRAN** – guitar, keyboards, vocals / **RIC JOHNSTON** – bass, guitar (from The WATCHMEN) / **RICHARD STUVERUD** – drums

			not iss.	Tim/Kerr
Dec 95.	(cd-ep) *<T/K 78>* **PILOT**		-	

– Another day has begun / The blue / Fork for a tongue.

			not iss.	Elektra
May 96.	(cd) *<83012-2>* **WHEN THE DAY HAS BROKEN**		-	

– Cloud covered figure 8 / Belong / Cheers, disappear / Asunder various / Distant star / Guitar store / No separation / Full of sunshine (this ain't the day) / When the day has broken / Don't want to lose you / Zoom / Crazy sleeper / Making my way back to you / Be.

			not iss.	Mercury
1998.	(cd) *<7004357052-2>* **STRANGERS WALTZ**		-	

– Strange powers / Swing / She sits in sunlight / Undigo bleeds the sun / West Texas wind / Jesus at my elbow / 600 miles / 2 stars / Tambourine waltz / Goodnight / Man made waltzes / Greenwood waltz.

DIANOGAH

Formed: Chicago, Illinois, USA ... early 1995 by JAY RYAN, JASON HARVEY and KIP MCCABE. The band came from the same left-field territory as fellow Chicago post-rockers, TORTOISE and TRENCHMOUTH, although their actual sound was very different. Originally appearing as a mainly instrumental unit made up of two bassists and a drummer they debuted later in 1995 with the experimental singles, '100% TREE' and

'GARDEN AIRPLANE TRAP'; later re-issued on the aptly-titled EP 'OLD MATERIAL, NEW FORMAT' (1998). Following these singles but predating the aforementioned compilation was their inaugural LP, 'AS SEEN FROM ABOVE' (1997), which showcased the trio's amazing ability to create rich and sonorous music from their basic rhythm instruments; it also featured subdued vocal work from RYAN. In the ensuing period, the group featured on several compilations, worthy of note was their subsequent appearance on the JOHN McENTIRE (of TORTOISE fame) soundtrack 'Reach The Rock'. The turn of the millennium saw DIANOGAH put out their sophomore album 'BATTLE CHAMPIONS' which benefitted from the experienced hand of STEVE ALBINI at the production tiller, while the band again managed to find new arrangements and patterning for their sparse instrumentation. Two years on and the group returned with their masterwork, the third full-length offering 'MILLIONS OF BRAZILIANS', also with McENTIRE in tow. The sound on this record was also bolstered by some guest spots from the COCTAILS' JOHN UPCHURCH – and RACHEL GRIMES of the RACHELS fame – with added instrumentation in the shape of synthesizers and six-string guitar.

Album rating: AS SEEN FROM ABOVE (*7) / BATTLE CHAMPIONS (*6) / (MILLIONS OF BRAZILIANS) (*7)

JAY RYAN – vocals, bass / **JASON HARVEY** – bass / **KIP McCABE** – drums

				not iss.	Actionboy 300
1995.	(7")	**100% TREE. / BUILDING A PLAYPEN**		-	
1995.	(7")	**GARDEN AIRPLANE TRAP. / EUCALYPTUS**		-	

Ohio Gold   not iss.

Oct 97. (cd) *(OHIOGOLD 002CD)* **AS SEEN FROM ABOVE**
– Plankton and krill / What is your landmass? / Seeing stars / Broken magnet halves / Colby / Between the ship and the land / Lone tree point / Spiral bound / Shogun. *(re-iss. Oct99 on 'Hefty'; HEFTY 006)*

not iss.   Hi Ball

1999. (7") **SUPER TINY ELECTRIC CAR. / (split w/ The LOG LETTERS)**

not iss.   Swedish

1999. (7"; as TEAM DIANOGAH) **MY BROTHER WORE BROWN. / I'M A SWEDE HEART**

––– both JAY + JASON now added to guitar to bass-playing

Southern   Southern

May 00. (cd/lp) *<18578>* **BATTLE CHAMPIONS**
– Kaisakunin / At the mercy of the mustang / Time for a game of stick / Sometimes there are birds / Indie rock Spock ears / Emerson / They have monkeys like we have squirrels / Eating cake / Work / My brother wore brown / Sometimes there used to be birds.

Feb 01. (7") *<18586-7>* **HANNIBAL. / A BEAR EXPLAINS THE RIGHT AND WRONG WAYS TO PUT ON A SHIRT, SHOES, PANTS AND A CAP**

Apr 02. (cd) *<18589-2/-1>* **(MILLIONS OF BRAZILIANS)**
– Wrapping the lamb, sir / Maria, which has got her heart completely fucked up / The smallest Chilean / American dipper / Flat panda / Take care, Olaf / Pinata oblongata / Goto Dengo loses the war / Pitufina / The sky came down to the rooftops.

– compilations, etc. –

1998. (cd-ep) *My Pal God; <MPG 027>* **OLD MATERIAL, NEW FORMAT** (early singles)

DIESELHED

Formed: Arcata, California, USA ... early 90's by VIRGIL SHAW, ATOM ELLIS, DANNY HEIFETZ, SHON McALINN and ZACHARY HOLTZMAN. Their work was normally placed within the alt-country bracket, which as open ended as it is, fails to convey the powerful and eclectic crossing of genres the band achieved. Although definitely fitting in with the country rock scene, the Bay Area crew loaded their music with punk sensibilites. They also had a real genius for quirky lyricism which would not always be at home in Nashville. However, it was refreshing in its honest sense of fun, and this playfulness being an important part of their make-up and great for inducing the live audiences to their side. It came as no surprise then that HEIFETZ spent the other half of his musical life in San Francisco category-disturbing group, MR BUNGLE. Signing to 'Amarillo' records the 'HED debuted in 1994 with their eponymous LP, 'DIESELHED', a great first outing which, although it got lost in itself at points, heralded a major new talent on the scene. DIESELHED were quick not to let the dust settle on this belief, bringing out their sophomore full-length set, 'TALES OF A BROWN DRAGON', the following year. With this set the group honed down some of their lengthier outbursts, producing what still stands out as one of their finest outings. Now with a name carved out for themselves as a multi-talented band willing to travel, they managed to attract the aid of Dusty Wakeman, an engineer who had carved a career working with DWIGHT YOAKAM. He produced their third album, 'SHALLOW WATER BLACKOUT' (1997). WAKEMAN's influence pushed the record towards the country end of the scale, although the band's musical maturity and defiance proved that it would always be an interesting listen. They were most certainly not going to be apeing anybody else's oeuvre. Riding on the back of this triumph the band toured with the hugely influential rock'n'roller, LINK WRAY. DIESELHED's fourth LP, 'ELEPHANT REST HOME' (1999), followed, and as the title suggested, displayed a more chilled, laid back, funky honky-tonk styling, although with no let down in quality. The millennium saw the release of their fifth full-set, 'CHICO AND THE FLUTE', and it seemed that the alt-country outfit were finding it hard to put a foot wrong.

Album rating: DIESELHED (*6) / TALES OF A BROWN DRAGON (*7) / SHALLOW WATER BLACKOUT (*7) / ELEPHANT REST HOME (*5) / CHICO AND THE FLUTE (*7)

ZACHARY HOLTZMAN – vocals / **VIRGIL SHAW** – vocals / **ATOM ELLIS** – guitar / **SHON McALINN** – / bass / **DANNY HEIFETZ** – drums (of MR. BUNGLE)

not iss.   Amarillo

1993. (7"m) *<AMAR 580>* **FORKLIFT TEST. / PEELIN' OUT / A-1 STEAK SAUCE**

Feb 94. (cd) *<ACM 590>* **DIESELHED**
– Hashbrowns / Poodle's ear / Sergio Taurus / B A band / Happy donut / Cloud of diesel / A-1 / 5 shots / Hot VW's / Greyhound / Macrame x-mas cards / Ice chest. *<re-iss. Oct96; same>*

Nov 95. (cd) *<ACM 601>* **TALES OF A BROWN DRAGON**
– Brown dragon / Butcher boy / Wedding song / Gravy boat / Wipe down the vinyl / Pizza box / M and M / Fork lift test / Aladdin's lamp / Baby song / Snow blind in the liquor store.

Sep 97. (cd) *<ACM 608>* **SHALLOW WATER BLACKOUT**
– Fog it up / Produce section / Yellow kitchen / Inches of air / Tea leaves / Betsy / Carving soap / Asphalt bib / Safety glass / Blue Hawaiian.

Bongload   Bongload

Feb 99. (cd) *<(BL 36CD)>* **ELEPHANT REST HOME**
– Tying flies / Trucker's alibi / Cold duck / Futon song / Lap dance / Life beyond eureka / Red chair / Twin falls / Corrine.

Mar 01. (cd) *<(BL 49CD)>* **CHICO AND THE FLUTE**   Oct00
– Prelude / Frank / Brownie / Tidepool / Froggy con saw / Gentle grooming / Homemade shoes / Marlboro man / Starting all over / Interlude / Bright lights / Thick sugary smell / Outerlude / Tag it up / Chico and the flute.

Ani DiFRANCO

Born: 23 Sep'70, Buffalo, New York, USA. Having learned to sing and play guitar at an early age, DiFRANCO began playing professionally after a move to the centre of New York. As fiercely independent and enterprising as she was talented, DiFRANCO set up her own 'Righteous Babe' imprint for the release of her eponymous debut album. Issued in 1990 as an American-only release, the album had originally been on sale at live shows before demand soon outstripped supply and necessitated a larger operation. Featuring the cream of the apparently massive catalogue of songs she'd built up throughout her teens, the record's intimate acoustic confessionals went down a storm with both militant lesbians and straight down the line folk/rock fans. Openly bisexual herself, the tattooed, pierced and shaven-headed DiFRANCO steadily built up a diehard following of kindred spirits through a punishing tour schedule. 1991's 'NOT SO SOFT' was another bare bones acoustic affair dealing in heartfelt sexual politics although it wasn't until the release of the more instrumentally rich 'IMPERFECTLY' (1992) and 'PUDDLE DIVE' (1993), that DiFRANCO began to draw attention from major labels. Standing by her DIY ethos, she released her most widely acknowledged album to date in 'OUT OF RANGE' (1994). Again embellishing her rhythmic acoustic guitar playing with eclectic instrumental textures, the record set the scene for her breakthrough opus, 'NOT A PRETTY GIRL'. With girl power very much on the agenda in the mid-90's, DiFRANCO finally gained recognition as one of America's foremost female commentators alongside the likes of LIZ PHAIR, HEATHER NOVA, etc. The one-woman powerhouse also finally clinched a UK deal with 'Cooking Vinyl', while 1996's acclaimed 'DILATE' gave DiFRANCO her first Top 100 US chart placing. Following on from 1997's well received double set, 'LIVING IN CLIP', she scored her biggest success to date with near Top 20 US album, 'LITTLE PLASTIC CASTLES' (1998). 1999 proved a busy year for DiFRANCO as she released both the solo set, 'UP UP UP UP UP UP' and a collaborative effort with UTAH PHILLIPS entitled 'FELLOW WORKERS'. While the latter was an alt-folk history of the beleaguered US working class, ANI was back on familiar, if unerringly downcast and mercilessly self-critical, territory with 'TO THE TEETH', her third long player of 1999. Yet however much the singer seems to exorcise her demons through music, it seems there are more waiting in the wings. 'REVELLING: RECKONING' (2001) found DiFRANCO's self-confession and apocalyptic worldview as uncompromising as ever, proving that integrity, at least, is not a quality she's lacking.

Album rating: ANI DiFRANCO (*6) / NOT SO SOFT (*6) / IMPERFECTLY (*7) / PUDDLE DIVE (*7) / LIKE I SAID – SONGS 1990-1991 compilation (*7) / OUT OF RANGE (*7) / NOT A PRETTY GIRL (*8) / DILATE (*7) / MORE JOY, LESS SHAME (*5) / THE PAST DIDN'T GO ANYWHERE with Utah Phillips (*5) / LIVING IN CLIP (*8) / LITTLE PLASTIC CASTLE (*7) / UP UP UP UP UP UP (*6) / FELLOW WORKERS with Utah Phillips (*5) / TO THE TEETH (*6) / REVELLING – RECKONING (*7)

ANI DiFRANCO – vocals, guitar

Haven   Righteous Babe

Nov 89. (cd) *<RBR 001CD>* **ANI DiFRANCO**
– Both hands / Talk to me now / Slant / Work you way out / Dog coffee / Lost woman song / Pale purple / Rush hour / Fire door / The story / Every angle / Out of habit / Letting the telephone ring / Egos like hairdos. *(UK-iss.Jul95; same)* *(re-iss. Jun97 on 'Cooking Vinyl'; COOKCD 112)*

1991. (cd) *<RBR 002CD>* **NOT SO SOFT**
– Anticipate / Rockabye / She says / Make me stay / On every corner / Small world / Not so soft / Roll with it / Itch / Gratitude / Whole night / The next big thing / Brief bus stop / Looking at the holes. *(UK-iss.Sep97 on 'Cooking Vinyl'; COOKCD 133)*

1992. (cd) *<RBD 003CD>* **IMPERFECTLY**
– What if no one's watching / Fixing her hair / In or out / Every state line / Circle of light / If it isn't her / Good, bad, ugly / I'm no heroine / Coming up / Make them apologize / Waiting song / Served faithfully / Imperfectly. *(UK-iss.Jul95; same)*

Ani DiFRANCO (cont)

Jul 93. (cd/c) *(HAVEN CD/MC 002)* <*RBR 004 CD/C*> **PUDDLE DIVE**
– Names and dates and times / Anyday / 4th of July / Willing to fight / Egos like hairdos / Back around / Blood in the boardroom / Born a lion / My IQ / Used to you / Pick yer nose / God's country. *(re-iss. Jan95; same)*

Jul 94. (cd) <*RBR 005CD*> **LIKE I SAID: SONGS 1990-1991**
(re-recorded early tracks)
– Anticipate / Rockabye / Not so soft / Roll with it / Work your way out / Fire door / Gratitude / Whole night / Both hands / She says / Rush hour / Out of habit / Lost woman song / Talk to me now / Slant.

                                                                                  Haven Righteous Babe

Jan 95. (cd/c) *(HAVEN CD/MC 3)* <*RBR 006CD*> **OUT OF RANGE**   Jul94
– Buildings and bridges / Out of range / Letter to a John / Hell yeah / How have you been / Overlap / Face up and sing / Falling is like this / Out of range / You had time / If he tries anything / Diner.

                                                                   Righteous Babe Righteous Babe

Nov 95. (cd) <*RBR 007CD*> **NOT A PRETTY GIRL**   Jul95
– Worthy / Tiptoe / Cradle and all / Shy / Sorry I am / Light of some kind / Not a pretty girl / The million you never made / Hour follows hour / 32 flavors / Asking too much / This bouquet / Crime for crime. *(UK-iss.Jan97 on 'Cooking Vinyl'; COOKCD 113)*

                                                               Cooking Vinyl Righteous Babe

Jul 96. (cd) *(COOKCD 103)* <*RBR 008CD*> **DILATE**   87 May96
– Untouchable face / Outta me, onto you / Superhero / Dilate / Amazing grace / Napoleon / Shameless / Done wrong / Going down / Adam and Eve / Joyful girl.

Dec 96. (m-cd) *(COOKCD 119)* <*RBR 010CD*> **MORE JOY, LESS SHAME**
– Joyful girl / Joyful girl / Joyful girl / Joyful girl / Shameless / Both hands.

Jan 97. (cd-s) *(FRYCD 049)* **OUTTA ME ONTO YOU / SHY**

Apr 97. (cd; UTAH PHILLIPS & ANI DiFRANCO) *(COOKCD 124)* <*RBR 009CD*> **THE PAST DIDN'T GO ANYWHERE**   Oct96
– Bridges / Nevada City, California /Korea / Anarchy / Candidacy / Bum on the road / Enormously wealthy / Mess with people / Natural resources / Heroes / Half a ghost town / Holding on.

Jun 97. (d-cd) *(COOKCD 122)* <*RBR 011CD*> **LIVING IN CLIP (live)**   Apr97
– Whatever / Wherever / Gravel / Willing to fight / Shy / Joyful girl / Hide and seek / Napoleon / I'm no heroine / Amazing grace / Anitpate / Tiptoe / Sorry I am / Diner – Slant / 32 flavors / Out of range / Untouchable face / Shameless / Distracted / Adam and Eve / Fire door / Both hands / Out of habit / Every state line / Not so soft / Travel tips / Wrong with me / In or out / We're all gonna blow / Letter to a John / Overleaf.

Feb 98. (cd) *(COOKCD 140)* <*RBR 012CD*> **LITTLE PLASTIC CASTLE**   22
– Little plastic castle / Fuel / Gravel / As is / Two little girls / Deep dish / Loom / Pixie / Swan dive / Glass house / Independence day / Pulse.

Jan 99. (cd) *(COOKCD 173)* <*RBR 013CD*> **UP UP UP UP UP UP**   29
– Tis of thee / Virtue / Come away from it / Jukebox / Angel food / Angry anymore / Everest / Up up up up up / Know now then / Trickle down / Hat shaped hat.

Mar 99. (cd-s) *(FRYCD 079)* **NOT ANGRY ANYMORE / (mixes; album / extended)**

May 99. (cd; ANI DiFRANCO & UTAH PHILLIPS) <*RBR 015CD*> **FELLOW WORKERS**
– Joe Hill (instrumental) / Stupid's song / The most dangerous woman / Stupid's pledge / Direct action / Pie in the sky / Shoot or stab them / Lawrence / Bread and roses / Why come? / Unless you are free / I will not obey / The long memory / The silence that is me / Joe Hill / The saw-playing musician / Dump the bosses / The internationale.

Nov 99. (cd) *(COOKCD 190)* <*RBR 017CD*> **TO THE TEETH**   76
– To the teeth / Soft shoulder / Wish I may / Freak show / Going once / Hello Birmingham / Back back back / Swing / Carry you around / Cloud blood / Arrivals gate / Providence / I know this bar.

                                                             Righteous Babe Righteous Babe

Jul 00. (cd-ep) *(74873 17020-2)* <*RBR-CD 20*> **SWING SET**
– Swing (radio set) / Swing (album version) / To the teeth (shoot-out remix) / Do re me (live) / When I'm gone / Hurricane.

Apr 01. (d-cd) <*(RBRCD 024)*> **REVELLING / RECKONING**   50
– Ain't that the way / O.K. / Garden of simple / Tamburitza lingua / Marrow / Heartbreak even / Harvest / Kazoointoit / Whatall is nice / What how when where (why whoo) / Fierce flawless / Rock paper scissors / Beautiful night / Your next bold move / This box contains . . . / Reckoning / So what / Prison prism / Imagine that / Flood waters / Grey / Subdivision / Old old song / Sick of me / Don't nobody know / School night / That was my love / Revelling / In here.

– compilations, etc. –

Nov 94. (cd) *Tradition & Moderne; (T&M 105)* **WOMEN IN (E)MOTION FESTIVAL**
<*US-iss.Jun98 on 'Imprint'; 28376*>

DIGGERS

Formed: Methil, Fife, Scotland . . . early 90's by ALAN MOFFAT and CHRIS MIEZITIS. After fruitlessly attempting to ply their classic indie-guitar wares around the less than sympathetic environs of Methil, Leven and surrounding Fife backwaters, the duo relocated to Glasgow where their approach was more in tune with the prevailing 'Bellshill Sound'. Completing the line-up with JOHN ESLICK and HANK ROSS, the band received encouraging support prior to a hiccup in their career as the former was laid off for six months following a car accident. Subsequently signed to 'Creation', The DIGGERS took more than three years to come up with a debut album, 'MOUNT EVEREST'. Finally surfacing in 1997, the record revealed no great surprises soundwise with an archetypal 'Creation' indie sound vaguely akin to The BLUETONES if not quite so assured, commentators drawing on the ever reliable BEATLES for comparisons; the harmony-fuelled CS&N or HALL & OATES were more accurate. • **Note:** The DIGGERS who issued an EP on 'Death Becomes Me' were not the same band.

Album rating: MOUNT EVEREST (*4)

ALAN MOFFAT – vocals, bass / **CHRIS MEIZITIS** – vocals, rhythm guitar / **JOHN ESLICK** – lead guitar / **HANK ROSS** – drums

                                                 Creation Creation

Aug 96. (7") *(CRE 226)* **PEACE OF MIND. / TANGLED WEB**
(cd-s+=) *(CRESCD 226)* – Get it.

Oct 96. (7"/c-s) *(CRE/+CS 234)* **NOBODY'S FOOL. / LIFE'S ALL WAYS**
(cd-s+=) *(CRESCD 234)* – Here and there.

Feb 97. (7"/c-s) *(CRE/+CS 259)* **O.K. ALRIGHT. / ON THE LINE**
(cd-s+=) *(CRESCD 259)* – Holiday Inn.

Mar 97. (cd/lp) *(<CRE CD/LP 193>)* **MOUNT EVEREST**
– Circles / Peace of mind / Waking up / Nobody's fool / Come on easy / Downbeat / East coast / O.K. alright / Hormonious / Passport to Rec / They said I'd know / Up against it.

——— split later in the year

DIMMER
(see under ⇒ STRAITJACKET FITS; 80's section)

DIM STARS
(see under ⇒ HELL, Richard; 70's section)

DIRTBOMBS

Formed: Detroit, Michigan, USA . . . 1998 by the multi-talented MICK COLLINS, who changes the line-up of the group depending on his mood at the time. Anybody would be forgiven for thinking that The DIRTBOMBS were a fresh-faced entity that followed JACK WHITE et al, as he dragged the New Wave of garage rock by the balls and into the new millennium. Well, suffice to say, it was really MICK COLLINS, lead singer/guitarist with The DIRTBOMBS, an all-around renaissance man, who started the ball rolling in the beginning. His back catalogue is a new kind of math, and every discographer's worst nightmare (believe us!). Starting in 1981, the young COLLINS, who had been raised listening to Stevie Wonder and Marvin Gaye, joined a soul/funk group U-BOAT (as an organist!). The collective disbanded after almost two years (never releasing anything either), and following a brief stint as drummer for faux-punk troupe The FLOOR TASTERS, COLLINS finally put together his own outfit, aptly titled The GORIES. Perhaps one of the longest running of COLLINS' wavering musical projects, the band – featuring DAN KROHA and drummer PEG – played late-night jangly funk/garage, and kicked the proverbial shit out of most local white college blues bands (COLLINS later commented: "At the time I was thinking, 'Am I the only brother in this?'"). The GORIES issued three albums and a handful of 7" singles, the best of which was the excellent 'THAT'S THE VIEW FROM HERE', a blues-funk stomper featuring COLLINS' classic soulful vocals, and the ALEX CHILTON-produced set 'I KNOW YOU FINE, BUT HOW YOU DOIN' (1991). The group's final album was to be 'OUTTA HERE' (1994), before COLLINS indulged in the art-noise nonsense of YETI SANCTION. Subsequently he formed BLACKTOP with DARIN LIN WOODS, ALEX CUERVO and JANET WALKER, with the collective issuing two LP's, 'I'VE GOT A BAAAD FEELING ABOUT THIS' (1995) and the flawed 'UP ALL NIGHT' (1995), before COLLINS got fed-up and moved onto something new – KINGSOUND QUARTET (with TIM KERR, ALEX CUERVO and STEPHANIE FRIEDMAN). He also instigated the rise of The SCREWS (keeping up?) with KERRY DAVIS and JIMMY HOLE. A pretty hardcore, grind-house punk collective, the group issued two sets; 1999's '12 NEW HATE FILLED CLASSICS' and the inferior 'SHAKE YOUR MONKEY' (2001). Which brings us onto The DIRTBOMBS, COLLINS' most recent collaboration. The group, who got swept up with the 'New Detroit Sound' movement in the early stages of this century, and who released 'HORNDOG FEST' and the indisputable 'ULTRAGLIDE IN BLACK' in 2001 and kicked up a whole loada' fuss with the music press. Playing fuzzed-out soul and funk covers from the seventies and sixties (including Wonder's 'LIVING FOR THE CITY' and Gaye's 'KUNG FU') this was COLLINS going back to his childhood and the songs that he listened to while growing up. The group changed its line-up thirteen times during the two years that they'd been around (members included TOM PORTER, JIM DIAMOND, PAT PANTANO and BEN BLACKWELL), and regularly had more than two drummers or bassists. Meanwhile, COLLINS was said to be making a garage rock cover album of funk classics, entitled 'I SING THE BOOTIE ELECTRIC'. The only brother in this? You betta' believe it! • **Covers:** Dirtbombs:- HATE (Stoics) / GIVE ME SOME MONEY (Spinal Tap) / BOOGIE CHILLUN (John Lee Hooker) / IDOL WITH THE GOLDEN HEAD (Coasters) / TO FIND OUT (Keggs) / Blacktop:- HERE I AM (Captain Beefheart) / SEARCHIN' (Coasters) / King Sound Quartet:- SPACE IS THE PLACE (Sun Ra) / Dirtbombs:- I'LL BE IN TROUBLE (Smokey Robinson) / MAYBE YOUR BABY (Stevie Wonder) / NOISE IN THE WORLD (Beat) / INSECURE . . . ME? (Soft Cell) / ODE TO A BLACK MAN (Phil Lynott) / NATURAL MAN (Lou Rawls) / BY MY SIDE (Elois) / I STARTED A JOKE (Bee Gees) / MY LOVE FOR YOU (ESG) / + others from second set.

Album rating: Gories: HOUSEROCKIN' (*6) / I KNOW YOU FINE, BUT HOW YA DOIN' (*6) / OUTTA HERE (*6) / Blacktop: I'VE GOT A BAAAD FEELING ABOUT THIS (*6) / UP ALL NIGHT (*6) / King Sound Quartet: THE GET-DOWN IMPERATIVE mini (*5) / Dirtbombs: HORNDOG FEST (*6) / ULTRAGLIDE IN BLACK (*8)

GORIES

MICK COLLINS (b.18 Dec'65) – vocals, guitar (ex-U-BOATS, ex-FLOOR TASTERS, ex-MAN RAY MAN) / **DAN KROHA** (b.30 May'65) – rhythm guitar, vocals / **MARGARET ANN "PEG(GY)" O'NEILL** (b.29 Jul'67) – drums

not iss.   Wanghead With Lips

1989. (lp) <WH 009> **HOUSEROCKIN'**
 – Feral / I think I've had it / Charm bug / Boogie chillun / I'll go / Hidden charms / Sovereignty flight / You'll be mine / You done got wrong / Sister Ann / Give me love / Let me hear the choir sing. <re-iss. 1990 on 'EFA'; LP-17314-08> (UK/French-iss.1990 on 'Fan Club – New Rose'; FC 077 – NR 340) (re-iss. May94 on 'Crypt'; crypt 041)

New Rose   not iss.

1990. (7") (NEW 141 – NR 100) **NITROGLYCERINE. / MAKIN' LOVE**
1991. (lp) (ROSE 219) **I KNOW YOU FINE, BUT HOW YOU DOIN'**
 – Hey hey, we're the Gories / You make it move / Detroit breakdown / Stranded / Goin' to the river / Early in the morning / Thunderbird ESQ / Nitroglycerine / Let your daddy ride / Six cold feet / Smashed / Ghostrider / Chick-inn / View from here. (re-iss. Jun94 on 'Crypt' crypt-42)

not iss.   In The Red

1991. (7"purple) <ITR 003> **HERE BE THE GORIES**
 – Telepathic / Hate.

not iss.   Sub Pop

1992. (7") <SP 134> **GIVE ME SOME MONEY. / YOU DON'T LOVE ME**

not iss.   Estrus

1992. (7",7"clear) <ES 724> **BABY SAY UNH! / IDOL WITH THE GOLDEN HEAD**

not iss.   Giant Claw

1992. (7") (GCS 005) **TO FIND OUT. / ICHIBAN**

not iss.   Crypt

1992. (lp/cd) <crypt 30> **OUTTA HERE**
 – He's doin' it / There but for the grace of God go I / Outta here / Can't catch up with you / Crawdad / Omologato / I got eyes for you / Telepathic / Trick bag / Drowning / Rat's nest / 48 hours / Great big idol with the golden head / Ichiban.

not iss.   Get Hip

1995. (7"m) <GH 173> **YOU LITTLE NOTHING. / CASTING MY SPELL / CHARM BAG**

— disbanded well before above

– compilations, etc. –

Sep 94. (cd) *Crypt; (04241)* **I KNOW YOU HOUSEROCKIN'**

BLACKTOP

MICK COLLINS with **DARIN LIN WOOD** – guitar, vocals / **ALEX CUERVO** – bass / **JANET WALKER** – drums

In The Red   In The Red

Jun 95. (7") <ITR 26> **MOJO KITTY. / HOT LIPS & SWIVEL HIPS**
Dec 95. (lp/cd) <(ITR 27/+CD)> **I'VE GOT A BAAAD FEELING ABOUT THIS**   Jun95
 – Blacktop (intro) / Tornado love / I think it's going to rain / Planet Earth (goddamn!) / Mojo Kitty / Blazing streets / From beyond / Here I am (her I always am) / Confusion / The grave / No one knows you're a dog / Flagpole hill / Your pretty face (is goin' to Waukeegan) / Blacktop (outro).

not iss.   Au-Go-Go

Dec 95. (7") <ANDA 182> **HERE I AM (HERE I ALWAYS AM). / SEARCHIN'**
Jan 96. (cd) <ANDA 188> **UP ALL NIGHT**
 – I think it's going to rain / Tornado love / Here I am, I always am / 44 blues / Planet Earth (goddamn) / Bahia / Mojo Kitty / Keep on doggin' me / Let me go home, whiskey / Blazing streets / Goin' / She's mine, all mine.

— had already gave up some time in June 1995

– compilations, etc. –

1997. (d7"ep) *In The Red; <ITR 051>* **WE DESIST!**
 – Hide and go seek (pt.1) / Hide and go seek (pt.2) / Self-destruct sequence / Baby.

KING SOUND QUARTET

COLLINS + CUERVO with **TIM KERR** – guitar / **STEPHANIE PAIGE FRIEDMAN** – drums

not iss.   Estrus

1996. (7",7"orange) <ES 787> **ANNIHILATE THIS WEEK. / MEMPHIS TRAIN**

In The Red   In The Red

May 98. (m-lp) <(ITR 052)> **THE GET-DOWN IMPERATIVE**   Nov97
 – I wouldn't put it past you / Innebriation '63 / I want to / White streak / Sheer terror / Space is the place.

DIRTBOMBS

MICK COLLINS – vocals, guitar / **DANA SPICER** – bass, fuzz / **TOM LYNCH** – bass / **CHRIS FACHINI** – drums / **PAT PANTANO** – drums

not iss.   Sympathy F

1996. (7") <SFTRI 423> **HIGH OCTANE SALVATION. / BROKE IN DETROIT (AGAIN)**

In The Red   In The Red

1997. (7"ep) <ITR 43> **ALL GEEKED UP**
 – Don't bogue my high / Infrared / I'm saving myself for Michelle Nicols (No.3) / I'll be in trouble.
1998. (7") <HM 001> **MAYBE YOUR BABY. / THEME FROM THE DIRTBOMBS**
 (above issued on 'High Maintenance') (below on 'Some Assembly Required')
1998. (7") <L 50442> **STUCK UNDER MY SHOE. / NOISE IN THE WORLD**

Sep 98. (lp/cd) <(ITR 55/+CD)> **HORNDOG FEST**
 – Vixens in space / I can't stop thinking about it / Granny's little chicken / Bittersweet romance song / Armageddon double feature (lovesick blues #4) / She blinded me with playtex / A brief treatise on the discovery of antimatter / Pheremone smile / My heart burns with deeps of lurve / Burnt to cinders / Fox box / Shake!! shivaree.
2000. (7") <SSLD 005> **HEADLIGHTS ON. / JOLENE**
 (above issued on 'Solid Sex Lovie Doll' records and below issued for 'Multiball' fanzine' #19)
2000. (7") <XTR 005> **CEDAR POINT '76. / White Stripes: HANDSPRINGS**
May 01. (lp/cd) <(ITR 79/+CD)> **ULTRAGLIDE IN BLACK**
 – Chains of love / If you can want / Underdog / Your love belongs under a rock / I'll wait / Livin' for the city / The thing / Kung Fu / Ode to a black man / Got to give it up / Livin' for the weekend / I'm qualified to satisfy you / Do you see my love (for you growing).
2001. (7"ep,7"brown-ep) <hate 20> **BRUCIA I CAVI**
 – They saved Einstein's brain / Temp / Insecure . . . me? / Brucia i cavi.
 (above issued on 'Hate' records, below issued on 'Sweet Nothing')
Oct 01. (7") <7SN 005> **ODE TO A BLACK MAN. / NATURAL MAN**
 (above issued on 'Zerox' records)
2002. (7"white) <Z45 010> **BY MY SIDE. / I STARTED A JOKE**

DIRTY THREE

Formed: Melbourne, Australia ... 1992 by WARREN ELLIS, MICK TURNER and JIM WHITE, all already established in various bands including FUNGUS BRAINS, BLACKEYED SUSAN, BUSLOAD OF FAITH and VENOM P. STINGER. The instrumental trio played bars and clubs mainly as a side project to the aforementioned outfits and eventually their impressive tightknit musical gymnastics won them favour among the Australian press. A demo tape eventually worked its way across the globe to a small Boston indie, 'Poon Village', who subsequently issued the mini-set as 'SAD AND DANGEROUS' late in '94. This helped them secure support slots to PAVEMENT on their North American tour, which, in turn, spurred promoters to book them for that year's 'Lollapalooza' festival. NICK CAVE had been a celebrity fan for over a year now and he proved it by accompanying The DIRTY THREE on piano while they performed Carl Dreyer's silent movie, 'The Passion Of Joan Of Arc', at London's National Film Theatre. The punk crooner also collaborated with the trio on an 'X-Files' TV soundtrack album entitled 'Song In The Key Of X', while ELLIS and CAVE later co-wrote a song for the latter's soap-ish (so pure) pop buddy, KYLIE MINOGUE. On the vinyl front, the DIRTY THREE were establishing themselves with each release. Signing to 'Big Cat' records ('Touch & Go' in the US), they issued two sets, 'THE DIRTY THREE' (1995) and 'HORSE STORIES' (1996). Squeezed inbetween these well-received gems was a collaboration with WILL OLDHAM on his 'Arise Therefore' (PALACE) album. A couple of years passed until the release of their STEVE ALBINI-produced 1998 set, 'OCEAN SONGS' (on ROBIN GUTHRIE's new imprint, 'Bella Union', was heralded as their finest hour yet. Around the same time, both TURNER and WHITE augmented CAT POWER on her 'MOONPIX' set. The year 2000 clocked up another long-player, 'WHATEVER YOU LOVE, YOU ARE', an at times restrained work of art that experimented with melodious chamber rock jettisoning the violin to the forefront. TURNER subsequently founded his own label, 'King Crab' (MARQUIS DE TREN were one of the first signings), while ELLIS went on to join NICK CAVE & THE BAD SEEDS. • **Covered:** KIM'S DIRT + OBVIOUS IS OBVIOUS (Kim Salmon) / RUNNING SCARED (Roy Orbison).

Album rating: SAD AND DANGEROUS (*5) / THE DIRTY THREE (*6) / HORSE STORIES (*6) / OCEAN SONGS (*7) / UFKUKO mini (*5) / WHATEVER YOU LOVE, YOU ARE (*6)

WARREN ELLIS – electric violin, piano-accordion, etc / **MICK TURNER** – guitar (ex-MOODISTS) / **JIM WHITE** – drums, percussion

not iss.   Poon Village

Dec 94. (cd) <27> **SAD AND DANGEROUS**
 – Kim's dirt / Killy Kundane / Jaguar / Devil in the hole / Jim's dog / Short break / Turk reprise / You were a bum deal / Warren's waltz / Turk. (UK-iss.Apr96 on 'Big Cat' lp/cd; ABB 107/+CD)

Big Cat   Touch & Go

Aug 95. (lp/cd) (ABB 93/+CD) <TG 147/+CD> **THE DIRTY THREE**
 – Indian love song / Better go home now / Odd couple / Kim's dirt / Everything's fucked / Last night / Dirty equation.
Sep 96. (lp/cd) (ABB 115/+CD) <TG 165/+CD> **HORSE STORIES**
 – 1000 miles / Sues last ride / Hope / I remember a time when once you loved / At the bar / Red / Warren's lament / Horse / I knew it would come to this. (UK d-lp-iss.Sep00 on 'Touch & Go'; same as US)

Bella Union   Touch & Go

Sep 98. (cd) (BELLACD 3) <TG 193> **OCEAN SONGS**   May98
 – Sirena / Restless waves / Distant shore / Authentic celestial music / Backwards voyager / Last horse on the sand / Sea above, sky below / Black tide / Deep waters / Ends of the earth. <US cd+=> – UFKUKO
Sep 98. (7") (NAR 001) **A STRANGE HOLIDAY. / (other track by SCENIC)**
 (above issued on 'Narwhal') (below on 'Anchor & Hope')
1998. (cd-ep) <AHX 01S> **SHARKS (live tour)**
 – Obvious is obvious / Two a.m. / Rope / Running scared.
Nov 98. (m-cd) (BELLACD 6) **UFKUKO**
 – To aster / Mihelkos arm / Cast adrift / Three wheels / Wish I could.

Mar 00. (cd) (BELLACD 16) <TG 223> **WHATEVER YOU LOVE, YOU ARE**
– Some summers they drop like flys / I really should've gone out last night / I offered it up to the stars & the night sky / Some things I just don't want to know / Steller / Lullabye for Christie.

— in April 2000, DIRTY THREE contributed several tracks for the original soundtrack movie, 'Praise'.

— ELLIS has since turned up for NICK CAVE & THE BAD SEEDS

DISCO INFERNO

Formed: Camden, London, England . . . early 1989 by IAN CRAUSE, PAUL WILLMOTT and ROB WHATLEY with the initial assistance of DANIEL GISH (of BARK PSYCHOSIS fame), who departed within their first year of gigging. DI's unfortunate short existence and lack of airplay is a real musical tragedy. Within their five-year lifespan, the group went from disciples of the British post-rockers like JOY DIVISION and WIRE to creating a technologically influenced pop hybrid that had taken indie music to new and uncharted sonic waters. Along with NICK ALLPORT of 'Cheree Records' the band formed 'Che' records at the beginning of the 90s and used the imprint to issue their debut 7", 'ENTERTAINMENT' (1990), following this up with their first LP, 'OPEN DOORS, CLOSED WINDOWS' (1991) and the EP 'SCIENCE'. These outings were later put together for the compilation album 'IN DEBT' (1992), aptly titled as it clearly showed the influence of DI's post-punk forebears, but more importantly it showed the enormous talent that the young band had and the directions it was later to take. By 1992 the band's 7" 'SUMMER'S LAST SOUND' was already hailing the experimental digital arena in which the band were moving. Unfortunately their imprint collapsed, although they were wisely scooped up by the hugely influential 'Rough Trade', and within a short space of time the group put out the singles 'A ROCK TO CLING TO' (1993) and 'THE LAST DANCE', which both gleaned them glowing reviews in the British musical press. The same year saw the issue of their masterpiece, the album 'D.I. GO POP' (1994) showcasing their clever use of sampling to complement and create amazing musical soundscapes; a sophomore effort any electronica band would be proud of. The following year saw the band release several more EPs, notably 'IT'S A KID'S WORLD' with its great sampling of the opening drum from IGGY POP's 'Lust For Life'. Unfortunately, although their third album proper 'TECHNICOLOUR' (1996) was again technically breathtaking, it had also seen musical differences spring up amongst the now disbanded group, CRAUSE and WHATLEY going on the next year to form FLOORSHOW; CRAUSE also went solo post-millennium.

Album rating: OPEN DOORS, CLOSED WINDOWS mini (*5) / D.I. GO POP (*6) / IN DEBT compilation (*5) / TECHNICOLOUR (*6)

IAN CRAUSE – vocals, guitar / **PAUL WILLMOTT** – bass / **ROB WHATLEY** – drums

Che / not iss.

Jan 92. (7") (che 1) **ENTERTAINMENT. / ARC IN ROUND**
Mar 92. (m-lp) (che 2) **OPEN DOORS, CLOSED WINDOWS**
– Emigre / Interference / Leisuretime / Set sail / Hope to God / Freethought / Bleed clean / Next in line / Incentives.
1992. (12"ep) **SCIENCE**
– Waking up / Glancing away / Fallen down the wire / No edge, no end.

Cheree / not iss.

1992. (12"/cd-s) (cheree 28 T/CDS) **SUMMER'S LAST SOUND. / LOVE'S STEPPING OUT**

Rough Trade Bar/None

Jul 93. (12"/cd-s) (R 298-0/-3) **A ROCK TO CLING TO> / FROM THE DEVIL AND TO THE DEEP BLUE SEA**
(12") (R 298XX) – (remixes).
Nov 93. (12"ep/cd-ep) (R 303-0/-3) **THE LAST DANCE**
– The last dance / D.I. go pop / The long dance / Scattered showers.
Feb 94. (cd/lp) (R 307-2/-1) <40> **D.I. GO POP**
– In sharky water / New clothes for the new world / Starbound: All burnt out and nowhere to go / A crash at every speed / Even the sea sides against us / Next year / A whole wide world ahead / Footprints in snow.
May 94. (12"ep/cd-ep) (R 315-0/-3) **SECOND LANGUAGE EP**
– Second language / The atheist's burden / At the end of the line / A little something.
Oct 94. (12"/cd-s) (R 335-0/-3) **IT'S A KID'S WORLD. / A NIGHT ON THE TILES / LOST IN FOG**
Jul 96. (cd) (R 410-2) **TECHNICOLOUR**
– Technicolour / Things most fast / I'm still in love / Sleight of hand / Don't you know / It's a kid's world / When the story breaks / Can't see through it / Over and over.

— retired from the scene after above, until . . .

Tugboat / not iss.

Sep 99. (cd-ep) (TUGCD 011) **THE MIXING IT SESSION**
– Shark / Elephant / Tortoise / Shrew / Bird / Rats.

– compilations, etc. –

Sep 95. (cd) Che; (che 4cd) / Carrot Top; <6> **IN DEBT** Mar95
– Entertainment / Arc in round / Broken / OPEN DOORS, CLOSED WINDOWS:- tracks / SCIENCE:- tracks.

IAN CRAUSE

Tugboat / not iss.

Nov 00. (7") (TUGS 025) **ELEMENTAL. / IF YOU'RE LOOKING TO FIND ME**
(cd-s+=) (TUGSCD 025) –

Acuarela / not iss.

Aug 02. (cd-s) (NOIS 023) **HEAD OVER HEELS / TIED UP IN KNOTS / DOWNSTREAM** – Spain

DISCOUNT

Formed: Vero Beach, Florida, USA . . . early '95 by schoolmates ALISON MOSSHART, RYAN SEAGRIST and BILL NESPER. DISCOUNT released their first album of sun-drenched pop/punk in 1996. The songs on 'ATAXIA'S ALRIGHT TONIGHT' were immediate and fun jam-packed with infectious hooks and raucous melodies. The release of their second album, 'HALF FICTION' (1998), confirmed that this was a band who wanted their music to evoke no more than simple pleasure, it was another collection of 3-minute throwaway, uncomplicated, punk songs done to great effect. The follow-up EP was a slight departure and a homage to a surprising influence. 'LOVE BILLY' (1998) entirely comprised of BILLY BRAGG songs yet played in DISCOUNT's trade mark, high-energy way. The group released a final album, 'CRASH DIAGNOSTIC' (2000), before splitting up. Vocalist ALISON MOSSHART relocated to London and created the altogether darker band, The KILLS, alongside JAMIE HINCE, whom she met a few years previously. The edgy PJ HARVEY-inspired EP, 'BLACK ROOSTER', was their first release for 'Dim Mak' ('Domino' in the UK), which whetted our lips for the forthcoming 'KEEP ON THE MEAN SIDE' album.

Album rating: ATAXIA'S ALRIGHT TONIGHT (*5) / HALF-FICTION (*7) / LOVE, BILLY mini (*5) / CRASH DIAGNOSTIC (*6) / SINGLES COLLECTION VOL.1 compilation (*6)

ALISON MOSSHART – vocals / **RYAN SEAGRIST** – guitar / **JAMES** – bass / **BILL NESPER** – drums

not iss. / own label

1995. (c) **MOM LIED TO ME**

Liquid Meat / Liquid Meat

1996. (7"ep) **WONDER PULLED ME UNDER**
Jun 97. (cd) <(LM 016CD)> **ATAXIA'S ALRIGHT TONIGHT** Jul96
– Waiting by the wayside / Malarie's mission / K.V. T-shirt / Milly / Lights out / Streets / The sun comes up / Her last day / No surprise / Tomorrow will be / Everybody everybody / The end of the world. <(re-iss. 1999 US/Mar01 UK on 'New American Dream'; NAD 1904CD)>
Jun 97. (7"ep) <LM 018> **IT'S BEEN YEARS / SUCCESSFULLY DELERIOUS. / (others by J CHURCH)**

not iss. / Mighty Toy

1997. (7"ep) <2> **ALL TOO OFTEN**
— split a single with CIGARETTEMAN (unknown)

not iss. / La Maison Grande

Jun 98. (12") <19> **NO DOUBT. /**

Kat / not iss.

Aug 98. (cd/lp) (KAT 23 CD/LP) **HALF-FICTION**
– Half fiction / Clap and cough / Torn jeans / Am I missing something / City bleach / Pocket bomb / Keith / Toxic home / Soup / Usual bad / Dreamt this was a castle / On the counter / Stitch / Is it OK. <(re-iss. 1999 US/Mar01 UK on 'New American Dream'; NAD 1905CD)>

Goodlife / not iss.

Mar 99. (7") (ED 035) **split w/ AS FRIENDS RUST**

Impresario / Fueled By Ramon

Apr 99. (m-cd) (IMPCD 001) **LOVE, BILLY**
– Accident waiting to happen / Waiting for the great leap forwards / A Pict song / Help save the youth of America / North Sea bubble.

Speedowax / not iss.

Apr 99. (7") (ATOM 011) **split w/ BEAUTY SCHOOL DROPOUT**
— **TODD ROCKHILL** – bass; repl. JAMES

Rugger Bugger / not iss.

Jun 99. (7"ep) (DUMP 047) **OPEN ENDED AERIAL EP**
– Slant invention / Aerial / Most brutal criminal.

New American Dream / New American Dream

Mar 00. (cd) <(AD 1911)> **CRASH DIAGNOSTIC** Jan00
– Broken to blue / Age of splitting / Math won't miss you / Harder to tell / (untitled) / Aerial / Behind curtain # / T.V. kiss / Sleeping motor boy / Apostrophe / Black and white / Hit / (untitled) / Medical / The kill fix.
Oct 00. (lp) (SEEP 030LP) **split w/ J CHURCH**
(above issued on 'Rugger Bugger')

— split in 2000; SEAGRIST teamed up with AMANDA RIN (of BIS) to form The KITCHEN, while MOSSHART became part of The KILLS

– compilations, etc. –

Mar 02. (cd) New American Dream; <(NAD 1912CD)> **SINGLES COLLECTION VOL.1**
Oct 02. (cd) New American Dream; <(NAD 1913CD)> **SINGLES COLLECTION VOL.2**

KILLS

ALISON MOSSHART (aka VV) – vocals / **JAIME HINCE** (aka HOTEL) – guitar (ex-SCARFO)

Domino / Dim Mak

Aug 02. (10"ep/cd-ep) (RUG 144 T/CD) <DM 036CD> **BLACK ROOSTER** Jun02
– Cat claw / Black rooster / Wait / Dropout boogie (live) / Glum.

DISKOTHI Q

Formed: Upland, California, USA . . . 1992 by brothers PETER HUGHES, KEVIN HUGHES, KEVIN TRAPP was soon to the line-up. Issuing limited edition cassette-only records in the early 90's, this lo-fi pop combo delivered their debut album, 'THE WANDERING JEW', in 1994 on the 'Shrimper' imprint. Collecting a huge fanbase in their native California, the trio released a handful of EP's and singles before embarking on a European tour, which for some unknown reason, ended in disaster. They began work on their sophomore set, which was also plagued by misfortune; in the end, the group decided to name it after Kevin Costner's crap-tacular 'WATERWORLD' (1997) – because they'd nearly gone bankrupt due to a massive over-budget. Surprisingly, the album was a fine piece of work, worthy of entering high in any Lo-Fi Top 50 polls. However, the follow-up 'SAD TRUTHS' was shelved and the group disintegrated (bar two volumes of "FOOTBALL ANTHEMS"), with PETER HUGHES establishing his own 'Sonic Enemy' imprint, as well as collaborating with the brilliant MOUNTAIN GOATS and NOTHING PAINTED BLUE. TRAPP was last spotted in Israel, of all places.

Album rating: WANDERING JEW (*7) / WATERWORLD (*4)

PETER HUGHES – vocals, guitar / **KEVIN HUGHES** – bass / **KEVIN TRAPP** – drums

 not iss. Shrimper

Feb 95. (cd) <lp/cd> <SHR 55/+CD> **WANDERING JEW**
– Most eligible bachelor / Tulsa imperative / Leap cat leap / Goping to Nick's / Kidney / Other lover's waltz / Chandra Mukhi / Loozers / Satch Carlson / Supersqualor / Ahs.

Apr 97. (cd) <SHR 86CD> **WATERWORLD**
– Great expectations / Imperial anthem / Pomp and circumstance / To face the truth / Albatros / Witness protection program / Leigh can't leave / Vacancy / I hope you don't / Argentine drinking song / Ovelay ockray.

 not iss. Sonic Enemy

1999. (cd) <3> **THE FOOTBALL ANTHEMS: NATIONAL CONFERENCE**
– Saints / Rams / Falcons / Panthers / 49ers / Bears / Buccaneers / Lions / Packers / Vikings / Eagles / Cowboys / Redskins / Cardinals / Giants / Los Angeles.

2000. (cd) <3> **THE FOOTBALL ANTHEMS: AMERICAN CONFERENCE**
– Bills / Jets / Dolphins / Colts / Patriots / Jaguars / Ravens / Titans (oilers) / Bengals / Steelers / Browns / Raiders / Chargers / Seahawks / Chiefs / Broncos.

— PETER HUGHES continued with The MOUNTAIN GOATS and went solo; DISKOTHI Q released other cassettes on 'Shrimper'

DISMEMBERMENT PLAN

Formed: Washington DC, USA ... 1st January 1993 by TRAVIS MORRISON, JASON CADDELL, ERIC AXELSON and STEVE CUMMINGS. A highly ambitious quartet who were rather wrongly placed within the emo rock category. Their musicianship and songwriting ability pushed their sound through synth-based alternative pop to soul-tinged melodies to raw rock as inspired by their native hardcore scene. Perhaps the best touchstones for the band were the genre-bending TALKING HEADS and the PIXIES. The band debuted with the 7", 'CAN WE BE MATURE?' (1994), issuing their exclamatory debut LP, '!', a year later on indie imprint 'DeSoto'. A vital sounding set with more serene moments amongst the swirl which took it away from being another heavy alternative rock effort. Following this effort, sticksman CUMMINGS was replaced by the more versatile drummer JOE EASLEY. Their ensuing sophomore effort, '. . .IS TERRIFIED' (1997), was another interesting piece that although containing the high energy of punk did not stray into simplicity. It also attracted the attention of major label 'Interscope' who put out the DP's EP, 'ICE OF BOSTON' (1998); its title track had been included on the former album release. Their third full-length offering, 'EMERGENCY AND I' (1999), capably demonstrated the band's growth in confidence and maturity, displaying their willingness to explore the many styles they quite obviously were into – standout track undoubtedly being 'YOU ARE INVITED'. Moving on from here, the outfit teamed up with band, JUNO, to put out the aptly-titled 'SPLIT RELEASE' (2001), prior to issuing their fourth and perhaps best LP, 'CHANGE', later that same year. An altogether more chilled affair, it skillfully displayed the band's breadth as well as MORRISON's lyrical adroitness.

Album rating: "!" (*5) / . . .IS TERRIFIED (*5) / EMERGENCY & I (*7) / CHANGE (*7)

TRAVIS MORRISON – vocals / **JASON CADDELL** – guitar / **ERIC AXELSON** – bass / **STEVE CUMMINGS** – drums

 not iss. Alcove

Apr 94. (7"m) **CAN WE BE MATURE**

 DeSoto DeSoto

Sep 95. (cd) <DI 13> **"!"**
– Survey says / The things that matter / The small stuff / Ok joke's over / Soon to be an ex Quaker / I'm going to buy you a gun / If I don't / Wouldn't you like to know? / 13th and Euclid / Fantastic! / Onward, fat girl / Rusty. (UK-iss.Mar02; same as US)

— JOE EASLEY – drums; repl. CUMMINGS

Mar 97. (cd) <DI 20> **. . .IS TERRIFIED**
– Tonight we mean it / That's when the party started / The ice of Boston / Academy award / Bra / Do the standing still / This is the life / One too many blows to the head / It's so you / Manipulate me / Respect is due. (UK-iss.Mar02; same as US)

Jan 98. (7") <DI 22> **WHAT DO YOU WANT ME TO SAY? / SINCE YOU DIED**

Oct 98. (cd-ep) <95036> **THE ICE OF BOSTON**
– The ice of Boston / The first anniversary of your last phone call / Just like you / Spider in the snow.
(above issued on 'Interscope')

May 00. (cd) <DI 34> **EMERGENCY & I** Oct99
– A life of possibilities / Memory machine / What do you want me to say? / Spider in the snow / The jitters / I love a magician / You are invited / Gyroscope / The city / Girl o'clock / 81/2 minutes / Back and forth.

May 01. (cd-ep; split) <DI 38> **JUNO & THE DISMEMBERMENT PLAN**
– The Dismemberment Plan get rich (w/ JUNO) / (other 3 by JUNO).

Oct 01. (cd) <(DI 42)> **CHANGE**
– Sentimental man / The face of the earth / Superpowers / Pay for the piano / Come home / Secret curse / Automatic / Following through / Time bomb / The other side / Ellen and Ben.

DISSOLVE
(see under ⇒ MONTGOMERY, Roy; 80's section)

DIVINE COMEDY

Formed: Londonderry, Northern Ireland ... 1990 by bishop's son, NEIL HANNON, JOHN McCULLAGH and KEVIN TRAYNOR. Moving across the water to London, the three signed to maverick indie label, 'Setanta', releasing a SEAN O'NEILL (That Petrol Emotion)-produced debut, 'FANFARE FOR THE COMIC MUSE' (1990). A mini-set, it was followed by two further EP's, before the extroverted HANNON took over the reins as McCULLAGH and TRAYNOR bailed out. Free to pursue his own eccentric muse, HANNON steered The DIVINE COMEDY away from trad indie-rock towards a more self-consciously cultured approach which suggested the influence of everyone from SCOTT WALKER to JARVIS COCKER, in a cod-romantic ANDREW LLOYD-WEBBER-esque fashion of course! His first step towards educating the alternative pop scene came in the shape of 1993's 'LIBERATION' album, his debonair charisma in full effect on tracks such as 'EUROPOP', 'BERNICE BOBS HER HAIR' and 'I WAS BORN YESTERDAY'. His next set of songs, 'PROMENADE' (1994), was a loose concept affair and featured the Irish comedian, SEAN HUGHES, who provided verbal support on the track, 'THE BOOKLOVERS'. The name, DIVINE COMEDY, came to the attention of 'Father Ted' loving music fans after the instrumental, 'SONGS OF LOVE', was used as the theme tune to the popular Channel 4 programme. HANNON also co-wrote another ditty for the second series of the show; the downright silly 'My Beautiful Horse' was the singing priests' (Ted and Dougal) entry for the Eurovision Song Contest!!! In 1996, HANNON (together with his new DIVINE COMEDY recruits) released his most perfectly conceived pop masterpiece to date in 'CASANOVA', the Roger Moore of rock crooning his way through a dapper set of richly orchestrated diamonds. Duly encrusted into the Top 50, the album contained such memorably tongue-in-cheek hits as 'SOMETHING FOR THE WEEKEND', 'BECOMING MORE LIKE ALFIE' and 'THE FROG PRINCESS'. Now a firm critical fave, The DIVINE COMEDY (well, HANNON) had two more Top 20 successes with 'A SHORT ALBUM ABOUT LOVE' (a mini-set) and 'EVERYBODY KNOWS (EXCEPT YOU)' (a single). In August '98, "the Leslie Thomas" of indie-pop/rock, HANNON/DIVINE COMEDY had his first Top 10 album, 'FIN DE SIECLE', a record that boasted three further hits including 'GENERATION SEX' and 'NATIONAL EXPRESS'; a stop-gap UK Top 3 'best of' package, 'A SECRET HISTORY', was delivered the following year. The aptly titled 'REGENERATION' (2001) displayed a wholesale change of tack as HANNON and Co employed RADIOHEAD producer Nigel Godrich and ditched the arch theatricality of old for a more forthright, if not exactly earnest, musical and lyrical approach. A UK Top 20 success bolstered by the hit singles 'BAD AMBASSADOR' and 'LOVE WHAT YOU DO', the album suggested that the impish Irish chameleon was sufficiently savvy to carry the whole thing off. • **Covered:** THERE IS A LIGHT THAT NEVER GOES OUT (Smiths) / MIRANDA + LAST STAND IN METROLAND (Michael Nyman).

Album rating: FANFARE FOR THE COMIC MUSE mini (*4) / LIBERATION (*6) / PROMENADE (*7) / CASANOVA (*8) / A SHORT ALBUM ABOUT LOVE (*7) / FIN DE SIECLE (*7) / A SECRET HISTORY – THE BEST OF THE DIVINE COMEDY (*7) / REGENERATION (*6)

NEIL HANNON (b. 7 Nov'70) – vocals, guitar, bass, piano, etc. / **JOHN McCULLAGH** – bass, vocals / **KEVIN TRAYNOR** – drums

 Setanta Setanta

Aug 90. (m-cd/m-lp) (SET CDM/LPM 002) **FANFARE FOR THE COMIC MUSE**
– Ignorance is bliss / Indian rain / Bleak landscape / Tailspin / Rise and fall / Logic vs. emotion / Secret garden.

Nov 91. (12"ep) (SET 008) **TIMEWATCH. / JERUSALEM / THE RISE AND FALL**

Feb 92. (12"ep) (SET 011) **EUROPOP EP**
– New wave / Intifada / Monitor.
(cd-ep+=) (SET 011CD) – Timewatch / Jerusalem / The rise and fall.

— now HANNON solo after the other two departed

Jul 93. (7"ep) (CAO 008) **LUCY. / THE POP SINGER'S FEAR OF THE POLLEN COUNT / I WAS BORN YESTERDAY**

Aug 93. (cd/c/lp) (SET CD/MC/LP 011) **LIBERATION**
– Festive road / Death of a supernaturalist / Bernice bobs her hair / I was born yesterday / Your daddy's car / Europop / Timewatching / The singer's fear of the pollen count / Queen of the south / Victoria Falls / Three sisters / Europe by train / Lucy. (re-iss. Aug96; same)

Oct 93. (7"pic-d-ep) (DC 001) **INDULGENCE No.1**
– Untitled melody / Hate my way / Europe by train.

Mar 94. (cd/c/lp) (SET CD/MC/LP 013) **PROMENADE**
– Bath / Going downhill / The booklovers / A seafood song / Geronimo / Don't look down / When the lights go out all over Europe / The summerhouse / Neptune's daughter / A drinking song / Ten seconds to midnight / Tonight we fly. (re-iss. Aug96 & Aug97; same)

DIVINE COMEDY (cont)

Aug 94. (7"ep) (DC 002) **INDULGENCE No.2**
– A drinking song / Tonight we fly (live) / When the lights go out all over Europe.

—— now one-man band **NEIL HANNON** and a large ensemble of musicians including main band; **STUART 'PINKIE' BATES** – hammond organ / **JOBY TALBOT** – piano, arranger / **IVOR TALBOT** – guitar / **BRYAN MILLS** – bass / **MIGUEL 'MIGGY' BARRADAS** – drums

Apr 96. (cd/c/lp) (SET CD/MC/LP 025) <36863> **CASANOVA** [48]
– Something for the weekend / Becoming more like Alfie / Middle-class heroes / In & out of Paris & London / Charge / Songs of love / The frog princess / A woman of the world / Through a long & sleepless night / Theme from Casanova / The dogs & the horses.

—— <above issued on 'Tristar' in the US>

Jun 96. (c-s) (SETMC 026) **SOMETHING FOR THE WEEKEND / SONGS OF LOVE** (theme from 'Father Ted') [14]
(cd-s+=) (SETCD 026) – Birds of Paradise farm / Love is lighter than air.

Aug 96. (7"/c-s) (SET/+MC 027) **BECOMING MORE LIKE ALFIE. / YOUR DADDY'S CAR (live)** [27]
(cd-s+=) (SETCD 027) – Untitled melody (acoustic) / The dogs & the horses (acoustic).

Nov 96. (c-s) (SETMC 032) **THE FROG PRINCESS / MOTORWAY TO DAMASCUS** [15]
(cd-s+=) (SETCD 032) – A woman of the world / Lucy (demo).
(cd-s) (SETCDL 032) – ('A'side) / Something before the weekend / Neptune's daughter / Tonight we fly.

Feb 97. (m-cd/m-c) (<SET CD/MC 036>) **A SHORT ALBUM ABOUT LOVE** [13]
– In pursuit of happiness / Everybody knows (except you) / Someone / If . . . / If I were you (I'd be through with me) / Timewatching / I'm all you need.

Mar 97. (cd-ep) (SETCDA 038) **EVERYBODY KNOWS (EXCEPT YOU) / MAKE IT EASY ON YOURSELF (live) / A DRINKING SONG (live) / SOMETHING FOR THE WEEKEND (live)** [14]
(cd-ep) (SETCDB 038) – ('A'side) / Johnny Mathis' feet (live) / Your daddy's car (live) / Europe by train (live).
(cd-ep) (SETCDC 038) – ('A'side) / Bath (live) / Tonight we fly (live) / Middle class heroes (live).

—— In April '98, The DIVINE COMEDY were part of a NOEL COWARD tribute album in which a single, 'I'VE BEEN TO A MARVELLOUS PARTY' was taken. It hit No.28 and was backed with a Shola Ama & Craig Armstrong track

—— added **ROB FARRER** – percussion

	Setanta	Imprint
Aug 98. (cd/c) (SET CD/MC 057) <111813> **FIN DE SIECLE** [9]		Dec98

– Generation sex / Thrillseeker / Commuter love / Sweden / Eric the gardener / National express / Life on Earth / The certainty of chance / Here comes the flood / Sunrise. (also ltd-cd; SETCDL 057)

Sep 98. (7") (SET 050) **GENERATION SEX. / POSTCARD TO ROSIE** [19] Nov98
(cd-s) (SETCDA 050) <114195> – ('A'side) / London Irish / Time lapse.
(cd-s) (SETCDB 050) <114197> – ('A'side) / Chasing sheep is best left to shepherds / Little acts of kindness.

	Setanta	Tristar
Nov 98. (c-s) (SETMC 067) **THE CERTAINTY OF CHANCE / MARYLAND ELECTRIC RAINSTORM** [49]		Mar99

(cd-s) (<SETCD 067>) – ('A'side) / Last stand in Metroland / Miranda.
(cd-s) (<SETCD 067>) – ('A'side) / Dead only quickly / Knowing the ropes.

Jan 99. (c-s) (SETMC 069) **NATIONAL EXPRESS / THE HEART OF ROCK AND ROLL** [8]
(cd-s) (SETCDA 069) – ('A'side) / Going downhill fast / Radioactivity.
(cd-s) (SETCDB 069) – ('A'side) / Famous / Overstrand.

Aug 99. (c-s) (SETMC 070) **THE POP SINGER'S FEAR OF THE POLLEN COUNT / JACKIE** [17]
(cd-s) (SETCDA 070) – ('A'side) / With whom to dance / Eric the gardener.
(cd-s) (SETCDB 070) – ('A'side) / This side of paradise / Vapour trail.

Aug 99. (cd/c) (SET CD/MC 100) <51080> **A SECRET HISTORY – THE BEST OF THE DIVINE COMEDY** (compilation) [3] Sep99
– National express / Something for the weekend / Everybody knows (except you) / Generation sex / Becoming more like Alfie / The summerhouse / Your daddy's car / The pop singer's fear of the pollen count / The frog princess / Gin soaked boy / Lucy / Songs of love / In pursuit of happiness / I've been to a marvellous city / The certainty of chance / Too young to die / Tonight we fly.

Nov 99. (c-s) (SETMC 071) **GIN SOAKED BOY / EUROPOP (live)** [38]
(cd-s) (SETCDA 071) – ('A'side) / Songs of love / I am.
(cd-s) (SETCDB 071) – ('A'side) / Geronimo (livd) / My lovely horse.

	Parlophone	Nettwerk
Feb 01. (c-s) (TCR 6554) **LOVE WHAT YOU DO / SOUL TRADER / GET ME TO A MONASTERY** [26]		

(cd-s) (CDRS 6554) – (first 2 tracks) / You / ('A'-video).
(cd-s) (CDR 6554) – (first & third tracks) / ('A'-Deadly Avenger mix).

Mar 01. (cd/c) (531761-2/-4) <30237> **REGENERATION** [14]
– Timestretched / Bad ambassador / Perfect lovesong / Note to self / Lost property / Eye of the needle / Love what you do / Dumb it down / Mastermind / Regeneration / The beauty regime.

May 01. (7") (R 6558) **BAD AMBASSADOR. / LIFE ON EARTH (live)** [34]
(cd-s) (CDRS 6558) – ('A'side) / Edward the confessor / U.S.E. / ('A'video).
(cd-s) (CDR 6558) – ('A'live) / Sweden (live) / Pictures of matchstick men (live).

Oct 01. (cd-s) (CDRS 6561) **PERFECT LOVESONG / NO EXCUSES / LES JOURS TRISTES** [42]
(cd-s) (CDR 6561) – ('A'side) / Thinking the unthinkable / Oh yeah.

DIVISION OF LAURA LEE

Formed: Sweden . . . September 1997 by HAKAN JOHANSSON, HENRIK ROSTBERG, PER STALBERG and JONAS GUSTAVSSON. Due in most part to their shared country of upbringing, DIVISION OF LAURA LEE (LAURA LEE was a soul singer!) were compared to R&B-punks, The HIVES, and although sharing a sound that favoured garage punk and rock sounds, they differed foremostly in the group's wider sonic pallette, combining alternative pop stylistics, and the math rock brand inspired by the Washington D.C. movement of such luminaries as FUGAZI. Debuting in 1998, with the EP, 'THERE IS A FIRST TIME FOR EVERYTHING', the band kept themselves busy with a heavy touring schedule, and the release of their initial full-length outing, 'AT THE ROYAL CLUB' (1999). The following few years saw the band ink a deal with Swedish imprint, 'Burning Heart' (joining the HIVES on the roster), and sending out the single, 'PRETTY ELECTRIC' in 2001 to widespread acclaim, where previous fame had been bound to their native environs. Not resting on their laurels, DOLL issued their second LP, 'BLACK CITY' (2002), a record displaying their songwriting maturity with a range of alt-rock happenings in the mix.

Album rating: AT THE ROYAL CLUB (*5) / BLACK CITY (*7)

PER STALBERG – vocals, guitar / **HENRIK ROSTBERG** – guitar, vocals / **JONAS GUSTAVSSON** – bass, vocals / **HAKAN JOHANSSON** – drums

	not iss.	own label
1998. (7"ep) **THERE IS A FIRST TIME FOR EVERYTHING**	-	- Sweden
1998. (7"ep) **split w/ MILEMARKER**	-	-

	not iss.	Carcrash
1999. (7"ep) **split w/ IMPEL**	-	-

	not iss.	own label
1999. (cd) (none) **AT THE ROYAL CLUB**	-	- Sweden

	Burning Heart	Burning Heart
Nov 01. (cd-ep) (<BHR 138-2>) **PRETTY ELECTRIC**	-	

– Number one / Pretty electric / The truth is fucked.

Feb 02. (cd/lp) (<BHR 146-2/-1>) **BLACK CITY**
– Need to get some / We've been planning this for years / Number one / Trapped in / Access identity / I guess I'm healed / The truth is fucked / Black city / I walk on broken glass / Second rule is / Pretty electric / Wild and crazy.

Apr 02. (cd-ep) (<BHR 148-2>) **NEED TO GET SOME / UPSIDE DOWN / I GUESS I'M HEALED (demo)** | | Jul02

—— (Jun'02) **DAVID OJALA** – guitar; repl. HENRIK

Nov 02. (cd-s) (BHR 160-2) **BLACK CITY / LOVELESS / THE TRUTH IS FUCKED (demo)** | | -

DNTEL (see under ⇒ STRICTLY BALLROOM)

DODGY

Formed: Hounslow, London, England . . . early 1990 by vocalist/bassist NIGEL CLARK, guitarist ANDY MILLER and drummer MATTHEW PRIEST. With DJ, CHRIS SLADE, they set up The Dodgy Club in a London bar, where they cultivated a grassroots fanbase over the course of the summer. Just over a year later, DODGY embarked upon their first national jaunt, christened the 'Word Of Mouth' tour in recognition of its unconventional nature; their fans had to phone up prospective promoters and venues to find out where they were playing (well dodgy!). After initial 7" singles on their own 'Bostin' label, they were snapped up by 'A&M', the major releasing two quickfire follow-ups in Spring '93, 'WATER UNDER THE BRIDGE' and 'LOVEBIRDS', the latter a Top 75 entry. The TURTLES to Oasis's BEATLES, DODGY's hazy shade of peace-pipe pop also incorporated the songwriting quality of SQUEEZE or CROWDED HOUSE. 'THE DODGY ALBUM' bounced onto the shelves that summer, although their spliff-friendly spirituality wasn't an immediate success and charming singles such as 'I NEED ANOTHER' and 'HOMEGROWN' went virtually unnoticed. A year later, DODGY's camper van sound made inroads into the Top 50; two hit singles, 'MELODIES HAUNT YOU' and the evocative 'STAYING OUT FOR THE SUMMER' preceded a second set, 'HOMEGROWN', although the critics remained unconvinced. 'SO LET ME GO FAR' and 'MAKING THE MOST OF' both broke their Top 30 duck and were followed by a re-issue of 'STAYING OUT FOR THE SUMMER', actually released in the summer this time around and a deserved Top 20 smash as Brit-pop gripped the nation. Now summer festival specialists, DODGY had finally found their sunkissed niche and a third album, 'FREE PEACE SWEET' (1996) was released to critical acclaim and major Top 10 success; the record also spawned four Top 20 singles, the pick of the bunch being the Top 5, 'GOOD ENOUGH'. However, after 'EVERY SINGLE DAY' hit the Top 40 in Autumn '98 and an accompanying 'best of' package failed to meets sales expectations, NIGEL bailed out. MILLER and PRIEST carried on regardless and by Spring the following year a new singer DAVE BASSEY was found. Augmented by NICK ABNETT and CHRIS HALLAM, DODGY were one of the first bands to release a single through the internet (yes, the music industry was indeed getting a major shake-up). A whole album's worth of new material, 'REAL ESTATE' followed in 2001 on their own 'Bostin' label, laying the breezy pop of DODGY mk 1 to rest with a brace of rough diamonds polished by the gin-soaked petulance of new boy BASSEY. • Covered: I CAN'T MAKE IT (Small Faces) / REVOLUTION (Beatles) / BACK INTO YOUR LIFE (Love Affair).

Album rating: THE DODGY ALBUM (*7) / HOMEGROWN (*6) / FREE PEACE SWEET (*8) / ACE A'S AND KILLER B'S compilation (*7)

NIGEL CLARK (b.18 Sep'66, Redditch, England) – vocals, bass, guitars / **ANDY MILLER** (b.18 Dec'68) – lead guitar, vocals / **MATTHEW PRIEST** (b. 3 Apr'70) – drums, vocals, percussion

	Bostin	not iss.
Sep 91. (7") (BTN 001) **SUMMER FAYRE. / ST. LUCIA**		-
Nov 91. (7") (BTN 002) **EAST WAY. / SEEMS LIKE A BAD DAY**		-

(cd-s+=) (BTN 002CD) – Groove song (St. Lucia demo) / See the way.

DODGY (cont) — THE GREAT INDIE DISCOGRAPHY — The 1990s

Apr 92. (7"black & white) *(BTN 003)* **THE BLACK AND WHITE SINGLE:- black side: WORTH THE BLOOD. / white side: THE ELEPHANT** ☐ -
(12"black & white+=) *(BTN 003X)* – Worth the blood (full).
(cd-s++=) *(BTN 003CDS)* – The D-Club versions; See the way / Jungle dark dance bath / Elevators goin' up / 4am nocturnal / Watch the sun go down.

—— added 4th member **CHRIS SLADE** – DJ, keyboards

A&M   A&M

Mar 93. (7"/c-s) *(AM/+MC 196)* **WATER UNDER THE BRIDGE. / IT'S BEEN SO LONG** ☐ -
(12"+=/cd-s+=) *(AM Y/CD 196)* – She wants my loving / Valuable fool.
Apr 93. (7"/c-s) *(AM/+MC 0177)* **LOVEBIRDS. / BIG BROWN MOON** 65 -
(12"+=/cd-s+=) *(AM Y/CD 0177)* – Sylvia's bedroom / Smashed up in a flat.
Jun 93. (cd/c/lp) **THE DODGY ALBUM** 75 -
– Water under the bridge / I need another / Lovebirds / Satisfied / Grand old English oak tree / Stand by yourself / As my time goes by / Never again / Cold tea / We're not going to take this anymore.
Jun 93. (7"mustard-ep/c-ep) *(580 317-7/-4)* **I NEED ANOTHER. / IF I FALL / HENDRE DHU** 67 -
(12"ep+=/cd-ep+=) *(580 317-1/-2)* – Never again (campfire version).
Oct 93. (7"ep/c-ep) *(580 414-7/-4)* **HOMEGROWN E.P.** ☐ -
– Don't go back (to the beaten track) / Home grown / Let's wait till we get there.
(10"ep+=/cd-ep+=) *(580 415-0/-2)* –

—— now without CHRIS and back to trio

Jul 94. (7"ep/c-ep) *(580 676-7/-4)* **THE MELOD-E.P.: MELODIES HAUNT YOU. / THE SNAKE** 53 -
(12"+=) *(580 676-1)* – Don't go back (to the beaten track).
(cd-s++=) *(580 676-2)* – Summer fayre. *(re-iss. Jul97; same)*
Sep 94. (7"blue/c-s) *(580 788-7/-4)* **STAYING OUT FOR THE SUMMER. / LOVEBIRDS (original)** 38 -
(cd-s+=) *(580 797-2)* – As time goes by (demo) / Back to life.
(cd-s) *(580 789-2)* – ('A'side) / A summer's day in mid-January / Don't you think / Colour me with paints. *(re-iss. Jul97; same)*
Oct 94. (cd/c/lp) *(<540 282-2/-4/-1>)* **HOMEGROWN** 43 -
– Staying out for the summer / Melodies haunt you / So let me go far / Crossroads / One day / We are together / Whole lot easier / Making the most of / Waiting for the day / What have I done wrong? / Grassman. *(re-iss. Jun95, hit No.28)*
Dec 94. (c-s) *(580 903-4)* **SO LET ME GO FAR / DON'T LET GO DON'T LET GO (U.K. R.I.P.)** 30 -
(12"+=/cd-s+=) *(580 905-1/-2)* – So let me Wobble Jah / The elephant (the Balaphon-a-bing bong immigrant mix).
(cd-s) *(580 903-2)* – ('A'side) / I need another (live) / Satisfied (live) / Melodies haunt you (live). *(re-iss. Jul97; same)*
(above featured JAH WOBBLE – bass) (below featured The KICK HORNS)
Feb 95. (7"pic-d/c-s) *(580 986-7/-4)* **MAKING THE MOST OF. / FAISONS AU MIEUX (YES, IT'S IN FRENCH)** 22 -
(cd-s+=) *(580 987-2)* – The Ludlow sessions part 1: Spent all my time running / All the time in the world.
(cd-s) *(580 989-2)* – ('A'extended) / The Ludlow sessions part 2: Watch out watcha doin' / This is ours / (Get off your) High horse. *(re-iss. Jul97; same)*
Jun 95. (c-s) *(581 092-4)* **STAYING OUT FOR THE SUMMER (mixed up in 95) / SATISFIED (live)** 19 -
(cd-s) *(581 093-2)* – ('A'side) / (Your love keeps lifting me) Higher and higher / Crossroads (live) / Melodies haunt you (live).
(cd-s) *(581 095-2)* – ('A'side) / Waiting for the day (live) / One day (live) / (Get off your) High horse (live). *(re-iss. Jul97; same)*

—— now with guest (4th member) **RICHARD PAYNE** – keyboards

May 96. (7"white/c-s) *(581 624-7/-4)* **IN A ROOM. / OUTCLUBBING** 12 -
(cd-s) *(581 625-2)* – ('A'side) / Self doubt / Long life (acoustic) / Jungle UK (no rest in peace). *(re-iss. Jul97; same)*
Jun 96. (cd/c/lp) *(<540 573-2/-4/-1>)* **FREE PEACE SWEET** 7 ☐
– Intro / In a room / Trust in time / You've gotta look up / If you're thinking of me / Good enough / Ain't no longer asking / Found you / One of those rivers / Prey for drinking / Jack the lad / Long life / U.K.R.I.P. / Homegrown.
Jul 96. (7"/c-s) *(581 814-7/-4)* **GOOD ENOUGH. / NUTTERS** 4 -
(cd-s+=) *(581 815-2)* – Speaking in tongues / Lovebirds on Katovit. *(re-iss. Jul97; same)*
Nov 96. (7"/c-s) *(581 998-7/-4)* **IF YOU'RE THINKING OF ME. / IN A ROOM (acoustic)** 11 -
(cd-s) *(581 998-2)* – ('A'side) / Pebblemilljam / Forever remain / Good enough (version). *(re-iss. Jul97; same)*
Mar 97. (7"/c-s) *(582 132-7/-4)* **FOUND YOU. / STAND BY YOURSELF** 19 -
(cd-s) *(582 133-2)* – ('A'side) / I can't make it / Revolution.

Polygram   Polygram

Sep 98. (c-s) *(MERMC 512)* <*582737*> **EVERY SINGLE DAY / THE BRIDGE / MOSTAR KEEP SHINING** 32 ☐ Nov98
(cd-s) *(MERCD 512)* – (first two tracks) / Look up.
(cd-s) *(MERDD 512)* – (first & third tracks) / Staying out for the summer.
Oct 98. (cd/c) *(<541 018-2/-4>)* **ACE A'S AND KILLER B'S** (compilation) 55 ☐ Nov98
– Every single day / Staying out for the summer (summer 95) / Water under the bridge / Good enough / Melodies haunt you / Big brown moon / Found you / Self doubt / In a room / Making the most of / If you're thinking of me / Lovebirds / (Get off your) High horse / So let me go far / Grassman / Ain't no longer asking / The elephant. *(<also d-cd; 541 019-2>)*

—— **DAVE BASSEY** – vocals (ex-MUSTARD) repl. NIGEL who went solo
—— **NICK ABNETT** – bass + **CHRIS HALLAM** – keyboards (were added)
—— a single, 'BACK INTO YOUR LIFE' was available in August '99 through the internet only:- www.dodgy.co.uk

Bostin'   not iss.

Jul 01. (cd) *(BTNCD 005)* **REAL ESTATE** ☐ -
– Featherweight and monkeyface / Come to bed / (We all need a little) Lifting / Rag doll / Vision / You shouldn't wear shorts / Right idea / Clean / Feather cuts (remix) / Be free.
Sep 01. (7") *(BTN 006)* **(WE ALL NEED A LITTLE) LIFTING. / LILLIES IN THE DOLLS HOUSE** ☐ -
(cd-s+=) *(BTNCD 006)* – Kimberley.

Julie DOIRON (see under ⇒ ERIC'S TRIP)

DOLEFUL LIONS

Formed: Chicago, Illinois, USA … 1996 by brothers JONATHAN and ROBERT SCOTT, JOE CAPARO and TONY STIGLITZ. Soon after formation the band moved to Chapel Hill, North Carolina, and after some gigging, managed to gain the assistance of noted knob-twiddler MITCH EASTER to work on their debut LP, 'MOTEL SWIM' (1998). This set was a fairly run-of-the-mill indie guitar affair bar the standout track 'THE SOUND OF COLOGNE' which referenced the highly influential Krautrock scene, but as a whole the LP hardly stood as forewarning of the stranger movements of the band that were to come. ROBERT SCOTT and STIGLITZ departed soon after this outing, their respective positions being filled by AMY PALAZZOLO and DAVE JACKSON for their next album 'RATS ARE COMING! THE WEREWOLVES ARE HERE!' (1999), which signalled a move into the more psychedelic regions of alternative rock which fitted well with the obsession with B-movie horror exemplified by the title and song tracks. SCOTT was also becoming even more of the mainman of the operation as evidenced by their next full-length offering 'SONG CYCLOPS, VOL.1' (2000). On this set SCOTT pre-recorded all his guitar and vocal tracks in his house and later presented it to the band to add just a smattering of backing, making for a dark and disturbing listen. Perhaps due to a reaction against the insular sound of this piece DL's fourth album, 'OUT LIKE A LAMB' (2002) was a far more open affair with great swathes of guitar and rhythm sections to be heard, producing possibly the peak of their recorded output. This last indie pop-esque number also included the handywork of new member AYNSLEY PIRTLE.

Album rating: MOTEL SWIM (*6) / RATS ARE COMING! THE WEREWOLVES ARE HERE! (*7) / SONG CYCLOPS VOLUME ONE (*5) / OUT LIKE A LAMB (*7)

JONATHAN SCOTT – vocals, guitar / **JOE CAPARO** – guitar, vocals / **ROBERT SCOTT** – bass / **TONY STIGLITZ** – drums

Parasol   Parasol

May 98. (cd) <*(PARCD 032)*> **MOTEL SWIM** ☐ ☐
– The sound of Cologne / Respirator / One revolution (around the world) / A viper in hiding / Motel swim / Gulliver diver / Advanced Japanese candlestick man / Hang around in your head / All winter long / Down tiger, down tiger.

—— **AMY PALAZZOLO** – bass; repl. ROBERT
—— **DAVE JACKSON** – drums, keyboards; repl. STIGLITZ

Oct 99. (cd) <*PARCD 051*> **THE RATS ARE COMING! THE WEREWOLVES ARE HERE!** - ☐
– I miss the kings / Ocean stars / In the early morning aviaries of Marathon / Sweet driller killer / The rats are coming! the werewolves are here! / Airline histories / The contrarian / Destroy all the monsters / Drillerkiller / Hoshizaki cubestar soldier.

—— now down to just **JONATHAN SCOTT** (+ JACKSON)

Oct 00. (cd) <*(PARCD 060)*> **SONG CYCLES VOLUME ONE** ☐ ☐
– Charles Starkweather vs. Sasquatch / My summer with ghosts / Gimghoul numerologist / Spacecraft marooned in the gorillaworld / The red top lounge flesheaters / Demon sounds / Hercules in the haunted world / Sung sawn song / Now you're a witch! / Turkish Star Wars / Sparks fly for magnemite / We three kings of Orient are / Contact beyond the mirror room / A walk in the sun / Deep inside the genie's lamp / Chinese rockets / Baptized in bees / Jamie conjures demons / Breather bulls / The marauding ghouls / Goodnight, Graceland / Charles Starkweather versus Sasquateh.

—— added **AYNSLEY PIRTLE** – bass

Broken Horse   Parasol

Nov 02. (cd) *(BKHCD 001)* <*PARCD 082*> **OUT LIKE A LAMB** ☐ ☐ Jul02
– Saturday mansions / Stand in the colosseum / I can take you to the sun / Surfside motel (live with The Miskatonic University Orchestra) / 1723 / Out like a lamb / Dear Lazarus / Sunshine Spartacus / Tanah lot / When we were wolves / Texas is beautiful / Graveyards of swallows.

DO MAKE SAY THINK

Formed: Montreal, Canada … 1997 by CHARLES SPEARIN, guitarist JUSTIN SMALL and JAMES PAYMENT, with the addition of multi-instrumentalist OHAD BENCHETRIT, JASON MacKENZIE and drummer DAVE MITCHELL. Although mainly talked about in the same breath as fellow label mates and close friends GODSPEED YOU BLACK EMPEROR!, DO MAKE SAY THINK had been wielding the same post-rock, experimental axe for almost as long as their aforementioned Canadian cousins. The only difference being that DMST, also known to rock-out on occasions, were more from the JOHN McENTIRE school of avant garde than, say, BIG BLACK or SLINT. But enough of naming names, this close-knit collective have carried their own steam since self-releasing their eponymous debut early in 1998, which was later remixed and re-issued by 'Constellation'. An angular swirl of synths and electric guitars, this was a good starting point for the band who would out-do themselves come the arrival of their second set, 'GOODBYE ENEMY AIRSHIP THE LANDLORD IS DEAD' (2000). An explosion of jazz, rock and lonesome melodies, the group fused samples, live drumming, brass accompaniment and heavy distorted guitars to what would become a landmark album in experimental rock. With its DIY artwork (artist unknown), and long drawn-out spacy atmospherics, in parts it sounded like HAWKWIND with, well, more wind! The best was yet to come, however, when the six-piece gave birth to the sublime and sparse 'AND YET AND YET' (2002), with its harsh/soft overtures and psychedelic, static and finely-tuned electric orchestrations.

Album rating: DO MAKE SAY THINK (*7) / GOODBYE ENEMY AIRSHIP THE LANDLORD IS DEAD (*7) / AND YET AND YET (*6)

OHAD BENCHETRIT – guitar, bass, sax, flute / **JASON MACKENZIE** – keyboards, effects / **DAVID MITCHELL** – drums / **JAMES PAYMENT** – drums / **JUSTIN SMALL** – guitar / **CHARLES SPEARIN** – bass, guitar, trumpet

			Constellation	Constellation
Oct 98.	(cd) <*cst 05d*>	**DO MAKE SAY THINK**	☐	☐

– 1978 / Le'Espalace / If I only / Highway 420 / Dr Hooch / Disco and haze / Onions / The fare to get there.

Aug 99.	(12") <*(RESONANT 01)*>	**BESIDES EP**	☐	☐

(above issued on 'Resonant')

Mar 00.	(lp/cd) <*cst 010/+cd*>	**GOODBYE ENEMY AIRSHIP THE LANDLORD IS DEAD**	☐	☐

– When the day chokes the night / Minmin / The landlord is dead / The apartment song / All of this is true / Bruce E Kinesis / Goodbye enemy airship.

Mar 02.	(cd/lp) <*cst 020-2/-1*>	**AND YET AND YET**	☐	☐

– Classic noonlanding / End of music / White light of / Chinatown / Reitschule / Soul and onward / Anything for now.

DON CABALLERO

Formed: Pittsburgh, Pennsylvania, USA ... 1992 by MIKE BANFIELD, DAMON CHE, PAT MORRIS and IAN WILLIAMS, this line-up featuring on the release of their debut album 'FOR RESPECT' in 1993. DON CABALLERO offered rock fans something different with their energetic instrumental music led by drummer CHE and featuring fantastic guitar duels between WILLIAMS and BANFIELD. The group's second album 'DON CABALLERO 2' (1995) further enhanced their reputation, with CHE in particular emerging as one of the most promising mainstream drummers around. In the same year, CHE also displayed his skills as a guitarist and vocalist after releasing the album 'SONGS FOR THE TERRESTRIALLY CHALLENGED' with his off-shoot band THEE SPEAKING CANARIES. DON CABALLERO returned in 1998 with the album 'WHAT BURNS NEVER RETURNS', a record which saw the group stretching their abilities still further. The music on the album abandoned conventional structures but was held together with the seemingly telepathic understanding between the group members who each delivered a virtuoso performance. A singles compilation followed in 1999 before the group bowed out with the, slower paced, 'AMERICAN DON' album in 2000. CHE returned in 2002 with his new group BELLINI and their ferocious debut album, 'SNOWING SUN'.

Album rating: FOR RESPECT (*6) / DON CABALLERO 2 (*7) / WHAT BURNS NEVER RETURNS (*6) / SINGLES BREAKING UP (VOL.1) compilation (*7) / AMERICAN DON (*6) / Bellini: SNOWING SUN (*6) / Thee Speaking Canaries: SONGS FOR THE TERRESTRIALLY CHALLENGED (*5)

DAMON CHE – drums / **IAN WILLIAMS** – guitar / **MIKE BANFIELD** – guitar / **PAT MORRIS** – bass

			not iss.	Chunklet
1992.	(7") <*#11*>	**WALTOR. / SHUMAN CENTER 91**	-	☐
			not iss.	Pop Bus
1992.	(7"m) <*005*>	**LUCKY FATHER BROWN. / BELTED SWEATER / SHOE SHINE**	-	☐
			not iss.	Broken Giraffe
1992.	(7") <*BG 002*>	**UNRESOLVED KARMA. / PUDDIN' IN MY EYE**	-	☐
			not iss.	Third Gear
1993.	(7") <*3G-04*> **ANDANDANDANDANDANDANDANDAND. / FIRST HITS**		-	☐
			City Slang	Touch & Go
Sep 93.	(7") <*TG 119*>	**OUR CABALLERO. / MY TEN YEAR OLD LADY IS GIVING IT AWAY**	☐	☐

(cd-s+=) (*efa 04922-03*) – Unresolved karma / First hits.

Oct 93.	(lp/cd) (*efa 04929-1/-2*) <*TG 120/+CD*> **FOR RESPECT**	☐	☐

– For respect / Chief Sitting Duck / New laws / Nicked and liqued / Rocco / Subdued confections / Got a mile, got a mile, got an inch / Our Caballero / Bears see things pretty much the way they are / Well built road / Belted sweater. (*re-iss. Dec98; same as US*)

			Touch & Go	Touch & Go
Sep 95.	(lp/cd) <(*TG 143/+CD*)>	**DON CABALLERO 2**	☐	☐

– Stupid puma / Please Tokio, please this is Tokio / Dick suffers is furious with you / Cold knees (in April) / P, P, P, antless / Repeat defender / Rollerblade success story / No one gives a hoot about faux-ass nonsense.

Apr 98.	(7") <*TG 181*>	**TREY DOG'S ACID. / ROOM TEMPERATURE LOUNGE**	-	☐
Jun 98.	(d-lp/cd) <(*TG 185/+CD*)>	**WHAT BURNS NEVER RETURNS**	☐	☐

– Don Caballero 3 / In the absence of strong evidence to the contrary, one may step out of the way of the charging bull / Delivering the groceries at 138 beats per minute / Slice where you live like pie / Room temperature suite / The room in perforated lines / From the desk of elsewhere go / June is finally here.

Jan 99.	(cd) <(*TG 184CD*)>	**SINGLES BREAKING UP VOL.1** (compilation)	☐	☐

– Lucky Father Brown / Belted sweater / Shoe shine / Unresolved kharma / Puddin' in my eye / My ten year old lady is giving it away / Our Caballero / Andandandandandandandandand / First hits / No more peace and quiet for the warlike / If you've read Dr. Adder then you know what I want / Trey dog's acid / Room temperature lounge.

—— now without BANFELD

Sep 00.	(d-lp/cd) <(*TG 218/+CD*)>	**AMERICAN DON**	☐	☐

– Fire back about your new baby's sex / The Peter Criss jazz / Haven't lived afro pop / You drink a lot of coffee for a teenager / Ones all over the place / I never like you / Details on how to get iceman on your license plate / A lot of people tell me I have a fake British accent / Let's face it pal, you didn't need that eye surgery.

—— split 2001; WILLIAMS carried on with side-project STORM & STRESS

BELLINI

GIOVANNA CACCIOLA – vocals (of UZEDA) / **AGOSTINA TILOTTA** – guitar / **MATTHEW TAYLOR** – bass / **DAMON CHE** – drums

			Monitor	Monitor
Sep 02.	(cd) <(*MON 011*)>	**SNOWING SUN**	☐	Aug02

– A short tale – Medusa / Furious / Rut row / Patience and passion in brown gloves / Conflict between the fire and the wet wood / On the road to Roscoe Lee / Marranzano / Spilled red salsa in black coffee / We crossed the ocean to see the snowing sun / Redtail hawk / The best song on a starship.

THEE SPEAKING CANARIES

DAMON CHE – vocals, guitar / **KARL HENDRICKS** – bass (of KARL HENDRICKS TRIO) / **NOAH LEGER** – drums

			not iss.	Scat
Jan 95.	(cd/lp) <*SCAT 39 CD/LP*>	**SONGS FOR VTHE TERRESTRIALLY CHALLENGED**	-	☐

– Houses and houses of perfectness / Summer's empty resolution / Terrestrial – Famous no space / Guitar strings for a holocaust / Hall of force – Gone bad – So glad – Reprise / Little ice queen / Super hit / El rancho / Any three days / Secrets / Our war on cool (pt.2) / When cats fight – Let loose on me / De-effect – Diminished.

Tanya DONELLY (see under ⇒ BELLY)

DONNAS

Formed: Palo Alta, California, USA ... 1996 initially as speed-metal outfit ELECTROCUTE by eighth graders, DONNA A (aka BRETT), DONNA R (aka ALLISON), DONNA F (aka MAYA) and DONNA C (aka TORRY). Retreading the blitzkrieg bop pioneered by the RAMONES twenty years earlier, the four DONNAS came on like a latter day RUNAWAYS minus the pop glamour. Unrelenting punk-rock with a capital P, the girls' eponymous debut album (written and produced by their svengali, DARRIN RAFFAELLI) surfaced on the tiny 'Superteem' imprint in '97, a frantic document of teen rebellion revelling in the usual US high school cliches. Subsequently becoming part of the 'Lookout' stable (which launched GREEN DAY and others), The DONNAS toured the States and Japan promoting a follow-up set, 'AMERICAN TEENAGE ROCK'N'ROLL' (1998). Now writing themselves, the DONNAS delivered their third set, 'GET SKINTIGHT', the following year. The girls came of age with 'DONNAS TURN 21' (2001) although musically and lyrically they were still fumbling around behind the proverbial bike shed looking for cheap thrills. If they could only translate the sexual ambition of '40 BOYS IN 40 NIGHTS' into some form of musical ambition then they wouldn't have to rely on a Judas Priest cover ('LIVING AFTER MIDNIGHT') to bolster their now cliche'd sound. For 'SPEND THE NIGHT' (released late 2002), The DONNAS welded their metallic rock with basic punk rock, like a modern day AC/DC fronted by JOAN JETT. • **Covered:** DRIVE IN (Beach Boys) / DA DOO RON RON (Crystals) / WIG WAM BAM (Sweet) / SCHOOL'S OUT (Alice Cooper).

Album rating: THE DONNAS (*5) / AMERICAN TEENAGE ROCK'N'ROLL MACHINE (*6) / TURN 21 (*7) / SPEND THE NIGHT (*7)

DONNA A. (b. BRETT ANDERSON) – vocals / **DONNA R.** (b. ALLISON ROBERTSON) – guitar / **DONNA F.** (b. MAYA FORD, 8 Jan'79) – bass / **DONNA C.** (b. TORRY CANSTELLANO, 8 Jan'79) – drums

			not iss.	Superteem
1997.	(lp) **THE DONNAS**		-	☐

– Hey, I'm gonna be your girl / Let's go Mano! / Teenage runaway / Lana and Stevie / I'm gonna make him mine (tonight) / Huff all night / I don't wanna go / We don't go / Friday fun / Everybody's smoking cheeba / Get rid of that girl / Drive in / Do you wanna go out with me / Rock'n'roll boy / High school yum yum / A boy like you / Let's rab. <*cd-iss. Aug98 on 'Lookout'+= singles tracks; LK 201CD*> – Let's go Mano! / Last chance dance / I wanna be a unabomber / Da doo ron ron / I don't wanna go to school / I wanna rock'n'roll tonight.

			Lookout	Lookout
Jan 98.	(7") <*(LK 196)*>	**ROCK'N'ROLL MACHINE. / SPEEDIN' BACK TO MY BABY**	☐	☐
Feb 98.	(cd/lp) <*(LK 191 CD/LP)*>	**AMERICAN TEENAGE ROCK'N'ROLL MACHINE**	☐	Jan98

– Rock'n'roll machine / You make me hot / Checkin' it out / Gimmie my radio / Outta my mind / Looking for blood / Leather on leather / Wanna get some stuff / Speed demon / Shake in the action.

Feb 99.	(7") <*(LK 214)*> **split w/ TOILET BOYS**	☐	☐
Jun 99.	(cd/lp) <*(LK 225 CD/LP)*> **GET SKINTIGHT**	☐	May99

– Skintight / Hyperactive / You don't wanna call / Hook it up / Doin' donuts / Searchin' the streets / Party action / I didn't like you anyway / Get outta my room / Well done / Get U alone / Hot boxin' / Too fast for love / Zero.

			Epitaph	Epitaph
Jan 01.	(cd) <*(6611-2)*>	**TURN 21**	☐	☐

– Are you gonna move it for me? / Do you wanna it? / 40 boys in 40 nights / Play my game / Midnite snack / Drivin' thru' my heart / You've got a crush on me / Little boy / Don't get me busted / Police blitz / Hot pants / Gimme a ride / Livin' after midnight / Nothing to do.

			Lookout	Atlantic
Apr 01.	(cd-s) <*1045-7/-2*>	**40 BOYS IN 40 NIGHTS. / WIG WAM BAM / SCHOOL'S OUT**	☐	-
Oct 02.	(cd/lp) (*LK 288 CD/LP*) <*83567*>	**SPEND THE NIGHT**	☐	☐

– It's on the rocks / Take it off / Who invited you / All messed up / Dirty denim / You wanna get me high / I don't care (so there) / Pass it around / Too bad about your girl / Not the one / Please don't tease / Take me to the backseat / 5 o'clock in the morning. (*cd+=*) – (interviews, the making of & a video).

DONOVAN

Born: DONOVAN PHILIP LEITCH, 10 May'46, Maryhill, Glasgow, Scotland. At the age of 10, his family moved to Hatfield, England. In 1964, while playing small gigs in Southend, he was spotted by Geoff Stephens and Peter Eden, who became his managers. Later that year, after performing on the 'Ready Steady Go!' pop show over three consecutive weeks, the denim-clad beatnik signed to 'Pye'. His debut single, 'CATCH THE WIND' (issued the same time as DYLAN's 'The Times They Are A-Changin'), saw him break into the Top 5, later reaching Top 30 in America where he was enjoying the fruits of a burgeoning career. His follow-up, 'COLOURS', also made the Top 5 in the summer of '65, as did the debut album, 'WHAT'S BIN DID AND WHAT'S BIN HID'. Later in the year, the 'UNIVERSAL SOLDIER' EP saw DONOVAN begin to develop his uncompromising anti-war stance, a theme which he touched on with his second album, 'FAIRYTALE'. Initially heralded as Britain's answer to BOB DYLAN, he began to build on his folk/pop roots, progressing into flower-power with 'SUNSHINE SUPERMAN' in 1966. The album of the same name (issued only in the States) saw DONOVAN hit a creative high point and included the much revered, 'SEASON OF THE WITCH'. At the beginning of '67, the single 'MELLOW YELLOW' was riding high in the American hit parade, and 'EPISTLE TO DIPPY' soon followed suit. In the meantime, 'MELLOW YELLOW', was given a belated UK release (making Top 10), while its similarly titled parent album (again only issued in the US), hit No.14. 'SUNSHINE SUPERMAN', a UK compilation lp of both aforementioned albums, made the Top 30 in the middle of '67. His label, 'Pye', followed the same marketing strategy with his next UK album, the double 'A GIFT FROM A FLOWER TO A GARDEN', which was in actual fact, two US-only lp's in one. During this highly prolific period, which saw him inspired by the transcendental meditation of guru Maharishi Mahesh Yogi, he released two sublime pieces of acid-pop in 'THERE IS A MOUNTAIN' and 'JENNIFER JUNIPER'. The momentum continued with, 'HURDY GURDY MAN', another classic sojourn into psychedelia which hit Top 5 on both sides of the Atlantic.

Album rating: WHAT'S BIN DID AND WHAT'S BIN HID (*7) / CATCH THE WIND (*6) / FAIRYTALE (*7) / SUNSHINE SUPERMAN (US version; *7) / MELLOW YELLOW (*6) / A GIFT FROM A FLOWER TO A GARDEN (*7; WEAR YOUR LOVE LIKE HEAVEN; *5 – FOR LITTLE ONES; *4) / DONOVAN IN CONCERT (*4) / HURDY GURDY MAN (*6) / DONOVAN'S GREATEST HITS compilation (*7)

DONOVAN – vocals, acoustic guitar, harmonica with **BRIAN LOCKING** – bass / **SKIP ALLEN** – drums / **GYPSY DAVE** (b. DAVID MILLS) – kazoo, etc.

			Pye	Hickory
Mar 65.	(7") (7N 15801) <1309>	CATCH THE WIND. / WHY DO YOU TREAT ME LIKE YOU DO	4	23 Apr65
May 65.	(7") (7N 15866) <1324>	COLOURS. / TO SING FOR YOU	4	61 Jun65
May 65.	(lp) (NPL 18117) <123>	WHAT'S BIN DID AND WHAT'S BIN HID <US title 'CATCH THE WIND'>	3	30

– Josie / Catch the wind / Remember the Alamo / Cuttin' out / Car car * (riding in my car) / Keep on truckin' / Goldwatch blues / To sing for you / You're gonna need somebody on your bond / Tangerine puppet / Donna Donna * / Ramblin' boy *(re-iss. Jul68 on 'Marble Arch';)* – (omitted *)

Sep 65.	(7") <1338>	UNIVERSAL SOLDIER. / DO YOU HEAR ME	–	53
Sep 65.	(7"ep) (NEP 24219)	THE UNIVERSAL SOLDIER EP	13	–

– Universal soldier / The ballad of a crystal man / Do you hear me now* / The war drags on.

Oct 65.	(lp) (NPL 18128)	FAIRYTALE	20	85 Dec 65

– Colours * / To try for the sun / Sunny Goodge street / Oh deed I do / Circus of sour / The summer day reflection song / Candy man / Jersey Thursday / Belated forgiveness plea / Ballad of a crystal man / Little tin soldier * / Ballad of Geraldine. *(re-iss. Mar69 on 'Marble Arch';)* – (omitted *). *(re-iss. Feb91 on 'Castle' cd/c; CLA CD/MC 226)*

Nov 65.	(7") (7N 15984)	TURQUOISE. / HEY GYP (DIG THE SLOWNESS)	30	–
Nov 65.	(7") <1375>	YOU'RE GONNA NEED SOMEBODY ON YOUR BOND. / THE LITTLE TIN SOLDIER	–	–
Jan 66.	(7") <1402>	TO TRY FOR THE SUN. / TURQUOISE	–	–
Feb 66.	(7") (7N 17067)	JOSIE. / LITTLE TIN SOLDIER	–	–
Apr 66.	(7") (7N 17088)	REMEMBER THE ALAMO. / THE BALLAD OF A CRYSTAL MAN	–	–

DONOVAN plus **JOHN CAMERON** – piano, harpsicord / **HAROLD McNAIR** – flute

			Pye	Epic
Jul 66.	(7") (7N 17241) <10045>	SUNSHINE SUPERMAN. / THE TRIP	2	1 Jun66
Sep 66.	(lp; mono<stereo>) <LN 24217><BN 26217>	SUNSHINE SUPERMAN	–	11

– Sunshine Superman / Legend of a girl child Linda / The observation / Guinevere / Celeste / Writer in the Sun / Season of the witch / Hampstead incident / Sand and foam / Young girl blues / Three kingfishers / Bert's blues. *(UK-iss.Feb91 on 'Beat Goes On' cd/c; BGO CD/MC 68)* *(cd re-iss. Oct96 on 'EMI Gold'; CDGOLD 1066)*

Nov 66.	(7") <10098>	MELLOW YELLOW. / SUNNY SOUTH KENSINGTON	–	2
Jan 67.	(7") <10127>	EPISTLE TO DIPPY. / PREACHIN' LOVE	–	19
Feb 67.	(7") (7N 17267)	MELLOW YELLOW. / PREACHIN' LOVE	8	–
Feb 67.	(lp; mono<stereo>) <LN 24239><BN 26239>	MELLOW YELLOW	–	14

– Mellow yellow / Writer in the Sun / Sand and foam / The observation / Bleak city woman / House of Jansch / Young girl blues / Museum / Hampstead incident / Sunny South Kensington. *(cd-iss. Oct93 on 'Sony Europe';)*

Jun 67.	(lp) (NPL 18181)	SUNSHINE SUPERMAN -(compilation of last 2 US albums)	25	–
Oct 67.	(7") (7N 17403) <10212>	THERE IS A MOUNTAIN. / SAND AND FOAM	8	11 Sep67

DONOVAN retained **HAROLD** and in came **TONY CARR** – percussion / **CANDY JOHN CARR** – bongos **CLIFF BARTON** – bass / **KEITH WEBB** – drums / **MIKE O'NEIL** – keyboards / **MIKE CARR** – vibraphone / **ERIC LEESE** – electric guitar

Dec 67.	(7") <10253>	WEAR YOUR LOVE LIKE HEAVEN. / OH GOSH	–	23
Dec 67.	(lp; mono)<stereo> <LN 24349><BN 26349>	WEAR YOUR LOVE LIKE HEAVEN	–	60

– Wear your love like Heaven / Mad John's escape / Skip-a-long Sam / Sun / There was a time / Oh gosh / Little boy in corduroy / Under the greenwood tree / The land of doesn't have to be / Someone's singing / Song of the naturalist's wife / The enchanted gypsy.

KEN BALDOCK – bass repl. BARTON, LEESE, WEBB, O'NEIL + MIKE CARR

Dec 67.	(lp; mono<stereo>) <LN 24350><BN 26350>	FOR LITTLE ONES	–	

– Voyage into the golden screen / Isle of Islay / The mandolin man and his secret / Lay of the last tinker / The tinker and the crab / Widow with shawl (a portrait) / The lullaby of spring / The magpie / Starfish-on-the-toast / Epistle to Derroll.

Feb 68.	(7") (7N 17457) <10300>	JENNIFER JUNIPER. / POOR COW	5	26
Apr 68.	(d-lp-box; mono/stereo) (NPL/NSPL 20000) <L2N6/B2N 171>	A GIFT FROM A FLOWER TO A GARDEN	13	19

– (contains 2 US Dec67 albums boxed) *(cd-iss. Jul93 & Jun97 on 'Beat Goes On'; BGOCD 194)*

May 68.	(7") (7N 17537) <10345>	HURDY GURDY MAN. / TEEN ANGEL	4	5
Sep 68.	(lp; mono/stereo) (NPL/NSPL 18237) <BN 26420>	DONOVAN IN CONCERT (live)		18 Jul68

– Isle of Islay / Young girl blues / There is a mountain / Poor cow / Celeste / The fat angel / Guinevere / Widow with shawl (a portrait) / Preachin' love / The lullaby of Spring / Writer in the Sun / Rules and regulations / Pebble and the man / Mellow yellow. *(re-iss. May91 & Apr97 on 'Beat Goes On' cd/c/lp; BGO CD/MC/LP 90)* *(cd-iss. Nov94 on 'Start';)* *(re-iss. cd Jan96 on 'Happy Price'; HP 93432)*

Oct 68.	(7") <10393>	LALENA. / AYE, MY LOVE	–	33
Oct 68.	(lp) <BN 26420>	HURDY GURDY MAN	–	20

– Jennifer Juniper / Hurdy gurdy man / Hi, it's been a long time / Peregrine / The entertaining of a shy girl / Tangier / As I recall it / Get thy bearings / West Indian lady / Teas / The river song / The Sun is a very magic fellow / A sunny day.

Nov 68.	(7") (7N 17660)	ATLANTIS. / I LOVE MY SHIRT	23	–
Feb 69.	(7") <10434>	ATLANTIS. / TO SUSAN ON THE WEST COAST WAITING	–	7
				35
Mar 69.	(lp) (NPL/NSPL 18283) <BXN 26439>	DONOVAN'S GREATEST HITS (compilation)		4

– Epistle to Dippy / Sunshine Superman / There is a mountain / Jennifer Juniper / Wear your love like Heaven / Season of the witch / Mellow yellow / Colours / Hurdy gurdy man / Catch the wind / Lalena. *<re-iss. 1972; PE 26439> <re-iss. 1973; BN 26836> (re-iss. Sep79 on 'CBS-Embassy' lp/c; CBS/40 31759) (cd-iss. Aug90 on 'Epic';)*

DOVES

Formed: Manchester, England . . . 1998 out of dance/rave outfit, SUB SUB, by JIMI GOODWIN, along with brothers JEZ and ANDY WILLIAMS. After the hectic turbulence of the house scene in the late 80's/early 90's, SUB SUB protagonist GOODWIN rocketed straight into the number 5 spot with 'AIN'T NO USE (AIN'T NO LOVE)', which predictably ruined any future respect given to the man. A shambolic, rushed released debut album, 'FULL FATHOM FIVE' (1993), sent GOODWIN into hiding for four years (during which he cropped up on various material by TRICKY and BERNARD SUMNER). In 1998, a new direction forced out the 'CEDAR' EP, which The DOVES issued on their own 'Casino' label. Sounding similar to OASIS and heavy rivals SHACK, frontman GOODWIN did his best to capture the essence and mad-for-it-ness that he'd experienced during the early 1990's. However, the music lacked interest, and, although long drawn and enterprising at times, the tired trio sounded as magnificent as RADIOHEAD without any transmitter. With two further singles under their belt, 'Heavenly' records ('Astralwerks' in the US) gave The DOVES a lucrative signing-on deal, the single 'THE CEDAR ROOM' and its parent debut album, 'LOST SOULS', both making healthy chart positions in spring 2000. The feted DOVES were now darlings of Britain's emotional indie scene, ranking alongside major players such as COLDPLAY, STARSAILOR and troubadour DAVID GRAY. However, come the release of their sophomore album 'THE LAST BROADCAST' (2002), the bearded troupe of musing musicians had formally eclipsed any of the above in terms of musical and lyrical integrity. Taking its name from the 1998 "mocumentary", which was said to have inspired 'The Blair Witch Project', '...BROADCAST' generated emotional intensity from its dreamlike artwork to GOODWIN's vocals. The single, 'THERE GOES THE FEAR', used child-like guitar melodies and striking orchestral accompaniment courtesy of SEAN O'HAGAN (The HIGH LLAMAS), not to mention a tripped-out video to boot. Where most bands fall flat on their face come album Number deux, the DOVES had simply evolved into something splendid and sublime – well, like a pristine dove, walking amongst a flock of dirty pigeons that currently litter Britain's indie scene. • **Note:** Not to be confused with an early 90's DOVES who issued one album, 'Affinity', in 1991.

Album rating: LOST SOULS (*6) / Sub Sub: FULL FATHOM FIVE (*5)

SUB SUB

JIMI GOODWIN – vocals, guitar / **JEZ WILLIAMS** – vocals, guitar / **ANDY WILLIAMS** – vocals, drums

		Rob's	not iss.
Jun 92.	(12"ep) *(12ROB 7)* **COAST EP**		-
	– Coast / Inside of this / Inside out / Past.		
Mar 93.	(7"/c-s; as SUB SUB featuring MELANIE WILLIAMS) *(7/C ROB 9)* **AIN'T NO LOVE (AIN'T NO USE. / (parkside mix)**	3	-
	(12"+=/cd-s+=) *(12/CD ROB 9)* – ('A'mixes; piano / on the house).		
Feb 94.	(7"/c-s) *(7/C ROB 19)* **RESPECT. / (original)**	49	-
	(12"+=/cd-s+=) *(12/CD ROB 19)* – ('A'-DaSilva – McCreedy + acid) / ('A'-primetime).		
Aug 94.	(c-s) *(CROB 29)* **ANGEL / SOUTHERN TREES (instrumental)**		-
	(12"+=/cd-s+=) *(12/CD ROB 29)* – ('A'-Deep love + Primetime).		
	(12") *(12ROB 29X)* – ('A'mixes).		
Sep 94.	(cd/c/lp) *(CD/C/LP ROB 30)* **FULL FATHOM FIVE**		-
	– Coast / Angel / Valium jazz / Southern trees / Inside of this / Ain't no love (ain't no use) / Flute / Swamp / Respect / Past.		
Jan 95.	(12"/cd-s) *(12/CD ROB 39)* **SOUTHERN TREES (7" + 12" mixes). / JAGGERNATH / NORTHERN TREES**		-

— wisely decided to take some time out

DOVES

— same line-up

		Casino	not iss.
Nov 98.	(10"ep) *(CHIP 001)* **CEDAR EP**		-
	– The cedar room / Rise / Zither.		
—	the track, 'GUTTER GIRL', featured on the V/A Manchester compilation EP, 'Everyone Knows Everyone Else' alongside JANE WEAVER and ANDY VOTEL		
May 99.	(cd-ep) *(CHIP 002CD)* **SEA EP**		-
	– Sea song / Breakmegently (incidently) / Darker.		
Aug 99.	(10"/cd-s) *(CHIP 003/+CD)* **HERE IT COMES. / MMET ME AT THE PIER / ACOUSTIC NO.1**	73	

		Heavenly	Astralwerks
Mar 00.	(10"/cd-s) *(HVN 95 10/CD)* **THE CEDAR ROOM. / ZITHER / KAREN**	33	-
Apr 00.	(d-lp/cd) *(HVNLP 26/+CD)* *<ASW 50248 LP/CD>* **LOST SOULS**	16	Oct00
	– Firesuite / Here it comes / Break me gently / Sea song / Rise / Lost souls / Melody calls / Catch the sun / The man who told everything / The cedar room / Reprise / A house.		
May 00.	(10"/cd-s) *(HVN 96 10/CDS)* **CATCH THE SUN. / VALLEY / DOWN TO SEA**	32	-
	(cd-s) *(HVN 96CD)* – ('A'side) / Crunch / Lost in watts.		
Oct 00.	(7") *(HVN 98)* **THE MAN WHO TOLD EVERYTHING. / YOUR SHADOW LAY ACROSS MY LIFE**	32	-
	(c-s+=/cd-s+=) *(HVN 98 CS/CD)* – Firesuite.		
	(cd-s) *(HVN 98CDS)* – ('A'side) / Rise (live) / Suitnoise.		

		Heavenly	Capitol
Apr 02.	(10") *(HVN 111-10)* **THERE GOES THE FEAR. / HIT THE GROUND RUNNING**	3	-
	(cd-s) *(HVN 111CD)* – ('A'side) / ('A'-video).		
Apr 02.	(d-lp/cd) *(HVNLP 35/+CD)* *<12232>* **THE LAST BROADCAST**	1	83
	– Intro / Words / There goes the fear / M62 song / Where we're calling from / N.Y. / Satellites / Friday's dust / Pounding / The last broadcast / The sulphur man / Caught by the river.		
Jul 02.	(10") *(HVN 116-10)* **POUNDING. / SATELLITES (Soulsavers remix) / M62 SONG (Four Tet remix)**	21	-
	(cd-s) *(HVN 116CD)* – ('A'side) / Far from grace / Northenden / ('A'-video).		
Oct 02.	(10") *(HVN 126-10)* **CAUGHT BY THE RIVER. / SULPHUR MAN (Rebelski remix) / WHERE WE'RE CALLING FROM (Hebden Bridge remix)**	29	-
	(cd-s) *(HVN 126CD)* – ('A'side) / Hit the ground running / Willow's song / ('A'-video).		

DRAGS

Formed: Albuquerque, New Mexico, USA ... mid-90's by CJ PRETZEL and LORCA SHALOM. The pair had both done musical time together in SWIZZLE STICKS, but left to form their punk revival trio, The DRAGS. After some raucous gigs in the early 90's, the threesome debuted with 7", 'I LIKE TO DIE', and followed this up with the singles, 'ANXIETY' and 'WELL WORTH TALKING ABOUT'. By the mid-90's, they had caught the ear of the 'Estrus' label, who put out their initial EP, 'DRAGSPLOITATION ... NOW!', which heralded this MC5-meets-NEW YORK DOLLS outfit to the greater record buying public. This was followed up two years later with the release of their premier LP, 'STOP ROCK AND ROLL', which although highly derivative, was still an enjoyable and vital listen especially with a running time of just less than twenty minutes. A year on and KEITH decided to hang up his sticks, which prompted the label 'eMpTy' to release the compilation album '45 X 3' (1999), which bunched together earlier singles and rarities. • **Covered:** ROSALYN (Pretty Things) / SLICK'S LIVIN IT UP AT THE BOTTOM OF THE SEA (Peechees) / SIX AND CHANGE (Pagans) / DON'T NEED YOU ANYMORE (Rumblers) / BABY YOU'RE SO REPULSIVE (Crime) / NIGHT RIDER (Kim Fowley) / COMMUNICATION BREAKDOWN (Led Zeppelin).

Album rating: DRAGSPLOITATION ... NOW! mini (*5) / STOP ROCK & ROLL (*5) / 45 x 3 compilation (*6) / SET RIGHT FIT TO BLOW CLEAN UP mini (*5)

CJ PRETZEL – vocals, guitar / **LORCA SHALOM** – bass / **KEITH** – drums

		not iss.	Resin
1995.	(7"m) *<RO 13>* **I LIKE TO DIE. / MINDBENDER / SEVEN DOLLAR BOLONGA**	-	

		not iss.	Rat City
1995.	(7") *<RC 9>* **WELL WORTH TALKING ABOUT. / ROSALYN**	-	

		not iss.	eMpTy
1995.	(7"m) *<MTR 309>* **ANXIETY. / FLYING SAUCER ROCK'N'ROLL / ELONGATED MAN**	-	

		Estrus	Estrus
Nov 95.	(m-cd/10"m-lp) *<ES 110 CD/LP>* **DRAGSPLOITATION ... NOW!**		Oct95
	– Dragsploitation now / Can't change my style / Teenage invasion / Don't need you anymore / Mr. Undertaker / Allergic reaction / 10th man theme / My girlfriend's in the F.B.I.		
1996.	(7") *<LOUD 15>* **CONSPIRACY. / THAT GIRL IS COMING AROUND**	-	
	(above issued on 'One Louder', below on 'G.I. Productions')		
1996.	(7") *<G.I. 007-7>* **RADIO DISAPPEARS**	-	
	– Slick's livin it up at the bottom of the sea / (other by PEECHEES).		
Apr 97.	(lp/cd) *<ES 1239>* **STOP ROCK & ROLL**		Jul97
	– Bacon striptease / Who's got the electricity / Explosives / Iron curtain rock / Tastes like poison / Anti-satisfaction / Private eye / Leopard skin / Not so good luck charm / Conspiracy / Cannible / Siento muy bien.		
1997.	(7"ep) *<087 – issue #36>* **PRESENTS ... (live at the Fireside Bowl, Chicago, Illinois, USA, 5/3/97)**	-	
	– Allergic reaction / Feel real good / I like to die / Iron curtain rock / Yeah, yeah, yeah, yeah, yeah / My girlfriend's in the FBI.		
	(above "VM Live" fanzine freebie issued 'V.M.L.', below on 'eMpTy')		
Jun 99.	(7") *<MTR 370>* **I KILLED ROCK AND ROLL (YO MATO ROCK Y ROLL). / BLACKLIGHT (LA LUZ DE NEGRA)**	-	
Nov 99.	(7") *<(KRS 331)>* **BOMBSHELTER. / NEW YORK, CALIFORNIA, WHEREVER**		
	(above issued on 'Kill Rock Stars')		
Jan 00.	(cd/cd) *<(ES 1263/+CD)>* **SET RIGHT FIT TO BLOW CLEAN UP**		
	– This is the sound of hard rock / Dirty little bird / The kick fighter / Night rider / Modern man / Jet lag / Amplifier blues / No matter what shape (your head is in) / FM shades / Black light / Communication breakdown / Drags gotta have it.		

– compilations, etc. –

Sep 99.	(lp/cd) *eMpTy;* *<(MTR 379/+CD)>* **45 x 3**		Aug99
	– Six and change / Slicks livin' it up at / Shovel fight / Conspiracy / That girl is coming around / Baby you're so repulsive / Well worth talking about / Rosalyn / I like to die / Mind bender / Seven dollar balogna / Allegro reaction / Feel real good / I like to die / Iron curtain rock / Yeah, yeah, yeah / My girlfriend's in the FBI / Tarantula / Treat me right / Anxiety / Flying saucer RnR / Elongated man.		

DRAIN
(see under ⇒ BUTTHOLE SURFERS; 80's section)

Nick DRAKE

Born: 19 Jun'48, Burma. He moved to Britain in the mid 50's, first to Tamworth-in-Ardon then Stratford. Already a budding singer-songwriter by the time he reached Cambridge University, he was discovered playing a gig by ASHLEY HUTCHINGS of Fairport Convention, who, in turn, introduced him to Witchseason Productions head JOE BOYD. Bowled over by his talent, BOYD helped him sign to 'Island', who released debut album 'FIVE LEAVES LEFT' in '69. The album highlighted his precocious talent and painful sensitivity, the music possessing a remarkable maturity not in keeping with DRAKE's young years. The melancholic resonance of DRAKE's voice and his crystalline guitar playing were complemented by delicate string arrangements, the effect one of understated intensity. After moving to London, DRAKE recorded the classic 'BRYTER LAYTER' in 1970 with BOYD again producing a cast of musicians that included RICHARD THOMPSON and JOHN CALE. The album boasted a jazzier flavour which saw DRAKE in a slightly more positive frame of mind. Ironically, like its predecessor, the album failed to sell in any great quantity. Due to his crippling shyness, DRAKE found live work too difficult, passing up the opportunity to promote his music. He fell into a deep depression, no doubt frustrated at his lack of success and inability to do something about it. After a spell in Europe he returned to record his tortured masterpiece, 'PINK MOON'. Recorded in just two nights, its spare, haunting songs were cloaked in regret and disillusionment. The bleak tone only let up occasionally as DRAKE attemted to exorcise his demons over a skeletal acoustic backing. Once again, the album was a commercial failure and DRAKE's mood blackened further, although he did begin work on a new album in 1973. He spent time in France with singer/friend FRANCOISE HARDY and his bouts of depression diminished when he decided to live there permanently. However, this didn't last long and he sadly overdosed on anti-depressants on 25th November 1974, a tragic end to a troubled but brilliant career. A questionable coroner's verdict was "Death By Suicide". The subsequent interest in DRAKE's work led to various compilations being released, including the excellent 'FRUIT TREE' boxed set. His music entrances more listeners with each passing year, a belated recognition that recently saw him grace the cover of 'Mojo' magazine. • **Trivia:** His sister Gabrielle was a TV actress in the 70's/80's 'Crossroads' soap.

Album rating: FIVE LEAVES LEFT (*8) / BRYTER LAYTER (*9) / PINK MOON (*9) / HEAVEN IN A WILD FLOWER posthumous (*7) / FRUIT TREE – THE COMPLETE RECORDED WORKS collection (*9) / TIME OF NO REPLY (*7) / WAY TO BLUE – AN INTRODUCTION TO NICK DRAKE compilation (*9)

NICK DRAKE – vocals, guitar, piano with **RICHARD THOMPSON** – guitar / **DANNY THOMPSON** – double bass / **PAUL HARRIS** – keyboards / **CLAIRE LOWTHER** and **ROCKY DZIDZORNU**, plus 15-piece orchestra.

		Island	Antilles
Sep 69.	(lp) *(ILPS 9105)* <*AN 7010*> **FIVE LEAVES LEFT**		

– Time has told me / River man / Three hours / Day is done / Way to blue / Cello song / The thoughts of Mary Jane / Man in a shed / Fruit tree / Saturday sun. *(cd-iss. Feb87; CID 9195)* *(re-iss. cd May89 & Jun00; IMCD 8)* *(lp re-iss. Jan00 on 'Simply Vinyl'; SVLP 163)*

— retained **RICHARD** bringing in other (FAIRPORT CONVENTION members: **DAVE PEGG** – drums / **DAVE MATTACKS** – bass. Also sessioned **PAUL HARRIS, RAY WARLEIGH, CHRIS McGREGOR**.

Nov 70. (lp) *(ILPS 9134)* <*7028*> **BRYTER LAYTER**
– Introduction / Hazey Jane II / At the chime of a city clock / One of these things first / Hazey Jane I / Bryter layter / Fly / Poor boy / Northern sky / Sunday. *(cd-iss. May87; CID 9134)* *(re-iss. cd Oct89 & Jun00; IMCD 71)* *(lp re-iss. Jun99 on 'Simply Vinyl'; SVLP 94)*

NICK DRAKE – vocals, guitar (totally solo)

Feb 72. (lp) *(ILPS 9184)* **PINK MOON**
– Pink moon / Place to be / Road / Which will / Horn / Things behind the sun / Know / Parasite / Ride / Harvest breed / From the morning / Voice from the mountain / Rider on the wheel / Black eyed dog / Hanging on a star. *(cd-iss. Apr90 & Jun00; IMCD 94)* *(lp re-iss. Feb00 on 'Simply Vinyl'; SVLP 172)*

— NICK had put down some tracks for new album, when on 25th Nov'74, he overdosed on medication/drugs.

– compilations, others, etc. –

1972.	(lp) Island; <9307> **NICK DRAKE** (69-70 material)
Apr 79.	(3xlp-box) Island; (NDSP 100) **FRUIT TREE – THE COMPLETE RECORDED WORKS** – (contains all 3 albums)

May 85. (lp/c) Island; (ILPS 9826) **HEAVEN IN A WILD FLOWER**
– Fruit tree / Cello song / Thoughts of Mary Jane / Northern sky / River man / At the chime of a city clock / Introduction / Hazey Jane I / Hazey Jane II / Pink moon / Road / Which will / Things behind the sun / Time has told me. *(cd-iss. Apr90; IMCD 91)*

Aug 86. (4xlp-box) *Hannibal / Rykodisc; (HNBX 5302)* **FRUIT TREE**
– (all 3 lp's, plus 1987 album) *(4xcd-box-iss.Dec91; HNCD 5402)(+=)* – TIME OF NO REPLY / Fruit tree / Fly / Man in a shed / Thoughts of Mary Jane.

Mar 87. (lp/cd) *Hannibal / Rykodisc; (<HNBL/HNCD 1318>)* **TIME OF NO REPLY**
– Time of no reply / I was made to love magic / Joey / Clothes of sand / Man in a shed / Mayfair / Fly / The thoughts of Mary Jane / Been smoking too long / Strange meeting II / Rider on the wheel / Black eyed dog / Hanging on a star / Voice from the mountain.

Jun 94. (cd)(c/lp) Island; (IMCD 196)(ICM/ILPM 2082) <1386> **WAY TO BLUE – AN INTRODUCTION TO NICK DRAKE**
– Cello song / Hazey Jane I / Way to blue / Things behind the sun / River man / Poor boy / Time of no reply / From the morning / One of these things first / Northern sky / Which will / Hazey Jane II / Time has told me / Pink moon / Black eyed dog / Fruit tree.

Nov 99. (cd-ep) *Sonic Book; <SB 20>* **THE SWEET SUGGESTIONS OF THE PINK MOON**
– When day is done / Saturday sun / Way to blue / Time has told me.

Jun 00. (lp) *Anthology; <ANT 1521>* **TAMWORTH IN ARDEN**

DRESSY BESSY

Formed: Denver, Colorado, USA . . . 1996 by TAMMY EALOM, who had instigated various small local bands and even spent time in The MINDERS and SISSY FUZZ. Alongside DARREN ALBERT and ROB GREENE, DRESSY BESSY debuted in 1997 with the 7" 'ULTRA VIVID COLOR', unleashing on the world their revisionary musing on classic 60's pop mixing with a good dose of 90's lo-fi sensibilities, akin to the 'Elephant 6' coterie of artists. The following year saw the issue of their first EP, 'YOU STAND HERE', which was sonically bolstered by the presence of EALOM's boyfriend, JOHN HILL (of APPLES IN STEREO). HILL contributed further to DB's sound producing their initial album, 'PINK HEARTS YELLOW MOONS' the following year. A fine debut set of lovely guitar pop melodies, although kept from straying down the path of twee by just the right pinch of grrrl riot sensibilities from EALOM. Succeeding this issue was another piece of pleasant pop tunery in the shape of stop-gap EP 'CALIFORNIA' (2000), aptly-titled for its summery BEACH BOYS-stylings and similar subject matter, but again their temporal distance and indie affectations kept this from being all too derivative. Their sophomore album, 'SOUND GO ROUND' (2002) did not wander too far from DRESSY BESSY's established formula, providing another piece of well-written and intentionally naive sounding pop.

Album rating: PINK HEARTS YELLOW MOONS (*6) / SOUND GO ROUND (*5)

TAMMY EALOM – vocals, guitar, keyboards (ex-40th DAY, ex-MINDERS, ex-SISSY FUZZ) / **ROB GREENE** – bass / **DARREN ALBERT** – drums, percussion

		not iss.	Little Dipper
Jul 97.	(7"m) <*001*> **ULTRA VIVID COLOR. / FUZZY / SAID YOU WOULD**	–	

— added **JOHN HILL** – guitar, melodia (of APPLES IN STEREO)

		not iss.	unknown
1998.	(7"ep) **YOU STAND HERE EP**	–	
		Kindercore	Kindercore
Nov 98.	(cd/lp) <*(KC 23 CD/LP)*> **PINK HEARTS YELLOW MOONS**		Sep99

– I found out / Just like Henry / Lookaround / Little TV / Jenny come on / If you should try to kiss her / Extra-ordinary / Makeup / Big vacation / You stand here / My Maryanne. *(UK cd-iss. Sep01 on 'Track & Field'; HEAT 03)*

Mar 01. (cd-ep) <*(KC 60CD)*> **THE CALIFORNIA EP**   Nov00
– California / Some better days / Super everything / Hangout wonderful / In the morning.

Feb 02. (7") *(LANE 11)* **split w/ SALOON**
(above on 'Track & Field')

Feb 02. (cd/lp) <*(KC 69 CD/LP)*> **SOUND GO ROUND**
– I saw cinnamon / Tag / There's a girl / Just being me / That's why / Oh mi amour / Buttercups / Maybe laughter / Big to do / All these colors / Flower jargon / Fare thee well / Carry-on. *(re-iss. Apr02 on 'Track & Field' cd/lp; HEAT 07/+LP)*

DRIBBLING DARTS OF LOVE
(see under ⇒ SNEAKY FEELINGS; 80's section)

DRIFT
(see under ⇒ EYELESS IN GAZA; 80's section)

DRIVE LIKE JEHU
(see under ⇒ ROCKET FROM THE CRYPT)

DROP NINETEENS

Formed: Boston, Massachusetts, USA . . . 1991 by former classmates GREG ACKELL and CHRIS ROOF, who subsequently added STEVE ZIMMERMAN, MOTOHIRO YASUE and PAULA KELLEY. Securing a UK deal via 'Virgin'-offshoot, 'Hut', DROP NINETEENS debuted in 1992 with the tongue-in-cheek 'WINONA' single. The attendant album, 'DELAWARE' (1992), followed in the grand tradition of schizophrenic Bostonian alternative guitar acts, sugary harmonies (courtesy of PAULA), a smattering of MY BLOODY VALENTINE-style noise and SONIC YOUTH/PIXIES guitar mangling thrown in for good measure. The record also included a cover of Madonna's 'ANGEL' alongside their own 'MY AQUARIUM' – the accompanying 'YOUR AQUARIUM' EP carried an appalling version of 'MANDY' (yes, once sung by Mr. MANILOW himself!). Well timed as they were to fit in with the prevailing grunge craze, the band nevertheless struggled to make significant headway in the UK market. Dramatic personnel changes (only ACKELL and ZIMMERMAN remained, the others being replaced by JUSTIN CROSBY, MEGAN GILBERT and PETE KOSPLIN) preceded the follow-up album, 'NATIONAL COMA' (1993), which fell on similarly deaf ears despite some positive critical noises.

Album rating: DELAWARE (*6) / NATIONAL COMA (*6)

GREG ACKELL – vocals, guitar / **MOTOHIRO YASUE** – guitar / **PAULA KELLEY** – vocals, guitar / **STEVE ZIMMERMAN** – bass, vocals / **CHRIS ROOF** – drums

		Hut	Caroline
Jul 92.	(12") *(HUT 019T)* **WINONA. / MY AQUARIUM**		–
Jul 92.	(cd/c/lp) *(CDHUT/HUTMC/HUTLP 4)* <*CAROL 1723-2/-4*> **DELAWARE**		

– Delaware / Ease it Halen / Winona / Kick the tragedy / Baby wonder's gone / Happen / Reberrymemberer / Angel / My aquarium. *(cd+=)* – Fish dream.

Oct 92. (10"ep/cd-ep) *(HUT EN/CD 22)* <*1469*> **YOUR AQUARIUM E.P.**
– My aquarium (second time around) / Mandy / Nausea / Movie.

— **MEGAN GILBERT** – guitar, vocals; repl. YASUE

— **JUSTIN CROSBY** – guitar; repl. KELLEY who formed HOT ROD

— **PETE KOSPLIN** – drums; repl. ROOF

Oct 93.	(12"/cd-s) *(HUT T/CD 39)* **LIMP. / TEMPEST / SEA ROCK**		–
	(12"+=/cd-s+=) *(HUT T/CD 39)* –		
Oct 93.	(cd/c/lp) *(CDHUT/HUTMC/HUTLP 14)* <*CAROL 1943-2/-4*> **NATIONAL COMA**		

– Limp / All swimmers are brothers / Skull / Cuban / Rot winter / Martini love / 7-8 / Franco inferno / My hotel deb / Moses Brown / Superfeed / The dead / Royal.

— split soon after above

DRUGSTORE

Formed: London, England . . . 1992 by Brazilian-born ISOBEL MONTEIRO and L.A. exile, MIKE CHYLINSKI. After trying in vain to find a suitable vocalist, MONTEIRO decided to take on the role herself, developing her earthy purr over a couple of early singles. The first of these, 'ALIVE', appeared on the band's own 'Honey' label while 'MODERN PLEASURE' was released as part of the 'Rough Trade' Singles Club series, the attendant press buzz leading to a deal with 'Go! Discs'. Recruiting third member, DARON ROBINSON, the band began work on an eponymous debut album which eventually surfaced in Spring '95, alternating pockets of brooding melody with squalling sheets of feedback in trademark DRUGSTORE fashion. The VELVET UNDERGROUND and MAZZY STAR were the most common reference points, MONTEIRO's tales of life's harsher lessons delivered in darkly seductive style. Although they didn't exactly have the standard Brit-pop credentials, the band were awarded an NME Single Of The Week award for accompanying single, 'SOLITARY PARTY GROOVER', while the album itself made the Top 40. A further single, 'FADER' made the Top 75 although the 'INJECTION' EP failed to chart. A move to 'Roadrunner' rejuvenated their fortunes, the 'EL PRESIDENT' single (featuring a guest vocal spot for THOM

DRUGSTORE (cont)

YORKE) denting the UK Top 20 in spring '98. The long-awaited follow-up album, 'WHITE MAGIC FOR LOVERS' (1998), meanwhile, may have hit the Top 50 but failed to win over many new fans. Resurfacing on 'Global Warming' records early in 2001, DRUGSTORE dispensed a new album, 'SONGS FOR THE JET SET'; single 'SONG FOR THE LONELY' being a particular highlight. • **Songwriters:** MONTEIRO main writer, some with group except SHE DON'T USE JELLY (Flaming Lips) / TEENAGE KICKS (Undertones) / COMMUNICATION BREAKDOWN (Led Zeppelin).

Album rating: DRUGSTORE (*6) / WHITE MAGIC FOR LOVERS (*5) / SONGS FOR THE JET SET (*6) / COLLECTOR NO.1 (*5)

ISOBEL MONTEIRO – vocals, bass / **DARON ROBINSON** – guitar, vocals / **MIKE CHYLINSKI** – drums

			Honey	not iss.
Apr 93.	(ltd-7")	*(HON 1)* **ALIVE. / GRAVITY**		-

			Rough Trade Sing. Club	not iss.
Nov 93.	(ltd-7")	*(45rev 24)* **MODERN PLEASURE. / ASCENDING**		-

			Honey – Go! Discs	Go! Discs – London
Sep 94.	(7")	*(HON 3)* **STARCROSSED. / ACCELERATE**		-
	(10"+=/cd-s+=) *(HON T/CD 3)* – Fader (4 track demo version).			
Jan 95.	(7")	*(HON 4)* **NECTARINE. / ANAESTHASIA**		-
	(10"+=/cd-s+=) *(HON T/CD 4)* – Jelly (acoustic).			
Jan 95.	(ltd-one-sided-7"freebie) *(HON 5)* **DRIVING**			-
Mar 95.	(7")	*(HON 6)* **SOLITARY PARTY GROOVER. / STARCROSSED (Isabel's demo)**		-
	(12"/cd-s) *(HON X/CD 6)* – ('A'side) / Get inside my head / Electric light / Spacegirl.			
Apr 95.	(cd/c/lp) *(<828556-2/-4/-1>)* **DRUGSTORE**	31	-
	– Speaker 12 / Favourite sinner / Alive / Solitary party groover / If / Devil / Saturday sunset / Fader / Super glider / Baby astrolab / Gravity / Nectarine / Accelerate. <US cd+=> – Starcrossed. (lp w/free 7", cd w/free cd-s) – SOLITARY PARTY GROOVER (acoustic). / BABY ASTROLAB (acoustic)		
May 95.	(7"m) *(HON 7)* **FADER. / REBOUND / UNDER THE MOON**	72	-
	(12"/cd-s) *(HON X/CD 7)* – ('A'side) / French devil / Slide / Sugar sugar (4 track demo).		
Oct 95.	(7"ep/cd-ep) *(HON 8/+CD)* **INJECTION / HEART OF HONEY. / SHE DON'T USE JELLY (electric version) / GRAVITY (Terry Edwards mix)**		-
Dec 95.	(one-sided-7"freebie) *(DXMAS 95)* **X-MAS AT THE DRUGSTORE**		-
1996.	(ltd-7"freebie) *<dot 001>* **PERFECT MOVIE. / Girl Of The Year: MANIFOLD**		-
	(above issued on 'Big White Dot' records)		
Nov 96.	(7"/c-s) *(HON/+MC 10)* **MONDO CANE. / WHAT EVERY GIRL SHOULD KNOW / MONDO CANE (acoustic)**		-
	(cd-s) *(HONCD 10)* – ('A'side) / No more tears / The adventures of Isabel.		
——	added **IAN BURDGE** – cello		

			Roadrunner	Roadrunner
Apr 98.	(7")	*RR 2236-7)* **EL PRESIDENT. / LIVIA**	20	-
	(cd-s+=) *(RR 2236-3)* – Eveything a girl should have.		
	(cd-s) *(RR 2236-9)* – ('A'side) / The night the Devil came to me / Perfect movie.		
May 98.	(cd/c/lp) *(<RR 8711-2/-4/-1>)* **WHITE MAGIC FOR LOVERS**	45	Jun98
	– Say hello / Mondo cane / El president / Sober / I know I could / Spacegirl / Never come down / Song for Pessoa / I don't wanna be here without you / White magic for lovers / Tips for travelling / The funeral (but most of all). *(hidden track+=)* – Everything a girl should have. *(cd re-iss. Aug00; same)*		

			Roadrunner	Imprint
Jun 98.	(7"colrd) *(RR 2230-7) <9013>* **SOBER. / WAIT**	68	Jan99
	(cd-s+=) *(RR 2230-3)* – Offside (demo).		
	(cd-s) *(RR 2230-9)* – ('A'side) / Cover me / The funeral (demo).		
Sep 98.	(cd-s) *(RR 2224-3)* **SAY HELLO (extended) / EL PRESIDENT (Portuguese version) / PRINCESS AND THE BEAST**		-

			Global Warming	not iss.
Oct 00.	(10"ep) *(WARM 10)* **I WANNA LOVE YOU LIKE A MAN / ALLEGRO MA NON TROPPO / THE WAY TO MEDINA**		-
	(cd-ep) *(WARMCD 10)* – (first 2 tracks) / Don't hurt yourself.		
Feb 01.	(cd) *(GLOBCD 6)* **SONGS FOR THE JET SET**		-
	– Baby don't hurt yourself / Song for the lonely / I wanna love you like a man / Navegando / The party is over / Hate / Little girl / Wayward daughter / Thin air / Allegro ma non troppo / Flying down to Rio.		
May 01.	(cd-s) *(WARMCD 11)* **SONG FOR THE LONELY / I KNOW I COULD / MAN BIRD MACHINE (demo)**		-
Oct 01.	(cd-s; free at gigs) *(WARMCD 15)* **BABY DON'T HURT YOURSELF / BABY DON'T HURT YOURSELF (French version) / THE PARTY IS OVER (live, White session)**		-
Apr 02.	(cd) *(GLOBCD 11)* **COLLECTOR NO.1** (rarities collection)		-
	– Say hello / Tourniquet / Starcrossed / What every girl should know / Gravity / Devil / Wayward daughter / Untitled – Daron sings / Mike talks / When the bottle is dry / 1000 blue caribou / Accelerate / El presidente / Xmas in the Arctic Pole.		

DRUMS & TUBA (see under ⇒ PAUL NEWMAN)

DRUNK

Formed: Richmond, Virginia, USA ... 1995 by guitarist and vocalist RICK ALVERSON. After 1997's blissfully quiet debut, 'A DERBY SPIRITUAL', this alt-country outfit became subsequently adored come their follow-up set, the blue-toned, heartfelt 'TO CORNER WOUNDS' (1998). If the sentimental hindrance of 'TO CORNER ...' did not intend to follow in the footsteps of softcore outfit The RADAR BROTHERS, then it certainly meant to echo the rich and lo-fi balance of The PALACE BROTHERS. If anything, the set was downright hopeful in its conquest; songs of love scatter the deck of a ship lost in a storm, and the cabin crew are singing laments next to a pale white candle. Mandolin, harmonica, finely picked guitar and the rasping (almost silent at times) vocals of ALVERSON were also present on their third album's

('RAISED TOWARD') most touching moments, notably the warm, but worn, 'THE PEELED BIRCH' and the haunting solidarity of 'CARVED SLOPE'. The sublime ensemble issued a further EP that year (1999), the beautiful 'PHINEAS GAGE'. Their fourth set, 'TABLESIDE MANNERS' (2000), found them lacking in sparkle, eleven sobering Lo-Fi pieces showed there was cracks in the, er ... Pavement. What remains now is a lost, dream-like and glazed set of musicians waiting for their big break in the 21st century. If pigs had wings! • **Covered:** RAKE (Townes Van Zandt) / ONE OF US CANNOT BE WRONG (Leonard Cohen) / JOHN HARDY (trad.).

Album rating: A DERBY SPIRITUAL (*7) / TO CORNER WOUNDS (*7) / RAISED TOWARD (*6) / TABLESIDE MANNERS (*4)

RICK ALVERSON – vocals, guitar / **VIA NUON** – guitar / **J.T. YOST** – accordion, organ / **RUSSELL COOK** – drums

			Jagjaguwar	Jagjaguwar
May 97.	(cd) *<(JAG 2)>* **A DERBY SPIRITUAL**		Jan97
	– Collarbone / Indeliberate matrimony / Coming home / Hand on deck / Germany skies / Gideon's trumpet / Window sill / Gizmo / A nip for Kitty / Fraulein / Drunk bed / Mental illness (leads to romance) / Roanoke.		
May 98.	(cd) *<(JAG 7)>* **TO CORNER WOUNDS**		Apr98
	– Carved slope / Council's lawn / Andrei Rublev / The peeled birch / Epoxy / As we go down together / The bark of the body / Spit / Rake / Bonitov / Montana daylight / Cold eel 1917.		
Mar 99.	(cd) *<(JAG 10)>* **RAISED TOWARD**		Feb99
	– Miscellany / Scaffold / Violent day / Epiphany of St. Thomas / I, Lilith / Equal parts both / Cupboard / One of us cannot be wrong / Chatter / All souls day / A mere passer-by / A notice to range users / A tether's length.		
Jul 99.	(cd-ep) *<(JAG 15)>* **PHINEAS GAGE EP**		-
	– As the world burns / The waltz as antidote? / The outside family / A last walk around the grounds / John Hardy / Appendix.		
Feb 00.	(cd) *<(JAG 16)>* **TABLESIDE MANNERS**		Jan00
	– Bouyant sinker / Dorothea / Cold afternoon / Mutual friend / Forfeit / Truancy / Queen of Venice / Our host / As the world burns / Upholstery / Soreness of legs.		
Oct 00.	(7") *<(JAG 23)>* **THE ROUND COUPLE. / ST. TERESA**		

DUB NARCOTIC SOUND SYSTEM
(see under ⇒ BEAT HAPPENING; 80's section)

DUBREQ (see under ⇒ SPARE SNARE)

DUBSTAR

Formed: Newcastle, England ... 1994 by ex-JOANS members; CHRIS WILKIE and STEVE HILLIER, who soon recruited singer, SARAH BLACKWOOD. With help from manager Graham Robinson, DUBSTAR secured a deal with Parlophone outlet 'Food' (home to BLUR). In June 1995, they had their first chart appearance with 'STARS' and grew to be an alternative pop favourite of '95. Dreamy experimental Euro-pop lying somewhere between SAINT ETIENNE and The PET SHOP BOYS, the band's debut STEPHEN HAGUE-produced album, 'DISGRACEFUL' (1995), also displayed a talent for biting lyrical realism, this winning combination at its most bittersweet on the Top 20 hit, 'NOT SO MANIC NOW'. A re-issued 'STARS' followed it into the charts soon after, while 'ELEVATOR SONG' made the Top 30. A second album, 'GOODBYE' (1997), was much in the same formula and spawned a further two hits, 'NO MORE TALK' and 'CATHEDRAL PARK'.

Album rating: DISGRACEFUL (*6) / GOODBYE (*5)

SARAH BLACKWOOD – vocals / **CHRIS WILKIE** – guitar / **STEVE HILLIER** – programmer

			Food	Polydor
Jun 95.	(cd-s) *(CDFOOD 61)* **STARS (mixes; original / sky / mother dub / search & destroy full vox / sweet tooths DJs excursion)**	40	-
	(12") *(12FOOD 61)* – ('A'mixes; sky / search & destroy / way out west / mother dub / original).		
Sep 95.	(c-s) *(TCFOOD 67)* **ANYWHERE / DON'T BLAME ME**	37	-
	(cd-s+=) *(CDFOOD 67)* – ('A'mixes; parkside / crunch chill).		
	(12") *(12FOOD 67)* – ('A'side) / ('A'-KLM extended klub mix) / ('A'-KLM millenium klub) / ('A'-parkside mix).		
Oct 95.	(cd/c) *(CD/TC FOOD 13)* **DISGRACEFUL**	33	-
	– Stars / Anywhere / Just a girl she said / Elevator song / The day I see you again / Week in week out / Not so manic now / Popdorian / Not once, not ever / St. Swithin's Day / Disgraceful. *(re-iss. Jul96 with free remixes cd; FOODCOR 13)*		
Dec 95.	(c-s) *(TCFOOD 71)* **NOT SO MANIC NOW / IF IT ISN'T YOU**	18	-
	(cd-s+=) *(CDFOOD 71)* – Song No.9 / Certain sadness.		
	(cd-s) *(CDFOODS 71)* – ('A'side) / ('A'-mixes; way out west / mother's whole dub / way out west prophecy dub).		
	(12"+=) *(12FOOD 71)* – ('A'-mother's moonshine mix).		
Mar 96.	(c-s) *(TCFOOD 75)* **STARS / EXCUSE ME FATHER**	15	-
	(cd-s+=) *(CDFOODS 75)* – Starfish / Bow wow now (we know).		
	(cd-s) *(FOODCD 75)* – ('A'mixes; original / Motiv 8 radio / sonic star dub / way out west).		
	(12"+=) *(12FOOD 75)* – ('A'-klubstar).		
Jul 96.	(c-s) *(TCFOOD 80)* **ELEVATOR SONG / ANYWAY**	25	-
	(cd-s+=) *(CDFOODS 80)* – The view from here / A northern bride.		
	(12"/cd-s) *(12/CD FOOD 80)* – ('A'mixes; original / d'Still more 4 food / Biff and Memphis club / d'Still 4 food).		
Jul 97.	(c-s/cd-s) *(TC/CD FOOD 96)* **NO MORE TALK / UNCHAINED MONOLOGUE / LA BOHEME / GOODBYE**	20	-
	(cd-s) *(CDFOODS 96)* – ('A'side) / Stars (acoustic) / Elevator song (acoustic) / Not once, not ever (acoustic).		

DUBSTAR (cont)

Sep 97. (c-s) *(TCFOOD 104)* **CATHEDRAL PARK / CATHEDRAL PARK (Dirty Rotten Scoundrels mix) / NO MORE TALK (Jamie Myerson breakout mix)** — 41 / -
(cd-s+=) *(CDFOOD 104)* – ('A'-environmental science remix pt.1).
(cd-s) *(CDFOODS 104)* – ('A'side) / Let down / This is my home / In my defence.
Sep 97. (cd/c) *(CD/TC FOOD 23)* <31453 7691-2/-4> **GOODBYE** — 18 / -
– I will be your girlfriend / Inside / No more talk / Polestar / Say the worst thing first / Cathedral park / It's over / View from here / My start in Wallsend / It's clear / Ghost / Can't tell me / Wearchest / When you say goodbye / Let's go. <US-iss. featured different tracks + some from UK debut>
Jan 98. (c-ep/cd-ep) *(TCFOOD/CDFOODS 108)* **I WILL BE YOUR GIRLFRIEND / STARS / NOT SO MANIC NOW / ANYWHERE** — 28 / -
(cd-s) *(CDFOOD 108)* – ('A'mixes by Dillon & Dickons vocal / Deadly Avenger / Sol Brothers / SDS Inc. / Steve Hillier).
May 00. (cd-s) *(CDFOODS 128)* **I (FRIDAY NIGHT) / I LOST A FRIEND / ELIZABETH TAYLOR AND RICHARD BURTON** — 37 / -
(cd-s) *(CDFOOD 128)* – ('A'mixes; original / DJ Jurgen radio / DJ Jurgen extended / Friday nite).
(c-s) *(TCFOOD 128)* – ('A'original / DJ Jurgen extended / Steve Hillier).
Aug 00. (cd-s) *(CDFOODS 153)* **THE SELF SAME THING / RESTRICTED MAIL (featuring GARY NUMAN) / AND WHEN YOU LAUGH (featuring IAN BROUDIE) / VICTORIA** — ☐ / -
Aug 00. (cd) *(FOODCD 30)* **MAKE IT BETTER** — ☐ / -
– Take it / I / The self same thing / Mercury / Stay / Another world / When the world knows your name / The arc of fire / Believe in me / I'm conscious of myself / Rise to the top / Swansong.

DUMP (see under ⇒ YO LA TENGO; 80's section)

Baxter DURY

Born: 8 Nov'72. Wingrave, Buckinghamshire, England. Son of legendary New Wave/Punk hero IAN DURY, BAXTER decided at first that he would not follow his father's footsteps into the record industry. Unfortunately though, academics was also quickly ruled out, as by his mid-teens he had already been thrown out of several schools. Although BAXTER did continue his schooling under the watchful eye of one of dad's pals (unfortunately IAN DURY was now headlong into his film career; filming for Roman Polanski's 1986 film 'Pirates'), the ominously nicknamed, The Sulphate Strangler, who had been one of the touring crew for LED ZEPPELIN. As much as he tried to resist it, music was obviously born into BAXTER, and by the late 90's he had begun to pen some tunes with BEN GALLAGHER, son of another mate of his father's, MICKEY, a BLOCKHEAD and former LOVING AWARENESS member. At this time he also worked on several low key independent films, while also working in a shop. Unfortunately, a fated record deal with 'Island' came to nothing, and it looked like BAXTER might never be heard. Until that is, he made pals with GEOFF TRAVIS of legendary indie 'Rough Trade', who gave him a deal at the turn of the millennium. In fact, one of his first live spots was a moving rendition of 'MY OLD MAN' at the wake for his father in April 2000. Soon afterwards, he relocated to Austin, Texas to take some time out for songwriting, and aided by such luminaries as GEOFF BARROW and ADRIAN UTLEY (both of PORTISHEAD fame) plus RICHARD HAWLEY (from PULP), BAXTER debuted with the EP, 'OSCAR BROWN'. A year on, he returned with the LP 'LEN PARROT'S MEMORIAL LIFT', which announced a new talent on the scene and showcased his dark blend of folk and ambient rock.

Album rating: LEN PARROT'S MEMORIAL LIFT (*6)

BAXTER DURY – vocals, acoustic guitar, keyboards, etc / with verious session people

Rough Trade Rough Trade

Jun 01. (cd-ep) *(RTRADESCD 017)* **OSCAR BROWN EP** — ☐ / -
– Oscar Brown / Tupac's down / Stray dogs.
Jul 02. (cd/lp) *(RTRADE CD/LP 050)* <83210> **LEN PARROT'S MEMORIAL LIFT** — ☐ / ☐
– Beneath the underdog / Oscar Brown / Lucifer's grain / Fungus hedge / Auntie Jane / Gingham smalls 2 / Bachelor / Len Parrot's memorial lift / Boneyard dogs.
Oct 02. (cd-s) *(RTRADESCD 066)* **GINGHAM SMALLS / LUCIFER'S GRAIN** — ☐ / -

DYLANS

Formed: Sheffield, England . . . early 1990 by COLIN GREGORY (formerly of 1,000 VIOLINS), JIM RODGER and ANDY CURTIS. Adding QUENTIN JENNINGS and GARRY JONES, the hopelessly retro 60's-styled outfit cashed in on the "baggy" scene with a major label deal courtesy of 'R.C.A.'. However after only one flop single and the recruitment of CURTIS's replacement, ANDY COOK, the harmony-laden band were relegated to Beggars Banquet offshoot, 'Situation 2'. Now officially a bonafide indie band, The DYLANS released a further couple of BEATLES-tinged singles prior to the Stephen Street-produced eponymous debut album. Internal tensions subsequently led to further changes, JONES and JENNINGS making way for newcomers CRAIG SCOTT and IKE GLOVER respectively. A long-awaited second album, 'SPIRIT FINGER' (1994), was virtually ignored, with the music scene favouring more up to date sounds.

Album rating: THE DYLANS (*6) / SPIRIT FINGER (*5)

COLIN GREGORY – vocals, bass (ex-1,000 VIOLINS) / **ANDY CURTIS** – guitar / **JIM RODGER** – guitar / **QUENTIN JENNINGS** – keyboards / **GARRY JONES** – drums

R.C.A. not iss.

Jan 91. (7") *(RCA 2806)* **GODLIKE. / LEMON AFTERNOON** — ☐ / -
(cd-s+=) *(RCACD 2806)* – My hands are tied / Lemon afteregg mix 1.

—— **ANDY COOK** – guitar; repl. CURTIS

Situation 2 Beggars Banquet

May 91. (7") *(SIT 78)* **MY HANDS ARE TIED. / LEMON AFTERNOON** — ☐ / -
(cd-s+=) *(SIT78CD)* – Lemon afteregg mix / My hands are still tied.
Aug 91. (7") *(SIT 81)* **PLANET LOVE. / MINE** — ☐ / -
(cd-s+=) *(SITU 81CD)* – Skywalk / ('A'demo version).
Oct 91. (lp/cd) *(SITU 33/+CD)* <61054-2/-4> **THE DYLANS** — ☐ / -
– She drops bombs / Planet love / I hope the weather stays fine / Sad rush on Sunday / No coming down / Mine / Particle ride / Ocean wide / Godlike / Mary Quant in blue / Love to / Indian sun.
May 92. (7") *(SIT 90)* **MARY QUANT IN BLUE. / I HOPE THE WEATHER STAYS FINE (remix)** — ☐ / -
(12"ep+=/cd-ep+=) **QUANT E.P.** *(SIT 90 T/CD)* – You won't last long without me / Deluxe reverse (submarine mix II).

—— **CRAIG SCOTT** – drums; repl. JONES

—— **IKE GLOVER** – keyboards; repl. JENNINGS

Beggars Banquet Atlantic

Nov 93. (12"/cd-s) *(BBQ 22 T/CD)* **GRUNGE / WISEBIRD. / PARTIAL RANCH / NERVE HUTCH** — ☐ / -
Mar 94. (12"/cd-s) *(BBQ 29 T/CD)* **I'LL BE BACK TO HAUNT YOU. / POINTS = PRIZES / PEACE BOMB BABY** — ☐ / -
Apr 94. (cd) *(BBQCD 144)* <92341> **SPIRIT FINGER** — ☐ / ☐
– Grudge / Children of the flame / Kill rave / Just one big plastic hassle / Hell no / Smarter than you / I'll be back to haunt you / Wise bird / Live in the know / How little you know / Get it together / Two tomorrows.

—— disappeared after their lack of success.

THE GREAT INDIE DISCOGRAPHY — The 1990s

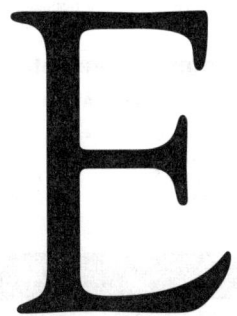

EARL BRUTUS

Formed: London, England ... 1992 by ex-WORLD OF TWIST keyboard-player, NICK SANDERSON, JAMIE FRY (none other than the brother of ABC's MARTIN FRY), ROB MARCHE and GORDON KING (the latter also from the WORLD OF TWIST). An unlikely but surprisingly effective combination of KILLING JOKE/FALL-like intensity and GLITTER BAND stomp!, EARL BRUTUS self-financed a debut single, 'LIFE'S TOO LONG', on their own 'Icerink' label. After a long-awaited follow-up in '95!, 'BONJOUR MONSIEUR' (for the 'Royal Mint' imprint), they almost immediately signed to Radio One/Music Week journo, Steve Lamacq's 'Deceptive' label and proceeded to churn out a series of sleazy singles prior to their debut album, 'YOUR MAJESTY ... WE ARE HERE' (1996). The EARL's bolstered their claim to indie high society by being tipped for the top by none other than soft-porn mag, Club International (don't ask me how I found this out!?). Moving on to 'Fruition' records, the band treated their ever-growing cult following with a further string of near excellent singles beginning late in '97 with 'THE S.A.S. AND THE GLAM THAT GOES WITH IT'. It was a highlight from the following year's much talked about second long-player, 'TONIGHT YOU ARE THE SPECIAL ONE'.

Album rating: YOUR MAJESTY ... WE ARE HERE (*8) / TONIGHT YOU ARE THE SPECIAL ONE (*7)

NICK SANDERSON – vocals, keyboards (ex-WORLD OF TWIST) / **JAMIE FRY** – keyboards, vocals / **ROB MARCHE** – guitar / **GORDON KING** – keyboards, drum machine (ex-WORLD OF TWIST)

		Icerink	not iss.
Jun 93.	(cd-s) *(DAVO 7 CD)* **LIFE'S TOO LONG. / VALLEY OF THE SLIMKINGS / LIFE'S TOO LONG**		–
		Royal Mint	not iss.
Sep 95.	(7"red) *(MINT 001)* **BONJOUR MONSIEUR. / ON ME, NOT IN ME**		–
		Deceptive	not iss.
Dec 95.	(7"etched) *(BLUFF 020)* **SINGLE SEATER XMAS**		–
Mar 96.	(7"m) *(BLUFF 025)* **NAVYHEAD. / NORTH SEA BASTARD / 48 TRASH**		–
	(cd-s+=) *(BLUFF 025CD)* – Navyhead (Union Street).		
Jun 96.	(7"m) *(BLUFF 030)* **LIFE'S TOO LONG. / MOTOROLA / I LOVE EARL BRUTUS**		–
	(cd-s+=) *(BLUFF 030CD)* – Life's too long (Flash Vs Tarkus).		
Sep 96.	(7"m/cd-s) *(BLUFF 032/+CD)* **I'M NEW. / LIKE QUEER DAVID / MONDO ROTUNDA**		–
Sep 96.	(cd/lp) *(BLUFF 036 CD/LP)* **YOUR MAJESTY ... WE ARE HERE**		–
	– Navyhead / I'm new / Male milk / On me, not in me / Don't leave me behind mate (Thelemix TM) / Black speedway / Motorola / Shrunken head (curtsy) / Blind date / Life's too long / Karl Brutus. *(cd+=)* – Singer seater Xmas.		
Mar 97.	(7"one-sided) *(BLUFF 039)* **PURCHASING POWER**		–
		Fruition	not iss.
Oct 97.	(7"clear) *(FRU 5)* **THE S.A.S. AND THE GLAM THAT GOES WITH IT. / MIDLAND RED**		–
	(cd-s+=) *(FRUCD 5)* – The Scottish.		
Jan 98.	(7") *(FRU 6)* **COME TASTE MY MIND. / SUPERSTAR**		–
	(cd-s+=) *(FRUCD 6)* – Nice man in a bubble / William.		
May 98.	(7") *(FRU 7)* **UNIVERSAL PLAN. / GYPSY CAMP BATTLE**		–
	(cd-s+=) *(FRUCD 7)* – TV tower / Bonjour monsieur.		
	(cd-s) *(FRUDX 7)* – ('A'live) / The S.A.S. and the glam that goes with it (live) / Come taste my mind (live) / Nicotine stains (live).		
Jun 98.	(cd/lp) *(FRU CD/LP 1003)* **TONIGHT YOU ARE THE SPECIAL ONE**		–
	– The S.A.S. and the glam that goes with it / Universal plan / Midland red / God, let me be kind (bitterfeld) / Come taste my mind / Second class war / Your majesty, we are here / Don't die Jim / 99p (take me away) / East / Edelweiss (blown away) / Male wife.		
May 99.	(7"/cd-s) *(FRUT 5 S/CD)* **LARKY. / TEENAGE OPERA**		–

E.A.R. (see under ⇒ EXPERIMENTAL AUDIO RESEARCH)

EARLY DAY MINERS

Formed: Bloomington, Indiana, USA ... late 90's out of ATIVIN by core members DANIEL BURTON RORY LEITH, JOE BRUMLEY was soon added and they have a number of session friends who appear on their albums and on tour. The group released their first album, 'PLACER FOUND', in 2000, a bleak soundscape evoking images of a lonely, desolate, world, with fractured instrumentation, hushed vocals and an overbearing sombre tone. The band were subsequently given the opportunity to visualise the mood they were creating on the 2002 split collaboration, 'STATELESS', with UNWED SAILOR and film-maker CHRIS BENNETT. The film was abstract and bleak, showing images of broken down vacation spots and wasted landscapes which served to enhance the music perfectly. Just when the band had begun looking like a one-trick pony, they surprised the music world with the release of 'LET US GARLANDS BRING' (2002). Ornate and uplifting, the band's decision to introduce cellos, violins and vocal harmonies, lifted the music to a new level and allowed them to show what they were capable of; EARLY DAY MINERS' sound was now technicolor rather than the previous dark, monochrome efforts.

Album rating: PLACER FOUND (*5) / LET US GARLANDS BRING (*7)

DANIEL BURTON – vocals, guitar / **ROY LEITCH** – drums / **JOE BRUMLEY** – guitar

		not iss.	Western Vinyl
Apr 00.	(cd) <8> **PLACER FOUND**	–	
	– Placer found / East Berlin at night / Texas cinema / In these hills / Stanwix / Longwall / Desert cantos.		
		Great Vitamin Mystery	Great Vitamin Mystery
Feb 02.	(cd; split w/ UNWED SAILOR) *(TGVM 002)* **STATELESS**		
	– The ninth ward / Scandinavian comfort / Treeline / Mosaic / Chandelier.		
—	there were also a few single releases on Swiss 'Zeal' records.		
—	plus **MATT LINBLOM** – bass / **MOLLY KIEN** – cello / **MAGGIE POLK** – violin		
		Secretly Canadian	Secretly Canadian
May 02.	(cd) *<(SC 71CD)>* **LET UD GARLANDS BRING**		
	– Centralia / Santa Carolina / Offshore / Silvergate / Summer ends / Autumn wake / Light in August / Upstate *[d-lp-only]* / A common wealth. *<(d-kp-iss. on 'Western Vinyl'; WV 15)>*		

EARWIG

Formed: Brighton, England ... early 90's by KIRSTY YATES, SERGEI TARDO, with the addition of sequencer/percussionist DIMITRI VOULIS. Not to be confused with the ultra rare EVERYTHING EARWIG, who had a handful of hard-to-find releases out in the early 90's, this beachcombing trio played stripped-down electronica and ambient music, eventually mutating into the group INSIDES after the release of a bag full of interesting EP's and their debut 'UNDER MY SKIN I AM LAUGHING' (1994). As INSIDES, YATES and TARDO signed to 4 a.d.'s 'Guernica' offshoot, issuing the haunting 'EUPHORIA' (1993). This was followed by the unsolicited delivery of a 38-minute self-proclaimed "mood piece", 'CLEAR SKIN' (1994), prompting the duo to sign with 'Third Stone' after some animosity was borne towards 'Guernica' and its boss Ivo Watts-Russell. All was quiet from the INSIDES/EARWIG camp, until 2000 when the summery, laid-back jazz of 'SWEET TIP' was unfettered. Abandoning their multi-layered atmospheric textures for something quite sweetly refined, INSIDES had taken a stab at the electro-pop genre, mixing in woodwind with live instrumentation sections.
• **Note:** watch out for another EARWIG from Columbus, Ohio fronted by LIZARD McGEE.

Album rating: PAST compilation (*6) / UNDER MY SKIN I AM LAUGHING (*7) / Insides: EUPHORIA (*6) / CLEAR SKIN (*6) / SWEET TIP (*5)

KIRSTY YATES – vocals, bass, guitar / **DIMITRI VOULIS** – guitar, drums, programming / **SERGEI TARDO** – guitars, piano

		La-Di-Da	Caroline
1991.	(12"ep) *(LADIDA 011)* **HARDLEY**		–
	– Blind stupid and desperate / Her stupid face / It's the waiting I can't stand / Both of us screaming.		
1992.	(12"ep) *(LADIDA 017)* **MIGHT**		–
	– Driving you mad, slowly / Everything's just fine / Sour song / You don't even come close.		
1992.	(12"ep) *(LADIDA 019)* **SUBTRACT (YOUR FRIENDS)**		–
	– Your friends / Out of my hands over my head / Slit.		
1992.	(12"/cd-s) *(LADIDA 021)* **EVERY DAY SHINES. / I NEED FEEL**		–
1992.	(cd) *(LADIDA 022CD)* **PAST** (compilation)		–
	– Both of us screaming / Her stupid face / It's the waiting I can't stand / Driving you mad, slowly / Everything's just fine / Sour song / You don't even come close / Your friends / Out of my hands, over my head / Slit. *(re-iss. Jul94; same)*		
1992.	(lp/cd) *(LADIDA 024/+CD) <CAROL 9402>* **UNDER MY SKIN I AM LAUGHING**		Nov94
	– Every day shines / Safe in my hands / When you're quiet / Scraped out / We could be sisters / Never be lonely again / Sickhair. *(re-iss. Jul94; same)*		

INSIDES

KIRSTY YATES + JULIAN TARDO (DIMITRI also producer)

		Guernica	4 a.d.
Oct 93.	(cd) *(GU 4) <45486-2>* **EUPHORIA**		
	– Walking in straight lines / Bent double / Darling effect / Distractions / Relentless / Skin divers / Carly Simon / Yes / Skykicking.		
Feb 94.	(cd) *(GU 7)* **CLEAR SKIN**		–
	– Clear skin.		
		Third Stone	not iss.
May 00.	(cd) *(STONE 040CD)* **SWEET TIP**		–
	– Magic box / Dazzled slightly / Take a sippa da drink / All life long / Joy / Grand prix / LV N B LVD / Sleep it off, lady / Nothing could be sweeter / Any comments? / Wash n wear hair / Hold this in your heart / Bossy nuevo / Blue nimbus / It's about that time / What can I tell you? / (untitled).		

719

EAST RIVER PIPE

Formed: Astoria, New York, USA ... 1989 as the musical alias of F.M. CORNOG. A hard luck story to beat most hard luck stories, FRED's (as he was then known) hard-bitten adventures were the stuff of scriptwriters' dreams. Born and raised in Suffolk, Virginia and Summit, New Jersey, the self-effacing CORNOG went through numerous menial jobs before succumbing to alcoholism and eventual homelessness. Attracted by the lure of a new start in the Big Apple, the budding singer-songwriter gravitated towards New York where he eked out an existence as a street/subway busker. His fortunes changed however, when his "guardian angel", BARBARA POWERS fell in love, first with his music and then the man himself. She subsequently moved him in to her Queen's, NY apartment, where she provided him with a basic home studio while also taking on the task of publicising and distributing his recordings. So named because FM equated his artistic output with the shit coming out of an NY sewer, EAST RIVER PIPE officially came into existence with the mail-order only demo cassettes, 'EAST RIVER PIPE' (1989), 'POINT OF NO MEMORY' (1990) and 'I USED TO BE KID COLGATE' (1991). Released on his/her own imprint, 'Hell Gate', these caught the attention of UK indie, 'Sarah', who duly issued his debut 7", 'HELMET ON' in Spring '93. A surprise Melody Maker single of the week, it helped boost ERP's obscure profile for future releases, 'SHE'S A REAL GOOD TIME' and the mini-set, 'GOODBYE CALIFORNIA' (1993). Now on the up and up, CORNOG also found a wider outlet for his records in America, 'Merge' handling the Stateside release of the acclaimed 'POOR FRICKY' (1994) a year after it appeared on UK shelves. Compared to everyone from LOU REED, BIG STAR and ELLIOTT SMITH to ROBERT FORSTER and BILL CALLAHAN, there was no mistaking the Lo-Fi heritage of FRED's one-man band although his surprisingly upbeat style set him apart. Resurfacing in '96 on the 'Shinkansen' label (UK only), EAST RIVER PIPE stuck to his trademark down-at-heel charm for that year's 'MEL' album; sewer(ly) it was only a matter of time before his talents will be more widely acknowledged. With 1999's 'THE GASOLINE AGE', CORNOG had come of age. From the opening, 'SHINY, SHINY PIMPMOBILE', to 'KING OF NOTHING NEVER' and 'ATLANTIC CITY (GONNA MAKE A MILLION TONIGHT' his goofball charm was never better. A man of the streets, indeed.

Album rating: GOODBYE CALIFORNIA mini (*6) / SHINING HOURS IN A CAN compilation (*6) / POOR FRICKY (*7) / EVEN THE SUN WAS AFRAID mini (*5) / MEL (*7) / THE GASOLINE AGE (*8)

F.M. CORNOG – vocals, guitar / with a drum machine

		Sarah	Hell Gate
1989.	(c) **EAST RIVER PIPE**	-	
1990.	(c) **POINT OF MEMORY**	-	
1991.	(c) **I USED TO BE KID COLGATE**	-	
1991.	(7") <HG-9101> **AXL OR IGGY. / HELMET ON**	-	
1992.	(7") <HG-9201> **MY LIFE IS WRONG. / SHE'S A REAL GOOD TIME**	-	
1993.	(7") <HG-9202> **MAKE A DEAL WITH THE CITY. / PSYCHIC WHORE**	-	
May 93.	(7") (SARAH 075) **HELMET ON. / HAPPYTOWN**		-
	(cd-s+=) (SARAH 075CD) – Axl or Iggy.		
Jun 93.	(7") (SARAH 078) **SHE'S A REAL GOOD TIME. / MY LIFE IS WRONG**		-
	(cd-s+=) (SARAH 078CD) – Times Square go-go boy.		
Sep 93.	(10"m-lp/m-cd) (SARAH 405/+CD) **GOODBYE CALIFORNIA**		-
	– Firing room / Silhouette town / Dogman / When will your friends all disappear? / Bernie Shaw / Psychic whore / 40 miles / Make a deal with the city.		
1993.	(7") <HG-9301> **FIRING ROOM. / HEY, WHERE'S YOUR GIRL?**	-	
1994.	(7") **AH DICTAPHONE. /**	-	
	<re-iss. 1994 on 'Merge'; >		

		Sarah	Merge
Jan 95.	(7"m) <MRG 076> **BRING ON THE LOSER. / FAN THE FLAME / SLEEPING WITH TALLBOY**	-	
Nov 94.	(cd) (SARAH 621CD) <MRG 081> **POOR FRICKY**		Jan95
	– Bring on the loser / Metal detector / Here we go / Put-down / Superstar in France / Keep all your windows tight tonight / Ah dictaphone / Walking the dog / Marty / Crawl away / Hey, where's your girl? / Powerful man / When the ground walks away. (re-iss. Feb00 on 'Merge' lp/cd+=; MRG 081/+CD) – Make it real / Million, trillion / Sleeping with tallboy / Hide my life away from you / Fan the flame (instrumental).		
May 95.	(10"m-lp/m-cd) (SARAH 407/+CD) **EVEN THE SUN WAS AFRAID**		-
	– Here we go / Marty / Sleeping with tallboy / Hide my life away from you / Fan the flame / When the ground walks away / Powerful man / Fan the flames.		
Nov 96.	(cd-ep) <MRG 110> **KILL THE ACTION / THE WAY THEY MURDERED ME / MINDCRACKER**	-	

		Shinkansen	Merge
Nov 96.	(7") (SHINKANSEN 6) **MIRACLELAND. / KING OF NOTHING EVER / MINDCRACKER**		-
Dec 96.	(cd) (SHINKANSEN 7CD) <MRG 111CD> **MEL**		Oct96
	– The club isn't open / I am a small mistake / Spotlight / Beautiful worn-out love / New York crown / Kill the action / We're going to nowhere / Lonely line away / Prettiest whore / Guilty as charged / Take back the days / Life is born today. (re-iss. Feb00 on 'Merge' lp/cd; MRG 111/+CD)		
Jul 99.	(7") (MUSE 006) **CYBER CAR. / BabyBird: DRUNK CAR**		-
	(above issued on 'Easy Tiger', US on 'Hell Gate')		

		Merge	Merge
Aug 99.	(cd) <(MRG 164CD)> **THE GASOLINE AGE**		
	– Shiny, shiny pimpmobile / Hell is an open door / Cybercar / Wholesale lies / My little rainbow / Party drive / King of nthing never / 14th street boys stolen car club / All you little suckers / Astrofarm / Down 42nd street to the light / Atlantic city (gonna make a million tonight) / Don't hurry. (re-iss. Jul00; same)		

– compilations, etc. –

1994.	(cd) Ajax; <041> **SHINING HOURS IN A CAN** (early material)	-	
	– Make a deal with the city / My life is wrong / Helmet on / Happytown / Axl or Iggy / Psychic whore / Firing room / Silhouette town / Dogman / When will your friends all disappear? / Bernie Shaw / 40 miles / Times Square go-go boy / She's a real good time / Woody's car. <(re+UK cd-iss. Mar02 on 'Merge'; MRG 203CD)>		

EASY

Formed: Jonkoping, Sweden ... 1990 by JOHAN HOLMLUND, TOMMY ERICSON, TOMMY JONSSON, RIKARD JORMIN and ANDERS PETERSSON. After recording a demo directly from their first live gig in 1989, the band were unexpectedly snapped up by the UK branch of New York noise specialists, 'Blast First'. Routinely mentioned in the same breath as JESUS & MARY CHAIN, EASY combined caterwauling guitar abuse, pockets of low-rent melody and a curiously Swedish self-deprecating charm, winning over British audiences on their support dates with The CHARLATANS. Debut album, 'MAGIC SEED' (1990), had already given indie fans a taste of what to expect, the band's No.1 rule of not taking themselves too seriously paying off in the UK but affording them a cautious reaction at home where critics were reportedly suspicious of their Blighty success. They subsequently split after a brief association with 'Snap'.

Album rating: MAGIC SEED (*6)

JOHAN HOLMLUND (b.13 Jul'65) – vocals / **TOMMY ERICSSON** (b.23 Mar'66, Umea, Sweden) – guitar / **ANDERS PETERSSON** (b.12 Nov'65) – guitar, keyboards / **RIKARD JORMIN** (b. 2 Aug'65) – bass / **TOMMY JONSSON** (b.15 Jun'66, Vasterik, Sweden) – drums

		Blast First	Mute
Oct 90.	(lp/c/cd) (BFFP 57/+C/CD) <9 61125-1/-4/-2> **MAGIC SEED**		1991
	– He brings the honey / Cloud chamber / Horoscope / Dam sugar / Sunny day / Land diving / Between John & Yoko / #25 / Pleasure cruise / Magic seed.		
Jan 91.	(cd-s) (BFFP 61CD) **HE BRINGS THE HONEY / #25**		-
Jun 91.	(cd-s) (BFFP 65CD) **HOROSCOPE / FLAMINGO V / APPLES FOR YOU**		-

		Snap	not iss.
Aug 93.	(cd-s) (SNAPC 012) **NEVER SEEN A STAR / REACH OUT, YVONNE / NEW SPRING**		-
Apr 94.	(12") (SNAPT 023) **LISTEN TO THE BELLS** (mixes; Fortran 5 - radio / Quant / Fortran 5 - master).		-
May 94.	(cd-s) (SNAPC 021) **IN BLACK AND WHITE / SAY GOODBYE TO HOLLYWOOD**		-

— disbanded when little interest was shown in them

EASYWORLD

Formed: Eastbourne, England ... 1997 by multi-instrumentalist DAV FORD, bassist JO and drummer GLENN. Indie-pop trio EASYWORLD's members met at college in Eastbourne, but due to a lack of opportunities in their home town, they relocated to London, around the same time as 'Fierce Panda' released their debut album 'BETTER WAYS TO SELF DESTRUCT' in 2001. Impressing 'Jive' records (er, home to BRITNEY SPEARS), they subsequently signed, and then released the catchy power-pop single 'BLEACH', followed by second album 'THIS IS WHERE I STAND' (in June 2002). It was a confident, glossy package of tunes, similar at times to MUSE, JJ72 and ASH. Highlights like 'JUNKIES AND WHORES' and 'YOU AND ME', were however let down by mediocre songwriting elsewhere on the set.

Album rating: BETTER WAYS TO SELF DESTRUCT (*6) / THIS IS WHERE I STAND (*5)

DAV FORD – guitar, vocals / **JO** – bass / **GLENN** – drums

		Fierce Panda	not iss.
Feb 01.	(7") (ning 103) **HUNDREDWEIGHT. / YOU MAKE ME WANT TO DRINK BLEACH**		-
	(cd-s+=) (ning 103cd) – All I ever had.		
Jul 01.	(cd) (ching 01cd) **BETTER WAYS TO SELF DESTRUCT**		-
	– Lights out / Hundredweight / Junkies and whores / Someone do something / Stain to never fade / U make me want to drink bleach (stylophone mix) / Try not to think / Compilation blues. (re-iss. Mar02; same)		

		Jive	not iss.
Mar 02.	(7") (925337-7) **TRY NOT TO THINK. / EVERYONE KNOWS**		-
	(cd-s+=) (925337-2) – She's something else.		
May 02.	(7") (925355-7) **BLEACH. / PEOPLE WHO DON'T CLIMB LADDERS ...**	67	-
	(cd-s+=) (925355-2) – Lights out.		
Jun 02.	(cd) (922337-2) **THIS IS WHERE I STAND**		-
	– Armistice / Try not to think / 100 weight / Junkies and whores / This is where I stand / A stain to never fade / Demons / By the sea / Bleach / You and me / You were right.		
Sep 02.	(7") (925409-7) **YOU AND ME. / RIGHT THING**	57	-
	(cd-s) (925409-2) – ('A'side) / Little sensation / Hopelessly devoted to you.		
	(cd-s) (925410-2) – ('A'side) / Better ways to self destruct / ('A'video).		

ECHOBELLY

Formed: London, England . . . 1992 by Anglo-Asian, SONYA AURORA MADAN, alongside co-writer and guitarist, GLENN JOHANSSON, ALEX KEYSER and ANDY HENDERSON. With MADAN's BLONDIE-esque vocals set to a SMITHS-style musical backdrop, ECHOBELLY were one of Brit-pop's early leading lights, debuting in late '93 with the 'BELLYACHE' EP. Adding former CURVE guitar abuser, DEBBIE SMITH (who had initially filled in for the injured JOHANSSON on a tour of the States with MORRISSEY, one of their biggest fans apparently!) and signing to the independent 'Fauve' label, the band released a debut album, 'EVERYONE'S GOT ONE' (as in EGO), in summer '94. Its jagged indie pop and intelligent, aware lyrics drew considerable critical acclaim and, combining studied cool with a vaguely PC agenda, MADAN became something of a female figurehead for the genre along with LOUISE WENER (SLEEPER) and JUSTINE FRISCHMANN (ELASTICA). A Top 10 UK hit, the album's success spurred them on to greater things as the Britpop phenomena reached its zenith in the summer of '95. That year's follow-up set, 'ON', was a bigger budget affair which nevertheless still managed to capture ECHOBELLY's abrasive immediacy, the record making the UK Top 5. The songwriting was as caustic as ever, singles 'KING OF THE KERB' and 'DARK THERAPY', making the Top 30. By the release of 1997's 'LUSTRA', however, the Britpop bubble had long since burst and, along with acts such as SLEEPER, ECHOBELLY seemed to be at the sharp end of the backlash. Out for the count for around four years, ECHOBELLY (SONYA, ANDY and GLENN) sprung back into action for 2001's comeback set, 'PEOPLE ARE EXPENSIVE'. A marked improvement on their lack-'LUSTRA' set and released on their own 'Fry Up' imprint, it nevertheless failed to generate any new fanbase. But they were back at least.

Album rating: EVERYONE'S GOT ONE (*6) / ON (*5) / LUSTRA (*4) / PEOPLE ARE EXPENSIVE (*5) / I CAN'T IMAGINE THE WITHOUT ME – THE BEST OF ECHOBELLY compilation (*7)

SONYA AURORA MADAN – vocals / **GLENN JOHANSSON** – guitar / **ALEX KEYSER** – bass, piano / **ANDY HENDERSON** – drums

Pandemonium / not iss.

Nov 93. (12"ep/cd-ep) *(PANN/+CD 001)* **BELLYACHE**
– Give her a gun / Call me names / England swings.
Jan 94. (12"ep/cd-ep) *(PANN/+CD 002)* **BELLYACHE / SLEEPING HITLER. / GIVE HER A GUN / I DON'T BELONG HERE**
(re-iss. May94; PANN/+CD 003)

Fauve-Epic / Epic

Mar 94. (7"/c-s) *(FAUV 001/+C)* **INSOMNIAC. / TALENT** — 47
(12"+=) *(FAUV 001T)* – ('A'mix).
(cd-s++=) *(FAUV 001CD)* – Centipede.

—— added **DEBBIE SMITH** – guitar noise

Jun 94. (7"/c-s) *(FAUV 002/+C)* **I CAN'T IMAGINE THE WORLD WITHOUT ME. / VENUS WHEEL** — 39
(12"+=/cd-s+=) *(FAUV 002 T/CD)* – Sober.
Aug 94. (cd/c/lp) *(FAUV 3 CD/C/LPS) <66775>* **EVERYONE'S GOT ONE** — 8 — Oct94
– Today tomorrow sometime never / Father, ruler, king, computer / Give her a gun / I can't imagine the world without me / Bellyache / Taste of you / Insomniac / Call me names / Close . . . but / Cold feet warm heart / Scream.
Oct 94. (cd/c-s/12") *(FAUV 004/+C/T)* **CLOSE . . . BUT. / SO LA DI DA** — 59
(cd-s+=) *(FAUV 004CD)* – I can't image the world without me (live) / Cold feet warm heart (live).

Fauve-Epic / Work–Columbia

Aug 95. (c-s) *(FAUV 5C)* **GREAT THINGS / HERE COMES THE SCENE** — 13
(cd-s+=) *(FAUV 5CD)* – God's guest list / On turn off.
(cd-s) *(FAUV 5CDX)* – ('A'side) / On turn on / Bunty / One after 5 a.m.
Sep 95. (cd/c/lp) *(FAUV 6 CD/C/LP) <67368>* **ON** — 4 — Oct95
– Oar fiction / King of the kerb / Great things / Natural animal / Go away / Pantyhose and roses / Something hot in a cold country / Four letter word / Nobody like you / In the year / Dark therapy / Worms an angels.
Oct 95. (c-s) *(FAUV 7C)* **KING OF THE KERB / CAR FICTION (French)** — 25
(cd-s+=) *(FAUV 7CD)* – On turn on (acoustic) / Natural animal (acoustic).
(cd-s) *(FAUV 7CDX)* – ('A'live) / I can't imagine the world without me (live) / Insomniac (live) / Great things (live).
Feb 96. (7"blue-ep/c-ep/cd-ep) *(FAUV 8/+C/CD)* **DARK THERAPY / WE KNOW BETTER. / ATOM / ALOHA LOLITA** — 20

—— (Aug'95) **JAMES HARRIS** – bass; repl. KEYSER

—— in Mar'97, SONYA MADAN featured on the (US male producer) LITHIAM (UK Top 40) single, 'Ride A Rocket'

Epic / Epic

Aug 97. (c-s/cd-s) *(664815-4/-2)* **THE WORLD IS FLAT / HOLDING THE WIRE / THE WORLD IS FLAT (mix)** — 31
(cd-s+=) *(664815-5)* – Drive myself distracted / Falling flame.
Oct 97. (c-s) *(665245-4)* **HERE COMES THE BIG RUSH / MOUTH ALMIGHTY** — 56
(cd-s+=) *(665245-2)* – Tesh.
(cd-s) *(665245-5)* – ('A'mixes).
Nov 97. (cd/c) *(<488967-2/-4>)* **LUSTRA** — 47
– Bulldog baby / I'm not a saint / Here comes the big rush / Iris art / The world is flat / Everyone knows better / Wired on / O / Bleed / Paradise / Angel B / Lustra.

—— **SONYA, ANDY + GLENN** returned with guests **SIMON ROBINSON** – bass + **KEN CAMPBELL** – keyboards

Fry Up / not iss.

Jan 01. (cd-ep) *(FRYUPCD 001)* **DIGIT**
– Kali yuga / Digit / Kathmandu / A map is not the territory.
May 01. (cd-s) *(FRYUPCD 002)* **TELL ME WHY / I AM AWAKE / WHEN I SEE RED**
May 01. (cd) *(FRYUPCD 003)* **PEOPLE ARE EXPENSIVE**
– Fear of flying / Tell me why / Down to earth / People are expensive / Digit / Dying / Kali yuga / Everything is all / A map is not the territory / Ondine / Point Dume.
Oct 01. (cd-s) *(FRYUPCD 004)* **KALI YUGA (remix) / SLEEPING HITLER (re-recorded) / I DON'T BELONG HERE**

– compilations, etc. –

Jun 01. (cd) *Sony TV; (502427-2)* **I CAN'T IMAGINE THE WORLD WITHOUT ME – THE BEST OF ECHOBELLY**
– I can't imagine the world without me / Insomniac / Call me names / Great things / The world is flat / Here comes the big rush / We know better / King of the kerb / Cold feet warm heart / Atom / Close but . . . / Father ruler king computer / Bellyache / Iris art / Give her a gun / Today tomorrow sometime never / Car fiction (French version) / Dark therapy.

ECHOBOY

Formed: Nottingham, England . . . 1998 by former mod crazy HYBRIDS frontman, RICHARD WARREN. The previous year – along with DARREN SHELDON and LOUIS DIVITO – the trio delivered a handful of singles and an eponymous album before being unceremoniously dumped by their label, 'Heavenly'. Taking an alternative option for his next project, the 26 year old established ECHOBOY the following year, having walked out on The HYBRIDS after a gig with PAUL WELLER. Then WARREN's electronica passion began. Fusing KRAFTWERK with ROBERT PALMER, fuzzy techniques and 12 minute long psychedelia, ECHOBOY issued a collection of singles and EP's, the eponymous 'ECHOBOY' being among the best of the crop. WARREN was also very prolific when choosing record labels, 'Mute' records (home of ADD N TO X, NICK CAVE, etc) issuing the EP, 'FRANCES SAYS THE KNIFE IS ALIVE', while 'Earworm' released 'SCENE 30' and 'For Us' delivered 'PURE NEW WOOL'; each setting a strong case for why this former SMALL FACES fanatic should not have been misunderstood. Having apparently turned down an invitation to join OASIS, the year 2000, kicked off with WARREN's debut ECHOBOY album proper, appropriately titled 'VOLUME 1', a fine exploration in the moodier side of electronic-pop. 'VOLUME 2' (also issued in 2000), was a little more subdued than its predecessor, although it did have its refining moments courtesy of 'TELSTAR RECOVERY' and 'SIOBHAN'. In September 2002, ECHOBOY released the single, 'AUTOMATIC EYES', a track from his/their forthcoming set in 2003.

Album rating: ECHOBOY mini (*7) / VOLUME ONE (*6) / VOLUME TWO (*5) / Hybrids: THE HYBRIDS (*6)

HYBRIDS

RICHARD WARREN – vocals, guitar / **DARREN SHELDON** – bass / **LOUIS DIVITO** – drums

Heavenly / not iss.

Jun 97. (10"ep/cd-ep) *(HVN 71 10/CD)* **TAKE YOU DOWN EP**
– Seventeen / Reeling / Peter take me down / The only ones (part 2).
Sep 97. (7") *(HVN 75)* **STRANDED. / FREEDOM FIGHTER**
(cd-s+=) *(HVN 75CD)* – Morning song.
Dec 97. (7") *(HVN 78)* **24. / WHERE I WANT TO BE**
(cd-s+=) *(HVN 78CD)* – Tell me.
Feb 98. (7") *(HVN 80)* **SEE ME THROUGH. / GOOD**
(cd-s+=) *(HVN 80CD)* – You / The only ones (Peel session).
Mar 98. (lp/c/cd) *(HVNLP 20/+MC/CD)* **THE HYBRIDS**
– Ball of twine / 24 / I'm coming out / See me through / Call me blue / The only ones (acoustic) / Born yesterday / The wanderers / Stranded / Words / Suzy Parker / I feel the weight. *(lp w/ free 7"; HVN 83)* – PETER TAKE ME DOWN. / TELL ME

Spectre Nocturnus / not iss.

Sep 98. (7") *(NOC 1)* **ON THE END OF THE 7th DAY. / COLD MOON OVER BLACK WATER: YASNALA**

—— disbanded after above

ECHOBOY

—— **RICHARD WARREN / LEE HORSLEY + LEONI + MR. MOORE**

Point Blank / not iss.

Jul 98. (cdep) *(BLANK 1CD)* **FLASHLEGS (SUITE)**
– Flashlegs (suite) / Flesh / Flight 21.
Feb 99. (m-cd) *(BLANK 2CD)* **ECHOBOY**
– Flashlegs (suite) / Flesh / Scene 30 / Wrap / Daylight / Flight 21 / Mountain song / Signs.

Earworm / not iss.

Mar 99. (10") *(WORM 42)* **SCENE 30. / VITAMINS AND OIL**

For Us / not iss.

May 99. (d7"ep) **PURE NEW WOOL. /**

Mute / Mute

Sep 99. (d10"ep/cd-ep) *(10/CD MUTE 237)* **FRANCES SAYS THE KNIFE IS ALIVE EP**
– Frances says the knife is alive / Canada / Touched / Slow down Sheena.
Feb 00. (12") **CONSTANTINOPLE. / USHERETTES**
Mar 00. (cd/lp) *(CD+/STUMM 180) <9123>* **VOLUME 1** — — May00
– 55 / Kit and Holly / Model 352 / Broken hearts / Constantinople / Crocodile milk / Walking / Contact.
Apr 00. (7") *(MUTE 246)* **KIT AND HOLLY. / EAST SHEEN**
(cd-s) *(CDMUTE 246)* – ('A'side) / Sixteen drums / Don't cross the sea.

ECHOBOY (cont)

Sep 00. (12"ep/cd-ep) *(12/CD MUTE 256)* **TELSTAR RECOVERY**
– Telstar recovery / Moving / Pressure drop / Scarab major 3000.
Sep 00. (cd/lp) *(CD+/STUMM 192)* <9142> **VOLUME 2** Nov00
– Turning on / Telstar recovery / Kelly's truck / Siobhan / Make the city the sound / Schram and the sheddle 262 / Sudwestfunk No.5 / Circulation / High pitch needs.
May 01. (12"ep/cd-ep) *(12/CD MUTE 257)* **TURNING ON**
– Turning on / Every household should have one / I'll always remember / Shortwave.
(12") *(L12MUTE 257)* – ('A'mixes).
Sep 02. (7") *(MUTE 277)* **AUTOMATIC EYES. / I LOVE YOU**
(cd-s) *(CDMUTE 277)* – ('A'side) / So far away / Blackened country.

– compilations, etc. –

Apr 01. (d-cd) *Mute; (ECHOBOYCD 1/2)* **VOLUME ONE / VOLUME TWO**

EGGMAN (see under ⇒ BOO RADLEYS)

EGGS

Formed: Arlington, Richmond, Virginia, USA ... 1990 by ANDREW BEAUJAN and a cast of players including GRENADINE trombonist, ROB CHRISTIANSEN, who was introduced to ANDREW through mutual acquaintance, MARK ROBINSON (of UNREST, GRENADINE and boss of the 'Teenbeat' imprint). Signed to the latter label, the loose aggregate debuted with the 'BRUISER' set in early '92, an adventurous record that took indie guitar-pop as a canvas and adorned it with everything from Latin-styled pop to off-kilter brass flourishes behind BEAUJAN's parched vocals. Having already poached a series of drummers from local peers, the band's backstage shenanigans began resembling a SPINAL TAP-style scenario as they went through more sticksmen than a Welsh colliery marching band. The following year, the basic trio of BEAUJAN, CHRISTIANSEN and new bassist EVAN SHURAK issued a rare UK single, 'THE GOVERNMENT ADMINISTRATOR', while also winning over fans and artists alike via their slot on the Lollapalooza tour. Recorded at the American University in Virginia (where ROB slogs away at his day job), an exhaustive second album, 'TEENBEAT 96 EXPLODER' (1994) made little compromise to commercial considerations with a near 20-track marathon of skewed pop. After the EGGS went sunny side down, CHRISTIANSEN formed his own outfit, VIVA SATELLITE!, the albums 'NISHMA' and 'EXTRA EYE' coming out in '96 and '97 respectively. The man's next project was The SISTERHOOD OF CONVOLUTED THINKERS, virtually a collaboration with singing wife JEANNINE DURFEE. Signed to 'Darla' records, SOCT released an eponymous set in 1999 before setting off to Japan to record sophomore effort 'UME SOUR' (2001) – the title of a Japanese plum drink. Described as quarky and strange, the 'THINKERS drew their inspiration from the ambient Orient and Broadway musicals fused into one synthetic indie framework.

Album rating: BRUISER (*7) / TEENBEAT 96 EXPLODER (*7) / HOW DO YOU LIKE YOUR LOBSTER compilation (*6) / Viva Satellite!: NISHMA (*5) / IN EXTRA EYE (*5) / the Sisterhood Of Convoluted Thinkers: THE SISTERHOOD OF CONVOLUTED THINKERS (*6) / UME SOUR (*7)

ANDREW BEAUJAN – guitar, vocals / **JONATHON RICKMAN** – guitar, vocals / **DAVE PARK** – bass / **MARIANNE McGEE** – French horn / with 5th member **ROB CHRISTIANSEN** – trombone, guitar (of GRENADINE)

                not iss. Teenbeat

Sep 91. (7") <*TEENBEAT 66*> **SKYSCRAPER. / OCELOT**
May 92. (cd/lp) <*TEENBEAT 76 CD/V*> **BRUISER**
– Spaceman / John's bar Mitzvah / Opener / It's hard to be an egg / Cushion / Theme from Bob / Hippie purple / Bruiser / Ebenezer / President / Ocelot (party mix) / This party never ends. *(UK-iss.Sep94; same)*

                not iss. Positive Force

1992. (7") **ERIN GO BRAGH! / IN STATE**

                not iss. Jade Tree

Jan 93. (7"ep) **JADE TREE EP**
– It's hard to be an egg / Sugar babe.

                not iss. Landspeed

Feb 93. (7") **THE OBLIVIIST PART ONE. / BAKED ALASKA**

                not iss. Hemiola

Mar 93. (7") **THE GOVERNMENT ADMINISTRATOR. / SUGAR BABE**

                Simple Machines Simple Machines

May 93. (7") <*smwh 4*> **ROLL AWAY THE STONE. / Jonny Cohen & The Shoetrees: Xmas Trees Everywhere** Apr93

— **ANDREW + ROB** recruited **EVAN SHURAK** – bass; to repl. PARK

                Teenbeat Teenbeat

Dec 93. (7") **A PIT WITH SPIKES. / A SPARKLING MIX**
Feb 94. (cd/c/d-lp) <*TEENBEAT 96 CD/C/LP*> **EGGS TEENBEAT 96 EXPLODER**
– Eggs Teenbeat 96 exploder, let's go! / Why am I so tired all the time? / Er in go bragh / Music without keys No.3 / Ampallang / Side division / March of the triumphant elephants / Claire's snakes / Pit with spikes / Evanston, Il. / Willow, willow / Eggs TNBT 96 XPLDR How're you doing? / Side division / Minestrone / Saturday's cool / Maureen's beans / Conchita / Side division / Oblivist part 3 / Rollercoaster / Music without keys No.7 / Salsa garden / Eggs Teenbeat 96 exploder bye bye!
Sep 94. (7") <*TEENBEAT 136*> **GENETIC ENGINEERING. / EGGS WHFS THEME #2**
Jul 95. (cd) <*TB 156CD*> **HOW DO YOU LIKE YOUR LOBSTER?**
(compilation of early singles)

— they broke-up (sorry!)

VIVA SATELLITE!

— **CHRISTIANSEN** with **IAN JONES** – guitars + **PAIGE SMITH** – vocals / **DAN MORRISSEY**

                not iss. Happy Go Lucky

1994. (7") <*HAPPY 002*> **TRAVAILLE SUR LE FILLE. / LE VIN EST MAL**

                Teenbeat Teenbeat

Nov 94. (7") <*TB 146*> **LEONARDO (ACT 1). / LEONARD (ACT 2)**
Jan 96. (cd) <*TB 186*> **NISHMA**
– The legend of how salt water Taffy came to be / Detente in four movements / Timebomb / Project Nishma / Supreme courting / The great bird of the galaxy / Moses.

— added **DAN MORRISSEY** – guitar, keyboards, vocals

Oct 97. (cd) <*TB 246*> **IN EXTRA EYE** Sep97
– Theme / Landing song / Dwight, the crude, but loveable, bastard / Bridget and her father / Meeting I / Meeting II / Secret wedding plans / Three's company / Halted at the altar / Paranoid / Coda / Theme electronique.

— CHRISTIANSEN was to join the short-lived GAZETTEERS

SISTERS OF CONVOLUTED THINKERS

ROB CHRISTIANSEN + JEANNINE DURFEE with session people incl. **JONATHON RICKMAN, STEVE SILVERSTEIN, JIM COURSEY, PEAT BIBY**, etc.

                Darla Darla

Mar 99. (cd) <*(DRL 083)*> **THE SISTERHOOD OF CONVOLUTED THINKERS** Jul99
– Action 98 / Ramanhat nbaddah / Raaaahhh! / Warrenton 1 / Sable / Klaus McGurdy's mechanized clock / Time piece / Just look at the building . . . it stands / Pablo, deepsea awuanautics mausoleum / Timing is correct / A goof plays on the roof / I will / Investor relations / Doors and humming. *(lp-iss.on '555'; 555LP 6)*
Apr 00. (7"ep) *(555/22)* **LUNCHDATE EP**
(above issued on '555')
Feb 01. (cd) <*(DRL 112CD)*> **UME SOUR**
– Ami-Chan, Mai-Chan / Ne-ne Ami-Chan / Lunchdate / Song for Tony and Ian / Tottori made / Nen-ga-joo / Yakusoku (a promise) / Armstrong archer / Sayuri / The rainbow.

EGGSTONE

Formed: Malmo, Sweden ... 1986 by PER SUNDLING, PATRIK BARTOSCH and MAURITS VARLSSON. Working hard to get their break through constant touring and recording demos, EGGSTONE finally self-financed their debut 7", 'BUBBLEBED', in 1991. After a second indie retro-pop single for 'Supersound', 'SHOOTING TIME', they signed a deal with Sweden's top independent, 'Snap', re-issuing the aforementioned EP as '...AT POINT LOMA'. Also in 1992, the first fresh fruits of their labour came courtesy of two further releases, the EP '...IN LEMON GROVE' and the CD-album '...IN SAN DIEGO', the latter containing a homeland radio hit, 'CAN'T COME CLOSE ENOUGH'. With producer Michael Blair at the controls, they released their sophomore set, 'SOMERSAULT' (1994), this time Japan heralding their talent while making 'WATER' a healthy hit. Although never quite fulfilling their potential in other countries such as the UK (like fellow countrymen/women The CARDIGANS and The WANNADIES had achieved), EGGSTONE managed to brighten up the life of many a Scandic pop fan and were known as "the godfathers of Swedish pop". Further long-players, 'VIVE LA DIFFERENCE!' (1997) and 'CA CHAUFEE EN SUEDE AVEC EGGSTONE' (1999), have kept the band and their twee fanbase amused.

Album rating: EGGSTONE IN SAN DIEGO (*7) / SOMERSAULT (*5) / VIVE LA DIFFERENCE! (*5) / CA CHAUFEE EN SUEDE AVEC EGGSTONE (*5) / SPANISH SLALOM compilation (*5)

PER SUNDING – vocals, bass / **PATRIK BARTOSCH** – guitar / **MAURITS CARLSSON** – drums

                Supersound not iss.

1991. (7"m) *(ESTS 01)* **BUBBLEBED. / HAVE YOU SEEN MARY / SEE THE GOOD TIMES** Sweden
1991. (7"ep) *(ESTS 02)* **SHOOTING TIME** Sweden
– Shooting time / Wrong heaven / My trumpets / Doesn't matter. *(re-iss. 1992 as 'EGGSTONE AT POINT LOMA' on 'Snap' 12"ep/cd-ep; SNAP T/C 2)*

                Snap Critique

1992. (cd-s) *(SNAPC 7)* **EGGSTONE IN LEMON GROVE** Sweden
– Can't come close enough / Those words / Diesel smoke / Have you seen Mary.
Nov 92. (cd) *(SNAP 002)* **EGGSTONE IN SAN DIEGO**
– Ooh ooh ma ma mine / Shooting time / Those words / Sun king / Have you seen Mary / Suffocation at sea / Wrong heaven / Go back / Can't come close enough / If you say / Beach boy / She's perfect / See the good things. *(lp-iss.1997 on 'Vibrafon'; VIBRLP 1)*
May 94. (cd) *(SNAP 009)* <*CR 15427*> **SOMERSAULT** Oct94
– Against the sun / It's not the rain / Hang on to your eco / Good morning / Desdemona / The dog / Water / Luck / Cornflake crown / Split / Happiest fool. *(lp-iss.1997 on 'Vibrafon'; VIBRLP 2)*
Jun 94. (cd-s) *(SNAPC 20)* **WATER / ANAETHESIA** Sweden

                Vibrafon not iss.

May 96. (cd-s) *(VIBRCD 16)* **SUMMER AND LOOKING FOR A JOB / BRASS** Sweden
Dec 96. (cd-s) *(VIBRCD 21)* **NEVER BEEN A BETTER DAY / A BETTER DAY** Sweden
Feb 97. (cd)(lp) *(VIBRCD 19)(VIBRLP 3)* **VIVA LE DIFFERENCE!** Sweden
– Head around / Supermeaningfeetlyless / Birds in cages / Never been a better day / Taramasalata / Il trascurato / April and May / Marabous / Still all stands still / Neil.
Apr 97. (cd-ep) *(VIBRCD 31)* **APRIL AND MAY / WAITING FOR THE BELL / PENGUIN / MIZU** Sweden
Oct 97. (cd-s) *(VIBRCD 25)* **BIRDS AND CAGES / EL BLUES DEL TIJUANA** Sweden

Jun 99. (cd) (<30512-2>) **CA CHAUFFE EN SUEDE AVEC EGGSTONE** (Tricatel / not iss. – May01)
– Waiting for the bell / Still all stands still / Against the sun / If you say / Summer and looking for a job / See the good things / Good morning / She's perfect / Marabous / Wrong heaven / Beach boy / Shooting time / Penguin / Sun king / The dog / Birds in cages / Brass / Taramasalata / Mizu.

— split after above

– compilations, others, etc. –

Apr 99. (cd) *Siesta; (SIESTA 82CD)* **SPANISH SLALOM**
– April and May / Summer and looking for a job / My trumpets / The dog / A better day / Birds in cages / If you say / She's perfect / Dreamer / Desdemona / Brass / Good morning / Diesel smoke / Wrong heaven / Still all stands still / Supermeaningfectyless / Water / Penguin.

18th DYE

Formed: Copenhagen, Denmark . . . early 1992 by Berlin-born SEBASTIAN BUTTRICH, Dane PIET BENDSTEN and half-German/half-Dane/South American-raised blonde HEIKE RADEKER. Meeting while on holiday in the Danish capital, the trio set about touring the rest of Europe before unleashing their debut set 'DONE' (1992), which still upheld the cut'n'paste hostility while adding BUTTRICH's soothing vocals to give it an eerie sense of control. Their UK debut for 'Che', the single 'WHOLE WIDE WORLD', was a celebratory Berlin-inspired tune with deep lyrics and aggressive bass under violent chaos. One year later (1995), and without hesitation, the cosmopolitan 3-piece released a second album proper under the strange title of 'TRIBUTE TO A BUS' on 'Matador' (home of PAVEMENT and SOLEX). The long-player had its crucifying sonic assaults but veered towards the VELVET UNDERGROUND's 'White Light – White Heat' with some beautiful mellow tracks squeezed in between RADEKER's crunching bass. The album was also mixed and recorded by former BIG BLACK, RAPEMAN and SHELLAC contributor STEVE ALBINI, whose credits include varieties so diverse as LOW and NIRVANA, so you can imagine what the finished product sounded like. • **Covered:** ISN'T IT A PITY (Galaxie 500).

Album rating: DONE (*6) / CRAYON mini (*4) / TRIBUTE TO A BUS (*7)

HEIKE RADEKER – vocals, bass / **SEBASTIAN BUTTRICH** – guitar, vocals / **PIET BENDSTEN** – drums

Cloudland / not iss.
Nov 92. (cd/lp) *(RAIN 003 CD/LP)* **DONE** – / – Danish
– Merger / Whole wide world / 9 out of 10 / Dive / Either / Club Madame / To a sunny day / Can you wink? / Stupidity / Club / Tumbling down / Girls boots / Tar. *(UK-iss.Jun94 on 'Che' cd/lp; che 12 cd/lp) <US-iss.Nov94 on 'Matador' cd/10"lp; OLE 117-2/-1>*
Oct 93. (m-cd/m-lp) **CRAYON** – / – Danish
– Aug. / 16 ink / Ray / Mystics II / Crank / Nuit N. *(<UK/US-iss.Dec94 on 'Matador'; OLE 118-2/-1>)*

Che / Quixotic
Apr 94. (7") *(che 10)* **WHOLE WIDE WORLD. / FRAGILE STARS**
May 94. (7"m) *<QX 013-7>* **HEY, WHY NOT? / COFFEE CUP REVISITED. / DIVE** – / –

Che / Matador
Jul 94. (7"m) *(che 15)* **DIVE. / CAN YOU WINK / PLUMBING**
Jan 95. (7"m) *(che 25) <OLE 137>* **PLAY W/ YOU. / GOUT S.F. / F** / May95
Mar 95. (cd/c/lp) *(che 26 cd/mc/lp) <OLE 125-2/-4/-1>* **TRIBUTE TO A BUS** / Apr95
– Glass house failure / Sole arch / Only burn / Play with you / Label / No time – 11 (spectators) / Poolhouse blue / Go! song / D. / Galeer / Mitsuo downer / Easy (& how we got there 1st).

Flowershop / not iss.
Jul 95. (7') **F H 4. / TRAINS AND BOATS AND PLANES**

— split later that year; BUTTRICH + BENDTSEN formed KIKKERT (later TEST – MILK IN MY LANGUAGE) while RADEKER became part of EVONIKE (no records issued UK/US)

– compilations, etc. –

1999. (cd) *Extreme Sports Armchair Enthusiast;* **LEFT** (leftovers, b-sides, demos and covers) – / – Danish
– Fragile stars / It feels like I'm in love / Coffee cup revisited / Poolhouse blue (demo version) / Only burn / Pour / Can U wink? (demo) / Mystics II (by PORT FRIENDLY) / Aug. (by HEADBUTT) / Merger (by SHOULD) / Sole arch (by NASA DUDE) / F 4 / Trains and boats and planes / Plumbing and soon forgetting / Merger / Nuit N / I was good / Axis / 55 / Isn't it a pity.

18 WHEELER

Formed: Glasgow, Scotland . . . early 90's by SEAN JACKSON, NEIL HALLIDAY, ALAN HAKE and DAVID KEENAN. A Glasgow band in the firmly established mould and a prime contender for Alan McGee's Creation offshoot label, 'August', 18 WHEELER emerged in 1993 with an eponymous EP prior to the cutesy indie-pop of the 'NATURE GIRL' single. This was followed by the country-ish 'SUNCRUSH', the DINOSAUR JR.-esque guitar squall of 'KUM BACK' and the TEENAGE FANCLUB impression, 'THE REVEALER', prior to the release of debut album, 'TWIN ACTION' in 1994. A trainee TEENAGE FANCLUB wouldn't be such a bad description for this lot in fact, preoccupied as they are with airy harmonies, sugary melodies and a fixation for the classic American triple-B i.e. The BYRDS, The BEACH BOYS and BIG STAR (plus the obligatory GRAM PARSONS factor, the lads even including what is presumably a tribute track, 'GRAM'). No bad thing if you're after a pleasant listen – and 'PROCK SHAKE' really hits the mark – but hardly a contender for a Mercury music prize. With the addition of extra guitarist STEVE HADDOW, follow-up set, 'FORMANKA' (1995), was grungier and relatively more adventurous, even employing strings on the moody instrumental title track. Still, by this point 18 WHEELER had been well and truly eclipsed at 'Creation' by a certain OASIS, the same Manc hopefuls that had supported them only a few years ago in Glasgow! Seemingly destined to forever linger in the Caledonian margins along with The PASTELS, WHITEOUT, The GYRES etc. etc., 18 WHEELER would've needed a tank of rocket fuel if they were to have any hope of breaking through.

Album rating: TWIN ACTION (*4) / FORMANKA (*5) / YEAR ZERO (*3)

SEAN JACKSON – vocals, guitar, bass, piano / **ALAN HAKE** – bass, vocals, guitar, Moog / **NEIL HALLIDAY** – percussion, vocals, guitars, synth / **DAVID KEENAN** – was an early member, before he formed the TELSTAR PONIES

August-Creation / not iss.
May 93. (12"ep/cd-ep) *(caug 005 t/cd)* **18 WHEELER EP**
Sep 93. (12"ep/cd-ep) *(caug 006 t/cd)* **NATURE GIRL. / PILLOW FIGHT / GOLDEN CANDLES**
Dec 93. (12"ep/cd-ep) *(caug 010 t/cd)* **SUNCRUSH / YER EYES. / FALLING OUT OF LOVE / SOME THINGS LAST A LONG TIME**

Creation / not iss.
May 94. (7") *(CRE 148)* **KUM BACK. / POTS OF TEA**
(cd-s+=) *(CRESCD 148)* – Alness curls / Pond life.
Jul 94. (7") *(CRE 188)* **THE REVEALER. / HUGGY BEAR**
(cd-s+=) *(CRESCD 188)* –
Jul 94. (cd/c/lp) *(CRECD/CCRE/CRELP 164)* **TWIN ACTION**
– Sweet tooth / Nature girl / Kum back / Golden candles / The revealer / Honey mink / Gram / Prock shake / Hotel 167 / Suncrush / Frosty hands / Life is strange / I won't let you down / Wet dream.

— added **STEVEN HADDOW** – guitar (was backing vocalist on debut)
Apr 95. (7"/cd-s) *(CRE/+SCD 198)* **BODDHA. / FORMANKA**
May 95. (cd/lp) *(CRE CD/LP 181)* **FORMANKA**
– Boddha / Drought / Steel guitars / Cartoon / The bottle / Formanka / Winter grrrl / Pretty ugly / The track / John the revelator. *(free cd/lp w/ above) (CRED CD/LP 181L)*
Jun 95. (7") *(CRE 209)* **STEEL GUITARS. / SOUNDS**
(cd-s+=) *(CRESCD 209)* – Truth drug / Zombie zombie.
Aug 96. (12") *(CRE 219T)* **THE HOURS AND THE TIMES / ('A'-Ultra Living mix). / BEYOND THE VALLEY OF THE HOURS AND THE TIMES / ('A'-the A&R guys mix – Danny Saber)**
(cd-s) *(CRESCD 219)* – ('A'side) / ('A'-William Orbit porcupine mix) / ('A'-Scissorkicks nutscape navigator mix).
Sep 96. (c-s) *(CRECD 232)* **CRABS / ('A'-Eyes on stalks mix)**
(12"+=)(cd-s+=) *(CRE 232T)(CRESCD 232)* – ('A'-Fis night fell mix) / ('A'-The Hooded claw mix).
Nov 96. (12") *(CRE 241T)* **PROZAC BEATS. / TASH**
(cd-s+=) *(CRESCD 241)* – Fuck easy listening / ('A'version).
Mar 97. (12") *(CRE 249T)* **STAY / STAY (Strange L'Escargot mix). / STAY (Big Kahuna mix) / STAY (Dr. Rockit mix)** 59 / –
(cd-s) *(CRESCD 249)* – ('A'side) / ('A'-Radio Orbit mix) / ('A'-Strange L'escargot mix) / Grease (wide receiver aural exciter mix).
(cd-s) *(CRESCD 249X)* – ('A'side) / ('A'mixes; Stereo odessey / Big Kahuna / Dr.Rockit / album).
Mar 97. (cd/lp) *(CRE CD/LP 192)* **YEAR ZERO**
– The hours and the times / Crabs / Stay / Grease / Prozac beats / The ballad of Paul Verlaine / Everythings dead / Retard / Blue eyed son / Den dagen, den sorgen / Planesong.
Apr 97. (c-s) *(CRECS 255)* **GREASE / THE BALLAD OF PAUL VERLAINE (Bentley Rhythm Ace mix)**
(12"+=)(cd-s+=) *(CRE 255T)(CRESCD 255)* – ('A'-Wide receiver heavy goods mix) / ('A'-M.C. ARR grass in Piccadilly mix).

— split after above

EIGHTIES MATCHBOX B-LINE DISASTER

Formed: Brighton, England . . . 1998 by GUY McKNIGHT, MARC NORRIS, ANDY HUXLEY, SYM GHARIAL and drummer TOM DIMANTEPOULO. A mish-mash of skull-busting sonics and frantic gothic rock'n'roll, The EIGHTIES MATCHBOX B-LINE DISASTER (an actual vintage 1940's hot-rod) would, probably, "fuck your mother" if they had the chance. They began playing riotous shows in their native Brighton, but since it wasn't a very rock'n'roll town these days, the group busted out and on to vinyl via the independent 'MORNING HAS BROKEN' single. They finally signed to 'M.C.A.' at the beginning of 2002. They issued the incestuous single 'CELEBRATE YOUR MOTHER' that September, a song so debased it actually sounded like The BIRTHDAY PARTY on crack (if that's possible); although singer McKNIGHT would deny it, his voice was an almost dead ringer of CAVE's. What followed? More debauchery; a twelve-track album entitled 'HORSE OF THE DOG' (2002) – that was under twenty-eight minutes long – evoked the same trashy scuzz-ball rockin' blues of The CRAMPS. A tour with The PARKINSONS followed which was said to have ended in happy chaos. Lock up your daughters because The EMB-LD want to "invent rock"!

Album rating: HORSE OF THE DOG (*8)

GUY McKNIGHT – vocals / **MARC NORRIS** – guitar / **ANDY HUXLEY** – guitar / **SYM GHARIAL** – bass / **TOM DIAMANTEPOULO** – drums

8 STOREY WINDOW

Formed: London, England... early 90's by Boston-born CHRIS CONKLIN, a British resident since 1987. He initially employed his songwriting skills in SPINNING JENNY before hooking up with ex-JANE POW drummer, ANDY CRISP and bassist STEVE GEORGE. Following a couple of EP's in 1992 (the second of which opened with 'I THOUGHT YOU TOLD ME EVERYTHING'), the trio supported LEVITATION, the TERRY BICKERS connection serving them well a year on as the feted guitarist played and co-produced on their 1994 eponymous debut album for 'Ultimate'. By this point in time, STEVE had been substituted by JOHN LODGEPATCH, the aforementioned 'I THOUGHT...' one of the record's melancholy high spots alongside the accompanying single, 'I WILL'. Lyrically downbeat but occasionally vertigo-inducing in a NIRVANA-esque kind of way, 8 STOREY WINDOW couldn't quite elevate themselves to the dizzying heights reached by KURT COBAIN and Co.

Album rating: 8 STOREY WINDOW (*5)

CHRIS CONKLIN – vocals, guitar, keyboards (ex-SPINNING JENNY) / **ANDY CRISP** – drums, vocals, keyboards (ex-JANE POW) / **STEVE GEORGE** – bass

			Mad Minute	not iss.
May 92.	(12"ep)	(MADMIN 001) **E.P.**		–
Sep 92.	(12"ep)	(MADMIN 003) **E.P. 2**		–
		– I thought you told me everything / etc		

— CONKLIN + CRISP added **JOHN LODGEPATCH** – bass / guest **TERRY BICKERS** – guitar, producer (of LEVITATION) / **STEVE TOTERDELL** – backing vocals

			Ultimate	Atlantic
Feb 94.	(7")	(Topp 020) **I WILL. / HOLIDAY 1**		–
	(12"+=/cd-s+=) (Topp 020 T/CD) – Holiday 2.			
Apr 94.	(cd/c/lp)	(Topp CD/MC/LP 006) <4077> **8 STOREY WINDOW**		Oct95
	– I will / Close to the sky / Screaming waterfalls / I thought you told me everything / Next to nothing / Already gone / What you like / Flower hill / Laughing at yourself.			
Nov 94.	(7"red)	(Topd 030) **WHAT YOU LIKE. / IT'S BEEN DONE**		–
	(cd-s+=) (Topp 030cd) – We took a long step years ago.			
Mar 95.	(7")	(Topp 032) **I WILL. / HOLIDAY 1**		–
	(cd-s+=) (Topp 032cd) – Holiday 2.			

— disbanded soon after above

ELASTICA

Formed: London, England... October '92 by JUSTINE FRISCHMANN, who had been an embryonic member of SUEDE, with then boyfriend, BRETT ANDERSON. Signing for the new 'Deceptive' label in 1993, JUSTINE and Co (namely DONNA MATTHEWS, ANNIE HOLLAND and JUSTIN WELSH) collected critical acclaim from the music press for their debut 45, 'STUTTER'. Their (early '94) follow-up, 'LINE UP', gave them a UK Top 20 and made American labels take note. 'Geffen' soon took up the option for worldwide sales as all awaited 1995's tip for the top and their first album. New wave of the new wave featuring fuzzgun WIRE-like guitars, their blatant plagiarism didn't go without notice when they had to settle out of court with WIRE for the use of 'Three Girl Rhumba' riff on the 'CONNECTION' hit. Soon after this, The STRANGLERS were paid out of court for 'No More Heroes'-esque backing on another hit, 'WAKING UP' (however bassist, JEAN-JAQUES BURNEL, is said to be a great fan). Finally released in Spring '95, their eponymous debut album went straight into the UK charts at No.1, ELASTICA's spkiy, punk-inspired sound the toast of Brit-pop's golden year with FRISCHMANN as the scene's uncrowned ice queen. Although HOLLAND departed in summer '95, it was almost a year before replacements were found in SHEILA CHIPPERFIELD conspicuous by their absence from the recording front. FRISCHMANN subsequently refused any more press interviews following the media circus surrounding her relationship with BLUR frontman, DAMON ALBARN. The only action from the ELASTICA camp of late was the ME ME ME project (featuring STEPHEN DUFFY, Blur's ALEX JAMES and CHARLIE BLOOR) who scored a UK Top 20 hit in summer '96 with 'HANGING AROUND'. Early in '99 and despite rumours of their demise, ELASTICA were still around in one way or another. By that summer, JUSTINE, JUSTIN, 1996 acquisition DAVID BUSH, new players PAUL JONES and MEW (who took DONNA's place) plus the returning ANNIE (who replaced SHEILA CHIPPERFIELD) made up the 6-piece that were back in August '99. To coincide with a new EP/mini-set release (recorded between 1996-99) entitled, er, 'ELASTICA', the band were more than happy to return to the limelight playing the Leeds and Reading festivals. Of the six tracks (which were incidently not eligible for the charts!), probably the highlight was the number 'HOW WE WROTE ELASTICA MAN', a FALL song with MARK E. on guesting vocals. As the century came to a close, ELASTICA were in the studio polishing off a long-awaited sophomore set... That album did indeed arrive in 2000, 'THE MENACE' undergoing countless false starts and the attentions of numerous producers before finally seeing the light of day. Patient fans expecting another dose of addictive razor-pop hits were to be disappointed as JUSTINE and Co enmeshed themselves in the oblique, angular dissonance of their art-punk progenitors. Only a minor hit single, 'MAD DOG', was forthcoming and the band split in October 2001 after a swansong 45 for 'Wichita' records. • **Songwriters:** FRISCHMANN lyrics / group compositions. • **Trivia:** DAMON ALBARN (as DAN ABNORMAL – anagram) played keyboards on their debut album and featured with them on Top Of The Pops.

Album rating: ELASTICA (*8) / ELASTICA mini (*5) / THE MENACE (*6)

JUSTINE FRISCHMANN (b.1968, Twickenham) – vocals, rhythm guitar (ex-SUEDE) / **DONNA MATTHEWS** (b. Newport, Wales) – vocals, guitar / **ANNIE HOLLAND** (b. Brighton, England) – bass / **JUSTIN WELCH** (b. Nuneaton, England) – drums (ex-SUEDE)

			Deceptive	Sub Pop
Oct 93.	(7")	(BLUFF 003) <SB 275> **STUTTER. / PUSSYCAT**		Aug94
Jan 94.	(7")	(BLUFF 004) **LINE UP. / VASELINE**	20	
	(12"+=/cd-s+=) (BLUFF 004 T/CD) – Rockunroll / Annie (both John Peel sessions).			

			Deceptive	D.G.C.
Oct 94.	(7"/c-s)	(BLUFF 010/+C) **CONNECTION. / SEE THAT ANIMAL**	17	–
	(12"+=/cd-s+=) (BLUFF 010 T/CD) – Blue (demo) / Spastica.			
Feb 95.	(7"/c-s)	(BLUFF 011/+C) **WAKING UP. / CAR WASH**	13	–
	(12"+=/cd-s+=) (BLUFF 011 T/CD) – Car wash / Brighton rock.			
Mar 95.	(cd/c/lp)	(BLUFF 014 CD/C/LP) <24728> **ELASTICA**	1	66
	– Line up / Annie / Connection / Car song / Smile / Hold me now / S.O.F.T. / Indian song / Blue / All-nighter / Waking up / 2:1 / Vaseline / Never here / Stutter.			
Mar 95.	(c-s)	<19385> **CONNECTION / GLORIA**	–	53

— In Jul'95, they guested on 'Sub Pop' 4x7"box-set 'HELTER SHELTER'.

Jun 95.	(10"gold-ep/cd-ep) <DGC 10/CD 22001> **STUTTER / ROCKUNROLL. / 2:1 (1 F.M. evening session) / ANNIE (John Peel session)**	–	67

— ANNIE departed in August '95, and was replaced nearly a year later by **SHEILA CHIPPERFIELD** – bass / **DAVID BUSH** – keyboards (ex-FALL).

— ELASTICA were back in '99; JUSTINE, JUSTIN, DAVID and the returning ANNIE recruited **PAUL JONES** – guitar (ex-LINOLEUM) who repl. DONNA + MEW – keyboards (ex-HEAVE)

Aug 99.	(12"ep/cd-ep) (BLUFF 071 T/CD) **ELASTICA EP**		–
	– How we wrote Elastica man / Nothing stays the same / Miami nice / KB / Operator / Generator.		
	(above was ineligible for the singles chart)		

			Deceptive	Atlantic
Apr 00.	(cd/lp)	(BLUFF 075 CD/LP) <83386> **THE MENACE**	24	
	– Mad dog / Generator / How he wrote Elastica man / Image change / Your arse my place / Human / Nothing stays the same / Miami nice / Love like ours / KB / My sex / The way I like it / Da da da.			
Jun 00.	(7")	(BLUFF 077) **MAD DOG. / SUICIDE**	44	–
	(cd-s+=) (BLUFF 077CD1) – Bush baby.			
	(cd-s) (BLUFF 077CD2) – ('A'mixes) / ('A'video).			

			Wichita	not iss.
Nov 01.	(7")	(WEBB 0265) **THE BITCH DON'T WORK. / NO GOOD**		–

— ELASTICA split late in October 2001

– compilations, etc. –

Nov 01.	(cd) Strange Fruit; (SFRSCD 101) **THE RADIO 1 SESSIONS**		–

ME ME ME

JUSTIN WELCH + ALEX JAMES (Blur), STEPHEN DUFFY + CHARLIE BLOOR

			Indolent	not iss.
Aug 96.	(c-s/cd-s)	(DUFF 005 C/CD) **HANGING AROUND / HOLLYWOOD WIVES / TABITHA'S ISLAND**	19	–

ELBOW

Formed: Bury, Manchester, England... 1994 by GUY GARVEY, RICHARD JUPP, CRAIG POTTER, his brother MARK POTTER and PETE TURNER. Shortlisted for the Mercury Music Prize, this bittersweet collective were living proof that the Manchester music scene didn't just comprise of arrogant guitar bands kissing the feet of major labels. That said, ELBOW have mostly been kicked in the face by the majors: 'Island' dropped them as did 'E.M.I.'. But thankfully, they came bounding back to astound us with their melancholic blend of (in their own words) "prog rock, without the solos". It began when all five members met at college and frequented local haunts before they attracted the watchful eye of 'Island'. This in turn led to their debut EP, 'THE NOISEBOX', its title track 'POWDER BLUE' gaining a spot in John Peel's Festive 50 late '98. Independent record label 'Uglyman' raised the money to fund the EP's 'THE NEWBORN' and 'ANY DAY NOW', two breezy, rousing tracks heir to TURIN BRAKES, KINGS OF CONVENIENCE and the spiralling New Acoustic Movement. The acclaim for the tracks was phenomenal, with music journos citing ELBOW as the millennium's answer to RADIOHEAD (if there was such a thing!). This led to the release of their debut set 'ASLEEP IN THE BACK' (2001), an album of inspired beauty and elegance. Tracks such as 'POWDER BLUE' and 'CAN'T STOP' made you wonder what the major labels were thinking when they gave them the proverbial elbow. The album, unsurprisingly, was nominated for a Mercury music prize while it also managed a few weeks in the Top 20.

Album rating: ASLEEP IN THE BACK (*8)

ELBOW (cont)

GUY GARVEY – vocals / **CRAIG POTTER** – organ / **MARK POTTER** – guitar / **PETE TURNER** – bass / **RICHARD JUPP** – drums

			Soft	not iss.
Jan 98.	(ltd-cd-ep) **THE NOISEBOX EP**		☐	-

– Powder blue / Red / George lassoes the Moon / Theme from Munroe Kelly / Can't stop.

			Uglyman	not iss.
Aug 00.	(cd-ep) (*UGLY 20*) **THE NEWBORN EP**		☐	-

– Newborn / Kisses / Bitten by the tailfly / None one.

| Jan 01. | (cd-ep/10"ep) (*UGLY 25/+V*) **ANY DAY NOW EP** | | ☐ | - |

– Any day now / Wurzel / George lassoes the moon / Don't mix your drinks.
(cd-s) (*UGLY 25VID*) – ('A'-video).

			V2	V2
Apr 01.	(7") (*VVR 501615-7*) **RED. / VUM GARDA**		36	-

(cd-s+=) (*VVR 501615-3*) – About time.
(cd-s) (*VVR 501615-8*) – ('A'side) / Crow (acoustic) / Newborn (acoustic).

| May 01. | (cd/d-lp) (<*VVR 101588-2/-1*>) **ASLEEP IN THE BACK** | | 14 | Jun01 |

– Any day now / Red / Little beast / Powder blue / Bitten by the tailfly / Newborn / Don't mix your drinks / Presuming Ed (rest easy) / Coming second / Can't stop / Scattered black and whites. *(cd re-iss. Feb02; VVR 101901-2)*

| Jul 01. | (cd-s) (*VVR 501616-3*) **POWDER BLUE / SUFFER / ABOUT TIME (acoustic)** | | 41 | - |

(cd-s) (*VVR 501616-8*) – ('A'side) / Red (session) / Powder blue (Andy Votel mix).

| Oct 01. | (12"/cd-s) (*VVR 501617-6/-3*) **NEWBORN. / LUCKY WITH DISEASE / PRESS YOUR LIPS (NEWBORN)** – El Presidente remix | | 42 | - |

(cd-s) (*VVR 501617-8*) – ('A'side) / One thing that was bothering me / None one.

| Feb 02. | (cd-s) (*VVR 501870-3*) **ASLEEP IN THE BACK / COMING SECOND / STUMBLE** | | 19 | - |

(cd-s) (*VVR 501870-8*) – ('A'side) / Coming second (Misery Lab mix) / Stumble.

ELECTRAFIXION
(see under ⇒ ECHO & THE BUNNYMEN; in 80's section)

ELECTRASY

Formed: West Country, England . . . 1997 by STEVE ATKINS, NIGEL NISBET and ALI McKINNELL, who invited ALEX MEADOWS, PAUL PRIDMORE and JIM HAYDEN into the fold. Like many outlandish rock groups, the conception of ELECTRASY is a hyperbolated myth, with stories ranging from the tad ludicrous to the utterly insane; according to the band, their bassist was rescued from prison in a Blues Brothers-esque car chase conundrum and vocalist McKINNELL was saved from the peril of drug rehab . . . yeah right!). However, if truth were to have its wicked way in the world of rock, listeners of the pop/rock, post-techno band in question would simply realise that the cheeky 5-piece felt the need to create a macabre background which befitted their mish-mash style of weirdy rock. The first example of this being 'LOST IN SPACE', a Top 60 tune which in 1998 outsized APOLLO 440's minimal efforts. Radio stations could not get enough of the hybrid intensity of swirling guitars and the downright inexplicable use of samples, which had record companies questioning the ethics of pop. 'MORNING AFTERGLOW', their sophomore single, reached the Top 20 by reputation only, it was evident that the population had succumbed to ELECTRASY's questionable charm. The debut album 'BEAUTIFUL INSANE' (1998) followed, although this fell on its knees due to disappointing reviews and lack of promotion. It had seemed, judging by the current popularity of other mix'n'match groups like The BETA BAND, that ELECTRASY fans had grown somewhat fed-up with the troupe's confusing laboratory antics. Nevertheless, they sprang back with the double A-side single, 'BEST FRIEND'S GIRL' / 'WASTED FIXATION', as devotees awaited their next instalment.

Album rating: BEAUTIFUL INSANE (*6)

ALI McKINNELL – vocals / **STEVE ATKINS** – guitar / **NIGEL NISBET** – guitar / **PAUL PRIDMORE** – drums / **ALEX MEADOWS** – bass / **JIM HAYDEN** – keyboards, samples, etc.

			M.C.A.	not iss.
Jun 98.	(7"/c-s) (*MCS/+C 40171*) **LOST IN SPACE. / I GOT U**		60	-

(cd-s+=) (*MCSTD 40171*) – Cosmic crusader.

| Aug 98. | (c-s) (*MCSC 40184*) **MORNING AFTERGLOW / QUEEN OF THE CRIMSON NILE (honky tonk version)** | | 19 | - |

(cd-s+=) (*MCSTD 40184*) – Lost in space (summer of love mix).

| Sep 98. | (cd/c) (*MCD/MCC 60051*) **BEAUTIFUL INSANE** | | 48 | - |

– Lost in space / Queen of the crimson Nile / Strawberry sunrise / Nineteen / Best friend's girl / Morning afterglow / Chemical angel / Miracle / Beautiful insane / Angel / Demented / Today's the day.

| Nov 98. | (c-s) (*MCSC 40195*) **BEST FRIEND'S GIRL / WASTED FIXATION** | | 41 | - |

(cd-s+=) (*MCSTD 40195*) – Future funk squad's threesome (radio mix) / Get the monk out.
(cd-s) (*MCSXD 40195*) – ('A'-Fat Nanny radio edit) / ('A'edit) / Cabaret of love.

			Arista	Arista
Dec 00.	(cd) (<*07822 14644-2*>) **IN HERE WE FALL**		☐	Sep00

– Renegades / Naked / Morning afterglow / Dazed and confused / Bussed out / Cosmic castaway / Special forces / Foot soldiers / In here we fall / Angel / Cry.

—— (May'01) now without HAYDEN
—— Arista dropped them in February 2002

ELECTRELANE

Formed: Brighton, England . . . 1999 by VERITY SUSMAN, EMMA GAZE, RACHEL DALLEY and guitarist MIA CLARKE. This all-female space rock quartet began life as a verse-chorus-verse indie pop band, releasing two singles in quick succession, 'FILM MUSIC' and 'LE SONG', the latter for 'Fierce Panda'. For their post-millennium work they moved on to something more experimental after they grew bored of the restrictive indie template. After creating their independent 'Let's Rock!' label, the group began piecing together what was to become 'ROCK IT TO THE MOON' (2001), a pulsating mixture of breakbeats, atmospherics, STEREOLAB inter-fusions and riot-grrrl mentality. To coincide with this set, the group issued the 'BLUE STRAGGLER' single on 'Skint' records.

Album rating: ROCK IT TO THE MOON (*7)

MIA CLARKE – guitar, vocals / **VERITY SUSMAN** – keyboards, guitar, vocals / **RACHEL DALLEY** – bass, vocals / **EMMA GAZE** – drums, percussion, vocals

			Indenial	not iss.
May 00.	(7") (*INDENIAL 1*) **FILM MUSIC. / COME ON**		☐	-

			Fierce Panda	not iss.
Jul 00.	(7") (*NING 098*) **LE SONG. / U.O.R.**		☐	-

			Let's Rock!	Mr. Lady
Dec 00.	(7"/cd-s) (*LROCK 01/+CDS*) **GABRIEL. / JOHN WAYNE**		☐	-
Apr 01.	(7") (*LROCK 02*) **BLUE STRAGGLER. / I LOVE YOU MY FARFISA**		☐	-

(cd-s+=) (*LROCK 02CDS*) – ('A-Jagz Kooner mix).

| Apr 01. | (cd/d-lp) (*LROCK 03 CD/LP*) <22> **ROCK IT TO THE MOON** | | ☐ | 2002 |

– The invisible dog / Long dark / Gabriel / Film music / Blue straggler / Many peaks / Le song / Sparkakiade / U.O.R. / The boat / Mother.

| Sep 01. | (7") (*LROCK 04*) **FILM MUSIC. / (version)** | | ☐ | - |

(cd-s+=) (*LROCK 02CDS*) – (2 Echoboy remixes).

| Apr 02. | (12"/cd-s) (*LROCK 05 T/CDS*) **I WANT TO BE THE PRESIDENT EP** | | ☐ | - |

– I want to be the president / I only always think / I've been your fan since yesterday.

ELECTRIC COMPANY (see under ⇒ MEDICINE)

ELECTRIC SOFT PARADE

Formed: Brighton, England . . . 1998 by brothers TOM and ALEX WHITE, who then enlisted MATT THWAITES and STEVE LARGE. Originally called FIXED ASCENT and then The FELTRO MEDIA (the latter issued a few demos including 'NEON OF THE CITY' in August '99), the band subsequently settled on being called The SOFT PARADE. A promising debut single 'SILENT TO THE DARK' hit the shops in spring 2001, and a follow-up 'EMPTY AT THE END' broke the UK Top 75 later in the year. The lads then added "ELECTRIC" to the moniker after discovering there already existed a DOORS cover band of the same name. 'THERE'S A SILENCE' nearly cracked the Top 50 and paved the way for media interest for their debut album 'HOLES IN THE WALL' (2002). The Top 40 record was a more than competent homage to their musical influences whilst also managing to sound contemporary. Clearly influenced by 1960's psychedelia the band offered something different to the increasingly faceless Brit-pop movement. ELECTRIC SOFT PARADE and their 'Arista'-backed label 'DB' re-mixed and re-promoted both their first two SOFT PARADE 45's and they duly went Top 40.

Album rating: HOLES IN THE WALL (*8)

ALEX WHITE (b. 1982) – vocals, guitar / **STEVE LARGE** – keyboards / **MATT THWAITS** – bass / **TOM WHITE** (b. 1985) – drums

			DB – Arista	not iss.
Apr 01.	(7"/cd-s; as SOFT PARADE) (*DB 004 SP7/CD7*) **SILENT TO THE DARK. / SOMETHING'S GOT TO GIVE**		☐	-
Jul 01.	(7"/red/cd-s/cd-s; as SOFT PARADE) (*DB 006 SP7/CD7/CD7JC*) **EMPTY AT THE END. / SUMATRAN**		65	-
Oct 01.	(7"/silver) (*DB 007SP7*) **THERE'S A SILENCE. / ON THE WIRES**		52	-

(cd-s+=/cd-s+=) (*DB 007 CD7/CDJ7*) – Broadcast.

| Feb 02. | (cd/d-lp) (*DB 002 CD+/LP*) **HOLES IN THE WALL** | | 35 | - |

– Start again / Empty at the end / There's a silence / Something's got to give / It's wasting me away / Silent to the dark / Sleep alone / This given line / Why do you try so hard to hate me / Holes in the wall / Biting the soles of my feet / Red balloon for me. *(re-iss. Aug02; DB 002CDLPX)*

| Mar 02. | (7"/blue) (*DB 008SP7*) **SILENT TO THE DARK II. / STAY WHERE YOU ARE** | | 23 | - |

(cd-s+=) (*DB 008CD7*) – ('A'-original video).
(cd-s) (*DB 008CDE7*) – ('A'side) / Hove park / Blitzed 6-4.

| May 02. | (7") (*DB 009SP7*) **EMPTY AT THE END (re-recording). / THIS GIVEN LINE** | | 39 | - |

(cd-s+=) (*DB 009CD7*) – The loop.
(cd-s+=) (*DB 009CDE7*) – Aerial roots.

| Sep 02. | (7") (*DB 013SP7*) **SAME WAY, EVERY DAY (BITING THE SOLES OF MY FEET). / POEMS** | | ☐ | - |

(cd-s+=) (*DB 013CD7JC*) – Zero return.
(cd-s) (*DB 013CD7*) – ('A'side) / Stop / Mood swing.

ELECTRIC SOUND OF JOY

Formed: East Midlands, England ... 1996 by frontman, GREG KURCEWICZ and musicians, DAN HAYHURST, BEN RODGERS, SCOTT NICHOLAS and JOHN REVILL. In the Spring of '98, after two 'Earworm' 45's shifted their limited copies, the 5-piece were the talk of A&R men vying for their signatures. However, conflict and pressure led to GREG bailing out leaving behind the remaining four to create a new CLUSTER-esque sound of pop/rock electronica. A third single, 'FOOD OF THE RANGE', was released on the new 'Foundry' imprint in the Autumn of '98, the majors having lost interest for the time being. An uncompromising eponymous debut album in 1999 was lauded by the Melody Maker. Their developing musak was even more enterprising on the following year's EP, 'DAUGHTERS OF DESTRUCTION', back-up tracks 'BERDOO' and 'DISEMBOOGIE', showing diverse contrasts ranging from analogue synths and avant-funk.

Album rating: ELECTRIC SOUND OF JOY (*6)

GREG KURCEWICZ – vocals / **BEN RODGERS** – keyboards / **SCOTT NICHOLAS** – guitar / **DAN HAYHURST** – bass / **JOHN REVILL** – drums

		Earworm	not iss.
Jul 97.	(ltd-7") *(WORM 5)* **TOTAL TURN. / OUR FLAG**		-
Sep 97.	(ltd-7") *(WORM 9)* **PLAY AWAY. / BUILDING BLOCKS**		-

— now without GREG

		Foundry	Foundry
Oct 98.	(ltd-12"ep) *(FR 001T)* **FOOD OF THE RANGE. / COUNTRY PIANO / MUSICLAND**		-
Sep 99.	(cd) *(<FR 005CD>)* **ELECTRIC SOUND OF JOY** – Familyman / Night & day / Don't waste time / Into the heart of tomorrow / Okay Oko / Hot cars / Mysteries of love / (untitled bonus tracks).		Jun00
Oct 00.	(cd-ep) *(FR 008CD)* **DAUGHTERS OF DESTRUCTION / BERDOO / DISEMBOOGIE / EXTRA FEET**		-

ELECTRO GROUP

Formed: Sacramento, Northern California, USA ... 1993 by bassist IAN HERNANDEZ and guitarist TIM JACOBSON. After the demise of shoegazing-influenced first band GRAHAM CRACKER CYCLONE, who never put out any records, HERNANDEZ and JACOBSON collaborated with a few other local amusing wannabe-musos (including a 6'5" YES fan who insisted on playing an electric drum set pre-programmed with guitar sounds, and DIPSOMANIAC DAVE, who stole the master tapes of their studio recording before evaporating forever like a puddle of lager in the dryburn desert sun) before settling on sticks-man MATT HULL in 1996. With full rhythm section in place the trio set about carving out a signature searing shoegazer sound. The band self-released their well-received first 7" 'THE LIFTER' in October 1998 before it was picked up and re-released by 'Omnibus' (who would put out their subsequent releases) a scant three months later. ELECTRO GROUP became noted for their angular, brash, chaotic-yet-delicate cuts-to-the-sonic-bone cuts, building on their good reputation by the release of another 7", 'THE LINE OF SIGHT' (2000) before their full-length debut 'A NEW PACIFICA' (2002). '...PACIFICA' was feted for its use of such disparate elements as indie melodies, falsetto vocals, xylophone-cutting-like-a-shark's-fin through the choppy waters of otherwise chaotic songs, off-beat drumbeats, surrealistic samples, electronic loops and Moog synthesizer licks. Flattering comparisons to vintage MY BLOODY VALENTINE abounded. JACOBSON would also perform in his other band TRACE as well as helping out friends ROCKETSHIP in the studio by playing instruments for them, but ELECTRO GROUP and TRACE were always his main musical squeezes.

Album rating: A NEW PACIFICA (*5)

TIM JACOBSON – vocals, guitar / **IAN HERNANDEZ** – bass / added **MATT HULL** – drums

		not iss.	own label
Oct 98.	(ltd-7") *<OMNI 018>* **THE LIFTER. / GREEN MACHINE** *<re-iss. Jan99 on 'Omnibus'; OMNI 018>*	-	

		Omnibus	Omnibus
Jan 00.	(cd) *<1612>* **A NEW PACIFICA** – Trigger – Repeat – Hold / La ballena alegria / If you could see / Line of sight / Cyrna ruka / Reprise / Continental / 4, 5 and 7 / Can't remember / A new Pacifica / Biped Last flight of Fantazma Gordo / 19.5 / Manimal + red lectroid orchestra. *<(UK + re-iss. Apr01 & Apr02 cd/lp; OMNI 27 A/B)>*	-	
Mar 00.	(ltd-7") *<OMNI 021>* **THE LINE OF SIGHT. / ALLSTAR**	-	

ELECTRONIC
(see under ⇒ NEW ORDER; in 80's section)

ELECTROSCOPE

Formed: Glasgow, Scotland ... April 1996 by radio broadcaster JOHN CAVANAGH and GAYLE, apparently in an attic room while tinkering with vintage recording equipment. Among CAVANAGH's stash of retro gear are gramophones, Farfisa organ and reel to reel tapes, all of which are utilised in creating their unique otherworldly music. Impossible to pigeonhole, the nearest journalists have got to their sound has involved namechecking the likes of SYD BARRETT-era PINK FLOYD and others sixties-type psychedelicists. Prolific in their wilfully obscure endeavours, the pair delivered a plethora of lovingly-crafted cassettes, singles/EP's (some split), albums, etc. The pick of these came in the shape of bewitchingly diverse full-length sets, 'HOMEMADE ELECTROSCOPE' (1997) and 'JOURNEY TO THE CENTRE OF THE ELECTROSCOPE' (1999). Having already covered Pink Floyd's 'CHAPTER 24', they earmarked a handful of GEOFF GODARD songs for 2000; he apparently penned for producer JOE MEEK. The 'SCOPE also appeared on countless V/A sets alongside even more obscure acts than themselves.

Album rating: WHERE THE OSCILLOSCOPE MEETS THE MAGIC EYE (*6) / HOMEMADE ELECTROSCOPE (*6) / SPLIT (*5) / JOURNEY TO THE CENTRE OF THE ELECTROSCOPE (*5)

GAYLE – (ex-ADVENTURES IN STEREO, ex-HEFNER, ex-DELGADOS, ex-SCREECH OWLS, ex-PLANET CLAIRE) / **JOHN CAVANAGH** – (ex-HEFNER)

		Boa	not iss.
Aug 96.	(c) *(HISS 8)* **WHERE THE OSCILLOSCOPE MEETS THE MAGIC EYE** – Wattle and weave / Ugaldugal / Octal starvision / Lament for the lost 70 / Pan pose / RPM overload / Soldering for beginners / Freespirit frequency / Rattle of the bees / Telephone suicide / Weave and wattle.		-

		Wurlitzer Jukebox	not iss.
Nov 96.	(7"ep) *(WJ 19)* **THE VANISHING PULSAR PLANET** – Space travel / Orion alignment / Welcome to Planet Barrett / Harmonic hiatus.		-
Mar 97.	(7"ep) *(WJ 23)* **SOMMERZO** – Walk the plank / Storm warning / On the seventh day of May / Fisher, dogger, German bight.		-
Aug 97.	(lp/cd) *(WJ 27/+CD)* **HOMEMADE ELECTROSCOPE** – Virtual Vega / Listen to prowlers / Fusee chain / Night flight to nowhere / Tunguska / Roter kamm / December woods / Battle lines are redrawn / Joe having a new world / Swan song sung / Mesmeric underground / Space travel 103 / Earth loop / The trumpet from outer space / Dunwich.		-
Feb 98.	(7",7"brown) *(WORMSS 2)* **SHAME CHANGED HIS PIGMENTATION. / (other side by Mount Vernon Arts Lab)**		-

		Tinseltones	not iss.
Apr 98.	(7") *(TINT 10)* **FOLLOW THE RAINBOW. / CHAPTER 24**		-

		Lissys	not iss.
Oct 98.	(7"ep; with SUZANNE RHATIGAN) *(LISS 30)* **UNHAPPY SOUL. / MAGIC LANTERN SHOW / HORACE BACHELOR'S METHOD / IF YOUR SHIP**		-

		Oggum	not iss.
Feb 99.	(7"ep) *(Og 4)* **WEE BALDY / NORTH UTSHIRE, SOUTH UTSHIRE. / (other tracks by Longstone)**		-

		Boa	not iss.
Apr 99.	(7") *(HISS 14)* **OUT ON THE EDGE OF TIME. / GLYCERINE GOLD**		-
Jul 99.	(7"ep) *(LYK 002)* **SPLIT SINGLE** – Where penguins are a force for good / Turbine / (other tracks by Stasola). (above iss. on 'Lykill', below on 'Rocket Racer' – 'Airborne Virus')		-
Jul 99.	(lp; shared with MINMAE) *(RR 006LP – AV 002LP)* **SPLIT LP** – Cloud ear / Squink / Witch's hat / Ears will spin / Kildonan / Velvet twilight / Someday you / Toledo trio / Molten you, gamma me / (other side by MINMAE).		-
Sep 99.	(lp/cd) *(HISS 16/+CD)* **JOURNEY TO THE CENTRE OF THE ELECTROSCOPE** – This is a box, a musical box / In the fog / Eight arms to drown you / Between two worlds / Gorse / Aradora star / Velvet shades / Friends in exile / Smile / Will morning never come? / Phase shift / Chalumeau / Lifetime flyte / Aphelion / Quartzite / Shamash / December moods / Curiously euphonic / Harbour.		-
May 00.	(7") *(HISS 18)* **JUST LIKE GEOFF** – Sky men (with MOUNT VERNON ARTS LAB) / CASTAWAY STONES: My friend Bobby.		-
Jul 00.	(7") *(KYLIE 056)* **CREPUSCULISNO. / (B-side by Echo Of Your Love: I Didn't Care)** (above iss.on 'Kylie Prod.', below issued on 'Octane Grammaphon')		-
Oct 00.	(7") *(OCT 1)* **EARTH & AIR. / WARSER GATE: Fire & Water**		-

— they have also contributed a plethora of individual cuts on various V/A compilations; they should surface one day on their own collection

ELF POWER

Formed: Athens, Georgia, USA ... mid-90's by multi-talented songwriter/musician/vocalist ANDREW RIEGER and the equally talented multi-instrumentalist LAURA CARTER. Their band formed part of the 'Elephant 6' imprint, although to call it just this seemed a bit of a disservice as it was more of a breeding ground and cross-pollinating arena for lo-fi indie bands. Other luminaries of this establishment included OLIVIA TREMOR CONTROL, NEUTRAL MILK HOTEL, and APPLES (IN STEREO). One of the great strengths of this label, and a great initial help to ELF POWER, was the willingness of the other groups to lend their artistic hands in the works of the others. The duo's debut LP, 'VAINLY CLUTCHING AT PHANTOM LIMBS' (1995) served to show that they were adamantly going to take their own alternative course up the musical river. The album was perhaps held back at points by its defiantly lo-fi approach, but at others this recording style served to enhance the emotions with the album, and the surrealism which would mark them out in their musical career. The following year the band recruited BRYAN HELIUM and AARON WEGELIN on bass and drums respectively, and released the EP 'THE WINTERHAWK'. The next three years saw the band reach the heights they were destined for with their two greatest full-length outings, 'WHEN THE RED KING COMES' (1997) and 'A DREAM IN SOUND' (1999). The former took a trip into the psychedelic concept album with song titles and cover art inspired by fantasy novels, and equally far-out music, lyrics, and choice of instrumentation. The latter LP stayed with the abstract subject matter of the former but with a warmer emotional depth, and a much cleaner sound from the mixing desk of DAVE FRIDMANN. The turn of the century produced another accomplished piece from the band, 'THE WINTER IS COMING', which is certainly more analogous to 'A DREAM IN SOUND' but without this record's experimental impact. The band's fifth LP came with the brief title of 'CREATURES' (2002), and introduced the listener to a strange concept-like album of RIEGER's otherworldly imagination, and was again a hit with the critics. The same year also saw the release of an album of covers, 'NOTHING'S GOING TO HAPPEN'. • **Covered:** UPSIDE DOWN (Jesus & Mary Chain) / HOT LOVE (T. Rex) / COTTON CROWN (Sonic Youth) / YOU MAKE ME DIE (Wild Billy Childish) / FELT GOOD TO BURN (Flaming Lips) / LISTENING TO THE HIGSONS (Robyn Hitchcock) / NEEDLES IN THE CAMELS EYE (Eno) / NOTHING'S GOING TO HAPPEN (Tall Dwarfs) / WHY I CAN'T TOUCH IT (Buzzcocks) / PAY TO CUM (Bad Brains) / NEVER TALKING TO YOU AGAIN (Husker Du).

Album rating: VAINLY CLUTCHING AT PHANTOM LIMBS (*4) / WHEN THE RED KING COMES (*6) / A DREAM IN SOUND (*6) / THE WINTER IS COMING (*5) / CREATURES (*6) / NOTHING'S GOING TO HAPPEN covers (*5)

ANDREW RIEGER – vocals, bass, guitar, wind, percussion, keyboards / **LAURA CARTER** – keyboards, vocals, zanzithophone, etc

	not iss.	Drug Racer
Nov 95. (lp) <PLACEBO 01> **VAINLY CLUTCHING AT PHANTOM LIMBS**		-

– Pioneer mansion / Temporary arms / All your experiments / Finally free / Drug store / Loverboy's demise / Slither hither / Circular malevolence / When the serpents approach / Surgery / Vainly clutching at phantom limbs / Arachnid dungeon attack / Grand intrusion call / Monster surprise / Heroes and insects / The winter hawk / Exalted exit wound. *(UK-iss.Nov96; same as US)* <(re-iss. Jun00 on 'Arena Rock' cd/lp; AR 013 CD/LP)>

— added **BRYAN HELIUM** – bass / **AARON WEGELIN** – drums / and a plethora of 'Elephant 6' session people

	not iss.	Kindercore
Oct 96. (7"ep) <007> **THE WINTER HAWK EP**	-	

– Grand intrusion call / Heroes and insects / The winter hawk / Exalted exit wound.

	Arena Rock	Arena Rock
Dec 97. (cd) <(AR 007)> **WHEN THE RED KING COMES**		Oct97

– Step through the portal / Into the everlasting time / Frightened singers / Secret ocean / Arrow flies close / Icy hands will never melt away / When the red king comes / Separating fault / Spectators / Introducing cosmic space / Bengal parade / Needles in the camels eye / . . . Silver lake / It's been a million years. *(re-iss. Aug99; same)*

Mar 99. (cd-ep) <(LA 009CD)> **COME ON EP**
– Upside down / Hot love / Cotton crown / You make me die / Felt good to burn / Listening to the Higsons / The separating fault (remix).
(above issued on 'Lil Army')

May 99. (cd) <(AR 010)> **A DREAM IN SOUND**
– Will my feet still carry me home / High atop the silver branches / Willowy man / Olde tyme waves / Jane / All the passengers / We dream in sound / Carnival / The well / Noble experiment / Simon (the bird with the candybar head) / Rising and falling in a little world / O what a beautiful dream / Interlude 87. *(lp-iss.Aug99; AR 010LP)* (re-iss. Mar01 & Jan02 on 'Shifty Disco'; SHIFTY 0102)

	Sugar Free	Sugar Free
Oct 00. (cd/lp) <(SF 021 CD/LP)> **THE WINTER IS COMING**		

– Embrace the crimson tide / Skeleton / The great society / The winter is coming / Wings of light / The sun is forever / People underneath / Green sea days / The naughty villain / Leopard's teeth / Birds in the backyard / 100,000 telescopes / The albatross. *(cd re-iss. Jan02 on 'Shifty Disco'; SHIFTY 0105)*

	Shifty Disco	Spin Art
Oct 00. (cd-s) (DISCO 0010) **JANE / NEEDLES IN THE CAMELS EYES**		-
Apr 01. (cd-s) (DISCOQUICK 8) **HIGH ATOP THE SILVER BRANCHES / YOU MAKE ME DIE**		-

— now without BRYAN HELIUM

Apr 02. (cd-s) (DISCOQUICK 17) **THE NAUGHTY VILLAIN / GREAT SOCIETY / DANDY IN THE UNDERWORLD**
May 02. (cd) (SHIFTY 0205) <SPIN 106> **CREATURES**
– Let the serpent sleep / Everlasting scream / The creature / Palace of the flames / The modern mind / Visions of the sea / Things that should not be / Three seeds / The haze / Unseen hand / The creature (pt.2). *(lp-iss.Jul02 on 'Luna'; LUNA 060)*
Nov 02. (cd-s) (DISCOQUICK 21) **LET THE SERPENT SLEEP**

– compilations, etc. –

Oct 02. (cd) *Orange Twin;* <(OTR 11CD)> **NOTHING'S GOING TO HAPPEN**
– Nothing's going to happen / Why I can't touch it / Shadows in vain / Weird on the avenue / Pay to cum / Hybrid moments / Never talking to you again / I walked with the zombie / Unforced peace / I love the living you / Upside down / Hot love / Cotton crown / You make me die / Felt good to burn / Listening to the Higsons.

EL HOMBRE TRAJEADO

Formed: Glasgow, Scotland . . . 1996 by vocalist HUBBY, STEVIE JONES and STEF SINCLAIR; BEN JONES was added after their debut 45 in the Autumn of '97, 'MOONUNIT MANUAL'. Translating the 'smart' name roughly as 'the man in the suit', this post rock outfit issued further special edition singles during '98 (some split with such indie luminaries as LUNGLEG and THE KARELIA) before embarking on fully-fledged tours across the ocean with peers SEBADOH and The DELGADOS. Not surprisingly, DJ John Peel was impressed too. He proudly marched the band into his session studio pronto(!). This gave EL HOMBRE TRAJEADO a chance to literally hypotise the audience with their trippy, sparse but clever TORTOISE-esque angular rock. Imagine SLINT doing a spot on Blue Peter, or even a day in the life of a drug-fuelled JOHN McENTIRE – with the lights switched off of course(!). EL HOMBRE subsequently released their long awaited debut set entitled 'SKIPAFONE' (1998), on trendy Scots label 'Guided Missile'. Tracks like 'NOFA' displayed the visual genius of EHT through soundscapes represented by staccato guitars, inane mumblings and – used to humourous effect – cowbells. 'LIKE QUICKSAND' developed minimalist strumming and lazy bass guitar to brilliant effect. Track 'NEOPRENE' found its way on to the 'GLASGOW EP', which was shared with others including MOGWAI, YUMMY FUR and the aforementioned THE KARELIA. Following after a few delays, the sophomore effort, 'SACCADE' (2000), a signing masterstroke for producer JAMIE WATSON at Edinburgh's hot-to-trot label, 'Human Condition'. EL HOMBRE TRAJEADO (pronounced EL HOM-BRAY TRA-CHEE-AH-DOH, for exotics everywhere) simply repeated the same tried and tested formula, albeit with fresh textures set to a deranged and dislocated style. Like TORTOISE, EHT didn't have an oral message per say, the music spoke for itself.

Album rating: SKIPAFONE (*8) / SACCADE (*7)

HUBBY – vocals, guitar / **STEVIE JONES** – bass / **STEF SINCLAIR** – drums

	Flotsam & Jetsam	not iss.
Sep 97. (7") (SHaG 015) **MOONUNIT MANUAL. / LOGO**		-
Apr 98. (7") (SHaG 13.06) **Club Beatroot Part Six**		-

– Nofo / (other track by LUNG LEG)
(above released in conjunction with 'The 13th Note')

— added **BEN JONES** – keyboards, DJ-ing

Jun 98. (7") (SHaG 019) **LIKE QUICKSAND. / (other track by THE KARELIA)**

	Guided Missile	not iss.
Sep 98. (7") (GUIDE 28) **SKIPAFONE. / SLEEP DEEP**		-
Oct 98. (cd) (GUIDE 33CD) **SKIPAFONE**		-

– Like quicksand / Skipafone / Nofo / Neoprene / Varispeed / Bit faster / Nearly a week nearly awake / Logo / Sleep deep.

— also in Nov'98, EL HOMBRE TRAJEADO (with the track 'NEOPRENE') split the 'Glasgow' EP with MOGWAI, the KARELIA and YUMMY FUR; released on 'Plastic Cowboy' *(Plastic 005)*

Sep 99. (10"ep/cd-ep) (GUIDE 32/+CD) **SHOPLIFT EP**
– Scrivener / Shopfitting / Babosa / Elhombre reworked by Auto Cade.

	Jonathon Whiskey	not iss.
Aug 00. (7") (CLYDE WHISKEY 12) **L'AMUSIA. / (other track by IMMENSE)**		-

	Human Condition	not iss.
Oct 00. (cd) (HCCD 0031) **SACCADE**		-

– i-330 / Dos / Shout out / Jetsuit / Dylar / Saccade / Double blind / Chapperon / Dig this big crux / Halo.

	Sickroom Gramaphonic Collective	not iss.
Nov 01. (7") (SGC 011) **SARDINES. / (other track by Sputniks Down)**		-

ELLIS ISLAND SOUND (see under ⇒ WEATHER PROPHETS)

EMBRACE

Formed: Bradford/Huddersfield, England . . . 1993 by Irish-ancestry songwriting brothers, DANNY (lyrics) and RICHARD McNAMARA (the music), who enlisted the rhythm team of STEVE FIRTH and MIKE KEATON. After the stunning OASIS-esque grandeur of the early '97 debut, 'ALL YOU GOOD GOOD PEOPLE', for the 'Fierce Panda' set-up, they signed to Virgin offshoot, 'Hut'. The band made an immediate impact on the singles chart with the EP, 'FIREWORKS', increasing their chart exposure with the summer '97 follow-up, 'ONE BIG FAMILY'. However, the pop nation finally clutched them to their proverbial bosom with the re-issue of 'ALL YOU GOOD GOOD PEOPLE', which cracked the Top 10 in the Autumn. The following year, the much vaunted songwriting siblings scored a further two Top 10 hits, 'COME BACK TO WHAT YOU KNOW' and 'MY WEAKNESS IS NONE OF YOUR BUSINESS', both taken from their chart-topping debut album, 'THE GOOD WILL OUT'. Towards the end the decade and with part-timer MICKEY DALE now their official 5th member, EMBRACE previewed their forthcoming sophomore set via a Top 20 hit, 'HOOLIGAN'. When it finally arrived, 'DRAWN FROM MEMORY' (2000) revealed a more mature band, conscious of their more overblown tendencies and determined to pare their sound down somewhat. Thus the Britpop-inspired orchestration which characterised this album's predecessor wasn't quite so conspicuous, although the record's highlights were still centered around soul searching balladry such as the title track. In the event, 'DRAWN FROM MEMORY' (2000), in addition to making the UK Top 10 itself, spawned a further three hits in the shape of 'YOU'RE NOT ALONE', 'SAVE ME' and 'I WOULDN'T WANNA HAPPEN TO YOU'. Although the worst excesses of orchestration had been reined in, EMBRACE seemed to be working with the philosophy that if it ain't broke, don't fix it. If so, it was an ethos that ensured them a Top 10 placing for 'IF YOU'VE NEVER BEEN' (2001), along with two singles: the Top 20 'WONDER' and 'MAKE IT LAST'.

Album rating: THE GOOD WILL OUT (*8) / DRAWN FROM MEMORY (*6) / IF YOU'VE NEVER BEEN (*6) / FIREWORKS: SINGLES 1997-2002 compilation (*7)

DANNY McNAMARA – vocals / **RICHARD McNAMARA** – guitar, vocals / **STEVE FIRTH** – bass / **MIKE KEATON** – drums, vocals

EMBRACE (cont)   THE GREAT INDIE DISCOGRAPHY   The 1990s

		Fierce Panda	not iss.
Feb 97.	(ltd-7") (NING 29) **ALL YOU GOOD GOOD PEOPLE. / MY WEAKNESS IS NONE OF YOUR BUSINESS**	-	-

		Hut	Geffen
May 97.	(c-ep/12"ep/cd-ep) (HUT C/T/CD 84) **FIREWORKS EP** – The last gas / Now you're nobody / Blind / Fireworks. (12"ep re-iss. Nov98; same)	34	-
Jul 97.	(c-ep/12"ep/cd-ep) (HUT C/T/CD 86) **ONE BIG FAMILY EP** – One big family / Dry kids / You've only got to stop to get better / Butter wouldn't melt. (12"ep re-iss. Nov98; same)	21	-
Oct 97.	(c-ep/12"ep/cd-ep) (HUT C/T/DX 90) **ALL YOU GOOD GOOD PEOPLE EP** – All you good good people (extended) / You won't amount to anything – this time / The way I do / Free ride. (12"ep re-iss. Nov98; same) (cd-ep) (HUTCD 90) – ('A' radio edit) / One big family (Perfecto mix) / ('A'-Fierce Panda version) / ('A'-orchestral mix).	8	-
May 98.	(c-s) (HUTC 93) <95132> **COME BACK TO WHAT YOU KNOW / LOVE IS BACK** (12"+=/cd-s+=) (HUT T/DX 93) – If you feel like a sinner / Perfect way. (cd-s) (HUTCX 93) – ('A'side) / Butter wouldn't melt (live) / Dry kids (live) / ('A'orchestral).	6	Jul98
Jun 98.	(cd/c/d-lp) (CDHUT/HUTMC/HUTDLP 46) <25165> **THE GOOD WILL OUT** – Intro / All you good good people / My weakness is none of your business / Come back to what you know / One big family / Higher sights / Retread / I want the world / You've got to say yes / Fireworks / The last gas / That's all changed forever / Now you're nobody / The good will out.	1	Jul98
Aug 98.	(7") (HUT 103) **MY WEAKNESS IS NONE OF YOUR BUSINESS. / FEELINGS I THOUGHT YOU SHARED** (c-s+=/cd-s+=) (HUT C/CD 103) – Don't turn your back on love. (cd-s) (HUTDX 103) – ('A'live) / Higher sights (live) / Retread (live). (12"ep re-iss. Nov98; HUTT 103)	9	-
Nov 98.	(12"ep) (HUTT 107) **THE GOOD WILL OUT. / BUTTER WOULDN'T MELT (live) / DRY KIDS (live) / BLIND**		
—	added p/t (now f/t) 5th member **MICKEY DALE** – keyboards (ex-CUD)		

		Hut	E.M.I.
Nov 99.	(c-s/cd-s) (HUT C/CD 123) **HOOLIGAN / I'VE BEEN RUNNING / I CAN'T FEEL BAD ANYMORE** (cd-s) (HUTDX 123) – ('A'side) / Like a believer / With the one who got me here.	18	-
Mar 00.	(cd-s) (HUTCD 126) **YOU'RE NOT ALONE / BROTHERS AND SISTERS / HAPPY AND LOST** (cd-s/12"+=) (HUT DX/T 126) – ('A'side) / Come on and smile / Tap on your shoulder.	14	-
Mar 00.	(cd/c/lp) (CDHUT/HUTMC/HUTLP 60) <849014> **DRAWN FROM MEMORY** – The love it takes / You're not alone / Save me / Drawn from memory / Bunker song / New Adam new Eve / Hooligan / Yeah you / Liars tears / I wouldn't wanna happen to you / I had a time.	8	-
May 00.	(c-s/12"/cd-s) (HUT C/X/CD 133) **SAVE ME / GET ON BOARD / STILL SO YOUNG** (cd-s) (HUTDX 133) – ('A'side) / ('A'mixes).	29	-
Aug 00.	(7") (HUT 137) **I WOULDN'T WANNA HAPPEN TO YOU. / 3 IS A MAGIC NUMBER** (cd-s+=) (HUTCDX 133) – Top of the heap. (12"++=) (HUTT 133) – First cut / I know what's going on. (cd-s) (HUTCD 133) – ('A'side) / First cut / I know what's going on.	23	-
Aug 01.	(c-s/cd-s) (HUT C/CD 142) **WONDER / ANYWHERE YOU GO / EVERYDAY** (cd-s) (HUTDX 142) – ('A'side) / Today / Caught in a rush.	14	-
Sep 01.	(cd/c/lp) (CDHUT/HUTMC/HUTLP 68) <810973> **IF YOU'VE NEVER BEEN** – Over / I hope you're happy now / Wonder / Many will learn / It's gonna take time / Hey, what you trying to say / If you've never been in love with anything / Make it last / Happiness will get you in the end / Satellites.	9	Oct01
Nov 01.	(cd-s) (HUTCD 144) **MAKE IT LAST / FIGHT YER CORNER / IT'S YOU I MAKE FOR** (cd-s) (HUTDX 144) – ('A'side) / ('A'-orchestral) / Giving forgiving and giving in / What you've never had you'll never have.	35	-
Mar 02.	(cd) (CDHUT 74) <812083> **FIREWORKS: SINGLES 1997-2002** (compilation) – All you good good people / You're not alone / Come back to what you know / Make it last / 3 is a magic number / One big family / My weakness is none of your business / I wouldn't wanna happen to you / Save me / Hooligan / The good will out / Wonder / Fireworks.	36	

EMF

Formed: Cinderford / Forest of Dean, Gloucestershire, England . . . late '89 by Oxford graduate IAN DENCH and JAMES ATKIN, DERRY BROWNSON, ZAC FOLEY, MARK DE CLOEDT and scratcher/DJ, MILF. After their 4th gig, they were spotted by ABBO (from former goth punks, UK DECAY) and his girlfriend, LINDA, who helped get them signed to 'E.M.I.' subsidiary, 'Parlophone' in March '90. Late that year, their debut single, 'UNBELIEVABLE', broke into the UK Top 3 and early the following year, they set about taking both sides of the Atlantic by storm. Similar in style, to say, JESUS JONES, or an uptempo DEPECHE MODE, EMF's brattish blend of indie dance and funky pop saw them hailed as the great white hopes of British music for as long as it took their teenybop fanbase to find someone new (i.e. not that long!). ATKIN's posh-accented whine was a bit much to take over the stretch of a whole album, although, spurred by the success of further singles, 'I BELIEVE' and 'CHILDREN', 'SCHUBERT DIP' (1991) was one of the year's biggest selling sets; it even did well in American where 'UNBELIEVABLE' had topped the charts. Touted as spearheading a second "British Invasion" along with JESUS JONES and Co., EMF's assault soon surrendered to the machinations of the music business as follow-up album,

'STIGMA' (1992) saw them making an ill-advised attempt at big boys' rock. Its heavier approach only succeeded in alienating their original fanbase, the band's apparent attempt to lighten up their image with a VIC REEVES and BOB MORTIMER collaboration (a Top 3 cover of The Monkees 'I'M A BELIEVER') not enough to prevent 'CHA CHA CHA' from virtually stiffing. Subsequently dropped by their label, EMF faced the inevitable and jacked it in. However, the story didn't quite finish there as DENCH resurfaced a few years later with his new trio, WHISTLER. Also comprising former disco singer, KERRY SHAW, and violin player JAMES TOPHAM, the group signed to the 'Wiiija' label and released a trio of singles (among them the music press fave, 'IF I GIVE YOU A SMILE') and an eponymous debut album in 1999. As starkly different to EMF as it was possible to get, the album's, pared-down folk-tinged indie-pop coalesced around SHAW's beguiling lullaby of a vocal. The band followed up with 'FAITH IN THE MORNING' (2000), another sweet treat that developed their easier-going approach. Sadly, on the 3rd of January 2002, IAN's old mucker, ZAC FOLEY, died. • **Covered:** LOW SPARK OF THE HIGH HEELED BOYS (Traffic) / SHADDAP YOU, FACE (Joe Dolce) / I'M A BELIEVER (Monkees) / STRANGE BREW (Cream). / WHISTLER:- AT SEVENTEEN (Janis Ian) / I JUST DON'T KNOW WHAT TO DO WITH MYSELF (hit; Dusty Springfield) / BLUE, RED AND GREY / ALL APOLOGIES (Nirvana). • **Trivia:** EMF was rumoured to stand for ECSTASY MOTHER FUCKERS, but later claimed to be EPSOM MAD FUNKERS.

Album rating: SCHUBERT DIP (*5) / STIGMA (*7) / CHA CHA CHA (*4) / EPSOM MAD FUNKERS: THE BEST OF EMF compilation (*6) / Whistler: WHISTLER (*6) / FAITH IN THE MORNING (*6)

JAMES ATKIN (b.28 Mar'67) – vocals / **IAN DENCH** (b. 7 Aug'64) – guitar, keyboards (ex-APPLE MOSAIC) / **DERRY BROWNSON** (b. DERRAN, 10 Nov'70) – samples, percussion (ex-LAC's) / **ZAC FOLEY** (b. ZACHARY, 9 Dec'70) – bass (ex-IUC's) / **MARK DE CLOEDT** (b.26 Jun'67) – drums (ex-ZU) / plus **MILF** – DJ scratcher

		Parlophone	E.M.I.
Oct 90.	(c-s/7") (TC+/R 6273) **UNBELIEVABLE. / EMF (live)** (12"+=/cd-s+=) (12R/CDR 6273) – ('A'-Cin City sex mix).	3	-
Jan 91.	(c-s/7") (TC+/R 6279) **I BELIEVE. / WHEN YOU'RE MINE** (12"+=/cd-s+=) (12R/CDR 6279) – Unbelievable (funk mix).	6	-
Mar 91.	(c-s) <50350> **UNBELIEVABLE** / ('A'-Cin City Sex mix)	-	1
Apr 91.	(c-s/7") (TC+/R 6288) **CHILDREN. / STRANGE BREW (live remix)** (12"+=) (12R 6288) – Children (mix). (cd-s+=) (CDR 6288) – Children – Battle for the minds of North Amerika. (7"ep+=) (RX 6288) – (live versions).	19	-
May 91.	(cd/c/lp) (CD/TC/PCS 7353) <96238> **SCHUBERT DIP** – Children / Long summer days / When you're mine / Travelling not running / I believe / Unbelievable / Girl of an age / Admit it / Lies / Long time. (re-iss. Mar94 cd/c; same) (Oct00 re-iss. on 'EMI Gold'; CDP 796238-2)	3	12
Aug 91.	(c-s/7") (TC+/R 6295) **LIES. / HEAD THE BALL** (12"+=/cd-s+=) (12R/CDR 6295) – ('A'mix).	28	-
Sep 91.	(c-s) <50363> **LIES / STRANGE BREW (live)**	-	18
Apr 92.	(7"ep) (SGE 2026) **UNEXPLAINED** – Getting through / Far from me / The same. (12"ep+=/cd-ep+=) (12/CD SGE 2026) – Search and destroy.	18	-
Sep 92.	(c-s/7") (TC+/R 6321) **THEY'RE HERE. / PHANTASMAGORIC** (12"+=) (12R 6321) – ('A'remix). (cd-s+=) (CDR 6321) – Low spark of the high heeled boys.	29	-
Sep 92.	(cd/c/lp) (CD/TC/PCSD 122) <80348> **STIGMA** – They're here / Arizona / It's you that leaves me dry / Never know / Blue highs / Inside / Getting through / She bleeds / Dog / The light that burns twice as bright . . .	19	-
Nov 92.	(c-s/7") (TC+/R 6327) **IT'S YOU. / DOF (Foetus mix)** (cd-s+=) (CDR 6327) – (2 other 'A'-Butch Vig mixes). (cd-ep) (CDRS 6327) – It's you (Orbital mix) / The light that burns twice as bright . . . (mix) / They're here (mix).	23	-

		Parlophone	Parlophone
Feb 95.	(c-s) (TCR 6401) **PERFECT DAY / ANGEL** (cd-s+=) (CDR 6401) – I won't give into you / Kill for you (lo-fi mix). (12"+=) (12R 6401) – ('A'-Temple of boom remix) / ('A'-Chris & James epic). (cd-s) (CDRS 6401) – ('A'side) / ('A'-Chris & James mix) / ('A'-Black One mix) / ('A'-Toytown mix).	27	-
Mar 95.	(cd/c) (<CD/TC PCSD 165>) **CHA CHA CHA** – Perfect day / La plage / The day I was born / Secrets / Shining / Bring me down / Skin / Slouch / Bleeding you dry / Patterns / When will you come / West of the Cox / Ballad o' the bishop / Glass smash Jack.	30	
Apr 95.	(c-s) (TCR 6407) **BLEEDING YOU DRY / TOO MUCH / EASY / PERFECT DAY (acoustic)** (cd-s) (CDRS 6407) – (first 3 tracks) / Shining (acoustic). (cd-s) (CDR 6407) – ('A'side) / I pushed the boat out so far it sank / Patterns (acoustic).		-
Jun 95.	(c-s/7"; EMF and REEVES & MORTIMER) (TC+/R 6412) **I'M A BELIEVER. / AT LEAST WE'VE GOT OUR GUITARS** (cd-s) (CDR 6412) – ('A'side) / At this stage I couldn't say / ('A'-Unbelievable mix) / La plage (mix).	3	-
Oct 95.	(c-s) (TCR 6416) **AFRO KING / UNBELIEVABLE** (cd-s+=) (CDR 6416) – Children / I believe. (cd-s) (CDRS 6416) – ('A'side) / Too much / Easy / Bring me down.	51	-

— split not long after the relative failure of the above single. DENCH returned in 1998 with a new outfit (see further below)

– compilations, etc. –

| 1998. | (cd,c; shared with JESUS JONES) EMI Capitol special; <19641> **BACK 2 BACK** | - | - |
| Jun 01. | (d-cd) Parlophone; (533543-2) **EPSOM MAD FUNKERS: THE BEST OF EMF** | | - |

WHISTLER

IAN DENCH – multi-instruments / **KERRY SHAW** – vocals / **JAMES TOPHAM** – viola (ex-BRIAN ENO)

		Wiiija	Wiiija
May 98.	(7") *(WIJ 084)* **RARE AMERICAN SHOES. / THINGS YOU NEVER SAY**	□	-
	(cd-s+=) *(WIJ 084CD)* – Thinking it's over.		
Sep 98.	(7") *(WIJ 091)* **IF I GIVE YOU A SMILE. / GOT WHAT YOU WANTED**	□	-
	(cd-s+=) *(WIJ 091CD)* – Song about you.		
Feb 99.	(7") *(WIJ 096)* **DON'T JUMP IN FRONT OF MY TRAIN. / FOR REAL**	□	-
	(cd-s+=) *(WIJ 096CD)* – Tender years.		
Mar 99.	(cd/lp) *(<WIJ CD/LP 1087>)* **WHISTLER**	□	
	– If I give you a smile / Don't jump in front of my train / Closing time / Emily / The end / Rare American shoes / Heaven help me / Pulling the strings / Natalie's song / Please don't love me anymore.		
Sep 99.	(10"ep/cd-ep) *(WIJ 104 T/CD)* **INTERMISSION e.p.**	□	-
	– At seventeen / I just don't know what to do with myself / Blue, red and grey / All apologies.		
Sep 00.	(7") *(WIJ 125)* **HAPPINESS. / EVEN LESS**	□	-
	(cd-s+=) *(WIJ 125CD)* – Small world.		
Oct 00.	(cd) *(<WIJ 1112CD>)* **FAITH IN THE MORNING**	□	□ Jan01
	– Happiness / Thank you / You and me / Faith in the morning / Sad songs / Don't forget me forever / Little boulders / Watches of Switzerland / It's not too late / Solitude / I felt a funeral / I saw you.		

Brian ENO

Born: BRIAN PETER GEORGE ST.JOHN LE BAPTISTE DE LA SALLE ENO, 15 May'48, Suffolk, England. After leaving art school, where he fronted heavy group MAXWELL DEMON, he joined ROXY MUSIC in 1971. Contributing greatly to their image and sound on the albums, 'ROXY MUSIC' & 'FOR YOUR PLEASURE', he left due to a dispute over their increasingly pop-rock orientated direction. His first post-ROXY venture was '(NO PUSSYFOOTING)' in 1973 with ROBERT FRIPP (of KING CRIMSON). This was nothing more than extreme experimentation of synth-electronics and treated guitar. However, it did provide art lovers with a photo-shot of ENO & FRIPP in a multi-mirrored room. His first solo work in early 1974, 'HERE COME THE WARM JETS', disappointed the critics, who gave it the thumbs down, bar one gem, 'BABY'S ON FIRE'. He released two more greatly improved efforts for 'Island' before he formed his own label in 1975, appropriately titled 'Obscure'. Preceding this, in a fit of depression, he joined The WINKIES for a short tour during Feb-Mar'74, but departed after being diagnosed with a collapsed lung. He recovered to find himself on an 'Island records' concert bill on '1st JUNE, 1974', alongside stablemates KEVIN AYERS, NICO and JOHN CALE. The following year, he was hit by a car, which caused slight but not lasting brain damage. 1975's 'ANOTHER GREEN WORLD' represented the fruition of ENO's aural experimentation, sculpting instrumental, insidiously melodic soundscapes while the title track was subsequently used as the theme tune for the BBC TV arts series, 'Arena'. 'BEFORE AND AFTER SCIENCE' (1977) was an equally brilliant, if colder sounding, tapestry of sonic delights. Around this time, ENO began working with DAVID BOWIE on a trilogy of lp's that included 'LOW' (1977) and 'HEROES' (1977), while the following year he hooked up with TALKING HEADS, producing three of their albums during the period 1978-'80. He also collaborated with DAVID BYRNE on the ethnic-flavoured 'MY LIFE IN THE BUSH OF GHOSTS' (1981). With 'AMBIENT 1: MUSIC FOR AIRPORTS' (1978), ENO created an innovative classic while 'APOLLO: ATMOSPHERES AND SOUNDTRACKS' (1983) was a beguiling fusion of country and ambient, the gorgeous 'DEEP BLUE DAY' belatedly cropping up on the 'TRAINSPOTTING' (1996) soundtrack. After initially collaborating with Canadian producer/engineer DANIEL LANOIS for production duties on such early 80's projects as 'THE PEARL' (a HAROLD BUDD/ENO album), the two worked wonders on U2's seminal 'UNFORGETTABLE FIRE' (1984). ENO clocked up further U2 production credits on 'THE JOSHUA TREE' (1987) and 'ACHTUNG BABY' (1991), scooping a joint Grammy (with LANOIS) in 1992 for the latter. The same year saw the release of a long awaited ENO solo album, 'NERVE NET', which took its cue from the burgeoning ambient techno scene. Throughout the 90's, this electronic auteur has continued to work on a dizzying array of music and other multi media projects, even publishing a volume of diaries in 1996, 'A YEAR WITH SWOLLEN APPENDICES'. The balding genius once described himself as a non-musician who just turned dials and switches. Maybe, but he happens to turn the right dials and switches, and this technically brilliant ambient experimentalist's obscure new musak is possibly a direct link to what listeners will appreciate in the 21st century. • **Songwriters:** All composed by ENO. • **Trivia:** His 1977 song 'KING'S LEAD HAT' was in fact an anagram of TALKING HEADS. ENO has also done session and production work for JOHN CALE (1974-75), ROBERT WYATT (1975), ROBERT CALVERT (1975), DAVID BOWIE (1977) / DEVO (1978) / TALKING HEADS (1978-80) / U2 (1985-91 with Daniel Lanois) / etc.

Album rating: NO PUSSYFOOTIN' with Fripp (*2 at the time – *6 now!?) / HERE COME THE WARM JETS (*7) / TAKING TIGER MOUNTAIN (BY STRATEGY) (*7) / ANOTHER GREEN WORLD (*9) / DISCREET MUSIC (*6) / EVENING STAR with Fripp (*2 at the time – *5 now!?) / BEFORE AND AFTER SCIENCE (*8) / CLUSTER AND ENO with Cluster (*6) / AFTER THE HEAT with Moebius & Roedelius (*6) / MUSIC FOR FILMS (*6) / AMBIENT 1: MUSIC FOR AIRPORTS (*7) / AMBIENT 2: THE PLATEAUX OF MIRROR with Harold Budd (*5) / FOURTH WORLD VOL.1: POSSIBLE MUSICS with Jon Hassell (*6) / MY LIFE IN THE BUSH OF GHOSTS with David Byrne (*8) / AMBIENT 4: ON LAND (*7) / APOLLO, ATMOSPHERES & SOUNDTRACKS with Daniel Lanois & Roger Eno (*8) / THE PEARL with Harold Budd & Daniel Lanois (*5) / THURSDAY AFTERNOON (*6) / HYBRID with Michael Brook & Daniel Lanois (*5) / VOICES with Roger Eno (*5) / MORE BLANK THAN FRANK compilation (*7) / DESERT ISLAND SELECTION compilation (*7) / MUSIC FOR FILMS 2 (*6) / WRONG WAY UP with John Cale (*7) / NERVE NET (*6) / THE SHUTOV ASSEMBLY (*6) / :NEROLI: (*5) / SPINNER with Jah Wobble (*6) / THE DROP (*5)

FRIPP & ENO

ROBERT FRIPP – guitar of KING CRIMSON / **BRIAN ENO** – synthesizers, instruments

		Island-Help	Antilles
Nov 73.	(lp) *(HELP 16) <7007>* **(NO PUSSYFOOTING)**	□	□
	– The heavenly music corporation / Swastika girls. *(re-iss. Oct77 on 'Polydor'; 2343 095) (re-iss. Jan87 on 'E.G.' lp/cd; EGED/EEGCD 2)*		

ENO

now solo with guest session people, including ROXY MUSIC musicians and ROBERT FRIPP, CHRIS SPEDDING, PAUL RUDOLPH and others.

		Island	Island
Jan 74.	(lp/c) *(ILPS/ICT <9268>)* **HERE COME THE WARM JETS**	26	
	– Needles in the camel's eye / The paw paw Negro blowtorch / Baby's on fire / Cindy tells me / Driving me backwards / On some faraway beach / Black rank / Dead finks don't talk / Some of them are old / Here come the warm jets. *(re-iss. Mar77 on 'Polydor'; 2302 063) (re-iss. Jan87 on 'E.G.' lp/c/cd; EG LP/MC/CD 11) (cd re-iss. Mar91; same)*		
Mar 74.	(7") *(WIP 6178)* **SEVEN DEADLY FINNS. / LATER ON**	□	□
	guests incl. PORTSMOUTH SINFONIA ORCHESTRA, PHIL COLLINS – drums / etc.		
Nov 74.	(lp/c) *(ILPS/ICT <9309>)* **TAKING TIGER MOUNTAIN (BY STRATEGY)**	□	□
	– Burning airlines give you so much more / Back in Judy's jungle / The fat lady of Limbourg / Mother whale eyeless / The great pretender / Third uncle / Put a straw under baby / The truth wheel / China my China / Taking tiger mountain. *(re-iss. Mar77 on 'Polydor'; 2302 068) (re-iss. Jan87 on 'E.G.' lp/c/cd; EG LP/MC/CD 17) (cd re-iss. Mar91; same)*		
Aug 75.	(7") *(WIP 6233) <036>* **THE LION SLEEPS TONIGHT (WIMOWEH). / I'LL COME RUNNING**	□	□
	now with FRIPP (3) / COLLINS (3) / JOHN CALE – viola (2) / PAUL RUDOLPH (3) / PERCY JONES – bass (3) / ROD MELVIN – piano (3) / BRIAN TURRINGTON – bass, piano (1)		
Sep 75.	(lp/c) *(ILPS/ICT <9351>)* **ANOTHER GREEN WORLD**	□	□
	– Sky saw / Over Fire Island / St. Elmo's fire / In dark trees / The big ship / I'll come running / Another green world / Sombre reptiles / Little fishes / Golden hours / Becalmed / Zawinul / Lava / Everything merges with the night. *(re-iss. Mar77 on 'Polydor'; 2302 069) (re-iss. Jan87 & Mar91 on 'E.G.' lp/c/cd; EG LP/MC/CD 21)*		

		Obscure	Antilles
Nov 75.	(lp) *(OBS 3) <7030>* **DISCREET MUSIC**	□	□
	– Discreet music 1 & 2 / Three Variations on canon in D major; a) Fullness of wind – b) French catalogues – c) Brutal ardour. *(re-iss. Jan87 on 'EG-Editions' lp/c/cd; EGED/EGEDC/EEGCD 23)*		

FRIPP & ENO

collaborate again.

		Help-Island	Antilles
Dec 75.	(lp) *(HELP 22) <7018>* **EVENING STAR**	□	□
	– Wind on water / Evening star / Evensong / Wind on wind / An index of metals. *(re-iss. Oct77 on 'Polydor'; 2343 094) (re-iss. Jan87 on 'E.G.' lp/cd; EGED/EEGCD 3)*		
	For the next couple of years he worked with 801 (PHIL MANZANERA's band). He also produced his own 'Obscure' label, discovering people including PENGUIN CAFE ORCHESTRA, MICHAEL NYMAN, MAX EASTLEY & DAVID TOOP, HAROLD BUDD plus JAN STEELE / JOHN CAGE. More commercially he also played on and produced 1977 albums by DAVID BOWIE, TALKING HEADS, ULTRAVOX.		

BRIAN ENO

		Polydor	Island
Dec 77.	(lp) *(2302 071) <9478>* **BEFORE AND AFTER SCIENCE**	□	□ May78
	– No one receiving / Backwater / Kurt's rejoiner / Energy fools the magician / King's lead hat / Here he comes / Julie with . . . / By this river / Through hollow lands / Spider and I. *(re-iss. Jan87 on 'E.G.' lp/c/cd; EG LP/MC/CD 32) (cd re-iss. Mar91; same)*		
Jan 78.	(7") *(2001 762)* **KING'S LEAD HAT. / R.A.F. (by "ENO & SNATCH")**	□	

		Polydor	E.G.
Sep 78.	(lp) *(2310 623) <EGS 105>* **MUSIC FOR FILMS**	55	□
	– M386 / Aragon / From the same hill / Inland sea / Two rapid formations / Slow water / Sparrowfall 1 / Sparrowfall 2 / Sparrowfall 3 / Quartz / Events in dense fog / There is nobody / A measured room / Patrolling wire borders / Task force / Alternative 3 / Strange light / Final sunset. *(privately pressed 1976 on 'EG'; EGM 1) (re-iss. Jan87 on 'E.G.' lp/c/cd; EGED/EGEDC/EEGCD 5)*		

		Ambient	P.V.C.
Mar 79.	(lp/c) *(AMB/+C 001) <7908>* **AMBIENT 1: MUSIC FOR AIRPORTS**	□	□
	– 1'1 / 2'1 / 1'2 / 2'2. *(re-iss. Jan87 on 'E.G.' lp/c/cd; EGED/EGEDC/EEGCD 17)*		
	Early in '79, ENO and MOEBIUS & ROEDILIUS (from CLUSTER) released album 'AFTER THE HEAT' *(Sky 021)*		
	Late in 1979, ENO collaborated with trumpeter JON HASSELL on album 'FOURTH WORLD VOL.1: POSSIBLE MUSICS' on 'E.G.'; *EGED 007)*		

Brian ENO (cont)

—— next with **HAROLD BUDD** – piano

	E.G.-Ambient	E.G.

Apr 80. (lp; ENO & BUDD) *(EGAMB 002)* <*EGS 107*> **AMBIENT 2: THE PLATEAUX OF MIRRORS**
– First light / Steal away / The plateau of mirror / Above Chiangmai / An arc of doves / Not yet remembered / The chill air / Among fields of crystal / Wind in lonely fences / Failing light. *(re-iss. Jan87 on 'EG')*

—— next with DAVID BYRNE, vocalist and instrumentalist w/ TALKING HEADS

	E.G.	Sire

Feb 81. (lp/c; BRIAN ENO & DAVID BYRNE) *(EG LP/MC 48)* <*6093*> **MY LIFE IN THE BUSH OF GHOSTS** — 29 / 44
– America is waiting / Mea culpa / Regiment / Help me somebody / The Jezebel spirit / Qu'ran / Moonlight in glory / The carrier / A secret life / Come with us / Mountain of needles. *(re-iss. Jan87 on 'E.G.' lp/c/cd; EG LP/MC/CD 48)*

May 81. (7"; BRIAN ENO & DAVID BYRNE) *(EGO 1)* **THE JEZEBEL SPIRIT. / REGIMENT**
(12"+=) *(EGOX 1)* – Very very hungry (Qu'ran).

Mar 82. (lp/c) *('EG-Editions'; EGED/+C 20)* **AMBIENT (4): ON LAND** — 93
– Lizard point / The lost day / Tal coat / Shadow / Lantern marsh / Unfamiliar wind / A clearing / Dunwich Beach, Autumn 1960. *(cd-iss. Jan87 on 'E.G.'; EEGCD 20)*

Jul 83. (lp; BRIAN ENO with DANIEL LANOIS & ROGER ENO) *(EGLP 53)* **APOLLO: ATMOSPHERES & SOUNDTRACKS**
– Under stars / The secret place / Matta / Signals / An ending (ascent) / Under stars II / Drift / Silver morning / Deep blue day / Weightless / Always returning / Stars. *(re-iss. Jan87 & Mar91 on 'E.G.' lp/c/cd; EG LP/MC/CD 53)*

	EG-Editions	not iss.

Aug 84. (lp; HAROLD BUDD & BRIAN ENO with DANIEL LANOIS) *(EGED 37)* **THE PEARL**
– Late October / A stream with bright fish / The silver ball / Against the sky / Lost in the humming air / Dark-eyed sister / Their memories / The pearl / Foreshadowed / An echo of night / Still return. *(re-iss. Jan87 on 'E.G.' lp/c/cd; EG LP/MC/CD 37)*

—— In 1984, he released 2 albums 'BEGEGNUNGEN I & II' with MOEBIUS, ROEDILUS & PLANK.

Aug 85. (lp/c; MICHAEL BROOK with BRIAN ENO & DANIEL LANOIS) *('EG-Editions'; EGED/+C 41)* **HYBRID**
– Hybrid / Distant village / Mimosa / Pond life / Ocean motion / Midday / Earth floor / Vacant. *(re-iss. Nov86 on 'E.G.' lp/c/cd; EG LP/MC/CD 41)*

Aug 85. (lp; ROGER ENO with BRIAN ENO) *('EG-Editions'; EGED 42)* **VOICES**
– A place in the wilderness / The day after / At the water's edge / Grey promenade / A paler sky / Through the blue / Evening tango / Recalling winter / Voices / The old dance / Reflections on I.K.B. *(re-iss. Jan87 on 'E.G.' lp/c/cd; EG LP/MC/CD 42)*

Jan 87. (lp/cd) *(EG LP/CD 64)* **THURSDAY AFTERNOON**
– Thursday afternoon. *(1 track only) (re-iss. cd Mar91; same)*

ENO / CALE

(collaboration JOHN CALE – vocals, multi-)with ROBERT AHWAI – rhythm guitar / DARYL JOHNSON – bass / NEIL CATCHPOLE – violin / RONALD JONES – drums, tabla / DAVE YOUNG – guitars, bass

	Land	Opal-Warner

Oct 90. (lp/c/cd) *(AS/+C/CD 12)* <*7599 26421-1/-4/-2*> **WRONG WAY UP**
– Lay my love / One word / In the backroom / Empty frame / Cordoba / Spinning away / Footsteps / Been there done that / Crime in the desert / The river. *(re-iss. Jul92; same)*

Nov 90. (12"ep/cd-ep) *(LANDHO 4)* <*9 40001-1/-2*> **ONE WORD. / GRANDFATHER'S HOUSE / PALAQUIN**

BRIAN ENO

	Opal-WEA	Opal-Warner

Jul 92. (7") *(48496-7)* <*9 40539-2*> **FRACTIAL ZOOM. / ('A'-Moby mix)**
(12"+=) *(48496-1)* – (4 mixes).
(cd-s++=) *(48496-2)* – (another mix) / The roil, the choke.

Sep 92. (cd/c) <*9362 45033-2/-4*> **NERVE NET** — 70
– Fractial zoom / Wire shock / What actually happened? / Pierre in mist / My squelchy life / Decentre / Juju space jazz / The roil, the choke / Ali click / Distributing being / Web.

Oct 92. (7") *(40618-7)* <*9 40650-2*> **ALI CLICK (Beirut mix). / ('A'-Rural mix)**
(12"+=) *(40618-1)* – ('A'-Markus Draws + Grid mixes).
(cd-s) *(40618-2)* – ('A'side) / ('A'-Markus Draws + Grid mixes) / ('A'-trance long darkly mad mix) / ('A'-trance instrumental).

Nov 92. (cd/c) <*9362 45010-2/-4*> **THE SHUTOV ASSEMBLY**
– Triennale / Alhondiga / Markgraph / Lanzarote / Francisco / Riverside / Innocenti / Stedelijk / Ikebukero / Cavallino.
(above music inspired by Moscow painter Sergei Shutov)

—— Around the same time as above, he lectured at Sadler's Wells, and is the brunt of NME jokes as Professor Eno.

	All Saints	Caroline

Jun 93. (cd) *(ASCD 015)* <*6600-2*> **:NEROLI:**
– :Neroli:
above's long piece of music was used in hospitals for childbirth!

—— Sep 94; he was credited on JAMES' ltd.album 'WAH WAH'.

	All Saints	Gyroscope

Oct 95. (lp/c/cd; BRIAN ENO & JAH WOBBLE) *(AS/+C/CD 023)* <*8190 6614-2*> **SPINNER** — 71
– Where we lived / Like organza / Steam / Garden recalled / Marine radio / Unusual balance / Space diary 1 / Spinner / Transmitter and trumpet / Left where it fell.

	All Saints	Thirsty Ear

Jun 97. (cd) *(ASCD 032)* <*6603-2*> **THE DROP**
– Slip dip / But if / Belgiam drop / Cornered / Black drop / Out-out / Swanky / Coasters / Blissed / M.C. Organ / Boomcubist / Hazard / Rayonism / Dutch blur / Back clack / Dear world / Iced world.

– his compilations, others, etc. –

on 'E.G.' unless mentioned otherwise

Apr 82. (d-c; FRIPP & ENO) *(EGDC 2)* **NO PUSSYFOOTIN' / EVENING STAR**

Nov 83. (10xlp-box) *(EGBS 002)* **WORKING BACKWARDS 1983-1973**
– (first 9 lp's, plus MUSIC FOR FILMS VOL.2 / + RARITIES m-lp:- Seven deadly finns / The lion sleeps tonight / Strong flashes of light / More volts / Mist rhythm)

Mar 86. (lp/c) *(EG LP/MC 65)* **MORE BLANK THAN FRANK**
(cd-iss. Jun87 & Mar91; EGCD 65)

Jan 87. (cd) *(EGCD 65)* **DESERT ISLAND SELECTION**
– Here he comes / Everything merges with the night / I'll come running (edit) / On some faraway beach (edit) / Spirits drifting / Back in Judy's jungle / St. Elmo's fire / No one receiving / Julie with . . . / Taking tiger mountain (edit) / 1'1.

Jan 87. (lp/c) *EG-Editions; (EGED/+C 35)* **MUSIC FOR FILMS 2**
– The dove / Roman twilight / Matta / Dawn, marshland / Climate study / The secret place / An ending (ascent) / Always returning 1 / Signals / Under stars / Drift / Study / Approaching Taidu / Always returning 2.

Mar 89. (cd-s) *(CDT 41)* **ANOTHER GREEN WORLD / DOVER BEACH / DEEP BLUE DAY / 2'1**

Dec 89. (3xc-box)(3xcd-box) *(EG BM/BC 7)* **ISLAND VARIOUS ARTISTS**
– (ANOTHER GREEN WORLD / BEFORE AND AFTER SCIENCE / APOLLO)

Nov 93. (3xcd-box) Virgin; *(ENOBX 1)* **BRIAN ENO** (collaborations)

Nov 93. (3xcd-box) Virgin; *(ENOBX 2)* **BRIAN ENO 2** (collaborations)

Feb 94. (cd/c) Venture; *(CD/TC VE 920)* **THE ESSENTIAL FRIPP AND ENO**

Oct 94. (3xcd-box) Virgin; *(TPAK 36)* **THE COMPACT COLLECTION**

—— ENO contributed 2 tracks on live lp 'JUNE 1st, 1974' with KEVIN AYERS, NICO and JOHN CALE. He also with brother ROGER and DANIEL LANOIS provided one track to DUNE film (1984). For albums by CLUSTER & ENO; see CLUSTER.

ENON

Formed: New York, USA . . . late 1999 by JOHN SCHMERSAL, formerly a member of geek-rockers BRAINIAC. After a few indie single releases as a solo project, SCHMERSAL linked up with RICK LEE and STEVE CALHOON of SKELETON KEY to form a trio. Before the release of their debut album 'BELIEVO!' (2000), ENON became a four-piece, with the addition of MATT SCHULTZ, and the replacement of CALHOON by TOKO YASUDA, previously with BLONDE REDHEAD. Heavy on experimentation, 'BELIEVO!' was an exercise in lo-fi indie-pop, reminiscent of BECK, although less accessible. For their second album, 'HIGH SOCIETY', released in 2002, ENON moved from 'See Thru' to the mightier 'Touch & Go' stable, formerly the home of BRAINIAC. 'HIGH SOCIETY' proved a more rounded effort than 'BELIEVO!', even approaching, at times, a sound both poppy and melodic.

Album rating: BELIEVO! (*5) / HIGH SOCIETY (*7)

JOHN SCHMERSAL – vocals, guitar (ex-BRAINIAC)

—— in 1999, ENON self-financed a few unknown singles

—— added **RICK LEE** – guitar, keyboards (ex-SKELETON KEY) / **TOKO YASADA** – percussion; repl. STEVE CALHOON (ex-SKELETON KEY)

	not iss.	See Thru

Mar 00. (cd) <*3*> **BELIEVO!**
– Rubber car / Cruel / Conjugate the verbs / Believo! / Come into / Matters gray / Get the letter out / World in a jar / For the sum of it / Elected / Biofeedback.

—— added **MATT SCHULTZ** – bass

	Self Starter	not iss.

Jul 01. (7") *(PSP 012)* **LISTEN WHILE YOU TALK. /**

	Touch & Go	Touch & Go

Jun 02. (lp/cd) <*(TG 235/+CD)*> **HIGH SOCIETY**
– Old dominion / Count sheep / In this city / Window display / Native dumb / Leave it to rust / Disposable parts / Sold! / Shoulder / Pleasure and privilege / Natural disasters / Carbonation / Salty / High society / Diamond raft.

ERASE ERRATA

Formed: Oakland, San Francisco, California, USA . . . late 1999 by JENNY HOYSTON, SARA JAFFE, ELLIE ERICKSON and BIANCA SPARTA. ERASE ERRATA discovered they had a real collective spirit after beginning to jam together in a spare room at HOYSTON and SPARTA's apartment. The group dynamic was such that they claimed to have written ten tracks in half an hour, which is certainly believable in light of their subsequent live performances, which would become characterized by their intuitive and instinctive playing (and matching monochrome dresses). In late 2000, they toured with MELT BANANA and LE TIGRE, and then issued a split-single with New York band BLACK DICE, on the 'Troubleman' imprint. The following year saw the release of the excellent, vociferous 'OTHER ANIMALS'. ERASE ERRATA's debut LP was brimming with anger and attitude, although there was patently intellect and skill behind their subversive BEEHEART-meets-FALL sonic assaults (most evident on 'HOW TO TELL YOURSELF FROM A TELEVISION'). In 2002, they released another split-single, this time with electro act, NUMBERS, and played live in the UK, including a support slot alongside the legendary FUGAZI.

Album rating: OTHER ANIMALS (*7)

JENNY HOYSTON – vocals, trumpet / **SARA JAFFE** – guitar / **ELLIE ERICKSON** – bass / **BIANCA SPARTA** – drums

			not iss.	Toyo
2001.	(cd-s) <toyo 678>	**THE STRUCTURE OF SCIENTIFIC MISCONCEPTIONS / THE SYSTEM OF SCIENTIFIC MISCONSTRUCTIONS**	-	

			Tsk Tsk	Troubleman
Sep 01.	(7") <TMU 080>	**split w/ BLACK DICE**	-	
Aug 02.	(cd) (TSK 001CD) <TMU 081>	**OTHER ANIMALS**		Oct01

– Tongue tied / Billy mummy / Delivery / 1 minute / Marathon / Other animals are #1 / High society / (untitled) / French Canadia / How to tell yourself from a television / Fault list / C. Rex / Walk don't fly / Dexterity is #2 / (untitled).

			Tigerbeat	not iss.
Aug 02.	(3"cd-ep) (MEOW 047)	**split w/ NUMBERS**		-

– Retreat, the most familiar, extensive, I bet! / Thief detests the criminal / (other two by the NUMBERS).

ERIC'S TRIP

Formed: Moncton, New Brunswick, Canada ... June 1990 by JULIE DOIRON-CLAYTOR, CHRIS THOMPSON, RICK WHITE and ED VAUGHAN (the latter replaced by MARK GAUDET in November 1991), all veterans of the Canadian indie scene. Despite naming themselves after a SONIC YOUTH track, the quartet traded in a slightly more melodic style of Lo-Fi punk/indie-pop than the NY noisesters, showcasing their sound on a series of early cassette demos and mini-sets over the period 1990-92. A surprise signing to 'Sub Pop', the band released a preliminary single, 'SONGS ABOUT CHRIS', for the label in spring '93, interspersing a debut album proper, 'LOVE TARA' with a further mini-set ('PETER') and 12" EP ('PORTHOLE TO DIMENTIA') for different labels. The prolific release schedule continued the following year with yet another EP, 'THE GORDON STREET HAUNTING' and a full length album, 'FOREVER AGAIN', the latter a marathon near-20 song affair reveling in a characteristically amateurish but often head spinningly addictive brand of noise-pop. Yet with such a limited musical scope, it came as little surprise when the band finally split with the various members going on to different projects on the local underground scene; their swansong set was 1996's 'PURPLE BLUE'. DOIRON's solo work (including an album as BROKEN GIRL) was issued on her own 'Sappy' independent, the latter being the stamping ground for acts such as ELEVATOR TO HELL, MOONSOCKET and SNAILHOUSE. Alongside DAVE SHOUSE, HOWE GELB, DOUG EASLEY and DAVIS McCAIN, JULIE and 'Sub Pop' records delivered her next album, 'LONELIEST IN THE MORNING' (1997), a record with sparse instrumentation that carried her ahead of the likes of AIMEE MANN or CAT POWER. 'JULIE DOIRON AND THE WOODEN STARS' (2000) – accompanied by The Wooden Stars whom she backed on their 'The Moon' LP – was straight-laced indie rock even sadder than her last efforts but worthy of a Canadian Juno Award. With the French language and bands taking an unusual upsurge since the advent of UK act STEREOLAB (led by LAETITIA SADIER), the brittle singer delivered her first Francophone long-player, 'DESORMAIS' (2001). Less obscure and back to basics was the rushed-released 'HEART AND CRIME' (2001), a record (also on 'Jagjaguwar') that showed her in solitary tender mood with little or no accompaniment. At the time of writing JULIE is still living with her three children and artist/painter husband JON CLAYTOR (who has worked on many of her LP sleeves) in Montreal Quebec, having moved there from New Brunswick.

Album rating: PETER mini (*6) / LOVE TARA (*6) / FOREVER AGAIN (*7) / PURPLE BLUE (*5) / Broken Girl: BROKEN GIRL (*6) / Julie Doiron: LONELIEST IN THE MORNING (*6) / JULIE DOIRON AND THE WOODEN STARS (*7) / DESORMAIS (*5) / HEART AND CRIME (*6)

JULIE DOIRON-CLAYTOR (b.1971) – vocals, bass / **CHRIS THOMPSON** – guitar (ex-DANG) / **RICK WHITE** – vocals, guitar (ex-BLOODSTAIN)

			not iss.	independent
Dec 90.	(c)	**ERIC'S TRIP**	-	
Apr 91.	(c-ep)	**CATERPILLARS**	-	
Aug 91.	(c-ep)	**DROWNING**	-	
Jan 92.	(c)	**WARM GIRL**	-	

— **MARK GAUDET** – drums (ex-PURPLE KNIGHT, ex-WHOREMOANS, ex-NO EXPLANATION) repl. VAUGHAN

			not iss.	N.I.M.
Apr 92.	(7"ep)	**BELONG**	-	

			not iss.	Murder
Apr 93.	(m-cd/m-c) <MUR 002>	**PETER**	-	

– Need / Listen / Tangles / Haze / Happens all the time / Deeper. (UK-iss.Jun93 on 'Sub Pop' m-lp/m-cd; SP/+CD 102/274)

			Sub Pop	Sub Pop
May 93.	(7"ep) <SP 87-258><SP 205>	**SONGS ABOUT CHRIS**		Apr93

– Hurt / Sloan song / Listen / Dinosaurs.
(cd-ep+=) (SPCD 87-258) – Mirror / Sand.

| Jul 93. | (12"ep) | **JULIE AND THE PORTHOLE TO DIMENTIA** | - | |

— <above issued on 'Sappy'>

| Nov 93. | (lp/c/cd) (SP/+MC/CD 115-293) <SP 234-A/B> | **LOVE TARA** | | |

– Behind the garage / Anything you want / Stove / Follow / Secret for Julie / Belly / Sunlight / June / To know them / Spring / Frame / May 11 / My room / Blinded / Allergic to love.

| Feb 94. | (7") <SHINE 045> | **OPENING SONG. / FLOAT** | - | |

(above issued on 'Summershine')

— around this time they also secured 2 splits 45's with SLOAN and MOVIOLA

| Jun 94. | (7"ep/cd-ep) <(SP/+CD 266)> | **THE GORDON STREET HAUNTING EP** | | |

– I'm so near here / Lightly feeling / Nevergrow / Departure song / You're always right.

| Oct 94. | (lp/cd) (SP/+CD 136-336) <SP/+CD 268> | **FOREVER AGAIN** | | |

– New love / This way out / About you / Girlfriend / Always there / Stupidest thing / December '93 / Thoroughly / My bed is red / View master / Cloudy / My chest is empty / Run away / Waiting all day / Let go / Hate song / Feeling around / Forever again.

| Aug 95. | (7"ep) <sunss 022> | **ON THE ROAD SOUTH** | - | |

– The road south / Smoke / I exist.
(above issued on 'Sonic Unyun')

| Feb 96. | (lp/cd) <(SP/+CD 333)> | **PURPLE BLUE** | | |

– Introduction into the . . . (pts.1-4) / Hourly / Sixteen hours / Universe / Eyes shut / Alone and annoyed / Lighthouse / Spaceship opening / Universal dawn / One floor below / Now a friend / Soon, coming closer / Not yours / Sun coming up / Beach.

— split after above JULIE DOIRON went solo (originally under the pseudonym, BROKEN GIRL) while GAUDET re-joined PURPLE KNIGHT, WHITE formed ELEVATOR TO HELL and THOMPSON to MOONSOCKET

– compilations, etc. –

| Feb 94. | (7"ep) Derivative; <DUH 011> | **WARM GIRL** | - | |

– Warm girl / Window / So easier last time / My chest is empty (part one) / The future.

| Oct 97. | (cd) Sonic Unyon; <017> | **LONG DAY'S RIDE** (early material) | - | |
| 2001. | (cd) Teenage USA; <teen 025> | **THE ERIC'S TRIP SHOW (live from 1991-1996)** | - | |

– Stove / Beach / My bed is red / Universal dawn / You're always right / Anytime you want / Girlfriend / Feeling around / Smoke / Sun coming up / Sunlight / Listen / Happens all the time / Frame / Smother / Near here / My room / Sloan song / Blinded / Burn / Belong / The beauty was all froze.

JULIE DOIRON

— - vocals, guitars, piano, drums, etc

			not iss.	home made
1991.	(c)	**DOG LOVE PART I**	-	

			not iss.	Sappy
1993.	(c)	**DOG LOVE PART II**	-	
1995.	(7"; as BROKEN GIRL)	**NORA**	-	

– The book song, his girlfriend / Dance music.

| May 96. | (cd; as BROKEN GIRL) | **BROKEN GIRL** | - | |

– Dance music / Elevator show / Crumble / Soon, coming closer / August 10 / Taller beauty / Grammy / Grew smaller / Happy lucky girl / Sorry story.

— now with **DOUG EASLEY** – pedal steel guitar, etc / **HOWE GELB** – guitars, keyboards, etc (of GIANT SAND) / **DAVE SHOUSE** – guitars, bass, piano (of GRIFTERS)

			Sub Pop	Sub Pop
Sep 97.	(lp/cd) <(SP/+CD 398)>	**LONELIEST IN THE MORNING**		Aug97

– So fast / Dance me / Sorry (part I) / Tell you again / Explain / Crying baby / Sweeter / Tonight, we sleep / Mother / Love to annoy / Creative depression / Sorry (part II) / Condescending you / Le soleil.

— now with **DAVE DRAVES** – piano, vocals

			Sappy	Sappy
May 99.	(cd-ep) <TREE 13>	**WILL YOU TILL LOVE ME?**		

– He will forget / Again, again / Stay now, then go / Will you still love me in December? / For me. (re-iss. Oct02 on 'Jag Jaguwar'; JAG 56)

— the **WOODEN STARS:- MIKE FEUERSTACK** – guitar / **JULIEN BEILLARD** – bass / **ANDY McCORMACK** – drums

| Feb 00. | (cd) <TREE 23> | **JULIE DOIRON AND THE WOODEN STARS** | | |

– The last time / Gone gone / The longest winter / The best thing for me / In this dark / Drums and horns / Dance music / Au contraire / Seven / The second time / Sweeter. <re-iss. 2002 on 'Jag Jaguwar'; JAG 57>

			not iss.	Plumline
Apr 00.	(7")	**WHO WILL BE THE ONE. / TOO MUCH**	-	

			Jag Jaguwar	Jag Jaguwar
Oct 01.	(cd) <(JAG 40CD)>	**DESORMAIS**		Aug01

– Ce charmant coeur / La jeune amoureuse / Faites de beaux reves / Don't ask / Le piano / Tu es malades / Au contraire / Pour toujours / Penses-donc (tu es seule) / Faites de beaux reves.

| Nov 01. | (cd) <(JAG 42CD)> | **HEART AND CRIME** | | |

– Wintermits / Too much / Shivers + crickets / All their broken hearts / Sending the photographs / I broke his heart / The sugary is over / Who will be the one? / The one you love / I love to dance / It's okay to stare / Oh these walls.

ESKA

Formed: Strathblane, Glasgow, Scotland ... 1993 by youngsters CHRIS MACK and COLIN KEARNEY who met in their local music (instrument) shop. With drummer STUART BRAITHWAITE on board (he's now sonic guitarist with MOGWAI), the trio's early experiments were apparently too avant-garde for latecomer KENNY MacLEOD. Upon his arrival, the bass man knocked the songs into shape and the first results emerged in the form of late 1995's 'TRUCKING AND PAVING'. Released by GRAHAM KEMP (of URUSEI YATSURA) on his own 'Modern Independent' imprint, the track wore its US noise influences proudly on its sleeve ... hardly surprising, given KEARNEY's petulant claim to dislike any music pre-1980 (with the exception of SUPERTRAMP). At least MACK had apparently been listening to his dad's record collection, his "challenging" singing sounding uncannily like LEONARD COHEN (albeit on a bender with PAVEMENT). A couple of lo-fi 7"ers followed before BRAITHWAITE went off to create sonic masterpieces with MOGWAI, replacement WILLIE MONE making his debut on 1996's 'RUNNING ON SUM SIX DEW' single. A further EP, 'LAST MAN ON THE

MOON' (on London-based 'Scared Of Girls'), appeared in Autumn '97 before a gap of more than three years preceded a long awaited ESKA debut album, 'INVENT THE FORTUNE' (2000). CHRIS MACK was also leader of the JAMES ORR COMPLEX (who issued the EP, 'FIGA' for 'Rock Action') and has worked with EL HOMBRE TRAJEADO.

Album rating: INVENT THE FORTUNE (*6)

CHRIS MACK – vocals, guitar / **COLIN KEARNEY** – guitar, vocals / **KENNY MacLEOD** – bass / **STUART BRAITHWAITE** – drums

	Modern Ind	not iss.
Nov 95. (7"m) *(MIR 003)* **TRUCKING AND PAVING. / THESE ARE THE DRY YEARS / FALSE START**		-

	Flotsam & Jetsam	not iss.
Feb 96. (7"ep) *(SHaG 002)* **SPLIT SINGLE** – In the bottle / Aristotle / (other 2 tracks by the Poison Sisters).		-

	Love Train	not iss.
May 96. (7") *(PUBE 10)* **Ill PIKE. / LET'S FENCE!**		-

— BRAITHWAITE took up his MOGWAI post full-time; new drummer **WILLIE MONE**

Oct 96. (7") *(PUBE 15)* **RUNNING ON SUM SIX DEW. / NOVA SCOTIA**		-

	Scared Of Girls	not iss.
Sep 97. (7"ep) *(GIRL 004)* **LAST MAN ON THE MOON** – Last man on the Moon / Finding it hard to do so little / Dustkicker / Ligercone.		-

— now with new drummer **HOPPY** (ex-HERNANDEZ); briefly

	Gringo	not iss.
Oct 00. (cd) *(WAAT 008CD)* **INVENT THE FORTUNE** – Goodbye to victories / Blast theory / From springboard to highdive / Knives, slowing / The ghosts invade / Between kings / ESP does work / The unbelievable snow of 1999.		-

	D & C	not iss.
Feb 02. (cd-ep) *(DCCD 006)* **THE CASE WRAPPED UP** – The case wrapped up / Flag etiquette / Lost map – lost orders / Criterium 75.		-

JAMES ORR COMPLEX

CHRIS MACK with various

	RockAction	not iss.
Nov 01. (7"ep/cd-ep) *(ROCKACT 8/+CD)* **FIGA EP** – Million men / Good prophecy / Eagle / Slip into slumber / O conde.		-

ESP SUMMER (see under ⇒ HIS NAME IS ALIVE)

ESSEX GREEN

Formed: Brooklyn, New York, USA ... summer 1997 by ex-GUPPYBOY members CHRIS ZITER, SASHA BELL, JEFF BARON and MIKE BARRET. Vermont- based GUPPYBOY released their one and only album 'JEFFERSONVILLE' in 1997. Their sound was typical of the Americana folk music being produced by such acts as WILCO at the time. It was earthy and atmospheric, employing instruments such as mandolins and banjos, which served to give the album a timeless quality. After the four members had relocated to Brooklyn, they enlisted drummer TIM BARNES and re-launched themselves as The ESSEX GREEN. The group released their first single in the spring of 1999, quickly followed by the album 'EVERYTHING IS GREEN'. With their new name, the band had taken on an entirely different musical direction. 'EVERYTHING IS GREEN' was an authentic sounding stab at 1960's psychedelia, a musical style with which the band appeared much more comfortable and capable of playing. Their self-titled EP released in 2000 continued to pilfer from all the essential "summer of love" groups whilst remaining fresh and original sounding. As a side-project, BARON, ZITER and BELL teamed up with MIKE BARRETT and ZACHARY WARD to form The SIXTH GREAT LAKE. A return to the sound of GUPPYBOY, their debut album 'UP THE COUNTRY' (2001) was heavily influenced by the likes of The BAND and NEIL YOUNG.

Album rating: Guppyboy: JEFFERSONVILLE (*5) / Essex Green: EVERYTHING IS GREEN (*7) / THE ESSEX GREEN mini (*6) / Sixth Great Lake: UP THE COUNTRY (*6)

GUPPYBOY

CHRIS ZITER – vocals, guitar / **SASHA BELL** – vocals, keyboards / **JEFF BARON** – guitar / **MIKE BARRETT** – bass

	not iss.	Sudden Shame
1997. (cd) <*019*> **JEFFERSONVILLE** – Washington Square / Trouble / Seventh avenue / The a.m. / Avalon ballroom / Ball in the sky / Affection / Twisted / Holiday / New Orleans / Cam 2 / Snow song / Wendy / Urb's lament / Berry girl.	-	

ESSEX GREEN

— added **TIM BARNES** – drums

	Kindercore	Kindercore
Mar 00. (cd/lp) <*(KC 034 CD/LP)*> **EVERYTHING IS GREEN** – Primrose / The playground / Mrs. Bean / Grass / Saturday / Big green tree / Tinker (she heard the news) / Everything is green / Sixties / Sun / Carballo.		Nov99

	Elephant 6	Elephant 6
Jun 00. (m-cd) <*(E6 019CD)*> **THE ESSEX GREEN** – Fabulous day / Trees / Chester / New Orleans / Bald.		Apr00

— BELL + BARON moonlighted with LADYBUG TRANSISTOR; although The ESSEX GREEN were back in 2003 after their The SIXTH GREAT LAKE outings

SIXTH GREAT LAKE

JEFF BARON, CHRIS ZITER, SASHA BELL, MIKE BARRETT + ZACHARY WARD

	Kindercore	Kindercore
Apr 01. (cd/lp) <*(KC 063/+LP)*> **UP THE COUNTRY** – Duck pond / Across the northern border / Up the country / The ballad of a sometimes traveler / Cannon beach / Descending star / Blue / Last in line / You make the call / Shade of love / 27 forever / Spin your wheels / 300 miles / Rockin' chair / Lovely today.		Mar01

ETERNALS (see under ⇒ TRENCHMOUTH)

ETHER

Formed: Blackwood, Caerphilly, Wales ... early 1996 by songwriter RORY MEREDITH, plus BRETT SAWMY and GARETH DRISCOLL. Allegedly hard-drinking lads, they were rumoured to have come to blows with the Chippendales, amid tales of general hotel debauchery. It was only a matter of time before they were signed to a major, 'Parlophone' picking them up after an indie debut on 'Regal'. However chart success eluded them, despite the soulful indie-pop of their 1997 singles 'IF YOU REALLY WANT TO KNOW' and 'SHE COULD FLY'. The following year saw two further 45's, 'WATCHING YOU' and 'BEST FRIEND', both taken from their long-awaited inaugural set, 'STRANGE' (1998). • **Note:** An entirely different ETHER (i.e. AMELIA NILES FAIRWEATHER and SEBASTIAN ARCHER) had a few albums between 1993-1998.

Album rating: STRANGE (*6)

RORY MEREDITH – vocals, guitar / **GARETH DRISCOLL** – vocals, bass / **BRETT SAWMY** – drums

	Regal	not iss.
Oct 96. (7") *(REG 12)* **HE SAY YEAH. / WHEN SHE WOKE**		-

	Parlophone	not iss.
Jun 97. (c-s/7") *(TC+/R 6468)* **IF YOU REALLY WANT TO KNOW. / JULIE** (cd-s+=) *(CDR 6468)* – Rome yo-yo.		-
Oct 97. (c-s/7") *(TC+/R 6481)* **SHE COULD FLY. / BATHROOM** (cd-s+=) *(CDR 6481)* – Now I'm ready.		-
Mar 98. (c-s) *(TCR 6491)* **WATCHING YOU / STRANGE (acoustic) / PROMISE THE EARTH** (cd-s) *(CDR 6491)* – (first two tracks) / Dogs life. (cd-s) *(CDRS 6491)* – (first & third tracks) / He say yeah (demo).	74	-
Jun 98. (7") *(R 6496)* **BEST FRIEND. / GETTING OFF ON T.V.** (cd-s+=) *(CDR 6496)* – One good reason.		-
Jul 98. (cd/c) *(4 94182-2/-4)* **STRANGE** – She could fly / Watching you / I love her anyway / He say yeah / Wasting time / When she woke / Best friend / If you really want to know / The world that she sees / Roadworks / Without you / Strange.		-

— disbanded after above

ETHYLINE (see under ⇒ SCREECHING WEASEL)

ETHYL MEATPLOW (see under ⇒ GERALDINE FIBBERS)

EUGENIUS (see under ⇒ VASELINES; in 80's section)

EUPHONE

Formed: Chicago, Illinois, USA ... 1994 by multi-instrumentalist RYAN RAPSYS, as an experimental progressive jazz/rock solo project. RAPSYS was previously a member of GAUGE, and remained concurrently involved with HEROIC DOSES. A hugely talented drummer, his live performances as EUPHONE were characterised by the audacious combination of only drums, a keyboard and a sequencer. It wasn't until 1997 that EUPHONE's eponymous debut album was released (on Chicago's 'Hefty' label). The nine-track LP comprised material from his earliest recordings. Its blend of discerning instrumentation and infectious beats, form a placid and immensely satisfying album. EUPHONE's next offering was 1998's 'BREAKING PAROLE' EP. With extra guitars from BILL DOLAN, ' ...PAROLE' is another fine collection, containing seven relatively short compositions on a slightly funkier edge, like 'THE SUN THEME' with its rousing bass. EUPHONE soon became a duo, with RAPSYS recruiting HEROIC DOSES band-mate NICK MACRI as a permanent member, and together they constructed EUPHONE's second album, 'CALENDAR OF UNLUCKY DAYS' (1999). There are more styles and influences present here – like Caribbean, Latin and dub – and a greater emphasis on production, resulting in a more layered depth of sound. Released a year later, third album 'HASHIN' IT OUT' finds RAPSYS in fine form on the drums, although the more experimental vibe leads to an inconsistency of outcome. Self-produced fourth LP, 2002's 'THE LAKEWOOD', featured EUPHONE's third permanent member, keyboardist JEREMY JACOBSEN – enhancing their overall sound and continuing a run of accomplished, challenging albums.

Album rating: EUPHONE (*6) / THE CALENDAR OF UNLUCKY DAYS (*5) / HASHIN' IT OUT (*4) / THE LAKEWOOD mini (*5)

RYAN RAPSYS – drums, keyboards, synthesizer (of HEROIC DOSES)

			Tiny Superhero	Tiny Superhero
Sep 97.	(cd) <(SUPERCD 006)>	**EUPHONE**		May97

– Island I'd love to live on / Red, blue, yellow / Two basic colors / From an unpublished letter / Message from Touhy Bay / Ko-ko / Weatherbeaten / My boatship / Oiseaux.

			Hefty	Hefty
Jan 99.	(cd-ep) <(HEFTY 003CD)>	**BREAKING PAROLE**		

– The sun theme / Passport / A hundred times and more / I did not say may be not / Nasal evidence / Little warbles / New dusk policy.

—— added **NICK MACRI** – bass (of HEROIC DOSES)

			Jade Tree	Jade Tree
May 99.	(lp/cd) <(JT 1041/+CD)>	**THE CALENDAR OF UNLUCKY DAYS**		

– Bought then sold / Fallout / Broken gourd / Su 10 #1 / Apostolic 6 as close to cold / As close to cold / Needle and crate / Cindy you hate to eat / Wickedness / Playboy.

Oct 00.	(lp/cd) <(JT 1054/+CD)>	**HASHIN' IT OUT**		

– Gyrations / Press on / Where's the B? / Newscast / Bad ascending I do you up / Oh you ache / Weekend / Shut it / Nick is Ryan / Honey, I'll be home by suppertime / My ladies can't remember the eighties / Confirmation of suspicions.

—— added **JEREMY JACOBSEN** – keyboards (of 5 STYLE)

			Bubblecore	Bubblecore
Jun 02.	(m-cd/m-lp) (efa 22050-2/-1) <25>	**THE LAKEWOOD**		Apr02

– The Lakewood burning bad boy / Tools of love / The Baldwin wipeout / Homodulations / Fanfare / Countdown / Passing notes.

EVEN AS WE SPEAK

Formed: Sydney, Australia ... early 90's by songwriter MARY THERESE BERNADETTE WYER, ROB IRWIN, PAUL CLARKE, JULIAN KNOWLES and two others who all made their new abode the in English resort of Brighton. EVEN AS WE SPEAK were an eclectic, oddball collection of strange pop video makers, cyber avant garde composers, children's television presenters and psychotics(!). They founded when key member THERESE had decided that she wanted a change in Sydney's corporate music scene. Hoping to be the next BIRTHDAY PARTY (well, not quite!), the ensemble debuted with the World Music-esque single, 'BEAUTIFUL DAY', before issuing their first album for UK label 'Sarah' in '93, 'FERAL POP FRENZY'. With ballads, swooning international music, VELVET UNDERGROUND-like lo-fi pop and a small bit of ambient techno, oiled in a production coating that could have even spiked NICK CAVE's dry bourbon. Add a slow acoustic version of NEW ORDER's 'BIZARRE LOVE TRIANGLE' and you had the ingredients of a strange entangled fold. Well, maybe not. Because they made as little impact here as they did on their own patch, the troupe deciding to throw the last shrimp on the barbee and retreat back to where the sun always shines bright in the sky.

Album rating: FERAL POP FRENZY (*5)

MARY THERESE BERNADETTE WYER – vocals / **PAUL CLARKE** – guitar / **ROB IRWIN** – bass / **JULIAN KNOWLES** – programmer / + 2 others

			Sarah	not iss.
Oct 90.	(7"ep) (SARAH 037)	**GOES SO SLOW / BLUE SUBURBAN SKIES. / BIZARRE LOVE TRIANGLE / NOTHING EVER HAPPENS / A STRANGER CALLS**		-
Jul 91.	(7"m) (SARAH 049)	**ONE STEP FORWARD. / MUST BE SOMETHING ELSE / BEST KEPT SECRET**		-
Dec 91.	(7") (SARAH 059)	**BEAUTIFUL DAY. / NOTHING MUCH AT ALL**		-
Feb 93.	(lp/cd) (SARAH 614/+CD)	**FERAL POP FRENZY**		-

– Beelzebub / Beautiful day / Falling down the stairs / Zeppelins / Anybody anyway / Love is the answer / To see you smile / Straight as an arrow / Squid / One thing / Sailor's graves / Spirit of progress / Criple creek / Swimming song / One step forward / Drown / O.G.T.T.

Jul 93.	(7") (SARAH 079)	**BLUE EYES DECEIVING ME. / (ALL YOU FIND IS) AIR**		-

(cd-s+=) (SARAH 079CD) – Getting faster.

—— went silent after above and returned to Australia

EVERCLEAR

Formed: Portland, Oregon, USA ... 1991 by former teenage junkie, ART ALEXAKIS (he gave up alcohol, drugs and nicotine in June '84). Coming from a broken home, he was also dogged by the drug deaths of his girlfriend and older brother, George. At the turn of the decade, ART was involved in two bands, The EASY HOES (lp released 'Tragic Songs Of Life' on 'Shindig') and COLORFINGER (cd issued 'Deep In The Heart Of The Beast In The Sun' – a demo cassette was also issued with future EVERCLEAR tracks!). Another founder member, CRAIG MONTOYA (other two, STEVEN BIRCH and SCOTT CUTHBERT) helped produce their debut indie album, 'WORLD OF NOISE', in 1994 and after rave reviews they were whisked away by 'Capitol' A&R man PERRY WATTS-RUSSELL. It was alleged that they were released from the indie, only when the gun-totting ALEXAKIS convinced the boss to let them go. By Spring '96 (and now with GREG EKLUND who had replaced CUTHBERT and BIRCH), their second album, 'SPARKLE AND FADE', had climbed into the US Top 30. A stylish anti-drug affair, it was described as ELVIS COSTELLO fused with LED ZEPPELIN, HUSKER DU or NIRVANA! ALEXAKIS and Co. returned in 1998 with a third set proper (the previous year's 'WHITE TRASH HELL' consisted of outtakes), 'SO MUCH FOR THE AFTERGLOW', the US Top 40 album almost spawning another UK Top 40 single, 'EVERYTHING TO EVERYONE'. While many of the tail-end grunge acts imploded before the 90's were through, EVERCLEAR entered the new millennium with their most ambitious project to date, a two-volume concept set exploring ALEXAKIS' divorce. 'SONGS FROM AN AMERICAN MOVIE, VOL.1: LEARNING HOW TO SMILE' (2000) covered the dating years with a peppy soundtrack inspired by the A.M. pop/rock of the frontman's youth (including a cover of Van Morrison's timeless 'BROWN EYED GIRL'). 'SONGS FROM AN AMERICAN MOVIE, VOL.2: GOOD TIME FOR A BAD ATTITUDE' (2000), meanwhile, hit the shelves a few months later and documented the dream turning sour. Unsurprisingly, the music was harder and the subject matter heavier as ALEXAKIS exorcised the pain of lost love and broken friendship. • **Covered:** HOW SOON IS NOW (Smiths).

Album rating: WORLD OF NOISE (*6) / SPARKLE AND FADE (*9) / SO MUCH FOR THE AFTERGLOW (*7) / SONGS FROM AN AMERICAN MOVIE VOL.1: LEARNING HOW TO SMILE (*7) / SONGS FROM AN AMERICAN MOVIE VOL.2: GOOD TIME FOR A BAD ATTITUDE (*5)

ART ALEXAKIS (b.12 Apr'62) – vocals, guitar / **STEVEN BIRCH** – guitar / **CRAIG MONTOYA** (b.14 Sep'70) – bass, vocals / **SCOTT CUTHBERT** – drums, vocals

			not iss.	Tim/Kerr
Oct 93.	(7",7"colrd) <TK 937055>	**NERVOUS & WEIRD. / ELECTRA MADE ME BLIND**	-	

(cd-ep+=) <TK 93CD57> – Drunk again / Lame / Connection / Slow motion genius (instrumental).

Nov 93.	(cd/lp) (FIRE CD/LP 46) <TK 59>	**WORLD OF NOISE**	-	

– Your genius hands / Sick & tired / The laughing world / Fire maple song / Pennsylvania is . . . / Nervous and weird / Malevolent / Sparkle / Trust found / Loser makes good / Invisible / Evergleam. <US re-iss. Nov94 on 'Capitol' cd/c; 30562-2/-4> (UK-iss.Feb95 on 'Fire' cd/lp; FIRE CD/LP 46)

			Fire	Capitol
Nov 94.	(cd-ep) <58255>	**FIRE MAPLE SONG EP**	-	

– Fire maple song / Detroit / 1975 / Blondes / Pacific wonderland (instrumental) / Fire maple song (acoustic version).

Feb 95.	(cd-ep) (BLAZE 77CD)	**FIRE MAPLE SONG EP**		-

– Fire maple song / Loser makes good / Lame / Connection.

—— **GREG EKLUND** (b.18 Apr'70) – drums, vocals; repl. CUTHBERT + BIRCH

Nov 95.	(7") <23261-7>	**HEROIN GIRL. / AMERICAN GIRL**	-	

(cd-s+=) <23261-2> – Annabella's song / Nahalem (alt. mix).

			Capitol	Capitol
Mar 96.	(cd/c/lp) (CDTC/TC+/EST 2257) <30929>	**SPARKLE AND FADE**		25 May95

– Electra made me blind / Heroin girl / You make me feel like a whore / Santa Monica / Summerland / Strawberry / Heartspark dollar / The twistinside / Her brand new skin / Nehalem / Queen of the air / Pale green stars / Chemical smile / My sexual life. (cd-cd re-iss. Jun98; CDESTX 2257) – (extra tracks).

Apr 96.	(cd-ep) <58538>	**HEARTSPARK DOLLARSIGN / HEROIN GIRL (acoustic) / SIN CITY / HAPPY HOUR**	-	85
May 96.	(7"clear) (CL 773)	**HEARTSPARK DOLLARSIGN. / LOSER MAKES GOOD (live)**	48	-

(cd-s+=) (CDCL 773) – Sparkle (live).
(cd-s) (CDCLS 773) – ('A'side) / Pennsylvania is . . . (live) / Nervous & weird (live).

Aug 96.	(7") (CL 775)	**SANTA MONICA (WATCH THE WORLD DIE). / AMERICAN GIRL (KDGE version)**	40	-

(cd-s+=) (CDCL 775) – Strawberry (KDGE version) / Fire maple song (KDGE version).
(cd-s) (CDCLS 775) – ('A'side) / Heroin girl (KDGE version) / Summerland (KDGE version) / Sin city.

Sep 96.	(cd-s) <promo>	**YOU MAKE ME FEEL LIKE A WHORE / AMERICAN GIRL (live) / LIKE BRANDON DOES (by Klinger)**	-	

—— added **CHRIS BIRCH** – guitar

Mar 98.	(cd/c) <(36503-2/-4/-1)>	**SO MUCH FOR THE AFTERGLOW**	63	33 Oct97

– So much for the afterglow / Everything to everyone / Ataraxia / Normal like you / I will buy you a new life / Father of mine / One hit wonder / El distorto de melodica / Amphetamine / White men in black suits / Sunflower / Why don't I believe in God / Like a California king.

Apr 98.	(7") (CL 799)	**EVERYTHING TO EVERYONE. / OUR LIPS ARE SEALED**	41	

(cd-s+=) (CDCL 799) – What do I get / ('A'-CD-Rom video).
(cd-s) (CDCLS 799) – ('A'side) / Walk don't run / Search and destroy / Santa Monica heroin (CD-Rom video).

Jul 98.	(cd-ep) <85592>	**I WILL BUY YOU A NEW LIFE EP**	-	

– I will buy you a new life / So much for the afterglow (live) / Heroin girl (live) / Local god (live).

Nov 98.	(cd-ep) <86181>	**FATHER OF MINE EP**	-	70

– Father of mine / So much for the afterglow (live) / Heroin girl (live) / Local god (live).

Aug 00.	(cd) (527864-2) <97061>	**SONGS FROM AN AMERICAN MOVIE VOL.1 – LEARNING HOW TO SMILE**	51	9 Jul00

– Songs from an American movie (part 1) / Here we go again / AM radio / Brown eyed girl / Learning how to smile / The honeymoon song / Now that it's over / Thrift store chair / Otis Redding / Unemployed boyfriend / Wonderful / Annabella's song.

Oct 00.	(c-s) (TCCL 824) <58870>	**WONDERFUL / FATHER OF MINE (remix) / I'M ON YOUR TIME**	36	11 Aug00

(cd-s+=) (CDCLS 824) – ('A'-CD-ROM video)>

Mar 01.	(cd-s) (CDCL 827)	**AM RADIO / I'M ON YOUR TIME / SANTA MONICA (live from Woodstock)**		-
Apr 01.	(cd) (530419-2) <95873>	**SONGS FROM AN AMERICAN MOVIE VOL.2 – GOOD TIME FOR A BAD ATTITUDE**	69	Nov00

– When it all goes wrong again / Slide / Babytalk / Rock star / Short blonde hair / Misery whip / Out of my depth / The good witch of the north / Halloween Americana / All f**ked up / Overwhelming / Song from an American movie (part 2).

EVERCLEAR (cont)

– compilations, etc. –

Aug 95. (cd) *Imprint; <97633>* **LIVE FROM TORONTO** (live)
Apr 97. (m-cd) *Fire; (MCD 45)* **WHITE TRASH HELL**
– Heroin girl (demo) / Detroit / 1975 / Blondes / Pacific wonderland (instrumental) / For Pete's sake / Fire maple song (acoustic). *(re-iss. May02; SFIRE 009CD)*

EVERLASTING THE WAY
(see under ⇒ JUNE OF 44)

EXHAUST
(see under ⇒ GODSPEED YOU BLACK EMPEROR!)

EXILE INSIDE (see under ⇒ MY LIFE STORY)

EXPERIMENTAL AUDIO RESEARCH
(see under ⇒ SPACEMEN 3)

EXPERIMENTAL POP BAND
(see under ⇒ BRILLIANT CORNERS; in 80's section)

EXTRA GLENNS (see under ⇒ MOUNTAIN GOATS)

FABULOUS

Formed: London, England ... 1991 by NME journalist turned frontman, SIMON DUDFIELD, alongside NME photographers, MARTIN GOODACRE and RUSSEL UNDERWOOD, the line-up being completed by the rhythm section of RONNIE and HODGE. Managed by their assistant editor, James Brown (although they were sadly lacking in the soul/charisma factor defined by his namesake!), the lads certainly weren't short of publicity/hype potential although they did resort to SEX PISTOLS/MALCOLM McLAREN-style tactics to get attention (i.e. stealing a carpet from the offices of 'E.M.I.'). If that wasn't enough to prove their punk-rock credentials, they underlined their rebel status by securing the services of PETE WATERMAN on their second single, 'PERSONALITY RECESSION'. They had already issued their debut, 'DESTINED TO BE FREE', on the fledgling 'Heavenly' label in late '91, a supposed reaction to the drug euphoria of the rave/baggy generation. It would be a further eighteen months or so before the release of the aforementioned follow-up, a third single, 'DEAD FRIENDS', all but sealing their less than fabulous career later that year. Maybe they shouldn't have given up their day jobs. Ah! music journalists ... who loves them?

Album rating: never released any

SIMON DUDFIELD – vocals / **MARTIN GOODACRE** – guitar / **RUSSEL UNDERWOOD** – guitar / **RONNIE** – bass / **HODGE** – drums

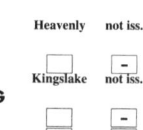

Nov 91. (ltd-7") *(HVN 11)* **DESTINED TO BE FREE. / THERE'S A RIOT GOIN' ON (INSIDE HER PRETTY HEAD)**
Jun 93. (12") *(SE 17)* **PERSONALITY RECESSION. / PRE-FLYING MEDALLIONS**
Nov 93. (7"ep) *(KLR 002)* **DEAD FRIENDS EP**
—— disbanded in 1994

FAINT

Formed: Omaha, Nebraska, USA ... 1994 by TODD BAECHLE (vocals, synthesizer), brother CLARK (drums) and bassist JOEL PETERSON. Initially known as NORMAN BAILER, they performed their lo-fi pop tunes in local coffee houses. Some of this early material made it onto a couple of split discs, and a cassette released through 'Saddle Creek' (then 'Lumberjack' records). The early incarnation of The FAINT, along with bands like BRIGHT EYES and CURSIVE, would come to propel a lively Omaha music scene. The FAINT began in earnest around 1998, with the release of a two-track promo CD; MATT BOWEN added to the line-up. These tracks were reworked, and later in 1998 appeared on the FAINT's debut LP 'MEDIA'. The songs on 'MEDIA' covered a diversity of styles and influences – Brit-pop, the CURE, acoustic folk – but all within the general parameters of indie-rock. After a national tour in support of the set, The FAINT – with BOWEN (significantly) replaced by keyboard/synth player JACOB THIELE – began moving in a different direction. The first half of 1999 saw them write and record a collection of new songs, this time with an emphasis on electronics, dance-beats and keyboard hooks. This new collection was 'BLANK-WAVE ARCADE' and showcased an unquestionably '80s influenced and driven FAINT sound – and it proved a winning move for the band. Tracks such as 'SEX IS PERSONAL', 'VICTIM CONVENIENCE' and 'SEALED HUMAN' showcased their transformation into progressive innovators, and contained incisive lyrics dealing with sexuality and mass consumption. Touring extensively following the release of 'BLANK-WAVE ...', The FAINT blew audiences away with their relentless energy and live light show. In January they recruited guitarist DAPOSE – who had recently disbanded Omaha death metal act LEAD – and although seeming like an unlikely union, DAPOSE brought a punk-rock attitude to the set-up. On third album 'DANSE MACABRE', released later in 2001, The FAINT continued their '80s dance-beat explorations, although this time with a darker edge. It was just as compelling – and critically acclaimed – as 'BLANK-WAVE ...', and became one of 'Saddle Creek's biggest-sellers. They followed 'DANSE ...' with more touring and a 12" of re-mixes. Meanwhile, JOEL P was concocting his own lo-fi solo project under the name of BROKEN SPINDLES. Retro-kitch and decidedly electronica, the man has released one eponymous solo set for 'Tiger Style' in 2002.

Album rating: MEDIA (*5) / BLANK-WAVE ARCADE (*6) / DANSE MACABRE (*5) / Broken Spindles: BROKEN SPINDLES (*6)

FAINT (cont)

TODD BAECHLE – vocals, synthesizer / **CLARK BAECHLE** – drums (guitarist/vocalist of PARK AVE) / **JOEL PETERSON** – bass

	not iss.	Saddle Creek
1995. (7"ep; as NORMAN BAILER w/ Various Artists) <LBJ 09> **Music Me All Over**	-	

— added **MATT BOWEN** – bass, vocals (PETERSON now on guitar)

	not iss.	Saddle Creek
Mar 98. (cd) <LBJ 21> **MEDIA**	-	

– Syntax lies / Some incriminating photographs / As the doctor talks / Tandem: city to city / Repertoire of uncommon depth / Typing: 1974-2048 / Lullaby for the . . . / Acting: on-campus television / (Getting/Giving the lock) / Armorous in bauhuas fashion / There's something not as valid when the scenery is a postcard / An allusion passes through the bar / Defy the ailments.

— **JACOB THIELE** – synthesizer, vocals; repl. BOWEN

Jun 99. (7") <LBJ 25> **THE FAINT / EX-ACTION FIGURES**	-	
Nov 99. (cd) <LBJ 28> **BLANK-WAVE ARCADE**	-	

– Sex is personal / Call call / Worked up so sexual / Cars pass in cold blood / Casual sex / Victim convenience / Sealed human / In concert / The passives.

May 00. (12"ep) <LBJ 33> **BLANK-WAVE ARCADE** (remixes by other artists)	-	

— added **DAPOSE** (b. MIKE DAPPEN) – guitar (ex-LEAD)

Aug 01. (cd/lp) <LBJ 37> **DANSE MACABRE**	-	

– Agenda suicide / Glass danse / Total job / Let the poison spill from your throat / Your retro career melted / Posed to death / The conductor / Violent / Ballad of a paralysed citizen.

	Gold Standard	not iss.
Oct 01. (cd-s) (GSL 47CD) **MOTE/DUST** (12"iss.May02; GSL 47)		-

	Fierce Panda	not iss.
Feb 02. (cd-s) (NING 117CD) **AGENDA SUICIDE / WORKED UP SO SEXUAL / SEX IS PERSONAL** (remix)		-

BROKEN SPINDLES

JOEL PETERSON – multi / plus **MIKE MOGIS** – guitar

	Tiger Style	Tiger Style
Sep 02. (cd/lp) <(TS 030 CD/LP)> **BROKEN SPINDLES**		

– Videosection / Downtown venues / A dinner party ambience / The love of foreign film / Matte / Empty bottle / The oldest accident / Connection in progress / The illness / Gamey / Twitching and restless.

FAIRWAYS

Formed: San Francisco, California, USA . . . late 90s by ex-SKYPARK members singer/guitarist BRENT KENJI, guitarist ANDREW LEAVITT and JEN COHEN; who were later joined by KEIKO KAYAMOTO and ZAC STANLEY. After building up a strong fanbase by playing live, The FAIRWAYS released their debut album 'IS EVERYTHING ALRIGHT' (2000). This eclectic musical tapestry, woven from smiley guitars, organs, horns and tambourines, won many admirers for its effortless brand of uplifting upbeat indie pop. Listening to the 10 songs comprising the running time, you couldn't help but be left with a sharksharp grin carved across your features by the end, with critics comparing The FAIRWAYS with the light, wistful, dreamy sonics of BELLE & SEBASTIAN and HOLIDAY (AMY LINTON of AISLERS SET and JAMIE McCORMICK (ex-CIAO BELLA) helped out with musical chores). The band released a split EP with the aforementioned AISLERS SET later on in 2000, as well as the split EP 'PERMANENT VACATION' with Japanese combo THREE BERRY ICE CREAM. STANLEY left the band in 2002 and was replaced by drummer, DEANNA.

Album rating: IS EVERYTHING ALL RIGHT? (*6)

SKYPARK

BRENT KENJI – vocals, guitar / **JEN COHEN** – keyboards / **ANDREW LEAVITT** – guitar (ex-NEW BAD THINGS)

	not iss.	Shelflife
Sep 98. (m-cd) <LIFE 6> **SUMMER DAYS ARE FOREVER**	-	

– Bicycle boy / Secret hideaway / Summer days are forever / Morse code / She is me / Countryside.

FAIRWAYS

KENJI, COHEN + LEAVITT recruited **KEIKO KAYAMOTO + ZAC STANLEY**

	not iss.	Matinee
May 00. (7"m) <Matinee 9> **DARLING, DON'T YOU THINK? / NOWHERE TO GO / THIS IS FAREWELL**	-	

	not iss.	Dogpaint Japan
May 00. (cd-ep) **PERMANENT VACATION EP**	-	

– Fine day / Winter song / (others by THREE BERRY ICE CREAM).

	not iss.	Paris Caramel
Jun 00. (cd) <007> **IS EVERYTHING ALL RIGHT?**	-	

– A song for Jenni / Secretive girl / Close to me / Quarter to seven / Postcard picture / KLM line / Get it right / Darling, don't you think? / Phthalo blue / Let's go.

— **DEANNA** – drums; repl. ZAC

	not iss.	Yakamashi
Nov 00. (7") <TIB 4> **THE RAIN FELL DOWN. /** (other by AISLERS SET)	-	

— COHEN joined The AISLERS SET in 2000

Th' FAITH HEALERS

Formed: Camden, London, England . . . late 80's by ROXANNE STEPHEN and TOM CULLINAN, who expanded the line-up with BEN HOPKIN and JOE DILWORTH (the latter also drummer with STEREOLAB). Along with STEREOLAB and PJ HARVEY, Th' FAITH HEALERS were one of the first bands on the roster of the (then) new indie label, 'Too Pure' (run by Richard Roberts and Paul Cox), for whom they released their debut EP, 'POP SONG', in 1990. Several further EP's hit the shops during the next couple of years, a debut album proper (not counting compilation, 'L') was finally released under the title of 'LIDO' in 1992. Well received by the music press for its repetitive, experimental lurch'n'roll (drifting between STEREOLAB and HAWKWIND!), the record saw th' HEALERS fashioning their own unique hybrid of post-modern nostalgic rock. Yet the group would only complete one further set, 'IMAGINARY FRIEND' (1993), bowing out the following year with a shared single, 'S.O.S.' flipped with MAMBO TAXI. Main songwriter, CULLINAN, subsequently re-surfaced with a new band, QUICKSPACE SUPERSPORT, although the line-up went through an initial period of instability before stabilising around SEAN NEWSHAM, WENDY HARPER, MAX CORRADI and BARRY STILLWELL after the release of a debut single in early '95. Although CULLINAN initiated his own 'Kitty Kitty Corporation' imprint, the band also recorded for 'Love Train' and 'Domino', the nouveau Kraut-rockers quickly dropping the sporty side of their moniker with the release of an eponymous set in '96. Over the course of the next two years (and now with a new line-up of CULLINAN, NEWSHAM, NINA PASCALE, PAUL SHILTON and CHIN), two further albums hit the shops, the singles compilation 'SUPO SPOT' (1997) and the experimental 'PRECIOUS FALLING' (1998). Now on 'Matador' records, the group delivered their most accessible release to date, 'THE DEATH OF QUICKSPACE' (2000) – a prophetic title as it turned out. Effortlessly hypnotic, yet at times easy and sweet, it had loads of highlights, none more so than the epic 'CLIMBING A HILL'. TOM CULLINAN subsequently resurfaced as the mysterious DOUGAL REED, re-recording and releasing the complete (Fleetwood Mac) – 'RUMOURS' album to a bewildered but entertained audience. • **Covered:** MOTHER SKY (Can) / etc. • **Trivia:** ROXANNE guested on MOOSE's 'XYZ' album in 1992.

Album rating: 'L' compilation (*6) / LIDO (*7) / IMAGINARY FRIEND (*5) / Quickspace: QUICKSPACE (*6) / SUPO SPOT compilation (*6) / PRECIOUS FALLING (*6) / THE DEATH OF QUICKSPACE (*6) / Dougal Reed: RUMOURS (*6)

ROXANNE STEPHEN – vocals / **TOM CULLINAN** – guitar / **BEN HOPKIN** – bass / **JOE DILWORTH** – drums (also of STEREOLAB)

	Too Pure	Elektra
Jul 90. (12"ep) (PURE 2) **POP SONG. / DELORES / SLAG**		-
Feb 91. (12"ep) (PURE 3) **A PICTURE OF HEALTH**		-

– Gorgeous blue flower in my garden / Not a God / God.

Jan 92. (12"ep) (PURE 6) **IN LOVE**		-

– Reptile smile / Super / Lovely.

Jun 92. (lp/cd) (PURE/+CD 12) <61425> **LIDO**		

– This time / Word of advicer / Hippy hole / Don't Jones me / Love song / Mother sky / It's easy being you / Spin half.

Oct 92. (12"ep/cd-ep) (PURE/+CD 15) **MR. LITANSKI**		-

– Oh baby / Moona-Inna-Joona / My loser / Reptile smile.

Feb 93. (cd-ep) (PURECD 18) <66327> **DON'T JONES ME / GORGEOUS BLUE FLOWER / OH BABY / MY LOSER**		
Oct 93. (lp/cd) (PURE/+CD 27) <61585> **IMAGINARY FRIEND**		Jan94

– Sparkingly chime / Heart fog / See-saw / Kevin / The people / Curly lips / Everything, all at once forever / Run out groove.

	Clawfist	not iss.
Mar 94. (7") (XPIG 23) **S.O.S. /** ('B'side by Mambo Taxi)		-

— split soon after above

– compilations, etc. –

Apr 92. (cd) Too Pure; (31023) / Warners; <43019> **'L'** (singles compilation)		Jul95

QUICKSPACE SUPERSPORT

— **TOM CULLINAN** – vocals, guitar / **SEAN NEWSHAM** – bass / **WENDY HARPER** – vocals, guitar / **BARRY STILLWELL** – keyboards / **MAX CORRADI** – drums

	Kitty Kitty Corporation	not iss.
Feb 95. (7") (CHOOSY 001) **QUICKSPACE HAPPY SONG (NO.1). / UNIQUE SLIPPY**		-

	Love Train	not iss.
Aug 95. (7") (PUBE 04) **FOUND A WAY. / DO IT MY OWN WAY**		-

	Domino	not iss.
Oct 95. (12"ep/cd-ep) (RUG 40 T/CD) **SUPERPLUS EP**		-

– Proplus / Scubaplus / Standard 8.

	Kitty Kitty Corporation	not iss.
Apr 96. (7") (CHOOSY 004) **FRIEND. / WHERE HAVE ALL THE GOOD TIMES GONE**		-

— **NINA PASCALE** – vocals, guitar; repl. WENDY

Jun 96. (cd-ep) (CHOOSY 005) **RISE EP**		-

– Rise / Docile / Riseteen sixtynine.

— after the shuffle, MAX CORRADI joined indie supergroup, SNOWPONY

Th' FAITH HEALERS (cont) THE GREAT INDIE DISCOGRAPHY   The 1990s

QUICKSPACE

— **CULLINAN + NEWSHAM + PASCALE** recruited **PAUL SHILTON** – keyboards / **CHIN** – drums

Kitty Kitty Corporation / Slash

Nov 96. (lp/cd) (CHOOSY 006/+CD) <422-828-924> **QUICKSPACE** — Nov97
 – Swisher / Song for someone / Quasi-pfaff / Mousetail * / Winona / Docile one / Docile two. <US repl.* with> – Rise / Friend.
Jun 97. (lp/cd) (CHOOSY 008/+CD) **SUPO SPOT** (compilation of early singles) – -
 – Happy song No.1 / Unique slippy / Extra plus / Found a way / Do it my own way / Whiff and spoof song / Exemplary swishy / Friend / Where have all the good times gone / Song for NME.
1997. (7") (E 182) **AMIGO. / RISE** – -
 (above issued on 'Elefant')
Nov 97. (12"ep/cd-ep) (CHOOSY 010/+CD) **THE PRECIOUS MOUNTAIN EP** – -
 – Precious mountain / You used my death as a pretext to go running / Ennio's blues.
May 98. (7") (CHOOSY 011) **HADID. / QUEEN OF THE DOWNS** – -
Jul 98. (7"ep/cd-ep) (CHOOSY 014/+CD) **PRECIOUS LITTLE EP** – -
 – Quickspace happy song (No.2) / Ming / Hadid / Queen of the downs.
Aug 98. (cd) (CHOOSY 013CD) **PRECIOUS FALLING** – -
 – Death + Annie / Take away / Mouse / 7 like that / Quickspace happy song #2 / Hadid / Melo / Minors / Cola Lola / Obvious / Walk me home / Mountain waltz / Goodbye precious mountain.

Kitty Kitty / Matador

Apr 00. (lp/cd) (CHOOSY 020/+CD) <OLE 433> **THE DEATH OF QUICKSPACE** — Mar00
 – The lobbalong song / They shoot horses don't they / Climbing a hill / Munchers no munchers / Gloriana / The munchers / A rose / Lob it / 4.

DOUGAL REED

aka **TOM CULLINAN** – vocals, instruments

Kitty Kitty / not iss.

Aug 01. (lp/cd) (CHOOSY 024/+CD) **RUMOURS** – -
 – Second hand news / Dreams / Never going back again / Don't stop / Go your own way / Songbird / The chain / You make loving fun / I don't want to know / Oh daddy / Gold dust woman.

FAITH OVER REASON

Formed: Croydon, Surrey, England ... early 1990 by MOIRA LAMBERT, who recruited BILL LLOYD, SIMON ROOTS and MARK WILSHER. Signed to 'Big Cat', the band released their eponymous debut EP in summer 1990, showcasing LAMBERT's emotive vocals (which graced the original 1990 version of ST. ETIENNE's 'Only Love Can Break Your Heart') and even attempting a version of Nick Drake's sublime 'NORTHERN SKY'. A second EP, 'BILLY BLUE', and an album of demos, 'EYES WIDE SMILE' (1991) followed before the band was put on ice as LAMBERT began a college course. With the addition of TEBO STEELE (as a replacement for ROOTS), a revamped FAITH OVER REASON re-emerged in summer '94 with a belated third EP, 'BLIND'. STEELE had already began to carve himself out a role as chief songwriter and the guitarist ended up penning most of the material on debut album, 'EASY' (1994). Produced by STEPHEN MALKMUS (mainman with labelmates, PAVEMENT), the album was met with mixed reviews as many critics bemoaned the fact that STEELE's guitar was often pushed way too far up in the mix, negating the vocal atmospherics provided by LAMBERT. Despite subsequent high profile support gigs with the likes of PAVEMENT and JEFF BUCKLEY, the musical differences eventually led to a split in the ranks, STEELE, LLOYD and WILSHER forming SOUP while LAMBERT carried on under the FAITH OVER REASON banner; although she later employed the services of former SUNDAYS sticksman, PATRICK HANNAN (aka PATCH), although no new material was forthcoming until 1998. The pair became OVA and recruited JOHN IACIAFANO (ex-DRUGSTORE) and FLOYD JENSEN for a debut single, 'UNIVERSAL AUDIO'. The following year, an album for 'Global Warming' was shelved and MOIRA broke up the group.

Album rating: EYES WIDE SMILE (*5) / EASY (*5)

MOIRA LAMBERT (b.13 Oct'70, Chichester, England) – vocals, acoustic guitar (ex-ST.ETIENNE) / **SIMON ROOTS** (b. 1 Sep'70) – guitar / **BILL LLOYD** (b.17 Mar'71, London) – bass, keyboards / **MARK WILSHER** (b. 1 May'70) – drums

Big Cat / not iss.

Jul 90. (12"ep) (ABB 17T) **FAITH OVER REASON EP** – -
 – Believing in me / Northern sky / Fallen / Evangeline.
Aug 91. (12"ep/cd-ep) (ABB 23 T/SCD) **BILLY BLUE EP** – -
 – Billy Blue / Move closer / High in the sun / Ice queen.
Sep 91. (lp/cd) (ABB/+CD 27X) **EYES WIDE SMILE** (demos) – -
 – Lullabye (mother love) / Sofya / So free / Northern sky / Song for Jessica / Evangeline / Not so / Eyes wide smile / Fallen.
— (late '91) **TEBO STEELE** – guitar; repl. ROOTS
Jul 94. (12"ep/cd-ep) (ABB 58 T/SCD) **BLIND EP** – -
 – Blind / Easy on me / Love is blind / Come.
Aug 94. (lp/cd) (ABB 63/+CD) **EASY** – -
 – Blind / Unsure / Too soon / Love is blind / Alone again / I've been told / Let the sun in / Work hard / Half asleep / So slow / My own child / Some things.
— LAMBERT was left holding the group name and although she recruited PATCH from The SUNDAYS, the outfit subsequently vanished after releasing nothing; the rest formed SOUP, who did likewise

OVA

MOIRA LAMBERT – vocals acoustic guitar / **PATRICK 'PATCH' HANNAN** – drums (ex-SUNDAYS) / **JOHN IACIAFANO** – guitar (ex-DRUGSTORE) / **FLOYD JENSEN** – double bass

Big Cat / not iss.

1998. (7") (ABB 143) **UNIVERSAL AUDIO. / TREAT ME LIKE A WOMAN** – w-drawn

Global Warming / not iss.

Aug 98. (cd-s) (WARMCD 1) **UNIVERSAL AUDIO / TREAT ME LIKE A WOMAN / LITTLE SECRETS** – -
— **ALAN GIBSON** – double bass; repl. FLOYD
— **NICK RYE** – drums; repl. PATRICK
— an album for 'Global Warming' was shelved and they split late '99

FAMILY CAT

Formed: Yeovil, Somerset, England ... 1988 by PAUL FREDERICK, STEPHEN JELBERT, TIM McVEY, JOHN GRAVES and KEVIN DOWNING. Despite the rather naff moniker, The FAMILY CAT became early 90's critical favourites if never quite managing to convince record buyers. Signed to indie label, 'Bad Girl', in 1989, the group scored an NME Single Of The Week with their debut single, 'TOM VERLAINE' – a thrilling tribute to the much revered TELEVISION guitar guru – but a rush-released mini-set, 'TELL 'EM WE'RE SURFIN'' (1989) failed to translate the power of their live work and the band were left facing the frustration which would dog them throughout their career. Following a further two singles, 'REMEMBER WHAT IT IS THAT YOU LOVE' and 'A PLACE WITH A NAME' (they had recently moved to London), the band moved on to 'Dedicated', finally proving what they were made of with a show stopping display of six string manipulation at the 1991 Reading Festival. The subsequent single, 'COLOUR ME GREY' featured none other than a young PJ HARVEY on backing vocals and consolidated their return to form, setting the scene for an impressive second album, 'FURTHEST FROM THE SUN' (1992). Yet despite gushing praise for the sterling, star spangled guitar melodies on offer, indie fans voted with their feet and once again, The FAMILY CAT were left in the commercial doghouse. The advent of grunge and the resulting focus on all things American only served to further marginalise the band and when a similarly obscure fate befell another fine, if more resigned third effort, 'MAGIC HAPPENS' (1994), these West Country stalwarts eventually returned to their proverbial baskets.
• **Covered:** BUS STOP (Hollies) / I MUST HAVE BEEN BLIND (Tim Buckley) / LEAN ON ME (I WON'T FALL OVER) (Carter The Unstoppable Sex Machine).

Album rating: TELL 'EM WE'RE SURFIN' mini (*6) / FURTHEST FROM THE SUN (*7) / MAGIC HAPPENS (*8)

PAUL FREDERICK – vocals, guitar / **STEPHEN JELBERT** – lead guitar / **TIM McVAY** – rhythm guitar / **JOHN GRAVES** – bass / **KEVIN DOWNING** – drums

Bad Girl / not iss.

Jul 89. (7"flexi) (BGRIFC 01) **TOM VERLAINE (demo version)** – -
 (12"ep+=) (BGRLT 01) – Gabriel's wings / Octopus.
Sep 89. (m-lp) (BGRMLP 001) **TELL 'EM WE'RE SURFIN'** – -
 – Albert Hoffman's bike / Final mistake / Sandbag your heart / Slept in clothes / From the city to the sea / Taken by surprise / Endless cigarette / Gabriel's wings. (cd-iss. Mar90; BGRLCD 001)
May 90. (7") (BGRL 003S) **REMEMBER WHAT IT IS THAT YOU LOVE. / PUSH COMES TO SHOVE** – -
 (12"+=/cd-s+=) (BGRL 003 T/SCD) – ('A' extended).
Aug 90. (12"ep/cd-ep) **A PLACE WITH NO NAME. / CONCRETE / PASSAWAY / THEME FROM THE FAMILY CAT** – -
Sep 91. (12"ep/cd-ep) (BGRL 009 T/SCD) **COLOUR ME GREY. / I MUST HAVE BEEN BLIND / GREAT UGLY PLACE** – -
 (above featured POLLY JEAN HARVEY on vocals)
 (below deleted in one day and issued on 'Clawfist')
Dec 91. (7"ep/12"ep/cd-ep) **JESUS CHRIST. / CHILL OUT YE MERRY GENTLEMEN / CHRIST JESUS / JESUS KARAOKE CHRIST (instrumental)** – -

Dedicated / Dedicated

May 92. (7") (FCUK 001) **STREAMROLLER (pt.1). / STEAMROLLER (pt.2)** – -
 (12"+=/cd-s+=) (FCUK 001 T/CD) – What we talk about when we talk about love / Across the universe.
Jun 92. (cd/c/lp) (DED CD/MC/LP 007) <66041> **FURTHEST FROM THE SUN** 55 Jan93
 – Too many late nights / Colour me grey / Prog one / Furthest from the sun / Steamroller / Keep it to yourself / With a war / River of diamonds / Gameshow / Fire music. (with free ltd-7"/cd+=) – Kolombus / Montague Terrace (in blue).
Sep 92. (12"ep/cd-ep) (FCUK 002 T/CD) **RIVER OF DIAMONDS (re-navigated). / SANDBAG YOUR HEART (re-bagged) / TOM VERLAINE (re-bereted)** – -
 (12"with free ltd-7") – Tom Verlaine.
Aug 93. (7"purple) (FCUK 003) **AIRPLANE GARDENS. / ATMOSPHERIC ROAD** 69 -
 (12"+=/cd-s+=) (FCUK 003 T/CD) – Amazing hangover.
Oct 93. (7") (FCUK 004) **SPRINGING THE ATOM. / PROG 4** – -
 (12"+=/cd-s+=) (FCUK 004 T/CD) – Happy to be here.

Dedicated-RCA / R.C.A.

May 94. (7"clear/c-s) (74321 20843-7/-4) **WONDERFUL EXCUSE. / UNWIELDY WORLD** 48 -
 (cd-s+=) (74321 20843-2) – Sign of the blood cell / Propeller blades.
 (12") (74321 20843-1) – ('A' side) / Counting crosses (acoustic) / Gameshow (acoustic) / ('A'-acoustic).

FAMILY CAT (cont)   THE GREAT INDIE DISCOGRAPHY   The 1990s

May 94. (cd/c/lp) (<74321 20466-2/-4/-1>) **MAGIC HAPPENS** Feb95
- Wonderful excuse / Amazing hangover / Move over I'll drive / Your secrets will stay mine / Airplane gardens / Gone, so long / Hamlet for now / Goldenbook / Rockbreaking / Springing the atom / Blood orange / Nowhere to go but down.

Jul 94. (7"green-ep/c-ep) (74321 22007-7/-4) **GOLDENBOOK EP** 42 –
- Goldenbook / Bring me the head of Michael Portillo / Springing the atom (acoustic) / River of diamonds (acoustic).
(7"gold-ep) (74321 22007-0) – (1st track) / Goldenboot / Old faithful.
(cd-s) (74321 22007-2) – (1st track) / Blood orange (acoustic) / Gone to Heaven.

— split towards the end of '94

Geoff FARINA (see under ⇒ KARATE)

Jay FARRAR (see under ⇒ UNCLE TUPELO)

FAT TULIPS

Formed: Peterborough, England ... 1987 by guitarist/songwriter MARK D and singer SARAH C. With the release of debut flexi-disc 'YOU OPENED UP MY EYES', came the departure of SARAH C, and MARK D's relocation to Nottingham. Hooking up with drummer MATT JOHNSON, singer KATIE KEEN, bassist PAULIE and Scots-born guitarist KATY 'SHEGGI' CLARKSON, the 'TULIPS recorded debut single 'WHERE'S CLARE GROGAN NOW?' in 1989, although KEEN soon left, which led to CLARKSON assuming vocals. Now a settled quartet, they released the 'FOUR SONGS FOR SIMON' EP in late 1989, and followed that with 'FERENSWAY' in 1990, both on the 'Heaven ' label (run by MATT). The FAT TULIPS' melodic indie-pop – comparable with the likes of HEAVENLY and CONFETTI – had garnered them a small, dedicated following, and was performed at regular gigs around the UK. After more EPs, a tour of Germany, and the long-awaited release of debut album 'STARFISH', the TULIPS' finally split in 1994, feeling they were "getting a bit old for this sort of thing". Together with friend VANESSA, CLARKSON went on to form the MELONS. Producing three singles – including the tuneful 'FROM HELL TO HELSINKI' in 1995 – the MELONS' sound was a little less frantic, and more refined, than the TULIPS'. The FAT TULIPS' track 'SO UNBELIEVABLE!' was actually used as a backing track on the Nickelodeon TV series 'The Adventures of Pete & Pete'. • **Covered:** TO CUT A LONG STORY SHORT (Spandau Ballet) / IS THAT LOVE (Squeeze) / + Confetti ANYONE CAN MAKE A MISTAKE (Wedding Present) / IT'S KINDA FUNNY (Josef K).

Album rating: STARFISH (*6)

SARAH C. – vocals / **MARK D.** (b. MARK RANDALL) – guitar

Sweet William / not iss.

1987. (7"flexi) **YOU OPENED UP MY EYES**

— **KATIE KEEN** – vocals; repl. SARAH

— added **SHEGGI CLARKSON** (b. KATY, Glasgow, Scotland) – guitar, vocals / **MATT JOHNSON** – drums/ **PAULIE H** – bass

Heaven / not iss.

1989. (7"m) (HV 01) **WHERE'S CLARE GROGAN NOW? / SO SURREAL / TO PUT IT BLINDLY**

— when KATIE left SHEGGI took over vocals

1990. (7"ep) (HV 02) **FOUR SONGS FOR SIMON EP**
May 91. (7"ep) (HV 04) **FERENSWAY EP**

Spindly Killer Fish / not iss.

1990. (7"flexi) (FLX) **AMELIA**
1990. (7"split) **A GIRL CALLED SUICIDE. / (other by Spinning Jennies)**

Windmill / not iss.

1991. (7"flexi) (WINDMILL 001) **ANGELS AMONGST US (with other artists: Applicants / Haywains / Paintbox)**

Marineville / not iss.

Dec 91. (7"ep) (MARINE 1) **THE TULIP EXPLODES EP**
- Treason / Reward / Passionate friend.

Sunday / not iss.

Dec 91. (7"m) (SUNDAY 001) **TAKE ME BACK TO HEAVEN. / ON THE SEVENTH DAY / REACH FOR THE SKY**
Jan 92. (7"flexi-ep) (SUNDAY 010) **SUNDAY HEAVEN FLEXI**
- What do you do? / To cut a long story short / CONFETTI: Bridge 61 / Diet.
May 92. (7"ep) (SUNDAY 011) **EARLY YEARS EP**
- Rainbow sky / You opened up my eyes / On Virgin Isles.

Vinyl Japan / not iss.

Sep 92. (12"ep/cd-ep) (TASK 08/+CD) **NOSTALGIA EP**
- Nostalgia / Deadhead baby / Last to know / Into space / Copper.
Jul 94. (cd/lp) (ASK CD/LP 034) **STARFISH**
- So unbelievable / A world away from me / Ribs / The sweetest child / Chainsaw / I promise you / My secret place / Double decker bus / Clumsy / If God exists / Big toe / Nothing less than you deserve / Letting go / The death of me / Never.
1993. (7"m) (SUNDAY 014) **ALBIE. / DANCE TO THE SUN / IS THAT LOVE**
(above on 'Sunday' records)
Aug 94. (7"m) (PAD 011) **DRIVING ME WILD. / LIKE CHRISTMAS / SURELY**
Aug 94. (7") (PAD 012) **NEW SPRING RITES FOR SARAH. / CONFESSIONS OF AN ENGLISH GIRL**
(above 2 singles re-iss. Sep94 on cd-ep; TASK 023)

— split later in '94; SHEGGI had already formed The MELONS

CONFETTI

MARK D plus **JULIE**

Heaven / not iss.

Dec 91. (7"ep) (HV 06) **HABERDASHER EP**

Sunday / not iss.

May 92. (7"ep) (SUNDAY 012) **SEA ANEMON EP**

Marineville / –

1992. (7"ep) (MARINE 4) **PRESENTI EP**

Vinyl Japan / not iss.

Sep 94. (cd) (ASKCD 039) **RETROSPECTIVEL EP**
- Who's big and clever now / It's kinda funny / Yes please / Tomorrow who knows / Warm / Jenny / Bridge 61 / Diet (remix) / Whatever became of Alice and Jane / Here again / River Island / Nothing II / Corduroy / Anyone can make a mistake / Once more.

SLUMBER

unknown with aq FAT TULIPS member

Sunday / not iss.

1993. (7"ep) (SUNDAY 020) **HOLY & IV EP**
- The thirteenth day of Christmas / I'll never know.

Vinyl Japan / not iss.

Nov 93. (12"ep/cd-ep) (TASK/+CD 021) **SLEEP EP**
- Sleepy avenue / What did you do / Remember me / Wasteland.

Wishing Chair / not iss.

1990's. (7") (WC 001) **TOO MUCH THE SAME. / VIOLET**

MELONS

SHEGGI – guitar / **VANESSA** – vocals / + 2

Heaven / not iss.

Apr 94. (7"flexi) (HV 07) **SHOW ME WISHES WORTH THAN THESE**

Damaged Goods / not iss.

Sep 95. (7"m) (DAMGOOD 79) **FROM HELL TO HELSINKI. / SEE IF I DON'T / THAT SUNSHINE**
Mar 96. (7"m) (DAMGOOD 91) **FAST LANE. / LITTLE DEATH WISHES / LOSING IT**

Picked Egg / not iss.

1997. (7") (EGG 1) **BLACK AND BLUE. / ESKIMO**

— SHEGGI moved to New York

FAUST

Formed: Hamburg, Germany ... 1970 by producer UWE NETTELBECK, who was given money to assemble a collective of musicians in his Wumme studios. These numbered RUDOLF SOSNA, HANS-JOACHIM IRMLER, JEAN-HERVE PERON, GUNTER WUSTHOFF and ARNULF MEIFERT; the latter being replaced by WERNER DIERMEYER in 1971. Following in the footsteps of CAN, TANGERINE DREAM and AMON DUUL II, they became an integral part of the burgeoning underground "krautrock" scene. Early recordings for 'Polydor', although strikingly innovative, failed to gain any widespread commercial appeal outside Germany. However, 'THE FAUST TAPES' (a 'Virgin' sampler of unreleased tunes) introduced them to the UK and sold a respectable quantity due to its 49p price-tag. This unfortunately disqualified it from chart returns. Inspired by a myriad of influences that took in everything from KARL-HEINZ STOCKHAUSEN to The BEATLES to The MOTHERS OF INVENTION, they left conventional song structures at the starting gate. Instead they opted for a continuous collage of musical set pieces which nevertheless had the potential to be great 3-minute songs. Alternately delighting and disgusting audiences, they were prone to playing pinball machines and wielding pneumatic drills on stage. They toured this bizarre spectacle around Europe after Richard Branson's 'Virgin' issued 'FAUST IV' while in 1974, they recorded an album with American minimalist TONY CONRAD (he had earlier been in The DREAM SYNDICATE; part of JOHN CALE's pre-VELVET days). Eventually FAUST faded away into obscurity but were re-called for a one-off gig at London's Marquee on the 25th of October '92. Their comeback albums, 'RIEN' and 'YOU KNOW FAUST', were issued between 1996-1997 and they were lined up for another rare live appearance at the Edinburgh Festival. • **Trivia:** UWE also produced for SLAPP HAPPY. Were and still are one of JULIAN COPE's (ex-TEARDROP EXPLODES) fave bands.

Album rating: FAUST (*7) / FAUST SO FAR (*8) / THE FAUST TAPES (*5 at the time – *8 now!?) / FAUST IV (*5) / MUNICH & ELSEWHERE collection (*5) / 71 MINUTES OF FAUST compilation (*7) / RIEN (*4) / YOU KNOW FAUST (*6) / LIVE IN EDINBURGH – AUGUST 1997 (*6) / FAUST WAKES NOSFERATU (*5) / RAVVIVANDO (*7)

RUDOLF SOSNA – guitar, keyboards / **HANS-JOACHIM IRMLER** – organ / **WERNER DIERMEIER** – drums; repl. ARNULF MEIFERT who contributed to recordings in 1971 / **JEAN-HERVE PERON** – bass / **GUNTER WUSTHOFF** – saxophone, synthesizer

Polydor / not iss.

Jan 72. (clear-lp) (2310 142) **FAUST**
- Why don't you eat carrots / Meadow meal / Miss Fortune. (re-iss. Oct79 as 'FAUST ONE' on 'Recommended'; RRA 1) (cd-iss. Nov96 on 'Klangbad'; KLANG 01) (cd re-iss. Jul01 on 'ReR'; RERF 6)
Jul 72. (lp) (2310 196) **FAUST SO FAR**
- It's a rainy day, sunshine girl / On the way to Abamae / No harm / So far / Mamie is blue / I've got my car and my T.V. / Picnic on a frozen river / Me back space . . . / . . . In the spirit. (re-iss. Oct79 on 'Recommended'; R.R.TWO) (cd-iss. Jul01 on 'ReR'; RERF 7)
Aug 72. (7") (2001 299) **IT'S A BIT OF A PAIN. / SO FAR**
(re-iss. 1979 on 'Recommended'; RR 2)

	Caroline	not iss.
1972. (lp; by TONY CONRAD & FAUST) (C 1501) **OUTSIDE THE DREAM SYNDICATE**	□	-

– From the side of man and womankind / From the side of woman and mankind. (cd-iss. Feb94 on 'Southern'; LITHIUM 2) <(cd re-iss. Apr98 on 'Table Of Elements'; LITHIUM 6)>

	Virgin	not iss.
1973. (lp) (V 2004) **FAUST IV**	□	-

– Krautrock / The sad skinhead / Jennifer / Just a second (starts like that!) / Picnic on a frozen river, deuxieme tableux / Giggy smile / Lauft . . . heisst das es lauft oder es kommt bald . . . lauft / It's a bit of a pain. (cd-iss. Oct92 & Jul97; CDV 2004) <US cd-iss. Oct92 on 'Caroline'; CAROL 1885-2>

1973. (lp) (VC 501) **THE FAUST TAPES** (rec. 1971-73; tracks were originally untitled)

– Flash-back Caruso / J'ai mal aux dents (I have a toothache) / Humphrey Bogart / Doctor Schwitters / 7/5/4 / Los Hideros / Finnish Autumn / Stretch out / Der baum (the tree) / Ma chambre (my room). (re-iss. 1980 on 'Recommended'; RRA 6) (cd-iss. Apr91 as 'THE LAST ALBUM'; RERF 2CD) (cd re-iss. Feb94 & Jun96 & Dec01 on 'ReR'; RERF 2CD)

— added **PETER BLEGVAD** – guitar, clarinet, vocals

— disbanded in 1973 and PETER BLEGVAD went solo. However, they (**IRMLER, DEIRMEIER + PERON**) did re-form in 1990 for a Prinzenbar, Hamburg concert and London Marquee gig on 25th October '92

	Recommended	Recommended
Jan 97. (cd) (<RERF 3CD>) **YOU KNOW FAUST**	□	Feb97

– Hurricane / Tenne laufen / C pluus / Pause / Irons / Cendre / Sixty sixty / Winds / Liebeswehen / Elektron 2 / Ella / Pause / Men from the Moon / Der pfad / Noizes from Pythagoras / Na sowas / L'oiseau / Huttenfreak / Teutonentango. (lp-iss.Feb98 on 'Klangbad'; KLANGBAD 1) (re-iss. Oct98 on 'Recommended'; F 4CD)

— the trio added **KEIJI HAINO + MICHAEL MORLEY + STEVEN WRAY LOBDELL** – guitars / **JIM O'ROURKE** – tapes

	Table Of Elements	Table Of Elements
Jun 97. (cd) (<CHROMIUM 24>) **RIEN** (rec. 1995)	□	1996

– Rien / untitled / Long distance calls in the desert / Eroberung der stille, teil II / untitled / Eroberung der stille, teil I / Fin.

— Table Of The Elements also split a 45 with SLAPP HAPPY, 'SORT OF'

— DIERMEIER, IRMLER + LOBDELL recruited **MICHAEL STOLL** – bass / **LARS PAUKSTAT** – percussion

	Klangbad	EFA
Nov 97. (cd) (FAUSTLIVECD 1) <KLANGF 2> **LIVE IN EDINBURGH - AUGUST 1997 (live)**	□	□

– (untitled tracks). (re-iss. Dec97 on 'Think Progressive'; EFA 03560-2) (re-iss. Mar99; C 8326)

Mar 98. (cd)(lp) (C 8173)(FL 15) <3558> **FAUST WAKES NOSFERATU**

– Ausbruch nach Rumanien / Verwirrung / Telepathia / Kampf der machte / Das unheil breitet sich aus / Die entscheidung.

— added **ULRIKE HELMHOLZ**

Apr 99. (cd) (EFA 36000-2) **RAVVIVANDO**

– Ein neuer tag / Carousel II / Wir brauchen dich #6 / Four plus seven means eleven / Take care / Spiel / Dr' hansl / Apokalypse / D.I.G. / Du weist schon / Livin' Tokyo / T-electronique.

Nov 01. (cd-s) (efa 06283-2) **WIR BRAUCHEN DICH 6 (Dave Ball & Ingo Vauk remixes)**

Mar 02. (cd/lp) (efa 06289-2/-1) **FREISPIEL** (remixes)

– compilations, others, etc. –

on 'Recommended' unless mentioned otherwise

Mar 80. (7"ep) (RRI 15) **EXTRACTS FROM FAUST PARTY 3**
1980. (lp; with SLAPP HAPPY) (RR 5) **CASABLANCA MOON** (or ACNALBASAC NOOM)
Sep 86. (lp) (RR 25) **MUNICH AND ELSEWHERE (live)**
Nov 92. (cd) (RERF 1CD) **71 MINUTES OF FAUST** (out-takes 1971-1975)

– Munic A / Baby / Meer / Munic B / Don't take roots / Faust party 3 / Party 2 / Party 8 / Spalter / Party 5 / Party 1 / Party 3 / Party 6 / Party 4. (re-iss. Feb94 & Jun96 & Dec01; same)

Oct 96. (cd) (RERHCD 2) **KIRK**
Jun 97. (cd) (RER 25) **RETURN OF A LEGEND**
Dec 97. (cd) Table of Elements; (CHROMIUM 26) **FAUST CONCERTS VOL.1 (live at Prinzenbar, Hamburg 1990)**

– As tu ton ticket? / Legendare gleichgultigkeit / The sad head / Haarscharf / Schempal buddha / 13/8 / Rainy day / Volitaire / Rien.

Dec 97. (cd) Table Of Elements; (CHROMIUM 27) **FAUST CONCERTS VOL.2 (live at the Marquee, London 1992)**

– Opening of the Marquee / Abamae / Das (s)tier part 1: as tu ton tickets? / Das (s)tier part 2: (Du rouge du bleu / Dying pigs / Viel obst / Stadtluft / Axel goes straight / Pentatonische kinderlied / Promotion / Ex..cess.

Jun 98. (lp) (RERFV 3) **THE BBC SESSIONS** (cd-iss. Jul01; RERF 5)

Nov 00. (5xcd-box) ReR; (RERFB 1) **THE WUMME YEARS**

FIELD MICE

Formed: Mitcham, South London, England . . . 1987 by ROB WRATTEN and MARK DOBSON, who recruited HARVEY WILLIAMS (of ANOTHER SUNNY DAY) after relocating to Bristol and signing with the local 'Sarah' label. The FIELD MICE fast gained a reputation for being the ultimate in "indie tweeness" with their label and nearly every band subsequently signed to it derided by the music press in the same sneering manner. Nevertheless, the indie establishment disdain was matched by an equally intense adoration from their sizeable fan base who snapped up a string of pastoral, largely acoustic singles and EP's including 'SENSITIVE', 'IF YOU NEED SOMEONE' and 'I CAN SEE MYSELF ALONE FOREVER'. The turn of the decade saw the group fleshing out their sound with the addition of ANNEMARI DAVIES (ROB's girlfriend at the time) and MICHAEL HISCOCK, the more sonically adventurous 'SKYWRITING' (1990) mini-set still failing to convince the band's critics. Even a sterling cover of the band's 'KISS & MAKE UP' by the soon-to-be-suffocatingly-trendy SAINT ETIENNE didn't reverse the band's image problem and after a further handful of singles and a belated full length album, 'FOR KEEPS' (1991) the FIELD MICE went to ground for good. After a brief period as YESTERDAY SKY, the band re-formed under the moniker NORTHERN PICTURE LIBRARY, recruiting friends BOBBY and CHRIS to help them record 93's acclaimed alternative album, 'ALASKA'. Influenced by ST. ETIENNE's sublime, grand scale melody, the group lulled their way through the set which referred, mostly, to WRATTEN's agoraphobic disorder. However, the ensemble were to sparkle and fade when they stopped releasing anything after single 'PARIS' due to the fact that WRATTEN had split up with lover ANNEMARI. A tribute to the novel 'The Story Of O', TREMBLING BLUE STARS was a hybrid vehicle for WRATTEN and ST. ETIENNE's arranger IAN CATT. Through albums 'HER HANDWRITING' (1996) and 'LIPS THAT TASTE OF TEARS' (1998), the troubled frontman reflected on his relationship with his aforementioned ex. Lyrically explicit, the songs may well have sounded like LOW or late YO LA TENGO, as they breezed though the emotional and personal strains of breaking up.

Album rating: SNOWBALL mini (*5) / SKYWRITING (*6) / FOR KEEPS (*6) / COASTAL compilation (*6) / Northern Picture Library: ALASKA (*7) / Trembling Blue Stars: HER HANDWRITING (*7) / LIPS THAT TASTE OF TEARS (*5) / BROKEN BY WHISPERS (*5) / ALIVE TO EVERY SMILE (*6)

ROB WRATTEN (b. 5 Aug'66, Carshalton, Surrey, England) – vocals / **MARK DOBSON** (b.27 Apr'65, Hartlepool, England) – drums / **HARVEY WILLIAMS** (b.31 Dec'65, Cornwall, England) – guitar (of ANOTHER SUNNY DAY)

	Sarah	not iss.
Nov 88. (7"ep) (SARAH 012) **EMMA'S HOUSE / WHEN YOU SLEEP. / FABULOUS FRIEND / THE LAST LETTER**	□	-
Feb 89. (7") (SARAH 018) **SENSITIVE. / WHEN MORNING COMES TO TOWN**	□	-
Oct 89. (10"m-lp) (SARAH 402) **SNOWBALL**	□	-

– Let's kiss and make up / You're kidding aren't you / End of the affair / Couldn't feel safer / This love is not wrong / Everything about you / White / Letting go.

Nov 89. (7") (SARAH 024) **IF YOU NEED SOMEONE. / THE WORLD TO ME**
Nov 89. (7"m) (SARAH 025) **ANYONE ELSE ISN'T YOU. / BLEAK**
Feb 90. (7"one-sided) (CAFF 2) **I CAN SEE MYSELF ALONE FOREVER / EVERYTHING ABOUT YO U**
(above on 'Caff' records)

— added **ANNEMARI DAVIES** (b. 9 Feb'71, Oxfordshire, England) – guitar, keyboards / **MICHAEL HISCOCK** (b.24 Feb'66, Carshalton) – bass

Jul 90. (m-lp) (SARAH 601) **SKYWRITING**
– Canada / Clearer / It isn't forever / Below the stars / Humblebee / Triangle.

Sep 90. (10"ep) (SARAH 038) **SO SAID KAY EP**
– Landmark / Quicksilver / Holland Street / Indian Ocean / So said Kay.

Jan 91. (7") (SARAH 044) **SEPTEMBER'S NOT SO FAR AWAY. / BETWEEN HELLO AND GOODBYE**

Aug 91. (lp/c/cd) (SARAH 606/+C/CD) **COASTAL** (compilation)
– September's not so far away / So said Kay / The last letter / Sensitive / This is not wrong / If you need someone / Anyone else isn't you / Couldn't feel safer / Let's kiss and make up / Below the stars / Quicksilver / When morning comes to town / It isn't forever / Between hello and goodbye.

Sep 91. (12"ep) (SARAH 057) **MISSING THE MOON. / A WRONG TURN AND RAINDROPS / AN EARLIER AUTUMN**

Oct 91. (lp/cd) (SARAH 607/+CD) **FOR KEEPS**
– Five movements / Star of David / Coach station reunion / This is not here / Of the perfect kind / Tilting at windmill / Think of these things / Willow / And before the first kiss / Freezing point.

— split late 1991 after ANNEMARI couldn't play live

– compilations, etc. –

Jan 98. (cd) Shinkansen; <SHINK 9CD> **WHERE'D YOU LEARN TO KISS THAT WAY?**

NORTHERN PICTURE LIBRARY

ANNEMARI, ROB + MARK with live to repl. former:- **BOBBY** – guitar / **CHRIS** – bass

	Vinyl Japan	Vinyl Japan
Sep 93. (12"/cd-s) (TASK/+CD 006) **LOVE SONG FOR THE DEAD CHE (mix). / THE WAY THAT STARS DIE**	□	-
Oct 93. (cd/lp) (ASK CD/LP 023) <6522> **ALASKA** <US-title 'NORTHERN PICTURE LIBRARY'>	□	

– Untitled No.1 / Into the ether / Catholic Easter colours / Glitter spheres / Insecure / Dreams and stars and sleep / Lucky / L.S.D. icing / Truly madly deeply / Isn't it time you faced the truth? / Untitled No.2 / Skylight / Of traffic and the ticking / Lucky (reprise) / Monotone.

Jun 94. (12"ep/cd-ep) (TASK/+CD 025) **BLUE DISSOLVE EP**
– Dear faraway friend / Here to stay / Untitled No.3 / Breaking.

	Sarah	not iss.
Oct 94. (7") (SARAH 094) **PARIS. / NORFOLK WINDMILLS**	□	-
Oct 94. (7") (SARAH 095) **LAST SEPTEMBER'S FAREWELL KISS. / SIGNS**	□	-

(cd-s+=) (SARAH 095CD) – Paris / Norfolk windmills.

— split when ROB and ANNEMARI broke up

FIELD MICE (cont)

TREMBLING BLUE STARS

BOB WRATTON with **IAN CATT** – arranger (ex-SAINT ETIENNE)

Shinkansen / Shinkansen

Apr 96. (7") *(SHINKANSEN 1)* **ABBA ON THE JUKEBOX. / SHE'S ALWAYS THERE**

May 96. (cd) *(<SHINKANSEN 3CD>)* **HER HANDWRITING** — Dec96
 – A single kiss / For this one / What can I say to change your heart? / Abba on the jukebox / The far too simple beauty / Less than love / Less than love (reprise) / Do people ever? / Last summertime's obsession / A London story / Saffron, beautiful and brown-eyed / Nobody but you / Two Octobers / To keep your heart whole.

—— added **HARVEY WILLIAMS** (ex-ANOTHER SUNNY DAY)

Nov 97. (7") *(SHINKANSEN 8)* **THE RAINBOW. / THOUGH I STILL WANT TO FALL INTO YOUR ARMS**
 (cd-s+=) *(SHINKANSEN 8CD)* – She's always there / The rainbow (long version).

Feb 98. (cd) *(<SHINKANSEN 10CD>)* **LIPS THAT TASTE OF TEARS**
 – All I never said / Headlights / Never loved you more / The rainbow / Made for each other / Letter never sent / I'm tired I've tried / You've done nothing wrong really / Old photographs / Never loved you more 2 / Deserve / Cecilia in black and white / Tailspin / Farewell to forever.

—— **MICHAEL HISCOCK** – bass; repl. HARVEY

Aug 99. (7"blue) *(SHINKANSEN 18)* **DOO-WOP MUSIC. / NOW THAT THERE'S NOTHING IN THE WAY**

Oct 99. (cd-ep) *(SHINKANSEN 20CD)* **DARK EYES EP**
 – Dark eyes / A slender wrist / Her world beneath the waves / Half in love with leaving.

Shinkansen Sub Pop

Mar 00. (cd) <70504> **BROKEN BY WHISPERS**
 – Ripples / She just couldn't say / Sometimes I still feel the bruise / To leave it now / Fragile / I no longer know anything / Back to you / Birthday girl / Snow showers / Sleep / Dark eyes.

Jun 00. (cd-ep) *(SHINKANSEN 23CD)* **SHE JUST COULDN'T SAY / FIND HER GONE / SMOKE AND STEAM / WHERE NORFOLK MEETS LINCOLNSHIRE**

—— **BOB** next with **ANNEMARI DAVIES** (ex-PICTURE CENTER) / plus **HARVEY WILLIAMS** – guitar, keyboards / **BETH ARZY** – vocals (of ABERDEEN) / **KERIS HOWARD** – bass (ex-BRIGHTER) + **JONATHAN ACKERMAN** – drums

Sep 01. (cd-ep) *(SHINKANSEN 31CD)* **THE GHOST OF AN UNKISSED KISS**
 – The ghost of an unkissed kiss / As long as she's needed / Before we know it / While your heart is still beating.

Oct 01. (cd) *(SHINKANSEN 33CD) <SP 559>* **ALIVE TO EVERY SMILE**
 – Under lock and key / With every story / Haunted days / Here all day / Until the dream gets broken / St. Paul's Cathedral at night / The ghost of an unkissed kiss / Maybe after all / Ammunition / Little gunshots / (untitled).

Apr 02. (cd-s) *(SHINKANSEN 35CD)* **SLOW SOFT SIGHS / HOME AND DRY / IT'S EASIER TO SMILE**

FIEND (see under ⇒ TELSTAR PONIES)

FIGURINE (see under ⇒ STRICTLY BALLROOM)

FIREWATER

Formed: USA .... 1996 by former COP SHOOT COP frontman, TOD ASHLEY, and a host of veteran alt-rock musicians including ex-JON SPENCER, ex-JESUS LIZARD and former SOUL COUGHING members that were always bound to be an interesting prospect. The strangely titled debut 'GET OFF THE CROSS, WE NEED THE WOOD FOR THE FIRE', achieved little in making a name for the band but, at the same time, encouraged many to mix punk with other sounds (notably tango, Latin-jazz, accordion and sax music), making it difficult for critics to pigeonhole the different influences involved (a problem they have with similar artist BECK). 'THE PONZI SCHEME' followed up the latter in 1998, the interweaving textures and noticeable directions remained intact with a brilliant homage to gangster and western movies segued inbetween. • **Note:** Not to be confused with the FIREWATER of 1986 who issued the countrified 'Brand New Vintage'.

Album rating: GET OFF THE CROSS, WE NEED THE WOOD FOR THE FIRE (*5) / THE PONZI SCHEME (*7)

TOD A. (b. ASHLEY) – vocals (ex-COP SHOOT COP) / **DUANE DENISON** – guitar (of JESUS LIZARD) / **YUVAL GABAY** – drums (of SOUL COUGHING) / **KURT HOFFMAN** – saxophone, accordion (ex-JON SPENCER BLUES EXPLOSION, ex-ORDINAIRES, ex-CONGO NORVELL) / **JENNIFER CHARLES** – vocals (of ELYSIAN FIELDS) / **JIM KIMBALL** – drums (ex-MULE, ex-LAUGHING HYENAS) / **HAHN ROWE** – violin (ex-HUGO LARGO, ex-FOETUS)

Jetset Jetset

Apr 97. (cd) *<(TWA 4CD)>* **GET OFF THE CROSS, WE NEED THE WOOD FOR THE FIRE** — Oct96
 – Some strange reaction / Bourbon nd division / Refinery / When I burn this place down / Circus / I am the rain / Balaliaka / Drunken Jew / Mr. Cardiac / Snake eyes and boxcars / One of those / Hold on slow John.

—— added **DAVE QUIMET** – keyboards, trombone

Mar 98. (cd) *<(TWA 11CD)>* **THE PONZI SCHEME**
 – The Ponzi's theme / Green light (in stereo) / Dropping like flies / Caroline / Whistling in the dark / Isle Of Dogs / El Borracho (Ponzi's relapse) / Another perfect catastrophe / So long, Superman / I still love you, Judas / Knock 'em down / Drunkard's lament.

FITZ OF DEPRESSION

Formed: Olympia, Washington, USA ... 1987 by MIKEY DEES, who recruited CRAIG BECKER, and JIM KOONTZ to rattle out some hardcore tinged punk sounds. In true indie style the boys released their debut eponymously titled EP on their own label 'Mumblesomething' records and whipped off just 300 copies. KOONTZ was soon replaced on bass by RYAN VON BARGEN who lasted an equally short time, managing before his replacement by JUSTIN WARREN in late 1991, to strum out the rhythm for FOD's sophomore release, the 7" single 'THE AWAKENING'. WARREN took on the revolving door slot only to find that after several more single releases, including the ELVIS COSTELLO B-side cover 'PISSBUTT / RED SHOES' single, he too had spun round to face the exit. In stepped BRIAN SPARHAWK in 1993 who was to remain their longest serving bass player. The following year FOD released their debut album, 'LET'S GIVE IT A TWIST', which was a competent piece of no thrills, rammed-down-your-throat punk. Several singles followed and, as with many of the smaller indie bands, spots on label and genre compilations. 1996 saw the release of their sophomore full-length outing, 'SWING', which didn't take many more risks than its predecessor although with a slightly more humorous and party edge. Unfortunately, increasing problems in helmsman and main songwriter DEES' personal life became too much to bear and thus led to the break-up of FOD in 1997. However the band did resurface briefly with DEES, BECKER, and WARREN back on bass, to support SOUL BRAINS (formerly BAD BRAINS; disagreements with their label had led to the name-change) on tour. Yet for FOB this was shortly aborted mid-tour; rumours circulating from the frontman, DEES, had it that the others were pining too hard for home-life. • **Covered:** RED SHOES + MIRACLE MAN + WELCOME TO THE WORKING WEEK (Elvis Costello) / 867-5309 (Tommy Tutone) / GLAD ALL OVER (Dave Clark Five) / I'M THE MAN (Joe Jackson).

Album rating: LET'S GIVE IT A TWIST (*5) / SWING (*6)

MIKEY DEES – vocals, guitar / **JIM KOONTZ** – bass / **CRAIG BECKER** – drums

not iss. Mumblesomething

Nov 89. (ltd-7"green-ep) <none> **FITZ OF DEPRESSION "PILLS" EP**
 – Crank shaft / Stud / Black death / Life of pain / Tons of poop / Cloans / Soal / C'mon-n-love-me. <re-iss. 1992 on 'K'; >

—— **RYAN VON BARGEN** – bass; repl. KOONTZ

not iss. Meat

Jul 91. (ltd-7"yellow) <Flesh 75> **THE AWAKENING. / WAITING FOR YOUR LOVE / I'M A POSER**

Jan 93. (10"ep) <FleshLP 1> **10" EP** (rec. 12/16/91)
 – Mighty me / Fear / The awakening / Everybody and their dog / Raw sewage / Think of words / H / Punk-a-rooni.

—— **JUSTIN WARREN** – bass; repl. BARGEN

not iss. Blatant

Nov 92. (7") <BLAT 005> **PISSBUTT. / RED SHOES**

not iss. Negative Feedback

Jun 93. (7") <none> **JENNY – 867-5309. / TAKE IT AWAY**

—— **BRIAN SPARHAWK** – bass (ex-TON TON BOA) repl. WARREN

K K

Oct 94. (7") <(IPU 47)> **LIE. / GLAD ALL OVER**

Fire K

Jan 95. (cd/lp) *(FIRE CD/LP 44)* <K 31> **LET'S GIVE IT A TWIST** — Jul94
 – Power shack / Slip shot / Setting in a room / See me, hear me / Young & free / Lie / Never quite my enime / I can see your house / Heavy doody / Grilled cheese / Before it's true / Big machine.

Feb 95. (7"blue) *(7SM 4)* **SEE ME, HEAR ME. / MIRACLE MAN**

Apr 95. (10"ep) *(BLAZE 86)* **YOUNG AND FREE**
 – Young and free / Take it away / Lie / Mask.

Yo Yo Kill Rock Stars

1995. (7") *(YOYO 7-2)* **I'M THE MAN. / WELCOME TO THE WORKING WEEK**

Jan 96. (7") <KRS 252> **SEEMINGLY VAGUE. / TOO RIPE**

K K

May 96. (cd/lp) *<(KCD/KLP 41)>* **SWING** — Apr96
 – We three / My good name / Form a line / No movie tonight / Time to leave / Connect the dot / She wants to know / Mind over matter / House or home / I can't / New disgrace / Shimmy.

—— disbanded some time in 1997

– compilations, etc. –

Oct 95. (cd-ep) *Negative Feedback; <NF 004>* **PIGS ARE PEOPLE TOO**
 – Jenny – 867-5309 / Take it away / The big machine / Mask / Gotten sly.

FIVER

Formed: Modesto, California, USA ... 1993 by DAVID WOODY and LUIS FREGOSO, originally gigging around as a trio with a varying third member. Two years later in 1995, the band swelled to six with the inclusion of CHRIS DOUD, ZACH EGENBERGER, SEAN DUNCAN and DAN LILLIE. Debuting with LP 'EVENTUALLY SOMETHING COOL WILL HAPPEN' (1998), the band were immediately getting the attention of the alternative music press, not least for the fact that the album was produced by GRANDADDY singer, JASON LYTLE. The set showcased the band's leaning towards the quirky indie rocking of PAVEMENT but with the insular and loner lyrics of peers SPARKLEHORSE. Although WOODY and EGENBERGER were still hitting the books at university, it did not stop the band from issuing

FIVER (cont)

their sophomore album 'STRINGS FOR SATELLITES' (2000), with KYLE STATHAM (from FUCK) this time at the production helm. Following this outing the group's star really seemed to be in the ascendancy as more and more of their shows sold out; the music scribbler's praise kept flowing with an expectant eye open for their third full-piece 'HERE IT COMES' (2002). This did not stray from its forebears but nevertheless showed the band were settling in nicely to a niche in the West Coast indie rock scene.

Album rating: EVENTUALLY SOMETHING COOL WILL HAPPEN (*6) / STRINGS FOR SATELLITES (*6) / HERE IT COMES (*5)

DAVID WOODY – vocals, guitar / **LUIS FREGOSO** – bass / added **CHRIS DOUD** – guitar / **SEAN DUNCAN** – keyboards / **DAN LILLIE** – keyboards / **ZACH EGENBERGER** – drums

Devil In The Woods / Devil In The Woods

Mar 00. (cd) <(DIW 021)> **EVENTUALLY SOMETHING COOL WILL HAPPEN** – Aug98
– Horse pill vector / Pretty Kitty / Builder / Feragogo / Tiger beat / Smoothie / Chalet motel / Turn down the pancake / One mile an hour / Snowball. (re-iss. Feb01 on 'Fierce Panda'; NONG 017CD)

Jun 00. (cd) <(DIW 033)> **STRINGS FOR SATELLITES**
– Turning your back on the bull / Don't tell me how to rock, I'm for here / Mini-bunny / The Devil is undeniably real / The launch / Fun summer drinks / Past from the future / Please form 1 line / This is up / Theme from lo-down. (re-iss. May01 on 'Fierce Panda'; NONG 19CD)

May 01. (7") (NING 106) **CHALET MOTEL. / MINI-BUNNY** –
(above issued on 'Fierce Panda')

May 02. (cd) <(DIW 048)> **HERE IT COMES** – Apr02
– Speeds of light / Buildings and homes / Tiny waves / The only ones / Every light is gone out / Warriors / Desires of the laser age / O fearless one / Haunted us / On our way.

5 STYLE

Formed: Wicker Park, Chicago, Illinois, USA ... 1995 by BILL DOLAN (guitar), JEREMY JACOBSEN (keyboards), LEROY BACH (bass) and JOHN HERNDON (drums). This hugely talented quartet released their self-titled debut album later in 1995. Their contemporary funk placed emphasis firmly on unhinged instrumentation, unlike so much indie-rock/funk that has become so increasingly commercially oriented. '5 STYLE' starts as it means to continue – a shout of "come on!" leads into the rollicking, melodic opener 'DEEP MARSH'. The album continues in floor-stomping fashion – other highlights include 'OUTTA SPACE CANOE RACE' and 'WAITING FOR THE ECLIPSE' – although the tempo is abated for 'I TOLD YA' and 'SURE IS HOT'. The funk on display is patently rooted in the late-'60s and '70s, but has more in common with the raw, organic sound of Southern Funk and the METERS, as opposed to the production sheen of PARLIAMENT. The fervour and frankness of 5 STYLE's debut propelled them to the fore-front of contemporary funk. Sadly it would be several years before any further 5 STYLE activity, as the band members set off to pursue new or concurrent ventures. BILL DOLAN sang with punk act AMERICAN STANDARD, although more significantly played guitar with indie "supergroup" HEROIC DOSES. Forming in January 1997, HEROIC DOSES also included EUPHONE mastermind and multi-instrumentalist RYAN RAPSYS and several bass players over time, including JESUS LIZARD's DAVID WM. SIMS, although C-CLAMP's NICK MACRI provided most bass parts on their self-titled debut LP, released in 1998. 'HEROIC DOSES' was an album of experimental and instrumental indie-rock; skillful, and at times inspired. At the same time JEREMY JACOBSEN moonlighted as the LONESOME ORGANIST, releasing two albums – 'COLLECTOR OF CACTUS ECHO BAG' (1997) and 'CAVALCADE' (1999). JACOBSEN's solo work allowed him to fully express his multi-instrumental dexterity – mixing instruments such as guitar, organ, piano and saxophone. Meanwhile, HERNDON had been with his band TORTOISE, and BACH with ISOTOPE 217. 5IVE STYLE (with a slight variation on their moniker) reunited in 1999, and created 'MINATURE PORTRAITS', their sound remained rooted in METERS inspired funk, although they incorporated other styles and elements – like electronics, prog-rock and reggae dub – creating another excellent album.

Album rating: 5 STYLE (*6) / MINIATURE PORTRAITS (*5) / Lonesome Organist: COLLECTOR OF CACTUS ECHO BAG (*6) / CAVALCADE (*6) / Heroic Doses: HEROIC DOSES (*5)

BILL DOLAN – guitar (vocalist of AMERICAN STANDARD) / **JEREMY JACOBSEN** – keyboards (of EUPHONE) / **LeROY BACH** – bass, keyboards (of UPTIGHTLY) / **JOHN HERNDON** – drums (of TORTOISE)

Sub Pop / Sub Pop

Aug 95. (7") <(SP 282)> **KIKI'S COOKOUT. / HOT BOX!**

Sep 95. (lp/cd) <(SP 309/+B)> **5 STYLE**
– Deep marsh / Hard Afro rubalon / Once around the park / Round up / I told ya / Outta space canoe race / Apple pie / Waiting on the eclipse / Freddy flakeout / Sure is hot.

1997. (7") <SP 394> **SHE'S HUMANOID. / BURNING AIRLINES GIVE YOU SO MUCH MORE** –

LONESOME ORGANIST

aka **JEREMY JACOBSEN** – vocals, multi

Thrill Jockey / Thrill Jockey

Sep 97. (lp/cd) <(THRILL 044/+CD)> **COLLECTOR OF CACTUS ECHO BAG**
– The lost oar / Catching flys with my teeth / Chasing the wheelbarrel / The Lonesome Organist theme / Ratt advance on the Windsor Deluxe / The sing song /

Let me be your man / King of the rail model 1895 trainset / The dragon song / You be Blake / Make me less lonesome / End of the road / Wind up bird / Clock song / 6 volt / Tip toe / My first piano / Miel Silvestre / Blue stew / Departing the sturdy ship.

Apr 99. (lp/cd) <(THRILL 067/+CD)> **CAVALCADE**
– The storm past by / Balloon race phenomenon / The low strike / Cranked up too hard / The steam crow / Dirty plight / Vibe sequencer / Fly on my plate / New age vamp / Flew out my window / Boing / Lonesome hobo squaw / All of those dirty swine / At the wingfest / Vine parade / Lap steel.

HEROIC DOSES

BILL DOLAN – guitar / **RAN RAPSYS** – drums (of EUPHONE) / **NICK MACRI** – bass (of HEROIC DOSES) repl. KURT NIESMAN + WM. SIMS

Aug 98. (lp/cd) <(SP/+CD 432)> **HEROIC DOSES** – Jun98
– On the corner / Gimme less friction / Reggie, is it? / Pushy girl / Crystals / Heroic theme song / Married to the scene / The mad spackler / Ollie oxen free / Blank ship / Is she queer / Manic kraut rock / Euphonix.

— **MATT LUX** – bass; repl. MACRI who continued with C-CLAMP

FIVE STYLE

— re-formed with same original line-up

Aug 99. (cd) <(SPCD 479)> **MINIATURE PORTRAITS**
– Mythical numbers / Marmy the count / Father time / The lost oar / Here we go / Pledge drive / Wrong about you / Hit the decks / The fancy dance in Jeremy's pants / Sailor girl song / Pet the cow / Playful sounds for hostile grounds.

— JACOBSEN was to join EUPHONE in 2002

FLAKE MUSIC (see under ⇒ SHINS)

FLAMINGOES

Formed: Hitchin, Hertfordshire, England ... Spring 1993 by identical twin brothers, JUDE and JAMES COOK, who completed the line-up with off-kilter drummer KEVIN MATTHEWS (an ex-dustman). Taking flight to the capital, the lads won a talent competition run by DJ, Gary Crowley, stirring up even more publicity when they played the celebrated New Art Riot gig alongside THESE ANIMAL MEN and S*M*A*S*H towards the end of the year. The following February, The FLAMINGOES unleashed their vinyl debut in the shape of 7" single, 'THE CHOSEN FEW', already being tipped for the top by such unlikely organs as the News Of The World. Yet another band harking back to the year of 1977 when The CLASH and The JAM ruled the pop charts, the feathered ones had no reservations about airing their suitability to wipe the floor with the New Wave of neo-Mod Brit-pop acts. Signed to 'Pandemonium', the trio released the 'TEENAGE EMERGENCY' EP (the title track having already netted them the aforementioned award) and a further single, 'DISAPPOINTED', both highlights from their forthcoming debut album, 'PLASTIC JEWELS' (1995). However, just as things looked promising for the hell-raising lads, they rather mysteriously disappeared from view. • **Note:** Not to be confused with another outfit of the same name who had a few singles released on dance label, Rob's, either end of '93.

Album rating: PLASTIC JEWELS (*6)

JUDE COOK (b.1970) – vocals, guitar / **JAMES COOK** (b.1970) – bass, vocals / **KEVIN MATTHEWS** – drums

La La Land / not iss.

Feb 94. (7") (LALA 002) **THE CHOSEN FEW. /** –

Pandemonium / Big Pop

Jul 94. (12"ep/cd-ep) (PANN/+CD 005) **TEENAGE EMERGENCY** –
– Teenage emergency / Running away / Six burning seven / Everyone makes mistakes.

Oct 94. (7") (PANN 006) **DISAPPOINTED. / DISTORT** –
(cd-s+=) (PANNCD 006) – London's laughing.

Feb 95. (cd/c/lp) (PANN CD/MC/LP 007) **PLASTIC JEWELS** –
– Disappointed / Teenage emergency / Safe / Try it on / Absent fathers, violent sons / Winter / Scenester / The chosen few / Unstable / Suicide bridge / Last of the big spenders / It's been a thrill. <US cd-iss. Sep96 on 'Big Pop'+=; 610> – Tonight is killing me (by JUDE) / Distort boy (by JUDE).

Mar 95. (12"ep/cd-ep) (PANN/+CD 008) **SCENESTER. / SUBURBAN SINNERS / TOUGH AGAIN** –

— split after above single

FLAMING STARS

Formed: Camden, London, England ... late 1994 out of the EARLS OF SUAVE (who released one single, 'IN MY DREAMS') by vocalist/keyboard player MAX DECHARNE (previously the drummer with GALLON DRUNK), drummer JOE WHITNEY, bassist PAUL DEMPSEY and guitarist JOHNNY JOHNSON (the latter two from THEE HEADCOATS and the STINGRAYS). Taking their moniker from an ELVIS PRESLEY movie and adding a fifth member, guitarist MARK HOSKING, the group embarked on a series of dates while also featuring on Radio One sessions including the obligatory John Peel and Mark Radcliffe shows. The FLAMING STARS remained on the EARLS' label, 'Vinyl Japan', several singles/EP's over the course of '95/'96 leading up to the drink-soaked vignettes of debut album, 'SONGS FROM THE BAR ROOM FLOOR' (1996). Two further sets were released the following year, namely 'BRING ME THE REST OF ALFREDO GARCIA' (a singles

FLAMING STARS (cont)

compilation) and 'SELL YOUR SOUL TO . . .'. The FLAMING STARS returned on top form in 1999 with the brilliant 'PATHWAY', displaying the group's usual flair for inserting distorted instrumentations into bruised little pop songs. A diversion could be heard on 2001's follow-up, 'A WALK ON THE WIRED SIDE', with the band making some sort of deliberate decision to become more broody – like CAVE's early BAD SEED days. 'SUNSET & VOID' (2002), however, was arguably their finest creation, with DECHARNE adding piano to his warped and twisted love songs. Stand-out tracks included the skull-busting 'CASH 22' and the rather eerie 'MANSION HOUSE BLUES'.

Album rating: SONGS FROM THE BAR ROOM FLOOR (*6) / BRING ME THE REST OF ALFREDO GARCIA compilation (*6) / PATHWAY (*6) / THE SIX JOHN PEEL SESSIONS collection (*6) / SELL YOUR SOUL TO . . . (*6) / A WALK ON THE WIRED SIDE (*7) / GINMILL PERFUME (*7) / SUNSET & VOID (*6)

MAX DECHARNE – vocals, keyboards (ex-GALLON DRUNK) / **JOHNNY JOHNSON** – guitar (ex-THEE HEADCOATS, ex-STINGRAYS) / **PAUL DEMPSEY** – bass (ex-THEE HEADCOATS, ex-STINGRAYS) / **JOE WHITNEY** – drums

Vinyl Japan / Vinyl Japan

Apr 94. (7"; as EARLS OF SUAVE) *(PAD 016)* **IN MY DREAMS. / SOMEBODY BUY ME A DRINK**

— added **MARK HOSKING** – guitar

Mar 95. (7"ep)(cd-ep) *(PAD 023)(TASKCD 049)* **HOSPITAL, HEAVEN OR HELL EP**
– Kiss tomorrow goodbye / Davy Jones' locker / Like trash / Revenge.

Jul 95. (7") *(PAD 028)* **THE FACE ON THE BAR ROOM FLOOR. / GET CARTER**

Dec 95. (7"ep)(cd-ep) *(PAD 030)(TASKCD 054)* **MONEY TO BURN EP**
– Money to burn / Bandit country / A hell of a woman / New shade of black.

May 96. (7"ep)(cd-ep) *(PAD 031)(TASKCD 056)* **DOWNHILL WITHOUT BRAKES EP**
– Downhill without brakes / Broken heart / Eat your heart out / Burnt out wreck of a man.

Jun 96. (cd/lp) *(ASK CD/LP 062)* **SONGS FROM THE BAR ROOM FLOOR**
– The face on the bar room floor / Forget my name / You can lie / Who's out there? / Burnt out wreck of a man / Bring me the rest of Alfredo Garcia / Kiss tomorrow goodbye / The ballad of the walking wounded / Downhill without brakes / Theme from dog instruction / Back of my mind / Down to you / Oncoming train / Tubs twist / Like trash / 3 a.m. on the bar room floor.

Nov 96. (7") *(PAD 34)* **TEN FEET TALL. / SPAGHETTI JUNCTION**

Mar 97. (cd) *(ASKCD 067)* **BRING ME THE REST OF ALFREDO GARCIA** (compilation)
– Bring me the rest of Alfredo Garcia / Money to burn / Bury my heart at Pier 13 / Like trash / Get Carter / New shade of black / Ten feet tall / A hell of a woman / The face on the bar room floor / Bandit country / Downhill without brakes / Revenge / Broken heart / Davy Jones' locker / 3 a.m. on the bar room floor / Kiss tomorrow goodbye / Eat your heart out / Spaghetti junction / Burnt out wreck of a man.

Apr 97. (7") *(PAD 035)* **BURY MY HEART AT PIER 13. / DOWN TO YOU**

Oct 97. (cd) *(<ASKCD 076>)* **SELL YOUR SOUL TO . . .** Mar99
– Sweet smell of success / Blood money / London after midnight / The street that never closes / I remembered to forget to remember / New hope for the dead / Find yourself another drunk / Don't need the sunshine / What you want / Just too bad / Don't mean a thing if you haven't got the king / Better than that / The day the Earth caught fire.

Apr 98. (7"ep/cd-ep) *(PAD/TASKCD 59)* **SWEET SMELL OF SUCCESS EP**
– Sweet smell of success / The day the Earth caught fire / Never missed you tonight / A place in the sun.

May 99. (cd/lp) *(ASK CD/LP 83)* **PATHWAY**
– Breaking down / Only tonight / Coffin Ed & Grave Digger Jones / Sixteen coaches long / Maybe one day / Lit up like a Christmas tree / Once bitten, twice shy / Malice doesn't live here anymore / Running out of time / House of dreams / Sing sing / Eight miles down / Black mask / Just how it feels / The ghost of Baghdad / The last picture show.

Jun 00. (cd) *(<ASKCD 111>)* **THE SIX JOHN PEEL SESSIONS** (collection)
– Kiss tomorrow goodbye / The face on the bar room floor / Broken heart / Like trash / Tubs twist / Forget my name / Downhill without brakes / Who's out there? / Back of my mind / 3 a.m. on the bar room floor / Bury my heart at Pier 13 / Just too bad / Sweet smell of success / London after midnight / Better than that / Blood money / The street that never closes / New hope for the dead / Only tonight / Running out of time / Sing sing / Just how it feels / Lit up like a Christmas tree / Breaking down / What do I get? / Coffin Ed & Grave Digger Jones / The last picture show.

Jan 01. (7") *(PAD 71)* **YOU DON'T ALWAYS WANT WHAT YOU GET. / SATURDAY NIGHT SPECIAL**

Jan 01. (cd/lp) *(<ASK CD/LP 121>)* **A WALK ON THE WIRED SIDE** Mar01
– Right face right time / You don't always want what you get / Grabber George / Absent without leave / Action / Crime and vision / Some things you don't forget / She says she says / The villain / Out of the past / Over and done / Meet the guv'nor / Leaving town / Sleepless nights / The dead don't care / More than enough / Tinnitus blues / Another shade of blue / Swimming the length of this bar.

Jun 01. (7") *<PAD 73>* **SOME THINGS YOU DON'T FORGET. / ONLY TONIGHT**

Alternative Tentacles / Alternative Tentacles

Oct 01. (7") *(VIRUS 267)* **ONE LONELY NIGHT. / DAYS LIKE THIS**

Oct 01. (lp/cd) *(<VIRUS 268/+CD>)* **GINMILL PERFUME**
– Like trash / Ten feet tall / Who's out there / Some things you don't forget / Only tonight / Bury my heart at PIer 13 / The last picture show / New hope for the dead / You don't always get what you want / Blood money / Face on the bar room floor / A place in the sun / Bring me the rest of Alfredo Garcia / Coffin Ed and Grave digger Jones / Kiss tomorrow goodbye.

Vinyl Japan / Vinyl Japan

Aug 02. (7") *(PAD 79)* **A LITTLE BIT LIKE YOU. / THE MAN WHO WOULD B.B. KING**

Sep 02. (cd/lp) *(<ASK CD/LP 139>)* **SUNSET & VOID** Oct02
– A little bit like you / Cash 22 / Baby steps / Mansion house blues / Sands, flamingo, Desert Inn / Midnight train / Sunset & void / House of the setting sun / Killjoy / Mexican roulette / The waiting game / Five for the road / Killer in the rain / The long walk home / Night must fall.

FLASHPAPR (see under ⇒ THOMAS, Fred)

FLIES INSIDE THE SUN

Formed: New Zealand . . . 1993 by KIM PIETERS and PETER STAPLETON via ROY MONTGOMERY's DADAMAH's one-off ensemble; the same pair were also part of a free-noise supergroup with The DEAD C's BRUCE RUSSELL – two sets 'Last Glass' (1994) and 'Sex/Machine' (1999). Joined by BRIAN CROOK (of The RENDERERS and ex-TERMINALS) and DANNY BUTT, FLIES INSIDE THE SUN forked out a deal with the US-based 'Kranky' imprint, turning out debut ' . . .AN AUDIENCE OF OTHERS (INCLUDING HERSELF)' in 1995; think PERE UBU and The DEAD C. Now without CROOK, FLIES UNDER THE SUN released an eponymous sophomore set, their second for 'Metonymic' having delivered a CD, 'SEDIMENT' as RAIN. A part noise/part ambient/part-improv recording, it was unfortunately cluttered by too many musical spooks. The original quartet reunited for two post-millennium efforts, 'CACTUS SKY' (2000) and 'LE MAL D'ARCHIVE' (2001), although the former was nearly roasted when master tapes escaped being burnt in a fire; STAPLETON and PIETERS had also moonlighted with their own project, SLEEP.

Album rating: . . .AN AUDIENCE OF OTHERS (AND HERSELF) (*6) / SEDIMENT as Rain (*7) / FLIES INSIDE THE SUN (*7) / CACTUS SKY (*6) / LE MAL D'ARCHIVE (*5) / Sleep: ENFOLDED IN LUXURY (*6) / GHOSTWRITING (*6)

KIM PIETERS – vocals, bass (ex-DADAMAH) / **PETER STAPLETON** – percussion, drums, lyrics (ex-PIN GROUP, ex-VICTOR DIMISICH BAND, ex-TERMINALS, ex-DADAMAH) / **BRIAN CROOK** – guitar, synth (ex-TERMINALS, of RENDERERS) / **DANNY BUTT** – guitar, synth

not iss. / Kranky

1995. (cd) *<KRANKY 008>* **. . .AN AUDIENCE OF OTHERS (AND HERSELF)**
– Mother kiss / The man with no arms / Absent and erotic lives / Icarus / Sleepwalk / The afternoon blind.

— now without CROOK who remained with The RENDERERS

Metonymic / not iss.

1996. (cd; as RAIN) *(MET 001)* **SEDIMENT** NewZ
– Dragonfly / Coma / Lost angel memory / Radii / Secrets of a rented island / The blindfold test / Violet stains red / Corridor.

1996. (cd) *(MET 002)* **FLIES INSIDE THE SUN** NewZ
– Casanovas / Living in the world / Devil / She passes by / Burn / Detour.

— **BRIAN CROOK** – guitar, organ, synth; returned to repl. KIM

2000. (cd) *(MET 007)* **CACTUS SKY** NewZ
– The birth of sand and gravel / Green hearted orange / A spy in your love / Cry of weight / The black ship / In the shadow of mysterious succulents / Farenheit / Plateau.

2001. (cd) *(MET 009)* **LE MAL D'ARCHIVE** NewZ
– Nightsky / In memory of forgetting / May 1968 / The flowers are dreaming.

SLEEP

aka **STAPLETON + PIETERS**

Metonymic / not iss.

1999. (cd) **ENFOLDED IN LUXURY** NewZ
2001. (cd) **GHOSTWRITING** NewZ
– Ether / Checkpoint / Filterline / Salt / The field / Who said the surface was flat / Perfume.

FLIN FLON (see under ⇒ UNREST)

FLOWCHART

Formed: Philadelphia, Pennsylvania, USA . . . 1994 by SEAN O'NEAL, the mastermind and inspiration behind FLOWCHART. O'NEAL became a recognized figure within the Philadelphia dance music scene, picking up local residencies, gradually widening his appeal, and soon landing gigs and filling dance floors worldwide. His playlists ranged from techno-pop, to deep house and ambient, with O'NEAL consistently experimenting and pushing the boundaries of the techno sound. Concurrently, he ran the 'Fuzzy Box' and 'Tuning Spork' independents, and with regular releases, these would also come to have a major impact upon the Philly underground scene. Teaming up with BRODIE BUDD (and temporarily CRAIG BOTTEL), 1995's 'MULTI-PERSONALITY TABLETOP VACATION' was FLOWCHART's first album release, and appeared on the 'Carrot Top' label. A collection of experimental electro-pop tunes, it immediately prompted comparisons with the sound of STEREOLAB, and even featured the track 'NEW RADIOLAB RIP-OFF'. The apparent STEREOLAB influence seemed but a distant memory with 1996's 'TENJIRA' EP, which saw FLOWCHART successfully exploring the droning beats and bleeping effects of Japanese electronica such as contemporaries SUGARPLANT. With BUDD departing, O'NEAL enlisted ERIN ANDERSON for FLOWCHART's second LP, 'CUMULUS MOOD TWANG' (1997). The layering of beats and samples remained, but the overall quality was more dreamy and soothing, and further enhanced FLOWCHART's reputation. Third album, 'COMMERCIAL', released in 1999, was further evidence of O'NEAL's passion for sonic experimentation, this time involving several collaborators, and adding elements like drum'n'bass and 60s-pop, creating a collection of real diversity. 2000's 'GEE BEE' EP contained a floor-stomping title track, and the ambient-trance number, 'MANDERINE', complete with a re-mix by Philadelphia's TLEILAXU.

Album rating: MULTI-PERSONALITY TABLETOP VACATION (*4) / CUMULUS MOOD SWING (*7) / COMMERCIAL with Holland (*5) / WISHWORM (*6)

SEAN O'NEAL – vocals, electronics / **BRODIE BUDD** – electronics / **CRAIG BOTTEL** – electronics

		Carrot Top	Carrot Top
Oct 95.	(cd) <SAKI 008> **MULTI-PERSONALITY TABLETOP VACATION**	-	

– Hero wine / Metro survey / Laser printer workshop / Fossil experiment delayed / Neronization of igloos / New radiolab rip-off / Shun to wonder / The digit do-bop / Do oscillators have wings. (UK-iss.Nov97; same)

— now without BOTTEL

| Aug 96. | (12"ep/cd-ep) <SAKI 012/+CD> **EVERGREEN NOISE IS FLEXIBLE EP** | - | |
| Nov 96. | (7") (MOTOR 011) **SIDESHOW ALL THE WAY. / DAINTY PILGRIMAGE** | | - |

(above issued on 'Motorway', below on 'Darla')

| Dec 96. | (12"ep/cd-ep) (BLISS 01/+CD) <25> **TENJIRU EP** | | Nov96 |

– Nationwide sleep disorder / Tenjira / El glacier-O / Soaring somewhat high like the retroman.

| Jun 97. | (cd-s) <(Singe 012)> **HALLOW SKY. / THIS IS WHERE THE STORY ENDS** | | |

(above issued on 'Burnt Hair', below on 'Black Bean & Placenta')

| Jun 97. | (12"ep/cd-ep) <(BBPTC 060/+CD)> **...THE SPIRIT OF KENNY G** | | |

– The spirit of Kenny G / Glorious and prosperous / E-flarepop / Drunken mini-musik / No microchips. (re-iss. Nov97; BAPX 1)

| Jun 97. | (7") (TB 02) **split w/ MALL** | | - |

(above issued on 'Blind OR')

— **ERIN ANDERSON** – electronics; repl. BUDD

| Sep 97. | (d-lp/cd) <(SAKI 017 1/CD)> **CUMULUS MOOD SWING** | | |

– Envelopment continuum / Another word explodes / Rain boa bye / Platform cloud / Yosho / Rust a la glare / Grain of apology / Icicles and clipboards.

		100 Guitar Mania	not iss.
Oct 97.	(7"; split w/ ECTOGRAM) (100GM 21) **STOLEN ECSTASY VOL.4**		-

– Norton / ECTOGRAM: All behind the witch tower.

		Wurlitzer Jukebox	not iss.
Feb 98.	(7") (WJ 028) **FLUTTER BY BUTTERFLY. / OSHKOSH WONDERBOY**		-

		Darla	Darla
Mar 99.	(cd-ep/d12"ep; as FLOWTRON) <(DRL 076 CD/LP)> **TICKLE MY DOLPHIN**		

– Tickle my dolphin / Fiending / Tickle my dolphin (Flowdub mix) / Tickle my dolphin (initial framework mix) / Tickle my dolphin (Flow down mix) / Tickle my dolphin (dolphin safe tuna mix) / Ode to Ian.

| Jul 99. | (cd; as HOLLAND and FLOWCHART) <(DRL 093)> **COMMERCIAL** | | |

– (untitled 1-10).

		Endorphin	not iss.
Jun 99.	(12"ep; as FLOWCHART & PACIFICA / MALL) (ENDOR 002) **HANGIN' WITH THE HOMOS EP**		-
Oct 00.	(12"ep/cd-ep) (ENDOR 005/+CD) **GEE BEE EP**		-

– Gee bee / Manderine / Manderine (mix).

| Jun 01. | (d-lp/cd) (ENDOR 006/+CD) **WISHWORM** | | |

– Pubic tango / Wish upon a jawn / Ka-bloom / Fig Newton / Ocra booty / Mmmarch / Flowers 'n' stars / Wishful thinking / Red I / Mishledoe / Comfortable hunger / Hahaha.

| Jan 02. | (7") (NOJ 005) **FUNNY TURN. /** | | |

(above on 'Darla')

| Nov 02. | (m-lp) (ENDOR 007) **SHOEGAZER TECHNO** | | - |

FLOWERED UP

Formed: London, England ... mid 1989 by LIAM MAHER, who recruited younger brother JOE along with TIM DORNEY, JOHN TUVEY and MICK LEADER. Touted as the cheeky-cockney answer to the scally charm of Manchester's HAPPY MONDAYS, FLOWERED UP lurched onto the "baggy" scene of summer 1990 in a blaze of hype with their debut single, 'IT'S ON'. Released by the fledgling 'Heavenly' label, the single grazed the Top 60 as the indie-dance craze reached its zenith, FLOWERED UP subsequently taking their already semi-legendary live show – complete with BEZ-style dancer/mascot, BARRY MOONCULT – on the road. Seemingly primed for big things, the group ran into problems following Heavenly's distribution deal with 'London', although by the release of their third single, 'TAKE IT' (co-written with JOE STRUMMER), they were in the Top 40. While the much anticipated debut album, 'A LIFE WITH BRIAN', was subsequently held up, the record eventually surfaced in Spring '91, breaking the UK Top 30 and receiving glowing praise for its good-natured vignettes of London bad boys living the high life. Eventually released in Spring '92 as part of a new deal with 'Columbia' following 'London's decision not to handle it, 'WEEKENDER' proved to be both FLOWERED UP's defining moment and their premature epitaph. A twelve minute-plus celebration of ecstasy culture hedonism, the single has since become regarded as one of the movement's most accurate portrayals and was even the basis for an accompanying short film. Despite the track's critical acclaim and Top 20 success, FLOWERED UP's precarious existence ceased the following year, their penultimate effort a cover of Right Said Fred's 'DON'T TALK JUST KISS', recorded for a 'Heavenly' charity EP. Mysteriously, FLOWERED UP resurfaced for a further one-off single in 1994, 'A BETTER LIFE', before permanently going to ground. • **Trivia:** Their flowery dancer, BARRY MOONCULT covered The Troggs' 'WILD THING'.

Album rating: A LIFE WITH BRIAN (*6)

LIAM MAHER – vocals / **TIM DORNEY** – keyboards (repl. SIMON, who formed SLY & LOVECHILD) / **JOE MAHER** – guitar / **JOHN TUVEY** – drums (repl. other JOHN) / **ANDY JACKSON** – bass

		Heavenly	not iss.
Jul 90.	(7") (HVN 3) **IT'S ON. / IT'S ON – SONIA**	54	-

(12") (12HVN 3) – ('A'side) / It's bloody on (it's on mix) / It's still on (dub).
(10"etched) (10HVN 3) – IT'S ON – FEEL PAIN
(cd-s) (CDHVN 3) – ('A'side) / It's on and on (not much like the Happy Mondays mix) / It's on John.

| Nov 90. | (12"/cd-s) (12/CD HVN 7) **PHOBIA (extended). / FLAPPING / PHOBIA (paranoid mix)** | 75 | - |

(re-iss. May91 as 7"; HVN 7) – (1st two tracks only).

		London	London
Apr 91.	(7"/c-s) (FUP 1/+C) **TAKE IT. / I'LL BE YOUR DOG**	34	-

(12"+=) (FUP 1T) – Phobia (live).
(cd-s+=) (FUP 1CD) – ('A'mixes).

| Aug 91. | (7"/c-s) (FUP 2/+C) **IT'S ON (re-recorded). / EGG RUSH (vox ANNA HAIGH)** | 38 | - |

(12"+=/cd-s+=) (FUP 2 T/CD) – Take it (live).

| Aug 91. | (cd/c/lp) <(828 244-2/-4/-1)> **A LIFE WITH BRIAN** | 23 | |

– Sunshine / Take it / Mr. Happy reveller / Hysterically blue / It's on / Silver plan / Phobia / Egg rush / Doris ... is a little bit partial / Crackerjack.

— **MICKEY LEADER** – bass; repl. ANDY

		Heavenly	Columbia
Apr 92.	(12"one-sided/cd-s) (HVN 16/+CD) **WEEKENDER**	20	-

(12") (HVN 16X) – WEATHERALL'S WEEKENDER (Andy Weatherall remix).
(re-iss. Oct02 on 'Heavenly'; VJAY 27)

— In Oct'92, they did a version of RIGHT SAID FRED's 'DON'T TALK JUST KISS' on an 'Heavenly' artists EP. Proceeds were given to the Terence Higgins trust. Other tracks 'DEEPLY DIPPY' (Rockingbirds) + 'I'M TOO SEXY' (St.Etienne). Disbanded sometime in 1993, MAHER went back to work as a cassette/bootleg seller in Camden market.

| Jul 94. | (12") (HVN 38) **A BETTER LIFE. / ('A'mixes)** | | - |

— after FLOWERED UP officially split, DORNEY helped form REPUBLICA

FLUF

Formed: Seattle, Washington, USA ... 1992 by San Diegoans, O and JOHNNY DONHOWE (formerly of OLIVELAWN). The two recruited drummer MILES GILBERT and issued the mindless punk/pop album 'THE COMPACT DISC IS WEAK: MANGRAVY / SHOOTING PUTTY AT THE MOON (1993). This was a highly confusing debut set as it came under three titles (stated above but always recognised as 'MANGRAVY'). 'HOME IMPROVEMENTS' was delivered the following year and, again, it saw the HUSKER DU influenced 3-piece trying to make a stab at the irritating new wave of American punk. Bassist JOSH HIGGINS joined the line up for an overall disappointing third album 'WAIKIKI' (1997), where the band tried on an indie rock formula, that, in the end didn't work to their advantage. The last release from FLUF was 1998's 'ROAD RAGE'; the group being on "fuckophonic sound!" apparently. • **Covered:** ENTIRE (Spinnanes) / SHEELA NA GIG (PJ Harvey) / SONG IN D (Overwhelming Colorfast).

Album rating: MANGRAVY – SHOOTING PUTTY AT THE MOON (*5) / HOME IMPROVEMENTS (*4) / THE CLASSIC YEARS compilation (*6) / WAIKIKI (*4) / ROAD RAGE (*4)

OLIVELAWN

O – vocals, guitar / **JOHNNY DONHOWE** – bass / **EDDIE GLASS** – drums

		not iss.	Instant Noise
1990.	(7") <001> **INSTANT PUNK ROCK SONG. /**	-	
		not iss.	Nemesis
1990.	(7") <15> **4 IS GREATER THAN 2. /**	-	
1990.	(7") <20> **CAT'S FARM. /**	-	
1991.	(cd) <25> **SAP**	-	
		not iss.	Headhunter
1992.	(cd/lp) <HED 012-2/-1> **SOPHO-MORE JINX!**	-	

– Hate / Major label blues / Too slow / Beautiful feeling / 555 / I only love myself / Earthquake / Trick or treat / Burner / Heard it on the X / Season in Hell.

FLUF

O + **JOHNNY** recruited **MILES GILLETT** – drums

		Headhunter	Headhunter
—	issued a number of 7" singles		
Jul 93.	(cd/c) <(HED 018 CD/MC)> **COMPACT DISC IS WEAK: MANGRAVY / SHOOTING PUTTY AT THE MOON**		

– Degrader / Peanut butter / Hashin' it out / Kim Thaylis paw / Hecho del diable / Little baby / 10 x this / Redemption song / Time over / Long Beach / Bart / Flight of sperm.

| Sep 94. | (cd/c) <HED 032 CD/C> **HOME IMPROVEMENTS** | - | |

– Sticky bun / RK wins / Nirvana, brass ring / Rooked / Page 3 + 1 / Snapper / Stuffed animal / Power / Twister / Token instrumental / Broke / Tried / Mark Andrea.

| 1995. | (cd/c) <HED 050 CD/C> **THE CLASSIC YEARS** (singles compilation) | - | |

– 24-7 years / Dumpling / Skyrocket / One trick pony / Entire / The troll song / Lobster tree / Rod widdler / Sheela na gig / Song in D / All the fuckers live in Newport beach / Waffles.

FLUFFY

Formed: London, England . . . 1994 by AMANDA E. ROOTES, BRIDGET JONES, ANGIE ADAMS and PANDORA ORMSBY-GORE, the latter making way for new bassist HELEN STORES. The latest bunch of tough-nut girlies to pick up guitars and take on the boys at their own game, FLUFFY were initially accused of being talentless posh birds on the musical make. Dressing down in provocative mini-skirted grunge chic, the lassies had NME journos frothing at the mouth, especially when they proved their working class credentials. Taking their musical cue from ELASTICA, HOLE or even the GERMS, the feisty punkettes released their debut single, 'HYPERSONIC', in the Autumn of '95. With the hype machine still in overdrive, they released a second single, 'HUSBAND', scraping into the Top 60 the following February; the label, 'Tim/Kerr' subsequently issued it in America, where the girls recorded the '5 LIVE' EP shortly after. Landing themselves a lucrative contract with 'Virgin', they finally made it onto Top Of The Pops with single, 'NOTHING', a minor hit which previewed the accompanying debut album, 'BLACK EYE' (1996). Despite featuring a guest spot from the FOO FIGHTERS' PAT SMEAR, the record failed to live up to the publicity they'd already generated and with a final flop single, 'I WANNA BE YOUR LUSH', FLUFFY became yesterday's bunnies. • **Covered:** I'M A BOY (Who).

Album rating: BLACK EYE (*6)

AMANDA E. ROOTES – vocals, guitar / **BRIDGET JONES** – guitar / **HELEN STORES** – bass; who repl. PANDORA ORMSBY-GORE / **ANGIE ADAMS** – drums

		Parkway	Tim/Kerr
Sep 95.	(7") *(PARK 003)* **HYPERSONIC. / CROSSDRESSER**		
	(cd-s+=) *(PARK 003CD)* – Psychofudge.		
Feb 96.	(7") *(PARK 006)* <135> **HUSBAND. / DENY EVERYTHING**	58	May96
	(cd-s+=) *(PARK 006CD)* – Cheap.		

		Enclave	not iss.
Jul 96.	(10"ep/cd-ep) *(58571-1/-2)* **5 LIVE (live in New York)**		-
	– I wanna be your lush / Deny everything / Psychofudge / Bed of vomit / Scream.		

		Virgin	Capitol
Sep 96.	(7") *(VS 1614)* **NOTHING. / SCREAM (live)**	52	-
	(cd-s+=) *(VSCDT 1614)* – Laphog.		
	(7") *(VSX 1614)* – ('A'side) / I'm a boy.		
Oct 96.	(cd/c) *(CDV/TCV 2817)* <53020> **BLACK EYE**		
	– Nothing / Hypersonic / Black eye / Scream / I wanna be your lush / Crossdresser / Psychofudge / Too famous / Technicolour yawn / Cosmetic dog / Crawl / Husband / Dirty old bird / Cheap. *(lp on 'Enclave'; ENC 53020-1)*		
Jun 97.	(7") *(VS 1631)* **I WANNA BE YOUR LUSH. / BED OF VOMIT (live)**		-
	(cd-s) *(VSCDT 1631)* – ('A'side) / Reanimator / ('A'live).		
	(cd-s) *(VSCDX 1631)* – ('A'side) / Sick things / Deny everything.		

—— looked to have split after above

FLYING MEDALLIONS

Formed: London, England . . . 1992 by ALEX and his motley crew of feisty nutters; he broke his ankle during a stagedive following a fracas at their debut gig. Re-forming the group with fellow frontman CHRISTIAN, guitarist TOM WILLIAMS, drummer JASON TOKAR, Scots bassist DOUGIE PALOMPO and extras TASHA and STU (both on vocals), ALEX and the 'MEDALLIONS returned to the fold early in 1994. That summer, they delivered no less than three singles, although the latter two were somewhat overshadowed by the controversy stirred by their debut double-A single, 'RAPIST' / 'PAEDOPHILE'. Influenced by SNUFF, The DEAD KENNEDYS and LEATHERFACE (if the BEASTIE BOYS were three up front the FLYING M's were four!), the zany skate-punk 7-piece opened for the likes of OASIS and riled up audiences so much, they left before the bewildered headliners took stage. To promote their forthcoming first album, 'WE LOVE EVERYBODY AND EVERYTHING'S GREAT' (1994), they posed outside Soho sex shops and indeed did anything, everything & everybody for a laugh (so to speak). However, tragedy was to strike the band the following September, when their tour bus crashed while returning from a gig/festival in Belgium. 25 year-old DOUGIE suffered head injuries and died on the 16th of September that year. His infectious charm and anti-Tory stance (with humour one must add) sadly would be missed by his anarchic chums, the result being that The FLYING MEDALLIONS bravely took flight from the music world after a brief comeback early in '96. In 1999 (after featuring on a 'Fierce Panda' V/A compilation), the punk-rockers released two further singles, 'ADDICT' and 'LEMON' and supported OFFSPRING.

Album rating: WE LOVE EVERYBODY AND EVERYTHING'S GREAT (*6)

ALEX – vocals / **CHRISTIAN** – vocals / **TOM WILLIAMS** – guitar / **DOUGIE PALOMPO** (b. JOHN DOUGLAS PALOMPO, 1969, St. Andrews, Scotland) – bass / **JASON TOKAR** – drums / **TASHA** – vocals / **STU** – vocals

		Acupuncture	not iss.
Jul 94.	(7") *(JITM 1)* **RAPIST. / PAEDOPHILE**		-
Aug 94.	(7") *(JIZ 02)* **BOYRACER. / HOOLIGAN**		-
Sep 94.	(7"green) *(JIZ 03)* **GLUEY. / WORDS FOR WINDOWS**		-
	(cd-s+=) *(JIZD 03)* – Rapist (Tipper Gore mix).		
Oct 94.	(cd/c/lp) *(JIZ CD/C/LP 1)* **WE LOVE EVERYBODY AND EVERYTHING'S GREAT**		-
	– Boyracer / Rapist / Cow puncher / Gangsta / Gluey / Words for windows / Death metal / Paedophile / Hooligan / Super model / Magazine love / Crusty / Sharon.		

—— tragically, DOUGIE died on the 16th of September, 1995 and the band split after a brief return early in '96. Three years later, the group were back again with a new bass player

		Yassaba	not iss.
May 99.	(7"one-sided-colrd) *(YAS 011)* **ADDICT**		-
	(cd-s+=) *(YACD 011)* – Nicky / Ageism.		
Nov 99.	(7"colrd) *(YAS 012)* **LEMON. / CONSPIRACY**		-
	(cd-s+=) *(YACD 012)* – Addict (live).		

FLYING SAUCER ATTACK

Formed: Bristol, England . . . 1992 by DAVE PEARCE and RACHEL BROOK, who had just dropped out of LYNDA'S STRANGE VACATION. The duo's initial releases consisted of limited singles for the 'Heartbeat' imprint, the first of these, 'SOARING HIGH' appearing in '93. Specialising in arty Lo-Fi psychedelia, FSA were influenced by everything from SYD BARRETT, SPACEMEN 3 and ambient Krautrockers such as CAN and POPOL VUH to JOHN COLTRANE-esque experimental jazz. In 1994, the pair signed to 'Domino' ('Drag City' in the States), debuting later in the year with the single 'LAND BEYOND THE SUN'. Around the same time, they played their first live gigs, augmented by ex-LYNDA'S STRANGE VACATION members, MATT ELLIOT and KATE WRIGHT; the former worked under the THIRD EYE FOUNDATION banner, releasing 'SEMTEX' in '96, while he, RACHEL and KATE had surfaced as MOVIETONE. By this point, FSA had already released two compilation sets, 'DISTANCE' (1994) and 'CHORUS' (1995) issued either side of a follow-up album proper, 'FURTHER' (1995). Continuing with their idiosyncratic aural experimentation, PEARCE and BROOK released a further batch of 45's, while recording another album, 'NEW LANDS' (1997). FLYING SAUCER ATTACK and their soothing vocalist DAVE PEARCE issued the spacy, ambient and, at times, industrial set 'MIRROR' in 2000. Oozing with late-night mellowness, the set (and its weird artwork) displayed a number of tracks which seem to have been dedicated to various elements of space, earth and time. For example, you'd be forgiven for thinking tracks such as 'RIVERS', 'ISLANDS' and 'CHEMICALS' had floated into a smokey haze. Whereas 'DARK WINDS' and 'TIDES' promptly grounded the listener with its muffled feedback and pinching electronica.
• **Songwriters:** PEARCE or duo, except OUTDOOR MINER (Wire) / THE DROWNERS (Suede).

Album rating: FLYING SAUCER ATTACK (*7) / DISTANCE compilation (*8) / FURTHER (*7) / CHORUS compilation (*7) / NEW LANDS (*6) / MIRROR (*6)

DAVE PEARCE – slide guitar, etc / **RACHEL BROOK** – vocals, multi

		Heartbeat	VHF
Mar 93.	(ltd-7") *(FSA 6)* **SOARING HIGH. / STANDING STONE**		-
Jun 93.	(ltd-7") *(FSA 61)* **WISH. / OCEANS**		-
Nov 93.	(lp) *(FSA 62)* <VHF 11CD> **FLYING SAUCER ATTACK**		Aug94
	– My dreaming hill / A silent tide / Moonset / Make my dream / Wish / Popol Vuh 2 / The drowners / Popol Vuh / Still / The season is ours.		
	(cd-iss. Aug94 & Nov95 & Dec96 on 'V.H.F.'; same as US)		

—— added **MATT ELLIOT** (piano) + **KATE WRIGHT** (vocals)

		Domino	VHF
Oct 94.	(ltd-7"/7") *(RUG 23/+X)* **LAND BEYOND THE SUN. / EVERYWHERE WAS EVERYTHING**		-
Oct 94.	(cd/lp) *(WIG CD/LP 12)* <VHF 14CD> **DISTANCE** (singles compilation)		
	– Oceans / Standing stone / Crystal shade / Instrumental wish / Distance / November mist / Soaring high / Oceans 2.		

		Planet	not iss.
Apr 95.	(ltd-7") *(PUNK 008)* **BEACH RED LULLABY. / SECOND HOUR**		-

		Domino	Drag City
Apr 95.	(cd/lp) *(WIG CD/LP 20)* <DC 69> **FURTHER**		
	– Rainstorm blues / In the light of time / Come and close my eyes / For silence / Still point / Here I am / To the shore / She is the daylight.		
Sep 95.	(7") *(RUG 41)* **OUTDOOR MINER. / PSYCHIC DRIVING**		-
	(cd-s+=) *(RUG 41CD)* – Land beyond the sun / Everywhere was everything.		
Nov 95.	(cd/lp) *(WIG CD/LP 22)* <DC 87CD> **CHORUS** (compilation of singles & sessions)		-
	– Feedback song / Light in the evening / Popol Vuh III / Always / Feedback song (demo) / Second hour / Beach red lullaby / There but not there / February 8th / There dub.		
1996.	(7") <RAPT45 05> **AT NIGHT. /** Jessamine: **FROM HERE TO NOW OTHERWISE**	-	
	(above on 'Enraptured')		
Nov 96.	(cd-s)<12"> *(RUG 48CD)* <DC 109> **SALLY FREE AND EASY / THREE SEAS**		
Dec 96.	(m-cd) <DC 117> **DISTANT STATION**	-	
	– Part one / Part two.		
Jan 97.	(12"ep/cd-ep; as FLYING SAUCER ATTACK & ROY MONTGOMERY) (<VHF 26/+CD>) **GOODBYE EP**		
	– Goodbye / And goodbye / Whole day.		
	(above issued on 'V.H.F.')		

FLUF (cont) — continued from previous page:

		Goldenrod	not iss.
Jan 97.	(7") *(GR 56)* **split w/ J CHURCH**		

		Headhunter	M.C.A.
Jun 97.	(lp/cd) *(HED 70/+CD)* <11568> **WAIKIKI**		Mar97
	– Skip beat / Got everything / Pushin' back days / Bump / Chooser / Of the Bo / TV anthem / Sweet dough / Class action / Chocolate / Pipe bomb / Batwing / Gift of.		

		Honest Don's	Honest Don's
Aug 98.	(lp/cd) <(DON 017/+CD)> **ROAD RAGE**		
	– J'n it on the net / Leo and George / Livin' it up / Not that kind / Hang out / Fuck up / If I could feel good / Ocean / Wake up / Just like you / Garden weasle / $79 / Something's wrong / You and I agree.		

—— JOSH HIGGINS – bass; repl. JOHNNY

FLYING SAUCER ATTACK (cont)   THE GREAT INDIE DISCOGRAPHY   The 1990s

Sep 97. (7") *(RUG 57)* **COMING HOME. / HOPE**
Oct 97. (cd/lp) *(WIG CD/LP 38)* <*DC 137*> **NEW LANDS**
 – Past / Present / Up in her eyes / Respect / Night falls / Whole day song / Sea / Forever.

—— now just **PEARCE** when BROOK concentrated on MOVIETONE

                                                    Flying
                                                    Saucer
                                                    Attack   Drag City
Nov 99. (clear-lp/cd) *(FSA 64/+CD)* <*DC 177*> **MIRROR**   Jan00
 – Space 1999 / Suncatcher / Islands / Tides / Chemicals / Dark wind / Wintersong / Rivers / Dust / Rise / Starcity.

FLY PAN AM (see under ⇒ GODSPEED YOU BLACK EMPEROR!)

FOEHN

Formed: London, England . . . 1997 by former THIRD EYE FOUNDATION member, DEBBIE PARSONS. Combing the depths of modern day technology for fresh sounds/samples to augment her multi-talented array of conventional musical instrumentation, PARSONS broke free from contemporary barriers as she served up her psychedelic drum'n'bass soundtracks. Beginning with mini-set, 'INSIDEOUT' (1997), and going full-steam ahead with multi-layered long-players, 'SILENT LIGHT' (1999) and 'HIDDEN CAMERA SOUNDTRACKS' (2000), DEBBIE's atmospheric world displayed a love of sketchy, lo-fi electronica in a way post-MY BLOODY VALENTINE outfits such as FLYING SAUCER ATTACK and her aforementioned THIRD EYE FOUNDATION had also positively demonstrated. However, PARSONS took a hiatus after the latter 'Fat Cat'-records effort.

Album rating: INSIDEOUT EYES mini (*6) / SILENT LIGHT (*6) / HIDDEN CAMERA SOUNDTRACKS (*6)

DEBBIE PARSONS – vocals, multi-instruments, samples

                                         Swarf   Swarf
                                         Finger   Finger
Nov 97. (m-lp) *(<SF 016>)* **INSIDEOUT EYES**   May98
Dec 99. (cd) *(<SF 037CD>)* **SILENT LIGHT**   Jun00
 – Claustrophobic conversations / Tearing apart / Forgotten dreams fade black at me / Insect disco / Lament / No need to speak / Zima Okno Wschod / The streets & conversations are empty / I'd reach across the stars & cry for you / Extract from films / Lonely fights / Who chose you / Race me to the end / Memories grate in my mind / I don't believe a word you say / The world it has to do with the world . . . / Photographs of frozen fears / Times moves like slow beats / Can't seem to find my way / Czerwowy Wschod / You make me sick.

                                         Fat Cat   Fat Cat
                                         Splinter   Splinter
Mar 00. (cd) *(<FAT/SP 01>)* **HIDDEN CINEMA SOUNDTRACKS**   Apr00
 – To the forgotten forest deep in space / Chagrin d'amour / We tear at each other's hearts / A wild face pours words on the last beach / Chase in an empty space / Someone / Carousel beneath the sea / This time was in a dream / Shining secrets / The celebration ceases to impress / Built up to falling / Creep and hide / Seven thirty / We live in a sea of sound / Collapsing / Yellow star / So full up on emptiness / I really love high winds / Into the darkness and stars / Suddenly he realised he could fly / Like I'd been on a long journey / Pour vous timide voyou / Thanks for saying goodbye / Piano clatter / Without wings / Isolate / I almost touch / One day music came from the skies.
2000. (7"; split w/ CHASM) *<TP7 E6>* **EMILIANA VS FOEHN / CHASM**

—— FOEHN and DEBS have now called it a day

FOIL

Formed: Fauldhouse, West Lothian, Scotland . . . 1995 out of guitar-rockers The NAKED SEE (who issued two singles for 'Human Condition', 'NOTHING'S LOST' and 'FACELESS') and MUTINY STRINGS by frontman/guitarist HUGH DUGGIE, guitar-man COLIN McINALLY, bassist SHUG ANDERSON and drummer JIM ANDERSON. Spreading their word via a gig at London's Underground venue early the following year, the band were picked up by Paul Taylor, who signed them to Mute-backed imprint '13th Hour'. That summer, their debut single, 'REVIVING GENE', hit the shops and was noted for its unmistakable STEREOPHONICS-meets-SUGAR hooklines. Over the course of the next 18 months, FOIL giftwrapped a string of other, equally impressive 45's which previewed their first long-player, 'SPREAD IT ALL AROUND' (1998). Witty, barbed and exquisitely catchy, the set highlighted the aforementioned singles, 'ARE YOU ENEMY?', 'A PLACE TO HIDE' and a remixed 'REVIVER GENE', plus the comical 'ACID KEWPIE'. With new drummer ALAN LINDLAY on board, FOIL returned in 2000, although follow-up album, 'NEVER GOT HIP', did exactly as its title suggested.

Album rating: SPREAD IT ALL AROUND (*7) / NEVER GOT HIP (*6)

NAKED SEE

PADDY – vocals, guitar / **COLIN McINALLY** – guitar / **MOONEY** – bass / **JIM ANDERSON** – drums

                                         Human
                                         Condition not iss.
Aug 93. (7") *(HC 004)* **NOTHING'S LOST. / NEVER SO NEAR**
Sep 94. (cd-ep) *(HC 006)* **FACELESS EP**
 – Faceless / Endgames / Night-town / The journey.

FOIL

—— **HUGH DUGGIE** – vocals, guitar; repl. PADDY
—— **SHUG ANDERSON** – bass; repl. MOONEY

                                         13th Hour   Mute
Jul 96. (7") *(HOUR 8)* **REVIVER GENE. / SNECK**
 (cd-s+=) *(CDHOUR 8)* – In the ground.
Oct 96. (7") *(HOUR 9)* **LET IT GO BLACK. / MAN OVERBOARD**
 (cd-s+=) *(CDHOUR 9)* – Spleen / Voodoo autograph.
May 97. (7") *(HOUR 10)* **ARE YOU ENEMY? / GOIN' DOWN**
 (cd-s+=) *(CDHOUR 10)* – Denny.
Sep 97. (7"blue) *(HOUR 11)* **A PLACE TO HIDE. / DON'T COME AROUND**
 (cd-s+=) *(CDHOUR 11)* –
Nov 97. (7"green) *(HOUR 13)* **REVIVER GENE. / SEDATE ME**
 (cd-s+=) *(CDHOUR 13)* – Hey you / Play dead.
Jan 98. (cd/lp) *(13TH CD/LP 5)* <*MUS 25-2*> **SPREAD IT ALL AROUND**   Mar98
 – A.C. rocket / High wire / Acid kewpie / Control freak / Penicillin / A place to hide / Soup / Don't come around / Are you enemy? / Coup d'etat / Reviver gene / Carstairs.

—— **ALAN LINDLAY** – drums; repl. JIM
May 00. (7") *(HOUR 14)* **I'LL TAKE MY CHANCES. / UNDERTOW**
 (cd-s+=) *(CDHOUR 14)* – Careering / Reviving gene (CD-Rom).
Jun 00. (cd/lp) *(<13TH CD/LP 6>)* **NEVER GOT HIP**
 – Never got hip / Easy life and ignominy / Superhero No.1 / End of the world / Groundwork / Half life bunker / British East India Co. trafficker / Weird kid / I'll take my chances / The ghost of Vernon Howell / Claremont junction optimist.
Oct 00. (7") *(HOUR 15)* **SUPERHERO NO.1. / BAD GIRLFRIEND / HONESTY FIT**
 (cd-s) *(CDHOUR 15)* – ('A'side) / World is weird / Curse of me / Forget to breathe / Stranger's almanac.

FOLK IMPLOSION (see under ⇒ SEBADOH)

FONTANELLE (see under ⇒ JESSAMINE)

FOO FIGHTERS

Formed: Seattle, Washington, USA . . . April/May '94, after the death of KURT COBAIN (Nirvana), by drummer turned singer/guitarist DAVE GROHL. He subsequently brought in COBAIN stand-in, PAT SMEAR, along with NATE MANDEL and WILLIAM GOLDSMITH, taking the group name from the mysterious lights reported by pilots during World War II. Continuing the UFO concept, the group founded their own 'Roswell' label, (funded by 'Capitol') and debuted in the summer of '95 with UK Top 5 single, 'THIS IS A CALL'. More harmonic and positively life-affirming than NIRVANA (comparisons were inevitable), The FOO FIGHTERS offered up one of the most exciting debuts of the year; while the lyrics may have been somewhat cryptic, the obvious grunge influences were tempered with an infectious, pop-hardcore rush that was impossible to resist. The album sold well on both sides of the Atlantic, with GROHL & Co heading out on a successful series of festival dates. Work on the Gil Norton-produced follow-up, 'THE COLOUR AND THE SHAPE', got off to a difficult start with initial sessions in Seattle being scrapped. Further problems arose with the departure of sticksman GOLDSMITH halfway through recording, although GROHL subsequently completed the drum parts and the record was finally released in Spring '97 to rave reviews. Outpacing even the debut, The FOO FIGHTERS had come on leaps and bounds in the songwriting department, their rich post-grunge tapestry markedly more diverse. With good old romantic love as the driving theme of the record, the likes of the heart-rending (UK Top 20) 'EVERLONG' took starry-eyed, melodic distortion-pop to new (neck) hair-raising limits (complete with 'Evil Dead'-style video for that true-love atmosphere!), while more mellow musings like 'WALKING AFTER YOU' (used on the movie 'X-Files: Fight The Future') and 'DOLL' suggested GROHL was gaining enough confidence in his writing to chill out and reflect rather than continually going for the jugular. The group's growing self-belief was confirmed by some storming festival sets, while the album later came out top in rock 'bible', 'Kerrang!'s yearly critic's poll. After GROHL's brief expedition into film score work (with soundtrack 'TOUCH' being issued mid-'98), the band inked a deal with 'R.C.A.' and were ready to unleash a third album. 'THERE IS NOTHING LEFT TO LOSE' (1999), which disappointed no one with its melodic, HUSKER DU/PIXIES-inspired rock tunes, especially the hit 'LEARN TO FLY' (although I hear RUSH's 'Finding My Way' every time). GROHL and the mighty FOO FIGHTERS went straight to No.1 in October 2002, courtesy of album, 'ONE BY ONE', a clean, polished-up rock album that seemed to be lacking any kind of sparkle or charisma or just plain damn rawness. Top 10 hit, 'ALL MY LIFE' was very reminscent of the thrash-attack of QUEENS OF THE STONE AGE (well, GROHL had joined as drummer!), while elsewhere on the album, ballads were stuck clumsily alongside clean-cut out-and-out rock songs, and with no attempt made at rekindling the punk spirit. In short, papa GROHL's gonna have to get a brand new bag. Whenever! • **Covers:** OZONE (Kiss) / GAS CHAMBER (Angry Samoans) / BAKER STREET (Gerry Rafferty). • **Trivia:** GREG DULLI (Afghan Whigs) played guitar on 'X-static'.

Album rating: FOO FIGHTERS (*8) / THE COLOUR AND THE SHAPE (*9) / TOUCH soundtrack by Dave Grohl (*6) / THERE IS NOTHING LEFT TO LOSE (*8) / ONE BY ONE (*6)

FOO FIGHTERS (cont)

DAVE GROHL (b.14 Jan'69, Warren, Ohio) – vocals, guitar / **PAT SMEAR** – guitar (ex-GERMS) / **NATE MENDEL** – bass / **WILLIAM GOLDSMITH** – drums (both of SUNNY DAY REAL ESTATE)

			Roswell	Roswell
Jun 95.	(7",7"red)	(CL 753) **THIS IS A CALL. / WINNEBAGO**	5	-
	(12"luminous+=/cd-s+=) (12/CD CL 753) – Podunk.			
Jun 95.	(cd/c/lp)	(CD/TC+/EST 2266) <34027> **FOO FIGHTERS**	3	23

– This is a call / I'll stick around / Big me / Alone + easy target / Good grief / Floaty / Weenie beenie / Oh, George / For all the cows / X-static / Wattershed / Exhausted.

Sep 95.	(c-s/7"red) (TC+/CL 757) **I'LL STICK AROUND. / HOW I MISS YOU**	18	-
	(12"+=/cd-s+=) (12/CD CL 757) – Ozone.		
Nov 95.	(c-s/7"blue) (TC+/CL 762) **FOR ALL THE COWS. / WATTERSHED (live at Reading)**	28	-
	(cd-s+=) (CDCL 762) – 'A'-live at Reading).		
Mar 96.	(c-s/7"white) (TC+CL 768) **BIG ME. / FLOATY (BBC session) / GAS CHAMBER (BBC session)**	19	-
	(cd-s+=) (CDCL 768) – Alone + easy target (BBC session).		

—— **TAYLOR HAWKINS** – drums (of-ALANIS MORISSETTE) repl. GOLDSMITH

Apr 97.	(7") (CL 788) **MONKEY WRENCH. / THE COLOUR AND THE SHAPE**	12	-
	(cd-s+=) (CDCLS 788) – Up in arms (slow version).		
	(cd-s) (CDCL 788) – ('A'side) / Down in the park / See you (acoustic).		
May 97.	(cd/c/lp) (CD/TC+/EST 2295) <58530> **THE COLOUR AND THE SHAPE**	3	10

– Doll / Monkey wrench / Hey Johnny Park / My poor brain / Wind up / Up in arms / My hero / See you / Enough space / February stars / Everlong / Walking after you / New way home.

Aug 97.	(7"blue) (CL 792) **EVERLONG. / DRIVE ME WILD**	18	-
	(cd-s+=) (CDCL 792) – See you (live).		
	(cd-s) (CDCLS 792) – ('A'side) / Requiem / I'll stick around (live).		

—— now without SMEAR who was repl. by **FRANZ STAHL** (ex-SCREAM)

Jan 98.	(7"red) (CL 796) **MY HERO. / DEAR LOVER**	21	-
	(cd-s+=) (CDCL 796) – Baker Street (BBC session). (with enhanced cd+=) – Everlong (video) / Monkey wrench (video).		
Jun 98.	(cd; by DAVE GROHL) <(7243 855632-25)> **TOUCH** (music from the motion picture)		

– Bill Hill theme / August Murray theme / How do you do / Richie Baker's miracle / Making popcorn / Outrage / Saints in love / Spinning newspapers / Remission my ass / Scene 6 / This loving thing / Final miracle / Touch.
above featured guests LOUISE POST + JOHN DOE plus BARRETT JONES keyboards + ERIC RICHARDS slide guitar

Aug 98.	(7"/c-s/cd-s) (E 4100/+C/CD) **WALKING AFTER YOU (remix). / (Ween: Beacon Light)**	20	-

(above from the movie, 'X-Files: Fight The Future' on 'Elektra')

—— now trio of GROHL, MENDEL + HAWKINS/ added on tour **CHRIS SHIFLETT** – guitar (ex-NO USE FOR A NAME)

		R.C.A.	R.C.A.
Oct 99.	(c-s) (74321 71308-4) <album cut> **LEARN TO FLY / HAVE A CIGAR**	21	19
	(cd-s+=) (74321 71308-2) – Iron and stone.		
	(cd-s+=) (74321 71310-2) – Make a bet.		
Nov 99.	(cd/c/lp) <(07863 67892-2/-4/-1)> **THERE IS NOTHING LEFT TO LOSE**	10	10

– Stacked actors / Breakout / Learn to fly / Gimme stitches / Generator / Aurora / Live-in skin / Next year / Headwires / Ain't it the life / M.I.A.

Mar 00.	(cd-ep) (74321 74958-2) **GENERATOR EP**	-	-
	– Generator / Ain't it the life (two meter Dutch session) / Floaty (two meter Dutch session) / Fraternity / Breakout (live).		
	(cd-ep) <74321 74617-2> – ('A'side) / Learn to fly (live in Australia) / Stacked actors (live in Australia) / Breakout (live).		
Sep 00.	(7") (74321 79012-7) **BREAKOUT. / STACKED ACTORS (live)**	29	-
	(cd-s+=) (74321 79011-2) – Monkey wrench.		
	(cd-s) (74321 79010-2) – ('A'side) / Iron and stone / Learn to fly (live).		
Dec 00.	(7"/c-s) (74321 80926-7/-4) **NEXT YEAR. / BIG ME (live/session)**	42	-
	(cd-s+=) (74321 80926-2) – Next year (live/session).		
	(cd-s) (74321 80927-2) – ('A'side) / Baker street (live/session) / ('A'-CD-ROM).		
Oct 02.	(7") (74321 97315-7) **ALL MY LIFE. / SISTER EUROPE**	5	-
	(cd-s+=) (74321 97314-2) – Win or lose / ('A'-video).		
	(cd-s) (74321 97315-2) – ('A'side) / Danny says / One.		
Oct 02.	(cd/lp) (74321 97348-2/-1) <68008> **ONE BY ONE**	1	3

– All my life / Low / Have it all / Times like these / Disenchanted lullaby / Tired of you / Halo / Lonely as you / Overdrive / Burn away / Come back.

FOR CARNATION (see under ⇒ SLINT)

FOREVER PEOPLE
(see under ⇒ RAZORCUTS; in 80's section)

FOR SQUIRRELS

Formed: Gainsville, Florida, USA ... early 1993 by JON FRANCIS VIGLIATURA IV, BILL WHITE, TRAVIS MICHAEL TOOKE and JAY RUSSELL. These ill-fated alt-rockers already had two independently released CD's ('BAYPATH RD.' and 'PLYMOUTH') under their belts and were on the verge of making their major label debut when two of the band members, JACK and BILL, were fatally injured in a car smash on the 8th of September 1995 . The aforementioned album, 'EXAMPLE', was issued on '550/Epic' the following month and spent a respectable four weeks in the Top 200. Although RUSSELL's replacement, JACK GREIGO was also seriously injured, he and TOOKE decided to carry on playing, completing the devastated line-up with the addition of new bass player, ANDY LORD.

A low-key set, 'NEVER BET THE DEVIL YOUR HEAD', was delivered in '97.

Album rating: BAYPATH RD. (*6) / EXAMPLE (*6) / NEVER BET THE DEVIL YOUR HEAD (*4)

JON FRANCIS VIGLIATURA IV – vocals / **BILL WHITE** – guitar / **TRAVIS MICHAEL TOOKE** – guitar / **JAY RUSSELL** – drums

			not iss.	Subrosa
Jan 94.	(cd) <EP-101> **BAYPATH RD.**		-	

– Flagboy / Kabaret / Go on up / Kill the birds / R.O. / Nathaniel's song / Unicycle / Plymouth / Left behind / 3.

Dec 94.	(cd-ep) <EP-102> **PLYMOUTH EP**	-	

– Flagboy / Kabaret / Go on up / Kill the birds / Plymouth.

—— **JACK GREIGO** – drums; repl. RUSSELL

—— On the 8th of September 1995, VIGLIATURA and WHITE were killed in an automobile accident in which GREIGO also suffered a broken back

		not iss.	550 – Epic
Oct 95.	(cd/c) <BK 67150-2/-4> **EXAMPLE**		

– 8:02 PM / Orangeworker / Superstar / Mighty K.C. / Under Smithville / Long live the king / The immortal dog and pony show / Stark pretty / Disenchanted / Eskimo sandune.

—— although the remaining two carried on after above disaster (added **ANDY LORD** – bass)

Jul 97.	(cd) <BK 67846> **NEVER BET THE DEVIL YOUR HEAD**	-	

– World's greatest lover / Rollercoaster / Damn the youth / Antigen fiend / The life inside me killed this song / Buzzard / Aerial / Never the best / Murder an angel / Madness is genius by design / pleH / Lullaby to the enemy / Pretend.

FOR STARS

Formed: San Francisco, California, USA ... 1998 by MIKE YOUNG, CHRISTINA PREJA, CARLOS FORSTER, TOMMY CASEY, DAN PARIS and MIKE FUNK. Loosely playing together for one year, this sad-core collective issued their self-titled debut album in 1999 without almost any formal introduction. Hot on its heels, the group delivered 'WINDOWS FOR STARS' in the same year, a much more developed set, it included pitch-perfect instrumentation and some of the best lyrics written by a young American band, courtesy of the moody FORSTER. In early 2000, FUNK was replaced with NICK FRITAS and the group squeezed out another transcient beauty in the shape of 'WE ARE ALL BEAUTFUL PEOPLE' (2001). Some may be in the gutter, but when it came to FS, they were definitely looking up to the stars . . .

Album rating: FOR STARS (*6) / WINDOWS FOR STARS (*7) / WE ARE ALL BEAUTIFUL PEOPLE (*5)

CARLOS FORSTER – vocals, guitar / **CHRISTIAN PREJA** – bass / **MIKE YOUNG** – guitar / **DAN PARIS** – keyboards / **MIKE FUNK** – drums / **TOMMY CASSEY** – percussion

		Laundry Room	Full Frequency Range
Feb 99.	(cd) (LRR 9611-2) <FFR 3> **FOR STARS**		

– Cowboys lost at sea / Movies / Playing at a party / We be friends / Lot like me / Field of fire / N.Y. gets cold / Don't it feel good / Rain, thunder / Come along / Aging.

		not iss.	Future Farmer
Oct 99.	(cd) <FF 006> **WINDOWS FOR STARS**	-	

– Spectators / Sorry / Whose idea / Go ahead / Burn the buildings / Catholic school / Bleu / Run from me / The kissing scene / Golden boy / Compliment me, baby. *(UK-iss.Jun01; same as US)*

		Acuarela	Acuarela
Dec 00.	(cd-ep) <(NOIS 014)> **AIRLINE PEOPLE**		

– At the end of the world / Brown skin saint / Motorway / The racecar driving scene / Airline people.

		Shifty Disco	not iss.
Mar 01.	(cd-s) (DISCO 0103) **SPECTATORS**		-

—— now without FUNK

		Munich	Future Farmer
Jun 01.	(cd) (MRCD 218) <FF 011> **WE ARE ALL BEAUTIFUL PEOPLE**		

– Wires / I got connected / How it goes / Back in France / Beautifully . . . / In open plains / The astronaut song / People party / Ony star / There was a river / If I could.

FOSCA (see under ⇒ ORLANDO)

FOUNTAINS OF WAYNE

Formed: New York City, New York, USA ... 1995 by the songwriting team of ADAM SCHLESINGER and CHRIS COLLINGWOOD, who met at Williams College in Massachusetts in 1987. ADAM, also of the revered outfit IVY, helped form the 'Scratchie' label with D'ARCY of The SMASHING PUMPKINS, the former having already recorded under the moniker of PINNWHEEL alongside CHRIS. Other moonlighting shenanigans included penning 'THAT THING YOU DO' for mock outfit The WONDERS, which featured in the movie of the same name starring Tom Hanks. FOW signed to 'Atlantic' in '96 and achieved some degree of success with debut single, 'RADIATION VIBE', a taste of retro 60's BEACH BOYS-esque pop with an edgy 90's slant. Their eponymous debut followed later that summer, a fine collection of power-pop akin to a heavier LEMONHEADS. The slightly wanton, 'UTOPIA PARKWAY' (1999), was too clean-cut and all-American for some, their Modern Rock tunes, 'DENISE' and 'RED DRAGON TATTOO' (both singles), pop puree for college kids into 'Happy Days' nostalgia.

Album rating: FOUNTAINS OF WAYNE (*8) / UTOPIA PARKWAY (*6)

ADAM SCHLESINGER (b.1968) – vocals, guitars / **CHRIS COLLINGWOOD** (b.1968) – vocals, guitar / live work:- **JODY PORTER** – bass (ex-BELLTOWER) / **BRIAN YOUNG** – drums (of The POSIES)

		Atlantic	Atlantic
Mar 97.	(7"/c-s) (A 5626/+C) **RADIATION VIBE. / KARPET KING**	32	-
	(cd-s+=) (A 5626CD) – Janice's party / Imperia.		
Apr 97.	(7"/c-s) (A 5612/+C) **SINK TO THE BOTTOM. / CAN'T GET IT OUT OF MY HEAD**		-
	(cd-s+=) (A 5612CD) – Kid gloves.		
May 97.	(cd/c) <(7567 92725-2/-4)> **FOUNTAINS OF WAYNE**	67	
	– Radiation vibe / Sink to the bottom / Joe Rey / She's got a problem / Survival car / Barbara H. / Sick day / I've got a flair / Leave the biker / You curse at girls / Please don't rock me tonight / Everything's ruined.		
Jul 97.	(7"/c-s) (AT 0004/+C) **SURVIVAL CAR. / COMEDIENNE**	53	-
	(cd-s+=) (AT 004CD) – I want you around (4-track demo).		
Oct 97.	(7"/c-s) (AT 0016/+C) **BARBARA H. / PLACES**		-
	(cd-s+=) (AT 0016CD) – She's got a problem (live).		
Dec 97.	(7"/c-s) (AT 0020/+C) **I WANT AN ALIEN FOR CHRISTMAS. / THE MAN IN THE SANTA SUIT**	36	-
	(cd-s+=) (AT 0020CD) – Haunukah under the stars.		
Mar 99.	(7"/c-s) (AT 0053/+C) **DENISE. / I KNOW YOU WELL**	57	-
	(cd-s+=) (AT 0053CD) – I'll do the driving.		
May 99.	(7"/c-s) (AT 0067/+C) **RED DRAGON TATTOO. / TODAY'S TEARDROPS**		
	(cd-s+=) (AT 0067CD) – Nightlight.		
May 99.	(cd/c) <(7567 83177-2/-4)> **UTOPIA PARKWAY**		
	– Utopia parkway / Red dragon tattoo / Denise / Hat and feet / The valley of malls / Troubled times / Go, hippie / A fine day for a parade / Amity gardens / Laser show / Lost in space / Prom theme / It must be summer / The senator's daughter.		
Sep 99.	(7"/c-s) (AT 0074/+C) **TROUBLED TIMES. / YOU'RE JUST NEVER SATISFIED**		
	(cd-s+=) (AT 0074CD) – These days.		

— JODY is currently in a side project The ASTROJET while FOW (minus BRIAN) have been on tour in 2002

FOUR TET (see under ⇒ FRIDGE)

FRANK & WALTERS

Formed: Cork, Ireland ... 1990 by young brothers PAUL and NIALL LINEHAM plus neighbour ASHLEY KEATING. Signed to the Celtic-friendly 'Setanta' label, the trio debuted their charmingly eccentric musical wares on 1991's 'THE FRANK AND WALTERS EP', 'Father Ted'-style power pop vignettes of everyday rural Irish life in stark contrast to the grunge/baggy dominated indie scene of the day. A follow-up EP, 'THE FRANK AND WALTERS 2', offered up more of the same and boasted the infamous 'FASHION CRISIS HITS NEW YORK' – although by this point the lads had moved to home of the Wombles, Wimbledon! – forever the band's defining moment and the track which saw them adopted as a kind of mascot by the indie press. A subsequent switch to 'Go! Discs' saw the lads hit the UK Top 50 for the first time with the EDWYN COLLINS-produced 'HAPPY BUSMAN' EP, the ex-ORANGE JUICE man also overseeing their much anticipated 'TRAINS, BOATS AND PLANES' (1992) debut album. With many previously available tracks, the record wasn't exactly essential listening and only scraped into the Top 40; stretching the FRANK & WALTERS concept over a whole album was probably too much too soon. Yet help was at hand courtesy of twee master, IAN BROUDIE (of The LIGHTNING SEEDS), who remixed 'AFTER ALL' and turned it into a near Top 10 hit. But even BROUDIE's deft touch couldn't secure a Top 40 placing for a revamped 'FASHION CRISIS . . .', as the band were looking increasingly bereft of original ideas and wearing thin the patience of a fickle music press. Returning homewards to think again was probably the best option although their long awaited return found them back with 'Setanta', the label issuing a slow-burning follow-up album, 'GRAND PARADE' (1997). After the latter's strident power-jangling, The FRANK & WALTERS belatedly discovered the wonders of technology on 'BEAUTY BECOMES MORE THAN LIFE' (1999): there were still echoes of U2, but in this case latter-day U2 rather than the bombastic 80's version. With 'GLASS' (2001), meanwhile, the Irishmen further refined their sound and seemed at last to have outgrown the musical petulance and tendency to overperform which characterised their earlier releases. • **Songwriters:** Group except; FUNKY COLD MEDINA (Tone Loc) / I'M A BELIEVER (The Monkees) / LOVE IS IN THE AIR (John Paul Jones) / CEMETERY GATES (Smiths).

Album rating: TRAINS, BOATS AND PLANES (*6) / GRAND PARADE (*6) / BEAUTY BECOMES MORE THAN LIFE (*6) / GLASS (*5) / THE FRANK AND WALTERS compilation (*6)

PAUL LINEHAM – vocals, bass / **NIALL LINEHAM** – guitar / **ASHLEY KEATING** – drums

		Setanta	not iss.
Jul 91.	(12"ep) (SET 007) **THE FRANK AND WALTERS E.P. 1**		-
	– Walters trip / Frank's night / Michael / Never ending staircase.		
Oct 91.	(12"ep) (SET 009) **THE FRANK AND WALTERS (E.P. 2)**		-
	– Fashion crisis hits New York / Rasputin / Daisy chain / Angela Cray.		
	(c-ep+=/cd-ep+=) (SET 009 MC/CD) – E.P. 1 (tracks).		
		Go! Discs	London
Jan 92.	(7") (HOO-HA 1) **WE ARE THE FRANK AND WALTERS. / HUMPHREY**		-
Mar 92.	(7") (HOO 2) **HAPPY BUSMAN. / THE WORLD CARRIES ON**	49	-
	(c-ep+=/12"ep+=/cd-ep+=) (HOO MC/X/CD 2) – Humphrey / If you're still waiting.		
Sep 92.	(7"/c-s) (HOO/+MC 3) **THIS IS NOT A SONG. / DAVY CHASE**	46	-
	(12"+=/cd-s+=)(w/free 7"clear+=) (HOO X/CD 3)(HOO HA 4) – Laurence Olivier / Happy busman (live).		
Oct 92.	(cd/c/lp) (828402-2/-4/-1) **TRAINS, BOATS AND PLANES**	36	
	– This is not a song / Walters trip / Trainspotters / After all / Happy busman / Fashion crisis hits New York / Daisy chain / John and Sue / Bake us a song / Time / High is low. (re-iss. Jul93; same) (cd re-iss. Sep02 on 'Setanta'; SETCD 117)		
Nov 92.	(cd/c) <162-351 005-2/-4> **THE FRANK AND WALTERS** (3 EP's collection)		-
Dec 92.	(c-ep/cd-ep) (HOO MC/CD 4) **AFTER ALL / THE DAY BEFORE THE WORLD ENDED / THE TURQUOISE GARDENS / MICHAEL (live)**	11	
	(12"ep) (HOOX 4) – (first 3 tracks) / Funky cold Medina.		
	(cd-ep) (HOCCD 4) – ('A'side) / Love is in the air / I'm a believer / Funky cold Medina.		
Apr 93.	(7"ep/c-ep/cd-ep) (HOO/+MC/CD 5) **FASHION CRISIS HITS NEW YORK / TIME (acoustic). / FRANK'S RIGHT / NEVER ENDING STAIRCASE**	42	-
	(cd-s) (HOACD 5) – ('A'side) / Rasputin / Daisy chain / Angela Cray.		
		Setanta	Go! Discs
Jul 96.	(7"ep/cd-ep) (HOO/+CD 6) **INDIAN OCEAN / PATHWAYS. / YOU CAN'T TAKE TOO MUCH NOTICE / RESTRAINT**		-
	(cd-s+=) (HOOCD 6) – You can't take too much notice / Restraint.		
Aug 96.	(7"ep/cd-ep; w-drawn) (HOO/+CD 7) **COLOURS. / SURRENDER TO WIN. / YOU ASKED ME / LAST TRAIN HOME**		-
Mar 97.	(cd-s) (SETCD 051) **COLOURS / SURRENDER TO WIN / YOU ASKED ME**		-
Jun 97.	(cd) (SETCD 054) <828823> **GRAND PARADE**		
	– Colours / Indian Ocean / Little dolls / Russian ship / I suppose / Saturday night / How can I exist? / Mrs. Xavier / Have you ever / Tony Cochrane / Landslide / Lately.		
Jun 97.	(c-s/cd-s) (SET MC/CDA 055) **HOW CAN I EXIST? / FAST ANTHONY (TONY COCHRANE) / LAST TRAIN HOME**		-
	(cd-s) (SETCDB 055) – ('A'side) / Indian Ocean (acoustic) / Little dolls.		
		Setanta	Red Ink
Jul 97.	(cd-ep) <WK 36457> **INDIAN OCEAN EP (live)**		-
	– Indian Ocean / Restraint / Pathways / Last train home / Fast Anthony / Little dolls (acoustic).		
1998.	(7"blue-ep) (ER 191) **FOUR SONGS EP SINGLE CLUB**		-
	– Indian Ocean (acoustic) / Little dolls (acoustic) / Pathways / Restraint. (above issued on 'Elefant')		
Oct 99.	(cd-s) (SETCD 064) **PLENTY TIMES / OPEN UP / FALLING OUT OF LOVE**		-
Oct 99.	(cd) (SETCD 065) <WK 45714> **BEAUTY BECOMES MORE THAN LIFE**		
	– Plenty times / Stop / Woman / Simple times / 7.30 / Let me know / Something happened to me / Time we said goodnight / Today / Take me through this life / Don't stop / Castaway / Until the end. (cd w/cd+=; SETCD 65-2) – Colours / Daisy chain / Indian Ocean / Fashion crisis hits New York / How can I exist.		
Feb 00.	(7"m) (SET 074) **SOMETHING HAPPENED TO ME. / SOMETHING HAPPENED TO ME (acoustic) / TIME WE SAID GOODNIGHT (live)**		Jul02
	(cd-s) (<SETCD 074>) – ('A'side) / Take me through this life (remixed by Kevin Shields) / An elegant chaos.		
Oct 00.	(cd) (SETCD 079) **GLASS**		-
	– Underground / Isn't it time / New York / 6 becomes 9 / Sinking / Talking about you / Paradise / Ancestors / Forgiveness / Facing silence / I will be king / Looking for America.		
Jan 01.	(7") (SET 082) **UNDERGROUND. / ROCK AND ROLL**		-
	(cd-s) (SETCD 082) – ('A'side) / Pistons / Simple times (Sean O'Hagan remix) / ('A'-video).		

– compilations, etc. –

Aug 02.	(cd) Setanta; (<SETCD 104>) **THE FRANK AND WALTERS** (compilation)		Oct02
	– Colours / Plenty times / Fashion crisis hits New York / This is not a song / How can I exist / New York / After all / Walters trip / Indian Ocean / Underground / Daisy chain / Time we said goodnight / Tony Cochrane.		

Paula FRAZER (see under ⇒ TARNATION)

FREAKWATER (see under ⇒ ELEVENTH DREAM DAY; in 80's section)

FREAKY REALISTIC

Formed: Peckham, London ... 1991 by singer-songwriter JUSTIN ANDERSON and Texan rapper, MICHAEL LORD (ex-NASTY GROOVE). Hooking up with foxy Japanese vocliast, AKI OMORI, the pair set out to realise their 70's inspired, space-themed, genre blurring musical vision. Armed with only synths, samplers and toy rayguns, the trio beamed up a series of funky singles for 'Polydor' over the course of '92/'93, beginning with underground club favourite, 'SOMETHING NEW – COSMIC LOVE VIBES'. This was quickly followed by 'KOOCHIE RYDER' and 'LEONARD NIMOY' which became minor chart hits. DEE-LITE had already covered similar territory much more successfully however and by the release of FREAKY REALISTIC's debut album, 'FREALISM' (1993), the dayglo hippie-indie-pop that had characterised the charts of the early 90's had already begun to dissipate.

Album rating: FREALISM (*5)

FREAKY REALISTIC (cont)

JUSTIN ANDERSON – songwriting/vocals / AKI OMORI – vocals / MICHAEL LORD – rapper/vocals

		Polydor	not iss.
Nov 92.	(cd-s) *(FRECD 1)* **SOMETHING NEW – COSMIC LOVE VIBES** (mixes; radio / full frealistic / fat planet / dubrosa)		-
	(12"+=) *(FREAX 1)* – ('A'-clubby rapino mix)		
Mar 93.	(cd-s) *(FRECD 2)* **KOOCHIE RYDER** / ('A'-fat planet mix) / ('A'-boomshanka flying mix – part 1) / **THE MOST**	52	-
	(12"/cd-s) *(FRE AX/DD 2)* – ('A'mixes; boomshanka flying parts 1 & 2) / full frealistic / sugarsweet part 1 & 2 / fat planet)		
Jun 93.	(cd-s) *(FRECD 3)* **LEONARD NIMOY / LEONARD NIMOY** (global grooves breakfast club 106 mix) / **BIG PICTURE / FREAKY BLUE**	71	-
	(cd-s) *(FREDD 3)* – ('A'mixes; E-Bloc elustrious fatt guitar frenzy / E-Bloc elustrious fatt bass frenzy / extended / global grooves breakfast club 106 / king of the freaky jungle / L.S. Diezel).		
Oct 93.	(cd/d-lp) *(517 919-2/-1)* **FREALISM**		-
	– Frealism / Something new – Cosmic love vibes / Koochie ryder / Love that loves / Leonard Nimoy / Reach / Salivate special / Trickle in / Imaginary pavillions / Make it happen / Sooner / The most / This is Freaky Realistic / Frealism (reprise). (lp w/free 12"+=) – Something new – Cosmic love vibes (the clubby rapino mix) / Something new – Cosmic love vibes (dubrosa mix) / Koochie ryder (boomshanka flying mix part 1) / Koochie ryder (fat planet mix) / Leonard Nimoy (E-bloc elustrious fatt guitar frenzy / Leonard Nimoy (global grooves breakfast club 106 mix).		
Dec 93.	(cd-s) *(FRECD 4)* **REACH / SOMETHING NEW – COSMIC LOVE VIBES / LEONARD NIMOY / SOONER**		-
	(cd-s) *(FREDD 4)* – ('A'mixes; can can / D-street / joy for life) / Koochie ryder (boomshanka flying mix part 1).		
	(12") *(FREAX 4)* – ('A'mixes; extended / joy for life / can can / D-street).		

— when MICHAEL departed nothing more was heard from the outfit; JUSTIN later formed MAINS IGNITION who released 'SPARKY'S BOMBSCHOOL' in 2000

FREE DESIGN

Formed: New York City, New York, USA ... 1966 by Delevan, NY-born DEDRICK siblings CHRIS (a multi-talented instrumentalist), BRUCE and SANDY. Although fairly ignored by the charts of their time, the group's gossamer, sugary sound became hugely influential for the throngs of twee and chamber pop bands that sprung up in the nineties. Their beginnings as a group and a family were steeped in music, via their father, ART, being a respected trombonist and arranger for Vaughn Monroe. Inspired by the impact they made on the city's folk circuit the threesome, with the assistance of dad, made a demo recording which caught the ear of experienced producer and orchestrator, Enoch Light, who subsequently notched them on to his 'Project 3' label. Almost immediately, the newly formed group released the LP, 'KITES ARE FUN' (1967), with the title track being their first single. The 7" reached No.114 on the Billboard pop chart (although it did breach the Top 40 adult contemporary chart) and incredibly was to be their biggest chart success. The album showcased the beautiful baroque pop of The FREE DESIGN, with lovely and adroit string and horn arrangements. As well as including the CHRIS penned classics 'UMBRELLAS' and 'WHEN LOVE IS YOUNG', it also comprised brilliant takes on such timeless classics as the Beatles' 'MICHELLE' and Simon & Garfunkel's 'THE 59TH STREET BRIDGE SONG (FEELIN' GROOVY)'. Easily the equal of contemporary harmony based peers in the shape of The MAMAS & THE PAPAS and The ASSOCIATION, the 'DESIGN nevertheless failed to see any rewards. The newly graduated sister, ELLEN, bolstered the group's vocal sound on their second album 'YOU COULD BE BORN AGAIN' (1968), which again showcased the DEDRICK family's undoubted musical skills. Highpoints included their own tune 'A LEAF HAS VEINS' and the wonderful reading of Duke Ellington's 'I LIKE THE SUNRISE'. Unfortunately this offering refused again to give them the chart attention that it merited, causing them to write and record the wry, '2002 – A HIT SONG', in response to the record buying public's ignorance. This track was included on their third full-length offering, 'HEAVEN / EARTH' (1969). Changing their tack, the band marketed themselves towards the children's market, a la The PARTRIDGE FAMILY, on their fourth album, 'SING FOR VERY IMPORTANT PEOPLE' (1970). Thankfully this was not a path they continued, coming back towards the AOR market with the LP, 'STARS / TIME / BUBBLES / LOVE' issued the same year. By the sixth album 'ONE BY ONE' (1972), the family was still in fine musical fettle, wandering into new areas exemplified by the funky 'LIKE TO LOVE' and the album standout 'FRIENDLY MAN'. Unfortunately though, this was to be the last record for 'Project 3' who dropped them the next year. The DEDRICK's took this as a sign to rethink and move to Canada, where things did not really improve; CHRIS recorded the unreleased solo album, 'BE FREE', and as a family they put down their seventh full-length offering, 'THERE IS A SONG' (1973), for 'Ambrotype'. They disbanding two years later. CHRIS did continue in the musical field with the formation of the STAR SCAPE SINGERS and songwriting, while arrangement work for CANADIAN BRASS as well as a host of work in film and television music kept him busy. By the final decade of the twentieth century, it seemed that the dust had settled on the FREE DESIGN output, although their name-checking and disciple-type worship by a host of young indie bands from CORNELIUS to STEREOLAB meant that the record industry again took notice of them; a compilation 'KITES ARE FUN: THE BEST OF FREE DESIGN' was unleashed in 1998. Due to the renewed interest the original trio of CHRIS, SANDY and BRUCE re-formed, writing and recording new material for the album release 'COSMIC PEEKABOO' (2001), which they dedicated to the memory of their other sister STEFANIE. This set saw them return to their former glories and amusingly featured the partner hit to '2002 – A HIT SONG', in the shape of 'THE HOOK'. The group also made a sterling contribution to the BEACH BOYS tribute LP 'Caroline Now!', with the fittingly chosen cover 'ENDLESS HARMONY'.

• **Covered:** ELEANOR RIGBY (Beatles) / TIME AND LOVE (Laura Nyro) / HAPPY TOGETHER (Bonner & Gordon) / BUTTERFLIES ARE FREE (. . . Schwartz) / CALIFORNIA DREAMIN' (Mamas & The Papas) / YOU ARE MY SUNSHINE (Jimmie Davis – Charles Mitchell) / IF I WERE A CARPENTER (Tim Hardin) / MEMORIES (Davis – Strange) / WHERE DO I GO (from 'Hair') / HURRY SUNDOWN (Hugo Montenegro) / RAINDROPS KEEP FALLING ON MY HEAD (Bacharach & David) / TOMORROW IS THE FIRST DAY OF THE REST OF MY LIFE (Courtney – Link) / LIGHT MY FIRE (Doors) / etc.

Album rating: KITES ARE FUN: THE BEST OF THE FREE DESIGN compilation (*7) / COSMIC PEEKABOO (*6) / THE VERY BEST OF FREE DESIGN compilation (*7)

CHRIS DEDRICK – multi-instruments / **BRUCE DEDRICK** – vocals / **SANDY DEDRICK** – vocals / + session people

		Project 3	Project 3
1967.	(7") *<45-1324>* **KITES ARE FUN. / THE PROPER ORNAMENTS**	-	-
1967.	(lp) *<33-5019>* **KITES ARE FUN** – Kites are fun / Make the madness stop / When love is young / The proper ornaments / My brother Woody / The 59th Street bridge song (feelin' groovy) / Don't turn away / Umbrellas / Michelle / Never tell the world / A man and a woman / Stay another season.	-	-
1968.	(7") *<45-1331>* **YOU BE YOU AND I'LL BE ME. / NEVER TELL THE WORLD**	-	-
1968.	(7") *<45-1336>* **UMBRELLAS. / I FOUND LOVE**	-	-

— added **ELLEN DEDRICK** – vocals

1968.	(7") *<45-1345>* **MAKE THE MADNESS STOP. / ELEANOR RIGBY**	-	-
1968.	(lp) *<33-5031>* **YOU COULD BE BORN AGAIN** – You could be born again / A leaf has veins / California' dreamin' / The windows of the world / Eleanor Rigby / Quartet No.6 in D minor / I like the sunrise / I found love / Daniel dolphin / Happy together / Ivy on a windy day / An elegy.	-	-
1968.	(7") *<45-1347>* **CLOSE YOUR MOUTH (IT'S CHRISTMAS). / CHRISTMAS IS THE DAY**	-	-
1969.	(7") *<45-1350>* **YOU COULD BE BORN AGAIN. / A LEAF HAS VEINS**	-	-
1969.	(lp) *<33-5037>* **HEAVEN / EARTH** – My very own angel / Now is the time / If I were a carpenter / You be you and I'll be me / Girls alone / 2002 – a hit song / Summertime / Where do I go / Hurry sundown / Memories / Dorian benediction.	-	-
1969.	(7") *<45-1356>* **WHERE DO I GO. / GIRLS ALONE**	-	-
1969.	(7") *<45-1358>* **DORIAN BENEDICTION. / SUMMERTIME**	-	-
1969.	(7") *<45-1366>* **2002 – A HIT SONG. / HURRY SUNDOWN**	-	-
1970.	(7") *<45-1370>* **BUTTERFLIES ARE FREE. / MY VERY OWN ANGEL**	-	-
1970.	(7") *<45-1387>* **DON'T CRY, BABY. / TIME AND LOVE**	-	-
1970.	(lp) *<33-4006>* **SING FOR VERY IMPORTANT PEOPLE** – Don't cry, baby / Can you tell me how to get to Sesame Street / Children's waltz / Scarlet tree / Little cowboy / Love you / Ronda go 'round / Bubbles / Daniel dolphin / Kites are fun / Lullaby.	-	-
1970.	(lp) *<33-5045>* **STARS / TIME / BUBBLES / LOVE** – Bubbles / Tomorrow is the first day of the rest of your life / Kije's ouija / Butterflies are free / Stay off your frown / Starlight / Time and love / I'm a Yogi / Raindrops keep falling on my head / Howdiadoo (fly me down) / That's all people / Close your mouth (it's Christmas).	-	-
1971.	(7") *<45-1404>* **A FRIENDLY MAN. / STAY OFF OF YOUR FROWN**	-	-
1972.	(lp) *<33-5061>* **ONE BY ONE** – One by one / Felt so good / Friendly man / Light my fire / Like to love / You are my sunshine / Go lean on a river / Going back / Love me / Friends (thank you all) / Christmas is the day.	-	-

— CHRIS issued a solo, 'BE FREE' (1972)

— disbanded in 1975 after one set for 'Amrotype', 'THERE IS A SONG' (1973); CHRIS became part of STAR SCAPE SINGERS

— (2000) CHRIS, SANDY + BRUCE re-formed

		Marina	Marina
Mar 01.	(cd) *<(MA 52)>* **COSMIC PEEKABOO** – Peekaboo / Younger son / McCarran airport / Destiny / Springtime / Listen / The hook / Music room / The only treasure / Day breaks / Perfect love.		-

– compilations, etc. –

Apr 98.	(cd) *Siesta; (SIESTA 68CD)* **BUBBLES**		-
Jul 98.	(cd) *Varese Sarabande; <5954>* **KITES ARE FUN: THE BEST OF THE FREE DESIGN** – Kites are fun / I found love / Bubbles / My brother Woody / 2002 – a hit song / Stay another season / Felt so good / Kije's ouija / My very own angel / Never tell the world / A man and a woman / Love you / Howdiadoo (fly me down) / Now is the time / You are my love.	-	-
Apr 99.	(cd/10"d-lp) *Siesta; (SIESTA 84 CD/LP)* **RAINDROPS**		-
Sep 99.	(cd/10"d-lp) *Siesta; (SIESTA 104 CD/LP)* **UMBRELLAS**		-
Sep 01.	(cd) *Cherry Red; <(CDMRED 194)>* **THE VERY BEST OF FREE DESIGN** – Chorale / Kites are fun / Bubbles / I found love / My brother Woody / Never tell the world / Love me / Love you / I wanna be there / Daniel dolphin / Starlight / 2002 – a hit song / Children's waltz / One by one / You are my sunshine / You could be born again / Kije's ouija / Love does not die / Tomorrow is the first day of the rest of my life.		

FREEHEAT
(see under ⇒ JESUS & MARY CHAIN; 80's section)

FREE KITTEN
(see under ⇒ SONIC YOUTH; in 80's section)

FRENCH KICKS

Formed: Brooklyn, New York, USA ... 1998 by Washington D.C. lads, MATT STINCHCOMB, JAMIE KRENTS and NICK STUMPF. On relocating to New York in the late part of the decade they met frontman JOSH WISE and became The FRENCH KICKS. 1999 saw their eponymously-titled debut EP hit the local shops and cause enough of a stir to keep the band in touring, leading them to a more fully-fledged contract with both 'Star Time' (Stateside) and ALAN McGEE's new label, 'Poptones' (in the UK); both labels keen to pick up artists doing the growing garage rock/proto-punk revival trip, a la The WHITE STRIPES and The STROKES. Putting out their sophomore EP, 'YOUNG LAWYER' in 2001, the band showed they had the energy and growing adeptness at catchy rock riffery. Their follow-up debut LP, 'ONE TIME BELLS', built upon this, with no falling back in vitality, and an added increase in songwriting prowess and performance.

Album rating: YOUNG LAWYER mini (*5) / ONE TIME BELLS (*7)

JOSH WISE – vocals, guitar / **MATT STINCHCOMB** – vocals, guitar / **NICK STUMPF** – vocals, drums / **JAMIE KRENTS** – bass

		not iss.	My Pal God
Oct 99.	(cd-ep) <032> **THE FRENCH KICKS** – Arena / White / Take in water / So many cakes.	–	

		Poptones	Star Time
Sep 01.	(m-cd) (MC 5051CD) <1> **YOUNG LAWYER** – Young lawyer / Living room is empty / Arena [UK-only] / The 88 / Call our hands / Destro / White [UK-only] / So many cakes [UK-only] / Piano.		Apr01

		Star Time	Star Time
May 02.	(cd) <(10)> **ONE TIME BELLS** – Wrong side / When you heard you / Down now / Crying just for show / Close to modern / 1985 / Right in time / Trying whining / One time bells / Where we went off / Sunday night is fair.		

— signed to 'Shifty Disco' in the UK, although 'WRONG SIDE' was shelved

FRENTE!

Formed: Melbourne, Australia ... early 90's by songwriters, ANGIE HART and SIMON AUSTIN alongside TIM O'CONNOR and ALISTAIR BARDEN (although MARK PICTON replaced the latter after a few singles). FRENTE! (Spanish for "front") were one of the more interesting musical exports to arrive from down under, eschewing the usual rock/pop predictability for a more experimental folky pop sound. Following a debut EP, 'LABOUR OF LOVE' on 'Flying Nun' subsidiary, 'White', the band signed to 'Mushroom' and issued their debut set, 'MARVIN THE ALBUM', in Spring '94. A focal point was undoubtedly the blonde-bobbed HART, an Antipodean hybrid of The CARDIGANS' NINA PERSSON, DUBSTAR's SARAH BLACKWOOD and SUZANNE VEGA, singing her cryptic, world-weary lyrics against a skeletal backing of often acoustic guitar, piano, rhythm section and sound effects. The record's cover of New Order's 'BIZARRE LOVE TRIANGLE' subsequently entered the US Top 50 although strangely, FRENTE! struggled to make any headway in Britain. Augmented by CAMERON McVEY (BOOGA BEAR) and STEVE GRIPA HOPWOOD, FRENTE!'s 1996 follow-up set, 'SHAPE', was another fine effort, again dominated by HART's haunting vocals. The album also featured possibly their most experimental track to date, 'SIT ON MY HANDS', uncannily reminiscent of territory once explored by The BEATLES on the likes of 'Sgt. Peppers' and 'Abbey Road'. • **Covered:** HERE YOU COME AGAIN (Mann-Weil) / SOMETHIN' STUPID (hit; Frank & Nancy Sinatra) / BLUE (Joni Mitchell).

Album rating: MARVIN THE ALBUM (*5) / SHAPE (*6)

ANGIE HART (b. 1971) – vocals / **SIMON AUSTIN** (b. 1966) – guitars, piano, vocals / **TIM O'CONNOR** – bass / **ALISTAIR BARDEN** – drums, percussion

		Thumbprint	not iss.
1991.	(7"ep/c-ep/cd-ep) (WHI 003/002/001) **WHIRLED** – Love and terror / Oh brilliance / Last to know / Labour of love / Risk / Baby blue sychophant / Testimony / Discipline and deep water. (UK-iss.Oct93; same)		–

		Mushroom	Alex
1992.	(cd-ep) (D 11125) **CLUNK** – Ordinary angels / Book song / Seamless / Paper, bullets and walls / Nadi.		–
1993.	(cd-ep) (D 11352) <4831> **NO TIME / THINKING DARLING / BLUE / NO TIME / FACE LIKE A SPIDER**		Nov94
1994.	(cd-ep) (D 11608) **LONELY / EXPLODE / GET REAL**		

		Mushroom	Mammoth
1994.	(m-cd) <MR 056> **LABOUR OF LOVE** – Labour of love / Testimony / Not given lightly / Paper, bullets, walls / Risk / Bizarre love triangle / Oh brilliance.	–	
Apr 94.	(7"ep/c-ep/cd-ep) (S/C/D 12063) **ACCIDENTLY KELLY STREET / MANY WINGS / HERE YOU COME AGAIN / SOMETHIN' STUPID**		–

May 94.	(cd/c) (TVD/TVC 93367) <92390> **MARVIN THE ALBUM**		75
	– Girl / Accidently Kelly Street / Most Beautiful / No time / Cuscatlan / Pretty friend / Lonely / Reflect / Explode / See – Believe / Labour of love / Ordinary angels / Dangerous.		
Aug 94.	(7"/7"colrd/c-s) (S/SR/C 11839) <98274> **BIZARRE LOVE TRIANGLE. / TESTIMONY** (cd-s+=) (D 1839) – Risk.		49 Apr94
Feb 95.	(7"clear/cd-s) (SP/D 11968) **ORDINARY ANGELS (remix / original / ayonarra mix) / MOST BEAUTIFUL (live acoustic)**		–

— **BILL McDONALD** – bass, guitar; repl. O'CONNOR

Jul 96.	(7"/7"pic-d) (S/SX 2001) **HORRIBLE. / THE DESTROYER** (cd-s+=) (D 2001) – Bill's o'bubblin'.		–
Sep 96.	(7"blue) (S 1451) **WHAT'S COME OVER ME. / I MISS YOU** (cd-s+=) (DX 1451) – Ruby's arms. (cd-s) (D 1451) – ('A'mixes) / A real miracle.		–
Oct 96.	(cd/c/lp) (D/C/L 93429) <980123> **SHAPE**		Jul96
	– Sit on my hands / Horrible / Goodbye goodguy / Burning girl / Clue / Harm / Air / Jungle / So mad / Safe from you / The destroyer / What's come over me / Calmly.		

— split after above

FRETBLANKET

Formed: Stourbridge, West Midlands, England ... 1992 by teenage "yoof" rockers WILL COPLEY, CLIVE POWELL, DAVE and MATT. They began playing in a band when they were no more than 14, earning a reputation by performing to a crowd of floppy-fringed, WONDER STUFF obsessed, early 90's indie kids in their school hall. Picked up by the NME in 1993, the band went on to record and release their debut EP, becoming just one of the annoying surge of jangly indie guitar pop bands that flooded the British music scene in the days of pre-Brit pop. Although songs on their EP sounded like NED'S ATOMIC DUSTBIN's (who they supported) earlier releases, the band could not escape that indie catchment. FRETBLANKET reckoned they'd be "Brilliant" by their third set ... well, we're still waiting for it. A second set, 'HOME TRUTHS FROM ABROAD' (1998), did however target a more grown-up audience, its BUSH-like ambience giving them some hope for the future.

Album rating: JUNKFUEL (*4) / HOME TRUTHS FROM ABROAD (*5)

WILL COPLEY – vocals, guitar / **CLIVE POWELL** – guitar / **DAVE** – bass / **MATT** – drums

		Neck Mohican	not iss.
1992.	(12"ep) (NECK 001EP) **BETTER THAN SWIMMING EP**		–
1993.	(cd-ep) (NECK 002EP) **CURTAINSVILLE EP** – Curtainsville / Sleep through everything / What you know / You're welcome.		–

		Rockville	not iss.
Jun 93.	(7"ep) **HANG GLIDE / TWISTED**		–
Feb 94.	(7"ep/cd-ep) (ROCK 6137-7/-2) **TWISTED EP** – Twisted / Sleep through everything / Captain invisible / You're welcome.		–

		Polydor	Polygram
Aug 94.	(cd/c) (<521997-2/-4>) **JUNKFUEL** – Twisted / Song in B / Junkfuelled / Transmission / Direct approach / I'm going to buy a hang glider / Now we're 30 / 1941 / Drag / Curtainsville / Big fat ugly / Sleep through everything / You're welcome.		
Sep 94.	(cd-ep) **SONG IN B** – Song in B / What do you know / Slow train coming / 28 feet tall.	–	
Feb 98.	(cd/c) <537494> **HOME TRUTHS FROM ABROAD** – Into the ocean / Why can't I sleep / Supercool / Killer in a former life / Hammer and tongues / Black tambourine / Modern man / Moneyspin / Accident in route / Abandon ship / Green is green / Me and the stars.	–	

FRIDGE

Formed: Putney, London, England ... 1995 by former classmates, KIERAN HEBDEN, ADEM ILHAN and SAM JEFFERS. Lucky enough to sign a deal almost immediately with Trevor Jackson's 'Output', FRIDGE dished out their first vinyl helping in the shape of 7", 'LOJEN', followed closely by debut album (a double!), 'CEEFAX' (1997). Obviously turned on by the ever expanding list of outfits experimenting in the post-rock grey area of indie electronica, FRIDGE clearly liked to chill out to ambient noodling in the vein of TORTOISE and ROME. A busy year for the cool teenagers, they would go on to deliver another two singles, the radio-friendly 'ANGLEPOISED' and a shared effort with ADD N TO (X). Precociously prolific, the FRIDGE boys passed their critical exams with early 1998's 'SEMAPHORE', a brooding, intoxicating series of undulating anti-rock frequencies that endeared them to more discerning indie fans. A neat overview of the band's career trajectory was presented later that year with the 'SEVENS AND TWELVES' singles compilation. Member KIERAN HEBDEN, meanwhile concentrated on his own FOUR TET project, right about the time when other members of FRIDGE were attending college. A strange mix between folk, electronica and post-rock, FOUR TET's debut release was the 35-minute long 'THIRTYSIXTWENTYFOUR' (1998), a fascinating slide of musical genres, mostly hip-hop and electronica based, with breakbeats, voice samples/loops, sirens and sound effects et al. HEBDEN's first album proper was the eclectic and mellow 'DIALOGUE' issued in 1999. Acoustic guitars, thumb pianos and a whole host of weird instruments collided with the scathing electronic drum samples, all to startling effect. FRIDGE, meanwhile, continued pushing out their own hybrid of electro-indie sounds, 'EPH' (1999) highlighted by the opener 'ARK'. FOUR TET issued the double A-

FRIDGE (cont)

side 'CALAMINE' / 'GLASSHEAD' (the latter being one of his greatest achievements in music, a transcending, hallucinogenic 11-minute adventure in stereo) and a collaboration with elecro-wizard POLE before returning with the excellent sophomore album 'PAUSE' (2001). Possibly one of the best albums of the year, 'PAUSE' carried on in the same vein as 'DIALOGUE', but with HEBDEN more focused on the hazy, dreamy, folk aspect of his music. With 'UNTANGLE' and 'TWENTY THREE', the listener could just imagine driving along a coast-line on a warm clear afternoon, gazing at the sea; whereas the heavy dud-electronic of standout track 'NO MORE MOSQUITOES' reminded people that FOUR TET's music, although 70% organic, was still deeply rooted in experimental electronica. In the same year, FRIDGE regrouped to record 'HAPPINESS' (2001), the follow-up to 1999's 'EPH'. A humble and minimalistic album from the outset, FRIDGE managed to escape the 'post-rock' tag by using less jazzy instrumentations and a more un-plugged theme. The tracks did what it said on the tin; 'MELODICA AND TROMBONE' was just that, while 'CUT UP PIANO AND XYLOPHONE' was a short poignant piece of music played for the saddest of hearts.

Album rating: CEEFAX (*5) / SEMAPHORE (*7) / SEVENS AND TWELVES double compilation (*7) / EPH (*6) / HAPPINESS (*8) / Four Tet: DIALOGUE (*8) / PAUSE (*9)

KIERAN HEBDEN – guitar, samples / **ADEM ILHAN** – bass, keyboards / **SAM JEFFERS** – drums, trombone

Output / not iss.

Jan 97. (7") *(OPR 5)* **LOJEN. / MORE EDH4800 (PHASE SHIFTER)**
Mar 97. (d-lp/cd) *(OPR 6/+CD)* **CEEFAX**
– EDM / Helicopter / Tricity / More EH4-800 / FDM / Robots in disguise / EDM 2 / Oracle / EDM 3 / Zed ex ay-ti-wan. *(cd re-iss. Jul98 & Nov99 & Dec01; same)*
Sep 97. (12"ep) *(OPR 9)* **ANGLEPOISED**
– Anglepoised / Astrozero / Simple harmonic motion / Concert in your house / Config.
Nov 97. (one-sided-12") *(OPR 10)* **ASTHMA**
Nov 97. (ltd-12") *(Piao! 10)* **ASTHMA. / (other track by Add N To (X)**
(above issued on 'Piao!' records)
Feb 98. (7"ep) *(OPR 11)* **LIGN EP**
– Lign / For force / Must be magic.
(12"ep) *(OPR 11T)* – ('A'extended) / Sequioia / The traps / Fisa.
Feb 98. (d-lp/cd) *(OPR 12/+CD)* **SEMAPHORE**
– Cassette / Furniture boy / A slow / Motorbus / Teletexed / Chroma / Low fat diet / Swerve and spin / Curdle / Lign / Stamper / There is no try / Michael Knight. *(cd re-iss. Dec01; same)*
May 98. (12"; w/7") *(OPR 15D)* **ORKO. / DISTANCE // IT'S ALL ON / JESSICA**
Aug 98. (one-sided-7"; as FRIDGE + D) *(SOUL 22)* **INDEGUISE**
(above issued on 'Soul Static')
Oct 98. (d-cd) *(OPRCD 19)* **SEVENS AND TWELVES** (compilation)
– Anglepoised / For force / Astrozero / Jessica / Single harmonic motion / Lign (extended) / It's all on / EH4-800 (phase shifter) / Sequoia // Orko / The traps / Concert in your house / Must be magic / Asthma / Fisa / Config / Lojen / Distance. *(re-iss. Dec01; same)*

Earworm / not iss.

Oct 98. (7") *(WORM 37)* **DEADLY CUBE. / (track by Portal)**

Go! Beat / not iss.

May 99. (12"/cd-s) *(GOB X/CD 15)* **KINOSHITA. / TERASAKA**
Jun 99. (cd/lp) *(GOB 16 CD/LP)* **EPH**
– Ark / Meum / Transience / Of / Tuum / Bad Ischl / Yttium / Aphelion. *<US cd-iss. Apr02 on 'Temporary Residence – Brainwashed'+=; 48>* – Kinoshita / Terasaka / Of (version) / Of (remix) / Of (edit) / Of (dub) / Ark (Herberts fully flooded mix) / Bad Ischl (Patrick Pulsinger mix).
Jul 99. (12"ep/cd-ep) *(GOB X/CD 17)* **OF EP**
– Of (version / remix / edit / dub).

not iss. / Box Theory

Nov 99. (cd-s) **PLUXUSVSFRIDGEVSPLUXUS**
– Take or leave it.

Text / Temporary Residence

Sep 01. (cd/d-lp) *(TEXT 002 CD/LP)* <43> **HAPPINESS**
– Melodica and trombone / Drum machines and glockenspiels / Cut up piano and xylophone / Tone guitar and drum noise / Five four child voice / Sample and clicks / Drum bass sonics and edit / Harmonics / Long singing.

FOUR TET

KIERAN HEBDEN – instruments, etc.

Output / not iss.

Jul 97. (7"; as 4T RECORDINGS) *(OPR 7)* **DOUBLE DENSITY. / LIKE SIAMESE FIGHTING FISH**
Aug 98. (d12"ep/cd-ep) *(OPR 14)* **THIRTYSIXTWENTYFIVE**
– (part one) / (part two).
Jan 99. (12"ep) *(OPR 20)* **MISNOMER EP**
– Misnomer (long version) / Aying / Fume / Charm.
Feb 99. (lp/cd) *(OPR 21/+CD)* **DIALOGUE**
– Space of two weeks / Chiron / Alambradas / 3.3 degrees from the pole / Misnomer / Liquefaction / She scanned / Calamine / The butterfly effect. *(cd+=)* – Aying / Fume / Charm. *(re-iss. May01; same)*
May 99. (12") *(LOEP 09)* **RIVERS BECOME OCEANS. / Rothko: RIVERS BECOME OCEANS (COLOUR DEFINES THE CITYSCAPE)**
(above issued on 'Lo Recordings')
Jul 99. (12"/cd-s) *(OPR/+CD 24)* **GLASSHEAD. / CALAMINE (radio mix)**

Leaf / not iss.

Jun 00. (12"ep) *(DOCK 20)* **POLE v FOUR TET ep**
– Heim (by POLE remixed by FOUR TET) / Cload (by FOUR TET) / Cload (by FOUR TET remixed by POLE) / Heim (by POLE).

Domino / Domino

May 01. (cd/lp) *(<WIG 94 CD/LP>)* **PAUSE**
– Glue of the world / Twenty three / Harmony one / Parks / Leila came round and we watched a video / Untangle / Everything is alright / No more mosquitoes / Tangle / You could ruin my day / Hilarious movie of the 90's. *(d-cd-iss. Jan02 +=; WIGCD 94X)* – PAWS
Jun 01. (12"ep/cd-ep) *(RUG 126 T/CD)* **NO MORE MOSQUITOES. / FLON / LOOK AFTER YOUR MERMAIDS / WARMER PLACES**
Dec 01. (12"ep) *(RUG 130T)* **PAWS**
– Glue of the other world (remix) / Hilarious movie of the 90's (Koushik funny flick remix) / Hilarious movie of the 90's (Manitoba remix) / No more mosquitos (boom bip remix).
May 02. (7") *(RUG 139)* **I'M ON FIRE (pt.1). / I'M ON FIRE (pt.2)**

FRIENDS OF BETTY (see under ⇒ RED RED MEAT)

FRIENDS OF DEAN MARTINEZ

Formed: Arizona, USA ... 1995 by BILL ELM, who invited GIANT SAND sideliners JOHN CONVERTINO and JOEY BURNS to the fold; VAN CHRISTIAN and TOM LARKINS were also featured on debut set while HOWE GELB and BRIDGET KEATING were there or thereabouts. This often kitschy, if not slightly ironic collective drew from a wide range of musical influences from 60's surf, rockabilly, glitter-covered lounge and sprawling desert guitar. Of course, you couldn't expect more from such an eclectic bunch, who, let's face it, had pretty much shaped the alt-country scene. 'SHADOW OF YOUR SMILE' was issued in 1995, and many CALEXICO fans would eventually hear most of this dusty style on the group's first three releases. It also helped that legend and alt-crooner HOWE GELB stepped in to play some piano on the record, giving it an overall Tex-Mex kinda feel. Two years down the line and the ensemble resurfaced with the brilliant 'RETROGRADE', a homage to the lounge acts and the many mangy dogs that littered the west. In it, BILL ELM took pride in displaying his steel guitar prowess, and ultimately went on to take free rein on the group's next effort 'ATARDECER' (1999), for which he wrote the majority of songs. But the group's next release was 2000's 'A PLACE IN THE SUN'. Highly emotive and beautifully arranged, the set equalled the likes of DIRTY THREE and MOGWAI (in their quieter moments) for sheer cinematic sound-scape. 'BROKEN BELL', an orchestra driven lament, and 'WHEN YOU'RE GONE', a simple sombre folk tune, had sceptics of the band running for cover under the "terrain-tial" downpour of proverbial loveliness. FRIENDS OF DEAN MARTINEZ, like many "hip" troupes from the desert, really deserved the recognition and attention they received from music fans and the press alike. After all, it's music to swoon by and with bassman BRAD FOREMAN in place in 2001, they delivered another set, 'WICHITA LINEMAN'. • **Covered:** I WISH YOU LOVE (Charles Trenet) / MISTY (Errol Garner) / UGLY BEAUTY (Thelonius Monk) / THE SHADOW OF YOUR SMILE (Johnny Mandel) / SEASHELLS + RATTLER + MONTE CARLO (Farina Brothers) / LONESOME (Henry Mancini) / THE WARMTH OF THE SUN (Beach Boys) / I WILL WAIT FOR YOU (Denny-Gimbel-LeGrand) / WICHITA LINEMAN (Jimmy Webb) / TENNESSEE WALTZ (King-Stewart).

Album rating: THE SHADOW OF YOUR SMILE (*5) / RETROGRADE (*5) / ATARDECER (*6) / A PLACE IN THE SUN (*7) / WICHITA LINEMAN (*5)

BILL ELM – steel guitar / **JOHN CONVERTINO** – vobes / **JOEY BURNS** – guitar / **VAN CHRISTIAN** – drums / **TOM LARKINS** – percussion

Sub Pop / Sub Pop

Jul 95. (7") *(SP 291)* **POLENA. / SEASHELLS**
Sep 95. (lp/cd) *<(SP/+CD 306)>* **THE SHADOW OF YOUR SMILE** Aug95
– All the pretty horses / I wish you love / House of pies / Chunder / Armory park / Dwell / El tiradito / Given the time / Swamp cooler / Blood of the earth (or the sun sets red in the west) / Misty / Ugly beauty / The shadow of your smile / Per sempre. *(cd re-iss. Sep01; same)*
Jan 96. (7") *<SP 334>* **CORDOVA. / MONTE CARLO**
Sep 97. (cd) *<(SPCD 375)>* **RETROGRADE** Jun97
– Rattler / Lonesome / Fresca / Cabeza de Mojado / Nile blues / Westbound #11 / Ask the dust / Monte Carlo / False Serpentine compassion / The warmth of the sun / I will wait for you / Retrograde. *(re-iss. Sep01; same)*

— when CONVERTINO + BURNS (+ CHRISTIAN) returned to GIANT SAND commitments, **ELM + LARKINS** recruited **MIKE SEMPLE** – guitars / **GRAHAM REYNOLDS** – keyboards / **TERRY OUBRE** – sitar, guitar / **DAVE LACHANCE** – drums / + TOSCA STRING QUARTET

Knitting Factory / Knitting Factory

Jul 99. (cd) *<(KFR 234)>* **ATARDECER** Mar99
– Quickening / Ethchlorvynol / La fin de l'ete / Otra vez / Inner sanctum / Casa mila / Atardecer / Twilight sleep / Contact / Spoonie (dark side of the spoon) / Coppertone. *(re-iss. Sep01; same)*
May 00. (cd) *<(KFR 261)>* **A PLACE IN THE SUN** Feb00
– A place in the sun / White lake / Siempre que / When you're gone / Summertime / Broken bell / Nothing at all / Aluminium / Pistola agua / Broken / Another place in the sun.

— **BRAD FOREMAN** – bass; repl. LARKINS + REYNOLDS + OUBRE

Glitterhouse / Glitterhouse

May 01. (cd) *<(GRCD 520)>* **WICHITA LINEMAN**
– Intro / Overload / Alternate theme / Main theme / In the wire / Incidental / Tennessee waltz / Through the whine / Wichita lineman / For all time.

— added **MIKE HARDWICK + CONRAD CHOUCROUN + CHRIS SMITH**

— late in 2001, two low-key sets, 'ATRASAR' and 'LIVE AT CLUB 2' were issued in German; probably through 'Glitterhouse'

FROM BUBBLEGUM TO SKY
(see under ⇒ CIAO BELLA)

Edith FROST

Born: 18 Aug'64, San Antonio, Texas, USA. FROST spent her early life moving with her family from her birthplace to the state capital, Austin, and also living for a time across the border in Guadalajara, Mexico. Seeking a change, her college days finished, she crossed the country and settled in Brooklyn, New York, where she found work as a computer programmer. Her day job managed to see her by, and allow her to indulge her musical passions, which she did with some fervour, playing with three country-derived acts; EDITH AND HER ROADHOUSE ROMEOS, MARFA LIGHTS, and The HOLLER SISTERS, although it was the nineties that would see her musical ambitions bear fruit. Due to an admiration for the country experimentations of WILL OLDHAM, FROST posted some demo material to his imprint, 'Drag City'. A bold move which culminated in the inking of a deal, and the label releasing her eponymous debut EP in 1996. She wasted no time in following this up with her first full-length outing, 'CALLING OVER TIME' (1997). The set was bolstered by the additional help of musical luminaries from GASTR DEL SOL, and was a more than competent debut into the alt country-rock scene. FROST proved that she not only had more songs in her, but was prepared to experiment further, with the release of her sophomore LP, 'TELESCOPIC' (1998). This added new dimensions to her sound, not least an indie-pop flavour, and some noticeable psychedelic elements for good measure. Worth a mention as well, is the beautifully evocative EP, 'LOVE IS REAL' (1999), which also pleads praise for her collaborators from the Chicago bands, ELEVENTH DREAM DAY, The COCTAILS, and PINETOP SEVEN (FROST had moved, and settled, in the "windy city" in the early nineties, following a divorce from her husband). Many of these musical aides continued their support into her third full-length set, 'WONDER WONDER' (2001), which showcased a further maturing in FROST's songwriting abilities, and along with some high class production work, the indie/country pop feel made this a worthwhile and accessible listen.

Album rating: CALLING OVER TIME (*7) / TELESCOPIC (*6) / WONDER WONDER (*7)

EDITH FROST – vocals / with **BILL NEUBAUER** – guitar

			Drag City	Drag City
Apr 96.	(cd-ep) <DC 78> **EDITH FROST**		–	

– Evangeline / Blame you / My god insane / Waiting room.

— now with **JIM O'ROURKE** + **DAVID GRUBBS** (of GASTR DEL SOL) + **RICK RIZZO** (of ELEVENTH DREAM DAY) + **SEAN O'HAGAN** (of HIGH LLAMAS)

Jun 97.	(lp/cd) <(DC 89/+CD)> **CALLING OVER TIME**			Apr97

– Temporary loan / Follow / Calling over time / Denied / Pony song / Too happy / Wash of water / Shadows / Thine eyes / Give up your love / Albany blues.

Jun 97.	(7") (TRDSC 007) **ANCESTORS. / SECRETS**		–	

(cd-s+=) (TRDSCCD 007) – Cold and on my mind.
(above issued on 'Trade 2')

Oct 98.	(lp/cd) <(DC 150/+CD)> **TELESCOPIC**			

– Walk on the fire / On hold / Light / Very earth / You belong to no one / Telescopic / Falling / Bluish bells / Through the trees / My capture / Tender kiss / Are you sure?

Jul 99.	(cd-s) <(DC 172)> **LOVE IS REAL / BETWEEN US / THE LAST ONE**			
Jul 01.	(lp/cd) <(DC 209/+CD)> **WONDER WONDER**			

– True / Cars and parties / Who / Wonder wonder / Hear my heart / The fear / Dreamers / Further / Merry go round / Easy to love / Honey please / You're decided.

FROSTED AMBASSADOR
(see under ⇒ OLIVIA TREMOR CONTROL)

FRUIT
(see under ⇒ KITCHENS OF DISTINCTION; 80's section)

FUCK

Formed: Oakland, California, USA . . . 1993 by TIMMY PRUDHOMME, KYLE STATHAM, TED ELLISON and GEOFF SOULE when, strangely enough, they all met in a cell! This abruptly titled quartet released their debut single 'MONKEY BEAUTY SHOTGUN' in 1994, subsequently following that with a host of 12" singles and compilation LP's, which heightened controversy surrounding their taboo-riden name. 'PRETTY . . . SLOW' appeared in 1996 under three different record labels, including the band's own, 'Rhesus'. The album did not sound like anything the coarse name suggested; slow moving ballads and country melodies haunted the technics of this set, as if The COWBOY JUNKIES had sprinkled their fairy dust all over the enigmatic ensemble. 'BABY LOVES A FUNNY BUNNY' appeared the same year, this time with a more brash, indie rock aproach, which suited their following label choice. The 1997 set 'PARDON MY FRENCH' saw FUCK sign to the aforementioned 'Matador', earning the unshakeable comparison to lo-fi losers PAVEMENT. Continuing the pattern, 'CONDUCT' was immediately delivered the following year and spawned humorous 1950's throw back tune 'MONKEY DOLL' and punk favourite 'ALICE, ALL I WANT IS ALICE'. They finally lived up to their moniker with, 'CUPID'S CACTUS' (2001), which featured the track, 'PANTIES OFF'.

Album rating: PRETTY . . . SLOW (*5) / BABY LOVES A FUNNY BUNNY (*6) / PARDON MY FRENCH (*7) / CONDUCT (*6) / CUPID'S CACTUS (*6) / GOLD BRICKS collection (*6)

TIMMY PRUDHOMME – vocals / **KYLE STATHAM** – guitar, violin / **TED ELLISON** – bass, piano / **GEOFF SOULE** – drums

		not iss.	Rhesus
1994.	(c) <none> **FUCK**	–	– demo
1994.	(7"ep) **MONKEY BEAUTY SHOTGUN**	–	

– Monkey does his thing / Beauty remains / Shotgun (h)ours.

1995.	(7"ep) **LIKEYOU BUTTERFLY SOMEWHERES**	–	

– Like you / Crush a butterfly / Somewheres else.

		not iss.	Walt – Rhesus – Esther
Mar 96.	(cd) <WALT 008> **PRETTY . . . SLOW**	–	

– Wrongy wrong / I am your king / Hide face / In the corner / From Heaven / One eye out the door / Monkey does his thing / Pretty pretty / Shotgun (h)ours. (UK-iss.May97; same as US)

		not iss.	Academy Of Chess & Checkers
1996.	(7") **FISH OR FRY / FUCK**	–	

– Elysian fields / Last thing / Dawnjii poo.

		Normal	Walt – Lamplighter
Feb 97.	(cd) (NORMAL 204CD) <WLR 2229> **BABY LOVES A FUNNY BUNNY**		Oct96

– Boy meets girl / Swinger / Love me 2 / Flight of the mongeese / Tired / 22 no / Nice burg, lettuce / Talent, OR / Ballet high / Part of me / Rococo / Like you / Loosened mind? / Crush a butterfly / Whimper and cry. (re-iss. Jun97; same as US)

		not iss.	Jagjaguwar
1997.	(7") <JAG 04> **FUCK MOTEL. / TETHER**	–	
		Matador	Matador
Jun 97.	(cd/lp) <(OLE 261-2/-1)> **PARDON MY FRENCH**		

– Li'l Hilda / Fuck motel / Le serpent / Bestest friend / Compromise / One lb of in / La jolla / For Lori / Raggy rag / Tether / Dirty brunette / To my gurl / Thoroughfare / Sometimes / Am I losin' / Scribble dibble.

1998.	(7") **TOCOTRONIC / FUCK**		

– Diapers / Mighty mouse, sir.

Sep 98.	(cd/lp) <(OLE 314-2/-1)> **CONDUCT**		

– The thing / Drinking artist / Straddle / Monkey doll / Italy / Stumble inn / My melting snowman / Laundry shop / Get over him / Alice, all I want is Alice / Stupid band / Never comin' back / Twist off / Gimme some / Stray / Gone / Blind beauty.

		Pan-o-rama	not iss.
Sep 98.	(7") (PAN 6694) **FLAPPER. / (other by Moxie)**		–
		not iss.	Vaccination
1999.	(7") **MELT. / (split w/ MUmble And Peg)**	–	
		not iss.	Cool Beans
2000.	(7") split w/ **PEE**	–	

– Agent 389 / Me so horny / Question your love.

		Speakerphone	Speakerphone
Aug 00.	(ltd-7"brown) <(DIAL 001)> **BLIND BEAUTY. / MADE UP LAST NIGHT**		Nov99
		Smells Like	Smells Like
Feb 01.	(cd) <(SLR 044)> **CUPID'S CACTUS**		

– Glass charms / High / Someday aisle / Dandelion ditch / Melt / Panties off / San Jacinto / Awright / It's unbelievable / Never alone / Flowers / Respond / How do you do, Mr. Do / Oshun / Cobra lullaby.

– compilations, etc. –

Jun 01.	(cd) Homesleep; <(REC 2006)> **GOLD BRICKS** (rare singles, etc.)		Nov01

– Diapers / Made up last night / Beauty remains / Flapper / Hide face / Elysian fields / Mighty Mouse sir / Blind beauty / Situation / She's a rainbow / Brazen / Last thing / Ten grains / Sweater / Bone for the baby / Question your love / D + A / Golden arm / Agent 389 / Me so horny / Dawnjii poo / You're a mean one Mr. Grinch / Somewhere's else / Aviary like you (video) / Monkey doll (video).

FUDGE

Formed: Richmond, Virginia, USA . . . 1990 by TONY AMMENDOLIA, DAVID JONES and MIKE SAVAGE (drums); the three initially started out with ENGINE NO.9, alongside DANI SICILIANO on bass. The quartet released one single, 'SLEEP' / 'WATERFALL', in 1991, before SICILIANO left, and the others continued as FUDGE. They then wrote and rehearsed together for over a year before they found a suitable replacement bass player – with STEVE VENABLE joining in 1992. The following year, they released debut LP 'THE FEROCIOUS RHYTHM OF PRECISE LAZINESS' (the title of an E.E. Cummings poem), which went on to sell 10,000 copies and led to a tour with punk legends the BUZZCOCKS. At this stage FUDGE were largely influenced by early-'90s British shoegazing, with a hazy, dreamy sound, although frequently incorporating a reggae dub-style groove. The BUZZCOCKS tour appeared to have had a profound effect on FUDGE, because second album 'SOUTHSIDE SPEEDWAY' – recorded immediately after – was a collection of high-tempo punk-pop tunes. Unfortunately for FUDGE, their new material was neither original nor inspiring, and consequently failed to sell, with the band splitting-up some time after.

Album rating: THE FEROCIOUS RHYTHM OF PRECISE LAZINESS (*5) / SOUTHSIDE SPEEDWAY (*4)

TONY AMMENDOLIA – vocals, guitar / **DAVID JONES** – guitar, fuzz bass, vocals / **DANI SICILIANO** – bass / **MIKE SAVAGE** – drums

		not iss.	Bus Stop
1991.	(7"; as ENGINE No.9) <BUS 008> **SLEEP. / WATERFALL**	–	

— **STEVE VENABLE** – bass, vocals; repl. DANI

1992.	(7") <BUS 013> **ASTRONAUT. / DRIVE**	–	

1992.	(7"ep) <ANT 01> **BOMB POP EP**	not iss.	Brilliant
1992.	(7") <SPR 101> **WAYSIDE. / GIRLWISH**	not iss. – Quigley	Superfly – Caroline
Mar 93.	(cd/c/lp) (QUIG D/M/L 2) <CAROL 1731> **THE FEROCIOUS RHYTHM OF PRECISE LAZINESS** – Oreo dust / Jr. High blur / Peanut butter / Mystery machine / Mull / Wayside / Pez / Astronaut / 20-nothing dub / Drive / Snowblind.		
Apr 94.	(cd) <CAROL 1749> **SOUTHSIDE SPEEDWAY** – Tree fort stash / Dart GT / It's morning, already / Patty Hearst machine gun / Our Francis III / Southside speedway / Feather splitter / Lucky's tightest t-shirt / Car stereo blast off / Superstar junky / Shirts & skins.	–	
—	split after above; SAVAGE and VENABLE formed CHERRY 2000 and released 'TAINT' in 1998		

FUKUYAMA

Formed: based- Dunblane, Scotland . . . Spring 1997 by GANGER moonlighters, guitarist CRAIG B and NATASHA NORAMLY. Naming themselves after the philosopher Francis Fukuyama, the duo followed a suitably esoteric post-Rock path on their only existing two EP's, 'GO BY SOUND' and 'WELCOME TO DISH'. Amicably splitting with both FUKUYAMA and GANGER, CRAIG B went on to set up his own outfit, AEREOGRAMME. According to the man himself, the debut single 'TRANSLATIONS' (issued on their own 'Babi-Yaga' imprint) was an attempt to match the excellence of the RED HOUSE PAINTERS and AMERICAN MUSIC CLUB. The music took a harder turn with the arrival of drummer MARTIN SCOTT (joining CRAIG B and bassist CAMPBELL McNEIL), staking out post-Hardcore territory on further EP's, 'AEREOGRAMME' and 'HATRED'. Towards the end of 2000, after a healthy reception at both the Reading and Leeds festivals, the trio were back with a new EP, 'GLAM CRIPPLE', for the 'Chemikal Underground' fukd i.d. series.

Album rating: Aereogramme: A STORY IN WHITE (*6)

NATASHA NORAMLY – bass, vocals, 303 synth, drums (of GANGER) / **CRAIG B** – guitar, drums, 303 synth (of GANGER)

		Wurlitzer Jukebox	not iss.
Oct 97.	(7"ep) (WJ 38) **GO BY SOUND EP** – Dog gone / Quit and walk away / Silverlining / Antidote / Alessandra and her electric fan / Magic spell / . . . For a few uncrossed miles.		–
		Liquefaction	not iss.
Mar 98.	(7"ep) (DUSKE 2) **WELCOME TO DISH EP** – I like you already / Argument / Into arc / Toby gets busted / Water comes too quickly / . . . So I challenge you.		–
—	CRAIG split from FUYUYAMA and GANGER to form his own act . . .		

AEREOGRAMME

CRAIG B – guitar, vocals / **CAMPBELL McNEIL** – bass

		Babi-Yaga	not iss.
Jun 99.	(7"ep) (YAGA 002-7) **TRANSLATIONS** – Salvation / The long walk home.		–
—	added **MARTIN SCOTT** – drums		
Sep 99.	(7") (YAGA 001) **HATRED. / THE ART OF BELIEF**		–
Nov 99.	(7"ep) (YAGA 003) **AEREOGRAMME EP**		–
		Chemikal Underground	Matador
Oct 00.	(12"ep/cd-ep) (CHEM 046/+CD) **fukd i.d. #1: GLAM CRIPPLE EP** – Fuel to burn / The ocean red / Fireworks / Fireworks (Gabriel's 13th dream mix).		–
Aug 01.	(12"ep/cd-ep) (CHEM 052/+CD) **WHITE PAW EP** – Zionist timing / Motion / Messenger / The art of belief.		–
Sep 01.	(cd/lp) (CHEM 053 CD/LP) <OLE 533> **A STORY IN WHITE** – The question is complete / Post-tour pre-judgement / Egypt / Hatred (new version) / Zionist timing / Sunday 3:52 / Shouting for Joey / A meaningful existence / Descending / Will you still find me? <US cd+=> – Motion / Messenger / The art of belief.		Oct01

FURTHER

Formed: Sierra Madre, California, USA . . . mid 1990'S by JOSH SCHWARTZ and brothers BRENT and DARREN RADEMAKER. The trio were already familiar to the music world having released two albums under the guise of SHADOWLAND. Their 1989 self-titled debut and 'THE BEAUTY OF ESCAPING' the following year, were both likeable, 1960's oriented, records. The band's influences were as obvious as they were confusing. Both albums tried to encompass all the sounds of rock's heyday ranging from LED ZEPPELIN to the BEACH BOYS and consequently the albums sounded a little cluttered. The demise of SHADOWLANDS led to the formation of two new bands. DARREN RADEMAKER and JOSH SCHWARTZ formed SUMMER HITS along with REX 'TARATEXT' THOMPSON and DADDY D. The band released a number of singles between 1992 and 1996, which were eventually compiled on 'BEACHES AND CANYONS' in 1997, before releasing the album 'HOT SKIN' in 1999. FURTHER were prolific in their output, releasing an album or EP almost annually. The group were obviously keen for success as they had now abandoned the sixties influenced sound of previous incarnations and jumped onto the nearest bandwagon. FURTHER were derivative of a number of American indie rock bands popular at the time, NIRVANA, SONIC YOUTH, and DINOSAUR JR. to mention a few. FURTHER released their debut album 'GRIPTAPE' in 1993, followed by 'SOMETIMES CHIMES' in 1994 and two EP's 'GRIMES GOLDEN' and 'DISTANCE' in 1995. By the time the band released their final album, 'NEXT TIME WEST COAST', they were trying to accommodate all their influences from the sixties through to the nineties and even included a cover of the PRIMAL SCREAM song 'YOU'RE JUST DEAD SKIN TO ME'. The RADEMAKER brother's resistance to being categorised took another twist with the formation of The TYDE. Formed in 1998, the outfit were compared to bands such as LLOYD COLE & THE COMMOTIONS and released the album 'ONCE' in 2001. • **SHADOWLAND covered:** Dylan's 'IT'S ALL OVER NOW, BABY BLUE'.

Album rating: Shadowland: SHADOWLAND mini (*5) / THE BEAUTY OF ESCAPING (*6) / Further: GRIPTAPE (*5) / SOMETIMES CHIMES (*5) / NEXT TIME WEST COAST mini (*6) / Summer Hits: BEACHES AND CANYONS 1992-1996 compilation (*7) Tyde: ONCE (*7)

SHADOWLAND

DARREN RADEMAKER – vocals, guitar / **BRENT RADEMAKER** – bass, vocals / **EDDIE K** – guitars / **RICHIE CLOSE** – piano, keyboards / **KEVIN FITZGERALD** – drums / + session people

		WEA	Geffen
1989.	(m-lp/m-c/m-cd) <1-/4-/2-24273> **SHADOWLAND** – Wink of an eye / Imitation of life / It's all over now, baby blue / Indigo blue / Sweet mystery.	–	
Aug 90.	(cd/c/lp) (7599 24286-2/-4/-1) **THE BEAUTY OF ESCAPING** – Miss yesterday / She's shooting fireworks / Hypnotised / Heroin eyes / Garden of Eden / My escape / Something on your mind / Evil that you do / The deepest indigo blue / Sweet mystery.		
—	**DARREN + BRENT** formed . . .		

FURTHER

DARREN + BRENT plus **JOSH SCHWARTZ** – drums

		not iss.	Kirbdog
1992.	(7") <kirbdog 16> **I WANNA BE A STRANGER** – They said it couldn't happen here . . . and it didn't / New York's not alright even if you like saxophones.	–	
		not iss.	Bongload
1993.	(7") <bl 3> **FILLING STATION. / THE SAD TRUTH**	–	
		not iss.	Standard
1993.	(7") <sr 75> **BORN UNDER A GOOD SIGN** – Generic 7 / Greasy 2.	–	
		Ball Product – Creation	Xmas
Aug 93.	(cd) (SHED 003CD) <chr 105> **GRIPTAPE** – Overrated / Filling station / Flounder (Ubel) / Real gone / Gimme indie fox / Still [cd-only] / Smudge / Greasy / Bazooka / Fix its broken / Fantastic now / Under and in / The death of an A+R man / Westward ho.		
1994.	(7"ep) <chr 107> **SURFING POINTERS** – Surfing pointers / The daily planet / Reach / New risen / Penelope tree.	–	
1994.	(cd) <chr 109> **SOMETIMES CHIMES L.P.** – Surfing pointers / Generic 7 / Duck pond / Ferrets and weasels / Brian and Ray / She lives by the castle 2 / The kindergarten set / Phase out / J.O.2 / Unstuck / Sometimes too / Poineer 10 / Isabel / Jaded ball / Doof amuz 6 (the love machine) / Going to Glendora / Traction in the rain / Ride / Big spoon / Katdancer / Sickness / Organ donor / furtherdoh.jr-q / Alternative ulcer / New glass / Untitled.	–	
		Fingerpaint	Fingerpaint
Oct 94.	(10"m-lp/m-cd) <(FP 004/+CD)> **GRIMES GOLDEN EP** – California bummer / Inert pieces / Quiet riot grrrl / Summer shorts / Artificial freedom / 20 pages / This time around / Teenage soul / . . .Vs (Livingston Seagull).		
		Boxing Day	not iss.
1995.	(7"ep) **THE FURTHER JOHN PEEL SOUNDS** – 1993 / Modern problems / Who am I? / Misinformed youth / She bangs the drugs.		–
		Lissy's	not iss.
1995.	(d7") (liss 4) **DISTANCE. / SPRINGFIELD MODS // SPHERES OF INFLUENCE. / SEA-A-SUKA-TIKA**		–
		not iss.	100 Guitar Mania
1996.	(m-cd) <100GM 15> **NEXT TIME WEST COAST** – Be that as it may / Victim rock / Grandview skyline / Badgers (part II) / Friends and enemies / Stranger than silver / You're just dead skin to me / Way too much.	–	– Japan
		Fierce Panda	not iss.
1997.	(7") (NING 28) **THE FAKERS & THE TAKERS. / CATALINA**		–
—	after they split, DARREN + BRENT formed The TYDE (the latter + JOSH moonlighted with BEACHWOOD SPARKS)		

SUMMER HITS

TARTAREX (b. REX THOMPSON) – vocals, bass / **DADDY D** (DARREN RADEMAKER) – guitar / **JOSH SCHWARTZ** – drums

		not iss.	Small-Fi
1992.	(7") <small-fi 3> **GROOVIER DRUGS. / CALIFORNIA SUMMER**	–	
		not iss.	Orgasm
1994.	(7"m) (spasm 05) **HONEY MACHINE. / CARMEL FEELIN' / DO YOU KNOW CIDNEY?**	–	– French
		not iss.	Silver Girl
1996.	(7") <silver 016> **1000 MOMENTS OF NATURAL FLOATATION** – Laetitia / Lift off / Mod cinema.	–	
		100 Guitar Mania	not iss.
Jun 96.	(7"blue) (100GM 14) **AWAY FROM THE CITY. / (other by SPARE SNARE)**	– Xmas	– Japan Xmas
Sep 97.	(cd) <(X-ARC 015)> **BEACHES AND CANYONS 1992-96** (compilation) – Stony creation / Honey machine / Preference / Groovier drugs / California summer / Maximum bum ride / Away from the city / Modern cinema / Beaches and canyons / Sandy hair / Thin / Laetitia / Lift off / Spanish films / Moto-guzzi / Carmel feelin'.		

FURTHER (cont) — THE GREAT INDIE DISCOGRAPHY — The 1990s

			not iss.	Vovolo
1999.	(12"ep) <*lo 1208*> **SWEET VACUUM CLEANER**		-	

– Sweet vacuum cleaner / Ain't no grease allowed / Dirty bad flash / Hot skin.

TUGBOAT 3001 a.d.

aka **DARREN RADEMAKER**

			not iss.	Little Mafia
1995.	(7"ep) <*lm 008*> **FIRST TELL ME YOUR NAME**		-	

– First tell me your name / Indian rocks / The fakers and the takers / Teenage boys need revolution too / I was almost a mountain goats song.

TYDE

DARREN RADEMAKER – vocals, guitar / **BRENT RADEMAKER** – bass, vocals / **DAVE SCHER** – organ, steel guitar / plus **BENJAMIN KNIGHT** – guitar / **ANN DO** – synthesizers

		Track & Field	Track & Field
Jan 01.	(7") *(LANE 04)* **STRANGERS AGAIN. / IMPROPER**		
Feb 01.	(7") *(LISS 37)* **ALL MY BASTARD CHILDREN. /**		
	(above issued on 'Lissys')		
Apr 01.	(cd) <*(HEAT 01)*> **ONCE**		Mar01

– All my bastard children / New confessions / Strangers again / Get around too / North county times / The dawn / Improper / Your tattoos / Silver's okay Michelle. <*lp-iss.on 'Orange Sky'; OS 2201*>

—— **CHRIS GUNST** (of BEACHWOOD SPARKS) was also a member

		Rough Trade	Sanctuary
Jul 02.	(7") *(RTRADES 056)* **BLOOD BROTHERS. / CRYSTAL CANYONS**		-

(cd-s+=) *(RTRADESCD 056)* – Play it as it lays.

FUTURE BIBLE HEROES
(see under ⇒ MAGNETIC FIELDS)

FUTURE PILOT AKA

Formed: Glasgow, Scotland ... 1996 by ex-SOUP DRAGONS man SUSHILL K DADE, who'd also had spells with TELSTAR PONIES (also ran 'Via Satellite' records) while still being part of The BMX BANDITS. Breaking free from all other collaborations, DADE, who was now practically a bonafide connoisseur of the Glaswegian indie scene, issued his striking debut single, 'WE SHALL OVERCOME', on 'Creeping Bent' records in 1997. Slightly misleading in places, the single displayed a very Eastern/Asian theme, with carnival drums pounding a steady beat against the voices of Indian children. However, second single 'MEDITATION RAT' (which was a collaboration with ALAN VEGA) and his early minglings with The PASTELS, were more ambient and delivered a crossover psychedelic feel. Two more singles were issued in '98/'99; one featuring BILL WELLS (appearing on the oh-so-cool 'Domino' sub-imprint 'Series 500') and the other double-A side with NATIONAL PARK and SHOMPA RAGA BHAIVAN – both just as impressive as the other. The debut album, 'FUTURE PILOT A.K.A VS A GALAXY OF SOUND' (1999), catapulted him into the indie/remixer terrain with songs fusing jazz, soul and funk – a definite change from his early 'DRAGONS days. The album brought together such independent heavyweights as CORNERSHOP, BILL WELLS, FALL guru BRIX SMITH, 60's throwback KIM FOWLEY, ALAN VEGA (of SUICIDE) and THE PASTELS, all in one sweltering, groovified brew(!). Early 2001, SUSHIL and Co took off once again, releasing for 'Geographic' records, the difficult second set, 'TINY WAVES MIGHTY SEA'. A hybrid of Indian-style mantra-folk, MERCURY REV-esque transcendental rock and the usual indie meanderings, the set was well received by a varied cosmopolitan audience who were well aware of the inclusion of STUART DAVID (BELLE & SEBASTIAN) and others.

Album rating: ...VS A GALAXY OF SOUND (*8) / TINY WAVES MIGHTY SEA (*7)

SUSHIL K DADE with other various singers:- A-side w/ **RANJIT NAGAR** (New Delhi schoolchildren) / B-side w/ **KIM FOWLEY**

		Creeping Bent	not iss.
Jul 97.	(7") *(bent 025)* **WE SHALL OVERCOME. / NIGHT FLIGHT TO MEMPHIS**		-
Nov 97.	(7"; by FUTURE PILOT A.K.A. & ALAN VEGA) *(bent 029)* **MEDITATION RAT. / BAD VIBRATIONS (by Mount Vernon Arts Lab & Scientific Support Dept)**		-

		Series 500	not iss.
May 98.	(12"; by FUTURE PILOT A.K.A. & The PASTELS) *(SER 507)* **HURRICANE FIGHTER PILOT. / THE GATES TO FILM CITY (w/ Two Lone Swordsmen)**		-

—— in Apr'99, the FUTURE PILOT A.K.A. teamed up with the BILL WELLS OCTET on the eponymous 'Domino' set.

		Earworm	not iss.
Jan 99.	(7") *(WORMSC 4)* **NATIONAL PARK VERSUS FUTURE PILOT A.K.A. / FUTURE PILOT A.K.A. VERSUS SHOMPA RAGA BHAIVAN**		-

		Sulphur	Beggars Banquet
Apr 99.	(d-cd/d-lp) *(SUL CD/LP 001)* <*85016*> **FUTURE PILOT A.K.A. Vs A GALAXY OF SOUND**		

– The gates to film city (w/ TWO LONE SWORDSMEN) / Pink city (w/ BILL WELLS) / Indians at N.A.S.A. (w/ BRIX SMITH) / Rest be thankful (w/ JAMES KIRK) / World wide web – We shall overcome (w/ RANJIT NAGAR) / Teri mitti bani (w/ CORNERSHOP) / Departure lounge (w/ DIGITAL COW) / Pink returns (w/ BILL WELLS) / Innocent railway (w/ JAMES KIRK) / Meditation rat (w/ ALAN VEGA) / Theme from "Buzz" (w/ 50htz) / Fresh milk! (w/ SCANNER) / Night flight to Memphis (w/ KIM FOWLEY) / Pink Money (w/ BILL WELLS) / Japan (w/ SUCKMONSTER) / Message from control tower (w/ JOWE HEAD) / Hurricane fighter pilot (w/ PASTELS) / Lee Jun fan (w/ INYO SAN) / Pink prophet (w/ BILL WELLS) / Sterling (w/ NATIONAL PARK).

		Geographic	not iss.
Dec 00.	(7") *(GEOGRAPHIC 9)* **DARSHAN. / OM NAMA SHIVAYA**		-
Jan 01.	(cd/lp) *(GEOGRAPHIC 6 CD/LP)* **TINY WAVES MIGHTY SEA**		-

– Maid of the loch / Ananda is the ocean / Witchi Tai to Darshan / Beautiful dreamer / Darshan returns / Shree ram, Jai ram / Opel waters / Beat of a drum / Radhika / Om nama shivaya / Strength of the sea / Prayer for Ananda.

Apr 01.	(7") *(GEOG 7)* **BEAT OF A DRUM. / MOUNT KALLASH**		-

(cd-s+=) *(GEOG 7CD)* – Om namah shivaya.

FUXA

Formed: Detroit, Michigan, USA ... 1995 by former WINDY & CARL member, RANDALL NIEMAN who teamed up with RYAN ANDERSON (ex-ASHA VIDA). Having both set up independent labels ('Mind Expansion', 'An I', etc), NIEMAN and ANDERSON collaborated on a series of 7" singles/EP's, the cream of these collected on 1996's debut set, '3 FIELD ROTATION'. Very much in the retro space-rock tradition, FUXA were orbiting a vintage musical world of analogue Moog synths, Hammond, etc, lying somewhere between SPACEMEN 3 and HAWKWIND. Later in the year, fresh material surfaced in the shape of 'VERY WELL ORGANIZED', the pair taking a smoother flightpath into trance-inducing spacey ambience. 'ACCRETION' (1998), was certainly no radical change from its blissed out predecessors, while 'INFLIGHT AUDIO' (1999) saw NIEMAN – and the soon departing ANDERSON – guaranteeing FUXA fans their ambient fix. NIEMAN's post-millennium outlook on life through his proverbial studio pod gave us another enterprising delivery. 'FUXA 2000' (er, 2000) – featuring vocals by The TELESCOPES' STEPHEN LAWRIE – continued their futuristic, blissed-out pop tradition and even saw a cover of Suicide's 'GIRL' with SONIC BOOM guesting. Another TELESCOPES member, JOANNA DORAN (also a guest on FUXA's last effort), was on show for 2002's 'SUPERCHARGED' effort, NIEMAN's organic approach to a pot pourri of jazzy, psychedelic and post-rock sounds, setting the mind controls for a post-KEVIN SHIELDS/MY BLOODY VALENTINE world.

Album rating: 3 FIELD ROTATION (*5) / VERY WELL ORGANIZED (*7) / ACCRETION (*6) / INFLIGHT AUDIO (*5) / FUXA 2000 (*6) / SUPERCHARGED (*6) / THE MODIFIED MECHANICS OF THIS DEVICE collection (*5)

RANDALL NIEMAN – guitar, Moog synth, samples (ex-WINDY & CARL) / **RYAN ANDERSON** – drums, Moog, bass / with also **JESSE PERCIVAL** – drums

		not iss.	Burnt Hair
Jul 95.	(7"green-ep) <*SINGE 004*> **FREE YOUR SOUL**	-	

– Main sequence diffusion / Photon / Lajolla / Subway / Free your soul / First abductions.

		not iss.	Colorful Clouds For Acoustics
1996.	(7") *(DV 002)* **OPELWERKS. / (other by AZUSA PLANE)**	-	

(UK-iss.Jan98 on 'Doorstep Vinyl'; DV 002)

		I – Che	I – Mind Expansion
Sep 96.	(cd/maroon-d-lp) <*(IRE 101-2/-1)*> **3 FIELD ROTATION** (compilation)		Jan96

– " " / 100 white envelopes / Tokearian parade / Main sequence diffusion / Photon / Lajolla / Subway / Free your soul / First abductions / Dreamlanding / The anvil.

Sep 96.	(7") *(LISS 15)* **split w/ Stereolab**		-

(above issued on 'Lissys', below issued on 'Astral Lanes')

Oct 96.	(7"white) *(ALR 702)* **CLEARLESS. / (split w/ Orange Cakemix)**		-

Mar 97.	(cd/3x12") <*(IRE 106-2/-2)*> **VERY WELL ORGANIZED**		Nov96

– At your leisure / Latitude – Longitude / Unexplained transmission repair / Witness to natural invention / 3 cp / Pangaea / Outer drive / Pleasant orbitings / Homonym hymn / Unified frequency.

		Darla	Darla
Jan 97.	(7") <*(DRL 027)*> **CITY. / Bright: METRO**		
Jun 97.	(12"ep/cd-ep) <*(DRL 033/+CD)*> **VENOY: bliss out v.5**		Aug97

– Overture 1 / Overture 2.

		I – Che	not iss.
Aug 98.	(12"ep) <*(IRE 206-1)*> **GREEN FIELD EP**		-

– Green field / What if a taxpayer died? / Third abductions / Project radiate / Silent industry.

—— **ERIC MORRISON** – drums; repl. PERCIVAL

		Mind Expansions	Mind Expansions
May 98.	(d-lp/cd) <*ME 024/+CD*> **ACCRETION**		

– Standing under U / Second abduction / City / Metro / Some Soviet sation / Convective envelope / Karmaloop / Landings / Tonality / Spruce. *(re-iss. Apr99; same)*

		I – Che	I – Che
Oct 99.	(cd/lp) <*(IRE 401-2/-1)*> **INFLIGHT AUDIO**		

– Intro (welcome to the Fuxa) / Limited sight distance / Sky high / U.S. airspace / RTM radio / Rocketship / Bzzz / Greenfield / Outro.

—— **NIEMAN** solo + next with **STEPHEN LAWRIE** – vocals (of TELESCOPES) / **GABE McDONOGH** – bass / **ERIK KASSAB** – Moog

		Rocket Girl	Rocket Girl
Mar 00.	(7"orange) *(RGIRL 014)* **TECHNO LIGHT. / IT'S MASHED POTATO TIME**		-

Nov 00. (cd) (RGIRL 024) <69824> **FUXA 2000**
– Rainy day dream away / Techno light / Amber gambler / Detroit / Today / Girl / Workerbee 5000 / Strange news from the angels / Rainy day dream away (instrumental).

	Ochre	not iss.
Mar 01. (m-cd; split) (OCH 048) **FUXA VERSUS ECTOGRAM**	☐	-

May 01. (cd-ep; as ADD N TO FU(X)A) (RGIRL 22) <69822> **AND ANOTHER THING!**	☐	☐ Jun02

(above on 'Rocket Girl')

––––– NIEMAN with DREW PETERS – drums / + STEPHEN LAWRIE + JOANNA DORAN – vocals

	Mind Expansion	Mind Expansion
Jan 02. (7") <(ME 2001)> **HIDE AWAY.** / Fuxa & Sonic Boom: **GIRL**	☐	☐

	Rocket Girl	Rocket Girl
Feb 02. (cd) (RGIRL 033CD) <69833> **SUPERCHARGED**	☐	☐

– Hide away / Supercharged / 420 / It was you / The formula / We could be together / In your dreams / A little time alone.

– compilations, etc. –

Mar 02. (cd) *Antenna; (ANTENNA 001CD)* **THE MODIFIED MECHANICS OF THIS DEVICE**
– Girl (radio edit) / Opel / Kids toy / Sitar – Tone / Bowie beat / Bzzz (extended) / Willow run / Run / Construction / Whiskaz / Kid bits / Sky high / 3rd abductions / What if a taxpayer died?

FUZZY

Formed: Boston, Massachusetts, USA . . . early 90's by HILKEN MANCINI, CHRIS TAPPIN and WINSTON BRAMAN. Boosted by the addition of LEMONHEADS drummer, DAVE RYAN – who'd come on board after checking out the band at the LEMONHEADS' studio – FUZZY secured a series of dates backing DINOSAUR JR. As it turned out, RYAN was absent with touring commitments to his other band, fill-in sticksman, "TOM THE MONK", proving a less than suitable replacement as TAPPIN and BRAMAN came to the brink of onstage fisticuffs. Help came in the unlikely form of SOUL ASYLUM man, DAVE PIRNER, the band's reputation saved from ruin before they'd even released their eponymous debut album. The accompanying single, 'FLASHLIGHT', narrowly missed an NME Single Of The Week award, while FUZZY's femme spangle-pop secured them a place – with indie ballad, 'CHRISTMAS' – on 'Fierce Panda's girl-powered Various Artists EP, 'FROM GREER TO ETERNITY'. In 1996, they moved on up to 'East West' (through 'Tag' records) and delivered a follow-up, 'ELECTRIC JUICES'. The Boston bratesses were back in 1999 with 'HURRAY FOR EVERYTHING', tripping the sonic fantastic with a clutch of bright-eyed, fuzzy-tailed tunes celebrating the simplicity of girlish-power rather than riot grrrl power.

Album rating: FUZZY (*6) / ELECTRIC JUICES (*7) / HURRAY FOR EVERYTHING (*5)

HILKEN MANCINI – vocals / **CHRIS TAPPIN** – vocals, guitar / **WINSTON BRAMAN** – bass / **DAVID RYAN** – drums (of LEMONHEADS)

	not iss.	H.A.C.
1993. (cd-ep) <HAC 23> **HALF A COW**	-	☐

– Bill / Four wheel friend / Girlfriend / Got it / Lemon rind / Country song.

	Seed	Seed
Jun 94. (7"m) (SEED 009) **FLASHLIGHT. / THURBER / COUNTRY SONG**	☐	☐
Jul 94. (cd/lp) <(14254-2/-1)> **FUZZY**	☐	☐

– Flashlight / Bill / Postcard / Now I know / 4 wheel friend / Almond / Lemon ring / Rock song / Intro / Sports / Severe / Got it / Surfing / Girlfriend.

Apr 95. (7") (SEED 011) **LEMON RIND. / CHRISTMAS**
(cd-s+=) (SEEDCD 011) – Thurber.

	East West	Tag-Atlantic
May 96. (cd/c) <(7567 92626-2/-4)> **ELECTRIC JUICES**	☐	☐

– Glad again / Drag / Throw me a bone / Girl don't tell me / Miss the mark / Ileeper / Flavor / It started today / One request / Someday / Pop a dime / Uncut / Christmas.

	not iss.	Catapult
Apr 99. (cd) <16> **HURRAY FOR EVERYTHING**	-	☐

– Band of gold / Are you living / True colors / Gave into you / Summer is gone / Never be replaced / Dead end day / Cage / All hung up / Over the edge / Motorcycle / Losing end.

G

Serge GAINSBOURG

Born: LUCIEN GINZBERG, 2 Apr'28, Paris, France. The son of Russian Jewish immigrants, GAINSBOURG attended art college and initially tried to scrape a living as a painter. To supplement his income, he worked nights as a bar pianist before being snapped up for an unwilling singing role in the musical 'Milord L'Arsoille'. Reluctant to take to the stage himself (partly due to his less than conventionally handsome appearance), GAINSBOURG felt more comfortable as a songwriter, composing for major-league French stars such as SACHA DISTEL and JOHNNY HALLIDAY. Nevertheless, he ventured into the studio himself in the late 50's for debut album, 'DU CHANTE A LA UNE!' (1958), following it up with 'NO.2' (1959), 'L'ETONNANT SERGE GAINSBOURG' (1961), 'NO.4' (1962), 'GAINSBOURG CONFIDENTIEL' (1964) and 'GAINSBOURG PERCUSSIONS' (1964). Although these weren't great successes (outside France) in their own right, his material was exposed to English audiences via the likes of DIONNE WARWICK and PETULA CLARK. A close association with French actress/sex symbol BRIGITTE BARDOT inspired some of GAINSBOURG's finest work, the pair cutting a series of celebrated duets including 'BONNIE & CLYDE' and 'HARLEY DAVIDSON'. Even the infamous 'JE T'AIME . . . MOI NON PLUS' was penned for BARDOT who subsequently declined to perform it. Instead, the increasingly wayward Frenchman duetted on the track with another actress-cum-sex-kitten, JANE BIRKIN. Released as a single on 'Fontana' in July 1969, this breathy ode to sweaty love was banned by the BBC although it crowned the UK chart all the same (in October '69 the 'Major Minor' re-issue was No.1 while its identical counterpart was still in the charts having made No.2!); it even made the Top 60 in the USA. 1971's 'HISTOIRE DE MELODY NELSON' album found GAINSBOURG preoccupied with life's darker side (MELODY was a 14-year old girl with whom the writer – as narrator – was having an affair!), a trait which would become more pronounced as his reputation grew ever more lecherous and provocative. His concept-type sets in the the mid-70's were weird to say the least. From 1973's 'VU DE L'EXTERIEUR' – with its fart joke song ('DES VENTS DES PETS DES POUM') – to 75's Adolf Hitler concept! 'ROCK AROUND THE BUNKER' and 'L'HOMME A TETE DE CHOU' ('THE MAN WITH A CABBAGE HEAD'), all were extremely shocking and OTT; LOU REED meeting 50's rock'n'roll was how one could describe it. 1979's cod-reggae 'AUX ARMES ET CETERA' (his only UK release) was also diverse, SLY & ROBBIE giving it their Jamaican dub treatment. SERGE even recorded a concept album about male prostitutes, 'LOVE ON THE BEAT' (1984), which updated 'HARLEY . . .' as 'HARLEY DAVID SON OF A BITCH'. Also guaranteed to shock was a duet with his daughter (actress Charlotte Gainsbourg), 'LEMON INCEST'; the Gallic Jew going a little astray even by his standards. Controversy was SERGE's middle name, while appearances on French chat shows were often accompanied by outrageous comments and remarks; actor Oliver Reed must have been watching. A pillar of the French anti-establishment, GAINSBOURG's hard-drinking lifestyle eventually caught up with him on 2nd March 1991 when he died of heart complications.

Best CD compilation: DE GAINSBOURG A GAINSBARRE boxed-set (*9)

THE GREAT INDIE DISCOGRAPHY | The 1990s

GALAXIE 500

Formed: Boston, Massachusetts, USA ... mid-80's by ex-Harvard College student, DEAN WAREHAM, along with NAOMI YANG and DAMON KRUKOWSKI. The trio soon relocated to New York where they met KRAMER (ex-BUTTHOLE SURFER and Shimmy Disc label boss), who produced their 1987 album, 'TODAY'. Two years later, they signed to 'Rough Trade' and with KRAMER at the controls yet again, unleashed their flawed epic, 'ON FIRE' (1989). Lo-Fi anti-rock psychedelia reminiscent of JONATHAN RICHMAN being backed by The VELVET UNDERGROUND, the album's minimalist appeal subsequently gained the band many fans in the UK, although their homebase critics lambasted WAREHAM's limited vocals at every opportunity. He and the other two (DAMON & NAOMI) went their separate ways early in 1991 after their third album, 'THIS IS OUR MUSIC' (1990), failed to cut much critical ice. WAREHAM went on to produce his mates, MERCURY REV ('Car Wash Hair' EP), before becoming part of 'Elektra'-signed indie supergroup, LUNA. After a patchy, unsettling debut, 'LUNAPARK' (1992), his band – who comprised JUSTIN HARWOOD (ex-CHILLS) ans STANLEY DEMESKI (ex-FEELIES) – made good with the more enchanting 1994 follow-up, 'BEWITCHED', a record which enticed veteran VELVET UNDERGROUND guitarist, STERLING MORRISON, out of retirement. Another famous guest was TOM VERLAINE (ex-TELEVISION), a major influence on the band's sound (similar to GALAXIE 500, although a little lighter and jazzier) alongside LOU REED. A further two albums, 'PENTHOUSE' (1995) and 'PUP TENT' (1997), also pleased the faithful, STEREOLAB's LAETITIA SADIER guesting on the former. Meanwhile, DAMON & NAOMI (also known as PIERRE ETOILE around the early 90's) remained with KRAMER, the man producing their 1992 debut album, 'MORE SAD HITS'. As well as helping out on two mid-90's albums, 'NO EXCESS IS ABSURD' and 'WILL THEY TURN YOU ON OR WILL THEY TURN ON YOU', with their friends (WAYNE ROGERS and KATE BIGGAR) in retro-psychedelic outfit, MAGIC HOUR, D&N released a follow-up 'Sub Pop' album, 'THE WONDROUS WORLD OF ...' (1995). It would be a few more years before a third long-player, 'PLAYBACK SINGERS', appeared on 'Rykodisc' in 1998. LUNA ran into trouble with 'Elektra', however, on the eve of releasing their fifth album proper, and were subsequently dropped from the label. The album didn't appear until one year later, titled 'THE DAYS OF OUR NIGHTS' (1999), a beautiful odessey into the sparkling, warming world of DEAN WAREHAM, which included a stripped-down cover of Guns n' Roses 'SWEET CHILD O' MINE'. An unexpected concert album followed, 'LUNA LIVE' (2001), recorded at the '9:30 Club' in Washington and New York's 'Knitting Factory', and which also saw the replacement of bassist JUSTIN HARWOOD – who left to look after his young daughter – with BRITTA PHILLIPS (Ultrababyfat). The group also recorded perhaps their 'career best' with DAVE FRIDMANN of MERCURY REV (and others), entitled 'ROMANTICA' (2002). A sweet, transcendental album, FRIDMANN's production and occasional keyboards embraced WAREHAM's cynically sensitive songs, coupled with his excellent musicianship and his group's sublime instrumentation. Meanwhile, ex-GALAXIE 5000 casualties DAMON & NAOMI issued the moody and mystical ' ... WITH GHOSTS' (2000), and also followed in the footsteps of LUNA, releasing their own concert album, 'SONG TO THE SIREN: LIVE IN SAN SEBASTIAN' (2002), only backed by Japanese psychedelic noisecore band GHOST. • **Songwriters:** Group, except CHEESE AND ONIONS (Rutles) / VICTORY GARDEN (Red Crayola) / LISTEN, THE SNOW IS FALLING (Yoko Ono) / DON'T LET OUR YOUTH GO TO WASTE (Jonathan Richman) / HERE SHE COMES NOW (Velvet Underground) / CEREMONY (New Order) / ISN'T IT A PITY (George Harrison). LUNA covered INDIAN SUMMER (Beat Happening) / RIDE INTO THE SUN (Velvet Underground) / THAT'S WHAT YOU ALWAYS SAY (Dream Syndicate) / SEASON OF THE WITCH (Donovan) / OUTDOOR MINER (Wire) / NO REGRETS (Tom Rush) / THANK YOU FOR SENDING ME AN ANGEL (Talking Heads) / IN THE FLESH (Blondie) / WAITING ON A FRIEND (Rolling Stones) / NEON LIGHTS (Kraftwerk). CAGNEY & LACEE covered BORDERLINE (Madonna) / BE MINE (Martin Rev) / LOVIN' YOU (Minnie Riperton) / SIX FEET OF CHAIN + BY THE WAY (Lee Hazlewood) / THE LAST GOODBYE (Marty Robbins) / GREYHOUND GOIN' SOMEWHERE (Lee Dorsey) / FOR THE SAKE OF THE CHILDREN (Baskin-Reicheg) / MEMPHIS (Otis Blackwell) / I'M NOT SAYIN' (Gordon Lightfoot). MAGIC HOUR covered AMERICA (Traffic Sound). DAMON & NAOMI covered: TRANSLUCENT CARRIAGES (with Tom Rapp) / LIFE WILL PASS YOU BY (Chris Darrow) / WHISPERING PINES (Band) / WHO AM I? (... McDonald).

Album rating: TODAY (*8) / ON FIRE (*7) / THIS IS OUR MUSIC (*8) / GALAXIE 500 boxed compilation (*8) / COPENHAGEN live (*5) / Luna: LUNAPARK (*6) / BEWITCHED (*8) / PENTHOUSE (*7) / PUP TENT (*6) / THE DAYS OF OUR NIGHTS (*6) / LIVE (*6) / ROMANTICA (*7) / CLOSE COVER BEFORE STRIKING (*6) / Damon & Naomi: MORE SAD SONGS (*6) / THE WONDROUS WORLD OF ... (*6) / PLAYBACK SINGERS (*6) / DAMON & NAOMI WITH GHOST (*7) / SONG TO THE SIREN: LIVE IN SAN SEBASTIAN (*6) / Cagney & Lacee: SIX FEET OF CHAIN (*5) / Magic Hour: NO EXCESS IS ABSURD (*6) / WILL THEY TURN YOU ON OR WILL THEY TURN ON YOU (*6)

(MICHAEL) DEAN WAREHAM (b. 1 Aug'63, Wellington, New Zealand) – vocals, guitar / **NAOMI YANG** (b.15 Sep'64) – bass, vocals / **DAMON KRUKOWSKI** (b. 6 Sep'63) – drums, percussion

		not iss.	Aurora
May 88.	(7",7"blue) <AU 001> **TUGBOAT. / KING OF SPAIN**	-	
Feb 89.	(lp) <AU 002> **TODAY**	-	

– Flowers / Pictures / Parking lot / Don't let our youth go to waste / Temperature's rising / Oblivious / It's getting late / Instrumental / Tugboat. *(UK-iss.Sep89 on 'Schemer' lp/cd+=; 8905/+CD)* – King of Spain / Crazy. *(UK re-iss. Oct89 on 'Shimmy Disc' cd/lp; SDE 8908/+LP)* *(UK re-iss. Sep91 on 'Rough Trade' lp/c/cd; ROUGH/+C/CD 266)* *(cd re-iss. Apr97 on 'Rykodisc'+=; RCD 10356)* – King of Spain.

		Rough Trade	Rough Trade
Oct 89.	(lp/c/cd) (ROUGH/+C/CD 146) <ROUGHUS 74/+C/CD> **ON FIRE**		

– Blue thunder / Tell me / Snowstorm / Strange / When will you come home / Decomposing trees / Another day / Leave the planet / Plastic bird / Isn't it a pity. *(re-iss. Sep91 w/cd-ep+=; ROUGH 146L)* – Blue thunder / Victory garden / Ceremony / Cold night. *(cd re-iss. Apr97 on 'Rykodisc'+=; RCD 10357)*

| Feb 90. | (12"ep/cd-ep) (RTT 246/+CD) **BLUE THUNDER / VICTORY GARDEN. / CEREMONY / COLD NIGHT** | | - |
| Jun 90. | (7"ltd) (CAFF 8) **RAIN (live). / DON'T LET OUR YOUTH GO TO WASTE (live)** | | |

(above 45 on 'Caff' records)

| Sep 90. | (12"/cd-s) (RTT 249/+CD) / Gasatanka; <6083> **FOURTH OF JULY. / HERE SHE COMES NOW** | | |
| Oct 90. | (lp/c/cd) (ROUGH/+C/CD 156) <ROUGHUS 86/+C/CD> **THIS IS OUR MUSIC** | | |

– Fourth of July / Hearing voices / Spook / Summertime / Way up high / Listen, the snow is falling / Sorry / Melt away / King of Spain, part two. *(other cd-iss. ; CDR 156L)* *(cd re-iss. Apr97 on 'Rykodisc'+=; RCD 10358)* – Here she comes now.

– In Spring '91, DEAN WAREHAM departed to work on solo project and guest for MERCURY REV. DAMON & NAOMI became PIERRE ETOILE and went into studio with Boston various musicians.

– compilations, etc. –

on 'Rykodisc' unless mentioned otherwise

| Sep 96. | (4xcd-box) <(RCD 10355)> **GALAXIE 500** | | |

– (TODAY / ON FIRE / THIS IS OUR MUSIC / UNCOLLECTED).

| Apr 97. | (cd) <(RCD 10363)> **COPENHAGEN** | | |

– Decomposing trees / Fourth of July / Summertime / Sorry / When will you come home / Spook / Listen, the snow is falling / Here she comes now / Don't let our youth go to waste. *(re-iss. Jun99; same)*

| Sep 98. | (cd) <(RCD 10445)> **THE PORTABLE GALAXIE 500** | | |

– Blue thunder / Flowers / When will you come home / Listen the snow is falling / Sorry / Fourth of July / Don't let our youth go to waste / Strange / Another day / Snowstorm / Summertime (live) / Tugboat.

DEAN WAREHAM

– augmented by JUSTIN HARWOOD (Chills), JIMMY CHAMBERS (Mercury Rev) + BYRON GUTHRIE (Ultra Vivid Scene)

		Mint Tea	not iss.
Feb 92.	(12"/cd-s) (MINT 6 T/CD) **ANESTHESIA. / I CAN'T WAIT / TOMATO PEOPLE**		-

LUNA

DEAN WAREHAM – vocals, guitar / **JUSTIN HARWOOD** – bass (ex-CHILLS) / **STANLEY DEMESKI** – drums (ex-FEELIES)

		Rough Trade	Rough Trade
Jan 92.	(12"ep/cd-ep) (R 2973/+CD) **INDIAN SUMMER / EGG NOG. / RIDE INTO THE SUN / THAT'S WHAT YOU ALWAYS SAY**		

		Elektra	Elektra
Aug 92.	(12"ep/cd-ep) (EKR 169 T/CD) **SMILE / SLASH YOUR TIRES. / HEY SISTER (demo) / ROLLERCOASTER**		-
Mar 93.	(c-ep/cd-ep) <61472-4/-4> **SLIDE EP**	-	

– Slide / Indian summer / Ride into the sun / That's what you always say / Hey sister / Rollercoaster.

| Aug 92. | (cd/c/lp) <7559 61360-2/-4/-1)> **LUNAPARK** | | |

– Slide / Anaesthesia / Slash your tires / Crazy people / Time / Smile / I can't wait / Hey sister / I want everything / Time to quit / Goodbye / We're both confused.

– added **SEAN EDEN** – guitar

| Mar 94. | (cd/c) <(7559 61617-2/-4)> **BEWITCHED** | | |

– California (all the way) / Tiger Lily / Friendly advice / Bewitched / This time around / Great Jones Street / Going home / Into the fold / I know you tried / Sleeping pill.

		Beggars Banquet	Elektra
Apr 95.	(12"ep/cd-ep) (BBQ 56 T/CD) **BONNIE AND CLYDE EP**		-

– Bonnie and Clyde (the Bonnie Parker version) / Chinatown / Thankyou for sending me an angel / Bonnie and Clyde (the Clyde Barrow version).
above w/ guest **LAETITIA SADIER** – vocals (of STEREOLAB)

| Aug 95. | (cd/c/dp) (BBQ CD/MC/LP 178) <61807> **PENTHOUSE** | | |

– Chinatown / Sideshow by the seashore / Moon palace / Double feature / 23 minutes in Brussels / Lost in space / Rhythm king / Kalanazoo / Hedgehog / Freakin' and peakin' / Bonnie and Clyde (the Clyde Barrow version).

GALAXIE 500 (cont)

Nov 95. (7") *(BBQ 59)* **HEDGEHOG. / 23 MINUTES IN BRUSSELS / NO REGRETS**
(cd-s+=) *(BBQ 59CD)* – Happy New Year.

— **LEE WALL** – drums; repl. DEMESKI

Mar 96. (cd-ep) *<KAR 036-2>* **LUNA EP**
– Sideshow by the seashore / Thankyou for sending me an angel / The moviegoer / It's bringing you down / The enabler / No regrets.
<above issued on 'No.6'>

— HARWOOD also joined supergroup, TUATARA, with PETER BUCK of R.E.M.

Sep 96. (10"ep/cd-ep) *(BBQ 302 TT/CD)* **SEASON OF THE WITCH / INDIAN SUMMER. / LOST IN SPACE / 23 MINUTES IN BRUSSELS**

Apr 97. (ltd.7") *(TRDSC 005)* **IN THE FLESH. / EARLY MORNING**
(above on 'Trade 2') <below on 'Radiation'>

Jun 97. (7"colrd) *<RARE 027>* **OUTDOOR MINER. / ROLL IN THE SAND**

Jun 97. (7") *(BBQ 313)* **IHOP. / WORDS WITHOUT WRINKLES**
(cd-s+=) *(BBQ 313CD)* – Fuzzy wuzzy.

Jul 97. (cd/c/lp) *(BBQ CD/MC/LP 194)* <62055> **PUP TENT**
– IHOP / Beautiful view / Pup tent / Bobby Peru / Beggar's bliss / Tracey I love you / Whispers / City kitty / Creeps / Fuzzy wuzzy.

Sep 97. (7"clear) *(BBQ 319)* **BOBBY PERU. / BOB LA FLAMBEUR / DANCE WITH ME**
(cd-s) *(BBQ 319CD)* – (first 2 tracks) / In the flesh / Beggar's bliss (demo).

Jul 98. (cd-ep) *(BBQ 322CD)* **BEAUTIFUL VIEW / BOBBY PERU (US radio edit) / CALIFORNIA ALL THE WAY**

1998. (7") *<RS 004>* **DANCE WITH ME. / (other side by WAKE OOLOO)**

— *<above on 'Rocker! Supernova'> <below on 'Sub Pop'>*

1998. (7"yellow) *<SP 438>* **EVERYBODY'S TALKIN'. / FUZZY WUZZY (demo)**

Apr 99. (7") *(BBQ 334)* **SUPERFREAKY MEMORIES. / NEON LIGHTS**
(cd-s+=) *(BBQCD 334)* – The bad vibe merchant.

May 99. (cd/lp) *(BBQ CD/LP 209)* <90003> **THE DAYS OF OUR NIGHTS** Oct99
– Dear diary / Hello little one / The old fashioned way / Four thousand days / Seven steps to Satan / Superfreaky memories / Math wiz / Words without wrinkles / The rustler / U.S. out of my pants! / The slow song / Sweet child o' mine.

— **BRITTA PHILLIPS** (b.11 Jun'63, Boyne City, Missouri) – bass (ex-BELLTOWER) repl. HARWOOD who returned to New Zealand

Mar 01. (cd) *(BBQMCD 218)* <17> **LIVE (live)** Feb01
– Bewitched / Chinatown / Friendly advice / Pup tent / Sideshow by the seashore / Anaesthesia / Tiger lily / 4000 days / Hello little one / Moon palace / Lost in space / 23 minutes in Brussels / 4th of July / Bonnie and Clyde.

Apr 02. (cd) *<TWA 44CD>* **ROMANTICA**
– Lovedust / Weird and woozy / Black postcards / Black champagne / Swedish fish / Renee is crying / Mermaid eyes / 1995 / Rememories / Dizzy / Orange peel / Romantica.

Oct 02. (cd) *<TWA 51CD>* **CLOSE COVER BEFORE STRIKING**
– Astronaut / Waiting for a friend / Teenage lightning / Drunken whistler / Alibi / New Haven comet / Neon lights / Lovedust (video) / 1995 (video).

CAGNEY & LACEE

— aka **WAREHAM** and his wife **CLAUDIA SILVER**

1995. (7") *<KAR 034>* **TIME. / BY THE WAY (I STILL LOVE YOU)**

Mar 97. (cd) *<KAR 041-2>* **SIX FEET OF CHAIN**
– Be mine / Lovin' you / Six feet of chain / The last goodbye / By the way / Greyhound goin' somewhere / For the sake of the children / Memphis / I'm not sayin'.

Nov 98. (one-sided-7"white) *(WORMSS 3)* **BORDERLINE / ORANGE**

DAMON & NAOMI

Jul 91. (12"ep/cd-ep; as PIERRE ETOILE) *(R 272-0/-3)* **IN THE SUN. / NINETEEN SIXTY-NINE / THIS CAR CLIMBED MT. WASHINGTON**
(re-iss. Jun97 on 'Elefant'; ER 306)

Nov 92. (lp/c/cd) *<(SHIMMY 058/+MC/CD)>* **MORE SAD HITS**
– E.T.A. / Little red record co. / Information age / Laika / This car climbed Mt. Washington / Astrofiamanne / Boston's daily temperature / (Scene change) / Sir Thomas and Sir Robert / Once more / This changing world / Memories. *<cd re-iss. Oct98 on 'Rykodisc'; RCD 10439/>*

Nov 95. (lp/cd) *(SP 322/+B)* **THE WONDROUS WORLD OF DAMON & NAOMI**
– In the morning / New historicism / Tour of the world / Forgot to get high / Pyewacket / Life will pass you by / Who am I? / New York City / Pandora's box / How long / Whispering blues.
<(cd re-iss. Oct98 on 'Rykodisc'; RCD 10440)>

— DAMON & NAOMI joined up with MAGIC HOUR (see further below)

Aug 97. (7") *(WORM 3)* **THE NAVIGATOR. / AWAKE IN A MUDDLE**

Apr 98. (cd) *(RCD 10438)* <SP 425> **PLAYBACK SINGERS**
– Turn of the century / Eye of the storm / In the sun / Navigator / I'm yours / Kinetoscope / Awake in a muddle / We're not there / Translucent carriages.

— next with Japanese group the GHOST:- **KAZUO OGINO, MASAKI BATOH + MICHIO KURIHARS**

Sep 00. (cd; as DAMON & NAOMI WITH GHOST) *<(SPCD 501)>* **DAMON & NAOMI WITH GHOST**
– Mirror phase / The new world / Judah and the Maccabees / Blue moon / Great wall / I dreamed of the Caucasus / Don't forget / Tanka / Eulogy to Lenny Bruce.
(lp-iss.Oct00 on 'Drag City'; DC 206)

— KURIHARI was still included (+ credited!) in line-up

Apr 02. (cd) *<(SPCD 592)>* **SONG TO THE SIREN: LIVE IN SAN SEBASTIAN (live in Spain)**
– Judah and the Maccabees / The new world / Eye of the storm / Song to the siren / The navigator / The great wall / I dreamed of the Caucasus / New York City / Tanka / Turn of the century / Love. *(w/ free DVD)*

MAGIC HOUR

— **WAYNE ROGERS** – vocals (from TWISTED VILLAGE & CRYSTALIZED MOVEMENTS stable) / **KATE BIGGAR** / **DAMON KRUKOWSKI** / **NAOMI YANG**

Dec 93. (7") *<TW 1028>* **HEADS DOWN. / (part 2)**

Sep 94. (10"ep) *(che 18)* **AFTER TOMORROW. / WORLD OF ONE / PERMANENT GREEN LIGHT**

Oct 94. (cd/lp) *(che 20 cd/lp)* *<TW 1031>* **NO EXCESS IS ABSURD**
– Isn't a way / Always leaving never / Sally free and easy / After tomorrow / Lower / World of one / The last mistake / Heads down #2.

May 95. (7") *(che 29)* **I HAD A THOUGHT. / AMERICA**

Jun 95. (cd/lp) *(che 30 cd/lp)* *<TW 1035>* **WILL THEY TURN YOU ON OR WILL THEY TURN ON YOU**

Dec 96. (cd) *<TW 1039>* **SECSESSION96**
– Sunset one / Rosebud / Sunrise / Sunset two.

GALLON DRUNK

Formed: Turnpike Lane, London, England ... late 80's by JAMES JOHNSTON and MIKE DELANIAN along with ex-EARLS OF SUAVE man, MAX DECHARNE and early drummer NICK COOMBE. Replacing the latter with maestro of the maracas, JOEY BYFIELD, GALLON DRUNK swaggered onto an indie stage dominated by the fag-end of the baggy scene and limp-wristed shoegazers; pausing only to grease back their quiffs and dust down their vintage suits, JOHNSTON & Co. proceeded to unleash the most violent, paranoid, unholy racket this side of The BIRTHDAY PARTY. After a clutch of early singles on their manager's 'Massive' label, the band signed to London indie, 'Clawfist'. Rolling in on a crescendo of distorted bass and exploding in a howl of organ abuse and clenched-teeth threats, 'SOME FOOLS MESS' was quintessential GALLON DRUNK (if you only ever buy one GALLON DRUNK record etc ....). It was also a much heralded NME Single Of The Week, paving the way for a debut album, 'YOU, THE NIGHT AND THE MUSIC' (1992). When this lot weren't spitting out their trademark cocktail of twisted blues/R&B, New Orleans voodoo and amphetamine fuelled rockabilly (LINK WRAY comes to mind), they were partial to a bit of low-rent lounge crooning; ok, JOHNSTON was never going to be NEIL DIAMOND and they never pulled it off with quite the same panache as The TINDERSTICKS but covers of Lee Hazelwood's 'LOOK AT THAT WOMAN' and Neil Sedaka's 'SOLITAIRE' remain compulsive listening. These tasty nuggets can be found hiding on the B-side of the searing 'BEDLAM' single, TERRY EDWARDS' baritone sax adding depth to what was basically a sharpened-up, groovier take on 'SOME FOOLS ...'. The best track by some measure on 'FROM THE HEART OF THE TOWN' (1992), it only served to underline the impression that they couldn't quite keep the pedal to the metal over a whole album. Still, GALLON DRUNK cruising was infinitely preferable to the bloodless indie pap of the day and grimy Big Smoke sketches like 'ARLINGTON ROAD' made a mockery of BLUR's subsequent oi! guv! pastiche. A mark of the man's underrated talents, JOHNSTON was signed up for touring duties with NICK CAVE during the BAD SEED's Lollapalooza '94 jaunt, no doubt a more entertaining proposition than GALLON DRUNK's disastrous gig at Glasgow's King Tut's the previous year (when some f***wit in the audience persisted in pulling the leads and caused JOHNSTON to storm off after about two songs). 1994 also saw JOHNSTON and EDWARDS cut the musical accompaniment for a spoken word album ('DORA SAUREZ') by crime writer, Derek Raymond while GALLON DRUNK the band eventually emerged from the pub in 1995 with an EP, 'THE TRAITOR'S GATE'. By this point the line-up was JOHNSTON, DELANIAN, BYFIELD alongside newcomers IAN WATSON, ANDY DEWER and IAN WHITE, this combination working on the long awaited third set, 'IN THE LONG STILL NIGHT'. Released on 'City Slang' in '96, the record revealed a more sober GALLON DRUNK; while the songwriting was probably stronger – highlights being the storming lead track, 'TWO CLEAR EYES' and the celluloid funk-noir of 'THE BIG PAYOFF', gone was the gloriously filthy sound, JOHNSTON's mumbled menace and the delirious sense of impending chaos that characterised the band's early work. Despite overwhelmingly positive reviews, a subsequent decision that GALLON DRUNK had reached its ultimate conclusion led to the band's official dissolution in '97. Of late, JOHNSTON has found a new outlet for his manic energy, linking up with EDWARDS to form J.J. STONE, who stormed the alternative dancefloors in 1998 (con)fusing unlikely elements of SPIRITUALIZED and QUINCY JONES. The JOHNSTON/EDWARDS axis was to be the basis of a regrouped GALLON DRUNK (along with a new rhythm section of JERRY COTTINGHAM and IAN WHITE), recruited

by Greek film director, Nikos Triandafyllidis, to cut the soundtrack for his 1999 thriller, 'Black Milk'. With their penchant for cinematic grooves and an obvious career-long fixation with ENNIO MORRICONE, the opportunity to record a film score was never likely to be squandered. On the contrary, it ranked as one of the band's most seamless efforts to date; JOHNSTON and EDWARDS' dark, sinuous incantations had never sounded so elegantly menacing. JOHNSTON himself was to make it on to the big screen in 2001 with a part in Ken Russell's 'The Fall of the Louse Usher' while a long awaited GALLON DRUNK studio album, 'FIRE MUSIC' (2002) – featuring Dylan's 'SERIES OF DREAMS' – confirmed that they were still one of the most potent and underrated forces in alternative music. • **Covered:** RUBY (Silver Apples) / SILVER WINGS (Merle Haggard) / TO LOVE SOMEBODY (Bee Gees) / HEAVEN HOLDS ALL MY TREASURES (Hank Williams).
• **Trivia:** JOE BYFIELD had brief spell with MY BLOODY VALENTINE, and drummer MAX DECHARNE also played keyboards with The PYROS (FRANK TOVEY's outfit!).

Album rating: YOU, THE NIGHT AND THE MUSIC (*6) / FROM THE HEART OF TOWN (*7) / TONITE... THE SINGLES BAR compilation (*7) / IN THE LONG STILL NIGHT (*7) / BLACK MILK (*6) / FIRE MUSIC (*5) / BEAR ME AWAY double compilation (*6)

JAMES JOHNSTON – vocals, guitar, organ / **MIKE DELANIAN** – bass / **NICK COOMBE** – drums

Gallon Drunk / not iss.

May 90. (ltd-7") (GAL 003) **SNAKEPIT. / PLEASE GIVE ME SOMETHING**

— added p/t **GARY BONNEYFACE** – maracas

Clawfist / Rykodisc

Nov 90. (7") (HUNKA LURVE 1) **RUBY. / US AND COUSIN EMMY**

— **MAX DECHARNE** – drums / **JOE BYFIELD** – maracas; repl. NICK + GARY

Mar 91. (7") (HUNKA 002) **DRAGGIN' ALONG. / MISERLOU**
Jul 91. (7") (HUNKA 003) **THE LAST GASP. / THE WHIRLPOOL**
Oct 91. (7"ep/12"ep/cd-ep) (HUNKA+/12/CD 006) **SOME FOOLS MESS. / ROLLING HOME / MAY THE EARTH OPEN HERE**
Feb 92. (cd/lp) (HUNKA CDL/LP 001) <RCD/RCS 10258> **YOU, THE NIGHT ... AND THE MUSIC (GALLON DRUNK)** Sep92
– Rev up – T.P.A. / Some fool's mess / Just one more / Two wings mambo / You, the night... and the music / Gallon drunk / Night tide / Eye of the storm / Tornado.
Jul 92. (cd/lp) (HUNKA CDL/LP 002) <RCD/RCS 10257> **TONITE... THE SINGLES BAR** (compilation)
– The last grasp (safety) / Rolling home / Snakepit / Miserlou / Ruby / Draggin' along / May the Earth open here / Please give me something / The whirlpool / Gallon drunk.
Oct 92. (7") (HUNKA 011) **BEDLAM. / LOOK AT THAT WOMAN**
(12"+=/cd-s+=) (HUNKA+/12/CD 011) – Solitaire.

— recruited **TERRY EDWARDS** – saxophone, organ, trumpet, harmonica (ex-HIGSONS, solo artist)

Clawfist / Sire

Apr 93. (cd/lp) (HUNKA CD/LP 005) <25269> **FROM THE HEART OF TOWN** 67
– Jake on the make / Arlington Road / Not before time / Keep moving on / Bedlam / You should be ashamed / End of the line / Loving alone / Push the boat out / Paying for pleasure. (w/free 20 minute live cd/lp) **LIVE AT MADISON SQUARE GARDENS)** – Just one more / Some fool's mess / Two wings mambo. (lp+=) – Silver wings / The Amsterdam run.
May 93. (12"ep/cd-ep) (HUNKA 018/+CD) **YOU SHOULD BE ASHAMED. / THE AMSTERDAM RUN / SILVER WINGS**
Oct 93. (ltd-7") (XPIG 21) **KNOWN NOT WANTED. / (b-side by Tindersticks)**

— in Dec'93, GALLON DRUNK featured on V/A 10"ep, 'SAVAGE SOUNDTRACKS FOR SWINGING LOVERS' on 'Blue Eyed Dog'; a month later JOHNSTON and Co provided words, etc for the 'DORA SUAREZ' soundtrack

IAN WHITE – drums; repl. MAX who formed FLAMING STARS as frontman (added on some tracks **IAN R. WATSON** – guitar, trumpet + **ANDY DEWAR** – percussion)

Gallon Drunk / not iss.

Dec 95. (cd-ep) (GDR 001) **THE TRAITOR'S GATE**
– Traitor's gate / Some cast fire / Chain of gold / Bear me away.

City Slang / City Slang

Sep 96. (7") (EFA 04985-7) **TWO CLEAR EYES. / MR. SLINKY'S**
(cd-s+=) (EFA 04985-2) – Fade away / My spent love.
Sep 96. (<EFA 04982-2/-1>) **IN THE LONG STILL NIGHT**
– Two clear eyes / Up on fife / It's all mine / Eternal tide / The road ahead / The big payoff / Take this poison / Some cast fire / Geraldine / Get ready... / To love somebody / In the long still night.
Mar 97. (7") (EFA 04986-7) **TO LOVE SOMEBODY. / COME UNTO ME**
(cd-s+=) (EFA 04986-2) – The shakedown / Heaven holds all of my treasures.

J.J. STONE

— aka **JAMES JOHNSTON** with **IAN WHITE** + **TERRY EDWARDS**

Itchy Teeth / not iss.

Aug 98. (12"/cd-s) (ITCHY 12/CD 001) **HURRICANE (mixes; PK radio / original / PsychedeliaSmith & PK Salty goodness) / ITCHY TEETH**

GALLON DRUNK

— returned after a long hiatus, the line-up being **JOHNSTON, WHITE, EDWARDS** + new bassman **JEREMY COTTINGHAM**; guest singer **PAVLINA MICHAILIDOU**

F.M. / not iss.

Jan 00. (cd-ep) (FM 2300) **BLOOD IS RED**
– Blood is red (radio edit) / Hurricane (new version) / Theme from Black Milk (instrumental) / Hurricane (video).
Mar 00. (cd) (FM 1134) **BLACK MILK** (original soundtrack)
– Theme from Black Milk / Hurricane (new version) / Every second of time / Blood is red / The funeral / Can you feel it / Now and forever / At my side / Prostitute / Hypnotised / Every second of time (instrumental) / One more time / Lament.

— now without **EDWARDS**

Sweet Nothing / not iss.

Nov 01. (7") (7SN 010) **THINGS WILL CHANGE. / RUSTLER**
(cd-s) (7SN 010CD) – ('A'side) / Out of sight / The greasy Caesar / I've been waiting / Up on fire (live).
Mar 02. (cd/lp) (SNCD/SNLP 012) **FIRE MUSIC**
– Outside of love / Out of sight / Things will change / In this moment / Everything's alright / Forget all that you know / Just one word / Fire music (pt.1) / Fire music (pt.2) / Series of dreams.
Nov 02. (d-cd) (SNCD 020) **BEAR ME AWAY** (compilation 1992-2002)

– compilations, others, etc. –

Nov 92. (cd/lp; shared with BREED) Strange Fruit; (SFMCD 213) / Dutch East India; <DEI 8414> **CLAWFIST – THE PEEL SESSIONS**
– Ruby / Some fool's mess / Drag '91 / Two wings mambo.

GANGER

Formed: Glasgow, Scotland ... early 1995 by two bassists! GRAHAM GAVIN and STUART HENDERSON, plus drummer JAMES A YOUNG and guitarist LUCY McKENZIE; STEVEN CLARK (aka SCI-FI STEVEN of BIS) augmented the Krautrock-inspired instrumental combo on their 1996 debut, 'HALF NELSON.ep'. A debut of infinite, spaced-out experimentalism, its finale was the 20-minute epic 'JELLYNECK'. Still on their FAUST, NEU! and ASH RA TEMPEL trip, GANGER walked the musical plank once more via the 'Domino' (Series 500) EP, 'THE CAT'S IN THE BAG...THE BAG'S IN THE RIVER', the basic 4-piece having added MARTIN ALLEN on keyboards. A further addition to the line-up came in the form of sax player CAROLINE KRAABEL, taking her place for the band's third single, the Jamie Watson-produced 'HOLLYWOOD LOAF'. After the obligatory singles compilation, GANGER re-shuffled once again, this time HENDERSON and YOUNG bringing in fresh creative blood CRAIG B and NATASHA NORAMLY. Gradually leaving behind their Germanic sprawls, they initiated their own brand of sonic architecture with the 2-minute! 'GEOCITIES' single, following it up with some fresh material for 'Domino' ('Merge' in the US) in the shape of 'WITH TONGUE TWISTING WORDS'. Shortly afterwards (in July '98), GANGER belatedly released their debut album proper, 'HAMMOCK STYLE', a Stateside jaunt alongside spiritual brethren MOGWAI increasing their street cred. However, the busy-busy CRAIG B (simultaneously a member of FUKUYAMA with NATASHA) couldn't be held down for long, subsequently lifting off with his new project, AEREOGRAMME. 1999's 'CANOPY' finally put the lid on GANGER's career, the group disbanding shortly after its release.

Album rating: FORE compilation (*6) / HAMMOCK STYLE (*6)

STUART HENDERSON – bass, effects, keyboards / **GRAHAM GAVIN** – bass, guitar / **JAMES A. YOUNG** – drums / **STEVEN CLARK** – drums (of BIS) / **LUCY McKENZIE** – clarinet, guitar, keyboards

Vesuvius / not iss.

Apr 96. (12"ep) (POMP 004) **HALF NELSON.ep**
– Guts and bravoodoo / Drummer's arms and bionic thumbs / Jellyneck.

— **MARTIN ALLEN** – keyboards; repl. SCI-FI STEVEN who continued with BIS

Planet / not iss.

Sep 96. (12"ep) (punk 014) **THE CAT'S IN THE BAG... THE BAG'S IN THE RIVER**
– Anomovieshot / Smorgasbord / Missile that back-fired.

— added **CAROLINE KRAABEL** – saxophone

Series 500 / not iss.

Dec 96. (12"ep) (ser 504) **HOLLYWOOD LOAF. / PRISONER OF MY EYEBALL / SMORGASBORD (Third Eye Foundation version)**

Domino / Merge

Apr 97. (cd/d-lp) (WIG CD/LP 30) **FORE** (compilation of EP's)
– Hollywood loaf / Missile that back-fired / Drummer's arms and bionic thumbs / Smorgasbord / Fore / Jellyneck / Anomovieshot / Prisoner of my eyeball.

— (Sep'97) **HENDERSON + YOUNG** recruited **CRAIG B** – guitar, vocals + **NATASHA NORAMLY** – bass (ex-FUKUYAMA) to repl. others

Feb 98. (7") (WJ 16) **GEOCITIES. / ALESSANDRA AND HER WESTERN FAN**
(above issued on 'Wurlitzer Jukebox')
Jun 98. (12"ep/cd-ep) (RUG 61/+CD) **WITH TONGUE TWISTING WORDS EP**
– With tongue twisting words / Hammock style / Baby cats and jaws / Hope.

— (first track above was recorded with GRAHAM, MARTIN + CAROLINE)
Jul 98. (cd/lp) (WIG CD/LP 47) **HAMMOCK STYLE**
– Cats, dogs and babies jaws / Upye / Capo (south of Caspian) / First thing in the morning / What happened to the king happened to me / Blau / Lid of the stars.

— **CRAIG B** (also of FUKUYAMA with NATASHA) left to form AEREOGRAMME

GANGER (cont) — THE GREAT INDIE DISCOGRAPHY — The 1990s

Dec 99. (cd-ep) *(GUIDE 38)* **CANOPY** (Guided Missile / not iss.)
 – Canopy / State conversation / Now we have you / Hai! / Standing on the shoulders of giants.

—— GANGER disbanded sometime in 1999

GARAGELAND

Formed: Auckland, New Zealand . . . 1993 by JEREMY EADE, ANDREW GLADSTONE, MARK SILVEY and his sister DEBBIE. Named after their number one CLASH song, the messy indie quartet signed to the cult 'Flying Nun' label in 1994, issuing the harmonic (but slightly warped) 'COME BACK' EP at the begining of '95. This debut offering, from such a low-key antipodean band, sounded as if STEVE MALKMUS (of PAVEMENT fame) had rammed an electric drill through SONIC YOUTH's amps, causing a mass ecological power surge on both sides of the equator. Their second outing, 'LAST EXIT TO GARAGELAND', was slightly more mainstream in the sense that it featured mature guitar clasps, catchy sing-a-long choruses and soaring melodies that would certainly keep your mother occupied. Many of their older fanbase preferred their earlier stuff. Like many NZ outfits before them, they found it difficult to bridge the expanse between their brand of indie rock'n'roll and Britain's lineage of iconic masters of rock. After a second set, 'DO WHAT YOU WANT' (1999), songwriter EADE was left to run the show, albeit with fresh guitarist DAVE GOODISON. The album 'SCORPIO RIGHTING' was on the wall by 2001, their obvious take-on STONES-esque rifferamas were praised by US-based mags such as Billboard and Rolling Stone, although the UK jury was out for the time-being at least.

Album rating: LAST EXIT TO GARAGELAND (*6) / DO WHAT YOU WANT (*6) / SCORPIO RIGHTING (*5)

JEREMY EADE – vocals, guitar / **MARK SILVEY** – bass / **ANDREW GLADSTONE** – drums / **DEBBIE SILVEY** – guitar

May 96. (7") *(FN 335)* **COME BACK. / POP CIGAR** (Flying Nun / Flying Nun Nov96)
 (cd-ep) <*(FNCD 335)*> – ('A'side) / Shouldn't matter but it does / Bus stops / What will you do? / Struck / Something's got a hold / Cut it out. *(re-iss. Jun97 on 'Discordant' 7"ep/cd-ep; CORD S/D 007)*

Nov 96. (7") *(FN 358)* **FINGERPOPS. / SOMETHING'S GOT A HOLD**
 (cd-s+=) *(FNCD 358)* – The floribundaimpetigo experience / Cherry cola vodka.

May 97. (7") *(FN 392)* **POP CIGAR. / WHAT WILL YOU DO?**
 (cd-s+=) *(FNCD 392)* – Fay Ray / Struck.

Sep 97. (cd-ep) *(FNCD 405)* **FEEL ALRIGHT EP** (— / NewZ)
 – Feel alright / Nude star / Fingerpops / Beelines '97 / Comeback '97.

Oct 97. (cd) *(CORDD 009)* <*70001*> **LAST EXIT TO GARAGELAND** (Discordant / Foodchain)
 – Intro / Fingerpops / Classically diseased / Nude star / Pop cigar / Beelines to Heaven / Come back / Fire away / Tired and bored / I'm looking for what I can't get / Never gonna come around here again / Return to you / Jesus I'm freezing / Fay Ray. *(NZ-iss.Jun96 on 'Flying Nun'; FNCD)*

Oct 97. (cd-s) *(CORDS 010)* **NUDE STAR (the Moulder mix) / (mixes)**

Jan 98. (7") *(CORDS 012)* **BEELINES TO HEAVEN. / BUS STOPS**
 (cd-s+=) *(CORDD 012)* – Cut it out / Bus trips.

Apr 98. (7") *(CORDS 013)* **FINGERPOPS. / SHOULDN'T MATTER BUT IT DOES**
 (cd-s+=) *(CORDD 013)* – I'm looking for what I can't get (XFM radio version).

Jun 99. (cd-ep) *(FNCD 422)* **THE NOT EMPTY EP** (Flying Nun / Foodchain — / NewZ)
 – Not empty / Trashcans / Allison / Rearrange / Favourite little star.

Oct 99. (cd) *(FNCD 423)* <*54448-2*> **DO WHAT YOU WANT** (— / Nov98)
 – Love song / Trashcans / You will never cry again / Not empty / Kiss it all goodbye / Good luck / What you gonna do? / Get even / Good morning / Burning bridges / Jean / Middle of the evening / End of the night. *(UK-iss.Oct02 on 'Foodchain'; same as US)*

—— **JEREMY** recruited **DAVE GOODISON** – guitar

Jun 01. (cd-s) *(FNCD 453)* **GONE / TREASURE TROVE / THE DARKEST HEARTS** (— / NewZ)

Oct 01. (cd) *(FNCD 452)* <*70006-2*> **SCORPIO RIGHTING** (— / Oct02)
 – Life is so sweet / Get some / Been around / Crazy / Superstars / Carry me south / High way / Gone / Rock and roll heart / Believe in you / Who the hell do you think you are? / Shine. *(bonus cd+=)* – acoustic:- Superstars / Trashcans / Jean / Beelines to Heaven / Rock and roll heart / Kiss it all goodbye.

GARBAGE

Formed: Madison, Wisconsin, USA . . . 1994 by BUTCH VIG, DUKE ERIKSON and STEVE MARKER, out of the ashes of FIRE TOWN and SPOONER. BUTCH's latter ham-pop/rock act, had been on the go since early 1978 and released their debut ep 'CRUEL SCHOOL' a year later <Boat; SP 4001>. Another soon followed, 'WHERE YOU GONNA RUN?' <Boat; SP 3001>, before an album, 'EVERY CORNER DANCE' surfaced in '82; <Mountain Railroad; HR 8005>. BUTCH then set up his own studio and produced KILLDOZER, before giving SPOONER another outing with the album 'WILDEST DREAMS' <Boat; SP 1004>. In 1986, their final flop 45, 'MEAN OLD WORLD' <Boat; SP 1018>, made BUTCH form FIRE TOWN, with old buddy STEVE MARKER and co-songwriter DOUG ERIKSON. A few singles, 'CARRY THE TORCH' <7-89242> and 'RAIN ON YOU' <7-89204>, appeared from the 'Atlantic' stable alongside albums 'IN THE HEART OF THE HEART COUNTRY' <Boat; 1013 / re-iss. Atlantic; 81754> & 'THE GOOD LIFE' cd/lp; <781945-2/-1>. In 1989/90, BUTCH re-formed with the original line-up of SPOONER, DUKE ERIKSON, DAVE BENTON, JEFF WALKER and JOEL TAPPERO, to release one-off comeback cd 'THE FUGITIVE DANCE' <Dali-Chameleon; 89026>. He was then to find fame in production work for greats like NIRVANA, SONIC YOUTH, SMASHING PUMPKINS, NINE INCH NAILS and U2, before coming across Edinburgh-born vixen SHIRLEY MANSON fronting the band ANGELFISH on MTV. The new-look GARBAGE contributed the electro-goth of 'VOW' to a 'Volume' various artists compilation and this ended up as their limited edition debut 45 in 1995. By that year's summer, they had signed to Geffen's 'Almo Sounds' (UK 'Mushroom') records, which helped them break into the UK Top 50 with 'SUBHUMAN'. Success finally came with the 'ONLY HAPPY WHEN IT RAINS' single, a grungey, more tuneful affair that retained the goth overtones, MANSON weaving her deep throat vocals around the melody like a spider's web. She was an obvious focal point for the group; on their Top Of The Pops debut the singer made like a brooding, 90's incarnation of CHRISSIE HYNDE while the rest of the band remained comfortably anonymous in uniform black. The eponymous debut album, released later that year, was a mixed bag of styles that worked fairly effectively. Subsequent single, 'QUEER', kind of summed up the GARBAGE ethos, a deceptively poppy number featuring a MANSON vocal positively dripping with loathing, self or otherwise. GARBAGE continued their rise to the top of the pile with a UK chart-topping second set, 'VERSION 2.0', masterfully treading the finest of lines between alternative credibility and outright mainstream success; the hits kept on coming with 'PUSH IT', 'I THINK I'M PARANOID' and 'SPECIAL' all making the UK Top 20. After the phenomenal success of their previous albums, the group re-united in the studio to record their third album proper, the strange and often confused 'BEAUTIFUL GARBAGE' (2001). A slice of every popular genre imaginable, the set offered the listener a wide range of uncommercial tracks, shot through with MANSON's sexual imagery and VIG's scorching production techniques. The sassy 'SILENCE IS GOLDEN' saw MANSON taking some hints from feminine hero PJ HARVEY, while 'SHUT YOUR MOUTH' and hit single 'ANDROGYNY' were classic GARBAGE and would have fitted anywhere on the group's debut album. 'CHERRY LIPS (GO BABY GO!)' was the surprise track out of them all; a funky, sexy take-on of new wave, which just proves that GARBAGE may have a few tricks up their sleeves yet. • **Covered:** KISS MY ASS (Vic Chesnutt) / WILD HORSES (Rolling Stones) / sampled the CLASH's 'Train In Vain' on 'STUPID GIRL'.

Album rating: GARBAGE (*8) / VERSION 2.0 (*7) / BEAUTIFUL GARBAGE (*6)

SHIRLEY MANSON (b. 3 Aug'66, Edinburgh, Scotland) – vocals, guitar (ex-GOODBYE MR MACKENZIE) / **STEVE MARKER** – guitar, samples, loops / **DUKE ERIKSON** (b. DOUG) – guitar, keyboards, bass / **BUTCH VIG** (b. BRYAN VIG, Viroqua, Wisconsin) – drums, loops, efx

Mar 95. (7") *(CORD 001)* <*89000*> **VOW. / VOW (Torn Apart version)** (Discordant / AlmoSounds — / 97 Jul95)

Aug 95. (s7"/7") *(SX/S 1138)* <*89001*> **SUBHUMAN. / £1 CRUSH** (Mushroom / AlmoSounds 50 / —)
 (cd-s+=) *(D 1138)* – Vow.

Sep 95. (7"/c-s/cd-s) *(SX/C/D 1199)* <*89002*> **ONLY HAPPY WHEN IT RAINS. / GIRL DON'T COME / SLEEP** (29 / 55 Feb96)

Oct 95. (cd/c/2x45rpm-lp/6x7"box) *(D/C/L/LX 31450)* <*80004*> **GARBAGE** (6 / 20 Aug95)
 – Supervixen / Queer / Only happy when it rains / As Heaven is wide / Not my idea / A stroke of luck / Vow / Stupid girl / Dog new tricks / My lover's box / Fix me now / Milk. *(d-lp re-iss. Sep99 on 'Simply Vinyl'+=; SVLP 123)* – Dumb (live) / Stupid girl (live) / Temptation waits (live) / Vow (live).

—— on above **MIKE KASHAN** – bass / **PAULI RYAN** – percussion

Nov 95. (7") *(SX 1237)* <*89003*> **QUEER. / QUEER (Adrian Sherwood remix)** (13 / Mar96)
 (silver-cd-s) *(D 1237)* – ('A'side) / Trip my wire / ('A'-The very queer dub-bin mix) / ('A'-The most beautiful girl in town mix).
 (gold-cd-s) *(DX 1237)* – ('A'side) / Butterfly collector / ('A'-Rabbit in the Moon remix) / ('A'-Danny Saber remix).

Mar 96. (7") *(SX 1271)* **STUPID GIRL. / DOG NEW TRICKS (pal mix)** (4 / —)
 (red-cd-s+=) *(D 1271)* – Driving lesson / ('A'-Red Snapper mix).
 (blue-cd-s+=) *(DX 1271)* – ('A'side) / Alien sex fiend / ('A'-Dreadzone dub) / ('A'-Dreadzone vox).

Jul 96. (c-s) <*89004*> **STUPID GIRL / DRIVING LESSON** (— / 24)

Nov 96. (7") *(SX 1494)* <*89007*> **MILK (The wicked mix). / MILK (the Tricky remix)** (10 / —)
 (cd-s) *(D 1494)* – Milk (the wicked mix featuring TRICKY) / ('A'-Goldie's completely trashed remix) / ('A'-original version) / Stupid girl (Tees radio mix by TODD TERRY).
 (cd-s) *(DX 1494)* – Milk (the wicked mix featuring TRICKY) / ('A'-Massive Attack classic remix) / ('A'-Rabbit in the moon udder remix) / Stupid girl (the Danny Saber remix).

May 98. (c-s) *(MUSH 28MCS)* <*89014*> **PUSH IT / LICK THE PAVEMENT** (9 / 52)
 (cd-s+=) *(MUSH 28CDS)* – ('A'-Boom Boom Satellites remix).
 (3"cd-s) *(MUSH 28CDSX)* – ('A'side) / Thirteen.

May 98. (cd/c/lp) *(74321 55410-2/-4/-1)* <*80018*> **VERSION 2.0** (1 / 13)
 – Temptation waits / I think I'm paranoid / When I grow up / Medication / Special / Hammering in my head / Push it / The trick is to keep breathing / Dumb / Sleep together / Wicked ways / You look so fine. *(d-cd-iss. Jun99; MUSH 29CDX)*

Jul 98. (c-s) *(MUSH 35MCS)* <*40035*> **I THINK I'M PARANOID / DEADWOOD** (9 / —)
 (cd-s+=) *(MUSH 35CDS)* – Afterglow.
 (cd-s) *(MUSH 35CDX)* – ('A'side) / ('A'extended) / ('A'-Purity mix).

GARBAGE (cont)

	(3"cd-ep+=) *(MUSH 35CDXXX)* – (all of the above).			
Oct 98.	(c-s) *(MUSH 39MCS)* <827> **SPECIAL / THIRTEEN X FOREVER**	15	52	Nov98
	(cd-s+=) *(MUSH 39CDS)* – ('A'-Brothers In Rhythm mix).			
	(cd-s+=) *(MUSH 39CDSX)* – ('A'side) / Medication (acoustic) / Push it (Victor Calderone remix).			
	(3"cd-s) *(MUSH 39CDSXXX)* – (all 5 above).			
Jan 99.	(c-s) *(MUSH 43MCS)* **WHEN I GROW UP / CAN'T SEEM TO MAKE YOU MINE**	9		
	(cd-s+=) *(MUSH 43CDS)* – ('A'-Danny Tenaglia club mix).			
	(cd-s+=) *(MUSH 43CDSXXX)* – Tornado / ('A'-Danny Tenaglia club).			
	(cd-s+=) *(MUSH 43CDSX)* – ('A'side) / Tornado / Special (Rickidy raw mix).			
May 99.	(c-s) *(MUSH 49MCS)* **YOU LOOK SO FINE / SOLDIER THROUGH THIS**	19		
	(cd-s+=) *(MUSH 49CDS)* – ('A'-Fine Young Cannibals remix).			
	(cd-s+=) *(MUSH 49CDSX)* – ('A'side) / Get busy with the fizzy / ('A'-Eric Kupper mix).			
	(3"cd-s) *(MUSH 49CDSXXX)* – ('A'side) / ('A'-Fine Young Cannibals mix) / ('A'-Eric Kupper mix) / ('A'-Plaid mix).			
Nov 99.	(c-s/cd-s) *(RAX C/TD 40)* **THE WORLD IS NEVER ENOUGH** (mixes; original / UNKLE / Ice Bandits)	11		
	(above from Bond movie of the same name – issued on 'Radioactive')			
Sep 01.	(c-s) *(MUSH 94CDS)* **ANDROGYNY / BEGGING BONE / ANDROGYNY (Felix Da Housecat 'thee glitz remix')**	24	-	
	(cd-s) *(MUSH 94CDX)* – ('A'side) / ('A'-Neptunes remix) / ('A'-Architechs remix).			
Oct 01.	(cd/c/lp) *(MUSH 95 CD/MC/LP)* <493115> **BEAUTIFUL GARBAGE**	6	13	
	– Shut your mouth / Androgyny / Can't cry these tears / Till the day I die / Cup of coffee / Silence is golden / Cherry lips (go baby go!) / Breaking up the girl / Drive you home / Parade / Nobody loves you / Untouchable / So like a rose.			
Jan 02.	(cd-s) *(MUSH 98CDSE)* **CHERRY LIPS / CHERRY LIPS (Roger Sanchez tha S man's release mix)**	22	-	
	(cd-s+=) *(MUSH 98CDSX)* – Enough is never enough.			
	(cd-s) *(MUSH 98CDS)* – ('A'side) / Use me / ('A'-Howie B remix) / ('A'-video).			
	(12") *(MUSH 98T)* – ('A'-Roger Sanchez tha S man's release mix) / ('A'-mauve dark vocal mix with accapella mix).			
Apr 02.	(cd-s) *(MUSH 101CDS)* **BREAKING UP THE GIRL / CANDY SAYS / BREAKING UP THE GIRL (Brothers In Rhythm remix) / BREAKING UP THE GIRL (video)**	27	-	
	(cd-s) *(MUSH 101CDSX)* – ('A'version) / Happiness (p.2) / ('A'-Tino Maas remix).			
	(cd-s) *(MUSH 101CDSXXX)* – ('A'-acoustic version) / Confidence / Cherry lips (go go jam; Eli Janey remix).			
Sep 02.	(cd-s) *(MUSH 106CDS)* **SHUT YOUR MOUTH / SEX NEVER GOES OUT OF FASHION / SHUT YOUR MOUTH (jolly scary music mix) / SHUT YOUR MOUTH (video)**	20	-	
	(cd-s) *(MUSH 106CDSX)* – ('A'side) / April tenth / ('A'-Jags Kooner full vocal mix).			
	(cd-s) *(MUSH 106CDSXXX)* – ('A'side) / I'm really into techno / Wild horses (live).			

Sue GARNER (see under ⇒ **RUN ON**)

GAS HUFFER

Formed: Seattle, Washington, USA ... 1989 by MATT WRIGHT, TOM PRICE, DON BLACKSTONE and JOE NEWTON. 'FIREBUG' was the group's first release through punk imprint 'eMpTy', following through with the 'ETHYL' EP in early 1990. The band went on to record and deliver their debut LP 'JANITORS OF TOMORROW' one year later, bagging some of the best reviews for a punk album that year. Critics described their unique sound as NEIL YOUNG and WILLIE NELSON joining the CRAMPS for a one-off collaboration. Two further sets, 'INTEGRITY, TECHNOLOGY AND SERVICE' (1992) and their 'Epitaph' debut, 'ONE INCH MASTERS' (1994) helped them establish themselves in the vast growing US indie/punk scene. 1996 saw the outfit dedicating a song to the aforementioned NELSON, the subversivly titled 'Twisted Willie' (however, many read too far between the lines!), whilst a fourth set, 'THE INHUMAN ORDEAL OF SPECIAL AGENT GAS HUFFER' was just as bizarre. Their best work was still yet to come, so, while waiting for the excellent 'JUST BEAUTIFUL MUSIC' (1998) to arrive, GAS HUFFER found sanctuary in the blessed BRIAN WILSON-styled DEL-LAGUNAS, who have managed to release a handful of singles. GAS HUFFER, meanwhile, plotted their long-awaited comeback via a fresh album, 'THE REST OF US' (2002), complete with production by the great JACK ENDINO. • **Covered:** YOU STUPID ASSHOLE (Angry Samoans) / BAD GUY REACTION (Rezillos).

Album rating: JANITORS OF TOMORROW (*6) / INTEGRITY, TECHNOLOGY AND SERVICE (*5) / ONE INCH MASTERS (*5) / THE INHUMAN ORDEAL OF SPECIAL AGENT GAS HUFFER (*6) / JUST BEAUTIFUL MUSIC (*7) / THE REST OF US (*5)

MATT WRIGHT – vocals / **TOM PRICE** – guitar, vocals / **DON BLACKSTONE** – bass, vocals / **JOE NEWTON** – drums, vocals

		not iss.	Black Label
1989.	(7") <7230> **FIREBUG. / JESUS WAS MY ONLY FRIEND**	-	
1991.	(7"ep) <BLR 009> **ETHYL EP**		-
	– I want to kiss you / Eat U hole / Bucknaked / Mouthful.		

		not iss.	eMpTy
Feb 92.	(cd) <MT 145> **JANITORS OF TOMORROW**	-	
	– Nisqually / Shoe factory / Night train to Spokane / Going to Las Vegas / Dangerous drifter / Robert / Mistake / All that guff / Lizard hunt / Insidious / Love comes creeping / Compromise in the dark / Girl, I need your love (right now). *(UK-iss.Mar93 on 'Musical Tragedies'; efa 11345CD)* – I want to kiss you / Eat you whole / Buck naked / Mouthful / Firebug / Jesus was my only friend.		
1992.	(7") <SFTRI 171> **MOLE. / BODY BUZZ**	-	-
	(above on 'Sympathy For The Record Industry', below on 'Overground')		
1992.	(7") <over 26> **KING OF HUBCAPS. / (other by the FASTBACKS)**	-	-
Nov 92.	(7") <MT 166> **KNIFE MANUAL. / (other by MUDHONEY)**	-	-
	(cd-ep+=) <MT 166CD> – You stupid asshole / (other by MUDHONEY).		
Feb 93.	(cd) <MT 181> **INTEGRITY, TECHNOLOGY AND SERVICE**	-	-
	– George Washington / Bad vibes / Overworked folk hero guy / Uncle! / Piano movers / In the Gras / Bomb squad / Do the Brutus / Remove the shoe / I.T.S. credo / Where the wolfmen lurk / Moon mission / Sandfleas. *(UK-iss.Sep95 on 'Musical Tragedies'; efa 11373CD)*		

		Musical Tragedies	Sub Pop
Apr 93.	(cd-ep) *(efa 11396CD)* <SP 163> **BEER DRINKIN' CAVEMEN FROM MARS / HOT CAKES!**		-

		not iss.	Hayseed
1993.	(7"ep) <HS 91192> **WASHTUCAN HOE-DOWN**	-	
	– Night train to Spokane / Bad guy reaction / Neanderthal.		

		not iss.	Gearhead
1993.	(7") <RPM 001> **BAD GUY REACTION. / (other by SUPERCHARGER)**	-	

		not iss.	Sympathy..
1994.	(7") <SFTRI 294> **TERACH ME TO KILL. / (other by RED AUNTS)**	-	

		Musical Tragedies	eMpTy
May 94.	(7"ep) *(EFA 12380-7)* <MT 271> **THE SHRILL BEEPS OF SHRIMPS EP**		
	– BMX / Bedtime for freaky / Boot check / Java jet pack.		
	(cd-ep+=) <Au-Go-Go; ANDA 170> – King of hubcaps / Spinning discs o' fire / Psycho devil girl / According to Hoyle.		

		Epitaph	Epitaph
Sep 94.	(cd/c/lp) <(E 86439-2/-4/-1)> **ONE INCH MASTERS**		
	– Crooked bird / Mr. Sudbuster / More of everything / Stay in your house 14th & Jefferson / Walla walla bang bang / Appendix gone / Chicken foot what's in the bag? / Hand of the nomad / Quasimodo '94 / No smoking action – Adventure / Goat no have.		
Feb 96.	(cd/c/lp) <(E 86459-2/-4/-1)> **THE INHUMAN ORDEAL OF SPECIAL AGENT GAS HUFFER**		
	– You are not your job / Fall of the kingfish / Sixty three hours / Mosquito stomp / Carolina hot foot / Matt's mood / Smile no more / Tiny life / Double-O-bum / Sin of sloth / Numbnuts cold / Discovery park / Money: 1, Fun: 0 / Plant you now.		
1996.	(7") <LRR 023> **OOH OOH OOH. / FLAMING STAR**	-	
	(above issued on 'Lance Rock')		
May 98.	(cd/c/lp) <(E 6511-2/-4/-1)> **JUST BEAUTIFUL MUSIC**		Apr98
	– Rotten egg / Beware of Viking / One the side / Is that for me? / Clay pigeon / Old man winter / Hacked / Last act / Princess / Don't panic / Jungles of Guam / Surgeons / Mr. Inbetween / Cut the check / Bridge to the 21st century / You may have already won.		

		not iss.	Au-Go-Go
1999.	(7") <ANDA 249> **ROTTEN EGG. / OLD SUMMERTIME**	-	

		Estrus	Estrus
Mar 02.	(lp/cd) <(ES 1287/+CD)> **THE REST OF US**		
	– The rest of us / Thje day the bottom fell out / Dig that, do that / Aldedly blues / Ghost in the lighthouse / Lexington nightlife / Glass bottom boat / Goodbye crescent / Third party man / Horse and wagon / I'm so delighted / Ink dries / Berlin to New York, 1937 / Babytown.		

GASTR DEL SOL (see under ⇒ **SQUIRREL BAIT**; in 80's section)

GATE (see under ⇒ **DEAD C.**; in 80's section)

Rebecca GATES (see under ⇒ **SPINANES**)

GAUNT

Formed: Columbus, Ohio, USA ... mid-90's by main songwriter JERRY WICK, ERIC BARTH, JOVAN KARCIC, and JEFF REGENSBURGER. After dropping out of a course in violin at Kent State University, WICK got himself a job at indie label, 'Used Kids', and played in the rock outfit, BLACK JU JU. However he soon longed for his own band, and duly formed GAUNT, quickly releasing a spilt 7" with fellow group, NEW BOMB TURKS. BARTH took his bow at this point and was replaced by JIM WEBER (from NEW BOMB TURKS), who only lasted with his new band for the release of two further singles, the second of which 'JIM MOTHERFUCKER' (1992), was labelled after his nickname. Hardly having been gone, BARTH was back in the GAUNT mix for their debut full-length outing, 'WHITEY THE MAN', released on the nascent indie imprint, 'Thrill Jockey'. After several more singles and compilation appearances, the pop-punksters followed up their debut album with 'SOB STORY' (1994), making use of the experienced, STEVE ALBINI on production duties. Having written and recorded more than enough tunes for one album, GAUNT were able to use the shelved material for their third set, 'I CAN SEE YOUR MOM FROM HERE', put out the following year. The Columbus boys were by now gaining much attention in the indie and alternative arena, much due to their blend of pop-punk and eighties metal stylings. Attracting the attention of 'Amphetamine Reptile', GAUNT recorded their fourth full-length set, 'YEAH, ME TOO', with the assitance of TIM MAC (of HALO OF FLIES fame) on knob-twiddling. MAC and the band had a successful partnership, which continued for two further albums. Another LP, 'KRYPTONITE' (1996), soon followed, again heightening the band's appeal, especially as they had begun to move into a more melodic pop vein. This set also signaled a big shift in the group's rhythm section, with BARTH and REGENSBURGER being replaced by BRETT FALCON and SAM BROWN respectively. The music world's attention to GAUNT was exemplified by MTV signing the band up to do the title tune for their 'Buzzkill' program and major,

'Warner Bros' signing them in 1997. Unfortunately this opportunity was to turn sour, as the sales of their sixth set, 'BRICKS AND BLACKOUTS' (1998), were deemed not good enough in the cut and thrust world of the major labels. Thus the band were duly dropped, and this in turn led to their disintegration soon afterwards. Tragically, founder and frontman, JERRY WICK, was killed in a traffic accident in Columbus on the 10th January, 2001.

Album rating: SOB STORY mini (*5) / I CAN SEE YOUR MOM FROM HERE (*5) / YEAH, ME TOO compilation (*7) / KRYPTONITE (*5) / BRICKS AND BLACKOUTS (*6)

JERRY WICK (b. 1967, Parma, Ohio) – vocals, guitar, keyboards / **JOVAN KARCIC** – guitar, vocals / **ERIC BARTH** – bass / **JEFF REGENSBURGER** – drums

		not iss.	Datapanik
1991.	(7"ep) <datapanik #7> **VOLCANO / VALENTINE. / (2 by NEW BOMB TURKS)**	-	

— **JIM MOTHERFUCKER** (b. WEBER) – bass (of NEW BOMB TURKS) repl. BARTH (although not on all)

| 1992. | (7"ep) <#13> **FIELDER'S CHOICE** – Pollution / Revolution / Suzi. | - | |

		not iss.	Anyway Stuff
1992.	(7") <Stuff 001> **JIM MOTHERFUCKER. / SPINE** <re-iss. 1993 on 'Get Hip'; GH 158>	-	

— **ERIC BARTH** returned to repl. WEBER (back to 'TURKS)

		Crypt	Thrill Jockey
1992.	(10"ep) <Thrill 002> **WHITEY THE MAN** – Silly watches / Back-off / Salvation Army / Ignored / Whitey / USA / Jim Motherfucker.	-	
1993.	(7") <Thrill 008> **THE POP SONG. / NO HOPE**	-	
1993.	(7") <DD 003> **OHIO. /** (other by the BEAVERS) (above issued on 'Demolition Derby') (below on 'Bag Of Hammers')	-	
1993.	(7") <BOH 018> **GOOD, BAD, HAPPY, SAD. / QUALITY OF ARMOR**		
1993.	(7") <SCP 002> **SOLUTION. / BLACK CAT** (above issued on 'Snap Crackle Punk'; with Speed Kills magazine)		
Jul 94.	(m-cd) (CR 51) <Thrill 015> **SOB STORY** – Fear / Now I know / Wait until / Lies / Each and every side effect / Solution / Frustration / Lies / Oh wait . . . / No hope.		
Oct 94.	(7") (potash 2-7) **TURN TO ASH. / FLYING** (above issued on 'Potential Ashtray')		-
Nov 94.	(cd) (CR 52) <Thrill 17> **I CAN SEE YOUR MOM FROM HERE** – I don't care / Rich kid / Turn to ash / Ohio / Scandals / Purple heart / Greatest days / Jerkin' yourself around / Weekend / Hangover / Worry / Manson-Nixon line / Dead man's coat / Revolution to spite your face.		
Apr 96.	(cd) <THRILL 28> **KRYPTONITE** – Kryptonite / Savior breath / Hope you're happy / Transistor sister / Bust / Hand in pants / Deranged / Bored girls / Beggin' 4 it genre / A.W.O.L. / Superman / $1,000 joke.	-	

— **BRETT FALCON** – bass; repl. BARTH
— **SAMMY BROWN** – drums; repl. REGENSBURGER

		not iss.	Warners
Apr 98.	(cd) <46856> **BRICKS AND BLACKOUTS** – Anxiety / 97th tear / Mixed metals / Different drum machine / Glitter / Bricks / Pop song / Don't tell / Maybe in the next world / Far away / Duh / Powder keg variety / On fire / Honor roll / Dancin' when you're down.	-	

— sadly, on the 10th of January, WICK was killed on his bicycle

– compilations, etc. –

| Dec 95. | (cd)(lp) Amphetamine Reptile; (ARRCD 66009)<(AMREP 41)> **YEAH, ME TOO** – Yeah, me too / Now / Justine / Insangel / Hit the ground / Richard generation / Just leave / Breakin' down / Frank Stein / Give up. | | Nov95 |

GAY DAD

Formed: Sunninghill, Berkshire, England . . . 1995 by CLIFF JONES and BAZ CROWE, who had been playing in a group together since their pre-pubescent days. Experimenting with progressive and psychedelic rock in the beginning, the two protagonists parted their separate ways as adulthood beckoned. JONES became a regular contributor to 'The Face' and 'Mojo' while CROWE set up his own publication cult 'CREATOR'. It wasn't until 1995 that the duo put plan into action and debuted on a London stage (with a line-up that comprised of JONES, CROWE and former medical student NIGEL HOYLE on vocals), however the gig was a tad shambolic. Despite this uneasy inauguration JONES marked the occasion claiming it to be a turning point for the group and took to some intensive re-shaping, recruiting JAMES RISEBORO on keyboards. In late '97, the new GAY DAD entered a London studio to record three new tracks: 'DESIRE', 'OH JIM' and 'TO EARTH WITH LOVE'; all were later included on the debut album. When the three track demo was unleashed into A&R hands many believed it to be the work of an obscure 70's pop/rock outfit. The press, however, were slightly sceptical about the demo and had convinced themselves that a troupe of session musicians were generating a pre-meditated joke at their expense! This theory was dampened when GAY DAD signed to 'London' records in September 1998 and released the Glam pop rock-out single 'TO EARTH WITH LOVE' early the following year. Radio stations couldn't get enough of this new arrival and would give any excuse to play the record. Its spacey keyboards and "fab" guitars weren't of the esoteric kind, on the other hand, its poignant piano break remained as the only true delightful aspect of the song. But as the public were catching a glimpse of the trademark 'Walking Man' posters that had been littered all over the major cities the more the GAY DAD hype was overflowing. Frontman, JONES, who looked and sounded like a soap opera bad guy received attention from closet indie kids who hailed him as their new guitar hero pin-up. A spot in the Top 10, hyperbolised reviews and a controversial name all prompted the looming success of the group. This was all but a positive prediction. The cheesy first album proper, 'LEISURE NOISE', only reached a disappointing Top 20. Even worse, singles 'JOY!' and 'OH JIM' virtually bombed, forcing the band to blame their failure on lack of airplay. The pretentious JONES reckoned that this hadn't phased the band. In September 1999, the group returned to the studio to work on the follow-up and set their sights upon a publicity stunt that included a giant Wicker Man, a load of bad reviews and the "Cleansing of GAY DAD". When it eventually arrived, few could've considered 'TRANSMISSION' (2001) worthing the wait, floundering as it was in a grating cul de sac of cliched 70's glam-rock motifs. Unsurprisingly, the album veered far from the commercial map although they did manage a semi-hit in 'NOW, ALWAYS AND FOREVER'.

Album rating: LEISURE NOISE (*6) / TRANSMISSION (*5)

CLIFF JONES – vocals / **JAMES RISEBORO** – keyboards, guitar / **CHARLEY STONE** – guitar / **NIGEL HOYLE** – bass / **BAZ CROWE** (b. NICHOLAS) – drums

		London	Sire
Jan 99.	(10"/c-s) (LON T/CS 413) **TO EARTH WITH LOVE. / US ROACH** (cd-s+=) (LONCD 413) – 51 Pegasus. (cd-s) (LOCDP 413) – ('A'extended) / How it might end / Soft return.	10	-
May 99.	(10") (LONT 428) **JOY! / DESIRE** (cd-s+=) (LONCD 428) – Sly. (cd-s) (LOCDP 428) – ('A'side) / Electrogeist / Twelve. (c-s) (LONCS 428) – ('A'side) / Electrogeist / Sly.	22	-
Jun 99.	(cd/c/lp) (556103-2/-4/-1) <31070> **LEISURE NOISE** – Dimstar / Joy! / Oh Jim / My son Mystic / Black ghost / To Earth with love / Dateline / Pathfinder / Different kind of blue / Jesus Christ.	14	Sep99
Aug 99.	(c-s) (LONCS 437) **OH JIM / BINGO NATION** (cd-s+=) (LONCD 437) – Uva. (cd-s) (LOCDP 437) – ('A'side) / To Earth with love (demo) / Lieb ist fur immer.	47	-

— now without STONE who might've been repl. by ANDY BELL (ex-HURRICANE #1) had he not been poached by OASIS

		B-Unique	Thirsty Ear
Mar 01.	(7") (BUN 004) **NOW, ALWAYS AND FOREVER. / JOY (live)** (cd-s+=) (BUN 004CDS) – ('A'side) / Estigon / God has moved on. (cd-s) (BUN 004CDX) – ('A'side) / Surprise party / Captains of industry.	41	-
Jun 01.	(7") (BUN 005) **HARDER FASTER. / NIGHT CLUB (demo)** (cd-s) (BUN 005CDS) – ('A'side) / Without sound / Live at the barfly (video).		-
Sep 01.	(7") (BUN 009-7) **TRANSMISSION. / SAILING BY** (cd-s) (BUN 009CDS) – ('A'side) / Art since 1978 / Dead man. (cd-s) (BUN 009CDX) – ('A'side) / Aim of the game / Young heart attack.	58	-
Sep 01.	(cd) (BUN 010) <57117> **TRANSMISSION** – Transmission / Now, always and forever / Nightclub / Harder faster / Plane going down / All my life / Breathe / Dinosaur / Shoot freak / Keep it heavy / Everything changes / Promise of a miracle.		Jan02

GAZETTEERS (see under ⇒ VEHICLE FLIPS)

GAZE (see under ⇒ TIGER TRAP)

GEAR (see under ⇒ CHESTERFIELDS; 80's section)

GEEK (see under ⇒ TSUNAMI)

GENE

Formed: Watford, England . . . Summer 1993 by MARTIN ROSSITER and three ex-members of GO HOLE and then SP!N (STEVE MASON, MATT WINGLEY (JAMES) and KEVIN MILES). SP!N were indie raves (mixing style of STONE ROSES and JIMI HENDRIX) for three years from 1988, before (on the 23rd March '91) a motorway accident left them shattered and unable to continue as a group for some time. Their tour manager, their soundman and their bassman, JOHN MASON (STEVE's older brother) were all seriously injured, with the latter having to be replaced by KEVIN MILES. In 1992, they found ROSSITER from gay disco group, DROP, finally debuting with 'FOR THE DEAD' in the Spring of '94. Both they and their label, 'Costermonger', were then picked up by 'Polydor', who issued Top 60 single, 'BE MY LIGHT, BE MY GUIDE'. Another couple of singles, 'SLEEP WELL TONIGHT' and 'HAUNTED BY YOU' followed, before the band finally released their debut album, 'OLYMPIAN' in Spring '95. With ROSSITER's effete tales of bedsit angst, alienation and despair and SMITHS-style musical approach, GENE polarized opinion. Fans found much to savour in the record's grooves, the vitality of singles giving way to a more reflective, downbeat ambience that characterised much of the album. It went Top 10 in the UK, spawning further singles with the title track and the re-released, 'FOR THE DEAD'. The latter was accompanied by an odds and sods compilation, 'TO SEE THE LIGHTS' (The SMITHS did the same a decade earlier), while a follow-up set proper, 'DRAWN TO THE DEEP END', hit the shelves about a year later. A busy few years were ahead for perhaps one of Britain's most underrated indie groups, and it started with the release of 1999's peculiar

'REVELATIONS'. Becoming a father had obviously changed ROSSITER's outlook on things and the way he wrote songs as most tracks on the album consisted of warm melodies, sweeping vocals and poignant lyrics. Although not a patch on 97's 'DRAWN TO THE DEEP END', tracks such as 'THE BRITISH DISEASE', 'MAYDAY' and the single 'AS GOOD AS IT GETS' displayed the band's ability to compose good solid songs (helped by the fact HUGH JONES stepped in to produce the album). The following year, the group packed their bags to play a handful of low-key shows in Los Angeles resulting in 'RISING FOR SUNSET', a recollection of those live dates. The band, as tight as ever, gracefully strolled through tracks such as 'LONDON CAN YOU WAIT?' (accompanied by a host of sing-along Americans), 'AS GOOD AS IT GETS' and 'WHERE ARE THEY NOW?'. The song title 'AS GOOD AS IT GETS' was appropriately used as the name for GENE's 'best of . . .' package, which arrived in 2001, and almost five months later they issued 'LIBERTINE', a sweeping, string-laden orchestral based set that surprised fans and critics alike with its touch of delicacy. • **Songwriters:** Group penned except DON'T LET ME DOWN (Beatles) / I SAY A LITTLE PRAYER (Burt Bacharach) / WASTELANDS (Jam) / NIGHTSWIMMING (R.E.M.).

Album rating: Sp!n: IN MOTION (*5) / Gene: OLYMPIAN (*7) / TO SEE THE LIGHTS (*6) / DRAWN TO THE DEEP END (*6) / REVELATIONS (*6) / RISING FOR SUNSET (*5) / AS GOOD AS IT GETS: THE BEST OF GENE compilation (*7) / LIBERTINE (*6)

GO HOLE

LEE CLARKE (b.20 Jan'63, Cleethorpes, England) – vocals, guitar / **STEVE MASON** (b.17 Apr'71, Pontypridd, Wales) – guitar / **JOHN MASON** (b. 8 Aug'67, Bristol, England) – bass / **MATT WINGLEY** (b. MATT JAMES, 20 Sep'65) – drums

	Big Pot	not iss.
Aug 87. (7") *(GONE 1)* **FLIGHT OF ANGELS. / SPANISH FLY**		-

SP!N

	Foundation	not iss.
Aug 90. (12"ep) *(TEL 7T)* **SCRATCHES (IN THE SAND). / SHAFTED / EAST**		-
(cd-ep+=) *(TFL 7CD)* – ('A'radio edit).		
Feb 91. (12"ep) *(TEL 9T)* **LET'S PRETEND / (part 2). / MANIFESTO OF LOVE / LET'S PRETEND (JIMI'S DEAD)**		-
(cd-ep+=) *(TFL 9CD)* – ('A'radio edit).		
Jul 91. (lp/c/cd) *(FOUND 3/+MC/CD)* **IN MOTION**		-
– Many sides of you / Let's pretend / Everything / Ask me / Shafted / Sweet / Colour of your eyes / Mary / Scratches (in the sand) / Sister Pearl.		

—— **KEV MILES** – bass repl. JOHN who after transit accident left and travelled around the country and then France as a bohemian poet.

Nov 91. (12"ep/cd-ep) *(TELO 12 T/CD)* **HOT BLOOD**		-
– Fifteen minutes / I'm getting out / Landslide / You're my worst nightmare.		

—— **MARTIN T. FALLS** (b.15 May'70, Cardiff, Wales) – vocals repl. LEE

—— disbanded 1992 after a recent member bailed out

GENE

MARTIN ROSSITER (b.1970, Cardiff, Wales) – vocals, keyboards / **STEVE MASON** – guitars / **KEVIN MILES** – bass / **MATT JAMES** – drums, percussion

	Costermonger-Polydor	Polydor
Apr 94. (7") *(COST 1)* **FOR THE DEAD. / CHILD'S BODY**	76	-
Aug 94. (7") *(COST 2)* **BE MY LIGHT, BE MY GUIDE. / THIS IS NOT A CRIME**	54	-
(cd-s+=) *(COST 2CD)* – I can't help myself.		
Oct 94. (7"/c-s/cd-s) *(COST 3/+MC/CD)* **SLEEP WELL TONIGHT. / SICK, SOBER AND SORRY / HER FIFTEEN YEARS**	36	-
Feb 95. (7"/c-s/cd-s) *(COST 4/+MC/CD)* **HAUNTED BY YOU. / DO YOU WANT TO HEAR IT FROM ME / HOW MUCH FOR LOVE**	32	-
Mar 95. (cd/c/lp) *(GENE 1CD/1MC/1LP)* <52-7662> **OLYMPIAN**	8	Jun95
– Haunted by you / Your love, it lies / Truth, rest your head / A car that sped / Left-handed / London, can you wait? / To the city / Still can't find he phone / Sleep well tonight / You haven't slept / We'll find our own way. *(cd re-iss. Mar99; 527446-2)*		
Jun 95. (7"blue) *(SP 294)* **BE MY LIGHT, BE MY GUIDE. / I CAN'T HELP MYSELF**		
(above on 'Sub Pop' UK & feat. on 'HELTER SHELTER' box-set)		
Jul 95. (7"/c-s) *(COST 5/+MC)* **OLYMPIAN. / I CAN'T DECIDE IF SHE REALLY LOVES ME / TO SEE THE LIGHTS**	18	-
(cd-s+=) *(COST 5CD)* – Don't let me down.		
Nov 95. (m-cd) <31457 9247-2> **GENE**	-	
– Sleep well tonight / I can't help myself / This is not my crime / Child's body / The olympian.		
Jan 96. (7") *(7COST 6A)* **FOR THE DEAD (version). / CHILD'S BODY**	14	-
(7"+=/c-s+=) *(COST 6/+MC)* – Sick, sober & sorry (live).		
(cd-s) *(COST 6CD)* – ('A'side) / Sick, sober & sorry (live) / Truth rest your head (live).		
Jan 96. (cd/c/d-lp) *(GENE 2LP/2MC/2CD)* <8249> **TO SEE THE LIGHTS** (compilation of rare, live & bootleg material)	11	
– Be my light, be my guide / Sick, sober & sorry / Her fifteen years / Haunted by you (live – Helter Skelter) / I can't decide if she really loves me / To see the lights / I can't help myself / A car that sped (Radio 1 session) / For the dead (version) / Sleep well tonight (live – Forum) / How much for love / London, can you wait? (Radio 1 session) / Child's body / Don't let me down (Radio 1 session) / I say a little prayer (live – Glastonbury) / Do you want to hear it from me / This is not my crime / Olympian (live – Forum) / Child's body (live – Forum). *(cd re-iss. Mar99; 529807-2)*		

	Polydor	A&M
Oct 96. (7"/c-s) *(575689-7/-4)* **FIGHTING FIT. / DRAWN TO THE DEEP END**	22	-
(cd-s+=) *(575689-2)* – Autumn stone.		
Jan 97. (7"/c-s) *(COS TS/MC 10)* **WE COULD BE KINGS. / DOLCE / GABBANA OR NOWT**	17	-
(cd-s+=) *(COSCD 10)* – Wastelands.		
Feb 97. (cd/c/d-lp) *(GENE CD/M/L 3)* <537104> **DRAWN TO THE DEEP END**	8	Mar97
– New amusements / Fighting fit / Where are they now? / Speak to me someone / We could be kings / Whi I was born / Long sleeves for the summer / Save me, I'm yours / Voice of the father / Accidental / I love you, what are you? / Sub rosa.		
May 97. (7") *(COSTS 11)* **WHERE ARE THEY NOW? / CAST OUT IN THE SEVENTIES**	22	-
(cd-s+=) *(COSCD 11)* – Nightswimming.		
(cd-ep) **LIVE AT THE ROYAL ALBERT HALL EP** *(COSDD 11)* – ('A') / Save me, I'm yours / Voice of the father / Sub Rosa.		
Jul 97. (7"/c-s) *(COS TS/MC 12)* **SPEAK TO ME SOMEONE. / AS THE BRUISES FADE**	30	-
(cd-s) *(COSCD 12)* – ('A'side) / Ship song / Drawn to the deep end.		
(cd-s) *(COSDD 12)* – ('A'side) / New amusements / Olympian.		
Feb 99. (7") *(COSTS 14)* **AS GOOD AS IT GETS. / TOASTING THE UNION**	23	-
(cd-s+=) *(COSCD 14)* – Man on Earth.		
(cd-s) *(COSDD 14)* – ('A'side) / All night / To all who sail on her.		
Mar 99. (cd/c/lp) *(GENE C/M/L 4)* **REVELATIONS**	25	-
– As good as it gets / In love with love / Love won't work / The British disease / Fill her up / Something in the water / Mayday / Angel / The looker / Little child / Stop / The police will never find you / You'll never walk again.		
Apr 99. (7") *(COSTS 15)* **FILL HER UP. / PASS ON TO ME**	36	-
(cd-s+=) *(COSCD 15)* – Touched by the hand of havoc.		
(cd-s) *(COSDD 15)* – ('A'side) / Common as air / Slice.		

	Contra	Contra
Jun 00. (cd) (<*CONRA 1CD*>) **RISING FOR SUNSET (live)**		Aug00
– Does he have a name (excerpt) / Fill her up / The British disease / Where are they now? / London, can you wait? / Mayday / As good as it gets / Your love, it lies / Rising for sunset / For the dead / Be my light, be my guide / Speak to me someone / Olympian / You'll never walk again / Somewhere in the world. *(re-iss. Sep01 on 'Snapper'; SMMCD 634)*		
Oct 01. (cd-ep) *(CONTRACDS 1)* **IS IT OVER? / SUPERMARKET BOMBSCARE / LITTLE DIAMOND / WHO SAID THIS WAS THE END?**	-	-
Oct 01. (cd) *(CONTRA 2CD)* **LIBERTINE**	-	-
– Does he have a name? A simple request / Is it over? / O lover / Let me rest / We;ll get what we deserve / Walking in the shadows / Yours for the taking / You / Spy in the clubs / Somewhere in the world.		

– compilations, etc. –

1996. (cd) *Hispanolo;* <040> **IF THE DRESS FITS: THE UNOFFICIAL COMPILATION**	-	-
May 01. (cd) *Costermonger;* (549741-2) **AS GOOD AS IT GETS: THE BEST OF GENE**		-
– As good as it gets / For the dead / Fighting fit / Olympian / We could be kings / Sleep well tonight / Fill her up / You'll never walk again / Where are they now? / Haunted by you / London, can you wait? / Speak to me someone / Mayday / I can't help myself / Drawn to the deep end / Be my light, be my guide / A town called Malice.		

GENEVA

Formed: Aberdeen, Scotland ... late 1992 (briefly as SUNFISH) by DOUGLAS CASKIE, STEVEN DORA, STUART EVANS, KEITH GRAHAM and ex-journalist ANDREW MONTGOMERY (with The Sunday Post!). Eventually after only a few gigs, they were spotted by 'Nude' records (home to the likes of SUEDE), where they released their stunning debut, 'NO ONE SPEAKS', which bubbled under the Top 30 singles chart late '96. Around the same time, they secured a support slot on a BLUETONES' tour, exposing the angelic, high-pitched vox of MONTGOMERY, a hybrid of BILLY MacKENZIE, THOM YORKE, IAN ASTBURY or even, God forbid, an 80's style alternative rock version of MORTEN HARKET! During the first half of '97, the singles, 'INTO THE BLUE' and 'TRANQUILLIZER', both went Top 30 and featured on their soaringly spiritual Top 20 album, 'FURTHER'. After a few years away from the public eye, GENEVA returned at the turn of the decade with two minor hits, 'DOLLARS IN THE HEAVENS' and 'IF YOU HAVE TO GO', both taken from sophomore set, 'WEATHER UNDERGROUND' (2000). • **Songwriters:** Most by DORA and MONTGOMERY, a few by MONTGOMERY, GRAHAM and one with EVANS.

Album rating: FURTHER (*8) / WEATHER UNDERGROUND (*5)

ANDREW MONTGOMERY – vocals / **STEVEN DORA** – guitar / **STUART EVANS** – guitar / **KEITH GRAHAM** – bass / **DOUGLAS CASKIE** – drums

	Nude	Sony
Oct 96. (7"/c-s) *(NUD 22 S/MC)* **NO ONE SPEAKS. / WHAT YOUR SHRINK SAYS**	32	-
(cd-s) *(NUD 22CD)* – ('A'side) / Closer to the stars / Keep the light on.		
Jan 97. (7"/c-s) *(NUD 25 S/MC)* <78594> **INTO THE BLUE. / AT THE CORE**	26	Jun97
(cd-s) *(NUD 25CD)* – ('A'side) / Riverwatching / Land's End.		
May 97. (7") *(NUD 28S)* **TRANQUILLIZER. / DRIFTWOOD**	24	-
(cd-s) *(NUD 28CD1)* – ('A'side) / Dead giveaway / Strung out on you.		
(cd-s) *(NUD 28CD2)* – ('A'side) / Michaelmas / Compulsive love disorder.		

Jun 97.	(cd/c/lp) *(NUDE 7 CD/MC/LP)* <68156> **FURTHER**	20	Aug97

– Temporary wings / Into the blue / The god of sleep / Best regrets / Tranquillizer / Further / No one speaks / Worry beads / Fall apart button / Wearing off / Nature's whore / In the years remaining.

Aug 97.	(7") *(NUD 31S)* **BEST REGRETS. / SELFBELIEF**	38	-

(cd-s) *(NUD 31CD1)* – ('A'side) / Feel the joy / Raymond Chandler.
(cd-s) *(NUD 31CD2)* – ('A'side) / Last orders / The god of sleep (demo).

Nov 99.	(7") *(NUD 46S)* **DOLLARS IN THE HEAVENS. / ECHO CHAMBER**	59	-

(cd-s) *(NUD 46CD1)* – ('A'side) / Faintest tremor in the weakest heart / She's so familiar.
(cd-s) *(NUD 46CD2)* – ('A'side) / When you close your eyes / Museum mile (Dave Fridmann mix).

Feb 00.	(cd-s) *(NUD 49CD1)* **IF YOU HAVE TO GO / HAVE YOU SEEN THE HORIZON LATELY? (Aloof mix) / VOSTOK**	69	-

(cd-s) *(NUD 49CD2)* – ('A'side) / Mindreading / Dollars in the heavens (CD-video).

Mar 00.	(cd/d10"lp) *(NUDE 15 CD/LP)* **WEATHER UNDERGROUND**		

– Dollars in the heavens / If you have to go / Killing stars / Museum mile / Amnesia valley / Morricone / Guidance system / Cassie / Rockets over California / A place in the sun / Have you seen the horizon lately?

GENTLE WAVES (see under ⇒ BELLE AND SEBASTIAN)

GERALDINE FIBBERS

Formed: Los Angeles, California, USA … 1992 by former ETHYL MEATPLOW and NEON VEIN singer, CARLA BOZULICH (real name!), who enlisted DANIEL KEENAN, WILLIAM TUTTON, KEVIN FITZGERALD and BRONWYN ADAMS. Making a departure from her noisy industrial/dance early work, CARLA used the GERALDINE FIBBERS as a vehicle to explore the common ground between American roots music and stark, blues-influenced punk. Signed to the local 'Sympathy For The Record Industry' label, the 'FIBBERS made their debut in '94 by previewing their heavily country influenced mini-set, 'GET THEE GONE' (1994). Subsequently signing to 'Virgin', CARLA and Co delivered their first album proper, 'LOST SOMEWHERE BETWEEN THE EARTH AND MY HOME' in 1995, revamping some of their earlier tracks and drawing comparisons with long-lost cowpunkers, X. A few years later, NELS CLINE was drafted in for the departing KEENAN, the resulting 'BUTCH' (1997) featuring a more robust guitar-rock sound and even attempting a cover of Can's 'YOU DOO RIGHT'. The usual major label woes ensued as 'Virgin' reportedly encouraged CARLA to split from her band and record a more listener-friendly solo album. In the event, almost the exact opposite happened. Although the band were put permanently on the backburner, BOZULICH's new project, SCARNELLA (in tandem with CLINE) was anything but commercial. Their eponymous 1998 debut was also something of a departure from the pseudo-roots sound of the GERALDINE FIBBERS, inspired by an American road trip and crafted in the spirit of experimental extemporizing. • **Covered:** JOLENE (Dolly Parton) / BLUE CROSS (Beck) / THE GRAND TOUR (Canned Heat) / FANCY (Bobbie Gentry) / PILLS (Bo Diddley) / HANDS ON THE WHEEL (Rainravens) / IF DRINKIN' DON'T KILL ME (Beresford-Sanders) / KISS OF FIRE (Allen-Hill).

Album rating: GET THEE GONE – THE GERALDINE FIBBERS mini (*5) / LOST SOMEWHERE BETWEEN THE EARTH AND MY HOME (*6) / BUTCH (*6) / Scarnella: SCARNELLA (*5) / Ethyl Meatplow: HAPPY DAYS, SWEETHEART (*6)

CARLA BOZULICH – vocals, guitar (ex-ETHYL MEATPLOW) / **DANIEL KEENAN** – lead guitar, vocals / **WILLIAM TUTTON** – upright bass, vocals / **KEVIN FITZGERALD** – drums, banjo / **BRONWYN ADAMS** – violin (ex-CRIME & THE CITY SOLUTION)

		Hut	Sympathy F
Oct 94.	(10"m-lp) <SFTRI 314> **GET THEE GONE**	-	-

– Get thee gone / Jolene / Marmalade / Outside of town / Blue cross / Mary / The grand tour. <re-iss. Feb97 as 'WHAT PART OF "GET THEE GONE" DON'T YOU UNDERSTAND?'+=; SFTRI 481> – Fancy / They suck / She's a dog / Pills / The smaller song / Hands on the wheel / If drinkin' don't kill me / Kiss of fire / The grand tour.

Jan 95.	(7") *(HUT 49)* **MARMALADE. / GET THEE GONE**		-
Jan 95.	(m-cd) *(DGHUTM 22)* **THE GERALDINE FIBBERS**		-

– (tracks same as 'GET THEE GONE' but in different order)

— **JULIE FOWELLS** – violin; repl. ADAMS (on below A-side)

Mar 95.	(ltd-7") *<JB 003>* **THEY SUCK. / FANCY**	-	

(above issued on 'Big Jesus Enterprises')

— **JESSY GREENE** – violin, viola, vocals; repl. FOWELLS

		Hut	Virgin
Jul 95.	(7") <SFTRI 384> **DRAGON LADY. / BIRTHDAY BOY**	-	-
Jul 95.	(cd/c) *(CDHUT/HUTMC 28)* <40602-2> **LOST SOMEWHERE BETWEEN THE EARTH AND MY HOME**		

– Lilybelle / The small song / Marmalade / Dragon lady / A song about walls / House is falling / Outside of town / The French song / Dusted / Richard / Blast off baby / Get thee gone.

Aug 95.	(7") *(HUT 60)* **DRAGON LADY. / BITTER HONEY**		-

(cd-s+=) *(HUTCD 60)* – Birthday boy.

— **NELS CLINE** – guitar (ex-NELS CLINE TRIO) repl. KEENAN

		Virgin America	Virgin America
Oct 97.	(cd) *(CDVUS 133)* <44419-2> **BUTCH**		Jul97

– California tuffy / Toybox / I killed the cuckoo / Trashman in furs / Swim back to me / Seven or in 10 / Claudine / Folks like me / Pet angel / Butch / Arrow to my drunken eye / You doo right / The dwarf song / Heliotrope. <US d-lp on 'Sympathy For The Record Industry'; SFTRI 507>

— the group have since split; CARLA had already guested on MIKE WATT's 'Ball-Hog Or Tugboat?' in '95

SCARNELLA

CARLA + NELS

		Smells Like	Smells Like
Nov 98.	(cd) *<(slr 027)>* **SCARNELLA**		

– Underdog / Release the spring / Improvisation #4 / The most useless thing / Dandelions / Improvisation #3 (safari youth) / Snowy (about a cat) / Death by northwest / Improvisation #1 (the bag of hair) / A millennium fever ballad.

– CARLA's pre-'FIBBERS work –

ETHYL MEATPLOW

CARLA alongside **HAROLD BAREFOOT SANDERS III** – guitar + **JOHN 'WEE-WEE NAPIER** – drums (KEENAN guested on the track, 'Suck')

		Dali – Chameleon	Dali – Chameleon
Apr 93.	(12") *<66305>* **QUEENIE. /**	-	
Oct 93.	(cd) *<(3704 61354-2)>* **HAPPY DAYS, SWEETHEART**		

– Opening precautionary instructions / Suck / Devil's Johnson / Car / Queenie / Close to you / Tommy / Mustard requiem / Abazab / Ripened peach / Feed / Rise / For my sleepy lover / Sad bear.

GERBILS

Formed: Athens, Georgia, USA … mid 90's by SCOTT SPILLANE, JOHN D'AZZO and WILL WESTBROOK; ROSS BEACH and PENNY BURBANK were soon added (BEACH, SPILLANE and D'AZZO had originally teamed up in the early nineties outfit, SMILIN' JOE FISSION, with JOHN FERNANDES of OLIVIA TREMOR CONTROL fame). The GERBILS, originally recording demos as a quintet, soon trimmed down to the threesome of SPILLANE, D'AZZO, and WESTBROOK, before actually committing their sound to the stores. Their intelligent, quirky, lo-fi indie-pop sound soon got them hallmarked within the label and musical collective, 'Elephant 6', which contained a group of bands of the likes of OLIVIA TREMOR CONTROL, ELF POWER, and APPLES (IN STEREO), who were tied by their cross-band collaboration, and fairly mutual adherence to paired down recording techniques. After several single releases, the trio, debuted with their first full-length set, 'ARE YOU SLEEPY?' (1998), a competent piece of weird and wonderful melodious indie pop. This was followed three years later by their sophomore album, 'THE BATTLE OF ELECTRICITY', which, although no less reasonable in quality to its predecessor, suffered at the hands of critics, who found it lacking the originality of the collective's bigger bands.

Album rating: ARE YOU SLEEPY? (*6) / THE BATTLE OF ELECTRICITY (*4)

SCOTT SPILLANE – vocals, guitar / **WILL WESTBROOK** – bass / **JOHN D'AZZO** – drums (guitarist ROSS BEACH + cellist PENNY BURBANK – of AZALIA SNAIL left after initial demos)

		Spare Me	Spare Me
May 97.	(7") *<(SPARE 3)>* **GRIN. / CRAYON BOX**		

		Hidden Agenda	Hidden Agenda
Oct 97.	(7") *<(AHA 001)>* **OLIVIA'S GLUE. / IS SHE FIONA?**		
Mar 98.	(cd) *<(AHA 006)>* **ARE YOU SLEEPY?**		

– Sunshine soul / Is she Fiona / Crayon box / Penny waits / Fluid / Wet host / Glue / Ted doesn't mind / Walnuts / Lead / Grin. *<(lp-iss.May98; AHA 008)>* (lp re-iss. Aug98 on 'Earworm'; WORM 33)

		Earworm	not iss.
Apr 98.	(7") *(WORM 14)* **LUCKY GIRL. / BIG WHITE LIMO**		-

— all three moonlighted with NEUTRAL MILK HOTEL and OLIVIA TREMOR CONTROL / added guest BILL DOSS (of latter)

		Orange Twin	Orange Twin
Oct 01.	(lp/cd) *<(OTR 06/+CD)>* **THE BATTLE OF ELECTRICITY**		

– Are you underwater / I / The air we share / Lucky girl / II / Fail to mention / III / Meteoroid from the sun strikes a deal weirdo / IV / A song of love / V / The white sky / VI / VII / Snorkel / The battle of electricity / Share again / VIII.

Lisa GERMANO

Born: 1 Jan'58, Mishawaka, Indiana, USA. Having learned the piano at an early age, LISA later landed the job of backing violinist with both JOHN MELLENCAMP and BOB SEGER. Working on her own material in her spare time, she continued to earn a living as a session musician for the likes of IGGY POP before self-financing her debut album, 'ON THE WAY DOWN FROM MOON PALACE' (1991). A stark departure from her work with MELLENCAMP, the record was characterised by a dark atmospheric sensitivity that drifted between dreamlike reverie and unsettling intimation, although her folky roots were never far from the surface. 'Capitol' obviously noted her potential, signing her up for 1993's eponymous follow-up wherein LISA exorcised her darkest demons but failed to connect with mainstream record buyers. Released in Britain as 'HAPPINESS' for IVO's '4 a.d.', the record was more warmly received by UK listeners eager for female singer-songwriter angst. 1994's 'GEEK THE GIRL', meanwhile, was a pseudo-concept affair charting the emotional and sexual development of an adolescent girl against a more musically adventurous backdrop. Of late, the moody chanteuse has been as prolific as ever, working with GIANT SAND mainman, HOWE GELB as OP8 and releasing two further sets, 'EXCERPTS FROM A LOVE CIRCUS' (1996) and 'SLIDE' (1998). Both sets continued to explore the grey areas and subterranean dead ends of human emotional experience, the former dissecting love's labyrinthine contradictions in the kind of cryptically allusive fashion GERMANO specializes in. 'SLIDE's slightly less claustrophobic, if no less painfully acute observations were nevertheless marked by as lighter musical touch.

Album rating: ON THE WAY DOWN FROM MOON PALACE (*5) / LISA GERMANO – HAPPINESS (*6) / GEEK THE GIRL (*7) / EXCERPTS FROM A LOVE CIRCUS (*7) / SLIDE (*6)

LISA GERMANO – vocals, piano, violin, etc / with **KENNY ARONOFF** – drums

not iss.   Major Bill

1991. (cd/c) <*191-2/-4*> **ON THE WAY DOWN FROM MOON PALACE**
– On the way down from the moon palace / Guessing game (or the music business) / Blue Monday / Calling / Hangin' with a dead man / Screaming angels dancing in your garden / Riding my bike / Simply Tony / Dig my own grave / Cry baby / Bye bye little doggie / The other one / Dark irie. *<cd re-iss. on 'Egg' records> (UK cd-iss. Feb99 on 'Koch Int.'; 37999-2)*

—— added a plethora of session people

not iss.   Capitol

Jul 93. (cd) <*98691*> **LISA GERMANO**
– Bad attitude / Destroy the flower / Puppet / Everyone's victim / Energy / Cowboy / Happiness / The Earth / Around the world / Sycophant / Miamo-tutti / The dresses song / The darkest night of all.

4 a.d.   4 a.d.

Jan 94. (cd-ep) <*74005*> **INCONSIDERATE BITCH**
– Happiness / Energy / Puppet / Sycophant / (Late night) Dresses.

Apr 94. (cd)(lp/c) *(CAD 4005CD)(CAD/+C 4005)* <*45593*> **HAPPINESS** ('LISA GERMANO' remixed, etc.)
– Around the world / You make me want to wear dresses / Happiness / Bad attitude / Sycophant / Miamo-tutti / Energy / Cowboy / Puppet / These boots are made for walkin' / Breathe across Texas / Everyone's victim / The darkest night of all. *(cd re-iss. Jul98 +=; GAD 4005CD)* – INCONSIDERATE BITCH

Oct 94. (cd) *(CAD 4017CD)* <*45758*> **GEEK THE GIRL**
– My secret reason / Trouble / Geek the girl / Just geek / Cry wolf / ...A psychopath / Sexy little girl princess / Phantom love / Cancer of everything / A guy like you / ...Of love and colors / Stars. *(cd re-iss. Jul98; GAD 4017CD)*

Aug 96. (7") *(AD 6019)* **SMALL HEADS. / FUN, FUN FOR EVERYONE** (acoustic)
(cd-s+=) *(BAD 6019CD)* – Tom, Dick and Harry / Messages from Sophia (instrumental).

Sep 96. (lp/cd) *(CAD 6012/+CD)* <*46217*> **EXCERPTS FROM A LOVE CIRCUS**
– Baby on the plane / A beautiful schizophrenic / Bruises "where's Miamo-tutti? by DOROTHY / I love a snot / Forget it, it's a mystery / Victoria's secret "just a bad dream" by Miamo-tutti / Small heads / We suck / Lovesick / Singing to the birds / Messages from Sophia "there's more kitties in the world than just Miamo-tutti" by LISA and DOROTHY / Big, big world. *(cd+=)* – Fun, fun for everyone / Tom, Dick and Harry / Message from Sophia (instrumental). *(cd re-iss. Jul98 +=; GAD 6012CD)*

Sep 97. (12") <*8*> **LOVESICK (Underdog remix). / LOVESICK**
—— <above was issued in US on 'Output'>

In June '97, LISA subsequently teamed up with GIANT SAND who had become OP8. They released a one-off set, 'SLUSH'.

Oct 98. (cd) *(CAD 8014CD)* <*78014*> **SLIDE**   Jul98
– Way below the radio / No color here / Tomorrowing / Electrified / Slide / If I think of love / Crash / Wood floors / Turning into Betty / Guillotine / Reptile.

GET UP KIDS

Formed: Kansas City, Missouri, USA . . . 1994 by RYAN POPE, ROBERT POPE, JIM SUPTIC and MATT PRYOR. 1996 saw these nineties punk pop-emo rockers begin their recording debut in an indie flash releasing three singles on three different labels; 'A NEWFOUND INTEREST' on 'Contrast', 'SHORTY' on 'Huey Prodhon' and 'ALL STARS' on 'Doghouse'. It was the latter of these labels that wasted no time in releasing the band's debut album, 'FOUR MINUTE MILE', the following year. This release was given quite a nod by the critics for its sincere and infectious lyrics and smart punky-pop sounds; a new and engaging voice on the scene. That year also saw them on a joint tour with fellow emo-rockers, BRAID, who they released a split 7" with, 'I'M A LONER, DOTTIE, A REBEL' (1998). GUP didn't rest on their laurels long, 1999 being a busy year for the group, with the recruitment of JAMES DEWEES on keyboards, the release of EP 'RED LETTER DAY' and more touring to support their second full-length outing, 'SOMETHING TO WRITE HOME ABOUT'. The album was what it said on the cover, as far as the music press were concerned. GUP had surpassed themselves in combining catchy melodies with crunchy punk sounds, all overseen by earnest, unaffected lyrics, and with the addition of DEWEES's input, their individual voice only got stronger. Cemented as a leading light within their genre, the group got to tour with other leading luminaries WEEZER and GREEN DAY in 2001. The following year they released their third album, 'ON A WIRE', which after much raucous touring is recognisably more muted than their earlier output, but no less so in quality. With nearly every indie/emo group having a second job outside the confines of their own band, The GET UP KIDS were no exception. MATTHEW PRYOR and ROBERT POPE (with also JAKE CARDWELL and ALEX BRAHL) found time to hit the public with two sets as The NEW AMSTERDAMS, 'NEVER YOU MIND' (2000) and 'PARA TODA VIDA' (2002) – MOULD, BARLOW and MALKMUS have indeed a lot to answer for.
• **Covered:** CLOSE TO ME (Cure) / SUFFRAGETTE CITY (David Bowie) / REGRET (New Order) / ALEC EIFFEL (Pixies) / ON WITH THE SHOW (Motley Crue) / BURNED BRIDGES (Coalesce) / BEER FOR BREAKFAST (Replacements).

Album rating: FOUR MINUTE MILE (*6) / RED LETTER DAY mini (*6) / SOMETHING TO WRITE HOME ABOUT (*7) / EUDORA compilation (*5) / ON A WIRE (*5) / New Amsterdams: NEVER YOU MIND (*6) / PARA TODA VIDA mini (*5)

JIM SUPTIC – vocals, guitar / **MATTHEW PRYOR** – guitar, vocals / **RYAN POPE** – drums / **ROBERT POPE** – bass

not iss.   Huey Proudhon

May 96. (7") **SHORTY. / THE BREATHING METHOD**

not iss.   Contrast

May 97. (7") **LOVE TELLER**
– A newfound interest in Massachusetts / Off the wagon.

Doghouse   Doghouse

Aug 97. (7"blue) <*DOG 45*> **WOODSON. / SECOND PLACE**
(cd-ep+=) <*DOG 45CD*> **ALL STARS** – A newfound interest in Massachusetts / Off the wagon. *(UK-iss.Apr00 as 'WOODSON' 7"ep/cd-ep; same as US)*

Oct 97. (cd) <*(DOG 47CD)*> **FOUR MINUTE MILE**   Sep97
– Coming clean / Don't hate me / Fall semester / Stay gold, ponyboy / Lowercase West Thomas / Washington Square park / Last place you look / Better half / No love / Shorty / Michele with one L. *(re-iss. Sep98 & Apr00 lp/cd; DGH 47/+CD) (re-iss. Oct01 on 'Golf'; CDHOLE 038) (lp re-iss. Jun02 on 'Defiance'; DEFIANCE 036)*

Feb 98. (7") <*#4*> **I'M A LONER, DOTTIE, A REBEL. / (other by BRAID)**
(above issued on 'Tree' records)

Jul 99. (10"ep/cd-ep) <*(DOG 63/+CD)*> **RED LETTER DAY**
– One year later / Red letter day / Forgive and forget / Anne Arbour / Mass pike. *(re-iss. Apr00; same) (re-iss. Oct01 on 'Golf'; CDHOLE 039) <(lp re-iss. Jun02 on 'Defiance'+=; DEFIANCE 037)>* – WOODSON

not iss.   Sub Pop

1999. (7") <*SP 451*> **10 MINUTES. / ANNE ARBOUR**

—— added **JAMES DEWEES** – keyboards, vocals

Vagrant   Doghouse

Oct 99. (cd/lp) *(VR 340CD)* <*DOG 66/+LP*> **SOMETHING TO WRITE HOME ABOUT**   Sep99
– Holiday / Action and action / Valentine / Red letter day / Out of reach / Ten minutes / Company dime / My apology / I'm a loner, Dottie, a rebel / Long goodnight / Close to home / I'll catch you. *(re-iss. Nov99 on 'Doghouse'; same as US) (cd re-iss. Mar00 on 'Epitaph'; 6587-2)*

Oct 99. (7") *(VR 341)* **split w/ ANNIVERSARY**
(also iss.Oct99 on 'Heroes & Villains'; HV 002)

May 00. (cd-s) *(1030-2)* **ACTION AND ACTION /**
(above on 'Epitaph')

Dec 00. (7") <*(VR 351)*> **split w/ ROCKET FROM THE CRYPT**

Nov 01. (7") *(SN 08)* **BURNED BRIDGES. / (split w/ COALESCE)**
(above issued on 'Second Nature')

Vagrant   Vagrant

Nov 01. (cd/lp) <*(VR 357 CD/LP)*> **EUDORA** (compilation)
– Up on the roof / Suffragette city / Central standard time / Close to me / Forgive and forget / Regret / Beer for breakfast / Newfound Mass / Alec Eiffel / Impossible outcomes / On with the show / 10 minutes / Anne Arbour / Burned bridges / I'm a loner Dottie, a rebel / Shorty / The breathing method.

May 02. (cd/lp) <*(VR 370 CD/LP)*> **ON A WIRE**
– Overdue / Stay gone / Let the reigns go loose / Fall from grace / Grunge pig / High as the moon / All that I know / Walking on a wire / Wish you were here / Campfire Kansas / The worst idea / Hannah hold on. *<(cd re-iss. Aug02 on 'Universal'; 910370-2)>*

NEW AMSTERDAMS

MATTHEW PRYOR – vocals, guitar / **ROBERT POPE** – bass / **ALEX BRAHL** – guitar / **JAKE CARDWELL** – drums

Vagrant   Vagrant

Sep 00. (lp/cd) <*(VR 347/+CD)*> **NEVER YOU MIND**
– Every double life / Lonely hearts / Proceed with caution / Slow down / Goodbye / Idaho / Drama queen / Make me change my mind / When we two parted / Never treat others / I won't run away.

—— **PRYOR** now totally on his own

Jan 02. (cd) <*VR 360CD*> **PARA TODA VIDA**
– My old man had a pistol / Picture in the paper / Son of a prophet / Stay on the phone / That side of me / Four more years / Forever leaving / Adeline, out of tune / All ears / Losing you.

GHOST CLUB (see under ⇒ 3Ds)

C. GIBBS GROUP (see under ⇒ MORNING GLORIES)

GIBSON BROS.

Formed: Columbus, Ohio, USA . . . 1984 by DON HOWLAND (ex-GREAT PLAINS), JEFF EVANS, DAN DOW, and ELLEN HOOVER. The GB's – not to be confused with late nineties bluegrass revivalists of the same name, or for that matter to the seventies Caribbean salsa rock band from Martinique who sang 'Cuba' – legacy to the alternative scene was considerable, with their punky and frenetic rockabilly, country rock blues stylings, sometimes dubbed succinctly as 'psychobilly', they inspired such indie luminaries as JON SPENCER BLUES EXPLOSION, ROYAL TRUX, and MULE. The band's debut album cassette, 'BUILD A RAFT' (1986) came out to little response, but since then became a hard-to-get release. The band subsequently signed to 'Homestead', who released their next two LPs, 'BIG PINE BOOGIE', and 'DEDICATED FOOL'. The latter of these releases also signaled the departure of DOW and HOOVER, who were supplanted by the WORKDOGS rhythm piece, made up of SCOTT JARVIS, and ROB KENNEDY for the fourth full-length outing, 'PUNK ROCK DRIVIN' SONG OF A GUN'. With the release of this set in the early nineties the GB's were already established as an interesting and innovative outfit, which aided them in getting the assistance of JON SPENCER and CRISTINA MARTINEZ for their live shows. These musicians were now in their ascendancy but had been influenced by the GB's sound, and their contribution to it is showcased on the fifth album, 'THE MAN WHO LOVED COUCH DANCING' (1991). SPENCER stayed on with the band for their sixth and final set, 'MEMPHIS SOL TODAY', which they had the coup of recording at Memphis' shrine-like Sun Studios. After their subsequent demise EVANS went on to form '68 COMEBACK, which continued the GB's punky roots rock mission. Needless to say JON SPENCER got together his BLUES EXPLOSION, and went on to greater things. HOWLAND teamed up with RICH LILLASH to form BASSHOLES, although LILLASH departed soon after the duo's debut LP, and was replaced by BIM THOMAS. Their sound was an eclectic nineties fusion of country, rock and folk, although with its roots always in the blues, exemplified by the fine sets, 'BLUE ROOTS' and 'LONG WAY BLUES'. • **Covers:** CHICKEN HEARTED (Bill Justis) / SHAKIN' ALL OVER (Johnny Kidd) / LET'S WORK TOGETHER (Wilbert Harrison) / etc. / '68 COMEBACK:- BO DIDDLEY 1969 (Bo Diddley) / TOCACCO ROAD (J.D. Loudermilk) / SLOP JAR BLUES (Jelly Roll Kings) / BULLMOOSE (Bobby Darin) / BOOGIE WOOGIE COUNTRY GIRL (Ashby-Pomus) / BLAME IT ON TIME (Charlie Feathers) / AIN'T IT DOWN (trad) / EVERGREEN (Roy Orbison) / SHAKE YOU HIPS (Slim Harpo) / GET RHYTHM (Johnny Cash) / BOOMERANG (Gene-Wayne) / BENDING LIKE A WILLOW TREE (Lowell Fulson) / LIKE ANY OTHER KIND (Barnes-Cupid) / WALL (...Hart) / LET IT ROCK (Chuck Berry) / THE WAY I WALK (... Scott) / MY GIRL JOSEPHINE (Fats Domino) / PINK PEDAL PUSHERS (Carl Perkins) / HOY HOY (... Stacy) / ROUTE 66 (Bobby Troup) / etc. / Bassholes: JUDGE HARSH BLUES + MOODY (.... Lewis) / INTERZONE (Joy Division).

Album rating: BUILD A RAFT (*3) / BIG PINE BOOGIE (*5) / DEDICATED FOOL (*7) / PUNK ROCK DRIVIN' SON OF A GUN (*5) / THE MAN WHO LOVED COUCH DANCING (*5) / MEMPHIS SOL TODAY! (*6) / '68 Comeback: MR. DOWNCHILD (*5) / SINGLES COLLECTIONS compilation (*5) / A BRIDGE TOO FUCKIN' FAR (*5) / LOVE ALWAYS WINS (*6)

DON HOWLAND – vocals, guitar (ex-GREAT PLAINS) / **JEFFREY EVANS** – guitar, banjo, vocals / **DAN DOW** – guitar / **ELLEN HOOVER** – drums

not iss.   Old Age
1986. (c) **BUILD A RAFT**

Homestead Homestead
Feb 89. (lp) <*HMS 119-1*> **BIG PINE BOOGIE** Nov88
– Casey Jones / Rhythm & booze / Thy burdens are greater than mine / Moon twist / Poor me / Sugartail rock / Big pine boogie / Rovin' dope peddler / Bo Diddley pulled a boner / Skull & crossbones / Ride a coal black mare / Satanville.
Apr 89. (lp/c) <*HMS 141-1/-4*> **DEDICATED FOOL**
– Dedicated fool / No way to get along / Tight Capris / Poor white trash / Caught in a dream / The sperm count / I'm so worried / Dirt preacher / Swank / Lost track of time / Lone wild bird / Trying to get you.

―― **ROB KENNEDY** – bass, vocals (of WORKDOGS) repl. DOW
―― **SCOTT JARVIS** – drums (of WORKDOGS) repl. HOOVER
1990. (lp/c) <*HMS 154-1/-4*> **PUNK ROCK DRIVIN' SONG OF A GUN**
– C.C. rider / Richard Cur / Rubber room / Moody river / Giddy-up-go / Amanda / Let's rodeo / Chicken hearted / Talk Italian to me / Gonorrhea / Shakin' all over.

―― **JON SPENCER** – guitar (of BLUES EXPLOSION) repl. KENNEDY
―― **ROSS JOHNSON** – drums; repl. JARVIS
1991. (lp/c/cd) <*HMS 163-1/-4/-2*> **THE MAN WHO LOVED COUCH DANCING**
– Intro – Kansas City / Roadrunner / I'm drifting / Hip shake / Louis Collins / Are U lonesome 2-nite? / The man who loved couch dancing / Memphis beat / Intro / Broke down engine / Rhythm and booze / Big guitar / Walkin' bum / Coal black mare. <*cd+=>* – (extra track).
Nov 92. (7"ep) <*HMS 170-7*> **MEAN MISTREATER EP**
– Cat drug in / Girl can't help it / Soul deep.

―― **CHRISTINA MARTINEZ** – was also a live member

not iss.   Sympathy F
1993. (cd) <*SFTRI 176*> **MEMPHIS SOL TODAY!**
– Memphis chicken / Barbara / Lil' hand, big gun / Cat drug in / I feel good, little good / I had a dream / Coming up / You walked in the room / Let's work together / Down in the alley / I'll follow her blues / My huckleberry friend / Naked party.

―― split after above

– compilations, etc. –

Aug 96. (cd) *In The Red*; <*ITR 34*> **COLUMBUS SOUL '85**
Apr 96. (cd) *In The Red*; <*ITR 35*> **ONE NIGHT ONLY**

'68 COMEBACK

JEFFREY EVANS – vocals, guitar / **DAN BROWN + ROSS JOHNSON** – guitars + drums / **JEFF BOUCK** – drums

not iss.   P.C.P.
1990's. (7") <*014*> **HIGH SCHOOL CONFIDENTIAL. / BOPPIN' HIGH SCHOOL BABY**

not iss.   Get Hip
1990's. (7") <*168*> **FLIP, FLOP & FLY. / HE'S MY EVERYTHING**

Sympathy F   Sympathy F
Apr 94. (cd) <*SFTRI 277*> **MR. DOWNCHILD**
– Bo Diddley 1969 / Don't judge me bad / Richman, Richman / Tobacco Road (part 1) / Tobacco Road (part 2) / Monk / Mr. Downchild / Otto Wood the bandit / Slop jar blues / String you wear / Greenback blues / Bullmoose / Boogie woogie country girl / Blame it on time / Ain't it down.
Jun 94. (7") <*SFTRI 292*> **TOBACCO ROAD (part 1). / HEDZAZ**
Aug 94. (cd) <*SFTRI 321*> **SINGLES COLLECTIONS** (compilation)
Jan 96. (7"box) (*SFTRI 1390*) **SOMEDAY MY PRINCE WILL COME. /**

―― **NICK DIABLO** – guitar; repl. BROWN

Jun 98. (cd/d-lp) <(*SFTRI 422 CD/LP*)> **A BRIDGE TOO FUCKIN' FAR** May98
– Clean Young 16 / '68 / You walked in the room / Shotgun saw / Evergreen / Shake you hips / Get rhythm / Muddy boots / Boomerang / Bending like a willow tree / Like any other kind / Wall / King's road / That's how my mind works / In the company of kings / Let it rock / The way I walk / My girl Josephine / Pink pedal pushers / Hoy hoy / Route 66.
Apr 99. (cd/lp) <(*SFTRI 574*)> **LOVE ALWAYS WINS**
– Love always wins / Grits ain't groceries / My babe / Tongue-tied Jill / Sitting on top of the world / Big boss man / Polaroid portrait / Dark cloud / What'd I say / Little pig / Dimples / Hound dog / Strange things are happening every day / Tragedy.

BASSHOLES

DON HOWLAND – vocals, guitar / **JON WAHL** – organ, sax, harmonica / **BIM THOMAS** – drums

not iss.   Revenant
1992. (cd) <*REV 204*> **BLUE ROOTS**
– Judge harsh blues / Nakema / I can tell by the way you smell / It's so easy / Light bulb boogie / Stack o' Lee and Billy Lyons / Bald headed woman blues / Sleepy man blues / Cigarette blues / Missing linkster / Candyman blues / Titanic blues / Love cry blues. <*re-iss. Aug97; same*> (*UK-iss.Nov97; same as US*)

In The Red   In The Red
Jan 95. (lp/cd) <*ITR 25/+CD*> **HAUNTED HILL!**
– Haunted hill / 20-20 vision / Cockroach blues / Fear and a hand full of sand / Puddin tame / Grief bird / When want becomes needs / Christine / Pneumonia / Nothing at all / Long gone Dillinger / Evil Devil blues / Retardolude / Reefer and glo-worms / Hokey pokey / John Henry / Big moon boogie.
Apr 97. (7") <*ITR 31*> **LION'S SHARE. / JESUS BOOK**
Jul 97. (lp/cd) <*ITR 49/+CD*> **DEAF MIX, VOL.3**
– Ear candle boogie / Bowling ball / Florida bus / Serena's song / Swimming blues / (Gonna) Write me a letter / Basshole luv theme / Daughter / Cornfield again / Wife blues / Hospital bus / In the red seats / Ovenbird.

not iss.   Bag Of Hammers
1990's. (7") <*BOH 021*> **PROBLEM. / CHANGES HAD TO COME**

―― now a duo of HOWLAND +

– compilations, others, etc. –

Jun 98. (cd/lp) *Matador*; <(*OLE 305-2/-1*)> **LONG WAY BLUES / 1996-1998** Apr98
– Big carnival overture / Or was it just a dream / She shimmy wobble / Long way blues / Hail bop / Lightswitch / Cabooseman blues / Afrodite / Knocked out on my lawn / Joan dark / Ass welt boogie / Angel of death / Turpentine.
Sep 98. (d-lp/cd) *In The Red*; <*ITR 59/+CD*> **WHEN MY BLUE MOON TURNS RED AGAIN**
– Microscope feeling / I saw beauty / Platform blues / Born to die / Cockroach blues / Florida bus / Bowling ball / She came on the bus / Interzone / Evil eagle / Hell blues / 7 days / For the river / Swimming blues / Virginia valley blues / Jack and the king's new ground / Judge harsh blues / Moody / Girls girls girls / Nakema / (I'm gonna) Write me a letter.
Mar 00. (lp/cd) *Sympathy For The Record Industry*; <*SFTRI 587*> **SECRET STRENGTH OF DEPRESSION**

WORKDOGS

ROB KENNEDY + SCOTT JARVIS

not iss.   Sympathy F
1993. (cd) <*SFTRI 212*> **WORKDOGS IN HELL**
– Eulogy regrets / Little boys with big guitars / More than an apology / Nine hundred seventy dogs / Realm of the censors / Solo #8 / Death of the Workdogs / The house that drugs built / Kill 'em, eat 'em, fuck 'em / * / Litany of complaints – Satan is real.
1994. (m-lp) <*SFTRI 248*> **ROBERTA**
– Roberta / Jane gone / Rob K.'s money crazy boogie / Naked giveaway / Moon goin' down / A woman is more than a box we come in.
Jan 95. (cd) <*SFTRI 301*> **OLD**
– Stimulant / Painting the Devil's office again / Back in the days / Brave new blues / Robert Kennedy blues / The facts of life / Back on the night of May 27, 1977 / Too young to die / Little Joe / Old.

GIGOLO AUNTS

Formed: Potsdam, New York, USA ... 1981 as SNIPER by DAVE GIBBS, brothers PHIL and STEVE HURLEY and PHIL BROUWER. After running a gamut of different monikers (including MARAUDER and ROSETTA STONE), the lads settled on the GIGOLO AUNTS following a suggestion by GIBBS' father who'd conceivably heard the SYD BARRETT track of the same name. Now basing themselves in Boston, Massachusetts, the power-pop quartet set to work on their debut album, 'EVERYBODY HAPPY' (1988). Inactive for the next few years (apart from a follow-up set, 'TALES FROM THE VINEGAR SIDE'), GIBBS guested for the VELVET CRUSH on a 1992 British tour in the interim, a chance meeting with 'Creation' supremo ALAN McGEE leading to a UK deal (with 'Fire') for the GIGOLO AUNTS. A trio of BYRDS-esque power-pop singles surfaced over the course of the next year, 'COPE', 'GUN' and 'MRS. WASHINGTON', all three featuring on their long-awaited third album, 'FLIPPIN' OUT' (1993); amid encouraging reviews and a considerable degree of hype, the 'AUNTS were taken on by 'R.C.A.' in the States, where the album was released the following Spring. One of the album's stand-out tracks, 'WHERE I FIND MY HEAVEN', saw the band achieve a modicum of belated fame after it was used in the film, 'Dumb And Dumber', although its subsequent Top 30 status in the UK (Spring '95) came after BBC2 adopted the song as the theme tune to sit-com, 'Game On'. Names such as The ICICLE WORKS, CROWDED HOUSE, the RASPBERRIES and BIG STAR continually cropped up in reviews, the good-time harmony merchants (DAVE and PHIL) even turning down a chance to play in the much-publicised 1993 reformation of the last-named outfit. Surprisingly, the GIGOLO AUNTS were conspicuous by their absence from the music scene of the mid to late 90's, only a mini-cd, 'LEARN TO PLAY GUITAR', emerging in 1997. The subsequent departure of PHIL, together with the replacement of BROUWER with FRED ELTRINGHAM, preceded the release of the belated 'MINOR CHORDS AND MAJOR THEMES' (1999). Perhaps these changes had affected the chemistry of the band as the youthful, power-pop spunk of yore was seemingly buried in a pristine production. 'PACIFIC OCEAN BLUES' (2002), meanwhile, seemed to strike a diplomatic balance between the two, older, wiser but still willing to let all hang out musically, as also witnessed on their other set that year, 'THE ONE BEFORE THE LAST'. • **Covered:** ASK (Smiths) / CAN YOU GET TO THAT (Funkadelic) / FLIPPIN' OUT (V. Casey) / WINDSOR DAM (Big Dipper) / SERIOUS DRUGS (BMX Bandits) / I AM THE COSMOS (Chris Bell) / THE GIRL FROM YESTERDAY (Alan Vega).

Album rating: EVERYBODY HAPPY (*5) / TALES FROM THE VINEGAR SIDE (*5) / FULL ON BLOOM mini (*6) / FLIPPIN' OUT (*7) / LEARN TO PLAY GUITAR mini (*5) / WHERE I FIND MY HEAVEN compilation (*6) / MINOR CHORDS AND MAJOR THEMES (*4) / THE ONE BEFORE THE LAST (*4) / PACIFIC OCEAN BLUES (*5)

DAVE GIBBS – vocals, guitar / **PHIL HURLEY** – guitar / **STEVE HURLEY** – bass / **PAUL BROUWER** – drums

		not iss.	Twin Tone – Coyote
1988.	(lp) <TTC 88146> **EVERYBODY HAPPY**	-	

– Summertime evening / Avalanche / Slipping away / Marble statue / Outside inside / Her face contorted / I can see / Coming clean / People walk up / Not for me / Holy Toledo / Is everybody happy?

		not iss. Fire	Impossible Summerville
1990.	(lp) <020> **TALES FROM THE VINEGAR SIDE**	-	- Spain

		Fire	Alias
Oct 92.	(7") (BLAZE 58) **COPE. / BLOOM**		

(cd-s+=) (BLAZE 58CD) – Stark gone / That's o.k.

Jan 93.	(7"m) <A 057S> **BLOOM. / SERIOUS DRUGS / STARK GONE**		
Mar 93.	(7") (BLAZE 61) **GUN. / TAKE ME ON**	-	

(cd-s+=) (BLAZE 61CD) – Sled / Walk among us.

Jul 93.	(m-cd) <A 051D> **FULL ON BLOOM**	-	

– Bloom / Serious drugs / That's o.k. / Little Carl / Walk among us / Take me on. <re-iss. Jul93 on 'King'; KICP 340>

Aug 93.	(7"clear) (7SM 001) **MRS. WASHINGTON. / SERIOUS DRUG**		

		Fire	King
Oct 93.	(cd/c/lp) (FIRE CD/MC/LP 35) <KICP 417> **FLIPPIN' OUT**		-

– Cope / Where I find my Heaven / Lullaby / Easy reader / Figurine / Mrs. Washington / Bloom / Gun / Pin cushion / Flippin' out. *(lp w/ free 7";)* – WHERE I FIND MY HEAVEN. / THAT'S O.K. <US re-iss. Apr94 on 'R.C.A.'+=; 66392-2/-4/-1> – FULL ON BLOOM (UK re-iss. May95 +=; same)

Apr 94.	(7"/c-s) (BLAZE 68/+MC) **MRS. WASHINGTON. / SERIOUS DRUGS**	74	

(12"/cd-s) (BLAZE 68 T/CD) – ('A'side) / Can you get to that / Windsor dam / Supernova crush.

Apr 95.	(7"/c-s) (BLAZE 87/+MC) **WHERE I FIND MY HEAVEN (remix). / RIDE ON BABY RIDE ON (acoustic)**	29	-

(cd-s+=) (BLAZE 87CD) – Lemon peeler / Serious drug.

—— **FRED ELTRINGHAM** – drums; repl. BROUWER
—— **JON SKIBIC** – guitar; repl. PHIL

		Wicked Disc	Wicked Disc
Sep 97.	(m-cd) <(WIC 1007)> **LEARN TO PLAY GUITAR**		Feb97

– Kinda girl / Wishing you the worst / Sway / Slow / Rocking chair / The sun will rise again.

		E Pluribus Unum	E Pluribus Unum
Oct 99.	(cd) <(41206-2)> **MINOR CHORDS AND MAJOR THEMES**		Feb99

– C'mon / Everyone can fly / Half a chance / Super ultra wicked mega love / You'd better get yourself together, baby / Everything is wrong / The big lie / Simple thing / Rest assured / For a moment / Fade away / Residue. *(hidden track +=)*

		Bittersweet	Bittersweet
May 02.	(cd) (BS 002CD) **THE ONE BEFORE THE LAST**		-

– The girl from yesterday / Kay and Michael / The shift to superoverdrive / To whoever / Sulk with me / Hey lucky / Kinda girl / Wishing you the worst / Sway / Slow / Rocking chair / The sun will rise again.

Oct 02.	(cd) <(BS 010CD)> **PACIFIC OCEAN BLUES**		Apr02

– Hello / Mr. Tomorrow / Even though (the one before the last) / Let go! / Pacific Ocean blues / Lay your weary body down / Stay / Only you / Once in a while / My favourite regret / Maybe the change will do us good. *(hidden track +=)*

– compilations, etc. –

Jun 98.	(cd) Reactive; (REMCD 528) / Nectar; <549> **WHERE I FIND MY HEAVEN (THE BEST OF THE GIGOLO AUNTS)**		1997

Astrud GILBERTO

Born: 30 Mar'40, Salvador, Bahia, Brazil. With the quirkiness of fate that seems to characterise all defining moments in pop history, ASTRUD GILBERTO was plucked from obscurity and coerced into singing purely because she happened to be in the right studio at the right time and, more importantly, spoke a little English. Of course, it helped that her husband was one of the founding fathers of the bossa nova movement, the new wave whose spray was as light as a feather but whose seismic impact on both the Brazilian and North American music scene was akin to that of a tsunami. Guitarist/singer João Gilberto, together with songwriters Antonio Carlos (Tom) Jobim and Vinícius de Moraes were at the centre of a mini-revolution which had inspired some of the most complex and subtle music to yet be filed under the banner of 'pop'. Utilising unconventional harmonic structures and chord changes yet doing it in such a way that it massaged the senses like a soporific spring shower, these artists permanently altered the course of Brazilian music and exercised a huge worldwide influence, especially in the field of jazz. With her teasingly sensual, playfully girlish vocals and dusky, exotic looks, João's wife Astrud inadvertently became both the face and the voice that bossa presented to the English-speaking world. In 1963 she'd gone along to a studio session for the 'Getz / Gilberto' album (ostensibly to accompany her husband) where one of the songs being rehearsed was the Jobim/De Moraes composition, 'Garota de Ipanema'. At the prompting of either Stan Getz or producer Creed Taylor (who wanted some English sung on the album), ASTRUD stepped up to the mic to deliver the English lyric Norman Gimbel had added to the song, in graceful, gender-subverting counterpoint to her husband's Portuguese and Getz' cool, insouciant sax. As 'GIRL FROM IPANEMA', the song hit the US Top 5 (UK Top 30) the following year, going on to become one of the most well known and widely played compositions of the 20th century. The 'Getz/Gilberto' album, also released in 1964 (and which received three Grammys), featured another beguiling ASTRUD vocal on 'CORCOVADO (QUIET NIGHTS OF QUIET STARS)', proving 'GIRL . . .' wasn't a one-off fluke. It was the beginning of a delicious, bittersweet musical romance. The reluctant international star was subsequently recorded numerous times by Taylor, most effectively singing Jobim/Moraes material but trying her hand at a variety of (not always entirely complementary) styles as was the mid-60's want. 'THE ASTRUD GILBERTO ALBUM WITH ANTONIO CARLOS JOBIM' (1965) featured one of her most haunting Jobim interpretations, 'AGUA DE BEBER'; even when singing scat, the babe from Bahia projected a serene yet compelling vulnerability which bore the unmistakable stamp of saudade. Singing in English, her endearing accentuation and unique phrasing lent itself to the unlikeliest of material: her 1969 cover of Chicago's 'BEGINNINGS' remains a delightful revelation, the Eumir Deodato-arranged 'WINDY' a kitschy pleasure. Her talents even attracted the legendary Gil Evans, with whom she worked on 'LOOK TO THE RAINBOW' (1966). While ASTRUD continued to record and tour well after bossa's heyday, her classic 60's sound and image were to influence a plethora of British indie acts (from TALULAH GOSH to STEREOLAB) in thrall to the twee factor and lounge cred inherent in her music. Her voice has often been described as childlike and perhaps it is, at least in the sense that it never sounds dated. Indeed, it's that effortless freshness which will no doubt ensure that further generations of artists continue to draw inspiration from Ipanema's favourite daughter. ASTRUD is still going strong today as her latest album, 'JUNGLE' (2002), will testify; she was also inducted to the "International Latin Music Hall Of Fame" in April 2002.

Best Albums: LOOK TO THE RAINBOW (*8) / THE SILVER COLLECTION (*8)

GIRL OF THE WORLD
(see under ⇒ CAT'S MIAOW!)

GIRLS AGAINST BOYS

Formed: Washington DC, USA . . . 1988 out of LUNCHMEAT, then SOUL SIDE (2/3 albums for 'Dischord') by SCOTT McCLOUD, ALEXIS FLEISIG and JOHNNY TEMPLE. ELI JANNEY, who had been the latter act's soundman joined as the band evolved into GIRLS AGAINST BOYS (drummer BRENDAN CANTY was also part of the part-time band before he joined FUGAZI, while AMY PICKERING was also involved). Their brand of hardcore industrial rock was first sampled on the 'Adult Swim' debut, 'NINETIES Vs. EIGHTIES' (1990), although it was their second set a few years later, 'TROPIC OF SCORPIO', that tested the waters. SCOTT subsequently moved to New York to try out film school, the others joining as they signed with 'Touch & Go'. Three albums of considerable European success were delivered during the mid 90's, 'VENUS LUXURE NO 1 BABY' (1993), 'CRUISE YOURSELF' (1994) and 'HOUSE OF GVSB' (1996), before their bass-heavy gutter sound was wanted by major 'Geffen'. In 1998, the 'BOYS were on the threshold of mini-stardom with their sixth set, 'FREAK*ON*ICA', an album full of sexual sleaze and of course, noise. After their major label cuffufel (which resulted in the band being dropped), GIRLS AGAINST BOYS delivered one of their finest albums to date (on the 'Jade Tree' imprint) in the form of 'YOU CAN'T FIGHT WHAT YOU CAN'T SEE' (2002), a chugging thrash soundtrack for banging yr head off the walls and shouting until yr lungs capsized. Tracks such as 'ALL THE RAGE', the jolting scuzz-ball mish-mash of 'KICKING THE LIGHTS' and Ted Niceley's schizo production were just three reasons to listen. • **Covered:** SHE'S LOST CONTROL (Joy Division).

Album rating: NINETIES VS. EIGHTIES mini (*5) / TROPIC OF SCORPIO (*6) / VENUS LUXURE NO.1 BABY (*7) / CRUISE YOURSELF (*6) / HOUSE OF GVSB (*7) / FREAK*ON*ICA (*6) / YOU CAN'T FIGHT WHAT YOU CAN'T SEE (*6) / Soul Side: SOON COME HAPPY compilation (*6)

SOUL SIDE

SCOTT McCLOUD (b.1968) – vocals, guitar / **JOHNNY TEMPLE** (b.1968) – bass / **ALEXIS FLEISIG** (b.1967) – drums

		Dischord	Dischord
Aug 88.	(lp) <(DISCHORD 29)> **TRIGGER**		Dec87

– Baby / Trigger / Forgiveness / Name is mind / War / K.T.T.K. / Pocket hurts / Problems faced.

Jun 89. (7"m) <(DISCHORD 34)> **BASS. / 103 / OTHERSIDE**
Jan 90. (m-lp) <(DISCHORD 38)> **HOT BODI-GRAM**
– God city / What do you know about that / Punch the geek / Clifton wall / New slow fucky / Pembroke / Hatemusic / New fast fucky / Kill / Bad show / A love supreme / Crazy.

—— in 1991, SOUL SIDE issued d7"ep live recordings, '18 ANY USE OF THE ROPES' for the 'komista' imprint in Germany

Feb 91. (cd) <(DISCHORD 51)> **SOON COME HAPPY** (compilation of all work above) — Nov90

—— had already evolved into ...

GIRLS AGAINST BOYS

McCLOUD, TEMPLE, FLEISIG + ELI JANNEY (b.1967) – sampler bass (keyboards) / plus **AMY PICKERING** (angel vocals) + **BRENDAN CANTY** (drums, organ) also on debut; CANTY joined FUGAZI

		Adult Swim	Adult Swim
Nov 90.	(m-cd) <AS 3CD> **NINETIES vs. EIGHTIES**	-	

– Stay in the car / Jamie / Kitty-yo / Move / Angels / Skind.

Dec 92. (cd/c/lp) <(AS 4 CD/C/V)> **TROPIC OF SCORPIO**
– My night of pleasure (with the mudjacking contractors) / Wow wow wow / Matching wits with flaming Frank / Can't do anything but I love you, babe / Wasting away / Plush / Everything I do seems to cost me $20 / Taste all the fruit / Little buccaneer / Everywhere I go I seem to spend $20.

		Touch & Go	Touch & Go
May 93.	(7") <(TG 115)> **BULLETPROOF CUPID. / SHARKMEAT**		
Jun 93.	(lp/c/cd) <(TG 117/+C/CD)> **VENUS LUXURE NO.1 BABY**		

– In like Flynn / Go be delighted / Rockets are red / Satin down / Let me come back / Learned it / Get down / Bulletproof Cupid / 7 seas / Billy's one stop / Bughouse.

May 94. (7") <(TG 129)> **SEXY SAM. / I'M FROM FRANCE**
(cd-s+=) <(TG 129CD)> – Stay in the car / My night of pleasure / Rockets are red / Sharkmeat.

Sep 94. (7") <(TG 137)> **(I) DON'T GOT A PLACE. / MAN RAY OF LOVE**

Oct 94. (lp/c/cd) <(TG 134/+C/CD)> **CRUISE YOURSELF**
– Tucked-in / Cruise your new baby fly self / Kill the sexplayer / (I) Don't got a place / Psychic know-how / Explicitly yours / From now on / Raindrop / The royal lowdown / My martini / Glazed-eye.

Feb 95. (cd-ep) <(TG 140CD)> **KILL THE SEXPLAYER / SEXY SAM (live) / LEARNED IT (live) / LET ME COME BACK (live)**

Sep 95. (7"white/cd-s) <(HUT 61/+CD)> **SHE'S LOST CONTROL. / (other by Miranda)**

Feb 96. (7"etched) <(TG 160)> **SUPER-FIRE**
(10"+=) <(TG 160-10)> – Viva Roma Star / Cash machine.
(cd-s+=) <(TG 160CD)> – If glamour is dead / Cash machine.

Mar 96. (lp/c/cd) <(TG 149/+C/CD)> **HOUSE OF GVSB**
– Super-fire / Click click / Crash 17 (x-rated car) / Disco six six six / Life in pink / TheKindaMzkYouLike / Vera Cruz / AnotherDroneInMyHead / Cash machine / Wilmington / Zodiac love team. (re-iss. Jun98; same)

Nov 96. (cd-ep) <(TG 166CD)> **DISCO SIX SIX SIX / DISTRACTED (RVS #7) / DO IT LIKE DIAMONDS / BLACK LEATHER / KEEP YER PANTS ON**

		Radiopaque	Radiopaque
Mar 97.	(cd; shared with GUIDED BY VOICES) <(RR 13CD)> **8 ROUNDS**		Jul97

– Learned it / Vera Cruz / Disco six six six / Kill the sexplayer / (others by GUIDED BY VOICES).

		Geffen	Geffen
May 98.	(cd/d-lp) <(GED/GEF 25156)> **FREAK*ON*ICA**		

– Park avenue / Pleasurized / Psycho future / American black hole / Roxy / One firecracker / Speedway / Exorcisto / Vogue thing / Push the fader / Exile / Cowboy's orbit.

		Geffen	Akashic
Jun 98.	(7"/cd-s) <(GFS/+TD 22335)> <AKR 06> **PARK AVENUE. / AMERICAN WHITE DWARF** (Miami Bassomatic remix) / **EPR**		

		Akashic	Akashic
Dec 98.	(7"blue) <(AKR 07)> **ROXY (WHATEVER). / VOGUE THING (squalophonic remix)**		
Feb 99.	(7") <(AKR 08)> **PSYCHO FUTURE. / MAGATTRACTION**		

		Jade Tree	Jade Tree
May 02.	(lp/cd) <(JT 1074/+CD)> **YOU CAN'T FIGHT WHAT YOU CAN'T SEE**		

– Basstation / All the rage / 300 looks for summer / Tweaker / Miami skyline / Resonance / BFF / Kicking the lights / One perfect thing / The come down / Let it breathe.

GITS

Formed: Ohio, USA ... 1986 by sharp lyricist MIA ZAPATA, co-songwriter JOE SPLEEN, STEVE MORIARTY, and MATT DRESDNER. After gigging for several years in their homestate, this in-your-face punk band moved to Seattle, Washington, to join in the city's blossoming music scene, which would, within a few years, cause a rock revolution, spearheaded by such luminaries as NIRVANA and PEARL JAM. Although the grunge sound did inform that of the GITS, they managed to stay fairly on their punk course, not least due to ZAPATA's strong and feisty on- and off-stage personality. For this reason the band were placed centre stage of the movement known as 'riot grrrl', despite being three quarters male in make-up, and this labelling certainly didn't do their appeal any harm. Initially ignored by the record industry, the GITS released their own debut LP 'FRENCHING THE BULLY' (1992). This set was hard-hitting punk, and brought them a notable following, due in parts to their rip-roaring stage appeal, ZAPATA taking the lion's share of credit for this. The band set to on a follow-up set, but were stopped in their tracks by the horrific events in the evening of 7th, July, 1993; ZAPATA was brutally raped and killed after leaving a bar in her adopted city. The heinous incident sent shockwaves through the musical community, resulting in the setting up of 'Home Alive', founded by drummer VALERIE AGNEW (of 7 YEAR BITCH fame) and artist Stacey Westcott. The aim of the group was to teach and aid people in various forms of resistance to physical violence. They managed several fund-raising gigs, and the release of the various artists compilation, 'The Art Of Self-Defense' (1994), which featured among others, NIRVANA, PEARL JAM and JOAN JETT. The remaining GITS finished off and released the album, 'ENTER THE CONQUERING CHICKEN' (1994), which they had been working on with ZAPATA. Although obviously slightly incomplete, the set does remain a beautiful sentiment to their erstwhile singer. Two further releases followed, 'KINGS AND QUEENS' (1996), and 'SEAFISH LOUISVILLE' (1996). The former was a recording of an early gig in Ohio in 1988, and showcased the phenomenal act they were live, the latter featured added live material and other unheard pieces. It is also worth mentioning that the remaining GITS were joined by JOAN JETT in 1995 to do a memorial gig for ZAPATA, the amalgamation also resulted in the release of an LP under the name, EVIL STIG (which was GITS LIVE backwards).

Album rating: FRENCHING THE BULLY (*7) / ENTER: THE CONQUERING CHICKEN (*5) / KINGS & QUEENS compilation (*5) / posthumous: SEAFISH LOUISVILLE (*5)

MIA ZAPATA – vocals / **JOE SPLEEN** – guitar / **MATT DRESDNER** – bass / **STEVE MORIARTY** – drums

		C/Z	C/Z
Dec 92.	(lp/cd) <(CZ 051/+CD)> **FRENCHING THE BULLY**		

– Absynthe / Another shot of whiskey / Insecurities / Slaughter of Bruce / Kings and queens / It all dies away / While you're twisting, I'm still .... / untitled / Wingo lamo / Cut my skin, it makes me human / Here's to your fuck / Second skin.

—— during 1993 (their follow-up was due), MIA was raped and murdered

Mar 94. (cd/c) <CZ 076 CD/C> **ENTER: THE CONQUERING CHICKEN** -
– Bob (cousin O.) / Guilt within your head / Seaweed / A change is gonna come / Precious blood / Beauty of the rose / Drunks / Italian song / Social love I / Social love II / Spear and magic helmet / Drinking song / Sign of the crab. <lp-iss.1995 on 'Broken Rekids'; 20>

—— disbanded for obvious reasons

– compilations, etc. –

Jun 96. (cd) *Broken Rikids; <44>* **KINGS & QUEENS** -
– Eleven / Cut my skin, it makes me human / Running / Look right through me / It all dies anyway / Monsters / It doesn't matter / Snivelling little rat faced git / Still you don't know what it's like / Tempt me / Gitsumental (breaks) / Kings & queens / Ain't got no right / Loose / Graveyard blues.

Oct 00. (cd) *Broken Rekids; <87>* **SEAFISH LOUISVILLE (live)** -
– Whirlwind / Seaweed / Absynthe / Another shot of whiskey / Insecurities / Slaughter of Bruce / Precious blood / While you're twisting, I'm still breathing / (untitled) / Social love / It doesn't matter / Kings and queens / Wingo lamo / Here's to your fuck / Second skin / Daily bread.

GLASS ONION (see under ⇒ TRAVIS)

GLITTERBOX

Formed: London, England ... late 1993 by JONNY GREEN, MILES HESELTINE and MARK SERVAES, who met at a college in Norwich, deciding there and then to start a band without the knowledge of how to play an instrument (who said punk was dead!). Early the following year, the three recruited TONY HOLLAND and subsequently played a disastrous solitary gig at a pub in London before retreating to their day jobs. Resurfacing with some of their own material early in '95, JONNY, MILES and TONY came up with the group name, SHE, eventually coaxing MARK to return from his new home in Barcelona. Annoyed by UK record labels who could not pigeonhole them between rock and indie, they sent demos to the States, the result being that A&R men quickly flew over to size them up; 'Atlantic' won the battle. However, luck was not on their side, when, in 1996, 'Death Row' all-female R&B act, SHE, threatened legal action (sleeping and fishes are two words that come to mind!?). Having already finished off the recording of their debut album, the release was delayed while the band came up with a new moniker, GLITTERBOX. However, yet more problems ensued as JONNY was hit by a throat virus which kept him out of the game for half a year. In August '97, the quartet finally released a single, 'YOU CAN'T LIVE ON MARS', its lack of appeal seeing the band downshift to Atlantic's subsidiary, 'Radar' for subsequent releases. Early the following year, the first of these, 'SCARED OF ALL THE WORLD', hit the shops and another, 'HOUDINI' preceded the long-awaited and nearly cancelled album, 'TIED AND TANGLED'. This was an overdue piece of Britrock-pop taking a whole list of influences including The MANICS, AFGHAN WHIGS and even TALKING HEADS!

Album rating: TIED & TANGLED (*7)

JONNY GREEN – vocals, guitar / **MILES HESELTINE** – guitar, vocals / **TONY HOLLAND** – bass / **MARK SERVAES** – drums, percussion

		Atlantic	Atlantic
Aug 97.	(7") *(AT 005)* **YOU CAN'T LIVE ON MARS. / MOTORCYCLE SONG**		
	(cd-s+=) *(AT 005CD)* – Roller skates.		
		Radar	Atlantic
Feb 98.	(7") *(SCAN 28)* **SCARED OF ALL THE WORLD. / I'M YOUR MONSTER**		-
	(cd-s+=) *(SCANCS 28)* – Your ghost.		
Apr 98.	(7") *(SCAN 29)* **HOUDINI. / SUNK**		-
	(cd-s) *(SCANCS 29)* – ('A'side) / Still breathing / Illuminate you / Promises.		
May 98.	(cd) *(SCANCD 30) <83021-2>* **TIED & TANGLED**		Oct97
	– Houdini / Scared of all the world / Woody Allen / Superman / I can wait / You can't live on mars / Jesus song / Summersong / Step inside / Sit back and watch her fly / Tonight to Hell.		
–––	split some time after above		

GLO-WORM (see under ⇒ BLACK TAMBOURINE)

GNAC

Formed: Manchester, England . . . around 1995 as the recording name of solo instrumentalist, MARK TRANMER, the moniker coming from a short story by Italian novelist, Italo Calvino. TRANMER's output comes from the strain of pop music that produced more ambient, mood creating music, a reason why his work is often placed in the category of "imaginary film" soundtracks. Touchstones in this area for his output are the cinema music of MICHAEL NYMAN, ENNIO MORRICONE, and MICHEL LEGRAND. GNAC's experimental guitar-work and instrumentation is also closely analogous to that of DURUTTI COLUMN's VINI REILLY, a similarity which never seems to escape the critics. TRANMER's musical career kicked off in the mid-nineties, with the release of several singles on differing indie labels, including the imprints, 'Liquefaction' and 'Earworm'. His atmospheric soundscaping reached the attention of Paris-based label, 'Vespertine', who TRANMER inked a deal with in 1997. His new label brought him to wider attention on their compilation release, 'An Evening In The Company Of . . .'. More importantly, for TRANMER's ascendancy, this release also featured the music of ROGER QUIGLEY. Due to their shared musical views, the duo met and formed the partnership known as MONTGOLFIER BROTHERS, QUIGLEY's vocals sitting well with TRANMER's instrumentation. Meanwhile, TRANMER's GNAC alias continued to be fruitful, with the release of his debut LP, 'FRIEND SLEEPING', in 1999. This was followed up by the compilation album, 'SEVENS' (2000), on imprint 'Rocket Girl', which needless to say from the title, collected together earlier GNAC singles. At about this time, ALAN McGEE, of 'Creation' label-fame, had just begun new indie imprint, 'Poptones', in order to take a new, less commercial direction from his earlier venture. The MONTGOLFIER BROTHERS' work fitted nicely into McGEE's recent concept, thus one of the label's earliest signings, and releases, was the duo's debut full-length outing, 'SEVENTEEN STARS' (2000), which had originally seen the light of day on the, now out-of-service, 'Vespertine' label. 'Poptones' also issued GNAC's third full-length set, 'BISCUIT BARREL FASHION' the following year. QUIGLEY meanwhile, kept himself busy, teaming up with DAVE SHERMAN, under the moniker, TRANSFIGURATION, to release the instrumental album, 'ALPHA TAPES' (2001). The MB's came back together the next year for their second set, 'THE WORLD IS FLAT', another well crafted piece of pop experimentation.

Album rating: FRIEND SLEEPING (*6) / SEVENS compilation (*6) / BISCUIT BARREL FASHION (*5) / Montgolfier Brothers: SEVENTEEN STARS (*6) / THE WORLD IS FLAT (*7)

MARK TRANMER – vocals, guitar

		Amberley	not iss.
May 98.	(7"mauve-ep) *(amy 007)* **IN MAUVE**		-
	– Our distance / Ves 004 / Le grand illusion.		
		Earworm	not iss.
Aug 98.	(7"beige) *(worm 29)* **THE MOUSTACHE. / ARMCHAIR THRILLER**		-
		Kooky	Darla
Nov 98.	(7"green) *(kooky 007)* **A TANGLE WITH . . . / THE BROKEN FALL**		-
Jan 99.	(ltd-12") **OUR DISTANCE (sweet trip mix). / OUR DISTANCE (futureboi mix)**	-	-
		Liquefaction	not iss.
Mar 99.	(7"blue) *(duske 9)* **HENNEBERT SLEEVE. / THE MAN WITH THE LAUGH LIKE A RUSTY HINGE**		-
		Acetone	not iss.
Apr 99.	(7"clear) **18th CENTURY QUIZ SHOW. / THE TRIALS OF DR PANGLOSS**	-	- French
		Vespertine	not iss.
Jul 99.	(cd) *(VES 010)* **FRIEND SLEEPING**		-
	– Friend sleeping / Hennebert sleeve / Continental balcony twilight / Ice cream van / Nanami togarashi / Stepping aside / A vantage point is the top of a tree / Plink / Bad self portrait / Fin. *(re-iss. Dec01; same)*		
		Rocket Girl	Rocket Girl
Oct 99.	(cd) *(<RGIRL 7CD>)* **SEVENS** (compilation)		Jun00
	– Le grand illusion / The broken fall / Armchair thriller / Another fine mess / 1958 / Difficult love / A tangle with . . . / The moustache / Heliotrope / Our distance / Ves 004 / Soviet bureau / Repetition / And now it's so much colder.		
		Poptones	not iss.
Mar 01.	(cd) *(MC 5028CD)* **BISCUIT BARREL FASHION**		-
	– Annonay / Bad dancers collide / Thrill of gambling / Biscuit barrel fashion / I think I think too much too / Neen scene / Joseph Michel and Jacques Etienne / Superintendent battle arrives / Uncomfortable modes of transport / Annonay for the second time / 18th century quiz show / Amstel diamond fraudsters / Gardens of brown and LeNotre / Constraints / Voltaire's inference.		

		Octane Gramophone	not iss.
May 01.	(7") *(OCT 2)* **split w/ SMOOTH OPERATOR**		-

MONTGOLFIER BROTHERS

aka **ROGER QUIGLEY** (vocals) + **MARK TRANMER** (instruments)

		Vespertine	not iss.
Apr 99.	(cd) *(VES 008) <QS 5001>* **SEVENTEEN STARS**		2000
	– Time spent passing / Even my mind can't tell you / Pro celebrity standing around / Four days / Seventeen stars / Low tide / In walks a ghost / Une chanson du Crepescule / Between two points / Fin. *(<re-iss. Sep00 on 'Poptones'; MC 5001 CD/LP>)*		
		Poptones	Poptones
May 01.	(7") *(MC 50015)* **PRO CELEBRITY STANDING AROUND. /**		
Aug 02.	(cd) *(<MC 5057CD>)* **THE WORLD IS FLAT**		
	– 2.55 Newbury / The understudy / Be selfish / The world is flat / The second takes forever / Swings and roundabouts / Dream in organza / I couldn't sleep, either / Think once more / Inches away.		

the GO

Formed: Detroit, Michigan, USA . . . 1998 by vocalist BOBBY HARLOW, alongside an ever-changing line up of bassists, guitarists and drummers, including originals JOHN KRAUTNER, MARK FELLIS and MATT HATCH; STEVE NAWARA and WHITE STRIPES frontman JACK WHITE were also present and correct at various times. After playing support for ? & THE MYSTERIANS, the group of R&B noisekins were signed to 'Sub Pop', issuing the straight-up, no bullshit album 'WHATCHA DOIN' (1999). Not bad for a trendy thrash rock group who indulged in feedbacked, scuzz rock noise on occasion. Oh, and a great chance to hear early material from the little known MR JACK WHITE.

Album rating: WHATCHA DOIN' (*7)

BOBBY HARLOW – vocals / **JOHN KRAUTNER** – guitar / **STEVE NAWARA** – guitar / **DAVE BUICK** – bass; repl. MATT HATCH who joined The SIGHTS / **MARK FELLIS** – drums

		Sub Pop	Sub Pop
Oct 99.	(lp/cd) *<(SP/+CD 478)>* **WHATCHA DOIN'**		Sep99
	– Meet me at the movies / Summer sun blues / Keep on trash / You can get high / It might be bad / Suzy don't leave / Get you off / Tired of the night / But you don't know / Whatcha doin' / On the corner / Time for moon.		
–––	NAWARA went on to play for ELECTRIC SIX as DISCO; **KEN TUDRICK** – guitar, vocals was added to HARLOW, KRAUTNER (bass) + FELLIS		

		Lizard King	not iss.
Nov 02.	(7") *(LIZARD 001X)* **CAPRICORN. / GROWED UP WRONG**		-
	(cd-s+=) *(LIZARD 001)* – Come back / Hey Linda.		

GOD BULLIES

Formed: Kalamazoo, Michigan, USA . . . 1985 by vocalist MIKE HARD and three other angry young men, TOMMY SHANNON, MIKE CORSO and ADAM BERG. Similar in some respects to The CRAMPS, The BUTTHOLE SURFERS and The STOOGES, the band gained a deal with US label, 'Amphetamine Reptile' (home of HALO OF FLIES, THROWN UPS and subsequently, HELMET), for whom they released a handful of releases from 1987's 'FEAR & PAIN' single to 1991's double-7", 'JOIN SATAN'S ARMY'. Three years on, 'Alternative Tentacles' took up the reins for what was to become their swansong set, 'KILL THE KING' (1994).

Album rating: MAMA WOMB WOMB (*5) / PLASTIC EYE MIRACLE mini (*5) / DOG SHOW (*5) / WAR ON EVERYBODY (*5) / KILL THE KING (*4)

MIKE HARD – vocals / **DAVID LIVINGSTONE** – guitar; repl. TOMMY SHANNON (in 1986) / **MIKE CORSO** – bass / **ADAM BERG** – drums (ex-DEBAUCHED)

		not iss.	Mad Queen
1988.	(7") *<MQ45 01>* **ALL I WANT IS MY MAMMA. / SEX POWER MONEY**	-	
		Amphetam. Reptile	Amphetam. Reptile
1989.	(7") *<Scale 11>* **FEAR AND PAIN. / KICK IT TO SLEEP**		
1989.	(lp) *(ARR 1/58) <89157-1>* **MAMA WOMB WOMB**		
	– Act of desire / Creepy people / O shit / Fear and pain / What reason / The godfather moves / To Arkansas, part 1 / Follow the leader / Sex power money / Red blood / All I want is my mamma / What are you looking for.		
Feb 90.	(m-lp) *(ARR 7/71)* **PLASTIC EYE MIRACLE** (half studio/half live)		
	– It's over / You cry now / She's wild / Plastic eye miracle / Freefall – Act of desire / Like it like that / Live sex (mamma).		
–––	added **MARY KATE MURRAY + TABATHA PREDOVICH** – backing vocals		
Nov 90.	(cd/lp) *(ARR 9/87) <89181-2/-1>* **DOG SHOW**		
	– Let's go to hell / Monster Jesus / Cemetary / I am invisible / Buddha / The godfather goes to hell (part 2) / 2 + 2 / Do it again / Shallow grave / Like it like that / Abigail.		
1990.	(d7") *<Scale 31>* **JOIN SATAN'S ARMY. / PREACHER MAN // YOU SEXY THING. / WHICH WAY YOU GOIN' BILLY**	-	
Dec 91.	(lp/cd) *(ARR 180/+CD) <amrep 006>* **WAR ON EVERYBODY**		
	– Book report time / I want to kill you / Ordinary man / Automaker / Long way home / Peace and love / Senojmot / Magical butterfly / Pet monkey / Andre / Safety zone / Saw you dead.		
–––	<they also featured one track on Various EP, 'Ugly American Overkill'; Scale 34>		
–––	**TONY OLIVERI** – drums (ex-COWS) repl. BERG who joined the short-lived HAND OVER HEAD		

	not iss.	Sympathy F
1992. (7") <SFTRI 130> **HOW LOW CAN YOU GO? / RUBY (desert storm mix)**

—— added the returning **TOMMY SHANNON** – guitar

—— **ADAM BERG** also returned to repl. OLIVERI

	Alternative Tentacles	Alternative Tentacles
Oct 94. (cd) <(VIRUS 152CD)> **KILL THE KING**
– Neighborhood kid / King of sling / How many times / Detain my brain / She's wild / Pretty on the inside / Space kid zoom / You have been warned / It's him / Artificial insemination by Aliens / Hate. (re-iss.Nov97; VIRUSUK 152)

—— now without LIVINGSTONE who continued with TEENAGE LARVAE; they released one 10" min-CD, 'Songs For Pigs' <SFTRI 203>

	Radical	Radical
Nov 95. (7") <(RDL 008-7)> **MILLENNIUM. / I FORGOT WHERE I LIVE**

—— **BRIAN DOWNEY** – drums; repl. BERG

—— after they disbanded SHANNON joined THRALL who released the album, 'Chemical Wedding' for 'Alternative Tentacles' <VIRUS 189>

– compilations, others, etc. –

1992. (ltd-7") *ASP Records; <asp 001>* **TELL ME. / CREEPY PEOPLE**
(above was recorded in 1986 with original line-up)

GOD IS MY CO-PILOT

Formed: New York City, New York, USA ... 1990 by CRAIG FLANAGIN and SHARON TOPPER. Harking back to the late 70's when sonic noise terrorists such as The POP GROUP, ESSENTIAL LOGIC and HALF JAPANESE were at the cutting edge, GIMC-P updated the form in typically experimental NY style. Lauded as the American equivalent of Riot Grrl campaigners HUGGY BEAR, FLANAGIN and TOPPER combined controversial, howling, gender-bending lyrics with a rhythmic, breakneck jazzcore assault that was initially showcased on debut album, 'SPEED YR TRIP' (1992). The same year's 'I AM NOT THIS BODY', confirmed their reputation as genre blurring funsters with an eye for the bizarre and an uncompromising social outlook. One of their biggest fans was John Peel, who invited the band onto his Radio One show for a handful of sessions between '93 and '95. Meanwhile, the group (who now included bassist FLY and twin-drummers, MICHAEL EVANS and DAN BROWN) went full steam ahead with their prolific release schedule, working with the likes of JOHN ZORN.

Album rating: SPEED YR TRIP (*6) / I AM NOT THIS BODY (*7) / STRAIGHT NOT (*5) / HOW TO BE (*5) / TIGHT LIKE FIST (*5) / MIR SHLUFN NISHT (*5) / SEX IS FOR MAKING BABIES (*6) / PUSS 02 (*6) / THE BEST OF GOD IS MY CO-PILOT compilation (*6) / GET BUSY (*5)

SHARON TOPPER – vocals / **CRAIG FLANAGIN** – guitar, bass, etc / with **ALEX KLEIN** – bass / **SIOBHAN DUFFY** – drums, vox organ / + others at various times

	not iss.	The Making Of Americans
1991. (7"ep) <1> **SONGS OF PRAISE**
– 4 steps down the Rd to trouble / I pulled up to park / Iko / Better get it in yr soul.

1991. (7"ep) <2> **REFUSED MEDICAL ATTENTION**
– Refusal / Replicant / Rent rant.

1992. (7"blue-ep) **ON A WING AND A PRAYER**
– Almost not / I hate my friends / Pussybox / I'm not the one / Well no wonder.
(above & below issued on 'Funky Mushroom')

1992. (7"yellow-ep) **GENDER IS AS GENDER DOES**
– Handsome Molly / I hate girls / Sun, wind / Submissive.

1992. (lp) <3> **SPEED YR TRIP**
– Little ghosts / Down down baby / They often look Fr. / In too deep / Angels in the air / Los mas sabrosa / No cross no crown / Anyone but you / Fat / C-etait une J. fille / Home / Woman enough / On lust / Catheter / Drave / Late last night / Comfort / Zonnebloem / Kingdom of the flesh / Hair in mouth / Poke / I surrender complete to Anne / Wipe that smirk off yr face / Got what / Brought up short / Scratch and sniff. (cd-iss. Apr95 on 'Les Disques Du Soleil'; DSA 54237) (UK-iss.Nov96 on 'Runt'; RUNT 16)

1992. (lp) <4> **I AM NOT THIS BODY**
– List / Angels in the air / Heaven / Smooch / Thunder, perfect mind / Invisible rocket / Kissing frenzy / Grizzly gizzard / Fierce beast / 2 meats / Crushing a girl / Said and done / Out in the streets / Lonesome highway / Very very / This situation / Joan / God knows / The truth be told / Adrenalin jitters / Looken for a fat girl / Seashell / Liz Cohen caught looking / Theresa says / You up / Well / Animal rights / Southwestern jazz / The day I owned the sky / To yr scattered bodies go / You smell like sex / Tight and low / Anthem / That's how I like it. <cd-iss. Apr95 on 'Les Disques Du Soleil; DSA 54236> (UK-iss.Nov96 on 'Runt'; RUNT 15)

	not iss.	Ajax
Feb 93. (7"ep) **HOW I GOT OVER**
– If I were Theresa / What's natural / I kill kids / Suliko / How I got over / Backstab.

	not iss.	Blackout!
May 93. (7"ep) **MY SINISTER HIDDEN AGENDA**
– Straight not / Eye contact / Suck on some ice / Bicycle girls / Sound of wings.

	not iss.	Dark Beloved Cloud
May 93. (7"clear-ep) <DBC 008> **WHEN THIS YOU SEE REMEMBER ME**
– Frauen U. nichtfrauen / Can't stop now / Hey churla / Jackalope hunting / Linear B.

Aug 93. (7") <DBC 017> **ILLUSION OF SECRECY**
– Vot vot ja niin niin / We signify.

	not iss.	Seze
Jun 93. (7"ep) **PISSING & HOOTING**
– Ich will dich essen / Femme thang / Losy highway / Lonesome Elliott.

	not iss.	Outpunk
Jul 93. (7"ep) **GOD IS MY CO-PILOT / FIFTH COLUMN split**
– Probable cause / Life under occupation / Held down / FIFTH COLUMN: Don't.

Aug 93. (cd/c/lp) **STRAIGHT NOT**
– Any # / Haul away / My earliest memory / Fruta si cancer no / We signify / Safety fast / Girl in a car singing along w/ the radio / Don't say my name / Star of the County Down / Pump action / Absent parent / She's so butch / I saw Helen's tits / Mid-air refueling / A little game / Youth / Tierhelden / Drave / Don't fuck / Both ways / Tom Sawyer " the center of the earth / Lost / Mieluummin onnellinen kuin kuuluisa / Someone's always telling you how to behave / Well / Danny boy.

	not iss.	Quinnah
Aug 93. (10"m-lp) **GETTING OUT OF BORING TIME, BITING INTO BORING PIE**
– Starch & chafe / Defer to avert / Stop / Plaid skirts – Well you needn't / Ant circus / Move the Moon / Sifter / 2 amis / "Bicycle girls" / Use – Mention / Looks like it feels / Look in & you'll see who I wish to love me / Funeral horse / Furbearing (mammal mambo).

—— following album incl. a plethora of session people

	not iss.	Knitting Factory
Sep 93. (cd) <KFWCD 148> **TIGHT LIKE FIST: LIVE RECORDING (live)**
– Angels in the air / Handsome Molly / Eye contact / Get it / Katrinan Luala / Sun, wind / Heavy layer / Sound of wings / Crushing a girl / Lead w/ yr chin / Bicycle girls / Ot azoi – Igneous ejaculation / 2 meats beat as 1 / Miinan Laulu / Zonnebloem / Sleep not / Tourschr. – How I got over / Role model / Backstab / Lou explains it / Oyfn nil / Any # / Fierce beast / I'm not gonna lie / Smooch / Khad gad yo / Heaven / 4 steps / Pornography and rape / Make you feel / Home / Frauen U. nichtfrauen / Farm recording / Straight not / That's how I like it / encore:- Firecracker / Iko / Jailhouse / Can't stop now. (UK-iss.Feb95; same)

	not iss.	Shrimper
Oct 93. (c) **WHAT DOCTORS DON'T TELL YOU**
– Heavier air / Lullaby / Opened wide / Then / Finnegans wake / When do I see the lightning / Every night / Close my eyes / Walk the cat / To be or have not / Mechant / Interlocking / Hey mister / Girls waiting / Porcupine homily / Bludgeon / An Irish airman forsees his death / Vanessa / Say the L word / I pulled up to park.

	not iss.	Finnish
Nov 93. (7") **YKT FLOT!**
– Iko Iceland / Jolalag.

	not iss.	Hedonist
Jan 94. (7"flexi) **MORE PRETTY GIRLS THAN ONE**

—— with now **FLY** – bass / **DAN BROWN** + **MICHAEL EVANS** – drums

	Soul Static Sound	Making Of America
May 94. (7"ep) <SOUL 3> **"SHARON QUITE FANCIES JO" EP**
– Loudmouth! / 55,151 / Double zero / 1000 lost souls.

Jun 94. (lp)<cd> <SOUL 4> <11> **HOW TO BE** — Apr96
– Carte celeste / Madly they did ride / Turkischer / X-yrs / Rubber or leather / Le 21 Janvier 1793 / Take one / Scourge / Honest / Strange things / Stella / Best friends / 3 times fast / Can't / Don't go crazy, go to sleep / Kittybait / Pornography & rape / Zocher eich radaknu et hahora / Pygmy dream / Reading Dick / Le corps sans merci / Honey ant song / You are my sunshine.

	Rough Trade Sing. Club	not iss.
May 94. (7"ep) (7) **THIS IS NO TIME TO BE FRAIL!**
– Childhood dreams of abduction and mutilation / Thank you, just thank you / Kiss & tell / I cream.

	not iss.	Ajax
Aug 94. (7"ep) <AJAX 035> **KITTYBAIT 5song EP**
– Turk blurt / Firecracker / My earliest memory / Cat Power love song – Ala Mee.

—— In 1994 also, the track 'BUTCH FLIP' featured on a split EP with MELT-BANANA below with **ELLIOT SHARP & ANTHONY COLEMAN**; most trad songs

	Avant	Avant
Jan 95. (cd) <(AVAN 032)> **MIR SHLUFN NISHT** — Dec94
– Vot vot ja niin niin / Hora / Tan Liz Cohane / Tuppasuita / Dayenu / Miyimalel / Double Dutch / Piramidn / B'nai! / Like – Park / We don't sleep / Raketa pisztoly / Miinan Laulu / Katrussya / Tantsukolena fin / Nya skor / Sissy dog / Khad gad yo / Churla / Palmcore / Hatikvah / Mia geht nach bodega / Oyfn nil / Tantsukolena yid.

	Runt	Runt
Jan 95. (7"ep) <(RUNT 3)> **AN APPEAL TO REASON**
– Steal yr girlfriend / Hutzulka / Kendine gel / Backstab.

—— line-up:- **FLANAGIN, TOPPER, MICHAEL EVANS** – drums / **OTTO KENTROL** – bass / **ANDY DOGFACE** – guitar, viola, vocals / **JENNY WADE** – bass / **DAVID SIMONS** – drums / **ZOE TOBIER** – vocals / **FLY** – vocals

—— **LAURA CROMWELL** – drums (appeared again) as did others

	Disques Du Soleil	Disques Du Soleil
Jan 95. (cd) <(DSA 54033)> **SEX IS FOR MAKING BABIES** — Dec94
– Tombstone / Runt hunt / A fly / In the forest / Tsifatelli / Interrogation / Sex is for making babies / What a goddess / High plains / Wetting the bed / Blue yodel #21 / (Fly) Tanja / Be nice to yr parents / Mechant / Work is love / Runt / Start / About how I hate the boys / Then phat / Kantele / Imaginary friend / Sissy dog / Little red moon / Fat children.

	not iss.	Trash Can
1995. (7"ep) **OOTKA SA POIKA VAI TYTTO?**
– Caught looking / Flesh made word / Laulu X / Pillu Laulu.

	not iss.	The Making Of Americans
1995. (cd; as GODCO) **NEKO NO AKUBI: NIHON NO FI (live)** — tour
– Neko no akubi / U doet me pijn / Mexican parade / T for Texas / Sound of wings / Certain snails / Steal yr girlfriend / Place on ground – Light fuse – Get away / Pa Janvier / Compliance / Eyes of Satan / Ethno techno squeako skweeko / My bicycle gang / Smooth & clean / Not no / Mambo no sampo / Katrussja / Valse du chat / Fall back / Crawdad song.

	Guided Missile	not iss.
Nov 95. (7"ep; GODCO split with GAG) (GUIDE 003) **GROW YOUR OWN COUNTRY WIDE PRIMARY SCHOOL BAND E.P.**
– (3 by GAG) / Girl-crazy girl / Bjorkfruits.

GOD IS MY CO-PILOT (cont) THE GREAT INDIE DISCOGRAPHY The 1990s

Disques Du Soleil / Disques Du Soleil

Dec 95. (cd; as GODCO) <*(DSA 54041)*> **PUSS 02**
– Dance / Pocketful of sugar / Duck duck duck goose / Coffee & cake / Secrets / Chicken reel / 9 1/2 out of 10 / Morton gets the urge / At home / Did it / Slow dismemberment / Pretty spoiled / Numbness & tingling / Careless love / Quinie Q / Cool / Asoi! / Puss in boots / Haiku A / . . .meanwhile . . . / Can't be what I am / Batgirl gets a C-section / Cunla / Musica caliente / Smooth & clean / Hallowed ground / Sex is for making babies / Teenage boyfriend / Jackie 60.

Miguel / not iss.

May 97. (m-cd) *(MIGUEL 1)* **CHILDREN CAN BE SO CRUEL** -
– Three times fast / I tanz Jo net / Zonnebloem / Hai cium dong / Get in / Chat valse / Gras och granbarr / Je suis totally d'accord.

not iss. / Dark Beloved Cloud

1997. (ltd-cd) <*DBC 210*> **JE SUIS TROP CONTENT: A GODDESS MICROPILOT TOUR (live)** -
– Abducted by aliens / Leave you alone / Eat the machine / Pretty spoiled / Akastos es suru csardas / Love w/ an F / Laisse tomber les filles / Chase scene / Boxstitch / Je suis satisfait / Sabbatical / Hello stranger / Belle / Por-de-sol sobre guarda / Tarsjusz.

Atavistic / Atavistic

Nov 98. (cd) <*(ALP 87CD)*> **GET BUSY**
– Menarche / Leave you alone / Chase scene / Far more attractive / Monkeys / Domestic partner / Kleines eisstuck / Lunch / Gras och granbarr / Shift and flicker / I can't dance / Hutulka / Nya skor / Abducted by aliens.

— looked to have split after above CD

– compilations, etc. –

Dec 95. (cd) *Meldac Corp;* **HISTORY OF MUSIC: VOLUME 1, 1989-1991** -
– (all EP's from 'SONGS OF PRAISE' to 'THIS IS NO TIME TO BE FRAIL!')

Feb 96. (cd) *Meldac Corp;* **HISTORY OF MUSIC: VOLUME 2, 1991-1993** -
– (all EP's from 'SHARON QUITE FANCIES JO' to 'GETTING OUT OF . . .')

Nov 96. (cd) *Atavistic;* <*(ALP 82CD)*> **THE BEST OF GOD IS MY CO-PILOT**
– Behave / Caught looking / Hutzulka / Totally wired / Queer disco anthem / Steal yr girlfriend / Kiss & tell / Pillu laulu / Flesh made word / Butch flip / Mezinke skip / Kendine gel / Girl-crazy girl / Bjorkfruits / Childhood daydreams of abduction and mutilation / I cream / Backstab / Rubber or leather (remix) / Laulu X / Thank you, just thank you / Queer disco anthem (remix) / Behave (remix).

Jan 97. (cd) *Strange Fruit;* (<*SFRSCD 004*>) **THE PEEL SESSIONS ('93, '94, '95)** Jun99
– Kiss & tell / 2 meats / Boxstitch / Disco by night / Katrussja / I pulled up to park / U doet me pjin / Boris / 55,151 / Moleskin / Quinie Q / Kurdish list laulu / Code & submit / I love my love with an F / Lead with your chin.

GODRAYS (see under ⇒ SMALL FACTORY)

GODSPEED YOU BLACK EMPEROR!

Formed: Mile End district, Montreal, Canada . . . 1994 by EFRIM and MAURO (the original pair issuing a very limited 33 copy cassette, 'ALL LIGHTS FUCKED ON THE HAIRY AMP DROOLING'). Enlarging the outfit to a 9-piece collective and enlisting DAVE, AIDAN GIRT, BRUCE, THIERRY, NORSOLA and SOPHIE with STEPH, SYLVIA, COLIN, CRISTOPHE, JESSE, DAN C, SHANEABERG, PETER and AMANDA making up contributors at various times. Revolting against the "pay to play" system that many of the local establishments employed, the ensemble took to playing empty warehouses and other such venues, enabling them to gain popularity among the more alternative centred individuals in their town. In 1996, GYBE! retreated to Hotel2Tango (a mythological apartment which certain members of the band were said to occupy), putting down material with the assistance of Chemical Daryl at his Chemical Sound studio. Broke again, they obtained free reel to reel tape from a friend and remixed their old material, adding two tracks and sequencing their efforts at Mile End studio. The result was the devastatingly bleak 'F#A#oo' album, issued in limited numbers in the summer of '98 for 'Constellation', harbouring the attention of Chicago-based cult experimental imprint, 'Kranky' for UK and US release. From its post-apocalyptic opener 'THE DEAD FLAG BLUES' (with the memorable spoken dialogue of 'The Car's On Fire And There's No Driver At The Wheel And The Sewers Are All Muddied With A Thousand Lonely Suicides And A Dark Wind Blows . . .') segued together with the eerie rumbling effects on the self-explanatory 'SLOW MOVING TRAINS' cruising into the epic tour de force of 'THE COWBOY' (a landscape of spiralling David Lynch-esque peaks that quite literally tickle the ears into orgasmic proportions on headphone experience!) and uplifted by the bright and folky denouement of its 'OUTRO'. The album's second piece, 'EAST HASTINGS', fades into the broken ramblings of a distressed street anarchist (see below) complaining "NOTHING'S ALRITE IN OUR LIFE" lamented by distant bagpipes and overlapped with soft vibrato acoustics and paranoid MOGWAI meets TANGERINE DREAM (their cinematic period!) slow burning crescendo culminating with ear-bashing orchestral avant-metal. Section two of this lengthy piece, 'THE SAD MAFIESE', navigated the psyche into further headbusting headphone gymnastics with its plucking harmonics swaying continuously like a rocking chair uneasy in a derelict porch. The track's third instalment, 'DRUGS IN TOKYO – BLACK HELICOPTER', was arguably the most disturbing piece of the set, its Oriental chimes festooned between sounds of bees trapped in a generator. Song(!) number three, 'PROVIDENCE', begins with a doubtful riddle lecturing about the current state of America linking that with the end of time, waking up to a sunrise owned by (BRIAN) ENO. Each of its four pieces were like a homage to late 60's/early 70's experimental rock (i.e. PINK FLOYD) battling on a stranger plateau of military percussion and space-age guitars. The following Spring, the group (now with new guitarist ROGER TELLIER-CRAIG) returned with 'SLOW RIOT FOR NEW ZER0 KANADA E.P.' an unusual two-track mini-set that again stunned audiences and critics alike. Soft violins, rattling guitars, orchestrated crescendoes and bizarre vox-pops were all the standard on opening track, 'MOYA', while the deeply negative 'BBF3' (named eponymously after the aforementioned street/soapbox anarchist, Mister Blaise Bailey Finnegan the third!) attacked world society and all its corruptive forces. Arguably this band were the most promising act to hit the year 2000, ironically it's everything that they rebel against. During all the hype and journo commotion, ROGER'S side-project, FLY PAN AM, took off on their campaign of climax-enduced minimalist (s)Lo-Fi, the result being a well-received eponymous album in October '99. GODSPEED . . . had now secured such a reputation on the leftfield scene that tours were being sold-out all over Europe and America, with film director Oliver Stone requesting to use the band's old music in a film, they politely declined. EFRIM, SOPHIE and NORSOLA established A SILVER MT. ZION, just one of the many militant groups which were springing up around Canada from the GODSPEED camp. They issued their debut album 'HE HAS LEFT US ALONE . . . BUT SHAFTS OF LIGHT STILL GRACE THE CORNERS OF OUR ROOM' (2000), a beautiful lament for what the band called "a falling/fallen world". The music was slow burning with the first few tracks backed by post-apocalyptic religious rantings, thundering piano and dashing strings. Later EFRIM sang (accompanied only by his fragile piano) about the collapse of capitalism. The set was a truly dazzling affair, with the eerie loop and drone of '13 ANGELS CIRCLING AROUND MY BED' being a particular treasure. MOLACES, 1-SPEED BIKE, EXHAUST and FLY PAN AM all issued equally brilliant albums in the time it took GODSPEED to complete the recording of their eagerly awaited sophomore set, 'LIFT YR. SKINNY FISTS LIKE ANTENNAS TO HEAVEN' (2000), a roaring 2-CD set that astounded and bewildered fans and critics alike. The set boasted some of the most poignant and musically mature tracks in the history of rock, outing any Prog-rock band with semi-classical pieces evoking sadness, hope and worry. It was a wonder GODSPEED had even made a record this non-conformist, this loud, this brash and still get away with releasing it in such a mafia-like music industry. So triumphant was their glory that when the words 'freedom can be achieved' flashed at the end of their shows, it was almost as if GODSPEED had been sent from the heavens themselves to save mankind from dull, unimaginative music. 'MONHEIM', their most powerful track evoked the same crescending substance as 'BBF111' on the 'SLOW RIOT . . .' EP. 'SHE DREAMT SHE WAS A BULLDOZER, SHE DREAMT SHE WAS ALONE IN AN EMPTY FIELD' began with sweeping violins, distorted guitar before crashing unannounced into a full on rock-out, before fading into a beautiful middle section reminiscent of "empty wet streets at dawn". Perhaps the most effective piece was 'THE BUILDINGS THEY ARE SLEEPING NOW', just a drone of feedback that sounded like Chinese symbols being played with violin bows, to create a stark and haunting sound. The members of GODSPEED excelled themselves once again by issuing the remarkable 'BORN INTO TROUBLE AS THE SPARKS FLY UPWARD' (2001), a joint collaboration between A SILVER MT. ZION (now renamed THE SILVER MT. ZION MEMORIAL ORCHESTRA) and The TRA-TRA-LA-LA-LA BAND. On one particular track EFRIM sings "Musicians are cowards . . .", providing the whole basis for GODSPEED as not just a collective from Montreal but as a philosophy; be brave, be free, help one another, don't let the greediness of man ruin our communities. Other musicians may be cowards, but GODSPEED suggested that they were all the above and no sell-out – a true democratic group of musicians. Anybody who was lucky enough to live in their time should be grateful, and for those who weren't, there's always the future. In 2002, along with fractions of FLY PAN AM and HANGED UP, GODSPEED collaborated on 'SINGS REIGN REBUILDER', under the collective nom de plum of SET FIRE TO FLAMES. The LP (with gorgeous packaging as standard) was mostly a collection of fragmented field recordings, taped around Vancouver and Montreal, respectively. Using brass, reed and a whole host of eerie guitar effects and strange percussion instruments, SET FIRE TO FLAMES had delivered the most sonically poetic album of the year. Like GODSPEED's 'SKINNY FISTS . . .' offering, instrumentals collided with broken down noises and bizarre, but always welcoming, voices which faded in and drifted out of the recording. Meanwhile, in Chicago, the band themselves were perfecting five long pieces with legendary producer STEVE ALBINI, which would eventually end up as 'YANQUI U.X.O.' (2002), meaning un-coordinated cluster bombs, dropped by American planes in the Gulf War. The set, from its quietly building opener, to the scary swirling percussion orientated ending was a sight to behold. ALBINI, as usual had just left the microphones on to tell it like it was: pure live orchestrations for a "falling/fallen world". But this time the Black Emperors weren't messing about. Firstly, they knew a war was imminent, and from the military-funded major label berating on the back cover to the blitzing beauty and sadness of 'ROCKETS FALL ON ROCKET FALLS' (with added clarinets, reeds and stand up bass to brilliant effect), 'YANQUI U.X.O.' was a deliberate warning to us of the brutality that was about to ensue. Years ago, GODSPEED YOU BLACK EMPEROR! were deemed by music critics as just a "cinematic orchestra for a post apocalyptic generation". Their music and what they stood for has never been more relevant.

Album rating: ALL LIGHTS FUCKED ON THE HAIRY AMP DROOLING (*5) / F#A#oo (*9) / SLOW RIOT FOR NEW ZER0 KANADA mini (*8) / LIFT YR. SKINNY FISTS LIKE ANTENNAS TO HEAVEN! (*7) / YANQUI U.X.O. (*7) / Exhaust: 230596 (*5) / EXHAUST (*6) / Fly Pan Am: FLY PAN AM (*7) / Silver Mt. Zion: HE HAS LEFT US ALONE... (*7) / BORN INTO TROUBLE AS THE SPARKS FLY UPWARD (*7) / 1-Speed Bike: DROOPY BUTT BEGONE! (*4) / Set Fire To Flames: SINGS REIGN REBUILDER (*6)

EFRIM – guitar, tape loops / **MAURO** – bass

_{not iss.   not listed}

Dec 94. (ltd-c) <none> **ALL LIGHTS FUCKED ON THE HAIRY AMP DROOLING** – Canada
– Drifting intro open / Shot thru tubes / Three three three / When all the furnaces exploded / Beep / Hush / Son of a diplomat, daughter of a politician / Glencairn 14 / $13.13 / Loose the idiot dogs / Diminishing shine / Random luvly moncton blue(s) / Dadmomdaddy / Frames per second / Revisionist alternatif wounds to the hair-cut hit head / Ditty for Moya / Buried ton / And the hair guts shine / Hoarding / Deterior 23 / All angels gone / Deterior 17 / Deterior three / Devil's in the church / No job / Dress like shit / Perfumed pink corpses from the lips of Ms. Celine Dion.

— added **DAVE** – guitar, tape loops / **AIDAN GIRT** – percussion, drums (also of EXHAUST) / **BRUCE** – percussion, glockenspiel / **THIERRY** – bass / **NORSOLA** – cello / **SOPHIE TRUDEAU** – violin

_{Kranky   Kranky}

Jun 98. (cd)<lp> <(KRANKY 27CD)><cst 003> **F#A#oo** – Aug97
– The dead flag blues: 1. The dead flag blues, 2. Slow moving trains, 3. The cowboy, 4. (; Outro) / East Hastings: 1. "Nothing's alrite in our life" – Dead flag blues (reprise), 2. The sad Mafiese, 3. Drugs in Tokyo – Black helicopter / Providence: 1. Divorce and fever, 2. Dead mothery, 3. Kicking horse on broken hill, 4. String loop manufacturer during downpour.

— added **ROGER TELLIER-CRAIG** – guitar

Apr 99. (m-lp/m-cd) <(KRANKY 34/+CD)><cst 006> **SLOW RIOT FOR NEW ZER0 KANADA E.P.** – Mar99
– Moya / BBF3 (voice by Mister Blaise Bailey Finnegan the third).

— <above releases also on 'Constellation' in Canada>

Sep 99. (7",7"white) <MAZE 01> **SUNSHINE & GASOLINE. / Fly Pan Am: L'ESPACE AU SOL EST REDESSINE PAR DES IMMENSES PANNEAUX BLEUS** –

— <above issued for 'aMAZEzine!' fanzine>

Oct 00. (d-cd)(d-lp) <(KRK 43D)><cst 012> **LIFT YR. SKINNY FISTS LIKE ANTENNAS TO HEAVEN!** 66
– Lift yr. skinny fists like antennas to heaven / Gathering storm / Il pleut amourir (+ clatters like worry) / Welcome to Barco AM/PM ... / Cancer towers on Holy road hi-way / Terrible canyons of state / Atomic clock / World police and friendly fire / (...+ the buildings they are sleeping now) / Murray Ostril: they don't sleep anymore on the beach / Monheim / Broken windows, locks of love pt.III / Moya sings "baby-o" / Edgyswingsetacid / Glockenspiel duet recorded on a campsite in Rhineback, N.Y. / Attention... mon ami... fa-lala-lala-la-la (55-St.Laurent) / She dreamt she was a bulldozer, she dreamt she was alone in an empty field / Deathkamp drone / (Antennas to heaven ...).

Nov 02. (cd/d-lp) <cst 024-2/-1> **YANQUI U.X.O.**
– 09-15-00 / 09-15-00 / Rockets fall on Rocket Falls / Motherfucker = redeemer / Motherfucker = redeemer.

EXHAUST

AIDAN GIRT – drums, etc / **GORDON KRIEGER** – bass, clarinet, (some) guitar / **MIKE ZABITSKY** – tape loops

_{Constellation   Constellation}

Oct 96. (c) <none> **230596**
– Cat face / Hork pitou / Wool fever dub / That cost you $116 / High Aidan diminished by fists / The bass and the trouble / Free shuttle from Bifteck / Bubbles will harm Nick / Tripolar depression.

Aug 98. (lp) <cst 004> **EXHAUST**
– A history of guerilla warfare / Metro Mile End / Homemade maggot beer / We support Iran in their bid to win the 1998 World Cup / Two years on welfare / This is our (borrowed) equipment Wool fever / A medley of late night buffet commercials / Winterlude / The black horns of H2T. <(cd-iss. Aug00; cst 004cd)>

FLY PAN AM

ROGER TELLIER-CRAIG – guitar / **J.S.** – bass (ex-WISIGOTH) / **JONATHAN** – guitar / **FELIX** – drums

_{Constellation   Constellation}

Oct 99. (3-sided-lp/cd) <(cst 008/+cd)> **FLY PAN AM**
– L'espace au sol est redesine par d'immeses panneaux bleus / Et aussi L'eclairge de plastique au centre de tout ces compartiments lateraux / Dans ses cheveux soixante circuits / Bibi a nice, 1921 / Nice est en feu!

Oct 00. (12"ep/cd-ep) <(cst 011 v/cd)> **SEDATIFS EN FREQUENCIES ET SILLONS**
– De cercle en cercle ... / Efferant – Afferant / Stereo stupefiant – (micro sillons).

SILVER MT. ZION

EFRIM, THIERRY + SOPHIE with guests **AIDAN, GORDON KRIEGER, SAM SHALABI** (of The Shalabi Effect) – guitar

Mar 00. (lp/cd; as A SILVER MT. ZION) <(cst 009/+cd)> **HE HAS LEFT US ALONE BUT SHAFTS OF LIGHT SOMETIMES GRACE THE CORNERS OF OUR ROOMS ...**
– Broken chords can sing a little / Sit in the middle of three galloping dogs / Stumble and then rise on some awkward morning / Movie (never made) / 13 angels standing guard 'round the side of your bed / Long march rocket or doomed airliner / Blown out joy from Heaven's mercied hole.

— the trio plus **BECKIE, IAN ILAVSKY** (of SACKVILLE, of SOFA, of RE:) + **JESSICA**, etc.

Oct 01. (10"d-lp/cd; as The SILVER MT. ZION MEMORIAL ORCHESTRA & TRA-LA-LA BAND) <cst 018/+cd> **BORN INTO TROUBLE AS THE SPARKS FLY UPWARD**
– Sisters! brothers! small boats of fire are falling from the sky! / This gentle hearts like shot bird's fallen / Built then burnt (hurrah! hurrah!) / Take these hands and throw them in the river / Could've moved mountains / Tho you are gone I still often walk w/ you / C'mon come on (loose an endless longing) / The triumph of our tired eyes.

1-SPEED BIKE

AIDAN GIRT solo

Oct 00. (cd/lp) <(cst 014 cd/v)> **DROOPY BUTT BEGONE!**
– The day that Mauro ran over Elwy Yost / Seattle – Washington – Prague 00-68 – Chicago – Nixon – Reagan circle-fighting ma / Yuppie restaurant-goers beware because this song is for the dishwasher / Just another jive-assed white colonial theft / Why are all the doges dying of cancer? / My kitchen is Tianamen Square / Any movement that forgets about class is a bowel movement / (untitled).

SET FIRE TO FLAMES

AIDAN + SOPHIE

_{Alien8   Alien8}

Oct 01. (cd/d-lp) <(CD/LP 130701)> **SINGS REIGN REBUILDER**
– I will be true / Reign rebuilder (head) / Vienna arcweld / Fucked gameplan / Rigid tracking / Steal compass / Drive north / Disappear / Wild dogs of the thunderbolt / They cannot lock me up ... / Ohama / There is no dance in frequency and balance / Cote d'Abrahams room tone / What's going on / Love song for 15 Ontario / In jur gutted two track / When I first get to Phoenix / Shit heap Gloria of the new town planning / Jesus / Pop / Esquimalt harbour / Two tears in a bucket / Fading lights are fading / Reign rebuilder (tall out).

GODSTAR

Formed: Canberra, Australia ... 1991 by ex-PLUNDERERS man NIC DALTON, with an ever-changing backing section of wandering musicians who littered DALTON's records for the first half of the 1990's. Following The PLUNDERERS' demise (and the fall of its various off-shoots, such as CAPTAIN DENIM and HIPPY DRIBBLE), GODSTAR issued their striking debut EP, the adrenaline-fuelled 'THE BRIGHTEST STAR' (1992), which included the track 'KITCHEN', later covered by The LEMONHEADS on 'It's A Shame About Ray'. Talking of EVAN DANDO and his jangly guitar pop exploits, he invited DALTON to join The LEMONHEADS on their 1992 tour of Europe, after which GODSTAR issued their debut album, 'SLEEPER' (1993). In 1994, DALTON began to concentrate on his hobbies and life-long ambitions; owning and running his own record label ('Half A Cow') and second-hand bookshop. He subsequently toured with GODSTAR (including the line-up of SMUDGE's ALISON GALLOWAY and TOM MORGAN, plus The HUMMINGBIRD's ROYBN ST. CLARE) and pasted together their sophomore set 'COASTAL' (1995), while in various locations (and countries!) with a batch of different musicians (including a turn from DANDO himself). The result was a well-oiled follow-up, perfectly displaying DALTON's use of power-pop punk indie, and his extremely melodic, tonally-tuned vocals. However, the man himself had given up the ghost with GODSTAR; the loose collective issued a mixed-bag of stuff in the form of 'SEPTEMBER' (1997) delivered under the moniker of GODSTAR REMAINDER, with DALTON moving on to form The KOMBI NATION, and undoubtably a whole host of spin-offs and spin-ons.

Album rating: SLEEPER (*7) / COASTAL (*5) / SEPTEMBER (*6) / WAY OUT JIM compilation (*6)

NIC DALTON – vocals, multi (ex-LEMONHEADS) / **TOM MORGAN** – guitar, vocals (of SMUDGE) / **ALISON GALLOWAY** – bass, drums, vocals (of SMUDGE)

_{Half A Cow   not iss.}

1992. (7"ep) (HAC 11) **THE BRIGHTEST STAR** – Austra
– The brightest star / Valentine tour / When Rosemary smiles / Way out Jim.

1993. (cd-ep) (HAC 14) **BAD BAD IMPLICATIONS – THE CHEMCRAZE EP** – Austra
– Bad bad implications / End of day / You treat me like a kid / Charter me / Babe rainbow / The best of friends / Every now and then.

1993. (cd-ep) (HAC 21) **LIE DOWN FOREVER** – Austra
– Lie down forever / Plummet / Sleeper / It's down to you to make it up to me / Turn around.

_{Ruggerbuggemot iss.}

1993. (7"ep) <DUMP 17> **GLASGOW**
– Look-a-like / When the sun goes down / Smothered / Doubledecker bus.

_{not iss.   Bus Stop}

1993. (7"ep) <BUS 029> **THE BRIGHTEST STAR**
– The brightest star / Valentine tour / Kitchen / Every now and then.

— added **ROBYN ST CLARE** – bass (of HUMMINGBIRDS)

_{Taang!   Taang!}

Dec 93. (d10"lp/cd) <(TAANG 79/+CD)> **SLEEPER** – Oct93
– Ersatz / Bad bad implications / Little bit about / Single / Everything you give me breaks / Wigram / Forgotten night / Lie down forever / The brightest star / Had the time of my life / Stranger / Days gone by / Something unplanned / Every now and again. (d10"+=) – My the mind / Poncho.

Mar 94. (cd-ep) <T 81> **LIE DOWN FOREVER**
– Lie down forever / Sleeper / Kitchen / It's down to you to make it up to me / Dead sad night / Turn around.

Jun 94. (cd-ep) <T 85> **SINGLE**
– Single / Butterfly knife / Way out Jim / Rain 14 / When Rosemary smiles / It's my turn.

_{not iss.   Bus Stop}

1994. (7"ep) <BUS 037> **FOUR SEVENTY EP**
– Love and trucks / Sunshower / Load / Mr. Austin.

GODSTAR (cont) — THE GREAT INDIE DISCOGRAPHY — **The 1990s**

		Elefant	not iss.
1994.	(7"ep; as the GODSTAR REMINDER) *(E 184)* **TAKE THE MONEY AND RUN EP**	-	- Spain

– Peanut butter / Speak memory speak / Girl most likely to succeed / Papas Fritas.

		Half A Cow	not iss.
1995.	(cd-ep) *(HAC 40)* **PUSHPIN / SEEING STARS EP**	-	- Austra

– Pushpin / Seeing stars / Blessed out clown / Needle pulling thread / That certain smile.

1995.	(cd) *(HAC 42)* **COASTAL**	-	- Austra

– Mistletoe revenge / Pushpin / Another spring, another love / Friend of a friend / It's hard to love a drunk / Out of my mind / Seeing stars / Table for one / Mathrock boy / Fly me to the moon / Go now / Coastal / Enter No.3 / Theme from "Annandale 2038" – Lula. (w/ free cd 'LOVE AND DEATH' +=; HAC 43) – And other planets / Forever snowing inside / Duje daisy / Watch out bicycle / Zillar.

1995.	(cd-ep) *(HAC 48)* **TABLE FOR ONE EP**	-	- Austra

– Table for one / High anxiety / Your ego's out of control / Rock your baby / Angela.

1996.	(cd-s; as the GODSTAR REMINDER) *<005>* **HAS SHE GOT YOUR TIME NOW? / UNREQUITED / ANDROID**	-	

(above issued on 'Blind')

1997.	(cd; as the GODSTAR REMINDER) *(HAC 60)* **SEPTEMBER**	-	- Austra

– Girls on the avenue / Stuck like gum / Mr. Austin / Load / Sunshower / Love and trucks / Dead sad night / Rain 14 / Mongoloid / Corey / Drop twenty / Pacman / Autumnal eyes / Every now and again.

—— split in September 1997; DALTON (also of SNEEZE with TOM MORGAN of SMUDGE) + ST. CLARE were also part of LOVE POSITIONS

– compilations, etc. –

1998.	(cd) *100 Guitar Mania; <100GM 2>* **WAY OUT JIM**	-	- Japan

– Valentine tour / You treat me like a kid / Every now and then / Look-a-like / It's down to you to make it up to me / Way out JIm / Stuck like gum / Butterfly knife / When Rosemary smiles / Sleeper / Babe rainbow / Rain 14 / Smothered / Best of friends / It's my turn / Kitchen / Charter me.

GODZUKI

Formed: Detroit, Michigan, USA . . . 1993 by SCOTT MICHALSKI, DION FISCHER, ERIKA HOFFMAN and CHRIS 'CRISPY' FACHINI. The group had cut their musical teeth playing in various Michigan-based bands such as the alt-country outfit, The VOLEBEATS, HIS NAME IS ALIVE, and FACHINI's former band, TEACH ME TIGER. The quartet came together to create what they dubbed 'science rock', an experimental mixing of nineties style noise-pop with synth-orientated eighties new wave. Following the issue of several singles, the band put out their debut album, 'TRAIL OF THE LONESOME PINE' (1996), aided by the triple-pronged production skills of DAVE TRUMFIO (of PULSAR fame), FACHINI's old HIS NAME IS ALIVE comrade, WARREN DEFEVER and OUTRAGEOUS CHERRY's MATTHEW SMITH. The knob-twiddler's assistance alone managed to gain the band a following in their home state and DEFEVER stayed on board to contribute his knowledge to the group's EP, 'FREE WADE'. The mini album was so-called, as it featured the saxophone work of WADE THE FREE JAZZ SAXOPHONIST, producing a sophisticated and mature blended sound. Their pleasing sophomore full-length effort, 'YOUR FUTURE' (1998), proved that the band certainly were not sitting back on their local success.

Album rating: TRAIL OF THE LONESOME PINE (*6) / YOUR FUTURE (*7)

ERIKA HOFFMAN – vocals, bass / **CHRIS 'CRISPY' FACHINI** – guitar (of DIRTBOMBS, ex-ROCKET 455) / **DION FISCHER** – guitar / **SCOTT MICHALSKI** – drums / plus **COREY REDHAGE** – guitar

		not iss.	March
1995.	(7"green) *<MAR 014>* **TOAST. / GLEASON ROCKET**	-	
1995.	(7") **12 INCH DANCE MIC. / (Pinion by ASHA VIDA)**	-	

(above issued on 'Binavsic')

Feb 96.	(7"m) *<MAR 019>* **POINSETTIA. / CITRUS / TRAIL OF THE LONESOME PINE**		
Mar 96.	(cd) *<MAR 020>* **TRAIL OF THE LONESOME PINE**		

– Pollen, U.S.A. / No song / Sunday man / Gleason rocket / Orange red, bright blue / (untitled) / Old number 7 / Poinsettia / Tractor driver / Auto-haze / 12x / Do the sputnic / Canary.

Mar 97.	(cd-ep) *<(GS 003)>* **FREE WADE**		

– Majic UFO / Brown city / Prophecy of Wade / Nature channel.
(above on 'Go Sonic / Time Stereo', below on 'Disques Twist Top')

1998.	(7") *<TT 02>* **LES TEMPS DE L'AMOUR. / (other by OUTRAGEOUS CHERRY)**	-	
Nov 98.	(cd) *<MAR 036>* **YOUR FUTURE**		

– Your future / Love crown / Count the rings / He'd turn us up / I feel like moth / Apple gate / Rock 4 – Rock 5 / Haunted valley / Tele-fone / Sew my hand / The leap / Who's gonna hold the rope.

		not iss.	Motorway
1999.	(7") *<motor 020>* **YOUR FUTURE. / OUR BEARS ELECTRIC?**	-	

TEACH ME TIGER

CRISPY FACHINI

		not iss.	Fantastic
1999.	(7"m) *<FAN 009>* **REMEMBER ME REMEMBER U / HOW CAN I STOP LOVING U (pt.1). / BEDROOM DUB**	-	

		not iss.	Motorway
2000.	(7") *<motor 029>* **WON'T YOU COME AROUND. / A LOVE THAT TRUE**	-	

GO HOLE (see under ⇒ GENE)

GO KART MOZART (see under ⇒ FELT; in 80's section)

GOLDBLADE (see under ⇒ MEMBRANES; 80's section)

GOLDEN SMOG

Formed: Minneapolis, Minnesota, USA . . . 1989 out of SKIDMARK T-SQUARE & Q-STOCK, by alternative country stars-to-be, DAN MURPHY (SOUL ASYLUM), GARY LOURIS (JAYHAWKS) and KRAIG JOHNSON (RUN WESTY RUN). Another SOUL ASYLUM frontman, DAVE PIRNER joined as an honorary member, in fact he became their drummer and back-up singer, although the drum parts on record were mainly taken up by CHRIS MARS (REPLACEMENTS). An EP of covers was delivered to mixed reviews as they all put the project on hold as their full-time commitments were coming to fruition. When the supergroup returned to the fold for 1996's debut album, 'DOWN BY THE OLD MAINSTREAM', the outfit had added two further stars, MARC PERLMAN (another JAYHAWKS member) and JEFF TWEEDY (from WILCO). Americana was the subject matter for these songwriters of note, y'alternative was now the phrase on the media's lips and by 1998 (with the addition of JODY STEPHENS of BIG STAR), they had issued what was thought to be the year's best country-rock set, 'WEIRD TALES'. • **Covered:** COWBOY SONG (Thin Lizzy) / SHOOTING STAR (Bad Company) / SON (Michelangelo) / EASY TO BE HARD (from 'Hair') / BACKSTREET GIRL (Rolling Stones) / SHE DON'T HAVE TO SEE YOU (Paterson-Strickland).

Album rating: DOWN BY THE OLD MAINSTREAM (*6) / WEIRD TALES (*8)

DAN MURPHY – vocals, guitar, keyboards (of SOUL ASYLUM) / **GARY LOURIS** – guitar, vocals (of JAYHAWKS) / **KRAIG JOHNSON** – vocals, guitar, piano (of RUN WESTY RUN) / added **DAVE PIRNER** – backing vocals (of SOUL ASYLUM) / **CHRIS MARS** – drums (of REPLACEMENTS)

		not iss.	Crackpot
Dec 92.	(cd-ep) *<1219>* **ON GOLDEN SMOG**	-	

– Son (we've kept the room just the way you left it) / Easy to be hard / Backstreet girl / Shooting star / Cowboy song. (UK-iss.Jan96 on 'Rykodisc'; RCD 30348)

—— **NOAH LEVY** – drums (of HONEYDOGS) repl. MARS

—— added **MARC PERLMAN** – bass, guitar, vocals (of JAYHAWKS) / **JEFF TWEEDY** – vocals, guitar, harmonica, bass (of WILCO)

		Rykodisc	Rykodisc
Feb 96.	(cd/c) *<(RCD/RAC 10325)>* **DOWN BY THE OLD MAINSTREAM**		

– V / Ill-fated / Pecan pie / Yesterday I cried / Glad and sorry / Won't be coming home / He's a dick / Walk where he walked / Nowhere bound / The friend / She don't have to see you / Red headed step child / Williamton angel / Radio king.

—— **JODY STEPHENS** – drums (of BIG STAR) repl. LEVY + PIRNER (back to SOUL ASYLUM)

Oct 98.	(cd/c) *<(RAD/RAC 10446)>* **WEIRD TALES**		

– To call my own / Looking forward to seeing you / Until you came along / Lost love / If I only had a car / Jane / Keys / I can't stop from talking / Reflections on me / Making waves / White shell road / Please tell my brother / Fear of falling / All the same to me / Jennifer save me.

Holly GOLIGHTLY

Born: London, England. When HOLLY courted THEE HEADCOATS' drummer BRUCE BRAND, he and the legendary BILLY CHILDISH invited her to sing live at a gig, which prompted the latter to set-up a sister group, THEE HEADCOATEES (out of The DELMONAS), to his already well-established combo. Now with GOLIGHTLY at the helm, they issued stark garage rock, similar to most three-chord garage bands of Detroit (it was no surprise then that the group had several records out on 'Sympathy For The Recording Insdustry'). After six albums of raunchy fun-blasted noise (with the ever impending presence of CHILDISH), THEE HEADCOATEES issued 'SISTERS OF SUAVE' (1999), a "best of" collection which catalogue'd the band's triumphs, plus a few oddball covers (The Sonics, The Ramones, etc.) and should be considered as a starting point for those who are curious. GOLIGHTLY herself departed from the group in 1995, but still kept in close contact with CHILDISH. She debuted with her solo outing 'THE GOOD THING' in 1995, displaying a terrific vocal range, plus a diverse mix of musical influences including folk, blues, free-jazz, and, of course, rock and roll. GOLIGHTLY was also very open about her musical influences; she has covered songs by people such as Ike Turner, Bill Withers and Chicago blues legend Willie Dixon. Through the years GOLIGHTLY has issued a number of LP's, EP's and singles on an abundance of labels. However, her two best cuts came in the form of 1999's 'IN BLOOD', for which she recorded once again with her mentor CHILDISH (and a record which saw them frequently duetting) and the breezy acoustic affair, 'DESPERATE LITTLE TOWN' (2001), which marked new territory for GOLIGHTLY as it contained hardly any musical accompaniment. • **Covered:** THEE HEADCOATEES covered songs by BILLY CHILDISH and others including TEENAGE KICKS (Undertones) / PINHEAD (Ramones) / CARA-LIN + I WANT CANDY (Feldman-Goldstein-Gotteher) / SHADOW (Lurkers) / CA PLANE POUR MOI (Plastic Bertrand) / WHEREVER YOU ARE (Malane-Morrison) / her second set contained a plethora of covers:- SALLY GO ROUND THE ROSES (Phil Spector) / IF I COULD JUST BE LOVED BY YOU (Kirkland-Thomas) / MELLOW DOWN EASY + HOLD

Holly GOLIGHTLY (cont)

ME BABY (Willie Dixon) / I CAN'T STAND IT (. . . McAllister) / CANDY MAN (Fred Neil) / LOOK FOR ME BABY (. . . Davis) / DON'T LIE TO ME (. . . Whittaker) / TROUBLES ON MY MIND (. . . Turner) / GETTING MIGHTY CROWDED (. . . McCoy) / SAND (Lee Hazlewood) / MARY-ANN (Link Wray) / GOOD ENOUGH (Mudhoney) / HIT TIME (. . . Pragnell) /

Album rating: THE GOOD THINGS (*5) / LAUGH IT (ALL) UP (*5) / PAINTED ON (*6) / UP THE EMPIRE compilation (*5) / SERIAL GIRLFRIEND (*6)

THEE HEADCOATEES

HOLLY GOLIGHTLY – vocals / **LUDELLA BLACK** – vocals / **BONGO DEBBIE** – vocals / **KYRA LaRUBIA** – vocals / with **BRUCE BRAND** – drums + **TUB** – bass

not iss.   Sympathy..

1991. (7") <SFTRI 151> **WE GOT SEVEN INCHES BUT WE WANTE TWELVE**
– Fish pie / Cum into my mouth.

Damaged Goods   Get Hip

1991. (lp) <GH 1011> **GIRLSVILLE**
– Wild man / When the night comes / Stolen love / Round every corner / Run for your life / Give it to me / Dirty old man / Melvin / The first plane home / Meet Jacqueline / Boysville / Money.

1992. (7") (DAMGOOD 4) **DAVEY CROCKETT. / YOUNGBLOOD**

Hangman's Daughter   not iss.

Aug 92. (7"ep) (LYNCH 001EP) **SECT EP**

Vinyl Japan   not iss.

Aug 92. (7") (FAD 1) **MY BOYFRIEND'S LEARNING KARATE. / MESS OF POTTAGE**

Aug 92. (cd/lp) (ASK CD/LP 11) **HAVE LOVE WILL TRAVEL**
– Have love will travel / Baby please / Don't try and tell me / Gotta get inside that boy's mind / Mess of pottage / You know you can't resist / Louis Riel / Baby come closer / Come into my life / Tear it to pieces / Something went wrong / Big boss man / My boyfriend's learning karate / I'm gonna make you mine.

Dec 93. (7"pic-d) (DAM 12) **SANTA CLAUS. / EVIL THING**
(above on 'Damaged Goods' & below single on 'Munster')

Oct 94. (7") (07768-1) **GOTTA MOVE. / AUTOMATIC LOVE**

Oct 94. (cd/lp) (ASK CD/LP 045) **BALLAD OF THE INSOLENT PUP**
– What once was / This heart / Pretend / Ballad of the insolent pup / You'll be sorry now / All my feelings denied / It's bad / When you stop loving me / Two hearts beating / No respect / Again and again / Now is not the best time / I was led to believe / You'll never do it baby.

Jul 95. (7") (PAD 018) **BALLAD OF THE INSOLENT PUP. / SPINELESS LITTLE SHIT**

Sympathy F   Sympathy F

Jul 96. (7") <(SFTRI 332)> **I'M HAPPY. / PARK IT UP YOUR ARSE**

Mar 97. (m-lp/m-cd) <(SFTRI 463/+CD)> **PUNK GIRLS**
– Punk girl / Don't wanna hold your hand / Billy B. Childish / Teenage kicks / You're right, I'm wrong / Pinhead / Cara Lin / Punk boy / Stick & stones / Ca plane pour moi.

Sep 97. (7") <SFTRI 485> **CA PLANE POUR MOI. / THE PRIZE**

Vinyl Japan   Vinyl Japan

Jan 98. (cd) <ASK 65CD> **BOZSTIK HAZE**
– We are Thee Headcoatees / Name your own poison / I need loving / Speak to me / Just like a dog / Never to go back / Bozstik haze / Baby-teeth Marge / He's in disguise / You ruined my night's rest / I want Candy / We are Thee Headcoatees (reprise).

May 99. (cd/lp) (<ASK CD/LP 84>) **HERE COMES CESSATION**
– You say that you love me / All night long / Hurt me / An image of you / Help out / Road runner / Here comes cessation / Is there any chance of you coming into my life / You're gonna get what's coming / True to you / Keep your big mouth shut / I want it.

– compilations, etc. –

Jun 99. (cd/lp) Damaged Goods; (<DAMGOOD 161 CD/LP>) **THE SISTERS OF SUAVE**   Jul00
– Davey Crockett / Ca plane pour moi / Santa Claus / I gotta move / Ballad of the insolent pup / Johnny Jack / Swallow my pride / Spineless little shit / Headcoat girl / My boyfriend's learning karate / I'm happy / Evil thing / Strychnine / Come into my mouth / Young blood / Jackie Chan does kung fu.

—— THEE HEADCOATEES also releasaed several split singles/EP's (most w/ THEE HEADCOATS – see Wild Billy CHILDISH)

HOLLY GOLIGHTLY

Vinyl Japan   not iss.

Aug 94. (7"ep)(cd-ep) (PAD 013)(TASKCD 031) **JIGGY JIGGY WITH HOLLY GOLIGHTLY EP**
– Hold me baby / Good enough / High time / Until I find you.

Damaged Goods   Damaged Goods

Jun 95. (cd/lp) (<DAMGOOD 65 CD/LP>) **THE GOOD THINGS**   Oct95
– Virtually happy / Listen / Wherever you are / Good things / Expert / Comedy time / Hold on / Without you / Anyotherway / Ride #2 / Every word / Last time / Charm / Headstart.

Sep 95. (7") (DAMGOOD 75) **VIRTUALLY HAPPY. /**

Vinyl Japan   not iss.

Feb 96. (7"ep)(cd-ep) (PAD 026)(TASKCD 045) **MARY-ANN EP**
– This happens / Candle song / If I should ever leave / Mary-Ann.

Jun 96. (7") (KETCH 15UP) **NO BIG THING. /**
(above issued on 'Hangman's Daughter')

Sep 96. (lp) (ASKLP 056) **LAUGH IT UP**
– Sally go round the roses / I could just be loved by you / Mellow down easy / I can't stand it / Candy man / Look for me baby / Don't lie to me / Too much going for you / It's all over now / Troubles on my mind / Getting mighty crowded / You ain't no big thing / Sand / Hold me baby. (cd-iss. Aug97 as 'LAUGH IT ALL UP'+=)/<US cd-iss. Mar99 +=; ASKCD 074>) – This happens / If I should ever leave / Mary-Ann / Good enough / Hit time.

Super Electro   not iss.

Oct 96. (7") (SE7 10) **GIRL IN THE SHOWER. /**

Oct 96. (7") (SE7 11) **PINKY PLEASE COME BACK. /**

Damaged Goods   not iss.

Nov 96. (7") (DAMGOOD 110) **COME THE DAY. / YOU**
—— her band now:- **BRUCE BRAND** – drums, guitar / **DAN MELCHIOR** – guitar, vocals (ex-BILLY CHILDISH collaborator) / **MATT RADFORD** – double bass / **GEORGE SUEREF** – mouth harp, vocals

Sympathy F   Sympathy F

Feb 97. (d7"ep) (<SFTRI 471>) **BELIEVE ME**

Aug 97. (lp/cd) (<SFTRI 474/+CD>) **PAINTED ON**
– Run cold / Indeed you do / I let my daddy do that / For all this / Painted on / Length of pipe / One more fact / Snake eyed / One kiss / Anyway you like it.

Feb 98. (lp/cd) (<SFTRI 506/+CD>) **UP THE EMPIRE** (singles compilation)
– Won't go out again / I can't stand it / Come the day / No big thing / If I should ever leave / Ride / Troubles / Eye for an empty heart / Big bass man / Believe me / Look for me baby / It's all over / Mellow down easy.

Damaged Goods   Damaged Goods

Nov 98. (cd/lp) (<DAMGOOD 156 CD/LP>) **SERIAL GIRLFRIEND**
– I can't be trusted / You shine / Want no other / Your love is mine / Grandstand / Clean in two / Down down down / Come the day / Serial girlfriend / My own sake / Where can I go / 'Til I get / Now.

Mar 00. (cd/lp) (<DAMGOOD 180 CD/LP>) **GOD DON'T LIKE IT**
– I hear you / Feel something / Give me back time / I don't know / Overtaking / Nothing you can say / Easy on me / Here beside you / Second place / Can't stand to see your face / Use me.

Sympathy..   Sympathy..

Jan 01. (cd/lp; as HOLLY GOLIGHTLY & DAN MELCHIOR) (<SFTRI 591 CD/LP>) **DESPERATE LITTLE TOWN**
– Directly from my heart / I'll follow her / Why don't you love me / All I want / Don't pass the hat around / Lifering / I'm feeling good / Further on up the road / Desperate little town / One of mine.

– compilations, etc. –

May 01. (cd/lp) Damaged Goods; (<DAMGOOD 189 CD/LP>) **THE MAIN ATTRACTION** (actually a re-release of 1995/6 recording)
– So far up there / I thought wrong / Just once / Dropsy / If I should ever leave / The sign / An eye for an empty heart / Kind of everything / Better of me / Fallapart / Seashells / Gullible's travels.

Sep 01. (cd/d-lp) Damaged Goods; (<DAMGOOD 190 CD/LP>) **SINGLES ROUND UP**

GOMEZ

Formed: Southport, England . . . 1997 originally as GOMEZ, KILL, KILL THE VORTEX by college lads BEN OTTERWELL, TOM GRAY, IAN BALL, PAUL BLACKBURN and OLLY PEACOCK. A home-recorded tape of the band found its way into the hands of record shop worker and former COMSAT ANGELS member, STEVE FELLOWS, who almost immediately became their manager. He in turn set up time in a Sheffield rehearsal studio in which he invited a plethora of A&R men to witness the unique talent of the band. After a fortnight, over thirty record labels were showing signs of interest, although FELLOWS and his protegees opted for Virgin offshoot, 'Hut'. Their early 70's to early 90's sound – like a hybrid of LOWELL GEORGE, GRATEFUL DEAD and BECK – was much in debt to the bluesy whisky-throated chords of lead singer, BEN, whose boyish, bespectacled look stunned an unsuspecting but appreciative audience on their debut single, '78 STONE WOBBLE'. It was their first UK Top 50 entry and was pursued a month later – in April '98 – by their classic debut album, 'BRING IT ON'. A critical and soon-to-be commercial success, its highlights were the tracks, 'GET MILES' (gruffly reminiscent of The BEATLES' 'Come Together'), 'WHIPPIN' PICCADILLY' and 'GET MYSELF ARRESTED', all of which helped it win the much lauded Mercury prize early in '99. Later that year, two brand-new GOMEZ tracks 'BRING IT ON' (surprisingly not a part of the debut!) and 'RHYTHM & BLUES ALIBI' hovered around the Top 20, while parent follow-up set, 'LIQUID SKIN' (1999) smashed in at No.2. On reflection, the band might've been better to wait a little longer. Good on GOMEZ though, as it says a lot for a band who release a fresh set of songs every year – here's hoping America could be their next prize. Prior to that difficult third album, GOMEZ stopped the proverbial gap with 'ABANDONED SHOPPING TROLLEY HOTLINE' (2000). Ostensibly a collection of the usual B-sides, live material and outtakes, this record merely served to underline GOMEZ's talent by transcending the implied second division quality of such material. Indeed, this could almost have been a third album proper in its own right save for the fact there are no obvious singles. 'IN OUR GUN' (2002) was a welcome return from GOMEZ. Still not surpassing the initial brilliance of their debut, the boys had a good shot at recreating that timid, stoned and gruff sound. Even more stoned here, with a lot of dub influences thrown in for good measure, these romantic-orientated ballads didn't seem too out of place (i.e. the title track). However, the production was as smooth as a polished stone, and the songs could get a little too Americana for their own good. Despite these small gripes, GOMEZ delivered one of the most enjoyable and entertaining records of the year.

Album rating: BRING IT ON (*9) / LIQUID SKIN (*7) / ABANDONED SHOPPING TROLLEY HOTLINE collection (*6) / IN OUR GUN (*6)

BEN OTTERWELL – vocals / **IAN BALL** – guitar, vocals, harmonica (ex-SEV) / **TOM GRAY** – keyboards, vocals, guitar, multi / **PAUL BLACKBURN** – bass / **OLLY PEACOCK** – percussion

Hut   Virgin

Mar 98. (cd-s) (HUTCD 95) **78 STONE WOBBLE / WHO'S GONNA GO TO THE BAR / STEVE McCROSKI**   44
(12"+=/c-s+=) (HUT T/C 95) – Wham bam.

Date	Format / Catalogue	Title	Chart	Re-iss
Apr 98.	(cd-c/d-lp) (CDHUT/HUTMC/HUTDLP 49) <45592>	**BRING IT ON**	11	May98

– Get miles / Whippin' Piccadilly / Make no sound / 78 stone wobble / Tijuana lady / Here comes the breeze / Love is better than a warm trombone / Get myself arrested / Free to run / Bubble gum years / Rie's wagon / The comeback.

Jun 98. (c-s) (*HUTC 97*) **GET MYSELF ARRESTED / THE COWBOY SONG** 45 -
(12"+=/cd-s+=) (*HUT T/CD 97*) – Flavours / Old school shirt.

Aug 98. (c-s) (*HUTC 105*) <95293> **WHIPPIN' PICCADILLY / PUSSYFOOTIN'** 35 Nov98
(12"+=/cd-s+=) (*HUT T/CD 105*) – Pick up the pieces.

Jun 99. (c-s/cd-s) (*HUT C/CD 112*) **BRING IT ON / DIRE TRIBE / M57** 21 -
(cd-s) (*HUTDX 112*) – ('A'side) / Chicken bones / Step inside.
(12"+=) (*HUTT 112*) – (all 5 tracks above).

Aug 99. (c-s/cd-s) (*HUT C/CD 114*) **RHYTHM & BLUES ALIBI / THE BEST IN THE TOWN / SO** 18 -
(cd-s) (*HUTDX 114*) – ('A'-Pre-mellotron version) / ZYX / Tijuanalaska (Tijuana lady – live version).
(12"+=) (*HUUT 114*) – (all 6 tracks above).

Sep 99. (cd/c/d-lp) (CDHUT/HUTMC/HUTDLP 54) <48218> **LIQUID SKIN** 2 -
– Hangover / Revolutionary kind / Bring it on / Blue moon rising / Las Vegas dealer / We haven't turned around / Fill my cup / Rhythm & blues alibi / Rosalita / California / Devil will ride.

Nov 99. (c-s/cd-s) (*HUT C/CD 117*) **WE HAVEN'T TURNED AROUND / FLIGHT / ROSEMARY** 38 -
(cd-s/12") (*HUT DX/T 117*) – ('A'mix) / Gomez in a bucket (a seaside town made of ice cream slowly melting) / Emergency surgery.

Sep 00. (cd/c/lp) (*CDHUTX/HUTMCX/HUTLP 64*) <50260> **ABANDONED SHOPPING TROLLEY HOTLINE** (collection) 10 Oct00
– Shitbag 9 / Bringin' your lovin' back here / Emergency surgery (remix) / Hit on the head / Flavors / 78 stone shuffle (BBC live session) / We haven't turned around (x-ray version) / Buena vista / Shitbag / Steve McCroski (BBC live session) / Wharf me / High on liquid skin / Rosemary (BBC live session) / Cowboy song / Getting better.

Mar 02. (7") (*HUT 149*) **SHOT SHOT. / SILHOUETTES** 28 -
(cd-s+=) (*HUTCD 149*) – Coltrane.
(cd-s) (*HUTDX 149*) – Shot shot (folk shot) / Air hostess song / Pop juice.

Mar 02. (cd/d-lp) (*CDHUT/HUTDLP 72*) <811950> **IN OUR GUN** 8 -
– Shot shot / Rex Kramer / Detroit swing 66 / In our gun / Even song / Ruff stuff / Sound of sounds / Army dub / Miles end / Ping one down / 1000 times / Drench / Ballad of nice and easy.

Jun 02. (7") (*HUT 154*) **SOUND OF SOUNDS. / PING ONE DOWN** 48 -
(cd-s+=) (*HUTCD 154*) – Where are your friends / ('A'video).
(cd-s) (*HUTDX 154*) – ('B'side) / ('A'instrumental) / Click click / ('B'video).

– compilations, etc. –

Oct 02. (d-cd) *Hut;* (543175-2) **IN OUR GUN / ABANDONED SHOPPING TROLLEY HOTLINE**
Oct 02. (d-cd) *Hut;* (543416-2) **LIQUID SKIN / BRING IT ON**

GOOD LIFE (see under ⇒ CURSIVE)

GORIES (see under ⇒ DIRTBOMBS)

GORILLAZ (see under ⇒ BLUR)

GORKY'S ZYGOTIC MYNCI

Formed: Carmarthen, South Wales … early 1991 by EUROS CHILD, RICHARD JAMES and JOHN LAWRENCE. Naming themselves after the Russian writer MAXIM GORKY, they were signed to the Bangor-based 'Ankst' label by owner ALUN LLWYD and issued their 1992 debut 45, 'PATIO'. Two years later, their first album 'TATAY', found favour in the indie circuit, while they toured supporting The FALL (The GORKY's were banned in some Welsh clubs for combining the Welsh and English language!). A youthful Welsh-language psychedelic/folk/pop-rock outfit, they were largely influenced by the likes of The INCREDIBLE STRING BAND, early SOFT MACHINE, or the even medieval, GRYPHON. Two brilliant singles were released in 1995; 'MISS TRUDY' (from 'LLANFROG' EP) and the classic 'IF FINGERS WERE XYLOPHONES', while they progressed with their second album proper, 'BWYD TIME', in 1995 (another in 1994; 'PATIO' was demos, etc from '91-93). Early in '96, they inked a deal with the major 'Fontana' label, through A&R man Steve Greenberg. Their first single for the label, the excellent 'PATIO SONG', was their initial breakthrough into the UK Top 50. In April '97, this song and 15 others, were featured on their best offering to date, the trippy 'BARAFUNDLE' which included the excellently folky 'SOMETIMES THE FATHER IS THE SON'. The following year, with cult glory seemingly at their feet, the GORKY'S released their fifth proper album, 'GORKY 5', a comparatively disappointing effort which, with mediocre reviews, only managed one week in the Top 75. After being dropped by Mercury in '99, they hooked up with Beggars Banquet subsidiary 'Mantra', only for JOHN LAWRENCE to become disillusioned just days before signing. However, a new-line (with RHODRY PUGH in tow) promoted the much-improved 'SPANISH DANCE TROUPE' (1999), the Catalonian-inspired title track scraping into the Top 50. By the time GORKY'S had issued the brilliant and timeless mini-set, 'THE BLUE TREES' (2001), their sound had mellowed so much it was hardly recognisable. The set included eight songs, all produced by GORWELL OWEN (his poignant diary entry about 'Bambi', written when he was nine years-old is worth the album alone), were written by CHILDS

with the occasional track by JAMES. But what remained standard on the album was the acoustic reverberation of mandolins, violins, pianos, strummed guitars and songs about summer. So folksy and introverted was the title track that once the piano trills began you had forgotten that you were listening to the champions of Welsh Indie, and instead convinced yourself that you had put on something by NICK DRAKE. 'THE SUMMER'S BEEN GOOD FROM THE START' saw CHILDS reminiscing over blue skies and green fields while a country-blues fiddle quietly wailed over the acoustic guitar. If GORKY'S had been invited to play on MTV's 'Unplugged', this is what it would've sounded like. The sunny theme was denoted even further when the group issued the album 'HOW I LONG TO FEEL THAT SUMMER IN MY HEART' (2001), a more back-to-basics for the MYNCI's. However, this wasn't a bad thing as tracks such as 'CAN MEGAN' and 'HOW I LONG' (which ends up turning into a kind of homage to the seventies, with its brass-led outro) still evoked the calm heard on 'BLUE TREES'. If 'SPANISH DANCE TROUPE' amazed music listeners with its complex structure and blinding ambiguity, then with 'HOW I LONG …' and the beyond-sublime 'BLUE TREES', GORKY'S ZYGOTIC MYNCI had re-invented their own wheel. • **Songwriters:** Mostly EUROS CHILDS, some by or with JOHN LAWRENCE (until his departure) and RICHARD JAMES, and a few by MEGAN. Covered; A DAY IN THE LIFE (Beatles) / WHY ARE WE SLEEPING? (Soft Machine) / O CAROLINE (Matching Mole).

Album rating: TATAY (*6) / PATIO (*5) / BWYD TIME (*6) / INTRODUCING … compilation US (*6) / BARAFUNDLE (*9) / GORKY 5 (*6) / SPANISH DANCE TROUPE (*7) / THE BLUE TREES mini (*7) / HOW I LONG TO FEEL THAT SUMMER IN MY HEART (*8)

EUROS CHILDS – vocals, keyboards, synthesizer / **RICHARD JAMES** – guitars, bass / **JOHN LAWRENCE** – bass, guitars, keyboards / **SION LANE** – keyboards / **STEFFAN** – violin

			Mynci	not iss.
1991.	(c) (001)	**ALLUMETTE**		-

— **OSIAN EVANS** – drums; repl. SION + STEFFAN

			G.Z.M.	not iss.
1992.	(c) (none)	**PEIRIANT PLESER**		-

— added **MEGAN CHILDS** – violin

			Ankst	not iss.
Oct 93.	(10"lp;ltd) (ANKST 40)	**PATIO**		-

– Peanut dispenser / Lladd eich gwraig / Dafad yn sirad / Mr Groovy / Ti! Moses / Barbed wire / Miriam o Farbel / Oren, mefus a chadno / Gwallt rhegi Pegi / Sally Webster / Diamonds o Monte Carlo / Siwt nofio. *(re-iss. Jan95 & Apr97 cd+=/c+=; ANKST 055 cd/c)* – Blessed are the meek / Reverend Oscar Marzaroli / Oren, mefus a chadno / Dean ser / Siwmper heb grys / Llenni ar gloi / Anna apera / Siwf nofio / Hi ar gan.

Mar 94. (cd/c) (*ANKST 047 cd/c*) **TATAY**
– Thema o cartref (Theme from home) / Beth sy'n digwydd i'r fuwch (What happens to the cow?) / Tatay / Y ffordd oren (Orange way) / Gwres prynhawn (Afternoon heat) / Amsermaemaiynbod (When May comes) – Cinema / O, Caroline / Naw.e.pimp (Nine for a pimp) / Kevin Ayers / When you hear the captain sing / O, Caroline II / Tatay (moog mix) / Anna apera:- a. Anna apera – b. Gegin nos (Night kitchen) – c. Silff ffenest (Window sill) – d. Backward dog. *(re-iss. Apr97; same)*

Jun 94. (7") (*ANKST 048*) **MERCHED YN GWALLT EI GILYDD. / BOCS ANGELICA / WHEN YOU LAUGH AT YOUR OWN GARDEN IN A BLAZER**
(cd-s+=) (*ANKST 048cd*) – Mewn. *(re-iss. Apr97; same)*

Nov 94. (7") (*ANKST 053*) **THE GAME OF EYES. / PENTREF WRTH Y MOR**
(cd-s+=) (*ANKST 053cd*) – Cwpwrdd sadwrn. *(re-iss. Apr97; same)*

— **EUROS ROWLANDS** – percussion, drums; repl. EVANS

Mar 95. (10"ep/cd-ep) (*ANKST 056/+cd*) **LLANFWROG EP**
– Miss Trudy / Eira / Methu aros tan haf / Why are we sleeping? *(re-iss. Apr97; same)*

Jun 95. (7"w-drawn) (*ANKST 058*) **GEWN NI GORFFEN. / 12 IMPRESSIONISTIC SOUNDSCAPES**

Jul 95. (lp/c/cd) (*ANKST 059/+c/cd*) **BWYD TIME**
– Bwyd time / Miss Trudy / Paid cheto ar Pam (Don't cheat on Pam) / Oraphis yndelphie / Eating salt is easy / Gewn ni gorffen (Let's finish) / Iechyd da (Good health) / Ymwelwyr a gwrachod (Visitors and witches) / The telescope and the bonfire / The man with salt hair / The game of eyes / Blood chant / Ffarm-wr. *(re-iss. Apr97; same)*

Nov 95. (7") (*ANKST 064*) **IF FINGERS WERE XYLOPHONES. / MOON BEATS YELLOW**
(cd-s+=) (*ANKST 064cd*) – Pethau. *(re-iss. Apr97; same)*

Jul 96. (10"ep/cd-ep) (*ANKST 068/+cd*) **AMBLER GAMBLER EP**
– Lucy's hamper / Heart of Kentucky / Sdim yr adar yn canu / 20. *(re-iss. Apr97; same)*

			Fontana	Polygram
Aug 96.	(cd) <532818-2>	**INTRODUCING …** (compilation)		

– Merched ya neod gwalt eu gilydd / If fingers were xylophones / PenTree WRTH Y mor / Games of eyes / Kevin Ayers / Miss Trudy / Why are we sleeping? / Y ffordd oren / Meth aros tan haf / Era / Iechyd da / The moon beats yellow.

Oct 96. (7") (*GZMX 1*) **PATIO SONG. / NO ONE LOOKED AROUND** 41 -
(cd-s+=) (*GZMCD 1*) – Morwyr o hyd in lladd eu hun ar y tir.

Mar 97. (7"/c-s/cd-s) (*GZM/+MC/CD 2*) **DIAMOND DEW. / QUEEN OF GEORGIA / TEARS IN DISGUISE** 42 -

Apr 97. (cd/c) (534 769-2/-4) <536122> **BARAFUNDLE** 46
– Diamond dew / The barafundle bumbler / Starmoonsun / Patio song / Better rooms … / Heywood lane / Pen gwag glas / Bola bola / Cursed, coined and crucified / Sometimes the father is the son / Meirion Wylit / The wizard and the lizard / Miniature kingdoms / Dark night / Hwyl fawr i pawb / Wordless song.

Jun 97. (7"/c-s) (*GZM/+MC 3*) **YOUNG GIRLS & HAPPY ENDINGS. / DARK KNIGHT** 49 -
(cd-s) (*GZMCD 3*) – Marching ants.

May 98. (7") (*GZM 4*) **SWEET JOHNNY. / UN HOGYN UN HOGAN DRIST** 60 -
(cd-s+=) (*GZMCD 4*) – Mifi Mihafan.

GORKY'S ZYGOTIC MYNCI (cont)

Aug 98. (7") *(GZM 5)* **LET'S GET TOGETHER (IN OUR MINDS) . / TONIGHT** — 43 / -
(cd-s) *(GZMCD 5)* – ('A'side) / Billy and the sugarloaf mountain / Hwiangerdd mair.

Aug 98. (cd/c/lp) *(558 822-2/-4/-1)* **GORKY 5** — 67 / -
– The tidal wave / Dyle fi / Let's get together (in our minds) / Tsunami / Not yet / Only the sea makes sense / Softly / Frozen smile / Sweet Johnny / Theme from Gorky 5 (Russian song) / Hush the warmth / Catrin.

	Mantra	Beggars Banquet
Sep 99. (7") *(MNT 047)* **SPANISH DANCE TROUPE. / (DO THE) CHICKEN IN THE JUNGLE**	47	-

(cd-s+=) *(MNT 047CD)* – The Johnny Cash lawsuit song.

Oct 99. (cd/c/lp) *(MNT CD/MC/LP 1015) <81015>* **SPANISH DANCE TROUPE**
– Hallway / Poodle rockin' / She lives on a mountain / Drws / Over and out / Don't you worry / Faraway eyes / The fool / Hair like monkey teeth like dog / Spanish dance troupe / Desolation blues / Murder ballad / Freckles / Christmas eve / The humming song.

—— (Jun'99) now without JOHN who formed the INFINITY CHIMPS (after partly recording with GZM on above) **RHODRY PUGH** (took his place)

Feb 00. (7") *(MNT 052)* **POODLE ROCKIN'. / FLU MUSIC** — 51 / -
(cd-s+=) *(MNT 052CD)* – Girl I've always known.

Oct 00. (m-cd/m-lp) *(MNT CDM/LP 1023) <81023>* **THE BLUE TREES** — / Feb01
– The blue trees / This summer's been good from the start / Lady fair / Foot and mouth '68 / Wrong turnings / Fresher than the sweetness in water / Face like summer / Sbia ar y seren.

—— **EUROS & MEGAN CHILDS + EUROS ROWLANDS** recruited **RICHARD JAMES** – guitar, vocals / **GORWEL OWEN** – piano / **PETER RICHARDSON** – bass / **RHODRI PHU** – drums / plus **ASHLEY COOKE, ANDY FUNG, NORMAN BLAKE + JASPER**

Sep 01. (7") *(MNT 64)* **STOOD ON GOLD. / MY HONEY** — 65 / -
(cd-s+=) *(MNT 64CD)* – Out on the side.

Sep 01. (cd/lp) *(MNT CDM/LP 1025) <81025>* **HOW I LONG TO FEEL THAT SUMMER IN MY HEART** — / Oct01
– Where does yer go now? / Honeymoon with you / Stood on gold / Dead-aid / Can Megan / Christina / Easy love / Let those blue skies / These winds are in my heart / How I long / Her hair hangs long / Hodgeston's hallelujah.

GO SAILOR (see under ⇒ TIGER TRAP)

GOTHIC ARCHIES (see under ⇒ MAGNETIC FIELDS)

GOYA DRESS

Formed: London, England ... 1994 by main songwriter and string arranger, ASTRID WILLIAMSON (who was actually born in the Shetlands), together with Minneapolis-born TERRY DE CASTRO and lone male SIMON PEARSON. Signed to 'Nude' (home of SUEDE, with whom they toured), GOYA DRESS issued a trio of EP's over the course of a year, 'BEDROOM CINEMA', 'RUBY' and 'GLORIOUS', showcasing WILLIAMSON's glacial vocals against a moody, textured, slo-core backdrop and drawing comparisons to THROWING MUSES, LIZ PHAIR, et al. However, only a solitary long-player, 'ROOMS' (1996) was to surface before the band returned to their disparate roots.

Album rating: ROOMS (*5)

ASTRID WILLIAMSON (b. Shetland, Scotland) – vocals, guitars, piano / **TERRY DE CASTRO** – bass, vocals / **SIMON PEARSON** – drums

	Nude	not iss.
Apr 95. (12"ep/cd-ep) *(NUD 13 T/CD)* **BEDROOM CINEMA ep**		-

– If I know / Strange death / King Thong / Jinxed.

Sep 95. (12"ep/cd-ep) *(NUD 18 T/CD)* **RUBY ep**
– Ruby Ruby / Valentina / In me / Closer.

Apr 96. (12"ep/cd-ep) *(NUD 19 T/CD)* **GLORIOUS ep**
– Glorious / Dusted down / 20th century box / Glorious (piano version).

May 96. (cd/c/lp) *(NUDE 5 CD/MC/LP)* **ROOMS**
– Sweet dreams for you / Crush / Scorch / Rooms / Greatest secret / Glorious / Any John / Katie stood on the benches / Picture this / The maritime waltz.

Jul 96. (7"/cd-s) *(NUD 20 S/CD)* **CRUSH. / TO ALL MY GIRLFRIENDS / THE MARITIME WALTZ (megaphone)**

—— split after above and ASTRID went solo; TERRY DE CASTRO + SIMON PEARSON would later resurface with CINERAMA (see WEDDING PRESENT)

GRANDADDY

Formed: Modesto, California, USA ... 1992 by ex-skater, JASON LYTLE, who, with the help of HOWE GELB (of GIANT SAND), found a sympathetic ear at 'Big Cat' records. The line-up around this time also included JIM FAIRCHILD, TIM DRYDEN, KEVIN GARCIA and AARON BURTCH, although it took time aplenty to finally emerge with debut release, the mini-set, 'A PRETTY MESS BY THIS ONE BAND'. 'UNDER THE WESTERN FREEWAY' followed in '98, another based on classic West Coast Americana, their BRIAN WILSON/MERCURY REV-esque sound marked them out as the Sunday drivers of the alt-country brigade. JASON LYTLE and his band of beardy brothers returned one year after the release of the 'BROKEN DOWN COMFORTER COLLECTION' with perhaps the best album of the year, 'THE SOPHTWARE SLUMP' (2000). As prog and as concept as you can get, 'THE SOPHTWARE SLUMP' began with what could only be described as an American Lo-Fi version of 'Paranoid Android' entitled 'HE'S SIMPLE, HE'S DUMB, HE'S THE PILOT'. On it LYTLE sang "How's it going 2000 man, I heard all of your controls were jammed ...", and continued the theme of man against machine through the entirety of the set. Backed by FAIRCHILD's psychedelic, effect-laden guitar and DRYDEN's electric piano, that doubled up as a space-age synth, LYTLE wandered like a lost child in a daunting sc-fi mountain landscape singing eleven sad songs about drunken robots, smashed up computers, lost love and ultimately, hope, all in his unsure NEIL YOUNG/DANIEL JOHNSON-esque croon. Tracks 'HEWLETT'S DAUGHTER' and 'THE CRYSTAL LAKE' must've been two of the best psychedelic pop songs ever written, whereas on 'CHARSANDGRAFS', the band cranked up all of their instruments for what sounded like progressive grunge. In turn, a humble band who were thought to only make sad, sun-blasted Lo-Fi had created one of the strongest concept albums since 'Ok Computer'. Even if it was pitched somewhere between the aforementioned set, THE FLAMING LIPS' 'The Soft Bulletin' and MERCURY REV's 'Deserters Songs', the biggest compliment the listener could've paid GRANDADDY was by saying that it sounded mostly like them.

Album rating: A PRETTY MESS BY THIS ONE BAND mini (*6) / UNDER THE WESTERN FREEWAY (*8) / THE BROKEN DOWN COMFORTER COLLECTION compilation (*8) / THE SOPHTWARE SLUMP (*9) / CONCRETE DUNES collection (*5)

JASON LYTLE – vocals / **JIM FAIRCHILD** – guitar / **TIM DRYDEN** – keyboards / **KEVIN GARCIA** – bass / **AARON BURTCH** – drums

	not iss.	Big Jesus
Apr 94. (c) *<none>* **COMPLEX PARTY COME-ALONG THEORIES**	-	
1994. (7") *<none>* **COULD THIS BE LOVE. / KIM, YOU BORE ME TO DEATH**	-	
1994. (7") *<none>* **TASTER. / NEBRASKA**	-	

	Big Cat	Will
1995. (c) *<w-drawn>* **DON'T SOCK THIS TRYER**	-	-
Apr 96. (m-cd) *<041>* **A PRETTY MESS BY THIS ONE BAND**		-

– Away birdies with special sounds / Taster / Peeano / Kim you bore me to death / Pre Merced / Gentle spike resort / Egg hit and Jack too.

1997. (7"ep) *<none>* **MACHINES ARE NOT SHE E.P.** — / mail-o
– Levitz / For the dishwasher / Lava kiss / Wretched songs / Sikh in a Baja VW bug / Fentry. <re-iss. 1998 on 'Big Cat'; ABB 128P>

Feb 98. (7") *(ABB 157S)* **EVERYTHING BEAUTIFUL IS FAR AWAY. / FOR THE DISHWASHER**
(cd-s+=) *(ABB 157SCD)* – Glass dusty.

Mar 98. (7"/cd-s) *(ABB 161S/+CD)* **LAUGHING STOCK. / G.P.C. / 12-PAK 599**

Apr 98. (lp/cd) *(ABB 152/+CD) <33646>* **UNDER THE WESTERN FREEWAY** — / Oct97
– Nonphenomenal lineage / A.M. 180 / Collective dreamwish of upper class / Summer here kids / Laughing stock / Under the western freeway / Everything beautiful is far away / Poisoned at Hartsy Thai food / Go progress chrome / Why took your advice / Lawn and so on. *(cd re-iss. Aug00; ABB 100248-2)*

May 98. (7"/cd-s) *(ABB 162S/+CD)* **SUMMER HERE KIDS. / LEVITZ (BIRDLESS) / MY SMALL LOVE**

Oct 98. (7") *(ABB 500 350-7)* **A.M. 180. / HERE**
(cd-s) *(ABB 164SCD)* – ('A'side) / For the dishwasher.

	V2	V2
Sep 99. (7"ep) *<27612>* **SIGNAL TO SNOW**		

– Hand crank transmitter / Jeddy's 3's poem / MGM grand / Protected from the rain.

May 00. (cd) *(VVR 101225-2) <27068>* **THE SOPHTWARE SLUMP** — 36 /
– He's simple, he's dumb, he's the pilot / Hewlett's daughter / Jed the humanoid / The crystal lake / Chartsengrafs / Underneath the weeping willow / Broken household appliance national forest / Jed's other poem (beautiful ground) / E. Knievel interlude (the perils of keeping it real) / Miner at the dial-a-view / So you'll aim toward the sky. *(re-iss. Aug00 +=; VVR 101225-8)* – THE CRYSTAL LAKE tracks *(d-cd iss.Nov00 +=; VVR 101389-8)* – OUR DYING BRAIN tracks *(d-cd iss.Feb01 +=; VVR 101613-2)* – SIGNAL TO SNOW tracks

May 00. (7") *(VVR 501301-7)* **THE CRYSTAL LAKE. / OUR DYING BRAIN**
(cd-s+=) *(VVR 501301-3)* – First movement / Message send: ID#5646766.

Aug 00. (7") *(VVR 501433-7)* **HEWLETT'S DAUGHTER. / LFO** — 71 / -
(cd-s) *(VVR 501433-3)* – ('A'side) / XD-data-II / Street bunny.
(cd-s++=) *(VVR 501465-3)* – Wonder why in L.A. / ('A'mix).
(cd-s) *(VVR 501465-8)* – ('A'side) / Wonder why in L.A. / Chartsengrafs.

Nov 00. (12"/cd-s) *(VVR 501493-6/-3)* **HE'S SIMPLE, HE'S DUMB, HE'S THE PILOT. / WIVES OF FARMERS / N. BLENDER**

Jan 01. (7") *(VVR 501515-7)* **THE CRYSTAL LAKE. / RODE MY BIKE TO MY STEPSISTER'S WEDDING** — 38 / -
(cd-s) *(VVR 501515-3)* – ('A'side) / Moe Bandy mountaineers / She-deleter.
(cd-s) *(VVR 501515-8)* – ('A'-chilly mix) / What can't be erased / I don't want to record anymore.

– compilations, etc. –

1996. (cd) *none; <none>* **THE WINDFALL VARIETAL** — - / -

Jun 99. (cd) *Big Cat; (ABB 100569-2)* **THE BROKEN DOWN COMFORTER COLLECTION** — / -
– (A PRETTY MESS BY THIS ONE BAND / MACHINES ARE NOT SHE).

Oct 02. (cd) *Lakeshore; <(LAK 33690CD)>* **CONCRETE DUNES** — / Feb02
– Why should I want to die / My small love / 12-pak-599 / Wretched songs / Levitz / For the dishwasher / Sikh in a baja VW bug / Lava kiss / Fentry / Gentle spike resort / Away birdies with spacial sounds / Kim you bore me to death / Pre merced / Taster / Egg hit and Jack too.

GRAND MAL (see under ⇒ ST*JOHNNY)

GRANDPABOY (see under ⇒ REPLACEMENTS)

Chick GRANING (see under ⇒ ANASTASIA SCREAMED)

GRANT LEE BUFFALO

Formed: North Hollywood, California, USA ... 1991 by GRANT LEE PHILLIPS (vocals, guitar), PAUL KIMBLE (bass, piano, vocals) and JOEY PETERS (drums, percussion) who had all played together in SHIVA BURLESQUE before splitting the group to concentrate on a new project, GRANT LEE BUFFALO, partly named after lead singer PHILLIPS. After BOB MOULD released 'FUZZY' as a one-off 7" on his own label, the band came to the attention of 'London'-offshoot, 'Slash', making their major label debut with an album, 'FUZZY' (1993). A compelling hybrid of country-rock, folk and feedback hum, the set was lauded by the press, PHILLIPS' incisive lyrics cutting at the heart of America's broken dreams and drawing comparisons to NEIL YOUNG, The WATERBOYS and The DOORS. The album was also praised by MICHAEL STIPE of R.E.M. (spiritual forebears), who pronounced it his favourite release of the year. After a mini album, 'BUFFALONDON EP' (1993), featuring live versions of some of the debut's most sublime tracks ('JUPITER AND TEARDROP', 'THE SHINING HOUR'), the band released 'MIGHTY JOE MOON' (1994), a set that employed a richer sonic tapestry without losing the raw impact of the debut. At times, PHILLIPS sounded like a more organic EDDDY VEDDER while on songs like 'IT'S THE LIFE', the effect was akin to a countryfied JAMES (decidedly more palatable in reality than on paper!) The breezy melancholy of 'HONEY DON'T THINK' was a highlight, as was 'ROCK OF AGES', rolling the final credits to the album's widescreen sweep. The band's third effort, 'COPPEROPOLIS' (1996), was even more ambitious, embellishing the sound with strings and mellotron amongst other instrumental exotica. The lyrics were more entrenched in threadbare Americana than ever, PHILLIPS invoking the spirit of WOODY GUTHRIE in his sensitive portraits of his country's often tragic past. With JON BRION on keyboards and RAMI JAFFE on organ, not to mention the guest efforts of MICHAEL STIPE and ROBYN HITCHCOCK, 1998's 'JUBILEE' proved a suitably exultant finale to GRANT LEE BUFFALO's illustrious career, PHILLIPS' songwriting having matured sufficiently to warrant a sustainable solo career. Thus did 'LADIES' LOVE ORACLE' (2000) rank as one of the finest singer-songwriter efforts of that year; shorn of a backing band, PHILLIPS' songs were thrown into the kind of informal relief that they'd perhaps always cried out for. Likewise the following year's 'MOBILIZE' (2001), which confirmed the man's status as one of the finest American songwriters of his generation. • **Covered:** BURNING LOVE (hit; Elvis Presley).

Album rating: FUZZY (*8) / MIGHTY JOE MOON (*7) / COPPEROPOLIS (*6) / JUBILEE (*5) / STORM HYMNAL: GEMS FROM THE VAULT OF ... collection (*7) / Grant Lee Phillips: LADIES' LOVE ORACLE (*6) / MOBILIZE (*7)

GRANT LEE PHILLIPS (b. 1 Sep'63, Stockton, Calif.) – vocals, guitars / **PAUL KIMBLE** – bass, piano, vocals, producer / **JOEY PETERS** – drums, percussion

	Singles Only Label	not iss.
Dec 91. (7") *(SOL 227)* **FUZZY. / WE'RE COMING DOWN**		–

	Slash – London	Slash – Reprise
Jun 93. (cd/lp) *(828 389-2/-1) <45217>* **FUZZY**	74	Feb93

– The shining hour / Jupiter and teardrop / Fuzzy / Wish you well / The hook / Soft wolf tread / Stars n' stripes / Dixie drug store / America snoring / Grace / You just have to be crazy. *(cd re-iss. Sep97; same)*

Aug 93. (7") *(LAS 45)* **AMERICA SNORING. / WISH YOU WELL** | | –
(12"+=/cd-s+=) *(LAS H/CD 45)* – The hook / Burning love.
Sep 93. (7") *(LAS 46)* **FUZZY. / STARS & STRIPES** | | –
(12"+=/cd-s+=) *(LAS H/CD 46)* – Dixie drugstore (Ju Ju mix) / I will take him.
Nov 93. (12"ep/cd-ep) *(LAS H/CD 47)* **BUFFALONDON EP** | | –
– Jupiter and teardrop / Wish you well / Soft wolf tread / The shining hour.
Sep 94. (cd/c) *(828 541-2/-4) <45714>* **MIGHTY JOE MOON** | 24 |
– Lone star song / Mockingbirds / It's the life / Sing along / Mighty Joe Moon / Demon called Deception / Lady Godiva and me / Drag / Last days of Tecumseh / Happiness / Honey don't think / Side by side / Rock of ages.
Oct 94. (cd-ep) *(LASHCD 49)* **MOCKINGBIRDS / ORPHEUS / GOODNIGHT JOHN DEE** | | –
(12"ep+=) *(LASHX 49)* – Let go of my hand.
(cd-ep+=) *(LASPD 49)* – (first track) / Let go of my hand / We're coming down.
May 96. (12"ep/cd-ep) *(LAS H/CD 55)* **HOMESPUN / ARMCHAIR. / COMES TO BLOWS / CRASHING AT CORONA** | | –
Jun 96. (cd/c/lp) *(828 760-2/-4/-1) <46250>* **COPPEROPOLIS** | 34 |
– Homespun / The bridge / Arousing thunder / Even the oxen / Crackdown / Armchair / Bethlehem steel / All that I have / Two and two / Better for us / Hyperion and sunset / Comes to blows / Only way down.

— 3rd member **DAN ROTHCHILD** – bass; repl. KIMBLE
— additional **JON BRION** – keyboards / **RAMI JAFFE** – organ
— guests included ROBYN HITCHCOCK, MICHAEL STIPE & E (of The EELS)

Jun 98. (cd) *(556 048-2) <46879>* **JUBILEE** | |
– APB / Seconds / Change your tune / Testimony / Truly, truly / Superslomotion / Fine how'd ya do / Come to mama, she say / 8 mile road / Everybody needs a little sanctuary / My, my, my / Crooked rice / Jubilee / The shallow end.

— disbanded mid-1999

– compilations, etc. –

Oct 01. (d-cd) *WEA; <(0927 41064-2)>* **STORM HYMNAL – GEMS FROM THE VAULT OF ...** | |
– Fuzzy / The shining hour / Jupiter and teardrop / Stars n' stripes / Lone star song / Mockingbirds / Honey don't think / Happiness / Bethlehem steel / Homespun / Two and two / Truly, truly / Testimony / My, my, my / The shallow end / We're coming down / The shining hour (alt.) / Wish you well (alt.) / Soft wolf

tread (alt.) / I will take him / Let go of my hand / Orpheus / Goodnight John Dee / Halloween / Gold chain drag / Crashing at Corona / Mr. Know-it-all / Were you there / Where do we go from here.

GRANT LEE PHILLIPS

(first) solo in BRION's basement studio

	not iss.	Magnetic Field
Feb 00. (cd) *<none>* **LADIES' LOVE ORACLE**	–	

– You're a pony / Heavenly / Squint / Don't look down / Flamin' shoe / Folding / Lonesome serenade / Nothin' is for sure / St. Expedite. *<re-iss. Aug02 on 'Rounder'+=; 431031>* – Snow flakes.

	Cooking Vinyl	Zoe – Rounder
Mar 02. (cd-s) *(FRYCD 122)* **SPRING RELEASED /**		–
Apr 02. (cd) *(COOKCD 232) <431021>* **MOBILIZE**		Jul01

– See America / Humankind / Love's mystery / Sadness soot / We all get a taste / Spring released / Lazily drowning / Like a lover / Mobilize / Beautiful dreamers / Sleepless lake / April chimes.

GRAPE
(see under ⇒ CHESTERFIELDS; see 80's section)

GRASSHOPPER & THE GOLDEN CRICKETS
(see under ⇒ MERCURY REV)

David GRAY

Born: 1970, Manchester, England. As a young boy of nine, GRAY moved to Wales (Solva) with his family where he found the joys of guitar playing while taking in the local punk and folk scene. In 1992 (through manager/A&R man Rob Holden), he signed to Virgin offshoot, 'Hut' and issued his debut set 'A CENTURY ENDS' (1993), which brilliantly displayed his tender and sparse songwriting skills. 'FLESH' (1994) appeared one year later, by now, GRAY had made a promising name for himself, attracting a huge cult following around Britain and Europe. The aforementioned album was not bad for somebody who was still learning his trade, comparisons to DYLAN, EDDIE VEDDER and MIKE SCOTT were bandied about like confetti at a wedding. The acoustic guitars, bouncing pedal steel and occasional piano made stand out tracks 'WHAT ARE YOU NOW', 'FALLING FREE' and 'NEW HORIZONS' levitate above some recent attempts at melancholic music, proving GRAY to be one of Britain's best kept secrets and filing him along with assets THOM YORKE and RICHARD ASHCROFT. 'SELL, SELL, SELL' (1996) was perhaps too proverbial for its own good and thus it didn't gain enough exposure to hit the shops in the UK. Nevertheless, it still received some airplay from Radio One's Steve Lamaque and went on to sustain GRAY's reputation in the alt-music world. It was 1999's 'WHITE LADDER' (on new imprint 'iht' through 'eastwest') which caught the attention of music critics and audiences alike. A fine album in every sense, GRAY took us into the underworld of his soul ... and deeper, with tracks 'SAIL AWAY' and Soft Cell's 'SAY HELLO WAVE GOODBYE' bringing something delicate and strangely human to the work. Easily the highlight from the set was 'BABYLON', a chart flop first time around although album opener 'PLEASE FORGIVE ME' slightly compensated for this, clocking in at No.72. Aaah! what a difference a year can make. Now signed to 'east west', the single 'BABYLON' was re-issued to a wider audience and after massive playlisting it finally peaked at No.5. A resurrected 'WHITE LADDER' also climbed the charts post-millennium, rising to No.1 a whole year later. A newcomer of sorts (tell that to the struggling 30-something troubadour!), GRAY proceeded to have three further hits during 2001, 'PLEASE FORGIVE ME', 'THIS YEARS LOVE' and 'SAIL AWAY'. The tender singer/songwriter returned in 2002 to issue 'A NEW DAY AT MIDNIGHT', an altogether more thoughtful and intimate set than 'WHITE LADDER'. It included the soaring piano lament 'SEE YOU ON THE OTHER SIDE', a deep but nevertheless uplifting feel through GRAY's psyche. Another surefire hit with fans was the song 'BE MINE', a slight hark back to GRAY's earlier days. But it was the bitterly bitter-sweet sound of his piano on the frosty ballad 'DECEMBER' which set him apart from many copyists.

Album rating: A CENTURY ENDS (*6) / FLESH (*6) / SELL, SELL, SELL (*6) / WHITE LADDER (*9) / LOST SONGS 95-98 collection (*6) / THE EP'S 1992-1994 ALBUM collection (*5) / A NEW DAY AT MIDNIGHT (*7)

DAVID GRAY – vocals, guitar, keyboards / with **NEILL MacCOLL** – guitar, mandolin, vocals / **ROBIN MILLAR** – guitar / "FAMOUS DAVE" ANDERSON – keyboards / **STEVE SIDELNYK** – programming

	Hut	Caroline
Nov 92. (12"/cd-s) *(HUT/+CD 23)* **BIRDS WITHOUT WINGS. / L'S SONG / THE LIGHT**		–
Mar 93. (12"/cd-s) *(HUT/+CD 27)* **SHINE. / BRICK WALLS / THE RICE**		–
Apr 93. (cd/c/lp) *(CDHUT/HUTMC/HUTLP 9) <CAROL 1739>* **A CENTURY ENDS**		Nov93

– Shine / A century ends / Debauchery / Let the truth sting / Gathering dust / Wisdom / Lead me upstairs / Living room / Birds without wings / It's all over. *(cd re-iss. Jul01; CDHUTX 9)*

Jul 93. (12"/cd-s) *(HUT/+CD 32)* **WISDOM. / LOVERS / 4AM** | | –

— with MacCOLL plus **ANDY METCALFE** – hammond organ / **SIMON EDWARDS** + **DAVID NOLTE** – bass / **ROY DODS** – drums / **CLUNE** – drums, vocals, keyboards, bass, co-writer

David GRAY (cont)

			Hut	not iss.
Sep 94.	(cd/c)	*(CDHUT/HUTMC 17)* **FLESH**		

– What are you? / The light / Coming down / Falling free / Mystery of love / Lullaby / New horizons / Loves old song / Flesh. *<US cd-iss. Jul00 on 'Vernon Yard'; 39770> (cd re-iss. Jul01; CDHUTX 17)*

— now with different session people incl. **CLUNE + TIM BRADSHAW**

			E.M.I.	not iss.
Apr 96.	(cd)	*(7243 8 37357)* **SELL, SELL, SELL**	-	- Europe

– Faster, sooner, now / Late night radio / Sell, sell, sell / Hold on to nothing / Everytime / Magdalena / Smile / Only the lonely / What am I doing wrong? / Gutters full of rain / Forever is tomorrow is today / Folk song. *(UK-iss.Jul00; CDEMC 3755) <US-iss.Sep00 on 'Nettwerk'; >*

— GRAY with **(Mc)CLUNE** + 3rd p/t co-writer/producer, **POLSON**

			Iht	A.T.O.
Mar 99.	(cd)	*(ihtcd 001) <21539>* **WHITE LADDER**		Jan00

– Please forgive me / Babylon / My oh my / We're not right / Nightblindness / Silver lining / White ladder / This years love / Sail away / Say hello wave goodbye. *(re-iss. Apr00 on 'eastwest'; 8573 82983-2)* – hit No.2 – No.1 a year later! *<US re-iss. Aug00 on 'R.C.A.'; 69351>* – hit No.35

Mar 99.	(cd-s)	*(ihtcds 001)* **THIS YEARS LOVE / NIGHTBLINDNESS / OVER MY HEAD**		-
Jul 99.	(cd-s)	*(ihtcds 002)* **BABYLON / LEAD ME UPSTAIRS (live) / NEW HORIZONS (live)**		-
Nov 99.	(12")(cd-s)	*(ihtv 001)(ihtcds 003)* **PLEASE FORGIVE ME. / PLEASE FORGIVE ME (Paul Hartnoll remix)**	72	-

			eastwest	R.C.A.
Jun 00.	(c-s/cd-s)	*(EW 215 C/CD1) <radio cut>* **BABYLON / TELL ME MORE LIES / OVER MY HEAD**	5	57 Nov00
	(cd-s+=)	*(EW 215CD2)* – ('A'-video).		
Oct 00.	(c-s)	*(EW 219C)* **PLEASE FORGIVE ME / (Paul Hartnoll remix)**	18	-
	(cd-s+=)	*(EW 219CD)* – Babylon (live at the Point) (video).		
Mar 01.	(c-s/cd-s)	*(EW 228 C/CD1)* **THIS YEARS LOVE (strings remix) / FLAME TURNS BLUE / THE LIGHTS OF LONDON**	20	-
	(cd-s)	*(EW 228CD2)* – ('A'live) / Roots of love / Tired of me.		
Jul 01.	(c-s)	*(EW 234C)* **SAIL AWAY (club mix)**	26	-
	(cd-s+=)	*(EW 234CD)* – ('A'-Rae & Christian remix).		
Dec 01.	(cd-s)	*(EW 244CD)* **SAY HELLO WAVE GOODBYE (mixes)**	26	-
Oct 02.	(cd)	*(5046 61658-2) <68154>* **A NEW DAY AT MIDNIGHT**	1	17 Nov02

– Dead in the water / Caroline / Long distance call / Freedom / Kangaroo / Last boat to America / Real love / Knowhere / December / Be mine / Easy way to cry / The other side.

| Dec 02. | (cd-s) | *(EW 259CD)* **THE OTHER SIDE / LORELEI / DECIPHER** | 35 | - |

– compilations, etc. –

| Jul 00. | (cd) | *iht; (IHTCD 002) / A.T.O.; <69375>* **LOST SONGS 95-98** | | Apr01 |

– Flame turns blue / Twilight / Hold on / As I'm leaving / If your love is real / Tidal wave / Falling down the mountainside / January rain / Red moon / A clean pair of eyes / Wurlitzer. *(re-iss. Feb01 on 'eastwest' cd/c; 8573 86953-2/-4)* – hit No.7

Jul 01.	(cd)	Hut; *(CDHUT 67)* **THE EP'S 1992-1994 ALBUM**	68	
Oct 02.	(d-cd)	Hut; *(543413-0)* **FLESH / A CENTURY ENDS**		-
Oct 02.	(d-cd)	Hut; *(543414-0)* **SELL, SELL, SELL / THE EP'S 1992-1994 ALBUM**		-

GREAT OUTDOORS
(see under ⇒ FARMER'S BOYS; in 80's section)

Adam GREEN (see under ⇒ MOLDY PEACHES)

GREEN DAY

Formed: Rodeo, nr. Berkeley, California, USA ... early 90's out of The SWEET CHILDREN by BILLY JOE ARMSTRONG and MIKE DIRNT. When TRE COOL replaced BILLY JOE's sister ANA on drums, they became GREEN DAY, this line-up releasing their debut LP, '39 / SMOOTH', which was recorded in under 24 hours. Their third album, 'DOOKIE' (their first for 'Reprise'), was a surprise US smash in 1994 due to its college/MTV favourite, 'BASKET CASE'. Retro punk-rock for young Americans (and now older Brits) who missed out on BUZZCOCKS, DICKIES, RAMONES (and even earlier 60's pop outfit, the MONKEES), GREEN DAY became a phenomenon in the States; like the SEX PISTOLS' revolution all over again, without the danger, unpredictability and raw excitement. Instead we got formulaic, annoyingly and yes, inanely catchy punk retreads that took you way back to '77. Still, the multi-millions who bought the record ensured that GREEN DAY were indeed radio-friendly unit shifters. A follow-up set, 'INSOMNIAC' (1995), was another massive seller, although it had to compete with the hordes of equally faceless acts clogging up the charts with similar material. A fifth set, 'NIMROD' (1997), made sure they were still in touch with their fanbase, the tried and tested formula again getting them into the Top 10. The album also spawned a surprise hit single in the shape of a rare ballad, 'TIME OF YOUR LIFE (GOOD RIDDANCE)', geeing the band on to er, express their more feminine side, or at least their less frantic side. With 'WARNING' (2000), GREEN DAY went ahead and exorcised those pop demons which had clearly been haunting them since way back when. By investing their punk-pop formula with a measure of melodic sparkle and a hint of vintage 60's flavour, the 3-chord thumpers had come up with their most consistently listenable album to date. • **Songwriters:** Lyrics; BILLIE JOE, group songs except TIRED OF WAITING FOR YOU (Kinks). • **Trivia:** DIRNT guested on The SCREAMING WEASEL album, 'How to Make Enemies And Irritate People'. BILLIE JOE was also a member of PINHEAD GUNPOWDER, who released an album, 'Jump Salty', plus a few EP's (also for 'Lookout').

Album rating: 39/SMOOTHED OUT SLAPPY HOUR compilation (*5) / KERPLUNK! (*5) / DOOKIE (*7) / INSOMNIAC (*6) / NIMROD (*6) / WARNING (*6) / INTERNATIONAL SUPERHITS compilation (*7) / SHENANIGANS compilation (*6)

BILLIE JOE ARMSTRONG (b.17 Feb'72, San Pablo, Calif.) – vocals, guitar / **MIKE DIRNT** (b. PRITCHARD, 4 May'72) – bass, vocals / **TRE COOL** (b. FRANK EDWIN WRIGHT III, 9 Dec'72, Germany) – drums (ex-LOOKOUTS) repl. JOHN KIFTMEYER who had repl. AL SOBRANTE

			not iss.	Lookout
Apr 89.	(7"ep)	*<LK 17>* **1000 HOURS EP**	-	

– 1000 hours / Dry ice / Only of you / The one I want. *(UK-iss.Dec94; as above)*

| Apr 90. | (lp/c/cd) | *<LO 22/+CS/CD>* **39 / SMOOTH** | - | |

– At the library / Don't leave me / I was there / Disappearing boy / Green day / Going to Pasalacqua / 16 / Road to acceptance / Rest / The judge's daughter / Paper lanterns / Why do you want him? / 409 in your coffeemaker / Knowledge / 1000 hours / Dry ice / Only of you / The one I want / I want to be alone. *<re-iss. Nov91 lp/c/cd; LOOKOUT 22/+CD> (UK-iss.Sep94 as '1,039 SMOOTHED OUT SLAPPY HOURS'; as above) (cd re-iss. Aug97 on 'Epitaph'; 6522-2)*

| Mar 90. | (7"ep) | *<LK 35>* **SLAPPY EP** | - | |

– Paper lanterns / Why do you want him? / 409 in your coffeemaker / Knowledge. *(UK-iss.Sep94; as above)*

| Dec 91. | (lp) | *<LOOKOUT 46>* **KERPLUNK!** | - | |

– 2000 light years away / One for the razorbacks / Welcome to Paradise / Christie Road / Private ale / Dominated love slave / One of my lies / 80 / Android / No one knows / Who wrote Holden Caulfield? / Words I might have ate. *(UK-iss.Sep94 on 'Lookout' lp/cd+=; LOOKOUT 46/+CD)* – Sweet children / Best thing in town / Strangeland / My generation. *(by SWEET CHILDREN and released US 1990 on 'Skene') (cd re-iss. Aug97 on 'Epitaph'; 6517-2)*

			Reprise	Reprise
Feb 94.	(cd/c)	*<(9362 45529-2/-4)>* **DOOKIE**		2

– Burnout / Having a blast / Chump / Longview / Welcome to Paradise / Pulling teeth / Basket case / She / Sassafras roots / When I come around / Coming clean / Emenius sleepus / In the end / F.O.D. *(cd+=)* – (hidden track). *(re-dist.Oct94 on green-lp soon hit UK No.13; 9362 45795-2/-4)*

Jun 94.	(7")	*(W 0247)* **LONGVIEW. / ON THE WAGON**		-
	(10"/cd-s)	*(W 0247 T/CD)* – ('A'side) / Going to Pasalacqua (infatuation) / F.O.D. (live) / Christy Road (live).		
Aug 94.	(7"green/c-s)	*(W 0257/+C)* **BASKET CASE. / TIRED OF WAITING FOR YOU**	55	-
	(cd-s+=)	*(W 0257CD2)* – On the wagon / 409 in your coffeemaker.		
	(cd-s)	*(W 0257CD)* – ('A'side) / Longview (live) / Burnout (live) / 2000 light years away (live).		
Oct 94.	(c-s)	*(W 0269C)* **WELCOME TO PARADISE. / CHUMP (live)**	20	-
	(12"green+=/cd-s+=/cd-s+=)	*(W 0269 T/CD/CDX)* – Emenius sleepus.		
Jan 95.	(7"green/c-s)	*(W 0279/+C)* **BASKET CASE. / 2,000 LIGHT YEARS AWAY (live)**	7	-
	(cd-s+=)	*(W 0279CD)* – Burnout (live) / Longview (live).		
Mar 95.	(7"/c-s)	*(W 0278/+C)* **LONGVIEW. / WELCOME TO PARADISE (live)**	30	-
	(cd-s+=)	*(W 0278CD)* – One of my lies (live).		
May 95.	(7"pic-d/c-s)	*(W 0294/+C)* **WHEN I COME AROUND. / SHE (live)**	27	-
	(cd-s+=)	*(W 0294CD)* – Coming clean (live).		
Sep 95.	(7"red/c-s)	*(W 0320/+C)* **GEEK STINK BREATH. / I WANT TO BE ON T.V.**	16	-
	(cd-s+=)	*(W 0320CD)* – Don't want to fall in love.		
Oct 95.	(cd/c/lp)	*<(9362 46046-2/-4/-1)>* **INSOMNIAC**	8	2

– Armatage Shanks / Brat / Stuck with me / Geek stink breath / No pride / Bab's Uvula who? / 86 / Panic song / Stuart and the Ave. / Brain stew / Jaded / Westbound sign / Tight wad hill / Walking contradiction.

Dec 95.	(7")	*(W 0327X)* **STUCK WITH ME. / WHEN I COME AROUND (live)**	24	-
	(c-s+=)	*(W 0327C)* – Jaded (live).		
	(cd-s)	*(W 0327CD)* – ('A'side) / Dominated love slave (live) / Chump (live).		
Jun 96.	(c-s)	*(W 0339C)* **BRAIN STEW / JADED / TIME OF YOUR LIFE (GOOD RIDDANCE)**	28	-
	(cd-s+=)	*(W 0339CD)* – Do da da.		
	(brain-shaped cd-s++=)	*(W 0339CDX)* – Brain stew (radio).		
Sep 97.	(c-s)	*(W 0424C) <43945>* **HITCHIN' A RIDE / SICK**	25	Jun98
	(cd-s+=)	*(W 0424CD)* – Espionage.		
Oct 97.	(cd/c)	*<(9362 46794-2/-4)>* **NIMROD**	11	10

– Nice guys finish last / Hitchin' a ride / The grouch / Redundant / Scattered / Worry rock / Desensitized / All the time / Platypus (I hate you) / Last ride in / Jinx / Haushinka / Walking alone / Suffocate / Uptight / Take back / King for a day / Good riddance / Prosthetic head.

Jan 98.	(c-s)	*(W 0430C) <43974>* **TIME OF YOUR LIFE (GOOD RIDDANCE) / DESENSITIZED**	11	Jun98
	(cd-s+=)	*(W 0430CD1)* – Rotting.		
	(cd-s)	*(W 0430CD2)* – ('A'side) / Suffocate / You lied.		
Apr 98.	(7")	*(W 0438)* **REDUNDANT. / THE GROUCH (live)**	27	-
	(cd-s+=)	*(W 0438CD1)* – Paper lanterns (live).		
	(cd-s)	*(W 0438CD2)* – ('A'side) / Reject all American (live) / She (live).		
Sep 00.	(c-s)	*(W 532C)* **MINORITY / BRAT (live)**	18	-
	(cd-s+=)	*(W 532CD)* – 86 (live).		
	(7"ep iss.Nov00 on 'Adeline'+=; ADELINE 013) – Jackass.				
Oct 00.	(cd/c)	*<(9362 48030-2/-4)>* **WARNING**	4	4

– Warning / Blood, sex and booze / Church on Sunday / Fashion victim / Castaway / Misery / Deadbeat holiday / Hold on / Jackass / Waiting / Minority / Macy's day parade. *<US version+=; 47857>* – Brat (live) / 86 (live). *<(lp; 9362 47613-1)> <US lp-iss.Oct00 on 'Adeline'; ADELINE 012>*

Dec 00.	(7"orange)	*(W 548)* **WARNING. / SUFFOCATE**	27	-
	(c-s+=/cd-s+=)	*(W 548 C/CD2)* – Outsider. *(7"iss.Feb01 on 'Adeline'; ADELINE 014)*		
	(cd-s)	*(W 548CD1)* – ('A'side) / Scumbag / I don't want to know if you are lonely.		
Oct 01.	(cd-s)	*(W 570CD)* **WAITING / MACY'S DAY PARADE / BASKET CASE**	34	-
	(cd-s)	*(W 570CDX)* – ('A'side) / She / F.O.D.		

Nov 01. (cd/c) <(9362 48145-2/-4)> **INTERNATIONAL SUPERHITS** (compilation) [15] [40]
– Maria / Poprocks and coke / Longview / Welcome to paradise / Basket case / When I come around / She / J.A.R. (Jason Andrew Relva) / Geek stink breath / Brain stew / Jaded / Walking contradiction / Stuck with me / Hitchin' a ride / Good riddance (time of your life) / Redundant / Nice guys finish last / Macy's day parade.

Jul 02. (cd/c) <(9362 48208-2/-4)> **SHENANIGANS** (B-sides, etc, compilation) [32] [27]
– Suffocate / Desensitized / You lied / Outsider / Don't wanna fall in love / Espionage / I want to be on T.V. / Scumbag / Tired of waiting for you / Sick of me / Rotting / Do da da / On the wagon / Ha ha you're dead.

GREENHORNES

Formed: Cincinnati, Ohio, USA ... 1998, by CRAIG FOX, BRIAN OLIVE, PATRICK KEELER, JACK LAWRENCE and keyboardist JARED McKINNEY. This R&B, quasi 'STONES-esque blues rockers, have been frequently linked with the Detroit garage rock scene, although originally hailing from the midwest. They issued their first album on 'Prince' records, 'GUN FOR YOU' (1999), and have since become one of America's indie garage rock darlings. Their debut, featuring FOX (formerly of the sinister NEVADA DEATH BAND) and his roughed-out vocals, coupled with that of the band's scuzzy KINKS-esque power-chord blues rock, enticed 'Telstar' (US) records to give them a chance. In confirmation of their 60's garage roots, The GREENHORNES' eponymous sophomore set (2001) included a plethora of cover songs – The Animals' 'INSIDE – LOOKING OUT' and The Spencer David Group's 'HIGH TIME BABY' just to mention two – plus a host of original garage blues stonkers like 'SHADOW OF GRIEF' and the aggressive testosterone led 'LIES'. The album prompted 'Sopranos' actor and national rock DJ, STEVIE VAN ZANDT, to invite the band onto the hugely popular gangster show for a brief cameo appearance, after which their cult status soared and the group found a home in the busy musical underground of the Detroit garage rock scene. This is where they recorded their third LP, 'DUAL MONO' (2002), a swinging country rock'n'roll set (think 'STONES 'Let It Bleed' or an early stetson-clad RAY DAVIES) that saw guitarist ERIC STEIN replace OLIVE and McKINNEY, after a supposed internal bust-up. Now championed by the US and British (surprise, surprise) press, the group embarked on a world tour and recruited part-time vocalist HOLLY GOLIGHTLY along the way. • **Covered:** WAKE ME, SHAKE ME (Blues Project) / LOST WOMAN (Yardbirds) / etc.

Album rating: GUN FOR YOU (*5) / THE GREENHORNES (*7) / DUAL MONO (*7)

CRAIG FOX – vocals / **BRIAN OLIVE** – guitar / **PATRICK KEELER** – drums / **JACK LAWRENCE** – bass / **JARED McKINNEY** – organ, vocals

                                              not iss. Deary Me
1998. (7") <DM 0012> **THE END OF THE NIGHT. / NO MORE**
                                              not iss. Prince
1999. (cd) <PRD 4299> **GUN FOR YOU**
– The end of the night / No more / Good times / Wake me, shake me / Hold me / My baby's alright / No friend of mine / Show me love / So cold / What a fool / Going to the river / I've been down.

                                              not iss. Italy
2000. (7") <IR 009> **STAYED HOME LAST NIGHT. / SHADOW OF GRIEF**
                                            Telstar Telstar
Sep 01. (lp/cd) <(TSR 042/+CD)> **THE GREENHORNES**   Mar01
– Can't stand it / Shadow of grief / Stay away girl / Inside looking out / It's my soul / Let me be / Lies / Nobody loves you / Lonely feeling / High time baby / Shame and misery / Can't you see.

    ERIC STEIN – guitar; repl. OLIVE + McKINNEY
Nov 02. (cd/lp) <(TR 045 CD/LP)> **DUAL MONO**   Oct02
– Satisfy my mind / The way it's meant to be / Three faint calls / It returns / Hard times / Too much sorrow / You'll be sorry / There is an end / It's not real / Don't come running to me / Pigtails and kneesocks / Gonna get me someone.

GRENADINE
(see under ⇒ UNREST; 80's section)

GRIFTERS

Formed: Memphis, Tennessee, USA ... 1990 out of A BAND CALLED BUD by DAVE SHOUSE, SCOTT TAYLOR and TRIPP LAMKINS, who were joined by STAN GALLIMORE after their radical name change. Debuting with the 'DISFIGUREHEAD' EP, these lo-fi noise terrorists differed from peers like ROYAL TRUX in that their sound was mired in the roots music of the American south. Following another breakneck blast of alt-rock distortion, 'SO HAPPY TOGETHER' (1992), The GRIFTERS took their feet off the accelerator for 1993's 'ONE SOCK MISSING'. Issued on their own 'Shangri-La' imprint, the record drew comparisons with a more extreme 'Stones circa 'Exile On ...'. A further couple of low-key releases (including 'CRAPPIN' YOU NEGATIVE' and the mini-set 'EUREKA') preceded a prestigious signing to 'Sub Pop', taking the time to polish up their sound without losing the rough hewn charm on 1996's 'AIN'T MY LOOKOUT'. A follow-up set, 'FULL BLOWN POSSESSION' (1997), saw them once again put down'n'dirty rock'n'roll through the lo-fi shredder. While TAYLOR moonlighted with his combo, HOT MONKEY, DAVID SHOUSE got his THOSE BASTARD SOULS project underway and recorded the almost solo effort '21st CENTURY CHEMICAL' (1996). Intentionally a record that couldn't fit on any GRIFTERS albums, '21st ...' led SHOUSE on to a support slot with SEBADOH, where he recruited MATT FIELD (former RED RED MEAT), JOAN WASSER and KEVIN MARCH (both formerly of The DAMBUILDERS) and FLAMING LIPS keyboardist STEVEN DROZD as a permanent live combo. Guitarist MICHAEL TIGHE (a musician in JEFF BUCKLEY's band), joined after the death of the aforementioned soul singer. Touched by the loss of BUCKLEY, the new formated 'BASTARD SOULS released 'DEBT AND DEPARTURE' (1999) through Virgin offshoot label, 'V2'. A "spiritual" record indeed, the set could be compared to the stark imagery of GIANT SAND or HAZELDINE; hushed guitars and tumbleweeds graced some of the album's quieter moments, example being ballad 'THE LAST THING ...', while SHOUSE and Co managed to uphold the drunken rock'n'roll trait with 'TRAIN FROM TERMINAL BOREDOM', which was so ablaze with passion you'd have to spit on it!

Album rating: SO HAPPY TOGETHER (*6) / ONE SOCK MISSING (*8) / CRAPPIN' YOU NEGATIVE (*7) / EUREKA mini (*5) / AIN'T MY LOOKOUT (*6) / FULL BLOWN POSSESSION (*6) / Hot Monkey: MORE THAN LAZY (*5) / Those Bastard Souls: 21st CENTURY CHEMICAL (*6) / DEBT & DEPARTURE (*7)

DAVE SHOUSE – guitar, vocals / **SCOTT TAYLOR** – vocals, guitar / **TRIPP LAMKINS** – bass
                                              not iss. Doink
1988. (c; as A BAND CALLED BUD) <none> **DAD**

    —— split a 7"flexi, 'SHARK' with The MARTINI AGE for 'Kreature Comforts'
    —— added **STAN GALLIMORE** – drums
Jan 90. (7"ep) <doink 003> **DISFIGUREHEAD EP**
– Disfigurehead / Need you / Reason enough / How long?
Aug 90. (7"ep) <D 1023> **THE KINGDOM OF JONES EP**
– Encrusted / Another song / Snake oil / Daydream riot.
                                            Sonic Noise Sonic Noise
Apr 92. (cd/lp) <(SON 002-2/-1)> **SO HAPPY TOGETHER**
– Dry bones / Hate / Tot / Clot / The want / Oar. (cd+=) – Love explosion / 10,000 / Meanwhile / Wreck.
                                            not iss. Shangri-la
Jun 92. (7"m) <shangi-la 002> **SODA POP. / DIVINE / SHE BLOWS BLASTS OF STATIC**
Dec 92. (7") <shangri-la 003> **COROLLA HOIST. / THUMBNAIL SKETCH**
                                            Southern Shangri-La
Jun 93. (cd/c/lp) (18511-2/-4/-1) <shangri-la 004> **ONE SOCK MISSING**   Apr93
– Bummer / She blows blasts of static / Shark / Teenage Jesus / 'Side / #1 / Tupelo moan / Wonder / Corolla hoist / Encrusted / The casual years / Sain / Just passing out. (cd+=) – I arise.
Aug 93. (7") <darla 01> **HOLMES. / JUNKIE BLOOD**
(above issued on 'Darla') (below issued on 'Simple Machines')
Oct 93. (7") <SMWH 10> **UNDER THE GROUND. / (other by Crain)**
Mar 94. (7") <shangri-la 006> **BRONZE CAST. / CONFIDENTIAL**
May 94. (cd/lp) (18519-2/-1) <shangri-la 008> **CRAPPIN' YOU NEGATIVE**
– Rats / Maps of the sun / Dead already / Black fuel incinerator / Skin man palace / Arizona / Felt-tipped over / Holmes / Get outta that spaceship and fight like a man / Piddlebach / Bronze cast / Junkie blood / Here comes Larry / Cinnamon.
                                            not iss. Cherry Smash
1994. (7") <CS 103> **DILDOZER. / (other by Fluffy Kitty)**
    —— in '94, one track 'I'M DRUNK' appeared on a GUIDED BY VOICES single
                                            Sub Pop Sub Pop
Nov 94. (7") <SP 278> **QUEEN OF THE TABLE WATERS. / RETURN TO CINDER**
                                            not iss. Derivative
Apr 95. (7") <018> **STREAM. / COAT OF SILENCE**
                                            not iss. Sonic Noise
May 95. (10"ep/cd-ep) <SON 013> **THE EUREKA E.P.**
– Eureka IV / His Jesus song / Slow day for the cleaner / Whatever happened to Felix Cole / Founder's day parade / Banjo / X-ray hip.
                                            Sub Pop Sub Pop
Feb 96. (7") <SP 339> **LAST MAN ALIVE. / PARTING SHOT**
Feb 96. (lp/cd) <(SP/+CD 327)> **AIN'T MY LOOKOUT**
– Covered with flies / Parting shot / Mysterious friends / Boho – Alt / Pretty notes / Day shift / The last man alive / My apology / Straight time / Return to cinder / Give yourself to me / Fixed in the sky / Radio city suicide.
Feb 96. (12"/cd-s) (ALPHA 12/CD 001) **AIN'T MY LOOKOUT. /**
(above issued on 'Alpha-Sub Pop') (below on 'Super 8')
Apr 96. (7") <frame 08> **SLIPKNOT. / SUBTERRANEAN DEATH RIDE BLUES**
Aug 97. (7") <SP 382> **WICKEDTHING. / ORGAN GRINDER**
Nov 97. (lp/cd) <(SP/+CD 402)> **FULL BLOWN POSSESSION**   Sep97
– Re-entry blues / Fireflies / Spaced out / Centuries / Sweetest thing / Happy / Wickedthing / Blood thirsty lovers / Hours / You be the stranger / Cigarette / Contact me now.

– compilations, etc. –

Jan 97. (10"m-lp/m-cd) Shangri-la; <025> **THE KINGDOM OF JONES**
– (DISFIGUREHEAD + THE KINGDOM OF JONES)

HOT MONKEY

    —— **SCOTT TAYLOR** and Co.
                                            not iss. Shangri-la
Apr 94. (7") <Shangri-la 005> **SHARK. / DEPENDS**
Aug 94. (7") <Shangri-la 007> **SAIN. / (other by Linda Heck)**
1995. (10"ep) <Shangri-la 009> **LAZY**
Jan 96. (m-cd) <2> **LION**
– Blue moon / Arizona / Another song / For you / Bringdown / Dogshit / Salt lick / Sew / Nothin' at all / Green can o' peas / Baby loves on me / Need you / X-ray spex.
(above issued on 'Personal Favorite')

GRIFTERS (cont)

Sep 96. (cd) <Shangri-la 020> **MORE THAN LAZY**
– Favors / That certain thing / 4 eyes / Steam / Wheel / Sometimes / Monty Carlo / Hide-n-seek / Wait up / Dandy lion / Other ideas / Strap / Sooner / I won't tell / Meat truck / Hours / Think I love you / Dinosaur angel / Sain.

THOSE BASTARD SOULS

DAVID SHOUSE – vocals, guitar

	Darla	Darla
Sep 97. (lp/cd) <(DRL 011/+CD)> **20th CENTURY CHEMICAL**		Nov96

– Introducing Those Bastard Souls / These things will slay you every time / Curious state I'm in / Subterranean death ride blues (pt.2) / Train from terminal boredom / !#*@#*! / Dirty looks / Good luck split town today / Remembering Sophie Rhodes / What am I gonna do now / Top ten zen offenders / 21st century chemical.

—— added **MATT FIELD** – bass (ex-RED RED MEAT) / **JOAN WASSER** – violin (ex-DAMBUILDERS) / **MICHAEL TIGHE** – guitar (ex-JEFF BUCKLEY) / **KEVIN MARCH** – drums (ex-DAMBUILDERS) / 6th member **STEVEN DROZD** – keyboards (of FLAMING LIPS) also played on below

	V2	V2
Jan 00. (cd) (VVR 100759-2) <27051> **DEBT & DEPARTURE**		Jul99

– The last thing I ever wanted was to show up and blow your mind / Telegram / Has anybody seen her / Train from terminal boredom / Debt & departure / Up to you / Curious state / The wake of your flood / Remembering Sophie Rhodes / Dirty looks / Spaced out.

GRIMBLE GRUMBLE

Formed: Chicago, Illinois, USA . . . 1995 by CHRISTINE, SALEEM, MIKE J., RUBEN RIOS and MIKE P. Naming themselves after a character in an early PINK FLOYD track, 'The Gnome', GRIMBLE GRUMBLE released their debut 45, 'SECOND MIND' (a split with AZUSA PLANE), in 1996. A year later, the wigged-out psychedelic 5-piece – fuse SPACEMEN 3 and MY BLOODY VALENTINE – delivered their self-titled follow-up which opened with 'ODYSSEY AND ORACLE', a track also featured on their eponymous first LP for 'Won't Go Flat' records in '98. GG continued to work from the studio – with various sets, etc. 'UFO'S AND VISITATIONS' (1999) and '. . .I ONCE HAD A DREAM' (1999) – right up to their split at the start of the millennium.

Album rating: GRIMBLE GRUMBLE (*5)

CHRISTINE – vocals, bass / **REUBEN RIOS** – guitar, Moog synthesizer, noises / **MIKE J.** – guitar / **SALEEM** – guitar / **MIKE P.** – percussion

	Enraptured	Enraptured
Nov 96. (7") <(RAPT45 06)> **SECOND MIND. / (other track by Azusa Plane)**		
	Burnt Hair	Burnt Hair
May 97. (10"ep) <(SINGE 013)> **GRIMBLE GRUMBLE EP**		

– Odyssey and oracle / Gossip, numbers and theories / The only point of entry.

	Won't Go Flat	Bouncing
Mar 98. (cd)(lp) (GS 007CD)(ARE 1) <Head-14> **GRIMBLE GRUMBLE**		1999

– The only point of entry / Odyssey and oracle / Gossip, numbers and theories / Introduction / Let it take you were it will / Harmonic transmission / Blistered / Ubermorgenfallsdiesonnescheint (cup up #5).

	Amberley	not iss.
May 98. (7") (AMY 002) **FUCKED IN THE HEAD. / RETURN**		
	not iss.	Ochre
1999. (cd) **UFO'S AND VISITATIONS**		
	Audio Information Phenomenon	Audio Information Phenomenon
Apr 99. (7") <(AIP 009)> **SENSELESS. / LEFT OUT**		
	not iss.	Rocket Racer
1999. (cd) **. . . I ONCE HAD A DREAM**	–	
	not iss.	Bouncing Corp.
2000. (7") <splash 14> **SAD. / THE ONLY POINT OF ENTRY**	–	

—— disbanded after above

David GRUBBS
(see under ⇒ SQUIRREL BAIT; 80's section)

GUITAR WOLF

Formed: Tokyo, Japan . . . late 80's by SEIJI, BILLY and drummer TORU. In the beginning their low-down dirty punk rock never reached further than the coasts of Japan. But as word of mouth spread the more intrigued American labels became aware of this cult phenomenon. 'WOLF ROCK' and 'KUNG FU RAMONE' (their two Japanese imports from the mid 90's) were finally released by US distributers following the band's live notoriety. After a riotous in-store performance at an anonymous record shop in New York, the talent scouts from 'Matador' duly signed the band to their imprint. 'MISSILE ME!' (1996) was the first GUITAR WOLF album ready for international unveiling. Trashy guitars and Japanese vocals, screaming out from underneath the noise, could be heard on this unusual release. The following two sets, 'PLANET OF THE WOLVES' (1997) and 'JET GENERATION' (1999) sounded no different. The band played like a spunky group of teenagers who had just received their first instruments, cranked up the distortion and let it rip . . . and in the process, not really caring about the consequences. • **Covers:** (I CAN'T GET NO) SATISFACTION (Rolling Stones) / MOTORCYCLE LEATHER BOY (Oblivians) / LET'S GET HURT (Teengenerate) / RUMBLE (Link Wray) / SOMETHIN' ELSE + SUMMERTIME BLUES (Eddie Cochran).

Album rating: WOLF ROCK (*5) / KUNG FU RAMONE (*5) / MISSILE ME! (*5) / PLANET OF THE WOLVES (*5) / JET GENERATION (*7)

SEIJI – guitar / **BILLY** – bass / **TORU** – drums

—— issued 2 Japanese-only albums

	Bag Of Hammers	not iss.
Oct 94. (7") (BAG 025) **SOMETHIN' ELSE**		–

– (I can't get no) Satisfaction / Thunders guitar.

	not iss.	Goner
1995. (lp) <1 GONE> **WOLF ROCK**	–	

(UK-iss.Aug98; same)

| 1995. (lp) **KUNG FU RAMONE** | – | |

	Matador	Matador
Nov 96. (cd/lp) <(OLE 219-2/-1)> **MISSILE ME!**		

– Missile me! / Hurricane rock / Kung Fu Ramone culmination tactic / Can nana fever / Midnight violence rock'n'roll / Link wray man / Guitar star / Racing rock / Jet rock'n'roll / Devil stomp / Jet blues / Venus drive.

Sep 97. (7") (OLE 271) **KAWASAKI Z II 750 ROCK'N'ROLL. / MIDNIGHT VIOLENCE ROCK'N'ROLL**

| Jun 98. (cd/lp) <(OLE 248-2/-1)> **PLANET OF THE WOLVES** | | Oct97 |

– Kawasaki Z II 750 rock'n'roll / Planet of the wolves / Invader ace / Motorcycle leather boy / Far East man / Wild zero / Planet heart / Energy Joe / Jett love / (I can't get no) Satisfaction / Kung Fu Ramone's passion / Let's get hurt / All through the night Buttobase!! / Rumble.

Jun 99. (cd/lp) <(OLE 331-2/-1)> **JET GENERATION**
– Jet generation / Fujiyama attack / Kaminari one / Kung Fu Ramone / Teenage U.F.O. / Cosmic space girl / Roaring blood / Gakulan rider / Refrigerator zero / Shimane slim / Cyborg kids / Summertime blues / Can nana fever.

GUMBALL
(see under ⇒ B.A.L.L.; see 80's section)

GUPPYBOY (see under ⇒ ESSEX GREEN)

GUSTER

Formed: West Somerville, Massachusetts, USA . . . 1992 (originally as GUS) by RYAN MILLER, ADAM GARDNER and BRIAN ROSENWORCEL. Formed: Boston, USA . . . 1992, when RYAN MILLER met ADAM GARDENER, subsequently recruiting BRIAN ROSENWORCEL while all three were studying at Tufts University. They began experimenting with styles of music that had been prominent influences, but managed to secure the traits of traditional blue grass pop before embarking on a small college tour. They issued the debut independent album 'PARACHUTE' (1995) to much critical acclaim, as the Boston Globe cited the release as the "best debut album of 1995". Word was initially spreading about this sub-PRESIDENTS OF THE USA across the Internet and through gratified crowds (who had witnessed GUSTER's bizarre and infamous on-stage antics). The band adopted an acoustic pop vibe with not much variation: producer MIKE DENNEEN brought the flavours of GUSTER's two-guitars-one-drum approach, adding subtle bass lines to match MILLER's infectious choruses. Their sophomore set, 'GOLDFLY', was issued in 1997, at the height of the band's popularity. They were nominated for a Best Live Act award at the Boston Music Awards, and had a strange cult devoted to promoting their material called "The Guster Reps". The trio signed to 'Sire' records in 1998 for the release of the disappointing, major label debut 'GONE AND LOST FOREVER', which had its quirky moments of humorous folly, but on the whole remained banal; 'Sire' records also re-released their unflinching 'GOLDFLY'. 2003 should a see a long-awaited comeback set 'KEEP IT TOGETHER'.

Album rating: PARACHUTE (*5) / GOLDFLY (*6) / LOST AND GONE FOREVER (*5)

RYAN MILLER – vocals, guitar / **ADAM GARDNER** – vocals, guitar / **BRIAN ROSENWORCEL** – percussion / + a plethora of session people

	not iss.	Aware
Nov 95. (cd) <101> **PARACHUTE**	–	

– Happiness in NYC / Baby hold on / Laigh I could learn to love / Easy tonight / Give back yourself / How I know / Ironsides / Matter / Breathe / Movie star mom / Letterbox / Never closer than that / Down / Clear day / Superstar / Goin' our way / Juainy.

Mar 97. (cd) <107> **GOLDFLY**
– Great escape / Demons / Perfect / Airport song / Medicine / X-ray eyes / Grin / Getting even / Bury me / Rocket ship. <re-iss. 1998 on 'Hybrid'; 20006>

	not iss.	Sire
Sep 99. (cd) <31064> **LOST AND GONE FOREVER**	–	

– What you wish for / Barrel of a gun / Either way / Fa fa / I spy / Center of attention / All the way up to Heaven / Happier / So long / Two points for honesty / Reiny day.

GUTTERBALL
(see under ⇒ DREAM SYNDICATE; in 80's section)

GUV'NER

Formed: New York City, New York, USA . . . 1993 by songwriting live-in couple, CHARLES GANSA and his Washington-born missus CHRISTINA 'PUMPKIN' WENTZEL. Notorious for their dislike of British food and culture, the lo-fi, acoustically-awashed GUV'NER came over as the bastard love child of YO LA TENGO and SONIC YOUTH. On the subject of the latter, GANSA and doe-eyed lover WENTZEL impressed THURSTON MOORE so

much that he financed the band's debut album, 'HARD FOR MEASY FOR YOU' in 1994 and released it through his 'Ecstatic Peace' imprint. Recruiting drummer JAMIE LAWRENCE, the ensemble took a little time over their follow up, 'THE HUNT' (1996). With DANNY TUNICK as new sticksman, a more clearly developed sound was evident on this beautiful lo-fi (JULIE CAFRITZ and DON FLEMING-produced) sophomore effort, which still had a sting in its tail due to it's ever so occasional guitar break or loud drum. A shift to 'Merge' helped the cult New Yorkers gain publicity and reverence for their third set, 'SPECTRAL WORSHIP', which was released the following year.
• **Covered:** HELP ME (Joni Mitchell).

Album rating: HARD FOR MEASY FOR YOU (*6) / THE HUNT (*6) / SPECTRAL WORSHIP (*6)

CHRISTINA 'PUMPKIN' WENTZEL – vocals, bass / **CHARLES GANSA** – vocals, guitar / with on session **JAMIE LAWRENCE** – drums

			not iss.	Gap Year
1993.	(7") <19467> **SHE DOG STOMP. / THESPIAN GIRL**		– Wiiija	– Ecstatic Peace
Nov 94.	(cd/lp) (WIJ 39 CD/V) <45> **HARD FOR MEASY FOR YOU**			
	– Drummer want-ad / No big deal / Red velvet chair / Little bitch on the phone / Bridge under water / Almond roca / Making headlines / Go to sleep / Wild couple / Touch wood / Amplitudem. (cd+=) – I will get you / Thespian girl / She dog stop.			
			Wiiija	Merge
Oct 94.	(7"ep) (WIJ 38) **CURRY FAVOR EP**			–
	– Making headlines / I will get you / Thespian girl / She dog stop.			

– **MICHAEL ROHATYN** – drums, co-producer; repl. JAMIE
Feb 95. (7"ep) (WIJ 044V) <MRG 82> **KNIGHT MOVES EP**
 – Jousters do it knightly / Baby's way cruel / Cameo.

– **DANNY TUNICK** – drums; repl. MICHAEL
Jul 96. (cd-ep) <MRG 112> **BREAK A PROMISE / ME IN SUN / LUCKY LADYBUG** – –
Aug 96. (cd/10"lp) (WIJ CD/LP 57) <MRG 109> **THE HUNT** Jun96
 – Motorcycle man / Stone's throw / She's evil / Nazarene / Your majesty / Tom tom / Break a promise / Feet on wood / Southern baptist w/ sparklers / Leave me be / Rockbending / Ghost of your controllership.
Aug 96. (7") (WIJ 59) **BREAK A PROMISE. / LUCKY LADYBUG** –
Dec 96. (7") (WIJ 62) **SHE'S EVIL. /** –
Jun 97. (m-cd/m-lp) (FISHNO 2 CD/LP) **IN THE FISHTANK** –
 – Concord jets / Help me / Now is not the time to love / Whose eyes? / Jungle bells / You lie. <US-iss.May99; same as US>
 (above issued on 'Konkurrent')

		Merge	Merge
Aug 98.	(cd) <(MRG 142CD)> **SPECTRAL WORSHIP**		
	– Spectral worship / Chereza / Love the lamp / Wounded birds and vampires own the edge / Anaphelact / Coozwax / Jealous girl / Time rarely stands still / Anything / Difficulty in openness / Someone else / Spectral workshop / Welcome.		

GYRES

Formed: Blantyre, Lanarkshire, Scotland ... 1995 by brothers ANDY and PAUL McLINDEN, together with PETER LYONS, MARK McGILL and PAT FLAHERTY. Blessed with opportunities that many (more deserving) young Scottish bands would jump at, The GYRES were lucky enough to be docu-filmed during their gestation period. They were also jammy enough to land an arena support slot to BOWIE, promoting their first three singles, 'BREAK', 'POP COP' and 'ARE YOU READY', in style. Released on the 'Sugar' label, the latter two tracks hit the Top 75, although a long lay-off meant these OASIS clones failed to break through with the 'FIRST' (1997) album.

Album rating: FIRST (*3)

ANDY McLINDEN – vocals / **PAUL McLINDEN** – guitar, vocals / **PETER LYONS** – guitar, vocals / **MARK McGILL** – bass / **PAT FLAHERTY** – drums

		Sugar	not iss.
Jan 96.	(7") (SUGA 7V) **BREAK. /**	–	–
Apr 96.	(7"/c-s) (SUGA 9 V/T) **POP COP. / A FOOL TO FOLLOW**	71	–
	(cd-s+=) (SUGA 9CD) – Sooner or later.		
Jun 96.	(7"/c-s) (SUGA 11/+T) **ARE YOU READY. / A MILLION MILES**	71	–
	(cd-s+=) (SUGA 11CD) – Top of the tree.		
Jul 97.	(7") (SUGA 17V) **SLY. / CONTACT DAY**		–
	(7") (SUGA 17VX) – ('A'side) / Sleepless nights.		
	(cd-s++=) (SUGA 17CD) – (all 3 tracks).		
Aug 97.	(cd/lp) (SUGA 16 CD/LP) **FIRST**		–
	– Sly / Hi-fi driving / Break / A million miles / Hooligan / Are you ready? / Falling down / On a roll / I'm alright / Pop cop / Downtime.		

– split after poor response to the above set

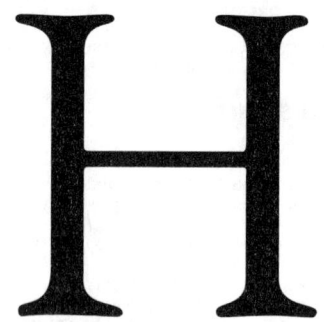

Petra HADEN (see under ⇒ that dog.)

Neil Michael HAGERTY (see under ⇒ ROYAL TRUX)

Luke HAINES (see under ⇒ AUTEURS)

HAIR & SKIN TRADING CO.

Formed: London, England ... 1991 by LOOP members, NEIL McKAY and JOHN WILLS, originally as a side project. Recruiting NIGEL WEBB, they went full-time upon the demise of LOOP and signed a deal with 'Situation 2'. Setting to work with producer ROLI MOSIMANN (ex-SWANS), they delivered their debut set, 'JO IN NINE G HELL' (1992), an out of control CAN meets FAUST affair carrying on in the darkly experimental tradition of their former outfit. The following year, the trio moved upstairs to 'Beggars Banquet', although the resulting album, 'OVER VALENCE' (1993), was met with slightly less enthusiasm. Retreating to lick their wounds after being dropped by the label, HAIR & SKIN TRADING CO. returned after an extended musical manicure with an outtakes album, 'PSYCHEDELIC MUSIQUE' (1995).

Album rating: JO IN NINE G HELL (*5) / OVER VALENCE (*5) / PSYCHEDELIC MUSIQUE collection (*5)

NEIL McKAY – bass (ex-LOOP) / **JOHN WILLS** – drums (ex-LOOP, ex-SERVANTS) / **NIGEL WEBB** – guitar

		Situation 2	Beggars Banquet
Apr 92.	(12"ep/cd-ep) **GROUND ZERO EP**		–
Apr 92.	(cd) (SITU 40CD) <66136> **JO IN NINE G HELL**		Dec92
	– Elevenate / Flat truck / Torque / Monkies / Kak / Where's gala / Ground zero / $1000 pledge / The final nail / Pipeline.		

		Beggars Banquet	Atlantic
Jul 93.	(10"ep/cd-ep) (BBQ 16 T/CD) <95983> **GO ROUND / DEEPS. / A MINE / SYMBOLS**		Oct93
Sep 93.	(cd) (BBQCD 141) <92324> **OVER VALENCE**		
	– On again off again / Go round / K-funk / Loa / F.D.M. / Machine gun / Take control / Carrier wave / Levers / Lock-up / Take control II / Sub surface / Static.		
Oct 93.	(12"ep/cd-ep) (BBQ 23 T/CD) **LOA**		–
	– Bath song / Snowballs.		

– had already disbanded

– **compilations, etc.** –

May 95. (cd/lp) Freek; (<FRR 11 CD/LP>) **PSYCHEDELIC MUSIQUE (LAVA SURF KUNST)** (outtakes from '92-'93)

HALF-HANDED CLOUD

Formed: Knoxville, Tennessee, USA ... 2000 as the writing and recording name of ex-WOOKIEBACK member, JOHN RINGHOFER. An eccentric composer, H-HC's blend of indie pop and multi-instrumentals, made for a good listen, especially if you had Attention Deficit Disorder, as the majority of his tunes clocked in at around a minute. His extreme alternative stance placed him near the musical collective's, 'Elephant 6', output in its avant-garde stance, although the christian sub-text of his music, made him closer to the likes of DANIELSON FAMILE, whose line-up also helped out on his LPs. H-HC's debut album, 'LEARNING ABOUT YOUR SCALE' (2001), which included 25 songs in the same amount of minutes, showcased RINGHOFER's ability as a pop tunesmith; his willingness to experiment with a large number of instruments was also apparent. This vein was tapped again, with not too much change, on his sophomore full-length set, 'WE HAVEN'T JUST BEEN TOLD, WE HAVE BEEN LOVED' (2002), although here RINGHOFER expanded his transitory aesthetic style a little, cramming 24 tracks into just over half an hour.

Album rating: LEARNING ABOUT YOUR SCALE mini (*6) / WE HAVEN'T JUST BEEN TOLD, WE HAVE BEEN LOVED (*7)

JOHN RINGHOFER – vocals, multi-instruments

HALF-HANDED CLOUD (cont)	THE GREAT INDIE DISCOGRAPHY	The 1990s

Oct 01. (m-cd) <SF 004> **LEARNING ABOUT YOUR SCALE** — Sounds Familyre / Sounds Familyre
 – Worlds in speech, now in reach! / Let's build a planet / Look how we made these people / Eating bad-bad fruit / Serpent head crushed / Baby moon / If before we were coughing / Can't even breathe on my own two feet / Hope for clean theme / Stew burnt-burn / Don't want to be dirty / Make us clean / Put a new life in me / Rewire my desire / We must be ploughed-up / So busted before your righteous throne / Tanning beds to shine your love / Holy pouch shoe guidance / Make me all petered-out / Three to guide us where we've never been / Three to guide us where we've never been / Three to guide us where we've never been / The body binds us / Secret Christ costume / To love like the father and son love each other.

—— next with **DAVID SMITH** – snare drums / **SUFJAN STEVENS**

Oct 02. (cd) <(SF 008)> **WE HAVEN'T JUST BEEN TOLD, WE HAVE BEEN LOVED**
 – In holy pursuit / One song in seven rests: Tuck us in, father – Our first full day was spent in rest – Running late for bed – That you may be gracious – There remains a rest – I got a-rested – Work isn't what it seemed to be / These crowns we wear / Hey advocate / Pressing into it / I'm the blinder / So-so sorry teacher / We don't know how it grows / Worry-in the waves / Sailing the veil-boat / We are not orphaned / Those who are saved say, "I'm lost" / Dear John / Samuel sleeps where the ark lays / We're very greatly loved / Even the sparrow'd be arrowed / Drowning chariot / Baldy knees.

HALF STRING

Formed: Arizona, USA ... 1991 by frontman BRANDON CAPPS, along with MATT (guitar), KIMBER (drums) and TIM (bass). HALF STRING's guitar-led dream-pop sound owes much to early-mid '90s British shoegazers like RIDE and MY BLOODY VALENTINE (as did many alternative bands to emerge from Arizona). A 1995 compilation, 'ECLIPSE OVAL HUE', featured their first three EP's, including stand-out track 'HUE'. Their debut album, 'A FASCINATION WITH HEIGHTS' (released in 1996), maintained their dream-pop orientation, although remaining, like the sound of contemporaries OCEAN BLUE, distinctly American.

Album rating: ECLIPSE OVAL HUE collection (*6) / A FASCINATION WITH HEIGHTS (*6)

BRANDON CAPPS – vocals, guitar / **MATT** – guitar / **TIM** – bass / **KIMBER** – drums

 not iss. / Independent Project

Dec 93. (7"ep) <IP 042> **ECLIPSE**
 – Eclipse / Maps for sleep / Arc-fold.
Jul 94. (7") <IP 047 – TX 001> **OVAL. / SUN LESS SEA**
Sep 94. (cd-ep) <IP 048CD> **TRIPPED UP BREATHING**
 – Evergreen / Quiet like seeds / Slipknot / Brief as photographs.
Dec 95. (cd-ep) <IP 52> **ECLIPSE OVAL HUE** (compilation)
 – Hue / Oval / Sun less sea / Pelican / Slow engine kill over / Eclipse / Maps for sleep / Arc-fold.
Oct 96. (cd) <IP 57> **A FASCINATION WITH HEIGHTS**
 – Shell life / Backstroke / Hurrah? / (...) / Departures / A fascination with heights / Momentum / Lolligag / The apathy parade / Numbers and fingers.

—— split early in 1997

Toni HALLIDAY (see under ⇒ CURVE)

HALO BENDERS
(see under ⇒ BEAT HAPPENING; see 80's section)

HALO BIT (see under ⇒ SMALL FACTORY)

Neil HALSTEAD (see under ⇒ SLOWDIVE)

HAMFISTED (see under ⇒ SPARE SNARE)

HANDSOME FAMILY

Formed: Chicago, Illinois, USA ... 1993 by songwriter BRETT SPARKS, his wife and co-conspirator RENNIE SPARKS plus third bespectacled member, drummer MIKE WERNER. The husband and wife team were the Gomez and Morticia (or even a distorted, updated version of TIMBUK 3!) to the GEORGE JONES and TAMMY WYNETTE of classic Nashville, although BRETT and RENNIE's sound was, well ... er ... miles apart. Born of acute personal difficulties, The HANDSOME FAMILY's music set against a background of strife; BRETT suffered a mental breakdown attempting to write his own bible!, while RENNIE was the "school freak" who immersed herself in literature (Greek classic, 'The Iliad', is apparently her favourite). From the onset, the trio toured extensively promoting their early releases, 'ODESSA' (1995), 'MILK AND SCISSORS' (1996) and foreign mini-set 'INVISIBLE HANDS' (1997), dark country tales and lifesize plastic animals unsettling audiences in both North America and Europe. Initially aided by co-producer DAVE TRUMFIO, the band of renegade "true country" folk were augmented on the aforesaid releases by studio helpers, et all. Recorded on collaborator JEFF TWEEDY's (WILCO/UNCLE TUPELO) mobile studio, 1998's pioneering (in every sense of the word!) 'THROUGH THE TREES' kicked-off with the delightfully disturbing 'WEIGHTLESS AGAIN'. These peerless lyrics describe their 'Dead Man' emotions; "This is why people O.D. on pills, And jump ... from the Golden Gate Bridge, Anything to feel weightless again".

Cloaked in the gothic GORDON LIGHTFOOT/BILLY BRAGG-esque vocals of BRETT, The HANDSOME FAMILY's mournful tales of tragic 19th century Wild West folklore conjure up cinematic images of barren canyons and Red Indian ghosts dancing on General Custer's grave. The gothic husband and wife team returned in 2001, with the deliciously bleak, but achingly tender 'TWILIGHT', which was their first album not to be recorded in a studio (it was made in their house on a computer, apparently). However, despite a usual turn of brilliance, there were faults within the set; sometimes the lyrics seemed too complex for the simplistics of BRETT's music ... such as the opener 'SNOW WHITE DINER' which tried to tell a rather moving story, only to be ruined by the singer's off-kilter voice and lyrics that didn't really fit around the guitar part. But these were minor qualms and the LP delivered the standard backwoods humour, with 'ALL THE TV'S IN TOWN' being a particular highlight. In 2002 they issued 'LIVE AT SCHUBA'S TAVERN', a rather good live album, that was initially intended for diehard fans, although all of the classics turned up in one way or another and the banter was not bad either! • **Covers:** BARBARA ALLEN (Merle Travis), etc.

Album rating: ODESSA (*5) / MILK AND SCISSORS (*5) / INVISIBLE HANDS mini (*5) / THROUGH THE TREES (*8) / DOWN IN THE VALLEY compilation (*8) / IN THE AIR (*6) / TWILIGHT (*6) / LIVE AT SCHUBA'S TAVERN (*5)

BRETT SPARKS – vocals, guitar, keyboards / **RENNIE SPARKS** – bass, vocals / **MIKE WERNER** – drums / with additional musicians DAVE TRUMFIO – acoustic guitar, keyboards, co-producer / MICHAEL HAGLER – guitar / STEVE THOMAS – pedal steel

 not iss. / Carrot Top

Jan 95. (cd) <SAKI 005CD> **ODESSA**
 – Here's hopin' / Arlene / Pony / One way up / Water into wine / Giant ant / Everything that rises must converge / Gorilla / The last / Claire said / Moving furniture around / Big bad wolf / She awoke with a jerk / Happy harvest. (German-iss.Jan96 on 'Scout'; SR 1004) (UK-iss.Oct99 & Oct01; same as US)

—— the trio's guests included MICHAEL, DAVE, HARRY TRUMFIO, DARRELL SPARKS and MARK STRUZYNSKI

Feb 96. (cd) <SAKI 011CD> **MILK AND SCISSORS**
 – Lake Geneva / Winnebago skeletons / Drunk by noon / The house carpenter / The Dutch boy / The king who wouldn't smile / Emily Shore 1819-1839 / 3-legged dog / #1 country song / Amelia Earhart vs. the dancing bear / Tin foil / Puddin' fingers. (German-iss.Sep96 on 'Scout'; SR 1011) (UK-iss.Oct99 & Oct01; same as US)

—— now without WERNER who retired from music

 Scout / not iss.

Sep 97. (m-lp) (SR 1012) **INVISIBLE HANDS** — — German
 – Tin foil / Cathedrals / Grandmother waits for you / Bury me here / Barbara Allen / Birds you cannot see. <(re-iss. Oct99 & Oct01 on 'Carrot Top'; SAKI 016CD)>

—— the husband and wife duo added guests DAVE, JEFF TWEEDY, JESSICA BILLEY, DAVE SMITH and DAVE WINER

 Loose / Carrot Top

Apr 98. (cd) (VJCD 105) <SAKI 20CD> **THROUGH THE TREES** / Jan98
 – Weightless again / My sister's tiny hands / Stalled / Where the birch trees lean / Cathedrals / Down in the ground / The giant of Illinois / Down in the valley of hollow logs / I fell / The woman downstairs / Last night I went out walking / Bury me here / My ghost.

Aug 99. (7") (MAG 025) **MY BEAUTIFUL BRIDE. / (other by Sackville)** — — Canada
 (above issued on 'Magwheel')

 Vinyl Junkie / Carrot Top

Oct 99. (cd) (VJCD 110) **DOWN IN THE VALLEY** (compilation) —
 – Tin foil / My sister's tiny hands / Lake Geneva / Weightless again / No.1 country song / Giant of Illinois / Drunk by noon / Don't be scared / House carpenter / Arlene / Woman downstairs / Cathedrals / Moving furniture around / Dutchboy.

Feb 00. (cd) (VJCD 112) <SAKI 23CD> **IN THE AIR**
 – Don't be scared / The sad milkman / In the air / A beautiful thing / So much wine / Up falling Rock Hill / Poor, poor Lenore / When that helicopter comes / Grandmother waits for you / Lie down / My beautiful bride.

Oct 01. (cd) (VJCD 126) <SAKI 27CD> **TWILIGHT**
 – The snow white diner / Passenger pigeons / A dark eye / There is a sound / All the TV's in town / Gravity / Cold, cold, cold / No one fell asleep alone / I know you are there / Birds you cannot see / The white dog / So long / Peace in the vallet once again.

– compilations, others, etc. –

Jul 02. (cd) D.C.N.; <(DCN 1005CD)> **LIVE AT SCHUBA'S TAVERN**
 (live in Chicago, December 2000)
 – Amelia Earhart vs. the dancing bear / The good toothpicks / So much wine / The Czar bar / Tin foil / A beautiful thing / Vienna sausage hotline / The giant of Illinois / My sister's tiny hands / Names for all his shirts / Cathedrals / Weightless again / Bony bread / Winnebago skeletons / Drunk by noon / Magic balls (introduction) / The sad milkman / Magic balls (conclusion) / I know you are there / Down in the ground / Arlene / Moving furniture around / Freebird / My ghost / The woman downstairs.

HANGED UP (see under ⇒ SACKVILLE)

HANGOVERS

Formed: London, England ... mid 90's as a multi-faceted, veteran indie supergroup featuring GINA BIRCH (ex-RAINCOATS), IDA AKESSON (ex-TRAM), SIMON FISHER TURNER (ex-KING OF LUXEMBOURG), JOHN FRENETT (of LAIKA) and JOE DILWORTH (ex-TH' FAITH HEALERS). With a line-up of such fortitude, it looked like The HANGOVERS would get their heads around anything, and after two 1997 singles, 'SOHO' and 'DUCK NONSENSE' (the latter for 'Kill Rock Stars'), things looked soberingly bright. However, outside commitments left only GINA and IDA to look after a revolving door outfit (which now included DAVE BARBE, ex-ADAM &

THE ANTS) to record and release their debut album, 'SLOW DIRTY TEARS' (1998). It was such a pity that this was The HANGOVERS' only long-playing delivery as the set itself was fresh, mature and danceable, all at the same time.

Album rating: SLOW DIRTY TEARS (*7)

GINA BIRCH – vocals, guitar, sampling (ex-RAINCOATS, ex-DOROTHY, ex-RED CRAYOLA) / **IDA AKESSON** – keyboards, sampling (ex-TRAM) / **JOE DILWORTH** – drums (of STEREOLAB, ex-TH' FAITH HEALERS) / **JOHN FRENETT** – bass (of LAIKA) / **SIMON FISHER TURNER** – guitar, keyboards (ex-KING OF LUXEMBOURG)

		Rough Trade	not iss.
1997.	(7") (45REV 42) **SOHO. / SORRY**		
		Smoke	Kill Rock Stars
Nov 97.	(7") (FUME 001) **DUCK NONSENSE. / I'M GLAD I'M ME TODAY**		-

— GINA + IDA added new members **DAVE BARBE** – guitar (ex-ADAM & THE ANTS, ex-BOW WOW WOW, ex-BEATS INTERNATIONAL, ex-REPUBLICA) / **MARY DEIGAN** – bass (ex-VOODOO QUEENS) / + guest **PHIL LEGG** – keyboards

Apr 98.	(cd) (FUME 002A) <KRS 295> **SLOW DIRTY TEARS**		May98

– Duck song / I'm glad I'm me today / Sweetest pain / Hello moon / Soho / I feel like . . . / Sorry / I hate you / We had a really smashing time / Phone / Drink / Monster / Sitting on top of the world.

May 98.	(7") <KRS 307> **SITTING ON TOP OF THE WORLD. / WE HAD A REALLY SMASHING TIME**	-	

— The HANGOVERS have since split up

Ed HARCOURT

Born: EDWARD HARCOURT-SMITH, 14 Aug'77, East Sussex, England. Known for his youthfulness and eager talent, this musing troubadour erupted into the pages of critics come his first release 'MAPLEWOOD' (2000). An edgy and sometimes frustrating mini-album, HARCOURT ambitiously recorded the whole thing on a 4-track, and appeared to be running through a cornfield on the cover sleeve. There were certain elements that suggested he was in love with the romanticism of TOM WAITS' lush Americana; tracks such as the gruff hobo dirge 'BECOME MISGUIDED', with its plinky-plonky banjo and obsure drifting lyrics et al, gave HARCOURT the confusing tag of "new country", when clearly it was the old one he was really obsessed with. Jazzy, late-nighter 'ATTABOY, GO SPIN A YARN' showcased his tender vocal muscles, while 'WHISTLE OF A DISTANT TRAIN' harked back to DONOVAN's 'Summer Day Reflections' period. After supporting SPARKLEHORSE on a brief tour, HARCOURT recorded his sophomore release, 'HERE BE MONSTERS' (2001) for 'Heavenly' records. More technically improved, the album went on to receive rave reviews, and earned HARCOURT a 'Mercury Music Prize' nomination. It was also a pleasant surprise to hear muted trumpets, soft strings and whispering piano all included on the set. A true enigma and one to watch out for in 2003 . . .

Album rating: MAPLEWOOD mini (*5) / HERE BE MONSTERS (*7)

ED HARCOURT – vocals, keyboards, guitars, multi / with **HADRIAN GARRARD** – multi

		Heavenly	Capitol
Nov 00.	(lp/cd) (HVNLP 27/+CD) **MAPLEWOOD**		

– Hanging with the wrong crowd / I've become misguided / Apple of my eye / Attaboy go spin a yarn / He's a building a swamp / Whistle of a distant train.

— added **LEO ABRAHAMS** – guitars / + strings

Jun 01.	(7") (HVN 101) **SOMETHING IN MY EYE. / HERE BE MONSTERS**		-

(cd-s+=) (HVN 101CD) – T-bone tombstone.

Jun 01.	(lp/cd) (HVNLP 31/+CD) <37688> **HERE BE MONSTERS**		Jul01

– Something in my eye / God protect your soul / She fell into my arms / Those crimson tears / Hanging with the wrong crowd / Apple of my eye / Beneath the heart of darkness / Wind through the trees / Birds fly backwards / Shanghai / Like only lovers can.

Sep 01.	(7") (HVN 104) **SHE FELL INTO MY ARMS. / I'VE BECOME MISGUIDED**		-

(cd-s+=) (HVN 104CD) – When Americans come to London.

Jan 02.	(7") (HVN 107) **APPLE OF MY EYE. / WEARY AND BLEARY EYED**	61	-

(c-s/cd-s) (HVN 107 CS/CD) – ('A'side) / The last of the troubadours / Little silver bullet.

Francoise HARDY

Born: 17 Jan'44, Paris, France. Already a competent singer/songwriter by the time she'd graduated from college, HARDY was courted by various French labels before signing for 'Vogue' in late '61. An almost immediate hit in her native country, she first came to international attention the following year with the swaying romanticism of 'TOUS LES GARCONS ET LES FILLES', a classic pop record that made the UK Top 40 and went on to sell in excess of a million copies in Europe. FRANCOISE HARDY's delicate, often hauntingly atmospheric style stood in stark contrast to the showy glitz that characterised the work of many of the day's major domestic artists while reflecting a wider range of influences from French torch balladeers to US girl groups and folk-rock. 1964 saw the release of 'TOUS LES GARCONS . . .' in English (available on a rare eponymous EP), HARDY's cute, girlish phrasing reminiscent of ASTRUD GILBERTO's attempts at translating her native Portuguese. The mid-60's marked her most creatively fertile period with the likes of the chiming 'CE PETITE COEUR', 'ET MEME' and 'ALL OVER THE WORLD' (the English version of 'DANS LE MONDE ENTIER'), the latter marking her first and only UK Top 20 entry. With 'MA JEUNESSE FOUT LE CAMP' (1967), HARDY moved towards a more sophisticated ballad style, the piano/strings arrangement of 'IL N'Y A PAS D'AMOUR HEUREUX' bringing her trademark dreamy melancholy to the fore. Late 60's albums such as 'COMMENT TE DIRE ADIEU' and 'FRANCOISE HARDY EN ANGLAIS' also saw her increasingly concentrating on cover material and – as the title of the latter might suggest – the international market. Stunningly beautiful but often crippled by stage fright, she found a kindred sensitive soul in tragic English singer/songwriter NICK DRAKE with whom she spent some time in Paris in the early 70's. Despite her shyness, HARDY appeared in a handful of Roger Vadim films and has also worked as a fashion model. While her international fame waned in the 70's, HARDY's huge popularity in her native France remained undimmed releasing several well-quoted albums. In 1994, Brit-pop faves BLUR invited her to back them on the French-version of 'TO THE END'. With 1996's indie-orientated 'LE DANGER' (on 'Virgin'), she proved she was far from being out of touch.

Best CD compilation: LES CHANSONS D'AMOUR (*7)

HARMONY ROCKETS (see under ⇒ MERCURY REV)

HARRY CREWS (see under ⇒ LUNCH, Lydia; 70's section)

HARVEST MINISTERS

Formed: Dublin, Ireland . . . early 90's by singing songwriter WILLIAM MERRIMAN, along with co-vocalist MAEVE ROCHE, PADRAIG McCALL, AINGEALA DeBURCA, MARK BYRNE and PAT DILLON. The HARVEST MINISTERS ploughed their blend of rootsy, indie-pop via three melodic 7"ers, 'YOU DO MY WORLD THE WORLD OF GOOD', '6 O'CLOCK IS ROSARY' and 'IF IT KILLS ME AND IT WILL', for the seminal 'Sarah' imprint, capped off by their Americana-meets-twee LP, 'LITTLE DARK MANSION' (1993). The tag of twee-folk was ever so slightly removed when the ensemble signed to London-based Irish imprint, 'Setanta', for two further albums, 'A FEELING MISSION' (1995) and 'ORBIT' (1997) – where are they now?

Album rating: LITTLE DARK MANSION (*5) / A FEELING MISSION (*6) / ORBIT (*5)

WILLIAM MERRIMAN – vocals, guitars / **MAEVE ROCHE** – vocals / **PADRAIG McCALL** – multi / **AINGEALA DeBURCA** – violin / **MARK BYRNE** – bass / **PAT DILLON** – drums

		Sarah	Widely Distributed
Jun 92.	(7") (SARAH 064) **YOU DO MY WORLD OF GOOD. / PETTICOATS**		-
Oct 92.	(7") (SARAH 068) **6 O'CLOCK IS ROSARY. / THE FIRST STAR**		-
Aug 93.	(7") (SARAH 084) **IF IT KILLS ME AND IT WILL. / CAN'T GO IT ALONE**		-

(cd-s+=) (SARAH 084CD) – You do my world the world of good / 6 o'clock is rosary.

Sep 93.	(lp/c/cd) (SARAH 616/+MC/CD) <26> **LITTLE DARK MANSION**		Sep95

– Grey matters / Railroaded / Forfeit trials / Little dark mansion / Silent house / I gotta lie down / Fictitious Christmas / A river wedding / Rug / When you have a faint heart / I hang from a great big oak / Dominique / Don't you ever.

		Setanta	Bar/None
May 95.	(cd/c/lp) (SET CD/MC/LP 019) <60> **A FEELING MISSION**		Oct95

– That won't wash / I've a mind / A drowning man / Temple to love / Dealing with a kid / Cleaning out the store / The only seat of power / An innopportune girl / She's buried / Modernising the new you / Mental charge / A secret way. (c+=) – Happy to abort. (cd++=) – Out of costume.

— **MERRIMEN, BYRNE + DeBURCA** now with **JOHN PARISH** – guitars, keyboards, drums, producer / **ANDY FITZPATRICK** – keyboards

		Setanta	Setanta
Jan 97.	(cd) (<SETCD 033>) **ORBIT**		

– Think about me more / I never raised my voice to you / A feeling mission / Stop doubting Thomas / Reluctant volunteer / Object of your affections / Orbit / Ballad of Lady Yarmouth / Our destinies were intertwined / Don't give a cent (to the charities of hope).

— disbanded after above

PJ HARVEY

Born: POLLY JEAN HARVEY, 9 Oct'69, Corscombe, nr. Yeovil, England. Born to music-loving hippie parents, HARVEY was acquainted with music and musicians from an early age. Her first songwriting experience was with rootsy outfit The POLEKATS, HARVEY later joining Somerset-based group AUTOMATIC DLAMINI, who had been around for some five years. Numbered in their ranks were ROBERT ELLIS on drums, JOHN PARISH (ex-THIEVES LIKE US) on guitar and vocals (both ex-HEADLESS HORSEMEN; alongside bassist DAVE DALLIMORE). With bassist JAMIE ANDERSON, they finally released a well-received debut EP, 'THE CRAZY SUPPER', in June '86 on the 'D For Drum' label (DLAM 1). PARISH also went into production work for The CHESTERFIELDS and BRILLIANT CORNERS. Early members of AUTOMATIC DLAMINI included ex-CLEANERS FROM VENUS keyboard man and future rock critic GILES SMITH, and IAN OLLIVER. 1987 was their busiest year, releasing a single, 'I DON'T KNOW YOU BUT . . .' / 'I'VE NEVER BEEN THAT COLOUR ANYWHERE BEFORE' (DLAM 2) / 7"+12" 'ME AND MY CONSCIENCE' for 'Idea' (IDEA+T 009), and album, 'THE D IS FOR DRUM' (on 'Idea' IDEALP 001). ELLIS departed soon after and POLLY finally convinced PARISH to let her play guitar, sax and contribute backing vocals. Unfortunately, recordings (i.e. 12" 'WATER', an album, 'HERE CATCH SHOUTED HIS FATHER') didn't quite reach the retail stage. In August 1992, the group released 'FROM A DIVA TO A DIVER' (BOT/+CD 04), after which PARISH took time out to produce WALL OF VOODOO and play with ENSENADA JOYRIDE, whose 'Hey Lady' POLLY has always wanted to cover. She then turned up on GRAPE's single 'BABY IN A PLASTIC BAG' and two tracks by The FAMILY CAT; 'COLOUR ME GREY' and 'RIVER OF DIAMONDS'. With ELLIS and OLLIVER, she had already formed PJ HARVEY in 1991, and they signed for 'Too Pure'. With POLLY on vocals, their first release, 'DRESS', immediately caught the attention of JOHN PEEL and achieved the dubious honour of a Melody Maker single of the week. A driving, primal howl of a record, it introduced HARVEY's lyrical preoccupation with the darker corners of female sexuality, a theme continued with 'SHEELA-NA-GIG' (without OLLIVER who was subsequently replaced by STEPHEN VAUGHAN) in early '92. The single hit the UK Top 75 and and there was enough of a buzz around the band for the debut album, 'DRY', to reach the fringes of the Top 10. HARVEY's impact had been immediate, her raw, defiantly individual interpretation of feminism sparking much debate in the music press, especially after an NME cover shot in which she appeared topless, back to the camera. Signing to 'Island', PJ HARVEY began work on the Steve Albini (ex-BIG BLACK)-produced follow-up, 'RID OF ME', which went Top 3 upon its release in the Spring of '93. As one might expect from the man who gave us 'Songs About Fucking', Albini's production didn't exactly make for an easy listen, HARVEY turning in her most ferocious performance to date. With the likes of 'LEGS', 'MAN SIZE' and 'RUB TILL IT BLEEDS', the singer continued to explore the contradictory and unsavoury aspects of sexuality/relationships with unparallelled feminine fury. Following the departure of ROB ELLIS, HARVEY assembled a backing band that incluuded JOHN PARRISH (guitar, ex-AUTOMATIC DLAMINI), NICK BAGNALL (keyboards/bass), JOE GORE (guitar) and ERIC FELDMAN (keyboards) and JEAN-MARC BUTTY (drums). In 1995, with FLOOD and BAD SEED, MICK HARVEY on production duties, she/they unleashed HARVEY's finest work to date, 'TO BRING YOU MY LOVE', which also hit the US Top 40 and was nominated for a UK "Mercury" award. A more balanced affair, HARVEY's dark rage chose to simmer below the surface this time around, creating the feeling of creeping unease that runs through much of NICK CAVE's work (her new acquaintance!?). In 1996, she gave JOHN PARISH a full credit on their dual album 'DANCE HALL AT LOUSE POINT', which sold relatively poorly. As well as featuring on TRICKY's 'Broken Homes' single, 1998 saw the release of 'IS THIS DESIRE?', the singer's most introspective, inscrutable work to date. Recorded amid a period of retreat from the vagaries and distractions of the rock world, the album's relatively restrained textures suggested an artist in transition. This was confirmed with the release of the widely acclaimed 'STORIES FROM THE CITY, STORIES FROM THE SEA' (2000), an album – a Mercury prize contender – with the energy of New York (where it was partly written), and the visceral thrill of self discovery coursing through its glamorous veins. Many commentators mentioned PATTI SMITH, a reference that HARVEY would be unlikely to dispute given the cathartic power she wielded throughout. • **Songwriters:** POLLY, and covers; HIGHWAY 61 (Bob Dylan) / DADDY (Willie Dixon) / BALLAD OF THE SOLDIER'S WIFE (Kurt Weill).

Album rating: DRY (*9) / RID OF ME (*8) / TO BRING YOU MY LOVE (*9) / DANCE HALL AT LOUSE POINT with John Parish (*5) / IS THIS DESIRE (*6) / STORIES FROM THE CITY, STORIES FROM THE SEA (*9)

POLLY HARVEY – vocals, guitar, cello, violin, organ / **IAN OLLIVER** – bass / **ROBERT ELLIS** (b.13 Feb'62, Bristol, England) – drums, vocals

	Too Pure	Indigo
Oct 91. (12"ep) (*PURE 5*) **DRESS. / WATER** (demo) / **DRY** (demo) (cd-iss. Mar92; PURECD 5)		-

— **STEPHEN VAUGHAN** (b.22 Jun'62, Wolverhampton, England) – bass repl. OLLIVER who returned to brief reformation of AUTOMATIC DLAMINI

Feb 92. (lp"ltd.) (*PURE S8*) **SHEELA-NA-GIG. / JOE** (demo) | 69 | - |
(12"+=/cd-s+=) (*PURE 8/+CD*) – Hair (demo).
Mar 92. (lp/cd/s-lp) (*PURE 10/+CD/D*) <*ING 5001*> **DRY** | 11 | Jun92 |
– Oh my lover / O Stella / Dress / Victory / Happy and bleeding / Sheela-na-gig / Hair / Joe / Plants and rags / Fountain water. (*s-lp w/ free 'Demonstration' lp; PURED 10*)

	Island	Island
Apr 93. (7"/c-s) (*IS/CIS 538*) **50FT QUEENIE. / REELING / MAN-SIZE** (demo)	27	-
(12"+=/cd-s+=) (*12IS/CID 538*) – Hook (demo).		
Apr 93. (cd/c/lp) (*CID/ICT/ILPS 8002*) <*514696*> **RID OF ME**	3	May93

– Rid of me / Missed / Legs / Rub 'til it bleeds / Hook / Man-size sextet / Highway '61 revisited / 50ft Queenie / Yuri-G / Man-size / Dry / Me-Jane / Snake / Ecstasy.

Jul 93. (12"ep/cd-ep) (*12IS/CID 569*) **MAN-SIZE. / WANG DANG DOODLE / DADDY** | 42 | - |

— drummer ELLIS departed after above.
Oct 93. (cd/c/lp) (*IMCD/ICT/ILPM 2079*) <*518450*> **4-TRACK DEMOS** (demos) | 19 | Nov93 |
– Rid of me / Legs / Reeling / Snake / Hook / 50ft Queenie / Driving / Ecstasy / Hardly wait / Rub 'til it bleeds / Easy / M-bike / Yuri-G / Goodnight.

— POLLY now with **JOHN PARISH** – drums, guitar / **JOE GORE** (b. San Francisco) – guitar (ex-TOM WAITS) / **NICK BAGNALL** – keyboards, bass / **ERIC FELDMAN** (b. San Francisco) – keyboards (ex-CAPTAIN BEEFHEART) / **JEAN-MARC BUTTY** (b. France) – drums

Feb 95. (7"ep/12"ep/cd-ep) (*IS/12IS/CID 607*) **DOWN BY THE WATER. / LYING IN THE SUN / SOMEBODY'S DOWN, SOMEBODY'S NAME** | 38 | - |
Feb 95. (cd/c/lp) (*CID/ICT/ILPS 8035*) <*524085*> **TO BRING YOU MY LOVE** | 12 | 40 |
– To bring you my love / Meet ze monsta / Working for the man / C'mon Billy / Teclo / Long snake moan / Down by the water / I think I'm a mother / Send his love to me / The dancer. (*re-iss. d-cd Dec95 w/ extra B-sides; CIDZ 8035*)
Jul 95. (12"/cd-s) (*12IS/CID 614*) **C'MON BILLY. / DARLING BE THERE / MANIAC** | 29 | - |
(cd-s+=) (*CIDX 614*) – One time too many.
Oct 95. (7"pic-d) (*IS 610*) **SEND HIS LOVE TO ME. / LONG TIME COMING** (session) | 34 | - |
(cd-s+=) (*CID 610*) – Harder.
(cd-s) (*CIDX 610*) – ('A'side) / Hook (live) / Water (live).

— Enjoyed more chart success on duet with NICK CAVE; 'Henry Lee' single released early '96.

JOHN PARISH & POLLY JEAN HARVEY

— with **JEREMY HOGG** – guitar / **ERIC DREW FELDMAN** – bass, keyboards (ex-CAPTAIN BEEFHEART) / **ROB ELLIS** – drums

	Island	Island
Sep 96. (cd/c/lp) (*CID/ICT/ILPS 8051*) <*524278*> **DANCE HALL AT LOUSE POINT**	46	

– Girl / Rope bridge crossing / City of no sun / That was my veil / Urn with dead flowers in a drained pool / Civil war correspondent / Taut / Un cercle autour du soleil / Heela / Is that all there is / Dance hall at Louse Point / Lost fun zone.
Nov 96. (7") (*IS 648*) **THAT WAS MY VEIL. / LOSING GROUND** | 75 | - |
(12"+=/cd-s+=) (*12IS/CID 648*) – Who will love me now? / Civil war correspondent (Global Communications mix).

— ELLIS joined 'Too Pure' outfit, LAIKA

PJ HARVEY

— In 1998, she featured with TRICKY on his 'Broken Homes' single.

	Island	Polygram
Sep 98. (7") (*IS 718*) <*572408*> **A PERFECT DAY ELISE. / SWEETER THAN ANYTHING / INSTRUMENTAL #3**	25	Oct98
(cd-s) (*CID 718*) – (first & third tracks) / The Northwood.		
(cd-s) (*CIDX 718*) – (first two tracks) / The bay.		
Sep 98. (cd/c/lp) (*CID/ICT/ILPS 8076*) <*524563*> **IS THIS DESIRE?**	17	54

– Angelene / Sky lit up / Wind / My beautiful Leah / A perfect day Elise / Catherine / Electric light / Garden / Joy / River / No girl so sweet / Is this desire?
Jan 99. (7") (*IS 730*) **THE WIND. / NINA IN ECSTASY 2** | 29 | |
(cd-s+=) (*CID 730*) – The faster I breathe, the further I go.
(cd-s) (*CIDX 730*) – ('A'side) / Rebecca / Instrumental No.2.
Oct 00. (cd/c/lp) (*CID/ICT/ILPS 8099*) <*548144*> **STORIES FROM THE CITY, STORIES FROM THE SEA** | 23 | 42 Nov00 |
– Big exit / Good fortune / A place called home / One line / Beautiful feeling / The whores hustle and the hustlers whore / This mess we're in / You said something / Kamikaze / This is love / Horses in my dreams / We float. (*cd+=*) – This wicked tongue.
Nov 00. (7") (*IS 769*) **GOOD FORTUNE. / 66 PROMISES** | 41 | - |
(cd-s+=) (*CID 769*) – Memphis.
(cd-s) (*CIDX 769*) – ('A'side) / Memphis / 30.
Feb 01. (7") (*IS 771*) **A PLACE CALLED HOME. / KICK TO THE GROUND** (demo) | 43 | - |
(cd-s) (*CID 771*) – ('A'side) / As close as this / My own private revolution.
Oct 01. (7") (*IS 785*) **THIS IS LOVE. / ANGELINE** (live) | 41 | - |
(cd-s) (*CID 785*) – ('A'side) / You said something / Place called home (live).

HARVEY DANGER

Formed: Seattle, Washington, USA . . . 1991 by local students SEAN NELSON, JEFF J. LINN, AARON HUFFMAN and EVAN SULT. The lads played grunge covers at local parties until 1996 when producer John Goodmanson was drafted in to flesh out their alt-rock sound. A debut album, 'WHERE HAVE ALL THE MERRYMAKERS GONE?', was originally issued on New York's indie imprint 'Arena Rock' in 1997 before the quartet were picked up by 'Slash' the following year. Summer '98 saw HARVEY DANGER make their UK debut with the Top 60 'FLAGPOLE SITTA' single, a bouncy but lyrically barbed geek-rock effort with a melodic singalong factor in the vein of the dB's and the REPLACEMENTS. The album had already been re-issued a month earlier in the States where its slow-burning chart progress eventually saw it breach the Top 75. 'KING JAMES VERSION' (2000) offered up more of the same with expertly aimed lyrical potshots at no doubt deserving targets while the likes of MARC OLSEN and GRANT LEE PHILLIPS chimed in on the more mature efforts.

Album rating: WHERE HAVE ALL THE MERRYMAKERS GONE? (*6) / KING JAMES VERSION (*5)

HARVEY DANGER (cont)

SEAN C. NELSON – vocals / **JEFF J. LIN** – guitar / **AARON HUFFMAN** – bass / **EVAN SULT** – drums

		Arena Rock	Arena Rock
May 98.	(cd) <(AR 006)> **WHERE HAVE ALL THE MERRYMAKERS GONE?**		Jul97

– Carlotta Valdez / Flagpole sitta / Woolly muffler / Private helicopter / Problems and bigger ones / Jack the lion / Old hat / Terminal annex / Wrecking ball / Radio silence. <(re-iss. Aug98/Jun98 on 'Slash'; 314 556002-2)> – hit US No.70

		Slash	Slash
Jul 98.	(7"/c-s) (LASH/LASCS 64) <570261> **FLAGPOLE SITTA. / BALLAD OF THE TRAGIC HERO (PITY AND FEAR)**	57	Sep98

(cd-s+=) (LASCD 64) – Wrecking ball.

		not iss.	Sire
Sep 00.	(cd) <31143> **KING JAMES VERSION**	–	

– Meeting the remarkable men (show me the hero) / Humility on parade / Why I'm lonely / Sad sweetheart of the rodeo / You miss the point completely, I get the point exactly / Authenticity / (Theme from) Carjack Fever / Pike St. – Park slope / This is the thrilling conversation you've been waiting for / Loyalty BLDG / Underground / The same as being in love.

HASH JAR TEMPO
(see under ⇒ MONTGOMERY, Roy; in 80's section)

Juliana HATFIELD

Born: 27 Jul'67, Wiscarset, Maine, USA. After fronting a high school covers band, HATFIELD met her future musical collaborators, JOHN STROHM and FREDA LOVE BONER, while studying at Boston's Berklee College of Music. The trio subsequently formed The BLAKE BABIES, releasing a debut mini-set, 'NICELY, NICELY' (1987), on the independent 'Chewbud' label (licensed to BILLY BRAGG's 'Utility' imprint in the UK). Not straying too far from the established Boston sound, the group's indie strumming brought comparisons with early R.E.M. and THROWING MUSES, although HATFIELD's distinctive girly vocals marked them out from the pack. The LEMONHEADS connection was there from the start, STROHM having previously played alongside EVAN DANDO and Co.; DANDO became a BLAKE BABY temporarily for a second mini-set, 'SLOW LEARNER' (1989), before returing to The LEMONHEADS as a drummer. Signing with 'Mammoth', The BLAKE BABIES subsequently released a full length set, 'EARWIG' (1990), an expanded version of their earlier release, while a follow-up, 'SUNBURN' (1992), upped the grunge factor and increased their already burgeoning college fanbase. After a further mini-set, the acclaimed 'ROSY JACK WORLD' (1992), the band surprised the music press by announcing a split; HATFIELD sang and played on The LEMONHEADS' breakthrough set, 'It's A Shame About Ray' (1992) album, before cutting her own solo album, 'HEY BABE', the same year. Despite the record's merits, the press were more concerned with the nitty gritty of her much publicised relationship with DANDO and the revelation that she was still a virgin at 25. Undeterred, the singer formed The JULIANA HATFIELD THREE (along with DEAN FISHER and TODD PHILIPS), signed to 'East West' and released a second solo set, 'BECOME WHAT YOU ARE' (1993), developing her hard-edged GO-GO's sound against lyrics which were as disarmingly angst-ridden as ever. A third set, 'ONLY EVERYTHING' (1995), packed more of a punch although its downbeat tone was obviously symptomatic of HATFIELD's continuing struggles; mirroring the personal strife of former beau, DANDO, HATFIELD suffered a nervous breakdown later that year. After an album ('GOD'S FOOT') was shelved by 'Mammoth', she severed ties with the label and returned in '97 with a six-song mini-set, 'PLEASE DO NOT DISTURB', a stop-gap until her first full-set for three years, 'BED' (1998). Her emotions at full stretch, it was nevertheless a decent enough jangle/grunge-pop outing, but strictly for the fans; two years on and her loyal supporters had to choose between two albums, the classy, return-to-basics 'BEAUTIFUL CREATURE' or the sonically wayward 'TOTAL SYSTEM FAILURE' (the latter as JULIANA'S PONY).
• **Covered:** TEMPTATION (Grass Roots) / SEVERED LIPS (Dinosaur Jr) / EVERY BREATH YOU TAKE (Police) / ONLY LOVE CAN BREAK YOUR HEART (Neil Young).

Album rating: Blake Babies: NICELY, NICELY mini (*6) / EARWIG (*7) / SUNBURN (*7) / ROSY JACK WORLD (*5) / INNOCENCE AND EXPERIENCE compilation (*8) / Juliana Hatfield: HEY BABE (*8) / BECOME WHAT YOU ARE (*7) / ONLY EVERYTHING (*6) / BED (*5) / BEAUTIFUL CREATURE (*6) / TOTAL SYSTEM FAILURE as Juliana's Pony (*4) / GOLD STARS 1992-2002 collection (*5)

BLAKE BABIES

JULIANA HATFIELD – vocals, guitar / **JOHN STROHM** (b.23 Mar'67, Bloomington, Indiana) – guitar (of-LEMONHEADS) / **FREDA LOVE BONER** (b. 3 ep'67, Nashville, Tennessee) – drums

		Utility	Chewbud
Dec 87.	(m-lp) <CBTW-001> **NICELY, NICELY**	–	

– Wipe it up / Her / Tom & Bob / A sweet burger lp / Bye / Let them eat chewy granola bars / Julius fast body / Better'n'you / Swill and the cocaine sluts. (UK-iss.Oct94 on 'Mammoth' cd/c; MR 0086-2/-4)

— added **EVAN DANDO** – bass, vocals (of-LEMONHEADS)

Jul 89.	(m-lp/cd) (UTIL/UTICD 6) **SLOW LEARNER**		–

– Lament / Grateful / Your way on the highway / Take your head off my shoulder / Rain / From here to Burma / Putta my head. (re-iss. Mar93 as 'BLAKE BABIES' cd/lp; same)

— now without DANDO who returned to The LEMONHEADS as drummer!

		Mammoth	Mammoth
Mar 90.	(cd/lp) <(MR 0016-2/-1)> **EARWIG**		1989

– Cesspool / Dead and gone / Grateful you / You don't give up / Your way on the highway / Rain / Lament / Alright / Loose / Take your head off my shoulder / From here to Burma / Don't suck my breath / Outta my head / Steamy Gregg / Not just a wish. (cd-iss. Oct92; same)

Mar 92.	(cd/lp) <(MR 0022-2/-1)> **SUNBURN**		1990

– I'm not your mother / Out there / Star / Look away / Sanctify / Gimme some girl in a dish / I'll take anything / Watch me now I'm calling / Gimme some mirth / Kiss and make up / A million years.

Nov 92.	(m-cd/m-lp) <(MR 0025-2/-1)> **ROSY JACK WORLD**		Jun91

– Rosy Jack world / Temptation eyes / Downtime / Take me / Nirvana.

— HATFIELD joined The LEMONHEADS on mid-92 album 'IT'S A SHAME ABOUT RAY', before forming The JULIANA HATFIELD three. STROHM and BONER had already formed ANTENNA, who released for same label 'SWAY' album mid-92 and eponymous album Mar93.

– compilations, etc. –

Oct 93.	(cd) Mammoth; <(MR 0058-2)> **INNOCENCE AND EXPERIENCE**		

– Wipe it up / Rain / Boiled potato / Lament / Cesspool / You don't give up / Star / Sanctify / Out there / Girl in a box / I'm not your mother / Temptation eyes / Downtime / Over and over.

JULIANA HATFIELD

— with **EVAN DANDO + JOHN WESLEY HARDING** (b. WESLEY HARDING STACE, 22 Oct'65, Hastings, England) – guitar, vocals

		Mammoth	Mammoth
Jul 92.	(12"ep/cd-ep) <MR 0041-1/-2> **FOREVER BABY / NIRVANA / EVERYBODY LOVES ME BUT YOU. / RAISANS / TAMARA**	–	
Aug 92.	(cd/c/lp) <(MR 0035-2/-4/-1)> **HEY BABE**		Mar92

– Everybody loves me but you / Lost and saved / I see you / The lights / Nirvana / Forever baby / Ugly / No outlet / Quit / Get off your knees / No answer.

Nov 92.	(12"ep/cd-ep) <(MR 0045-1/-2)> **I SEE YOU / UGLY RIDER. / HERE COMES THE PAIN / FEED ME**		

JULIANA HATFIELD three

— **JULIANA HATFIELD** – vocals, guitar / **DEAN FISHER** – bass / **TODD PHILIPS** – drums (ex-BULLET LaVOLTA)

— guests **PETER HOLSAPPLE** – keyboards (ex-dB's) / **DENNY FONGHEISER** – percussion ('Mammoth' now taken over by the majors)

		East West	Atco
Aug 93.	(cd/lp) <(4509 93529-2/-1)> **BECOME WHAT YOU ARE**		44

– Supermodel / My sister / This is the sound / For the birds / Mabel / A dame with a rod / Addicted / Feelin' Massachusetts / Spin the bottle / President Garfield / Little pieces / I got no idols.

Sep 93.	(7"/c-s) (YZ 767/+C) **MY SISTER. / PUT IT AWAY**	71	

(10"+=/cd-s+=) (YZ 767 T/CD) – A dame with a rod (demo) / Ruthless.

Nov 93.	(7"ep/c-ep/10"ep/cd-ep) (YZ 791/+C/EP/CD) **FOR THE BIRDS / HELLO, MY NAME IS BABY. / I GOT NO IDOLS)piano version) / BATWING**		
Aug 94.	(c-s) (YZ 819C) **SPIN THE BOTTLE / MY DARLING**		–

(10"+=/cd-s+=) (YZ 819 TE/CD) – My sister (acoustic) / Nirvana.

Nov 94.	(c-s) <64207> **SPIN THE BOTTLE** / (track by Ethan Hawke)	–	97

(above issued US on 'RCA', and from the film 'Reality Bites')

Mar 95.	(c-s) (YZ 916C) **UNIVERSAL HEART-BEAT / GIRL IN OLD BLUE VOLVO DISOWNS SELF**	65	–

(10"+=/cd-s+=) (YZ 916 TE/CD) – Where would I be without you / Yardsailing.

Mar 95.	(c-s) <98179> **UNIVERSAL HEART-BEAT / WHERE WOULD I BE WITHOUT YOU**	–	84
Mar 95.	(cd/c) <(4509 99886-2/-4)> **ONLY EVERYTHING**	–	59

– What a life / Fleur de lys / Universal heart-beat / Dumb fun / Live on tomorrow / Dying proof / Bottles and flowers / Outsider / Ok Ok / Congratulations / Hang down from Heaven / My darling / Simplicity is beautiful / You blues.

— In August '95, JULIANA suffered a nervous breakdown and took a rest from the music business until '96/'97

— now with **MIKE LEAHY** – guitar / **TODD PHILIPS** – drums

		not iss.	Bar/None
Oct 97.	(m-cd) <100> **PLEASE DO NOT DISTURB**	–	

– Sellout / Trying not to think about it / As if your life depended on it / Give me some of that / Get off / Edge of nowhere.

— now with various session people

		Cherry Red	Zoe
Sep 98.	(cd) (CIAO 001CD) <431001> **BED**		Aug98

– Down on me / I want to want you / Swan song / Sneaking around / Backseat / Live it up / You are the camera / Running out / Bad day / Let's blow it all.

		Zoe	Zoe
Jul 00.	(cd) (ZOE 1011) <431011> **BEAUTIFUL CREATURE**		May00

– Daniel / Close your eyes / Choose drugs / Cool rock boy / Don't rush me / Slow motion / Might be in love / Somebody's waiting for me / Until tomorrow / The easy way out / Hotels / When you loved me / Cry in the dark / Every breath you take / When you loved me.

— next with **MICKEY WELSH** – bass + **ZEPHAN COURTNEY** – drums

Jul 00.	(cd; as JULIANA'S PONY) (ZOE 1012) <431012> **TOTAL SYSTEM FAILURE**		May00

– White trash / Metal fume fever / Housebody / Road wrath / Let's get married / Breeders / My protegee / Total system failure / The victim / Using you / Leather pants / Noblesse oblige / Ten foot pole.

Oct 02. (cd) *(ZOE 1029)* <*431029*> **GOLD STAR 1992-2002: THE JULIANA HATFIELD COLLECTION** (compilation) □ □ Jun02
– Everybody loves me but you / My sister / Spin the bottle / Universal heartbeat / Fleur de lys / Mountain of love / Fade away / Sellout / Live it up / Sneaking around / Somebody is waiting for me / Cry in the dark / Houseboy / My protegee / Every breath you take / Only love can break your heart / Don't walk away / Your eyes / We will rise again / Table for one.

HAVEN

Formed: Cornwall, England... 1996 by GARY BRIGGS and NAT WASON who met in a Penzance record store; rhythm section IWAN GRONOW and TOM LEWIS were soon recruited. Named after a local holiday resort, the band began gigging around their nascent county until they were scooped up by former SMITHS manager, JOE MOSS, who brought the boys back to Manchester, where they were set up with a regular slot at the city's Night & Day club. Due to their managerial connections the boys (now with JACK MITCHELL replacing LEWIS) also had the fortune of backing-up gigs for JOHNNY MARR's band, the HEALERS and the likes of BADLY DRAWN BOY. May 2001 saw the band debut with the EP 'TIL THE END' (2001), which gleaned them the attention of the British music press, which was further excited by raunchy single 'BEAUTIFUL THING' (2001). The following year saw the band settle down to some studio time with MARR at the production helm, their reward coming with the release of their second 7" 'LET IT LIVE', Parent album, 'BETWEEN THE SENSES' (2002), showcased their adroit indie guitar pop akin to their peers COLDPLAY and STARSAILOR and recalling the glory days of THE VERVE. • **Note:** Not to be confused with the HAVEN who issued 'The Road'.

Album rating: BETWEEN THE SENSES (*6)

GARY BRIGGS – vocals / **NAT WASON** – guitar / **IWAN GRONOW** – bass / **JACK MITCHELL** – drums; repl. TOM LEWIS

			Radiate	Virgin
May 01.	(cd-ep/7"ep)	*(RDT/+S 1)* **TIL THE END EP**	□	–
		– Til the end / Beautiful thing / Speakers corner / Feel your way.		
Jul 01.	(7")	*(RDTS 2)* **BEAUTIFUL THING. / THROUGH IT ALL**	□	–
		(cd-s+=) *(RDT 2)* – Lying tongue.		
Sep 01.	(7")	*(RDTS 3)* **LET IT LIVE. / COMES A CHANGE**	72	–
		(cd-s+=) *(RDT 3)* – Last dance.		
Jan 02.	(7")	*(RDTS 4)* **SAY SOMETHING. / OUTSIDE**	24	–
		(cd-s+=) *(RDT 4)* – Sleep.		
		(cd-s) *(RDTX 4)* – ('A'side) / Tear it down / No sound.		
Feb 02.	(cd/lp)	*(RDT CD/LP 1)* <*12836*> **BETWEEN THE SENSES**	26	□ Aug02
		– Beautiful thing / Where is the love / Say something / Out of reach / Still tonight / I need someone / Til the end / Lately / Let it live / Is this bliss / Keep on giving in / Holding on. <*US cd+=*> – – Sleep / Outside.		
Apr 02.	(7")	*(RDTS 6)* **TIL THE END. / MAY CHANGE**	28	–
		(cd-s+=) *(RDT 6)* – Downtime / Say something (live acoustic) / ('A'-video).		
		(cd-s) *(RDTX 6)* – ('A'side) / ('A'-alternate Johnny Marr version) / ('A'-Steve Lamacq evening session).		

Richard HAWLEY (see under ⇒ LONGPIGS)

HAYDEN

Born: HAYDEN DESSER, 1971, Toronto, Ontario, Canada. This enigmatic and wilfully obscure singer/songwriter caused something of a stir on the alt-country underground with his debut set, 'EVERYTHING I LONG FOR', drawing comparisons to the likes of WILL OLDHAM, BECK and HOWIE GELB. Initially released on tiny Canadian label, 'Hardwood/Sonic Unyon', the record was a hauntingly downbeat trawl through torn and frayed acoustic Americana with occasional bouts of grizzled grunge, all set, of course, to a lyrical world view of gritted-teeth realism/miserabilism. Vocally, the man occasionally sounded like he'd been gargling with razorblades yet it was difficult to ignore the high, lonesome spectre of NEIL YOUNG throughout the record, especially bearing in mind the Toronto connection. Although HAYDEN subsequently signed a worldwide deal with M.C.A. offshoot label, 'Outpost', (possibly the most mysterious man in the alt-country canon released follow-up set, 'MOVING CAREFUL', on the 'Sonic Unyon' imprint later the same year. After the release of 'THE CLOSER I GET' (1998) album, HAYDEN embarked on a tour with JULIANA HATFIELD. He was later dropped by 'Outpost'. The reluctant musician turned to recluse, and was barely seen out of his home town after the major-label fiasco. However, internet fanbases kept a torch burning and in 2001, HAYDEN issued the sparsely beautiful 'SKYSCRAPER NATIONAL PARK', on only 100 limited, hand-pressed CDs. The demand grew bigger and the album was given a full release (HAYDEN had recorded it without a record deal in tow), where it ended up in many 'Best Of Year' polls. Its floating reverence, matched with HAYDEN's worn but testy vocals made the album an underground alt. country classic. Following his new found success, HAYDEN issued the sold-out Toronto show 'LIVE AT CONVOCATION HALL' LP in September of 2002, which perfectly re-created the intensity of his damaged songs. • **Covered:** GOUGE AWAY (Pixies) / TELL ME WHY (Neil Young).

Album rating: EVERYTHING I LONG FOR (*7) / THE CLOSER I GET (*5) / SKYSCRAPER NATIONAL PARK (*6) / LIVE AT CONVOCATION HALL (*6)

HAYDEN DESSER – vocals, guitar, piano / with **JOAO CARVALHO** (some) drums

			not iss.	Hardwood
1996.	(7"ep)	**MILD AND HAZY**	–	□

			M.C.A.	Outpost-MCA
May 96.	(cd/c)	<*(OPD/OPC 30000)*> **EVERYTHING I LONG FOR**	□	□
		– Bad as they seem / In September / We don't mind / Tragedy / Stem / Skates / I'm to blame / Assignment in space with Rip Foster / Driveway / Hardly / You were loved / When this is over / My parent's house / Lounging.		
—	(orig.iss.1995 in Canada on 'Hardwood-Sonic Unyon')			

			Sonic Unyon	Sonic Unyon
Dec 96.	(m-cd)	<*(SUNCD 032)*> **MOVING CAREFUL**	□	□ May97
		– Pots and pans / Stride / Middle of July / Old fashioned way / Half of me / Choking / You are all I have.		

			not iss.	Landspeed
1997.	(7")	**CARRY ON MENTALITY**	–	– Canada
—	now with a plethora of session people			

			not iss.	Outpost-MCA
May 98.	(cd)	<*30006*> **THE CLOSER I GET**	–	□
		– The closer I get / Stride / The hazards of sitting beneath palm trees / Bullet / Waiting for a chance to see her / Two doors / Between us to hold / Better off inside / Instrumental with mellotron / Memphis / Nights like these / You are all I have / I'll tell him tonight.		

			Vinyl Junkie	Badman
Sep 02.	(cd)	*(VJCD 132)* <*BRCD 981*> **SKYSCRAPER NATIONAL PARK**	□	□
		– Street car / Dynamite walls / Steps to miles / I should have been watching you / Long way down / Tea pad / All in one move / Bass song / Carried away / Looking for you in me / Lullaby. *(re-iss. Oct02; same as US)*		
Sep 02.	(cd)	<*BRCD 977*> **LIVE AT CONVOCATION HALL (live)**	–	□
		– Street car / I should have been watching you / Steps into miles / The hazards of sitting beneath palm trees / Holster / Middle of July / Between us to hold / I'm to blame / Bass song / We don't mind / Stem / Two doors / I don't think we should ever meet / Woody / Long way down / All in one move / Bad as they seem / Lullaby / Pots and pans / Trees lounge / Tell me why / Carried away.		

Annie HAYDEN (see under ⇒ SPENT)

HEARTWORMS (see under ⇒ VELOCITY GIRL)

Reverend Horton HEAT

Born: JIM HEATH, Corpus Christi, Dallas, Texas. Initially conceived as a one-off gospel send-up, the hick REVEREND scoured the proverbial music biz congregation for a rhythm section of JIMBO WALLACE and TAZ BENTLEY. A hard-drinking, pot-smoking, card-gambling, women-chasing, bar-brawling kinda guy, The REVEREND's high-octane, CRAMPS-esque punkabilly sermons presented him as the 'Sub Pop' generation's answer to 50's wildman, JERRY LEE LEWIS. The preacher man's vinyl christening, 'SMOKE 'EM IF YOU GOT 'EM', certainly kicked up an unholy racket upon its release late in '91, whipping his boys into a beer-soaked rock'n'roll frenzy. The musical equivalent of tearing down Route 66 in a stolen Cadillac convertible high on Jack Daniels and Holy Water, 1993's 'THE FULL CUSTOM GOSPEL SOUNDS' even outstripped most of his heathen peers in the alternative/grunge sphere; the trio (with SCOTT CHURILLA replacing TAZ) were to support SOUNDGARDEN in '94. Subsequently making a pact with the Dev.. sorry, 'Interscope', The REV's next ten commandments (well er, thirteen actually!) came in the shape of the AL JOURGENSEN-produced 'LIQUOR IN THE FRONT' (1994), although the title was surely open to interpretation. Finally getting through to the non-believers and sinners among the American public, the REV hit the US Top 200 with his 1996 set, 'IT'S MARTINI TIME' (containing a cover of Bill Haley's 'ROCK THE JOINT'), a record that critically fell on its knees and suggested that the drink-saddled HEAT was in need of a bit of musical "heeeeaaling" himself. Likewise, 1998's 'SPACE HEATER', indicated that the REVEREND's reliable but increasingly predictable brand of metallic rockabilly was closer to anachronism than evangelism – praise the Lord! Likewise the PAUL LEARY-produced 'SPEND A NIGHT IN THE BOX' (2000), stripped back the flab and got right back to that old time rockabilly religion without any of the sinful studio distractions of the modern world. 'LUCKY 7' (2002), meanwhile, had the good RHH getting holier than thou, or at least holier than a stand-up bassist (JIMBO) should be. There were no doubt glasses of moonshine toasted all round as tracks such as 'LIKE A ROCKET' roared out of the blocks as the Daytona 500 theme song. • **Covered:** FOLSOM PRISON BLUES (Johnny Cash) / THE ENTERTAINER (Scott Joplin).

Album rating: SMOKE 'EM IF YOU GOT 'EM (*7) / THE FULL CUSTOM GOSPEL SOUNDS (*8) / LIQUOR IN THE FRONT (*6) / IT'S MARTINI TIME (*4) / SPACE HEATER (*5) / HOLY ROLLER compilation (*7) / SPEND A NIGHT IN THE BOX (*6) / LUCKY 7 (*5)

REVEREND HORTON HEAT (b. JIM HEATH) – vocals, guitar / **JIMBO WALLACE** – stand-up bass / **TAZ BENTLEY** – drums

			not iss.	Four Tot
1988.	(7"red)	**BIG LITTLE BABY. / BULLET**	–	–

			Sub Pop	Sub Pop
Dec 90.	(7",7"blue)	<*SP 96*> **PSYCHOBILLY FREAKOUT. / BABY YOU-KNOW-WHO**	□	□
Nov 91.	(10"lp,c,cd)	<*(SP 25-177)*> **SMOKE 'EM IF YOU GOT 'EM**	□	□
		– Bullet / I'm mad / Bad reputation / Put it to me straight / Marijuana / Baby, you-know-who / Eat steak / Love whip. *(cd+=/c+=)* – It's a dark day / Big dwarf rodeo / Psychobilly freakout / D for Dangerous.		

Reverend Horton HEAT (cont)

Apr 93.	(lp/cd) *(SP/+CD 248)* <*SP 202/+B*> **THE FULL CUSTOM GOSPEL SOUNDS**

– Wiggle stick / 400 bucks / The Devil's chasing me / Livin' on the edge (of Houston) / You can't get away from me / Beer / Big little baby / Lonesome train whistle / Bales of cocaine / Loaded gun / Nurture my pig! / Gin and tonic blues. *(cd re-iss. Sep98; same as US)*

May 94.	(7") <*SP 125-308*> **CALIENTE. / (other side by SUPERSUCKERS)**

── **SCOTT CHURILLA** – drums; repl. TAZ

Interscope Interscope

Jun 94.	(cd-s) **ONE TIME FOR ME. / MARIJUANA (live) / NUTURE MY PIG (live)**
Jul 94.	(cd/c) <*(6544 92364-2/-4)*> **LIQUOR IN THE FRONT**

– Big sky / Baddest of the bad / One time for me / Five-o Ford / In your wildest dreams / The entertainer / Rockin' dog / Jezebel / I can't surf / Liquor, beer and wine / I could get used to it / Cruisin' for a bruisin' / Yeah right. *(cd re-iss. Jul96; IND 92364)*

── added guests **TIM ALEXANDER** – keyboards + **DAN PHILLIPS** – steel guitar

Dec 96.	(cd/c) <*(INTD 90065-2/-4)*> **IT'S MARTINI TIME** — Jul96

– Big red rocket of love / Slow / It's martini time / Generation why / Slingshot / Time to pray / Crooked cigarette / Rock the joint / Cowboy love / Now, right now / Spell on me / Or is it just me / Forbidden jungle / That's showbiz.

Sep 98.	(cd) <*(INTD 90168)*> **SPACE HEATER**

– The price of San Jacinto / Lie detector / Hello Mrs. Darkness / Jimbo song / Revolution under foot / Starlight lounge / Goin' manic / Mi amor / For never more / Prophet stomp / Native tongue of love / Couch surfin' / Cinco de Mayo / Texas rock-a-billy rebel / Baby I'm drunk / Space heater.

Oct 98.	(cd-s) <*(IND 97357)*> **LIE DETECTOR / STARLIGHT LOUNGE**

not iss. Fun-Guy

Jul 99.	(7") **KING. / GIRL IN BLUE**

Time Bomb Time Bomb

Mar 00.	(7") **IT WAS A VERY GOOD YEAR. / SUE JACK DANIELS**
Apr 00.	(cd) <*(70930 43534CD)*> **SPEND A NIGHT IN THE BOX** — Mar00

– Spend a night in the box / Big D boogie woogie / Sleeper coach driver / The girl in blue / Hand it to me / Sue Jack Daniels / I'll make love / It hurts your daddy bad / The bedroom again / KIng / Whole lotta baby / The millionaire / Unlucky in love / The party in your head.

Artemis – Artemis – Epic Epic

Mar 02.	(cd) *(507540-2)* <*5112-2*> **LUCKY 7**

– Los gringos like a party / Like a rocket / Reverend Horton Heat's big blue car / Galaxy 500 / What's reminding me of you / The tiny voice of reason / Duel at the two o'clock bell / Go with your friends / Ain't gonna happen / Suicide doors / Remember me / Show pony / Sermon on the Jimbo / You've got a friend in Jimbo.

– compilations, etc. –

Aug 99.	(cd) *Sub Pop*; <*(SPCD 450)*> **HOLY ROLLER** — Apr99

– Big sky / Baddest of the bad / Wiggle stick / Big red rocket of love / Bales of cocaine / Bath-water blues / Lie detector / 400 bucks / Marijuana / It's Martini time / Baby I'm drunk / Where in the world did you go with my toothbrush / Bad reputation / One time for me / Now, right now / Slow / Love whip / Jimbo song / Big little baby / Cowboy love / In your wildest dreams / Eat steak / Folsom Prison blues / The entertainer.

HEATMISER (see under ⇒ SMITH, Elliott)

Angie HEATON (see under ⇒ CORNDOLLY)

HEAVENLY (see under ⇒ TALULAH GOSH; see 80's section)

HEAVENS TO BETSY (see under ⇒ SLEATER-KINNEY)

HEAVY STEREO

Formed: Durham, England . . . 1993 by songwriter GEM ARCHER, alongside PETE DOWNING, NEZ (aka NEIL) and NICK JONES. Although they spent two years at 'Food' records under a different moniker, their release sheet remained blank until they became HEAVY STEREO. Having moved from the home of BLUR to the stable of OASIS ('Creation'), they hit the Top 50 in mid '95 with the debut single, 'SLEEP FREAK'. Despite their name, the band were revealed to be glam-rock devotees influenced by BOLAN or even the SWEET. The following year saw further minor hits, 'SMILER', 'CHINESE BURN' and 'MOUSE IN A HOLE', the latter's relative failure putting paid to any commercial hopes for their debut album, 'DEJA VOODOO' (1996). Further strife befell the band at that year's Phoenix Festival (July '96), when NICK was bitten in the arm (not too seriously) by a one-legged crusty. A month later, NEZ was also attacked by an unknown assailant, suffering a broken nose, broken ribs and concussion.

Album rating: DEJA VOODOO (*6)

GEM (b. COLIN MURRAY ARCHER) – vocals, guitar (ex-CONTENDERS, ex-WHIRLPOOL) / **PETE DOWNING** – lead guitar / **NEZ** (aka NEIL) – bass / **NICK JONES** – drums, percussion, vocals

Creation not iss.

Jul 95.	(7"red/c-s) *(CRE/+CS 203)* **SLEEP FREAK. / MAGIC SPONGE**	46	-
	(cd-s+=) *(CRESCD 203)* – Pleasure dip.		
Oct 95.	(7"purple/c-s) *(CRE/+CS 213)* **SMILER. / CARTOON MOON**	46	-
	(cd-s+=) *(C-CRE 213)* – Wonder fools.		
Feb 96.	(7"/c-s) *(CRE/+CS 218)* **CHINESE BURN. / WORM BRAIN**	45	-
	(cd-s+=) *(CRESCD 218)* – Big apple pie.		
Aug 96.	(7"/c-s) *(CRE/+CS 230)* **MOUSE IN A HOLE. / NO SMALL PRINT**	53	
	(cd-s+=) *(CRESCD 230)* – Freedom bug.		
	(cd-s) *(CRESCD 230X)* – ('A'live) / Smiler (live) / Cartoon moon (live) / Chinese burn (live).		
Oct 96.	(cd/lp) *(CRE CD/LP 85)*(*C-CRE 185*) **DEJA VOODOO**		-

– Chinese burn / Cartoon moon / Deja voodoo / Tell yer ma / Crown of thoughts / Mouse in a hole / Bangers and mash / Deep fried heart / Reaching for heaven / Keep up / Planet empty / Shooting star.

── disbanded after above; GEM later joined OASIS

HEAVY VEGETABLE (see under ⇒ PINBACK)

Chris HEAZLEWOOD (see under ⇒ KING LOSER)

HEFNER

Formed: East London, England . . . late '96 by the Hugh Hefner (Playboy mogul)-monikered trio of songwriter DARREN HAYMAN, ANTHONY HARDING and JOHN MORRISON. Similar in approach to BUILT TO SPILL, they worked on perfecting their fragile meanderings over three very rare independent singles. Early the following year, they found a home at 'Too Pure', the resulting 'HEFNER SOUL' EP immediately converting new fans. After two more instalments of heartbreaking, SOFT BOYS-esque lyricism, the indie press were beginning to take note, hooking onto the excellent debut set, 'BREAKING GOD'S HEART', its jazzy, fragile alternative-soul a critical success. HAYMAN and Co returned with 'THE FIDELITY WARS' in 1999, a bitter, scathing, relationship break-up record, set to the usual tune of HEFNER's indie guitar musings. 2000 saw the delivery of 'BOXING HEFNER', a B-sides and rarities set, along with the ironically titled 'WE LOVE THE CITY', a brutal attack on London's middle-class and elite, not to mention the monarchy, the government and the media. Which would lead us then to . . . 'DEAD MEDIA' (2001), a more concentrated effort to bring down Max Clifford and Co through blistering indieness. • **Note:** The 12" releases on 'Inertia' ('CAR CHASE' and 'AN EVENING WITH HEFNER') were in fact, not theirs.

Album rating: BREAKING GOD'S HEART (*8) / THE FIDELITY WARS (*7) / BOXING HEFNER collection (*5) / WE LOVE THE CITY (*6) / DEAD MEDIA (*7) / Ant: A LONG WAY TO BLOW A KISS (*5)

DARREN HAYMAN – vocals, guitar / **JOHN MORRISON** – bass / **ANTHONY HARDING** – drums

Sticky not iss.

1996.	(c-ep) *(STICKY 17)* **THE DEVOTION CHAMBER EP**		-

– May God protect your home / The sweetness lies within / I stole a bride / You've been prayed for. *(re-iss. Nov97; same)*

Boogie Wonderland not iss.

Apr 97.	(7") *(BWL 020)* **A BETTER FRIEND. / CHRISTIAN GIRLS**		-
Feb 98.	(7") *(BWL 023)* **LEE REMICK. / SCHOOLGIRLS KNEES**		-

Too Pure Too Pure

Mar 98.	(10"ep) *(PURE 64X)* **THE HEFNER SOUL EP**		

– Flowers / A hymn for the coffee / Broodmare / The girl from the coast / More Christian girls.

May 98.	(7") *(PURE 80S)* **PULL YOURSELF TOGETHER. / CHRIST**		-
	(cd-s+=) *(PURE 80CDS)* – Smoking girlfriend / Wicker girl.		
Jul 98.	(cd/lp) <*PURE 83 CD/LP*> **BREAKING GOD'S HEART**		Nov98

– The sweetness lies within / The sad witch / A hymn for the postal service / Love will destroy us in the end / The librarian / God is on my side / Another better friend / Love inside the stud farm / Tactile / Eloping.

Jul 98.	(7") *(PURE 84S)* **LOVE WILL DESTROY US IN THE END. / BLIND GIRL WITH HALO**		-
	(cd-s+=) *(PURE 84CDS)* – Destroyed cowboy falls / Goethe's letter to Vic Chestnutt.		
Oct 98.	(7") *(PURE 87S)* **THE SWEETNESS LIES WITHIN. / HELLO KITTEN**		-
	(cd-s+=) *(PURE 87CDS)* – Normal Molly / A hymn for Berlin.		
Feb 99.	(7") *(STICKY 23)* **THE HYMN FOR THE ALCOHOL. / MY ART COLLEGE DAYS ARE OVER**		-
	(above issued on 'Sticky', below on 'Acuarela')		
Feb 99.	(cd-ep) *(AFF 005)* **THE HEFNER HEART EP**		-

– Mary Lee / The hymn for the things we didn't do / Karen / The hymn for Thomas Courtney Warner / The heart of Portland Oregon.

Jun 99.	(7") *(PURE 92)* **THE HYMN FOR THE CIGARETTES. / GRANDMOTHER DIES**		-
	(cd-s+=) *(PURE 92CDS)* – Lisa and me / You need a mess of help to stand alone.		
Jun 99.	(cd/lp) <*PURE 93 CD/LP*> **THE FIDELITY WARS**		Sep99

– The hymn for the cigarettes / May God protect your heart / The hymn for the alcohol / I took her love for granted / Every little gesture / The weight of the stars / I stole a bride / We were meant to be / Fat Kelly's teeth / Don't flake out on me / I love only you.

Oct 99.	(7") *(PURE 98)* **I TOOK HER LOVE FOR GRANTED. / BELLY FULL OF BABIES**		-
	(cd-s+=) *(PURE 98CDS)* – To hide a little thought.		
Feb 00.	(cd-ep) *(FIDO 001CDS)* **REVELATIONS EP**		-

– Nobody knows / Dragnet for Jesus / He got better things for you / Turtle dove. (above issued on 'Top Dog')

Too Pure Beggars . . .

Mar 00.	(7") *(PURE 95S)* **CHRISTIAN GIRLS. / WE DON'T CARE WHAT THEY SAY ABOUT US**		-
	(cd-s+=) *(PURE 95CDS)* – Fear.		
Apr 00.	(cd/lp) *(PURE 99 CD/LP)* <*80099-2*> **BOXING HEFNER** (B-sides, rarities, etc)		

– Christian girls / Lee Remick / Pull yourself together / Blind girl with halo / Hello kitten / Destroyed cowboy falls / The hymn for the coffee / Mary Lee / The hymn for the things we didn't do / To hide a little thought / The science fiction / Twisting Mary's arm. *(cd+=)* – We don't care what they say.

Aug 00. (7") *(PURE 108S)* **GOOD FRUIT. / GOOD FRUIT (Piano Magic remix) / GOOD FRUIT (Wisdom Of Harry remix)** | 50 | - |
(cd-s) *(PURE 108CD1)* – ('A'side) / Jubilee / Blackhorse road.
(cd-s) *(PURE 108CD2)* – ('A'side) / I will make her love me / Seafaring.

Oct 00. (7") *(PURE 111S)* **GREEDY UGLY PEOPLE. / (Baxendale remix)** | 64 | - |
(cd-s) *(PURE 111CD1)* – ('A'side) / Milkmaids / Kate Cleaver's house.
(cd-s) *(PURE 111CD2)* – ('A'side) / Everything's falling apart / Don't give up on us baby / ('A'-electric sound of joy mix).

Oct 00. (cd/lp) *(PURE 106 CD/LP) <80106-9>* **WE LOVE THE CITY** | | Nov00 |
– We love the city / The greedy ugly people / Good fruit / Painting and kissing / Hold me closer / Don't go / The greater London radio / As soon as you're ready / Your head to toes. *(d-cd+=; PURE 106CDLTD)* **BBC PEEL SESSIONS** – I took love for granted (video) / Good fruit (video) / Greedy ugly people / She can't sleep no more / The cure for evil / The day that Thatcher dies.

Jan 01. (7") *(PURE 112S)* **HALF A LIFE. / (other by MURRY THE HUMP)** | Too Pure - | Too Pure - |

Aug 01. (7") *(PURE 118S)* **ALAN BEAN. / (munit remix)** | 58 | - |
(cd-s) *(PURE 118CDS1)* – ('A'side) / Horror show / Better man.
(cd-s) *(PURE 118CDS2)* – ('A'side) / Just take care / Charlie girl.

Sep 01. (cd/lp) *(<PURE 115 CD/LP>)* **DEAD MEDIA**
– Dead media / Trouble kid / Junk / When the angels play their drum machines / Union chapel bay / China crisis / Alan Beam / Peppermint taste / The mangle / The king of summer / The nights are long / Treacle / Half a life / Waking up to you / Home.

Oct 01. (7") *(PURE 123-5)* **TROUBLE KID (Appliance mix). / TROUBLE KID (Darren Hayman mix)**

Feb 02. (10"ep/cd-ep) *(PURE 125 X/CDS) <80125>* **THE HEFNER BRAIN** | | May02 |
– When the angels play their drum machine (mothership mix) / Dark hearted discos / Baggage reclaim song / Can't help losong you / All I'll ever need.

ANT

ANTHONY HARDING solo

Fortune & Glory | not iss.

Apr 02. (cd) *(FORCDALB 107)* **A LONG WAY TO BLOW A KISS** | | - |
– Trick / Maybe love will return / Any girl can make me smile / History / When I need you to / Waste the days away / A long way to blow a kiss / I always hurt the one that I love / Every drop of rain / Today as yesterday / April rain.

HELEN LOVE

Formed: Swansea, Wales ... 1992 by the all-female trio of HELENE (yes, Helene) LOVE and her companions, SHEENA and ROXY. Having met up at design college, they began to rehearse in HELENE's mum's kitchen; this cosy family affair continued as SHEENA's brother dispatched a demo of their cutie indie-pop to 'Damaged Goods'. The track in question, 'FORMULA ONE RACING GIRLS' was released on the label in summer '93, while a second 7"-only single 'SHEENA'S IN LOVE WITH JOEY RAMONEY', was a tribute to their US punk hero. The RAMONES frontman always seemed to crop up in future 45's (of which there was no shortage!), compiled on the albums, 'RADIO HITS' (1994) and 'RADIO HITS VOL.2' (1997). Although they never played a gig until 1995, the girls are staunch advocates of the 7 inch single and general indie traditionalism, subsequently signing to 'Che' in '97 where they finally broached the British Top 75 a year later with the hopefully titled 'LONG LIVE THE UK MUSIC SCENE'. • **Trivia:** ASH covered their song, 'PUNKBOY'.

Album rating: SUMMER POP PUNK POP mini (*5) / RADIO HITS compilation (*5) / RADIO HITS VOL.2 compilation (*5) / LOVE AND GLITTER, HOT DAYS AND MUSIC (*5) / RADIO HITS, VOL.3 compilation (*5)

HELENE LOVE – vocals, guitar / **SHEENA** – guitar, keyboards / **ROXY** – bass, drum machine / **MARK** – casio keyboards

Damaged Goods | Damaged Goods

Jul 93. (ltd-7"pink) *(DAMGOOD 18)* **FORMULA ONE RACING GIRLS. / RIDING HI**
(re-iss. 1997 on ltd-7"red)

Oct 93. (ltd-7"green) *(DAMGOOD 27)* **(SHEENA'S IN LOVE WITH) JOEY RAMONEY. / GREATEST FAN**

Dec 93. (ltd-7"green; split with WAT TYLER) *(DAMGOOD 33)* **XMAS SINGLE: HAPPIEST TIME OF THE YEAR**

Jun 94. (ltd-7"blue) *(DAMGOOD 38)* **PUNK BOY. / PUNK BOY 2**

Jul 94. (ltd-10"pink-m-lp) *(DAMGOOD 42)* **SUMMER POP PUNK POP**
– Love; kiss; run; sing; shout; jump! / Rollercoasting / Rockaway Beach for me, Heartbreak Hotel for you / Summer pop radio / So hot / Golden summer. *(re-iss. Sep98; same)*

Oct 94. (cd) *(DAMGOOD 51CD)* **RADIO HITS** (compilation)
– Formula One racing girls / Riding hi / Joey Ramoney / Greatest fan / Punk boy 1 / Punk boy 2 / Love; kiss; run; sing; shout; jump! / Rollercoasting / Rockaway Beach for me, Heartbreak Hotel for you / Summer pop radio / So hot / Golden summer. *(yellow lp-iss.Mar97; DAMGOOD 51) (re-iss. Sep97 & Sep98 lp/cd; same)*

Apr 95. (ltd-7"pink) *(DAMGOOD 61)* **BUBBLEGUM. / LET'S GO**
(re-iss. Sep97; same)

Dec 95. (ltd-7"white) *(DAMGOOD 80)* **AHEAD OF THE RACE. / DIET COKE GIRL**
(cd-s+=) *(DAMGOOD 80CD)* – Rollercoasting (alt.take).

Jan 96. (ltd-7"blue) *(DAMGOOD 89)* **BEAT HIM UP. / SUPER BOY, SUPER GIRL**
(cd-s+=) *(<DAMGOOD 89CD>)* – Matthew Kaplan superstar.

May 96. (7"flexi) *(WJ 4)* **IL FAIT BEAU. / (other artist)**
(above issued on 'Wurlitzer Jukebox')

Jun 96. (ltd-d7"white/orange/cd-ep) *(<DAMGOOD 95/+CD>)* **WE LOVE YOU. / GIRL ABOUT TOWN // WE LOVE YOU (version 2). / PUNK BOY**

Mar 97. (green-lp/cd) *(DAMGOOD 117/+CD)* **RADIO HITS VOL.2** (compilation)
– Bubblegum / Let's go / Ahead of the race / Diet coke girl / Rollercoasting / Beat him up / Super boy, super girl / Matthew Kaplan superstar / Il fait beau / We love you / Girl about town / We love you (version 2). *(re-iss. Sep97 & Sep97; same)*

Che | Che

Sep 97. (ltd-7"pink) *(Che 72)* **DOES YOUR HEART GO BOOM. / SO IN LOVE WITH YOU**
(cd-s+=) *(Che 72cd)* – Yeah yeah we're Helen Love / Put your foot on the fuzzbox baby.

Aug 98. (7") *(Che 82)* **LONG LIVE THE UK MUSIC SCENE. / SUNBURST SUPER KAY** | 65 | - |
(cd-s+=) *(Che 82cd)* – Great in Formula One.

Mar 00. (cd/lp) *(<Che 87 cd/lp>)* **LOVE AND GLITTER, HOT DAYS AND MUSIC**
– Shifty Disco girl / Jump up and down / Atomic beat boy / Who stole the starz / 2000mph girl / Love and glitter, hot days and muzik / Does your heart go boooooooomm / Happy hardcore / Bigbigkiss / MC5 / Punk boy / Better set your phasers to stun. *(re-iss. Sep01 on 'Damaged Goods' cd+=/lp+=; DAMGOOD 202 CD/LP)* – (1999 New York radio session):- Automatic disco club / MC5 / Bigbigkiss / Jump up and down.

Apr 00. (12") *(Che 88)* **DOES YOUR HEART GO BOOM (Cuban Boys mix). / NUMBER ONE FANTASTIC DAY**

May 00. (7"/cd-s) *(Che 89/+cd)* **SHIFTY DISCO GIRL. / KING OF KUNG FU / LEADER OF THE PACK**

Jun 00. (7"/cd-s) *(Che 90/+cd)* **JUMP UP AND DOWN. / ATOMIC BEAT BOY / BIG PINK CANDYFLOSS HAIRCUT**

Damaged Goods | Damaged Goods

Mar 02. (ltd-one-sided-7") *(DAMGOOD 206)* **MERRY CHRISTMAS I DON'T WANNA FIGHT**

Mar 02. (cd/lp) *(DAMGOOD 203 CD/LP)* **RADIO HITS VOL.3** (compilation)
– Does your heart go boom / So in love with you / Yeah yeah we're Helen Love / Put your foot on the fuzzbox baby / Long live the UK music scene / Sunburst super Kay / Great in Formula One / Shifty Disco girl / King of kung fu / Leader of the pack / Jump up and down / Atomic beat boy / Big pink candyfloss haircut / Does your heart go boom (Cuban Boys remix) / Number one fantastic day.

HELIUM

Formed: Boston, Massachusetts, USA ... late '92 out of CHUPA (a band that featured JULIANA HATFIELD's brother, JASON) by SHAUN KING DEVLIN, BRIAN DUNTON and former AUTOCLAVE member, MARY TIMONY. The HELIUM trio debuted in '93 with the self-financed single, 'THE AMERICAN JEAN' (a track that subsequently appeared on V/A compilation, 'End Of The Trail, Vol.II'), closely followed by another import-only 7", 'HOLE IN THE GROUND'. Signing to 'Matador' after an A&R scramble, TIMONY furthered her hardline feminist agenda on 1994's mini-set, 'PIRATE PRUDE'. Drawing comparisons to MADDER ROSE, the record was characterised by the singer's sinister, childlike vocals against a churning, turgid musical backing. A full-length set, 'THE DIRT OF LUCK', followed in '95, although by the time of the record's release, DUNTON had made way for ASH BOWIE (moonlighting from POLVO). TIMONY's vocal capabilities were further strengthened on 1997's 'THE MAGIC CITY', although the overall impression was as uncompromising as ever. The previous year, TIMONY had been exercising her vocal chops and literate lyricism in pseudo supergroup, MIND SCIENCE OF THE MIND, together with SHUDDER TO THINK's bassist NATHAN LARSON, DAMBUILDERS' stringswoman JOAN WASSER and drummer KEVIN MARCH. All in all, she'd served a varied apprenticeship for her inevitable solo venture, 'MOUNTAINS' (2000). Confirming the preoccupation with myth and fantasy which had begun to manifest itself on HELIUM's final effort, the record's proggy, folk-ish flourishes and determinedly opaque lyrical conceits demanded (and, in part, rewarded) considerable persistence on the part of the listener. TIMONY continued her flight into fantasy on 2002's 'THE GOLDEN DOVE', again couching her painfully introspective musings in antiquated yet vivid imagery and adorning them with delicate musical baroque.

Album rating: PIRATE PRUDE mini (*5) / THE DIRT OF LUCK (*7) / THE MAGIC CITY (*6) / Mary Timony: MOUNTAINS (*6) / THE GOLDEN DOVE (*6)

MARY TIMONY – vocals, guitar / **BRIAN DUNTON** – bass / **SHAUN KING DEVLIN** – drums (ex-DUMPTRUCK)

not iss. | Warped

May 93. (7") *<WR 002>* **THE AMERICAN JEAN. /** | - | |

not iss. | Pop Narcotic

Jul 93. (7") *<narc 004>* **HOLE IN THE GROUND. / LUCY** | - | |

Matador | Matador

May 94. (m-cd/m-lp) *<(OLE 078-2/-1)>* **PIRATE PRUDE** | | Apr94 |
– Baby vampire made me / Wanna be a vampire too, baby / XXX / OOO / I'll get you, I mean it / Love $$$ / Surprise ending.

Dec 94. (7") *<OLE 116-7>* **PAT'S TRICK. / GHOST CAR** | - | - |

Apr 95. (cd/lp) *<(OLE 124-2/-1)>* **THE DIRT OF LUCK**
– Pat's trick / Trixie's star / Silver angel / Baby's going underground / Medusa / Comet #9 / Skeleton / Superball / All the X's have wings / Oh the wind and the rain / Honeycomb / Flower of the apocalypse.

Sep 95. (7") *<(OLE 144-7)>* **SUPERBALL. / WHAT INSTITUTION ARE YOU FROM?**
(cd-s+=) *<(OLE 144-2)>* – Lucky charm / #12 l'enfant / I am a witch.

HELIUM (cont)

—— **ASH BOWIE** – bass (of POLVO) repl. DUNTON

Apr 97. (cd-ep) <OLE 225> **NO GUITARS EP**
 – Silver strings / Dragon #2 / The king of electric guitars / Sunday / 13 bees / The riddle of the chamberlin.

Sep 97. (cd/lp) <(OLE 195-2/-1)> **THE MAGIC CITY**
 – Vibrations / Leon's space song / Ocean of wine / Aging astronauts / Medieval people / Lady of the fire / Lullaby of the moths / The revolution of hearts (pts.1 & 2) / Ancient cryme / Cosmic rays / Devil's tear / Clementine / Blue rain soda / Walk away.

MARY TIMONY

with **ASH BOWIE** – percussion / **JOHN McENTIRE** – synths

	Matador	Matador
Apr 00. (cd/lp) <(OLE 363-2/-1)> **MOUNTAINS**		Mar00

 – Dungeon dance / Poison moon / I fire myself / The bell / Painted horses / The hour glass / Bees / The golden fruit / Whisper from the tree / 1542 / Valley of one thousand perfumes / Tiger rising / An-deluzion / The fox and hound / Rider on the stormy sea.

—— with help from **AL WEATHERHEAD** – guitar, etc / etc

May 02. (cd/lp) <(OLE 521-2/-1)> **THE GOLDEN DOVE**
 – Look a ghost in the eye / The mirror / Blood tree / Dr. Cat / The owl's escape / Musik and charming melodee / 14 horses / Magic power / The white room / Ant's dance / Dryad and the mule / Ash and Alice.

– MARY TIMONY's early work –

AUTOCLAVE

MARY TIMONY – vocals, guitar / **CHRISTINA BILLOTTE** – bass, vocals / **NIKKI CHAPMAN** – guitar, vocals / **MELISSA BERKOFF** – drums, bass

	not iss.	Mira – Dischord
Oct 90. (7"ep) <DIS 60.5> **GO FAR**	-	
May 91. (10"ep) <DIS 65.5> **AUTOCLAVE**	-	

—— BILLOTTE would later be a part of SLANT 6 and QUIX*O*TIC

Aug 97. (cd) <(DIS 108CD)> **AUTOCLAVE** (compilation)
 – Go far / I'll take you down / It's not real life / Dr. Seuss / Still here / Hot spurr / Vision / Bulls eye / I'll take you down / Summer / Paper boy.

HELLACOPTERS

Formed: Stockholm, Sweden ... 1994 by drummer/songwriter turned guitarist, NICKE ANDERSON (aka NICK ROYALE), as a stop-gap project while his regular band, The ENTOMBED, tried to obtain a new record deal. NICKE enlisted the help of childhood chum, ROBERT ERIKSSON (bass), ASK DREGEN (guitarist of the BACKYARD BABIES) and drummer KENNY HAKANSSON (drums), indulging his passion for bluesy, anthemic punk/metal in the vein of MC5 or KISS. The mainman subsequently made this bunch a full-time project in '97 after finally leaving his beloved ENTOMBED. It was on the 14th & 15th of June that year that The HELLACOPTERS were to support their heroes KISS in Stockholm. Significantly more prolific than ANDERSON's previous outfit, the airborne metallers released a plethora of 45's (on various labels, including their own 'White Jazz') alongside three albums, 'SUPERSHITTY TO THE MAX!' (1996), 'PAYIN' THE DUES' (1997) and 'DISAPPOINTMENT BLUES' (1998). Further sets, 'GRANDE ROCK' (1999), 'HIGH VISIBILITY' (2000) and 'BY THE GRACE OF GOD' (2002) witnessed the Swedes going from strength to strength, shaving down the rougher edges and further refining their revisionary take on 70's rock yet losing none of their sharpness or earthy power in the process.
• **Covered:** THE CREEPS (Social Distortion) / I GOT A RIGHT (Iggy & The Stooges) / LOW DOWN SHAKIN' CHILLS (Nomads) / AIN'T NOTHIN' TO DO (Dead Boys) / AMERICAN RUSE (MC5) / WORKING FOR MCA (Lynyrd Skynyrd) / A MAN AND A HALF (Wilson Pickett) / HER STRUT (Bob Seger) / GIMME SHELTER (Rolling Stones) / I WANT A LIP (April Stevens) / IT'S ALL MOVING FASTER (Electric Frankenstein) / IT'S TOO LATE (New York Dolls) / ANGEL DUST (Venom) / CITY SLANG + HEAVEN (Sonic Rendezvous Band) / SPEED FREAK (Motorhead) / 455 SD + TIME TO FALL (Radio Birdman) / YOU'RE TOO GOOD (TO ME BABY) (Silky Hargreaves) / MASTER RACE ROCK (Dictators) / A HOUSE IS NOT A MOTEL (Love) / BULLET (Misfits) / TELEVISION ADDICT (Victims) / EVIL WOMEN (Black Sabbath) / ALL AMERICAN MAN (Kiss) / UNGROUNDED CONFUSION (Flaming Sideburns) / COLD NIGHT FOR ALLIGATORS (Roky Erickson) / STAB YOR BACK (Damned) / GET READY + WHOLE LOTTA SHAKIN' GOIN' ON IN MY HEART (SINCE I MET YOU) (Smokey Robinson) / YOU LEFT THE WATER RUNNING (Rick Hall, Oscar Franck & Dan Penn).

Album rating: SUPERSHITTY TO THE MAX! (*7) / PAYIN' THE DUES (*7) / DISAPPOINTMENT BLUES mini collection (*5) / GRANDE ROCK (*7) / HIGH VISIBILITY (*8) / BY THE GRACE OF GOD (*7)

NICKE ANDERSON (aka NICK ROYALE) – vocals, guitar (of/ex-ENTOMBED) / **ASK DREGEN** – guitar / **ROBERT ERIKSSON** – bass / **KENNY HAKANSSON** – drums

	Psych-out	not iss.
Feb 95. (7") (Psych 001) **KILLING ALLAN. / FERRYTALE / THE CREEPS**		-

	Freak Scene	not iss.
Dec 95. (7"ep) (Freak 3) **1995. / TILT CITY / FREESPEEDIN'**		-
(re-iss. Jan98 on 'Get Hip'; GH 201)		

	White Jazz	not iss.
Jun 96. (cd/clear-lp) (JAZZ 001 CD/LP) **SUPERSHITTY TO THE MAX!**		-

 – (Gotta get some action) Now! / 24h hell / Fire fire fire / Born broke / Bore me / It's too late [lp-only] / Tab / How could I dare / Didn't stop us / Random riot / Fake baby / Ain't no time / Such a blast / Sprock in my rocket. (cd re-iss. Jan98; same) (cd re-iss. Apr98 on 'Toy Factory'; TFCK 87143) <US-iss.Nov98 on 'Man's Ruin'; MR 22>

Oct 96. (7",7"red) (Pon 007) **WHAT ARE YOU. / LOWDOWN / ANOTHER PLACE**	-	- Sweden

(above issued on 'Planet Of Noise')

Oct 96. (clear-d7"ep/cd-ep) (WJ 002CD) **(GOTTA GET SOME ACTION) NOW! / FREEWAY TO HELL / GHOUL SCHOOL / LOW DOWN SHAKIN' CHILLS**
(re-iss. Dec97; same)

Nov 96. (7") (BA 001) **MISANTHROPIC HIGH. / I GOT A RIGHT**
(above single on 'Bad Afro')

Aug 97. (10"/cd-s; shared with GLUECIFER) (JAZZ 666/+CD) **RESPECT THE ROCK**
 – You are nothing / Kick this one slow / Another place.

—— in Aug'97, they also collaborated with ELECTRIC FRANKENSTEIN on the 7" EP for 'Frank' records; Frank 004

—— added **BOBBY LEE FLETT** – piano

Sep 97. (cd/purple-lp) (JAZZ 004 CD/LP) **PAYIN' THE DUES**
 – You are nothin' / Like no ther man / Looking at me / Riot on the rocks / Hey! / Soulseller / Where the action is / Twist action / Colapso nervioso / Psyched out and furious. (bonus live lp/cd+=) – Action de grace / You are nothin' / Disappointment blues / Born broke / Alright already now / Down right blue / City slang [lp-only] / (Gotta get some action) Now! / Soulseller. (cd re-iss. Apr98 on 'Toy Factory'; TFCK 87142)

Nov 97. (7") (SP 003) **RIOT ON THE ROCKS. / TELEVISION ADDICT**	-	- Sweden

(above issued on 'Safety-Pin')

Apr 98. (7") (7JAZZ 008) **SOULSELLER. / AIN'T NOTHIN' TO DO**
(cd-s) (JAZZ 008CD) – (same as above).

Jul 98. (7") (7JAZZ 010) **HEY! / HER STRUT**
(cd-s+=) (JAZZ 010CD) – (same as above).

—— now without DREGEN who was still in the BACKYARD BABIES

	Flapping Jet	not iss.
Jul 98. (7",7"pic-d) (FJ 007) **LIKE NO OTHER MAN. / GIMME SHELTER**		-

	Munster	not iss.
Aug 98. (7"blue) (7112) **CITY SLANG. / BORN BROKE**		-
(re-iss. Nov99; same)		

	Estrus	Estrus
Aug 98. (7",7"colrd) (<ES7 122>) **LOOKING AT ME. / ROCK HAMMER**		

	Rocketdog	not iss.
Nov 98. (7") (RD-07001) **ROCK'N'ROLL JIHAD**		-

 – Times are low / NITWITZ: Jackass.

	Bang	not iss.
Dec 98. (7"colrd) (BANG 004) **DIRTY WOMEN**		-

 – I got the shakes / Evil woman.

	Anyway	not iss.
Mar 99. (7") (AWR 49) **LOWERED PENTANGLES. / (other by New Bomb Turks)**		-

	Man's Ruin	Sub Pop
Mar 99. (cd; split with GLUECIFER) (MR 117) <SP 476> **RESPECT THE ROCK AMERICA**		

 – American ruse / Working for MCA / A man and a half / Her strut / Doggone your bad luck soul / (others by GLUCIFER). (re-iss. Aug00; same)

Mar 99. (10"ep) (MR 155) **DOGGONE YOUR BAD LUCK SOUL**
 – (same tracks as above).

	Butcher's Hook	not iss.
Mar 99. (7") (HOOK 004) **A HOUSE IS NOT A MOTEL. / (other by the Powder Monkeys)**		-

—— guests on below were **SCOTT MORGAN** – lead guitar, vocals + **DANIEL REY** – lead guitar

	Sub Pop	Sub Pop
Apr 99. (7") <(SP 454)> **DOWN RIGHT BLUE. / THANKS FOR NOTHING**		

	White Jazz	Sub Pop
May 99. (cd/lp) (JAZZ 016 CD/LP) <SP 474> **GRANDE ROCK**		Jun99

 – Action de Grace / Alright already now / Move right out of here / Welcome to Hell / The electric eel index / Paul Stanley / Angel dust [lp-only] / The Devil stole the beat from the Lord / Dogday mornings / Venus in force / 5 vs. 7 / Lonely / Renvoyer.

Aug 99. (7"/cd-s)<7"pic-d> (7JAZZ 021/+CD) <SP 477> **THE DEVIL STOLE THE BEAT FROM THE LORD. / HOLIDAY CRAMPS / BE NOT CONTENT**		Aug99

Oct 99. (7"/cd-s) (7JAZZ 023/+CD) **MOVE RIGHT OUT OF HERE. / HEART OF THE MATTER**
(cd-s+=) (JAZZ 023CDL) – Makes it alright / The Devil stole the beat from the Lord (live).
(10"++=) (JAZZ 023) – Alright already now (live).

	Gearhead	not iss.
Jun 99. (7") (none) **CRIMSON BALLROOM. / (other by Rocket From The Crypt)**	-	- fanz
Jul 99. (7") (none) **DISAPPOINTMENT BLUES. / (split w/ BLA TAGET)**	-	- Norway

—— added **ROBERT 'STRINGS' DAHLQVIST** – guitar
(below was a shared effort with the QUADRAJETS)

	not iss.	Estrus
Oct 99. (7") <ES7 144> Quadracopters: **THINK IT OVER. /** Hellajets: **I WASN'T BORN IN A HALLWAY**	-	

Feb 00. (7"; as SCOTT MORGAN & THE HELLACOPTERS) <SP 483> **SLOW DOWN TAKE A LOOK. / 16 WITH A BULLET**

	Munster	Munster
Nov 99. (7") (MR 7112) **CITY SLANG. / BORN BROKE**	-	

	Safety Pin	Safety Pin
Jun 00. (7") (SP 017) **MASTER RACE ROCK. /** Powder Monkeys: **TWO TUB MAN**		-

			Universal	Polygram
Oct 00.	(cd-s) *(158 349-2)* **TOYS AND FLAVORS / A CROSS FOR CAIN**		-	-

(7"-iss. on 'Sweet Nothings'; 7SN 002)

Oct 00.	(cd) *(159 737-2)* <*1003*> **HIGH VISIBILITY**			Mar01

– Hopeless case of a kid in denial / Baby borderline / Sometimes I don't know / Toys and flavours / You're too good (to me baby) / Throw away heroes / So song unheard / Truckload of nuthin' / A heart without a home / No one is gonna do it for you / I wanna touch / Hurtin' time / Envious. *(d-lp-iss.Oct00 on 'Sweet Nothing'; SNLP 006)*

Jan 01.	(10"m-lp)(m-cd) (<*FRO 1003*>)(<*AFROCD 008*>) **WHITE TRASH SOUL** (split w/ FLAMING SIDEBURNS)			

– Whole lotta shakin' goin' on in my heart (since I met you) / Get ready / Ungrounded confusion / (others by the FLAMING SIDEBURNS).
(above issued on 'Bad Afro')

Jan 01.	(cd-s) *(158 553-2)* **HOPELESS CASE OF A KID IN DENIAL / COLD NIGHT FOR ALLIGATORS / (I'M A) STEALER**		-	- Sweden
Mar 01.	(cd-ep) (<*158801-2*>) **FLIGHTCASE** <US title 'THE HELLACOPTERS'>			

– Hopeless case of a kid in denial / A cross for Cain / Cold night for alligators / (I'm a) Stealer / Like no other man (live).

May 01.	(cd-s) *(158 782-2)* **NO SONG UNHEARD / HAVE MERCY ON THE CHILDREN / YOU LEFT THE WATER RUNNING**		-	- Sweden
Mar 01.	(7") *(fr-017)* **STAB YOR BACK. / Adam West: NEAT NEAT NEAT**			

(above + below issued on 'Fandango')

Sep 01.	(7"; as NICKE ROYALE) *(fr-023)* **BURT WARD LAW. /**			
Nov 02.	(cd) (<*64998-2*>) **BY THE GRACE OF GOD**			Sep02

– By the grace of God / All new low / Down on freestreet / Better than you / Carry me home / Rainy days revisited / It's good but it just ain't right / U.Y.F.S. / On time / All I've got / Go easy now / The exorcist / Pride.

– compilations, others, etc. –

Sep 98.	(cd) *Au-Go-Go;* (<*ANDA 246CD*>) **DISAPPOINTMENT BLUES** (B-sides)			

– Long gone losers / Freeway to Hell / Heaven / Speed freak / Disappointment blues / Ferrytale / 455 SD. *(lp-iss.Oct98; ANDA 246) (re-iss. Nov98 on 'White Jazz' 10"lp/cd; JAZZ 015 LP/CD)*

Jan 99.	(7"pic-d) *007;* <*#20*> **IT'S NOT A LONG WAY DOWN. / FREEDOM TO HELL (live) / LONG GONE LOSERS (live)**		-	- mail-o
Feb 99.	(7") *Fandango;* <*fr-015*> **TWIST ACTION. / FAKE BABY**			tour
Jan 02.	(m-cd) *Universal;* <*1027*> **GEEKSTREAK**			
Feb 02.	(m-lp) *Sweet Nothing;* (12N 007) **THE HELLACOPTERS**			

– Have mercy on the children / Cold night for alligators / I'm a stealer / You left the water running / Like no other man (live) / A house is not a motel.

Apr 02.	(d-lp) *Sweet Nothing;* (SNLP 017) / *Gearhead;* <*34*> **THE CREAM OF THE CRAP VOL.1**			

Karl HENDRICKS TRIO

Formed: Pittsburgh, Pennsylvania, USA ... early 90's by namesake KARL HENDRICKS and sidekick rhythm players TIM PARKER and TOM HOFFMAN. Having abandoned his former grungy outfit, SLUDGEHAMMER, singer/guitarist HENDRICKS opted for the indie-rock route via a series of self-financed demo cassettes. From this humble background came next the inaugural debut LP, 'BUICK ELECTRA' (1992), which led on to further moody, autobiographical sets such as 'SOME GIRLS LIKE CIGARETTES' (1992), '. . .SINGS ABOUT MISERY AND WOMEN' (1994), 'A GESTURE OF KINDNESS' (1995) and 'FOR A WHILE, IT WAS FUNNY' (1996); KARL even took time out to play bass for THEE SPEAKING CANARIES with DON CABALLERO's DAMON CHE. Having already inked a deal with 'Merge' records, The KARL HENDRICKS TRIO once again submitted another decent, but not groundbreaking set, 'DECLARE YOUR WEAPONS' (1998).

Album rating: BUICK ELECTRA (*5) / SOME GIRLS LIKE CIGARETTES (*5) / THE KARL HENDRICKS TRIO SINGS ABOUT MISERY AND WOMEN (*5) / A GESTURE OF KINDNESS (*4) / FOR A WHILE, IT WAS FUNNY (*5) / DECLARE YOUR WEAPONS (*6)

KARL HENDRICKS (b. 1970) – vocals, guitar / **TIM PARKER** – bass / **TOM HOFFMAN** – drums

			not iss.	Peas Kor
1992.	(lp) **BUICK ELECTRA**		-	

– Dead flowers / Heart gone wrong / The last bus / Stupidhead / Painted my heart / She was hot / All that's left / Dumber than I look / I don't wanna be in love / Orange Nehi / Heart of steel / Nowhere but here / She's the shit / Fuck shit up / Beergasm / Ride you home. *(UK-iss.Feb95 on 'Grass'; GROW 38-2)*

			not iss.	Big Ten Rex
1992.	(10"lp) **SOME GIRLS LIKE CIGARETTES**		-	

– Some girls like cigarettes / Pittsburg's hottest babes / It could be a miracle / It could be a miracle (pt.2) / Baseball cards / Smartypants / If this song was a cigarette / Ducky / The last thing you'll ever do for me / How's the cat? <*cd-iss. Apr95 on 'Merge'; MRG 94*>

			not iss.	Mind Curve
1992.	(7") **BASEBALL CARDS. / SMARTYPANTS**		-	
1993.	(7") **CHECKING YOU OUT. / VALENTINE MELODY**		-	
			not iss.	Egg-Yolk
1994.	(7") **CATCH THE WIND. / (other by MOTHRA)**		-	
			Fire	Fiasco
Jun 94.	(cd/lp) *(FIRE CD/LP 39)* <*107*> **THE KARL HENDRICKS TRIO SINGS ABOUT MISERY AND WOMEN**			Oct93

– Get out your hankies for this one / Do you like to watch me sob? / Romantic stories from the war / Distant relations / Flowers avenue / I don't need your shit / Women and strangers / You're a bigger jerk than me / I didn't believe in gravity / You can't argue with cash / You're the man / You poor miserable fool.

1995.	(cd) <*109*> **A GESTURE OF KINDNESS**		-	

– Foolish words of a woman in love / The official shape of beauty / The scoffer's reply / What you're queen of now / Four babes in a Pontiac / The dress you bought in Cleveland / King beds and morning coffee / Desperate drunken artist / Breathtaking first novel / A gesture of kindness / Your damned impertinence.

— **LEN JARABECK** – bass; repl. PARKER

			not iss.	Merge
Apr 93.	(7") <*MRG 93*> **WHAT EVERYONE ELSE CALLS FUN. / A BOY WHO PLAYS WITH DOLLS**		-	
1996.	(cd) <*MRG 107*> **FOR A WHILE, IT WAS FUNNY**		-	

– Naked and high on drugs / A boy who plays with dolls / Somewhere a weekend of sin / Coming in September / Nogales by Tuesday / The hearts of Spaniards everywhere / Spock is depressed / Pale lips / Apologies for crying / How can you dance?

1997.	(7") **THE WORST COFFEE I'VE EVER HAD (pt.2). / OUT ON THE WEEKEND**			
Feb 98.	(cd/lp) <*MRG 137*> **DECLARE YOUR WEAPONS**		-	

– Like John Travolta / A letter to the coach / Surrender on demand / Your lesbian friends / Know more about jazz / The policeman's not your friend / When will the goddamn poor wise up? / The colonel feels all right / The smile that made you give up / The worst coffee I've ever had.

— (late 1998) **CHRIS EMERSON** – drums; repl. HOFFMAN

— added **MATT JENCIK** – guitar

— (late 2001) **KARL** plus **CAULEN KRESS** – bass + **JAKE LEGER** – drums

— The KHT are about to issue a new set in 2003

HENRY'S DRESS

Formed: Albuquerque, New Mexico, USA ... 1993 by AMY LINTON and MATT HARTMAN (alternating singing/guitar/drum duties), and bassist HAYYIM. When LINTON was accepted into the San Francisco Art Institute, the trio relocated west, while debut single '1620', was released on 'Slumberland' records'. Following a split single with TIGER TRAP, 1995 saw the release of the eponymous 'HENRY'S DRESS' eight-track 10" EP, featuring songs recorded in 1993 and 1994. Beginning to create a buzz amongst the West Coast indie community, they were approaching a very distinctive indie-rock sound, and style, drawing comparisons with SONIC YOUTH, amongst others. Using pedals and distortion combined with LINTON's dreamy vocals, HENRY'S DRESS create a haunting, melancholic sound; fully in evidence on slow-burner 'THREE'. The acclaimed 1996 LP, 'BUST 'EM GREEN', displayed real signs of maturity and progression. An album of quick-fire mod-art-punk-pop, featuring a dozen tracks in just over 25 minutes, its strengths are its simplicity, immediacy, and attitude. This was to be HENRY'S DRESS' final release, and after touring with ROCKETSHIP they split-up, with HAYYIM going on to record as UAKACHAKA GUITAH, and LINTON forming The AISLERS SET. Initially working solo, LINTON soon recruited TRACK STAR's WYATT CUSICK (guitar), POUNDSIGN#'s ALICIA VANDENHEUVAL (bass), and SCENIC VERMONT's YOSHI NAKAMOTO (drums). Essentially all LINTON's own work, AISLERS debut LP 'TERRIBLE THINGS HAPPEN' (1998) contrasts the WHO inspired indie-pop, with hushed, heart-broken vocals. Employing JEN COHEN on keyboards, AISLERS SET's 2000 LP 'THE LAST MATCH' followed a similar indie-pop path, successfully drawing on even more 60s influences and sounds. LINTON also teamed up with STEWART ANDERSON to form SPLIT, releasing a 1999 EP of lo-fi, home-recorded guitar pop. • **Covered**: Aislers Set: YEH YEH (Georgie Fame) / BALLOON SONG (14 Iced Bears).

Album rating: HENRY'S DRESS mini (*5) / BUST 'EM GREEN (*7) / Aislers Set: TERRIBLE THINGS HAPPEN (*6) / THE LAST MARCH (*7)

AMY LINTON – vocals, drums (ex-GO SAILOR) / **MATT HARTMAN** – guitar / **HAYYIM** – bass

			Slumberland	Slumberland
1994.	(7") <*WISH 2*> **1620. / STUMBLE**			
Mar 95.	(7") <*SLR 33*> **split w/ TIGER TRAP**			
Apr 95.	(10"m-lp/m-cd) <*SLR 34/+CD*> **HENRY'S DRESS**		-	

– Definitely nothing / Title forthcoming / Sally wants / (You're my) Radio one / "A" is for cabbage / Three / Feathers / You killed a boy for me.

Dec 96.	(lp/cd) <*(SLR 54/+CD)*> **BUST 'EM GREEN**			Mar96

– The way she goes / Target practice / Winter '94 / Hey Allison / Treefort / Get yourself together / Jimmy / Sunshine proves all wrongness / All this time for nothing / Zero-zero-zero / Not today / Self starter.

			not iss.	Omnibus
1997.	(7") <*OMNI 008*> **ALL THIS TIME FOR NOTHING. / (other by FLAKE)**		-	

— split in 1996, HAYYIM went solo as UAKACHAKA GUITAH, AMY formed ...

AISLERS SET

AMY LINTON – vocals, multi / with some guests

			Slumberland	Slumberland
Jul 98.	(lp/cd) <*(SL 55/+CD)*> **TERRIBLE THINGS HAPPEN**			

– Friends of the heroes / California / Holiday gone well / Alicia's song / I've been mistreated / Mary's song / Why baby / Long division / London Madrid / Cocksure whistler / Army street / Falling backwards / Jaime's song / My boyfriend (could be a Spanish man).

— added **JEN COHEN** – keyboards (of The FAIRWAYS)

			555	Slumberland
Mar 99.	(7") *(555/15)* <*SLR 52*> **BEEN HIDING. / FIRE ENGINES**			
Apr 99.	(7") <*WISH 7*> **THE WALK (part 1). / (other by POUNDSIGN)**		-	

HENRY'S DRESS (cont) — THE GREAT INDIE DISCOGRAPHY — The 1990s

Apr 99. (7") <FAN 012> **NOT TOO YOUNG TO GET MARRIED. / (other by POUNDSIGN)**
(above issued on 'Fantastic' records)

1999. (7"ep; as AMY LINTON) <SLR 64> **AMY LINTON / STEWART ANDERSON split**
– The lights are out / Romance, baby I don't care (STEWART ANDERSON) / Hipsters, scenesters, teenstars and fakers / I cut my tooth on one just like you (STEWART ANDERSON).

Oct 00. (7") (555/30) **HEY LOVER. / (other by The HOW)**

—— added **WYATT CUSICK** – multi, vocals (of TRACK STAR) / **ALICIA VANDEN HEUVEL** – bass (of POUNDSIGN) / **YOSHI NAKAMOTO** – drums (of SCENIC VERMONT)

	Fortuna Pop!	Slumberland
Sep 00. (cd) (FPOP 23) <SLR 062CD> **THE LAST MATCH**		

– The way to Market station / Hit the snow / Chicago New York / One half laughing / Been hiding / Balloon song / Lonely side of town / The last match / Christmas song / The walk / The red door / Fairnt chairnt / We give up / Bang bang bang. (lp-iss.Jul00 on '555'; 555/3)

Oct 00. (one-sided;7") <WISH 8> **HAPPY HOLIDAYS FROM THE AISLERS SET AND SLUMBERLAND RECORDS**

Nov 00. (7") (TIB 4) **YEH, YEH. / (other by the FAIRWAYS)**
(above issued on 'Yakamashi')

Apr 01. (7"ep) (FPOP 27) <SLR 66> **THE RED DOOR. / SUMMERS REPRISE / WARM GIRLS (live)**

	Suicide Squeeze	Jul01 not iss.

Apr 01. (7") (S 015) **ACTION, ATTRACTION, REACTION. / CLOUDS WILL CLEAR**

HENTCHMEN

Formed: Caniff, Detroit, Michigan, USA ... autumn 1992, by JOHN SZYMANSKI and MIKE LATULIPPE (under the monikers of JOHNNY VOLARE and TIM V. EIGHT). A largely influential hammond organ-driven garage rock band, which owed more to the SSMALL FACES than MC5, The HENTCHMEN were just one of many bands connected to the Detroit garage scene (which all seemed to lead back to MICK COLLINS – of The DIRTBOMBS and The GORIES). Surviving mostly without a bassist for their entire career and known to be quite prolific if not flippant (SZYMANSKI had his fingers in many pies including PAYBACKS, DETROIT COBRAS and The WILDBUNCH – latter currently The ELECTRIC SIX), the group had recorded four albums during the 90's; '...ULTRA HENTCH' (1994), 'CAMPUS PARTY' (1995), 'BROAD APPEAL' (1997) and 'MOTORVATIN'' (1998). In 1999, WHITE STRIPES frontman and general Detroit garage knockabout, JACK WHITE, joined the group briefly as their bassist. It was with WHITE that The HENTCHMAN issued the ultra rare (and now extremely expensive) 'HENCH-FORTH' EP (1999), before going off to join random groups – see above – in their city's musical community. After a three-year gap, they re-formed for the minor masterpiece 'THREE TIMES INFINITY', which fused RAMONES-style riffs with ARTHUR LEE and RAY DAVIES licks. • Covered: DON'T YOU JUST KNOW IT (Smith-Vincent) / OH BABYDOLL + IT DON'T TAKE BUT A FEW MINUTES + COUNTY LINE (Chuck Berry) / NEVER MET A GIRL LIKE YOU BEFORE (Kinks) / SINCE I LAST SAW YOU (Fick ...) / DIMPLES (John Lee Hooker) / MUSH MOUTH MILLIE (Bo Diddley) / THUNDER EXPRESS (Comma-Drake) / SLOW DOWN (...Williams) / RED HOT CAR (Holiday-Verne) / RAININ' IN MY HEART (Slim Harpo) / SOME OTHER GUY (...Barrett) / PSYCHO DAISIES (Yardbirds) / LUCILLE (Little Richard) / SHIMMY SHAKE (Devo) / TEENAGE LETTER (Renald Richard).

Album rating: ...ULTRA HENTCH (*5) / CAMPUS PARTY (*5) / BROAD APPEAL (*6) / MOTORVATIN' (*5) / THREE TIMES INFINITY (*7)

JOHNNY VOLARE (aka JOHN SZYMANSKI) – vocals, organ / **TIM V. EIGHT** – guitar, vocals / **CHRIS HANDYSIDE** – drums

	not iss.	Front Porch
1993. (7"ep) <FPR 1> **NERVOUS RECK EP**		

– Nervous reck / Cindybeth / Henthbeat / Creepdog.

1993. (7"ep) <FPR 2 – HH 1004> **THE BREATHER**
– Red pony tail / The breather / Get out of my way (right now).
(above was a shared released with 'Happy Hour')

	Norton	Norton
1994. (7"m) <45-025> **HOT ROD MILLIE. / OUR LITTLE RENDEZVOUS / RAWHIDE**		
Sep 94. (cd/lp) <C+/ED 237> **...ULTRA HENCH**		

– Fly catcher / Don't you just know it / Find me a girl / Nervous reck / County line / Plumbline stomp / Never met a girl like you before / Get outta my way / Chicks & cars / Mothball / Five year itch / Red ponytail / Hot rod Millie / Hentchbeat / Blue bull blues / Since I last saw you.

1994. (7"m) <FPR 3> **GIRL FROM JACKSON. / BRAND NEW PORCH / OH BABYDOLL**
(above issued on 'Front Porch', below on 'Estrus')

1995. (7"ep) <ES 768> **YPSILANTI'S NEWEST HITMAKERS**
– Two tone Belair / 20 girls / Porch recker.

1995. (7"m) <45-034> **SO MANY GIRLS. / MEAN '37 / FARFISA & THE AIRLINE**

1995. (7"m) <GH 176> **MY CATALINA. / CONTAGION / BY THE OLD MILL STREAM**
(above issued on 'Get Hip', below on 'Hillsdale')

1995. (7"m) <HR 011> **RED HOT CAR. / WOLF WAGON / OIL LEAK**

Dec 95. (cd/lp) <C+/ED 245> **CAMPUS PARTY**
– Campus party / Dimples / Every girl I see / I got wheels / Mush mouth Millie / Diesel / Bag of tricks / Traction / So many girls / J-5 / Mess around with you / Thunder express / Brown bomber / School's a drag / Scare tactic / Get in my car and drive.

1995. (7"m) <099> **GRAVEL-BITE. / IT DON'T TAKE BUT A FEW MINUTES / THE PASSERBY**
(above issued on '1 + 2', below on 'Verboten')

1996. (7"ep) (none) **PORTRAIT OF THE HENTCHMEN** — German
– Larry / New contagion / Michigan blues / Cindy Beth / Our man Flint.

1997. (7"m) <LZ 037> **RAININ' IN MY HEART. / MUTE / GIRL FROM JACKSON**
(above issued on 'Larsen' records)

—— **MIKE "AUDI" LATULLIPE** – drums; repl. HANDYSIDE

1997. (7") <45-057> **RED RIVER ROCK. / WHY DID GOD MAKE GIRLS**

Nov 97. (cd/lp) <(C+/ED 257)> **BROAD APPEAL** — Sep97
– Michigan blues / Slow down / Casmere and campau / Chrissy rides again / Half step away / Exit 154 / Old enough to drive / Four eyed buick / Red hot car / Lookin' for a girl / Shadow play / Leaving the Highlands / My Catalina / Nothing to say / Celibate stroll / Lucille.

Nov 98. (cd/lp) <C+/ED 264> **MOTORVATIN'**
– Polish lady / Life story / Rat bones / Take me back to the arcade / Poor Sherilee / Naked sister / West side brat / Elektra / (Cryin' just like) Otis / Two tone Blair (live) / Half step away (live) / Every girl I see (live) / Yesterday's trash (live) / Leaving the Highlands (live) / Hot rod Millie (live) / Take a good look (live) / So many girls (live).

—— added guest **JACK WHITE** – bass (of WHITE STRIPES)

1998. (7") <IR 004> **SOME OTHER GUY. / PSYCHO DAISIES**

Jan 99. (m-lp) <IR 008> **HENTCH-FORTH**
– Yesterday's trash / L.A.M.F. / Automatic / Gawker delay / Me and my monotone / Big screen lover / Little no more / Carry me home / R&R cancer.
(above 2 issued on 'Italy' records)

Nov 99. (7") <45-068> **COME ON SANTA. / MERRY CHRISTMAS BABY**

1999. (7") <GRS 109> **HAM AND OIL. / CLUB WAGON**

2000. (7") <DET.002> **TEENAGE LETTER. / CREEP OF THE YEAR**
(above 2 on 'Gas' and D-wrecked' respectiv..., below on 'Keystone')

2000. (7"ep) <KEY 1-EP> **ONE UP!**
– Old lady (down the road) / Cut out / LaSabre radar / Messed up (my brain).

—— SZYMANSKI moonlighted with The PAYBACKS, The DETROIT COBRAS and The WILBUNCH (later ELECTRIC SIX) on various releases

Nov 02. (cd/lp) <C+/ED 294> **THREE TIMES INFINITY**
– Straight up / Makin' out / Brain power / Broke down / Shimmy shake / April / LeSabre radar / Front porch entertainers / At the phone / Beat that / Pack up and go / Teenage letter.

Stephen HERO
(see under ⇒ KITCHENS OF DISTINCTION; 80's section)

HEROIC DOSES (see under ⇒ 5 STYLE)

HERON

Born: ROB HERON, Liverpool, England. Scouser, PAUL HERON, is the mastermind behind HERON's bluesy lo-fi sounds – effectively a one-man band. ROB was inspired to produce his own music firstly by PRINCE, and then by BECK. Becoming a prolific songwriter, he released two 7" singles on his own label 'Cracked Analogue', before the arrival of his debut LP, 'THE BROWN ROOM', in early 2002 (and now on the 'Hut' label). Completely self-written, recorded and produced, the set was an exquisite fusion of blues, hip-hop, electro and techno, containing stand-out tracks like the haunting 'WE GET HIGH' and the funky 'PUNK MUTHAFUCKA'. A minor masterpiece, and surely one of the debuts of 2002.

Album rating: THE BROWN ROOM (*7)

ROB HERON – vocals, instruments

	Cracked Analogue	not iss.
Jun 01. (7") (CA 001) **B SIDES VOL 1**		

– Umbrella / Punk muthafucka.

Nov 01. (7") (CA 002) **B SIDES VOL 2**
– Juke box saloon / Lemon aid.

	Hut	not iss.
Mar 02. (cd/lp) (HUT CD/LP 73) **THE BROWN ROOM**		

– J-funk / I want 2 know / Umbrella / Jukeboxsaloon / We get high / Punk muthafucka / Keyboard song / Cracked analogue / I'll B your alibi / Every little thing.

HER SPACE HOLIDAY

Formed: San Mateo, California, USA ... 1994 by MARC BIANCHI as a solo project and creative channel for his electronic dream-pop. Multi-instrumentalist BIANCHI is the mastermind behind the 'Audio Information Phenomenon' label and a former member of bands MOHINDER, CALM, INDIAN SUMMER; he also worked with BRIGHT EYES. HER SPACE HOLIDAY's first release was a 1996 12", 'AUDIO ASTRONOMY', which contained spaced-out electronica combined with the sonic assault of shoegazing, and could clearly be linked to the sounds of SLOWDRIVE and MY BLOODY VALENTINE. HER SPACE HOLIDAY recordings from between 1996-98 formed 2000's 'ASTRONAUTS ARE SLEEPING' (released on Milwaukee's 'No Karma' label). HSH had two further releases in 2000, the 'SILENT FILMS' EP and the swooning double-disc 'HOME IS WHERE YOU HANG YOURSELF'; with BIANCHI's girlfriend KEELY involved in the

production process. Subdued vocals and harmonies, mesh with guitars, samples and electronic beats to create an air of solemn ambience, although it failed to enter uncharted musical territory. The following year also saw the release of an EP, 'ELECTRONIC SUNRISE' and an LP, 'MANIC EXPRESSIVE'. BIANCHI's mastery of sound production is fully evident on 'MANIC . . .'.
• **Covered:** GIGANTIC (Pixies).

Album rating: AUDIO ASTRONOMY (*5) / HOME IS WHERE YOU HANG YOURSELF (*6) / MANIC EXPRESSIVE (*6)

MARC BIANCHI – vocals, multi-electronics

not iss. Trainbridge

Jun 96. (lp) **AUDIO ASTRONOMY**
– Slow down smile / Through the eyes of a child / Gravity fails us / Pictures of music / One million galaxies / Dreaming / Skyliner / Hair cut short / Crazy (studio). <US cd-iss. Nov 02 on 'Tiger Style'+=; TS 24> – Wish list / Indie car / Sick at best.

1998. (7") **split w/ URBAN LEGENDS** *not iss. Audio Information Phenomenon*

1999. (7") <AIP 6> **ELECTRONIC SUNRISE. / (other by FLOWCHART)** *not iss. Clover*

1999. (7") **SLIDE GUITARS. /** *not iss. Japan Motorway*

1999. (7") **WISH LIST. /** *not iss. Bravenoise*

1999. (cd-ep) **SOMETHING BLUE** *not iss. Dogprint*

Nov 99. (cd-ep) <8> **SILENT FILMS**
– Silent films / Skyline / The unbelievable broadcast / All my old friends / Gigantic.

— added **KEELY** – vocals

Wichita Tiger Style

Jul 00. (cd/lp) (WEBB 002/+LP) <TS 7> **HOME IS WHERE YOU HANG YOURSELF** Jun00
– Home is where you hang yourself / Snakecharmer / Through the eyes of a child / A matter of trust / The doctor and the DJ / Sleeping pills / Famous to me / Can you blame me / Sugar water / Homecoming / Misery loves company. *(cd w/ free cd+=)* – Godspeed (by ASPERA AD ASTRA) / Contrast and compare (by BRIGHT EYES) / Sounds just like an ocean (by NOVASONIC DOWN HYPERSPACE) / Smile decoy (by MICROMARS) / Singing arc lamp (by MAHOGANY) / And things are mostly ghosts (by DUSTER) / Famous to me (hurtful kid mix).

Sep 00. (7") (WEBB 005S) **THE DOCTOR AND THE DJ. / (other by BRIGHT EYES)**
(cd-s+=) (WEBB 005SCD) – Making words work / Hurtful kid.

Jul 01. (cd; by Various Artists) (WEBB 017) **AMBIDEXTROUS**
(mixed by HER SPACE HOLIDAY)

Oct 01. (cd) (WEBB 022) <TS 17> **MANIC EXPRESSIVE**
– Manic expressive (enter) / Lydia / The ringing in my ears / Polar opposite / Key stroke / Spectator sport / Hassle free harmony / Perfect on paper / Manic expressive (exit).

Nov 01. (cd-s) (WEBB 021SCD) **KEYSTROKE (awayteam mix) / MICROFILMED / HASSLE FREE HARMONY (bench remix)**

– compilations, etc. –

Jan 99. (cd) *Skylab Operations;* **THE ASTRONAUTS ARE SLEEPING (VOL.1)**

Jan 99. (cd) *No Karma;* <011> **THE ASTRONAUTS ARE SLEEPING (VOL.2)**
– These days / Crazy / Sunday drivers / Slide guitars and moving cars / Count on the days / Audiophase / 1939 / You know why I lie / Homecoming / Ceilingstars.

HERZFELD (see under ⇒ McCARTHY; in 80's section)

HE SAID (see under ⇒ WIRE; 70's section)

HEX (see under ⇒ CHURCH; in 80's section)

HIGH

Formed: Manchester, England . . . late 80's by ex-member of The STONE ROSES, ANDY COUZENS. Recruiting a line-up of JOHN MATTHEWS, SIMON DAVY and CHRIS GOODWIN, COUZENS attempted to secure his band a place in the lucrative 'Madchester' scene which his former bandmates had unwittingly helped form and from which they'd assumed near legendary status. Signed to 'London' in the rush to find the "next big thing" from Manchester, The HIGH achieved minor chart success at the dawn of the 90's with their first three singles. Trading in a melodic yet predictable retro, quasi psychedelic "baggy" sound encompassing the likes of The LA's, The BYRDS and of course The STONE ROSES, COUZENS & Co. finally cracked the Top 30 in early '91 with a revamped version of their debut single, 'BOX SET GO'. Yet by this point the press were sharpening the knives for one of the most vicious backlashes of the 90's and as the debut album, 'SOMEWHERE SOON' (1990) languished in relative obscurity, The HIGH's inextricable link with the scene was to be their downfall. The band at least had a sense of humour, titling their second album, 'HYPE' (1992) even as it almost instantly hit the bargain bins along with excess copies of The FARM's debut.

Album rating: SOMEWHERE SOON (*6) / HYPE (*4)

JOHN MATTHEWS (b.23 Sep'67, Torquay, Devon, England) – vocals / **ANDY COUZENS** (b.15 Jul'65) – guitar (ex-STONE ROSES, ex-BUZZCOCKS FOC) / **SIMON DAVY** (b.24 Jan'67) – bass / **CHRIS GOODWIN** (b.10 Aug'65) – drums (ex-BUZZCOCKS FOC, ex-INSPIRAL CARPETS)

London not iss.

Jun 90. (7"/c-s) (LON/+CS 261) **BOX SET GO. / P.W.A.**
(12"+=/cd-s) (LON X/CD 261) – P.W.A. (instrumental).

Aug 90. (7"/c-s) (LON/+CS 272) **UP AND DOWN. / MAKE IT HAPPEN** 53
(12"+=/cd-s+=) (LON X/CD 272) – Bombay mix.

Oct 90. (7"/c-s) (LON/+CS 280) **TAKE YOUR TIME. / Bombay mix – live** 56
(12"/cd-s) (LON X/CD 280) – ('A'side) / ('B'-full length).
(12") (LONXP 280) – ('A'side) / Box set go / A minor turn (live).

Oct 90. (cd/c/lp) (828 224-2/-4/-1) **SOMEWHERE SOON** 59
– Box set go / Take your time / This is my world / Rather be Marsanne / So I can see / A minor turn / Dreams of Dinesh (a.k.a. Bombay mix) / Up and down / P.W.A. / Somewhere soon.

Jan 91. (7"/7"g-f/c-s) (LON/+G/CD 286) **BOX SET GO (remix). / BOX SET GO (original) / P.W.A. (instrumental)** 28
(12"/cd-s) (LON X/CD 286) – (first 2 versions) / Up & down / This is my world.
(7"ep) (LONP 286) – ('A'live) / So I can see (live) / This is my world (live) / P.W.A. (live).

Mar 91. (7"/c-s) (LON/+CS 297) **MORE . . . / FOUR THIRTY / MAKE IT HAPPEN** 67
(12"+=/cd-s+=) (LON X/CD 297) – Blue tourist.
(10") (LONP 297) – More . . . (madness) / More . . . / Blue tourist.

Aug 92. (7"/c-s/12"/cd-s) (LON/+CS/X/CD 324) **BETTER LEFT UNTOLD. / HICKORY SMOKE / JOUSTABOUT**

Sep 92. (cd/c/lp) (828 354-2/-4/-1) **HYPE**
– Better left untold / The healer / Sweet liberty / This is your life / Let nothing come between us / Goodbye girl / Keep on coming / Slowly happens here / Can I be / Lost and found.

Feb 93. (12"ep/cd-ep) (LON X/CD 333) **SWEET LIBERTY. / THIS IS YOUR LIFE (the wonderknob session) / BETTER LEFT UNTOLD (the wonderknob session)**

— split after the hype had faded

HIGH BACK CHAIRS

Formed: Washington D.C., USA . . . 1989 by songwriter PETER HAYES and his laid back veteran sidekicks, CHARLES BENNINGTON, JIM SPELLMAN, CHARLES STECK and JEFF NELSON. With ELI JANNEY (of GIRLS AGAINST BOYS) upholstering/engineering their early sound, their comfy twee power-pop (with illustrations of er, squirrels on the sleevework courtesy of bass player, STECK), managed to release only a couple of mini-sets for FUGAZI-connected label, 'Dischord'. Er, sofa so good. The aforementioned 'OF TWO MINDS' (1991) and 'CURIOSITY AND RELIEF' (1992), were high-class HIGH BACK CHAIRS short-players, although the 'CHAIRS split in '93; SPELLMAN joined VELOCITY GIRL.

Album rating: OF TWO MINDS mini (*6) / CURIOSITY AND RELIEF mini (*5)

PETER HAYES – vocals, guitar / **CHARLES BENNINGTON** – guitar, vocals / **JIM SPELLMAN** – guitar / **CHARLES STECK** – bass, vocals / **JEFF NELSON** – drums, vocals

Dischord Dischord

Jan 92. (m-cd/m-c/m-lp) <(DIS 56 CD/C/V)> **OF TWO MINDS** Nov91
– Miles to inches / Take away / Swear / Wild / Kiss & tell / Doldrums / Afterlife / Cannon fodder.

Oct 92. (7") <(DIS 74V)> **SHARE. / ONE SMALL STEP**

Nov 92. (m-cd/m-c) <(DIS 75CD/CS)> **CURIOSITY AND RELIEF**
– Share / One small step / Dream of a day / Unending / Fuj / Summer.

— went into hibernation after above; SPELLMAN joined VELOCITY GIRL while HAYES formed WONDERAMA (2 singles for 'Ajax')

HIGH FIDELITY
(see under ⇒ SOUP DRAGONS; in 80's section)

HIGH LLAMAS

Formed: London, England . . . 1991 by Irish-born, ex-MICRODISNEY co-leader, SEAN O'HAGAN. Following his split with former songwriting partner and future FATIMA MANSIONS man, CATHAL COUGHLAN, O'HAGAN spent the bulk of the ensuing three years crafting his first solo work, 'HIGH LLAMAS' (1990). Released on retro specialist, 'Demon', the record was the toast of classic West Coast pop connoiseurs, critics already mentioning O'HAGAN's work in the same breath as BRIAN WILSON (a constant reference point for reviewers over the course of HIGH LLAMAS/O'HAGAN's career). Confusingly enough, by the release of 1992's mini-set, 'APRICOTS', he'd decided to promote his backing musicians (JOHN FELL, MARK PRINGLE and old MICRODISNEY man, TOM FENNER) to full band status, naming the project the HIGH LLAMAS. An eagerly anticipated full-length follow-up, the very BEACH BOYS-esque 'GIDEON GAYE', finally appeared in 1994 (the Europe-only 'SANTA BARBARA' album was also released in '94 although it was subsequently re-issued in the UK after O'HAGAN signed to 'V2' in the late '90's), its luxuriant, hypnotic blend of orchestration and harmonies suggesting that O'HAGAN's part-time work with STEREOLAB had been at least as much of an influence as his penchant for vintage transatlantic sounds. Another superlative-heavy critical reception led to a Stateside deal with 'Epic', while O'HAGAN set up his own 'Alpaca Park' label to re-issue the album in the UK the following year. 1996's 'HAWAII' set was even more ambitious, a kitsch, pseudo-psychedelic mesh of O'HAGAN's favourite things very much in the BEACH BOYS' late 60's/early 70's mould. After the band had finally secured a British major label deal with Richard Branson's new 'V2' label, two further HIGH LLAMAS albums, 'COLD AND

BOUNCY' and 'LOLLO ROSSO', appeared in 1998. The 'LLAMAS issued the very disappointing 'SNOWBUG' in 1999, but made up for it with the delivery of 2000's psychedelic 'BUZZLE BEE', an album much in the same vein of late 60's shimmering Californian sunburst classics such as 'Pet Sounds'. And with titles such as 'NEW BROADWAY', 'TAMBOURINE DAY' and 'SLEEPING SPRAY', why not?

Album rating: HIGH LLAMAS (*6) / APRICOTS mini (*5) / SANTA BARBARA (*5) / GIDEON GAYE (*6) / HAWAII (*6) / COLD AND BOUNCY (*6) / LOLLO ROSSO (*7) / SNOWBUG (*4) / BUZZLE BUG (*6)

SEAN O'HAGAN – vocals, guitar, keyboards (ex-MICRODISNEY) / with **JOHN FELL** – bass / **TOM FENNER** – drums (ex-MICRODISNEY) / **MARK PRINGLE** – piano, bass

Demon — not iss.

Sep 90. (lp/c/cd; by SEAN O'HAGAN) *(FIEND/+C/CD 90)* **HIGH LLAMAS**
– Perry Como / Edge of the sun / Pretty boy / Hoping you would change your mind / C'mon let's go / Paint & pets / Doggy / Half face cut / Trees / Have you heard the latest news. *(cd re-iss. Jul98 on 'Diabolo'; DIAB 866)*

— SEAN joined STEREOLAB on a part-time basis while continuing with his own band **JOHN BENNETT + ROB ALLUM** + others

Plastic — not iss.

Jan 92. (m-cd/m-lp) *(PLAS CD/LP 003)* **APRICOTS**
– Travel / Banking on karma / Birdies sing / Period music / Black balloon / Apricots. *(cd re-iss. Dec95; same)*

Jacky Boy — not iss.

Dec 92. (cd) *(none)* **SANTA BARBARA** — French
– Put yourself down / Birdies sing / Banking on karma / Market traders / Travel / Taximan's daughter / Period music / Holland / Apricots. *(UK-iss.Jan98 on 'V2'; VVR 100108-2) <US-iss.Jan98 on 'V2'; 27011>*

Target — Epic

Apr 94. (cd) *(TGT 012CD)* **GIDEON GAYE**
– Giddy strings / Dutchman / Giddy and gay / Easy rod / Checking in, checking out / Goat strings / Up in the hills / The goat looks on / Taog skool no / Little collie / Track goes by / Let's have another look / Goat. *(re-iss. Feb95; same) (re-iss. Jul95 on 'Alpaca Park' cd/c/lp; CD/MC/LP WOOL 1)*

Alpaca Park — Alpaca Park

Jun 95. (c-s) *(WOOLM 1)* **CHECKING IN, CHECKING OUT / APRICOTS**
(12"+=/cd-s+=) *(WOOL/+D 1)* – Cropduster.

Mar 96. (cd/c/lp) *(CD/MC/LP WOOL 2) <27004>* **HAWAII**
– Cuckoo casino / Sparkle up / Literature is fluff / Nomads / Snapshot pioneer / Ill-fitting suits / Recent orienteering / The hot revivalist / Phoney racehorse / Dressing up the old Dakota / D.C.8 / Doo-wop property / Theatreland / A friendly pioneer / Cuckoo's out / Peppy / There's nobody home / The hokey curator / Campers in control / Double drift / Island people / Incidentally N.E.O. / Tides / Nomad strings / Pilgrims / Rustic vespa / Folly time / Hawaiian smile / Untitled. *(cd re-iss. Jan98 on 'V2'; VVR 100109-2) (d-cd re-iss. Apr98 +=; 27004-2)* – NOMADS

Jun 96. (12"ep/cd-ep) *(WOOL T/D 2)* **NOMADS EP**
– Might as well be Dumbo / Cropduster / Mini-management / Chimes of a city clock / Literature is fluff / 3 frame offset.

V2 — V2

Jan 98. (cd/d-lp) *(VVR 100073-2/-1) <27007>* **COLD AND BOUNCY**
– Twisto teck / Sun beats down / Hiball Nova Scotia / Tilting windmills / Glide time / Bouncy glimmer / Three point scrabble / Homespin rerun / Painters paint / Evergreen vampo / Showstop hip hop / Over the river / End on tick tock / Didball / Jazzed carpenter / Lobby bears.

Mar 98. (7") *(VVR 500146-7)* **SUN BEATS DOWN. / SHOWSTOP**
(cd-s+=) *(VVR 500146-3)* – Stop trainer.

Oct 98. (cd/lp) *(VVR 100258-2/-1) <27034>* **LOLLO ROSSO**
– Showstop hic hup / Homespin rerun / Homerun ubershow / Mini-management / Space raid remix / Reflections in a plastic glass / Milting tindmills.

Sep 99. (7") *(VVR 500937-7)* **COOKIE BAY. / HARMONIUM**
Oct 99. (cd/d-lp) *(VVR 100897-2/-1) <27063>* **SNOWBUG**
– Bach ze / Harper's romo / Hoops Holley / Cookie Bay / Traids / The American scene / Go to Montecito / Janet jangle / Amin / Dalton's star / Cotton to the bell / Green coaster / Cut the dummy loose.

— now with guest **MARY HANSEN** – vocals (of STEREOLAB)

Duophonic Super — V2

Oct 00. (cd/lp) *(DS45CD/DS33 28) <70085>* **BUZZLE BEE**
– Passing bell / Pat mingus / Get into the galley shop / Switch pavilion / Tambourine day / Sleeping spray / New Broadway / Bobby's court. *<(lp-iss.Nov00 on 'Drag City'; DC 191)>*

HIS NAME IS ALIVE

Formed: Livonia, Michigan, USA ... 1987 by WARREN DEFEVER (also of group, ELVIS HITLER) alongside schoolfriends, ANGELA CAROZZO and KARIN OLIVER. Over the course of the next few years they issued a series of self-financed recordings, the last of which, 'EUTECTIC', was a commission for Detroit's Harbinger Dance Company. Subsequently snapped up by arty UK indie label, '4 a.d.', HIS NAME IS ALIVE made their British debut with the avant-garde, pseudo-gothic experimentalism of the 'LIVONIA' (1990) album. Sounding something like the COCTEAU TWINS fused with ENO, the record found DEFEVER feeding his guitar flurries and folky strumming through an echo chamber, the resulting sonic debris melting into OLIVER's graceful harmonies. Follow-up set, 'HOME IS IN YOUR HEAD' (1991), continued in a similarly dark vein, focusing, as ever, on the more disturbing aspects of human nature, while 'THE DIRT EATERS' EP featured a surprising coice of cover material in Rainbow's 'MAN ON THE SILVER MOUNTAIN' alongside the HNIA classic, 'WE HOLD THE LAND IN GREAT ESTEEM'. 1993's more upbeat 'MOUTH BY MOUTH', meanwhile, divided the songs between HNIA and sister act, confusingly enough also titled the DIRT EATERS; the result was a complementary collection of raucous DE guitar workouts alongside the glacial ambience and haunting harmonies of the HNIA material. The product of a songwriting partnership between DEFEVER and new collaborators, SMITH and IAN MASTERS (ex-PALE SAINTS), 1996's 'STARS ON E.S.P.' was HIS NAME IS ALIVE at their most accessible, turning in a collection of largely acoustic, BEACH BOYS influenced folk-pop. Two years later, DEFEVER changed direction once more on the rockier 'FORT LAKE', the likes of 'WISH I HAD A WISHING RING' sounding like a scuzzier SKUNK ANANSIE! Along with LOVETTA PIPPEN and FRED THOMAS (of FLASHPAPR), DEFEVER was back challenging music styles again courtesy of 2001's 'SOMEDAY MY BLUES WILL COVER THE EARTH', a groove-friendly excursion into contemporary urban-pop territory.

Album rating: LIVONIA (*8) / HOME IS IN YOUR HEAD (*7) / MOUTH BY MOUTH (*7) / KING OF SWEET out-takes (*5) / STARS ON E.S.P. (*8) / FORT LAKE (*6) / ALWAYS STAY SWEET compilation (*7) / SOMEDAY MY BLUES WILL COVER THE EARTH (*6) / ESP Summer: MARS IS A TEN (*6)

WARREN DEFEVER (b.1969) – guitar, bass, vocals, samples / **KARIN OLIVER** – vocals, guitar / **ANGELA CAROZZO** – vocals

not iss. — Nonhnia1

1987. (c-ep) **RIOTOUSNESS AND POSTROPHE**
1987. (lp) **HIS NAME IS ALIVE**
1988. (c) **I HAD SEX WITH GOD**
1988. (lp) **EUTECTIC**

4 a.d. — Rykodisc

Jun 90. (lp/cd)(c) *(CAD 0008/+CD)(CADC 0008) <10244>* **LIVONIA**
– As we could ever / E-Nicolle / If July / Some and I / E-Nicolle / Caroline's supposed demon / Fossil / Reincarnation / You and I have seizures / How ghosts affect seizures / How ghosts affect relationships / Darkest dreams. *(cd re-iss. Jul98; GAD 0008CD)*

— CAROZZO departed and was repl. by **DENISE JAMES** – vocals / **MELISSA ELLIOTT** – guitar / **JYMN AUGE** – guitar / **DAMIAN LANG** – drums

Sep 91. (lp/cd)(c) *(CAD 1013/+CD)(CADC 1013) <20243>* **HOME IS IN YOUR HEAD** — Jul92
– This week / Eyes were / Charmer / Hope (song of schizophrenia) / Feathers (song of schizophrenia) / Well (song of schizophrenia) / Something / Ice / Are we still married? / Put your finger in your eye / Home / Why people disappear / Eyes are / Birds / Chances are we are mad / Mescalina / Sitting / Very bad / Beautiful / Tempe / Spirit / Fish eye / Dreams. *(cd re-iss. Jul98; GAD 1013CD)*

Apr 92. (12"ep/cd-ep) *(BAD 2005/+CD)* **THE DIRT EATERS EP**
– Man on the silver mountain / Are we still married? / Is this the way the tigers? / We hold the land in great esteem.

4 a.d. — 4ad-Warners

Apr 93. (lp/cd)(c) *(CAD 3006/+CD)(CADC 3006) <45214>* **MOUTH BY MOUTH**
– Baby fish mouth / Lip / Cornfield / In every Ford / Lord, make me a channel of your peace / Drink, dress and ink / Where knock is open wide / Can't go wrong without you / Jack rabbits / Sort of / Sick / Blue moon / Ear / Lemon ocean / The torso / The dirt eaters. *(cd re-iss. Jul98; GAD 3006CD)*

— **DEFEVER with SMITH + IAN MASTERS** (ex-PALE SAINTS)

May 96. (7") *(AD 6007)* **UNIVERSAL FREQUENCIES. / SUMMER OF ESP**
(cd-s+=) *(BAD 6007CD)* – Up your legs forever / Your word against mine.

Jun 96. (lp/cd) *(CAD 6010/+CD) <46207>* **STARS ON E.S.P.** — Jul96
– Dub love letter / This world is not my home / Bad luck girl / What are you wearing tomorrow / The bees / What else is new list / Wall of speed / Universal frequencies / The sand that holds the lakes in place / I can't live in this world anymore / Answer to rainbow at midnight / Famous goodbye king / Across the street / Movie. *(cd re-iss. Jul98 +=; GAD 6010CD)* – NICE DAY EP

Apr 97. (7"ep; with LITTLE PRINCESS) *(MOTOR 016)* **PET FARM EP**
(above on 'Motorway' & below on 'Friendly Science')

Aug 97. (7") *(FS 02)* **SOUND SYSTEM WANTS IT SWEET. /**
Nov 97. (cd-ep) *<46838>* **NICE DAY**
– Nice day / Baby you feel me up / Hot / Crashed up on the corner / Whale, you ease my mind / Drive around the clock.

Jun 98. (cd) *(CAD 8009CD) <97673>* **FT. LAKE** — Aug98
– Don't glue the world / Everything takes forever / Waitress / No hiding place down her / Can't always be loved / Wish I had a wishing ring / Red haired girl / A spirit needs a spirit too / Up your legs forever / How it got to be / Always turn me on / Rock'n'roll girl from rock'n'roll / Last American blues.

Aug 98. (7"m) *(AD 8015)* **CAN'T ALWAYS BE LOVED. / CAN'T WAIT FOREVER / WISH I HAD A WISHING RING (first one 04:09)**
(cd-s) *(BAD 8015CD)* – ('A'side) / Wish I had a wishing ring (uncut 17:14).

Feb 99. (cd) *<79002>* **ALWAYS STAY SWEET** (compilation)
– Are you coming down this weekend? / Her eyes were huge things / E-Nicolle / If July / How ghosts affect seizures / Chances are we are mad / As we could ever / Are we still married? / Why people disappear / Blue moon / Cornfield / Home is in your head / Underwater / Home in life Great Eastern / Last one / Sitting still moving still staring . . . / The sand that holds the lakes in place / In every Ford / Baby fish mouth / The dirt eaters / Man on the silver mountain.

— **DEFEVER with LOVETTA PIPPEN + FRED THOMAS**

Jul 01. (cd) *(CAD 2101CD) <72101>* **SOMEDAY MY BLUES WILL COVER THE EARTH** — Aug01
– Nothing special / Interlude / Happy blues / Solitude / Write my name in the groove / Your cheating heart / Our last affair / One year / Interlude / Karin's blues / Are we still married? / Someday my blues will cover the earth / Last time.

– others, etc. –

1993. (ltd-cd) *Perdition Plastics; <NONHNIA 7>* **KING OF SWEET** (out-takes, etc)
1995. (cd) *Time Stereo; <1227>* **SOUND OF MEXICO** (live)
Sep 96. (cd) *Time Stereo; <12228>* **GREAT LAKES STATE BLUES** (live)
1999. (cd) *Time Stereo;* **RADIO LP**
2000. (cd) *Time Stereo;* **IN THE EAST**
2000. (cd) *Time Stereo;* **WHEN THE STARS REFUSE TO SHINE**

ESP SUMMER

WARREN DEFEVER + IAN MASTERS

        not iss.   **Perdition Plastics**

1995. (10"m-lp) *<PER 005>* **ESP SUMMER**
– Everything grows together / When it shows / No tomorrow / Let's be together today / I'm taking care of you / United friendly.

1996. (cd; as E.S.P. CONTINENT) **MARS IS A TEN**
– Sticky sun / Web of dream / Simple eye / More water / Golden heart of the year / Land of 102 / Your hands / On you / Splinters / Last time hand / When leaves are gone / No June. *(UK-iss.May97 as 'ESP SUMMER'; same as US)*

        unknown   *not iss.*

1997. (7"ep; as ESP NEIGHBOURHOOD) *(FS 01)* **BAD VIBRATIONS E.P.**
– Golden heart of the year / Bad vibrations / Another thought / Pen = symphony.

HIVES

Formed: Fagersta, Sweden ... 1993 by NICHOLAUS ARSON, his brother HOWLIN' PETE ALMQVIST – later, CHRIS DANGEROUS, DR. MATT DESTRUCTION AND VIGILANTE CARLSTROEM were added to the line-up. Owing as much style and zeitgeist to The STOOGES, The KINKS and The ROLLING STONES as The STROKES did, this punky, mod-looking collective were banging out quasi-garage rock tunes before The STROKES had even left private school. In hindsight, possibly the only reason The HIVES became so popular after four years of industry/consumer ignorance was because of the Garage rock explosion during the summer of 2001, but, unlike the dull-ish LOU REED drone of The STROKES, The HIVES partied like it was 1969 ... and boy did they rock some! Clad in Al Capone gangster uniform (black suit, white tie, naturally), The HIVES originally began playing rock'n'roll to annoy the commercial punk pundits who sifted around their hometown of Fagersta. After an inaugural EP in '96 ('OH LORD! WHEN? HOW?'), the quintet issued their debut album 'BARELY LEGAL' in September 1997 and practically became local heroes, selling-out clubs and venues and rocking up a storm with the Swedish music press. Soon the word spread like wildfire around Scandinavia and The HIVES issued 'aka I-D-I-O-T' as a mini-set at the beginning of '98. A thrash blend of rawk'n'roll and punk, the release was to be the band's last for almost two years as they began to experience management problems. However, this break turned out to be a blessing in disguise as they re-emerged in 2000 with a killer album and a re-invented, semi-fictional history involving a mysterious MONKEES-esque manufacturing. 'VENI VIDI VICIOUS' smacked the European music press in the face with its screeeeeching guitars, fuzz-bass and hollering, but nobody seemed to be paying any attention – for now. The British music buying public missed the soaring KINKS driven anthems that were 'HATE TO SAY I TOLD YOU SO' and 'MAIN OFFENDER' the first time around when they were issued as singles in 2000 and 2001, but thanks to a Garage-rock revival, a few TV promos and ALAN McGEE (now boss at the newly-formed 'Poptones' imprint), The HIVES legacy was finally realised with the premiere of their "Best Of ..." compilation 'YOUR NEW FAVOURITE BAND' (2001, and a title taking a subtle dig at the histrionic coverage that The STROKES received in the NME). The two aforementioned singles were re-released the following year to – hurrah! – critical acclaim, which just shows that sometimes you can't just lead a horse to the water, you have to make it drink the damn thing as well. • **Trivia:** Their mysterious 6th member/writer, FITZSIMMONS was actually mainman PETE who seemingly took the name of his old school teacher.

Album rating: BARELY LEGAL (*7) / a.k.a. I-D-I-O-T mini (*5) / VENI VIDI VICIOUS (*8) / YOUR NEW FAVOURITE BAND (*8)

HOWLIN' PETE ALMQVIST – vocals / **NICHOLAUS ARSON** (b. ALMQVIST) – guitar / **VIGILANTE CARLSTROEM** – guitar / **DR MATT DESTRUCTION** – bass / **CHRIS DANGEROUS** – drums

        Burning Heart   **Gearhead**

Jun 96. (cd-ep) *(JABSCD 001)* **OH LORD! WHEN? HOW?**
– You think you're so darn special / Cellblock / Some people / How will I cope with that? / Bearded lady / Let me go.

Sep 97. (cd) *(BHR 068CD)* **BARELY LEGAL**
– Well, well, well / a.k.a. I-D-I-O-T / Here we go again / I'm a wicked one / Automatic schmuck / King of asskissing / Hail hail spit n' drool / Black Jack / What's that spell? ... go to hell! / Theme from ... / Uptempo venomous poison / Oh Lord! when? how? / The stomp / Closed for the season. *<(US+re-iss. cd/lp-iss.Mar01/Jan02 on 'Gearhead'; RPM 030 CD/LP)>*

Mar 98. (m-cd,m-lp) *(BHR 072) <RPM 023>* **a.k.a. I-D-I-O-T**
– a.k.a. I-D-I-O-T / Outsmarted / Untutored youth / Fever / Mad man / Numbers. *(re-iss. Mar01 on 'Gearhead' m-lp/m-cd; same as US)*

Apr 00. (cd/lp) *(BHR 107-2/-1) <82005-2>* **VENI VIDI VICIOUS**   Sep00
– The Hives – declare guerre nucleaire / Die, all right! / A get together to tear it apart / Main offender / Outsmarted / Hate to say I told you so / The Hives – introduce the metric system in time / Find another girl / Statecontrol / Inspection wise 1999 / Knock knock / Supply and demand. *(lp re-iss. Jul02 on 'Gearhead'; RPM 040LP)(hit US No.63)*

Dec 00. (7"/cd-s) *(BHR 122-2) <RPM 024/+CD>* **HATE TO SAY I TOLD YOU SO. / DIE, ALL RIGHT! / THE HIVES ARE LAW, YOU ARE CRIME**
(re-iss. Jan02 on 'Gearhead'; same as US)

Sep 01. (cd-s) *(BHR 134-2)* **MAIN OFFENDER / LOST AND FOUND / HOWLIN' PELLE TALKS TO THE KIDS**

        Poptones   **Poptones**

Sep 01. (7") *(MC 50555)* **SUPPLY AND DEMAND. / THE STOMP**

Oct 01. (cd) *(<MC 5055CD>)* **YOUR NEW FAVOURITE BAND** (compilation)   Apr02
– Hate to say I told you so / Main offender / Supply and demand / Die, all right! / Untutored youth / Outsmarted / Mad man / Here we go again / a.k.a. I-D-I-O-T / Automatic schmuck / Hail hail spit n' drool / Hives are law you are crime. *(cd+=)* – Main offender (video) / Hate to say I told you so (video) / a.k.a. I-D-I-O-T (video) / Die, all right! (video). *(re-dist.Jan02)* – hit UK No.7. *(lp-iss.Mar02; MC 5055LP)*

Nov 01. (7") *(7SN 006)* **MAIN OFFENDER. / LOST AND FOUND / HOWLIN' PELLE TALKS TO THE KIDS**
(above issued on 'Sweet Nothing') (re-iss. Dec01 on 'Big Wheel' 7"/cd-s; BWR 0248/+CD)

Feb 02. (7") *(BHR 1058-7)* **HATE TO SAY I TOLD YOU SO. / UPTEMPO VENOMOUS POISON**   23   86
(cd-s+=) *(BHR 1057-2)* – Gninrom ytic kcorknup.
(cd-s) *(BHR 1059-2)* – ('A'side) / Fever / Barely homosapien.
(above issued on 'Burning Heart') (below on 'Hard On' records)

Mar 02. (7"ep; split w/ PRICKS) *(HARDON 2)* **3:30 PUNK ROCK CITY MORNING / GNINROM YTIC KCOR KNUP 3:30 / NUMBERS. / (other side by The Pricks)**

May 02. (7") *(MC 5076S)* **MAIN OFFENDER. / LOST AND FOUND**   24
(cd-s+=) *(MC 5076SCD)* – Hate to say I told you so (live on Top Of The Pops + video).

Oct 02. (cd-s) *(MC 5078SCD)* **DIE, ALL RIGHT! / SUPPLY AND DEMAND**

HOGGBOY

Formed: Sheffield, England ... January 2000 by HOGG, HUGH (aka 'SMIFF'), BAILEY and RITCHIE. After a chance meeting of HOGG and SMIFF on the top deck of a No.53 bus in their home city, the two decided to get together in a band and brought BAILEY and RITCHIE in to complete the line-up. Playing a kind of energetic garage rock hybrid, the boys soon relocated to London where with the assistance of PULP's RICHARD HAWLEY, the band recorded their debut 7", 'SO YOUNG' (2001). The single stalled for a while until it was championed by Radio One DJ Steve Lamacq; the British music community were no doubt begging for some homegrown rock talent to compete with the likes of The HIVES and The STROKES. HOGGBOY's sophomore single, 'SHOULDN'T LET THE SIDE DOWN', appeared in spring 2002 and was followed by promotional touring, where the band garnered more publicity appearing with the likes of The WHITE STRIPES and the aforementioned STROKES. Their ensuing debut set, 'OR 8?', was a competent affair, but not likely to knock their foreign rivals off their NME pedestal. The set was also helped by the assistance of veteran producer CHRIS THOMAS.

Album rating: OR 8? (*5)

HOGG – vocals, guitar / **HUGH 'SMIFF'** – guitar / **BAILEY** – bass / **RITCHIE** – drums

        Sobriety   *not iss.*

Jan 02. (7") *(SOB 2)* **SO YOUNG. / CALL ME SUCK**
Apr 02. (7"/cd-s) *(SOB 4/+CDA)* **SHOULDN'T LET THE SIDE DOWN. / URGH!!!**   74
Jul 02. (7"/cd-s; w-drawn) *(SOB 10/+CD)* **LEFT AND RIGHT**
Sep 02. (7"/cd-s) *(SOB 12/+CD)* **UPSIDE DOWN. / TITILATION**
Oct 02. (cd) *(SOB 13CD)* **OR 8?**
– Left and right / Upside down / Don't get lost / Urgh!!! / Call me suck / Gonna take me a while / Death of a friend? / So young / Shouldn't let the side down / 1:10 / Mile high club.

HOLE

Formed: Los Angeles, California, USA ... late 1989 by COURTNEY LOVE (bizarrely enough, a two-piece indie band of the same moniker – see under LOIS – surfaced with a few 45's a year later!) and six foot plus guitarist and Capitol records employee, ERIC ERLANDSON. LOVE, who had previously worked as an exotic dancer and an actress (she appeared in the 1986 punk movie, 'Sid & Nancy') and played alongside JENNIFER FINCH (L7) and KAT BJELLAND (Babes In Toyland) in a band called SUGAR BABY DOLL, was also involved in an early incarnation of FAITH NO MORE. Taking the name HOLE from a line in Euripides' Medea, they placed an ad in a local paper, 'Flipside', finding a bassist and drummer, namely JILL EMERY and CAROLINE RUE. In the Spring of 1990, HOLE released the 'RAT BASTARD' EP, subsequently relocating to the burgeoning Seattle area. Early the following year, 'Sub Pop' issued the 'DICKNAIL' EP, the band duly signing to 'Caroline' records for their debut album, 'PRETTY ON THE INSIDE'. Produced by KIM GORDON and DON FLEMING, it hit the lower regions of the US charts, the record being voted album of the year by New York's Village Voice magazine. A harrowing primal howl of a record, LOVE's demons were confronted mercilessly on such psyche-trawling dirges as 'TEENAGE WHORE' and 'GARBAGE MAN'. Around the same time, LOVE's relationship with NIRVANA's KURT COBAIN, was the talk of the alternative rock world, the singer subsequently marrying him in February '92, giving birth to their daughter, Frances Bean, later that summer. The following year, with newcomers PATTY SCHEMEL (drums) and KRISTEN PFAFF (bass), the group secured a deal with the David Geffen Company ('D.G.C.'), much to the dismay of MADONNA who wanted HOLE for her newly formed 'Maverick' label. In Spring 1994, LOVE finally celebrated a UK Top 20 album, 'LIVE THROUGH THIS', although its success was overshadowed by the shocking suicide of KURT on the 8th of April. She subsequently held a memorial two days later, hailing everyone there to call him an asshole.

More press coverage followed later that summer, when PFAFF was found dead in her bath on the 16th June (it was believed to be another tragic drug related death). Despite the press circus surrounding LOVE, the band played a rather disappointing Reading Festival stint in August that year, her at times lethargic vox letting some of the more discerning fans down (EVAN DANDO of The LEMONHEADS was rumoured to be her new boyfriend, although a number of lucky people – including DANDO – were privy to her womanly charms – both of them – when she "flashed" at the side of the stage). With a new bassist, MELISSA AUF DER MAUR, the group released two UK hits, 'DOLL PARTS' and 'VIOLET', LOVE certainly back on top form with her incendiary Top Of The Pops performances (LYDIA LUNCH eat your heart out!?). Back in the news again, she was fined for assaulting BIKINI KILL's KATHLEEN HANNA, LOVE and SCHEMEL conversely taking three security guards to court following an alleged assault incident while signing autographs stagefront at a GREEN DAY concert in Lakefront Arena (yet more column inches were devoted to the controversial singer in August '96, when LOVE was acquitted of a stage assault nine months previous on two teenage fans in Florida). More recently, LOVE has played down her wild child character, exchanging the Seattle grunge mantle for a more respectable Hollywood career. This was largely down to her acclaimed roles in the movies, 'Feeling Minnesota' and more so with the controversial, 'The People Vs. Larry Flint'. On the recording front, only a lone version of FLEETWOOD MAC's 'GOLD DUST WOMAN' has surfaced (this was included on the film soundtrack from 'The Crow II: City Of Angels'). In '98, COURTNEY (and HOLE) was once again writing new material, this time with BILLY CORGAN of the SMASHING PUMPKINS, although a dispute over who actually wrote what the public thought were collaborations was subsequent tabloid news. The album in question, 'CELEBRITY SKIN' (1998), was worthy of its Top 10 placing although a little commercialised for some. The following year (in November), MELISSA bailed out of the band and more shocking still was that she joined COURTNEY's old pal CORGAN in The SMASHING PUMPKINS.
• Covers: STAR BELLY sampled DREAMS (Fleetwood Mac) + INTO THE BLACK (Neil Young) / DO IT CLEAN (Echo & The Bunnymen) / CREDIT IN THE STRAIGHT WORLD (Young Marble Giants) / HUNGRY LIKE THE WOLF (Duran Duran) / SEASON OF THE WITCH (Donovan) / HE HIT ME (IT FELT LIKE A KISS) (Goffin-King) / IT'S ALL OVER NOW, BABY BLUE (Bob Dylan). 'I THINK THAT I WOULD DIE' was co-written w / KAT BJELLAND (Babes In Toyland). • Note: Not to be confused with band who released in the late 80's; OTHER TONGUES, OTHER FLESH (LP) and DYSKINSIA (12") both on 'Eyes Media'.

Album rating: PRETTY ON THE INSIDE (*7) / LIVE THROUGH THIS (*9) / MY BODY, THE HAND GRENADE collection (*6) / CELEBRITY SKIN (*7)

COURTNEY LOVE (b. MICHELLE HARRISON, 9 Jul'65, San Francisco, Calif.) – vocals, guitars / **ERIC ERLANDSON** (b. 9 Jan'63) – guitars / **JILL EMERY** – bass, vocals / **CAROLINE RUE** – drums

		not iss.	Sympathy F
Jul 90.	(7"white-ep) <SFTRI 53> **RETARD GIRL. / PHONEBILL SONG / JOHNNIES IN THE BATHROOM** (UK-iss.cd-ep Sep97 +=; SFTRI 53CD) – Turpentine.	-	

		not iss.	Sub Pop
Apr 91.	(7"colrd-various) <SP 93> **DICKNAIL. / BURNBLACK**	-	

		City Slang	Caroline
Aug 91.	(7"colrd-various) (EFA 04070-45) **TEENAGE WHORE. / DROWN SODA** (12"+=/cd-s+=) (EFA 04070-02/-03) – Burnblack.		
Oct 91.	(cd/c/lp-some red) (EFA 0407-2/-C/-1) <SLANG 012> **PRETTY ON THE INSIDE** – Teenage whore / Babydoll / Garbage man / Sassy / Goodsister – bad sister / Mrs. Jones / Berry / Loaded / Star belly / Pretty on the inside / Clouds. (re-iss. Sep95; same)	59	Jul91

—— **LESLEY** – bass repl. JILL / **PATTY SCHEMEL** (b.24 Apr'67, Seattle Washington) – drums repl. CAROLINE

		City Slang	D.G.C.
Apr 93.	(7") (EFA 04916-45) **BEAUTIFUL SON. / OLD AGE** (12"+=/cd-s+=) (EFA 04916-02/-03) – 20 years in the Dakota.	54	-

—— **KRISTEN PFAFF** – bass, piano, vocals repl. LESLEY

| Mar 94. | (7"some pink) (EFA 04936-7) **MISS WORLD. / ROCK STAR (alternate mix)** (cd-s+=) (EFA 04936-2) – Do it clean (live). | 64 | |
| Apr 94. | (cd/c/lp;some white) (EFA 04935-2/-4/-1) <24631> **LIVE THROUGH THIS** – Violet / Miss World / Plump / Asking for it / Jennifer's body / Doll parts / Credit in the straight world / Softer, softest / She walks on me / I think that I would die / Gutless / Rock star. (re-iss. cd/lp Mar95 on 'Geffen'; GED/GEF 24631) | 13 | 52 |

—— KRISTEN was found dead in her bath 16th June 1994. COURTNEY, ERIC + PATTI continued and later recruited **MELISSA AUF DER MAUR** (b.17 Mar'72, Montreal, Canada) – bass. As HOLEZ (HOLE + PAT SMEAR of GERMS) they released tribute GERMS cover 'CIRCLE 1' on 'Dutch East India' Mar95.

		Geffen	D.G.C.
Nov 94.	(c-s) <19379> **DOLL PARTS / PLUMP (live)**	-	58
Apr 95.	(7") (GFS 91) **DOLL PARTS. / THE VOID** (cd-s) (GFSTD 91) – Hungry like the wolf (live). (cd-s) (GFSXD 91) – ('A'side) / Plump (live) / I think that I would die (live) / Credit in the straight world (live).	16	-
Jul 95.	(7") (GFS 94) **VIOLET. / OLD AGE** (7"colrd) (GFSP 94) – ('A'side) / He hit me (it felt like a kiss). (cd-s++=) (GFSCD 94) – Who's porno you burn (black).	17	

Nov 96.	(etched-d7") (573164-7) **GOLD DUST WOMAN. / (NY LOOSE: Spit)** (above 45 was a limited edition on 'Polydor' UK, 'Hollywood' US)		
Sep 98.	(7"/c-s) (GFS/+C 22345) <radio play> **CELEBRITY SKIN. / BEST SUNDAY DRESS** (cd-s+=) (GFSTD 22345) – Dying (original demo).	19	85
Sep 98.	(cd/c/lp) <(GED/GEC/GEF 25164)> **CELEBRITY SKIN** – Celebrity skin / Awful / Hit so hard / Malibu / Reasons to be beautiful / Dying / Use once & destroy / Northern star / Boys on the radio / Heaven tonight / Playing your song / Petals. (special cd w/tour cd Jun99 +=; IND 90385) – Pretty on the inside / Heaven tonight / Northern star / Awful / Paradise city / Celebrity skin.	11	9
Jan 99.	(7") (GFS 22369) <radio cut> **MALIBU. / DRAG** (cd-s+=) (GFSTD 22369) – It's all over now, baby blue. (cd-s) (GFSCX 22369) – ('A'side) / Celebrity skin (live) / Reasons to be beautiful (live).	22	81

		Interscope	Interscope
Jun 99.	(7") (INTS7 97098) **AWFUL. / VIOLET (live)** (cd-s) (INTDE 97099) – ('A'side) / Miss World (live) / Celebrity skin (CD-Rom video). (cd-s) (INTDE 97098) – ('A'side) / She walks on me (live) / Malibu (CD-Rom video).	42	

– compilations, etc. –

| Oct 95. | (m-cd) Caroline; <1470> **ASK FOR IT** (radio session) | - | |
| Sep 97. | (cd/c/lp) City Slang; <(EFA 04995-2/-4/-1)> **MY BODY, THE HAND GRENADE** – Turpentine / Phonebill song / Retard girl / Burn black / Dicknail / Beautiful son / 20 years in Dakota / Miss World / Old age / Softer softest / He hit me (it felt like a kiss) / Season of the witch / Drown soda / Asking for it. | | Oct97 |

HOLIDAY FLYER

Formed: Roseville, California, USA . . . 1992 by brother/sister combo JOHN and KATIE CONLEY. Putting out a handful of singles in the early to mid 90's the twosome debuted with the LP, 'TRY NOT TO WORRY' (1995), which showcased their cutesy male/female, harmony-based twee indie-pop. A musical case which they furthered with their sophomore full-length set, 'THE RAINBOW CONNECTION', released two years later. This release was true to the pleasant pop genre with a lot of emotional subject matter and well thought-out lyrical content, marked out from its contemporaries by the enhancing sibling dynamics. For their next EP, 'BLUE HARVEST', released a year later, the band had grown to a threesome with the assistance of VERNA BROCK (of BEANPOLE and ROCKETSHIP fame) on bass. A year on and another member in the shape of MICHAEL YOAS had joined the fold and he helped to bolster the sound further on their third full-length effort 'YOU MAKE US GO'. The set displayed the band's un-self-conscious syrupy approach; full of tracks about love and break-up, but beneath its seemingly naive exterior showed an outfit maturing in its own musical abilities. Two years on and true to form HOLIDAY FLYER had acquired another member, JIM RIVAS, who had also seen time in ROCKETSHIP. He helped to round off their sound on the fourth LP, 'I HOPE' (2001), which benefitted from the presence of experienced knob-twiddler, LARRY CRANE.

Album rating: TRY NOT TO WORRY (*4) / THE RAINBOW CONFECTION (*5) / YOU MAKE US GO (*5) / I HOPE (*5) / Sinking Ships: OUT OF KEY HARMONY (*5)

JOHN CONLEY – vocals, guitar / **KATIE CONLEY** – vocals, drums

		not iss.	Fingerpaint
1993.	(7") <#3> **SNOWBALLING. /**	-	

		not iss.	Silver Girl
Sep 95.	(cd) <SG 021> **TRY NOT TO WORRY** – Everyday I get to see you / Is it hard to stay away? / Runaround / Can we overcome this? / Especially the ones without / Secondhand / Count my steps home / Lost at sea / Happy hour friends / Wrap the covers over my head / Let go / Weigh on me / If I can't see through / I didn't wish for you to be wrong.	-	

		Darla	Darla
Apr 96.	(cd-ep) <DRL 17> **THE BIG CALIFORNIA SOUND** – Sweet and sour / Don't go back again / Answer / Bonus 1 2 3.		

—— added **VERNA BROCK** – flute, bass, cello (of CALIFORNIA ORANGES)

		not iss.	Silver Girl
1997.	(cd) <SG 030> **THE RAINBOW CONFECTION** – Three times might be nice / Leaving us alone / Tore myself / Can I steal your heart away / Coming back to this / This town / Same / Don't paint angry / Things that made you blue / How come / Better there than here / Take me away.	-	

		Darla	Darla
Apr 98.	(cd-ep) <(DRL 058CD)> **BLUE HARVEST** – It's not every day / California / Hello blue / Convincing story / Now that you're gone / It shouldn't hurt so bad.		
1998.	(7") <PCT 005> **split w/ BEANPOLE** (above issued on 'Papercut')		

—— added **MIKE YOAS** – bass

| Sep 99. | (cd/lp) <(DRL 088 CD/LP)> **YOU MAKE US GO** – How when or where / Closer valley road / Movies / Nothing's wrong / Still here / Guts / Nobody follow me / Joke's on me / Be alright / Anyway / When will I ever learn / Surprised. | | |

—— added **JIM RIVAS** – drums (of ROCKETSHIP)

| Sep 01. | (cd) <DRL 119> **I HOPE** – Up at night / Trouble / Trains / Out of here / Falling apart at the seams / Strange / Green envy / Signals and traffic signs / Long story short / Invincible. | - | |

—— split October 2002

SINKING SHIPS

JOHN CONLEY + ZAC DAMON plus **VERNA BROCK** – bass, vocals + **ROSS LEVINE** – drums, vocals

		Darla	Darla
Nov 02.	(cd) <*(DRL 128CD)*> **OUT OF KEY HARMONY**		Oct02

– You can't push me away / It always ends the same / Give me my year back / What did I do / I'll fly anywhere / Back to the start / If we don't escape / Out of key harmony / Laughable / Complicate everything / Stars so bright.

Chris HOLMES

Born: 1971, Chicago, Illinois, USA. A musical jack-of-all-trades, CHRIS HOLMES (obviously NOT the blonde-maned, spandex-wearing one-time guitarist with schlock-rockers, WASP!) was apparently inspired by PRINCE's virtuosity, collecting and mastering an eclectic array of instruments while attending the University Of Chicago. The bespectacled intellectual also hosted his own Uni radio programme on aliens and conspiracy theory, his sci-fi obsession influencing his first musical outfit, SABALON GLITZ (named after a Dr. Who character!). Although formed in 1992 as a synth-based solo project inspired by space-rockers, HAWKWIND, no material would be commercially released until HOLMES secured a deal with 'Atlantic' in the mid-90's. Side by side with this, he was also operating a second space-themed enterprise, ASHTAR COMMAND, although as yet no official releases have materialised. The multi-faceted American had also been writing a wealth of 60's influenced psychedelic pop songs, the cream of which were released in summer 1996 as the 'DAN LOVES PATTI' album. Recorded with a full band (SARA DOMINIS, BARBARA GRETSCH, JIM NEWBERRY, MICHAEL KIRTS, HILARY RACHEL PORISS and DARCY VAUGHN) and issued under the YUM-YUM moniker, the record drew much praise for its orchestral sweeps, oblique complexity and strange melancholy vocals; in Britain, the record was released early in 1997 under his own name, UK audiences unlikely to get confused with the aforementioned ageing headbanger. Previous to all this was the aforementioned unfettering of the SABALON GLITZ set, 'UFONIC' (1995), HOLMES' homage to MY BLOODY VALENTINE, PINK FLOYD and early POPOL VUH.

Album rating: Yum-Yum: DAN LOVES PATTI (*6) / Sabalon Glitz: UFONIC (*5)

YUM-YUM

CHRIS HOLMES – vocals, guitar, multi / with **SARA DOMINIS** – vocals / **BARBARA GRETSCH** – vocals / **JIM NEWBERRY** – organ / **HILARY RACHEL PORISS** – violin / **DARCY VAUGHN** – viola / **MICHAEL KIRTS** – percussion, drums, vocals

		Atlantic	Tag-Atlantic
Nov 96.	(c-s/cd-s) *(A 5652 C/CD)* **APIARY / RAINBOW CONNECTION**		
Feb 97.	(cd; as YUM-YUM; in US-only) <*(7567 92710-2)*> **DAN LOVES PATTI**		May96

– I'm not telling / Apiary / Dan loves Patti / Doot-doot / Train of thought / Sister / Cross my heart / Ring / Jealous of the stars / Uneasy / Words will fail / Lament.

| Apr 97. | (c-s/cd-s) *(A 5617 C/CD)* **DOOT DOOT** | | - |

SABALON GLITZ

CHRIS HOLMES – multi / **ROB KAEDING** – guitars / **RICK WHITE** – percussion

		not iss.	Trixie
Oct 95.	(cd) *(ORG 016)* <8> **UFONIC**	-	-

– Hammer of the witches / Time traveller / The forge of Vulcan / Superchiasmic nucleus / Forest / The lonesome death of Elijah P. Woods / Dance of the firewalker / Ufonic. *(UK-iss.Feb98 on 'Organico'; ORG 016)*

HOLY CHILDHOOD

Formed: New Jersey, USA ... 1997 principly by DANNY LEO (formerly of NATIVE NOD), PETER KERLIN and NAWI AVILA, although recording and touring could see the band's number swell with a large number of accompanists and contributors. Some notable help was provided by LEO's brother TED (of CHISEL fame), JODI BUONNAMO (from the SECRET STARS) and GIBB SLIFE (who played with the LAPSE, interestingly fronted by LEO's other brother, CHRIS). After signing a deal with 'Gern Blandsten', the trio set about recording and releasing their debut LP, 'UP WITH WHAT I'M DOWN WITH', with the assistance of NICHOLAS VERNHES on production. The album showcased the group's unique indie mix of pop, soul, blues and folk stylings achieved via a mass of instrumentation and a great deal of ingenuity in combining these sounds to create an extremely competent and individual product.

Album rating: UP WITH WHAT I'M DOWN WITH (*7)

DANNY LEO – vocals, guitar (ex-NATIVE NOD) / **PETER KERLIN** – bass / **NAWI AVILA** – saxophones / with at times TED LEO (ex-CHISEL), JODI BUONNANNO (ex-SECRET STARS) + GIBB SLIFE

		not iss.	Gern Blandsten
May 00.	(cd) <*GERN 048CD*> **UP WITH WHAT I'M DOWN WITH**	-	

– Shame / I better be careful or I'll be understood by everybody / Fat Tuesday everyday! / I'm going to the airport / Narragansett night life / The shaker aesthetic / Emma Flood, my best friend / Sometimes I feel like a motherless child / Ambivalent blues / The Holy Childhood meets its maker on a mystery hill.

HONEYBUNCH

Formed: Providence, Rhode Island, USA ... 1987 by JEFF UNDERHILL, an American obsessed by the relatively recent British indie/twee-pop. Along with the rhythm section of PETER HIMMELMAN and CHRISTINE BAIRD, HONEYBUNCH caressed and cuddled their way into Stateside hearts via several independently released 7"ers, opening their musical account with 1989's 'HEY BLUE SKY!' for 'Bus Stop' records. "Cuddlecore" was certainly at its height in the mid-90's when the trio divided, leaving behind a posthumous CD collection, 'HOME TRIALS: 1987-1995'; UNDERHILL's fascination for twee settled with his subsequent move to VELVET CRUSH.

Album rating: TIME TRIALS: 1987-1995 compilation (*8)

JEFFREY UNDERHILL – vocals, guitar / **PETER HIMMELMAN** – bass, vocals / **CHRISTINE BAIRD** – drums

		not iss.	Bus Stop
1989.	(7") <*BUS 004*> **HEY BLUE SKY! / WARTS AND ALL**	- not iss.	Slumberland
1990.	(7") <*DRYL 005*> **CANDY BREATH. / ARM IN ARM / NO MORE I TOLD YOU SO'S**	-	
1991.	(7"flexi) <*FLW 001*> **CROOKED MILE** (above issued on 'Four Letter Words')	-	
1991.	(7") <*DRYL 014*> **MINE YOUR OWN BUSINESS. / REMEMBER YOU ALWAYS**	- not iss.	Summershine
1991.	(7") <*SHINE 018*> **WALKING INTO WALLS. / MINE YOUR OWN BUSINESS**	- not iss.	Milky Way
1991.	(7"flexi) <*none*> **NOTHING BUT TROUBLE**	- not iss.	Four Letter Words
1992.	(7"flexi) <*FLW 009*> **ENDURE ME**	- not iss.	K
1994.	(7") <*IPU 51*> **COUNT YOUR BLESSINGS. / TAPEWORM**	-	

── split in 1995; UNDERHILL joined VELVET CRUSH

– compilations, etc. –

| Oct 97. | (cd) *Elefant; (ER 1037)* / *Summershine;* <*SHINE-US 12*> **TIME TRIALS 1987-1995** | | Apr96 |

– Hey blue sky / Warts and all / Candy breath / Arm in arm / No more I told you so's / My contribution to the greenhouse effect / These dark days / Sticks & stones / Mine your own business / Remember you always / Walking into walls / Endure me / Time trials / Count your blessings / Always someone else's shadow / The great divide / I won't stand in your way / Tapeworm.

HONEYRIDER

Formed: San Diego, California, USA ... mid-90's by songwriter GARY STRICKLAND. The name came from, needless to say, the character name of the legendary part played by Ursula Andress in the Bond movie, 'Dr.No'. It was not without reason either as HONEYRIDER's stock themes involved sun-kissed babes, beaches, and sunshine. Anyone thinking of the BEACH BOYS? Although HONEYRIDER does not sound like BRIAN WILSON's crew, STRICKLAND definitely pays homage to them conceptually; with short upbeat power-pop bursts, although sonically more akin to the alternative sound of the late seventies than the early sixties. HONEYRIDER first saw the light of the record shops in single form, 'DRUGSTORE SHOOT-OUT' (1996) for the indie label 'Candy Floss'. Also appearing on this track was LISAH, the singer from local indie pop band RED DYE £5. STRICKLAND then moved to British label, 'Damaged Goods' who released several more of his singles, before collecting all of these together and beefing them out to release HONEYRIDER's debut LP 'ALL SYSTEMS GO!' in 1998. At this point STRICKLAND made his European move, relocating to Germany to work for a record firm, but soon he moved to England where he had been going sporadically on recording missions. In the millennium HONEYRIDER released their second full-length outing, 'SPLASHDOWN' on which STRICKLAND was aided by ROBIN HILL, PETRINKA DRASOVIC, and playing both bass and producing the album was former PRIMITIVES member, PAUL SAMPSON. During this time STRICKLAND went homeward to the sunny beaches of California, but would return to record in England when his muse gave him new tunes. • **Covered:** SURFIN' SAFARI (Beach Boys).

Album rating: ALL SYSTEMS GO (*4) / SPLASHDOWN (*5) / SUNSHINE SKYWAY (*6)

GARY STRICKLAND – vocals, guitar, multi / with **LISAH** – guest vocals (of RED DYE #5)

		not iss.	Candyfloss
1996.	(7",7"green) <*CFR 11*> **DRUGSTORE SHOOTOUT.** /	- Damaged Goods	Damaged Goods
Sep 96.	(7") *(DAMGOOD 105)* **ENDLESS SUMMER. / GALAXY GIRL**		-
Aug 97.	(7") *(DAMGOOD 127)* **SUMMER'S ALMOST GONE. / RADIO HEATWAVE**		-
Jul 98.	(cd/lp) *(DAMGOOD 138 CD/LP)* **ALL SYSTEMS GO!** (compilation)		-

– Endless summer / Turn me on / Summer's almost gone / Galaxy girl / Radio heatwave / Drugstore shoot-out / The subterraneans / Spacegirl / Superstar love machine / She gets around / Lovesick / Veronica / Bikini meltdown / Summertime action girls.

── **STRICKLAND** now with **PETRINKA DRASOVIC** – rhythm guitar / **PAUL SAMPSON** – bass (+ producer) / **ROBIN HILL** – drums

| Jul 99. | (7") *(DAMGOOD 168)* **STARCROSSED SUMMER. / CALIFORNIA U.S.A.** | | - |
| Jan 00. | (m-lp/m-cd) <*(DAMGOOD 177/+CD)*> **SPLASHDOWN** | | - |

– Pleasure beach / California USA / Sweeter than sunshine / Destination planet love /

HONEYRIDER (cont)

California dreams / Supersonic Cindy / Rollercoaster / You made me hate the Beach Boys / Waiting for the sun / Won't look back / Lovely young thing / Summer of my life / Starcrossed summer / Gina.

Jan 01. (7") (DAMGOOD 187) **CALIFORNIA DREAMS. / SURFIN' SAFARI**
(cd-s) (DAMGOOD 187CD) – ('A'side) / The summer scene / In the distance.

2001. (12") <011> split w/ **The Bristols**
(above on 'Trippin' Elephant')

Orange Sky / Orange Sky

Aug 02. (lp/cd) <(OS 2204/+CD)> **SUNSHINE SKYWAY**
– Suncoast / Depths of nowhere / Are you clear? / Madeira moon / Bavarian streets / Hello Tokyo / Sunshine skyway / Drowning in countryside / Coolest girl in school / Summer love affair / Summer girl / Diamond doll.

HOOD

Formed: Leeds, England ...1990 by and revolving around the principle founding members, brothers CHRISTOPHER and RICHARD ADAMS, with collaboration of varying degrees by musicians, ANDREW JOHNSON, CRAIG TATTERSALL, NICOLA HODGKINSON, JOHN EVANS and STEPHEN ROYLE. Self-taught musicians and producers, the brothers ADAMS embarked on an innovative journey in pop/rock experimentalism, inspired initially by sonic investigators, DISCO INFERNO, and BARK PSYCHOSIS. The HOOD combined an eclectic use of instrumentation with samples and electronica, crossing boundaries into the genres of hip hop, and being a forerunner of the latter experiments of UK groups such as RADIOHEAD. The HOOD came out strongly in 1992 with the release of the hard to get hold of debut single, 'SIRENS'. This was followed up, after another 7" outing, 'OPENING INTO ENCLOSURE' (including the amusingly titled track, 'I DIDN'T THINK YOU WERE GOING TO HIT ME IN THE FACE'), two years later with their debut LP, 'CABLED LINEAR TRACTION'. This earlier set was more closely associated with the indie rock sound, although the nascent inventiveness of the band could be heard. A string of further singles were issued, leading up to the release of their sophmore full-length album, 'SILENT '88' (1996). This set and its follow-up, 'STRUCTURED DISASTERS' (1997), showcased the band's progressive outlook in full-swing. The following years album, 'RUSTIC HOUSES, FORLORN VALLEYS', seemed to get a little lost in the alleyways of experimentalism, but was still a commendable release, and may well have contributed to their fifth set, 'THE CYCLE OF DAYS AND SEASONS' (1999), unfortunately not getting an initial stateside release. Meanwhile the ADAMS boys, supplemented their musical leanings, with the running of club nights, 'Freedom Sounds in Pub', and 'Echoleila'. The added elements of DJing and mixing, directed HOOD's sound towards the areas of sampling and remixing, and greater collaboration with other likeminded parties. This was probably best explored on their long-player, 'COLD HOUSE' (2001), which fuses electronica with gritty trip-hop beats, spacerock and the likes of rappers DOSE ONE and WHY?, from cLOUDDEAD, in the mix. • **Note:** not the same HOOD who had releases on 'Crepescule'.

Album rating: CABLE LINEAR TRACTION (*5) / SILENT '88 (*4) / STRUCTURED DISASTERS collection (*6) / RUSTIC HOUSES, FORLORN VALLEYS (*5) / THE CYCLE OF DAYS AND SEASONS (*6) / COLD HOUSE (*8)

CHRISTOPHER ADAMS – instruments / **RICHARD ADAMS** – instruments / with at various times **NICOLA HODGKINSON + ANDREW JOHNSON + CRAIG TATTERSALL + JOHN EVANS**

Fluff / not iss.

Sep 92. (ltd-7"ep) (HONEY 4) **LIVE LINES CAN KILL**
– Sirens / Fault / Your sixth sense.

Aug 93. (ltd-7"ep) (HONEY 6) **OPENING INTO ENCLOSURE**
– I didn't think you were coming to hit me in the face / In the trap of doing / Choosing a grimace.

Hedonist / not iss.

Mar 94. (ltd-7"flexi) (CAKE 002F) **57 WHITE BREAD**
– My last August / Experimental film-making.

1994. (ltd-lp) (ARC 01) **CABLED LINEAR TRACTION**
– Norfolk / Evening return / (little pictures) / The hay harvest had special charms / An oblique view of an irrationally happy time / Small town prejudices / Abstracting electricity / A spell of rain / Fades to end a day / Fashion mistakes of the decade / Summers last annual / Coastal driftings / British radars / Church, circular / Be nice to everyone at all times (with a few important exceptions) / Highly competitive cut throat world / Hurt [not on cd] / Untitled #2 / A thinly veiled excuse for something more. (<cd-iss. Apr99 on 'Slumberland'; SLR 46CD>)

—— in 1993/94, The HOOD also appeared on limited 7" flexis w/ HEM and HULA HOOP/BLAIRMAILER

Sticky / not iss.

Sep 94. (c; by The HOOD / MEREDITH) (STICKY 08) **NOISE, WARMTH & UNASSUMING GRACE**
– Trust me I'm a stomach / Irradiate forthwith / My Autumn days / The piano is an object / A pleasure deferred / Former miner / A job well done / August charge / Rusted airline / Choosing a grimace / Rural colours / Field day / The fateful nature of joy / Present architecture (sic) / My hollow head / Sea shelter / Token travellers.

Orgasm / not iss.

1995. (7"ep) (ORGASM 08) **A HARBOUR OF THOUGHTS / DISAPPOINTED / UNEVEN CONVERSATION SHOULD POINT TO CAUSE. / FORCED BY THE REASONING HAND / JOHN CLYDE-EVANS / SILO CRASH**

555 Record / not iss.

1995. (5x7"box) (555-01) **LEE FAUST'S MILLION PIECE ORCHESTRA**
– Biochemistry revision can wait / England's fine fields / I've forgotten how to live / Rocck? I can't even spell the word / Dismissed army brought us knives / One way negative friend utilisation / Stricken office worker.

Orange / not iss.

1995. (7"ep) (none) split w/ **CARMINE**
– Clues to our past and future existence / Myself / Failed medic.

Earworm / not iss.

1996. (ltd-7"ep) (WORM 1) **SECRETS NOW KNOWN TO OTHERS**
– Forhead / Crow blown west / Beware! falling ox / I'm turning into a cart / Further woodland / 20x / Visions of old machinery / Sometimes doomed / You should never feel alone in this world / Crushed by life.

Love Train / not iss.

Oct 96. (7") (PUBE 11) **I'VE FORGOTTEN HOW TO LIVE. / THE WEATHER SIDE OF THE STONE MILL TOWER / DIMENSIONS T.B.A.**

Slumberland / Slumberland

Dec 96. (lp/cd) (<SLR 59/+CD>) **SILENT '88**
– The field is cut / Hood northern / Delusions of worthlessness / At last! riots on Spofforth Hill / 5 / Rural colours / Western skies / Deny deny deny / Smash your head on the cubist jazz / The hidden ambience of a lost art / Being beaten up / Silent '88 / Outro / Intro / Documenting crop rotations / I hate you now / Her innocent stock of words / Trust me, I'm a stomach / Resonant 1942 / Sometimes I worry / 21 / Downpour / The fields are divided. (w/ free 7"+=) – Love is dead but never buried / Empty canvas / Silent years / untitled.

Domino / Aesthetics

Nov 97. (7") (RUG 60) **USELESS. / THE SEA AGAINST THE SAND**
Jan 98. (cd/lp) (WIG CD/LP 42) **RUSTIC HOUSES, FORLORN VALLEYS**
– S.E. rain patterns / Boer farmstead / The light reveals the place / Your ambient voice / The leaves grow old and fall and die / Diesel pioneers.

1998. (ltd-7") (ROCKET 04) **THE YEAR OF OCCASIONAL LULL. / FOG PROJECTIONS**
(above issued on 'Rocket Racer', below on 'Happy Go Lucky')

Apr 98. (ltd-7") (HAPPY 12) **FILMED INITIATIVE. / AS EVENING CHANGED THE DAY**

Jun 98. (10"ep) (555 11) **THE HOOD EP**
– (The) Weight / Fallen farmer / We are not to ptomote / Impossible calm / Feel the rush (coming in from the avant garde) / I know what to sqaunder / Mast-on-hill / Collapsing climate soul.
(above issued on '555 Recordings')

Apr 99. (cd/lp) (WIG CD/LP 61) **THE CYCLE OF DAYS AND SEASONS**
– Western housing concerns / September brings the autumn dawn / In iron light / How can you drag your body blindly through / Houses tilting towards the sea / Roads lead northwards / The cliff edge of workaday morality / (The Hood is finished).

2000. (ltd-7") <4> **[HOOD] / STEWARD**
– I can't find my brittle youth / Song of the sea / (others by STEWARD).
(above issued on 'Jonathon Whiskey')

Mar 01. (7"ep/cd-ep) (RUG 121/+CD) <13> **HOME IS WHERE IT HURTS / THE FACT THAT YOU FAILED. / COLD FIRE WOODS OF WESTERN LANES / THE WORLD TOUCHES TOO HARD / IT'S BEEN A LONG TIME SINCE I WAS LAST HERE**

Nov 01. (cd/lp) (WIG CD/LP 102) <17> **COLD HOUSE**
– They removed all trace that anything had ever happened here / You show no emotion at all / With branches bare / Enemy of time / The winter hit hard / I can't find my brittle youth / This is what we do to sell out(s) / The river curls around the town / Lines low to frozen ground / You're worth the whole world.

Apr 02. (cd-ep) (RUG 140CD) **YOU SHOW NO EMOTION AT ALL / ACROSS THE LONELY WRITING SIDE / PAINTING THE TOWN RED / GHOST BY JAPAN / YOU SHOW NO EMOTION AT ALL (video)**

– compilations, others, etc. –

May 97. (lp/cd) Happy Go Lucky; (HAPPY 10/+CD) **STRUCTURED DISASTERS**
– Swan finer / Sirens / Your sixth sense / Silo crash / A dead day / I didn't think you were going to hit me in the face / Toel bow / Choosing a grimace / My last August / Experimental filmaking / Experiments in science / Fears grow / Dismissed army brought us knives / One way negative friend utilisation. (w/ free 7"+=) – I said yes unwise yet again / 70's manual worker / Doubts slowly fade / How bad can it be.

Feb 99. (12"ep) Dropbeat; (SPL 008) **REMIXES EP**
– (by THIRD EYE FOUNDATION / HORSE OPERA / SPYMANIA / TWISTED SCIENCE).

Oct 00. (10"ep) (555LP 24) **HOOD VERSUS DUO 14 REMIX PROJECT**
– Sun on wrought iron / Steeped in history / Tuesday 2pm / My last resting place.

HOOVER

Formed: Washington, D.C., USA ... summer '92 by the short-lived line-up of FRED ERSKINE, CHRIS FARRAL and two main vocalists/musicians, AL DUNHAM and JOE McREDMOND. Unfairly dismissed at the time as the poor man's FUGAZI, HOOVER released two independent 45's before unsurprisingly signing to 'Dischord' (run by the FUGAZI team). A debut LP, 'THE LURID TRAVERSAL OF ROUTE 7' (1994), was however, to be their only output for the seminal emo-core imprint as they disbanded in the spring of '94. McREDMOND and ERSKINE subsequently resurfaced with CROWNHATE RUIN, but they too had had an all too brief affair with the musical world courtesy of one LP, 'UNTIL THE EAGLE GRINS' (1996). After a spell with REGULAR WATTS and ALBILENE, DUNHAM and his old buddies plugged in the HOOVER trio once again – minus JUNE OF 44 bound ERSKINE – for another release, the mini-EP 'HOOVER' (1998).

Album rating: THE LURID TRAVERSAL OF ROUTE 7 (*5) / Crownhate Ruin: UNTIL THE EAGLE GRINS (*4) / Hoover: HOOVER (*4)

AL DUNHAM – vocals, guitar / **JOE McREDMOND** – vocals, guitar / **FRED ERSKINE** – bass, vocals / **CHRIS FARRAL** – drums

—— released 2 unknown singles for their own label

Feb 94. (lp/c/cd) <DIS 89/+C/CD> **THE LURID TRAVERSAL OF ROUTE 7**   *not iss.*   *Dischord*
– Distant / Pretender / Shut / Route 7 / Regulator watts / Father / Cable / Letter / Cuts like drugs. *(cd+=)* – Return / Private / Dries.

— DUNHAM formed REGULATOR WATTS (two hardcore/punk albums, 'THE AESTHETICS OF NO-DRAG' + 'MERCURY' in 1997 and 1998 respectively)

CROWNHATE RUIN

ERSKINE + McREDMOND with **VIN NOVARA** – drums
    not iss.   *Dischord*

Apr 96. (cd) <DIS 98> **UNTIL THE EAGLE GRINS**
– Ride your ride / Late arriving rock dudes / Stretched too thin / In the four years to come / Every minutes sucker / Tornado season finale / Better still if they don't know / Piss alley / You will wish me dead / Blood relative.

HOOVER

— re-formed with same line-up except JUNE OF 44 bound ERSKINE
    Slowdime   *Slowdime*

Mar 98. (m-lp/m-cd) <(SLOWDIME 9/+CD)> **HOOVER**   Feb98
– T.N.T. / New five drive / Breather resist / Weeds / Relectrolux – electrodub.

HOPEWELL

Formed: Hopewell Junction, New York, USA ... 1993 by brothers JUSTIN and JASON RUSSO, with also DALIA GARIH and WHIP (aka J MERRIT). All through the mid to late 90's, the band put out a string of singles on varied indie imprints, showcasing their brand of up-front psychedelic space-rock. Although comparisons were made between them and eccentric luminaries in the shape of HARMONY ROCKETS and MERCURY REV, who the RUSSO boys joined in early 1998, there was a distinct difference in their sounds; HOPEWELL going for a louder, more stadium-orientated affair, a feat which must have rubbed off on MERCURY REV's comeback extravaganza 'Deserter's Songs'. Their own debut LP, 'CONTACT', was also released in '98, displaying their songwriting prowess and instrumental adeptness on such standouts as 'LOVE SWEET CANCER'. As well as their other musical duties, the RUSSO's managed to follow this record up with the sophomore LP proper, 'THE CURVED GLASS'. and several EPs including the brilliant 'PURPLE BALLON', for which they had the added bonus of MERCURY REV's SEAN MACKIOWIAK (aka GRASSHOPPER) in attendance. Also during the brothers RUSSO's involvement with DONAHUE, GRASSHOPPER et al, WHIP managed to find time to issue a solo album. • **Covered:** PARANOID (Black Sabbath).

Album rating: CONTACT (*7) / PURPLE BALLOON mini (*6) / THE CURVED GLASS (*5)

JASON RUSSO – vocals, guitar (of HARMONY ROCKETS) / **JUSTIN RUSSO** – keyboards, vocals, samples (of HARMONY ROCKETS) / **WHIP** (RENE BO) – bass / **DALIA GARIH** – drums
    Burnt Hair   *Burnt Hair*

1995. (7") <singe 8> **JIM LAFFIN. / (other by WINDY & CARL)**
    not iss.   *Priapus*
1996. (7",7"red) <pria 005> **STRANGER. / PARANOID**
    Burnt Hair   *Burnt Hair*
Jun 98. (cd) <singe 017cd> **CONTACT**
– Love sweet cancer / Drop / Purple balloon / Waste / Jim Laffin / Stranger / You / This little light.

— the RUSSO's joined live MERCURY REV
    Priapus   *Priapus*

Dec 98. (m-cd) <pria 012> **PURPLE BALLOON**
– Purple balloon / Lift / Sunny days / Passover, Christmas, and the best day ever / Anthema / Memories.
Oct 99. (12") <(pria 013)> **ANTHEMA (coincidental gospel version). / (other track by PLANETARIUM)**
Nov 99. (12"box; with other) <pria 014> **PIECES OF A UTOPIAN PUZZLE**
– Memorial acclamation / Moon man / Light & water goodnight.

— **RENE BO** – bass; repl. WHIP (released two for 'Priapus')
    Zeal   *Zeal*

Oct 00. (7") <(ZEAL 002)> **IN THE SMALL PLACES. / SUNNY DAYS (egoless mix)**
    Cutty Shark   *Priapus*

May 01. (cd-s) (REL 011CD) **SAFE AS MILK / CONTACT / THE CURVED GLASS**
May 01. (cd) (REL 009CD) **THE CURVED GLASS**   Jan01
– The angel is my watermark / In the small places / There is something / There is nothing / Safe as milk / Moonman / Lazy day / Memorial acclamation B / Christmas now / The fish / Watermark (reprise) / Light & water goodnight.
Sep 01. (cd-s) (REL 012CD) **THE ANGEL IS MY WATERMARK / A KISS / INCANTATIO**

HOPE BLISTER
(see under ⇒ THIS MORTAL COIL; in 80's section)

HOPPER

Formed: London, England ... 1992 by RACHEL MORRIS, PAUL SHEPHERD, CHRIS BOWERS and MATT ALEXANDER, who met at the capital's 'Brain Club'. Signed to 'Damaged Goods', the band bounced onto the scene with a single, 'HUNTER', followed in summer '94 with the equally promising 10" EP, 'BABY OIL APPLICATOR'. MORRIS's feisty attitude turned the head of 'Factory (Too)' boss, Tony Wilson, who signed the quartet up for a series of singles and a debut album, 'ENGLISH AND FRENCH' (1996). While the earlier released 'WASTED' single kicked and snarled like a chained rottweiler, producer BERNARD BUTLER (ex-SUEDE) overlayed the band's sweet'n'sour guitar attack with lofty string touches and lent the album (their one and only) a more accessible sheen.

Album rating: ENGLISH AND FRENCH (*5)

RACHEL MORRIS – vocals / **PAUL SHEPHERD** – guitar / **CHRIS BOWERS** – bass / **MATT ALEXANDER** – drums
    Damaged Goods   *not iss.*

Jan 94. (7") (DAMGOOD 29) **HUNTER. / DEPTH**
Jul 94. (10"ep) (DAMGOOD 39) **BABY OIL APPLICATOR**
– Baby oil applicator / Fifteen / Won't hurt a bit / Shine / Sugary.
    Factory Too   *not iss.*

Jul 95. (7") (FAC 2.05) **WASTED. / DOUBLE JOY**
(cd-s+=) (FACD 2.05) – So damn clever / Dangerous men.
May 96. (7"/cd-s) (FAC 2.22/+CD) **BAD KID. / CHEAP JACK**
Jul 96. (7") (FAC 2.32) **RIDICULOUS DAY. / E.S.P.**
(cd-s+=) (FAC 2.32) – Weeping Mary.
Jul 96. (cd/c/lp) (FAC D/MC/T 2.10) **ENGLISH AND FRENCH**
– Bad kid / Placebo / Nice set up / Oh my heartless / 'Cause I rock / Someone phoned / Germolene / Ridiculous day / 4 good byes / Interference / Homesick / English and French / Wasted / Joytown. *(cd+=)* – (untitled instrumental).
Mar 97. (7") (FAC 2.12) **OH MY HEARTLESS. / AUDITORIUM / WASTED (the Chopper Squad mix)**
(cd-s+=) (FACCD 2.12) – Interference.
(above was scheduled for release in Nov'95; but unissued)

— disbanded in 1998

HORMONES

Formed: London, England ... 1996 by Dublin-born MARC CARROLL, who had led Irish trio, PUPPY LOVE BOMB. The latter outfit were part of the 'Rough Trade' stable for a brief period in 1994, releasing the singles, 'NOT LISTENING' and 'BOBBY MILK EP, before splitting the following year. Moving to the English capital, a mutual friend introduced the guitar-wielding frontman to his new mate to-be, JIMI BOLIN, JEZ HOUSDON and PAT WALTERS. The HORMONES made their debut on 'Trade 2' with the single, 'ARE YOU WITH US', a unique fusion of NIRVANA, the BEACH BOYS and a hint of Irish folk! Signed to Richard Branson's ever-expanding punk-pop-metal label, 'V2', the group embarked upon a prolific singles release schedule culminating with the debut album, 'WHERE OLD GHOSTS MEET', in the summer of '98.

Album rating: WHERE OLD GHOSTS MEET (*6)

MARC CARROLL – vocals, guitar / **JIMI BOLIN** – guitar / **JEZ HOUSDON** – bass / **PAT WALTERS** – drums
    Trade 2   *not iss.*

Sep 96. (7"/cd-s) (TRDSC/+CD 001) **ARE YOU WITH US? / THE DEVIL GOES TO MOSCOW (GOOD TO KNOW YOU)**
    V2   *Imprint*
Jul 97. (7") (VVR 500041-7) **THIS IS THE SOUND. / LOVE THE GIRL**
(cd-s+=) (VVR 500041-3) – Bitched, balloxed and bewildered / G'night, g'luck (I'm going home).
Mar 98. (7"ep/cd-ep) (VVR 500125-7/-3) **STAY AHEAD / GOOD TO KNOW YOU. / PATTERNS / TIRED OLD SOULS**
May 98. (7") (VVR 500158-7) **DON'T LET THEM GET YOU DOWN. / BE WHAT YOU ARE**
(cd-s+=) (VVR 500158-3) – Ballad of a drifter (let's go home) / Oh Lord, sometimes I could die.
Jul 98. (7"/cd-s) (VVR 500189-7/-3) **MR. WILSON. / BARK AND BITE / ONLY ONES**
Aug 98. (cd/lp) (VVR 100165-2/-1) <112031> **WHERE OLD GHOSTS MEET**
– Stay ahead / Don't let them get you down / This is the sound / Radio stars / Mr. Wilson / A house by the hill / All we thought / Dig like merry hell / Someplace somewhere / The kisser / Feel alright / Where old ghosts meet.

– MARC's early days –

PUPPY LOVE BOMB
    Rough Trade   *not iss.*

May 94. (7") (R 320-7) **NOT LISTENING. / ALL WORTHWHILE**
(12"+=/cd-s+=) (R 320-0/-3) – Almost a saint / Swapping cards.
Oct 94. (d7"ep/cd-ep) (R 334-9/-3) **BOBBY MILK EP**
– Blind / Here again / Liar (re-recorded) / Tight lipped.

HOTALACIO
(see under ⇒ FLUX OF PINK INDIANS; see 80's section)

HOT HOT HEAT

Formed: Victoria, British Columbia, Canada ... 1999 by MATT MARNIK, STEVE BAYS, PAUL HAWLEY and DUSTIN HAWTHORNE. The band began as guitar-less new wave/punk revival rock outfit, using disturbing synthesizer sound and pounding bass to create a lively and vital piece of alt rock while carving their space out amongst their more garage rock obsessed peers.

This early sound was probably best witnessed on subsequent compilation, 'SCENES ONE THROUGH TO THIRTEEN' (2002), which collected material from the period from about 2000 through to 2001. The following year saw the departure of frontman MARNIK, who was replaced by guitarist DANTE DECARO. This led the band's sound down a punkier road as evidenced on the EP, 'KNOCK KNOCK KNOCK', released on the influential 'Sub Pop' indie imprint. A packed year of touring ensued to support this record and their subsequent debut album, 'MAKE UP THE BREAKDOWN' (2002) which, with its non-stop synth-punk attack, led to a major deal with 'Warner Bros' by the year end.

Album rating: SCENES ONE THROUGH THIRTEEN compilation (*6) / MAKE UP THE BREAKDOWN (*7)

MATT MARNIK – vocals, guitar / **STEVE BAYS** – keyboards / **DUSTIN HAWTHORNE** – bass, vocals / **PATRICK HAWLEY** – drums

Apr 00. (7"red-ep) <ACHE 001> **HOT HOT HEAT**
– Fashion fight pause / Tourist in your town / Matador at the door / Spelling live backwards. (UK-iss.Sep02; same)

Nov 00. (lp) <ACHE 002> **HOT HOT HEAT / THE RED LIGHT STING**
– Case that they gave me / Haircut economics / Circus maximus / Tokyo vogue / I blew a fuse in my personality / (others by RED LIGHT STING).

Jun 01. (7"ep) **HOT HOT HEAT** *Monoton Studios*
– Keep my name out of your mouth / Word to water / Paco Pena.

Feb 02. (cd) <(OHEV 009CD)> **SCENES ONE THROUGH THIRTEEN** (compilation)
– Keep my name out of your mouth / Word to water / Haircut economics / The case that they gave me / Paco Pena / Circus maximus / I blew a fuse in my personality / Tokyo vogue / Fashion fight pause / Spelling live backwards / Matador at the door / Tourist in your own town / You're ruining it for everyone.

—— **DANTE DECARO** – vocals, guitar; repl. MATT

Jul 02. (cd-ep) <(SPCD 594)> **KNOCK KNOCK KNOCK** *Sub Pop* / *Sub Pop* Apr02
– Le le low / 5 times out of 100 / Have a good sleep / Touch you touch you / More for show. <(12"ep iss.Oct02; SP 594)>

Oct 02. (lp/cd) <SP/+CD 599> **MAKE UP THE BREAKDOWN**
– Naked in the city again / No, not now / Get in or get out / Bandages / Oh, godamnit / Aveda / This town / Talk to me, dance with me / Save us S.O.S. / In Cairo.

HOT MONKEY (see under ⇒ GRIFTERS)

HOT PURSUIT (see under ⇒ TUSCADERO)

HOT ROD (see under ⇒ REVOLVER)

HOT ROD CIRCUIT

Formed: Auburn, Alabama, USA . . . late-1990s by ANDY JACKSON, CASEY PRESTWOOD, JAY RUSSEL and WES CROSS (drums). HOT ROD CIRCUIT were previously known as ANTIDOTE, and released an album, 'MR. GLENBOWSKI', which won them 'Best Unsigned Band Of 1998' by Musician Magazine. Despite this accolade, they relocated to Connecticut and became HOT ROD CIRCUIT, signing to 'Triple Crown' in the process for the release of their debut album in September 1999. 'IF I KNEW NOW WHAT I KNEW THEN' instantly established them as venerable purveyors of post-grunge indie-rock, alongside contemporaries like WEEZER and AT THE DRIVE-IN (whom HOT ROD CIRCUIT toured with in support of the album). 'WEAK WARM' and 'REMOVER' displayed blistering guitars, and an intelligence of songwriting equal to any such guitar rock of the late-'90s. 'IF IT'S COOL WITH YOU IT'S COOL WITH ME' (released a year later) and 'SORRY ABOUT TOMORROW' (2002) consolidated their position within the higher echelons of US indie-rock, a position achieved courtesy of their hugely impressive debut.

Album rating: MR. GLENBOWSKI as Antidote (*6) / IF I KNEW NOW WHAT I KNEW THEN (*5) / IF IT'S COOL WITH YOU IT'S COOL WITH ME (*7) / SORRY ABOUT TOMORROW (*5) / BEEN THERE, SMOKED THAT collection (*4)

ANDY JACKSON – vocals, rhythm guitar / **CASEY PRESTWOOD** – lead guitar, vocals / **JAY RUSSEL** – bass, vocals / **WES CROSS** – drums

1998. (lp; as ANTIDOTE) **MR. GLENBOWSKI** *not iss.* / *own label*

May 00. (cd) <(TC 1401CD)> **IF I KNEW NOW WHAT I KNEW THEN** *Triple Crown* / *Triple Crown* Sep99
– Weak warm / Irish car bomb / Slacker / Remover / Chemistry / Medicated lungs / Achy breaky hockey hair / Good intentions / Chinese cuts / Low.

Oct 00. (cd) <(TC 1402CD)> **IF IT'S COOL WITH YOU IT'S COOL WITH ME** Sep00
– Radio song / Supersad / Two hand touch / The power of the vitamins / Cool with me / Versatility / This is not the time or place / Smithsonian liver / Flight 89 (North American) / You kill me / What's left standing. (re-iss. Jun02; same)

May 01. (cd-ep) <LOI 007> **HOT ROD CIRCUIT / THIS YEAR'S MODEL** *Law Of Inertia* / *not iss.*
– Visible distance / God's gift to old tricks / Patty Hearst machine gun / What's left standing.

Mar 02. (cd/lp) <VR 364 CD/LP> **SORRY ABOUT TOMORROW** *Vagrant* / *Vagrant*
– The pharmacist / At nature's mercy / Radiation suit / Safely / Now or never / Cool for one night / Knees / Let's go home / Consumed by laziness / Get what you want / The night they blew up the moon. (cd re-iss. May02 on 'B-Unique'; BUN 023)

Nov 02. (cd-s) (BUN 26CDS) **THE PHARMACIST / SAFELY / ACHEY BREAKY HOCKEY HAIR / THE PHARMACIST (live video)** *B-Unique* / *not iss.*

– **compilations, etc.** –

Nov 02. (cd) *Triple Crown*; <TC 1403CD> **BEEN THERE, SMOKED THAT**
– Very best friend / Slacker / Blurry 17 / Hi-tech lip gloss / Richardsimmons / Sadie Hawkins / Understood / Grocery store / The greatest disappointment / Master control program / Power of vitamins (live) / This one's for Randy (live) / Hi-tech lip gloss (live) / Patty Hearst machine gun (live) / Sin city / Blank.

HOT SNAKES (see under ⇒ ROCKET FROM THE CRYPT)

HOVERCRAFT

Formed: Seattle, Washington, USA . . . early 90's by medical students RYAN (aka CAMPBELL 2000) and BETH LIEBLING (aka SADIE 7"). Although appearing out of the cities grunge boom the band turned away in part from this sound, to produce an experimental, progressive hard rock instrumental sound. It would be wrong to say they turned completely back towards the prog-rock of bands like HAWKWIND, but they used this kind of innovation combined with a SONIC YOUTH-esque punkiness to produce some unique recordings. The outfit debuted in 1996 with the single, 'ZERO ZERO ZERO ONE' (issued on their 'Repellent' label), and the self-titled EP, 'HOVERCRAFT', introducing their weird and wonderful sonicscapes to the music world. Touring followed with the aid of PEARL JAM's frontman, EDDIE VEDDER (on drum duty!), who was also LIEBLING's husband. Their debut full-length outing, 'AKATHISIA' (1997), followed a year later with the help of KARL 3-30, on drums. Later that same year, the set was also reworked to produce the remix set, 'VAGUS NERVE/DE-ORBIT'. Not resting long, these aural scientists hit out with their third piece, 'EXPERIMENT BELOW', which although not the most accessible piece, was nonetheless a worthwhile one for those who chose to immerse themselves in it.

Album rating: AKATHISIA (*7) / EXPERIMENT BELOW (*7)

RYAN (CAMPBELL 2000) – guitar / **BETH LIEBLING (SADIE 7")** – instruments / **JEROME 230** (aka EDDIE VEDDER) – drums

Apr 96. (7"ep) <(REP 001-7)> **ZERO ZERO ZERO ONE** *Repellent* / *Repellent* 1995

—— **CARL 3-30** – drums; repl. VEDDER who continued with PEARL JAM

Aug 96. (10"ep) (BRRC 10060) <REP 002> **HOVERCRAFT** *Blue Rose* / *Repellent* Jul96
– Stereo specific polymerization / Thixotropic.

Jan 97. (cd) (BFFP 135CD) <69029> **AKATHISIA** *Blast First* / *Mute* Feb97
– Quiet room (44) / Angular momentum / Haloperidol / Vagus nerve / De-orbit burn.

Aug 97. (12") (BFFP 134S) <69041> **Scanner remixes: VAGUS NERVE / DE-ORBIT BURN**

—— added **DASH 11** – drums; repl. CARL

Mar 99. (lp/cd) (BFFP 160/+CD) <69080> **EXPERIMENT BELOW** Sep98
– Anthropod / Phantom limb / Transmitter down / Endoradiosonde / Benzedrine / Wire trace / Epoxy.

—— disbanded after above

H.P. ZINKER

Formed: Innsbruck, Austria . . . 1988, although founding members, HANS PLATZGUMER and FRANK PUEMMEL took flight to New York in July '89 where they subsequently based themselves permanently after completing national service. After playing the still-going-strong CBGB's club, the duo came to the attention of NY producer Wharton Tiers, who produced a debut mini-album, ' . . .AND THERE WAS LIGHT', early in 1990. In the event, the record didn't gain an official UK release until summer '91, by which time the pair had replaced their drum machine with real live jazz-loving drummer, DAVE WASIK. They also had a second album, 'BEYOND IT ALL' (1990) and covers EP 'THE SUNSHINE CD' (1991) under their belts, both released on Brit indie label, 'Roughneck'. The latter boasted a cameo appearance by chief LEMONHEAD, EVEN DANDO (on the track, 'TO ONE IN PARADISE') whom the band met when playing DANDO's hometown of Boston. That said, there was little similarity between the two bands, HP ZINKER trading in a noised-up hybrid of BEEFHEART, the HEARTBREAKERS and the 'CHILI PEPPERS, PLATZGUMER openly citing his love for, and the influence of, heads down heavy metal on his guitar playing and writing style. Possibly a little too dense and schizophrenic for the average indie fan, the Euro trio called it a day after a further three albums, 'HOVERING' (1991), 'PERSEVERANCE' (1992) and 'AT THE MOUNTAINS OF MADNESS' (1995). After PLATZGUMER moved back to Europe and commit to an electronically-friendly solo career, he re-formed HPZ in 2002. • **Covered:** DANCING DAYS (Led Zeppelin) / SUNSHINE + TO ONE IN PARADISE (Peter Tolley) / TAKE FIVE (Dave Brubeck) / BILLION DOLLAR BABIES (Alice Cooper).

Album rating: . . .AND THERE WAS LIGHT mini (*6) / BEYOND IT ALL (*7) / HOVERING (*5) / PERSEVERANCE (*5) / STAYING LOOSE: a compilation (*6) / AT THE MOUNTAINS OF MADNESS (*5)

HANS PLATZGUMER – vocals, guitar / **FRANK PUEMMEL** – bass / + a drum machine in '89 (repl. by drummer **DAVID WASIK**)

	Roughneck	Matador
Feb 90. (m-lp) <OLE 001> **...AND THERE WAS LIGHT**	-	□

– Dancing days / My days seem to be long / Sip of death / Hurdles on my way / Sunshine / Down in the basement. *(UK-iss.Jul91 on 'Roughneck' m-cd/m-lp; NECK CD/LP 004)*

	Roughneck	Fire
May 90. (7") <OLE 002> **THE KNOW-IT-ALL. / SIP OF DEATH**	□	□
Oct 90. (cd/lp) (NECK CD/LP 003) <8> **BEYOND IT ALL**	□	□

– Me and my misery / Schwindling / Sometimes I just don't feel like talking / I don't know what's going on / Die todesdrodge / The offense / Sunbeam First Ave.

May 91. (10"ep/cd-ep) <10> **THE SUNSHINE CD**	□	□

– Sunshine / To one in Paradise / Take five.

Oct 91. (cd/c) (NECK CD/MC 006) **HOVERING**	□	-

– Das testament: The shelling / The attack / Wounded / Epilog / Our precious love / Fish are burning / Abandoned feelings / The floating mind / Flug nach Alpha Centauri.

--- PEUMPEL departed + was repl. by **STEPHAN APICELLA** (aka STEVIE APATHETIC) – guitar (ex-SKUNK) / added **ANDI HALLER** – bass

Mar 92. (10"ep/cd-ep) **THE REASON EP**	□	-

– Reason / My days seem to be long / Reason (4-track demo).

Jun 92. (10"ep/cd-ep) (HYPE 16 T/CD) **THE MYSTERIOUS GIRL EP**	□	-

– Mysterious girl / Billion dollar babies / Trampled to death / The last hug.

	Roughneck	Thrill Jockey
Sep 92. (cd/lp) (NECK CD/LP 010) <6001> **PERSEVERANCE**	□	□

– Invitation / Warzone city / Reason / Trapped / Mysterious girl / Soulmate / A million sparks are riding my mind / Twister / Desperate moves / Mirror / Now that you're gone.

--- **UVEY BATRUEL** – bass; repl. ANDY (on some below)

	Roughneck	Energy
Nov 93. (cd) (NECKCD 14) <81105> **STAYING LOOSE – A COMPILATION** (compilation)	□	□

– Reason / Billion dollar babies / Trapped / Our precious love / Soulmate / Hurdles on my way / Fish are burning / Die todesdrodge / To one in Paradise / The know-it-all / Mysterious girl / Flug nach Alpha Centauri / Sunshine / Mirror / My days seem to be long / Warzone city / Trampled to death / Sunbeam First Ave.

--- had split for a while but re-formed for below

Feb 95. (cd) <81113> **AT THE MOUNTAINS OF MADNESS**	-	□

– The shack / The breed / Birch / Override / Mountains of madness / Undeniable / Woman is away / Good times / The hunting / Sister / Waz / Anxiety / Fortress of fears / The oov / Stalker.

--- disbanded; HANS returned to Europe for a solo career

HUCKLEBERRY

Formed: Edinburgh, Scotland . . . Autumn 1996 by long-time school friends VIC GALLOWAY (guitar) and JAMES WRIGHT (bass), who were raised in the village of Kingsbarns, near St.Andrews. They grew up together and bonded over their love of music – firstly ADAM & THE ANTS, then 2-Tone, Punk, Indie, Reggae, etc – and witnessed their first gig together in 1985 at the Edinburgh Playhouse watching The DAMNED. After leaving school in 1991, the pair formed the seminal MIRACLEHEAD alongside drummer STU BASTIMAN and vocalist CLIFF SIMMS, although this popular outfit collapsed when the latter pursued a college career. WRIGHT and GALLOWAY went their separate ways and played in various combos (KHARTOUM HEROES and AGAPAPA), although they met up again in 1996 and decided to form another group with the aim of sounding like a VIOLENT FEMMES-esque Punk busking band. After auditioning and finally teaming up with DAVE SIMANDI, it became apparent that their songwriting and the latter's drumming was more rock-orientated and less acoustic so they searched for another musician to complete the line-up and sound. This came in the form of REUBAN TAYLOR, a classically trained pianist and budding Hammond organ player who defied logic with his amazing speed and dexterity on the chunky keys – he was a must and agreed to sign up! The name HUCKLEBERRY was decided upon – for its ambiguous nature (only a C&W band would call themselves that!). After a few months (and their first recording, the 'HALO JONES' EP), SIMANDI was superseded by their old pal, BASTIMAN. Their first stroke of luck was meeting enthusiastic entrepreneur, PAUL MUSTARDE, whose vision, dedication and support to HUCKLEBERRY's cause was certainly worth its weight in gold. He set up 'Copper' records in early '97 and began promoting the band's material as best a small independent could possibly do. For the next year or two, HUCKLEBERRY and 'Copper' delivered a number of infectious but unhinged Ska-punk singles, 'THE IDIOT-LISTENING' EP, 'MOROCCO' and 'THE LIVES OF THE SAINTS', while an album, 'HARD LUCK STORIES' was issued in summer '98. PAUL eventually became disillusioned with the music business and abandoned Copper before moving to New Zealand. During this period, the weird but wonderful act that was HUCKLEBERRY – who were best described as Loungecore Garage-rock meeting JETHRO TULL/IAN ANDERSON gurning with a chainsaw – received airplay via Evening Sessions and Peelie, while the Student Radio Network and Tip Sheet were also supportive. Touring Scotland, England and France (they played 'T In The Park', 'Reading' and 'Trans Musicales' festivals), the HUCK's also supported the likes of CARTER USM, the WANNADIES, SPACE and The SUPERNATURALS. However, the year 1999 saw the band undergoing some rigid personnel changes, CYMON ARETZ took over from BASTIMAN, while WRIGHT took off for a more rootsy solo career under the names J WRIGHT PRESENTS and JAMES YORKSTON (the latter has supported JOHN MARTYN). It was also the year that GALLOWAY managed to secure himself a rather tasty job as a Radio One DJ co-presenting the (Evening) Session in Scotland. And thus HUCKLEBERRY were put on hold for a while. To add another weird twist, MUSTARDE's brother STEVE joined on bass in 2000 and since then the band have been honing their style and sound. The songs were now heavier and even more unhinged, with a Prog-rock/psychedelic feel, although retaining their classic Hammond textures and rawk-y guitar; all witnessed during gigs at the Glasgow Green festival and subsequent support slots to NOMEANSNO, MAN OR ASTROMAN? and URUSEI YATSURA. Having just recorded a new album (due to be released in 2003) at West Granton's (Edinburgh) Chamber Studios, HUCKLEBERRY look set to take on the UK music biz, if not the world.

Album rating: HARD LUCK STORIES (*6)

VIC GALLOWAY (b. MICHAEL, Kingsbarns, Fife) – vocals, guitars, etc / **JAMES WRIGHT** (b. Kingsbarns) – bass, vocals, acoustic guitar, concertina / **REUBEN TAYLOR** – piano / **DAVE SIMANDI** – drums

	Hooj Choons	not iss.
Nov 96. (cd-ep) (HJEP 1) **HALO JONES ep**	□	-

– Halo Jones / Pablo the donkey / Virtues / Hothead.

--- **STU BASTIMAN** – drums, percussion (ex-MIRACLEHEAD) repl. DAVE

	Copper	not iss.
Jun 97. (7"ep/cd-ep) (COPP EP2 V1/CD) **THE IDIOT-LISTENING E.P.**	□	-

– Sink with me / The man who wanted a new head / Flying kites for Christ / Coffee.

Apr 98. (7"ep/cd-ep) (COPP S5/+CD) **MOROCCO**	□	-

– Morocco / Morocco – Wreckage Inc. mix / Nervous situations / Count it over.

Jun 98. (7"m) (COPP S6UP) **THE LIVES OF THE SAINTS. / A MIGHTY SAINT / A MIGHTY FISH (Grove House sessions)**	□	-

(cd-ep+=) (COPP 6CD) – Le petit Hispanic.

Jun 98. (cd) (COPPLP 7CD) **HARD LUCK STORIES**	□	-

– Pablo the donkey / Ugly / Morocco / Marvellous sons / Flying kites for Christ / The lives of the saints / Easily led / The short Hispanic / Shake off your bones / Learning Latin / Bellyache / Paper faith.

--- **CYMON ARETZ** – drums (ex-CONEY ISLAND CYCLONE) repl. BASTIMAN

--- **STEVE MUSTARDE** – vocals, bass; repl. WRIGHT who went solo as JAMES YORKSTON

--- (Oct'01) **ALAN MUSTARDE** – bass; repl. STEVE

--- expect something soon; as soon as VIC gets off the radio!

HUGGY BEAR

Formed: Brighton, England . . . 1992 as a girl/boy group of neo-feminists. With a line-up comprising of JO JOHNSON, NIKI ELLIOT, KAREN, CHRIS and JON, HUGGY BEAR spearheaded the UK 'Riot Grrrl' movement aimed at tackling misogynism and breaking down the illusory barriers between the sexes. Although their intentions might have been honourable, much of the message and the music was buried under an avalanche of (partly self-created) media hype and controversy. Signed to 'Wiiija' (home of CORNERSHOP, SILVERFISH, etc), HUGGY BEAR released a couple of 7" EP's in the latter half of '92, namely 'RUBBING THEE IMPOSSIBLE TO BURST' and 'KISS CURL FOR THE KID'S LIB. GUERILLAS', the former opening with the inflammatory 'KATHOLIC KUNT'. The following year, they found themselves in the news again after objecting to a feature on Channel 4's 'The Word' (they had actually performed their new single, 'HER JAZZ', on the show that night), the band embroiled in an alleged bust-up with security. A shared lp, 'OUR TROUBLED YOUTH / YEAH YEAH YEAH' – with fellow femme agitators, BIKINI KILL – surfaced later that year, an anarchic fusion of The POISON GIRLS and The DOLLY MIXTURES. Meanwhile, JO and NIKI found time to collaborate with members of another likeminded outfit, CEE CEE BEAUMONT; naming themselves BLOOD SAUSAGE, the group issued an EP (an NME Single Of The Week) and a 10" LP, 'HAPPY LITTLE BULLSHIT BOY' (1993). A busy year all round, HUGGY BEAR dodged the press backlash and defiantly delivered another 7"-only EP and a 10"mini-set, TAKING THE ROUGH WITH THE SMOOCH', both featuring the RSPCA-worrying 'SHAVED PUSSY POETRY'. With the 'Riot Grrrl' movement soon to be overtaken by the diluted corporate equivalent of Girl Power (yeah yeah yeah, right), HUGGY BEAR became extinct after 1994's 'WEAPONRY LISTENS TO LOVE'.

Album rating: OUR TROUBLED YOUTH shared (*6) / TAKING THE ROUGH WITH THE SMOOCH (*6) / WEAPONRY LISTENS TO LOVE (*5) / Blood Sausage: HAPPY LITTLE BULLSHIT BOY (*6)

JO JOHNSON – vocals, bass (ex-THEE ELEMENT OF CRIME) / **NIKI ELLIOT** – vocals / **CHRIS** – vocals (ex-THEE ELEMENT OF CRIME) / **JON SLADE** – guitar (ex-ALMOST RINGO, ex-COMET GAIN, ex-MAST, ex-SMALL THINGS) / **KAREN** – drums

	Wiiija	Kill Rock Stars
Sep 92. (7"ep) (WIJ 16) **RUBBING THEE IMPOSSIBLE TO BURST**	□	-

– Katholic kunt / Jupiter supercone / Snail messenger loss / Single bullets.

Dec 92. (7"ep) (WIJ 18) **KISS CURL FOR THE KID'S LIB. GUERILLAS**	□	-

– Sizzle meet / Carn't kiss / Derwin / Concrete life.

Feb 93. (7"ep) (TROUBLE 001) **HER JAZZ. / WORDCORE // PRAYER / PRO NO FROM NOW**	□	-

(above & below each jointly issued on 'Catcall-Wiiija')

Mar 93. (lp; with BIKINI KILL) (PUSS 001) <KRS 206> **OUR TROUBLED YOUTH / YEAH YEAH YEAH**	□	□

– Jupiter re-entry / My song No.1 / T-shirt tucked in / Blow dry / Nu song / Into the mission / Hopscortch / Aqua girl star / February 14. // (+ 7 tracks by BIKINI KILL).

HUGGY BEAR (cont) — THE GREAT INDIE DISCOGRAPHY — The 1990s

1993. (7"ep) **LONG DISTANCE LOVERS**
– Steppin' on bugs / Limit 2 surf / Tuff luvin / Code fucker.
(above issued on 'Gravity')
Aug 93. (7"ep) *(WIJ 023)* **DON'T DIE**
– Dissthenic penetration / Teen tightens / No sleep till . . . / Shaved pussy poetry / Pansy twist.
Sep 93. (10"lp/cd) *(BOMB 015/+CD)* <KRS 214CD> **TAKING THE ROUGH WITH THE SMOOCH**
– Dissthenic penetration / Sizzle meat / Shaved pussy poetry / Pansy twist / Concrete life / Pro no from now / Prayer / Her jazz / Teen tightens / Derwin / No sleep / Carn't kiss. *(cd re-iss. Apr00; same as US)*
Sep 94. (cd-ep) *(11)* **MAIN SQUEEZE** — Austra
– Children absent from Heaven says / Red flipper #2 / My best kiss.
(above issued on Australia' 'Fellaheen' records)
Nov 94. (cd/lp) *(WIJ 037 CD/V)* <KRS 236CD> **WEAPONRY LISTENS TO LOVE**
– Immature adolescence / F*** your heart / Face down / Warning rails / On the wolves tip / Erotic bleeding / Sixteen and suicide / Obesity and speed / Insecure offenders / Why am I a lawbreaker / Local arrogance. *(cd re-iss. Apr00; same as US)*

— after they disbanded, KAREN joined The PHANTOM PREGNANCIES, JON joined I'M BEING GOOD and CHRIS went to SKINNED TEEN who released the 'KARATE HAIRDRESSER' EP

BLOOD SAUSAGE

JO JOHNSON – bass, drums / **NIKI ELLIOT** – drums, vocals / plus **DALE SHAW** – vocals, guitar / **OWEN THOMAS** – guitar, percussion (also of CEE CEE BEAUMONT) / **A.J.W. BOURTON** – guitar, bass, flute, keyboards (also of CEE CEE BEAUMONT)

Wiiija / K

Feb 93. (7"ep) *(WIJ 020V)* **TOUCHING YOU IN WAYS THAT DON'T FEEL COMFORTABLE / WHAT LAW AM I BREAKING NOW? / FUCK YOU AND YOUR UNDERGROUND / KNOCK OUT DROPS / THE GIRL WHO KISSED HIS FACE LIKE A CLOCK**
Jul 93. (10"lp) *(WIJ 024V)* **HAPPY LITTLE BULLSHIT BOY**
Nov 93. (7"m) <IPU 043> **DENIS LAVANT. / FEEDER / LIVING IN A HAUNTED HOUSE**

HULA BOY (see under ⇒ BOYRACER)

HUM

Formed: Champaign, Illinois, USA . . . 1989 by JEFF DIMPSEY, TIM LASH, BRYAN ST. PERE and MATT TALBOTT. Enterprising and self-reliant, HUM built up a grassroots following through heavy touring while initiating their own label, '12 Inch Records', for the release of debut album, 'ELECTRA 2000' (1993). A few years later, a follow-up set, 'YOU'D PREFER AN ASTRONAUT' was bubbling under the US Top 100; released on 'R.C.A.' ('Dedicated' in the US), the record set layers of mid-paced, muscular guitar against TALBOTT's complex, cryptic lyrics to compelling effect. In early '98, HUM were back with a third long-player, 'DOWNWARD IS HEAVENWARD', carrying on in much the same vein. DIMPSEY subsequently concentrated his energies on side project NATIONAL SKYLINE, a conglomerate which featured various former members of the band CASTOR. One of these, JEFF GARBER, was to remain with the group long-term, painstakingly putting an eponymous debut album together with DIMPSEY in his home studio after a round of initial performances. Finally seeing the light of day in 2000, the record's minimalist, experimental approach was indicative of its incubation period and testament to the pair's fertile collective imagination. While DIMPSEY left soon after the record's release (to be replaced by COMPOUND RED man, JIM MINOR), he was back in the driving seat for a sophomore effort, 'THIS EQUALS EVERYTHING' (2001), if anything an even more inspired and subtly executed series of left field pop compositions.

Album rating: ELECTRA 2000 (*5) / YOU'D PREFER AN ASTRONAUT (*6) / DOWNWARD IS HEAVENWARD (*5) / National Skyline: NATIONAL SKYLINE mini (*5) / EXIT NOW mini (*5) / THIS EQUALS EVERYTHING (*5)

MATT TALBOTT (b.27 Jun'67, Geneseo, Illinois) – vocals, guitar / **TIM LASH** (b.16 Jun'74) – guitar / **JEFF DIMPSEY** (b.23 May'67) – bass (ex-POSTER CHILDREN) / **BRYAN ST. PERE** (b. 2 Apr'66, Evergreen Park, Illinois) – drums

not iss. / 12-Inch Records

Oct 93. (cd) <TIN 007> **ELECTRA 2000**
– Iron clad Lou / Pinch and roll / Shovel / Pewter / Scraper / Fire head / Sun dress / Double dip / Winder. *(hidden track+=)* – Diffuse. *(UK-iss.Sep97 & Oct01 on 'Martians Go Home'+=; MGH 001)* – Diffuse.

Dedicated / R.C.A.

Feb 96. (7"green) *(HUM 001)* **STARS. / STARS (version)**
(cd-s) *(HUM 001CD)* – ('A'side) / Boy with stick / Baby, baby.
Mar 96. (cd/lp) *(DED CD/LP 023)* <66577> **YOU'D PREFER AN ASTRONAUT** — Apr95
– Little dipper / The pod / Stars / Suicide machine / The very old man / Why I like the robins / I'd like your hair long / I hate it too / Songs of farewell and departure. *(originally issued in the UK Oct95 as lp on '12 Inch Inch Records'; TIN 012)*
May 96. (7") *(HUM 002)* **THE POD. / MS LAZARUS**
(cd-s+=) *(HUM 002CD)* – Firehead.
Jan 98. (cd) <67446> **DOWNWARD IS HEAVENWARD**
– Isle of the cheetah / Comin' home / If you are to bloom / Ms. Lazarus / Afternoon with the Axolotis / Green to me / Dreamboat / The inuit promise / Apollo / The scientists.

— they have since disbanded

NATIONAL SKYLINE

JEFF DIMPSEY – bass, etc / **JEFF GARBER** – vocals, guitar (ex-CASTOR) – **DEREK NIEDRIGHAUS** + **NICKY MACRI** were also early members

Hidden Agenda / Hidden Agenda

Jun 00. (m-cd) <(AHA 015)> **NATIONAL SKYLINE** — Apr00
– Metropolis / Tropical depression 3 / L'nuh / Aia / Karolina / Icemeasure / Kandles.

File 13 / File 13

Nov 00. (m-cd) <(FT 33)> **EXIT NOW**
– October / Identity crisis / Ghosts / Karolina II.

— added **JIM MINOR** – guitar (ex-COMPOUND RED)

May 01. (cd) <FT 36> **THIS EQUALS EVERYTHING**
– Some will say / Reinkiller / A million circles / Day on the beach / Morse code / A night at the drugstore / Make it stop / Cadence of water / The look / Granstanding.

HUMPERS

Formed: Long Beach, California, USA . . . 1990 by SCOTT DERBERT DRAKE and JEFF FIELDHOUSE who were ex-guitarists from the SUICIDE KINGS. Abandoning guitar for full-time vocals (or to put it bluntly; downright shouting), The HUMPERS – with JIMI SILVEROLI, BILLY BURKS and JAYBIRD BLAKE – found overwhelming success in Yugoslavia (of all places!) where the now collectable 'MY MACHINE' was issued. The band's sound emanated around edgy-hardcore punk witnessed some ten years previous by Cleveland's The PAGANS. 1994, however, saw them find a label where they recorded their second set 'JOURNEY TO THE CENTRE OF YOUR WALLET'. Two LPs ('LIVE FOREVER OR DIE TRYING' and 'PLASTIQUE VALENTINE') followed before the band signed to notorious punk imprint 'Epitaph' in 1997. • **Covered:** ROCKET REDUCER No.62 (MC5) / BUMMER BITCH (Freestone) / 96 TEARS (? & The Mysterians) / MOTORHEAD (Motorhead) / PROTEX BLUE (Clash).

Album rating: POSITIVELY SICK ON 4th STREET (*7) / JOURNEY TO THE CENTRE OF YOUR WALLET (*5) / LIVE FOREVER OR DIE TRYING (*5) / PLASTIQUE VALENTINE (*5) / EUPHORIA, CONFUSION, ANGER AND REMORSE (*5)

SCOTT "DELUXE" DRAKE – vocals (ex-SUICIDE KINGS) / **JEFF FIELDHOUSE** – bass, guitar (ex-SUICIDE KINGS) / **BILLY BURKS** – guitar / **JAYBIRD BLAKE** – bass / **JIMI SILVEROLI** – drums

Mean Dog / not iss.

1990. (lp) *(492-90)* **MY MACHINE** — Yugos
– Baby '89 / Kill sister kill / Whips and chains / Planet Earth / St. Jon / Miracle mile / Black cats / My machine / S.O.B. story / Sunday, Sunday / 3D glasses / Losers club.

not iss. / Listen Loudest

1991. (lp; as SUICIDE KINGS) <none> **HIGH & MIGHTY**
– Take yer machine / Slut / Switchblade / Cadillac boogie / Faster than the speed of love / Better go now / Digging a ditch / Suicide king / Bad blood / Back sass baby / Bad love / Bummer bitch / You're so inconvenient / Smash & grab. <cd-iss. 1996 on 'Sonic'+=; SRCD 0010> – 96 years / Take yer medicine (alt.) / Love it / Dum & stoopid / Bad boy / Fist fight.

not iss. / Dionysus

1991. (7") <IDO 74543> **HEY SHADOW. / INSECT LIBERATION**

not iss. / Sympathy F

1991. (7") <SFTRI 084> **BABY '89. / ST. JON**
1993. (cd) <SFTRI 216> **POSITIVELY SICK ON 4th STREET**
– Murder city revolution / Up yer heart / Psycho repairman / Hey shadow / Drunk tank / War is hell / Rocket and the retards / Soul surgeon / Cops and robbers / Unsafe at any speed / Zombie / Insect liberation / Rocket reducer No.62 / Apocalypse girl / Death threat machine.
1993. (7",7"yellow) <BOH 020> **SPACE STATION LOVE. / THIS MEASLY DIMENSION**
(above issued on 'Bag Of Hammers') (below on '1+2 records')
1994. (7") <45063> **SARCASMATRON. / MY GAME**
1994. (cd) <SFTRI 282> **JOURNEY TO THE CENTRE OF YOUR WALLET**
– This measly dimension / Freak magnet / You give good headache / (I'm) Watching you / Space station love / Bombs away / Dope on a rope / Dead last / Blow / Do the wrong thing / Crank call / Up yer heart / Motorhead.
1995. (7") <ID 074558> **DEAD LAST. / SUPER POWER**
(above issued on 'Dionysus', below on 'Hate')
1995. (10"ep) <HATE 1> **A TOUCHING DATE**
– The kid with the replaceable head / Communist pussy / Irradescent itch / (other 3 by TEMPORAL SLUTS).

— **MITCH CARTWRIGHT** – bass; repl. BLAKE

May 96. (10"m-lp/m-cd) <SFTRI 344/+CD> **CONTRACTUAL OBLIGATION**
– Wake up and lose / Protex blue / 13 forever / My machine / Say goodbye / Fable of love / Loser's club. *(m-cd+=)* – Fast, fucked and furious / For lovers only. *(UK-iss.Jul98; same as US)*
Jun 96. (7") <SFTRI 351> **FAST, FUCKED AND FURIOUS. / FOR LOVERS ONLY**

— **MARK "ANARCHY" LEE** – guitar; repl. FIELDHOUSE

Epitaph / Epitaph

1996. (cd/c/lp) <8644-2/-4/-1> **LIVE FOREVER OR DIE TRYING**
– Wake up and lose / Soul surgeon / Sarcasmatron / Fast, fucked and furious / Beyond belief / Migraine shack / Don't wanna be your pal / Loser's club / Space station love / World of hurt / Protex blue / Drunk tank / 13 forever / Apocalypse girl / You drive me bats / Rocket and the retards / Anarchy juice.
Jan 97. (7") <JR 7> **MUTATE WITH ME. / DUMMY GOT A HUNCH**
(re-iss. May98 on 'Nitro'; 16807-7)
(above issued on 'Junk', below on 'Sympathy For The Record Industry')
Feb 97. (7",7"sha-pic-d) <(SFTRI 490-7)> **PLASTIQUE VALENTINE. / FUCKING SECRETARIES**

Feb 97. (cd/c/lp) <(6483-2/-4/-1)> **PLASTIQUE VALENTINE**
– Plastique valentine / For lovers only / Amemia / Mutate with me / Fable of luv / Make-up / Sick of tomorrow today / Here comes nothing / With a whip / Dummy got a hunch / Chump change / Say goodbye / Mongrel train.
1997. (7"purple) <SP 002> **CALIFORNIA SUN. / MONGREL TRAIN**
(above issued on 'Safety Pin')
Apr 98. (cd/c/lp) <(8652-2/-4/-1)> **EUPHORIA, CONFUSION, ANGER AND REMORSE**
– Steel-toed sneakers / Shortcut to nowhere / Kaiser Bill / Fucking secretries / The Devil's magic pants / Peggy Sue got buried / No you don't / Ghetto in the sky / Ten inches higher / No escape / You dirty rat / Fistful of zen.
—— disbanded and DRAKE + BURKE formed the VICE PRINCIPALS (one set in 2000 for 'Sympathy..'; 'AFTER SCHOOL WITH ...')

– compilations, etc. –

Apr 96. (12"ep/cd-ep) Hell Yeah; <34> **THIS IS ... THE SAVAGE YOUNG HUMPERS – THE DIONYSUS YEARS**
– Hey shadow / Insect liberation / Cops and robbers / Black cats / Dead last / Superpower.

HUNGRY GHOSTS

Formed: Nth Fitzroy, Melbourne, Australia ... mid 90's by the shy and mysterious J. BONEHAM, T. HOWDEN and JON BROOKS, all inexperienced in the world of rock ... so far. Under the wing of producer ROWLAND S. HOWARD (ex-BIRTHDAY PARTY) and engineer LINDSAY GRAVINA, the starving trio recorded their eponymous debut early 1997, although it didn't hit UK shores until the very last months of the millennium. GODSPEED, MOGWAI and bleak spaghetti westerns conjured up what the band might've been listening to over their patient, unassuming lifespan. Once the album had started, the listener was blindly led into a world inhabited only by empty streets and vacant bars. 'THE MAN WHO COULD NOT KILL', in all of its gothic integrity, reminded us of a dark, faceless stranger wandering the haunted allies in a town with no name. 'NOWNESS', had all of the authenticity of early DIRTY THREE works: among it's slow and brooding percussion, glockenspiels glistened like stars in the clear sky. Although, end track 'RELIEF' was the show stealer with its clumsy, horse-footed accordion and dancehall guitar which left the listener relieved that, for once, all had ended well. Subsequently hooking up with SONIC YOUTH drummer, STEVE SHELLEY, who, had witnessing a live gig in New York, they recorded an album for his 'Smells Like Records' label. The result was the eerie 'ALONE, ALONE' (2000), a kind of sequel to their eponymous album of er, yore. Again, it's a one-horse town, only the horse is nowhere to be seen; creepy instrumentals weave in and out of each other, and at certain points even give MOGWAI and GODSPEED ... a run for their money. Perhaps the best cut is 'I DON'T THINK OF YOU ANYMORE, BUT I DON'T THINK ABOUT YOU ANYLESS', a chiming dirge accompanied by pump-organ and shimmering guitar. • **Note:** not to be confused with THE HUNGRY GHOST.
Album rating: HUNGRY GHOSTS (*7) / ALONE, ALONE (*6)

J. BONEHAM / T. HOWDEN / JOHN BROOKS – instruments

	Reliant – Fiido	not iss.
Oct 99. (cd) (NC 170004) **HUNGRY GHOSTS**		–

– Man who refused to kill / A joke's a joke / Nowness / Hannah / Plaster of Paris / Peak / Snake (swallowing a flower) / Desert / Blood / Relief. (re-iss. Jul00; same)

	Smells Like	Smells Like
Jun 00. (cd) <(slr 039)> **ALONE, ALONE**		

– Back for more I go / Trying to lift a rock with a bottle on your head / (interlude) / Reading your mail / No prior convictions / (untitled) / Alone alone / I don't think about you anymore but, i don't think about you anyless / (interlude) / Float / Coma / Remember what it was like to float / Nothing has to happen / (interlude) / Blackout.

HUNGRY I
(see under ⇒ EYELESS IN GAZA; in 80's section)

HURRICANE #1

Formed: Oxford, England ... 1996 by former RIDE guitarist and songwriter, ANDY BELL. Having procured his new recruits from a variety of disparate sources (i.e. WILL PEPPER from THEE HYPNOTICS, ALEX LOWE – via a newspaper ad placed by Creation boss ALAN McGEE – a former boxer from Glasgow and GAZ from the crowd at a BELL solo gig), the band changed their name to HURRICANE #1 to avoid confusion with another similarily named act. In the Spring of '97, Creation records released 'STEP INTO MY WORLD', which stormed into the Top 30. They gained further exposure via an appearance at The Brighton Essential Music Festival before hitting the charts again with follow-up, 'JUST ANOTHER ILLUSION'. Their third 45, 'CHAIN REACTION', also made the UK Top 30 and preceded their fairly cliched self-titled album, which although nearly hitting the Top 10, failed to carve out a distinctive sound to set it apart from the legions of sub Brit-pop no-hopers. To end a fairly successful year, the live favourite, 'STEP INTO MY WORLD' was given the remix treatment resulting in their highest chart position so far, 19. • **Trivia:** BELL married Creation solo artist IDHA in the mid 90's.

Album rating: HURRICANE #1 (*5) / ONLY THE STRONGEST WILL SURVIVE (*4)

ALEX LOWE (b.1965, Blairgowrie, Scotland) – vocals / **ANDY BELL** (b.11 Aug'70, Cardiff, Wales) – lead guitar, keyboards, vocals (ex-RIDE) / **WILL PEPPER** – bass (ex-THEE HYPNOTICS) / **GARETH FARMER** – drums, percussion

	Creation	Alex-Warners
Apr 97. (7"/c-s; as HURRICANE) (CRE/+C 253) <6097> **STEP INTO MY WORLD. / DON'T LOOK AWAY**	29	May98
(cd-s+=) (CRESCD 253) – Smoke rings.		
Jun 97. (7"; as HURRICANE) (CRE 264) <6042> **JUST ANOTHER ILLUSION. / TOUCHDOWN**	35	Feb98
(cd-s+=) (CRESCD 264) – Slapshot.		
(cd-s) (CRESCD 264X) – ('A'mixes; original / Midfield General #10 / PC Kahuma).		
Aug 97. (7") (CRE 271) **CHAIN REACTION. / KEEP WALKING**	30	–
(cd-s+=) (CRESCD 271) – Why don't you do it?		
(cd-s) (CRESCD 271X) – ('A'mixes; original / ceasefire / lunatic calm / coolest-sugarrush).		
Sep 97. (cd/c/lp) (CRECD/CCRE/CRELP 206) <46763> **HURRICANE #1**	11	Oct97
– Just another illusion / Faces in a dream / Step into my world / Mother Superior / Let go of the dream / Chain reaction / Lucky man / Strange meeting / Monday afternoon / Stand in line.		
Oct 97. (cd-s) (CRESCD 276) **STEP INTO MY WORLD (radio edit of Perfecto mix) / STEP INTO MY WORLD (original) / IF YOU THINK IT'S EASY / NEVER MIND THE RAIN**	19	–
(cd-s) (CRESCD 276X) – ('A'mixes; Perfecto / Kahuna / Perfecto dub / Get it together).		
Feb 98. (cd-s) (CRESCD 285) **ONLY THE STRONGEST WILL SURVIVE / ONLY THE STRONGEST WILL SURVIVE (radio) / I BELIEVE IN MAGIC / SLOW SPEED**	19	–
(cd-s) (CRESCD 285X) – ('A'mixes; radio / Farley and Heller / James Lavelle / Dub Pistols).		
	Creation	Imprint
Oct 98. (cd-s) (CRESCD 303) <111580> **RISING SIGN / THE PRICE WE PAY (acoustic) / BULLET TRAIN (NAGOYA)**	47	Nov98
(cd-s) (CRESCD 303X) – ('A'mixes; radio / Olmec heads ascension / Cuba).		
Mar 99. (cd-s) (CRESCD 309) **THE GREATEST HIGH / SWEET INSANITY / SAY IT'S FOREVER**	43	–
(cd-s) (CRESCD 309X) – ('A'radio) / ('A'-side) / Rising sign (My Bloody Valentine mix).		
Apr 99. (cd/c/lp) (CRE CD/MC/LP 237) **ONLY THE STRONGEST WILL SURVIVE**	55	–
– Intro / N.Y.C. / The greatest high / Remote control / Price that we pay / Separation Sunday / Rising sun / Only the strongest will survive / Long way down / Twilight world / Come alive / What do I know / Afterhours / Outro – NYC2.		
Jun 99. (cd-s) (CRESCD 316) **REMOTE CONTROL / DON'T WORRY / INDIAN WATER SONG**		–
(cd-s) (CRESCD 316X) – ('A'side) / ('A'-Big Audio Dynamite sound system groove mix) / Twilight world (Rae & Christian remix).		

—— split later in the year with BELL subsequently joining OASIS

HYBRIDS (see under ⇒ ECHOBOY)

HYDROPLANE (see under ⇒ CAT'S MIAOW)

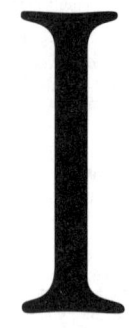

I AM KLOOT

Formed: Manchester, England ... early 1999 by gig promoter JOHN BRAMWELL, PETE JOBSON and ANDY HARGREAVES. After a one-off 45, 'TITANIC', for the enterprising indie outlet, 'Uglyman', the trio signed to 'Wall Of Sound' offshoot, 'We Love You'. Two further singles, 'TWIST' and 'DARK STAR', preceded a glowing GUY HARVEY (ELBOW)-produced debut album, 'NATURAL HISTORY' (2001), a weird but wonderful acoustic indie-folk record inspired by the likes of SOFT BOYS maverick, ROBYN HITCHCOCK.

Album rating: NATURAL HISTORY (*7)

JOHN BRAMWELL – vocals, guitar / **PETE JOBSON** – guitar, bass, vocals / **ANDY HARGREAVES** – drums, percussion

		Uglyman	not iss.
Nov 99.	(7") *(UGLY 16)* **TITANIC. / TO YOU**		-
		We Love You	not iss.
May 00.	(7") *(AMOUR 004S)* **TWIST. / 86 TV'S**		-
	(cd-s+=) *(AMOUR 004D)* – 86 TV's (video).		
Feb 01.	(7") *(AMOUR 009S)* **DARK STAR. / TO YOU**		-
	(cd-s+=) *(AMOUR 009D)* – Titanic.		
Apr 01.	(cd/lp) *(AMOUR 005 CD/LP)* **NATURAL HISTORY**		-
	– To you / Morning rain / Bigger wheels / No fear of falling / Loch / Storm warning / Dark star / Stop / Sunlight hits the snow / Twist / 86 TV's / Because.		
Jul 01.	(7") *(AMOUR 011S)* **MORNING RAIN. / PROOF**		-
	(cd-s+=) *(AMOUR 011D)* – Twist (live).		

I AM THE WORLD TRADE CENTER
(see under ⇒ KINCAID.)

ICARUS LINE

Formed: Hollywood, Los Angeles, California, USA ... 1996 by punk kids JOE CARDAMONE, LANCE ARNAO, ALVIN DeGUZMAN, AARON NORTH and finally settling with drummer JEFF WATSON. This group of BLACK FLAG-inspired youngsters had been playing in various punk outfits during the early-to-mid 90's. After tragedy struck with the death of three close band members, The ICARUS LINE slowly began to form, developing a mutual love for good punk rock and a solid hatred for commercial music. Dressed uniformly in black shirts with thin red ties, the newly-formed troupe began organising local shows supporting the DESCENDENTS, which usually ended in chaos much like The BIRTHDAY PARTY shows of the early 80's. They released a handful of singles on the varying labels 'Hellcat' and 'Buddyhead', which eventually caught the attention of 'Crank!', who issued the brilliant 'RED AND BLACK ATTACK' EP, named in favour of their striking stage clothes. The sonic punk rock, with waves of feedback and CARDAMONE's unscathing vocals earned the group a cult following in their native LA. They also bravely decided to rage against the mainstream; apparently they broke into 'Interscope' vice-president and meat-headed LIMP BIZKIT frontman FRED DURST's office and infiltrated his cabinet of red hats (yes, according to the band's website he actually has one!). Other alleged debauchery included posting DURST's mobile number on the internet, trashing the late STEVIE RAY VAUGHAN's guitar at a gig in the Hard Rock Cafe and infuriating The STROKES by writing "$ucking Dick$" on the side of their tourbus. All of this punk-rock disturbance was eschewed, however, come the delivery of the 'LINE's debut album 'MONO' (2001), which was produced by metal-man Alex Newport. Somewhat akin to being bludgeoned by blunt meat-cleaver. In other words, a minor punk-rock masterpiece. • **Covered:** 1970 + L.A. BLUES (Stooges).

Album rating: MONO (*8)

JOE CARDAMONE – vocals / **AARON NORTH** – guitar / **ALVIN DeGUZMAN** – guitar / **LANCE ARNAO** – bass / **JEFF WATSON** – drums

		New American Dream	New American Dream
Mar 00.	(cd-ep) *<(AD 1901)>* **THE RED AND BLACK ATTACK**		Aug99
	– The suicide pact / Separate the sounds / Last night all my teeth fell out / And the sad thing is . . .		
		Crank!	Crank!
May 01.	(cd) *<(CRC 036CD)>* **MONO**		
	– Love is happiness / You make me nervous / L.O.S.T. / Enemies in high places / In lieu / Feed a cat to your cobra / Oh faithless / Please fire me / Keep your eyes peeled / Best two out of three / Rape of the Holy Mother / S.P.M.C. *<(lp-iss.Jun01 on 'Buddyhead'; BUDDY 004)>* (re-iss. Feb02 on 'Sweet Nothing'; SNCD 010)		
		Sweet Nothing	not iss.
Feb 02.	(7") *(7SN 008)* **FEED A CAT TO YOUR COBRA. / 1970 (Peel session version)**		-
	(cd-s+=) *(CSSN 008)* – S.P.M.C. (Peel session version) / Kill Cupid with a nailfile.		

— **TROY BOY** – drums; repl. WATSON

IDA

Formed: New York City, New York, USA ...1992 by DANIEL LITTLETON and ELIZABETH MITCHELL. Both members already had quite an impressive track-list in the alternative rock world. LITTLETON had been a member of Maryland punk band, The HATED, and went on from there to play with a succession of bands, including, CHOKE, SLACK, and THREE SHADES OF DIRTY. MITCHELL had sown her musical oats singing alongside LISA LOEB, whom LITTLETON would also aid in her solo career. IDA originally signed to JENNY TOOMEY's (of TSUNAMI fame) label, 'Simple Machines' (LITTLETON had worked with TOOMEY while in SLACK), who released the duo's debut album, 'TALES OF BRAVE IDA' (1994). A great opener for the band, forefronting their muted folk-pop style with the addition of cello work by JULIA KENT, which is not the least reason that the band drew comparisons with such luminaries as NICK DRAKE. The following year saw the release of the infectious single, 'IT'S NOT ALRIGHT', which was followed up by their second full-length outing, 'I KNOW ABOUT YOU' (1996). This album introduced LITTLETON's brother, MICHAEL, to the fold on drums, who had previously played with HASSASSINS. The accompanying beat certainly lifted this album, but it is also the added sophistication of the tunes and lyrics that made this release surpass its forerunner, and be regarded as one of IDA's best. 1997 saw the band grow again with the inclusion of BEEKEEPER bass-player, KARLA SCHICKELE, who not only bolstered IDA's rhythm section, but on their third LP, 'TEN SMALL PACES', released that same year, wrote several tracks and sang alongside DANIEL LITTLETON and MITCHELL. This piece ranked alongside 'I KNOW . . .' in the band's canon, and included some great covers; notably a homage to Neil Young's 'EVERYBODY KNOWS THIS IS NOWHERE'. A year on (and around the same time as an IDA RETSIN FAMILY "ALBUM" collaboration, and the group was still in a soaring creative curve with the release of the EP, 'LOSING TRUE', with five quality tunes on board. 1999 saw the band go back to a duo for the album 'YOU ARE MY FLOWER'. This was not a permanent shift but more of a project to create a piece for both children and adults, and was a series of bluesy, folk and country covers beautifully delivered by IDA's original twosome. The making of this album may have also been pushed to the fore by the less than ideal wranglings the group were having with major label, 'Capitol', who would have been releasing work by them that year. This was probably linked to DAN LITTLETON's musical moonlightings in 1999, alongside TREY MANY (who, in fact, married MITCHELL later that year) of HIS NAME IS ALIVE and, former bandmate TOOMEY, in LIQUORICE. Unfortunately MICHAEL LITTLETON left IDA that same year, although his drumming can still be heard on their fifth album, 'WILL YOU FIND ME' (2000), released on 'Tiger Style' records; actually tracks rescued from their disastrous deal of the previous year. Again this was a fine piece with such stand-out tracks as 'MAYBELLE'. IDA continued strongly and rapidly with the release of their sixth set, 'THE BRAILLE NIGHT', the following year. This was again a critical success, and the loss of MICHAEL LITTLETON, was nicely made up for by the expert bolstering of IDA PEARLE and ZACH WALLACE on violin and upright bass respectively. • **Covered:** GOLDEN HOURS (Eno) / I WANT TO SEE THE BRIGHT LIGHTS TONIGHT (Richard & Linda Thompson) / WHEN U WERE MINE + DIRTY MIND (Prince) / MENDOCINO (Doug Sahm) / THE PAIN OF LOVING YOU (Dolly Parton & Porter Wagoner) / etc

Album rating: TALES OF BRAVE IDA (*6) / I KNOW ABOUT YOU (*7) / TEN SMALL PACES (*7) / IDA RETSIN FAMILY ALBUM VOL.1; as Ida Retsin Family (*5) / YOU ARE MY FLOWER (*5) / WILL YOU FIND ME (*6) / THE BRAILLE NIGHT (*6)

DAN LITTLETON – vocals, guitar (ex-HATED, ex-THREE SHADES OF DIRTY, ex-CHOKE, ex-SLACK; one lp for 'C/Z' in 1990, 'Deep Like Space') / **ELIZABETH MITCHELL** – vocals, guitar (ex-LISA LOEB & NINE STORIES)

		Simple Machines	Simple Machines
Oct 94.	(cd) *<smr 37>* **TALES OF BRAVE IDA**	-	
	– F boyfriend / Temping / Post prom disorder / Slow dance / Coupons / Shotgun / Doll face / Accidents / Dog show / Nick Drake / Equator / Looking through the glass / Vacation / Baroque boyfriend.		
Jul 95.	(7") *<smr 39>* **IT'S NOT ALRIGHT. / THANK-YOU**	-	

— added **MICHAEL LITTLETON** – drums (ex-HASSASSINS)

May 96.	(cd) *<smr 47>* **I KNOW ABOUT YOU**	-	
	– Little things / Back burner / Tellings / Thank-you / Downtown / Treasure chest / Requator / When I was now / August again / Plans / 95 north / Goodnight.		

— added **KARLA SCHICKELE** – bass, vocals (ex-BEEKEEPER)

Sep 97.	(cd) *<smr 54>* **TEN SMALL PACES**		
	– Hilot / Les etoiles secretes / Fallen arrow / The weight / Everybody knows this is nowhere / Blue moon of Livonia / Shoe-in / Poor dumb bird / Golden hours / Ashokan reservoir / Drunk aviator / Do you remember / Purely coincidental / Dream date / Capo.		
Oct 97.	(7"m) *<smr 55>* **POOR DUMB BIRD. / I WANT TO SEE THE BRIGHT LIGHTS TONIGHT / WHEN U WERE MINE**		

IDA (cont)

				not iss.	Tree
1998.	(7") <TRR 9.1> **POST PROM DISORDER. / (other by The DEADWOOD DEVINE)**			-	

			not iss.	Muss My Hair
Jul 98.	(cd; as IDA RETSIN FAMILY) <5567> **IDA RETSIN FAMILY ALBUM VOLUME 1**		-	

– 3 chords for Greta / Tales of the brave Ida / The pitter patter / Be careful / Log ride / The great south river / Sad song Wisconsin / SAve me a place / Scrump. (above featured RETSIN: **TARA JANE O'NEIL + CYNTHIA NELSON**)

			not iss.	Bingo
Nov 98.	(cd-ep) <5> **LOSING TRUE**		-	

– Best of the belated / Tiger dare / 6 year old girl tap dancing on the wing of / Crooked teeth / Turn me on.

— IDA also released a single split with VERMONT

— now without MICHAEL (now a trio)

			not iss.	Last Affair
1999.	(cd) <001> **YOU ARE MY FLOWER**		-	

			Tiger Style	Tiger Style
Jul 00.	(cd/lp) <TS 005 CD/LP> **WILL YOU FIND ME**		-	

– Down on your back / Maybelle / This water / Shrug / The radiator / Shotgun / Turn me on / Man in mind / Past the past / Georgia / Triptych / Firefly / Encantada / Don't get sad. (UK-iss.Aug01; same)

— added **IDA PEARLE** – violin + **ZACH WALLACE** – upright bass

Jul 01.	(cd) <TS 012> **THE BRAILLE NIGHT**			Jun01

– Let's go walking / Ignatia amara / Arrowheads / So long / Blizzard of '78 / So worn out / The braille night / Gladiolas / Ocean of glass / Moves through the air.

– compilations, etc. –

2000.	(ltd-cd) In-Sound; <11> **LIVE AT CARNEGIE HALL, THE ALBUM (live, 1997-1999)**	-	
Mar 02.	(cd) Time Stereo; <(TST 1021)> **SHHH** (remixes)	-	

IDAHO

Formed: Los Angeles, California, USA ... 1991 by frontman/singer JEFF MARTIN along with the uptight JOHN BERRY. This strange and soft-core duo debuted in 1993 with 'THE PALMS' EP and the much acclaimed album 'YEAR AFTER YEAR'. While supporting The RED HOUSE PAINTERS, IDAHO's drummer and guitarist BERRY left to pursue other musical projects. The lo-fi group/duo heralded a second album 'THIS WAY OUT' (1995), which collected battered'n'bruised numbers from a weep-core country, where JIM PUTNAM and other slo-fi originators were head of a supreme government. With the addition of TERRY BORDEN, MARK LEWIS and DAN SETA, JEFF MARTIN re-shaped the IDAHO plan. Early in 1996, 'THREE SHEETS OF WIND', was a distinct improvement on their slo-core noodlings of previous efforts, tracks such as 'SHAME' and 'POMEGRANATE BLEEDING' were obvious highlights. Retaining only SETA, MARTIN wasted no time in releasing 'THE FORBIDDEN' EP, their first for 'Buzz' records. 'ALAS' (1998) followed on from 'THREE SHEETS ...', adding seasoned drummer JOEY WARONKER (as third member) in the process and showcasing a guest spot from HOLE's MELISSA AU DER MAR. A stop-gap 'concert' set, 'PEOPLE LIKE US SHOULD BE STOPPED' – from live shows 1993 onwards – was a testament to their sonically-enhanced early days, while they subsequently founded their own 'Idaho' imprint. 'HEARTS OF PALM' (2000) and 'LEVITATE' (2001) – the latter with new drummer ALEX KIMMEL – took melancholic lo-fi to another dimension, their subtle use of sparse, mournful instrumentation, virtually on a plane of its own.

Album rating: YEAR AFTER YEAR (*6) / THIS WAY OUT (*6) / THREE SHEETS TO THE WIND (*7) / ALAS (*6) / PEOPLE LIKE US SHOULD BE STOPPED live collection (*5) / HEARTS OF PALM (*6) / LEVITATE (*6) / WE WERE YOUNG AND WE NEEDED THE MONEY outtakes (*6)

JEFF MARTIN (b. 1964) – vocals, guitar / **JOHN BERRY** (b. 1964) – guitar, drums

			Quigley	Caroline
Jun 93.	(cd-ep) <CAROL 1472> **THE PALMS**		-	

– Creep / Fall around / Gone / You are there.

Oct 93.	(cd/lp) (QUIG D/L 4) <CAROL 1736> **YEAR AFTER YEAR**			

– God's green earth / Skyscrape / Gone / Here to go / Sundown / Memorial day / One Sunday / The only road / Let's cheat / Save / Year after year / Endgame.

— now down to **JEFF MARTIN** (+ session drummers) when BERRY left

Oct 94.	(c-s) <HREC 3> **DRIVE IT / SWEEP**		-

(cd-s+=) <HRECD 3> – A ten to noon / Red snake.
(above also licensed to 'Hi-Rise' in the UK)

Jan 95.	(cd/lp) (QUIG D/L 7) <CAROL 1757> **THIS WAY OUT**		

– Drop off / Drive it / Weird wood / Fuel / Still / Sweep / Glow / Taken / Crawling out / Zabo / Forever.

— added **DAN SETA** – guitars / **TERRY BORDEN** – bass / **MARK LEWIS** – drums (also on early sessions)

		Caroline	Caroline
Apr 96.	(7") <7CAR 001> **POMEGRANATE BLEEDING. / RIGHT ESCAPE**		-

(cd-s+=) <CDCAR 001> – Shame.

Apr 96.	(cd/lp) <CAROL 001 CD/LP> <CAROL 7500> **THREE SHHETS TO THE WIND**		Feb96

– If you dare / Catapult / Pomegranate bleeding / Shame / Stare at the sky / No ones watching / Alive again / Sound awake / Glass bottom / Get you back.

		Fingerpaint	Fingerpaint
Feb 97.	(10"ep) <(FP 07)> **BAYONET EP**		Nov95

– The worm / Sliding past / Losing light / Only maybe.

— now down to **MARTIN + SETA** (**JOHN GOLDMAN** – bass)

		Buzz	Buzz
Apr 97.	(cd-ep) <(BUZ 12)> **THE FORBIDDEN EP**		Mar97

– The thick and the thin / Hold everything / Goldenseal / Apricots to Armagnac / Bass crawl.

— added **JOEY WARONKER** – drums (ex-SPAIN, of BECK)

Mar 99.	(cd) <(BUZ 16CD)> **ALAS**		Sep98

– Jump up / Tensile / You'll get to the bottom of this / Scrawny / Only in the desert / Run but you ran / Clouded / Yesterday's unwinding / Leaves upon the water.

		Idaho	Idaho
Oct 00.	(cd) <(IDA 0022)> **HEARTS OF PALM**		

– To be the one / Hearts of palm / Down in waves / This cloud we're on / Happy times / Dum dum / Astrida / Evolution is cold / Alta dena / Before you go / Under.

(3rd member) **ALEX KIMMEL** – drums; repl. WARONKER

Oct 01.	(cd) <IDA 0032> **LEVITATE**	-	

– Wondering the fields / 20 years / For granted / On the shore / Levitate (pt.2) / Santa Claus is weird / Orange / Come back home / Carousel / Casa mia / Levitate.

– compilations, etc. –

Aug 00.	(cd) Idaho; <(IDA 0012)> **PEOPLE LIKE US SHOULD BE STOPPED: IDAHO LIVE VOL.1 (live 1993 ...)**		Jul00

– Intro / Here to go / Fall around / Star / Creep / Gone / Tear / God's green earth / You are there / Segue #5 / Segue #6 / Autumn in Paris.

Oct 02.	(cd) Idaho; <(IDA 0042)> **WE WERE YOUNG AND WE NEEDED THE MONEY** (outtakes)		Sep02

– Social studies / Teeth marks / This day / Come over / Shoulder back / Flat top / Breathe / A second chance / Straw dogs / Signs of life / Much closer now / Spiral / Nothing wrong / Stayin' out in front / Traces / Carefully turning / Drown.

IDHA

Born: IDHA OVELIUS, 22 May'72, Sodertalje, Sweden. Having been a fully paid up Goth living in London at the turn of the decade (80's/90's), the stunning redhead's fortunes took a turn for the better after chancing upon her future boyfriend/husband, ANDY BELL, at a RIDE concert. Inspired to take up the guitar herself, IDHA subsequently found herself on the roster of 'Creation' (home to RIDE), co-writing some of her debut album, 'MELODY INN' (1994) with BELL. Also boasting ex-(SMALL) FACES keyboard man, IAN McLAGAN, the record was a rootsy, countrified affair featuring an array of choice cover versions (i.e. Gram Parsons' 'HICKORY WIND' and 'SAFE AT HOME' side by side with Tim Hardin's 'RED BALLOON'). Later that year, another high profile guest artist, EVAN DANDO, was to feature on the EP, 'A WOMAN IN A MAN'S WORLD', while BELL again shared the songwriting duties on slightly improved follow-up set, 'TROUBLEMAKER' (1997). • **Covered:** COMING DOWN (Byrd-Moskowitz)

Album rating: MELODY INN (*6) / TROUBLEMAKER (*7)

IDHA – vocals, guitar / with **IAN McLAGAN** – Hammond organ, piano / **CREEDENCE J. WRIGHT** – Hammond organ

		Creation	Tristar
Jan 94.	(cd/c/lp) (CRECD/C-CRE/CRELP 160) <66925 66191-2> **MELODY INN**		

– High over Hollywood / Red balloon / From me to you / More love / Another door / Stockholm / All my loving / Hickory wind / Get undressed / Safe at home / Music carries on.

Apr 94.	(12"ep)(cd-ep) (CRE 161T)(CRESCD 161) **GET UNDRESSED / DO RIGHT BY ME. / SHE / COMING DOWN**		-
Oct 94.	(cd-ep) (CRESCD 166) **A WOMAN IN A MAN'S WORLD**		-

– Ooh la la / A song for you / Willin' / Going to Mexico / I'm losing more than I'll ever have / She.

— now with **ANDY BELL** – guitar (ex-RIDE, of HURRICANE #1) / **TONY BARBER + ALAN WHITE**

May 97.	(7") (CRE 265) **SORRY SORRY. / HEY HONEY**		-

(cd-s+=) (CRESCD 265) – Downtown.

Jul 97.	(7") (CRE 268) **GOING DOWN SOUTH. / SWEET 16**		-

(cd-s+=) (CRESCD 268) – Fire in the sky.

Aug 97.	(cd/lp) (CRE CD/LP 184) **TROUBLEMAKER**		-

– Sorry sorry / Always been with you / Going down south / Still alive / Mercy me / Sweet September / Me and Johnny / Troublemaker / Fields of Avalon / Just moved in.

— IDHA has been a little quiet of late

IDLEWILD

Formed: Edinburgh, Scotland ... late '95 by RODDY WOOMBLE, ROD JONES and COLIN NEWTON, each having a penchant for noise veterans, SONIC YOUTH and FUGAZI. Having met at a party, the erstwhile students whittled away their revision time with ramshackle rehearsals, eventually channelling their frustrations into a debut single, 'QUEEN OF THE TROUBLED TEENS'. Famously financed by a student loan (and issued on their own 'Human Condition' imprint), the track was championed by Radio One DJ Steve Lamacq, duly rescuing the band from eternal toilet gig hell and setting in motion the mechanics of A&R overload. A follow-up single, 'CHANDELIER', appeared on 'Fierce Panda' while an acclaimed mini-album on 'Deceptive', 'CAPTAIN', kickstarted '98 and became their final fully fledged indie release prior to a deal with 'Food'. Somewhere along the way the band also picked up bassist BOB FAIRFOULL and began to coax some melancholic tunefulness from the blizzard of sound and fury that characterised their youthful approach. 'A FILM FOR THE FUTURE' announced their major label arrival in fittingly convulsive style, the first of many minor hits which

IDLEWILD (cont)

have cemented the band's reputation as one of Scotland's most talked about and possibly most dedicated sonic abusers. Their highly anticipated first album proper, 'HOPE IS IMPORTANT' (late '98), made the UK Top 60 and the band's steady rise proves that noisy guitars never go out of fashion. '100 BROKEN WINDOWS' (2000) might've been the casualties of noise, perhaps. But surprisingly enough, the four-piece turned the screeching guitars down for this commercially-orientated release. The single, 'THESE WOODEN IDEAS' unveiled another side to the band that used to literally knee-cap themselves on stage. Still, with its edge intact 'LITTLE DISCOURAGE' found IDLEWILD adopting an REM-esque style (circa 1995), and 'THERE'S A GLORY IN YOUR STORY' saw them unplugging their guitars altogether. Still, this set could make ears bleed if played at the correct volume. They toned it down, however, for their next release, the bleakly entitled 'THE REMOTE PART' (2002), an album which flirted with a lot of influences; from the Top 20, AZTEC CAMERA-inspired single 'YOU HELD THE WORLD IN YOUR ARMS' to the punky R.E.M. 'Murmur'-era led 'AMERICAN ENGLISH'. The same formula (seen on the latter LP) remained with 'I NEVER WANTED', a soft, heartfelt acoustic number and even a bit of spoken-word on 'THE REMOTE PART'. The album also crashed into the UK charts at No.3, providing one of Scotland's premier rock bands with the recognition they've been striving for since their musical birth.

Album rating: HOPE IS IMPORTANT (*7) / 100 BROKEN WINDOWS (*7) / THE REMOTE PART (*8)

RODDY WOOMBLE (b.13 Aug'76) – vocals / **ROD JONES** (b. 3 Dec'76) – guitar / **COLIN NEWTON** (b.18 Apr'77) – drums / **PAUL TIPLER** (helped out on) bass

		Human Condition	not iss.
Mar 97.	(7") (HC 0017) **QUEEN OF THE TROUBLED TEENS. / FASTER / SELF HEALER** *(re-iss. Jan98; same)*		–

— **BOB FAIRFOULL** (b. 6 Aug'76) – bass; repl. PAUL

		Fierce Panda	not iss.
Dec 97.	(ltd-7") (NING 42) **CHANDELIER. / I WANT TO BE A WRITER**		–

		Deceptive	not iss.
Jan 98.	(m-cd) (BLUFF 058CD) **CAPTAIN** – Self healer / Annihilate now / Captain / Last night I missed all the fireworks / Satan polaroid / You just have to be who you are.		–
Feb 98.	(7") (BLUFF 057) **SATAN POLAROID. / HOUSE ALONE**		–

		Food	Odeon-EMI
Apr 98.	(7") (FOOD 111) **A FILM FOR THE FUTURE. / MINCE SHOWERCAP (part I)** (cd-s+=) (CDFOOD 111) – What am I going to do?	53	–
Jul 98.	(7") (FOOD 113) **EVERYONE SAYS YOU'RE SO FRAGILE. / MINCE SHOWERCAP (part II)** (cd-s+=) (CDFOOD 113) – Theory of achievement.	47	–
Oct 98.	(7") (FOOD 114) **I'M A MESSAGE. / MINCE SHOWERCAP (part III)** (cd-s+=) (CDFOOD 114) – This is worse. (cd-s) **THE SESSIONS EP** (CDFOODS 114) – ('A'live) / Satan polaroid (live) / You've lost your way (live).	41	–
Oct 98.	(cd/c/lp) (497132-2/-4/-1) <9504> **HOPE IS IMPORTANT** – You've lost your way / A film for the future / Paint nothing / When I argue I see shapes, / I am happy to be here tonight / Everyone says you're so fragile / I'm a message / You don't have the heart / Close the door / Safe and sound / Low light.	53	
Feb 99.	(7") (FOOD 116) **WHEN I ARGUE I SEE SHAPES. / (1903-70) / CHANDELIER (10.15 version)** (cd-s) (CDFOOD 116) – (first 2 tracks) / Last night I missed all the fireworks (live). (cd-s) (CDFOODS 116) – (first & third tracks) / Palace flophouse.	19	–
Sep 99.	(7") (FOOD 124) **LITTLE DISCOURAGE. / BROKEN WINDOWS** (cd-s+=) (CDFOOD 124) – A-Tone. (cd-s) (CDFOODS 124) – ('A'side) / You don't have the heart (live) / 1990 – night-time.	24	–
Mar 00.	(7") (FOOD 127) **ACTUALLY IT'S DARKNESS. / MEET ME AT THE HARBOUR** (cd-s+=) (CDFOODS 127) – West Haven. (cd-s) (CDFOOD 127) – ('A'side) / Forgot to follow / It'll take a long time.	23	–
Apr 00.	(cd/c/lp) (FOOD CD/TC/LP 32) <65397> **100 BROKEN WINDOWS** – Little discourage / I don't have the map / These wooden ideas / Roseability / Idea track / Let me sleep (next to the mirror) / Listen to what you've got / Actually it's darkness / Rusty / Mistake pageant / Quiet crown / The bronze medal.	15	May00
Jun 00.	(7") (FOOD 132) **THESE WOODEN IDEAS. / THERE'S GLORY IN YOUR STORY** (c-s) (TCFOOD 132) – ('A'side) / When the ship comes in. (cd-s+=) (CDFOODS 132) – (three tracks above). (cd-s) (CDFOOD 132) – ('A'side) / Actually it's darkness (acoustic) / Rescue.	32	–
Oct 00.	(7") (FOOD 134) **ROSEABILITY. / RUSTY (the poop soldier mix)** (cd-s+=) (CDFOOD 134) – A thousand. (cd-s) (CDFOODS 134) – ('A'side) / I've only just begun / Self healer (live acoustic version) / ('A'-CD-Rom).	38	–

		Parlophone	E.M.I.
Apr 02.	(7") (R 6575) <55078-2> **YOU HELD THE WORLD IN YOUR ARMS. / A DISTANT HISTORY** (cd-s+=) (CDR 6575) – I was made to think it. (cd-s) (CDRS 6575) – ('A'side) / All this information / No generation.	9	May02
Jul 02.	(7") (R 6582) **AMERICAN ENGLISH. / POOR THING** (cd-s+=) (CDR 6582) – These are just years / ('A'-CD-video). (cd-s) (CDRS 6582) – ('A'side) / The nothing I know / We always have to impress.	15	–
Jul 02.	(cd/lp) (540243-2/-1) **THE REMOTE PART** – You held the world in your arms / A modern way of letting go / American English / I never wanted (I am) What I am not / Live in a hiding place / Out of routine /	3	–

Century after century / Tell me ten words / Stay the same / In remote part – Scottish fiction.
| Oct 02. | (7") (R 6587) **LIVE IN A HIDING PLACE. / GREAT TIMES WASTED** (cd-s+=) (CDR 6587) – Everything flows / ('A'-video). (cd-s) (CDRS 6587) – ('A'side) / Found that essence rare / I'm happy to be here tonight (live). | 26 | – |

— FAIRFOUL had already departed the previous month

– compilations, etc. –

| Oct 02. | (d-cd) Parlophone; (543148-2) **100 BROKEN WINDOWS / HOPE IS IMPORTANT** | | – |

IDYLL SWORDS (see under ⇒ POLVO)

James IHA (see under ⇒ SMASHING PUMPKINS)

IKARA COLT

Formed: Whitechapel, London, England . . . 1999 by CLAIRE INGRAM, PAUL RESENDE, bassist JON BALL and drummer DOMINIC YOUNG. This dark electronic rock band, who came to the attention of John Peel and Steve Lamacq after a superb gig at Dublin Castle, went on to become one of the most promising acts of 2002. However, back in 1999 the band were struggling to be heard, with demo after demo refused by record companies. They finally issued two singles, 'SINK VENICE' and 'ONE NOTE' on the 'Fantastic Plastic' label in 2001, and set to work on their debut album, to be entitled 'CHAT AND BUSINESS' (2002). A compendium mix of strange influences (SONIC YOUTH, WIRE, FUGAZI, JOY DIVISION and hints of Japanese noisecore MELT BANANA), the group toured with fellow British rockers The PARKINSONS and EIGHTIES MATCHBOX B-LINE DISASTER, drawing comparisons to another dark retro experimental band from across the ocean, INTERPOL.

Album rating: CHAT AND BUSINESS (*6)

PAUL RESENDE – vocals / **CLAIRE INGRAM** – guitar / **JOHN BALL** – bass / **DOMINIC YOUNG** – drums

		Fantastic Plastic	not iss.
May 01.	(cd-s) (FPS 026) **SINK VENICE. / AT THE LODGE / ESCALATE**		–
Oct 01.	(7") (FP7 027) **ONE NOTE. / SURF #2** (cd-s+=) (FPS 027) – Kite.		–
Feb 02.	(7") (FP7 029) **RUDD. / YOUR VAIN ATTEMPTS** (cd-s+=) (FPS 029) – Memory.	72	–
Mar 02.	(cd/lp) (FPCD/FPLP 005) **CHAT AND BUSINESS** – One note / Rudd / Bishop's son / City of glass / Pop group / Belgravia / Sink Venice / After this / At the lodge / Here we go again / May B 1 day. (cd+=) – (video clip show).		–
Sep 02.	(d7"ep/cd-ep) (FP7/FPS 031) **BASIC INSTRUCTIONS EP** – Bring it to me / May B 1 day (part 2) / Don't they know / Panic / May B 1 day (part 1).		–

IMAGINARY FRIEND (see under ⇒ BUDDHA ON THE MOON)

IMPERIAL DRAG (see under ⇒ JELLYFISH)

INBREDS

Formed: Kingston, Ontario, Canada . . . early '92 by songwriter MIKE O'NEILL and DAVE ULRICH. Launching their own 'P.F.' label the same year with a Canadian-only demo cassette, 'DARN FOUL DOG', The INBREDS initiated a steady release schedule that saw them issuing a 7" EP, 'LET'S GET TOGETHER', a CD-EP, 'EGROG' and their first full album, 'HILARIO' (1993) over the course of a year. A subsequent round of touring brought the band's distorted, minimalist Lo-Fi sound to a bigger audience, ensuring a higher profile for follow-up album, 'KOMBINATOR' (1994). A prestigious support slot to BUFFALO TOM helped them secure a licensing deal with soon-to-be 'Atlantic' subsidiary, 'Tag', who re-issued the aforementioned second set a year and a half later. 1996's 'IT'S SYDNEY OR THE BUSH' revealed a satisfying broadening of their musical horizons with the addition of guitars and even brass to their sparse blueprint. 'WINNING HEARTS' (1997), meanwhile, found the band bowing out with what was perhaps the most consistently listenable album in their patchy canon.

Album rating: HILARIO (*6) / KOMBINATOR (*5) / IT'S SYDNEY OR THE BUSH (*4) / WINNING HEARTS (*5)

MIKE O'NEILL (b. 1970) – vocals, bass / **DAVE ULRICH** (b. 1970) – drums

		not iss.	Proboscis Funkstone
Feb 92.	(c-ep) <PF#001> **DARN FOUL DOG** – Prince / Landlord / Smote / Second chance / Fine.	–	Canada
Jun 92.	(7"ep) <PF#004> **LET'S GET TOGETHER** – Russ / Granpa's heater / Derailleur.	–	Canada
Jan 93.	(cd-ep) <PF#005> **EGROG EP** – Carnival / Final word / Link / T.S. Eliot / Winter / Late movie / Bub.	–	Canada
Mar 93.	(cd-ep) <PF#008> **DARN FOUL DOG E.P.** (compilation of 'DARN FOUL DOG' & 'LET'S GET TOGETHER')	–	Canada

Apr 93. (7"ep) <PF#009> **SHERMANS / INBREDS split** – (2 by The SHERMANS) / Tell the truth / He never.		–	– Canada
Jun 93. (cd) <PF#012> **HILARIO** (compilation & 7 new songs) – Matterhorn / Russ / Noah's cage / Good taste / He never / Granpa's heater / Late movie / Thin / Prince / T.S. Eliot / Final word / Oliver / Smote / Tell the truth / Landlord / Carnival / Derailleur / Bub / Fine / T.S. Eliot (Youth mix) / Farmboy.		–	– Canada
Aug 94. (cd) <PF#017> **KOMBINATOR** – Kimbinator / Round 12 / You will know / Any sense of time / Turn my head / Dale says / She's acting / Scratch / Link / Dangerous / Don't try so hard / Cruise control / Last flight / Amelia Earhart. <(US/UK-iss.Aug95/Jan96 on 'Tag-Atlantic' cd/lp; 92606-2/-1)>		–	– Canada

		not iss.	Summershine
1995. (7") <020> **YELVERTON HILL. / CATHY'S CLOWN**		– Seed-Tag	– not iss.

		Tag – Atlantic	not iss.
Oct 95. (7"ep/cd-ep) (TAG 001/+CD) **YOU WILL KNOW / MATTERHORN. / HE NEVER / TELL THE TRUTH / SHE'S ACTING**			

		not iss.	Probiscus Funkstone
Jan 96. (cd-s) (95650-2) **ANY SENSE OF TIME / DERAILLEUR / OLIVER / CARNIVAL**			

		not iss.	Tag
1996. (7"; split) <PF#023> **NORTH WINDOW. / (a track by Plumtree)**		–	– Canada
Nov 96. (cd) <030> **IT'S SYDNEY OR THE BUSH** – North window / Wanna be your friend / Drag us down / When you're angry / Final word / Cut my throat / My favourite satellite / Sad sack / Do you really / Wind picks up / Reason why I'm sad.		–	– Canada

		not iss.	Murderecords
1997. (cd) <97210> **WINNING HEARTS** – Attitude / Every time I turn around / Is it the right time / Never be the same / Get along / Moustache / Take the path / Yelverton hill / This train I ride / Sometimes / The runaround / You remain unchanged / White caps.		–	– Canada

—— disbanded in July '98

INNER SLEEVE

Formed: London, England . . . early '98 by former "shoegazers" SIMON SCOTT on words (ex-SLOWDIVE and CHARLOTTES drummer!) and bassist RUSSELL BARRETT (ex-CHAPTERHOUSE), along with PAUL FYFE and BERLIN OTTO. Firing their first musical shots through the barrel of stalwart indie label, 'Fierce Panda', via the track 'COME ALIVE' (on a split single w/ DAWN OF THE REPLICANTS), INNER SLEEVE were the next pretenders to the shoegazing throne, albeit several years too late. Luscious, atmospheric and mellow were three adjectives laid at their door by music critics after reviewing their follow-up 45, 'LET ME DOWN' and parent album, 'LOOKING UP' (1999). Whatever happened to? . . .

Album rating: LOOKING UP (*6)

SIMON SCOTT – vocals (ex-SLOWDIVE, ex-CHARLOTTES) / **RUSSELL BARRETT** – bass (ex-CHAPTERHOUSE, ex-BIKINIS) / **PAUL FYFE** – guitar / **BERLIN OTTO** – drums

		Fierce Panda	not iss.
Aug 98. (cd-s) (NING 59CD) **GOING DOWN THE TUBES WITH . . .** – Come alive / (other track by DAWN OF THE REPLICANTS).			–
Dec 98. (7") (NING 064) **LET ME DOWN. / OVER**			–
Mar 99. (cd) (NONG 007CD) **LOOKING UP** – Come alive / Let me down / Smile / Over / Time of your life / It's gone / Bombarey 7 / Inside / Luminous.			–

—— the band split later in year

INSIDES (see under ⇒ EARWIG)

INSPIRAL CARPETS

Formed: Manchester, England . . . 1980 initially as The FURS, by schoolboy GRAHAM LAMBERT. He was joined in the mid-80's by STEPHEN HOLT, TONY WELSH and CHRIS GOODWIN. In 1986, as The INSPIRAL CARPETS, they replaced GOODWIN and WELSH with CRAIG GILL, DAVE SWIFT and CLINT BOON. Early in '87, they recorded a version of 'GARAGE' for a 7" flexi-disc given free with 'Debris' magazine. After gigs supporting the WEDDING PRESENT, JAMES, STONES ROSES and The SHAMEN, they issued their official debut, the 'PLANE CRASH EP' in mid-'88 for indie, 'Playtime' records. Early in 1989, they set up their own 'Cow' label, after their distributors, 'Red Rhino', went bust. At the same time, HOLT and SWIFT left to form The RAINKINGS, and were replaced by HINGLEY and WALSH. After a late 1988 recording, 'TRAIN SURFING EP', was issued, they recorded the 808 STATE-produced 'JOE' single/EP. A year later, they had their first UK Top 50 entry with 'MOVE', which led to Daniel Miller of 'Mute' records taking on both band and label. In April 1990, they broke into UK Top 20 with the poignant single, 'THIS IS HOW IT FEELS', pushing their debut album, 'LIFE', to No. 3. A heavy, organ-orientated psychedelic-pop group, their music lay somewhere between The DOORS and The FALL. The INSPIRAL CARPETS continued with a run of hit singles that included, 'SHE COMES IN THE FALL', 'CARAVAN' and 'DRAGGING ME DOWN', the latter two featured on the Top 5 album, 'THE BEAST INSIDE' (1991). The following year, with a further clutch of hit singles under their belt, they scraped into the Top 20 with 'REVENGE OF THE GOLDFISH', a weaker effort. A year of reflection in 1993 preceded a return to form with a MARK E. SMITH (The Fall) collaboration 45, 'I WANT YOU' (and featured on a certain TV ad). This helped the album, 'DEVIL HOPPING', reach the Top 10 but when their next single, 'UNIFORM', failed to even dent the Top 50, they were unceremoniously dropped by their label, 'Mute'. The band split soon after, leaving behind the customary cash-in compilation. The man behind their trademark keyboard sound eventually struck out on his own with The CLINT BOON EXPERIENCE, accompanied by RICHARD STUBBS aka STUBBSY, KATHRYN STUBBS aka SISTA STUBBS, PAPA T aka TONY THOMPSON, MATT HAYDEN and MOOSE. After a trio of singles on 'Rabid Badger' (namely 'ONE WAY I CAN GO', 'WHITE NO SUGAR' and 'COMET THEME #1'), the outfit signed to 'Artful' for a further single, 'CAN'T KEEP A GOOD MAN DOWN' (featuring Manchester's very own MARK E) and debut album, '(THE COMPACT GUIDE TO) POP MUSIC AND SPACE TRAVEL' (1999). Poking fun at various easy targets, the album was a more easy-going listening experience after the intensity of The INSPIRALS, BOON and co delivering a millennial follow-up in the shape of 'LIFE IN TRANSITION' (2000). • **Songwriters:** Group penned except; 96 TEARS (? & The Mysterians) / GIMME SHELTER (Rolling Stones) / TAINTED LOVE (Soft Cell) / PARANOID (Black Sabbath). • **Trivia:** To promote debut album, they employed the services of the Milk Marketing Board who ran a TV ad on their bottles. Early 1990, they penned 'THE 8.15 FROM MANCHESTER' (theme) from children's Saturday morning TV show.

Album rating: LIFE (*8) / THE BEAST INSIDE (*7) / REVENGE OF THE GOLDFISH (*6) / DEVIL HOPPING (*5) / THE SINGLES compilation (*8) / Clint Boon Experience: (THE COMPACT GUIDE TO) POP MUSIC & SPACE TRAVEL (*7) / LIFE IN TRANSITION (*6)

GRAHAM LAMBERT (b.10 Jul'64, Oldham, England) – guitar / **STEPHEN HOLT** – vocals / **DAVE SWIFT** – bass repl. TONY WELSH / **CRAIG GILL** (b. 5 Dec'71) – drums repl. CHRIS GOODWIN who joined ASIA FIELDS (later BUZZCOCKS F.O.C. and The HIGH) / added **CLINT BOON** (b.28 Jun'59, Oldham) – organ, vocals (ex-INCA BABIES)

		Playtime	not iss.
Jul 88. (7"ltd.) (AMUSE 2) **KEEP THE CIRCLE AROUND. / THEME FROM COW** (12"ep+=) **PLANE CRASH EP** (AMUSE 2T) – Seeds of doubt / Garage full of flowers / 96 tears.			–

		Cow	not iss.
Mar 89. (12"ep) (MOO 2) **TRAIN SURFING** – Butterfly / Causeway / You can't take the truth / Greek wedding song.			–

—— **TOM HINGLEY** (b. 9 Jul'65, Oxford, England) – vocals (ex-TOO MUCH TEXAS) repl. HOLT who formed RAINKINGS **MARTIN WALSH** (b. 3 Jul'68) – bass (ex-NEXT STEP) repl. SWIFT who formed RAINKINGS

May 89. (12"ep) (MOO 3) **JOE. / COMMERCIAL MIX / DIRECTING TRAFFIK / COMMERCIAL RAIN**			–
May 89. (c;ltd) (DUNG 4) **DEMO CASSETTE** (rec.Dec'87) – Keep the circle around / Seeds of doubt / Joe / Causeway / 26 / Inside my head / Sun don't shine / Theme from Cow / 96 tears / Butterfly / Garage full of flowers.			–
Aug 89. (7") (DUNG 5) **FIND OUT WHY. / SO FAR** (12"+=/cd-s+=) (DUNG 5 T/CD) – Plane crash (live).			–
Oct 89. (7"/s7") (DUNG 6/+X) **MOVE. / OUT OF TIME** (12"+=/cd-s+=) (DUNG 6 T/CD) – Move in.		49	–

		Cow-Mute	Elektra
Mar 90. (7") (DUNG 7) <66581> **THIS IS HOW IT FEELS. / TUNE FOR A FAMILY** (12"+=/cd-s+=) (DUNG 7 T/CD) – ('A'extended) / Seeds of doubt. (c-s+=) (DUNG 7MC) – ('A'extended) / Whiskey. (12") (DUNG 7R) – ('A'-Robbery mix) / ('B'drum mix).		14	
Apr 90. (lp/c/cd) (DUNG 8/+C/CD) <60987> **LIFE** – Real thing / Song for a family / This is how it feels / Directing traffik / Memories of you / Many happy returns / Memories of you / She comes in the fall / Monkey on my back / Sun don't shine / Inside my head / Move * / Sackville. (cd+= *) <US++=> – Commercial rain / Weakness / Biggest mountain / I'll keep it in mind.		2	Oct90
Jun 90. (7") (DUNG 10) **SHE COMES IN THE FALL. / SACKVILLE** (12"+=/cd-s+=) (DUNG 10 T/CD) – Continental reign (version). (12"+=) (DUNG 10R) – ('A'acappella version).		27	–
Nov 90. (7"ep/12"ep) (DUNG 11/+T) **ISLAND HEAD** – Biggest mountain / I'll keep it in mind / Weakness / Gold to . . . (cd-ep+=) (DUNG 11CD) – Mountain sequence.		21	
Mar 91. (7") (DUNG 13) <66543> **CARAVAN. / SKIDOO** (7"/12") (DUNG 13 R/T) – ('A'side) / ('B'-Possession mix). (cd-s) (DUNG 13CD) – ('A'-What noise rethink mix) / ('B'side).		30	Apr91
Apr 91. (lp/c/cd) (DUNG 14/+C/CD) <61089> **THE BEAST INSIDE** – Caravan / Please be cruel / Born yesterday / Sleep well tonight / Grip / Beast inside / Niagara / Mermaid / Further away / Dreams are all we have.		5	May91
Jun 91. (7"/c-s) (DUNG/+C 15) **PLEASE BE CRUEL. / THE WIND IS CALLING YOUR NAME** (12"+=/cd-s+=) (DUNG 15 T/CD) – St.Kilda (version).		50	–
Feb 92. (7") (DUNG 16) **DRAGGING ME DOWN. / I KNOW I'M LOSING YOU** (12"+=/cd-s+=) (DUNG 16 T/CD) – (2 other 'A'mixes).		12	–
May 92. (7") (DUNG 17) **TWO WORLDS COLLIDE. / BOOMERANG** (12"+=/cd-s+=) (DUNG 17 T/CD) – ('A'-Mike Pickering remix).		32	–
Sep 92. (7") (DUNG 18) **GENERATIONS. / ('A'remix)** (c-s) (DUNG 18C) – Lost in space again. (12"/cd-s) (DUNG 18 T/CD) – ('A'side) / She comes in the fall (live) / Move (live) / Directing traffik (live). (cd-s) (DUNG 18CDR) – ('A'side) / Joe (live) / Commercial rain (live) / Butterfly (live).		28	–
Oct 92. (lp/c/cd) (DUNG 19/+C/CD) <61397> **REVENGE OF THE GOLDFISH** – Generations / Saviour / Bitches brew / Smoking her clothes / Fire / Here comes the flood / Dragging me down / A little disappeared / Two worlds collide / Mystery / Rain song / Irresistable force.		17	
Nov 92. (c-ep/12"ep) (DUNG 20 C/T) **BITCHES BREW / TAINTED LOVE. / BITCHES BREW (Fortran 5 remix) / IRRESISTABLE FORCE (Fortran 5 mix)**		36	–

INSPIRAL CARPETS (cont)

(cd-ep+=) *(DUNG 20CD)* – Mermaid (live) / Born yesterday (live) / Sleep well tonight (live).
(cd-ep+=) *(DUNG 20CDR)* – Dragging me down (live) / Smoking her clothes (live) / Fire (live).

— parted company with 'Cow' co-founder/manager Anthony Boggiano.

May 93.	(7"/c-s) *(DUNG 22/+C)* **HOW IT SHOULD BE. / IT'S ONLY A PAPER MOON**	49	-
	(12"+=/cd-s+=) *(DUNG 22 T/CD)* – I'm alive.		
Jan 94.	(7"/c-s) *(DUNG 23/+C)* **SATURN 5. / PARTY IN THE SKY**	20	-
	(cd-s+=/12"+=) *(DUNG 23 T/CD)* – ('A'mixes).		
	(cd-s) *(DUNG 23CDR)* – ('A'side) / Well of seven heads / Two cows / Going down.		
Feb 94.	(7"/c-s; by INSPIRAL CARPETS featuring MARK E. SMITH) *(DUNG 24/+C)* **I WANT YOU. / I WANT YOU (version)**	18	-
	(cd-s+=) *(DUNG 24CD)* – We can do everything / Inside of you.		
	(cd-s+=) *(DUNG 24CDR)* – ('A'side) / Dragging me down / Party in the sky / Plutoman		
Mar 94.	(lp/c/cd) *(DUNG 25/+C/CD)* <61632> **DEVIL HOPPING**	10	-
	– I want you / Party in the sky / Plutoman / Uniform / Lovegrove / Just Wednesday / Saturn 5 / All of this and more / The way the light falls / Half way there / Cobra / I don't want to go blind. *(w/ free ltd-cd of 'BBC SESSIONS' or free ltd.red-10"lp)*		
Apr 94.	(7"/c-s/cd-s) *(DUNG 26/+C/CD)* **UNIFORM. / PARANOID**	51	-
	(cd-s) *(DUNG 26 CDR)* – ('A'side / Paranoid (Collapsed Lung mix).		
Aug 95.	(7"m) *(DUNG 27L)* **JOE (acoustic). / SEEDS OF DOUBT / WHISKEY**	37	-
	(7"m) *(DUNG 27R)* – Joe (live) / Sackville (live) / Saviour (live).		
	(cd-s) *(DUNG 25CD)* – ('A'side) / I want you / I'll keep it in mind / Tainted love.		
Sep 95.	(cd/c/d-lp) *(CD/C+/MOOTEL 3)* <9010> **THE SINGLES** (compilation)	17	
	– Joe / Find out why / Move / This is how it feels / (extended) / She comes in the fall / Commercial reign / Sackville / Biggest mountain / Weakness / Caravan / Please be cruel / Dragging me down / Two worlds collide / Generations / Bitches brew / How it should be / Saturn 5 / I want you / Uniform.		

— had already been dropped from the 'Mute' roster late in 1994

– compilations, etc. –

Jul 89.	(12"ep/cd-ep) *Strange Fruit; (SFPS/+CD 072) / Dutch East India;* <8305> **THE PEEL SESSIONS**		
	– Out of time / Directing traffic / Keep the circle around / Gimme shelter.		
Aug 92.	(cd/10"lp) *Strange Fruit; (SFRSCD 082) / Dutch East India;* <8502> **THE PEEL SESSIONS**		

— also released import 7"colrd/12"colrd/pic-cd-s 'GIMME SHELTER'.

CLINT BOON EXPERIENCE!

— **BOON** with **MATT HAYDEN** – guitar / **RICHARD STUBBS** – bass, trumpet / **KATHRYN STUBBS** – keyboards / **TONY THOMPSON** – drums

		Rabid Badger	not iss.
Aug 98.	(12"/cd-s) *(NANG 004)* **ONLY ONE WAY I CAN GO. / TIGER WOODS, ASTRONAUT / PRESLEY ON OLDHAM STREET**		-
Nov 98.	(7") *(NANG 006)* **WHITE NO SUGAR. / NOT ENOUGH PURPLE, TOO MUCH GREY**		-
	(cd-s+=) *(NANG 006CD)* – Philip Glass, astronaut.		
Apr 99.	(7") *(NANG 008)* **COMET THEME NO.1. / 17 . . . AND OVER**		-
	(cd-s+=) *(NANG 008CD)* – Andrew Gill, astronaut.		

		Artful	not iss.
Aug 99.	(7") *(7ARTFUL 31)* **YOU CAN'T KEEP A GOOD MAN DOWN. / NOW I WANNA BE YOUR DOG (featuring MARK E. SMITH)**		-
	(cd-s+=) *(CDARTFUL 31)* – ('A'-karaoke mix).		
Sep 99.	(cd/lp) *(ARTFUL CD/LP 25)* **(THE COMPACT GUIDE TO) POP MUSIC & SPACE TRAVEL**		-
	– Presley on Oldham Street / Comet theme number one / White no sugar / Not purple enough, too much grey / Only one way I can go / Tiger Woods: astronaut / You can't keep a good man down / This night will see me falling / Push me back down / The cool people who know who the cool people are / The biggest horizon / Andy Gill; astronaut.		
Oct 99.	(7") *(7ARTFUL 32)* **WHITE NO SUGAR. / NOT ENOUGH PEOPLE, TOO MUCH GREY (live)**	61	-
	(cd-s+=) *(CDARTFUL 32)* – You can't keep a good man down.		
	(cd-s) *(CDXARTFUL 32)* – ('A'mixes; New improved Bascombe blend – radio / Mark 1 / original classic formula).		
Jan 00.	(7") *(7ARTFUL 33)* **THE BIGGEST HORIZON. / THE BIGGEST HORIZON, THE DROP (Hedrock mix)**	70	-
	(cd-s+=) *(CDARTFUL 33)* – ('A'-unplugged Hedrock mix).		
Jul 00.	(7") *(7ARTFUL 34)* **DO WHAT YOU DO (EARWORM SONG). / (same version)**	63	-
	(cd-s) *(CDXARTFUL 34)* – ('A'side) / Life in transition / Only one way I can go.		
Nov 00.	(cd) *(ARTFULCD 36)* **LIFE IN TRANSITION**		-
	– This is the sound / Life in transition / Climbing back inside the dream / Cool vacation / Do what you do (earworm song) / 17 & over! / Radio Fritz commercial / Kids get kicks / Me I'm just a girl / The Frankie generation / It's always summertime / The craziest diamond / Somewhere in time / In chaos I see.		

INTERNATIONAL AIRPORT

Formed: Glasgow, Scotland . . . 1996 as the sole brainchild of TOM CROSSLEY, a part-timer with winsome indie-folkers APPENDIX OUT. For some reason, possibly because they numbered a Japanese bass player, AKI (of INCENCE), or more likely because they had a track featured on a Japanese V/A CD (see below), INTERNATIONAL AIRPORT made their vinyl debut courtesy of Eastern label, 'Osaka Lanes'; the line-up at this time was bolstered by STEPHEN, ROBBIE, CARI and JULIE. The EP in question, 'CRUNK INTO UP', was also a V/A affair and led to a one-off deal with Chicago's 'All City' imprint. The resulting 'AIRPORT SONGS' EP featured a mesmerising rendition of Ennio Morricone's 'UNA STANZA VUOTA', and even prompted one journalist to make a comparison with The RED KRAYOLA. APPENDIX OUT man, ALI ROBERTS, continued the free exchange of ideas by becoming part of INTERNATIONAL AIRPORT for the millennial 'NOTHING WE CAN CONTROL' album, a record that was also enlivened by the presence of TORTOISE's JOHN McENTIRE.

Album rating: NOTHING WE CAN CONTROL (*5)

TOM CROSSLEY – guitar, vocals, keyboards, drums (of APPENDIX OUT) / **STEPHEN** – guitar, vocals / **ROBBIE** – melodica, guitar / **CARI** – keyboards / **AKI** – bass (of INCENSE) / **JULIE** – drums

— early in '98, Japanese mag 'Beikoku-Ongaku' issued the 'Dream On' CD which featured the track, 'CHORDAMOL'.

		Osaka Lanes	not iss.
Apr 98.	(7"ep) *(HONEY 001)* **CRUNK INTO UP**	-	- Japan!
	– Blue wheel / (other artists are Honey Skoolmates / Disco Girl / Tirolean Tape).		

— In Jan'99, another Japanese V/A compilation, 'Crunk Into Up, Volume 2', for 'LD&K' featured the 'AIRPORT track, 'MOUNTAIN MUSIC'.

		All City	All City
May 99.	(7"ep) <*(ac 11)*> **AIRPORT SONGS EP**		Oct98
	– Strident hi-fi / Una stanza vuota / Melodica 1.		

— next with now full-time **ALI ROBERTS** – multi (of APPENDIX OUT)

		Geographic	Overcoat
Oct 00.	(cd/lp) *(geographic 2 cd/lp)* <*oc 06*> **NOTHING WE CAN CONTROL**		
	– Western / Moving water / Mountain music / Primo or Dutch / Vale of twisted sendal / Remnant kings / De menging van Bruin en Groen / Does chocolate live here / Gold strike / Icerink / Melodica 2 / Cyclionic lanes.		

(INTERNATIONAL) NOISE CONSPIRACY
(see under ⇒ REFUSED)

INTERPOL

Formed: New York City, New York, USA . . . 1998 by students DANIEL KESSLER, CARLOS DENGLER, and an old acquaintance PAUL BANKS. After some early gigging in the millennium the band settled on the inclusion of drummer SAM FOGARINO, they were then set for a busy 2001. In that year, in true indie fashion, the band delivered on their own an EP, as well as another EP on the Scottish imprint 'Chemikal Underground' on the 'fukd i.d.' run. The group could also be found on several compilations not least the British indie label Fierce Panda's 'Clooney Tunes'. INTERPOL was garnering interest in the music press both in their stateside homeland and in the UK; they toured Britain in April, and took the well-trodden track of alternative acts by appearing on the, need it be said, legendary John Peel slot on Radio 1. Comparisons were being bandied around by the music hacks, not least of which was their likeness to celebrated Mancunian post-New Wavers The CHAMELEONS. The darker tones of the band's material did echo back to MARK BURGESS' et al's melancholy output, but it would have been wrong to have taken this analogy too far, as INTERPOL also ran in the tradition of many of the great American East-coast alternative acts. These New Yorkers were brought to the attention of 'Matador', who signed them up in 2002, and released a triple-track single in the early summer of that year. Hot on its heels came the release of their debut album 'TURN ON THE BRIGHT LIGHTS' (2002). Fairly despondent stuff was showcased here but, in mood, rather than quality, which on the whole was promising. Thus more rave reviews followed, not least by NME, who had them play in their UK touring NME awards show at the beginning of 2003.

Album rating: TURN ON THE BRIGHT LIGHTS (*8)

DANIEL KESSLER – vocals, guitar / **PAUL BANKS** – guitar, vocals / **CARLOS DENGLER** – bass, keyboards / **SAM FOGARINO** – drums; repl. GREG

		Chemikal Underground	Chemikal Underground
Dec 00.	(12"ep/cd-ep) (<*CHEM 047/+CD*>) **fukd i.d. #3: PDA**		
	– PDA / Precipitate / Roland / 5.		

		Matador	Matador
Jul 02.	(7"ep/cd-ep) <*(OLE 546-7/-2)*> **THE INTERPOL EP**		Jun02
	– PDA / NYC / Specialist.		
Aug 02.	(cd/lp) <*(OLE 545-2/-1)*> **TURN ON THE BRIGHT LIGHTS**		
	– Untitled / Obstacle 1 / NYC / PDA / Say hello to the angels / Hands away / Obstacle 2 / Stella was a diver and she was always down / Roland / The new / Leif Erikson.		
Nov 02.	(7") *(OLE 570-7)* **OBSTACLE 1. / OBSTACLE 2 (Peel session)**	72	-
	(cd-s) *(OLE 570-2)* – ('A'side) / PDA (KCRW session) / Hands away (Peel session).		

IRVING

Formed: Bay Area, San Francisco, California, USA . . . 1998 by ALEX CHURCH, BRIAN CANNING, STEVEN SCOTT, BRENT TURNER and SHANA LEVY. CHURCH, CANNING and SCOTT had previously got together earlier in the year to play at a local art show and soon after teamed up with TURNER and LEVY under the IRVING moniker. Their shared love of 60's garage and melodious pop meant their output was a varied form of dream pop written by all the members, which gave each song some kind of distinction outwith their overall style. After performing around their native California, most notably with OF MONTREAL from the 'Elephant 6' music collective, which the band's sound had much in common with, they gained larger exposure playing at the CMJ music happening in New York in 2000. Fortunately they also gleaned the ear of ANDY PALEY, who worked with them on their debut full-length offering, 'GOOG MORNING BEAUTIFUL' (2002). This showcased their talent for penning and playing melodious dreamy pop, but also being able to rock it up when needs be.

Album rating: GOOD MORNING BEAUTIFUL (*5)

STEVEN SCOTT – guitar / **BRIAN CANNING** – guitar / **ALEX CHURCH** – bass / **SHANA LEVY** – keyboards / **BRENT TURNER** – drums

	not iss.	Eenie Meenie
Sep 02. (cd) <*MARS 006*> **GOOD MORNING BEAUTIFUL**	-	-

– Climbing mountain tops / Eyes adjust to light / L-O-V-E / Sleepy inside / Did I ever tell you I'm in love with your girlfriend / Holiday / March was fair at best / Turn of the century / Heading north / A very frivolous distribution of sundries / Faster than steam.

—— **AARON BURROWS** – keyboards; repl. SHANA (to LET'S GO SAILING)

ISOTOPE 217 (see under ⇒ TORTOISE)

IVY (N.Y.C.)

Formed: New York City, New York, USA ... 1993 by French expatriot (from the late 80's) DOMINIQUE DURAND along with ANDY CHASE. After a solitary recording they invited former BELLTOWER (and soon-to-become Oscar nominated FOUNTAINS OF WAYNE frontman) bassist ADAM SCHLESINGER to their indie-pop combo, releasing 45, 'GET ENOUGH', in the summer of '94. Their debut single was quickly followed with the mini-album, 'LATELY', which bordered on bland pop, however it was saved by DURAND's sexy and mysterious foreign vocals. Early in '95, the trio issued 'REALISTIC' to much deserved attention, and annoyingly being constantly mistaken for the East Anglian band of the same name. The album maintained guitar-pop sensibility with a clean cut, no mistakes, DIY production, bringing justice to the excellent pop tracks 'DYING STAR' and the haunting 'EVERYDAY'. 1997 (and now on major label 'Atlantic') saw the release of, arguably, the band's best work 'APARTMENT LIFE', a collage of dreamy 60's inspired indie rock set against SCHLESINGER's and CHASE's rhythmic and vocal efforts. DURAND's lisping voice still remained, most probably providing a catalyst for the pre-FOUNTAINS OF WAYNE-period of rock. Setting up their 'Stratosphere Sound' studio courtesy of JAMES IHA (SMASHING PUMPKINS), DURAND and CHASE – who'd married in the interim – produced their third, long-awaited album, 'LONG DISTANCE' (2001). However, this nearly didn't see the light of day as a fire, resulting in extensive damage (to the studio and their purse-strings) caused delay after delay. With a sense of irony however, tracks such as 'ONE MORE LAST KISS' and a cover of The Blow Monkeys' 'DIGGING YOUR SCENE', showcased their evolving love of trip-hop (think MORCHEEBA). Now an integral part of 'Nettwerk' records, they subsequently delivered a covers set, 'GUESTROOM' (2002), featuring ... • **Covers:** LET'S GO TO BED (Cure) / KITE (Justin Hayward) / SAY GOODBYE (Papas Fritas) / STREETS OF YOUR TOWN (Go-Betweens) / I DON'T KNOW WHY I LOVE YOU (House Of Love) / ONLY A FOOL WOULD SAY THAT (Steely Dan) / L'ANAMOUR (Serge Gainsbourg) / BE MY BABY (Ronettes) / I GUESS I'M JUST A LITTLE TOO SENSITIVE (Edwyn Collins). • **Note:** not to confused with East Anglian IVY who released records for 'Sarah' and 'Noisebox' c.mid-90's.

Album rating: REALISTIC (*6) / APARTMENT LIFE (*7) / LONG DISTANCE (*5) / GUESTROOM (*6)

DOMINIQUE DURAND – vocals / **ANDY CHASE** – guitar / **ADAM SCHLESINGER** – bass (ex-BELLTOWER, of FOUNTAINS OF WAYNE)

	Seed	Seed
May 94. (7"white) (*SEED 008*) **GET ENOUGH. / DRAG YOU DOWN**		-
Jun 94. (10"m-lp/m-cd) <(*95913-1/-2*)> **LATELY**		

– Wish it all away / Twisting / I hate December / Can't even fake it / Too sensitive [UK] / I guess I'm just a little too . . . [US]

—— added **MIKE VIOLA** – guitar / **JULIUS KLEPACZ** – drums

Apr 95. (7") (*SEED 012*) **DON'T BELIEVE A WORD. / BY MYSELF**		-
(cd-s+=) (*SEED 012CD*) – Get enough / Ordinary man.		
May 95. (cd/lp) <(*14253-2/-1*)> **REALISTIC**		Feb95

– Get enough / No guarantee / Decay / 15 seconds / Everyday / Point of view / Don't believe a word / Beautiful / Shallow / In the shadows / Dying star / Over.

	Atlantic	Atlantic
Nov 96. (cd-s) <*7697 120109-2*> **I HATE DECEMBER / I HATE DECEMBER (extended) / I HATE DECEMBER**	-	
Feb 98. (7"/c-s) (*AT 0023/+C*) **THE BEST THING. / SLEEPING LATE**		
(cd-s+=) (*AT 0023CD*) – ('A'mixes).		

	Epic	Atlantic
Apr 99. (cd/c) (*492831-2/-4*) <*83042-2*> **APARTMENT LIFE**		Oct97

– The best thing / I've got a feeling / This is the day / Never do that again / I get the message / Baker / You don't know anything / Ba ba ba / Get out of the city / These are the things about you / Quick, painless and easy / Back in our town.

	Nettwerk	Nettwerk
Jul 01. (cd-s) <*6700 30213-2*> **EDGE OF THE OCEAN (remix) / EDGE OF THE OCEAN (album version)**	-	
Sep 01. (cd) <(*6700 30218-2*)> **LONG DISTANCE**		Jul01

– Undertow / Disappointed / Edge of the ocean / Blame it on yourself / While we're in love / Lucy doesn't love you / Worry about you / Let's stay inside / Midnight sun / I think of you / Hideaway / One more last kiss / Digging your scene.

May 02. (10"ep/cd-ep) (*33139-1/-2*) **EDGE OF THE OCEAN EP**		-

– Edge of the ocean / Hideaway (alternative version) / Only a fool would say that (alternative version).

	not iss.	Minty Fresh
Sep 02. (cd) <*70045*> **GUESTROOM**	-	

– Let's go to bed / Kite / Say goodbye / Streets of your town / I don't know why I love you / Only a fool would say that / Digging your scene / L'anamour / Be my baby / I guess I'm just a little too sensitive.

JACK

Formed: Cardiff, Wales . . . 1994 by then teenager ANTHONY REYNOLDS and MATTHEW SCOTT, who subsequently enlisted others RICHARD ADDERLEY, GEORGE WRIGHT, COLIN WILLIAMS and PATRICK PULZER. After a move to London, the sextet signed a deal with maverick indie label, 'Too Pure', scoring a Melody Maker Single Of The Week towards the end of '95 with their debut 7", 'KID STARDUST' (a tribute to cult writer, Charles Bukowski). Enhancing their lush sound with the addition of cellist, AUDREY MORSE, the band created a minor stir with early '96's 'WINTERCOMESSUMMER', a track centering on girlfriend/boyfriend violence. A third single, 'WHITE JAZZ', previewed the band's inaugural long-player, 'PIONEER SOUNDTRACKS' (1996); it was hardly a coincidence that the record was overseen by Peter Walsh, a one-time producer for SCOTT WALKER, a JACK icon alongside moodmeisters such as NICK CAVE and JACQUES BREL. Following a collaboration, 'HOW TO MAKE LOVE, VOL.1' (1997) as JACQUES, with fellow BREL afficionado, MOMUS, frontman REYNOLDS reunited with his JACK cohorts for a second set, 'THE JAZZ AGE' (1998). Inspired by a lineage that could be drawn through SCOTT WALKER, BRYAN FERRY and The MONOCHROME SET, REYNOLDS and his JACK crew produced something of a quintessentially English masterpiece. Following a rather playful and literary JACQUES sophomore effort, 'TO STARS' (2000), the real JACK stood up for two further sets, the mini 'LA BELLE ET LA DISCOTHEQUE' (2000) and 'THE END OF THE WAY IT'S ALWAYS BEEN' (2002).

Album rating: PIONEER SOUNDTRACKS (*7) / THE JAZZ AGE (*7) / LA BELLE ET LA DISCOTHEQUE mini (*5) / THE END OF THE WAY IT'S ALWAYS BEEN (*5) / Jacques: HOW TO MAKE LOVE VOLUME 1 (*6) / TO STARS (*6)

ANTHONY REYNOLDS – vocals, guitar, keyboards / **MATTHEW SCOTT** – guitar / **RICHARD 'DICKO' ADDERLEY** – guitar / **GEORGE WRIGHT** – keyboards / **COLIN WILLIAMS** – bass / **PATRICK PULZER** – drums, percussion

Too Pure   American

Nov 95. (ltd-7") *(PURE 049)* **KID STARDUST. / I DIDN'T MEAN IT MARIE**

——— added 7th member **AUDREY MORSE** – cello

Jan 96. (7") *(PURE 052)* **WINTERCOMESSUMMER. / HEY! . . . JOSEPHINE**
(cd-s+=) *(PURECD 052)* – I was drunk in the underworld / Biography of a first son *[hidden]*.
Apr 96. (7") *(PURE 053)* **WHITE JAZZ. / THE BALLAD OF MISERY AND HEAVEN**
(cd-s+=) *(PURECD 053)* – Ballad for a beautiful blonde eye / Morning light *[hidden]*.
Jun 96. (lp/cd) *(PURE/+CD 055) <9 43073-2>* **PIONEER SOUNDTRACKS**
– . . .Of lights / Wintercomessummer / White jazz / Biography of a first son / Filthy names / I didn't mean it Marie / F.U. / Dress you in mourning / Hope is a liar.
Aug 96. (7") *(PURE 059)* **BIOGRAPHY OF A FIRST SON. / FOR LUNA**
(cd-s+=) *(PURECD 059)* – The seventh day / Kid Stardust.
Jan 98. (7") *(ER 176)* **ENAMORATE DE MI OTRA VEZ. / CINEMATICO**
(above issued on 'Elefant')
Jun 98. (7") *(PURE 079S)* **3 O'CLOCK IN THE MORNING. / LOLITA ELLE**
(cd-s+=) **LOLITA EP** *(PURE 079CDS)* – The ballad of swing and solar / The jazz age *[hidden]*.
Aug 98. (lp/cd) *(PURE 072/+CD)* **THE JAZZ AGE**
– 3 o'clock in the morning / Pablo / My world vs. your world / Saturday's plan / Nico's children / Lolita Elle / Cinematic / Steamin' / Love and death in the afternoon / Half cut wholly yours.
Oct 98. (7"ep) *(PURE 081)* **STEAMIN'. / FALL IN LOVE WITH ME AGAIN / LAST MOMENTS IN THE MIND OF DANNY SAMMY JR**
(cd-s) *(PURE 081CDS)* – ('A'side) / Yuka's life / You will forget me / When my landlord dies *[hidden]*.

Acuarela   not iss.

Jul 00. (m-cd) *(NOIS 1007)* **LA BELLE ET LA DISCOTHEQUE**
– Disco-cafe society / Sometimes / A bachelor in London / Sometimes (reprise) / Whilst high, I had this premonition / When your hair becomes lighter than air *[hidden]*.

Crepescule   Crepescule

Apr 02. (cd-s) *(TWI 1119)* **THE EMPEROR OF NEW LONDON / BOYFRIENDS AND GIRLFRIENDS / THE EMPEROR OF NEW LONDON (instrumental)**
May 02. (cd) *(TWI 1121)* **THE END OF THE WAY IT'S ALWAYS BEEN**
– The end of the way it's always been / The emperor of new London / With you I'm nothing / Disco-cafe society / That's the way we make it / Maybe my love doesn't answer anything in you anymore / Sleeping makes me thirsty / Sometimes / No north left.

JACQUES

aka **ANTHONY REYNOLDS + MATTHEW SCOTT** with **KIRK LAKE** (others include **NICK CURRIE** (MOMUS))

——— a single, 'FIVE FINGER DISCOUNT' was credited to KIRK LAKE & JACQUES

Setanta   Setanta

Apr 97. (cd) *(<SETCD 058>)* **HOW TO MAKE LOVE (VOLUME 1)** Jul02
– Tonight, you and me, through the gates of the world / Death of an ex-lover / We can, we will / Two lovers / Morning light / Dressing for winter / Her cello / When I was king / Disillusioned with the light from a dead and distant star / The crack in the ceiling / Somewhere / The harvest is over.
Nov 99. (7") *(MMBS 71)* **I DON'T KNOW WHY I LOVE YOU. / THEME FROM "LOVED AS A CHILD BUT NOT SO MUCH NOW"**
(cd-s) *(MMBS 71CD)* – ('A'side) / London loves you / I won't let you down / Morning light (live in Paris).
(above issued on 'Mistemacbari' of Argentina)

——— next with **REYNOLDS, SCOTT** plus **BRYAN MILLS** – bass (of DIVINE COMEDY) / **JAMES LANG** – keyboards (ex-JACK) / **STEVE BEES** – drums / **WILL FOSTER** – piano (ex-DELICATESSEN, ex-LODGER)

May 00. (7") *(SET 076)* **BLUE PARTY. / DEAD LOVE** Jul02
(cd-s) *(SET 076CD)* – ('A'side) / When you kill me / Beauty and me.
Jun 00. (cd) *(<SETCD 075>)* **TO STARS** Jul02
– So long, my blue valentine / Blue party / The orchestra that I loved / This is what you do / The day before you came / Sad in the sun / To stars / It'll never happen again / London loves you / I won't let you down.

Acuarela   not iss.

Nov 02. (cd-ep) *(NOIS 025)* **ROMANTIC**
– Primera parada / Serenade / All of me loves a little piece of you / Winterpollen / Last night in Tremorfa.

JACK DRAG

Formed: Boston, Massachusetts, USA . . . around 1994 beginning as a side-project for experienced and talented musician and producer JOHN DRAGONETTI. The output of JACK DRAG epitomises the alternative movement, coursing and mixing through many genres without being truly pinned down to any of them. DRAGONETTI's strength is his amazing aural imagination and the skill to translate this onto tape in the studio. In this way many critics make analogy between him and BECK, but comparisons are slightly redundant in this divergent field. 1994 saw JACK DRAG's first release with the single 'VELOUR', and over the next few years he released another single and a couple of albums, notably the eponymously titled 'JACK DRAG' (1996). There was some great stuff there, establishing DRAGONETTI's love of experimentation and psychedelia. For the next LP JD was bolstered courtesy of JOE KLOMPUS and JASON SUTTER on bass and drums respectively. This skilled rhythm section helped to increase the sonic investigations of the head honcho, and highlight his undoubted proficiency on the guitar, making 'UNISEX HEADWAVE' (1997) an oxymoronic album, being all over the place, and at the same time, harmonious. Although it was the release of 'DOPE BOX' (1998) the following year that brought the group to wider public attention, with such differing stand-out tracks as 'PSYCHO CLOGS' and 'SEEM SO TIRED'. After releasing, what appears to be a foray into the world of sound effects, remixing, and lab-testing different beats on EP 'JUNIOR COMMUNIST CLUB', aided by fellow knob-twiddler PETER DUCHARME, DRAGONETTI again took JD down the solo road with 'SOFT SONGS LP: AVIATING' (2000). This was certainly not to say it was anything like mainstream rock, on the contrary he used lo-fi recording techniques to bring out a more honest, and in turns, emotive sound. A few years later and JACK DRAG released the considerably bouncier and leftfield pop full-length outing, 'THE SUN INSIDE' (2002), which also showcased the mixing skills of DAN NAKAMURA on the big beat track 'FM ROYALTY'.

Album rating: JACK DRAG (*5) / UNISEX HEADWAVE (*5) / DOPE BOX (*5) / SOFT SONGS LP: AVIATING (*6) / THE SUN INSIDE (*6)

JOHN DRAGONETTI – vocals, guitars, electronics / with **JOE KLOMPUS** – bass / **FRED ELTERINGHAM** – drums

not iss.   Summerville

1994. (7") **VELOUR. / GREEN CHERRIES**

not iss.   Devil's Weed

1995. (c) **THE MANY MANY SONGS OF SAD BOY**
1996. (7") **LOOP. / DEBUTANTE AND TALL BUILDINGS**

not iss.   Hep-cat

Apr 96. (cd) *<10008>* **JACK DRAG**
– Velour / Loop / Hail the caffeine dream / Should've told / Dope box / There was a moon / Friends / Raincoat / Space 67 / Bright day.

——— **JASON SUTTER** – drums; repl. FRED

Jun 97. (cd) *<10015>* **UNISEX HEADWAVE**
– Unisex headwave / Nilla wafer / Cha cha / Screw / Surfin' le Charles / "Hey Rod, what's the word?" / Tattoo / Bad mood / Freakin' in Calistone / Veenus.

JACK DRAG (cont)

		not iss.	Summerville
1997.	(7") **VELOUR. / GREEN CHERRIES**	-	

— JASON SUTTER – drums; repl. FRED

		not iss.	A&M
Sep 98.	(cd) <540909> **DOPE BOX**	-	

– Debutante / Psyco clogs / Seem so tired / Dope box / Sinner's delight / Surfin' the Charles / Where are we / Tall buildings / Best friend / Distorto toy-drum love / I feel really o.k. / Kung fu dub.

		not iss.	Scientific
1999.	(cd-s; as JUNIOR COMMUNIST CLUB) **FREEDOM OF SPEED**	-	

– Ultrabollywood / Ultrasound.
(above aka JOHN DRAGONETTI solo)

		Shifty Disco	Sugar Free
Jun 00.	(cd-s) **AT THE SYMPHONY, I COULD BE / LOVING YOU (in mellow acid style)**		-
Aug 00.	(cd) <19> **SOFT SONGS LP: AVIATING**		Jun00

– Aviating / We could've been big / 1000 dancing people with sub-machine guns / Wow! (dig the no scene) / Interlude / Crazy / Future is now: yesterday / At the symphony, I could be / An evening at the Boston music awards / Only, only one (pt.1-2).

		Shifty Disco	Shifty Disco
Feb 01.	(cd-ep) (DISCOQUICK 9) **WE COULD'VE BEEN BIG / NOW OR NEVER / MIND IS ON FIRE**		-
May 02.	(cd) (SHIFTY 0204) **THE SUN INSIDE**		

– My favorite hole / FM royalty / Smile on fire / The sun inside / April / Happy songs of Lata / Gettin' high with Jesus / Now or never / Her voice made the angels in Hell sing / She's my kind of boy / Eighteen / I could never let you go / Beer helps us cope / Home is where?

| Jul 02. | (cd-ep) (DISCOQUICK 14) **SMILE ON FIRE / FM ROYALTY / SHE TRIPS OUT WITH THE PINK FLOYD / FM ROYALTY (the Jack Lord Jones remix)** | | - |
| Oct 02. | (cd-ep) (DISCOQUICK 19) **FM ROYALTY / SPOOKY / MY MOTHER WAS BORN IN DETROIT AND THEN AGAIN IN DELHI** | | - |

JACK FROST
(see under ⇒ CHURCH; in 80's section)

JACKIE-O MOTHERFUCKER

Formed: New York City, New York, USA . . . 1994 by multi-instrumentalists and lynch pin members TOM GREENWOOD and JEF BROWN. The band were a collective of various contributors and inspirations. Although there was no determined stereotypical band set up, their ensemble members brought their musical styles and instrumentation to the table for a feast of differing styles and opinions. Signed originally to Portland, Oregon, label 'Imp' records, they released three albums of their musical hybrid. 'ALCHEMY' (1995), 'CROSS POLLENIZATION' (1996), and 'FLAT FIXED' (1998). All displayed the band's varying and free formed approach to song writing. Combining elements of free jazz improvisation, folk, and psychedelic rock to name but three main ingredients, these albums demonstrated JOMF's ability to delve into varying genres and produce results. It wasn't until they signed with larger label, 'Road Cone', that they gained greater attention, aiding the further development of their style. The LP, 'FIG.5', released by their new label in late 2000, gained favourable comparisons to the legendary 'Trout Mask Replica' set by CAPTAIN BEEFHEART. Further releases of 'WOW' (2000), and 'THE MAGICK FIRE MUSIC' (2001), continued the trend for experimentation. Although the release of 'LIBERATION' in 2001, saw a slight change in style from the previous offerings; a subdued sound without diluted it.

Album rating: ALCHEMY – SHIT TO GOLD (*6) / CROSS POLLINATE (*6) / FLAT FIXED (*6) / FIG. 5 (*8) / WOW (*6) / THE MAGICK FIRE MUSIC (*6) / LIBERATION (*7) / CHANGE (*6)

TOM GREENWOOD – vocals, multi (ex-RAILROAD JERK) / **JEF BROWN** – multi / with **JESSE CARROT** – drums / **HONEY OWENS** – guitar / **ANDY CVAR** – multi / **JOHN FLAMING + NESTOR BUCKET** – saxophones

		not iss.	Imp
1995.	(lp) <IMP JO> **ALCHEMY – SHIT TO GOLD**	-	
1996.	(lp) **CROSS POLLINATE**	-	
1998.	(d-lp) **FLAT FIXED**	-	

— GREENWOOD + BROWN recruited **BRIAN FOOTE** – bass, electronics / **BARRY HAMPTON** – basses, percussion, flute / **PATRICK ALVEREZ** – flute, percussion

		Roadcone	Roadcone
May 00.	(cd) <(ROCO 024)> **FIG. 5**		Jan00

– Analogue skillet / Native Einstein / Your cells are in motion / Go down, old Hannah / Amazing grace / Beautiful September (we are going there) / Chiapas! I must go there! / Michigan Avenue social club / Madfame Curie.

| 2000. | (lp) **WOW** | | - |

(above issued on 'Fisheye', below on 'Ecstatic Peace')

| 2001. | (d-lp) **THE MAGICK FIRE MUSIC** | - | |

— **BROOKE CROUSER** – multi; repl. FOOTE + ALVEREZ

| Oct 01. | (cd) <(ROCO 031)> **LIBERATION** | | |

– Peace on earth / Ray-o-graph / Northern line / In between / Something on your mind / Tea party / The pigeon / Pray.

		Textile	not iss.
2002.	(12") **split w/ ACCENT ON SCIENCE**		- French
		Tcid Allepha	not iss.
Sep 02.	(cd/lp) (TCD/TLP 2) **CHANGE**		-

– Everyday / Sun ray harvester / 7 / 777 (tombstone massive) / Bus stop. (cd+=) – Feast of the Mau Mau / Fantasy hay co op / Breakdown.

JACKNIFE LEE (see under ⇒ COMPULSION)

JACKOFFICERS
(see under ⇒ BUTTHOLE SURFERS; in 80's section)

JACOB'S MOUSE

Formed: Bury St.Edmunds, Suffolk, England . . . 1991 by identical twins, HUGO and JEBB BOOTHBY alongside singing drummer SAM MARSH. Formed when the lads had barely reached puberty, the band had rather murky heavy metal beginnings, churning out STATUS QUO numbers until a chance TV sighting of Scots noisemongers The DOG FACED HERMANS turned their musical world around. Older and wiser, the trio made their vinyl debut in 1990 with the 'Dot' EP, issued on their own indie label, 'Liverish' and the proud winner of a Single Of The Week award from Sounds. A string of high profile support slots ensued including prestigious dates with NIRVANA, the band most widely mentioned when tackling any objective description of the JACOB'S MOUSE sound. While many noted the similarity with NIRVANA's 'Nevermind', the Bury St.Edmunds camp pointed out that debut album, 'NO FISH SHOP PARKING' (1992) – released on the band's own 'Blithering Idiot' label – had actually been recorded before the NIRVANA landmark had been released. Still, in terms of attitude and melodic, CARTER USM-style blitzkrieg spirit, there was a definite musical kinship, indie label 'Wiiija' finally signing them after intially turning the band down. Another EP, 'TON UP', surfaced later that year, as did a follow-up album, 'I'M SCARED' (1992), the lyrical intensity matching the sonic barrage note by searing note. Two more EP's, 'GOOD', and 'GROUP OF SEVEN', appeared in 1993 and while the predicted indie domination never quite materialised, 1995's 'RUBBER ROOM' album was testament to their talents.

Album rating: NO FISH SHOP PARKING (*6) / I'M SCARED (*6) / WRYLY SMILERS compilation (*6) / RUBBER ROOM (*5)

HUGO BOOTHBY – guitar / **JEBB BOOTHBY** – bass / **SAM MARSH** – vocals, drums

		Liverish	not iss.
Jan 91.	(12"ep) (LIVES 001) **THE DOT**		-

– Sign / Enterprise / Hey dip sugar / Ho-hum / Microfish. (re-iss. Oct94; same)

		Blithering Idiot	Frontier
Feb 92.	(lp/cd) (BLIT 001/+CD) <34646> **NO FISH SHOP PARKING**		

– Tumbleswan / Twist / She is dead / A place to go / Carfish / Caphony / Justice / The vase. (cd+=) – Ghetto queen / Company news. (cd re-iss. Sep94; same)

		Wiiija	Frontier
Sep 92.	(12"ep/cd-ep) (WIJ 15 V/CD) **TON-UP**		-

– Oblong / This room / Motorspare / Fridge.

| Apr 93. | (cd/lp) (WIJ 21 CD/V) <31058-2/-1> **I'M SCARED** | | |

– Kettle / Deep canvas lake / This room / Zig zag / Solo / Coalmine dig / Thin sound / Ash tray / Body shop / Box hole / Colum. (cd+=) – Oblong / Motorspare / Fridge. (re-iss. Sep93 on green-lp)

Oct 93.	(7"ep/cd-ep) (WIJ 26 V/CD) **GOOD. / DUSTY / LIP AND CHEEK**		-
Nov 93.	(7"ep/cd-ep) (WIJ 27 V/CD) **GROUP OF SEVEN. / PALACE / SAG BAG**		-
Apr 94.	(7"ep/cd-ep) (WIJ 32 V/CD) **FANDANGO WIDEWHEELS. / B12 MARMITE / 3 POUND APATHY / KEEN APPLE**		-
Sep 94.	(cd/lp) (JCOB 001 CD/V) **WRYLY SMILERS** (compilation)		-

– Good / Dusty / Lip and cheek / Group of seven / Palace / Sag bag / Fandango widewheels / B12 marmites / 3 pound apathy / Keen apple.

| Feb 95. | (7"one-sided) (LTD 001) **HAWAIIAN VICE** | | - |
| Feb 95. | (cd/lp) (WIJ 40 CD/V) **RUBBER ROOM** | | - |

– Kuff prang / Hawaiian vice / Public oven / James John Robert / Foam face / Snivelling / Hostile / Rubber room / Club scare / Domstic / Poltergeist / Blither.

— split later in the year when the twins went off to college

MACHISMO

SAM MARSH with a few others

		Recline	not iss.
May 96.	(7") (RECLINE 01) **MY NARGHILE. / LOW SOUL**		-

— released one hard-to-get single as their follow-up

JACQUES (see under ⇒ JACK)

JALE

Formed: Halifax, Nova Scotia, Canada . . . Spring '92 by the all-girl line-up of JENNIFER STEIN, ALYSON MacLEOD, LAURA PIERCE and EVE HARTLING, taking their moniker from the first letter of each member's christian name. Having all attended the same art school, the bespectacled librarian-like ladies decided to try their hand at alternative pop-rock, borrowing instruments from classmates and intially playing PIXIES/BREEDERS covers at parties. Making quick progress, they soon began writing their own material (as a group effort) and issued their debut 7", 'AUNT BETTY', in 1992. This led to the inclusion of a track on the 'Sub Pop' sampler, 'Never Mind The Molluscs', the JALE birds subsequently signing a bonafide deal with the label (having turned down 'Island') and releasing a further couple of singles prior to a debut album, 'DREAMCAKE' (1994). Intelligent, fresh and exciting, the record combined the sweet-lipped harmonies of classic pop with the kick of

ELASTICA and dark undercurrent of THROWING MUSES, the highlights of which could be witnessed live on that summer's trial-by-fire L7 tour and Reading Festival appearance. Barring a US-only EP, the group kept a low profile until 1996's well-received follow-up set, 'SO WOUND', by which time MacLEOD had been replaced by a guy(!), MIKE BELITSKY. The subsequent departure of HARTLING the following year looked to have put paid to the band for good, until, that is . . . some remaining JALE-birds (i.e. JENNIFER, LAURA and er, MIKE) premiered the short-lived VEES project.

Album rating: DREAMCAKE (*6) / SO WOUND (*7)

EVE HARTLING – vocals, guitar / **JENNIFER STEIN** – guitar / **LAURA PIERCE** – bass, vocals / **ALYSON MacLEOD** – drums, vocals

		not iss.	Cinnamon Toast
1992.	(7"ep) **AUNT BETTY ep** – I lied / Twisted / Sweetness.	-	
		not iss.	Derivative
1993.	(7"ep) <*DUH 008*> **SORT OF GRAY** – Emma / Brother. *(UK-iss.Nov96; same)*	-	
		not iss.	Genius
1993.	(7") <*015*> **GOLD LEATHER WITH HEEL DETAIL** – Steppin' out / River (acoustic).	-	
		Sub Pop	Sub Pop
Jun 94.	(7"/cd-s) *(SP/+CD 134-331)* <*SP 235*> **3 DAYS. / PROMISE**		
Aug 94.	(cd/lp) <*(SP 256A/127-317)*> **DREAMCAKE** – Not happy / Nebulous / 3 days / To be your friend / Again / River / I'm sorry / Mend / Unseen guest / Love letter / Emma / Promise.		Jul94
1995.	(cd-ep) <*018*> **CLOSED EP** – Nine years now / Wash my hands / Jesus loves me / Long way home / Double edge.	-	

––– <above issued on 'Murderchords'>

MIKE BELITSKY – drums; repl. ALYSON who joined HARDSHIP POST

| May 96. | (7"ep/cd-ep) <*(SP/+CD 346)*> **HEY HEY**
– Hey hey / All ready / Leave it alone / Coincidence / Bluestreak. | | |
| Jun 96. | (lp/cd) <*(SP/+CD 350)*> **SO WOUND**
– Ali / Hey hey / Signs of life / All ready / Tumble / Blue / Mosquito / Storm / Drag / Back on track / Over you / Despite / Superstar. | | |

––– HARTLING departed in August 1997, the band became . . .

VEES

––– were **JENNIFER + LAURA + MIKE** + added guest guitarists **MICHAEL BEGIN + MATT MURPHY**

		not iss.	Murderecords
Nov 97.	(cd-ep) <*0032*> **THE VEES** – Chicago lights / A / Denied / Seven thirty / Circumstance.	-	

––– note: the VEES on 'Rockhouse' were an all-male quartet

Denise JAMES

Born: Detroit, Michigan, USA. Formerly under the wing of WARREN DEFEVER and his outfit, HIS NAME IS ALIVE, DENISE gathered a slimline back-up (i.e. MATTHEW SMITH on production and instruments plus SCOTT MICHALSKI on drums) to help out on her eponymous 2001 debut for ALAN McGEE's 'Poptones' imprint. Coated with massive amounts of reverb, DENISE's vocals were akin to one-time VU chanteuse, NICO.

Album rating: DENISE JAMES (*6)

DENISE JAMES – vocals (ex-HIS NAME IS ALIVE, ex-DIRT EATERS) / with **MATTHEW SMITH** – guitars, bass, organ (ex-OUTRAGEOUS CHERRY, ex-SLUMBER PARTY, ex-The GO) / **SCOTT MICHALSKI** – drums

		Poptones	not iss.
Sep 01.	(cd) *(MC 5030CD)* **DENISE JAMES** – Who sent you love / No start tonight / Could you love me / Fourth of July / Darlin' / In dreams / Everywhere / Forty men / I know why you made her cry / Leave me lonely / I still long for you.		-

JAMES ORR COMPLEX (see under ⇒ ESKA)

JANE POW

Formed: Southampton, England . . . 1988 by brothers ANDREW and RICHARD STARKE, VINCENT KALLETT, RUPERT HANN, PETER DALE and GREG MacDERMOTT. Although the band's sound was clearly influenced by the British mod music of the late sixties and its later disciples like The JAM, they worked their own unique sound by combining this passion with electonica and unusual instrumentation plus structure, to create a kind of psychedelic revival meets Brit-pop sensibility. Debuting in 1989 with the singles, 'SAFE' and 'GOOD MORNING' (for 'Ambition' records), the band moved to 'Target' the following year for the release of their inaugural LP, 'STATE'. This was a competent first set which defied the pretentiousness that many of the American neo-psyche bands fell into. The band actually saw a Stateside release with the US indie label 'Slumberland', who put out their single, 'WARM ROOM', in 1991. Their sophomore full-length outing 'LOVE IT, BE IT!' (1993), displayed the promise of its predecessor, but evidently not enough for the group who had already parted ways in late 1992. Unfortunately for them their star was on the alternative ascent in the States, exemplified by their American imprint issuing the combined first two albums on a single CD. Noteworthy was RICHARD STARKE's later musical apparition in the electronic based outfit, FIRING BULLETS.

Album rating: STATE (*5) / LOVE IT, BE IT! (*6)

RICHARD STARKE – vocals, guitar / **ANDREW STARKE** – guitar / **VINCENT KALLETT** – guitar / **PETER DALE** – keyboards / **RUPERT HANN** – bass / **GREG MacDERMOTT** – drums

		Ambition	not iss.
1989.	(7") *(AMB 002)* **SAFE. / THAT'S ME GIRL**		-
1990.	(7"flexi) *(AMB 004)* **WHY AM I HERE. / (other by GIRL OF MY BEST FRIEND)**		-
1990.	(12") *(AMB 005)* **GOOD MORNING. /**		-
		Target	not iss.
Oct 90.	(lp) *(PGT 001)* **STATE**		-
		Slumberland	not iss.
Mar 91.	(7") *(DRYL 006)* **WARM ROOM. / SHUT DOWN**		-
		Marineville	not iss.
1992.	(7") *(MARINE 2)* **SANITIZED. / MORNINGSIDE**		-
		Slumberland	Slumberland
Jul 93.	(cd) <*SLUM 025*> **LOVE IT, BE IT!** – Sanitized / It's on it's way / Walker / Get by / Soundbarrier / Shutdown / 90's / Love it, be it / Track 9 / Playpower / Morningside / Out of it / On hold / Through / Latitude / Take / Jack boot / Warm room / Bophia green / Fruity. *(includes +=) –* STATE		Apr96

––– had already disbanded in '92; STARKE formed FIRING BULLETS

Bill JANOVITZ (see under ⇒ BUFFALO TOM)

JANUARY

Formed: London, England . . . 1999 by Australian-born singer-songwriter SIMON McLEAN (formerly of JUPITER and SCALA), with JONNY WOOD, JONNY MATHERS and SARAH PEACOCK (also ex-SCALA). Sadcore, lo-fi like MY BLOODY VALENTINE-meets-NICK DRAKE-meets-TEENAGE FANCLUB, the quartet delivered their debut single, 'ALL TIME', in er, January 2000. Described as an altar-boy singing the blues, McLEAN and his spacy team of canyon rockers signed a contract with ALAN McGEE's 'Poptones' imprint, releasing 'EYES ALL MINE' later that year. Tipped for great things, JANUARY finally issued their first album, the Mads Bjerke-produced 'I HEARD MYSELF IN YOU' (2001), a record to play on a sunny day sitting on a porch. If only . . .

Album rating: I HEARD MYSELF IN YOU (*7)

SIMON McLEAN – vocals, guitar / **SARAH PEACOCK** – slide guitar, keyboards / **JONNY WOOD** – bass, violin / **JONNY MATHERS** – drums

		One Day Rover	not iss.
Jan 00.	(7") *(ROVER 01)* **ALL TIME. / I HEARD MYSELF IN YOU**		-
		Poptones	not iss.
Nov 00.	(7") *(MC 5018S)* **EYES ALL MINE. / LISTEN TO THE BAND**		-
Feb 01.	(cd) *(MC 5018CD)* **I HEARD MYSELF IN YOU** – All time / Through your skies / Contact light / I heard myself in you (part 2) / Invisible lines / Sequences start / Eyes all mine / Projections / Falling in / Fused.		-
May 01.	(7") *(MC 5045S)* **FALLING IN. / SEQUENCE START** (cd-s+=) *(MC 5045SCD)* – ('A'-extended album) / ('A'-version).		-

JAPANCAKES

Formed: Athens, Georgia, USA . . . 1997 by ERIC BERG whose wish it was to form a 10-man collective who would play an unrehearsed, 45 minute, concert entirely in d chord. As unlikely as it might seem conceptual experiments such as this netted them a recording deal with 'Kindercore' and the group released their debut 'IF I COULD SLEEP IN DALLAS' in 1999. Working in the studio allowed the group, which now featured NICK BIELLI, TODD KELLY, HEATHER McINTOSH, JOHN NEFF and SCOTT SOSEBEE amongst others, to experiment further and deliver musical landscapes which had greater tonal variation than could be produced at their live shows. The 2000 follow up 'DOWN THE ELEMENTS' was an organic ambient effort and far more musical than their debut had been. The group continued to build on this with the release of their next two albums 'THE SLEEPY STRANGE' (2001) and 'BELMONDO' (2002) which with richly textured instrumentation seemed more soulful than the more common electronic ambient music available.

Album rating: IF I COULD SEE DALLAS (*7) / DOWN THE ELEMENTS (*6) / THE SLEEPY STRANGE (*6) / BELMONDO (*6)

ERIC BERG – producer / with **ANDY BAKER** – engineer / plus guitarists **JOHN NEFF + RYAN BERG + TIM BERG + HEATHER McINTOSH + TODD KELLY + BRENT RACKLY + NICK BIELLI + BRIAN TEASLEY + MISCHO McKAY + SCOTT SOSEBEE**

		Kindercore	Kindercore
Sep 99.	(cd) <*KC 031CD*> **IF I COULD SEE DALLAS** – Now wait for last year / Elevator headphone / Vocode-inn / Toomsuba / A short mile / Pole tricks / Elephants / Westworld / Baker beats / Dallas / Allah rahka.	-	

––– ERIC still with **McINTOSH, BIELLI, RACKLY, R. BERG + NEFF + KELLY**

Apr 00.	(cd/lp) <*(KC 037 CD/LP)*> **DOWN IN ELEMENTS** – Version / A.W. Sonic / Sputnik / Down the elements.		
Mar 01.	(cd/lp) <*(KC 058 CD/LP)*> **THE SLEEPY STRANGE** – The waiting / Disconnect the cables / This year's beat / Vanishing point / Soft n ez / The sleepy strange / Vinyl fever.		Feb01
		Darla	Darla
Apr 02.	(cd/lp) <*(DRL 123 CD/LP)*> **BELMONDO** – And begun / Handguns and firearms / Theme for a film / Always stuck with leaving / Duluth / Another.		Feb02

JAWBOX

Formed: Washington DC, USA ... summer '89 by ex-GOVERNMENT ISSUE mainman, J. ROBBINS, who, over the course of the next year enlisted BILL BARBOT, KIM COLETTA and ZACHARY BAROCAS. Older than, and untypical of (both lyrically and musically) many 'Dischord' bands, a label for whom they signed during the early 90's and for whom KIM had previously worked, JAWBOX nevertheless won respect from both their peers and the press. After releasing two albums, 'GRIPPE' (1991) and 'NOVELTY' (1992) for IAN MacKAYE's fiercely independent operation, JAWBOX were tempted by the greater opportunities available as a new addition to Atlantic's new sideline, 'Tag' (although they remained independent in the UK via 'City Slang'). Early in '94, the quartet made their major label debut with the acclaimed 'FOR YOUR OWN SPECIAL SWEETHEART', previewed by the laid-back post-grunge reflections of the 'SAVORY' single. Yet by the release of 1996's eponymous fourth set, the buzz had died down and JAWBOX had become yet another casualty of the US major label Grunge goldrush. By the time of the group's final demise in 1997, ROBBINS had already begun working on new material with ex-GOVERNMENT ISSUE (a band ROBBINS had also played in) and WOOL sticksman PETE MOFFETT. JAWBOX stalwart BARBOT completed the trio and they took the name BURNING AIRLINES, their expansive, melodic noise-pop unveiled for public consumption on 1999's acclaimed 'MISSION: CONTROL!' album. BARBOT, in particular, was instrumental in shaping the band's sound, his previously unheard bass-playing talent shoring up a solid, fluid groove behind the infectious lead runs and incisive lyrics. Which is why follow-up set, 'IDENTIKIT' (2001), recorded after BARBOT's untimely departure, reverted in part to treading old water first charted back in the JAWBOX days. The most obvious casualty was the invigorating sense of melody which had so enlivened the debut, leaving a competent but hardly compelling impression. • **Covered:** SOMETHING MUST BREAK (Joy Division) / SOUND ON SOUND (Big Boys) / CORNFLAKE GIRL (Tori Amos) / I'VE GOT YOU UNDER MY SKIN (Cole Porter) / STATIC (Tar) / LOW (R.E.M.) / IT'S EXPECTED I'M GONE (Minutemen) / MEATHOOK (Cure) / AIRWAVES DREAM (Buzzcocks).

Album rating: GRIPPE (*5) / NOVELTY (*5) / FOR YOUR OWN SPECIAL SWEETHEART (*7) / JAWBOX (*5) / MY SCRAPBOOK OF FATAL ACCIDENTS compilation (*7) / Burning Airlines: MISSION: CONTROL! (*6) / IDENTIKIT (*5)

J. ROBBINS – vocals, guitar, Hammond organ (ex-GOVERNMENT ISSUE) / **(W.C.3db)**
BILL BARBOT – guitar, vocals, sax, Hammond organ / **KIM COLETTA** – bass, vocals / **ZACHARY BAROCAS** – drums

			not iss.	DeSoto – Dischord
Apr 90.	(7"white-ep) <JA 2 – 45.5>	**JAWBOX**	-	
– Tools and chrome / Secret history / Ballast / Twister.				
			Dischord	Dischord
May 91.	(cd/c/lp) <(DIS 52 CD/C/V)>	**GRIPPE**		
– Freezerburn / Impossible figure / Tools and chrome / Paint out the light / Consolation prize / Grip / Ballast / Something must break / Green-line delayed / Bullet park / Manatee bound / Footbinder. (cd+=) – JAWBOX ep (re-iss. Jun94; same)				
Jun 91.	(7") **AIRWAVES DREAM. / (other by Jawbreaker)**		-	
(above issued on 'Selfless' records)				
Jan 92.	(7") <DIS 61> **TONGUES. / ONES & ZEROS**		-	
May 92.	(cd/c/lp) <(DIS 69 CD/C/V)> **NOVELTY**			
– Cutoff / Tracking / Dreamless / Channel 3 / Spiral fix / Linkwork / Chump / Static / Spit – Bite / Send down / Tongues / Ones and zeros. (re-iss. Jun94; same)				
			Touch & Go	Touch & Go
Feb 93.	(7") <(DIS 77V)> **MOTORIST. / JACKPOT PLUS!**			
Apr 93.	(7"; shared w/ TAR) <(TG 113)> **STATIC X2**			
			City Slang	DeSoto
Jun 93.	(7") <EJ 6> **SAVORY. / Edsel: PENALUMA**		-	
Sep 93.	(7") <WH 9> **FALK. / (other by Crackerbash)**		-	
(above on 'Simple Machines')				
Feb 94.	(7") (EFA 04931-7) **SAVORY. / SOUND ON SOUND**			-
(cd-d+=) (EFA 04931-2) – Lil' shaver / 68.				
			City Slang	Atlantic
Mar 94.	(cd/lp) (EFA 04932-2/-1) <82555> **FOR YOUR OWN SPECIAL SWEETHEART**			Jan94
– FF=66 / Savory / Breathe / Motorist / LS/MFT / Cooling card / Green glass / Cruel swing / Jackpot lus! / Chicago piano / Reel / U-trau / Whitney walks.				
May 95.	(7") <JA 11> **ABSENTER. / CHINESE FORK TIE**		-	
(above issued on 'DeSoto')				
Jun 96.	(cd/lp) (EFA 04981-2/-1) <92707-2/-4> **JAWBOX**			
– Mirrorful / Livid / Iodine / His only trade / Chinese fork tie / Won't come off / Excandescent / Spoiler / Desert sea / Empire of one / Mule – Stall / Nickel nickel millionaire / Capillary life / Absenter. (cd hidden track+=) – Cornflake girl.				

—— disbanded the following Spring

– compilations, etc. –

Dec 95.	(10"lp/cd; shared with LEATHERFACE) *Your Choice Live;* <(YCLS 23/+CD)> **YOUR CHOICE LIVE**		Sep95
Nov 98.	(cd) *DeSoto;* <JA 23> **MY SCRAPBOOK OF FATAL ACCIDENTS**	-	
– Static / Tongues / Chinese fork tie / Cooling card / 68 / Apollo amateur / Under glass / Low strung / The big shave / Dreamless / Bullet park / Won't come off (live) / Mirrorful (live) / Desert sea (live) / Savory (live) / I've got you under my skin / Sound on sound / Static / Low / It's expected I'm gone / Metahook / Airwaves dream.		

BURNING AIRLINES

J. ROBBINS – vocals, guitar / **BILL BARBOT** – bass, vocals / **PETE MOFFETT** – drums (ex-GOVERNMENT ISSUE, ex-WOOL)

			De Soto	De Soto
Aug 98.	(7") <BA 24> **CARNIVAL. / SCISSORING**		-	
Oct 98.	(7") <(BB 27)> **BACK OF LOVE. / Braid: ALWAYS SOMETHING THERE TO REMIND ME**			
Apr 99.	(cd) <(BU 30)> **MISSION: CONTROL!**			Feb99
– Carnival / Wheaton calling / Pacific 231 / Scissoring / Escape engine / My pornograph / Meccano / 3 sisters / Flood of foreign capital / Crowned / Sweet deals on surgery / I sold myself in.				
Mar 00.	(7") <(THK 066)> **DELUXE WAR BABY. / (a track by At The Drive In)**			
(above issued on 'Thick')				
——	**MIKE HARBIN** – bass; repl. BARBOT			
May 01.	(cd) <(BU 36)> **IDENTIKIT**			
– Outside the aviary / Morricone dancehall / A lexicon / A song with no words / All sincerity / The surgeon's house / The deluxe war baby / Everything here is very new / Paper crowns / Blind trial / Identikit / Election-night special / Tastykake / Earthbound / Dear Hilary.				

—— added on tour **BEN PAPE** – keyboards, guitar

JAWBREAKER

Formed: Santa Monica, California, USA ... 1988 by songwriter BLAKE SCHWARZENBACH and ADAM PFAHLER, the high school mates soon being joined by CHRIS BAUERMEISTER. JAWBREAKER subsequently came into existence with the addition of CHRIS BAUERMEISTER, a fellow student SCHWARZENBACH had met while studying at New York University. Although PFAHLER was attending film school in Los Angeles at the time, the trio managed sporadic recording sessions which resulted in a clutch of singles and EP's. An independently released (on the 'Shredder' label) debut album, 'UNFUN', arrived in 1989, its stark, deeply introspective lyrics and intelligent punk-pop/proto grunge sound heralding the arrival of an exciting new talent. 'BIVOUAC' (1992) and '24-HOUR THERAPY' (1993) garnered the band a sizeable underground following, their muscular chords and literate songwriting attracting the attention of NIRVANA who secured their support services for a number of dates on the 'In Utero' tour. Yet bad luck seemed to stalk JAWBREAKER, both in terms of personal health problems and misdirected criticisms from both inside and outside the grunge scene. A subsequent deal (allegedly of the multi-million dollar variety) with 'Geffen' resulted in 'DEAR YOU' (1995), a record which hardly compromised their principled approach yet failed to break through alongside the likes of GREEN DAY et al. • **Covered:** YOU DON'T KNOW ... + PACK IT UP (Chrissie Hynde / Joan Jett) / PRETTY PERSUASION (R.E.M.)/ INTO YOU LIKE A TRAIN (Psychedelic Furs).

Album rating: UNFUN (*6) / BIVOUAC (*6) / 24 HOUR REVENGE THERAPY (*5) / DEAR YOU (*7) / LIVE 4/30/96 (*6) / ETC collection (*6)

BLAKE SCHWARZENBACH – vocals, guitar / **CHRIS BAUERMEISTER** – bass / **ADAM PFAHLER** – drums

			not iss.	Shredder
Nov 89.	(cd) <7> **UNFUN**		-	
– Want / Seethruskin / Fine day / Incomplete / Imaginary war / Busy / Softcore / Driven / Wound / Down / Gutless / Drone / Lawn / Crane / Eye-5.				
1991.	(7") <(SHREDFIFTY)> **BUSY.**			
			not iss.	Selfless
Jun 91.	(7") **WITH OR WITHOUT U2. / Jawbox: AIRWAVES DREAM**		-	
			Tupelo	Tupelo
May 92.	(m-lp) <(TUPLP 35-1)> **CHESTERFIELD KINGS**			1991
Nov 92.	(cd/c/lp) <(TUP 38-2/-4/-1)> **BIVOUAC**			1991
– Shield your eyes / Big / Chesterfield kings / Sleep / Donatello / Face down / P.S. New York is burning / Like a secret / Tour song / You don't know ... / Pack it up / Parabola / Bivouac. (re-iss. Nov99 on 'Communion' lp/cd; COMM 38/+CD)				
1993.	(cd-ep) <10> **split w/ SIMIAN**		-	
– Caroline / Rich / Kiss the bottle / Equalized / With or without you.				
(above issued on 'No Idea')				
Feb 94.	(cd/c/lp) <(TUP 49-2/-4/-1)> **24 HOUR REVENGE THERAPY**			1993
– The boat dreams from the hill / Indictment / Boxcar / Outpatient / Ashtray monument / Condition Oakland / Ache / Do you still hate me? / West Bay invitational / Jinx removing / In sadding around.				
			not iss.	D.G.C.
Sep 95.	(cd/c) <24831> **DEAR YOU**		-	
– Save your generation / I love you so much it's killing us .... / Fireman / Accident prone / Chemistry / Oyster / Million / Lurker II: Dark son of night / Jet black / Bad scene, everyone's fault / Sluttering / Basilica / (untitled track).				

—— disbanded after a final gig in April '96; BLAKE formed JETS TO BRAZIL

– compilations, etc. –

Nov 99.	(cd) *Blackball;* <(BBALL 002)> **LIVE 4/30/96** (live)		
– Jinx removing / Save your generation / Ashtray monument / Accident prone / Boxcar / Gemini / Parabola / For Esme / Shirt.			
Aug 02.	(cd) *Blackball;* <(BB 003)> **ETC**		Jul02
– Shield your eyes / Equalized / Caroline / Better half / Split / Gutless / With or without U2 / Fantastic planet / Rich / Peel it the fuck down / Pretty persuasion / Kiss the bottle / First step / Friends back east / Sea foam green / Housesitter / Into you like a train / Sister / Friendly fire / Boxcar.			

JAZZ CANNON (see under ⇒ MADDER ROSE)

J CHURCH

Formed: Bay Area, San Francisco, California, USA ... 1992, the all-male trio (one Oriental) stemming from CRINGER; aka songwriter LANCE HAHN and GARDNER FUSUHARA. These pop-punk boys, named after their nearby public transport route, definitely had good musical precedents coming, as they did, from legendary indie band CRINGER. The duo employed several drummers through their early years as J CHURCH, one of their longest lasting being REED BURGOYNE who joined them in 1994. Several years and 7"'s after their conception the band released their debut LP 'QUETZALCOATL' (1993), which was on the whole fairly good, but surpassed by their second full-length outing, the bouncy and vivacious 'PROPHYLAXIS', released the following year. The same year saw them releasing 'CAMELS, SPILLED CORONA AND THE SOUND OF MARIACHI BANDS', on 'Broken Rekids' which nicely collected together early singles for the lazier and more economically minded fan. 1995 saw the release of EP 'THE PROCESSION OF SIMULCRA / MAP PRECEDES TERRITORY', a short stop-gap release, although the band didn't leave the die-hards wanting too much; releasing another singles compilation, 'NOSTALGIC FOR NOTHING' that same year, and the high-point album of their career, 'ARBOR VITAE'. Released on HAHN's own 'Honey Bear' imprint, this LP combined mature subject matter, not always a strength in the pop-punk market, with vital and energetic rocking. The next year saw no let down in quality with the release of 'DRAMA OF ALIENATION', which continued on with their brisk lo-fi punky outbursts. After these two great efforts the group didn't release another album for several years, although the singles kept coming. Notable from this period was the 7" 'NOTHING CITY' (1997) which was taped during a visit to the UK, and among other things had the backing singing of HARRIET from a certain Glasgow band. The same year also saw the departure and replacement of BURGOYNE by ANDEE CONNORS, formerly of A MINOR FOREST. Another year, and another singles compilation, 'ALTAMONT '99' followed and also the withdrawal of founding member FUSUHARA and long-standing drummer, CONNORS, who were supplanted by JEFF BURSLEY, and former JAWBREAKER, ADAM PFAHLER, respectively. After a small period with no full-length releases the millennium saw the band put out 'ONE MISSISSIPPI', which although retaining their traditional stylings also saw a slight departure into more experimental regions. 2001 saw the release of yet another singles and covers collection, which rocked-up versions of several ELO tracks and a loud and punky take on 'YOU'RE THE ONE THAT I WANT' from the musical, 'Grease', with HAHN's Danny singing alongside KELLY GREEN from COCKPIT's Sandy; the band forefronting their sense of humour on this one. • **Covered:** ASSHOLE (Beck) / SEA OF PEARLS (Seam) / GIRLFRIEND IN A COMA (Smiths) / CREEP (Radiohead) / COOL GUITAR GIRL (Heavenly) / NOT GIVEN LIGHTLY (Chris Knox) / LIVING WITH THE DREAMING BODY (Poi Poi Pondering) / NO DOVES FLY HERE (Mob) / PLANET EARTH (Duran Duran) / AT THE END OF THE M1 (Wat Tyler) / THE LAST OF THE INTERNATIONAL PLAYBOYS (Morrissey) / IF WE WAIT (Guided By Voices) / DA DA DA (Trio) / TURN TO STONE + TELEPHONE LINE + SWEET TALKIN' WOMAN + DON'T BRING ME DOWN (Electric Light Orchestra) / YOU'RE THE ONE THAT I WANT (John Travolta & Olivia Newton-John) / KILL SURF CITY (Jesus & Mary Chain) / HARVEST (Neil Young) / PEOPLE ARE SCARED (Subhumans).

Album rating: QUETZALCOATL (*5) / PROPHYLAXIS (*6) / CAMELS, SPILLED CORONA AND THE SOUND OF MARIACHI BANDS compilation (*6) / NOSTALGIC FOR NOTHING compilation (*6) / ARBOR VITAE (*7) / THE DRAMA OF ALIENATION (*6) / WHOREHOUSE: SONGS AND STORIES mini compilation (*5) / CAT FOOD (*4) / ALTAMONT '99 collection (*5) / ONE MISSISSIPPI (*5) / MEATY, BEATY, SHITTY SOUNDING compilation (*3) / PALESTINE collection (*4)

LANCE HAHN – vocals, guitar / **GARDNER FUSUHARA** – bass / **AARON** – drums

		Damaged Goods	Allied
1991.	(7") **SAID SHE WOULDN'T SACRIFICE** – Bomb / Sacrifice / Commodity.	-	
1992.	(7") <ALLIED 22> **J TOWN REVISITED** – Favorite phrase / JONESTOWN: We are all prostitutes.		-
1992.	(7"ep) <SKIP 10> **THIS SONG IS FOR KATHI** – November / Katrina and Paul / Kathi / Girl in a magazine. (above issued on 'Broken Rekids')	-	

in 1992, 'MISERY' featured on V/A comp 7"ep, 'This Is Fiucked . . .'

| 1993. | (cd-ep) <ALLIED 25> **YELLOW, BLUE AND GREEN /**
– Yellow, blue and green / Open road / In vain (live) / November (live) / Bomb (live). | | - |

BRENDAN – drums; repl. AARON

1993.	(cd/lp) <ALLIED 27> **QUETZALCOATL** – Bottom rung / Good judge of character / Blister / Yellow, blue and green / New book / In vain / Hate so real / Cilantro / Open road / Disappear / Limp / Concede / What could I have done / Made life simple.		-
Jun 93.	(7"one-sided) (DUMP 014) **SLEEP / COOL GUITAR GIRL** (above issued on 'Rugger Bugger')		-
Jul 93.	(7"ep) (DAMGOOD 20) **NO ONE HAS A FUTURE** – Mariachi bands / November (live) / Bomb (live).		-
1993.	(ltd-7"m) **TRAVELLERS. / MISERY / HAD IT RIGHT**	-	
1993.	(ltd-7"m) **MY FAVORITE PLACE. / PLANET EARTH / NIGHT TIME** (above 2 issued on 'Honey Bear') (below on 'Word Of Mouth – Humble')	-	
1993.	(7"ep) **CREEP. / GIRLFRIEND IN A COMA / LINES** <re-iss. 1995 on 'Broken Rekids'; SKIP 45>	-	
1993.	(7"yellow) <DB 01> **SHE HAS NO CONTROL** – Made life simple / What could I have done.	-	
1993.	(7"ep) <DB 04> **SHE NEVER LEAVES THE NEIGHBORHOOD** – Good judge of character / Financial zone / Priest. (above 2 issued on 'Dead Beat')	-	
1994.	(7") **CRAZY LADY ON MARKET STREET. / (other by SMALL 23)** (above on 'Honey Bear')	-	

REED BURGOYNE – drums; repl. BRENDAN

| 1994. | (cd) <ALLIED 42> **PROPHYLAXIS**
– Foreign films / No surprise / Lucidity / Financial zone / New dreams broken / Picture this / Marge Schott / Why I liked Bikini Kill / Chemicals / Letter to a friend / I can't be nice to you / Priest. (lp-iss.1994 on 'Broken Rekids'; SKIP 25> (w/free 7")
– SACRIFICE (live). / WHAT COULD I HAVE DONE (live). | - | |

		Damaged Goods	Broken Rekids
Apr 94.	(7"ep) <SKIP 19> **TIDE OF FATE EP** – Tide of fate / Panama / No doves fly here. (cd-ep+=) <19> – Sleep / Cool guitar girl / Birthday.		-
May 94.	(10"ep) (DAMGOOD 37) **A MILLION BROKEN STEREOS** – Tide of fate / Panama / No doves fly here / Birthday / Travelers.	-	
1994.	(7"ep) <SD 001> **IF I'M LONELY / AT THE END OF THE M1. / (other 3 by WAT TYLER)** (above issued on 'Suspect Device')	-	
Feb 95.	(7",7"white) <SKIP 35> **IVY LEAGUE COLLEGE. / BAND YOU LOVE TO HATE / MARIE PROVOST**		-
Jul 95.	(d7"ep; pale blue + green) (DAMGOOD 77) **LAMA TEMPLE** – Lama temple / On dying alone / About the she / You almost feel sad / As I lie . . . / Not given lightly / Living with the dreaming body.	-	

		Jade Tree	Jade Tree
Jul 95.	(10"ep) <(JT 019)> **THE PRECESSION OF SIMULACRA: THE MAP PRECEDES TERRITORY** – Fascist radio / Case number / High / Jennifer Jason Leigh / Stupid lesson / Lama temple. (cd-ep+=) <(JT 019CD)> – Part of the problem / Why I liked Bikini Kill / Tea time.		Apr95

		not iss.	Allied
Nov 95.	(cd-ep) <ALLIED 60> **ANALYSIS, YES, VERY NICE** – At the cannery / Analysis, yes, very nice / Radical chic / Zero = zero / Beverly Hills / Kill your boss. (UK-iss.May97 as 10"pic-d-ep; ALLIED 085)	-	

		Rugger Bugger	Honey Bear
1995.	(7"m) **YOUR SHIRT. / I WOULD FOR YOU / TRANSVESTITE SHOW**	-	
1995.	(7"ep) <HB 8> **ALONE AT NIGHT EP** – Nostalgic for nothing / If I'm lonely . . . / At the end of the M1.		-
1995.	(7"ep) **ASSHOLE** – Asshole / Pointless pointing / Sea of pearls / Earthquake song.	-	
1995.	(7"ep) <DB 07> **J CHURCH / SERPICO split** – Mistake – Missed / UFOs will crash / Hypothesis / SERPICO: Sunset square. (above issued on 'Dead Beat')	-	
Nov 95.	(lp)<cd> <SEEP 15> <HB 11> **ARBOR VITAE** – Cigarettes kill / Racked / Drinking down / Church on fire / Your shirt / Without a single word / Contempt for modesty / Swallow / Smoke in my face / Waiting on the ground / Mr. Backrub / Stinking seas / Switzerland [lp-only] / Transvestite show [cd-only]. (UK cd-iss. Dec96 on 'Honey Bear'; same as US)		

		not iss.	Vagrant
Dec 95.	(7"m) <VAG 2> **RACKED. / MARY'S MOVING OUT / YOU FUCKING TRICK** (UK-iss.Feb97; same as US)	-	

		not iss.	Goldenrod
1996.	(7") **J CHURCH / FLUF split** – If we wait . . . / Contempt for modesty / FLUF: Assmunch.	-	

		Spiral Objective	not iss.
1996.	(7"m) **WAITING ON THE GROUND. / AYN RAND IS DEAD / COLLEGE STATION**	-	- Austra

		Honest Don's	Honest Don's
Nov 96.	(cd/c/lp) <(DON 003 CD/MC/LP)> **THE DRAMA OF ALIENATION** – Simple gesture / Smell it rot / Alone when she dies / Undisputed king of nothing / Secrets / Santa Cruz / Parts unknown / Crop circles / Colors lie / You're on your own / The dramatic history of a boring town / Static.		

		Suspect Device	Suspect Device
Dec 96.	(7"ep) <(SDR 002)> **CROP CIRCLES / ALONE WHEN SHE DIES. / (other 2 by WAT TYLER)**		

		Crackle!	Crackle!
Jan 97.	(7"m) (CAT 011) **THE DRAMATIC HISTORY OF A BORING TOWN. / 8:28 / BACK TO HAWAIIAN**		

		Liquid Meat	Liquid Meat
Jun 97.	(7"ep) <(LM 018)> **(I WANT TO SEE) FAYE WONG / WHAT WILL I DO. / (other 2 by DISCOUNT)**		

		Rumblestrip	not iss.
Aug 97.	(7"m) (RSTR 009) **THE UNDISPUTED KING OF NOTHING. / I HAVE TO ADMIT / SNOT RAGS**		

		not iss.	Dead Beat
1997.	(7"ep) <DB 15> **PLASTIC / YOU MAY NEVER. / (other 2 by LESS THAN JAKE)**	-	

		not iss.	Marigold
1998.	(7"ep; as CILANTRO) **EMPTY SODA CAN** – Empty soda can / Symbols / Colonial Hong Kong / Seventeen / Everybody laughs / Now you realize. (above was down to LANCE solo)	-	

ANDEE CONNORS – drums (ex-A MINOR FOREST) repl. BURGOYNE

		Damaged Goods	Damaged Goods
Jul 98.	(7"m) (DAMGOOD 151) **TURN TO STONE. / YOU'RE THE ONE THAT I WANT / PART OF THE PROBLEM** (7"m) (DAMGOOD 151X) – ('A'side) / Kill surf city / Lemon zinger. (cd-s) (DAMGOOD 151CD) – ('A'side) / Telephone line / Winter comes again / Indignation.		-

J CHURCH (cont)

Oct 98.	(cd/lp) <(DAMGOOD 150 CD/LP)> **CAT FOOD**		-	Nov98

– Heroic trio / Sound gut Smiley / My favourite place / More Faye / All girl band / Versace killer / Asha Blake / City by the bay / L.A. / Well earnced reputation / Violent motions created / Turn to stone.

                                                                                                      Helter Skelter *not iss.*

Jul 99. (10"ep/cd-ep) *(NOW 1398/+CD)* **TRAVELS IN HYPER REALITY EP**

– L.A. / Rock'n'roll museum / Soliloquy / I will savor this / Lost in a silent stare / A well earned reputation / I've got a crazy feeling / Names and planes and thesis / Nowhere / To the moon.

— **JEFF BURSLEY** – bass; repl. FUSUHARA

— **ADAM PFAHLER** – drums (ex-JAWBREAKER) repl. CONNORS

                                                                                                 Honest Don's *Honest Don's*

Jul 00. (d-lp/cd) <(DON 029/+CD)> **ONE MISSISSIPPI**

– No jazz / New York Times book review / The track / Where the trains go / Sunshine / Quickstep / Your mother / She says / Never happy / She's so mean / Diet coke / Imaginary friends / Anybody / I reach for her hand / The doctor / Cut the shit / Leni Riefenstahl's tinder box / Sadie Mae glutz / Jane, Vanessa and I / Gulf breeze, Florida / The Devil and I / Rich and young and dumb / J Church sucks / Reaching for Thoreau / Christmas lights / Stars are exploding.

          not iss. *Loveboat*

Sep 00. (7") **LENI RIEFENSTAHL'S TINDER BOX. / CLOSING TIME IN AN EARLY TOWN / HARVEST**

          not iss. *Traffic Violation*

2001. (ltd-7") **FUCK YOU. I'M CRAIG & IT'S MY BIRTH-DAY**

– Nostalgic for nothing / (other by CONTRA).

          not iss. *Snuffy Smile*

2001. (7"ep) **J CHURCH / MINORITY BLUES BAND** split

– People are scared / Petrograd / (other 2 by MINORITY BLUES BAND).

          not iss. *Christophers*

2002. (ltd-7"white-ep) **HAWAII**

– Hawai'i / War / 3 cops cars / (other 2 by PETROGRAD).

– compilations, etc. –

Apr 94. (pic-lp/cd) *Broken Rekids;* <*SKIP 17/+CD*> **CAMELS, SPILLED CORONA AND THE SOUND OF MARIACHI BANDS** (singles, etc)

Nov 95. (cd/lp) *Broken Rekids;* <(*SKIP 037CD*)> **NOSTALGIC FOR NOTHING** (singles collection)   Oct95

– My favorite place / Ivy league college / Tide of fate / Sleep / On dying alone / About the she / As I lie . . . / You almost feel sad / Not given lightly / Living with the dreaming body / Cool guitar girl / No doves fly here / Birthday / Panama / Band you love to hate / Mary Provost / Planet Earth / Night time / The last of the famous international playboys / Sweet and soup plums / Mistake – Missed / UFO's will crash / Hypothesis / Nostalgic for nothing / If I see you . . . / At the end of the M-1.

Sep 96. (m-lp/m-cd) *Damaged Goods;* <(*DAMGOOD 103/+CD*)> **WHOREHOUSE: SONGS & STORIES**   Jul00

– New year / Simple gesture / San Francisco thespians (pt.2) / Over compensation / Best served cold / Thirty second song / Guitar center / Asshole / Nothing worth knowing / Accentuated nothing / The overwhelming smell / My lie.

1996. (7"ep) *V.M. Live;* <*issue #15*> **V.M. LIVE presents J CHURCH 7/14/95 Fireside Bowl – Chicago, IL**

– Lama temple / Fascist radio / Foreign films / Why I liked Bikini Kill / No surprise / November.

Apr 97. (t7"ep/cd-ep) *Damaged Goods;* (*DAMGOOD 120/+CD*) **MY FAVOURITE PLACE. / WILLIAM TELL SUICIDE NOTE / YOUNG MOTHER // NOTHING CITY. / DA DA DA / TRAFFIC JAM // PARKAS AND FLAGS. / DESPERATION EVERY OTHER NIGHT / YOU FEEL LIKE A FOOL**

Jul 97. (cd) *Startracks;* (*STAR 4914-2*) **THE ECSTASY OF COMMUNICATION**

– Bottom rung / Good judge of character / Yellow, blue and green / November / Kathi / My favourite phrase / The sound of maraichi bands / Foreign films / No surprise / Why I liked Bikini Kill / Fascist radio / Lame people / My favourite place / Ivy league college / Sleep / Panama / Band you love to hate / Nostalgic for nothing / Analysis, yes, very nice / Kill your bos / Walking on the ground / Cigarettes kill / Racked / Stinking sea. *(re-iss. Oct98; same)*

Sep 98. (cd) *Au-Go-Go;* <*243*> **ALTAMONT '99** (live-in-studio)

– I would for you / Transvestite show / Your shirt / Switzerland / Without a single word / Church on fire / Lines / Creep / Girlfriend in a coma / Racked / Mary's moving on / You fucking trick / The dramatic history of a boring town / 8:28 / Waiting on the ground / Ayn Rand is dead / College station / Undisputed king of nothing / Snot rags / I have to admit . . . / If we wait . . . / Contempt for modesty / Faye song / What should I do? / Plastic / You might never / Crop circles / Alone when she dies.

Oct 00. (lp; split w/ DISCOUNT) *Rugger Bugger;* (*SEEP 030LP*) **ELO / BILLY BRAGG**

Aug 01. (cd) *Honey Bear;* <*26*> **MEATY, BEATY, SHITTY SOUNDING**

2001. (7"ep) *Beat Bedsit;* **ASPHYXIA BY SUBMERSION / FUCK SCHOOL. / (other 2 by ANNALISE)**

Oct 02. (cd) *Honey Bear;* <*41*> **PALESTINE** (demos, etc)

– Underground #1 / The star hotel / At the crossroads of Hell / Star of the show / The state of things / Sam Rivers / Underground #2 / Blase / Jazz Butcher on a work night / Not proud of the USA / Dora and Lili / The legend of Rita / Tricky / Underground #3.

— note: there are other 7"split singles; mainly foreign

CRINGER

LANCE + GARDNER

          not iss. *Vinyl Comm*

1990. (lp) <*VC 12*> **TIKKI TIKKI TEMBO, NO SA REMBO, CHARI BARI RUCHI, PIP PERI PEMBO**

– A song about Hawaii / Russia / Sunday / Peace and harmony / The dumb song / Anti-climax / El Salvador / Berlin wall / Walk in closet / Two friends / Just the same / This town / Take back the night II / Carmen / Sentient / Funk song / Zen Hana Hou / Perversion / Ed's song / Workaholic / Alone / Sword / Corrupt / In solitary witness / National hero – Garbage and trash / Example / Nowhere to run / McElligot's pool / Zen flesh zen blues.

Oct 93. (cd) <*VC 46*> **GREATEST HITS, VOL.1** (compilation of early 45's)

– Cottleston pie / Rain / If I had your pen / Triangle, pt.2 / Pay to play / Hooked on junk / Despair ends / Burn down the forest / Sword / Blasphemous / Carmen / Cocktail molotov / Stump / Confession / Two friends / Ballad of a handgun / Step back / Sunday / Understand / Play / Petrograd / A song about Hawaii / Waste away / Another day / Signals / (untitled).

JEEVAS (see under ⇒ KULA SHAKER)

Peter JEFFERIES (see under ⇒ THIS KIND OF PUNISHMENT)

JELLYFISH

Formed: Pleasanton, San Francisco, California, USA . . . 1990 out of BEATNIK BEACH by ANDY STURMER and JASON FALKNER, alongside brothers CHRIS and ROGER MANNING. Updating power-pop in day-glo retro style, JELLYFISH were a shrewd investment by 'Charisma', which in turn, employed the services of veteran disco producer, Albhy Galuten, more famous for his work on the 'Saturday Night Fever' soundtrack. The kitschy 4-piece became the toast of muso types and pop fans alike with their classic debut 45, 'THE KING IS HALF UNDRESSED', a surprise UK Top 40 hit. The track was a fairly representative taster for their 1990 debut album, 'BELLYBUTTON', critics marvelling over the band's clever combination of BEACH BOYS/10CC/QUEEN harmonies and BEATLES-style intricacies. After a further handful of minor hits, including US breakthrough, 'BABY'S COMING BACK', JELLYFISH were stung by the departure of two founding members, CHRIS and JASON (the latter was to become a well respected solo artist in his own right). Replacing them with ERIC DOVER and TIM SMITH, the band resurfaced in Spring 1993 with possibly their finest three minutes, 'GHOST AT NUMBER ONE', another UK Top 50 hit and lifted from the accompanying near Top 20 second set, 'SPILT MILK'. Amid a rising tide of rumours, JELLYFISH were finally left high and dry as ROGER MANNING undertook two separate projects, the tongue-in-cheek covers album, 'The MOOG COOKBOOK' (1996) and cult glam-pop/rock outfit, IMPERIAL DRAG, with frontman, ERIC DOVER. The latter band released an eponymous album for 'Columbia' in '96 which featured a minor UK hit, 'BOY OR A GIRL'; MANNING continued earning a crust as a member of UMAJETS.
• **Songwriters:** STURMER, or most with MANNING, except covers; NO MATTER WHAT (Badfinger) / LET 'EM IN + JET (Paul McCartney & Wings).

Album rating: BELLYBUTTON (*8) / SPILT MILK (*6) / Roger Manning: ROGER MANNING (*5) / Moog Cookbook: MOOG COOKBOOK (*5) / Imperial Drag: IMPERIAL DRAG (*5)

ANDY STURMER – vocals, drums, keyboards / **JASON FALKNER** (b.1968) – guitar (ex-THREE O'CLOCK) / **CHRIS MANNING** – bass / **ROGER MANNING** – keyboards, vocals

                                                                Charisma – Virgin *Charisma*

Jan 91. (7"/c-s) (*CUS S/C 1*) **THE KING IS HALF UNDRESSED. / CALLING SARAH**   39

(12"+=/cd-s+=) (*CUS X/DG 1*) – The man I used to be.

Feb 91. (c-s) <*98837*> **BABY'S COMING BACK / THE KING IS HALF UNDRESSED**   -   62

Mar 91. (cd/c/lp) (*CDCUS/CUSMC/CUSLP 3*) <*91400*> **BELLYBUTTON**   - Nov90

– The man I used to be / That is why / The king is half undressed / I wanna stay home / She still loves him / All I want is everything / Now she knows is wrong / Bedspring kiss / Baby's coming back / Calling Sarah. *(free 12"w/ lp + on c+=/cd+=)* – No matter what / Medley live:- Let 'em in – That is why / The king is half undressed (live) / Jet (live) / Now she knows she's wrong (live). *(re-iss. Feb92 cd/c; CDCUX/CUSMX 3)*

Apr 91. (7"/c-s) (*CUS S/C 2*) **BABY'S COMING BACK. / ALL I WANT IS EVERYTHING** (live)   51   -

(12"+=/cd-s+=) (*CUS X/DG 2*) – No matter what (live).

Jul 91. (7"ep) (*CUSS 3*) **THE SCARY-GO-ROUND EP**   49

– Now she knows she's wrong / Bedspring kiss / She still loves him (live) / Baby's coming back (live).

(12"ep) (*CUSX 3*) – (1st-2 tracks) / The man I used to be (live) / Calling Sarah (live).

(cd-ep) (*CUSDG 3*) – (1st-2 tracks) / Let 'em in – That is why (live) / The king is half undressed (live).

Oct 91. (7"/c-s) (*CUS S/C 4*) **I WANNA STAY HOME. / JET (live)**   59

(10"+=/cd-s+=) (*CUS T/DG 4*) – Now she knows she's wrong (live).

— now a duo of **ANDY + ROGER** after the departure of CHRIS + JASON (the latter joined The GRAYS for one album, 'Bo Sham Bo', before going solo with the much improved 'Elektra' set, 'JASON FALKNER PRESENTS ANOTHER UNKNOWN', in 1996)

— added **ERIC DOVER** – guitar / + **TIM SMITH** – bass, vocals / and guest guitarists **LYLE WORKMAN** + **JON BRION** / additional bass – **T-BONE**

Apr 93. (7"/c-s) (*CUS S/C 10*) **THE GHOST AT NUMBER ONE. / ALL IS FORGIVEN**   43

(cd-s+=) (*CUSDG 10*) – Worthless heart / Ignorance is bliss.

(cd-s) (*CUSCD 10*) – ('A'side) / Watchin' the rain / Family tree.

May 93. (cd/c/lp) (*CDCUS/CUSMC/CUSLP 20*) <*86459*> **SPILT MILK**   21

– Hush / Joining a fan club / Sabrina, paste & Plato / New mistake / The glutton of sympathy / The ghost at mumber one / Bye, bye, bye / All is forgiven / Russian hill / He's my best friend / Too much, too little, too late / Brighter day.

Jul 93. (7"/c-s) (CUS S/C 11) **NEW MISTAKE. / HE'S MY BEST FRIEND** — 55
(cd-s+=) (CUCDG 11) – All is forgiven / Russian Hill (demos).
(cd-s) (CUSCD 11) – ('A'side) / Sabrina, Paste & Patto (demo) / The man I used to be (demo) / Bedspring kiss (demo).
—— split-up after above

– compilations, etc. –

Jan 99. (cd) *Charisma;* <51048> **GREATEST HITS**
Jun 02. (4xcd-box) *Not Lame;* <(NLA 007)> **FAN CLUB**

ROGER MANNING

S.S.T. / S.S.T.

Dec 88. (lp/c/cd) <(SST 203 LP/CA/CD)> **ROGER MANNING**
– The #14 blues / The pearly blues / The lefty rhetoric blues / The hitch-hikers' blues / The west valley blues / strange little blues / The airport blues / The #16 blues / The #17 blues / Blues for the chosen few / The 1010 blues / The Sicilian train blues. *(re-iss. Aug93 on 'Shimmy Disc' cd/c/lp; SHIMMY 067 CD/MC/LP)*

MOOG COOKBOOK

ROGER MANNING + BRIAN KEHEW – both keyboards, synths

Restless / Restless

Jun 96. (cd) <(72914-2)> **THE MOOG COOKBOOK**
– Black hole sun / Buddy Holly / Basket case / Come out and play / Free fallin' / Are you gonna go my way / Smells like teen spirit / Even flow / The one I love / Rockin' in the free world.

IMPERIAL DRAG

—— formed 1994 by **ROGER JOSEPH MANNING JR.** – keyboards, vocals / **ERIC DOVER** – vocals, guitar (ex-SLASH'S SNAKEPIT) / **JOSEPH KARNES** – bass, vocals / **ERIC SKODIS** – drums, vocals

Columbia / Work-Sony

Aug 96. (cd/c) (484178-2/-4) <67378> **IMPERIAL DRAG**
– Zodiac sign / Boy or a girl / Crosseyed / The man in the moon / "Breakfast" by tiger (kiss it all goodbye) / Playboy after dark / Illuminate / Spyder / Overnight sensation / The salvation army band / Dandelion / Stare into the sun / Scaredy cats and egomaniacs.
Sep 96. (cd-ep) (663299-2) **BOY OR A GIRL / HEY HONEY PLEASE / MOTHER NATURE / SHE CRIES ALL NIGHT** — 54
—— they split in 1997; MANNING subsequently joined Atlanta semi-supergroup, UMAJETS, with TIM SMITH, ROB ALDRIDGE, releasing 'DEMOLOTION', early '98

JELLYFISH KISS

Formed: Huddersfield, England . . . 1988 by DAVID LALJEE and NICK. The pair issued a debut album, 'GASOLINE JUNKIE', the following year before relocating to Leeds and becoming a trio with the addition of bassist/vocalist, JOHN GALVIN. Signing a one-off deal with 'Demon', JELLYFISH KISS cut a follow-up album, 'PLANK', in 1990, although their psychedelic hardcore sound was more suited to the environs of New York where they recorded 'ANIMAL RIGHTS' with 'Shimmy Disc' boss, KRAMER later that year. However, things went badly awry when on tour (26th November, 1991) to support their 4th album, 'STORMY WEATHER', they were attacked and stung for over £5,000 worth of equipment. • **Covered:** I'M STICKING WITH YOU (Velvet Underground).

Album rating: GASOLINE JUNKIE (*4) / PLANK (*5) / ANIMAL RIGHTS (*4) / STORMY WEATHER (*4)

NICK – vocals / **DAVID LALJEE** – guitar / **CHIL** – drums, percussion

Longpig / not iss.

Jul 89. (lp) (LPIG 001) **GASOLINE JUNKIE**
—— added **JOHN GALVIN** – bass, vocals

Demon / not iss.

Jun 90. (lp/cd) (FIEND/+CD 190) **PLANK**
– Crazy bong / Melo / A.C. 801 A / Burn / La ronde (Viennese waltz) / Soul apart / Pre-mortem / Astro Z / Off the floor! (cd+=) – (6 alt. versions).

Shimmy Disc / Shimmy Disc

Dec 90. (lp)(cd) (<SHIMMY 038>)(<SDE 9028>) **ANIMAL RIGHTS**
– Sinbad / Screwed up papers / Regular folk / Little red car / DEad / Big talk / Overdone / Underground / Wave goodbye / Muttonhead / Zero tolerance / I really do / Crazy bong / Burn / Mello.
Oct 91. (cd) (<SHIMMY 047CD>) **STORMY WEATHER**
– First signs / A quiet word / Mad cow / Mr. Station / Secret party / Ends of invitation / Miffy / Let the day / Ms. Marmalade / C.Y. street rap.

Longpig / not iss.

May 92. (7"ep) **BIG DRIVING EP**
—— split after above

JENNIFERS (see under ⇒ SUPERGRASS)

JESSAMINE

Formed: Galion, Ohio, USA . . . 1992 by REX RITTER, DAWN SMITHSON, ANDY BROWN and MICHAEL FAETH. Moving wholesale to the more sympathetic climes of Seattle, the quartet released a one-off single, 'YOUR HEAD IS SO SMALL IT'S LIKE A . . .' for 'Sub Pop' in '94 before signing to 'Kranky' (home of LABRADFORD). The first phase of the band's interstellar drone-pop experimentation came in the shape of 1995's 'JESSAMINE', harking back to the heady days of SPACEMEN 3's tripped-out sound manipulation. Appropriately enough, the latter band's co-pilot, SONIC BOOM (i.e. SPECTRUM), would subsequently work with JESSAMINE on a collaborative mini-CD, 'A POX ON YOU' (the title track a cover of a Silver Apples track). Their second long-player, 'THE LONG ARM OF COINCIDENCE' (1996), followed in much the same heavy-lidded vein, seeing a UK release – along with the debut – in spring '97. A singles compilation, 'ANOTHER FICTIONALIZED HISTORY', surfaced later in the year, prior to a third and final album, 'DON'T STAY TOO LONG' (1998). Following on from another split CD, this time with offshoot E.A.R. for the live 'LIVING SOUND' (1999), RITTER and BROWN formed FONTANELLE alongside PAUL DICKOW, CHARLIE SMYTH, BRIAN FOOTE, MICHAEL FAETH and MAT MORGAN. Harmonic and groove-friendly post-rock fusing CAN and MILES DAVIS, the FONTs have delivered three hypnotic electronic sets, 'FONTANELLE' (2000), 'F.' (2001) and 'STYLE DRIFT' (2002).

Album rating: JESSAMINE (*7) / A POX ON YOU with Spectrum (*6) / THE LONG ARM OF COINCIDENCE (*6) / DON'T STAY TOO LONG (*5) / ANOTHER FICTIONALIZED HISTORY compilation (*7) / LIVING SOUND split w/ E.A.R. (*5) / Fontanelle: FONTANELLE (*6) / F. (*4) / STYLE DRIFT (*5)

REX RITTER – vocals, guitar / **DAWN SMITHSON** – vocals, bass / **ANDY BROWN** – keyboards / **MICHAEL FAETH** – drums

not iss. / Sub Pop

Nov 94. (7") <SP 0279> **YOUR HEAD IS SO SMALL IT'S LIKE A LITTLE LIGHT. / SOON THE WORLD OF FASHION**

Kranky / Kranky

May 95. (lp/cd) <(KRANK 003/+CD)> **JESSAMINE**
– Another fictionalized history / Secret / Royal jelly eye cream / Ordinary sleep / Inevitably / Cellophane / / You have ugly talents, Martha / One trick pony / Don't you know that yet? / Lisboa. *(re-iss. Mar97; same)*
May 96. (m-cd; shared JESSAMINE & SPECTRUM) (ORBIT 003CD) **A POX ON YOU**
– A pox on you / Satellite / Radiophonic (musique concrete) Opus 3 / Satellite (reprise).
(above issued on 'Space Age') (below on 'Enraptured')
1996. (7") <RAPT45 05> **FROM HERE TO NOW OTHERWISE. / (other side by Flying Saucer Attack)**
Nov 96. (7") (DRL 014) **SEAGREEN. / (split w/ TRANSPARENT THING)**
(above issued on 'Darla')
Mar 97. (lp/cd) <(KRANK 012/+CD)> **THE LONG ARM OF COINCIDENCE** — Sep96
– Say what you can / . . .Or what you mean / Periwinkle / Step down / You may have forgotten / Polish countryside / Schisandra / The long arm of coincidence makes my radio connections / All the same.
Sep 98. (lp/cd) <(KRANK 030/+CD)> **DON'T STAY TOO LONG**
– Elsewards / It was already Thursday / Pilot-free ignition / Continuous / Corrupted endeavor / Burgundy / Hand held.
—— they disbanded in '99

– compilations, etc. –

Sep 97. (cd) *Histrionic;* <(HIST 1CD)> **ANOTHER FICTIONALIZED HISTORY**
– Cheree / Reflections / (I'm not afraid of) Electricity / Your head is so small it's like a little light / Soon the world of fashion will take and interest in these proceedings / Oscillations / It shouldn't take so long for a man to drown / Air from another world / The moon is made of cheese / From hereto and now otherwise / Live at off the record. *(d-lp-iss.Jan98; HIST 1LP)*
Apr 99. (cd; by JESSAMINE & E.A.R.) *Histrionic;* <(HIST 2CD)> **LIVING SOUND (live)** — Dec99
– Living sound (parts 1-7).

FONTANELLE

RITTER + BROWN added **PAUL DICKOW** – Farfisa organ (of EMERGENCY, of STRATEGY) / **BRIAN FOOTE** – keyboards (of NUDGE) / **CHARLIE SMYTH** – guitar / **MICHAEL FAETH** – drums / **MAT MORGAN** – drums (of NUDGE)

Kranky / Kranky

Jun 00. (cd/lp) <(KRANK 42 CD/LP)> **FONTANELLE** — May00
– Picture start / Niagara / Reflex vs parallax / The telephone fade / 29th & going / Counterweight.
May 01. (cd) <(KRANK 48)> **F.**
– Fulcrum / Corrective lenses / Charm and strange / Slow January / Return envelope / Floor tile / Walking with Mercer.
Nov 02. (cd) <(KRANK 56 CD/V)> **STYLE DRIFT**
– Intersticies / Just, go, crazy / Scissure / James going / Style drift / Red light, green light / Monday morning.

JETPLANE LANDING

Formed: Sussex, England . . . 2000 by former (grungy) CUCKOO members ANDREW FERRIS, JAMIE BURCHELL and his brother RAIFE. The group tore up the rule book for starting a band by first recording their album, 'ZERO FOR CONDUCT' (2001) in a makeshift studio in the BURCHELL's parents' garage. This DIY method served them well offering the album an unintentional lo-fi sound that complemented their unique folk/punk fusion. Having released the album on their own 'Smalltown America' label, the group booked venues in Ireland. The first concert was a support slot for the group SUNSHINE and, amazingly, was also the first time ANDREW FERRIS had sung in front of a live audience. The band secured a deal with 'Yoga Boy' records who released the single, 'THIS IS NOT REVOLUTION ROCK', in 2001, before re-releasing the album in 2002.

Album rating: Cuckoo: BREATHING LESSONS (*5) / Jetplane Landing: ZERO FOR CONDUCT (*6)

CUCKOO

RUARI O'DOHERTY – vocals, bass / **ANDREW FERRIS** – guitar / **JASON FLOOD** – guitar / **BRIAN DEERY** – drums

Geffen / not iss.

- Jan 98. (7") *(GFS 22312)* **NON SEQUITUR. / SEE THROUGH**
  (cd-s+=) *(GFSTD 22312)* – Brim.
- Mar 98. (7"m) *(GFS 22329)* **WHAT'S IT ALL ABOUT. / SOMETHING I AM NOT / OUT OF HABIT**
  (cd-s+=) *(GFSTD 22329)* – Coasting.
- Jul 98. (7"m) *(GFS 22342)* **BLACKMAIL / CEO BREAKDOWN (demo) / FOR A WEEK OR TWO (acoustic)**
  (cd-s) *(GFSTD 22312)* – ('A'side) / Most peculiar way of leaving / Big mistake (acoustic) / Cartoon moves.
- Jul 98. (cd) *(GED 25162)* **BREATHING LESSONS**
  – Big mistake / Central / Gold and silver / Blackmail / For a week or two / Don't wanna get up / What's it all about / Non sequitor / Assume / Potential / Wink of sleep / Pocket friends.

— **JAMIE BURCHELL** – bass; repl. FLOOD – before they split

JETPLANE LANDING

ANDREW FERRIS – vocals, guitar (ex-CUCKOO) / **JAMIE BURCHELL** – bass (ex-CUCKOO) / **RAIFE BURCHELL** – drums

Yogaboy / Smalltown America

- Sep 01. (cd-ep) *<STA 002>* **JETPLANE LANDING**
  – Tiny bombs / Summer ends / The boy you love to hate / An upheaval.
- Oct 01. (7") *(YOB 002) <STA 003>* **THIS IS NOT REVOLUTION ROCK. / ATOMS DREAM IN TECHNICOLOUR**
- Feb 02. (7") *(YOB 004) <STA 004>* **SUMMER ENDS. / SLEEPS WITH THE LIGHTS ON**
- Mar 02. (cd) *(YOB 005) <STA 001>* **ZERO FOR CONDUCT**
  – Tiny bombs / This is not revolution rock / Underground queen / Summer ends / End of the night / What the argument has changed / The boy you love to hate / The last thing I should do / Interstate five / Atom dreams in technicolour / A miracle of science.
- Jun 02. (cd-ep) *(INFEC 118CDS)* **SEAFOOD / JETPLANE LANDING split**
  – What the argument has changed / Summer ends / (2 by SEAFOOD).
  (above issued on 'Infectious')
- Oct 02. (cd-ep) *(YOB 006) <STA 006>* **ELS QUATRE GATS**
  – Acrimony / Lights out / My fundamental flaw / An upheaval.

JETS TO BRAZIL

Formed: New York, USA ... 1997 by ex-JAWBREAKER frontman BLAKE SCHWARTZENBACH, ex-TEXAS IS THE REASON drummer CHRIS DAILY and former HANDSOME vocalist/guitarist JEREMY CHATELAIN. Cult supergroup JETS TO BRAZIL carried a certain weight of expectation when recording their debut album 'ORANGE RHYMING DICTIONARY' (1998), SCHWARZENBACH in particular was still revered by the punk community. The band, of course, went completely against type and delivered a set of folk pop songs. With SCHWARZENBACH's raspy vocals rising above delicate guitar playing it was reminiscent of one of MARK LANEGAN's solo departures from The SCREAMING TREES. Their second effort, 'FOUR CORNERED NIGHT' (2000), was on the same trajectory, although the band were clearly becoming more comfortable in their new roles and the songs sounded less formulaic and more heartfelt. In between completing this album and recording their next, bassist CHATELAIN found time to pen a few songs and record an album with guests including his JETS TO BRAZIL band mates and a host of ex-metallic punks such as THEO KOGAN (of the LUNACHICKS) and CHRIS TRAYNOR (of HELMET). This collective came together as CUB COUNTRY and the album 'HIGH UINTA HIGH' was another reminder that punks have a sensitive side. Ahh, nice! 'PERFECTING LONELINESS' (2002) was a further progression for JETS FROM BRAZIL and saw a greater maturity in the musicianship.

Album rating: ORANGE RHYMING DICTIONARY (*7) / FOUR CORNERED NIGHT (*6) / PERFECTING LONELINESS (*6) / Cub Country: HIGH UINTA HIGH (*6)

JEREMY CHATELAIN – vocals, bass (ex-HANDSOME) / **BLAKE SCHWARZENBACH** – guitar, keyboards (ex-JAWBREAKER) / **CHRIS DALY** – drums, percussion (ex-TEXAS IS THE REASON)

Jade Tree / Jade Tree

- Oct 98. (d-lp/cd) *<(JT 1038/+CD)>* **ORANGE RHYMING DICTIONARY**
  – Crown of the valley / Morning new disease / Resistance is futile / Starry configurations / Chinatown / Sea anemone / Lemon yellow black / Conrad / King medicine / I typed for miles / Sweet avenue.
- Aug 00. (lp/cd) *<(JT 1052/+CD)>* **FOUR CORNERED NIGHT**
  – You're having the time of my life / One summer last fall / Air traffic control / Pale new dawn / In the summers when you really know / Empty picture frame / Little light / "Your x-ray have just come back from the doctor and we think we know what the problem is" / Milk and apples / Mid-day anonymous / ******* / Orange rhyming dictionary / All things good and nice.
- Oct 02. (lp/cd) *<JT 1079/+CD>* **PERFECTING LONELINESS**
  – The frequency / You're the one that I want / Cat heaven / Perfecting loneliness / Lucky charm / Wish list / Psalm / Autumn walker / Further north / William Tell override / Disgrace / Rocket boy.

CUB COUNTRY

JEREMY CHATELAIN with **BLAKE + CHRIS** plus **CASHE TOLMAN** (of RIVAL SCHOOLS) / **THEO KOGAN** (of LUNACHICKS) / **CHRIS TRAYNOR** (of ORANGE 8mm) / **NICK MACRI** (of EUPHONE)

not iss. / Jade Tree

- Feb 02. (cd) *<JT 1068CD>* **HIGH UINTA HIGH**
  – Could be the moon / St. Louis / Hit the roof / O great telephone / High uinta high / Faithful soldier / Butterfly / Through my window / Your old street / What would you say to me? / Hollow sidewalks.

JETT BRANDO
(see under ⇒ ALL NATURAL LEMON & LIME FLAVORS)

JIMMY EAT WORLD

Formed: Tempe, Arizona, USA ... 1993 by JIM ADKINS, TOM LINTON, MITCH PORTER and ZACH LIND. Having begun life as a METALLICA covers band, the quartet soon developed a more lugubrious, melodic post-grunge sound as evidenced on their independently released debut 7". An eponymous album quickly followed as did a slew of split singles with the likes of CHRISTIE FRONT DRIVE and BLUEPRINT. Subsequently signed to 'Capitol', the group released 'STATIC PREVAILS' as their major label debut in 1996. Their contract nevertheless allowed for indie releases and they issued an eponymous five track EP in 1998 as a taster for the acclaimed 'CLARITY' (1999), a blinding, infused album of pure rock energy. Hailed by music journos as "the official Emo boys", the group settled on playing their abrasive, no bullshit, straight up rock'n'roll. But this wasn't three-chord idiot rock, oh no! JIMMY EAT WORLD incorporated intelligent lyrics and swirling, prolonged instrumentals, akin to the good ol' days of FUGAZI and straight-edged punk. After a split mini-album with Australian rockers JEBEDIAH, the group were dropped by majors 'Capitol'. They headed back into the studio and self-financed their sophomore set 'BLEED AMERICAN', later to be re-titled 'JIMMY EAT WORLD' (2001), after the 9/11 terrorists attacks. With runaway single 'The MIDDLE' blasted all over MTV, and the growing popularity of emo-core, the 'EAT WORLD found themselves a distribution deal with Geffen/Spielberg label 'Dreamworks'. The album subsequently catapulted them into the mainstream and they are said to be currently recording its long-awaited follow-up. • **Covered:** NEW RELIGION (Duran Duran) / SPANGLE (Wedding Present) / LAST CHRISTMAS (Wham) / FIRSTARTER (Prodigy).

Album rating: JIMMY EAT WORLD (*4) / STATIC PREVAILS (*5) / CLARITY (*6) / SINGLES compilation (*6) / BLEED AMERICAN (*7)

JIM ADKINS – vocals, guitar / **TOM LINTON** – vocals, guitar / **MITCH PORTER** – bass / **ZACH LIND** – drums

not iss. / Wooden Blue

- 1994. (7"ep) **ONE, TWO, THREE, FOUR**
  – What would I say to you now / Speed read.
- 1994. (cd) **JIMMY EAT WORLD**
  – Chachi / Patches / Amphibious / Splat out of luck / House arrest / Usery / Wednesday / Crooked / Reason 346 / Scientific / Cars.
- 1995. (7") **OPENER. / 77 SATELLITES**
  <re-iss. 1995 on 'Jimmy Eat World'; >
- 1995. (7") **DIGITS. / (other by CHRISTIE FRONT DRIVE)** *not iss. / Ordinary*
- Nov 95. (7") **BETTER THAN OH. / (other by EMERY)** *not iss. / Abridged*
- Dec 95. (7"ep) **CHRISTMAS CARD / UNTITLED. / (other 2 by BLUEPRINT)**

— **RICK BURCH** – bass; repl. PORTER

not iss. / Capitol

- Jul 96. (cd/c) *<32404>* **STATIC PREVAILS**
  – Thinking, that's all / Rockstar / Claire / Call it in the air / Seventeen / Episode IV / Digits / Caveman / World is static / In the same room / Robot factory / Anderson Mesa. (UK cd-iss. Jul02 on 'E.M.I.'+=; 539615-2) – Rockstar (video).
- 1996. (7"ep) **LESS THAN JAKE / JIMMY EAT WORLD split**
  – Rockstar / Call it in the air / Seventeen / (other 3 by LESS THAN JAKE).

— in 1997, the track 'CRUSH' featured on a 7" split alongside SENSEFIELD + MINERAL

- 1998. (7"ep) **JIMMY EAT WORLD / JEJUNE split**
  – What I would say to you now / Speed read / (other 2 by JEJUNE).
  (above issued on 'Big Wheel Recreation') (below on 'Fueled By Ramen')
- Oct 98. (cd-ep) *<FBR 020CD>* **JIMMY EAT WORLD**
  – Lucky Denver mint / For me this is heaven / Your new aesthetic (demo) / Softer / Roller queen. (UK-iss.Apr99; same as US)
- Feb 99. (cd) *<55950>* **CLARITY**
  – Table for glasses / Lucky Denver mint / Your new aesthetic / Believe in what you want / Sunday / Crush / 12.23.95 / Ten / Just watch the fireworks / For me this is Heaven / Blister / Clarity / Goodbye sky harbor. (UK-iss.Jul02 on 'E.M.I.'+=; 539616-2) – Lucky Denver mint (video).

Big Wheel / Big Wheel

- Oct 00. (3x7"/cd-ep) *<(BWR 0232/+CD)>* **JEBEDIAH & JIMMY EAT WORLD**
  – The most beautiful things / No sensitivity / Cautioners / (other 3 by JEBEDIAH).

Universal / Dreamworks

- Aug 01. (cd) *(450348-2) <450334>* **BLEED AMERICAN** — 54 Jul01
  – Bleed American / A praise chorus / The middle / Your house / Sweetness / Hear you me / If you don't, don't / Get it faster / Cautioners / The authority song / My sundown / Splash, turn, twist *[UK+lp-only]*. <lp-iss.on 'Grand Royal'; GR 99> <(re-prom.Nov01 & Feb02 as 'JIMMY EAT WORLD'; same)> – (hit No.62)
- Oct 01. (cd-s) *(450897-2)* **BLEED AMERICAN / SPLASH, TURN, TWIST / YOUR HOUSE (demo) / THE AUTHORITY SONG (demo) / BLEED AMERICAN (video)**

Nov 01. (7") *(450878-7)* **SALT SWEAT SUGAR. / YOUR HOUSE (demo)** | 60 | - |
(c-s) *(450878-4)* – ('A'side) / Splash, turn, twist.
(cd-s+=) *(450878-2)* – ('A'-video).
Dec 01. (7") **LAST CHRISTMAS. / FIRESTARTER** | - | - |
(above issued on 'Better Looking' records)
Jan 02. (7"/c-s) *(450848-7/-4)* **THE MIDDLE. / A PRAISE CHORUS** | 26 | - |
(cd-s) *(450848-2)* – ('A'side) / If you don't, don't / Game of pricks / ('A'video).
Jun 02. (7") *(450832-7)* **SWEETNESS. / CLARITY (live)** | 38 | - |
(cd-s) *(450833-2)* – ('A'side) / Blister (live) / Your new acoustic (live).
(cd-s) *(450834-2)* – ('A'side) / A praise chorus (live) / Lucky Denver mint (live).

– compilations, etc. –

Aug 01. (cd) *Big Wheel;* <*(BWR 0230CD)*> **SINGLES** | | |
– Opener / 77 satellites / What would I say to you now / Speed read / Spangle / H Ramina / Christmas card / Untitled / Carbon scoring / Digits. *(cd re-iss. Oct01 on 'Golf' +=; CDGOLF 049)* – If model / Most beautiful things / Cautioners.

JIM'S SUPER STEREOWORLD (see under ⇒ CARTER THE UNSTOPPABLE SEX MACHINE)

JJ72

Formed: Dublin, Ireland . . . 1997 by MARK GREANEY and percussionist FERGAL MATTHEWS. The pair met whilst attending Belvedere College and struck up a friendship after MATTHEWS complimented GREANEY on his "cool" coat. They also shared a similar intrest in music: NIRVANA, MUDHONEY and JOY DIVISION are cited as primary influences. The only thing missing was a bassist, and after sifting through Dublin's directory of musicians, young actress HILARY WOODS was quickly recruited. The newly formed trio subsequently cut a demo tape entitled 'OXYGEN' and sent it to assorted radio stations and record companies. Progress was undoubtably slow, but surely the group (and their ubiquitous name) started making waves within the music industry. They signed to 'Lakota' records mid 1999 and issued the single 'OCTOBER SWIMMER', a swirling hybrid of indie guitar, pop punk and fuzz grunge all backed by GREANEY's melodic vocals. Comparisons to ASH were obvious, although there was definitely a hint of R.E.M. (strictly their 'Monster' period) in there too, although GREANEY would deny this in the NME. Various other singles emerged over the next couple of years, notably 'SNOW' and a re-issue of the demo 'OXYGEN' before the release of their eponymous debut album in 2000. Although the album boasted many delicious tracks, the group seemed to be hiding in their rehearsal room for now. JJ72 followed their critically acclaimed debut with the not-so-strong 'I TO SKY', a pop record bursting with radio-friendly melodies and a keen eye for intrumentation and production. GREANEY, once again did his best BONO impression and the album's producer, FLOOD, gave a clean, crisp sound that detracted from the group's heavier, more abrasive rock. Still, tracks 'I SAW A PRAYER' and 'HALF THREE' managed to keep within the JJ72 mould.

Album rating: JJ72 (*7) / I TO SKY (*6)

MARK GREANEY – vocals, guitar / **HILARY WOODS** – bass, vocals / **FERGAL MATTHEWS** – drums

	Lakota	Sony
Nov 99. (cd-s) *(LAK 0011CD)* **OCTOBER SWIMMER / IMPROV / GHERKIN**		-
Feb 00. (7")(cd-s) *(LAK7 0014)(LAK 0014CD)* **SNOW. / WILLOW / FRESH WATER**		-
May 00. (7")(cd-s) *(LAK7 0015)(LAK 0015CD)* **LONG WAY SOUTH. / SNOW (acoustic) / EARTHLY DELIGHTS**	68	-
Aug 00. (7")(cd-s) *(LAK7 0016)(LAK 0016CD1)* **OXYGEN. / ASTORIA / OXYGEN (live)**	23	-
(cd-s) *(LAK 0016CD2)* – ('A'side) / Desertion / Long way south (live).		
Aug 00. (cd/lp) *(LAK CD/LP 017)* <*85825*> **JJ72**	16	
– October swimmer / Undercover angel / Oxygen / Willow / Surrender / Long way south / Snow / Broken down / Improv / Not like you / Algeria / Bumble bee.		
Oct 00. (7")(cd-s) *(LAK7 0018)(LAK 0018CD1)* **OCTOBER SWIMMER. / GUIDANCE / BLACK-EYED DOG**	29	-
(cd-s) *(LAK 0018CD2)* – ('A'side) / Blood tests / Bumble bee (live).		
Jan 01. (7")(cd-s) *(LAK7 0019)(LAK 0019CD1)* **SNOW / WOUNDED / SURRENDER (original demo)**	21	-
(cd-s) *(LAK 0019CD2)* – ('A'side) / Gherkin / Oxygen (CD-Rom).		

	Columbia	not iss.
Sep 02. (7") *(673159-7)* **FORMULAE. / DREAM'D IN A DREAM**	28	-
(cd-s+=) *(673159-2)* – ('A'demo) / ('A'video).		
(cd-s) *(673159-5)* – ('A'side) / Alabaster ocean / Higher than gods.		
Oct 02. (cd) *(509529-2)* **I TO SKY**	20	-
– Nameless / Formulae / I saw a prayer / Serpent sky / Always and forever / Brother sleep / Sinking / 7th wave / Half three / Glimmer / City / Olche mhaith.		

JOAN OF ARC

Formed: Chicago, Illinois, USA . . . mid-90's by former CAP'N JAZZ alum, TIM KINSELLA, his brother MIKE and SAM ZURICK. Looking for a change in direction after the break-up of their former hardcore/emo band, they found it with the inclusion of JEREMY BOYLE and ERIC BOCEK. This quintet moved steadily into the more experimental regions of alternative rock, eschewing standard song structures for freeform compositions with a new bent towards the use of electronics, sound effects, and samples. Their debut full-length outing, 'A PORTABLE MODEL OF JOAN OF ARC' (1997), came after a year which included an acclaimed tour with THE PROMISE RING (which was the other group to form from the erstwhile players of CAP'N JAZZ), and was met by mixed reviews although most critics sided towards applauding their novel course. This initial release set the tone for what was to be JOA's career highlight released the following year, 'HOW MEMORY WORKS' (1998). With this album JOA managed to get the right balance between their more avant-garde leanings and an accessible sound. Although KINSELLA's vocals could be erractic at moments, this album did manage to prove that he deserved his job. Unfortunately the same could not be said for JOA's third album, 'LIVE IN CHICAGO' (1999), released the following year. It seemed that pretension and arty musical meanderings had been mistaken for intellectual content and interesting song structures, which was a pity judging by the artistic promise of the band. Sad to say but the situation deteriorated somewhat again with the release of 'THE GAP' at the turn of the century. This album attempted again to hit a high intellectual level but unfortunately contained none of the band's earlier wit which had prevented the tone from becoming tiresome, which is what on the whole happened here with the lyrics and music. The same can be said of 'HOW CAN ANYTHING SO LITTLE BE ANY MORE' (2001), but then again many of the songs were from the same recording session as 'THE GAP'. After this JOA went silent for a period and the original CAP'N JAZZ TRIO of MIKE and TIM KINSELLA, and SAM ZURICK teamed up with another former CAP'N JAZZ player, VICTOR VILLARREAL, to form the OWLS. With this incarnation the quartet drew back towards a much more solid rock format as seen on their eponymously named debut album of 2001. This outing attracted some much needed critical praise not least for the beautiful guitar work which sounded the return of VILLARREAL to the original fold, but also for the return to songwriting form. Previously to his time well spent in The OWLS (and now only a guest with JOAN OR ARC), MIKE instigated two bands, indie-darlings AMERICAN FOOTBALL (who released their eponymous set in '99) and OWEN who've so far delivered two further LP's for 'Polyvinyl', 'OWEN' (2001) and 'NO GOOD FOR NO ONE NOW' (2002).

Album rating: Cap'n Jazz: ANALPHABETAPOLOTHOLOGY compilation (*6) / Joan Of Arc: A PORTABLE MODEL OF JOAN OF ARC (*5) / HOW MEMORY WORKS (*7) / LIVE IN CHICAGO 1999 (*5) / THE GAP (*4) / HOW CAN ANYTHING BE SO LITTLE ANY MORE mini (*4) / the Owls: THE OWLS (*6) / American Football: AMERICAN FOOTBALL (*5) / Owen: OWEN (*7) / NO GOOD FOR NO ONE NOW (*6)

CAP'N JAZZ

DAVEY VONBOHLEN – vocals, guitar / **SAM ZURICK** – bass / **TIM KINSELLA** – drums (later vocals, guitar) / **MIKE KINSELLA** – drums; repl. VONBOHLEN who formed The PROMISE RING

—— released several singles all contained on below

– compilations, etc. –

Apr 97. (cd) *Man With The Gun;* *(MWG 002CD)* **KITES, KUNG FU, BANANA PEELS WE'VE SLIPPED ON, AND EGG SHELLS WE'VE TIPPY TOED OVER** | | - |
– Little league / Oh messy life / Puddle splashers / Flashpoint: catheter / In the clear / Yes, I am talking to you / Basil's kite / Bluegrass / Planet Shhh / The sands've turned purple / Precious / Que suerte!
Jun 97. (lp) *Tiny Superhero;* *(SUPERLP 001)* **SCHMAP'N SCMAZZ** | | - |
Jan 98. (d-cd) *Jade Tree;* <*(JT 1036CD)*> **ANALPHABETAPOLOTHOLOGY** | | |
– Little league / Oh messy life / Puddle splashers / Flashpoint: catheter / In the clear / Yes, I'm talking to you / Basil's kite / Bluegrassish / Planet Shhh / The sands've turned people / Precious / Que suerte! / Take on me / Tokyo / Ooh do I love you / Hey ma, do I hafta choke on these / Forget who we are / Olerud / We are scientists! / Sea tea / Troubled by insects / Rocky Rococo / In the clear / Soria / No use for a piano player / Scary kids scaring kids! / Bluegrass / Winter wonderland / AOK / Geheim / Sergio valente / Easy driver / Theme to "90210" / Ooh do I love you.

JOAN OF ARC

TIM KINSELLA – vocals, guitar / **ERIC BOCEK** – guitar / **JEREMY BOYLE** – keyboards, guitar / **SAM ZURICK** – bass / **MIKE KINSELLA** – drums

	Jade Tree	Jade Tree
Oct 96. (7"ep; as JEANNE D'ARC) <*(JT 1028)*> **METHOD AND SENTIMENT**		
– Didactic prom / Please sleep / Trial at Orleans.		
May 97. (7") *(18544-7)* **BUSY BUS, SUNNY SUN. / STEMINGWAY & HEINBECK**		
(above issued on 'Southern')		
Jul 97. (lp/cd) <*(JT 1033/+CD)*> **A PORTABLE MODEL OF JOAN OF ARC**		Jun97
– I love a woman (who loves me) / The hands / Anne Aviary / Let's wrestle / Romulans! Romulans! / Post coitus rock / Count to a thousand / How wheeling feels / In Pompeii / Caliban / In Pamplona / I was born / (I love a woman) Who loves me.		
May 98. (lp/cd) <*(JT 1037/+CD)*> **HOW MEMORY WORKS**		May98
– Honestly now / Gin & platonic / To've had two of / This life cumulative / A pale orange / White out / So open; hooray / A name / Osmosis doesn't work / God bless America / A party able model of.		

—— **TIM KINSELLA + BOYLE** recruited **TODD MATTEI** + guest drummers incl. **MIKE KINSELLA**

May 99. (d-lp/cd) <*(JT 1042/+CD)*> **LIVE IN CHICAGO 1999** | | |
– It's easier to drink on an empty stomach (than eat on a broken heart) / Who's afraid of Elizabeth Taylor? / If it feels good, do it / Live in Chicago 1999 (I'm 5 senses) None of them common / Me (plural) / I'm certainly not pleased with my options for the future / When the parish school dismisses and the children running sin / Thanks for Chicago, Mr. James / (In fact I'm) Pioneering new emotions / Better d'ed than read / Sympathy for the Rolling Stones / All until the greens reveal themselves at dawn.

JOAN OF ARC (cont)

— added **MATT CLARK**

Sep 00. (colrd-lp/cd) <JT 1053/+CD> **THE GAP**
– (You) [I] Can not see (you) [me] as (I) [you] (can) / As black pants make cat hairs appear / Knife fights every night / John Cassavetes, Assat Shakur, and Guy Debord walk into a bar . . . / Another brick at the gap (part 2) / Zelda / "Pleasure isn't simple" / Me and America (or) The united colors of the gap / Your impersonation this morning of me last night / Outside the gap.

May 01. (m-lp/m-cd) <JT 1057/+CD> **HOW CAN ANYTHING BE SO LITTLE ANY MORE**
– Leaving needn't take long / Ne mosquitos pass / We neither hide nor seek / Most at home in motels / My cause is noble and just / My fight is necessary / / What if we are not after all, all destined for greatness? / I'll show you, I'll show you all.

OWLS

TIM KINSELLAS + **MIKE KINSELLA** + **SAM ZURICK** + **VICTOR VILLARREAL** (guitar)

                                                                  Jade Tree Jade Tree

Aug 01. (lp/cd) <JT 1059/+CD> **THE OWLS**
– What whorse you wrote Id on / Anyone can have a good time / I want the quiet moments of a party girl / Everyone is my friend / I want the blindingly cute to confide in me / For Nate's brother whose name I never knew / Life in the hair salon – Themed bar on the island / Holy fucking ghost.

— JOAN OF ARC re-formed in 2002

AMERICAN FOOTBALL

MIKE KINSELLA – vocals, bass, guitar / **STEVE HOLMES** – guitar / **STEVE LAMOS** – drums, trumpet

                                                                  Polyvinyl Polyvinyl

Oct 98. (cd-s) <PRC 019> **THE ONE WITH THE TAMBOURINE / LETTERS AND PACKAGES / FIVE SILENT MILES**

Sep 99. (cd) <PRC 025CD> **AMERICAN FOOTBALL**
– Never meant / The summer ends / Honestly? / For sure / You know I should be leaving soon / But the regrets are killing me / I'll see you when we're both not so emotional / Stay home / The one with the wurlitzer.

OWEN

MIKE KINSELLA – vocals, multi

                                                                  Polyvinyl Polyvinyl

Oct 01. (cd) <PRC 43CD> **OWEN**   Sep01
– That which wasn't said / Most days and / Most nights / Accidentally / Declaration of incompetence / You should do it now while it's on your mind / Dead men don't lie / Places to go / Think about it.

Nov 02. (cd) <PRC 55CD> **NO GOOD FOR NO ONE NOW**
– Nobody's nothing / Everyone feels like you / Poor souls / The ghost of what should've been / Good deeds / I'm not going anywhere tonight / Take care of yourself.

JOCASTA

Formed: London, England . . . Autumn '94 by the much-travelled TIM ARNOLD, together with former school friend, JACK REYNOLDS, ANDY LEWIS and ADRIAN MEEHAN. Taking their mythological moniker from the Greek legend of Oedipus, the lads lubricated their musical partnership with infamous drinking sessions around their favourite Soho haunts. Initially forming their own label ('V4'), they released their debut single, 'GO', in Spring '96, resulting in much hype from the London-based music press. Following a further single, 'CHANGE ME', JOCASTA were the subject of a surprise signing to 'Epic', the label subsequently re-issuing both tracks as a build up to their debut album, 'NO COINCIDENCE' (1997). Basically an unstartling US-influenced Brit-pop band with strings attached (well, they did employ a 22-piece orchestra!), JOCASTA were never destined to achieve the historical fame of their namesake.

Album rating: NO COINCIDENCE (*5)

TIM ARNOLD – vocals / **JACK REYNOLDS** – guitar / **ANDY LEWIS** – bass / **ADRIAN MEEHAN** – drums

                                                                 V4   not iss.

Mar 96. (7") (V4V 001) **GO. / TRAPPED (demo)**
(cd-s+=) (V4V 001CD) – Try it (demo).

May 96. (7") (V4V 002) **CHANGE ME. / THE LAND OF DO AS YOU PLEASE**
(cd-s+=) (V4V 002CD) – Not related.

                                                                 Epic   not iss.

Nov 96. (7"red/c-s) (663767-7/-4) **SOMETHING TO SAY. / SWINGS AND ROUNDABOUTS**
(cd-s+=) (663767-2) – Mesmerizing Milla / Don't know when to stop.

Feb 97. (7"blue) (664141-7) **GO. / STOP TO THINK**   50
(cd-s+=) (664141-2) – Clean ash / The land of do as you please.
(cd-s) (664141-5) – ('A'side) / Something to say (session) / Change me (session).

Apr 97. (7"purple) (664390-7) **CHANGE ME. / PORTION OF MY HEART**   60
(cd-s+=) (664390-5) – Only no one / The skin we're in.
(cd-s) (664390-2) – ('A'side) / Relativity / Best of both worlds / The apple and the strawberry.

Jun 97. (cd/c) (487861-2/-4) **NO COINCIDENCE**
– Laughing / Go / Life in a day / Change me / Actress / Leave the light on / Something to say / Single as hell / Perfect / Face you / Crackbaby / Inside out.

— JOCASTA have now disbanded

JOHNBOY

Formed: Austin, Texas, USA . . . 1991 by BARRY STONE, TONY BICE and JASON MEADE. Not a band destined for the alt-rock mainstream, JOHNBOY were picked up by local label, 'Trance Syndicate' (also home of CRUNT amongst others), who issued their debut album, 'PISTOLSWING' (1993). A nihilistic blast of mutant R&R, the record caught the ear of both BOB MOULD (who offered them a support slot) and STEVE ALBINI, the latter working on their 1994 follow-up, 'CLAIM DEDICATION'.

Album rating: PISTOLSWING (*6) / CLAIM DEDICATION (*5)

BARRY STONE – guitar, vocals / **TONY BICE** – bass, vocals / **JASON MEADE** – drums

                                                             not iss.   Undone

1992. (7") **CALYX. /**   Trance Trance
                                                               Syndicate Syndicate

Jun 93. (lp/cd) <TR 16/+CD> **PISTOLSWING**
– Admiration / Sourmouth / Sunday two / Pistolswing / Hold / Freestanding / New Jersey roadbase / Yellow / I.

Sep 94. (lp/cd) <TR 27/+CD> **CLAIM DEDICATION**   Aug94
– Shortstack / Quick to drain / Driving reservoirs up noses / 10 W 40 / Chair / Genius / Pivotal / Lorac / Flung circles.

— disbanded after above

Mike JOHNSON
(see under ⇒ DINOSAUR JR.; in 80's section)

Will JOHNSON (see under ⇒ CENTRO-MATIC)

Freedy JOHNSTON

Born: 1961 . . . on a farm in rural Kinsley, Kansas. JOHNSTON began writing songs at university, moving to the more sympathetic climes of New York in the mid 80's. Securing a deal with indie label, 'Bar/None' ('Demon' in the UK), JOHNSTON released his debut album in 1990. Although acclaimed by critics for its pithy, keenly observed lyrics and downbeat authenticity, the singer/songwriter found a more appreciative audience in Europe than the States. Famously financed by the sale of the family farm, follow-up set, 'CAN YOU FLY' (1992) suggested that JOHNSTON's self belief was anything but misguided. Released on 'Rough Trade' in Britain, the record's wide-eyed, broken-down charm marked JOHNSTON out as one of America's most promising young singer/songwriters, even if his rootsy authenticity didn't sit well with the prevailing grunge craze. A stopgap EP, 'UNLUCKY' (featuring a wholly appropriate cover of Jimmy Webb's 'WICHITA LINEMAN'), followed in '93 prior to JOHNSTON moving on up to major label status and releasing third set, 'THIS PERFECT WORLD', on 'Elektra'. Produced by Butch Vig, the record was a deeply satisfying and emotive series of character sketches from the fringes of American culture, encapsulating the idea of the songwriter as spokesperson for the downcast and dispossessed. Although the critics raved once more, FREEDY's genius surprisingly seemed to bypass the bulk of the record buying public. A shame, as 1997's 'NEVER HOME' was another masterful collection of short story style creations brought to life by the emotive empathy and unique musical vision of their author. Produced in part by T-BONE BURNETT, 'BLUE DAYS BLACK NIGHTS' (1999) was in contrast a decidedly more introspective affair, distilling the essential essence of songwriter as confessor and confidente against monochromatic, elegiac guitar textures. The yang to its predecessor's yin, 'RIGHT BETWEEN THE PROMISES' (2001) signalled that JOHNSTON had presumably exorcised his demons to a sufficient degree to allow him to carry on where he left off pre-millennium. Surprisingly effusive and unerringly positive, the record even found JOHNSTON indulging in an irony-free cover of Edison Lighthouse's 70's confection, 'LOVE GROWS (WHERE MY ROSEMARY GOES)'.

• **Covered:** BUS STOP (Hollies) / WICHITA LINEMAN (Jimmy Webb) / NIGHT AND DAY (Cole Porter).

Album rating: THE TROUBLE TREE (*6) / CAN YOU FLY (*6) / THIS PERFECT WORLD (*8) / NEVER HOME (*7) / BLUE DAYS BLACK NIGHTS (*6) / RIGHT BETWEEN THE PROMISES (*6)

FREEDY JOHNSTON – vocals, guitar / with various personnel

                                                                  Demon Bar/None

Nov 90. (cd) (FIENDCD 208) <18> **THE TROUBLE TREE**
– Innocent / Down on the moon No.1 / No violins / That's what you get / Fun ride / Gina / Nature boy / Bad girl / After my shocks / Tucumcari / Down on the moon No.2 / Little red-haired girl.

                                                                  Rough Trade Bar/None

Apr 92. (cd/c/lp) (R 287-2/-4/-1) <24> **CAN YOU FLY**
– Trying to tell you I don't know / In the new sunshine / Tearing down this place / Remember me / Wheels / Lucky one / Can you fly / Responsible / Mortician's daughter / Sincere / Down in love / California thing / We will shine. (re-iss. Sep93 on 'Elektra' cd/c; 7559 61587-2/-4)

Aug 93. (cd-ep) <AHAON 024> **UNLUCKY EP**
– The lucky one / Death of stars / For a lost key / Caroline / Wichita lineman / The lucky one (demo).

                                                                  Elektra Elektra

Jul 94. (cd/c) <(7559 61655-2/-4)> **THIS PERFECT WORLD**   Jun94
– Bad reputation / Evie's tears / Can't sink this town / This perfect world / Cold again / Two lovers stop / Across the avenue / Gone like the water / Delores / Evie's garden / Dissapointed man / I can hear the laughs.

Nov 94. (c-s) <64495> **BAD REPUTATION**

Freedy JOHNSTON (cont)

Mar 97. (cd) <(7559 61920-2)> **NEVER HOME** Feb97
– On the way out / I'm not hypnotised / Western sky / One more thing to break / He wasn't murdered / You get me lost / Hotel seventeen / Gone to see the fire / Seventies girl / If it's true / Something's out there.

Sep 99. (cd) <(7559 62263-2)> **BLUE DAYS BLACK NIGHTS** Jul99
– Underwater life / The farthest lights / While I wait for you / Pretend it's summer / Changed your mind / Caught as you look away / Moving on a holiday / Until the sun comes back again / Depending on the night / Emily.

Aug 01. (cd) <7559 62652> **RIGHT BETWEEN THE PROMISES** –
– Broken mirror / Waste your time / Love grows (where my Rosemary grows) / That's alright with me / Radio for heartache / Back to my machine / Arriving on a train / Save yourself, city girl / Anyone / In my dream.

– compilations, others, etc. –

2000. (ltd-cd) Singing Magnet; <SM 07> **LIVE AT 33 1/3** –
– The mortician's daughter / Until the sun comes back again / The lucky one / Dolores / Emily / Western sky / Night and day / Bus stop / Wichita lineman / Radio for heartache.

Oct 01. (cd) Bar None; <121> **THE PRIMITIVE YEARS** –

JOLT (see under ⇒ SENSELESS THINGS)

JONATHAN FIRE*EATER

Formed: New York, USA ... mid 90's having all attended a private school in Washington DC. STEW, PAUL, WALT, TOM and MATT eventually secured a semi-permanent residency at NY's The Continental club. In 1995, their debut album was made available at gigs, creating a buzz which led to a single on the 'P.C.P.' label. Stardom beckoned after David Geffen's 'Dreamworks' secured their signature, the mini-cd, 'TREMBLE UNDER BOOM LIGHTS', finally surfacing late in 1996. This was issued in Britain having signed to 'Deceptive' (home of ELASTICA) and kicked up a storm with its comparisons to The BIRTHDAY PARTY and The CRAMPS (the latter, at one time having numbered their new-found buddy KID CONGO). In the event, the band's much heralded debut album, 'WOLF SONGS FOR LAMBS' (1997) displayed all the wilful, perverse individuality they'd become known for yet its corrosive, mutant blues was never going to shift the amount of units required by a major like 'Dreamworks'. Following their subsequent 1998 break-up, LUPTON performed in a solo guise while the remaining members, WALTER, PAUL and MARK, soldiered on as TODAY OKAY (along with ex-RECOYS musicians, HAMILTON LEITHAUSER and PETER BAUER). By 2001, the 5-piece were now billed as The WALKMEN, their styles now ranging from U2 to TELEVISION with say, a post-punk ghost of late producer JOE MEEK at the controls – if only? After an eponymous EP emerged (opening with classy 'WAKE UP'), the bombastic WALKMEN polished off their quirky and exuberant debut full-length, 'EVERYONE WHO PRETENDED TO LIKE ME IS GONE' (2002).

Album rating: TREMBLE UNDER BOOM LIGHTS (*8) / WOLF SONGS FOR LAMBS (*6) / Walkmen: EVERYONE WHO PRETENDED TO LIKE ME IS GONE (*6)

STEWART LUPTON (b.1975) – vocals / **PAUL MAROON** – guitar / **WALTER MARTIN** – organ / **THOMAS FRANK** – bass / **MATT BARRICK** – drums

P.C.P.   P.C.P.
Sep 95. (7"/cd-s) <(PCP 028-7/-2)> **THE PUBLIC HANGING OF A MOVIE STAR. / THE CAKEWALK / WHEN PRIME WAS A HIT**

Deceptive   Medicine
Oct 96. (7") (BLUFF 037) **GIVE ME DAUGHTERS. / SEARCH FOR CHERRY RED** –

Jan 97. (m-cd) (BLUFF 038CD) <79603> **TREMBLE UNDER BOOM LIGHTS** Jun95
– The search for cherry red / Make it precious / Give me daughters / Beautician / Winston Plum: undertaker / When Prince was a kid. (lp-iss.Oct97 on 'Crippled Dick'; EFA 04396-1) (cd re-iss. Mar98 on 'Crippled Dick'; CDHW 044)

Deceptive   Dreamworks
Aug 97. (7") (BLUFF 048) **WHEN THE CURTAIN CALLS FOR YOU. / A NIGHT IN THE NURSERY** –
(cd-s+=) (BLUFF 048CD) – Don't forget me.

Sep 97. (cd/lp) (BLUFF 049 CD/LP) <50024> **WOLF SONGS FOR LAMBS** Oct97
– When the curtain calls for you / Shape of things that never come / This is my room / There is no love like that / Bi-polar summer / I've changed hotels / Everybody plays the mime / These little monkeys / Station coffee / Night in the nursery / In-patient talent show.

Feb 98. (7") (BLUFF 059) **THESE LITTLE MONKEYS. / TOMORROW'S NEWS TONIGHT** –
(cd-s+=) (BLUFF 059CD) – The city never sleeps.

— disbanded in August '98

WALKMEN

WALTER MARTIN – vocals, organ / **PAUL MAROON** – guitars / **MATT BARRICK** – drums / **HAMILTON LEITHAUSER** – vocals (of RECOYS) / **PETER BAUER** – bass (of RECOYS)

not iss.   Star Time
Aug 01. (cd-ep) <STAR 4> **THE WALKMEN** –
– Wake up / We've been had / The crimps / Summer stage. (UK lp-iss.Aug02 on 'Troubleman'; TMU 94LP)

Mar 02. (cd) <STAR 7> **EVERYONE WHO PRETENDED TO LIKE ME IS GONE** –
– They're winning / Wake up / Everyone who pretended to like me is gone / Revenge wears no wristwatch / The blizzard of '96 / French vacation / Stop talking / We've been had / Roll down the line / That's the punch line / It should take a while / Rue the day / I'm never bored.

Troubleman   Troubleman
Sep 02. (cd) <TMU 95CD> **THE WALKMEN / CALLA** –
– Look out the window / Here comes another day / (other 2 by CALLA).

Stephen JONES (see under ⇒ BABYBIRD)

JULIE RUIN (see under ⇒ BIKINI KILL)

JUMBO

Formed: Newcastle, England ... 1998 by RICHARD MacLEAN, BEN WILKINSON, JOHN LEE, STEVE MARSHALL and ANDREW HODSON. Hailing from an area in Geordieland where local bands obsessively played cover songs, the weirdo 5-piece took to doing the absolute opposite by composing the most trippy, wigged-out psychedelic sounds – not heard since The FLAMING LIPS' 'Oh My Gawd!'. JUMBO (who apparently took their name from a lost BEE GEES classic ... or, erm, a rather large sausage in chip shops) issued a 2-track single, 'BRIGHTEN UP' (1999), on the 'Bright Orange Biscuit' label. The band proceeded to tour (frightening the audience with their million-part-structured songs) and subsequently promised eager listeners an album under the working title of 'CB MAMAS' in the summer of '99. With many critics defining them as Britain's answer to the 'LIPS, JUMBO were back with another cut'n'paste-style pot pourri of sounds (Krautrock-psych and lo-fi pop) courtesy of sophomore set, 'JUMBO' (2001). • **Note:** A different JUMBO released the 1998 cd, 'The Best Of Jumbo (Turn On To Love)'.

Album rating: CB MAMAS (*5) / JUMBO (*6)

RICHARD MacLEAN – vocals, guitar / **BEN WILKINSON** – guitar / **JOHN LEE** – keyboards / **STEVE MARSHALL** – bass / **ANDREW HODSON** – drums

Bright Orange Biscuit   not iss.
Oct 98. (ltd-7") (BROB 001) **WELCOME IN PIECES** –
Apr 99. (ltd-7") (BROB 002) **BRIGHTEN UP. / H.O.N. HONEY** –
Sep 99. (cd)(lp) (BROBCD 003)(BROB 003V) **CB MAMAS** –
– Sirocco / Sunrise 3000 / 12 traditions / Brighten up / The pleasant blue sky radiation company / H.O.N. honey / Welcome in pieces / Wet denim / Punk bubble / Good looking experiment.

Earworm   not iss.
May 01. (7"ep) (WORM 73) **DOUBLE SUPER BUZZ** –
– Double super buzz / Meet your bones / I always believed in the cunt / Alphabet soup.

Cargo   not iss.
Aug 01. (cd) (CUK 0032) **JUMBO** –
– Double super buzz / The cunt won't start / Man part / I love my body / Roulette / Everybodys gonna get get me / Daddy coo coo / Strike anywhere / My husband's my motivator / Views from the south / Pigmy FM / Co-pilot was a cooler / The Devil may care.

JUNE OF 44

Formed: Louisville, Kentucky, USA ... 1994. Consisting of JEFF MUELLER, FRED ERSKINE, SEAN MEADOWS (of SONORA PINE) and DOUG SCHARIN, this rattling folk-rock ambient group debuted with 'ENGINE TAKES TO WATER' (1995), a sweet, if not ripe, avant jazz experimentation which dabbled in SLINT dynamics and WILL OLDHAM/PALACE lo-fi integrity. Their sophomore set, 'TROPICS & MERIDIANS' (1996) saw a transition to SLINT's own Kentucky label, 'Touch & Go' as comparisons to The FOR CARNATION and TORTOISE were thrown at the band's equally more developed second long-player. Harbouring complex structures and sour guitars as well as peaceful and harmonic methods, two other albums later ('FOUR GREAT POINTS' and 'ANAHATA') surfaced by the band. JUNE OF 44 were apparently still unphased by criticism as they issued their bravest and most uncynical album to date, the brooding 'FISH 6', which featured the lonely whispers of MUELLER and an orchestra of mariachi trumpets and dizzy violins. With MUELLER forming SHIPPING NEWS with JASON NOBLE, SEAN MEADOWS subsequently conceived EVERLASTING THE WAY, a short-lived affair that produced two dreamy, mediterranean-styled releases, the eponymous 'EVERLASTING THE WAY' EP and 'LONG STRETCH – MOTORCYCLE – HYMN – HIGHWAY' (2000). Not content with this outlet for his prolific songwriting, MEADOWS assembled a new project, The LETTER E, along with CHRIS HARVEY (of REX and PULLMAN), JOSH MATTHEWS (of BLUE MAN GROUP) and ENIS SEFERSAH; the experimental math-rock album, 'NO.5IVE LONGPLAYER' (2000), was the outcome of this side-project.

Album rating: ENGINE TAKES TO WATER (*5) / TROPICS AND MERIDIANS (*5) / THE ANATOMY OF SHARKS mini (*5) / FOUR GREAT POINTS (*7) / ANAHATA (*6) / IN THE FISHTANK (*5) / Everlasting The Way: LONG STRETCH – MOTORCYCLE – HYMN – HIGHWAY (*5) / the Letter E: NO.5IVE LONGPLAYER (*6)

SEAN MEADOWS – vocals, guitar (of SONORA PINE) / **JEFF MUELLER** – vocals, guitar / **FRED ERSKINE** – bass / **DOUG SCHARIN** – drums (also of REX, of H.I.M., of DIRECTIONS IN MUSIC)

Jun 95. (lp/cd) <(QS 32/+CD)> **ENGINE TAKES TO THE WATER**
– Have a safe trip, dear / June Miller / Pale horse sailor / Mindel / I get my kicks for you / Mooch / Take it with a grain of salt / Sink it busted.

JUNE OF 44 (cont)

Jun 96. (lp/cd) <(QS 44/+CD)> **TROPICS AND MERIDIANS**
– Anisette / Lusitania / Lawn bowler / June leaf / Arms over arteries / Sanctioned in a birdcage.
Jan 97. (10"m-lp/m-cd) <(QS 40/+CD)> **THE ANATOMY OF SHARKS**
– Sharks and sailors / Boom / Seemingly endless summer.
Jan 98. (lp/cd) <(QS 54/+CD)> **FOUR GREAT POINTS**
– Of information and belief / Dexterity of luck / Cut your face / Doomsday / Does your heart beat slower / Lifted bells / Shadow pugilist / Air #17.
Jun 99. (cd) <QS 64CD> **ANAHATA**
– Wear two eyes (boom) / Escape of the levitational trapeze artist / Cardiac atlas / Equators to bi-polar / Recorded syntax / Southeast of Boston / Five bucks in my pocket / Peel away velleity.

Konkurrent / Konkurrent

Oct 99. (lp/cd) <(FISH 6/+CD)> **IN THE FISHTANK**
– Pregenerate / Generate / Henry's revenge / Modern hereditary dance steps / Every free day a good day / Degenerate.

– compilations, others, etc. –

Jan 01. (7") *B-Core; (BC 066)* **SOUTH EAST OF BOSTON. / DEXTERITY OF LUCK (live)**

EVERLASTING THE WAY

SEAN MEADOWS – vocals, bass, etc.

not iss. Magic Eye

1999. (cd-ep) <016> **EVERLASTING THE WAY**
– Calle de la Palma / A polite drunk / Boat to Portugalete / Nothing I'm proud of.

Monitor Monitor

May 00. (cd) <(MON 003)> **LONG STRETCH – MOTORCYCLE – HYMN – HIGHWAY**
– Volcanic sunrise / Another birthday / From solar exodus (sunburst) / One month window / 555 / Once the ocean floor / Crown the day / To star implosion (anti-Nova) / Hung up and don't know why / Day after the last / Bastimentos by dug out.

LETTER E

SEAN MEADOWS – guitars / **CURTIS HARVEY** – guitar, piano, accordion (of REX, of PULLMAN) / **JOSH MATTHEWS** (of BLUE MAN GROUP) / **ENIS SEFERSAH**

Tiger Style Tiger Style

Oct 00. (cd/lp) <(TS 009/+LP)> **NO.5IVE LONGPLAYER**
– Alushta / Better days / Plains / Mary Bahtyarli / Events / Isabella / Block and tackle.

B-core B-core

Jan 01. (cd-ep) <(BC 069CD)> **THE LETTER E EP**
– On the corner / Number 2 / Goodbye / Bess in Bejing.

JUNIOR VARSITY

Formed: Nacogdoches, Texas, USA . . . around 1995 by KIM HAMMOND and MATT MURILLO. The group were definitely on the alternative strand of pop music, although what they were playing was once extremely mainstream, namely innocent fifties American teen tunes, about drive-in movie theatres and first-loves, although JV add their nineties ironic stance, although that is not to say this shines through so much in the music, but more in the two cheerleaders and one geek live show. In the early days of the band they were supplemented on guitar by SEAN MCMANUS, and with the help of local DJ, BUTCHIE CORDELL, they managed to get a deal with indie label, 'Peek-A-Boo' in 1996, who released their debut 7", 'ICE CREAM SOCIAL'. Over the next four years the band continued to tour with much success, especially around the college fraternities, with their self-styled name for their genre, 'frat-hop', and releasing a handful of singles on various independent labels, and appearing on more compilations. During this time MCMANUS was replaced by former guitarist with fellow Texan indie band, THE JEWWS, REBECCA WHITLEY. The millennium saw the release of their debut LP 'BAM BAM BAM!', which featuring tunes like 'DANCE, FRANNY, DANCE' and 'POP SOCKS', was no change from form. Although the album features 14 tracks it is under a half-hour in length, so apart from not getting tedious, it is a good fun blast of a bygone era without the static crackling.

Album rating: TAKING CARE OF YOU (BLISS OUT VOL.10) (*6) / BAM BAM BAM! mini (*6)

MATT MURILLO – drums, vocals / **SEAN McMANUS** – guitar, vocals / **KIM HAMMOND** – bass, vocals / + **DJ BUTCHIE CORDELL**

not iss. Peek-A-Boo

1996. (7"ep) **GO! TO THE ICE CREAM SOCIAL**

not iss. Twist Like This

1997. (7"ep) **PEP RALLY ROCK**

not iss. Remedial

1998. (7"ep) **JUVENILE**

not iss. NGOO

1999. (7") **PANTHER VS. JUNIOR VARSITY**

— **REBECCA WHITLEY** – guitar, vocals; repl. SEAN

Peek-A-Boo Peek-A-Boo

Mar 00. (lp/cd) <(BOO 1206/+CD)> **BAM BAM BAM!**
– Bam b-b-bam bam bam / Lafayette (rock city) / Poppa burger / Dance, Franny, dance / So great / Mark Lochridge twist / Switch sides / Pop socks / My boyfriend / Pin monkey / Alley cat / Can't take it no more / Woodpecker stomp / Package store.

not iss. Twist LIke This

2000. (7") **BAM BAM BAM!**

not iss. She's Gone

2001. (7") **split w/ KUNG FU MONKEYS**

JUNIOR VARSITY KM

Formed: San Francisco, California, USA . . . mid 90's by electronics wizard, KENRIC McDOWELL. Fusing ambient techno with indie space-pop, JUNIOR VARSITY KM (named so, due to indie-popsters JUNIOR VARSITY taking similar moniker) released a handful of releases for 'Darla' records. From the 'STYLE OF LIFE' EP in '97 on to the 'TELEDISC' volumes in 1999, KEN's work experimentated with most genres.

Album rating: TAKING CARE OF YOU (*5) / TELEDISC DISCO 1 (*5) / TELEDISC DISCO 2 (*4)

KENRIC McDOWELL – electronics

Darla Darla

Nov 97. (12"ep) *(DRL 051)* **STYLE FOR LIFE EP**
– Friendly friends / Transbay tube / Gardener / Asleep symphony / The party where you cry.
Mar 98. (d-lp/cd) <(DRL 056/+CD)> **TAKING CARE OF YOU (BLISS OUT VOL.10)** *Oct99*
– You're fabulous! / Suspension bridge / Regarder / Fourshadowing / The injury / Sea of tranquility / Brothers and sisters / Waiting for the big.
Jun 98. (12"ep/cd-ep) *(DRL 064/+CD)* **YOU'RE FABULOUS!**
– You're fabulous / Imasu ka? / You're fabulous (mixes; Paradise / Minty cut / Blissful thinking).
Jun 98. (12"ep) *(DRL 065)* **FOURSHADOWING EP**
Mar 99. (m-lp/m-cd) <(DRL 081/+CD)> **TELEDISC DISCO 1** *Jul99*
– Lower the shields, ponce / Inhale / Snow / Natives of the new world.
Mar 99. (m-lp/m-cd) *(DRL 082/+CD)* **TELEDISC DISCO 2** *Jul99*
– City sleepwalker / Boprosthesis / Caribou / Towards a psychedelic beat.
Apr 99. (12"ep) *(DRL 086)* **MATCHMAKER VIA REMIXOLOGY VOL.3 EP**

Black Bean & Placento Tape Club / not iss.

Jul 99. (12"ep) *(ACME 78)* **THE DOWNTEMPO EP**

JUNIPER (see under ⇒ MONDO CRESCENDO)

JUPITER AFFECT (see under ⇒ THREE O'CLOCK)

Damien JURADO

Born: Seattle, Washington, USA. Arriving on the Seattle music scene in the mid-1990s (via small-time outfits, COOLIDGE, CUPCAKES, FLOWERMOUTH, MOONBOY and LO-LIFE), singer/songwriter JURADO gradually acquired a local following, largely due to the exposure of some self-released cassettes, including 'LEADED', 'TRAILER PARK RADIO' and 'GASOLINE'. His work was brought to the attention of the 'Sub Pop' label by fan JEREMY ENIGK, frontman with SUNNY DAY REAL ESTATE. Having signed, and released two singles, 'TRAMPOLINE' and 'MOTORBIKE', his debut LP 'WATERS AVE S.' arrived in early 1997. A prolific songwriter, JURADO selected thirteen tracks to showcase his skill for indie-folk storytelling. Crooning fictional tales, and affecting personal struggles, 'WATERS . . .' was an assured debut from JURADO. If further confirmation of his talent as a singer/songwriter was required, then 1999's 'REHEARSALS FOR DEPARTURE' provided it. Lyrical, plaintive and intimate, it painted an often bleak portrait of urban middle-class America. With instrumentation provided by friends, there was also a diversity of styles and sounds – with the honky-tonk 'HONEY BABY' and the dreamy 'SATURDAY'. JURADO's 2000 follow-up was an odd and audacious collection of old recordings from second-hand boom boxes and answering machines, without any music. Returning to more conventional urban-folk with 'GHOST OF DAVID' (also 2000), and now drawing comparisons with artists like TOM WAITS and NICK DRAKE, JURADO was even more melancholic and reflective on 'GHOST OF DAVID'; which was as compelling as 'REHEARSALS . . .'. He upped the tempo with 2002's 'I BREAK CHAIRS', exploring indie-pop and rock, and with the majority of tracks, using his backing band GATHERED IN SONG to full effect.

Album rating: WATERS AVE S. (*6) / REHEARSALS FOR DEPARTURE (*7) / GATHERED IN SONG mini (*5) / POSTCARDS AND AUDIO LETTERS collection (*5) / GHOST OF DAVID (*6) / I BREAK CHAIRS (*6)

DAMIEN JURADO – vocals, guitars / with various back-up

not iss. Casa Recording

1994. (c) **LEADED**
1995. (c) **TRAILER PARK RADIO**
1995. (c) **GASOLINE**

Sub Pop Sub Pop

Nov 95. (7"ep) <SP 0335> **MOTORBIKE EP**
Jul 96. (7") <SP 0364> **TRAMPOLINE**
– Rollerskating queen / Pigtails.
Nov 97. (lp/cd) <(SP/+CD 374)> **WATER AVE S.** *Jan97*
– Wedding cake / Angel of May / Treasures of gold / Yuma, Az. The joke is over / Space age mom / Circus, circus, circus / Hell or highwater / Independent / Purple anteater / Sarah / Halo friendly / Water Ave S.

Rykodisc Sub Pop

Mar 99. (cd) *(RCD 10382)* <SPCD 440> **REHEARSALS FOR DEPARTURE** *Feb99*
– Ohio / Tragedy / Curbside / Honey baby / Eyes for window / Letters & drawings / Love the same / Saturday / Tornado / Rehearsals for departure.

Damien JURADO (cont)

		Made In Mexico	Made In Mexico
Mar 99.	(m-cd) <*MEX 003CD*> **GATHERED IN SONG**	-	

– Chevrolet / Simple hello / Happy birthday John / East Virginia / To those who will burn . . . (*UK-iss.Apr01; same as US*)

Jun 00. (cd) <(*MEX 009CD*)> **POSTCARDS AND AUDIO LETTERS**
(collection)
– Robert 1972 / Angel 1972 / Christmas 1983 / Christmas 1983 (pt.2) / "Hi Dawn, this is Phil" / Waking Dawn / At the airport / "Our kid is getting hurt".

		not iss.	Summershine
2000.	(7") <*017*> **HALO FRIENDLY. / OCEAN SHORES 97 / LONG DISTANCE**		

		Sub Pop	Sub Pop
Oct 00.	(cd) <(*SPCD 507*)> **GHOST OF DAVID**	-	Sep00

– Medication / Desert / Johnny go riding / Great today / Tonight I will retire / Ghost of David / Parking lot / Rearview / Paxil / Walk with me / December / Rosewood casket / Ghost in the snow.

Feb 02. (etched-12"ep) <(*BTV 041*)> **FOUR SONGS**
– Spitting teeth / How I broke my legs / The killer / Flowers in the yard.
(above issued on 'Burnt Toast Vinyl')

—— next with **ERIC FISHER** – keyboards, guitar, glockenspiel + **ANDREW MYERS** – drums, glockenspiel

Mar 02. (cd; as DAMIEN JURADO & GATHERED IN SONG)
<(*SP/+CD 571*)> **I BREAK CHAIRS** Feb02
– Paper wings / Dancing / Birdcage / Inevitable / Air show disaster / Never ending tide / Big deal / The way you look / Castles / Like Titanic / Parade / Lose my head.

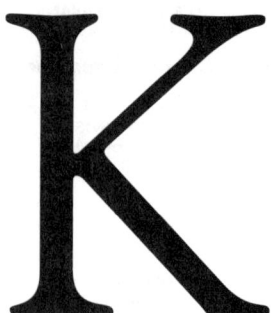

KAIA (see under ⇒ TEAM DRESCH)

KARATE

Formed: Boston, Massachusetts, USA ... 1992 by guitarist and vocalist GEOFF FARINA, bassist EAMONN VITT, and drummer GAVIN McCARTHY. After a year of practice and rehearsal, they played their first gig in December 1993. 1994 saw KARATE establish themselves within the Boston alternative music scene, and release first single, 'DEATH KIT', on The Self-Starter Foundation. Meanwhile, the talented FARINA, with best friend JODI BUONANNO, had also formed The SECRET STARS in 1993. This romantic-folk outfit came to include several East Coast indie figures, like GEORGE HALL and TED LEO. After self-releasing 'THE SECRET STARS' cassette in 1994, they were signed by the 'Shrimper' label, the collection being re-released a year later. It would be another few years before further SECRET STARS material appeared, because FARINA would concentrate his energies on KARATE, developing their indie-rock sound potential. In 1995 they became a quartet, and with the addition of bassist JEFF GODARD (leading to VITT's move to second guitar), they released second single, 'THE SCHWINN', a split-disc with his own band, The LUNE. KARATE's eponymous debut LP (released in 1996 on the 'Southern' label) was raw, jagged indie-rock, showing signs of promise, and some real highlights, like 'BAD TATTOO'. The following year's 'IN PLACE OF REAL INSIGHT' marked a definite progression for the band, with tighter construction and the emergence of a jazz influence (FARINA studied jazz guitar at college), although it was around this time VITT departed. With 1998's 'THE BED IS THE OCEAN', KARATE had unmistakably absorbed jazz as a major element of their sound, and FARINA had clearly expanded his vocal range – demonstrated on 'NOT TO CALL THE POLICE'. 1998 was a busy year for FARINA, with the release of his debut solo album, 'USONIAN DREAM SEQUENCE', completed by the SECRET STARS releasing second LP 'GENEALOGIES'. Somewhere between KARATE and The SECRET STARS, GEOFF FARINA solo has a gentle, country feel, continued through his second solo offering, 'REVERSE ECLIPSE' (2001). The man's jazzy groove explorations with KARATE continued on fourth album, 'UNSOLVED' (2000) and 2002's ROBERT SMITH-influenced 'SOME BOOTS'.

Album rating: KARATE (*5) / IN PLACE OF REAL INSIGHT (*6) / THE BED IS THE OCEAN (*5) / UNSOLVED (*4) / CANCEL – SING mini (*6) / SOME BOOTS (*4) / Secret Stars: SECRET STARS (*6) / GENEALOGIES (*7) / Geoff Farina: USONIAN DREAM SEQUENCE (*6) / REVERSE ECLIPSE (*5) / BLOBSCAPE (*5)

GEOFF FARINA – vocals, guitar / **EAMONN VITT** – bass / **GAVIN McCARTHY** – drums

		not iss.	Self-Starter
1994.	(7") **DEATH KIT. / NERVE**	-	

—— added **JEFF GODDARD** – bass (VITT now on second guitar)

		not iss.	unknown
1995.	(7") **THE SCHWINN. / (split w/ The LUNE)**	-	
		Southern	Southern
Mar 96.	(cd/lp) <(*18534-2/-1*)> **KARATE**		

– Gasoline / If you can hold your breath / Trophy / What is sleep? / Bad tattoo / Every sister / Bodies / Caffeine or me? (*cd+=*) – (hidden track).

Apr 97. (cd/lp) <(*18543-2/-1*)> **IN PLACE OF REAL INSIGHT**
– This, plus slow song / New martini / Wake up, decide / It's 98 stop / New new / The new hangout condition / On cutting / Die die / Today or tomorrow.

—— now without EAMONN VITT

Apr 98. (7") **OPERATION: SAND. / EMPTY THERE** -
Nov 98. (cd/lp) <(*18554-2/-1*)> **THE BED IS THE OCEAN**
– There are ghosts / The same stars / Diazapam / The last wars / Bass sounds / Up nights / Fatal strategies / Outside the drtama / Not to call the police.

Nov 00. (cd) <(*18584-2*)> **UNSOLVED** Oct00
– Small fries / The lived-but-yet-named / Sever / The roots and the ruins / Number six / One less blues / The halo of the strange / The angels just have to show / This day next year.

Mar 02. (m-cd) <(*18594-2*)> **CANCEL / SING**
– Cancel / Sing.

Sep 02. (cd/lp) <(*18599-2/-1*)> **SOME BOOTS**
– Original spies / First release / Ice or ground? / South / In hundreds / Airport / Baby teeth / Corduroy / Remain relaxed.

KARATE (cont)

SECRET STARS

GEOFF FARINA – vocals, guitar / **JODI BUONANNO** – guitar

Shrimper / Shrimper

Dec 96. (lp/cd) <(SHR 80/+CD)> **SECRET STARS** / Aug 96
- Vague / Life of submission / Whisper: eye / Andy and girls / Alienation #3 / The kids can't maintain / Jumpstart #1 / Snowday / Whisper: heart / Aufheben / Untitled 2 / Sleep, star / Jumpstart / Your life to live / This new garage / Psychic intrusion / Darstellung / Moving song / Zombie samba / Femmes damness.
(above was actually self-released earlier on tape)

Mar 98. (lp/cd) <(SHR 107/+CD)> **GENEALOGIES** / Feb 98
- Haphazard joy / Shoe in / Melt / N29, it's alright / Can U feel it? / The four senses / Serc / Sister, brother / Trance hall storm / 5,000,000,000 / Some Sinatra / The mode-E / The vitamin-V / We have been schooled by / Release form / Back in the car.

not iss. / March

Jul 98. (7"ep) **ABNER LOUIMA** – /

— FARINA + BUONANNO have since shelved the project

GEOFF FARINA

Southern / Southern

Mar 98. (cd) <(18550-2)> **USONIAN DREAM SEQUENCE**
- As you are right / $48 / The most recent imaginary / Car / The United States / Not about a birthday / Usonian dream sequence / The same way / Eventually / Midlantic schemes / For now / Dries / Window seats.

— accompanied by **JOSH LaRUE** – guitar (of the SORTS)

Feb 01. (cd) <(18583-2)> **REVERSE ECLIPSE**
- Special diamonds / The left-handed way / Fire / Henningson or Hemingway / Gravity / Pordeone plaster / Soon in tents / The rights / Only yellows / The Dianne eraser / Olive or otherwise / One percent / Fixable.

not iss. / Kimchee

Jul 02. (cd) <15> **BLOBSCAPE** – /
- Feign elsewhere / Slurphy / Fiction (part 1) / Prototype / Chewable resources / Blobscape / Fake mysterious Lisas / Fiction (part 2) / Hibye / Excerpt / Peanut butter faction / Some details / Universal Indians / Near – Miss Generator / Piss / Ouliponic.

the KARELIA

Formed: Glasgow, Scotland ... late 1996 out of rock/jazz outfit, The BLISTERS by singer ALEX HUNTLEY. Since 1994, the modest, unassuming ALEX was responsible for the '13th Note' club, which was the stamping ground for up and coming acts such as BIS, MOGWAI and URUSEI YATSURA. However, along with band members ALAN WYLIE and GLEN THOMSON (Greek drummer TASSOS BOBOS was added towards the end of '96 – the band even using the name of a Greek cigarette!), the KARELIA took off almost immediately having been signed (as The BLISTERS) to 'Roadrunner'! by Ruth Robinson after a Bucketful Of Bands contest at the Barrowlands. Prog/techno rock with IGGY-voxed overtones, their diverse jazzy film-noir Lo-fi was certainly a change from anything around at the time. Debut album, 'DIVORCE AT HIGH NOON' (1997) found some favour in the indie inkies, although live ALEX was HANNON, COCKER and even BID (the MONOCHROME SET singer to the uninitiated!) rolled into one brassy musical empire. HUNTLEY was also one of the team responsible for The AMPHETAMEANIES, a 10-piece Ska outfit into chaos and fun.

Album rating: DIVORCE AT HIGH NOON (*6)

BLISTERS

ALEX HUNTLEY – vocals, guitar / **ALAN WYLIE** – trumpet, keyboards / **GLEN THOMSON** – bass

Moden Independent / not iss.

Apr 95. (7"burgundy) (mir 001) **A DULL THOUGHT IN ITSELF. / (other track by Urusei Yatsura)** / –

— after the BLISTERS folded **TASSOS BOBOS** – (was on) drums

the KARELIA

Roadrunner / Roadrunner

Feb 97. (cd-ep) (RR 2280-3) **A SMOOTH TASTE OF THE KARELIA** / –
- Say try / Des veaux ca taille nous une / Life in a barrat garret / Garavurghty butes.

Apr 97. (cd) (RR 8823-3) **DIVORCE AT HIGH NOON** / –
- Divorce at high noon / Love's a cliche / Say try / To his dietres / Life in a Barrat Garret / Crazy irritation / Remorse at high noon / Dancing along the nekrotaphion / Devil rides Hyndland / Infinite duration / Nostalgia / Tension / Bleach yours / Exaggeration / Garavaughty butes.

Nov 97. (cd-s) (RR 2253-3) **LOVE'S A CLICHE / LOVE'S A THROWAWAY CLICHE / LOVE'S A MORBID CLICHE / LOVE'S A RELENTLESS CLICHE** / –

Flotsam & Jetsam / not iss.

May 98. (7") (SHaG 13.07) **Club Beatroot Part Seven** / –
- Summer in Spain / (other track by the Poison Sisters).
(above was released in conjunction with 'The 13th Note')

Jun 98. (7") (SHaG 019) **VISION IN A WORLD WITHOUT SPECTACLES. / (other track by El Hombre Trajeado)** / –

— Nov'98 and signed to 'Guided Missile', the band appeared on a 'Glasgow' d7"EP (with track 'NEW YEAR IN NEW YORK') alongside MOGWAI, YUMMY FUR and EL HOMBRE TRAJEADO. The KARELIA also contributed the track 'THE ONLY DIFFERENCE' to the labels' V/A comp 'Hits & Missiles'. Early in 2000, THE KARELIA shared an EP, '15 Minutes With The Smiths', alongside three Argentinian groups; GRAND PRIX, FUN PEOPLE and ULTRAMAR.

KATASTROPHY WIFE
(see under ⇒ BABES IN TOYLAND)

Matt KEATING

Born: Boston, Massachusetts, USA. Having cut his teeth playing guitar and piano at the old Boston Mafia Club (yes, actually run by the Mafia), MATT formed his first band, CIRCLE SKY, in the latter half of the 80's. Developing a tried and tested singer-songwriter approach (similar to ELLIOTT SMITH, MARK KOZELEK and LEONARD COHEN) through working on street corners and undergrounds/subways, the man finally released his first solo set, 'TELL IT TO YOURSELF' (1993), having signed earlier to 'Alias' records. His sophomore LP, 'SCARYAREA' (1994), also went a little unnoticed but KEATING persevered, ultimately receiving rave reviews for his follow-up effort, 'KILLJOY' (1997). Deeper and analytic of the people around him, the record's highlights were 'EMILY' (his girlfriend), 'THE L WORD' (about a drug induced nervous breakdown) and 'WHILE WE FIDDLE' (covering right-wing politics). MATT subsequently took some time to reflect while also trying to find another record contract. In 2001, he was lured into ALAN McGEE's new independent, 'Poptones' label, who delivered his long-awaited fourth set, 'TILT A WHIRL', arguably slightly better than his previous LP with great moments such as 'SUCCESSFUL' (a limited single) and 'WINDOW BOOTH'.

Album rating: TELL IT TO YOURSELF (*5) / SCARYAREA (*6) / KILLJOY (*7) / TILT A WHIRL (*7)

MATT KEATING – vocals, guitar, piano / with sessioners

Alias / Alias

Jun 93. (lp/c/cd) <(A 035/+C/D)> **TELL IT TO YOURSELF** / Jan 93
- Sanity in the asylum / Don't suffer in silence / When you don't have to work / A little talk / Lonely blues / Arrangements / Show me how / '92 / Nostalgia / So near, so far / Lost again / Hard place to be.

Jun 93. (7") <(A 037-5)> **SANITY IN THE ASYLUM**
- Pull some strings / Hand me downs (acoustic).

Sep 93. (cd-ep) <(A 052)> **SATAN SINGS EP**
- Sanity in the asylum / Pull some strings (demo) / When you don't have to work (live) / A little talk (live) / Lonely blue (live).

Oct 94. (cd/c/lp) <(A 069 D/C/LP)> **SCARYAREA**
- Boxed Inn / McHappiness / I thought I heard my head exploding / Way to go / Pull some strings / The wrong god / Opportunist / Never fit in / Late October / Your other face / All the rest / A sudden way of nothing' feelin'.

Feb 96. (cd-ep) <(A 092D)> **CANDY VALENTINE** / Jan 96
- Candy valentine (live) / Lonely blue (live) / Emily / That kind of girl / All the rest (live).

Apr 97. (cd) <(A 093D)> **KILLJOY**
- Killjoy / Don't go the road alone / Bowery heights / The fruit you can't eat / Emily / You and me and this TV / Just to feel something / By the way / A roundabout way to get wise / While we fiddle / The L word / Happy again.

— next w/ **GARY MAURER** – bass + **MARK BROTTER** – drums

Poptones / Future Farmer

Jun 01. (cd) (MC 5046CD) <25291> **TILT A WHIRL** / 2000
- Sunday song / Man overboard / As bas as it lasts / Jacksonville / Successful / Not today / On closer inspection / Window booth / Believe it / Executioner / Float away / It's a shame / Beautiful / Anyway / Bad things will happen.

Aug 01. (7") (MC 5046S) **SUCCESSFUL. / WINDOW BOOTH (piano version)** / –

KENICKIE

Formed: Tyne & Wear, Sunderland, England ... August '94 by songwriters JOHNNY XAVERRE and MARIE DU SANTIAGO, along with LAUREN LE LAVERNE (JOHNNY's younger sister) and EMMY-KATE MONTROSE. After releasing two indie 7"er's, the second being, 'COME OUT 2NITE', in early '96 on the influential 'Fierce Panda' label. Their fusion of radical punk-pop and femme-power endeared them to 'Creation', KENICKIE subsequently turning their noses up at the offer in favour of a more lucrative deal with 'Emidisc'. This shrewd move paid off with a Top 50 hit, 'PUNKA', re-issued a year later when it fared a little better. In fact, 1997 saw KENICKIE become regular chart fixtures with no less that two Top 30 hits, 'IN YOUR CAR' and 'NIGHTLIFE', plus a Top 10 album, 'AT THE CLUB'. Early in '99 (after their demise late the previous year), EMMY-KATE and MARIE were back at the helm of a new 5-piece, ROSITA, although only one single surfaced later in the year. Meanwhile, the other siblings founded the band CHRIS; LAVERNE had also become a TV presenter on BBC select's 'Alphabet Show'. • **Covers:** SAVE YOUR KISSES FOR ME (Brotherhood Of Man).

Album rating: AT THE CLUB (*6) / GET IN (*5) / THE JOHN PEEL SESSIONS mini (*6)

LAUREN LE LAVERNE – vocals, guitar, keyboards, etc / **MARIE DU SANTIAGO** – lead guitar, vocals, keyboards / **EMMY-KATE MONTROSE** – bass, vocals, keyboards, trumpet / **X** (b. JOHNNY XAVERRE) – drums, keyboards, percussion

Slampt Underground / not iss.

Jun 95. (7"ep) (SLAMPT 31) **CATSUIT CITY** / –
- Rama lama lama / Private Buchowski / Come in / Snakebite / My nites out! / SK8BDN song / Perfect plan / Jellybean 8.

Fierce Panda / not iss.

Feb 96. (7"ep) (NING 16) **SKILLEX E.P.** / –
- Come out 2nite / How I was made / Scared of spiders / Acetone.
(above was originally issued as 7" double-A; first 2 tracks)

KENICKIE (cont)

		Emidisc	Warners
Sep 96.	(c-s/7") (TC+/DISC 001) **PUNKA. / COWBOY SONG**	43	-
	(cd-s+=) (CDDISC 001) – Drag race / Walrus.		
Nov 96.	(c-s/7") (TC+/DISC 002) **MILLIONAIRE SWEEPER. / PERFECT PLAN 9T6**	60	-
	(cd-s+=) (CDDISC 002) – Kamikaze Annelids / Girl's best friend.		
Jan 97.	(7") (DISC 005) **IN YOUR CAR. / CAN I TAKE U 2 TO THE CINEMA?**	24	-
	(cd-s+=) (CDDISCX 005) – I'm an agent.		
	(cd-s) (CDDISC 005) – ('A'side) / Private Buchowski / Killing fantasy.		
Apr 97.	(7") (DISC 006) **NIGHTLIFE. / J-P**	27	-
	(cd-s+=) (CDDISCX 006) – Eat the angel.		
	(cd-s) (CDDISC 006) – ('A'side) / Kenix / Skateboard song.		
May 97.	(cd/c) (7243-8-56147-2/-4) <46552> **AT THE CLUB**	9	
	– In your car / People we want / Spies / How I was made / Brother John / Millionaire sweeper / Robot song / Classy / Punka / Nightlife / P.V.C. / Come out 2nite / I never complain / Acetone.		
Jun 97.	(7"pic-d) (DICS 007) **PUNKA. / LIGHT OUT IN A PROVINCIAL TOWN**	38	-
	(7") (DISC 007) – ('A'side) / Waste you.		
	(cd-s) (CDDISC 007) – (3 tracks above).		
	(cd-s) (CDDISCS 007) – ('A'side) / Brighter shade of blue / We can dream.		

		E.M.I.	Imprint
May 98.	(7"clear) (TCEM 513) **I WOULD FIX YOU. / PACKED IN**	36	-
	(cd-s+=) (CDEMS 513) – I would fix you (Mint Royale mix).		
	(cd-s+=) (CDEMS 513) – Rough boys & modern girls / ('A'-DJ Downfall mix).		
	(12") (12EM 513) – ('A'-Mint Royale mix) / Rough boys & modern girls.		
Aug 98.	(7") (EM 520) **STAY IN THE SUN. / HOORAY FOR EVERYTHING**	43	-
	(c-s+=) (TCEM 520) – Save your kisses for me.		
	(cd-s+=) (CDEM 520) – ('A'-Fridge remix).		
	(cd-s) (CDEMS 520) – ('A'side) / ('A'-Maxwell Implosion Influenza mix) / Save your kisses for me.		
Aug 98.	(cd/c) (495851-2/-4) <113438> **GET IN**	32	
	– Stay in the sun / Lunch at Lassiters / I would fix you / 60's bitch / Run me over / And that's why / Magnatron / Weeknights / Psychic defence / 5 a.m. / 411 (la la la) / Something's got to give. (cd+=) – Disco Xmas on the dole.		

—— brought in DOT ALLAN (b. Scotland) – keyboards + GRAHAM CHRISTIE – drums (JOHNNY X now on guitar)

—— split in October '98; LAVERNE became a TV presenter

– compilations, etc. –

Aug 99.	(m-cd) (SFRSCD 085) **THE JOHN PEEL SESSIONS**		-
	– Drag race / Millionaire sweep / PVC / How I was made / Scared of spiders / Acetone / Can I take you to the cinema / Come out 2night.		

ROSITA

EMMY-KATE MONTROSE + MARIE DU SANTIAGO with **DOT ALLAN** – keyboards / **MATT McGINN** – guitar / **PADDY PULTZER** – drums

		For Us	not iss.
Aug 99.	(7") (FU 009) **LIVE IT DOWN. / IF YOU'VE HEARD**		-
		Zubizaretta	not iss.
Apr 00.	(7"/cd-s) (ZUB 006/+CD) **SANTA POCA'S DREAM. / DOWN HERE / DEMON**		-

—— ROSITA looked to have split

KENNY PROCESS TEAM

Formed: Chiswick, London, England ... around 1994 by KEV PLUMMER, MATT ARMSTRONG and DAVE ROSS. The trio, led principally by PLUMMER's songwriting developed over a short recording career a unique blend of progressive, experimental rock, flavoured with surf-pop, and the kind of sounds expected to be found in sixties action flick soundtracks. They were favourably compared to the great sonic entrepreneur, CAPTAIN BEEFHEART, especially for taking their brand of instrumental rock into the more classical realms. KPT's innovative style first saw the light of the record shop shelves with the release of the LP, 'SURFIN' WITH KENNY PROCESS TEAM' (1995), on the pioneering indie imprint, 'Hemiola'. Noteworthy on this album was the drum sound, which went by way of the old phrase, "necessity is the mother of invention", as ROSS had to learn how to play with sticks that were split lengthways in order not to disturb neighbours as KPT practised. Aided by second guitarist, SIMON DEEWOGAB, they toured globally, although this partnership ended in 1997, when DEEWOGAB fell foul of a fairly gory accident in the Netherlands. The remaining trio were unfortunate that several ventures they proposed never found legs, namely stateside touring, and a regular slot at a London club night, which never got off the ground. Thus the band drifted off the musical map. A posthumous release, '94-97' (1999), brought together the band's one and only album, together with an unreleased live album, 'KENNY PROCESS TEAM IN CONCERT', keeping the legacy smouldering. • **Trivia:** 'MOUSE IN THE HOLE', was a brilliant track on Guided Missile V/A set 'Hits & Missiles'.

Album rating: SURFIN' WITH (*4) / 94-97 compilation (*4)

KEV PLUMMER – guitar / **MATT ARMSTRONG** – bass / **DAVE ROSS** – drums / added **SIMON DEEWOGAB** – 2nd guitar

		Hemiola	not iss.
Oct 95.	(lp) (HEM 009) **SURFIN' WITH**		-
	– Team international / Driving test / Romans / Surf logic / Romance today / Farewell my darling / Magic wife / Open sesame / Sweet heart / Cats and dogs / Out of town / Old folks / Hooray for Gilligan / Surfin' / Grown man / Jugs McGinty / I'm in the team.		

		Guided Missile	not iss.
Aug 97.	(7") (GUIDE 21) **GIRLS. /**		-

—— split in 1997

– compilations, etc. –

Oct 99.	(cd) Bingo; <BIN 006> **94-97**	-	
	– (SURFIN' WITH tracks) / Bundle / The Windsors / Fantastic four / Armchair getting / Bionic eyes / Mystery lights / The song we don't like / I.D.K. / Fingernails / Tug / Tantrums / Ta-wit to-woo / Girls.		

KEPONE

Formed: Richmond, Virginia, USA ... early 90's by the imposingly bearded MICHAEL BISHOP, along with TIM HARRISS and SETH HARRIS, taking the group name from a dangerous chemical manufactured by a local firm (previously detailed by musical mentor JELLO BIAFRA on The DEAD KENNEDYS' 'Kepone Factory'). Signed to noted US indie label, 'Quarter Stick', the band premiered their blend of idiosyncratic yet powerful mutant punk-blues on the debut album, 'UGLY DANCE' (1994). Like a downhome JESUS LIZARD, they flavoured their music and especially their lyrics with a Deep South small-town weirdness. Now without SETH – who was replaced by EDWARD JEFFERSON TRASK – KEPONE issued a second set, 'SKIN' (1995), which was followed by 1997's acclaimed eponymous album.

Album rating: UGLY DANCE (*6) / SKIN (*6) / KEPONE (*7)

MICHAEL BISHOP – vocals, bass / **TIM HARRISS** – guitar, vocals / **SETH HARRIS** – drums

		Tenderizer	Tenderizer
Jun 93.	(7") <(TZR 002)> **HENRY. / PRISONERS**		May93
		not iss.	Alternative Tentacles
Dec 93.	(7") <VIRUS 144> **295. / PHOBIC**	-	
		Quarter Stick	Quarter Stick
Aug 94.	(lp/cd) <(QS 27/+CD)> **UGLY DANCE**		
	– Loud / Dickie boys / Leadbreath / Brainflower / Some pig / Henry / Shit talk / Fly bop / Wrong / Eenie meenie / Sick river / Silly Sally / Ugly dance.		

—— **EDWARD JEFFERSON TRASK** – drums; repl. SETH

Sep 95.	(lp/cd) <(QS 33/+CD)> **SKIN**		Aug95
	– Knifethrower / Velveteen / Blue-devil / Stay down / Ed's sad party / Idiot ball drop / Superfucker / Prisoners / Left Eskimo / Thin solution.		
Oct 96.	(7") <(QS 45)> **THE GHOST. / Pegboy: DANGERMARE**		
Apr 97.	(cd) <(QS 46CD)> **KEPONE**		Mar97
	– Bring it down / Joe / Pointless / Ghost / Liner hymn / Thaw / Clicking jam / Leave your bones / I am an alien / Slow build / Jimmy Spit / Scrub / Virginia creeper / Dead pop ideal.		

—— disbanded after above

KHAYA

Formed: Edinburgh, Scotland ... 1996 by DAN MUTCH, GREG DODGSON, JOHN MACKIE and RICHIE ANDERSON. An early spot on local radio led to the quartet contributing a handful of tracks to 'S.L.' compilation album, 'It's A Life Sentence ...' in 1997, the same year they released a debut single proper, 'SUMMER/WINTER SONG'. With an enthusiastic response from the likes of Steve Lamacq, John Peel and Jo Whiley, the band were spurred on to bigger and better things. These included a follow-up single, 'TWO SONGS BY KHAYA', a performance at the Edinburgh Fringe's 'Planet Pop' festival and the recruitment of a mini string section (violinist CAROLINE EVANS and cellist PETE HARVEY). The fruits of their labour paid off with 1998's debut album, 'WE'VE GOT RHYMES 4 X LIKE THESE', a record that generated enough interest for a live performance on Radio Scotland and much airplay on Radio One's Evening Session. A subsequent Peel session was followed by abortive sessions for a second album, the band eventually knuckling down at Chamber Studios in Granton where they recorded 'AVOIDANCE' (1999). Again the record brought widespread critical acclaim with reviewers mentioning the likes of BELLE & SEBASTIAN and PAVEMENT. ARAB STRAP meets STEPS may be just a bridge too far in an attempt to describe their hook-laden sound but successive rounds of sold out gigs are testament to KHAYA's appeal. A new mini-set, 'THE LOST FEELING', was released early in 2001.

Album rating: WE'VE GOT RHYMES 4 X LIKE THESE (*6) / AVOIDANCE (*6) / THE LOST FEELING mini (*6) / Desc: UP HERE IN THE HEAT (*7)

DAN MUTCH – vocals, guitar / **GREG DODGSON** – keyboards / **JOHN MACKIE** – bass / **RICHIE ANDERSON** – drums

		sl	not iss.
May 97.	(cd; Various Artists) (lone 01) **It's A Life Sentence ...**		-
	– Here / It couldn't be worse / Snow song / (tracks.. other artists).		
Nov 97.	(7") (lone 02) **SUMMER/WINTER SONG. / I GET UPSET AT ALL THE RIGHT THINGS / M-MENU**		-
Apr 98.	(7") (lone 04) **TWO SONGS BY KHAYA**		-
	– Duet / Boy, girl dependence.		

—— added **CAROLINE EVANS** – violin / **PETE HARVEY** – cello

		Koala Music	not iss.
Nov 98.	(cd) (KMCD 003) **WE'VE GOT RHYMES 4 X LIKE THESE**		-
	– M-menu / Love and whips / Sing-a-song / Wives and lovers / We've got rhymes / Fever / Edward and Merlin / Baby, don't bother / Sportsday / Ground.		

Mar 99. (10"blue-ep) *(KMVS 005)* **LOVE AND WHIPS EP** (acoustic)
– Swap boots / It's worth trying / DAN MUTCH – Swap boots.

—— now with **RUAIRIDH** – guitar (on tour)

Nov 99. (cd) *(lone 05)* **AVOIDANCE**
– Rag / Do the thing / Avoidance / Take off / This is the most sad song / Western theme tune / Wild friends / Husbands / Music is 4 pussies Morning sounds / Baby, you terrify me.

Mar 00. (7"ep) *(lone 07)* **DO THE THING BY KHAYA**
– Do the thing / Dan and Greg / John and Richie.

Feb 01. (m-cd) *(lone 09)* **THE LOST FEELING**
– The vampires / I hate fucking / Death 2 numbers / More argument / The lost feeling / Acoustic guitar.

DESC

DAN MUTCH + HELENA MacGILP

Apr 02. (cd) *(lone 12)* **UP HERE IN THE HEAT**
– I look after / Up here / City gallery / Untitled / Joy / Decision / Forgiveness.

KID SILVER (see under ⇒ ROLLERSKATE SKINNY)

KILLER TWEEKER BEES (see under ⇒ BLACK FLAG; 70's section)

KILLS (see under ⇒ DISCOUNT)

KINCAID.

Formed: Brooklyn, New York, USA ... mid 1990's by DAN GELLAR, RYAN LEWIS, GREG HARNELINK, PAT VALENTINE and SEAN RAWIS; the group released their debut album 'GOOD CITIZEN OF THE MONTH' through the LEWIS, GELLAR owned 'Kindercore' album, having already relocated to Athens, Georgia. It is always a worry when you hear an album is going to be released as a result of industry nepotism; however, after listening to KINCAID it was immediately apparent that this was a band of real quality. The album's opening track 'NOBODY'S BEEN HERE' was an exquisitely played, joyous pop song brimming with optimism which served as a template for the rest of the album. The constantly uplifting tone of the album never became tiresome as the intricate melodies ensured that theirs was something new to discover with each listen. The group released the relatively disappointing 'play SUPER HAWAII' in 1999 before disbanding. In 2001 GELLER returned alongside AMY DYKES in the unfortunately named group I AM THE WORLD TRADE CENTER. Although the group released their debut album 'OUT OF THE LOOP' two months before the September 11th terrorist attack on the twin towers, they still faced a considerable backlash for choosing to stick with the name afterwards. The release of their second album 'TIGHT CONNECTION' in 2002 provoked outrage amongst sections of the American public.

Album rating: GOOD CITIZEN OF THE MONTH (*7) / play SUPER HAWAII (*6) / I Am The World Trade Center: OUT OF THE LOOP (*6) / TIGHT CONNECTION (*5)

GREG HARMELINK – vocals, guitar, organ, horns / **DAN GELLER** – guitar, vocals, programming / **SEAN RAWLS** – keyboards, vocals, synthesizers, accordion, banjo / **PATRICK VALENTINE** – bass, vocals / **RYAN LEWIS** – drums, vocals, guitar

Kindercore Kindercore

Jan 97. (7") *<KC 001>* **COOL JETS BABY. / PORTALES**

—— with JOE CHRISTMAS, KINCAID collaborated on 'ELEANOR ROOSEVELT' for a 'Kindercore' (KC 005) 7" compilation

Aug 97. (cd) *<(KC 010)>* **GOOD CITIZENS OF THE MONTH**
– Nobody's been here / MMR / Me to be / Cool jets baby / Babyhood / Brown's Bridge road / Great America / Super elfin lipstick / Hwy 100 / Fox river sanctuary / Tuesday / Atl atl / Gloucester City, New Jersey / Storm king.

May 00. (cd) *<(KC 033)>* **play SUPER HAWAII**   Nov99
– Solid, Jackson / Super Hawaii / Parachute / California 2012 / Keskesay / Plot #36 / Bells will ring / Benjamin / Tyme machine / Holland day parade / Semi-circle / There's an ocean / How long has it been / Alaska.

—— the quintet split after above

I AM THE WORLD TRADE CENTER

DAN GELLER – instruments / **AMY DYKES** – vocals

Kindercore Kindercore

Jul 00. (m-lp) *(KC 042LP)* **HOLLAND TUNNEL**
Sep 00. (m-lp) *(KC 047LP)* **AURORA BOREALIS**

Track & Field   Kindercore

Jan 02. (7") *(LANE 08)* **LOOK AROUND YOU. / SHOOT YOU DOWN**

Mar 02. (cd) *(HEAT 05) <KC 038>* **OUT OF THE LOOP**   May01
– Metro (Brooklyn mix) / Me to be / Sounds so crazy / Look around you / Light delay / Inside your head / Holland tunnel / Flute loops / Auroa Borealis / You don't even know her / September / Move on / Analogous / Metro (Athens mix).

—— in Mar'02, the duo split a 7"single, 'LOVELESS SUNDAY', with PHOFO

Kindercore Kindercore

Aug 02. (cd) *<(KC 075)>* **TIGHT CONNECTION**   Jul02
– The postcard / Big star / Believe in me / Shoot you down / Pretty baby / Hold on to my lines / Call me / Can't take the heat / California dreaming again / Dancing alone / Soiree.

KING ADORA

Formed: Birmingham, England ... 1998 by MATT BROWNE and MARTYN NELSON; after placing an ad ROBERT GRIMMIT and DAN DABROWSKI were soon drafted in. Taking their cue from glam sleazoids The NEW YORK DOLLS, PUSSY GALORE and er, SUEDE, KING ADORA set out their musical stall by playing to enthusiastic crowds in and around their Midlands base. 'Superior Quality' records subsequently took them on board, issuing their debut 45, 'BIONIC' in the spring of 2000. A year later on its reappearance, it would scrape into the UK Top 30, their highest position so far as previous singles 'SUFFOCATE', 'SMOULDER' and 'BIG ISN'T BEAUTIFUL' had all hovered around the Top 75. KING ADORA's inaugural album release, 'VIBRATE YOU', also managed a place in the Top 30 to coincide with 'BIONIC's re-emergence. Mascara and rock were once again in vogue.

Album rating: VIBRATE YOU (*6)

MATT BROWNE – vocals / **MARTYN NELSON** – guitar / **ROBERT GRIMMIT** – bass / **DAN DABROWSKI** – drums

Superior Quality   not iss.

May 00. (7"/cd-s) *(RQS 007/+CD)* **BIONIC. / THE LAW**
Jul 00. (7") *(RQS 008)* **BIG ISN'T BEAUTIFUL. / SCREAM AND SHOUT**
(cd-s+=) *(RQS 008CD)* – Comfortable.

Oct 00. (cd-s) *(RQS 009)* **SMOULDER / EGO / LOVED**   62
Feb 01. (7") *(RQS 011)* **SUFFOCATE. / ACE FACE**   39
(cd-s+=) *(RQS 011CD)* – Smoulder (video).
(cd-s) *(RQS 011DD)* – ('A'side) / Into space / Drink don't think / ('A'-video).

May 01. (7") *(RQS 012)* **BIONIC. / DON'T TRUST THE ONES YOU LOVE**   30
(cd-s+=) *(RQS 012CD)* – Big isn't beautiful (absolute zero remix).
(cd-s) *(RQS 012DD)* – ('A'side) / Freak / ('A'-CD-ROM).

May 01. (cd/lp) *(RQS 013 CD/LP)* **VIBRATE YOU**   30
– Smoulder / Bionic / Big isn't beautiful / Friday night explodes / Aftertime / The law / Whether / We are heroes / SuperMuffDiver / Asthmatic / Music takes you / Suffocate. (cd+=) – Scream and shout / Aceface / Exclusive film footage:- Smoulder / Bionic / Suffocate / Big isn't beautiful.

Jul 01. (12"/cd-s; w-drawn) *(RQS 014/+CD)* **FRIDAY NIGHT EXPLODES**

KING BISCUIT TIME (see under ⇒ BETA BAND)

KING KONG

Formed: Louisville, Kentucky, USA ... 1989 by ex-SLINT and Kentucky's underground regular, ETHAN BUCKLER, who recruited AMY GREENWOOD, WILLIE MacLEAN and percussionist RAY RIZZO. After recording SLINT's Albini-produced debut 'Tweez' in 1989, BUCKLER moved onto side-project KING KONG, issuing 7" singles on imprints 'Trash Flow' and 'Homestead' respectively. 'OLD MAN ON THE BRIDGE' was released to minor acclaim in 1991, while its uptempo dance/rhythm lo-fi bass-driven beats proved to be a hit with the too-cool-for-college crowd, prompting the ensemble to tour US universities. BUCKLER and Co moved to Chicago's 'Drag City' label and issued the 'conceptual' 'FUNNY FARM' LP, which saw the group make a concentrated effort to include storyline and narrative in their work. With BUCKLER's dead-pan sung/spoken vocals and KING KONG's backing section playing some seriously funky dance-rock, the band were invited to perform on Lollapalooza's second stage, and got a mention in the trendy music style-mag, 'Spin'. KING KONG continued with the very ape sounding 'ME HUNGRY' (1995), a stomper of a record that would enlighten even the most crazed dance fan. 'KINGDOM OF KONG' (1997) followed, and after a strenuous tour of Europe, the group indefinitely disengaged and BUCKLER took on a full-time job washing dishes in a restaurant (BRIAN McMAHON, also of SLINT and The FOR CARNATION was also working in a grocery shop at this point). However, SLINT casualty and fellow Louisville comrade, DAVID PAJO coaxed BUCKLER out of retirement in 2000, and KING KONG re-formed to play Headliner's Music Hall in 2001 with PAJO's PAPA M outfit. One year later and the quakes were resounding in the American indie world; the KING was back – namely in the form of the partly NEIL HAGERTY-produced 'THE BIG BANG' (2002).

Album rating: OLD MAN ON THE BRIDGE (*4) / FUNNY FARM (*6) / ME HUNGRY (*5) / KINGDOM OF KONG (*5) / BREEDING GROUND collection (*4) / THE BIG BANG (*4)

ETHAN BUCKLER – vocals, guitar (ex-SLINT) / **AMY GREENWOOD** – vocals / **WILLIE MacLEAN** – bass / **RAY RIZZO** – drums

not iss.   King Kong

1989. (7"m) *<none>* **MOVIE STAR. / THE CAMEL SONG / CHICKEN SHIT**
<re-iss. Jun95 on 'Drag City'; DC 72>

not iss.   Trash Flow

1990. (7") *<04>* **BRING IT ON. /**

not iss.   Homestead

Nov 91. (lp/c/cd) *<HMS 167/+C/CD>* **OLD MAN ON THE BRIDGE**
– Mama mama / The man / Business man / Lifesaver blues / Rolling O / Foolish turkey / Big rock friend / Old man on the bridge / I'm free.

Drag City   Drag City

Aug 93. (lp/cd) *<DC 33/+CD>* **FUNNY FARM**
– Funny farm / Dirty city rainy day / Scooba dooba diver / Uh-oh / Here I am / Bad cat blues / Tornado song / King Kong / White horse / Island paradise. (UK cd-iss. Dec96; same as US)

KING KONG (cont)

Aug 94. (7") <DC 58> **HOT DOG DAYS. / RED HOT LOVIN'**
Oct 95. (lp/cd) <DC 67/+CD> **ME HUNGRY**
– Animal / To love a yak / Danger / Teardrop / Beastie bear / Ten long years / White stuff / Me hungry / The crow. (UK cd-iss. Dec96; same as US)
Oct 97. (lp/cd) <DC 122/+CD> **KINGDOM OF KONG**
– Kingdom of Kong / Games / Floor, door, I don't wanna party anymore / Imposter monsters / Horny toad / Nature of the flow / Energy / Basketball / Mars / Funky monkey.
Apr 02. (cd) <DC 212CD> **THE BIG BANG**
– The big bang / What lies beyond? / Deep blue sea / Space travel / Black hole / Planet Kong on the radar screen / We are the people of Kong / Life.

– compilations, etc. –

Nov 01. (cd) *Sea Note*; <(SNCD 9)> **BLEEDING GROUND**
– Bleeding ground / Paint my face / Scooba dooba diver / Sumaki walker / Lolly pop / Party girl / Bad cat / Experiment / Horny toad w/Dalphine / Stripper / Stalker / Red stuff / Tear drop / Funny farm / Flying turkey / Meters / Dance of the ducks / Tornado / A day at the submarine race.

KING LOSER

Formed: Dunedin, Christchurch, New Zealand ... 1995 by CHRIS HEAZLEWOOD, a veteran of a host of antipodean post-rock bands including first real project, The SFERIC EXPERIMENT, in the late 80's. Alongside SEAN O'REILLY and CELIA "PAVLOVA" MANCINI who'd replaced original LESLEY PARIS, KING LOSER musically surfed their way through three above par albums, 'SONIC SUPER FREE HI-FI' (1994), 'YOU CANNOT KILL WHAT DOES NOT LIVE' (1996) and 'CAUL OF THE OUTLAW' (1997). Meanwhile, HEAZLEWOOD also found time to deliver several solo releases including 1997's 'CASH GUITAR'.

Album rating: SONIC SUPER FREE HI-FI (*6) / YOU CANNOT KILL WHAT DOES NOT LIVE (*6) / CAUL OF THE OUTLAW (*5) / Sferic Experiment: EIGHT MILES collection (*5) / Chris Heazlewood: CASH GUITAR (*5)

SFERIC EXPERIMENT

CHRIS HEAZLEWOOD – vocals, guitar **SEAN O'REILLY** – guitar / **GAVIN SHAW** – vocals, guitar / **GREG CAIRNS** – guitar

Xpresswway not iss.

1988. (c) (X/WAY 14) **BUNNY LIVER** – / – NewZ

—— after their split in 1989 GAVIN formed CHILDREN'S TELEVISION WORKSHOP; HEAZLEWOOD guested for DEAD C ...

1990. (c; as HEAZLEWOOD) (X/WAY 23) **HELLMOUTH** – / – NewZ

– compilations, etc. –

Mar 96. (cd) *Drunken Fish*; <DF 16> **EIGHT MILES** ('BUNNY LIVER' plus outtakes)
– A stranger aversion to blue / Psychofish / Gordon is sad / Too many people / Funeral march / Joff's song / The ghost / Punk / A shitty little ditty / The Devil comes to town / Grated violin – White rain / Lemmy from Motorhead is in our heads / Butthole Maria / Let all mortal flesh be silent / Vogalishness / Who does what? / Stoner jazz / High St. / Ancient / Dead person viola.

KING LOSER

—— added **LESLEY PARIS** – drums (ex-LOOK BLUE GO PURPLE)

Flying Nun not iss.

1992. (7"m; as OLLA) (FN 214) **SEPTIC HAGFISH / DITCH. / DON'T FALL TOO HARD / OLLA PUTRIDO** – / – NewZ

—— **CELIA 'PAVLOVA' MANCINI** – bass, organ, synthesiser / **PETER JEFFERIES** – drums (ex-THIS KIND OF EXPERIMENT); repl. LESLEY

1995. (7") (FN 283) **STAIRWAY TO HEAVEN. / EXIT THE KING** – / – NewZ

—— **TRIBAL THUNDER** (b. LANCE STRICKLAND) – drums; repl. JEFFERIES

1995. (cd) (FN 299) **SONIC SUPER FREE HI-FI** – / – NewZ
– Neurons / Shadow on my trail / Surf lost / Most avid sonic spectrum / Pretty pretty / Dick Dale / Never a thought / Surfarama / Vultura / Dawn / Spy 1 / Dead fish / Stairway to heaven / Exit the king. (orig.iss.1994 on 'Turbulence')

Feb 96. (lp/cd) (FN/+CD 309) **YOU CANNOT KILL WHAT DOES NOT LIVE** – / –
– Centre of things / '76 comeback / Morning dew / Shake yr wings / Stowing away / Song remains the same / Tribal Thunder theme / Jungle beat / You follow / Misirlou / Broken man / Flippin' the bird / Everything is forgotten / Ten rays.

1996. (7"; by SF) (FN 357) **SUPRASF EP** – / – NewZ
– Catwalk / Semi – Sleepy hollow.
(above SF is virtually SEAN's outfit with CHRIS)

1996. (7"; by CELIA MANCINI) (FN 360) **KIASU. / SUCKED IN ROCK AND ROLL CUNTS – BORN TO BE WILD** – / – NewZ

Apr 97. (cd) (FNCD 382) **CAUL OF THE OUTLAW** – / –
– Troubled land / 1692 / Band on the run / Cyclonic vibration / Situation / Alien presence / New age power / Solid sky nine / Lazenby's folly / Shadow / Change the locks / Four from the dark side.

1997. (7") (FN 394) **TROUBLED LAND. / POW WOW** – / – NewZ
(cd-s+=) (FNCD 394) – Vamp kamp / Down from doves.

—— disbanded in 1997

CHRIS HEAZLEWOOD

Flying Nun not iss.

1993. (7"m; as HEAZLEWOOD) (FN 222) **SURF'S UP IN MALIBU. / NO FEAR OF FALLING / SKRONK** – / – NewZ

1995. (7"; as HEAZLEWOOD) (FN 354) **BADGE OR MEDALLION. / SPEED / AERO** – / – NewZ
1997. (cd) (FNCD 398) **CASH GUITAR** – / – NewZ
– Surf's up in Malibu / Backwards trip / Badge or medallion / Euro disco / Move it / How many times / Dawn / 1969 ok / Running fast / Aero / Bad girls / Stowing away / Filthy little world / Throb / Set the limit / John apology / The thunder theme / International smoker / Everything is forgotten.

Turbulence not iss.

1990's. (7"; as HEAZLEWOOD) (004) **THEY SLAUGHTER SMALL CHILDREN. / MY FRIEND TOLD ME / FILTHY LITTLE WORLD** – / – Belgium

not iss. Crawlspace

1990's. (7"ep; as HEAZLEWOOD) <003> **INTRODUCING THE RON ASHETON CLUB** – / –

KINGMAKER

Formed: Hull, England ... late 1990 by ex-TOMBSTONE GRAFFITI members, LOZ HARDY (the main songwriter) and MILES HOWELL. Subsequently recruiting JOHN ANDREW, the band made their vinyl debut with the 'CELEBRATED WORKING MAN' EP, released on their own 'Sacred Heart' label. Impressive enough to get the band signed to 'Chrysalis'-offshoot, 'Scorch', the record was followed by a 7", 'WHEN LUCY'S DOWN' and another EP, 'TWO HEADED, YELLOW BELLIED HOLE DIGGER', prior to a debut album, 'EAT YOURSELF WHOLE' (1991). While the band initially found favour with the press, KINGMAKER subsequently became an easy target for critical hatchet-jobs on the premise that they represented all that was ordinary about indie-pop. Not that the band suffered too much as a result, their natural constituency of WONDER STUFF/CARTER USM-type fans not likely to pay too much attention to journalistic snobbery. Early '92 saw KINGMAKER bag their first Top 40 hit while the debut's title track made the Top 20 six months later, follow-up album, 'SLEEPWALKING' (1993) finding HARDY's lyrical invective as succinct and razor sharp as it had ever been. A further two minor hits followed in 'QUEEN JANE' and 'SATURDAY'S NOT WHAT IT USED TO BE' but KINGMAKER's star eventually faded with the onset of Brit-pop in the mid-90's. While Spring '95's 'YOU AND I WILL NEVER SEE THINGS EYE TO EYE' scraped a Top 40 placing, the accompanying album, 'IN THE BEST POSSIBLE TASTE', sank like a stone and KINGMAKER finally called it a day later that year. • **Covered:** LADY MADONNA (Beatles).

Album rating: EAT YOURSELF WHOLE (*7) / SLEEPWALKING (*6) / TO HELL WITH HUMDRUM mini part compilation (*5) / IN THE BEST POSSIBLE TASTE (*5) / BLOODSHOT & FANCY FREE compilation (*6)

LOZ HARDY (b.LAWRENCE, 14 Sep'70) – vocals, guitar / **MILES HOWELL** (b.23 Jan'71, Rugby, England) – bass (ex-RAIN) / **JOHN ANDREW** (b.27 May'63, Hull, England) – drums

Sacred Heart not iss.

Jan 91. (12"ep) (NONE 1) **THE CELEBRATED WORKING MAN / LITTLE MISS KINGMAKER. / FREEWHEELIN' / POCKETS OF ST.MALACHI**
(re-iss. Feb92; same)

Scorch – Chrysalis Chrysalis

Apr 91. (c-s/7") (TC+/SCORCH 1) **WHEN LUCY'S DOWN. / WHERE YOU STAND**
(12"+=/cd-s+=) (12/CD SCORCH 1) – High as a kite / Join the human race.

Aug 91. (12"ep/cd-ep) (12/CD SCORCH 2) **TWO HEADED, YELLOW BELLIED HOLE DIGGER. / THIS TIME THIS TOWN THIS SEA. / WONDERFUL GARDEN / POCKETS OF ST. MALACHI (live)**

Sep 91. (cd/c/lp) (<CCD/ZCHR/CHR 1878>) **EAT YOURSELF WHOLE** 69
– Revelation / Really scrape the sky / Two headed, yellow bellied hole digger / Hard times / Loveless-defamed / When Lucy's down / Wave / Lady Shakespeare's bomb / Everything in life / High as a kite. (re-dist.Feb92) – hit No.29

Jan 92. (7"ep) (SCORCH 3) **IDIOTS AT THE WHEEL EP** 30
– Really scrape the sky / Every teenage suicide / Strip away.
(12"ep+=/cd-ep+=) (12/CD SCORCH 3) – Revelation (Bombay mix).

Mar 92. (12"ep/cd-ep; w-drawn) (12/CD SCORCH 4) **KILLJOY WAS HERE EP**
– Eat yourself whole / Highway's gate / Pyjama girl.

May 92. (c-s/7") (TC+/SCORCH 5) **EAT YOURSELF WHOLE. / PYJAMA GIRL** 15
(12"+=/cd-s+=) (12/CD SCORCH 5) – Highway's gate.

Oct 92. (12"ep/cd-ep/7"ep) (12/CD+/SCORCH 6) **ARMCHAIR ANARCHIST / EVERYTHING'S CHANGED (SINCE YOU'VE BEEN TO LONDON). / KISSING UNDER ANAESTHETIC** 47

Apr 93. (c-ep/7"ep) (TC+/SCORCH 8) **10 YEARS ASLEEP. / BROADMOOR HOTEL / DON'T COME OVER / I'M IN LOVE** 15
(cd-ep) (CDSCORCH 8) – ('A'side) / Genuine liar / Lady Madonna / When Lucy's down (live).
(cd-ep) (CDSCORCHS 8) – ('A'side) / Shiver / High as a kite (live) / Hard times (live).

May 93. (cd/c/lp) (<CD/TC+/CHR 6014>) **SLEEPWALKING** 15
– Playground reality / Armchair anarchist / Queen Jane / Sad to see you go / Help yourself / Tomorrow's world / 10 years asleep / Honesty kills / Sequinned thug / Sleepwalking in the five o'clock shadow / Stay free / Pyromaniacs anonymous.

Jun 93. (7"/7"s) (SCORCH/+P 9) **QUEEN JANE. / SICK AND ANGRY CHILDREN** 29
(12"+=) (12SCORCH 9) – Flesh phobia / Sequinned thug ('92 version).
(cd-s) (CDSCORS 9) – ('A'side) / Your place / Electric Sue.
(cd-s) (CDSCORCH 9) – ('A'side) / No way out / Sequinned thug ('92 version).

KINGMAKER (cont)

Oct 93. (cd-ep) (CDSCORCH 10) **SATURDAY'S NOT WHAT IT USED TO BE / ARMCHAIR ANARCHIST (live) / HIGHWAY'S GATE (live) / FREEWHEELIN' (live)** [63] [-]
(10") (10SCORCH 10) – (1st track) / Eat yourself whole (live) / Everything's changed (since you've . . .) (live) / Every teenage suicide (live).

Nov 93. (m-cd/m-c/m-lp) (CD/TC+/CHR 6055) **TO HELL WITH HUMDRUM** (part compilation) [ ] [-]
– Saturday's not what it used to be / Never too high to fall / Lies before kisses / Loose lips sink ships / Ten years asleep / Honesty kills / Sleepwalking (in the five o'clock shadow) / Queen Jane.

Apr 95. (c-s) (TCSCORCH 11) **YOU AND I WILL NEVER SEE THINGS EYE TO EYE / BITCH OF A SON / YOU OF ALL PEOPLE** [33] [-]
(cd-s) (CDSCORCHS 11) – ('A'side) / When Lucy's down / Queen Jane / Saturday's not what it used to be.
(cd-s) (CDSCORCHS 11) – ('A'side) / Friends in low places / S*T*A*R / Warm heart, cold feet.

Apr 95. (cd/c/lp) (<CD/TC+/CHR 6098>) **IN THE BEST POSSIBLE TASTE** [ ] [-]
– In the best possible taste (part 2) / You and I will never see things eye to eye / Hey, birdman / Frustrated gangster / Story of my life / Sometimes I think she takes me along just for the ride / One false move / Side by side / A fool like you / End of the line / In the best possible taste (part 1).

May 95. (7"pink) (SCORCHS 12) **IN THE BEST POSSIBLE TASTE (part 2). / AMATEUR'S LULLABY / IF YOU WERE MINE** [41] [-]
(cd-s) (CDSCORCH 12) – ('A'side) / Two headed yellow bellied hole digger / Sad to see you go / Never too high to fall.
(cd-s) (CDSCORCH 12) – ('A'side) / Backroom boys / Another bad dose of home truths / Dissatisfaction guaranteed.

—— split October 1995

– compilations, etc. –

Sep 98. (cd) *EMI Gold;* (CDCHRM 104) **BLOODSHOT & FANCY FREE (THE BEST OF & THE REST OF KINGMAKER)** [ ] [-]
– 10 years asleep / Armchair anarchist / Really scrape the sky / You and I will never see things eye to eye / Hard times / Two headed yellow bellied hole digger / Freewheeling / Everything's changed (since you've been to London) / Queen Jane / When Lucy's down / In the best possible taste / High as a kite / Frustrated gangster / Honesty kills / Don't come over.

KINGSBURY MANX

Formed: Chapel Hill, North Carolina, USA . . . 1998 by KEN STEPHENSON, BILL TAYLOR, RYAN RICHARDSON and SCOTT MYERS. This extremely intimate group, who came from a long line of delicate US indie musos (YO LA TENGO, The BYRDS, RADAR BROS., JIM O'ROURKE), tip-toed onto the indie scene in 1999, before the Garage rock revival had exploded and magazines didn't make you feel guilty about listening to slo-core. The group, who all met at school, drifted away during college, and reformed only to be approached by ex-'Thrill Jockey' A&R man Howard Greynolds, who asked to put their debut album out on his freshly established 'Overcoat' imprint. The result was the eponymous 'KINGSBURY MANX' LP (2000), which was released to glowing reviews and was hailed as one of the finest debuts of the new millennium. The quietly realized set breezed through songs like DONOVAN on an air glider; beautiful harmonies, twinkling pianos and floaty guitars all made the mould. It didn't take the group long to follow this mysterious debut with the psychedelic 'LET YOU DOWN' (2001), which was akin to The RADAR BROS 'Singing Hatchet', in terms of melody and structure. Emotionally more realized than the debut album, once songs like 'PORCHLIGHT', 'BABY YOU'RE A DEAD MAN' and the sublime ballad 'SLEEPING ON THE GROUND' had wormed their way into your brain, there was no turning back.

Album rating: THE KINGSBURY MANX (*7) / LET YOU DOWN (*8)

KEN STEPHENSON – guitar, vocals / **BILL TAYLOR** – guitar, vocals / **SCOTT MYERS** – bass, keyboards / **RYAN RICHARDSON** – drums, vocals

Overcoat Overcoat

Jan 00. (lp/cd) <(OC 04/+CD)> **THE KINGSBURY MANX** [ ] [ ]
– Pageant square / Regular hands / Piss diary / Cross your eyes / Blue Eurasians / Hawaii in ten seconds / How cruel / Fields / New old friend blues / Whether or not it matters / Fanfare / Silver trees. *(cd re-iss. Sep00 on 'City Slang'; 20169-2)*

City Slang Overcoat

Sep 01. (cd/lp) (20185-2/-1) <OC 9CD> **LET YOU DOWN** [ ] [ ]
– Let you down / Porchlight / Simplify / Et tu, kitte? / Rustic stairs / Sleeping on the ground / Patterns shape the mile / Courtyard waltz / Arun / The new evil / Baby you're a dead man / Do what you're told.

KINGS OF CONVENIENCE

Formed: Bergen, Norway . . . 1999 by English speaking EIRIK GLAMBEK BOE and trivial pursuit genius ERLEND OYE, their first major appearances being at several European Festival dates with sideline project The PEACHFUZZ. If a band were ever to be awarded 'Best Mellow Group', the prestigious gong would most certainly go to KINGS OF CONVENIENCE, with their late summer strummings and a prolific collection of tea-sipping songs. Imagine the kind of album BELLE & SEBASTIAN would make if they were shipped off to a health spa for the weekend courtesy of whispering Bob Harris, and you'd be close. According to their 'life story', the duo weren't always a tightly-knit collective from the fjord terrain of central Norway. After some jamming sessions (including the use of plastic flutes for instruments), SKOG, which was their original moniker, became distant and unfocused, with various members pursuing mundane jobs and enrolling in banal college courses. It wasn't until late '99 that BOE and OYE finally reformed, piecing together some old material that seemed to be forever lost in a quiet kingdom. The pair moved to Greenstead, just outside of London, and began work on what was to become their debut album. 'KINGS OF CONVENIENCE' (2000) appeared on the US-based 'Kindercore' imprint, and provided music hacks with the slogan to describe the current trend of NAM – New Acoustic Music. If "quiet was the new loud", then KINGS OF CONVENIENCE were, er . . . the kings! With a slight change in tracking order, the debut set was virtually re-issued as, wait for it, 'QUIET IS THE NEW LOUD', early in 2001. From opener, and debut British single 'TOXIC GIRL', to the beautiful simplicity of 'WEIGHT OF MY WORDS', it was not difficult to tell that the duo were strictly bedsit. Like ERIC MATTHEWS or NICK DRAKE, their acoustic love songs sounded exquisite when graced with a piano or trumpet; however the real magic lay in the uptempo guitar strumming and OYE's gentle voice. Some of the set was coffee'n'chat/background music, only to be played on possibly a Sunday morning in the vain hope of recovering from a hangover – most of it was pure soothing bliss that surprisingly deserved to top the Norwegian charts. Best mellow band ever? Well, I think we know who the award goes to . . .

Album rating: KINGS OF CONVENIENCE (*7) / QUIET IS THE NEW LOUD (*8) / VERSUS (*5)

EIRIK GLAMBEK BOE – vocals, guitars (also drums, piano) / **ERLEND OYE** – guitars, harmony vocals (also drums, percussion)

Ellet not iss.

1999. (cd-ep) **TOXIC GIRL / LEANING AGAINST THE WALL / DAYS I HAD WITH YOU / INSTRUMENTAL** [-] [-] Norway

2000. (cd-ep) **FAILURE / I DON'T KNOW WHAT I CAN SAVE YOU FROM / SURPRICE ICE** [-] [-] Norway

Kindercore Kindercore

Jun 00. (cd) (KC 046) **KINGS OF CONVENIENCE** [ ] [ ]
– Toxic girl / I don't know what I can save you from / Leaning against the wall / Brave new world / An English rose / Days I had with you / Parallel lines / Winning a battle, losing the war / Surprise me. *(re-iss. Mar01; same)*

Source not iss.

Oct 00. (d7"ep/cd-ep) (SOUR V/CDS 011) **PLAYING LIVE IN A ROOM EP** [ ] [-]
– Toxic girl / Singing softly to me / Into the ring of fire / Parr-a-pluie / Until you understand.

Jan 01. (cd/lp) (SOUR CD/LP 019) **QUIET IS THE NEW LOUD** [72] [-]
– Winning a battle, losing the war / Toxic girl / Singing softly to me / I don't know what I can save you from / Failure / The weight of my words / The girl from back then / Leaning against the wall / Little kids / Summer on the westhill / The passenger / Parallel lines.

Feb 01. (7") (SOURV 018) **WINNING A BATTLE LOSING THE WAR. / (Andy Votel remix)** [ ] [-]
(cd-s) (SOURCDS 018) – ('A'side) / Manhattan skyline / Enjoy.

Apr 01. (7") (SOURV 025) **TOXIC GIRL. / ONCE AROUND THE BLOCK** [44] [-]
(cd-s+=) (SOURCDS 025) – ('A'-Monte Carlo 1963 version) / Little kids (live) / ('A'-video).
(cd-s) (SOURCDSE 025) – ('A'side) / Gold for the price of silver / Winning a battle losing the war (J. Walk remix).

Jun 01. (12") (SOURT 037) **I DON'T KNOW WHAT I CAN SAVE YOU FROM (Royksopp remix). / (Royksopp instrumental)** [ ] [-]

Jul 01. (7") (SOURV 036) **FAILURE. / (Alfie version)** [63] [-]
(cd-s+=) (SOURCD 036) – I don't know what I can save you from (Royksopp remix) / ('A'-video).
(cd-s) (SOURCDX 036) – ('A'side) / Eternal / Free fallin'.

Oct 01. (cd/lp) (SOUR CD/LP 040) **VERSUS** (remixes) [ ] [-]

Oct 01. (12"ep) (SOURT 044) **WEIGHT OF MY WORDS (Four Tet remixes) / LITTLE KIDS (Ladytron fruits of the forest mix) / GIRL FROM BACK THEN (Riton remix)** [ ] [-]

KING SOUND QUARTET (see under ⇒ DIRTBOMBS)

KINKS

Formed: Muswell Hill, London, England . . . 1963 by brothers RAY and DAVE DAVIES, who recruited PETER QUAIFE from The RAVENS. With help from managers Robert Wace and Grenville Collins, they met Larry Page who gave them the name KINKS late '63. He also arranged demos, which were soon heard by American SHEL TALMY, securing them a deal with 'Pye' early '64. Two singles flopped, but the third, 'YOU REALLY GOT ME', stormed the top spot in the UK, soon breaking into US Top 10. With its scuzzy, propulsive guitar riff, the song is oft cited as one of the first real "heavy rock" records, although it's debatable whether RAY DAVIES would admit to inspiring a multitude of poodle-maned Van Halen soundalikes. A top selling eponymous lp followed, as did a series of Top 10 sixties singles, including two more UK No.1's, 'TIRED OF WAITING FOR YOU' and 'SUNNY AFTERNOON'. As RAY's songwriting developed, the band moved to a quieter, more reflective sound, his camp, semi-detached vocals complementing the wry observations and quintessential Englishness of the lyrical themes. Come 1967, when every band worth their weight in spiked sugarcubes were looking towards the 'East', Davies looked no further than his proverbial back garden. 'SOMETHING ELSE', with its heartfelt eulogies to a mythical England past, still stands as the Kinks' greatest moment, the aching melancholy of 'WATERLOO SUNSET' its crowning glory. Davies' nostalgic bent continued on 1968's 'THE KINKS ARE THE VILLAGE GREEN PRESERVATION SOCIETY', an enchanting concept album that reached ever further into a faded history of rural simplicity.

KINKS (cont) — THE GREAT INDIE DISCOGRAPHY — The 1990s

It also included the KINKS' sole dalliance with psychedelia, 'WICKED ANNABELLA', a Brothers Grimm-like fairytale come nightmare fantasy. DAVIES' lyrical obsessions were given centre stage once more on 'ARTHUR (OR THE DECLINE OF THE ROMAN EMPIRE)' (1969) wherein the rosy hue of the past was contrasted with the grey decline of modern day Britain.

Album rating: THE KINKS – YOU REALLY GOT ME (*6) / KINDA KINKS (*5) / KINKS-SIZE (*6) / THE KINK KONTROVERSY (*5) / KINKS KINKDOM (*5) / THE KINKS GREATEST HITS! compilation (*8) / FACE TO FACE (*8) / LIVE AT KELVIN HALL (*5) / SOMETHING ELSE BY THE KINKS (*7) / VILLAGE GREEN PRESERVATION SOCIETY (*8) / ARTHUR (OR THE DECLINE AND FALL OF THE BRITISH EMPIRE) (*8)

RAY DAVIES (b.21 Jun'44) – vocals, guitar / **DAVE DAVIES** (b. 3 Feb'47) – guitar, vocals / **PETER QUAIFE** (b.31 Dec'43, Tavistock, Devon) – bass with session drummers

			Pye	Cameo
Mar 64.	(7") *(7N 15611) <308>* **LONG TALL SALLY. / I TOOK MY BABY HOME** <US re-iss. Nov64; 345>		-	Apr64

			Pye	Reprise
May 64.	(7") *(7N 15636)* **YOU STILL WANT ME. / YOU DO SOMETHING TO ME**		-	-
Aug 64.	(7") *(7N 15673) <0306>* **YOU REALLY GOT ME. / IT'S ALRIGHT**		1	7 Sep64

— **MICK AVORY** (b.15 Feb'44) – drums was now used although he joined 9 months previously

Oct 64.	(lp) *(NPL 18096) <6143>* **THE KINKS** <US-title 'YOU REALLY GOT ME'> – Beautiful Delilah / So mystifying / Just can't go to sleep / Long tall Shorty / You really got me / Cadillac / Bald headed woman / Revenge / Too much monkey business / Revenge / I've been driving on Bald mountain / Stop your sobbing / Got love if you want it. *(re-iss. Jan67 on 'Golden Guinea'; GGL 0357) (re-iss. May80 as 'YOU REALLY GOT ME'; NSPL 18615) (re-iss. Oct87 on 'P.R.T.' lp/c/cd; PYL/PYM/PYC 6002) (cd re-iss. Dec89 on 'Castle'; CLACD 155)*	3	29 Dec64
Oct 64.	(7") *(7N 15714) <0334>* **ALL DAY AND ALL OF THE NIGHT. / I GOTTA MOVE** *(re-iss. Oct84 on 'P.R.T.'; KIS 003) (re-iss. Jan88 on 'P.R.T.'; PYS 4)*	2	7 Dec64
Jan 65.	(7") *(7N 15759) <0347>* **TIRED OF WAITING FOR YOU. / COME ON NOW**	1	6 Mar65
Mar 65.	(lp) *<6158>* **KINKS-SIZE** – Tired of waiting for you / Louie Louie / I've got that feeling / Revenge / I gotta move / Things are getting better / I gotta go now / I'm a lover not a fighter / Come on now / All day and all of the night.	-	13
Mar 65.	(lp) *(NPL 18112) <6173>* **KINDA KINKS** – Look for me baby / Got my feet on the ground / Nothin' in the world can stop me worryin' 'bout that girl / Naggin' woman / Wonder where my baby is tonight / Tired of waiting for you / Dancing in the street / Don't ever change / Come on now / So long / You shouldn't be sad / Something better beginning. *(re-iss. Oct87 on 'P.R.T.' lp/c/cd; PYL/PYM/PYC 6003) (cd re-iss. Dec89 on 'Castle'; CLACD 156)*	3	60 Aug65
Mar 65.	(7") *(7N 15813) <0366>* **EVERYBODY'S GONNA BE HAPPY. / WHO'LL BE THE NEXT IN LINE** <above 45 flipped over in the States with B-side hitting No.34>	11	Apr65
May 65.	(7") *(7N 15854) <0379>* **SET ME FREE. / I NEED YOU**	9	23 Jun65
Jul 65.	(7") *(7N 15919) <0409>* **SEE MY FRIENDS. / NEVER MET A GIRL LIKE YOU BEFORE**	10	
Nov 65.	(7") *<0420>* **A WELL RESPECTED MAN. / MILK COW BLUES**	-	13
Nov 65.	(7") *(7N 15981) <0454>* **TILL THE END OF THE DAY. / WHERE HAVE ALL THE GOOD TIMES GONE**	6	50 Mar66
Nov 65.	(lp) *(NPL 18131) <6197>* **THE KINK KONTROVERSY** – Milk cow blues / Ring the bells / Gotta get the first plane home / When I see that girl of mine / Till the end of the day / The world keeps going round / I'm on the island / Where have all the good times gone / It's too late / What's in store for me / You can't win. *(re-iss. Oct87 on 'P.R.T.' lp/c/cd; PYL/PYM/PYC 6004) (cd re-iss. Dec89 on 'Castle'; CLACD 157)*	9	95 Apr66
Dec 65.	(lp) *<6184>* **KINKS KINKDOM** – Well respected man / Such a shame / Wait 'til the summer comes along / Naggin' woman / Who'll be the next in line / Don't you fret / I need you / It's all right / Louie Louie.	-	47
Feb 66.	(7") *(7N 17064) <0471>* **DEDICATED FOLLOWER OF FASHION. / SITTING ON MY SOFA**	4	36 May66

— **JOHN DALTON** – bass deputised on tour for QUAIFE while injured

Jun 66.	(7") *(7N 17125) <0497>* **SUNNY AFTERNOON. / I'M NOT LIKE EVERYBODY ELSE**		1	14 Aug66
Aug 66.	(lp) *<6217>* **THE KINKS GREATEST HITS** (compilation) – Dedicated follower of fashion / Tired of waiting for you / All day and all of the night / You really got me / Well respected man / Who'll be the next in line / Everybody's gonna be happy / Till the end of day / Set me free / Something better beginning.		-	9

— **JOHN DALTON** sessioned between 66-69, QUAIFE's photo on covers

Oct 66.	(lp; mono/stereo) *(NPL/NSPL 18145) <6228>* **FACE TO FACE** – Party line / Rosy won't you please come home / Dandy / Too much on my mind / Session man / Rainy day in June / House in the country / Sunny afternoon / Holiday in Waikiki / Most exclusive residence for sale / Fancy / Little Miss Queen of Darkness / You're looking fine / I'll remember. *(re-iss. Oct87 on 'P.R.T.' lp/c/cd; PYL/PYM/PYC 6005) (cd re-iss. Dec89 on 'Castle'; CLACD 158)*		12	Feb67
Nov 66.	(7") *(7N 17125) <0540>* **DEAD END STREET. / BIG BLACK SMOKE**		5	73 Jan67
May 67.	(7") *(7N 17321)* **WATERLOO SUNSET. / ACT NICE AND GENTLE**		2	-
May 67.	(lp; mono/stereo) *(NPL/NSPL 18191) <6260>* **LIVE AT KELVIN HALL** (live in Glasgow) <US-title 'THE LIVE KINKS'> – Till the end of the day / I'm on an island / You really got me / All day and all of the night / You're looking fine / Sunny afternoon / Dandy / Come on now / Milk cow blues – Batman theme – Tired of waiting for you. *(re-iss. Oct87 on 'P.R.T.' lp/c/cd; PYL/PYM/PYC 6007) (cd re-iss. Dec89 on 'Castle'; CLACD 160)*			Sep67
Jun 67.	(7") *<0587>* **MR. PLEASANT. / HARRY RAG**		-	80
Sep 67.	(7") *<0612>* **WATERLOO SUNSET. / TWO SISTERS**		-	
Oct 67.	(lp; mono/stereo) *(NPL/NSPL 18193) <6279>* **SOMETHING ELSE BY THE KINKS** – David Watts / Death of a clown / Two sisters / No return / Harry Rag / Tin soldier man / Situation vacant / Love me till the sun shines / Lazy old sun / Afternoon tea / Funny face / End of the season / Waterloo sunset. *(re-iss. Oct87 on 'P.R.T.' lp/c/cd; PYL/PYM/PYC 6006) (cd re-iss. Dec89 on 'Castle'; CLACD 159)*		35	Feb68
Oct 67.	(7") *(7N 17400) <0647>* **AUTUMN ALMANAC. / MR. PLEASANT**		3	
Apr 68.	(7") *(7N 17468) <0691>* **WONDERBOY. / POLLY**		37	
Jul 68.	(7") *(7N 17573) <0762>* **DAYS. / SHE'S GOT EVERYTHING**		12	
Jul 68.	(lp; mono/stereo) *(NPL/NSPL 18233) <6327>* **THE KINKS ARE THE VILLAGE GREEN PRESERVATION SOCIETY** – Village green preservation society / Do you remember Walter / Picture book / Johnny Thunder / The last of the steam powered trains / Big sky / Sitting by the riverside / Animal farm / Village green / Starstruck / Phenomenal cat / All my friends were there / Wicked Annabella / Monica / People take pictures of each other. *(re-iss. Nov85 on 'Flashback-PRT'; FBLP 8091) (re-iss. Oct87 on 'P.R.T.' lp/c/cd; PYL/PYM/PYC 6008) (cd re-iss. Dec89 on 'Castle'; CLACD 161) (cd re-iss. Feb97 on 'Original Recordings'; ORRLP 005)*			
Apr 69.	(7") *(7N 17724) <0743>* **PLASTIC MAN. / KING KONG**		31	
Apr 69.	(7") *<0806>* **STARSTRUCK. / PICTURE BOOK**		-	

— **JOHN DALTON** (b.21 May'43) – bass officially repl. QUAIFE

Jun 69.	(7") *<0847>* **WALTER. / VILLAGE GREEN PRESERVATION SOCIETY**		-	
Jun 69.	(7"; b-side by KINKS featuring DAVE DAVIES) *<7N 17776>* **DRIVIN'. / MINDLESS CHILD OF MOTHERHOOD**		-	
Sep 69.	(7") *(7N 17812)* **SHANGRI-LA. / THIS MAN HE WEEPS TONIGHT** (above initially had 'LAST OF THE STEAM-POWERED TRAINS' on B-side)		-	
Oct 69.	(lp) *(NSPL 18317) <6366>* **ARTHUR (OR THE DECLINE AND FALL OF THE BRITISH EMPIRE** – Victoria / Yes sir, no sir / Some mother's son / Brainwashed / Australia / Shangri-la / Mr. Churchill says / She bought a hat like Princess Marina / Young and innocent days / Nothing to say / Arthur. *(re-iss. Oct87 on 'P.R.T.' lp/c/cd; PYL/PYM/PYC 6009) (cd re-iss. Oct89 on 'Castle'; CLACD 162)*			
Dec 69.	(7") *(7N 17865) <0847>* **VICTORIA. / MR. CHURCHILL SAYS**		33	-
Jan 70.	(7") *<0863>* **VICTORIA. / BRAINWASHED**		-	62

KINKY MACHINE (see under ⇒ RIALTO)

KITCHEN (see under ⇒ BIS)

KITEMONSTER (see under ⇒ ASTRID)

K-LINE (see under ⇒ STUPIDS)

KNIFE IN THE WATER

Formed: Austin, Texas, USA … July 1997 by LAURA KRAUSE, BILL McCULLOUGH, AARON BLOUNT, MARK NATHAN and CISCO RYDER. Soon after coming together, the band found some small success at a self-organised gathering of bands, which emboldened them to take their musical mission further. A year later this culminated in the release of their debut LP, 'PLAYS ONE SOUND AND OTHERS' (1998). This outing showcased their unique alternative rock sound, blending space rock stylistics with smatterings of country, provided in large part by McCULLOUGH's pedal steel guitar, which gained them comparisons to the likes of progressive country rock master, GRAM PARSONS. From this predominantly lo-fi affair, the band hit the technological age with a bang, courtesy of their second full-length set, 'RED RIVER', coming two years on from its predecessor. Despite the recording upgrade, KITW's music stayed sincere, eccentric and on the whole, highly competent.

Album rating: PLAYS ONE SOUND AND OTHERS (*7) / RED RIVER (*6)

AARON BLOUNT – vocals, guitar / **LAURA KRAUSE** – vocals, organ / **BILL McCULLOUGH** – pedal steel guitar / **MARK NATHAN** – bass / **CISCO RYDER** – drums

		not iss.	Western Vinyl
1998.	(7") **SLAVERY. / REDBIRD**	-	

		Knife In The Water	Knife In The Water
Apr 99.	(cd) *<(KW 9801CD)>* **PLAYS ONE SOUND AND OTHERS** – One sound / Swallows / Seat of pity / Married woman / Norma / Come on cotton / Sent you up / Muse / Careering. *(UK-iss.Mar00 on 'Glitterhouse'; GRCD 470)*		Nov98

		All City	All City
May 00.	(7") *<(AC 13)>* **SUNSET MOTEL. / 2 SPADES**		

		Glitterhouse	Overcoat
Jul 00.	(cd) *(GRCD 489) <26105>* **RED RIVER** – Watch your back / Rene / Machine to Tulsa / Party / Sundown, sundown / Promenade / Nevada spider / Young blood in the river / Broad daylight / Nightingales of Evelyn. *<(lp-iss.Jun00 on 'Overcoat'; OC 05LP)>*		Jun00

		Peek-A-Boo	not iss.
Apr 02.	(m-cd) *(BOO 1003CD)* **CROSSPROSS BELLS EP** – From the catbird seat / Exploding seagulls / A lesson / Crosshair chapel / When trouble goes to seed.		-

KO AND THE KNOCKOUTS

Formed: Detroit, Michigan, USA ... 2000 by KO SHIH, who was a part-time bassist for The COME ONS, along with other Detroit "connections" (she shared a flat with MEG WHITE and was a bartender at hip Detroit venue 'Magic Stick'). SHIH was approached by LONG GONE JOHN (a legendary figure in the Detroit recording scene), to add something to his compilation of young Detroit music. SHIH recruited EDDIE BARANEK of The Sights and recorded the track 'BLACK AND BLUE', which fitted aptly onto the 'Sympathetic Sounds Of Detroit' sampler. One year later, the newly composed group's self-titled album was issued on 'Sympathy For The Record Industry' and featured JEFF KLIEN on drums. The set, just what you'd expect from a messy Detroit garage rock trio, included guest performances by members of The DIRTBOMBS, The VON BONDIES and R&B-fixated DETROIT COBRAS, et al.

Album rating: KO AND THE KNOCKOUTS (*7)

KO SHIH – vocals, bass (of The COME ONS) / **EDDIE BARANEK** – bass (of The SIGHTS) repl. STEVE NAWARA (of The GO) / **JEFF KLEIN** – drums

			Sympathy F	Sympathy F
Mar 02.	(lp/cd) <(SFTRI 657/+CD)>	**KO AND THE KNOCKOUTS**		Jan02

– Cry no more / Go-getter / Wasted all those tears / Set me free / You're on my mind / You did it / It's alright / If I / I really hate you / Twisting postman / I wanna (see you again) / Black and blue.

KOMEDA

Formed: Sweden ... 1991 by LENA KARLSSON, MATTIAS NORDLANDER, MARCUS HOLMBERG and his brother JONAS. Apparently named in tribute to the late, great jazzman, Kryzstof Komeda, this kitschy, twee-pop foursome, comprising LENA KARLSSON, MATTIAS NORDLANDER, MARCUS HOLMBERG and brother JONAS HOLMBERG, released their 'POP PA SVENSKA' debut in 1993. While also working under the banner of PROJEKTOR 7 (for soundtracks only), KOMEDA released a handful of singles/EP's and two STEREOLAB-like full-length sets, 'THE GENIUS OF KOMEDA' (1996) and 'WHAT MAKES IT GO?' (1998). However, with The CARDIGANS raking in all the attention and sales, the futuristic KOMEDA gave up the ghost.

Album rating: POP PA SVENSKA (*5) / THE GENIUS OF KOMEDA (*4) / WHAT MAKES IT GO? (*6)

LENA KARLSSON – vocals / **MATTIAS NORDLANDER** – guitar / **MARCUS HOLMBERG** – bass / **JONAS HOLMBERG** – drums

			North Of No South	Minty Fresh	
1993.	(cd) (NONS 04)	**POP PA SVENSKA**	-	-	Sweden

– Oj vilket Liv! / Bonjour tristesse / Sen sommar / Ad fontes / Vackra kristaller / Medicin / Feeling fine / Vals pa skare / Snurrig bossanova / Stjarna / Glod / En promenix / Borgo / Mod.

1995.	(cd-ep) (NONS 20)	**PLAN 714 TILL**	-	-	Sweden

– Fuego de la vida / Herbamore / Som I fjol / En spricka I taket.

1996.	(cd-s) (NONS 31-2)	**ROCKET PLANE (MUSIC ON THE MOON) / NEW NEW NO**	-	-	Sweden
1996.	(cd-s) (NONS 39-2)	**BOOGIE WOOGIE / ROCK'N'ROLL**	-	-	Sweden
Mar 97.	(cd) (NONS 26-2) <MF 18>	**THE GENIUS OF KOMEDA**			Sep96

– More is more / Fire / Rocket plane (music on the Moon) / Boogie woogie / Rock'n'roll / Disko / Top star / Light o' my life / If / Frolic / In orbit / Arbogast / New new no.

May 98.	(cd) (NONSCD 65) <70028>	**WHAT MAKES IT GO?**			Apr98

– Binario / It's alright, baby / Curious / Cul de sac / Living things / Flabbergast / Campfire / Happyment / Our hospitality / Focus / A simple formality.

Jun 98.	(cd-s) (NONS 67)	**IT'S ALRIGHT, BABY / MUSHROOM / THE SOUND OF FEELING**	-	-	Sweden

– compilations, etc. –

Aug 98.	(cd-ep) Imprint; <111802>	**A SIMPLE FORMALITY** (the Dot remixes)			
Mar 01.	(cd) Minty Fresh; <70040>	**POP PA SVENSKA / PLAN 714 TILL**			

KOSTARS (see under ⇒ LUSCIOUS JACKSON)

KOUFAX

Formed: Detroit, Michigan, USA ... 1999 by ROBERT SUCHAN, SEAN GROGAN, DAVE SHETTLER and ANDREW CAMERON. Taking their moniker from Sean Koufax, a pitcher with the Los Angeles Dodgers, the group debuted with their brand of synthesizer-dominated emo-pop and 80s post-punk revivalism on the eponymously-titled EP, 'KOUFAX' (1999). Although the mini-set perhaps played too heavily on electronica there did exist moments of seventies-style rock guitar to play off against it. Fortunately for them, The GET UP KIDS saw their potential and managed to get their label, 'Heroes & Villains', to take them under their wing for the issue of debut LP, 'IT HAD TO DO WITH LOVE' (2000). This set displayed a band that was willing to ditch more of the guitar noodling and suffered slightly due to this, as the sound was too sterile for the majority of indie listeners. Following this record, the outfit brought in the further assistance of JARED ROSENBERG, who aided their heavy promotional touring that ensued. By the time they sat down to work on their sophomore LP, 'SOCIAL LIFE' (2002), the band had pared-down to a quartet following the departure of GROGAN and CAMERON; the fourth position being filled by BEN FORCE. Whether it was the line-up change or the tide change in music with the massive growth of garage rock revival acts, aka The STROKES and The HIVES, their second set duly put forth some great guitar rocking moments yet with the same underladen keyboard work ... thus making it a more balanced and rounded sound which put it streets ahead of their former efforts.

Album rating: IT HAD TO DO WITH LOVE (*4) / SOCIAL LIFE (*6)

ROBERT SUCHAN – vocals, guitar / **SEAN GROGAN** – keyboards / **ANDREW CAMERON** – bass, keyboards / **DAVE SHETTLER** – drums, synthesizer, vocals

			Doghouse	Doghouse
Nov 99.	(12"ep/cd-ep) <(DOG 065/+CD)>	**KOUFAX**		Oct99

– A soundwave sound / Living alone / Going to happen / So long to you and I.

			Vagrant	Vagrant
Sep 00.	(lp/cd) <(VR 349/+CD)>	**IT HAD TO DO WITH LOVE**		

– Out of your element / Move out, move on / Minor chords / It had to do with love / Out of your element (reprise) / Going to happen / Offering advice / Living alone / Work will never end / Over it.

— **JARED ROSENBERG** – keyboards; repl. CAMERON + GROGAN

Oct 02.	(lp/cd) <VR 374/+CD>	**SOCIAL LIFE**	-	

– Let us know / Break it off / Social life / Saturdays alone / Come back to life / So put on / Brightside / Younger body / Simply passing time / Adultery / So long to good times.

Mark KOZELEK
(see under ⇒ RED HOUSE PAINTERS)

KRAFTWERK

Formed: Dusseldorf, Germany ... 1969 as ORGANISATION by RALF HUTTER, FLORIAN SCHNEIDER-ESLEBEN and three others, namely BUTCH HAUF, FRED MONICKS and BASIL HAMMOND. After one CONRAD PLANK-produced album, 'TONE FLOAT', for 'R.C.A.' in 1970, the pair broke away to form KRAFTWERK (German for POWERPLANT), with KLAUS DINGER and THOMAS HOMANN. After one album for 'Philips', RALF & FLORIAN became KRAFTWERK, releasing the 1973 album (titled after their Christian names) for 'Vertigo' in the process. In 1974, they added KLAUS ROEDER & WOLFGANG FLUR, issuing their magnus-opus 'AUTOBAHN'. This UK & US Top 5 album contained a 22-minute title track, which, edited into 3 minutes, also became a hit. The next album, 'RADIO ACTIVITY' (which was also issued on their own 'Kling Klang' label in Germany), disappointed most and failed to secure a Top 50 placing. In 1978, they were back in the UK Top 10 at least, with an excellent return to form, 'THE MAN MACHINE'. In the early 80's, they enjoyed another hit album, 'COMPUTER WORLD', and a run of UK hit singles, one of which, 'THE MODEL' (from 1978 lp) made the top spot. A projected album by the name of 'TECHNOPOP', was pencilled in for release in 1983 and allegedly 'E.M.I.' were even supplied with artwork. The record never appeared, and of course, given KRAFTWERK's reclusive reticence, no explanation was offered. The same year, however, the band did release a one-off 12" single, 'TOUR DE FRANCE', no doubt inspired by HUTTER's preoccupation with cycling. It was to be another three years before the band released a full album, the disappointing 'ELECTRIC CAFE'. By this point the band were starting to tread water, an assumption that seemed to be confirmed when fans had to wait another five years for 'new' material. 'THE MIX', released in 1991, was actually an album of reworkings of old tracks, a bit of a hit and miss affair which failed to deliver any original pieces per se. Both BARTOS and FLUR had left the band before the album's release, allegedly sick of the laboriously slow and detailed recording process and the band's reclusive inertia. Despite a reputation for a disciplined working ethos, the band remain defiantly distant from the music industry. Their studio apparently possesses neither fax nor phone, they've no management and they've turned down all offers of remix work and collaborations. Whether they can remain on the cutting edge in such a vacuum remains to be seen and for the moment, their Guru-like status is based on past glories, sounds that continue to permeate almost all strands of pop culture, now more than ever. It's testament to their towering influence that despite releasing no new material for more than a decade, they headlined the Tribal Gathering dance festival in the late 90's. This robotic electronic rock act with minimalist synth-tunes, being at times (on stage!) twiddled by dummies, were more inspirational than their contemporaries TANGERINE DREAM. KRAFTWERK became a major influence for ULTRAVOX!, GARY NUMAN, DAVID BOWIE '77, JEAN-MICHEL JARRE, SIMPLE MINDS, OMD, etc. Back on the musical autobahn for the new millennium, KRAFTWERK released a German-only single, 'EXPO 2000'. • **Songwriters:** RALF & FLORIAN. • **Trivia:** They have been sampled by many, including AFRIKA BAMBAATAA on his single, 'Planet Rock'.

Album rating: Organisation: TONE FLOAT (*4) / Kraftwerk: KRAFTWERK (HIGHRAIL) (*4) / KRAFTWERK 2 (VAR) (*4) / RALF AND FLORIAN (*5) / AUTOBAHN (*8) / RADIOACTIVITY (*4) / TRANS-EUROPE EXPRESS (*8) / THE MAN MACHINE (*8) / COMPUTER WORLD (*7) / ELECTRIC CAFE (*4) / THE MIX remixes (*5)

ORGANISATION

RALF HUTTER (b.1946, Krefeld, Germany) – electric organ, strings / **FLORIAN SCHNEIDER-ESLEBEN** (b.1947, Dusseldorf)– flute, echo unit, strings / **BUTCH HAUF** – bass, percussion / **FRED MONICKS** – drums / **BASIL HAMMOND** – percussion, vocals

			R.C.A.	not iss.
Aug 70.	(lp) (SF 8111)	**TONE FLOAT**		-

– Tone float / Milk float / Silver forest / Rhythm salad / Noitasinagro.

KRAFTWERK

HUTTER + SCHNEIDER with **KLAUS DINGER** – guitar, keyboards / **THOMAS HOMANN** – percussion

			Philips	not iss.
1971.	(lp) *(6305 058)* **KRAFTWERK**		–	– German
	– Ruckzuck / Stratowargius / Megaherz / Vom Himmel hoch.			

— **HUTTER + SCHNEIDER** trimmed to a duo. (DINGER and HOMANN formed NEU!)

1972.	(lp) *(6305 117)* **KRAFTWERK 2**	–	– German
	– Klingklang / Atem / Strom / Spule 4 / Wellenlange / Harmonika.		

		Vertigo	Vertigo
Nov 72.	(d-lp) *(6641 077)* **KRAFTWERK** (2 German lp's combined)		
Nov 73.	(lp) *(6360 616)* **RALF & FLORIAN**		
	– Elektrisches roulette (Electric roulette) / Tongebirge (Mountain of sound) / Kristallo (Crystals) / Heimatklange (The bells of home) / Tanzmusik (Dance music) / Ananas symphonie (Pineapple symphony). *<US-iss.Sep75; 2006>*		

— added **KLAUS ROEDER** – violin, guitar / **WOLFGANG FLUR** – percussion

Nov 74.	(lp/c) *(6360/ 620)* <2003> **AUTOBAHN**	4	5
	– Autobahn / Kometenmelodie 1 & 2 (Comet melody) / Mitternacht (Midnight) / Morgenspaziergang (Morning walk). *(re-iss. Mar82 on 'E.M.I.' lp/c; EMC/TC-EMC 3405); hit 61 UK) (re-iss. Jun85 on 'Parlophone' lp/c; AUTO/TCAUTO 1) (cd-iss. Jun87 & Aug95 on 'E.M.I.'; CDP 746153-2)*		
Feb 75.	(7") *(6147 012)* **AUTOBAHN. / KOMETENMELODIE**	11	–
Feb 75.	(7") <203> **AUTOBAHN. / MORGENSPAZIERGANG**	–	25
Jul 75.	(7") *(6147 015)* **KOMETENMELODIE 2. / KRISTALLO**	–	–
Jul 75.	(7") <204> **KOMETENMELODIE 2. / MITTERNACHT**	–	–

— In Oct'75, **KARL BARTOS** – percussion repl. ROEDER

		Capitol	Capitol
Nov 75.	(lp/c) *(<EST/TC-EST 11457>)* **RADIO-ACTIVITY**		
	– Geiger counter / Radio-activity / Radioland / Airwaves / (intermission) / News / The voice of energy / Antenna / Radio stars / Uran / Transistor / Ohm sweet ohm. *(re-iss. Jun84 on 'Fame' lp/c; FA 413103-1/-4) (re-iss. 1985 on 'E.M.I.' lp/c; EMS/TC-EMS 1256) (cd-iss. May87 on 'E.M.I.' lp/c; CDP 746474-2) (re-iss. Aug87 on 'E.M.I.' lp/c; ATAK/TCATAK 104) (re-iss. cd Apr94 on 'Cleopatra';) (re-iss. cd Apr95 on 'E.M.I.';)*		
Feb 76.	(7") *(CL 15853)* <4211> **RADIO-ACTIVITY. / ANTENNA**		
Apr 77.	(lp/c) *(<EST/TC-EST 11603>)* **TRANS-EUROPE EXPRESS**		
	– Europe endless / The hall of mirrors / Showroom dummies / Trans-Europe express / Metal on metal / Franz Schubert / Endless endless. *(in Feb82, they hit UK No.49 Feb82) (re-iss. 1985 on 'E.M.I.' lp/c; ATAK/TCATAK 5) (re-iss. Jun86 on 'Fame' lp/c; FA 413151-1/-4) (cd-iss. May87 on 'E.M.I.'; CDP 746473-2) (re-iss. cd Apr94 on 'Cleopatra';)*		
Apr 77.	(7") *(CL 15917)* **TRANS-EUROPE EXPRESS. / EUROPE ENDLESS**		–
Aug 77.	(7") *(CLX 104)* **SHOWROOM DUMMIES. / EUROPE EXPRESS**		
May 78.	(7") <4460> **TRANS-EUROPE EXPRESS. / FRANZ SCHUBERT**	–	67
May 78.	(lp/c) *(<EST/TC-EST 11728>)* **THE MAN MACHINE**	9	
	– The robots / Spacelab / Metropolis / The model / Neon lights / The man machine. *(re-iss. Mar85 on 'Fame' lp/c; 413118-1/-4) (re-iss. Jul88 on 'Fame' cd/c/lp; CD/TC/FA 3118) (cd-iss. Apr94 on 'Cleopatra'; CLEO 5877CD) (re-iss. cd/c Apr95 on 'E.M.I.'; CD/TC EMS 1520) (cd re-iss. Jun97 on 'E.M.I.'; CDCNTAV 4)*		
May 78.	(7") *(CL 15981)* **THE ROBOTS (edit). / SPACELAB**		
Jun 78.	(7") <4620> **NEON LIGHTS. / THE ROBOTS**	–	
Sep 78.	(7"/12"luminous) *(CL/12CL 15998)* **NEON LIGHTS. / TRANS-EUROPE EXPRESS / THE MODEL**	53	
Nov 78.	(12"m) *(CL 16098)* **SHOWROOM DUMMIES. / EUROPE ENDLESS / SPACELAB**		

		E.M.I.	Warners
Apr 81.	(7") *(EMI 5175)* <49723> **POCKET CALCULATOR. / DENTAKU**	39	
	(12"+=) *(12EMI 5175)* – Numbers.		
	(c-s) *(TCEMI 5175)* – ('A'extended) / ('A'side) / Numbers.		
May 81.	(lp/c) *(EMC/TC-EMC 3370)* <3549> **COMPUTER WORLD**	15	72
	– Pocket calculator / Numbers / Computer-world / Computer love / Home computer / It's more fun to compute. *(re-iss. Apr95 cd/c; CD/TC EMS 1547)*		
Jun 81.	(7"/12") *(EMI/12EMI 5207)* **COMPUTER LOVE. / THE MODEL**	36	–
	(Dec81; flipped over, hit UK No.1) (re-iss. May84; G45 16)		
Jun 81.	(7") <49795> **COMPUTER LOVE. / NUMBERS**	–	–
Feb 82.	(7") *(EMI 5272)* **SHOWROOM DUMMIES. / NUMBERS**	25	–
	(12"+=) *(12EMI 5272)* – Pocket calculator.		

— (In May'83, they had album 'TECHNO POP' cancelled)

Jul 83.	(7") *(EMI 5413)* <29342> **TOUR DE FRANCE. / TOUR DE FRANCE** (instrumental)	22	
	(c-s+=/12"+=) *(TC/12 EMI 5413)* – ('A'version).		
Aug 84.	(7") *(EMI 5413)* **TOUR DE FRANCE (remix). / TOUR DE FRANCE**	24	
	(12"+=) *(12EMI 5413)* – ('A'instrumental).		
Oct 86.	(7"/ext.12") *(EMI/12EMI 5588)* **MUSIQUE NON-STOP. / MUSIQUE NON STOP (version)**		
Nov 86.	(lp/c)(cd) *(EMD/TC-EMD 3370)(CDP 746416-2)* <25525> **ELECTRIC CAFE**	58	
	– Boom boom tschak / Techno pop / Musique non stop / The telephone call / Sex object / Techno pop / Electric cafe. *(cd re-iss. Aug95; CDEMS 1546)*		
Feb 87.	(7") *(EMI 5602)* <28441> **THE TELEPHONE CALL. / DER TELEFON ANRUF**		
	(12"+=) *(12EMI 5602)* – House phone.		

— **FRITZ HIJBERT** repl. WOLFGANG FLUR

May 91.	(c-s/7") *(TC+/EM 192)* **THE ROBOTS (re-recorded). / ROBOTRONIK**	20	
	(12"+=) *(12EM 192)* – ('A'album version).		
	(cd-s+=) *(CDEM 192)* – Robotnik.		
Jun 91.	(cd/c/d-lp) *(CD/TC+/EM 1408)* **THE MIX** ('91 remixes)	15	
	– The robots / Computer love / Pocket calculator / Dentaku / Autobahn / Radioactivity / Trans-Europe express / Abzug / Metal on metal / Homecomputer / Musique non-stop. *(cd re-iss. Aug95; CDEM 1408)*		
Oct 91.	(c-s/7") *(TC+/EM 201)* **RADIOACTIVITY (Francois Kevorkian remix). / ('A'-William Orbit mix)**	43	
	(12"+=/cd-s+=) *(12/CD EM 201)* – ('A'extended).		

— In Jul'91, BARTOS and FLUR formed their own project, ELEKTRIC

Dec 99.	(12"/cd-s) *(EXPO 1/+CD)* **EXPO 2000** (mixes)		–
	(above issued on German 'Kling Klang')		
Mar 00.	(12"/cd-s) *(12EM/CDEM 562)* **EXPO 2000** (mixes)	27	

– compilations, others, etc. –

on 'Vertigo' unless mentioned otherwise

Oct 75.	(lp) *(6360 629)* **EXCELLER 8**		–
Oct 80.	(7") *(CUT 108)* **AUTOBAHN. / (b-side by BEGGAR'S OPERA)**		–
Apr 81.	(lp) *(6449 066)* **ELEKTRO KINETIC**		–
May 81.	(7") *(VER 3)* **KOMETENMELODIE 2. / VON HIMMEL HOCH**		–

<In the US compilation lp 'THE ROBOTS' on 'Capitol'; 9445>

Apr 94.	(cd) *Cleopatra; (CLEO 6843CD)* **SHOWROOM DUMMIES**		
	(re-iss. May97; same)		
Apr 94.	(cd) *Cleopatra; (CLEO 5761-2)* **THE MODEL (The Best Of Kraftwerk 1975-1978)**		
Mar 97.	(12") *Discopromo; (D 762)* **NUMBERS**		
Mar 97.	(12") *Discopromo; (D 801)* **TOUR DE FRANCE**		
May 97.	(d-cd) *Cleopatra; (CLEO 9416-2)* **THE CAPITOL YEARS**		
Oct 99.	(12"/cd-s) *E.M.I.; (887421-0/-6)* **TOUR DE FRANCE** (mixes)	61	

KRAY CHERUBS
(see under ⇒ ART ATTACKS; 70's section)

KREIDLER (see under ⇒ TO ROCOCO ROT)

KULA SHAKER

Formed: Highgate, London, England ... mid 90's out of mods The KAYS by CRISPIAN MILLS. They initially played down the fact his mother was the famous English actress Hayley Mills (daughter of Sir John Mills) and father being director, Roy Boulting. In the late 80's, CRISPIAN and ALONZA BEVIN set up a school group, The LOVELY LADS, later becoming The OBJECTS. In 1995, after jointly winning the 'In The City' new band competition and a Glastonbury appearance, KULA SHAKER (now with PAUL WINTER-HART and JAY DARLINGTON) signed to 'Columbia', through A&R man Ronnie Gurr. They debuted that Xmas with the limited edition single, 'TATTVA'. Their first single proper, 'GRATEFUL WHEN YOU'RE DEAD', was a tribute of sorts to the late, great JERRY GARCIA and earned them their first Top 40 hit. Their follow-up, a re-vamped version of 'TATTVA', fared even better, making the Top 5. 'HEY DUDE', the next single, kept up the momentum, reaching No.2 following a blinding 'T In The Park' appearance in Scotland (they returned there in 1997 as headliners). CRISPIAN MILLS' songwriting was heavily influenced by a combination of classic 60's psychedelia and grandiose 70's rock, much in evidence on their debut album 'K' (1996). Relying on similar Eastern influences as 'TATTVA', 'GOVINDA' was another slice of elaborate, but cliched psychedelia, while 'HUSH' (1997) was workman-like in its similarity to the DEEP PURPLE version of the JOE SOUTH original. KULA SHAKER continued to musically spar with their tried and tested cod-mod/psychedelia, a Top 3 single in '98, 'SOUND OF DRUMS', testament to just that. The track was also included on their Bob Ezrin-produced sophomore set, 'PEASANTS, PIGS & ASTRONAUTS' (1999), a pretentious set of good-time cosmic rock'n'roll that gave ammunition to the gun-toting music journos all ready to shoot them down at any opportunity. Two further Top 20 singles, 'MYSTICAL MACHINE GUN' and 'SHOWER YOUR LOVE', marked the end for CRISPIAN and his chums as the band split that September. The frontman was expected to go solo but chose instead to form trad-rock trio, the JEEVAS who released a few singles prior to their debut album, '1 2 3 4' (2002). • **Covered:** BALLAD OF A THIN MAN (Bob Dylan).

Album rating: K (*7) / PEASANTS, PIGS & ASTRONAUTS (*5) / Jeevas: 1 2 3 4 (*4)

CRISPIAN MILLS (b.18 Jan'73) – vocals, guitars / **ALONZA BEVIN** (b.24 Oct'70) – bass, piano, tabla, vocals / **JAY DARLINGTON** (b. 3 May'69, Sidcup, England) – keyboards / **PAUL WINTER-HART** (b.19 Sep'71) – drums

		Columbia	Columbia
Dec 95.	(ltd; 7"/cd-s) *(KULA 71/CD1)* **TATTVA (Lucky 13 mix)/ HOLLOW MAN (part II)**		–
Apr 96.	(c-s) *(KULAMC 2)* **GRATEFUL WHEN YOU'RE DEAD – JERRY WAS THERE. / ANOTHER LIFE**	35	–
	(cd-s+=) *(KULACD 2)* – Under the hammer.		
Jun 96.	(7") *(KULA 3)* **TATTVA. / TATTVA ON ST. GEORGE'S DAY / DANCE IN YOUR SHADOW**	4	–
	(cd-s) *(KULACD 3)* – (first & third tracks) / Moonshine / Tattva (lucky 13).		
	(cd-s) *(KULACD 3K)* – (second & third tracks) / Red balloon (Vishnu's eyes).		

KULA SHAKER (cont)

Aug 96. (7"/c-s) *(KULA/+MC 4)* **HEY DUDE. / TROUBLED MIND** — 2 / —
(cd-s+=) *(KULACD 4)* – Grateful when you're dead (Mark Radcliffe session) / Into the deep (Mark Radcliffe session).
(cd-s) *(KULACD 4K)* – ('A'side) / Tattva / Drop in the sea / Crispian reading from the Mahabharata.
Sep 96. (cd/c/lp) *(SHAKER CD/MC/LP 1)* <67822> **K** — 1 / Oct96
– Hey dude / Knight on the town / Temple of the everlasting light / Govinda / Smart dogs / Magic theatre / Into the deep / Sleeping jiva / Tattva / Grateful when you're dead – Jerry was there / 303 / Start all over / Hollow man (parts 1 & 2). *(also ltd-cd; SHAKER CD1K)*
Nov 96. (c-s) *(KULAMC 5)* **GOVINDA / GOKULA** — 7 / —
(cd-s+=) *(KULACD 5)* – Hey dude (live) / Alonza Bevan's The Leek.
('A'-Hari & St.George mix-cd-s+=) *(KULACD 5K)* – ('A'-Monkey Mafia Pigsy's vision) / ('A'-Monkey Mafia Ten to ten version).
(7"mail-order+=) *(KULA 75)* – Temple of everlasting light.
Feb 97. (c-s) *(KULAMC 6)* **HUSH / RAAGY ONE (WAITING FOR TOMORROW)** — 2 / —
(cd-s+=) *(KULACD 6)* – Knight on the town (live) / Smart dogs (live).
(cd-s+=) *(KULACD 6K)* – Under the hammer (hold on to the magical key) / Govinda (live).

—— (all above cd-singles were re-iss. Jul98; *KULA 71-76CD*)

Jul 97. (cd-ep) <68514> **SUMMER SUN EP** — — / —
– Govinda / Gokula / Dance in your shadow / Raagy one (waiting for tomorrow) / Moonshine / Troubled mind.
Apr 98. (c-s) *(KULA 21MC)* **SOUND OF DRUMS / HURRY ON SUNDOWN (HARI OM SUNDOWN)** — 3 / —
(cd-s+=) *(KULA 21CD)* – Reflections of love / Fairyland (featuring DON PECKER).
(cd-s+=) *(KULA 21CDX)* – The one that got away / Smile.
Feb 99. (c-s) *(KULA 22MC)* **MYSTICAL MACHINE GUN / GUITAR MAN** — 14 / —
(cd-s+=) *(KULA 22CD)* – Prancing bride.
(cd-s) *(KULA 22CDX)* – ('A'side) / Avalanche / Holy river.
Mar 99. (cd/c/lp) *(SHAKER 2 CD/MC/LP)* **PEASANTS, PIGS & ASTRONAUTS** — 9 / —
– Great Hosannah / S.O.S. / Mystical machine gun / Radhe radhe / I'm still here / Shower your love / 108 battles / Sound of drums / Timeworn / Last farewell / Golden avatar / Namami nanda nandana.
May 99. (c-s) *(KULA 23MC)* **SHOWER YOUR LOVE / GOODBYE TIN TERRIERS** — 14 / —
(cd-s+=) *(KULA 23CD)* – Sound of drums (live).
(cd-s) *(KULA 23CDX)* – ('A'side) / The dancing flea / Light of the day.

—— disbanded in September '99

JEEVAS

CRISPIAN MILLS / DAN McKINNA / ANDY NIXON

Cowboy / Epic

Jul 02. (7"m) *(COW 001)* **SCARY PARENTS. / SHE SPEAKS / MEET THE JEEVAS** — / —
Sep 02. (7"m) *(COW 002)* **VIRGINIA. / TEENAGE BREAKDOWN (acoustic) / MEET THE JEEVAS (part 2)** — / —
(cd-s) *(COWCD 002)* – ('A'side) / Stoned love / Old friends new faces (live).
Sep 02. (cd) *(COWCD 003)* <150> **1 2 3 4** — / Oct02
– Virginia / Ghost cowboys in the movies / You got my number / What is it for? / Once upon a time in America / Don't say the good times are over / Scary parents / Teenage breakdown / Silver apples / She speaks / Edge of the world / America (demo).

KUSTOMIZED (see under ⇒ VOLCANO SONS)

Ben KWELLER (see under ⇒ RADISH)

KYOKO (see under ⇒ BEATNIK FILMSTARS)

L

LABRADFORD

Formed: Richmond, Virginia, USA ... 1991, by MARK NELSON and CARTER BROWN. They set-up CARTER's Moog synthesizer in MARK's house and eventually acquired gigs supporting low-grade Virginia punk bands. In 1992, Chicago-based label 'Kranky' took up an option to sign them, subsequently releasing 'PRAZISION LP' in 1993. Drummerless Krautrock revivalists likened to CLUSTER, SPACEMEN 3 and MAIN, LABRADFORD specialised in creating space-rock dreamscapes and ambient drones of uneasy-listening while resurrecting the nearly forgotten Moog. After the album's cult success, they retreated back home, although the pair were lured back to sign for the UK arm of New Zealand-based, 'Flying Nun'. The label subsequently released a follow-up set, 'A STABLE REFERENCE' (1995), – with bassman ROBERT DONNE – the music press hailing it as one of the year's most essential releases. In November '96, 'Blast First' issued their eponymous third effort to similar acclaim, their increasingly minimalist tendencies moving them to even cut the song titles of 1997's 'MI MEDIA NARANJA' down to single letters.

Album rating: PRAZISION LP (*7) / A STABLE REFERENCE (*8) / LABRADFORD (*8) / MI MEDIA NARANJA (*7) / E LUXO SO (*7) / FIXED::CONTEXT (*6)

CARTER BROWN – synthesizers / **MARK NELSON** – vocals, guitars, tapes

not iss. / Retro

1992. (7") <8> **EVERLAST. / PRESERVE THE SOUND OUTSIDE** — / —

not iss. / Kranky

1993. (cd,d-lp) <krank 001> **PRAZISION LP** — / —
– Listening in depth / Accelerating on a smoother road / Splash down / Disremembering / Experience the gated oscillator / Soft return / Sliding grass / C of people / New listening / Gratitude / Skyward with motion / Everlast. *(UK-iss.Feb96 & Sep98 on 'Flying Nun' lp/cd; FN/+CD 342)*

—— added **ROBERT DONNE** – bass (ex-BREADWINNER)

not iss. / Merge

1995. (7") <mrg 062> **JULIUS. / COLUMNA DE LA INDEPENDENCIA** — / —

Flying Nun / Kranky

Jun 95. (lp/cd) *(FN/+CD 329)* <krank 006> **A STABLE REFERENCE** — / —
– Mas / El Lago / Streamlining / Banco / Eero / Balanced on it's own flame / Star City, Russia / Comfort / SEDR 77.

Duophonic / not iss.

Feb 96. (10") *(ds45-12)* **SCENIC RECOVERY. / UNDERWOOD 5IVE** — / —

Blast First / Kranky

Nov 96. (lp/cd) *(BFFP 136/+CD)* <krank 013> **LABRADFORD** — / —
– Phantom channel crossing / Midrange / Pico / The cipher / Lake speed / Scenic recovery / Battered. *(cd re-iss. Sep98 on 'Flying Nun'; FNCD 329)*
Jun 97. (12") <(TR 60)> **THE KAHANEK INCIDENT VOL.3** — / Aug97
– Virginia (remixed by STARS OF THE LID) / Texas (by STARS OF THE LID – remixed by LABRADFORD).
(above release on 'Trance Syndicate')
Oct 97. (lp/cd) *(BFFP 144/+CD)* <krank 023> **MI MEDIA NARANJA** — / —
– S / G / WR / C / I / V / P.
May 99. (d-lp/cd) *(BFFP 157/+CD)* <krank 037> **E LUXO SO** — / —
– Recorded and mixed at Sound of Music, Richmond, Va. / With John Morand and assisted by Brian Hoffa. / Dulcimers played by Peter Neff, strings played / by Chris Johnston, Craig Markva, Jamie Evans, / and Jonathan Morken. Photo provided by / Let O'Steen. Design assistance by John Piper.
Nov 00. (10"lp; split w/ SURFERS OF ROMANTICA) *(EERIE 18)* **ENE** (remixes) — / —
(above issued on 'Eerie Materials')
Feb 01. (lp/cd) *(BFFP 167/+CD)* <krank 047> **FIXED::CONTENT** — / —
– Twenty / Up to Pizmo / David / Wren.

LADYBUG TRANSISTOR

Formed: Brooklyn, New York, USA ... 1994 by GARY OLSON, EDWARD POWERS (+ two others), the group debuting in 1996 with 'MARLBOROUGH FARMS' album. Although the band's musical abilities were never in question, they were clearly influenced by the sound of PAVEMENT and let themselves down by making this too apparent rather than concentrating on the development of their own identity. The group endured personnel changes at almost every stage of their career; however, rather than allowing this to become a set-back, the group turned it to their advantage. Having lost their guitarist and bass player, OLSON recruited the far more influential siblings JENNIFER and JEFF BARON, and consequently their second album 'BEVERLY ATONALE' (1997) had a much more individual sound. The group continued to build on this with their 1999 release 'ALBEMARLE SOUND'. By now the LT's sound

was leaning more towards orchestral sixties pop, a genre the group were more comfortable and capable of recreating whilst managing to retain their own personality. The 2001 release 'ARGYLE HEIR' saw the group finally reach their potential. The lush arrangements on the record leant themselves perfectly to the dreamy melodies that the group were now effortlessly producing.
• **Covered:** MASSACHUSETTS (Bee Gees).

Album rating: MARLBOROUGH FARMS (*5) / BEVERLEY ATONALE (*6) / THE ALBEMARLE SOUND (*7) / ARGYLE HEIR (*6)

GARY OLSON – vocals, guitar, keyboards / **EDWARD POWERS** – drums / +2

			not iss.	Sit'n'spin
1995.	(cd)	**MARLBOROUGH FARMS**	-	

– The wheel / (Theme to) Lout / Magic forest report / Sneedle / Seadrift / Blaze / 95 miles per hour / Land / Twice in a lifetime / Song for vocoder & trumpet. <re-iss. Oct96 on 'Park'n'ride'; 1>

—— **JENNIFER BARON** – guitar (of SATURNINE) / **JEFF BARON** – bass; repl. originals

			not iss.	After Hours
Jan 97.	(7")	**INTRO – RUSHES OF PURE SPRING. / (others by Portastatic + Land Of The Loops)**	-	

			Merge	Merge
Mar 97.	(lp/cd) <(MRG 121/+CD)> **BEVERLEY ATONALE**			Feb97

– Here is your space / Rushes of pure spring / Windy / Swedish Libra and you / This order is tall / Music for tennis courts / Your wagging tail / Stuck / Forest marching son / The occasional / It will be a lifetime / Thoughts of you / The Swedish Libra II.

—— **SAN FADYL** – drums (ex-INDIVIDUAL FRUIT PIE; one set 'Lay-By Lullaby' in 1997) repl. POWERS

—— added **SASHA BELL** – keyboards, flute (of ESSEX GREEN)

Jan 99.	(7") <MRG 141> **TODAY KNOWS. / MASSACHUSETTS**		-
Mar 99.	(lp/cd) <(MRG 154/+CD)> **THE ALBEMARLE SOUND**		

– Oriental boulevard / Six times / Meadowpark arch / Today knows / The great British spring / Like a summer rain / The swimmer / Cienfuegos / The automobile song / Oceans in the hall / Vale of cashmere / Aleida's theme. (cd re-iss. Aug02 on 'Pointy'; POINT 006CD)

			Pointy	Merge
Jul 01.	(cd) (POINT 005CD) <MRG 489> **ARGYLE HEIR**			May01

– Fires on the ocean / Echoes / Perfect for shattering / Going up north (icicles) / Wooden bars / Catherine Elizabeth / Nico norte / Words hang in the air / Fjords of winter / In a certain place / Brighton bound / The reclusive hero / The glass pane / Caton gardens.

—— in 2001, they issued official bootleg, 'LIVE AT THE AMIGO'

			Elefant	not iss.
Aug 02.	(7") (ER 226) **BRIGHTON BOUND. / CIENFUEGOS (CICADA SONATA)**		-

LADYTRON

Formed: Liverpool, England . . . mid-1998 by DANIEL HUNT and REUBEN WU who travelled together across Asia and Europe, where they met female vocalist MIRA AROYO on a train in Bulgaria. MIRA's friend HELEN MARNIE was recruited as second vocalist and keyboard player and the collective finally settled on a name, taken from the title of an early ROXY MUSIC song. The group began practising and recording (namely their debut single 'HE TOOK ME TO A MOVIE' – for £50) and developed a style crossed somewhere between the indie rock chic of ELASTICA and the swirling keyboard driven electronica of CABARET VOLITAIRE or KRAFTWERK. An EP, 'COMMODORE ROCK' was issued in 2000 to much praise and the 'TRON prepared themselves for first-album proper '604' (2001). A playfully detached album of bleeps and pips, the quartet fused rock/electronica and brightly sexual vocals with strong driven house beats and DIY-disco pop. Live, the two front women looked bored out of their skulls and gave off the aura of two trendy, self-assertive style-mag models. But their music was not to falter their image; 'CSKA SOFIA' was BROADCAST stripped down to their essence, and 'I'M WITH THE PILOTS' proved to be electronic loveliness. A year later and LADYTRON had recorded 'LIGHT AND MAGIC' which veered towards darker analogue fiddling, such as contemporaries ADD N TO (X). • **Note:** not to be confused with 'Shimmy Disc' act, THE LADYTRON.

Album rating: 604 (*7) / LIGHT & MAGIC (*7)

MIRA AROYA – vocals / **HELEN MARNIE** – vocals, keyboards / **REUBEN WU** – keyboards, rhythm / **DANNY HUNT** – keyboards / plus 5th member **JOHN LEVI** – bass

			Invicta Hi-Fi	not iss.
Jul 99.	(12"m) (LIQ 005) **HE TOOK HER TO A MOVIE. / OLIVETTI JERK / HE TOOK HER TO A MOVIE (surreal Madrid mix)**		-

			Tricatel	not iss.
Mar 00.	(10"ep) (TRIEP 25002) **COMMODORE ROCK**		-

			Invicta Hi-Fi	Emperor Norton
Jul 00.	(cd-s) (LIQ 008CD) **PLAYGIRL / COMMODORE ROCK / HE TOOK HER TO A MOVIE**		
Jul 00.	(cd-ep) <EMN 7034CD> **COMMODORE ROCK**	-	

– Play girl / Commodore rock / Miss Black / Paco!

Nov 00.	(12"ep/cd-ep) (LIQ 011/+CD) **MU-TRON EP**		-

– Another breakfast with you / Paco! / USA vs white noise / Playgirl (snap ant version).

Feb 01.	(7"/cd-s) (LIQ 012/+CD) **THE WAY THAT I FOUND YOU. / HOLIDAY 601 / MISS BLACK**		-
Apr 01.	(d-lp/cd) (LIQ 014/+CD) <EMN 7037CD> **604**			Feb01

– Mu-tron / Discotraxx / Another breakfast with you / CSKA Sofia / The way that I found you / Paco! / Commodore rock / Zmeyka / Play girl / I'm with the pilots / This is our sound / He took me to a movie / Laughing cavalier / Ladybird / Jet age / Skools out . . . (cd re-iss. Sep02; same as US)

Nov 01.	(cd-s) (LIQ 777CD1) **PLAY GIRL (mixes; album / king of Woolworths coming down / I Monster Northern Lites)**		-

(cd-s) (LIQ 777CD2) – ('A'mixes; Felix*thee grooveretro radio / Zombie Nation / Simian playboy).

			Emperor Norton	Emperor Norton
Sep 02.	(cd/d-lp) (<EMN 7058 CD/LP>) **LIGHT & MAGIC**		

– True mathematics / Seventeen / Flicking your switch / Fire / Turn it on / Bluejeans / Cracked LCD / Black plastic / Evil / Startup chime / NuHorizons / Cease2xist / Re:agents / Light & magic / The reason why.

			Telstar	not iss.
Nov 02.	(12"/cd-s) (12/CD STAS 3284) **SEVENTEEN (mixes; original / the droyds / Soulwax / radio)**	68	-

LAETO

Formed: Dundee, Scotland . . . mid-1998 by FRASER SIMPSON, ANDREW SMITH, KEVIN D BLACK (he left after only a week but returned to the fold in '99) and ROBBIE 'DES TROY' COOPER, one-time mucker of ALEX CHARLES in the short-lived NEUROLA; the latter also worked with the man's MAGNETIC NORTH POLE (the group that is) until he took up this hotter post full-time. A year playing the toilet circuit finally payed off when LAETO were rewarded with support slots to FUGAZI and IDLEWILD. A debut EP for 'Evol' entitled 'FIELDSETTINGS' (recorded towards the end of 1999), was a Lo-Fi part-sonic attempt at sounding somewhere between MOGWAI and FUGAZI, while the flip side 'CAR – LOW' was pure sonic. By the time their first album (for 'Guided Missile') 'MAKE US MILD' (2000) was released, their grizzly instrumental rock was finally kicking in.

Album rating: MAKE US MILD (*6)

FRASER SIMPSON – vocals, guitar / **ANDREW SMITH** – guitar / **KEVIN D BLACK** (b. KEVIN GILLIES, 11 Nov'82) – bass / **ROBBIE 'DES TROY' COOPER** – drums (ex-NEUROLA, of/ex-MAGNETIC NORTH POLE)

			Evol	not iss.
Jan 00.	(7") (evol 08) **FIELDSETTINGS. / CAR – LOW**		-

			Guided Missile	not iss.
Mar 00.	(cd) (GUIDE 39CD) **MAKE US MILD**		-

– Rowan guerilla / Tears on the golf course / A / Wild nature crank / B / For the driver / C / Histrography / D / El Topo.

—— KEVIN GILLIES has since joined YESSA DE PASO who've now become LOKI

LAGWAGON

Formed: Goleta, South California, USA . . . 1990 initially as SECTION 8 by JOEY CAPE and various others. As with many latter day punk acts of their ilk, LAGWAGON underwent almost constant personnel upheaval with a line-up of JOEY, CHRIS, SHAWN, JESSE and DERRICK in place for their 1992 debut album, 'DUH'. The fact it was released on 'Fat Wreck Chords' only served to confirm the band were pitched squarely in the NOFX camp of head-on, harmonised hardcore and more than occasional lyrical buffoonery. Which isn't to say they were incapable of tackling meatier issues, as the likes of 'ISLAND OF SHAME' – from sophomore effort, 'TRASHED' (1994) – attested. 1995's 'HOSS' attempted a more serious approach, leaving out the puerile cover versions and opting for starker song titles. The self deprecating theme behind 'DOUBLE PLAIDINUM' (1997) at least suggested that as a group, LAGWAGON knew the limits of their potential. By the release of the latter set – which featured erstwhile POSIES guitarist KEN STRINGFELLOW – their revolving door line-up included a couple of renegades from RICH KIDS ON LSD (DAVE RAUN and CHRIS) who both played on 1998's 'LET'S TALK ABOUT FEELINGS'. • **Covered:** BAD MOON RISING (Creedence Clearwater Revival) / BROWN EYED GIRL (Van Morrison) / etc. • **Trivia:** CAPE (on guitar!) and DAVE RAUN also moonlight with punky covers star band, ME FIRST AND THE GIMME GIMMES, who've released two albums in '97 and '99.

Album rating: DUH (*7) / TRASHED (*6) / HOSS (*6) / DOUBLE PLAIDINUM (*5) / LET'S TALK ABOUT FEELINGS (*6) / LET'S TALK ABOUT LEFTOVERS outtakes (*5)

JOEY CAPE – vocals / **CHRIS** – guitar / **SHAWN** – guitar / **JESSE** – bass / **DERRICK** – drums

			Fat Wreck Chords	Fat Wreck Chords
1992.	(cd/c/lp) <FAT 502 CD/MC/LP> **DUH**	-	

– Tragic vision / Folied again / Bury the hatchet / Angry days / Noble end / Child inside / Bad moon rising / Beer goggles / Inspector Gadget / Parents guide to living / Mr. Coffee / Of mind and matter / Stop whining / Lag wagon.

Feb 94.	(cd) <(FAT 513-2)> **TRASHED**		

– Island of shame / Lazy / Know it all / Stokin' the neighbors / Give it back / Rust / Goin' south / Dis'chords / Coffee and cigarettes / Brown eyed girl / Whipping boy / No one / Bye for now.

Nov 95.	(cd/c/lp) <(FAT 532 CD/MC/LP)> **HOSS**		

– Kids don't like to share / Violins / Name dropping / Bombs away / Move the car / Sleep / Sick / Rifle / Weak / Black eyes / Bro dependent / Razor burn / Shaving your head / Ride the snake.

—— **DAVE RAUN** – drums, percussion (ex-RICH KIDS ON LSD, of ME FIRST AND THE GIMME GIMMES) repl. DERRICK / **KEN STRINGFELLOW** – guitar (ex-POSIES) repl. SHAWN

Aug 97.	(cd/c/lp) <FAT 558 CD/MC/LP> **DOUBLE PLAIDINUM**	-	

– Alien 8 / Making friends / Unfurnished / One thing to live / Today / Confession / Bad scene / Smile / Twenty-seven / Choke / Failure / To all my friends.

—— **CHRIS** – guitar (ex-RICH KIDS ON LSD) repl. STRINGFELLOW

Nov 98. (10"lp/cd) <(FAT 578/+CD)> **LET'S TALK ABOUT FEELINGS**
– After you my friend / Gun in your hand / Leave the light on / Change despair / Train / Hurry up and wait / Everything turns grey / Love story / Messengers / Kids are all wrong / May 16 / Owen Meaney.

— LAGWAGON will return for an album in spring '03

– compilations, etc. –

Feb 00. (cd) *My Records*; <(MR 8056-2)> **LET'S TALK ABOUT LEFTOVERS**
– Feedbag of truckstop poetry / Narrow straits / Burn that fridge when we get to it / Losing everyone / Jimmy Johnson / Eat your words / Want / Bring on the dancing horses / Randal gets drunk / Raise a family / Restrain / No one like you / Brodeo / Wind in your sail / Over the hill / Defeat you / Layman's terms / Jazzy Jeff / The champ / Demented rumours / Truth and justice / No conviction / Jaded ways.

LAIKA

Formed: London, England ... early '94 by ex-MOONSHAKE pair, MARGARET FIEDLER and JOHN FRENETT, along with that band's former producer, GUY FIXSEN. Completing the line-up with LOU CICCOTELLI and 5th member LOUISE ELLIOTT, LAIKA took their name from the first dog in space and set about creating otherworldly sounds in line with their label, Too Pure's eclectic music policy. Keen to expound on the inter-related nature of life, philosophy graduate, FIEDLER, explained that LAIKA's driving force was an attempt to break down the illusive musical barriers between indie, dance technology and the avant-garde. The first results came in the shape of 1994's debut album, 'SILVER APPLES OF THE MOON', a multi-layered, CAN meets TRICKY (FIEDLER's ghostly vocal reminiscent of the latter's sidekick, NICOLETTE) affair bringing 70's Krautrock/pop up to date. A month or two after its completion, former PJ HARVEY drummer, ROB ELLIS came into the fold and, by the release of their follow-up set, 'SOUNDS OF THE SATELLITES' (1997), FRENETT had made way for percussion man, ALONZO MENDOZA. Another experimental fusion of pop electronics and haunting avant-jazz, a definite highlight was 'SHUT OFF / CURL UP', a subversive alternative cousin to MADONNA's 'Justify My Love' (!). With 'GOOD LOOKING BLUES' (2000), FIEDLER's dark, sonorous vocals were given higher prominence, as impermanent and ethereal an ingredient in LAIKA's sonic stew as the hypnotic electronica and quilted rhythms with which they've patented their sound. • **Covered:** GERMAN SHEPHERDS (Wire). • **Note:** no relation to LAIKA & THE COSMONAUTS on 'Upstart' records.

Album rating: SILVER APPLES OF THE MOON (*7) / SOUNDS OF THE SATELLITES (*7) / GOOD LOOKING BLUES (*6)

MARGARET FIEDLER – vocals, samples, etc (ex-MOONSHAKE) / **GUY FIXSEN** – guitar, bass, etc / **LOU CICCOTELLI** – drums, percussion / **JOHN FRENETT** – bass (ex-MOONSHAKE) / plus **LOUISE ELLIOTT** – flute, sax

	Too Pure	Warners
Oct 94. (cd) *(purecd 042)* <43010> **SILVER APPLES OF THE MOON**		Feb95

– Sugar daddy / Marimba song / Let me sleep / Itchy & Scratchy / Coming down glass / If you miss / 44 robbers / Red river / Honey in heat / Thomas / Spider happy hour.

— added **ROB ELLIS** – drums, piano, percussion (ex-PJ HARVEY) — **ALONZO MENDOZA** – vibraphone; repl. FRENETT

Jan 97. (2x12") *(pure/+cd 067)* **BREATHER. / LOOKING FOR THE JACKALOPE / ('A'&'B'mixes)**

Feb 97. (d-lp/cd) *(pure/+cd 062)* <31002> **SOUNDS OF THE SATELLITES**
– Prairie dog / Breather / Out of sight and snowblind / Almost sleeping / Starry night / Bedbugs / Martinis on the Moon / Poor gal / Blood + bones (moody mix) / Shut off – Curl up / Spooky Rhodes / Dirty feet + giggles.

Sep 97. (12"ep/cd-ep) *(pure 071 rt/cds)* **ALMOST SLEEPING / PRAIRIE DOG (Maxwell House mix). / SHUT OFF – CURL UP (Cabbage Boy mix) / BREATHER (Luke Vibert mix)**

	Too Pure	Too Pure
Feb 99. (7") *(pure 091s)* **UNEASY. / LIE LOW**		-

(cd-s+=) *(pure 091cds)* – Single word.

Jan 00. (12") *(pure 101t)* **BLACK CAT BONE. / BADTIMES** | | - |

Feb 00. (lp/cd) (<*pure 089/+cd*>) **GOOD LOOKING BLUES** | | Apr00
– Black cat bone / Moccasin / T. street / Uneasy / Good looking blues / Windows' weed / Glory cloud / Go fish / Badtimes / Knowing too little / Lie low / A single word.

May 00. (7") *(pure 103s)* **BADTIMES. / HE KNOWS**
(cd-s+=) *(pure 103cds)* – Longwave.

Kirk LAKE

Born: 1964, Notting Hill Gate, London, England. Looking like a cross between tortured martyr JEFF BUCKLEY and a man who is, ahem, "a little bit woo and a little bit wey", the penfriend of Charles Bukowski (who had very much influenced his music and writing) began his musical explorations when he joined the rather sloppy outfit SHAKEDOWN with SUEDE drummer SIMON GILBERT in the early 90's. The postman-cum-author debuted with 1995's 'SO YOU GOT ANYTHING ELSE?', a collection of spoken word tracks that featured members of SONIC BOOM and The BOO RADLEYS, which sounded extremely similar to some of NICK CAVE's narrated performances. The dark and moody youngster dragged himself back into the world of music once again in 1997 with the TINDERSTICKS-esque 'THE BLACK LIGHTS', appearing on hip indie 'Che'. ANTHONY and MATTHEW from London-based JACK (going under the nom de plume JACQUES for this release only) helped our down-on-his-luck hero as did SPACEMEN 3 and MARTIN CARR. The one major flaw on the album was that LAKE attempted singing for the first time, which, in context, might've been a bad thing. Returning to the fold for 2002's eponymous debut set for 'Dreamy' records, LAKE covered familiar territory (i.e. melancholic poetry set to lo-fi music) and kept his maverick eccentricity alive and kicking.

Album rating: SO, YOU GOT ANYTHING ELSE? mini (*5) / THE BLACK LIGHTS (*5) / KIRK LAKE (*6)

KIRK LAKE – vocals/words / with **SONIC BOOM** (ex-SPACEMEN 3) / **MARTIN CARR** (of BOO RADLEYS)

	Che	not iss.
Apr 95. (m-cd/m-lp) *(che 27 cd/lp)* **SO, YOU GOT ANYTHING ELSE?** (spoken word)		-

— next with **ROY MONTGOMERY** (organ) + **TOM HODGES** (saxophone)

	I – Che	not iss.
Aug 96. (cd) *(IRE 103-2)* **THE BLACK LIGHTS** (remixes from debut)		-

– Aggravated TDA / Finish your drink so I can get your glass to the wall – There's something / Clay vs. Tyson (DMX Krew remix) / Hooligan night (band version) / Baddest man on the planet / Dementia pugilistica / Looking for Dylan Thomas.

— now w/ backing from group **JACK** (aka **MATTHEW + ANTHONY**)

Apr 97. (7"; as KIRK LAKE / JACQUES) *(IRE 205-7)* **FIVE FINGER DISCOUNT. / ALL THE CLOCKS HAVE STOPPED** | | - |
(cd-s+=) *(IRE 205-2)* – 10,000 dog / Dementia pugilistica.

	4M	not iss.
Nov 97. (7") *(MSR 001)* **A BEAUTIFUL ENDING. /**		-

— In Jul'98, KIRK collaborated with ROY MONTGOMERY on his 'Rocket Girl' single, 'LONDON IS SWINGING BY HIS NECK' (RGIRL 3)

— KIRK LAKE would subsequently provide some extra vox for JACQUES

	Dreamy	not iss.
May 02. (cd) <*rem 010cd*> **KIRK LAKE**		-

– I'll take it as read / Nothing to no one / A beautiful ending / Painted horses / Interlude / Morphology / Everyday lingers / The adventures of an abstract detective / The wedding song / The end of music.

L/A/L (see under ⇒ LOVE AS LAUGHTER)

LAMBCHOP

Formed: Nashville, Tennessee, USA ... 1992 initially as POSTERCHILD by KURT WAGNER, the 90's country-lounge answer to 60's icons, CAT STEVENS and TIM HARDIN. His hesitant but heavy-lidded vocal monotone sat perfectly against the lethargic drowsiness of the country-jazz played by his large backing ensemble. Although they could hardly be termed rock, LAMBCHOP emerged from the flourishing alternative roots scene with an album on 'Merge' ('City Slang' UK) 'I HOPE YOU'RE SITTING DOWN' (1995). A post-modern cousin of CHET ATKINS (although at times at least twice removed!), the record revealed WAGNER's love of vintage string-laden production and his penchant for beer-soaked, meandering tales of ordinary madness. Early the following year, KURT and LAMBCHOP delivered another collection of near comatose country vignettes, 'HOW I QUIT SMOKING', this time around wrapped up in a classic 70's Nashville production sheen courtesy of arranger, John Mock. One of the record's highlights, 'THE MAN WHO LOVED BEER', was issued as the first LAMBCHOP single and has since been adopted as author, Martin C. Strong's theme tune. Joking aside, 1996 also saw the release of a third set, the critically acclaimed live/festival (1995) recorded 'HANK', relaxzzzed audiences no doubt giving WAGNER and Co the first ever horizontal standing ovation. A third studio album, meanwhile, sauntered onto the scene in 1997, the LAMBCHOP man surely being just a tad ironic in naming it 'THRILLER', although opening cuts, 'MY FACE YOUR ASS' and 'YOUR SUCKING FUNNY DAY', raised the pulse a little. Prolific as ever, WAGNER and his entourage (they had all worked on VIC CHESNUTT's 'The Salesman & Bernadette') returned in 1998 with possibly his/their best album to date, 'WHAT ANOTHER MAN SPILLS', featuring croonsome classic, 'THE SATURDAY OPTION', alongside a few covers by F.M. CORNOG (i.e. EAST RIVER PIPE) and one by Curtis Mayfield, 'GIVE ME YOUR LOVE'. The country-soul meets disco connection carried on to the acclaimed 'NIXON' (2000) wherein WAGNER's impenetrable songwriting was transformed into (relatively) more intelligible but no less fascinating observations on life's essential minutiae. As for the album title, it was apparently inspired by the infamous ex-American President, LAMBCHOP kindly supplying a reading list of related material on the sleeve. Take for instance minor hit, 'UP WITH PEOPLE' – complete with their hilarious and overlooked "Nixon" video – and opener 'THE OLD GOLD SHOE'; surely this was truly the album that set WAGNER and Co apart from anything remotely similar. LAMBCHOP returned with their most intimate and mature album to date, the breezy 'IS A WOMAN' in early 2002. If 'NIXON' was a Saturday night out on the town, then 'IS A WOMAN' was most certainly the sleepy Sunday morning afterwards. WAGNER muted the soul-thang to give us soft croaky songs, reminiscent of 70's RANDY NEWMAN. The tracks, all recorded bare-bones, like delicate little ornaments, also displayed WAGNER's impending talent which makes you wonder if this man was writing songs thirty years ago, he would be a living legend by now. MARK NEVER's production and spacey guitar was impeccable, with the last track even sliding into a reggae riff. Bloody marvellous.

LAMBCHOP (cont) — THE GREAT INDIE DISCOGRAPHY — The 1990s

Album rating: I HOPE YOU'RE SITTING DOWN (*6) / HOW I QUIT SMOKING (*7) / HANK (*7) / THRILLER (*6) / WHAT ANOTHER MAN SPILLS (*7) / NIXON (*9) / IS A WOMAN (*8)

KURT WAGNER – vocals, guitar / **BILL KILLEBREW** – guitar / **MARC TROVILLION** – bass / **STEVE GOODHUE** – drums / **ALLEN LOWREY** – percussion / **JONATHAN MARX** – clarinet, trumpet / **SCOTT CHASE** – washboard, maracas

		not iss.	Thump Audio
1992.	(7"ep; as POSTERCHILD) <1> **AN OPEN FRESCA / A MOIST TOWELETTE.** / (other two by Crop Circle Hoax)	-	

		City Slang	Merge
1992.	(7") <MRG 048> **NINE. / MOODY FUCKER**	-	
1994.	(7") <02> **MY CLICHE. / LORETTA LUNG** (re-iss. 1999 on Spanish label 'Elefant'; ER 15913-69)	-	
—	<above on 'Sunday Driver'>		
Aug 94.	(7") <MRG 066> **SOAKY IN THE POOPER. / TWO KITTENS DON'T MAKE A PUPPY**	-	
1994.	(7") **IT'S IMPOSSIBLE.** / (other track by NONPAREILS AND BARTLEBEES) (above on 'Contrast International') <below on 'Bloodsucker'>	-	
1995.	(7"ep) <19846> **I CAN HARDLY SPELL MY NAME / THE SCARY CAROLER.** / (other tracks by CYOD)	-	

line-up WAGNER, CHASE, MARX, TROVILLION, LOWREY, KILLEBREW + GOODHUE added **PAUL NIEHAUS** – lap steel guitar, trombone, vocals / **JOHN DELWORTH** – organs / **DEANNA VARAGONA** – vocals, alto sax, banjo, cello / **MIKE DOSTER** – bass (on 1)

Mar 95.	(cd/d-lp) (efa 04953-2/-1) <MRG 70> **I HOPE YOU'RE SITTING DOWN / JACK'S TULIPS**		Sep94
	– Begin / Betweemus / Soaky in the pooper / Because you are the very air he breathes / Under the same moon / I will drive slowly / Oh, what a disappointment / Hellmouth / Bon soir, bon soir / Hickey / Breathe deep / So I hear you're moving / Let's go bowling / What was he wearing? / Cowboy on the moon / The pack-up song. (cd re-iss. May00; 8403530)		
1995.	(7") <7003-7> **YOUR LIFE AS A SEQUEL. / SMUCKERS**	-	
—	<above on 'Mute America'> <below issued for 'I-sore 5' club'>		
1996.	(5") <#1> **SCARED OUT OF MY SHOES.** / (other track by Spent)	-	
Jan 96.	(cd/d-lp) (efa 04969-2/-1) <MRG 97> **HOW I QUIT SMOKING** – For which we are truly thankful / The man who loved beer / The militant / We never argue / Life's little tragedy / Suziequ / All smiles and mariachi / The scary caroler / Smuckers / The militant / Garf / Your life as a sequel / Theone / Again.		
Apr 96.	(7"m)(cd-s) (efa 04974-45)(efa 04977-03) **THE MAN WHO LOVED BEER. / ALUMNI LAWN / BURLY & JOHNSON**		
—	added guest **HANK TILBURY** – banjo		
Jul 96.	(m-cd/10"m-lp) (efa 04979-2/-1) <MRG 108> **HANK (live)** – I'm a stranger here / Blame it on the brunettes / The tin chime / Randi / Doak's need / Poor bastard. (cd+=) – I sucked my boss's dick. below by VIC CHESNUTT, DAVE LOWERY, KURT WAGNER + PAUL NIEHAUS		
1996.	(7") <25075> **A LOOSE CONFEDERATION OF SATURDAY CITY-STATES** – Plagarism / How can I face tomorrow.	-	
—	added **PAUL BIRCH JR., MARKY NEVERS, ALEX McMANUS + JOHN CATCHINGS** ; to repl. STEVE + BILL		
Jul 97.	(7") <(MRG 124)> **CIGARETTIQUETTE. / MR. CRABBY** (above & below 45's released on 'Merge' only)		
Sep 97.	(7") <(MRG 126)> **WHITEY. / PLAYBOY, THE SHIT**		
Sep 97.	(cd/lp) (efa 04998-2/-1) <MRG 130> **THRILLER** – My face your ass / Your fucking sunny day / Hey, where's your girl / Crawl away / Gloria Leonard / Thriller / The old fat robin / Superstar in France.		
Nov 97.	(cd-ep) (efa 0870-03) **YOUR SUCKING FUNNY DAY / THE PETRIFIED FLORIST / THE THEME FROM THE NEAL MILLER SHOW**		-
—	added **DENNIS CRONIN, MIKE GRIFFITH, VIC CHESNUTT + TONY CROW**		
Sep 98.	(cd/lp) (efa 08711-2/-1) <MRG 146> **WHAT ANOTHER MAN SPILLS** – Interrupted / The Saturday option / Shucks / Give me your love (love song) / Life #2 / Scamper / It's not alright / N.O. / I've been lonely for so long / Magnificent obsession / King of nothing never / The theme from the Neil Miller show.		
Nov 98.	(ltd-12") <fu 003> **GIVE ME YOUR LOVE (LOVE SONG) - Doppergange remix. / ('A'-album & Doppelganger instrumental)**		
—	<above on City Slang's 'For Us' records, below on own label>		
Dec 98.	(cd-s) <none> **CHRISTMAS TIME IS HERE / CHRISTMAS TIME IS HERE**	-	- radio
Apr 99.	(ltd-7") <(ER 198)> **LA DISTANCIA DESCE ELLA HASTA ALLI (THE DISTANCE FROM HER TO THERE). / THE BOOK I HAVEN'T READ** (above issued on Spanish 'Elefant 6') (below on 'Third Gear')		-
—	**MATT SWANSON** – bass + **DENNIS CRONIN** – trumpet, cornet; repl. KILLEBREW + CATCHINGS + CHESNUTT + GRIFFITH		
Nov 99.	(7") (3G 23) **UP WITH PEOPLE.** / Dump: Die For The Memory		-
—	Nov'99, KURT WAGNER was credited on an EP, 'Chester' with JOSH ROUSE		
Feb 00.	(cd/lp) (20152-2/-1) <MRG 175> **NIXON** – The good old shoe / Grumpus / You masculine you / Up with people / Nashville parent / What else could it be? / The distance from her to there / The book I haven't read / The petrified florist / The butcher boy.	60	
May 00.	(7") (20165-7) **UP WITH PEOPLE. / MISS PRISSY** (cd-s+=) (20159-2) – ('A'-remix by Zero 7). (12") (20159-6) – ('A'side) / ('A'-remix by Zero 7) / ('A'-reprise by Zero 7).	66	-
Feb 02.	(cd/d-lp) (20190-2/-1) <MRG 504> **IS A WOMAN** – The daily growl / The new cobweb summer / My blue wave / I can hardly spell my name / Autumn's vicar / Flick / Caterpillar / D. Scott Parsley / Bugs / The old matchbook trick / Is a woman.	38	
May 02.	(cd-s) (20196-0) **IS A WOMAN / THE NEW COBWEB SUMMER (Schneider TM Lanzarote remix) / IS A WOMAN (Alpha remix) / IS A WOMAN (Maxwell implosion rework) / IS A WOMAN (video)**		-

LAND OF NOD

Formed: Cheltenham, England ... 1998 out of ELEGANT CHAOS (mid-80's), LUCID DREAM (early to mid 90's outfit on ECHO & THE BUNNYMEN's label 'Euphoric'; released 'PURE PUNK' in March '97) and REVERB. LAND OF NOD were a duo comprising ANT WALKER on guitar and DAVE BATTERSBY on bass, complete with a drum machine. The pair – with at times DAVID WRENCH – were obviously inspired by "Krautrock" (mainly FAUST) and honed-in their personal musical experiments via space-rock outlet, 'Ochre'. Albums such as 'TRANSLUCENT' (1999) and 'TIMELESS POINT' were two starter-kits from a batch of average brain-numbing recordings; think GODSPEED, LABRADFORD and STARS OF THE LID. WALKER is also the man behind the similarly wigged-out PULSAR and LAKE SCENE, who were part of the 'Ochre' team.

Album rating: TRANSLUCENT (*5) / TIMELESS POINT (*5) / MONT VENTOUX mini (*5) / ARCHIVE collection (*7) / INDUCING THE SLEEP SPHERE (*7)

ANT WALKER – guitar / **DAVE BATTERSBY** – bass / + others incl. **DAVID WRENCH** – synthesizer, piano, cello / + others

		Ochre	not iss.
Jun 95.	(ltd-12"ep; Various Artists) (OCH 002) **Voyage To The Cosmic Underworld: Volume One** – Floating around in the bubblebuzz / (other artists).		-
Mar 96.	(ltd-12"ep) (OCH 007) **SEEING INTO THE GREAT VOID / REVOID.** / (split w/ The BASS CADETS)		
Jan 98.	(ltd-7"clear) (OCH-PRO 003) **SPIRAL.** / (other by ECTOGRAM)		
Jul 98.	(ltd-10"claret) (OCH 023) **MASAKI. / CHRONICLE BLUEPRINT #1 / EXPONENTIAL**		
Feb 99.	(cd) (OCH 007LCD) **TRANSLUCENT** – The land of Nod (sunrise) / Quadrant zero / Exponential #2 / Filtration / Parabolic velocity / Objective reality / Ephemeral / Missing mass / Luminosity / The land of Nod (earthrise). (re-iss. Nov00; same)		
Jan 00.	(7"blue) (RAPT45 25) **CHRONICLE BLUEPRINT #2. / LAKE MERRIT** (above issued on 'Enraptured')		-
Sep 00.	(cd) (OCH 022LCD) **TIMELESS POINT** – Ice station Nod / Timeless point / Signs of life / Second sight / Reality channel / Conventional grid pattern / Tropical dust cloud / Masaki / Alternate / Noose of ice.		-
Jul 01.	(m-cd) (SILBER 015) **MONT VENTOUX** – Orientation point / San Juan capistrano / Altitude / Sommet / Anqueutil / Mont Ventoux. (above issued on 'Silber')		
Feb 02.	(d-cd) (OCH 029LCD) **ARCHIVE: 02** (compilation 1995-2001) – Floating around in the bubblebuzz / Seeing into the great void / Revoid (Bass Cadets remix) / Interceptor #1 (demo) / Interceptor #2 (demo) / Spiral / Exponential / Chronicle blueprint #1 / Masaki / Escape velocity / Chronicle blueprint #3 / C.O.B.E. / Ice station Nod (original) / Bubblebuzz // The Land Of Nod – Earthrise (out-take) / Quadrant zero (out-take) / Objective reality (out-take) / Noose of ice (live) / Drop / Chronicle blueprint #2 / Lake Merrit / Ice station Nod (live) / Reality channel (live) / Chronicle blueprint (live) / Orientation point (live) / Noose of ice (live) / Mont Ventoux edit (live) / The Land Of Nod – Earthrise (live).		
Dec 02.	(cd) (OCH 036LCD) **INDUCING THE SLEEP SPHERE** – Half light / Elevator / A sequence of speed / Close to conscious / Loose contact / Radiate / Le sonnet a Mont Vertoux / Change of mind / Shimmering / Eddy / Inducing the sleep sphere.		-

LAPSE

Formed: New Jersey, USA ... 1997 by guitarist CHRIS LEO and bassist TOKO YASUDA. They had long been fixtures on the indie scene, with LEO having performed in scream therapy crunch rockers NATIVE NOD; YASUDA had been in sonic avant-garde combo BLONDE REDHEAD. Both men also were in VAN PELT, and they would transpose certain elements of this band to their work in The LAPSE to continue with the alternative sound they had started to develop there. The LAPSE, however, would be a much more esoteric affair than the fairly straightforward heavy rock VAN PELT, with experimental tunes operating far beyond the more linear arrangements of the duo's earlier project. LEO'S lyrics range from poetic to concise to gibberish on both LAPSE albums, 'BETRAYAL' (1998) and 'HEAVEN AIN'T HAPPENIN'' (2000), and his soft-spoken vocals are interestingly complemented by his musical partner's turns on the mic, with her mix of soft sibilant hisses and howls. No matter which sonic guise the two collaborators choose to come in, they are always intensely interesting listening.

Album rating: Native Nod: TODAY PUBERTY, TOMORROW THE WORLD (*7) / Van Pelt: STEALING FROM OUR FAVORITE THIEVES (*5) / THE SULTANS OF SENTIMENT (*6) / the Lapse: BETRAYAL (*6) / HEAVEN AIN'T HAPPENING (*5)

NATIVE NOD

CHRIS LEO – vocals, guitar / **DANNY LEO** – drums, vocals

		not iss.	Gern Blandsten
1994.	(7"m) <GERN 9-7> **BREAD. / HIGH TIDE IN ALASKA / BACK TO MIMSEY**	-	-
1995.	(7") <GERN 24-7> **LOWER G.I. BLEED. / RUNNER**	-	-

LAPSE (cont)

1995. (cd) <GERN 22CD> **TODAY PUBERTY, TOMORROW THE WORLD** (compilation)
– Bread / High tide in Alaska / Back to Mimsey / Answers / Crossing / Tangled / Mr. President / Lower G.I. bleed / Runner.

— after their split, DANNY formed the HOLY CHILDHOOD and his brother TED's short-lived The SIN-EATERS

VAN PELT

CHRIS LEO – vocals, guitar / **BRIAN MARYANSKI** – guitar / **SEAN GREENE** – bass / **NEIL O'BRIAN** – drums

Gern Blandsten / Gern Blandsten

May 96. (lp/cd) <(GERN 25/+CD)> **STEALING FROM OUR FAVORITE THIEVES**
– His steppe is my prairie / It's a suffering / Shame on you / Magic fantasy / You are the glue / Simone never had it this good / His saxophone is my guitar / It's new to me / Turning twenty into two.

— **TOKO YASUDA** – bass (ex-BLONDE REDHEAD) repl. SEAN who joined The SIN-EATERS

Oct 97. (cd/lp) <(GERN 030 CD/V)> **SULTANS OF SENTIMENT**
– Nanzen kills a cat / The good, the bad and the blind / Yamato (where people really die) / My bouts with pouncing / Don't make me walk my own log / The young alchemists / We are the heathens / Pockets of pricks / Let's make a list / Do the lovers still meet at the Chiang Kai – Shek memorial?

— disbanded late 1998

not iss. / Art Monk

Nov 98. (7"ep) <18> **THE VAN PELT**
– The speeding train / Evil high / The democratic teacher's union.

LAPSE

CHRIS LEO + **TOKO YASUDA** plus **DAVID LETO** – drums

Gern Blandsten / Gern Blandsten

Oct 98. (lp/cd) <(GERN 37/+CD)> **BETRAYAL**
– The betrayal / Excessive exposure / Infinite me / Hide your daughters / People wouldn't shoot up if it didn't feel good / The a, b, c, and d's of fascism / The threat / 3 people wide at all times / Mentabolism / From destructive urges reason emerges / Consent / The speeding train / This is not pure aesthetic / We must move backwards to progress.

— **HARRISON HAYNES** – drums; repl. LETO

Southern / Southern

Mar 00. (cd/lp) <(18572-2/-1)> **HEAVEN AIN'T HAPPENIN'**
– Buffet / S.O.S. / I vow for now / Cell yielding cell / H'a'chi / Basilico basilica / Aerial / Dragonflies / Fruit / Into the psychanteum, Chris & Toko.

— now without YASUDA who joined ENON with JOHN SCHMERSAL; **LEO** continued with (2000/01) **GARY KEATING** – bass + **ADAM WADE** – drums (ex-SHUDDER TO THINK, ex-JAWBOX)

LARMOUSSE

Formed: Cumbernauld, Scotland ... 1997 by the duo of CLIFF HENDERSON and SCOTT WALLACE, who set up a rehearsal studio in their garage; apparently on the same estate as the 1980 movie, Gregory's Girl, was filmed. After a few years tucked away from the rigours of normal day life, LARMOUSSE emerged with a 60-minute demo tape, which they duly sent to their favourite indie imprint, 'City Slang' (home of TO ROCOCO ROT and LAMBCHOP). Impressed with their Lo-Fi, avant-rock meanderings, the label despatched their mixing genius, GUY FIXSEN (of LAIKA), who sorted out all the loose ends, especially a 16-minute feedback piece. Early in 2000, an etched 12" of the 10-minute+ epic, 'A UNIVERSAL HELLO', was dispatched promptly to the public. TORTOISE, MOGWAI and JIM O'ROURKE were artistes thrown at them as musical references, although the subtle, tempered beauty of LARMOUSSE oozed more than just the basic and simple acoustic electronica. The eagerly-awaited eponymous debut set – released towards the end of 2000 – disappointed little or no one, from the opening soundscape 'STATIC PHASE' to the final dreamy fourth track, 'TAPE', this was sheer, uninhibited genius.

Album rating: LARMOUSSE (*8)

CLIFF HENDERSON + **SCOTT WALLACE** – instruments, vocals, etc

City Slang / City Slang

Mar 00. (12"etched) (<20155-6>) **A UNIVERSAL HELLO**
Nov 00. (cd) (<20162-2>) **LARMOUSSE**
– Static phase / A universal hello / Relics & artefacts / Tape.

LASSIE FOUNDATION

Formed: Los Angeles, California, USA ... mid 90's by latecomers to the shoegazing tradition, JULIE MARTIN, ANDREW PRICKETT, WAYNE EVERETT and FRANK LENZ. Inspired by everyone from the BEACH BOYS to RIDE, The LASSIE FOUNDATION (what a truly awful name) released a few EP's, 'CALIFORNIA' and 'DIVE BOMBER', before we were treated to full-length, 'PACIFICO' (1999); a fine set made even better when re-released with a re-arranged track listing in the UK a year later. 'EL REY' (from the EP 'EL REY' and also in 1999) was used on the wedding episode of 'Buffy The Vampire Slayer', and it looked like the 'FOUNDATION would carry on with soundtrack work after the release of film score, 'I DUEL SIOUX AND THE ALE OF SATURN' (2001).

Album rating: PACIFICO (*6) / EL REY mini (*5) / THE EL DORADO LP (*6) / PACIFICO UK (*7) / I DUEL SIOUX AND THE ALE OF SATURN soundtrack (*6)

JULIE MARTIN – vocals / **ANDREW PRICKETT** – guitar, recorder / **WAYNE EVERETT** – drums / **FRANK LENZ** – drums / **JEREMY WOOD** – drums

not iss. / Velvet Blue

1996. (cd-ep) <402> **CALIFORNIA**
– I can be her man / I'm stealin' to be your one in a million / Laid with cool / Walking spinning backing free / Save yourself and watch you win.

1997. (7") **I'M STEALIN' TO BE YOUR ONE IN A MILLION. / SAVE YOURSELF AND WATCH YOU WIN** (original demo version)

1998. (cd-ep) <VBM 032> **DIVE BOMBER**
– Dive bomber / You are infinity / She's the coming sun (live) / I can be her man (live) / I'm stealin' to be your one in a million (live).

not iss. / Shogun Sounds

1999. (cd) **PACIFICO**
– Dive bomber / She's the coming sun – She's long gone / Bounties as kisses / Crown of the sea / I got the rock and roll for you / You are infinity / Come on, and let your limelight shine / Bombers' moon / The Moon won't let you wait / El rey.

GrandTheft Autumn / Anisette

1999. (m-cd) <3> **EL REY**
– El Rey / Promise ring / I'm stealin' to be your one in a million (a new chic version) / Conquer me / Crown of the sea / I can be her man.

2001. (cd) **THE EL DORADO LP**
– As good as gold / Every line has let you inside of me / You can't deny a broken heart / The sweet release / Let your boy come back / The battle of Vernon / Through and through powersurge / City of industry / Brand new beat / Hero / Vive les animaux.

GrandTheft Autumn / GrandTheft Autumn

Oct 00. (cd/lp) <(GTA 012 CD/LP)> **PACIFICO**
– Scapa flow / Dive bomber / Crown of the sea / She's the coming sun – She's long gone / Come on, let your lime light shine / El Ray / The Moon won't let you wait / Kisses as bounties / I've got the rock and roll for you / Bombers moon / You are infinity.

Aug 01. (cd; split w/ DURALUXE) <(GTA 013CD)> **I DUEL SIOUX AND THE ALE OF SATURN** (music from the film soundtrack)
– Good ctimes comin' my way / Look all ways / The psalm of the strongest man / All together now / The golden state / You could shoot me down / (other 6 tracks by DURALUXE).

LAZER BOY

Formed: London, England ... 1995 by DAVID LAZONBY (not ambient/dance man, DAVE LAZENBY!), along with his girlfriend keyboardist, KIM BIRTWELL. After writing a few songs together they enlisted the help of MICK DALE, STEVE GOODWIN (both from CUD) and indie veteran, CHRIS TROUT. The extremely weird LAZONBY began his quest for pop stardom when he toured Eastern Europe with his saxophone as a busker. After the man released a jazz album (one which he later admitted was "shit"), the self-confessed songsmith moved to Newcastle and London (after a brief spell as a dogs body in a record shop) before writing the pop nouveau single 'CRAZY BUSINESS'. Afterwards he recruited the aforementioned musicians and retreated to the studio to record his first opus. Time was evidently well spent when the band issued the lo-fi/sci-fi epic album, 'FORGET NOTHING' (1996), which sounded like The FLAMING LIPS – if they had recorded in space at 125 revolutions per second. Daring cresendos with a slight hint of MERCURY REV-psychedelia and an arena of sounds were all included on this wayward journey through the musical macabre set to LAZONBY's baritone vocals. • **Trivia:** LAZONBY was also a member of COPING SAW until 1998.

Album rating: FORGET NOTHING (*6) / THE FALLEN WORLD (*6) / THE MAN ON THE STREET WHERE HE LIVES (*5)

DAVID LAZONBY – vocals, multi / **KIM MARIE BIRTWELL** – keyboards / **CHRIS TROUT** – guitar (ex-KILGORE TROUT, ex-AC TEMPLE, ex-SPOONFED HYBRID, of BEAR) / **MICK DALE** – bass (ex-CUD) / **STEVE GOODWIN** – drums (ex-CUD)

Vespertine / not iss.

Feb 96. (10"m-lp; split w/ QUIGLEY) (VES 001) **SPRING WILL BE A LITTLE LATE ...**
– Blues for Donald / All the gang's here / Shaky Bob's theme / Where be pop (2 with QUIGLEY).

Chute / not iss.

May 96. (7") (CHUTE 006) **AYE AYE CAPTAIN. / (other by SPARE SNARE)**

Freek / Freek

Jun 96. (cd) (<FRR 021>) **FORGET NOTHING**
– It's your train / Aye aye captain / 27-100 / Mathilda Marlene / Mi gato pequeno / You'll never no / Crazy business / Forget nothing / A tomorrow person / Shaky Bob's theme / Vortex girl from Hell / Shortwave but why / My love is like a rainbow baby.

Vespertine / not iss.

Oct 96. (7") (VES 003) **A SCAN FOR LIFE. / ST. IVES VORTEX-ON-SEA**

Che / not iss.

Nov 96. (7") (che 063) **LOVE IS AMARILLO. / Zambonis: AVALANCHE**

— DALE who joined EMBRACE

Probe Plus / not iss.

Jul 97. (cd) (PROBEUP 44CD) **THE FALLEN WORLD**
– Fallen world overture / Atom / A normal life / Lazer fox / Chemical / How do you like those apples / The shopping centre whistler / Forget nothing (computerized Trout version) / 100-173 / Pray / Fallen world finale.

—— added **TOM ALEXANDER** – keyboards

	Rocket Soul	not iss.
Feb 99. (cd) *(RSM 1)* **THE MAN ON THE STREET WHERE HE LIVES**	☐	-

LAZYCAME
(see under ⇒ JESUS & MARY CHAIN; in 80's section)

LEAVES

Formed: Reykjavik, Iceland ... early 2000 by former MOWER guitarist ARNAR GUDJONSSON, HULLUR HAUSON, ARNUR OLAFSSON, BJARNI GRIMSSON and ANDRI ASURIMSSON. Iceland's answer to the likes of COLDPLAY or MUSE, their debut single 'BREATH' – released early in 2002 – was welcomed by fans of what ALAN McGEE described as "bed wetter" music. Nevertheless, follow up singles 'RACE' and 'CATCH', both taken from the parent debut album 'BREATH', served to further enhance the reputation of music being produced by Icelandic outfits. Past efforts by the likes of BJORK and SIGUR ROS, to mention but a few, had already gone a long way to reversing the view that bands from any part of Europe were capable of nothing better than cheesy, eurovision, electro pop. 'BREATH' delivered a tender and accomplished set of songs, atmospheric yet with a prevailing pop sensibility. I'm booking my holidays north this year.

Album rating: BREATHE (*7)

ARNAR GUDJONSSON – vocals (ex-MOWER) / **ARNAR OLAFSSON** – guitar, accordion / **ANDRI ASURIMSSON** – keyboards / **HULLUR HAUSON** – bass / **BJARNI GRIMSSON** – drums

	B-Unique	not iss.
Jan 02. (7") *(71762-7)* **BREATHE. / FAVOUR**	☐	-
(cd-s+=) *(71762-2)* – Alone in the sun.		
May 02. (7") *(BUN 020-7)* **RACE. / ALRIGHT**	66	-
(cd-s+=) *(BUN 020CDS)* – Perfect.		
Aug 02. (7") *(BUN 029-7)* **CATCH. / (others by The CORAL + ELECTRIC SOFT PARADE)**	☐	-
(cd-s) *(BUN 029CDS)* – ('A'side) / Tomorrow never knows / (+1).		
Aug 02. (cd) *(0927 48739-2)* **BREATHE**	71	-
– I go down / Catch / Silence / Breathe / Crazy / Epitaph / Alone in the sun / Deep blue sky / Suppose / Race / We.		
Oct 02. (7") *(BUN 037-7)* **SILENCE. /**	☐	-
(cd-s+=) *(BUN 037CDS)* –		

LE COUPE

Formed: San Francisco, California, USA ... late 90's by STACY MICHELSON and JOSH MOORE. Their brand of sweet electronically under-pinned indie pop first saw the light in the record shops on the fittingly-titled post-millennial 'Shelflife' records compilation, 'You Make Me Smile', with their 'OUR WAY' track. The indie imprint quickly put out their debut 7", 'ALL I HEAR', which showcased the band's dreamy pop sensibilities with MICHELSON's luscious vocals being key above the underlying drum machine rhythms. Following this release, LE COUPE found their way on to several other indie collections, notably for 'Just For A Day' and 'Contact' records, as well as being featured on a complimentary CD for Japanese magazine, Beikoku Ongaku. With their SAINT ETIENNE-style doped-out pop in full swing, the duo put out their eponymously-titled album 'LE COUPE' (2001), utilising the help of fellow musicians including DWAYNE PALASEK and CHAD CALDER. Displayed on this set was a mature and optimistic songwriting approach and more of the same enhancing romantic dynamics between MOORE and MICHELSON. The pair could also be found on their mother label's ORCHESTRAL MANOEUVRES IN THE DARK homage compilation doing OMD's early 'PRETENDING TO SEE THE FUTURE'.

Album rating: LE COUPE (*6)

STACY MICHELSON – vocals / **JOSH MOORE** – guitar / + a drum machine

	not iss.	Shelflife
Mar 00. (7"m) *<life 017>* **ALL I HEAR. / MILKY TEA / PLANE**	-	☐
—— added **CHAD CALDER** – bass / **DWAYNE PALASEK** – trumpet		
Oct 01. (cd) *<life 026>* **LE COUPE**	-	☐
– It will never work out / Forget about it / You showed me / Stars in the movies / Plane / Saved up / Better way / When I think / Second to no one / Safe.		

Arthur LEE (see under ⇒ LOVE)

LE MANS

Formed: San Sebastian, Spain ... 1986 as AVENTURAS DE KIRLIAN by JONE GABARAIN, IBON ERRAZKIN, TERESA ITURRIOZ and drummer PERU IZETA. The band played simple, melodic guitar driven pop, issuing a self-titled mini-set in 1989, before being dropped by Madrid's thriving indie label 'D.R.O.'. The ensemble stuck together and changed their name to LE MANS, meanwhile IZETA switched to guitar and new percussionist GORKA OCHOA joined. Four years had passed and by 1993 the group had independently recorded their first album proper, 'LE MANS', a record which eventually was released on 'Elefant'. Unhappy with their musical direction, the group quickly recorded its follow-up, 'ENTRESEMANA' (1994), which saw the quintet's first use of strings and a diverse musical outlook, nabbing snippets from bands such as MY BLOODY VALENTINE and echoing the songwriting styles of LEONARD COHEN (only in Spanish!). An unannounced remix album, 'ZEBRINA' followed, and thus began LE MANS' exploration into electronica, trance and the occasional ambience. 'SAUDADE' (1996) justified this jolting switch; a dense, macabre indulgence into trip-hop, matched with some haunting arrangements and a crackling production. However, the end was soon nigh as the troupe's final album, 'AQUI VIVA YO' (1998), was delivered to great acclaim on both sides of the Atlantic. It featured some of their best work – tightly-knit arrangements with less of an experimental standpoint. The group parted company, with IBON ERRAZKIN the only member to continue recording.

Album rating: LE MANS (*5) / ENTRESEMANA mini (*6) / ZERBINA mini remixes (*6) / SAUDADE (*6) / AQUI VIVIA YO (*7)

JONE GABARAIN – vocals / **IBON ERRAZKIN** – guitar / **TERESA ITURRIOZ** – bass / **PERU IZETA** – drums

	D.R.O.	not iss.
May 89. (m-lp; as AVENTURAS DE KIRLIAN) **AVENTURAS DE KIRLIAN**	-	- Spain
—— (1991) added **GORKA OCHOA** – drums (PERU now guitar)		

	Elefant	not iss.
Nov 93. (lp/cd) *(ER 1005/+CD)* **LE MANS**	-	- Spain
– Un rayo de sol / Jersey Ingl S / Juan / Por tres a os / Astronautas / Al bulevar / El cielo / El nuevo cantante / H.E.L.L.O. / Lucille / Pescado y vino / Manzanas y naranjas.		
Dec 94. (m-lp/m-cd) *(ER 1020/+CD)* **ENTRESEMANA**	-	- Spain
– Con Peru en la playa / La tarea / A la hora del cafe / Entresemana / San Martin / Mejor dormir / Cancion de si tu me quieres / Perezosa y tonta.		
Nov 95. (m-lp/m-cd) *(ED 002/+CD)* **ZERBINA** (remixes)	-	- Spain
1996. (12"/cd-s) *(ED 004/+CD)* **JONATHAN JEREMIAH. / LUCIEN (instrumental) / AMA HIL ZAIGU**	-	- Spain
Apr 96. (d10"lp/cd) *(ER 1023/+CD)* **SAUDADE**	-	- Spain
– Desacierto / Cancion de puede ser / Oh Romeo, Romeo! / Lucien / Travesia / Dry Martini / Saudade / Orlando / Paramour.		
1996. (7") *(ER 169)* **DRY MARTINI.**	-	- Spain
1997. (7") *(ER 188)* **MI NOVELA AUTOBIOGRAFICA. / REVELACION**	-	- Spain
(cd-s+=) *(ER 312)* – La balada de la primavera / Catastrofe N17.		
1997. (7") *<GR 007>* **UN RAYO DE SOL. / AMA HIL ZAIGU**	-	☐
(above & below issued on 'Grimsey')		
1997. (cd) *<GR 008>* **LE MANS / ENTRESEMANA** (compilation)	-	☐
1998. (cd-ep) *(ER 314)* **YIN YANG**	-	- Spain
– Yin yang / Jueves / Hay que ver / Belleza arrebatadora.		
May 99. (d-lp/cd) *(ERE 1058/+CD)* **AQUI VIVIA YO**	-	-
– Cancion de todo va mal / Buenos dias corazon / El amor / Aqui vivia yo / No vino, estaba enferma o de vacaciones / Balalaika / La princesita / Yin yang / Papa negro / No me abrurnes amor / Una mujer expansiva / Mi novela autobiografica / Ay que triste estoy! / Sic transit Gloria Mundi.		

—— split after above; ERRAZKIN went solo in a lounge/cocktail mood

Don LENNON

Born: Boston, Massachusetts, USA. LENNON's musical career began as the lead singer with local band The UMPTEENS. In 1997, after a few years together – and a few minor releases – LENNON quit to pursue a solo career. He entered the studio with producer SEAN DRINKWATER, and recorded solo debut 'MANIAC', which was released later in 1997 on the 'Martin Philips' label. His quirky, folk-pop songs and deadpan delivery led to comparisons with JONATHAN RICHMAN, and saw him begin to achieve some notoriety within the indie community – simplicity was the key for LENNON – musically and lyrically. Although hiring drummers, bassists, and saxophonists, he performed all vocals, guitar and keyboards himself. His lyrics were playful and charming, evident on tracks like 'TURN THE LIVING ROOM INTO A DANCE FLOOR' and 'BEST FRIENDS FOREVER'. DON's eponymous second LP – this time produced by PETE WEISS – was released in 1999; then came his best release to date – 2002's 'DOWNTOWN' (now on Indiana's 'Secretly Canadian' label). LENNON takes no prisoners on this hilarious/serious album. It was teeming with pop culture references, and contained tracks poking fun at DAVE MATTHEWS, LENNY KRAVITZ and JOHN CALE, in a seamless blend of the sublime and the ridiculous.

Album rating: MANIAC (*5) / DON LENNON (*6) / DOWNTOWN (*8)

DON LENNON – vocals, guitar / with various session people

	Martin Philip	Martin Philip
Dec 97. (cd) *(MP 001CD) <415127>* **MANIAC**	☐	Feb98
– Definition of love / Grad student / Dance music / Best friends forever / I walk right by / Talking to girls / Party all the time / Cool to be alone / Party coordinator / Party in September / Get moving / I need friends / Take back the night / Turn the living room into a dance floor. *(re-iss. Oct01; same)*		
1999. (cd) **DON LENNON**	-	☐
– My debut album / Hang out with my friends / DI'97 / Ich heisse Don / Bass guitar / Double dong / One rock·band / Halloween / Get to know my neighbors / My favorite rock group / Not the same / The women who run with the wolves / Field of dreams / The need to sing.		

Don LENNON (cont)

Apr 02. (cd) <(SC 62CD)> **DOWNTOWN** — Secretly Canadian / Secretly Canadian
– Really Dave Matthews / John sex / Matthews comes alive / Lenny Kravitz and Lisbon / The Boston music scene / Gay fun / Jean-Michel / Mekons come to town / The night Kramer met Ann / John Cale.

LENOLA

Formed: New Jersey, USA ... 1994 by lynch-pin member JAY LAUGHLIN, and a later expansion which included former bandmate SEAN BYRNE, DAVID GRUBB, SEAN COLAN and JAY's brother CHRIS. Wearing their alternative-pop influences (a la MERCURY REV and FLAMING LIPS) on their sleeve, the band debuted with a handful of 7"s including 'TARRED DOG SAVED' and their debut LP, 'THE LAST 10 FT. OF THE SUICIDE MILE' (1996) on their own imprint 'Tappersize'. This initial offering showed the noise pop direction the band were heading courtesy of winning melodies and hooks washed over by MY BLOODY VALENTINE-esque feedback reverb. Not wasting much time, the group put out their sophomore album, 'THE SWERVING CORPSE' the following year, a record which showcased the band's confidence to stretch out their sonic range and add some more unique touches. With a nod to the record collector, the outfit put out the dual compilation EPs 'THE DAY THE LAUGHTER SMELLED' (1998) and 'THE RESURRECTION OF THE CLOSE-UP ON THE MAGIC SPOT' (1998), which collected together stop-gap material. Their third full-length piece, 'MY INVISIBLE NAME' (1999), tracked their continuing musical improvement and was succeeded two years later by their best effort to date, 'TREAT ME TO SOME LIFE'.

Album rating: THE LAST 10 FT. OF THE SUICIDE MILE (*5) / THE SWERVING CORPSE (*5) / MY INVISIBLE NAME (*5) / TREAT ME TO SOME LIFE (*6)

JAY LAUGHLIN – vocals, guitar / **CHRIS LAUGHLIN** – keyboards / **DAVID GRUBB** – guitar / **SCOTT COLAN** – bass / **SEAN BYRNE** – drums

Tappersize Tappersize

Nov 94. (7") <TPZ 1> **DISCOUNT OATMEAL. / GREEDO**
Jul 95. (7",7"red) <TPZ 2> **TARRED DOG SAVED. / FRISBEE WEEKEND**
Jan 96. (7"m) <L 196> **I SHARED A ROUTE WITH JIM / SLAP ME. / (other by THE ASTEROID #4)**
(above issued on 'Lounge')
Aug 96. (cd) <TPZ 3> **THE LAST 10 FT. OF THE SUICIDE MILE**
– Shared a route / Patches / Z-frame / Pipebomb / Rat circle / Twice twice / Brand new less / Helen / Riding greens / Gorilla arm.
Oct 97. (cd) <(TPZ 4)> **THE SWERVING CORPSE**
– Warm dog over the fence / Super guns / Good luck with it / Spazco / Test disaster / Martin song / Track this / Plates must spin / Horse vs. tank / Center of the red leaf pine / Subtraction: addiction's tricky pal / Curses will fly / Jimothy.
1998. (7"ep) <FUZ 9> **THE RESURRECTION OF THE CLOSE-UP ON THE MAGIC SPOT**
– Lights on the hut / I'm as nude as the day is long / The resemble a keg / Track this (left) / Customs (right).
(above issued on 'Fuzzy Box', below on 'Blackbean & Placenta')
1998. (one-sided-12"ep) <ACME 43> **THE DAY THE LAUGHTER SMELLED**
– Lenny puff / It's 1 a.m., Bob is up / Pause & serve / Peat gatherers honeymoon / I'm in your band / The cold is coming on.
Apr 99. (cd) <TPZ 020> **MY INVISIBLE NAME**
– Jet row / Unsettling down / Who made me bleed like this? / Your stars / Baby loves headrub / Round Sunday / Dust from your skin / Frukus / Something for Brown / Bring yourself home / Stood up by a cold front / Blessed me.

Earworm Merrimac

1999. (7") <MMC 1> **HIDDEN WHEEL. / (other by PHOTON BAND)**
Jun 00. (one-sided-7"yellow) (WORM 65) **SLIPPING UNDER THE SHADOWS**

Tappersize-File 13 / Tappersize-File 13

Nov 00. (cd-ep) <(TPZ 12 – FT 31.5)> **THE ELECTRIC TICKLE** — Oct00
– Slipping under the shadows / Driving over to your house / Black eyes / Small shin splints / Inside the golden days of missing you.
Mar 01. (cd) <FT 32> **TREAT ME TO SOME LIFE**
– First floor killer / Do you want to see a volcano? / Cast your lines / Lazy eye / Derelict organ / White-lined knuckle landing / I don't mean / Slipping under the shadows / Come back to retreat / Come down / Medicine glow / Silver credentials.

not iss. Tappersize-Devil In The Woods

Oct 01. (cd-ep; split w/ FIVER) <TPZ 14.5 – DIW 45> **DR. PICKLEFEATHER'S ELECTRIC SOOTHING-MUSIC AND CALMATIVE**
– (track by FIVER) / As far as I can throw you / (track by FIVER) / What's this fight about? / (track by FIVER) / Eye in the sky.

not iss. 2nd Story

Oct 01. (7"clear) <SS 1> **KEEP COMING BACK. / BEFORE THE RING**

Ted LEO / PHARMACISTS
(see under ⇒ CHISEL)

LEOPARDS

Formed: Glasgow, Scotland ... mid-90's by veterans of the early 80's 'Postcard' scene, CAMPBELL OWENS (ex-AZTEC CAMERA), MICK SLAVEN (ex-JAZZATEERS) and SKIP REID, the former two having recently split from PAUL QUINN AND THE INDEPENDENT GROUP. The LEOPARDS fused psychobilly surf and goth (play that geetar, man!), witnessed on a legendary debut gig at Postcard records Fin de Siecle club supporting The NECTARINE No.9. The spotted ones subsequently became one of the first signings to the 'Creeping Bent' stable and, having appeared on the inaugural 'A Leap Into The Dark' (bent 001), they unleashed their debut summer '95 single, 'BURNING'. Further support slots with the SECRET GOLDFISH, SPACEHOPPER and English punk bard VIC GODARD (all stablemates at '...Bent'), earned them a higher profile around the indie circuit, while a plethora of releases in 1997 made sure they weren't about to change their proverbial spots. The album, 'THEY TRIED STAYING CALM' (1997), and split 45's with ADVENTURES IN STEREO and APPENDIX OUT, looked set to put these fiery cats back into the spotlight. However, a proposed collaboration with old mucker, GODARD, has yet to materialise; though they'd have to reform.

Album rating: THEY TRIED STAYING CALM (*6)

MICK SLAVEN – vocals, guitar (ex-JAZZATEERS, ex-PAUL QUINN) / **CAMPBELL OWENS** – bass (ex-AZTEC CAMERA, ex-PAUL QUINN) / **SKIP REID** – drums

Creeping Bent / not iss.

Jun 95. (7") (bent 003) **BURNING. / LITERALLY BURNING**
Mar 97. (7") (bent 007) **SURF ON. / DERAILED BY MAD DOG**

w-drawn

Jun 97. (7") (bent 019) **THEME E. / (track by Adventures In Stereo)**
(cd-ep+=) (bent 019cd) – (tracks by the Revolutionary Corps & Spacehopper). (re-iss. Dec00; same)
Jun 97. (cd) (bent 021cd) **THEY TRIED STAYING CALM**
– Ju ju girl / Surf on / Motorcycle baby / Theme E / Burning / Starlings / Always on your side / Vendetta machine / Cutting a short dog / Carried by six / Full moon light / Derailed by mad dog / Piney's prayer / Being wowed. (re-iss. Dec00; same)
Sep 97. (7") (bent 027) **CUTTING A SHORT DOG. / (other track by Appendix Out)**
Mar 98. (7") (bent 031) **STARLINGS. / V MACHINE: BACK TO CRUISING SPEED**

—— the group split after above

LES SAVY FAV

Formed: Brooklyn, New York, USA ... 1995 by TIM HARRINGTON, SYD BUTLER, SETH JABOUR and GIBB SLIFE. The group toured continuously for two years before being picked up by 'Sub-Pop' and releasing debut EP 'RODEO' and debut album '3/5' in the same year. The album was in equal parts tensely aggressive and emotionally moving with fuzzy anxious guitars making way for haunting melodies. Vocalist HARRINGTON's clever use of flirting between the English and French languages is also extremely effective. LES SAVY FAV continued to impress with the release of albums 'CAT AND THE COBRA' (1999) and mini 'ROME (WRITTEN UPSIDE DOWN)' the following year. Part of the charm of the group was the sketchiness of their albums; however as their reputation had grown so had their recording budget and this was evident on their third full album 'GO FORTH'. Released in 2001, this was the group's most fully realised album to date. Unfortunately being afforded the luxury to polish their sound worked against them and this release missed the tension of their previous efforts.

Album rating: 3/5 (*6) / THE CAT AND THE COBRA (*6) / GO FORTH (*5)

TIM HARRINGTON – vocals / **SETH JABOUR** – guitar / **GIBB SLIFE** – guitar / **SYD BUTLER** – bass / **PATRICK MAHONEY** – drums

not iss. Sub Pop

1997. (7") <SP 411> **RODEO. / BLACKOUTS ON THURSDAY**
(UK-iss.Apr01; same as US)

not iss. Self-Starter

1997. (lp,cd) <PSP 003> **3/5**
– Intro / New teen anthem / Cut it out / Pluto / Cassolette / Scout's honor / Je t'aime / Raise buildings / Blackouts / False starts.
1998. (cd-s) **REFORMAT. / REFORMAT (live)**

not iss. DeSoto

Jan 99. (7") <LE 28> **OUR COASTAL HYMN. / BRINGING US DOWN**
(UK-iss.Feb01; same as US)

—— **HARRISON HAYNES** – drums; repl. MAHONEY

not iss. French Kiss

Dec 99. (cd) <1> **THE CAT AND THE COBRA**
– The orchard / We've got boxes / Who rocks the boat / Wake up! / Roadside memorial / Dishonest Don (part 1) / Dishonest Don (part 2) / The end / This incentive / Reformat / Titan. <lp-iss.Dec99 on 'Self-Starter'; PSP 009> (UK-iss.Aug00 on 'Southern'; 18575-2)

Southern Southern

Aug 00. (cd-ep/12"ep) <(18581-2/-1)> **ROME (WRITTEN UPSIDE DOWN)** — Jul00
– I.C. timer / Asleepers union / In these woods / Hide me from next February / Rome.

X-Mist not iss.

May 01. (7") (XM 063) **REPROBATE'S RESUME. / NO SLEEVES**

—— now without SLIFE

LES SAVY FAV (cont)

	Southern	French Kiss
Sep 01. (cd/lp) *(18590-2/-1)* <5> **GO FORTH**	☐	☐

– Tragic monsters / Reprobate's resume / Crawling can be beautiful / Disco drive / The slip / Daily dares / One to three / Pills / Adopduction / No sleeves / Bloom on demand.

Mar 02. (cd-s) *(18597-2)* **split w/ MARS VOLTA + APES** ☐ -

LE TIGRE (see under ⇒ BIKINI KILL)

LETTER E (see under ⇒ JUNE OF 44)

LETTERS TO CLEO

Formed: Boston, Massachusetts, USA ... 1990 by frontwoman, KAY HANLEY, along with SCOTT RIEBLING, GREG McKENNA, MICHAEL EISENSTEIN and STACY JONES. Enthusiastic, young and fresh-faced (well, KAY anyway!), these US wannabe Brit-poppers made their debut in 1994 via Stateside imprint, 'CherryDisc' with the 'AURORA GORY ALICE' album. After one of the record's tracks, 'HERE AND NOW', hit the US Top 60 the following Spring (after being aired on US TV series, 'Melrose Place'), 'Warners/Giant' re-promoted the debut set, which bubbled under the US Top 100. The hastily put together follow-up set, 'WHOLESALE MEATS AND FISH', arrived in August that year, failing to do the band any favours in the power-pop market place despite spawning another minor hit, 'AWAKE'. A new drummer, TOM POLCE, was posted in 1996 after JONES had been despatched to VERUCA SALT, the band's newly bolstered sound showcased on 'GO!' (1997). • **Covered:** SECRET AGEN (Lee Hazlewood) / DREAMS (Fleetwood Mac) / YOU DIRTY RAT (. . . Chesterman).

Album rating: AURORA GORY ALICE (*5) / WHOLESALE MEATS AND FISH (*4) / GO! (*5) / SISTER early work (*5)

KAY HANLEY (b. New England, USA) – vocals / **MICHAEL EISENSTEIN** – guitar / **GREG McKENNA** – guitar / **SCOTT RIEBLING** – bass / **STACY JONES** – drums

	not iss.	CherryDisc
1994. (cd) <24598> **AURORA GORY ALICE**	-	☐

– Big star / I see / Rim shak / Wasted / Get on with it / Here and now / From under the dust / Mellie's comin' over / Come around / Step back. <re-prom.Mar95 by 'Giant'; same> (UK-iss.Apr95 on 'China' cd/c; WOL CD/MC 1057)

	China	Warners
Mar 95. (7"/c-s) *(WOK/+MC 2049)* <17913> **HERE AND NOW. / BIG STAR**	☐	56
(cd-s+=) *(WOKCD 2049)* –		
Jan 96. (7") *(WOK 2069)* <17823> **AWAKE. / ACID JED**	☐	88 Aug95
(cd-s+=) *(WOKCD 2069)* – You dirty rat.		
Jan 96. (cd) *(WOLCD 1068)* <24613> **WHOLESALE MEATS AND FISH**	☐	Aug95

– Demon rock / Fast way / Jennifer / Awake / Laudanum / Acid Jed / Pizza cutter / St. Peter / Little Rosa / Do what you want, yeah / He's got an answer / I could sleep (the wuss song).

— **TOM POLCE** – drums; repl. JONES who joined VERUCA SALT

	not iss.	Warners
Oct 97. (cd/c) <24688-2/-4> **GO!**	-	☐

– I got time / Because of you / Anchor / Find you dead / Veda very shining / Co-pilot / Go! / Sparklegirl / Alouette & me / I'm a fool / Disappear.

— split in 2000 after HANLEY (as Mary Magdalene) earlier went into Boston Rock Opera version of Jesus Christ Superstar; a solo set, 'CHERRY MARMALADE' was available from August 2002

– compilations, etc. –

Nov 98. (cd) Wicked Disc; <1010> **SISTER** - -
– I see / Sister / Pete beat / He's stayin' / Clear blue water / Never tell / Boy / Green eggs / You dirty rat / Secret agent / Dreams.

LEVELLERS

Formed: Brighton, England . . . early '88 by MARK CHADWICK, JEREMY CUNNINGHAM, CHARLIE HEATHER, JON SEVINK and ALAN MILES. Taking their name from the English political radicals of the 17th Century, The LEVELLERS were one of the most successful and consistent bands to emerge from the free festival/crusty scene, building up a loyal grassroots fanbase with their raggle-taggle blend of folk and punk. After Phil Nelson took over as manager the following year, he released a couple of raw EP's on his own 'Hag' imprint, before the band signed to European label, 'Musidisc', and began work on a debut album with WATERBOYS producer, Phil Tennant. While 'A WEAPON CALLED THE WORD' helped introduce their rootsy assault to a larger audience, the band subsequently broke from their contract and signed to 'China', while MILES was replaced by songwriter/guitarist, SIMON FRIEND. Another hectic UK tour followed and by Autumn '91, The LEVELLERS' popularity was such that the 'LEVELLING THE LAND' album made the Top 20 with only the support of minor hit single, 'ONE WAY'. With a more accessible anthemic rock/folk approach, the album took the band's defiantly pro-earth, pro-equality philosophy overground and into the mainstream, 'BATTLE OF THE BEANFIELD' commemorating the famous festival stand-off between hippies and police. In Spring '92, The LEVELLERS scored their biggest hit to date with the 'FIFTEEN YEARS' EP, almost making the Top 10, while they chose to end the year with a series of 'Freakshows' combining the likes of fellow agit-poppers, CHUMBAWAMBA with such established crusty pastimes as juggling and fire-eating. The following year's eponymous album missed the No.1 spot by a whisker, spawning a trio of Top 20 singles in 'BELARUSE', 'THIS GARDEN' and the lovely 'JULIE'; although The LEVELLERS were now rather unlikely but fully fledged pop stars, they also became embroiled in a war of words with the music press and fellow musicians. Not that this affected their popularity one iota, the band finally topping the UK charts with 'ZEITGEIST' (1995) as they found themselves surfing the new wave of enthusiasm for British music in general. 'MOUTH TO MOUTH' (1997) – their final output for 'China' – and 'HELLO PIG' (2000) – their first on 'East West' – kept the fans reletively happy for a while, and even 2002's 'GREEN BLADE RISING' – on punk's final outpost, 'Eagle', kept the wolf from the door. Certainly one of the UK's more conscientious bands, The LEVELLERS are sadly part of a dying breed who still believe that music and politics are a feasible combination. • **Songwriters:** Group compositions except; THE DEVIL WENT DOWN TO GEORGIA (Charlie Daniels Band) / TWO HOURS (McDermott) / GERM FREE ADOLESCENCE (X-Ray Spex) / PRICE OF LOVE (Everly Brothers) / HANG ON TO YOUR EGO (Pixies). • **Trivia:** The FENCE released one single in May '87 on 'Flag'; FROZEN WATER / EXIT.

Album rating: A WEAPON CALLED THE WORD (*7) / LEVELLING THE LAND (*8) / THE LEVELLERS (*6) / ZEITGEIST (*5) / HEADLINES, WHITE LINES, BLACK TAR RIVERS – BEST LIVE (*6) / MOUTH TO MOUTH (*5) / ONE WAY OF LIFE (THE BEST OF . . .) compilation (*8) / HELLO PIG (*5) / GREEN BLADE RISING (*5)

MARK CHADWICK – vocals, guitar, banjo (ex-FENCE) / **JEREMY CUNNINGHAM** – bass, bazouki / **CHARLIE HEATHER** – drums / **JON SEVINK** – violin (ex-FENCE) / **ALAN MILES** – vocals, guitar, mandolin, harmonica

	Hag	not iss.
May 89. (12"ep) *(HAG 005)* **CARRY ME**	☐	-
– Carry me / What's in the way / The lasy days of winter / England my home.		
Oct 89. (12"ep) *(HAG 006)* **OUTSIDE INSIDE. / HARD FIGHT / I HAVE NO ANSWERS / BARREL OF A GUN**	☐	-

	Musidisc	not iss.
Apr 90. (7") *(105 577)* **WORLD FREAK SHOW. / BARREL OF A GUN (acoustic)**	☐	-
(12"+=) *(108 936)* – What you know.		
Apr 90. (cd/c/lp) *(10557-2/-4/-1)* **A WEAPON CALLED THE WORD**	☐	-

– World freak show / Carry me / Outside-inside / Together all the way / Barrel of a gun / Three friends / I have no answers / No change / Blind faith / The ballad of Robbie Jones / England my home / What you know. (cd re-iss. Jan01 on 'Universal'; E 15397-2)

Oct 90. (7") *(106897)* **TOGETHER ALL THE WAY. / THREE FRIENDS (re-mix)** (Arfa mix short version)	☐	-
(12"+=) *(106896)* – Cardboard box city / Social insecurity.		

— **SIMON FRIEND** – guitars, vocals repl. ALAN.

	China	Elektra
Sep 91. (7"/c-s) *(WOK/+MC 2008)* **ONE WAY. / HARD FIGHT (acoustic) / THE LAST DAYS OF WINTER**	51	-
(12"+=/cd-s+=) *(WOK T/CD 2008)* – ('A'-Factory mix) / The Devil went down to Georgia.		
Oct 91. (lp/c/cd) *(WOL/+MC/CD 1022)* <61325-1/-4/-2> **LEVELLING THE LAND**	14	May92

– One way / The game / The boatman / The liberty song / Far from home / Sell out / Another man's cause / The road / The riverflow / Battle of the beanfield. (cd re-iss. Jul99; 4509 96100-2)

Nov 91. (7"/c-s) *(WOK/+MC 2010)* **FAR FROM HOME. / WORLD FREAK SHOW (live)**	71	-
(12"+=/cd-s+=) *(WOK T/CD 2010)* – Outside inside (live) / The boatman (live) / Three friends (live).		
May 92. (c-ep/10"pic-d-ep/12"ep/cd-ep) *(WOK MC/X/T/CD 2020)* **15 YEARS / DANCE BEFORE THE STORM. / RIVERFLOW (live) / PLASTIC JEEZUS**	11	-
Jun 93. (c-s) *(WOKMC 2034)* **BELARUSE / SUBVERT (live at Trancentral) / BELARUSE RETURN**	12	-
(12"+=/cd-s+=) *(WOK T/CD 2034)* – Is this art?		
Sep 93. (lp/c/cd) *(WOL/+MC/CD 1034)* <61532> **THE LEVELLERS**	2	☐

– Warning / 100 years of solitude / The likes of you and I / Is this art? / Dirty Davey / This garden / Broken circles / Julie / The player / Belaruse. (cd re-iss. Jul99; 4509 95908-2)

Oct 93. (7"pic-d/c-s) *(WOK P/MC 2039)* **THIS GARDEN. / LIFE (acoustic)**	12	-
(12"+=/cd-s+=) *(WOK T/CD 2039)* – ('A'-Marcus Dravs remix) / ('A'-Banco De Gaia remix).		
May 94. (7"clear-ep/c-ep/10"pic-d-ep/cd-ep) *(WOK/+MC//CD 2042)* **THE JULIE EP**	17	-

– Julie (new version) / English civil war / Warning (live) / 100 years of solitude / The lowlands of Holland.

Jul 95. (7"pic-d/c-s) *(WOKP 2059)* **HOPE ST. / LEAVE THIS TOWN**	12	-
(7"pic-d) *(WOKPX 2059)* – ('A'side) / Miles away.		
(cd-s+=/c-s++=) *(WOK CD/MC 2059)* – Busking on Hope Street.		
Aug 95. (lp/c/cd) *(WOL/+MC/CD 1064)* <61887> **ZEITGEIST**	1	☐

– Hope St. / The fear / Exodus / Maid of the river / Saturday to Sunday / 4.am / Forgotten ground / Fantasy / P.C. Keen / Just the one / Haven't made it / Leave this town / Men-an-tol. (cd re-iss. Jul99; 0630 11597-2)

Oct 95. (7"/c-s/cd-s) *(WOK/+MC/CD 2067)* **FANTASY. / SARA'S BEACH / SEARCHLIGHTS (extended)**	16	-
(below featured JOE STRUMMER (ex-CLASH) on piano)		
Dec 95. (7"ep/c-ep/cd-ep) *(WOK/+MC/CD 2076)* **JUST THE ONE / A PROMISE. / YOUR 'OUSE / DRINKING FOR ENGLAND**	12	-
Jul 96. (7"ep/c-ep/cd-ep) *(WOK/+MC/CD 2082)* **EXODUS – LIVE (live)**	24	-

– Exodus / Another man's cause / Leave this town / P.C. Keen.

LEVELLERS (cont)

Aug 96. (cd/c) *(WOL CDX/MC 1074)* **HEADLIGHTS, WHITE LINES, BLACK TAR RIVERS – BEST LIVE (live)** [13] [-]
– Sell out / Hope St. / 15 years / Exodus / Carry me / The boatman / 3 friends / Men-an-tol / The road / One way / England my home / England my home / Battle of the beanfield / Liberty / The riverflow. *(cd re-iss. Jul99; 0630 15783-2)*

Aug 97. (c-s/c-d-s) *(WOK MC/CD 2088)* **BEAUTIFUL DAY / BAR ROOM JURY / ALL YOUR DREAMS** [13] [-]
(cd-s) *(WOKCDX 2088)* – ('A'side) / Germ free adolescence / Price of love / Hang on to your ego.

Aug 97. (lp/c/cd) *(WOL+/MC/CD 1084)* **MOUTH TO MOUTH** [5] [-]
– Dog train / Beautiful day / Celebrate / Rain and snow / Far away / C.C.T.V. / Chemically free / Elation / Captains' courageous / Survivors / Sail away / Too real. *(cd re-iss. Jul99; 0630 19856-2)*

Oct 97. (c-ep/cd-ep) *(WOK MC/CD 2089)* **CELEBRATE / RAIN & SNOW (The White Mountain Yarn mix) / SEA OF PAIN / SURVIVORS** [28] [-]
(cd-s) *(WOKCDX 2089)* – ('A'side) / Men-an-tol (live acoustic) / 4 + 20 / Ring of fire.

Dec 97. (12"ep/c-ep/cd-ep) *(WOK/+MC/CD 2090)* **DOG TRAIN / LAST DAYS OF WINTER. / CARRY ME / WHAT'S IN THE WAY** [24] [-]

Mar 98. (12"ep/c-ep/cd-ep) *(WOK/+MC/CD 2091)* **TOO REAL (mixes; Steve Osborne / Morcheeba / Indian Rope Man / Lean Fiddler / Morcheeba instrumental / Bliss)** [46] [-]

Oct 98. (7"/c-s) *(WOK/+MC 2096)* **BOZOS. / DON'T YOU GRIEVE** [44] [-]
(cd-s) *(WOKCD 2096)* – Plastic factory.
(cd-s) *(WOKCDR 2096)* – ('A'side) / New York mining disaster 1941 / Supercharger (heavy mental mix).

Oct 98. (cd/c) *(052173-2/-4)* **ONE WAY OF LIFE (THE BEST OF . . .)** (compilation) [15] [-]
– One way / What a beautiful day / Fifteen years / Shadow on the sun / Hope street / Belaruse / Celebrate / Too real (12"mix) / Bozos / Carry me / Fantasy / Julie / Dog train / Far from home / Just the one. *(ltd.d-cd+=)* – Far from home / Just the one / PC Keen / Sell out / Hope Street / 15 years / Men-an-to. *(cd re-iss. Jun02; 3984 25099-2)*

Jan 99. (c-s) *(WOKMC 2102)* **ONE WAY (new version). / ANGEL** [33] [-]
(cd-s+=) *(WOKCD 2102)* – Windows.
(cd-s) *(WOKCDX 2102)* – ('A'side) / England my home / I have no answers.

East West   not iss.

Aug 00. (c-s) *(EW 218C)* **HAPPY BIRTHDAY REVOLUTION / SURPRISINGLY EASY!** [57] [-]
(cd-s+=) *(EW 218CD)* – Best part of the day.

Sep 00. (cd/c/lp) *(8573 84339-2/-4/-1)* **HELLO PIG** [28] [-]
– Happy birthday revolution / Invisible / The weed that killed Elvis / Edge of the world / Do it again tomorrow / Walk lightly / Voices on the wind / Sold England / Modern day tragedy / Dreams / 61 minutes of pleading / Red sun burns / Gold and silver.

Eagle   Eagle

Sep 02. (7") *(EHAG7 001)* **COME ON. / WELCOME TO TOMORROW** [44] [-]
(cd-s+=) *(EHAGXA 001)* – Vanished.
(cd-s) *(EHAGXS 001)* – ('A'side) / Hooligan / Tranquil blue.

Sep 02. (cd) *(EHAGCD 002)* <20000> **GREEN BLADE RISING** [ ] [Feb03]
– Four winds / Falling from the tree / Pretty target / Come on / Pour / Aspects of spirit / Wild as angels / Believers / A chorus line / Not what we wanted / Wake the world. *(other cd++; EHAGLT 002)* – Come on (dub).

– compilations, etc. –

Jan 92. (7") *Musidisc; (105 557)* **WORLD FREAK SHOW (remix). / WHAT YOU KNOW** [ ] [-]
(12"+=/cd-s+=) *(10893 6/2)* – Barrel of a gun / What you know.

Mar 93. (lp/c/cd) *China; (WOL 1035/+MC/CD)* **SEE NOTHING, HEAR NOTHING, DO SOMETHING** (early material) [ ] [-]

May 01. (cd) *Hag; (HAG 005)* **SPECIAL BREW** [ ] [-]

LEVITATION

Formed: London, England ... 1989 by main songwriter, TERRY BICKERS, who had just split less than amicably with GUY CHADWICK and his HOUSE OF LOVE. Hooking up with DAVE FRANCOLLINI (ex-SOMETHING PRETTY BEAUTIFUL), they invited seasoned indie campaigners, CHRISTIAN 'Bic' HAYES, BOB WHITE and JOE ALLEN to join. Signed to 'Ultimate' records, they lived up to the hype with the release of their debut EP, 'COPPELIA', in 1991, an intense affair highlighting BICKERS' swirls of sensuround sound and guitar effects. Later that year, LEVITATION proved it wasn't a fluke with a second EP, 'AFTER EVER BE', the two collected together as 'THE COTERIE ALBUM' (early 1992). Prior to its release, the quintet became the first outfit to issue a 7" ('SQUIRREL') for the 'Rough Trade Singles Club' series, which led to them signing a full album deal with the label ('Capitol' in the States). LAURENCE O'KEEFE had by now taken the place of JOE ALLEN, making his debut on the incendiary UK Top 50 album, 'NEED FOR NOT' (1992), produced by TIM SMITH (of The Cardiacs) and featuring former MAGAZINE guitarist, JOHN McGEOGH, in a guest capacity. LEVITATION must have been literally floating on air after signing a major record deal with 'Chrysalis'. However, after only one poorly received single, 'EVEN WHEN YOUR EYES ARE OPEN', BICKERS took off to pursue his own wayward muse (he subsequently contributed to the debut album by OEDIPUSSY). The remaining members (HAYES, FRANCOLLINI and O'KEEFE) struggled on with new frontman, STEVE LUDWIN, although the chemistry of their prime line-up was missing on the Australian-only set, 'MEANWHILE GARDENS' (1994). After spells with HEATHER NOVA, the aforementioned trio re-emerged to critical acclaim in the late 90's as DARK STAR, HAYES, O'KEEFE and FRANCOLLINI forming the band during a live SONIC YOUTH experience. Maintaining their love of noisy psychedelia, DARK STAR surfaced late in '98 with the groundbreaking 'GRACEADELICA' EP.

Album rating: THE COTERIE ALBUM compilation (*6) / NEED FOR NOT (*7) / MEANWHILE GARDENS (*4) / Dark Star: TWENTY TWENTY SOUND (*7)

TERRY BICKERS – vocals, guitar (ex-HOUSE OF LOVE, ex-COLENSO PARADE) / **CHRISTIAN 'Bic' HAYES** – guitar (ex-CARDIACS) / **BOB WHITE** – keyboards, vocals / **JOE ALLEN** – bass / **DAVE FRANCOLLINI** – drums (ex-SOMETHING PRETTY BEAUTIFUL)

Ultimate   Capitol

Feb 91. (7") *(TOPP 003)* **NADINE. / SMILE** [ ] [-]
(12"+=/cd-ep+=) **COPPELIA EP** *(TOPP 003 T/CD)* – Paid in kind / Rosemary Jones.

Aug 91. (7"ep/12"ep/cd-ep) *(TOPP 005/+T/CD)* **AFTER EVER BE EP** [ ] [-]
– Firefly / Attached / Bedlam.

Jan 92. (cd/lp) *(TOPP CD/LP 001)* <C2/C4 97959> **THE COTERIE ALBUM** (compilation) [ ] [ ]
(re-iss. Jul94; same)

Rough Trade Sing. Club   not iss.

1991. (7") *(45REV 1)* **SQUIRREL. / IT'S TIME** [ ] [ ]

— **LAURENCE O'KEEFE** – bass (ex-JAZZ BUTCHER) repl. JOE

Rough Trade   Capitol

Feb 92. (cd-ep) *(R 285-3)* **WORLD AROUND / JAY / USHER** [ ] [ ]
May 92. (cd/c/lp) *(R 286-2/-4/-1)* <C2/C4 98501> **NEED FOR NOT** [45] [ ]
– Against nature / World around / Hangnail / Resist / Arcs of light and dew / Pieces of Mary / Smile / Embedded / Coterie.

Chrysalis   Chrysalis

Apr 93. (12"ep/cd-ep) *(12/CD CHS 3972)* **EVEN WHEN YOUR EYES ARE OPEN. / EVERGREEN / MANTRA** [ ] [ ]

— Later in 1993, BICKERS announced his departure, although an album 'MEANWHILE GARDENS' was recorded for the Australian label 'Festival' (D-31018). He was replaced by **STEVE LUDWIN** – vocals. Meanwhile, BICKERS formed The CRADLE in 1995, while a few years later, HAYES, FRANCOLINI and O'KEEFE formed DARK STAR after spells in HEATHER NOVA, production work and DEAD CAN DANCE respectively. An entirelt different LEVITATION issued a CD in '97 entitled, 'Nous Ka Woule'.

DARK STAR

— **HAYES + O'KEEFE + FRANCOLINI**

E.M.I.   not iss.

Oct 98. (10"ep/cd-ep) *(10EM/CDEM 523)* **GRACEADELICA EP** [ ] [-]
– Graceadelica / The crow song / New model worker / Solitude song.

Apr 99. (cd) *(497201-2)* **TWENTY TWENTY SOUND** [ ] [-]
– Ninety six days / I am the sun / About 3am / Vertigo / Graceadelica / Disaffection / Lies / What in the world's wrong / Sound of awake.

Jun 99. (7") *(EM 545)* **ABOUT 2 A.M. / GEE ST.** [50] [-]
(cd-s) *(CDEMS 545)* – ('A'side) / Henry Beckett / Light years.
(cd-s) *(CDEM 545)* – ('A'mixes) / S.P.A.M.

Jan 00. (7") *(EM 556)* **GRACEADELICA. / DIRTY** [25] [-]
(cd-s) *(CDEM 556)* – ('A'side) / What in the world's wrong (session) / Vertigo (session).
(cd-s) *(CDEMS 556)* – ('A'side) / ('A'-video).

May 00. (7") *(EM 566)* **I AM THE SUN. / BUGS** [31] [-]
(cd-s) *(CDEM 566)* – ('A'side) / What in the world's wrong.
(cd-s) *(CDEMS 566)* – ('A'side) / Graceadelica / Birds.

LIARS

Formed: Brooklyn, New York, USA ... late 2000 by bassist PAT NOECKER and drummer RON ALBERSTON, a rhythm section from Nebraska. A press ad attracted Australian ANGUS ANDREW and guitarist/drum-machine programmer AARON HEMPHILL, who joined to complete the band. Exhibiting sound-roots as varied as The FALL and JAWBOX, The LIARS released their debut 'Gern Blandsten' (later re-released by 'Blast First/Mute') album in 2001 under the wonderfully long-winded title 'THEY THREW US ALL IN A TRENCH AND STUCK A MONUMENT ON TOP'. On this album the band would throw group sing-a-long-chorus punk, deep-bass-funk and computer keypads into an angry, intelligent, experimental groove. The 30-minute final soundslab 'THE DUST THAT MAKES THE MUD' (like to use five words where one would do, do these lads) grinds to a halt after starting off as attitude-laden maximum rock'n'roll before changing gears to end up as sample-sprayed hip-hop.

Album rating: THEY THREW US ALL IN A TRENCH AND STUCK A MONUMENT ON TOP (*7)

ANGUS ANDREW (b. Melbourne, Australia) – vocals / **AARON HEMPHILL** (b. Los Angeles) – guitar / **PAT NOECKER** (b. Nebraska) – bass / **ROB ALBERTSON** (b. Nebraska) – drums

Gern Blandsten   Mute

Feb 02. (lp/cd) *(GERN 059/+CD)* <9187> **THEY THREW US ALL IN A TRENCH AND STUCK A MONUMENT ON TOP** [ ] [Oct01]
– Grown men don't fall in the river, just like that / Mr. you're on fire Mr. / Loose nuts on the velandrome / The garden was created and outside / Tumbling walls buried me in the debris with ESG / Nothing is ever lost or can be lost my science friend / We live NE of Compton / Why midnight walked but didn't ring her bell / This dust makes that mud. *(re-iss. Aug02 on 'Blast First'; BFFP 172/+CD)*

Jul 02. (12"ep/cd-ep) <9184> **MAGICAL** [-] [ ]
– Pillars were hollow and filled with candy so we down them / Every day is a child with teeth / Grown men don't fall in the river, just like that.

2002. (cd-ep) **WE NO LONGER KNEW WHO WE WERE**

Blast First   not iss.

Nov 02. (10"ep/cd-ep) *(BFFP 174/+CD)* **FINS TO MAKE US MORE FISH-LIKE** [ ] [-]

LIBERTINES

Formed: Bethnal Green, London, England . . . 2001 by CARL BARAT, PETE DOHERTY, both of whom shared guitar and vocal duties, along with the rhythm section of JOHN HASSALL on bass guitar and GARY POWELL on drums. Having secured a deal with 'Rough Trade', The LIBERTINES arrived on the music scene in 2002 by way of their debut single 'WHAT A WASTER'. Instantly they were compared with other groups such as The STROKES, The WHITE STRIPES and The HIVES who were, jointly, seen as the frontrunners in an emerging garage rock scene. The group were quickly recognised as serious contenders with the release of another, assured, single 'I GET ALONG', almost immediately followed by the debut album 'UP THE BRACKET' (2002). A blend of aggressive, catchy, melodies that THE JAM would be proud of and a scuzzy guitar sound not unlike The STOOGES, the band's first long player demanded that you pay attention. The entire album brims with confidence and attitude, however, 'BOYS IN THE BAND', 'TIME FOR HEROES', and, third single and title track, 'UP THE BRACKET' are particularly rousing. It is no coincidence that the album was produced by MICK JONES of The CLASH as like their punk classics 'London Calling' and 'Give 'Em Enough Rope' this is music for trouble makers.

Album rating: UP THE BRACKET (*7)

CARL BARAT – vocals, guitar / **PETE DOHERTY** – vocals, guitar / **JOHN HASSALL** – bass / **GARY POWELL** – drums

			Rough Trade	Sanctuary
Jun 02.	(7") *(RTRADES 054)* **WHAT A WASTER. / I GET ALONG**		37	-
	(cd-s+=) *(RTRADESCD 054)* – Mayday.			
Sep 02.	(7") *(RTRADES 064)* **UP THE BRACKET. / BOYS IN THE BAND**		29	-
	(cd-s+=) *(RTRADESCD 064)* – Skag & bone man.			
	(cd-s) *(RTRADES 064X)* – ('A'side) / The Delaney / Plan A.			
Oct 02.	(cd/lp) *(RTRADE CD/LP 065)* <83213> **UP THE BRACKET**		35	
	– Vertigo / Death on the stairs / Horror show / Time for heroes / Boys in the band / Radio America / Up the bracket / Tell the king / The boy looked at Johnny / Begging / The good old days / I get along. <US cd+=> – What a waster / Mayday.			

LIBERTY CAGE (see under ⇒ MEN THEY COULDN'T HANG; in 80's section)

LIBIDO

Formed: Bergen, Norway . . . 1995 by EVEN JOHANSEN, CATO EIKELAND and JORGEN LANDHAUGH. Described by some sections of the press as Brit-pop for Scandinavians, these lusty young English-speaking lads were signed to 'Fire' on the strength of a demo cassette. After making their vinyl debut in June '97 with the 'BLOW' single, the trio played the Phoenix festival the following month, showcasing their feisty melodic indie-pop to the sunburnt hordes. Musically lying somewhere between OASIS and The LA'S, LIBIDO attracted further media coverage with the 'SUPERSONIC DAYDREAM' single, even hitting the UK Top 60 early in '98 with 'OVERTHROWN'. The accompanying album, 'KILLING SOME DEAD TIME' (1998), didn't perform so well, the Bergen boys not exactly firing on all cylinders. • **Note:** Not to be confused with the dance act of the same name who had releases on 'Hooj Choons' and 'Top Banana'.

Album rating: KILLING SOME DEAD TIME (*6)

EVEN JOHANSEN – vocals, guitar / **CATO EIKELAND** – bass / **JORGEN LANDHAUGH** – drums (ex-SUNFLOWER)

		Fire	Velvel
Jun 97.	(7") *(BLAZE 113)* **BLOW. / GOD'S GUEST LIST**		-
	(cd-s+=) *(BLAZE 113CD)* – Ashamed and afraid (demo).		
—	'IN MY SHADOW' featured on a 'Fierce Panda' 7"ep V/A, 'Blees His Little Cotton Socks' alongside CROCKETTS, CASSIUS and POHODA + MASSEY		
Sep 97.	(7") *(BLAZE 116)* **SUPERSONIC DAYDREAM. / ANNIE'S SONG**		-
	(cd-s+=) *(BLAZE 116CD)* – Inner beauty is a lame comfort when you're fuck bored – Television devine.		
Jan 98.	(7") *(BLAZE 119)* **OVERTHROWN. / LYING THROUGH HER TEETH**	53	-
	(cd-s+=) *(BLAZE 119CD)* – Man inside my head.		
	(cd-s) *(BLAZE 119CDX)* – ('A'side) / Choking / Time of the month.		
Feb 98.	(cd/c) *(FIRE CD/MC 62)* <79743> **KILLING SOME DEAD TIME**		Mar98
	– Overthrown / Supersonic daydream / Strange news / Crash out / In my shadow / Blow / Remarkably abnormal (good intentions) / Revolving / Molest me / Comfort / God's guest list / Magic mushroom night.		
Mar 98.	(7") *(BLAZE 121)* **REVOLVING. / HURRY SLOWLY**		-
	(cd-s+=) *(BLAZE 121CD)* – Television devine II.		
	(cd-s) *(BLAZE 121CDX)* – ('A'side) / Arm pit veins / Monotony.		
—	LIBIDO looked to have disbanded		

LIBRANESS (see under ⇒ POLVO)

LIFE WITHOUT BUILDINGS

Formed: Glasgow, Scotland . . . mid-1999 by English-born SUE TOMPKINS, CHRIS EVANS (no, not that one), WILL BRADLEY and lone Scotsman ROBERT JOHNSTON. The quartet were all students at the Glasgow School Of Art (like TRAVIS before them) and came together through a shared appreciation of PUBLIC IMAGE LTD and TELEVISION (probably unlike TRAVIS before them). Signed to Rough Trade outlet, 'Tugboat', on the back of their debut London gig, LIFE WITHOUT BUILDINGS (incidentally, named after a JAPAN b-side) released 'THE LEANOVER' as their first single in Spring 2000. Enjoying airplay from both Radio One and XFM, LWB went on to cut two higher profile singles, 'IS IS AND THE I.R.S.' and 'YOUNG OFFENDERS', and a full-length set, 'ANY OTHER CITY' (2001).

Album rating: ANY OTHER CITY (*6)

SUE TOMPKINS – vocals / **ROBERT JOHNSTON** (b.22 Apr'73, Scotland) – guitar / **CHRIS EVANS** – bass / **WILL BRADLEY** – drums

		Tugboat	not iss.
Mar 00.	(7") *(TUGS 018)* **THE LEANOVER. / NEW TOWN**		-
Jun 00.	(7"/cd-s) *(TUGS/+CD 019)* **IS IS AND THE I.R.S. / LET'S GET OUT**		-
Nov 00.	(7"/cd-s) *(TUGS/+CD 026)* **YOUNG OFFENDERS. / DAYLIGHTING**		-
Feb 01.	(cd/lp) *(TUG CD/LP 023)* **ANY OTHER CITY**		-
	– PS exclusive / Let's get out / Juno / The leanover / Young offenders / Philip / Envoys / 14 days / New town / Sorrow.		

LIFT TO EXPERIENCE

Formed: Denton, Texas, USA . . . 1997 by JOSH "BEAR" BROWNING and JOSH "BUCK" PEARSON. Both met while still attending college and with an unknown drummer, they issued an eponymous EP. Their drummer subsequently flitted to join a local band leaving BROWNING and PEARSON the job to find another percussionist. ANDY "THE BOY" YOUNG, a son of a preacher from New Orleans who had only been in the city for four weeks, was asked to join the band, problem being that he wasn't old enough to legally enter any of the other members' local pub haunts, hence the condesending middle title. YOUNG was not the only son of a preacher, which could explain the band's fascination with religion: PEARSON'S father was also a bible puncher whose ideas took a sinister turn, resulting in a family divorce. The newly assembled group played the Texas circuit, gathering a local fanbase until in 2000, with the help of COCTEAU TWINS (and former Grangemouth resident) ROBIN GUTHRIE, LIFT TO EXPERIENCE recorded their album 'THE TEXAS-JERUSALEM CROSSROADS' (2001), a biblical epic of a record that incorporated many styles from gothic blues rock to MOGWAI-esque cinematic post-rock. PEARSON's eerie and often brooding vocals shone best on tracks 'JUST AS WAS TOLD' and the mesmerising 'WITH CRIPPLED WINGS'. The rest of the band conjured up some devilish accompaniment with their twisted guitar hooks reminscent of early SLINT, or late MY BLOODY VALENTINE. Perhaps if Jesus was amongst the rednecks and freaks circulating the dusty roads of Texas, and just happened to be in a gothic biblical rock band, then LIFT TO EXPERIENCE would be the holy grail which he would drink from.

Album rating: THE TEXAS-JERUSALEM CROSSROADS (*8)

JOSH "BEAR" BROWNING – bass **JOSH PEARSON** – guitar / + drummer who left to MANDARIN before recording

		not iss.	Random Precision
1997.	(cd-ep) *<001>* **LIFT TO EXPERIENCE**	-	
	– Falling from cloud 9 / Liftin on up.		

ANDY "THE BOY" YOUNG – percussion; repl. drummer

		Bella Union	Bella Union
May 01.	(d-cd) *<(BELLACD 23)>* **THE TEXAS-JERUSALEM CROSSROADS**		Jun01
	– Just as was told / Down came the angels / Falling from cloud 9 / With crippled wings / Waiting to hit / The ground so soft / These are the days / When we shall touch / Down with the prophets / To guard and to guide you / Into the storm. (d-lp-iss.Mar02; BELLAV 23) (d-cd re-iss. Nov02; same)		
Dec 01.	(cd-ep) *<(BELLACD 33)>* **THESE ARE THE DAYS / WITH THE WORLD BEHIND / FALLING FROM CLOUD 9**		Apr02

LILYS

Formed: Boston, Massachusetts, USA . . . early 90's by KURT HEASLEY, who now lives in Hartford, Connecticut. He/they recorded their first album, 'IN THE PRESENCE OF NOTHING' in 1992, a noisily rough affair in the mould of MY BLOODY VALENTINE. A few singles for 'Slumberland' and 'Summershine' were delivered prior to the 1994 mini-set, 'A BRIEF HISTORY OF AMAZING LETDOWNS'. It featured the lead track, 'GINGER', the guitar intro soon to be used on the CK1 (Calvin Klein) commercial. A second, more accomplished set, 'ECCSAME THE PHOTON BAND' came out at the end of '94 and was picked up by UK 'Che' records, who licensed its release in Britain, having found KURT in Denver playing bass for APPLES IN STEREO. In 1996, after extensive touring around the States and Europe, they issued their third album, 'BETTER CAN'T MAKE YOUR LIFE BETTER', which highlighted a retro "new wave" approach, especially on the classy MONKEES-esque pop tune, 'A NANNY IN MANHATTAN'. In fact a year later, at the end of '97, the song was discovered by fan, Roman Coppola (son of director, Francis Ford Coppola), who used a new remixed version on a Levi commercial. This gave the song a fresh lease of life, helping it to soar high in the UK charts early the following year (the highest position so far for 'Che', although this was through Seymour Stein at Warners). The LILYS returned in spring 1999 with 'THE 3 WAY', a back-to-basics, psychedelic pop set that harked back to the days of SMALL FACES, The WHO and The ACTION. However, much couldn't be said for their specially-released electronica follow-up, 'ZERO POPULATION GROWTH', straight from 'Darla' records' "BLISSED OUT" series. A record too far as their absence from music has since proved.

Album rating: IN THE PRESENCE OF NOTHING (*5) / A BRIEF HISTORY OF AMAZING LETDOWNS mini (*7) / ECCSAME THE PHOTON BAND (*7) / BETTER CAN'T MAKE YOUR LIFE BETTER (*6) / THE 3 WAY (*5) / ZERO POPULATION GROWTH (*3)

KURT HEASLEY (b. 1971) – vocals, guitars, etc / with various musicians incl. **TONY EMMENDOLIO + DAVE JONES** (members of VELOCITY GIRL, SUDDENLY, TAMMY! and The ROPERS)

		not iss.	Slumberland
Mar 91.	(7") <DRYL 007> **FEBRUARY FOURTEENTH. / THREW A DAY**	-	
Sep 92.	(cd/lp) <SLR 20 CD/LP> **IN THE PRESENCE OF NOTHING**	-	

– There's no such thing as black orchids / Elizabeth colour wheel / Collider / Tone bender / Preiscope / It does nothing for me / Snowblinder / The way snowflakes fall / Claire hates me. *(re-iss. Jun00 on 'Spin Art' lp/cd; SRT 80002/+CD)*

		not iss.	Summershine
Mar 94.	(7"ep/cd-ep) <SHINE 33> **TONE BENDER**	-	

– Tone bender / Eskimo / Threw a day / February fourteenth.

		SpinArt	SpinArt
Mar 94.	(10"m-lp/m-cd) <SPART 11/+CD> **A BRIEF HISTORY OF AMAZING LETDOWNS**		

– Ginger / Ycjcyaqfrj / Any place I've lived / Jenny, Andrew and me / Dandy / Evel Knievel. *(UK-iss.Feb98; same as US)*

— KURT recruited **MIKE DEMING** – organ, bass, etc / **DAVE FRANK** – drums / **RICH COSTEY** – synthesizer, producer

| Jan 95. | (cd/lp) <(SPART 43-2/-1)> **ECCSAME THE PHOTON BAND** | | Dec94 |

– High writer at home / Day of the monkey / FBI and their Toronto transmitters / The turtle which died before knowing / The hermit crab / Overlit canyon (the obscured wingtip memoir) / Hubble / Kodiak (reprise) / Radiotricity / Your guest and host. *(UK cd re-iss. Jun00; SRT 80043)*

— current line-up; **KURT HEASLEY + TORBEN PASTORE** – guitar / **TIMOTHY WEIDMAN** – keyboards / **THOM MONAHAN** – bass / **AARON FIRE SPERSKE** – drums

		Che	Primary-Sire
Apr 96.	(7") *(che 51)* **RETURNS EVERY MORNING. / TOUCH THE WATER**		-
Sep 96.	(cd/lp) *(che 52 cd/lp)* <61956> **BETTER CAN'T MAKE YOUR LIFE BETTER**		

– Cambridge California / A nanny in Manhattan / Shovel into spade kit / Elevator is temporary / Can't make your life better / Who is moving / Tennis system (and its stars) / Daz en el Hogar / Bring up the stamp / Sammael sea / Returns every morning. *(cd re-iss. Mar98 on 'Warners'; 3984 22461-2)*

| Nov 96. | (7") *(che 65)* **A NANNY IN MANHATTAN. / MORE THAN THAT IS DESERVED** | | - |
| Dec 96. | (7"ep) *(sp 356)* **WHICH STUDIES THE PAST? EP** | | - |

– Welfare murder plot / Baby's a dealer.
(above released on 'Sub Pop')

| Apr 97. | (cd-ep) <63956-2> **SERVICES (FOR THE SOON TO BE DEPARTED) EP** | - | |

– Hark, an open channel / The energy channel (Tayt variation) / Icy water, water everywhere / The first half second / Pookah / The gravity free atmosphere of MSA.

| Feb 98. | (7"/c-s) *(che 77/+c)* **A NANNY IN MANHATTAN. / THE FIRST HALF SECOND** | 16 | |

(cd-s+=) – *(che 77cd)* – Hark, the open energy channel is icy water, water everywhere / The gravity free atmosphere of MSA.

| Apr 99. | (cd) <31048> **THE 3 WAY** | - | |

– Dimes makes dollars / Socs hip / Accepting applications at university / And one (on one) / Leo Ryan (our pharoah's slave) / Solar is here / The spirits merchant / The lost victory / The generator / A tab for the holiday.

		Darla	Darla
May 99.	(m-cd/m-lp) <(DRL 091 CD/LP)> **ZERO POPULATION GROWTH** (Bliss Out – Volume 15)		Jul99

– The escape / The law / Windows / You win / Lharper laws / Back again.

– compilations, etc. –

| Jun 00. | (cd/lp) *Tiger Style;* <(TS 002 CD/LP)> **ASPERA AD ASTRA / THE LILYS split** (rec.1995) | | May00 |

– Elsa / Coby / Timber / Hymn / (others by ASPERA AD ASTRA).

| Nov 00. | (12"ep/cd-ep) *File 13;* <(FT 34/+CD)> **SELECTED** | | |

– Any several Sundays / Touch the water / Peerless / Won't make you (sleepy) / Peerless II.

LINOLEUM

Formed: London, England . . . 1991 by CAROLINE FINCH and PAUL JONES after a meeting in King's Road. Three years on the songwriting pair added EMMA TORNERO and DAVE NICE and signed to CMO (managers of BLUR and ELASTICA) but maintained an independent stance when they set up their own label, 'Lino Vinyl'. 'DISSENT / TWISTED', issued in 1996, had a sleeve made entirely from (yep, you guessed it) linoleum and was pressed up on a 1000 copies only. Due to the success of the debut single, LINOLEUM returned again, the second single 'SMEAR' (which, like the previous, was a limited edition affair) sold out within days. The quartet were compared to the likes of ELASTICA (whom they toured with, funnily enough) and forgotten indie girl-power protagonists LUSH. This Brit pop comparison was certainly matched by the time their debut set, 'DISSENT' (1997), appeared. This weak, self-indulgent effort didn't survive any unwelcome criticism, sinking like a heavy trademark NOEL GALLAGHER-esque Union Jack guitar under the currents of more contemporary, original music. After a one-off split 45 with SING SING for 'Fierce Panda' in early '99, LINOLEUM – with GAVIN PEARCE replacing ELASTICA-bound PAUL – returned the following year with 'THE RACE FROM THE BURNING BUILDING' (2000), a set that featured their version of The Passions' 'I'M IN LOVE WITH A GERMAN FILMSTAR'.

Album rating: DISSENT (*5) / THE RACE FROM THE BURNING BUILDING (*5)

CAROLINE FINCH – vocals, guitar / **PAUL JONES** – guitar / **EMMA TORNERO** – bass / **DAVE NICE** – drums

		Lino Vinyl	Geffen
Apr 96.	(ltd-7") *(LINO 001)* **DISSENT. / TWISTED**		-
Jun 96.	(ltd-7") *(LINO 002)* **SMEAR. / TIRED**		-

(cd-s+=) – *(LINO 002CD)* – Cellophane.

| Apr 97. | (7") *(LINO 003)* **ON A TUESDAY. / THIS GAME** | | - |

(cd-s+=) – *(LINO 003CD)* – Swim.

| Jun 97. | (7") *(LINO 004)* **MARQUIS. / FLAWED** | | - |

(cd-s+=) – *(LINO 004CD1)* – Shine brightly.
(cd-s) – *(LINO 004CD2)* – ('A'side) / On a Tuesday / Smear / Twisted.

| Jul 97. | (cd/c) *(LINO 005 CD/MC)* <25130> **DISSENT** | | Jun97 |

– Marquis / Dissent / Dangerous shoes / On a Tuesday / Stay awhile / Restriction / Ray Liotta / She's sick / Twisted / Beds / Unresolved / Smear / Ether.

		Fierce Panda	not iss.
Jan 99.	(7"/cd-s) *(NING-NING 66/+CD)* **YOU'RE BACK AGAIN. / Sing Sing: I CAN SEE YOU**		-

— **GAVIN PEARCE** – guitar; repl. PAUL who joined ELASTICA

| Jun 00. | (7") *(NING 093)* **I'M IN LOVE WITH A GERMAN FILM STAR. / SIRENS** | | - |
| Jul 00. | (cd) *(NONG 015CD)* **THE RACE FROM THE BURNING BUILDING** | | - |

– You're back again / Black dress / Don't come down / Sirens / 29 / I'm in love with a German film star / Libertine / Sing to me / Till daylight found them / This scene / Fin.

— LINOLEUM looked to have split after a non-appearance at the Reading Festival

---

LIQUORETTE (see under ⇒ **CORNDOLLY**)

LIQUORICE (see under ⇒ **TSUNAMI**)

LITTLE RED ROCKET (see under ⇒ **AZURE RAY**)

LITTLE VILLAGE (see under ⇒ **LOWE, Nick; 70's section**)

LLAMA FARMERS

Formed: Greenwich, London, England . . . 1996 by BERNIE SIMPSON, his 14 year-old sister, JENNI and two other school friends BROOKE ROGERS and WILLIAM BRIGGS who all, apparently in their own words, played in the "shitiest band in the school". Rumour had it that this cheeky punk-pop outfit started their fully-fledged odyssey when ROGERS lied to BERNIE, claiming he could play the drums. After a few gigs in their native town, the band somehow managed to blag themselves a support slot with DAVE GROHL's vehicle The FOO FIGHTERS. The LLAMA's supposedly signed on the dotted line after a record label drinking bash ended in sheer madness. Apparently, they topped the main stage bill at Glastonbury before their name alone, and managed to convince punters that they were "rockin'" due to the infectiousness of 1998's debut single, 'PAPER EYES'. The LLAMA FARMERS' first album appeared in June 1999 under the R.E.M. parody title, 'DEAD LETTER CHORUS', having already breached the UK Top 75 with singles, 'BIG WHEEL' (their classiest piece so far!) and 'GET THE KEYS AND GO'. However, the aforementioned set didn't possess any range or scope, only wallowing in GREEN DAY-esque silliness. From a band who claimed that they didn't like the SEX PISTOLS, they owed much to the 70's filthy idols. Their use of raw angst punk had turned slightly sour by cliched elderly ethics. 'JESSICA' remained the only true song on the set worth pricking your ears up for, the rest, however, was as tame as Roger Rabbit strumming a noisy guitar. The LLAMA FARMERS tightened up their grunge-meets-Brit-pop sound on their sophomore set, 'EL TOPPO' (2000), a decent enough record that might've gone gold a decade earlier.

Album rating: DEAD LETTER CHORUS (*5) / EL TOPPO (*6)

BERNIE SIMPSON – vocals, guitar / **JENNI SIMPSON** – bass, vocals / **WILLIAM BRIGGS** – guitar / **BROOKE ROGERS** – drums

		Fierce Panda	not iss.
May 98.	(7") *(NING 49)* **PAPER EYES. / PVC**		-
Jul 98.	(7"/cd-s) *(NING 58/+CD)* **ALWAYS ECHOES. / JESSICA / YELLOW**		-

LLAMA FARMERS (cont)   THE GREAT INDIE DISCOGRAPHY   The 1990s

		Beggars Banquet	Beggars Banquet
Jan 99.	(7") *(BBQ 333)* **BIG WHEELS. / MULTI-COLOURED CURTAINS**	67	-
	(cd-s+=) *(BBQ 333CD)* – We've gone wrong.		
May 99.	(7") *(BBQ 335)* **GET THE KEYS AND GO. / ICE LUNGS**	74	-
	(cd-s+=) *(BBQ 335CD)* – Weightless.		
Jun 99.	(cd/lp) *(BBQ CD/LP 212)* <80212> **DEAD LETTER CHORUS**		Nov99
	– Get the keys and go / Lull / Pomoco / Zorillo / When we were friends / Big wheels / Jessica / Yellow / P.V.C. / Always echoes / Forgot to breathe / Kill will / Picture.		
Aug 99.	(7") *(BBQ 338)* **YELLOW. / I DON'T WANT TO TALK ABOUT IT**		-
	(cd-s+=) *(BBQ 338CD)* – Dead letter chorus.		
Apr 00.	(7") *(BBQ 345)* **SAME SONG. / MOVIE**		-
	(cd-s+=) *(BBQ 345CD)* – Reflector.		
Sep 00.	(7") *(BBQ 346)* **SNOW WHITE. / CERTAIN SQUARE**		-
	(cd-s+=) *(BBQ 346CD)* – Waz.		
Oct 00.	(cd/lp) *(BBQ CD/LP 217)* <80217> **EL TOPPO**		Jan01
	– El Toppo / Snow white / Dodgy fudge / Postcards and moonrock / Feathers / Note on the door / Same song / Ear the C / You bore me / Movie. *(hidden track+=)* – Do you remember the time, we got drunk and . . .		
Feb 01.	(7") *(BBQ 351)* **NOTE ON THE DOOR. / LITTLE BUGS**		-
	(cd-s+=) *(BBQ 351CD)* – 7even twists clockwise / Postcards and moonrocks (XfM session) / Note on the door (XfM session).		

LODGER

Formed: London, England . . . 1997 by the indie supergroup line-up of DANNY GOFFEY (of SUPERGRASS) and his collaborative songwriting girlfriend, PEARL LOWE (ex-POWDER), who enlisted two former members of DELICATESSEN, NEIL CARLILL and WILL FOSTER. An unusual set-up due to the fact that DANNY was moonlighting with permission from his aforementioned group and record label, although no publicity was allowed. Stranger still was the fact that PEARL and NEIL took on a barbed vocal tete-a-tete, a NANCY SINATRA and LEE HAZLEWOOD for the 90's you could say! This was much in evidence on their excellent debut single, 'I'M LEAVING', its dual counterplay helping it to scrape into the Top 40. A follow-up, 'ALWAYS ROUND HERE', was much of the same although not faring as well in the commercial world of pop.

Album rating: WALK IN THE PARK (*4)

PEARL LOWE – vocals (ex-POWDER) / **NEIL CARLILL** (b. 1966) – vocals (ex-DELICATESSEN) / **WILL FOSTER** (b. 1973) – bass (ex-DELICATESSEN) / **DANNY GOFFEY** (b. 1975) – drums (of SUPERGRASS)

		Island	Imprint
Apr 98.	(c-s/7") *(C+/IS 693)* **I'M LEAVING. / CIAO**	40	-
	(cd-s+=) *(CID 693)* – Jacko's baby.		
Jun 98.	(7") *(IS 704)* **ALWAYS ROUND HERE. / SEE ME ROUND**		-
	(cd-s+=) *(CID 704)* – Many mistakes.		
	(cd-s) *(CIDX 704)* – ('A'side) / Safe (instrumental) / Not in a million tears.		
Aug 98.	(7") *(IS 713)* **SMALL CHANGE. / DRUNK**		-
	(cd-s+=) *(CID 713)* – Eric.		
	(cd-s) *(CIDX 713)* – ('A'side) / Compass point / Toby said kick me.		
Sep 98.	(cd) *(CID 8073)* <120494> **WALK IN THE PARK**		Nov98
	– I'm leaving / Always round here / The girl's in love with me / Bones / LOve is the game / Old ways / Cold breeze / Top gear luv / Small change / Stepped on / Ciao / Safe.		

–––– LODGER left the building after above set

Jason LOEWENSTEIN (see under ⇒ SEBADOH)

LOFTUS (see under ⇒ RED RED MEAT)

LOFTY PILLARS (see under ⇒ BOXHEAD ENSEMBLE)

LOIS

Born: LOIS MAFFEO, Phoenix, Arizona, USA. LOIS' musical origins derive mainly from the town she was to make her base, Olympia, Washington, where she began studying at Evergreen State College in 1981. It was here that she ran an increasingly popular radio show, 'Your Dream Girl', on the local station KAOS. Her program focused on female rock and punk, and in so doing got her labelled, especially in later years, as from the 'riot grrrl' movement, something which she was not totally comfortable with, but was not constrained by either. But it was not until around 1987, when she taught herself guitar, that LOIS actually decided to make, rather than just play, the music. Her first outfit The CRADLE ROBBERS, begun with REBECCA GATES (later of SPINANES fame) did not last long, LOIS moving swiftly on to form COURTNEY LOVE (not to be confused with the infamous HOLE member of the same name), with drummer PATRICK MALEY. This coupling was more fruitful than her first venture, but only just; the duo split in 1991 after releasing several singles, although the quality of these early pieces gave LOIS a nice stepping stone into her solo career. It was at this point she dropped MAFFEO, and began to bill herself as LOIS, using an assortment of musicians to aid her live, and in the studio. An early collaborator was MOLLY NEUMAN, of BRATMOBILE fame, who appeared on her debut LP, 'BUTTERFLY KISS' (1992). A competent opening set, showcasing LOIS' blossoming songwriting talent, and punk-edged folk pop work. NEUMAN stayed on the drum-stool to aid with sophomore album, 'STRUMPET', released by Olympia based 'K' records in 1993. Touring, and the release of the live set, 'LOWRIDER' (1994) followed, before LOIS teamed up with TIGER TRAP sticskwoman, HEATHER DUNN, to issue her third full-length outing, 'BET THE SKY' (1995), to even greater praise from the indie music press. More quality was to follow with the release of fourth LP 'INFINITY PLUS' (1996), featuring some excellent guest appearances, notably ALAN SPARHAWK of LOW, and a beautiful duet with ELLIOTT SMITH on the track, 'ROUGHER'. The millennium saw LOIS retracing her steps to the duo format, teaming up with FUGAZI drummer, BRENDAN CANTY, to create the paired down beauty 'THE UNION THEMES'. • **Covered:** THE WAY I FEEL INSIDE (Rod Argent).

Album rating: BUTTERFLY KISS (*7) / STRUMPET (*6) / BET THE SKY (*6) / INFINITY PLUS (*5) / Lois Maffeo & Brendan Canty: THE UNION THEMES (*6)

COURTNEY LOVE

LOIS MAFFEO – vocals, guitar / **PAT MALEY** – drums

		not iss.	K
1990.	(7"m) <*IPU 12*> **UNCRUSHWORTHY. / SUNNY DAY / MOTORCYCLE BOY / THE 2nd MOST BEAUTIFUL GIRL IN THE WORLD**	-	
1991.	(7"m) <*IPU 22*> **HIGHLIGHTS. / SHANAKO / DISAPPEARING LESSONS**	-	

		not iss.	Feel Good All Over
1991.	(7"m) **HEY! ANTOINETTE. / STRIPMINE / MY LAST NIGHT**	-	

–––– disbanded late in '91, MALEY ran the 'Yo-Yo' label

LOIS

LOIS – vocals, guitar / with **STUART MOXHAM** – bass (ex-YOUNG MARBLE GIANTS) / **MOLLY NEUMAN** – drums (of BRATMOBILE)

		K	K
1992.	(7") <*IPU 30*> **PRESS PLAY AND RECORD. / LONG TIME GONE**		-
1992.	(lp) <*KLP 15*> **BUTTERFLY KISS**		-
	– Davey / Narcissus / Press play and record / Staring at the sun / Valentine / Stroll always / Spray / Never last / Bonds in seconds / Sorora / Look who's sorry. <(cd-iss. Nov95; KCD 15)>		

–––– now with **STEVE PETERS** – guitar / **DONNA DRESCH + STEPHEN IMMERWAHR** – bass

1993.	(7") <*IPU 40*> **THE TROUBLE WITH ME. / PAGE TWO**		-
1993.	(lp/cd) <*KLP/LCD 21*> **STRUMPET**		-
	– Evening in Paris / Diopter / Return (your turn) / The trouble with me / Sugar rush / Wet eyes / From a heart / Danger UXB / Strumpet MC / The way I feel inside. *(UK-iss.Nov95; same)*		

–––– now with **AMY FARINA** – drums

Jul 93.	(7") <*JULY*> **INDIE. / (other by NOTHING PAINTED BLUE)**		-
	(above issued on 'Simple Machines', below on 'Slabco')		
1994.	(c) **LOWRIDER** (live)		-
	– Wet eyes / The trouble with me / Uncrushworthy / Highlights / Long time gone / Valentine / Hawaiian baby (with The SPINNANES) / Girlfriend in a coma / Davey / Press play and record / Narcissus / Valentine / Stroll always / Spray / Strumpet / The way I feel inside.		

–––– now with **BRENDAN CANTY** – guitar / **JOHN GOODMANSON** – bass

Jan 95.	(lp/cd) <*KLP/KCD 36*> **BET THE SKY**		-
	– Charles Atlas / Shy town / Cover yr. eyes / Transatlantic telephone call / Wrestling an angel / Flamer / The western / Unattached / Steal heat / February 15. *(UK-iss.Nov95; same as US)*		
Apr 95.	(cd-ep) <*K 37*> **SHY TOWN EP**		-
	– Shy town / Grass widow / Hey! Antoinette / Page two / St. What's-her-name.		

–––– now with **BRENDAN + / HEATHER DUNN** – drums (of TIGER TRAP)

Aug 96.	(cd-ep) <*K 57*> **SNAP SHOT RADIO**		-
	– My souvenir / Northern soul / Tell her / No style / Not funny, ha-ha.		
Oct 96.	(lp/cd) <(*KLP 58/+CD*)> **INFINITY PLUS**		-
	– Rougher / Sunrise semester / 2 hearts / R.S.V.P. / Not funny, ha-ha / Capital A / A summer long / Silent auction / Bridge burner / Lucky in a way.		

		not iss.	Kill Rock Stars
Mar 00.	(cd; as LOIS MAFFEO & BRENDAN CANTY) <*KRS 356*> **THE UNION THEMES**	-	
	– These parts / Being blind / How I came to know / Best believe / You love your wounds / Hollow reed / Give faith / Con job / Handwriting / Monument.		

LONE PIGEON

Formed: St. Andrews, Fife, Scotland . . . 1997 as the concept of GORDON ANDERSON, one-time embryonic member/songwriter of The BETA BAND. After helping conceive the aforementioned musical baby for around two years (1994 – mid'96), he had to leave the group in London (their newfound base) due to ill-health. While GORDON struggled to regain enough strength to return to the band, his songs ('Dry The Rain', 'Dogs Got A Bone' and more recently 'The Cow's Wrong') were making the grade for THE BETA BAND; it seemed fate had dealt the singer/songwriter a cruel hand. However, with a collection of songs at his command, THE LONE PIGEON secured a fresh deal with Bury St.Edmunds-based 'Bad Jazz' records (licensed through his own 'Fence' imprint). Fence had delivered the very rare 'MOSES' and '28 SECRET TRACKS' releases between 1997 and 2000. In March 2001, the first few were delivered via the EP, 'TOUCHED BY TOMOKO', a Lo-Fi/WILL OLDHAM eat-yer-heart-out, mix'n'match array of melancholy weirdness; this boy was back in town.

Album rating: CONCUBINE RICE mini (*7)

LONE PIGEON (cont)

GORDON ANDERSON – vocals, instruments (ex-BETA BAND)

		Fence	not iss.

- 1997. (ltd-dat) *(fnc 303)* **MOSES**
  – Time is a white rabbit / Heaven tree / The womblight / My distant friends on Earth / Waiting / Summertime beeswing / If I find her / Born in the light of a Sunday / Rocks / Sitting on a toadstool / The Sol / Transformers / Long way down / Various gnome tracks / I came on home / Ants.
- 2000. (ltd-4xc-box) *(fnc 302)* **28 SECRET TRACKS**
  – Maheema / I'm going down / Love will grow upon the walls / Space / Man from Nazareth / Mean old mind of man / Shadow of a distant past – Scottish heart / Smoke / She came along (big fat song) / Tootle poem deafness / Waterfall (1) / Osaka castle instrumental / Pernickity jack tar deejay / Victoria's song / Rise little baby rise – Broken face / FUKEM / T.Rex teenager / Tiger alley / Sitting on a cloud / We have walked so far / Waterfall (2) / Pernickity jack tar deejay / In the summer of '64 / Can I hold back the tears? / Who are they Iain? / All in the dark can you light me? / I'm tired and I'm happy / Roundabout.

		Bad Jazz – Fence	not iss.

- Mar 01. (7"ep) *(Bebop 31 – fnc 304)* **TOUCHED BY TOMOKO EP**
  – Summertime beeswing / Touched by Tomoko / Empty town / The mean old mind of man / Waterfall.
- Nov 01. (7"ep) *(Bebop 33 – fnc 305)* **ROCKS / YOU THINK ONLY BOATS CAN SINK. / James Yorkston & The Athletes: St. Patrick**

		Fence	Domino

- Jun 02. (m-cd) *(fnc 306)* **CONCUBINE RICE**
  – Concubine rice / King Creosote's wineglass symphony / The road up to Harlow Square / Heaven come down / Beatmix chocbar wrap / Waterfall / Old Mr. Muncherman / Melonbeard / Lonely vagabond / Oh Catherine / Bona fide world / The rainking / Concubine rice. *(lp-iss.Jul01 on 'Sketch'; SKETCH 00124) (re-iss. Sep02 on 'Domino'; WIGCD 109)*

LONESOME ORGANIST (see under ⇒ 5 STYLE)

LONG FIN KILLIE (see under ⇒ BOWS)

LONGPIGS

Formed: Sheffield, England … 1993 by mainman, CRISPIN HUNT, RICHARD HAWLEY, SIMON STAFFORD and DEE BOYLE. The band's career got off to a less than encouraging start when a car crash left CRISPIN in a coma, their problems compounded when a deal with the UK arm of 'Elektra' went awry; they were effectively prevented from recording and playing live for two years, that is, until lawyer, John Stratham, bailed them out. With an album's worth of previously recorded GIL NORTON-produced material in limbo, LONGPIGS eventually secured a new contract with 'Mother', re-recording their debut and soon breaking into the UK Top 75 with their second single, 'SHE SAID'. Finally released in the Spring of '96, 'THE SUN IS OFTEN OUT' spawned a handful of classy hit singles ('FAR', 'ON & ON', a re-issued 'SHE SAID' – Top 20 and 'LOST MYSELF') calling to mind the heady swagger of SUEDE, AUTEURS and occasionally the dark majesty of RADIOHEAD. Why it took three and a half years for a follow-up was anybody's guess. A disastrous American tour which resulted in plenty of fights between HUNT and DEE BOYLE (who had allegedly found God) might have been to blame – the latter was unceremoniously ousted from the band early in '99 while a single 'SWIM' failed to materialise. That "difficult" second album, 'MOBILE HOME', finally hit the shops and the UK Top 40 in October '99; The LONGPIGS were at long last getting back to work. However, just as things took an upturn, the bitter BOYLE was reported to have stuck a glass into HUNT's face after they bumped into each other at a PRETENDERS gig; the frontman received six stitches. With The LONGPIGS out of the way and after augmenting PULP on tour, RICHARD HAWLEY embarked on a solo career, releasing the eponymous 'RICHARD HAWLEY' mini set in spring 2001. Heartworn, and sweet with lush melodies, the record paved the way for a sophomore release, 'LATE NIGHT FINAL' (2001); he was also supporting the likes of COLDPLAY and chums, PULP, while providing songs for LEE HAZLEWOOD and ELVIS tribute sets.

Album rating: THE SUN IS OFTEN OUT (*7) / MOBILE HOME (*7) / Richard Hawley: RICHARD HAWLEY mini (*5) / LATE NIGHT FINAL (*7)

CRISPIN HUNT – vocals, guitar / **RICHARD HAWLEY** – guitar, vocals / **SIMON STAFFORD** – bass, piano / **DEE BOYLE** – drums, vocals (ex-CHAKK)

		Mother	Polygram
Mar 95.	(7") *(MUM 63)* **HAPPY AGAIN. / SALLY DANCES**		-
Jul 95.	(7"/c-s) *(MUM/+C 66)* **SHE SAID. / TAKE IT ALL** (cd-s+=) *(MUMCD 66)* – Devoted / Juicy.	67	-
Oct 95.	(7"red/c-s) *(MUM/+C 68)* **JESUS CHRIST. / SWEETNESS** (cd-s+=) *(MUMCD 68)* – Vagina song / Whiteness.	61	-
Feb 96.	(7"/c-s) *(MUM/+C 71)* **FAR. / BLAH BLAH BLAH** (cd-s+=) *(MUMCD 71)* – Amateur dramatics / Far (Sheffield version).	37	-
Apr 96.	(7"ep/c-ep/cd-ep) *(MUM/+C/CD 74)* <569238> **ON & ON / YOUR FACE. / DOZEN WICKED WORDS / SLEEP**	16	Jan97
May 96.	(cd/c/lp) *(MUM CD/MC/LP 9602)* <531542> **THE SUN IS OFTEN OUT** – Lost myself / She said / Far / On and on / Happy again / All hype / Sally dances / Jesus Christ / Dozen wicked words / Elvis / Over our bodies.	26	
Jun 96.	(7") *(MUM 77)* **SHE SAID. / FLARE IS METEOR** (c-s+=/cd-s+=) *(MUM C/CD 77)* – Soap opera credo / Tendresse. (cd-s) *(MUMXD 77)* – ('A'side) / I lost myself / Far / On and on.	16	-
Sep 96.	(7"/c-s) *(MUM/+C 82)* **LOST MYSELF. / FLOSS** (cd-s+=) *(MUMCD 82)* – Wonder drug / When you're alone.	22	-
Mar 97.	(7"/c-s/cd-s) *(MUM/+C/CD 90)* **SWIM** (above could well have been withdrawn)		-
Sep 99.	(7") *(MUM 113)* **BLUE SKIES. / HEADACHES** (cd-s+=) *(MUMCD 113)* – Seventies just passing over. (cd-s) *(MUMXD 113)* – ('A'side) / I love you / On and on.	21	-
Oct 99.	(cd/c) *(MUM CD/C 9901)* **MOBILE HOME** – The Frank sonata / Blue skies / Gangsters / Free toy / Baby blue / Dance baby dance / Miss believer / I lied I love you / Keep the light alight / Speech bubble / Dog is dead / Loud and clear / In the snow.	33	-
Nov 99.	(7") *(MUM 114)* **THE FRANK SONATA. / AS A GIRL** (cd-s+=) *(MUMCD 114)* – New York. (cd-s) *(MUMXD 114)* – ('A'side) / ('A'-Echoboy remix) / ('A'-My Way remix).	57	-

— they split in 2000; HAWLEY sessioned for PULP on 'We Love You'

RICHARD HAWLEY

with his own session people

		Setanta	Setanta
Apr 01.	(m-cd) (<*SETCD 087*>) **RICHARD HAWLEY** – Coming home / Bang to rights / Sunlight / Caravan / Naked in Pitsmoor / Time has made a change / Happy families.		Jul01
Jul 01.	(cd-s) *(SETCD 090)* **COMING HOME / CANED / CHEAP SPANISH WHINE**		-
Oct 01.	(cd-s) *(SETCD 088)* <*123*> **LATE NIGHT FINAL** – Something is . . .! / Baby, you're my light / Love of my life / The nights are cold / Can you hear the rain, love? / Lonely night / Precious sight / No way home / Cry a tear for the man in the moon / Long black train / The light at the end of the tunnel (was a train coming the other way).		Jan02
Feb 02.	(cd-s) *(SETCD 096)* **BABY, YOU'RE MY LIGHT / SICKPAY / BABY'S BACK**		-
Jul 02.	(ltd-cd-s) **THAT'S ALRIGHT MAMA**		-

P.W. LONG'S REELFOOT (see under ⇒ MULE)

LOOPER

Formed: Glasgow, Scotland … by BELLE & SEBASTIAN member STUART DAVID, who made his debut with the 'Sub Pop'-endorsed single 'IMPOSSIBLE THINGS' prior to issuing the electronica-based album, 'UP A TREE' in 1999. Fusing the twee of B&S with bleeping house beats and an assortment of weird instruments, 'UP A TREE' impressed indie fans of the North on its inaugural outing. What started as a side project, however, turned into something more full-time as DAVID departed from B&S in 2000 to concentrate on LOOPER's second full-set, 'THE GEOMETRID' (2000), a record that boasted a cleaner, polished version of 'UP A TREE'. More of a companion piece, tracks such as 'MONDO '77' and 'MY ROBOT' proved that DAVID had a keen ear for dance, house and FOUR TET-inspired folktronica. His third release, the brooding 'THE SNARE' (which also played as an imaginary soundtrack to his novel 'PEACOCK JOHNSON' – and the title of track four), divided audiences with its midnight jazz and eerie PORTISHEAD-esque drones. Appearing once again, video artist KARN DAVID, guitarist RONNIE BLACK and the sinister saxophonist EVIL BOB all contributed to the album's dark blend of slow-burning, tripped-out styles, that would've felt more at home on a TRANSCIENT WAVES album than something by a Scottish indie guru.

Album rating: UP A TREE (*7) / THE GEOMETRID (*5) / THE SNARE (*6)

STUART DAVID – voice, programmer, keyboards, guitars / w/ **WEE KARN (DAVID)** + **RONNIE BLACK**

		Jeepster	Sub Pop
Jul 98.	(7") <*SP 446*> **IMPOSSIBLE THINGS. / SPACEBOY DREAM No.3**	-	
Feb 99.	(10"ep/cd-ep) *(JPR 10/CDS 010)* **BALLAD OF RAY SUZUKI. / RAY'S GOLDEN FIST (bananahand mix) / SUZUKI'S BIG RIP-OFF (twintub remix)**		-
Mar 99.	(cd/lp) *(JPR CD/LP 005)* <*SP 453*> **UP A TREE** – The treehouse / Impossible things / Burning flies / Festival '95 / Ballad of Ray Suzuki / Dave the Moon man / Quiet and small / Colombo's car / Up a tree again / Back to the treehouse.		
Oct 99.	(10"/cd-s) *(JPR 10/CDS 015)* **UP A TREE AGAIN. / WHO'S AFRAID OF Y2K?**		-

— added **SCOTT TWYNHOLM** – sampler

May 00.	(10"/cd-s) *(JPR 10/CDS 017)* **MONDO '77 / (ALL OF) THESE THINGS (Are Available At Tony's Textiles mix)**		-
May 00.	(cd/col-lp) *(JPR CD/LP 009)* <*SP 499*> **THE GEOMETRID** – Mondo '77 / On the flipside / Modem song / Uncle Ray / Puddle monkey / These things / Bug rain / My robot / Tomorrow's world / Money hair.		

— next featured **MICK COOKE, ISOBEL CAMPBELL, MARGARET SMITH, DEBBIE POOLE, DAVID CAMPBELL** + arranger **CHRIS LAUTERBACH**

		Mute	Mute
Jun 02.	(cd-s) *(CDMUTE 273)* **THE SNARE / PEACOCK'S FALL / PEACOCK'S APPEAL** (10") *(10MUTE 273)* – ('A'side) / Arrow / Peacock Johnson (original).		
Jun 02.	(cd/lp) *(CD+/STUMM 195)* <*9181*> **THE SNARE** – The snare / Sugarcane / New York snow / Peacock Johnson / Driving myself crazy / Lover's leap / Good girls / She's a knife / This evil love / Fucking around.		
Nov 02.	(cd-s) *(CDMUTE 274)* **SHE'S A KNIFE / SHE'S A KNIFE (Ladytron vs Looper mix) / ALL DIAMONDS (Phipps mix)**		-

Mary Lou LORD

Born: 1967, Salem, Massachusetts, USA. Despite briefly attending Boston's Berklee Music College, LORD paid her dues the hard way as a street busker after relocating to London. Upon her return to Boston, she was spotted by the 'Kill Rock Stars' label, releasing a debut single, 'ABOUT A BOY', in 1994. There was much speculation that the lyrics referred to KURT COBAIN, a one-time close friend of MARY's; the singer subsequently became the focus of COURTNEY LOVE's ire as the HOLE frontwoman openly criticised LORD in the press. Preferring to concentrate on her music, the songstress delivered an eponymous mini-set in early '95, its knowing – some from hero THE BEVIS FROND – lyrics and bittersweet indie-folk instigating a major label A&R scramble. Eventually opting for 'Sony' subsidiary, 'Work', LORD was augmented by an impressive cast of alternative luminaries (including ELLIOTT SMITH, MONEY MARK, JULIANA HATFIELD and the BEVIS FROND's NICK SALOMAN) on her belated debut full length album, 'GOT NO SHADOW' (1998). Branching out from her trademark acoustic strum, she pumped up the volume with a newly electrified sound that bore the polished hallmarks of a major label recording budget, LORD covering tracks by SALOMAN. The queen of cover versions again raided her record collection for her 2000 split EP with SEAN NA NA, sweetening up Lucinda Williams' 'HARD ROAD' amongst others. It was a case of more of the same on 'LIVE CITY SOUNDS' (2001), a set documenting LORD's return to the subway busking culture which spawned her and which LORD recorded herself. The covers rarely branched out from the tried and tested folk/rock/indie axis, lending the record a reliable if somewhat one dimensional sheen. • **Covered:** ANDALUCIA (John Cale) / SMELLS LIKE TEEN SPIRIT (Nirvana) / ONLY BUSINESS (Rain Parade) / THAT'S THE WAY (Led Zeppelin) / THE LUCKY ONE (Freedy Johnston) / SHAKE SUGAREEE (Elizabeth Cotten) / I'M TALKING TO YOU (Jimmy Bruno) / THAT KIND OF GIRL (Matt Keating) / I FIGURED YOU OUT (Elliott Smith) / SUNSPOT SUNWATCH (Pete Droge) / CINDERELLA BACKSTREET (Pater Laughner) / BANG BANG (Martin) / I DON'T WANT TO GET OVER YOU (Magnetic Fields) / THIRTEEN (Big Star) / 1952 VINCENT BLACK LIGHTNING + BEESWING + FROM GALWAY TO GRACELAND (Richard Thompson) / HALF RIGHT (Heatmiser) / SHE'S STILL BEWITCHING ME (Green Pajamas) / ST. SWITHINS DAY + ONTARIO, QUEBEC AND ME + ON THE AVENUE (Billy Bragg) / THUNDER ROAD (Bruce Springsteen) / BY THE TIME IT GETS DARK (Sandy Denny) / SAYONARA (Pogues) / RICOCHET IN TIME + POLAROIDS (Shawn Colvin) / OUR WORST ENEMY (Richard Harris) / ETERNAL CIRCLE + YOU'RE GOING TO MAKE ME LONESOME WHEN YOU GO (Bob Dylan) / SPEEDING MOTORCYCLE (Daniel Johnston) / POWER TO THE PEOPLE (John Lennon) / BIRTHDAY BOY (Ween) / SUGAR, SUGAR (Berry-Kim) / JUMP (Van Halen) / OUTDOOR MINER (Wire) / etc. + a plethora of BEVIS FROND (aka NICK SALOMAN) songs.

Album rating: MARY LOU LORD mini (*6) / GOT NO SHADOW (*6) / LIVE CITY SOUNDS (*6)

MARY LOU LORD – vocals, guitar

		not iss.	Deep Music
1992.	(c) <DM 011> **REAL**	-	

– Andalucia / Smells like teen spirit / Thirteen / Not necessarily the bubonic plague / St. Swithins day / Eternal circle / Memories of you / Can you fool / Please be with me / Only business / Walkin on air / That's the way / London bridges.

— she also released a demo tape, 'TSWL (TO SIR WITH LOVE)' in 1993

		Kill Rock Stars	Kill Rock Stars
1993.	(7") <KRS 217> **SOME JINGLE JANGLE MORNING (WHEN, I'M STRAIGHT). / WESTERN UNION DESPERATE (version 1 & 2)**		
Jan 95.	(m-cd/m-lp) <(KRS 238 CD/EP)> **MARY LOU LORD**		

– The lights are changing / Helsinki / That kind of girl / He'd be a diamond / The bridge / I'm talking to you / His indie world / Speeding motorcycle.

| Jan 97. | (7"m) <KRS 264> **MARTIAN SAINTS! / SALEM '76 / I FIGURED YOU OUT** | - | |

(cd-ep+=) <KRS 264CD> – Sunspot stopwatch / Cinderella backstreet.

— next – like above – with a plethora of session people incl. NICK SALOMAN, ELLIOTT SMITH, ROGER McGUINN, MONEY MARK, JOSH FREESE, etc

		Work-Sony	Work-Sony
Nov 97.	(cd-ep) <OSK 2917> **MIND THE GAP**		

– His indie world / I figured you out / Some jingle jangle morning (when I'm straight) / Subway.

| Jan 98. | (cd) <(OK 67574)> **GOT NO SHADOW** | | |

– His latest flame / Western union desperate / The lights are changing / Seven sisters / Throng of Blowtown / Lucky one / She had you / Some jingle jangle morning / Shake sugaree / Two boats / Supergun / Down along the sea / Subway. <US w/ free cd-ep+=; OSK 5098> **THE PACE OF CHANGE** – 1952 Vincent black lightning / Book / Ontario, Quebec and me / On the avenue.

		not iss.	Kill Rock Stars
Jan 00.	(cd-ep) <KRS 350> **MARY LOU LORD / SEAN NA NA split**	-	

– Bang bang / Hard road / Aim low / (3 others by SEAN NA NA).

— next with **NICK SALOMAN** – instruments (of BEVIS FROND)

		Rubric	Rubric
Apr 02.	(cd-s) <(RUB 32)> **SPEEDING MOTORCYCLE / RIGHT ON 'TILL DAWN / DRIVEN AWAY**		Jan01
Apr 02.	(cd) <(RUB 30CD)> **LIVE CITY SOUNDS (live)**		Jan01

– I don't want to get over you / She had you / Thirteen / 1952 Vincent black lightning / Half right / She's still bewitching me / Ontario, Quebec and me / His lamest flame /

Beeswing / Thunder road / By the time it gets dark / Sayonara / Ricochet in time / Our worst enemy / You're going to make me lonesome when you go / Speeding motorcycle.

LORELEI

Formed: Arlington, Virginia, USA ... 1990 by SMITHS and Dischord fan and 17 year-old teenager STEPHEN GARDENER (son of that town's mayor!) and the much older DAVIS WHITE, a JOE JACKSON fan who was said to have joined because he fancied the former's sister. At first a 5-piece (including a female singer, GINA YI), the aforementioned pair signed to 'Slumberland' (after an appearance on the 'Rough Trade' compilation, 'End Of The Trail'). With 20 year-old vocalist MATT DINGEE (a BEACH BOYS fan!) in tow, they completed their second EP, 'ASLEEP' (their debut 'SOMETIMESMETHINKS' was delivered in February '92), a dreamy melodic piece of weird shoegazing beauty that deserved better fortune. Carrying on this formula, LORELEI finally hit the destruct button after a slightly disappointing 'EVERYONE MUST TOUCH THE STOVE' (1995) set. • **Covered:** OSCILLATIONS (Silver Apples).

Album rating: EVERYONE MUST TOUCH THE STOVE (*5)

GINA YI – vocals / **STEPHEN GARDENER** – bass / **DAVIS WHITE** – mandolin / **DAVE CERF** – guitar / **PETER BIBY** – drums

		Slumberland	Slumberland
Feb 92.	(7"ep) <DRYL 12> **SOMETIMESMETHINKS / EVERYTHING'S GONE RAIN. / THE BITTER AIR**	-	

— **STEPHEN + DAVIS (now drums)** recruited **MATT DINGEE** – vocals, guitar (DAVE later joined THRENODY ENSEMBLE)

| Oct 93. | (7",7"red) <SLR 32> **ASLEEP** | - | |

– Mostly I sleep / Float my bed.
(cd-ep+=) <SLR 32CD> – The sky is falling / Caterwaul.

| Sep 95. | (cd/lp) <SLR 44 CD/LP> **EVERYONE MUST TOUCH THE STOVE** | - | |

– Today's shrug / Quiet staid debt / Thigh for a leg / Throwaway / Inside the crimelab / Day [cd-only] / Newsprint / Windmill / Stop what you're doing [cd-only] / Pillar.

— split after each member took off to other parts of the States; MATT became TEXTILE SOUNDS after a spell with SABINE while STEPHEN formed CHESSIE and DAVIS worked under The GLASS BOTTOM BOATS moniker

LOTHARS (see under ⇒ ABUNAI!)

LOTION

Formed: New York, USA ... 1991 by TONY ZAJKOWSKI, BILL FERGUSON, JIM FERGUSON and ROB YOUNGBERG. Veterans of the alternative scene (TONY, BILL and ROB had been playing in bands since meeting up at Syracuse Uni in the 80's), the LOTION lads started out as Madchester devotees before realising that New York's social/cultural climate just wasn't right for beany hats and floppy middle partings. Instead, they looked to homegrown legends like R.E.M. and HUSKER DU for inspiration, releasing a debut single, 'HEAD', on KRAMER's 'Kokopop' label in early '93. Entering the studio later that summer with ULTRA VIVID SCENE mainman, KURT RALSKE, at the production helm, they began work on their acclaimed debut set, 'FULL ISAAC'. The record eventually emerged in Spring '94 on the 'SpinArt' label to almost universally positive reviews, subsequently notching up an album of the year award in the 'Village Voice' and generally reducing music journalists to gibbering wrecks. While the band cited the obscure MIRACLE LEGION and the not so obscure LEO SAYER(!) as influences, there was no denying the freshness of their post-grunge musical pot-pourri that effortlessly moved between stinging noise assault and goosebump melancholy. British fans wondering what all the fuss was about were saved from stumping up import prices after 'Big Cat' signed LOTION for the UK, Creation head honcho, Alan McGee having allegedly passed them up. The band were also praised for their contribution to 'Chairman Of The Board' (1994), a Frank Sinatra tribute album wherein LOTION convincingly crooned their way through 'FLY ME TO THE MOON'. Released on 'Warners' in the States, 'NOBODY'S COOL' (1995) was an impressive follow-up set that again met with encouraging reviews and boasted sleeve notes by cult writer, Thomas Pynchon. Later the same year, they released the 'AGNEW FUNERAL' EP before taking a lengthy sabbatical, eventually returning in 1998 with 'THE TELEPHONE ALBUM' (1998).

Album rating: FULL ISAAC (*7) / NOBODY'S COOL (*6) / THE TELEPHONE ALBUM (*6)

TONY ZAJKOWSKI – vocals, guitar / **JIM FERGUSON** – guitar / **BILL FERGUSON** – bass / **ROB YOUNGBERG** – drums

		Kokopop	Kokopop
Dec 92.	(cd-s) <KOKO 6CD> **HEAD. / SHE IS WEIRD CITY / PEACHTREE**	-	
Dec 93.	(7"ep/cd-ep) <(KOKO 14/+CD)> **TEAR EP**		

– Tear / Chrome PKG / 22+ / Really drunk.

		Big Cat	SpinArt
Mar 94.	(lp/cd) (ABB 60/+CD) <SPART 27> **FULL ISAAC**		

– Tear / Dr. Link / Paas / Boost / Long / Pajamas / Around / Head / Dock Ellis / She is weird city / Love theme from Santo Gold.

| Aug 94. | (12"ep/cd-ep) (ABB 66 T/SCD) **AROUND EP** | | - |

– Around / Juggernaut / Gardening your wig / Treat me.

LOTION (cont)

				Big Cat	Warners
Jun 95.	(lp/cd)	(ABB 89/+CD) <24643>	**NOBODY'S COOL**		

– Dear sir / New Timmy / Sad part / Rock chick / Blind for now / Enormous room / Sandra / Juggernaut / Namedropper / Dalmacia 007 / Precious Tiny / Switch.

				SpinArt	SpinArt
Oct 95.	(12"ep/cd-ep)	<SPART 45/+CD>	**AGNEW FUNERAL EP**		

– Marijuana Vietnam / Walk away Renee / Switch / Famous redheads / Treat me.

| Mar 98. | (lp/cd) | <(SPART 58/+CD)> | **THE TELEPHONE ALBUM** | | |

– Rich cop / Poor cop / Feedback queen / I love me / No.99 / Mr. Mosquito / Glorified / Mr. President / My name is Prince / Drop dead / West of here / Blackjack / 5th fret – Distant cousin. (re-iss. Jun00 lp/cd; SRT 80058/+CD)

— LOTION have since disbanded

LOUD FAMILY
(see under ⇒ GAME THEORY; in 80's section)

LOVE

Formed: Los Angeles, California, USA . . . early '65 originally as The GRASS ROOTS, by ARTHUR LEE and former BYRDS roadie BRYAN MacLEAN. The contrasting songwriters recruited JOHN ECHOLS, KEN FORSSI and DON CONKA (the latter being replaced by SNOOPY PFISTERER). When another band of the same name made the US charts, they became LOVE, soon signing to Jac Holzman's 'Elektra' records. In 1966, they released a snarling cover of Burt Bacharach's 'MY LITTLE RED BOOK', nearly breaking it into the US Top 50. With The LEAVES beating them to the US Top 40 on a cover of 'HEY JOE', LOVE opted instead for a British release, although it failed to chart. Soon after, an eponymous album hit the shops, a fairly competent folk-rock set that nevertheless contained the classics, 'SIGNED D.C.', 'CAN'T EXPLAIN' and the two singles. Around the same time, the band scored their only Top 40 success with the galloping HENDRIX-like psych-out of '7 AND 7 IS'. Early in 1967, they followed up with the classic, 'DA CAPO' album, containing the ambitious 20-minute 'REVELATION' alongside such timeless jewels, 'ORANGE SKIES', 'SHE COMES IN COLORS', 'STEPHANIE KNOWS WHO', 'THE CASTLE' and the previous 45. Shacked-up in LEE's Hollywood mansion, the band eventually emerged with 'FOREVER CHANGES', often cited as one of the greatest albums of all-time. A psychedelic tour de force, it combined acoustic musings, Latin rhythms and the eerily surreal LEE-penned lyrics. Almost every track was flawless and it remains one of rock's great mysteries why the album's two singles, 'ALONE AGAIN OR' and 'ANDMOREAGAIN', failed to chart. Equally baffling was the fact that the album only made the highest position of No.154, while in Britain it hit the Top 30. The band recorded a further brilliant single, 'YOUR MIND AND WE BELONG TOGETHER', before LEE sacked the rest of the group "cause they couldn't cut it". He subsequently formed a "new" LOVE with JAY DONELLAN, JIM HOBSON, FRANK FAYAD, GEORGE SURANOVICH and some additional members. This line-up cut a fourth album, the disappointing 'FOUR SAIL', following it up with two others in the early 70's, 'OUT HERE' and 'FALSE START'. Eventually LEE was again left on his own, leading him to carve out a solo career, the album 'VINDICATOR' (1972) being released to a lukewarm reception. He re-created yet another LOVE in 1974, fans again bitterly disappointed with a commercial set that even unadvisedly touched on disco! After various other re-unions in the late 70's, LEE released a self-titled solo effort in 1981, before going AWOL again. In the early 90's, with renewed LOVE interest, LEE re-formed the group for a re-union album, 'ARTHUR LEE AND LOVE'. The 90's weren't exactly kind to this revered eccentric, LEE being diagnosed with Parkinson's Disease and, more recently, receiving a 12-year sentence for firearms offences. His former partner, born-again christian BRYAN MacLEAN (who had virtually retired in 1970, although he did pen songs for his half-sister MARIA McKEE and country-star PATTY LOVELESS) tragically died of a suspected heart attack on Christmas Day, 1998. ARTHUR LEE quietly re-formed LOVE for a series of live concerts in the late 90's, 'ELECTRICALLY SPEAKING' (2001), was document of some of these. • **Trivia:** In 1970, LEE was about to initiate a supergroup, BAND AID (not the charity) with STEVE WINWOOD and HENDRIX, but JIMI died on September '70. In 1973, he recorded an album, 'BLACK BEAUTY' for 'Buffalo' records. This was shelved, although illegal bootlegs did surface.

Album rating: LOVE (*6) / DA CAPO (*8) / FOREVER CHANGES (*10) / FOUR SAIL (*6) / OUT HERE (*4) / FALSE START (*4) / REEL TO REAL (*4) / LOVE LIVE (*4) / ARTHUR LEE AND LOVE (*4) / COMES IN COLOURS compilation (*8) / LOVE STORY 1966-1972 compilation (*8) / ELECTRICALLY SPEAKING: LIVE IN CONCERT (*5) / FIVE STRING SERENADE (*6) / Bryan MacLean: IFYOUBELIEVEIN (*6) / posthumous CANDY'S WALTZ (*5)

ARTHUR LEE (b. ARTHUR TAYLOR PORTER, 1945, Memphis, Tennessee) – vocals, guitar (ex-LAG'S, ex-AMERICAN FOUR) / **BRYAN MacLEAN** (b.1947) – guitar, vocals / **JOHN ECHOLS** (b.1945, Memphis) – lead guitar (ex-LAG'S) / **KEN FORSSI** (b.1943, Cleveland, Ohio) – bass (ex-SURFARIS) / **ALBAN 'SNOOPY' PFISTERER** (b.1947, Switzerland) – drums; repl. DON CONKA

				London	Elektra
Mar 66.	(7")	<45603>	**MY LITTLE RED BOOK. / A MESSAGE TO PRETTY**	-	52
Jun 66.	(7")	(HLZ 10053)	**HEY JOE. / MY LITTLE RED BOOK**		-
Sep 66.	(7")	(HLZ 10073) <45605>	**7 AND 7 IS. / NO. FOURTEEN**		33 Aug66

				Elektra	Elektra
Sep 66.	(lp; mono/stereo)	<(EKL/EKS 7-4001)>	**LOVE**		57 Jul66

– My little red book / A message to Pretty / Softly to me / Emotions / Gazing / Signed D.C. / Mushroom clouds / Can't explain / My flash on you / No matter what you do / You I'll be following / Hey Joe / Coloured bells falling / And more. (re-iss. Jan72 lp/c; K/K4 42068) (re-iss. Feb87 on 'Edsel'; ED 218) (cd-iss. Feb93 & Dec93; 7559 74001-2) <(cd re-iss. Sep01 +=; 8122 73567-2)> – LOVE (stereo). <(lp re-iss. Jan02 on 'Sundazed'; SCLP 5100)>

— added **MICHAEL STUART** – drums (ex-SONS OF ADAM) ('SNOOPY' now on keyboards) + **TJAY CANTRELLI** – saxophone

| Dec 66. | (7") | (EKSN 45010) <45608> | **SHE COMES IN COLOURS. / ORANGE SKIES** | | |
| Feb 67. | (lp; mono/stereo) | <(EKL/EKS 7-4005)> | **DA CAPO** | | 80 |

– Stephanie knows who / Orange skies / Que vida / 7 and 7 is / The castle / She comes in colors / Revelation. (re-iss. Jan72 lp/c; K/K4 42011) (cd-iss. 1989 on 'WEA'; 974005-2) <(lp re-iss. Jan02 on 'Sundazed'; SCLP 5101)>

| Mar 67. | (7") | <45613> | **QUE VIDA (edit). / HEY JOE** | - | - |
| Sep 67. | (7") | (EKSN 45016) | **THE CASTLE. / SOFTLY TO ME** | | - |

— Reverted to a quintet when 'SNOOPY' and TJAY left. (latter to DOMINIC TROIANO)

| Jan 68. | (7") | <45629> | **ALONE AGAIN OR (edit). / A HOUSE IS NOT A MOTEL** | - | |
| Jan 68. | (7") | (EKSN 45024) | **ALONE AGAIN OR. / BUMMER IN THE SUMMER** | | - |

(re-iss. Oct70; 2101-019)

| Feb 68. | (lp; mono/stereo) | <(EKL/EKS 7-4013)> | **FOREVER CHANGES** | 24 | Jan68 |

– Alone again or / A house is not a motel / Andmoreagain / The daily planet / Old man / The red telephone / Maybe the people would be the times or between Clark and Hilldale / Live and let live / Good honor man he sees everything like this / Bummer in the summer / You set the scene. (re-iss. Jan72 lp/c; K/K4 42015) (cd-iss. Jul88 on 'WEA'; 7559 60656-2) <(cd re-mast.Feb01 +=; 8122 73537-2)> – Hummingbirds (demo) / Wonder people (I do wonder) (alt.) / Alone again or (alt.) / You set the scene (alt.) / Your mind and we belong together (alt.) / Your mind and we belong together (single) / Laughing stock (single). <(lp re-iss. Jan02 on 'Sundazed'; SCLP 5102)>

| Mar 68. | (7") | (EKSN 45024) | **ANDMOREAGAIN. / THE DAILY PLANET** | | - |
| Sep 68. | (7") | (EKSN 45038) <45633> | **YOUR MIND AND WE BELONG TOGETHER. / LAUGHING STOCK** | | |

— ARTHUR LEE dismissed others and recruited new people below **JAY DONELLAN (LEWIS)** – guitar / **JIM HOBSON** – keyboards / **FRANK FAYAD** – bass / **GEORGE SURANOVICH** – drums

— augmented by **PAUL MARTIN** and **GARY ROWLES** – guitar plus **DRACKEN THEAKER** – keyboards (ex-CRAZY WORLD OF ARTHUR BROWN)

| Nov 69. | (lp) | <(EKS 74049)> | **FOUR SAIL** | | Sep69 |

– August / Your friend and mine – Neil's song / I'm with you / Good times / Singing cowboy / Dream / Robert Montgomery / Nothing / Talking in my sleep / Always see your face. (re-iss. Jan72 lp/c; K/K4 42030) (re-iss. Nov87 on 'Thunderbolt'; THBL 047) (cd-iss. Jun88; CDBT 047)

| Mar 70. | (7") | (EKSN 45086) | **I'M WITH YOU. / ROBERT MONTGOMERY** | | |

				Harvest	Blue Thumb
May 70.	(d-lp)	(SHDW 3-4) <BTS 9000>	**OUT HERE**	29	Dec69

– I'll pray for you / Abalony / Signed D.C. / Listen to my song / I'm down / Stand out / Discharged / Doggone / I still wonder / Love is more than words or better late than never / Nice to be / Car lights on in the day time blues / Run to the top / Willow willow / Instra-mental / You are something / Gather round. (re-iss. Jul88 on 'Big Beat' lp; WIKA 69) (cd-iss. Jul90; CDWIKA 69)

| May 70. | (7") | <BLU-7 106> | **I'LL PRAY FOR YOU. / STAND OUT** | - | - |
| Nov 70. | (7") | (HAR 5030) <BLU-7 116> | **KEEP ON SHINING. / THE EVERLASTING FIRST** | | |

— **GARY ROWLES** now full time; repl. JAY

| Jan 71. | (lp) | (SHVL 787) <BTS 8822> | **FALSE START** | | Dec 70 |

– The everlasting first / Flying / Gimi a little break / Stand out / Keep on shining / Anytime / Slick Dick / Love is coming / Feel daddy feel good / Ride that vibration. (cd-iss. Jul92 on 'Beat Goes On'; BGOCD 127) (cd re-iss. Apr94 on 'One Way'; MCAD 22029)

| Mar 71. | (7") | (HAR 5014) | **STAND OUT. / DOGGONE** | | - |

ARTHUR LEE

— a solo venture with BAND AID: **FAYAD** and new men **CHARLES KARP** – guitar / **CRAIG TARWATER** – guitar / **CLARENCE McDONALD** – keyboards / **DON PONCHA** – drums / + guest **DAVID HULL** – bass

				A&M	A&M
Aug 72.	(lp)	(AMLS 64356) <SP 4356>	**VINDICATOR**		

– Sad song / You can save up to 50% / Love jumped through my window / Find somebody / He said she said / Everytime I look up / Everybody's gotta live / He knows a lot of good women / You want change for your re-run / Hamburger breath stinkfinger / Ol' morgue mouth / Busted feet. (cd-iss. Apr97; 540697-2)

| Aug 72. | (7") | <1361> | **EVERYBODY'S GOT TO LIVE. / LOVE JUMPED THROUGH MY WINDOW** | - | - |
| Nov 72. | (7") | <1381> | **SAD SONG. / YOU WANT TO CHANGE FOR YOUR RE-RUN** | - | - |

LOVE

— **ARTHUR LEE** recruited **MELVIN WHITTINGTON** + **JOHN STERLING** – guitar / **SHERWOOD AKUNA** + **ROBERT ROZENO** – bass / **JOE BLOCKER** – drums

				R.S.O.	R.S.O.
Dec 74.	(7")	<SO 502>	**TIME IS LIKE A RIVER. / WITH A LITTLE ENERGY**	-	-
Jan 75.	(7")	(2090 151)	**TIME IS LIKE A RIVER. / YOU SAID YOU WOULD**		-
Jan 75.	(lp)	(2394 145) <SO 4804>	**REEL TO REAL**		

– Time is like a river / Stop the music / Who are you? / Good old fashioned love / Which witch is which / With a little energy / Singing cowboy / Be thankful for what you got / You said you would / Busted feet / Everybody's gotta live.

Mar 75. (7") <SO 506> **YOU SAID YOU WOULD. / GOOD OLD FASHIONED DREAM**

ARTHUR LEE

— solo again, using loads of session people

Da Capo / not iss.

1977. (7"ep) (CAP 001) **I DO WONDER / JUST US. / DO YOU KNOW THE SECRET? / HAPPY YOU**

Beggars Banquet / Rhino

Jul 81. (lp) (BEGA 26) <RNLP 020> **ARTHUR LEE**
– One / I do wonder / Just us / Happy you / Do you know the secret / One and one / Seven and seven is / Mr. Lee / Bend down / Stay away from evil / Many rivers to cross.

— LOVE re-formed in Autumn '91, with **ARTHUR LEE, DON CONKA, SHUGGIE OTIS** – guitar / **MELLAN WHITTINGTON** – guitar / **SHERWOOD AKUNA** – bass

New Rose / not iss.

May 92. (cd/lp) (ROSE CD/LP 288) **ARTHUR LEE AND LOVE**
– Five string serenade / Somebody's watching you / Twenty on my way / You're the prettiest song / I believe in you / Ninety miles away / Seventeen / Love saga / The watcher / Passing by. (re-iss. May94; 422214)

— ARTHUR was diagnosed with Parkinson's Disease in the early 90's (see biog above)

LOVE

ARTHUR LEE – vocals, guitar / **MELVAN WHITTINGTON** – guitar / **SHERWOOD AKUNA** – bass / **GARY STERN** – drums

Yeaah / Yeaah

Jun 01. (cd) <(YEAAH 49)> **ELECTRICALLY SPEAKING: LIVE IN CONCERT** (live) — Nov01
– Alone again or / My little red book / 7 and 7 is / Orange skies / Signed DC / The everlasting first / Andmoreagain / Hey Joe / She comes in colors / Everybody's gotta live – Instant karma / That's the way it goes / Signed DC / Andmoreagain / Little wing.

Last Call / Last Call

Oct 01. (cd; as ARTHUR LEE & LOVE) <(306986-2)> **FIVE STRING SERENADE**
– Five string serenade / Somebody's watching you / Twenty on my way / You're the prettiest song / I believe in you / Nonety miles away / Seventeen / Love saga / Watcher / Passing by.

– LOVE compilations etc. –

on 'Elektra' unless mentioned otherwise

Aug 70. (7") <45700> **ALONE AGAIN OR. / GOOD TIMES** — 99
Dec 70. (lp) (2469 009) <EKS 74049> **LOVE REVISITED** Aug70
(re-iss. Jan72 lp/c; K/K4 42091) <(re-iss. Jan02 on 'Sundazed'; SCLP 5104)>
Feb 73. (lp/c) (K/K4 32002) **LOVE MASTERS**
– My little red book / Signed D.C. / Hey Joe / 7 and 7 is / Stephanie knows who / Orange skies / Que vida / The castle / She comes in colours / Laughing stock / Your mind / And we belong together / Old man / The Daily Planet / A house is not a motel / Andmoreagain / Alone again or.
Jul 73. (7") (K 12113) **ALONE AGAIN OR. / ANDMOREAGAIN**
(re-iss. Apr84; G 9740)
Sep 76. (7") (K 12231) **ALONE AGAIN OR. / THE CASTLE**
1980. (lp) Rhino; <RNLP 800> **THE BEST OF LOVE**
1981. (pic-lp) Rhino; <RNDF 251> **LOVE LIVE** (live)
1982. (lp) M.C.A.; <27025> **STUDIO / LIVE**
(UK cd-iss. Apr94 on 'One Way'; MCAD 22036)
1986. (lp) Rhino; <RNLP 70175> **GOLDEN ARCHIVE**
Jan 93. (cd) Raven; (RVCD 29) **COMES IN COLOURS**
– My little red book / Can't explain / Message to pretty / Softly to me / Hey Joe / Signed D.C. / And more / 7 and 7 is / No.14 / Stephanie knows who / Orange skies / Que vida / The castle / She comes in colors / Alone again or / Andmoreagain / Old man / A house is not a motel / Daily planet / Live and let live / Laughing stock / Your mind and we belong together / August / (Arthur Lee interview). (re-iss. Feb99; same)
May 00. (cd/lp) by ARTHUR LEE & SHACK) Viper; <(VIPER 3 CD/LP)> **LIVE IN LIVERPOOL 1992** (live)

BRYAN MacLEAN

— solo recordings between 1966-82 + 1970's respectively

Sundazed / Sundazed

Nov 97. (cd) <(SC 11051)> **IFYOUBELIEVEIN**
– Barber John / Fresh hope / Kathleen / Orange skies / Strong commitment / Alone again or / Tired of sitting / Blues singer / Friday's party / People / Claudia / If you believe in / Orange skies (2nd version) / Alone again or (2nd version) / She looks good / Old man.
Oct 00. (cd) <SC 11076> **CANDY'S WALTZ**
– I can't remember / Most of us / Special joy / Love will be here / Candy's waltz / Always I wanted / Castle waltz / Hip-hip hooray / Claudia / Husband and father / If this is love / Claudine's samba / Candy's waltz (live) / Kathleen (live) / You could be here / Soon / Darlin / Love in the end / We'll be together again / (Bryan MacLean interview).

LOVE AS LAUGHTER

Formed: Seattle, Washington, USA . . . 1994 by SAM JAYNE, a one-time member of LYNC (with also JAMES BERTRAM and DAVE SCHNEIDER) were Olympia-based emo punks who managed to releases a series of singles and one LP, 'THESE ARE NOT FALL COLORS' (1994), before JAYNE founded LOVE AS LAUGHTER. 1996's

'THE GREKS BRING GIFTS' album was a SAM JAYNE solo project in all but name. One-man touring soon took its toll however and in early 1998, L/A/L became a 4-piece band, JAYNE enlisting friends, DAVE SCHNEIDER (from the aforementioned LYNC), JESSICA ESPELETA and his girlfriend LESLIE. This line-up completed a second set, '*1 USA', a rockier affair that broke from the lo-fi roots. In 2001, LOVE AS LAUGHTER (a return to their old moniker) delivered yet another rousing set of songs courtesy of LP, 'SEA TO SHINING SEA', probably their best offering to date.

Album rating: Lync: THESE ARE NOT FALL COLORS (*7) / REMEMBERING THE FIREBALLS (PART 8) compilation (*6) / Love As Laughter: THE GREKS BRING GIFTS (*5) / L/A/L: *1 USA (*6) / DESTINATION 2000 (*6) / Love As Laughter: SEA TO SHINING SEA (*7)

LYNC

SAM JAYNE – vocals, guitar / **JAMES BERTRAM** – bass / **DAVE SCHNEIDER** – drums

not iss. / Magic Pail

1992. (7"m) <001> **PIGEONS. / ELECTRICITY / PATHETIC**

not iss. / Magic Pail – Land Speed

1993. (7") <002> **PAN. / MHz**

– / K

1994. (lp) <KLP 30> **THESE ARE NOT FALL COLORS**
– B / Perfect shot / Silver spoon glasses / Pennies to save / Clay fighter / Cue cards / Angelfood fodder and vitamins / Heroes and heroines / Turtle / Uberrima fides.
1994. (7") <IPU 41> **TWO FEET IN FRONT. / LIGHTBULB SWITCHES**

— disbanded after recording above set

– compilations, etc. –

Aug 97. (lp/cd) <(KLP/KCD 73)> **REMEMBERING THE FIREBALL (PART 8)**
– Pigeons / Friend / Hands and knees / Electricity / Pathetic / Two feet in front / MHZ / Pan / Pennies to save / Firestarter / Turtle / Lightbulb switch / Can't tie yet / The last song (live).

LOVE AS LAUGHTER

SAM JAYNE – vocals, guitar, etc (ex-BECK) / with **DIANA ARENS + STEVE 'THE WIZARD' DORE**

not iss. / own label

1994. (c) <none> **MIX TAPE**
– My lovely radiophile / Mediks / Trapeze artist / Motor dance / This isn't the deal / Sleeves / Queen of Venus / She carries matches / Catch me / Visions / Downtown.
1994. (c) <none> **CLEAR SKY = BLUE DYE**
– CLEAR SKY = Cigarette constellations / Atrium / Coping strategies / The spokesmodel / Backpack / My neglected his shirt / Zookeeper vows / Knock for mokl / Featherweight champ / Royal jelly / BLUE DYE = Pirate song / TV / An interest in science at an early age / Fireballs of vitamins / The "revolution" boys eat apple pie / Accolade / You are an example / My body and home will be destroyed just like everyone else's / No one heard us / Rock song / Avengeful wishes / Changeling.

K / K

Feb 96. (cd) <(KLP 51CD)> **THE GREKS BRING GIFTS** Jan96
– It's only Lena / TTFL / You gotta bug / Keep your shade / Uninvented trumpets / Next time you fall apart / The youth are plastic / Singing sores make perfect swords / A tune and a comfortable ride / Let's talk radar / I am seldom reared / High noon / Eeyore crush it / Half-assed / Kung Fu exercise fountain / If I ever need someone like you.
Feb 96. (7"ep) <IPU 64> **PLANET OF CHILDREN**
– My lovely radiophile / 2 chs lrg fry / My lovely radiophile 2 / My lovely radiophile 3 / Chicken space / Deep monster thought eexplodofry / My lovely radiophile 4.

— **SAM / + MARK HAMILTON** – drums

Aug 96. (7") <IPU 71> **DO YOU BELIEVE IN ALIEN BOREDOM? / IDOL WORSHIP! IDOL WORSHIP! WE OFFER SLEEP TO YOU!**
Nov 96. (7") <IPU 76> **WIRED / BONUS NOISE. / (other by the Seductive)**
Dec 96. (7"m) <IPU 77> **I'M A BEE. / WAITING / I DON'T KNOW WHERE I AM**

L/A/L

— split a single with RINGFINGER around this stage

— **SAM** added **KOBL NEWELL** – drums

K / K

Jan 98. (7"ep) <IPU 82> **4 SONG EP**
– Fever / Snapshots of Cairo / Instruments of death / California dreamin'.

— **SAM** added **JESSICA ESPELETA** – guitar / **DAVE SCHNEIDER** – drums (ex-LYNC) / **LESLIE** – bass

Feb 98. (cd) <(KLP 76CD)> ***1 USA** Jan98
– Old gold / #1 U.S.A. / I'm a bee / Slow river fever / Vacation / Tonight / Puger sound sanitation / PhoBias. <US cd+=> – (below EP)

— now with **BRANDON ANGLE** – bass, guitar / **RYAN DAVIDSON** – bass / **ZEKE HOWARD** – drums, guitar

Sub Pop / Sub Pop

Oct 99. (lp/cd) <(SP/+CD 490)> **DESTINATION 2000** Sep99
– Stay out of jail / Aftermath / Margaritas / On the run / Destination 2000 / Stakes avenue / Statuette / Freedom dop / Demon contacts / Body double / Untitled / Untitled.
Nov 00. (7") <(SP 547)> **MY CASE. /**
Sep 01. (cd) <(SPCD 531)> **SEA TO SHINING SEA**
– Coast to coast / Temptation island / Sam Jayne = dead / Put it together / Miss direction / My case / Druggachusetts / French heroin / The square / E.H.
Oct 01. (7") <(SP 576)> **TEMPTATION ISLAND. /**

LOVE BATTERY

Formed: Seattle, Washington, USA ... 1990 by RON NINE (ex-ROOM NINE), KEVIN WHITWORTH (ex-CRISIS PARTY), DAVE DEDERER, and JASON FINN. Taking their moniker from a track by punk-heroes, BUZZCOCKS, the band emerged amid the west-coast grunge explosion forefronted notably by NIRVANA and PEARL JAM, and were perhaps unfairly submerged beneath it. The band's sound mixed the post-punk grunge idiom with a penchant for psychedelic pop; showcased by some excellent guitar wizardry from WHITWORTH, and lyrical fun from NINE. 1990 saw the release of LB's debut album, 'BETWEEN THE EYES', a great opener which wore its psyched-out influences on its sleeve. A few years on, and the group put out their sophomore set, 'DAYGLO' (1992). This was certainly their career high, unfortunately not receiving the attention it deserved, due in part to the focus on the other native musical cohorts of Seattle. This release also marked the departure of DEDERER, who went on to form PRESIDENTS OF THE UNITED STATES OF AMERICA, with the aid of FINN, although he continued to split his time between LB and this new venture. DEDERER's place was ably filled by BRUCE FAIRWEATHER, who had cut his teeth in the cult grunge bands, GREEN RIVER and MOTHER LOVE BONE. Unfortunately FAIRWEATHER's inclusion could not save LB's third full-length outing, 'FAR GONE' (1993), from being a bit of a disappointment in comparison to their erstwhile offerings. The Washington state boys picked it up with the set, 'STRAIGHT FREAK TICKET' (1995), although only really in parts, making it more of a short note home from the critics, than the lauded praise they should have received for 'DAYGLO'. A long break soon followed for LB, in which time FINN left to be replaced by DAN PETERS, of MUDHONEY and SCREAMING TREES fame. Blasting back with their fifth set 'CONFUSION AU GO GO' (1999), the band seemed to be in full swing and willing to push their boundaries. Although it is certainly a notable album, filling out their potential, it came too late to receive the kind of respect it might have gleaned had LB kept their quality steady throughout.

Album rating: BETWEEN THE EYES (*5) / DAYGLO (*7) / FAR GONE (*4) / STRAIGHT FREAK TICKET (*5) / CONFUSION AU GO GO (*7)

RON NINE – vocals, guitar / **KEVIN WHITWORTH** – guitar / **TOMMY 'BONEHEAD' SIMPSON** – bass / **JASON FINN** – drums

		Tupelo	Sub Pop
Oct 89.	(7",7"red) <SP 45> **BETWEEN THE EYES. / EASTER**	-	
Nov 90.	(cd/c) (TUP CD/MC 22) <SP 69 B/A> **BETWEEN THE EYES**		Jan90

– Between the eyes / Easter / Highway of souls / Orange / Two and two / Before I crawl / Ibiza bar. <US cd+=> – 67 / Wings / Shellshock. (UK-iss.Mar94; same as US)

---- **JIM TILLMAN** – bass (+ on above); repl. SIMPSON

| Mar 92. | (lp/cd) <(SP 185/+CD)> **DAYGLO** | | |

– Out of focus / Foot / Damaged / See your mind / Side (with you) / Cool school (trance of thought) / Sometimes / Blonde / Dayglo / 23 modern stories.

---- **BRUCE FAIRWEATHER** – bass (ex-GREEN RIVER, ex-MOTHER LOVE BONE) repl. TILLMAN

		not iss.	Atlas – Polygram
1995.	(cd,c) <527152> **STRAIGHT FREAK TICKET**	-	

– Fuzz factory / If it wasn't me / Harold's pink room / Brazil / Nehru jacket / Perfect light / Red onion / Sunny Jim / Straight freak show / Angelhead / Waylaid / Drowning sun / Silent treatment.

		not iss.	Atlantic
Apr 95.	(c-s/cd-s) <124034> **NEHRU JACKET / ILLUMINATED MAN / RED ONION / PLEASE BEFORE YOU GO**	-	

---- split when FINN left to join The PRESIDENTS OF THE UNITED STATES OF AMERICA and SIMPSON joined ALCOHOL FUNNYCAR; LOVE BATTERY re-formed in 1998 when the POTUSA outfit broke up.

---- **DAN PETERS** – drums; was added (JASON still a member)

		not iss.	C/Z
May 99.	(cd) <C/Z 92> **CONFUSION AU GO GO**	-	

– Confusion au go go / One small step / Snipe hunt / Corporate memo / Colorblind / Get on da big foot / Dead boys / Hollow body / Cute one / Punks want rights / Transcendental fornication / Guilty of every thing / Monkey brain / Faithfull.

LOVE CORPORATION
(see under ⇒ BALL, Edward; 70's section)

LOVEJOY (see under ⇒ BLUEBOY)

LOVELETTER
(see under ⇒ KING OF LUXEMBOURG; 80's section)

LOVESICK (see under ⇒ THOMAS, Fred)

LOVE SPIT LOVE
(see under ⇒ PSYCHEDELIC FURS; in 80's section)

LOVES UGLY CHILDREN

Formed: Christchurch, New Zealand ... 1991 by guitarist/ vocalist SIMON McLAREN, bass player FLOSS and drummer JASON YOUNG. This power pop trio were already well regarded in the New Zealand underground scene, having released the blistering EP, 'PURGE', before they were signed to 'Flying Nun' in 1994. The group subsequently unleashed the uncompromising EP 'COLD WATER SURF' the same year and impressed critics with their ability for producing music of such ferocity whilst still managing to retain infectious, melodic hooks. The group followed this with the demented, full-length debut, 'CAKEHOLE' in 1995. Again the group succeeded in delivering songs which felt as though they were blistering your skin whilst simultaneously applying a soothing ointment. The group stuck with the same formula for their 1997 album, 'SHOWERED IN GOLD', however the songs were not of the same standard as previous efforts.

Album rating: CAKEHOLE (*5) / SHOWERED IN GOLD (*5)

SIMON MacLAREN – vocals, guitar / **FLOSS** (FLORA McLAREN) – bass / **JASON YOUNG** – drums, vocals

		Flat City	not iss.
1994.	(cd-ep) (fc 003) **PURGE EP**	-	- NewZ

– Love you dead / You take me there / Flesh-hook / Nebula. (hidden track+=) – (extra track).

		Flying Nun	not iss.
Jan 95.	(7") (FN 307) **SENSELESS. / 13.2.94**		-
	(cd-ep) (FNCD 307) **COLD WATER SURF** – ('A'side) / You don't know / Falling down / City that shines / Space suit.		
Oct 95.	(7") (FN 336) **PERSONAL WORLD. / SHALLOW**		-
	(cd-s) (FNCD 336) – ('A'side) / Fear and loathing / Jesus Christ Satan / Eating the cheese.		
Nov 95.	(lp/cd) (FN/+CD 324) **CAKEHOLE**		-

– Messing things up / Here comes stupid / Superficial semi-automatic / Hothead / I couldn't help you / Totally down / Surf Nazis must die / Mind control / Alter ego / Fear and loathing / Latest product / Personal world / Get the facts right / I found my thrill / Day of the dogs.

Jun 96.	(7") (FN 355) **SUCK. / DESTROY THE CITY**		-
	(cd-s+=) (FNCD 355) – Rockpig / Headin' south.		
Oct 97.	(cd) (FNCD 380) **SHOWERED IN GOLD**	-	- NewZ

– Coming 4 you / Sixpack / Pump it baby / Voodoo girl / Motorbike girl / Junkfood / Damaged goods / You don't hate me / Seven / Don't need a reason / Suck / It's in my blood.

---- disbanded after above

LOW

Formed: Duluth, Minnesota, USA ... late 1993 by Mormons ALAN SPARHAWK, his wife MIMI PARKER and third member, JOHN NICHOLS (replaced by ZAK SALLY after debut). Their early efforts, 'I COULD LIVE IN HOPE' (1994) and 'LONG DIVISION' (1995), were more or less ignored, although critics pricked up their ears for the low-key Lo-Fi/ambient classic, 'THE CURTAIN HITS THE CAST' (1996). LOW subsequently completed a few UK gigs to promote it during that summer and later cut a single for the legendary 'Sub Pop', 'VENUS'. The trio delivered a further two sets, namely 'SONGS FOR A DEAD PILOT' (1997) and 'ONE MORE REASON TO FORGET' (1998), described as "sad-core" in the music tabloids; it also featured 17-minute track, 'DO YOU KNOW HOW TO WALTZ?'). 1999 saw the return of the trio and the release of their 5th and best work to date, the bruised and ultra sensitive 'SECRET NAME' album. Recorded over a 7-day period with West Coast rock throwback and ex-BIG BLACK frontman STEVE ALBINI riding the faders, the band had hit a new creative peak with this warm and whispering alternative classic. Tracks such as 'SOON' and the harmonic 'MISSOURI' evoked blissful sensation and echoed tingling country heir to GRAM PARSONS. Others like 'TWO-STEP' and 'I REMEMBER' could easily be compared to a CARPENTERS ballad or something reminising GALAXIE 500. Meanwhile, ZAK SALLY moonlighted with another minimalist trio, ENEMYMINE (along with MIKE KUNKA of GODHEADSILO and DANNY SASAKI), recording an eponymous mini-set for Calvin Johnson's 'K' imprint. Towards the end of the millennium, LOW came up with 'THE CHRISTMAS EP', which featured four brand new tracks and cover of four traditional hymns that would peacefully send the children off to sleep by the fire come the festive season. Prolific as always, LOW returned in 2001 with their most accessible album to date, the haunting 'THINGS WE LOST IN THE FIRE'. The album, produced by Steve Albini once again, saw the group head towards a more uptempo, song-based direction, although tracks such as 'WHITETAIL', 'JULY' and 'CLOSER' still upheld the LOW watermark. But songs 'DINOSAUR ACT' (issued as a single) and 'WHORE' stepped towards a rockier area, with fuzz guitar being used in the latter, in amongst the soaring vocals of PARKER, SPARHAWK and the crashing drums. Not as poignant or as beautiful as 'SECRET NAME' (every track was a classic), 'THINGS WE LOST IN THE FIRE' demonstrated the group's abilities to write great compositions, while still maintaining the sad-core motif that had became so synonymous with the group. A split EP was issued in April the same year with underground artist K and although LOW were on top form (produced by WARN DeFEVER), it was really K's tremendous contribution that shone most on the set. In another bizarre but brilliant twist in LOW's direction, the band issued a cover single of the Smiths' 'LAST NIGHT I DREAMT THAT SOMEBODY LOVED ME', which could've almost been better than the original, with strings fusing into crashing crescendos and PARKER's and SPARHAWK's vocals sounding as strange and as powerful as always. It's also worth mentioning the B-side track 'BECAUSE YOU STOOD STILL'; how did something so incredible get omitted from an album? LOW returned in September of 2002 with the delicately crafted 'TRUST', a slightly unadorned set, from the usually consistently reliable group. The album, which saw LOW delve deeper into sparse and darker terrain, may have been saved from droning obscurity by PARKER's light vocals and the group's undeniable knack for writing beautiful songs, no matter how dark and eerie. • **Songwriters:** Group except SUNSHINE (Mitchell – Davis) / JACK SMITH (Supreme Dicks) / Transmission (Joy Division) / LONG LONG LONG (George Harrison) / DOWN BY THE RIVER (Neil Young) / LAST NIGHT I DREAMT THAT SOMEBODY LOVED ME (Smiths) / LITTLE DRUMMER BOY + BLUE CHRISTMAS + SILENT NIGHT + TAKING DOWN THE TREE (trad).

Album rating: I COULD LIVE IN HOPE (*7) / LONG DIVISION (*8) / THE CURTAIN HITS THE CAST (*7) / SECRET NAME (*8) / THINGS WE LOST IN THE FIRE (*8) / TRUST (*6)

ALAN SPARHAWK – vocals, guitar / **JOHN NICHOLS** – bass / **MIMI PARKER** – vocals, drums

Aug 94. (cd) <(QUIGD 5)> **I COULD LIVE IN HOPE** — Quigley / Quigley
– Words / Fear / Cut / Slide / Lazy / Lullaby / Sea / Down / Drag / Rope / Sunshine.
1994. (cd-ep) <shine 48CD> **LOW** — not iss. / Summershine
– Below & above / Lazy / Words / Caroline / Tired.

― **ZAK SALLY** – bass; repl. NICHOLS

1995. (cd) <YARDCD 014> **LONG DIVISION** — Vernon Yard / Vernon Yard
– Violence / Below and above / Shame / Throw out the line / Swingin' / See-through / Turn / Caroline / Alone / Streetlight / Stay / Take. (UK-iss.Feb97; same)
Feb 96. (cd-ep) (FLATSCD 24) **TRANSMISSION EP**
– Transmission / Bright / Cardine / Hands / Jack Smith / Untitled.
(above issued on 'Vernon Yard' UK)
May 96. (cd-ep) <(YARD 022CD)> **FINALLY**
– Anon / Tomorrow one / Prisoner / Turning over.
Aug 96. (d-lp/cd) <YARD/+CD 018> **THE CURTAIN HITS THE CAST**
– Anon / The plan / Over the ocean / Mom says / Coat tails / Standby / Laugh / Lust / Stars gone out / Same / Do you know how to waltz / Dark. (d-lp+=) – Prisoner / Tomorrow one.
Nov 96. (7"/cd-s) <(YARD 024/+CD)> **OVER THE OCEAN. / CIOLENCE / BE THERE**
Sep 97. (7") <(SP 392)> **VENUS. / BOYFRIEND** — Sub Pop / Sub Pop
Oct 97. (7") (WJ 44) **IF YOU WERE BORN TODAY (A SONG FOR LITTLE BABY JESUS). / BLUE CHRISTMAS** — Wurlitzer Jukebox / not iss.
Oct 97. (m-lp/m-cd) <(KRANKY 021/+CD)> **SONGS FOR A DEAD PILOT** — Kranky / Kranky
– Will the night / Condescend / Born by the wires / Be there / Landlord / Hey Chicago.
May 98. (7") (TUG 001) **JOAN OF ARC. / LONG LONG LONG** — Tugboat / Kranky
(re-iss. Aug99 on 'Tugboat'; same)
Jul 98. (cd) (INR 1040CD) **ONE MORE REASON TO FORGET**
– Be there / Venus / Condescend / Landlord / Over the ocean / Do you know how to waltz? / Shame / If you were born today (song for the little baby jesus).
(above issued on 'Bluesant Musak')
Feb 99. (7") (TUGS 006) **IMMUNE. / I REMEMBER**
Apr 99. (cd/d-lp) (TUG CD/LP 007) <KRANKY 035> **SECRET NAME**
– I remember / Starfire / 2-step / Weight for water / Missouri / Don't understand / Soon / Immune / Lion – Lamb / Days of . . . / Will the night / Home.
Nov 99. (m-cd) <(TUGCD 014 – LOWXMASD 1)> **CHRISTMAS**
– Just like Christmas / Long way around the sea / Little drummer boy / If you were born today / Blue Christmas / Silent night / Taking down the tree / One special gift.
May 00. (12"/cd-s; with SPRINHEEL JACK) (TUGS/+CD 017) **BOMBSCARE EP**
– Bombscare / Hand so small / So easy (so far) / The way behind.
Oct 00. (7") (TUGS 024) **DINOSAUR ACT. / OVERHEAD**
(cd-s+=) (TUGSCD 024) – Don't carry it all.
Feb 01. (cd/lp) (TUG CD/LP 027) <KRANKY 046> **THINGS WE LOST IN THE FIRE**
– Sunflower / Whitehall / Dinosaur act / Medicine magazines / Laser beam / July / Embrace / Whore / Kind of girl / Like a forest / Closer / Funny noise / In metal. (lp+=) – Overhead / Don't carry it all.
Apr 01. (7"ep; shared w/ K) <15> **THOSE GIRLS** — not iss. / Tiger Style
– (track by K) / Those girls / Venus / (track by K).
Oct 01. (7") (RTRADES 033) <CKM 003> **LAST NIGHT I DREAMT THAT SOMEBODY LOVE ME. / BECAUSE YOU STOOD STILL** — Rough Trade / Chairkicker's Music
(cd-s+=) (RTRADESCD 033) – Dinosaur act (dub).
Mar 02. (7") <(MM 01)> **split w/ VIBRACATHEDRAL**
(above issued on 'Misplaced') (re-iss. Sep02; same)
Sep 02. (cd/d-lp) (RTRADE CD/LP 061) <KRANKY 52> **TRUST** — Rough Trade / Kranky
– (That's how you sing) Amazing grace / Canada / Candy girl / Time is the diamond / Tonight / The lamb / In the drugs / Last snowstorm of the year / John Prine / Little argument with myself / La la la song / Point of disgust / Shots & ladders.
Oct 02. (7"/cd-s) (RTRADES/+CD 058) **CANADA. / FEARLESS**

– compilations, etc. –

Jul 98. (cd) Vernon Yard; <YARD 27> **OWL** (LOW remixes by other artists)
– Down / Annon (spore) / Over the ocean / Laugh / Anon (pollen) / Do you know how to waltz / Over the ocean / Words.
May 01. (cd/lp; shared with DIRTY THREE) In The Fishtank; (FISH 7 CD/LP) **IN THE FISHTANK**
– I hear . . . goodnight / Down by the river / Invitation day / When I called upon your seed / Cody / Lordy.

LOWCRAFT

Formed: Portland, Oregon, USA . . . out of short-lived ABSINTHE by NATHAN KHYBER, KEITH SOMMERS, BRADY WOODCOCK, BILLY LA GRAND and PETER NOONE (the latter having replaced original CLARK STILES). Their debut 'ONE OF US' (for 'Disco Volante'), heralded a bright beginning for young starlets from America who were now plying their trade in London. Further 45's 'FUN WITH FLASHLIGHTS' and 'TRANSCENDENTAL MELTDOWN' preceded a slightly disappointing first full-length outing, 'MANTICORE' (1999); the poor man's, in fact, the very poor man's RADIOHEAD, although a glam-laden PSYCHEDELIC FURS also come to mind.

Album rating: MANTICORE (*5)

NATHAN KHYBER – vocals / **KEITH SOMMERS** – guitar / **BRADY WOODCOCK** – guitar / **CLARK STILES** – bass / **BILLY LA GRAND** – drums

Oct 98. (cd-ep; as ABSINTHE) **SPOONS** — not iss. / Stiles
– Divine / Happy in my pants / Angel in the snow / Inch away from Heaven / Porn star [hidden track].

― **PETER NOONE** – bass; repl. STILES

Feb 99. (7") (DVS 1001VS) **ONE OF US. / BOOKS & BOTTLES** — Disco Volante / not iss.
(cd-s) (DVS 1001CD) – ('A'side) / All the rage / Both sides of the sun.
May 99. (7") (DVS 1002VS) **FUN WITH FLASHLIGHTS. / BEFORE THE ENDING COMES**
(cd-s+=) (DVS 1002CD) – Trembling.
Aug 99. (7") (DVS 1003VS) **TRANSCENDENTAL MELTDOWN. / PORN STAR**
(cd-s) (DVS 1003CD) – ('A'side) / Strictly chemical / She's flying on.
Aug 99. (cd) (DVA 5001CD) **MANTICORE**
– Inch away from Heaven / One of us / Strong wind / All the rage / Trembling / Transcendental meltdown / Happy in my pants / Tree mantra / Divine angel / Avalon / Porn star.

― looked to have split towards the end of the millennium

Alex LOWE

Born: c.1975, Blairgowrie, Perthshire, Scotland. Abandoning a career in boxing (he once landed LIAM GALLAGHER a few punches!), ALEX answered a newspaper advertisement (placed by fellow-Scot, ALAN McGEE) apparently looking for a singer to reactify the career of one-time RIDE songwriter/guitarist, ANDY BELL. In 1996, along with WILL PEPPER (ex-THEE HYPNOTICS) and GARETH 'GAZ' FARMER, the aforementioned pair became Oxford-based HURRICANE – ne HURRICANE #1. McGEE's 'Creation' imprint subsequently delivered a string of chart-hitting singles, 'Step Into My World' (twice, counting the remixed version), 'Just Another Illusion' and 'Chain Reaction', all taken from the Brit-pop band's near Top 10 eponymous set released in September 1997. However, by the time of their sophomore long-player in '99, 'Only The Strongest Will Survive', HURRICANE #1 was blowing more cold than hot. Since yon time, ALEX was in the studio devising his next, much improved solo assault. The new millennium started out well enough after he landed a three-album deal with the Japanese outlet of 'Sony/Epic'. He'd sent them a demo of recordings he'd made in a Turiff (Aberdeenshire) studio with long-time friend and producer, STEVE RANSOME; ALEX was living in a £10,000 caravan just outside Blairgowrie. Surprisingly, his debut album 'DREAMCATCHER' (released in October 2000) rocketed up the Japanese charts, boosted by a chart-topping single, 'TAKE ME BACK' – a Hurricane #1, indeed. A sophomore set came in the form of 'BOYS UNITED NEVER DIE YOUNG', issued in September 2001. A slighty more chilled-out indie venture, opener 'FLIGHT TO NOWHERE' employed the same song structure seen on LOWE's previous work, with jangling guitars, pianos and lush orchestrations.

Album rating: DREAMCATCHER (*7) / BOYS UNITED NEVER DIE YOUNG (*7)

ALEX LOWE – vocals, guitar / with various people

Oct 00. (cd) **DREAMCATCHER** — not iss. / Sony/Epic Japan
– I'll be on my way / Across the waves / Sperk the truth / Think of you that way / Coming down / Take me back / Sleepless standing in the rain / I do believe / Go and tell the world / Your love / Hey bulldog.
Sep 01. (cd) (12FTCD 2) **BOYS UNITED NEVER DIE YOUNG** — 12ft Wide / not iss.
– Flight from nowhere / Between times / Just the same / Darling boy / Fields (come along) / All my life / So is it time / A new beginning ends / Now I know it's right / It's understood / End.

LOWGOLD

Formed: London, England . . . 1998 by main songwriter DARREN FORD and DAN SYMONS. If Britain had a thriving alt country scene then it was quite certain that LOWGOLD, a group who almost didn't see their debut album make it onto the shop floor, were the driving force. Named after the brief translation of a Nordic word meaning 'of hidden worth', FORD and SYMONS met in a university bar and after two tracks were quickly recorded, the pair sent the demo tape to 'Nude' records (home of SUEDE). 'Nude' asked them to perform live and the duo had to quickly recruit MILES WILLEY and SCOTT SIMON for one weeks rehearsal. Luckily for them, the record company virtually signed the group on the spot. Unluckily for the record company, however, they were experiencing major finanical difficulties and LOWGOLD's dreamy debut 'JUST BACKWARDS OF SQUARE' was shelved. It appeared some two years later with mixed reactions from the British music press, although it did hit the Top 40 (as did the single, 'BEAUTY DIES YOUNG'). Some tipped the band to go on to do great things in the new year, others just saw them as imitators of "cool" American Lo-Fi. Whatever, the ensemble still managed to be compared to BADLY DRAWN BOY, GRANDADDY and The RED HOUSE PAINTERS and were far more interesting than some tabloid-y music-journos made them out to be. • **Covers:** SHE DARKED THE SUN (Dillards).

Album rating: JUST BACKWARDS OF SQUARE (*7)

DARREN FORD – vocals, guitar / **DAN SYMONS** – guitar / **MILES WILLEY** – bass / **SIMON SCOTT** – drums

			Nude	not iss.
Jul 00.	(10"ep/cd-ep) (NUD 50 T/CD) **THE 108 EP**			-
	– In amber / Can't say no / The feelings / God willing.			
Sep 00.	(7"/cd-s) (NUD 52 S/CD1) **BEAUTY DIES YOUNG. / PLEASE BE GOOD TO ME / SILVER OCEAN**		67	-
Jan 01.	(7"/cd-s) (NUD 53 S/CD1) **MERCURY. / EDDIE LEJEUNE / IF PEOPLE WERE VINYL (featuring TUX)**		48	-
Feb 01.	(cd/lp) (NUDE 17 CD/LP) **JUST BACKWARDS OF SQUARE**		33	-
	– Golden ratio / Beauty dies young / Mercury / Out of reach / Back here again / Counterfeit / Never alone / In amber / Open the airwaves / Less I offer / Into the void.			
Apr 01.	(7") (NUD 55S) **COUNTERFEIT. / WHATEVER YOU THINK, YOU'RE WRONG**		52	-
	(cd-s+=) (NUD 55CD1) – Atlantic Pacific.			
	(cd-s) (NUD 55CD2) – ('A'side) / She darked she sun / Remission time.			
Aug 01.	(7") (NUD 59) **BEAUTY DIES YOUNG. / END OF THE MATTER**		40	-
	(cd-s) (NUD 59CD1) – ('A'side) / Can't say no / Coming strong.			
	(cd-s) (NUD 59CD2) – ('A'-Graham Coxon mix) / Make over, make up / I'd rather fuck up than miss out.			

L7

Formed: Los Angeles, California, USA . . . 1986 by DONITA SPARKS (guitar/vocals) and SUZI GARDNER (guitar/vocals). Recruiting seasoned L.A. punk veteran JENNIFER FINCH on bass and drummer ANNE ANDERSON, the band signed for the small 'Epitaph' label. The feisty punk-metal noise of their 1988 eponymous debut attracted the attention of the now-famous 'Sub Pop' label the following year, DEE PLAKAS replacing ANDERSON and 'SMELL THE MAGIC' (1990) fuelling the band's growing cult reputation. 1990 also saw the girls touring with a relatively unknown NIRVANA, L7's infamous onstage antics almost causing as much of a stir as the headliners. The band were soon snapped up by 'Slash', hitting the UK Top 20 in 1992 with the pop-grunge of the 'PRETEND WE'RE DEAD' single. This was closely followed by the 'BRICKS ARE HEAVY' album, a hard hitting collision of girl power grunge and ultra hard line, often humorous, post-feminist lyrics. The band caused further uproar later that year when DONITA exposed her womanly charms on 'The Word', having already blessed that year's Reading Festival audience with a used tampon. Irreverent yet committed, L7 also formed 'Rock For Choice', a pro-abortion pressure group which won unprecedented support in the male-dominated environs of the music business. 'HUNGRY FOR STINK' (1994) was equally blistering, the frenetic 'FUEL MY FIRE' later covered by The PRODIGY on their landmark 'THE FAT OF THE LAND' album. 'THE BEAUTY PROCESS: TRIPLE PLATINUM' (1997) marked FINCH's final fling with the band before she left to form LYME, the record's move into harder rocking territory signalling a new era for L7 as they attempted to chart the uncertain waters of the post-grunge era. With first GRETA BRINKMAN and then GAIL GREENWOOD at the helm, they went on to record 'SLAP-HAPPY' (1999), an album which came in for some critical flak for sounding too one dimensional. More satisfying for longtime fans was the live set, 'OMAHA TO OSAKA', a visceral aural document culled from various Japanese club dates. • **Songwriters:** Group or SPARKS penned except THREE DAYS (Willie Nelson).

Album rating: L7 (*6) / SMELL THE MAGIC mini (*6) / BRICKS ARE HEAVY (*8) / HUNGRY FOR STINK (*6) / THE BEAUTY PROCESS: TRIPLE PLATINUM (*6) / FROM OSAKA TO OMAHA (*6) / SLAP-HAPPY (*6) / THE BEST OF L7 compilation (*7)

DONITA SPARKS (b. 8 Apr'63, Chicago, Illinois) – vocals, guitar / **SUZI GARDNER** (b. 1 Aug'60, Altus, Oklahoma) – guitar, vocals / **JENNIFER FINCH** (b. 5 Aug'66) – bass, vocals / **ANNE ANDERSON** (b.Chicago) – drums repl.by **ROY KOUTSKY**

		not iss.	Epitaph
Dec 88.	(lp/c/cd) <E 86401-1/-4/-2> **L7**	-	
	– Bite the wax tadpole / Cat-o'-nine-tails / Metal stampede / Let's rock tonight / Uncle Bob / Snake handler / Runnin' from the law / Cool out / It's not you / I drink / Ms. 45. (UK-iss.Jun92; same)		

(DEMETRA) DEE PLAKAS (b. 9 Nov'60, Chicago) – drums repl. ROY

		Glitterhouse	Sub Pop
Jan 90.	(7",7"green) <SP 58> **SHOVE. / PACKIN' A ROD**	-	
	(UK-iss.Jan91 on 'Sub Pop'; EFA 08105)		
Nov 90.	(12"ep,12"purple-ep) <SP 79> **SMELL THE MAGIC**		Aug90
	– Shove / Til the wheels fall off / Fast'n'frightening / (Right on) Thru / Deathwish / Broomstick. (cd-ep Oct95+= ; SPCD 79) – Packin' a rod / Just like me / American society.		

		Slash	Slash
Mar 92.	(7"red/c-s) (LASH/LACS 34) **PRETEND WE'RE DEAD. / SHIT LIST**	21	
	(12"+=/cd-s+=) (LASHX/LASCD 34) – Lopsided head / Mr. Integrity.		
Apr 92.	(cd/c/lp) (828 307-2/-4/-1) <26784> **BRICKS ARE HEAVY**	24	
	– Wargasm / Scrap / Pretend we're dead / Diet pill / Everglade / Slide / One more thing / Mr. Integrity / Monster / Shit list / This ain't pleasure.		
May 92.	(7"green) (LASH 36) **EVERGLADE. / FREAK MAGNET**	27	
	(12"+=/cd-s+=) (LASHXP/LASHCD 36) – Scrap.		
Sep 92.	(7"/c-s) (LASH/LACS 38) **MONSTER. / USED TO LOVE HIM**	33	
	(12"+=/cd-s+=) (LASHX/LASCD 38) – Diet pill.		
Nov 92.	(7"/c-s) (LASH/LACS 42) **PRETEND WE'RE DEAD. / FAST 'N' FRIGHTENING (live)**	50	-
	(cd-s+=) (LASCD 42) – (Right on) Thru / Shove / Shit list / Diet pill.		

– L7 appeared as CAMEL LIPS group in the film 'Serial Mom'.

Jun 94.	(7"colrd/12"colrd) (LASH/LASCS 48) **ANDRES. / BOMB**	34	
	(cd-s+=) (LASCD 48) – (KRXT radio interview).		
Jul 94.	(cd/c/lp) <(828 531-2/-4/-1)> **HUNGRY FOR STINK**	26	
	– Andres / Baggage / Can I run / The bomb / Questioning my sanity / Riding with a movie star / Stuck here again / Fuel my fire / Freak magnet / She has eyes / Shirley / Talk box.		

– After recording 1996 album, FINCH left to form LYME. She was repl. by **GRETA BRINKMAN** who appeared on next album, before **GAIL GREENWOOD** (ex-BELLY) took over

Feb 97.	(cd/c) <(828 868-2/-4)> **THE BEAUTY PROCESS: TRIPLE PLATINUM**		
	– Beauty process / Drama / Off the wagon / I need / Moonshine / Bitter wine / Masses are asses / Bad things / Must have more / Non existant Patricia / Me, myself and I / Lorenza, Giada, Alessandra / Guera.		
Feb 97.	(c-s/cd-s) <17403/43834> **OFF THE WAGON / GUERA / PUNK BROKE (MY HEART)**		

		Man's Ruin	Man's Ruin
Jan 99.	(cd) <(MR 146CD)> **FROM OSAKA OR OMAHA**		Dec98
	– L7 medley – Overture: Fast and frightening / Bad things / Must have more / Deathwish / Slide / Bitter wine / Drama / Non-existant Patricia / Pattylean / El Whatusi / Shitlist / Andres / Fast and frightening / Off the wagon / Little one / Lorenza, Giada, Allesandra.		

		Bongload	Bongload
Aug 99.	(cd/lp) <(BL 43 CD/V)> **SLAP-HAPPY**		
	– Crackpot baby / On my rockin' machine / Lackey / Human / Livin' large / Freeway / Stick to the plan / War with you / Long green / Little one / Freezer burn / Mantra down.		

– compilations, etc. –

Mar 00.	(cd) Slash; <(8573 82064-2)> **THE BEST OF L7: THE SLASH YEARS**		May00
	– Pretend we're dead / Mr Integrity / Monster / Everglade / Andres / Fuel my fire / Freak magnet / Can I run / Bad things / Off the wagon / Moonshine / Bitter wine.		

LUCKSMITHS

Formed: Melbourne, Australia . . . early 1993 by TALI WHITE, MARTY DONALD and MARK MONNONE. The band gradually eased themselves into the music business with the limited edition 'FIRST TAPE' which caused a stir in the Australian underground scene. The following year saw the release of the EP 'BOONDOGGLE'. It was in 1995 the band began to gather real momentum with the delivery of the understated yet effective debut album 'GREEN BICYCLE CASE'. The album's sparse arrangements and wistful vocals made for compelling listening. Without compromising the quality of their music the band managed to sustain their prolific output and released two further albums in as many years. 'WHAT BIRD IS THAT' (1996) and 'A GOOD KIND OF NERVOUS' (1997). Both of these albums were breezy and intimate sounding and showed that The LUCKSMITHS were growing in confidence as lyricists. A lengthy European tour afforded the band greater skills as musicians and consequently enabled them to deliver a more complete sound. The culmination of this was to be heard on two 1999 mini albums 'HAPPY SECRET' and 'STARING AT THE SKY'. On these albums the band bravely sacrificed features of their music that had endeared them to their fans in the first place. The bouncy melodies and occasionally silly lyrics of earlier efforts were triumphantly replaced by the stronger and more evocative sound of a band to be reckoned with. It would be another two years before the band would release another full length album. The gorgeous 'WHY THAT DOESN'T SURPRISE ME' (2001) delivered everything that was promised by the pair of 1999 mini albums.

Album rating: BOONDOGGLE mini (*6) / FIRST TAPE mini (*5) / THE GREEN BICYCLE CASE (*6) / WHAT BIRD IS THAT? (*5) / A GOOD KIND OF NERVOUS (*6) / HAPPY SECRET (*6) / STARING AT THE SKY mini (*5) / WHY THAT DOESN'T SURPRISE ME (*6) / WHERE WERE WE? compilation (*7)

TALI WHITE – vocals, percussion / **MARTY DONALD** – guitar / **MARK MONNONE** – bass

			Candle	not iss.
1993.	(m-c) *(Luc 01)* **FIRST TAPE**		-	Austra

– Cliched title for Kris / Cat in sunshine / Adolescent song of mindless devotion / Run spot run / Weatherboard / Andrew's pleasure / Remote control / Tale of two cities / Birthday present for Katrina / Scottsdale / English murder mystery.

1994. (m-cd) *(Luc 02)* **BOONDOGGLE** – / Austra
– Victor trumper / Clever Hans / Summer town / Tree / 21 / Umbrella / The baker's wife / Fridge magnet song.

1995. (m-cd) *(Luc 03)* **THE GREEN BICYCLE CASE** – / Austra
– Jewel thieves / Motorscooter / The Tichborne claimant / Spond / Two storeys / Detective agency / Thomas and Martha / Mezzanine / William and Mary / Only angels have wings / Aviatrix / From here to maternity.

1996. (cd) *(Luc 04)* **WHAT BIRD IS THAT?** – / Austra
– Shine on me / Silver friends / Off with his cardigan! / Macintyre / Snug / Putt putt / Day in the city / Housewarming / The drunkest man in the world / Twenty-two / Jennifer Jason / Danielle Steel / Frisbee / I am about to sail.

1996. (7"ep) *(Luc 05)* **MACINTYRE** – / Austra
– Macintyre / Get well now / Shine on me / Are you having a good time?

Drive-In   Drive-In

1997. (7") *<DRIVE 13>* **THE INVENTION OF ORDINARY EVERYDAY THINGS. / UP**

May 98. (cd) *<(DRIVE 21)>* **A GOOD KIND OF NERVOUS**
– Caravanna / Under the rotunda / Train robbers' wives / World encyclopedia of twentieth century murder / The invention of ordinary everyday things / Punchlines / Guess how much I love you / Columns o' steam / Up / Wyoming / Little athletics.

Oct 98. (7"m) *(MATINEE 4) <DRIVE 28>* **UNTIDY TOWNS. / PIN CUSHION / EDWARD, SANDWICH HAND**

Mar 99. (7"m) *(MATINEE 8) <DRIVE 32>* **SOUTHERNMOST. / BEER NUT / PAPER PLANES**
(above singles on 'Matinee' UK)

May 99. (cd) *<(DRIVE 35)>* **HAPPY SECRET**
– Untidy towns / Pin cushion / Edward, sandwich hand / Abdication! / The art of cooking for two / Don't come with me / A great parker / Southernmost / Beer nut / Paper planes.

Matinee   Drive-In

Jan 99. (d7"ep; Various Artists) *(MATINEE 5)* **A Smike Took Over**
– I've got it and it's not worth having / (other acts inc. BOYRACER)

Mar 00. (m-cd/10"m-lp) *(MAT CD/LP 004)* **STARING AT THE SKY**
– Smokers in love / I can't believe it's not better / I.E., e.g., etc. / The golden age of aviation / Before the sun came up / The opposite of coffee.

Oct 00. (cd-ep) *(MATINEE 018CD)* **T-SHIRT WEATHER**
– T-shirt weather / TMRW vs. y'day / Deep sea diving suit / Southernmost.

Jul 01. (7") *(MATINEE 027)* **FRIENDLESS SUMMER. / GOODNESS GRACIOUS**

Fortuna
Pop   Drive-In

Sep 01. (7") *(FPOP 28)* **THE CASSINGLE REVIVAL. / MYOPIC FRIENDS**

Oct 01. (cd) *(FPOP 32) <DRIVE 52>* **WHY THAT DOESN'T SURPRISE ME** Mar01
– Music to hold hands to / Synchronised sinking / The great dividing range / Beach Boys medley / Broken bones / First cousin / Don't bring your work to bed / Fear of rollercoasters / Harmonicas and trams / The forgetting of wisdom / Self-preservation / How to tie a tie / All the recipes I've ever ruined / The year of living languorously.

Sep 02. (cd) *(MATCD 19 – FPOP 39)* **WHERE WERE WE?**
(compilation)
– The cassingle revival / Myopic friends / A downside to the upstairs / Can't believe my eyes / I prefer the twentieth century / T-shirt weather / TMRW vs. y'day / Southernmost / Even Stevens / The great dividing range (demo version) / Friendless summer / Goodness gracious / Welcome home / Mars.

Oct 02. (cd-s) *(MATINEE 42)* **MIDWEEK MIDMORNING / POINT BEING / REQUIEM FOR THE PUNTERS CLUB**

LUCKY PIERRE (see under ⇒ ARAB STRAP)

LUCKY SPERMS
(see under ⇒ HALF JAPANESE; 70's section)

LUGWORM

Formed: Glasgow, Scotland . . . 1994 by vocalist SUNNI CARO, guitarist DEP DOWNIE, bassist GRAHAM GAVIN and drummer/trumpeter! STEVIE DUNBAR. There was a time in the mid-90's that LUGWORM must've wondered – when they would ever manage to get a record released (apart from featuring on V/A compilations). However by Spring '97, the band had two singles in the indie shops, the first 'TE LO DIR'O!' (pronounced "Telaw a deraw") was actually recorded in May '95 for BIS' 'teen-c recordingz', the second for 'Guided Missile' was a shared affair with likeminded BIS and PINK KROSS. The latter English-based imprint was also responsible for a subsequent track, 'EL LOCO BOOGALOO' (from their V/A 'Hits & Missiles' album), by which time DUNBAR was replaced by drummer DEMPSEY. If you'd mixed the POP GROUP with the RAINCOATS you'd be close to the LUGWORM sound – short, to-the-point, quirkiness was the order of day.

SUNNI CARO – vocals / **DEP DOWNIE** – guitar / **GRAHAM GAVIN** – bass, vocals / **STEVIE DUNBAR** – drums, trumpet

teen-c!   not iss.

Mar 97. (7") *(SKETCH 002)* **TE LO DIR'O! EP**
– Biodegradable disco / Toby Mangel / Sweaty says / Barmitzvah.

Guided
Missile   not iss.

Apr 97. (7"ep) *(GUIDE 011)* **split**
– Rococ negro / Harrap ageing fast / (2 by BIS with PINK KROSS).

—— . . . **DEMPSEY** – drums; repl. DUNBAR

—— might've released a few more split singles before their split

LULLABY FOR THE WORKING CLASS

Formed: Omaha, Nebraska, USA . . . 1994 by MIKE MOGIS and TED STEVENS; later inclusions being MIKE's brother A.J. and SHANE ASPEGREN. Touting their mixture of singer/songwriter material in the alternative country/folk vein with chamber-pop style backing around the New York gig circuit, the band managed to garner the attention of 'Bar-None' records, who issued their debut LP, 'BLANKET WARM', in 1996. A set similar in mood to the highly talented later work of WILL OLDHAM, the band nevertheless managed to carve out an individual place in the hearts of the alternative press and fans with their unique use of added violin work which gave the album its atmospheric strength. Their undoubted talent and foresight opened the door for fellow Nebraskans with like-minded sounds in the shape of bands like COMMANDER VENUS and WE'D RATHER BE FLYING, as the record buying public searched for more sonic nuggets from their state of origin. Fortunately the critics didn't have to wait long, with their second set, 'I NEVER EVEN ASKED FOR MORE', turning up a year later. This was followed by a sound third offering, 'SONG' (1999), which also featured the adroit violin playing of the staple collaborator TIFFANY KOWALSKI. Unfortunately, this record was also to be their last, as the band drifted off for various side-projects; MIKE and ASPEGREN could be found contributing to the acclaimed SONGS: OHIA release 'Ghost Tropic' (2000) and STEVENS replaced the departing PEDERSEN in indie rock outfit, CURSIVE, as well as helping out bandmate TIM KASHER in his other musical outfit, The GOOD LIFE. Yet by 2001, STEVENS had brought nearly all the old gang together again for his new direction, MAYDAY. This project saw an all-star alt-rock cast with A.J. and MIKE, KOWALSKI, BRIGHT EYES' CONOR OBERST and members of AZURE RAY coming together to issue the LP, 'OLD BLOOD' (2001). The set was a fine return to LFTWC form and ploughed a similar vein, with some lovely sea shanty stylings and flamenco guitar flavours added to boot.

Album rating: BLANKET WARM (*6) / I NEVER EVEN ASKED FOR LIGHT (*5) / SONG (*6) / Mayday: OLD BLOOD (*6)

TED STEVENS – vocals, guitar / **MIKE MOGIS** – guitars, banjo, mandolin, etc / **A.J. MOGIS** – bass / **SHANE ASPEGREN** – drums

Rykodisc   Bar/None

Sep 96. (cd/lp) *(RCD/RALP 10372) <86>* **BLANKET WARM**
– Good morning / Honey, drop the knife / Turpentine / Spreading the evening sky with crows / Boar's nest / Eskimo song duel / Three peas in a pod / Rye / Queen of the long-legged insects / The drama of your life / February North 24th St. / The wounded spider / Good night.

Sep 97. (cd/lp) *(RCD/RALP 10426) <93>* **I NEVER ASKED FOR A LIGHT**
– Show me how the robots dance / Irish wake / Jester's siren / Hypnotist (song for Daniel H.) / In honor of my stumbling / This is as close as we get / The sunset & the electric bill / Bread crumbs / Descent / The man vs. the tide.

—— added **TIFFANY KOWALSKI** – violin

Saddle   Saddle
Creek   Creek

Nov 99. (lp) *<(LBJ 27)>* **SONG** Sep99
– Expand, contract / Inherent song / Asleep on the subway / Seizures / Non serviam / Sketchings on a bar room napkin / Kitchen song / Ghosts / Still life.

—— STEVENS joined CURSIVE; MIKE + A.J. became studio engineers

MAYDAY

TED STEVENS – vocals, guitar / **TIFFANY KOWALSKI** – violin / **MIKE + A.J.** – engineers, instruments / **CONOR OBERST** – guitar (of BRIGHT EYES) / **MARIA TAYLOR** – vocals (of AZURE RAY) / **ORENDA FINK** – vocals (of AZURE RAY) / + **ANDY LeMASTER**

not iss.   Saddle
Creek

May 02. (cd) *<LBJ 44>* **OLD BLOOD**
– Cinquefoils / Come home / Captain / Tone – Atone – Atonal / Lullaby for the sleeping elephant / I know moonlight / Confession / Pilot / Temple – Temporary – Extempore – Tempo – Domes . . .

LUNA (see under ⇒ GALAXIE 500)

LUNACHICKS

Formed: Brooklyn, New York, USA . . . 1988 by THEO KOGAN, BECKY WRECK, SQUID SID, GINA and SINDI. Reportedly recommended to the influential indie label, 'Blast First' by NY noisemongers, SONIC YOUTH, LUNACHICKS were a garish explosion of colour and scuzzy punk/grunge, North Eastern cousins to the likes of BABES IN TOYLAND and L7. The sassy grunge girls weren't afraid of controversy, taking the name of their debut album, 'BABYSITTERS ON ACID' (1990) from a real-life incident (when a drug-crazed babysitter phoned her employers to tell them their child would be ready and cooked for them arriving back. She was obviously arrested! Sick), the crazed fem-rockers bashing out a racket that would probably scare most black-hearted Norwegian metallers. Their live show was equally raucous, the intergalactic noise terrorists subsequently releasing a slightly improved follow-up set in 1993, 'BINGE PURGE'. Switching labels to 'Go Kart' and replacing BECKY with CHIP, the band staggered on with a further two releases, 'JERK OF ALL TRADES' (1995) and 'PRETTY UGLY' (1997). Following the obligatory live 'DROP DEAD . . .' in '98, The LUNACHICKS were back creating musical havoc in the studio, the results being their fifth set 'LUXURY PROBLEM' (1999). • **Covers:** NOISE ANNOYS (Buzzcocks) / THE PASSENGER (Iggy Pop).

Album rating: BABYSITTERS ON ACID (*5) / BINGE AND PURGE (*6) / JERK OF ALL TRADES (*6) / PRETTY UGLY (*6) / DROP DEAD LIVE (*5) / LUXURY PROBLEM (*5)

THEO KOGAN – vocals / **SINDI** – guitar / **GINA** – guitar / **SQUID SID** – bass / **BECKY WRECK** – drums

			not iss.	own label
1988.	(7") <none>	**C.I.L.L. / PLUGG**	-	-
1988.	(7") <none>	**SUSHI A LA MODE. /**		

Blast First / Plan 9 – Caroline

Apr 89.	(d7"ep/cd-ep) (BFFP 44/+CD) **SUGAR LUV. / GET OFF THE ROAD // MAKIN' IT (WITH OTHER SPECIES). / JAN BRADY**		
Nov 89.	(lp/c/cd) (BFFP 52/+C/CD) <2105> **BABYSITTERS ON ACID** <US-title 'LUNACHICKS'> – Jan Brady / Glad I'm not yew / Babysitters on acid / Makin' it (with other species) / Mabel rock / Theme song / Born 2B mild / Pin eye woman 665 / Cookie core / Octopussy / Sugar luv / Complication. (re-iss. Oct90; same) <(cd re-iss. Mar01 on 'Go Kart'; GK 059CD)>		
Apr 90.	(7") (BFFP 55) **COOKIE MOSHTER. / COMPLICATION**	Zuma	Safe House
Aug 92.	(12"ep/cd-ep) <2105> **APATHETIC EP**	-	
Mar 93.	(lp/cd) (ELUNA 1/+CD) <SH 2107-1/-2> **BINGE AND PURGE** – Apathetic / Plugg / P.S. Hell / Binge and purge / Mom / Superstrong / This is serious / Whole lotta B.S. / 2 bad 4 U / 11 / Rip U / C.I.L.L. (re-iss. Mar96 on 'SPV'; SPV 0844543-2) (re-iss. Nov96 on 'Safe House' cd/lp; SH 2107-2/-1)		Sep92

		not iss.	Sympathy..
1993.	(7") **SHIT FINGER DICK. / LIGHT AS A FEATHER (STIFF AS A BOARD)**	-	-

Go Kart / Go Kart

Oct 95.	(cd/lp) <(GK 013/+CD)> **JERK OF ALL TRADES** – Drop dead / Fingerful / F.D.S. / Light as a feather / Edgar / Dogyard / Butt plugg / Bitterness Barbie / Deal with it / Brickface and Stucco / Jerk off all trades / Spoilt / Ring and run / Fallopian rhapsody / Insomnia / Why me. (UK-iss.May97; same)		May95
Feb 97.	(cd) <(GK 024CD)> **PRETTY UGLY** – Yeah / Thrown it away / The day Squibs gerbil died / Dear Dotti / Mr. Lady / Spork / What's left / Gone kissin' / Don't want you / Baby / #%@!* / Wing Chun / MMM donuts / Missed it.		
Nov 98.	(cd/d-lp) <(GK 042 CDLP)> **DROP DEAD LIVE (live)** – Yeah / FDS / The day Squid's gerbil died / Gong kissin / Fingerful / Thrown it away / Don't want you / Jerk of all trades / Wing Chun / Bitterness Barbie / Drop dead / Donuts / Passenger / Buttplug / Crash / Dear Dotti / #%@!* / Spoilt.		Aug98
Aug 99.	(lp/cd) <(GOKART 051/+CD)> **LUXURY PROBLEM** – Less teeth more tits / Luxury problem / I'll be the one / Crash / Terror firmer / Say what you mean / Nowhere fast / Bad ass bitch / Shut you out / Cumming into my own / Hope to die / Knuckle sandwich / The return of Brickface & Stucco / Subway / Down at the pub.		

LUNCHBOX

Formed: Berkeley, California, USA . . . 1994 by singer/songwriter/guitarist TIM BROWN, bassist DONNA McKEAN and drummer MARTY KELLY, although BROWN and McKEAN would form the core of LUNCHBOX, with several drummers coming and going over the following years. Clearly taking early inspiration from British bands like the JAM and the BUZZCOCKS, they released the 'LUNCHBOX' LP in 1996 on San Francisco label 'Not Happy'. The record contained fifteen rollicking three-chord punk-pop numbers, but was blighted by uneven songwriting and clumsy production. After a three-year gap, second album 'MAGIC OF SOUND' was proof that LUNCHBOX had addressed their shortcomings, and sought a more mature variation and approach. Now sounding more like contemporaries STEREOLAB, with the incorporation of electronics, organs and keyboards, the set was boosted by the polished indie-pop production from CIAO BELLA's JAMIE McCORMICK. 'MAGIC . . .' contained several excellent tracks, like the atmospheric opener 'IN MY WORLD'. On follow-up 'EVOLVER', released in 2002, LUNCHBOX were more experimental, adding distortion and a greater depth of instrumentation.

Album rating: LUNCHBOX (*5) / THE MAGIC OF SOUND (*6) / EVOLVER (*5)

TIM BROWN – vocals, guitar / **DONNA McKEAN** – vocals, bass / **MARTY KELLY** – drums; repl. JON BRAHM +/or HUGH HOWIE

		not iss.	Smile
Oct 95.	(12") <902-1> **EASTERN INFLUENCE**	-	

not iss. / Not Happy

1996.	(cd) <005> **LUNCHBOX** – Oh did I? / What you love / Three speed / In it for you / Out of sight / Everybody / Up to you / Slowly I turned / Fight or flight / Generic / Reprise / I don't care / Leave me alone / Insane / TV tray.	-	

— **SHANNON HANDY** – drums; repl. KELLY

		Motorway	not iss.
Jul 99.	(7") (MOTOR 32) **3.2.1. /**	-	Japan

Magic Marker / Magic Marker

Oct 99.	(cd) <(MMA 005)> **THE MAGIC OF SOUND** – In my world / Ordinary day / Lotion / Just because / A special feeling / Wanna reach you / Little things / Still life / So much about you / I need more time / Episode.		Jul99

— **MARIO HERNANDEZ** – drums (ex-CIAO BELLA) repl. HANDY

Oct 01.	(7"ep) **GLOW LIKE THERE'S NO TOMORROW** – Satellite / I could have been someone else / Fernruf / Gravity.	-	
Jan 02.	(cd) <MMA 019> **EVOLVER**	-	
	– Evolver / Particle – Wave / Letter from Overend / Tone poem / Temperature is a constant / .06 / Sleeping is not dreaming / Gravity / .09 / Weekling / Sea life / (untitled).		

555 / not iss.

Apr 02.	(m-cd) (555CD 33) **SUMMER'S OVER** – Letter from Overend / Everything's ok / So everyday / Summer's over / Tigerstripe / Beauty supply / Anti-me.		-

LUNE

Formed: Boston, Massachusetts, USA . . . 1998 by KARATE man, JEFF GODDARD, and two other equally experimentally-minded mates, BRAD WHITE and MARK ROMANO. The LUNE delivered a couple of average jazzed-up indie releases for 'Aesthetics', 'ON THE CUTTING ROOM FLOOR' and 'the mini 'SILL' (both issued in '99) before GODDARD left to pursue his other musical duties.

Album rating: ON THE CUTTING ROOM FLOOR (*6) / SILL mini (*5) / BLAMELESS (*6)

JEFF GODDARD – bass, trumpet (of KARATE) / **BRAD WHITE** – acoustic guitar, vocals / **MARK ROMANO** – drums, piano

		Aesthetics	Aesthetics
Jun 99.	(cd/lp) <(AST 001 CD/LP)> **ON THE CUTTING ROOM FLOOR** – The hook / Pain and pleasure at the failure of Will / Fast / Get along / That night / What no brings / Old trumpet / Lucky / Basically, a life of crime / The decision / Young and full of poison / When the woods came.		
Oct 99.	(m-cd) <(AST 003CD)> **SILL** – That / The blues instrumental / Seatbelt / No, no / Back to the well / Near the place of asking / In me.		

— GODDARD now left to concentrate on KARATE

		Crow Point	not iss.
Apr 01.	(cd) (CP 01) **BLAMELESS** – Pussy galore.		-

LUNGFISH

Formed: Baltimore, Maryland, USA . . . early 90's by DANIEL HIGGS, ASA OSBORNE, JOHN CHRIEST and MITCHELL FELDSTEIN. The band's sound was fairly and squarely from the post-hardcore and punk fields, but with a good deal of emo thoughtfulness, best encapsulated by the lyricism of HIGGS, who was one of the major reasons the band stood out from their peers. The frontman was so lyrically fruitful that he was not to be confined solely to vinyl, but also published a tome of his erratic poetry, 'The Doomsday Bonnet'. Early on the band inked a deal with indie label, 'Dischord', who released their debut LP, 'TALKING SONGS FOR WALKING' (1991), and sophomore piece, 'RAINBOWS FROM ATOMS' (1993) to little public response. It was not until the release of their third full-length set, 'PASS & STOW' (1994), that the critics sat up and began to take notice. It was mainly due to the group finding the equilibrium between HIGGS' words, and the music. Their first two albums had tended towards too great an emphasis on the vocal, which had got them noticed in art-rock circles, but had overshadowed their sound. After finding this balance LUNGFISH were not going to throw it away, emphasised by the release of two solid albums in a row, 'SOUND IN TIME' (1996), and the magnificently dark, 'INDIVISIBLE' (1997). These releases also saw the introduction of SEAN MEADOWS to the fold, replacing CHRIEST on bass. By now the band were getting well established in the indie and alternative market, and had the time and clout to set up their own label, 'Walker' records. HIGGS also took time out to work with his brother, ALEX on a musical offshoot, CONE OF LIGHT, culminating in the release of the experimental, 'MAGIC EYE'. The revolving door bass place also went another revolution, with the replacement of MEADOWS by NATHAN BELL. Busy as the group were they still managed to release another competent piece in the shape of 'ARTIFICIAL HORIZON' (1998), which they followed up the next year with 'THE UNANIMOUS HOUR'. Both of these albums were good, but they had not really broken any new musical ground for the band. They did not really break this status quo with the release of 'NECROPHONES' in the millennium, which although popular with their fanbase, was not really moving on from the sounds the group had been pushing in the mid-nineties.

Album rating: TALKING SONGS FOR WALKING (*5) / RAINBOWS FROM ATOMS (*5) / PASS AND STOW (*6) / SOUND IN TIME (*5) / INDIVISIBLE (*5) / ARTIFICIAL HORIZON (*6) / THE UNANIMOUS HOUR (*7) / NECROPHONES (*6)

DANIEL HIGGS – vocals / **ASA OSBORNE** – guitar / **JOHN CHRIEST** – bass / **MITCHELL FELDSTEIN** – drums

		Dischord	Dischord
1992.	(lp/c/cd) <DIS 65/+C/CD> **TALKING SONGS FOR WALKING** – Friend to a friend in the endtime / Broadcast / Descender / Samuel / Kissing / Reveal me / My foll heart / One face / Non dual bliss / Put your hand in my hand / Come clean / Put your halo on / Ain't no color / Not only long ride too high / Parthogenesis / Devilhead / Nothing is easy / Fambly.	-	
Mar 93.	(7") <(WHFEB)> **FEBRUARY. / (other by The TINKLERS)** (above issued on 'Simple Machines')		
Jun 93.	(lp/c/cd) <DIS 78/+C/CD> **RAINBOWS FROM ATOMS** – Instrument / Mother made me / Abraham Lincoln / Animal man / Fresh air cure / Creation story / Axiomatic / Open house / 8.14.2116 / You might ask me what / Seek sound shelter.		
Sep 94.	(lp/c/cd) <(DIS 92 CD/C/V)> **PASS & STOW** – Cleaner than your surroundings / Straightaway / Washing away / At liberty to say / The trap gets set / Computer / Highway sweetheart / Astronaut's prayer / Idiot vehicle / One way all the time / In praise of amoral phenomena / Gorilla monsoon / The evidence / Terminal crush.		

LUNGFISH (cont)

—— **SEAN MEADOWS** – bass; repl. CHRIEST
Feb 96. (lp/cd) <(DIS 97 V/CD)> **SOUND IN TIME**
– Constellations / To whom you were born / Jonah / Solid state / X-ray the pharaoh / Signpost / Sphere of influence / The cipher / Panic and hysteria / Constellations.
Apr 97. (lp/cd) <(DIS 106 V/CD)> **INDIVISIBLE**
– Indivisible / You did not exist / E=Fu / Urania / Organ harvest / Yellow sun / Tick tock / Cut to fit the mouth / Fill the days / Sin to live.
—— **NATHAN BELL** – bass; repl. MEADOWS
May 98. (lp/cd) <(DIS 115/+CD)> **ARTIFICIAL HORIZON**
– Black helicopters / Oppress yourself / Amnesiac / Love will ruin your mind / Ann the word / Slip of existence / Free state / Truth cult / Shed the world / Pray for the living / Light for all.
Jul 99. (lp/cd) <(DIS 117/+CD)> **THE UNANIMOUS HOUR**   May99
– Space orgy / Web of mirrors / Searchlight / Vulgar theories / God's will / Mated / Metatron / Sands of time / Return to the caves / Hallucinatorium.
Nov 00. (cd/lp) <(DIS 119 CD/V)> **NECROPHONES**
– The words / The way / Necrophones / All day and all of the night / Blue sky / Hanging bird / Shapes in space / Sex war / Cross road / Eternal nightfall / Occult vibrations / Infinite daybreak.

LUNG LEG

Formed: Glasgow, Scotland . . . early 1994 by feisty females JANE EGYPT, ANNIE SPANDEX, MO-MO and Cockney drummer JADE GREEN. Taking us back fifteen years to the end of the 70's (i.e. KLEENEX, the RAINCOATS, etc), LUNG LEG first came to light via crowd-pleasing appearances at the city's '13th Note' venue – stamping ground too for URUSEI YATSURA, The DELGADOS and the similar BIS. During this 'Riot Grrr' spell, LUNG LEG managed to please journos of the Melody Maker, who duly awarded them Singles Of The Week for both the debut EP, 'THE NEGATIVE DELINQUENT AUTOPSY' and the follow-up 'SHAGG THE TIGER'. 1996/7 saw the girls support the likes of SONIC YOUTH, MAKE UP and BIKINI KILL, all of whom were impressed by LUNG LEG's spunky array of indie 7"ers, the best of which, 'THEME PARK', was issued on 'Guided Missile'. Like SHONEN KNIFE getting their nose-wiped by YUMMY FUR, the aforementioned 'THEME PARK' was a retro-fied Riot Grrr/Punk classic. Coinciding with a support slot to 'Vesuvius' label mates YUMMY FUR, LUNG LEG (with male drummer TODD now replacing JADE) delivered their long-awaited debut set, 'MAID TO MINX', in the summer of '97. Further promotion came via top slots at T In The Park, although this would be one of their last outings with MO-MO who was superseded by ex-DICK JOHNSON guitarist PHILLIPA SMITH. However, after another fresh spate of 45's between '98 and '99, LUNG LEG croaked their last breath and high-tailed it into obscurity.

Album rating: MAID TO MINX (*6) / HELLO SIR compilation (*6)

JANE EGYPT – vocals, bass / **MO-MO** (aka MONICA QUIM) – vocals, guitar / **ANNIE SPANDEX** – vocals, guitar / **JADE GREEN** – drums, vocals

Piao! / *not iss.*

Oct 94. (7"ep) *(PIAO! 2)* **THE NEGATIVE DELINQUENT AUTOPSY EP**
– Punk pop travesty / Milk & water / Eek! / Anatomy of a dolly bird / secret / Dirty plotte / Friends.
Jul 95. (7"ep) *(PIAO! 5)* **SHAGG THE TIGER EP**
– Small screen queen / Edith Massey / Kung Fu on the internet / Accident / Butt sister.

Basketcase / *not iss.*

Dec 95. (7"; shared) *(FLOP 02)* **Easter Egg-splosion**

Nana / *not iss.*

1996. (7"; shared) *(NANA 1)* **ASTRAL ANGORA. /**
—— (mid-1996) **TODD** – drums, percussion, theramin, vocals (ex-HECK) repl. JADE

Vesuvius / *not iss.*

May 97. (7"m) *(POMP 010)* **RIGHT NOW BABY. / WHISKY A-GO-GO / A DIFFERENT KIND OF LOVE**
May 97. (7") *(GUIDE 17)* **THEME PARK. / CHOP CHOP**
(above issued on 'Guided Missile')
Jul 97. (cd/lp) *(POMP CD/LP 007)* **MAID TO MINX**
– Previous condition / Theme park / Disco biscuit / The shaver / Maid to minx / Right now baby / Viva by spectacula / Lonely man / F.S.R. / Kung Fu on the internet '97 / Lust for leg. <US-iss.& re-mast.May99 on 'Southern'; 18555>
—— (mid-97) **PHILLIPA SMITH** – guitar (ex-DICK JOHNSON) repl. MO-MO

Flotsam & Jetsam – The 13th Note / *not iss.*

Apr 98. (7") *(SHaG 13.06)* **Club Beatroot Part Six**
– Por que tevas / (other track by EL HOMBRE TRAJEADO)

Vesuvius / *not iss.*

Jul 98. (7") *(POMP 016)* **KRAYOLA. / (other track by the MAKE-UP)**

Southern / *Southern*

Mar 99. (7") *(<18560-7>)* **MAID TO MINX. / JUANITA**

– compilations, etc. –

Nov 97. (10"m-lp/m-cd) *Kill Rock Stars; (<KRS 259/+CD>)* **HELLO SIR** (compilation of early EP's)   May97

LUPINE HOWL

Formed: London, England . . . 1999. Following the success of the SPIRITUALIZED album 'Ladies And Gentlemen . . .' frontman JASON PIERCE made the shock move of sacking key members of the band. The three casualties for PIERCE's strop, MIKE MOONEY, SEAN COOK and JON MATTOCK soon picked themselves up and returned as LUPINE HOWL. A single, 'VAPOURIZER', kicked off the new millennium in fine style, and after another, 'BRONZAGE', they inked a deal with 'Beggars Banquet'. Their debut album, 'THE CARNIVOROUS LUNAR ACTIVITIES OF LUPINE HOWL' (2001), was well received in some quarters, most seeing it as an attempt to ambush their former boss's market share. Without the guidance of PIERCE, the songs lacked any really quality and even the best of the bunch would have struggled to appear on a SPIRITUALIZED B-side. Their second offering 'THE BAR AT THE END OF THE WORLD' (2002) saw them trying to escape the shadow of their former band; however, this new direction meant they now sounded like a poor man's CHARLATANS. The album was a bland collection of songs unidentifiable from a plethora of other bands on the circuit at the time.

Album rating: THE CARNIVOROUS LUNAR ACTIVITIES OF LUPINE HOWL (*5) / THE BAR AT THE END OF THE WORLD (*5)

MIKE MOONEY – guitar, keyboards, synthesizer / **SEAN COOK** – bass, vocals, synthesizer / **JON MATTOCK** – percussion, drums

Vinyl Hiss / *not iss.*

Jan 00. (12"/cd-s) *(VHISS 12/CD 001)* **VAPORIZER. / MEXICAN CANTINA**   68   -
Jun 00. (12") *(VHISS12 002)* **BRONZAGE (mixes)**
(cd-s) *(VHISSCD 002)* – ('A'side) / Voodoo raygun.

Beggars Banquet / *Beggars Banquet*

Oct 00. (7") *(BBQ 347)* **125. / TIRED**   Feb01
(cd-s+=) *(BBQ 347CD)* – Swell.
Feb 01. (cd-ep) *<81347>* **125**
– 125 / Vaporizer / Tired / Swell / Bronzage / Mexican cantina / Voodoo raygun.
Apr 01. (cd/lp) *(BBQ CD/LP 2190 <80219>* **THE CARNIVOROUS LUNAR ACTIVITIES OF LUPINE HOWL**   Aug01
– Vaporizer / Sniff the glue / 125 / Carnival / Lonely roads / Sometimes / Planet X / This condition / The jam that ate itself. (other cd; BBQCD 219X)
Mar 02. (12") *(BBQ 357T)* **VAPORIZER. (3D mix)**
(cd-s+=) *(BBQ 357CD)* – You get inside me.
Sep 02. (7") *(BBQ 362)* **DON'T LOSE YOUR HEAD. / SIGNING OFF**
Oct 02. (cd/lp) *(BBQ CD/LP 230) <80230>* **THE BAR AT THE END OF THE WORLD**
– A grave to go to / Don't lose your head / Can you forgive me? / The pursuit of pleasure / Gravity's pull / Centre of the universe / Trust me? / Signing off / Burning stars / All I can do.

LUSCIOUS JACKSON

Formed: New York City, New York, USA . . . 1991 by JILL CUNNIFF and GABRIELLE GLASER (both main songwriters), plus KATE SCHELLENBACH (an early BEASTIE "BOY"). In fact, LJ signed to the latter band's Capitol subsidiary, 'Grand Royal', releasing the acclaimed debut set, 'IN SEARCH OF MANNY', in 1992. The last word in alternative indie hip-hop, the record fused ungainly rock/pop with NY street suss to impressive effect. 1994 saw the release of their first full-length set, 'NATURAL INGREDIENTS', although critics were not so enamoured this time around. They returned three years later with a new member, VIVIAN TRIMBLE and 'FEVER IN FEVER OUT', their most consistent, mature release to date. Produced by the esteemed DANIEL LANOIS (aided by TONY MANGURIAN), the record was big on ambient atmospherics and shifted its fair share of units on both sides of the Atlantic, spawning their first hit single, 'NAKED EYE'. VIVIAN and JILL had already found time to produce a one-off JOSEPHINE WIGGS-produced set, 'CLASSICS WITH A K' (1996), as KOSTARS, an album which matched anything the LUSCIOUS girls were achieving. With the original trio subsequently channeling their thoughts around LUSCIOUS JACKSON once again, the group released what was to become their final set, 'ELECTRIC HONEY' (1999), a record which bubbled under the US Top 100 for some time.

Album rating: IN SEARCH OF MANNY (*8) / NATURAL INGREDIENTS (*5) / FEVER IN FEVER OUT (*7) / ELECTRIC HONEY (*6) / Kostars: CLASSICS WITH A K (*6)

JILL CUNNIFF – vocals, bass, guitar / **GABRIELLE GLASER** – vocals, guitar / **KATE SCHELLENBACH** – drums (ex-BEASTIE BOYS)

Big Cat / *Grand Royal – Capitol*

May 93. (m-lp/m-cd) *(ABB 46X/+CD) <GR 001 – 27582>* **IN SEARCH OF MANNY**   Nov92
– Let yourself get down / Life of leisure / Daughters of the kaos / Keep on rockin' it / She be wantin' it more / Bam-bam / Satellite. (cd re-iss. Aug95; same) (re-iss. Apr97 on 'Grand Royal' lp/cd; same as US)

Capitol / *Grand Royal – Capitol*

Jun 94. (12"/cd-s) *<GR 007 – 58220>* **CITYSONG / CITYSONG (supernatural mix). / ENERGY SUCKER / RADIATING**
Aug 94. (cd/c/lp) *(CD/TC+/EST 2234) <GR 009 – 28356>* **NATURAL INGREDIENTS**
– Citysong / Deep shag / Angel / Strongman / Energy sucker / Here / Find your mind / Pele Merengue / Rock freak / Rollin' / Surprise / LP retreat.
Mar 95. (c-s) *(TCCL 739) <GR 011>* **DEEP SHAG / CITYSONG**   69   Jan95
(12"+=/cd-s+=) *(12/CD CL 739)* – Daddy.
Oct 95. (c-s)<12"/cd-s> *(TCCL 758) <GR 017 – 58372>* **HERE / BAM BAM (live)**   59   Jun95
(cd-s) *(CDCL 758)* – ('A'side) / Queen of bliss.
(cd-s) *(CDCLS 758)* – ('A'mixes) / Surprise (live).
—— added **VIVIAN TRIMBLE** – keyboards, vocals
Mar 97. (12"/cd-s) *(12/CD CL 786) <GR 036> 58619>* **NAKED EYE. / ('A'mixes)**   25   36   Oct96
(cd-s) *(CDCLS 786)* – ('A'side) / Banana's box / Foster's lover.

LUSCIOUS JACKSON (cont)

Apr 97. (cd/lp) (CD+/EST 2290) <GR 038 – 35534> **FEVER IN FEVER OUT** — 53 — 72 Oct96
— Naked eye / Don't look back / Door / Mood swing / Under your skin / Electric / Take a ride / Water your garden / Soothe yourself / Why do I lie? / One thing / Parade / Faith / Stardust.

Jul 97. (12") </1122> **UNDER YOUR SKIN. /** — -
— VIVIAN left to form DUSTY TRAILS with JOSEPHINE WIGGS (ex-BREEDERS, etc.) for one eponymous set in 2000 for 'Atlantic'

Jun 99. (c-s/cd-s) (TC/CD CL 813) **LADYFINGERS / GRIDLOCK / UNDER YOUR SKIN (Bentley Rhythm Ace mix)** — 43 —
(cd-s) (CDCLS 813) – ('A'side) / To sir with love ('A'-Americruiser mix).

Jul 99. (cd) <(4 96084-2)> **ELECTRIC HONEY** — Jun99
— Nervous breakthrough / Ladyfingers / Christine / Alien lover / Summer daze / Sexy hypnotist / Friends / Devotion / Fantastic fabulous / Gypsy / Beloved / Country's a callin' / Space dive / Fly / Lover's moon. (lp-iss.on 'Grand Royal'; GR 073)

Jul 99. (7") <(GR 074)> **LADYFINGERS. / TO SIR WITH LOVE**
— disbanded the following spring

KOSTARS

JILL CUNNIFF – vocals, acoustic guitar / **VIVIAN TRIMBLE** – vocals, acoustic guitar, keyboards

Grand Royal / Grand Royal

Nov 95. (7"m) <GR 20> **HEY COWBOY. / FRENCH KISS / DON'T KNOW WHY (YOU WENT AWAY)** — - -
Apr 96. (lp/cd) <GR 25/+CD> **CLASSICS WITH A K** — - -
— Never so lonely / Jacqueline / Red umbrella / Jolene on the freeway / One sunny day / Hey cowboy / Reverend / Mama never said / Don't know why / French kiss.

LUSH

Formed: Camberwell, London, England … October '88 by girls MIKI BERENYI (half-Japanese / half-Hungarian) and EMMA ANDERSON, plus lads STEVE RIPPON and CHRIS ACLAND. After supports slots to DARLING BUDS, etc, they signed to top independent label '4.a.d.' in 1989 (MERIEL BARHAM was also a member before she joined The PALE SAINTS). A 1989 debut EP, 'SCAR', introduced the band's delicate wash of sound, all hazy guitar effects and celestial harmonies; immediately hailed by the press as one of the front runners in the 'shoegazing' scene, the band even attracted the attentions of ROBIN GUTHRIE (of 'shoegazing' forebears, COCTEAU TWINS) who produced a follow-up, the 'MAD LOVE' EP. Along with MY BLOODY VALENTINE, RIDE etc., LUSH were now the toast of the UK indie scene, while also enjoying minor success in Europe and America. A further EP, 'BLACK SPRING', followed in Autumn '91 prior to the departure of RIPPON. With former NME employee, PHIL KING (ex-FELT, SERVANTS etc.) drafted in as a replacement, the band eventually completed work on a debut album, 'SPOOKY'. Issued to a mixed critical reaction in early '92, the record reached the UK Top 10 despite complaints about the suffocating GUTHRIE production. Nevertheless, the scene which had spawned LUSH was dying on its feet (still staring at its shoes, presumably) with the influx of American grunge and the group took time out to reconsider their approach. The resultant follow-up, 'SPLIT' (1994), was well received by fans but failed to break the band out of the indie margins. Finally, with the advent of Britpop, LUSH re-emerged with a more straightforward, spiky pop sound, the fey vocal affectations of old giving way to unashamed cockney wide-girl attitude on the 'LADYKILLERS' single while 'SINGLE GIRL' was as breezy as anything they'd ever recorded. An album, 'LOVELIFE', made the Top 10 later that summer and although older fans might've mourned the haunting textures of old, the simple approach suited them down to the ground. Yet this mini-revival in the band's fortunes was tragically marred later that year when the 30-year old CHRIS ACLAND took his own life. • **Songwriters:** MIKI and EMMA, except HEY HEY HELEN (Abba) / FALLIN' IN LOVE (Dennis Wilson) / OUTDOOR MINER (Wire) / LOVE AT FIRST SIGHT (Young Marble Giants) / I WANNA BE YOUR GIRLFRIEND (Rubinoos). • **Trivia:** In 1990, they all posed topless for an NME cover shot, although they were given the body paint treatment.

Album rating: SPOOKY (*8) / GALA (*7) / SPLIT (*6) / LOVELIFE (*8) / CIAO! 1989-1996 compilation (*7)

MIKI BERENYI (b.18 Mar'67) – vocals, guitar / **EMMA ANDERSON** (b.10 Jun'67) – guitar, vocals / **STEVE RIPPON** – bass / **CHRIS ACLAND** (b. 7 Sep'66, Lancaster, England) – drums

4 a.d. / Nesak

Oct 89. (m-lp/m-c/m-cd) (JAD/+C 911/+CD) <911> **SCAR** — -
— Baby talk / Thoughtforms / Scarlet / Bitter / Second sight / Etheriel.
Feb 90. (12"ep/c-ep/cd-ep) (BAD/+C 0003/+CD) **MAD LOVE EP** — 55 —
— De luxe / Leaves me cold / Downer / Thoughtforms.

4 a.d. / 4 a.d.-Reprise

Oct 90. (7"/c-s) (AD/+C 0013) **SWEETNESS AND LIGHT. / BREEZE** — 47 —
(12"+=/cd-s+=) (BAD 0013/+CD) – Sunbathing.
Dec 90. (lp/c/cd) (CAD/+C 0017/+CD) <26463> **GALA** — - -
— Sweetness and light / Sunbathing / Breeze / De luxe / Leaves me cold / Downer / Baby talk / Thoughtforms / Scarlet / Bitter / Second sight / Etheriel / Hey hey Helen / Scarlet (alt.take).
Sep 91. (7"/c-s) (AD/+C 1016) <40231> **NOTHING NATURAL. / GOD'S GIFT** — 43 —
(12"ep+=/cd-ep+=) (BAD 1016/+CD) – 'BLACK SPRING EP' – Fallin' in love / Monochrome.
Dec 91. (12"ep/10"ep/c-ep)(cd-ep) (BAD/+D/C 2001)(BAD 2001CD) **FOR LOVE / STARLUST. / OUTDOOR MINER / ASTRONAUT** — 35 —
— Although on above + below recording RIPPON had left Oct'91.

Jan 92. (lp/d-10"lp/c)(cd)(s-cd) (CAD/+D/C 2002)(CAD/+D 2002CD) <26798> **[SPOOKY]** — 7 —
— Stray / Nothing natural / Tiny smiles / Covert / Ocean / For love / Superblast! / Untogether / Fantasy / Take / Laura / Monochrome.
— RIPPON was replaced by **PHIL KING** (b.29 Apr'60) – bass (ex-SEE SEE RIDER, ex-APPLE BOUTIQUE, ex-FELT)

4 a.d. / Warners

May 94. (7") (AD 4008) **HYPOCRITE. / LOVE AT FIRST SIGHT** — 52 —
(12"+=/cd-s+=) (BAD 4008/+CD) – Cat's chorus / Undertow.
May 94. (7") (AD 4010) **DESIRE LINES. / WHITE WOOD** — 60 —
(12"+=)(cd-s+=) (BAD 4010/+CD) – Girl's world / Lovelife (suga bullit remix).
Jun 94. (lp/c/cd) (CAD/+C 4011/+CD) <45578> **SPLIT** — 19 —
— Light from a dead star / Kiss chase / Blackout / Hypocrite / Lovelife / Desire lines / The invisible man / Undertow / Never-never / Lit up / Stardust / When I die.
Jan 96. (7"clear) (AD 6001) **SINGLE GIRL. / SWEETIE** — 21 —
(cd-s) (BAD 6001CD) – ('A'side) / Tinkerbell / Outside world / Cul de sac.
(cd-s) (BADD 6001CD) – ('A'side) / Pudding / Demystification / Shut up.
Feb 96. (7"green) (AD 6002) **LADYKILLERS. / I WANNA BE YOUR GIRLFRIEND** — 22 —
(cd-s) (BAD 6002CD) – ('A'side) / Matador / Ex / Dear me.
(cd-s) (BADD 6002CD) – ('A'side) / Heavenly / Carmen / Plums and oranges.
Mar 96. (clear-lp/c/cd) (CAD/+C 6004/+CD) <46170> **LOVELIFE** — 8 —
— Ladykillers / Heavenly nobodies / 500 / I've been here before / Papasan / Single girl / Ciao! / Tralala / Last night / Runaway / The childcatcher / Olympia.
— JARVIS COCKER (Pulp) featured vox with MIKI on the track 'Ciao!'.
Jul 96. (7"red) (AD 6009) **500 (SHAKE BABY SHAKE). / I HAVE THE MOON** — 21 —
(cd-s+=) (BAD 6009CD) – Piledriver / Olympia (acoustic).
(cd-s) (BADD 6009CD) – ('A'side) / I'd like to walk around your mind / Kiss chase (acoustic) / Last night (hexadecimal dub mix).

— Sadly on the 17th of October '96, 30 year-old ACLAND committed suicide after returning from the States and splitting with his girlfriend. LUSH virtually gave up with the group after that. A dance group of the same name issued a single, 'GOLD', late '97 (nothing to do with the real LUSH). In 1998, EMMA teamed up with vocalist, LISA O'NEILL, to form SING-SING, debuting that year with a single, 'FEELS LIKE SUMMER'. It was released on the indie label, 'Bella Union' (with help of COCTEAU TWINS' ROBIN GUTHRIE and SIMON RAYMONDE), when EMMA couldn't find a new one after severing her association with '4 a.d.'.

– compilations, etc. –

Mar 01. (cd) 4 a.d.; (GAD 2K22CD) <70022> **CIAO! 1989-1996**
— Ladykillers / Single girl / Ciao! / 500 (shake baby shake) / Light from a dead star / Hypocrite / Desire lines / Lovelife / When I die / Nothing natural / Untogether / For love / Monochrome / De-luxe / Sweetness and light / Thoughtforms / Etheriel.

LYNC (see under ⇒ LOVE AS LAUGHTER)

LYNNFIELD PIONEERS

Formed: Brooklyn, New York, USA … 1995 by DAN COOK, MIKE JANSON and JOHN PAUL 'J.P.' JONES (no, not that one!). Named as an ode to COOK's school football team, the cheeky neo "New Wave" punk outfit earned their claim to fame when they released their 'LAMB COMP' EP in early 1997. Committed to full-time touring, LYNNFIELD PIONEERS created a promising response in the underground indie scene. After a few singles, the full-length 'emerge' was cut, leading to a lucrative (well in punk circles!) 'Matador' signing. Many were astounded by the album's comic sound that might've possibly made The BEASTIE BOYS proud. COOK sang like a whining DAVID THOMAS (PERE UBU frontman) on amphetamine while JONES banged at his kit with skill and grace although still managing to sound similar to a hyperactive child. Follow-up, 'FREE POPCORN' (1999), contained the ultra-"groovy" 'MAXIMUM SUNSHINE', COOK abusing his organ(!) while singing something about "Bad vibrations" (man!). An unreleased track ('WIND-BLOWN') was included on their label's 10th anniversary album, the song referring back to 90's grunge while sounding similar to the zeitgeist of ASH or possibly MUDHONEY (with a dodgy clarinet tooting away in the back ground for good measure!).

Album rating: emerge (*7) / FREE POPCORN (*6)

DAN COOK – vocals, multi, Moog synthesizer / **MIKE JANSON** – guitar / **JOHN PAUL 'J.P.' JONES** – drums, etc
— released a few unknown singles

not iss. / Lambshop

Jan 97. (m-cd) <16004> **LAMB COMP EP** — -
— Latoya / Contact high / Yos to go / Newport / Sabbatical / Shopping / Automatic / One hand.

Matador / Matador

Nov 97. (cd/lp) <(OLE 242-2/-1)> **emerge** — Oct97
— Go for a ride / Add it up / Bad luck baby / Unlucky stars / Get off your feet / Last last time / Outside in / Superceded / Not for long / Cynthia / Cool calm serene / Bus / Lucite / Louis III.

— **BRAD TRAUAX** – bass; repl. JANSON

Jun 99. (cd/lp) <(OLE 342-2/-1)> **FREE POPCORN** — May99
— Astral plane / Accolades / Time to get dumb / Maximum sunshine / Anamaxamander / Free popcorn / Exoskeletons / Crossfade / Real / Wide open spaces / Feels so good / Get into it.

MACHISMO (see under ⇒ JACOB'S MOUSE)

Bryan MacLEAN (see under ⇒ LOVE)

MACROCOSMICA (see under ⇒ TELSTAR PONIES)

MADDER ROSE

Formed: Greenwich Village, New York, USA . . . 1991 by MARY LORSON and BILLY COTE, together with MATT VERTA-RAY and JOHNNY KICK. With the release of an eponymous debut EP on 'Rockville' in Spring '93, the VELVET UNDERGROUND comparisons flew thick and fast while the UK music press hailed them as the next big thing. Picked up by 'Atlantic' subsidiary, 'Seed', the group released their debut album, 'BRING IT DOWN', in summer '93. Again, the influences of NY forebears such as VU and TELEVISION were obvious although the guitar noise was contrasted with an emerging rootsiness and LORSON's high register harmonies were reminiscent of SUZANNE VEGA. By the release of follow-up set, 'PANIC ON' (1994), LORSON had developed even further as a songwriter, stamping her presence over much of the material and acting as a catalyst in effecting a more melodic, haunting sound. The album also took MADDER ROSE to the outer fringes of the UK Top 50 while the title track and the hypnotic 'CAR SONG' made the Top 75. With VERTA-RAY having departed around the time of the album's release, a replacement bassist, CHRIS GIAMMALVO, was recruited in time for the attendant touring commitments. Strangely, MADDER ROSE were conspicuous by their absence, until that is 1997's comeback set, 'TRAGIC MAGIC'. The band subsequently parted company with 'Atlantic' and re-emerged in 1999 with the acclaimed 'HELLO JUNE FOOL', an inscrutable, at times claustrophobic instalment of slow burning, pre-millennial psychedelia with career-best vocal performances from LORSON. The latter found an additional outlet for her talents in side project SAINT LOW (also featuring JENNIE STEARNS, ZAUN MARSHBURN, MICHAEL STARK, JOE MYER and STAHL CASO), whose moody, candlelit musings were showcased on an eponymous 2000 debut and 'TRICKS FOR DAWN', two years later. LORSON also found the time to duet with EVAN DANDO and take the mic for erstwhile MADDER ROSE compadre BILLY COTE's moonlighting project, The JAZZ CANNON. A more singular labour of love than MADDER ROSE, this was effectively a vehicle for COTE's tentative forays into the world of multi-layered, alterna-electronica. A debut album, 'AMATEUR SOUL SURGERY', appeared in 2000. • **Covered:** I WANNA SLEEP IN YOUR ARMS (Jonathan Richman) / RULER OF MY HEART (. . . Neville).

Album rating: BRING IT DOWN (*7) / PANIC ON (*8) / TRAGIC MAGIC (*6) / HELLO JUNE FOOL (*6) / Saint Low: SAINT LOW (*6) / TRICKS FOR DAWN (*5)

MARY LORSON – vocals, guitar, keyboards / **BILLY COTE** – guitars, bass, vibes / **MATT VERTA-RAY** – bass, rhythm guitar, slide guitar, organ, violin, vibes / **JOHNNY KICK** (b. RICK KUBIC) – drums, keyboards, vocals, vibes

		Rockville	Seed
Mar 93.	(7"ep/12"ep/cd-ep) *(ROCK 6100-7/-1/-2) <14238-2>* **MADDER ROSE** – Swim / Z / I wanna sleep in your arms / Amnesia / Baby gets high / Take it away. *(cd-ep re-iss. Apr97; same)*		

		Seed	Seed
May 93.	(7"ep/cd-ep) *(SEED 003/+CD)* **BEAUTIFUL JOHN / BABY GETS HIGH. / LIGHTS GO DOWN / TAKE IT AWAY**		
Jun 93.	(cd/c/lp) *<(14229-2/-4/-1)>* **BRING IT DOWN** – Beautiful John / While away / Bring it down / 20 foot red / Swim / Lay down low / Altar boy / Lights go down / (Living a) Daydream / Sugarsweet / Razor pilot / Waiting for engines / Pocket fulla medicine.		
Oct 93.	(7") *(SEED 006)* **SWIM (remix). / LIKED YOU MORE (WHEN YOU WERE HIGH)** (12"+=) *(SEED12 006)* – Z. (cd-s++=) *(SEECD 006)* – Amnesia.		

		Atlantic	Atlantic
Mar 94.	(7") *(A 8301)* **PANIC ON. / ONE ARMED BANDIT** (10"+=/cd-s+=) *(A 8301 TE/CD)* – Mad dog.	65	
Mar 94.	(cd/c/lp) *<(7567 82581-2/-4/-1)>* **PANIC ON** – Sleep, forever / Car song / Panic on / What Holly sees / Almost lost my mind / Drop a bomb / Ultra anxiety (teenage style) / Happy new year / Day in, day out / Margaret / Foolish ways / Black eye town / When you smile / Mad dog.	52	
Jul 94.	(7"/c-s) *(A 7256/+C)* **CAR SONG. / JENNY TAKE A RIDE** (10"+=/cd-s+=) *(A 7256 TE/CD)* – The widow song / Holiday.	68	-

— (Feb'94) **CHRIS GIAMMALVO** – bass; repl. MATT who joined SPEEDBALL BABY

Apr 95.	(7") *(SEED 014)* **THE LOVE YOU SAVE. / DIANE** (cd-s+=) *(SEEDCD 014)* – No avail / Ruler of my heart. (above issued on 'Seed')		-
Jun 97.	(cd/c) *<(7567 83009-2/-4)>* **TRAGIC MAGIC** – My star / Real feel / Float to the top / Hung up in you / Delight's pool / (She's a) Satellite / Peter and Victor / Best friend / Scenes from "Starbright" / Midnight on the dot / Don Greene / Not perfect. *(cd re-iss. Jan99 on 'Cooking Vinyl'+=; COOKCD 167)* – Narco / Jailbird.		
Aug 97.	(7") *(A 5438)* **MY STAR. / LILI MARLENE** (c-s) *(A 5438C)* – ('A'side) / Peter and Victor. (cd-s++=) *(A 5438CD)* – See her every night.		-

		Cooking Vinyl	Thirsty Ear
Jul 99.	(7") *(FRY 086)* **OVERFLOW. / LILI MARLENE** (cd-s+=) *(FRY 086CD)* – Overflow (Overload mix).		-
Aug 99.	(cd) *(COOKCD 181) <57072>* **HELLO JUNE FOOL** – Feels like summer / Overflow / Hotel / Fade / Goodbye June fool / Something / You remember / Should have known / Talking to myself / Train / Dark rain.		Jul99

SAINT LOW

aka **MARY LORSEN** with **JENNIE STERNS** – vocals / **MICHAEL STARK** – piano / **JOE MYER** – violin / **STAHL CASO** – bass / **ZAUN MARSHBURN** – drums

		Cooking Vinyl	Thirsty Ear
Jul 00.	(cd) *(COOKCD 198) <57089>* **SAINT LOW** – Anywhere / On the outside / Johnson city / Crash / Tall trees / Keep an open mind / Only one / A thing or two / Dreamland / Walk on by / Spanish moss / After the fall.		
Mar 02.	(cd) *(COOKCD 224)* **TRICKS FOR DAWN** – Planet pleasant grove / Morningless dreamer / Friends I have been drinking / Oh regret / Interlude / Strange gift / Anything can happen / Your lament / Blast off / Accelerate / A long way down (with EVAN DANDO) / Tricks for dawn.		-

JAZZ CANNON

BILLY COTE solo project w/ **DON GREENE + MARY LORSEN**

		Function 8	Function 8
Dec 98.	(12") *<89176>* **DADDY RIDE. / THE RESONANT PRIEST**	-	
Oct 00.	(cd) *<(FER 88809-2)>* **AMATEUR SOUL SURGERY** – Tell it to the hi-rise / Shere Khan / Wyyr pt dub / Daddy ride / Where you are, star / (Last days) In Candy's room / Blackie's echo box (R.I.P.) / Killed at party / TTT2 / Thinly veiled / The resonant priest.		Jul00

MADISON ELECTRIC (see under ⇒ VERONICA LAKE)

MAD SCENE (see under ⇒ CLEAN; in 80's section)

MAGIC DIRT

Formed: Geelong, Australia . . . 1993 by vocalist ADALITA SRSEN, guitarist DAVE THOMAS, bassist DEAN TURNER and drummer ADAM ROBERTSON. After generating interest via a cover of 'HEROIN' for a VELVET UNDERGROUND tribute album, MAGIC DIRT released two early EPs, 'SIGNS OF SATANIC YOUTH' (1994) and 'LIFE WAS BETTER' (1995). Their eponymous debut LP (released on the 'Dirt' label in 1996) was a compilation of material from these two EPs. Subsequently supporting revered contemporaries DINOSAUR JR., HOLE, PAVEMENT and SONIC YOUTH, MAGIC DIRT's raw, fuzzed-out indie-rock was now making waves, ensuring a major label bidding war for their signatures. Choosing 'Warner Bros.', late 1996 saw the release of 'FRIENDS IN DANGER', which contained hard-rocking ballads and stand-out track 'I WAS CRUEL'. Third LP, 'YOUNG AND FULL OF THE DEVIL' (1998), marked their further development, and 2000's 'WHAT ARE ROCK STARS DOING TODAY?' proved to be their best work to date. • **Covered:** KICK OUT THE JAMS (MC5).

Album rating: MAGIC DIRT (*7) / FRIENDS IN DANGER (*6) / YOUNG AND FULL OF THE DEVIL (*7) / WHAT ARE ROCK STARS DOING TODAY (*7)

ADALITA SRSEN – vocals / **DAVE THOMAS** – guitar / **DEAN TURNER** – bass / **ADAM ROBERTSON** – drums

		Au-Go-Go	Dirt
1994.	(cd-ep) *(ANDA 167)* **SIGNS OF SATANIC YOUTH** – Touch that space / Eat your blud / Supertear / Choker / Redhead.	-	- Austra
1995.	(cd-ep) *(ANDA 180)* **LIFE WAS BETTER . . . WHEN I USED TO BE A WETTER** – Daddy / Ice / Amoxycillin / Fairy park / He-man / Untitled.	-	- Austra
Feb 96.	(cd) *<DIRT 021>* **MAGIC DIRT** (compilation) – Redhead / Eat your blud / He-man / Ice / Supertear / Daddy / Fairy park / Choker / Goofy gumb / Touch that space / Amoxycillin. *(re-iss. Oct97 on 'Subway'+=; 3820342-2)* – Sea / Fearless fly.	-	

		Au-Go-Go	Warners
Jul 96.	(10"m) *(ANDA 202)* **I WAS CRUEL. / YOU WON'T KNOW / INSERT YOUR OWN TITLE**	-	- Austra
Sep 96.	(cd/c/lp) *(ANDA 206CD) <46276-2/-4/-1>* **FRIENDS IN DANGER** – Friends in danger / Heavy business / Pristine Christine / Bodysnatcher / Dylans lullaby / Sparrow / Shovel / Fear / Befriended fallen angel / I was cruel. *(UK-iss.Jun98 on 'Headhunter' cd/lp; HUK 004 CD/LP)*		- Austra

		not iss.	Man's Ruin
Oct 96.	(10"m) *(MR 057)* **I WAS CRUEL. / SHE-RIFF / YOU WON'T KNOW**	-	-

MAGIC DIRT (cont) — THE GREAT INDIE DISCOGRAPHY — The 1990s

				Au-Go-Go	Au-Go-Go
Sep 97.	(cd-ep)	(<ANDA 211CD>)	**SPARROW**		

– Sparrow / Shovel / Dean wants to go home / Redhead (live) / Pristine Christine (live) / (untitled).

				-	- Austra
May 98.	(cd-ep)	(ANDA 235CD)	**RABBIT WITH FANGS**		

– Rabbit with fangs / These drugs are really starting to fuck me over / He-man (live) / Amoxycillin (live) / Rabbit with fangs (live).

				-	-
Jun 98.	(cd)	(ANDA 237CD)	**YOUNG AND FULL OF THE DEVIL**		

– Babycakes / She-riff / Rabbit with fangs / Shrinko / What have I done? / These drugs are really starting to fuck me over / Short + slack / X-ray / Ascot red / Babycakes you always freeze me up.

				-	- Austra
Jul 98.	(cd-ep)	(ANDA 240CD)	**SHE-RIFF**		

– She-riff / Peom / Delay / Sparrow (live) / Sea (live).

				Warners	not iss.
Oct 00.	(cd)	(8573 85003-2)	**WHAT ARE ROCK STARS DOING TODAY**	-	- Austra

– City trash / Teenage vampire / Dirty jeans / Pace it / Competition girl / Nightingale / Rockstars / Come on the scene / Supagloo / For a second / Smoulder. (*UK-iss.Jun02 on 'Sweet Nothing' cd/d-lp; SNCD/SNLP 016*)

				-	- Austra
Apr 01.	(cd-ep)	(86747)	**PACE IT / 9 OUT OF 10 / ISOTOPE / NOW OR NEVER**		

MAGICDRIVE

Formed: Edinburgh, Scotland . . . mid-90's by Inverness-born heavy drinkers (or was that lager?) DAVE ROBERTSON and JEFF HALLAM, who flitted from the capital and found DAVID JACK, KATE GRIEVE and JANE BORDWELL. Blending a speedy mixture of Power-pop and quickfire rock, this eccentric quintet emerged from indie's darker undergrowth and into beaming sunlight with their debut single 'HAD TO BE YOU' (issued on 'Fierce Panda' in 1997). The petite ROBERTSON, supported by the New Wave elements of his fellow band members, began the strange ballad with a weird opening line and proceeded through this eclectic piece with an organic mix of oboes and flutes courtesy of talented backing singer JANE BORDWELL. The single subsequently prompted a major signing to 'Fontana', although one extremely poppy single, 'BANG 2 RIGHTS', surfaced from this transaction. Another year on and another label, Aberdeen-based 'Lithium' released 'HOTEL TRANSMISSION', but the combo's everyday ambition of appearing on Top of the Pops was wearing thin.

Album rating: WHAT'S THE BEEF (*5)

DAVE ROBERTSON – vocals, guitar / **DAVID JACK** – bass / **JEFF HALLAM** – drums / **KATE GRIEVE** – oboe, flute, backing vocals / **JANE BORDWELL** – oboe, flute, backing vocals

				Fierce Panda	not iss.
Feb 97.	(7")	(NING 032)	**HAD TO BE YOU. / MAMMOGRAM**		
				Fontana	not iss.
Jun 98.	(7")	(NAD 2)	**BANG 2 RIGHTS. /**		-
	(cd-s+=)	(NADCD 2)	–		
				Lithium	not iss.
Mar 99.	(7"ep/cd-ep)	(LITH 003/+CDS)	**HOTEL TRANSATLANTIQUE EP**		

– The case / Japanese school girl / Overture / Hairy girl.

| Sep 99. | (7"ep/cd-ep) | (LITH 006/+CDS) | **GRAND HOTEL EP** | | - |

– Oh Christina / Anyway you want it / Argo / Houses of the Ole.

— although DAVID JACK joined PILOTCAN in 2000, MAGICDRIVE had not split. In fact, the man himself released a solo trip-hop release the following July.

				Knife Fighting Monkey	not iss.
Jul 02.	(cd)	(KFM 004)	**WHAT'S THE BEEF**		

– Very French . . .? / I don't wanna go out / Pimento / By the balls / She's got a hold on me / What would your daddy say? / Water titrure / Do not adjust your mind / Utopia / Argonaut song / What's the beef?

MAGIC HOUR (see under ⇒ GALAXIE 500)

MAGICK HEADS (see under ⇒ BATS; see 80's section)

MAGNAPOP

Formed: Atlanta/Athens, Georgia, USA . . . 1988 out of HOMEMADE SISTER and SWELL by LINDA HOPPER and RUTHIE MORRIS, plus SHANNON MULVANEY and DAVID McNAIR who had recently departed from the group OH-OK (the latter act numbered DAVID PIERCE, MATTHEW SWEET and LINDA STIPE – sister of MICHAEL STIPE – in their ranks!). With the production skills and industry experience of R.E.M. figurehead, MICHAEL STIPE, on their side, the band won a fanatical following in the Benelux countries with their debut single, 'SUGARLANDS' (a Top 20 hit in the Netherlands). Another early supporter was ex-HUSKER DU man, BOB MOULD, who produced their ensuing eponymous 1992 debut album. The two man/two woman combination proved a winning formula with HOPPER's insinuating, accusatory vocals sparking off a grunge-pop chemistry and occasionally bringing to mind prime THROWING MUSES. Their failure to secure an American major deal meant that European alternative label, 'Play It Again Sam', remained their home for a further two albums, 'HOT BOXING' (1994) and 'RUBBING DOESN'T HELP' (1996). Yet the band couldn't seem to translate their continental success into substantial British or American sales despite continuing critical support. • **Songwriters:** HOPPER-MORRIS penned except; SONG NUMBER ONE (Fugazi).

Album rating: MAGNAPOP (*7) / HOT BOXING (*6) / RUBBING DOESN'T HELP (*5)

OH OK

LINDA HOPPER – vocals, noises (ex-TANZPLAGEN) / **LYNDA STIPE** – bass (ex-TANZPLAGEN) / **DAVID PIERCE** – drums (ex-TANZPLAGEN); note:- TANZPLAGEN released one single in 1981 with MICHAEL STIPE but without HOPPER

				not iss.	D.B.
1982.	(7"ep)	<DB 63>	**WOW MINI ALBUM**	-	

– Lilting / Brother / Playtime / Person.

— **DAVID McNAIR** – drums; repl. PIERCE

— added **MATTHEW SWEET** – guitars, vocals

| 1983. | (12"ep) | <DB 69> | **FURTHERMORE WHAT** | | |

– Such n such / Guru / Choukoutien / Straight / Giddy up / Elaine's song.

— LINDA would join HOLIDAY in 1987; they released one EP, 'Hello'.

MAGNAPOP

LINDA HOPPER – vocals / **RUTHIE MORRIS** – guitar / **SHANNON MULVANEY** – bass / **DAVE McNAIR** – drums

				not iss.	Safety Net
1991.	(7"; as HOMEMADE SISTER)	**RIP THE WRECK. / MERRY**	-		
				not iss.	Solid
Feb 92.	(7")	<none>	**MERRY. / COMPLICATED**		
				Play It Again Sam	Play It Again Sam
Jun 92.	(12"ep/cd-ep)	(BIAS 228/+CD)	**SUGARLAND**		

– Merry / Garden / Skinburns / Snake.

| Jul 92. | (lp/c/cd) | <(BIAS 220/+MC/CD)> | **MAGNAPOP** | | Oct92 |

– Garden / Guess / Ear / 13 / Spill it / Chemical / Favourite writer / Complicated / Merry.

| Aug 93. | (12"ep/cd-ep) | (BIAS 243/+CD) | **KISS MY MOUTH EP** | | |

– Texas / Lay it down / Precious / Nowhere.

| Jan 94. | (12"ep/12"white-ep/cd-ep) | (BIAS 257/+X/CD) | **SLOWLY, SLOWLY / SONG NUMBER ONE. / HERE IT COMES / PUFF** | | - |

| Feb 94. | (lp/c/cd) | (BIAS 251/+MC/CD) <53909> | **HOT BOXING** | | Jul94 |

– Slowly, slowly, Texas / Lay it down / Here it comes / Piece of cake / Free mud / Leo / The crush / Ride / In the way / Idiot song / Get it right / Emergency / Skinburns.

| May 94. | (12"ep/cd-ep) | (BIAS 267 X/CD) | **LAY IT DOWN. / SLOWLY, SLOWLY (demo) / THE CRUSH (demo) / PIECE OF CAKE (demo)** | | - |

— McNAIR was repl. by temp **JOSH FREESE** – drums

| Feb 96. | (7"ep/cd-ep) | (BIAS 287 7/CD) | **FIRE ALL OF YOUR GUNS AT ONCE** | | - |

– Come on inside / Voice without a sound / Down on me / Hold you down.

| Apr 96. | (7") | (BIAS 297-7) | **OPEN THE DOOR. / RE-HAB** | | - |
| | (cd-s+=) | (BIAS 297CD) | – True love. | | |

| May 96. | (cd/red-lp) | (BIAS 321 CD/LP) <53992> | **RUBBING DOESN'T HELP** | | |

– This family / I don't care / Open the door / Come on inside / Down on me / An apology / My best friend / Juicy fruit / Firebrand / Cherry bomb / Radio waves / Snake / Dead letter.

| Sep 96. | (cd-s) | (BIAS 307CD) | **THIS FAMILY (Mark Freegard remix) / THIS FAMILY (album version)** | | - |

— MAGNAPOP have since disbanded but could be back in 2003

MAGNETIC FIELDS

Formed: 1990 . . . by STEPHIN MERRITT, who based his underground one-man outfit in Boston, Massachusetts. A prolific singer/songwriter (writes more than 100 songs a year!), the experimental minimalist with a penchant for pop – ABBA and BRIAN WILSON were obvious influences! – released a plethora of albums during the first half of the 90's. The first of these, 'DISTANT PLASTIC TREES' (1990/91), found him working with a cast of collaborators (CLAUDIA GONSON and SAM DAVOL) that would remain fairly constant over the next few years. Their kitschy yet lovelorn and desolate second set, 'THE WAYWARD BUS', was easily their best, although it was their last with singer, SUSAN ANWAY. Taking over vocal duties, STEPHIN was revealed to be a kind of lugubrious, lo-fi LEONARD COHEN on electro-pop pills. His/their next two long-players, 'HOLIDAY' (1994) and 'THE CHARM OF THE HIGHWAY STRIP' (1994/5), further developed the nomadic spirit possessing STEPHIN's muse. His first of many side projects, The 6ths, utilized the eclectic vocal talents of such underground indie figureheads as LOU BARLOW, MITCH EASTER and BARBARA MANNING, to name but a few on the 1995 album, 'WASPS NESTS' (one of the last albums on Tony Wilson's now defunct UK imprint, 'Factory'). Reprising the MAGNETIC FIELDS moniker, STEPHIN delivered another instalment of wayward synth-pop, 'GET LOST' (1996), the openly gay schizophrenic retiring from the limelight before re-inventing himself – at first as the short-lived The GOTHIC ARCHIES and then as The FUTURE BIBLE HEROES alongside ever faithful sidekick, CLAUDIA. Remaining with 'Setanta' records, the pair added a third member, CHRIS EWEN, for the 'MEMORIES OF LOVE' album in the first half of '98. STEPHIN MERRITT became rather busy over a three-year period, beginning with the release of his brilliant MAGNETIC FIELDS set '69 LOVE SONGS' (1999); a sprawling three-disc set, which introduced his lyricly whimsical songs, paired with the group's sparse instrumentations, it was possibly one of the most ambitious "love" records ever! In September of 2000, he joined his band The 6THS and delivered 'HYACINTHS & THISTLES', plus a solo soundtrack affair for the film 'EBAN & CHARLEY' (2002), which some criticised as being too morbid. FUTURE BIBLE HEROES, his

MAGNETIC FIELDS (cont)   THE GREAT INDIE DISCOGRAPHY | The 1990s |

electro-ambient offshoot with CHRISTOPHER EWEN dropped the album 'ETERNAL YOUTH', also in 2002.
Album rating: DISTANT PLASTIC TREES (*6) / THE WAYWARD BUS (*8) / HOLIDAY (*7) / THE CHARM OF THE HIGHWAY (*6) / GET LOST (*6) / 69 LOVE SONGS (*7) / the 6ths: WASPS' NESTS (*7) / HYACINTHS AND THISTLES (*6) / Future Bible Heroes: MEMORIES OF LOVE (*7) / ETERNAL YOUTH (*7) / Stephin Merritt: EBAN & CHARLEY soundtrack (*5)

STEPHEN MERRITT – keyboards, guitar / **CLAUDIA GONSON** – percussion / **SAM DAVOL** – cello, flute / **SUSAN ANWAY** – vocals

Red Flame   not iss.
Feb 91. (cd/c) *(RFCD/RFC 3)* **DISTANT PLASTIC TREES**
 – Railroad boy / Smoke signals / You love to fail / Kings / Babies falling / Living in an abandoned firehouse with / Tar-heel boy / Falling in love with the wolfboy / Josephine / 100,000 fireflies.

not iss.   Harriet
Sep 91. (7") *<HARRIET 07>* **100,000 FIREFLIES. / OLD ORCHARD BEACH**

not iss.   PoPuP
Jan 92. (cd) **THE WAYWARD BUS**
 – When you were my baby / The saddest story ever told / Lovers from the moon / Candy / Tokyo a go-go / Summer lies / Old orchard beach / Jeremy / Dancing in your eyes / Suddenly there is a tidal wave. *<re-iss. Jan95 on 'Merge' +=; MRG 75>*
 – DISTANT PLASTIC TREES *(UK-iss.Nov00; same as US/tracks)*

not iss.   Feel Good All Over
Apr 92. (7"ep) *<FGAO 7007>* **THE HOUSE OF TOMORROW**
 – Young and insane / Technical (you're so) / Love goes home to Paris in the Spring / Either you don't love me or I don't.
 (cd-ep+=) *<FGAO 007>* – Alien being. *<(UK + re-iss. Jan99 on 'Merge'; MRG 152CD)>*

Dec 92. (7"m) *<HARRIET 017>* **LONG VERMONT ROADS. / ALIEN BEING / BEACH-A-BOOP-BOOP**
 (above issued on 'Harriet')

— now without SUSAN (STEPHIN took over vocals)
1994. (cd) *<FGAO 26>* **HOLIDAY**
 – BBC radiophonic workshop (short instrumental) – Desert island / Deep sea diving suit / Strange powers / Torn green velvet eyes / Flowers she sent and the flowers she said she sent / Swinging London / In my secret place / Sad little moon / The trouble I've been looking for / Sugar world / All you ever do is walk away / In my car / Take ecstasy with me. *<UK + re-iss. Feb99 on 'Merge'; MRG 151CD)>*

— added **JOHN WOO** – guitar

Setanta   Merge
Aug 95. (cd/lp) *(SET CD/LP 021) <MRG 55CD>* **THE CHARM OF THE HIGHWAY STRIP**   Dec94
 – Lonely highway / Long Vermont roads / Born on a train / I have the moon / Two characters in search of a country song / Crowd of drifters / Fear of trains / When the open road is closing in / Sunset city / Dust bowl. *<UK + re-iss. Nov00 on 'Merge'; same as US)>*

Dec 95. (7") *<MRG 73>* **ALL THE UMBRELLAS IN LONDON. / RATS IN THE GARBAGE OF THE WESTERN WORLD**
Mar 96. (cd) *(SETCD 023) <MRG 91CD>* **GET LOST**
 – Famous / The desperate things you made me do / Smoke and mirrors / With whom to dance? / You and me and the moon / Don't look away / Save a secret for the moon / Why I cry / Love is lighter than air / When you're old and lonely / The village in the morning / All the umbrellas in London / The dreaming moon. *(also other cd; SETCD 023L) <(UK + re-iss. Nov00 on 'Merge'; same as US)>*

Merge   Merge
Aug 98. (7") *<(MRG 143)>* **I DON'T BELIEVE YOU. / WHEN I'M NOT LOOKING YOU'RE NOT THERE**
Sep 99. (cd) *<(MRG 166CD)>* **69 LOVE SONGS VOLUME 1**
 – Absolutely cuckoo / I don't believe in the sun / All my little words / A chicken with its head cut off / Reno Dakota / I don't want to get over you / Come back from San Francisco / The luckiest guy on the Lower East Side / Let's pretend we're bunny rabbits / The cactus where your heart should be / I think I need a new heart / The book of love / Fido, your leash is too long / How fucking romantic / The one you really love / Punk love / Parades go by / Boa Constrictor / A pretty girl is like . . . / My sentimental melody / Nothing matters when we're dancing / Sweet-lovin' man / The things we did and didn't do.
Sep 99. (cd) *<(MRG 167CD)>* **69 LOVE SONGS VOLUME 2**
 – Roses / Love is like jazz / When my boy walks down the street / Time enough for rocking when we're old / Very funny / Grand Canyon / No one will ever love you / If you don't cry / You're my only home / (Crazy for you but) Not that Crazy / My only friend / Promises of eternity / World love / Washington, D.C. / Long-forgotten fairytale / Kiss me like you mean it / Papa was a rodeo / Epitaph for my heart / Asleep and dreaming / The sun goes down and the world goes dancing / The way you say good-night / Abigail, belle of Kilronan / I shatter.
Sep 99. (cd) *<(MRG 168CD)>* **69 LOVE SONGS VOLUME 3**
 – Underwear / It's a crime / Busby Berkeley dreams / I'm sorry I love you / Acoustic guitar / The death of Ferninand de Saussure / LOve in the shadows / Bitter tears / Wi' nae wee bairn ye'll me beget / Yeah! oh, yeah! / Experimental music love / Meaningless / Love is like a bottle of gin / Queen of the savages / Blue you / I can't touch you anymore / Two kinds of people / How to say goodbye / The night you can't remember / For we are the king of the boudoir / Strange eyes / Xylophone track / Zebra.
Sep 99. (3xcd-box) *<(MRG 169CD)>* **69 LOVE SONGS** (compilation)
 (re-iss. May00 on 'Circus'; CIRCUSCD 003)

the 6THS

STEPHIN MERRITT with guest vocalists (see below)

Factory Too   Polygram
Jul 95. (cd/c) *(FAC D/MC 206) <828592>* **WASPS' NESTS**   Mar95
 – BARBARA MANNING: San Diego zoo / STEPHIN MERRITT: Ageing spinsters / MARY TIMONY: All dressed up in dreams / DEAN WAREHAM: Falling out of love (with you) / AYAKO AKASHIBA: Winter in July / MITCH EASTER: Pillow fight / MAC McCAUGHAN: Dream hat / GEORGIA HUBLEY: Movies in my head / LOU BARLOW: In the city in the rain / AMELIA FLETCHER: Looking for love in the hall of mirrors) / ROBERT SCOTT: Heaven in a black leather jacket / ANNA DOMINO: Here in my heart / MARK ROBINSON: Puerto Rico way /

JEFFREY UNDERHILL: You can't break a broken heart / CHRIS KNOX: When I'm out of town.

— next with singers (see below) and musicians **DANIEL HANDLER, IDA PEARLE, CHRIS EWEN + MAGNETIC FIELDS**

Circus   Merge
Sep 00. (cd) *(CIRCUSCD 005) <MRG 485>* **HYACINTHS AND THISTLES**
 – MOMUS: As you turn to go / SALLY TIMMS: Give me back my dreams / BOB MOULD: He didn't / MELANIE: I've got New York / DOMINIQUE A: Just like a movie star / SARAH CRACKNELL: Kissing things / MIHO HATORI: Lindy Lou / CLARE GROGAN: Night falls like a grand piano / NEIL HANNON: The dead only quickly / GARY NUMAN: The sailor in love with the sea / MARC ALMOND: Volcana! / ODETTA: Waltzing me all the way home / KATHERINE WHALEN: You you you you you / MISS LILY BANQUETTE: Oahu.

GOTHIC ARCHIES

— **STEPHIN MERRITT** solo

not iss.   Hello
Mar 96. (cd-ep) **LOOMING IN THE GLOOM**
 – The abandoned castle of my soul / Your long white fingers / The dead only quicky / In a cave / City of the damned.

not iss.   Merge
Oct 97. (cd-ep) *<MRG 127>* **THE NEW DESPAIR**
 – It's useless to struggle / City of the damned / Abandoned castle of my soul / Your long white fingers / Ever falls the twilight / The tiny goat / In a cave.

FUTURE BIBLE HEROES

— **STEPHIN + CLAUDIA GONSON** recruited **CHRISTOPHER EWEN** (ex-FIGURES ON A BEACH)

Setanta   Slow River
Mar 98. (7") *(SET 059)* **LONELY DAYS. / HOPELESS**
 (cd-s) *(SETCD 059)* – ('A'side) / Love is blue / How to get laid in Japanese / Berlin on $10 a day.
Apr 98. (cd) *(SETCD 056) <slr 24>* **MEMORIES OF LOVE**   May97
 – Lonely days / She-devils of the deep / Hopeless / Death opened a boutique / You pretend to be the moon / Blonde adonis / But you're so beautiful / You, you never knew / Real summer / Memories of love / You steal the scene.

Merge   Merge
Jul 00. (cd-ep) *<(MRG 178CD)>* **I'M LONELY (AND I LOVE IT) / MY BLUE HAWAII / CAFE HONG KONG / GOOD THING I DON'T HAVE ANY FEELINGS / HOPELESS (remix)**

not iss.   Instinct
Aug 02. (cd) *<608>* **ETERNAL YOUTH**
 – Losing your affection / The slow fade / Doris Daytheearthstoodstill / A thousand lovers in a day / Bathysphere / I'm a vampire / From some dying star / Viennese lift / Smash the beauty machine / The control room / Find an open window / Kiss me only with your eyes / Jakarta / No river / Cartoon / The world is a disco ball.

STEPHIN MERRITT

Sketchbook   Merge
Feb 02. (cd) *(SKETCH 002) <MRG 505>* **EBAN & CHARLEY**   Jan02
 (soundtrack)
 – Mother / Some summer day / O Tannenbaum / Poppyland / Drowned sailors / Maria Maria Maria / Titles / This little ukelele / Tea party / Tiny flying player pianos / Mother remembered / Victorian robotics / Water torture / Greensleeves / Stage rain.

MAGNETIC NORTH POLE

Formed: Dundee, Scotland … summer 1998 out of the short-lived NEUROLA, by Birmingham lad ALEX CHARLES and ROBBIE 'DES TROY' COOPER (the latter became only temporary as his own band, LAETO, were taking off). ALEX was also an ex-member of 'Earworm' outfit, MAPS OF JUPITER, and played for six months with the aforementioned LAETO; he still contributes on a regular basis. However, before all of this, ALEX independently issued a handful of cassettes under the BIKESHED moniker before setting up his own N.Pole Soundlab Recordings (@ L Appleyard, Ground Left, 67 Dens Road, Dundee, DD3 7HZ); he also promotes the local 'unscene' music festival. Enlisting the help of MIQUETTE BREITENBACH, RONNIE WALLACE (ex-NEW PANS PEOPLE, ACTOR SCREAM, MOMA, etc) and ROBBIE, MAGNETIC NORTH POLE set about trying to conquer the South. Described as SIMON AND GARFUNKEL meeting SONIC YOUTH (surely not!), MNP issued a series of split releases which included some of their own work. Newcomers to the line-up STUART GILLIES and CLAIRE THORNTON have since become YESSA DE PASO. ALEX CHARLES soon resurfaced after a spell in Canada with e-mail girlfriend DOMINIQUE; she would be part of his new project THEE MOTHS alongside old buddy RONNIE (although others such as drummer GAV, bassist KAT and guitarists HILARY and JAMES).

Album rating: NOISE ROOM split w/ Southall Riot (*5)

BIKESHED

ALEX CHARLES – vocals, guitar

Independent   not iss.
May 95. (c) *(none)* **BIKESHED**   – mail-o
Aug 95. (c) *(none)* **SOAP STAR: HOME / AWAY**   – mail-o
Sep 95. (c) *(none)* **THE ENJOYMENT OF STEREO WITH . . .**   – mail-o
Jul 96. (c) *(none)* **USE WEAPONS WHERE YOU CAN**   – mail

MAPS OF JUPITER

ALEX CHARLES with **RICHIE** – guitar / **AIMI** – drums, vocals / **CLAIRE THORNTON** – bass, vocals

	Earworm	not iss.
Mar 98. (7"ep) *(WORM 19)* **SIX STEREO RECORDINGS . . .**		-

– Maybe it all came true / Wait / Angled and poised / Sleeping / My excuse / Something special.

— when they split, all but ALEX formed The ELECTRIC COMPANY; RICHIE moved on to TACOMA RADAR

MAGNETIC NORTH POLE

ALEX CHARLES – vocals, guitar / **MIQUETTE BREITENBACH** – guitar, drums, vocals / **RONNIE WALLACE** – bass / **ROBBIE COOPER** aka **DES TROY** – drums (of LAETO)

	N.Pole Soundlab	not iss.
Nov 98. (7"ep; split) *(POLE 001)* **SOUNDS IN YOUR HEAD (VOL.1)**		-

– Caterpillar / (tracks by other bands).

— in Apr'99, MNP contributed to the double-CD V/A compilation, 'The Tell Tale Signs Of Earworm' (WORM 43).

	Earworm	not iss.
Jun 99. (lp; split w/ SOUTHALL RIOT) *(WORMSS 6)* **NOISE ROOM**		-

– Caterpillar (pt.2) / Sleep, sleep / etc

— **JOHN** – drums (ex-WILDERNESS CHILDREN, ex-WILD HOUSE, ex-NEW PANS PEOPLE, ex-GERILS) repl. ROBBIE who continued with LAETO

— **STUART GILLIES** – guitar, vocals; repl. MIQUETTE

— **CLAIRE THORNTON** – bass, vocals; repl. RONNIE

— in March-May 2000, MNP contributed tracks to a handful of V/A cassette compilations, including 'The Eric's Trip Show' (on 'Paperhearts'), 'Nobody Lives There Anymore Vol.1' (for 'Tayside') and 'We'll Cross That Bridge When We Get There' (+ CD on 'Tangerine Tapes')

	N.Pole Soundlab	not iss.
Aug 99. (cd-ep; by Various Artists) *(POLE 002)* **EP**		-
Feb 00. (cd-s; by MY ITALICS) *(POLE 006)* **RED IS NEXT TO GREEN. / LONGWAVE**		-
May 00. (cd-ep; split w/ LAETO, etc) *(POLE 015)* **WE STARTED WITH OVER 100 MEMBERS**		-

– (SPRAYDOG / NUBIA / PHARISETS + DIRTY ROSY).

– As far as here the river is deep / (other artists).

— STUART + CLAIRE have since formed YESSA DE PASO

THEE MOTHS

ALEX CHARLES, DOMINIQUE + RONNIE with others

	Tiny Pop	not iss.
Feb 01. (cd/c) **THE NEED**		-

MAGOO

Formed: King's Lynn, Norfolk, England . . . . 1991 by ANDREW RAYNER, ADAM BLACKBOURN, OWEN TURNER and DAVID BAMFORD. Finally signing to the appropriately titled 'Noisebox' label, these Lo-Fi pop alchemists began making a name for themselves with the first of three EP's, 'MUDSHARK', in Spring '95. A year on MAGOO had a further two under their belt, 'ROBOT CARNIVAL' and the seven track 7", 'EYE SPY'. Taking their cue from transatlantic experimentalists like GUIDED BY VOICES, MAGOO thrived on the sonic possibilities inherent in combining distortion, noise and melody. As such they were an obvious choice for up and coming Scottish indie institution, 'Chemikal Underground', already home to MOGWAI, ARAB STRAP and The DELGADOS. By the time they'd signed up in early '97, the group had been reduced to a trio following the departure of ADAM, two part-time members, CHRIS THORPE-TRACEY and CHRIS WYATT helping out on their debut album, 'THE SOATERAMIC SOUNDS OF MAGOO' (1997). The following year, they took on the task (along with MOGWAI) of covering a classic BLACK SABBATH track – MAGOO's choice being the highly unlikely 'BLACK SABBATH' – on the split CD single, ' . . . .. DO THE ROCK BOOGALOO'. Returning to the headspinning creative spark of their own material, the Norfolk lads released a second album proper, 'VOTE THE PACIFIST TICKET TODAY' (1998), six months on from a 'Noisebox' singles compilation, 'CLOSE CONTINENTAL D.N.A.'. After a lengthy two and a half year hiatus, MAGOO returned to the fold via 'REALIST WEEK' (2001), their first for 'Global Warming'. This certainly left SABBATH comparisions cold at the front door, relying this time on well-crafted blissed-out psychedelic epics such as 'EAST POLAR OPPOSITES CAN DREAM'.

Album rating: THE SOATERAMIC SOUNDS OF MAGOO (*7) / VOTE THE PACIFIST TICKET TODAY (*7) / CLOSE CONTINENTAL D.N.A. compilation (*6) / REALIST WEEK (*7)

ANDREW RAYNER – vocals, guitar, bass, piano / **ADAM BLACKBOURN** – guitar, bass / **OWEN TURNER** – guitar, effects / **DAVID BAMFORD** – drums

	Noisebox	not iss.
Mar 94. (7"ep; Various Artists) *(nbx 006)* **Backwater Three**		-
May 95. (7"ep) *(nbx 013)* **MUDSHARK EP**		-
Sep 95. (7"ep) *(nbx 016)* **ROBOT CARNIVAL EP**		-

– Don't stop to think / (others by COMPACT PUSSYCAT + The JOEYS).

– Tom, Lou and me / Elsie's skinny arms / Pop your mouth.

– Robot carnival / Sampa calmida (Land of joy) / Candle buddha / Rocket to Spector City.

— the track, 'PEANUT BOY', appeared on a various artists EP, 'Now That's What I Call Noisebox' *(nbx 018)*

Apr 96. (7"yellow-ep) *(nbx 020)* **EYE SPY EP**		-

– Eye spy / Motel mining / Soaterama / Polka party No.2 / Silver screen / Word is out / Diving bell.

— the track, 'GOLDWYN', appeared on a 'Fierce Panda' collection, 'Songs About Picniking' *(ning 018)*

— ADAM left the band

— the track, 'STRUCK A CHORD', appeared on a various artists cd, 'C96'

— ADAM was replaced by two part members **CHRIS THORPE-TRACEY** – guitar, bass, organ / **CHRIS WYATT** – drums, effects

	Chemikal Underground	Beggars Banquet
Mar 97. (7"ep/cd-ep) *(Chem 011/+cd)* <85006> **A TO Z AND BACK AGAIN EP**		Jun97
Apr 97. (lp/cd) *(Chem 012/+cd)* <85008> **THE SOATERAMIC SOUNDS OF MAGOO**		Sep97

– A to Z and back again / The big comeback starts here / Some dark action / Baxter Preminger / It's good for you.

– The starter's gun / A to Z and back again / Your only friend / Telling you lies / Red lines (are fine) / The guilt club / The advantage of noise / Have you heard? / The social event of the year / Soaterama / The queen of the 8-bus singers / It's not going to stop / Hello . . . / Playing cards with the stars / British cars / This red earth / Say goodnight. *(cd+=/+free-7"ep)* – Lonely legionaire / Careering dice (a loose dear Santa) / Melodra / Bebe alights / Dutch dynamico / Train of thought.

Jun 97. (7"ep/cd-ep) *(Chem 016/+cd)* **RED LINES (ARE FINE) EP**		-

– Red lines (are fine) / A perfect vision: a) The priority transmission, b) A perfect vision, c) Joint venture.

Dec 97. (ltd-7"colrd-ep) *(ER 157)* **TREMOR, TREMOR, TREMOR / PEANUT BOY (mix). / CANDLE BUDDHA / ROBOT CARNIVAL**		-

(above 45 released on 'Elefant') (below on 'Fierce Panda')

Mar 98. (cd-s;split) *(NING 47CD)* **. . ... DO THE ROCK BOOGALOO**		-

– Black sabbath / Sweat Leaf (by MOGWAI)

Jun 98. (7"ep/cd-ep) *(Chem 025/+cd)* **HOLY SMOKE. / PINK DUST / A MEETING OF MINDS**		-
Sep 98. (7"ep/cd-ep) *(Chem 028/+cd)* **SWISS BORDER ESCAPE. / SWITCHED AROUND / I FORGOT ALL THE THINGS I EVER KNEW**		-
Nov 98. (cd/lp) *(Chem 030 cd/lp)* **VOTE THE PACIFIST TICKET TODAY**		-

– Vote the pacifist ticket today / Pink dust / Swiss border escape / Get on it superhero / Acid goldbar / The casino effect / Billion dollar brain / Holy smoke / Keep it pure / My vote is you / Cable tuned and sabre toothed / The spectre closes in / Implicate the targets – Airmen afraid.

	Global Warming	not iss.
Jul 01. (7"m/cd-s) *(WARM 013/+CD)* **EAST POLAR OPPOSITES CAN DREAM. / SKYLIGHT SONG / EYES WIDE OPEN**		-
Aug 01. (cd/lp) *(GLOB CD/LP 010)* **REALIST WEEK**		-

– Realist week / East polar opposites can dream / Motorama / Nastro adhesivo / Milk freaks / You make the surprise / The high castle / Knowledge is power / Powerman / 2 dearborn / Only test with guarantees / Revolution of the planets.

Oct 01. (7"/cd-s) *(WARM 014/+CD)* **KNOWLEDGE IS POWER. / REPETITIVE GOLD**		-

	Star Harbour	not iss.
Jun 02. (cd-s) *(disco 0205)* **THE BIG COMEBACK STARTS HERE / WIVES OF FARMERS / 2 DEARBORN**		-

– compilations, etc. –

Mar 98. (cd) *Noisebox; (nbx 036)* **CLOSE CONTINENTAL D.N.A. {NOISEBOX 94-96}**		-

– Eye spy / Motel mining / Soaterama / Struck a chord / Polka party No.2 / Silver screen / Word is out / Diving bell / Goldwyn / Robot carnival / Sampa calmida (Land of joy) / Candle buddha / Rocket to Spector city / Are you alright? / Pop your mouth / Tome, Lou and me / Elsie's skinny / Peanut boy / On a beach . . .

MAIDS OF GRAVITY

Formed: Los Angeles, California, USA . . . 1993 by ED RUSCHA and JIM PUTNAM, both straight out of rock outfit MEDICINE, they recuited drummer IRWIN. Named after an unconscious band (in that RUSCHA had dreamed about them), MAIDS OF GRAVITY played highly melodic psychedelic sludge-grunge, a kind of MELVINS-meets-MUDHONEY crossover that was taken to the next level come their self-titled debut, cut for 'Vernon Yard' in 1994. In the coming months, MOG toured extensively and supported the likes of English rockers BUSH. Their heady brand of fuzz-pop, coupled with the vocal harmonies of RUSCHA and PUTNAM, set them apart from the many Seattle grunge copycats, earning the trio quite a cult reputation in their native California. Their sophomore release, the JOHN CALE-produced 'THE FIRST SECOND' (1996), had a more sun-baked feel, with the BRIAN WILSON overtures creeping out from under the distorted melodies and the hazey jams. By this point, PUTNAM had swapped his electric guitar for acoustic and piano and formed The RADAR BROTHERS, a home-recorded weep-core trio. RUSCHA kept ploughing his field of psych rock, and enlisted EUGENE GORESTER and MARK KAY.

Album rating: STRANGE CHANNEL mini (*5) / MAIDS OF GRAVITY (*4) / THE FIRST SECOND (*6)

ED RUSCHA – vocals, guitar (ex-MEDICINE) / **JIM PUTNAM** – guitar (ex-MEDICINE) / **IRWIN** – drums

	Virgin	Vernon Yard
Apr 95. (m-lp/m-cd) *(VUSMLP/CDVUSM 85)* **STRANGE CHANNEL**		

– Your ground / Slave & rule / Moonspiders / Taste. *(cd+=)* – In other words. <US cd-iss. Jul00; same as UK>

MAIDS OF GRAVITY (cont)

May 95. (7") *(VUS 90)* **ONLY DREAMING. / SHE HIT THE SPOT**
(12"+=/cd-s+=) *(VUS T/CD 90)* – Burnt down.

—— **CRAIG LEVITZ** – drums, percussion; repl. IRWIN

Nov 95. (cd) *<VYD 010 – 40178>* **MAIDS OF GRAVITY**
– 20th Century zen / Only dreaming / Introverted skies / Moonspiders / A sad one / Alright / Your ground / Play inside / Windows / Where on earth / Shimmering / Hold on / (untitled) / (untitled).

                                                                                                      Vernon Yard / Vernon Yard

Mar 97. (cd) *<(VYD 019)>* **THE FIRST SECOND**   Nov96
– Half awake / Don't you disagree / The light you gave / No room / Another one / Golden harm / Can't lose / Looks the same / Islands / Live and die / In the days / Don't have to be.

—— added **EUGENE GORESTER** – guitar + **MARK KAY** – bass

—— MOG split + PUTNAM continued with The RADAR BROS.

MAIN (see under ⇒ LOOP; in 80's section)

MAJESTIC

Formed: San Francisco, California, USA … 1995. Originally billed as MAJESTIC 12, the departure of vocalist JANA WITTREN led to the group being re-named. Although the band had a revolving cast of protagonists (there could be as many as thirteen in the group at any one time) there were a number of more permanent fixtures:- SCOTT SCHULTZ, JAROND GIBBS and the two pairs of siblings AAMON and AARON WATENE, and RON and STEVE BERRETT. Their debut album, 'LIVE IT UP' (1999), benefitted greatly from their vast pool of musicians. Although the album was rooted in indie pop the multi-layered effect provided by the keyboards and horn section leant them a sound of their own. A second album, 'WAKE UP, COME OUT AND PLAY' (2001), continued the good work, the music now even more intricate and impressive.

Album rating: LIVE IT UP! (*6) / WAKE UP, COME OUT AND PLAY! (*6)

SCOTT SCHULTZ – vocals / **JANA WITTREN** – vocals / **JAROND GIBBS** – guitar / **AAMON WATENE** – guitar / **RON BERRETT** – piano / **STEVE BERRETT** – wurlitzer / **AARON WATENE** – drums / + others

                                                                      not iss. / 5HQ

Jun 97. (7"; as MAJESTIC 12) *<009-439>* **RESONANT EVIL. / KENNEDY**

                                                                       not iss. / Quiddity

Nov 97. (7"; as MAJESTIC 12) *<QUID 12>* **LOST AND FOUND. / COLD WIND**

—— now without JANA who formed The ARROGANTS (with three McFERSON brothers, JAYD, JEFFREY and JON); released a set for 'Shelflife'

                                                                      Shelflife / Shelflife

Apr 98. (7",7"colrd) *<life 002>* **NOTHING ON T.V. / HOLLOW / CLOSER**

May 99. (cd) *<life 007>* **LIVE IT UP!**
– Bub / Wonderful / Overcoat / Little bird / Rainbow connection / Say dee la / Harry / Sleep / Before I came / Killing time / Hula hoop.

—— added **RUTH SCHULTZ + SARAH WINDES** – vocals / **PETER QUINNEL** – drums

Nov 01. (cd) *<life 027>* **WAKE UP, COME OUT AND PLAY!**
– Tumbling / Sunday driver / Come out and play / Name / Chocolate milk / It's alright / Tennis racket / I was wrong / Almost awake / Malibu U. / On and on / Wake up.

MAKE-UP

Formed: Washington DC, USA … Spring '88 initially as NATION OF ULYSSES. This sharp-suited politi-core terrorist outfit consisted of JAMES CANTY, TIM GREEN, STEVE KRONER, STEVE GAMBOA plus the "sassy" frontman, IAN SVENONIUS. Until their demise in the Autumn of '92, NOU issued two IAN MacKAYE-produced albums, '13-POINT PROGRAM TO DESTROY AMERICA' (1991) and 'PLAYS PRETTY FOR BABY' (1992). CANTY, SVENONIUS and GAMBOA formed the short-lived CUPID CAR CLUB with former FRUMPIES bassist, MICHELLE MAE, although the name was thankfully shelved for the more basic MAKE-UP. Like JON SPENCER BLUES EXPLOSION and ROCKET FROM THE CRYPT rolled into one, their legendary "greaseball" stage shows were recorded for posterity in the guise of their debut release, 'DESTINATION: LOVE – LIVE! AT COLD RICE' (1996). 'Dischord' (home of MacKAYE's FUGAZI) delivered one more set, 'AFTER DARK' (1997), before they released 'SOUND VERITE' (1997), for 'K' records (NOU guitarist, TIM GREEN, had worked for the label since the split). The ROYAL TRUX-produced 'IN MASS MIND' (1998) and the following year's 'SAVE YOURSELF', found the band making giant leaps in both their songwriting and their sonic reach, kicking up a veritable storm of soulful garage and, on the latter, covering the chilling folk/blues standard, 'HEY JOE' (previously made famous, of course, by JIMI HENDRIX). The ROYAL TRUX connection was still on show (i.e. NEIL HAGERTY) with SVENONIUS and MAE's next project, WEIRD WAR. In spring 2002, the trio manifested their own brand of sexed-up R&R via a rousing eponymous collection. • **Covered:** BLACK WIRE (MC5).

Album rating: Nation Of Ulysses: 13-POINT PROGRAM TO DESTROY AMERICA (*5) / PLAYS PRETTY FOR BABY (*6) / Make-Up: DESTINATION: LOVE – LIVE! AT COLD RICE (*6) / AFTER DARK (*6) / SOUND VERITE (*5) / I WANT SOME compilation (*7) / SAVE YOURSELF (*7) / Weird War: WEIRD WAR (*7)

NATION OF ULYSSES

IAN SVENONIUS – vocals, trumpet / **TIM GREEN** – guitar / **STEVE KRONER** – guitar / **STEVE GAMBOA** – bass / **JAMES CANTY** – drums

                                                                    Dischord / Dischord

1991. (7"ep) *<DIS 46>* **THE SOUND OF YOUNG AMERICA. / CHANNEL 1 ULYSSES / ATOM BOMB**

Sep 91. (cd/c/lp) *<DIS 57 CD/C/V>* **13-POINT PROGRAM TO DESTROY AMERICA**
– Spectra sonic sound / Look out! soul is back / Today I met the girl I'm going to marry / Ulythium / A kid who tells on another kid is a dead kid / Cool senior high school (fight song) / Diptheria / Aspirin kid / Hot chocolate city / P. Power / You're my Miss Washington, D.C. / Target: U.S.A. / Love is a bull market. *(cd+=)* – The sound of young America / Channel One Ulysses / Atom bomb. *(UK-iss.Feb97; same as US)*

Oct 92. (cd/c/lp) *<(DIS 71 CD/C/V)>* **PLAYS PRETTY FOR BABY**
– N-sub Ulysses / A comment on ritual / The hickey underworld / Perpetual motion / Machine / N.O.U. future-vision / Hypothesis / 50,000 watts of goodwill / Maniac dragstrip / Last train to cool / Shakedown / Mockingbird, yeah! / Depression III / S.S. Explorer / The kingdom of Heaven must be taken by storm.

—— disbanded when supposedly one of them (possibly KRONER begat a baby)

– compilations, etc. –

Nov 00. (cd/lp) *Dischord;* *<(DIS 124/+LP)>* **THE EMBASSY TAPES**
(rec. September 1992)
– Introduction / Uptight / R.O.T.T.E.N. / A.P.E. embassy / Hex-proof / Outline for hangout / Gimme disaster / Shakedown (party) / Last train to cool / P-power (pt.II).

MAKE-UP

IAN SVENONIUS – vocals / **STEVE GAMBOA** – drums / **MICHELLE MAE** – bass, vocals (ex-FRUMPIES) / **JAMES CANTY** – drums, organ

                                                                   not iss. / Black Gemini

Mar 95. (7") *<#1>* **BLUE IS BEAUTIFUL. / TYPE U BLOOD**

Apr 95. (7") *<#2>* **TRANS-PLEASANT EXPRESS / ABNSENCE OF RHYTHM. / (split w/ the META-MATICS)**

                                                                   not iss. / Time Bomb

Jul 95. (7"ep) *<128>* **split w/ SLANT 6**
– We're having a baby / This is . . . young vulgarians / (2 by SLANT 6).

                                                                     not iss. / K

Aug 95. (7") *<DN 106>* **R.U.A. BELIEVER. / (other by DUB NARCOTIC)**

                                                                   Dischord / Dischord

Apr 96. (cd/lp) *<(DIS 99 CD/V)>* **DESTINATION: LOVE – LIVE! AT COLD RICE (live)**
– Intro "Hold it" / Here comes the judge / You + I vs. the world / They live by night / Bring the birds down / Don't mind the mind / Evidence is everywhere / We can't be contained / Introductions / Don't step on the children / How pretty can U get / R U a believer (part 2) / International airport / We gotta get offa this rock / So . . . chocolatey – Destination: love / Outro "Hold it".

Oct 96. (7") *<(TBI 38)>* **SUBSTANCE ABUSE. / UNDER THE IMPRESSION**
(above issued on 'Time Bomb' in Japan)

Feb 97. (cd/lp) *<DIS 105 CD/V>* **AFTER DARK**
– Spoken intro / Prelude to comedown – Can I hear U say . . . ?? / Blue is beautiful / At the tone . . . (the time will be) / We can't be contacted / Gospel 2000 / Vs. culture / We're having a baby / Make up is: lies / R U a believer / The final comedown / Don't mind the mind / Here comes the judge.

                                                                        K / K

Mar 97. (lp/cd) *<KLP 64/+CD>* **SOUND VERITE**
– If they come in the morning / Make up is: lies / At the tone, the time will be / Tell it like it will be / What's the rumpus? / Gospel 2000 / Hot coals / Gold record (part 1) / Gold record (part 2) / Have U got the new look.

Oct 97. (7") *<(IPU 85)>* **FREE ARTHUR LEE. /**

Jan 98. (7") *(ACMU 1)* **WADE IN THE WATER. / GOSPEL 2000** (designer remix)
(above on 'All City' & below on 'Woo Me')

Mar 98. (7") *(WOOME 001)* **UNTOUCHABLE SOUND. / I DIDN'T MEAN 2 TURN U ON**

Apr 98. (cd/lp) *<DIS 113 CD/V>* **IN MASS MIND**
– Black wire (part 1) / Live in the rhythm hive / Joy of sound / Watch it with that thing / Drop the needle / Earth worm (part 1) / Do you like gospel music? / Come up to the microphone / Centre of the earth / (I've heard about) Saturday nite / Earth worm (part 2) / Time machine / Caught up in the rapture / Black wire (part 2).
(above issued on 'Dischord')

Jul 98. (7") *(POMP 16)* **POW! TO THE PEOPLE. / (other by LUNGLEG)**
(above on 'Vesuvius' records) (below on 'K')

Jul 98. (7") *<IPU 86>* **U R MY INTENDED. / THE CHOICE**

Aug 98. (7") *<SD 016>* **split w/ CRANIUM**
(above on 'Slowdime' below on 'Giant Claw')

Jan 99. (7") *<GCS 019>* **I WANT SOME. / POW! TO THE PEOPLE**

Mar 99. (d-lp/cd) *<KLP 92/+CD>* **I WANT SOME** (compilation)
– Pow! to the people / I want some / Walking on the dune / The choice / Born on the floor / Hey! Orpheus / Grey motorcycle / Every baby cries the same / I am if . . . / Little black book / Blue is beautiful / Trans-pleasant express / Type-U blood / We're having a baby / This is . . . young vulgarians / R U a believer / Free Arthur Lee / Untouchable sound / I didn't mean 2 turn U on / Wade in the water / Substance abuse / Under the impression / Have U heard the tapes?

Apr 99. (7") *<IPU 91>* **BORN ON THE FLOOR. / LITTLE BLACK BOOK**

May 99. (12"ep) *<SLOWDIME 20>* **EVERY BABY CRIES THE SAME**
(above issued on 'Slowdime')

Oct 99. (cd/lp) *<KLP 105/+V>* **SAVE YOURSELF**
– Save yourself / White belts / The bells / The steps / I am Pentagon / Call me mommy / Feelin' man / C'mon, let's spawn / Hey Joe.

—— The MAKE-UP split at the turn of the millennium

WEIRD WAR

SVENONIUS + MAE plus **NEIL HAGERTY** (of ROYAL TRUX)

		Domino	Drag City
Aug 02.	(cd/lp) *(WIG CD/LP 110) <DC 205CD>* **WEIRD WAR**		Jun02

– Baby it's the best / Chicago charlemagne / Who's who / Fin rat / Grass / Ibex club / Name names / Burgers and fries / I live in a dream / Pick up the phone and ball / Family cong / Weird war / Man is money.

MALE NURSE

Formed: Edinburgh, Scotland ... 1993 by vocalist KEITH FARQUHAR and ALAN CRICHTON, along with a more settled line-up in 1994 consisting of ALASTAIR MacKINVEN, short-stay ANDREW HOBSON, PAUL CARTER on drums and RICHARD RAINEY on bass; it was at this stage KEITH decided to relocate to Baltimore and vocalist BEN WALLERS (from sister group, COUNTRY TEASERS) was drafted in to fill his shoes. A demo tape was duly recorded of this line-up, although drummer MARK DEAS deputised on this occasion. THE MALE NURSE were put on hold temporarily until 1996 when the AWOL FARQUHAR returned to duty, meanwhile WALLERS and CRICHTON were both serving time with the aforementioned COUNTRY TEASERS. After a succession of drummers, around a dozen to be exact, LAWRENCE WORTHINGTON was drafted in. London-based "superindie" imprint, 'Guided Missile', released their first offering in 1997, 'GDR'. A rush-released sophomore 45, 'MAGIC CIRCLE IN THE SKY', was next up for grabs; imagine The FALL with IRVINE WELSH contributing lyrics and you'll be just about there. Their third single, 'MY OWN PRIVATE P. SWAYZE', saw FARQUHAR and his crew hitting a critical peak, while the band also appeared on the 'Hits & Missiles' V/A compilation; the track being the 1997 recorded 'CATWALK'. When CRICHTON left due to ill-health in October '98, THE MALE NURSE also took time off work. Sadly, CRICHTON, who was recovering from opiates addiction, died in February '99; the coroner's verdict was misadventure. However, the story was not yet over, as BEN, ALASDAIR and LAWRENCE had settled in to be a bigger part of COUNTRY TEASERS.

Album rating: never released any

KEITH FARQUHAR – vocals / **BEN WALLERS** – guitar, vocals (also of COUNTRY TEASERS) / **ALAN CRICHTON** – guitar (also of COUNTRY TEASERS) / **ALASTAIR MacKINVEN** – bass / **LAWRENCE WORTHINGTON** – drums; repl. a succession of drummers incl. MARK DEAS + PAUL CARTER

		Guided Missile	not iss.
Jun 97.	(7") *(GUIDE 14)* **GDR. / I'M A MAN**		-
Jul 97.	(7") *(GUIDE 19)* **MAGIC CIRCLE IN THE SKY. / WHAT DOES WOMAN WANT?**		-

— ANDREW HOBSON – (or AM or LW above repl. CRICHTON who left then died '99)

| May 98. | (7") *(GUIDE 25)* **MY OWN PRIVATE P. SWAYZE. / DEEP FRIED** | | - |

— disbanded in October 1998; ALASDAIR and LAWRENCE had already joined BEN's group The COUNTRY TEASERS; sadly ALAN was to die in February '99. THE MALE NURSE re-formed once again after the millennium.

		Stupid Cat	not iss.
Apr 00.	(7") *(SCAT 05)* **TOWER. / (other track by Gilded Lil)**		-

Stephen MALKMUS (see under ⇒ PAVEMENT)

MAMBO TAXI

Formed: London, England ... mid '91 by DELIA and ANDREA, together with Ohio-raised ELLA and Belgian-born LENNIE. These young, boisterous, garage-punk, all-girl feminists took their name from a cab in the cult movie, 'Women On The Verge Of A Nervous Breakdown' and were virtually The RAINCOATS and The SHANGRI-LA'S fused into one. A handful of singles into the proceedings, MAMBO TAXI paid their rhythmic fares via one solitary set, 'IN LOVE WITH ...' (1994).

Album rating: IN LOVE WITH ... (*4)

LENNIE (b. Belgium) – vocals, bass / **ELLA** – guitar / **ANDREA** – keyboards / **DELIA** – guitar / **ANJALI** – drums

		Clawfist	not iss.
Jan 93.	(7") *(HUNKA 013)* **PROM QUEEN. / INSECURE**		-

— now with new drummer when ANJALI formed Asian all-female band VOODOO QUEENS (ELLA also joined part-time)

Jun 93.	(7"ep/cd-ep) *(HUNKA 019/+CD)* **POEMS ON THE UNDERGROUND / A TO E. / INSECURE / PROM QUEENS**		-
Oct 93.	(7"ep/cd-ep) *(HUNKA 020/+CD)* **DO YOU ALWAYS DRESS LIKE THAT IN FRONT OF OTHER PEOPLE'S BOYFRIENDS? / I WANT TO MARRY A SERIAL KILLER / SEA MONSTER**		-
May 94.	(cd) *(HUNKA CDL7)* **IN LOVE WITH ...**		-

– Tom / Kiss kiss kiss / Belgian blues / 2 nice boys / Happy Claire / (Push that) Pram (under the train) / Evangelical / Screaming in public / Poems on the underground / Reasons to live / Insecure / My room / Velvet youth.

		Echostatic	not iss.
Nov 95.	(d7") *(ECHO 5-6)* **TOM. / Breed: FEVERISH**		-

MANIC STREET PREACHERS

Formed: Blackwood, Caerphilly, Wales ... 1988 by JAMES DEAN BRADFIELD (vocals, guitar) and cousin SEAN MOORE (drums). With the addition of former school friends NICKY WIRE (bass) and RICHEY EDWARDS (rhythm guitar), the line-up was complete and the band set about recording their self-financed debut single, 'SUICIDE ALLEY'. The group began to attract attention with the release of the 'NEW ART RIOT' EP (1990), derivative but impassioned neo-punk which drew interest more for the band's defiant slurs on a range of targets (fellow musicians were shown no mercy) than its musical content. While the band looked the part (low rent glamour chic) and namechecked all the right people (RIMBAUD, The CLASH, etc.), their philosophy of kill your idols and then burn out, smacked of contrivance to say the least. When journalist STEVE LAMACQ said as much in an interview with EDWARDS in 1991, the guitarist proceeded to carve '4 REAL' into his arm with a razor, upping the ante in the band's already precarious relationship with the music press and causing furious debate between doubters and obsessive fans. The group proceeded to release a couple of raging singles on 'Heavenly', 'MOTOWN JUNK' and the stinging 'YOU LOVE US' (aimed at the press), before signing to 'Columbia' in 1991. After a couple of minor hits, 'STAY BEAUTIFUL' and 'LOVE'S SWEET EXILE', the MANICS cracked the Top 20 with a re-released 'YOU LOVE US', their much anticipated debut album, 'GENERATION TERRORISTS' following in February 1992. A sprawling double set, it kicked convincingly against the pricks, lashing out at such deserving targets as high street banks ('NAT WEST-BARCLAYS-MIDLAND-LLOYDS') and our beloved monarch ('REPEAT'). The band also proved they had a way with melody and songwriting in the soaring melancholy of 'MOTORCYCLE EMPTINESS'. Despite their original well intentioned claims to break up after the debut, the band rather predictably toured the album and began work on a new collection, 'GOLD AGAINST THE SOUL' (1993). Lacking the vicious kick of the debut, the record nevertheless contained some fine moments in the likes of 'LA TRISTESSE DURERA (SCREAM TO A SIGH)' and 'LIFE BECOMING A LANDSLIDE', reaching No.8 in the album charts. The MANIC STREET PREACHERS continued to court controversy with NICKY WIRE making his infamous comments about MICHAEL STIPE at the 1993 Reading Festival. The following year RICHEY EDWARDS' depression, self-mutilation and anorexia reached a head, the guitarist eventually admitted to a clinic for several weeks. His trauma was detailed in the harrowing '4st 7lb' from their third album, 'The HOLY BIBLE' (1994), a dark night of the soul which centred on such grim topics as Nazi genocide. Then, on 1st February '95, with EDWARDS apparently recovered, he went AWOL from his London hotel. A fortnight later, his abandoned car was found at the Severn Bridge, and rumours of suicide abounded. Even after a protracted police search, there was no trace of the guitarist and at the time of writing , he is still missing. Numerous sightings have since been reported, most notably in Goa, India although the Police have continued to draw a blank. The remaining members eventually decided to carry on, contributing a poignant 'RAIN DROPS KEEP FALLING ON MY HEAD' to the 1995 Warchild charity album, 'HELP', and releasing their fourth album, 'EVERYTHING MUST GO' (1996). The group's most accomplished work to date, the record was preceded by their biggest hit single (No.2), the bitter 'A DESIGN FOR LIFE'. Embellished with soaring strings and lavish arrangements, the band scored with a succession of brilliant songs including 'AUSTRALIA' and the title track, compositions that were almost transcendant in their emotive power, the memory of EDWARDS never far away. It seemed that at last the MANIC STREET PREACHERS had lived up to their early boasts and in early 1997 their talent was recognised when 'EVERYTHING MUST GO' won the coveted Mercury Music Award. The top of the singles chart was the only place the MANICS hadn't been. This was remedied late summer '98 when 'IF YOU TOLERATE THIS YOUR CHILDREN WILL BE NEXT' made No.1, a taster from their massive selling parent album, 'THIS IS THE TRUTH TELL ME YOURS' (1998). Classic anthems such as 'THE EVERLASTING', 'YOU STOLE THE SUN FROM MY HEART', and 'TSUNAMI', also became top selling in the UK charts, although what was happening to their records in America? Not that the staunchly socialist MANICS gave a fig for their Stateside oblivion, content to become the first Western rock band to play in Communist Cuba, that longtime thorn in Uncle Sam's bloated side. No need to ask then, what 'BABY ELIAN' was all about given the Cuba vs USA tussle of summer 2000. The latter track was served up for 'KNOW YOUR ENEMY' (2001), the band's sixth album and one of their most accomplished to date. The almost STOOGES-style savagery of 'FOUND THAT SOUL' (a dual Top 10 single released simultaneously with 'SO WHY SO SAD') set the tone, a blistering punk/garage track that put many of the so called American nu-metal/punk groups to shame and served as a timely reminder of how good angry rock music can be when it comes from the gut and not the marketing strategy. 'OCEAN SPRAY', in contrast, was a poignant homage to JAMES' mum's battle with cancer, Ocean Spray being a brand of cranberry juice used to combat the disease. Yet this album was primarily a politicised affair, again railing against the evils of the USA in the likes of 'FREE SPEECH WON'T FEED MY CHILDREN' and 'LET ROBESON SING', a tribute to the forgotten entertainer/political activist. They may be guilty of naivety, bombast and even double standards but few bands of the modern era write, play and perform with the emotional and political intensity, the dignity and the humbleness of The MANIC STREET PREACHERS; Britain's anaemic music scene (never mind the USA) needs this band now more than ever. • **Covered:** IT'S SO EASY (Guns N' Roses) / UNDER MY WHEELS (Alice Cooper) /

SUICIDE IS PAINLESS (Theme from 'Mash') / CHARLES WINDSOR (McCarthy) / THE DROWNERS (Suede) / STAY WITH ME (Faces) / WROTE FOR LUCK (Happy Mondays) / RAINDROPS KEEP FALLING ON MY HEAD (Bacharach-David) / VELOCITY GIRL (Primal Scream) / TAKE THE SKINHEADS BOWLING (Camper Van Beethoven) / I CAN'T TAKE MY EYES OFF YOU (hit; Andy Williams) / TRAIN IN VAIN (Clash).

Album rating: GENERATION TERRORISTS (*8) / GOLD AGAINST THE SOUL (*9) / THE HOLY BIBLE (*9) / EVERYTHING MUST GO (*9) / THIS IS MY TRUTH TELL ME YOURS (*8) / KNOW YOUR ENEMY (*7) / FOREVER DELAYED – GREATEST HITS compilation (*8)

JAMES DEAN BRADFIELD (b.21 Feb'69, Newport) – vocals, guitar / **RICHEY JAMES EDWARDS** (b.27 Dec'69) – rhythm guitar / **NICKY WIRE** (b. NICHOLAS JONES, 20 Jan'69, Tredegar) – bass / **SEAN MOORE** (b.30 Jul'70, Pontypool) – drums

S.B.S. not iss.

- Aug 89. (7") (SBS 002) **SUICIDE ALLEY. / TENNESSEE (I FEEL SO LOW)** — / —

Damaged Goods not iss.

- Jun 90. (12"ep) (YUBB 4) **NEW ART RIOT.** — / —
  – New art riot / Stip it down / Last exit on yesterday / Teenage 20-20. (re-iss. Dec91, Jul93 + Sep96, 12"pink-ep/cd-ep; YUBB 4 P/CD)

Heavenly not iss.

- Jan 91. (12"ep/cd-ep) (HVN8 12/CD) **MOTOWN JUNK. / SORROW 16 / WE HER MAJESTY'S PRISONERS** 92 / —
- May 91. (7") (HVN 10) **YOU LOVE US. / SPECTATORS OF SUICIDE** 62 / —
  (12"+=/cd-s+=) (HVN 10 12/CD) – Starlover / Strip it down (live).

Caff not iss.

- Jul 91. (7") (CAFF 15) **FEMININE IS BEAUTIFUL: NEW ART RIOT. / REPEAT AFTER ME** — / —

Columbia Columbia

- Jul 91. (7") (657337-7) **STAY BEAUTIFUL. / R.P. McMURPHY** 40 / —
  (12"+=/12"w-poster/cd-s+=) (657337-6/-8/-2) – Soul contamination.
  (US-cd-ep+=) – Motown junk / Sorrow 16 / Star lover.
  (cd-ep re-iss. Sep97 on 'Epic' hit No.52; MANIC 1CD)
- Nov 91. (7") (657582-7) **LOVE'S SWEET EXILE. / REPEAT** 26 / —
  (12"+=/cd-s+=) (657582-6/-2) – Democracy coma.
  (12"ltd.++=) (657582-8) – Stay beautiful (live).
  (cd-ep re-iss. Sep97 on 'Epic' hit No.55; MANIC 2CD)
- Jan 92. (7"/c-s) (657724-7/-4) **YOU LOVE US. / A VISION OF DEAD DESIRE** 16 / —
  (12"+=) (657724-6) – It's so easy (live).
  (cd-s++=) (657724-2) – We her majesty's prisoners.
  (cd-ep re-iss. Sep97 on 'Epic' hit No.49; MANIC 3CD)
- Feb 92. (pic-cd/cd/d-c/d-lp/pic-d-lp) (471060-0/-2/-4/-1/-9) <52474> **GENERATION TERRORISTS** 13 / —
  – Slash 'n' burn / Nat West-Barclays-Midland-Lloyds / Born to end / Motorcycle emptiness / You love us / Love's sweet exile / Little baby nothing / Repeat (stars and stripes) / Tennessee / Another invented disease / Stay beautiful / So dead / Repeat (UK) / Spectators of suicide / Damn dog / Crucifix kiss / Methadone pretty / Condemned to rock'n'roll. *(cd re-iss. Jan99; same)*
- Mar 92. (7"/c-s) (657873-7/-4) **SLASH 'N' BURN. / AIN'T GOING DOWN** 20 / —
  (12"+=) (657873-6) – Motown junk.
  (cd-s+=/gold-cd-s++=) (657873-2/-0) – ('A'version).
  (cd-ep re-iss. Sep97 on 'Epic' hit No.54; MANIC 4CD)
- Jun 92. (7"/c-s) (658083-7/-4) **MOTORCYCLE EMPTINESS. / BORED OUT OF MY MIND** 17 / —
  (12"pic-d+=) (658083-8) – Under my wheels.
  (cd-s++=/s-cd-s++=) (658083-2/-9) – Crucifix kiss (live).
  (cd-ep re-iss. Sep97 on 'Epic' hit No.41; MANIC 5CD)
- Sep 92. (7"/cd-s) (658382-7/-2) **THEME FROM M.A.S.H. (SUICIDE IS PAINLESS). / ('b'side by 'Fatima Mansions' – Everything I Do (I Do It For You)** 7 / —
- Nov 92. (7") (658796-7) **LITTLE BABY NOTHING. / SUICIDE ALLEY** 29 / —
  (12"+=/cd-s+=) (658796-6/-2) – Yankee drawl / Never want again.
  (cd-ep re-iss. Sep97 on 'Epic' hit No.50; MANIC 6CD)
- Jun 93. (c-s) (659337-4) **FROM DESPAIR TO WHERE. / HIBERNATION** 25 / —
  (12"+=) (659337-6) – Spectators of suicide (Heavenly version).
  (cd-s+=) (659337-2) – Star lover (Heavenly version).
- Jun 93. (cd/c/lp/pic-lp) (474064-2/-4/-1/-9) <57386> **GOLD AGAINST THE SOUL** 8 / —
  – Sleepflower / From despair to where / La tristesse durera (scream to a sigh) / Yourself / Life becoming a landslide / Drug drug druggy / Roses in the hospital / Nostalgic pushead / Symphony of tourette / Gold against the soul.
- Jul 93. (7"/c-s) (659477-7/-4) **LA TRISTESSE DURERA (SCREAM TO A SIGH). / PATRICK BATEMAN** 22 / —
  (12"+=) (659477-6) – Repeat (live) / Tennessee.
  (cd-s+=) (659477-2) – What's my name (live) / Slash'n'burn (live).
- Sep 93. (7"/c-s) (659727-7/-4) **ROSES IN THE HOSPITAL. / US AGAINST YOU / DONKEY** 15 / —
  (cd-s+=) (659727-2) – Wrote for luck.
  (12") (659727-6) – ('A'side) / (5-'A' mixes).

Epic Epic

- Feb 94. (c-s) (660070-4) **LIFE BECOMING A LANDSLIDE / COMFORT COMES** 36 / —
  (12"+=) (660070-6) – Are mothers saints.
  (cd-s++=) (660070-2) – Charles Windsor.
- Jun 94. (7"/c-s) (660447-7/-4) **FASTER. / P.C.P.** 16 / —
  (10"+=) (660447-0) – Sculpture of man.
  (cd-s++=) (660447-2) – New art riot (in E-minor).
- Aug 94. (10"/c-s) (660686-0/-4) **REVOL. / TOO COLD HERE** 22 / —
  (cd-s+=) (660686-2) – You love us (original Heavenly version) / Love's sweet exile (live).
  (cd-s) (660686-5) – ('A'side) / (3 live at Glastonbury tracks).

—— RICHEY booked himself into a health clinic, after wasting himself down to 5 stone.

- Aug 94. (cd/c/pic-lp) (477421-2/-4/-0) <66967> **THE HOLY BIBLE** 6 / —
  – Yes / Ifwhiteamericatoldthetruthforonedayit'sworldwouldfallapart / Of walking abortion / She is suffering / Archives of pain / Revol / 4st 7lb / Mausoleum / Faster / This is yesterday / Die in the summertime / The intense humming of evil / P.C.P.
- Oct 94. (10"/c-s) (660895-0/-4) **SHE IS SUFFERING. / LOVE TORN US UNDER (acoustic)** 25 / —
  (cd-s+=) (660895-2) – The drowners / Stay with me (both live w/ BERNARD BUTLER).
  (cd-s) (660895-5) – ('A'side) / La tristesse durera (scream to a sigh) / Faster (Dust Brothers remixes).

—— RICHEY was now fully recuperated... but on 1st Feb '95, he went AWOL again after walking out of London's Embassy Hotel at 7 that morning. Two weeks later, his car was found abandoned and after police frogmen searched the Severn, it was believed he might be dead. By the end of 1995, with RICHEY still missing, the group carried on as a trio.

—— Meanwhile, BRADFIELD produced the debut of NORTHERN UPROAR.

- Apr 96. (c-s) (663070-4) **A DESIGN FOR LIFE / BRIGHT EYES (live)** 2 / —
  (cd-s) (663070-2) – ('A'side) / Mr Carbohydrate / Dead passive / Dead trees and traffic islands.
  (cd-s) (663070-5) – ('A'side) / ('A'-Howard Grey remix) / ('A'-Apollo 440 remix) / Faster (Chemical Brothers remix).
- May 96. (cd/c/lp) (483930-2/-4/-1) <67709> **EVERYTHING MUST GO** 2 / —
  – Elvis impersonator: Blackpoool pier / A design for life / Kevin Carter / Enola - alone / Everything must go / Small black flowers that grow in the sky / The girl who wanted to be God / Removables / Australia / Interiors (song for Willem De Kooning) / Further away / No surface at all.
- Jul 96. (c-s) (663468-4) **EVERYTHING MUST GO / RAINDROPS KEEP FALLING ON MY HEAD (live)** 5 / —
  (cd-s) (663468-2) – ('A'side) / Hanging on / Black garden / No-one knows what it's like to be me.
  (cd-s) (663468-5) – ('A'side) / ('A'-Stealth Sonic Orchestra remix) / ('A'-Chemical Brothers remix).
- Sep 96. (c-s) (663775-4) **KEVIN CARTER / EVERYTHING MUST GO (acoustic)** 9 / —
  (cd-s) (663775-2) – ('A'side) / Horses under starlight / Sepia / First republic.
  (cd-s) (663775-5) – Kevin Carter busts loose (Jon Carter remix) / ('A'-Stealth Sonic Orchestra mixes).
- Dec 96. (c-s) (664044-4) **AUSTRALIA / A DESIGN FOR LIFE (live)** 7 / —
  (cd-s) (664044-2) – ('A'side) / Velocity girl / Take the skinheads bowling / I can't take my eyes off you (acoustic).
  (cd-s) (664044-5) – ('A'side) / ('A'-Lionrock remix) / Motorcycle emptiness (Stealth Sonic Orchestra version).

Epic Virgin

- Aug 98. (c-s) (666345-4) **IF YOU TOLERATE THIS YOUR CHILDREN WILL BE NEXT / KEVIN CARTER (live)** 1 / —
  (cd-s) (666345-2) – ('A'side) / Prologue to history / Montana Autumn '78.
  (cd-s) (666345-5) – ('A'-Massive Attack remix) / ('A'-The Class Reunion Of The Sunset Marquis mix; aka David Holmes).
- Sep 98. (cd/c/lp) (491703-2/-4/-1) <47579> **THIS IS MY TRUTH TELL ME YOURS** 1 / —
  – The everlasting / If you tolerate this your children will be next / You stole the sun from my heart / Ready for drowning / Tsunami / My little empire / I'm not working / You're tender and you're tired / Born a girl / Be natural / Black dog on my shoulder / Nobody loved you / S.Y.M.M. *(cd re-iss. Nov02; 491703-6)*
- Nov 98. (c-s) (666686-4) **THE EVERLASTING / SMALL BLACK FLOWERS THAT GROW IN THE SUN (live at Nunex)** 11 / —
  (cd-s) (666686-2) – ('A'side) / Blackholes for the young / Valley boy.
  (cd-s) (666686-5) – ('A'extended) / ('A'-Deadly Avenger's Psalm 315) / ('A'-Stealth Sonic Orchestra mix).
- Mar 99. (c-s) (666953-4) **YOU STOLE THE SUN FROM MY HEART / IF YOU TOLERATE THIS YOUR CHILDREN WILL BE NEXT (live)** 5 / —
  (cd-s) (666953-2) – ('A'side) / Socialist serenade / Train in vain (live).
  (cd-s) (666953-5) – ('A'mixes by David Holmes & Mogwai).
- Jul 99. (c-s) (667411-4) **TSUNAMI / MOTOWN JUNK (live)** 11 / —
  (cd-s) (667411-2) – ('A'side) / Buildings for dead people / A design for life (video).
  (cd-s) (667411-5) – ('A'mixes by Cornelius & Stereolab).
- Jan 00. (c-s) (668530-4) **THE MASSES AGAINST THE CLASSES / CLOSE MY EYES** 1 / —
  (10"+=/cd-s+=) (668530-6/-2) – Rock and roll music.
- Feb 01. (c-s) (670832-4) **SO WHY SO SAD / YOU STOLE THE SUN FROM MY HEART (live from Cardiff Millennium Stadium 31st December 1999)** 8 / —
  (cd-s) (670832-2) – ('A'side) / ('A'-Avalanche remix) / Pedestal.
- Feb 01. (7") (670833-7) **FOUND THAT SOUL. / THE MASSES AGAINST THE CLASSES (live)** 9 / —
  (cd-s) (670833-2) – ('A'side) / Locust valley / Ballad of the Bangkok Novotel.
- Mar 01. (cd/c/lp) (501880-2/-4/-1) <10113> **KNOW YOUR ENEMY** 2 / —
  – Found that soul / Ocean spray / Intravenus agnostic / So why so sad / Let Robeson sing / The year of purification / Wattsville blues / Miss Europa disco dancer / Dead martyrs / His last painting / My Guernica / The convalescent / Royal correspondent / Epicentre / Baby Elian / Freedom of speech won't feed my children. *(untitled hidden track+=) (cd re-iss. Nov01; same)*
- Jun 01. (c-s) (671253-4) **OCEAN SPRAY / OCEAN SPRAY (Ellis Island mix)** 15 / —
  (cd-s) (671253-2) – ('A'side) / The groundhog days / Just a kid.
  (cd-s) (671253-5) – ('A'-Medicine mix) / ('A'-Kinobe mix).
- Sep 01. (12") (671773-6) **LET ROBESON SING. / ('A'-Ian Brown mix) / ('A'-thee glitz mix by Felix Da Housecat)** 19 / —
  (cd-s+=) (671773-5) – ('A'video).
  (cd-s) (671773-2) – ('A'-side) / Masking tape / Didn't my Lord deliver Daniel / ('A'-video).
- Oct 02. (cd-s) (673166-2) **THERE BY THE GRACE OF GOD / AUTOMATIK TEKNICOLOUR / IT'S ALL GONE / ('A'video)** 6 / —
  (cd-s) (673166-5) – ('A'-side) / Unstoppable salvation / Happy ending.
- Oct 02. (cd/lp) (509551-2/-1) <87029> **FOREVER DELAYED – GREATEST HITS** (compilation) 4 / —
  – A design for life / Motorcycle emptiness / If you tolerate this your children will be next / La tristesse durera (scream to a high) / There by the grace of God / You

love us / Australia / You stole the sun from my heart / Kevin Carter / Tsunami / Masses against the classes / From despair to where / Door to the river / Everything must go / Faster / Little baby nothing / M.A.S.H. (suicide is painless) / So why so sad / Everlasting / Motown junk. *(d-cd+=; 509551-9)* – (remixes).

MANIFESTO
(see under ⇒ EMBRACE; in 80's section)

Roger MANNING (see under ⇒ JELLYFISH)

MAN OR ASTRO-MAN?

Formed: Auburn, California, USA . . . 1992 by COCO THE ELECTRONIC MONKEY WIZARD, BIRDSTUFF, STARCRUNCH and DR. DELECTO & HIS INVISIBLE VAPORTRON. After the release of 'IS IT . . . MAN OR ASTRO MAN', this weirdy, post-Ed Wood influenced sci-fi rock group have released over nine albums in total, ranging from the bizarre 'LIVE TRANSMISSION FROM URANUS' (1995) to the absurdly queer 'DESTROY ALL ASTROMEN' (1994). Described as sci-fi surf rock (can there be such a thing?!), 'MAN? certainly had stamina; when after the deliverance of three albums in 1995, 'PROJECT INFINITY', 'INTRAVENOUS TELEVISION CONTINUUM' and the aforementioned 'LIVE TRANSMISSION . . .', the band kept on coming up with NASA-sampled quirky rock, only matched by conceptual albums such as 'The Point' and that RESIDENTS favourite 'Eskimo'. 1996 saw the band shift to 'Touch & Go' records where they released the 'EXPERIMENTAL ZERO' album and another move in 1997 led to the inuendos continuing with 'WHAT REMAINS INSIDE A BLACK HOLE'. Possibly the ensemble's finest work was to emerge from the great pits of outta space after the second 1997 release 'MADE FROM TECHNETIUM', matched only by a a brilliant and musically competent 'EEVIAC: OPERATIONAL INDEX & REFERENCE GUIDE' (1999). The strange fruitiness of this ninth set proved to be more than just a pip-pip-whizz-bang soundscape of electronica. It rivalled such contemporary groups as ADD N TO (X) and the various stream of 'Warp' bands. The record was certainly avant-garde, instrumental space-rock at its prime, as was their next effort, 'SPECTRUM OR INFINITE SCALE' (2000), simple, to-the-point robotic rock. • **Covers:** JOURNEY TO THE STARS (Ventures) / DESTINATION VENUS (Rezillos) / DEUCES WILD (Link Wray) / BOMBORA + ALPHA SURFARI (Surfaris) / TIME BOMB (Avengers IV) / MACH ONE (Chancellors) / XL-3 (Phantoms) / TACO WAGON (Dick Dale) / MANTA RAY (Pixies) / GOLDFINGER (John Barry) / WAR OF THE SATELLITES (Danny Hamilton) / MYSTERY SCIENCE 3000 + JETSON'S + MUNSTER'S themes (various) / TELEVISION MAN (Talking Heads) / etc.

Album rating: IS IT . . . MAN OR ASTRO-MAN? (*7) / DESTROY ALL ASTROMEN! (*5) / YOUR WEIGHT ON THE MOON mini (*5) / LIVE TRANSMISSIONS FROM URANUS (*4) / PROJECT INFINITY (*5) / INTRAVENUS TELEVISION CONTINUUM (*6) / EXPERIMENT ZERO (*5) / WHAT REMAINS INSIDE A BLACK HOLE (*5) / MADE FROM TECHNETIUM (*5) / EEVIAC: OPERATIONAL INDEX & REFERENCE GUIDE (*8) / A SPECTRUM OF INFINITE SPACE (*5)

COCO THE ELECTRONIC MONKEY WIZARD – electric bass / **STAR CRUNCH** – guitar, vocals / **BIRDSTUFF** – drums, voice / **DR. DELECTO & HIS INVISIBLE VAPORTRON** (b. JASON RUSSELL) – bass

		not iss.	Homo Habilis
1992.	(7"blue-ep) <HH 701> **POSSESSION BY REMOTE CONTROL** – Eric Estrotica / Landlocked / Adios Johnny Bravo / Joker's wild.	-	

		One Louder	Estrus
1993.	(blue-lp/cd) <ES 129/+CD> **IS IT . . . MAN OR ASTRO-MAN?** – Taxidermist surf / Invasion of the Dragonmen / Nitrous burn out / Clean up on aisle #9 (turn up the monitors) / Journey to the stars / Cowboy playing dead / Illidium Q-36 / Sadie Hawkins atom bomb / The human calculator / Organ smash / Cattle drive / Escape through the air vent / Rudy's lounge / Mermaid love / Eric Estrotica / Alien visitors. *(UK-iss.Jul95; same as US)*	-	
1993.	(7"ep) <LRR 008> **SUPERSONIC TOOTHBRUSH HELMET** – Bermuda Triangle shorts / The vortex beyond / Caffeine trip / The heavies. *(UK-iss.Jan98; same as US)* (above issued on 'Lance Rock') (below issued on 'Lucky')	-	
1993.	(7"ep) <LKY 009> **CAPTAIN HOLOJOY'S SPACE DINNER** – The universe's only intergalactic radioactive breakfast bar / Taco wagon / Holojoy's interlude / Mystery meat / Space potatoes / You can't get good riblets in space.	-	
1993.	(7"ep) *(LOUD 1)* **MISSION INTO CHAOS!** – Name of numbers / Of sex and demise / Madness in the streets / Within a Martian heart / Point blank.		
1994.	(cd/lp) <ES 1215 CD/LP> **DESTROY ALL ASTROMEN!** – Reverb 10,000 / Name of numbers / Popcorn crabula / A mouthful of exhaust / Of sex and demise / Joker's wild / Intoxica / Mystery meat / The heavies / Madness in the streets / Espanto del futuro / Mystery science theater 3000 love theme / Landlocked / Bombora / Gargantua's last stand / You can't get good riblets in space / Bermuda Triangle shorts / Taco wagon / The vortex beyond / Destination Venus / Time bomb / The shadow knows. *(UK-iss.Jul95; same as US)* <US cd re-iss. 1996 on 'Bird Cage'; 11782>	-	
1994.	(7"ep) <GH 167> **THE VARIOUS BOSS SOUNDS FROM BEYOND THE REACHES . . . AND THEN SOME** (split w/ HUEVOS RANCHEROS) – A mouthful of exhaust / Rovers / (other 2 by HUEVOS RANCHEROS). (above issued on 'Get Hip') (below on 'Worrybird')	-	
1994.	(7") <WOE 22> **split w/ TEENAGE CAVEMEN** – Bombora / Surf terror / (other 2 by above).	-	

— they also split a tour gig EP with GIRLS AGAINST BOYS

Aug 94.	(10"pink-m-lp/m-cd) *(LOUD/LOUDER 4)* **YOUR WEIGHT ON THE MOON** – Rocketship XL-3 / Special agent Conrad Uno / Electrostatic brainfield / Shockwave / Taser guns mean big fun / Space patrol / Happy fingers / Destination Venus / Polaris.		-
Sep 94.	(7"orange-ep) <ES 751> **ASTRO LAUNCH** – Philip K. Dick in the pet section of Wal-Mart / The man from U.N.C.L.E. / Transmissions from Venus '94 / Time bomb. (above also issued on 'Estrus') (below issued on 'Demolition Derby')		
Oct 94.	(7"ep) *(DD 012)* **THE BRAINS OF THE COSMOS** – Electrostatic brainfield / Mach one / XL-3 / Cowboy playing dead (live).		
Dec 94.	(7"green-ep) <ES 765> **INSIDE THE HEAD OF . . . MR. ATOM** – Sferic waves / Inside the atom / Put your finger in the socket / 24 hours.		-
Feb 95.	(7"yellow-ep) <ES 769> **WORLD OUT OF MIND** – Escape velocity / Tomorrow plus X / Max Q / The Quatermass phenomenon.		-

— **CAPTAIN ZENO** – rhythm guitar; repl. DELECTO

Mar 95.	(lp/cd) *(LOUD/LOUDER 6)* **LIVE TRANSMISSIONS FROM URANUS** – Intro sample / Transmissions from Uranus / Time bomb / Special agent Conrad Uno / Sferic waves / Destination Venus / Names of numbers / A mouthful of exhaust / Cowboy playing bombora / Mystery science theatre 3000 love theme / Gargantua's last stand / Surfari / Rovers / Manta ray / Max Q / Man fron F.U.C.K. Y.O.U. / Eric Estrotica / Nitrous burn out. <US cd re-iss. Feb97 on 'Touch & Go'; TG 170>		-
May 95.	(7"clear-ep) *(LOUD 5)* <HH 711> **RETURN TO CHAOS** – Secret agent Conrad Uno / POint blank / Goldfinger.		

— <above issued on 'Homo Habilis' US>

Jul 95.	(lp/cd) *(LOUD/LOUDER 8)* **INTRAVENOUS TELEVISION CONTINUUM** – Immersion static / Put your finger in the socket (maximum voltage version) / Nitrous burn out 2012 / Tetsuwan atomu / Max Q (Nielson rating video version) / Max Q – untitled (reverse sync moog version) / Jetson's theme / Invasion of the Dragonmen / Bionic futures / Tomorrow plus X (time travel through sleep deprivation mix) / Out of limits / Calling Hong Kong / Munster's theme / Principles unknown / Everyone's favorite Martian / Deuces wild / Cool your jets. <US-iss.1996 on 'Bird Cage'; 11783> <re-iss. 1997 on 'Touch & Go'; TG 213>		-
Jul 95.	(cd/lp) <(ES 1221 CD/LP)> **PROJECT INFINITY** – Escape velocity / Sferic waves / (untitled – classified) / Transmissions from Venus / Max Q / Inside the atom / Philip K. Dick in the pet section of a Wal mart / Put your finger in the socket / Complex 34 / The man from U.N.C.L.E. / Tomorrow plus X / Manta ray / Point blank / Special agent Conrad Uno / Alpha Surfari / Mach one. (above also issued on 'Estrus' UK)		
1995.	(7"clear-ep) <shake 709> **MAN OR ASTRO-MAN? IN ORBIT** – Complex 34 / Alpha surfari / Manta ray / Space helmet. (above issued on 'Shake It') (below on 'Sympathy For . . .')		
1995.	(7") <SFTRI 250> **POLARIS. / WAR OF THE SATELLITES** *(UK-iss.Jul98; same as US)*		-
1995.	(7"flexi) <sexi flexi 002> **free w/ Monster Magazine** – The gargantua's last stand / The shadow knows / Creature in the surfer's lagoon / Espanto del futuro. (above issued on 'Kronophonic', below for Fear & Loathin)		
1995.	(one-sided-7") <rcrpa 12> **ESPANTO DEL FUTURO**		-
1995.	(7") **NEEDLES IN THE HAYSTACK** – Radio Fission / Calling Hong Kong. (above issued on 'East Side') (below on 'Gearhead')		-
1996.	(7") <rpm 005> **split w/ CHROME** – 4,000,000.37 miles (breaking the sdanity barrier).		-
Feb 96.	(7"ep) <ES 783> **THE SOUNDS OF TOMORROW** – The evil sounds of Planet Spectra / The wayward meteor / Green-blooded love / The powerful fully-transistorized Dick Tracy two-way wrist radio.		-

		Loud	Touch & Go
Feb 96.	(7"ep/cd-ep) *(LOUD/+ISH 10)* <TG 159/+CD> **DELUXE MEN IN SPACE** – Maximum radiation level / U-Uranus / March of the androids / Super rocket rumble / Configuration 9 / Rhombics.		
Apr 96.	(lp/cd) *(LOUD/LOUDER 12)* <TG 157 LP/CD> **EXPERIMENT ZERO** – Stereo phase test / Television fission / DNI / Planet collision / Big trak attack / 9 volt / Evil plans of Planet Spectra / Anoxia / Maximum radiation level / King of the monsters / Cyborg control / Test driver / Television man / Z-X3 / Principles unknown / The space alphabet.		
Jan 97.	(7"ep) <(DR 003)> **UFO'S AND THE MEN WHO FLY THEM!** – 9-volt (rechargable version) / The sound waves, reversing / Italian movie theme / HIgh wire. (above issued on 'Drug Racer')		Nov96

— **DEXTER X** – rhythm guitar repl. CAPTAIN ZENO

May 97.	(10"ep/cd-ep) *(LOUD/+ISH 23)* <TG 167/+CD> **1000X EP** – Miracle of genuine pyrex / Specify gravity / Like a giant microwave / Man made of Co2 / Universe city / 100 individual magnets / With automatic shut off.		
Jun 97.	(7") *(XPIG 28)* **KING OF THE MONSTERS. / BIRD'S STUFF** (above issued on 'Clawfist')		
Sep 97.	(lp/cd) *(LOUD/LOUDER 25)* <TG 180> **MADE FROM TECHNETIUM** – Message from the LP/CD / Lo Batt / Jonathan Winters Frankenstein / Don't think what Jack / Junk satellite / 10 years after World War 4 / A saucerful of sucrets / Breathing iron oxide / Muzak for cybernetics / Structo (Mr. Microphone mixup) / The sound waves reversing / Theoretical sounds of slow motion / Static cling (theme from) / Evert 1 Pipkin / Weightless at zero return / Quasi*man *[lp-only]*.		

— now without STARCRUNCH

		Touch & Go	Touch & Go
Dec 98.	(7") <TG 199> **DEUS EX MACHINA** – Cuts and volts / Drainingtheirbatteries.	-	
Apr 99.	(cd/lp) <(TG 189 CD/LP)> **EEVIAC: OPERATIONAL INDEX & REFERENCE GUIDE, INCLUDING OTHER MODERN COMPUTATIONAL DEVICES** – Interstellar hardrive / D:contamination / U-235 – PU-239 / Domain of the human race / Theme from EEVIAC / A reversal of polarity / Fractionalized reception of		

a scrambled transmission / Engines of difference / Psychology of A.I. (numbers follow answers) / Krannoyask-26 / Within the mainframe, impaired vision from inoperarable cataracts can become a new impending nepotism / As estrelas Agora Elas estao mortas – Myopia. *(pic-lp iss.Jan01; 1029-1)*

				Astro-Fonic	not iss.
1999.	(d7"ep) *(AF 001)* **INSIDE THE HEAD OF JOHN PEEL**			☐	-

– Stereo waves / (classified) / Inside the head of John Peel / Max Q.

				Epitaph	Touch & Go
Sep 00.	(cd/10"d-lp) *(6603-2/-1)* <*TG 906*> **A SPECTRUM OF INFINITE SCALE**			☐	☐

– Pathway to the infinite / Song of the two-mile linear particle accelerator Stanford University, Stanford California / Preparation clont / Curious constructs of stem-like devices which now prepare themselves to be thought of as fingers / Um espectro sem escala / Many pieces of large fuzzy mammals gathered together at a curve and schmoozing with a brick / (trapazoid – untitled) / Very subtle elevators / Within one universe there are millions / Spectograph reading of the varying phantom frequencies of chronic, incurable tinnitus / A simple text file / Obligatory part 2 song in which there is no presently existing part 1, nor the plans to make one / Multi-variational stimuli of sub-turgid foci covering cross evaluative techniques for cognitive analysis of hypersignificant graph peaks following those intersubjective modules having biodegradable seepage.

		not iss.	Loch Ness
2000.	(7") <*TMA 008*> split w/ JONNY & THE SHAMEN	-	☐

– compilations, etc. –

Jan 97. (cd) *Au-Go-Go; <(ANDA 191)>* **WHAT REMAINS INSIDE A BLACK HOLE?** ☐ -
– The universe's only intergalactic radioactive breakfast bar / The Quatermass phenomenon / Eric Estrotica (live in space) / War of the satellites / Rovers / 24 hours / Squad car (live in space) / Surf terror / Transmission from Venus / Reverb 1000 / Caffeine trip / Polaris / Adios Johnny Bravo / The vortex beyond / Within a Martian heart.

Jul 01. (cd) *Estrus; <(ES 1278CD)>* **BEYOND THE BLACK HOLE** ☐ -
– The wayward meteor / Rovers / The Quatermass phenomena / Polaris / The vortex beyond / 24 hrs. / Surf terror / The powerful fully-transistorized Dick Tracy two-way wrist radio / Reverb 1000 / Transmissions from Venus / Green-blooded love / Within a Martian heart.

MANSUN

Formed: Chester, England . . . 1995 originally as MANSON by songwriter PAUL DRAPER, DOMINIC CHAD (both from Wales), STOVE, THE HIB and MARK STENT. After one single under this moniker ('TAKE IT EASY CHICKEN'), they caused a minor rumpus with the legal team of notorious killer CHARLES MANSON. The band claimed their name was taken from a VERVE b-side, 'A MAN CALLED SUN', deliberately slightly altering it to avoid court action. With name change now complete, they issued their follow-up, 'SKIN UP PIN UP'. A month later with the help of A&R man, Keith Wozencroft, they were part of Parlophone's enviable roster. Their blend of melodic, alternative rock, was described as a 90's indie update of TEARS FOR FEARS. Two UK Top 40 hits appeared as the EP's, 'ONE' & 'TWO' in 1996, paving the way for further successes, 'STRIPPER VICAR' and 'WIDE OPEN SPACE'. The year 1997, began on a high note with a Top 10 hit, the charmingly titled 'SHE MAKES MY NOSE BLEED' and a No.1 album, 'ATTACK OF THE GREY LANTERN'. Ambitious in its stylistic diversity, it contained additional Top 20 hits, 'TAXLO$$' and 'CLOSED FOR BUSINESS'. In the summer of '98, MANSUN were back in the hit parade with two EP's, 'LEGACY' (their eighth in the series) and 'NINE' (leading in with 'BEING A GIRL'), both taken from their pseudo-concept follow-up album, 'SIX', which, spookily enough, reached the same number in the charts. MANSUN returned in summer 2000 with their new set, the very average 'LITTLE KIX'. An overly produced, post-Britpop disappointment, MANSUN seemed content with not only isolating fans, but isolating their music itself with cringeworthy tracks such as 'UNTIL THE NEXT LIFE' and 'WE ARE THE BOYS'. The orchestral aspect remained, but after the melancholy dabblings of 'ATTACK OF THE GREY LANTERNS', 'LITTLE KIX' seemed like the metaphorical difference between a limousine and a horse and cart. Rumour had it that the group were planning to work with Ibiza dance guru PAUL OAKENFOLD. Let's hope he can fix what went so wrong. • **Covers:** RAILINGS (Howard Devoto). Everyone Must Win was co-written with the ex-MAGAZINE frontman.

Album rating: ATTACK OF THE GREY LANTERN (*8) / SIX (*7) / LITTLE KIX (*5)

PAUL DRAPER (b. Flint, Wales) – vocals, guitars, piano, synthesizer / **DOMINIC CHAD** (b. Bangor, Wales) – lead guitar, piano, vocals, synthesizer / **STOVE KING** – bass / **THE HIB** – drums / **MARK 'SPIKE' STENT** – beatbox

		Regal	not iss.
Sep 95.	(7"; as MANSON) *(REG 2)* **TAKE IT EASY CHICKEN. / ('A'version)**	☐	-

(above also issued on own 'Sci Fi Hi Fi' label; MANSON 1)

Nov 95. (7"white) *(REG 3)* **SKIN UP PIN UP. / FLOURELLA** ☐ -
(cd-s+=) *(REG 3CD)* – Take it easy chicken.

— early '96, MARK suddenly departed

		Parlophone	Sony
Mar 96.	(cd-ep/c-ep/7"ep) *(CDRS/TCR/R 6430)* **MANSUN – ONE**	37	-

– Egg shaped Fred / Ski jump nose / Lemonade secret drinker / Thief.

Jun 96. (cd-ep/c-ep/7"ep) *(CD/TC+/R 6437)* **MANSUN – TWO** 32 -
– Take it easy chicken / Drastic sturgeon / The greatest pain / Moronica.

— lost another member when THE HIB quit

— **ANDIE RATHBONE** – drums; repl. temp. JULIAN (ex-KINKY MACHINE)

Sep 96. (7"clear) *(R 6447)* **STRIPPER VICAR. / NO ONE KNOWS US** 19 -
(cd-ep+=) *(CDR 6447)* **THREE EP** – An open letter to the lyrical trainspotter / Things keep falling off buildings.
(cd-ep) *(CDRS 6447)* **THREE EP** – ('A'side) / The edge / Duchess.

Nov 96. (7"white) *(R 6453)* **WIDE OPEN SPACE. / REBEL WITHOUT A QUILT** 15 -
(cd-s+=) *(CDR 6453)* **FOUR EP** – Vision impaired / Skin up pin up.
(cd-s) *(CDRS 6453)* **FOUR EP** – ('A'side) / The gods of not very much / Moronica (acoustic) / Lemonade secret drinker (acoustic).

Feb 97. (7"red) *(R 6458)* **SHE MAKES MY NOSE BLEED. / THE HOLY BLOOD AND THE HOLY GRAIL** 9 -
(cd-s+=) *(CDRS 6458)* **FIVE EP** – Live open space / Drastic sturgeon (live).
(cd-s) *(CDR 6458)* **FIVE EP** – ('A'side) / The most to gain / Flourella / ('A'acoustic).

Feb 97. (cd/c/d-lp) *(CD/TC+PCS 3787)* <*67935*> **ATTACK OF THE GREY LANTERN** 1 -
– The Chad who loved me / Mansun's only love song / Taxloss / You, who do you hate? / Wide open space / Stripper vicar / Disgusting / She makes my nose bleed / Naked twister / Egg shaped Fred / Dark Mavis.

May 97. (cd-ep) *(CDR 6465)* **SIX EP** 15 -
– Taxloss / Grey lantern / Taxloss (Lisa Marie Experience remix).
(cd-ep) *(CDRS 6465)* – ('A'side) / The impending collapse od it all / Ski jump nose (live) / Wide open space (acoustic).
(12"ep) *(12R 6465)* – ('A'mixes:- John '00' Fleming remix / album version / Slam remix / Gaudi remix).

Oct 97. (7"clear) *(R 6482)* **CLOSED FOR BUSINESS. / EGG SHAPED FRED (acoustic)** 10 -
(cd-s) *(CDR 6482)* **SEVEN EP** – ('A'side) / K.I.Double.S.I.N.G. / Everyone must win / The world's still open.
(cd-s) *(CDRS 6482)* **SEVEN EP** – ('A'side) / Dark Mavis (acoustic) / Stripper vicar (live) / Taxloss (video for PC or Mac).

Jun 98. (c-ep) *(TCR 6497)* <*57396*> **LEGACY EP (EIGHT EP)** 7 Aug98
– Legacy / Wide open space (the Perfecto remix) / The acoustic collapse of it all / Ski jump nose (acoustic).
(cd-ep) *(CDR 6497)* – ('A'side) / Wide open space (the Perfecto remix) / GSOH / Face in the crowd.
(cd-ep) *(CDRS 6497)* – ('A'side) / Can't afford to die / Spasm of identity / Check under the bed.

Aug 98. (c-ep) *(TCR 6503)* **NINE EP** 13 -
– Being a girl (part 1) / Wide open space (Trouse Enthusiasts mix) / Mansun's only acoustic song.
(cd-ep) *(CDR 6503)* – ('A'side) / Railings / Been here before.
(cd-ep) *(CDRS 6503)* – ('A'side) / Hideout / Wide open space (Trouser Enthusiasts mix).

Sep 98. (cd/c/d-lp) *(96723-2/-4/-1)* <*69748*> **SIX** 6 Apr99
– (Part one):- Six / Negative / Shotgun / Inverse Midas / Anti-everything / Fall out / Serotonin / Cancer (interlude) / Witness to a murder (part two) / (Part two):- Television / Special – Blown it (delete as appropriate) / Legacy / Being a girl.

Oct 98. (7") *(R 6508)* **NEGATIVE. / MANSUN'S ONLY LIVE SONG** 27 -
(cd-s) *(CDR 6508)* – ('A'side) / I deserve what I get / Take it easy chicken (live).
(cd-s) *(CDRS 6508)* – ('A'side) / When the wind blows / King of beauty.

Feb 99. (7") *(R 6511)* **SIX. / BEING A GIRL (parts 1 & 2) / LIVE TELEVISION** 16 -
(cd-s) *(CDR 6511)* – ('A'side) / But the trains run on time / What's it like to be hated.
(cd-s) *(CDRS 6511)* – ('A'side) / Church of the drive thru Elvis / But the trains run on time.

Jul 00. (c-s) *(TCR 6544)* **I CAN ONLY DISAPPOINT U / REPAIR MAN / MY IDEA OF FUN** 8 -
(cd-s) *(CDR 6544)* – (first 2 tracks) / Decisions decisions.
(cd-s) *(CDRS 6544)* – (first & third tracks) / Golden stone.

Aug 00. (cd/c/d-lp) *(527782-2/-4/-1)* **LITTLE KIX** 12 -
– Butterfly (a new beginning) / I can only disappoint U / Comes as no surprise / Electric man / Love is . . . / Soundtrack 4 2 lovers / Forgive me / Until the next life / Fool / We are the boys / Goodbye.

Nov 00. (c-s/cd-s) *(TCR/CDRS 6550)* **ELECTRIC MAN / I CAN ONLY DISAPPOINT U (Perfecto mix) / ELECTRIC MAN (acoustic)** 23 -
(cd-s) *(CDCHS 6550)* – ('A'side) / Drifters / Apartment.

Jan 01. (c-s) *(TCR 6553)* **FOOL / I'VE SEEN THE TOP OF THE MOUNTAIN** 28 -
(cd-s+=) *(CDRS 6553)* – Promises.
(cd-s) *(CDR 6553)* – ('A'side) / Fade in time / Black infinite space.

– compilations, etc. –

Oct 02. (d-cd) *Parlophone; (543150-2)* **ATTACK OF THE GREY LATTERN / LITTLE KIX** ☐ -

MANTARAY

Formed: Braintree, Essex, England . . . 1993 by the trio of CHRIS LATTER, bassist DAVE STANDEN and drummer SIMON. Despite vociferously denying any association with the New Wave Of New Wave scene, MANTARAY made their debut on 'Fierce Panda's celebrated 'Shagging In The Streets' EP back to back with THESE ANIMAL MEN and S*M*A*S*H. Soon making a name for themselves in the press with their rent-a-quote opinions, The JAM-loving neo-Mod throwbacks subsequently signed to the 'Dead Dead Good' label, debuting in late '94 with a couple of singles, 'INSOMNIAC'S DREAM' and 'ADORATION'. Dismissing mainstream party politics, the power Brit-pop trio instead took a more individualistic lyrical stance which nevertheless failed to mask the average quality of the songwriting on debut album, 'SOME POP' (1994). Only two further singles surfaced in as many years before MANTARAY signed a major record deal with 'Fontana', only to let down both fans and critics alike with comeback single, 'KNOW WHERE TO FIND YOU' and follow-up album, 'THE REDS AND THE BLUES' (1997). • **Note:** A different MANTARAY released the 'Numinous Island' CD for 'Silent' in October '95 (SR 9592CD).

MANTARAY (cont)

Album rating: SOME POP (*5) / THE REDS AND THE BLUES (*4)

CHRIS LATTER – vocals, guitar / **DAVE STANDEN** – bass / **SIMON** – drums

Dead Dead Good / not iss.

- Sep 94. (7"orange) *(GOOD 25)* **INSOMNIAC'S DREAM. / HARD**
  (cd-s+=) *(GOOD 25CD)* – Self centre.
- Oct 94. (7"blue) *(GOOD 26)* **ADORATION. / PAINFUL**
  (cd-s+=) *(GOOD 26CD)* – Sad.
- Nov 94. (cd/c/yellow-lp) *(GOOD CD/MC/LP 3)* **SOME POP**
  – Adoration / Alive & well / When you say yes / All you want / Insomniac's dream / Closet hetero / Greatest living soul / Bullet proof / Hide & seek / Up all night / Without doubt / If you were a girl / My own way / Jumped up.
- Feb 95. (7"red) *(GOOD 30)* **HIDE & SEEK. / HERE FOR THE RIDE**
  (cd-s+=) *(GOOD 30CD)* – (2 tracks).
- Apr 96. (7") *(GOOD 36)* **I DON'T MAKE PROMISES. / DEATH OF ME**
  (cd-s+=) *(GOOD 36CD)* – (1 track).

Fontana / not iss.

- Feb 97. (7") *(MAN 1)* **KNOW WHERE TO FIND YOU. / TIME WITH THE ANGELS**
  (cd-s+=) *(MANCD 1)* – Unstuck.
- May 97. (7") *(MAN 2)* **PATIENT MAN. / TRUST TO FATE**
  (cd-s+=) *(MANCD 2)* – Full circle.
  (cd-s) *(MANDD 2)* – ('A'side) / I know you too well / Pollen.
- May 97. (cd/c) *(534205-2/-4)* **THE REDS AND THE BLUES**
  – Know where to find you / I don't make promises / Always tomorrow / Look after myself / Just a ride / Something special / Everybody looks the same / Rise above it all / Blackburn / Behind the clouds / Patient man / Don't believe in me.

— the band have since split

MAPS OF JUPITER
(see under ⇒ MAGNETIC NORTH POLE)

MARBLES (see under ⇒ APPLES IN STEREO)

April MARCH

Born: ELINOR BLAKE, 21 Apr'65, New York City, New York, USA. MARCH's musical career took many twists and turns, through the styles of French sixties pop to nineties dance beats, mixed in with her dual career as a cartoon animator. After graduating from high school in 1983, which had included a life-altering school exchange in France, MARCH moved back to her home city and began work as a jobbing cartoonist with Archie Comics, and within three years had gained enough experience to be moulding an animated figure of MADONNA for her 'Who's That Girl' promo video. The following year her musical ambitions also came to fruition with the formation of the PUSSYWILLOWS, with two fellow females, LISA and er, LISA. The following year they issued their one and only album, 'SPRING FEVER', which showcased covers in an early sixties girl group styling. This led to the event of MARCH's small band singing with RONNIE SPECTOR at Madison Square Gardens in the winter of 1990. From a massive high, came the low; the breakup of the band the next year (although MARCH's animation work was still going strong). She was enlisted to work for 'The Ren and Stimpy Show', which resulted in a move to Los Angeles. Here her musical leanings once again came to the fore, as she began to record as APRIL MARCH. She released her debut solo single, 'VOO DOO DOLL' in 1992. Alongside this venture MARCH formed the SHITBIRDS, issuing their debut musical dropping in the form of 7", 'FLUNKY'. Following these minor successes, MARCH released her first solo debut LP, 'GAINSBOURGSION', which, as evidenced by the title, showcased her love of sixties Euro-pop and SERGE GAINSBOURG. A year later came SHITBIRDS' initial full-length set, 'FAMOUS RECORDING ARTISTS', which sadly also marked the disbanding of the outfit. But this did not seem to dent MARCH's musical ascendancy as she released her sophomore solo set, 'PARIS IN APRIL' (1996), and put together yet another group, the HAVES. This outfit saw their first LP, 'SUPERBANYAR', hit the Japanese record shops in 1997 on 'Nippen Columbia', while MARCH's solo work continued to see success with another two consecutive albums being issued by 'Sympathy For The Record Industry'. This took her up to the end of the decade and the issue of full-length outing, 'CHROMINANCE DECODER' on hip-hop production DUST BROTHERS' 'Ideal' records. • **Covered:** SHITBIRDS:- NOT OF THIS EARTH (Angry Samoans) / THERE WAS A TIME (Hard-Ons) / YOU SAID THAT (Vanda-Young) / BEEF BALOGNA (Lee Ving) / BABY WHAT'S NEW (Barry Houk).

Album rating: Pussywillows: SPRING FEVER! (*4) / Shitbirds: OH JOY! mini (*4) / FAMOUS RECORDING ARTISTS compilation (*5) / April March: CHICK HABIT mini (*6) / PARIS IN APRIL (*7) / SINGS ALONG WITH THE MAKERS (*6) / APRIL MARCH AND LOS CINCOS (*6) / LESSONS OF APRIL MARCH compilation (*3) / CHROMINANCE DECODER (*6)

PUSSYWILLOWS

APRIL MARCH – vocals / **LISA** – vocals / **LISA** – vocals

not iss. / Telstar

- Sep 88. (m-lp) *<TR 003>* **SPRING FEVER!**

— disbanded early in Feb '91, she sessioned for JONATHAN RICHMAN, etc

SHITBIRDS

— **APRIL SHITBIRD** – vocals / **PHIL SHITBIRD** – guitar / **REV. SCOTT SHITBIRD** – bass / **ULI SHITBIRDSKY** – drums / added later **CAESAR + RICHARD SHITBIRD** – bass

not iss. / Pop Llama

- 1992. (7"m) *<PL7-36>* **THEME FROM SHITBIRD / FLUNKY. / I WANT YOU**

not iss. / Sympathy F

- 1993. (10"m-lp) *<SFTRI 193>* **OH JOY!**
  – Theme from Shitbird / Oh joy / Not of this earth / There was a time / You said that / Beef balogna / Baby what's new / Scheissebird.
- 1994. (5") *<SFTRI 311>* **FASTER AND SHORTER. / UNTERSCHALL**
- 1994. (7"ep) *<SFTRI 312>* **split w/ SIMON & THE BAR SINISTERS**
  – Kickback 1812 / Canadian carwash / (other 2 by SIMON & THE BAR . . .)
- 1995. (7"; as THE HAVES) *<SFTRI 370>* **COAL BLACK. /**
- Feb 96. (cd) *<SFTRI 421>* **FAMOUS RECORDING ARTISTS**
  (compilation of singles)

— SHITBIRDS disbanded after above and APRIL formed The HAVES

APRIL MARCH

— had already become a solo artist

not iss. / Kokopop

- Jun 92. (7"ep/cd-ep) *<KOKO 10/+CD>* **VOO DOO DOLL**
  – Voo doo doll / Kooky / Stay away from Robert Mitchum / How to land a man / It's laughing.

— with **ANDY PALEY** – organ, percussion, etc / **JONATHAN RICHMAN** – guitar / **STEVE SAVITSKY** – bongos, drums / **FRANK MACCHIA** – saxophone / etc

Eurovision / not iss.

- Jan 94. (cd) **GAINSBOURGSION!**

French Sympathy F / Sympathy F

- Oct 95. (m-lp/m-cd) *<SFTRI 398/+CD>* **CHICK HABIT**
  – Laisse tomber les filles / Deux garcons pour une fille / Caribou / Temps de l'amour / Chanson de prevert / Tu mens / Cet air-la / Chick habit.
- Oct 96. (lp/cd) *<(SFTRI 456/+CD)>* **PARIS IN APRIL** Sep96
  – Chick habit / Poor Lola / While we're young / Brainwash (part 2) / Moto shagg / Land of go / Chanson de prevert / Laisse tomber les filles / Tu mens / Temps de l'amour / Pauvre Lola / Fille a la moto / Temps des yoyos / Chez les ye-ye.
  below MAKERS were her pseudonymous backing band
- Apr 97. (lp/cd) *<(SFTRI 434/+CD)>* **APRIL MARCH SINGS ALONG WITH THE MAKERS**
  – Dreams don't come true / I just might crack / Try to cry / Sometimes sometimes / Sad little bug / Explosion / I'm alone / Let him try / Bust out.

— now backed by the band, LOS CINCOS
- May 98. (lp/cd) *<(SFTRI 491/+CD)>* **APRIL MARCH AND LOS CINCOS**
  – Theme for the Lima cafe / Last train to Christmas / Olive green / Moon is blue / Some things just stick in your mind / Bebert / Winter cave / Last train to Christmas.

Edel / Ideal

- Nov 98. (cd) *<009>* **LESSONS OF APRIL MARCH** (compilation)
  – Kneesocks / Sugar / Garcon glacon / Theme from Lime cafe / Chick habit / Caribou / Olive green dictionary / Winter cave / Cet air la / Le temps de l'amour / Stay away from Robert Mitchum / Jesus and I love you.

— next was a collaboration with writers **BERTRAND BERGALAT** – guitar, multi + **PHILLIPE AUCLAIR** – guitar / + many on session

- Aug 99. (cd) *(0100082MAM) <810010>* **CHROMINANCE DECODER** Feb99
  – Garden of April / Sugar / Knee socks / Charlatan / Mignonette / Chrominance decoder / Garcon glacon / Mickey et Chantal / Pas pareil / Mon petit Ami / Mon petit cowboy / Martine / Ideal standard / Keep in touch / Superbagneres / Nothing new / Sugar / No parachute.
  (above was issued in 1998 Japan as 'SUPERBANYAIR')

MARINE RESEARCH
(see under ⇒ TALULAH GOSH; in 80's section)

MARION

Formed: Macclesfield, Manchester, England . . . 1992 by JAIME HARDING, TONY GRANTHAM and PHIL CUNNINGHAM, who had been together in numerous teenage bands since the mid-80's. Beefing up the sound with the rhythm section of JULIAN PHILLIPS and MURAD MOUSSA, MARION issued a one-off 1994 debut, 'VIOLENT MEN', for 'Rough Trade'. This led to 'London' records taking over the reins, the group going from strength to strength throughout '95 and the STEPHEN STREET/AL CLAY-produced album, 'THIS WORLD AND BODY' scraping into the UK Top 10. Trawling the same sub-SMITHS territory as the likes of GENE, HARDING and Co. enjoyed a brief period of singles success culminating in the UK Top 20 re-issue of 'SLEEP' zzz . . . However, JAIME's heroin and cocaine habit took its toll, the band's lengthy hiatus resulted in the difficult second – JOHNNY MARR-produced – album syndrome, in that of 'THE PROGRAM' (1998), selling poorly.

Album rating: THIS WORLD AND BODY (*6) / THE PROGRAM (*4)

JAIME HARDING (b. 1975) – vocals, harmonica / **TONY GRANTHAM** – guitar, piano / **PHIL CUNNINGHAM** – guitar / **JULIAN PHILLIPS** – bass / **MURAD MOUSSA** – drums, percussion

Rough Trade / not iss.

- May 94. (7") *(RT 319-7)* **VIOLENT MEN. / TOYS FOR BOYS**
  (cd-s+=) *(RT 319-3)* – Today and tonight.

London / Polygram

- Feb 95. (7") *(LON 360)* **SLEEP. / FATHER'S DAY** 53
  (12"+=/cd-s+=) *(LON X/CD 360)* – Moving fast.

Date	Format	Cat#	Title	Chart UK	Chart US
Apr 95.	(7"/c-s)	(LON 366)	**TOYS FOR BOYS. / DOWN THE MIDDLE WITH YOU**	57	-
	(cd-s+=)	(LONCD 366)	– Changed for the same.		

—— **NICK GILBERT** – bass; repl. PHILLIPS who joined ELECTRAFIXION

Date	Format	Cat#	Title	UK	US
Oct 95.	(7"yellow/c-s)	(LON 371)	**LET'S ALL GO TOGETHER. / LATE GATE SHOW**	37	-
	(cd-s+=)	(LONCD 371)	– The only way (live).		
Jan 96.	(7"red/c-s)	(LON/+CS 377)	**TIME. / CHANCE**	29	-
	(cd-s+=)	(LONCD 377)	– Let's all go together.		
Jan 96.	(cd/c/lp)	(<828695-2/-4/-1>)	**THIS WORLD AND BODY**	10	
			– Fallen through / Sleep / Let's all go together / Wait / The only way / I stopped dancing / All for love / Toys for boys / Time / Vanessa / Your body lies / My children. *(lp w/ free 7")*– VIOLENT MEN		
Mar 96.	(7"yellow/c-s)	(LON/+CS 381)	**SLEEP (remix). / WAITING FOR ON-ONE**	17	-
	(cd-s+=)	(LONCD 381)	– Violent men.		
	(cd-s)	(LOCDP 381)	– ('A'acoustic) / Wait (acoustic) / Time (acoustic).		
Feb 98.	(7")	(LON 403)	**MIYAKO HIDEAWAY. / SPEECHLESS**	45	-
	(cd-s+=)	(LONCD 403)	– We love everything.		
	(ext; cd-s)	(LOCDP 403)	– ('A'side) / Minus you / Promise Q.		
Apr 98.	(7")	(LON 409)	**SPARKLE. / PRESENT**		-
	(cd-s+=)	(LONCD 409)	– Journey to the centre / Miyako hideaway.		
	(cd-s)	(LONPD 409)	– ('A'side) / Psycho killer / Our place.		
Aug 98.	(cd/c)	(828994-2/-4)	**THE PROGRAM**		-
			– The smile / Miyako hideaway / Sparkle / Is that so? / What are we waiting for? / Strangers / The powder room plan / The program / All of these days / Comeback.		

—— disbanded in May 1999; JAIME continued with the new MARION while TONY formed CHALK

MARK FOUR (see under ⇒ CREATION)

MARS VOLTA (see under ⇒ AT THE DRIVE-IN)

MASTERS OF THE HEMISPHERE

Formed: Athens, Georgia, USA ... 1996 by lynch-pin members, SEAN RAWLS and BREN MEAD, with the addition of RYAN LEWIS. The former two had in fact met years earlier at high school, where they had been playing in a number of outfits such as EAT RICE ON FRIDAY and LINUS. They also found time to run a small imprint, 'Everybody's Wearing Them'. This partnership split for a short period as MEAD moved to New Mexico due to family commitments. Regrouping in Athens, the boys soon met up with 'Kindercore' label boss, LEWIS, who joined them for the birth of MOTH, although he was soon replaced on drums by JEFF GRIGGS (ex-MENDOZA LINE). Following the debut EP, 'GOING ON A TREK TO ICELAND', in the summer of 1997, the trio were bolstered by the introduction of ADRIAN FINCH. This release, like their ensuing eponymously-titled mini-LP, 'MASTERS OF THE HEMISPHERE' (1999), displayed their love of twee indie-pop stylings, showcasing their talent for the melodious song structures of this genre. Pushed forth by the ambitious nature of RAWLS and MEAD, MOTH released the concept LP, 'I AM NOT A FREEMDOOM', the following year – which was issued with a comic (the idea and music based itself within the environs of children's cartoons, with a battle of goodie and baddie creatures on an imaginary island). The sound was also heavily informed by the psychedelic musings of late sixties BEACH BOYS. A competent and well-thought out piece, the boys nevertheless turned towards a heavier, maturer pop style with their third full-length outing, 'PROTEST A DARK ANNIVERSARY' (2002).
• **Covered:** SECOND HAND NEWS (Fleetwood Mac).

Album rating: MASTERS OF THE HEMISPHERE mini (*6) / I AM NOT A FREEMDOOM (*6) / PROTEST A DARK ANNIVERSARY (*7)

SEAN RAWLS – vocals, guitar / **BREN MEAD** – vocals, guitar / **JEFF GRIGGS** – drums; repl. RYAN LEWIS

Date	Format	Cat#	Title	not iss.	Kindercore
Jun 97.	(7"ep)	<KC 012>	**GOING ON A TREK TO ICELAND**	-	
			– Bat / On the streets, the key.		

				not iss.	Happy Happy Birthday To Me
1998.	(7"ep)	<none>	**MAY**	-	
			– Silence / Raindrops / All you had to write.		

				not iss.	Gentlemen
1999.	(7")	<none>	**BETTER THINGS. / DIE MUSTAFA DIE**	-	

				not iss.	dcbaltimore 2012
1999.	(7"ep)	<DCB 004>	**PERMANENT STRANGER EP**	-	
			– Summertime, that's when the good times start / Permanent stranger / When people were younger / Time passes slowly / Chance of growing apart / Uncola.		

—— added **ADRIAN FINCH** – multi

				Kindercore	Kindercore
Sep 99.	(cd/lp)	<KC 026/+LP>	**MASTERS OF THE HEMISPHERE**		
			– West Essex / Billy Mitchell / Saucy foreign lass / Meteor / Everybody knows Canada / Map / She plays guitar / Your ship looks like a captain. *(UK-iss.Jul00; same as US)*		
Aug 00.	(cd/lp)	<KC 039/+LP>	**I AM NOT A FREEMDOOM**		
			– So what about Freemdoom / Who is this dog? / The dog who controls people's lungs / The new commotion / Gogar's roo / Freemdoom's lab / The new Freemdoom / The sun in the afternoon / Summer in Krone Ishta / Mal needs to talk about the things he wants to say / Mal's thores / Calm calm coma / The fearsome duo.		

				Cherry Red	Kindercore
Apr 02.	(cd)	(SDWR 1) <KC 073CD>	**PROTEST A DARK ANNIVERSARY**		
			– Anything anything / 200 heads / Sailboat kite / Local government / Take time / Rules of life / All your winning numbers / Give me something clearly / In the morning / The gauntlet / Summer with you. *(re-iss. Sep02; same)*		

—— the group split late in 2002

Eric MATTHEWS

Born: 12 Jan'69, Gresham, Portland, Oregon, USA. A one time student of the San Francisco Conservatory classical music college, MATTHEWS' first love was trumpet although his penchant for classic orchestral pop and his decision to take up the guitar eventually led him to the thriving alternative music scene in Boston, Massachusetts. There, he hooked up with SEBADOH's LOU BARLOW and BOB FAY, with whom he cut an obscure EP in 1993 under the name of BELT BUCKLE. Subsequently finding a musical foil in Australian ex-MOLES leader, RICHARD DAVIES, MATTHEWS found an outlet for his lush arranging/instrumental talent as one-half of the acclaimed duo, The CARDINAL. Although they only lasted one album – an eponymous 1994 effort – the publicity generated helped MATTHEWS secure a solo deal with Seattle label, 'Sub Pop'. Hardly a typical signing for the former bastion of grunge, MATTHEWS surpassed all expectations with his 1995 solo debut, 'IT'S HEAVY IN HERE', a darkly luxuriant sequence of exquisitely arranged and executed orchestral pop. Showcasing a breathy, wistful vocal style that frequently brought comparisons with NICK DRAKE, MATTHEWS showed himself to be a master pop craftsman, layering trumpets, chiming guitars and melancholy string flourishes in a manner reminiscent of past masters like BRIAN WILSON, VAN DYKE PARKS and the largely unsung ROBERT KIRBY (NICK DRAKE's string arranger on his first two albums). Despite boasting a more extensive array of guest musicians, follow-up set, 'THE LATENESS OF THE HOUR' (1997) lost little of the debut's focus or sense of continuity, consolidating MATTHEWS' position as grand master of modern baroque pop for the thinking indie fan. • **Covered:** A CERTAIN KIND (Soft Machine).

Album rating: IT'S HEAVY IN HERE (*8) / THE LATENESS OF THE HOUR (*7)

ERIC MATTHEWS – on usual instruments & vocals (also conducts orchestra & produces) musicians mostly **JASON FALKNER** – guitars, bass / **STEVE HANFORD** – drums

				Sub Pop	Sub Pop
Nov 95.	(lp/c/cd)	<(SP/+MC/CD 312)>	**IT'S HEAVY IN HERE**		
			– Fanfare / Forging plastic pain / Soul nation select them / Faith to clay / Angels for crime / Fried out broken girl / Lust takes time / Hop and tickle / Three-cornered moon / Distant mother reality / Flight and lion / Poison will pass me / Sincere sensation / Fanfare (reprise).		
Feb 96.	(7")	<(SP 319)>	**FANFARE. / LIDS, NAILS, SCREWS**		
	(cd-s+=)	<(SPCD 319)>	– A certain kind / Distant mother reality (S H mix).		

—— now with **JASON FALKNER** – guitar, bass, piano, drums / **WES MATTHEWS** – guitar, bass, piano / **GREGG WILLIAMS** – drums, percussion / **TONY LASH** – drums, percussion, piano / **SPOOKEY RUBEN** – bass / plus others **DON SCHWARTZ** – bass / **ANDREW SHAW** – sax / **STEVEN HANFORD** – drums / **STEVEN MATTHEWS** – acoustic guitar

Nov 97.	(lp/cd)	<(SP 404/+CD)>	**THE LATENESS OF THE HOUR**		
			– Ideas that died that day / My morning parade / Pair of cherry / To clear the air / Yes, everyone / Everything so real / Becomes dark blue / The pleasant kind / Gilded cages / dopeyness / Since the wheel free / Festival fun / No gnashing teeth.		

—— ERIC has been a little conspicuous by his absence

matt pond PA

Formed: Philadelphia, Pennysylvania, USA ... 1998 by lynch-pin member and former MEL'S ROCKPILE member, MATT POND, with the added assistance of JOSH KRAMER, JIM HOSTETTER, SEAN BYRNE and ROSIE McNAMARA-JONES. Debuting in '98 with 'DEER APARTMENTS', their skillful and wistful chamber pop got a proverbial pat on the back when they won a competition of un-contracted bands on the internet. MATT POND P.A. followed this success up with their LP, 'MEASURE' (2000), a record that heralded their undoubted talent and POND's skills as an arranger of a multitude of instrumentation including french horns, flutes, cellos and violins. Although tapping into similar veins like peers LULLABY FOR THE WORKING CLASS the group's sound never really showed the same kind of melancholic broodiness as this outfit, tending instead towards a slightly more extroverted poppier feel. The following year saw the mini-release, 'I THOUGHT YOU WERE SLEEPING' hit the shops, followed by touring duties with the likes of TED LEO and ASPERA AD ASTRA. By the middle of 2002, POND had changed his line-up retaining only HOSTETTER from the original and adding EVE MILLER (from the RACHELS), JIM KEHOE, MATT RAISCH and MIKE KENNEDY for the third full-length offering 'THE GREEN FURY' (2002). Albeit with a changed roster, the set proved to be one of their finest offerings, with standout tracks in the shape of 'PROMISE THE BITE' and 'CITY PLAN'. As well as putting out a further sound album 'THE NATURE OF MAPS' with MATT POND P.A. that same year, the busy POND also manged to find time to pen work for OXYGEN NETWORK.

Album rating: DEER APARTMENTS (*6) / MEASURE (*6) / THE GREEN FURY (*7) / THE NATURE OF MAPS (*6)

MATT POND – vocals, guitar, keyboards / **JOSH KRAMER** – guitar, bass / **ROSIE McNAMARA-JONES** – violin / **JIM HOSTETTER** – cello / **SEAN BYRNE** – drums, percussion

matt pond PA (cont) — THE GREAT INDIE DISCOGRAPHY — The 1990s

		not iss.	own label
1998.	(cd) **DEER APARTMENTS**	-	

- For sale / Fortune flashlight / Perfect fit / The lettuce / Stars and scars / Green pennies / Deer season / Electric / Corn stalks / Riser two / Possibilities of summer / Hunter / Bad idea / Full as full / Apology.

		File 13	File 13
Oct 00.	(cd) <*(FT 31)*> **MEASURE**		

- Measure 1 / The sound and the words / The hollows / Green grass / Measure 2 / Sugar house / New fall / Competition / Flying through the scenery / The price of spring / It's over.

— **MATT + HOSTETTER** added **MIKE KENNEDY** – drums

Apr 01.	(cd-ep) <*FT 37*> **I THOUGHT YOU WERE SLEEPING**	-	

- Other countries / Put your hair down / St. Andrew's / I thought you were sleeping / Sleeping.

— the trio added **JIM KEHOE** – guitar / **EVE MILLER** – cello (of RACHEL'S) / **MATT RAISCH** – bass

		not iss.	Polyvinyl
Jan 02.	(cd) <*PRC 48*> **THE GREEN FURY**	-	

- Canadian song / Measure 3 / Neighbor's new yard / City plan / Promise the bite / Silence / This is Montreal / A part of the woods / A new part of town / Jefferson / Crickets / It becomes night / Copper mine.

Oct 02.	(cd) <*PRC 52*> **THE NATURE OF MAPS**	-	

- Fairlee / No more / The party / Closer / New Kehoe NJ / Close map / No more (again) / Summer is coming / A well of tires / A million middhe fingers / Promise the party / Athabasca.

MAYDAY
(see under ⇒ LULLABY FOR THE WORKING CLASS)

MAZARIN

Formed: Philadelphia, Pennsylvania, USA ... 1999 by former AZUSA PLANE cohort, QUENTIN STOLTZFUS. After the release of the damaged psych rock outing 'WHEATS' (1999), MAZARIN's indie debut 'WATCH IT HAPPEN' was issued in 2000. Mixing GUIDED BY VOICES' reaming guitar-pop and YO LA TENGO's fuzzy psychedelic grunge, STOLTZFUS had created an energetic minefield of a record, encompassing the greatest song you've never heard, 'CHASING THE GIRL'. A year later and he was back, this time with a more instrumentally solid LP, 'A TALL TALE STORYLINE' (2001). The bleak winter must have turned STOLTZFUS somewhat, as his dark lyrics (song title: 'SUICIDE WILL MAKE YOU HAPPY') were coupled with distorted banjo, cello and eerie guitar effects. Not forgetting his high falsetto vocal parts, that, at points, sounded as if RUSH's GEDDY LEE was being thrust into a helium generator.

Album rating: WATCH IT HAPPEN (*5) / A TALL TALE STORYLINE (*6)

QUENTIN STOLTZFUS – vocals, guitars, keyboards, samples / with **BRIAN McTEAR** – guitar, bass, keyboards, producer / **JAY LAUGHLIN** – guitar / **MATT WERTH** – bass / **SEAN BYRNE** – drums, percussion, slide guitar, vocals

		Rocket Girl	Victoria
Dec 99.	(7"blue) *(RGIRL 11)* **WHEATS. / JOHN CAGE'S BOX OF FEATHERS**		-
Feb 00.	(cd) *(RGIRL 15CD)* **WATCH IT HAPPEN**		Jun00

- Chasing the girl / I should be sleeping / 500 repetitions once a week from 13 to 17 / Wheats / Henry Darger / Deed to drugs / Progress is lovely / December's coming / Sicily / Green lane / Watch it happen. <*(lp-iss.Jul00; RGIRL 15)*>

Jul 00.	(7") *(RGIRL 20)* **CHASING THE GIRL. / THE DIVINE LORRAINE**		-

		Rocket Girl	SpinArt
Sep 01.	(lp/cd) *(RGIRL 29/+CD)* <*SPIN 97*> **A TALL TALE STORYLINE**		

- Go home / Suicide will make you happy / What sees the sky / 2.22.1 / A tall tale storyline / To keep things moving / RJF variation / My favourite green hill / Bend / Flying arms for driving / Limits of language. *(re-iss. Feb02; same)*

Feb 02.	(7") *(RGIRL 34)* **SUICIDE WILL MAKE YOU HAPPY. / FLYING ARMS FOR DRIVING**		-

MAZINGA PHASER

Formed: Denton, Texas, USA ... 1995 by JESSICA NELSON, COLE WHEELER, MIKE THORNEBERRY, ERIC HERMEYER and WANZ DOVER. The highly experimental psychedelic chamber pop quintet spent much of their time in the studio working on the complex arrangements for their LP releases, exemplified by their debut, 'CRUISING IN THE NEON GLORIES OF THE NEW AMERICAN NIGHT' (1996). The set showcased their space rock credentials and was full of atmospheric sonic investigation through common pop instrumentation and electronica. Their sophomore LP, 'ABANDINALLHOPE', appeared the next year after another heavy session in the recording booth. It was not to be superceded for three years until the emergence of third full-length offering, 'DISSATISFIED CUSTOMERS OF HALLUCINATION'. In the hiatus period between their second and third albums lynch-pin member DOVER departed, leaving NELSON to take up the captaining role; the band's sound unfortunately suffered due to this as it waded into ever more tedious areas. DOVER went on to study electro-acoustic sound studies at the University of North Texas and also occupied his time with the outfit, The FALCON PROJECT.

Album rating: CRUISING IN THE NEON GLORIES OF THE NEW AMERICAN NIGHT (*8) / ABANDINALLHOPE (*7) / DISSATISFIED CUSTOMERS OF HALLUCINATION (*6)

JESSICA NELSON – vocals, keyboards / **MWANGA "WANZ" DOVER** – guitar, programming / **ERIC HERMEYER** – guitar / **COLE WHEELER** – bass / **MIKE THRONEBERRY** – drums

		not iss.	Aether
1996.	(lp) <*002*> **CRUISING IN THE NEON GLORIES OF THE NEW AMERICAN NIGHT**	-	

- New journeys / Grey area / Infinity for now / Katia (my enchantress) / Ling Ling and pepper / Dub sonic / Glass of glycerine / Alice Coltrane (it doesn't matter) / Third arm. *(UK cd-iss. Nov98 on 'Womb Tunes'; MAZPHA 007)*

		Idol	Idol
Apr 98.	(cd) <*(ID 011)*> **ABANDINALLHOPE**		Nov97

- A diamond in shrink wrap / Japanese space opera / (Infinity) for now / Jack Luther / Hot weird / Sterno sky / Duke and duchess / Dream of lost rivers / Kitten of the sleep / Valsalva headgear / (untitled).

— now without DOVER who released 'THE REVENGE OF SONIC SOULAR; as The FALCON PROJECT

Nov 99.	(cd-ep) <*ID 016*> **COUNTING BREATHS**	-	

- Counting breaths / Manhattan hoedown / Glass of glycerine.

Jul 00.	(cd) <*ID 019*> **DISSATISFIED CUSTOMERS OF HALLUCINATION**	-	

- Time is its own revenge / Dissatisfied customers of hallucination / Blue sparkle barchetta / Scattered, smothered and covered / Apoclypso / Alpha jerk / Wee-gee / Counting breaths / Afflux I / Afflux II.

— disbanded after above

MAZZY STAR

Formed: Santa Monica, Los Angeles, California, USA ... by Paisley Underground veteran, DAVID ROBACK and the young HOPE SANDOVAL. She had met him around six years previous after a friend, KENDRA SMITH (erstwhile member of RAINY DAY alongside ROBACK), had introduced the pair. SANDOVAL initially joined ROBACK's band, OPAL, a short-lived affair which came to a premature end after a tour in '87. The couple were reunited at the beginning of '89 as MAZZY STAR, a darkly languid, soft-VELVETS style project which fused haunting folk/country and dreamy psychedelia to mesmerising effect. The resulting album, 'SHE HANGS BRIGHTLY' (1990), surprised many in the rock world, although it was their 1993 set, 'SO TONIGHT THAT I MIGHT SEE' which cracked the US Top 50. An even more soporific set of stoned acoustic rock, the album even spawned a near Top 40 hit with the gorgeously melancholy 'FADE INTO YOU'. Fans had to wait another three long years before their next fix, 'AMONG MY SWAN' delighting the faithful if not exactly taking any risks. MAZZY STAR's inevitable split was eventually made official and the ever alluring SANDOVAL subsequently paired up with another figure long lost in the rock hinterlands, ex-MY BLOODY VALENTINE man COLM O'CIOSOIG. Naming themselves HOPE SANDOVAL & THE WARM INVENTIONS, the duo re-emerged in 2000 with a debut EP, 'AT THE DOORWAY AGAIN'. Fragile, featherlight and ever so slightly folky, these acoustic sketches, occasionally embellished with subtle stings, set the tone for 2001's full length 'BAVARIAN FRUIT BREAD', featuring covers such as The Jesus & Mary Chain's 'DROP' and Leonard Cohen's 'SUZANNE' as well as contributions from folk legend BERT JANSCH. • **Covers:** BLUE FLOWER (Slapp Happy) / I'M GONNA BAKE MY BISCUIT (McCoy) / I'M SAILIN' (Lawler) / FIVE STRING SERENADE (. . . Lee) / GIVE YOU MY LOVIN' . RAINY DAY covered I'LL KEEP IT WITH MINE (Bob Dylan) / SLOOP JOHN B (Beach Boys) / I'LL BE YOUR MIRROR (Velvet Underground). • **Trivia:** HOPE SANDOVAL guested on The JESUS & MARY CHAIN's 1994 single, 'SOMETIMES ALWAYS'.

Album rating: SHE HANGS BRIGHTLY (*6) / SO TONIGHT THAT I MIGHT SEE (*8) / AMONG MY SWAN (*6) / Hope Sandoval & The Warm Inventions: BAVARIAN FRUIT BREAD (*5) / Rainy Day: RAINY DAY (*6) / Opal: HAPPY NIGHTMARE BABY (*7) / EARLY RECORDINGS compilation (*6)

RAINY DAY

DAVID ROBACK – guitar, vocals, piano, bass (ex-RAIN PARADE) / **WILL GLENN** – violin, cello (of RAIN PARADE) / **MICHAEL QUERICO** – vocals, bass, guitar (of THREE O'CLOCK) / **MATT PIUCCI** – guitar (of RAIN PARADE) / **KENDRA SMITH** – bass, vocals + **KARL PRECODA** – guitar + **DENNIS DUCK** – drums (3 of DREAM SYNDICATE) / **ETHAN JAMES** – keyboards / + **SUSANNA HOFFS** + **VICKI PETERSON** – backing vocals (of BANGLES)

		Rough Trade	Llama
Apr 84.	(lp) *(ROUGH 70)* <*E-1024*> **RAINY DAY**		

- I'll keep it with mine / John Riley / Flying on the ground is wrong / Sloop John B. / Holocaust / On the way home / I'll be your mirror / Rainy day, dream away.

Jun 84.	(7") *(RT 140)* **I'LL KEEP IT WITH MINE. / HOLOCAUST**		-

OPAL

DAVID ROBACK / + KENDRA SMITH – bass

		One Big Guitar	not iss.
1986.	(12"ep) *(OBG 002T)* **NORTHERN LINE. / EMPTY BOTTLES / SOUL GIVER**		-

— split but left compilation below . . .

		not iss.	S.S.T.
Sep 87.	(lp/c/cd) <*SST/+C/CD 103*> **HAPPY NIGHTMARE BABY**	-	

- Rocket machine / Magick power / Revelation / A falling star / She's a diamond / Supernova / Siamese trap / Happy nightmare baby / Soul giver. <*(re-iss. May93; same)*>

— when KENDRA left ROBACK, he introduced friend **HOPE SANDOVAL** – vocals, guitar (ex-GOING HOME); disbanded sometime in '88

Nov 89. (cd/c/lp) (CD/C+/ROUGH 128) **EARLY RECORDINGS** — Rough Trade / not iss.
– Empty box blues / She's a diamond / My only friend / Empty bottles / Grains of sand / Brigit on Sunday / Northern line / Strange delight / Fell from the sun / Harriet Brown / Lullabye / All souls. (cd+=) – Hear the wind blow.

MAZZY STAR

ROBACK + HOPE SANDOVAL – vocals (ex-GOING HOME)

Rough Trade / Capitol

Apr 90. (cd/c/lp) (CD/TC+/R 158) <C2/C4 96508> **SHE HANGS BRIGHTLY** — / Feb91
– Halah / Blue flower / Ride it on / She hangs brightly / I'm sailin' / Give you my lovin' / Be my angel / Taste of blood / Ghost highway / Free / Before I sleep. (re-iss. May93 + Sep94 on 'Capitol' cd/c; CD/TC EST 2196)

Capitol / Capitol

Oct 93. (cd/c/lp) (CD/TC+/EST 2206) <98253> **SO TONIGHT THAT I MIGHT SEE** — 68 / 36
– Fade into you / Bells ring / Mary of silence / Five string serenade / Blue light / She's my baby / Unreflected / Wasted / Into dust / So tonight that I might see. (re-iss. Jun94; same)

Aug 94. (c-s) <58286> **FADE INTO YOU / HALAH** — - / 44
(cd-s) <58121> – ('A'side) / I'm gonna take my biscuit / Under my car / Bells ring.

Aug 94. (cd-s) (CDCL 720) **FADE INTO YOU / BLUE FLOWER / I'M GONNA BAKE MY BISCUIT** — 48 / -
(10") (10CL 720) – ('A'side) / Five string serenade / Under my car / Bells ring (acoustic)

—— The track 'TELL ME NOW' featured in the film 'Batman Forever' and was also on B-side of U2's 'Hold Me, Kiss Me, Kill Me!'.

Oct 96. (7"/cd-s) (CL/CDCLS 781) **FLOWERS IN DECEMBER. / TELL YOUR HONEY / HAIR AND SKIN** — 40 / -
(cd-s) (CDCL 781) – ('A'side) / Ride it on (live) / Had a thought.

Nov 96. (cd/c) (CD/TC+/EST 2288) <27224> **AMONG MY SWAN** — 57 / 68 Oct96
– Disappear / Flowers in December / Rhymes of an hour / Cry cry / Take everything / Still cold / All your sisters / I've been let down / Roseblood / Happy / Umbilical / Look on down from the bridge.

—— ROBACK has since went into production work for BETH ORTON

HOPE SANDOVAL & THE WARM INVENTIONS

SANDOVAL – vocals / + **COLM O'CIOSOIG** – guitar, bass, drums, keyboards (ex-MY BLOODY VALENTINE)

Rough Trade / not iss.

Dec 00. (12"ep/cd-ep) (RTRADES/+CD 008) **AT THE DOORWAY AGAIN**
– Around my smile / Charlotte / Sparkly / At the doorway again.

Oct 01. (cd/lp) (RTRADE CD/LP 031) <83201> **BAVARIAN FRUIT BREAD**
– Drop / Suzanne / Butterfly mornings / On the low / Baby let me / Feeling of gaze / Charlotte / Clear day / Bavarian fruit bread / Around my smile / Lose me on the way. (+ hidden track)

Apr 02. (cd-s; w-drawn) (RTRADESCD 042) **ON THE LOW**

Sep 02. (cd-s) (RTRADESCD 059) <83205> **SUZANNE / I THOUGHT YOU'D FALL FOR ME / THESE THINGS / FRIENDS OF A SMILE**

John McENTIRE (see under ⇒ TORTOISE)

McLUSKY

Formed: Cardiff, Wales ... 1999 by JONATHAN CHAPPLE, MATTHEW HARDING and ANDREW FALKOUS. Seen as a saviour of the British alternative rock scene when their debut LP, 'MY PAIN AND SADNESS IS MORE SAD AND PAINFUL THAN YOURS', appeared post-millennium, the trio had a lot of expectations on their young shoulders. From the title to the music, the band displayed their pop-punk credentials, combining both wit and integrity to create a competent first effort that fought back against the pseudo-angst of the American nu-metal invasion. The UK alternative music press liked what they heard on the whole, while the band were compared to pop-punk luminaries, The PIXIES. Emboldened by this support, the Welsh lads hired the help of veteran indie producer, STEVE ALBINI, to aid them with their sophomore album, 'McLUSKY DO DALLAS' (2002) ... a fine effort that through its noisy dynamics made up for where the member's individual skills may have been lacking.

Album rating: MY PAIN AND SADNESS IS MORE SAD AND PAINFUL THAN YOURS (*6) / McLUSKY DO DALLAS (*7)

ANDREW FALKOUS – vocals, guitar / **JONATHAN CHAPPLE** – bass / **MATTHEW HARDING** – drums

Fuzzbox / not iss.

Sep 00. (cd-ep) (FZBX 004) **RICE IS NICE**
– Rice is nice / White liberal on white liberal action / The Murphy syndrome / Provincial song.

Nov 00. (cd) (FZBX 006) **MY PAIN AND SADNESS IS MORE SAD AND PAINFUL THAN YOURS**
– Joy / Friends stoning friends / White liberal on white liberal action / Rice is nice / Flysmoke / Rock vs. single parents / She come in pieces / (Sometimes) I have to concentrate / When they come tell them no / You are my sun / Rods on crutches / Problems posing as solutions / Mi-o-mai / Medium is the message / World Cup drumming. (re-iss. Jun02; same)

Boobytap / not iss.

Aug 01. (cd-s) (BOOB 008CD) **WHO YOU KNOW / LOVESONG FOR A MEXICAN**

Too Pure / Too Pure

Nov 01. (7") (PURE 121S) **LIGHTSABRE COCKSUCKING BLUES. / NO COVERS**

Mar 02. (7") (PURE 124S) **TO HELL WITH GOOD INTENTIONS. / BEACON FOR PISSED SHIPS**
(cd-s+=) (PURE 124SCD) – The habit that kicks itself / No covers.

Apr 02. (cd/lp) (<PURE 117 CD/LP>) **McLUSKY DO DALLAS**
– Lightsabre cocksucking blues / No new wave no fun / Collagen rock / What we've learned / Day of the deadringers / Dethink to survive / Fuck this band / To hell with good intentions / Clique application form / The world loves us and is our bitch / Alan is a cowboy killer / Gareth Brown says / Cheses / Who you know.

Sep 02. (7") (PURE 130S) **ALAN IS A COWBOY KILLER. / RANDOM CELEBRITY INSULT GENERATOR**
(cd-s+=) (PURE 130SCD) – Exciting whistle-ah / Friends stoning friends.

MEDAL

Formed: Oxford, England ... 1998 by one-time DAISIES, JAMIE HYATT, MARK GILLES, DANIEL KEMP and SIMON 'LEMMY'. The aforementioned outfit had been around for about five years (releasing single 'IF I WAS BARRY WHITE'), MEDAL finally getting off the starting blocks after the introduction on keyboards of a songwriting partner for JAMIE, RICHARD BRINCKLOW. This became the start of the group's legacy; singles 'ORDINARY' and 'POSSIBILITY' becoming property of giant label 'Polydor'. These earned much publicised airplay from Radio One as well as journalistic comparisons to moody, influential rockers, THE VERVE. MEDAL's debut set, 'DROP YOUR WEAPON', appeared in the summer of '99 and, rather disappointingly, didn't live up to former expectations. Its spacy guitars, sci-fi ridden technics and broken lyrics rattled through the set like a brigade of dog-eared, slow-burning indieites on a rocketship to God knows where. A promotional tour with The BLUETONES and The DANDY WARHOLS only hyperbolated those Brit-pop sentiments, watering the eyes of audiences who expected something a little different. In other cases the set displayed a delicate and moody Sunday morning blue, the unappropriately-named 'GETTING UP' acquired the tenderness of say, WITNESS, who the band quite possibly owed a debt to. 'UP HERE FOR HOURS' (another single release) sported the king of lo-fi freedom (which influenced BLUR on their '13' album), where as opening track, 'IS YOUR SOUL IN YOUR HEAD', delivered soul-tingled melodies with a rasp, reverberating guitar. Now on their own imprint, 'El Producto' (named after one of their songs on 'DROP YOUR WEAPON'), MEDAL presented the public with a second set, 'STUNTMAN' (2001).

Album rating: DROP YOUR WEAPON (*5) / STUNTMAN (*5)

DAISIES

JAMIE HYATT – vocals, guitar / **MARK WILLIS** – guitar / **DANIEL KEMP** – bass / **SIMON 'LEMMY' WICKSON** – drums

Regal / not iss.

May 96. (7") (REG 6) **IF I WAS BARRY WHITE. /**

—— changed their moniker below

MEDAL

—— added **RICHARD BRINCKLOW** – keyboards

Polydor / A&M

Apr 98. (7") (569656-7) **ORDINARY. / JAGGEDY DOORS**
(cd-s+=) (569657-2) – Assault on interlude / Porno song.

Mar 99. (7"blue) (563560-7) **POSSIBILITY. / DR. HOOK**
(cd-s+=) (563561-2) – ('A'-Away team mix).

May 99. (7") (563822-7) **UP HERE FOR HOURS. / MARK FOLK**
(cd-s+=) (563823-2) – Drop your weapon.
(cd-s) (563825-2) – ('A'side) / In your soul in your headphones / A.P.E.

Jun 99. (cd/lp) (559902-2/-1) <7403> **DROP YOUR WEAPON** — / Apr00
– Is your soul in your head / Up here for hours / Monkey man / Outside / Visit your local taxidermist / Possibility / Ponceby Smythe / Porno song / El producto / Getting up.

Aug 99. (d7"ep/cd-ep) (561195-7/-2) **PORNO SONG EP**
– Porno song / Don't go there / Saturday night special / Get Spencer / Malfunction.
(cd-s+=) (561196-2) – ('A'-enhanced CD).

—— **OLLIE** – bass; repl. KEMP

El Producto / not iss.

Oct 00. (cd-s) (ELP 001) **FINGERPRINTS / BARRY 2 GARY / AIR FRANCE**

May 01. (cd-s) (ELP 003) **STUNTMAN / PICKSTRUM / BEHEMOTH BE HE BUTTERFLY**

Jun 01. (cd) (ELP 002CD) **STUNTMAN**
– Thermoking / Stuntman / Bernie winter gardens / Behemoth be he butterfly / Fingerprints / 10,000 / Daggers hill / Ambassador / Gloria victis / Drum spring.

MEDALARK 11 (see under ⇒ BODINES; in 80's section)

MEDICINE

Formed: Los Angeles, California, USA ... spring 1991 by BETH THOMPSON, BRAD LANER, JIM PUTTNAM, JIM GOODALL and ED RUSCHA (son of the pop artist of the same name). All were seasoned campaigners on the local music scene: LANER had previously formed New York noise experimentalists DEBT OF NATURE as well as the band

MEDICINE (cont)

STEAMING COILS (his CV also boasted a stint with SAVAGE REPUBLIC) while, in contrast, GOODALL had performed as part of a latter day line-up of the 'BURRITOS. After securing initial airplay on Rodney Bingenheimer's West Coast radio show, the group were signed to UK uber-indie label, 'Creation' ('American Recordings' in the States) for an eponymous debut EP. Attempting to combine the classic sounds of West Coast Americana with Krautrock and MBV-style guitar atmospherics, MEDICINE dispensed a pretty gloomy prescription with their inaugural album, 'SHOT FORTH SELF LIVING', in '92. The following year, the darkly addictive quintet mixed up the medicine, so to speak, on remix set, 'THE BURIED LIFE', although it would be another two years before the appearance of their second album proper, 'HER HIGHNESS' (1995). After their subsequent split, PUTNAM found a degree of success in both MAIDS OF GRAVITY and The RADAR BROS. With the creative juices and mutant melodies increasingly hard to come by, the aforementioned split was to serve the rampantly creative LANER especially well. No sooner had MEDICINE divided than he unveiled his experimental solo debut, 'A PERT CYCLIC OMEN', released under the ELECTRIC COMPANY moniker. He subsequently hooked up with former TOOL bass player PAUL D'AMOUR, REPLICANTS keyboardist, CHRIS PITMAN and FAILURE's GREG EDWARDS to release a one-off album, 'FREE MARS', under the name LUSK. While this project became increasingly bogged down amidst legal hassles, LANER concentrated on his own noised-up, fuzz-pop formula under the AMNESIA banner. The overlooked 'CHERRY FLAVOURED NIGHT TIME' (1997) and 'LINGUS' (1998) albums, the latter with string arrangments courtesy of BECK's pop, functioned as a kind of coda to LANER's indie rock career as he became increasingly enmeshed in the world of electronica. The likes of 'STUDIO CITY' (1998), 'OMAKASE' (1999), 'EXITOS' (2000) and 'SLOW FOOD' (2001) found the erstwhile guitar mangler enthralled by the possibilities of abstract electronic sound, progressively phasing out even regular rhythmic structures for an approach which bordered on the most austere form of esoteric minimalism. The confusingly (no doubt deliberately) titled 'GREATEST HITS' (2001), meanwhile, let a clutch of producers associated with LANER's label, 'Tigerbeat6', loose on the man's material.

Album rating: SHOT FORTH SELF LIVING (*7) / THE BURIED LIFE (*5) / HER HIGHNESS (*5) / Electric Company: A PERT CYCLIC OMEN (*6) / STUDIO CITY (*7) / OMAKASE (*6) / EXITOS (*5) / SLOW FOOD (*5) / 62-56 mini (*6) / Amnesia: CHERRY FLAVOR NIGHT TIME (*5) / LINGUS (*5)

BETH THOMPSON (b.12 Jun'67, St. Louis, Missouri) – vocals (ex-FOUR WAY CROSS) / **BRAD LANER** (b. 6 Nov'66) – vocals, guitar (ex-SAVAGE REPUBLIC, ex-STEAMING COILS) / **JIM PUTNAM** (b.30 Sep'67, Hollywood, Calif.) – guitar (ex-SDF, ex-BUS ENGINES, ex-MAGIC BEARD) / **ED RUSCHA** (b.14 Dec'68, Inglewood, Calif.) – bass (ex-SDF, ex-MAGIC BEARD, ex-PITA HAWKS, ex-MAIDS OF GRAVITY, ex-DUMB SPEEDWAY CHILDREN) / **JIM GOODALL** (b. 9 May'52, Burbank, Calif.) – drums (ex-FLYING BURRITO BROTHERS, ex-CANADIAN SWEETHEART, ex-ROGER McGUINN)

	Creation	Def American
Aug 92. (12"ep)(cd-ep) *(CRE 135T)(CRESCD 135)* **MEDICINE EP**		
– Aruca / Onion flower / The powder / World hello.		
Oct 92. (lp/cd) *(CRE LP/CD 142)* <45067> **SHOT FORTH SELF LIVING**		
– One more / Aruca / Defective / A short happy life / 5ive / Sweet explosion / Queen of tension / Miss Drugstore / The Christmas song.		
Feb 93. (12"ep)(cd-ep) *(CRE 141T)(CRESCD 141)* **5IVE E.P.**		–
– 5ive / Title baby II / Time 6 / Wrought.		

	American	Warners
Nov 93. (cd/lp) *(ARB CD/LP 5)* <45443> **THE BURIED LIFE**		
– The pink / Babydoll / Slut / She knows everything / Something goes wrong / Never click / Fried awake / Beneath the sands / Emmeline / I hear / Live it down / The earth is soft and white.		
Jan 94. (12"/cd-s) *(ARB 3 T/CD)* **NEVER CLICK. / WHILE / TIL I DIE**		
Jun 94. (12"ep/cd-ep) *(ARB 6 T/CD)* <45609> **TIME BABY 3** <US-title 'SOUNDS OF MEDICINE'>		
– Time baby 3 / Little Miss Drugstore / She knows everything / Little slut / Zelzah / Lime 6.		
Oct 95. (cd) *(74321 28757-2)* <43016> **HER HIGHNESS**		
– All good things / Wash me out / Candy Candy / Feel nothing at all / A fractured smile / Farther dub / Further down / Aarhus / Seen the light alone / Heads.		

the band went off on their own projects, PUTNAM to MAIDS OF GRAVITY and The RADAR BROS while LANER formed the ELECTRIC COMPANY and AMNESIA

	not iss.	Next Century
Jun 98. (12") <12-013> **I'M SICK. / BLEACH**	–	

ELECTRIC COMPANY

BRAD LANER – synthesizers, guitars

	not iss.	Warners
Aug 95. (cd) <43053> **A PERT CYCLIC OMEN**		
– P.A. intercomcycle / Polymeric accent / Elm crypt oceanic / A pert cyclic omen / Electro am cynic / Come circa plenty / Cyclic peematron / In compact celery / Cyclopean metric / I can cop my tercel.		

	not iss.	Trance Syndicate
Jun 97. (12"; split w/ FURRY THINGS) *<TR 58>* **KAHANEK INCIDENT, VOL.2**	–	

— added **KEN GIBSON** – keyboards, co-writer (on 3)

	not iss.	Polygram
Mar 98. (cd) *<524482>* **STUDIO CITY**	–	
– Arbor sirens / Star klang / Darken an' slobbering / Greenland / Throb ear / Second serve / Appendix / Born algebra skinned / Yard disturb / Soundcard.		

	VinComms.	VinComms.
Apr 99. (cd) *<(VC 166)>* **OMAKASE**		
– +++ / A cereal Syria / Lab errand / Andy Linear / Randy alien / Blare / Pha / ++ / Half tiger / Bald perhaps foamy / + / Minidisco / Ear chute / Surgical past.		

	Tigerbeat6	Tigerbeat6
Nov 00. (cd) *<(MEOW 005)>* **EXITOS**		
– Wednes 3 / Around / Entered / Archive 5 / Heart / Through / Octelcogopod / Thursa2 / Mentioned / Oufui / () / Knotted / Known / 170.		
Apr 01. (cd) *<(ZIQ 039)>* **SLOW FOOD**		
– A / Un pocky / Yresbo / Men's pocky / New imbalance / Mainly seconds / Watch yrself / Postwils / New type of funny / Culillo / Oiyaho / Forty-sixed / I'm in a Mazda / As am I / Que pena.		
(above issued on 'Planet Mu')		
Aug 01. (m-cd) *<(MEOW 019)>* **62-56**		Jul 01
– Sun stroke / Hyperion / Local doppler / Slamang / Test card / Simi valley radar / New hearing A / Something akin to living / New hearing B / Kidblesserfromblelectriccompany / Eye induction.		
Oct 01. (cd) *<(MEOW 032)>* **GREATEST HITS** (remixes by LANER & other artists)		
Oct 01. (lp) *<(MEOW 033)>* **GREATEST HITS COMPANION VOL.1**		
Oct 01. (lp) *<(MEOW 034)>* **GREATEST HITS COMPANION VOL.2**		

	Sun Moon	not iss.
Aug 02. (12"; by ELECTRIC COMPANY & INSIGHT) *(LDR 3006)* **RESPECT LIFE**		–

AMNESIA

BRAD LANER – guitars, etc / **MATT DEVINE** – guitar / **JOSH LANER** – drums

	not iss.	Supreme
Mar 97. (cd) *<531088>* **CHERRY FLAVOR NIGHT TIME**	–	
– Internal / Drained / Stay awake / If you come around / Wrong with me / Blind me / Undergarden song / Slice / Homing / Mind is slow / Cherry flavor night time.		

— **JUSTIN MELDAL-JOHNSEN** – bass; repl. DEVINE

	not iss.	Polygram
Jun 98. (cd) *<524527>* **LINGUS**	–	
– Love story / Drop down / Swimming lessons / Salty / Let you down again / I'll wait forever more / Train try / Sensual corgi / Handful of lies / Pastry dog / Mind your head / Turtle song / Leaving.		

ME FIRST AND THE GIMME GIMMES

Formed: Hollywood, California, USA ... 1996 by frontman SPIKE SLAWSON with the help of – on their debut full-set at least! – top hardcore punk friends FAT MIKE (of NOFX) on bass, JOEY CAPE (of LAGWAGON) on guitar, DAVE RAUN (also of LAGWAGON) on drums and CHRIS SHIFLETT (of NO USE FOR A NAME) on guitar. SPIKE was employed at MIKE's label, 'Fat Wreck Chords', and it was there the supergroup (of sorts!?) delivered a series of cover singles under the name of their associated songwriter ('DENVER', 'DIAMOND', 'BILLY', 'BARRY', 'ELTON', etc). Some of these were included on their funpacked debut album, 'HAVE A BALL' (1997), alongside work once(!) classic by JAMES TAYLOR, CARLY SIMON, JACQUES BREL – enough said. Not content with giving us one ball, they decided to give us two, by releasing a follow-up album, 'ARE A DRAG' (1999), in which this time they chose to destroy Broadway/Hollywood musicals (or just simply music!) • **Note:** The ME FIRST on 'Broken' records – who released a single 'Pinkie' and album 'Awful Friendly' (in '97) – were not the same outfit.

Album rating: HAVE A BALL (*5) / ARE A DRAG (*4) / BLOW IN THE WIND (*6)

SPIKE SLAWSON – vocals / **JOEY CAPE** – guitar (of LAGWAGON) / **CHRIS SHIFLETT** – guitar (of NO USE FOR A NAME) / **FAT MIKE** – bass (of NOFX) / **DAVE RAUN** – drums (of LAGWAGON)

	Fat Wreck Chords	Fat Wreck Chords
May 96. (7") *<(FAT 531-7)>* **DENVER**		Nov95
– Country road / Leaving on a jet plane.		
1996. (7") **BILLY**	–	
– Only The Good Die Young / Uptown girl.		
(above issued on 'Epitaph')		
May 97. (cd/c/lp) *<(FAT 554 CD/MC/LP)>* **HAVE A BALL**		
– Danny's song / Leaving on a jet plane / Me and Julio down by the schoolyard / One tin soldier / Uptown girl / I am a rock / Sweet Caroline / Seasons in the sun / Fire and rain / Nobody does it better / Mandy / Rocket man.		
Jun 97. (7") *<(HR 624-7)>* **DIAMOND**		
– Sweet Caroline / America.		
(above issued on 'Hopeless' records, below on 'Kung Fu')		
Jun 97. (7") *<(KFS 700-2)>* **PAUL**		
– Me and Julio down by the schoolyard / I am a rock.		
1997. (7") **BARRY**	–	
– Mandy / I write the songs.		
(above issued on 'Side One Dummy ...')		
Feb 99. (7") *<(DON 20)>* **ELTON**		
– Don't let the sun go down on me / Rocket man.		
(above issued on 'Honest Don's')		

— **JAKE JACKSON** – guitar (of SWINGIN' UTTERS) repl. CHRIS who later joined The FOO FIGHTERS

Apr 99. (cd/lp) *<(FAT 586 CD/LP)>* **ARE A DRAG**		
– Over the rainbow / Don't cry for me Argentina / Science fiction double feature / Summertime / Favorite things / Rainbow connection / Phantom of the opera song / I sing the body electric / It's raining on prom night / Tomorrow / What I did for love / Stepping out.		

ME FIRST AND THE GIMME GIMMES (cont)   THE GREAT INDIE DISCOGRAPHY   The 1990s

May 99. (7"ep) <(LK 219)> **GARF**
— The boxer / I am a rock.
(above issued on 'Lookout!', below on 'Alternative Tentacles')
May 99. (7") <(VIRUS 226)> **IN YOUR BARCALOUNGER**
— Fire and rain / You've got a friend.
Mar 01. (7") <(BYO 071)> **SHANNON**
— Runaway / Hats off to Larry.
(above issued on 'B.Y.O.')
Mar 01. (lp/cd) <(FAT 820/+CD)> **BLOW IN THE WIND**
— Blowin' in the wind / Sloop John B / Wild world / Who put the bomp / Elenor / My boyfriend's back / All my loving / Stand by your man / San Francisco / I only want to be with you / Runaway / Will you still love me tomorrow / Different drum.
Apr 01. (7") <(15841-7)> **STEVENS**
— Wild world / Father and son.
(above issued on 'Nitro')
May 01. (cd-ep) <50200> **TURN JAPANESE**
— The times they are a-changin' / The boxer / You've got a friend / Blowin' in the wind / Don't let the sun go down on me.
— also available in 7"box-set, 'BOB' which featured 'Blowin' in the wind' + 'The times they are a-changin''

MEICES

Formed: San Francisco, California, USA ... early 90's by JOE REINEKE, STEVE BORGERDING and drummer MARC TURNER. This college post-punk band joined forces when they dismembered themselves from a catalogue of similar troupes before embarking on a bedroom and basement tour with snot-rock buddies GREEN DAY. The MEICES issued the fuzz-pop/rock long player, 'GREATEST BIBLE STORIES EVER TOLD' (1992), which saw the band incorporate a mixture of raw garage rock and cheesy punk fledged from the RAMONES school-of-cool. The follow-up album, 'TASTES LIKE CHILDREN' (1994), was a refreshing change from the mindless American punk riff-o-ramas that had existed on the aforementioned debut. The set was backed by the splendid single, 'THAT GOOD ONE', which, was probably played on every college radio station through 1994's summer semester. Just as things were looking bright for the three menacing rascals, a shift to 'Polygram' laid pressure upon the shoulders of the MEICES when they forced out the uncertain 'DIRTY BIRD' album in 1996. Their accessible punk could still be heard throughout the set's stronger moments, with REINEKE's adolescent vocals carrying a whole host of previously unheard violins, mushy strings and weeping ballads that did not fit the group's character. The MEICES subsequently split after the album's release, REINEKE with JASON KREVEY, JEFF ROUSE and NABIL AYERS almost immediately forming ALIEN CRIME SYNDICATE. After a disastrous stint in L.A. (c. 1998), which resulted in a major label bust-up and a shelved album, ACS escaped to Seattle where they recorded and released the album, 'DUST TO DIRT' (2000). 'Warner Bros.' finally relinquished the master tapes of the aforementioned recording to 'Will' records) and 'FROM THE WORD GO' was also delivered in 2000. With MIKE SQUIRES on board to replace KREVEY, the REPLACEMENTS/URGE OVERKILL-type ACS released their next set, 'XL FROM COAST TO COAST' (2002). • **Covered:** HE'S WAITING (Sonics). • **Trivia:** The members of the group were exiled from Nebraska when they started a riot by throwing smoke bombs on stage during the main band's set.

Album rating: GREATEST BIBLE STORIES EVER TOLD (*5) / PISSIN' IN THE SINK compilation (*5) / TASTES LIKE CHICKEN (*7) / DIRTY BIRD (*5) / Alien Crime Syndicate: DUST TO DIRT (*5) / FROM THE WORD GO (*5) / XL FROM COAST TO COAST (*6)

JOEY REINEKE – vocals, guitar / **STEVIE BORGERDING** – bass / **MARC TURNER** – drums, vocals

	not iss.	Musical Tragedies
1992. (cd/c) <MT 205-2/-4> **GREATEST BIBLE STORIES EVER TOLD**	-	

– Alex put something in his pocket / La la land / Push you down / Don't let the soap run out / Near ya / This way / Pissin' in the sink / Didn't wanna / Number one / Hey little punker / 40 miles / (untitled). (UK-iss.Sep94 on 'eMpTy' cd/lp; EFA 11382-2/-1)

	not iss.	eMpTy
1990's. (7") <164> **DON'T LET THE SOAP RUN OUT. /**	-	

	not iss.	Word Of Mouth
1990's. (7") <004> **WORDS. / ONE HAND**	-	

	not iss.	Me and the Mouse
1993. (cd) **PISSIN' IN THE SINK** (compilation)	-	

– Pissin' in the sink / Hey little punker / This way / It's Oakland / Sweet dreams / Drunk / Cheap cig's / How bout' now / Where you get on / Bad posture couch.

	Deceptive	External
Nov 94. (7") (BLUFF 008) **THAT GOOD ONE. / CRASH '94 / ONE TIME ONLY**		-
Feb 95. (cd/lp) (BLUFF 013 CD/LP) <607-124008> **TASTES LIKE CHICKEN**		Nov94

– That good one / Daddy's gone to California / All time high / Light 'em up / Slide / Until the weekend / Lettuce is far out / The big shitburger / Untruly / Hopin' for a ride / Now / That other good one. (cd+=) – Don't let the soap run out / Alex put something in his pocket / Pissin' in the sink / Number one.

— new drummers **SHAWN TRUPEAU + APOLLO 9 + TOM GALBRAITH**

	London	Polygram
Feb 96. (cd/c/lp) <(828681-2/-4/-1)> **DIRTY BIRD**		

– Wow / Disenchanted eyes / Hold it / Uncool / Wings / Harry / Yeah / Monday mood / Helping me along / Hey fella / Rosies on the dole / Leave me alone / Well I . . .

— disbanded some time in '97

ALIEN CRIME SYNDICATE

JOEY REINEKE – vocals, guitar / **JASON KREVEY** – guitar / **JEFF ROUSE** – bass / **NABIL AYERS** – drums

	not iss.	American Pop
2000. (cd-ep) **SUPERNATURAL EP**	-	

	Collective Fruit	Collective Fruit
May 00. (cd) <(COL 025)> **DUST TO DIRT**		Mar00

– Take me to your leader / What I said / Outerspace / Some kind of way / I want it all / Tripping up to the clouds / Nothing beats the surf in / Do it again / Pimpin' the land / Here with you / Always running / Atmosphere. (re-iss. Mar02; same)

	not iss.	Will
Aug 00. (cd) <3367-2> **FROM THE WORD GO**	-	

– Take me to your leader / Land we made up / Supergirl / When I get home / Outerspace / Always running / Trippin' up to the clouds / In a dream / Atmosphere / Another time / Everything around / Earthgirls are cool / Revolving.

— **MIKE SQUIRES** – guitar, vocals; repl. KREVEY

	not iss.	V2
Jul 02. (cd) <27128> **XL FROM COAST TO COAST**	-	

– Ozzy / Break the record / My happy ending / Stronger / Figure it out / Not today / Softly / Ya blink it's / Careless / Is it U / We are.

Rose MELBERG (see under ⇒ TIGER TRAP)

MELODIE GROUP (see under ⇒ WINDMILLS)

MELODY UNIT

Formed: Seattle, Washington, USA ... late 1990's by KEVIN KELLY and MARK SALVADALENA along with three of their friends. The band was originally called URSA MINOR but they were forced to change it to The MELODY UNIT upon discovering they shared their moniker with another act. Early in their career the group experienced a number of personnel changes. Firstly there was the introduction of bass player TIM KAPPER and a keyboardist as replacements for the release of their 1998 debut EP 'WAX CYLINDER'. In the year between the release of the EP and their full length debut 'ODDS AGAINST TOMOROW', the group had parted company with the keyboard player and recruited singer JESSICA FOLSOM and guitarist DAVID WENTWORTH. The inclusion of a female vocalist and second guitarist afforded the album a greater depth and tonal range than that which had appeared on the previous EP. The album was a mixture of layered instrumental and vocal led pop songs in the same vein as shoegazing bands such as RIDE and MY BLOODY VALENTINE. A second, more impressive album 'CHOOSE YOUR OWN ADVENTURE' followed in 2001.

Album rating: ODDS AGAINST TOMORROW (*5) / CHOOSE YOUR OWN ADVENTURE (*7)

KEVIN KELLY – vocals, guitar, keyboards / **TIM KAPPERT** – bass / **MARK SALVADALENA** – drums, percussion / **PETER LYNCH** – keyboards / added **DAVID WENTWORTH** – guitar

	not iss.	unknown
1998. (7"ep) **WAX CYLINDER EP**	-	

— disgarded LYNCH for new guest vocalist **JESSICA FOLSOM**

	not iss.	101
1999. (cd) <001> **ODDS AGAINST TOMORROW**	-	

– Nutation / The fugue / With the domestics / Spy song / Daffodil 11 / Campfire autopsy / Theme from frolic / Doc Ellis / The hallucinogenic toreador / Echovirus.

	not iss.	Hidden Agenda
2000. (7") **KONA SONG. / SNOQUALMIE**	-	
2001. (cd) <27> **CHOOSE YOUR OWN ADVENTURE**	-	

– Suite for Caesar / Go (or not go) / Kona song / April New Year / Prepare the juggernaut / Nine / Welcome back tomorrow / Snoqualmie / Nutation 1.

MELONS (see under ⇒ FAT TULIPS)

MEL-O-TONES (see under ⇒ WALKING SEEDS)

MELT (see under ⇒ HAGAR THE WOMB; in 80's section)

MELT-BANANA

Formed: Osaka, Japan ... 1992 by lead singer YASUKO O, guitarist AGATA and bassist RIKA. From the same stable as lunatic noise-core experimentalists The BOREDOMS, MELT BANANA have been scaring the crap out of audiences and listeners since their incarnation on their debut 'SPEAK SQUEAK CREAK' (1995). After signing to 'Skin Graft' in 1996 experimental producers STEVE ALBINI (of SHELLAC) and JIM O'ROURKE (GASTR DEL SOL) stepped in to help MELT-BANANA, recording and mixing the album 'SCRATCH OR STITCH' (1996), in Chicago. Literally a melting pot of noise, this brilliantly arranged and frantically recorded noise-epic added another experimental classic to Japan's back catalogue of madness (MERZBOW metallers, etc). They subsequently delivered 'CHARLIE' (1998) before re-releasing their cassette-only DIY introduction set 'CACTUSES COME IN (THE) FLOCKS' (recorded in 1994 for 'Chocolate Monk', re-issued in '99). A live album surfaced in 1999 entitled 'MXBX 1998: 13,000 MILES AT LIGHT VELOCITY', which showcased the group's furious live performance – one which was of legendary status by this point. 'TEEN SHINY' (2000) kept their momentum high, while 'Simpsons' creator Matt Groening recently cited them as one of the most interesting groups who are currently playing music. He even invited them to perform at the US version of indie festival 'All Tomorrow's Parties'. ALBINI also booked them for a heart-stopping performance when he curated the British equivalent in 2002.

Album rating: CACTUSES COME IN (THE) FLOCKS (*5) / SPEAK SQUEAK CREAK (*5) / SCRATCH OR STITCH (*6) / CHARLIE (*4) / MXBX 1998: 13,000 MILES AT LIGHT VELOCITY (*5) / TEEN SHINY (*5)

YASUKO ONUKI – vocals / **AGATA ICHIRO** – guitar / **RIKA HAMAMOTO** – bass / **TOSHIAKI SUDOH** – drums

Chocolate Monk / not iss.

1994. (c) **CACTUSES COME IN (THE) FLOCKS**
– Just grub & run / Talk like pop / Shining hatcher / F pt.1 / To the core / F pt.2 / Shuuuuuuuuuuu . . . / Bunny wasted a month waiting / Party-hat / Shouting about love / Sonic turtle / Bored elephant / Up and down, 1, 2, 3 . . . / 1 to 11 / Dried up water park / How to say "rip them off". repeat after me / Interval . . . / Locoweed in the bottle / Ketchup-mess / We love choco-pa! / No way to hear / We had tails in the old days / So far so bad so what? / Frog swims the river down giggling / I hate it! (long version) / Who cares? / Fmfyyf / Pie war / Ants living in a narrow box / Crayfish song / 6 feet long for her neck / Picnic with panic (long version). (*<cd-iss. Sep99/Nov99 on 'A-Zap' cd/lp; AZCD/AZLP 02>*)

not iss. Charnel

1994. (7"ep) <CHS 5> **HEDGEHOG** – Japan
– Stick out / So unitilial rule / Mind thief / Screw, loose / Scrubber / Pierced eye.

not iss. Skingraft

1994. (7"m) <GR 24> **IT'S IN THE PILCASE. / RUSH & – >WARP / PICNIC IN PANIC** – Japan

not iss. H.G. Fact

1994. (7"ep) <HG 024> **split with GOD IS MY CO-PILOT** – Japan
– (GOD IS MY PILOT track) / Ketchup-mess / First defy / Iguana in trouble.

1995. (7"ep) <HG 042> **split with DISCORDANCE AXIS** – Japan
– (six DISCORDANCE AXIS tracks) / Buddhism core / hangnail (let it go) / No one wants next one / Sicklist on fire / One dimentional / Not D. but M, also S.

not iss. Anti-Music

1995. (7"ep) <none> **split with PENCILCHECK** – Japan
– Mind thief (live) / P-pop-slop (live) / (PENCILNECK tracks).

not iss. Nux Organisation

Aug 95. (cd) <9> **SPEAK SQUEAK CREAK**
– Tail in garbage (Tedepake) / R.R.AGG. / In X out = bug / Scrubber / So unifial rule / Dust head / Teaspoon of salt / Stick out / Mouse is a biscuit / 55 hands need to cut down / P-pop-slop / Smell the medicine / Switch / P.B.D. / Mind thief / Chicken headed racoon dog / Cry for more fish / Screw loose / Cook cool Kyau Kuru / Scissor quiz / Too many to dispose / Blandished hatman / Cut off / Pierced eye. (*UK-iss.May01 on 'A-Zap' cd/lp; AZ 04 CD/LP*)

Skingraft Skingraft

Apr 96. (lp/cd) (<GR 34/+CD>) **SCRATCH OR STITCH**
– Plot in a pot / Scratch or stitch / Sick zip everywhere / Disposable weathercock / Ten dollars a pile / Ketchup-mess / Buzzer #P / Rough dogs have bumps / Iguana in trouble / It's in the pillcase / Test: Ground 1 / Zoo, no vacancy / A finger to hackle / Type B for me / His name is Mickey (at last she got him . . .) / Back to the womb / I hate it / What do you slaughter next? / Eye-Q trader / Dig out! / Contortion out of confusion / Pigeons on my eyes (go to bed!!).

not iss. Fire Inc.

Jun 96. (10"ep) **MELT-BANANA / STILLUPPSTEYPA split** – Japan
– Bad gut missed fist / It's not my fault / Neck on me / Stop the cook-cu test / No doubt / Scooped brain in a cup / Capital 1060 / How to parlare / I say "shoot!" / Minus-minus-to one / Call me please – 6824 / Popsy teeth in red / Blackout screened / To be continued? / STILLUPPSTEYPA: Important anti-art dances.

not iss. Destroy All Music

1996. (7"ep) <MZG 3253> **split with TARGET SHOPPERS** – Japan
– Making fuss, fuss, fuss / Turtle vs. bunny (who won?) / Pig to dog / Bird-like monkey in cave, singing in drops / (others by TARGET SHOPPERS).

not iss. Gentle Giant

1996. (7") <GG 703> **$10 A PILE (ax version)** – Japan

Slap A Ham / Slap A Ham

Oct 97. (7"ep) <(SAH 39)> **ELEVENTH**
– Wedge / Seesaw semiology / Cough coughed coughing / Q for quinine / Bird like monkey part 2 (calling on the cliff) / Least clipper / Baby buggy spitted / Drill the dentist.

– also split records w/ PLAINFIELD + XEROBOT

not iss. H.G. Fact

1998. (7"ep) <HG 097> **DEAD SPEX** – Japan
– Dead spex / Sonic brain burst / Ethar twisted / Shoot the Moon.

not iss. Kool Pop

1998. (7") **WREST THE FIST (JUST FOR REFLECTION). / (other by KILLOUT TRASH)** – Japan

A-Zap / A-Zap

Oct 98. (cd/lp) (<AZCD/AZLP 01>) **CHARLIE**
– Introduction for Charlie / Circle-Jack (chase the magic words, lego lego) / Spathic!! / Tapir's flown away / F.D.C. for short / Taen taen taen / Cannot / Area 877 (Phoenix mix) / Giggle on the stretcher / Section eight / Drug store / Stimulus for revolting virus / Excess / Chipped zoo on the wall, wastes in the sky . . .

Tzadik Tzadik

Jan 99. (cd) (<TZACD 7219>) **MXBX 1998: 13,000 MILES AT LIGHT VELOCITY (live)** Feb99
– Scratch or stitch / R.R.AGG. / Wedge / Seesaw semiology / Circle-Jack (chase the magic words, ...) / Sick zip everywhere / Disposable weathercock / Mind thief / Blandished hatman / Ihuana in trouble / Tapir's flown away / His name is Mickey (at last she got . . . .) / We love Choco-Pa / Some kind of I.D. / Stick out / Scrubber / Screw loose / So unfilial rule / Spathic! / Picnic in panic / It's in the pillcase / Surfin' USA / Bad gut missed fist / Ketchup-mess / Plot in a pot.

A-Zap A-Zap

Nov 00. (cd/lp) <AZ 03 CD/LP> **TEENY SHINY**
– Free the bee / Flash cube, or eyeball / Lost in mirror / First contact to Planet Q / Warp, back spin / Third attack / Cub, not cube / Flip and hit / Bright splat (red point, black dot) / Skit closes, windy / Moon flavor.

not iss. Passacaglia

2001. (8"ep) **split with THREE STUDIES FOR A CRUCIFIXION** – Japan
– Who did it? who dig it? / Dog in lost / 2 knees / Puddle float / Quite free / And I . . . / (2 by THREE STUDIES FOR A CRUCIFIXION).

MELYS

Formed: Betws-y-Coed, Conwy, Wales . . . mid 90's when vocalist ANDREA PARKER and guitarist PAUL ADAMS bet £10 they couldn't sing or write electronic music; the jury was out until the release of their debut EP, 'FRAGILE', in 1996. Having been joined by GARETH HUSBAND and CARYS JONES, The MELYS (pronounced "Melisth" and meaning sweet) released another 45, 'CUCKOO', while the track 'CYSUR', featured on 'Ankst' label's V/A EP compilation, 'SC4 Makes Me Want To Smoke Crack Volume Two'. John Peel and Mark Radcliffe loved them, playlisting their 'Arctic' debut single 'DIWIFR' (pronounced "Dewither" – 'having no wires'); they signed the new contract on top of Snowdon. Electro-pop fusing both Welsh and English lyrics – think YOUNG MARBLE GIANTS and CAN – they delivered inaugural set, 'RUMOURS AND CURSES' (1998), before changing labels again, this time to 'Sylem'. The bitter/sweet EP 'BABY TORNADO' was issued the following year, while sophomore set, 'KAMIKAZE' (2000), delivered more of the same treatments. The MELYS are still going strong and with the release of CD-single, 'SO GOO', it looks bright for them in 2003.

Album rating: RUMOURS AND CURSES (*7) / KAMIKAZE (*6) / SUIKERSPIN compilation (*7)

ANDREA PARKER – vocals / **PAUL ADAMS** – guitar / **CARYS JONES** – keyboards / **GARETH HUSBAND** – drums

Ankst not iss.

Dec 96. (12"ep/cd-ep) (ANKST 072/+CD) **FRAGILE**
– Let yourself scream / Noeth / Puppet / Adeiladu fi.

Apr 97. (7") (ANKST 075) **CUCKOO. / NI DDISGYNNA'R ADERYN**
(cd-s+=) (ANKSTCD 075) – Fried.

Arctic not iss.

Mar 98. (7") (FROST 104) **DIWIFR. / IN LOVE WITH DANIELLE STEEL**
(cd-s+=) (FROST 104CD) – Paper, stone, scissors.

Jun 98. (cd) (KOLD 102CD) **RUMOURS AND CURSES**
– Achilles heel / Diwifr / Acid queen / Painfully thin / Hatchesput / Fade away (for the last time) / Lemming / When you put Leonard Cohen on / Ambulance chaser / Misunderstand me / Hope you cry yourself to sleep / Martyroshka.

Aug 98. (7") (FROST 106) **LEMMING. / WHEN THE SUN WENT OUT**
(cd-s+=) (FROST 107CD) – Hedfan.

Nov 98. (7") (FROST 107) **AMBULANCE CHASER. / YOUR 'FUCK ME' EYES**
(cd-s+=) (FROST 107CD) – ('A'-meatwagon mix).

Sylem not iss.

Jun 99. (cd-s) (SYLEMCD 001) **BABY TORNADO / ELENYA / PENYSGAFN**

Nov 99. (cd-ep) (SYLEMCD 002) **SLAGGING OFF TOURISTS E.P.**
– Disco pig / Mae'n amser I newid / Porn myself / Chasing again.

May 00. (cd) (SYLEMCD 004) **KAMIKAZE**
– Protect and survive / Porn myself / Then there was one / Sumimasen / Lullaby / You should have been there / Baby tornado / Magneswim / Tiny bombs / Waiting to fall / Dirty whore / Can y gegin.

Nov 00. (cd-s) (SYLEMCD 007) **UN DARLLENWR LWCUS / ALL PLAYED OUT / BEAUTIFUL BREAKDOWN**

May 01. (7") (SYLEM 008) **I DON'T BELIEVE IN YOU. / (other track by SEEDLING)**

Nov 01. (cd-s) (SYLEM 009) **CHINESE WHISPERS / WATERCOLOUR / GWERTHPAWR**

Nov 02. (cd-s) (SYLEM 011) **SO GOO**

– released comeback set early 2003

– compilations, etc. –

Feb 02. (cd) *Transformed Dreams;* (DREAM 20) **SUIKERSPIN**
– Disco pig / You should have been there / I don't believe in you / Chinese whispers / Baby tornado / Un darllenwr lwcus / Cuckoo / Puppet / Porn myself / All played out / Mae'namser I newid'.

ME ME ME (see under ⇒ ELASTICA)

Ric MENCK (see under ⇒ VELVET CRUSH)

MENSWE@R

Formed: Camden, London, England . . . 1994 by JOHNNY DEAN, CHRIS GENTRY and STUART BLACK, who subsequently completed the line-up with SIMON WHITE and TODD PARMENTER (the latter being replaced by MATT EVERITT in 1994). The following year, they scored their first of three major UK hits with the WIRE-sounding, 'DAYDREAMER'. Other influences of BLUR and the MONKEES were apparent on the other two 'STARDUST' and 'SLEEPING IN', both taken from the Top 10 album, 'NUISANCE' (1995). However, two further chart appearances with 'BEING BRAVE' and 'WE LOVE YOU' (both in '96) were the last with EVERITT, who has since been replaced by former roadie, TUD. • **Trivia:** CHRIS GENTRY is (still?) the boyfriend of DONNA from ELASTICA.

Album rating: NUISANCE (*6)

JOHNNY DEAN (b.12 Dec'71) – vocals / **SIMON WHITE** – guitar, vocals / **CHRIS GENTRY** (b.23 Feb'77) – guitars / **STUART BLACK** – bass, acoustic guitar / **MATT EVERITT** – drums, percussion; repl. TODD PARMENTER

		Laurel-London	London
Apr 95.	(7"/cd-s) *(LAU/+CD 4)* **I'LL MANAGE SOMEHOW. / SECONDHAND**	49	-
Jun 95.	(7"/c-s) *(LAU/+MC 5)* **DAYDREAMER. / GENTLEMAN JIM**	14	-
	(cd-s+=) *(LAUCD 5)* – Around you again.		
Sep 95.	(7"/c-s) *(LAU/+MC 6)* **STARDUST. / DAYDREAMER (dub dreamer)**	16	-
	(cd-s+=) *(LAUCD 6)* – Back in the bar / Satellite.		
Oct 95.	(cd/c/lp) *(<828 676-2/-4/-1>)* **NUISANCE**	11	-
	– 125 West 3rd Street / I'll manage somehow / Sleeping in / Little Miss Pinpoint eyes / Daydreamer / Hollywood girl / Being brave / Around you again / The one / Stardust / Piece of me / Stardust (reprise). *(cd re-iss. Mar00; 8573 81951-2)*		
Nov 95.	(7"/c-s) *(LAU/+MC 7)* **SLEEPING IN. / SUNDAY DRIVER**	24	-
	(cd-s+=) *(LAUCD 7)* – Now is the hour / 26 years.		
Mar 96.	(7") *(LAU 8)* **BEING BRAVE. / PUBLIC IMAGE**	10	-
	(cd-s+=) *(LAUCD 8)* – Sunlight on the moon / This will be our year.		
	(cd-s) *(LAUDP 8)* – ('A'side) / I'll manage somehow (live) / Daydreamer (live) / Stardust (live).		
Aug 96.	(c-s) *(LAUMC 11)* **WE LOVE YOU / CRASH**	22	-
	(cd-s+=) *(LAUCD 11)* – Phat kid music (demo) / Hanging in the blue sky (demo).		
	(cd-s) *(LAUDP 11)* – ('A'side) / The one (live) / Sleeping in (live) / Little Miss Pinpoint eyes (live).		

— **TUD** – drums (ex-roadie) repl. EVERITT (to MONTROSE AVENUE)

MERCURY PROGRAM

Formed: Gainseville, Florida, USA ... August 1997 by SANDER TRAVISANO, TOM RENO and DAVE LEBLEU. MERCURY PROGRAM's sound came from the experimental post-rock canon a la TORTOISE and the COCTAILS, although leaning towards more noise than the feedback orientated stylings associated within this genre. Hitting out with the debut 7", 'LIGHTS OUT IN GEORGIA', the group followed this up with their eponymously-titled inaugural LP, 'MERCURY PROGRAM' (1999). Garnering the attention of indie label 'Tiger Style', the band – with new recruit in the shape of WHITNEY TRAVISANO – quickly followed up their opener with the sophomore album, 'FROM THE VAPOR OF GASOLINE' (2000). This was a fairly decent set, although not really catching the band in their stride. The ensuing mini-set, 'ALL THE SUITS BEGAN TO FALL OFF' (2001), saw the band begin to have more confidence in their sonic investigations via more skilled use of their tools. Their musical star continued in the ascendancy with their third full-length offering, 'A DATA LEARN THE LANGUAGE' (2002), a record which witnessed the band ditching vocals and looking towards electronica to fill the gap on this jazz tinged number; they were also ably assisted by producer Andy Baker.

Album rating: MERCURY PROGRAM (*5) / FROM THE VAPOR OF GASOLINE (*5) / ALL THE SUITS BEGAN TO FALL OFF mini (*7) / A DATA LEARN THE LAUNGUAGE (*6)

TOM RENO – vocals, guitar, vibraphone / **SANDER TRAVISANO** – bass, drums / **DAVID LEBLEU** – drums, vibraphone

		not iss.	Boxcar
1998.	(7") **LIGHTS OUT IN GEORGIA.** /	-	
1998.	(7") split w/ **VERSAILLES**	-	
Jul 99.	(cd) **MERCURY PROGRAM**	-	
	– In from the sea / Travelling at night / Over this land / From Athens to Rome / Childers / This hits home / Miles among miles / Southwest.		

— added **WHIT TRAVISANO** – keyboards, vibraphone

		Tiger Style	Tiger Style
Jun 00.	(cd) *<(TS 003)>* **FROM THE VAPOR OF GASOLINE**		May00
	– The sea is in here / Re-inventing a challenge for machines / Leaving Capitol City for good / Nazca lines of Peru / Every particle of the atmosphere / From the vapor of gasoline / Fastest way through the south / Down on your own lung / The vortex east / Highways like veins.		
Apr 01.	(m-cd) *<(TS 013)>* **ALL THE SUITS BEGAN TO FALL OFF**		
	– The secret to quiet / There are thousands sleeping in peace / Marianas / Undiscovered genius of the Mississippi Delta / A delicate answer.		
Sep 02.	(cd) *<(TS 029)>* **A DATA LEARN THE LANGUAGE**		
	– Tequesta / Fragile or possibly extinct / Slightly drifting / Egypt / To/from Iceland / You yourself are too serious / Gently turned on your head / Sultans of el Sur.		

MERCURY REV

Formed: Buffalo, New York, USA ... 1988 by JONATHAN DONAHUE, DAVID BAKER, GRASSHOPPER (aka SEAN MACKIOWIAK), DAVE FRIDMANN, JIMY CHAMBERS and SUZANNE THORPE, who claimed they had all met while attending a psychiatric hospital. Admittedly, their sound, which came about by playing their own soundtrack to nature TV programmes! ('VERY SLEEPY RIVERS' indeed) was certainly deliciously deranged enough for this explanation of their secret history. Just over two years of rehearsals passed (DONAHUE, co-producer FRIDMANN and GRASSHOPPER were part-time members of FLAMING LIPS and utilised some spare studio time), before they finally surfaced with the mini-lp, 'YERSELF IS STEAM' (1991). Perhaps most immaculate marriage of searing noise and crystalline pop ever committed to vinyl, this freaky guitar-angst rock classic mixed up psychedelia, noise, film dialogue and exhilarating experimentation in a way only previously matched by The FLAMING LIPS; other indie influences were also apparent (i.e. BIRTHDAY PARTY, STUMP, VERY THINGS and MY BLOODY VALENTINE). The inspired opening salvo of 'CHASING A BEE', 'SYRINGE MOUTH' and 'CONEY ISLAND CYCLONE', alone was enough to give the album a resounding thumbs-up by the British press and record buying public alike. Later that year, the 'CAR WASH HAIR' EP/track (recorded with DEAN WAREHAM of GALAXIE 500), further convinced commentators of MERCURY REV's volatile genius although squabbling and widely publicised, wildly unpredictable live shows led to break-up rumours. These were subsequently quashed when the band were snapped up by 'Beggars Banquet', a follow-up album, 'BOCES' (1993), carrying on in the established schizophrenic mould but too often straying into wanton self-indulgence at the expense of conventional tunes. However, it did satisfy some punters by becoming their first record to hit the UK Top 50. The following year, the band's infamous in-fighting reach a head as the proverbial time-honoured musical differences led to the wayward BAKER pursuing a noisier career of his own as SHADY. Although a solitary MERCURY REV single, 'EVERLASTING ARM', appeared in summer '94 (featuring ALAN VEGA of SUICIDE), it would be another long year before the release of 'SEE YOU ON THE OTHER SIDE' (1995), although by this time the first chapter of MERCURY REV's maverick career had already drawn to a close. While critics marvelled over the album's more accessible but wonderfully eclectic pop-jazz experiments, DONAHUE and GRASSHOPPER were in the process of completing a debut album, 'PARALYZED MIND OF THE ARCANGEL VOID' (1995) for their revamped side-project, HARMONY ROCKETS. A few years later, the pair resurrected the MERCURY REV moniker with a complete new cast (namely ADAM SNYDER, JUSTIN RUSSO, JASON RUSSO and JEFF MERCEL), although the subsequent return of THORPE, FRIDMANN and CHAMBERS (SNYDER was retained) resulted in a more fully-fledged reformation. V.I.P. HARMONY ROCKETS guests, LEVON HELM and GARTH HUDSON of The BAND, were also brought on board for the album no one thought was possible, 'DESERTER'S SONGS' (1998). Issued on Richard Branson's new imprint, 'V2' ('Epic' in the States), the record was widely hailed as THE album of the year as MERCURY REV enjoyed one of the critical rebirths of the decade. Older and wiser, the band (or THE BAND, take your pick!) had possibly stumbled upon what GRAM PARSONS really meant when he dreamt of his 'cosmic American music', a wistful (in a far-out sort of way) melange of quixotic pop, spacey orchestration and lullaby romanticism quite possibly unlike anything you've ever heard. If long-time fans were hoping to hear the anarchic spark of old they were in for a drastic shock, tracks such as 'TONITE IT SHOWS', 'OPUS 40', 'DELTA SUN BOTTLENECK BLUES' and 'ENDLESSLY', meandering to a more mature muse, the latter even incorporating their own heavy-lidded interpretation of traditional carol, 'Silent Night'. A couple of months previous to the album's release, GRASSHOPPER & His GOLDEN CRICKETS (including flautist, SUZANNE THORPE) had taken their own, more off-beat journey into the psychedelic musical galaxy with the album, 'THE ORBIT OF ETERNAL GRACE'. After recovering from the trailblazing glory of 'DESERTER'S SONGS', many fans and critics were pondering over the group's next release: how were they going to match the previous album? How would they write songs now that their woe and grief had disappeared thanks to their new found glory? MERCURY REV, however, answered both of these questions on the eve of the release of their fifth album, the epic 'ALL IS DREAM' (2001). A kaleidoscope of drifting thoughts, strange orchestral lulls, and dark, uncertain things that creeped around in the shadows, the set displayed all of the usual REV decorations, only with a brooding overtone. Darker than their last set, the record opened with the soaring, heart-wrenchingly poignant 'DARK IS RISING' (the unofficial sequel to 'HOLES') – a piano led wander into DONAHUE's subconscious, with aching violins and unnormally high choir voices that sounded like a collaboration between a broken-down NEIL YOUNG and a drunken SCOTT WALKER. Elsewhere on the album, 'DROP IN TIME', 'TIDES OF THE MOON' and 'HERCULES' were all fine demonstrations by the group that they hadn't lost any of their musical ambition (especially FRIDMANN, who was surely becoming the PHIL SPECTOR of the independent movement). If 'DESERTER'S SONGS' was the soundtrack to a sad children's Christmas movie, then 'ALL IS DREAM' was pitched somewhere between a classic romantic period drama and a high-tension adventure set in a faraway land.
• Covered: IF YOU WANT ME TO STAY (Sly Stone) / SHHH – PEACEFUL (Miles Davis) / DEADMAN (Alan Vega) / RAINDROPS KEEP FALLING ON MY HEAD (Bacharach & David) / HE WAS A FRIEND OF MINE (Bob Dylan) / SILVER STREET (Nikki Sudden) / MOTION PICTURES (Neil Young) / OBSERVATORY CREST (Captain Beefheart) / I KEEP A CLOSE WATCH (John Cale) / STREETS OF LAREDO (Marty Robbins) – The HARMONY ROCKETS covered I'VE GOT A GOLDEN TICKET (from 'Charlie & The Chocolate Factory') / L'APOCALYPSE DES ANIMAUX (Vangelis) / etc..

Album rating: YERSELF IS STEAM (*8) / BOCES (*6) / SEE YOU ON THE OTHER SIDE (*8) / DESERTER'S SONGS (*9) / ALL IS DREAM (*8) / Harmony Rockets: PARALYZED MIND OF THE ARCANGEL VOID (*6) / Grasshopper & The Golden Crickets: THE ORBIT OF ETERNAL GRACE (*7)

DAVID BAKER – vocals / **JONATHAN DONAHUE** – vocals, guitar (ex-FLAMING LIPS) / **SEAN 'Grasshopper' MACKIOWIAK** – guitar / **DAVID FRIDMANN** – bass / **JIMY CHAMBERS** – drums / **SUZANNE THORPE** – woodwind

Feb 91. (cd/c/blue-lp) <(MINT CD/C/LP 4)> **YERSELF IS STEAM** *Mint Films | Mint Films*
– (Rocket): Chasing a bee / Syringe mouth / Coney Island cyclone / Blue and black / Sweet oddysee of a cancer cell t' th' center of yer heart / (Harmony): Frittering / Continuous trucks and thunder under a mother's smile / Very sleepy rivers. *(re-iss. Nov92 on 'Beggars Banquet' as d-cd+=/d-c+=/d-lp+=; BBQ CD/MC/LP 125)*
LEGO MY EGO – If you want me to stay / Shhh – Peaceful – Very sleepy rivers / Frittering / Coney Island cyclone / Car wash hair / Syringe mouth / Blood on the moon / Chasing a girl (inside a car). *<US cd re-iss. Nov92 on 'Columbia'; 53030> (re-iss. Feb99 +=; same)* – Space patrol / Uh . . . it's out there / I better hold my pants back on / My mom is coming over. *(d-cd-iss. Jul02; MINTCD 0045)*

Nov 91. (12"ep/cd-ep) <(MINT 5 T/CD)> **CAR WASH HAIR** (The Bee's Chasing me) full pull / **CHASING A BEE** (demo) / **CONEY ISLAND CYCLONE** (demo) *Rough Trade | not iss.*

Apr 92. (7") *(45REV 6)* **IF YOU WANT ME TO STAY. / THE LEFT-HANDED RAYGUN OF PAUL SHARITS (RETIREMENT JUST LIKE THAT)** *Beggars Banquet | Columbia*

Nov 92. (12"/cd-s) *(BBQ 1/+CD)* <74717> **CHASING A BEE. / CONEY ISLAND CYCLONE**

Mar 93. (10"/cd-s) *(BBQ 5 T/CD)* <74907> **THE HUM IS COMING FROM HER. / SO THERE** (with ROBERT CREELY) *| Apr93*

May 93. (7") *(BBQ 14)* **SOMETHING FOR JOEY. / THREE SPIDER'S EGGS** (live)
(12"+=) *(BBQ 14/+T)* – Suzanne peels out.
(cd-s++=) *(BBQ 14CD)* – Noise. *(re-iss. Jul93)*

Jun 93. (cd/c/lp) *(BBQ CD/MC/LP 140)* <53217> **BOCES** 43 |
– Meth of a rockette's kick / Trickle down / Bronx cheer / Boys peel out / Downs are feminine balloons / Something for Joey / Snorry mouth / Hi-speed boats / Continuous drunks and blunders / Girlfren.

Jul 93. (cd-ep) <CSK 5532> **SOMETHING FOR JOEY / SO THERE / BOYS PEEL OUT / VERY SLEEPY RIVERS / (Ron Jeremy interview)**

Feb 94. (cd-ep) <77112> **BRONX CHEER / THERE'S SPIDER EGGS IN BUBBLA YHUM / SUZANNE PEELS OUT**

— now without BAKER who re-surfaced as SHADY, releasing towards the end of '94, a solo album, 'WORLD' (for 'Beggars Banquet' UK, 'Atlantic' US), which included members of SWERVEDRIVER, ROLLERSKATE SKINNY, Th' FAITH HEALERS, SHARKBOY and BOO RADLEYS. A single, 'NARCOTIC CANDY' was taken from it with a subsequent single, 'PEARLS', coming out a year later.

Jun 94. (12"white/cd-s) *(BBQ 37 T/CD)* **EVERLASTING ARM. / DEADMAN**

May 95. (cd/c/lp)(pic-lp) *(BBQ CD/MC/LP 176)(BBQ 176P)* <64362> **SEE YOU ON THE OTHER SIDE** *| Sep95*
– Empire state (Sun House in excelsis) / Young man's stride / Sudden ray of hope / Everlasting arm / Racing the tide / Close encounters of the 3rd grade / A kiss from an old flame (a trip to the Moon) / Peaceful night.

— split late '94, as DONAHUE and GRASSHOPPER were already moonlighting as the HARMONY ROCKETS. The former and MERCURY REV collaborated on The CHEMICAL BROTHERS 'Dig Your Own Hole' track, 'Private Psychedelic Reel'.

HARMONY ROCKETS

— **DONAHUE + GRASSHOPPER** plus **LEVON HELMS + GARTH HUDSON** (The BAND) (they also guested on MERCURY REV's comeback album) / **ZOOT ROLLO HORN** (ex-CAPTAIN BEEFHEART) *Rockville | Rockville / Big Cat | Big Cat*

Jun 93. (7") *(ROCK 6113-7)* **SKELETON MAN. /**

Oct 95. (lp/cd) <(ABB 90/+CD)> **PARALYZED MIND OF THE ARCHANGEL VOID** *| Sep98*
– Paralyzed mind of the archangel void.
 Big Cat | No.6
Oct 97. (cd-s) *(ABB 151SCD)* <45> **I'VE GOT A GOLDEN TICKET EP** *| Nov98*
– I've got a golden ticket / L'apocalypse des animaux / Tale scendeva l'etternale adore / I've got a golden ticket (version) / I've got a golden ticket (extended).

MERCURY REV

— **JONATHAN + GRASSHOPPER** reformed the band in the summer of '97 with **ADAM SNYDER** – keyboards / **JUSTIN RUSSO** – keyboards / **JASON RUSSO** – bass / **JEFF MERCEL** – drums

— by 1998, **SNYDER** was the only person that **JONATHAN + GRASSHOPPER** retained, bringing back **DAVE FRIDMANN, SUZANNE THORPE + JIMY CHAMBERS**
 V2 | Epic
Oct 98. (cd/lp) *(VVR 100277-2/-1)* <27027> **DESERTER'S SONGS** 27 | Sep98
– Holes / Tonite it shows / Endlessly / I collect coins / Opus 40 / Hudson line / The happy end (the drunk room) / Goddess on a hiway / The funny bird / Pick up if you're there / Delta sun bottleneck stomp. *(also on special cd; VVR 100379-2)*

Nov 98. (7") *(VVR 500332-7)* **GODDESS ON A HIWAY. / RAGTAG** 51 | –
(cd-s+=) *(VVR 5000332-3)* – I only have eyes for you.

Jan 99. (12") *(VVR 500541-6)* **DELTA SUN BOTTLENECK STOMP. ('A'-Chemical Brothers mix) / ENDLESSLY** (instrumental) 26 |
(cd-s) *(VVR 500541-3)* – (first two tracks) / Vampire blues (live).
(cd-s) *(VVR 500616-3)* – ('A'side) / Holes (live) / Isolation (live).

May 99. (7") *(VVR 500696-7)* **OPUS 40. / MOTION PICTURES** (live) 31 | –
(cd-s) *(VVR 500697-3)* – ('A'side) / He was a friend of mine (live) / Raindrops keep falling on my head (live).
(cd-s) *(VVR 500696-3)* – ('A'side) / He was a friend of mine (live) / Tonite is shows (live).

Aug 99. (7") *(VVR 500849-7)* **GODDESS ON A HIWAY. / CAROLINE SAYS** 26 | –
(cd-s) *(VVR 500849-3)* – ('A'side) / I don't wanna be a soldier / Car wash hair (live).
(cd-s) *(VVR 500849-8)* – ('A'side) / I dreamt / Very sleepy rivers (live).

Aug 01. (cd/lp) *(VVR 101752-2/-1)* <27106> **ALL IS DREAM** 11 |
– The dark is rising / Tides of the Moon / Chains / Lincoln's eyes / Nite and fog / Little rhymes / A drop in time / You're my queen / Spiders and flies / Hercules.

(cd re-iss. Apr02 w/free cd+=; VVR 101752-0) – Saw song (live) / Hercules (live) / Little rhymes (live) / Nite and fog (video) / The dark is rising (video) / (interview documentary).

Sep 01. (7") *(VVR 501772-7)* **NITE AND FOG. / NITE AND FOG** (demo) 47 | –
(cd-s) *(VVR 501772-3)* – ('A'side) / A drop in time (demo) / Serpentine.
(cd-s) *(VVR 501772-8)* – ('A'side) / Cool waves / Nite & fog (alt. version feat. boys choir).

Jan 02. (cd-s) *(VVR 501871-3)* **THE DARK IS RISING / NOCTURNE IN C# MINOR – OPUS 27 NO.1 / PLANET CARAVAN** 16 |
(cd-s) *(VVR 501871-8)* – ('A'side) / Spiders and flies (live) / Blues skies.

Jul 02. (cd-s) *(VVR 501978-3)* **LITTLE RHYMES / CHAINS (Peter Stillman mix) / I KEEP A CLOSE WATCH** 51 |
(cd-s) *(VVR 501978-8)* – ('A'side) / Observatory crest / Streets of Laredo.

GRASSHOPPER AND THE GOLDEN CRICKETS

with **SUZANNE THORPE** – flute, co-producer (of MERCURY REV) + others
 Beggars Banquet | Beggars Banquet
Jul 98. (7") *(BBQ 325)* **SILVER BALLOONS. / SOLAR POWERED HORNET BEYOND THE SHADOWS OF OVERLOOK MOUNTAIN**
(cd-s+=) *(BBQ 325CD)* – ('A'mix).

Aug 98. (cd/lp) *(BBQ CD/LP 201)* <80201> **THE ORBIT OF ETERNAL GRACE**
– Silver balloons / The ballad of the one-eyed angelfish / O-ring (baby talk) / Nickel in a lemon / The orbit of eternal grace / September's fool / Univac bug track / Smpte for the Devil / N.Y. avenue playground / Sketches of Saturn (love in space) / Midnight express / N.Y. avenue playground (reprise).

Stephin MERRITT (see under ⇒ MAGNETIC FIELDS)

MEXICO 70

Formed: Windsor (Thames Valley), England . . . late 80's by ex-FELT member, MICK BUND, a veteran of many other outfits including PRIMAL SCREAM, BOCCA JUNIORS and his own AIRSTREAM. Along with RICKY VAN SPALL (also an AIRSTREAM pilot), DARREN CHRISTIAN and vocalist VICKY, MEXICO 70 – named after the host/year of the World Cup – delivered a couple of 'Cherry Red' EP's, 'VALENCIA' and 'WONDERFUL LIE', prior to a slightly disappointing debut JOHN RIVERS-produced long-player, 'THE DUST HAS COME TO STAY' (1992). Inspired by sixties acts like The KINKS, with leanings to the lads rock of OASIS, MEXICO 70 furthered their discography by releasing two follow-up sets, 'SING WHEN YOU'RE WINNING' (a record probably shelved) and 'IMPERIAL COMET HOUR' (1996). • **Covered:** CORTEZ THE KILLER (Neil Young).

Album rating: THE DUST HAS COME TO STAY (*5) / SING WHEN YOU'RE WINNING (*5) / IMPERIAL COMET HOUR (*7)

MICK BUND – vocals, guitar (ex-FELT, of-AIRSTREAM, ex-BOCCA JUNIORS, ex-PRIMAL SCREAM) / **JOHN SNELL** – guitar / **RICKY VAN SPALL** – drums (ex-METRO TRINITY, of-AIRSTREAM) / **DARREN CHRISTIAN** – bass / **VICKY** – vocals / + a drummer
 Cherry Red | not iss.
Jun 91. (12"ep/cd-ep) *(12/CD CHERRY 117)* **VALENCIA EP**
– What's in your mind / Find someone else to play "Misty for you" / You make it worse / All day long.

Jan 92. (12"ep/cd-ep) *(12/CD CHERRY 120)* **WONDERFUL LIE EP**
– Wonderful lie / I feel fine / Drug is the love / Queen of swords.

Jul 92. (cd) *(CDBRED 101)* **THE DUST HAS COME TO STAY**
– Wonderful lie / Just like we never came down / What's in your mind / Sacred heart / I feel fine / Drug is the love / All day long / Find someone else to play "Misty For You" / Always by your side / Queen of swords / Heaven in your eyes / Make it right / Worthless. *<US-iss.Jul95 on 'Big Pop'; 110>*
 Inertial | not iss.
May 93. (cd-s) *(ERTMEX 1)* **WORTHLESS. / HEAVEN IN YOUR EYES**

Oct 93. (12"/cd-s) *(ERTMEX 2-12/CD2)* **EVERYWHERE. / I WANT YOU / CORTEZ THE KILLER**

— **BUND** recruited **MARK BARRETT** – lead guitar / **GUIDO MULLIGAN** – bass / **RICK DUCE** – drums
 not iss. | Big Pop
Sep 95. (cd-ep) <BP 111> **SOMETHING FOR THE WEEKEND EP**
– I want you (acoustic) / Everywhere / I feel fine / I want you / The road movie in you.

Oct 96. (cd) <BP 120> **IMPERIAL COMET HOUR**
– Every hour / I want you / Till you've spoken / Best & Hurst / It'll never happen again / In time / Hate for you / So do I / Road movie in you / Me all over / Days can't touch you now / Little tears / Jimmy McGriff / Jet century horses.

— BUND retired the group after above

MICE (see under ⇒ ALL ABOUT EVE; 80's section)

MIDGET

Formed: Stamford, Lincolnshire, England . . . 1995 out of The SMOKIN' LIZARDS by the youthful trio of RICHARD GOMBAULT, ANDY HAWKINS and LEE MAJOR (no, not the six million dollar man!). Taking up the punky-pop sound normally peddled by ASH, GREEN DAY and SUPERGRASS, the lads inked a deal with 'Radarscope' in '96. Early the following year, MIDGET delivered a sort of tribute debut, 'KYLIE AND

JASON' (MINOGUE and DONOVAN), the first in a series of eight singles released over the course of the next two years. Their first album proper, 'JUKEBOX' (had already issued mini-cd, 'ALCO-POP!') hit the shops in the summer of '98 and showed they had promise if nothing else. • **Covered:** DAYDREAM BELIEVER (Monkees) / SENSES WORKING OVERTIME (Xtc). • **Note:** 'THE TOGGLE SWITCH' CD on 'Au-Go-Go' in March '97 was not theirs, nor were releases on 'Pet Sounds'.

Album rating: ALCO-POP! mini (*6) / JUKEBOX (*6)

RICHARD GOMBAULT – vocals, guitar / **ANDY HAWKINS** – bass / **LEE MAJOR** – drums

		Radarscope	Sire
Jan 97.	(7") (TINY 1) **KYLIE AND JASON. / PATHETICALLY DEVOTED TO YOU**		-
Mar 97.	(7") (TINY 2) **CAMOUFLAGE. / FIRST THING IN THE MORNING**		-
	(cd-s+=) (TINYCDS 2) – So damn creepy.		
May 97.	(7"blue) (TINY 3) **WELCOME HOME JELLYBEAN. / DOROTHY**		-
	(cd-s+=) (TINYCDS 3) – Wendyhouse.		
	(cd-s) (TINYCDS 3X) – ('A'side) / Solitudinational / Family man / How?		
Aug 97.	(7") (TINY 4) **OPTIMISM. / STILL**		-
	(cd-s+=) (TINYCDS 4) – Bleached Queenie.		
	(cd-s) (TINYCDS 4X) – ('A'side) / You're back again / Meeting the parents / The way things turn out.		
Nov 97.	(m-cd) (TINYCDS 5) **ALCO-POP!**		-
	– Kylie and Jason / Why have cotton? / Camouflage / The pop song / So damn creepy / Silly little rich cow / Welcome home Jellybean / Wendyhouse / Parting shot.		
Jan 98.	(7") (TINY 6) **ALL FALL DOWN. / DESIGNER FRIEND**	57	-
	(cd-s) (TINYCDS 6) – ('A'side) / Daydream believer / Heavier than a really heavy thing.		
	(cd-s) (TINYCDS 6X) – ('A'side) / Tigger had a good idea / The victim.		
Mar 98.	(7") (TINY 7) **INVISIBLE BALLOON. / OPTIMISM (acoustic)**		-
	(cd-s) (TINYCDS 7) – ('A'side) / Three little words / All fall down (demo).		
	(cd-s) (TINYCDS 7X) – ('A'side) / Prince Valium / Kevin's girl.		
Jun 98.	(7") (TINY 8) **THE DAY OF YOUR LIFE. / INVISIBLE BALLOON (demo)**		-
	(cd-s) (TINYCDS 8) – ('A'side) / Senses working overtime / Kylie and Jason (live) / ('A'album version).		
	(cd-s) (TINYCDS 8X) – ('A'side) / The good, the bad and the beautiful / Parting shot (live) / ('A'album version).		
Jun 98.	(cd/c) (TINY CD/MC 9) <31024> **JUKEBOX**		Jul98
	– Invisible balloon / Ben wants to be a secret agent / The day of your life / Magic lamp / You cope / The one who should save me / All fall down / On the run / Canada / A guy like me / Optimism / The way things turn out.		

– compilations, etc. –

Aug 98.	(cd) Imprint; <111979> **B-SIDE TRACKS** (compilation)	-	

MIDWAY STILL

Formed: Bexleyheath, South London, England . . . early 90's as The MELON PITS by PAUL THOMPSON, DECLAN KELLY and JOHN/JAN KANOPKA. Vaguely crusty indie-rockers following in the wake of CARTER USM, MEGA CITY 4 etc., MIDWAY STILL enjoyed a brief period of media enthusiasm as the music press cast around blindly trying to locate a new scene following the demise of both the baggy and shoegazing movements. The band were also given vocal support via John Peel, the DJ airing the band's impressive 'Roughneck' debut single, 'I WON'T TRY'. Characterised by THOMPSON's gravel-throated growl atop a roughly hewn yet melodic guitar sound, MIDWAY STILL's US-influenced appeal (HUSKER DU and NEIL YOUNG) saw their DON FLEMING-produced debut album, 'DIAL SQUARE' (1992) notch up respectable sales in the independent market and win over the cynicism of hardened hacks. Fickle as ever, the press soon forgot about them as the full force of the Seattle grunge wave hit Britain, leaving MIDWAY STILL, and their follow-up effort, 'LIFE'S TOO LONG' (1993), washed up on the shores of indifference. After a 7-year hiatus, THOMPSON and Co were back with the shockingly-titled 'FUCK YOU'. Nice. • **Covered:** YOU MADE ME REALISE (My Bloody Valentine) / WOW (Captain America).

Album rating: DIAL SQUARE (*6) / LIFE'S TOO LONG (*4)

PAUL THOMPSON – vocals, guitar / **JOHN/JAN KANOPKA** – bass / **DECLAN KELLY** – drums, percussion

		Roughneck	not iss.
Aug 91.	(7") (HYPE 10) **I WON'T TRY. / APPLE**		-
	(12"+=/cd-s+=) (HYPE 10 T/CD) – Daynight.		
Oct 91.	(7") (HYPE 13) **WISH. / YOU MADE ME REALISE**		-
	(12"+=/cd-s+=) (HYPE 13 T/CD) – Everywhere I look / Who are you.		
Mar 92.	(7") (HYPE 15) **BETTER THAN BEFORE. / IN FRONT OF YOU**		-
	(12"+=/cd-s+=) (HYPE 15 T/CD) – I won't try (lazy version) / What you said (shimmyglitter mix).		
Apr 92.	(cd/c/lp) (NECK CD/MC/LP 8) **DIAL SQUARE**		-
	– Found / Better than before / Me in you / Gun / Making time / Killing time / Come down / Make a start / What you said / Wish / Brand new / Sweat / Heaven.		
Nov 92.	(tour-7") (HYPE 18) **WOW. / (other by CAPTAIN AMERICA)**	-	-
Feb 93.	(10"ep/cd-ep) (HYPE 19 T/CD) **SLUGABED EP**		-
	– Just get stuck / Abnegate / Three five nine / Still get by.		
May 93.	(7") (HYPE 23) **COUNTING DAYS. / MOD SONG NO.2**		-
	(cd-s+=) (HYPE 23CD) – Fragments.		
Jun 93.	(cd/lp) (NECK CD/LP 12) **LIFE'S TOO LONG**		-
	– Jamie and Gigi / Lies / Straight line / Out pf view / Sell these ears / Counting days / Kemper / Disappear / Cyclops / Summercide / Strange how / Goodbye. (lp		

w/free 7"; HYPE 26) – FLY ME TO THE MOON. / A DAY IN THE LIFE OF A SHOWGIRL

—— split in 1994, although they were back in 2000
—— **BRAD AITCHISON** – drums (ex-SPEED CIRCUS) repl. KELLY
—— **RUSSELL LEE** – bass; repl. JOHN/JAN

		Antipop	not iss.
Dec 00.	(cd-ep) (ANTI 004CD) **FUCK YOU / SINCE YOU'VE BEEN GONE / COUNTING DAYS (bongo version) / FUCK YOU (jazz version)**		-

MIGHTY WAH! (see under ⇒ WAH!)

MIIGHTY FLASHLIGHT
(see under ⇒ RITES OF SPRING; 80's section)

MILKY WIMPSHAKE

Formed: Heaton, Newcastle upon Tyne, England . . . 1996 by RAMONES-obsessed PETE DALE, with CHRISTINE and MS. JOEY RAMONE (not relation, of course!). Not just an old school punk enthusiast, DALE played a vital role during the incarnation of the North's thriving inide punk rock scene, running the 'Slampt Underground' label and being involved in a collection of bands; PUSSYCAT TRASH (who have a best of, '1992-95: THE BRAT YEARS'), the overtly political RED MONKEY (check 1998's 'MAKE THE MOMENT and '99's 'DIFFICULT IS EASY') and AVOCADO BABY, respectively. During his stint fronting PUSSYCAT TRASH, DALE formed the post-modern punk band MILKY WIMPSHAKE and issued a handful of 7" singles in the mid 1990's, the most unlikely of the bunch – a cover of Daniel Johnston's 'TRUE LOVE WILL FIND YOU IN THE END'. The trio delivered the album 'BUSROUTE TO YOUR HEART' (1996), a flamboyant, pogo-y spin on international affairs, with a trashy rhythm section that made The CRAMPS look comparitively camp. Having not received much attention or acclaim for this brilliant debut, MILKY WIMPSHAKE grew quiet. They didn't do much in the way of music; with DALE running 'Slampt . . .', he kept busy managing and producing other bands, and eventually MS. JOEY RAMONE fell by the wayside. However, after a switch to America's 'Troubleman' label and a freshly recruited drummer (in the form of GRANT), the dubious 'WIMPSHAKE managed to record again and issued the jangling 'LOVERS NOT FIGHTER' in 2002.

Album rating: Pussycat Trash: "THE BRAT YEARS: 1992-1995" COMPLETE DISCOGRAPHY CD compilation (*6) / Avocado Baby: A MILLION AND NINE AND SEX AND GUM AND STUFF compilation (*5) / Milky Wimpshake: BUSROUTE TO YOUR HEART (*6) / Red Monkey: MAKE THE MOMENT (*6) / DIFFICULT IS EASY (*5) / GUNPOWDER, TREASON AND PLOT (*6) / Milky Wimpshake: LOVERS NOT FIGHTERS (*6)

PETER DALE – vocals, guitar / with MILKY WIMPSHAKE: **CHRISTINE** – bass, vocals / **MS. JOEY RAMONE** – drums

		Slampt Underground	not iss.
1993.	(c) (SLAMPT 6) **SONGS OF ZOOM AND BUZZ**		-
	– Not zombie / Fake fool / Pressure cooker boy / You're shaken / I'm stirred / Palm of my hand / Drum beat zoom / Hey! brother mine / True love will find you in the end / Shells and shoes.		
Oct 94.	(7"ep) (SLAMPT 24) **THE DEVIATION AMPLIFICATION SPIRAL EP**		-
	– Clicking it / Roll a disco / Shaved head thrills / Chewing broken glass / Yeah, it's true.		
Apr 96.	(7"ep) (SLAMPT 40) **LOVE SONGS FOR PUNK ROCKERS**		-
	– Cheque card / Kickstart affair / My heart beats faster than techno / Milk maid.		
May 97.	(lp/cd) (SLAMPT 48/+CD) **BUSROUTE TO YOUR HEART**		-
	– I wanna be seen in public with you / '77 punk rock boy / I love you, you weirdo / Electric shock / It might sound dramatic / Bar code punk / Palm of my hand / Mon couer bat plus rapidement que la techno / Noam Chomsky versus the Ramones / Ex boyfriend / Nightclub voyeur cliche / Bedroom love song / Golgo 13 / Latr expectations / Phone bill fear / Blow out at 80 miles per hour.		
Aug 97.	(cd) (SLAMPT 54) **SEVEN UNLUCKY SEVENS** (compilation of 7" EP's)		-

—— **GRANT** – drums; repl. MS. JOEY

		Liebellous	not iss.
Aug 99.	(7") (LIE 01) **HOME IS WHERE THE HATE IS. / ITCHY FEET**		-

		Ferric Mordant	not iss.
Feb 00.	(7") (FE 05) **DIALLING TONE. / TRUE LOVE WILL . . .**		-

		Fortuna Pop	Troubleman
Apr 02.	(cd) (FPOP 34) <TMU 75CD> **LOVERS NOT FIGHTERS**		
	– Scrabble / Philosophical boxing gloves / Dialling tone / Do what I have to / Second generation middle-class dropout / White liberal guilt / Newport / Didn't we? / Lemonade / Jack ass / Bourgeois blues '99 / Too much, too drunk / Etymology / Lovers not fighters.		

PUSSYCAT TRASH

PETE DALE / + RACHEL HOLBORROW – bass (of HUGGY BEAR)

		Slampt Underground	Troubleman Unlimited
May 94.	(7"ep) (SLAMPT 16) **LA LA OVULAR**		-
	– Exhibit "A" / Crush-o-matic / Secret rocket / Ultraism / Stupid nothing.		
Oct 94.	(lp/cd) (SLAMPT 25/+CD) **NON-STOP HIP-ACTION**		-
	– Existentialism / Punk xerox connections / I need science fiction / Galore / Style B: Rogue robots / Zombie beat / Pussycat Trash vs. Jarvis Cocker / Fuc / Big sulk / Mock style examinations / Viva la punka / Fake heart / Dumb crush / Tattoo / Spacesuit in a supermarket / Style A: Resistence is useful / Where will we strike next?.		

MILKY WIMPSHAKE (cont)

Apr 01. (cd) <TMU 48CD> "THE BRAT YEARS: 1992-1995"
COMPLETE DISCOGRAPHY CD (compilation)
– NON-STOP HIP-ACTION / Positive bomb / Girlfriend / Hot bed / Squid joke / Un soul less / Doris / Alien shake / Kiss! kiss! / Pussycat stomp / Exhibit "A" / Crushomatic / Secret rocket / Ultraism / Stupid nothing / 1, 2, 3, 4 / Overture / Queen bee empire / Object to I-dent / Blessing mix-up / Itchee Scratchee / Implicated in crime / Abrupt to the point of rudeness / Wish fulfillment.

AVOCADO BABY

PETE DALE

Slampt Underground / not iss.

1993. (7"ep) (SLAMPT 10) QUEEN BOY AND THE KING GIRL

Paper Plane / not iss.

1994. (7"ep) (super vinyl 01) VOLUMPTUOS AND SUPREME

Beekeeper–Shakedown / not iss.

1996. (7"ep) (none) FOOLISH AND PUNK

– compilation –

Jul 95. (lp) *Slampt Underground; (SLAMPT 32)* A MILLION AND NINE AND SEX AND GUM AND STUFF (44 tracks)

RED MONKEY

PETER DALE (as VITAMIN P) + **RACHEL** (as RK FUSEE) + **MARC** (as M.E. CHA CHA)

Apr 97. (7"ep) (SLAMPT 47) DO WHAT YOU FEEL (FEEL WHAT YOU DO)
Sep 97. (lp) (SLAMPT 50) MAKE THE MOMENT
– Activity book / Pro choice / Litmus test / Rationale showdown / Cakey pig / The converse / Not for rent / Missy / Equate this / Fake dagger day / The way I peel oranges / No negative / Luxury / (untitled) / (untitled) / (untitled) / (untitled). *(re-iss. Mar98 on 'Troubleman Unlimited' lp/cd; TMU 28/+CD)*

Kill Rock Stars / not iss.

1998. (7"ep) (KRS 305) RED MONKEY
– (Ain't nothing but a) Incendiary device / Make a mess / The exact geographical centre of me.

Slampt Underground / Troubleman Unlimited

1999. (7"ep) <TR 0025> THE TIME IS RIGHT EP
– Chewing gum / Weight of should / Teenagers are boring / Trespass.
Jun 99. (cd) (SLAMPT 57) <TMU 32CD> DIFFICULT IS EASY
– This medium is not the message / Bike song / Paper crown / Straight lines don't fit / My bed and ancestry / Waiting for now / Kissing with tongues / Power and dependence / In her own write / Glitterglue and 1/3 / Gioco in le demensioni.
Oct 01. (lp/cd) (<TMU 068/+CD>) GUNPOWDER, TREASON AND PLOT
– The jazz step forwards / Spoken time / Essential nutrients / Bloody Mary / Baking and dirt / From ground down / Courage in this now / Sewing / Not certain positive / Navigation.

MILLTOWN BROTHERS

Formed: Colne, Lancashire, England ... early '88 by brothers MATT and SIMON NELSON (who had originally called themselves The WORD ASSOCIATION), the group completed by BARNEY JAMES, JAMES FRASER and NIAN BRINDLE. After a few releases – including the original of 'WHICH WAY SHOULD I JUMP' – on their own 'Big Round' imprint, the MILLTOWN BROTHERS were signed to 'A&M' by A&R man, Sean O'Sullivan in 1990. Basically an acoustic/keyboard outfit influenced by R.E.M. and The GO-BETWEENS, the band initially flopped with 'APPLE GREEN' before breaking through early the following year with a revamped version of the easy-rocking 'WHICH WAY ...' single. The accompanying album, 'SLINKY' (1991), showed definite promise, although with subsequent singles hovering around the Top 50 mark, their second division status was confirmed. Amid protracted difficulties over the musical direction of new material, follow-up set, 'VALVE' (1993), was delayed. As a preview to the album's release, the 'BROTHERS scored their last (minor) hit with a cover of Bob Dylan's 'IT'S ALL OVER NOW BABY BLUE'; the cd-EP actually featured three other DYLAN classics, namely 'POSITIVELY 4th STREET', 'HURRICANE' and 'I SHALL BE RELEASED'.

Album rating: SLINKY (*6) / VALVE (*4) / THE BEST OF THE MILLTOWN BROTHERS compilation (*6)

MATTHEW NELSON – vocals / **SIMON NELSON** – guitar (ex-BLUE BERLIN) / **BARNEY JAMES** – keyboards / **JAMES FRASER** – bass / **NIAN BRINDLE** – drums

Big Round / not iss.

Feb 89. (7") (BIGR 101) COMING FROM THE MILL 1989
– Roses / We've got time.
(12"+=/cd-s+=) (BIGR 101 T/CD) – Something on my mind.
Oct 89. (7") (BIGR 104) WHICH WAY SHOULD I JUMP. / SILVER TOWN
(12"+=) (BIGR 104T) – Why should I.

Orea Milltown / not iss.

Apr 90. (12"/cd-s) (MTOWN 001/+CD) SEEMS TO ME. / NATURAL / SEEMS TO ME (take 2)

A&M / A&M

Oct 90. (7") (AM 704) APPLE GREEN. / WHEN IT COMES
(12"+=/cd-s+=) (AMY/AMCD 704) – My favourite place.
Jan 91. (7"/c-s) (AM/+MC 711) WHICH WAY SHOULD I JUMP. / DIPLOMAT 38
(12"+=) (AMY 711) – Knives and forks / Drop out.
(cd-s+=) (AMCD 711) – Drop out / Natural.
(10"box+=) (AMT 711) – Natural / Silver town.

Mar 91. (cd/c/lp) (395346-2/-4/-1) <5346> SLINKY 27
– Apple green / Here I stand / Sally Ann / Which way should I jump? / Real / Nationality / Never come down again / Something cheap / Seems to me / Sandman.
Apr 91. (7") (AM 758) HERE I STAND. / DON'T BREATHE IN 41
(cd-s+=) (AMCD 758) – Jack Lemmon.
(12"++=) (AMX 758) – Something on my mind.
Jun 91. (7"/c-s) (AM/+MC 787) APPLE GREEN. / WE'VE GOT TIME 43
(12"+=/cd-s+=) (AMY/AMCD 787) – So you want to be a writer / Drop like a stone.
(12") (AMX 787) – ('A'side) / Sally Ann (acoustic) / Nationality (demo) / Something cheap (demo).
May 93. (7") (580 269-7) TURN OFF. / WORLDWIDE 55
(12"+=) (580 269-6) – Got this feeling.
(cd-s) (580 271-2) – ('A'side) / Caroline / Rosemary Page / Alice.
Jul 93. (7") (580 330-7) IT'S ALL OVER NOW BABY BLUE. / SWEET NOTHING 48
(cd-s) (580 331-2) – ('A'side) / Roses / Which way should I jump (original) / Seems to me.
(10"/cd-s) (580 333-0/-2) – ('A'side) / Positively 4th Street / Hurricane / I shall be released.
Aug 93. (cd/c/lp) (540 132-2/-4/-1) VALVE
– When it comes / Turn off / Killing all the good men, Jimmy / Pictures (round my room) / Turn me over / Trees / Sleepwalking / Falling straight down / Crawl with me / Someday / It's all over now baby blue / Cool breeze. *(cd re-iss. May95; same)*
Sep 93. (etched-7") (580 384-7) SLEEPWALKING / FEE FIE FOE FUM
(cd-s+=) (580 385-2) – You don't know me no more / Long time.
(cd-s) (580 387-2) – ('A'side) / Everybody knows / Can't find the time / Freedom song.
— they disbanded after above; re-formed 10 years later ...

– compilations, etc. –

Nov 99. (cd) *Spectrum; (554 207-2)* THE BEST OF THE MILLTOWN BROTHERS
– Apple green / Here I stand / Sally Ann / Which way should I jump? / Nationality / Never come down again / Something cheap / Seems to me / Sandman / Real / Turn off / It's all over now baby blue.

MINDERS

Formed: Denver, Colorado, USA ... 1995 by British expatriate songwriter, MARTYN LEAPER, who, with the help of APPLES IN STEREO man ROBERT SCHNEIDER, issued the mostly band-less affair 'COME ON AND HEAR!' on 'Elephant 6' in 1996. LEAPER assembled a proper group with JEFF ALMOND, REBECCA COLE and JEFF RICHARDSON, and they released their second EP, 'PAPER PLANE' in 1997, along with 'ROCKET 58' (by which point RICHARDSON had been relaced with MARC WILLHITE). The indie-jangle pop of The MINDERS' debut set, 'HOORAY FOR TUESDAY' (1998), was hugely successful with the PAVEMENT crowd, and ended up at the top of many 'end-of-the-year' polls. However, the group fell apart in late '98, with LEAPER and COLE flitting to Oregon and obtaining a new batch of musicians – ADAM GOLDMAN, BRYCE EDWARDS and RACHEL BLUMBERG. The early single compilation set 'CUL-DE-SACS & DEAD ENDS' surfaced in 1999, followed by their sophomore 'DOWN IN FALL' (2000), a brilliant, musically colourful album, cram-packed full of 60's influences and a keen ear for instrumentation and songwriting. With good reviews and sold out tours across America and Europe, The MINDERS were on a roll; they delivered the sparkling retro pop of 'GOLDEN STREET' in 2001, minus the contributions of GOLDMAN, EDWARDS and BLUMBERG (overshadowed here with yet another line-up change, adding drummer HUTCH HARRIS and STEPHEN MALKMUS regular JOANNA BOLME).

Album rating: HOORAY FOR TUESDAY (*6) / CUL-DE-SACS & DEAD ENDS compilation (*7) / DOWN IN FALL mini (*5) / GOLDEN STREET (*5)

MARTYN LEAPER – vocals, guitar / with producer/on session **ROBERT SCHNEIDER** (of APPLES IN STEREO)

Elephant 6 / Elephant 6

Apr 96. (7"ep) <E6 004> COME ON AND HEAR!! EP
– Build / Almost arms / Chatty Patty. *(UK-iss.Jan97; same)*
— added **JEFF ALMOND** – guitar / **JEFF RICHARDSON** – bass / **REBECCA COLE** – drums
Jan 97. (7"ep) <(E6 006)> PAPER PLANE. / SALLY / BIG MACHINE Sep96
— **MARC WILLHITE** – bass; repl. RICHARDSON

not iss. / 100 Guitar Mania

Oct 97. (7"yellow) <100GM 31> ROCKET 58. / BETTER THINGS / WEIGH THE ANCHOR

SpinArt / SpinArt

Sep 98. (lp/cd) <(SPART 64/+CD)> HOORAY FOR TUESDAY
– Hooray for Tuesday / Pauline / Joey's pez / Comfortably tucked up inside / Yeah yeah yeah / Our man in Bombay / I've been wondering / More and more / Pass it around / Red bus / Bubble / Frida.
Aug 99. (7"ep) (WORM 38) THE MINDERS EP
(above issued on 'Earworm' as was below, but jointly)
— **LEAPER + COLE** recruited **ADAM GOLDMAN** – lead guitar / **RACHEL BLUMBERG** – keyboards / **BRYCE EDWARDS** – bass
Sep 99. (cd)(lp) <(SPART 76CD)>(WORM 47) CUL-DE-SACS & DEAD ENDS (compilation)
– Build / Almost arms / Chatty Patty / Paper plane / SAlly / Big machine / Rocket 58 / Better things / Weigh the anchor / Now I can smile / Black balloon / Hand me downs / Bicycle / Step right up / As good as you are / Waterlooville / Time vs. length.
Dec 00. (m-cd) <(SPART 86CD)> DOWN IN FALL Oct00
– Young and with it / On and on / Time machine / The loneliest of faces / Helen.
Jun 01. (lp/cd) <(SPART 89/+CD)> GOLDEN STREET Mar01
– Golden street / Light / Treehouse / Hand on heart / We never shout / Give me strength / Right as rain / Instrumental / Sleeping through everything / If you're lonely / Middle of the part / Nice day for it / Easy now.
Apr 02. (7") EMPTY BUBBLE. / (other by TOBIN SPROUT)

THE GREAT INDIE DISCOGRAPHY — The 1990s

Takako MINEKAWA

Born: 3 Jun'69, Japan. TAKAKO MINEKAWA was a child star in her native Japan, appearing on TV and in movies. Pursuing her interest in music, she formed the group LOLITA with college friends. In 1990, LOLITA became FANCY FACE GROOVY NAME – and included the now-popular KAHIMI KARIE – then after playing with several more acts, MINEKAWA decided to go it alone. She was unlike most Japanese female-led pop acts or artists because her approach was very individual and personal. Her debut solo LP, 'CHAT CHAT', made a virtue of her individuality. Her cutesy, girlish voice and frivolity were unmistakably rooted in Japanese pop, and her own compositions – like 'MIMI' – reflected this, but they sat side-by-side with covers including Mike Oldfield's 'MOONLIGHT SHADOW' and Eddie Cochran's 'SUMMERTIME BLUES'; Black Sabbath even receive a credit note. She followed 'CHAT CHAT' with the '(A LITTLE TOUCH OF) BAROQUE IN WINTER' EP later in '95, before the arrival of second album 'ROOMIC CUBE', in 1996. Largely a collaboration with her friends of BUFFALO DAUGHTER, the 'ROOMIC CUBE' was the conceptual space where MINEKAWA's musical creativity would blossom and flourish. Her delicate, minimal songwriting and music was expanded upon by BUFFALO DAUGHTER's noisy effects and funk/rock tendencies – like on 'KLAXON!' and '1.666666'. 'SLEEP SONG' and 'NEVER / MORE' are plainly and affectedly MINEKAWA's, and 'T.T.T. (TURNTABLE TENNIS)' is a successful blend of both styles. 'RECUBED', released in 1998, was an EP of 'ROOMIC ...' remixes, by friends including the PULSARS, TRANS AM, and BUFFALO DAUGHTER. MINEKAWA's third LP, 'CLOUDY CLOUD CALCULATOR', followed later in 1998. It represented a real development in her songwriting, full of invention and humour, with an airy electro/futuristic feel, displaying a patent love of KRAFTWERK ('KRAFTPARK', 'KANGAROO POCKET CALCULATOR'). The 1999 EP, 'XIMER', like 'RECUBED', was a collection of remixes, this time by the likes of CORNELIUS, OVAL and KID LOCO. Her next LP, 'FUN 9' (also 1999), was brimming with confidence and featured co-production from CORNELIUS and DJ ME DJ YOU. 'MAXI ON!' (2000) further distends her productive relationships with (again) CORNELIUS, DJ ME DJ YOU and BUFFALO DAUGHTER.

Album rating: CHAT CHAT (*5) / ROOMIC CUBE (*7) / CLOUDY CLOUD CALCULATOR (*6) / FUN 9 (*7) / MAXI ON mini (*5)

TAKAKO MINEKAWA – vocals, guitars, etc / + guests

			not iss.	Polystar
Jun 95.	(cd) <PSCR 5381>	**CHAT CHAT**	–	– Japan

– I love / Summertime blues / (untitled) / Clover / Moonlight shadow / My love / Drive my car / Gotta pull myself together / Circling Times Square I love (instrumental) / Mimi / Love.

Dec 95.	(cd-ep) <PSCR 5429>	**(A LITTLE TOUCH OF) BAROQUE IN WINTER**	–	– Japan

– Jesu, joy of man's desiring / La valse grise / Snow frolic.

May 96.	(cd) <PSCR 5476>	**ROOMIC CUBE ...A TINY ROOM EXHIBITION**	–	– Japan

– Sleep song / Fantastic cat / Never – More / Klaxon! / Wooooog (instrumental) / Dessert song / Destron / Pop up squirrels (instrumentals) / 1.666666 / Rainy song / T.T.T. (turntable tennis) (instrumental) / Fabie ... white / More pop up squirrels (instrumental). <US-iss.Feb97 on 'What Are?'; 63028>

Feb 97.	(12"ep) <PSCR 5577>	**ATHLETICA**	–	– Japan

– Metromusica / Slow flow mole / Klaxon! (new tipe) / Fabie (1,2,3 exercise) / Fabie (1,2,3 beat it).

			not iss.	March
Mar 97.	(7") <MAR 025>	**FANTASTIC CAT. /**	Emperor Norton	Emperor Norton

			Emperor Norton	Emperor Norton
Aug 98.	(12"ep/cd-ep) <EMN 7009/+CD>	**RECUBED** (remixes by V/A)	–	

– Fantastic cat / 1.666666 / Klaxon! / Dessert song / T.T.T. (turntable tennis) / Sleep song.

Oct 98.	(cd/lp) <EMN 7010 CD/LP>	**CLOUDY CLOUD CALCULATOR**	–	

– Micro mini cool / Milk rock / Phonoballoon song / Cat house / Cloud chips / Kraftpark (micro trip club) / Kangaroo pocket calculator / Black forest / International velvet / Cloud cuckoo land / Telstar.

Jul 99.	(m-cd/m-lp) <(EMN 7019-2/-1)>	**XIMER** (remixes by V/A)		Jun99

– Milk rock / Telstar / Black forest / International velvet / Cloud cuckoo land (acoustic) / Phonoballoon song. (re-iss. Aug00 +=; EMN 11LP) – Black forest / Cat house.

Feb 00.	(cd/lp) <(EMN 7022 CD/LP)>	**FUN 9**		Aug99

– Gently waves / Plash / Flow in a tide / Fantastic voyage / Tiger / Shh song / Spin spider spin / Flash / Fun 9 (French) / Soft graffiti / Fancy work funk. (cd+=) – Etoufee . . .

Jan 01.	(cd/lp) <(EMN 7036 CD/LP)>	**MAXI ON**		Nov00

– Maxi on! / Lullaby of grey / A report on an investigation / Brioche / Picnic at Loose Rock / Follow my dreams / Sleeping bag.

MINK LUNGS

Formed: Brooklyn, New York, USA . . . 1998 by JENNIFER HOOPES and GIAN CARLO FELEPPA, work-mates at a diner in the Hamptons district. Together with FELEPPA's half-brother TIM, they began writing and rehearsing, inspired by the music of The PIXIES and The FLAMING LIPS. Moving from San Francisco to New York, drummer TOM GALBRAITH completed the line-up, allowing them to proceed with recording. Their New York live debut came in April 1999, and was followed by gigs at the Mercury Lounge and Brownies, while supporting slots with LUNA and DELTA 72 soon followed. Now signed to the 'Arena Rock' label, their debut album 'THE BETTER BUTTON' was released in 2001. A quirky and varied indie-rock collection, the album included elements of folk, witnessed on 'REMAINING LOYAL'; although overall it lacked cohesion. The MINK LUNGS also played the South By Southwest Festival and scored an independent film, 'Sore Losers'.

Album rating: THE BETTER BUTTON (*6)

JENNIFER HOOPES – vocals, guitar / **GIAN CARLO FELEPPA** – vocals, guitar / **TIM FELEPPA** – bass / **TOM GALBRAITH** – drums

			Rykodisc	Arena Rock
Sep 02.	(cd) (RCD 16009) <AR 19>	**THE BETTER BUTTON**		May02

– I sell love / Silent sex / Watch yourself / Think of me / Synthersizer baby / Your nose lights up the dark / Widths and longths / Oscillator / Snail / Blue and creme car / Skin or no skin / Peep show / Remaining loyal / Demon power of Hell / Who loves you dear?

MINTY

Formed: London, England . . . 1993 by fashion icon, artist, musician and legendary clothes designer LEIGH BOWERY, together with fellow designer and club-owner RICHARD TORRY. After moving from Australia to London's cold streets in the early eighties, BOWERY soon created a striking reputation with the city's "art" set, due to his extravagant, wild sense of dress and his exuberant 'Factory'-esque taste in art. He met TORRY in the iconic gay club 'Taboo' and soon the pair had hatched a plan; to re-invent performance art with a slick slab of subjective art, theatrics and music, all rolled into one. Coined MINTY, which is gay slang for someone who is aloof and hyper-sensitive, BOWERY and TORRY recruited MATTHEW GLAMORRE, DANIELLE MINNS, sampler HONOLULU, LEIGH's wife NICOLA and MIRANDA SEX GARDEN's TREVOR SHARPE. They began playing London's gay and transvestite clubs, including 'Madame Jojos' and 'Smashing Live', where they courted notoriety for their outlandish stage antics, coupled with art nonsense and a tac-sharp visual flair (one can only imagine!). However, before the group issued their first single, 'USELESS MAN' (1995), some of MINTY had disbanded – MINNS and HONOLULU were quickly replaced with NEIL KACZOR and MATT FISHER, with the inclusion of Elizabeth Bunny's guitarist STEADY. The group toured Europe with their wonderfully camp stage show, and, after securing a regular spot in Soho's 'Freedom Cafe', their live performance was shut-down by the authorities on December 27th, 1994. LEIGH tragically died four days later (New Year's eve) from the HIV infection, thrusting friends, admirers, and band members into mourning. 'USELESS MAN' was issued posthumously in 1995, reaching the No.2 spot in the Netherlands, and, along with loose art collective OFFSET, TORRY and the surviving MINTY members toured once again and issued the frankly bonkers (but great) album 'OPEN WIDE' in 1997. Meanwhile, MINNS, FISHER and SHARPE formed The SERVANT, while MATTHEW GLAMORRE established the dark industrial "speed-core" nite club 'Harder, Faster, Louder' and LEIGH's wife, NICOLA BOWERY had reclusively settled down to live as an artist and a full-time mother.

Album rating: OPEN WIDE (*6)

LEIGH BOWERY (b. 1961) – vocals / **RICHARD TORRY** – guitar / **MATTHEW GLAMORRE** (b. HARDERN) – keyboards / **NICOLA BOWERY** – vocals / **MATT FISHER** – bass; repl. DANIELLE MINNS / **NEIL KACZOR** – keyboards + **STEADY** – guitar; repl. HONOLULU (samples) / **TREVOR SHARPE** – drums

			Candy	not iss.
Feb 95.	(12"/cd-s) (CAN 1 V/CD)	**USELESS MAN** (mixes; version / The Grid / King Rocker / Dis-cuss / Subversion)		–

– sadly, on the 31st December, LEIGH died of an AIDS-related illness
NICOLA + MATTHEW took over vocal chores

			Sugar	not iss.
Dec 95.	(12"/cd-s) (SUGA 6 V/CD)	**PLASTIC BAG** (mixes; version / partycrashers / foil-wrapped / French movie) / **MINTY** (live)		–
Apr 96.	(12"ep/cd-ep) (SUGA 10 V/CD)	**THAT'S NICE!**		–

– That's nice / Partychasers (mix) / Student union (mix) / Add in to X (mix) / Minty (mix).

			Candy	not iss.
Jul 97.	(cd/lp) (CAN 2 CD/LP)	**OPEN WIDE**		–

– Procession / Minty / That's nice / Plastic bag / Useless man / Homage / Manners mean / King size / Hold on / Nothing / Homme Aphrodite (part 1) / Homme Aphrodite (part 2) / Dream / Art? / Jeremy.

– MINTY disbanded in 1997; GLAMORRE continued with his OFFSET project

MINUS 5
(see under ⇒ YOUNG FRESH FELLOWS; in 80's section)

MIRANDA SEX GARDEN

Formed: London, England . . . early 90's by 19 year-olds, KATHARINE BLAKE and KELLY McCUSKER, both classically trained musicians (at Harrow's Purcell Music School) with piercing falsetto voices. Together with violinist JOCELYN WEST, the pair spent the early part of their career busking around the capital, performing madrigals ("16th-17th century part song for unaccompanied voices" according to the dictionary) to impressed passers by. BARRY ADAMSON was sufficiently bewitched to secure the girls an

MIRANDA SEX GARDEN (cont)

appearance on his 'Delusion' soundtrack, the group – completed by keyboard player BEN GOLOMSTOCK and percussionist TREVOR SHARPE – subsequently joining ADAMSON as part of the diverse 'Mute' roster. Complete with gothic typeface and arty photography, the haunting 'GUSH FORTH MY TEARS' served as the debut MIRANDA SEX GARDEN single in 1991 as the trio went on to support BLUR. An avant-ambience mix courtesy of ORB man, THRASH, provided an interesting juxtaposition between austerity and modernity, the press reacting with a mixture of bemusement and surprise amid charges of pretentiousness as debut album, 'MADRA' (1991) hit the shops. Mini-set, 'IRIS', followed in 1992 while a further two full length albums, 'SUSPIRIA' (1993) and 'FAIRYTALES OF SLAVERY' (1994) – remaining member KATHARINE now with DONNA McKEVITT, BEN GOLOMSTOCK and TREVOR SHARPE – put paid to any ideas of classical prudishness as BLAKE explored sado-masochism and allegedly performed semi-naked at fetish clubs. • **Songwriters:** Group except; GUSH FORTH MY TEARS (William Holborne) / SEE AMARYLLIS SHAMED (Michael West) / FULL FATHOM FIVE (Robert Johnson) / MY FUNNY VALENTINE (Hart-Rogers) / IN HEAVEN (Ivers-Lynch) / HAVANA LIED (Brecht-Weill).

Album rating: MADRA (*6)

KATHARINE BLAKE – vocals, percussion, violin, keyboards / **JOCELYN WEST** – vocals, some instruments / **KELLY McCUSKER** – vocals, strings, keyboards, etc

	Mute	Mute-Elektra
Jun 91. (7") (MUTE 123) <66497> **GUSH FORTH MY TEARS. / SEE AMARYLLIS SHAMED**		
(12"+=) (12MUTE 123) – ('A'-Danny Rampling mix) / ('A'-Thrash & Paul Kendal mix).		
(cd-s+=) (CDMUTE 123) – ('A'-A Cappella mix) / ('A'-remix).		
Jul 91. (cd/c/d-lp) (CD/C+/STUMM 91) <61126> **MADRA**		

– Seek sweet content / While joyful springtime lasteth / Go wailing accents / Gush forth my tears / Fly not so fast / The nightingale / Lady those eyes / Through my carriage be but careless / All creatures now are merry minded / Full fathom five / See Amaryllis shamed // It was a lover and his lass / Those sweet delightful lillies / Ah, look upon these eyes / If it be love / Away, thou shalt not love me / How merrily we live / Sweet Kate / This love is but a wanton fit / Sure there is no god of love / See my own sweet jewel / When first I saw thee / The silver swan / Sweet honey-sucking bees.

May 92. (cd/c/m-lp) (CD/C+/STUMM 97) <61277> **IRIS**
– Lovely Joan / Falling / Fear / Blue light / Iris.

— **KATHARINE + DONNA** brought in **BEN GOLOMSTOCK** – keyboards / **DONNA McKEVITT** – violin / **TREVOR SHARPE** – percussion / etc

Jan 93. (12"ep/cd-ep) (12/CD MUTE 139) **PLAY. / INFERNO (version II) / MY FUNNY VALENTINE**

Feb 93. (cd/c/lp) (CD/C+/STUMM 112) <61460> **SUSPIRIA**
– Ardera sempre / Open eyes / Sunshine / Distance / Play / In Heaven / Bring down the sky / Feed / Inferno / Willie Biddle / Ah his amazing maggot / My funny valentine.

Mar 93. (12"ep/cd-ep) (12/CD MUTE 154) **SUNSHINE / WILLIE BIDDLE. / FEAR (live) / MUFF DIVING SIZE QUEEN**

— **KATHARINE, BEN, TREVOR** with newcomer **HEBZIBAH SESSA** – strings, keyboards

Apr 94. (12"ep/cd-ep) (12/CD MUTE 163) **PEEP SHOW. / THE WOODEN BOAT / FREEZING**

May 94. (cd/c/lp) (CD/C+/STUMM 129) <61666> **FAIRYTALES OF SLAVERY**
– Cut / Fly / Peep show / Wooden boat / Havana lied / Cover my face / Transit / Freezing / Serial angels / The wheel / Intermission / Monk song / Fairytale about slavery.

— disbanded after above

MODEST MOUSE

Formed: Issaquah, Washington, USA... 1993 by ISAAC BROCK, ERIC JUDY and JEREMIAH GREEN. After magnum practice sessions in a confined space called the "Shed" (a, erm, shed that was built by BROCK next to his mother's mobile home in their trailer park) the weirdo-trio entered the dark and mysterious circle of CALVIN JOHNSON (and his 'K' imprint'), cutting their first self-titled single in his 'Dub Narcotic' studio. A move to the 'Up' label was to follow, and the release of two further sets; 'THIS IS A LONG DRIVE FOR SOMEBODY WITH NOTHING TO THINK ABOUT' and 'INTERSTATE 8' in 1996. Never making their minds up, and shifting to 'K' once again, the 3-piece released 'THE FRUIT THAT ATE ITSELF' and the more superior 'LONESOME CROWDED WEST' (1997), which contained the fabulous 'HEART COOKS BRAIN', a song for which the term "Slacker" could have been invented. The track had all the ingredients to become a generation-x anthem, with kooky scratching, lo-fi guitars, SLINT-like vocals, chicken noises and the lyrics: "I'm on my way to god knows, I don't care/in this place that I call home, the hours go fast and the days go so slow." The tracks on 'THE FRUIT THAT ATE ITSELF' rambled on in certain places and JOHNSON's deliberate messy production did the band no justice, certainly adding zero credibility to their name. BROCK and chums returned in 2000, issuing their major label ('Sony') debut 'THE MOON AND ANTARTICA', a wayward mix of downbeat, spacy lo-fi, jinxed-up no wave; The PIXIES show their looming influence as ever. Light rock/pop songs such as 'GRAVITY RIDES EVERYTHING' and the immensely enjoyable 'WILD PACK OF FAMILY DOGS' were immediate highlights. BROCK once again reminded us of how unique his voice was, because, like STIPE and CORGAN, there is no denying that he sounds like no-one else, with his trademark abrasive, broken-down lisp. The group also issued two previously unreleased sets; 2000's B-side and rarity collection 'BUILDING NOTHING OUT OF SOMETHING', and a brilliant

THE GREAT INDIE DISCOGRAPHY — The 1990s

"lost" album, 'SAD SAPPY SUCKER' (2001). The latter, supposedly recorded in 1994 (!) by 'K' record's CALVIN JOHNSON, was shelved and thought to have been destroyed. It played like JOHNSON's previous BECK effort 'One Foot In The Grave', all ramshackle recording and coughs and background noises. It also featured the ultra-rare 7" single 'WORMS VS. BIRDS", and a collection of BROCK's answerphone songs. But if his genius hadn't yet been fully realized then the delivery of 2002's 'SHARPEN YOUR TEETH' set, under the bizarre moniker UGLY CASANOVA (sounds more like a UK garage rap artist, than a fumbling indie hero), then all hope was lost. Issued to tremendous critical acclaim, BROCK insisted that the songs on the album were derived from a bunch of tapes left at 'Sub Pop's headquarters by a crazed MODEST MOUSE fan named Edgar Graham. A likely story indeed! It was, in fact, the work of BROCK, TIM RUTILI (of RED RED MEAT) and the recent CALIFONE, PALL JENKINS (from BLACK HEART PROCESSION) and post-rock producer BRIAN DECK (TORTOISE, The SEA AND THE CAKE). A soft, gliding addition to the alt country hall of fame, the set shone with ballads from a nowhere place, where the roads were dusty and every day is like a Sunday. 'CAT FACES', 'PACIFICO' and 'SO LONG TO THE HOLIDAYS' displayed moments of brilliance, but its 'HOTCHA GIRLS', with its catchy acoustic guitar riff, building orchestral movement and psychedelic click-track beats that made it one of the most uplifting and mournful songs of BROCK's career. A true gem of an album.

Album rating: THIS IS A LONG DRIVE FOR SOMEONE WITH NOTHING TO THINK ABOUT (*6) / INTERSTATE 8 mini (*6) / THE FRUIT THAT ATE ITSELF mini (*7) / THE LONESOME CROWDED WEST (*8) / THE MOON & ANTARTICA (*7) / SAD SAPPY SUCKER exploitation (*5) / Ugly Casanova: SHARPEN YOUR TEETH (*7)

ISAAC BROCK – vocals, guitar / **ERIC JUDY** – bass / **JEREMIAH GREEN** – drums

	not iss.	K
1994. (7"ep) <IPU 58> **BLUE CADET-3, DO YOU CONNECT?**	-	

– Blue cadet-3, do you connect? / Dukes up / Woodgrain / It always rains on a picnic / 5,4,3,2,1 ... lisp off.

	Sub Pop	Sub Pop
Feb 96. (7"m) <SP 338)> **BROKE. / WHENEVER I BREATHE OUT / POSITIVE NEGATIVE**		
(re-iss. Aug99; same)		

	not iss.	Up
Feb 96. (lp/cd) <UP 27/+CD> **THIS IS A LONG DRIVE FOR SOMEONE WITH NOTHING TO THINK ABOUT**	-	

– Dramamine / Breakthrough / Custom concern / Might / Lounge / Beach side property / Ionizes and atomizes / Head south / Dog paddle / Novocain stain / Tundra – Desert / Ohio / Exit does not exist / Talking shit about a pretty sunset / Make everyone happy – Mechanical birds / Space travel is boring. (lp+=) – Edit the sad parts / A manic depressive named laughing boy.

Nov 96. (m-lp/m-cd) <UP 35/+CD> **INTERSTATE 8**
– Interstate 8 / All night diner / Sleepwalking (couples only dance prom) / Tundra – Desert / Edit the sad parts.

	K	K
Jun 97. (m-lp/m-cd) <(KLP 63/+CD)> **THE FRUIT THAT ATE ITSELF**		

– Waydown / Dirty fingernails / Sunspots in the house of the late scapegoat / The fruit that ate itself / Summer / Karma's payment.

	Suicide Square	Suicide Square
Jan 98. (7") <(SS 003)> **LIFE OF ARCTIC SOUNDS. / MEDICATION**		Nov97
	Up	Up
Feb 98. (lp/cd) <(UP 44/+CD)> **THE LONESOME CROWDED WEST**		Oct97

– Teeth like God's shoeshine / Heart cooks brain / Convenient parking / Lounge (closing time) / Jesus Christ was an only child / Doin' the cockroach / Cowboy Dan / Trailer trash / Out of gas / Long distance drunk / Shit luck / Truckers atlas / Polar opposites / Bankrupt on selling / Styrofoam boots – It's all nice on ice, alright. (lp+=) – Baby blue sedan.

Feb 98. (7") <(UP 47)> **OTHER PEOPLE'S LIVES. / GREY ICE WATER**

Jul 98. (12"/cd-s) <(UP 58/+CD)> **WHENEVER YOU SEE FIT / ('A'-DJ Dynomite) / Omega (mixes by 764 HERO)**
(re-iss. 12" with 764 HERO on 'Suicide Squeeze'; SSQ 008)

	not iss.	Sub Pop
Oct 98. (7") **NEVERENDING MATH EQUATION. / WORKIN' ON LEAVIN' THE LIVIN'**	-	
	Matador	Sony
Jul 99. (7") (OLE 382-7) **HEART COOKS BRAIN. / SHIT LUCK**	-	-
Jun 00. (12"ep) <UP 90> **NIGHT ON THE SUN**	-	

– Night on the sun / You're the good things (it's alright to die) / Wild pack of family dogs / Dark center of the universe / Your life.
(above issued on 'Up')

Jul 00. (cd/d-lp) (OLE 450-2/-1) <EK 063871> **THE MOON & ANTARTICA** | | Jun00
– 3rd planet / Gravity rides everything / Dark center of the universe / Perfect disguise / Tiny cities made of ashes / A different city / The cold part / Alone down there / The stars are projectors / Wild packs of family dogs / Paper thin walls / I came as a rat / Lives / Life like weeds / What people are made of.

Nov 00. (12"ep) (OLE 464-1) **WILFUL SUSPENSION OF DISBELIEF / NIGHT ON THE SUN. / I CAME AS A RAT (LONG WALK OFF A SHORT DOCK) / YOU'RE THE GOOD THINGS** | | -

– compilations, others, etc. –

Feb 00. (lp/cd) <(UP 73/+CD)> **BUILDING SOMETHING OUT OF NOTHING** | | Jan00
– Never ending math equation / Interstate 8 / Broke / Medication / Workin' on leavin' the livin' / All nite diner / Baby blue sedan A life of arctic sounds / Sleepwalkin' / Grey ice water / Whenever I breathe out / Other people's lives.

Apr 01. (cd) <K; <(KLP 131CD)> **SAD SAPPY SUCKER** (rec.1994)
– Worm vs. birds / Four fingered fisherman / Wagon ride return / From point A to point B / Path of least resistance / It always rains on a picnic / Dukes up / Think

MODEST MOUSE (cont)

long / Every penny fedcat / Mice eat cheese / Race car grin you ain't no landmark / Red hand case / Secret agent X-9 / Blue cadet-3, do you connect? / Call to dial a song / 5,4,3,2,1 lisp off / Woodgrain / BMX crash / Sucker betru / Black blood and old newagers / SWY / Australopithecus / Sin gun chaser.

UGLY CASANOVA

ISAAC BROCK – vocals / **BRIAN DECK** – multi / **TIM RUTILI** – fiddle, guitar, keyboards, vocals (of CALIFONE, of RED RED MEAT) / **PALL A. JENKINS** – guitar, keyboards, vocals (of BLACK HEART PROCESSION) / **JOHN ORTH** – drums (of HOLOPAW)

			Sub Pop	Sub Pop
Jun 02.	(d-lp/cd) <(SP 552/+CD)> **SHARPEN YOUR TEETH**			May02

– Barnacles / Spilled milk factory / Parasites / Hotcha girls / (no song) / Diamonds on the face of evil / Cat faces / Ice on the sheets / Beesting / Pacifico / Smoke like ribbons / Things I don't remember / So long to the holidays.

MOGWAI

Formed: Glasgow, Scotland ... 1995 by DOMINIC AITCHISON, STUART BRAITHWAITE (also of ESKA) and MARTIN BULLOCH. In the Spring of '96, the band debuted with 'TUNER' / 'LOWER', a precursor to the band's double whammy NME Singles Of The Week, 'SUMMER' and 'NEW PATHS TO HELICON'. Early in 1997, they signed to the suffocatingly hip Glasgow-based 'Chemikal Underground' (home of BIS and friends, ARAB STRAP), the first outing being 'THE 4 SATIN EP'. A fine collection of their early singles was released a month later in June, although another label was responsible. That summer, the new 5-piece MOGWAI (complete with JOHN CUMMINGS and former TEENAGE FANCLUB member, BRENDON O'HARE) alternately bludgeoned/charmed the NME tent at Scotland's premier festival 'T In The Park' with their striking hybrid of SONIC YOUTH, METALLICA and pre-'Blue Monday' NEW ORDER! The feverishly anticipated "proper" debut album, 'MOGWAI YOUNG TEAM' was released late '97 to rave reviews, also scraping into the Top 75. Stunningly dynamic, the record shifted seamlessly from tranquil, bleakly beautiful soundscapes to brain scrambling white noise and sledgehammer riffing. Prime examples were 'LIKE HEROD', 'WITH PORTFOLIO' and 'MOGWAI FEAR SATAN', while 'TRACY' was a near 10-minute collage of drifting, childlike charm segueing into a taped phone conversation. Another track, 'R U STILL IN 2 IT', featured the mumbling vocal talents of ARAB STRAP's AIDAN MOFFAT. Prior to the album's release, O'HARE was summarily dismissed, apparently for yapping his way through an ARAB STRAP gig (tsk, tsk!). 1998 was indeed a busy year for the "young team", five releases hitting the shops between March and August and nearly all making the Top 75. The first of these, ' ..... DO THE ROCK BOOGALOO' was a split affair with fellow noisemongers MAGOO, the title not an EP but the "un"-covering of two classic BLACK SABBATH tracks, MOGWAI having a laugh with 'SWEET LEAF'. 'FEAR SATAN' was then chosen for the remix treatment (MY BLOODY VALENTINE's the highlight), while a full album, 'KICKING A DEAD PIG: MOGWAI SONGS REMIXED', was all their best tunes reworked by others including ARAB STRAP, KID LOCO and ALEC EMPIRE. 'Chemikal Underground' put their two-pennith in by issuing the 'NO EDUCATION = NO FUTURE (FUCK THE CURFEW)' ep, while 'TEN RAPID' was an early singles collection. The following March (with newcomer pianist BARRY BURNS now a fully-fledged member) 'COME ON DIE YOUNG' was the gangland war cry they chose as the title of their more sedate second album proper. A hard album indeed, in the sense that it took time to "get into" (probably due to the slight omission of their characteristic sonic crescendos), it unearthed a softer, more delicate style which was rewarded with a Top 30 entry. Opening with 'PUNK ROCK:' (complete with IGGY POP archive interview as voiceover), the Slo-Fi 'CODY' and the sludgedelic 'HELP BOTH WAYS, the album proved the young MOGWAI were top of the class; 'EX-COWBOY' and the emotional MORRICONE-inspired finale 'PUNK ROCK / PUFF DADDY / ANtICHRISt' were also noteworthy. Towards the end of '99, they delivered a self-titled EP, attributing 'STANLEY KUBRICK' as the lead track. 'BURN GIRL PROM QUEEN', an excellent diversion from the 'WAI featured the Cowdenbeath Brass Orchestra to eerie effect. Perhaps the best career move a band of their status could make, 'ROCK ACTION' (2001), saw MOGWAI reach new musical heights with their first release on their own 'Southpaw' label. The album, named after the band's other record label, focused its attention on the subtler side of life. It gladly took advice from the DAVID PAJO (who appears on the record) school of experimental rock, evoking his recent PAPA M meanderings. With its harmonic use of banjos, lap-steel and orchestra, the album harked back to the aforementioned 'STANLEY KUBRICK' EP. 'SINE WAVE' was briefly melodic, with hints of warped guitar static and BULLOCH's tom-toms adding an abrasive edge to the mix. '2 RIGHTS MAKE A WRONG' is quietly SLINT-ish, with the odd-kilter signature tune thrown in for good measure. But it's 'DIAL: REVENGE' with SUPER FURRY ANIMALS vocalist GRUFF RHYS which makes the album. His lingering Welsh vocals proved to be a catalyst for the overall structure of the album, and the emotions that surface during the intensified verse-chorus-verse of the song. Preceding the album by a few weeks was an unusual and unique appearance at Rothesay in the Isle Of Bute for 500 lucky fans who could afford the ferry and the entrance fee. • **Covered:** HONEY (Spacemen 3).

Album rating: MOGWAI YOUNG TEAM (*9) / KICKING A DEAD PIG: MOGWAI SONGS REMIXED (*7) / TEN RAPID compilation (*8) / COME ON DIE YOUNG (*9) / ROCK ACTION (*9)

pLasmatroN (b. STUART BRAITHWAITE) – guitar, vocals (also of ESKA, until Autumn '86) / **DEMONIC** (b. DOMINIC AITCHISON) – bass / **bionic** (b. MARTIN BULLOCH) – drums

		Rock Action	not iss.
Feb 96.	(ltd-7") (RAR 001) **TUNER. / LOWER**		
		Che	not iss.
May 96.	(ltd-7"green) (che 61) **ANGELS VERSUS ALIENS. / (other side by DWEEB)**		
		Love Train	not iss.
Sep 96.	(ltd-7"; "CAMDEN CRAWL II") (PUBE 011) **A PLACE FOR PARKS. / (other artists)**		
Oct 96.	(ltd-7"; "TEN DAY WEEKEND") (PUBE 012) **I AM NOT BATMAN. / (other artists)**		
Nov 96.	(ltd-7") (PUBE 014) **SUMMER. / ITHICA 27 o 9**		
		Wurlitzer Jukebox	not iss.
Jan 97.	(ltd-7") (WJ 22) **NEW PATHS TO HELICON**		

– Helicon 1 / Helicon 2.

  added **Cpt. Meat** (aka JOHN CUMMINGS) – guitar

		Chemikal Underground	Jetset
May 97.	(12"ep/cd-ep) (chem 015/+cd) <TWA 14CD> **4 SATIN EP**		

– Superheroes of BMX / Now you're taken / Stereo Dee. <US++> – Guardians of space. (re-iss. Apr99; same)

  added **+the relic+** (aka BRENDAN O'HARE – piano (of-MACROCOSMICA, ex-TEENAGE FANCLUB, ex-TELSTAR PONIES)

Oct 97.	(cd/d-lp) (chem 018 cd/lp) <7> **MOGWAI YOUNG TEAM**	75	

– Yes! I am a long way from home / Like Herod / Radar maker / Tracy / Summer (Priority version) / With portfolio / R u still in 2 it / A cheery wave from stranded youngsters / Mogwai fear Satan. (re-iss. Apr99; same)

| Feb 98. | (7") (ShaG 13.05) **Club Beatroot Part Four** | | - |

– Stereo Dee (live) / (other side by Ph FAMILY)
(above issued on 'Flotsam & Jetsam – 13th Note')

  now without O'HARE, who was sacked (see above)

| Mar 98. | (7"; split w/ MAGOO) (NING 47CD) **..... DO THE ROCK BOOGALOO** | 60 | - |

– Black Sabbath (by MAGOO) / Sweet leaf.
(above issued on 'Fierce Panda', below 2 for 'eye q' / US 'Jetset')

| Apr 98. | (cd-ep) (eyeuk 032cd) **FEAR SATAN remixes** | 57 | - |

– Mogwai remix / U-ziq remix / Surgeon remix / My Bloody Valentine remix. (re-iss. Apr99; same)

| May 98. | (cd/d-lp) (eyeuk cd/lp) <TWA 13 CD/LP> **KICKING A DEAD PIG: MOGWAI SONGS REMIXED** | | Jun98 |

– Like Herod (Hood remix) / Helicon 2 (Max Tundra remix) / Summer (Klute's weird winter remix) / Gwai on 45 (Arab Strap remix) / A cheery wave from stranded youngsters (Third Eye Foundation tet offensive remix) / Like Herod (Alec Empire's face the future remix) / Mogwai fear Satan (Surgeon remix) / R U still in to it? (DJ Q remix) / Tracy (Kid Loco's playing with the young team remix) / Mogwai fear Satan (Mogwai remix). (re-iss. Apr99; same) (cd re-iss. Sep01 on 'Chemikal Underground'; CHEM 057CD)

| Jun 98. | (12"ep/cd-ep) (chem 026/+cd) <111230> **NO EDUCATION = NO FUTURE (FUCK THE CURFEW) e.p.** | 68 | - |

– Xmas steps / Rollerball / Small children in the background. (re-iss. Apr99; same)

  In Nov'98, their track 'I CAN'T REMEMBER' featured on the 'Glasgow' V/A EP along with EL HOMBRE TRAJEADO, the KARELIA and the YUMMY FUR

  added **BARRY BURNS** – piano, flute, guitar

		Chemikal Underground	Matador
Mar 99.	(d-lp/cd) (chem 033/+cd) <OLE 365> **COME ON DIE YOUNG**	29	

– Punk rock: / Cody / Helps both ways / Year 2000 non-compliant cardia / Kappa / Waltz for Aidan / May nothing but happiness come through your door / Oh! how the dogs stack up / Ex-cowboy / Chocky / Christmas steps / Punk rock – Puff Daddy – ANtICHRISt.

| Oct 99. | (12"ep/cd-ep) (chem 036/+cd) <OLE 412> **MOGWAI e.p.** | | |

– Stanley Kubrick / Christmas song / Burn girl prom-queen / Rage: man. (re-iss. Sep01 as 'MOGWAI+6'+=; CHEM 056CD) – Xmas steps / Rollerball / Small children in the background / Superheroes of BMX / Now you're taken / Stereodee.

		Southpaw	Matador
Apr 01.	(cd/lp) (PAW CD/LP 001) <OLE 490> **ROCK ACTION**	23	

– Sine wave / Take me somewhere nice / O I sleep / Dial: revenge / You don't know Jesus / Robot chant / 2 rights make 1 wrong / Secret pint.

May 01.	(12"ep) <OLE 522-1> **D TO E / DRUM MACHINE. / (other 2 by Bardo Pond)**	-	- tour
		Rock Action	Matador
Oct 01.	(cd-s) (ROCKACTCD 10) <OLE 538> **MY FATHER MY KING**		

– compilations, etc. –

| Aug 98. | (cd) Rock Action; (ROCKACTCD 5) / Jetset; <TWA 05LP> **TEN RAPID (collected recordings 1996-1997)** | | Aug97 |

– Summer / Helicon 2 / Angels versus aliens / I am not Batman / Tuner / Ithica 27 o 9 / A place for parks / Helicon 1 / End.

MO-HO-BISH-O-PI

Formed: London, England ... early 1996 by Cardiff University fine art students, MARTIN BIMROSE and RICHARD ARNOLD (both minor veterans of various outfits), along with MIKE CARTER (ex-QUARTER FOIL). BIMROSE apparently arrived at the weird group moniker (an extinct exotic bird from Hawaii) while browsing through a Readers Digest in a doctor's surgery. As you do. Fusing elements of The FLAMING LIPS, PAVEMENT and BECK, MO-HO-BISH-O-PI released a series of homemade cassettes before finally delivering their debut proper, the 'TWO TIER WATER SKIER' EP, in August 1999. Described by most as lo-fi, slacker rock with glitter courtesy of stage costumes (i.e. Elvis suits, wigs, false beards), the trio released two further singles, 'SMOKE YOURSELF THIN' and 'VITAMIN E(P)', before cracking open the champagne with major label, 'V2'. However, with single after single (including 'HEAR THE AIR' twice!) not breaking through, and an album, 'VAGUE US' (2001), plummeting sales wise, it looked as though the MO-HO's would be taking a similar flight path to its namesake bird.

Album rating: VAGUE US (*6)

MARTIN BIMROSE – vocals, guitar (ex-CHOPPER, ex-SUKI) / **MIKE CARTER** – bass, vocals (ex-QUARTER FOIL) / **RICHARD ARNOLD** – drums, vocals (ex-FLETCH F FLETCH SHEPHERD)

		own label	not iss.
1997.	(ltd; c-ep) *(none)* **SCARECROW RECORDINGS**		-

– Belinda "middle" bit / Lands my town / Sir Gerri / Roast beef (live) / 2 (two) minute man (live).

1997.	(ltd; c-ep) *(none)* **FOR YOUR HEALTH**		-

– Another planet's records / Frisco disco / Lindy hop / Lands my town / Sir Gerri / Beauty cream.

1998.	(ltd; c-s) *(none)* **A11 NON-CLASSIFIED**		-

– 22nd tyme / Sheik ills / Another planet's records.

		Seriously Groovy	not iss.
Aug 99.	(cd-ep) *(LLL 2080)* **TWO TIER WATER SKIER**		-

– Smoke yourself thin / Another planet's records / Beauty cream / B blond / 22 time.

–––– in 1999, the track 'KATE IS COOL' featued on 'Fierce Panda' V/A compilation, 'Otter Than July'

		FF Vinyl	not iss.
Oct 99.	(7") *(FF 03)* **SMOKE YOURSELF THIN. / FINGERS FOR EYES**		-
Jan 00.	(cd-ep) *(FFZINC 004)* **VITAMIN E(P)**		-

– Fall apart / Take a target / Prosthetic groove / Vacuum / Gay fad.

		V2	not iss.
Jun 00.	(7") *(VVR 501351-7)* **HEAR THE AIR. / DON'T R.I.P. MY FACE**		-
	(cd-s+=) *(VVR 501351-3)* – Totally uninspired.		
Oct 00.	(7") *(VVR 501352-7)* **DROP JAW. / SWITCH TO POSITIVE**		-
	(cd-s+=) *(VVR 501352-3)* – Checkout.		
Mar 01.	(7") *(VVR 501590-7)* **PLAYBOY. / FISH + VISITORS**		-
	(cd-s+=) *(VVR 501590-3)* – Mt – 400v.		
May 01.	(12"/cd-s) *(VVR 501620-6/-3)* **NAMES, (FOR NAMELESS THINGS). / PUBLIC FOX / BURN THE BATTERIES**		-
Sep 01.	(7") *(VVR 501724-7)* **HEAR THE AIR. / BUTTERFLIES**		-
	(cd-s+=) *(VVR 501724-3)* – Three things.		
Sep 01.	(cd) *(VVR 101589-2)* **VAGUE US**		-

– Maverick / Vague us / Fista blista / Kids on cake / Hear the air / Drop jaw / Over seXXXed / E to C / Playboy / A moment too soon / The push ((parts 1, 2 and 3) / Names, (for nameless things) / All your health / Navel in a suitcase / Harpers.

MOISTBOYZ (see under ⇒ WEEN)

MOJAVE 3 (see under ⇒ SLOWDIVE)

MOLDY PEACHES

Formed: New York, USA . . . late 90's by ADAM GREEN and his partner KIMYA DAWSON. After meeting somewhere on the Lower East Side, this pair of pedigree Lo-Fi champions began writing songs after KIMYA fell in love with ADAM's childish post-grunge songs. The pair began writing and playing together with the assistance of a non-permanant backing group. After falling under the spell of the 'Anti-folk' scene in NYC, the charitable 'Rough Trade' offered to issue the album 'GREATEST HITS' (not in fact a 'best of') before the brilliant eponymous 'MOLDY PEACHES' hit the shops in April 2001. Embarrassingly Lo-Fi, the set consisted of a plethora of songs recorded mostly on a four-track. The opener 'LUCKY NUMBER NINE' was reminiscent of a hip, folksy VELVET UNDERGROUND, while the immature but poignant 'JORGE REGULA' used WAR's 'LOW RIDER' to bizarre and astounding effect. Amongst the gems were 'DOWNLOADING PORN WITH DAVO', a faux bebop track with jangly pianos et al and very rude lyrics indeed, 'WHO'S GOT THE CRACK?', a SOTW in the NME and 'LAZY CONFESSIONS', the latter could've been lifted straight from BECK's 'One Foot In The Grave' album. Sure, the lyrics were a bit childish (not to mention the costumes), and the music a tad loose, but the MOLDY PEACHES proved that content over style was more interesting than a polished A&R produced record with no soul. KIMYA and ADAM maintained their indie cool without once washing the grime from under their fingernails. With the MOLDY ones taking a brief sabbatical in 2002, ADAM GREEN found time to put together his eponymous solo debut (released in the US as 'GARFIELD'). Anti-folk and at times romantic, the GREEN album showed a mellower, reflective mood that was reminiscent of the days of TIM HARDIN, LEONARD COHEN or PHIL OCHS.

Album rating: MOLDY PEACHES (*7) / Adam Green: ADAM GREEN (*5)

ADAM GREEN – vocals, guitars / **KIMYA DAWSON** – vocals / with various friends/guests **BRIAN PILTIN** – bass, vocals / **JACK DISHEL** – guitar, drums, vocals / **STEVE ESPINOLA** – piano / **DREW BLOOD** – piano, vocals / **CHRIS BARRON** – guitar / **KURT FELDMAN** – drums / **DENISE KOLEDA** – bass / **ADAM GOLDSTEIN** – vocals / **HOLLIS SMITH** – vocals

		Rough Trade	Sanctuary
Mar 01.	(cd/lp; w-drawn) *(RTRADE CD/LP 013)* **GREATEST HITS**	-	-
Apr 01.	(one-sided-7") *(RTRADES 016)* **WHO'S GOT THE CRACK? / NYC'S LIKE A GRAVEYARD**		-
Apr 01.	(cd/lp) *(RTRADE CD/LP 014)* <83200> **MOLDY PEACHES**		Sep01

– Lucky number nine / Jorge Regula / What went wrong / Nothing came out / Downloading porn with Davo – All I ever think about is drowning / These burgers / Steak for chicken / On top / Greyhound bus / Anyone else but you / Little Bunny Foo Foo / The ballad of Helen Keller & Rip Van Winkle / Who's got the crack? / Lucky charms / D.2. boyfriend / I forgot / Lazy confessions / NYC's like a graveyard / Goodbye song.

Apr 02.	(cd-s) *(RTRADESCD 047)* **COUNTY FAIR / RAINBOWS**		-

ADAM GREEN

		Rough Trade	Sanctuary
Apr 02.	(cd) *(RTRADECD 051)* <83206> **ADAM GREEN** <US-title 'GARFIELD'>		Oct02

– Apples, I'm home / My shadows tag on behind / Bartholomew / Mozzarella swastikas / Dance with me / Computer show / Her father and her / Baby's gonna die tonight / Times are bad / Can you see me. <US+=> – Dance with me / Bleeding heart / Computer show.

Nov 02.	(cd-s) *(RTRADESCD 062)* **DANCE WITH ME / BLEEDING HEART / COMPUTER SHOW**		-

MOLES (see under ⇒ DAVIES, Richard)

MOLLY HALF HEAD

Formed: Manchester, England . . . 1992 out of mysterious beginnings by PHIL MURPHY and ANDY PICKERING who subsequently recruited PAUL BARDSLEY and NEIL DALY. Despite an A&R stampede at that year's 'In The City' music biz conference, the quartet ended up signing with local indie label, 'Playtime', through whom they issued a debut single, 'TASTE OF YOU'. Complaining to the music press that the dole were still on their backs, the band put their money where their mouth was and discounted the single for UB40 card holders. Musically, the band traded in inventive but unpretentious alternative pop with a leftfield streak compared to fellow Manc mavericks, MAGAZINE (whose track, 'THE LIGHT POURS OUT OF ME', they later covered), while lyrically, BARDSLEY was located somewhere between the impenetrability of MARK E. SMITH and the colourful laddishness of SHAUN RYDER. A further two singles, 'JUST' and 'BARNY', previewed a debut album, 'SULK' (1993), although the media hype had obviously failed to impress the average indie fan and the anticipated breakthrough never really materialised. Nevertheless, the band were given a second chance by 'Columbia', re-emerging in 1995 (by which time DALY had been replaced with GRAHAM ATKINSON) with an OASIS-friendly comeback single, 'BREAKING THE ICE'. Unfortunately, it failed to cut any ice in the charts although MOLLY HALF HEAD did manage to scrape into the Top 75 with subsequent single, 'SHINE'. The accompanying album, meanwhile, 'DUNCE' (1995), failed miserably and MOLLY HALF HEAD were soon out on their ear.

Album rating: SULK (*6) / DUNCE (*6)

PAUL BARDSLEY – vocals / **PHIL MURPHY** – guitar / **NEIL DALY** – bass / **ANDY PICKERING** – drums

		Playtime	Columbia
Mar 93.	(7"one-sided) *(AMUSE 015L)* **TASTE OF YOU**		-
	(10"+=/cd-s+=) *(AMUSE 015 T/CD)* – Treehouse steps / Vivid Whitsun.		
May 93.	(7") *(AMUSE 018)* **JUST. / TOE TO SAND**		-
	(10"+=/cd-s+=) *(AMUSE 018 T/CD)* – The light pours out of me.		
Sep 93.	(7") *(AMUSE 019L)* **BARNY. / SUCKING BLANKETS**		-
	(10"+=/cd-s+=) *(AMUSE 019 T/CD)* – Aeroplane mother / ('A'-Bernard Chevron mix).		
Nov 93.	(cd/c/lp) *(AMUSE 020 CD/MC/LP)* <64296> **SULK**		Feb94

– Vivid whitsun / Barny / Promote / Just / Arty breakfast / Bone idle / Spectacle clear / Taste of you / Hopscotch / Inkwell / Writing time / Ginger Pat's avenue / Toe to sand.

–––– **GRAHAM ATKINSON** – bass; repl. NEIL

		Columbia	Columbia
Feb 95.	(c-s) *(661216-4)* **BREAKING THE ICE. / BLISTERED**		-
	(10"+=) *(661216-0)* – Airwaves.		
	(cd-s++=) *(661216-2)* – Ginger Pat's avenue.		
May 95.	(7"clear) *(662073-7)* **SHINE. / PUMP IT UP**	73	-
	(cd-s+=) *(662073-5)* – Stay as you are / 1 DY.		
	(cd-s) *(662073-2)* – ('A'side) / Exactly / P.G. / Are 'friends' electric.		
Jul 95.	(cd/c/lp) *(<478314-2/-4/-1>)* **DUNCE**		

– Breaking the ice / Natures slice / Aisle 8 / Shine / Dunce / Caprio / Heaton's bliss / What will come / Seat on teak / Meccano / Who buys.

–––– split some time later

MONACO
(see under ⇒ NEW ORDER; in 80's section)

MONDO CRESCENDO

Formed: Washington D.C., USA . . . 1995 by JENNIFER TAYLOR, MIKE HAMMEL (ex-ROPERS) and drummer DOUGLAS ARMOUR. The trio had already released a couple of singles under the name, JUNIPER, before relocating to San Francisco in 1997 and adopting the moniker the MONDO CRESCENDO. The band released their debut EP 'GET FADED' through the 'Blackbean & Placenta Tape Club' label in 1998. The EP was six songs of straightforward sun-kissed indie pop which were elevated above the rest of the pack by TAYLOR's blissful vocals. The group's first album, 'YOUNG, NAKED AND VERY WITH IT', arrived the following year and showed the band had developed as musicians without losing any of their ability for producing infectious uplifting tunes. Sadly for their fans this was to be The MONDO CRESCENDO's last outing, however TAYLOR and HAMMEL did go on to form The VEXERS who are scheduled to release an album in 2003.

Album rating: GET FADED (*5) / YOUNG, NAKED AND VERY WITH IT (*7)

JUNIPER

JENNIFER TAYLOR – vocals, guitar / **SCOTT** – bass / drummer

		not iss.	A Turntable Friend
1996.	(7"blue) <TURN 31> **YOU DON'T HIDE SO WELL. / ANNA THEMA**	–	
1996.	(7") <ORG 002> **MAKING GERARD SMILE. /**	not iss.	Orange Fantastic
1997.	(7") <FAN 005> **THINK AND DIE THINKING. / SUMMER ON MY MIND**	not iss.	–

MONDO CRESCENDO

JENNIFER TAYLOR – vocals, guitar / **MICHAEL HAMMER** – bass (ex-ROPERS) / **DOUGLAS ARMOUR** – drums

		not iss.	Train Bridge
1998.	(7") **A BOY AND HIS ITCH. / NO REASON WHY**	–	
		Blackbean & Placenta	Blackbean & Placenta
May 98.	(7") <ACME 49> **CALIFORNIA SUN. / ON THE BEACH**		–
Jun 98.	(m-cd) <BBP 92> **GET FADED** – (I don't care / The sun don't shine no more / Baby / Spaceship terrific / Shhh / La surf noire / Heaven only knows.		–
Nov 99.	(cd) <(BBP 150)> **YOUNG, NAKED AND VERY WITH IT** – Free / 3 little words / Check it on out / Just kiss me / Who's holding you tonight? / True / The other side / What kind of friend / Bluejeans / The flame / Love light.		

—— TAYLOR + HAMMER later formed The VEXES

MONGERS (see under ⇒ POLICECAT)

MONGOOSE (see under ⇒ SECRET GOLDFISH)

MONKEYWRENCH (see under ⇒ MUDHONEY; 80's section)

MONOGRAPH

Formed: North London, England . . . early 1998 by multi-instrumentalist and singer-songwriter ROB CRUTCHLEY. They issued his debut EP, 'PAPER MUSEUM', on the 'Shinkansen' imprint in mid 1998. Initially just himself, he recruited friends MARTINE and CLIVE, with GETHYN JORDAN, SURAIN LOKUGE and STEVE McNAIRN, delivering the single, 'PLEASE DON'T BE AFRAID OF ANYTHING' (1999), before embarking on a toilet-tour of London's underground indie venues. John Peel was impressed with the combo's downbeat indie-guitar musings and offered to record them in session at the beginning of 1999. An impressive, home-recorded album would follow, entitled 'LORELEI' (2000), which perfectly showcased CRUTCHLEY's songwriting abilities – however, he was now a man without a band as the remainder of the group had tired of live performances in small venues. CRUTCHLEY decided to start anew. In mid-2000, he entered the studio once more, under the supposedly long-term moniker PACIFIC RADIO and issued a seven song mini-set in September of that year.

Album rating: LORELEI (*5) / PACIFIC RADIO mini (*4)

ROB CRUTCHLEY – vocals, multi / with help from **MARTINE ROBERTS** – backing vocals / **CLIVE PAINTER** – keyboards

		Shinkansen	not iss.
Jun 98.	(7"ep) (SHINKANSEN 11) **PAPER MUSEUM** – International Klein blue / Cheering, applause / Brevity thing / Paper museum.		–
Feb 99.	(7"m) (SHINKANSEN 15) **PLEASE DON'T BE AFRAID OF ANYTHING. / STRANGE DISEASE / A STORY TIME HAS TOLD US** (cd-s+=) (SHINKANSEN 15CD) – PAPER MUSEUM EP.		–

—— ROB with live band **STEVE McNAIRN** – guitar / **SURAIN LOKUGE** – bass / **GETHYN JORDAN** – drums

| Sep 99. | (7"m) (SHINKANSEN 19) **DON'T GIMME SHELTER. / HOLDING ON IN COLOUR / PALE LIGHT** | | – |
| Oct 99. | (cd) (SHINKANSEN 21) **LORELEI**
 – Something that you do / Speaking clearly / An afterthought / The river / Last word to the underdog / To be loved / Our sometime star / Don't gimme shelter / Long stretch / New league of nations / Your perfect world / I can't help it / Finding new rest for the ghost / Bring on the lonely hearts / Gallant losers. | | – |

PACIFIC RADIO

—— CRUTCHLEY + McNAIRN + PAINTER

| Sep 00. | (m-cd) (SHINKANSEN 27) **PACIFIC RADIO**
 – Slow refrain 1 / Downwind / Pop heart / You don't understand / Head start for nothing / The rain comes down / Slow refrain 2. | | – |

MONO MEN

Formed: Bellingham, Washington, USA . . . 1990 by garage rock enthusiasts DAVE CRIDER, LEDGE MORRISETTE, AARON ROEDER and ex-GAME OF VULTURES man JOHN MORTENSEN. This prolific band of crazy, rude, trashy revivalists were named in homage to the short-lived surf-punk quartet The READY MEN, who played head-stomping liquor-fuelled rock in the early sixties. Not only were the MONO MEN responsible for some of the sleaziest grindcore retro-rock of the 1990's, but they also ran their own 'Estrus' empire and the annual Garage Shock music and movie festival, up in Washington.

After 1990's widely ignored 'STOP DRAGGIN' ME DOWN', they issued an album of thrash instrumentals, called, erm, 'SHUT THE FUCK UP!' (1993). In the same year they delivered the DIY punk album 'BENT PAGES', in which the ensemble re-issued some of their early singles and delivered some weird but brilliant covers. 'SIN & TONIC' was dropped in 1994, proceeded by the concert set 'THOSE MONO MEN RECORDED LIVE! AT TOM'S STRIP-N-BOWL', in which the listener could hear the rumble of bowling pins in the foreground (the show was actually put on for a friend's bachelor party). In between that and the covers album 'TEN COOL ONES' (1995) the group delivered 'HAVE A NICE DAY, MOTHERFUCKER', which was to be their final LP in 1997, before CRIDER and ROEDER formed WATTS with CHRIS DEGON and JEFF BRAIMES and recorded their self-titled debut (1999). Like the lunacy and ubiquitousness of MAN OR ASTROMAN?, The MONO MEN frequently cropped up on the early-to-mid 90s indie scene. And gawddamn, they rocked! • **Covers:** RAT FINK (Nomads) / THE BOSS (Rumblers) / AIN'T NO FRIEND OF MINE (. . . Sparkles) / MR. ELIMINATOR (Dick Dale) / SHAKIN' ALL OVER (Johnny Kidd) / 54-40 OR FIGHT (Dead Moon) / I'M BRANDED + SWITCHBLADE + JACK THE RIPPER + COMANCHE + RUMBLE + RUN CHICKEN RUN (Link Wray) / HE'S WAITIN' + BOSS HOGG + THE WITCH (Sonics) / CATALINA + LIE DETECTOR (Wild Billy Childish) / GONNA MISS ME (13th Floor Elevators) / DRAGSTRIP (Fender Benders) / RUN DOWN (Saints) / SIGNED D.C. (Love) / YOU MUST BE A WITCH (Lollipop Shoppe) / OVER THE EDGE (Wipers) / THE WIMP (Dils) / etc.

Album rating: STOP DRAGGIN' ME DOWN (*5) / SHUT THE FUCK UP! (*6) / BENT PAGES compilation (*7) / SIN AND TONIC (*8) / WRECKER! (*4) / LIVE! AT TOM'S STRIP-N-BOWL (*6) / TEN COOL ONES compilation (*6) / HAVE A NICE DAY, MOTHERFUCKER (*5)

DAVE CRIDER – vocals, guitar / **MARX WRIGHT** – guitar, vocals / **LEDGE MORRISETTE** – bass / **AARON ROEDER** – drums

		Estrus	Estrus
1989.	(7") <ES 71> **BURNING BUSH. / RAT FINK**	–	
1990.	(7") <ES 74> **I DON'T CARE. / JEZEBEL**	–	
1990.	(cd) <ESCD 1R> **STOP DRAGGIN' ME DOWN** – Stop draggin' me down / Right now / The boss / Ain't no friend of mine / No way back / I don't care / Dead end / That's her / Girl / Stay awake / Fate / Reptile / Daylight / Pete's spango / Burning bush. (UK-iss.Sep94; same as US)		
1991.	(7"ep) <ES 718> **BOOZE EP** – Watch outside / Catalina / Rumble.	–	
1992.	(7"m) <SFTRI 164> **TOOK THAT THING. / SHAKIN' ALL OVER / MR. ELIMINATOR** (above issued on 'Sympathy For The Record Industry', below on 'Rekkids')	–	
1992.	(7") <rekkids 003> **HE'S WAITING. / BOSS HOG**	–	
1992.	(7") <scat 020> **AWAY. / PEACE OF MIND** (above issued on 'Scat', below on 'September Gurls')	–	
1992.	(7"m) <SGs 005> **ONE SHOT. / 54-40 OR FIGHT / RESET**	–	
1992.	(7"m) <SCAP 011> **REMIND ME. / THAT'S YOUR PROBLEM / I'M BRANDED** (above issued on 'Screaming Apple', below on 'Lucky')	–	
1992.	(7"m) <LKY 004> **DON'T KNOW YET. / LIE DETECTOR / JACK THE RIPPER**	–	
1992.	(7") <SP 159> **SKIN & BONES. / COMANCHE** (above issued on 'Sub Pop', below on 'Lance Rock')	–	
1992.	(7") <LRR 005> **JUST A GIRL> / OVER THE EDGE**	–	

—— **JOHN MORTENSEN** – guitar (ex-GAME OF VULTURES) repl. WRIGHT

Mar 93.	(7") <(RR 072-7)> **I'M HANGING. / (other by YOUNG FRESH FELLOWS)** (above issued on 'Rise') (below on 'Au-Go-Go')		
1993.	(7") <ANDA 163> **LAST STRAW. / CRUSTER'S THEME**	–	
1993.	(m-cd) <ES 101> **SHUT THE FUCK UP!** – Wrecker! / Phantom on Lane 12 / Little Miss 3-B / Switchblade / Reset / Warm piston / Mr. Eliminator / Rumble.		
1993.	(7") <036> **WRECKER! / 'TIL THE END OF THE DAY** (above issued on '1+2' records, below on 'Demolition Derby')	–	
1993.	(7") <DD 002> **DRAGSTRIP. / (other by APEMEN)**	–	
1994.	(cd) <ESD 1218> **SIN AND TONIC** – Mystery girl / Slammer / Hexed / One more time / Waste o' time / Skin & bones / Monster / Powerage woman / Afterglow / Scotch / No way / Can't understand.		
1994.	(7") <dig 704> **SEE MY SOUL. / AS FOR TOMORROW** (above issued on 'Dig', below on 'Lucky')	–	
1994.	(7"ep) <E.L. 002> **DAS MONOMEN LOST IN EUROPE (live)** – One shot / Over the edge / Boss Hog / Testify.	–	
1994.	(7") <ES 752> **MYSTERY GIRL. / SIN AND TONIC**	–	
Sep 94.	(cd) <(ESD 123)> **WRECKER!** – Watch outside / Your eyes / Last straw / One shot / Took that thing / He's waiting / Swampland / See my soul / Tomahawk / Testify / Just a girl / Don't know yet / I'm hangin' / Remind me / I'm hangin'.		
Oct 94.	(7") <SMUT 001> **HEXED. / SKIN & BONES** (above issued on 'Trash Shity Rekids', below on 'Impossible')		
1995.	(7") <IMPS 006> **POWERAGE WOMAN. / GYPSY WOMAN**		
1995.	(7") <HS 95753> **SLAMMER. / SIGNED D.C.** (above issued on 'Helter Skelter', below on 'El Diablo')	–	
1995.	(7") **CAN'T UNDERSTAND. / TESTIFY**	–	
Jun 95.	(lp/cd) <(ES 108/+CD)> **LIVE! AT TOM'S STRIP-N-BOWL (live)** – Hexed / Mystery girl / Lie detector / Phantom on Lane 12 / Watch outside / T.S.B. / Just a girl / One shot / Testify / Waste o' time.		
1996.	(7") <ES 782> **ANOTHER WAY GIRL** – Another way / Behind bars.	–	
1996.	(7") <RPM 004> **KICK OUT THE JAMS. / (other by GIRL TROUBLE)** (above issued on 'Gearhead', below on 'Man's Ruin')	–	

MONO MEN (cont)

Date	Format	Cat#	Title		
1996.	(7")	<MR 013>	**MONSTER. / YOU MUST BE A WITCH**	–	
1996.	(7"ep)	<ES 788>	**CROSS ALLEY STOMP (live)**	–	
			– Wrecker! / Rumble / One more time / Remind me.		
1996.	(7")	(NBT45 26)	**WASTE O' TIME. / RUN DOWN**	–	
			(above issued on 'Next Big Thing')		
Sep 97.	(cd/lp)	<(ES 1234 CD/LP)>	**HAVE A NICE DAY, MOTHERFUCKER**		
			– Off my back / Murder city nights / Rev it up / Hate your way / Another way / Back at you / The wimp / Feel alright / Sin #1 / Stand back / Hey (you with the face) / Get a clue.		

not iss.   *Pure Vinyl*

1998.	(7"orange-ep)	<PV 011>	**HATE YOU WAY**	–	
			– Hate your way / Off my back / Rev it up / Sin #1.		

―― split up after above

– compilations, etc. –

1993.	(cd)	*Estrus*; <9301-2>	**BENT PAGES** (singles)	–	
			– The witch / Catalina / Lie detector / Daylight / Right now / Over the edge / etc. (UK-iss.May87 on 'Au-Go-Go' lp/cd; ANDA 215/+CD)		
1996.	(7"m)	*Estrus*; <ES 701>	**BURNING BUSH. / RAT FINK / DON'T TREAD ON ME**		
Sep 96.	(cd/lp)	*Scat*; <54>	**TEN COOL ONES** (covers)		
			– Kick out the jams / 54-40 or fight / You're gonna miss me / The way you touch my hand / Gypsy women / Run chicken run / Hey little bird / Already gone / As for tomorrow / Return of the rat.		

WATTS

DAVE + AARON were joined by **CHRIS DeGON** – bass + **JEFF BRAIMES** – vocals (ex-MAVEN)

Estrus   *Estrus*

Aug 99.	(cd)	<(ES 1258)>	**WATTS**		
			– Cool American / Misery / Goddamn devil / Co'mon and drug me / Monkey chain / Tarantula / Star fukka / Sweet invicta / Outta my mind / Kings of jackin' you around.		

MONROE MUSTANG

Formed: Norman, Oklahoma, USA ... (but based Texas) early 1990's by JASON STOUT, BRIAN BARRY and TAYLOR HOLLAND, the trio recruiting former PILOT SHIPS members MIKE and CHRIS LINNEN before releasing their 1996 debut single 'I WAS EIGHTEEN, IT WAS HATE'. The following year saw another single release 'GUIDED BY WUSSES' (a slight dig at GBV, no doubt), however it was not until 1998 that the band delivered their first full-length album 'PLAIN SWEEPING THEMES FOR THE UNPREPARED'. The album was jammed with melodic lo-fi indie rock songs, however, it failed to deliver anything modern in the sense that The BEATLES to APPLES (IN STEREO) had covered all that ground. The group's second album, 'THE ELEPHANT SOUND' (1999), showed a slight improvement in terms of the complexity of their songs but primarily it was just basic psychedelic indie rock. • **Covered:** WAITING (Pete Townshend).

Album rating: PLAIN SWEEPING THEMES FOR THE UNPREPARED (*5) / THE ELEPHANT SOUND (*7) / DE AVONDEN 091099 mini (*4)

JASON STOUT + BRIAN BARRY + TAYLOR HOLLAND / MIKE LINNEN + CHRIS LINNEN

not iss.   *Framed!*

1996.	(7"m)	<4963>	**I WAS EIGHTEEN, IT WAS HATE. / SPY / MAUDE**	–	

not iss.   *Ata-Glance*

1997.	(7")		**GUIDED BY WUSSES. / CARCRASH HEAD**	–	

Trance Syndicate   *Trance Syndicate*

Jul 98.	(lp/cd)	<(TR 68/+CD)>	**PLAIN SWEEPING THEMES FOR THE UNPREPARED**		
			– Waking up / I was eighteen, it was hate / Elephant sound / The bees / Candidate / We aren't the stars / Incredible eagle / Vinyl / Veronica / TN spirit of the wild / Overplayed / The charges / Wusses / Opus.		

Jagjaguwar   *Jagjaguwar*

Jun 99.	(cd)	<(JAG 011CD)>	**THE ELEPHANT SOUND**		May99
			– Dee / Been choppin' that mountain a thousand . . . / Uninspired / Cat – Moth / Lie / Bottle rocket / Veronica (orange) / The elephant sound 424.		
Sep 00.	(m-cd)	<(JAG 24CD)>	**DE AVONDEN 091099 (live acoustic)**		
			– Evening / Lie / Uninspired / Waiting / Mountain / Overplayed / Crepescule.		

Emperor Jones   *Emperor Jones*

Nov 00.	(cd-ep)	<(EJ 34CD)>	**I AM THE ONLY RUNNING FOOTMAN**		
			– F.L.N.W.K. / Weren't gone / Spirits of unfreedom / Your shapeless head / The Ford Chevy debate.		

MONSTERLAND

Formed: Danbury, Connecticut, USA ... 1992 by THOM MONAHAN, GREG VEGAS and TODD CRONIN. MONSTERLAND formed under slightly unusual circumstances when the two founding members (MONAHAN and VEGAS) were still working in the ladies section of Macy's in their sleepy home town. After a debut 7", 'BLANK' – followed by their first for 'SpinArt', 'PEANUT BUTTER KARMA' – KURT RALSKE (of ULTRA VIVID SCENE) was brought in to produce the 'LOSER FRIENDLY' EP. Still unable to work as a unit full-time, the harsh rock trio released their first full-length album, 'DESTROY WHAT YOU LOVE' (1993), which had seen FUGAZI producer TED NICELY ride the faders for what is the only MONSTERLAND album. The sound was melodic but visceral alternative indie-rock, lying between NIRVANA and LEMONHEADS. FUGAZI could be heard in the dimly lit backdrop, although the guitar pop riffs surrounded a softer SONIC YOUTH, much like their mini-set follow-up, 'AT ONE WITH TIME' (1994). Sadly, the band could have received a welcome niche within the market, but instead, were sectioned along with the cycle of grungy wannabes in the height of West Coast rock. • **Covered:** FISH EYE (Bailter Space).

Album rating: DESTROY WHAT YOU WANT (*7) / AT ONE WITH TIME mini (*5)

THOM MONAHAN – vocals, bass / **GREG VEGAS** – guitar, vocals / **TODD CRONIN** – cymbals, drums

Serial Killer   *SpinArt*

Mar 92.	(7")	<SPART 008>	**PEANUT BUTTER KARMA. / WHY DID I FALL FOR YOU?**	–	
Apr 92.	(7")	<FATAL 1>	**PEANUT BUTTER KARMA. / SUNBURN**	–	–
Jan 93.	(7"maroon)	<MUDD 3>	**BLANK. / China Pig: MAGGIE**	–	
			(above issued on 'Mudd Industries')		
Jun 93.	(10"ep/cd-ep)	<SPART 009>	**LOSER FRIENDLY EP**	–	
			– Magazine / Chris' clone / Store 28 / Sunshine and piss / Presence dear (I'm always touched by your) / 244-250.		

Seed-Atlantic   *Seed-Atlantic*

Oct 93.	(7")	<(SEED 005)>	**INSULATION. / TOTALLY WIRED**		
Nov 93.	(cd/c/lp)	<(14236-2/-4/-1)>	**DESTROY WHAT YOU LOVE**		Aug93
			– Insulation / Rid of you / Lobsterhead / Nobody loves you / Car on fire / Twice at the end / At one with time / Fish eye / Crashing teenage crush / Angel scraper / Bursitis.		
Mar 94.	(m-cd/m-lp)	<(95928-2/-1)>	**AT ONE WITH TIME**		
			– At one with time / Jane Wiedlin used to be a Go-Go / Your touch is uncomfortable to me / Chewbacca / Blank / Girlfriend on drugs.		

―― disbanded in the mid-90's

MOOG COOKBOOK (see under ⇒ JELLYFISH)

MOONEY SUZUKI

Formed: New York City, New York, USA ... late 1996 by JOHN PAUL RIBAS, GRAHAM TYLER, SAMMY JAMES JR. and WILL ROCKWELL. Playing classic proto-punk flair like the great forefather figures of MC5 and The STOOGES, the band were never going to go far wrong as they kept to the basic format and dropped any ironical retro-looking stance. 'SUZUKI spent the following few years gigging and partying, rock'n'roll style around their native city, before debuting with the eponymously-titled single, 'MOONEY SUZUKI' in 1999. The next year saw the release of their debut LP, 'PEOPLE GET READY', only just predating the international renewed interest in R&R that would ride in with fellow New Yorkers, The STROKES. The MOONEY SUZUKI bettered their honest brand of punky R&B with their sophomore set, 'ELECTRIC SWEAT' (2002), their integrity and energy putting paid to critics who saw them as mimics of a pre-gone era.

Album rating: PEOPLE GET READY (*6) / ELECTRIC SWEAT (*7)

SAMMY JAMES JR. – vocals, guitar / **GRAHAM TYLER** – guitar / **JOHN PAUL RIBAS** – bass / **WILL ROCKWELL** – drums

not iss.   *Self-Starter*

1998.	(7"ep)	<PSP 004>	**TAKING ME APART**	–	
			– A simple life / Taking me apart / Lookout!		

not iss.   *Sonic Unyon*

1998.	(7"ep)		**LOVE IS EVERYWHERE**	–	
			– Love is everywhere / I say I love you / Don't answer / Guitdown!		

not iss.   *own label*

1999.	(cd-ep)		**THE MOONEY SUZUKI EP**	–	
			– And begin / I say I love you / Half of my heart / My dear persephone / Turn my blue sky black / Your love is a gentle whip.		

not iss.   *Telstar*

1999.	(7"m)	<TR 036>	**YOUR LOVE IS A GENTLE WHIP. / TURN MY BLUE SKY BLACK / BABIES IN THE CRADLE**		

Estrus   *Estrus*

Sep 00.	(lp/cd)	<(ES 1273/+CD)>	**PEOPLE GET READY**		
			– Singin' a song about today / Right about now / Make my way / Make you mine / Half of my heart / Everything's gone wrong / I say I love you / Do it / My dear persephone / Yeah you can / Oh no / Everytime.		

Gammon   *Gammon*

Apr 02.	(7"/cd-s)	<(GR 2105/+CD)>	**OH SWEET SUSANNA. / SAY MAN, WHAT TIME IS IT?**		
May 02.	(cd)	<(GR 2101CD)>	**ELECTRIC SWEAT**		
			– Electric sweat / In a young man's mind / Oh sweet Susanna / A little bit of love / It's not easy / Natural fact / It's showtime (part 2) / I woke up this mornin' / The broken heart / Electrocuted blues. <d-lp-iss.Aug02; GR 2101>		

Estrus   *Estrus*

Jun 02.	(7")	<(ES7 162)>	**HOT. / SHITTER**		

MOONFLOWERS

Formed: Bristol, England ... 1987 by THE REVEREND SONIK RAY alongside SMOKIN' SAM, JESSIE JAMES VERNON, ELECTRIC PUSSY, DOUGAL MacSHAGGER and ELMO. After a debut EP, 'WE DIG YOUR EARTH', in summer '89 and a cover of Sly Stone's 'GET HIGHER' on 'Heavenly' the following year, RAY formed his own label, 'Pop God'. He quickly signed local lads, The FAMILY who released their own mini-lp while The MOONFLOWERS themselves were afforded free publicity and ensuing hype after appearing in court for not paying the dreaded Poll Tax. A few months later – to promote their limited 7"single, 'WARSHAG' – the latter day hippies were again a talking point after appearing naked (hand over parts) in the NME. Despite their dedication to the free festival circuit and community benefit work, their prolific release schedule continued apace and a long awaited debut album, 'HASH SMITS', appeared towards the tail end of '91. Influenced by a freaky hybrid of US West Coast psychedelic pop, GONG weirdness, GEORGE CLINTON's colourful funk experimentation, dub reggae and even ZODIAC MINDWARP, MOONFLOWERS were clearly out on a musical limb. As for playing the music business game, the band were content to communicate with the media by hand-written letter and defiantly refused to be lumped in with any music press-created scene. A couple of 1992 covers EP's showed the band weren't lacking a sense of humour while a follow-up album, 'FROM WHALES TO JUPITER BEYOND THE STARS OF RAINBOHEMIA' (1993) preached a new, unceasingly optimistic hippy gospel for the crusty generation. 1995's 'SHAKE IT TOGETHER' EP, meanwhile, was something of a minor classic, a possible precursor to the stoned genius of The BETA BAND. The lead track was taken from the longest titled album in history 'WE WOULD FLY AWAY ...' (see discography), the MOONFLOWERS last epistle before their mid-90's demise. After a period busking in France (at times as the RAINBOHEMIANS), the group returned to the studio for Japanese-only LP's. Meanwhile, JESSE VERNON was carving out his own solo sojourn via MORNING STAR who as a duo/trio/quintet/30-piece, released a few indie gems; SEAN O'NEILL and his SOLAR MUMUNS played gigs in and around Bristol. Tragically, on the 1st of June 2002, TOBY PASCOE died. • **Covered:** NORWEGIAN WOOD (Beatles) / ARMAGEDDON TIME (Clash) / TIGHTEN UP (Archie Bell & The Drells) / I JUST CAN'T BE DISCOMAN TODAY (Damned) / NAIMA (John Coltrane). • **Trivia:** All their mothers sang backing vocals on their last 1991 EP.

Album rating: HASH SMITS (*6) / FROM WHALES TO JUPITER BEYOND THE STARS OF RAINBOHEMIA (*6) / WE WOULD FLY AWAY ... (*6) / THE BLACK BEETLES AND WHITE BIRD collection (*5) / BRAINWASHING AND HEARTISTS BLUE LIFE STRIPES (*5) / DON'T JUST SIT THERE ... FLY (*5) / Morning Star: MORNING STAR (*5) / MY PLACE IN THE DUST (*5)

THE REVEREND SONIK RAY (b. SEAN O'NEILL) – vocals, guitar / **SMOKIN' SAM** (b. SAM BURNS) – keyboards, saxophone, vocals / **JESSIE JAMES VERNON** (b. DAVE VERNON) – guitar / **ELECTRIC PUSSY** (b. YODDOM POPE) – drums / **DOUGAL MacSHAGGER** (b. PAUL WATERWORTH) – bass / **ELMO** – DJ

Electric Stars / not iss.

Jul 89. (7"ep/12"ep) *(EST/+T 1)* **WE DIG YOUR EARTH EP**
 – Rock'n'roll / My baby don't love me anymore / All or nothing / Johnny.

— **PRAISE THE ELECTRIC MOONCHILLUM** (b. TOBY PASCOE) – percussion, vocals; repl. ELMO

Heavenly / not iss.

Oct 90. (12") *(HVN 5-12)* **GET HIGHER. / ('A'-Rather large in the Bristol area mix) / ('A'-dub mix by Mark Lusardi)**

Pop God / not iss.

Jan 91. (12"etched) *(PGTT 003)* **WARSHAG**
May 91. (7"etched) *(PGTT 7)* **FIRE**
 (12"+=) *(PGTT 7)* – Bring me down gently / I want to dill you.
Oct 91. (12"ep) *(PGTT 010)* **GROOVEPOWER EP**
 – Groovepoer (Big) / Groovepower (Fast) / Groovepower (Dub).
Dec 91. (cd/lp) *(PG CD/LP 012)* **HASH SMITS**
 – Rock'n'roll / We dig your earth / Warshag / Fire / I want to dill you / Dub time / My baby / Groovepower / Back where I belong / Get higher.
May 92. (12"ep/cd-ep) *(PG TT/CD PGTT 15)* **TIGHTEN UP ON THE HOUSEWORK BROTHERS AND SISTERS EP**
 – Brothers and sisters / Housework / Tighten up.
Nov 92. (12"ep/cd-ep) *(PGTT 023)* **THE COVERS EP**
 – I've just got to be discoman today / Armageddon time / Tighten up / Norwegian wood.

— **GINA GRIFFIN** – violin, viola, vocals; repl. POPE

Jun 93. (cd/c/lp) *(PG CD/MC/LP 025)* **FROM WHALES TO JUPITER BEYOND THE STARS OF RAINBOHEMIA**
 – There we will find the sun / Connotation vibration / Goldmine / Ug / Smile and the face of evil and dance / Share your food / Planet Dodo / Song for summer / Serpents of the deep / Come by ours, love / Dreamlovers / Jupiter / Stick and bow.
May 95. (12"ep/cd-ep) *(PG TT/CD 032)* **SHAKE IT TOGETHER / SOUL HEAVY. / DUB IT TOGETHER / I WOULD LIKE TO SEE EGYPT ONE OF THESE DAYS**
May 95. (cd/d-lp) *(PG CD/LP 034)* **WE WOULD FLY AWAY (WE COULD FLY AWAY NEVER LOOK BACK AND LEAVE THE WORLD TO SPIN SILENTLY IN A SUICIDE PACT AND ALL THE COLOURS AND SOUNDS THAT PASS THROUGH US IN SPACE FALL DOWN TO THE EARTH AND PUT A MILE ON IT'S FACE)**
 – Future alien / What is going to happen / Nopar king / The world leaves the world / Shake it together / Revolution / Path of the free / White bird / Sun and Moon / The winkstress / Friends / If you feel like / Colours and sounds / Keepers of the fire / The world's most famous unknown people.

Crue-l / not iss.

1997. (cd) *(KYTHMAK 035DA)* **BRAINWASHING AND HEARTISTS BLUE LIFE STRIPES** – Japan
 – Cairo disco / Goldmine / Pink girl / We are stars / Titanium mountain / Losing you / Spirits / Naima / Skydancer / Let it rain.

— now without PAUL

P-Vine / not iss.

2000. (cd) *(PCD 24022)* **DON'T JUST SIT THERE ... FLY** – Japan
 – Baba Yaga and the revolution / Apple blossom / Morning pipe / Fast friends / House of the silver hare / The river is flowing / I love your eyes / Ambience genial / Don't just sit there ... fly / Little bird / What is love but a moment in time.

— sadly, on the 1st of June 2002, TOBY PASCOE passed away

– compilations, etc. –

1996. (cd) *Crue-l; (KYTHMAK 021DA)* **BLACK BEETLES AND WHITE BIRD** – Japan
 – Colours and sounds / Connotation vibration / Get higher / Warshag / Lighten-up / Norwegian wood / Dub it together / Armagideon time / Planet Dodo / Housework / Fire / I would like to see Egypt one of these days.
2002. (cd) *Colour And Sounds;* **DIRTY AND LOST (EPS COLLECTION)** – Japan
 – Rock'n'roll / My baby / All or nothing / Johnny / Get higher / Bring me down gently / Groovepower (Dub) / Groovepower / Disco man / Armagideon time / Who do you love / Norwegian wood / Tighten-up / Housework / Shake it together / Soul heavy / I would like to see Egypt (one of these days).

MORNING STAR

JESSE VERNON + Co incl. **JIM BARR** + **JOHN PARRISH**

Angels Egg / not iss.

Jun 98. (7") *(MFSBAE 033S)* **DANCE WITH YOU. / BISCUITS IN BED**

Swarf Finger / not iss.

Feb 99. (cd) *(SF 031CD)* **MORNING STAR**
 – When we love again / Dance with you / Travelling highway song / If you're gonna rain / Shining / In all this sleep / Where is my lover in the morning / Cruel cruel world / Strangers looking for love / What is this thing called love.

Sink & Stove / not iss.

Oct 01. (cd) *(SASR 5CD)* **MY PLACE IN THE DUST**
 – I heard beauty calling / Hereafter / Morning star / Humming song / Peace beyond all ages / I hear the waves / This is for you / Gravity / Come with me / Keepers of the fire.

SOLAR MUMUNS

SEAN O'NEILL – acoustic guitar / **NEIL SMITH** – guitar / **PETE JUDGE** – trumpet / + a bass player + 3 female singers incl. **RASHA** (from MOOZ)

2002. (cd) *(mail-o)* **BREAKING WATERS** – web

MOONSHAKE
(see under ⇒ WOLFHOUNDS; in 80's section)

MOOSE

Formed: London, England ... Spring 1990 by RUSSELL YATES, KEVIN 'MOOSE' McKILLOP and DAMIEN WARBURTON (LINCOLN FONG was to become a member mid '91 after short-lived recruit MICK CONROY decamped to STEREOLAB). One of the prime movers in the shoegazing scene of the early 90's, MOOSE stood out from the glacial-guitar pack by dint of their country/folk stylings; the initial three debut EP's ('THE JACK', 'COOL BREEZE' and 'REPRISE') suggested hints of what was to come although it was 1992's impressive 'XYZ' album – released on 'Virgin' subsidiary, 'Hut' – which had critics reaching for the thesaurus. Produced (partly naked, according to the sleeve!) by US veteran, MITCH EASTER (and augmented by DOLORES from The CRANBERRIES and ROXANNE of Th' FAITH HEALERS), the album combined the obligatory guitarscapes with a rootsy twang and subtle strings. Granted, RUSSELL's rather fey vocal style – pitched somewhere between MORRISSEY and DAMON ALBARN – wasn't exactly an ideal bed partner for the country hoedown of 'SOON IS NEVER ENOUGH' yet it worked just fine on mellower numbers like 'DON'T BRING ME DOWN' and the canter through Fred Neil's 'EVERYBODY'S TALKIN'. Unfortunately for MOOSE, the scene they'd played a large part in forming was already on its last legs by this time and inevitably they ended up taking the same one-way ticket to obscurity as CHAPTERHOUSE, SLOWDIVE, LUSH etc. (although the latter outfit did enjoy a subsequent reincarnation). Recorded for Euro label, 'Play It Again Sam', 1993's 'HONEY BEE' album saw MOOSE move even further away from their indie beginnings yet despite positive press from some loyal critics, both the record and MOOSE themselves sank without trace. 'LIVE A LITTLE, LOVE A LOT' (1996) did an admirable but ultimately futile job of reminding a disinterested press and largely ignorant public that MOOSE were not only alive and kicking but had taken on the mantle of classic songwriting revisionists as effortlessly as sliding on a comfortably worn pair of Levis. Despite gathering dust for a couple of years, 'HIGH BALL ME!' (2000) was perhaps even more impressive in its acoustic-based breeziness, subtly paying homage to past masters while revelling in its own, exquisitely arranged pop fare. • **Trivia:** The PIXIES' KIM DEAL produced their debut single. RUSSELL was also part of STEREOLAB live act in Spring 1991, while McKILLOP does the same for SEE SEE RIDER.

Album rating: XYZ (*8) / HONEY BEE (*6) / LIVE A LITTLE, LOVE A LOT (*5) / HIGH BALL ME! (*6)

MOOSE (cont)

RUSSELL YATES – vocals, guitar / KEVIN McKILLOP – guitar / DAMIEN WARBURTON – drums

		Hut	Virgin
Mar 91.	(12"ep/cd-ep) *(HUT T/CD 3)* **THE JACK E.P.**	□	-

– Jack / Ballad of Adam and Eve / Boy / I'll take tomorrow.

Jun 91. (7") *(HUT 5)* **SUZANNE. / BUTTERFLY COLLECTOR**
(12"ep+=/cd-ep+=) **COOL BREEZE** *(HUT T/CD 5)* – Untitled love song / Speak to me.

── LINCOLN FONG – bass; repl. MICK CONROY who joined STEREOLAB then formed TREETOP

Nov 91. (7"ep/12"ep/cd-ep) *(HUT/+T/CD 8)* **REPRISE EP**
– Last night I fell again / This river will never run dry / Do you remember? / Reprise.

Jan 92. (m-cd) *(HUTCD 11)* <96266> **SONNY AND SAM** (1991 ep's)

── RICHARD THOMAS – drums (ex-JESUS & MARY CHAIN, ex-DIF JUZ) repl. DAMIEN

Aug 92. (7") *(HUT 020)* **LITTLE BIRD (ARE YOU HAPPY IN YOUR CAGE)? / THERE I GO AGAIN**
(12"+=) *(HUT 020T)* – Theme from 'Ace Conroy'.
(cd-s++=) *(HUT 020CD)* – ZYX.

Sep 92. (cd/c/lp) *(HUT CD/MC/LP 55)* **XYZ**
– Soon is never soon enough / I'll see you in my dreams / High flying bird / Screaming / Friends / XYZ / Slip & slide / Little bird / Don't bring me down / Polly / The whistling song / Everybody's talking / Sometimes loving is the hardest thing.
(cd+=/c+=/free-7"w-lp) – This river is nearly dry (live).

		Cool Badge	not iss.
Feb 93.	(12"ep/cd-ep) *(CB 001 T/CD)* **LIQUID MAKE-UP EP**		

– I wanted to see you to see if I wanted you / There's a place / Ramon.

── added ROXANNE STEPHEN, JOE DILWORTH, RUSSELL FONG + STEVEN YOUNG

		Play It Again Sam	not iss.
Sep 93.	(12"ep/cd-ep) *(BIAS/+CD 254)* **UPTOWN INVISIBLE / CALL IT WHAT YOU WANT, ANYTHING. / NEVERGREEN / TOWER OF CRUMBS**		-

Oct 93. (cd/lp) *(BIAS 260 CD/LP)* **HONEY BEE**
– Uptown invisible / Meringue / Mondo cane / You don't listen / Joe Courtesy / Asleep at the wheel / I wanted to see you to see if I wanted you / Around the warm bed / Stop laughing / Dress you the same / Hold on. (lp w /free lp)

Mar 94. (12"ep/cd-ep) *(BIAS 264/+CD)* **BANG BANG EP**
– I wanted to see you to see if I wanted you / Welcome to the mind of Mr. Breeders / Following in my own footsteps / Sexy M.O.R. (take your clothes off).

Feb 96. (cd) *(BIAS 320CD)* **LIVE A LITTLE, LOVE A LOT**
– Play God / The man who hanged himself / First balloon to Nice / Rubdown / Poor man / Eve in a dream / Old man Time / Love on the dole / So much love so little time / Last of the good old days / Regulo 7.

── YATES + McKILLOP with guest MIKI BERENYI – vocals (of LUSH)

		not iss.	Nickel And Dimes
Apr 00.	(cd) <*001*> **HIGH BALL ME!**	-	

– A staring point / Can't get enough of you / Keeping up with you / Lily la tigresse / Won't look for love / High ball me baby! / The only man in town / Pretend we never met / There's a place / Wonder where I'll go / Twelve new ways to fly.

MORELLA'S FOREST

Formed: Dayton, Ohio, USA … mid-90's by SYDNEY RENTZ, SHAWN JOHNSON, SEAN McCORKLE and his brother NATE. Playing the type of dreamy, female-fronted power-chord indie pop of the likes of LUSCIOUS JACKSON, MORELLA'S FOREST released a few self-financed singles before debuting with their 'ULTRAPHONIC HISS' (1996) LP. It was not as experimental as the title suggested, in fact, it was a surprise that the album didn't spawn at least three hit singles – with RENTZ's vocals sometimes matching that of sk8ter-girl AVRIL LAVIGNE (only much more self-realised and not as moot). 1996 saw the delivery of EP 'HANG OUT' and then later, the disappointing sophomore set, 'SUPER DELUXE', before the group took a turn in musical direction. They recruited ex-BRAINIAC keyboardist JOHN SCHMERSAL and issued the psychedelic pop record 'FROM DAYTON WITH LOVE' (1998). It was produced by Keith Cleversley and boasted a set of sun-kissed songs, straight from the beach of bittersweet acid-pop. In 2001 SCHMERSAL was replaced with organist ED LACY for the recording of the more polished 'TINY LIGHTS OF HEAVEN' (2001), again produced by Cleversley. • **Covered:** KIDS IN AMERICA (Kim Wilde).

Album rating: SUPER DELUXE mini (*5) / ULTRAPHONIC HISS (*5) / FROM DAYTON WITH LOVE (*6) / TINY LIGHTS OF HEAVEN (*5)

SYDNEY RENTZ – vocals, guitar / SHAWN JOHNSON – guitar, keyboards / SEAN McCORKLE – bass / NATE McCORKLE – drums

		Tooth & Nail	Tooth & Nail
Jun 96.	(m-cd) <*TNR 1029CD*> **SUPER DELUXE**	-	□

– Hang-out / Lush of group / Wonder boy / Superstar / Oceania / Fizzle kiss / Puppy luv / Glowing green / Stargazer / Curl.

Jun 96. (cd-ep) <*TNR 1039CD*> **HANG-OUT EP**
– Hang-out / Pasty white / Voices carry / Art of love.

Oct 96. (cd) <*TNR 1063CD*> **ULTRAPHONIC HISS**
– Candy necklace kind of love / Glitter / Butter scotch boy / Tangerine drops / Pastel straws / Hula hoop / Big orange bubble / Lime velvet love seat / Silver syrup / 30 sec. wheely / Gate called beautiful.

── added JON SCHMERSAL – keyboards (ex-BRAINIAC)

Sep 98. (cd) <(*TNR 1109CD*)> **FROM DAYTON WITH LOVE**
– Water's overhead / Falling / Waiting / Separate / 1:30 afternoon / Bounty hunter / Living on takeout / Instrumental / One glorious night / Kids in America.

── SYDNEY + SHAWN recruited new rhythm section

		Endearing	Endearing
Sep 02.	(cd) <(*NDR 036*)> **TINY LIGHTS OF HEAVEN**		

– Running / Shining stars / Choppy / Lullaby / Love is blind / Sand and the sea / Some other time / Gentle go the hours / Hopeless / Never let go.

MORNING GLORIES

Formed: New York, USA … early 90's by C. (CHRISTIAN) GIBBS and cohorts. Issuing an eponymous debut album in 1993, The MORNING GLORIES were catapulted into strange cultism as eager fans demanded an album. One year later, the Blues'n'Grunge 3-piece delivered an outstanding self titled mini-set, mixing bland melodies with abrasive rock. Along with the critically lauded 'MANY MOODS' (1995), The MORNING GLORIES released their second set 'FULLY LOADED', a disappointing, quickly assembled album that, in many ways, owed much to FAITH NO MORE. A two year delay passed and the band eventually delivered 'LET THE BODY HANG' (1997), spelling the end for the indie pop MG's. However, key songwriter and frontman GIBBS returned with a (C. GIBBS GROUP) project album, 'TWENTY NINE OVER ME', in spring 1999.

Album rating: MORNING GLORIES (*5) / FULLY LOADED (*6) / LET THE BODY HANG (*5) / C. Gibbs Group: TWENTY NINE OVER ME (*5)

CHRISTIAN GIBBS – vocals, guitar / NICHOLAS PALUMBO – bass / KENNY SAVELSON – drums

		not iss.	Kokopop
1992.	(7"pink) <*002*> **CHAPTER OF WILLS. /**	-	□
		Burnt Sienna	Headhunter
Sep 94.	(cd) <*HED 031*> **MORNING GLORIES**	-	

– Pink fog assertion / Stranglehold / Cowboy song / Hollow / Coming down / Home / Demon / Blues / Augustina rules.

		Radarscope	Cargo
Oct 94.	(7") *(BSRV 5663)* **TOWER. / AVERAGE CROWD PLEASER**		-
Sep 95.	(7") *(SCAN 005)* **ELIZABETH. / PENNY SOUVENIR**		-
Sep 95.	(cd/lp) *(SCAN CD/LP 006)* <*46*> **FULLY LOADED**		

– Fully loaded / In my cold room / Elizabeth / Friendly song / Tower / My health / Fluorescence / Tire iron serenade / Jazz / Penny souvenir / Sweet side of Jesus.

		Headhunter	Headhunter
Jul 97.	(cd) <(*HED 069*)> **LET THE BODY HANG**		

– Tattoo ruins / Memphis / Little blue man / Methods / Slow retreat / B.B. gun / One out of three / Peeling off the blood that sticks / Hickory / Mascara / Expired.

── disbanded after above

The C. GIBBS GROUP

with a plethora of musicians incl. JOEY PETERS, GREG LEISZ, RAMI JAFFEE, CHUCK FINDLEY, PAUL FOX and DENNY FONGHEISER

		not iss.	Atlantic
Apr 99.	(cd) <*83169*> **TWENTY NINE OVER ME**	-	

– Cut my spirit dry / Drag the ashes / Animal criminals / House in a bottle / Lay on the fire / Ellen Terry / Twenty nine over me / Sincerity's ground / Down on Rivington / Milk / Slowly creeping smile / Bruises to claim / Cash / Photography.

MORNING STAR (see under ⇒ MOONFLOWERS)

MORPHINE

Formed: Boston, Massachusetts, USA … 1990 out of TREAT HER RIGHT by MARK SANDMAN and DANA COLLEY, who subsequently added drummer JEROME DUPREE. Certainly not your average Boston indie band, MORPHINE employed a musical set-up that defied standard rock convention; while SANDMAN offered up subtle, often treated vocals and a pioneering two-string bass played like a bottleneck guitar, COLLEY contributed breathless baritone/tenor sax over DUPREE's spare, jazzy backbeat. The trio quickly made their mark with an independently released US-only debut album, 'GOOD' (1992), the record drawing across the board praise from America's alternative media network and resulting in a long term deal with 'Rykodisc'. The label subsequently gave it a new lease of life as well as releasing the set in Britain where MORPHINE were also fast rising cult stars. Although new drummer BILLY CONWAY was soon to replace DUPREE, the musical chemistry was even stronger than ever on 1993's follow-up, 'CURE FOR PAIN', another inspired set of avant blues/jazz. Two years on, MORPHINE had the critics intoxicated yet again with, 'YES' (1995) a more spontaneous album that swung between low-key introspection and upfront affirmation. One of the few alt-rock acts to be honoured with a 'DreamWorks' contract (US-only), SANDMAN and Co finally eased their way into chart territory (Top 75) via their fourth album, 'LIKE SWIMMING' (1997). Just as MORPHINE looked to be on the verge of something big, tragedy struck on the 3rd of July 1999, when frontman SANDMAN had a fatal heart attack while onstage in Italy. At the time of his death, the band had almost completed work on a fourth album, 'THE NIGHT', which SANDMAN had largely produced. Finally released in early 2000, the record was a fitting epitaph to the man, employing more varied but no less haunting instrumentation which served to magnify MORPHINE's patented sense of unease. Another, wholly different tribute to SANDMAN was released in 2000 in the shape of 'BOOTLEG DETROIT'. Slightly different to the usual official bootleg favoured by some bands, this was actually recorded by a member of the audience during a Detroit show on MORPHINE's 'Cure For Pain' tour. While the quality was never going to match a professional live release, the original tapes were mastered by SANDMAN before his death and give an intimate insight into what made this band tick.

MORPHINE (cont)

Album rating: GOOD (*7) / CURE FOR PAIN (*6) / YES (*8) / LIKE SWIMMING (*8) / B-SIDES AND OTHERWISE compilation (*7) / THE NIGHT (*5) / BOOTLEG DETROIT posthumous (*5)

MARK SANDMAN (b. 1952) – vocals, 2-string bass (ex-TREAT HER RIGHT) / **DANA COLLEY** – saxophones / **JEROME DUPREE** – drums

                                                not iss. Accurate-Distortion

Jan 92. (cd/c) <1001-2/-4> **GOOD**
 – Good / Saddest song / Have a lucky day / You speak my language / You look like rain / Do not go quietly unto your grave / Lisa / Only one / Test tube baby / Shoot'm down / Other side / I know you (pts.1 & 2). <(cd re-iss. Sep92=US/Jul93=UK & Apr97 on 'Rykodisc'; RCD 10263)>

                                                Rykodisc Rykodisc

─── **BILLY CONWAY** – drums (ex-TREAT HER RIGHT) repl. JEROME

Jan 94. (cd/c) <(RCD/RACS 10262)> **CURE FOR PAIN**   Sep93
 – Dawna / Buena / I'm free now / All wrong / Candy / Head with wings / In spite of me / Thursday / Cure for pain / Mary, won't you call my name / Let's take a trip together / Sheila / Miles Davis' funeral. <(cd re-iss. Apr97; same)>
Jan 94. (cd-s) <RCD 51033> **CURE FOR PAIN / DOWN LOVE'S TRIBUTARIES / SHAME / MY BRAIN**
Mar 94. (cd-ep) <(RCD 51035)> **BUENA / SHAME / MORPHINE PROFILE – INTERVIEW**
Mar 94. (7") <(RA7 1036)> **THURSDAY. / MARY WON'T YOU CALL MY NAME? (live)**
 (cd-s+=) <(RCD5 1036)> – You look like rain.
Mar 95. (7") <(RA7 1046)> **SUPERSEX. / I KNOW YOU**
 (cd-s+=) <(RCD5 1046)> – All wrong.
Apr 95. (cd/c/lp) <(RCD/RAC/RALP 10320)> **YES**
 – Honey white / Scratch / Radar / Whisper / Yes / All your way / Supersex / I had my chance / Jury / Sharks / Free love / Gone for good. <(cd re-iss. Apr97; same)>
Jun 95. (7"clear) <(RA7 1047)> **HONEY WHITE. / BIRTHDAY CAKE**
 (cd-s+=) <(RCD5 1047)> – Lucky day / Sunday afternoon weightlessness.

                                              Rykodisc DreamWorks

Mar 97. (cd/c) RCD/RAC 10362 <50009> **LIKE SWIMMING**   67
 – Lilah / Potion / I know you (part 3) / Early to bed / Wishing well / Like swimming / Murder for my money / French lines with pepper / Empty box / Eleven o'clock / Hanging on a curtain / Swing it low.
May 97. (cd-s) (RCD5 1057) **MURDER FOR MY MONEY / KEROUAC**
Jan 99. (cd-s) <RCD 1131> **ELEVEN O'CLOCK / KEROUAC / ELEVEN O'CLOCK / VIRGIN BRIDE / ANITA**

─── disbanded when SANDMAN died on the 3rd of July '99

Jan 00. (cd) (RCD 10499) <450056> **THE NIGHT**   Feb00
 – The night / So many ways / Souvenir / Top floor, bottom buzzer / Like a mirror / A good woman is hard to find / Rope on fire / I'm yours, you're mine / The way we met / Slow numbers / Take me with you.

– compilations, etc. –

on 'Rykodisc' unless mentioned otherwise
Sep 97. (cd) <(RCD 10387)> **B SIDES AND OTHERWISE**
 – Have a lucky day / All wrong (live) / I know you (live) / Bo's veranda / Mile high / Shame / Down love's tributaries / Kerouac / Pulled over the car / Sunday afternoon weightlessness / Virgin bride / Mail / My brain.
Sep 00. (cd) <(RCD 10495)> **BOOTLEG DETROIT (live 1993)**
 – Intro / Come along / Dana intro / Mary / Banter #1 / Candy / Sheila / Billy intro / Claire / My brain / Banter #2 / Head with wings / Cure for pain / You speak my language / Thursday / Banter #3 / You look like rain / Buena.
Sep 01. (cd; as ORCHESTRA MORPHINE) Accurate; (OM 1) **LIVE ON TOUR (live)**
 – The night / So many ways / Souvenir / Good woman / The way we met / Not like that / I know you (part 3) / Rope / Top floor / Cook / Take me with you.

Ennio MORRICONE

Born: 11 Oct'28, Rome, Italy. A graduate of Rome's Conservatory Of Santa Cecilia, MORRICONE initially worked in radio before he began scoring films in the early 60's. Although he'd already worked with other directors on various Italian westerns, it would be his subsequent partnership with "Spaghetti Western" king, Sergio Leone, which would both revolutionise the concept of the film soundtrack and transform him into a cult figure. While Leone's unshaven, existential gunslingers aimed point blank at the heart of the great Western myth, MORRICONE conjured up the striking soundtracks to their invariably short lives and the unforgiving, sun-parched terrain they roamed in. Masterfully arranging seemingly incongruous instrumentation into a dazzling, seamless whole, MORRICONE employed everything from rattlesnake castanets and heartbreaking mariachi horns to thundering church organ, ghostly harmonica, jews harp and grunting native indian-style chants. Add to this his basic recipe of sweeping orchestration and echo-soaked, DUANE EDDY-style guitar twang and you had a musical vista unparalleled in the history of film. What's more, the likes of 'A FISTFUL OF DOLLARS', 'FOR A FEW DOLLARS MORE' and the sublime 'ONCE UPON A TIME IN THE WEST' don't even need the visual accompaniment. As contemporary sounding today as they undoubtedly were back then, these records have such hauntingly potent imagery locked in their collective grooves you need only don a set of headphones and close your eyes. This fertile period also produced the theme MORRICONE is most readily identified with even today, 'THE GOOD, THE BAD AND THE UGLY' (1968). Originally released as 'IL BUONO, IL BRUTTO, IL CATTIVO' in 1966, the theme was subsequently covered by HUGO MONTENEGRO who took it to the top of the UK chart (US No.2) and was duly inspired to record a whole album's worth of classic MORRICONE material. The Italian's incredibly prolific output (even the man himself doesn't know how many films he's worked on though it's rumoured to be in excess of 500!) continued throughout the 70's as he moved away from Westerns and worked with the cream of the world's directors. In 1972, he composed the theme to a film version of Mikhail Bulgakov's brilliant satirical novel, 'The Master And Margarita' (by Yugoslav director, Aleksander Petrovic) while 1977 saw him scoring 'Exorcist' follow-up, 'THE HERETIC'. Yet serious mainstream recognition didn't arrive until 1981 when the BBC dug up an obscure single from three years previous, 'CHI MAI'. Used as the theme tune to their 'Life & Times Of David Lloyd George' period drama, the track was a surprise No.2 UK hit. Starring Robert De Niro in a lead role, 'ONCE UPON A TIME IN AMERICA' (1984) was another massive soundtrack success for MORRICONE, while he subsequently went on to win an Oscar for 'THE MISSION' (1986) which utilised Native Indian melodies to haunting effect. In addition to these high profile projects, he spent the 80's and 90's working on all manner of obscure and not so obscure films, many of them in his native Italy. A seismic influence on modern music, the spectre of MORRICONE can be heard in the work of artists as diverse as NICK CAVE, GALLON DRUNK, MORPHINE, PORTISHEAD, TINDERSTICKS and JOHN ZORN.

Album rating (selective): A FISTFUL OF DOLLARS (*8) / FOR A FEW DOLLARS MORE (*7) / THE GOOD, THE BAD AND THE UGLY (*8) / ONCE UPON A TIME IN THE WEST (*9) / BURN (*7) / EXORCIST II: THE HERETIC (*6) / ONCE UPON A TIME IN AMERICA (*6) / THE MISSION (*8) / THE UNTOUCHABLES (*6) / RAMPAGE (*6) / CASUALTIES OF WAR (*7) / CINEMA PARADISO (*6) / DISCLOSURE (*5) / WOLF (*7) / FILM MUSIC BY ENNIO MORRICONE compilation (*7)

ENNIO MORRICONE – composer / credited with ORCHESTRA

                                                RCA Victor RCA Victor

Jun 67. (lp; mono/stereo) (RD/SF 7875) <1135> **A FISTFUL OF DOLLARS** (soundtrack)
 – Titoli / Almost dead / Square dance / The chase / The result / Without pity / Theme from a fistful of dollars / "A Fistful Of Dollars" suite.
1967. (7") (RCA 1596) **A FISTFUL OF DOLLARS. / THE MAN WITH NO NAME**
1967. (lp) **FOR A FEW DOLLARS MORE** (soundtrack)   –   – Italian
 – La resa dei conti / Osservatori osservati / Il vizio di uccidere / Il colpo / Addio colonnelo / Per qualche dollaro in piu / Poker d'assi / Carillion. (UK-iss.1970 w/ 'A FISTFUL OF DOLLARS' on 'RCA Camden'; CDS 1052) (c-iss.May74; CAM 411)
1967. (7") (RCA 1634) **FOR A FEW DOLLARS MORE. / LA RESI DEI CONTI**

                                                U.A. U.A.

Oct 68. (lp; stereo/mono) (S+/ULP 1197) <5172> **THE GOOD, THE BAD AND THE UGLY** (soundtrack)   4 Feb68
 – The good, the bad and the ugly – main title (Il buono, il brutto, il cattivo)/ The sundown (Il tramonto) / The strong (Il forte) / The desert (Il deserto) / The carriage of the spirits (La carrozza dei fantasmi) / Marcia (Marcetta) / The story of a soldier (La storia de un soldato) / Marcia without hope (Marcetta senza speranza) / The death of a soldier (Morte de un soldato) / The ecstasy of gold (L'estasi dell'oro) / The trio – main title (Il triello). (re-iss. May85 on 'E.G.' lp/c; EG 260582-1/-4) (<cd-iss. Sep88 on 'EMI Manhattan'; CDP7 48408-2>) (cd re-iss. Jul93 on 'Silva Screen'; 46408-2)

─── New York-born composer HUGO MONTENEGRO also went US Top 10 with a collection of the above three soundtracks – the man also took the title track to No.2 (Feb'68) & No.1 (Sep'68) in the US & UK respectively. Around the same time, HUGO also scored with another Clint Eastwood-starring movie, 'Hang 'Em High'.

1969. (7") (UP 35004) **PROFESSIONAL GUN. / PACO**

                                                R.C.A. not iss.

1969. (lp) **ONCE UPON A TIME IN THE WEST** (soundtrack) – – Italian
 – Once upon a time in the west / As a judgement / Farewell to Cheyenne / The transgression / The first tavern / The second tavern / Once upon a time in the west (reprise) / Man with a harmonica / A dimly lit room / Bad orchestra / The man / Jill's America / Death rattle / Finale. (UK-iss.Jul78 lp/c; PL/PK 31387) (re-iss. Oct83 lp/c; NL/NK 70032) (cd – iss.Jun88; ND 71704) (cd re-iss. Feb90 on 'Silva Screen'; 4736.2)
1969. (7") (RCA 1892) **ONCE UPON A TIME IN THE WEST. / FINALE**
 (re-iss. Oct79; PB 6197)

MOST (see under ⇒ **SPIREA X**)

MOTOR LIFE CO.

Formed: Largs, Scotland ... early 1995 by SEAN GUTHRIE, MATT GILFEATHER, CHRIS GROVE and Helensburgh-raised BEN ELLIS; their "More To Life" company was indeed a play on words. After a few grungy, noisecore 45's on their own 'Pendejo' imprint, namely 'MY MAIL ORDER THAI BRIDE' and 'BE A HERO', MOTOR LIFE CO. played some dynamic underground live gigs. In 1998, after supporting such indie luminaries as ARAB STRAP, MOGWAI and AC ACOUSTICS, the quartet finally let loose their first album, the mini-set, '(BIRDSTYLE)'. Opening with the accompanying 7", 'TROD ON YOUR HEAD-MINE', the set was both fragile and sonic courtesy of SEAN, MATT and BEN seemingly all fighting over the one mic; the BEACH BOYS they were not.

Album rating: (BIRDSTYLE) mini (*6)

SEAN GUTHRIE – guitar, vocals / **MATT GILFEATHER** – guitar, vocals / **BEN ELLIS** – bass, vocals / **CHRIS GROVE** – drums

                                                Pendejo not iss.

Nov 95. (7") (PEN 01) **MY MAIL ORDER THAI BRIDE. / FELL ILL**
Oct 96. (7") (PEN 02) **BE A HERO. / SWERVE, THEN FREE REVERSE**

MOTOR LIFE CO. (cont) — THE GREAT INDIE DISCOGRAPHY — The 1990s

			mei mei	not iss.
Jul 98.	(7")	*(mei 002)* **TROD ON YOUR HEAD-MINE. / SHOW THE COSMOS**	□	–
Sep 98.	(m-cd)	*(mei 003CD)* **(BIRDSTYLE)**	□	–

– Trod on your head-mine / In the Lee of a steeple / Airshot / Miguel the dinted / More fuel for future fires / 20k.

―― unsure what became of them; probably failed the M.O.T.

MOUNTAIN GOATS

Formed: California, USA . . . 1991 by JOHN DARNIELLE, who was working as a nurse when he issued a cassette-only album for tiny label 'Shrimper'. As the years progressed, DARNIELLE, now somewhat of a DANIEL JOHNSTON figure in his Californian musical community, produced further cassette albums and various 7" singles, all recorded onto a crude ghettoblaster and all displaying his intricate guitar and vocal work. His first album proper (CD, that is) was to be titled 'SWEDEN' and was delivered in 1995 to critical acclaim. Again, entirely recorded on his stereo, DARNIELLE introduced what was to become classic MOUNTAIN GOATS motifs on the album; the now "famed" 'Going To . . .' set of songs and the equally frequented 'Songs For . . .'. This debut set included the first of many oddball cover songs to come – Steely Dan's 'FM', and a bloody good version at that! The same year, 'ZOPILOTE MACHINE' was released. It contained a host of brilliant tracks including 'ALPHA SUN HEAT' and the wonderful 'GOING TO GEORGIA'. The album also saw DARNIELLE maintain the raw taped production, which echoed BECK's '95 effort 'One Foot In The Grave', and helped push the Lo-Fi envelope further into the 90's (GRANDADDY, NEUTRAL MILK HOTEL and PAVEMENT were certainly taking notes). DARNIELLE and a couple of his musical buddies (PETER HUGHES, ALLEN CALLACI) moved into the studio for their mini-album release, 'NINE BLACK POPPIES' (1995), some of these tracks being home-recorded. Featured on the set was the simple ballad 'I KNOW YOU'VE COME TO TAKE MY TOYS AWAY' and a cover of Refrigerator's 'LONESOME SURPRISE', dueted with the aforementioned CALLACI (over the phone, me thinks!). 1996 and 1997 saw The MOUNTAIN GOATS turn moody with their albums 'NOTHING FOR JUICE' (co-written and sung with RACHEL WARE and issued on 'Ajax') and 'FULL FORCE GALESBURG', a medative, slightly melancholic album that would see a three-year hiatus for this mostly prolific one-man-band. DARNIELLE returned in 2000 – with members of LULLABY FOR THE WORKING CLASS and BRIGHT EYES on his sleeve – for the brilliant, scatter-brain release of 'THE CORONER'S GAMBIT'. Another rambling 'GOATS special (yes, it was back to the Ghettoblaster), DARNIELLE made sure that his songs were given the proper treatment, albeit with the background tape-hiss making a welcome appearance. As was the case with his side project, the legendary EXTRA GLENNS, which saw himself and NOTHING PAINTED BLUE's FRANKLIN BRUNO play San Francisco's 'Noise Pop Festival' and deliver the album 'MARTIAL ARTS WEEKEND', something that had apparently been in the pipeline for ten years! In 2002, The MOUNTAIN GOATS unfettered a ton-weight equivalent of material, beginning with 'ALL HAIL TO THE WEST' (check out the hilarious 'THE BEST EVER DEATH METAL BAND IN DENTON'), three excellent retrospective compilations; 'PROTEIN SOURCE OF THE FUTURE . . . NOW!', 'BITTER MELON FARM' and 'GHANA', plus the group's fully-recorded studio album, 'TALLAHASSEE'. So, if The MOUNTAIN GOATS have never had the courtesy of being a part of your life, then now's the time to catch up . . .

Album rating: SWEDEN (*6) / BEAUTIFUL RAT SUNSET mini (*5) / NINE BLACK POPPIES mini (*7) / ZOPILOTE MACHINE (*6) / NOTHING FOR JUICE (*6) / FULL FORCE GALESBURG (*5) / THE CORONER'S GAMBIT (*6) / ALL HAIL WEST TEXAS (*6) / PROTEIN SOURCE OF THE FUTURE . . . NOW! collection (*6) / BITTER MELON FARM collection (*6) / GHANA collection (*6) / TALLAHASSEE (*6) / Extra Glenns: MARTIAL ARTS WEEKEND (*6)

JOHN DARNIELLE – vocals, guitar, tapes / with others incl. **PETER HUGHES** – vocals / **RACHEL WARE** – vocals

			not iss.	Shrimper
1991.	(c)	**TABOO VI: THE HOMECOMING**	–	□
1992.	(c)	**THE HOUND CHRONICLES**	–	□
1992.	(7"ep)	**SONGS FOR PETRONIUS**	–	□
			not iss.	Ajax
1993.	(7"ep)	**CHILE DE ARBOL**	–	□
			not iss.	Sonic Enemy
1993.	(c)	**TRANSMISSIONS TO HORACE**	–	□
			not iss.	Shrimper
1993.	(c)	**HOT GARDEN STOMP**	–	□
			not iss.	Ajax
1994.	(cd) <AJAX 36> **ZOPILOTE MACHINE**		–	□

– Alpha incipienis / Azo tle Nelli in Tlalticpac? / Alpha sun hat / The black ice cream song / Sinaloan milk snake song / We have seen the enemy / Standard bitter love song #7 / Quetzalcoatl eats plums / Orange ball of love / Orange ball of hate / Bad priestess / Going to Bristol / Young Caesar 2000 / Going to Lebanon / Grendel's mother / Song for Tura Santana / Alpha in Tauris / Going to Georgia / Quetzalcoalt is born.

			not iss.	Theme Park
1994.	(7"ep)	**PHILYRA**	–	□
			not iss.	Car In Car
1994.	(c)	**TAKING THE DATIVE**	–	□
			not iss.	Sing Eunuchs
1994.	(7"ep)	**WHY YOU ALL SO THIEF**	–	□
			not iss.	Oska
1994.	(c)	**YAM, THE KING OF CROPS**	–	□

			not iss.	Walt
1995.	(7"ep; with ALASTAIR GALBRAITH) **ORANGE RAJA, BLOOD ROYAL**		–	□
			not iss.	Sonic Squid
1995.	(7"ep)	**SONGS FOR PETER HUGHES**	–	□
			Emperor Jones	Emperor Jones
Nov 95.	(m-cd) <*EJ 02CD*> **NINE BLACK POPPIES**		□	□ Oct95

– Cubs in five / Going to Utrecht / Cheshire county / Chanson du bon chose / Pure money / I know you've come to take my toys away / Nine black poppies / Stars fell on Alabama / Lonesome surprise (live).

			not iss.	Cassiel
1995.	(7"ep)	**SONGS ABOUT FIRE**	–	□
			not iss.	Shrimper
1995.	(lp/cd) <*SHR 68/+CD*> **SWEDEN**		–	□

– The recognition scene / Downtown Seoul / Some Swedish trees / I wonder where our love has gone / Deianara crush / Whole wide world / Flashing lights / Sept 19 triple X love! love! / Going to Queens / Tahitianambrosia maker / Going to Bolivia / Tollund man / California song / Snow crush killing song / Send me an angel / Neon orange glimmer song / FM / Prana ferox / Cold milk bottle. *(UK-iss.Dec96; same as US)*

Jan 96.	(m-cd) <*SHR 99CD*> **BEAUTIFUL RAT SUNSET**	–	□

– Itzcuintli-Totzli days / New star song / Song for Cleomenes / Sendero luminoso verdero / Song for Mark and Joel / Going to Maryland / Seeing daylight / Resonant bell world. *(UK-iss.Dec96; same as US)*

			not iss.	Ajax
Aug 96.	(cd) <*AJAX 56*> **NOTHING FOR JUICE**		–	□

– Then the letting go / Heights / Alpha double negative: Going to Catalina / Hellbound on my trail / Blueberry frost / Alabama nova / Moon and sand / I will grab you by the ears / It froze me / Full flower / Million / Going to Bogota / Orange ball of pain / Going to Kansas / Waving at you / Going to Reykjavik / I Corinthians 13: 8-10 / Going to Scotland.

			not iss.	Little Mafia
1997.	(7"ep; split w/ FURNITURE HUSCHLE) **TROPICAL DEPRESSION**		–	□

―― **ALASTAIR GALBRAITH** repl. WARE

			Emperor Jones	Emperor Jones
Nov 97.	(lp/cd) <*EJ 11/+CD*> **FULL FORCE GALESBURG**		□	□ Jun97

– New Britain / Snow owl / West Country dream / Masher / Chinese house flowers / Ontario / Down here / Twin human highway flares / Weekend in western Illinois / Us mill / Song for the Julian calendar / Maize stalk drinking blood / Evening in Stalingrad / Minnesota / Original air-blue-gown / It's all here in Brownsville.

			not iss.	YoYo
1998.	(one-sided-12"ep) **NEW ASIAN CINEMA**		□	–

– Cao Dai blowout / Narakaloka / Golden jackal song / Treetop song.

2000.	(one-sided-12"ep) **ISOPANISAD RADIO HOUR**	–	□

―― now with **SIMON JOYNER + LULLABY FOR THE WORKING CLASS**

			Absolutely Kosher	Absolutely Kosher
Jan 01.	(cd/lp) <*AK 012/+1*> **THE CORONER'S GAMBIT**		□	□ Oct00

– Jaipur / Elijah / Trick mirror / Island garden song / The coroner's gambit / Baboon / Scotch grove / Horser Adish road / Family happiness / Oinions / Blue jays and cardinals / Shadow songs / There will be no divorce / Insurance fraud #2 / The Alphonse mamb / We were patriots.

			not iss.	Nursecall
2001.	(3"cd-ep) **ON JUHU BEACH**		–	□
			Emperor Jones	Emperor Jones
Feb 02.	(cd) <*(EJ 41CD)*> **ALL HAIL WEST TEXAS**		□	□

– The best ever death metal band in Denton / Fall of the star high school running back / Color in your cheeks / Jenny / Fault lines / Balance / Pink and blue / Riches and wonders / The mess inside / Jeff Davis county blues / Distant stations / Blues in Dallas / Source delay / Absolute lithops effect.

			not iss.	YoYo
2002.	(one-sided-12"ep) **DEVIL IN THE SHORTWAVE**		–	□

―― **DARNIELLE** still retained **PETER HUGHES**

			4 a.d.	4 a.d.
Nov 02.	(7") *(AD 2208)* **SEE AMERICA RIGHT. / NEW CHEVROLET IN FLAMES**		□	–

(cd-s+=) *(BAD 2208CD)* – Design your own container garden.

Jan 03.	(cd) *(CAD 2215CD)* <*72113*> **TALLAHASSEE**	□	□ Nov02

– Tallahassee / First few desperate hours / Southwood plantation road / Games shows touch our lives / The house that dripped blood / Idylss of the king / No children / See America right / Peacocks / International small arms traffic blues / Have to explode / Old college try / Oceanographer's choice / Alpha rats nest.

– compilations, etc. –

on 'Beads Of Sweat' unless mentioned otherwise

Aug 02.	(cd) <*(3BOS 1001)*> **PROTEIN SOURCE OF THE FUTURE . . . NOW!**	□	□ Apr02

– Going to Tennessee / Pure heat / Hand ball / The window song / Night of the mules / Going to Malibu / Billy The Kid's dream of the magic shoes / Fresh berries for you / Alphabetizing / Third snow song / The monkey song / Love cuts the strings / Pure honey / Duke Ellington / Seed song / Quetzalcoatal comes through / Omega blaster / Coco-yam song / Alagemo / Two thousand seasons / Chinese rifle song / Yam, the king of crops / Alpha Omega.

Aug 02.	(cd) <*(3BOS 1002)*> **BITTER MELON FARM**	□	□ Apr02

– Noche del guajolote / Going to Bangor / Against Agamemnon / Going to Cleveland / Early spring / Historiography / No, I can't / Alpha desperation march / Going to Monaco / Star dusting / Teenage world / Going to Santiago / Sail on / Black Molly / Rain song / The bad doctor / Alpha double negative: Going to Catalina / Pure intentions / The lady of Shanghai / Pure love / Song for an old friend / Snow song / Faithless bacchant song / Short song about the 10 freeway / No, I can't / Song for Dana Plato / The sign.

Aug 02.	(cd) <*(3BOS 1003CD)*> **GHANA**	□	□ Apr02

– Golden boy / Pure gold / Papagallo / Song for John Davis / Stars around her / Going to Port Washington / Blood royal / The only thing I know / Raja vocative / Hatha hill / Going to Kirby Sigston / Please come home to Hamngatan / The last day of Jimi Hendrix's life / Orange ball of peace / Standard bitter love song #8 / Chino love

MOUNTAIN GOATS (cont) — THE GREAT INDIE DISCOGRAPHY — The 1990s

song 1979 / Wrong! / Alpha Gelida / Wild Palm City / The Anglo-Saxons (live) / Flight 717: Going to Denmark / The admonishing song / Anti music song / Going to Hungary / Earth air water trees / Creature song / Pure sound / Going to Maine / Noctifer Birmingham / Leaving home.

EXTRA GLENNS

JOHN DARNIELLE + FRANKLIN BRUNO (of NOTHING PAINTED BLUE)

		Absolutely Kosher	Absolutely Kosher
Feb 02.	(cd) <(AK 017)> **MARTIAL ARTS WEEKEND**		

– Baltimore / All rooms cable a/c free coffee / Ultra violet / Twelve hands high / The river song / Somebody else's parking lot in Sebastopol / Memories / Going to Morocco / Going to Michigan / Terminal grain / Malevolent seascape Y / Going to Marrakesh.

MOUNT VERNON ARTS LAB

Formed: Glasgow, Scotland ... 1996 by the initially mysterious experimentalist, DREW MULHOLLAND. Inspired by the late, JOE MEEK, DANIEL MILLER (remember, The NORMAL) and the theremin, lab technician MULHOLLAND and his crew delivered a succession of noises and loops that would make any Kraut-rocker envious. Independent outlet, 'Via Satellite' (and at times 'Earworm') were behind MOUNT VERNON from the outset, a plethora of avant-garde/post-rock EP's being introduced to the public circa '97/'98; even Glasgow's 'Creeping Bent' got in on the act via V/A album, 'Electronic Lullabies', and track 'MV 3'. The latter also made an appearance on MVAL's first mini-set, 'GUMMY TWINKLE' (1998), a longwave/shortwave frequency collage of soundscapes that featured SONIC BOOM (aka PETE KEMBER) and NORMAN BLAKE (of TEENAGE FANCLUB). Subsequently inking a deal with 'Ochre' records, DREW embarked on selecting all sorts of minimalistic pocket symphonics, evidenced on their 23-minute collaboration, 'WARMINSTER', with PORTISHEAD's ADRIAN UTLEY. If improvised atmospherics were God, the MOUNT VERNON ARTS LAB would be Zeus, the 21st Century had arrived via satellite and via Ochre's 'ONE MINUTE BLASTS RISING TO THREE AND THEN DIMINISHING' (2000); DREW recorded this 100 feet below ground at the abandoned nuclear bunkers at Troywood, the man was indeed, wired up to the mains! This was followed by 2001's 'THE SEANCE AT HOBS LANE', a strange collection of songs inspired by "Victorian Skullduggery, outlaws, secret societies and subterranean experiences". The set also featured the talents of NORMAN BLAKE (TEENAGE FANCLUB), ISOBEL CAMPBELL (BELLE & SEBASTIAN), BARRY 7 (ADD N TO X) and PORTISHEAD's ADRIAN UTLEY and turned MULHOLLAND's keen sense of humour and fascination with weird subjects into one of the most interesting Scottish releases of the year.

Album rating: GUMMY TWINKLE (*6) / WARMINSTER mini with Adrian Utley (*6) / E FOR EXPERIMENTAL compilation (*6) / ONE MINUTE BLASTS RISING TO THREE AND THEN DIMINISHING (*6) / THE SEANCE AT HOBS LANE (*7)

DREW MULHOLLAND – electronics, etc

		Via Satellite	not iss.
May 97.	(10"ep) (V-Sat 008) **NOVA EP**		
Oct 97.	(7"ep) (WORM 007) **split**		-

– Window / CLOCKWORK: Exp.#1 / OMIT: Cold evolution.
(above issued on 'Earworm')

Oct 97.	(7"ep) (V-Satastra 1961) **TALVIN STARDUST EP**		-

– Talvin Stardust / The little velvet ladder / The mind field / Oram.

| Feb 98. | (7"ep) (V-Satastra 1972) **WILLIAM GREEN EP** | | |
| Feb 98. | (one-sided-7"brown) (WORMSS 2) **IMBER. / Electroscope: SHAME CHANGED HIS PIGMENTATION** | | - |

(above issued on 'Earworm')

| Sep 98. | (m-cd) (V-Sat 2525) **GUMMY TWINKLE** | | |

– Expo / William Green / Cabaret volt age / Live mains electricity / Mr. Astra / Shirts / Imber loop / Telek / MV 3 / Superpatch / (+ hidden track).

		Ochre	not iss.
Jun 99.	(m-cd; by ADRIAN UTLEY & MOUNT VERNON ARTS LAB) (OCH 040CD) **WARMINSTER**		-

– Warminster.

| Sep 99. | (cd) (OCH 13CD) **E FOR EXPERIMENTAL** (compilation 1996-1999) | | - |

– Arthur Cravan / Mania / The Third Eye Centre / Frenzy / Electrolumminessense / Imps . . . I am Lubbert Das / Andromeda / Lunar three / Feldspar / Via satellite / Bedlam / Scooby don't / The mind field / Window / Imber / Talvin Stardust / Oram / The little velvet ladder / William Green / Automatic frequency control / Magic carpet ride / Broadcasting / Der lumpenrocker / Bad vibrations.

| Nov 00. | (m-cd) (OCH 046) **ONE MINUTE BLASTS RISING TO THREE AND THEN DIMINISHING** | | - |

– One minute blasts rising to three and then diminishing.

		Via Satellite	not iss.
Aug 01.	(cd) (ASTRA 007) **THE SEANCE AT HOBS LANE**		-

MOVIETONE

Formed: Bristol, England ... 1994 initially as an offshoot of FLYING SAUCER ATTACK by its members KATE WRIGHT, RACHEL BROOK and MATT ELLIOTT along with FLORENCE LOVEGROVE and MATT JONES. England's very own answer to GALAXIE 500, the hushed and atmospheric MOVIETONE first issued a couple of 7" singles (for 'Planet') before recording and releasing their self-titled debut in 1995. The album impressed critics and fans of the new emerging lo-fi/sad-core scene, from which bands such as LOW, The FOR CARNATION and The RADAR BROS were already slowly emerging in America. The cult-ish 'Drag City' took notice and the quintet delivered another slow-burning set of songs entitled 'DAY AND NIGHT' (1997), this time, displaying WRIGHT's sensual and whispering vocals over the band's psychedelic-flavoured string pickings. MOVIETONE eventually took a break, returning three years later with a bruising third album-proper, 'THE BLOSSOM FILLED STREETS' (2000). A complex LP, built around a simple framework, MOVIETONE had, well, set the tone – or composed a soundtrack – to their own movie. As epic as anything MOGWAI had ever done and as emotionally challenging as WILL OLDHAM and his stable, who needed movies when you could invent your own?

Album rating: MOVIETONE (*6) / DAY AND NIGHT (*6) / THE BLOSSOM FILLED STREETS (*7)

KATE WRIGHT – vocals, guitar / **RACHEL BROOK** – clarinet / **FLORENCE LOVEGROVE** – viola / **MATT ELLIOTT** – piano / **MATT JONES** – percussion

		Planet	not iss.
Mar 94.	(7") (PUNK 003) **SHE SMILED MANDARIN LIKE. / ORANGE ZERO**		-
Oct 95.	(7") (PUNK 009) **MONO VALLEY. / UNDER THE 3000-FOOT RED CEILING**		-
Nov 95.	(lp/cd) (PUNK 010/+CD) **MOVIETONE**		-

– Chance is her opera / Heatwave pavement / Green ray / Orange zero / Late July / Darkness – Blue glow / Mono valley / Coastal lagoon / Alkaline eye / 3 a.m. walking smoking talking / Three fires / ?.

| Jun 96. | (7") (PUNK 013) **USELESS LANDSCAPE. / SUMMER** | | - |

		Domino	Drag City
Jul 97.	(7") (RUG 56) **SUN DRAWING. / MARINE OCEANO**		
Sep 97.	(cd/lp) (WIG CD/LP 36) <DC 141> **DAY AND NIGHT**		Dec97

– Sun drawing / Blank like snow / Useless landscape / Summer / Night of the acacias / Noche marina / The crystallisation of salt at night.

| Jul 00. | (cd/lp) (WIG CD/LP 79) <DC 193> **THE BLOSSOM FILLED STREETS** | | |

– Hydra / Star ruby / 1930's beach house / Year ending / The blossom filled streets / Porthcurno / Seagulls – Bass / In a marine light / Night in these rooms.

MUFFS
(see under ⇒ PANDORAS; in 80's section)

MULE

Formed: Ann Arbor/Detroit, Michigan, USA ... 1991 by PRESTON CLEVELAND, who, after his brief stint with WIG (on one EP, 'LYING NEXT TO YOU'), took the new moniker of P.W. LONG; alongside LAUGHING HYENAS' (for whom LONG's brother John Brannon fronted) KEVIN MUNRO and JIM KIMBALL. A thrash blues trio by nature, MULE unsuspectingly issued their robust, sleazy and downright swampy self-titled debut in 1992. Recorded by STEVE ALBINI and issued by 'Quarterstick', the set displayed LONG's rip-roaring vocals, coupled with dirty slide guitar and crashing tom-toms. KIMBALL departed in 1993, with drummer DANIEL JACOB WILSON replacing him for 1994's 'WRUNG' EP and the fraught and noisy sophomore 'IF I DON'T SIX'. However, MULE disbanded shortly afterwards, with P.W. going on the road to play mainly solo acoustic sets. It wasn't long before he joined another band, and, in 1997, P.W. LONG'S REELFOOT was established. JESUS LIZARD's MAC McNEILLY and touring bassist DAN MAISTER were on board for the recording of 1998's suberb 'PUSH ME AGAIN' set.

Album rating: MULE (*7) / IF I DON'T SIX (*6) / P.W. Long's Reelfoot: WE DIDN'T SEE YOU ON SUNDAY (*5) / PUSH ME AGAIN (*6)

P.W. LONG (b. PRESTON CLEVELAND) – vocals, guitar (ex-WIG) / **KEVIN MUNRO** (b. STRICKLAND) – bass (ex-LAUGHING HYENAS) / **JIM KIMBALL** – drums (ex-LAUGHING HYENAS)

		Quarter Stick	Quarter Stick
Feb 93.	(lp/cd) <(QS 15/+CD)> **MULE**		Nov92

– Mississippi breaks / What every white nigger knows / I'm hell / Drown / Now I truly understand / Mama's reason to cry / Lucky Sugarcane Zuzu.

| Mar 93. | (7") <(QS 16)> **I'M HELL. / TO LOVE SOMEBODY** | | |

— **DANIEL JACOB WILSON** – drums; repl. KIMBALL who joined DENNISON/KIMBALL TRIO (+ later JESUS LIZARD)

| Jun 94. | (12"ep/c-ep/cd-ep) <(QS 25/+C/CD)> **WRUNG EP** | - | |

– Ass / We know you're drunk / Searchlight / Rope and the cuckold.

| Sep 94. | (lp/c/cd) <(QS 29/+C/CD)> **IF I DON'T SIX** | | |

– Hayride / X & 29 / Beauteous / Nowhere's back / Obion / Hundred years / Spearfish / Piano / Pent.

— disbanded soon after above

P.W. LONG'S REELFOOT

— now with **DAN MAISTER** – bass (ex-HAIRMASTER) / **MAC McNEILLY** – drums (ex-JESUS LIZARD)

		Touch & Go	Touch & Go
Jun 97.	(cd) <(TG 178CD)> **WE DIDN'T SEE YOU ON SUNDAY**		

– My name / Aw bruiser / I'll be your angel / Shakin' feaars / Jelly / Temple / James / You would've never crawled alone / Tomorrow / Oleander / Bound to ride / Jack of diamonds.

| Jul 98. | (cd) <(TG 192CD)> **PUSH ME AGAIN** | | |

– Signifyin' honkey / Say it ain't so / Eagleeye / Fly trap lair / Pooh butt / Stand up! / Honey bee / Jane Dwim / Laughing eyes / State house / Yo' money.

MULL HISTORICAL SOCIETY

Formed: Glasgow, Scotland ... early in the year 2000 by COLIN MacINTYRE (son of KENNY MacINTYRE, the late and much missed political reporter for BBC Scotland), a man born and raised on the isle of Mull (Tobermory, to be exact). Having learned the guitar at an early age, he honed up on the music world by reading about, rather than listening to records; it was hard for him to obtain anything decent outside the Top 40. Writing a barrelload of songs (artwork complimented each one, apparently!), COLIN crossed the water to Glasgow and er, wrote some more. Abandoning other late 90's projects such as LOVE SICK ZOMBIES, WESTERNIZED and 7/11 (good names!), COLIN met up with like-minded bassist ALAN MALLOY (also from his hometown) and formed the MULL HISTORICAL SOCIETY (is there such a thing that already exists?). Towards the end of the year, the quartet (recent additions being COLIN 'SLEEPY' MacPHERSON and TONY SOAVE) unveiled their debut single for 'Tugboat', 'BARCODE BYPASS', a fine blend of MERCURY REV, BEACH BOYS and AZTEC CAMERA – 'Mull Of MacIntyre' anyone? Indeed. Moving on slightly and come the release of the group's debut set 'LOSS' (2001) – a universally praised homage to Glasgow (that's where most of the tracks were written) and an all-round great album – MacINTYRE's vocals did become a tad taxing on some tracks, but it was nothing that the music didn't make up for. 'PUBLIC SERVICE ANNOUNCER' opened the album with bursting, full-on guitars, heightening the pop factor to 11, whereas 'INSTEAD' offered up a quaint ballad, with a children's choir thrown in for good measure. The press had a field day over the album (and a minor hit 45, 'WATCHING XANADU'), which prompted the band to tour with the likes of The STROKES, TRAVIS and The MOLDY PEACHES, as well as being faves on the Glastonbury and T In The Park festivals.

Album rating: LOSS (*7)

COLIN MacINTYRE – vocals, guitar / **ALAN MALLOY** – bass / **COLIN 'SLEEPY' MacPHERSON** – keyboards / **TONY SOAVE** – drums

			Tugboat	not iss.
Nov 00.	(7"/cd-s)	(TUGS/+CD 28) **BARCODE BYPASS. / MULL HISTORICAL SOCIETY**	□	-
Mar 01.	(7"/cd-s)	(TUGS/+CD 29) **I TRIED. / SOME YOU WIN, SOME YOU LOSE**	□	-
			Rough Trade	not iss.
Jul 01.	(7"/cd-s)	(RTRADES/+CD 021) **ANIMAL CANNABUS. / UGLY BUILDINGS ARE BEAUTIFUL / INDUSTRIAL HANGERS**	53	-
			Blanco Y Negro	Beggars XL
Oct 01.	(cd/d-lp)	(0927 41307-2/-1) <85027> **LOSS**	43	□
		– Public service announcer / Watching Xanadu / Instead / I tried / This is not who we were / Barcode bypass / Only I / Animal cannabus / Strangeways inside / Mull Historical Society / Paper houses.		
Jan 02.	(7")	(NEG 138) **WATCHING XANADU. / PIGEON LOVESONG**	36	-
	(cd-s)	(NEG 138CD1) – ('A'side) / Pigeon fancier (by correspondence) / Don't suffer.		
	(cd-s)	(NEG 138CD2) – ('A'side) / Naked ambition at the E.P.A. / Sad old day to be down / ('A'-CD-Rom).		

MUMMIES

Formed: San Francisco, California, USA ... late 1988 by MAZ KATTUAH, TRENT RUANE, LARRY WINTHER and RUSSELL QUAN. Although their recorded output was not phenomenal in amount, the band's legacy was of great importance to the West Coast indie rock/punk scene. The Bay Area punksters, swabbed up in bandages, played out their DIY, lo-fi garage rock to ecstatic audiences. After a string of 7"s (both covers and originals) on various indie imprints, the band's debut full-length outing, 'THE MUMMIES PLAY THEIR OWN RECORDS' appeared in 1990. This set was not written as an album, and instead collected together the early singles recorded in the MUMMIES' paired down (with run-down equipment), inimitable way. The following year the group were dragged to the sterility of the studio, but after hearing the technologically enhanced sound it produced, they binned the material; although, as always, it did resurface sometime later on the bootleg, 'FUCK THE MUMMIES'. Within the same year the lads did in fact do another recording, 'NEVER BEEN CAUGHT' (1992), which in fact was their only real full-length outing, recorded as such. Unfortunately, by the time it hit the record shops, the following year, the band had taken their bow, and disbanded. This was not quite the end for the boys though, as fellow West Coast rockers, SUPERCHARGER, managed to persuade them to reform and support them on a European tour in 1993. The success of these gigs led the MUMMIES to do their own farewell tour in Europe. Later RUANE, QUAN, and KATTUAH took up positions in The PHANTOM SURFERS, while WINTHER joined the ORANGE PEELS. All the members also had various slots with other outfits.

Album rating: NEVER BEEN CAUGHT (*7) / PARTY AT STEVE'S HOUSE (*5) / RUNNIN' ON EMPTY VOL.1 compilation (*5) / RUNNIN' ON EMPTY VOL.2 compilation (*5)

LARRY WINTHER – lead guitar / **MAZ KATTUAH** – bass / **TRENT RUANE** – organ, saxophone / **RUSSELL QUAN** – drums

			not iss.	Pre-B.S.
1990.	(7"ep)	<P45-001> **THAT GIRL / TEST DRIVE. / I'M BIGGER THAN YOU / DIRTY ROBBER** (UK-iss.Oct96; same as US)	-	□
1990.	(7")	<P45-002> **FOOD, SICKLES AND GIRLS. / ONE BY ONE** (UK-iss.Oct96; same as US)	-	□
			not iss.	Estrus
1990.	(7")	<ES 79> **OUT OF OUR TREE. / TALL COOL ONE**	-	□
			not iss.	Regal Select
1990.	(7"ep)	<RS 01013> **SHITSVILLE** – A girl like you / That's mighty childish / (Doin') The Kirk / Die!		
			not iss.	Rekkids
1990.	(7")	<001> **SKINNY MINNIE. / YOU CAN'T SIT DOWN**	-	□
1992.	(7"ep)	<005> **GREG LOWERY & THE MUMMIES** – Food, sickles and girls / In and out / Shot down.	-	□
			not iss.	Sympathy F
1991.	(7"ep)	<SFTRI 110> **THE MUMMIES VS. THE WOLFMEN** – Land of 1000 dances / Victim of circumstances / (other 2 by WOLFMEN).	-	□
			not iss.	Planet Pimp
1992.	(7"ep)	<PP 002> **LARRY WINTHER AND HIS MUMMIES (live)** – The legend of Sleepy Hollow / I saw her in a mustang.	-	□
			not iss.	Estrus
1992.	(7"promo)	<ES 94017> **INTRODUCTION TO THE MUMMIES: PLAY THEIR OWN RECORDS! / HIGH HEEL SNEAKERS** <re-iss. 1995; ES 94017R>	-	□
			Hangman's Daughter	Telstar
Jul 92.	(lp)	(HANG 47UP) <TR 005> **FUCK CD'S ... IT'S THE MUMMIES** <US-title 'NEVER BEEN CAUGHT'>	□	□
		– Your ass (is next in line) / Stronger than dirt / Little Miss Tee-N-T / Come on up / Sooprize package for Mr. Mineo / Rosie [US-only] / Shot down / The ballad of Iron Eyes Cody / Skinny Minnie / She lied / The red cobra #9 / The Frisko freeze / Justine / Mariconda's a friend of mine [US-only] / The thing from Venus / Shut yer mouth / Jezebel [US-only]. (UK-iss.Mar98 as 'NEVER BEEN CAUGHT' on 'Telstar'; TR 005) <cd-iss. Oct02 on 'Telstar'+=; TR 005CD> – (You must fight to live) On the planet of .... / Whitecaps / I'm down / Your love / Uncle Willie.		
1992.	(7")	<TR 006> **STRONGER THAN DIRT. / YOUR LOVE**	-	□
			not iss.	Sympathy F
1993.	(7"ep)	<SFTRI 196> **(YOU MUST FIGHT TO LIVE) ON THE PLANET OF THE APES / WHITECAPS (pt.I). / WHITECAPS (pt.II) / I'M DOWN**	-	□
			not iss.	Demolition Derby
1993.	(7")	<DD 001> **LIVE AT CAFE THE PIT'S (live)** – What can I do / (other by SUPERCHARGER).	-	□
			not iss.	Pin-Up
1993.	(7"flex-ep)	<Pinup 93006> **THE MUMMIES VS. SUPERCHARGER TOUR '93** – I'm gonna kill my baby tonight / I should better be looking for Dangerman / (other 2 by SUPERCHARGER).	-	□
Mar 94.	(lp)	<Pinup 94012> **PARTY AT STEVE'S HOUSE** – Shake! / Big boy Pete / Caesar's gonna get in trouble you know / Don Gallucci's balls / I hear you laughing / You better stop / Babba diddy baby / Tough enough / Just one more dance / I don't like it / Duel / Zip a dee doo dah. (UK-iss.Oct98; same as US)	-	□
Oct 94.	(7")	<Pinup 94014> **GWENDOLYN. / BIG BOY PETE**	-	□

— WINTHER had now joined The ORANGE PEELS

– compilations, others, etc. –

1992.	(lp)	Estrus; <(ES 94015)> **:PLAY THEIR OWN RECORDS!** – That girl / Test drive / I'm bigger than you / Dirty robber / Food, sickles and girls / One by one / Out of our tree / Tall cool one / A girl like you / That's mighty childish / (Doin') The Kirk / Die! / Mashi / The fly / The house on the hill.	□	□
1996.	(d7"ep)	Estrus; <ESX 2> **DOUBLE DUMB ASS ... IN THE FACE** (es45001 + es45002 singles)	-	□
Oct 96.	(lp)	Estrus; <(ES 94016)> **RUNNIN' ON EMPTY VOL.1** (early + live recordings 1991) – One potato, two potato / The house on the hill / Die! / (They call me) Willie the wild one / The Mummies' theme / Shit / The double axe / Come on up / What a wat to die / The fly / Uncontrollable urge / Justine / Stronger than dirt / Skinny Minnie / One potato, two potato.	□	□
Jan 97.	(lp)	Estrus; <(ES 94018)> **RUNNIN' ON EMPTY VOL.2** (unreleased + bootleg stuff) – Down home girl / Food, sickles and girls / In and out / (You) Can't sit down / I'm gonna kill my baby tonight / (I should better be lookin' for) Dangerman / Uncontrollable urge / Girl U want / The fly / The ballad of Iron Eyes Cody / Just one more dance / Babba diddy baby / High heel sneakers.	□	□

MUPPET MULE (see under ⇒ SPARE SNARE)

MURDER CITY DEVILS

Formed: Seattle, Washington, USA ... 1997 by SPENCER MOODY, NATE MANNY, DANN GALLUCI, DEREK FUDESCO, COADY WILLIS and GABE. Veterans of Seattle's ever thriving rock scene (various members had previously played in local acts The UNABOMBERS, AREA 51 and The DEATHWISH KIDS), the 'DEVILS set out to prove that garage'n'roll was still alive and puking in the city even as grunge was taking its last breath. A couple of early singles, 'THREE NATURAL SIXES' and 'DANCE HALL MUSIC' preceded a deal with 'Sub Pop' imprint, 'Die Young Stay Pretty', through whom the band issued their 1997 eponymous debut album. A formative effort which introduced their patented brand of bleak, organ-fuelled retro punk, the record was haunted by the ghosts of The STOOGES, MC5 and The NEW YORK DOLLS. The JACK ENDINO-produced 'EMPTY BOTTLES, BROKEN HEARTS' (1999) further enhanced their reputation with many commentators citing them as the Seattle area's most promising newcomers. The biggest thrill of their short career came when PEARL JAM took them

MURDER CITY DEVILS (cont)

out as support on their 'Yield' tour, making the progression from sweaty clubs to stadiums literally overnight. By this point former HOLE keyboard woman, LESLIE HARDY had joined up, making her recording debut via the millennial 'IN NAME AND BLOOD' (2000). • **Covered:** CAN'T SEEM TO MAKE YOU MINE (Seeds) / I'LL COME RUNNING (Neil Diamond) / HYBRID MOMENTS (Misfits).

Album rating: MURDER CITY DEVILS (*5) / EMPTY BOTTLES, BROKEN HEARTS (*6) / IN NAME AND BLOOD (*7)

SPENCER MOODY – vocals / **NATE MANNY** – guitar / **DANN GALLUCCI** – guitar / **DEREK FUDESCO** – bass / **COADY WILLIS** – drums / + 7th member/roadie **GABE**

		not iss.	eMpTy
1997.	(7"m) <MTR 354> **DANCEHALL MUSIC. / JOHNNY THUNDERS / RIDE THE TRAIN**	-	

		Die Young	Die Young
Sep 97.	(lp/cd) <(DIE/+CD 001)> **MURDER CITY DEVILS**		Aug97

– Dance hall music / It's in my heart / Boom swagger room / Get off the floor / Flashbulb / Broken glass / Murder city roit / Sick of dreaming / Make it on my own / Tell you brother. *(re-iss. Aug01; same)*

		not iss.	Hopscotch
1998.	(7"red-ep) <#5> **THREE NATURAL SIXES**	-	

– Murder city riot / Broken glass / Officer / Halfman.

		Sub Pop	Sub Pop
May 99.	(lp/cd) <(SP/+CD 429)> **EMPTY BOTTLES, BROKEN HEARTS**		Nov98

– I want a lot now (so come on) / Dancin' shoes / 18 wheels / Left hand right hand / Ready for more / Cradle to the grave / Dear hearts / Hey sailor / Johnny Thunders / Stars in her eyes / Another round on you / Every shitty thing. *(re-iss. Aug01; same)*

—— added **LESLIE HARDY** – keyboards (ex-HOLE)

Oct 99.	(7"ep) <(SP 482)> **IN THIS TOWN / CAN'T SEEM TO MAKE YOU MINE. / (other 2 by GLUCIFER)**		
Jun 00.	(lp/cd) <(SP/+CD 497)> **IN NAME AND BLOOD**		

– Press gang / I drank the wine / Bunkhouse / Idle hands / Rum and whiskey / I'll come running / Demon brother / Lemuria rising / Somebody else's baby / In this town / No grave but the sea / Fields of fire. *(re-iss. Aug01; same)*

2000.	(7"orange/lightblue) <#03> **PRESS GANG. / (other by AT THE DRIVE-IN)**	-	

(above issued on 'Buddyhead')

Aug 01.	(10"m-lp/m-cd) <(SP/+CD 560)> **THELEMA**		

– That's what you get / Bear away / Midnight service at the mutter museum / One vision of May / Bride of the elephant man / 364 days.

MURRY THE HUMP

Formed: Aberystwyth, Ceredigion, Wales ... late 90's by singer/lyricist (in the MORRISSEY/JARVIS vain), MATTHEW EVANS, GWIAN ROWLANDS, BILL COYNE and CURIG HUWS. In the mid to late 1990's bands such as the SUPER FURRY ANIMALS and GORGY'S ZYGOTIC MYNCI had made the Welsh valleys an unlikely source for quality, left of centre, rule bending music. MURRY THE HUMP dutifully aided this movement and made their intent clear from the offset. Their debut single 'GREEN GREEN GRASS OF HOME' (an NME SOTW) was a neo-psychedelic humourous ode to their dope dealer. Later that same year another single 'THROWN LIKE A STONE' preceded the 'COLOURING BOOK' EP and already the group were being hailed as the best new band in Wales (and possibly the UK). 2001 saw the departure of bassist CURIG who was replaced by former TOPPER member SION GLYN. Now signings of 'Too Pure' records, the band were enjoying further adulation for the single 'THE HOUSE THAT USED TO BE A SHIP'. Their 2001 debut album 'SONGS OF IGNORANCE' was well received although many thought this was a band who had not yet realised their full potential. Frustrated by a lack of commercial success the MTH called it a day in September 2001. However, EVANS, ROWLANDS and GLYN did resurface the following year as The KEYS.

Album rating: SONGS OF IGNORANCE (*7)

MATTHEW EVANS (b. 2 May'75) – vocals, guitar / **GWION ROWLANDS** (b.16 Apr'76) – guitar, vocals / **CURIG HUWS** – bass / **BILL COYNE** (b.28 Feb'70) – drums

		Blue Dog	not iss.
1999.	(7") **GREEN GREEN GRASS OF HOME. / (other by GEORGEOUS FAME & THE 3 DEGREES)**		-

		Shifty Disco	not iss.
Sep 99.	(cd-s) (DISCO 9909) **THROWN LIKE A STONE / DON'T SLIP**		-

		Malthouse	not iss.
Nov 99.	(cd-ep) (MALT 001) **COLOURING BOOK E.P.**		-

– Colouring book / Cracking up / Blue bottle / Kebab or shag? / Pussy willow.

		Prim & Proper	not iss.
May 00.	(7") **SILVER SUIT. / BOOZE AND CIGARETTES**		-

—— **SION GLYN** – bass; repl. CURIG

		Pure	not iss.
Jan 01.	(7") (PURE 112S) **THE HOUSE THAT USED TO BE A SHIP. / (other by HEFNER)**		-
Mar 01.	(7") (PURE 114S) **CRACKING UP. / NO GIRL NO SEX**		-

(cd-s+=) (PURE 114CDS) – Travel.

May 01.	(7") (PURE 117S) **DON'T SLIP UP. / PIGS ON PARADE**		-

(cd-s+=) (PURE 117CDS) – Kebab or shag?

May 01.	(cd/lp) (PURE 116 CD/LP) **SONGS OF IGNORANCE**		-

– Green green grass / Cracking up / Thrown like a stone / Don't slip up / Colouring book / Valley girl / Booze & cigarettes / The house that used to be a ship / Five / New deal / Vodka & wine.

—— MURRY THE HUMP have now disbanded

MUSE

Formed: Teignmouth, Devon, England ... 1997 by MATTHEW BELLAMY, CHRIS WOLSTENHOLME and drummer DOMINIC HOWARD. After playing dingey pubs and damp basements, the 3-piece from the south-west arose when they debuted at the 'In The City' A&R field day in 1998. HOWARD's THOM YORKE-esque vox impressed record pedallers so much that they took the group to America to showcase them for MADONNA's record label 'Maverik' – home to The DEFTONES, ALANIS MORISSETTE and, erm, WANK. The 20-something indie kids released a John Leckie (knob-twiddler for RADIOHEAD, STONE ROSES and somebody called JOHN LENNON) produced EP entitled 'MUSE' at the beginning of 1999, which was only pressed on 999 copies (it can nowadays fetch up to £30). The EP sounded like many earlier RADIOHEAD efforts, with a little MY BLOODY VALENTINE twist thrown in for good measure. MUSE proceeded with the 'MUSCLE MUSEUM' EP and two singles 'UNO' and 'CAVE' before unveiling their debut set 'SHOWBIZ' in late '99. The album boasted nothing special (bar say, the track 'SUNBURN'), except that it may have contained some of the most melodramatic tracks since OASIS's 'WHAT'S THE STORY...'. It unleashed a new brand of genre that had the same ideology as Brit Pop: MOR – where have I heard this before? – rock. 2001 saw MUSE go from strength to strength via two major UK hit singles, 'PLUG IN BABY' and 'NEW BORN', both taken from their celebrated Top 3 sophomore set, 'ORIGIN OF SYMMETRY'. 2002 saw the release of the obligatory live/B-sides collection, 'HULLABALOO SOUNDTRACK', documenting a French concert performance and collecting various odd'n'sods for obsessives and completists. • **Note:** The MUSE who released the CD in '97 entitled 'Innocent Voices' were not the same band.

Album rating: SHOWBIZ (*7) / ORIGIN OF SYMMETRY (*7) / HULLABALOO SOUNDTRACK (*6)

MATTHEW BELLAMY – vocals, guitar / **CHRIS WOLSTENHOLME** – bass / **DOMINIC HOWARD** – drums

		Dangerous	not iss.
May 98.	(cd-ep) (DREXCDEP 103) **MUSE EP**		-

– Overdue / Cave / Coma / Escape.

Jan 99.	(cd-ep) (DREXCDEP 104) **MUSCLE MUSEUM EP**		-

– Muscle museum / Sober / Uno / Unintented / Instant messenger / Muscle museum #2.

		Mushroom	Warners
Jun 99.	(7"clear) (MUSH 50S) **UNO. / AGITATED**	73	-

(cd-s) (MUSH 50CDS) – ('A'side) / Jimmy Kane / Forced in.

Sep 99.	(7"clear) (MUSH 58S) **CAVE / CAVE (instrumental remix)**	52	

(cd-s+=) (MUSH 58CDS) – Twin.
(cd-s) (MUSH 58CDX) – ('A'side) / Host / Coma.

Oct 99.	(cd/md/c/lp) (MUSH 59 CD/MC/LP) <47382> **SHOWBIZ**	69	

– Sunburn / Muscle museum / Fillip / Falling down / Cave / Showbiz / Unintended / Uno / Sober / Escape / Overdue / Hate this & I'll love you. *(re-iss. Feb00; same)*

Nov 99.	(7") (MUSH 66S) **MUSCLE MUSEUM. / ('A'live acoustic)**	43	

(cd-s+=) (MUSH 66CDS) – Do we need this?
(cd-s) (MUSH 66CDSX) – ('A'extended) / Pink ego box / Con-science.

Feb 00.	(7") (MUSH 68S) **SUNBURN. / ('A'live)**	22	

(cd-s+=) (MUSH 68CDS) – Ashamed.
(cd-s) (MUSH 68CDSX) – ('A'side) / Yes please / Uno (live).

Jun 00.	(7"/c-s) (MUSH 72 S/MCS) **UNINTENDED. / RECESS**	20	

(cd-s+=) (MUSH 72CDS) – Falling down (live acoustic) / ('A'-CD-ROM).
(cd-s) (MUSH 72CDSX) – ('A'side) / Nishe / Hate this & I'll love you (live).

Oct 00.	(7") (MUSH 84S) **MUSCLE MUSEUM. / SOBER (The Saint remix)**	25	-

(cd-s+=) (MUSH 84CDS) – Sunburn (Timo Maas sunstroke remix).

		Mushroom	Mushroom
Mar 01.	(c-s) (MUSH 89MCS) **PLUG IN BABY / NATURE 1**	11	-

(cd-s+=) (MUSH 89CDS) – Execution commentary.
(cd-s) (MUSH 89CDSX) – ('A'side) / Spiral static / Bedroom acoustics.

Jun 01.	(7") (MUSH 92) **NEW BORN. / SHRINKING UNIVERSE**	12	-

(cd-s+=) (MUSH 92CDS) – Piano thing / ('A'-video).
(cd-s) (MUSH 92CDSX) – ('A'side) / Map of your head / Plug in baby (live).
(12") (MUSH 92T) – ('A'-Perfecto remix) / Sunburn (Timo Maas sunstroke remix).

Jun 01.	(cd/c/lp) (MUSH 93 CD/MC/LP) <40093> **ORIGIN OF SYMMETRY**	3	Jul01

– New born / Bliss / Space dementia / Hyper music / Plug in baby / Citizen erased / Micro cuts / Screenager / Dark shines / Feeling good / Megalomania.

Aug 01.	(7") (MUSH 96S) **BLISS. / THE GALLERY**	22	-

(cd-s+=) (MUSH 96CDS) – Screenager (live) / ('A'-CD-Rom).
(cd-s) (MUSH 96CDSX) – ('A'side) / Hyper chondriac music / New born (live) / ('A'-making of the video).

Nov 01.	(7") (MUSH 97S) **HYPER MUSIC. / FEELING GOOD (live)**	24	-

(cd-s+=) (MUSH 97CDS) – Shine / ('A'-video).
(cd-s) (MUSH 97CDSX) – ('A'live) / ('B'studio) / Please, please, please let me get what I want / ('B'video).

Jun 02.	(7") (MUSH 104S) **IN YOUR WORLD. / DEAD STAR**	13	-

(cd-s+=) (MUSH 104CDS) – Futurism / Dead star (video).
(cd-s+=) (MUSH 104CDSX) – Can't take my eyes off you / In your world (video).

Jul 02.	(d-cd) (MUSH 105CD) <65021> **HULLABALOO SOUNDTRACK (compilation + live)**	10	

– Forced in / Shrinking universe / Recess / Yes please / Map of your head / Nature 1 / Shine acoustic / Ashamed / The gallery / Hyper chondriac music // Dead star / Micro cuts / Citizen erased / Showbiz / Megalomania / Dark shines / Screenager / Space dementia / In your world / Muscle museum / Agitated.

MUSIC

Formed: Kippax, Leeds, England . . . 1999 by STUART COLEMAN, ADAM NUTTER, ROBERT HARVEY and PHIL JORDAN. Barely out of their teens, and with very little money, this impressive quartet issued a demo EP entitled 'TAKE THE LONG ROAD AND WALK IT' in 2001, which led Radio 1 DJ Steve Lamacq to give the group almost unlimited airtime on his evening shows. On the strengh of this demo, tiny label 'Fierce Panda' bought the rights to the EP and re-issued it on a limited run of 1,000 copies – they sold out in almost a fortnight. With COLEMAN's intense swagger and vocals to match, he seemed like the new generation's BEZ, only with a few more brain cells. The MUSIC's music, well, it wasn't as almighty as the ensemble's moniker would have you believe; rough, early VERVE came to mind along with, traces of JOY DIVISION and even MOGWAI on the track 'WALLS GET SMALLER' – basically a fusion of good old Northern glum. 'Hut' records eventually won the bidding war for the band in 2001, prompting them to issue their first EP proper 'YOU MIGHT AS WELL TRY TO FUCK ME', followed by 'THE PEOPLE' EP and eventually their cracking self-titled debut album in 2002.

Album rating: THE MUSIC (*8)

ROBERT HARVEY – vocals / **ADAM NUTTER** – guitar / **STUART COLEMAN** – bass / **PHIL JORDAN** – drums

		Fierce Panda	not iss.
May 01.	(ltd-7") (NING 107) **TAKE THE LONG ROAD AND WALK IT. / WAKKS GET SMALLER**	-	-

		Hut	Capitol
Nov 01.	(12"ep/cd-ep) (HUT T/CD 145) <546066> **YOU MIGHT AS WELL TRY TO FUCK ME EP**		Jan02
	– You might as well try to fuck me / Karma / Treat me right on / Too high.		
Apr 02.	(12"ep/cd-ep) (HUT T/CD 152) **THE PEOPLE EP**	-	-
	– The people / Let love be the healer / Life / Jag tune.		

		Hut	Virgin
May 02.	(cd-ep) <68381> **THE MUSIC**	-	-
	– Take the long road and walk it / The walls get smaller / You might as well try to fuck me / Karma / Too high / New instrumental (live).		

		Hut	Capitol
Aug 02.	(7") (HUT 158) <546023> **TAKE THE LONG ROAD AND WALK IT. / ALONE**	14	Jan02
	(cd-s+=) (HUTCD 158) – Raindance / ('A'-video).		
	(12"++=) (HUTT 158) – The walls get smaller.		
	(cd-s) (HUTDX 158) – ('A'side) / The walls get smaller / New instrumental / ('A'-original).		
Sep 02.	(cd/d-lp) (CDHUT/HUTDLP 76) **THE MUSIC**	4	-
	– The dance / Take the long road and walk it / Human / The truth has no words / Float / Turn out the light / The people / Getaway / Disco / Too high.		
Nov 02.	(7"/cd-s) (HUT/+CD 162) **GETAWAY. / DRAGON SONG**	26	-

MUSIC TAPES (see under ⇒ **CHOCOLATE USA**)

MUTTON BIRDS

Formed: Auckland, New Zealand . . . 1989 by DON McGLASHAN, a singer-songwriter with Scottish ancestry and former member of various obscure Kiwi outfits including The ERIC GLANDY MEMORIAL BIG BAND. With a line-up initially completed by fellow musical veterans, RUSS BURGE and DAVID LONG, prior to the addition of ALAN GREGG, they debuted with the NZ-only 'HEATER' EP in 1994 (the lead track a highlight from that year's eponymous debut set), revealing them to be darker, more experimental, cinematic cousins of countrymen, CROWDED HOUSE (especially on the haunting 'HE TURNED AROUND'). A further domestic single, 'ANCHOR ME' – lifted from the acclaimed, best selling 'SALTY' album – netted a major songwriting award and amid the ensuing acclaim, The MUTTON BIRDS secured a contract with Virgin subsidiary, 'Dindisc'. Their first long-player for the label, 'NATURE' was compiled from the deep, earthy early recordings on the first two albums, while the aforementioned 'ANCHOR ME' was re-issued as a UK single. 1996 saw the band release a broodingly impressive cover of Blue Oyster Cult's 'DON'T FEAR THE REAPER' (as the B-side to NZ-only single, 'SHE'S BEEN TALKING'); originally recorded for a film by Kiwi director, Peter Jackson, the track became a minor hit in Australia (where the band were signed to 'E.M.I.') and was subsequently tacked on to Aussie and Canadian versions of third album, 'ENVY OF ANGELS' (1997). Recorded at Rockfield studios in Wales, the latter set gave the band their first UK chart placing, scraping into the Top 75. • **Covered:** IT HAPPENED ONE NIGHT (Jody Harris) / A MAN AND A WOMAN (Front Lawn) / DON'T FIGHT IT MARSHA . . . (Blam Blam Blam).

Album rating: THE MUTTON BIRDS (*6) / SALTY (*6) / NATURE compilation (*6) / ENVY OF ANGELS (*7) / TOO HARD BASKET compilation (*6)

DON McGLASHAN – vocals, guitar / **RUSS BURGE** – drums / **ALAN GREGG** – bass / **DAVID LONG** – guitar

		Warners	not iss.	
May 92.	(c-s) (FLSC 400) **DOMINION ROAD / WHITE VALIENT**	-	-	NewZ
	(re-iss. Oct93 in Australia)			
Aug 92.	(c-s) (BAGSC 1002) **NATURE / DOMINION ROAD**	-	-	NewZ
Aug 92.	(c-s/c) (435300-2/-4) **THE MUTTON BIRDS**	-	-	NewZ
	– Dominion road / Your window / She's like a city / No plans for later / Before the breakthrough / White valient / Giant friend / Big fish / A thing well made / Nature. (re-iss. Feb94 in Australia)			
Nov 92.	(c-s) (877005-4) **GIANT FRIEND / SHE'S LIKE A CITY (live)**	-	-	NewZ
	(re-iss. Aug94 in Australia)			
Apr 93.	(c-s/cd-s) (877012-4/-2) **YOUR WINDOW / DOMINION ROAD / GIANT FRIEND**	-	-	NewZ
Feb 94.	(cd-s) **NATURE / A THING WELL MADE (live) / SHE'S LIKE A CITY (live)**	-	-	Austra
Feb 94.	(c-ep/cd-ep) (877019-4/-2) **THE HEATER EP**	-	-	Austra
	– The heater / The ballad of Kelvin / He turned around / It happened one night.			
Apr 94.	(c-ep/cd-ep) (877020-4/-2) **IN MY ROOM / YOU WILL RETURN / WELLINGTON**	-	-	Austra
Apr 94.	(cd/c) (839488-2/-4) **SALTY**	-	-	Austra
	– The heater / Ngaire / You will return / Wellington / In my room / When the wind comes round / Queens English / Salty my dear / There's a limit / Esther / No telling when / Anchor me / Too close to the sun / Don't forget it Marsha it's bigger than both of us.			
Aug 94.	(c-s/cd-s) (877021-4/-2) **NGAIRE / THE QUEEN'S ENGLISH (Annus Horribilis mix) / A MAN AND A WOMAN**	-	-	Austra
Sep 94.	(cd-s) (877023-2) **ANCHOR ME / THE HEATER (Careful With . . . version) / NGAIRE (version)**	-	-	Austra

		Dindisc	Virgin
Aug 95.	(c-s) (DINSC 148) **DOMINION ROAD / YOU WILL RETURN**	-	-
	(cd-s+=) (DINSD 148) – Wellington / Ngaire.		
Sep 95.	(cd) (CDVIR 39) **NATURE** (compilation of first two NZ albums)	-	-
	– Nature / Dominion road / Anchor me / The heater / Giant friend / Your window / White valient / In my room / A thing well made / The Queen's English / There's a limit / Too close to the sun.		
Feb 96.	(c-s) (DINSC 149) **ANCHOR ME / ESTHER / DON'T FIGHT IT MARSHA, IT'S BIGGER THAN BOTH OF US**	-	-
	(cd-s) (DINSD 149) – ('A'side) / When the wind comes round.		
Nov 96.	(c-s/cd-s) (877043-4/-2) **SHE'S BEEN TALKING / DON'T FEAR THE REAPER / FACE IN THE PAPER**	-	- Austra
Feb 97.	(c-s) (DINSC 157) **COME AROUND / WHEN THE WIND COMES ROUND**	-	-
	(cd-s+=) (DINSD 157) – Along the boundary / Face in the paper.		
	(cd-s) (DINSDX 157) – ('A'side) / Dominion road / Anchor me.		
Jun 97.	(cd/c) (CD/MC VIR 55) <842584-2> **ENVY OF ANGELS**	64	
	– Straight to your head / She's been talking / Trouble with you / April / Like this rain / Another morning / Ten feet tall / Come around / Crooked mile / While you sleep / Inside my skin / Envy of angels.		
Jun 97.	(c-s) (DINSC 160) **SHE'S BEEN TALKING / WHITE VALIANT**	-	-
	(cd-s+=) (DINSD 160) – Inbetween man.		
	(cd-s) (DINSDX 160) – ('A'side) / He turned around / The heater.		

– compilations, etc. –

Nov 95.	(d-cd/d-c) (471057-2/-4) **BOX OF BIRDS**	-	- Austra
	– (THE MUTTON BIRDS – GIANT FRIEND / SALTY).		
Dec 98.	(cd) Gravy Train; (GRAVY cd2) **"TOO HARD BASKET" – B SIDES AND BASTARDS**	-	-
	– It happened one night / He turned around / The ballad of Kelvin / Three minutes / So long / The heater (careful with . . . version) / The Queen's English (annus horribilis mix) / Cinema of unease – credit music / Don't fear the reaper / Ash Wednesday / Ranchslider / Answerphone / Face in the paper / Inbetween man / Along the boundary.		

MY BLOODY VALENTINE

Formed: Dublin, Ireland . . . 1984 by KEVIN SHIELDS and COLM O'CIOSOIG. Later the same year, the pair travelled to Germany where they hooked up with DAVE CONWAY and TINA to record a mini-lp, 'THIS IS YOUR BLOODY VALENTINE', for the small 'Tycoon' records. This was issued the following year although only 50 copies seem to have emerged (now very rare!). They subsequently moved to London, DEBBIE GOODGE replacing TINA for the recording of the 'GEEK!' EP on 'Fever'. After more 45's for 'Kaleidoscope' then 'Lazy' (home of The PRIMITIVES), the band really began to move away from their early twanging, IGGY POP-style sound following a move to 'Creation' in 1988 (masterminded by SLAUGHTER JOE FOSTER, ex-TV PERSONALITIES). With co-"vocalist", BILINDA BUTCHER now also on board, SHIELDS and Co. finally made the breakthrough in 1990 when the 'GLIDER' EP nearly went Top 40 in the UK, hot on the heels of the acclaimed 'ISN'T ANYTHING' (1988) album. The full extent of their pioneering guitar manipulation – responsible for a whole scene of "shoegazing" musical admirers, stand up RIDE, MOOSE, LUSH etc., etc. – was revealed as MBV released their most challenging and inventive track to date in 'TO HERE KNOWS WHEN' (from the Top 30 'TREMOLO' EP). Creating a whole new concept and language of sound, the song either enveloped the listener in blissful noise or just seemed out of bloody tune, there was no middle ground. 'LOVELESS' (1991), MBV's long awaited and much heralded follow-up, was a revelation. Its hypnotic, undulating noisescapes sounded not-of-this-earth and 'Creation' were saddled with an astronomical studio bill to match, almost going bankrupt as a result. They subsequently signed to 'Island' records, and 12(!!!) years on, fans are still awaiting some new product. Although MY BLOODY VALENTINE have arguably been the most influential indie band of the last decade and few doubt their potential to return with a masterpiece, their reclusive silence makes the late Stanley Kubrick appear prolific. Nevertheless, SHIELDS has surfaced occasionally as a remixer, notably for the single release of PRIMAL SCREAM's 'Stuka' and many more; he subsequently joined them in 2000. • **Songwriters:** SHIELDS writes most of material, with words after 1987 by BILINDA. Covered MAP REF 41 (Wire). • **Trivia:** A track, 'SUGAR', was given away free with 'The Catalogue' magazine of February '89.

Album rating: THIS IS YOUR BLOODY VALENTINE (*5) / ISN'T ANYTHING (*8) / ECSTASY AND WINE compilation (*7) / LOVELESS (*9)

MY BLOODY VALENTINE (cont)

KEVIN SHIELDS (b.21 May'63, Queens, New York) – guitar, vocals, occasional bass / DAVE CONWAY – vocals / COLM CUSACK (b. COLM MICHAEL O'CIOSOIG, 31 Oct'64) – drums / TINA – keyboards

			Tycoon	not iss.
1985.	(m-lp) *(ST 7501)* **THIS IS YOUR BLOODY VALENTINE**		-	- German

– Forever and again / Homelovin' guy / Don't cramp my style / Tiger in my tank / The love gang / Inferno / The last supper.

—— DEBBIE GOOGE (b.24 Oct'62, Somerset, England) – bass; repl. TINA

			Fever	not iss.
Apr 86.	(12"ep) *(FEV 5)* **GEEK!**			-

– No place to go / Moonlight / Love machine / The sandman never sleeps.

Jun 86.	(7") *(FEV 5X)* **NO PLACE TO GO. / MOONLIGHT**			

			Kaleidoscope Sound	not iss.
Oct 86.	(12"ep) *(KS 101)* **THE NEW RECORD BY MY BLOODY VALENTINE**			-

– Lovelee sweet darlene / By the danger in your eyes / On another rainy Sunday / We're so beautiful.

			Lazy	not iss.
Feb 87.	(7") *(LAZY 04)* **SUNNY SUNDAE SMILE. / PAINT A RAINBOW**			-

(12"+=) *(LAZY 04T)* – Kiss the eclipse / Sylvie's head.

—— BILINDA BUTCHER (b.16 Sep'61, London, England) – vocals, guitar; repl. CONWAY

Nov 87.	(m-lp) *(LAZY 08)* **ECSTASY**			-

– (Please) Lose yourself in me / The things I miss / I don't need you / Clair / (You're) Safe in your sleep / She loves you no less / Strawberry wine / Lovelee sweet darlene.

Nov 87.	(12"m) *(LAZY 07)* **STRAWBERRY WINE. / NEVER SAY GOODBYE / CAN I TOUCH YOU**			

			Creation	Relativity
Jul 88.	(7") *(CRE 055)* **YOU MADE ME REALISE. / SLOW**			

(12"+=) *(CRE 055T)* – Thorn / Cigarette in your bed / Drive it all over me. *(re-iss. Mar90 as cd-ep; CRECD 55)*

Oct 88.	(7") *(CRE 061)* **FEED ME WITH YOUR KISSES. / EMPTINESS INSIDE**			-

(12"+=) *(CRE 061T)* – I believe / I need no trust. *(re-iss. Mar90 as cd-ep; CRECD 61)*

Nov 88.	(lp/cd)(c) *(CRELP 040/+CD)(C-CRELP 040)* <1006> **ISN'T ANYTHING**			

– Soft as snow (but warm inside) / Lose my breath / Cupid come / (When you wake) You're still in a dream / No more sorry / All I need / Feed me with your kiss / Sue is fine / Several girls galore / You never should / Nothing much to lose / I can see it (but I can't feel it). *(free 7"w/ lp)* – INSTRUMENTAL. / INSTRUMENTAL <*US cd re-iss. 1993 on 'Warners'; 45231*> *(cd re-iss. Jan01; same)*

			Creation	Sire
Apr 90.	(7"ep/12"ep)(cd-ep) *(CRE 73/+T)(CRESCD 73)* <26313> **GLIDER**		41	

– Soon / Glider / Don't ask why / Off your face.

Feb 91.	(7"ep/12"ep)(cd-ep) *(CRE 085/+T)(CRESCD 085)* <40024> **TREMOLO**		29	Apr91

– To here knows when / Swallow / Honey power / Moon song.

Nov 91.	(cd/lp)(c) *(CRE CD/LP 060)(C-CRELP 060)* <26759> **LOVELESS**		24	

– Only shallow / Loomer / Touched / To here knows when / When you sleep / I only said / Come in alone / Sometimes / Blown a wish / What you want / Soon. *(cd re-iss. Jan01; same)*

—— During their long hiatus, KEVIN SHIELDS contributed (1996) to an album 'Beyond The Pale' by EXPERIMENTAL AUDIO RESEARCH. It also featured SONIC BOOM (ex-SPACEMEN 3), KEVIN MARTIN (of GOD) & EDDIE PREVOST (of AMM). Meanwhile, DEBBIE GOOGE teamed up with KATHERINE GIFFORD and MAX CORRADI to form SNOWPONY. In 2000, COLM finally reappeared in HOPE SANDOVAL & THE WARM INVENTIONS (she of MAZZY STAR fame).

– compilations, others, etc. –

Feb 89.	(lp/cd) Lazy; *(LAZY 12/+CD)* **ECSTASY AND WINE**			-

– Strawberry wine / Never say goodbye / Can I touch you / She loves you no less / The things I miss / I don't need you / Safe in your sleep / Clair / You've got nothing / Lose yourself in me.

MY FAVORITE

Formed: Long Island, New York, USA . . . 1990 by school friends, MICHAEL GRACE JR. and DARREN AMADIO, with the aid of ANDREA VAUGHAN, GILBERT AMAD and TOD (although rumour persists that this was actually a drum synthesizer). The quintet's joint love of the early eighties post-punk and new wave sound informed their music, but unlike much from this period, MY FAVORITE instill their songs with emotion that was sometimes subdued in favour of that aforementioned decade's swaggering pseudo-sophistication. Beginning in classic indie fashion, the band issued their debut, 'BRIGHTON RIOT' (1992) on tape, and off of their own backs; several singles followed, notably, 'THE INFORMERS & US' in 1996. Although this gained MY FAV attention in the alternative music press, it was to be another four years before their debut LP proper, 'LOVE AT ABSOLUTE ZERO' would appear. A competent piece, it was succeeded by the EP, 'JOAN OF ARC AWAITING TRIAL' two years later, which included some great additional help by the likes of VIKA PANANYUK and TARA EMELYE NEEDHAM. This release and their following EP, 'A CULT OF ONE', were conceived as two parts of a loose trilogy – the third being 'THE KIDS ARE ALL WRONG' – around the central character of Joan of Arc, and marked a good maturing of the band's style, showcased by the added instrumentation which they skillfully used to strengthen their sound, rather than cloud it.

Album rating: LOVE AT ABSOLUTE ZERO (*7)

MICHAEL GRACE JR. – vocals / DARREN AMADIO – guitar / ANDREA VAUGHN – vocals, keyboards / GILBERT AMAD – bass / TOD – drums

			not iss.	own label
1992.	(ltd-c) **BRIGHTON RIOT**		-	Swingset

			not iss.	Swingset
1994.	(7"ep) **THE LAST NEW WAVE RECORD**		-	

– Go kid go / Absolute beginners again / 1986.

			not iss.	Double Agent
1995.	(7"ep) <*DA 001*> **CULT HERO, COME HOME. /** (others artists:- ROSE MELBERG & DUSTIN RESKE, PAPAS FRITAS + ZAIUS)			

			not iss.	Harriet
1996.	(7"ep) **THE INFORMERS & US**		-	

– The informers / The detectives of suburbia / The informers part 2.

			not iss.	A Turntable Friend
1996.	(7") **WORKING CLASS JACKET. /** (other by MAD PLANETS)		-	

			Double Agent	Double Agent
Apr 96.	(7") <*TURN 28*> **MODULATE. /** (other by BOYRACER)		-	
1999.	(cd) <*DA 007CD*> **LOVE AT ABSOLUTE ZERO**		-	

– Absolute zero / Absolute beginners again / 17 Berlin / The truth about Lake Ronkonkama / Let's stay alive / Go kid go / Modulate / Party crashers / Between cafes / The informers / Working class jacket / You belong with us. *(UK-iss.Apr02; same as US)*

2001.	(cd-ep) <*DA 015CD*> **JOAN OF ARC AWAITING TRIAL**			-

– LP / Homeless club kids / Badge / White roses for blue girls.

2001.	(cd-ep) <*DA 018CD*> **A CULT OF ONE**			-

– Le monster / The suburbs are killing us / The black cassette / John Dark (a simulation).

2002.	(cd-ep) **THE KIDS ARE ALL WRONG**		-	

– Burning hearts / The radiation / Rescue us / The lesser saints.

MY LIFE STORY

Formed: London, England . . . 1990 by JAKE SHILLINGFORD and arranger AARON CAHILL. The son of artist/musician parents and cousin of noted producer, Warne Livesey, SHILLINGFORD decided on a course of pop stardom at an early age, forming his first band at high school. He subsequently secured work as an artist and DJ at Camden's Dingwall's club before hooking up with CAHILL and setting about realising his musical vision of glamorous, orchestral pop set to gritty lyrics. After a couple of years spent writing and performing low profile gigs around the capital, JAKE and Co. finally secured a deal with indie label, 'Mother Tongue'. The winner of a Single Of The Week award in both the NME amd Melody Maker, the debut 'MY LIFE STORY' EP introduced SHILLINGFORD's trademark cockney-style vocals and featured fans' favourite, 'YOU DON'T SPARKLE (IN MY EYES)', released as a single in its own right the following year. The subject of comparisons with everyone from 80's stars, ABC and The BLOW MONKEYS to 90's fops, DIVINE COMEDY and PULP, MY LIFE STORY were hailed as the perfect antidote to grunge scruffiness with the release of their highly praised debut album, 'MORNINGTON CRESCENT', in 1995. Seemingly unable to turn the acclaim into sales, JAKE was on the verge of throwing in the towel when 'Parlophone' came to the rescue, signing the band up and releasing what turned out to be their first Top 40 hit, '12 REASONS WHY I LOVE HER'. A third-time-lucky 'SPARKLE' followed into the Top 40 while JAKE's credentials as a self-styled Prince Of Suave were confirmed with 'THE KING OF KISSINGDOM'. All featured on follow-up album, 'THE GOLDEN MILE' (1997), as did future single, 'STRUMPET', the sad story of a fading groupie. Possibly too contrived to be everyone's cup of tea, MY LIFE STORY nevertheless make for an entertaining listen, especially in the live arena where their grandiose stage show incorporates the full-on orchestral experience. EXILE INSIDE was a fitting new moniker for the recently reclusive SHILLINGFORD who'd quietly abandoned his MLS project. With AARON CAHILL, on board to arrange and produce EXILE INSIDE (alongside a plethora of invited fans on their audience participation website), it looked quite promising for the retro-synth-pop duo. Their eponymous set in 2002 showed self-indulgence to be an unworthy attribute.

Album rating: MORNINGTON CRESCENT (*6) / THE GOLDEN MILE (*5) / JOINED UP TALKING (*5) / Exile Inside: EXILE INSIDE (*3)

JAKE SHILLINGFORD (b.15 May'66, Southend, England) – vocals / **AARON CAHILL** – instruments, arrangements / **OLLIE KRAUS** – cello, keyboards / **LUCY WILKINS** – vioiln / **BECKI DOE** – violin / **ROXANNA SHIRLEY** – trumpet / **RUTH THOMAS** – trumpet / **MARK BRADLEY** – trumpet / **BEN SPENCER** – saxophone

			Mother Tongue	not iss.
Oct 93.	(12"ep/c-ep/cd-e) *(MOTHER 2 T/MC/CD)* **GIRL A, GIRL B, BOY C / YOU DON'T SPARKLE (IN MY EYES). / STAR COLLIDING / YOU DON'T SPARKLE (BIG SCREEN SOUNDTRACK)**			-
Feb 94.	(7") *(MOTHER 3S)* **FUNNY HA HA. / THE LADY IS A TRAMP**			-

(12"+=/cd-s+=) *(MOTHER 3 T/CD)* – These words are haunting / Funny peculiar.

Apr 94.	(7") *(MOTHER 4S)* **YOU DON'T SPARKLE (IN MY EYES). / FIRST PERSON SINGULAR**			-

(12"+=/cd-s+=) *(MOTHER 4 T/CD)* – Stood amongst friends / You don't sparkle (quintet).

Jan 95.	(cd/lp) *(MOTHER CD/LP 1)* **MORNINGTON CRESCENT**			-
Jun 95.	(cd-ep) *(MOTHER 5CD)* **MORNINGTON CRESCENT COMPANION EP**			-

—— added **DANNY TURNER** – piano, harpsicord / **PAUL SIEPEL** – bass (ex-DIRECTION) / **SIMON WRAY** – drums, timpani

MY LIFE STORY (cont)

                                                          Parlophone Alex

Aug 96. (c-s/7") *(TC+/R 6442)* **12 REASONS WHY I LOVE HER. / LOVER'S RECIPE** — 32 / –
    (cd-s) *(CDR 6442)* – ('A'side) / Lady Somerset / Silent screaming / Heaven suitcase.

Oct 96. (7"clear) *(R 6450)* **SPARKLE. / EMERALD GREEN** — 34 / –
    (cd-s+=) *(CDRS 6450)* – Megaphone theology / ('A'-concert hall).
    (cd-s) *(CDR 6450)* – ('A'side) / Garden fence affair / 17 reasons why I lover her / ('A'-Jazz club).

Feb 97. (7") *(R 6457)* <6052> **THE KING OF KISSINGDOM. / A BOY CALLED DAYDREAM** — 35 / – Apr98
    (cd-s+=) *(CDR 6457)* – Sir Richard Steele.
    (cd-s) *(CDRS 6457)* – ('A'side) / Stuck up your own era / I love you like gala.

Mar 97. (cd/c/lp) *(CD/TC+/PCS 7386)* **THE GOLDEN MILE** — 36
    – 12 reasons why I love her / Suited and booted / Marriage blister / Strumpet / Claret / Mr. Boyd / King of Kissingdom / I dive (unanswered questions and questionable answers) / You can't unheat the apple / Sparkle / April 1st / November 5th / Duchess.

May 97. (7"yellow) *(R 6464)* **STRUMPET. / WELCOME TO MY ARCHIPELAGO** — 27 / –
    (cd-s+=) *(CDR 6464)* – The return of emerald green / Wallpaper.
    (cd-s) *(CDRS 6464)* – ('A'side) / Waiting to explode / I faced the music / March 9th.

Aug 97. (7") *(R 6476)* **DUCHESS. / SILENTLY SCREAMING** — 39 / –
    (cd-s+=) *(CDRS 6476)* – Suited and booted / Mr. Boyd.
    (cd-s) *(CDR 6476)* – ('A'side) / Birthday suit / Emerald green strikes back / Love scene.

Nov 97. (7") *(R 6485)* **YOU CAN'T UNEAT THE APPLE. / CHERRIES** — – / –
    (cd-s+=) *(CDRS 6485)* – Emerald green blah blah blah / History of the world on ice.
    (cd-s) *(CDR 6485)* – ('A'side) / Florence's theme / My sweet little death / Emerald green vs. Dr.Who.

                                                      I.T.R.   not iss.

Jun 99. (c-s) *(ITRC 001)* **IT'S A GIRL THING / EMERALD GREEN BLAH BLAH BLAH** — 37 / –
    (cd-s+=) *(ITR 001)* – Florence's theme.
    (cd-s) *(ITRX 001)* – ('A'side) / My sweet little death / E.G.M.C.M.X.C.I.X.

Oct 99. (7") *(ITRV 003)* **EMPIRE LINE. / I'M A STATISTIC** — 58 / –
    (cd-s+=) *(ITR 003)* – Paint it emerald green.
    (cd-s) *(ITRX 003)* – ('A'side) / Sleep / It's a boy thing.

Feb 00. (cd-s) *(ITR 007)* **WALK / DON'T WALK** — 48 / –
    (cd-s+=) *(ITRX 007)* – Holy deadlock / Cherries / Self defence mechanism.

Feb 00. (cd) *(ITRCD 003)* **JOINED UP TALKING**
    – Empire line / If you can't live without me then why aren't you dead yet? / It's a girl thing / Sunday tongue / Yes to everything / Walk – Don't walk / There's nothing for nobody and everybody wants to be someone / The new New Yorker / Neverland / Stalemate / Don't believe in love / Two stars.

— split late in 2000

EXILE INSIDE

JAKE SHILLINGFORD + AARON CAHILL

                                                      Exilophone not iss.

Aug 02. (cd) *(EI 034)* **EXILE INSIDE**
    – Anaesthesia / I can't feel anymore / Katrin / Exile inside / Disconcerto / Taylorville / She came to stay / Antiques / I hear echoes (when I scream) / Butterfly wings / The will to live / Goodbye / Katrin (French version).

MY VITRIOL

Formed: London, England ... 1998 by Sri Lankan-born singer/songwriter SOM WIJAY-WARDNER and his college mate RAVI KESAVARAM. Taking the name from Graham Greene's classic novel, 'Brighton Rock', the pair cut a 6-track demo EP entitled 'DELUSIONS OF GRANDEUR'. Although more than 200 CDR's were pressed up, less than a quarter were actually playable due to a technical hitch. Luckily, one of these found its way into the hands of Radio 1 DJ Steve Lamacq who duly aired a track on his Evening Session show. Further tracks appeared on compilation albums courtesy of the 'Org' and 'Abuse' labels while the former was to release a debut single proper, 'ALWAYS YOUR WAY' / 'PIECES' in late '99. By this point, the line-up had been completed by SETH TAYLOR and CAROLYN BANNISTER, the four-piece finally landing a deal with 'Infectious' amid much column inches and radio play. The new millennium began with a session for Radio One followed by a couple of live acoustic sessions for X-FM. A much anticipated debut album, 'FINELINES' (2000), hit the shelves in March to widespread acclaim with critics namechecking a host of US noise luminaries including SONIC YOUTH, DINOSAUR JR and SMASHING PUMPKINS. SOM, for his part, cited NIRVANA's 'Smells Like Teen Spirit' as the spark that ignited his much raved over musical bile. A subsequent series of single releases culminated in a Top 40 entry for a re-released 'ALWAYS ...' while the album nearly breached the Top 20. With a string of festival appearances lined up for summer 2001, MV look set to win over yet more punters with their self-confessed 'C.O.R.'; that's critic-orientated-rock to you ... • **Covers:** BREAKFAST (Kelly) / WAIT A MINUTE (Wipers) / OH FATHER (Madonna) / GAME OF PRICKS (Guided By Voices) / STATIC (Jawbox).

Album rating: FINELINES (*7)

SOM WIJAY-WARDNER (b.26 Dec'79) – vocals, guitar (ex-SHOCK SYNDROME) / **SETH TAYLOR** – guitar (ex-MINT 400) / **CAROLYN BANNISTER** – bass, vocals (ex-PRODUCT) / **RAVI KESAVARAM** – drums

                                                      Org   not iss.

Dec 99. (cd-ep) **ALWAYS YOUR WAY / PIECES / GROUNDED (demo)**

                                                     Infectious Epic

Apr 00. (7") *(INFECT 88S)* **LOSING TOUCH. / TONGUE TIED** — / –
    (cd-s+=) *(INFECT 88CDS)* – Breakfast (live/BBC). *(re-iss. Jan01)*

Jul 00. (7") *(INFECT 89S)* **CEMENTED SHOES. / WAIT A MINUTE** — 65 / –
    (cd-s+=) *(INFECT 89CDS)* – All of me. *(re-iss. Jan01)*

Oct 00. (cd-s) *(INFECT 94CDS)* **PIECES / SAFETY ZONES AND CRUMPLE ZONES** — 56 / –
    (cd-s) *(INFECT 94CDSX)* – ('A'side) / Another lie / Cemented shoes (live).

Feb 01. (7") *(INFECT 95S)* **ALWAYS: YOUR WAY. / SPOTLIGHTS** — 31 / –
    (cd-s+=) *(INFECT 095CDS)* – Game of pricks.
    (cd-s) *(INFECT 095CDSX)* – ('A'side) / Losing touch (acoustic) / It came crashing.

Mar 01. (cd/lp) *(INFECT 96 CDX/LP)* <85958> **FINELINES** — 24
    – Alpha waves / Always: your way / The gentle art of choking / Kohlstream / Cemented shoes / Grounded / C.O.R. / Infantile / Ode to the red queen / Tongue tied / Windows & walls / Taprobane / Losing touch / Pieces / Falling off the floor / Under the wheels. *(d-cd-iss. Jul02 +=; INFECT 96CDS)* – Deadlines / Wait a minute / Windows and walls (acoustic) / Safety zones and crumple zones / Vapour trails / Taproplane and losing touch (live) / Oh father / Spotlights / Moodswings / Game of pricks / Another lie / It came crashing / Static / Always your way (live) / Breakfast / All of me.

May 01. (cd-s) *(INFECT 97CDS)* **GROUNDED / OH FATHER / ALWAYS: YOUR WAY** — 29 / –
    (cd-s) *(INFECT 97CDSX)* – ('A'side) / Deadlines / Windows and walls (piano).

Jul 02. (cd-s) *(INFEC 107CDS)* **MOODSWINGS / THE GENTLE ART OF CHOKING (misery lab remix) / VAPOUR TRAILS** — 39 / –
    (cd-s) *(INFEC 107CDSX)* – ('A'mixes) / Vapour trails / ('A'-video).

THE GREAT INDIE DISCOGRAPHY — The 1990s

NADA SURF

Formed: Los Angeles, California, USA ... mid 90's out of BECAUSE BECAUSE BECAUSE by MATTHEW CAWS and DANIEL LORCA, who invited IRA ELLIOT to replace the original drummer. A veteran of the local indie scene and former music journo (with 'Guitar World'), CAWS took on the role of both frontman and songwriter, his tales of adolescent angst set to a SONIC YOUTH meets post-NIRVANA grunge sound. Almost immediately finding an audience among disaffected American youth, NADA SURF hit a raw nerve with the single, 'POPULAR', opening track on their moderately successful 'Elektra' debut album, 'HIGH/LOW' (1996). The aforementioned signature tune would become something of an albatross around their necks as a 1998 follow-up set, 'THE PROXIMITY EFFECT', suffered from minimal press interest. Just when they thought it safe to get back in the water, NADA SURF finally came up for air once more via the long-awaited "indie" set, 'LET GO' (2002).

Album rating: HIGH/LOW (*6) / THE PROXIMITY EFFECT (*5) / LET GO (*5)

MATTHEW CAWS – vocals, guitar / **DANIEL LORCA** – bass / **IRA ELLIOT** – drums (ex-FUZZTONES)

			not iss.	No.6
Mar 96.	(cd-ep) <38>	**KARMIC EP**	-	☐

– Telescope / Sea knows when / Everybody lies / Tree house / Nothing.

			Elektra	Elektra
Oct 96.	(cd/c) <(7559 61913-2/-4)>	**HIGH/LOW**	☐	63 Jul96

– Popular / Plan / Sleep / Psychic caramel / Stalemate / Hollywood / Zen brain / Icebox / Treehouse / Deeper well.

Feb 97.	(c-s) (EKR 231C) **POPULAR / PRESSURE FREE**	☐	☐
	(cd-s+=) (EKR 231CD) – Oh no.		
Jul 98.	(7") (DER 352) **DEEPER WELL. / PRESSURE FREE**		-
	(above issued on 'Deep Elm')		
Sep 98.	(cd/c) <(7559 61913-2/-4)> **THE PROXIMITY EFFECT**	☐	☐

– Hyperspace / Amateur / Why are you so mean to me? / Mother's day / Troublemaker / 80 windows / Bacardi / Bad best friend / Dispossession / Voices / Firecracker / Slow down / Robot. (cd re-iss. Oct00 on 'Subterfuge'; 21216CD)

		Heavenly	Barsuk
Sep 02.	(cd) (HVNLP 42CD) <29> **LET GO**	☐	☐ Oct02

– Blizzars of '77 / Happy kid / Inside of love / Fruit fly / Blonde on blonde / Hi-speed soul / Killian's red / The way you wear your head / Neither Heaven nor space / La pour ca / Treading water / Paper boats.

| Oct 02. | (7"/cd-s) (HVN 123/+CD) **THE WAY YOU WEAR YOUR HEAD. / NEITHER HEAVEN NOR SPACE** | ☐ | - |

NAKED SEE (see under ⇒ FOIL)

NANCY BOY

Formed: 1993, New York City, USA ... by offspring of 60's flower-power protagonist DONOVAN LEITCH, son of original MONKEES drummer, JASON NESMITH, nephew of unknown metallers (UFO), NIGEL MOGG and yet another son of, erm, factory worker MIKE WILLIAMS. The "son of" supergroup made their first appearance on Halloween after each member had duly committed themselves to various other useless projects in L.A. Their unique NEW YORK DOLLS-esque stage antics saw them being catogorised under "bi-sexual glam", a situation that similar artists THE DANDY WARHOLS found themselves under, a few years later. After the release of a cover of Gary Numan's 'ARE FRIENDS "ELECTRIC"', the 4-piece delivered the lazy and glossy 'PROMOSEXUAL' debut set in 1995. This "came out" just after the unfettering of nuance of the previous years' 45, 'JOHNNY CHROME AND SILVER'. Straight out of the pages of The Rocky Horror Show script, the album boasted such theatrical characters as 'Roman Emperor', 'Queen Wagon' and the aforementioned 'Johnny Chrome ...', tying them all up with a frilly pink stage rope to create one strange album. A year later (and the addition of keyboardist HOWARD HUGHES), the much improved self-titled set was issued. By coincidence, and mostly through the rise and rise of such bands as PLACEBO, SUEDE and MANSUN, the group found a new wave of fans locked away in the closet and unleashed before NANCY BOY's own glitter-laden eyes. Also, the famous PLACEBO song took the band's name and rocketed it into the lives of many.

Album rating: PROMOSEXUAL (*4) / NANCY BOY (*6)

DONOVAN LEITCH – vocals / **JASON NESMITH** – guitar, keyboards, vocals / **NIGEL MOGG** – bass / **MIKE WILLIAMS** – drums, percussion

		Equator Neverland	not iss.
Nov 94.	(7"/c-s) (NBOY S/MC 001) **JOHNNY CHROME & SILVER. / (interview + W.R.I.P. intro)**	☐	-
	(10"+=/12"+=/cd-s+=) (NBOY X/T/CD 001) – Roman emperor (live) / Oh 'eavens (live).		
Jun 95.	(c-s) (NBOYMC 002) **ARE 'FRIENDS' ELECTRIC / / YOU LOOKING AT MY PINT?**	☐	-
	(cd-s+=) (NBOYCD 002) – Johnny Chrome & Silver.		
	(cd-s) (NBOYCDR 002) – ('A'side & mixes; 3 am / Pacifica / album).		
Oct 95.	(cd/c) (BEND CD/MC 001) **PROMOSEXUAL**	☐	-

– Gender bender / New attitude / Johnny Chrome & Silver / Welcome to my world / Mr. Euro / Insecurity / Man inside your brain / It's hard / Are 'friends' electric? / Roman emperor / Oblivion.

		Elektra	Elektra
May 96.	(c/c) (7559 61895-2/-4) **NANCY BOY**	☐	-

– Deep sleep motel / Can you dig it? / Johnny Chrome & Silver / Sometimes / Colors / Foxtrot / Rocking chair / Dearest girl / I don't mind / Mother's ruin / W.R.I.P. / Ultrasex / You deserve a place.

Jun 96.	(c-s) (EKR 224C) **DEEP SLEEP MOTEL / AUTOMAKER WE**	☐	-
	(cd-s+=) (EKR 224CD) – Little worm / Did you see him.		
Aug 96.	(cd-s) **DEEP SLEEP MOTEL / JOHNNY CHROME & SILVER / ARE 'FRIENDS' ELECTRIC?**	-	☐

— split later in the year

NATIONAL PARK

Formed: Glasgow, Scotland ... 1997 by JOHN HOGARTY (ex-BMX BANDITS and ex-TELSTAR PONIES), SIMON SHAW, MICHAEL McGAUGHRIN and SCOTT WALKER (no, not that one!). Described by some as like GALAXIE 500 meeting FAUST, NATIONAL PARK issued their first vinyl-only release via Earworm's 1998 10", 'GREAT WESTERN'. HOGARTY, meanwhile, was branching out in other directions, mainly a one-off project, PHANTOM ENGINEER, with DAVID KEENAN and jazzman BILL WELLS. Settling back with the NATIONAL PARK, he and his crew collaborated with another 'Wedgie' fave THE FUTURE PILOT AKA. The track in question, 'NORMAN DOLPH'S MONEY', was about the person who funded the artwork for the VELVET UNDERGROUND's debut "banana" cover. Tributes were also forthcoming towards the end of '99, when the same pairing contributed 'STERLING' – aka the recently deceased STERLING MORRISON, to the '...Galaxy Of Sound' set.

Album rating: not released any

JOHN HOGARTY – / **SIMON SHAW** – / **SCOTT WALKER** – piano / **MICHAEL McGAUGHRIN**

		Earworm	not iss.
Aug 98.	(ltd-10") (WORM 30) **GREAT WESTERN. / SHAPES, STARS**	☐	-
Jan 99.	(7") (WORMSS 4) **NATIONAL PARK VERSUS FUTURE PILOT AKA**	☐	-

– Norman Dolph's money.

— SCOTT took off to join other acts, while NP found a new live guitarist **ALI ROBERTS** (of APPENDIX OUT) / **TOM CROSSLEY** (also of APPENDIX OUT + INTERNATIONAL AIRPORT) played piano recently

NATIONAL SKYLINE (see under ⇒ HUM)

NATION OF ULYSSES (see under ⇒ MAKE-UP)

NATIVE NOD (see under ⇒ LAPSE)

NAVIGATOR

Formed: Norwich, England ... 1994 by NICK MELIA, JENNY ROBOTTOM and SAM RICHARDS, while attending the city's university. The very antithesis of raucous indie guitar-pop, this experimental trio forged their delicate sound while testing the waters around the student circuit. Signed to the local 'Noisebox' label (home of MAGOO), they released a debut EP, 'KILLTAKER', in summer '96, its sedative appeal reminiscent of LABRADFORD or even "a Sunday morning MOGWAI", as one journalist commented. 'A LITTLE ASTRONOMY' followed later that year, another audibly obscured slice of mogadon-paced melancholia that whetted appetites for early '97's classically-influenced marathon, 'WHEN THE WIRES FALL'. NAVIGATOR mapped out further directions in minimalist stereo that summer with the 'ASSAY' EP, while a debut album, 'NOSTALGIE', finally arrived on new label, 'Swarf Finger' a full year later.

Album rating: NOSTALGIE (*6)

NICK MELIA – guitar, vocals / **JENNY ROBOTTOM** – bass, vocals / **SAM RICHARDS** – drums

		Noisebox	not iss.
Jun 96.	(7"ep/cd-ep) (NBX 022/+CD) **KILLTAKER. / SWING / WE WILL BURN TOGETHER**	☐	-
Oct 96.	(7"blue) (NBX 026) **A LITTLE ASTRONOMY. / AT THE END OF THE DAY**	☐	-
Feb 97.	(d7") (NBX 027) **WHEN THE WIRES FALL**	☐	-

NAVIGATOR (cont)   THE GREAT INDIE DISCOGRAPHY   The 1990s

Jun 97. (cd-ep) *(NBX 028CD)* **ASSAY EP**
— Assay / Diving bell / On all you hold sacred.
(7"ep+=) *(NBX 028)* – II.

Swarffinger / not iss.

Jul 98. (lp/cd) *(SF 032/+CD)* **NOSTALGIE**

—— NAVIGATOR have since gone AWOL

NAYSAYER (see under ⇒ RETSIN)

NECTARINE No.9
(see under ⇒ FIRE ENGINES; in 80's section)

NED'S ATOMIC DUSTBIN

Formed: Stourbridge, West Midlands, England ... late '87 by JOHN PENNEY, RAT, ALEX GRIFFIN, MAT CHESLIN, and DAN WARTON. The 'Sound of Stourbridge' along with neo-crustie contemporaries like THE WONDER STUFF and the more rhythmically inclined POP WILL EAT ITSELF, NED'S took their name from a character on BBC TV's infamous 'Goon Show'. The group didn't quite reach the same giddy heights, though, admittedly they gave it their best shot. With the dubious advantage of two bass players, the group developed an engagingly spiky indie-pop sound prone to bursts of manic guitar thrashing and the odd sample. After the underground success of the 'INGREDIENTS', 'KILL YOUR TELEVISION' and 'UNTIL YOU FIND OUT' EP's, the band were picked up by 'Sony' who jointly released all their forthcoming product on 'Furtive'. The NED'S major label debut, 'HAPPY', soared into the Top 20, while the album, 'GOD FODDER', made the Top 5. The group then embarked on a punishing touring schedule including an appearance at that bastion of indie-dom, The Reading Festival (where the ubiquitous NED's T-shirt was almost as de rigeur as the NIRVANA Dante's Inferno job). Further Top 20 singles followed with 'TRUST' and 'NOT SLEEPING AROUND', while that difficult second album, 'ARE YOU NORMAL' (1992) again made the UK Top 20. Yet while other Brit hopefuls like EMF and JESUS JONES were sparking proclamations of another full scale American invasion (where are they now?, a nation probably doesn't ask), NED'S couldn't seem to break the lucrative US market despite heavy touring. Maybe their sound was just too 'British' and anyhow, with the success of the aforementioned NIRVANA, the yanks were back on top of their game, the dream of a British invasion fading faster than sales of The FARM's 'SPARTACUS' album. In the three years prior to the release of 'BRAINBLOODVOLUME' (1995), the musical landscape of the UK had undergone a sea change in attitude, attitude, of course, being the operative word. The likes of NED'S were just no longer fashionable, despite the album being their most rounded and consistent to date. Inevitably, the band split the following year, another act, dare I say it, consigned to the dustbin of history. Who knows, maybe the lads will re-emerge in a BENTLEY RHYTHM ACE fashion, NED'S ATOMIC BREAKBEAT, anyone?

Album rating: GOD FODDER (*8) / ARE YOU NORMAL (*7) / BRAINBLOODVOLUME (*6)

JONN PENNEY (b.17 Sep'68) – vocals / **RAT** (b.GARETH PRING, 8 Nov'70) – guitar / **ALEX GRIFFIN** (b.29 Aug'71) – bass / **MAT CHESLIN** (b.28 Nov'70) – bass / **DAN WARTON** (b.28 Jul'72) – drums

Chapter 22 / not iss.

Mar 90. (12"ep) *(12CHAP 047)* **THE INGREDIENTS**
– Aim / Plug me in / Grey cell green / Terminally groovy.

Jul 90. (cd-ep/12"ep/7"ep) *(CD/12+/CHAP 048)* **KILL YOUR TELEVISION**   53
– Kill your television / That's nice / Sentence / Kill your remix.

Oct 90. (7") *(CHAP 52)* **UNTIL YOU FIND OUT. / FLEXIBLE HEAD**   51
(12"+=/cd-s+=) *(12/CD CHAP 52)* – Bite.

Furtive – Columbia / Columbia

Feb 91. (7"/c-s) *(656680-7/-4)* **HAPPY. / TWENTY THREE HOUR TOOTHACHE**   16
(12"+=/cd-s+=) *(656680-6/-2)* – Aim (at the Civic – live) / 45 second blunder.

Apr 91. (cd/c/lp) *(468112-2/-4/-1) <47929>* **GOD FODDER**   4   91
– Kill your television / Less than useful / Selfish / Grey cell green / Cut up throwing things / Capital letters / Happy / Your complex / Nothing like until you find out / You / What gives my son. *(re-iss. cd May95; same)*

Sep 91. (7") *(657462-7)* **TRUST. / FACELESS**   21
(12"+=/cd-s+=) *(657462-6/-2)* – Titch.

Feb 92. (c-s) *<74141>* **GREY CELL GREEN / TRUST**   –
(cd-s+=) *<73991>* – Titch / Faceless / Until you find out.

Apr 92. (cd-ep) *<74202>* **KILL YOUR TELEVISION. / TERMINALLY GROOVIE / SENTENCE / KILL YOUR REMIX**   –

Oct 92. (7") *(658386-7)* **NOT SLEEPING AROUND. / CUT UP**   19
(12"+=/cd-s+=) *(658386-6/-2)* – Scrawl.
(US c-s+=) *<74718>* – N.S.A. (NAD VS. NOX).

Oct 92. (cd/c/lp) *(472633-2/-4/-1) <53154>* **ARE YOU NORMAL?**   13
– Suave and suffocated / Walking through syrup / Legoland / Swallowing air / Who goes first / Tantrum / Not sleeping around / You don't want to do that / Leg end in his own boots / Two and two made five / Fracture / Spring / Intact.

Nov 92. (7") *(658816-7)* **INTACT. / PROSTRATE**   36
(10"+=) *(658816-0)* – NAD & NDX = Intact.
(12"+=/cd-s+=) *(658816-6/-2)* – Swiss legoland (live).

Furtive / Chaos

Mar 95. (c-s) *(661356-4)* **ALL I ASK OF MYSELF IS THAT I HOLD TOGETHER / CAPSIZE**   33
(12"+=) *(661356-6)* – ('A'-Just together mix) / ('A'-No answer mix).
(cd-s++=) *(661356-2)* – ('A'-In control mix).
(cd-s+=) *(661356-5)* – Take me to the cleaners / Premonition (need to know mix).

Jul 95. (7") *(662056-7)* **STUCK. / A TEMPTED FATE**   64
(cd-s+=) *(662056-2)* – ...To be right (acoustic) / ('A'acoustic).
(12") *(662056-6)* – ('A'side) / Premonition (as I thought mix) / Premonition (dirty caller mix).

Jul 95. (cd/c/lp) *(478330-2/-4/-1) <67040>* **BRAINBLOODVOLUME**
– All I ask of myself is that I hold together / Floote / Premonition / Talk me down / Borehole / Your only joke / Stuck / ...To be right / I want it over / Traffic / Song eleven could take forever.

—— disbanded October 1995

– compilations, etc. –

Jan 91. (lp/cd) *R.T.D. Euro; (1401183-1/-2)* **BITE** (imported)   72
Nov 94. (cd) *Sony Soho2; (477984-2)* **5.22** (B-sides, etc)
Feb 00. (cd) *Sony Soho2; (491411-2)* **THE BEST OF NED'S ATOMIC DUSTBIN**
Sep 01. (cd) *Gig; (GIG 1018-2)* **ONE MORE NO MORE (live)**
– Until you find out / Less than useful / Selfish / Intact / Stuck / Happy / Trust / Tantrum / Cut up / Song 11 / Grey cell green / Kill your television.

NEU!

Formed: Dusseldorf, Germany ...Autumn 1971 by breakaway KRAFTWERK members KLAUS DINGER and THOMAS HOMANN. The latter was soon deposed by MICHAEL ROTHER who appeared on NEU!'s classic eponymous 1972 debut, cut in a short space of time with legendary knob-twiddler, CONRAD PLANK; live gigs were augmented at the time by EBERHARD KRAHNEMANN, who had also guested for KRAFTWERK. After only three acclaimed underground albums, the aforementioned 'NEU!', the seminal 'NEU! 2' (1973) and 'NEU! '75', they split for a second time so that ROTHER could go solo; their first break was after 'NEU! 2' when ROTHER and the CLUSTER duo (of DIETER MOEBIUS and JOACHIM ROEDELIUS) created HARMONIA. Although ROTHER and DINGER went their respective separate ways (the latter to LA DUSSELDORF), they still found time to record one more set in the mid-80's, surprisingly titled 'NEU 4' – left in the can until 1996. Encompassing repetitive trance-rock and avant-garde improvisation, NEU! mined similar territory to early KRAFTWERK, AMON DUUL II or HAWKWIND (DAVE BROCK was a great fan). Along with the likes of CAN and FAUST, the band are held in high esteem by Krautrock connoisseurs, search out STEREOLAB records for examples.

Album rating: NEU! (*8) / NEU II (*8) / NEU '75 (*9) / BLACK FOREST GATEAU compilation (*9) / NEU! 4 (*5)

MICHAEL ROTHER (b. 2 Sep'50) – guitar, bass, keyboards, synths, percussion / **KLAUS DINGER** (b.24 Mar'46) – guitar, vocals, drums, keyboards (ex-KRAFTWERK)

U.A. / Billingsgate

Oct 72. (lp) *(UAS 29396) <1001>* **NEU!**
– Hallo Gallo / Sonderangebot / Weissensee / Jahresuebersicht / Im glueck / Negativland / Lieber honig. *(re-iss. May80 as 'HALLO GALLO' on 'Brain' Germany; 0040 145) (cd-iss. Jan98 on 'Germanofon'; 941025)*

Jan 73. (7") *(UP 35485)* **SUPER. / NEUSCHNEE**
Sep 73. (lp) *(UAS 29500)* **NEU! 2**
– Fur immer / Spitzenqualitat / Gedenkminute / Lila engel / Neuschnee / Super 16 / Neuschnee / Cassetto / Super 78 / Hallo exentrico / Super. *(cd-iss. Jan98 on 'Germanofon'; 941026)*

—— ROTHER joined HARMONIA, with CLUSTER members MOEBIUS + ROEDELIUS. They made two albums 'MUSIK VON HARMONIA' *(Brain; 1044)* & 'HARMONIA DELUXE' *(Brain 1073)*, before he returned to NEU!

—— added **HANS LAMPE + THOMAS DINGER** – drums (ex-KRAFTWERK)

Jun 75. (7") *(UP 35874)* **ISI. / AFTER EIGHT**
Jun 75. (lp) *(UAS 29782)* **NEU! '75**
– Isi / Seeland / Leb' wohl / Hero / E-Musik / After eight. *(cd-iss. May98 on 'Germanofon'; 941030)*

—— split after above; the DINGER's + LAMPE formed LA DUSSELDORF while ROTHER subsequently released a plethora of albums

– compilations, others, etc. –

Nov 82. (lp) *Cherry Red; (BRED 27)* **BLACK FOREST GATEAU**
– Hallo Gallo / Isi / E-Musik / Negativland / Seeland / Leb' wohl / After eight.

Dec 96. (cd) *Captain Trip; (CTCD 020)* **NEU! 4** (rec.mid-80's)
– Nazionale / Crazy / Flying Dutchman / Schaine welle (nice wave) / Wave naturelle / Good life (random – rough) / 86 commercial trash / Fly Dutch II / Danzing / Quick wave machineue / Bush – drum / La bomba (stop aparthijd worldwide) / Good life / Elanoizan.

Dec 96. (cd) *Captain Trip; (CTCD 045)* **1972 LIVE! (live)**
Jun 97. (cd) *Captain Trip; (CTCD 051)* **LA NEU DUSSELDORF**
Feb 98. (cd) *Captain Trip; (CTCD 086)* **LA NEU ZEELAND LIVE 1997**
Apr 98. (cd) *Captain Trip; (CTCD 087)* **REMBRANDT**
Jun 98. (cd) *Captain Trip; (CTCD 098)* **DIE WITH DIGNITY**
Jun 98. (d-cd) *Captain Trip; (CTCD 100-101)* **CHA CHA 2000 (live in Tokyo)**

NEUTRAL MILK HOTEL

Formed: Ruston, Louisiana, USA ... 1989 by singer-songwriter, JEFF MANGUM, along with WILLIAM CULLEN HART and BILL DOSS, although the latter two soon bailed out to form OLIVIA TREMOR CONTROL. Confusingly enough, however, this would be after NMH evolved out of Athens, Georgia outfits, CRANBERRY LIFE CYCLE and SYNTHETIC FLYING MACHINE, leaving MANGUM to flit once more, this time to Denver, Colorado. After a period helping out his Ruston-born buddy, ROBERT SCHNEIDER, in his outfit APPLES (IN STEREO), MANGUM finally got NEUTRAL MILK HOTEL underway, releasing a series of obscure singles and demos before signing to 'Merge' and releasing the single, 'EVERYTHING IS', following it up with a debut album, 'ON AVERY ISLAND' (1996). Apparently recorded on SCHNEIDER's bedroom four track and released in the UK on 'Fire', the record bore inevitable comparison with OLIVIA TREMOR CONTROL's 'Dusk At Cubist Castle', if only for its fantastical concept strangeness. Not as overtly psychedelic as the latter album but rampantly experimental, 'ON AVERY ISLAND' was a collision of seemingly spontaneous, barely formed musical ideas, samples and sound effects, underlaid by a frazzled pop genius and executed with delirious abandon. MANGUM continue to indulge his passion for conceptual weirdness with 1998's 'IN THE AEROPLANE OVER THE SEA', released this time around on 'Blue Rose'

Album rating: ON AVERY ISLAND (*7) / IN THE AEROPLANE OVER THE SEA (*6)

JEFF MANGUM – vocals, multi / with **ROBERT SCHNEIDER** – xylophone, etc / **HILARIE SIDNEY** – multi (of APPLES IN STEREO, of SECRET SQUARE) / **AARON REEDY** – multi / **RICK BENJAMIN** – trombone / **LISA JANSSEN** – bass (of SECRET SQUARE)

		not iss.	Elephant 6
1991.	(c) **INVENT YOURSELF A SHORTCAKE**	-	-
1992.	(c) **BEAUTY**	-	-
1993.	(c) **HYPE CITY**	-	-

		not iss.	Cher Doll
Nov 94.	(7") <Cher 002> **EVERYTHING IS. / SNOW SONG pt. one**	-	

— 'Cher Doll' also issued a few split singles which included the tracks 'UP AND OVER' and 'INVENT YOURSELF A SHORTCAKE'

		Fire	Merge
Jul 95.	(7") (BLAZE 79) **EVERYTHING IS. / SNOW SONG pt. one**		-
	(cd-s+=) (BLAZE 79CD) – Aunt Eggma blowtorch.		
Sep 96.	(cd) (FIRECD 53) <MRG 53> **ON AVERY ISLAND**		Mar96

– Song against sex / You've passed / Someone is waiting / A baby for Pree / Marching theme / Where you'll find me now / Avery Island – April 1st / Gardenhead – Leave me alone / Three peaches / Naomi / April 8th / Pree-sisters swallowing a donkey's eye. (UK+=) – Everything is / Snow song pt.1.

— now without JANSSEN

		Blue Rose	Merge
Jun 98.	(cd) (BRRC 1019-2) <MRG 136CD> **IN THE AEROPLANE OVER THE SEA**		Feb98

– The king of carrot flowers (pt. one) / The king of carrot flowers (pts. two and three) / In the aeroplane over the sea / Two-headed boy / The fool / Holland, 1945 / Communist daughter / Oh comely / Ghost / (untitled) / Two-headed boy (part 2). (UK re-iss. Nov00; same as US)

| Oct 98. | (7") (BRRC 1023-7) **HOLLAND, 1945. / ENGINE** | | - |

– compilations, others, etc. –

| Oct 01. | (cd-ep) Orange Twin; (OTR 05CD) **EVERYTHING IS / SNOW SONG (part 1) / AUNT EGGMA BLOWTORCH / TUESDAY MOON** | | - |

NEW AMSTERDAMS (see under ⇒ GET UP KIDS)

NEW BOMB TURKS

Formed: Columbus, Ohio, USA ... 1990 by Ohio University students ERIC DAVIDSON, JIM WEBER, MATT REBER and BILL RANDT. Akin to a fusion of IGGY POP, DEAD BOYS and The DWARVES, their brand of melody-fuelled punk was initially heard on US-only singles before they signed to 'Crypt' and issued a highly praised (in underground circles at least) debut album, '!!DESTROY-OH-BOY!!' (1993). A follow-up, 'INFORMATION HIGHWAY REVISITED' (1994), appeared a couple of years later to equally effusive praise and despite a resurgence in interest for nu-punk in the wake of grunge, the band's profile and sales remained low. 1995 saw the release of a collaboration with The ENTOMBED, misanthropically titled 'I HATE PEOPLE', as well as a double set, 'PISSIN' OUT THE POISON', which collected the group's early singles; including a plethora of covers (see below). Subsequently signing with the seminal 'Epitaph' label, the group released 'SCARED STRAIGHT' in 1996 and needless to say turned a tad heavier. While never really altering their blitzkrieg approach, the 'TURKS carried out musical misson after mission for the label, pretty much year in year out with the likes of 'AT ROPE'S END' (1998), 'THE BIG COMBO' (1999), 'NIGHTMARE SCENARIO' (2000) and most recently, 'THE NIGHT BEFORE THE DAY THE EARTH STOOD STILL' (2002). • **Covers:** SUMMER ROMANCE + JIVING SISTER FANNY (Rolling Stones) / I WANNA SLEEP (Modern Lovers) / BAD GIRL (New York Dolls) / CHRISTMAS (Phil Spector, etc) / YOUNGBLOOD (Wild Billy Childish) / JUST HEAD (Nervous Eaters) / DO THE POP (Radio Birdman) / BOTTLE ISLAND (Thomas Jefferson Slave Apartments) / JIM (Gaunt) / FEEL IT (Motorcycle Boy) / SEXUAL HEALING (Death Of Samantha) / JOB (Nubs) / JAGUAR RIDE (Electric Eels) / CHIP AWAY THE STONE (Supa) / I HATE PEOPLE (Anti-Nowhere League) / ROCK CITY USA + ACTION (Devil Dogs) / I DON'T NEED YOUR LOVIN' (Chocolate Watch Band) / MR. SUIT (Wire) / THIS PLACE SUCKS (Queers) / EJECTION (Hawkwind) / SPANISH ROSE (Cheater Slicks) / FUCK IT (Jim Swope & The Left) / ACTION (Knots).

Album rating: !!DESTROY-OH-BOY!! (*5) / INFORMATION HIGHWAY REVISITED (*7) / PISSIN' OUT THE POISON compilation (*6) / SCARED STRAIGHT (*7) / AT ROPE'S END (*6) / THE BIG COMBO compilation (*5) / NIGHTMARE SCENARIO (*6) / THE NIGHT BEFORE THE DAY THE EARTH STOOD STILL (*6)

ERIC DAVIDSON – vocals / **JIM "MOTHERFUCKER" WEBER** – guitar / **MATT REBER** – bass / **BILL RANDT** – drums

		not iss.	Datapanik
1991.	(7"ep) <datapanik #7> **split w/ GAUNT**	-	
	– Tail crush / Out of my mind / (other 2 by GAUNT).		
1992.	(7"ep) <datapanik #14> **SO COOL, SO CLEAN, SO SPARKLING CLEAR**	-	

– Cryin' into the beer of a drunk man / Just head / Let's dress up the naked truth / Do the pop. <re-iss. 1995 on 'Dog Meat'; DOG 063>

		not iss.	Get Hip
1993.	(7",7"purple) <GH 139> **I'M WEAK. / SUMMER ROMANCE**	-	

		not iss.	Munster
1993.	(7") <7046> **THE NEXT BIG THING**	-	

– Dragstrip riot / Cryin' into the beer of a drunk man. (UK-iss.Jul97 on 'Munster' DLM 179)

		not iss.	eMpTy
1993.	(7") <MT 228> **SO YOUNG, SO FAIR, SO DEBONAIR**	-	

– Got no proof / Polyester thinking cap.

		not iss.	Sympathy F
1993.	(7") <SFTRI 228> **TRYING TO GET BY. / LAST LOST FIGHT**	-	

		not iss.	Bag Of Hammers
1993.	(7") <BOH 012> **SHARPEN-UP TIME. / LAISSEZ FAIR STATE**	-	
1993.	(7") <BOH 016> **DEATHBEDSIDE MANNER. / (other by SINISTER SIX)**	-	

		Crypt	Crypt
Apr 93.	(lp/cd) (EFA 11560/+D) <CR-032> **!!DESTROY-OH-BOY!!**		

– Born Toulouse-Lautrec / Tail crush / Up for a downside / Tattooed apathethic boys / Dragstrip riot / We give a rat's ass / Runnin' on go / Lone gone sister / Mr. Suit / Let's dress up the naked truth / Hapless attempt / I want my baby ... dead? / Sucker punch. (cd+=) – I'm weak / Tryin' to get by / Cryin' into the beer of a drunk man. <re-iss. Feb00; same)>

Oct 93.	(7") (DAM 26) **BOTTLE ISLAND. / YOUNGBLOOD**		
	(above issued on 'Damaged Goods') (below on 'Demolition Derby')		
Nov 93.	(7"m) <DD 004> **I WANNA SLEEP. / JIM / UP FOR A DOWNSIDE**		
Dec 93.	(10"ep/cd-ep) <vroom 06> **DRUNK ON COCK**		

– American soul spiders / Grounded ex-patriot / Tall order / This place sucks / Who's afraid of Virginia Woolf. (above issued on 'Engine')

Feb 94.	(7") (EFA 402977) <HS 93736> **DOGS ON 45: ROCK CITY USA – ACTION – BACKSTAGE – ROCK CITY USA. / (other by the DEVIL DOGS)**		
	(above on 'Helter Skelter', below 'Sympathy For The Record Industry')		
Oct 94.	(7"pic-d) <(SFTRI 319)> **(GOTTA, GOTTA) SINKING FEELING. / FEEL IT**		
Oct 94.	(lp/cd) (EFA 11585-1/-2) <49> **INFORMATION HIGHWAY REVISITED**		

– It slips in / Bullish on / If I only could / Brother Orson Welles / T.A.S. / Fingernail chomp / Dented 'n' spent / Girl can't help it / (Gotta gotta) Sinking feeling / Grandpa atomic / Never will / Apocalyptic dipstick / Lyin' on our backs / I got you bitter end / Straight-on chaser. <re-iss. Feb00 & Apr02; same)>

Jun 95.	(7") (7mosh 32) **I HATE PEOPLE. / (other by The ENTOMBED)**		
	(above issued on 'Earache') (below on 'Rise')		
Jul 95.	(7") <RR 83> **MY HOPES ARE COPACETIC. / SEXUAL DREAMING**	-	

		Fat Wreck Chords	Fat Wreck Chords
Jul 96.	(7"m) <(FAT 542-7)> **STICK IT OUT. / (STILL) NEVER WILL / JOB**		

		Epitaph	Epitaph
Aug 96.	(cd/c/lp) <(86479-2/-4/-1)> **SCARED STRAIGHT**		

– Hammerless nail / Bachelor's high / Professional gangster / Cultural elite sign-up sheet / Jukebox lean / Jeers of a clown / Look alive jive / Staring down the gift horse / Shoot the offshoot / Drop what you're doin' / Telephone numbrrr / Wrest your hands.

Jun 97.	(7") (WAL 015) **PROFESSIONAL AGAINSTER. / JIVING SISTER FANNY**		-
	(above on 'Wallabies', below on 'Sympathy For The Record Industry')		
Mar 98.	(7") <(SFTRI 553)> **SNAP DECISION. / JAGUAR RIDE**		
Mar 98.	(cd/c/lp) <(6515-2/-4/-1)> **AT ROPE'S END**		

– Scapegoat soup / Snap decisions / Ally smile / So long silver lining / Veronica Lake / Defiled / Bolan's crash / Raw law / Minimum wages of sin / At rope's end / Common cold shoulder / Aspirin aspirations / Streamline yr skull.

| Mar 98. | (7"ep/cd-ep) (1001-7/-2) **VERONICA LAKE EP** | | - |

– Veronica Lake / Snap decision / Double Marlon (rough mix) / Don't Kimosabe me (demo).

Nov 98.	(7"ep/cd-ep) (1011-7/-2) **RAW LAW / SO LONG SILVER LINING (live) / HAMMERLESS NAIL (live) / TAIL CRUSH (live)**		-
1999.	(7"colrd) <aw 049> **ALL THE RIGHT PLACES. / (other by The HELLACOPTERS)**	-	
	(above issued on 'Anyway' below on 'Full Toss')		
1999.	(7",7"white) <TOSS 001> **GOOD ON YA BABY. / (other by The ONYAS)**	-	

NEW BOMB TURKS (cont)

Jun 00. (cd/lp) <(6561-2/-1)> **NIGHTMARE SCENARIO** — Apr00
– Point A to point blank / Automatic teller / End of the great credibility race / Too much / Killer's kiss / Continental cats / Spanish fly by night / The roof / Your beaten heart / Turning tricks / Wine and depression / Quarter to four / Untitled.
Dec 00. (10"colrd-ep) (1031-1) **THE BLIND RUN**
– End of the great credibility race / Turning tricks (Glynt mix) / Ad nauseum / Action.

—— **SAM BROWN** – drums (ex-GAUNT) repl. RANDT

Glazed   Safety Pin

Jan 02. (7") (GLZ 006) <SP 029> **SPANISH FLY BY NIGHT. / CHIP AWAY THE STONE** — 2001

Gearhead   Gearhead

Sep 02. (colrd-lp/cd) <(RPM 036/+CD) **THE NIGHT BEFORE THE DAY THE EARTH STOOD STILL**
– The night before the day the earth stood still / Statue of liberty / Pretty lightning / Hassle St. / Grifted / Rat feelings / Leaving town / Sick sermon / Don't bug me, I'm nutty / Constance Keane / Like ghosts / Ditch / The night before the day the earth stood still (reprise).

Sweet Nothing   not iss.

Nov 02. (7"m) (7SN 014) **PRETTY LIGHTNING. / BUCKEYE DONUTS / LAW OF THE LONG ARM**

– compilations, etc. –

1995. (12"ep) Anyway; <anyway 022> **LIVE '93**
– Taller order / Girl can't help it / Born Toulouse Lautrec / Grounded ex patriot / Deathbedside manner.
Oct 95. (d-lp/cd) Crypt; (EFA 11598-1/-2) <CR-058> **PISSIN' OUT THE POISON**
– Tail crush / Out of my mind / Cryin' in the beer of a drunk man / Just head / Let's dress up to the naked truth / Do the pop / Sucker punch / Spinnin' clock / Summer romance / The girl can't help it / Got no proof / Polyester thinking cap / Last lost fight / We need more / Sharpen-up time / Laissez faire state / Croonin' into the beer of a drunk man / Pist / Deathbedside manner / I wanna sleep / Youngblood / Taller order / Bad girl / Ejection / Christmas (baby please come home) / Anal swipe. <(re-iss. Feb00 & Apr02; same)>
Apr 99. (cd/lp) Dropkick; <(BEHIND 001/+LP)> **THE BIG COMBO (MORE SINGLES AND OTHER SWILL 1994-98)**
– Stick it out / Feel it / (Still) Never will / Slung jury / Bachelor's high / Professional againster / Jivin' sister Fanny / Streamline yr skull / Job / Veronica Lake / Don't kimosabe me / Fuck it / So long silver lining (live) / Hammerless nail (live) / Tail crush (live) / Eyes of Satan.

NEW END ORIGINAL
(see under ⇒ TEXAS IS THE REASON)

NEW FAST AUTOMATIC DAFFODILS

Formed: Manchester, England ... 1988 out of punk group PARIAH, with an initial line-up of guitarist DOLAN HEWISON, bassist JUSTIN CRAWFORD and drummer PERRY SAUNDERS, vocalist ANDY SPEARPOINT and precussionist ICARUS WILSON-KNIGHT joining later. In 1989, just as the 'Madchester' scene was crystallising, the group unleashed their indie 45, 'LIONS', reminiscent of the alternative funk-rock of the early 80's (i.e. PIGBAG, ACR, FIRE ENGINES or 23 SKIDOO) and heralded as the best debut for years. By late 1990, a fresh move to a new label ('Play It Again Sam') gave them a brief entry into the UK chart with a debut album, 'PIGEONHOLE', showcasing the band's diverse, often breakneck style and SPEARPOINT's intelligent, highly articulate lyrics. Produced by Craig Leon (FALL, RAMONES), 'BODY EXIT MIND' was a decidedly darker affair featuring the defiant likes of 'WHAT KIND OF HELL IS THIS' and 'HOW MUCH LONGER SHALL WE TOLERATE MASS CULTURE'. Following the record's release the band's moniker was subject to a slight abbreviation to NEW FADS, SPEARPOINT and Co. following a more rhythmic direction on their well-received 1995 release, 'LOVE IT ALL'. Produced by JEREMY ALLOM (MASSIVE ATTACK), the record further illustrated the band's willingness to experiment with diverse musical styles and ideas.
• **Songwriters:** Group penned except; I'M SET FREE (Velvet Underground).
• **Trivia:** Around mid'91, 20,000 copies of 'Getting Better' were mistakenly stolen by Basque separatists in Spain.

Album rating: PIGEONHOLE (*7) / BODY EXIT MIND (*8)

ANDY SPEARPOINT – vocals / **DOLAN HEWISON** (b.Newcastle) – guitar / **JUSTIN CRAWFORD** – bass / **PERRY SAUNDERS** – drums / **ICARUS WILSON-KNIGHT** – percussion

Playtime   not iss.

Jun 89. (12"ep) (AMUSE 4T) **LIONS / FATE DON'T FAIL ME NOW. / YOUR DREAMS, MY NIGHTMARES**
Oct 89. (12"ep/cd-ep) (AMUSE 6 T/CD) **MUSIC IS SHIT**
– Beam me up / Men without qualities / Music is shit (parts 1, 2 & 3) / Lions.
Mar 90. (7"one-sided) (AMUSE 7) **BIG**
(12"+=/cd-s+=) (AMUSE 7 T/CD) – ('A')instrumental) / Baka / ('A'-Baka mix).

Play It Again Sam   Elektra

Sep 90. (7") (BIAS 162-7) **FISHES EYES. / FISHES EYES (UNDERWATER)**
(ext;12"+=/cd-s+=) (BIAS 162/+CD) – White.
Nov 90. (lp/c/cd) (BIAS 185/+MC/CD) <61102> **PIGEONHOLE** 49 Jan91
– Get better / Fishes eyes / Working for him / Part 4 / Big / You were lying when you said you loved me / Amplifier / Reprise / Partial. (free-7") (BIAS 185X) – I'M SET FREE. / PENGUINS (cd re-iss. Sep93; same)
Apr 91. (7") (BIAS 193-7) **GET BETTER.**
(ext.12"+=) (BIAS 193) – I found myself in another room.
(ext.cd-s++=) (BIAS 193CD) – ('A'extended).

Nov 91. (7") (BIAS 199-7) **ALL OVER MY FACE. / WHY THE HARD MEN FAIL**
(12"/cd-s) (BIAS 199/+CD) – ('A'-split decision mix) / ('A'-off the road mix) / ('B'side).
Jan 92. (cd-s) <66510> **BIG /**
Aug 92. (7") (BIAS 219-7) **IT'S NOT WHAT YOU KNOW. / BEAUTIFUL**
(12"+=/cd-s+=) (BIAS 219/+CD) – Head on / Beatlemania.
Sep 92. (7") (BIAS 229-7) **STOCKHOLM (radio mix). / CANNES**
(12"+=/cd-s+=) (BIAS 229/+CD) – ('A'extended).
(10") (BIAS 229-LTD) – ('A'demo) / Hexagon spray / It's not what you know (demo).
Oct 92. (lp/c/cd) (BIAS 205/+MC/CD) <61398> **BODY EXIT MIND** 57 Mar93
– Bong / It's not what you know / Stockholm / I take you to sleep / Bruises / Kyphos / Beatlemania / What kind of Hell is this? / American money / Missing parts of famous people / Patchwork lies / Music. (cd+= cd-ep) – How much longer shall we tolerate mass culture? / Teenage combo / Exit body, exit mind.
Jan 93. (cd-ep) <61438> **BONG**
– Bong / It's not what you know / Head on / Beautiful / Cannes.

NEW FADS

—— change of name but same line-up

Sep 94. (12"m) (BIAS 249) **LIFE IS AN ACCIDENT. / EVERY ONCE IN A WHILE (Fuzzy Logic remix) / MAD POP**
(cd-s) (BIAS 249CD1) – (1st 2 tracks) / Aches and pains.
(cd-s) (BIAS 249CD2) – (1st & 3rd tracks) / PSV (VPL remix).
Nov 94. (10") (BIAS 269) **THESE FOOLISH THINGS. / EVERY ONCE IN A WHILE**
(cd-s+=) (BIAS 269CD) – Bassdrum (H.Nicholson mix) / Lions (live).
Jan 95. (cd/c/lp) (BIAS 285 CD/MC/LP) **LOVE IT ALL**
– These foolish things / Life is an accident / Left right / Every once in a while / Why waste your love / What I feel / Saxophone / Monday it is / P.S.V. / Kill my instincts / Souvenir.

—— disbanded after above; JUSTIN is now in his ONLY CHILD project

– compilations, others, etc. –

Jul 91. (m-lp/m-cd) Strange Fruit; (SFPMA/+CD 209) / Dutch East India; <8410> **THE PEEL SESSIONS** (19.12.89 – 11.11.90) Feb92
– Purple haze / Man without qualities II / Jaggerbog / Big II (instrumental) / Get better / Part 4 / Man without qualities I.

NEW PORNOGRAPHERS (see under ⇒ ZUMPANO)

NEW RADIANT STORM KING

Formed: Northampton, Massachusetts, USA ... 1990 and soon Amherst-based by PEYTON PINKERTON, MATT HUNTER, ELI MILLER and ELIZABETH SHARP. NEW RADIANT STORM KINGS endured a number of set backs during the early stages of their career. Having secured a deal with 'Rough Trade', they were preparing to release their debut album, 'ONE DAY RUST', in 1992, just as the label went belly up. This blow caused the departure of guitarist, MILLER, however the other three members persevered, eventually releasing 'MY LITTLE BASTARD SOUL' (1993) for 'Axis'. The album was largely disappointing, sounding like a poor man's DINOSAUR JR with songs chopping from quiet to noisy coupled with a dry, croaking vocal on top. The band were then faced with further disappointment when, again their record company collapsed. Showing their resilience once more, the group returned with another label and a much improved album 'RIVAL TIME' (1993), showing that the group had grown confident enough to reveal their own personalities. This leant the songs a lot more bite than there had been on their haphazard debut. The 1994 follow-up, 'AUGUST REVITAL', displayed further progress and the development of a pop sensibility; the band were now comfortable in their stride, releasing three quality albums, 'HURRICANE NECKLACE' (1996), 'SINGULAR NO ARTICLE' (1998) and 'WINTERS KILL' (2002) in the next six years. • **Covered:** I AM A SCIENTIST (Guided By Voices).

Album rating: MY LITTLE BASTARD SOUL (*5) / RIVAL TIME (*5) / AUGUST REVITAL (*7) / HURRICAN NECKLACE (*7) / SINGULAR, NO ARTICLE (*7) / WINTER'S KILL (*6)

PEYTON PINKERTON – vocals, guitar, keyboards / **MATT HUNTER** – vocals, bass, guitar, piano / **ELI MILLER** – guitar / **ELIZABETH SHARP** – drums, percussion, vocals

not iss.   Trixie

1991. (7") **SMEAR. / INDIANA JONES**

not iss.   Rough Trade

1992. (cd; w-drawn) **ONE DAY RUST**
<re-iss. 1998 as 'THE CASTLE'; see next debut>

—— now a trio and without ELI

not iss.   Axis

1993. (cd) <17> **MY LITTLE BASTARD SOUL**
– Assfault (part 2) / Every day is mother's day / El – Train / Gideon's room / Prozac / Snake eyes / Nevada / Surf king / Submariner / Queen Street device / Mad money / Christmas quaallude / Drowned / Infomniac / Space / Assfault (part 1) / Xanax / Trampoline. <re-iss. 2000 on 'Wormco'+=; 3> – THE CASTLE
1993. (7") **MADMONEY. / XANAX**
(above issued on 'Axis')

not iss.   Positive

1993. (cd) <207> **RIVAL TIME**
– Viral mind / The opposing engineer (sleeps alone) / Oil an impatient fuck / New math / Phonecall / Hazardville / Commercial / 511 little nightmares / Happy for the first time in weeks / Country box / Phonecall II / Do it for the sensitive guy.

NEW RADIANT STORM KING (cont)

			not iss.	Penny Farthing
1993.	(7"ep) **...AND THEN I'M GONE** – Back door / Hey baby / (2 by POLVO).		-	
			not iss.	Chunk
1993.	(7") <CH 453> **SUBWAY TOKEN (SAVE MY SOUL). / RIVAL TIME (VIRAL MIND) / THE LORD IS COMING**		-	
1993.	(7") split w/ SILVER JEWS – Rocket science / (other 2 by above group).		-	
			not iss.	Grass
1994.	(cd) <33> **AUGUST REVITAL** – Froglegs (I suppose) / Parking lot / Forty-seven / Go back and start / What it / Zelda / Self-helpless / St. Louis born again / Backdoor / Twenty chairs / Walk of shame / Misdirected energy. <re-iss. 1996; 13014>		-	

— **JEREMY SMITH** – drums (of NEW HARMFUL, of FIGGS) repl. SHARP who moonlighted with SKINNER PILOT before forming ILL EASE

| Jan 96. | (7") <CH 4520> **I AM A SCIENTIST. / (other by GUIDED BY VOICES)** (above issued on 'Chunk') | | - | |
| Oct 96. | (cd) <13043> **HURRICANE NECKLACE** – Honor roll / C/swoon / Lovers in Waco / Drool / Embry's crossroads / Maui / Combat chair / The kind ghost / Blood for a vase / Lost in the closet / Bastard song / What money? | | - | |

— **GARRETT FONTES** – drums; repl. SMITH

		Rainbow Quartz	Poster Girl
Apr 98.	(cd) (RQTZ 009) **SINGULAR, NO ARTICLE** – Correct liar / Barium springs / Founder's day / Occidental florist / Carry my chin / Secrets to better skin / Right scream / Pocket Greek chorus / Miranda / Leftover blues / Contentedly / Era died.		1999
Jun 02.	(cd) (RQTZ 070) <1047> **WINTER'S KILL** – In the spirit of distance / Golden parachute / Lesslie skyline / Colony falls / Vieja / Montague terrace / Constellation prize / Bombs and broccoli / Winter's kill / Small broken words / Your better half / View of a wedding through the Hubble telescope.		Apr02

NEW RISING SONS
(see under ⇒ TEXAS IS THE REASON)

NICE (see under ⇒ ASHTRAY BOY)

NIGHTBLOOMS

Formed: Netherlands ... 1987 by ESTHER SPRIKELMAN, HARRY OTTEN, PETRA VAN TONGEREN and manic drummer LEON MORSELT. After a few singles, such as the dizzy 'GO ELIZA' (in '88) and 'CRYSTAL EYES' (in 1990), this quartet of noisy prog-punks issued their self-titled debut album in 1993. A swirling rock opera of sorts, The NIGHTBLOOMS influences ranged schizoid-like from the weird experimental overtones of The BEATLES "White Album", to the effects laden supersonics of HAWKWIND or The MONKS (check the eight-and-a-half minute 'BUTTERFLY GIRL'). The group were never really that comfortable with each other (plus a melting-pot of diverse musical tastes), and, after issuing the rather disappointing '24 DAYS AT CATASTROPHE CAFE' (1994), they split up. SPRIKKELMAN and OTTEN began SAFE HOME and issued the striking 'YOU CAN'T UNDO WHAT'S ALREADY UNDID' (1996), an album which played out like an unauthorised tribute to MY BLOODY VALENTINE.

Album rating: THE NIGHTBLOOMS (*6) / 24 DAYS AT CATASTROPHE CAFE (*4) / Safe Home: YOU CAN'T UNDO WHAT'S ALREADY UNDID (*5)

ESTHER SPRIKKELMAN – vocals / **HARRY OTTEN** – guitar / **PETRA VAN TONGEREN** – bass / **LEON MORSELT** – drums

		Dingo	not iss.
1988.	(7") (D 1988) **GO ELIZA. / TOO LATE FOR TEARS**	-	- Dutch
		Fierce	Seed
Apr 90.	(7") (Fright 041) **CRYSTAL EYES. / NEVER DREAM AT ALL**		
Feb 92.	(12"/cd-s) (Fright 057/+CD) **BUTTERFLY GIRL** – Butterfly girl / Blue marbles / Crystal eyes / One weak moment. (re-iss. Jan93 on 'Paperhouse'; PAPER 021 T/CD)	-	-
Mar 92.	(lp/cd) (Fright 58/+CD) <14226> **THE NIGHTBLOOMS (live)** – 59 #1 / Slowly rising / Butterfly girl / Sisters / Blue marbles / 59 #2 / Starcatcher / Panicle / Thousand years / He's dead.		
Jun 92.	(one-sided-lp) (Fright 059) **LIVE (live)** – Crystal eyes / Starcatcher / 59#1 / Blue marbles / Go Eliza / One weak moment.	-	- mail-o
Jan 93.	(7"test) (Fright 062) **KOMT VRIENDEN IN HET RONDE**		
		Fire	Seed
Nov 92.	(d7") (BLAZE 59S) **STARCATCHER. / 59#2**		
Jun 93.	(7") (BLAZE 66) <SEED 4> **NEVER DREAM AT ALL. / IT'S ALL RIGHT** (cd-s+=) (BLAZE 66CD) – He's dead.		-
Sep 93.	(cd/lp) (FIRE CD/LP 34) <14237> **24 DAYS AT CATASTROPHE CAFE** – 24 days at Catastrophe cafe / Kiss and spell / Hold on / Hope for it fast, count on it slow / Make it rain / Never dream at all / Double speed / Everyone loves you / Shatterhand / Sweet rescue.		
1994.	(7") (7SM 2) **HOLD ON. / CHANGES**		-
Mar 95.	(12"/cd-s) (BLAZE 075/+CD) **LOVE IS GONE (mixes; outer sanctum / original / inner sanctum / radio)**		-

— split the following year; ESTHER + HARRY later formed ...

SAFE HOME

ESTHER SPRIKKELMAN – vocals, harmonium, organ + **HARRY OTTEN** – guitar / with **STEVE GREGORY** (ex-POOH STICKS)

		Sunday	not iss.
Mar 01.	(cd-ep) (SUN 890) **TRAVEL IN TIME** – Travel in time / Three steps closer / Dear Dusty / Strangers.	-	- Dutch
		Are There Angels In Space?	not iss.
Mar 01.	(ltd-7") (SAFE 1) **SLOW GIRL. / ARIES**	-	- Dutch
May 01.	(ltd-7") (SAFE 2) **NEXT TIME ON THE BACK OF A GOOSE. / THREE STEPS CLOSER**	-	- Dutch
Aug 01.	(ltd-7") (SAFE 3) **BIRTHDAY. / BOOTS**	-	- Dutch
Nov 01.	(ltd-7") (SAFE 4) **AS SHE WAS. / AFTER ALL THESE YEARS**	-	- Dutch
Mar 02.	(ltd-7") (SAFE 5) **MOORTOWN BLUEBAY. / EVERY OTHER SIGH**	-	- Dutch
		Sunday	not iss.
May 02.	(cd) (Sunday 930) **YOU CAN'T UNDO WHAT'S ALREADY UNDID** – Travel in time / Moortown bluebay / Next time on the back of a goose / Umble wumble / Thin tiny kind / Slow girl / Birthday / Sailor's choice / Boots / After all these years / Dear Dusty / Start of a holiday / Bloemen / As she was / Aries / Rickett's revenge / Three steps closer / Strangers.	-	- Dutch

90 DAY MEN

Formed: St. Louis, Missouri, USA ... mid 1995, by CHANDLER McWILLIAMS, BRIAN CASE and CAYCE KEY; the former was superseded by ROBERT LOWE. Their enigmatic moniker coming from a term used in a psychology textbook for offenders waiting for a sanity evaluation, 90 DM's output is similarly perplexing, described by some as "math rock", although it did not have the complete precision of this style, and mixed grungier post-hardcore elements into its puzzling stew. After moving to Chicago, and benefiting from the vibrant musical diaspora the city had to offer (and a handful of single releases on several indie imprints), the band issued their debut EP, '1975-1977-1998', to healthy critical reviews from the alternative press. Emboldened by this support the group followed this up with the initial full-length outing, '(IT (IS) IT) CRITICAL BAND', released in the millennia. This further showcased the band's desire to push the boundaries of indie rock, and to push themselves further out of easy categorization, while also proving that they had the talent to do so. Their star definitely seemed to be in the ascendancy with the issue, two years later, of sophomore effort, 'TO EVERYBODY', which not only was better offering than its competent predecessor, but also made better and more sustained use of the skills of new keyboardist, ANDY LANSANGAN.

Album rating: 1975-1977-1998 mini (*7) / (IT (IS) IT) CRITICAL BAND (*7) / TO EVERYBODY (*7)

BRIAN CASE – vocals, guitar / **ROBERT LOWE** – bass; repl. CHANDLER McWILLIAMS / **CAYCE KEY** – drums

		not iss.	Actionboy
1997.	(7") **IF YOU CAN BAKE A CAKE, YOU CAN BUILD A BOMB. /**	-	
		Rosewood Union	Temporary Residence
Aug 99.	(m-cd) (UNION 012) **1975-1977-1998** (US title '90 DAY MEN') – My trip to Venus / Sink potemken / Streamlines and breadwinners / Sweater queen / Hey, Citronella!		1998
		Boxfactory	not iss.
Apr 00.	(m-cd) (BFEP 013) **SPLIT EP with GOGOGOAIRHEART** – From one primadonna to another / Studio four / Methodist / Hypnotized / I knew / Who are the young? / International feel / Is this Berlin? / 4 your will.		-
		Southern	Southern
Nov 00.	(cd/lp) <(18577-2/-1)> **(IT (IS) IT) CRITICAL BAND** – Dialed in / Missouri kids cuss / From one primadonna to another / Super illuminary / Hans Lucas / Exploration vs. solution, baby / Sort of is a country in love / Jupiter and Lo.		Sep00
Jan 01.	(7") (18576-7) **SHE'S A SALT SHAKER. / ACTIVATE THE BORDERS**		

— added **ANDY LANSANGAN** – keyboards

| Mar 02. | (cd/lp) <(18592-2/-1)> **TO EVERYBODY** – I've got designs on you / Last night, a DJ saved my life / Saint Theresa in ecstacy / We blame Chicago / Alligator / A national car crash. | | Feb02 |

NIPS / NIPPLE ERECTORS (see under ⇒ POGUES)

NOCTURNAL PROJECTIONS
(see under ⇒ THIS KIND OF PUNISHMENT)

NO-MAN
(see under ⇒ PORCUPINE TREE; in 80's section)

NOONDAY UNDERGROUND

Formed: London, England ... 1997 by ex-ADVENTURES IN STEREO man SIMON DINE and female vocalist DAISY MARTEY. According to internet gossip, the low-key duo met in a pizza restaurant and, after a lengthy discussion about music, decided to record together. The result was the swinging beat-box psychedelia of the hush-hush 'SELF-ASSEMBLY' LP (2000). Quickly becoming a collector's item, due to the limited run of copies, 'Setanta' re-released it for mass consumption in 2001. Former mod and JAM man, PAUL WELLER, became a fan and championed the group as "the most influencial

NOONDAY UNDERGROUND (cont)

band of all-time". Well, their album might have been pretty darn impressive, but you've got to wonder what WELLER's been taking in his tea these days. The man himself found time to collaborate with the duo on a single.

Album rating: SELF-ASSEMBLY (*7) / SURFACE NOISE (*6)

DAISY MARTEY – vocals / **SIMON DINE** – DJ (ex-ADVENTURES IN STEREO)

M21   M.I.L.

Mar 00. (cd) *(M21CD 001)* <2003> **SELF-ASSEMBLY**
– The light brigade / London / Hello / Hush / The hooded claw / Marvellous / When you leave / Rock steady / Where have they gone / On Sunday noon / Inside / Never go away / We saw the midnight / The good old summer time / Wonderful tonight. *(re-iss. Sep00 cd/lp; M21 CD/LP 001) (re-iss. Sep01 on 'Setanta'; SETCD 089) (lp re-iss. Sep01 on 'Guided Missile'; GUIDE 45LP) <US re-iss. Sep01 on 'Bar/None'; 118>*

Sonic Syrup   not iss.

Jul 00. (7"purple) *(SSY45 002)* **WHEN YOU LEAVE. / THE HOODED CLAW**

Blow Up   not iss.

Feb 01. (7") *(BU 021)* **THE LIGHT BRIGADE. / HELLO**

Jonathan Whiskey   Liberation

Mar 01. (7")<cd-s> *(ULALAWHISKEY 21)* <LIBSP 40482> **LONDON. /**

Setanta   Bar/None

Apr 02. (12") *(SET 097T)* **WHEN YOU LEAVE (Jay-J remix). / WHEN YOU LEAVE (Jay-J dub)**
Sep 02. (7") *(SET 111)* **NOBODY BUT YOU. / HITCH YOUR WAGON TO THE STARS**
Sep 02. (cd) *(SETCD 109)* **SURFACE NOISE**
– Surface noise / Go it alone / That noonday sun / Nobody but you / Windmills / Boy like a timebomb / Friends of the garden (part 1) / I'll walk right on / When I fall / Friends of the garden (part 2) / Barcelona / Hitch your wagon to the stars / Thunder park / Closing time.
Nov 02. (7"/cd-s; w-drawn) *(SET 119/+CD)* **BOY LIKE A TIMEBOMB**   –   –

Stina NORDENSTAM

Born: 1969, Stockholm, Sweden. Inspired by jazz and classical from an early age (mainly JOHN COLTRANE and ERIK SATIE), STINA began writing her own material during adolescence, having survived the harrowing break-up of her parents' marriage. After leaving school, the elfin-like musical prodigy (she had mastered piano, violin and guitar!) cut her teeth in jazz outfit, The FLIPPERMEN. NORDENSTAM (now aged 21) signed to 'Telegram' and soon cut her debut album, 'MEMORIES OF A COLOUR', an acclaimed record of melancholy, monochromatic beauty which was deservedly picked up by Warners global offshoot, 'East West', in '92. A self-confessed depressive compared to movie director and fellow gloom-meister, Ingmar Bergman, NORDENSTAM was given the honour of playing for the Swedish parliament and royal family despite her maverick reputation. In 1994, she left behind the JONI MITCHELL and TORI AMOS comparisons by digging even deeper into her troubled psyche, unearthing a series of tragic tales frosted by her icy, deceivingly childlike vocals and coloured by the jazz textures of veteran, JON HASSELL. The following year, another veteran of the ambient/pop music world, VANGELIS, invited her to sing on his single, 'Ask The Mountains', although the collaboration didn't work out commercially. STINA's third album, 'DYNAMITE' (1996), saw the diminutive Swede take a mood swing of sorts away from her morbidly established mould towards a more forthright sound. 1998's 'PEOPLE ARE STRANGE' was one of those rare beasts, a covers album that actually adds (or, in this case, often subtracts) something to the originals, or indeed warps them beyond recognition. In her curious Scandinavian manner, NORDENSTAM tackled the likes of Prince's 'PURPLE RAIN' and Tim Hardin's 'REASON TO BELIEVE' with as little reverence as she was seemingly capable, twisting their structures and grafting on found sounds. The basic musical formula was extended on 'THIS IS STINA NORDENSTAM' (2002), a more accessible set of original material with guest contributions from the likes of SUEDE's BRETT ANDERSON.

Album rating: MEMORIES OF A COLOUR (*7) / AND SHE CLOSED HER EYES (*7) / DYNAMITE (*6) / PEOPLE ARE STRANGE (*6) / THIS IS STINA NORDENSTAM (*5)

STINA NORDENSTAM – vocals, guitar, piano, violin / with session people

East West   East West

Sep 92. (cd/c) *(<4509 90767-2/-4>)* **MEMORIES OF A COLOUR**
– Memories of a colour / The return of Alan Bean / Another story girl / His song / He watches her from behind / I'll be cryin' for you / Alone at night / Soon after Christmas / A walk in the park.
Mar 93. (cd-s) *(YZ 711CD)* **ANOTHER STORY GIRL. / A WALK IN THE PARK**   –
Mar 94. (7"/c-s) *(YZ 807/+C)* **LITTLE STAR. / FIRST DAY IN SPRING**   –
(cd-s+=) *(YZ 807CD)* – He watches her from behind.
Apr 94. (cd/c) *(<4509 93898-2/-4>)* **AND SHE CLOSED HER EYES**
– Little star / When Debbie's back from Texas / Viewed from the spire / Crime / Murder in Mairyland Park / So this is goodbye / Something nice / And she closed her eyes / Fireworks / Proposal / Hopefully yours / I see you again.
Sep 94. (c-s) *(YZ 853C)* **SOMETHING NICE / WHEN DEBBIE'S BACK FROM TEXAS**   –
(cd-s+=) *(YZ 853CD)* – Soon after Christmas.

– another 'East West' artist, VANGELIS, invited STINA to sing on their early '96 collaboration single, 'Ask The Mountains'.

Jul 96. (c-ep/10"ep/cd-ep) *(EW 055 C/TE/CD)* **THE PHOTOGRAPHER'S WIFE E.P.**   –
– I could still (be an actor) / Now when I see you / The things you said.
Mar 97. (10"/c-s/cd-s) *(EW 091 TE/C/CD)* **DYNAMITE. / GREETINGS FROM THE OLD WORLD**
Apr 97. (cd/c) *(<0630 15605-2/-4>)* **DYNAMITE**   Oct96
– Under your command / Dynamite / Almost a smile / Mary Bell / The man with the gun / This time John / C.Q.D. / Down Desire Avenue / Now that you're leaving.
Jun 97. (c-s/cd-s) *(EW 106 C/CD)* **LITTLE STAR / THE MAN WITH THE GUN**   –
Nov 98. (cd) <(3984 24506-2)> **PEOPLE ARE STRANGE**
– Sailing / I dream of Jeannie (with light brown hair) / Love hurts / Lonesome road / Bird on a wire / Purple rain / Swallow strings / Like a swallow / Reason to believe / I came so far for beauty / Come to me / People are strange.
Nov 98. (12"/cd-s) *(EW 189 T/CD)* **PEOPLE ARE STRANGE. / PEOPLE ARE STRANGE (Unkle remix)**

Independiente   Sony

Nov 01. (cd) *(ISOM 24CD)* <504118> **THIS IS STINA NORDENSTAM**
– Everyone else in the world / Trainsurfing / So Lee / The diver / Circus / Stations / Keen yellow planet / Lori glory / Welcome to happiness / Clothe yourself for the world / Sharon & Hope.

NORTHERN PICTURE LIBRARY
(see under ⇒ FIELD MICE)

NORTHERN UPROAR

Formed: Manchester, England ... 1994 by schoolfriends LEON MEYA, PK (aka PAUL KELLY), JEFF FLETCHER and KEITH CHADWICK. Not exactly one of Heavenly's deftest signings, this bunch were snapped up by the label on the strength of an 'In The City' industry showcase. Produced by JAMES DEAN BRADFIELD (of The MANICS) and released amid a veritable tidal wave of hype, 'ROLLERCOASTER' was a promising enough debut single in late '95. While the record stalled just outside the Top 40, the band had no such problems with follow-up, 'FROM A WINDOW', crashing into the Top 20 and drawing the tired and inevitable "next OASIS" predictions. While they might've espoused the same boorish philosophy as their Manc compatriots, they had neither the looks/attitude of LIAM nor the common-man songwriting talent of NOEL; one thing they did share was the ability to somehow splice soundalike fragments of rock'n'pop history into an easily consumed whole i.e. the echoes of MARVIN GAYE/TAMMI TERRELL classic, 'It Takes Two' and The STONE ROSES' 'She Bangs The Drum' on 'IN MY WORLD'. 1996's eponymous debut album confirmed matters, an enjoyable trad-rock romp along the obligatory SMALL FACES/WHO/CLASH/JAM lineage but hardly strong enough to justify the lads' well publicised boasting. Critics were divided on their merits although the music buying public voted with their feet and ensured that despite another respectable offering in 1997's 'TOMORROW, TODAY AND YESTERDAY', NORTHERN UPROAR fizzled out with merely a whimper along with Brit-pop itself. • **Songwriters:** Most by MEYA (or with KELLY) except MY MIND'S EYE (Small Faces) / I AM THE COSMOS (Chris Bell). • **Trivia:** LEON MEYA was called up for national service to the Spanish army although he only lived there during the first five years of his life!

Album rating: NORTHERN UPROAR (*6) / TOMORROW, TODAY AND YESTERDAY (*5)

LEON MEYA – vocals, bass / **PK (PAUL KELLY)** – guitar / **JEFF FLETCHER** – guitar, vocals / **KEITH CHADWICK** – drums, piano

Heavenly   Alex

Oct 95. (7"/c-s) *(HVN 047/+CS)* **ROLLERCOASTER. / SMOOTH GEEZER**   41   –
(cd-s+=) *(HVN 047CD)* – Rough boy / Waiting on (acoustic).
Jan 96. (7"/c-s) *(HVN 051/+CS)* **FROM A WINDOW. / THIS MORNING**   17   –
(cd-s+=) *(HVN 051CD)* – My mind's eye / Credibility.
Apr 96. (7"ep/c-ep/cd-ep) *(HVN 052/+CS/CD)* **LIVIN' IT UP / STONEFALL. / GOODBYE / IN MY WORLD**   24   –
May 96. (cd/c/lp) *(HVN CD/MC/LP 12)* **NORTHERN UPROAR**   22   –
– From a window / Rough boy / Town / Kicks / Breakthrough / Memories / Waiting on / Livin' it up / Head under water / Moods / Rollercoaster / Living in the red.
Jun 96. (7"/c-s) *(HVN 054/+CS)* <6053> **TOWN. / KICKS (acoustic)**   48   Apr98
(cd-s+=) *(HVN 054CD)* – Memories / I am the cosmos.
May 97. (c-s) *(HVN 73CS)* **ANY WAY YOU LOOK / BREAKING THE ICE**   36   –
(10"+=/cd-s+=) *(HVN 70-10/CD)* – I remember.
Aug 97. (7"/c-s/cd-s) *(HVN 73 7/CS/CD)* **A GIRL I ONCE KNEW /**   63   –
Aug 97. (cd/c/lp) *(HVN CD/MC/LP 19)* **TOMORROW, TODAY AND YESTERDAY**   –
– Any way you look / A girl I once knew / Down to me / What's it gonna be? / Blind / Goodbye / One of those things / Blown away / So much / More than this / Another day / I'm coming undone.
Nov 97. (7"/c-s) *(HVN 77/+CS)* **GOODBYE. / ON MY MIND**   –
(cd-s+=) *(HVN 77CD)* – Really feeling.

—   said goodbye the following year

NORTHSIDE

Formed: Manchester, England ... 1989 by DERMO (WARREN DERMODY), CLIFF OGIER and the WALSH brothers, TIMMY and PAUL. One of the many second division stragglers to follow in the 'Madchester' wake of The HAPPY MONDAYS and The STONE ROSES, the band were picked up by local indie institution, 'Factory', through whom they released a debut single, 'SHALL WE TAKE A TRIP'. The title alone was enough to fuel accusations of bandwagoneering and neither follow-up single, 'RISING STAR', nor the aptly named debut album, 'CHICKEN RHYTHMS' (1991) cut much ice with the critics. They didn't do much sales-wise either, the

NORTHSIDE (cont)

group sinking back into deepest, darkest Manchester along with the scene that spawned them as the press turned its attention to the more intelligent sounds of London shoegazing. • **Songwriters:** Group compositions, although they did Peter Gabriel's 'SOLISBURY HILL' on stage.

Album rating: CHICKEN RHYTHMS (*6)

WARREN 'Dermo' DERMODY – vocals / **TIMMY WALSH** – guitar / **CLIFF OGIER** – bass / **PAUL 'Walt' WALSH** – drums

		Factory	Geffen
May 90.	(7"/ext.12") *(FAC/12FAC 268)* **SHALL WE TAKE A TRIP. / MOODY PLACES**	50	-
Oct 90.	(7") *(FAC 298-7)* **MY RISING STAR. /** ('A'instrumental) (12"+=) *(12FAC 298)* – ('A' extended). (cd-s+=) *(FACD 298)* – Shall we take a trip / Moody places.	32	-
May 91.	(7") *(FAC 308-7)* **TAKE 5. / WHO'S TO BLAME** (instrumental) (12")(cd-s+=) *(12FAC 308)(FACD 308)* – ('A' version).	40	
Jun 91.	(cd)(lp/c) *(FACTD 310)(FACT 310/+C)* <24412> **CHICKEN RHYTHMS** – Take 5 / Weight of air / Funky Munky / A change is on it's way / Yeah man / Tour de world / Wishful thinking / Shall we take a trip / Who's to blame / Practice makes perfect.	19	

— disbanded later in the year. Another NORTHSIDE were around in the mid-90's and were mainly club/dance orientated

NOTHING PAINTED BLUE

Formed: Los Angeles, California, USA ... 1986 out of The BORN LEADERS by FRANKLIN BRUNO and KYLE BRODIE, along with various musicians coming in and out of the band over the years, including PETER HUGHES, BOB DURKEE and JOEY BURNS. Their sound borrowed from the early eighties post-punk, new wave staple and developed it into a well-crafted and sharp form of alternative power-pop akin to the smarter indie bands such as PAVEMENT and The MINUTEMEN. NPB began doing the college party circuit which helped them hone down their style. By the time they debuted in 1990 with the LP, 'A BABY, A BLANKET, A PACKET OF SEEDS', they were sounding like a fully-fledged and confident indie rock group in the midst of their careers. Following this up, they delivered the album, 'POWER TRIPS DOWN LOVER'S LANE' three years later, with full-length offering 'PLACEHOLDERS' (1994) coming hot on it heels. As well as the stable twosome of BRUNO and BRODIE, this set also featured the skilled guitar work of DURKEE with some unusual instrumentation coming in the shape of violins and the percussive beat of the congas. A fine piece with such standouts as 'DRINKING GAME' and 'RIGHTFUL ROCKER', the band gave an album that appealed to those who didn't want every track on the album to sound the same; moving from up front punky styles to more airy open pieces. The ensuing year saw the issue of the more off-the-wall EP, 'THE FUTURE OF COMMUNICATION' (1995), which collected together many rarer band recordings like 'VENGEFUL AS HELL' from a radio spot on Santa Monica's influential KCRW-FM, as well as previously released 7"s. The eponymous 'NOTHING PAINTED BLUE' LP hit the record shops to the double delight of their growing fanbase and the quality kept on rolling in with their next studio album 'THE MONTE CARLO METHOD' (1998), two recordings that showed that the band had lost none of its shine. While NPB took a little breather now and then, BRUNO issued a few solo releases, including limited-edition cassettes 'SUGGESTION BOX' (1991) and 'ETUDES FOR VOICE AND SMACKMASTER' (1993). His first widely-available release came courtesy of 'Simple Machines', who delivered 'A BEDROOM COMMUNITY' (1995). Of late (post-millennium), BRUNO has released two worthy solo efforts, 'KISS WITHOUT MAKEUP' (2000) and 'A CAT MAY LOOK AT A QUEEN' (2002); he also collaborated with MOUNTAIN GOATS mainman JOHN DARNIELLE on their EXTRA GLENNS album, 'MARTIAL ARTS WEEKEND' (2002). • **Covered:** LAB RAT BLUES (Mountain Goats) / ANTI-NOMINATION (Refrigerator).

Album rating: POWER TRIPS DOWN LOVERS' LANE (*4) / PLACEHOLDERS (*6) / THE FUTURE OF COMMUNICATIONS mini (*3) / EMOTIONAL DISCIPLINE compilation (*6) / THE MONTE CARLO METHOD (*7) / Franklin Bruno: A BEDROOM COMMUNITY (*5) / KISS WITHOUT MAKEUP (*6) / A CAT MAY LOOK AT A QUEEN (*7)

FRANKLIN BRUNO (b.29 Dec'68, Pomona, Calif.) – vocals, guitar, synthesizer, piano / **MIKE NEELON** – bass, vocals / **KYLE BRODIE** – drums

		not iss.	Jupa
Jan 90.	(lp) <1> **A BABY, A BLANKET, A PACKET OF SEEDS**	-	
Jan 90.	(7"ep) <2> **THE BELLYSPEAK EP**	-	

		not iss.	Anyway
1991.	(7") <aw 019> **AFTER THE HOUSE WARMING. / LOVE TO THE THIRD POWER**	-	

— **JOEY BURNS** – bass, vocals (of GIANT SAND) repl. NEELON

		Kokopop	Kokopop
Dec 92.	(7") <KOKO 1> **SWIVELCHAIR. / BLOOMING, BUZZING**	-	
Aug 93.	(cd/c/lp) <KOKOPOP 001 CD/MC/LP)> **POWER TRIPS DOWN LOVERS' LANE** – White bicycles / Peace dividend / Block colors / Officer angel / Campaign song / Register / Storefronts / Unscheduled train / Epistemophilia / Smothered / Scapegoat / Few / Rock and roll friend / Undeserving. <cd re-iss. Dec95 as 'NOTHING PAINTED BLUE'; same>		Jun93

		not iss.	Simple Machines
Jul 93.	(7") <JULY> **ANOTHER CHILD BRIDE. /** (other by LOIS)	-	

			Scat	Scat
	— **PETER HUGHES** – bass, vocals; repl. BURNS			
Oct 94.	(cd) <(SCT 37-2)> **PLACEHOLDERS** – Couldn't be simpler / Weak / Drinking game / Career day / Spread your poison / In May / Masonic eye / Ballwalker / Travel well / Rightful heir / Houseguest / Kissing booth / Can't F(X).			Aug94
Jul 95.	(cd-s) **ANTI-NOMINATION (split w/ REFRIGERATOR)** (above issued on 'Misha')		-	

— **JOEY BURNS** – bass; repl. PETER full-time after below

		Scat	Scat
Sep 95.	(7") <SCT 43> **NIACIN.** /	-	
Nov 95.	(m-cd/m-lp) <(SCT 47-2/-1)> **THE FUTURE OF COMMUNICATIONS** – Sorely tempted / A shakey start / Vengeful as hell / Lapped / (I'm a) Haunted house / The future of communications.		
May 97.	(cd) <(SCT 53> **EMOTIONAL DISCIPLINE** (singles compilation) – Go to waste / Up w/Upland / K for karnival / Let's kiss / Foundation slips / Few / Or do they? / Swivelchair / Blooming, buzzing / El Nino / Nig pink heart / Missed the point / Underserving / Sorely tempted / Lab rat blues / Going to Fontana / Another child bride / After the house warming / Love to the third power / Anti-nomination.	-	
Jan 99.	(cd) <(SCT 59CD)> **THE MONTE CARLO METHOD** – Willingness / Shameproof flirt / Collage elements / Modern again / Explorer scout / Cathexis / Niacin / 2nd class citizen / Spent / Developer's dream / I should be with you / Growth spurt / Off the face.		Aug98

FRANKLIN BRUNO

		not iss.	Shrimper
1991.	(c) **SUGGESTION BOX**	-	
1992.	(7") **HERMETIC GEOMETRY. /** (above issued on 'Baby Huey')	-	
1993.	(c) **ETUDES FOR VOICE AND SMACKMASTER**	-	
1994.	(7") **THE IRONY ENGINE. /** (above issued on 'Walt')	-	
1994.	(7") **SAND DOLLAR.** /	-	

— next with **BRODIE + NEELON**

		not iss.	Simple Machines
May 95.	(lp/cd) <smr 28/+cd> **A BEDROOM COMMUNITY** – Then again, maybe I won't / Ghost package / Cheat / The two of you / Uninsulated wall / The lonelysocks generation / Layered look / At Marsh ranch / Great fool / A frozen lake / Skipped a grade / (untitled) / For the firedrill / The death of Vaudeville.	-	

— next with **DAN SETA** – guitar + **LYLE HYSEN** – drums

		Absolutely Kosher	Absolutely Kosher
Jul 00.	(cd) <(AK 006)> **KISS WITHOUT MAKEUP** – A radial / Just because it's / Nurse / Beautiful right now / Thin, weak smile / Clean needle / Charlottesville / Nickname stuck / Shapeless things / Save a piece for me / Idiots / Narrow shoulders / Dia lara / (untitled).		Jun00

— next with **JOEY BURNS, KYLE BRODIE, DANIEL BRODO + TOMMY LARKINS**

| Oct 02. | (cd) <(AK 019)> **A CAT MAY LOOK AT A QUEEN** – Dashboard issues / Lies on your lips / Janet Shaw / I blame you / Tired of the west / Threadbare / A cat may look at a queen / Bulk removal truck / Callous / Dossier / Love's got a ghetto / Two purple shadows / Blue's the only color. | | Sep02 |

NOTWIST

Formed: Weilheim, Germany ... 1987 by the ACHER brothers, MARKUS and MICHA. A few years later, the pair found drummer MECKI MESSERSCHMID and completed their US hardcore influenced eponymous debut set. To obtain cash, the siblings played traditional drums and trumpets respectively at Dixieland jazz parties and weddings. Breaking from the hardcore and metal mould (early DINOSAUR JR, etc) on a number of albums, they marked a career change into alternative ambient-jazz on 1997's, '12' (which featured a cover of Robert Palmer's 'JOHNNY AND MARY'). Shortly afterwards they added the sampling delights of MARTIN GRETSCHMANN, who stuck around for a similar 'Duophonic' (home of STEREOLAB) release, 'SHRINK'. Meanwhile, the brothers moonlighted in the brassy, avant-jazz outfit, The TIED AND TICKLED TRIO. The NOTWIST returned on 'City Slang' records for another assortment of tunes, 'NEON GOLDEN' (2002).

Album rating: THE NOTWIST (*6) / NOOK (*6) / LIVE (*5) / 12 (*7) / SHRINK (*6) / NEON GOLDEN (*7)

MARKUS ACHER – guitar / **MICHA ACHER** – bass / **MECKI MESSERSCHMID** – drums

		Subway	not iss.
1990.	(colrd-lp/cd) *(3550003-1/-2)* **THE NOTWIST** – Is it fear? / Bored / Winter / Crack it open / Be reckless / K. das devil / One wasted / Agenda / I've not forgotten you / M. del terror / Seasons / Think for yourself / Nothing like you. *(UK-iss.Aug94; same)* <US-iss.May02 on 'Subway'; 602020>	-	- German

		Big Store	not iss.
1992.	(cd) *(BST 035)* **NOOK** – Belle de l'ombre / Walk on / Unsaid, undone / Welcome back / Nook / No love / The incredible change of our alien / This sorry confession / One dark love poem / The only thing we own / I'm a whale. *(UK-iss.Aug94; same)*	-	- German

		Your Choice	Your Choice
Aug 94.	(cd) <(YCLS 021)> **LIVE** (live) – Electric bear / Incredible change of our alien / Agenda / I've not forgotten you / Instrumental / Unsaid undone / M. del terror / Nook / One wasted / Nothing like you / 12.		

		Diversity	not iss.
Nov 95.	(cd) *(WACCY 014)* **THE NOTWIST** – Torture day / My phrasebook / Puzzle / M / Noah / My fault / The string / Instr. / 12. (above was given away free with a LOUP cd)	-	- German

			Zero Hour	Zero Hour
Jan 97.	(12"ep/cd-ep)	(ZERS 10014) **TORTURE DAY EP**		-

– Torture day / My phrasebook / The incredible change in our alien / No love.

			Community	Zero Hour
Jun 97.	(cd/d-lp)	(COM 1003216-2/-1) <2180> **12**		

– Torture day / My phrasebook / Puzzle / M / Noah / My faults / String / Instr. / 12 / The string / The incredible change of our alien / Johnny and Mary / Torture day "loup" / Noah. *(free cd w/cd+=)* – LOUP REMIXES – Torture day / 12.

—— added **MARTIN GRETSCHMANN** – samples, etc (of CONSOLE; one album – PAN OR AMA)

Jul 97.	(12"ep)	(COM 00923) <3181> **DAY 7 EP**		Oct98

– Dau 7 / Your signs / Noah (November '96 version) / Your signs (instrumental).

			Duophonic	Zero Hour
Sep 98.	(cd/lp)	(DS45CD/DS33 023) <3180> **SHRINK**		

– Day 7 / Chemicals / Another planet / Moron / Electric bear / No encores / N.L. / Shrink / Your signs / 0-4.

			-	-
Oct 98.	(12")	<3182> **CHEMICALS** (mixes)		City Slang / not iss.
Nov 01.	(12") **THRASHING DAYS**			-
Jan 02.	(12"/cd-s)	(20183-6/-2) **PILOT. / PILOT** (Console remix) / **DIFFERENT CARS AND TRAINS** (Loopspool version)		-
Feb 02.	(cd/lp)	(20184-2/-1) **NEON GOLDEN**		-

– One step inside doesn't mean you understand / Pilot / Pick up the phone / Trashing days / This room / Solitaire / One with the freaks / Neon golden / Off the rail / Consequence.

| Apr 02. | (12") | (20193-6) **PICK UP THE PHONE** (mixes) | | - |

Heather NOVA

Born: HEATHER FRITH, 6 Jul'68, Bermuda. HEATHER was raised on a sailboat around the Caribbean, an idyllic upbringing which allowed her plenty of time to sit around and learn the guitar. Moving to dry land at the age of 19, she studied film at art college in Providence, Rhode Island, subsequently finding a more permanent base in London after a spell in New York. After working on music for her own films and releasing a one-off 45 as HEATHER FRITH in 1990, NOVA found a kindred spirit in former KILLING JOKE/BRILLIANT bassman turned cult producer, YOUTH, who took the budding singer/songwriter under the wing of his own 'Butterfly' records. The resulting album, 'GLOW STARS' (1993), recorded at her own London home studio, received mixed but generally encouraging reviews and NOVA's growing reputation secured support slots to SUGAR/BOB MOULD, etc. A live mini-set, 'BLOW' (1993), filled in time between her next studio album, the acclaimed UK Top 75, YOUTH-produced 'OYSTER' (1994). Fusing together the pop-folk influences of her childhood with the more worldly-wise standpoint of a maturing wordsmith, HEATHER had created a thought-provoking collection of songs, not least the thorny document of domestic abuse, 'ISLAND'. After touring the world on the much vaunted NEIL YOUNG / PEARL JAM "Mirrorball" trek, she took time out to collect her thoughts before emerging on Richard Branson's new 'V2' imprint with 1998's Top 60 album, 'SIREN'. The subsequent tour, or at least one German date, was captured for posterity on 'WONDERLUST' (2000), a rootsy live document which went at least some way towards crystalising her magnetic stage persona and featured a moving coda of Springsteen's 'I'M ON FIRE'. Its title a tribute to her exotic origins, 'SOUTH' (2001), meanwhile, found a thirty-something NOVA exuding an aura of self contentment, resulting in her most accessible work to date. • Covered: MANY RIVERS TO CROSS (Jimmy Cliff) / LIKE A HURRICANE (Neil Young) / I'M ON FIRE (Bruce Springsteen).

Album rating: GLOW STARS (*6) / BLOW (*6) / OYSTER (*8) / LIVE FROM THE MILKY WAY mini (*5) / SIREN (*6) / WONDERLUST (*5) / SOUTH (*5)

HEATHER NOVA – vocals, guitar; with a few people on session

			Big Cat	not iss.
Nov 90.	(12"ep; as HEATHER FRITH)	(ABB 24T) **THESE WALLS EP**		-

– These walls / New love / Further than you / Flying as she falls. *(cd-ep iss.Feb97 as 'THE FIRST RECORDING'; ABB 132SCD)*

			Butterfly	not iss.
Apr 93.	(cd-ep)	(BSL 3) **SPIRIT IN YOU / GLOWSTARS / EAR TO THE GROUND / SHAKING THE DOLL**		-
May 93.	(cd/c/lp)	(BFL CD/MC/LP 002) **GLOW STARS**		-

– Bare / My fidelity / Spirit in you / Shell / Glow stars / Ear to the ground / Second skin / Mother tongue / All the way / Frontier / Shaking the doll / Talking to strangers. *(re-iss. Aug95 cd/c; same)*

| Oct 93. | (cd/c) | (BFLCD 008) <ABB 57 CD/C> **BLOW** (live) | | |

– Light years / Sugar / Maybe an angel / Blessed / Mother tongue / Talking to strangers / Shaking the doll. *(cd re-iss. Aug95 +=; BFLCD 8)* – Frontier / Doubled up. *(cd re-iss. Sep98 on 'Big Cat'; same as US)*

| Feb 95. | (c-s) | (BFLC 19) **WALK THIS WORLD / HOME** | 69 | - |

(cd-s+=) (BFLD 19) – Blind.
(12"++=) (BFT 19) – ('A'acoustic).

			Butterfly	Work–Columbia
Oct 94.	(cd/c)	(BFL CD/MC 12) <67113> **OYSTER**	72	

– Walk this world / Heal / Island / Throwing fire at the sun / Maybe an angel / Truth and bone / Blue black / Walking higher / Light years / Verona / Doubled up.

| Apr 95. | (m-cd) | <OK 67046> **LIVE FROM THE MILKY WAY** (live) | - | |

– Maybe an angel / Throwing fire at the sun / Talking to strangers / Sugar / Walking higher / Verona.

| Sep 95. | (c-s) | (BFLC 27) **MAYBE AN ANGEL / THROWING FIRE AT THE SUN** | | - |

(cd-s+=) (BFLDA 27) – Talking to strangers (live) / ('A'-Undertow mix).
(cd-s) (BFLDB 27) – ('A'side) / Verona / Heal / My fidelity.

| Apr 96. | (c-s) | (BFLC 34) **TRUTH AND BONE / BLUE BLACK** (live) | | - |

(cd-s+=) (BFLD 34) – Like a hurricane (live) / I'm on fire (live).

			V2	Sony
May 98.	(cd-s)	(VVR 5001188-3) **LONDON RAIN (NOTHING HEALS ME LIKE YOU DO) / GROW YOUNG** (acoustic) / **WATER FROM VINE** (acoustic)		-

(cd-s) (VVR 5001188-8) – ('A'side) / Ship song / LOndon rain (acoustic).

| Jun 98. | (cd) | (VVR 100187-2) <67953> **SIREN** | 55 | |

– London rain (nothing heals me like you do) / Blood of me / Heart and shoulder / What a feeling / Valley of sound / I'm the girl / Winterblue / I'm alive / Widescreen / Paper cup / Avalanche / Make you mine / Ruby red / Not only human.

| Feb 99. | (cd-s) | (VVR 500257-3) **HEART AND SHOULDER / DAYS AND NIGHTS / HEART AND SHOULDER** (acoustic) | | - |

(cd-s) (VVR 500257-8) – ('A'side) / Many rivers to cross / Nothing.

| Aug 00. | (cd) | (VVR 101324-2) **WONDERLUST** (live) | | - |

– Winter blue / Walk this world / Island / Heart and shoulder / Paper cup / London rain (nothing heals me like you do) / Not only human / Doubled up / Truth and bone / I'm the girl / Heal / Make you mine / Sugar / I'm on fire.

| Sep 01. | (cd-s) | (VVR 501736-3) **I'M NO ANGEL / MAN IN THE OCEAN / TESTED** (band version) / **IN THE GARDEN** | | - |

(cd-s) (VVR 501736-8) – ('A'side) / In the garden / Sweet November.

| Oct 01. | (cd) | (VVR 101735-2) <27121> **SOUTH** | | Dec01 |

– If I saw you in a movie / Talk to me / Virus of the mind / Like lovers do / Waste the day / Heaven sent / It's only love / I'm no angel / Help me be good to you / When somebody turns you on / Gloomy Sunday / Tested / Just been born.

| Mar 02. | (cd-s) | (VVR 501889-3) **VIRUS OF THE MIND / SWEET NOVEMBER / PAINT THE WORLD / WINTER BLUE** | | - |

NOVA MOB
(see under ⇒ HUSKER DU; in 80's section)

NOVAK STATE CONSPIRACY
(see under ⇒ VENUS FLY TRAP; in 80's section)

NOVOCAINE

Formed: Newport, Wales … 1994 by STEVE EVANS, RUSSELL EDWARDS, RICHARD JACKSON and BERT LEWIS. They made their vinyl debut that year with 'MODERN MAN', raw, gut-wrenching punk-grunge with turps-gargling vocals provided by EVANS. A follow-up, 'TENSION', appeared on the 'Townhill' label a year later, leading to a contract with the more experienced indie imprint, 'Fire'. NOVOCAINE injected even more energy into 1997 albums, the mini 'FRUSTRATION No.10' and 'NERVOUS DISPOSITION'; although the band were saddled with the usual NIRVANA or RADIOHEAD comparisons, they were hotly tipped for greater things in '98/'99 although they split soon after.

Album rating: FRUSTRATION No.10 mini (*6) / NERVOUS DISPOSITION (*7)

STEVE EVANS – vocals / **RICHARD JACKSON** – guitar / **RUSSELL EDWARDS** – bass / **BERT LEWIS** – drums

			Liberty Place	not iss.
Jun 94.	(7")	(LP 004) **MODERN MAN. / BRAIN**		-
			Townhill	not iss.
Jul 95.	(7")	(TIDY 002) **TENSION. / DADDY'S MONEY**		-
			Fire	Velvel
Nov 96.	(7")	(BLAZE 107) **CELLOPHANE WRAPPED NEW HEAD. / 'E'**		
Jan 97.	(m-cd)	(FIREMCD 61) <79742> **FRUSTRATION NO.10**		Oct97

– Brain / Cellophane wrapped new head / Modern man / Culture me / Sneaky servo? / Tension / Bedroom addict / Daddy's money.

| May 97. | (7") | (BLAZE 114) **MOTHER – FATHER. / IN MY HEAD** | | |

(cd-s+=) (BLAZE 114CD) – My big business.

| Jul 97. | (7") | (BLAZE 117) **STONEFACE / FLAMES** | | |

(cd-s+=) (BLAZE 117CD) – Bury the hate.

| Aug 97. | (cd) | (FIRECD 67) **NERVOUS DISPOSITION** | | |

– Walls / Mother – Father / Awake / Bittersoul / Stoneface / Frustration No.10 / Pondlife / Million miles / Sorry (scum like me) / Boring git / Waiting / Analyse / Horses / She knows nothing.

| Dec 97. | (7") | (BLAZE 118) **POND LIFE. / BEDROOM ADDICT** (alternative version) | | |

(cd-s+=) (BLAZE 118CD) – Astronaut / Modern man (radio version).

| Feb 98. | (7") | (BLAZE 120) **MILLION MILES. / YOU KNOW ME BETTER THAN THAT** | | |

(cd-s+=) (BLAZE 120CD) – Control / Asylum.

—— looked to have disbanded

NOW IT'S OVERHEAD (see under ⇒ AZURE RAY)

NUBILES

Formed: Oxford, England … 1994 by TARA MILTON, CHRIS NETTLETON, GEORGIO CURCETTI and DAN GODDARD (DANNY and GAZ – later of SUPERGRASS – were also original members). Propelled by the anti-hero revolutionary vision of mainman TARA MILTON, The NUBILES launched their first sonic attack on the mainstream with the incendiary 'LAYABOUT'. Veering between indie-pop melody and blitzkrieg guitar noise, the single was vaguely reminscent of RADIOHEAD, at least in spirit. The lovesick 'WITHOUT WAKING' followed a similar formula, building up to a raging climax of frustration and bitterness while B-side, 'A SAP'S GUIDE TO ROCK'N'ROLL' wasn't exactly short on sarcasm; you could tell MILTON had been through the music biz mill at least once before (with also-ran power mods, 5:30). Despite initial press acclaim, a further clutch of singles –

'TATJANA', 'I WANT TO BE YOUR KUNTE KINTE' and a revamped 'LAYABOUT' (PENNY SCHUELLER now on keyboards) – and a debut album, 'MINDBLENDER' (1998) were afforded only minimal interest.

Album rating: MINDBLENDER (*5)

TARA MILTON – vocals, bass (ex-FIVE THIRTY) / **GEORGIO CURCETTI** – guitar / **CHRIS NETTLETON** – keyboards, guitar, vocals / **DAN GODDARD** – drums, percussion, vocals, programming

		Lime Street	not iss.
Feb 95.	(7") (LS 01) **LAYABOUT. / MOTHER & FATHER**	☐	-
May 95.	(7") (LS 02) **WITHOUT WAKING. / A SAP'S GUIDE TO ROCK'N'ROLL**	☐	-
	(cd-s+=) (LS 02CD) – Toodle pip.		
Oct 95.	(7") (LS 03) **TATJANA (ALL OVER ME). / BIG CHILD**	☐	-
	(cd-s+=) (LS 03CD) – Chasing 10 (acoustic).		

–––– **PENNY SCHUELLER** – guitar, keyboards; repl. CHRIS

Jun 96.	(12") (LS 04) **I WANNA BE YOUR KUNTA KINTE.** / ('A'-Laura B gorgeousity mix)	☐	-
	(cd-s+=) (LS 04CD) – ('A'-Patterson subway mix).		
Mar 98.	(cd-ep) (LS 08) **LAYABOUT VS MINDBLENDER**	☐	-
	– Layabout / Mindblender / Teenage torso / Food and wine.		
May 98.	(cd) (LSCD 01) **MINDBLENDER**	☐	-
	– Mindblender / I want to be your Kunta Kinte / Bedbound / Stop the city / A sap's guide to rock'n'roll / Cerebral movies / A good talking to / Layabout / Null / Single mum Barbie / Cloaca maxima / Best friends, large fries and a diet coke / (unamed).		

–––– after their split, DAN joined the FOUR STOREYS

NUMBER ONE CUP

Formed: Chicago, Illinois, USA ... 1993 by SETH COHEN, MICHAEL LENZI and PAT O'CONNELL. Apparently conceived as a combination of GASTR DEL SOL, UNREST and STEREOLAB stylings, NUMBER ONE CUP was the brainchild of bespectacled intellectual, SETH COHEN, who was contacted by MICHAEL LENZI and PAT O'CONNELL after the pair read about his intentions in a local newspaper article. Signed to 'Flydaddy', the band released their debut album, 'POSSUM TROT PLAN', in Spring '96, to encouraging reviews. With an attention-span challenging twenty tracks, the appeal of the album lay in quieter moments such as 'STRANGE & SILENT STAIRCASE' and 'PATCH KIT', cheesy electric piano and COHEN's wonderfully off-the-cuff lyrics drawing the listener in. Among the noisier stuff, the synth enhanced, soaraway ba-ba-ba melodica of subsequent single, 'DIVEBOMB', was the cream of the crop, preceding the 'KIM CHEE IS CABBAGE' mini-set later that year. 1997 was equally prolific with a handful of singles (including a split affair with RED RED MEAT) and a follow-up album, 'WRECKED BY LIONS' (1997). NUMBER ONE CUP spilled out after one final outing, 'PEOPLE, PEOPLE, WHY ARE WE FIGHTING?' (1999). • **Covers:** THE MONKEY SONG (Mountain Goats) / TEENAGE KICKS (Undertones) / LITTLE JOHNNY JEWEL (Television).

Album rating: POSSUM TROT PLAN (*6) / KIM CHEE IS CABBAGE mini (*4) / WRECKED BY LIONS (*4) / PEOPLE, PEOPLE, WHY ARE WE FIGHTING? (*5)

SETH COHEN – vocals, guitar / **MICHAEL LENZI** – drums / **PATRICK O'CONNELL** – guitar / **JOHN PRZYBOROWSKI** – bass; repl. PAT 'TIGER' REIS + JENNI SNYDER

		not iss.	Sweet Pea
Jun 94.	(7") **CONNECTICUT. /**	-	☐
Sep 94.	(7"ep) **INDIE SOFTCORE DENIAL**	-	☐
1994.	(7") **THE MONKEY SONG. /**	-	☐

		Flydaddy	Flydaddy
Nov 95.	(cd) <(FLY 012)> **POSSUM TROT PLAN**	☐	Aug95

– Birth of a gasser / Just let go / Autumn lever / No particular style / 'Til Tuesday / Aspirin burns / Outboard motors / Why did you piss yourself? / Strange & silent staircase / Static / Divebomb / Pocket / Seminar for backward pupils / Let me know / Patch kit / Apple cider / Lustrous poppies / Ohio arts / She pays the numbers / & Nico.

		Blue Rose	Flydaddy
Feb 96.	(7"/c-s) (BRRC 1003-7/-4) **DIVEBOMB. / THE QUIET ASTRONAUT**	☐	-
	(cd-s+=) (BRRC 1003-2) – Lustrous poppies (German robot mix) / Joe the lion.		
Jul 96.	(7"/c-s) (BRRC 1005-7/-4) **JUST LET GO. / THE BLACK CHOPPERS' CRY**	☐	-
	(cd-s+=) (BRRC 1005-2) – Premium invisible.		
Nov 96.	(m-cd) <FLY 021-2> **KIM CHEE IS CABBAGE EP**	-	☐
	– Malcolm's X-ray picnic / Not quite reading / Caught sliding / The house is falling down / Stereo / High diver / As men will. (UK-iss.Apr00; same as US)		
Mar 97.	(7") (FLY 019-7) **THE TONGUE OF 2 AM. / Red Red Meat: Milk For The Mechanics**		-

		Blue Rose	Flydaddy
Mar 97.	(7") (BRRC 1014-7) **MONKEY SONG. / MALCOLM'S X-RAY PICNIC**	☐	-
	(cd-s+=) (BRRC 1014-3) – Not quite reading / High diver.		

–––– (MALCOLM'S X-RAY PICNIC also issued on 7" on 'Derivative')

May 97.	(7"red) (BRRC 1007-7) **EASE BACK DOWN. / PARIS**	☐	-
	(cd-s+=) (BRRC 1007-2) – The tongue of 2 a.m. / (+1).		
Jun 97.	(cd/lp) (BRRC 1013-2/-1) <FLY 018> **WRECKED BY LIONS**	☐	Mar97

– Ease back down / Backlit / Chisel / Paris / Bright orange fireball sun / Black choppers cry / Astronaut / Waiting on the lions / Maybe there's a highway / Tree song / Concordia / Malcolm's x-ray picnic / Flickers and flames / So inclined / Three miles from talent. (cd re-iss. Apr00; same as US)

Oct 97.	(7") (BRRC 1009-5) **MONEY PIT VOL.1. /**	☐	-

–––– **KURT VOLK** – bass; repl. PRZYBOROWSKI

		Cooking Vinyl	Flydaddy
May 99.	(7"m) (FRY 082) **REMOTE CONTROL. / TEENAGE KICKS / LITTLE JOHNNY JEWEL**	☐	-
May 99.	(cd) (COOKCD 179) <FLY 028> **PEOPLE PEOPLE WHY ARE WE FIGHTING**	☐	☐

– (Who awaits) The countdown? / Vintage male singer / High diver / Ice melts around my battery / What does it mean? / Canada disappears / 3 stars / Remote control / Caught on the crown / The low sparks / Unison bends / Why are we fighting?

N.Y. LOOSE

Formed: Manhattan, New York, USA ... 1993 as LOOSE by vocalist/guitarist, BRIJETTE WEST, DANNY NORDAHL and drummer JOHN MELVILLE. With another band already operating under that name, the pair were forced to prefix their moniker with NY prior to the release of a self-financed debut single, 'BITCH'. A potted history of streetwise punk/New Wave from the Big Apple's skool of kool, the track kicked the stagnant Grunge-fixated US indie squarely in the bollocks. BRIJETTE's tough-talking patter and feminist invective also had the critics chattering, some even daring to compare her with COURTNEY LOVE. Bolstering the line-up with two battle-scarred veterans of the NY scene, GARY SUNSHINE (formerly of the blistering but criminally overlooked CIRCUS OF POWER), BRIJETTE and Co delivered two further 45's, 'GREEN LIGHT SEMAPHORE' and 'SPIT', the latter a one-off for Chris Parry's offshoot label, 'Non-Fiction'. After a period of label-less instability, the hard-bitten quartet found a home at 'Hollywood' (well, the company, that is) and finally got round to freeing up a debut long-player, 'YEAR OF THE RAT', in '96. Containing a brilliant cover of the Velvet Underground's 'SUNDAY MORNING', although the set turned out to be their swansong.

Album rating: YEAR OF THE RAT (*6)

BRIJETTE WEST – vocals, guitar / **DANNY NORDAHL** – bass (ex-STIV BATORS) / **JOHN MELVILLE** – drums

		not iss.	Loose
1994.	(7") **BITCH. /**	-	☐

–––– added **GARY SUNSHINE** – guitar (ex-CIRCUS OF POWER)

		not iss.	Holy Plastic
1994.	(7") **GREEN LIGHT SEMAPHORE. /**	-	☐

		Non-Fiction	not iss.
Apr 95.	(7") (YES 12) **SPIT. / PRETTY SUICIDE**	☐	-

		Flipside	Flipside
Sep 95.	(m-cd) <(FLIP 70)> **LOOSEN UP**	☐	Apr95

– The desperate hopeful / Loosen up / James / The late 20th Century blues / Monolith kids.

–––– **WEST + NORDAHL** recruited **MARC DIAMOND** – guitar + **PETE LLOYD** – drums

		Polydor	Hollywood
Sep 96.	(cd) <(162049-2)> **YEAR OF THE RAT**	☐	☐

– Pretty suicide / Rip me up / Broken / Apathy is golden / Dragonfly / Sunday morning / Detonator / Song for Margo / Kiss my wheels / Hide / Trash the given chance / Spit.

–––– the group have since split

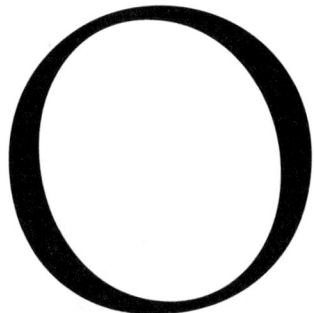

OASIS

Formed: Manchester, England ... summer 1992, by frontman LIAM GALLAGHER, rhythm guitarist PAUL 'BONEHEAD' ARTHURS, bassist PAUL McGUIGAN and drummer TONY McCARROLL. Initially called RAIN, they were soon joined by LIAM's older brother NOEL who had worked as a roadie for The INSPIRAL CARPETS. He was also a budding songwriter/guitarist with a concrete self-belief and after a year of rehearsals and occasional local gigs, they were signed by Creation's ALAN McGEE, after the eagle-eared Scotsman clocked them at a Glasgow gig in mid-1993. With a groundswell of interest not witnessed since the heady early days of The STONE ROSES, OASIS secured a near UK Top 30 placing with 'SUPERSONIC', a sneering, leering anthem with lyrics that SHAUN RYDER would've been proud to call his own. Later that summer the band released the follow-up, 'SHAKER MAKER', a rather tame effort in comparison which appeared to be modelled on the NEW SEEKERS' chestnut, 'I'd Like To Teach The World To Sing'. Nevertheless, what the single lacked in originality, it made up for in controversy and the stage was set for OASIS' first Top 10 hit, the classic 'LIVE FOREVER'. A life-affirming rush celebrating the strength of the human spirit, the song was lauded as single of the year, closely followed by the epochal debut album, 'DEFINITELY MAYBE' (1994). There were no maybes about it, this album defined an era in the same way that The SEX PISTOLS (an obvious influence) focused the frustrations of a generation with 'Never Mind The Bollocks', it's just a pity that the dubious 'Britpop' era spawned an interminable glut of production line indie chancers. The record opens on the same wave of freefall exhilaration as say, 'Exile On Main Street', (The ROLLING STONES were another oft cited influence), 'ROCK'N'ROLL STAR' with a palpable sense of what it actually means to want fame that badly. The feeling that this was "for real, man", never lets up until the last track fades, a visceral, exhaustive listen and one of the most consistent debut albums ever released. Another highlight from the album, the T.REX-esque nihilism of 'CIGARETTES AND ALCOHOL' was the next single, peaking at No.7 in late '94. Basically, OASIS were like all your favourite bands rolled into one, a kind of potted history of rock, NOEL having a unique talent for constructing classic songs that seemed somehow familiar yet annoyingly difficult to pin down. On top of this, LIAM was a natural, his piercing stare and cooly motionless stage presence coupled with his inimitably lethargic sneer a vital component of OASIS' rock'n'roll juggernaut. That Christmas the band narrowly missed No.1 with the string-laden, overtly BEATLES-esque 'WHATEVER', a poppier effort that hinted at the band's future direction. By this point, OASIS were a headline act, the scramble for tickets that accompanied any announcement of a gig becoming all too familiar over the next few years. As would the brothers' press profile, their loudmouth self-aggrandising and embarrassingly public fisticuffs becoming a regular feature of OASIS' increasingly cartoonish image. The first casualty of the well documented in-fighting was McCARROLL, his place in the drum seat subsequently filled by ALAN WHITE. The boasting was backed up by consistently strong material, however, and in the Spring of '95, OASIS deservedly scored their first No.1 with the soaring, yearning 'SOME MIGHT SAY'. The band's single releases had always been good value for money, the B-sides usually better than most indie bands' half-arsed lead tracks. This release was no exception, containing the affecting 'TALK TONIGHT' (NOEL on vocals) and the brilliant melodic noise of 'ACQUIESCE', arguably one of the group's finest tracks. Thus the stage was set for the media-created battle with the recently revitalised BLUR, both bands releasing a single simultaneously that August. In the event, despite the verbal jousting, BLUR took the top spot with 'Country House', OASIS forced to bite their tongue and, erm, 'ROLL WITH IT' at No.2. The Mancs had the last laugh, however, when their follow-up album '(WHAT'S THE STORY) MORNING GLORY' (1995) proceeded to sell multi-millions, catapulting OASIS into the musical stratosphere alongside U2 etc., something unheard of for a group who started out as, basically, another guitar band from Manchester. While the album lacked the serrated edge and amphetamine rush of the debut, the songwriting was once again faultless, tracks like 'WONDERWALL' (almost a Christmas No.1), 'DON'T LOOK BACK IN ANGER', and 'CHAMPAGNE SUPERNOVA' reflecting a newfound maturity and a more coffee-table friendly pop-rock sound. The rapid ascent of the GALLAGHER's continued the following year, with awards galore and a significant dent into the US market. The latter wasn't achieved without some cost to the band, however, as LIAM and NOEL had their most serious and most widely reported fracas to date, LIAM flying home midway through a US tour amid rumours that the band had split. It was merely a case of another day, another fight however, and the band went on to break British concert attendance records with two sell-out shows at Knebworth in August ('96). Early the following year, NOEL was the featured vocalist on The CHEMICAL BROTHERS' chart-topper, 'Setting Sun', effective psychedelia and right on. Return single in '97, 'D'YOU KNOW WHAT I MEAN?' hit No.1 and was reputed to have amassed UK sales of 162,000 copies on its first day of release (19th July). Shortly afterwards, their third album 'BE HERE NOW' was finally in the shops, the hype and media attention the record (and the brothers) received paying off big-time with a massive selling chart topper (No.2 in America). Probably its finest four minutes, 'STAND BY ME', surprisingly failed to make No.1, the album was also marked as a disappointment by some and was considered underwhelming to say the least. The posturing and epic feel of '(WHAT'S THE STORY) . . .' were still there but the record sounded like a parody of OASIS, if that's not a contradiction in terms. While the album broke records with its first day sales figures, it has hardly achieved the same momentum as its predecessor. A stop-gap collection of B-sides and rarities, 'THE MASTERPLAN' (1998), did little for any obsessed fan who already owned all the singles. In May '99, former drummer TONY McCARROLL won an out of court settlement of half a million – £18m for unpaid royalties was the figure he originally wanted. The old band took time out for the rest of the 90's (BONEHEAD and GUIGSY also bailed out), although the GALLAGHER brothers were never far away from controversy and the tabloids. 'STANDING ON THE SHOULDER OF GIANTS' (2000) proved that OASIS were in for the long haul, a studied, immaculately professional effort which indulged NOEL's passion for classic psychedelia while grafting on just enough contemporary flourishes to make it relevant. Hardly the rebellious ball of sonic phlegm we all knew and loved, then, but no doubt the first in a series of passable 30-something efforts designed to please their already ageing fanbase. Live set 'FAMILIAR TO MILLIONS' (2000) merely confirmed the fact, a Wembley Stadium gig which underlined the band's stodgy reliability. Even LIAM's wildcard rantings have become somewhat predictable if no less amusing. Previewed by the regal, spring-coiled riffing of 'THE HINDU TIMES', the much heralded 'HEATHEN CHEMISTRY' (2002) held few surprises save perhaps LIAM's charming, countrified 'SONGBIRD'. The rest was NOEL putting in a solid day at the office with reasonably efficient results; the requisite careworn ballad, 'LITTLE BY LITTLE' hit No.2, while the album itself hit No.1; yet big brother's insistence on a bombastic production did the band few favours. • **Songwriters:** NOEL, except I AM THE WALRUS + HELTER SKELTER (Beatles) / CUM ON FEEL THE NOIZE (Slade) / STREET FIGHTING MAN (Rolling Stones) / FEELIN' LONELY by Noel (Small Faces) / HEY HEY MY MY (INTO THE BLACK) (Neil Young). • **Trivia:** NOEL wrote 'SLIDE AWAY' on a Les Gibson guitar, which he bought from friend JOHNNY MARR (ex-Smiths) and which was once the property of PETE TOWNSHEND (The Who). After a long on-off relationship, LIAM married actress/singer, PATSY KENSIT. He has since divorced and is the beau of NICOLE APPLETON (of ALL SAINTS).

Album rating: DEFINITELY MAYBE (*10) / (WHAT'S THE STORY) MORNING GLORY? (*10) / BE HERE NOW (*7) / THE MASTERPLAN compilation (*7) / STANDING ON THE SHOULDER OF GIANTS (*6) / FAMILIAR TO MILLIONS (*5) / HEATHEN CHEMISTRY (*7)

LIAM GALLAGHER (b.21 Sep'72) – vocals / **NOEL GALLAGHER** (b.29 May'67) – guitar / **PAUL 'BONEHEAD' ARTHURS** (b.23 Jun'65) – guitar / **PAUL McGUIGAN** (b.19 May'71) – guitar / **TONY McCARROLL** – drums

		Creation	Epic
Apr 94.	(7") *(CRE 176)* <55332> **SUPERSONIC. / TAKE ME AWAY**	31	Jul94
	(12"+=) *(CRE 176T)* – I will believe (live).		
	(cd-s++=) *(CRECD 176)* – Columbia (demo).		
	(re-iss. Nov96 c-s repl.7" as so below; same); hit No.47)		
	(re-iss. Mar00 on 'Big Brother'; RKIDSCD 010)		
Jun 94.	(7"/c-s) *(CRE/+CS 182)* **SHAKERMAKER. / D'YER WANNA BE A SPACEMAN?**	11	–
	(12"+=) *(CRE 182T)* – Alive (demo).		
	(cd-s++=) *(CRECD 182)* – Bring it on down (live).		
	(re-iss. Nov96; same); hit No.48)		
	(re-iss. Mar00 on 'Big Brother'; RKIDSCD 011)		
Aug 94.	(7"/c-s) *(CRE/+CD 185)* **LIVE FOREVER. / UP IN THE SKY (acoustic)**	10	–
	(12"+=) *(CRE 185T)* – Cloudburst.		
	(cd-s++=) *(CRECD 185)* – Supersonic (live).		
	(re-iss. Nov96; same); hit No.42)		
	(re-iss. Mar00 on 'Big Brother'; RKIDSCD 012)		
Aug 94.	(cd/c/d-lp) *(CRE CD/MC/LP 169)* <66431> **DEFINITELY MAYBE**	1	58 Jan95
	– Rock'n'roll star / Shakermaker / Live forever / Up in the sky / Columbia / Supersonic / Bring it down / Cigarettes and alcohol / Digsy's dinner / Slide away / Married with children. *(d-lp+=)* – Sad song. *(re-iss. Nov96 as '. . .SINGLES BOX – SILVER' cd/5xcd-s-box; CREDM 001/002); hit No.23) (cd re-iss. Feb00; same) (re-iss. Mar00 on 'Big Brother' cd/md/c/lp; RKID CD/MC/MC/LP 006)*		
Oct 94.	(7"/c-s) *(CRE/+CS 190)* **CIGARETTES AND ALCOHOL. / I AM THE WALRUS (live)**	7	–
	(12"+=) *(CRE 190T)* – Fade away.		
	(cd-s++=) *(CRECD 190)* – Listen up.		
	(re-iss. Nov96; same); hit No.38)		
	(re-iss. Mar00 on 'Big Brother'; RKIDSCD 013)		
Dec 94.	(7"/c-s) *(CRE/+CS 195)* **WHATEVER. / (IT'S GOOD) TO BE FREE**	3	–
	(12"+=) *(CRE 195T)* – Slide away.		
	(cd-s++=) *(CRECD 195)* – Half the world away.		
	(re-iss. Nov96; same); hit No.34)		
	(re-iss. Mar00 on 'Big Brother'; RKIDSCD 014)		
—	after a punch-up McCARROLL left and was replaced by drummer **ALAN WHITE** (b.26 May'72, London) (ex-IDHA) and brother of STEVE WHITE (long-time sticksman with PAUL WELLER)		

OASIS (cont)

Apr 95. (7"/c-s) *(CRE/+CS 204)* **SOME MIGHT SAY. / TALK TONIGHT** `1` `-`
(12"+=) *(CRE 204T)* – Acquiesce.
(cd-s+=) *(CRECD 204)* – Headshrinker.
(re-iss. Nov96; same); hit No.40)
(re-iss. Mar00 on 'Big Brother'; RKIDSCD 015)

— their first 5 singles also re-entered UK Top 60 in Jun'95

Aug 95. (7"/c-s) *(CRE/+CS 212)* **ROLL WITH IT. / IT'S BETTER, PEOPLE** `2` `-`
(12"+=) *(CRE 212T)* – Rockin' chair.
(cd-s+=) *(CRECD 212)* – Live forever (live).
(re-iss. Nov96; same)hit No.55)
(re-iss. Mar00 on 'Big Brother'; RKIDSCD 016)

Oct 95. (cd/c/d-lp) *(CRE CD/MC/LP 189) <67351>* **(WHAT'S THE STORY) MORNING GLORY?** `1` `4`
– Hello / Roll with it / Wonderwall / Don't look back in anger / Hey now! / Some might say / Cast no shadow / She's electric / Morning glory / Champagne supernova. *(d-lp+=)* – Bonehead's bank holiday. *(re-iss. Nov96 as '…SINGLES BOX – GOLD' cd/5xcd-s-box; CREMG 001/002); hit No.24) (re-iss. Mar00 on 'Big Brother' cd/md/c/lp; RKID CD/MD/MC/LP 007)*

Oct 95. (7"/c-s) *(CRE/+CS 215)* **WONDERWALL / ROUND ARE WAY** `2` `-`
(12"+=) *(CRE 215T)* – The swamp song.
(cd-s+=) *(CRECD 215)* – The masterplan.
(re-iss. Nov96; same); hit No.36)
(re-iss. Mar00 on 'Big Brother'; RKIDSCD 017)

Jan 96. (cd-s) *<49K 78216>* **WONDERWALL / ROUND ARE WAY / TALK TONIGHT / ROCKIN' CHAIR / I AM THE WALRUS (live)** `-` `8`

— NOEL also part of one-off supergroup The SMOKIN' MOJO FILTERS alongside PAUL WELLER and PAUL McCARTNEY. They had Top 20 hit with 'COME TOGETHER'.

Feb 96. (7"/c-s) *(CRE/+CS 221)* **DON'T LOOK BACK IN ANGER. / STEP OUT** `1` `-`
(12"+=) *(CRE 221T)* – Underneath the sky.
(cd-s++=) *(CRECD 221)* – Cum on feel the noize.
(re-iss. Nov96; same); hit No.53)
(re-iss. Mar00 on 'Big Brother'; RKIDSCD 018)

Jul 96. (cd-s) *<34K 78356>* **DON'T LOOK BACK IN ANGER / CUM ON FEEL THE NOIZE** `-` `55`

— NOEL met up with great pensmith and fan! BURT BACHARACH who wanted to do a collaboration. He also refused to accept his Ivor Novello award for best songwriter of the year, after he was told it would be shared with rivals BLUR. In Aug'96, NOEL objected to The SMURFS releasing 'WONDERWALL' on their album.

Jul 97. (7"/c-s) *(CRE/+CS 256)* **D'YOU KNOW WHAT I MEAN? / STAY YOUNG** `1` `-`
(12"+=) *(CRE 256T)* – Angel child (demo).
(cd-s+=) *(CRESCD 256)* – Heroes.
(re-iss. Mar00 on 'Big Brother'; RKIDSCD 019)

Aug 97. (cd/c/lp) *(CRECD/CCRE/CRELP 219) <68530>* **BE HERE NOW** `1` `2`
– D'you know what I mean? / My big mouth / Magic pie / Stand by me / I hope I think I know / Girl in the dirty shirt / Fade in-out / Don't go away / Be here now / All around the world / It's gettin' better (man) / All around the world (reprise). *(re-iss. Mar00 on 'Big Brother' cd/md/c/lp; RKID CD/MD/MC/LP 008)*

Sep 97. (7"/c-s) *(CRE/+CS 278)* **STAND BY ME. / (I GOT) THE FEVER** `2` `-`
(12"+=) *(CRE 278T)* – My sister lover.
(cd-s+=) *(CRESCD 278)* – Going nowhere.
(re-iss. Mar00 on 'Big Brother'; RKIDSCD 020)

Jan 98. (7"/c-s) *(CRE/+CS 282)* **ALL AROUND THE WORLD. / THE FAME** `1` `-`
(12"+=) *(CRE 282T)* – Flashbox.
(cd-s++=) *(CRESCD 282)* – Street fighting man.
(re-iss. Mar00 on 'Big Brother'; RKIDSCD 021)

Nov 98. (cd/d-lp)(c) *(CRE CD/LP 241)(C-CRE 241) <69647>* **THE MASTERPLAN** (compilation) `2` `51`
– Acquiesce / Underneath the sky / Talk tonight / Going nowhere / Fade away / The swamp song / I am the walrus / Listen up / Rockin' chair / Half the world away / (It's good) To be free / Stay young / Headshrinker / The masterplan. *(cd re-iss. Feb00; same) (re-iss. Mar00 on 'Big Brother' cd/md/c/lp; RKID CD/MD/MC/LP 009)*

— now without BONEHEAD who left after supplying his part to the forthcoming album (GUIGSY also bailed out, his replacement being **ANDY BELL** (ex-HURRICANE #1, ex-RIDE)

— In Oct'99, LIAM GALLAGHER was credited with STEVE CRADDOCK (of OCEAN COLOUR SCENE) on the UK Top 10 (JAM) tribute double-A side single, 'CARNATION' (flipped with BUFFALO TOM and 'Going Underground')

— added **GEM ARCHER** – guitar (ex-HEAVY STEREO)

Big Brother   Epic

Feb 00. (7"/c-s) *(RKID/+CS 001)* **GO LET IT OUT. / LET'S ALL MAKE BELIEVE** `1` `-`
(12"+=)(cd-s+=) *(RKID 001T)(RKIDSCD 001)* – As long as they've got) Cigarettes in Hell.

Feb 00. (cd/c/lp) *(RKID CD/MC/LP 002) <63586>* **STANDING ON THE SHOULDER OF GIANTS** `1` `24` Mar00
– Fuckin' in the bushes / Go let it out / Who feels love? / Put yer money where your mouth is / Little James / Gas panic! / Where did it all go wrong? / Sunday morning call / I can see a liar / Roll it over.

Apr 00. (7"/c-s) *(RKID/+CS 003)* **WHO FEELS LOVE? / ONE WAY ROAD** `4` `-`
(12"+=)(cd-s+=) *(RKID 003T)(RKIDSCD 003)* – Helter skelter (live).

Jul 00. (7"/c-s) *(RKID/+CS 004)* **SUNDAY MORNING CALL. / CARRY US ALL** `4` `-`
(12"+=)(cd-s+=) *(RKID 004T)(RKIDSCD 004)* – Full on.

Nov 00. (d-cd/c/t-lp) *(RKID CD/MC/LP 005) <85267>* **FAMILIAR TO MILLIONS (live)** `5` `-`
– Fuckin' in the bushes / Go let it out / Who feels love? / Supersonic / Shakermaker / Acquiesce / Step out / Gas panic! / Roll with it / Stand by me / Wonderwall / Cigarettes and alcohol / Don't look back in anger / Live forever / Hey hey, my my (into the black) / Champagne supernova / Rock'n'roll star / Helter skelter. *(cd re-iss. Oct01; RKIDCD 005X)*

Apr 02. (7") *(RKID 23)* **THE HINDU TIMES. / JUST GETTING OLDER** `1` `-`
(12"+=)(cd-s+=) *(RKID 23T)(RKIDSCD 23)* – Idler's dream.

Jun 02. (7") *(RKID 24)* **STOP CRYING YOUR HEART OUT. / THANK YOU FOR THE GOOD TIMES** `2` `-`
(12"+=)(cd-s+=) *(RKID 24T)(RKIDSCD 24)* – Shout it out loud.

Jul 02. (cd/c/d-lp) *(RKID CD/MC/LP 25) <86586>* **HEATHEN CHEMISTRY** `1` `23`
– The Hindu times / Force of nature / Hung in a bad place / Stop crying your heart out / Songbird / Little by little / A quick peep / (Probably) All in the mind / She is love / Born on a different cloud / Better man.

Sep 02. (7") *(RKID 26)* **LITTLE BY LITTLE. / SHE IS LOVE** `2` `-`
(cd-s+=) *(RKIDSCD 26)* – My generation.

– compilations, etc. –

Mar 00. (cd) *Chrome Dreams; (ABCD 047)* **MAXIMUM OASIS (AN AUDIO BIOGRAPHY)** `-` `-`

OBABEN

Formed: Edinburgh, Scotland … 1998 by songwriter BEN WRIGHT, who studied medieval history at Edinburgh University. Taking their moniker from the Portuguese meaning, "Hey! Ben", OBABEN (basically BEN plus DOM GIBBESON and SAM) delivered their first Mediterranean offering, 'NINETEEN', towards the end of '99. Six months on (and with DOM GOUNDAR, ROB JENKINS, GERARD McLACHAN and a handful of violinists replacing SAM), their surprisingly fresh Jamie Watson-produced debut album for 'Human Condition', 'BLUE EYE' (2000), was met with indifferent reviews – imagine 'The Wicker Man' film set in a Spanish amphitheatre topped off with NEIL HANNON (DIVINE COMEDY) on lead vox and you wouldn't be quite close to their Med/indie-Folk. Follow-up, 'MARBLEHEAD' (2001), continued in the same romantic vein and it was to work out why this eclectic bunch hadn't broke through. Play OBABEN to someone you meet on a foreign holiday and confuse them by saying they come from Scotland(!).

Album rating: BLUE EYE (*8) / MARBLEHEAD (*6)

BEN WRIGHT – vocals, guitars / **DOM GIBBESON** – bass / **SAM** – drums

Human Condition   not iss.

Nov 99. (7") *(HC 0025)* **NINETEEN. / AUTUMN HEART** `-` `-`

— basically **BEN + DOM** with **ROB JENKINS** – lead guitar / **DOM GOUNDAR** – percussion / **GERARD McLACHAN** – drums / plus **GREG MICKELBOROUGH** – string arrangements / **JIM O'TOOLE + GAYLE SWANN + TAROT COUZYN + CARENZA HUGH-JONES** – violins / **LUCY HARDY + FRANCESCA DYMOND + JULIETTE RAWLINS + JOANNA HOWARD** – other vocals

May 00. (cd) *(HCCD 0028)* **BLUE EYE** `-` `-`
– Nineteen / Smash him up / Blink again / A letter / Autumn heart / Kyrie / Northern wind / Saranda / Blue eye.

Apr 01. (cd) *(HCCD 32)* **MARBLEHEAD** `-` `-`
– Intro / Beauty blinds / Sin descanso / Bar to bed / 5 a.m. / Blow up / EC4 / Blink again / Marblehead / Din-o-rush / Columbia road / Luke, who is he? / She tells tales / Sounds and signs / Outro.

May 01. (cd-ep) *(HCCD 33)* **BEAUTY BLINDS / TUESDAY MORNING / PISS TALKERS** `-` `-`

OBLIVIANS

Formed: Memphis, Tennessee, USA … summer '93 by JACK, GREG and ERIC 'OBLIVIAN' (YARBER, CARTWRIGHT and FRIEDL). Instrumentally interchangable, the average OBLIVIANS live set was characterised by much guitar and drum swapping as the trio belted out the filthiest blues/garage groove this side of one-time fellow 'Crypt'-kicker, JON SPENCER. The latter label was home to The OBLIVIANS' debut album, 'SOUL FOOD', a record that boasted warped interpretations of tracks by Lightnin' Hopkins, Dave Clark Five(!) and German one-hit wonders, Trio(!). Weird if not wonderful, the er… trio were wont to invent their own inter-band subdivisions, e.g. GREG OBLIVIAN & THE TIP TOPS, the pseudonymous moniker of 1998's 'HEAD SHOP'. Previous to this, the OBLIVIAN "brothers" had issued two further albums, 'POPULAR FAVOURITES' (1996) and 'PLAY 9 SONGS WITH MR. QUINTRON' (1997). Of late, JACK has found time between jobs as a dishwasher and crate-packer to be part of The COOL JERKS, a garage-punk outfit headed by FORREST HEWES. • **Songwriters:** JACK's 'SO LOW' album in late '98 featured a handful of covers including the New York Dolls' 'TRASH', Memphis Minnie's 'LET ME BE YOUR CHAUFFER' and Otis Rush's 'ALL YOUR LOVIN'.

Album rating: SOUL FOOD (*5) / POPULAR FAVOURITES (*5) / PLAY 9 SONGS WITH MR. QUINTRON mini (*4) / HEAD SHOP by Jack Oblivian (*4) / SO LOW by Jack Oblivian (*5) / THE BEST OF THE WORST 1993-1997 compilation (*7) / MELISSA'S GARAGE REVISITED (*6)

GREG "CARTWRIGHT" OBLIVIAN – guitar, drums, vocals / **ERIC "FRIEDL" OBLIVIAN** – guitar, drums, vocals / **JACK "YARBER" OBLIVIAN** – guitar, drums, vocals

not iss.   Goner

1993. (7"ep) *<2 Gone>* **CALL THE SHOTS EP** `-` `G`
– Vietnam war blues / Jim Cole / No reason to live.

1993. (c) <0 Gone – POB 103> **split w/ IMPALA**
— Cannonball / Make me blue / Nigger rich / Arabian interlude / Blew my cool / Nail driver / Bum a ride / Never change / Plate in my head / Black as coal / Mad lover / (other side by IMPALA).

not iss. Estrus

1994. (7"ep) <ES 756> **NOW FOR THE HARD OF HEARING FROM ... "BLOW THEIR COOL EP"**
— Motorcycle leather boy / Love killed my brain / Blew my cool / Song inside.

not iss. In The Red

1994. (7"m) <ITR 018> **STATIC PARTY. / AND THEN I FUCKED HER / NEVER CHANGE**

not iss. Sympathy..

1994. (10"lp) <SFTRI 304> **OBLIVIANS**
— Can't take another night / Happy blues / Never enough / Feel real good / Plate in my head / Five hour man / Shut my mouth / Show me what you like.

Crypt Crypt

Jan 95. (7") (EFA 11582-7) <CR 044> **SUNDAY YOU NEED LOVE. / JA JA JA**

Feb94

Feb 95. (cd/lp) (EFA 11589-2/-1) <CR 055> **SOUL FOOD**

May94

— Viet Nam war blues / And then I fucked her / Big black hole / Jim Cole / Mad lover / Sunday you need love / Never change / No reason to live / I'm not a sicko, there's a plate in my head / Blew my cool / Cannonball / Nigger rich / Bum a ride / Anyway you want it / Static party.

1995. (10"ep) <UDR 0008-10> **WALTER DANIELS PLAYS WITH MONSIEUR JEFFREY EVANS & THE OBLIVIANS AT MELISSA'S GARAGE**
— It don't take too much / Rockin' in the graveyard / Don't worry / Dearest darling / We're not in it to lose. <(lp/cd re-iss. Nov99 as 'MELISSA'S GARAGE REVISITED'+=; SFTRI 590/+CD)> – Someday my prince will come / The darker the berry / Sticks and stones / Bending like a willow tree.
(above on 'Undone') (below issued on 'Drug Racer')

Jan 96. (7") <(DR 001)> **GO! PILL-POPPER!**
— Pill popper pt.I & II (studio) / Pill popper pt.I & II (live).

1996. (7"m) <CR 053> **STRONG COME ON. / LET HIM TRY / BLACK SEPTEMBER**

Jul 96. (cd/lp) (EFA 12876-2/-1) <CR 065> **POPULAR FAVOURITES**

Oct96

— Christina / Trouble / Leather / Guitar shop asshole / Hey mama, look at sis / Part of your plan / Do the milkshake / The strong come on / She's a hole / Bad man / He's your man / Drill / You better behave / Pinstripe Willie / You fucked me up, you put me down / Emergency. *(cd re-iss. Apr02; same)*

Jul 96. (10"m-lp) <SFTRI 383> **SIX OF THE BEST**
— Clones / No time / What rocknroll is all about / Memphis creep / Something $ nothing / Big black hole / Can't afford you.
(above & below issued on 'Sympathy For The Record Industry')

Aug 96. (cd) <SFTRI 406> **THE SYMPATHY SESSIONS**
— Can't take another night / Happy blues / Never enough / Feel real good / Plate in my head / Five hour man / Shut my mouth / Show me what you like / Clones / No time / What rocknroll is all about / Memphis creep / Something $ nothing / Big black hole / Can't afford you / Kick your ass / No butter for my bread / Show me again.

Aug 96. (7") <SFTRI 412> **KISS YOUR ASS. / NO BUTTER FOR MY BREAD / SHOW ME AGAIN**

Jun 97. (m-lp/m-cd) (EFA/+CD 12892) <82> **PLAY 9 SONGS WITH MR. QUINTRON**
— Feel all right / Live the life / I may be gone / I don't wanna live alone / The final stretch / What's the matter now? / Ride that train / If mother knew / Mary Lou.

not iss. Hate

1997. (7") <hate 7> **KING LOUIE STOMP. / (other by TWO BO'S MANIACS)**

—— in 1998, they also split a single, 'THE JACK', w/ The CRIME KAISERS

– compilations, etc. –

on 'Sympathy For The Record Industry' unless mentioned otherwise

Sep 99. (d-lp/cd) <(SFTRI 584/+CD)> **THE BEST OF THE WORST: 1993-1997**
— Siamese purse / Alcoholic / Indian in me / Tear drop for you / Bald headed woman / Peepin' & hidin' / Don't haunt me / I got something to say / Lady, oh lady / Roadrunner / Hey ma, look at sis / Talk to me / Robot blues / Locomotion / Oh, how to do / Shut my mouth / Losing hand / Pill popper part I & II / Live the life / Alone again, or / Kick your ass / Mad lover / Blew my cool / Never change / Everybody but me.

JACK OBLIVIAN

—— with IMPALA = SCOTT BOMAR – bass / STUART SIKES – drums

Sympathy F Sympathy F

Feb 97. (m-lp/m-cd) <SFTRI 475/+CD> **AMERICAN SLANG**
— American slang / 2000 man / Hustler / Honey, I'm too old for you / Robot lover / Got the funky blues (pts. 1 & 2) / Out of tune / Am. slang (reprise).

Nov 98. (cd) <(SFTRI 535)> **SO LOW**
— Intro – Midnight hour queen / Shake it off / Trash / So low / Downtown / Let me be your chauffer / Mama don't get off / You made me crazy / Human being / All your lovin' / All the way down.

GREG OBLIVIAN & THE TIP TOPS

Mar 98. (lp/cd) <(SFTRI 513/+CD)> **HEAD SHOP**

Jan98

— Watching my baby get ready / Precious one / Twice as deep / Girl with the glasses / Beside you / Bad man / The man you need (close) / Self-indulgent asshole.

OCEAN BLUE

Formed: Hershey, Pennsylvania, USA . . . late 1986 by lyricist/singer, DAVID SCHELZEL, along with STEVE LAU and BOBBY MITTAN; ROB MINNIG being added soon after. From the outset the group seemed to have the right stuff to make it in the indie pop world. They had a good education in late 80's college favourites like ECHO AND THE BUNNYMEN, THE SMITHS, and U2, and were talented musicians and writers. Within two years of their high school conception OB had inked a deal with part- indie label, 'Sire', who released their eponymous debut LP, 'THE OCEAN BLUE' (1989). This was a competent piece which wore its British pop influences on its sleeve, and introduced SCHELZEL's and the bands love of a good melody. It also spawned the singles, 'BETWEEN SOMETHING AND NOTHING', and 'DRIFTING, FALLING', which gained notable airtime on the alternatives stations. Their second album, 'CERULEAN', appeared two years later, showcasing their mix of shoegazing indie with clear breezy melodic pop patterning. Again the band took another two years before releasing their third full-length outing, 'BENEATH THE RHYTHM AND SOUND'. The tweeked and clean production on this album heightened the band's commercial appeal, and made this release by far their most rewarding and lucrative piece, not least due to the single, 'SUBLIME', gaining much attention on MTV. While promoting the set, OB added the musical skills of OED RONNE to the roster. This was also the beginning of the end of LAU's participation with the band. He lasted on to the following year and the release of the EP 'PEACE AND LIGHT' (1994), which was also to be their last recording for 'Sire', and then departed. LAU later commented that his departure from the band was due to his homosexuality, which the rest of the group strongly dismissed as the cause. LAU went on to a successful career in studio production, and eventually to running 'Kinetic' records, and RONNE took over his responsibilities in OB. A contractual void followed for the boys, until they were picked up by 'Mercury', who issued their fourth album, 'SEE' (1996). Again this was a proficient piece which showed a growing maturity in their songwriting, although musically the years had not changed their sound much. Unfortunately the band again came unstuck as the deal with their new paymasters soon ended. Thus 1999 saw OB go all DIY, releasing their fifth full-length affair, 'DAVY JONES' LOCKER', in a limited run of 1000, through their own website. While touring, the band found that the fan-base was still there, and this support gleaned the attention of 'March' records, who signed them up and re-released the album in 2001. • **Covered:** THERE IS A LIGHT THAT NEVER GOES OUT (Smiths).

Album rating: THE OCEAN BLUE (*7) / CERULEAN (*5) / BENEATH THE RHYTHM AND SOUND (*6) / SEE (*5) / DAVY JONES' LOCKER (*5)

DAVID SCHELZEL – vocals, guitar / **STEVE LAU** – keyboards, sax, vocals / **BOBBY MITTAN** – bass / **ROB MINNIG** – drums

Warners Sire

Jul 89. (lp/c/cd) (K 925906-1/-4/-2) <25906> **THE OCEAN BLUE**
— Between something and nothing / Vanity fair / Drifting, falling / The circus animals / Frigid winter days / Just let me know / Love song / Ask me Jon / Awaking to a dream / The office of a busy man / Myron / A familiar face.

Feb 91. (cd/c) <26550> **CERULEAN**
— Breezing up / Cerulean / Marigold / A separate reality / Mercury / A question of travel / When life was easy / The planetarium scene / Falling through the ice / Ballerina out of control / Hurricane amore / I've sung one too many songs . . .

Warners Warners

Sep 93. (cd) <(9362 45369-2)> **BENEATH THE RHYTHM AND SOUND**

Aug93

— Peace of mind / Sublime / Listen, it's gone / Either/or / Bliss is unaware / Ice skating at night / Don't believe everything you hear / Crash / Cathedral bells / The relatives / Emotions ring.

Sep 93. (c-s) <18383> **SUBLIME**

Mar 94. (cd-ep) <41417> **PEACE AND LIGHT**
— Peace of mind / There is a light that never goes on (live) / Don't believe everything you hear (live) / Sea of green.

—— **OED RONNE** – keyboards; repl. LAU

not iss. Polygram

Oct 96. (cd/c) <532982> **SEE**
— Jouissance / Whenever you're around / Out here / Ways and means / My scream / Past future perfect / Slide / 1010 cloud deck / Behind / Bite your lip / Cloudy days / Bye.

not iss. Ocean Blue

Nov 99. (cd) <60044> **DAVY JONES' LOCKER**
— Ayn / Garden song / Denmark / My best friend / Cukaloris / Been down a lot lately / Consolation prize / Cake / Bottle yours / I can't see you / So many reasons / Do you still remember me? / It never, just might.

March March

Dec 00. (cd-ep) (MAR 064) **DENMARK EP**
— Denmark / Walk away / Sweetheart, you're surrounded / Mood swing.

Mar 01. (cd-ep) <MAR 074> **AYN**
— Ayn / Garden song (dawn at New Hope, PA) / Harlequin / New man from Chicago.

OCEAN COLOUR SCENE

Formed: Moseley, Birmingham, England . . .mid-'89 out of The FANATICS, by SIMON FOWLER, DAMON MINCHELLA and OSCAR HARRISON, who released a one-off '45 for the 'Chapter 22' label before recruiting BOYS' guitarist STEVE CRADOCK. In the summer of 1990, OCS found manager JOHN MOSTYN, who signed them to his new '!Phffft' stable. A debut track, 'SWAY', helped secure a joint venture with 'Phonogram' for a follow-up, 'YESTERDAY TODAY'. The latter track breeched the Top 50 in March '91, and, just when it seemed as if a breakthrough was imminent, '!Phffft' was sold during the recording of their JIMMY MILLER-produced debut album. Now on 'Fontana', the momentum was lost as they re-recorded the whole project, a 1992 re-issue of 'SWAY' and the follow-up, 'GIVING IT ALL AWAY' sinking without trace. In April, the aforementioned eponymous album finally surfaced, although it brought criticism for its over-cooked production. After another 45, 'DO YOURSELF A FAVOUR' bombed, the group subsequently found themselves without a recording contract and up to their necks in debt. Aided by lawyer, Michael Thomas, they were successful in persuading

OCEAN COLOUR SCENE (cont) THE GREAT INDIE DISCOGRAPHY The 1990s

Fontana's DAVE BATES to waive the million £'s they were still owing. OCS returned with a support slot to their newfound mate, PAUL WELLER, CRADOCK and FOWLER guested on his Autumn '93 classic 'Wildwood' album; CRADOCK subsequently became an integral part of WELLER's band over the course of the next year. Meanwhile in the summer of '94, OCEAN COLOUR SCENE supported OASIS and completed a 'Fontana' tour of the States supporting HOUSE OF LOVE and The CATHERINE WHEEL. A year later, all group members played for WELLER at some point, with CRADOCK and MINCHELLA guesting on his No.1 album, 'Stanley Road'. 1995 also saw the band recording their long-awaited follow-up album, having earlier signed to 'M.C.A.'. Early in '96 (with WELLER on organ), they scored their first of many Top 20 hits with 'THE RIVERBOAT SONG' (later chosen for Chris Evans' TFI Friday Show theme song). Dropping the indie-dance trappings of old, OCS adopted a heavier, funkier, white-soul/mod sound and a retro image to boot, dominating the charts in the wake of WELLER's massively successful return to a rootsier sound. 'YOU'VE GOT IT BAD' fared even better, followed by a BRENDAN LYNCH-produced album, 'MOSELEY SHOALS' (name of their own studio), which hit the UK Top 3. The record inevitably featured WELLER on a few other tracks and the man augmented the group on their 'Later With Jools Holland' spot. Two further Top 10 smashes, 'THE DAY WE CAUGHT THE TRAIN' (their classiest so far) and 'THE CIRCLE' were culled from the album, an odds'n'sods collection, 'B-SIDES, SEASIDES & FREERIDES' keeping their profile high prior to the release of new material. A couple of Top 5 hits, 'HUNDRED MILE HIGH CITY' and 'TRAVELLERS TUNE', preceded an Autumn '97 album, 'MARCHIN' ALREADY', a lesser work which nevertheless reached the top of the UK charts. An easy target for the critics, only time will tell whether OCS's retro-lite and almost wholly teenage audience can stay the course. 'ONE FROM THE MODERN' (1999), was the next Top 5 album on the retro production line, OCS defiantly standing by their Mod roots while opener and hit single, 'PROFITS IN PEACE', showed they were a caring type of band. 'SO LOW' was the next single. Enough said. Yet one suspects that while there is still an audience for OASIS there will still be an audience for OCEAN COLOUR SCENE, so indistinguishable are their respective markets. No surprise then that the admittedly fairly intoxicating 'UP ON THE DOWNSIDE' single made the UK Top 20, pushing the rather more workmanlike 'MECHANICAL WONDER' (2001) album into the Top 10. After ending the year on this relative high, the band released the obligatory festive period compilation which also reached the UK Top 20. • **Songwriters:** FOWLER lyrics / group music; except DO YOURSELF A FAVOUR (Stevie Wonder & Syreeta) / DAYTRIPPER (Beatles) / etc.

Album rating: OCEAN COLOUR SCENE (*6) / MOSELEY SHOALS (*8) / B-SIDES, SEASIDES & FREERIDES collection (*5) / MARCHIN' ALREADY (*6) / ONE FROM THE MODERN (*5) / MECHANICAL WONDER (*5)

FANATICS

SIMON FOWLER – vocals, acoustic guitar, harmonica / **DAMON MINCHELLA** – bass / **PAUL WILKES** – guitar / **OSCAR HARRISON** – drums, piano, vocals (ex- ECHO BASE) who recd. CAROLINE BULLOCK

		Chapter 22	not iss.
Mar 89.	(12"ep) (12CHAP 38) **SUBURBAN LOVE SONGS**		-
	– Suburban love songs / 1.2.3.4. / My brother Sarah / Tight rope.		

OCEAN COLOUR SCENE

STEVE CRADOCK – guitars, piano, vocals (ex-BOYS; late 80's mods) repl. WILKES

		!Phffft	not iss.
Sep 90.	(7") (FIT 001) **SWAY. / TALK ON**		-
	(ext-12"+=/ext-cd-s+=) (FITX/FITCD 001) – One of these days.		
Mar 91.	(7") (FIT 002) **YESTERDAY TODAY. / ANOTHER GIRL'S NAME / FLY ME**	49	
	(12"+=/cd-s+=) (FITX/FITCD 002) – No one says.		
		Fontana	not iss.
Feb 92.	(7") (OCSS 1) **SWAY. / MY BROTHER SARAH**		-
	(12"+=/cd-s+=) (OCS 112/CD1) – Mona Lisa eyes / Bellechoux.		
Apr 92.	(7") (OCSS 2) **GIVING IT ALL AWAY. / THIRD SHADE OF GREEN**		-
	(12"+=/cd-s+=) (OCS 212/CD2) – Flowers / Don't play.		
Apr 92.	(cd/c/lp) (<512269-2/-4/-1>) **OCEAN COLOUR SCENE**		Sep92
	– Talk on / How about you / Giving it all away / Justine / Do yourself a favour / Third shade of green / Sway / Penny pinching rainy Heaven days / One of these days / Is she coming home / Blue deaf ocean / Reprise. (re-iss. Sep96, hit UK 54)		
May 92.	(7") (OCSS 3) **DO YOURSELF A FAVOUR. / THE SEVENTH FLOOR**		-
	(12"+=/cd-s+=) (OCS 312/CD3) – Patsy in green / Suspended motion.		
		M.C.A.	M.C.A.
Feb 96.	(7"/c-s) (MCS/+C 40021) **THE RIVERBOAT SONG. / SO SAD**	15	-
	(cd-s+=) (MCSTD 40021) – Charlie Brown says.		
Apr 96.	(c-s) (MCSTD 40036) <55217> **YOU'VE GOT IT BAD / I WANNA STAY ALIVE WITH YOU**	7	Jul96
	(cd-s+=) (MCSTD 40036) – Robin Hood / Huckleberry Grove.		
	(cd-s) (MCSXD 40036) – ('A'demo / Here in my heart / Men of such opinion / Beautiful losers.		
Apr 96.	(cd/c/d-lp) (<MCD/MCC/MCA 60008>) **MOSELEY SHOALS**	2	
	– The riverboat song / The day we caught the train / The circle / Lining your pockets / Fleeting mind / Forty past midnight / One for the road / It's my shadow / Policeman and pirates / Downstream / You've got it bad / Get away.		
Jun 96.	(c-s) (MCSC 40046) **THE DAY WE CAUGHT THE TRAIN / THE CLOCK STRUCK 15 HOURS AGO**	4	-
	(cd-s+=) (MCSTD 40046) – I need a love song / Chicken bones and stones.		
	(cd-s) (MCSXD 40046) – ('A'acoustic) / Travellers tune / Justine.		
Sep 96.	(c-s) (MCSC 40077) **THE CIRCLE / MRS JONES**	6	-
	(cd-s+=) (MCSTD 40077) – Cool cool water / Top of the world.		
	(cd-s) (MCSXD 40077) – ('A'acoustic) / Chelsea walk / Alibis / Daytripper (live).		
Mar 97.	(cd/c/d-lp) (<MCD/MCC/MCA 60034>) **B SIDES • SEASIDES & FREERIDES** (compilation)	4	
	– Huckleberry grove / The day we caught the train (acoustic) / Mrs Jones / Top of the world / Here in my heart / I wanna stay alive with you / Robin Hood / Chelsea walk / Outside of a circle / The clock struck 15 hours ago / Alibis / Chicken bones and stones / Cool cool water / Charlie Brown says / Day tripper / Beautiful losers.		
Jun 97.	(7"/c-s) (MCS/+C 40133) **HUNDRED MILE HIGH CITY. / THE FACE SMILES BACK EASILY**	4	-
	(cd-s+=) (MCSTD 40133) – Falling to the floor / Hello Monday.		
Aug 97.	(7"/c-s) (MCS/+C 40144) <Alex 6055> **TRAVELLERS TUNE / SONG FOR THE FRONT ROW**	5	Apr98
	(cd-s+=) (MCSTD 40144) – On the way home / All God's children need travelling shoes.		
Sep 97.	(cd/c/d-lp) (<MCD/MCC/MCA 60048>) **MARCHIN' ALREADY**	1	
	– Hundred mile high city / Better day / Travellers tune / Big star / Debris road / Besides yourself / Get blown away / He's not talking / Foxy's folk faced / All up / Spark and Cindy / Half a dream away / It's a beautiful thing. (<also enhanced-cd; MCD 60053>)		
Nov 97.	(7"/c-s) (MCS/+C 40151) **BETTER DAY. / THE BEST BET ON CHINASKI**	9	-
	(cd-s+=) (MCSTD 40151) – On and on.		
Feb 98.	(7"/c-s) (MCS/+C 40157) **IT'S A BEAUTIFUL THING. / MARINERS WAY**	12	-
	(cd-s+=) (MCSTD 40157) – Going nowhere for a while / Expensive chair.		
	(above featured singer, P.P. ARNOLD)		
		Island	Ark 21
Aug 99.	(c-s/7") (C+/IS 757) **PROFIT IN PEACE. / IF YOU GET YOUR WAY**	13	-
	(cd-s+=) (CID 757) – Flood tide rising.		
Sep 99.	(cd/c/d-lp) (CID/ICT/ILPS 8090) **ONE FROM THE MODERN**	4	-
	– Profit in peace / So low / I am the news / No one at all / Families / Step by step / July / Jane she got excavated / Emily Chambers / Soul driver / The waves / I won't get grazed.		
	In Oct'99, STEVE CRADOCK was credited with LIAM GALLAGHER (of OASIS) on UK Top 10 (JAM) tribute double-A single, 'CARNATION' (flipped with 'Going Underground' by BUFFALO TOM)		
Nov 99.	(c-s/7") (C+/IS 759) **SO LOW. / HOPING YOU'RE MAKING IT TOO**	34	-
	(cd-s+=) (CID 759) – The inheritors.		
	(cd-s+=) (CIDX 759) – Soul driver / Jane she got excavated.		
Jun 00.	(c-s/7") (C+/IS 763) **JULY. / I AM THE NEWS**	31	-
	(cd-s+=) (CID 763) – ('A'-forza moderna mix).		
	(cd-s+=) (CIDX 763) – This understanding.		
Mar 01.	(c-s/7") (C+/IS 774) **UP ON THE DOWNSIDE. / THESE ARE THE ONES**	19	-
	(cd-s+=) (CID 774) – Take you back.		
Apr 01.	(cd/lp) (CID/ILPS 8104) <81007-2> **MECHANICAL WONDER**	7	May01
	– Up on the downside / In my field / Sail on my boat / Biggest thing / We made it more / Give me a letter / Mechanical wonder / You are amazing / If I gave you my heart / Can't get back to the bassline. (UK+=) – Something for me.		
Jul 01.	(7") (IS 779) **MECHANICAL WONDER. / FIRE ON THE WIND**	49	-
	(cd-s+=) (CID 779) – I was.		
Nov 01.	(cd/d-lp) (CID/ILPS 8111) <810077> **SONGS FOR THE FRONT ROW – THE BEST OF OCEAN COLOUR SCENE** (compilation)	16	
	– The riverboat song / The day we caught the train / One for the road / Circle / You've got it bad / Hundred mile high city / Better day / Travellers tune / Get blown away / It's a beautiful thing / Profit in peace / So low / July / Up on the downside / Mechanical wonder / Huckleberry grove / Robin Hood (live) / Crazy lowdown ways.		
	(d-cd+=; CIDD 8111) – LIVE AT STIRLING CASTLE		
Dec 01.	(7") (IS 787) **CRAZY LOWDOWN WAYS. / BEST FRIENDS AND LOVERS**	64	-
	(cd-s+=) (CID 787) – Come home.		

OCTOPUS

Formed: Shotts, Lanarkshire, Scotland ... 1995 by frontman MARC SHEARER and guitarist ALAN McSEVENEY. Disillusioned by the Glasgow indie scene, the pair took off to London with new recruits CAMERON MILLER (an old school mate) and OLIVER GRASSEL. Having played several gigs down south, OCTOPUS were eyeballed by DAVID FRANCOLINI (ex-LEVITATION drummer), who duly despatched their demo to Andy Ross at EMI's 'Food' offshoot. Immediately impressed (as he was with The SUPERNATURALS), Ross signed the band and issued their debut single, 'MAGAZINE', early in 1996. As a live act, OCTOPUS were joined on stage by four other members (tentacles, you could say) including harmonica-player NICK REYNOLDS, son of the Great Train Robber, Bruce Reynolds; a piece for the press/media at the time. OCTOPUS' sophomore effort, 'YOUR SMILE', complete with melodic, guitar-rock appeal, certainly brightened up the Top 50. That September, the band went one better and into the Top 40 courtesy of 'SAVED', although the accompanying debut album, 'FROM A TO B', was given short-shrift on several reviews. By 1997, all four were looking for other outlets.

Album rating: FROM A TO B (*5)

MARC SHEARER – vocals, guitar / **ALAN McSEVENEY** – guitar / **CAMERON MILLER** – bass / **OLIVER GRASSEL** – drums

OCTOPUS (cont) — THE GREAT INDIE DISCOGRAPHY — The 1990s

			Food	not iss.
Mar 96.	(7") (FOOD 68)	**MAGAZINE. / ADRENALINA**		-
	(cd-s+=) (CDFOOD 68) – (Untitled) / Unicorns and eiderdowns.			
Jun 96.	(7") (FOOD 78)	**YOUR SMILE. / KING FOR A DAY**	42	-
	(cd-s+=) (CDFOOD 78) – Catboy.			
Sep 96.	(7") (FOOD 84)	**SAVED. / I KNOW WHO I AM**	40	-
	(cd-s+=) (CDFOODS 84) – Guestlist.			
	(cd-s) (CDFOOD 84) – ('A'side) / No answer / What did you do today? / True, true, true.			
Sep 96.	(cd/c/lp) (FOOD CD/MC/LPX 18)	**FROM A TO B**		-
	– Your smile / Everyday kiss / If you want to give me more / King for a day / Adrenalina / Instrumental 1 / Jealousy / Magazine / From A to B / Instrumental 2 / Saved / Wait & see / Theme from Joy Pop / Night song / In this world.			
Nov 96.	(7") (FOOD 87)	**JEALOUSY. / THIS BOOK'S FOR YOU**	59	-
	(cd-s+=) CDFOODS 87) – Neon lights.			
	(cd-s) (CDFOOD 87) – ('A'side) / Everyday kiss (live) / Your smile / Theme from Yes Yes Yes.			

— disbanded the following year

OEDIPUSSY
(see under ⇒ PERFECT DISASTER; in 80's section)

OF MONTREAL

Formed: Athens, Georgia, USA . . . 1996 around the nucleus of songwriter KEVIN BARNES, with additional help provided by ELF POWER's BRYAN HELIUM and DEREK ALMSTEAD. OF MONTREAL were a second generation 'Elephant 6' outfit, a collective which included such bands as APPLES IN STEREO and OLIVIA TREMOR CONTROL. After leaving his native Athens following a relationship split with a woman of Montreal (hence the band's name), BARNES travelled around the northern cities of Minneapolis and Cleveland looking for suitable band mates to fulfil his weird musical ideas, eventually heading South and home where he recruited BARNES and ALMSTEAD. Debuting with the LP, 'CHERRY PEEL', (1997), BARNES heralded his unique talent on to the indie pop scene. The set – which remains one of the high points of the group's career – showed all the elements which would make them one of the more influential of their peers. Heavily influenced by the perfect pop melodies of the BEATLES and BEACH BOYS, OF MONTREAL also added their own dashes of revived psychedelia and circus type stylings. Hot on its heels was the EP, 'THE BIRD WHO ATE THE RABBIT'S FLOWERS' (1997) and the companion mini-effort 'THE BIRD WHO CONTINUES TO EAT THE RABBIT'S FLOWERS' (1997), which, although sound pieces, were not essential OF M, displaying more of their earlier lo-fi light garage pop sound; the latter contained a notable cover of the Who's 'DISGUISES'. At this point HELIUM departed to devote more time to his own sonic experimentalism with ELF POWER. The revolving door roster was kept strong with the introduction of DOTTIE ALEXANDER and JAMEY HUGGINS, although the group's sophomore full-length outing, 'THE BEDSIDE DRAMA: A PETITE DRAMA' (1998), was more of a one-man project for BARNES. The outfit's sound was bolstered by the multi-talented A.C. FORRESTER for their brilliant opus work 'THE GAY PARADE'. This set exemplified the perfection for which whimsical indie pop bands sought. It seemed that the band could do no wrong and as a nod to the fans they put out the compilation work, 'HORSE AND ELEPHANT EATERY (NO ELEPHANTS ALLOWED): THE SINGLES AND SONGLES ALBUM' (2000), which alongside their own material, also contained such beauties as their interpretation of KINKS' track 'THE WORLD KEEPS GOING 'ROUND'. This was followed by the not-quite-as-great nascent OF MONTREAL rarities collection, 'THE EARLY FOUR TRACK RECORDINGS' (2001); worthy of note is that each of these old tunes were given an amusing title relating to a fictional bathtime episode of the actor Dustin Hoffman. The same year also saw the delivery of the stellar album proper, 'COQUELICOT ASLEEP IN THE POPPIES: A VARIETY OF WHIMSICAL VERSE', a record which provided another good bout of BARNES' unpretentious weird and wonderful storytelling on tracks such as 'LECITHIN'S TALE OF A DNA EXPERIMENT THAT WENT TERRIBLY AWRY'. Their subsequent offering, 'ALDHILS ARBORETUM' (2002), witnessed an adroit turning towards a hookier filled pop rock sound. • **Covered:** I FELT LIKE SMASHING MY FACE THROUGH . . . . (Yoko Ono) / A SPOONFUL OF SUGAR (Gants).

Album rating: CHERRY PEEL (*6) / BEDSIDE DRAMA: A PETITE TRAGEDY (*6) / THE BIRD WHO CONTINUES TO EAT THE RABBIT'S FLOWERS compilation (*6) / THE GAY PARADE (*6) / HORSE & ELEPHANT EATERY compilation (*6) / THE EARLY FOUR TRACK RECORDINGS early demos (*4) / COQUELICOT ASLEEP IN THE POPPIES (*7) / ALDHILS ARBORETUM (*6)

KEVIN BARNES – vocals, guitar / with **BRYAN HELIUM** – bass (of ELF POWER) / **DEREK ALMSTEAD** – drums

			not iss.	Bar/None
Aug 97.	(cd) <AHAON 089>	**CHERRY PEEL**	-	
	– Everything disappears when you come around / Baby I can't stop your memory / When you're loved like you are / Don't ask me to explain / In dreams I dance with you / Sleeping in the beetle bug / Tim I wish you were born a girl / Montreal / This feeling (Derek's theme) / I was watching your eyes / Springtime is the season / At night trees aren't sleeping / You've got a gift.			
			Kindercore	Kindercore
Oct 97.	(7"ep/cd-ep) <KC 015/+CD>	**THE BIRD WHO ATE THE RABBIT'S FLOWER EP**	-	
	– You are an airplane / The inner light / When a man is in love with a man / If I faltered slightly twice / Disguises.			

— basically **BARNES** solo

Jun 98.	(cd) <KC 022CD>	**BEDSIDE DRAMA: A PETITE TRAGEDY**	-	
	– One of the very few of a kind / Happy yellow bumblebee / Little viola hidden in the orchestra / Sing you a love you song / Honeymoon in San Francisco / Cutie pie / Panda bear / Please tell me so / My darling, I've forgotten / If you feel you must go, don't go! / Just recently lost something of importance / The hollow room / It's easy to sleep when you're dead / In the army kid / Montreal makes me sad again.			
Aug 98.	(7"m) <100GN 29>	**NICKI LIGHTHOUSE. / DON'T ASK ME TO EXPLAIN / SCENES FROM MY FUNERAL**	-	
	(above issued on '100 Guitar Mania')			
Feb 99.	(cd) (KC 027CD)	**THE BIRD WHO CONTINUES TO EAT THE RABBIT'S FLOWER** (compilation)		-
	– (EP above) + / On the drive home / Secret ocean / Christmas is only good if you're not an animal / My favorite Christmas (in a hundred words or less).			

— ALMSTEAD (now on bass when HELIUM stuck with ELF POWER)

— added **DOTTIE ALEXANDER** – keyboards + **JAMIE HUGGINS** – drums

			Kindercore	Bar None
Jun 99.	(7"box-lp)<cd> (KC 029CD) <105>	**THE GAY PARADE**		Feb99
	– Old familiar way / Fun loving nun / Tulip baroo / Jacques Lamure / March of the gay parade / Neat little domestic life / A collection of poems about water / I'd be a yellow feathered loon / The autobiographical grandpa / The miniature philosopher / My friend will be me / My favorite boxer / Advice from a divorced gentleman to his bachelor friend . . . / A man's life flashing before his eyes while he and his wife drive . . . / Nickee Coco and the invisible tree / The gay parade outro.			
Nov 99.	(7") <HHBTM 003>	**A CELEBRATION OF H. HARE**		
	(above issued on '2000 Singles Club')			

— added **ANDY GONZALEZ** – guitar, percussion, violin, piano (of MARSHMALLOW COAST)

Jan 01.	(7"ep) <(KC 052)>	**ARCHIBALD OF THE BALDING SPARROWS**		Jun00
	– Cast in the haze / Craig's head hallucination / MARSHMALLOW COAST: David and the giant crabs.			
			Kindercore	Kindercore
Apr 01.	(cd/d-lp) <(KC 064/+LP)>	**COQUELICOT ASLEEP IN THE POPPIES: A VARIETY OF WHIMSICAL VERSE**		
	– Good morning Mr. Edminton / Peacock parasols / Look at the bell / An introduction for Isabell / Let's do everything for the first time forever / Rose Robert / It's a very starry night / Mimi Merlot / Butterscotching Mr. Lynn / Go call you mine / The events leading up to the collapse of Detective Dulllight / Penelope / A dreamy day of daydreaming of you / Hello from the inside a shell / Lethecin's tale of a DNA experiment . . . / It's just so / The frozen island / Upon setting on the frozen island, Lecithin presents . . . / Let's go for a walk / The hopeless opus or the great battle of the . . . (re-iss. Sep01; same)			
Jun 01.	(7") <KCSC 010>	**SEPTEMBER. / (other by LADYBUG TRANSISTOR)**		
Nov 01.	(7"; split w/ the late BP HELIUM) <Sebastian Whiskey 16> **INSIDE A ROOM FULL OF TREASURES A BLACK PYGMI HORSE'S HEAD POPS UP LIKE A PERISCOPE**		-	
	(above issued on 'Jonathon Whiskey')			
			Track & Field	Kindercore
Oct 02.	(lp/cd) (HEAT 10/+CD) <KC 076CD>	**ALDHILS ARBORETUM**		Sep02
	– Doing nothing / Old people in the cemetery / Isn't it nice? / Jennifer Louise / The blank husband epidemic / Pancakes for one / We are destroying the song / An ode to the noctural muse / Predictably sulking Sara / Natalie and Effie in the park / A question for Emily Foreman / Kissing in the grass / Kid without claws / Death dance of Omipapas and sons for you.			

– compilations, etc. –

Mar 00.	(cd) Bar/None; <112>	**HORSE AND ELEPHANT EATERY (NO ELEPHANTS ALLOWED)** (the singles & songles album)	-	
	– A celebration of H. Hare / Joseph and Alexander / The problem with April / Nicki Lighthouse / Was your face a head in the pillow case? / Julie the mouse / In the army kid / Buried with me / Spoonful of sugar / The world keeps going 'round / Scenes from my funeral / True friends don't want to do things like that / The you I created / Cast in the haze (been there four days). (UK lp-iss.Jul00 on 'Kindercore'; KC 045LP)			
Jan 01.	(cd) Kindercore; <KC 61>	**THE EARLY FOUR TRACK RECORDINGS**	-	
	– Dirty Dustin Hoffman needs a bath / Dustin Hoffman gets a bath / Dustin Hoffman thinks about eating the soap / Dustin Hoffman scrubs too hard and loses soap / Dustin Hoffman does not resist temptation to eat the bathtub / Dustin Hoffman's wife come home / Dustin Hoffman's wife seems suspicious about the absent tub / Dustin Hoffman feigns ignorance of missing bathtub / Dustin Hoffman's wife calls in detective to dust for porcelain particles on Dustin Hoffman's tongue / Dustin Hoffman's tongue taken to a police lab where it is used as toilet paper and reading material while on the toilet / Dustin Hoffman offers lame possible explanation for missing bathtub / Dustin Hoffman's wife makes a sarcastic remark, cuts the head off a duck, places it where the tub was and begins to growl / Dustin Hoffman becomes igdignant and wets himself / Dustin Hoffman quits bathroom and climbs a tree / Dustin Hoffman's children enter the bathroom / Dustin Hoffman's children don't enter the bathroom. (UK lp-iss.Feb01 as 'AN INTRODUCTION TO OF MONTREAL' on 'Earworm'; WORM 60)			

OH OK (see under ⇒ MAGNAPOP)

Will OLDHAM

Born: Louisville, Kentucky, USA. OLDHAM was raised by a large family (later his brothers would join him in THE PALACE BROTHERS) and began his dark, revered career as an actor in John Sayles' 1987 mining vehicle 'Matewan'. After a few more made-for-TV- movies, and a role in another bleedin' mining film, the repressed hillbilly for the 90's (at times compared to BECK!) photographed the front cover for SLINT's 'Spiderland', and for his troubles was awarded the assistance of McMAHAN and WALFORD on his debut album 'THERE IS NO ONE WHAT WILL TAKE CARE OF

YOU' (1993). A deep crooner by nature, OLDHAM, eased his way (however unsteady he sounds on guitar), into insular tales of death, sex and er . . . death in a small town community. Several country/gospel/folk albums appeared around 1992/3; the return to basics, 'PALACE' (1994) and 'VIVA LAST BLUES' (1995), showed a marked improvement in song structure and production value. Having drifted between 'Drag City' in the US and 'Domino' in the UK, PALACE made one last attempt at sounding sadder and deeper than LEONARD COHEN ('ARISE THEREFORE'), before OLDHAM persevered under his own name, releasing the, at times, unlistenable 'JOYA' (1997) and the rarities collection 'LOST BLUES AND OTHER SONGS' (also '97). Perhaps his most remarkable contribution to the music scene, 'I SEE A DARKNESS' (1999), was issued under the alias BONNIE 'PRINCE' BILLY, and saw OLDHAM take comic twists and turns throughout the set (sending his image up on an alarming scale). The album, recorded in a nondescript house, played like a beautiful ode to the Greek tragedy, whilst managing to substain a 'live' feel throughout. 'DEATH TO EVERYONE', possibly the finest track, was so bleak and sombre that it could quite literally make one roll around the ground with laughter by its sheer piss-take alone. His humour was further in evidenced on the sharp and commercially viable 'EASE DOWN THE ROAD' (2001), under the aforementioned BONNIE 'PRINCE' BILLY nom de plume. The set, mainly comprised of melancholy love songs, boasting a tight collective of musicians (namely CATHERINE IRWIN, DAVID PAJO, JON THEODORE and arty film-maker HARMONY KORINE) to accompany an even brighter, if not mellower interpretation of OLDHAM's troubled persona. Stand-out tracks included the poetic 'A KING AT NIGHT', 'JUST TO SEE MY HOLLY HOME', which sounded suspiciously like a church choir jamboree and the fleeting title track, with its banjos et al. A new lyrical direction was also present; gone were the morbid Sunday afternoon trials and tribulations of OLDHAM's psyche, these being replaced with affectionate, if not downright rude stanzas heir to ARAB STRAP or the POGUES. No wonder JOHNNY CASH is a fan.
Album rating: Palace: THERE IS NO-ONE WHAT WILL TAKE CARE OF YOU (*8) / PALACE – DAYS IN THE WAKE (*6) / VIVA LAST BLUES (*7) / ARISE THEREFORE (*7) / LOST BLUES AND OTHER SONGS collection (*8) / Will Oldham: JOYA (*6) / ODE MUSIC mini (*4) / GUARAPERO: LOST BLUES 2 collection (*5) / Bonnie 'Prince' Billy: I SEE A DARKNESS (*8) / EASE DOWN THE ROAD (*8) / MORE REVERY mini (*6)

PALACE BROTHERS

WILL OLDHAM – vocals, guitar / with **BRIAN McMAHAN** – guitar (of SQUIRREL BAIT and SLINT) / **BRITT WALFORD** – drums (of SLINT)

			Big Cat	Drag City
May 93.	(7") *(ABB 51S) <DC 25>*	**OHIO RIVER BOAT SONG. / DRINKING WOMAN**		
Jun 93.	(lp/cd) *(ABB/+CD 050) <DC 34>*	**THERE IS NO-ONE WHAT WILL TAKE CARE OF YOU**		

– Idle hands are the Devil's playthings / Long before / I tried to stay healthy for you / The cellar song / Pulpit / There is no-one what will take care of you / O Lord are you in need / Merida / King me / I had a good mother and father / Riding / O Paul. *(UK-lp re-iss. Jun97; same as US) (cd re-iss. Jan01 on 'Domino'; REWIGCD 008)*

— now OLDHAM completely solo

			Domino	Drag City
Dec 93.	(7") *<DC 37>*	**COME IN. / TRUDY LIES**	-	
May 94.	(7") *<DC 47>*	**HORSES. / STABLE WILL**	-	
Jun 94.	(cd-ep) *(RUG 21CD)*	**COME IN / HORSES / STABLE WILL / TRUDY DIES**		-
Sep 94.	(cd/c/lp) *(WIG CD/MC/LP 14) <DC 50>*	**PALACE** <aka 'DAYS IN THE WAKE'>		Aug94

– You will miss me when I burn / Pushkin / Come a little dog / I send my love to you / Meaulnes / No more workhouse blues / All is grace / Whither thou goest / (Thou without) Partner / I am a cinemagrapher. *<re-iss. Dec97 as 'DAYS IN THE WAKE'; same)>*

| Jan 95. | (m-cd/m-lp; as PALACE SONGS) *(WIG CD/LP 18) <DC 57>* | **HOPE** | | Nov94 |

– Agnes, queen of sorrow / Untitled / Winter lady / Christmastime in the mountains / All gone, all gone / Werner's last blues to blokbuster.

— with **PAUL OLDHAM** – guitar / **HAYDEN + JOHN STITH** – bass / **GORDON TOWNSEND** – drums

Mar 95.	(7") *<DC 61>*	**WEST PALM BEACH. / GULF SHORES**	-	
Jul 95.	(7") *<DC 71>*	**MOUNTAIN LOW. / (END OF) TRAVELING**	-	
Aug 95.	(12"ep/cd-ep; as PALACE SONGS) *(RUG 35 T/CD)*	**THE MOUNTAIN EP**		

– Mountain low / Gulf shores / (End of) Traveling / West Palm Beach.

— now with **BRYAN RICH** – guitar / **LIAM HAYES** – organ / **JASON LOWENSTEIN** – bass

| Aug 95. | (cd/c/lp; as PALACE MUSIC) *(WIG CD/MC/LP 21) <DC 65 – PR 4>* | **VIVA LAST BLUES** | | |

– More brothers rides / Viva ultra / Brute choir / Mountain low / Tonight's decision (and thereafter) / Work hard – play hard / New partner / Cat's blues / We all, us three, will ride / Old Jerusalem.

| Oct 95. | (7") *<DC 64 – PR 1>* | **O HOW I ENJOY THE LIGHT. / MARRIAGE** | - | |

— now simply as PALACE; with **NED OLDHAM** – bass / **DAVID GRUBBS** – piano / **MAYA TONE** – percussion, drums

| Apr 96. | (cd/c/lp) *(WIG CD/MC/LP 24) <DC 88>* | **ARISE THEREFORE** | | |

– Stablemate / Sucker's evening / Arise therefore / You have cum / Kid of Harith / Sun highlights / the lack in each / No gold digger / Disorder / Group of women / Give me children / Weaker soldier. *(also on ltd-cd; RUG 46CD)*

			not iss.	Palace
Jun 96.	(7") *<PR 13>*	**FOR MEKONS ET AL. / STABLE WILL**	-	

			Drag City	Drag City
Dec 96.	(7"; as PALACE MUSIC) *<(DC 91)>*	**LITTLE BLUE EYES. / THE SPIDER'S DUDE IS OFTEN THERE**		

WILL OLDHAM

— now under his own moniker

| Jan 96. | (7") *<DC 83>* | **EVERY MOTHER'S SON. / NO MORE RIDERS** | - | |
| Mar 97. | (7") *<(DC 118)>* | **PATIENCE. / TAKE HOWEVER LONG YOU WANT** | | |

			Domino	Drag City
Nov 97.	(cd/lp) *(WIG CD/LP 39) <DC 107>*	**JOYA**		Oct97

– O let it be / Antagonism / New gypsy / Under what was oppression / The gator / Open your heart / Richer / Be still and know God (don't be shy) / Apocalypse, no! / I am still what I meant to be / Bolden boke boy / Idea and deed.

			Palace	Acuarela
Oct 97.	(cd-ep) *(WILL 1CD) <AFF 002>*	**WESTERN MUSIC**		Mar98

– Always bathing in the evening / Western songs for J.L.L. / Three photographs / Jump in jump in, come in come in.

			Drag City	Drag City
Jun 98.	(12"/cd-s) *<(DC 100/+CD)>*	**BLACK/RICH MUSIC**		

– Do what you will do / Do what you will do / Risen Lord / Allowance / Allowance / Black/rich tune / Black/rich / Do what you will do.

| Jun 98. | (cd-ep) *<(DC 107X)>* | **LITTLE JOYA** | | |

– Prologue / Joya / Exit music for a dick.

| Jan 00. | (m-lp/m-cd) *<(DC 183/+CD)>* | **ODE MUSIC** | | |

– Ode #1 / Ode #2 / Ode #3 / Ode #4 / Ode #1a / Ode #1b / Ode #2a / Ode #5 / Ode #3a / Ode #4a.

| Oct 02. | (m-lp; as CONTINENTAL OP) *<(DC 195)>* | **SLITCH MUSIC** (original soundtrack) | | |

– compilations, etc. –

| Apr 97. | (cd/d-lp; as PALACE MUSIC) *Domino; (WIG CD/LP 33) / Drag City; <DC 110>* | **LOST BLUES AND OTHER SONGS** | | |

– Ohio river boat song / Riding / Valentine's day / Trudy dies / Come in / Little blue eyes / Horses / Stable will / Untitled / O how I enjoy the light / Marriage / West Palm Beach / Gulf shores / (End of) Travelling / Lost blues.

| Oct 97. | (7") *Skingraft; (GR 26)* | **SIDES 5-6** | | - |
| Feb 00. | (cd/lp) *Domino; (WIG CD/LP 74) / Drag City; <40111>* | **GUARAPERO: LOST BLUES 2** | | |

– Drinking woman / The spider's dude is often there / Gezundheit / Let the wires ring / Big balls / For the mekons et all / Stable Will / Every mother's son / No more rides / The risen Lord / Boy, have you cum / Patience / Take however long you want / Sugarcane juice drinker / Call me a liar / O Lord are you in need?

| Jan 02. | (one-sided-10"ep+book) *Konkurrent; (907857040-2)* | **FOREST TIME** | | |
| Oct 02. | (7") *Isota; (SODY 005)* | **WE ALL US THREE WILL RIDE. / BARCELONA** | | - |

BONNIE 'PRINCE' BILLY

with **BOB ARELLANO, COLIN GAGON, PAUL OLDHAM + PETER TOWNSEND**

— session people provided the backing for OLDHAM

			not iss.	All City Nomad
Apr 98.	(ltd-7"+purple) *<AC 7>*	**BLACK DISSIMULATION. / NO SUCH AS WHAT I WANT** (UK-iss.Feb00; same as US)	-	

			Domino	Palace
May 98.	(cd-s; tour) *(RUG 67CD)*	**I AM DRINKING AGAIN / DREAMING MY DREAMS**		-
Nov 98.	(cd-ep) *(RUG 81CD)*	**BLUE LOTUS FEET**		

– One with the birds / Southside of the world / When die song / I am the sky / Blue lotus feet / Pole star / Door of my heart.

| Jan 99. | (cd/lp) *(WIG CD/LP 59) <PR 22>* | **I SEE A DARKNESS** | | |

– A minor place / Nomadic revery (all around) / I see a darkness / Another day full of dread / Death to everyone / Knockturne / Madeleine- Mary / Song for the new breed / Today I was an evil one / Black / Raining in darling.

Jun 99.	(7") *<PR 20>*	**ONE WITH THE BIRDS. / SOUTHSIDE OF THE WORLD**		
1999.	(7"blue) *<SP 462>*	**LET'S START A FAMILY (BLACKS). / A WHOREHOUSE IN ANY HOUSE**	-	
1999.	(7") *<LF 075>*	**I CONFESS**	-	

— <above 2 on 'Sub Pop' & 'Lowfly' – below on 'Western'>

| Jul 00. | (7"m; as BONNIE "BLUE" BILLY) *(West 009)* | **LITTLE BOY BLUE** | | - |

– Little boy blue I / Little boy blue II / Blue boy.

| Sep 00. | (cd-s; as BONNIE PRINCE BILLY & THE MARQUIS DE TREN) *(RUG 109CD) <PR 24>* | **GET ON JOLLY** | | |

– 2/15 / 25 / 81 / 86 / 64 / 66.

— MARQUIS DE TREN included **MICK TURNER** (of DIRTY THREE)

| Dec 00. | (12"ep/cd-ep; as WILL OLDHAM & RYAN MURPHY) *(RUG 117) <DC 123>* | **ALL MOST HEAVEN** | | |

– Fall again / Fall and raise it on / Song of most / Song of all.

| Mar 01. | (cd) *(WIGCD 89) <PR 26>* | **EASE DOWN THE ROAD** | | Apr01 |

– May it always be / Careless love / A king at night / Just to see my holly home / At break of day / After I made love to you / Ease down the road / The lion lair / Mrs William / Sheep / Grand dark feeling of emptiness / Rich wife full of happiness. *(w/ free cd-ep+=; WIGCD 89X)* **BONNIE 'PRINCE' BILLY WITH MIKE FELLOWS, JAMES LO, AND MATT SWEENEY** – What's wrong with a zoo / I send my love to you / Stablemate.

			Temporary Residence	Temporary Residence
Jun 01.	(m-cd; as BONNY BILLY) *<(TRR 37)>*	**MORE REVERY**		2000

– Someone's sleeping / Sweeter than anything / Same love that made me laugh / A dream of the sea / Strange things / Just to see you smile.

2001. (cd-ep) <MAP 001> **GET THE FUCK ON JOLLY LIVE** [not iss. / Palace]
– XXV / II-XV / LXXXI / LXXXVI / LXIV / LXVI / XIII / CII.

OLIVELAWN (see under ⇒ FLUF)

OLIVIA TREMOR CONTROL

Formed: Athens, Georgia, USA ... 1992 out of CRANBERRY LIFE CYCLE and SYNTHETIC FLYING MACHINE by WILL CULLEN HART and BILL DOSS. A true lo-fi enigma, OTC emerged from the 'Elephant 6' musical collective, a kind of Wild Bunch for the US underground which also boasted NEUTRAL MILK HOTEL and APPLES (IN STEREO). OTC mainmen/singer-songwriters, HART and DOSS began playing together at school, developing their musical partnership at university. Together with childood friend, JEFF MANGUM, the pair formed CRANBERRY LIFE CYCLE after relocating to Athens, Georgia. Following the subsequent replacement of MANGUM with JOHN FERNANDES, the band changed name to SYNTHETIC FLYING MACHINE before finally adopting the OTC moniker just prior to the addition of PETE ERCHICK and ERIC HARRIS. Initiating their own 'Drug Racer' label, the band made their debut in 1994 with the 'CALIFORNIA DEMISE' EP. A concept affair influenced by 60's psychedelia, the record was the first part in an ongoing saga conceived by DOSS and HART as a pseudo film script. Follow-up EP, 'GIANT DAY' served as a link into the weird and wonderful complexities of OLIVIA TREMOR CONTROL's debut double set, 'DUSK AT CUBIST CASTLE' (1996). Released on 'Flydaddy' and previewed by two singles, 'THE OPERA HOUSE' and 'JUMPING FENCES', the record found DOSS and HART employing classic psychedelic techniques and fusing everything from space-rock to BYRDS-ian pop with cutting edge lo-fi noise. While many critics noted the influence of late 60's BEATLES and guiding spirit of BRIAN WILSON, a more contemporary comparison might've been SEAN O'HAGAN and his HIGH LLAMAS (had they grown up listening to PAVEMEMT!). Before their split in 1999, The OLIVIA TREMOR CONTROL still had one great record left in them, the hypnotic 'BLACK FOLIAGE: ANIMATION MUSIC VOLUME ONE', a swirling psychedelic pop record that harked back to their BLACK SWAN NETWORK releases; 'OLIVIA TREMOR CONTROL VS. BLACK SWAN NETWORK', 'DUSK AT CUBIST CASTLE' and 'LATE MUSIC VOL.1' (1997, and which infused taped descriptions of dreams with soundscapes and post-experimental ambience). After the combo had parted company, BILL DOSS could be heard on the 'AGE OF THE SUN' LP, under his sparkling psych-pop project The SUNSHINE FIX, released in 2001 on 'Elephant 6' offshoot imprint 'Emperor Norton'. Meanwhile, his other half (HART, of course) established CIRCULATORY SYSTEM with OTC members ERCHICK and HARRIS, alongside NEUTRAL MILK HOTEL's JEFF MAGNUM and classically-trained violinist HEATHER McINTOSH. The group had practically re-formed OTC, with HART's delicate experimentalism cropping-up once again on the ensemble's self-titled debut (2001). However, the most curious and interesting of all post-OTC releases was 'THE FROSTED AMBASSADOR' (1999), supposedly created by a man of the same name (it's 99.9% certain that the man in question is indeed ex-percussionist HARRIS). The silly story of the good AMBASSADOR went like this: he began in a 1977 psychedelic group, had a bad experience with the 80's music industry and moved to Belgium to "study toast". The most amusing thing about this homespun yarn was that the album itself was said to be found inside a shoe in a thrift store in Athens. Whatever, the set displayed minimal instrumentals using wind-up toys, glockenspiels and kiddies instruments that made it sound tiny and childlike – you never know, perhaps it was the kind of music created by an ex-80's icon who has strange dealings with toast ...

Album rating: DUSK AT CUBIST CASTLE (*7) / EXPLANATION II: INSTRUMENTAL THEMES AND DREAM SEQUENCES (*5) / OLIVIA TREMOR CONTROL VS BLACK SWAN NETWORK mini (*6) / BLACK FOLIAGE; ANIMATION MUSIC – VOLUME ONE (*7) / SINGLES AND BEYOND compilation (*6) / Black Swan Network: LATE MUSIC VOLUME 1 (*5) / Sunshine Fix: AGE OF THE SUN (*6) / Circulatory System: CIRCULATORY SYSTEM (*5) / Frosted Ambassador: THE FROSTED AMBASSADOR (*5)

WILL CULLEN HART – vocals, multi / **BILL DOSS** – vocals, multi / **PETE ERCHICK** – keyboards / **JOHN FERNANDES** – bass / **ERIC HARRIS** – drums

[not iss. / Elephant6]
1994. (7"ep) <E6 002> **CALIFORNIA DEMISE EP**
– California demise (pt.1) / California demise (pt.2) / A sunshine fix / Fireplace / Collage No.1.

[not iss. / Small Fi – No Life]
1994. (7") <small-fi 4> **split w/ APPLES (IN STEREO)**

[not iss. / Drug Racer]
1996. (7"ep) <DR 2> **THE GIANT DAY EP**
– The giant day / Shaving spiders / Princess turns the key to the cubist castle / Curtain call (part 3) / I'm not feeling human / The giant day (dusk). *(UK-iss.Jun97; same as US)*

[Blue Rose / Flydaddy]
Sep 96. (d-cd/d-lp) (BRRC 1008-2/-1) <FLY 17> **MUSIC FROM THE UNREALIZED FILM SCRIPT "DUSK AT CUBIST CASTLE"** [/ Aug96]
– The opera house / Frosted ambassador / Jumping fences / Define a transparent dream / No growing (exegesis) / Holiday surprise / Courtyard / Memories of Jacqueline 1906 / Tropical bells / Can you come down with us? / Marking time / Tracks 12-21: Green typewriters / Spring succeeds / Theme for a very delicious grand piano / I can smell the leaves / Dusk at Cubist castle / Gravity car / N.Y.C.-25. *(d-cd+=)* – EXPLANATION II

Oct 96. (cd-s) (BRRC 1011-2A) **THE OPERA HOUSE / BLACK SWAN RADAR**
(cd-s) (BRRC 1011-2B) – ('A'side) / Capillary radar.
(d7"+=) (BRRC 1011-7) – (above tracks) / Black swan radar (with enveloping bicycle folds).

May 97. (12"ep/cd-ep) (BRRC 1015-6/-3) **JUMPING FENCES**
– Jumping fences / Optical atlas / The language of stationary travellers / Green typewriters (outer themes).

Nov 97. (cd) <(FLY 017X)> **EXPLANATION II (INSTRUMENTAL THEMES AND SEQUENCES)**
– (9 untitled tracks). *(re-iss. Oct98 & Jun99; same)*

[Blue Rose – Flydaddy – V2 / V2]
Oct 98. (12"ep/cd-ep) (BRRC 500459-6/-3) **HIDEAWAY**
– Hideaway / Combinations / Can you come down with us?

Mar 99. (cd/d-lp) (BRRC 100578-2/-1) <FLY 27> **BLACK FOLIAGE; ANIMATION MUSIC – VOLUME ONE**
– Opening / A familiar noise called "train director" / Combinations / Hideaway / Black foliage – animation 1 / Combinations / The sky is a harpsicord canyon / A sleepy company / Grass canons / A new day / Combinations / Black foliage – animation 2 / I have been floated / Paranormal echoes / Black foliage – animation 3 / A place we have been to / Black foliage (itself) / The Sylvan screen / The bark and below it / Black foliage – animation 4 / California demise 3 / Looking for quiet seeds / Combinations / Mystery / Another set of bees in the museum / Black foliage – animation 5 / Hilltop procession.

– **compilations, others, etc.** –

Aug 00. (cd/lp) *Emperor Norton*; <(EMN 7033 CD/LP)> **...PRESENTS: SINGLES AND BEYOND**
– Love Athena / Today I lost a tooth / California demise (pt.1) / California demise (pt.2) / A sunshine fix / Fireplace / Collage #1 / Beneath the climb / I won this dog at the Driftwood reunion carnival / Christmas with William S. / The giant day / Shaving spiders / The princess turns the key to cubist castle / Curtain call (pt.3) / I'm not feeling human / The giant day (dusk) / Late music 2 / Gypsum oil field fire / King of the claws / The ships.

BLACK SWAN NETWORK

aka **WILLIAM CULLEN HART, BILL DOSS, PETE ERCHICK + JOHN FERNANDES**

[Camera Obscura / not iss.]
Aug 97. (cd) (CAM 003CD) **LATE MUSIC VOL.1**
– One / Two / Three / Four / Five / Six / Seven.

[Flydaddy / Flydaddy]
Jun 98. (m-cd) <(FLY 030)> **OLIVIA TREMOR CONTROL VS. BLACK SWAN NETWORK (A.K.A. THE TOUR EP)** [/ 1997]
– Introduction / Theme from Airplane Avenue / Flags of symphony / Morning drones / Neuron trains backfire – Tape splice prelude / Dusk at cubist castle closing theme.

– In '97, the also released an untitled "dream tape" (2 tracks).

SUNSHINE FIX

BILL DOSS – vocals, multi / with **SCOTT SPILLANE** – guitars, trumpet, etc / **ERIC HARRIS** – drums

[Kindercore / Kindercore]
Aug 00. (cd-ep) <(KC 054)> **THE FUTURE HISTORY OF THE SUNSHINE FIX**
– The sound around you / The many keys to reunion / Last night I had a dream (said I had a dream last night) / Future history and the irrelevance of time / Beaconary words ...

[Elefant / Elefant]
Sep 01. (7") <(U 50706)> **SUNSHINE FIX**

– DOSS now with **DEREK ALMSTEAD** – bass, drums / and a plethora of musicians

[Emperor Norton / Emperor Norton]
Oct 01. (cd) <(EMN 7048CD)> **AGE OF THE SUN**
– Age of the sun / Ultraviolet orchestra / That ole sun / Everything is waking / Digging to China / A better way to be / An illuminated array / See yourself / Inside the nebula / Hide in the light / Sail beyond the sunset / A 93 million mile moment / Mr. Summer day / 72 years / Cycles of time / Le roi-soleil.

CIRCULATORY SYSTEM

WILLIAM CULLEN HART – vocals, multi / **PETE ERCHICK** – keyboards / **ERIC HARRIS** – drums / **JEFF MANGUM** – drums, vocals (of NEUTRAL MILK HOTEL) / **HEATHER McINTOSH** – cello / etc.

[Cloud / Cloud]
Jan 02. (cd) <(CLD 001)> **CIRCULATORY SYSTEM** [/ Aug01]
– Yesterday's world / Prehistoric / Diary of wood / Outside blasts / Joy / The lovely universe / Round / Inside blasts / Illusion / Waves of bark and light / Now / A peek / Fingers / Days to come (in photographs) / Symbols and maps / The pillow / Stars / Should a cloud replace a compass? / Time or dateline / How long? / Your parades / Forever.

FROSTED AMBASSADOR

ERIC HARRIS – drums, etc

[Kindercore / Kindercore]
May 00. (cd) <(KC 030)> **THE FROSTED AMBASSADOR**
– (12 untitled tracks).

OLYMPIC DEATH SQUAD (see under ⇒ UNREST)

ONEIDA

Formed: Brooklyn, New York, USA ... mid-90's by PAPA CRAZY aka PCRZ, BOBBY MATADOR aka FAT BOBBY, HANOI JANE aka BABY JANE and KID MILLIONS. Committed garage revivalists with a typically experimental NY edge, ONEIDA combine hard-driving retro punk and R&B with frazzled free jazz and even elements of Krautrock. Having built up a

ONEIDA (cont)

healthy reputation amongst the city's music cognoscenti, the band made their vinyl debut in 1997 with 'A PLACE CALLED EL SHADDAI'S'. A second independently released album, 'ENEMY HOGS', followed in 1999 while a prolific start to the new millennium saw the release of both the 'COME ON EVERYBODY LET'S ROCK' set and 'STEEL ROD' EP, the latter featuring a cover of Creedence Clearwater Revival's 'SINISTER PURPOSE'. While fine tuning their streak of often savagely ironic humour, neither this nor its successor 'ANTHEM OF THE MOON' (2001) diverged from the established musical assault. In stark contrast, 'EACH ONE TEACH ONE' (2002) was a forcible and in large part, effective attempt at broadening the band's musical resources. A double set, the record's first disc was unashamed in its nod to classic Krautrock, zoning out on percolating riffs over two lengthy compositions. The second disc was no less experimental but considerably more concise, ranging through stripped down primitivism and psyched-out claustrophobia over a more easily digestible seven tracks.

Album rating: A PLACE CALLED EL SHADDAI'S (*6) / ENEMY HOGS (*5) / STEEL ROD mini (*5) / COME ON EVERYBODY LET'S ROCK (*6) / ANTHEM OF THE MOON (*5) / EACH ONE TEACH ONE (*7)

(PCRZ) PAPA CRAZY – vocals, guitar / **(FAT) BOBBY MATADOR** – keyboards / **HANOI (BABY) JANE** – bass / **KID MILLIONS** – drums

		Turnbuckle	Turnbuckle
Dec 97.	(cd) <(TB 009)> **A PLACE CALLED EL SHADDAI'S** – Hieronymous / Go there / Salad days / Medium cool / Gandhi for now / Dog days / Ballad of Vaurice / El Shaddai's.		
Nov 98.	(7") **BEST FRIENDS. / THE LAND OF BUGS**		

		Turnbuckle	Jagjaguwar
Oct 99.	(cd) <(TB 018)> <JAG 29> **ENEMY HOGS** – Whitney fortress / Primanti Bros. / Bombay fraud / Give up ... and move on / Little red dolls / Ginger (bein' free) / Turn it: up (loud) / Gettin' it on / Hard workin' man / Quest for two / Fourth eye / Wicked servant. (hidden track+=) – O.L.B. (re-iss. Apr01 on 'Jagjaguwar'; same as US)		

		Jagjaguwar	Jagjaguwar
Nov 99.	(7") <(JAG 14)> **split w/ Songs: Ohia**		
Aug 00.	(m-cd) <(JAG 25)> **STEEL ROD** – XXY / Steel rod / Tennessee / Helltrain / Sinister purpose.		Nov00
Nov 00.	(cd) <(JAG 27)> **COME ON EVERYBODY LET'S ROCK** – I love rock / Major havoc / Pure light invasion / Legion of scags / Doin' business in Japan / Snow machine / Slip inside this house / Power animals / Fat Goggy's black thumb.		
Sep 01.	(cd) <(JAG 38CD)> **ANTHEM OF THE MOON** – New head / All arounder / Geometry / Rose and Licorice / Almagest / Still rememberin' hiding in the snow / Dead worlds / People of the north / The wooded world / Ballad of impervium / To seed and flower / Double lock your mind.		
Feb 02.	(7") <(JAG 31)> **ANTHEM OF THE MOON. / Brother JT: Children Of The Sun**		
Oct 02.	(cd) <(JAG 48CD)> **EACH ONE TEACH ONE** – Sheets of Easter / Antibiotics / Each one teach one / People of the north / Number nine / Sneak into the woods / Rugaru / Black chamber / No label. — (originally iss.d-lp May02 on 'Version City'; VERC 03)		

ONE LADY OWNER

Formed: Manchester, England ... 1998 when a demo tape of singer STEVE DOUGHERTY's songs were passed onto the band, KID DYNAMO, via manager DEREK RYDER (father of BLACK GRAPE's SHAUN), who himself was tipped off by a mutual friend (the latter had met the frontman holidaying in Sri Lanka). Upon his return, DOUGHERTY was searched out by KID DYNAMO (ROD SMITH, CHESY, NATHAN SUDDERS and aptly named drummer BO JOHN BONHAM WALSH) and almost immediately signed to Alan McGee's 'Creation' records. Nearing the end of '98, they debuted with a classy, raucous single, 'WHEELKINGS 1973', an ambitious beginning and possibly the metallic answer to stablemates, OASIS.

Album rating: THERE'S ONLY ME (*6)

STEVE DOUGHERTY – vocals / **ROD SMITH** – guitar / **CHESY** – keyboards / **NATHAN SUDDERS** – bass / **BO JOHN BONHAM WALSH** – drums

		Creation	not iss.
Nov 98.	(7") (CRE 307) **WHEELKINGS 1973. / WEIRD DREAMS** (cd-s+=) (CRESCD 307) – Acceleration.		-
Mar 99.	(7") (CRE 310) **I DO NEED YOU. / TRICK CHEST** (cd-s+=) (CRESCD 310) – There's only we.		-
May 99.	(7"/cd-s) (CRE/+SCD 319) **POLICE CAR SEX. / WORLD X / FICTION FUELED CON**		-
Jun 99.	(cd/lp) (CRE CD/LP 245) **THERE'S ONLY WE** – Weird dream / Wheelkings 1973 / I haven't been to San Francisco / Cathode queen / Police car sex / MPH is everything / Planet XXX / Car crash / Trick chest / Blue chrome zoo / I do need you.		-

— OLO subsequently disbanded

1-SPEED BIKE
(see under ⇒ GODSPEED YOU BLACK EMPEROR!)

OOBERMAN

Formed: Liverpool, England ... 1997 by former Bradford-born schoolmates, DANNY POPPLEWELL and ANDY FLETT. Moving to Merseyside, they acquired ANDY's little brother STEVE, along with ALAN KELLY and SOPHIA CHURNEY (the latter from a placed ad in a shop window!). The five-piece set their sights high by recording a demo which aroused indie protagonist and BLUR guitarist GRAHAM COXON. He quickly snapped the band up, issuing the 'SUGAR BUM' single on his enterprising 'Transcopic' label. The brilliant second release, 'SHORLEY WALL' EP, generated so much interest (on radio play only), that sales went from 1000 to a staggering 10 times that amount in the space of two months. The EP sounded like a collage of broken dreams and promises, with BEATLES-esque guitars, whispering partly spoken lyrics and an ambience that would make MERCURY REV blush. A single, 'BLOSSOM'S FALLING', was released by 'Independiente' in May '99, securing a place in the UK Top 40 and was followed by the critically acclaimed eccentric debut album, 'THE MAGIC TREEHOUSE'. After a one-off single ('DOLPHIN BLUE') for 'Rough Trade', OOBERMAN kicked in again with their second set, the mini 'RUNNING GIRL' (2001) – this time for 'RotoDisc'. If you liked your pop lush and twee but intelligent, OOBERMAN seemed to be dishing it out like confetti.

Album rating: THE MAGIC TREEHOUSE (*7) / RUNNING GIRL mini (*6)

DANNY POPPLEWELL – vocals / **SOPHIA CHURNEY** – vocals, keyboards / **ANDY FLETT** – guitar / **STEVE FLETT** – bass / **ALAN KELLY** – drums

		Transcopic	not iss.
May 98.	(7") (Tran 002) **SUGAR BUM. / TEARS FROM A WILLOW**		-

		Tugboat	not iss.
Nov 98.	(12"ep/cd-ep) (TUGS/+CD 003) **SHORLEY WALL EP** – Shorley wall / Today's the day (part 1) / Serotonin smile / A place I call home / Why did my igloo collapse? / Live again (don't die father) / Honeydew. (cd+=) – (secret track).		

		Independiente	not iss.
Apr 99.	(7") (ISOM 26S) **BLOSSOMS FALLING. / THE THINGS I HAVE LOST** (cd-s) (ISOM 26MS) – ('A'side) / Gray / 13.	39	-
Jul 99.	(12") (ISOM 30T) **MILLION SUNS. / STEVE TROOPER** (cd-s) (ISOM 30MS) – ('A'side) / Sur la plage / Pa3uh Budut Coh. (cd-s) (ISOM 30MS) – ('A'side) / Dodo was made for Heaven / When summer's gone.	43	-
Oct 99.	(7") (ISOM 37S) **TEARS FROM A WILLOW. / IGLOO II: YELLOW SNOW** (cd-s) (ISOM 37MS) – ('A'side) / Moth to a flame / Danny boy.	63	-
Oct 99.	(cd/c/lp) (ISOM 13 CD/MC/LP) **THE MAGIC TREEHOUSE** – Million suns / Blossoms falling / Sur la plage / Roro blue / Tears from a willow / Bees / Sugar bum / Rolle me in cotton / Physics disco / The magic treehouse / Amazing in bed / My baby's too tall and thin / Shorley wall / Silver planet. (hidden CD-ROM tracks)		
Mar 00.	(7") (ISOM 41S) **SHORLEY WALL. / BUSTER** (cd-s) (ISOM 41MS) – ('A'side) / Wasteland of souls / Blossoms falling (acoustic version). (cd-s) (ISOM 41SMS) – ('A'side) / Golden fall / Tears from a willow (Sound 5's disko 77 mix).	47	-

		Rough Trade	not iss.
Dec 00.	(7") (RTRADES 009) **DOLPHIN BLUE. / DANNY BOY (live)** (cd-s) (RTRADESCD 009) – ('A'side) / C'est la vie (c'est la meme chose) / Laughter lines.		

		RotoDisc	March
Oct 01.	(m-cd) (ROTOCD 001) **RUNNING GIRL** – Running girl / Flashing light at sunset / We'll know when we get there / Blink of an eye / Here come the ice wolves / Ghosts / The kitchen fire / Follow the sun / Alone at last. <US+=> – Dolphin blue / Running girl (Phantom 309 remix).		2002
Nov 01.	(7") (ROTO 001) **RUNNING GIRL (original mix). / RUNNING GIRL (Pierced Teen indie club mix).**		
May 02.	(cd-ep) (ROTOCD 002) **BLUEBELL MORNING EP** – Bluebell morning / Angel of Bradford / Souls of the northern lights / Miss U miss / Snakedance (original).		-
Aug 02.	(7") (ROTO 003) **BEANY BEAN. / BEHIND MY SHIELD** (cd-s) (ROTACDA 003) – ('A'side) / Just sittin here / Car song. (cd-s) (ROTACDB 003) – ('A'side) / Fly around the world / Heroes and villains.	79	-

OP8 (see under ⇒ GIANT SAND; see 80's section)

ORANGE CAKE MIX

Formed: Connecticut, USA ...early 1990's as the recording name of multi-talented, one-man band, songwriter JIM RAO. Throughout OCM's career RAO was extremely fruitful, putting out many homemade recordings on hard to get hold of cassettes, in which he combined his love of alternative pop with an eclectic mix of styles and use of instrumentation. He transcended the musical boundaries, from hard rocking to ambient sounds, but not always with the same degree of success. Amongst the many tapes RAO put down, OCM also released some larger projects on various indie labels, the first of which was the album, 'MORE MELLOW HITS' (1995) on 'Elefant'. A competent piece mixing electronica with more acoustic sounds, to make a fittingly individual sound. This fertile composer quickly followed this release with another full-length outing 'GRAPEFRUIT' (1996), and hot on its heels was the instrumental album, 'SILVER LINING UNDER WATER' (1997), released on 'Darla'. This latter output showed OCM's artistic flourishing compared to the more nascent earlier offerings, and gave a taste of what RAO was capable of. Thus it was no surprise that 'FLUFFY PILLOW', released the following year, was OCM's best offering to date. The album swung effortlessly between melancholic brooding tones to up-beat funkiness, and sometimes managed to combine both. The high OCM achieved on this album continued to some degree into the albums, 'BLUE ISLAND SOUND' (1997) and 'ANOTHER ORANGE WORLD' (1998). The latter of these showed that RAO was not just stuck in a love for 80's synthesizer-dominated pop, but had kept an artisic ear open for the changes that had been wrought by the 90's dance explosion. Unfortunately OCM's output on the whole tended to be teetering on the side of quantity rather than quality, though it was evident that RAO was capable of the latter. Thus the following years saw many lesser albums fall from OCM's creative tree, such as 'LOVECLOUD AND SECRET TAPE' (1999), and 'MICROCOSMIC WONDERLAND' (1999). The standard was picked up again with the release of 'DREAM WINDOW' (1999), which was a calibre above in production techniques, but did not stray too far from the intimacy of the bedroom pop sound. Slipping back into banal music machine mould OCM put out the full-length outing, 'A SHADOW OF ECLIPSE AND OTHER PHASES OF THE MOON' (2001), and other equally competent, but in the end forgettable releases, making most fans of RAO's work wish he would sit back and concentrate on putting out less, but better offerings. • **Covered:** I STARTED A JOKE (Bee Gees).

Album rating: MORE MELLOW HITS (*4) / GRAPEFRUIT (*4) / FLUFFY PILLOW (*6) / SILVER LINING UNDERWATER (*5) / ANOTHER ORANGE WORLD (*5) / LOVECLOUD & SECRET TAPES compilation (*4) / BLUE ISLAND SOUND (*4) / DREAM WINDOW (*7) / A SHADOW OF ECLIPSE AND OTHER PHASES OF THE MOON (*5)

JIM RAO – vocals, acoustic guitar, keyboards, electronics

Blackbean & Placenta / not iss.

May 95. (12"ep) <BBPTC 47> **LOOK FOR A PLACE IN THE SUN – AND FIND IT!**
– F.U.C. me / You really should be here alone with me / Capitalism never sleeps / Wish I was a ghost / Cream and sugar / So long ago / Stereo friendly. *(UK-iss.Nov97; BBPTC 72)*

Elefant / not iss.

Jun 95. (cd) <ER 1007> **MORE MELLOW HITS**
– Girl on the film / Faithful / Melanie knows why / Goodbye why / Glitter daze / If you were here / Like the sun / As days go by / We went to Graceland / Fall from grace / Anticipation / Before the summer fades away / Transcendental airways.

Black Bean & Placenta Tape Club / Black Bean & Placenta Tape Club

Jun 96. (one-sided;12") <BBPTC 17> **OBSERVATIONS OF TOMORROW AND TODAY**
– Closely guarded secrets * / Don't let tomorrow get in your way / Within / No shelter * / Stars in the sky / She won't fade out / See through you / Walls and doorways / Strange world out there *. <*2nd pressing omits * but +=*> – Anna Rainbow / Hilltop view.

Aug 96. (cd) <(BBPTC 24CD)> **GRAPEFRUIT**
– Feel so cold / When I need you most / Watching the cars / Snow White opinions / Mary Jane's world / Ready to fall / 90 day crash / Open up your heart / Suicide watch / L.A. dreamer / Tommy James / Val / How I feel / I sometimes wonder where you are / A wish to wonder / Lost in dreamland / Mercury turnpike cruiser.

Astrolane / not iss.

Oct 96. (7"white) *(ALR 702)* **CRISP LETTUCE / FAST FOOD PART 2. / (other by FUXA)**

— next feat. **VERNA BROCK**

Tinseltones / Tinseltones

Jan 97. (7") <(TT 001)> **37 SHADES OF BLUE. / BABY, IT'S IN THE STARS**

Darla / Darla

Jan 97. (cd) <(DRL 029)> **FLUFFY PILLOW**
– She's like a beautiful painting / Some kind of drug / Interlude for love / Feel your love / Sexylovemachine / The river flows to the sea / Space rotation (parts 1 & 2) / The ceiling effect / Beautiful icon / Kinmokusei / Closer all the time / Broken machine / Fuzzy pillow. <*re-iss. Jun98 on 'Fuzzy Box'; FUZ 005*>

Mar 97. (cd/lp) <(DRL 031-2/-1)> **SILVER LINING UNDERWATER: THE BLISS OUT VOL.3**
– Streetlights and stars / '67 Chevy Malibu / Like warm velvet static / Bird song / Out the door / The ballad of Sonny Jim / Glitch / Twilight sleep / Half-baked elegy / Alice Coltrane / The soul of trees / I honor the light that shines within you / Close to Heaven – Always by your side. <*w/ free 7"*>

Mar 97. (7"ep) *(BUS 047)* **RIVERS AND TREES EP**
– If you see me / Rivers and trees / Blank pages.
(above issued on 'Bus Stop') (below on 'Black Bean & Placenta')

Apr 97. (7") *(BBPTC 25)* **ANIMALS AND MACHINES (split w/ TRICYCLE POPSTAR)** Jan97
– Crystal lake / Sunday kind of girl.

Aug 97. (7"; as BEANMIX) <005> **YOU DON'T WANT ME ANYMORE. / SHELL OF A DREAMER / THE BRIGHTEST SUNRISE (w/ VERNA BROCK)**
(above issued on 'Myke Droner') (below issued on 'Elefant')

Aug 97. (cd) <ER 1034> **BLUE ISLAND SOUND** Feb97
– Deeper inside / Honeybee / Walls and doorways / Wonder ways / When I needed you most / The days of cherry red / When you touch me the whole world disappears / Art groupie / Godlight / Can't buy a miracle / Stars in the sky / Why think about tomorrow / Now I'm not afraid to say I love you anymore.

Sep 97. (7") <DRL 047> **HEAVEN IS RISING (remix). / WE CAN BELIEVE IN LOVE**

Sep 97. (cd/lp) <DRL 047-2/-1> **ANOTHER ORANGE WORLD**
– Your favorite coffee shop / Heaven is rising / Remember the summer / Waves in space / And I feel it coming on / Another wave / Krishna vision 3 / Still falling star / Get it together now / Jai guru Dev 2 / Invisible cosmic rays / Waiting for another light (to shine on me) / In the groove of your romantic soul.

Elefant / Elefant

Jul 97. (7"tan) *(ER 175)* **TAKE A HOLIDAY. / MR RABBIT AND HIS FURRY FRIENDS / DREAM COME TRUE**

Sep 97. (cd-ep) *(ER 307)* **LIKE WAVES IN SPACE EP** Jun97
– Honeybee / When the sky was falling down on you / Waves in space / Heavenly lane / Believe in me. *(UK re-iss. Oct00; same)*

not iss. / Tokuma

Jun 98. (cd) <TKCB 71383> **OCEAN RAINBOW** Japan
– Valentine love letter / Introversion / Small world we're living in / Water medley:- a) Holy stream (of consciousness) – b) A summer waterfall – c) Spirit of the river / A million dreams / Rothko / Music for dining / It won't be long until I see you again / Into the rising sun / Glorified abyss / Your sweet smile / I am still waiting for you to come home / Little baby star / Another frozen flower / Could it be I'm still falling in love with you / Santa Monica boulevard / Sleepytime song / Broken valentine.

not iss. / Black Bean & Placenta Tape Club

Nov 98. (7") <ACME 25> **WHEN THE SUN SHINES DOWN ON THE TOWN YOU LEFT BEHIND. / SKY BLUE OCEAN SONG** (split w/ DENVER)

Nov 98. (7") <ACME 27> **THE SKY IS EMPTY. / SECRET NATURE SINGS** (split w/ MANDORRIS)

Dec 98. (7") <ACME 31> **GOOD MORNING SHIVA** (split w/ METRONOME)

Jun 99. (5"; as BEANMIX) **THERE'S ALWAYS A LIGHT THAT SHINES. / SOMEONE TO LIVE FOR** (split w/ VERNA BROCK)

Audio Information Ensemble / Audio Information Ensemble

Mar 99. (10"m-lp/m-cd; as JIM RAO & HIS ORANGE CAKE MIX ORCHESTRA) <(AIP 008/+CD)> **MICROCOSMIC WONDERLAND: BEDROOM MUSIC VOLUME 1**
– Pacific ocean park / King of inertia / I just can't be without you again / I heard your whisper / Some sweetness / Wind painting.

Clover / Clover

Sep 99. (7"ep) <(CVR 709)> **BEACH FLOWER EP** Jan99
– Delicate angel / Delicate flower / Disco baby girl / Disco on the beach.

Nov 99. (cd) *Clover*; <(CLUS 40-2)> **DREAM WINDOW** Mar99
– When summer returns / Maybe it's all a dream / Void if otherwise unknown / Revelation at 3:33 a.m. / Dream wave tapestry (of stars) / POem for walrus / Sugar maple / Radio magic static / Dreaming of you / Blissful trip / Versus / Glaze / Long lost / Joy of painting / Sonic Surfer 2009 (dreaming in black and white) / Silver lining under water / She needs space (and time) / Song about floating down the river / Feel your desire / Plastic fish.

Sonic Syrup / not iss.

Oct 99. (7") *(SS 1)* **THERE ARE NO WORDS EP** (instrumental)
– Groove soul city / Impala / Beautiful superstar / Hopmeadow.

not iss. / Vividsound

Nov 99. (cd) <VRCD 3302> **PINK GRAPEFRUIT** Japan
– The space within / Ever after all / Still behind the clouds / Pink grapefruit / Lost my watch / Birthday cake / Something – Anything / The space without / Back to the island / Secret nature sings / Within / She can sail me to the stars / Mellow hit #4 / River of glass / Wash away.

not iss. / Black Bean & Placenta Tape Club

Mar 01. (cd) <none> **A SHADOW OF ECLIPSE AND OTHER PHASES OF THE MOON**
– Your favorite space journey / A wind wave takes me far away / First day of spring / Osaka morning sunshine / Someday never happens / Seeds and stones / Early morning space time / Mellow sun / Soul expression #3 / Westerly beaches / Sail back to yesterday / Dream window shade / The space I'm in / Soul expression #2 / Lost inside a dream of an ocean sun / The warm summer breeze and you.

not iss. / Twilight Furniture

May 02. (cd) <TF 002> **HARMONIES AND ATMOSPHERES**
– Zzzz / Andthenagain / Days of time and space / Clustertone / WAy out there / Less is more / The surrealist painter / Everywhere the light goes / Deluxe harmonia / Safe inside your sky / Thought balloon / Save for a rainy day / June moonbeams / Touch down Earth / Lost in the crowd.

– compilations, etc. –

Jul 97. (cd) *Black Bean & Placenta Tape Club*; <(BBPTC 83)> **LOVECLOUD AND SECRET TAPE** Jun97
– A gentle wind rushes through her hair / Going nowhere / Forever will be / A mixture of clouds and sun / Strawberry swirl / Pacific coast highway / Blue sky bar / Summer sunshine girl / Closely guarded secrets / Invisible chaos / Silly love songs / Valley of clay / Pacific coast highway revisited / Bedtime for the baby / The last time I saw God was when I looked into your eyes / Jai guru Dev / Emerald beach at sunset / Glitter daze (part 2).

ORANGE CAN

Formed: London, England ... early 1999 by brothers JASON and JAMES ASLETT, who soon recruited the help of RORY CLARKE, and LEE CATLIN. In true indie fashion the ASLETT boys set about making their debut at home using whatever instrumentation and recording equipment they had at hand. Their original idea had been to market this as a demo, but after indie imprint, 'Regal', got a hold of the 'ENTRANCE HIGH RISE' demo, they decided to release it as was the following year (2000). The record showcased the sibling's psychedelic indie pop leanings and brought them many comparisons to PINK FLOYD, although obviously with an early nineties Brit-rock slant. By the time of its release, the ASLETTS bolstered their duo-standing to a quartet (with the above mentioned players) and had issued the EP, 'ENGINE HOUSE'. In 2001, the lads released a second set, 'HOME BURNS', which was slightly disappointing compared its predecessor.

Album rating: ENTRANCE HIGH RISE (*6) / HOME BURNS (*5)

JASON ASLETT – vocals, guitar, piano / **JAMES ASLETT** – guitar / **LEE CATLIN** – bass / **RORY CLARKE** – drums; repl. original (unknown)

Regal / not iss.

Oct 99. (12"ep/cd-ep) *(REG 036/+CD)* **THE ENGINE HOUSE EP**
– In the bag / Down where she lies (reprise) / Bother boots / I don't mind / Light it up.

Mar 00. (lp/cd) *(REG 037/+CD)* **ENTRANCE HIGH RISE**
– High rise / Butterfly / Come on Easies / The big storm / Wheels rolling / Young man / Feed 'em up / Wheels movin' / Beat the sky / Diamonds / Softly / Wasted days / Monkey magic / We love you.

Apr 00. (12"/cd-s) *(REG 043/+CD)* **YOUNG MAN. / CLOSE KNIT FAMILY / HONEY**

ORANGE PEELS

Formed: Redwood City, Bay Area, San Francisco, California, USA . . . 1993 as ALLEN CLAPP AND HIS ORCHESTRA by namesake songwriter, along with LARRY WINTHER, JILL PRIES (ALLEN's wife) and BOB VICKERS. It is important at this point to give the more complex background history of this band. CLAPP, originally from Foster City, California, had played with WINTHER and MAZ KATTUAH in their school days but they had parted ways after several years; KATTUAH and WINTHER going onto to put together the rock outfit The MUMMIES. CLAPP also kept up his musical ambitions going for a few years, but in a more folk direction, in a acoustic duo. He also began doing some solo home-recordings, of which came a single, 'VERY PECULIAR FEELING' (1992), which KATTAUH, who by now had begun his own label, 'Four letter Words', released. This was enough to bring CLAPP to the attention of indie label, 'Bus Stop' who signed him up. It was about this time that CLAPP began trading himself as ALLEN CLAPP AND HIS ORCHESTRA, and released his debut album, 'ONE HUNDRED PERCENT CHANCE OF RAIN' (1994) under this slightly misleading moniker; CLAPP performed and wrote almost all the material on the album, aided in small part by his wife, PRIES. The album was a brilliant piece of bouncy lo-fi power pop, analogous to the early material of PAVEMENT and BLUR. Worth noting on the album, for the titles' humour value is, 'WHY STING IS SUCH AN IDIOT', which is a great riposte to that artist's song, 'If You Love Somebody, Set Them Free'. The following year CLAPP released an EP on 'Darla' records and was rejoined by WINTHER and KATTAUH. Now we are back to where we came in. The quartet played the San Francisco area for a year or two, in which period they also did some studio time. Unfortunately KATTUAH had some issues with the producer, Jeff Saltzmann, who they were working with at the time, and thus left, being replaced by former CEREBRAL CORPS drummer, BOB VICKERS. At which point the band switched names to the ORANGE PEELS. In 1997 the band released their debut set, 'SQUARE', on 'Minty Fresh', which followed on nicely from CLAPP's earlier solo work, in its loving use of clear-cut melodies and catchy hooks. The fans were kept waiting, but were probably not disappointed, with the groups sophomore effort, 'SO FAR' (2001), in as far as it really was a fairly unchanged sound to the former album. Bolstered by the renewed enthusiasm, caused by Bus Stop's re-issue of 'ONE HUNDRED PERCENT . . .', in the millennium, CLAPP again went solo; releasing 'AVAILABLE LIGHT' (2002). Again this was a competent slice of great pop songwriting, showcasing his mix of sixties and seventies rock-pop flavours, with a nineties aesthetic.

Album rating: Allen Clapp And His Orchestra: ONE HUNDRED PERCENT CHANCE OF RAIN (*5) / Orange Peels: SQUARE (*7) / SO FAR (*6) / Allen Clapp: AVAILABLE LIGHT (*6)

ALLEN CLAPP

		not iss.	Four Letter Words
1991.	(7"flexi) <FLW 002> **VERY PECULIAR FEELING. / The Bridge: MOTORCYCLE ANGEL**	-	
1991.	(7") <FLW 004> **A CHANGE IN THE WEATHER. /**	-	
1994.	(7"; Various Artists) <FLW 012> **In A Lonely Place**	-	
	– The apple of my eye / (other 2 by FURTHER + SIX CENTS AND NATALIE).		

		not iss.	Bus Stop
1992.	(7"m) <BUS 019> **SNOW IN THE SUN. / MYSTERY LAWN / HAPPY TO BE SAD**	-	
1994.	(lp; as ALLEN CLAPP AND HIS ORCHESTRA) <BUS 1002> **ONE HUNDRED PERCENT CHANCE OF RAIN**	-	
	– Why Sting is such an idiot / Something strange happens / Life before the breakdown / Scattered showers / Milky Way / She grins and waves goodbyes / Shopping mall disaster #1 / Evening time / Man and Superman / Blaze / Keep it simple. <cd-iss. 1999; BUS 1002CD>		

		not iss.	Elefant
1994.	(7") <ER 156> **BROWN FORMICA TABLE. / THE SUNSET**	-	

ORANGE PEELS

ALLEN CLAPP – vocals / **LARRY WINTHER** – guitar (ex-MUMMIES) / **JILL PRIES** – bass / **BOB VICKERS** – drums (ex-CEREBRAL CORPS) repl. JEFF SALTZMANN

		Minty Fresh	Minty Fresh
Sep 97.	(cd) <(MF 23)> **SQUARE**		Aug97
	– All the world could pass me by / Something strange happens / Get it right / I don't mind the rain / Take me over / Everybody's gone / Spaghetti-o western / She is like a rose / On the way to somewhere / Slow train / Didn't you know? / Man and Superman / Tex / Love coming down.		

		not iss.	Bus Stop
1999.	(7") <BUS 051> **A GIRL FOR ALL SEASONS. / THE PATTERN ON THE WALL**	-	
1999.	(cd-s; by ALLEN CLAPP) <BUS 055> **WHENEVER WE'RE TOGETHER / SAD SEPTEMBER / NIGHT FALLS**	-	
—	added **JOHN MOREMEN** – drums (BOB VICKERS now on guitar)		

		SpinArt	SpinArt
Feb 01.	(cd) <(SPART 088CD)> **SO FAR**		
	– Back in San Francisco / So far / You're so clever / Mazatlan – Shining bright / Redwood city / The pattern on the wall / Mystery lawn / Girl for all seasons / Lost in you – I can see the planets / Every single thing / The West Coast rain.		

ALLEN CLAPP

		March	March
Jun 02.	(cd) <(MAR 079)> **AVAILABLE LIGHT**		
	– Beautiful / Drop me a line / Whenever we're together / Solstice (song for David) / So right / High above the earth / While there's still time / Not gonna fake it / Tumble and fall / Open door / Just like yesterday / Big bright shiny yellow sun / Whenever we're together (reprise).		

ORANGER

Formed: San Francisco, California, USA . . . 1997 by JIM LINDSAY (formerly of STICK FIGURES), MIKE DRAKE (ex-OVERWHELMING COLORFAST) and CHAD DYER. The band's sound centered around their devotion to classic 60's psychedelia, likened alot to the BEACH BOYS' acid period, although inevitably tinged by the rock progressions of the nineties West Coast. Following a well received gig at a West Coast festival in 1997, they managed to get time to put down tracks in the studio. Around the same period DYER decided to take his bow, to be replaced by MATT HARRIS, who had played with DRAKE in OVERWHELMING COLORFAST. The newly-restored threesome's studio efforts eventually bore fruition, becoming their debut LP, 'DOORWAY TO NORWAY' (1998). The succeeding year saw the Bay Area trio get taken up by 'Amazing Grease' records, who subsequently re-promoted their debut album, and released their sophomore effort, 'THE QUIET VIBRATION LAND' (2000), a record which showcased the additional talent of recently acquired, multi-instrumentalist, PATRICK MAIN. • **Covered:** PORPOISE SONG (Monkees).

Album rating: DOORWAY TO NORWAY (*5) / THE QUIET VIBRATION LAND (*6)

MIKE DRAKE – vocals, guitar, keyboards (ex-OVERWHELMING COLORFAST) / **MATT HARRIS** – bass, vocals, keyboards, guitar (ex-OVERWHELMING COLORFAST) / **JIM LINDSAY** – drums, percussion (ex-STICK FINGERS) / **ALAN STEWART** – keyboards; repl. CHAD DYER (he was bass player until 1997)

		not iss.	Pray For Mojo
1998.	(white-lp) <none> **DOORWAY TO NORWAY**	-	
	– Mike Love not war / Eggtooth / Everything goes away / Wolfy / Donald, you're freaking out / Jettsett traveler / Telepathic waves / This snake will kill you. <(re+UK-iss.Jan00 on 'Amazing Grease' cd+=/lp; AG 04 CD/V)> – (Slow nerve action.		

		not iss.	Horsebrand
1999.	(7") **MIKE LOVE NOT WAR. / PORPOISE SONG**		

		Amazing Grease	Amazing Grease
1999.	(7"m) <AG 01> **CIRCLE GETS THE SQUARE. / BIZARRO / BLEEDING KNEECAPS**		
2000.	(7") <M-28> **NICE RIDE. / (other by ALIEN CRIME SYNDICATE)**	-	
	(above issued on 'm-theory')		
Oct 00.	(7"m) <(AG 07)> **BLUEST GLASS EYE SEA. / SPACE COLONY BOOGIE / THE AMAZING LIFE OF . . .**		

		Poptones	Amazing Grease
Nov 00.	(cd/lp) (MC 5023CD) <AG 06 CD/V> **THE QUIET VIBRATION LAND**		Sep00
	– Sorry Paul / Suddenly upsidedown / Lay down your head, child / A view of the city from an airplane / The quiet vibration land theme VII / Falling stars / Texas snow / Springtime / The mother of all my pain / Collapsed in the superdome / Stoney Curtis in reverse / The quiet vibration land theme VII / Green gold rolling skull / Straight love. (lp-iss.Dec00 on 'Amazing Grease'; AG 06V)		
May 01.	(7") (MC 500235) **TEXAS SNOW. / THE WINTER GARDENER**		-

ORGANISATION (see under ⇒ KRAFTWERK)

ORLANDO

Formed: London, England . . . 1994 by keyboard player/composer, RICHARD DICKON EDWARDS and his singing accomplice, TIM CHIPPING, a former funeral director. Conceived as an attempt to parody the archetypal girlie indie band, ORLANDO additionally consisted of SIMON KEHOE and STEPHEN JEFFERIS in its initial incarnation. As the sound gradually became heavier than EDWARDS had envisaged, he split the group before later reuniting with TIM and recording the 'REPRODUCTION IS POLLUTION' single for 'Sarah' under the moniker, SHELLEY, in Spring '95. Sinking without trace, the record's failure spurred on the duo to resurrect ORLANDO, bringing in backing musicians, NEIL TURNER and MIKE AUSTIN. In September '96, 'Blanco Y Negro' delivered their debut single proper, 'JUST FOR A SECOND', a mutton-dressed-as-lamb synth-pop effort that was shamelessly hyped as ORLANDO were placed firmly in the vanguard of the hopelessly contrived, Melody Maker-created 'Romo' scene. An embarrassing attempt to revive the early 80's 'New Romantic' movement, the kids stayed at home in their droves and the accompanying 'Club Skinny' package tour fell flat.

Hardly even built up before they were knocked down, ORLANDO were left licking their wounds among the wreckage of 'Romo' as debut album, 'PASSIVE SOUL' (1997), was virtually ignored. EDWARDS subsequently performed under the name FOSCA with various line-ups, releasing the self-produced EP, 'NERVOUS, LONDON' in late '99 before hooking up with long-term musical partner and former Brighton man, ALEX SHARKEY. With a line-up completed by RACHEL STEVENSON and SHEILA B, the group recorded the IAN CATT-produced 'ON EARTH TO MAKE THE NUMBERS UP' (2000). Released on indie label, 'Shinkansen', the record was preceded by 'THE AGONY WITHOUT THE ECSTASY' single. CATT was again at the helm for 2001's 'SUPINE ON THE ASTROTURF' EP and 'DIARY OF AN ANTIBODY' album (2002).

Album rating: PASSIVE SOUL (*6) / Fosca: ON EARTH TO MAKE THE NUMBERS UP (*5) / DIARY OF AN ANTIBODY (*5)

RICHARD DICKON EDWARDS (b. Bildeston, Suffolk, England) – keyboards, vocals / **SIMON KEHOE** – vocals, keyboards (left before debut) / added **TIM CHIPPING** (b. TIMOTHY MARK) – vocals / **STEPHEN JEFFERIS** – guitar (left before debut; formed CODY)

	Sarah	not iss.
Apr 95. (7"/cd-s; as SHELLEY) *(SARAH 098/+CD)* **REPRODUCTION IS POLLUTION. / PREJUDICE / HERO**		–

—— revived ORLANDO with **DICKON + TIM** plus augmentation from **NEIL TURNER + MIKE AUSTIN**

	Blanco Y Negro	not iss.
Sep 96. (c-s) *(NEG 91C)* **JUST FOR A SECOND / SOMETHING TO WRITE HOME ABOUT**		–
(12"+=/cd-s+=) *(NEG 91/+CD)* – ('A'mixes).		
Nov 96. (7"ep/c-ep/cd-ep) *(NEG 98/+C/CD)* **THE MAGIC EP**		–
– Don't kill my rage / Fatal / Up against it / Contained.		
Apr 97. (7"/c-s) *(NEG 101/+C)* **NATURE'S HATED. / SOMEDAY SOON**		–
(cd-s+=) *(NEG 101CD)* – ('A'mixes).		
Sep 97. (cd) *(0630 19718-2)* **PASSIVE SOUL**		–
– Introduction / Furthest point away / Just for a second / Nature's hated / On dry land / Contained / Afraid again / Happily unhappy / Don't sleep alone / Save yourself / Three letters / Here (so find me).		

—— EDWARDS disbanded ORLANDO in 1998

FOSCA

RICHARD DICKON EDWARDS – vocals, (some) guitar / with various musicians incl. **RACHEL STEVENSON** – synth, backing vocals

	Something Velvet	not iss.
Nov 99. (cd-ep) **NERVOUS, LONDON**		–

—— added **ALEX SHARKEY** – guitars, bass, keyboards, keyboards, vocals (ex-BRIGHTER, ex-HAL, of PINKIE) / **SHEILA B** – cello

	Shinkansen	not iss.
Jun 00. (cd-s) *(SHINKANSEN 25)* **THE AGONY WITHOUT THE ECSTASY / CONFUSED AND PROUD / WEIGHTLESS**		–
Oct 00. (cd) *(SHINKANSEN 26)* **ON EARTH TO MAKE THE NUMBERS UP**		–
– The agony without the ecstasy / It's going to end in tears (all I know) / The millionaire of your own hair / Storytelling Johnny / Assume nothing / Live deliberately / On Earth to make the numbers up / There is another country.		
Sep 01. (cd-ep) *(SHINKANSEN 32)* **SUPINE ON THE ASTROTURF EP**		–
– Supine on the astroturf / Square in the social circle / My body isn't me.		
Jun 02. (cd-ep) *(SHINKANSEN 36)* **SECRET CRUSH ON THIRD TROMBONE**		–
– Secret crush on third trombone / Diary of an antibody: entries 1-22 / Diary of an antibody: entries 23-30.		
Aug 02. (cd) *(SHINKANSEN 38)* **DIARY OF AN ANTIBODY**		–
– Secret crush on third trombone / Idiot savant / The director's cut / Oh well there's always reincarnation / Universal gatecrasher / Supine on the astroturf / I'm on your side / Letter to Saint Christopher / I know I have been happier / Rude esperanto.		

—— **KATE DORMAN** – keyboards; was added for live shows

Jim O'ROURKE

Born: 1969, Chicago, Illinois, USA. Tinkering with guitars at the age of six, O'ROURKE's subsequent career was hard to pinpoint as the soloist was so prolific in his future music. At university, the unique songwriter had composed enough material for a good few albums, collaborating with improvisational guitarist DEREK BAILEY on 'REMOVE THE NEED', 'TAMPER' and 'TERMINAL PHARMACY'. Whilst O'ROURKE contemplated a solo career, he also engaged in an ongoing experiment with rock troupe GASTR DEL SOL and worked as co-producer and co-writer for the German experimentalists FAUST (while maintaining a strong bond with post-angular rockers, TORTOISE). The man released the brilliant 'BAD TIMING' (on 'Drag City') which followed up 1997's quasi-acoustic 'HAPPY DAYS'. Springing back in early '99, he issued the "already-a" masterpiece 'EUREKA', a startling album that awoke new fans to JIM's ever existing genius. From the epic 7-minute plus opener, 'WOMEN OF THE WORLD' (a re-working of IVOR CUTLER'S comic opus, done O'ROURKE style of course!) through to the haunting piano and lap steel ballad 'GHOST SHIP IN A STORM', the bizarre artwork of a manchild holding a rabbit into his groin (!) didn't stop the word-of-mouth popularity surrounding the new SPIRIT-meets-FLOYD/NYMAN/TORTOISE long player. Following 1999's burst of maverick creativity that also saw the release of a collaborative effort with GUNTER MULLER ('SLOW MOTION') and an EP, 'HALFWAY TO A THREEWAY', O'ROURKE resurfaced in late 2001 with his third solo effort for 'Drag City', 'INSIGNIFICANCE'. Continuing in the spirit of his most recent work, the latter presented JIM's warped worldview in all its lovingly crafted, bittersweetly engaging glory.
• **Note:** A different JIM O'ROURKE released a few lp's ('Ar Hoelion Wyth' and 'Y Bont') between 1984 and '88.

Album rating: REMOVE THE NEED (*5) / TAMPER (*5) / TERMINAL PHARMACY (*6) / HAPPY DAYS (*5) / BAD TIMING (*7) / EUREKA (*8) / INSIGNIFICANCE (*8)

JIM O'ROURKE – vocals, guitar, etc

	Sound Of Pig	not iss.
1989. (c) **SOME KIND OF PAGAN**	–	– German
	audiofile	not iss.
1990. (c) **IT TAKES TIME TO DO NOTHING**	–	– German
	Generations Unlimited	not iss.
1990. (c-s; split w/ DAVID PRESCOTT) **FEY**	–	– German
	Enterpfuhl	not iss.
1991. (lp) **THE GROUND BELOW ABOVE OUR HEADS**	–	– German
	Sound Of Pig	not iss.
1991. (c) **SECURE ON THE LOOSE RIM**	–	– German
	Staalplaat	not iss.
1992. (d-cd) *(STCD 048)* **DISENGAGE**		– German
– Mere (parts 1, 2 & 3) // A young person's guide to drowning (parts 1 & 2). *(UK-iss.Feb96; same)*		
	La Legend Des Voix	not iss.
1992. (cd; with SYLLYK) **FRONTIERES?**	–	– German

—— joined ex-SQUIRREL BAIT member DAVID GRUBBS in the duo, GASTR DEL SOL

	not iss.	Metamkine
1993. (cd-ep) *(009)* **RULES OF REDUCTION**	–	
	not iss.	Complacency
1993. (cd-ep; JIM O'ROURKE / EDDIE PREVOST) *(9302)* **THIRD STRAIGHT DAY MADE PUBLIC**	–	
– Reason for eyelids / Two's company / A mean fiddle / On a slow mend.		
	not iss.	TableOfThe Elements
1993. (7") **MUNI. / MICHEL PICCOLI**	–	
	Extreme	not iss.
Nov 93. (cd) *(9)* **TAMPER**		– German
– Spirits never forgive / He felt the patient memory of a reluctant sea / Ascend through unspoken shadow. <re-iss. Nov95 on 'P-Vine'; 23008>		
Sep 94. (cd) *(18)* **REMOVE THE NEED**		– German
– Chicago one / Zurich one / Zurich two / Chicago two.		

—— In 1994, O'ROURKE collaborated with HENRY KAISER on the CD album, 'TOMORROW KNOWS WHERE YOU LIVE' for 'Victo'; VICTOCD 014

—— in the same year, O'ROURKE (+ DARIN GRAY of DAZZLING KILLMEN) formed one-off BRISE-GLACE and the album, 'WHEN IN VANITAS'

	not iss.	Soleilmoon
1994. (dat) **USE**	–	
	not iss.	TableOfThe Elements
1995. (7"; split w/ TONY CONRAD) **JAPANESE ROOM AT LA PAGODE**	–	
	not iss.	Tzadik
Dec 95. (cd) *<7011>* **TERMINAL PHARMACY**	–	
– Cede / (interlude) / Terminal pharmacy.		
	Revenant	Revenant
Feb 97. (cd) *<REV 101>* **HAPPY DAYS**		
– Happy days (47 mins). *(UK-iss.Nov97; same)*		

—— now with **JOHN McENTIRE** – drums / **JEB BISHOP** – trombone / **THYMME JONES** – trumpet

	Drag City	Drag City
Aug 97. (lp/cd) *<(DC 120/+CD)>* **BAD TIMING**		
– There's hell in hello, but more in goodbye / 94 the long way / Bad timing / Happy trails. *(cd re-iss. Jan01 on 'Domino'; REWIGCD 004)*		
	Some	not iss.
Mar 98. (10") *(SOME 08)* **PLEASE NOTE OUR FAILURE**		–
	not iss.	S.Y.R.
1998. (cd-ep; with SONIC YOUTH) **INVITO AL CIELO / HUNGARA VIVO / RADIO-AMATOROJ**	–	

—— now with **KEN CHAMPION** – piano / **JEB BISHOP** – trombone / **GLENN KOTCHKE** – drums / **DARIN GRAY** – bass / **JOAN MORRONE** – french horn / **ROB MAZUREK** – cornet / etc

	Domino	Drag City
Mar 99. (cd/lp) *(WIG CD/LP 62) <DC 162>* **EUREKA**		
– Prelude to 110 or 220 – Women of the world / Ghost ship in a storm / Movie on the way down / Through the night softly / Please patronize our sponsors / Something big / Eureka / Happy holidays.		
Jul 99. (cd; JIM O'ROURKE & GUNTER MULLER) *(4EARSCD 514)* **SLOW MOTION**		–
– Now all seen heard then forgotten / A faster silence / An Atlantean returned knows the value of stars.		
(above issued on 'For 4 Ears')		
Nov 99. (12"ep/cd-ep) *(RUG 103 T/CD) <DC 178>* **HALFWAY TO A THREEWAY / THE WORKPLACE. / NO SPORT, MARTIAL ART / FUZZY SUN**		Jun00
Sep 00. (cd; by JIM O'ROURKE & MATS GUSTAFSSON) *(INCUSCD 38)* **XYLOPHONEN VIRTUOSEN**		–
(above issued on 'Incus')		
Nov 01. (cd/lp) *(WIG CD/LP 104) <DC 202>* **INSIGNIFICANCE**		
– All downhill from here / Insignificance / Therefore, I am / Memory lame / Good times / Get a room / Life goes off.		
Feb 02. (promo-cd-s) *(RUG 135CD)* **THEREFORE, I AM**		–

Beth ORTON

Born: Dec'70, Norfolk, England. A one-time Buddhist nun (after her mother died of cancer), she was discovered in 1991/2 by WILLIAM ORBIT who saw her performing in a play. Her collaborative work with ORBIT (on the Japanese-only 'SUPERPINKYMANDY' CD) was subsequently heard by The CHEMICAL BROTHERS and RED SNAPPER, the former act employing her downbeat but poignant vocals on the 1995 'Exit Planet Dust' album track, 'Alive Alone'. The following year, she found herself on the books of 'Heavenly' records, delivering her debut album, 'TRAILER PARK' soon after. An affecting blend of fragile folk and subtle lo-fi trip-hop rhythms, it won praise from such diverse camps as Folk Roots magazine and Mixmag (it was even nominated for the 1997 Mercury Music Prize). The same year (1997), BETH's four singles scored successively higher chart placings, the re-released 'SHE CRIES YOUR NAME', revealing the melancholy depths of her NICK DRAKE/SANDY DENNY-esque muse. The lanky ORTON (she's 6 feet tall) ended the year on a high note, collaborating with her long-time hero, TERRY CALLIER on the Top 40 EP 'BEST BIT'. The princess of bedsitter music served up a second helping of rich, thought-provoking tunes in the shape of 1999's 'CENTRAL RESERVATION'. A deserved UK Top 20 success (with guest appearances from BEN WATT, BEN HARPER, DAVE ROBACK and DR. JOHN), BETH also made some headway in the States where she had befriended BECK (to namecheck but a few). Songs such as 'STOLEN CAR', the title track (both Top 40 hits) and 'STARS ALL SEEM TO WEEP' were emotionally and lyrically attuned like paintings set on the deepest canvas taking every colour imaginable from rainforest green to deepest silver. • **Songwriters:** Most with rhythm section FRIEND and BARNES, except SHE CRIES YOUR NAME; she co-wrote this with WILLIAM ORBIT. Covered IT'S NOT THE SPOTLIGHT (Bobby Bland; c.) / I WISH I NEVER SAW THE SUNSHINE (Spector – Greenwich – Barry) / DOLPHINS (Fred Neil).

Album rating: SUPERPINKYMANDY (*5) / TRAILER PARK (*8) / CENTRAL RESERVATION (*8) / DAYBREAKER (*6)

BETH ORTON – vocals, acoustic guitar (ex-SPILL); with **TED BARNES** – guitar (of JUNCTIONS) / **ALI FRIEND** – double bass (of RED SNAPPER) / **WILL BLANCHARD** – drums (of SANDALS) / guest **DAVID BOULTER** – harmonium / + string section

			not iss.	Toshiba
1993.	(cd) *(TOC 7984)* **SUPERPINKYMANDY**		–	Japan

– Don't wanna know about evil / Faith will carry / Yesterday's over / She cries your name / When you wake / Roll the dice / City blue / The prisoner / Where do you go / Release me.

			Heavenly	Dedicated
Jul 96.	(7"one-sided) *(HVN 56)* **I WISH I NEVER SAW THE SUNSHINE**			–
Sep 96.	(10"ep/cd-ep) *(HVN 60 10/CD)* **SHE CRIES YOUR NAME / TANGENT. / SAFETY / IT'S NOT THE SPOTLIGHT**			–
Oct 96.	(cd/c/lp) *(HVNLP 17 CD/MC/LP) <44007>* **TRAILER PARK**	68		

– She cries your name / Tangent / Don't need a reason / Live as you dream / Sugar boy / Touch me with your love / Whenever / How far / Someone's daughter / I wish I never saw the sunshine / Galaxy of emptiness.

Jan 97.	(10"ep/cd-ep) *(HVN 64 10/CD)* **TOUCH ME WITH YOUR LOVE. / PEDESTAL / GALAXY OF EMPTINESS**	60	–
Mar 97.	(c-ep/10"ep/cd-ep) *(HVN 65 CS/10/CD)* **SOMEONE'S DAUGHTER. / I WISH I NEVER SAW THE SUNSHINE / IT'S THIS I AM I FIND**	49	–
Jun 97.	(c-s) *(HVN 68CS)* **SHE CRIES YOUR NAME (1997 version) / IT'S NOT THE SPOTLIGHT**	40	–
	(10"+=/cd-s+=) *(HVN 68-10/CD)* – Bullet / Best bit.		

		Heavenly	Heavenly
Dec 97.	(c-ep; BETH ORTON featuring TERRY CALLIER) *(<HVN 72CS>)* **BEST BIT EP**	36	

– Best bit / Skimming stone / Dolphins.
(12"ep+=/cd-ep+=) *(<HVN 72 12/CD>)* – Lean on me.

— next with guitarist **BEN HARPER**

Mar 99.	(c-s) *(HVN 89CS)* **STOLEN CAR / PRECIOUS MAYBE**	34	
	(cd-s+=) *(HVN 89CD)* – I love how you love me.		
	(cd-s) *(HVN 89CD2)* – ('A'side) / Stars all seem to weep (shed version) / Touch me with your love (live).		
Mar 99.	(d-lp/c/cd) *(HVNLP 22/+MC/CD) <19038>* **CENTRAL RESERVATION**	17	

– Stolen car / Sweet decline / Couldn't cause me harm / So much more / Pass in time / Central reservation / Stars all seem to weep / Love like laughter / Blood red river / Devil song / Feel to believe / Central reservation.

Sep 99.	(cd-s) *(HVN 92CD1)* **CENTRAL RESERVATION. / CENTRAL RESERVATION (Spiritual Life – Ibadan remix) / CENTRAL RESERVATION (William Orbit remix)**	37	–
	(cd-s) *(HVN 92CD2)* – ('A'-Deep dish modern red rock mixes; remix edit / remix / 2000 dub).		
	(12") *(HVN 92-12)* – ('A'-Spiritual Life – Ibadan remix) / ('A'-Deep dish modern red rock 2000 dub).		
Jul 02.	(cd-ep) *(HVN 115CD)* **CONCRETE SKY EP**		–
	– Concrete sky / Ali's waltz / Bobby Gentry / Carmella (Four Tet remix).		
Jul 02.	(lp/cd) *(HVNLP 37/+CD) <39918>* **DAYBREAKER**	8	
	– Paris train / Concrete sky / Mount Washington / Anywhere / DAybreaker / Carmella / God song / This one's gonna bruise / Ted's waltz / Thinking about tomorrow.		
Nov 02.	(cd-s) *(HVN 125CDS)* **ANYWHERE / BEAUTIFUL WORLD / ANYWHERE (Two Lone Swordsmen remix) / ANYWHERE (video)**	55	–

OSTLE BAY (see under ⇒ TRASH CAN SINATRAS)

OTHER TWO (see under ⇒ NEW ORDER; in 80's section)

OUTRAGEOUS CHERRY

Formed: Detroit, Michigan, USA ... 1992 by MATTHEW SMITH (also leader of prolific roots-rock outfit, The VOLEBEATS), CHAD GILCHRIST, LARRY RAY and percussionist DEB AGNOLLI. This noisy, melodic, garage-rock quartet debuted in 1993 with the 7" single, 'PALE, FRAIL & LOVELY', and went on to churn out a plethora of albums in the same vein, beginning with 1994's eponymous 'OUTRAGEOUS CHERRY' set. In 1996, the group followed this moderately successful album with the DIY covers LP, 'STEREO ACTION RENT PARTY', including scuzzed-up versions of Prince's 'SIGN O THE TIMES', Television's 'DAYS', Scott Walker's 'BOY CHILD', 10cc's 'I'M NOT IN LOVE' and a whole host of bizarro renditions. Prolific as ever, they delivered the sixties-soundin' 'NOTHINGS GONNA CHEER YOU UP' in 1997, subsequently followed by a switch to the 'DF2K' imprint and the unfettering of 'OUT THERE IN THE DARK' (1999), an album widely considered to be the band's best. OUTRAGEOUS CHERRY turned space-rock and released their very first "space-opera", 'THE BOOK OF SPECTRAL PROJECTIONS' (2001) – a funky, visceral and noisy album from the outset, the combo's musical inhibitions had them playing garage PHILIP GLASS while unsuspectingly cranking their amps up to full volume. • **Covered:** MISTY MOUNTAIN (Silver Apples) / KEEP EVERYTHING UNDER YOUR HAT (Skip Spence).

Album rating: OUTRAGEOUS CHERRY (*6) / STEREO MACTION RENT PARTY (*5) / NOTHING'S GONNA CHEER YOU UP (*7) / OUT THERE IN THE DARK (*7) / THE BOOK OF SPECTRAL PROJECTIONS (*5)

MATTHEW SMITH – vocals, guitar / **LARRY RAY** – guitar / **CHAD GILCHRIST** – bass / **DEB AGNOLLI** – drums

		not iss.	March
1994.	(cd/c) *<MAR 010>* **OUTRAGEOUS CHERRY**	–	

– Pale frail lovely one / The stare / If someone loves you / 'Til I run out / West / Party's over / Ace 100 / Withdrawal / Overwhelmed / Bridge / Radio telephone operator procedures (part 2).

1995.	(7") *<MAR 013>* **ALL IN A CHAIN. / ALL IN A CHAIN (backwards)**	–	

		Third Gear	Third Gear
1995.	(ltd-7"purple) *<3G 06>* **PALE FRAIL LOVELY ONE. / IT ALWAYS RAINS**	–	
Jun 96.	(cd) *<3G 14>* **STEREO ACTION RENT PARTY**	–	

– Sign of the times / Days / Qui peut dire? / Song from the bottom of a well / Wonderful / Boy child / I'm not in love / Chinese white / Miss X / Reel around the Moon / Reel around the fountain / Some of them are old / A bunch of lonesome heroes / Make the world go away.

Jun 97.	(cd) *<3G 18>* **NOTHING'S GONNA CHEER YOU UP**		

– I've never seen your world / More than blue / Panavision 70 / Genevieve / Nothing's gonna cheer you up / You don't understand me / Jayne / The hypnotic eye / Nope / Where things belong / Strained.

		not iss.	Disques Twist Top
1998.	(7") *<TT 02>* **QUAND ON A QUE L'AMOUR. / (other by Godzuki)**	–	

		Del-Fi	Del-Fi
Aug 99.	(cd) *<(DF2K 2002)>* **OUT THERE IN THE DARK**		

– Georgie don't you know / Togetherness / Where do I go when you dream? / Corruptable / Eclipsed / Easy come, uneasy glow / Tracy / Only the easy way down / Song for Inoshiro Honda / A bad movie / It's always never / Out there in the dark / There's no escape from the infinite. (re-iss. Sep00 on 'Poptones'; MC 5003CD)

— (1999) **ARAN RUTH** – bass; repl. GILCHRIST

		not iss.	Mind Expansion
2000.	(cd-ep) *<016>* **X-RAYS IN THE CLOUDMINE**	–	

– Only your yesterdays / The book of dead time / Misty mountain.

		Poptones	Poptones
Jun 01.	(cd) *<(MC 5014CD)>* **THE BOOK OF SPECTRAL PROJECTIONS**		

– The book of spectral projections / Shadow of my universe / The unseen devourers / Fate's strange parade / The hour glass / Here where the stars are cracking up / Wide awake in the spirit world / My demon friend / Through parallel dimensions / It's only sorcery / The astral transit authority / History of magic / Of transparent versions / Is it time? / Everything's back to normal / When you emerge / Always less than changing / Electric child of witchcraft rising / Spectral sunrise / It's so nice to be here. *<US re-iss. Apr02 on 'Rainbow Quartz'; 1054>*

OVA (see under ⇒ FAITH OVER REASON)

OWEN (see under ⇒ JOAN OF ARC)

OWLS (see under ⇒ JOAN OF ARC)

OXES

Formed: Baltimore, Maryland, USA ... late 90's by guitarist NATALIO, guitarist MARC MILLER and drummer CHRISTOPHER FREELAND. Eccentric and conceptual, The OXES' experimental rock is delivered with attitude and follows a non-conformist manifesto. They are very much a band defined by their live performances. They perform music that appears improvisational (although isn't), using only their (wireless) guitars and drumkit, while standing on black boxes confronting the audience. In 1999, they released the single 'PANDA STRONG' (for the 'Reptilian' imprint), followed by a split set with BIG'N. And then in 2000, their eponymous debut LP settled them in, while follow-up, 'OXXXES' (2002), stirred up the angst. On record the OXES sound much like DON CABALLERO, although they do manage to translate some of their ideas, and style, onto the album. The OXES' main failing seemed to be their inability to recreate the intensity and originality of their live shows on to record.

Album rating: OXES (*6) / OXXXES (*7)

NATALIO FOWLER – vocals, guitar / **MARC MILLER** – guitar / **CHRISTOPHER FREELAND** – drums

			not iss.	Reptilian
1999.	(7"ep) <042> **PANDA STRONG / KAZ HAYASHI EP**		–	☐

– Panda strong / Kaz Hayashi / Challenger / Year long disaster.

			Monitor	Monitor
Jun 00.	(cd) <(MON 006)> **OXES**		☐	☐

– Dear spirit, I'm in France / I'm from Hell, open a windle / Panda strong / Your street vs. Wall Street / Horses are OK / And giraffe, natural enemies / Riki creem calls this one 'Chivas Regal'.

| May 02. | (cd/lp) <(MON 012 CD/LP)> **OXXXES** | ☐ | ☐ |

– Boss kitty / Half half and half / Kaz Hayashi '01 / Chyna, Chyna, Chyna / Tony Baines / Take and free Miami / Bees won / Russia is here.

P (see under ⇒ BUTTHOLE SURFERS; in 80's section)

PACIFIC RADIO (see under ⇒ MONOGRAPH)

PACK (see under ⇒ SPEAR OF DESTINY)

PALACE (see under ⇒ OLDHAM, Will)

PALE

Formed: Dublin, Ireland . . . 1992 by frontman MATTHEW DEVEREAUX. This eccentric Irish trio were a darker, quirkier CARTER THE UNSTOPPABLE SEX MACHINE. Propelled by DEVEREAUX's manic, madcap vocals, they signed to 'A&M' after releasing two independent tapes in Ireland. The typically frenetic 'DOGS WITH NO TAILS' – the PALE's take on the 'What Are Little Girls Made Of?' nursery rhyme – gave them a Simon Mayo Record Of The Week. It proved to be one of the highlights of debut album 'HERE'S ONE WE MADE EARLIER'. This collection contained a diversity of influences and sounds, including ska, disco, and Eastern European mandolins; but its originality often bordered on novelty.

Album rating: HERE'S ONE WE MADE EARLIER (*5)

MATTHEW DEVEREAUX – vocals / +2

			own label	not iss.
1990.	(c) *(none)* **WHY GO BALD?**		–	– Irish

– Shut up Venus / Butterfly / Dogs with no tails / Mother Nature is a man / Delirious / Opium poem / Willie song.

| 1991. | (cd) *(none)* **HAPPY RING HOUSE** | – | – Irish |

– I want to steal your car / Armadillo / Whales / Weela waile / Violins / Jamais / Moon / Bonedigger.

		Hot Press	not iss.
1991.	(7"flexi) *(none)* **MOON**	☐	–
		A&M	not iss.
1992.	(cd) *(none)* **HERE'S ONE WE MADE EARLIER**	☐	–

– Shut up Venus / Mother Nature is a man / I want to steal your car / Dogs with no tails / I don't love you half as much as you do / Butterfly / Violins / Bonedigger.

1992.	(cd-ep) **DOGS WITH NO TAILS / WHALES / ARMADILLO / WEELA WAILE**	☐	–
1992.	(cd-ep) **BUTTERFLY / MOON / JAMAIS**	☐	–
1992.	(cd-ep) **SHUT UP VENUS / UNLESS IT'S FROM YOU / OPIUM POEM / WILLIE SONG**	☐	–
1994.	(cd-ep) **RIPE EP**	☐	–

– Nought point zero (of a hero) / You is what you is / In me / Accident.

		own label	not iss.
1996.	(cd) *(none)* **CHEAPSIDE**	–	– mail-o

– Madame electric / Palate of the beast / Man Friday / Days like these / Shot them in pairs / Baliff / This parade / Not about art / I'm not surprised / Breakfastia / Mrs. Humble / Big Unkle Bill.

| 1997. | (cd) *(none)* **CRIPPLEGATE** | – | – mail-o |

– Dirty habits / Big turnaround / Anarchy as a birthright / Bad terms / Saturday's matinee / 1744 / Roberto's legs / Krying boy / D.I.Y.

| 1997. | (cd) *(none)* **SPUDGUN** | – | – Europe |

– Ladies and gentlemen / My eyes glaze over / Should've seen me / Downsizing / Cobweb / Dry powder / Disco inferno / Lucky boy / Little trinkets / Dying of the light / Plastic bag.

| 2000. | (cd) *(none)* **LONELY SPACE AGE** | ☐ | – |

– Million brilliant stars / Expecting zero / Gain from pain / Dave / Bulb / Pretty Victoria / Jumping beans / The gutter / Morning star avenue / Sacrifice a-go-go.

PALE SAINTS

Formed: Leeds, England . . . 1987 by IAN MASTERS, GRAEME NAYSMITH and CHRIS COOPER with occasional help from ASHLEY HORNER. Clocked by indie stalwart, '4 a.d.' at their debut London gig, this proto-shoegazing outfit were signed up at the same time as more successful peers LUSH, the two bands sharing a fondness for combining intense, abstract guitar textures and distortion with pop melodies in the mould of The CHAMELEONS or The BOO RADLEYS. Following a debut EP, 'BARGING INTO THE PRESENCE OF GOD', the band scraped a Top 40 placing for their debut album, 'THE COMFORT OF MADNESS' (1990). Initial acclaim gave way to rather harsh and unnecessary criticism in some quarters; while

PALE SAINTS (cont)

MASTERS' vocals could've done with a bit of a charisma boost, there was no denying the potential of their ideas and talent. With HORNER subsequently working full-time on his EDSEL AUCTIONEER project, female vocalist/guitarist MERIEL BARHAM added a new dimension to the band's sound and acted as a counterpoint to MASTERS. A second EP, 'HALF-LIFE', and a Top 75 cover of Nancy Sinatra's 'KINKY LOVE' preceded a follow-up album, 'IN RIBBONS' (1992). Highlights included the arpeggio atmospherics of 'HAIR SHOES' and the BARHAM-sung 'NEVERENDING NIGHT' yet by now all the shoegazing bands had been declared easy meat for a circling press and The PALE SAINTS were buried under the weight of the vicious backlash alongside SLOWDIVE, CHAPTERHOUSE etc. Even MASTERS had departed by the release of 'SLOW BUILDINGS' (1993), COLLEEN BROWNE sharing vocal duties with BARHAM, the latter having taken over songwriting duties. • **Songwriters:** Group penned except; REFLECTIONS FROM A WATERY WORLD (Slapp Happy) / FELL FROM THE SUN (Opal). • **Trivia:** PALE SAINTS issued a Japanese-only album in 1991 'MRS.DOLPHIN'. MERIEL guested on The BOO RADLEYS' 1993 album, 'Giant Steps'.

Album rating: THE COMFORT OF MADNESS (*8) / IN RIBBONS (*9)

IAN MASTERS (b.4 Jan'64, Potters Bar, Hertfordshire, England) – vocals, bass / **GRAEME NAYSMITH** (b. 9 Feb'67, Edinburgh, Scotland) – guitar / **CHRIS COOPER** (b.17 Nov'66, Portsmouth, England) – drums

		4 a.d.	4 a.d.-Warners
Sep 89.	(12"ep/cd-ep) *(BAD 910/+CD)* **BARGING INTO THE PRESENCE OF GOD**	□	-

– Sight of you / She rides the waves / Mother might.

— added **ASHLEY HORNER** – guitar

| Feb 90. | (lp/c/cd) *(CAD 0002/+C/CD) <7564>* **THE COMFORT OF MADNESS** | □ | 40 |

– True coming dream / Little hammer / You tear the world in two / The sea of sound / Way the world is / A deep sleep for Steven / Fell from the sun / Time thief / Insubstantial / Language of flowers / Sight of you. *(cd re-iss. Jul98; GAD 002CD)*

— **MERIEL BARHAM** (b.15 Oct'64, Germany) – guitar, vocals repl. HORNER who concentrated on own group EDSEL AUCTIONEER, whom he spent the last 2 years with

| Oct 90. | (12"ep/cd-ep) *(BAD 015/+CD)* **HALF-LIFE** | □ | - |

– Half-life remembered / Baby maker / Two sick sisters / A revelation.

Jun 91.	(7") *(AD 1009)* **KINKY LOVE. / HAIR SHOES**	72	-
	(12"ep+=/cd-ep+=) **FLESH BALLOON EP** *(CAD 1009/+CD)* – Hunted / Porpoise.		
Mar 92.	(lp/c/cd) *(CAD 2004/+C/CD) <26913>* **IN RIBBONS**	61	Apr92

– Throwing back the apple / Ordeal / Thread of light / Shell / There is no day / Hunted / Hair shoes / Babymaker / Liquid / Neverending night / Featherframe / A thousand stars bust open. *(free 12"w/lp as "The TINWISTLE BRASS BAND") (RIB 1)* **A THOUSAND STARS BUST OPEN. / A REVELATION**

| May 92. | (12"ep/cd-ep) *(BAD 2008/+CD)* **THROWING BACK THE APPLE** | □ | - |

– Throwing back the apple / Blue flower / Half-life remembered / Reflections from a watery world.

— **COLLEEN BROWNE** – bass, vocals (ex-PARACHUTE MEN) repl. MASTERS who formed SPOONFED HYBRID with CHRIS TROUT (ex-AC TEMPLE)

| Aug 94. | (12"ep/cd-ep) *(BAD 4013/+CD)* **FINE FRIEND. / SPECIAL PRESENT / MARIMBA / SURPRISE** | □ | - |
| Sep 94. | (lp/c/cd) *(CAD 4014/+C/CD) <45625>* **SLOW BUILDINGS** | □ | - |

– King Fade / Angel (will you be my) / One blue hill / Henry / Under your nose / Little gesture / Song of Solomon / Fine friend / Gesture of a fear / Always I / Suggestion. *(cd re-iss. Jul98; GAD 4014CD)*

— disbanded later in the year; MASTERS formed ESP SUMMER with IAN DEFEVER of HIS NAME IS ALIVE

PANOPLY ACADEMY . . .

Formed: Bloomington, Indiana, USA ... spring 1996 by NICK QUAGLIARA, RYAN HICKS, MARTY SPROWLES and DARIN GLENN. The post-punk madness of The PANOPLY ACADEMY GLEE CLUB (as they were initially monikered) had audiences squirming in their seats after the 'Secretly Canadian'-released debut 'RAH!' (1998). The sort of music you'd perhaps associate with snobby record shop owners (who look like STEVE ALBINI), arrogant hard-edged music journos and post-rock nutters, the ever-evolving quintet had much in common with their speed-metal/noisecore cousins (and labelmates) RACEBANNON. The only difference was, The PANOPLYs honed a sort of silly math-rock, coupled with screaming feedback noise and SPROWLES' barmy half-yodeling vocals. After the brilliant 'WHAT WE DEFEND' EP, the group issued their sophomore set 'CONCENTUS' (2000) under a slightly adjusted moniker The PANOPLY ACADEMY CORPS OF ENGINEERS. It was a cracked and continually unnerving set which dipped in between electronica, angular rock and noisecore, with the tracks seguing into one another without any pause. The off-kilter time-signatures (a la SLINT) and genuine unsettling sounds were recorded by Jim Kuckowski at 'Engine Room' studios, and had a strange and peculiar resonance. Subsequently (and another name change) The PANOPLY ACADEMY LEGIONNAIRES delivered their most scathing and unconventional set to date, 'NO DEAD TIME' (2001) – a sort of concept album (the old chestnut – man vs. machine), PAL were pushing the envelope with the Dan Burton (of Miners and Ativin)-produced LP. Perhaps as progressive and prolific as RADIOHEAD's 'OK Computer' and just as noisy as and as complicated as anything that The BOREDOMS, The GIZMOS or SCRATCH ACID have done, the listener would be forgiven for tearing off his ears after this sonic assault. And yet, the eerie rumbles and drones juxtaposed between tracks had a quiet contemplation about them. In whatever shape or form, The PANOPLY ACADEMY seemed to be the musical equivalent to hard drugs.

Album rating: RAH! (*6) / CONCENTUS (*6) / NO DEAD TIME (*6)

PANOPLY ACADEMY GLEE CLUB

DARIN GLENN – vocals, guitar, trombone / **MARTY SPROWLES** – guitar, vocals (ex-INTRO TO AIRLIFT) / **BEKKAH WALKER** – keyboards, samples, vocals / **NICK QUAGLIARA** – bass, vocals / **RYAN HICKS** – drums

		not iss.	LiLieL Copgn
1997.	(7") **ADMINISTRATION. / REMEDIAL SYMMETRY**	- not iss.	In All Directions
			Secretly Canadian	Secretly Canadian
1998.	(7") **CAMP KEEP THE QUIET. / (other by A MINOR FOREST)**	-	□
Jul 98.	(cd) *<SC 19CD>* **RAH!**		□

– Allies in insects / Flaminginestinaltrack / Hustle / Henenenaway / Dedache / The post-contest / Dine / The administration / Lake Sanoma / The cagey can speak / Our coordinates from orbit / The entrance of the candidate / Glossalalia / Pligthweaver / Quintet / Sweep / A justifiable trajectory / Somsuey / Blow / Awayteam / Rotherwood / Exquisite corpse.

| Oct 99. | (cd-ep) *<SC 25>* **WHAT WE DEFEND** | - | □ |

– Camp keep the quiet (version) / The Panoply Academy has nothing on you / Something steeped, something stowed / Six volts until good news / Where all the air goes / The dance of the precisely stricken.

PANOPLY ACADEMY CORPS OF ENGINEERS

— **PETE SCHREINER** – bass (ex-INTRO TO AIRLIFT drummer) repl. NICK

— released a special, '9/16/99' for 'LiLieL Copgn' in 2000

| Jun 00. | (cd) *<SC 33CD>* **CONCENTUS** | □ | • **Apr00** |

– Beating boring organ takes / Bogus breath / Rules of engagement / Cash in your coffin / The assist / 50% / Panic button pushers union / Nan nab nab / The entertainers / Tsk tsk.

PANOPLY ACADEMY LEGIONNAIRES

| Mar 01. | (7") *<SC 38>* **DIURNALLY YOURS. / NOCTURNALLY YOURS** | □ | □ |
| May 01. | (cd) *<SC 39CD>* **NO DEAD TIME** | - | □ |

– The 7th direction / Abattoir / The work it / Hushlife / Do you (want to) grind? / Eyesore to bedsore / I, Bloomingtonian / Thermonitor / Highlight & marginalia.

PANSY DIVISION

Formed: San Francisco, California, USA . . . 1991, when openly gay frontman, JON GINOLI, placed an ad in a newspaper looking for queer musicians into The Beatles, Buzzcocks and Ramones. He picked three like minded homosexuals, CHRIS FREEMAN, SALLY SCHLOSSTEIN and finally PATRICK GOODWIN, the self-professed "faggot quartet" getting around to releasing their debut album, 'UNDRESSED', in 1993. A couple more basic (s)punk rock sets appeared in the mid '90's before they slapped it on the table with a tongue-in-bum-cheek variation of an AC/DC number, 'FOR THOSE ABOUT TO SUCK COCK . . . WE SALUTE YOU'. The EP poked fun at two other covers of Judas Priest's 'BREAKING THE LAW' and Kiss's 'SWEET PAIN', while KIRK HAMMETT (don't tell anyone!) made a guest spot on 'HEADBANGER'. 1997's delightfully titled 'MORE LOVIN' FROM OUR OVEN' was another, fairly revealing collection of odds'n'sods, some tracks stretching back to GINOLI's earliest efforts before he'd even formed the band. A set of new songs, 'ABSURD POP SONG ROMANCE', followed in 1998. • **Covered:** TRASH (Roxy Music) / HOMESAPIEN (Pete Shelley) / THE BIGGEST LIE (Husker Du) / CRY FOR A SHADOW (Beat Happening) / JACK U OFF (Prince) / LOOSE (Stooges).

Album rating: UNDRESSED (*6) / DEFLOWERED (*5) / PILE UP compilation (*5) / WISH I'D TAKEN PICTURES (*6) / MORE LOVIN' FROM OUR OVEN (*6) / ABSURD POP SONG ROMANCE (*5)

JON GINOLI – vocals / **PATRICK GOODWIN** – guitar / **CHRIS FREEMAN** – bass / **SALLY SCHLOSSTEIN** – drums

		Lookout	Lookout
Feb 93.	(7"m) *<LOOKOUT 069>* **FEM IN A BLACK LEATHER JACKET. / HOMO CHRISTMAS / SMELLS LIKE QUEER SPIRIT**	-	□
Mar 93.	(cd) *<LOOKOUT 070CD>* **UNDRESSED**	-	□

– Versatile / Fem in a black leather jacket / Bunnies / Boyfriend wanted / The story so far / Hippy dude / Curvature / The cocksucker club / Crabby day / Luck of the draw / Rock and roll queer bar / Surrender your clothing / Anthem. *(UK-iss.Oct94; same as US)*

Jun 93.	(7"m) *<LOOKOUT 074>* **TOUCH MY JOE CAMEL. / HOMOSAPIEN / TRASH**	-	□
Jul 93.	(7") *<(OUT 006)>* **BILL AND TED'S HOMO ADVENTURE. / BIG BOTTOM**	□	Feb93
	(above issued on 'Outpunk')		
Feb 94.	(7"ep) *<LOOKOUT 085>* **I'VE NINE INCH MALES**	-	□

– Fuck buddy / The biggest lie / Cry for a shadow.

| Oct 94. | (cd) *<(LOOKOUT 087CD)>* **DEFLOWERED** | □ | Jun94 |

– Reciprocate / Groovy underwear / Anonymous / Fluffy city / James bondage / Negative queen / Denny / Rachbottomoff / Beercan boy / Kissed / A song of remembrance for old queers / Deep water / Not enough of you to go around / New pleasures / Homosapien.

		not iss.	eMpTy
Sep 94.	(7") *<MT 286>* **JACK U OFF. / STRIP YOU DOWN**	- K	K
Dec 94.	(7") *<(IPU 52)>* **JACKSON. / I REALLY WANTED YOU**	□	□

PANSY DIVISION (cont)

— rhythm section now **CHRIS BOWE + DAVID AYER**

		Damaged Goods	Lookout!
Jan 95.	(7"ep) <*LOOKOUT 109*> **JAMES BONDAGE EP** – James bondage / Real men / Flower / Denny (naked).	-	
Mar 95.	(cd) <*DAMGOOD 60CD*> (*LOOKOUT 110CD*) **PILE UP** (compilation) – I can't sleep / Ring of joy / Fuck Buddy / Cowboys are frequently secretly fond of each other / Flower / Cry for shadow / Real men / Bill & Ted's homosexual adventure / Jack you off / Strip U down / Jackson / Big bottom / Touch my Joe camel / The biggest lie / Denny (naked) / Femme fatale / Trash / Homo Christmas / C.S.F. / Smells like queer spirit.		Feb95

— now with drummer **DUSTIN DONALDSON**

		Lookout	Lookout
Jan 96.	(7"m) <*LOOKOUT 127*> **VALENTINE'S DAY. / HE COULD BE THE ONE / PRETTY BOY (WHAT'S YOUR NAME?)**	-	
Feb 96.	(lp/cd) <(*LOOKOUT 133/+CD*)> **WISH I'D TAKEN PICTURES** – Horny in the morning / Vanilla / I really wanted you / Dick of death / Expiration date / The summer you let your hair grow out / Wish I'd taken pictures / Pillow talk / This is your life / Don't be so sure / Kevin / The ache / Pee shy / Sidewalk sale.		
Aug 96.	(7"ep) <(*LOOKOUT 147*)> **FOR THOSE ABOUT TO SUCK COCK, WE SALUTE YOU EP** – For those about to suck cock, we salute you / Headbanger / Breaking the law / Sweet pain.		
Apr 97.	(7"ep) <(*LOOKOUT 174*)> **QUEER TO THE CORE EP** – Political asshole / I'm gonna be a slut / Two way ass / Expiration date (exp. 01/97).		
Sep 97.	(cd) <(*LK 175CD*)> **MORE LOVIN' FROM OUR OVEN** – I'm gonna be a slut / Manada / Pretty boy (what's your name?) / Hockey hair / Headbanger / Breaking the law / Political asshole / Male model / Valentine's day / Expiration date 01-97 / Summer you let your hair grow out (acoustic) / He could be the one / On any other day / Negative queen (stripped bare) / Sweet pain / One night stand / Two way ass / Bunnies (live) / Manada / Fem in a black leather jacket (demo) / The story so far (demo).		Jun97
Apr 98.	(7") **LOOSE. / (others by ADOLPH'S DOG + JOAN JETT & THE BLACKHEARTS)** (above issued on 'Royalty')	-	
Sep 98.	(cd) <(*LK 198CD*)> **ABSURD POP SONG ROMANCE** – (untitled) / February 17 / Sweet insecurity / It'll never be the same / Better off just friends / Too beautiful / (untitled) / Luv luv luv / (untitled) / The best revenge / Bad boyfriend / (untitled) / You're gonna need your friends / Tinted windows / (untitled) / Glenview / Used to turn me on / Obstacle course / Vicious beauty.		

— The PANSYs are about to release a comeback set in March 2003

PAPA M (see under ⇒ SLINT)

PAPAS FRITAS

Formed: Somerville, Massachusetts, USA ... 1993 by main songwriter TONY GODDESS, alongside girlfriend at-the-time, SHIVIKA ASTHANA and Houston-born KEITH GENDEL, who all met at Tufts University. Exploring paths once trod by The BEATLES, The BEACH BOYS and PHIL SPECTOR, they created a low-fi sonic sound which led to Chicago's 'Minty Fresh' label giving them a try-out. A couple of singles, namely 'PASSION PLAY' and 'WILD LIFE', previewed late 1995's critically acclaimed eponymous debut album, a record upon which the band's classic pop instincts came to the fore. A second set, 'HELIOSELF', surfaced a few years later, refining their sound and consolidating their wide ranging appeal. The long-awaited 'BUILDINGS AND GROUNDS' (2000) wasn't graced with a UK release, a shame as they've further carved out their own niche within the crowded sphere of indie-pop, no mean feat and one which has been achieved by an off-kilter talent, an obvious fondness for classic pop and a determination to create something fresh from eternally fresh music. • **Note:** The PAPAS FRITAS name is Spanish for "fried potatoes" and said phonetically "pop has freed us".

Album rating: PAPAS FRITAS (*6) / HELIOSELF (*6) / BUILDINGS AND GROUNDS (*7)

TONY GODDESS – vocals, guitar, piano / **KEITH GENDEL** – bass, vocals / **SHIVIKA ASTHANA** – drums, vocals

		not iss.	Sunday Driver
Feb 94.	(7"m) **FRIDAY NIGHT. / SMASH THIS WORLD / ANGEL**	-	

		Minty Fresh	Minty Fresh
May 95.	(7"green) <*MF 10*> **PASSION PLAY. / LAME TO BE**		-
Aug 95.	(cd-ep) (*MF 13*) **PASSION PLAY EP** – Passion play / Means / Howl / Radio days.		-
Nov 95.	(cd-s) (*MFP 1*) **WILD LIFE / AFTER ALL**		-
Jan 96.	(cd) <(*MF 14*)> **PAPAS FRITAS** – Guys don't lie / Holiday / Wild life / Passion play / TV movies / My revolution / Kids don't mind / Smash this world / Lame to be / Possibilities / My own girlfriend / Explain / After all.		Nov95
Apr 97.	(cd) <(*MF 22*)> **HELIOSELF** – Hey hey you say / We've got all night / Say goodbye / Small rooms / Rolling in the sand / Live by the water / Words to sing / Sing about me / Just to see you / Captain of the city / Weight / Starting to be it.		
Jun 97.	(cd-ep) (*MF 21-3*) **HEY HEY YOU SAY / HOLIDAY / WORDS TO SING (demo) / WE'VE GOT ALL NIGHT (live)**		-
Mar 00.	(cd) <*MF 35*> **BUILDINGS AND GROUNDS** – Girl / People say / Way you walk / Vertical lives / What am I supposed to do? / Far from an answer / I believe in fate / It's over now / Questions / Besides you / Another day / I'll be gone / Lost in a dream.	-	

PARADISE MOTEL

Formed: Hobart, Tasmania ... 1994 by main songwriter, CHARLES BICKFORD, plus MATTHEW AULICH, BJ AUSTIN, MATTHEW BAILEY and TIM O'SHANNESSY. To gain the attention a band needs to get on in the big wide world, they jumped ship to Melbourne, Australia, finding the beautifully bleak vocal talents of librarian turned professional singer, MERIDA SUSSEX. Like a fusion of the COCTEAU TWINS, MY BLOODY VALENTINE and the PIXIES, The PARADISE MOTEL recorded their debut album, 'LEFT OVER LIFE TO KILL' (1998), in a council squat CHARLES had been occupying at the time. Its subject matter was as uncomfortable and repressed as an emotionally sad life should be, although it seemed to possess a strange eerie tenderness not unlike that of other down under faves, DEAD CAN DANCE. Having subsequently moved to London, the band released their most deliciously downbeat album to date in 'FLIGHT PATHS' (1999), luxuriating in the kind of exquisitely swelling strings and moody, subtle arrangements that only such critically and commercially ignored bands can.

Album rating: LEFT OVER LIFE TO KILL (*6) / FLIGHT PATHS (*6)

CHARLES BICKFORD – guitar, vocals / **MERIDA SUSSEX** – vocals / **MATTHEW AULICH** – guitar / **BJ AUSTIN** – Hammond organ / **MATTHEW BAILEY** – bass / **TIM O'SHANNESSY** – drums

		Les Martin	not iss.
Jun 97.	(7") (*LESM 0027*) **THUMBELINA. / HISTORICAL**		-

		Infectious	not iss.
Feb 98.	(7") (*infect 46s*) **CALLING YOU. / LETTER TO A STRANGER** (cd-s) (*infect 46cds*) – ('A'side) / F heart / Jackstar / J star.		-
Mar 98.	(cd) (*infect 47cd*) **LEFT OVER LIFE TO KILL** – Calling you / Dead skin / Men who loved her / Watch illuminum / Skip bins / Desperate plan / Bad light / German girl / Ashes / Stones.		-
Apr 98.	(7") (*infect 53s*) **WATCH ILLUMINUM. / LONG DAY** (cd-s) (*infect 53cds*) – ('A'side) / Thin arms / Glitter / Circles.		-
Sep 98.	(7") (*infect 68s*) **HOLLYWOOD LANDMINES. / FIND NINETEENS** (cd-s) (*infect 68cds*) – ('A'side) / Candeline Brazil / Foxholes.		-
Mar 99.	(7") (*infect 69s*) **DRIVE. / ('A'-Mogwai mix)** (cd-s+=) (*infect 69cds*) – California.		-
Mar 99.	(cd) (*infect 65cd*) **FLIGHT PATHS** – Aeroplanes / Heavy weather / Derwent river star / Other things / Four degrees / Dead beats / Daniel / Drive / Cities / Caravan / Hollywood landmines / Find nineteens. (*re-iss. Sep99 w/ 'THE REWORKINGS RECORD'+=; INFECT 65cdx*) – Lee's trees (Lee Ranaldo remix) / Drive (Mogwai remix) / Hollywood landmines (Junpier remix) / Cities (Mark Eitzel remix) / Four degrees (Hefner remix) / Derwent river star (Echoboy remix) / BH rock (Bows remix). (*re-iss. Jan01; same*)		-

Richard PARFITT (see under ⇒ 60 FT. DOLLS)

PARIS ANGELS

Formed: Manchester/Liverpool, England ... 1989 by SCOTT CAREY, RIKKI TURNER, PAUL WAGSTAFF, SIMON WORRALL, who were subsequently joined by JAYNE GILL, MARK ADGE and computer wizard STEVEN TATJY BLAKE. Debuting with a self-financed cover of David Bowie's 'STAY', the band were picked up by independent label, 'Sheer Joy' and scooped an NME Single Of The Week award with follow-up track, 'PERFUME'. A further two tracks, 'SCOPE' and 'OH YES', garnered similar critical plaudits yet like so many bands of the era, PARIS ANGELS' marriage of indie guitars and dance dynamics was both a blessing and a curse, the "buzz" only lasting until the press decided the scene was no longer trendy. A thing which largely coincided with the major labels getting in on the act, 'Virgin' picking up The PARIS ANGELS only to see their investment fail to meet expectations as a minor charting debut album, 'SUNDEW' (1991) fell victim to a combination of the baggy backlash and the band's own hype.

Album rating: SUNDEW (*5)

RIKKI TURNER – vocals, wind / **JAYNE GILL** – vocals, percussion / **PAUL WAGSTAFF** – guitar / **SCOTT CAREY** – bass, harmonica / **MARK ADGE** – rhythm guitar, percussion / **SIMON WORRALL** – drums / **STEVEN TATJY BLAKE** – programming, effects

		own label	not iss.
Feb 90.	(7") **STAY**		-

		Sheer Joy	not iss.
Jun 90.	(7") (*SHEER 002*) **PERFUME. / MUFFIN 2** (12"+=) (*SHEER 002T*) – Perfume (all on you). (cd-s) (*SHEER 002CD*) – Perfume (loved up) / Pure / Perfume (all on you).		-
Oct 90.	(7") (*SHEER 004-7*) **SCOPE. / GIVE ME SOME MORE SCOPE** (12"/cd-s) (*SHEER 004 T/CD*) – Scope two / GBF.	75	-
Apr 91.	(7") (*SHEER 005-7*) **OH YES. / I UNDERSTAND** (12"+=/cd-s+=) (*SHEER 005 T/CD*) – ('A'-instrumental) / Too easy.		

		Virgin	not iss.
Jul 91.	(7"/c-s) (*VS/+C 1360*) **PERFUME (loved up). / PURE** (12") (*VS12 1360*) – ('A'-All do you mix) / ('B'-summer version). (cd-s) (*VSCD 1360*) – ('A'version).	55	-
Aug 91.	(cd/c/lp) (*CD/T+/V 2667*) **SUNDEW** – Eternity / Fade / Smile / Slippery man / What goes on / Perfume (all on you) / Perfume (loved up) / Louise / Breathless / Chaos (stupid stupid) / Purest values / Oh yes.	37	-
Sep 91.	(7"/c-s) (*VS/+C 1365*) **FADE. / FENCE** (cd-s) (*VSCD 1365*) – ('A'-Tag mix) / ('A'-Polo mix).	70	-

— split late 1991

John PARISH & POLLY JEAN HARVEY
(see under ⇒ HARVEY, PJ)

PARKINSONS

Formed: Coimbra, Portugal ... mid 1990's by singer ALFONSE PINTO, guitarist VICTOR TORPEDO and bassist PEDRO XAU. VICTOR and PEDRO were already legends in the Portuguese underground scene having released three albums between 1994 and 1998 on the 'Elevator Music' label; however it would be their offshoot band of the PARKINSONS that would gain them wider recognition. Riotous live shows and altercations with the law meant the PARKINSONS soon had a reputation as genuine punk rockers who lived by the genre's anarchistic code. The group (now US-based) were given greater credibility with an offer to play at JOEY RAMONE's birthday party plus support slots with the JON SPENCER BLUES EXPLOSION and The FALL. During these tours the group would often appear on stage naked and cause as much chaos as possible which had fans salivating at the prospect of their debut album. This would not arrive until they had relocated to the spiritual home of punk, London, and recruited former APOSTLES drummer CHRIS LOW. In 2002, the group eventually released the album 'A LONG WAY TO NOWHERE' (produced by JIM REID of the JESUS & MARY TRAIN), a record perfectly encapsulating the group's raucous live sound.

Album rating: A LONG WAY TO NOWHERE (*6)

ALFONSE PINTO – vocals / **VICTOR TORPEDO** – guitar (ex-TEDIO BOYS, ex-77) / **PEDRO XAU** – bass (ex-77) / **CHRIS LOW** (b. Edinburgh, Scotland) – drums (ex-APOSTLES)

			Fierce Panda	Elevator
Feb 02.	(cd)	*(NONG 23CD)* **A LONG WAY TO NOWHERE**	☐	☐ Apr02

– Too many shut ups / Primitive / Angel in the dark / Universe / Hate machine / Nothing to lose / Scientists / Bad girl. *<US+=>* – Pill (live). *(re-iss. Jul02; same)*

| Aug 02. | (7") | *(NING 121)* **STREETS OF LONDON. / BEDSIT CITY** | ☐ | - |

(cd-s) *(NING 121CD)* – ('A'side) / Sommerstown / Pill.

Gram PARSONS

Born: CECIL INGRAM CONNOR, 5 Nov'46, Winter Haven, Florida, USA. Through a privileged but traumatic childhood in Waycross, Georgia, during which his father, Coon Dog, committed suicide and his mother died of alcohol-related illness (on the day he graduated from high school), GRAM diverted himself with music; although his first love was country, the traditional preserve of white Southerners, GRAM was inspired to get up on stage after witnessing the hip-swivelling suave of ELVIS PRESLEY. Developing his talents in high-school covers outfits such as The PACERS and The LEGENDS, he was also sidelining with solo gigs and, through manager, Buddy Freeman, secured a appearance on a Greenville, South Carolina, TV Station. This in turn led to GRAM forming The SHILOS (having previously sang as a duo with KENT LAVOIE – aka hitmaker, LOBO), a fairly staid folk outfit who recorded a session for a Greenville campus radio station (released in 1979 on 'Sundown' as 'GRAM PARSONS – THE EARLY YEARS 1963-65') and with whom PARSONS penned his most fully realised song to date, 'ZAH'S BLUES'. Inevitably, the band fell by the wayside following GRAM's enrolment at Harvard in 1965; bypassing classes for the lure of the local music scene, he barely lasted six months, hooking up with local musicians, IAN DUNLOP, JOHN NUESE and MICKEY GAUVIN to form The LIKE and pioneering a synthesis of R&B, rock'n'roll and country which would would inform the remainder of PARSON's relatively short career. Around this time, GRAM spoke of having a deal with 'R.C.A.' and although it's widely believed he never recorded for the label, two tracks, 'CAN'T TAKE IT ANYMORE' and 'REMEMBER', have recently been unearthed (thanks to eagle-eyed archives man, Ron Maharg) from the label's vaults. The former a BYRDS-esque jangle calling to mind 'Chimes Of Freedom' and the latter a version of 'NOVEMBER NIGHTS' (a staple of The LIKE's live set never recorded under its original title but subsequently covered by actor Peter Fonda), these tracks may well have been recorded at the same time as the legendary lost Brandon De Wilde session, which GRAM & Co. are rumoured to have played on (the actor was a close confidante of the band and a regular at their new communal home in The Bronx, New York); through the continuing efforts of GP obsessive and all-round top man, Keith Munro, the songs might just be given an official release – subject to legal complexities – in the near future through 'B.M.G.'. Whatever, they're certainly more representative of the direction PARSONS was headed than the lame film theme, 'THE RUSSIANS ARE COMING', which served as a debut single in Spring '67. By this point trading under The INTERNATIONAL SUBMARINE BAND moniker, GRAM & Co. were encouraged by the experimentation of renegade country artists like BUCK OWENS and the hard-driving B-side, 'TRUCK DRIVING MAN' was a truer taste of what was to come. After another flop single for 'Columbia', 'SUM UP BROKE', the group relocated to L.A., where the West Coast scene was sending out cultural shockwaves around the world. Hobnobbing with the likes of the aforementioned Peter Fonda, the group blagged a cameo role in hippy flick, 'The Trip', for which they also recorded a track, 'LAZY DAYS' (it belatedly turned up on the second FLYING BURRITO BROTHERS album). As country wasn't yet hip with the L.A. set, the song was rejected and the band ended up lip-synching to music by the more suitably psychedelic ELECTRIC FLAG. Bearing out such iniquities with their heads held high, the group eventually secured a contract with L.A. producer LEE HAZLEWOOD's 'L.H.I.' records. But the INTERNATIONAL SUBMARINE BAND that signed up wasn't the same beast that had moved to California only a matter of months earlier. DUNLOP and GAUVIN, tired of waiting around and eager to move in a more R&B/rock direction, hooked up with BARRY TASHIAN and BILLY BRIGGS for the first, short-lived incarnation of The FLYING BURRITO BROTHERS. PARSONS and NUESE, meanwhile, pursued their idea of a pure country sound; JON CORNEAL, BOB BUCHANAN (co-writer of PARSONS' classic 'HICKORY WIND') and CHRIS ETHRIDGE all played on the resulting album, 'SAFE AT HOME' (1968) alongside Nashville veteran, EARL 'LES' BALL and pedal steel player, J.D. MANESS. While half the album was out and out country (including covers of Johnny Cash's 'I STILL MISS SOMEONE' and Merle Haggard's 'SOMEBODY ELSE YOU'VE KNOWN'), PARSONS was already in the process of creating something fresh and exciting with his original material; the little-boy-lost charm of 'BLUE EYES' was irresistible while the chugging 'LUXURY LINER' became something of a country-rock standard covered by EMMYLOU HARRIS amongst others, the whole record characterised by GRAM's quavering, frail but emotional depth-charge singing. Retrospectively hailed as the first ever country-rock album, it was nevertheless ignored at the time and to all intents and purposes, The BYRDS' 'Sweetheart Of The Rodeo' (1968) was the record which really introduced the concept to a wider public and more significantly, the rock and country establishments. With sales of 'SAFE AT HOME' barely registering, GRAM wasn't slow in taking up an invitation to join the band (The BYRDS), and, along with CHRIS HILLMAN, formed the main thrust of their move away from folk-rock to stone country. An album consisting almost wholly of cover versions, 'Sweetheart..'s only two originals were penned by PARSONS, the poignant 'ONE HUNDRED YEARS FROM NOW' and the aforementioned autumnal beauty of 'HICKORY WIND'. Ironically, GRAM's distinctive vocals were erased (in favour of ROGER McGUINN) on all but the latter track prior to release, the controversial reason given that PARSONS was still contracted to HAZLEWOOD (note-the original versions were belatedly released as part of The BYRDS' 1990 'C.B.S.' box set). Despite shaking up the Grand Ole Opry, drawing critical acclaim and setting in motion a return to roots music that would reverbate well into the 70's, GRAM, in what was already becoming a familiar career pattern, was quickly tiring of life as a BYRD. Following a messy departure on the eve of a South African tour (newfound buddies The ROLLING STONES were instrumental in persuading GRAM that such a venture was really like, not a hip thing to do, man), PARSONS flew back to L.A. and mused upon his fabled vision of a "Cosmic American Music". HILLMAN soon joined him and along with pedal steel maestro, SNEAKY PETE KLEINOW and old cohorts CORNEAL and ETHRIDGE, realised that vision and then some, with The FLYING BURRITO BROTHERS. Taking the name from the brief project put together by DUNLOP, GAUVIN etc, the group blended country, soul, R&B and rock into a seamless strand of Americana that to this day has never been bettered. Yet after only two albums (see The FLYING BURRITO BROTHERS section for the full lowdown on the band's trailblazing, hellraising heyday), PARSONS again bailed out, spending more and more time with KEITH RICHARDS; PARSONS influence on The 'STONES was obvious, from the reworked hoedown of 'Honky Tonk Woman' ('Country Honk') to the stoned backwoods bliss of their finest album, 'Exile On Main Street'. Although he was never credited, GRAM is rumoured to be floating around somewhere in the murk of the latter masterpiece, certainly spending enough time at RICHARDS' French villa/makeshift recording studio to lend the claims some weight. With his career in limbo, PARSONS eventually returned to L.A. in 1972 and began recording his first fully fledged solo album; unable to secure the production services of his hero, MERLE HAGGARD, GRAM did the next best thing and hired the man's recording engineer, Hugh Davies, leaving the lion's share of the knob-twiddling to another English friend, RIK GRECH (erstwhile FAMILY member and part of the short-lived BLIND FAITH). Employing ELVIS stalwarts such as JAMES BURTON and GLEN D. HARDIN, GRAM assembled a crack band with the angel-voiced EMMYLOU HARRIS at its epicentre; a struggling folk singer when PARSONS met her, HARRIS was the musical other half that he'd been searching for all his life and vice versa. PARSONS schooled her in the ways of cosmic country and her crystal pure soprano ringing against GRAM's flawed but impassioned holler remains one of the most sublime sounds ever laid down on vinyl. Grand claims perhaps, but the pairing's magic transformed well-worn standards like 'STREETS OF BALTIMORE' and 'WE'LL SWEEP OUT THE ASHES IN THE MORNING' into bittersweet soul food, highlights – along with the fragile 'A SONG FOR YOU' – of 'G.P.' (1973). Again the critics frothed (at least the ones who could recognise the talent, others were more sceptical of what PARSONS was trying to achieve) and again the public remained indifferent. Undeterred, GRAM, EMMYLOU and manager, Eddie Tickner, took advantage of Warner's (GRAM was now signed to 'Reprise') enthusiasm for a bonafide tour and set about forming a road band, The FALLEN ANGELS. Despite managing only eight shows in an incident-packed month which saw GRAM falling further into drug oblivion, the tour was by all accounts a freewheeling success if not exactly an effective promotional tool; fans still in their nappies when GRAM's ragged country roadshow came to town can get at least some idea of what the fuss was about via a live set recorded for broadcast over a Long Island, NY radio station; 'LIVE 1973 (live with The FALLEN ANGELS)' (1994). Back in L.A., his personal life continuing to unravel with each passing month, GRAM got it together one last time and, as he eagerly told his friends upon its completion, finally made the album he'd been hearing in his head for years. Although a hotch-potch of old and new, borrowed and blue, the songs on 'GRIEVOUS ANGEL' (1974) resonate as deeply as any in the history of country, or rock for that matter. GRAM's voice had taken on a new lease of life, his duets with HARRIS, 'HEARTS ON FIRE' and 'LOVE HURTS' blessed with the kind of spiritual intensity normally found in gospel music. Similarly, the PARSONS/HARRIS pairing transformed 'HICKORY WIND' from a wistful country ballad into a transcendant country ballad (despite its cheesy mock-live setting), while 'RETURN OF THE GRIEVOUS ANGEL' combined a Beat-cowboy narrative with soaring harmonies and a swooning chorus to mesmerising effect. If 'BRASS BUTTONS' and '$1000 WEDDING' were GRAM at his most intimately confessional, then closing track, 'IN MY HOUR OF DARKNESS', read like both a prayer of hope and an uncanny portent of GRAM's own death. Within a matter of weeks, road manager/professional nanny/best friend, Phil Kaufman, was driving out to the Joshua Tree monument, Arizona desert in a ramshackle hearse, GRAM's lifeless body in the back. GRAM PARSONS died on the 19th of September '73, officially from a drugs overdose although suspicion still surrounds the events that took place in the Joshua Tree Inn that night, where the singer was taking a break with friends prior to a scheduled tour. True to the pact they'd made (at the funeral of revered country picker, CLARENCE WHITE), Kaufman burned GRAM's body in the desert heat, a fitting end perhaps, for an artist who'd blazed his way through the musical consciousness like a comet. 'GRIEVOUS ANGEL' was finally issued posthumously in early '74, although seemingly (at least initially) not even GRAM's death could spark interest in his music. While EMMYLOU HARRIS went on to an impressive and successful career of her own, belatedly popularising some of GRAM's songs, the GRAM PARSONS legend has since taken on such mythical proportions that there's even an annual event held at Joshua Tree each year. Yet while the myth threatens to obscure the actual music, a cursory glance around the country/alt-country scene of today is proof enough that GRAM's vision has endured. The Brandon De Wilde tapes mentioned above have apparently just been discovered, although their exact content remains unclear at present.

Album rating: — International Submarine Band: SAFE AT HOME (*5) / Gram Parsons: G.P. (*8) / GREVIOUS ANGEL (*8)

Reprise Reprise

Jan 73. (7") <1139> **SHE. / THAT'S ALL IT TOOK** [-] [ ]

Mar 73. (lp) *(K 44228)* <MS 2123> **G.P.** [ ] [ ]
– Still feeling blue / We'll sweep out the ashes in the morning / A song for you / Streets of Baltimore / She / That's all it took / The new soft shoe / Kiss the children / Cry one more time / How much I've lied / Big mouth blues.

Mar 73. (7") *(K 14245)* **THE NEW SOFT SHOE. / SHE** [ ] [-]

Jan 74. (lp) *(K 54018)* <MS 2171> **GREVIOUS ANGEL** [ ] [ ]
– Return of the grevious angel / Hearts on fire / I can't dance / Brass buttons / $1000 wedding / Medley live from Northern Quebec:- (a) Cash on the barrelhead – (b) Hickory wind / Love hurts / Ooh Las Vegas / In my hour of darkness.

Jan 74. (7") <1192> **LOVE HURTS. / IN MY HOUR OF DARKNESS** [-] [ ]

— GRAM died on the 19th September '73 after recording 90% of above LP

PATTERN

Formed: Oakland, nr. San Francisco, California, USA . . . early 2000 by ex-PEECHEES man CHRIS APPELGREN, with ex-SAINT JAMES INFIRMARY guitarist JASON ROSENBERG, ANDY ASP, CARSON BELL and drummer JIM ANDERSON. A real skull-busting quintet, The PATTERN began issuing singles in the Bay Area (noted for its thriving punk scene) of Oakland, and racked up quite a local following. Their mini album, 'IMMEDIATELY' (2001) got the attention of college radios across America who blazed out thrash punk tracks such as, ahem, 'FINGER US' and the anthemic 'SUNNED THINGS SPEAK', all over college campuses. The group began work on their debut album proper, in between issuing the three EP's 'NON STOP', 'FEVERISH' and 'WET CIRCUIT CITY' (plus, replacing drummer ANDERSON with SCOTT BATISTE) and, in 2002, released the eagerly awaited 'REAL FEELNESS', a bruising punk-rock epitaph running just under half-an-hour. The PATTERN successfully managed to capture their live energy on this disc, with twelve speed-punk garage songs blasting from the speaker and APPELGREN's vocals reaching a nasal high . . . BLINK 182, they ain't! • **Covered:** CREAM PUFF WAR (Grateful Dead).

Album rating: IMMEDIATELY mini (*6) / REAL FEELNESS (*8)

CHRIS APPELGREN – vocals (ex-PEECHEES) / **JASON ROSENBERG** – guitar (ex-SAINT JAMES INFIRMARY) / **ANDY ASP** – guitar (ex-NUISANCE) / **CARSON BELL** – bass (ex-CUTZ) / **JIM ANDERSON** – drums (ex-TALK IS POISON, ex-BLACKFORK)

not iss. Gearhead

Jan 01. (7") <RPM 021> **NON-STOP** [-] [ ]
– No books! / My own age.

not iss. Alternative Tentacles

Apr 01. (7") <Virus 259> **WET CIRCUIT CITY** [-] [ ]
– Breakfast / Sunned things speak.

Wichita Lookout!

Jun 01. (m-cd/m-lp) <(WEBB 015/+LP)> <LK 276> **IMMEDIATELY** [ ] [ ] Sep01
– Finger us / Breakfast / Sunned things speak / Worse all the time / Mary's sister Margaret Jones / Untold.

Jul 01. (7"clear/colord) <(GSL 44)> **FEVERISH** [ ] [ ]
– Finger us / Worse all the time.
(above issued on 'G.S.L.')

Nov 01. (7") *(WEBB 025S)* **NO CARESS** [ ] [-]
– She's a libra / No books.
(cd-s+=) *(WEBB 025SCD)* – Untold.

— **SCOTT BATISTE** – drums (ex-YAPHET) repl. ANDERSON

Jul 02. (7") *(WEBB 032S)* **FRAGILE AWARENESS. / LADIES SPEAKING OUT** [ ] [-]
(cd-s+=) *(WEBB 032SCD)* – You or you (alt. version).

Aug 02. (cd/lp) *(WEBB 033/+LP)* <LK 285> **REAL FEELNESS** [ ] [ ] Sep02
– Fragile awareness / You or you / Nothing of value / Thunder us / Mary's sister / Selling submarines / She's a Libra / Last night called / Let's get important / The best hate the rest / Happy sarong / Rangefinder.

Oct 02. (7") *(WEBB 035S)* **NOTHING OF VALUE. / CREAM PUFF WAR** [ ] [-]
(cd-s+=) *(WEBB 035SCD)* – Abigail.

PAUL NEWMAN

Formed: Austin, Texas, USA . . . late 1995 by CRAIG McCAFFERY, PAUL NEWMAN and TONY NOZERO, originally as a three-piece, although soon after their conception they added EDWARD ROBERT to the mix. After honing their style on the live circuit, the quartet debuted in 1997 with their 7", ' . . .PLEASE WAIT DURING THE SILENCE', which was soon followed up by their inaugural LP, 'FRAMES PER SECOND'. The set showcased their mainly instrumental experimental take on the post-rock sound which gained them many comparisons to the likes of the early work of other sonic investigators, TORTOISE. The ensuing year saw the issue of their sophomore full-length offering, 'ONLY LOVE CAN BREAK YOUR HEART' (1998), which again captured a band that were at home with their instrumentals, and although the tracks could tend towards alternative meanderings it was nevertheless a very listenable effort. The musical side-projects of various members of the band meant that they became fairly far-flung from each other across the States, although it did not stop them getting it on for their third album, 'MACHINE IS NOT BROKEN', which they recorded in 1999. Unfortunately, due to the collapse of their imprint 'Trance Syndicate', it did not hit the record shops until two years later. Their new label, 'My Pal God', also put out the compilation offering 'RE-ISSUE! RE-PACKAGE! RE-PACKAGE! RE-EVALUATE THE SONGS' (2001), which collected together previously released singles and hard to get hold of material. As well as spending their time with the PAUL NEWMAN band set-up, various members also did time in other alternative acts; ROBERT played under the moniker CYRUS REGO, while NOZERO continued to perform in another instrumental outfit, DRUMS AND TUBA. Starting out as a twosome in Austin around 1995, they consisted of NOZERO and BRIAN WOLFF under the label JUST DRUMS AND TUBA, but had soon expanded to include guitarist NEAL McKEEBY (a former bandmate of WOLFF's in HOMINY BOP); at which point they aptly dropped the JUST. The group put out in quick succession the LPs, 'BOX FETISH' (1997) and 'THE FLYING BALLERINA' (1998), records which displayed their brass-based punky funk stylings. Their next full-length outing 'FLATHEADS AND SPOONIES' (1999), witnessed them add electronica to their established style and also saw the band move apart across the US. They were brought back together after a call to tour from an admirer of their sound, ANI DiFRANCO, who also went on to produce their fourth LP, 'VINYL KILLER' (2001). This set continued their fascination with electronica-based musings but also displayed their new found admiration for the Afro-funk sound of luminaries like Nigerian, FELA KUTI.

Album rating: FRAMES PER SECOND (*7) / ONLY LOVE CAN BREAK YOUR HEART (*6) / MACHINE IS NOT BROKEN (*6) / RE-ISSUE! RE-PACKAGE! RE-PACKAGE! RE-EVALUATE THE SONGS collection (*5) / Drums & Tuba: BOX FETISH (*5) / THE FLYING BALLERINA (*4) / FLATHEADS AND SPOONIES (*5) / VINYL KILLER (*6) / MOSTLY APE (*5)

PAUL A. NEWMAN – bass / **CRAIG McCAFFREY** – guitar, vocals / **ANTHONY NOZERO** – drums / **EDDIE ROBERT** – bass, keyboards, vocals

not iss. Twistworthy

May 97. (7") <3> **. . .PLEASE WAIT DURING THE SILENCE. / CLEAR BABY** [-] [ ]

Trance Syndicate Trance Syndicate

Jan 98. (lp/cd) <(TR 65/+CD)> **FRAMES PER SECOND** [ ] [ ]
– Elements of style / The real pro / Carl Sagan / Work to do / Astroglide / And white / Enter the empire of the ants.

Sep 98. (lp/cd) <TR 70/CD> **ONLY LOVE CAN BREAK YOUR HEART** [-] [ ]
– Seizure's fashion / Apollo Creed / Where are your hands now / Dawson 4, Oklahoma 0 / Curse you would / Arriving early / The new goth.

not iss. Temporary Residence

Sep 99. (7") <TRR 16> **WAY TO BREATHE, NO-BREATH. / (other by SONNA)** [-] [ ]

My Pal God My Pal God

May 00. (lp/cd) <(MPG 034/+CD)> **MACHINE IS NOT BROKEN** [ ] [ ] Feb00
– Eight-day wait / The cup is fierce / Perhaps you would be more comfortable / Order of operations / Under the golden horses / Hampton kids / Some common items you never notice / The pound or the fist.

Apr 01. (cd) <(MPG 042CD)> **RE-ISSUE! RE-PACKAGE! RE-PACKAGE! RE-EVALUATE THE SONGS** (compilation) [ ] [ ] Mar01
– Way to breath, no-breath / All black, all anal / Beeline to Mamou / Popcorn / Grady No.101 / I know my luck too well / December '91 or so / Where those ever cowboys boots . . . / Clear baby / . . .Please wait during the silence.

DRUMS & TUBA

ANTHONY NOZERO – drums, percussion, synths / **BRIAN WOLFF** – tuba, trumpet, trombone / **NEAL McKEEBY** – guitar

		not iss.	T.E.C. Tones
Nov 97.	(cd) <9733-2> **BOX FETISH**	-	

– Does it suck to be you / The inspector / Adventures of poo-poo and pee-pee / Carrots / Loteria / Open case / Kuc to luc / Gimpel the fool / 5.24.94 / In case / Meat / The butcher / Tuba song / No good with words / Close case / Curtains. <re-iss. Sep00 on 'My Pal God'+=; MPG 36CD> – Brief case / Out of case / Pete's dance.

Nov 98.	(cd) **THE FLYING BALLERINA**	-	

– Fists of spaghetti / Kermit / Chummus, a challah, and a whole lot of ... / The inspector returns / Lots of luc / Blazevitch / The flying ballerina / Scottie pippen / Boogie stop shuffle / Neal hamburger / God bows to math / Pig ears for Lily. <re-iss. Sep00 on 'My Pal God'+=; MPG 37CD> – Meter maid / Bertone / There is a monster.

		not iss.	My Pal God
Oct 99.	(cd) <MPG 33CD> **FLATHEADS AND SPOONIES**	-	

– The mummy / Dr. Small / 11 o'clock / The chicken / Green shirt / Fortunado / Flatheads and spoonies / The notorious rumpler.

		not iss.	Grey Flat
2000.	(7") **BORSCHT.** /	-	
		not iss.	own label
2000.	(cd-ep) **CAIRO EP**	-	

– The metrics / Breakfast w/ Melitis / Prowling / Cairo.

		Righteous Babe	Righteous Babe
Nov 01.	(cd) <(RBRCD 23)> **VINYL KILLER**		Jan01

– The diagram / The donkey and the walrus / Rayronus / The 100 attacks of dagger / Territory / Topolino / The sauce maker / Eli / The horse and the tree / Chapeau Russia / Prince meets the phantom / No accomodation for buffalo / Carlos the cat.

Sep 02.	(cd) <RBRCD 28> **MOSTLY APE**	-	

– Brian liaters / Igor Rosso / Sevens / The metrics / 4style / Elephants / Clashing / Air Con Dee / Super bee / Breakfast with Miletus / Goose geese / Magoo.

PAVEMENT

Formed: Stockton, California, USA ... 1989 by frontman STEPHEN MALKMUS and longtime friend/guitarist, SCOTT KANNBERG. They were soon joined by drummer GARY YOUNG (although this was initially a loose arrangement), the band recording their early US-only EP's at YOUNG's home studio, the first of which, 1989's 'SLAY TRACKS', was released on the self-financed 'Treble Kicker' label. A further two EP's, 'DEMOLITION PLOT J-7' and 'SUMMER BABE', together with a mini-lp, 'PERFECT SOUND FOREVER', were subsequently issued on the US indie, 'Drag City' over the course of the ensuing two years. The lo-fi, shambling charm of the likes of 'SUMMER BABE' eventually secured the band a UK deal with 'Big Cat' records, PAVEMENT consistently hitting the charts in Britain throughout their career. The debut album, 'SLANTED AND ENCHANTED' was finally released amid much anticipation in early 1992, its covertly melodic, avant-indie drawing inevitable but favourable comparisons with The PIXIES, The VELVET UNDERGROUND and even KING CRIMSON! Masterfully combining chaotic dischord and shards of crystalline harmony, the record's most compelling moments lay in the lazy melancholia of 'TRIGGER CUT' or 'ZURICH IS STAINED'. MALKMUS' brilliantly cryptic lyrics and offhand phrasing together with the twisted beauty of their music saw the band consistently dubbed as an American FALL. No bad thing, and besides, the band were carving out their own niche on the live circuit, by now augmented with extra sticksman, BOB NASTANOVICH and bassist MARK IBOLD, wildman YOUNG's infamous onstage antics an added attraction. The debut reached the lower reaches of the UK chart while a compilation of the early EP's, 'WESTING (BY MUSKET & SEXTANT)' (1993) made the Top 30. Prior to the release of the follow-up proper, 'CROOKED RAIN CROOKED RAIN' (1994), the band parted company on less than amicable terms with YOUNG, his replacement being STEVE WEST. This folk-ish record marked the band's most enticingly melodic affair to date, the keening 'CUT YOUR HAIR' single almost making the Top 40, the record itself reaching No.15 and cementing PAVEMENT's position as the crown kings of lo-fi. Although PAVEMENT failed to breach the Billboard chart, they built up a loyal following on the US underground scene on the back of constant touring, the defiantly experimental and diverse 'WOWEE ZOWEE!' (1995) proving that the band were making no concessions to radio programmers. There were still perfect PAVEMENT moments of stark beauty, as on the single, 'FATHER TO A SISTER OF THOUGHT'. While the album may have put off those after the immediate pop fix of 'CROOKED . . .', PAVEMENT's next release, the meditative 'BRIGHTEN THE CORNERS' (1997) took a different tack again. It was clear that MALKMUS' songwriting was fast maturing, his work taking on a new depth and resonance that eschewed the stylistic grab-bag of old for a more straightforwardly direct approach. Feted by the likes of BLUR, who had previously pooh-pooh'd the American scene, PAVEMENT remain one of music's most resolutely individual bands. In 1999 and with drummer GARY YOUNG back into the fray, the band scored their first Top 30 single, 'CARROT ROPE', one of highlights on their Top 20 album, 'TERROR TWILIGHT'. Unfortunately, they bowed out towards the end of the decade. The break-up of PAVEMENT hadn't effected MALKMUS that much, as in 2001 he issued his solo set 'STEPHEN MALKMUS'. Like a lost PAVEMENT album, this is probably the direction the band would have headed in, considering the tone of the joyful 'TERROR TWILIGHT' compared with that of the stuffy, cynically serious 'BRIGHTEN THE CORNERS'. The songs were delightful, with MALKMUS' half-spoken soft vocals matching that of the jangling, uptempo songs such as 'JO JO'S JACKET' and the irresistible 'TROUBBBLE'. There were still dark overtones; 'BLACK BOOK' had the slightly singular twang of a PAVEMENT song circa 'WOWEE ZOWEE', whilst 'CHURCH ON WHITE' saw MALKMUS sing his first love song since 'MAJOR LEAGUES' with beautiful integrity. It certainly wasn't Swedish Reggae, but whatever ideas MALKMUS had up in that head of his were faithfully communicated onto this album. • **Covered:** THE CLASSICAL (Fall) / THE KILLING MOON (Echo & The Bunnymen). • **Trivia:** MALKMUS produced early 90's album 'Eyes Wide Smile' for FAITH OVER REASON. BOB and STEVEN played on SILVER JEW's (David Berman) album 'Starlite Walter'.

Album rating: PERFECT SOUND FOREVER mini (*5) / SLANTED AND ENCHANTED (*7) / WESTING (BY MUSKET & SEXTANT) compilation (*8) / CROOKED RAIN CROOKED RAIN (*7) / WOWEE ZOWEE (*8) / BRIGHTEN THE CORNERS (*7) / TERROR TWILIGHT (*8) / Stephen Malkmus: STEPHEN MALKMUS (*8)

STEVEN MALKMUS (b. 30 May'66, Santa Monica, California) – vocals, guitar / **SCOTT "SPIRAL STAIRS" KANNBERG** – guitar, vocals

		not iss.	Treble Kicker
1989.	(7"ep) <TK 001> **SLAY TRACKS 1933-1969**	-	

– You're killing me / Box elder / Maybe maybe / She believes / Price yeah!.

— added **GARY YOUNG** (b.1953, Stockton) – drums

		not iss.	Drag City
1990.	(7"ep) <DC 2> **DEMOLITION PLOT J-7**	-	

– Forklift / Spizzle trunk / Recorder grot / Internal K-dart / Perfect depth / Recorder grot (rally).

— (Aug90) added **BOB NASTANOVICH** – drums

1991.	(10"m-lp) <DC 4> **PERFECT SOUND FOREVER**	-	

– Heckler spray / From now on / Angel carver blues – Mellow jazz docent / Drive by fader / Debris slide / Home / Krell vid-user.

— (mid '91) added **MARK IBOLD** (b. New York) – bass (ex-DUSTDEVILS)

Jan 92.	(7"ep) <DC 9> **SUMMER BABE (Winter version) / MERCY: THE LAUNDROMAT. / BAPTISS BLACKTICK / MY FIRST MINE / MY RADIO**	-	

		Big Cat	Matador
Mar 92.	(lp/c/cd) (ABB 034/+/CD) <OLE 038-2> **SLANTED AND ENCHANTED**	72	

– Summer babe (winter version) / Trigger cut – Wounded – Kite at: 17 / No life singed her / In a mouth of a desert / Conduit for sale / Chesleys little wrists / Loretta's scars / Here / Two states / Perfume-V / Fame throwa / Jackals, false grails – The lonesome era / Our singer / Zurich is stained.

Jul 92.	(7"/12"/cd-s) (ABB 35 S/T/SCD) <OLE 042> **TRIGGER CUT. / SUE ME JACK / SO STARK (YOU'RE A SKYSCRAPER)**		
Nov 92.	(12"ep/12"pic-d-ep/cd-ep) (ABB 38 T/P/SCD) <OLE 044> **WATERY, DOMESTIC EP**	58	

– Texas never whispers / Frontwards / Feed 'em to the (Linden) lions / Shoot the singer (1 sick verse).

| Mar 93. | (lp/c/cd) (ABB 40/+C/CD) <Drag City; DC 14> **WESTING (BY MUSKET & SEXTANT)** (first 4 US singles material) | 30 | |

(cd/lp re-iss. Sep98/Jan99 on 'Drag City'; same as US)

— **STEVE WEST** (b. Richmond, Virginia) – drums; repl. GARY YOUNG – solo (single; 'PLANET MAN' 94)

| Jan 94. | (7"/12"/cd-s) (ABB 55 S/T/CD) <OLE 082> **CUT YOUR HAIR. / CAMERA / STARE** | 52 | |
| Feb 94. | (lp/c/cd) (ABB 56/+C/CD) <OLE 079> **CROOKED RAIN CROOKED RAIN** | 15 | |

– Silence kit / Elevate me later / Stop breathin / Cut your hair / Newark wilder / Unfair / Gold sound Z / 5-4 = unity / Range life / Heaven is a truck / Hit the plane down / Fillmore jive. (s-lp w/free 7"; OLE 087) – HAUNT YOU DOWN. / JAM KIDS (cd re-iss. Feb02 on 'Domino'; REWIGCD 010)

Jul 94.	(7") (ABB 70S) **GOLD SOUNDZ. / KNEELING BUS**		-

(12"+=/cd-s+=) (ABB 70 T/SCD) – Strings of Nashville / The exit theory.

— line-up= **STEPHEN MALKMUS / MARK IBOLD / ROBERT NASTANOVICH / STEVE WEST / SPIRAL STAIRS (KANNEBERG) + FATAH RUARK**

Jan 95.	(7") (ABB 77S) **RANGE LIFE. / COOLIN' BY SOUND**		-

(12"+=/cd-s+=) (ABB 77 T/SCD) – Raft.

| Mar 95. | (7"/12") (ABB 86 S/T) <OLE 134> **RATTLED BY THE RUSH. / FALSE SKORPION / EASILY FOOLED** | | |

(cd-s+=) (ABB 86SCD) – Brink of the clouds.

| Apr 95. | (3-sided d-lp/c/cd) (ABB 84/+C/CD) <OLE 130> **WOWEE ZOWEE!** | 18 | |

– We dance / Rattled by the rush / Black out / Brinx job / Grounded / Serpentine pad / Motion suggests / Father to a sister of thought / Extradition / Best friends arm / Grave architecture / At & t / Flux = rad / Fight this generation / Kennel district / Pueblo / Half a canyon / Western homes.

| Jun 95. | (7"ep/12"ep/cd-ep) (ABB 91 S/T/SCD) <OLE 169> **FATHER TO A SISTER OF THOUGHT. / KRIS KRAFT / MUSSLE ROCK (IS A HORSE IN TRANSITION)** | | |
| Aug 95. | (7") <3G-08> **DANCING WITH THE ELDERS. / (other artist)** | | - |

— <above released on 'Third Gear'>

| Jan 96. | (cd-ep) (ABB 110SCD) <OLE 188CD> **PACIFIC TRIM EP:- GIVE IT A DAY / GANGSTERS & PRANKSTERS / SAGANAW** | | |

(7"ep+=) (ABB 110S) <OLE 188> – I love Perth.

— now without FATAH

		Domino	Capitol
Jan 97.	(7") (RUG 51) **STEREO. / BIRDS IN THE MAJIC INDUSTRY**	48	-

(cd-s) (RUG 51CD) – ('A'side) / Westie can drum / Winner of the . . .

| Feb 97. | (cd/c/lp) (WIG CD/MC/LP 31) <55226> **BRIGHTEN THE CORNERS** | 27 | 70 |

– Stereo / Shady lane / Transport is arranged / Date with IKEA / Old to begin / Type slowly / Embassy row / Blue Hawaiian / We are underused / Passat dream / Starlings of the slipstream / Infinite spark.

		Domino	Matador
Apr 97.	(7") *(RUG 53)* <*OLE 266*> **SHADY LANE (KROSSFADER). / UNSEEN POWER OF THE PICKET FENCE**	40	Jun97
	(cd-s) *(RUG 53CD)* – ('A'side) / Slowly typed / Cherry area.		
	(cd-s) *(RUG 53CDX)* – ('A'side) / Wanna mess you around / No tan lines.		

— drummer **GARY YOUNG** returned

		Domino	Matador
May 99.	(7") *(RUG 90)* **CARROT ROPE. / AND THEN**	27	-
	(cd-s) *(RUG 90CD1)* – ('A'side) / Harness your hopes / Roll with the wind.		
	(cd-s) *(RUG 90CD2)* – ('A'side) / Porpoise and the hand grenade / Rooftop rambler.		
Jun 99.	(cd/c/lp) *(WIG CD/MC/LP 66)* <*OLE 260*> **TERROR TWILIGHT**	19	95
	– Spit on a stranger / Folk jam / You are a light / Cream of gold / Major leagues / Platform blues / Ann don't cry / Billie / Speak, see, remember / The hexx / Carrot rope.		
Sep 99.	(cd-s) *(RUG 96CD1)* **MAJOR LEAGUES / YOUR TIME TO CHANGE / STUB YOUR TOE / THE CLASSICAL**		-
	(cd-s) *(RUG 96CD2)* – ('A'side) / The killing moon / ('A'demo) / Decouvert de soleil.		
	(d7"set) *(RUG 96)* – (all above).		

— KANNEBERG/STAIRS went on to form PRESTON SCHOOL OF INDUSTRY

STEPHEN MALKMUS

— solo with **JOHN MOEN** – percussion, drums

		Domino	Matador
Feb 01.	(cd/lp) *(WIG CD/LP 090)* <*OLE 444*> **STEPHEN MALKMUS**	49	-
	– Black book / Phantasies / JoJo's jacket / Church on white / The hook / Discretion grove / Troubbble / Pink India / Trojan curfew / Vague space / Jenny & the ess-dog / Deado.		
Apr 01.	(7") *(RUG 123)* **DISCRETION GROVE. / SIN TAX**	60	-
	(cd-s+=) *(RUG 123CD)* – Leisurely poison.		
Jul 01.	(7") *(RUG 128)* **JENNY & THE ESS-DOG. / ALIEN BOY**		-
	(cd-s+=) *(RUG 128CD)* – Keep the faith / That's what mama said.		
Dec 01.	(7") *(RUG 133)* **JO JO'S JACKET. / OPEN AND SHUT CASES**		-
	(cd-s) *(RUG 133CD)* – ('A'side) / Polish mule / The hook (live) / ('A'-CD-rom).		

PEACH COBBLER (see under ⇒ RUN ON)

PEDRO THE LION

Formed: Seattle, Washington, USA . . . 1995 by hardcore enthusiast and devout christian DAVID BAZAN (who also flirted with UNWED SAILOR, featuring JONATHAN FORD). After giving up on the hardcore scene, BAZAN issued the polar opposite to metal – a transcending mini-album named 'WHOLE' (1997), which featured six beautifully crafted songs, akin to LOW, IDA or the soft alt-country of HAYDEN. 'IT'S HARD TO FIND A FRIEND' appeared in 1998, and marked BAZAN's debut appearance on LP. Here was a collection of frankly humorous and damaged songs, matched with his minimalistic production and instrumentation; BAZAN, at times, sounded like a DANIEL JOHNSTON who was quietly at peace with himself. In 1999, recruiting BEN BRUBAKER and bassist JOSH GOLDEN, they recorded 'THE ONLY REASON I FEEL SECURE' in two sessions during 1998; the album was issued in 1999 for 'Jade Tree'. This leaning towards the more sonically adventurous side of BAZAN, paved the way for a more rockier insurrection (with BAZAN perhaps revisiting the olden days) – resulting in the stripped down tape-recorded lo-fi rock album 'WINNERS NEVER QUIT' in 2000. Two years later, BAZAN, now with the aid of multi-instrumentalist CASEY FOUBERT, returned to form with the lyrically hushed 'CONTROL', an album typically about faith.

Album rating: WHOLE mini (*5) / IT'S HARD TO FIND A FRIEND (*6) / THE ONLY REASON I FEEL SECURE (IS THAT I AM VALIDATED BY MY PEERS) mini (*6) / WINNERS NEVER QUIT (*5) / CONTROL (*6)

DAVID BAZAN – vocals, guitar

		not iss.	Tooth & Nail
Apr 97.	(m-cd/m-lp) <*1086*> **WHOLE**	-	
	– Nothing / Fix / Almost there / Whole / Lullaby / Hymn.		

		Made In Mexico	Made In Mexico
Jan 99.	(cd) <*MEX 002*> **IT'S HARD TO FIND A FRIEND**		Oct98
	– Of up and coming monarchs / The longer I lay here / Big trucks / Suspect fled the scene / Bad diary days / Longest winter / When they really get to know you you wiil run / Of minor prophets and their prostitute wives / The bells / Secret of easy yoke / The well / Promise. *(re-iss. Jul00; same)* <*(re-iss. Nov01 on 'Jade Tree' lp/cd; JT 1063/+CD)*>		

— **BAZAN** now with 1998:- **NICK PETERSON** – guitar + **BLAKE WESCOTT** – snare drums (or) 1999:- **JOSH GOLDEN** – bass + **BEN BRUBAKER** – drums

May 99.	(m-cd) <*MEX 006*> **THE ONLY REASON I FEEL SECURE (IS THAT I AM VALIDATED BY MY PEERS)**		
	– Criticism as inspiration / I am always the one who calls / Invention / Letter from a concerned follower / Be thou my vision. *(re-iss. Nov01 on 'Jade Tree'; JT 1064CD)*		

— **BAZAN** on his own again

		Jade Tree	Jade Tree
Apr 00.	(cd) <*JT 1046CD*> **WINNERS NEVER QUIT**		Mar00
	– Slow and steady wins the race / Simple economics / To protect the family name / A mind of her own / Never leave a job half done / Eye on the finish line / Bad things to good people / Winners never quit.		
Jun 00.	(cd-ep) <*SSQ 011*> **PROGRESS EP**	-	
	– June 18, 1976 / April 6, 2039 / Of up and coming monarchs / Letter from a concerned follower. *(UK-iss.Sep01 as 7"ep+book; same)*		
	(above on 'Suicide Squeeze')		

— **BAZAN** now with **CASEY FOUBERT** (of SELDOM)

Apr 02.	(lp/cd) <*JT 1072/+CD*> **CONTROL**		
	– Options / Rapture / Penetration / Indian summer / Progress / Magazine / Rehearsal / Second best / Priests and paramedics / Rejoice.		

PEECHEES

Formed: San Francisco, California, USA . . . 1994 by the cosmopolitan line-up of CHRISTOPHER APPELGREN, CARLOS CANEDO, ROP VASQUEZ and ex-BRATMOBILE sticksperson MOLLY NEUMAN. The general critical consensus on these shambolic art-punks was that their shortfall in musicality and originality redeemed itself with attitude aplenty and a healthy irreverence. Over a brace of 7" singles, mainly for the 'Kill Rock Stars' label, The PEECHEES proved that their ebullient racket was ripe for the picking while 'DO THE MATH' (1996), 'GAMES PEOPLE PLAY' (1997) and 'LIFE' (1999) all sneered with abandon. • **Covered:** WELL WORTH TALKIN' ABOUT (Drags) / NO HEART (Vibrators) / LOVE IS THE LAW (Suburbs) / SING LIKE ME (Elliott Smith).

Album rating: DO THE MATH (*5) / GAMES PEOPLE PLAY (*4) / LIFE (1994-1998) compilation (*5)

CHRISTOPHER APPELGREN (b. Kansas City, Missouri) – vocals / **CARLOS CANEDO** (b. Culiacan, Sinaloa) – guitar / **ROP VASQUEZ** (b. Metro Manila, Philippines) – bass / **MOLLY NEUMAN** (b. Washington, D.C.) – drums (ex-BRATMOBILE)

		Kill Rock Stars	Kill Rock Stars
Aug 94.	(7"ep) <*KRS 231*> **CUP OF GLORY**	-	
	– Cheap fun / Grease / Fine watch.		
1995.	(7"ep) <*LK 119*> **SCENTED GUM**	-	
	– Genuine article / Tea biscuit to show / Olive Oil.		
	(above issued on 'Lookout', below on 'Skinnie Girl')		
1995.	(7") <*SG 004*> **SPEND SOME TIME WITH . . .**		
	– Modern soul / LONG HIND LEGS: Kicking giant.		
Jan 96.	(lp/cd) <*KRS 255/+CD*> **DO THE MATH**	-	
	– Pepper / Do the math / I could have loved you / Mad doctor / On with Guayabera / Cloud fantasy / Cloud frenzy / Beer city / I don't know too / Tired imagery / The fascist lawn / Slick's living it up (on the bottom of the sea) / The animal. *(UK-iss.Apr00; same)*		
1996.	(7") <*G.I. 007-7*> **RADIO DISAPPEARS**	-	
	– Well worth talkin' about / The DRAGS: Slick's living it up.		
	(above on 'G.I. Productions', below issued on 'Rugger Bugger')		
Mar 97.	(7") <*(DUMP 041)*> **LOVE MOODS**		1996
	– New Moscow woman / Quadruple bypass.		
Sep 97.	(lp/cd) <*KRS 285/+CD*> **GAMES PEOPLE PLAY**		Aug97
	– An invitation / Antarticists / Lose the motorcade (and live it up) / The right reasons / One for the treble / To be counted / Everybody / Quadruple bypass / New Moscow woman / Can we check in? / Two for the bass / The restart / Return of the rock'n'roll nurse / Feel free / Brass tinsel.		
Dec 97.	(7") *(ROX 002)* **ANTARTICISTS. / LOVE IS THE LAW**		-
	(above issued on 'Roxy', below on 'Damaged Goods')		
Jul 98.	(7"pic-d) *(DAMGOOD 152)* **SING LIKE ME. / OTHER ICE AGE**		-

— disbanded late 1998; APPELGREN formed The PATTERN

– compilations, etc. –

Jan 99.	(cd) *Kill Rock Stars*; <*(KRS 315)*> **LIFE (1994-1998)**		
	– Cheap fun / Fine watch / Grease / Patty Coahuila / Genuine article / Tea biscuit to show / Tomfoolery / Olive Oil / Maintenance free / Modern soul / New Moscow woman / Quadruple bypass / Well worth talkin about / No heart / Love is the law / Other ice age / Sing like me / You are not. *(lp-iss.Feb99 on 'Damaged Goods'; DAMGOOD 160LP)*		

PEEPS INTO FAIRYLAND

Formed: Carnoustie, Scotland . . . summer 1996 by village boys MICHAEL ANGUS, PAUL HERBERT and GRAEME WILLIAMSON. Starting out as a dual songwriting team, ANGUS and HERBERT were quickly introduced to the stage-shy, but extremely talented WILLIAMSON. The quiet, brooding 4-piece (who had now added HAMISH FULFORD) recorded the 'THE WISE WITCH' 2-track EP in the summer of '98 and picked up acclaim from fellow Scottish songsmiths, IDLEWILD (who covered their grave-turning masterpiece, 'PALACE FLOPHOUSE', which takes its name from a passage in Steinbeck's 'Cannery Row'). This was followed by the exclusion of WILLIAMSON (as his stage fright overcame his ability to perform) and the drafting in of guitarist JEREMY MILLS and percussionist FERGUSON; after another single, 'MUDDY WATER' – for Bristol's 'Roisin' – MARTIN BATE would also come in as substitute for HAMISH (who had left to pursue the study of priesthood!). The 'RAIN AND WIRES' EP surfaced late in 1999, and having moved westward to Glasgow (a year earlier, in fact!), their GRANDADDY, PALACE and NICK DRAKE near impersonations were well accepted by the weep-core acoustic community. They were invited to record in Glasgow's 'Stuffhouse' studios, which resulted in their debut album, 'THE SHOT' (2000). Definitely underrated, the album continued the group's minimal/acoustic affair, with hushed and beautiful melodies; it was an album to send your children to sleep on a winter's night. In 2000 the band went through a difficult period after their tour van bizarrely exploded; MARTIN BATE divorced himself from the group in order to concentrate on his side-project STUPID ACTING SMART. Although the band were slightly dazed by this set-back they still managed to issue the brilliant 'HAPPINESS' LP in 2002. A collection of field-recordings and ballads, the group decided to split temporarily after the music press and the music-buying public took no interest in The PEEPS masterpiece. But, like LONE PIGEON and The RADAR BROTHERS, the group's floating melodics and lush arrangments were finding solace in the hearts of those cult record collectors who find a gem and tell their friends, who tell their friends . . . hopefully, not before long it'll have the beaming, underground reputation it deserves. • Trivia: 'Take a peep into Fairyland' is the title of a pop-up children's book which the group's moniker originated from.

Album rating: THE SHOT (*7) / HAPPINESS (*8)

MICHAEL ANGUS – vocals, drums, guitar / **PAUL HERBERT** – vocals, guitar, drums / **JEREMY MILLS** – guitar / **GRAEME WILLIAMSON** – guitar / **HAMISH FULFORD** – bass

Roisin / not iss.

Jul 98. (ltd-12"ep) (ROISIN 01) **THE WISE WITCH EP**
– Tales from the abbey / Wise witch of the moor slow rides backwards.

―― **JEREMY MILLS** – guitar + **D. JOHN FERGUSON** – drums, accordion; repl. GRAEME who retired from music scene

Feb 99. (7") (ROISIN 02) **MUDDY WATER. / LAST DAY**

―― **MARTIN BATE** – bass; repl. HAMISH who went into priesthood

D & C Recordings / not iss.

Dec 99. (cd-ep) (DC 002) **RAIN AND WIRES EP**
– Palace flophouse / Willow pattern / A drink to the hand / Fragment.
Sep 00. (cd) (DCCD 004) **THE SHOT**
– Home / Blackspot / Go out walking / Cat / When pictures move / Cloud formation / 3 step dancing / Muddy water / Autumn / Dawnsong / Lurches and swings / Counting song / Covering the sun.

―― now without MARTIN

Jan 02. (cd) (DCCD 005) **HAPPINESS**
– Intro / Tremble / Deaf by hands / Passing place / Sulliven from Elphin / Death by lions / Fear of flying / I count alone / Thoughts and lines.

PENTHOUSE

Formed: Camden, London, England . . . mid 90's by CHARLIE FINKE, JON FREE, GRAEME FLYNN and TIM CEDAR. What the 'STONES might've sounded like had they been born twenty, thirty, or even forty (!) years later, PENTHOUSE traded in a similar scabby vein of dirty, distorted blues as JON SPENCER, if a bit more lascivious. After the release of two independent 45's, 'RIPPED 'N' HAPPY' and 'GAS PORTER BLUES', they signed to 'World Domination', releasing their debut album, 'GUTTER EROTICA', in 1997. From the devilish sleaze of the cover art to the explicit nature of the lyrics, especially opening track/single, 'VOYEUR'S BLUES', the record was the aural equivalent of Soho at its seediest.

Album rating: GUTTER EROTICA (*6)

CHARLIE FINKE – vocals, mouth harp / **JON FREE** – guitar / **GRAEME FLYNN** – bass / **TIM CEDAR** – drums (ex-FURY THINGS, ex-LOVEBLOBS, ex-ACTION SWINGERS)

Kitty Kitty Corporation / not iss.

Nov 95. (7") (CHOOSY 002) **RIPPED 'N' HAPPY. / BABY PEELER**
Apr 96. (7") (CHOOSY 003) **GAS PORTER BLUES. / STUNG TRUNKS**

Syrup / not iss.

Jul 96. (ltd.7") (SYRUP 001) **LE STUNT. / Country Teasers: GETAWAY**

World Domination / Beggars Banquet

Apr 97. (7") (WDOM 33S) **VOYEUR'S BLUES. / PLATE OF SLAGS**
(cd-s+=) (WDOM 33SCD) – Le stunt / Tongue Kung Fu.
May 97. (lp/cd) (WDOM 34/+CD) <80206> **GUTTER EROTICA** Nov98
– Voyeur's blues / Gus' neck / La grotte d'amour / Road rash / The beauty in the beast / A deviant soiree / Harmonic surf spastic / Widow's chagrin / Mare Ingram's lament / The gin waltz / White coal / Lap dog shuffle / Face down. (re-iss. Apr98; same) (cd re-iss. Oct98 on 'Beggars Banquet'; BBQMCD 206)
Nov 97. (cd-ep) (CRH 00009) **RECKS EP**
– Baby pealer / Ript'n'happy / Gas porter blues / Strung trunks / Queen of sex / Behemoth.
(above single on 'Carcrashh') (re-iss. Jan99; CCRASH 004)
Apr 98. (12"ep/cd-ep) (PENT 001 T/CD) **REMIX EP**
– White coal / Voyeur's blues / Road rash / Lap dog shuffle.

Beggars Banquet / not iss.

Nov 98. (7") (BBQ 331) **VALLEY OF THE SOWS. / INSIDE SLICK**
(cd-s+=) (BBQ 331CD) – What meanders.
Jun 99. (cd/lp) (BBQ CD/LP 211) **MY IDLE HANDS**
– Creeper's reef / Valley of the sows / Man o' fire / Detunabilly / Petit song / The fool at blood gulley / Head of the wake / Giant haystacks / Nudie Ron / Lil' brown kisses / Beautiful be the indolent / Wot meanders / The 49th ton.

Butcher's Wig / not iss.

Nov 00. (7") (SYRUP 009) **WHITE SLAVE SPEAKS. / NIGHT JAR**

PERFUME

Formed: Leicester, England . . . late 1993 by MICK McCARTHY and TONY OWEN, who enlisted JOHNNY WADD. Having set up their own appropriately titled label, 'Aromasound', the whiffy wannabes made their debut with the single, 'YOGA', quite literally leaving a scented trail with a further two 45's, 'YOUNG' and 'LOVER'; the former actually smelled of perfume! Meanwhile, the lads built up their already swaggering confidence with a Jo Whiley session for Radio One and a tour supporting GENE whom PERFUME bore at least a passing musical resemblance. After another indie hit, 'YESTERDAY FOLLOWS TODAY', they got their one solitary sniff at chartland (No.71) with early '96's 'HAVEN'T SEEN YOU'. A year on, the band had signed to 'Big Star', previewing their belated debut album, 'ONE' (1997) with a re-issue of 'LOVER'.

Album rating: ONE (*7) / YESTERDAY RISING compilation (*7)

MICK McCARTHY – vocals, guitar / **TONY OWEN** – bass / **JOHNNY WADD** – drums

Aromasound / not iss.

Dec 93. (7") (AROMA 001) **YOGA. /**
Apr 94. (7") (AROMA 002) **YOUNG. / ANOINTED**
Jan 95. (7") (AROMA 003) **LOVER. / MORPHEUS**
(cd-s+=) (AROMA 003CDS) – Lover (acoustic) / Yoga.
Jul 95. (7") (AROMA 004) **YESTERDAY FOLLOWS YOU. / RISING STAR**
(cd-s+=) (AROMA 004CDS) – Aylestone lane / Walk into the wind.
Jan 96. (7"/c-s) (AROMA 005/+MC) **HAVEN'T SEEN YOU. / OPEN YOUR SHELL** 71
(cd-s+=) (AROMA 005CDS) – Walk like a god (live) / You've got something (live).
May 96. (7"/c-s) (AROMA 006/+MC) **CARVING YOUR NAME. / LOST IN YOU**
(cd-s+=) (AROMA 006CDS) – Climber / You kill me.

Big Star / not iss.

Feb 97. (7"/c-s) (STAR/+K7 103) **LOVER. / MORPHEUS**
(cd-s+=) (STARC 103) – Lover (acoustic) / Yoga.
Mar 97. (cd/c) (STAR C/K7 104) **ONE**
– I'm alive / Lover / Watch me bleed / You and I / As I go blind / Carving your name / Your life is now / One / Haven't seen you / I'm no saint / Changes / Fallen / Things that I love / Wild honey.
Mar 97. (7"/c-s) (STAR/+K7 106) **YOU AND I. /**
(cd-s+=) (STARC 106) –

– compilations, etc. –

Feb 98. (cd) Aromasound; (AROMALP 001CD) **YESTERDAY RISING**
– Yesterday follows you / Rising star / Morpheus / Yoga / Lost in you / Climber / L.I.P.S. / Perfume / Anointed / Aylestone lane.

PERMANENT GREEN LIGHT
(see under ⇒ THREE O'CLOCK)

PERNICE BROTHERS

Formed: Boston, Massachusetts, USA . . . 1996 by er, the PERNICE BROTHERS, songwriter JOE (formerly of 'Sub Pop' outfit, SCUD MOUNTAIN BOYS), who made three albums in the mid 90's) and his elder sibling BOB, who doubled the line-up with PEYTON PINKERTON and THOM MONAHAN (formerly of the NEW RADIANT STORM KINGS and The LILYS respectively). America's country-rock equivalent to TEENAGE FANCLUB, JOE and Co issued a couple of low key 45's before delivering a set of orchestra-laden tunes in the shape of 1998's 'OVERCOME BY HAPPINESS'. This featured JOE's homage to his poet hero, CHARLES SIMIC, on the track, 'WHEREIN OBSCURITY'; lushness was back in musical city.

Album rating: OVERCOME BY HAPPINESS (*6) / CHAPPAQUIDDICK SKYLINE as Chappaquiddick Skyline (*7) / BIG TOBACCO as Joe Pernice (*6) / THE WORLD WON'T END (*7)

JOE PERNICE – vocals, guitar (ex-SCUD MOUNTAIN BOYS) / **BOB PERNICE** – guitar, vocals / **PEYTON PINKERTON** – guitar / **THOM MONAHAN** – bass, vocals / + a 10-piece orchestra in the studio

Sub Pop / Sub Pop

Sep 97. (7") <SP 381> **JIMMY COMA. / MONKEY SUIT** Jan97
not iss. / Summershine
Dec 97. (7") <SHINEUS 21> **SQUARE WORLD. / IN PLAIN SIGHT**
Rykodisc / Sub Pop
May 98. (cd) (RCD 10447) <SPCD 427> **OVERCOME BY HAPPINESS**
– Crestfallen / Overcome by happiness / Sick of you / Clear spot / Dimmest star / Monkey suit / Chicken wire / Wait to stop / All I know / Shoes and clothes / Wherein obscurity / Ferris wheel.
Apr 00. (cd-s) (RCD 51058) **CLEAR SPOT**

CHAPPAQUIDDICK SKYLINE

JOE PERNICE plus **THOM + PEYTON** plus **LAURA STEIN, MIKE BELITSKY, JOHN CROOKE, JOE HARVARD + JENNIFER PIERCE**

Sub Pop / Sub Pop

Mar 00. (cd) <(SPCD 470)> **CHAPPAQUIDDICK SKYLINE** Jan00
– Everyone else is evolving / Solitary Swedish houses / Courage up / The two of you sleep / Breakneck speed / Theme to an endless bummer / Up in Michigan / Hundred dollar pocket / Nobody's watching / Knights of the night vol.1 / Leave me alone / Kidney shaped pool.

JOE PERNICE

―― with **PEYTON + THOM** plus **MATT HUNTER, LAURA STEIN, MIKE DALY, GORDON ZACHARIAS, DAVID REID + JEREMY SMITH**

Glitterhouse / Ashmont

Jul 00. (cd) (GRCD 488) <3> **BIG TOBACCO** Sep00
– Prince valium / The pill / Bum leg / Pipe bomb / I still can't say her name / Undertow / I break down / Hard to take v/ Second semester lesbian.

PERNICE BROTHERS

―― returned with the usual suspects

PERNICE BROTHERS (cont)

		Southpaw	Ashmont
May 01.	(7"m/cd-s) *(PAW SCDS 4)* **7:30. / UP THE DOWN ESCALATOR / OUR TIME HAS PASSED**	□	-
Jun 01.	(cd) *(PAWCD 5)* <4> **THE WORLD WON'T END** – Working girls (sunlight shines) / 7:30 / Our time has passed / She heightened everything / Bryte side / Let that show / Shaken baby / Flaming wreck / The ballad of Bjorn Borg / Endless supply / Cronulla breakdown.		
Sep 01.	(7"m/cd-s) *(PAW S/CDS 6)* **WORKING GIRL (SUNLIGHT SHINES). / MY OWN PERSONAL PSYCHIC / SHE FALLS APART**	□	-

Liz PHAIR

Born: 17 Apr'67, New Haven, Connecticut, USA. Chicago based, USA. After graduating in Art History, PHAIR concentrated full-time on her songwriting and, with the help of friend/COME guitarist, CHRIS BROKAW, eventually secured a contract with indie label, 'Matador' early in 1992. Hooking up with musicians BRAD WOOD, CASEY RICE and LEROY BACH, PHAIR translated her song sketches into a marathon double album, 'EXILE ON GUYVILLE', its title a typically PHAIR-esque play on the classic 'STONES album. An engagingly eclectic, often brazenly confessional affair, PHAIR had fashioned a folk-grunge mini-classic, fusing wry life-in-America / hard-hitting sexual lyrics with beautiful country harmonies in a similar vein to MAZZY STAR or THROWING MUSES. Critics loved it and in addition to the gushing reviews, PHAIR became the first woman since JONI MITCHELL (in 1974) to win the prestigious 'Village Voice' annual award. The sonic femme-thrust of 'SUPERNOVA' previewed follow-up, 'WHIP-SMART' (1994), a record that surprisingly received a less than enthusiastic response in comparison to its predecessor. While the album may have lacked a little of the debut's wayward charm, the songs were more focused and PHAIR's muse was as fertile, and occasionally as candid as ever (even if her much talked about stage-fright might've belied the bolshy, sexually liberated persona her music projected). While 1995 saw the release of a stop-gap odds'n'sods collection, 'JUVENILIA' (1995), it would be another three years before another studio set, 'WHITECHOCOLATESPACEEGG' (1998). Reaching the Top 40 in America, the album was once again the toast of the Rolling Stone readers, although her Lo-Fi ramblings sounded a tad similar to BELLY or even SLEATER-KINNEY for the more discerning Brits.

Album rating: EXILE IN GUYVILLE (*7) / WHIP-SMART (*8) / JUVENILIA compilation (*4) / WHITECHOCOLATESPACEEGG (*6)

LIZ PHAIR – vocals, guitar / **BRAD WOOD** – drums, percussion / **CASEY RICE** – guitar / **LEROY BACH** – bass

		Minty Fresh	not iss.
Aug 93.	(7") *(MF 4)* **CANARY. / CARNIVORE**	□	-
		Matador	Matador
Aug 93.	(cd/c/lp) <*(OLE 051-2/-4/-1)*> **EXILE IN GUYVILLE** – 6'1" / Help me Mary / Glory / Dance of the seven veils / Never said / Soap star Joe / Explain it to me / Canary / Mesmerizing / Fuck and run / Girls! girls! girls! / Divorce song / Shatter / Flower / Johnny Sunshine / Gunshy / Stratford-On-Guy / Strange loop.	□	Jun93
Sep 94.	(7") <*(OLE 103-7)*> <98206> **SUPERNOVA. / COMBO PLATTER**	□ Atlantic	78 Jul94 Atlantic
Sep 94.	(cd/c/lp) <*(7567 92429-2/-4/-1)*><*OLE 107*> **WHIP-SMART** – Chopsticks / Supernova / Support system / X-ray man / Shane / Nashville / Go west / Cince de Mayo / Dogs of L.A. / Whip-smart / Jealousy / Crater lake / Alice Springs / May queen.	□	27
Oct 94.	(7"/c-s) *(A 8224/+C)* **SUPERNOVA. / X-RAY MAN (remix)** (12"+=/cd-s+=) *(A 8224 T/CD)* – ('A'-clean version).	□	-
		Matador – Capitol	Matador – Capitol
Aug 98.	(cd/c/lp) <*(OLE 191 – 7243 8 53554-2/-4/-1)*> **WHITECHOCOLATESPACEEGG** – White chocolate space egg / Big tall man / Perfect world / Johnny Feelgood / Polyester bride / Love is nothing / Baby got going / Uncle Alvarez / Only son / Go on ahead / Headache / Ride / What makes you happy / Fantasize / Shitloads of money / Girls' room.	□	35

– compilations, etc. –

| Aug 95. | (d7"ep/cd-ep) *Matador*; <*(OLE 129-7/-2)*> **JUVENILIA** – Jealousy / Turning Japanese / Animal girl / California / South Dakota / Batmobile / Dead shark / Easy. | □ | - |

PHANTOM ENGINEER

Formed: Glasgow, Scotland ... early 1998 by the unlikely trio of DAVID KEENAN (ex-TELSTAR PONIES), JOHN HOGARTY (of NATIONAL PARK and ex-BMX BANDITS and TELSTAR PONIES) plus jazzman BILL WELLS. Described – and deservedly so – as "out there", PHANTOM ENGINEER were indeed indie improvisers of the Nth degree. A haunting, but nevertheless atmospheric eponymous debut, was delivered towards the end of 1998.

Album rating: PHANTOM ENGINEER (*6)

DAVID KEENAN – guitar (ex-TELSTAR PONIES) / **BILL WELLS** (b. Falkirk) – sax / **JOHN HOGARTY** – (of NATIONAL PARK, ex-BMX BANDITS, ex-TELSTAR PONIES briefly)

		Paperhouse	not iss.
Dec 98.	(cd) *(GHOST 001CD)* **PHANTOM ENGINEER** – Morton Bartlett's children / Sweetheart come / Western snowfall / BC52 / Arc of a jetplane / End of a holiday / Welcome home David.	□	-

PHANTOM SURFERS

Formed: San Francisco, California, USA ... 1988 by MEL "FROSTBITE" BERGMAN, JOHNNY "BIG HAND" BARTLETT, MIKE "DADDY LOVE" LUCAS and DANNY SEELIG. This none-too-serious attempt at bringing together a retro-garage surf outfit, only to fill in at the last minute for a band that pulled out of a college gig, turned out to be a surprisingly successful venture for BARTLETT and Co. The four men, who donned the stage in Lone Ranger's masks and played out the sort of landlocked surf-punk instrumentals that used to belong to the READY MEN, were faced with the possibility of becoming cult heroes. A batch of singles subsequently followed after the legendary gig, proceeded by 1992's crash'n'burn debut '18 DEADLY ONES'. Over the following years, the group issued a silly amount of singles, EP's and splits – some with legends such as DAVIE ALLAN and DICK DALE himself, and mostly on the proto-punk DIY label 'Lookout!'. The trashy 'EXCITING SOUNDS OF MODEL ROAD RACING' was delivered in 1995, then 'THE GREAT SURF CRASH OF '97', to the appropriately titled 'SKATERHATER' in 1998. But by this point, BARTLETT and SEELIG had parted with the group, only to be replaced by MAZ KATTUAH and RUSSELL QUAN. With the quartet now missing their two original masked men, things went rapidly downhill – they issued the downright terrible 'XXX PARTY' in 2000. A concept "comedy" album, it featured the group playing nasty instrumentals over the jokes of past-it comedians RUDY RAY MOORE and CLARENCE "BLOWFLY" REID. The jokes were so crap, they wouldn't even have the cheek to put them on a rude Spanish postcard, whereas the band, well, they just weren't the same. • **Covered:** BESAME MUCHO (Consuelo Velasquez) / + others incl. X-Files theme and a few more covers on real debut / SHEENA WAS A PUNK ROCKER (Ramones).

Album rating: 18 DEADLY ONES (*5) / ...PLAY THE SONGS OF THE BIG-SCREEN SPECTACULARS (*5) / THE EXCITING SOUNDS OF MODEL ROAD RACING (*6) / THE GREAT SURF CRASH OF '97 (*5) / SKATERHATER (*4) / A DECADE OF QUALITY CONTROL compilation (*6) / XXX PARTY (*3)

MEL BERGMAN – guitar / **JOHNNY BARTLETT** – guitar / **MIKE LUCAS** – bass / **DANNY SEELIG** – drums

		not iss.	Standard
1991.	(7") <SR 71> **BESAME MUCHO. / MOVE IT!**	-	□
		not iss.	Pre-B.S.
1991.	(7") <SS45 003> **NORTHWEST BUDGET ROCK MASSACRE** – Paradise cove / (other by The MUMMIES).	-	□
		not iss.	Norton
1992.	(lp) <ED 218> **EIGHTEEN DEADLY ONES!** – Pleasure point / 20,000 leagues under the surf / San Onofre / Horror beach / Monster from the surf / Sewer peak / Surfin' with the Vy / Legend of the phantom surfer / Wave hog / Palincar / Sandtrap stomp / Slots o' fun / Stiletto / 14 miles to Gotham / Theme from Dead West / Twist off / Jalama burger / Banzai run. *(UK-iss.Jun98; same as US)*	-	□
		not iss.	Sympathy F
1992.	(7") <SFTRI 168> **UNKNOWN MUSEUM STOMP. / ANDALUSIA**	-	□
		not iss.	Demolition
1992.	(7"ep) <DEMO 003> **HELL-BEACH PARTY** – El aguila / Squad car / (other 2 by The ROOFDOGS).	-	□

— added **TRENT RUANE** – organ, rhythm guitar

		not iss.	Estrus
1992.	(lp) <ES 125> **PHANTOM SURFERS PLAY THE SONGS OF THE BIG-SCREEN SPECTACULARS** – Bikini drag / Pursuit of the leather girls / Geronimo / L'ultima volta / Hush, hush sweet Charlotte / Batwoman vs. Ratfink / High wall / Bali hai / Big screen spectacular tonight / Eaffin' and surfin' / Gammera / The beach girls and the monster / Suffer / Popcorn.	-	□
1992.	(7"ep) <ES 713> **BANZAI WASHOUT EP** – Banzai washout / Orbitron / Aye, five gold / Erotica / Surf rider.	-	□

— now without TRENT

		not iss.	Drop-Out
1993.	(7") <DO-1/DO-2> **FLUTTER FOOT. / PLAYA RATON**	-	□
		Pin Up	not iss.
Oct 94.	(7"ep) *(PINUP 94013)* **SURFIN' / ROCKET TO EUROPE TOUR 1994** – Surfari / Dark eyes / Special message / (others by The ASTRONAUTS).	□	-
		Planet Pimp	Planet Pimp
1995.	(7"ep) <PPR 012> **SURVIVAL OF THE FATTEST EP** – Fuck surf music / Stop, listen & collaborate / Leprechauns / Dick!	□	□

— **MAZ KATTUAH** – guitar (ex-MUMMIES) repl. BARTLETT

— **RUSSELL QUAN** – drums; repl. SEELIG who joined The HI-FIVES

		not iss.	Hobby Hut
1995.	(cd) <hobbyhut 124> **THE EXCITING SOUNDS OF MODEL ROAD RACING** – Introduction / Everybody up / Death of a rookie / Schlock slot / Slotter on 10th avenue / Crossover tragedy / Rheostat rock / Pacific shores / A slot car named Desire / Turn Marshal / Stumps of mystery / Endurance rally / Final lap / (untitled). <(re-iss. Aug97 on 'Lookout!' cd/lp; LK 183 CD/LP)>	-	□
		not iss.	Crown
1996.	(lp/cd) <CST 5358> **PHANTOM SURFERS W/ DICK DALE (NOT REALLY ...)** – Stop that Cedric / Tell tale couch / Rochambeau / Tic-toc rock / Battle of little big hand / Skirfir / Fairest of them all / Wow! / The lonely mattress / Gas chamber / Try to hide me / Pretty little Lisa / Sloth in molasses / We'll never hear the end of it. (above featured DALE on a few tracks)	-	□
		Lookout!	Lookout!
Sep 96.	(lp/cd) <*(LOOKOUT 155/+CD)*> **THE GREAT SURF CRASH OF '97** – The great surf crash / Rootin' around for Ramona / Pygmy dance / Basset ballet / Single whammy / The cat came back / Ticker tape jungle / Medley:- X-Files – Stupid	□	□

Files / Ants in my pants / (I call my baby) D.D.T. / Holiday harbor / Babalou / Buy high, sell low / Yozora no hoshi / Out the window / No go Diggy-Di / Lancelot Link Wray.

Sep 96. (7") <LK 156> **ISTANBUL. / TOKYO TWIST** | - | |

Sep 98. (cd; as The PHANTOM SURFERS and DAVIE ALLAN) <(LK 204)> **SKATERHATER** | | |
– Curb job (skaterhater overture) / Sidewalk city / Devil dust / Sheena was a punk rocker / You meet the nicest people on a Harley / Supercycle (love theme from Skaterhater) / The end of a skater / Blues theme (vocal) / Grindhouse / (The sound of) Breaking glass / Arrow space / Skate and bait / Murder can be fun / Polyurethane / Drag run.

Apr 00. (cd/lp) <(LK 240 CD/LP)> **XXX PARTY** | | Mar00 |
– I know it when I hear it / Dick hickeys / The pioneers – Have a good funeral – Yellow neck will pay / The golden turd / Nantucket sleigh ride / Necro Sue / The crepitation contest / Tomato juice / The big dick club / Peach poussaye / Dolemites corner / Happiness is / The Phantom Surfers' alphabet / Business deal / Love is . . . / A funny thing happened to me on the way to the orgy / Sin in the suburbs / Special guest guffaws / Let's fist again / Summa pornographica.

– **compilations, etc.** –

Oct 99. (lp) *V8; (V8 002)* **A DECADE OF QUALITY CONTROL 1988-1999** | | |
– Phantom Surfers quality statement / The hearse – El aguila / Paradise cove / Skating red square / Six pack / Gypsy surfer / Lafayette / Klingons vs. Daleks / Surfari / Move it / Besame mucho / Playa raton / Flutterfoot / Shaving cream / Tie me kangaroo down.

Joel R.L. PHELPS

Born: Missoula, Montana, USA. JOEL R.L. PHELPS first earned recognition as a member of SILKWORM, however, it wasn't until he embarked on a solo career that his full potential was realised and he got to enjoy the acclaim that was heaped upon him. Accompanied by The DOWNER TRIO (ROBERT MERCER on bass and drummer WILLIAM HERZOG), PHELPS delivered his debut solo album, 'WARM SPRING NIGHTS', in 1995. The man's ragged guitar playing and nasal vocals, coupled with the rollicking rhythm section, immediately drew comparisons with NEIL YOUNG & CRAZY HORSE. The sombre tone of the album only served to enhance the parallels between PHELPS and YOUNG, however nobody could deny the fundamental quality of the songs. There was a three-year hiatus before PHELPS would release a second album. Simply titled '3', the record did nothing to harm the singer's reputation. The understanding between the three band members had reached such a level, the music sounded as though it was emanating from one organism. PHELPS had clearly developed more confidence in his vocal abilities and was stretching his voice to, almost, TIM BUCKLEY proportions. 'BLACKBIRD' released the following year was a blistering and intense affair reminiscent of the work he had done with SILKWORM. PHELPS' fourth album, 'INLAND EMPIRES' (2001), was a collection of cover versions featuring songs by FLEETWOOD MAC and STEVE EARLE amongst others, while JP delivered the songs with such soulful individuality. • **Covered:** EMERALD CITY (. . . Easdale) / GUNS OF BRIXTON (Clash) / etc.

Album rating: WARM SPRINGS NIGHT (*7) / 3 (*6) / BLACKBIRD (*5) / INLAND EMPIRES mini (*5)

JOEL R.L. PHELPS – vocals, guitar / **ROBERT MERCER** – bass / **WILLIAM HERZOG** – drums (latter two aka The DOWNER TRIO)

	not iss.	El Recordo
Oct 95. (cd) <3> **WARM SPRINGS NIGHT**	-	

– Counsel / All we want / Lady Lucero / Warm springs night / Ave Patricia / God bless the little pigs / The graze and the graves / There is not enough / OK Reno. *(UK-iss.Nov98 on 'Glitterhouse'; GRCD 394)*

JOEL R.L. PHELPS & THE DOWNER TRIO

	Pacifico	Pacifico
1997. (cd-ep) <PAC 05> **THE DOWNER TRIO**	-	

– Razorback / Good advice for dogs / At El Paso / Emerald city / Guns of Brixton.

Jun 98. (cd) <(PAC 07)> **3** | | |
– The way down / Rev Robert Irving / Hope's hit / Always glide / Give me back my animal / Who can I burn? / Chaplin's radiotelephone / Fifty / Alita Aleta / Lull.

Sep 99. (cd) <(PAC 10)> **BLACKBIRD** | | |
– Then slowly Kimm / I got a live one / Unless your tired of living / Get the chills / Invited / Lost continent / Blessed Salt Lake / Waiting in the water / Pourdelanes / Mega tonight / Landslide. *(re-iss. Mar01 on '12XU'; 12XU 0022)*

	12XU	Moneyshot
Feb 01. (m-cd) (12XU 0012) **INLAND EMPIRES**		Jan01

– Songbird / Our mother the mountain / Someday / Apology accepted / Now you are found. *(m-lp-iss.Mar01; 12XU 0021)*

Grant Lee PHILLIPS
(see under ⇒ GRANT LEE BUFFALO)

PHOTON BAND

Formed: Philadelphia, Pennsylvania, USA . . . mid 90's by ART DIFURIA, JEFF TANNER and SIMON NAGLE. Influenced by a plethora of 60's British psychedelic acts such as The KINKS, The WHO and BARRETT, The PHOTON BAND opened their lo-fi-esque musical account via debut 1996 single, '747 (DON'T WORRY)'. Whereas the similarly-motivated OLIVIA TREMOR CONTROL and The LILYS were cracking their respective neo-psych fields, the PHOTON BAND struggled a little with spacy albums such as 'ALL YOUNG IN THE SOUL' (1998), 'OH, THE SWEET, SWEET CHANGES' (2000) and 'IT'S A LOVELY PLANET' (2002).

Album rating: ALL YOUNG IN THE SOUL (*7) / OH, THE SWEET, SWEET CHANGES (*6) / OUR OWN ESP DRIVEN SCENE compilation (*6) / IT'S A LONELY PLANET (*5)

ART DIFURIA – vocals, guitar / **JEFF TANNER** – bass / **SIMON NAGLE** – drums

	Darla	Darla
Apr 96. (cd-s) <DRL 20> **747 (DON'T WORRY) / IT TO GET / MOVE DREAM**	-	
Mar 98. (7") <tpz 5> **SONGS TO BE PLAYED AT 3 A.M. IN SMOKE FILLED, DRAFTY, PRE-APOCALYPTIC END OF THE CENTURY WAREHOUSES BY MISTY-EYED YOUTH OF ALL AGES AS SATURDAY NIGHT TURNS INTO SUNDAY MORNING**	-	

– Turn of the century #2 / Turn of the century #1. (above issued on 'Tappersize')

Jun 98. (lp/cd) <(DRL 059/+CD)> **ALL YOUNG IN THE SOUL** | | Jul99 |
– Anything for you / Exactly what is weird / 10,000 buckets of rain / 2:37 a.m. / Crabapple Annie / 9 of dreams / Only lucky lonely / Jealousy / (The future's) Comin' round the bend / 23 old & tired / Free / January.

── **GARY PLOWMAN** – bass; repl. TANNER

Aug 00. (cd) <(DRL 105)> **OH, THE SWEET, SWEET CHANGES** | | |
– Genius / End of the week / Could it be? / Disillusuion / Runaways / It's happening now / Now it's over (and over) / Saturn returns again / She don't need lovin' – Snowflake in the sky / Maybe in November.

Aug 00. (cd) <(DRL 106)> **OUR OWN ESP DRIVEN SCENE (SINGLES AND COMPS & OUTTAKES '95-'00)** (collection) | | |
– Sitting on the sunn / Supertard / I don't need to be told / Rise above / I understand / Commercial for taking drugs / It to get (bike mix) / 747 (don't worry) / The darkest hour / Broken melody / You can never really have too much wine / End of the century #2 / Little wind / Would you believe / Saturn returns / The magic word / See what I see / Here come some changes.

2001. (ltd-lp) <DRL 114> **ALONE ON THE MOON** | - | |
Nov 02. (cd) <DRL 129> **IT'S A LONELY PLANET** | - | |
– Re-entry burn / It's a lonely planet / Outerspace / Out of synch, out of season, out of rhyme, out of reason / Indirection (school) / Paper plane / Dreamin II / If it's a beautiful day / Closer / We don't care anymore.

PIANO MAGIC

Formed: London, England . . . summer 1996 by mainstays GLEN JOHNSON and DICK RANCE. The oddly-titled PIANO MAGIC started as a casual activity with various members (RAECHEL LEIGH and DOMINIC CHENNELL among them) coming and going whenever they wished. However, the group now had very little recording time and several months went by without them recording together. JOHNSON spent the time remixing tracks previously recorded and also took to developing new material featured on the band's demo recording which was sent to 'Che' records. That November, the band released their debut single, 'WRONG FRENCH', issued on 'Che'-associated imprint, 'i'. The platter was a critical success receiving the prestigious SOTW from Melody Maker. Their minimalist electronica lay somewhere between KRAFTWERK and YOUNG MARBLE GIANTS; mototonik Krautrock with sweet'n'sour indie pop romance. The band then began to play venues with respected bands such as MOGWAI and THIRD EYE FOUNDATION. PIANO MAGIC were fast becoming a group one found hard to become familiar with as their line-ups constantly changed. A debut album, 'POPULAR MECHANICS', was delivered in autumn 1997, its childlike approach to instrumentation and interpretation led to one John Peel becoming an admirer. With further personnel changes (i.e. ALEXANDER PEARLS, JEN ADAM and EZRA FEINBERG), PM released a four track 12" EP, 'THE FUN OF THE CENTURY', in the winter months of '97. An album was not released for another eighteen months however, although fans were compensated by several classy singles/EP's including a split EP with LOW and TRANSIENT WAVES. The band now consisted of the ever present JOHNSON, alongside CHARLES WYATT, CHRIS OVENDEN and PAUL TRONBOHM. Finally released, 'A TRICK OF THE SEA' (1998) consisted of only two lengthy ambient tracks, both of which featured LUCY GULLAND (the girlfriend of OVENDEN). Not surprisingly, JOHNSON gave the band a little rest while he subsequently took PIANO MAGIC for a solo sojourn via 'MUSIC FOR ANNAHBIRD' and 'MUSIC FOR ROLEX'. JOHNSON had not given up on PIANO MAGIC as a band and decided later in '99 that the band was due a resurrection. JOHN CHEVES was enlisted to play guitar and MIGUEL MARIN answered an advertisement for a drummer; the latter was more than qualified having played in a successful Spanish indie band (he's now the brainchild of ARBOL). 'LOW BIRTH WEIGHT' was next off the production line, JOHNSON again utilising children's toys for instruments, while he assembled together CAROLINE POTTER, RAECHEL LEIGH and SIMON RIVERS. Being compared to the AWOL KEVIN SHIELDS (of MY BLOODY VALENTINE) was some accolade, although JOHNSON was certainly worthy of the highest merits. 'ARTISTS RIFLES' (2000) was a concept record of sorts, the trials of war being the theme and JOY DIVISION and THIS MORTAL COIL being soundtrack'd by Stanley Kubrick being (possibly) the inspiration. Talking of soundtracks, JOHNSON and his revolving-door musos were invited to lay down tracks for Bigas Luna on his film, 'SON DE MAR' (2001). This lush, intimate and ethereal set saw PIANO MAGIC on the roster of '4 a.d.' (where else!), their ambient nature suited for Ivo's rich stable. However, just when it looked like JOHNSON had conjured up a winning musical ticket to

PIANO MAGIC (cont)

indie stardom, PIANO MAGIC failed to win over the critics for follow-up, 'WRITERS WITHOUT HOMES' (2002). Solemn to the extreme, the 'MAGIC had run out of tricks – or had they?

Album rating: POPULAR MECHANICS (*6) / A TRICK OF THE SEA (*7) / LOW BIRTH WEIGHT (*8) / ARTISTS' RIFLES (*7) / SEASONALLY AFFECTIVE compilation (*7) / SON DE MAR (*7) / WRITERS WIITHOUT HOMES (*4)

GLEN JOHNSON – vocals, keyboards / **DICK RANCE** – instruments / **DOMINIC CHENNELL** – instruments / **RAECHEL LEIGH** – vocals

	i – Che	i – Che
Nov 96. (12"ep) *(IRE 107-1)* **WRONG FRENCH. / NON-FICTION / GENERAL ELECTRIC WITH FAIRY LIGHTS**	□	-
Mar 97. (12"ep) *(IRE 203-1)* **WINTERSPORT / CROSS COUNTRY. / ANGEL PIE / MAGIC TREE / MAGNETIC NORTH**	□	-

— now just **JOHNSON + CHENNELL**

Jun 97. (7") *(WJ 26)* **FOR ENGINEERS A. / FOR ENGINEERS AA** □ -
(above issued on 'Wurlitzer Jukebox')

— the original trio (+ RAECHEL) again added **HAZEL BURFITT** – vocals / **MARTIN COOPER** – bass, guitar, drums, etc. / **PAUL TORNBOHM + DAVID GRIFFITHS**

Nov 97. (cd/lp) (<*IRE 210-2/-1*>) **POPULAR MECHANICS** □ Sep97
 – Metal coffee / Wintersport – Cross country / Everything works beautifully (0.53) / Amongst Russian lathes and metal curls / Birth of an object / Revolving moth cage / To be swished – Dream of the ups driver / Freckled robot / Soft magnets / Wrong French / You've lost your footing in this world.

— added **ALEXANDER PERLS** – guitar / **JEN ADAM** – synthesizer, vocals / **EZRA FEINBERG**

	Piao!	not iss.
May 98. (12"ep) *(PIAO 12)* **THE FUN OF THE CENTURY** – The fun of the century / The sharpest knife in the drawer / Industrial cutie / I am the sub-librarian.	□	-
	Debut	not iss.
Aug 98. (7"clear) *(DEBT 001)* **FRENCH MITTENS. / Icebreaker: MELODY FOR NATO**	□	-
	Rocket Girl	not iss.
Oct 98. (7"; by LOW, TRANSIENT WAVES & PIANO MAGIC) *(RGIRL 4)* **SLEEP AT THE BOTTOM.** / (other track by Transient Waves)	□	-
	Lissy's	not iss.
Nov 98. (7"clear) *(LISS 32)* **MUSIC FOR ROLEX.** / (other side by Matmos)	□	-
	Darla	Darla
Nov 98. (lp/cd) (<*DRL 074/+CD*>) **A TRICK OF THE SEA** – A trick of the sea / Halloween boat. *(re-iss. Apr00; same)*	□	□
	Bad Jazz	not iss.
Dec 98. (7") *(BEBOP 09)* **MUSIC FOR ANNAHBIRD. / MUSIC FOR WASPS**	□	-

— **JOHNSON, ADAM, COOPER + PERLS** now with **CAROLINE POTTER + RAECHEL LEIGH + PETE ASTOR** – vocals

	Rocket Girl	Rocket Girl
Jun 99. (cd/beige-lp) (<*RGIRL 5 CD/LP*>) **LOW BIRTH WEIGHT** – Snowfall soon / Crown estate / Bad patient / The fun of the century / Birdy machine / Not fair / Dark secrets look for light / Snow drums / Shepherds are needed / I am the sub-librarian / Waking up.	□	□
Aug 99. (cd-ep) **MORT AUX VACHES EP** – Kingfisher – Grass / Greece / Birds / Trick / Winter. (above issued on 'Staalplaat', below on 'Acetone Singles Club')	-	- German
Sep 99. (7") *(010)* **AMONGST THE BOOKS, AN ANGEL. / C'EST UN MAUVEIS PRESAGE LORSQUE TON AMRESTE TOMBE**	-	- French

— **GABE** (was their third bass player)

Oct 99. (7"red) *(RGIRL 12)* **THERE'S NO NEED FOR US TO BE ALONE. / THE CANADIAN BROUGHT US SNOW** □ -
above single features **DARREN** – vocals (of HEFNER)

— **JOHNSON + POTTER** recruited **MIGUEL MARIN + PAUL TORNBOHM**

May 00. (lp/cd) *(RGIRL 19/+CD)* <69819> **ARTISTS' RIFLES** □ □
 – (1.16) / No closure / A return to the sea / (1.22) / You and John are birds / The index / (1.50) / Century schoolbook / Password / Artists' rifles.

— **JOHNSON + MARIN** recruited **JEROME TCHERNEYAN + ALASDAIR STEER**

	Acuarela	not iss.
Apr 01. (cd-s) *(NOIS 012)* **I CAME TO YOUR PARTY DRESSED AS A SHADOW / BLOOD AND SNOW / THE DROWNING OF ST. CHRISTOPHER**	□	-
	4 a.d.	4 a.d.
Aug 01. (cd) (<*MAD 2105CD*>) **SON DE MAR** (original soundtrack) – (parts 1-6).	□	□

— added **BERND JESTRAM + SIMON RAYMONDE** (piano, bass) + **ROBERT JOHNSTONE** (guitar)

Jun 02. (cd) (<*CAD 2209CD*>) **WRITERS WITHOUT HOMES** □ □
 – (Music won't save you from anything but) Silence / Postal / Modern Jupiter / 1.30 / The season is long / Certainty / Crown of the lost / It's the same dream that lasts all night / Dutch housing / Already ghosts / Shot through the fog.

— MIGUEL MARIN records under the moniker, **ARBOL**

– compilations, etc. –

Oct 01. (d-cd) *Rocket Girl; (RGIRL 31CD)* <69831> **SEASONALLY AFFECTIVE** □ □
 – Wrong French / Non-fiction / General electric with fairy lights / Wintersport – Cross country / Angel pie – Magic tree / Magnetic north / For engineers A / For engineers AA / The fun of the century / The sharpest knife in the drawer / Industrial cutie / I am the sub-librarian / Music for Rolex / Music for Annahbird / Music for wasps / Me at 19 / How does it feel? / French mittens / The biggest lie / Amongst the books, an angel / C'est un mauvais presage lorsque ton amreste a tombe / There's no need for us to be alone / The Canadian brought us snow / Sketch for Joanne / My password is a dead aunt's name.

PIE FINGER
(see under ⇒ FIRE ENGINES; in 80's section)

PILOT (see under ⇒ DHARMA BUMS)

PILOTCAN

Formed: Edinburgh, Scotland... mid-90's by leader KEIRON MELLOTTE, also subsequent founder of the capital's 'Evol' alternative nightspot every Friday. The singer/guitarist borrowed the group name from a FLAMING LIPS number, 'Pilot Can At The Queer Of God' and possibly too young to have noticed there was another 'Burgh band of a similar moniker – PILOT – who were top of the pops two decades previous. PILOTCAN – with also JOE HERBERT, KEVIN RAE and newest member STEVE MURGATOID in their ranks – were the first act to sign for STUART BRAITHWAITE's imprint, 'Rock Action'. KEIRON and Co had been (and still are) mutual friends with the MOGWAI guitarist having witnessed their friends WORMHOLE support idols TRUMAN'S WATER. With the ethos of FLAMING LIPS, SUPER FURRY ANIMALS and melodic traditional Rock much in their blood, PILOTCAN grew up in public as the wee gigs turned into bigger ones. Two 7" singles, 'RUSTY BARKER LEARNS TO FLY' and 'FIVE MINUTES ON A TUESDAY NIGHT', were the first fruits of their short-lived musical tenure in 1996; MELLOTTE and Co ended up paying for these releases themselves. The following year, KEIRON took PILOTCAN's US-biased indie-Rock and formed his own appropriately-billed 'Evol' label, where they were content making their PAVEMENT meets MUDHONEY meets SONIC YOUTH-styled assaults. P-CAN's 1997 single, 'LOSING MORE THAN MY FINGERS', previewed their Jamie Watson-produced parent album, 'SOCIALLY INEPT DISCO', a set that could well have fitted nicely into any American boy's CD collection. A second set, 'THE BOY WHO KNEW MAPS' (1999), fared a tad worse by comparison, although it did unearth another mighty 45, 'THE WORLD TURNS WITHOUT YOU' and the cheeky 'C(O)UNTRY SONG'. With KEIRON, JOE, STEVE, adding SCOTT MacDONALD (from I AM SCIENTIST) and new bassist DAVID JACK (of MAGICDRIVE), PILOTCAN worked as a tighter unit both live (supporting US outfit, NEW WET KOJAK) and in the studio. In Spring/Summer 2001, the new line-up emerged from the Substation at Cowdenbeath, where they had just completed their third and best set with MOGWAI producer Michael Brennan Jr.

Album rating: SOCIALLY INEPT DISCO (*7) / THE BOY WHO KNEW MAPS (*6)

KEIRON MELLOTTE – vocals, guitar / **JOE HERBERT** – guitar / **KEVIN RAE** – bass / **STEVE MURGATOID** – drums

	Rock Action	not iss.
Jun 96. (7") *(RAR 002)* **RUSTY BARKER LEARNS TO FLY. / FALLSFIRE**	□	-
Dec 96. (7") *(ROCKACT 04)* **FIVE MINUTES ON A TUESDAY NIGHT. / SOLID STATE (MORE SONGS ABOUT ME)**	□	-
	Evol	not iss.
Oct 97. (7") *(evol 4)* **LOSING MORE THAN MY FINGERS. / NON-TICKING CLOCKS**	□	-
Nov 97. (lp/cd) *(evol 2/+d)* **SOCIALLY INEPT DISCO** – Anakin / Greenie beanie / Spooning the grems / Losing more than my fingers / Dormouse, Sam and me / Weird sci-fi shit / Hal and Roger / Sky rocket / Non doctor / Explicit palaroids of a suicide / Decaying orbit around a dying star / Tinsel / Rainsong / 23 small trout (my hamster).	□	-
Mar 99. (cd-s) *(evol 6)* **THE WORLD TURNS WITHOUT YOU / CUM SHOTS / JUNKIE BLOOD**	□	-
May 99. (cd) *(evol 7cd)* **THE BOY WHO KNEW MAPS** – C(o)untry song / Las Vegas monkey / A blue print for Milton / Matinee coat / Circuit breaker or catalyst? / X-wing / Non-ironie surfactant / The world turns without you / Phone machine / Lipstuck / Caitlin / Under the western approach road. *(+ hidden track)*	□	-

— added **SCOTT MacDONALD** (b. Inverness) – guitar

— (late 2000) **DAVID JACK** – bass (of MAGICDRIVE) repl. KEVIN who became a civil servant!

PILOT SHIPS (see under ⇒ STARS OF THE LID)

PINBACK

Formed: San Diego, California, USA... early 1998 by multi-instrumentalists ROB CROW and ARMISTEAD BURWELL SMITH IV. The former had been an integral part of off-kilter art-rock quartet, HEAVY VEGETABLE, alongside ELEA TENUTA, TRAVIS NELSON and MANOLO TURNER, releasing a handful of sets for the 'Headhunter' imprint. ROB (and ELEA) subsequently formed THINGY, a slightly more melodious acquisition, and a band who issued two independent sets, 'SONGS ABOUT ANGELS, EVIL, AND RUNNING AROUND ON FIRE' (1997) and 'TO THE INNOCENT' (2000). Meanwhile, former alt-rocker ARMISTEAD (ex-3 MILE PILOT) teamed up with CROW to form PINBACK (with third member TOM ZINSER). An eponymous 1998 set was well-received leading to a bidding war which by all accounts never got off the ground and led to delays in recording. Late in 2001, they finally delivered their sophomore album, 'BLUE SCREEN LIFE', a record that fused emocore with ELLIOTT SMITH-style songwriting.

Album rating: Heavy Vegetable: THE AMAZING UNDERSEA ADVENTURES OF HEAVY VEGETABLE (*4) / FRISBE (*4) / MONDO AQUA KITTY compilation (*5) / Thingy: STARING CONTEST mini (*5) / SONGS ABOUT ANGELS, EVIL, AND

PINBACK (cont)

RUNNING AROUND ON FIRE (*5) / TO THE INNOCENT (*6) / Pinback: PINBACK (*5) / BLUE SCREEN LIFE (*7)

HEAVY VEGETABLE

ELEA TENUTA – vocals / **ROB CROW** – guitar, bass, piano, vocals / **TRAVIS NELSON** – bass, guitar, vocals / **MANOLO TURNER** – drums

			Cargo	unknown
Sep 94.	(7"ep)	(WAY 001) **A BUNCH OF STUFF EP**		

			Headhunter	Headhunter
1994.	(cd)	<HED 027CD> **THE AMAZING UNDERSEA ADVENTURES OF HEAVY VEGETABLE**		

– Thingy / Saloon / Eggy in a bready II / Doesn't mean shit / Myliebetz / Couch / Head rush / Listen to this song, kill pigs, and try to sue me / Eight / Dutch / Termites / Calling the toads / Krishna on the ledge / Black suit / Junior / Johnny Pig / Means less.

Oct 95.	(d-lp/cd)	<(HED 047/+CD)> **FRISBE**		Sep95

– Still moving / Cotton swab / Abducted by the work aliens / Crash / Poe / Song for Wesley / Sad mud song / Never forget / Intro / Bully / Tune Travis tune / On purpose / E – Or / Mushroom boy / Henry Mancini goes surfing / I owe you / Multiball / Dental / Daisy / Ducks at Ralphs / Spatula / Jackie Chan is a punk rocker / Pine / Fired / Tap / Stop / Radio / Going steady with the limes.

—— split and there were several other US singles; CROW became part of OPTIGANALLY YOURS (fronted by PEA HIX); and also released the solo FANTASY MISSION FORCE, releasing 'CIRCUS ATARI' EP in '97

– compilations, etc. –

Aug 98.	(cd)	Headhunter; (HED 058) **MONDO AQUA KITTY**		

– Love American style / Baby / Doesn't mean shit / St. Livingston / Slint on 4 / Green light gorilla / On purpose / Eggy in a bready / Perfect love / Excesses / Crash / Times up / Over two minutes / Saloon / Recycle song / Longsleeves (stupid motherfucker) / Daisy / Seesaw / Crackling Mexican Jesus candle / Love American style (acappella).

THINGY

ROB CROW – vocals, guitar / with **ELEA TENUTA** + **BRENT ASBURY** + **KENSETH THIBIDEAU** + **CAMERON JONES**

			Headhunter	Headhunter
Nov 96.	(m-cd)	<HED 66> **STARING CONTEST**	-	

– Disco blues / Thread and Karo / Pony! / Cutest baby / Revolution in a box / 1-800 / Candyland.

May 97.	(cd)	<(HED 67)> **SONGS ABOUT ANGELS, EVIL, AND RUNNING AROUND ON FIRE**		

– Destroy all music / SK5 / Olive drab / Thins / Honest / Fake / Numb / Cottingley fairies / Nosebleed / Evil shadow / Revolution in a box / Homework / Drugs / Fine / Window / Hit bottom / Semolina / Kessel run / Cutest baby / Wave of depression / Rental / Cut / Already Ivy / Nod / Light drizzle.

			Absolutely Kosher	Absolutely Kosher
Jan 00.	(cd)	<(AK 003)> **TO THE INNOCENT**		

– Mayday / Jabberwocky / Big dumb animal / S.S. eggshell / Blueprint / Hide and seek / Sunset / Plenty / Rope swing / Ketchup sandwich / O.B.1 / Letterbomb / 0+0 / Ballpoint pen / Molly / Chico vs. Fifa 96' / My room has a T.V. / Hydroplane / The long song at the end of the record.

PINBACK

ROB CROW – vocals, multi / **ARMISTEAD BURWELL SMITH IV** – vocals, multi (of 3 MILE PILOT) / **TOM ZINSER** – drums (of 3 MILE PILOT)

			Cutty Shark	Vinyl Comm.
Aug 98.	(cd)	<VC 147> **PINBACK**	-	

– Tripoli / Hurley / Charborg / Chaos engine / Shag / Loro / Crutch / Rousseau / Lyon / Montaigne. (UK-iss.Apr00 as 'THIS IS PINBACK' on 'Cutty Shark'; REL 002CD)

Apr 00.	(7")	(REL 005) **TRIPLOI. / HURLEY**		-

(cd-s+=) – (REL 005CD) – ('A'-mixes / Tin Foil / Starfish Pool)

			Cutty Shark	Tree
Dec 00.	(10"ep/cd-ep)	(REL 006/+CD) <15> **SOME VOICES**		Sep00

– Some voices / Trainer / Manchuria / June.

Nov 01.	(cd-s)	(REL 013CD) **PENELOPE / ANTI-HU / SEVILLE (demo)**	-	

			Cutty Shark	Ace Fu
Jan 02.	(cd)	(REL 010CD) <15> **BLUE SCREEN LIFE**		Oct01

– Offline PK / Concrete seconds / Boo / 88 tone / Penelope / Talby / XIY / Prog / Your sickness / Seville / West / Tres.

PINEHURST KIDS

Formed: Portland, Oregon, USA ... 1995 by JOE DAVIS and ROBLER KIND (both ex-FIVE TIMES FAST) with also CAL GATES (coincidentally, brother of REBECCA GATES of the influential SPINNANES). The group – under the moniker of DAVIS' native town in Idaho, where there had been an infamous chemical leak which affected the younger population of the town – debuted in 1997 with their DIY album, 'MINNESOTA HOTEL'. Their energetic emo-rock stylings on this opening set attracted the attention of indie imprint, '4-Alarm', who signed them up and put it out the following year. Bolstered by the addition of GENE POOL, the band went on a promotional tour, after which POOL departed and the rest of the band hit the studio to record their sophomore LP, 'VIEWMASTER', which although completed in early 1999 was not issued by their label until the following year. By this time KIND had also taken his bow and he was replaced by MARNIE MARTIN. New member, guitarist DEVON MORROW, also joined the band to record their third full-length offering, 'BLEED IT DRY' (2001). A lighter affair than their previous sets and helped by the added assistance of veteran knob-twiddler, LARRY CRANE, it was indeed their best to date.

Album rating: MINNESOTA HOTEL (*5) / VIEWMASTER (*5) / BLEED IT DRY (*6)

JOE DAVIS – vocals, guitar / **CAL GATES** – bass, vocals / **ROBLER KIND** – drums

			not iss.	own label
Jul 98.	(lp)	<1> **MINNESOTA HOTEL**	-	

– Switch / Johnny Mercer / Dump truck / The birds / Brick / Gatsby / New rung / So shiny / High water / Nuzzle / Jodi Foster. <cd-iss. 1999 on 'Four Alarm'; FAR 444CD>

—— added **GENE POOL** – guitar (he left during below recording)

			Four Alarm	Four Alarm
Mar 00.	(cd)	<(FAR 448CD)> **VIEWMASTER**		

– Burn alone / Lumper / Pretty whistle / Me wrong / Flicker / Short bus / Trepidation / Evil mirror / Viewmaster / Don't worry / Nothing no way.

—— **MARNIE MARTIN** – drums; repl. KIND

—— added **DEVIN MORROW** – guitar

			Barbaric	Barbaric
Jun 01.	(cd)	<(BAR 102)> **BLEED IT DRY**		

– Spinning out / The onceler / Rollover / I woke up / Big fight / All I know / Planet of the apes / Deconstruct / No show / Shepherd to lost sheep / Flashbulbs.

PINK FLOYD

Formed: London, England ... 1965 initially as The ABDABS by ROGER WATERS, RICHARD WRIGHT and NICK MASON, (with others; CLIVE METCALFE – bass, KEITH NOBLE and JULIETTE GALE on vocals). The latter three were dismissed, when the band enlisted SYD BARRETT and adopted the moniker PINK FLOYD (the name taken from bluesmen PINK ANDERSON and FLOYD COUNCIL). In March '66, they secured a residency at the Marquee Club, where their Sunday afternoon gigs were described as "spontaneous underground". Having played the UFO club late in 1966, they were subsequently signed to EMI's 'Columbia' records by their new management team of Peter Jenner and Andrew King. PINK FLOYD's March '67 debut outing, 'ARNOLD LAYNE' (about a transvestite washing-line thief), surprisingly escaped a BBC ban. One of the first missives from the psychedelic underground to reach the Top 20, it was characterised by SYD's whimsically affected vocals. On the 29th of April, they were top of the bill at Alexandria Palace's 14-hour Technicolour Dream, one of the psychedelic era's most infamous events. Their follow-up, 'SEE EMILY PLAY' (originally titled 'GAMES FOR MAY'), hit the Top 10, preceding their classic debut album, 'THE PIPER AT THE GATES OF DAWN' (a pioneering work in the sense that it contained no singles). The collection dominated by BARRETT's eccentric songwriting, it featured the cosmic 'ASTRONOMY DOMINE' alongside the acid-fuelled space-rock of 'INTERSTELLAR OVERDRIVE'. These were contrasted with idiosyncratic ramblings like 'BIKE', 'MATILDA MOTHER' and 'SCARECROW'. Their third 45, 'APPLES AND ORANGES', surprisingly flopped late in 1967, BARRETT's mental condition deteriorating rapidly due to his excessive use of LSD. He increasingly missed shows and studio sessions, PINK FLOYD bringing in DAVE GILMOUR (an old school-friend of SYD's) to compensate. In the April '68, BARRETT was asked to leave the group, retreating to a life of recluseness in his mother's Cambridge home.

Album rating: THE PIPER AT THE GATES OF DAWN (*9)

SYD BARRETT (b. ROGER KEITH BARRETT, 6 Jan'46) – vocals, guitar / **RICHARD WRIGHT** (b.28 Jul'45, London) – keyboards / **ROGER WATERS** (b. GEORGE WATERS, 9 Sep'44, Surrey, England) – bass, vocals, percussion / **NICK MASON** (b.27 Jan'45, Birmingham, England) – drums, percussion

			Columbia	Tower
Mar 67.	(7")	(DB 8156) <333> **ARNOLD LAYNE. / CANDY AND THE CURRANT BUN**	20	
Jun 67.	(7")	(DB 8214) <356> **SEE EMILY PLAY. / SCARECROW**	6	
Aug 67.	(lp; mono/stereo)	(SX/SCX 6157) **THE PIPER AT THE GATES OF DAWN**	6	-

– Astronomy domine / Lucifer Sam / Matilda mother / Flaming / Pow R. Toc H. / Take up thy stethoscope and walk / Interstellar overdrive / The gnome / Chapter 24 / Scarecrow / Bike. (re-iss. May83 on 'Fame' lp/c; FA/TCFA 3065) (cd-iss. Feb87; CDP 746384-2) (re-iss. Oct94 on 'E.M.I.' cd/c; CD/TC EMD 1073) (re-iss. Aug97 on 'E.M.I.' cd/lp hit UK No.44; CD+/EMD 1110)

Nov 67.	(lp)	<5093> **PINK FLOYD** (nearly as above)	-	
Nov 67.	(7")	(DB 8310) **APPLES AND ORANGES. / PAINTBOX**	-	
Jan 68.	(7")	<378> **FLAMING. / THE GNOME**	-	

—— added **DAVID GILMOUR** (b. 6 Mar'44, Cambridge, England) – guitar; who soon repl. BARRETT who later went solo

PINK KROSS

Formed: Glasgow, Scotland . . . late 1993 by day-glo Punks, GERALDINE KANE and JUDE BOYD, the latter inviting sister VIC BOYD to the fold as drummer and vocalist! Using drums like a war cry, VIC BLUE (as she was then named) banged her way through a tidal wave of seedy glam punk, reminiscent of BLONDIE or the NEW YORK DOLLS. Sporting feather boas, knee-high boots and all the sass a female punk act could muster, the trio picked up where the RUNAWAYS had left off. Singles 'DRAG STAR RACING QUEEN' and 'ABOMINATION' really exposed the spirit of these guitar-weilding vixens who incidently – as a joke – named themselves in tribute to Brit rockers REDD KROSS. VIC and Co later issued the single 'SCUMBAG', which, for all its glorious fuzz guitar and nihilistic lyrics, reminded a perhaps bored listener that another group could churn out trashy music from the land that was Retro. Much the same old story was evident on their low-key debut set, 'CHOPPER CHIX FROM VP HELL' (1998), which was issued by 'teen-c'. A terrible title from the Russ Meyer camp of crude, no doubt, the more discerning listener may find the head-stomping tribal drums a little too severe. On an indie/punk scale of one to ten, SHAMPOO being the worst at one and KENICKIE being ten, PINK KROSS just might be smack bang in the middle.

Album rating: CHOPPER CHIX FROM VP HELL (*5)

VIC BOYD – vocals, drums / **JUDE BOYD** – guitar / **GERALDINE KANE** – bass

Bouvier | not iss.

1994. (7"ep) **PUNK OR DIE EP** –
– Drag star racin' queen / No time for Bimbo / I'm gonna kill yr valentine / Pussy cat a go-go / Punk rock riot.

Gasatanka | not iss.

1995. (7"ep) **BIG BEAT JESUS CHEAT / CHOPPER CHIX (FROM TEENAGE HELL) / NOT COMIN BACK** –

Modern Ind | not iss.

Jan 96. (7"ep) *(MIR 004)* **THE ABOMINATION EP** –
– Abomination / Velocababy / Hot trash / Punkoutfit.

— **JANE STRAIN** – bass, vocals; repl. GERALDINE

Flotsam & Jetsam | not iss.

Oct 96. (7"ep) *(SHaG 7)* **THE ACTIVE DALMATION EP** –
– A-bomb prom / Wish I had a tail / Self obsessed mess.

— in Apr'97, PINK KROSS, BIS & LUGWORM all collaborated/sidelined on the 'POP SONG' single *(GUIDE 11)*

teen-c! | not iss.

Aug 97. (7"m) *(SKETCH 003)* **SCUMBAG. / HACKSAW / NOISE UP** –

Mar 98. (lp) *(SKETCH 005LP)* **CHOPPER CHIX FROM VP HELL** (compilation) –
– Tension toy / Do it Joseph / Scumbag / Slick lizard / Dinahmite / Supersucceeder / Smug / Hacksaw / Surfy pigeon / Dirty pigeon / Lobotomy bay / A-bomb prom / P.M.T. / Skinhead Pearson / Dragstar 2000 / Noise up / Egyptian / 99 star scam / Spooky dooky. *(cd-iss. Jul98; SKETCH 005CD)*

Flotsam & Jetsam | not iss.

Apr 98. (7") *(SHaG 13.05)* **Club Beatroot – Part Five (live series)** –
– Tension Toy / (other by the RADIO SWEETHEARTS)

Bouvier | not iss.

May 99. (cd-s) **DOGZ DINNER / + 2** –

— split and JUDE subsequently joined LUNG LEG

— note; they've also featured on a plethora of V/A comp albums/EP's

PIPE

Formed: Chapel Hill, North Carolina, USA . . . 1992 by RON LIBERTI, MIKE KENLAN, DAVE ALWORTH and CHUCK GARRISON (ex-SUPERCHUNK). Playing their own brand of heavy dirge-rock, the band debuted in 1992 with the EP 'BALL PEEN'. Unfortunately, although not long into their stride, KENLAN departed to concentrate his efforts on SMALL, his and GARRISON's other musical side project; he was replaced by BAD CHECK's CLIFTON LEE MANN. Their ensuing 7", 'YOU'RE SOAKING IT IN', was a sound effort but it was three more years until their debut LP, '6 DAYS TO BELLUS' (1995, hit the shops. A worthwhile gritty rock set which garnered the band touring duties alongside BAD BRAINS. The boys busily worked on and put out their sophomore full-length set, 'INTERNATIONAL CEMENT', the same year as well as the 7" 'PACEWAY PARK'. Following more tours, ALWORTH departed to head for the capital of grunge, Seattle. GREG ADAMS stepped up to take his place and the group put out their third album, 'SLOWBOY' (1997). Easily their career highlight, it became an underground garage rock revival touchstone. Unfortunately, providence was not to be in their favour, with the accidental injury of GARRISON cutting short their promotional tour alongside the influential The NEW BOMB TURKS. More bad luck was to follow when MANN was also put out of action for half a year due to ill-fated injury. KENLAN moved back in to take up MANN's position, although their morale was low and the group decided to call it quits in 1999. LIBERTI and MANN did however come back together in the new millennium under the mouthful of a moniker the GHOST OF THE BRITISH SOLDIER WHO LOVED TO ROCK, which was wisely abbreviated to GHOST OF ROCK. KENLAN continued his musical pursuits and joined ASHLEY STOVE in 2000. • **Covered:** WARSAW (Joy Division).

Album rating: 6 DAYS TIL BELLUS (*5) / INTL. CEMENT (*5) / SLOWBOY (*6)

RON LIBERTI – vocals / **MIKE KENLAN** – guitar / **DAVE ALWORTH** – bass / **CHUCK GARRISON** – drums (ex-SUPERCHUNK)

not iss. | Matt

1991. (7") **SUBMARINER. / (other by SMALL)** –

not iss. | Sonic Bubblegum

1992. (cd-ep) **BALL PEEN EP** –

— **CLIFTON LEE MANN** – guitar (ex-BAD CHECKS) repl. MIKE KENLAN; who stuck with SMALL 23

not iss. | Amish

1992. (7") *<001>* **YOU'RE SOAKING IN IT. / TROUBLE** –

not iss. | Merge

Apr 93. (7") *<MRG 037>* **ASHTRAY. / WARSAW** –
Apr 94. (7") *<MRG 054>* **HUMAN GUTTERBALL. / FIGURE 8** –

not iss. | Jesus Christ

1995. (cd) **6 DAYS TO BELLUS** –
Apr 96. (cd) *<8>* **INTL. CEMENT** –
– Recliner / Hooks & ladders / Lo boy / Spirit & vigor / Browntoblack / The stall / Inhalaciondecemento / Kirk's floor / What's happening now? / Eating, breathing / Hatred, ridicule and contempt / Raceway park / GBC.

not iss. | Amish

1996. (7") **RACEWAY PARK. / (other by RUBBERMAID)** –

— **GREG ADAMS** – bass; repl. ALWORTH

Merge | Merge

Jul 97. (lp/cd) *<(MRG 123/+CD)>* **SLOWBOY**
– Favorite dirty flavor / Spring training / Take it / Dead level / Magnet face / How the west was won / Chula / The beard / Getting good at sleeping / No action / Tighten up to go / I love you I kill you / Panic in the streets.

— when GARRISON + MANN both suffered hand injuries the band took a break; **MIKE KENLAN** – guitar; repl. MANN who formed The GHOST OF THE BRITISH SOLDIER . . . with LIBERTI

PLACEBO

Formed: South London, England . . . October '94 by the cosmopolitan pair of BRIAN MOLKO and STEFAN OLSDAL, who had attended the same school in Luxembourg. They met up again in a London tube having spent time in the States and Sweden respectively. Early the following year, they recruited Swedish drummer, ROBERT SCHULTZBERG, the trio subsequently becoming joint winners of the 'In The City' Battle Of The Bands competition. Late in '95, PLACEBO shared a one-off single, 'BRUISE PRISTINE', with the band, SOUP, on 'Fierce Panda' records. After only a handful of gigs, they signed for 'Deceptive' (home of ELASTICA), leading to tours with ASH, BUSH and WHALE. A solitary single later ('COME HOME'), MOLKO and Co., hit the proverbial jackpot via a deal with Virgin/Hut subsidiary, 'Elevator'. The openly bisexual, cross-dressing MOLKO, drew comparisons with 70's glam idols like BOLAN and BOWIE, the music, however, traded in the glitter for a darker listening experience. Taking the fast lane out of the post-grunge pile-up, they fused elements of avant-garde rock and cerebral metal, MOLKO's paint-stripping shrill drawing comparisons with Rush's GEDDY LEE and DAVID SURKAMP of the more obscure Pavlov's Dog. Their eponymous debut album was released in mid-'96 to a fawning music press, metal-mag Kerrang's strong support helping the record dent the UK Top 40. Hit singles 'TEENAGE ANGST' and the Top 5 'NANCY BOY', helped regenerate sales of a collection which many hailed as one of the years' best. In addition to the more incendiary tracks, the album also contained such hauntingly reflective songs as 'LADY OF THE FLOWERS' and 'HANG ON TO YOUR IQ'. PLACEBO – with STEVE HEWITT replacing SCHULTZBERG – were back with a bang (so to speak!) in the Autumn of '98, two blistering UK Top 5 singles in quick succession, 'PURE MORNING' and 'YOU DON'T CARE ABOUT US', premiering their equally superb sophomore set, 'WITHOUT YOU I'M NOTHING' – 'EVERY YOU EVERY ME' and collaborative title track with MOLKO's idol BOWIE, kept the band in high profile the following year. With 'BLACK MARKET MUSIC' (2000), MOLKO took his brooding sexual vision to its twisted climax on an album which ranks as one of PLACEBO's most darkly satisfying to date. Longtime fans will be glad to know that the ever androgynous frontman is still wrestling with his soiled demons, content to provide a mascara-smeared foil to the bloke-rock clogging up the music biz. • **Songwriters:** Group, except BIGMOUTH STRIKES AGAIN (Smiths) / 20TH CENTURY BOY (T.Rex) / JOHNNY & MARY (Robert Palmer).

Album rating: PLACEBO (*9) / WITHOUT YOU I'M NOTHING (*8) / BLACK MARKET MUSIC (*6)

BRIAN MOLKO (b. 1972) – vocals, guitars, bass / **STEFAN OLSDAL** (b. Sweden) – bass, guitars, keyboards / **ROBERT SCHULTZBERG** – drums, percussion, didgeridoo

Fierce Panda | not iss.

Nov 95. (7") *(NING 13)* **BRUISE PRISTINE. / (Soup: 'Meltdown')** –

Deceptive | not iss.

Feb 96. (7") *(BLUFF 024)* **COME HOME. / DROWNING BY NUMBERS** –
(cd-s+=) *(BLUFF 024CD)* – Oxygen thief.

Elevator | Caroline

Jun 96. (7") *(FLOOR 001)* **36 DEGREES. / DARK GLOBE** –
(cd-s+=) *(FLOORCD 001)* – Hare Krishna.
Jun 96. (cd/c/lp) *(CD/MC/LP FLOOR 002)* *<7575>* **PLACEBO** 40 | Jul96
– Come home / Teenage angst / Bionic / 36 degrees / Hang on to you IQ / Nancy boy / I know / Bruise pristine / Lady of the flowers / Swallow. *(re-dist.Jan97 hit UK No.5; same)*

PLACEBO (cont)

Sep 96.	(7"/cd-s) (FLOOR/+CD 003) **TEENAGE ANGST. / BEEN SMOKING TOO LONG / HUG BUBBLE**	30	-
	(7"m) (FLOORX 003) – ('A'-V.P.R.O. radio session) / Flesh mechanic (demo) / HK farewell.		
Jan 97.	(7") (FLOOR 004) **NANCY BOY. / SLACKERBITCH**	4	-
	(cd-s+=) (FLOORCD 004) – Bigmouth strikes again / Hug bubble.		
	(cd-s) (FLOORCDX 004) – ('A'side) / Eyesight to the blind / Swallow (Brad Wood mix) / Miss Moneypenny.		
May 97.	(c-s/cd-s) (FLOOR MC/CD 005) **BRUISE PRISTINE / THEN THE CLOUDS WILL OPEN FOR ME / BRUISE PRISTINE (One Inch Punch remix)**	14	-
	(cd-s) (FLOORCDX 005) – ('A'side) / Waiting for the sun of man / Serenity (Lionrock remix).		

—— **STEVE HEWITT** (b. Northwich, England) – drums; repl. SCHULTZBERG

<small>Elevator Hut</small>

Aug 98.	(cd-ep) (FLOORCD 6) **PURE MORNING / MARS LANDING PARTY / LEELOO**	4	-
	(cd-ep) (FLOORCDX 6) – ('A'-lp version) / Needledick / The innoceence of sleep.		
Sep 98.	(c-s/cd-s) (FLOOR C/CD 7) <95363> **YOU DON'T CARE ABOUT US / 20TH CENTURY BOY / ION**	5	-
	(cd-s) (FLOORDX 7) – ('A'side) / ('A'-Les Rhythmes Digitales remix) / ('A'-Howie B remix).		
Oct 98.	(cd/c/lp) (CDFLOOR/FLOORMC/FLOORLP 8) <46531> **WITHOUT YOU I'M NOTHING**	7	Nov98
	– Pure morning / Brick shithouse / You don't care about us / Ask for answers / Without you I'm nothing / Allergic (to thoughts of Mother Earth) / The crawl / Every you every me / My sweet prince / Summer's gone / Scared of girls / Burger queen.		
Jan 99.	(7") (FLOORLH 9) **EVERY YOU EVERY ME. / NANCY BOY (Blue Amazon remix)**	11	-
	(c-s+=/cd-s+=) (FLOORCD 9) – ('A'-Jimmy Cauty remix).		
	(cd-s) (FLOORDX 9) – ('A'side) / ('A'-Sneaker Pimps version) / ('A'-Brothers In Rhythm remix).		
Aug 99.	(cd-ep; featuring DAVID BOWIE) (FLOORCD 10) **WITHOUT YOU I'M NOTHING / ('A'-Unkle remix) / ('A'-Americruiser remix) / ('A'-Brothers In Rhythm remix)**	-	nochart
Jul 00.	(c-s/cd-s) (FLOOR C/CD 11) **TASTE IN MEN / THEME FROM FUNKY REVEREND / TASTE IN MEN (Alpinestars Kamikaze skimix)**	16	-
	(cd-s) (FLOORDX 11) – ('A'side) / Johnny & Mary / Taste in men (Adrian Sherwood Go Go dub mix).		
	(12"++=) (FLOORT 11) – (all above).		
Sep 00.	(c-s/cd-s) (FLOOR C/CD 12) **SLAVE TO THE WAGE / LENI / BUBBLEGUM**	19	-
	(cd-s/12"+=) (FLOOR DX/X 12) – ('A'-album version) / Holocaust / ('A'-Les Rythmes Digitales new wave mix).		
Oct 00.	(cd/c/lp) (CDFLOOR/FLOORMCX/FLOORLP 13) <10316> **BLACK MARKET MUSIC**	6	-
	– Taste in men / Days before you came / Special K / Spite & malice / Passive aggressive / Black-eyed / Blue American / Slave to the wage / Commercial for Levi / Haemoglobin / Narcoleptic / Peeping Tom.		
Mar 01.	(cd-s) (CDFLOOR 14) **SPECIAL K / DUB PSYCHOSIS / PASSIVE AGGRESSIVE (Brothers In Rhythm remix)**		-
	(12"+=) (TFLOOR 14) – Little Mo / Slave to the wage (I can't believe it's a remix).		
	(cd-s) (CDFLOORX 14) – ('A'-Timo Maas remix) / (above 2).		

PLANES MISTAKEN FOR STARS

Formed: Peoria, Illinois, USA ... 1997 by GARED O'DONNELL, MATT BELLINGER, AARON WISE and drummer MIKE RICKETTS. One of the many emo/hardcore groups from the 'Deep Elm' stable, PLANES MISTAKEN FOR STARS could've been mistaken themselves for some sort of weep-core indie group. But their nom de plume was misleading; this combo exploded venomously on their self-titled mini-set in 1998, with O'DONNELL's screeching guitar and howling vocals enough to send FRANK BLACK cowering. Boy, could he holler! This was mostly evident on the group's fractured DIY song-bag of a mini-album, 'KNIFE IN THE MARATHON' – a five track jugular juggernaut. After the departure of WISE in 2000, the group moved to Colorado and recruited JAMIE DRIER. In the same year, they issued a split EP, 'STAGGERSWALLOWSWELL' with labelmates The APPLESEED CAST and RACE CAR RIOT; the 'FUCK WITH FIRE' album followed in 2001.

Album rating: PLANES MISTAKEN FOR STARS mini (*4) / KNIFE IN THE MARATHON mini (*5) / FUCK WITH FIRE (*5)

GARED O'DONNELL – vocals, guitar / **MATT BELLINGER** – guitar / **AARON WISE** – bass / **MIKE RICKETTS** – drums

<small>Deep Elm Deep Elm</small>

Jun 99.	(m-cd) <(DER 377CD)> **PLANES MISTAKEN FOR STARS**		Apr99
	– Copper and stars / Division / The time is took / The past two / Somewhere in September / Standing still fast / Knuckle hungry / Where the arrow went out.		

—— **JAMIE DRIER** – bass; repl. WISE

Aug 99.	(cd-ep) <(DER 378CD)> **PLANES MISTAKEN FOR STARS / RACE CAR RIOT / APPLESEED CAST**		
	– Staggerswallowswell / (tracks by RACE CAR RIOT + APPLESEED CAST).		
Mar 00.	(m-cd) <(DER 383CD)> **KNIFE IN THE MARATHON**		
	– Scratching pounds / Leaning the room / Pillbox / Anthem / 66 crush.		

<small>No Idea not iss.</small>

Jul 01.	(lp/cd) (NIR 113/+CD) **FUCK WITH FIRE**		
	– Leveless / End me in Richmond / Funeral for a friend / Hollow point and whiskey / Bloody but unbowed / Fuck with fire / Rhythm dies / Sicillian smile / I'll see you in hell / Get burned.		

PLUSH

Formed: Chigaco, Illinois, USA ... 1994 by LIAM HAYES, a part-time keyboard-player with PALACE (aka WILL OLDHAM). The well-named PLUSH debuted early the following year with a fine 7" single, 'THREE-QUARTERS BLIND EYES', although it was the grandiose and symphonic flip-side, 'FOUND A LITTLE BABY', that created a mini-sensation. However, the introverted HAYES went into seclusion for a long period; stories were rife that he was spending time in a Californian commune. He was also rumoured to be working with an orchestra for his debut album, although this might have broken him financially. Late in 1997, he was back in action with a comeback single, 'NO EDUCATION', a balladesque, lo-fi number that was yet again acclaimed in some quarters. A tour in Australia with OLDHAM seemed to be going well, until he virtually disappeared once more. His debut album, 'MORE YOU BECOMES YOU' (a mini, compared to today's standards), finally reached the shops in the Autumn of '98, a hidden masterpiece that was actually recorded in 1995 (not the rumoured material mentioned above which was supposedly shelved).

Album rating: MORE YOU BECOMES YOU (*7)

LIAM HAYES (c.1960's) – vocals, piano, organ

<small>Domino Drag City</small>

Jan 95.	(7") (RUG 32) <DR 056> **THREE-QUARTERS BLIND EYES. / FOUND A LITTLE BABY**		

—— went into retreat for a while (see above)

Nov 97.	(7"/12") <(FLY 024/+T)> **NO EDUCATION. / SOARING AND BORING**		
	(above issued on 'Flydaddy') (re-iss. Aug98; same)		
Sep 98.	(cd/lp) (WIG CD/LP 50) <DC 070> **MORE YOU BECOMES YOU**		
	– Virginia / More you becomes you / (I didn't know) I was asleep / The party I / The party II / Soaring and boring / (See it in the) Early morning / Instrumental / Save the people / The sailor.		

PLUTO MONKEY
(see under ⇒ DAWN OF THE REPLICANTS)

POLAK (see under ⇒ ADORABLE)

POLARA

Formed: Minneapolis, Minnesota, USA ... mid 80's out of 27 VARIOUS by ED ACKERSON. An enigmatic psychedelic guitar-pop proposition, the latter outfit released a series of obscure but noteworthy long-players over the course of the late 80's/early 90's. For his new combo, POLARA, ED recruited JENNIFER JURGENS, JASON ORRIS and PETER ANDERSON, exploring more experimental avenues that drew on the pioneering fusion of 60's influences and punk once initiated by fellow Minneapolis sons, HUSKER DU. Surfacing on local institution, 'TwinTone', ACKERSON and Co debuted early in '95 with an impressive eponymous album that caught the ear of leading major alternative bastion, 'Interscope'. While not as compellingly innovative as their earlier work, subsequent albums, 'C'EST LA VIE' (1997) and 'FORMLESS – FUNCTIONAL' (1998), were still worthy of attention. Unfortunately, the relative decline in their creative fertility was more pronounced in the jaded 'JETPACK BLUES' (2002), the sound of a band who've seen it, done it, and somehow can't be bothered doing it again.

Album rating: 27 Various: HI. (*5) / YES, INDEED (*5) / APPROXIMATELY (*6) / UP (*4) / FINE (*4) / Polara: POLARA (*7) / C'EST LA VIE (*6) / FORMLESS – FUNCTIONAL (*4) / JETPACK BLUES (*5)

the 27 VARIOUS

ED ACKERSON – vocals, guitar, sitar, keyboards / **JED MAYER** – drums / with **JAY ORFF** – bass, vocals / **JERRY LEFKOWITZ** – guitar, vocals

<small>not iss. Susstones</small>

Mar 87.	(lp) <511> **HI.**	-	
	– Yes, indeed / Principal Percival / Furry creatures from the forest / The Gormleys will miss me / Temperamental artist / Lamentations / Colored world / Venetian blinds / Saturday night and Sunday morning / I'm in it / The fish (knows why).		
Jun 89.	(lp) <531> **YES, INDEED**	-	
	– Yes, indeed / If you can't trust death / The maggot's sermon / Stick it in it bake it / I was blown away / Mr Sun and Venus / Shine that smile / Wide-eyed girl / It seems I've seen / Feedtime for Martin / Far be it / Stone boat.		

<small>not iss. Clean</small>

Sep 90.	(cd) <TRG 89200> **APPROXIMATELY**	-	
	– I feel damage(d) / You look a treat / Deposit / I can't wait till the end of my days to get a sign from you girl / You reached me / Like the poison / Cold / Too long a day / Blue concourse / The things I wasn't supposed to see / Out of lungs.		

—— **ACKERSON** now with **MIKE REITER** – percussion / **BART BAKKER** – bass, vocals

Jan 92.	(cd) <TRG 89218> **UP (live)**	-	
	– Happening – Sometime / While you can / Lay it on, Elaine / Love somebody / Leave it / Never been told / Cavern eyes / Fare thee well / Whenever I'm gone / What to do? / Burned / Put me down / Doesn't matter to you.		
Jan 93.	(cd) <TRG 89226> **FINE**	-	
	– Turn on and on / You've got it bad / Swoop factor: 9000 / Down the line / Shag / Song for mire / Out of mohair / c/o Anne / Make it through / Song for Juliana / Up / Contrast.		

—— ACKERSON joined the touring line-up of ANTENNA until ...

POLARA

ED ACKERSON – vocals, guitar, bass, keyboards, synthesizer, etc / **JENNIFER JeRAE JURGENS** – vocals, guitar, organ, synthesizer / **JASON ORRIS** – bass, vocals / **PETER ANDERSON** – drums, percussion

		Clean – Restless	Clean – Restless
Feb 95.	(cd) <(CR 89276-2)> **POLARA**		

– Counting down / Allay / Source of light / Squelch / Listening now / Taupe / Avenue E / Anniversary 6 / One foot / a+b=y / State / Letter bomb.

		not iss.	Interscope
Nov 96.	(10"ep) <INT 97011> **PANTOMIME**	-	

– Pantomime / Idle hands / Light the fuse and run / Confusing times.
(cd-ep+=) <INTD 97011> – Pantomime (version).

| Apr 97. | (cd/c) <INTD 90074> **C'EST LA VIE** | - | |

– Transformation / Sort it out / Light the fuse and run / Quebecois / So sue me / Make it easy / Incoming / Elasticity / Idle hands / Other side / Pantomime / Shanghai bell. (cd-bonus+=) – Untitled.

— now without ORRIS

| Mar 98. | (cd) <INTD 90182> **FORMLESS – FUNCTIONAL** | - | |

– Whassup? / A brighter day / Trainwreck / Got the switch! / Halo / Peaking Charlie / I can believe / Semi-detatched / Verbing / Midtown greenway / Tread lightly / Corporate hegemony (smash the state!).

— added **DAN BOEN** – bass

		not iss.	Susstones
Oct 02.	(cd) <2501> **JETPACK BLUES**	-	

– Can't get over you / Jetpack blues / Is this it? / Sweep me away / Wig on / Obsolete / Hold on to the thread / Overboard / Other / The story so far / Eight by twelve.

POLICECAT

Formed: Edinburgh, Scotland . . . late 1993 initially as the part-time project of the PASTELS' JONATHAN KILGOUR. Recruiting twin brother, GORDON (who was also in The MONGERS), YVONNE SLAVEN, KATRINA DIXON and JOHN HARRINGTON (who replaced original bassist NEIL MITCHARD), POLICECAT were up and running for their debut maxi-single, 'DROWN', for 'Domino' in April '94. If you could imagine the CHILLS fused with surf-legend DICK DALE, you'd be close to their unique sound. The 'LARRY' EP, released the following year was of the indie-folk variety, The PASTELS and The VASELINES immediately come to mind. Meanwhile, POLICECAT's off-duty activities consisted of alter-ego ROYAL BRONCO – with bass players included DEKE PATTON, JEM ANDERTON and GILDED LIL's MALCY DUFF – and the Lo-Fo 'No-Fi' band, The MONGERS, who comprised RB/PC members GORDON and YVONNE with JEM and latterly JOHN. Adopting new monikers (i.e. MONSTER TRUX, leather-clad vixen JUICY DETROIT and LARD FREEWAY), the mongy cats released a couple of cheap mail-order cassettes of mainly outrageous avant-jazz; cool loungecore from the gutter it certainly wasn't. In 1997/98, POLICECAT were back on song, delivering two split singles for 'Creeping Bent', entitled 'AUTOMOBILE' and 'DARK HOLIDAY'. Ex-OFFHOOKS/THANES man CALVIN BURT was in place for their swansong single in '99, 'GIVE US THIS DAY' but the KILGOUR's left the scene of the crime when they were invited to join the ZEPHYRS.

Album rating: never released any

JONATHAN KILGOUR (b.21 Oct'68) – vocals, guitar / **GORDON KILGOUR** (b.21 Oct'68) – guitar, vocals (of The MONGERS) / **JOHN HARRINGTON** – bass, etc (of MY HUSTLER) / **YVONNE SLAVEN** – keyboards / **KATRINA DIXON** – drums

		Domino	not iss.
Apr 94.	(7"m) (RUG 19) **DROWN. / BOLDER / VOODOO HOEDOWN**		-

<US-iss.Jun96 on 'Derby'; >

— an assortment of drummers **SCOTT** plus **DEKE PATTON** repl. DIXON

| May 95. | (10"ep) (RUG 34T) **LARRY EP** | | - |

– Larry / Music for pleasure / Classy / Tram 22.

		Creeping Bent	not iss.
Jul 97.	(7") (bent 024) **AUTOMOBILE. / Secret Goldfish: GIVE HIM A GREAT BIG KISS**		-
Jun 98.	(7") (bent 034) **DARK HOLIDAY. / (other track by Appendix Out)**		-

— **CALVIN BURT** – drums (ex-OFFHOOKS) repl. DEKE PATTON

		not iss.	Fantastic
Jan 99.	(7") <010> **GIVE US THIS DAY. /**	-	

— a release on 'No-Fi' records was shelved when GORDON and JONATHAN formed The ZEPHYRS

MONGERS

MONSTER TRUX (aka GORDON KILGOUR) + **LARD FREEWAY** (aka JEM ANDERTON) / **JUICY DETROIT** (aka YVONNE SLAVEN) – synthesizer

		No-Fi	not iss.
1994.	(c-ep) (none) **HEY HEY WE'RE THE MONGERS**	-	- mail-o

– Leather-look lady / Bad milk / Jesus on a motorbike.

| Oct 95. | (c-ep) (none) **TABLE FOR THREE** | - | - mail-o |

– Broke-bottle blues / B-roq / UHT lounge.

— they had already added **JOHN HARRINGTON**

		Galvani	not iss.
Jan 99.	(7"ep) (MILK 001) **LEATHER-LOOK LADY. / (other two by APPENDIX OUT)**		-

POLVO

Formed: Chapel Hill, North Carolina, USA . . . early 90's by ASH BOWIE, DAVE BRYLAWSKI, STEVE POPSON and EDDIE WATKINS. Taking their cue from the complex, oblique noise experimentation once the domain of SONIC YOUTH and to a lesser extent, DINOSAUR JR and WIRE, POLVO often dismissed chorus/verse convention in favour of atonal guitar scree and sprawling stop-start song patterns. A deal with 'Merge' (licensed to 'Touch & Go' in the States) and a debut album, 'COR-CRANE SECRET' (1992), quickly established POLVO as one of the most challenging acts thrown up by the fertile Chapel Hill alternative scene. Working at a rate of almost an album a year, the quartet maintained an impressively prolific release schedule throughout the mid-90's while frontman ASH also found the time to moonlight for the band HELIUM. Following the band's split in 1998, DAVE went on to form IDYLL SWORDS, a studio based affair dedicated to creating inscrutable, ethnic meditations in keeping with a spirit of global identification. Utilising an impressive array of exotic instrumentation sourced from the far corners of the earth, the trio succeeded in achieving an understated fusion of disparate melodic and rhythmic elements which nevertheless eschewed the tired cliches of world music meets electronica. 'II' (2000) continued in a similar vein, updating the vision (if not the style and method) of say, The INCREDIBLE STRING BAND, for a world where distance has become meaningless. BOWIE, meanwhile, re-emerged himself (under the LIBRANESS moniker) in 2000 with 'YESTERDAY . . . AND TOMORROW'S SHELLS', an off-the-cuff, turbulent collection delineating the man's creative trajectory over the past half decade.

Album rating: CRO-CRANE SECRET (*6) / TODAY'S ACTIVE LIFESTYLES (*5) / CELEBRATE THE NEW DARK AGE mini (*5) / THIS ECLIPSE mini (*5) / EXPLODED DRAWING (*5) / SHAPES (*5) / Idyll Swords: IDYLL SWORDS (*6) / II (*6) / Libraness: YESTERDAY . . . AND TOMORROW'S SHELLS (*6)

ASH BOWIE – guitar, vocals / **DAVE BRYLAWSKI** – guitar, vocals / **STEVE POPSON** – bass, vocals / **EDDIE WATKINS** – drums

		not iss.	Kitchen Puff
1990.	(d7"ep) <puff 001> **POLVO**	-	

– Can I ride / Leaf / Lull / Totemic // Tread on me / Teen dream / Snake fist fighter.
<cd-ep iss.1992 on 'Jesus Christ'; JC 001>

		not iss.	Rockville
1991.	(7") <ROCK 6066-7> **VIBRACOBRA. / THE DRILL**	-	

		Touch & Go	Merge
Jun 92.	(7"ep) <MRG 021> **EL CID**	-	

– (2 tracks by ERECTUS MONOTONE) / In the hand, in the sieve.

| Jul 92. | (lp/cd) (TG 101/+CD) <MRG 22/+CD> **COR-CRANE SECRET** | | |

– Vibracobra / Kalgon / Bend or break / Can I ride / Sense of it / Ox scapula / Channel changer / In the hand, in the sieve / The curtain remembers / Well is deep / Duped.

| Apr 93. | (7"m) <MRG 038> **TILEBREAKER. / THE CHAMELEON / TIARA FETISH** | - | |
| May 93. | (lp/cd) (TG 114/+CD) <MRG 40/+CD> **TODAY'S ACTIVE LIFESTYLES** | | |

– Thermal treasure / Lazy comet / My kimono / Sure shot / Stinger (five wigs) / Tilebreaker / Shiska / Time isn't on my side / Action vs. vibe / Gemini cusp.

| Jan 94. | (7"ep) <PF 001> **. . .AND THEN I'M GONE** | - | |

– Two fists / All the cliches on Broadway / (2 by NEW RADIANT STORM KING).
(above issued on 'Penny Farthing')

| May 94. | (m-cd/t7"ep) (TG 133CD) <MRG 56 CD> **CELEBRATE THE NEW DARK AGE** | | |

– Fractured (like chandeliers) / City spirit // Tragic carpet ride / Solitary pet / Every holy shroud // Old Lystra / Virtual cold.

| Nov 95. | (m-cd) (TG 156CD) <MRG 095> **THIS ECLIPSE** | | |

– Bat radar / Bombs that fall from your eyes / Titan up / Production values / Title track.

		Touch & Go	Touch & Go
May 96.	(lp/cd) <(TG 162/+CD)> **EXPLODED DRAWING**		

– Fast canoe / Bridesmaid blues / Feather of forgiveness / Passive attack / Light of the moon / Crumbling down / Street knowledge / High-wire moves / Monolith / In this life / Secret's secret / Snowstorm in iowa / Purple bear / Taste of your mind / Missing receipts / When will I die / For the last time / In my dreams.

— ASH BOWIE also moonlighted with HELIUM

— **BRIAN WALSBY** – drums; repl. WATKINS

| Sep 97. | (cd/lp) <(TG 179 CD/LP)> **SHAPES** | | |

– Enemy insects / Fighting kites / Rock post rock / Golden ladder / Downtown dedication / Pulchritude / Twenty white tents / Everything in flames / D.D. (S.R.) / El Rocio / Lantern.

— split up in '98; BRYLAWSKI and BOWIE formed their own outfits

IDYLL SWORDS

DAVE BRYLAWSKI – guitars, vocals, etc / **CHUCK JOHNSON** – organ, guitars, vocals, etc. / **GRANT TENNILLE** – percussion, etc

		Communion	Communion
Jun 99.	(cd) <(COMM 52)> **IDYLL SWORDS**		May99

– Wild geese descend on level sands / Strawberry airwaves / The destination / Anhinga negra / Turistan – Night approach / Kehen yorum billa / Autumn in empire / Portals to a land / Silver silk / Dawn approach / Sagarika / When the train comes along / Birch eye waltz / Japanese lantern.

| Oct 00. | (cd) <(COMM 56)> **II** | | |

– Tantz / Lake palace / Escutcheon ascent – Biza's theme / Kashal in rag pilu / A bridge to a bridge / Ucalegon blues / Moab / Morning in miniature / Bani park / Abreaction / The Mezereon dynasty / Nile monitor / Steep creek.

LIBRANESS

ASH BOWIE – vocals, instruments

			Tiger Style	Tiger Style
Oct 00.	(cd/lp) <(TS 004/+LP)>	**YESTERDAY... AND TOMORROW'S SHELLS**		Sep00

– Intro / Face on backwards / You are my foreign film / No separation / The memory / Richard Petty / Hit the horizon / Grief mechanism / Deformed bridges / Paper raft / Totempole / 24 hrs. / New and old clouds.

POLYPHONIC SPREE

Formed: Dallas, Texas, USA ... 2000 by frontman/lyricist TIM DeLAUGHTER in a bizarre postscript to the ill-fated TRIPPING DAISY outfit after the death of his bandmate WES BERGGREN. The aforementioned TRIPPING DAISY began in 1991 by DeLAUGHTER, BERGGREN, MARK PIRRO and BRYAN WAKELAND and signing to 'Island', the band debuted with the 'BILL' album in 1994. Sporting a psychedelic punk/hard-rock sound similar to JANE'S ADDICTION (DeLAUGHTER's whining vocals a bizarre cross between PERRY FARRELL and LIAM GALLAGHER!), the group soon attracted a growing following on the American alternative scene. With media coverage also gathering strength, the band released a follow-up set, 'i am an ELASTIC FIRECRACKER' (complete with sleevework by deceased artist, Gugliemo Achille Cavellini) in early '96. The record was their most successful to date, scraping into the lower regions of the US Top 100, while the swaggering 'PIRANHA' single made the Top 75. A third album, 'JESUS HITS US LIKE AN ATOM BOMB' (1998), was a slightly disappointing set and sadder still was the untimely death of BERGGREN who o.d'd in 1999. With its twenty or so members (including PIRRO and DeLAUGHTER's loose open-door policy, the Dallas congregation were established when they issued a cassette-only mini-LP 'THE BEGINING STAGES OF...' (2000), before playing countless live shows around Texas. The independent label 'Good' issued the set, and, with their white sinuous robes, uplifting dreamy psychedelic gospel and quasi-religious overtones ("Jesus is love", and all that), the collective were soon becoming uber cult. It wasn't long before the British music press got their grubby little hands on the band – after all, they were still filthy with the overt favouritism and lazy handling of certain garage rock groups, it was refreshing to see around 23 robe-wearing happy Texans don the cover of a publication. The group added new material to their already existing mini-album and re-issued it as their debut LP 'THE BEGINNING STAGES OF...' (2002). The music it contained – all in sections – was that of strange, breezy psychedelic pop in the vein of MERCURY REV or The FLAMING LIPS, but with the general communal ethos applied by the likes of LAMBCHOP (who'd also boasted quite a line-up). After the clever pop/rock of TRIPPING DAISY, DeLAUGHTER obviously had strong intentions of creatiing joyful Americana; a sometimes ecstatic blend of gospel, pop and lo-fi with warm instrumentation and DeLAUGHTER's cracked vocals floating over the whole thing, The POLYPHONIC SPREE were a ray of sunshine that blasted into the often bleak world of American alt-rock.

Album rating: BILL (*5) / i am an ELASTIC FIRECRACKER (*8) / JESUS HITS US LIKE AN ATOM BOMB (*5) / Polyphonic Spree: THE BEGINNING STAGES OF... (*8)

TRIPPING DAISY

TIM DeLAUGHTER – vocals, guitar / **WES BERGGREN** – guitar / **MARK PIRRO** – bass / **BRYAN WAKELAND** – drums, percussion

			Island	Red Dragon St.
Jul 94.	(cd/c/lp) (CIRD/IRCT/IRLP 1001) <70392>	**BILL**		Nov92

– My umbrella / One through four / Lost and found / Change of mind / On the ground / The morning / Blown away / Brown-eyed pickle boy / Miles and miles of pain / Triangle. <cd re-iss. 1997 on 'Polygram'; 555002>

Jul 94.	(12"ep/cd-ep) (12IR/CIRD 102)	**MY UMBRELLA / IT'S SAFE, IT'S SOCIAL (live). / GET IT ON (live) / WE'RE ONLY GONNA DIE (live)**		

			Island	Island
Feb 96.	(c-s/7") (C+/IS 636)	**I GOT A GIRL. / MARGARITA TROPENZANDO**		-

(12"+=/cd-s+=) (12IS/CID 636) – Cause tomb shop / Noose.

Feb 96.	(cd/lp) (CIRD/IRLP 1004) <314-524 112-2>	**i am an ELASTIC FIRECRACKER**	95	Aug95

– Rocket pop / Bang / I got a girl / Piranha / Motivation / Same dress new day / Trip along / Raindrop / Step behind / Noose / Prick / High.

Mar 96.	(7") (IS 638)	**PIRANHA. / CREATURE**	72	-

(12"+=/cd-s+=) (12IS/CID 638) – High.

1997.	(m-cd) <531095>	**TIME CAPSULE**	-	

– Rise / Cause tomb shop / Creature / Boobie the clown / I'm a fish / Blue train.

added **ERIC DREW FELDMAN** – producer, multi (ex-CAPTAIN BEEFHEART, ex-FRANK BLACK)

Jul 98.	(cd) <(524518-2)>	**JESUS HITS US LIKE AN ATOM BOMB**		

– Field day jitters / Waited a light year / Sonic bloom / Bandaids for Mire / Mechanical breakdown / Your socks have no name / Geeareohdoubleyou / New plains medicine / Our drive to the sun – Can a man mark / Human contact / Pillar / 8 ladies / About the movies / Tiny men / Indian poker (pt.2 & 3).

			not iss.	Good
1999.	(cd-s) <GR 002>	**BEDHEAD. / (other by Centro-Matic)**	-	

— when WES died of a drug o.d. in 1999, TIM, MARK and BRYAN formed...

POLYPHONIC SPREE

TIM DeLAUGHTER – vocals / **MARK PIRRO** – bass / **BRYAN WAKELAND** – drums / **RYAN FITZGERALD** – guitar / **EVAN HISEY** – organ / **TOBY HALBROOKS** – theremin, electronics, whistle / **MARK McKEEVER** – keyboards, trumpet / **JEFF BOUCK** – percussion / **MIKE MELENDI** – percussion / **ANDREW TINKER** – french horn / **AUDREY EASLEY** – flute, piccolo / **JAMES REIMER** – trombone / **RICK RASURA** – classic harp / **LOGAN REESE** – trumpet / **RICK NELSON** – violin / **JENNIFER JOBE** – vocals / **MICHAEL TURNER + ROY IVY + JOHN VINEYARD + CHRISTY STEWART + JENNIE KELLY + KELLY REPKA + JESSICA JORDAN + JULIE DOYLE** – backing vocals

			Good	Good
Jul 02.	(cd) <(GR 004CD)>	**THE BEGINNING STAGES OF...**		Jun02

– Section 1 (Have a day – Celebratory) / Section 2 (It's the sun) / Section 3 (Days like this keep me warm) / Section 4 (La la) / / Section 5 (Middle of the day) / Section 6 (Hanging around the day – part one) / Section 7 (Hanging around the day – part two) / Section 8 (Soldier girl) / Section 9 (Light and day – Reach for the sun) / Section 10 (A long day). (re-iss. Sep02 on '679 Recordings' cd/lp; 5046 60918-2/-1)

			Fierce Panda	not iss.
Aug 02.	(cd-s) (NING 123CD)	**SOLDIER GIRL / SUN (section 2) / SOLDIER GIRL (string version) / SOLDIER GIRL (radio) / SOLDIER GIRL (section 8)**		-

			679 Recordings	not iss.
Oct 02.	(7") (679L 012)	**HANGING AROUND. / FIVE YEARS**	39	-

(cd-s+=) (679L 012CD1) – ('A'version) / ('A'-Video).
(cd-s) (679L 012CD2) – ('A'live) / What will be will be (live) / Soldier girl (live).

— now with **JOE BUTCHER** – sho-bud pedal steel, synyhs

POND

Formed: Portland, Oregon, USA ... early 90's by Alaskan (Juneau, to be exact) lads CHRIS BRADY and CHARLIE CAMPBELL, who met one time molecular biologist DAVE TRIEBWASSER on a trip to Seattle. All veterans of various underachieving amateur outfits despite their youthfulness, the trio surfed the initial North-Western grunge wave with a melodic, retro-influenced debut single for 'T/K', 'YOUNG SPLENDOR'. POND were subsequently thrown in at the deep end when 'Sub Pop' netted them for a long term deal, the band swimming among the alternative scene's bigger fish with early 1993's eponymous debut album. Presumably immersing themselves in their beloved Star Trek, POND later resurfaced in the mid-90's with their second set, 'THE PRACTICE OF JOY BEFORE DEATH' (1995). Signed to 'Sony' the following year, POND splashed out with their third and final album, 'ROCK COLLECTION' (1997), more grunge/SCREAMING TREES than indie-rock. After POND had split, BIRCH and CHRISTOPHER BRADY (of SPRINKLER and touring chums of EVERCLEAR) became musically drawn to one another, issuing the limited edition 'HOME RECORDINGS' under the moniker MANDARIN in 1999. Through the buzz of that cassette demo, 'Vagrant' records signed the duo, who were now billed as AUDIO LEARNING CENTER. They teamed up with fellow emo-hardcore man PAUL JOHNSON and issued the striking 'FRIENDSHIPS OFTEN FADE AWAY' (2002), a bitter and visceral record simmering over the brim with masculine energy and repressed sadness.

Album rating: POND (*5) / THE PRACTICE OF JOY BEFORE DEATH (*6) / ROCK COLLECTION (*6) / Audio Learning Center: FRIENDSHIPS OFTEN FADE AWAY (*6)

CHRIS BRADY – vocals, bass / **CHARLIE CAMPBELL** – vocals, guitar / **DAVE TRIEBWASSER** – drums, vocals (ex-THRILLHAMMER)

			not iss.	Tim/Kerr
Jan 92.	(7"green)	**YOUNG SPLENDOR. / TREE**	-	

			Sub Pop	Sub Pop
Nov 92.	(7"white) (SP 218) <SP 178>	**WHEEL. / CINDERS**		

(12"+=/cd-s+=) (SP/+CD 222) – Snowing.

Feb 93.	(lp/cd) (SP/+CD 66-233) <SP 186b>	**POND**		

– Young splendor / Perfect four / Gone / Agatha / Tree / Wheel / Spots / Foamy / Grinned / Filler.

Jul 94.	(7") <SP 263>	**MOTH. / YOU DON'T QUITE GET IT DO YOU, BUT YOU'RE THINKING HARD**		

Feb 95.	(7") <SP 146-366>	**SUNDIAL. / GLASS SPARKLES IN THEIR HAIR**		

Feb 95.	(lp/cd) (SP/+CD 143-357) <SPCD 265>	**THE PRACTICE OF JOY BEFORE DEATH**		Jan95

– Side road / Mubby's theme / Union / Magnifier / Patience / Ol' blue hair / Sundial / Glass sparkles in their hair / Van / Happy cow farm family / Carpenter ant / Artificial turf / Rock collection / Gagged and bound.

			not iss.	Sony
Apr 97.	(cd,c) <67630>	**ROCK COLLECTION**	-	

– Spokes / You're not an astronaut / Scoliosis / One day in the future / Twins / You're not a seed / Flawed / My dog is an astronaut though / Forget / Golden / Greyhound / Rebury me / Filterless / (untitled) / (untitled) / Ugly.

AUDIO LEARNING CENTER

CHRIS BRADY – vocals, bass / **STEVEN BIRCH** – guitar, vocals (ex-SPRINKLER; one 'Sub Pop' set in '92, 'More Boy, Less Friend')

			not iss.	own label
1999.	(7"ep; as MANDARIN)	**HOME RECORDINGS**	-	

— added **PAUL JOHNSON** – drums

			Vagrant	Vagrant
Mar 02.	(cd/lp) <(VR 361 CD/LP)>	**FRIENDSHIPS OFTEN FADE AWAY**		Feb02

– The shell / Hand me downs / Favorite / Winter / The dream / A dedication / Broken / Prescription / December / If you choose / I love robot.

PONY CLUB

Formed: Dublin, Ireland . . . summer 2001 by lone musician and ex-cab driver, MARK CULLEN. A songwriter for quite some time, CULLEN apparently gave up his day job and began writing what was to become his first release, the aptly-titled 'HOME TRUTHS', which appeared on the 'Setanta' label in 2002. A mixture of CHRISTY MOORE's Irish wit, coupled with BILL CALLAHAN's (SMOG) dry, sarcastic humour and downbeat guitar rock, CULLEN, in the form of PONY CLUB, careered through songs such as 'FUCK WITH MY HEART' and the excellent swipe at the music industry, 'MILLIONS LIKE US'. A couple of tracks on the album were co-written by the mysterious VIOLET WILLIAMS, but overall it's CULLEN's set. Indie gentry, MORRISSEY, seemed equally impressed, as he offered CULLEN a support slot on his concurrent American tour.

Album rating: HOME TRUTHS (*6)

MARK CULLEN – vocals, guitar

Setanta   Setanta

Mar 02. (cd) (<SETCD 091>) **HOME TRUTHS**   Jul02
– Fuck with my heart / CCTV / Stop / Single / The thing about men / Millions like us / Home is so sad / What did you expect / Tenderness / Happy families / Flakey wife / Afternoon drinking.

POPGUNS

Formed: Brighton, England . . . 1988 by lyricicst WENDY MORGAN, SIMON PICKLES, GREG DIXON and PAT WALKINGTON. Debut release, 'WHERE DO YOU GO' was recorded for flexidisc label, 'La Di Da', a split affair featuring the band, HOW MANY BEANS MAKE FIVE on the flip side. In April '89, indie label 'Way Cool' issued their debut proper, the 'LANDSLIDE' ep, the band subsequently jettisoning the drum machine in favour of sticksman, SHAUN CHARMAN (ex-Wedding Present). A second ep, 'WAITING FOR THE WINTER', followed later that year, its frantic yet melancholy title track the most promising shot from the POPGUNS' canon up to that point. Both EP's, together with 1990's 'SOMEONE YOU LOVE', were collected together on compilation set, 'EUGENIE' (1990), issued on the 'Midnight Music' label, while a bonafide debut album, 'SNOG' finally surfaced in 1991. Roundly acclaimed by the indie press, the album found MORGAN & Co.'s eager-beaver indie jangle finally coming of age, even if the 20-something angst remained. A further couple of EP's appeared later the same year although The POPGUNS went strangely silent for much of the early 90's, eventually staging a comeback in late '94 with an EP, 'STAR', for the '3rd Stone' label. A long awaited follow-up album, 'LOVE JUNKY', followed a few months later in early '95, although the press support wasn't offered a second time around. • **Covers:** HARLEY DAVIDSON (Serge Gainsbourg) / CAN I KICK IT? (A Tribe Called Quest) • **Songwriters:** Group. • **Trivia:** GENESIS P. ORRIDGE (late of PSYCHIC TV and THROBBING GRISTLE) guested on acclaimed debut 'SNOG'.

Album rating: EUGENIE compilation (*6) / SNOG (*8) / LOVE JUNKY (*6) / A PLUS DE CENT (*5) / ANOTHER YEAR, ANOTHER ADDRESS compilation (*7)

WENDY MORGAN – vocals / **SIMON PICKLES** – guitar / **GREG DIXON** – guitar / **PAT WALKINGTON** – bass / drum machine

La-Di-Da   not iss.

Nov 88. (7"flexi) (none) **WHERE DO YOU GO? / HOW MANY BEANS MAKE FIVE?**   –

Way Cool   not iss.

Apr 89. (12"ep) (MC 19T) **LANDSLIDE. / DOWN ON YOUR KNEES / LEAVE IT ALONE**   –

— SIMON CHARMAN – drums (ex-WEDDING PRESENT) repl. drum machine

Midnight Music   not iss.

Nov 89. (12"ep) (DONG 55) **WAITING FOR THE WINTER. / EVERY DREAM / BECAUSE HE WANTED TO**   –
Apr 90. (12"ep) (DONG 62) **SOMEONE YOU LOVE. / THOSE OTHER THINGS / DON'T SMILE**   –
Aug 90. (cd/c/lp) (CHIME 01.08) **EUGENIE** (singles compilation)   –
Mar 91. (12"ep/cd-ep) (DONG 68/+CD) **STILL A WORLD AWAY. / I'M SPOILING EVERYTHING / A WAY TO CONVINCE YOU**   –
Apr 91. (cd/c/lp) (CHIME 01.15) **SNOG**   –
– Still a world away / Where do you go / Put me through it / You must never know / Gone / Lightning / In my weed / Bye bye baby / Send me shame / Going under.
Jul 91. (12"ep/cd-ep) (DONG 71/+CD) **XXX EP**   –
– Put me through it / Living in sin / Can't ignore the train / Really gone.
Oct 91. (12"ep/cd-ep) (DONG 77/+CD) **CRAZY EP**   –
– Crazy / Gesture / Over your head.

3rd Stone   ZYX

Nov 94. (cd-ep) (STONE 013CD) **STAR / CRAZY / STAY ALIVE**   –
Feb 95. (cd/c) (STONE 016 CD/MC) <20307-2> **LOVE JUNKY**   Oct95
– (I'll) Take you down / Get out / Star / Second time around / Someone to dream of / Under starlight / A miserable boy / How to face it / Can I kick it? [US-only] / Here in Heaven / Over your head / So cold. (cd re-iss. Mar98; same)
May 95. (cd-ep) (STONE 019CD) **GET OUT / DAYBREAK / WHAT ARE YOU WAITING FOR?**   –
(12"ep+=) (STONE 019T) – Can I kick it?

Tall Poppy   not iss.

Feb 96. (cd) (POP 001CD) **A PLUS DE CENT**   –
– Harley Davidson (french version) / Star / Get out / Stay alive / So amazing / Crushed / What are you waiting for? / Daybreak / Can I kick it / Crazy / Gesture. (re-iss. Mar98; same)
Mar 96. (7") (POP 002S) **HARLEY DAVIDSON (French version). / HARLEY DAVIDSON (English version)**   –

— The POPGUNS have since split

– compilations, etc. –

Nov 96. (cd) *Cherry Red*; (<CDMRED 135>) **ANOTHER YEAR, ANOTHER ADDRESS – . . .THE BEST OF THE MIDNIGHT YEARS**   Jun00
– Because he wated to / Landslide / Waiting for the winter / Every dream / Someone you love / Still a world away / Put me through it / Can't ignore the train / You must never know / Gone / Lightning / Down on my knees / Leave it alone / Don't smile / Living in sin / Bye bye baby / Send me shame / Going under. (re-iss. Mar01; same)

POPINJAYS

Formed: Kentish Town, London, England . . . 1988 by WENDY ROBINSON and POLLY HANCOCK. Setting out to make sassy, sexy pop music as a reaction to the manufactured Stock, Aitken & Waterman fare of the day, the songwriting duo originally performed with the help of a drum machine, recruiting third member DANA BALDINGER prior to the inking of a contract with 'One Little Indian' (the deal sweetened by a supply of candy and biscuits!) and the release of debut single, 'DON'T GO BACK'. The latter was soon replaced by American-born ANNE ROGERS as they followed up with 'PLEASE LET ME GO' and feisty debut album, 'BANG UP TO DATE WITH THE POPINJAYS' (1990), the accompanying 'VOTE ELVIS' single going down well in the States and prompting an ill-fated American jaunt. With the subsequent addition of sticksman SEAMUS FEENEY, The POPINJAYS became a fully fledged, bonafide indie-pop band and proceeded to record the album they'd always been capable of in 'FLYING DOWN TO MONO VALLEY' (1992). Comparisons with VOICE OF THE BEEHIVE aside, the pop-brass cleverness and sing-song swooning of singles 'MONSTER MOUTH' and 'TOO JUNG' belied lyrics which ran deeper than their indie contemporaries, reflecting ROBINSON's belief in therapy and backing up her conviction that all pop lyrics are self analytical. This certainly seemed to be the case with 1994's 'TALES FROM THE URBAN PRAIRIE' set, a musical departure towards more rootsy territory inhabited by strumming introspection and beerglass melancholy. • **Covered:** I'M A BELIEVER (Monkees) / 59th STREET BRIDGE SONG (Simon & Garfunkel) / etc.

Album rating: BANG UP TO DATE . . . (*7) / FLYING DOWN TO MONO VALLEY (*5) / TALES FROM THE URBAN PRAIRIE (*5)

WENDY ROBINSON (b. 6 Apr'64, Huddersfield, England) – vocals / **POLLY HANCOCK** (b.16 Jul'64, Berkshire, England) – vocals, guitar / **EMMA** – bass / drum machine

Big Cat   not iss.

Aug 88. (12"m) (BBA 02) **DON'T GO BACK. / SO CLOSE / MOVE TO PERISH**   –

— DANA BALDINGER (b.26 Dec'63, California, USA) – bass; repl. EMMA

One Little Indian   Epic

Mar 90. (12") (40 TP12) **PERFECT DREAM HOME. / PLEASE LET ME GO**   –

— ANNE ROGERS (b.17 Oct'62, New York, USA) – bass; repl. DANA

Apr 90. (cd/lp) (TP CD/LP 28) **BANG UP TO DATE WITH THE POPINJAYS**   –
– Please let me go / Doctor fell / Rain / Hey! (back to the beginning) / Perfect dream home / I don't believe in anything / Thinking about the weather / Mr. Spacecase / Laughing at it all / Kissing cowboys. (cd re-iss. Jan99; same)

— next with guest CATHAL COUGHLAN (of FATIMA MANSIONS)

Oct 90. (12"ep/cd-ep) (45 TP12/7CD) <73021> **VOTE ELVIS**   Mar91
– Vote Elvis / Doctor fell / Thinking about the weather / Hey! (back to the beginning) / Fine lines.

— added **SEAMUS FEENEY** (b.19 Nov'64, Middlesex, England) – drums repl. machine / **BEN KESTEVEN** – bass (ex-AIRHEAD) repl. ANNE

One Little Indian   Epic

May 92. (7") (61 TP7) **MONSTER MOUTH. / SOMETHING ABOUT YOU**   –
(12"+=/cd-s+=) (61 TP 12/7CD) – Helicopter people (disco sex mix).
Jul 92. (7") (71 TP7) **TOO JUNG. / SUN**   –
(12"+=/cd-s+=) (71 TP 12/7CD) – Vote Elvis.
Aug 92. (lp/c/cd) (TPLP 38/+C/CD) <52822> **FLYING DOWN TO MONO VALLEY**   –
– Monster mouth / Too jung / The moon looks nice from here / Nothing / We love you / Vote Elvis / Sun / It doesn't matter / Snowblind / Getting better / See-saw. (cd re-iss. Jul01; same)
Nov 92. (7"/c-s) (81 TP7/+C) **I'M A BELIEVER. / 59th STREET BRIDGE SONG**   –
(12"+=/cd-s+=) (81 TP 12/7CD) – ('A'extended) / Rain.

One Little Indian   Sony

Jun 94. (lp/c/cd) (TPLP 48/+C/CD) <64383> **TALES FROM THE URBAN PRAIRIE**   –
– Queen of the parking lot / Feelin' / When I believed in you / Moonheart / Slowly I reach / Hurricane / Kentish town / Buffalo / Down / Drive the train. (cd re-iss. Jan99; same)

— disbanded after above

POPSICLE

Formed: Stockholm, Sweden ... early 90's by ANDREAS MATTSSON, FREDRIK NORBERG, KENNY VIKSTROM and PER-ARNE WIKANDER. Having already issued two albums (for 'M.N.W.') in Scandinavia, these UK indie-fixated Swedes finally gained a British release with 1993's award-winning 'LACQUER'. Despite ploughing the same furrow of upfront cutesy pop as countrymen, The WANNADIES and The CARDIGANS, POPSICLE never quite scaled the same chart-winning heights outside of their native Sweden. With ARVID LIND replacing VIKSTROM, the power-pop Vikings found a home with 'Warners' ('East West' UK) for 1995's 'ABSTINENCE' although they were back with homegrown imprint, 'Telegram', for subsequent releases. • **Covered:** Buzzcocks songs in '97.

Album rating: TEMPLATE mini (*5) / LACQUER (*6) / ABSTINENCE (*5) / POPSICLE (*5) / STAND UP AND TESTIFY (*5)

ANDREAS MATTSSON – vocals, guitar / **FREDRIK NORBERG** – vocals, guitar / **KENNY VIKSTROM** – bass / **PER-ARNE WIKANDER** – drums

		M.N.W.	not iss.
1991.	(c-s) **POPSICLE**	–	– Swedish
1992.	(m-cd) **TEMPLATE**	–	– Swedish
	– Ten / Wonderful / Blow up / Further / Loveflies / Never know.		
1992.	(cd-ep) **WHITSUN**	–	– Swedish
	– Undulate / True / Bird, live / Velveteen.		

		Snap	not iss.
Aug 93.	(cd-ep) *(SNAPC 014)* **HEY PRINCESS / BLOW UP / NEVER KNOW**		–
Sep 93.	(cd) *(SNAP 011)* **LACQUER** (compilation of above two CD's)		–
	– Hey princess / Popcorn / Undulate / How come we / Pale honey / Irreplaceable / She / Template / True / A song called Liberty / Bird / Sandy / Slow.		
Feb 94.	(cd-ep) *(SNAPC 018)* **UNDULATE / TRUE / VELVETEEN**		–

---- **ARVID LIND** – bass; repl. VIKSTROM

		East West	Warners
Feb 95.	(7"/c-s/cd-s) *(YZ 900 X/C/CD)* **MAKE UP. / EVERYTHING'S THE ONLY THING**		
Feb 95.	(cd/c) <*(4509 95679-2/-4)*> **ABSTINENCE**		
	– Mayfly / Sunkissed / Make up / Step inside my mind / Could be / Histrionics / Prussian blue / Spaniel / Diving bell / Join my stream / Soul lacquer drug / Join my stream / Smooth / Soft.		
Jun 95.	(c-s) *(YZ 943C)* **HISTRIONICS / MAYFLY**		
	(cd-s+=) *(YZ 943CD)* – Soul laquer drug / Smooth.		

		Telegram	not iss.
1996.	(cd-s) **THIRD OPINION**	–	– Swedish
1996.	(cd) *(13287)* **POPSICLE**	–	– Swedish
	– Good with us / Not forever / Speed it up / Please don't ask / Third opinion / Use my name / Sadly missing / American poet / A song ago / Soft / Power ballad #1 / Power ballad #3.		

		Warners	not iss.
1997.	(cd) **STAND UP AND TESTIFY**	–	– Sweden
	– I don't feel it / The price we pay / Train across the bridge / Vibrant days / Story of my life / By the time I get to understand you / Dry spot / That was summer / Genuine / Snow in July / The sweetest relief / Noise annoys / Lust lust / Lipstick / Why can't I touch it? / Something's gone wrong again.		

---- disbanded in '97

PORCUPINE TREE

Formed: London, England ... 1989 by STEVEN WILSON, a self-taught guitarist and pianist. He had originally surfaced in the duo, ALTAMONT (in 1983, aged 15), issuing the cassette, 'PRAYER FOR THE SOUL' (half solo, half with SI VOCKINGS on keyboards). Released on 'Acid Tapes', it featured lyrics by the label's owner, ALAN DUFFY, who later founded 'Imaginary' records. WILSON was also sidelining with the heavier KARMA, an outfit that released a few private tapes, 'THE JOKE'S ON YOU' (1983) and 'THE LAST MAN TO LAUGH' (1985), before splitting in 1986; several tracks from these were to take on a new lease of life with PORCUPINE TREE, an ambient retro-progressive/psychedelic outfit akin to PINK FLOYD fused with HAWKWIND and rave! STEVEN then compiled a progressive rock collection, 'Exposure', which featured several new bands alongside his own new project, NO MAN IS AN ISLAND EXCEPT THE ISLE OF MAN (with the track, 'From A Toyshop Window'). He shortened the moniker slightly to NO MAN for another compilation, 'Double Exposure', adding ex-PLENTY frontman, TIM BOWNESS, on the song, 'FAITH'S LAST DOUBT'. NO MAN continued for two years and issued a few items for 'Plastic Head', including a couple of tracks for the label's 'Expose It' V/A album. WILSON's next venture, PORCUPINE TREE (also with ALAN DUFFY), continued in much the same vein, releasing the cassette-only 'TARQUIN'S SEAWEED FARM' (which featured a PRINCE cover, 'THE CROSS'). Two more cassettes surfaced in the early 90's, namely 'LOVE, DEATH AND MUSSOLINI' and 'THE NOSTALGIA FACTORY', whose tracks appeared on the excellent debut album proper, 'ON THE SUNDAY OF LIFE', in 1992. A single, 'VOYAGE 34' (a 30 minute track!), was issued soon after while STEVEN continued with NO MAN, the one-man unit expanding into a band featuring members of JAPAN (i.e. STEVE JANSEN, RICHARD BARBIERI and MICK KARN). STEVEN returned the favour in 1994 when he featured on two of their post-JAPAN albums, 'Seed' and 'Stone To Flesh' (the latter without KARN). In 1996, PORCUPINE TREE were back on form with 'SIGNIFY', while WILSON's NO MAN project had signed to '3rd Stone', releasing the more commercial 'WILD OPERA'. PORCUPINE TREE subsequently signed to the 'Snapper/K-Scope' label for 'STUPID DREAM' (1999), a pointedly more expansive effort albeit couched in neo-prog terms, the undeniable influence of RADIOHEAD making itself felt both lyrically and musically. The band's seemingly inexorable drive towards accessibility continued with both 'LIGHTBULB SUN' (2000) and 'IN ABSENTIA' (2002), the former gilt edging some of the hooks to an unprecedented degree while still retaining WILSON's nose for opaque beauty and his gift for razor sharp irony, the latter achieving a hitherto unheard balance between the myriad facets of the PORCUPINE TREE sound. Reassuringly, WILSON, in tandem with BOWNESS and assorted crew, reserved his most compelling experimental energies for NO MAN, whose 'RETURNING JESUS' (2001) album made some exquisite ventures into ambient jazz territory, Brit legend IAN CARR guesting. • **NO MAN covers:**- COLOURS (Donovan).

Album rating: ON THE SUNDAY OF LIFE (*8) / UP THE DOWNSTAIR (*6) / THE SKY MOVES SIDEWAYS (*6) / SIGNIFY (*7) / COMA DIVINE (*6) / METANOIA outtakes (*5) / STUPID DREAM (*7) / LIGHTBULB SUN (*6) / VOYAGE 34: THE COMPLETE TRIP collection (*4) / RECORDINGS collection (*5) / STARS DIE: THE DELERIUM YEARS '91-'97 (*7) / IN ABSENTIA (*6) / No Man: LOVEBLOWS AND LOVECRIES (*6) / WILD OPERA (*6) / DRY CLEANING RAY (*5) / RETURNING JESUS (*6)

ALTAMONT

STEVEN WILSON + ALAN DUFFY

		Acid Tapes	not iss.
1983.	(c) *(TAB 004)* **PRAYER FOR THE SOUL**		–
1985.	(c) *(TAB 010)* **EVERYDAY HEROES** (compilation)		–

---- also with KARMA who also released private cassettes (see above).

NO-MAN

STEVEN WILSON – guitar, keyboards / **TIM BOWNESS** – vocals / **BEN COLEMAN** – violin

		Plastic Head	not iss.
Jun 89.	(12"ep; as NO MAN IS AN ISLAND) *(PLASS 012)* **THE GIRL FROM MISSOURI / FOREST ALMOST BURNING. / NIGHT SKY SWEET EARTH / THE BALLET BEAST**		–

		Hidden Art	not iss.
Jul 90.	(7") *(HA 4)* **COLOURS. / COLOURS** (remodelled)		–

		Probe Plus	not iss.
Nov 90.	(12"ep) *(PP 27T)* **COLOURS. / DRINK JUDAS / COLOURS** (remodelled)		–

		One Little Indian	not iss.
Jul 91.	(12"ep/cd-ep) *(57TP 12/7CD)* **DAYS IN THE TREES EP**		–
	– Days in the trees (Mahler / Ives / Bartok / Reich versions).		
Apr 92.	(m-lp/m-cd) *(TPLP 47 M/CD)* **LOVESIGHS – AN ENTERTAINMENT**		–
	– Heartcheat pop / Days in the trees (Mahler) / rink Judas / Heartcheat motel / Kiss me stupid / Colours / Iris Murdoch cut me up / Days in the trees (Reich).		

---- added JAPAN (RAIN TREE CROW) members **STEVE JANSEN** – drums / **RICHARD BARBIERI** – keyboards / **MICK KARN** – bass

Sep 92.	(12"ep/cd-ep) *(63TP 12/7CD)* **OCEAN SONG. / BACK TO THE BURNING SHED / SWIRL**		–
Jan 93.	(cd-ep mail-order) *(73TP 7CD)* **SWEETHEART RAW / BLEED / SAY BABY SAY GOODBYE**		–
Mar 93.	(12"ep/cd-ep) *(83TP 12/7CD)* **ONLY BABY** (Move For Me) **/ ONLY BABY** (Breathe For Me) **/ ONLY BABY** (Be For Me) **/ LONG DAY FALL**		–
May 93.	(d-lp/c/cd) *(TPLP 57/+C/CD)* **LOVEBLOWS AND LOVECRIES – A CONFESSION**		–
	– Loveblow / Only baby / Housekeeping / Sweetheart raw / Lovecry / Tulip / Break Heaven / Beautiful and cruel / Painting Paradise / Heaven's break. *(ltd.cd w/ free cd) (TPLP 57CDL)* LOVESIGHS		
Jun 93.	(12"/c-s) *(93TP 12/7CD)* **PAINTING PARADISE. / HEAVEN TASTE**		–

---- JAPAN members dislodged by ROBERT FRIPP (King Crimson) – guitar

Jun 94.	(d-lp/c/cd) *(TPLP 67/+C/CD)* **FLOWERMOUTH**		–
	– Angel gets caught in the beauty trap / You grow more beautiful / Animal ghost / Soft shoulders / Shell of a fighter / Teardrop falls / Watching over me / Simple / Things change.		

---- now without COLEMAN

		3rd Stone	3rd Stone
May 96.	(cd-ep) *(<STONE 026CD>)* **HOUSEWIVES HOOKED ON HEROIN / HIT THE CEILING / HOUSEWIVES HOOKED ON METHADONE** (Scanner mix) **/ URBAN DISCO / WHERE I'M CALLING FROM**		Jun96
Aug 96.	(cd) *(<STONE 027CD>)* **WILD OPERA**		
	– Radiant city / Pretty genius / Infant phenomenon / Sinister jazz / Housewives hooked on heroin / Libertino libretto / Taste my dream / Dry cleaning Ray / Sheep loop / My rival Trevor / Time travel in Texas / My revenge on Seattle.		
May 97.	(7"ltd) *(STONE 034S)* **DRY CLEANING RAY. / TIME TRAVEL IN TEXAS / WATCHING OVER ME**		–
Jun 97.	(cd) *(<STONE 035CD>)* **DRY CLEANING RAY**		
	– Dry cleaning Ray / Sweetside silver night / Jack the sax / Diet mothers / Urban disco / Punished for being born / Knightlinger / Evelyn (the song of slurs) / Sicknote.		
Aug 98.	(cd) *(<STONE 037CD>)* **CAROLINA SKELETONS**		
	– Carolina skeletons / Something falls / Close your eyes / Carolina.		

---- TIM BOWNESS also moonlighted with DARKROOM, the project releasing 'DAYLIGHT' in 1998

Feb 01.	(cd) *(<STONE 038CD>)* **RETURNING JESUS**		Mar01
	– Only rain / No defence / Close your eyes / Carolina skeletons / Outside the machine / Returning Jesus / Slow it all down / Lighthouse / All that you are.		

– compilations, etc. –

Jul 99.	(cd) *Material Sonori; (MASO 90111)* **SPEAK** (recorded for cassette 1989)		–

PORCUPINE TREE

STEVEN WILSON – guitar, keyboards, vocals

		Delerium	C&S
1991.	(ltd.c) *(DELC 0002)* **TARQUIN'S SEAWEED FARM** (originally very ltd.50 in 1989)	-	-

— LOVE, DEATH AND MUSSOLINI cassette released 1990 but only 10 copies.

1991.	(ltd.c) *(DELC 0003)* **THE NOSTALGIA FACTORY** (originally very ltd.50 in 1990)	-	
May 92.	(cd/d-lp) *(DELEC CD/LP 008D)* **ON THE SUNDAY SIDE OF LIFE**		-

– Music for the head / Jupiter island / Third eye surfer / On the Sunday side of life . . . / The nostalgia factory / Space transmission / Message from a self-destructing turnip / Radioactive toy / Nine cats / Hymn / Footprints / Linton Samuel Dawson / And the swallows dance above the sun / Queen quotes Crowley / No luck with rabbits / Begonia seduction scene / This long silence / It will rain for a million years. *(<cd+US-iss.Oct00; same>)*

Nov 92.	(12"ep/cd-ep) *(DELEC EP/CDEP 010)* **VOYAGE 34: PHASE 1. / PHASE 2**		-

— added **COLIN EDWIN** – bass / **CHRIS MAITLAND** – drums / **RICHARD BARBIERI** – keyboards

Jun 93.	(cd/lp) *(DELEC CD/LP 020)* **UP THE DOWNSTAIR**		-

– What are you listening to / Synesthesia / Monuments burn into moments / Always never / Up the downstair / Not beautiful anymore / Siren / Small fish / Burning sky / Fadeaway. *(cd re-mast.Oct00; same)*

Nov 93.	(12"ep) *(DELEC EP 007)* **VOYAGE 34 REMIX: PHASE 3 (Astralasia Dreamstate). / PHASE 4 (A New Civilisation)**		-

— added **RICK EDWARDS** – percussion

Oct 94.	(12"ep/cd-ep) *(DELEC EP/CDEP 032)* **STARS DIE. / MOONLOOP**		-
Oct 94.	(cd-ep) *<CS 2024-2>* **STARS DIE / MOONLOOP / ALWAYS NEVER**	-	
Jan 95.	(cd,pic-cd/lp/blue-lp) *(DELEC CD/LP 028/+L)* **THE SKY MOVES SIDEWAYS**		-

– The sky moves sideways (part one) / Dislocated day / Moon touches your shoulder / Prepare yourself / The sky moves sideways (part two). *(cd+=)* – Moonloop. *(cd re-mast.Oct00; same)*

Apr 96.	(12"ep) *(DELEC EP 049)* **WAITING PHASE 1 / WAITING PHASE 2. / COLOURFLOW IN MIND / FUSE THE SUN**		-

(cd-ep) *(DELEC CDEP 049)* – (Phase 1 & 2) / The sound of no-one listening.

Sep 96.	(cd/d-lp) *(DELEC CD/LP 045)* **SIGNIFY**		-

– Bornlivedie / Signify / Sleep of no dreaming / Pagan / Waiting phase one / Waiting phase two / Sever / Idiot prayer / Every home is wired / Intermediate Jesus / Light mass prayers / Darkmatter. *(d-lp+=)* – The sound of no-one listening. *(cd re-mast.Oct00; same)*

Oct 97.	(cd) *(DELECCD 067)* **COMA DIVINE**		-

– Bornlivedieintro / Signify / Waiting phase one & two / The sky moves sideways / Dislocated day / Sleep of no dreaming / Moonloop / Radioactive toy / Not beautiful anymore.

		Snapper	Snapper
Mar 99.	(cd) *(<SMACD 813>)* **STUPID DREAM**		Apr99

– Even less / Piano lessons / Stupid dream / Pure narcotic / Slave called Shiver / Don't hate me / This is no rehearsal / Baby dream in cellophane / Stranger by the minute / A smart kid / Tinto brass / Stop swimming.

Apr 99.	(7") *(SMAS7 103)* **PIANO LESSONS. / OCEANS HAVE NO MERCY**		-

(cd-s) *(SMASCD 103)* – ('A'side) / Ambulance chasing / WAke as gun.

Oct 99.	(7") *(SMAS7 107)* **STRANGER BY THE MINUTE. / HALLOGALLO**		-

(cd-s) *(SMASCD 107)* – ('A'extended) / Even less (part 2) / PIano lessons (video).

Nov 99.	(7") *(SMAS7 110)* **PURE NARCOTIC. / NINE CATS (acoustic)**		-

(cd-s) *(SMASCD 110)* – ('A'side) / Tinto brass (live) / Door to the river.

May 00.	(7") *(SMAS7 111)* **FOUR CHORDS THAT MADE A MILLION. / ORCHIDIA**		-

(cd-s) *(SMASCD 111)* – ('A'side) / Disappear / In formaldehyde.
(cd-s) *(SMAXCD 111)* – ('A'side) / Even less (extended demo).

May 00.	(cd) *(<SMACD 827>)* **LIGHTBULB SUN**		Jul00

– Lightbulb sun / How is your life today? / Four chords that made a million / Shesmovedon / Last chance to evacuate Planet Earth before it is recycled / Rest will flow / Hatesong / Where would we be / Russia on ice / Feel so low. *(re-iss. Feb01 +=; SMACD 841X)* – Piano lessons (video) / Buying new soul (edit) / Tinto brass (live) / Pure narcotic.

Jul 00.	(7") *(SMAS7 120)* **SHESMOVEDON. / NOVAK**		-

(cd-s) *(SMASCD 120)* – ('A'side) / Cure for optimism / Untitled.
(cd-s) *(SMAXCD 120)* – ('A'extended) / Russia on ice (demo).

— **GAVIN HARRISON** – drums; repl. CHRIS

		Lava – Atlantic	Lava – Atlantic
Jan 03.	(cd) *(<07567 83604-2>)* **IN ABSENTIA**		Sep02

– Blackest eyes / Trains / Lips of ashes / The sound of musak / Gravity eyelids / Wedding nails / Prodigal / 3 / The creator has a mastertape / Heartattack in a lay by / Strip the soul / Collapse the light into Earth.

– compilations, others, etc –

Aug 94.	(cd) *Magic Gnome; (MG 4299325)* **YELLOW HEDGEROW DREAMSCAPE**		-

– Mute / Landscape / Prayer / Daughters in excess / Delightful suicide / Split image / No reason to live, no reason to die / Wastecoat / Towel / Execution of the will of the Marquis De Sade / Track eleven / Radioactive toy / An empty box / The cross / Yellow hedgerow dreamscape / Music for the head. *(lp-iss.May00 on 'Gates Of Dawn'; GOD 005)*

Oct 94.	(10"m-lp) *Lazy; (LE 3094)* **STAIRCASE INFINITIES**		-

(cd-iss. Oct95 on 'Blueprint'; BP 217CD)

Jan 99.	(d10"ep) *Chromatic; (CHR 003)* **METANOIA** (outtakes 1995-96)		-

– Mesmer (pt.1) / Mesmer (pt.2) / Mesmer (pt.3) – Coma divine / Metanoia (pt.1) – Intermediate Jesus / Metanoia (pt.2) / Milan. *(<cd-iss. Mar02 on 'Delerium'+=; DELECCD 079>)* – Door to the river / Insignificance.

Oct 00.	(cd) *Delerium; (<DELECCD 034>)* **VOYAGE 34: THE COMPLETE TRIP**		
May 01.	(cd) *Snapper; (SMACD 840)* **RECORDINGS**		Jun00

– Buying new soul / Access denied / Cure for optimism / (untitled) / Disappear / Ambulance chasing / In formaldehyde / Even less / Oceans have no memory.

Mar 02.	(d-cd) *Snapper; (<SMADD 851>)* **STARS DIE: THE DELERIUM YEARS '91-'97**		

– Radioactive toy / Nine cats / And the swallows dance above the sun / The nostalgia factory / Voyage 34 / Synaesthesia / Phantoms / Up the downstair / Fadeaway / Rainy taxi / Stars die / Men of wood / The sky moves sideways (phase one) / Waiting / The sound of no-one listening / Colourflow in mind / Fuse the sky / Signify II / Every home is wired / Sever / Dark matter.

PORTASTATIC (see under ⇒ SUPERCHUNK)

POSIES

Formed: Seattle, Washington, USA … 1987 by ex-SKY CRIES MARY members, JONATHON AUER and KEN STRINGFELLOW. Influenced by the twin strands of classic 60's/70's Brit/US pop and the alternative rock sounds of their hometown, these budding retro merchants first set up their stall in 1989 with the cassette-only release, 'FAILURE'. Carefully re-arranging their sound with the addition of rhythm section DAVE FOX and MIKE MUSBURGER, the band were an unlikely signing to 'Geffen' for 1990's John Leckie-produced 'DEAR 23'. Although it didn't fit into the emerging Grunge zeitgeist, the album was the toast of critics who liked their Power-Pop as lush, fresh and fragrant as a newly picked bouquet. Inevitably, the band were compelled to slide inexorably into grungier but still relatively composed musical territory with the long-awaited DON FLEMING-produced third album, 'FROSTING ON THE BEATER' (1993). Equally inevitably, The POSIES' effeminate charm was partly buried although they did have a surprise minor UK hit with 'DEFINITE DOOR'. The latter's CD b-side featured a cover of Chris Bell's 'I AM THE COSMOS', both AUER and STRINGFELLOW having already followed in their idol's footsteps by joining a re-formed BIG STAR. In 1996, The POSIES confounded fans and critics alike by embracing Grunge wholesale on that year's disappointing 'AMAZING DISGRACE', the record featuring a tribute to another of their heroes, 'GRANT HART'. A few years later, after a solo album by STRINGFELLOW ('THIS SOUNDS LIKE GOODBYE'), the quartet issued their fifth and what looked to be their final effort, 'SUCCESS' (1998). By the time of the band's break-up in 1998, STRINGFELLOW already had a debut solo album, 'THIS SOUNDS LIKE GOODBYE' (1997), under his belt although he went on to form the short-lived SALTINE (who split with only a solitary EP to their name) and also helped out R.E.M. on tour. Yet the partnership between STRINGFELLOW and AUER proved too strong to simply be made redundant. The pair duly recorded the live 'IN CASE YOU DIDN'T FEEL LIKE PLUGGING IN' (2000), an intimate, acoustic date primed for long time fans. The duo also released an EP, 'FIND YOURSELF ALONE', in 2001 while STRINGFELLOW released his follow-up solo set, 'TOUCHED', the same year. • **STRINGFELLOW covered:** TAKE CARE (Big Star).

Album rating: FAILURE (*5) / DEAR 23 (*7) / FROSTING ON THE BEATER (*5) / AMAZING DISGRACE (*4) / SUCCESS (*5) / ALIVE BEFORE THE ICEBERG live (*5) / DREAM ALL DAY: THE BEST THE POSIES compilation (*7) / IN CASE YOU DIDN'T FEEL LIKE PLUGGING IN (*6) / AT LEAST AT LAST boxed set collection (*6) / Ken Stringfellow: THIS SOUNDS LIKE GOODBYE (*4) / TOUCHED (*6)

JONATHON AUER – vocals, guitar (ex-SKY CRIES MARY) / **KEN STRINGFELLOW** – vocals, guitar (ex-SKY CRIES MARY)

		not iss.	23
1989.	(c) *<none>* **FAILURE**	-	

– Blind eyes open / The longest line / Under easy / Like me too / I may hate you sometimes / Ironing Tuesdays / Paint me / Believe in something other (than yourself) / Compliment? / At least for now / Uncombined / What little remains. *(UK cd-iss. Feb95 on 'Pop Llama'; PLCD 2323)*

— added **DAVE FOX** – bass / **MIKE MUSBURGER** – drums

		Geffen	Geffen
Nov 90.	(cd/c/lp) *<(7599 24305-2/-4/-1)>* **DEAR 23**		

– My big mouth / Golden blunders / Apology / Any other way / You avoid parties / Suddenly Mary / Help yourself / Mrs. Green / Everyone moves away / Flood of sunshine. *(re-iss. Aug93 cd/c; GFLD/GFLC 19223) (cd re-iss. Nov96; GED 24305)*

Apr 91.	(cd-s) *<21631>* **SUDDENLY MARY / FEEL / SPITE AND MALICE**	-	
May 93.	(cd/c/lp) *<(GED/GEC/GEF 24522)>* **FROSTING ON THE BEATER**		

– Dream all day / Solar sister / Flavor of the month / Love letter boxes / Definite door / Burn & shine / Earlier than expected / 20 questions / When mute tongues can speak / Lights out / How she lied by living / Coming right along. *(cd re-iss. Oct95 & Feb98 & Aug99; GFLD 19298)*

Sep 93.	(7"/c-s) *(GFS/+C 50)* **DREAM ALL DAY. / HOW SHE LIED BY LIVING**		-

(12"+=/cd-s+=) *(GFST/+D 50)* – Ever since I was alone / Open every window.

Oct 93.	(7"mauve/c-s) *(GFS/+C 58)* **FLAVOR OF THE MONTH. / START A LIFE**		-

(cd-s+=) *(GFSTD 58)* – This one's taken.

Mar 94.	(7") *(GFS 68)* **DEFINITE DOOR. / SONG OF THE BAKER**	67	-

(cd-s+=) *(GFSTD 68)* – Ooh child / I am the cosmos.

Oct 94. (7"ep) *(ER 121)* **THIS IS NOT THE POSIES**
– Open every window / Farewell, typewriter.
(above issued on 'Elefant')

— AUER and STRINGFELLOW became part of a re-formed BIG STAR before returning to The POSIES, they later became part of MINUS 5 with YOUNG FRESH FELLOWS frontman, SCOTT McCAUGHEY

— **STRINGFELLOW + AUER** recruited **JOE SKYWARD + BRIAN YOUNG**

Apr 96. (c-s) *(GFSC 22128)* **PLEASE RETURN IT / SAD TO BE AWARE**
(cd-s+=) *(GFSTD 22128)* – Dream all day / Solar sister / Suddenly Mary.

Apr 96. (cd/c) *<(GED/GEC 24910)>* **AMAZING DISGRACE**
– Daily mutation / Ontario / Throwaway / Please return it / Hate song / Precious moments / Fight it (if you want it) / Everybody is a fucking liar / World / Grant Hart / Broken record / Certainty / Song #1 / Will you ever ease your mind. *<(lp-iss.Jul00 on 'Tim/Kerr'; 961213-1)>*

Apr 98. (cd) *<(PLCD 3232)>* **SUCCESS** — Pop Llama / Pop Llama / Feb98
– Somehow everything / You're the beautiful one / Fall apart with me / Placebo / Who to blame / Start a life / Friendship of the future / Grow / Farewell typewriter / Every bitter drop / Fall song. *<(re-iss. Jun00 on 'Houston Party'; HPR 004)>* *<(lp-iss.May01; HPVR 004)>*

— **AUER + STRINGFELLOW** as a duo

Oct 00. (m-cd) *<(CRC 232CD)>* **IN CASE YOU DIDN'T FEEL LIKE PLUGGING IN (live acoustic)** — Casa / Casa / Aug00
– Grant Hart / Every bitter drop / Flavor of the month / Suddenly Mary / (untitled) / Believe in something other (than yourself) / Solar sister / I may hate you sometimes / (Sick f's) / Please return it / Precious moments / (Brownie) / Throwaway.

Mar 01. (cd-ep/12"ep) *<(HPR/+V 037)>* **NICE CHEEKBONES AND A Ph.D.** — Feb01
– Matinee / Chainsmoking in the U.S.A. / With those eyes / No consolation / Lady friend.

– compilations, etc. –

Mar 00. (cd) *D.G.C.; <490555>* **DREAM ALL DAY – THE BEST OF THE POSIES**
– My big mouth / Golden blunders / Any other way / Suddenly Mary / Spite and malice / I am the cosmos / King Midas in reverse / Dream all day / Solar sister / Flavor of the month / Definite door / Coming right along / Going, going, gone / Ontario / Throwaway / Please return it / Sad to be aware / Everybody is a fucking liar / Flood of sunshine.

May 00. (cd) *Houston Party; <(HPR 012)>* **ALIVE BEFORE THE ICEBERG (live in Barcelona 1998)** — Feb00
– Somehow everything / Please return it / Dream all day / You're the beautiful one / Start a lie / Precious moments / Grant Hart / Flavor of the month / Everybody is a fucking liar / Broken record / Surrender / Throwaway.

May 01. (4xcd-box) *Not Lame; <(NLA 006)>* **AT LEAST AT LAST: DEMOS, LIVE RECORDINGS AND WHATNOT, 1987-1998** — 2000

KEN STRINGFELLOW

with various people on session

Nov 97. (m-lp/m-cd) *(MR/+CD 123)* *<AHA 1004CD>* **THIS SOUNDS LIKE GOODBYE** — Munster / Hidden Agenda / Oct97
– Here's to the future / Trans potato / Your love won't be denied / A short drumbreak / Bi-son / Too true / Anxiety ryder / Unfortunate threnody / Take care. *(cd re-iss. Feb98; same as US)*

May 01. (cd-s; as SALTINE) *<(HPR 016)>* **FIND YOURSELF ALONE / REVEAL LOVE / ANY SIGN AT ALL** — Houston Party / Houston Party

Aug 01. (7") *(MC 50495)* **DOWN LIKE ME. / AIRSCAPE** — Poptones / Manifesto

Sep 01. (cd) *(MC 5049CD) <42801>* **TOUCHED**
– Down like me / This one's for you / Find yourself alone / Sparrow / Reveal love / Uniforms / One morning / Spanish waltz / Fireflies / The lover's hymn / Here's to the future.

POSSIBILITIES

Formed: Athens, Georgia, USA . . . 1991 by CHRIS GREHAN, BOB SPIRES and MATT LANE. The band plugged away for almost a decade and had expanded to a 5-piece with the addition of JASON GONZALES and KEVIN LANE before the release of their self-titled debut in 1999. Listening to the record begged the question why it had taken them so long to be picked up. Their psychedelia-tinged alt-country sound was comparable to The FLAMING LIPS yet firmly marked with the group's own signature. It is a possible explanation, that working as a backing band for both JACK LOGAN and BOB McBRIDE on tours and albums in the mid to late 1990's had honed the groups talents. Their 2002 follow up 'WAY OUT' was another psychedelic guitar pop triumph worthy of challenging critical big hitters such as GRANDADDY or LAMBCHOP. After a slow start this group had suddenly realised that The POSSIBILITIES were limitless.

Album rating: THE POSSIBILITIES (*6) / WAY OUT (*7)

CHRIS GREHAN – vocals, guitar / **KEVIN LANE** – guitar, vocals / **BOB SPIRES** – bass, vocals / **MATT LANE** – drums, vocals / **JASON GONZALES** – keyboards, vocals

Jun 99. (cd) *<3>* **THE POSSIBILITIES** — not iss. / Backburner
– You don't mean it / Rely on you / Lie to you / Genius / Up your nose / Outside like a wallflower / Lost times / Dozen of dimes / Slow draw / Steady now / Stringing along / Counting the days / Next party / Don't look back.

2001. (7") **INVISIBLE. /** — not iss. / Seed & Feed

Jul 02. (cd) *<CD 081>* **WAY OUT** — not iss. / Parasol
– Invisible / Now and then you appear / Way out / Wouldn't take nothing / Braintree / Everywhere I look / Coming in waves / Tikki ball / Downtown dream / Starlight / Swing and sway / What makes you run.

POSSUM DIXON

Formed: Los Angeles, California, USA . . . 1989 by ROBERT ZABRECKY who recruited members from likely candidates playing at his Jabber Jaw club. Concocting an awkward but original sound drawing influences from the likes of TALKING HEADS, XTC, WIRE and The STRANGLERS, ZABRECKY self-financed the release of three US-only 45's. Trading in a similarly quirky lyrical vein as acts like THEY MIGHT BE GIANTS, the POSSUM DIXON muse drew on a quintessentially American strand of fantasy and distorted reality to entertaining effect. The major-label backed 'Interscope' were quick to snap them up and 1994 saw the release of an eponymous debut album, the accompanying 'NERVES' single featuring a bleep frenzy rendition of The Yardbirds' 'FOR YOUR LOVE' on the B-side. A few years on, the POSSUM posse were back in town, still casting around for a musical identity with the follow-up set, 'STAR MAPS' (1996). In 1998, POSSUM delivered their RIC OKASEK-produced long-player, 'NEW SHEETS', although this was to be their final effort.

Album rating: POSSUM DIXON (*6) / STAR MAPS (*5) / NEW SHEETS (*5)

ROBERT ZABRECKY – vocals, bass / **ROBERT O'SULLIVAN** – electric piano / **CELSO CHAVEZ** – guitar / **RICHARD TREUEL** – drums

1990. (7") **WATCH THE GIRL DESTROY ME. / FRIENDS** — not iss. / Freak Scene

1991. (7") **SISTER. / (other by BLACK ANGELS DEATH SONG)** — not iss. / Piece Of Mind

1992. (3x7"box) **MUSIC FOR A ONE BEDROOM APARTMENT** — not iss. / Pronto

1993. (7") **NERVES. / WHO YOU ARE** — not iss. / Surf Detective – Flipside

Mar 94. (7") *(A 8304)* **NERVES. / SHE DRIVES** — Interscope-Atlantic / Interscope-Atlantic
(12"+=/cd-s+=) *(A 8304 T/CD)* – For your love.

Apr 94. (cd/c) *<(6544 92291-2/-4)>* **POSSUM DIXON**
– Nerves / In buildings / Watch the girl destroy me / She drives / We're all happy / Invisible / Pharmaceutical itch / Executive slacks / Regina / John struck Lucy / Elevators. *(cd re-iss. Jul96; IND 92291)*

Jun 94. (7"/c-s) *(A 8297/+C)* **WATCH THE GIRL DESTROY ME. / EXECUTIVE SLACKS**
(12"+=/cd-s+=) *(A 8297 T/CD)* – Damn the rainbow.

1994. (cd-ep) **SUNSHINE OR NOIR**
– Farewell my lovely / Personals / Go west / Nameless / In buildings (live).

Jul 96. (cd) *<(IND 92625)>* **STAR MAPS**
– Go west / In her disco / Radio comets / Party tonight / Emergency's about to end / General electric / Crashing your planet / Personals / Reds / Skid marks / Artificial sunlight / Apartment song. *(lp-iss.Jun96 on 'Revelation'; REV 2625)*

1997. (d7"ep) **KCRW LIVE RECORD (live)**
(above issued on 'Surf Detective – Flat Earth')

Aug 98. (cd/c/lp) *<90221-2/-4/-1>* **NEW SHEETS**
– Songs from a box / Holding (Lenny's song) / Only in the summertime / Firecracker / New sheets / Always engines / Stop breaking me / Now what? / Plan B / Heavenly / Faultlines / What you mean / End's beginning.

— the group split in 1999

POSTER CHILDREN

Formed: Champaign-Urbana, Illinois, USA . . . 1987 by RICK VALENTIN and ROSE MARSHACK. These hyperactive punk-pop kids made an enterprising start to their career with a self-financed cassette-only releases, 'FLOWER PLOWER' and 'TOREADOR SQUAT' (1988), their DIY skills extending to artwork, T-shirts, tour promotion, etc. Securing the services of STEVE ALBINI, The POSTER CHILDREN completed their first album for 'Limited Potential', in the shape of 'FLOWER POWER' (1990) which was subsequently licensed to 'Frontier'. Drawing comparisons with The PIXIES, BITCH MAGNET and SLINT, The POSTER CHILDREN found admirers across the US alt-rock spectrum (where they had signed to 'Sire-Reprise'); the buzz soon spread across the water where Creation's Alan McGee was quick to spot their more than limited potential. While they never quite reached pin-up status, The POSTER CHILDREN did enjoy underground critical acclaim with a further two albums, 'DAISYCHAIN REACTION' (1992) and 'TOOL OF THE MAN' (1992/93). Soon to be given a higher priority by their Stateside label ('Warner Bros.'), the band's mid-90's albums, 'JUNIOR CITIZEN' (1995) and 'RTFM' (1997) were aimed at the alternative crossover audience who'd taken GREEN DAY to the top. Meanwhile, the quartet were hatching another plan, the post-progressive, textured TRANS AM-like SALARYMAN, who delivered a sole eponymous set in '97. Following their withdrawal from the world of major labels, The POSTER CHILDREN returned with the self-produced 'NEW WORLD RECORD' (1999), opening with a cover of Billy Bragg's 'ACCIDENT WAITING TO HAPPEN' and injecting an undercurrent of uncut funk into their indie stew. 'DDD' (2000), meanwhile, found the kids keeping on keeping on. • **Covered:** ISIS (Bob Dylan) / ACCIDENT WAITING TO HAPPEN (Billy Bragg) / DOWN IN THE DESERT (Thin White Rope) / I FEEL LOVE (Donna Summer).

POSTER CHILDREN (cont)

Album rating: DAISYCHAIN REACTION (*7) / FLOWER PLOWER compilation (*5) / TOOL OF THE MAN (*5) / JUNIOR CITIZEN (*6) / RTFM (*6) / NEW WORLD RECORD (*6) / DDD (*5) / Salaryman: SALARYMAN (*6) / KAROSHI (*5)

RICK VALENTIN – vocals, guitar / **ROSE MARSHACK** – vocals, bass / **RICK McCOLLUM** – guitar / **BRENDAN GAMBLE + SHANNON DREW** – drums

		not iss.	Limited Potential
1987.	(c-ep) <none> **FLOWER PLOWER**	-	
	– Dangerous life / Wanna / Byron's song / Eye.		
1988.	(c) <none> **TOREADOR SQUAT**	-	
	– Hollywood / Modern art / Evidence / She walks / 10,000 pieces / Question / Non-reggae song / Detective Tracy / Bump bump / Jeremy Straight / Rain on me.		

— added **JEFF DIMPSEY** – guitar

		not iss.	Twin/Tone
Jul 90.	(cd/lp) <89205> **DAISYCHAIN REACTION**	-	
	– Dee / Cancer / If you see Kay / L-O-V-E / Freedom rock / Space gun / Water / Want it / Carver's / Chain reaction / Frustration / Where we live. <re-iss. 1991 on 'Reprise'; 26947> (UK-iss.Jul92 on 'Creation' cd/lp; CRE CD/LP 131)		

		not iss.	Sub Pop
Oct 90.	(7") <SP 88> **THINNER, STRONG. / POINTED STICK**	-	

		Clawfist	not iss.
Aug 91.	(ltd-7") (FIST 10) **DOWN IN THE DESERT. / Thin White Rope: EYE**		-

— **JIM VALENTIN** – guitar; repl. JEFF who joined HUM (McCOLLUM also departed)
— **JOHN HERNDON** – drums; repl. GAMBLE + DREW

		Creation	Sire-Reprise
Feb 93.	(12"ep)(cd-ep) (CRE 152T)(CRESCD 152) **CLOCK STREET / EVERYTHING BURNS. / MATTER CRUSH / OUTSIDE IN**		-
Mar 93.	(cd/lp) (CRE CD/LP 155) <45178> **TOOL OF THE MAN**		Nov92
	– Dynamite chair / Tommyhaus / In my way / Clock street / Redline / Shotguns & pickups / Blatant dis / Idiot show / Outside in / Three bullets.		

— **HOWIE KANTOFF** – drums; repl. HERNDON

		Sire-Reprise	Sire-Reprise
Mar 95.	(cd/c) <(9362 45737-2/-4)> **JUNIOR CITIZEN**		
	– Get a life / Junior citizen / He's my star / Revolution year zero / The drug I need / New boyfriend / Wide awake / King for a day / Mustaine / Downwind / One of us.		
Apr 95.	(cd/c) <45772> **JUST LIKE YOU EP**		-
	– Not like you / Sick of it all / Voight / What's inside the box / Uther / Just like you.		
Apr 97.	(cd/c) <9362 46567-2/-4> **RTFM**		-
	– Blackdog / Ofor 1 / Music of America / Dreamsmall / Speedoflight / King of the hill / 21st century / Attack! / Sleep / Pearlygates / Afterglow / Happenseveryday.		

		SpinArt	SpinArt
Feb 99.	(cd) <SRT 80069CD> **NEW WORLD RECORD**	-	
	– Accident waiting to happen / 6x6 / Time to kill / Ankh / Mr. Goodnight / Chemicals / Straightline / Planet Earth / Good cop bad cop / Secret handshake / Wait and see / Deadman. (UK-iss.Jun99; same as US)		
Jun 00.	(cd) <(SRT 80081CD)> **DDD**		Feb00
	– This town needs a fire / Strange attractors / Daisy changed / Zero stars / Time share / Rock and roll / Persimmon / Elf / The old school and the new / Judge freeball / Silhouette / Perfect product / Peck n' paw.		

– compilations, etc. –

Feb 92.	(cd/c) Frontier; <(34633-2/-4)> **FLOWER PLOWER** (first 2 cassettes)		Sep91
	(cd re-iss. Oct00 on 'Parasol'; TIN 015)		

SALARYMAN

— a pseudonym for the quartet **RICK, JIM, ROSE + HOWIE**

		City Slang	City Slang
Jul 97.	(cd/lp) <(efa 04996-2/-1)> **SALARYMAN**		Feb97
	– Rather / Inca picnic / Voids + superclusters / New centurions / Burning at the stake / I need a monkey / Hummous.		
Dec 97.	(12"ep) (08703-6) **VOIDS + SUPERCLUSTERS EP**		
	– Voids + superclusters / Foral clock / Tilo / Pull a tube.		
Oct 99.	(7") (08725-7) **GRAZE THE UMBRA. / SUBLUXATION**		
Oct 99.	(cd/lp) <(08715-2/-1)> **KAROSHI**		
	– Strong holder / The companion / Thomas Jefferson Airplane / My hands are always in water / Monterey days / Malibu nights / Dull normal / Graze the umbra / Taca muerte / My dog has fleas / Craters of the national moon / Karoshi.		

#POUNDSIGN#

Formed: Bay Area, San Francisco, California, USA … 1993 by English-born STEPHEN VESECKY, ALICIA VANDEN HUEVEL (also of THE AISLERS SET) and BECKY BARRON. The trio issued the sparkling uber-indie pop of 'WAVELENGTH' in 1998. A moderate album, full of floating harmonies and oh-so-mellow Casio keyboards, the group would later eclipse it with the inclusion of bassist JAIME KNIGHT and their sophomore set 'UNDERNEATH THE MARQUEE'. Issued on California's 'Fantastic' records in 2002, the set displayed a thematic lay-out and an otherworldly use of new instruments; pianos, sitars, horns and synths cropped up quite a bit. This new and mature direction (all the band members had their turn to sing on the record), prompted #POUNDSIGN# to tour the entire US, citing New Orleans as their favourite state. A batch of new songs is said to be on their way …

Album rating: WAVELENGTH (*5) / UNDERNEATH THE MARQUEE (*6)

STEPHEN VESECKY (b. England) – vocals, guitar, organ, synthesizer, sitar / **ALICIA VANDEN HEUVEL** (b. Arkansas) – vocals, guitar, bass, synthesizer (of AISLERS SET) / **BECKY BARRON** – drums, vocals, guitar (of SCRABBEL)

		not iss.	Small-Fi
1995.	(7") <#5> **DISASTER. / (split w/ POASTAL)**	-	-
		not iss.	Fantastic
1996.	(7"m; some colrd) <FAN 003> **THE ALMONDY MANY. / BUTTON / OUR NEW WAYS**	-	
Apr 97.	(7") <BEL 01> **MICHIGAN. / ROOFTOPS**	-	
	(above issued on 'Belmondo Discs')		
Apr 98.	(lp/cd) <FAN 008/+CD> **WAVELENGTH**	-	
	– Isolation / Da da da / Telephone / It's so hard / Sundried / You're on your own / Lou Gehrig / Walking and talking / Tiny / Carry on.		
—	in 1999, 'CHICKEN SOUP' featured on 'Motorway' 7" EP compilation, 'How Embarrassing To Dance Like That'		
Apr 99.	(7") <FAN 012> **THE WEDDING. / (other by The AISLERS SET)**	-	
—	added **JAIME KNIGHT** – bass, vocals, guitar		
2002.	(cd) <FAN 016> **UNDERNEATH THE MARQUEE**	-	
	– Matinee Sunday / Vitamin Dee / The best day / Sheila / Piano song / S.L.C. / I had a nightmare (and you were in it) / Coffee flavoured friend / Tears / It's easy / Oh! Dolly.		

PRAM

Formed: Birmingham, England … 1990 by ROSIE CUCKSTON, who soon found kindred spirits, SAM OWEN, MATTHEW EATON and MAX SIMPSON. Taking their inspiration from cult femme punks, the RAINCOATS and the SLITS, PRAM wheeled out their self-financed debut mini-set, 'GASH', an impressive minimalist outing that caught the ever attentive ear of 'Too Pure'. Filling out their sound as drummer ANDY GARRETT replaced MAX, PRAM employed an array of toy instruments against CUCKSTON's haunting vocal style to create a sinister childlike atmosphere that served as a backdrop for the trials and traumas hinted at in their dark lyrics. The quartet also experimented with rhythm and repetition in a similar way to the likes of STEREOLAB, all the component parts coming scarily together on 1993's 'IRON LUNG' EP. Later that year, they finally unleashed their first full-length set, 'THE STARS ARE SO BIG, THE EARTH IS SO SMALL … STAY AS YOU ARE', an album that further explored the boundaries between spooky ambience and neo Kraut-rock. Come the mid-90's, PRAM were mapping out similar abstract, avant-jazz terrain to the likes of TORTOISE, raking in underground credit for albums, 'HELIUM' (1994) and especially 'SARGASSO SEA' (1995). However, a near three-year break between albums saw the band lose a bit of momentum on 1998's comeback set, 'NORTH POLE RADIO STATION'. While long time fans may have been disappointed by the stylistic volte-face, this was a distinct opportunity for newcomers to acquaint themselves with a decidedly more accessible PRAM aesthetic. Gone was the abrasiveness of yore, replaced by a fluid, jazzy approach further developed on the 1999's mini-set, 'TELEMETRIC MELODIES' and the exquisite millennial album, 'THE MUSEUM OF IMAGINARY ANIMALS' (2000). Another EP, 2001's cleverly titled 'SOMNILOQUAY', let loose the likes of ANDY VOTEL and PLONE for an impressive remix venture.

Album rating: GASH mini (*5) / THE STARS ARE SO BIG, THE EARTH IS SO SMALL … STAY AS YOU ARE (*7) / HELIUM (*6) / SARGASSO SEA (*7) / NORTH POLE RADIO STATION (*6) / TELEMETRIC MELODIES mini (*5) / THE MUSEUM OF IMAGINARY ANIMALS (*7) / SOMNILOQUY mini (*5)

ROSIE CUCKSTON – vocals, theremin / **SAM OWEN** – bass / **MATT EATON** – multi / **MAX SIMPSON** – keyboards, sampler

		Howl	not iss.
Apr 91.	(m-cd) **GASH**		-
	– Dead piano / Flesh / Inmate's clothes / I'm a war / Pram / Dirty children / Blue singer / The day the animals turned on the cars / Gooswalk / Sunset international / Bleed. <US-iss.Mar97 on 'World Domination'; 56>		

— **ANDY GARRETT** – drums; repl. MAX

		Too Pure	American
Feb 93.	(12"ep/cd-ep) (PURE 17/+CD) **IRON LUNG EP**		-
	– Cumulus / Water toy / Blue singer / Iron lung (version).		
Sep 93.	(lp/cd) (PURE/+CD 26) **THE STARS ARE SO BIG, THE EARTH IS SO SMALL … STAY AS YOU ARE**		-
	– Loco / Radio freak in a storm / Loredo Venus / Milky / Dorothy / In dreams you too can fly / The ray / Cape St. Vincent.		
May 94.	(12"ep/cd-ep) (PURE 35/+CD) **MESHES EP**		-
	– Life in the clouds / Chrysalis / The legacy band of Venus.		
	(ltd.12"ep) (PURE 35LTD) – Life in the clouds (remixes).		
Jun 94.	(lp/cd) (PURE/+CD 41) <43012> **HELIUM**		Feb95
	– Gravity / Dancing on a star / Nightwatch / Things left on the pavement / Windy / My father the clown / Blue / Little angel, little monkey / Meshes in the afternoon / Shadows.		
Sep 95.	(lp/cd) (PURE/+CD 46) <43021> **SARGASSO SEA**		
	– Loose threads / Little scars / Earthling and protection / Cotton candy / Three wild Georges / Serpentine / Crystal tips / Crooked tiles / Eels / Sea swells and distant squalls.		

		Duophonic	not iss.
1996.	(cd-ep) (AE 004) **MUSIC FOR YOUR MOVIES**		-
	– Silver nitrate / Sea jungle / Carnival of souls / Eggshells.		

		not iss.	Wurlitzer Jukebox
1997.	(7") (WJ 10) **OMNICHORD. / 60 YEARS OF TELEPHONEY**		-
		Domino	Merge
Mar 98.	(cd/lp) (WIG CD/LP 049) **NORTH POLE RADIO STATION**		
	– Omnichord / Cinnabar / El Topo / Bathysphere / Fallen snow / The clockwork lighthouse / Sleepy sweet / Cow ghosts / The doors of empty cupboards.		
Aug 98.	(12"ep/cd-ep) (RUG 037 T/CD) **SLEEPY SWEET / VERSION. / CINNABAR (PCM version) / CARNIVAL OF SOULS GOES TO RIO**		-
Aug 98.	(7") (KOOKY 004) **THE LAST ASTRONAUT. / CINNABAR**		-
	(above issued on 'Kooky')		

Apr 99.	(12"/cd-s) *(RUG 084 T/CD)* **KEEP IN A DRY PLACE AND AWAY FROM CHILDREN. / SPACE SIREN / SPACE IRON**	-
May 99.	(m-cd/m-lp) *(WIG CD/LP 065)* **TELEMETRIC MELODIES**	

– The last astronaut / Space siren / 60 years of telephoney / Loose threads (mix) / Cinnabar (instrumental mix) / Omnichord / Superchouete / Loose threads.

—— added **STEVE PERKINS** – drums (ex-BROADCAST)

Jun 00.	(7"/cd-s) *(RUG 110/+CD)* **THE OWL SERVICE. / THE MERMAIDS' HOTEL (sub aquatic refrain)**	-
Aug 00.	(cd/lp) *(WIG CD/LP 080)* <MRG 184> **THE MUSEUM OF IMAGINARY ANIMALS**	Sep00

– The owl service / Bewitched / Mother of pearl / Narwhal / A history of ice / The mermaids' hotel / Cat's cradle / A million bubbles burst / Picture box / Play of the waves.

| Jul 01. | (m-cd/m-lp) *(WIG CD/LP 095)* **SOMNILOQUY** | - |

– Mother pf pearl / The way of the mongoose / Monkeypuzzle / A clock without hands / Bewitched (Plone mix) / Play of the waves (balky mule mix) / Omnichord (Terry: funken mix) / The last astronaut (Andy Votel mix) / A million bubbles burst (Sir real mix).

—— PRAM are about to return with a new set in Jan'03, 'DARK ISLAND'

Sam PREKOP (see under ⇒ SEA AND CAKE)

PRESTON SCHOOL OF INDUSTRY

Formed: California, USA ... 2000 by ex-PAVEMENT guitarist SPIRAL STAIRS (aka SCOTT KANNBERG). After the hard slog that was PAVEMENT's 'Terror Twilight', KANNBERG and the rest of the group decided to call it a day (leader MALKMUS embarked on a solo career), with the estranged guitarist forming The PRESTON SCHOOL OF INDUSTRY). He recruited TOM WAITS and MOORE BROTHERS rhythm section ANDREW BORGER and JON ERICKSON with the trio signing to 'Matador' and issuing 'ALL THIS SOUNDS GAS' (2001). A simple, stark but beautiful album, the sheer quality of tracks on this set would make one wonder about the songwriting credentials within the PAVEMENT set. Interestingly enough, KANNBERG claimed that the songs featured on the album were orignally intended for 'Terror Twilight', but were harshly rejected by MALKMUS.

Album rating: ALL THIS SOUNDS GAS (*6)

SPIRAL STAIRS (b. SCOTT KANNBERG) – vocals, guitar (ex-PAVEMENT) / **JON ERICKSON** – bass (of MOORE BROTHERS) / **ANDREW BORGER** – drums

		Amazing Grease	Amazing Grease
Jul 01.	(cd-ep) <*(AG 12)*> **GOODBYE TO THE EDGE CITY**		

– Somethings happen always / Now to impress the goddess (part 2) / Spaces in between / Where you gonna go / Goodbye to the edge city. *(10"ep-iss.Oct01; AGV 12)*

		Domino	Matador
Jul 01.	(7") *(RUG 127)* **WHALEBONES. / MOST COMMON METHOD**		-

(cd-s) (RUG 127CD) – ('A'side) / To squash it for good / Imperial.

Aug 01.	(cd/lp) *(WIG CD/LP 096)* <OLE 520> **ALL THIS SOUNDS GAS**		

– Whalebones / Falling away / A treasure @ Silver Bank (this dynasty's for real) / Encyclopedia knowledge of / History of the river / Doping for gold / Solitaire / Blu son / Monkey heart and the horses' leg / The idea of fires / Take a stand – All this sounds gas. *(lp+=)* – Walls of grain / Suddenly stable.

| Oct 01. | (7") *(RUG 131)* **FALLING AWAY. / ANYTHING CAN HAPPEN** | | - |

(cd-s) (RUG 131CD) – ('A'side) / I've done nothing wrong / Toff.

Archer PREWITT (see under ⇒ COCTAILS)

PRISONSHAKE

Formed: Cleveland, Ohio, USA ... 1987 by DOUG ENKLER and ROBERT GRIFFIN, the latter founding his own fanzine which eventually evolved into a bonafide indie record label, 'Scat'. A series of Stateside 7"ers and two albums ensued over the course of the early 90's, one of these albums, 'FAILED TO MENACE', finally surfacing on 'Matador' as their UK debut. The band's US debut 'THE ROARING THIRD', appeared later that year, although it seems PRISONSHAKE have gone on extended parole since then. • Covered: EISBAER (Grauzone).

Album rating: THE ROARING THIRD (*6) / FAILED TO MENACE (*6)

DOUG ENKLER – vocals (ex-OFFBEATS) / **ROBERT GRIFFIN** – guitar / **CHRIS BURGESS** – bass / **SCOTT PICKERING** – drums, mandolin

		not iss.	Scat
Jan 89.	(c) <*scat A*> **11 SONG DEMO**	-	
Jan 89.	(c) <*scat B*> **LIVE**	-	
Jan 89.	(7") <*scat one*> **DEANNA. / SHOOK LIKE ROSES**	-	
Oct 89.	(4x7"box) <*scat three*> **SINGLES '87-'89**	-	
Apr 90.	(7") <*scat six*> **I'M REALLY FUCKED NOW. / (other by MY DAD IS DEAD)**	-	
Nov 90.	(7"+mag) <*scat 11*> **ALMOST CHRISTMAS**	-	
Jan 91.	(7") <*scat 12*> **THEN SHE PRAYED. / LITTLE PINK RIBBONS** (above issued on 'Rubber', below 'Sympathy For The Record Industry')	-	
1991.	(7"m) <*SFTRI 124*> **SOMEONE ELSE'S CAR. / (+2)**	-	
Oct 91.	(10"ep/cd-ep) <*scat 23*> **DELLA STREET**	-	

– Molly / From down here / London – Stuck in St. Louis, 1985.

Nov 91.	(7") <*scat 24*> **split w/ MY DAD IS DEAD**	-	

—— **BARRY BRANHAM** – bass + **TIM TOBIAS** – guitar; repl. rhythm

Mar 93.	(7"m) <*scat 30*> **2 SISTERS. / EISBAER / (+1)** *(UK-iss.Nov94 on 'Shake'; SAL 206)*	-	
Nov 93.	(lp/cd) <*scat 33*> **THE ROARING THIRD**	-	

– Kick up yer heels / Carthage burns! / Hurry / 2 sisters / Precious / Cigarette day / Quits / Always almost there / Asiento / Irene / Seemed a brilliant idea. *(UK-iss.Nov94 on 'Shake' lp/cd; SALD 209/+CD)*

		Matador	Matador
Jul 94.	(cd) <(OLE 085-2)> **FAILED TO MENACE**		

– Last time I looked / Either way evil eye / A brilliant idea / Ever and ever / Some chick you fucked / Stumble / Asiento / Cigarette day / (Not without) Grace / Nothing has to hurt / Humor.

		not iss.	Carcrashh
Apr 96.	(7") <*crashh 07*> **JIMJIMMYJIMJIM. / IGNITION** (above recorded 1994)	-	

		not iss.	Wabana
1997.	(7"m) <*ore 11*> **FUCK YOUR SELF ESTEEM. / (+2)**	-	

—— they have now disbanded

PROJECT (see under ⇒ UNREST)

PROLAPSE

Formed: Leicester, England ... 1991 by Scotsman MICK DERRICK and LINDA STEELYARD, who soon expanded the unit to a sextet/septet with the addition of DAVE JEFFREYS, PAT MARSDEN, DONALD ROSS-SKINNER, MICK HARRISON and TIM PATTISON. Having met during a drinking binge, the band played some initial shows in Hanover (or is it hangover?!), Germany, before signing to 'Cherry Red' and debuting with a JOHN ROBB-produced EP, 'CRATE' early in '94. An album, 'POINTLESS WALKS TO DISMAL PLACES', followed later in the year, a THROBBING GRISTLE/NME C-86! industrial guitar-mangling hybrid. Follow-up album, 'BACKSATURDAY' was notable for its 15-minute epic track, 'FLEX', a must hear for any 'Kraut-rock' fan. In 1997, after tours supporting PULP and STEREOLAB, PROLAPSE signed to Warner Brothers affiliated label, 'Radarscope', offering up their most accessible noisefest to date, 'THE ITALIAN FLAG'. Towards the end of the 90's, MICK turned up as guest of MOROCCO, on the 'Guided Missile' single, 'New Javelins'. A fourth long-player, 'GHOSTS OF DEAD AEROPLANES' saw them sign off for good. • **Covered:** LOVE LIKE ANTHRAX (Gang Of Four) / DIAMONDS O' MONTE CARLO (Gorky's Zygotic Mynci).

Album rating: POINTLESS WALKS TO DISMAL PLACES (*6) / BACKSATURDAY mini (*6) / THE ITALIAN FLAG (*7) / GHOSTS OF DEAD AEROPLANES (*5)

MICK DERRICK (b. Glasgow, Scotland) – vocals / **LINDA STEELYARD** – vocals / **DAVE JEFFREYS** – guitar / **PAT MARSDEN** – guitar / **DONALD ROSS-SKINNER** – keyboards / **MICK HARRISON** – bass / **TIM PATTISON** – drums

		Cherry Red	not iss.
Jan 94.	(7"ep) *(CHERRY 128)* **THE PROLAPSE 'CRATE' EP**		-

– Psychotic now / p.d.f. (Pete de Freitas) / Screws / Kilometrica banca.

Jun 94.	(cd-ep) *(CDCHERRY 133)* **PULL THRU BARKER: SONGS FOR GRANDPOPS MANTERFIELD**		-

– Pull thru Barker / Dirge / They slept in darkness / E.O.P.O. (end of part one).

Sep 94.	(7") *(CHERRY 135)* **DOORSTEP RHYTHMIC BLOC. / PILE TENT**		-

(cd-s+=) (CDCHERRY 135) – Muscovite parricide song / ('A'-concise version).

Oct 94.	(cd) *(CDBRED 116)* **POINTLESS WALKS TO DISMAL PLACES**		-

– Serpico (theme) / Headless in a beat motel / Surreal Madrid / Doorstep rhythmic bioc / Burgundy spine / Black death ambulance / Chili blown / Hungarian suicide song / Tina this is Matthew Stone. *(re-iss. Nov97; same)*

Dec 94.	(7") *(CHERRY 136)* **WHEN SPACE INVADERS WERE BIG. / LOVE LIKE ANTHRAX**		-

		Love Train	not iss.
Oct 95.	(7") *(PUBE 06)* **T.C.R. / IRRITATING RADIATOR**		-

		Lissys	Big Cat
Dec 95.	(m-lp/m-cd) *(LISS 8/+CD)* <1> **BACKSATURDAY**		Apr96

– Mein minefield, mine landmind / T.C.R. / Framen Fr. Cesar / Every night I'm mentally crucified / Zen nun deb / Irritating radiator / Drown radio therapy / Flexed / Strain contortion of bag. *(lp re-iss. Feb99; same)*

		Radarscope	Radarscope
Apr 97.	(7") *(scan 24)* **KILLING THE BLAND. / MOVE TO LIMIT SLABS**		-

(7"/cd-s+=) (scan x/cs 24) – Snappy horse / Fear of teeth.

Sep 97.	(7") *(scan 26)* **AUTOCADE. / TESTATION**		-

(7") (scan 26x) – ('A'-Didactic feral control) / Pro-loop.
(cd-s) (scancs 26) – (all 4).

Oct 97.	(cd/d-lp) <*scan cd/lp 25*> **THE ITALIAN FLAG**		

– Slash / Deanshanger / Cacophony No.A / Killing the bland / I hate the clicking man / Autocade / Tunguska / Flat velocity curve / Return of shoes / Day at death seaside / Bruxelles / Visa for Violet and Van / Three wooden heads.

Mar 98.	(7") *(scan 27)* **DEANSHANGER. / LIQUID COMPLIMENT**		-

(cd-s+=) (scancs 27) – Diamonds o' Monte Carlo / Deanshanger (Carlo Rama remix).

		Lissys	not iss.
Feb 99.	(12") *(LISS 17)* **FLEXED. / UNROADKILL**		-

		Cooking Vinyl	Cooking Vinyl
Apr 99.	(7") *(FRY 081)* **FOB.COM. / MARCONI'S WIFE**		-

(cd-s+=) (FRYCD 081) – Hairdryer.

May 99.	(lp/cd) *(COOK/+CD 177)* **GHOSTS OF DEAD AEROPLANES**		

– Essence of Cessna / Fob.com / Adiabatic / Cylinders v12 beats cylinders 8 / One illness / After after / Government of Spain / Planned obsolescence.

—— after they split, HARRISON formed EARS GO FFF!

CHA CHA 2000

MICK DERRICK + PAT MARSDEN with guests incl. **MARK HIBBETT, RUTH PO + JOCK SUPEREIGHT**

                                                                    Flighted
                                                                    Miskick   not iss.
Oct 97. (7") <FLICK 002> **TIRED LEGS AT THE END OF THE GAME. / Trout: GREEN AND WHITE**
(above was a tribute to Celtic F.C.)

                                                                    Lissy's   not iss.
Feb 99. (10"ep) (liss 3) **AUTOBAHN**
– Autobahn / Theme from Cha Cha 2000 / John Cage Barleycorn.

PROMISE RING

Formed: Milwaukee, Winsconsin, USA ... early 1995 by former CAP'N JAZZ frontman, DAVEY VONBOHLEN, along with JASON GNEWIKOW, SCOTT BESCHTA and DAN DIDIER (the latter two stemming from local acts, CEILISHRINE and NONE LEFT STANDING). Having secured a deal with 'Jade' records, the band released their debut EP, 'FALSETTO KEEPS TIME', in 1996. It was a confident and mature record filled with achingly sentimental pop songs played with infectious, boisterous, energy. In the same year, the group delivered their first full-length album 'THIRTY DEGREES EVERYWHERE' and proved their earlier EP was no fluke. The following year saw the release of singles compilation 'HORSE LATITUDES' and another album 'NOTHING FEELS GOOD'. With BESCHTA assuming most of the writing duties for The PROMISE RING, VONBOHLEN and DIDIER, along with PELE guitarist CHRIS ROSEANAU, started the side-project VERMONT as an outlet for their creativity. VERMONT'S debut album, 'LIVING TOGETHER' (1999), was less accessible than the music of The PROMISE RING, however repeat listening reveals it to be a tender and emotive record. VONBOHLEN and DIDIER flirted between the two groups, issuing PROMISE RING albums 'VERY EMERGENCY' (1999) and 'WOOD/ WATER' (2002) as well as 'CALLING ALBANY' by VERMONT (also in 2002).

Album rating: 30 DEGREES EVERYWHERE (*7) / THE HORSE LATITUDES part compilation (*6) / NOTHING FEELS GOOD (*6) / VERY EMERGENCY (*5) / WOOD – WATER (*5) / Vermont: LIVING TOGETHER (*6) / CALLING ALBANY (*5)

DAVEY VONBOHLEN – vocals, guitar (ex-CAP'N JAZZ) / **JASON GNEWIKOW** – guitar / **SCOTT BESCHTA** – bass / **DAN DIDIER** – drums

                                                                    not iss.   Foresight
May 93. (7") (HIP 7011) **WATERTOWN PLANK. / MINERAL POINT**
(UK-iss.Jul96 on 'Hipster'; HIP 7011)

                                                                    Jade Tree Jade Tree
Feb 96. (7"ep) <JT 1023> **FALSETTO KEEPS TIME EP**
– A picture postcard / Saturday / Scenes from Parisian life. (UK-iss.Jul00; same)
May 96. (7") <JT 1024> **E. TEXAS AVE. / (other by TEXAS IS THE REASON)**
(UK-iss.Jul00; same)
Sep 96. (lp/cd) <JT 1026/+CD> **30 DEGREES EVERYWHERE**
– Everywhere in Denver / Red paint / Heart of a broken story / Scenes from France / Anne you will sing / My firetower flame / Between Pacific coasts / A picture postcard / Somebody's done for / The sea of Cortez / Run down the waterfall / We don't like romance (instrumental). (UK-iss.Jul00; same)
Feb 97. (cd) <JT 1031> **THE HORSE LATITUDES** (part compilation)
– Watertown plank / Mineral point / A picture postcard / Saturday / Scenes from Parisian life / E. Texas Ave. / Miette / I never trusted the Russians.
Oct 97. (cd) <(JT 1035CD)> **NOTHING FEELS GOOD**
– Is this thing on? / Perfect lines / Red & blue jeans / Why did we ever meet / Make me a chevy / How nothing feels / A broken tenor / Raspberry rush / Nothing feels good / Pink chimneys / B is for Bethlehem / Forget me. (lp-iss.Jan98; JT 1035)

—— **SCOTT** now had an alternative surname: **SCHOENBECK**

Dec 98. (7"ep/cd-ep) <(JT 1040/+CD)> **BOYS AND GIRLS EP**   Oct98
– Tell everyone we're dead / Best looking boys / American girl.
Oct 99. (lp/cd) <(JT 1043/+CD)> **VERY EMERGENCY**   Sep99
– Happiness is all the rage / Emergency! emergency! / The deep south / Happy hour / Things just getting good / Living around / Jersey shore / Skips a beat (over you) / Arms & danger / All of my everythings.
May 00. (cd-ep) <JT 1048CD> **ELECTRIC PINK**
– Electric pink / Strictly television / American T.V. (V.01) (version one) / Make me a mix tape. (re-iss.Jun00 on 'Burning Heart'; BHR 109S)
                                                                    Anti   Anti
May 02. (cd) <8 6617-2)> **WOOD / WATER**   Apr02
– Size of your life / Stop playing guitar / Suffer never / Become one anything one time / Wake up April / Get on the floor / Half year sun / My life is at home / Letters to the far reaches / Bread and coffee / Say goodbye good / Feed the night. (10"lp on 'Foreign Leisure'; FORLE 001)
Jun 02. (7") (1068-7) **STOP PLAYING GUITAR. / YOU ONLY TELL ME YOU LOVE ME WHEN YOU'RE DRUNK**
(cd-s) (1068-2) – ('A'side) / All good souls / ('A'-album mix).

—— The PROMISE RING disbanded in October 2002

VERMONT

VONBOHLEN + DIDIER / + CHRIS ROSEANAU – guitar (of PELE)

                                                                    not iss.   unknown
1999. (7") **WE ONLY HAVE EACH OTHER IN THE NIGHT. / (other by IDA)**

                                                                    Kindercore Kindercore
Aug 99. (cd) <(KC 032)> **LIVING TOGETHER**
– Indiana Jones / Lightning tattoos / Broadway Joe / Where planes go down / Bee, leave me be / Tiny white crosses / Downtown heart / Old blue / My favorite legend / These dudes, they got a hand.
Feb 01. (cd-ep; split w/ CENTRO-MATIC) <006> **OPPORTUNITY**
– (3 by CENTRO-MATIC) / Lil' blonde hairs / What to do / Say something – 95 frowns.
(above issued on 'Quality Park')
Apr 02. (cd) <(KC 067)> **CALLING ALBANY**   Jan02
– Bells of saint alcohol / Chlorine chlorine / Ballad of Larry Bird / Stop sending me gas and electricity – Calling Jeus, call my mother / Where the wild drums are / Hello-goodbye sex / Screw-on shoes / Kill an hour / Arrest Harrison Ford! / The world doesn't ask you / Commodores 64 / I'd be happy as the world turning around you.

PSYCHED UP JANIS

Formed: Copenhagen, Denmark ... late 1989 by Sonderborg-raised SUNE and JAKOB. They relocated to Brighton, England after being signed up by producer, Craig Leon, the man obviously impressed to see them carrying on after the ceiling caved in at a Copenhagen gig in 1994. By this time, the trio (who had added drummer, MARTIN) had already released their self-financed Scandinavian-only debut EP, 'I DIED IN MY TEENS', a trippy sonic-country affair with similarities to HOLE, although lyrically way out. They had also signed to Swedish label, 'Metrognome-Replay', which released their LEON-produced debut album, 'SWELL', its worldwide critical success prompting a UK deal in 1995 with Island off-shoot, 'This Way Up'. The band made their British debut with the 'VANITY' EP early the following year, previewing the re-release of both the single, 'I DIED IN MY TEENS' and album 'SWELL'.

Album rating: SWELL (*7)

SUNE – vocals, guitar / **JAKOB** – bass / **MARTIN** – drums

                                                                    This Way
                                                                    Up   not iss.
Jan 96. (10"ep/cd-ep) (WAY 4688/4633) **VANITY EP**
– Vanity / Modest us / Punk song (live) / Flabbergaster (live).
Mar 96. (7") (WAY 4711) **I DIED IN MY TEENS. / SHOOT THE BREEZE**
(cd-s+=) (WAY 4733) – Dense high.
Mar 96. (cd/c/d-lp) (532031-2/-4/-1) **SWELL**
– Vanity / I died in my teens / Shudder / Modest us / Subsonic why / Swirl like you / Chandelier / Dead green summer / Reddening star / New 5 / They / Fragments.

—— (all above issued on Swedish 'Metrognome-Replay' a few years earlier)

PSYCLONE RANGERS

Formed: Allentown, Pennsylvania, USA ... 1992 by JONATHAN VALANIA, who recruited SCOTT DANTZER, MICHAEL VALLONE and RACE BANNON. One of the first signings to DAVE ALLEN's (ex-GANG OF FOUR) label, 'World Domination', the PSYCLONE RANGERS stormed on to the scene with 1994's 'FEEL NICE' set, featuring a reading of Jonathan Richman's 'I'M STRAIGHT'. As the name might suggest, the band's sound conjured up images of rural America's seedy underbelly, akin to a more updated, swamptrash CREEDENCE CLEARWATER REVIVAL (whose 'EFFIGY' they subsequently covered). A year later, the 'RANGERS posse were back in town for a follow-up Ian Caple-produced collection, 'THE DEVIL MAY CARE'. A third set, 'BEATIN' ON THE BAT POLE' (1996), confirmed their credentials as the 90's version of The GUN CLUB. • **Covered:** HONEY CUMS HOME (Eddie Pus) / BAD SEEDS (Beat Happening).

Album rating: FEEL NICE (*6) / THE DEVIL MAY CARE (*6) / BEATIN' ON THE BAT POLE (*6)

JONATHAN VALANIA – vocals / **SCOTT DANTZER** – guitar, vocals / **MICHAEL VALLONE** – bass / **RACE BANNON** – drums

                                                                    not iss.   Sympathy F
Mar 94. (7"ep) <SFTRI 264> **SWING, BABY, SWING EP**
– I want to be Jack Kennedy / Honey cums home / Bad seeds.
                                                                    World   World
                                                                    Domination Domination
May 94. (7"ep/cd-ep) <(WDOM 001/2 S/+CD)> **CHRISTIE INDECISION / I WANNA BE JACK KENNEDY. / BAD SEEDS / C.I.A.**
May 94. (lp/cd) <(WDOM 005/+CD)> **FEEL NICE**
– I wanna be Jack Kennedy / Spinnin' my head / Christie indecision / I feel nice / The hate noise / Stephen / Heaven / Riot girl / Bigger than a gun / Devil's down there / Perfect engine / You're not Edie Sedgewick.
Apr 95. (cd) <(WDOM 015CD)> **THE DEVIL MAY CARE**
– Deal / Ain't goin' down / Firenze / Tilt-a-whirl / Boyo / The awe song / Ehy the hell did I die? / I'm straight / Dejesus / Nazi mother / Dr. Softness / Mono town.

—— **DAN McKINNEY** – organ + **P.R. BEHLER** – bass; repl. VALLONE

May 96. (7") <(WDOM 25S)> **LITTLE MAN WITH A GUN IN HIS HAND. /**
Jul 96. (cd/lp) <(WDOM 036-2/-1)> **BEATIN' ON THE BAT POLE**
– Fuel city! / (Can you feel the) Kingdom comin' / Little man with a gun in his hand / For the sake of Ivy / Meth carnival / Tim, are you home?

PULLMAN

Formed: Chicago, Illinois, USA ... by seasoned alternative/Lo-Fi campaigners, CHRIS BROKAW (of COME), CURTIS HARVEY (of REX), DOUG McCOMBS (of TORTOISE and ELEVENTH DREAM DAY) and BUNDY K BROWN (of TORTOISE and DIRECTIONS IN MUSIC). Taking influences from such acoustic "folk" artists as JOHN FAHEY, NICK DRAKE and RY COODER, the supergroup of sorts delivered a much talked about debut set, 'TURNSTYLES & JUNKPILES', in 1998. Entirely instrumental, the album's atmospheric, textured guitar highlights included 'GRAVENHURST', penned by another former TORTOISE cohort, DAVID PAJO (now of AERIAL-M). A follow-up eventually surfaced in the form of 'VIEWFINDER' (2001) and while the major reference point was still concentrated, JOHN FAHEY-style, acoustic-based contructions, the additions of drums (courtesy of newcomer TIM BARNES) and selected electric instrumentation not altering the overall approach to any great extent.

Album rating: TURNSTYLES & JUNKPILES (*6) / VIEWFINDER (*7)

CHRIS BROKAW – guitars, percussion / **CURTIS HARVEY** – guitars, strings / **BUNDY K BROWN** (b. KEN) – guitar, bass / **DOUG McCOMBS** – bass

			Thrill Jockey	Thrill Jockey
Aug 98.	(lp/cd) <(THRILL 055/+CD)>	**TURNSTYLES & JUNKPILES**		

– To hold down a shadow / Barefoot / In a box, under the bed / Sagamore bridge / Gravenhurst / Lyasnya / Two parts water / Beacon and Kent / Deer hill / So breaks yesterday / Fullerton / Sunday morning traffic / Tall grass / With hands.

— added **TIM BARNES** – percussion, drums

Aug 01.	(cd/d-lp) <(THRILL 090/+LP)>	**VIEWFINDER**		

– Same grain with new wood / DElta one / Or, otherwise / Forty fingers / F.L.T. / Hatah / Isla Mujeres / Chicken smoked blanket / Bookends / Felucca / Quantum mechanic / Narrow canyon / Street light / Wire and one good shoe / Brewster road.

PULSARS

Formed: Chicago, Illinois, USA ... early 90's by DAVID TRUMFIO and his brother HARRY, both fuelled by electronic pop and indie music of the 80's – think DEPECHE MODE and The JESUS & MARY CHAIN. With several independent singles behind them, the pair signed to 'Almo Sounds' records and came up with the EP, 'SUBMISSION TO THE MASTERS' in 1996 and their eponymous album the following year. DAVID subsequently produced a number of highly-rated "indie" people including TAKAKO MINEKAWA.

Album rating: PULSARS (*6)

DAVID TRUMFIO – vocals, electronics / **HARRY TRUMFIO** – drums / + a plethora of session people

			not iss.	Sweet Pea
1995.	(7"ep) <SP 009>	**TEENAGE NITES**	–	

– Owed to a devil / 153 drive-in / Silicon teens / Teenage nites.

			Almo Sounds	Almo Sounds
Oct 96.	(cd-ep) <AMSDM 88002>	**SUBMISSION TO THE MASTERS**		

– Submission song / Chicago swingers / Cast iron dog / Owed to a devil / Das lifeboat.

Mar 97.	(cd) <AMSD 80011>	**PULSARS**		–

– Count off / Wisconsin / Tunnel song / Suffocation / Owed to a devil / Technology / Machine talk / Silicon teens / Save you / Lucky day (part 1) / Lucky day (part 2) / My pet robot / Runway / Submission song / Tales from tomorrow / Das lifeboat. (UK-iss.Sep98; ALMCD 58)

Jun 98.	(cd-s) (CDALM 53)	**SUFFOCATION / INLAND EMPIRE / LOGO**		

			not iss.	Pioneer
Dec 98.	(cd-ep) <PICP 3018>	**INLAND EMPIRE EP**	–	– Japan

– Romp & frolic / Inland empire / Logo / Perfect / The freeze / Suffocation (remix).

— the TRUMFIO brothers went into production work

PUNCH WAGON (see under ⇒ SUPERDRAG)

PUPPY LOVE BOMB (see under ⇒ HORMONES)

PURE MORNING (see under ⇒ CLINIC)

PURESSENCE

Formed: Oldham, Lancashire, England ... May '92 by JAMES MUDRICZKI, NEIL McDonald, KEVIN MATTHEWS and TONY SZUMINSKI. Inspired by, or even idolising the STONE ROSES after their legendary 1990 Spike Island concert, PURESSENCE embarked on their own creative sojourn. In the summer of '92, their first of three singles over the course of the following year, the 'PETROL SKIN' EP, was issued by Northern imprint, '2 Damn Loud'. However, it wasn't until Island's Toby Chalmers took control, that the band's indie-rock direction started to take shape. In 1995, signed to the aforementioned major, PURESSENCE found a larger fanbase with the much-improved 'I SUPPOSE' 45, having also supported MARION on tour. An eponymous debut set was in the shops by '96, although the track 'CASTING LAZY SHADOWS', should really have fared better when released as an accompanying single. However, the quartet finally made their long-awaited chart breakthrough when the track, 'THIS FEELING', burst into the UK Top 40 in 1998. Although the JOY DIVISION/MORRISSEY-laden, 'IT DOESN'T MATTER ANYMORE', just failed to do a similar feat, their second album, 'ONLY FOREVER', notched up sufficient sales. The high-pitched singer, JAMES, subsequently landed a bit part in the movie, 'Molly's Idle Ways', which starred SHAUN RYDER (of BLACK GRAPE), while the long-struggling PURESSENCE were happening big time in the Mediterranean sunspots of Greece and Israel. After an extended lay-off, the Manchester bombast merchants returned in 2002 with the 'PLANET HELPLESS' album. The strident feel of their previous work remained although they'd managed to shake off their reliance on more overt influences, taking more sonic risks than before and achieving the same effect even when taking their foot off the gas.

Album rating: PURESSENCE (*7) / ONLY FOREVER (*6) / PLANET HELPLESS (*5)

JAMES MUDRICZKI – vocals / **NEIL McDONALD** – guitar / **KEVIN MATTHEWS** – bass / **TONY SZUMINSKI** – drums

			Rough Trade	not iss.
Jun 92.	(7") (45rev 9)	**SIAMESE. / SCAPA FLOW**		–

			2 Damn Loud	not iss.
Jul 92.	(12"ep) (2DM 01)	**PETROL SKIN EP**		–

– Telekenesis / Suck the knife / Polystyrene snow / Petrol skin.

			Island	Island
Apr 93.	(12"/cd-s) (2DM/+CD 02)	**OFFSHORE. / NONE HANDED (demo) / MIST**		–
May 95.	(12"/cd-s) (12IS/CID 612)	**I SUPPOSE. / LET IT ALL GO / FREE FALL**		–
Nov 95.	(7") (IS 619)	**FIRE. / YOU'RE ONLY TRYING TO TWIST MY ARM**		–

(cd-s+=) (CID 619) – Allstar.

Apr 96.	(7") (IS 624)	**INDIA. / GUTTER GIRL**		–

(7"g-f) (ISG 624) – ('A'-cut 2) / LET DOWN
(cd-s+=) (CID 624) – Let down.

Apr 96.	(cd/c/lp) (CID/ICT/ILPS 8046) <524194>	**PURESSENCE**		–

– Near distance / I suppose / Mr. Brown / Understanding / Fire / Traffic jam in memory lane / Casting lazy shadows / You're only trying to twist my arm / Every house on every street / India.

Jun 96.	(7"/c-s) (ISG/CIS 639)	**TRAFFIC JAM IN MEMORY LANE. / DIFFERENT SAND**		–

(cd-s+=) (CID 639) – Sick of waiting.

Aug 96.	(7"/c-s) (IS/CIS 641)	**CASTING LAZY SHADOWS. / FIFTEEN YEARS**		–

(cd-s+=) (CID 641) – Half the way you were.

May 98.	(7") (IS 688)	**THIS FEELING. / THINK OF THE TIMES**	33	–

(cd-s+=) (CID 688) – Walk on by.
(cd-s) (CIDX 688) – ('A'side) / Near distance (demo) / Northern framing company (demo) / London in the rain.

Jul 98.	(7"/cd-s) (IS 703)	**IT DOESN'T MATTER ANYMORE. / ANOTHER DAY ANOTHER NIGHT / TAKE A RIDE**	47	–

(cd-s) (CIDX 703) – ('A'side) / Drone / Deathtrap.

Aug 98.	(cd/c/lp) (CID/ICT/ILPS 8064) <524478>	**ONLY FOREVER**	36	–

– Sharpen up the knives / This feeling / It doesn't matter anymore / Street lights / Standing in your shadow / All I want / Behind the man / Never be the same again / Hey hey I'm down / Past believing / Turn the lights out when I die / Gazing down.

Nov 98.	(7") (IS 722)	**ALL I WANT. / TURN THE LIGHTS (demo)**	39	–

(cd-s) (CID 722) – ('A'side) / Along the sure / This feeling.
(cd-s) (CIDX 722) – ('A'side) / Never be the same again / All I want (acoustic) / Casting lazy shadows (acoustic).

			Island	Universal
Sep 02.	(7") (IS 803)	**WALKING DEAD. / WALKING DEAD (instrumental)**	40	–

(cd-s) (CID 803) – ('A'side) / Moss Side lonely / Ironstone Izadora (Echoboy mix).
(cd-s) (CIDX 803) – ('A'side) / Only holy maybe / Emotion.

Oct 02.	(cd) (CID 8124) <63328>	**PLANET HELPLESS**		Dec02

– Walking dead / Prodigal son / How does it feel? / Analgesic love song / She's gotten over you / Make time / Planet helpless / Ironstone Izadora / You move me / Comfort when you smile / Stranger / Heart of gold / Throw me a line.

PUSHERMAN

Formed: London, England ... 1994 out of baggy crusties, $KAW by Anglo-American six-piece of ANDY FRANK and YANK, who enlisted MARTIN HOYLAND, TONY ANTONIO, HARRY HARRISON and BO ELLERY. Taken under the wing of OASIS manager, Marcus Russell and signed to 'Ignition' ('Sony' in the States), PUSHERMAN were groomed for alternative crossover stardom with a series of support slots with the VERVE. Late in '95, the groovy punk/funk posse delivered their debut EP, 'FIRST TIME', followed over the course of the ensuing year by a further batch of singles culminating with a debut long-player, 'FLOORED' (1996).

Album rating: FLOORED (*6)

ANDY FRANK – vocals / **YANK** – vocals, harmonica / **MARTIN HOYLAND** – guitar / **TONY ANTONIO** – guitar / **HARRY HARRISON** – drums / **BO ELLERY** – bass

			Ignition	Sony
Nov 95.	(12"ep/cd-ep) (IGN TVE/CDE 1)	**FIRST TIME EP**		–

– First time / Touch me / The aim indeed (live).

Mar 96.	(12"/cd-s) (IGN TV/SCD 7)	**SHOW ME SLOWLY. / 95% / FIRST TIME (live)**		–
May 96.	(7") (IGN 8)	**CHASE IT. / FAST CARS ARE DANGEROUS**		–

(cd-s+=) (IGNSCD 8) – Lonely road.

Sep 96.	(7") (IGN 10)	**THE AIM INDEED. / GET OFF MY DAY**		–

(cd-s+=) (IGNSCD 10) – It's just you.

Sep 96.	(cd/c/d-lp) (IGN CD/MC/LP 1) <67752>	**FLOORED**		

– Chase it / Sold / The aim indeed / So long ago / First time / Whole / Never coming back / Cos I lied / Show me slowly / Floored.

PUSH KINGS

Formed: Boston, Massachusetts, USA . . . mid 90's by brothers CARRICK MOORE GERETY and FINN MOORE, along with drummer MATT FISHBECK and bassist DAVID BENJAMIN. The group released a couple of PAVEMENT-influenced lo-fi pop rock singles before, in an apparent attempt to avoid being lost in the sea of bands doing the same thing, adopting a much more radio friendly approach. The group released their self-titled debut in 1997 and although they clearly had a knack for producing sweet melodies, the middle-of-the-road sound failed to capture the imagination. The equally banal mini album 'BLOWIN' UP' followed the same year before the band finally tried to ruffle some feathers with the 1998 full-length 'FAR PLACES'. This time the band included drum loops, scratching and breakbeats and suddenly they no longer sounded as though they were making music that your dad would buy. The band grew increasingly experimental with the 2000 release 'THE PUSH KINGS' (a mini-CD on 'Rebbel' records) and 'FEEL NO FADE' the following year. On both of these albums the band occasionally bite off more than they can chew – however it was good to see that they were trying.

Album rating: PUSH KINGS (*7) / BLOWIN' UP! mini (*5) / FAR PLACES (*7) / CRIME IN ACETATE: 1995-1997 compilation (*6) / THE PUSH KINGS mini (*3) / FEEL NO FADE (*3)

CARRICK MOORE GERETY – vocals, guitar / **FINN MOORE GERETY** – vocals, guitar / **DAVID BENJAMIN** – bass / **MATT FISHBECK** – drums

		not iss.	Chunk
1995.	(7") <CH45 15> **SLOW DOWN. / THIS IS NOT MONTE CARLO.** /		

		not iss.	Sealed Fate
1996.	(7") <SFR 001> **MACY, MACY. / POOL PLAYER**	-	
1996.	(7") <Slowball 02> **PARK. / JESSE JANOWITZ**	-	
	(above issued on 'Slowball') (below on 'Double Agent')		
Jan 97.	(7") <DA 003> **FLORIDA. / CUBAN GIRLS**	-	
Mar 97.	(cd/lp) <SFR 201/101> **PUSH KINGS**	-	
	– Nine straight lines / Pop phenomenon / Florida / Stay with her / D.J. / Mrs. McKean / Love in my heart / Raincoat renegade / European dreams / Songs of empire / Jenny G / Let's face it / Number ones / Be kind, be still, be near.		
Jan 98.	(m-cd) <SFR 003> **BLOWIN' UP!**	-	
	– Number ones / $$$ / Love won't desert us (famous) / Macy, Macy / Pool player / Riverdale.		
May 98.	(cd/lp) <SFR 007/+12> **FAR PLACES**	-	
	– Little star / Sunday on the west side / Lonely times / Shadows of San Francisco / Take me home / Diamonds aren't forever / The girl who only loves candy / The wild ones / Love takes flight / Orange glow / We don't have to say goodbye forever / 3012.		

		not iss.	Rebbel
2000.	(m-cd) **THE PUSH KINGS**	-	
	– Born stoned / Summer trippin / Beat girl / All my life / Honey come closer / Shake it up / Hello, I don't even know my own name / Party to end.		

		Le Grand Magistery	Le Grand Magistery
Oct 01.	(lp/cd) <(HRH 28/+CD)> **FEEL NO FADE**		Sep01
	– Summer trippin / Born stoned / Hands 2gether / Rocket 'n' ride / I hate everybody but you / Honey come closer / All my life / RAin on Duane / Beat girl (and me) / The minute / Panic button / Hello, I don't even know my own name / Touching / Shakeitup / Party to end / Runnin' from something.		

– compilations, etc. –

Mar 99.	(cd) Bandai Music: <APCY-8466> **CRIME IN ACETATE: 1995-1997**	-	- Japan
	– Queen of Spain / Spain / Overseas / Phony phone / Macy, Macy / Pool player / Memphis / Jesse Janowitz / Florida / Cuban girls / Waiting for Nina / Getting to the gopher / My little Pixie / New order #2.		

PUSSYCAT TRASH (see under ⇒ MILKY WIMPSHAKE)

PUSSYWILLOWS (see under ⇒ MARCH, April)

Q AND NOT U

Formed: Washington D.C., USA . . . late 1998 by CHRISTOPHER RICHARDS, HARRIS KLAHR, JOHN DAVIS and MATHIEU BOURLIQUE. Q & NOT U's relentless touring and energising razor-sharp power-pop meant that the group had already amassed a considerable fanbase before they were signed to 'Dischord' records in 2000. That same year the band – impressively – managed to capture the good time spirit of their live shows on their debut album, 'NO KILL NO BEEP BEEP'. The group spent most of the following year on the road, enhancing their reputation as a fearsome live band, albeit before the departure of bass player BOURLIQUE. Continuing as a three-piece the band became more experimental as they began to use an assortment of percussion instruments to fill the void left by the aforementioned BOURLIQUE. The group's brave decision to tamper with their sound was a triumphant success and afforded their 2002 album 'DIFFERENT DAMAGE' an enduring quality that was possibly missing from their debut.

Album rating: NO KILL NO BEEP BEEP (*7) / DIFFERENT DAMAGE (*7)

JOHN DAVIS – drums, percussion, vocals / **CHRISTOPHER RICHARDS** – guitars, vocals, bass, synths / **HARRIS KLAHR** – guitars, vocals, synths / **MATHIEU BOURLIQUE** – bass

		DeSoto	DeSoto
Jul 00.	(7"ep) <(QA 35)> **HOT AND INFORMED**		Apr00
	– And the Washington Monument blinks goodnight / Busy lights, busy carpet / Kiss distinctly American.		

		Dischord	Dischord
Jan 01.	(cd/lp) <(DIS 123 CD/V)> **NO KILL NO BEEP BEEP**		Nov00
	– A line in the sand / And the Washington Monument (blinks) goodnight / Fever sleeves / Hooray for humans / Kiss distinctly American / We heart our hive / Little sparkee / The more I get the more I want / Y plus white girl / Nice things everybody knows / Sleeping the terror code.		

— now without MATHIEU

May 02.	(7"/cd-s) (DIS 132 V/CD) **ON PLAY PATTERNS**		-
	– Ten thousand animal calls / Soft pyramids.		
Oct 02.	(cd/lp) <(DIS 133 CD/V)> **DIFFERENT DAMAGE**		
	– Soft pyramids / So many animal calls / Air conditions / Black plastic bag / Meet me in the pocket / This are flashes / Everybody ruins / Snow patterns / When the lines go down / O'no / No damage nocturne / Recreation myth.		

QUASI

Formed: Portland, Oregon, USA . . . mid 90's by former San Franciscans, SAM COOMES and JANET WEISS, both seasonal campaigners since 1989 for the likes of HEATMISER (ELLIOTT SMITH's old band) and SLEATER-KINNEY respectively. Trading in a unique hybrid of lo-fi drum'n'Hammond stylings, QUASI supported their old chum, ELLIOTT, in November to promote their second proper set, 'FEATURING "BIRDS"' (1998); previous albums being 'EARLY RECORDINGS' (1996) and 'R&B TRANSMOGRIFICATION' (1997). 1999's 'FIELD STUDIES' was another enlightening lesson on both the theory and practice of creating deceptively melodic, playful, cheeky and acerbic indie rock, the duo's deliciously discordant experiments whetting the appetite for more of the same. Newly signed to 'Touch & Go', the pair made sure that 'THE SWORD OF GOD' (2001) had been worth the wait, its barbed humour and savagely accurate satirising never really threatening to undermine the essential flawed genius of their joyful racket.

Album rating: EARLY RECORDINGS (*6) / R&B TRANSMOGRIFICATION (*7) / FEATURING "BIRDS" (*7) / THE SWORD OF GOD (*6)

SAM COOMES – vocals, keyboards, guitar (ex-HEATMISER, ex-DONNER PARTY, ex-MOTORGOAT) / **JANET WEISS** – vocals, drums (of SLEATER-KINNEY)

		not iss.	Key Op
Mar 96.	(cd) <23> **EARLY RECORDINGS**	-	
	– Two hounds / Superficial / Birds are bells / Lump of coal / Time flies by / Gaping holes / Hul neng / Homunculus / Monkey, mirror / Hairs / The egg / Rumpy / Digital delay / Mammon / Reverse coagulations / Op.7 / Pay me now, or pay me later / Unspeakable thing / Deep sleep. <re-iss. 2001 on 'Touch & Go'; TG 930>		

		Domino	Up
Mar 97.	(cd) <UP 40> **R&B TRANSMOGRIFICATION**	-	
	– Ghost dreaming / The ballad of mechanical man / In the first place / Bird's eye view / Two-faced / Ghost vs. vampire / R&B transmogrification / When I'm dead / Sugar / My coffin / Mama, papa, baby / Chocolate rabbit / Iron worm / Clouds.		

QUASI (cont)

Sep 98. (cd/lp) *(WIG CD/LP 55)* <*UP 54*> **FEATURING "BIRDS"**   Apr98
– Our happiness is guaranteed / I never want to see you again / Poisoned well / Happy prole / Sea shanty / It's hard to turn me on / Nothing from nothing / Tomorrow you'll hide / California / You fucked yourself / Ape self prevails / Please do / I give up / Birds / Repetition / Only success can fail me now.

— added guests **ELLIOTT SMITH** – bass / **BRENT ARNOLD** – strings / **FRANCES WOODS** – cello

Sep 99. (cd/lp) *(WIG CD/LP 69)* <*UP 72*> **FIELD STUDIES**
– All the same / The golden egg / The skeleton / The star you left behind / Empty words / Birds / A fable with no moral / Under a cloud / Me & my head / Two by two / It don't mean nothing / Bon voyage / Smile / Let's just go.

Aug 01. (7") *(RUG 129)* **THE SWORD OF GOD. / NOTHING NOWHERE**

Aug 01. (cd/lp) *(WIG CD/LP 097)* <*TG 927*> **THE SWORD OF GOD**
– Introduction / Fuck Hollywood / It's raining / Genetic science / The sword of God / A case of no way out / The curse of having it all / Seal the deal / From a hole in the ground / Little Lord Fontleroy / Goblins and trolls / Better luck next time / Nothing, nowhere / Rock and roll can never die.

Monica QUEEN (see under ⇒ THRUM)

QUICKSPACE (SUPERSPORT)
(see under ⇒ FAITH HEALERS, Th')

QUIX*O*TIC (see under ⇒ SLANT 6)

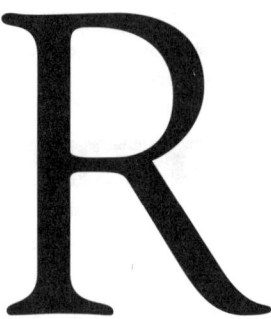

RACEBANNON

Formed: Indianapolis, Indiana, USA . . . 1996 by MICHAEL ANDERSON, JAMES BAUMAN, and DAVE BRITTS. These hardcore rockers were much lauded as the bright future of the genre, but they began slowly, gigging around their home city and not releasing their debut single until 1998; the same point at which they relocated to Bloomington where BAUMAN had begun attending the state university. Here the band flourished as they were outside the capital city's claustrophobic music scene, and in true indie fashion, they churned out various singles on small local imprints. They also developed their frantic stage presence, a must for any fledgling hardcore band. The group managed to attract the attention of area label, 'Secretly Canadian' who signed them up. Although, hardcore bands were not common currency for the label, they did well for the band, hooking them up with producer MIKE MOGIS, to work on their debut LP 'IN THE GRIPS OF THE LIGHT' (2002). The veteran knob-twiddler brilliantly captured the energy of the band on this album, something that can be quite a task with this live-orientated style. The accolade of hardcore's 'bright young things' did not seem to be an illusion. Under the commanding vocals of ANDERSON, the band pushed the boundaries of the genre; BRITTS used record decks, not in a conventional dance/hip-hop mixing sense, but to add another layer of sound to the performance. The band, both bravely and quickly, followed this up with the rock-opera concept piece 'SATAN'S KICKIN' YR DICK IN' (2002). Certainly a courageous undertaking for a young group, but one that they pulled off, by all accounts, pretty successfully. The story of a man trading his soul with the Devil, to become a famed female singer, and then having to reap what he sowed, is laid out competently and stays its course.

Album rating: IN THE GRIPS OF THE LIGHT (*8) / SATAN'S KICKIN' YR DICK IN (*7)

MICHAEL ANDERSON – vocals / **JAMES BAUMAN** – guitar

		not iss.	Electric Human Project
1998.	(6") **split w/ MARA'AKATE**	–	
		not iss.	Monotonstudio
1999.	(7") **THE DISEASE. /**	–	
		not iss.	Alone
2000.	(7") **CLUBBER LANG. / SATAN'S KICKIN' YER DICK IN (part 3)**	–	
2000.	(7") **IS TE MOST COMPLETE VOLUME OF THE MOTION OF THE PLANETS. /**	–	
2000.	(7") **MASTER CONTROL PROGRAM. /**	–	
		Secretly Canadian	Secretly Canadian
Feb 02.	(cd) <*(SC 63CD)*> **IN THE GRIPS OF THE LIGHT**		Jan02

– Fox boogie / Flip n' fuck / Go with the flow / Sober and sad / Electricity / Clubber Lang / Fuck yr obvious words / I'm yr egomaniac (in the grips of the light). *(lp-iss.Oct02 on 'Level Plane'; LP 34)*

— RACEBANNON split a CD with SONG OF ZARATHUSTRA, 'NEAR AND FAR VOL.2' for 'Backroad – Level Plane' <*BR 03*>

Nov 02. (cd) <*SC 79CD*> **SATAN'S KICKIN' YR DICK IN**
– (7 untitled tracks).

RACHEL'S

Formed: Louisville, Kentucky, USA . . . 1989 by JASON NOBLE and CHRISTIAN FREDERICKSEN who released the Christmas tape 'RACHEL'S HALO' in 1991. The group was then dormant for a number of years whilst NOBLE was playing in the group RODAN. They paired up again in 1994 and enlisted pianist RACHEL GRIMES, releasing their first proper album, 'HANDWRITING', the following year. The music was a compelling blend of modern classical music and experimental sounds featuring a chamber orchestra comprising of sixteen musicians. Their second album, 'MUSIC FOR EGON SCHIELE' (1996), was eponymously named after the tortured Austrian artist and was to provide the soundtrack to a play about his tragic life. The dramatic, haunting music of the RACHEL'S leant itself perfectly to the subject matter. The group produced more of this delicately complex music on the albums 'THE SEA AND THE BELLS' (1997) and 'SELENOGRAPHY' (1999). The 2000 released two-track EP 'FULL OF NIGHT' showed signs the group may be venturing towards an even more experimental sound. Having earlier co-written with JEFF MUELLER (of JUNE OF 44) on TV program 'This American Life', while finding another like-minded math-rockist KYLE CRABTREE, NOBLE formed SHIPPING NEWS (taking the name from a novel by E. Annie Proulx). In 1997, reports of their debut set were confirmed when the trio issued

'SAVE EVERYTHING', a half-rocking/half-calming record complete with waves of dramatic nautical connotations running through its repetitive bows. A long-awaited second set, 'VERY SOON, AND IN PLEASANT COMPANY' (2001), was, compared to their last effort, a little out of its depth.

Album rating: Rodan: RUSTY (*7) / Rachel's: HANDWRITING (*6) / MUSIC FOR EGON SCHIELE (*6) / THE SEA AND THE BELLS (*7) / SELENOGRAPHY (*7) / FULL ON NIGHT mini; split w/ Matmos (*5) / Shipping News: SAVE EVERYTHING (*7) / VERY SOON, AND IN PLEASANT COMPANY (*4)

RODAN

JASON NOBLE – guitar, vocals / **CHRISTIAN FREDERICKSON** – viola / **KEVIN COULTAS** – guitar, drums, vocals / **TARA JANE O'NEIL** – bass / **EVE MILLER** – cello

			not iss.	Three Little Girls
1993.	(7") <007> **HOW THE WINTER WAS PASSED. / MILK AND MELANCHOLY**		-	
			Quarterstick	Quarterstick
Apr 94.	(lp/cd) <(QS 24/+CD)> **RUSTY**			
	– Bible silver corner / Shiner / The everyday world of bodies / Jungle Jim / Gauge / Tooth-fairy retribution manifesto.			

— TARA JANE O'NEIL formed SONORA PINE and RETSIN

RACHEL'S

JASON NOBLE + CHRISTIAN FREDERICKSON plus **RACHEL GRIMES** – piano / + a plethora of rotating session people

Quarterstick Quarterstick

May 95. (lp/cd) <(QS 30/+CD)> **HANDWRITING**
– Southbound to Marion / M. Daguerre / Saccharin / Frida Kahlo / Seratonin / Full of night / Handwriting.
Feb 96. (lp/cd) <(QS 35/+CD)> **MUSIC FOR EGON SCHIELE**
– Family portrait / Egon & Gertie / First self-portrait series / Mime Van Osen / Second self-portrait series / Wally, Egon & models in the studio / Promenade / Third self-portrait series / Egon, Edith & Wally meet / Egon & Wally embrace & say farewell / Egon & Edith / Second family portrait.
Jan 97. (lp/cd) <QS 38/+CD> **THE SEA AND THE BELLS**
– Rhine & courtesan / The voyage of Camille / Tea merchants / Lloyd's register / With more air than words / All is calm / Cypress branches / Sirens / Night at sea / Letters home / To rest near to you / The blue-skinned waltz / His eyes.
Jun 99. (d-lp/cd) <(QS 55/+CD)> **SELENOGRAPHY**
– A French Galleasse / On demeter / The last night / Kentucky nocturne / Honeysuckle suite (sugar maple – elm – sweetgum) / Artemisia / Old road 60 / An evening of long goodbyes / Cuts the metal cold / The mysterious disappearance of Louis LePrince / Forgiveness / Hearts and drums.
May 00. (m-cd/m-lp; as RACHEL'S & MATMOS) <(QS 69 CD/LP)> **FULL ON NIGHT**
– Full on night (recension mix) / The precise temperature of darkness (remixed by MATMOS).

SHIPPING NEWS

JASON NOBLE – guitar, bass, vocals / **JEFF MUELLER** – vocals, guitar (of JUNE OF 44) / **KYLE CRABTREE** – drums, sounds effects

Quarterstick Quaretstick

Sep 97. (cd/lp) <(QS 50 CD/LP)> **SAVE EVERYTHING**
– Books on trains / Steerage / The photoelectric effect / All by electricity / At a venture / A true lover's knot.
May 98. (cd) <INITIAL 025CD> **split w/ METROSCHIFTER**
– (3 METROSCHIFTER tracks) / Nine bodies, nine states (live) / Books on trains (live) / Steerage (live). (UK-iss.Jul01; same as US)
Jan 01. (cd/lp) <(QS 65 CD/LP)> **VERY SOON, AND IN PLEASANT COMPANY**
– The march song / Actual blood / Simple halo / Nine bodies, nine states / Quiet victories / Contents of a landfill / How to draw horses. (re-iss. Jan02; same)
Oct 01. (cd-ep) <QS 73CD> **RMSN EP 1: CARRIER**
– Horrible bed versus sickening bridge / Paper lanterns / Cock-a-doodle-do.
Feb 02. (cd-ep) <QS 74CD> **RMSN EP 2: SICKENING BRIDGE**
– Haunted on foot / We start to drift / Now that your diamond-lined star is failing you, what fair silhouette would best suit this satellite.
Nov 02. (cd-ep) <QS 76CD> **RMSN EP 3: VARIEGATED**
– Dogs / Non-volant / Haymaker / You can't hide the mark inside / Untitled.

RADAR BROS.

Formed: San Fernando, California, USA ... summer '94 by former MEDICINE man, JIM PUTNAM (who also sidelined with MAIDS OF GRAVITY). Abandoning psychedelic noise for a life of reflective "sadcore", PUTNAM recruited a rhythm section of SENON GAIUS WILLIAMS and STEVE GOODFRIEND, cobbling together ragged strands of COWBOY JUNKIES, NEIL YOUNG and early 70's era BEACH BOYS on their eponymous late '95 debut mini-set. Approximately a year later, the trio emerged with a full-length album on 'Restless', confusingly enough again entitled simply 'THE RADAR BROS.', the record cementing – especially among UK critics – PUTNAM's reputation as a long lost musical cousin to the likes of SMOG's BILL CALLAHAN. Three years down the line and a difficult 9-month recording period, PUTNAM and his disciples returned with the strange and delicate 'THE SINGING HATCHET', produced and entirely composed by PUTNAM himself; the album was released through tartan label, 'Chemikal Underground' (home to MOGWAI, The DELGADOS, etc). The long-player was described as a "weep-core" masterpiece, its chirpy harmonies and melancholic minor scales breathed life back into the group and earned them an entry into the UK indie Top 20. From the slow burning 'TAR THE ROOFS' to the fatigue laden 'FIVE MILES', the album's emotional depth held no bounds, with the ridiculously brilliant 'THE PILGRIM' as the stand out track. PUTNAM and his band of troubadours returned to the 'Chemikal Underground' label in 2002, with their magnificent third set 'AND THE SURROUNDING MOUNTAINS'. One of the last great American independent bands (namechecked alongside The KINGSBURY MANX, CALIFONE and MODEST MOUSE), The RADAR BROS' music didn't hit the listener straight away, but insinuated itself into the subconscious and never went away. Songs such as 'ON THE LINE', bursting with musical flavour, and the eerie 'ROCK OF THE LAKE', left audiences reeling with its consistent piano harmonies and PUTNAM's tenterhook vocal harmonies.

Album rating: RADAR BROTHERS mini (*7) / THE RADAR BROS. (*7) / THE SINGING HATCHET (*8) / AND THE SURROUNDING MOUNTAINS (*7)

JIM PUTNAM (b.30 Sep'67) – vocals, guitar, keyboards (ex-MEDICINE) / **SENON GAIUS WILLIAMS** – bass / **STEVE GOODFRIEND** – drums

not iss. Never

Nov 95. (m-cd) <NR 4004> **RADAR BROTHERS**
– Hey / Into the hills / Friend / Long long time / Animals / Yukon. <re-iss. Aug97; same>

not iss. Restless

Oct 96. (cd) <72927-2> **THE RADAR BROS.**
– Lose your face again / Capital gain / Wise mistake of you / Stay / Supermarket pharmacy / On the floor / We're over here / Distant mine / Underwater culprits / This drive / Take stuff / Goddess.
Nov 96. (cd-ep) <72942-2> **STAY EP**
– Stay / Into the door / On the phone / The guests.

Chemikal Philips
Underground Media

Jul 99. (7") (chem 034) **OPEN OCEAN SAILING. / OLYMPIC GAMES**
Sep 99. (cd) (chem 035cd) <2> **THE SINGING HATCHET**
– Tar the roofs / Shifty lies / Shovelling sons / All the ghosts / Find the hour / You're on an island / The pilgrim / You've been hired / To be free again / Five miles / Open ocean sailing / Gas station downs.
Mar 00. (7"/cd-s) (chem 038/+cd) **SHOVELING SONS. / NO ONE LEFT / TO CARRY ME HOME**

Chemikal
Underground Merge

May 02. (lp/cd) (Chem 061/+cd) <MRG 509> **AND THE SURROUNDING MOUNTAINS**
– You and the father / On the line / This Xmas eve / Rock of the lake / Sisters / Uncles / Still evil / The wake of all that's past / Camplight / Mothers / Mountains / Morning song.

RADIAL SPANGLE

Formed: Oklahoma City, Oklahoma, USA ... 1991 by ALAN LAIRD, APRIL TIPPENS and RICHARD ENGLISH. Inspired by the redneck isolation of their dustbowl environment, LAIRD and Co befriended fellow musical mavericks, MERCURY REV, whose DAVID FRIDMANN and JONATHAN DONAHUE produced their debut album, 'ICE CREAM HEADACHE' (1993). There was one further connection between the bands in that both recorded first for the 'Mint Tea' label and later for 'Beggars Banquet', the 'BIRTHDAY' single being RADIAL SPANGLE's first effort for the latter imprint. A self-confessed archetypal middle class slacker, LAIRD admitted to being influenced by everything from The CARPENTERS to the MARQUIS DE SADE, the music an equally schizophrenic lunge between grating SONIC YOUTH-style noise and whimsical, SYD BARRETT-esque nursery pop. These tactics were employed to impressive effect on 1994's 'SYRUP MACRAME', after which the band dissolved; MERCURY REV also fell apart around the same time and while that group were reborn to great critical acclaim in the late 90's, RADIAL SPANGLE were left with only memories of their short-lived indie stardom.

Album rating: ICE CREAM HEADACHE (*6) / SYRUP MACRAME (*7)

ALAN LAIRD – vocals, guitar / **APRIL TIPPENS** – bass / **RICHARD ENGLISH** – drums

Mint Tea Mint Tea

May 93. (cd/lp) <(MINT CD/LP 8)> **ICE CREAM HEADACHE**
– Raze / Canopy and shoe / Dream problem / Drop / Snow / Birthday / Hand / Gutter chain / White paper basket / Copper.
Jul 93. (12"ep/cd-ep) (MINT 7 T/CD) **RAZE. / CURTAIN LEAF / SAPPHIRE**

Beggars Beggars
Banquet Banquet

Nov 93. (12"ep/cd-ep) (BEG 24 T/CD) **BIRTHDAY / TURPENTINE. / BIRTHDAY / SNOW**

— added **KENNEDY** – co-writer on 2 songs

Aug 94. (cd/lp) (BBQ CD/LP 163) <92476> **SYRUP MACRAME**
– Marble / Special love / Caf, 'fine / Busy hole / Cross your legs / Knees / New dress / Dragonfly / Patio furniture / Sunflower graveyard.

— disbanded after above

RADIO 4

Formed: New York City, New York, USA ... 1999 by ex-GARDEN VARIETY bassist ANTHONY ROMAN, along with TOMMY WILLIAMS, GREG COLLINS, PJ O'CONNER and GERALD GARONE. The group issued a three-track EP on the 'Gern Blandsten' imprint, before delivering their rough and hard-edged electro-dance-rock album 'THE NEW SONG AND DANCE' (2000), a record which was produced by Tim O'Heir and featured the minor club 12"er 'DANCE TO THE UNDERGROUND'. All phat (yes, with a 'ph') basslines and sinister grooves, clicks and squeaks, RADIO 4 sounded convincingly like ADD N TO X, only with a much funkier template. The group recorded demos in a dingy basement in 2001, which were later remixed by production prodigies DFA (Tim Goldsworth and James Murphy), who tweaked the album 'GOTHAM' which was issued in 2002 and was considered to be the best psychedelic rock/dance crossover since DEATH IN VEGAS' 'Contino Sessions'. It surely had more influences than that; the CLASH came to mind, as did BIG AUDIO DYNAMITE, or more recently Detroit electro-clash duo ADULT, in terms of noisy distorted breakbeats and fuzzed-up bass. But the real compliment was that, at the end of the day, RADIO 4 sounded like RADIO 4.

Album rating: NEW SONG AND DANCE (*6) / GOTHAM! (*8)

ANTHONY ROMAN – vocals, bass (ex-GARDEN VARIETY) / **TOMMY WILLIAMS** – guitar / **GREG COLLINS** – drums / **P.J. O'CONNOR** – percussion / **GERARD GARONE** – keyboards

Gern Blandsten / Gern Blandsten

Jan 00. (7"ep) *<GERN 042>* **RADIO 4 EP** [-] [ ]

May 00. (lp/cd) *<(GERN 047/+CD)>* **NEW SONG AND DANCE** [ ] [ ]
– How the stars got crossed / Buy and sell / Beat around the bush / Communication (no more room for) / Get set to fall out / Election day / Walls falling / Boy meets girl / We must be sure / Beautiful ride / New motive.

City Slang / Gern Blandsten

Sep 02. (7") *(20206-7)* **EYES WIDE OPEN. / RED LIGHTS** [ ] [-]

Oct 02. (cd/lp) *(20202-2/-1) <GERN 061CD>* **GOTHAM!** [ ] [ ] Feb02
– Our town / Start a fire / Eyes wide open / Struggle / Calling all enthusiasts / Save your city / Speaking in codes / Certain tragedy / Red lights / The movies / End of the rope / Pipe bombs / New disco.

Nov 02. (12"/cd-s) *(20212-6/-2)* **DANCE TO THE UNDERGROUND (mixes; radio / prance by the Faint / Playgroup / DFA)** [ ] [-]

RADIOHEAD

Formed: Oxford, England . . . 1988 by frontman THOM YORKE, guitarist ED O'BRIEN and bassist COLIN GREENWOOD with drummer PHIL SELWAY completing the line-up. Dubbing themselves ON A FRIDAY, the band began gigging around Oxford, subsequently boasting a triple guitar attack following the addition of COLIN's brother, JONNY. Initially, the group also fleshed out their sound with a couple of saxaphone players (though it's now difficult to imagine what that must have sounded like). With the various members trooping off to complete their respective educations, the RADIOHEAD story really began in the summer of '91 when the band got back together and adopted the aforesaid moniker (after a TALKING HEADS song). Signed to the ever vigilant 'Parlophone', the band enjoyed some airplay with their first release, a Spring '92 EP with 'PROVE YOURSELF' as the lead track. Next up was the seminal 'CREEP', an incendiary anthem for anyone who'd ever felt rejected/alienated (and let's face it, that's most of the population), the song stiffing first time round but subsequently kickstarting RADIOHEAD's career. The track also used the group's trademark soft bit/quiet bit dynamics to stunning effect, a method which would come to form the basis for some of the band's best tracks. In the meantime, RADIOHEAD eventually scraped in to the lower regions of the Top 40 with the abrasive 'ANYONE CAN PLAY GUITAR', the debut album, 'PABLO HONEY' making the UK Top 30 around the same time in early '93. Though it had its moments, the album lacked consistency with YORKE seemingly searching for some kind of vocal identity. While the record found enthusiastic champions in some sections of the music press, by and large, RADIOHEAD were passed over. All that changed, however, when 'CREEP' exploded in the States, the record obviously striking a deep chord with the multitudes who weren't part of the 'American Dream'. Taking the first flight over there, RADIOHEAD capitalised on this surprise success, the band treated like homecoming heroes and selling out concerts night after night. In a bizarre reversal of the standard process, this US success laid the groundwork for the re-release of 'CREEP' in the UK, where it became a Top 10 hit, sales of the album also enjoying a healthy re-invigoration. With such a universal theme, it was no surprise that the track was also a massive hit all over the world, RADIOHEAD finding themselves in the strange position of being international pop stars yet at the same time, regarded merely as a competent indie band in their home country. 'THE BENDS' (1995) convincingly silenced the doubters once and for all, a groundbreaking album with a spectral musical vision which rarely failed to take the breath away. Opening with the searing, reverbating 'PLANET TELEX' the record proceeded to juxtapose howling guitar menace against bleakly beautiful melodies, echoing synth and acoustic strumming, YORKE painting piercingly vivid images with his tortured musings on the nature of the human psyche. The fragile majesty of 'FAKE PLASTIC TREES' was RADIOHEAD at their most sublime, YORKE's ability to hit those high notes pivotal to the resigned melancholy of his vocals. The churning claustrophobia of 'BLACK STAR' sounded like the final fling of a condemned man, positively revelling in its own pain and misery, while the funereal 'STREET SPIRIT' was a ghostly coda, its award-winning video perfectly evoking the track's haunting feeling of time standing still. Basically, the album wiped the floor with the competition, laying waste to the snot-nosed chaff of Brit-pop and confirming that there was indeed a thinking man's alternative to OASIS. R.E.M. felt the same way, inviting the band to support them on tour later that year, something of a dream come true for RADIOHEAD who had long been massive fans of STIPE & Co. The summer of '95 also saw the release of the 'HELP' album, a project involving the cream of the British music scene with proceeds from album sales donated to the War Child charity (which raised money for war torn Bosnia). RADIOHEAD contributed 'LUCKY', a song apparently written about the band's newfound position as one of the most highly regarded group's in the world. Stunning though the track is, it sounds more like a dirge than a celebration, the searing guitar line evoking a feeling of utter desolation and emptiness. Probably the best example of YORKE's self-acknowledged struggle to sound anything other than melancholy, the track was one of many highlights on 'OK COMPUTER' (1997), RADIOHEAD's feverishly anticipated follow-up to the poll-topping 'THE BENDS'. A densely complex, almost initially impenetrable album, 'OK..' was a demanding beast, previewed by the wildly ambitious 'PARANOID ANDROID', a kind of post-prog symphony in three parts. The oscillating guitar vibration of 'AIRBAG' kicked off proceedings in much the same fashion as 'PLANET TELEX', but then things started getting weird. 'SUBTERRANEAN HOMESICK ALIEN' was truly adrift in space, the guitars twinkling and shimmering like tiny constellations, while with 'EXIT MUSIC (FOR A FILM)' (written for closing sequence of the revamped 'Romeo And Juliet' movie), YORKE's vocal was so eerily intimate, it sounded as if he was in the same room, the song building to a majestic climax via unearthly choral parts and swooning synths. 'LET DOWN' was an almost BYRDS-esque follow-up to 'CREEP', its pealing guitar and infectious melody framing a similar theme and creating what was conceivably the nearest the record came to conventional rock. Much of the album was vaguely reminiscent of the more cerebral moments on U2's 'Unforgettable Fire', although YORKE has never come so close to sounding like BONO as on 'CLIMBING THE WALLS', for once managing to avoid the bruised resignation that normally colours his voice. With 'NO SURPRISES', RADIOHEAD cleverly contrasted an almost child-like musical lullaby with lyrics expressing a hopeless world weariness. Of their contemporaries, only SPIRITUALIZED and MOGWAI were making music this far out, RADIOHEAD once again almost sweeping the board at the end of year polls and bravely taking rock music into the future rather than fawning over a Union Jack-clad past. With 'KID A' (2000) they took the music into the future with a vengeance; whether this was a brave new sonic world or a sterile wasteland of short-circuit experimentation remains a moot point. Maybe it should've been titled 'All That You CAN Leave Behind', YORKE and Co putting to bed the bruised beauty of their best work with brutal determination. The oblique, serrated electronica and disjointed dirgescapes offered up nothing in the way of redemptive miserabilism never mind a hook or a melody. Perseverance dragged brief snatches of genius screaming petulantly from the broodingly dense mix yet the effort was hardly relative to the meagre rewards on offer. More, YORKE's vocal, previously a thing of exotic desolation, begins to grate against the unremitingly bleak backdrop, reduced to one of the dismal whole's gratuitously mechanical constituent parts – in other words a classic! 'AMNESIAC' (2001) was an equally daunting if not quite so wilfully oppressive listen, its material drawn from the same sessions as its predecessor. Despite featuring the studio debut of established live favourites 'KNIVES OUT' and 'YOU AND WHOSE ARMY?', the album merely confirmed that RADIOHEAD had absolutely no intention of resuming normal service anytime soon. On the contrary, they kept up their new adrenaline-paced release schedule with 'I MIGHT BE WRONG: LIVE RECORDINGS' (2001), a clipped concert set again inspired by the template of 'KID A'.

Album rating: PABLO HONEY (*7) / THE BENDS (*10) / OK COMPUTER (*10) / KID A (*9) / AMNESIAC (*7) / I MIGHT BE WRONG: LIVE RECORDINGS mini (*5)

THOM YORKE (b. 7 Oct'68) – vocals, guitar / **ED O'BRIEN** (b.15 Apr'68) – guitar, vocals / **JON GREENWOOD** (b. 5 Nov'71) – guitar / **COLIN GREENWOOD** (b.26 Jun'69) – bass / **PHIL SELWAY** (b.23 May'67) – drums

Parlophone / Capitol

May 92. (c-ep/12"ep/cd-ep) *(TCR/12R/CDR 6312)* **DRILL EP** [ ] [ ]
– Prove yourself / Stupid car / You / Thinking about you.

Sep 92. (c-ep/12"ep/cd-ep) *(TCR/12R/CDR 6078)* **CREEP / LURCEE. / INSIDE MY HEAD / MILLION $ QUESTION** [ ] [-]

Feb 93. (c-ep/12"ep/cd-ep) *(TCR/12R/CDR 6333)* **ANYONE CAN PLAY GUITAR. / FAITHLESS, THE WONDER BOY / COKE BABIES** [32] [-]

Feb 93. (cd/c/lp) *(CD/TC+/PCS 7360) <81409>* **PABLO HONEY** [25] [32] Jun93
– You / Creep / How do you? / Stop whispering / Thinking about you / Anyone can play guitar / Ripcord / Vegetable / Prove yourself / I can't / Lurgee / Blow out.

Apr 93. (c-s,cd-s) *<44932>* **CREEP / FAITHLESS, THE WONDER BOY** [-] [34]

May 93. (c-ep/12"ep/cd-ep) *(TCR/12R/CDR 6345)* **POP IS DEAD / BANANA CO. (acoustic). / CREEP (live) / RIPCORD (live)** [42] [-]

Sep 93. (7") *(RS 6359)* **CREEP. / YES I AM** [7] [-]
(cd-s+=) *(CDR 6359)* – Blow out (remix) / Inside my head (live).
(12"clear) *(12RG 6359)* – ('A'-acoustic KROQ) / You (live) / Vegetable (live) / Killer cars (live).

Oct 94. (c-ep/12"ep) *(TCR/12R 6984) <58274>* **MY IRON LUNG / THE TRICKSTER / LEWIS (mistreated) / PUNCHDRUNK LOVESICK SINGALONG** [24] [ ]
(cd-s) *(CDRS 6394)* – (1st & 4th track) / Lozenge of love.
(cd-s) *(CDR 6394)* – (1st & 2nd track) / Permanent daylight / You never wash up after yourself.

Mar 95. (c-s) *(TCR 6405) <58537>* **HIGH & DRY / PLANET TELEX** [17] [ ] Feb96
(cd-s+=) *(CDR 6405)* – Killer cars / Planet Telex (LFO JD mix).
(cd-s+=) *(CDRS 6405)* – Maquiladora / Planet Telex (hexadecimal mix).
(12") *(12R 6405)* – Planet Telex (hexadecimal mix) / Planet Telex (LFO JD mix) / Planet Telex (hexadecimal dub) / High & dry.

Mar 95. (cd/c/lp) *(CD/TC+/PCS 7372) <29626>* **THE BENDS** [6] [88]
– Planet Telex / The bends / High & dry / Fake plastic trees / Bones (nice dream) / Just / My iron lung / Bulletproof . . .I wish I was / Black star / Sulk / Street spirit (fade out).

May 95. (c-ep/cd-ep) *(TCR/CDRS 6411) <58424>* **FAKE PLASTIC TREES / INDIA RUBBER / HOW CAN YOU BE SURE?** [20] [ ] Jul95
(cd-s) *(CDR 6411)* – ('A'side) / ('A'acoustic) / Bulletproof..I wish I was (acoustic) / Street spirit (fade out) (acoustic).

RADIOHEAD (cont)

Date	Format	Details	Chart1	Chart2
Aug 95.	(c-ep/12"ep) *(TCR/12R 6415)*	**JUST / PLANET TELEX (Karma Sun Ra mix) / KILLER CARS (mogadon mix)**	19	-
	(cd-s) *(CDR 6415)*	– ('A'side) / Bones (live) / Planet Telex (live) / Anyone can play guitar (live).		
Jan 96.	(7"white) *(R 6419)* <82523>	**STREET SPIRIT (FADE OUT). / BISHOP'S ROBES**	5	
	(cd-s+=) *(CDRS 6419)*	– Talk show host.		
	(cd-s) *(CDR 6419)*	– ('A'side) / Banana co. / Molasses.		
Feb 96.	(cd-s,cd-s) <58537>	**HIGH AND DRY / FAKE PLASTIC TREES**	-	78
Jun 97.	(7") *(NODATA 01)*	**PARANOID ANDROID. / POLYETHYLENE (PARTS 1 & 2)**	3	-
	(cd-s+=) *(CDNODATAS 01)*	– Pearly.		
	(cd-s) *(CDNODATA 01)*	– ('A'side) / A reminder / Melatonin.		
Jun 97.	(cd/c/d-lp) *(CD/TC+/NODATA 02)* <55229>	**OK COMPUTER**	1	21
		– Airbag / Paranoid android / Subterranean homesick alien / Exit music (for a film) / Karma police / Electioneering / Climbing up the walls / No surprises / Lucky / The tourist.		
Aug 97.	(cd-s) *(CDNODATA 03)*	**KARMA POLICE / CLIMBING UP THE WALLS (Fila Brazillia & Zero 7 mixes)**	8	
	(12"+=) *(12NODATA 03)*	– Meeting in the aisle.		
	(cd-s) *(CDNODATAS 03)*	– ('A'side) / Meeting in the aisle / Lull.		
Jan 98.	(12") *(12NODATA 04)*	**NO SURPRISES. / PALO ALTO**	4	
	(c-s+=/cd-s+=) *(TC/CD NODATA 04)*	– How I made my millions.		
	(cd-s) *(CDNODATAS 04)*	– ('A'side) / Airbag (live) / Lucky (live).		
Apr 98.	(m-cd) *(858701-2)*	**AIRBAG / PEARLY (remix) / MEETING IN THE AISLE / A REMINDER / POLYTHENE (parts 1 & 2) / MELATONIN / PALO ALTO**		-
		(above wasn't legitimate to chart in Britain)		
Apr 98.	(m-cd) <58071>	**AIRBAG / HOW AM I DRIVING (EP)**	-	56
Oct 00.	(cd/c) <2435 27753-2/-4>	**KID A**	1	1
		– Everything in its right place / Kid A / The national anthem / How to disappear completely / Treefingers / Optimistic / In limbo / Idioteque / Morning bell / Motion picture soundtrack.		
May 01.	(12") *(12FHEIT 45102)*	**PYRAMID SONG. / THE AMAZING SOUNDS OF ORGY / FAST TRACK**	5	-
	(cd-s) *(CDSHEIT 45102)*	– (first 2 tracks) / Trans Atlantic drawl.		
	(cd-s) *(CDFHEIT 45102)*	– (first & third tracks) / Kinetic.		
Jun 01.	(cd/c/d-lp) *(CD/TC/LP FHEIT 45101)* <32764>	**AMNESIAC**	1	2
		– Packt like sardines in a crushd tin box / Pyramid song / Pulk-pull revolving doors / You and whose army? / I might be wrong / Knives out / Morning bell / Amnesiac / Dollars & cents / Hunting bears / Like spinning plates / Life in a glasshouse.		
Aug 01.	(12"/cd-s) *(12/CD FHEIT 45103)*	**KNIVES OUT / CUTTOTH. / LIFE IN A GLASSHOUSE (extended)**	13	-
	(cd-s) *(CDSFHEIT 45103)*	– ('A'side) / Worrywort / Fog.		
Nov 01.	(m-cd/m-lp) *(CD/12 FHEIT 45104)* <36616>	**I MIGHT BE WRONG: LIVE RECORDINGS (live)**	23	44
		– The national anthem / I might be wrong / Morning bell / Like spinning plates / Idioteque / Everything in its right place / Dollars and cents / True love waits.		

RADISH

Formed: Greenville, Texas, USA . . . 1993 by 12 year-old BEN KWELLER. After recruiting his schoolfriend JOHN KENT and BRYAN BLUR, a codgerly late 20-something in comparison, they were subsequently the subject of a frantic major bidding war. 'Mercury' came out on top and an album, 'RESTRAINING BOLT' was completed by 1997. Akin to a fusion of Britpack counterparts, ASH and SYMPOSIUM, the band were the pop-grunge alternative to HANSON, girlie haircuts intact. The group garnered further kudos, purportedly being adored by COURTNEY LOVE and MADONNA. Now in his early twenties, KWELLER opted for a solo career, abandoning the goofball/punk attitude for alt-folk/rock and indie-pop. The first year of the new millennium saw his first musical delivery, the self-financed 'FREAK OUT, IT'S BEN KWELLER' EP, a record that secured enough interest from major-label 'B.M.G.' to come a-knocking. The fruits of the last half decade finally surfaced in 2002 as the 'SHA SHA' album, a melancholic, post-grunge effort from a very talented golden boy of rock.

Album rating: RESTRAINING BOLT (*5) / Ben Kweller: SHA SHA (*7)

BEN KWELLER (b.1982) – vocals, guitar / **BRYAN BLUR** (b.1968) – bass / **JOHN KENT** (b.1980) – drums

Date	Format	Details	Mercury	Polygram
1994.	(cd-s) <*demo*>	**DIZZY**	-	
1995.	(cd-s) <*demo*>	**HELLO**	-	
Oct 96.	(cd-s) <578680>	**DEAR AUNT ARCTICA / BEDTIME**	-	
Aug 97.	(7") *(MER 494)*	**LITTLE PINK STARS. / MAKE IT UP (demo)**	32	-
	(cd-s+=) *(MERCD 494)*	– The you in me (live) / Dear Aunt Artica (live).		
Sep 97.	(cd/c/lp) *(534 644-2/-4/-1)*	**RESTRAINING BOLT**		Apr97
		– Little pink stars / Simple sincerity / Falling and leaving / Dear Aunt Artica / Sugar free / Today's bargain / You in me / Still in wait / Promise / Apparation of purity / My guitar / Bedtime.		
Nov 97.	(7") *(MER 498)*	**SIMPLE SINCERITY. / LITTLE PINK STARS (live)**	50	-
	(cd-s+=) *(MERCD 498)*	– Dear Aunt Arctica (live) / Bedtime (live).		
	(cd-s) *(MERDD 498)*	– ('A'side) / Take my seashell (demo) / Sugar tree (live) / P girl (live).		

— RADISH split up and KWELLER went solo

BEN KWELLER

with **JOSH LATTANZI** – bass + **JOHN KENT** – drums

Date	Format	Details	not iss.	own label
2000.	(cd) <*none*>	**FREAK OUT, IT'S BEN KWELLER**	-	
		– BK baby / Walk on me / How it should be (sha sha) / Make it up / In other words / Lizzy / Problems.		

Date	Format	Details	679	B.M.G.
Mar 02.	(12"ep/cd-ep) *(679 004 TE/CD)*	**BEN KWELLER EP (live)**		-
		– Walk on me / Sweater song / Tomorrow / Superneat.		
Jun 02.	(10"ep/cd-ep) *(679 006 TE/CD)*	**EP PHONE HOME**		-
		– Launch ramp / How it should be (sha sha) / Debbie don't worry doll / Harriet's got a song / Falling.		
Jul 02.	(cd/lp) *(0927 47720-2/-1)* <07863 68114-2>	**SHA SHA**		Mar02
		– How it should be (sha sha) / Wasted and ready / Family tree / Commerce TX / In other words / Walk on me / Make it up / No reason / Lizzy / Harriet's got a song / Falling.		
Aug 02.	(7") *(679 009)*	**WASTED AND READY. / I DON'T KNOW WHY**		-
	(cd-s+=) *(679 009CD)*	– Problems.		

RAILROAD JERK

Formed: Trenton, New Jersey, USA . . . 1989 by MARCELLUS HALL and TONY LEE, adding CHRIS MULLER and JEZ ASPINALL the following year for their eponymous introductory album for 'Matador' records. A potpourri of rootsy rock that encompassed blues, messy punk and country, RAILROAD JERK subsequently delivered their sophomore album, 'RAISE THE PLOW' (1992) after a few more personnel adjustments; STEVE CERCIO for ASPINALL and ALEC STEPHEN for MULLER. The former would make way for DAVE VARENKA, prior to the release of their celebrated third full-set, 'ONE TRACK MIND' (1995). RAILROAD JERK mysteriously vanished for a five-year stretch until a one-off 'Sub Pop' single, after their fourth and final outing, 'THIRD RAIL' (1996). • **Covers:** PROBLEMS (Everly Brothers).

Album rating: RAILROAD JERK (*5) / RAISE THE PLOW (*5) / ONE TRACK MIND (*7) / THE THIRD RAIL (*6)

MARCELLUS HALL – vocals, guitar / **TONY LEE** – bass, vocals / **CHRIS MULLER** – guitar / **JEZ ASPINALL** – drums

Date	Format	Details	Raise The Roof	Matador
Aug 90.	(cd/lp) <*OLE 005-2/-1*>	**RAILROAD JERK**	-	
		– Don't be jealous / Old mill stream / Glamours bitch / Krismus / Talking Railroad Jerk blues / In my face / Participant / Ninety nine miles / Carnival / I'm not mad.		
Jul 91.	(7",7"red) <*OLE 022*>	**YOUNGER THAN YOU. / BALLAD OF JIM WHITE**	-	
1992.	(d7"ep) <*PCP 004*>	**MILK THE COW**		
		– All downhill / Problems / Ordinary nights / I am fine. (above issued on 'P.C.P.')		

— **STEVE CERCIO** – drums, percussion; repl. ASPINALL

— **ALEC STEPHEN** – guitar, vocals; repl. MULLER

Dec 92.	(cd/lp) *(PELLO 02-2/-1)* <*OLE 040-2/-1*>	**RAISE THE PLOW**	-	
		– These streets / Call me the son / Pin prick / During the war / Fixin' to die / In the main / I wanna sway you / Yes baby / You can't go back / Hanging around. (re-iss. Dec95 on 'Matador'; same as US)		
May 93.	(7"ep) <*walt 002*>	**02.20.93**		
		– Message to Maisie / Glamorous bitch / I don't wanna be your welcome mat. (above issued on 'Walt')		

— **DAVE VARENKA** – drums; repl. CERCIO

Date	Format	Details	Matador	Matador
Dec 93.	(d7"/cd-ep) <(OLE 067-7/-2)>	**WE UNDERSTAND / HALFWAY ACROSS. / IRENE / GRANDSTAND BLACKOUT**		Oct93
May 95.	(cd/lp) <(OLE 127-2/-1)>	**ONE TRACK MIND**		Mar95
		– Gun problem / Bang the drum / Rollerkoaster / Riverboat / What did you expect? / Home = hang / Forty minutes / The ballad of Railroad Jerk / Big white lady / Help yourself / You better go now / Some girl waved / Zero blues.		
Sep 95.	(7") <(OLE 149-7)>	**BANG THE DRUM. / HIGHWAY 80**		Jul95
	(cd-s+=) <(OLE 149-2)>	– Why don't we do it in the road / Home = hang / All down hill / In my face (pretty flower).		
Oct 96.	(cd/lp) <(OLE 199-2/-1)>	**THE THIRD RAIL**		
		– Clean shirt / Objectify me / You forgot / Natalie / You bet / Well / Dirty knuckle / Middle child / This is not to say I still miss you / Another nite at the bar / (I can't get) No sleep / Sweet librarian.		

— disbanded some time in '97

Mar 97.	(cd-ep) <(OLE 239-2)>	**SAUBERES HEMD**	-	- Europe
		– Sauberes hemd / Clean shirt / Hot potato / Switchyard / Crow cries.		

Date	Format	Details	not iss.	Sub Pop
2001.	(7"clear) <*SP 537*>	**RAILROAD JERK 2001**	-	
		– Old McNeil / Only one thing.		

RAIN

Formed: Huyton, Liverpool, England . . . 1988 by songwriters NED CLARK and COLIN MURPHY, alongside MARTIN CAMPBELL and TONY McGUIGAN, having luckily received a 6-figure sum from a local trade union centre. Friends and sometime musical compadres of legendary scousers The LA's, RAIN were signed to 'Columbia' – along with fellow Liverpudlians The REAL PEOPLE – at the tail end of '89, prompting much excitement among the press as commentators predicted big things for their BYRDSian three-part harmony trad-pop. After an ensuing 18 month lull – during which initial sessions with NICK LOWE were abandoned – RAIN eventually surfaced with debut album, 'A TASTE OF RAIN' (1991), justifying the early hype with a star-crossed collection of anthemic, bass-heavy power rock/pop drawing comparisons with the likes of CREAM and R.E.M. Critics weren't so enamoured with the record's cover art, however, a 70's heavy metal-style throwback shot of a moisture-soaked female torso framed off at the head and pubic area with the RAIN logo plastered over the breasts.

Album rating: A TASTE OF RAIN (*6)

NED CLARK – vocals, guitar / **COLIN MURPHY** – vocals, guitar / **MARTIN CAMPBELL** – bass, vocals / **TONY McGUIGAN** – drums

		Columbia	Columbia
Mar 91.	(7") *(656732-7)* **LEMONSTONE DESIRED. / OUTBACK BLUES**		-
	(cd-s+=) *(656732-2)* – Drive on (live).		
	(10"++=) *(656732-0)* – ('A'live).		
Jun 91.	(7") *(656981-7)* **A TASTE OF RAIN. / LAUGHING MAN**		-
	(12"+=/cd-s+=) *(656981-6/-2)* – Tumbledown.		
Jul 91.	(cd/c/lp) *(468442-2/-4/-1)* <*52437*> **A TASTE OF RAIN**		-
	– All I want / Going / The beat goes on / Lemonstone desired / Hold on / Here they are / A taste of rain / She's on fire / Mother Earth / Inside out. *(cd+=/c+=)* – Outback blues. *(cd re-iss. Feb96 as 'LIVERPOOL – THE CALM BEFORE THE RAIN'; 483660-2)* – (shared with The REAL PEOPLE album).		
Oct 91.	(7") *(657552-7)* **LEMONSTONE DESIRED. / GOING**		-
	(12"+=/cd-s+=) *(657552-6/-2)* – Outback blues.		
	(10"+=) *(657552-8)* – Drive on (live).		

— disbanded soon after above. Where are they now?

RAINER MARIA

Formed: Madison, Wisconsin, USA . . . 1995 by former EZRA POUND members KYLE FISCHER and WILLIAM KUEHN, alongside CAITHLIN DE MARRAIS. Having already released a self-financed cassette demo, the group were signed to the 'Polyvinyl' label and released a self-titled EP in 1997. A full-length album followed the same year, however the group struggled to make an impact on the music listening community who were probably fatigued with the Emo sound. 1999 saw the band take a step up in quality with the release of the EP, 'ATLANTIC', and the album 'LOOK NOW LOOK AGAIN', both of which managed to transcend the tired genre that the group were labelled with. The band were again impressive on the 2000 'HELL AND HIGH WATER' EP, but then allowed their standards to drop on the album 'A BETTER VERSION OF ME' (2001).

Album rating: PAST WORN SEARCHING (*4) / LOOK NOW LOOK AGAIN (*6) / A BETTER VERSION OF ME (*5)

KYLE FISCHER – vocals, guitar / **CAITHLIN DE MARRAIS** – vocals, bass / **WILLIAM KUEHN** – drums

		Polyvinyl	Polyvinyl
Aug 96.	(cd-ep) <*PRC 009*> **RAINER MARIA**	-	
	– Summer + longer / I love you too / Rain yr hand / Portland / Ian / Made in secret.		
Jan 97.	(7") <*PRC 013*> **NEW YORK: 1955**	-	
Dec 97.	(cd) <*PRC 016*> **PAST WORN SEARCHING**		
	– Tin foil / Half past April / Viva anger, viva hate / Always more often / Sickbed / Never in anger / New York, 1955 / Homeopathy / Put me to sleep.		
Apr 99.	(lp/cd) <*(PRC 024/+CD)*> **LOOK NOW LOOK AGAIN**		
	– Rise / Planetary / Broken radio / Feeling neglected? / Breakfast of champions / The reason the night is so long / Lost, dropped and cancelled / Centrifuge / I'm melting!		
Nov 99.	(cd-ep) <*PRC 029*> **ATLANTIC EP**	-	
	– There will be no night / Atlantic / Soul singer.		
Nov 00.	(7") <*PRC 038*> **HELL AND HIGH WATER. / PAPER SACK**	-	
Feb 01.	(lp/cd) <*(PRC 039/+CD)*> **A BETTER VERSION OF ME**		Jan01
	– Artificial light / Thought I was / Ceremony / The seven sisters / Save my skin / The content of Lincoln's pockets / Atropine / Spit and fire / Heel and high water.		
Nov 02.	(cd-s) <*PRC 056*> **EARS RING / ALCHEMY / AUTOMATIC**	-	

RAIN TREE CROW
(see under ⇒ JAPAN; 70's section)

RAPTURE

Formed: New York City, New York, USA . . . early 1998 by VITO ROCCOFORTE and LUKE JENNER. This experimental punk group released their debut album, 'MIRROR', in 1999 – think TELEVION, TALKING HEADS and PiL. The band's blistering three-minute sonic assaults may not have been to everyone's taste but they could not fail to grab your attention. In 2001 the group recruited bass player MATT SAFER and released the miniset, 'OUT OF THE RACES AND ONTO THE TRACKS' (for 'Sub Pop'), which had critics championing them as leaders of the post-New Wave revival. The following year the band became a four-piece with the inclusion of multi-instrumentalist, GABRIEL ANDRUZZI, and released their finest collection of songs on the 'HOUSE OF JEALOUS LOVERS' EP. • **Covered:** DUMB WAITERS (Psychedelic Furs).

Album rating: MIRROR mini (*5) / OUT OF THE RACES AND ONTO THE TRACKS mini (*5)

LUKE JENNER – vocals, guitar / **VITO ROCCOFORTE** – drums / + bassist

		not iss.	Gold Standard
1998.	(7") <*GSL 36*> **THE CHAIR THAT SQUEAKS. / DUMB WAITERS**	-	
	(UK-iss.Jul01 & Jul02; same as US)		

		Gravity	Gravity
Jan 99.	(m-lp/m-cd) <*(GRAVITY 36/+CD)*> **MIRROR**		
	– In finite clock! / Notes . . . / Olio / Frames frames frames / Mirror / Alienation / Dusk at Maureen's / Kid 606 in love with the underground.		

— **MATT SAFER** – bass; repl. original

		Sub Pop	Sub Pop
Jun 01.	(10"white-m-lp/m-cd) <*(SP/+CD 505)*> **OUT OF THE RACES AND ONTO THE TRACKS**		May01
	– Out of the races and onto the tracks / Modern romance / Caravan / The jam / The pop song / Confrontation. *(re-iss. Oct02; same)*		

		Output	not iss.
Apr 02.	(12") *(OPRDFA 001)* **HOUSE OF JEALOUS LOVERS. / HOUSE OF JEALOUS LOVERS (Morgan Geist remix)**		-
Jul 02.	(12") *(OPRDFA 003)* **OLIO. /**		-

REAL PEOPLE

Formed: Bootle, Liverpool, England . . . 1989 by songwriting brothers TONY and CHRIS GRIFFITHS, who had cut their teeth as JO JO AND THE REAL PEOPLE. The pair were joined by SEAN SIMPSON and TONY ELSON, and, after many impressive local gigs, signed to 'CBS-Columbia'. However, a subsequent trip to India swallowed up most of their advance and it wasn't until late 1990 that they issued their first single, 'WINDOW PANE' (re-issued and a hit a year later). Hyped as leading the vanguard of the new Scally sound alongside RAIN and The LA'S, the band crept ever closer to the Top 40 with each single release. These tracks were all lifted from their eponymous debut album, a disappointingly average collection of pop-indie which lacked the headspinning charm of contemporaries The LA'S. After parting company with their major label paymasters, The REAL PEOPLE laid low for a while before returning on their own terms in 1995.

Album rating: THE REAL PEOPLE (*5)

TONY GRIFFITHS (b. 7 Apr'66) – vocals, bass / **CHRIS GRIFFITHS** (b.30 Mar'68) – guitar, vocals / **SEAN SIMPSON** (b. 9 Oct'69) – guitar / **TONY ELSON** (b. 2 Jan'66) – drums

		Columbia	Relativity
Nov 90.	(7") *(656387-7)* **WINDOW PANE. / LOVE**		-
Feb 91.	(7") *(656612-7)* **OPEN UP YOUR MIND (LET ME IN). / WHO ARE YOU**	70	-
	(12"+=/cd-s+=) *(656612-6/-2)* – ('A' remix).		
Apr 91.	(7"m/cd-s) *(656787-7/-2)* **THE TRUTH. / GO AWAY (demo) / WE TAKE TEA**	73	-
May 91.	(cd/c/lp) *(468084-2/-4/-1)* <*88561 1080-2/-4/-1*> **THE REAL PEOPLE**	59	Jul91
	– Window pane / I can't wait / For you / The truth / Everyday's the same / Wonderful / Open up your mind (let me in) / She / In your hands / Looking at you / Words / Another day.		
Jun 91.	(7"m) *(656932-7)* **WINDOW PANE. / SEE THROUGH YOU / EVERYTHING MUST CHANGE**	60	-
	(12"+=) *(656932-6)* – ('A' extended).		
	(cd-s+=) *(656932-5)* – Begin (live).		
Jan 92.	(7") *(657698-7)* **THE TRUTH (remix). / WORDS (remix)**	41	-
	(cd-s+=) *(657698-2)* – Easy (remix).		
	(12"+=) *(657698-6)* – ('A' extended).		
	(7"ep) *(657698-0)* – ('A'side) / Breathe / Ashamed / Easy.		
May 92.	(7"/c-s) *(658006-7/-4)* **BELIEVER. / IF I'M A FOOL**	38	-
	(12"+=/cd-s+=) *(658006-6/-2)* – Sun shines down (demo) / Don't look now (demo).		
Jul 92.	(7"/cd-s) *(658195-7/-2)* **DREAM ON**	-	w-drawn

— RP were casualties of the music biz in the New Year, although they were back around the mid-90's.

		Egg	not iss.
Apr 95.	(cd-ep) *(1 EGG)* **RAYNERS LANE / SHE SAYS / LIFE'S SO STRANGE**		-
Jun 95.	(7"ep/cd-ep) *(2 EGG/+CD)* **BRING YOU DOWN**		-
	– Rolling stone / Bring you down / What's on the outside / Refugee / Lost in space.		

		MGL Granite	not iss.
Nov 95.	(7"m) *(MGGR7 9)* **EVERY VISION OF YOU. / I DON'T MIND / LOST IN SPACE**		-
	(cd-s+=) *(MGGRCD 9)* – Life is a bore.		
Jun 96.	(7"green/c-s) *(MGGR/+MC 18)* **ROLLING STONE. / REFUGEE**		-
	(cd-s+=) *(MGGRCD 18)* – Waiting for the world.		

— they finally disbanded after above

– compilations, etc. –

Feb 96.	(cd; shared with The RAIN) *Columbia; (483660-2)* **LIVERPOOL (/ THE CALM BEFORE THE STORM)**		-

RED AUNTS

Formed: South California, USA . . . 1991 by KERRY DAVIS, TERRI WAHL, DEBI MARTINI and LESLEY ISHINO. During the band's live shows audiences were initially turned off by the RED AUNTS' inability to play decent structured songs. However, that was to rapidly change when the outfit's "buzz" was circulating the San Francisco and Los Angeles punk scene in early 1993 (just around about the time US millionaire's GREEN DAY were playing bathrooms and living rooms!). Signed to 'Sympathy For The Record Industry' in 1994, the foul-mouthed cartoon punksters released their debut long-player, 'DRAG', following it up with the just as banal 'BAD MOTHERFUCKER 40 O-Z' a year later. These albums created enough reputation for the band, who eventually (after much probing from NOFX and The BOUNCING SOULS) signed to 'Epitaph' late 1995, issuing the 14 song/23 minute mini, '#1 CHICKEN'. The RED AUNTS continued with two more albums, the disappointing 'SALTBOX' (1996) and the much-improved 'GHETTO BLASTER' (1998).

Album rating: DRAG (*4) / BAD MOTHERFUCKER 40 O-Z (*5) / #1 CHICKEN (*7) / SALTBOX (*3) / GHETTO BLASTER (*6)

KERRY DAVIS – vocals, guitar / **TERRI WAHL** – vocals, guitar / **DEBI MARTINI** – bass / **LESLEY ISHINO** – drums

Sympathy F   Sympathy F

Apr 94. (cd) <SFTRI 237> **DRAG**
– Kung Fu kitten / Sleeping pill / Lethal Lolita / Hot rod / Sleeping in the wet spot / Route 66 fucker 6 / Lonely beer troops / Built for a barstool / Luz / Teach me to kill / My cat scratch / Sweet enough / Fly Ford comet – Ho choice / Sex zombie / Hard hearted Hannah.

Apr 95. (cd) <SFTRI 283> **BAD MOTHERFUCKER 40 O-Z**
– Silver moon hotel / Batman a go-go / Terri man / Die baby / Wasted / My Impala '65 / Brian has a car / Baby tough luck / Ice tea / Smoke / Monsterfucker – mothertrucker.

Epitaph   Epitaph

Mar 95. (m-cd/m-c/m-lp) <(E 86446-2/-4/-1)> **#1 CHICKEN**
– Freakathnon / Tin foil fish bowl / Hate / Detroit valentine / Krush / Satan / Roller derby queen / Willarell / When sugar turns to shit / Poker party / Peppermint Patty / Mota / Number one chicken / Netty.

Aug 96. (cd/c/lp) <(E 86473-2/-4/-1)> **SALTBOX**
– Whatever / I can't do anything right / Paco / All red inside / Suerte / Eldritch sauce / Fake modern / Handsome devil / The snake / Ruby (what I won't) / $5 / Palm tree swing / Bullet train / Goin' downtown.

Apr 98. (cd/lp) <(E 86528-2/-4)> **GHETTO BLASTER**
– I'm crying / Poison steak / The things you see, the things you don't / Midnight in the jungle / Exene / Fade in – fade out / Alright! / Who? / Skeleton hand / Wrecked / I'm bored with you / Cookin', cleanin' and cryin'.

RED CRAYOLA

Formed: Houston, Texas, USA … 1966 by MAYO THOMPSON with STEVE CUNNINGHAM and RICK BARTHELME. Signed to local label 'International Artists', they made two classy albums, 'PARABLE OF ARABLE LAND' and 'GOD BLESS THE RED CRAYOLA AND ALL WHO SAIL WITH IT' before disbanding. These consisted of textured, avant-garde psychedelia, a precursor to the likes of PERE UBU and TORTOISE. In 1972, MAYO released a solo album before moving to England five years later to resurrect the band. They signed to JAKE RIVIERA's 'Radar' label, debuting once again with a single, 'WIVES IN ORBIT'. The band also released a comeback album, 'SOLDIER TALK'. In the 80's, MAYO merged his ART & LANGUAGE outfit with RED CRAYOLA to release two albums for 'Rough Trade'; 'KANGAROO' & 'BLACK SNAKES'. MAYO then worked with The RAINCOATS and EPIC SOUNDTRACKS (ex-SWELL MAPS), before embarking on production work for The CHILLS. He relocated to Dusseldorff, Germany, where he completed the 1989 album, 'MALEFACTOR ADE'. This was augmented by RUDIGER CARL, for whom MAYO returned the compliment on his COWWS Quintet project. In 1994, THE RED KRAYOLA entourage (THOMPSON, JOHN McENTIRE, JIM O'ROURKE, DAVID GRUBBS et al) released yet another comeback album, the eponymous 'THE RED KRAYOLA', a pot-pourri experimental exercise for 'Drag City' (of all people). 'COCONUT HOTEL' in 1995 was not the follow-up it seemed but a 1967 RED CRAYOLA recording shelved by 'International Artists' – too weird man! Quirky and subjective to anything around at the time (MAYO was over 50 and reviled by electro-indie fans!), the 'KRAYOLA delivered the JOHN FAHEY-ish 'HAZEL' (1996). The ensemble of around 11 full/part-time members (including GRUBBS, GEORGE HURLEY and FREDERICK BARTHELME) challenged the buying public once again courtesy of 'FINGERPAINTING' (1999), a creative but largely disappointing workout.
• **Songwriters:** MAYO THOMPSON except a few covers. • **Trivia:** ROKY ERICKSON (13th Floor Elevators) guested on debut album.

Album rating: PARABLE OF ARABLE LAND (*7) / GOD BLESS THE RED CRAYOLA AND ALL WHO SAIL WITH IT (*7) / CORRECTED SLOGANS as Art & Language (*5) / SOLDIER TALK (*5) / KANGAROO? with Art & Language (*5) / BLACK SNAKES (*4) / THREE SONGS ON A TRIP TO THE UNITED STATES (*4) / MALEFACTOR ADE (*4) / COCONUT HOTEL the shelved follow-up (*3) / The Red Krayola: THE RED KRAYOLA (*6) / HAZEL (*5) / FINGERPAINTING (*4) / BLUES, HOLLERS AND HELLOS mini (*4) / Mayo Thompson: CORKY'S DEBT TO HIS FATHER (*5)

MAYO THOMPSON – vocals, guitar / **STEVE CUNNINGHAM** – bass / **RICK BARTHELME** – drums

not iss.   Int.Artists

1967. (lp) <IA-LP 2> **PARABLE OF ARABLE LAND (WITH THE FAMILIAR UGLY)**
– Free form freakout; (a) Hurricane fighter pilot – (b) Transparent radiation – (c) War sucks – (d) Pink stainless tail – (e) Parable of arable land / Former reflections enduring doubt. *(UK-iss.1978 on 'Radar'; RAD 12) (re-iss. Jan88 on 'Decal'; LIK 20) (UK cd-iss. Nov96 on 'Spalax'; 14887) (cd re-iss. Jul02 on 'Sunspot'; SPOT 507)*

— **TOMMY SMITH** – drums; repl. RICK (also added guest HOLLY PRITCHETT – vox)

1968. (lp) <ALP 7> **GOD BLESS THE RED CRAYOLA AND ALL WHO SAIL WITH HER**
– Say hello to Jamie Jones / Music / The shirt / Listen to this / Save the house / Victory garden / Coconut hotel / Sheriff Jack / Free piece / Ravi Shankar / Parachutist / Dairy maid's lament / Big / Leejol / Sherlock Holmes / Dirth of tilth / Tina's gone to have a baby / The jewels of the Madonna / Green of my pants / Night song. *(UK-iss.Jun79 on 'Radar'; RAD 16) (UK cd-iss. Nov96 on 'Spalax'; 14898) (lp re-iss. Mar99 on 'Get Back'; GET 534) (cd re-iss. Oct02 on 'Sunspot'; SPOT 521)*

— split in 1970

MAYO THOMPSON

with **FRANK DAVIS, JOE DUGAN, MIKE SUMLER, JIMMY NEWHOUSE, CARSON GRAHAM + ROGER ROMANO**

not iss.   Texas Revolution

1969. (lp) <2270> **CORKY'S DEBT TO HIS FATHER**
– The lesson / Oyster thins / Horses / Dear Betty baby / Venus in the morning / To you / Fortune / Black legs / Good brisk blues / Around the home / Worried worried. *<(cd-iss. 1994/UK Dec96 on 'Drag City'; DC 49)>*

ART & LANGUAGE / RED CRAYOLA

MAYO + JESS CHAMBERLAIN

not iss.   Music Language

1976. (lp) <1848> **CORRECTED SLOGANS**
– Maharashta / Keep all your friends / Imagination 1 & 2 / Coleridge vs. Martineau / An exemplification / Postscript to SDS infiltration / War dance 1 & 2 / An harangue / Ergastulum / The mistakes of Trotsky / The smophoriazusae / Louis Napoleon / Seven compartments / Petrichenko / Don't talk to sociologists / What are the inexpensive things the panel most enjoys an international / History / Organisation / It's an illusion / Penny capitalists / Plekhanov / Natura facit saltus.

RED CRAYOLA

In 1977, they re-formed with **MAYO + CHAMBERLAIN** / **+ CHRISSIE THOMPSON** (Mayo's wife) – vox / **PERE UBU: DAVID THOMAS** – vocals, **TONY MAIMONE** – bass, **ALLEN RAVENSTINE** – sax, **SCOTT KRAUSE** – drums, **TOM HERMAN** – guitar / **LORA LOGIC** – sax (of ESSENTIAL LOGIC) / **DICK CUTHELL** – trumpet

Radar   not iss.

Oct 78. (7"red) (ADA 22) **WIVES IN ORBIT. / YIK YAK**
Mar 79. (lp) (RAD 18) **SOLDIER TALK**
– March No.12 / On the brink / Letter bomb / Conspirator's oath / March No.14 / Soldier talk / Discipline / X / An opposition spokesman / Uh, knowledge dance / Wonderland.

— **MAYO, ALLEN + LORA** with **EPIC SOUNDTRACKS** – drums (ex-SWELL MAPS) / **GINA BIRCH** (of RAINCOATS) + **BEN ANNESLEY** – bass

Rough Trade   not iss.

Aug 79. (12") (RT 026) **MICRO CHIPS & FISH. / THE STORY SO FAR**

ART & LANGUAGE / RED CRAYOLA

Oct 80. (7") (RT 054) **BORN IN FLAMES. / SWORD OF GOD**
May 81. (lp)(c) (ROUGH 19)(COPY 005) **KANGAROO**
– Kangaroo / Portrait of V.L. Lenin in the style of Jackson Pollock (parts 1 & 2) / Marches nos.23, 24 & 25 / Born to win (transactional analysis with Gestalt experiments) / Keep all your friends / The milkmaid / The principles of party organisation / Prisoner's model / The mistakes of Trotsky / 1917 / The tractor driver / Plekhanov. *(c+=) –* An old man's dream / If she loves you. *(cd-iss. Dec96 on 'Drag City'; DC 80)*
Jul 81. (7") (RT 073) **AN OLD MAN'S DREAM. / THE MILKMAID**

RED CRAYOLA - ART & LANGUAGE

— **CHRIS TAYLOR** – drums; repl. EPIC, GINA + LORA

Recommended Ralph

Sep 83. (lp) (ALRC 1949) <002> **BLACK SNAKES**
– Black snakes / Ratman, the weight watcher / The sloths / The jam / Hedges / A portrait of V.L. Lenin in the style of Jackson Pollock (part 1) / Future pilots / A portrait of you / Words of love / Cafe twenty-one / Gynaecology in ancient Greece. *(cd-iss. Jun97 on 'Drag City'; DC 104CD)*

RED CRAYOLA

JESSE CHAMBERLAIN – drums; returned to repl. TAYLOR + ANNESLEY

Pure Freude   not iss.

1984. (lp) (PF36 CK18) **THREE SONGS ON A TRIP TO THE UNITED STATES (live)** — German
– Monster one / California girl / Caribbean postcard / Discipline / X / Wives in orbit / Ergastulum / A portrait of you. *(UK cd-iss. Jun97 on 'Drag City'; DC 105CD)*

— next with **ALBERT OEHLEN** – multi / **RUDINGER CARL** – reeds

Glass   not iss.

Mar 89. (lp/cd) (GLA LP/CD 035) **MALEFACTOR ADE**
– Extremism / Baby Jesus frog / Blue jeans / Steve McQueen's garden / Colour theory, No.4 / Franz Von Assisi / Sex machine / The coaster / Break a leg / T.B. – Tissues / Dope / The Alma fanfare / Colour theory, No.3. *<cd re-iss. 2000 on 'Drag City'; DC 45>*

RED KRAYOLA

— **MAYO THOMPSON** with **JIM O'ROURKE** – guitar (b. Chicago) / **JOHN McENTIRE** – drums (of TORTOISE) / **DAVID GRUBBS** – guitar / **TOM WATSON** – bass / **GEORGE HURLEY** – drums

Drag City   Drag City

Sep 94. (cd) <(DC 52)> **THE RED KRAYOLA**
– Jimmy Silk – Supper be ready / Pride / Book of kings / Pessimisty / Worms, worms, thirst / People get ready (the train's not coming) / If 'S' is / Miss X / Raspierre / Stand-up / Art-dog / I knew it / 101st / (Why) I'm so blase / The big macumba / Voodoo child / Suddenly. *(re-iss. Dec96; same)*

Jun 95. (12"/cd-s) <(DC 53/+CD)> **AMOR AND LANGUAGE**
– Stil de grain brun (Wendy Gondeln remix) / Stil de grain brun (radio edit) / Stil de grain brun. *(re-iss. Dec96; same) (re-iss. Feb02 on 'Ruminance'; RUM 013)*

Dec 95. (7") <(DC 86)> **CHEMISTRY. / FAREWELL TO ARMS**

— plus **MICHAEL BALDWIN / WERNER BUTTNER / LYNN JOHNSTON / HEI HAN KHIANG / ALBERT OEHLEN / STEPHEN PRINA / ELISA RANDAZZO / MARY LASS STEWART / CHRISTOPHER WILLIAMS**

RED CRAYOLA (cont)

Jan 97. (cd) <(DC 98CD)> **HAZEL** Nov96
– I'm so blase / Duck & cover / Duke of Newcastle / Decaf the planet / GAO / Larking / Jimmy too bad / Falls / We feel fine / 5123881 / Hollywood / Another song, another Satan / Boogie / Dad / Father Abraham / Serenade.

Apr 98. (7"+book) (EFA 07326-7) **SONGS FOR OHIO**
– I'm so blase / Father Abraham (alternate mix).
(above issued on 'Stewardess' records + Ohio fanzine)

Feb 99. (12") <(DC 119)> **FATHER ABRAHAM (remixes by TRANQUILITY BASS, SCHORSCH KAMERUN + WENDY GONDELN)**

— next with **DAVID GRUBBS, STEPHEN PRINA, GEORGE HURLEY + FREDERICK BARTHELME**

Jun 99. (cd) <9156-2> **FINGERPAINTING**
– George III / Bad medicine / A hybrid creature of greed, ignorance and powers of comprehension plays a vaulted drum kit . . . / Tears for example / There there Betty Betty / The greed of a clarinet that is puffy from crying gets tossed in butter and spread by notes / Vile vile grass / A sow with an abbess's bonnet is sitting on four rock-objects and singing along with them . . . / Mother / Out of a trombone that is divided lengthways by a partition of gold sound seven violins . . . / In my baby's Ruth, Sandy's drums with David & Shadwell, filthy lucre.

Sep 00. (m-lp/m-cd) <(DC 190/+CD)> **BLUES, HOLLERS AND HELLOS**
– Container of drudgery / (Never had a name) / Magnificence as such / Is there? / 6-5-3 blues. (cd+=) – (hidden track).

– compilations, etc. –

Apr 90. (cd) Decal; (CDLIK 65) **THE PARABLE OF ARABLE LAND / GOD BLESS THE RED CRAYOLA AND ALL WHO SAIL WITH IT**
(re-iss. Jan97 on 'Charly'; CDCRH 112) (re-iss. Jan02 on 'Snapper'; SNAP 049CD)

1996. (cd) Leiterwagen; (official bootleg) **DELIVERANCE** (rec. 1969-1996 + compiled by Wendy Gondeln – Albert Oehlen) – German

Dec 96. (cd) Drag City; <(DC 62)> **COCONUT HOTEL** (rec. 1967) Apr95
– Boards / Water pour / One-second piece (1-36) / Organ buildup / Vocal / Free guitar / One-minute imposition / Piano / Guitar.

Jan 99. (d-cd) Drag City; <(DC 92)> **LIVE 1967 (live)** Jul98
– (6 untitled tracks).

RED HOUSE PAINTERS

Formed: San Francisco, California, USA . . . 1989 by MARK KOZELEK (who had earlier sang in GOD FORBID) along with drummer ANTHONY KOUTSOS who he met in 1989, after moving from Ohio to Atlanta. Relocating once again, this time to San Francisco, the pair duly recruited guitarist GORDON MACK and bassist JERRY VESSEL. The outfit was basically KOZELEK's baby, however, and his writing and distictly melancholy musings dominated the group's work. Their debut album, 'DOWN COLOURFUL HILL', was virtually a bare demo which had arrived in the hands of '4 a.d.' supremo, Ivo Watts-Russell, via American Music Club miserabilist, MARK EITZEL. Spiritually akin to AMC, the debut showcased KOZELEK's moody pastel-rock introspections, downbeat but often hauntingly melodic. Though the press raved over it (comparisons were made with singer/songwriters like NEIL YOUNG and LOU REED), the album sold negligably. A further couple of RED HOUSE PAINTERS' releases followed in 1993, confusingly enough, both entitled 'RED HOUSE PAINTERS'. One was a spawling double set building on the wistfulness of the debut while the other was a mini-album featuring such endearing covers as Paul Simon's 'I AM A ROCK' and 'THE STAR SPANGLED BANNER'. It would be another two years before the group's next album, KOZELEK and Co. undertaking a rare UK tour, their first British dates since an early appearance at London's 'Borderline'. 'OCEAN BEACH' (1995) was a more robust set, KOZELEK illustrating the breadth of his influences with a YES cover, 'LONG DISTANCE RUNAROUND', no doubt a crime punishable by public flogging in most indie bands' book. Though the critical plaudits continued to roll in, the album again failed to sell in any great quantity. With a move to 'Island' in 1996, surely a better home for the sparse melancholy of the bulk of KOZELEK's material, the group released 'SONGS FOR A BLUE GUITAR?'. Unfortunately, KOZELEK became enmeshed in legal problems which effectively shelved The RED HOUSE PAINTERS release, 'OLD RAMON'. In the meantime, the singular singer/songwriter confounded many fans and critics with the independently released mini-set 'ROCK'N'ROLL SINGER' (2000). Chances are there can't be too many record collections around with a fair whack of both AC/DC and JOHN DENVER albums. It's also probably fair to say that no performers have ever attempted to cover both artists on the same record. All credit to KOZELEK then, who demonstrated that not only did he have a wide ranging taste but that he had a hitherto relatively unannounced and quite startling talent for interpreting other writers in ways they couldn't possibly have imagined. In addition to the title track, the aforementioned mini-set featured virtually unrecognisable covers of AC/DC's 'YOU AIN'T GOT A HOLD ON ME' and 'BAD BOY BOOGIE', transformed from balls-out rock'n'roll to fragile, suffering folk-blues. Denver's 'AROUND AND AROUND' was also turned upside down but in a different way. The very fact that KOZELEK has deemed Denver's work worthy of reinvestigation is significant in itself given that the late singer/songwriter is still the butt of many a joke and remains foolishly overlooked by many sneering critics. KOZELEK also masterminded 'Take Me Home: A Tribute to John Denver' as well as two compilations for an American AIDS charity, the Shanti Project. Following on from the EP, a full length solo release, 'WHAT'S NEXT TO THE MOON' (2001) went one better and featured a whole album's worth of AC/DC interpretations (including the three already released on the EP), proving that his virtual reinvention of Bon Scott, Angus and Malcolm Young's sweaty cock-rock muse was no fluke. The shelved 'OLD RAMON' eventually saw the light of day (via 'Sub Pop') in spring 2001 under The RED HOUSE PAINTERS moniker, revealing a lighter, dare we say exuberant side to the outfit's mournful oeuvre. Sub Pop also offered concert set, 'WHITE CHRISTMAS LIVE' (2001) available initially on a mail order only basis. • **Songwriters:** All by KOZELEK, except 'Dragonflies' by ROBYN RIEL-NAIL. Covers; STAR SPANGLED BANNER (US National Anthem) / SHOCK ME (Kiss). • **Trivia:** Their UK first gig (very rare) was at The Borderline in London in the Autumn of '92.

Album rating: DOWN COLORFUL HILL (*7) / RED HOUSE PAINTERS double-set (*9) / RED HOUSE PAINTERS mini-set (*6) / OCEAN BEACH (*7) / SONGS FOR A BLUE GUITAR (*6) / RETROSPECTIVE compilation (*8) / OLD RAMON (*7) / Mark Kozelek: ROCK'N'ROLL SINGER mini (*5) / WHAT'S NEXT TO THE MOON (*7)

MARK KOZELEK – vocals / **GORDON MACK** – guitar / **JERRY VESSEL** – bass / **ANTHONY KOUTSOS** – drums

	4 a.d.	4ad-Warners

Sep 92. (cd)(lp/c) (CAD 2014CD)(CAD/+C 2014) <45062> **DOWN COLORFUL HILL**
– 24 / Medicine bottle / Down colourful hill / Japanese to English / Lord kill the pain / Michael.

May 93. (cd)(d-lp/c) (DAD 3008CD)(DAD/+C 3008) <45256> **RED HOUSE PAINTERS** 63
– Grace cathedral park / Down through / Katy song / Mistress / Things mean a lot / Funhouse / Take me out / Rollercoaster / New Jersey / Dragonflies / Mistress (piano version) / Mother / Strawberry hill / Brown eyes.

Oct 93. (cd)(m-lp/c) (CAD 3016CD)(CAD/+C 3016) <45441> **RED HOUSE PAINTERS** 68
– Evil / Bubble / I am a rock / Helicopter / New Jersey / Uncle Joe / Blindfold / Star spangled banner.

Feb 94. (12"ep/cd-ep) (BAD 4004/+CD) **SHOCK ME / SHOCK ME (mix). / SUNDAYS AND HOLIDAYS / THREE-LEGGED CAT**

Mar 95. (cd)(c)(2x10"lp) (CAD 5005CD)(CADC 5005)(DAD 5005) <45859> **OCEAN BEACH**
– Cabezon / Summer dress / San Geronimo / Shadows / Over my head / Red carpet / Brockwell Park / Moments / Drop. (lp+=) – Long distance runaround.

	Island	Polygram

Jul 96. (cd/c) (CID/ICT 8050) <531061> **SONGS FOR A BLUE GUITAR**
– Have you forgotten / Song for a blue guitar / Make like paper / Priest alley song / Trailways / Feel the rain fall / Long distance runaround / All mixed up / Revelation Big Sur / Silly love songs / Another song for a blue guitar.

MARK KOZELEK

— with **TIM MOONEY** – instruments (of AMERICAN MUSIC CLUB)

	Badman	Badman

Jul 00. (m-cd) <(BRCD 993)> **ROCK'N'ROLL SINGER** Jun00
– Find me, Reuben Olivares / Rock'n'roll singer / You ain't got a hold on me / Metropol 47 / Around and around / Bad boy boogie / Ruth Marie.

Mar 01. (cd) <(BRCD 990)> **WHAT'S NEXT TO THE MOON** Jan01
– Up to my neck in you / Love at first feel / Love hungry man / Bad boy boogie / What's next to the moon / Walk all over you / You ain't got a hold on me / If you want blood / Riff raff / Rock'n'roll singer. (d-cd iss.Dec01 as 'IF YOU WANT BLOOD'+=; BRCD 982) – ROCK'N'ROLL SINGER

	Sub Pop	Sub Pop

Dec 01. (cd) <(SPCD 587)> **WHITE CHRISTMAS LIVE (live)**
– Rock'n'roll singer / Cruiser / Up to my neck in you / White Christmas / What's next to the Moon / Admiral Fell promises / Wop a din din / Shadows / Evil / Dragonflies / Things mean a lot / Three-legged cat.

RED HOUSE PAINTERS

— **KOZELEK + KOUTSOS + VESSEL** recruited **PHIL CARNEY**

	Sub Pop	Sub Pop

Apr 01. (cd) <(SPCD 565)> **OLD RAMON**
– Wop-a-din-din / Byrd Joel / Void / Between days / Cruiser / Michigan / River / Smokey / Golden / Kavita.

– compilations, etc. –

Jul 99. (d-cd) (DAD 9013CD) <79006> **RETROSPECTIVE** May99
– Shock me / Grace cathedral park / Katy song / Summer dress / New Jersey / Medicine bottle / Michael / San Geronimo / Bubble / Mistress / Drop / Evil / Rollercoaster / Funhouse / Waterkill / Uncle Joe / Helicopter / Brown eyes / Dragonflies / Japanese to English / Shock me (mix) / Over my head / Brockwell Park / Shadows / Mistress (piano version) / Summer dress / Instrumental.

RED KRAYOLA (see under ⇒ RED CRAYOLA)

RED MONKEY (see under ⇒ MILKY WIMPSHAKE)

RED RED MEAT

Formed: Chicago, Illinois, USA . . . 1990 as FRIENDS OF BETTY, by frontman/songwriter, TIM RUTILI (also a pop video maker for the likes of VERUCA SALT), GLYNIS JOHNSON, GLENN GIRARD and BRIAN DECK. A debut 45, 'SNOWBALL' and an LP 'FRIENDS OF BETTY' (1992) – the latter for 'Perishable' records – were issued to no great cheer. Tragedy was to subsequently beset the band when later in the year, GLYNIS

JOHNSON died of AIDS, her boyfriend RUTILI apparently unaware of her rapid ill-health; he had just previously sacked her from the band. As a tribute to JOHNSON, RED RED MEAT (with new replacement TIM HURLEY on board) continued, inspired and enthused by a recent support slot to new mates, The SMASHING PUMPKINS. Their eponymous 1993 'RED RED MEAT' debut didn't quite set the barbeque alight, although a deal with 'Sub Pop' won the band a wider audience. Brooding, laid-back and eerily melancholic, RED RED MEAT played at the opening New York party of controversial Spanish director Pedro Almodavar's film, 'Kika', although their Lo-fi psychedelic grunge-blues set wasn't quite appreciated by the arty dance crowd. A 1994 album, 'JIMMYWINE MAJESTIC', was highly regarded by many critics, a record they topped a year later with the semi-classic 'BUNNY GETS PAID'. Although a clutch of obscure singles and a fourth set, 'THERE'S A STAR ABOVE THE MANGER TONIGHT' (1997) appeared over the next two years, the band splintered when RUTILI and HURLEY (with newcomer BEN MASSARELLA) formed LOFTUS. Early in 1998, this short-lived project delivered their one and only album, 'LOFTUS', before the trio changed their name to CALIFONE, releasing a solitary eponymous mini-set on the 'Flydaddy' label later that year. Realising that all the members of RED RED MEAT had really just begun playing stripped electro-blues, and had really only changed their name, CALIFONE began work on their debut LP, 'ROOMSOUND' (2001 – and issued on RUTILI's 'Perishable' imprint). The set boasted a revolving-door cast of musicians from the Chicago indie set (TORTOISE, FRUITBATS, et al) and harked back to RED RED's early stoned acoustic blues sound, with the addition of keyboards and bleepy electronics. A limited edition EP entitled 'DECLARATION ONE' was delivered in 2002, and the mix'n'match combo were featured on the 'SOMETIMES GOOD WEATHER FOLLOWS BAD PEOPLE' compilation (also 2002) set of CALIFONE's early material. In autmun 2002, the group began work on their second LP proper, to be entitled 'QUICKSAND / CRADLESNAKES', RUTILI promised more hazey blues, with a sprinkling of free-form jazz instrumentals. • **Covered:** CARPET OF HORSES (Polara) / SAD PETER PAN with Smashing Pumpkins (Vic Chesnutt).

Album rating: Friends Of Betty: FRIENDS OF BETTY (*4) / Red Red Meat: RED RED MEAT (*6) / JIMMYWINE MAJESTIC (*6) / BUNNY GETS PAID (*7) / THERE'S A STAR ABOVE THE MANGER TONIGHT (*6) / Loftus: LOFTUS (*4) / Califone: CALIFONE mini (*5) / SOMETIMES GOOD WEATHER FOLLOWS BAD PEOPLE compilation (*5) / ROOMSOUND (*6)

FRIENDS OF BETTY

TIM RUTILI – vocals, guitar, keyboards, etc / **GLENN GIRARD** – guitar, etc (of CROWS) / **BRIAN DECK** – synthesizer, drums, percussion / **GLYNIS JOHNSON** – bass

			not iss.	unknown
1991.	(7")	**SNOWBALL. /**	-	-
			not iss.	Perishable
1992.	(lp) <PER 001>	**FRIENDS OF BETTY**	-	

RED RED MEAT

—— **TIM HURLEY** – bass, guitars, synthesizer; repl. JOHNSON who was sacked (she died of AIDS late in 1992)

			not iss.	Red Red Meat
1993.	(cd) <RRM 001>	**RED RED MEAT**	-	

– Robo sleep / Snowball / Molly's on the rag / Flossy / Idaho durt / Cellophane / Grief giver / Rabbit eyed / Hot nickety monkey / Nice round numbers / X-diamond cutter blues / Stare box. <(US/UK-iss.Oct94/Feb95 on 'Sub Pop'+=; 3)> – P.C.L.M. / Rubbing mirrors / Sand box.

			Sub Pop	Sub Pop
Sep 93.	(7") <(SP 232S)>	**FLANK. / LATHER**		
Mar 94.	(lp/cd)(c) <(SP/+CD 119-300)<(SP 243 A/B)>	**JIMMYWINE MAJESTIC**		

– Flank / Stained and lit / Braindead / Smokey Mtn. cool dip / Moon calf tripe / Cillamange / Ball / Lather / Rusted water / Gorshin / Dowser / Comes / Roses.

Oct 94.	(7"/10") <(SP 272)>	**IDIOT SON. / GAUZE**		

(10"+=) <(SP 139/343)> – Mouse-ish.

—— added former guest **BEN MASSARELLA** – drums; to repl. GIRARD

Oct 95.	(lp/cd) <(SP 318/+B)>	**BUNNY GETS PAID**		

– Carpet of horses / Chain chain chain / Rosewood, Wax, Voltz + Glitter / Buttered / Gauze / Idiot son / Variations on Nadia's theme / Oxtail / Sad cadillac / Taxidermy blues in reverse / There's always tomorrow.

Nov 96.	(7") (SP 376)	**THERE'S A STAR ABOUT THE MANGER TONIGHT. / WELCOME CHRISTMAS**		-
Feb 97.	(cd) <(SPCD 387)>	**THERE'S A STAR ABOUT THE MANGER TONIGHT**		

– Sulfur / There's a star above the manger tonight / Chinese balls / Second hand sea / All tied / Paul Pachal / Bury me / Airstream driver / Mecanix (from cold milk) / Quarter horses (B-slow) / Just like an egg on stilts.

			Generator	not iss.
Feb 97.	(7") <G 25>	**LISTENING NOW. / Polara: Carpet Of Horses**		
			Flydaddy	Flydaddy
Mar 97.	(7") <(FLY 019-7)>	**MILK FOR THE MECHANIC. / Number One Cup: THE TONGUE OF 2 AM**		

—— new bassist **MATT FIELDS** was also a member before joining GRIFTERS offshoot, THOSE BASTARD SOULS

LOFTUS

—— were formed by **TIM RUTILI + TIM HURLEY** plus **BEN MASSARELLA**

			Perishable	Perishable
Jan 98.	(cd) <(PERISH 03CD)>	**LOFTUS**		Jul00

– Raisin / Emma's rubber leg / Haywine / Stolen from a rifle clean brothel / King Carp in a Dan Ryan ditch / Theme from Loftus Nine / Nervous / Bell and hammer / Penguin boy's love story / When the electricity goues out in the submarine / Marlon Perkins / Cake / Blind.

CALIFONE

—— **RUTILI + MASSARELLA + HURLEY + DECK** with **DOUGLAS SCHARIN, BUNDY K. BROWN, PHIL SPIRITO + CURTIS HARVEY**

			Flydaddy	Flydaddy
Sep 98.	(m-cd) <(FLY 031)>	**CALIFONE**		

– On the steeple with the shakes (Xmas tigers) / Silvermine pictures / Pastry sharp / To hush a sick transmission / Dime fangs / Red food old heat / Down Eisenhower sun up w/mule.

			Road Cone	Road Cone
Mar 00.	(cd-ep) <(ROCD 025)>	**CALIFONE**		

– Electric fence / St. Martha let it fold / Beneath the yauchtsman / Don't let me die nervous / Docks Boggs.

			Glitterhouse	Perishable
Feb 01.	(cd) (GRCD 510) <PERISH 19>	**SOMETIMES GOOD WEATHER FOLLOWS BAD PEOPLE** (compilation)		Mar02

– CALIFONE mini / CALIFONE ep / To hush a sick transmission / When the snakehandler slips.

Jun 01.	(cd) (GRCD 527) <PERISH 15>	**ROOMSOUND**		Apr01

– Trout silk / Bottles and bones (shades and sympathy) / Fisherman's wife / Porno starlet vs. rodeo clown / Tayzee nub / Slow RT. hand / St. Augustine (a belly full of swans) / Wade in the water / Rattlesnakes smell like split cucumber / New black tooth.

Feb 02.	(cd) <mail-order>	**DECELERATION ONE**	-	-

– Handpainted halo – Ceiling / Rooftop – Static / Face under hat – Old streetside / Parade queen – Milk waltz – Dirt moon / Lakewater / Parachutes / Peel / Intro – Sleepy child asks for an orange / Monkey, cat, ballerina and hood escape from moving car – Clown loses head – Dog stays / Dog sold – Hangs from rearview mirror – Loosen and fall / Fruitstand floor – Ankle bite – Dog steals fallen orange – Broom / Night falls – Devil springs fully formed from spilt whiskey – Hellions assemble / Hell orchestra with dancers – Glass choir / Cat fights Devil – Hellions chase dog – Toy police chase hellions / Garlic head clown serenades ballerina crying vaseline tears / Dog feeds orange to sleepy child – Outro.

RED SLEEPING BEAUTY
(see under ⇒ ACID HOUSE KINGS)

Dougal REED (see under ⇒ FAITH HEALERS, Th')

REFUSED

Formed: Umea, Sweden ... 1991 by DENNIS LYXZEN, JONF BRANNSTROM, KRISTOFER STEEN and DAVID SANDSTROM. More often than not REFUSED are placed in the hardcore punk revival bracket, but they fuse together many styles including jazz movements and breakbeat, and unlike some of the punk revivalists of this period their anarchist sensibilities were fairly unquestionable. In many ways they were the forerunners of punky dance bands like The PRODIGY's later incarnation, although incomparable as far as political integrity goes. REFUSED became available to the record buying public with their EP, 'THIS IS THE NEW DEAL' (1993). Following this up the same year with their first full-length set, 'THIS JUST MIGHT BE . . . THE TRUTH' (1993). A period of three years elapsed, with several EP's released, before the band brought out another album, 'FAN THE FLAMES OF DISCONTENT' (1996). On this set they proved their adept musicianship, while never straying from the point of the songs, and the reason why they were doing it in the first place. Something which they continued on into their third full-piece, 'SHAPE OF PUNK TO COME' (1998). On this album though they really took off as far as punk-innovation was concerned; skilfully mixing the hardcore styles with lighter more dance-inspired passages. Unfortunately this record marked the end of the band as a unit. Although the musical creativity of the members did not finish there. REFUSED's frontman, LYXZEN, joined fellow punk-minded idealists LARS STROMBERG (from punk outfit SEPARATION), INGE JOHANSSON from punk art band THE FEMALE ANCHOR OF SADE, SARA ALMGREN from SAIDWAS and the DOUGHNUTS and LUDWIG ALMGREN (also from SAIDWAS) to form the anarcho-punky The (INTERNATIONAL) NOISE CONSPIRACY. (I)NC recorded and put out two full-length albums, 'THE FIRST CONSPIRACY' (1999) and 'SURVIVAL SICKNESS' (2000). The former was a collection of 7" singles the band had put out in 1999 on several different labels. The latter on 'Burning Heart' was conceived as a whole unit, and shows the band's mix of punk and hardcore styles with the British Mod sounds of the sixties. LYXZEN also found time in 1999 to write, record, and release, a single and album, 'SONGS IN THE KEY OF RESISTANCE' (1999), with his other outfit, LOST PATROL. With Swedish garage-punk (i.e. The HIVES, etc.) about to be unleashed to a young, unwary UK (and later US) audience raised on GREEN DAY and BLINK-182, The (INTERNATIONAL) NOISE CONSPIRACY delivered their second full-set, 'A NEW MORNING . . .' (2001). The anthemic and witty 'CAPITALISM STOLE MY VIRGINITY', 'BORN INTO A MESS' and nine other pro-Socialist tracks set out their post-millennium retro-political manifesto. What's next? 'Malmo's Burning'!

REFUSED (cont)

Album rating: THIS JUST MIGHT BE . . . THE TRUTH (*5) / SONGS TO FAN THE FLAMES OF DISCONTENT (*5) / THE SHAPE OF PUNK TO COME mini (*6) / (International) Noise Conspiracy: THE FIRST CONSPIRACY (*6) / SURVIVAL SICKNESS (*6) / A NEW MORNING (*8)

DENNIS LYXZEN – vocals / **JON F BRANNSTROM** – guitar / **KRISTOFER STEEN** – bass, guitar / **DAVID SANDSTROM** – drums

			House Of Kicks	not iss.
Oct 94.	(cd)	(STARTREC 372-2) **THIS JUST MIGHT BE . . . THE TRUTH**		-

– Intro / Pump the brakes / Trickbag / 5th freedom / Untitled / Strength / Our silence / Dust / Inclination / Mark / Tide / Button. *(re-iss. Jan95 on 'We Bite'; WB 3116CD) (re-iss. Sep97 on 'Burning Heart'; BHR 062CD)*

			Burning Heart	not iss.
Oct 94.	(cd-ep)	(BHR 002CD) **THIS IS THE NEW DEAL**		-

– Hate breeds hate / Break / Where's equality? / Soft / I wish.

1995.	(cd-ep)	**REFUSED LOVES RANDY**	-	- Sweden

– TV freak / Pump the brakes / Humanology / Re-fused.

1996.	(cd-ep)	**PUMP THE BRAKES EP**	-	- Sweden

– Pump the brakes / Perception / Strength / Who died.

			Equal Vision	Equal Vision
Mar 97.	(m-cd/m-lp)	(<EVR CD/LP 033>) **THE EVERLASTING EP**		

– Burn it / Symbols / Sunflower princess / Everlasting / I am not me / The real / Pretty face.

			Burning Heart	Victory
Sep 97.	(cd)	(BHR 061CD) <VR 40> **SONGS TO FAN THE FLAMES OF DISCONTENT**		Jun96

– Rather be dead / Coup d'etat / Hook, line and sinker / Return to the closet / Life support addiction / It's not O.K. / Crusader of hopelessness / Worthless is the freedom bought . . . . / This trust will kill again / Beauty / Last minute pointer / The slayer.

			Burning Heart	Epitaph
Mar 98.	(m-cd)	(BHR 071CD) <82001> **THE SHAPE OF PUNK TO COME**		Oct98

– Worms of the senses – Liberation frequency / The deadly rhythm / Summerholidays vs. punkroutine / Bruitist pome #5 / New noise / The Refused party program / Protest song '68 / Refused are fuckin' dead / The shape of punk to come / Tannhauser – Derive / The Apollo programme was a hoax.

			Burning Heart	Honey Bear
May 98.	(cd-ep)	(BHR 079CDS) <21> **THE NEW NOISE THEOLOGY EP**		Nov98

– New noise / Blind date / Poetry written in gasoline / Refused are fucking dead.

—— after they split, LYXZEN formed The LOST PATROL who released an eponymous set in 1999; 'SONGS IN THE KEY OF RESISTANCE' was issued in Nov'00 on 'Startracks'; (STAR 7842-2)

– compilations, etc. –

Sep 97.	(cd)	Burning Heart; (BHR 063CD) **THIS ALBUM CONTAINS OLD SONGS VOL.1**		-
Sep 97.	(cd)	Burning Heart; (BHR 064CD) **THIS ALBUM CONTAINS OLD SONGS VOL.2**		-

(INTERNATIONAL) NOISE CONSPIRACY

DENNIS LYXZEN – vocals, tambourine / **SARA ALMGREN** – guitar, tambourine, organ (ex-DOUGHNUTS, ex-SAIDIWAS) / **LARS STROMBERG** – guitar, vocals (ex-SEPARATION) / **INGE JOHANSSON** – bass, vocals (ex-FEMALE ANCHOR OF SADE) / **LUDWIG DAHLBERG** – drums (ex-SAIDIWAS)

			G-7	Epitaph
Jun 99.	(cd)	(G7 009CD) <82008> **THE FIRST CONSPIRACY**		-

– The first conspiracy / Abolish war / A new language / Do U know my name? / T.I.M.E.B.O.M.B. / The sin crusade / The blast-off / Young pretenders army / I swear if U do / Airports / Introduction to the . . . / Black mask. <US-iss.Apr01; same as UK> *(re-iss. Jan02; same) (re-iss. Jun02 on 'Burning Heart' cd/lp; BHR 149-2/-1)*

			Burning Heart	not iss.
Apr 00.	(lp/cd)	(BHR 106-1/-2) **SURVIVAL SICKNESS**		-

– I wanna know about U / The subversive sound / Smash it up / Survival sickness / The reproduction of death / Imposter costume / Intermission / Only lovers left alive / Do I have to spell it out / Will I ever be quiet / Enslavement blues / Ready steady go!

			Big Wheel	Big Wheel
Nov 00.	(7"ep/cd-ep)	(<BWR 0238/+CD>) **SMASH IT UP. / INNER CITY REJECTS / SLEEPING PILLS**		

			Sweet Nothing	Sub Pop
Mar 01.	(7")	(7SN 003) <SP 558> **THE REPRODUCTION OF DEATH. / THE TRANSMISSION / SIMALCRUA OVERLOAD**		May01

(cd-ep iss.May01 on 'Burning Heart'; BHR 123-2)

			Hopeless	not iss.
Oct 01.	(cd-s)	(5005) **CAPITALISM STOLE MY VIRGINITY / EVER FELT CHEATED? / UNITED BY HAIRCUTS**	-	- Sweden

			Burning Heart	Epitaph
Nov 01.	(cd/lp)	(BHR 137-2/-1) <82020> **A NEW MORNING**		

– A northwest passage / Up for sale / Bigger cages, longer chains / Breakout 2001 / A body treatise / Born into a mess / New empire blues / Capitalism stole my virginity / Last century promise / Dead language of love / A new morning, changing weather.

May 02.	(cd-s)	(BHR 144-2) **UP FOR SALE / WEIGHING WAR ON COMA / WRITTEN ON THE BOURGOIS BODY**		-
Jun 02.	(7")	(DESTROYER 15SV) **UP FOR SALE. / I'VE GOT SURVIVAL SICKNESS** (above on 'Must Destroy')		-
Nov 02.	(cd-ep)	(<BHR 158>) **BIGGER CAGES, LONGER CHAINS**		Jan03

– Bigger cages, longer chains / Beautiful so alone / Baby doll / Waiting for salvation / A textbook example / When words are not working.

REGULAR FRIES

Formed: North London, England . . . 1997 by graphic designer WILL BEAVAN, film-maker PAUL MOODY and music journalist ANDY STARKE, who completed the line-up with DAVE BROTHWELL, RICH LITTLE, PAT O'SULLIVAN and STEPHEN GRIFFIN. Touted as one of the leading lights of the much hyped "skunk" rock movement, The REGULAR FRIES revisited the old stamping ground of early 90's baggy stars like HAPPY MONDAYS and FLOWERED UP, although live the septet came into their own with a blinding kaleidoscope of light and sound. On the recording front, they shared/split a 'Fierce Panda' single later that year with fellow indie hopefuls, CAMPAG VELOCET. 'Rabid Badger' (the label, that is!) almost immediately delivered their debut single proper, 'DUST IT, DON'T BUST IT', a classy 12"only effort that featured the inimitable lyrics, "Hey Vanessa! ciao Tessa!!". After gigging up and down the country, The 'FRIES prised themselves away from fast-food outlets long enough to ink a deal with independent dance label, 'J.B.O.', who delivered two promising EP's, 'FREE THE REGULAR FRIES' and 'FRIES ENTERTAINMENT', in the second half of '98. The band went on to deliver their first proper LP, the brilliant 'ACCEPT THE SIGNAL' (1999), and in 2000 the mixed-bag fusion of 'WAR ON PLASTIC'. Co-produced by DAVE FRIDMANN (of MERCURY REV), the album featured a collaboration ('SMOKE & COKE') with legendary hip-hop artist KOOL KEITH, but that was only the start of it, as The REGULAR FRIES booted their way through every musical genre imaginable. As the band were trying to break the US, they had time to record their third set proper, 'BLUEPRINT FOR A HIGHER CIVILISATION' (2001).

Album rating: ACCEPT THE SIGNAL (*7) / WAR ON PLASTIC PLANTS (*6) / TRANSMISSIONS FROM THE WAR OFFICE VOL.1 mini (*4) / BLUEPRINT FOR A HIGHER CIVILIZATION (*5)

DAVE BROTHWELL – vocals / **RICH LITTLE** – vocals, percussion / **STEPHEN 'GRIFF' GRIFFIN** – guitars / **WILL BEAVAN** – keyboards / **PAT O'SULLIVAN** – bass / **PAUL MOODY** – synthesizer, vibes / **ANDY STARKE** – percussion

			Fierce Panda	not iss.
Nov 97.	(7"split)	(Ning 41) **DUST IT, DON'T BUST IT. / (other by CAMPAG VELOCET)**		-

			Rabid Badger	not iss.
Jan 98.	(12"ep)	(Nang 02) **DUST IT, DON'T BUST IT (full version) / SUPPOSED TO BE A GAS. / DUST IT, DON'T BUST IT (produced by Richard Fearless)**		-

			J.B.O.	not iss.
Sep 98.	(cd-ep)	(JNR 500353-3) **FREE THE REGULAR FRIES**		-

– Hypnosis / The prayer / New moon / Christopher Colombus / Ray's garage.

Dec 98.	(12"ep/cd-ep)	(JNR 500481-6/-3) **FRIES ENTERTAINMENT EP**		-

– Cyanide / Mars hotel / Cyanide (beach detective mix) / Mars hotel (psychonauts mix).

May 99.	(12")	(JBO 500481-6) **KING KONG. / ('A'-mixes; Kid Loco / Ellis Ellis Sound)**		-

(cd-s) (JBO 500481-8) – ('A'side) / ('A'-Kid Loco mix) / ('A'-Add N To X mix).
(cd-s) (JBO 500481-0) – ('A'side) / ('A'-Hitman mix) / ('A'-Maybe Mash Mam mix).

Jun 99.	(cd/c/lp)	(JBO 100750-2/-4/-1) **ACCEPT THE SIGNAL**		-

– Agar / Dust it / King Kong / The girls / Dream lottery / Can't face the animals / Swimming in someone's pool / Supposed to be a gas / The pink room / Wires / Anno Domini #1 / Anno Domini #2 / Cyanide / Mars hotel. *(cd+=/c+=)* – Cyanide (beach detective mix) / Mars hotel (psychonauts mix).

Oct 99.	(12"/cd-s)	(JBO 500816-6/-3) **DUST IT (short version) / VEGA / DUST IT (Brothers In Sound Jack Chicken mix)**		-
Aug 00.	(12"ep/cd-ep)	(JBO 501441-6/-3) **SMOKIN CIGARS WITH THE PHARAOHS EP**		-

– Africa take me back / Zachary Swan / Hells angle / Fused.

Oct 00.	(12"/cd-s)	(JBO 501506-6/-3) **SUPERSONICWAVES (COKE N SMOKE) feat. KOOL KEITH. / SUPERSONICWAVES (remix by JAMES Dean Bradfield and Dave Eringa) / PILLS**		-
Oct 00.	(cd/d-lp)	(JBO 101333-2/-1) **WAR ON PLASTIC PLANTS**		-

– The program / High as the music / Blown a fuse / Eclipse / London Eye / Brainticket / Voojoo / Hells angle / Coke n smoke / Radio virus / Africa take me back / The drowned world / Lost horizon / Peace treaty.

Jan 01.	(12"/cd-s; w-drawn)	(JBO 501535-0/-3) **ECLIPSE**	-	-

			Soft City	Sony
Mar 01.	(cd-ep)	(SOFTCD 1) **ECLIPSE EP**		-

– Eclipse / Loosen your mind (triple X / Internal flight / Brain ticket (Four Tet remix).

Jun 01.	(m-lp)	(SCR 006) **TRANSMISSIONS FROM THE WAR OFFICE VOL.1**		-

– Fused (Jagz Kooner mix) / Brain ticket (Four Tet mix) / Swimming in someone else's pool (instrumental) / I can't turn back (program – full version) / Mars Hotel (psychonauts instrumental remix).

Jul 01.	(cd)	(SOFTCD 2) <547670> **BLUEPRINT FOR A HIGHER CIVILIZATION**		-

– Blueprint / Big bang / Soft city / United states of mind / Emotional plane crase / Pink India / Weird school / Sister universe / Nothing on TV / Three / Africa take me back / (untitled).

Aug 01.	(12")	(SOFT 122) **AFRIKA (mixes)**		-

REINDEER SECTION

Formed: based – Glasgow, Scotland . . . by fellow Celt and full-time member of SNOW PATROL, GARY LIGHTBODY, adding to the eclectic mix militant members of the Scottish guitar army, MICHAEL BANNISTER, GARETH RUSSELL, WILLIE CAMPBELL, AIDAN MOFFAT, GILL MILLS, MICK COOKE, CHARLIE CLARK, MOGWAI's JOHN CUMMINGS, BOB KILDEA, COLIN MacINTYRE, JENNY REAVE and JONNY QUINN (also

REINDEER SECTION (cont)

of SNOW PATROL) . . . phew! Probably best described as GODSPEED YOU BLACK EMPEROR! for the thrift-store indie generation of the North (only a little less serious), the ensemble gathered together to record and arrange songs that LIGHTBODY had deemed too obscure for his SNOW PATROL team. Put together in a studio in Glasgow, 'Y'ALL GET SCARED NOW, YA HEAR!' (2001), displayed a whole host of interesting ideas thrown together by the eclectic members of such groups as BELLE & SEBASTIAN, ASTRID, ARAB STRAP and The MULL HISTORICAL SOCIETY. Spacy, punch-drunk love songs and slow-building instrumentals all shaped up to be the best collaboration this side of the Border. AIDAN MOFFAT's excellent lullaby 'NYTOL' told his usual narratives of lost love to brilliant effect. The gentle 'OPENING TASTE' set the scene for what was to follow; heartfelt melodics courtesy of EVA's JENNY REAVE and the floating beauty of ASTRID's own CAMPBELL and CLARKE's mellowed 'STING'. The group extended their line-up with the inclusion of RODDY WOOMBLE (IDLEWILD) and TEENAGE FANCLUB's NORMAN BLAKE come the single 'YOU ARE MY JOY'. This hit the shops just prior to their sophomore set 'SON OF EVIL REINDEER' (2002), a record that lacked the consistancy of their debut but had enough sparkle and stamina to make for some enlightened listening.

Album rating: Y'ALL GET SCARED NOW, YA HEAR! (*7) / SON OF EVIL REINDEER (*6)

GARY LIGHTBODY (b. Ireland) – guitar, keyboards, harmonica vocals (of SNOW PATROL) / **AIDAN MOFFAT** – vocals (of ARAB STRAP) / **JOHN CUMMINGS** – guitar (of MOGWAI) / **RICHARD COLBURN** – percussion (of BELLE & SEBASTIAN) / **MICK COOKE** – trumpet, flugelhorn (of BELLE & SEBASTIAN) / **JONNY QUINN** (b. Ireland) – drums (of SNOW PATROL) / **BOB KILDEA** – guitar (of BELLE & SEBASTIAN) / **GILL MILLS** – vocals (of EVA) / **GARETH RUSSELL** – bass (of ASTRID) / **WILBUR CAMPBELL** – guitars (of ASTRID) / **CHARLIE CLARKE** – gut string guitar / **MICHAEL BANNISTER** – keyboards, organ

	Bright	P.I.A.S.
Aug 01. (cd/lp) *(BSR 14/+V)* <2> **Y'ALL GET SCARED NOW, YA HEAR!**		Oct01

– Will you please be there for me / The opening taste / 12 hours it takes sometimes / Deviance / If there is I haven't found it yet / Fire bell / If everything fell quiet / I've never understood / Raindrop / Sting / Billed as single / Tout le monde / Nytol / The day we all died.

— added **RODDY WOOMBLE** – vocals (of IDLEWILD) / **NORMAN BLAKE** – vocals (of TEENAGE FANCLUB) / **IAIN ARCHER** (of CADET) / **NEIL PAYNE** (of ASTRID) / **MALCOLM MIDDLETON + COLIN MacPHERSON** (of ARAB STRAP) / **MARK McLELLAND** (of SNOW PATROL) / **SARAH ROBERTS** (of EVA) / **EUGENE KELLY (of VASELINES)** / **LEE GORTON + SAM MORRIS + BEN DUMVILLE** (of ALFIE) / **STACEY SIEVEWRIGHT + MARCUS MACKAY + PAUL FOX**

Jun 02. (7") *(BSR 22V)* **YOU ARE MY JOY. / BUDAPEST (demo)**   –
(cd-s) *(BSR 22)* – You are my joy (the freelance hellraiser "birds love the 80's" remix) / ('B'side).

Jun 02. (cd/lp) *(BSR 19/+V)* <7> **SON OF EVIL REINDEER**   Aug02
– Grand parade / Budapest / Strike me down / Your sweet voice / I'll be here when you wake / Where I fall / Cartwheels / Last song on the blue tape / Cold water / You are my joy / Who told you / Whodunnit?

RELICT (see under ⇒ CLIENTELE)

RENDERERS

Formed: New Zealand . . . late 80's by husband and wife BRIAN and MARYROSE CROOK (the former ex-TERMINALS). Alongside the experience of ROBBIE YEATS (ex-VERLAINES and DEAD C member) plus DENISE ROUGHAN, The RENDERERS chalked up several average albums from 1991's 'Flying Nun' debut, 'TRAIL OF TEARS'. Mixing blues and country with primitive sonic rock, The RENDERERS tried every angle to get their message through; further sets, 'THAT DOG'S HEAD . . .' (1995) and 'SURFACE OF JUPITER' (1996) were released by Chicago-based 'Ajax' records. However, 1998's first for 'Siltbreeze', 'A DREAM OF THE SEA', impressed many with its funereal trips laden with feedback and nightmarish lyrics. Spooky!

Album rating: TRAIL OF TEARS (*5) / BIGGER THAN TEXAS (*4) / THAT DOG'S HEAD IN THE GUTTER GIVES OFF VIBRATIONS (*5) / THE SURFACE OF JUPITER (*4) / A DREAM OF THE SEA (*7) / Brian Crook: BATHYSPHERE (*5)

MARYROSE CROOK – vocals, guitar / **BRIAN CROOK** – guitar, vocals (of TERMINALS) / **DENISE ROUGHAN** – bass, vocals / **ROBBIE YEATS** – drums (ex-VERLAINES, of the DEAD C)

	Flying Nun	not iss.
Jan 91. (lp/c) *(FN/+C 184)* **TRAIL OF TEARS**	–	– NewZ

– More dead than alive / Bigger than Texas / Trail of tears / Never drunk alone / Holiday in Dakota / Arizona / Burns like a brand / Old paint / Drink in my hand / Splitting atoms / Lone star burning / Liquor slicked highay / Cold fingerprints / I hear the Devil.

1991. (lp/c) *(FN/+C 185)* **BIGGER THAN TEXAS** – – NewZ
1992. (7") *(FN 254)* **TOUCH OF EVIL. / HOLING AT THE MOON** – – NewZ
	not iss.	Merge
1990's. (7") <*MRG 036*> **MILLION LIGHTS. / PRIMITIVE COUNTRY**	not iss.	Ajax

Jul 95. (cd) <*AJAX 42*> **THAT DOG'S HEAD IN THE GUTTER GIVES OFF VIBRATIONS**   –
– Unforgiven / So blind / Timebomb / Forbidden planet / Pure poison / Half life / Planet of pain / Shrunken heads / Underworld / Bloodsucker / Burning bible / On a night like this / It's sad.

Oct 96. (cd) <*AJAX 58*> **THE SURFACE OF JUPITER**   –
– Carnival / Outer Mongolia / Darkest way / Sleeping with the Devil / High seas / Mercury / Without eyes / Bottomless pit / all around the world / Moonflower / Like a virus / Death race / Drink.

	Siltbreeze	Siltbreeze
Oct 98. (cd) <*(SB 72)*> **A DREAM OF THE SEA**		

– Low to the ground / A dream of the sea / Out of the forest / Transparent black / Right from wrong / Dark continent / Great ships / Broken banks / Dimmer waters / Thin atmosphere.

BRIAN CROOK

	Metonymic	not iss.
1999. (cd) *(MEDI 003)* **BATHYSPHERE**	–	– NewZ

– Thunderbolt or fire / Psychic surgery / Valentina Tereshkova's recurring nightmare / Daggers / Leprosy / Living death / Best room in the house / I can't hear you / Aerobosoap / Apollo 13 / Echo on still waters / Space junk.

RENTALS (see under ⇒ WEEZER)

RESERVOIR (see under ⇒ SPACE NEEDLE)

RETSIN

Formed: New York, USA . . . 1993 by RODAN singer TARA JANE O'NEIL and her girlfriend CYNTHIA LYNN NELSON, who was also a member of the band RUBY FALLS. The duo signed to the 'Simple Machines' label and released their debut album 'SALT LICK' in 1995. The record featured a number of good ideas and at times the duo managed to create a real sense of atmosphere, however their songwriting ability was not developed enough to carry the entire album. The group's full-length debut, 'EGG FUSION', (1996) was similarly inconsistent as was the follow-up, 'SWEET LUCK OF AMARYLLIS' (1998). In the time between these two albums, O'NEIL had been further honing her songwriting skills with the band, SONORA PINE, who released their self-titled debut in 1996 and 'SONORA PINE II' the following year. When RETSIN returned in 2001 with 'CABIN IN THE WOODS', they had eventually found their groove and produced an elegant and engaging album that radiated fireside warmth. The 2001 follow-up EP, 'MONEY MONEY MONEY', felt more hastily constructed and once again the band had allowed sloppiness to seep in. Meanwhile, the pair found time to moonlight with NAYSAYER (run by ANNA PADGETT), an alt-country project with so-far, 2 average albums to their name, 'DEATHWHISKER' (2000) and 'HEAVEN, HELL OR HOUSTON' (2002).

Album rating: SALT LICK mini (*5) / EGG FUSION (*4) / SWEET LUCK OF AMARYLLIS (*5) / CABIN IN THE WOODS (*7) / the Sonora Pine: THE SONORA PINE (*6) / THE SONORO PINE II (*6) / Naysayer: DEATHWHISKER (*4) / HEAVEN, HELL, OR HOUSTON (*5)

TARA JANE O'NEIL – vocals, bass, acoustic guitar (ex-RODAN) / **CYNTHIA LYNN NELSON** – vocals, acoustic guitar, bass (of RUBY FALLS) / with **JOSH MADELL** – drums / **GEOFF TURNER** – guitar / **STEVE THORNTON** – trombone / **JENNIFER SHARPE** – slide guitar

	Simple Machines	Simple Machines
Oct 95. (m-lp/m-cd) <*smr 42/+cd*> **SALT LICK**	–	

– Hybrid ice princess / Mary B. / Hitched & caught / Pulp / Unsavory / Country style spoonin' / Valerium / Pink river.

May 96. (lp/cd) <*(smr 46/+cd)*> **EGG FUSION**   Mar96
– Fly south / Hottie titmouse / Loon / Foul / Kangaroo / BB / Tamale / Duck out / The pitter patter / Barefoot and stoned / Red wing / A duplex for sidewinders / Guilford / Bodega.

— in Jul'98, a collaboration with IDA as IDA RETSIN FAMILY released 'Ida Retsin Family Album, Volume 1'

— duo added **TODD COOK** – bass + **GRETA RITCHER** – drums

	Carrot Top	Carrot Top
Oct 98. (cd) <*SAKI 021CD*> **SWEET LUCK OF AMARYLLIS**	–	

– Lone star drive / The story of one party / Good morning bird / 5 down to 4 / Pope street / Swallow / What the Devil said / Never again blue / Song on foot / We are the rings / Stealing winks / Dad gone / Broken hearted wine. *(UK-iss.Dec99; same as US)*

— CYNTHIA recorded her second RUBY FALLS group set, 'HEROINES' (2000); her first was 'WHAT SHE DOES' in 1996

— guest now **IDA PEARLE** – violin / **LIZ MITCHELL** – accordion

Apr 01. (cd) <*(SAKI 025CD)*> **CABIN IN THE WOODS**
– Bright sunshine / The bitter bar corner / The good lady obstacle / Sepia shade / Land of the lost / Bug song / Berries / Ohayo mtn road / Carnival / Broke / A trite song / Dog and a butterfly / Tangerine moon / Southwater / Flatleaver.

	Acuarela	not iss.
Nov 01. (cd-ep) *(022)* **MOON MONEY MOON**	–	– Spain

– Duck out / Pauline and Susie / The moon fickle / Money song / Moonshine.

SONORA PINE

TARA JANE O'NEIL – vocals, bass, guitar / **KEVIN COULTAS** – drums, percussion / **SAMARA LUBELSKI** – violin / with guests on first; **RACHEL GRIMES** – piano (of RACHEL'S) / **SEAN MEADOWS** – organ, guitar, vocals

	Quarterstick	Quarterstick
May 96. (lp/cd) <*(QS 39/+CD)*> **THE SONORA PINE**		Mar96

– Owl's nest / Compass lure / The gin mills / Hoya carnosa / Goldmund / Ooltenah / The hook / Rungs / A couple of ones / One ring machine.

— guests **NORA CHRISTENSEN** – accordion + **NOEL BRATHER** – cello

Aug 97. (lp/cd) <*(QS 47/+CD)*> **THE SONORA PINE II**
– Eek / Claister / Long ago boy / Weak kneed / Shadows cut snapshot / Baby come home / Linda Jo.

NAYSAYER

ANNA PADGETT – vocals, guitar / **CYNTHIA NELSON** – guitar, drums, vocals, harmonica / **TARA JANE O'NEIL** – bass, guitar

			Carrot Top	Carrot Top
Mar 01.	(cd) <(SAKI 024)> **DEATHWHISKER**			Nov00

– Subway lullaby / Currency / Goodbye to hope / Fyf / Deathwhisker / Plans / Woman on 11th street / The truth / I'm not proud / Alamagordo / Medicine / Anna Pope sampler / Anna Silver school / Sick / Bumblebee in water / Bumblebee sequel / Quit song.

— added **WINK O'BANNON** – lap steel guitar (of FREAKWATER) / **MATTHEW SUTTON** – pedal steel guitar / **NOEL HAWLEY** – cello

Apr 02. (cd) <(SAKI 032)> **HEAVEN, HELL, OR HOUSTON**

– Dead end road / The naysayer / My bad blood / These boys / Break up / Hawaiian pool / 66 cicadas / Things to do / Envy and regret / I just left myself / Banned by the best / Heaven, Hell, or Houston.

REVENGE
(see under ⇒ NEW ORDER; in 80's section)

REVOLUTIONARY CORPS OF TEENAGE JESUS

Formed: Glasgow, Scotland ... 1995 by former ALTERED IMAGES guitarist/drummer STEPHEN LIRONI, a veteran of numerous short-lived indie-pop outfits (RESTRICTED CODE and FLESH) as well as a co-writer and producer of both BLACK GRAPE and SARAH CRACKNELL. REVOLUTIONARY CORPS OF TEENAGE JESUS (named after LIRONI was pipped at the post for his original choice of REVOLUTIONARY ARMY OF INFANT JESUS) was a considerably less accessible proposition than most of the above, essentially a LIRONI solo project with the added kudos of one ALAN VEGA. The former SUICIDE legend was alerted to LIRONI's activities after copping an earful of his debut single, a cover of SUICIDE classic, 'Frankie Teardrop'. The latter was released in early '96 on Glasgow's 'Creeping Bent' label while the subsequent songwriting partnership of VEGA and LIRONI bore fruit in the shape of 1997's 'PROTECTION RAT', issued as part of the 'Creeping Bent' singles club alongside the likes of ADVENTURES IN STEREO and SPACEHOPPER. A third single, 'PAY THA WRECK, MR MUSIC KING', appeared in Spring '99, in anticipation of debut album, 'RIGHTEOUS LITE' (1999). The record sounded pretty much how you'd expect with lashings of millennial electro-minimalist angst, American evangelist samples and droning/spoken vocals courtesy of the ever deadpan VEGA. A set of remixes entitled 'A BROOKLYN NIGHTMARE', surfaced later that year, the likes of FUTURE PILOT AKA, SCIENTIFIC SUPPORT DEPT. and MONGOOSE giving 'FRANKIE TEARDROP' the once over. LIRONI is still currently married to former ALTERED IMAGES starlet CLARE GROGAN.

Album rating: RIGHTEOUS LITE (*8)

STEPHEN LIRONI – machines (ex-RESTRICTED CODE, ex-ALTERED IMAGES, ex-FLESH) / **ALAN VEGA** – vocals (ex-SUICIDE)

		Creeping Bent	not iss.
Jan 96.	(12"ep; as the REVOLUTIONARY CORPS OF TEENAGE JESUS vs SUICIDE) (bent 005) **FRANKIE TEARDROP EP**		-

– Frankie Teardrop 126bpm / USA 95 / Womb #17 / Frankie Teardrop 114bpm.

Mar 96.	(12") (bent 011) **PROTECTION RAT. / SUPERMARKET**		-
Jun 97.	(cd-ep) (bent 019cd) **singles club #1**		-

– Protection rat / (other tracks by the Leopards, Adventures In Stereo and Spacehopper).

Mar 98.	(7") (bent 033) **WHO CARES WHO DIES. / (other side by the Nectarine No.9)**		-
Apr 99.	(12"/cd-s) (bent 043/+cd) **PAY THA WRECK, MR MUSIC KING. / SATURATION**		-
May 99.	(cd) (bent 045cd) **RIGHTEOUS LITE**		-

– Righteous lite / Protection lute / Daddy died / Pay tha wreck, Mr. music king / Money day / Puzz puzz / American / Motor cross / Who cares who dies / Sinister minister.

Nov 99.	(cd-s) (bent 051cd) **A BROOKLYN NIGHTMARE (mixes)**		-
Oct 00.	(cd) (bent 061cd) **A BROOKLYN NIGHTMARE** (remixes)		-

– Frankie Teardrop (mixes; by ... & SUICIDE / FUTURE PILOT AKA / RADIOGRAM / SCIENTIFIC SUPPORT DEPT / MONGOOSE / QUAD 90 / etc).

REVOLVER

Formed: Winchester, England ... Autumn 1990 by songwriter MAT FLINT, alongside NICK DEWEY and HAMISH BROWN, who all met in London. Having played their first gig at the end of that year, they secured a deal with Virgin off-shoot label, 'Hut', issuing a debut single, 'HEAVEN SENT AN ANGEL', the following summer. Quintessential "shoegazers", REVOLVER had all the qualities of a typical early 90's band, i.e. neo-psychedelic effects-laden guitars, fey vocals and almost-hooklines. A further couple of singles, 'CRIMSIN' and 'VENICE', preceded their 1992 debut album, 'BABY'S ANGRY', its watered down, RIDE-esque fare bearing the full brunt of the music press backlash; a cover of Strawberry Switchblade's 'SINCE YESTERDAY' didn't help matters. 1993's follow-up set, 'COLD WATER FLAT', on the other hand, impressed even the most jaundiced of rock journos with its more robust approach. However, the trio weren't really a hit with the wider indie public and following the parting shot of single, 'I WEAR YOUR CHAIN', REVOLVER bit the bullet and called it a day. MAT FLINT helped form HOT ROD with ex-DROP NINETEENS' PAULA KELLEY; he later joined DEATH IN VEGAS (as bassist). FLINT subsequently teamed up with girlfriend and erstwhile DROP NINETEENS chick, PAULA KELLEY, to form HOT ROD. Joined by JOHN DRAGONETTI and ERIC PAUL, the pair released a one-off album, 'SPEED DANGER DEATH' (1993). Hardly as glamorously perilous as the title might have suggested, the record nevertheless cruised along satisfyingly on post-shoegazing, noisemongering melodicism.
• **Covered:** SINCE YESTERDAY (Strawberry Switchblade). • **Note:** Not to be confused with the REVOLVER who issued 12" 'ABSORBER' in 2000.

Album rating: BABY'S ANGRY (*5) / COLD WATER FLAT (*7)

MAT FLINT – vocals, guitar, organ / **HAMISH BROWN** – bass / **NICK DEWEY** – drums

		Hut	Caroline
Aug 91.	(12"ep/cd-ep) (HUT T/CD 7) **'45'**		-

– Heaven sent an angel / Painting pictures / Molasses / Cherish.

Nov 91.	(7") (HUT 9) **CRIMSIN. / DON'T EVER LEAVE**		-
	(12"+=/cd-s+=) (HUT T/CD 9) – Drowning inside / Further away.		
Apr 92.	(7"blue) (HUT 14) **VENICE. / RED ALL OVER**		-
	(12"+=/cd-s+=) (HUT T/CD 14) – Since yesterday.		
May 92.	(cd/c/lp) (HUT CD/MC/LP 15) <CAROL 1722CD> **BABY'S ANGRY**		-

– Venice / Painting pictures / Red all over / Heaven sent an angel / Drowning inside / Molasses / Cherish / Since yesterday / Don't ever leave.

Feb 93.	(10"ep/12"ep/cd-ep) (HUT EN/T/CD 26) **CRADLE SNATCH / DON'T YOU WONDER WHY? / CRIMSIN / IF WE COULD SPEND SOME TIME**		-
Apr 93.	(cd/c/lp) (CD/TC+/HUT 8) <CAROL 1734> **COLD WATER FLAT**		-

– Cool blue / Shakesdown / Cradle snatch / I wear your chain / Nothing without you / Bottled out / Coming back / Cold water flat / Makes no difference all the same / Wave.

Jul 93.	(12"ep/cd-ep) (HUT T/CD 34) **I WEAR YOUR CHAIN (screaming mix) / CARRY ME AWAY. / BOTTLED OUT (acoustic) / RUINED**		-

— split after above

HOT ROD

PAULA KELLEY – vocals, guitar, keyboards (ex-DROP NINETEENS) / **MAT FLINT** – bass, vocals / **JOHN DRAGONETTI** – guitar / **ERIC PAULL** – percussion

		Caroline	Caroline
Aug 93.	(cd) (CARCD 25) <CAROL 1742> **SPEED DANGER DEATH**		

– Salt / Liar's liar / You're my own / I'll always know you / Tough / Firewalker / Soaking / Candy star / Waiting forever / Perplexed.

— MAT would later join DEATH IN VEGAS

Suzanne RHATIGAN

Born: Dublin, Ireland. Vocalist and songwriter SUZANNE RHATIGAN came to London in the early 80s with dreams and aspirations of becoming a respected British songwriter. She began session work for Pete Waterman and his company Stock, Aitken and Waterman, but after learning how to play piano and guitar she chose to hone her craft, finally recording her debut LP, 'TO HELL WITH LOVE', with FRED MAHER in 1992 (and, bizarrely, featuring the guest vocal talents of 'Red Dwarf's CRAIG CHARLES). The album received a few column inches, with the chanteuse being compared to SINEAD O'CONNOR, although, really, she sounded more like PJ HARVEY. RHATIGAN's distribution company 'Imago' went bust shortly after the delivery of the album, tipping the talented young lady into indefinite limbo. In 1995 she formed the group RHATIGAN with fellow musician PAUL MURPHY and a revolving-door cast of other players. The brilliantly harsh lo-fi turn of 'LATE DEVELOPER' (1996), heralded the voice of a scathing new talent in the British music scene, although the band were receiving very little press attention, due to the sickly attention given to the Brit-pop explosion. The group went on to record the mini set, 'BIG SICK' (2000) and the passionate EP, 'DIY' (2002), all issued on RHATIGAN's very own 'Cushy' label.

Album rating: TO HELL WITH LOVE (*6) / Rhatigan: LATE DEVELOPER (*6) / BIG STICK mini (*5)

SUZANNE RHATIGAN

SUZANNE – vocals, piano / with session people

		Imago	not iss.
Oct 92.	(c-s) (25019) **TO HELL WITH LOVE**		-
Mar 93.	(cd/c) (72787 21007-2/-4) **TO HELL WITH LOVE**		-

– To hell with love / Open up / The further in we go / Nearly 18 / The games we play / Indian summer / Don't talk / Shelter me / All you ever need / Daddy / Learning to cry / The spinner of years.

RHATIGAN

SUZANNE with **JOHN MORRISON** – bass / **BRYN BURROWS** – drums

		Org	not iss.
Jan 96.	(cd) (ORGAN 018CD) **LATE DEVELOPER**		-

– Late developer / Only joking / Happy / Traffic / Keeping us together / Scared / Not your girlfriend / Disconnected / Nonsense / Tonight / Dick / Hello.

Feb 96.	(c-ep) (ORGAN 019) **split w/ PURA VIDA**		-

Suzanne RHATIGAN (cont)   THE GREAT INDIE DISCOGRAPHY   The 1990s

Aug 96. (7") *(ORGAN 021)* **HAPPY. / Dream City: CRAWL**

── **PAUL MURPHY** – drums; repl. BURROWS

Cushy / not iss.

2002. (m-cd) **BIG STICK**
 – Big stick / Can't keep up / Julianne / Stabbed / King Dong / Envy of the gods / Requiescat.
2002. (cd-ep) **DIY**
 – That song / DIY / Older.

RIALTO

Formed: West London, England ... late '91 as KINKY MACHINE by LOUIS ELIOT and JULIAN FENTON, who enlisted the rhythm section of JOHN BULL and Swede MALCOLM, some of whom began their musical careers as faux-glam-rock poppers KINKY MACHINE, a group so undeniably kistch (think PULP and MOTT THE HOOPLE) that they landed four top 75 hits between 1993 and '94, donned some feather boas and subsequently toured with The MANICS STREET PREACHERS. The MACHINE issued an album entitled, ahem, 'BENT' (1995), that soon became eclipsed by the many other brash and shouty Brit groups, and really wasn't much good anyway. Management problems eventually led to the group's demise, although innovators ELIOT and BULL rounded up JULIAN TAYLOR, PETE CUTHBERT and TOBY HOUNSHAM and formed the deliciously camp RIALTO – whose moniker was derived from a decrepit chain of theatres in London. They played romantic/noir Brit ballads (with matching suits and ties and a style straight out of a David Bailey photo shoot) in the vein of Blur's 'To The End'; with melodramatic strings and vocal arrangements, coupled with songs about detectives, murder mysteries, lost love and passionate affairs, they delivered singles 'WHEN WE'RE TOGETHER' and 'UNTOUCHABLE' to major success in 1997. However, despite everything going rather swimmingly, record label 'East-West' dropped the ensemble in 1998, prompting them to shelf their self-titled debut album until another imprint would agree to release it. When 'China' offered to issue the set in July of '98, RIALTO obliged. But for some reason they didn't return to the music scene until two years later, when ELIOT and Co unfettered the mini-album 'GIRL ON A TRAIN'. By this point, HOUNSHAM had split, and the remaining four were left to finish their sophomore set, 'NIGHT ON EARTH' (2002), an album which saw the band do "a Radiohead", in terms of changing their musical style to suit the more experimental. • **Covered:** HELLO HELLO I'M BACK AGAIN (Gary Glitter).

Album rating: Kinky Machine: KINKY MACHINE (*5) / BENT (*4) / Rialto: RIALTO (*5) / NIGHT ON EARTH (*4)

KINKY MACHINE

LOUIS ELIOT – vocals, guitar / **JONNY BULL** – lead guitar / **MALCOLM PARDON** – bass / **JULIAN FENTON** – drums

Lemon / not iss.

Jul 92. (7") *(LEMON 3)* **GOING OUT WITH GOD. / CROOKED**
 (12"+=) *(LEMON 3T)* – (2 sessions).
Oct 92. (7") *(LEMON 4)* **SWIVELHEAD. / PRESIDENT YES-MAN**
 (12"+=) *(LEMON 4T)* – Going out with God (live) / Swivelhead (live).
 (cd-s+=) *(LEMON 4CD)* – (sessions).
Jan 93. (7"/10"etched) *(LEM/10LEM 006)* **SUPERNATURAL GIVER. / BLUE POLYTHENE** — 70
 (12"+=/cd-s+=) *(LEMON 006 T/CD)* – ('A'extended).

Oxygen-MCA / not iss.

May 93. (7"/c-s) *(GASP/+C 5)* **SHOCKAHOLIC. / MONDAYS CHILD** — 70
 (cd-s+=) *(GASPD 5)* – Crooked / ('A'demo).
 (10"+=) *(GASPV 5)* – ('A'rehearsal version) / Time bomb / Going out with God.
Jun 93. (cd/c/lp) *(MCD/MCC/MCA 10862)* **KINKY MACHINE**
 – Shockaholic / Candy deceit / Monkey on a string / Glitter bullets / Going out with God / Supernatural giver / Bring on the clones / Clever / Sister Magpie / Swivelhead. *(cd+=)* – Blue polythene.
Aug 93. (7") *(GASPC 9)* **GOING OUT WITH GOD / CROOKED** — 74
 (12"+=/cd-s+=) *(GASP T/D 9)* – Counting down to zero / Timebomb.
 (cd-s) *(GASXD 9)* – ('A'side) / Candy deceit / Yes man / Supernatural giver.
Jun 94. (c-s) *(GASPC 14)* **10 SECOND BIONIC MAN / PISSING IN THE SNOW** — 66
 (12"+=/cd-s+=) *(GASP V/D 14)* – Charlotte Rampling / Crashing the ambulance.
Sep 94. (c-s) *(GASPC 15)* **CUT IT DOWN / LITTLE BOY BLUE**
 (10"+=/cd-s+=) *(GASP V/D 15)* – Queen of the slums.
Oct 94. (cd/c/lp) *(MCD/MCC/MCA 11085)* **BENT**
 – 10 second bionic man / Gooseberry fool / Dolly mixture kid / Cut it down / Nosebleed / Lounge dummy / Pissing in the snow / Alsatians / Wet cigarettes / Christopher / Chemical lullaby / Last song.

East West / not iss.

Jun 95. (c-s) *(YZ 939C)* **LONDON CRAWLING / WAITING FOR THE WEEKEND**
 (12"+=/cd-s+=) *(YZ 939 T/CD)* – Hello hello I'm back again / Love like semtex.

── split in 1995, FENTON joined The LIGHTNING SEEDS

RIALTO

── **ELIOT + BULL** plus **JULIAN TAYLOR** – bass, vocals / **TOBY HOUNSHAM** – keyboards / **PETE CUTHBERT** – drums / **ANTHONY CHRISTMAS** – drums

Jealous / not iss.

1996. (cd-s) *(COUP 005)* **JEALOUS / (other track by Dogger)**

East West / not iss.

Mar 97. (c-s) *(EW 089C)* **WHEN WE'RE TOGETHER / VINEGAR VERA**
 (cd-s+=) *(EW 089CD)* – Los Angelenos.
Jun 97. (c-s) *(EW 107C)* **UNTOUCHABLE. / LIPSTICK LETTERS**
 (cd-s+=) *(EW 107C2)* – King of Karaoke.
 (cd-s) *(EW 107CD1)* – ('A'side) / Monday morning 5.19 / The red telephone.
 (above re-iss. Jan98, hit UK No.20; 10"= *EW 107TE*)
Oct 97. (c-s) *(EW 116C)* **MONDAY MORNING 5.19 / LITTLE COMEDIAN** — 37
 (cd-s+=) *(EW 116CD)* – Kieslowski.
Mar 98. (c-s/cd-s) *(EW 156 C/CD1)* **DREAM ANOTHER DREAM / THE HAND THAT USED TO FEED / SUBWAY** — 39
 (cd-s) *(EW 156CD2)* – ('A'side) / Wild is the wind / Playground songs.

China / not iss.

Jul 98. (c-s) *(WOKMC 2095)* **MONDAY MORNING 5.19 (widescreen mix) / THE UNDERDOGS**
 (cd-s+=) *(WOKCDR 2095)* – Skyscraper.
 (cd-s) *(WOKCD 2095)* – ('A'side) / Slow mo death below / Monday morning (orchestral soundtrack) / ('A'-CD-Rom).
Jul 98. (lp/c/cd) *(WOL/+MC/CD 1086)* **RIALTO** — 21
 – Monday morning 5.19 / Dream another dream / Broken Barbie doll / Summer's over / Untouchable / Hard candy / Quarantine / Lucky number / Love like semtex / When we're together / The underdogs / Milk of amnesia. *(cd re-iss. Jul99; 0630 19745-2)*
Oct 98. (7"/c-s/cd-s) *(WOK/+MC/CD 2099)* **SUMMER'S OVER (windswept version). / VINEGAR VERA / SKYSCRAPER** — 60
 (cd-s) *(WOKCDR 2099)* – ('A'side) / Slo-mo death blow / Los Angelenos.
Dec 98. (7"/c-s) *(WOK/+MC 2100)* **WHEN WE'RE TOGETHER. / VINEGAR VERA**
 (cd-s+=) *(WOKCD 2100)* – Los Angelenos.

── now without BULL + CHRISTMAS

Eagle / Koch Int.

Jun 01. (cd-s) *(EAGXS 191)* **ANYTHING COULD HAPPEN / FALLING IN LOVE / MONDAY MORNING 5.19 (French version)**
 (cd-s) *(EAGXA 191)* – ('A'side) / Remote control / The car that took my love away.
Jul 01. (cd) *(EAGCD 190)* <8369> **NIGHT ON EARTH**
 – London crawling / Anything could happen / Anyone out there? / Catherine's wheel / Idiot twin / Shatterproof / Brilliant fake / Three ring circus / Drive / Deep space / Underneath a distant moon. *<US+=>* – Someone that she used to know / Catherine's wheel.

RIDE

Formed: Oxford, England ... 1988 by local art college students MARK GARDENER, ANDY BELL and LAURENCE COLBERT. They drafted in STEVE QUERALT and journalist/manager Dave Newton who subsequently secured them some London gigs. These led to a deal with 'Creation' records and they released their eponymous debut EP early in 1990, the record quickly selling out of its limited number and squeezing into the UK Top 75. The disc showcased the band's spiralling guitar-scapes and contained an early classic in the cathartic 'DRIVE BLIND'. It was hotly pursued by two further Top 40 EP's, 'PLAY' and 'FALL', the latter containing their best track to date (at that point) in 'TASTE'. Come October, with the "shoegazing" scene in full flow, they nearly secured a Top 10 place with their stunning debut album, 'NOWHERE'. 1991 was spent in the studio (excluding Reading Festival), and the fruits were heard early in '92 on their superb 8-minute single 'LEAVE THEM ALL BEHIND'. This slow burning psychedelic epic gave them their first Top 10 entry and was a prelude to their second, more BYRDS-esque album, 'GOING BLANK AGAIN'. The record went Top 5, despite being derided by certain music critics. Frictions began to appear and it was thought a two-year sabbatical would solve the problem. BELL took time off to help out his Swedish wife and stablemate IDHA (OVELIUS) on her debut album. In 1994, RIDE were back with 'CARNIVAL OF LIGHT', but again they received lukewarm reviews. Early the next year, GARDENER took off to the States, leaving them all behind (ouch!). Their swansong, 'TARANTULA' was annoyingly deleted after one week, as BELL and GARDENER considered separate solo ventures.
• **Songwriters:** Lyrics MARK or ANDY / group compositions except covers EIGHT MILES HIGH (Byrds) / THE MODEL (Kraftwerk) / HOW DOES IT FEEL TO FEEL (Creation) / THAT MAN (Small Faces) / UNION CITY BLUE + ATOMIC (Blondie). • **Trivia:** In 1991, they headlined the Slough Music Festival in front of over 8,000 fans.

Album rating: SMILE (*7) / NOWHERE (*8) / GOING BLANK AGAIN (*7) / CARNIVAL OF LIGHT (*6) / LIVE LIGHT (*4) / TARANTULA (*6) / OX4: THE BEST OF RIDE compilation (*7)

MARK GARDENER – vocals, guitar / **ANDY BELL** (b.11 Aug'70, Cardiff, Wales) – guitar, vocals / **STEPHAN QUERALT** – bass / **LAURENCE COLBERT** – drums

Creation / Sire

Jan 90. (12"ep)(cd-ep) *(CRE 072T)(CRESCD 072)* **RIDE** — 71
 – Chelsea girl / Drive blind / Close my eyes / All I can see. *(re-iss. Oct90; same)*
Apr 90. (12"ep)(cd-ep) *(CRE 075T)(CRESCD 075)* **PLAY** — 32
 – Like a daydream / Silver / Furthest sense / Perfect time.
Jun 90. (m-cd,m-c) *<26390>* **SMILE** (first two EP's)
 – Chelsea girl / Drive blind / All I can see / Close my eyes / Like a daydream / Silver / Furthest sense / Perfect time. *(UK-iss.Nov92; CRECD 126) (cd re-iss. Sep01 on 'Ignition'; IGNCD 8)*
Oct 90. (12"ep)(cd-ep) *(CRE 087T)(CRESCD 087)* **FALL** — 34
 – Dreams burn down / Taste / Here and now / Nowhere.
Oct 90. (cd/lp)(c) *(CRE CD/LP 74)(CREC 74) <26462>* **NOWHERE** — 11 Dec90
 – Seagull / Kaleidoscope / Polar bear / Dreams burn down / In a different place / Decay / Paralysed / Vapour trail. *(cd+=)* – Taste / Here and now / Nowhere. *(cd re-iss. Sep01 on 'Ignition'; IGNCD 9)*
Jan 91. (cd-ep) *<40055>* **VAPOUR TRAIL**
Mar 91. (c-ep)(12"ep)(cd-ep) *(CRECS 100)(CRE 100T)(CRESCD 100)* **TODAY FOREVER** — 14
 – Unfamiliar / Sennen / Beneath / Today.

RIDE (cont)

Feb 92. (c-ep)(12"ep)(cd-ep) *(CRECS 123)(CRE 123T)(CRESCD 123)* <40332> **LEAVE THEM ALL BEHIND. / CHROME WAVES / GRASSHOPPER** — 9

Mar 92. (cd/2x12"lp)(c) (CRE CD/LP 124)(CCRE 124) <26836> **GOING BLANK AGAIN** — 5
– Leave them all behind / Twisterella / Not fazed / Chrome waves / Mouse trap / Time of her life / Cool your boots / Making Jusy smile / Time machine / OX4. *(cd re-iss. Sep01 on 'Ignition'; IGNCD 10)*

Apr 92. (c-ep)(12"ep)(cd-ep) *(CRECS 150)(CRE 150T)(CRESCD 150)* <40448> **TWISTERELLA / GOING BLANK AGAIN. / HOWARD HUGHES / STAMPEDE** — 36

— In Oct'93, 'Fright' records issued 'UNION CITY BLUE' *(FRIGHT 060) (re-iss. Apr97; same)*

Apr 94. (12"ep/12"clear-ep)(cd-ep) *(CRE 155T/+C)(CRESCD 155)* **BIRDMAN / ROLLING THUNDER 2. / LET'S GET LOST / DON'T LET IT DIE** — 38

Jun 94. (7"/c-s) *(CRE/+MC 184)* **HOW DOES IT FEEL TO FEEL? / CHELSEA GIRL** — 58
(12")(cd-s) *(CRES 184T/CRESCD 184)* – ('A'side) / Walkabout / At the end of the universe.

Jun 94. (pic-cd/d-lp/c) *(CRE CD/LP 147)(C-CRE 147)* <45610> **CARNIVAL OF LIGHT** — 5
– Moonlight medicine / 1000 miles / From time to time / Natural grace / Only now / Birdman / Crown of creation / How does it feel to feel? / Endless road / Magical spring / Rolling thunder / I don't know where it comes from. *(cd re-iss. Sep01 on 'Ignition'; IGNCD 11)*

Sep 94. (c-s) *(CRECS 189)* **I DON'T KNOW WHERE IT COMES FROM. / TWISTERELLA** — 46
(12")(cd-s) *(CRE 189T)(CRESCD 189)* – ('A'side) / Drive blind / From time to time / How does it feel to feel (live w / The CREATION).
(cd-s) *(CRESCD 189R)* – ('A'-Apollo 11 mix) / Moonlight medicine (ride on the wire mix by Portishead) / A journey to the end of the universe (version).

— split officially early '96. MARK citing ANDY's near takeover of vocal duties.

Feb 96. (12"ep/cd-ep) *(CRE 199T)(CRESCD 199)* **BLACK NITE CRASH** — 67

Mar 96. (cd/lp)(c) *(CRE CD/LP 180)(CCRE 180)* <61893> **TARANTULA** — 21
– Black nite crash / Sunshine – Nowhere to run / Dead man / Walk on water / Deep inside my pocket / Mary Anne / Castle on the hill / Gonna be alright / Dawn patrol / Ride the wind / Burnin' / Starlight motel. *(cd re-iss. Sep01 on 'Ignition'; IGNCD 12)* above was only available for 1 week only

— On the 30th of June '96, MARK GARDENER released his limited solo cd-single 'MAGDALEN SKY / CAN'T LET IT DIE (demo)' for Oxford-based 'Shifty Disco' *(DISCO 9706). (re-iss. Jun97; same)*

— split around the same time; ANDY BELL formed HURRICANE #1

– compilations, etc. –

Oct 95. (cd,c) *Elektra;* <61884> **LIVE LIGHT (live)** — —
– Seagull / Magical Spring / From time to time / Chelsea girl / Birdman / Only now / Leave them all behind / Let's get lost. *(UK-iss.Jul97 on 'Mutiny' cd/lp; 80002-2/-1)*

Sep 01. (3xcd-box) *Ignition;* (IGNCD 13) **BOXED SET** — —

Sep 01. (cd) *Ignition;* (<IGNCD 14>) **OX4: THE BEST OF RIDE** — —
– Chelsea girl / Drive blind / Like a daydream / Taste / Dreams burn down / Vapour trail / Unfamiliar / Leave them all behind / Twisterella / OX4 / Birdman / From time to time / How does it feel to feel? / I don't know where it comes from / Black nite crash.

RIG

Formed: California, USA ... 1992 by MR.IBARRA, MR.WABSCHALL and MR.PALACIOS. The US punks made their first appearance on the split 7-inch single with similar group OILER on the B-side. One year later they were subsequently signed to 'Cruz' records, subsequently releasing their debut album, the industrial, GREG GINN-produced, 'BELLY TO THE GROUND'. The last release from the 3-piece was 'KING OF THE SOFT SERVE', which contained a cover of the deliciously-titled 'MY SOFT VAGINA' (Bassin – Fergusson – Lebrun – Neves). • **Note:** A different RIG issued an eponymous lp for 'Capitol'.

Album rating: BELLY TO THE GROUND (*5) / KING OF THE SOFT SERVE (*5)

MR. IBARRA (b. CRAIG) – megaphone/vocals / **MR. WABSCHALL** – bass, vocals, programming / **MR. PALACIOS** – guitar, programming

		not iss.	Dead Good Cruz	Dead Cruz

1993. (12") <7> **SPANK. / (other by Oiler)** — — —

Feb 94. (lp/c/cd) <*(CRZ 035/+C/CD)*> **BELLY TO THE GROUND** — — —
– Mark 16:17 / Tania / Buried alive / Cattleaxe / Say that / Joe's alarm / Syphilis Diller / Personal service announcement / Miracle / Cut voice / 9-iron.

Jan 97. (cd) <*CRZ 039CD*> **KING OF THE SOFT SERVE** — — —
– American guey / Bleak / Ton of bricks / I'm through / Homo cholo – 410 / Sharp as a marble / Harvesting catastrophe / Going under / My island / Soft mouth vagina / My Uriah Heep / Going under.

— RIG have now split

RIVERDALES (see under ⇒ SCREECHING WEASEL)

RIZZO

Formed: Los Angeles, California, USA ... 1995 by JEN ABERCROMBIE and SARAH DeANGELIS, originally under the billing, MOPAR, although they soon changed this when they discovered they had both coincidentally played Rizzo in their school's version of the musical, 'Grease'. The twosome debuted with their pared-down drum'n'guitar punky indie pop on a split single with TULLYCRAFT on which they performed 'RENTAL RACCOON' (1997).

Their ensuing EP, 'SHYMASTER' (1998), proved that the girls were a force to be reckoned with, especially based on their riot-grrrl attitude. Their inaugural LP, 'PHONING IT IN', appeared three years later in 2001, and showcased a host of short punchy tracks delivered with brevity and skill, bar the near 15 minute onslaught of closer 'RASPBERRY BERET'.

Album rating: PHONING IT IN (*5)

SARAH DeANGELIS – vocals, drums / **JEN ABERCROMBIE** – guitar, vocals

		not iss.	Harriet

1997. (7") <40> **RENTAL RACCOON. / (other by TULLYCRAFT)** —

		not iss.	Cher Doll

1998. (7"m) <010> **SHYMASTER. / ROAD SONG / CATHY'S SONG** —

		not iss.	Sympathy F

May 01. (cd) <*SFTRI 639*> **PHONING IT IN** —
– The joke's on you / Long gone bon / Apple pancakes / Cathy / Lifetime guarantee / Spin this / Peter's sick / Noise boy / I know it's late / Right side of the tracks / Let it ride / Baby, you fucked up / Raspberry beret.

ROADSIDE MONUMENT

Formed: USA ... mid-90's by vocalists/guitarists DOUGLAS LORIG and MIKE DENTE; who initially recruited rhythm men TODD FLORENCE and JOEL METZGER. Their Northwest blend of emo-core and schizoid angst/sadcore found a home at 'Tooth & Nail' courtesy of debut LP, 'BEISE THIS BRIEF HEXAGONAL' (1996). However, things took a sharp turn when LORIG and the rest split leaving the former to enlist the aid of buddies JONATHAN FORD and MATTHEW JOHNSON to carry on the ROADSIDE MONUMENT name; JEFF BETTGER was soon added. The resulting album, 'EIGHT HOURS AWAY FROM BEING A MAN' (1997), surprised many except themselves, its lyrical, groove-friendly display a good example of math and emo. For 1998's 'I AM THE DAY OF CURRENT TASTE' (1998) – produced by J ROBBINS (of BURNING AIRLINES) – they tried the same moody/uptempo formula – but failed; their direction was going out of control. With ROADSIDE MONUMENT out of the way JONATHAN FORD took time to put his own career back in shape. With UNWED SAILOR (featuring members of PEDRO THE LION, EARLY DAY MINERS, etc.), he released the enlightened instrumental set, 'THE FAITHFUL ANCHOR' (2001).

Album rating: BESIDE THIS BRIEF HEXAGONAL (*6) / EIGHT HOURS AWAY FROM BEING A MAN (*7) / I AM THE DAY OF CURRENT TASTE (*5) / Unwed Sailor: THE FAITHFUL ANCHOR (*6)

DOUGLAS LORIG – vocals, guitar / **MIKE DENTE** – vocals, guitar / **TODD FLORENCE** – bass / **JOEL METZGER** – drums

		Tooth & Nail	Tooth & Nail

Nov 95. (7") **MY LIFE IS GREEN. /** — —

Apr 96. (cd) <*TNR 1049*> **BESIDE THIS BRIEF HEXAGONAL** — —
– Oh so fabled / Seed / A girl named Actually / Still / Prozac princess / Lobbyest / Immersion / Greek tragedy / Boasting in weakness / Mothered others.

— LORIG recruited **JONATHAN FORD** – vocals, bass (ex-MR. BISHOPS FIST) / **MATTHEW JOHNSON** – drums (ex-BLENDERHEAD) / + initial guest **JEFF BETTGER** – keyboards

Jun 97. (cd) <*TNR 1080*> **EIGHT HOURS AWAY FROM BEING A MAN** — —
– Sperm ridden burden / Eight hours away from being a man / John Wayne marina / Sunken anchor / Iowa backroads / Kansas city / Tired of living with people who are tired of living / Compressor district / Apartment over the peninsula / My hands are the thermometers.

1997. (7"ep) split w/ **PULLER** — —

Nov 97. (cd-ep) <*TNR 1098*> **ROADSIDE MONUMENT / FRODUS split** — —
– Nothing short of a comfortable situation / Tired of living with people who are tired of living / (two others by FRODUS)

Sep 98. (cd) <*(TNR 1119CD)*> **I AM THE DAY OF CURRENT TASTE** — —
– I am the day of current taste / OJ Simpson house auction / Taxi riding as an artform / Cops are my best customers / The life vest / Egos the size of cathedrals / This city is ruthless and so are you / Car vs. Semi, Semi wins every time.

— towards the end of the year, the group split

UNWED SAILOR

JONATHAN FORD – vocals, bass + **DAVID BAZAN** – drums (of PEDRO THE LION) / plus **KC WESCOTT** – guitar

		not iss.	Made In Mexico

Aug 99. (cd-ep) <*MEX 005*> **FIRECRACKER** —
– Firecracker / Ruby's wishes / Snowcaps / Once in a blue moon. *(UK-iss.May02 as 7"ep on 'Zeal'; ZSBTV 042)*

— FORD now with **NICK TSE** – guitar / etc.

		Lovesick	Lovesick

Sep 01. (cd) <*(LVSK 001)*> **THE FAITHFUL ANCHOR** — Aug01
– Last goodbyes / The house of hopes ... dreams ... and wishes / The faithful anchor / Our nights / Golden cities / Ruby's wishes / In the presence of thrones / Riddle of stars / The quiet hour.

— in early 2002, UNWED SAILOR collaborated with The EARLY DAY MINERS on the mini-set, 'Stateless'

Alasdair ROBERTS (see under ⇒ APPENDIX OUT)

ROCKET FROM THE CRYPT

Formed: San Diego, California, USA ... 1989 by half-Portuguese singer, SPEEDO (JOHN REIS), alongside PETEY X, ATOM, JC 2000 and ND. REIS left school and joined PITCHFORK, a hardcore band who rapidly evolved into DRIVE LIKE JEHU (other members of this outfit being RICK FROBERG, MIKE KENNEDY and MARK TROMBINO), the frontman continuing to moonlight for the latter outfit through his early career with the 'CRYPT. Kick-ass speedball R&R punks/greasers drawing on the earthiest of 50's tradition, ROCKET FROM THE CRYPT were as suave as Vegas-era ELVIS with the attitude and sound of their heroes, The MISFITS (who they initially supported). In a further bid to boost their street cred, RFTC also claimed to have opened for two of the most legendary figures in black music, JAMES BROWN and SUN RA. On the recording front, the lads issued a plethora of singles for various hip US underground labels (the tracks were later collected together for UK consumption as 'ALL SYSTEMS GO!'), along the way releasing a debut album, 'PAINT AS A FRAGRANCE' (1991) and picking up sax player, APOLLO NINE. They unearthed a second album, 'CIRCA: NOW!', a year later and although the ROCKET-fuelled formula varied little, there was an audible improvement in the musicianship. While their mid-90's release schedule was as prolific as ever, they finally settled on a long-term deal with 'Interscope' ('El-e-mental' in the UK) in 1995. Towards the end of that year, they finally made their critical breakthrough on the UK alt-rock scene with the 'SCREAM, DRACULA, SCREAM!' album. It also lent them a modicum of commercial success scraping into the UK Top 40 and spawning no less than three hit singles, the last of which, 'ON A ROPE', found them threatening the Top 10. In the best tradtion of the DEAD BOYS or the SAINTS, however, ROCKET FROM THE CRYPT were in their element on stage blasting out their visceral, three-chord mainline rock'n'roll, NME recognising their talent by bestowing upon them a Brat Award for Best Newcomer. In the summer of '98, the slicked-back six-piece resurfaced with their second major label album, 'RFTC', a slightly subdued, more pop/rock-orientated affair that only just scraped into the UK Top 75. Despite subsequently parting company with 'Interscope' in less than amicable circumstances as well as losing founding member ATOM, the band licked their wounds and came back stronger than ever with the independently released 'GROUP SOUNDS' (2001). By the time former BLACK HEART PROCESSION man MARIO RUBALCABA was eventually recruited as a permanent replacement for ATOM, SUPERCHUNK's JON WURSTER had already completed most of the album's drum parts. Yet such instability hardly affected the music, at least not in the negative sense, as SPEEDO and co ripped up the rock'n'roll rule book while simultaneously paying homage in their own bad-assed way to blues, country and gospel. Partly recorded in Memphis, the album's authentic feel was also enhanced by the piano of veteran producer Jim Dickinson. Having previously played together in experimental offshoot DRIVE LIKE JEHU (who were active in the early 90's), the pairing of REIS and RICK FROBERG formed the core of another side project, HOT SNAKES. Also featuring the rhythm section of GAR WOOD and JASON KOURKOUNIS, the group made their debut with 'AUTOMATIC MIDNIGHT' (2000). Greased up, revved up and metaphorically at least, messed up, the record's uncut rock'n'roll forced the competition off the road and made occasional detours into the left-field. 'SUICIDE INVOICE' (2002) offered a slightly more sinister, if no less breakneck ride, roaring out of the blocks with 'I HATE THE KIDS'. • **Songwriters:** Group, except GOLD (MC5) / TROUBLE + MASCULINE INTUITION (Music Machine). • **Trivia:** SPEEDO recently married ND's sister.

Album rating: PAINT AS A FRAGRANCE (*5) / CIRCA: NOW! (*5) / ALL SYSTEMS GO compilation (*7) / THE STATE OF THE ART IS ON FIRE mini (*5) / HOT CHARITY mini (*4) / SCREAM, DRACULA, SCREAM! (*8) / RFTC (*6) / ALL SYSTEMS GO 2 compilation (*7) / GROUP SOUNDS (*7) / Hot Snakes: AUTOMATIC MIDNIGHT (*6) / SUICIDE INVOICE (*7)

SPEEDO (b. JOHN REIS) – vocals, guitar / **ND** (aka ANDY) – guitar / **PETEY X** – bass, bass vocals / **ATOM** (aka ADAM) – drums / **JC 2000** (aka JAY) – trumpet, percussion, organ, vocals

			not iss.	Headhunter
Feb 91.	(lp/c/cd) <HED 003/+MC/CD>	**PAINT AS A FRAGRANCE**	–	

– French guy / Maybelline / Shy boy / Basturds / Velvet touch / Evil party / Stinker / Jiggy jig / Weak superhero / Thumbmaster. *(cd-iss. Mar93; same +UK)*

			Helter Skelter	not iss.
Jun 91.	(7"ep) <HS 92712>	**YUM KIPPERED EP**	–	– Italian

– Bad Ninja / Goodbye / Kill the funk (there will be no funk in Outer Space). *(UK-iss.Apr95 c-s/cd-s; same)*

			not iss.	Pusmort
Sep 91.	(7"red, etc) <200772>	**CUT IT LOOSE. / GLAZED**	–	

<re-iss. Aug92 d7" w/ SEPTIC DEATH 7" on Pusmort'>

— added **APOLLO NINE** (aka PAUL) – saxophone, vocals

			not iss.	Sympathy F
Jun 92.	(7"pic-d) <SFTRI 179>	**BOY CHUCKER. / JUMPER K. BALLS / LEFTY**	–	

<re-press.1994; same w/ diff. cover>

			not iss.	Sub Pop
Jun 92.	(7"blue-ep) <SP 154>	**NORMAL CARPET RIDE / WHERE ARE THE FUCKERS. / SLUMBER QUEEN / FLIP THE BIRD**	–	

			not iss.	Drunken Fish
Jul 92.	(one-sided-7"gold) <DF 02>	**GOLD**	–	

			not iss.	Standard
Oct 92.	(7") <SR 72>	**CHA CHA CHA. / (other track by DEADBOLT)**	–	

			not iss.	Merge
Nov 92.	(7") <MRG 035>	**PIGEON EATER. / (THE) PASTE THAT YOU LOVE**	–	

			Headhunter	Headhunter
Jan 93.	(lp/c/cd) <(HED 015/+MC/CD)>	**CIRCA: NOW!**		Nov92

– Short lip fuser / Hippy dippy do / Ditch digger / Don't Darlene / Killy kill / Hairball alley / Sturdy wrists / March of dimes / Little arm / Dollar / Glazed.

			not iss.	Drunken Fish
Apr 93.	(7",7"clear) <DF 05>	**PURE GENIUS. / LIFT AND LOVE**	–	

			not iss.	Pusmort
1993.	(7") <400777>	**CALL IT A COMPLEX. / (other by Radio Wendy Song)**	–	

			not iss.	SCP
1993.	(7"one-side) <SCP 001>	**SNAP CRACKLE PUNK**	–	

– Lie / Video radio man.

			not iss.	Merge
Feb 94.	(7") <MRG 049>	**BURN MOUTH OFF LIAR WITH PUNK MEAT BLAST**	–	

– UFO UFO UFO / Birdman.

			Bacteria Sour	Pusmort
May 94.	(7"ep) <SOUR 2V/3V>	**split w/ BLOODY THIRSTY BUTCHERS**		

– Cut it loose / On living and dying / Pressures on / (+3 by BTB).

			not iss.	Sympathy F
Apr 95.	(m-lp) <SFTRI 320>	**THE STATE OF THE ART IS ON FIRE**	–	

– Light me / A+ in arson class / Rid or ride / Human torch / Ratsize / Human spine / Trouble / Masculine intuition. *<cd-ep-iss.Nov96; SFTRI 320CD>*

1995.	(7") <SFTRI 373>	**PLAYS THE MUSIC MACHINE EP**		

– Trouble / Masculine intuition. *(UK-iss.Oct96; same as US)*

			not iss.	Perfect Sound
1995.	(7"clear; one-sided)	**TATTOO**	–	
1995.	(7"; fan club)	**I FLAME YOU**	–	

			El-e-mental	Interscope
Oct 95.	(m-lp) (ELM 27LP) <92595>	**HOT CHARITY**		Aug95

– Pushed / Guilt free / Poison eye / My arrow's aim / Feathered friends / Cloud over Branson / Lorna Doom / Shucks / Pity yr paws.

Dec 95.	(cd/c)<lp> (ELM 34 CD/MC) <92596-2/-4><Hed 54>	**SCREAM, DRACULA, SCREAM!**	40	Oct95

– Middle / Born in '69 / On a rope / Young livers / Drop out / Used / Ball lightning / Fat lip / Suit city / Heater hands / Misbeaten / Come see, come saw / Salt future / Burnt alive.

			El-e-mental	Interscope
Jan 96.	(7"/cd-s) (ELM 32 S/CD)	**BORN IN '69. / CIAO PATSY**	68	–
Apr 96.	(7"/c-s) (ELM 33 S/MC)	**YOUNG LIVERS. / BURNING ARMY MEN**	67	–

(cd-s+=) *(ELM 33CD)* – Lumps.

Sep 96.	(cd-ep) (ELM 38CD1)	**ON A ROPE / ALONE / WHO NEEDS YOU / YOUNG LIVERS (Mark Radcliffe session)**	12	–

(cd-ep) *(ELM 38CD2)* – ('A'-White Room version) / Allergic reaction / Transcendent crankiness / Suit city (Mark Radcliffe session).
(cd-ep) *(ELM 38CD3)* – ('A'-Ghetto box mix) / You and I / Intro – Don't Darlene (Mark Radcliffe session) / Lorna Doom (Mark Radcliffe session).

Jun 98.	(10"pic-d-ep) (ELM 47TPIC)	**WHEN IN ROME (DO THE JERK). / TARZAN / TIGER FEET TONITE**		–
Jul 98.	(cd/c/lp) (ELM 50 CD/MC/LP) <90167>	**RFTC**	63	Jun98

– Eye on you (with HOLLY GOLIGHTLY) / Break it up / I know / Panic scam / Made for you / Lipstick / You gotta move / Your touch / Let's get busy / Dick on a dog / Back in the state / When in Rome / Run kid run. *(also ltd-cd; ELM 50CDQ)*

Aug 98.	(10") (ELM 48TEN)	**LIPSTICK. / HOT HEART**	64	

(cd-s) *(ELM 48CDS1)* – ('A'side) / Heads are gonna roll / Cheetah.
(cd-s) *(ELM 48CDS2)* – ('A'side) / When in Rome (do the jerk) / Stranglehold.

— In Oct'98, the group were on a split 7" 'LUMPS' with JULIAN Y SUS HERMANOIS for 'Vinyl Communication' (VC 76)

Nov 98.	(7") (ELM 49S)	**BREAK IT UP. / TURKISH REVENGE**		–

(cd-s+=) *(ELM 49CDS1)* – Crack attack.
(cd-s) *(ELM 49CDS2)* – ('A'side) / U.S. Army / Raped by ape.

			Flapping Jet	Flapping Jet
Oct 99.	(12"ep; ltd-some blue) <(FJ 010)>	**CUT CAREFULLY & PLAY LOUD**		

– If the birds can fly / Blood robots / Waste it / Hot wired / Who let the snakes in?? *<re-iss. Aug00; FLAP 010>*

— in Oct'99, they split yet another single 'DELOREAN', this time with the Hellacopters for the 'Gearhead' fanzine #10

			Glazed	Glazed
Jan 00.	(7",7"gold,7"red) <(GLZ 001)>	**DANCING BIRDS**		Dec99

– Black eye / Bombs away.

— **MARIO RUBALCABA** – drums (ex-BLACK HEART PROCESSION) – + some JON WURSTER (ex-SUPERCHUNK) – repl. ATOM

— late in 2000, RFTC split a single w/ GET UP KIDS

			B-Unique	Vagrant
Jun 01.	(cd) (BUN 006) <352>	**GROUP SOUNDS**		

– Straight American slave / Carne voodoo / White belt / Out of control / Return of the liar / Heart of a rat / Venom venom / Savoir faire / S.O.S. / Dead seeds / This bad check is gonna stick / Spitting / Ghost shark.

– compilations, etc. –

Dec 93.	(lp/cd) *Sympathy For The Record Industry; (SFTRI 558/+CD)* / *Hedhunter; <Hed 023>* **ALL SYSTEMS GO**		

– Live the funk / Bad song Ninja / Goodbye / Boy chucker / Jumper K. balls / Lefty / Normal carpet ride / Where are the fuckers / Slumber queen / Flip the bird / Cha cha cha / Pressure's on / Pigeon eater / (The) Paste that you love / Pure genius / Lift and love / Press darlings / Filly fill again / Chantilly face. *(cd re-iss. Dec98; same)*

Oct 99.	(lp/cd) *Swami; <(SWA 2001/+CD)>* **ALL SYSTEMS GO 2**		

– Tarzan / UFO x3 / Birdman / Ciao Patsy / Heads are gonna roll / Cheetah / Turkish revenge / US aim / Raged by an age / Crack party / Stranglehold / 10 forward / Call it a clue / Cut it loose / Hot heart / I drink blood / Slow / Who

DRIVE LIKE JEHU

JOHN REIS – guitar / **RICK FROBERG** – vocals, guitar / **MIKE KENNEDY** – bass / **MARK TROMBINO** – drums

not iss.   Merge

1992. (7") <MRG 023> **HAND OVER FIST. / BULLET TRAIN TO VEGAS**

Headhunter Headhunter

Jan 93. (lp/cd) (HED/+CD 008)> **DRIVE LIKE JEHU**   Dec91
– Caress / Spikes to you / Step on chameleon / O pencil sharp / Atom Jack / If it kills you / Good luck in jail / Turn it off / Future home of Stucco monstrosity.

El-e-mental Cargo

May 94. (cd) (ELM 22CD) <EFA 17690-2> **YANK CRIME**
– Here come the Rome plows / Do you compute / Golden brown / Luau / Super unison / New intro / New math / Human interest / Sinews. *(lp-iss.Aug94 on 'Cargo'; HED 037)*

HOT SNAKES

JOHN REIS – vocals / **RICK FROBERG** – guitar, vocals / **GAR WOOD** – bass / **JASON KOURKOUNIS** – drums (of DELTA 72)

Swami   Swami

Apr 00. (lp/cd) <(SWA 2002/+CD)> **AUTOMATIC MIDNIGHT**   Feb00
– If credit's what matters I'll take credit / Automatic midnight / No hands / Salton city / 10th planet / Light up the stars / Our work fills the pews / Past lives / Mystery boy / Apartment O / Let it come. *(re-iss. Aug02 lp/cd; SWA 113/+CD)*

Jun 02. (lp/cd) <(SWA 111/+CD)> **SUICIDE INVOICE**
– I hate the kids / Gar forgets his insulin / Xox / Who died / Suicide invoice / Paid in cigarettes / Lax / Bye nancy boy / Paperwork / Why does it hurt / Unlisted / Ben Gurion.

ROCKETSHIP

Formed: Sacramento, California, USA ... 1993 by lynch-pin member DUSTIN RESKE with the assistance of JIM RIVAS, VERNA BROCK and HEIDI BARNEY. Short-lived but celebrated, the band's sixties pop stylings mixed well with their own nineties indie guitar and organ-biased work, to produce a pleasing and not too sugary sound. Their inaugural single, 'HEY, HEY, GIRL', heralded them onto the indie pop scene with a bang and made ready for their debut full-length offering, 'A CERTAIN SMILE, A CERTAIN SADNESS' (1996), a record which remained as a touchstone for its West Coast peers. Unfortunately, the band disbanded soon afterwards, with RESKE keeping the moniker going as mainly a solo project. He followed up the album with the 7", 'HONEY, I NEED YOU' (1997), and came back in 1999 with the slight sonic departure of the more atmospheric 12", 'GARDEN OF DELIGHTS'.

Album rating: A CERTAIN SMILE, A CERTAIN SADNESS (*6)

DUSTIN RESKE – vocals, guitar (ex-ROSEBUDS) / **HEIDI BARNEY** – keyboards / **VERNA BROCK** – bass (of HOLIDAY FLYER) / **JIM RIVAS** – drums

not iss. Bus Stop

May 94. (7"m) <BUS 034> **HEY, HEY, GIRL. / NAOMI AND ME / PEOPLE I KNOW**

not iss. Slumberland

Feb 96. (cd/lp) <SLR 40> **A CERTAIN SMILE, A CERTAIN SADNESS**
– I love you like the way that I used to do / Kisses are always promises / Heather, tell me why / Let's go away / I'm lost without you here / Carrie Cooksey / We're both alone / Friendship and love.

— now just down to **RESKE**

not iss. Bus Stop

Jan 97. (7") <BUS 057> **HONEY, I NEED YOU. / SHE'S GONNA MAKE ME CRY**

not iss. Jigsaw

May 97. (ltd-7"gold) <PZL 005> **GET ON THE FLOOR (AND MOVE IT). / ALL THE PLEASURES**

Drive-In Drive-In

Feb 99. (lp) <(DRIVE 26)> **ROCKETSHIP'S GARDEN OF DELIGHTS**

— RESKE and ROCKETSHIP have been a little conspicuous by their absence

ROCKINGBIRDS

Formed: Camden, London, England ... 1990 by former squatters, ALAN TYLOR, ANDY HACKETT, PATRICK ARBUTHNOT, SHAUN REID, DAVE GOLDING and former WEATHER PROPHETS drummer, DAVE MORGAN. The ROCKINGBIRDS soon signed on the dotted line for Jeff Barrett's 'Heavenly', the label releasing their debut, 'A GOOD DAY FOR YOU IS A GOOD DAY FOR ME', the following year. Its B-side, the harmony-happy 'JONATHAN, JONATHAN' (a tribute to that RICHMAN bloke), was later used as a follow-up in its own right in 1992, previewing the eponymous, CLIVE LANGER-produced debut album. Shouldered with the nigh on impossible task of rehabilitating country for the younger generation, the album was an enjoyable enough saunter down the dusty paths once trod by GRAM PARSONS, GENE CLARK, etc. That year, they also took part in the Cambridge Folk Festival, even venturing out to the country heartland of Texas to promote themselves as part of their Stateside deal with 'Sony'. Sadly, the indie scene wasn't ready to don their cowboy shirts just yet and bar a one-off V/A charity single – upon which they had to perform a version of Right Said Fred's 'DEEPLY DIPPY' – they failed to chart, subsequent EP's, 'FURTHER DOWN THE LINE' and 'ROCKINGBIRDS 'R' US', selling poorly. With GOLDING now moving on, the Camden country-rockers returned in '95 on 'Cooking Vinyl' with a belated EDWYN COLLINS-produced follow-up set, 'WHATEVER HAPPENED TO THE ROCKINGBIRDS'. Exactly. • **Covered:** YOUR GOOD GIRL'S GONNA GO BAD (Tammy Wynette) / IN TALL BUILDINGS (John Hartford) / OLDER GUYS (Parsons – Hillman) / etc.

Album rating: THE ROCKINGBIRDS (*6)

ALAN TYLOR – vocals, guitar / **ANDY HACKETT** – guitar / **PATRICK ARBUTHNOT** – pedal steel guitar / **DAVE GOLDING** – bass / **SHAUN REID** – percussion, vocals / **DAVE MORGAN** – drums (ex-LOFT)

Heavenly Sony

Sep 91. (7") (HVN 14) **A GOOD DAY FOR YOU IS A GOOD DAY FOR ME. / JONATHAN, JONATHAN**
(12"+=/cd-s+=) (HVN 14 12/CD) – Only one flower.

— (In Nov'91, with LESLIE SILVERFISH on vox, they released a single for 'Clawfist'; 'YOUR GOOD GIRL'S GONNA GO BAD')

Apr 92. (lp/cd) (HVN/+CD 2) **THE ROCKINGBIRDS**
– Gradually learning / Further down the line / Standing at the doorstep of love / Jonathan, Jonathan / The day my life begins / Searching / Restless / Times drives the truck / Halfway to comatose / In tall buildings / Only one flower / Drifting.

May 92. (7") (HVN 17) **JONATHAN, JONATHAN. / TIME DRIVES THE TRUCK**
(12"+=/cd-s+=) (HVN 17 12/CD) – Older guys.

Aug 92. (7") (HVN 21) **GRADUALLY LEARNING. / WHERE I BELONG**
(12"+=) (HVN 21-12) – Love has gone and made a mess of me.
(cd-s++=) (HVN 21CD) – ('A'-full version).

— (In Nov'92, with other 'Heavenly' acts, they released their version of 'DEEPLY DIPPY' on 'FRED EP' (HVN 19) (hit UK No.26)

Feb 93. (cd-ep) (HVN 027CD) **FURTHER DOWN THE LINE / SEARCHING (alternate mix) / HALFWAY TO COMATOSE (live) / DRIFTING (live)**

Jul 93. (12"ep/cd-ep) (HVN 031-12/-CD) **ROCKINGBIRDS 'R' US: THE HEAVENLY EP**
– Gladly . . . / I'm a little less lonely / It won't be long / Harden up your heart.

Oct 94. (7") (HVN 43) **BAND OF DREAMS. / EVERYBODY LIVES WITH US**

— now without GOLDING

Cooking Vinyl   not iss.

Apr 95. (lp/cd) (COOK 084/+CD) **WHATEVER HAPPENED TO THE ROCKINGBIRDS**
– Roll on forever / I like winter / Everybody lives with us / Band of dreams / We had it all / I woke up one morning / The high part / Bitter tear / Before we go to the end / Hell / Let me down slow.

— they disbanded after above

RODAN (see under ⇒ RACHEL'S)

ROLLERSKATE SKINNY

Formed: Dublin, Ireland ... early 90's by brothers KEN and GER GRIFFIN, together with JIMI SHIELDS (younger sibling of MY BLOODY VALENTINE's mainman, KEVIN SHIELDS) and STEVIE M. The lads subsequently set up home in Marble Arch/Wandsworth, London in 1992, making a name for themselves with the self-financed 'NOVICE' EP early the following year. Its 8-minute+ lead track, 'COMPLACENCY', was an ambitious beginning, suggesting they'd been listening to the awkward avant-noise of MERCURY REV or MY BLOODY VALENTINE. Beggars Banquet offshoot, 'Placebo' (also home of COME), were shrewd enough to pick them up, releasing a second 10" EP the following Spring, 'TROPHY'. Slightly less ferocious, the lead track, 'BOW-HITCH-HIKER', signalled a move towards a slightly more restrained PAVEMENT-style approach. This mapped out the sonic territory the band would explore throughout the subsequent debut album, 'SHOULDER VOICES' (1993) and EP, 'THRESHOLD'. The following year, ROLLERSKATE SKINNY actually supported spiritual cousins, PAVEMENT, on that summer's 'Lollapalooza' jaunt, the resulting upsurge in media coverage helping them find a home at 'Warners'. Complete with new drummer, CLIVE CARROLL (replacing JIMI), they finally unveiled their new material in the shape of early 1996's 'HORSE DRAWN WISHES'. In the event, their major label tenure was brief and following the band's split, KEN struck out on his own as KID SILVER. His critically acclaimed debut album, 'DEAD CITY SUNBEAMS' (1999), left behind the angular territory of old for the kind of broad brushstroke, sonic panorama only a musician who has been around the block a bit can conceive.

Album rating: SHOULDER VOICES (*6) / HORSE DRAWN WISHES (*6) / Kid Silver: DEAD CITY SUNBEAMS (*7)

KEN GRIFFIN – vocals (also keyboards) / **GER GRIFFIN** – guitar / **JIMI SHIELDS** – guitar, drums (also vocals, keyboards) / **STEVIE MURRAY** – bass (also guitar, keyboards)

Showbiz not iss.

Sep 92. (10"ep) (RSS 001) **NOVICE**
– Complacency / Crushy daughter.

Placebo Beggars Banquet

Apr 93. (10"ep) (PILL 5) **TROPHY**
– Bow hitch-hiker / Violence to violence / Trophy.

Oct 93. (cd/lp) (PILL CD/A 3) <92325-2/-4> **SHOULDER VOICES**   Feb94
– Miss leader / Violence to violence / Lunasa / Bring on stgmata / Bella / Ages / Bow hitch-hiker / Some give birth / Shallow thunder / Slave / So far down up to heaven.

Feb 94. (10"ep/cd-ep) *(PILL 9/+CD)* **THE "THRESHOLD" EP – ACCEPT MORALITY .... (& FREEDOM IS YOUR BONE)**
– Miss leader (remix) / Entropy / Goodbye balloon.

── **CLIVE CARROLL** – drums; repl. JIMI who formed LOTUS CROWN who issued one 'Reprise' set, 'CHOKIN' ON THE JOKES'

                                                WEA   Warners

Feb 96. (cd/c) *(<9362 45943-2/-4>)* **HORSE DRAWN WISHES**
– Swing boat yawning / Cradle burns / One thousand couples / Swab the temples / Speed to my side / All morning break / Man under glass / Shimmer son like a star / Angela starling / Ribbon fat / Thirsty European / Bells jar away.

May 96. (c-s) *(W 0349C)* **SPEED TO MY SIDE / GOOD NIGHT DIAMOND**
(12"+=/cd-s+=) *(W 0349 T/CD)* – Trial of witness.

── disbanded early in 1997

KID SILVER

aka **KEN GRIFFIN** with **BRYAN SYNOTT** – guitar / **CLIVE CARROLL** – programming
                                             Jetset   Jetset

Mar 99. (cd) *(<TWA 18CD>)* **DEAD CITY SUNBEAMS**
– Dead city sunbeams / Hey trespasser / Racing daylight / Don't start / 67 cities of light / My electric sky / 24 days of the lilac / Breadcrumbs / Devils and demons / Keep warm / Punchdrunk sweethearts / Don't bring tears to a table / Scarecrow / Layabout superstars.

ROPERS

Formed: Washington, D.C., USA ... 1991 by college friends DOUG BAILEY and MIKE HAMMEL, plus latterly, ALEX HACKER, whom the original duo had briefly played with in The LILYS, alongside 4th member, GREG PAVLOVCAK. Debuting in 1992 with the 7"ers 'SUNBATHE' and 'I DON'T MIND', the boys heralded their competent blend of jangly sixties style pop with JOY DIVISION-esque post punk to create a very nineties indie rock sound. Following these initial blasts, The ROPERS issued their eponymously titled EP two years later and hot on its heels came the well received full-length outing, 'ALL THE TIME' (1995), a record which showcased the band's lucid guitar-heavy sound on standouts such as the 'Slumberland' single 'REVOLVER' and track 'YOU HAVE THE LIGHT' – think psychedelic bands such as LOVE. HACKER departed the following year to be replaced by MIKE DONOVAN. However, by the time of the release of their sophomore LP, 'THE WORLD IS FIRE' (1997), the band had disbanded.

Album rating: ALL THE TIME (*4) / THE WORLD IS FIRE mini (*4)

DOUG BAILEY – vocals / **MIKE HAMMEL** – guitar / **GREG PAVLOVCAK** – bass / **ALEX HACKER** – drums
                                             Slumberland Slumberland

Jul 93. (7"ep) *<(SLUM 017)>* **SUNBATHE EP**
– Lost waiting / Waiting / It's so strange / Cool self.

Aug 93. (7"ep; Various Artists) *<ANT 09>* **Pearl EP**
– Sweet Lord I know / (other artists).
(above on 'Brilliant' records)

May 94. (7") *<SLUM 038>* **I DON'T MIND. / SEPTEMBER'S RAIN**
(cd-ep) *<SLR 38>* **THE ROPERS** – SUNBATHE EP

Jun 94. (7") *<WISH 5>* **PRETTY QUIET. / (other by BOYRACER)**

Aug 95. (7") *<SLR 53>* **REVOLVER. / TRANSPARENT DAY**

Oct 95. (lp/cd) *<SLR 50/+CD>* **ALL THE TIME**
– Revolver / Flash light / Rain / You have a light / Drive / Chained / Blind / Spider web / Tired / Mystery girl / (untitled).

── **MIKE DONOVAN** – drums; repl. HACKER
                                      A Turntable Friend Teenbeat

Jun 97. (m-lp/m-cd) *(TURN 33/+CD) <TEENBEAT 225>* **THE WORLD IS FIRE**   Aug97
– Drink you up / Please understand / Take your time / Home / Paste / These days / Dawn.

── disbanded after above; PAVLOVCAK later joined The SATURDAY PEOPLE

THESE ARE THE SOUNDS OF KALEIDOSCOPE

BAILEY + HAMMEL plus one member
                                            not iss. Foxyboy

Jul 02. (cd-ep) *<foxy 001>* **THESE ARE THE SOUNDS OF KALEIDOSCOPE**
– And there you go / Haven't got the time / The parallelogram / Sleep plenty.

ROSA MOTA

Formed: Camden, London, England ... 1992 by IAN BISHOP, SACHA GALVAGNA, JULIE D. RUMSEY, JUSTIN CHAPMAN and MICHELLE MARTI. Drawing sonic inspiration from BAUHAUS and ECHO AND THE BUNNYMEN, these noir art-rockers released their debut EP in '93 prior to their first full-length outing 'WISHFUL SINKING' in 1995. The set showcased their alternative rock edge but also displayed somewhat of a heavier guitar sound that gave flavours of THE VERVE's earlier space-rock dabblings. ROSA MOTA followed this up with their sophomore set, 'BIONIC' (1996), which built on and superseded the quality of its predecessor; CLARE GROGAN (ex-ALTERED IMAGES) made a guest appearance on this recording.

Album rating: DRAG FOR A DRAG mini (*5) / WISHFUL SINKING (*4) / BIONIC (*6)

IAN BISHOP – vocals, guitars, clarinet / **JULIE D. RUMSEY** – vocals, guitar / **SACHA GALVAGNA** – guitar, bouzouki / **MICHELLE MARTI** – bass, guitar, harmonica / **JUSTIN CHAPMAN** – percussion, clarinet
                                       Placebo not iss.

Jul 93. (m-cd/m-lp) *(PILLM CD/A 2)* **DRAG FOR A DRAG**
– Baby flower / Are we having fun yet? / Cold / Riverblind / Fucked / Roma.

1994. (7"pink) *(PILLS 7)* **STOP – START. / LEAVE THE PLANET**
                                         Flower Shop not iss.

1994. (7") *(FLOWER 002)* **FV 3431. / LITTLE WAYS**
                                         13th Hour Mute

Jan 95. (12"ep) *(HOUR 4)* **ASBESTOS FRENZ EP**
– Asbestos frenz / Little girl / I'll take your life / Scratch.

Jan 95. (cd/lp) *(13TH CD/LP 2) <9005>* **WISHING SINKING**
– Thintro / L'egoiste / Asbestos frenzy / Hopey / Unrequited love song / Big fat arms / Little white horse / Touched / Smack scratch / Always with wings / Got nuffin / Deepness / Stripped and bleeding. *(lp w/ free 12"+=)* – ASBESTOS FRENZY (edit) / ASBESTOS FRENZ (cement mix)

May 95. (cd-s) *(HOUR 5CD)* **HOPEY (re-recorded) / TRACTION**

Jan 97. (7"m) *(HOUR 7)* **SPACE JUNK. / STAR STRUCK / THENEZINE**
(cd-s+=) *(CDHOUR 7)* – Angel (French).

Feb 97. (cd/lp) *(13TH CD/LP 3) <69022>* **BIONIC**   Sep96
– From her to maternity / Shelf life / Victoria Falls / This grudge / Frostbitten / Pigeon / Space junk / Scenic layby / La chienne est dans l'arbre / Sometimes narcoleptic / Angel.

── disbanded after above

ROSITA (see under ⇒ KENICKIE)

Malcolm ROSS

Born: c.1960, Edinburgh, Scotland. In 1979, guitarist ROSS, PAUL HAIG, RON TORRANCE and GARY McCORMACK, were part of TV ART, a band that quickly evolved into JOSEF K when their roadie DAVE WENDELL replaced EXPLOITED bound McCORMACK. With the help of ROSS's buddy STEPHEN DALY (from The NU-SONICS, the soon-to-be ORANGE JUICE), JOSEF K delivered their own self-financed 45, 'Chance Meeting', a post-punk, atonal affair. Along with the aforementioned ORANGE JUICE, JK were one of the first acts to sign for the Glasgow-based "young sound of Scotland" imprint, 'Postcard' (run by ALAN HORNE). ROSS and the boys duly rattled off several singles and an album for the label before they sadly abandoned the band in 1982. With HAIG now a solo artist and the others in The HAPPY FAMILY, ROSS teamed up with his old pal DALY in ORANGE JUICE. Early in '84, MALCOLM became part of the third 'Postcard' outfit, AZTEC CAMERA, although this was curtailed when he and AZ's DAVE RUFFY joined forces with vocalist SUSAN BUCKLEY to form the short-lived HIGH BEES; the play on words moniker, a nickname for fans of Hibernian F.C. However, only one platter, 'SOME INDULGENCE', was released; it's seemingly very rare nowadays. In 1992, ROSS teamed up once again with DAVE WENDELL and formed the short-lived MAGIC CLAN with new drummer PAUL MALLINEN. Finding an outlet for his solo work through the German-based 'Marina', MALCOLM ROSS delivered his solo EDWYN COLLINS-produced debut, 'LOW SHOT' (1995), a record which also featured some of his MAGIC CLAN; ROBERT VICKERS (ex-GO-BETWEENS), STEPHEN DALY and DAVY WENDELL. A second, 'HAPPY BOY', recorded in '97, marked an appearance by BARRY ADAMSON, while MALCY co-wrote a few with former ORANGE JUICE cohort, DAVID McCLYMONT. To be honest, the albums were a little disappointing, possibly in hindsight vocalist/guitarist ROSS (with a sound not too dissimilar to EDWYN C) might've been better using an up and coming trained singer.

Album rating: LOW SHOT (*4) / HAPPY BOY (*3)

MALCOLM ROSS – vocals, guitars / with his DELANCY ST. GROUP and the MAGIC CLAN:- **ROBERT VICKERS, STEPHEN DALY + DAVY WENDELL**
                                           Marina Bus Stop

Sep 95. (cd) *(ma 14)* **LOW SHOT** <US-title 'MALCOLM ROSS'>   May96
– Low shot / Homestreet / Another year, another town / My avenger / Tried so hard / Hiram's dead / Big woman / Frogs and grass / One more day / Scarface / Round and round.

── now with **DOMINIC MURCOTT** – drums, vibes, percussion, programming / **SEAMUS BEAGHEN** – keyboards / **DAVE CHAMBERLAIN** – bass / **GED BARRY** – sax / **ANDREA SPAIN** – bass clarinet

Jan 98. (cd) *(ma 33)* **HAPPY BOY**
– Happy boy / Heavens doors / Big guitar / I really could / Traitors / Lunchbreak / Heartbroken all over again / Missing / She plays the drums / Slim Jim on the slippery slope.

ROXY MUSIC

Formed: Newcastle, England ... 1970 by art school graduate and teacher, BRYAN FERRY alongside GRAHAM SIMPSON. Early in 1971, they invited ANDY MACKAY and electronic wizard BRIAN ENO to join, finally settling with the debut album line-up a year later, when they added PHIL MANZANERA and PAUL THOMPSON. The concept of ROXY MUSIC was the brainchild of FERRY, who attempted to realise his vision of a musical equivalent to the pop art he'd become fascinated with at college. Fashioning the band in an outlandish hybrid of decadent glamour and future shock experimentalism, FERRY made sure ROXY MUSIC would be hot property after only a handful of gigs. At this point, the other prime mover behind ROXY MUSIC was BRIAN ENO, who shaped the band's pioneering sound by wrenching all manner of bizarre electronic noises from his mini-moog, feeding the rest of the instruments through an EMS modular synth and masterminding pre-recorded special effects. Signed to 'Island', the band released their self-titled debut in the summer of 1972. Produced by PETE SINFIELD (the KING CRIMSON lyricist), the album effortlessly fused FERRY's suave crooning, a pulsing rhythm section and ENO's inspired electronic experimentation, garnering rave reviews and defying any attempts to pigeonhole the band's sound. But it was the follow-up single, 'VIRGINIA PLAIN' (1972), which launched the band into pop stardom. A careering blast of avant-pop that managed to incorporate a lyric focusing on one of FERRY's surrealist paintings, the single breached the upper echelons of the charts. By this juncture, SIMPSON had been given his marching orders and the band went through a bewildering succession of personnel changes, FERRY retaining strict control throughout. After another top ten hit with 'PJAMARAMA' in 1973, ROXY MUSIC released their second album, 'FOR YOUR PLEASURE' later the same year. Juxtaposing the ironic wig-out of tracks like 'DO THE STRAND' and 'BEAUTY QUEEN' with the vivid desolation of 'IN EVERY DREAM HOME A HEARTACHE', the album distilled the essence of FERRY's original vision. ENO left soon after, his more extreme experimental leanings at odds with the direction in which FERRY wanted to take the band.

Album rating: ROXY MUSIC (*8) / FOR YOUR PLEASURE (*9) /

BRYAN FERRY (b.26 Sep'45, Washington, Durham, England) – vocals, piano / **ANDY MACKAY** (b.23 Jul'46, London, England) – saxophone, oboe, wind inst. / (BRIAN) **ENO** (b.15 May'48, Woodbridge, Suffolk, England) – synthesizers-keyboards / **GRAHAM SIMPSON** – bass, vocals / **PHIL MANZANERA** (b. PHILIP TARGETT-ADAMS, 31 Jan'51, London) – guitar (ex-QUIET SUN) repl. DAVID O'LIST (ex-NICE) who had repl. original ROGER BUNN (Jul'71). / **PAUL THOMPSON** (b.13 May'51, Jarrow, Northumberland, England) – drums repl. original DEXTER LLOYD (Jul'71).

		Island	Reprise
Jun 72.	(lp/c) (ILPS/ICT 9200) <RS 2114> **ROXY MUSIC**	10	

– Re-make/re-model / Ladytron / If there is something / 2 H.B. / The bob (medley) / Chance meeting / Would you believe? / Sea breezes / Bitters end. (re-iss. Feb77 on 'Polydor' lp)(c; 2302 048)(3100 348) (re-iss. Jan87 & Sep91 on 'EG' lp/c/cd+=; EG LP/MC/CD 6) – Virginia plain.

— (May'72) **RIK KENTON** (b.31 Oct'45) – bass repl. SIMPSON
Aug 72. (7") (WIP 6144) <1124> **VIRGINIA PLAIN. / THE NUMBERER** 4

— (Jan'73) **JOHN PORTER** – bass repl. KENTON who went solo

		Island	Warners
Mar 73.	(7") (WIP 6159) **PJAMARAMA. / THE PRIDE AND THE PAIN**	10	
Mar 73.	(lp/c) (ILPS/ICT 9232) <2696> **FOR YOUR PLEASURE**	4	

– Do the strand / Beauty queen / Strictly confidential / Editions of you / In every dream home a heartache / The bogus man / Grey lagoons / For your pleasure. (re-iss. Feb77 on 'Polydor' lp)(c; 2302 049)(3100 349) (re-iss. Jan87 on 'E.G.' lp/c/cd; EG LP/MC/CD 8) (cd+c.Sep91 on 'EG') (re-iss. Feb97 on 'E.M.I.'; LPCENT 19)

Jul 73. (7") <7719> **DO THE STRAND. / EDITIONS OF YOU** — —

— (Jul'73) **EDDIE JOBSON** (b.28 Apr'55, Billingham, Teeside, England) – keyboards, violin (ex-CURVED AIR) repl. ENO who went solo

---

ROYAL BRONCO (see under ⇒ POLICECAT)

ROYAL TRUX

Formed: Chicago, Illinois, USA . . . 1987 by Calvin Klein model and self-confessed junkie, JENNIFER HERREMA and PUSSY GALORE's NEIL HAGERTY, who had originally met in a New York sewer two years previously. Lo-fi avant-garde terrorists from the stable of BEEFHEART or ZAPPA that shifted more into The 'STONES (early 70's era), the difference being the sultry JANE BIRKEN style-vox of HERRERA. Following the junkie freeform chaos of earlier albums (by this point she had kicked her habit), the couple signed to 'Virgin'-offshoot, 'Hut' in 1994 and finally got it together for the most focused album of their career to date, the David Briggs-produced 'THANK YOU' (1995). Reportedly cleaned up and newly relocated to Virginia, HAGGERTY and HERREMA had created a work of hip swivelling, ground-in-the-dirt rock'n'roll drawing inevitable comparisons with the early 70's glory of The ROLLING STONES while recreating the spirit of such less readily remembered boogie merchants as BLACK OAK ARKANSAS and GRAND FUNK RAILROAD, the legendary 'TRUX musical bloody mindedness bubbling under the surface. An unlikely UK tour with TEENAGE FANCLUB helped raise their profile, yet perhaps not surprisingly, it seemed ROYAL TRUX weren't destined for mainstream indie success and following the release of 'SWEET SIXTEEN' (1997), the pair relocated to the more familiar surroundings of US indie label, 'Domino', issuing the 'ACCELERATOR' album in 1998. The aptly titled 'VETERANS OF DISORDER' (1999), meanwhile, provided a right ROYAL TRUX racket, or at least half of it did. Split fairly evenly between two and a half minute minor classics and a trio of longer noisefests, the album provided a bridge between old and new without losing any of the shambolic, subversive edge. In contrast, 'POUND FOR POUND' (2000) found HERREMA and HAGERTY once again kicking back in the musical equivalent of a battered old leather armchair, content to crank out bruised rock'n'roll free from the pressures of experimentation. HAGERTY's solo career was underway the following year via the 'NEIL MICHAEL HAGERTY' (2001) set, a worthy debut from 'Drag City' that paved the way for a second batch, 'PLAYS THAT GOOD OLD ROCK AND ROLL' (2002).

Album rating: UNTITLED – ROYAL TRUX (*4) / TWIN INFINITIVES (*4) / ROYAL TRUX (*5) / CATS AND DOGS (*6) / THANK YOU (*6) / SWEET SIXTEEN (*5) / ACCELERATOR (*6) / VETERANS OF DISORDER (*8) / POUND FOR POUND (*6) / HAND OF GLORY (*6) / Neil Michael Hagerty: NEIL HAGERTY (*6) / PLAYS THAT GOOD OLD ROCK AND ROLL (*5)

JENNIFER HERREMA – vocals / **NEIL HAGERTY** – guitar, vocals (ex-PUSSY GALORE) / with a few others

		not iss.	Royal
Jan 89.	(lp) <none> **UNTITLED – ROYAL TRUX**	–	

– Bad blood / Incineration / Strawberry soda / Hashish / Sanction Smith / Zero dok / Touch / Bits and spurs / Esso dame / Sice I bones / Gold dust / Jesse James / Andersonville / The set-up / Walking machine / Hawk'n around. <cd-iss. Dec96 as 'ROYAL TRUX' on 'Drag City'; DC 5CD> (UK cd-iss. Jan01 on 'Domino'; REWIGCD 003)

		not iss.	Vertical
1989.	(7"ep) <none> **SPIKE CYCLONE / NO FIXED ADDRESS. / BAGHDAD BUZZ / SUNFLAVOR**	–	

		not iss.	Drag City
1989.	(7") <DC 1> **HERO – ZERO. / LOVE IS . . .**		–
1990.	(d-lp/cd) <DC 3/+CD> **TWIN INFINITIVES**		

– Solid gold tooth / Ice cream / Jet pet / RTX – USA / Kool down wheels / Chances are the comets in our future / Yin Jim vs. the vomit creature / Osiris / (Edge of the) Ape oven / Florida Avenue theme / Lick my boots / Glitterbust / Funky yon / Ratcreeps / New York Avenue bridge. (UK-iss.Jan94 on 'Domino'; WIGCD 8)

		Domino	Drag City
Nov 92.	(cd) <DC 10CD> **ROYAL TRUX**		

– Air / Move / Hallucination / Junkie nurse / Sometimes / Lightning boxer / Blood flowers / Sun on the run. (UK-iss.Jun93 on 'Domino' cd/lp; WIG CD/LP 5)

Dec 92.	(7") <DC 21> **RED TIGER. / LAW MAN**		–
Feb 93.	(7") <DC 23> **STEAL YR FACE. / GETT OFF**		–
Jul 93.	(cd/lp) (WIG CD/LP 6) <DC 32CD> **CATS AND DOGS**		Jun93

– Teeth / The flag / Friends / The spectre / Skywood greenback mantra / Turn of the century / Up the sleeve / Hot and cold skulls / Tight pants / Let's get lost / Driving in that car (with the eagle on the hood).

| Aug 93. | (7") <DC 35> **BACK TO SCHOOL. / CLEVELAND** | | – |
| Oct 93. | (7"/cd) (RUG 8 T/CD) **DOGS OF LOVE EP** | | |

– Back to school / Chairman blow / Cleveland / Sincerely yours, confused.

| 1994. | (7") **CHAIRMAN BLOW. / SINCERELY YOURS, CONFUSED** | – | |

(above issued on 'Electroacoustic')

| Oct 94. | (7") (RUG 27) <DC 42> **MERCURY. / SHOCKWAVE RIDER** | | |

(UK-iss.May97; same as US)

— added **DAN BROWN** – bass / **CHRIS PYLE** – drums / **ROBBIE ARMSTRONG** – percussion / with guests RIAN MURPHY + DAVID BERMAN

		Hut	Virgin + Drag City
Feb 95.	(7") (HUT 50) **MAP OF THE CITY. / NATIONAL MOTHER**		–
Feb 95.	(cd)(c/lp) (CDHUT 23)(HUT MC/LP 23) <40141><DG 66> **THANK YOU**		

– A night to remember / The sewers of Mars / Ray O Vac / Map of the city / Granny grunt / Lights on the levee / Fear strikes out / (Have you met) Horror James / You're gonna lose / Shadow of the wasp.

| May 95. | (10"/cd-s) (HUT EN/CD 56) **YOU'RE GONNA LOSE. / HIBISCUS (live) / HOT AND COLD (live)** | | – |

— **KEN NASTA** – drums; repl. PYLE + ARMSTRONG

| Apr 97. | (cd) (CDHUT 43) <42752> **SWEET SIXTEEN** | | Feb97 |

– Don't try too hard / Morphic resident / Pickup / Cold joint / Golden rules / You'll be staying in romm 323 / Can't have it both ways / 10 days 12 nights / Microwave made / Sweet sixteen / I'm looking through you / Roswell seeds and stems / Pol Pot pie.

		Domino	Drag City
Apr 98.	(7"m) (RUG 065) **I'M READY. / P.T. 20 / MR CRUMP DON'T LIKE IT**		
Apr 98.	(cd/lp) (WIG CD/LP 045) <DC 145CD> **ACCELERATOR**		

– I'm ready / Yellow kid / The banana question / Another year / Juicy, juicy, juice / Liar / New bones / Follow the winner / Stevie (for Stevie S.).

| Jun 98. | (7") (RUG 069) **LIAR. / MONEY FOR NOTHING** | | – |

(cd-s+=) (RUG 069CD) – P.T. 20 / Mr. Crump don't like it.

| Aug 98. | (12"ep/cd-ep) (RUG 076 T/CD) <DC 154CD> **3 SONG EP** | | |

– Deafer than blind / The United States vs. one 1974 Cadillac El Dorado Sedan / Run shaker life.

— **HERREMA, HAGGERTY, NESTA, PYLE** plus **DAVID PAJO** – bass

| Aug 99. | (7") (RUG 097) **WATERPARK. / WATERPARK (version)** | | |

(cd-s) (RUG 097CD) – ('A'side) / Old Yank / The new, new bones.

| Sep 99. | (cd/lp) (WIG CD/LP 068) <DC 168CD> **VETERANS OF DISORDER** | | |

– Waterpark / Stop / The exception / Second skin / Witch's tit / Lunch money / !Yo se! / Sickazz dog / Coming out party / Blue is the frequency.

— **DAN BROWN** – bass; repl. PAJO (other commitments)

| Jan 00. | (12"ep/cd-ep) (RUG 105 T/CD) **RADIO VIDEO EP** | | |

– The inside game / Victory chimp episode 3 / Dirty headlines / Mexican comet / On my mind.

| May 00. | (12") (JAGZ 001T) **DIRTY HEADLINES** | | – |
| Jun 00. | (cd/lp) (WIG CD/LP 081) <DC 188CD> **POUND FOR POUND** | | |

– Call out to the lions / Fire hill / Platinum tips / Accelerator / Deep country sorceror / Sunshine and grease / Blind navigator / Teenage murder mystery / Small thief / Dr. Gone. <(lp-iss.Aug00 on 'Drag City'; DC 188)>

| Aug 00. | (7") (RUG 113) **SUNSHINE AND GREASE. / TEENAGE MURDER MYSTERY** | | – |

(cd-s+=) (RUG 113CD) – Zing zang / Dirty headlines (mix).

ROYAL TRUX (cont) — THE GREAT INDIE DISCOGRAPHY — The 1990s

― HAGERTY + HERREMA now with **MATT RAY** – guitar / **ANIL MELNICK** – organ / **TOMMY RAFFERTY** – drums, percussion

Oct 02. (cd/lp) *(WIG CD/LP 115)* <*DC 217CD*> **HANDS OF GLORY**
– Domo des burros boxing story / Electric boxing story / Four kings – Golden lament – Pots & pansy – K-9 to the core.

– compilations, etc. –

Nov 97. (d-cd/t-lp) *Domino; (WIG 040 CD/LP) <DC 93>* **SINGLES LIVE UNRELEASED** (rarities, etc)
– Esso dame / Mercury / No fixed address / Red tiger / Lucy Peaupaux / June night afternoon / Steal your face / Back to school / Faca amolada / Luminous dolphin / Spike cyclone / Vile child / Law man / Shockwave rider / Chairman blow / Womban / Cut you loose / Baghdad buzz / Hero – Zero / Statik Jakl / Gett off / Teeth / Cleveland / Theme from M*A*S*H / Strawberry soda / Sunflavor / Love is . . . / Ratcreeps / Hair beach / Sometimes / Signed, confused / Aviator blues.

Aug 00. (lp) *Drag City; <(DC 93)>* **SINGLES LIVE UNRELEASED**

NEIL MICHAEL HAGERTY

with various backing musicians

Mar 01. (cd/lp) *(WIG CD/LP 092)* <*DC 182*> **NEIL HAGERTY** Domino: / Drag City: Feb01
– Know that / Fortune and fear / Repeat the sound of joy / Kali, the carpenter / Whiplash in park / Creature catcher / I found a stranger / Oh to be wicked once again / Tender metal / The menace / Chicken, you can roost on the Moon.

Feb 02. (lp/cd) <*(DC 214/+CD)*> **PLAYS THAT GOOD OLD ROCK AND ROLL** Drag City / Drag City
– The storm song / Sayonara / Oklahoma township / Shaved c*nt / Rockslide / Louisa la Ray / Some people are crazy / Gratitude / It could happen again.

― HAGERTY soon helped to form WEIRD WAR (with MAKE-UP members, IAN SVENONIUS + MICHELLE MAE)

RUDE CLUB

Formed: Manchester, England . . . 1993 by songwriters CHRIS BRIDGETT and JANE PARKER, the latter a sassy female with MARK E/LIAM attitude. The pair spent their formative years as an acoustic duo, even finding a healthy support slot with The FALL. Recruiting the rhythm section of STEVEN TATJI and RICHARD GREEN, the quartet hogged their wares around the toilet circuit and found themselves locked in the crazy arms of some A&R hype. The RUDE CLUB quickly found sanctuary in MANIC STREET PREACHER's manager Martin Hall's 'Sacred' imprint, where the group spent a hard dollar enlisting ex-STONE ROSES manager, Steve Adge, and releasing anti-dictator (and anti-masculine) single, 'MEN IN SUITS' (1997). The band soon became a regular feature on the festival front, playing the likes of Reading and Glastonbury before issuing follow-up platter, 'FOUL MOUTH PUNTER'. The raw edged, blinding punk song sounded as if the mics had been left on while PJ HARVEY was in the middle of a primal scream therapy session. Third single, 'LOCUST', subsequently followed, although the band failed to deliver an album before they abruptly left the scene (rude by name, rude by nature!).

Album rating: never released any

JANE PARKER – vocals / **CHRIS BRIDGETT** – guitar / **STEVEN TATJI** – bass / **RICHARD GREEN** – drums

		Sacred	not iss.
Feb 97.	(7") *(SACRED 007)* **MEN IN SUITS. / NO ME**		-
	(cd-s+=) *(SACRED 007CD)* – Literary fuck.		
May 97.	(7") *(SACRED 010)* **FOUL MOUTH PUNTER. / DO NOT OPERATE**		-
	(cd-s+=) *(SACRED 010CD)* – Docile decay.		
Sep 97.	(7") *(SACRED 014)* **LOCUST. / POSSIBLE SIDE EFFECTS**		-
	(cd-s+=) *(SACRED 014CD)* – Itch.		

― disbanded without telling anyone

Legendary Jim RUIZ (Group)

Formed: Minneapolis, Minnesota, USA . . . 1992 by JIM RUIZ, a quirky JONATHAN RICHMAN type who recruited his brother CHRIS, his wife STEPHANIE, plus CHARLOTTE LA BONNE, MATT GERZEMA and BRYAN HANNA. A connoissieur of the ridiculous and quirky, songwriter JIM RUIZ decided one day to become an "anti-legend" and recorded a batch of light indie-pop gems, with a bizarre twist of Latin-flavoured lemon juice to the jam. His debut album 'OH BROTHER WHERE ART THOU?' (1995) displayed his chilled casio keyboard rhythms and the band's laid-back lounge guitar, plus JIM's kooky lyrics straight from the RICHMAN school of the stoned. They toured Europe and the US in striped pyjamas (no, really) before delivering their sophomore set 'SNIFF' in 1998, a record which showcased much of the same styles, only with thicker beats, better production and the inclusion of French pop icon KATERINE and The PULSERS. The band rightfully contributed to a GALAXIE 500 tribute album, entitled 'Snowstorm' in 2001.

Album rating: OH BROTHER WHERE ART THOU? (*5) / SNIFF (*6)

JIM RUIZ – vocals, guitar / **STEPHANIE WINTER-RUIZ** – backing vocals / **MATT GERZEMA** – guitar / **CHARLOTTE LA BONNE** – bass / **BRYAN HANNA** – drums / **CHRIS RUIZ** – keyboards

		Minty Fresh	Minty Fresh
May 95.	(7"colrd) <*(MF 8)*> **MIJ AMSTERDAM. / MINNEAPOLIS / JODY**		
Jun 95.	(cd) <*(MF 11)*> **OH BROTHER WHERE ART THOU?**		
	– Mij Amsterdam / My bloody Yugo / Stormtrooper / Spain / Be my valentine / Glad they're gone / Urban gentleman / Every other Sunday / She's gone away / Yes I do / Lucht / Oh porridge.		

― **JIM + STEPH + CHRIS** recruited **JOHN CROZIER** – guitar (of HANG-UPS) / **OLAF MEDUIS** – bass / **PETE ANDERSON** – drums

		Siesta	Minty Fresh
Apr 99.	(cd) *(SIESTA 86CD)* <*MF 27*> **SNIFF**		Jul98
	– Last time / Last summer / Big foot / Baby where art thou? / Until I met you / Katherine / Uncle Wieney / Goodbye to all that / Without you, gurl / My foolish heart / Bigfoot (I remember Wes) / Sound of music.		

― JIM + STEPHANIE have since abandoned the project, the latter helped form SHEBREWS, who've released one set, 'OFF WITH THEIR HEARTS' (2001)

RUMAH SAKIT

Formed: San Francisco, California, USA . . . 1998 by JOHN BAEZ, JEFF SHANNON, MITCH CHENEY and KENSETH THIBIDEAU. Neither hailing from Chicago or Canada, it was refreshing to see a post-punk/post-rock/post-whatever group playing screwed-up instrumentals, dowsed with a bit of humour. Taking their cues from KING CRIMSON, as well as GODSPEED YOU BLACK EMPEROR! and The OXES, RUMAH SAKIT (apparently pronounced "Room-uh-sac-eet") were too silly to be recorded by STEVE ALBINI, but serious enough not to be kicked out of the MOGWAI camp. Their debut set, 'RUMAH SAKIT' (2000), contained a plethora of swirling instrumentals, all clocking in at over four minutes and some reminiscent of Japanese noisecore groups such as The BOREDOMS and MELT BANANA. Their scathing follow-up, 'OBSCURED BY CLOWNS' (2002) – complete more PINK FLOYD conotations that you could wave a pointy stick at – took this template further, adding melodic pieces of purified ambience, plus a more extreme sonic assault, challenging contemporaries such as BLACK DICE to battle for the ethereal noise wig-out stakes. 'NO ONE LIKES A GRUMPY CRIPPLE' and 'ARE WE NOT SERIOUS? WE ARE RUMAH SAKIT' were two brilliant examples of great song titles, plus, just great songs!

Album rating: RUMAH SAKIT (*7) / OBSCURED BY CLOWNS (*5)

JOHN BAEZ + JEFF SHANNON + KENSETH THIBIDEAU + MITCH CHENEY – instruments, etc

		Temporary Residence	Temporary Residence
Jun 00.	(cd) <*(TRR 26CD)*> **RUMAH SAKIT**		
	– I can't see anything when I close my eyes / Scott and Jeremiah / Careful with that fax machine / Wind and wing / Bring on the cobras / Stomachache due to the sincere belief that the rest of the band is trying to kill me.		
Jul 02.	(cd) <*(TRR 49CD)*> **OBSCURED BY CLOWNS**		Jun02
	– Hello beginning, this is my friend . . . the end / New underwear dance / No one looks like a grumpy cripple / German clock / Obscured by clowns / Are we not serious? We are Rumah Sakit! / Sausage full of secrets "live" / Go horsey go "live" / Hello friend, this is my end . . . the beginning. (*lp-iss.Jul02 on 'Sickroom'; SRR 07*)		

– compilations, specials, etc. –

Jul 02.	(cd) *Errol; (WILK 005)* **LIVE – RECORDED AT THE BOOTOM OF THE HILL**		-

RUN ON

Formed: New York, USA . . . 1992 by husband and wife RICK BROWN (drummer) and SUE GARNER (singer, guitarist). BROWN and GARNER are veterans of the New York's various independent/underground music scenes, playing together in various groups for well over a decade. Often juggling commitments to different bands/projects, they played with art punk acts FISH & ROSES, INFORMATION and V-EFFECT, while GARNER also sang with VIETNAM, The LAST ROUND-UP and The SHAMS. Her trio The SHAMS – also featuring guitarist AMY McMAHON RIGBY and drummer AMANDA UPRICHARD – released an EP, 'SEDUSA' and an LP, 'QUILT' (both 1994), before splitting the same year. When FISH & ROSES disbanded, the pair linked up with former LOVE CHILD guitarist ALAN LICHT. RUN ON were now beginning to take shape, and after the release of 7" 'DAYS AWAY' – recorded with IRA KAPLAN of YO LA TENGO – they recruited a fourth permanent member, trumpeter DAVID NEWGARDEN. A former member of indie-rockers MAD SCENE, NEWGARDEN also worked for the 'Tzadik' label, and was a LOVE CHILD and FISH & ROSES fan. RUN ON began playing live, and then entered the studio to record the 'ON/OFF' EP, with production from GENE HOLDER (bassist with YO LA TENGO). 'ON/OFF' was released in 1995 on the 'Matador' label, which was formed by GERARD COSLOY – a friend from FISH & ROSES old label 'Homestead'. This release was a promising introduction to RUN ON's well-crafted, expansive sound. Debut LP, 'START PACKING', released in 1996, successfully blended intelligent (yet accessible) arrangements of jazz and rock, and featured GARNER's mutating, versatile voice. After touring with YO LA TENGO, The DIRTY THREE and TORTOISE, NEWGARDEN left, violinist KATIE GENTILE joined, and RUN ON headed back to the studio. On 'NO WAY', released in 1997, RUN ON further developed their jazz rhythms while incorporating

GENTILE's impressive playing – like on 'OUT FOR A WALK'. After two more 1997 EP releases, 'SCOOT' and 'SIT DOWN', GENTILE left to concentrate on her other band SPECIAL PILLOW. Finally, in 1998, BROWN and GARNER called it a day with RUN ON, and LICHT found other session work. The same year, GARNER released a solo album, 'TO RUN MORE SMOOTHLY', which utilised the sincerity of her voice with a collection of intimate ballads. Two further solo albums followed, 'STILL' (2000) and 'SHADYSIDE' (2002), with songwriting and instrumental assistance from BROWN.

Album rating: Fish & Roses: WE ARE HAPPY TO SERVE YOU (*7) / Shams: QUILT (*4) / Peach Cobbler: GEORGIA PEACH (*5) / Run On: START PACKING (*7) / NO WAY (*8) / Sue Garner: TO RUN MORE SMOOTHLY (*6) / STILL; with Rick Brown (*7) / SHADYSIDE (*6)

FISH & ROSES

SUE GARNER (b. Cave Spring, Georgia, USA) – vocals, guitar / **DAVID SUTTER** – bass / **RICK BROWN** – drums, percussion, vocals (ex-V-EFFECT)

			Homestead	Homestead
Jul 89.	(lp)	<(HMS 130)> **WE ARE HAPPY TO SERVE YOU**		
			not iss.	Twin/Tone
1990.	(lp)	<TTL 87123> **FISH & ROSES**	–	

— SUE would part of The LAST ROUNDUP; BROWN joined TIMBER

SHAMS

SUE GARNER – bass / **AMY McMAHON RIGBY** – guitar / **AMANDA UPRICHARD** – drums

			Matador	Matador
1993.	(cd/c/lp)	<OLE 028-2/-4/-1> **QUILT**	–	

– It'll all catch up to you / Stuck here on the ground / Dark angel / Dressed to kill / Only a dream / Ice tea / Watching the grass grow / File clerk blues / Down at the Texaco / Brown's diner / Time / Always with me.

| May 94. | (7") | (OLE 063-7) **THE SEDUSIA** | | |

– Voices in my head / Love me with your mind / Continuous play.

RUN ON

GARNER + BROWN recruited **ALAN LICHT** – guitar (ex-LOVE CHILD, ex-BLUE HUMANS)

			not iss.	Ajax
Nov 94.	(7"m)	<ajax 037> **DAYS AWAY. / ORDERING / WE'LL PLAY HOUSE**	–	

— added **DAVID NEWGARDEN** – trumpet, keyboards (of MAD SCENE)

			Matador	Matador
Jun 95.	(12"ep/cd-ep)	<(OLE 143-1/-2)> **ON/OFF**		

– Into the attic / Switch on / Pretty note / Water / Beat out.

| Nov 95. | (7") | <(OLE 178-7)> **MISCALCULATION. / A TO Z** | | |
| Mar 96. | (cd/lp) | <(OLE 153-2/-1)> **START PACKING** | | Feb96 |

– Tried / Baap / Go there / A to Z / Miscalculation / In strength / Xmas trip / Doesn't anybody love the dark / Tell me / You said / Coffee / Surprise.

| Feb 97. | (cd) | <(OLE 229-2)> **NO WAY** | | |

– Something sweet / Lab rats / As good as new / Look / Bring her blues / Half of half / Anything you say / Road / Days away / Out for a walk / Ropa vieja / Sinner man.

| 1997. | (cd-ep) | **SCOOT** | – | |

(above issued on 'Sonic Bubblegum')

— added **KATIE GENTILE** – violin

| Nov 97. | (cd-ep) | <(OLE 283-2)> **SIT DOWN** | | |

– Owe you / Go there / Xmas trip / Double Gemini / Half of half.

— split after above; LICHT went solo

SUE GARNER

with **GEORGIA HUBLEY** – drums (of YO LA TENGO) / **KATIE GENTILE + RICK BROWN**

			City Slang	Thrill Jockey
Mar 98.	(cd/lp)	<(08708-2/-1)> <THRILL 51CD> **TO RUN MORE SMOOTHLY**		Feb98

– Nightfall / Dear darling / Rose colored glue / Box and you / Glazed / Silver wings / Intuition / A life / Sense enough / Item's song / Something else / Goodbye / Continuous play.

			Thrill Jockey	Thrill Jockey
Jan 00.	(lp/cd; by SUE GARNER & RICK BROWN)	<(THRILL 065/+CD)> **STILL**		

– Synthbug / I like the name Alice / Asphalt road / Let us out / Absorbed / It's so hard / Damp spirit / Bomb squad / Swimmingly / Short and semi-sweet / Molly my / Fussy fuss.

— retained **BROWN** plus other guests

| Oct 02. | (cd) | <(THRILL 112)> **SHADYSIDE** | | Sep02 |

– Yes / Come again / Don't still the flicker / Day out / These old walls / Handful of grapes / Paint a design / Beach / Old woman / Tapas bar / Even now / It's gonna be.

PEACH COBBLER

SUE GARNER + RICK BROWN + DOMINIQUE GRIMAUD (guitars, etc) + **MONIQUE ALBA** (guitars, percussion, vocals, xylophone)

			not iss.	Ajax
Sep 95.	(cd)	<ajax 049> **GEORGIA PEACH**	–	

– Sunday / Indian giver / Come on in my kitchen / Peach / New Jersey breakdown / Queen of the hallway / White cat / Future blues / Early this morning / Moonlight on Georgia / Beyond colours / Children at C.B.G.B. / Distorted truth / Denver (after a snowstorm) / Music building breakdown / Robinson's island / White bird / Hard time killin' floor blues / Police dog blues / Song bird / Whistlin' blues.

Bruce RUSSELL (see under ⇒ DEAD C)

RUTH'S REFRIGERATOR
(see under ⇒ DEEP FREEZE MICE; in 80's section)

RYE COALITION

Formed: Jersey City, New Jersey, USA ... 1994 by RALPH CUSEGLIO, JON GONNELLI, DAVID LETO, HERB WILEY and JUSTIN MOREY. The band's sound moved from their more grungy hardcore beginnings through vital punk revival sounds to seventies style hard rock a la KISS, although always with the intention to produce all-out rawk. The 'COALITION debuted with the demo mini-album, 'THE DANCING MAN', in 1994, following this up with some touring on the New York gig circuit. Their progress towards proper recognition was slow due to the academic commitments of GONNELLI and CUSEGLIO; WILEY departed the band in 1996 for the same reasons. The subsequently reduced quartet put out several singles including a split 7" with the outfit KARP, before seeing their musical ambitions realised with the issue of debut LP, 'HEE SAW DHUH KAET', in 1997. The set showcased RC's more FUGAZI style leanings, and was a sound opener for the young band. MOREY was to bow out soon afterwards, being replaced by LETO on bass, whose brother GREG moved in for drum duties. Their next full-length offering, 'THE LIPSTICK GAME' (1999), displayed an altogether more confident band, who were not going to let go of their punk rock roots and who were prepared to try out a few quieter numbers like the acoustic underpinned 'TANGIERS' track. Meanwhile, MOREY returned just in time to let GREG go off and fulfil his student wants. The band slightly lost its way at this point, day jobs seemingly becoming of more relevance. Following a gig in the new millennium with SHELLAC and SEAM, the band again gave music another stab and inked a deal with 'Tiger Style', who issued their metal informed third full-length affair 'ON TOP' (2002); this was augmented by the experienced hand of veteran producer STEVEN ALBINI and the return of WILEY.

Album rating: HEE SAW DHUH KAET (*5) / THE LIPSTICK GAME (*7) / ON TOP (*6)

RALPH CUSEGLIO – vocals / **JON GONNELLI** – guitar / **JUSTIN MOREY** – bass (ex-MEREL) / **DAVID LETO** – drums (ex-MEREL) / **HERB WILEY** – guitar

			not iss.	Troubleman
Oct 96.	(m-lp; as RYE + split w/ KARP)	<TM 26> **KARP/RYE**		

– Sensation / Baby puts out old flames / Algebra of need / White Jesus of 114th Street / Romancing the Italian horn / (others by KARP).

— now without WILEY

			Gern Blandsten	Gern Blandsten
Oct 97.	(lp/cd)	<(GERN 029/+CD)> **HEE SAW DHUH KAET**		May97

– The higher the hair, the closer to God / 300 foxes / Nothing like a clean ashtray / Dressing up for the indictment / White Jesus of 114 St. / The buzzard / Fucking with beautiful posture / We ride / Iron fist velvet glove.

— **GREGG LETO** – drums; repl. MOREY (DAVID now bass)

| Jul 99. | (lp/cd) | <(GERN 040/+CD)> **THE LIPSTICK GAME** | | May99 |

– The prosthetic aesthetic / Thanksgiving day for cats / Baby's got a new flame / The dirty aristocrat / Amplification of the queen bee / The lipstick game / Tangiers / Digital crucifix / Bustled bride's last ride / Through the years.

— **JUSTIN MOREY** – bass; repl. GREGG (DAVID back to drums)

			Tiger Style	Tiger Style
Feb 02.	(7")	<TS 22> **ZZ TOPLESS. / SNOW JOB**	–	

— added the returning **HERB WILEY** – guitar, vocals

| Apr 02. | (cd/lp) | <(TS 23 CD/LP)> **ON TOP** | | Feb02 |

– One daughter hotter than one thousand suns / Stairway to the free bird on the way to the smokey water / Hot strikes / Stop eating while I'm smoking / Freshly frankness / Vacations / Heart of gold, jacket of leather / Born a monkey in the year of the snake / Switchblade sister: one touch nun / Honky, please!

THE GREAT INDIE DISCOGRAPHY — The 1990s

SABALON GLITZ (see under ⇒ HOLMES, Chris)

SACKVILLE

Formed: Montreal, Canada . . . 1994 by violinist GENEVIEVE HEISTEK, who added GABRIEL LEVINE, IAN IIAVSKY, HARRIS NEWMAN and PAT CONAN to the mix. The group, who were very busy in the mid 90's issuing, first, 'LOW EBB EP' (1996), then their sweeping debut album 'THESE LAST SONGS' (1998) and then a 7" split EP with mournful husband and wife duo The HANDSOME FAMILY, eventually joined Canada's most influential thriving independent label 'Constellation'. They must've felt at home, as this band, who had been making sweet and dark records for years, issued the fantastic 'THE PRINCIPLES OF SCIENCE' (1999), to much critical admiration. The mini set, comprising uplifting dirges backed by piano and fingerpicked guitar (much like their debut release), focused more on structure and melody, rather than on lyrics or musical interplay. That said there were some golden moments; JESSICA MOSS' timeless vocals on 'IF HIS SHADOW MOVES ON WATER' and the tonal logistics between NEWMAN's stand-up bass and CONAN's minimalistic drumming. SACKVILLE wasn't the only musical project HEISTEK had his teeth in, either. The sparse electric noise of HANGED UP (also on 'Constellation') was something of label importance when the duo issued two sets 'HANGED UP' (2000) and the caustic, explosive 'KICKER IN TOW' (2002), recorded by GODSPEED's EFFRIM.

Album rating: THE PRINCIPLES OF SCIENCE mini (*4) / Hanged Up: HANGED UP (*6) / KICKER IN TOW (*6)

GENEVIEVE HEISTEK – violin / **HARRIS NEWMAN** – bass / **GABRIEL LEVINE** – guitar, vocals / **IAN IIAVSKY** – keyboards, guitar / **PAT CONAN** – drums

	Car Tunes	Mag Wheels
Dec 96. (cd-ep) *(CARTCD 2) <mag 09>* **LOW EBB E.P.**		

– Messengers / Donkey song / William / Showcase showdown / Low ebb / Thomas / This thing I want, I know what I want / Cheap.
(re-iss. Nov98 on 'Glitterhouse'; GRCD 412)

Jan 98. (cd) *<mag 18>* **THESE LAST SONGS** — | – | – |
– Sydney mines / Clothesline / Good citizen / Upstate / Tie back yr hair / Lines & barriers / The frame-up / Bender / Invisible ink / Her ghost will one day rise again / Border towns / Pioneers.

— added guest **JESSICA MOSS** – vocals

	Constellation	Constellation
Jun 99. (m-cd/m-lp) *<(cst 07 d/v)>* **THE PRINCIPLES OF SCIENCE**		May99

– Gold dust / If his shadow moves on the water / Blue lips / Four-alarm fire / The principles of science.

	not iss.	Mag Wheel
Aug 99. (7") *<mag 25>* **split w/ The HANDSOME FAMILY**	–	– Canada

HANGED UP

GEN HEISTEK – viola / **ERIC CRAVEN** – drums, percussion

	Constellation	Constellation
May 00. (lp/cd) *<(cst 016/+cd)>* **HANGED UP**		

– Winternational / Propane tank / Powered by steam / New blue monda / Tapping / Czech disco (part 2) / Wilt / Bring yr scuba gear.

— added **HARRIS NEWMAN** – bass

Oct 02. (lp/cd) *<(cst 022/+cd)>* **KICKER IN TOW**
– Kinetic work / Sink / Losing your charm / View from the ground / Moment for the motion machine / No more bad future / Motorcycle muffler / Automatic spark control / Broken reel.

SAFE HOME (see under ⇒ NIGHTBLOOMS)

SAINT ETIENNE

Formed: North London, England . . . early 90's by music journo, BOB STANLEY and PETE WIGGS. Naming themselves after French football team, St. Etienne, after originally toying with the name, REARDON (the snooker player!), they signed to up-and-coming indie label 'Heavenly'. With MOIRA LAMBERT on vocals (borrowed from FAITH OVER REASON), the outfit's first vinyl foray was a sublime dub/indie-dance cover of Neil Young's 'ONLY LOVE CAN BREAK YOUR HEART'. Re-released after securing their first minor hit, 'NOTHING CAN STOP US', the track brought ST. ETIENNE to the attention of both the dance and indie scene. By this point however, a full-time vocalist (guest DONNA SAVAGE of the DEAD FAMOUS PEOPLE featured on their version of the Field Mice's 'KISS AND MAKE UP') had been recruited in the shape of SARAH CRACKNELL, whose sensuous, playful voice graced the bulk of 'FOXBASE ALPHA' (1991). A stunning debut album mixing and matching disco samples, trippy bass-lines and airy atmospherics into a pot-pourri of kitschy pop genius, the record was released to rave reviews and its relatively lowly chart position barely reflected its importance. With word now out, the group narrowly missed the UK Top 20 with their next single, 'JOIN OUR CLUB', although by early 1993 they found themselves bonafide pop stars when 'YOU'RE IN A BAD WAY' became their biggest hit to date. The accompanying album, 'SO TOUGH', cemented SAINT ETIENNE's position as top swoon-pop ironists, a masterfully sampledelic set featuring such classy compositions as 'HOBART PAVING', 'AVENUE' (also a Top 40 hit) and 'CALICO'. Following CRACKNELL's high profile collaboration with TIM BURGESS (Charlatans) for the Xmas hit, 'I WAS BORN ON CHRISTMAS DAY', the oufit completed their fourth set, 'TIGER BAY', a record which slightly disappointed their fan/fox base with its more experimental approach. Although the future of the group seemed in doubt with CRACKNELL working on solo material, a brilliant return to form with the 'HE'S ON THE PHONE' single boded well for the future. 1996 brought collaborations ('RESERECTION' with Frenchman ETIENNE DAHO), a club remix set ('CASINO CLASSICS') and a Top 40 solo single from SARAH CRACKNELL ('ANYMORE'). Her full length debut, 'LIPSLIDE' was released the following year to chart oblivion although SAINT ETIENNE were back within sniffing distance of the Top 10 with 1998's 'SYLVIE' single. As the track promised, 'GOOD HUMOUR' (1998) was a return to the song-based stucture of their debut, as knowingly and lovingly crafted as ever. In contrast, 'SOUND OF WATER' (2000) was more expansive, charting the depths of oceanic electronica while occasionally coming up for air, their pop instincts never far from the shimmering surface. In contrast, 'FINISTERRE' (2002) revisited, in part, the mix'n'match policy of old, succeeding in proving that they've still got that magpie eye for pop glitter if not exactly capturing the spirit of the early 90's. • **Songwriters:** STANLEY-WIGGS except a few with CRACKNELL plus outside covers WHO DO YOU THINK YOU ARE (Scott-Dyer) / MY CHRISTMAS PRAYER (Billy Fury) / WESTERN WIND (trad.) / STRANGER IN PARADISE (hit; Tony Bennett) / IS IT TRUE (Marc Bolan) / HOW I LEARNED TO LOVE THE BOMB (TV Personalities). • **Trivia:** Sang a version of RIGHT SAID FRED's 'I'M TOO SEXY' on a 1992 'Heavenly' compilation ep.

Album rating: FOXBASE ALPHA (*8) / SO TOUGH (*7) / YOU NEED A MESS OF HELP TO STAND ALONE compilation (*6) / TIGER BAY (*6) / TOO YOUNG TO DIE – THE SINGLES compilation (*7) / CASINO CLASSICS (*6) / GOOD HUMOUR (*6) / SOUND OF WATER (*6) / SMASH THE SYSTEM: THE SINGLES AND MORE 1990-1999 compilation (*7) / FINISTERRE (*5) / Sarah Cracknell: LIPSLIDE (*5)

BOB STANLEY (b.25 Dec'64, Horsham, Sussex) – keyboards / **PETE WIGGS** (b.15 May'66, Reigate, Surrey) – keyboards, synthesizers / **MOIRA LAMBERT** – vocals (of FAITH OVER REASON)

	white label	not iss.
1988. (12"; as the NEXT PROJECTED SOUND) *<none>* **BRUTAL GENERATION**		

	Heavenly	Warners
Jul 90. (7"/12") *(HVN 2/212)* **ONLY LOVE CAN BREAK YOUR HEART.** / ('A'version)		–

(12") *(HVN 212R)* – ('A'-A mix of two halves mix by Andy Weatherall) / The Official Saint Etienne world cup theme.

— **DONNA SAVAGE** – vocals (of DEAD FAMOUS PEOPLE) repl. MOIRA

Sep 90. (7"/12") *(HVN 4/412)* **KISS AND MAKE UP. / SKY'S DEAD** | | – |
(cd-s+=) *(HVN 412R)* – ('A'extended).
(12") *(HVN 4CD)* – ('A'mixes by Pete Helber incl. dub version).

— **SARAH CRACKNELL** – vocals (ex-solo artist) repl. DONNA

May 91. (7"/12") *(HVN 9/912)* **NOTHING CAN STOP US. / SPEEDWELL** | 54 | |
(cd-s+=) *(HVN 9CD)* – ('A'instrumental).
(12"++=) *(HVN 912R)* – ('B'-Flying mix) / ('B'-Project mix) / 3-D tiger.
below A-side featured MOIRA LAMBERT / B-side featured Q-TEE

Aug 91. (7"/12"/c-s) *(HVN 12/+12/+CS)* **ONLY LOVE CAN BREAK YOUR HEART. / FILTHY** | 39 | – |
(cd-s+=) *(HVN 12CD)* – ('A'-A mix of two halves).

Oct 91. (cd/c/lp) *(HVN CD/MC/LP 1) <26793>* **FOXBASE ALPHA** | 34 | Jan92 |
– This is Radio Etienne / Only love can break your heart / Wilson / Carnt sleep / Girl VII / Spring / She's the one / Stoned to say the least / Nothing can stop us / Etienne gonna die / London belongs to me / Like the swallow / Dilworth's theme.
(cd re-iss. Dec01; same)

Jan 92. (12"ep) *<0-40395>* **NOTHING CAN STOP US (mixes) / SPEEDWELL** | – | |

Feb 92. (c-s) *<19078>* **ONLY LOVE CAN BREAK YOUR HEART / STONED TO SAY THE LEAST** | – | 97 |
(12"+=) *<0-40196>* – ('A'mixes).

May 92. (7"/c-s) *(HVN 15/+CS)* **JOIN OUR CLUB. / PEOPLE GET REAL** | 21 | – |
(12"+=/cd-s+=) *(HVN 15 12/CD)* – ('A'-Chemically friendly zoom mix) / Scene '93.

Sep 92. (c-ep/12"ep/cd-ep) *(HVN 23 CS/12/CD)* **AVENUE / SOME PLACE ELSE. / PAPER / JOHNNY IN THE ECHO CAFE** | 40 | – |
(cd-s) *(HVN 23CDR)* – ('A'-Marshall mix) / ('A'-Venusian mix) (all remixed by A.R. KANE or GORDON KING).

— added **IAN CATT** – guitar, programmer

Feb 93. (7"/c-s) *(HVN 25/+CS)* **YOU'RE IN A BAD WAY. / CALIFORNIA SNOW STORY** | 12 | – |
(12"+=/cd-s+=) *(HVN 25 12/CD)* – Archway people / Duke Duvet.

Mar 93. (cd/c/lp) *(HVN CD/MC/LP 6)* <45166> **SO TOUGH** | 7 | - |
– Mario's cafe / Railway jam / Date with Spelman / Calico / Avenue / You're in a bad way / Memo to Pricey / Hobart paving / Leafhound / Clock milk / Conchita Martinez / No rainbows for me / Here come clown feet / Junk the morgue / Chicken soup. *(re-iss. Jun93 with free ltd.cd 'YOU NEED A MESS OF HELP TO STAND ALONE' compilation; HVN CDX 6)* – Who do you think you are / Archway people / California snow storm / Kiss and make up / Duke duvet / Filthy / Join our club / Paper / Some place else / Speedwell.

May 93. (7"/c-s) *(HVN 29/+CS)* **HOBART PAVING. / WHO DO YOU THINK YOU ARE** | 23 | - |
(12"+=/cd-s+=) *(HVN 29 12/CD)* – Your head my voice (voix revirement) / Who do you think you are (Quex-Rd) (Aphex Twin remixes).

Jun 93. (12"/cd-s) <40910> **WHO DO YOU THINK YOU ARE (mixes)** | - | - |

Dec 93. (7"/c-s) *(HVN 36/+CS)* **I WAS BORN ON CHRISTMAS DAY. / MY CHRISTMAS PRAYER** | 37 | - |
(12"+=/cd-s+=) *(HVN 36 12/CD)* – Snowplough / Peterloo. (above 'A' featured dual vocals with TIM BURGESS of The CHARLATANS)

Dec 93. (cd/c/lp) *(HVN CD/MC/LP 7)* **YOU NEED A MESS OF HELP TO STAND ALONE** | - | - |
– (see last album)

Feb 94. (7"/c-s) *(HVN 37/+CS)* **PALE MOVIE. / HIGHGATE ROAD INCIDENT** | 28 | - |
(12"/cd-s) *(HVN 37 12/CD)* – ('A'side) / ('A'-Stentorian dub) / ('A'-Secret Knowledge trouse assassin mix) / ('A'-Lemonentry mix).

Feb 94. (cd/c/lp) *(HVN CD/MC/LP 8)* <45634> **TIGER BAY** | 8 | Jun94 |
– Urban clearway / Former lover / Hug my soul / Like a motorway / On the shore / Marble lions / Pale movie / Cool kids of death / Western wind / Tankerville / Western wind / Boy scouts of America.

May 94. (7"/c-s) *(HVN 40/+CS)* **LIKE A MOTORWAY. / YOU KNOW I'LL MISS YOU WHEN YOU'RE GONE / SUSHI RIDER** | 47 | - |
(12"/cd-s) *(HVN 40 12/CD)* – ('A'side) / ('A'-Chekhov warp mix) / ('A'-David Holmes mix) / ('A'-Secret Knowledge mix) / ('A'-Motiv8 mix) / ('A'-Skin up, you're already dead) (Dust Brothers mix).

Sep 94. (c-ep/cd-ep) *(HVN 42 CS/CD)* <41591> **HUG MY SOUL / I BUY AMERICAN RECORDS / HATE YOUR DRUG / LA POUPEE QUI FAIT NON (NO, NO, NO) (live)** | 32 | - |
(12"ep) *(HVN 4012)* – ('A'side) / ('A'-Sure Is Pure) / ('A'-Motiv8) / ('A'-Secret Knowledge).
(cd-ep+=) *(HVN 42CDR)* – (above tracks) / ('A'-Juan "Kinky" Hernandez mix).

Feb 95. (fan club-cd) *(HVNCD 9)* **I LOVE TO PAINT** | - | - |
Heavenly M.C.A.

Oct 95. (c-s) *(HVN 50CS)* <55268> **HE'S ON THE PHONE / ('A'-Motiv8 mix)** | 11 | Jan96 |
(cd-s+=) *(HVN 50CDR)* – Cool kids of death (Underworld mix) / How I learned to love the bomb.
(cd-s) *(HVN 50CD)* – ('A'side) / Groveley Road / Is it true / The process.

Nov 95. (cd/c/d-lp) *(HVN CD/MC/LP 10)* **TOO YOUNG TO DIE - THE SINGLES** (compilation) | 17 | - |
– Only love can break your heart / Kiss and make up / Nothing can stop us / Join our club / People get real / Avenue / You're in a bad way / Who do you think you are / Hobart paving / I was born on Christmas day / Pale movie / Like a motorway / Hug my soul / He's on the phone. *(cd w/cd 'THE REMIX ALBUM'; HVN LP 10CDR)(+=)* – (9 remixes).

—— next with French dance artist ETIENNE DAHO and on 'Dindisc'/'Alex'US.

Jan 96. (m-cd; as ST. ETIENNE DAHO) *(DINSD 150)* <5567> **RESERECTION** | 50 | Feb96 |
– Reserection / Jungle pulse / A amours / Accident / Le baiser francais / Jungle pulse.

Oct 96. (d-cd/d-c/t-lp) *(HVNLP 16 CD/MC/LP)* **CASINO CLASSICS** | 34 | - |
– remixes by Chemical Brothers / PFM / Underworld / Way out West / Andrew Weatherall / Lionrock / David Holmes / Monkey Mafia / Death In Vegas / Sure Is Pure / Billy Nasty / Gordon King / Secret Knowledge / The Aloof / Broadcast / Aphex Twin / Primax / Psychonauts / Balearico. *(d-cd re-iss. Apr02; same)*

—— SARAH had already tried out a solo career

SARAH CRACKNELL

Gut   not iss.

Jul 96. (cd-s) *(CDGUT 3)* **ANYMORE / OH BOY, THE FEELING WHEN YOU HELD MY HAND / FIFTH FLOOR / ANYMORE** | 39 | - |
(cd-s) *(CXGUT 3)* – ('A'mixes; radio / 4anymore / Nino's liquid steel / Faster pussycat, kill kill).

Apr 97. (c-s/cd-s) *(CA/CD GUT 7)* **GOLDIE / EMPIRE STATE HIGH / AUSSIE SOAP GIRL / GOLDIE** | - | - |

May 97. (cd/c) *(GUT CD/MC 2)* **LIPSLIDE** | - | - |
– Ready or not / Desert baby / Coastal town / Home / Anymore / How far / Goldie / Taxi / Taking off for France / If you leave me / Penthouse girl, basement boy / Can't stop now.

—— SARAH also released, 'KELLY'S LOCKER' mini-cd in Japan Sep'00

SAINT ETIENNE

—— SARAH returned to the fold in 1997

Creation   not iss.

Jan 98. (7") *(CRE 279)* **SYLVIE. / ZIPCODE** | 12 | - |
(cd-s+=) *(CRESCD 279)* – Afriad to go home / Hill street connection.
(cd-s) *(CRESCD 279X)* – ('A'mixes; trouser enthusiasts tintinnabulation x2 / Stretch'n'Vern / Faze action Friday night boiler).

Apr 98. (c-s) *(CRECS 290)* **THE BAD PHOTOGRAPHER / HIT THE . . .** | 27 | - |
(cd-s+=) *(CRESCD 290)* – Swim swan swim / Madelaine.
(cd-s) *(CRESCD 290X)* – ('A'side) / 4.35 in the morning (Kid Loco remix) / Foto (Bronx Dogs mix) / Uri Geller bent my boyfriend (Add N To X mix).

May 98. (cd/lp) *(CRE CD/LP 225)* **GOOD HUMOUR** | 18 | - |
– Woodcabin / Sylvie / Split screen / Mr Donut / Goodnight Jack / Lose that girl / The bad photographer / Been so long / Postman / Erica America / Dutch TV. *(also ltd-cd; CRECD 225L)*

Kung Fu Fighting   not iss.

Feb 99. (ltd-7") *(CHANME 02)* **LOVER PLAY THE BASS. / CATNAP** | - | - |

Mantra   Sub Pop

May 99. (cd-ep) <SP 466> **PLACES TO VISIT** | - | - |
– Ivy house / 52 pilot / We're in the city / Artieripp / Sadie's anniversary / Half timbered / Garage for Gunther.

Sep 99. (ltd-7") *(AMY 009)* **SATURDAY. / (split w/ Fugu)** | - | - | French
(above issued on 'Amberley')

Mar 00. (12") *(MNT 053T)* **HOW WE USED TO LIVE. / ROSE NECK / RED SETTER** | - | - |
(cd-s+=) *(MNT 053CD)* – ('A'mixes; aim / aim instrumental / Dot Allison mix / Dot Allison instrumental).

—— In May'00, SAINT ETIENNE were credited on PAUL VAN DYK's UK Top 10 hit, 'Tell Me Why (The Riddle)'

May 00. (cd/c/lp) *(MNT CD/MC/LP 1018)* <SP 509> **SOUND OF WATER** | 33 | - |
– Late morning / Heart failed (in the back of a taxi) / Sycamore / Don't back down / Just a little overcome / Boy is crying / Aspects of Lambert / Downey, CA / How we used to live / The place at dawn.

Jun 00. (12"/cd-s) *(MNT 054 T/CD1)* **HEART FAILED (IN THE BACK OF A TAXI)** (mixes; futureshock vocal / Two Lone Swordsmen / Bridge & tunnel all not too well for Otto and Ulli) | 50 | - |
(cd-s) *(MNT 054CD2)* – ('A'side) / Thank you / Bar conscience.

Jan 01. (12") *(MNT 60T)* **BOY IS CRYING. / HOW WE USED TO LIVE (Paul Van Dyk mix)** | 34 | - |
(cd-s+=) *(MNT 60CD2)* – Northwestern (si.cut.db mix).
(cd-s) *(MNT 60CD1)* – ('A'side) / Northwestern / Shoot out the lights.

Mantra   Mantra

Aug 02. (cd-s) *(MNT 73CD)* **ACTION / ANDERSON / 7 SUMMERS** | 41 | - |
(cd-s/12") *(MNT 73 CD2/T)* – ('A'-Mr. Joshua edit/club) / ('A'-DJ Tiesto mix) / ('A'-Laub mix).

Oct 02. (cd/lp) *(<MNT CD/LP 1033>)* **FINISTERRE** | 55 | - |
– Action / Amateur / Language lab / Soft like me / Summerisle / Stop and think it over / Shower scene / The way we live now / New thing / B92 / The more you know / Finisterre.

– compilations, etc. –

Sep 01. (d-cd) *Columbia; (503427-2)* **SMASH THE SYSTEM (THE SINGLES AND MORE 1990-1999)** | - | - |
– Only love can break your heart / Kiss and make up / Nothing can stop us / Spring / Can't sleep / Filthy / Join our club / People get real / *(t-lp-iss.Sep02 on 'Simply Vinyl'; 512504-2)*

Oct 02. (12") *Heavenly; (VJAY 24)* **ONLY LOVE CAN BREAK YOUR HEART. / THE SEA** | - | - |

SAINT LOW (see under ⇒ MADDER ROSE)

SAINT SOPHIA

Formed: Boulder, Colorado, USA . . . late 90's by DEVON BRYAN, PETER BARNETT, BRENDAN CRICH and JESSELL AMS. After moving to Seattle, this futuristic electro-space-rock quartet set about recording a debut album, 'EXAMPLE: I DIE ON MY KNEES' (2000). Luxuriant yet austere in an ominous, filmic kind of way, their quasi-goth guitars and clipped drum machine rhythms nevertheless conspired in creating to a surprising accessibility on occasion. Their literate (both musically and in the wider sense of the word) brand of art-rock was further refined later that year on sophomore set, 'DEEP SWEET NOTHINGS NETWORK'.

Album rating: EXAMPLE: I DIE ON MY KNEES (*5) / DEEP SWEET NOTHINGS NETWORK (*5)

DEVON BRYANT – synthesizer, multi-instruments / **BRENDAN CRICH** – synthesizer, guitar, keyboards / **PETER BARNETT** – synthesizer, drums / **JESSELL AMS** – synths

not iss.   Little Girl Empire

2000. (cd) <LGE 001> **EXAMPLE: I DIE ON MY KNEES** | - | - |
– Cricket (paralyzed) / The rig is starting to rotate / Normalize sugarplum / The way to live is the way to die / Safer distances / Interactive media final / Spidering / Low elms.

—— now without JESSELL

2000. (cd) <LGE 002> **DEEP SWEET NOTHINGS NETWORK** | - | - |
– Seven going on eight (pt.1) / Cricket (paralyzed) / Trapline / The rig is starting to rotate / Low elms / Tesselations / Silverfish / Interoffice / Slowfade nightflower / Dream of a lost life / My sighing lens / Seven going on eight (pt.2).

SALAD

Formed: London, England . . . 1992 by ex-MTV presenter and fashion model, MARIJNE VAN DER VLUGT, along with fellow ex-film student and boyfriend, PAUL KENNEDY, PETE BROWN and ROB WAKEMAN. Releasing the 'KENT' EP in summer '93 on their own 'Waldorf' label, the band aroused immediate interest from the indie press with their raw-edged alternative pop/rock sound, artfully convoluted lyrics adding extra cred. After a further 12" single, 'DIMINISHED CLOTHES', SALAD were picked up by 'Island's new indie offshoot label, 'Island Red', subsequently making inroads into the indie charts with classy singles, 'ON A LEASH' and 'YOUR MA' before 'DRINK THE ELIXIR' made the lower regions of the Top 75 and the SHANGRI-LAS influenced 'MOTORBIKE TO HEAVEN' narrowly missed the Top 40. All were included on their long awaited debut album, 'DRINK ME', released amid much anticipation the following month. Its patented combination of ALL ABOUT EVE, The PRIMITIVES and BLONDIE was unusual in that

SALAD (cont)

the songwriting was divided almost equally between KENNEDY, VLUGT and WAKEMAN, a democratic approach which made for interesting, if not always satisfying listening. Although the record made the Top 20, SALAD couldn't keep up the momentum and a further single, 'GRANITE STATUE', failed to make the all important leap into the Top 40. After a solitary single in late '96, the band eventually released a follow-up, 'ICE CREAM', in summer '97, although by this point the press had newer fish to fry and SALAD, rather unfairly, appeared to be off the menu. • **Cover:** IT'S FOR YOU (Lennon-McCartney; hit for Cilla Black).

Album rating: DRINK ME (*8) / ICECREAM (*5) / SINGLES BAR compilation (*6)

MARIJNE VAN DER VLUGT – vocals, keyboards / **PAUL KENNEDY** – guitar, vocals / **PETE BROWN** – bass / **ROB WAKEMAN** – drums, samples

			Waldorf	not iss.
Jun 93.	(12"ep)	(WALD 001) **KENT EP**		-
	– Kent / The king of love / Heaven can wait / Mistress.			
Oct 93.	(12"/cd-s)	(WALD 002 T/CD) **DIMINISHED CLOTHES. / CLEAR MY NAME / COME BACK TOMORROW**		-

			Island Red	not iss.
Apr 94.	(7")	(IR 101) **ON A LEASH. / WHAT DO YOU SAY ABOUT THAT?**		-
	(12"+=/cd-s+=) (12IR/CIRD 101) – Planet in the ocean / Problematique.			
Jul 94.	(7")	(IR 103) **YOUR MA. / PLANK**		-
	(12"+=/cd-s+=) (12IR/CIRD 103) – Open.			
Feb 95.	(7"/c-s)	(IR/CIRS 104) **DRINK THE ELIXIR. / KISS MY LOVE**	66	-
	(12"+=/cd-s+=) (12IR/CIRD 104) – Julius / Diminished clothes (live).			
Apr 95.	(7"/c-s)	(IR/CIRS 106) **MOTORBIKE TO HEAVEN. / DIARY HELL**	42	-
	(cd-s+=) (CIRD 106) – I am December.			
May 95.	(cd/c/lp)	(CIRD/IRCT/IRLP 1002) **DRINK ME**	16	-
	– Motorbike to Heaven / Drink the elixir / Granite statue / Machine of menace / Overhear me / Shepherds' isle / Muscleman / Your ma / Warmth of the hearth / Gertrude Campbell / Nothing happens / No.1's cooking / A man with a box / Insomnia.			
Aug 95.	(7"/c-s)	(IR/CIRS 108) **GRANITE STATUE. / IT'S FOR YOU**	50	-
	(cd-s+=) (CIRD 108) – Ici les amigos.			
	(cd-s) (CIRDX 108) – ('A'side) / Rip goes love and lust / Roadsex.			

			Island	not iss.
Oct 96.	(7")	(IS 646) **I WANT YOU. / FLY IN A SHEET OF WINTER**	60	-
	(cd-s+=) (CID 646) – ('A'side) / Decade of the brain / Ugly fashion town.			
	(cd-s) (CIDX 646) – ('A'side) / One in the bag / A size more woman than her.			
May 97.	(7")	(IS 654) **CARDBOY KING. / MOTORBIKE TO HEAVEN (demo)**	65	-
	(cd-s) (CID 654) – ('A'side) / Bridesmaids' gimmicks / Down at Monty's.			
	(cd-s) (CIDX 654) – ('A'side) / One imitation smile / Moon above my shoulder.			
Jun 97.	(cd/c/lp) (CID/ICT/ILPS 8056) **ICECREAM**			
	– UV / Written by a man / Yeah yeah / Broken bird / Wanna be free / A size more woman than her / Cardboy king / Namedrops / Foreign cow / Terrible day / Wolves over Washington / The sky's our terminal.			
Aug 97.	(7")	(IS 660) **YEAH YEAH. / PALM TREE ON THE MOON**		-
	(cd-s+=) (CID 660) – Sleepwalking.			
	(cd-s) (CIDX 660) – ('A'side) / Lovesong / Party.			
—	SALAD have now split			

– compilations, etc. –

Jun 95. (cd) *Island Red;* (CIRM 1000) <23544> **SINGLES BAR**

SALAKO

Formed: Hull, England ... 1995 by JAMES WAUDBY, DAVID LANGDALE, LUKE BARWELL and THOMAS SPENCER. Taking their moniker from a Native American rain god, they joined the hallowed ranks of 'Jeepster' alongside critical faves, BELLE & SEBASTIAN, making a small but perfectly formed mark on the indie scene with summer '98's debut set, '"rE-inVentiNg; Punc.tU!at?iOn>:'. Annoyingly smart-arsed title aside, the album proved SALAKO to be psychedelic folksters for the 21st century, melding found-sound elements of GORKY'S ZYGOTIC MYNCI, SUPER FURRY ANIMALS and THE BETA BAND into one surprisingly melodic, lighter-than-air jamboree. Pick of the bunch was the single, 'GROWING UP THE NIGHT' or possibly 'THE MOONLIGHT RADIATES A PURPLE GLOW IN HIS WORLD', released in its own right later that year.

Album rating: "rE-inVentiNg; Punc.tU!at?iOn>: (*8) / MUSICALITY (*6)

JAMES WAUDBY – vocals / **DAVID LANGDALE** – guitar / **LUKE BARWELL** – bass / **THOMAS SPENCER** – percussion

			Jeepster	Imprint
Aug 98.	(7")	(JPR7 006) <112024> **GROWING UP IN THE NIGHT. / MY INTERNAL VISITOR**		Nov98
	(cd-s+=) (JPRCDS 006) – My booroo clow.			
Aug 98.	(cd/lp) (JPR CD/LP 002) <112032> **"rE-inVentiNg; Punc.tU!at?iOn>:**		
	– Each one unique / Words are not useful / Island life / Glass-bottom boat rides / For inspiration only / Colours merge and fly / Second age / Story of Bill / The moonlight radiates a purple glow in his world / In swoosh we trust / Sun and moon conspire / Go on then! enlighten me, why doncha? / Sunburst / Six part lullaby / Don't be afraid / When will be alone? / Porpoise sunlamp / In the morning / Growing up the night / Could things be the same.			
Nov 98.	(7")	(JPR7 008) **THE MOONLIGHT RADIATES A PURPLE GLOW IN HIS WORLD. / GO ON THEN! ENLIGHTEN ME, WHY DONCHA?**		-
	(cd-s+=) (JPRCDS 008) – Easy to love you.			
—	quartet augmented by MARISSA CLAUGHAN, MARTIN JONES + JOHN TAYLER			
Jul 99.	(7")	(JPR7 012) **THE BIRD AND THE BAG. /**		-
Jul 99.	(cd/lp)	(JRP CD/LP 008) **MUSICALITY**		-
	– The bird and the bag / Green is the colour of evil / Come! follow me / Truth in me / The cloning of Fudadeg Ulag / Arts and crafts / Devil's feet lullaby / Look left / Look right / Maybe we will find the divine cult / Do it yourself / Waiting and thinking / Bedtime astronomy / Finger exercise #1 / The cult of winter / I'll be there (when you're down) / Magicality.			
Dec 99.	(cd-ep)	(JPRCDS 014) **MAPPLETON SANDS EP**		-
May 00.	(cd-ep)	(JPRCDS 016) **VENTIMIGLIA 120899 EP**		-
	– Hull City tiger / 98.7 / The Queen's got a price on my life / I mamalian / Tales from the riverbed.			

			Elefant	not iss.
Aug 02.	(7"ep)	(ER 221) **LAND AND FREEDOM EP**		-
	– Look right / Six bridges / Morning after midnight / Sky at night.			
—	LUKE is no longer with the group			

SALARYMAN (see under ⇒ POSTER CHILDREN)

SALOON

Formed: Reading, England ... early '98 by multi-talented ADAM CRESWELL and MICHAEL SMOUGHTON, who almost immediately found singer AMANDA GOMEZ, ALISON COTTON and MATT ASHTON. SALOON quickly developed a unique futuristic pop sound, fusing electronics and samples, guitar feedback, and organic instrumentation. With their self-released four-track demo, 'LISA MILLENNIUM / CONQUISTADOR', and 7", 'FUTURISMO' (a split with LAZER GUIDED), SALOON began to acquire a following, and found a champion in DJ John Peel. Their progression continued with further single releases, numerous UK gigs, a 2001 Peel session, and culminated with the recording and release of debut album, '(THIS IS) WHAT WE CALL PROGRESS', in April 2002. With production from ANDREW PRINZ (a member of US labelmates, MAHOGANY), and multi-layered atmospherics, moogs, trumpets, glockenspiel and stylophone, SALOON have crafted an accomplished and mellifluous debut.

Album rating: (THIS IS) WHAT WE CALL PROGRESS (*6)

AMANDA GOMEZ – vocals / **ADAM CRESWELL** – bass, synthesizer, sampling / **ALISON COTTON** – viola / **MATT ASHTON** – guitar / **MICHAEL SMOUGHTON** – drums

			Belmondo	not iss.
Nov 98.	(7")	(none) **LISA MILLENNIUM. / CONQUISTADOR**		-

			Artists Against Success	not iss.
1999.	(7")	(AAS 023) **FUTURISMO. / (other by LAZER GUIDED)**		-

			Bearos	not iss.
Jul 00.	(7")	(BEAROS 013) **ELECTRON. / SUENO ESCOLAR**		-

			Amberley	not iss.
Aug 00.	(7")	(AMY 013) **SHOPPING. / SONG FOR HUGO**		-
Sep 00.	(7"m)	(AMY 016) **RESONANCES – SUIVEZ LA PISTE (Gag remix). / (others by MAHOGANY + CURTIS NEWTON)**		-

			Glamourpuss	not iss.
May 01.	(7")	(CAT 001) **IMPACT. / Sonic Catering Band: BODY POP**		-

			Track & Field	Darla
Sep 01.	(7")	(LANE 07) **FREEFALL. / MOVIMIENTO**		
Feb 02.	(7")	(LANE 11) **HAVE YOU SEEN THE LIGHT. / (other by DRESSY BESSY)**		
Apr 02.	(cd/lp)	(HEAT 04) <DRL 124 CD/LP> **(THIS IS) WHAT WE CALL PROGRESS**		
	– Plastic surgery / Bicycle thieves / Le weekend / Make it soft / Static / Girls are the new boys / 2500 Weldon Avenue / Across the great divide / My everyday silver is plastic / Victor Safronov.			
Oct 02.	(7"m)	(LANE 16) **GIRLS ARE THE NEW BOYS (version). / SOLITUDE / I AM THE CHEESE**		-

SAMMY

Formed: New York, USA ... 1993 by songwriters, LUKE WOOD and JESSE HARTMAN. Having worked in the NY offices of Geffen, WOOD was well placed to secure a US release (on STEVE SHELLEY's Geffen-backed subsidiary, 'Smells Like Records') for the pair's inuagural debut set, er 'DEBUT ALBUM' (1994), issued a year later in Britain on 'Fire' records. Moving upstairs to 'Geffen' and taking on new drummer, ALEXIS FLEISIG (to replace original TONY MAXWELL, who apparently went by the zany nickname of CORN), WOOD and HARTMAN concocted follow-up album, 'TALES OF GREAT NECK GLORY', the angular grooves and incoherent but skybound pop refrains contained within once again seeing SAMMY charged as PAVEMENT clones.

Album rating: DEBUT ALBUM (*4) / TALES OF GREAT NECK GLORY (*5)

JESSE HARTMAN – vocals, guitar / **LUKE WOOD** – guitar, bass / with also **TONY 'CORN' MAXWELL** – drums

			Fire	Smells Like
Nov 93.	(7")	<slr 004> **BABE COME DOWN. / ROACH GIRL**	-	
Jul 94.	(cd/lp) (FIRE CD/LP 40) <slr 005> **DEBUT ALBUM**		
	– Rudy / Hi-fi killers / Dim some / Shoot it around! / The turtle / Babe come down / Fantastic Sam / Rico & Carl / Evergladed / Royal flush / TZ queen / Room No.8 (DM 2).			
Sep 94.	(7"ep/cd-ep)	(BLAZE 72/+CD) **HI-FI KILLERS**		-
	– Hi-fi killers / Roach girl / Death motel / T'hell with me.			
Mar 95.	(7"ep/cd-ep)	(BLAZE 80/+CD) <slr 013> **KINGS OF THE INLAND EMPIRE**		Aug95
	– Inland empire / Majik man / Teen hour / Cracked up.			
Aug 95.	(7")	(BLAZE 83) **MAJIK MAN. / TRICK MAMMOTH**		-
	(cd-s+=) (BLAZE 83CD) – Kohut (little darlings) / East Coast blow-up.			

SAMMY (cont)

— **ALEXIS FLEISIG** – drums; repl. MAXWELL

	Fire	Geffen
May 96. (7") *(BLAZE 105)* **NEPTUNE AVENUE. / SLIM STYLE**		-
(cd-s+=) *(BLAZE 105CD)* – Lirr.		
Jun 96. (cd/lp) *(FIRE CD/LP 58)* <24962> **TALES OF GREAT NECK GLORY**		

– Possibly Peking / Encyclopedi-ite / Slim style / Neptune Ave. (ortho hi rise) / Buckle-up sunshine / Blue oyster bay / Chilling excerpts / Red lights flashing / Anything / Horse or ballet? / Kings pt. vs. steamboat.

Aug 96. (7") *(BLAZE 108)* **ENCYCLOPEDI-ITE. / PENCIL NECK**
(cd-s+=) *(BLAZE 108CD)* – Cafeteria hawker / Red lights flashing.

— SAMMY looked to have given up after above

Hope SANDOVAL & THE WARM INVENTIONS (see under ⇒ MAZZY STAR)

SANDY DIRT (see under ⇒ SOME VELVET SIDEWALK)

SARGE

Formed: Champaign, Illinois, USA ... December 1995 by singer/guitarist ELIZABETH ELMORE and bassist RACHEL SWITZKY; they later added drummer RUSS HORVATH. SARGE made their live debut in January 1996, and subsequent gigs ensured them an ardent local following. After signing with 'Mud', they released the punk-pop single, 'DEAR JOSIE, LOVE ROBYN', which reappeared some months later on a split-disc with SUPPORTING ACTRESS for 'Grand Theft Autumn'. The single was also one of the highlights of their debut LP, 'CHARCOAL', released in October '96. ELMORE's lively vocals and SMUDGE's buoyant drive divert from the often dark, troubled lyrics. Soon after recording 'CHARCOAL', HORVATH left and was replaced by CHAD ROMANSKI whose first SARGE duty was recording single, 'STALL', released in 1997. A year later, second album 'THE GLASS INTACT' proved to be SARGE's breakthrough record, and was met with widespread critical acclaim. Intelligent, impassioned and honest, ELMORE's faultless songwriting and vocals set the standard for '90s girl-punk. PAT CRAMER appeared on the album as second guitarist, but left shortly afterwards, being replaced by SUE ROTH. After more line-up changes, RACHEL SWITZKY left, with DEREK NIEDRINGHAUS replacing her, although ELMORE finally disbanded SARGE in December 1999 (with her law school finals looming). 2000's 'DISTANT' was a posthumous compilation of SARGE demos, covers, live recordings and a few ELMORE solo tracks. • **Covered:** TIME AFTER TIME (Cyndi Lauper) / THESE BOOTS ARE MADE FOR WALKIN' (Lee Hazlewood).

Album rating: CHARCOAL (*6) / THE GLASS INTACT (*7) / DISTANT collection (*5)

ELIZABETH ELMORE – vocals, guitar / **RACHEL SWITSKY** – bass / **RUSS HORVATH** – drums

	Mud	Mud
Mar 96. (7") <MUD 018> **DEAR JOSIE, LOVE ROBYN. / THE LAST BOY**		-
May 96. (7") <002> split w/ SUPPORTING ACTRESS (above issued on 'Grand Theft Autumn')	-	
Nov 96. (cd) <(MUDCD 019)> **CHARCOAL**		Oct96

– Smoke / Backlash / Dear Josie, love Robyn / Chicago / Crush / Bedroom / I don't / Another dear uncaught / The last boy.

— **CHAD ROMANSKI** – drums; repl. HORVATH

May 97. (7") <MUD 023> **STALL. / TIME AFTER TIME** — | —

— added **PATRICE CRAMER** – guitar

Mar 98. (cd) <(MUDCD 028)> **THE GLASS INTACT**
– Stall / A torch / Beguiling / Charms and Fegins / Homewrecker / Half as far / I took you driving / Fast girls / The first morning / Put in the reel / To keep you trained.

— **SUE ROTH** – guitar; repl. CRAMER

— **DEREK NIEDRINGHAUS** – bass (ex-CASTOR) repl. SWITSKY

Jul 00. (cd) <(MUDCD 043)> **DISTANT** (demos, live, etc.) | Apr00
– Detroit star-lite / The end of July / Clearer / Stall (live) / Fast girls (live) / Half as far (live) / Dear Josie, love Robyn (live) / Homewrecker (live) / The first morning (live) / These boots are made for walkin' / Last Christmas / Time after time / Distant / All my pland changed ...

— SARGE had already split the previous year

SATURDAY LOOKS GOOD TO ME (see under ⇒ THOMAS, Fred)

SATURDAY PEOPLE (see under ⇒ VELOCITY GIRL)

SATURN V (see under ⇒ RAZORCUTS)

SATURNINE

Formed: Williamsburg, Brooklyn, New York, USA ... 1992/93. Originally billed as SATURNINE 60, the band comprised JENNIFER BARON on guitar, MATT GALLAWAY on guitar and lead vocals, drummer JIM HARWOOD and bassist MIKE DONOFRIO. Having earned a record deal with the label 'Dirt', they released the singles 'ALMOST IMPOSSIBLE' and 'PLAYING BACKWARDS GAZE' in 1994. The following year saw the release of their debut EP 'AUTOGLIDER', which was seen as a promising effort although, perhaps, guilty of borrowing too obviously from sonic groove pioneers MY BLOODY VALENTINE. Later on that same year, with their moniker shortened to SATURNINE, the quartet released their debut album, the altogether more individual sounding 'WRECK AT PILLAR POINT' (1995). The will to experiment with sound and noise was still evident; however, the ambience of the album had much more in common with alternative country music heroes such as NEIL YOUNG, GRAM PARSONS and THE BYRDS. Their 1997 effort 'FLAGS FOR UNKNOWN TERRITORIES' was characterised by a more mainstream sound and was, consequently, overworked and disappointing. A change of record label coupled with a return to their preferred melancholic sound saw them return with the much improved 'MID THE GREEN FIELDS'. An album rich with atmosphere and well served by the inclusion of cello, piano, horns and flute. This creative rebirth was continued on the 1999 offering 'AMERICAN KESTREL' another, well crafted, confident collection of melodic, hopeful yet angst ridden, tunes. The next two years saw the departure of JENNIFER BARON – who went on to join LADYBUG TRANSISTOR – and another change of record label. SATURNINE managed to release 'PLEASURE OF RUINS' in 2001, but this was their weakest collection of songs to date and musically they had failed to progress. • **Covered:** PINK TURNS TO WASTE (Husker Du).

Album rating: WRECK AT PILLAR POINT (*7) / FLAGS FOR UNKNOWN TERRITORIES (*5) / MID THE GREEN FIELDS (*6) / AMERICAN KESTREL (*4) / PLEASURE OF RUINS (*4)

MATT GALLAWAY – vocals, guitar / **JENNIFER BARON** – guitar / **MIKE DONOFRIO** – bass / **JIM HARWOOD** – drums

	not iss.	own label
Mar 94. (7"; as SATURNINE 60) **ALMOST IMPOSSIBLE**	-	
	not iss.	Lounge
Jul 94. (7"; as SATURNINE 60) **PLAYING BACKWARDS GAZE. / RETREATING**	-	
	Dirt	Dirt
Nov 94. (cd-ep; as SATURNINE 60) **AUTOGLIDER EP**	-	

– Almost impossible / West / Nothing's matching / Wonder / Then again / Time of day / Half-truths / (untitled).

Aug 95. (7") **YOUR MAPS. / WEST (Live)** — | —
Oct 95. (cd) <DRT 019> **WRECK AT PILLAR POINT** — |
– This time, the best / Ground truth / Your maps / Summer was a waste / Mikes Co. / Broken / Slightly less than even / Reeling / Tell me lies later / Had enough / Mavericks / Give me reasons.

Feb 96. (7") **SUMMER WAS A WASTE. / PINK TURNS TO BLUE** — | —
Nov 96. (cd) <(DRT 031)> **FLAGS FOR UNKNOWN TERRITORIES**
– Elora / Ivan Boesky / The death of Hong Kong / Shine into the sky / Where are the crows? / Palomar / Traitors / Planes / The march of the Ides / Tailspin / Listing.

	not iss.	Victorialand
May 98. (cd) **MID THE GREEN FIELDS**	-	

– Buried ships / The raven / From the table to the place / Painting of life / The taste for water / St. Petersburg / There's a long long trail / The wooden room / Mid the green fields / The rain of ghosts / The clear / The field of the cloth of gold.

	Motorcoat	Motorcoat
Feb 00. (cd) <(MC 15)> **AMERICAN KESTREL**		Nov99

– Peace and rest / Trees / The wind is blowing like an outlaw / Old flowers / This world is made of fire / The future according to palm reading / Hollidaysburg / Tallis' canon / Neither lost nor stayed / One in a hundred / Miles was.

— **JOE PISANI** – keyboards; repl. BARON

Nov 01. (cd) <(MC 86)> **PLEASURE OF RUINS** | Oct01
– When we were anchors for the sun / Entertainment / The mad river / Picking up the pieces of the world / The history of Cleveland / JUicy whip / Apples / Mike's Co. #2 / Make way for a new parade / Theme song for a temporary worker / When I am a boatman.

SAVES THE DAY

Formed: New Jersey, USA ... 1997 by CHRIS CONLEY, DAVID SOLOWAY, TED ALEXANDER, EBEN D'AMICO and BRYAN NEWMAN (drums). They soon recruited producer Steve Evetts (who had worked with SEPULTURA) for debut album 'CAN'T SLOW DOWN', released in 1998. SAVES THE DAY's fresh and winsome punk-pop chronicles teenage highs and lows, although the set's lyrical naivety reflects its overall short-comings. Despite CONLEY's best efforts, it failed to ignite. 1999's 'THROUGH BEING COOL' proved a real turning point though, with SAVES THE DAY garnering critical acclaim, and a widening fan base. CONLEY's earnest lyrics and delivery were more refined, while the band had clearly upped the tempo and tightened things up – evident on album highlight 'THE LAST LIE I TOLD'. Now on the 'Vagrant' label, and with ROB SCHNAPF mixing, 'STAY WHAT YOU ARE' (2001), confirmed SAVES THE DAY's musical progress and increasing maturity. Tracks such as 'NIGHTINGALE' and 'JUKEBOX BREAKDOWN' contained a darkness and sorrow previously unexplored in their work.

Album rating: CAN'T SLOW DOWN (*4) / THROUGH BEING COOL (*6) / STAY WHAT YOU ARE (*7)

CHRIS CONLEY – vocals / **TED ALEXANDER** – guitar / **DAVID SOLOWAY** – guitar / **EBEN D'AMICO** – bass / **BRYAN NEWMAN** – drums

	not iss.	Immigrant Sun
1998. (cd-ep) <10> **I'M SORRY I'M LEAVING**	-	

– I'm sorry I'm leaving / Hold / Jessie and my whetstone / Take our cars now! / I melt with you.

SAVES THE DAY (cont)

		Equal Vision	Equal Vision
Sep 98.	(lp/cd) <(EVR 042CD)> **CAN'T SLOW DOWN**		Aug98

– Deciding / The choke / Handsome boy / Blindfolded / Collision / Three miles down / Always ten feet tall / Shoulder to the wheel / Nebraska bricks / Seeing it this way / Hot time in Delaware / Houses and billboards / Obsolete / Sometimes, New Jersey / Jodie.

Oct 99. (lp/cd) <(EVR 054/+CD)> **THROUGH BEING COOL**
– All-star me / You vandal / Rocks tonic juice magic / Holly, Hox forget me not / Third engine / My sweet fracture / The vast spoils of America / The last lie I told / Do you know what I love the most? / Through being cool / Banned from the black porch.

		Vagrant	Vagrant
Jul 01.	(cd) <(VR 356CD)> **STAY WHAT YOU ARE**		100

– At your funeral / See you / Cars & calories / Certain tragedy / Jukebox breakdown / Freakish / As your ghost takes flight / Nightingale / All I'm losing is me / This is not an exit / Firefly. *(re-iss. Mar02 on 'B-Unique'; BUN 017)*

		B-Unique	not iss.
May 02.	(7") (BUN 021-7) **AT YOUR FUNERAL. / UPS AND DOWNS**		-
	(cd-s+=) (BUN 021CDS) – At your funeral (video).		
Sep 02.	(7") (BUN 034-7) **FREAKISH. / CERTAIN TRAGEDY (live at the BBC)**		-
	(cd-s) (BUN 034-2) – ('A'side) / Firefly / ('A'-video).		

SCARCE (see under ⇒ ANASTASIA SCREAMED)

SCARFO

Formed: Andover, England ... 1994 by former art college students, JAIME HINCE, AL SAUNDERS and NICK PRIOR. Relocating to a squat in Deptford, London, the trio gigged around the capitol and released a one-off single for 'Fierce Panda', 'SKINNY'. Snapped up by 'Deceptive' (home to ELASTICA and PLACEBO), the band fused JAM-esque power-chords with US noise influences on late '95's eponymous debut mini-set. While a further two singles raised their profile, things were subsequently put on hold when AL was hit square-on by a car when leaving a pub. This near-fatal accident (which left AL in hospital limbo for a number of months) only served to fan the flames of their fiercely passionate attitude to music, as witnessed on their belated full-length album, 'LUXURY PLANE CRASH' (1997). That year also saw a couple of minor hit singles, 'ALKALINE' and 'COSMONAUT No.7', although by the release of 'A YEAR FROM MONDAY', the 12-month delay had put paid to the momentum. • **Covered:** READ ABOUT SEYMOUR (Swell Maps).

Album rating: SCARFO mini (*6) / LUXURY PLANE CRASH (*7)

JAIME HINCE – vocals, guitar / **NICK PRIOR** – bass / **AL SAUNDERS** – drums

		Fierce Panda	not iss.
May 95.	(7") (NING 08) **SKINNY. / LIFELINE**		-
		Deceptive	Broken Rekids
Nov 95.	(m-cd/m-lp) (BLUFF 017 CD/LP) <48> **SCARFO**		Oct96
	– Eyesore / Coin op / Skinny / Backwater / Car chase / Throw it all / Wailing words. <US+=> – Shuffling souls / Bingo England / Read about Seymour.		
Dec 95.	(7"etched) (BLUFF 022) **TUNNEL OF LOVE**		-
Apr 96.	(7"m) (BLUFF 028) **BINGO ENGLAND. / SHUFFLING SOULS / READ ABOUT SEYMOUR**		-
	(cd-s+=) (BLUFF 028CD) – Car chase (part 2).		
May 97.	(7") (BLUFF 041) **ELO. / FUJI**		-
	(cd-s+=) (BLUFF 041CD) – Porno.		
Jul 97.	(7") (BLUFF 044) **ALKALINE. / BRAZIL**	61	-
	(7") (BLUFF 044X) – ('A'side) / El Topo / Montserrat.		
	(cd-s++=) (BLUFF 044CD) – (all 4 tracks).		
Jul 97.	(cd/lp) (BLUFF 045 CD/LP) **LUXURY PLANE CRASH**		-
	– Elo / Jet samshed flat / Safecracker / Don't let go / Japanese cameras / Jazz cigarette / Cosmonaut No.7 / Pajo gear / Chomsky airport / U-feline / Prison architect.		
Oct 97.	(7") (BLUFF 053) **COSMONAUT No.7. / ALCATRAZ**	67	-
	(7"m) (BLUFF 053X) – ('A'side) / Assistant assassin / I want you.		
	(cd-s++=) (BLUFF 053CD) – (all 4 tracks above).		
Sep 98.	(7") (BLUFF 064) **A YEAR FROM MONDAY. / NOTHING DOING / SPECIAL COMMUNIQUES**		-
	(cd-s) (BLUFF 064CD) – ('A'side) / Off and on / Nothing doing.		

– after their split, JAIME met up with DISCOUNT's ALISON MOSSHART; they were to form The KILLS

SCENIC (see under ⇒ SAVAGE REPUBLIC; in 80's section)

SCHEER

Formed: Magherafelt, County Derry, N.Ireland ... 1990 by AUDREY GALLAGHER, NEIL CALDERWOOD, PADDY LEYDEN, PETER FLEMING and JOHN BATES. Following a self-financed debut single, 'DEMON', the band were picked up by U2's 'Mother' label as part of a development deal, resulting in the 'PSYCHOBABBLE' EP. Veteran indie label, '4 a.d.' were sufficiently impressed with the band's abrasive sound – memorably described as a cross between BJORK and the PIXIES – and hard gigging ways to offer them a fully fledged deal. The result was 1995's acclaimed 'SCHISM' EP, a record that saw SCHEER draw interest from both the indie and metal press, a testament to their crossover sound. Indeed, the long awaited debut album, 'INFLICTION' (1996) proved to be even heavier than their earlier material, carefully straddling the line between melody, noise and monster guitar licks.

Album rating: INFLICTION (*6) / ...AND FINALLY (*5)

AUDREY GALLAGHER – vocals / **NEAL CALDERWOOD** – guitar / **PADDY LEYDEN** – guitar / **PETER FLEMING** – bass / **JOHN BATES** – drums

		Son	not iss.
1993.	(cd-ep) (BUASC 293CD) **WISH YOU WERE DEAD**	-	- Irish
1994.	(cd-ep) (BUASC 294CD) **PSYCHOBABBLE**	-	- Irish
		Schism	not iss.
1995.	(7"promo) (SCHEER 1) **DEMON (demo). / HOWLING BOY (demo)**	-	- Irish
1995.	(cd-s) (SCHEER 4) **FIRST CONTACT / SEX KITTEN**	-	- Irish
		4 a.d.	Warners
Oct 95.	(12"ep/cd-ep) (BAD 5012/+CD) **SCHISM EP**		
	– Sometimes / You said / Babysize / Take you anywhere.		
Feb 96.	(7") (AD 6003) **SHEA. / YOU SAID (acoustic)**		-
	(cd-s) (BAD 6003CD) – ('A'side) / My world (live studio) / Demon (acoustic) / Nemesis (demo).		
Apr 96.	(7") (AD 6005) **WISH YOU WERE DEAD. / HANGING ON THE TELEPHONE**		-
	(cd-s+=) (BAD 6005CD) – Sad loved girl (acoustic) / Cannon (instrumental).		
May 96.	(cd)(lp/c) (CAD 6006CD)(CAD/+C 6006) <46108> **INFLICTION**		
	– Shea / Howling boy / Wish you were dead / In your hand / Demon / Babysize / Sad loved girl / Driven / Screaming / Goodbye. *(cd re-iss. Jul98; GAD 6006CD)*		
Feb 97.	(cd-s) (BAD 7006CD) **DEMON / OBSESSION / (GREEN ROOM) SEX KITTEN**		-

– disbanded after above

– compilations, etc. –

Dec 99.	(cd) Schism; (SCH 008) **...AND FINALLY**	-	- Irish

– Deadly serious / First contact / Face the sun / 6 a.m. / The one forgot / Say what you came to say / The healer / Idle time / Merey / Slowly / Suffocate / Where were you when the house burnt down / Secrets and lies / Say the word.

Fred SCHNEIDER (see under ⇒ B-52's; 70's section)

SCISSOR GIRLS

Formed: Chicago, Illinois, USA ... summer 1991 by AZITA YOUSSEFI, HEATHER MELOWIC and SUE ANNE ZOLLINGER. Although their respective roots lay in Washington D.C., Chicago's art school was where YOUSSEFI and MELOWIC first hooked up with ZOLLINGER. It was also where they met KELLY KUVO, who stepped in after ZOLLINGER's subsequent departure. A debut 7", 'PHY, DIABLO!' and an appearance on a various artists EP (alongside the likes of SLANT 6 and BASTRO) preceded a debut album, 'THE SCISSOR GIRLS TO: THE IMAGINARY LAYER ON SKELETONS' (1994), partly released by GOD IS MY CO-PILOT's label 'Quinnah'. Quite apart from its great title, sophomore set, 'WE PEOPLE SPACE WITH PHANTOMS' (recorded in 1994 but not released until 1996, on 'Atavistic') pushed the envelope a little further with regards to their ruptured proto-punk experiments, squaring bristling, angular guitar work and rhythmic non sequiturs with a wonderfully contrary aural allure. While ZOLLINGER departed soon after the record's recording, the aforementioned KUVO was only persuaded to come in when her immediate replacement, JAMES YOO, proved unsuitable. Initially stepping in for a tour, she joined up full-time and played on the 1996 10" single, 'SO YOU CAN START TO SEE WHAT S-T-A-T-I-C-L-A-N-D'. While a deal was signed with 'Atavistic', the group's subsequent break-up (late '96) meant that the label had to fall back on a singles compilation, 'HERE IS THE IS-NOT' (1997). MELOWIC went on to play with Chicago scenesters LAKE OF DRACULA while KUVO formed the short-lived SWEET THUNDER.

Album rating: WE PEOPLE SPACE THE PHANTOMS (*5) / HERE IS THE "IS-NOT" (*6)

AZITA YOUSSEFI – vocals, bass / **HEATHER MELOWIC** – drums / **SUE ANNE ZOLLINGER** – guitar

		not iss.	Monkeytech
1993.	(7") **PHY, DIABLO! /**	-	-

– featured on a V/A comp, 'Time Expired' alongside SLANT 6, RASTRO and DRINKING WOMAN

		not iss.	Quinnah
1994.	(10"lp) **THE SCISSOR GIRLS TO: THE IMAGINARY LAYER ON SKELETONS**	-	
	<cd-iss. 1995 on 'The Making Of Americans'; >		
		not iss.	own label
1994.	(7") **NEW TACTICAL OUTLINE SEC.1**	-	
1994.	(7") **NEW TACTICAL OUTLINE SEC.2**	-	

– (early '95) KELLY KUVO – drums (of DOT DOT DOT) repl. JAMES YOO who repl. ZOLLINGER

		not iss.	Load
Jun 96.	(10") <LOAD 007> **SO YOU CAN START TO SEE WHAT S-T-A-T-I-C-L-A-N-D**	-	

– the girls disbanded in October 1996; MELOWIC joined LAKE OF DRACULA while KUVO formed SWEET THUNDER

– compilations, etc. –

Feb 97.	(lp/cd) Atavistic; <(ALP 63/+CD)> **WE PEOPLE SPACE WITH PHANTOMS** (recorded 1994)		Apr96

– The sequential / A dedication to cronies and goats / In two acts / Vamps, here! / Dismemberment murder / Skeletal – Binary / World of unreal time / Forecast total brain shut-down / S. Mongers / Anti-fut nos.1,2 / (untitled).

SCORPIO RISING

Formed: Birkenhead, Liverpool, England ... 1989 by Manchester lads, MICKEY BANKS (frontman & lyricist), MARTIN ATHERTON, SPLOOTE, STEVE SOAR and COLIN OWENS. Taking their moniker from a 60's Kenneth Anger movie, the band set about combining the guitar assault of the Fraggle scene with the backbeat groove of the Baggy brigade. Unsurprisingly, the term 'Bagel' (another failed pigeon-hole attempt by the media) didn't really stick and in reality, the SCORPIO's were, if anything, more JAMES-ish. Initially produced by John A. Rivers, they toured supporting the NEDS, while releases came in the shape of two 1991 EP's for 'Chapter 22', 'STRANGEST TIMES' and 'THE WATERMELON'. A couple more singles, a mini-set, 'IF...' and a predictable press hype was enough to persuade 'Sire' that SCORPIO RISING were a commercialy viable proposition. However, the resulting 'PIG SYMPHONY' (1993) album failed to bring home the proverbial bacon, the SCORPIO's brief rise to fame cut short.

Album rating: IF... mini (*4) / ZODIAC KILLERS mini compilation (*4) / PIG SYMPHONY (*5)

MICKEY BANKS – vocals / **MARTIN ATHERTON** – guitar / **SPLOOTE** – guitar / **STEVE SOAR** – bass / **COLIN OWENS** – drums

Chapter 22 / Sire

May 91. (12"ep) *(12CHAP 56)* **STRANGEST TIMES EP**
– Strangest times / Turn you on / Bliss.
Sep 91. (12"ep/cd-ep) *(12/CD CHAP 59)* **THE WATERMELON EP**
– Watermelon / Malicious / Beautiful people.
Jan 92. (m-cd/m-c/m-lp) *(CHAP CD/MC/MLP 62)* **IF...**
– Freedom No.5 / Bliss / Rage on / Freedom thirteen / Honeykill / Disturbance (tidal version) / Watermelon.
Jul 92. (12"ep/cd-ep) *(12/CD CHAP 68)* **SATURNALIA. / DISTURBANCE / PEACE FROG**
(10"ep+=) *(10CHAP 68)* – Watermelon (Mark Goodier session).
Aug 92. (m-cd/m-c) *<2-/4-45115>* **ZODIAC KILLERS** (compilation)
– Saturnalia / Bliss / Freedom thirteen / Burn out / Watermelon / Beautiful people / Rage on / Disturbance.
Jan 93. (10"etched) *(10CHAP 71)* **SILVER SURFING / FOUNTAIN OF YOU**
(12"+=/cd-s+=) *(12CHAP/CHAPCD 71)* – Zero.

Sire / Sire

Jun 93. (cd/c) *(<9362 42570-2/-4>)* **PIG SYMPHONY**
– Talking backwards / Breathing underwater / Beautiful people / Watermelon / Oceanside / Silver surfing / Evelyn / Little pieces / Goofball / Sleeping sickness.
Aug 93. (7"/c-s) *(W 0197/+C)* **EVELYN. / IT'S OBVIOUS**
(cd-s+=) *(W 0197CD)* – Find your own way / Brutal deluxe.

— split after the commercial failure of above

SCOTT 4

Formed: South Newington, London, England ... 1996 by namesake, SCOTT BLIXEN, who, alongside JOHN MOODY and ED TILLEY (which makes 3 oddly enough!), blended a type of Stetson-rock; country, blues, hip-hop and lo-fi new wave. Inspired by The BYRDS' 'Sweetheart Of The Rodeo' and realising SPARKLEHORSE and BECK were selling loads of records, SCOTT 4 (named after a SCOTT WALKER album), delivered their 'Satellite' records debut, 'ELEKTRO AKOUSTIC AND VOLKMECHANIK', a 10" mini-album in 1997. Early the following year, the band received universal plaudits for their 'RECORDED IN STATE' album; country-rock was alive and kicking in London! Their sophomore set, 'WORKS PROJECT', followed singles 'JEANS RECORD' and 'CATASTROPHE' in 1999, marking a turn in direction for the folk'n'hop combo. Strings, steel guitars and samplers were added to the mix, making for a more rounded and accomplished record – in other words, SCOTT 4 had considerably developed and matured as a group. If more evidence was needed, it could be found on the blistering 10-minute EP split with MAGIC CAR, 'EUROPEAN PUNKS' (2002), a heady mix between prog and post rock, the set sounded like two bands drunk on their own insanity.

Album rating: RECORDED IN STATE (*7) / WORKS PROJECT (*6) / EUROPEAN PUNKS with Magic Car (*6)

SCOTT BLIXEN – vocals / **JOHN MOODY** – guitar / **ED TILLEY** – drums

Satellite / Imprint

Jun 97. (10"m-lp; with free 7") *(STL 004)* **ELEKTRO AKOUSTIC UND VOLKMECHANIK**
– East winter / Work / Afternoons / You set the scene / Broken stones / I've been tamed / Lucky strike / On off. *(re-iss. Jul98 lp/cd; STL 004/+CD)*
Dec 97. (7"ep/cd-ep) *(STL 008/+CD)* **DEUTSCHE LP RECORDS / STRING 'A'. / WITH DRINKING / ROBERT HARRY**
Feb 98. (lp/cd) *(STL 009/+CD) <112765>* **RECORDED IN STATE** Aug98
– Start-up / Deutsche LP records / East winter / Aspirins / Your kingdom to dust / Plane / Cheese fours / Miss Goddess nr.2 / Zilch / Choke bore / Philly's song.

V2 / not iss.

Jun 98. (12"/cd-s) *(VVR 500181-6/-3)* **YOUR KINGDOM TO DUST. / YOU SET THE SCENE**
May 99. (7"m/cd-s) *(VVR 500751-7/-3)* **CATASTROPHE. / AVIS RAILHOME / FAMISHED**
(cd-s) *(VVR 500751-8)* – Catastrophe (lp mix) / Wolfpack / I've been tamed.
Jun 99. (cd/d-lp) *(VVR 100801-2/-1)* **WORKS PROJECT**
– Catastrophe / Troubles 1-2-3 / Hallo doctor / Lefturno / Das junior / We're not robots / May last / Lilla B-boy lullaby / Scott 4 travel on electric trains / Applied for release / We scratched our names / Glass & steel / 7 days – I'll see ya / Konigskraft / Ancient & modern.
Sep 99. (cd-s) *(VVR 500914-3)* **LEFTURNO (new version) / LEFTURNO (Wiseguys remix) / SONY**

— in 2001, SCOTT & ED's dancd alter-ego MAN & WOMAN released 'SEX ON THE MINITEL'

SCOTT 4 & MAGIC CAR

Tiny Dog / not iss.

Jan 02. (cd) *(TDR 004)* **EUROPEAN PUNKS**
– European punks / Shiny cattle / For teens in the meantime / For teens in the springtime / Stillness / In the nursery at night and further on / In the time of pop & roll / Yellow main sequence / Valhalla.
May 02. (cd-s) *(TDR 005)* **MEANTIME / SHOOTING STAR / THE FIRST STEP**

SCREECHING WEASEL

Formed: Chicago, Illinois, USA ... mid-80's by 'Maximumrocknroll' columnist and RAMONES obsessed punk rocker BEN FOSTER (who soon adopted his WEASEL moniker). Although the line-up was to fluctuate wildly over the course of their career, the early 'WEASEL crew consisted – in addition to BEN himself – of JOHN JUGHEAD, STEVE CHEESE and VINNI BOVINE. An eponymous debut album arrived the following year on the 'Underdog' label, albeit in a limited pressing. More widely available was 'BOOGADABOOGADABOOGADA' (1989), by which point WARREN OZZFISH had joined up with BRIAN VERMIN following not long after (as replacements for BOVINE and CHEESE respectively). The pseudonymous japery continued unabated as OZZFISH was replaced by DANNY VAPID for a further string of EP's. With VAPID and VERMIN subsequently leaving to from SLUDGEWORTH, WEASEL temporarily split up the band only to later reform his shock punk-revival troops for a renewed assault on good taste: a line-up of WEASEL, JUGHEAD and VAPID were joined by new members DAVE NAKED and DAN PANIC for 'MY BRAIN HURTS' (1991). Further personnel changes ensued although a surprising surge in creativity saw the release of 'WIGGLE' (1992), 'RAMONES' (a cover of the entire classic debut by the infamous NY brudders) (1993), 'ANTHEM FOR A NEW TOMORROW' (1993) and 'HOW TO MAKE ENEMIES AND IRRITATE PEOPLE' (1994), the latter a farewell set recorded with the help of GREEN DAY's MIKE DIRNT. WEASEL then formed The RIVERDALES with VAPID and PANIC, a group which again took their influence from The RAMONES and were basically SCREECHING WEASEL in all but name. With JUGHEAD soon returning to the fold, the band reverted to the SCREECHING WEASEL moniker once more although this was to cause legal difficulties and eventually lead to yet another split. In the meantime, the 'BARK LIKE A DOG' album eventually found a sponsor in the shape of the 'Fat Wreck Chords' label. An umpteenth version of the 'WEASEL returned towards the turn of the decade with a further three albums, 'TELEVISION CITY DREAMS' (1998), 'EMO' (1999) and 'TEEN PUNKS IN HEAT' (2000). However, after the largely disappointing latter set, BEN WEASEL thought he would branch out on his solo career; 'FIDATEVI' in summer 2002 another inconsistent effort. • **Covered:** RAMONES numbers by the score plus I CAN SEE CLEARLY (Johnny Nash) / AIN'T GOT NO SENSE (Kerr-Lewis-Mahon-Stipanitz) / I THINK WE'RE ALONE NOW (Tommy James & The Shondells) / I FALL TO PIECES (Patsy Cline) / FUCK YOU (Subhumans) / SUSPECT DEVICE (Stiff Little Fingers) / DIRT (Stooges) / etc.

Album rating: SCREECHING WEASEL (*5) / BOOGADABOOGADABOOGADA! (*5) / MY BRAIN HURTS (*7) / WIGGLE (*6) / RAMONES (*5) / ANTHEMS FOR A NEW TOMORROW (*6) / HOW TO MAKE ENEMIES AND IRRITATE PEOPLE (*5) / KILL THE MUSICIANS compilation (*6) / BARK LIKE A DOG (*4) / TELEVISION CITY DREAMS (*4) / EMO (*5) / TEEN PUNKS IN HEAT (*3) / Ben Weasel: FIDATEVI (*4) / Riverdales: RIVERDALES (*3) / STORM THE STREETS (*5) / Sludgeworth: WHAT'S THIS (*4) / LOSERS OF THE YEAR (*5) / Ethyline: JITTERS (*5)

BEN WEASEL – vocals / **(JOHN) JUGHEAD** – guitar / **VINNIE BOVINE** – bass / **STEVE CHEESE** – drums

Shigaku / Underdog

1987. (lp) **SCREECHING WEASEL**
– Say no! to authority / Wanna die / Society / California sucks / Murder in the Brady house / I can't stand myself / My song / High ambitions / March of the lawnmowers / Leave me alone / Don't touch my car / 7-11 / Cows / Work. *(UK cd-iss. Jan98 on 'Vermiform'; VML 072) <(cd-iss. Feb99 on 'Liberation'+=; LIB 37813CD)>* – Wavin' gerbs / Liar / O.M.W. / Clean-cut ass-hole / Raining needles / B.P.D. / Experience the Ozzfish / Jockpunk / K-mart blues / Bates motel / Hardcore hippie / What is right / Yeah right / In the hospital / I feel like shit / I hate Led Zeppelin / American suicide / A political song for Screeching Weasel / Twinkie winkie / Stoned and stupid / Life sucks / I wanna be naked! / My right / Hey suburbia / Ashtray.

— **WARREN OZZFISH** – bass (ex-OZZFISH EXPERIENCE) repl. BOVINE

Wet Spots / Roadkill

Oct 88. (lp) *(WETLP 5) <001>* **BOOGADABOOGADABOOGADA!**
– Dingbat / Love / Zombie / This ain't Hawaii / We skate / Police insanity / Stupid over you / Runaway / I hate Led Zeppelin / My right / Nicaragua / Sunshine / I wanna be naked / Ashtray / American suicide / Psychiatrist / Mad at the paper boy / I love to hate / More problems / Supermarket fantasy / Holy hardcore / Professional distribution / Used cars / Hunter / I believe in UFO's / Hey suburbia. *<(re-iss./UK-iss.1993/Jan97 on 'Lookout!' lp/c/cd; LOOKOUT 62/+C/CD)>*

- **BRIAN VERMIN** – drums; repl. CHEESE
- **(SEWERCAP) DAN VAPID** (b. SCHAFER) – bass (ex-IGOR SKULLS, ex-GENERATION WASTE vocalist) repl. WARREN

		not iss.	Limited Potential

1989. (7"ep) <none> **PUNKHOUSE EP**
– Punkhouse / Fathead / Good morning / I need therapy / I think we're alone now / Something wrong. <re-iss. 1991 on 'No Budget'; > <re-iss. 1993 on 'Selfless'; 18>

- now without VERMIN
- split when VAPID joined SLUDGEWORTH
- **BEN** + **JUGHEAD** re-formed with **DAVE NAKED** (b. ROBINSON) who was subsequently repl. by **VAPID** (now on guitar, vocals) + **JOHN PERSONALITY** (b. SULLIVAN) – bass, vocals (who repl. GUB) / **DAN PANIC** (b. LUMLEY) – drums

not iss. / Shred Of Dignity

1991. (7"ep) **PERVO-DEVO**
– I wanna be a homosexual / She's giving me the creeps / I fall to pieces.

Lookout! / Lookout!

Nov 91. (lp/c/cd) <LOOKOUT 50/+C/CD> **MY BRAIN HURTS**
– Making you cry / Slogans / Guest list / Veronica hates me / I can see clearly / Cindy's on methadone / Science of myth / What we hate / Teenage freakshow / Kamala's too nice / Don't turn out the lights / Fathead / I wanna be with you tonight / My brain hurts. (UK-iss.Jan97; same as US)

Nov 92. (lp/c/cd) <LOOKOUT 63/+C/CD> **WIGGLE**
– Hanging around / I'm not in love / One step beyond / I was a high school psychopath / Crying in my beer / Slomotion / Like a parasite / Joanie loves Johnny / Second floor east / Automatic rejector / Jeannie's got a problem with her uterus / Sad little girl / Ain't got no sense / It's all in my head / Teenage slumber party / Danny is a wimp / Going home. (UK-iss.Jan97; same as US)

Selfless / Selfless

1992. (7"ep) <#9> **SNAPPY ANSWERS FOR STUPID QUESTIONS**
– My right / The science of myth / Jeannie's got a problem with her uterus / I was a high school psychopath / Danny is a wimp.

1992. (d7"ep; one pink) <#9.5> **HAPPY, HORNY, GAY AND SASSY (live)**
– (SNAPPY ANSWERS . . .) / My brain hurts / I wanna be a homosexual / Don't turn out the lights.

1993. (7"ep; split) **RADIO BLAST / THE GIRL NEXT DOOR**

- **JOE KING** – guitar, vocals; repl. JOHN P

Mar 93. (lp) <(SLFS 17)> **RAMONES** (covers)   Nov92
– Blitzkreig bop / Beat on the brat / Judy is a punk / I wanna be your boyfriend / Chainsaw / Now I wanna sniff some glue / I don't wanna go down to the basement / Loudmouth / Havana affair / Listen to my heart / 53rd & 3rd / Let's dance / I don't wanna walk around with you / Today your love, tomorrow the world. <(cd-iss. Nov98 as 'BEAT ON THE BRAT' on 'Lookout'+=; LK 213CD)> – (Nothing's gonna) Turn me off (of . . . .) / Pretty girls don't talk to me / I don't care anymore / Why'd you have to leave.

not iss. / V.M.L.

1993. (7"ep) **SCREECHING WEASELS / PINK LINCOLNS**
– Stab stab stab / Going home / (2 by PINK LINCOLNS).

- now without **JOE KING** (VAPID back to bass + BEN added guitar)

Lookout / Lookout

Aug 93. (7"ep) <LOOKOUT 73> **SCREECHING WEASEL / BORN AGAINST**
– El mozote / Funk this / (2 by BORN AGAINST).
(cd-ep+=) <LOOKOUT 73CD> – Chicago / (1 by BORN AGAINST).

Sep 93. (7"ep) <LOOKOUT 75> **YOU BROKE MY FUCKING HEART**
– The American dream / Mary was an anarchist / Around on you / Goodbye to you.

Oct 93. (lp/c/cd) <LOOKOUT 76/+C/CD> **ANTHEM FOR A NEW TOMORROW**
– I'm gonna strangle you / Falling apart / Leather jacket / Rubber room / Inside out / Peter Brady / I, robot / Every night / Totally / Three sides / I don't wanna be friends / Cancer in my body / Thrift store girl / Panic / Trance / Claire Monet / A new tomorrow. (UK cd-iss. Oct94 & Jan97; same as US)

- **MIKE DIRNT** – bass, vocals (of GREEN DAY) repl. VAPID

Mar 94. (7") <LOOKOUT 86> **SUZANNE IS GETTING MARRIED. / WAITING FOR SUSIE**

Sep 94. (lp/c/cd) <LOOKOUT 97/+C/CD> **HOW TO MAKE ENEMIES AND IRRITATE PEOPLE**
– Planet of the dupes / 86 / I love yer nuts on Monday / Johnny is that beer? / Slime pond / Burnt out squirrel / If I was Hugh / Nobody bites you / Da genitals / Smurf goddess / Kathy's not too light / Kathy's on the moon / I wrote ignatius J. Reilly. (UK cd-iss. Jun95 & Jan97; same as US)

- split early the following year

RIVERDALES

- were formed by **WEASEL (FOSTER), VAPID (SCHAFER) + PANIC (LUMLEY)**; latter also now a member of SQUIRTGUN and later COMMON RIDER

Sep 95. (cd/lp) <LOOKOUT/+LP 120)> **THE RIVERDALES**   Jul95
– Fun tonight / Judy go home / Wanna be alright / Back to you / Not over me / She's gonna break your heart / I think about you during the commercials / Rehabilitated / Plan 13 / Outta sight / In your dreams / Hampton beach.

Honest Don / Honest Don

Sep 97. (lp) <(HDN 00010)> **STORM THE STREETS**
– Make way / Mental retard / Don't let them beat my baby / Cementhead / Riverdale stomp / Dyna-mole / I will make it up to you / Blood on the ice / I don't wanna go to the party / Kick your head in / I accuse my parents / Boy in the plastic bubble / Give it up / I am not a freak.

SCREECHING WEASEL

- had re-formed inbetween above albums (trio + **JUGHEAD**)

Fat Wreck Chords / Fat Wreck Chords

Dec 96. (cd/c/lp) <FAT 547 CD/MC/LP)> **BARK LIKE A DOG**
– Get off my back / Cool kids / First day of summer / You'll be in my dreams today / You blister my paint / Stupid girl / Phasers on kill / Handcuffed to you / (She got) Electroshocked / It's not enough / I will always be there / You name is tattooed on my heart.

Vermiform / Vermiform

Jun 97. (7"ep) <(VMFM 31)> **FORMULA 27**
– (Nothing's gonna) Turn me off (of you) / Pretty girls don't talk to me / I don't care anymore / Why'd you have to leave.

Lookout! / Lookout!

Feb 98. (12"ep/cd-ep) <(LK 190/+CD)> **MAJOR LABEL DEBUT EP**   Jan98
– The last Janelle / D.I.Y. / Compact disc / Hey asshole / Racist society / Night breed.

Fat Wreck Chords / Fat Wreck Chords

Aug 98. (lp/cd) <(FAT 572/+CD)> **TELEVISION CITY DREAM**
– Count to three / Speed of mutation / Dummy up / Your morality / Dirty needles / Breaking point / Outside of you / We are the Generation X / Identity crisis / First day of winter / Plastic bag / I don't give a fuck / Only a test / Pervert at large / Burn it down.

Lookout! / Lookout!

May 99. (cd/lp) <(LK 227 CD/LP)> **EMO**
– Acknowledge / Sidewalk warrior / Static / Scene / Let go / Regroup / Passion / Linger / Last night / 2-7 split / On my own / Bark like a dog.

Dec 99. (7"pic-d-ep) **JESUS HATES YOU**
– Fuck you / Suspect device / Dirt.
(above issued on 'Probe' records)

Oct 00. (cd/lp) <(LK 257 CD/LP)> **TEEN PUNKS IN HEAT**   Sep00
– Bottom of the 9th / Gotta girlfriend / Too worked up / I'll stop the Rai / I love you / Molecule / 21 months / The first day of Autumn / Erection / I will always do / You're the enemy / I wanna fuck / Cat-like / Pauline / Things seem all fucked up today / Message in a beer bottle / You're sorry now / Don't want it / Six percent / The edge of the world.

– compilations, etc. –

Jun 95. (cd) Lookout!; <(LOOKOUT 95CD)> **KILL THE MUSICIANS**   Apr95
– Kamala's too nice / Punkhouse / Fathead / Good morning / I need therapy / I think we're alone now / Something wrong / This bud's for me / I wanna be a homosexual / She's giving me the creeps / I fall to pieces / Celena / Radio blast / Girl next door / Achtung / Judy is a punk / Chainsaw / Now I wanna sniff some glue / Havana affair / Soap opera / Stab stab stab / Six a.m. / Hey suburbia / American dream / Mary was an anarchist / Around on you / Goodbye to you / Veronica hates me / I can see clearly / Supermarket fantasy / Science of myth. <re-iss. Jan97; same)>

Feb 00. (d-cd) Lookout; <(LK 239CD)> **THANK YOU VERY LITTLE**
(demos, outtakes, etc)
– I hate old folks / Nothing matters / Crawl / Someday / I need therapy / Slogans / I wanna be a homosexual / Crying in my beer / Jeannie's got a problem with her uterus / Shirley's on methadone / Amy saw me looking at her boobs / 27 things I want to do to you / Every night (SONIC IGUANA version) / Totally / Nightbreed / Suzanne is getting married / Waiting for Susie / Lose the dink / Stuck out here / Suspect device / Fuck you / The prisoner / Can't take it / My own world / Tightrope / Dirt / You are my sunshine / Anchor // I love beer (live) / Around on you / Squeaky clean / Electroshock therapy / You're the enemy / (intro to live show 3.20.93) / Slogans / Cindy's on metadone / Teenage freakshow / Veronica hates me / I was a high school psychopath / I can see clearly / Joanie loves Johnny / Automatic rejector / Supermarket fantasy / Science of myth / I'm gonna strangle you / Hey suburbia / Totally / Inside out / Goodbye to you / Guest list / Eine kleine scheissenmusik.

BEN WEASEL

with **DAN VAPID** – guitar, bass, vocals / **MATT** – drums (of TEEN IDOLS)

Jul 02. (cd/lp) <(LK 282 CD/LP)> **FIDATEVI**
– Patience / The true heart of love / Fidatevi / Even pace / The ship / Strangers / Truth and beauty / Indecision / No expectations / Imperfect world / Responsibility / Take action / Water and waves / The rays of the sun.

SLUDGEWORTH

MATT BESSEMER – vocals / **ADAM WHITE** – guitar / **DAVE McLEAN** – guitar / **MIKE "STRAT" HOOTEN** – bass / **BRIAN "VERMIN" McQUAID** – drums

not iss. / Johann's Face

1992. (cd) <JFR 002> **WHAT'S THIS?**
– Never say never / Another day / Over and over / Two feet on the ground / Someday / Waste it away / What's this / Funk dungeon / Plunger / Tomato paste / Untitled backwards / Only one / Cry baby.

- **DAN SCHAFER** – vocals; repl. MATT

Lookout / Lookout

Nov 95. (cd) <(LOOKOUT 131CD)> **LOSERS OF THE YEAR**   Oct95
– Waste it away / Someday / Anytime / Only one / Another day / I analyze / Never say never / Follow / Over and over / She's no disposable / Cry baby / Nearest on to stand behind / Angry man / Two feet on the ground.

ETHYLINE

- **MATT, ADAM, MIKE, DAVE + BRIAN**

not iss. / Wild West

Nov 96. (cd/c) <7002> **JITTERS**
– Intro / Dry me out / D.U.I. / Black & blue / Wings / Crazy K's / Nicole / Free advice / Cum / Gawk / Quick fix / 10 foot pole / Five.

SCUD MOUNTAIN BOYS

Formed: Northampton, Massachusetts, USA ... 1991 originally as The SCUDS by JOE PERNICE, STEPHEN DESAULNIERS, BRUCE TULL and TOM SHEA. Eventually seeing the alt-country light after a few years banging out straight-down-the-line rock, the quartet recorded a debut cassette, 'PINE BOX', which was later given a limited CD release in the mid-90's on the miniscule 'Chunk' label. This was quickly followed up by 'DANCE THE NIGHT AWAY' (1995), their growing reputation enabling them to secure a deal with former grunge label, 'Sub Pop'. Graced with that peaceful, easy feeling, 1996's 'MASSACHUSETTS' was an unassuming but satisfying collection of acoustic, harmony-rich country-rock in the more traditional sense of the term. Despite glowing reviews and a wealth of material in the can, JOE would subsequently form The PERNICE BROTHERS, sibling BOB having already guested for the SCUD crew on the aforementioned swansong album.
• **Covered:** GYPSIES, TRAMPS AND THIEVES (hit; Cher) / PLEASE, MR. PLEASE (...Augustus) / WICHITA LINEMAN + WHERE'S THE PLAYGROUND SUSIE (Jim Webb) / HELEN (... Bonanno).

Album rating: PINE BOX (*6) / DANCE THE NIGHT AWAY (*6) / MASSACHUSETTS (*7) / THE ESSENTIAL ... collection (*7)

JOE PERNICE – vocals, guitar / **STEPHEN DESAULNIERS** – bass, vocals / **BRUCE TULL** – lap steel guitar, vocals / **TOM SHEA** – drums, mandolin

not iss.   Chunk

Nov 94. (7") <CH45 11> **TELEVISION. / Sittin' on the bottom of the world: STEVE WESTFIELD & THE SLOW BAND**
Jan 95. (c) **PINE BOX**
– Silo / Reservoir / Glacier bay / Peter Graves' anatomy / Freight of fire / Sweet Sally / Oklahoma! / Don't know how to tell her / Gypsies, tramps and thieves / There is no Hell (like the Hell on this Earth) / Wichita lineman / Please, Mr. please / Down in writing / Closing time.
Apr 95. (cd) <1007> **DANCE THE NIGHT AWAY**
– Freight of fire / One hand / Letter to Bread / Television / (She took his) Picture / Where's the playground, Susie? / Combine / Blood and bones / Silo / Sangre de Cristo / Kneeling / Fiery coffin / Helen.

Sub Pop   Sub Pop

Nov 95. (7") **KNIEVEL. / 1/2 WAY**
Jun 96. (lp/cd) <(SP/+CD 342)> **MASSACHUSETTS** Apr96
– In a ditch / Scratch ticket / Penthouse in the woods / Grudge **** / Big hole / Van drunk / Lift me up / Liquor store / A ride / Holy ghost / Cigarette sandwich / Massachusetts / Glass jaw / Knievel. *(cd re-iss. Jan02; same)*
— split when JOE formed The PERNICE BROTHERS

– compilations, etc. –

Apr 97. (d-cd) *Sub Pop*; <SP 389> **THE EARLY YEAR: PINE BOX & DANCE THE NIGHT AWAY**
Oct 01. (cd) *Discmedia*; (DEM 6120-2) **THE ESSENTIAL SCUD MOUNTAIN BOYS**
– Wichita lineman / Penthouse in the woods / In a ditch / Freight of fire / Kneivel / Cigarette sandwich / She took his picture / Scratch ticket / Scratch ticket / Grudge / Liquor store / Holy ghost / Sweet Sally / Silo / Combine / Lift me up / Helen / Please, Mr. Please / Where's the playground, Susie? / Massachusetts.

SEA AND CAKE

Formed: Chicago, Illinois, USA ... 1993 initially as a one-off part-time project by mainman, SAM PREKOP, along with ERIC CLARIDGE, the pair having frequently performed with the group, SHRIMP BOAT. For several years from '86 to '93, the aforementioned SHRIMP BOAT quartet (original line-up without CLARIDGE) were pioneers of Chicago's burgeoning post-rock scene, releasing proper LP's, 'SPECKLY' (1989), 'DUENDE' (1992) and the great 'CAVALE' (1993). PREKOP and CLARIDGE reunited as SEA AND CAKE, enlisting the help of guitarist ARCHER PREWITT and TORTOISE's head honcho, JOHN McENTIRE on drums to record their excellent eponymous debut in '94. Another deliciously different 'Thrill Jockey' release (licensed to 'Rough Trade' in the UK), the album floated along on a current of subtle pop-lite noodling, propelled by shifting Afro-Caribbean influenced backbeats. Further albums, 'NASSAU' (1995), 'THE BIZ' (1995) and 'THE FAWN' (1997), seamlessly enveloped the diverse strands of laid back neo-jazz, exotic rhythmic excursions, burbling electronica and post-rock experimentalism that underpins many of the projects connected with McENTIRE, PREKOP and the rest of the Chicago indie mafia. PREWITT proved himself a prolific artist in his own right with a clutch of solo albums running parallel to his SEA & CAKE duties. Beginning with 1997's highly praised 'IN THE SUN' and running through both 'WHITE SKY' (1999) and 'THREE' (2002), the loungemeister sculpted his own beguiling strand of left-field pop from his myriad of influences. PREKOP was also to subsequently surpass even his own previous high standards with a lauded solo debut, 'SAM PREKOP' (1999). Less reliant on the studio and more in tune with a purer pop aesthetic, the record utilised such local talent as CHICAGO UNDERGROUND DUO's CHAD TAYLOR and TOWN & COUNTRY's JOSH ABRAMS alongside his more regular sparring partners PREWITT and McINTIRE. The result was more tropical than experimental, revolving around jazzy, languorous, occasionally frisky rhythms with an overtly Brazilian flavour, PREKOP's low-key vocals trickling into the mix like condensation droplets on a cocktail glass. In fact, the record's balmy ambience carried over into the recording of 'OUI' (2000), The SEA & CAKE's long awaited fifth long player. A delicious marriage of organic and electronic, the record confirmed that while Chicago may be the windy city, its more talented musical inhabitants were set on recreating a completely different (musical) climate.

Album rating: Shrimp Boat: SPECKLY (*5) / DUENDE (*6) / CAVALE (*7) / The Sea And Cake: THE SEA AND CAKE (*8) / NASSAU (*7) / THE BIZ (*8) / THE FAWN (*7) / A BRIEF HISTORICAL RETROSPECTIVE compilation (*7) / OUI (*7) / Sam Prekop: SAM PREKOP (*6) / Archer Prewitt: IN THE SUN (*6) / WHITE SKY (*7) / GERROA SONGS mini (*5) / THREE (*7)

SHRIMP BOAT

SAM PREKOP – vocals, guitar / **IAN SCHNELLER** – guitar / **DAVID KROLL** – bass / **BRAD WOOD** – drums

not iss.   own label

1988. (c) <none> **SOME BISCUIT**
1988. (c) <none> **DAYLIGHT SAVINGS**

not iss.   Specimen

1989. (lp) **SPECKLY**

Rough Trade Bar/None

Mar 92. (cd/c/lp) <BARNONE 22-2/-4/-1> **DUENDE**
– Back to the Ukraine / Jing jing / Sad banjo / I swear, happy days are mine / River of wine / Duende / Sunday crawls along / Limerick / Duende / Rock me baby / Chimp / Bumblebees / New song waltz / Van Buren / Malva Rosita / Tartar's mark.
— **ERIC CLARIDGE** – bass; repl. KROLL
Jul 93. (cd/lp) (R 300-2/-1) <BARNONE 27-2/-1> **CAVALE**
– Pumpkin lover / Duende suite / Line song / Blue green misery / What do you think of love / Swinging shell / Creme brulee / I'll name it Sue / Free love overdrive / Dollar bill / Apples / Smooth ass / Small wonder / Oranges / Henny Penny.
— BRAD WOOD went into production (SMASHING PUMPKINS, etc), SCHNELLER formed FALSTAFF who issued one eponymous set in 1995 for 'Specimen'

SEA AND CAKE

SAM PREKOP – vocals, guitar / **ERIC CLARIDGE** – bass / **ARCHER PREWITT** (b. Frankfort, Kentucky) – guitar (of COCTAILS) / **JOHN McENTIRE** – drums (of TORTOISE)

Rough Trade   Thrill Jockey

Feb 94. (cd/lp) (R 310-2/-1) <THRILL CD/LP 016> **THE SEA AND CAKE**
– Jacking the ball / Polio / Bring my car I feel to smash it / Flat lay the waters / Choice blanket / Culabra cut / Bombay / Showboat angel / So long to the captain / Lost in autumn. *(re-iss. Apr02 on 'Thrill Jockey'; same as US)*

Lissy's   not iss.

Jan 95. (ltd-7"m) (LISS 1) **GLAD YOU'RE RIGHT. / TIGER PANTHER / CRIMSON WING**

Moll   Thrill Jockey

May 95. (cd/lp) (EFA 12112-2/-1) <THRILL CD/LP 21> **NASSAU** Jan95
– Nature boy / Parasol / A man who never sees a pretty girl that he doesn't love her a little / The world is against you / Lamont's lament / Soft and sleep / The cantina / Earth star / Alone, for the moment / I will hold the tea bag.
Oct 95. (cd/lp) (EFA 12115-2/-1) <THRILL CD/LP 026> **THE BIZ**
– The biz / Leeora / The kiss / Station in the valley / Darkest night / Sending / Escort / Aa assassin / The transaction / For minor sky. *(cd re-iss. Apr98 on 'Thrill Jockey'; TKCD 70951) (lp re-iss. Dec99 on 'Moll'; MOLL 15)*

Thrill Jockey   Thrill Jockey

Apr 97. (cd/lp) <(THRILL CD/LP 39)> **THE FAWN**
– Sporting life / The arguement / The fawn / The ravine / Rossignol / There you are / Civilise / Bird and flag / Black tree in the bee yard / Do now fairly well.
Sep 97. (12"ep/cd-ep) <THRILL 48/+CD> **TWO GENTLEMEN** (remixes)
– The Cheech Wizard meets Baby Ultraman in the cool blue cave (short stories about birds, trees and the sports life wherever you are) / Rinky-dink O.S. type rip / I took the opportunity to antique my end table / Early Chicago / The sewing machine.
Jun 98. (cd) <(TKCB 70952)> **A BRIEF HISTORICAL RETROSPECTIVE** (compilation)
– Jacking the ball / Flat lay the waters / Bombay / So long to the captain / Bring my car I feel to smash it / Showboat angel / Lost in autumn / Chainer / Nature boy / Parasol / A man who never sees a pretty girl that he doesn't love her a little / The world is against you / Alone, for the moment / The cantina / Earth star / Glad you're right.
Oct 00. (lp/cd) <(THRILL 086/+CD)> **OUI**
– Afternoon speaker / All the photos / You beautiful bastard / The colony room / The leaf / Everyday / Two dolphins / Midtown / Seemingly / I missed the glance.

SAM PREKOP

with **JIM O'ROURKE, ARTHUR PREWITT, CHAD TAYLOR, ROB MAZUREK, JOSH ABRAHMS + JOHN McENTIRE**

Thrill Jockey   Thrill Jockey

Feb 99. (lp/cd) <(THRILL 061/+CD)> **SAM PREKOP**
– Showrooms / The company / Practice twice / A cloud to the back / Don't bother / Faces and people / On such favors / The shadow / Smaller rivers / So shy.

SEAFOOD

Formed: London, England ... mid '97 by DAVID LINE and CHARLES MacLEOD, who recruited flatmates CAROLINE BANKS and KEVIN HENDRICK through an ad in the capital's premier exchange forum, 'Loot'. Twin-headed, youthful, shouty, pop noise merchants akin to a crossover of the PIXIES and SONIC YOUTH, SEAFOOD served up their first platter in the shape of early '98's 'SCORCHED COMFORT'. Having already been snapped up by cult indie launching pad, 'Fierce Panda', they delivered another fine 45 and a mini-cd, 'MESSENGER IN THE CAMP' (1998). At Reading '98, with CHARLES suffering some sort of hand injury, they reinterpreted ALED JONES' balls-clutching choirboy carol, 'WALKING IN THE AIR' (cockles and mussels, not so much alive alive-o!). The fishy Londoners continued their homage to classic Stateside alternativa with 'SURVIVING THE QUIET' (2000), with the likes of GIRLS AGAINST BOYS and MADDER ROSE again being none too subtle reference points. Both were to feature on 2001's

'WHEN DO WE START FIGHTING', the former's ELI JANNEY lending his not inconsiderable talents and the latter's MARY LORSON emphasising the band's emotionally taut undercurrent on 'WHAT MAY BE THE OLDEST'.

Album rating: MESSENGER IN THE CAMP mini compilation (*6) / SURVIVING THE QUIET (*7) / WHEN DO WE START FIGHTING (*6)

DAVID LINE – vocals, guitar / **KEVIN HENDRICK** – bass, vocals / **CHARLES McLEOD** – guitar / **CAROLINE BANKS** – drums

		Fierce Panda	Sony
Jan 98.	(7") (NING 45) **SCORCH COMFORT. / DIG**	☐	-
Mar 98.	(7"maroon) (KOOKYDISC 005) **PSYCHIC RAINY NIGHTS. / WE FELT MAROON** (above issued on 'Kooky' records)	☐	-
Jun 98.	(7"m) (NING 54) **PORCHLIGHT. / UKIAH / MAINTENANCE 1** (cd-s+=) (NING 54CD) – Maintenance 2. (7".re-iss. May00 on 'Silvertone'; ORE 27)	☐	-
Nov 98.	(m-cd) (NONG 06CD) **MESSENGER IN THE CAMP** (compilation) – Scorch comfort / Psychic rainy nights / Porchlight / Ukiah / Rot of the stars / Dope stars / We felt maroon / Dig. (re-iss. May00 +m-lp; NONG 06LP)	☐	-
Jun 99.	(7") (NING 72) **EASY PATH. / WALKING IN THE AIR (S.B.N. session)** (cd-s+=) (NING 72CD) – Duck and cover.	☐	-
Oct 99.	(7") (NING 83) **THIS IS NOT AN EXIT. / PEEPHOLE CRAFTS** (cd-s+=) (NING 83/+CD) – Demand mountains.	☐	-
Feb 00.	(cd/lp) (NONG 11 CD/LP) <1095> **SURVIVING THE QUIET** – Guntrip / Easy path / Belt / Dear leap the ride / This is not an exit / Led by bison / Toggle / Beware design / Folksong crisis / FSC II – The quiet. <US cd+=> – Peephole crafts / Walking in the air (evilated live session).	☐	Dec00
Feb 00.	(7") (NING 89) **BELT. / PEBBLE MULE** (cd-s+=) (NING 89CD) – Did you come in a car?	☐	-
May 00.	(7") (NING 95) **LED BY BISON. / TEETH HIDDEN** (cd-s+=) (NING 95CD) – What may be the oldest.	☐	-
		Infectious	Nettwerk
Jul 01.	(7") (INFEC 103S) **CLOAKING. / BOGGLE** (cd-s+=) (INFEC 1035CDS) – Clear keeping.	71	-
Jul 01.	(cd/lp) (INFECT 105 CD/LP) **WHEN DO WE START FIGHTING** – Splinter / Western battle / What may be the oldest / Pleasurehead / Cloaking / Similar assassins / People are underestimated / Desert stretched before the sun / In this light will you fight me / He collects dust. (special cd; INFECT 105CDX) (re-iss. Mar02 d-cd+=; INFEC 105CDB) **COURSEWORK** – Cloaking / In this light will you fight me? / Similar assassins / People are underestimated / What may be the oldest / Porchlight.	☐	Apr02
Dec 01.	(7") (INFEC 104S) **SPLINTER. / SPLINTER (Gerling remix)** (cd-s+=) (INFEC 104CDS) – Levitate me.	☐	-
Mar 02.	(7") (INFEC 113S) **WESTERN BATTLE. / BLUE BOLT** (cd-s+=) (INFEC 113CDS) – All slept.	☐	-
Jun 02.	(cd-ep; split w/ JETPLANE LANDING) (INFEC 118CDS) **PLEASUREHEAD / GUN TRIP (live) / (other 2 by JETPLANE LANDING)**	☐	-

SEAFRUIT

Formed: Sheffield, England ... 1998 by GEOFF BARRADALE (formerly of the WILD ORCHIDS and 80's synth-pop outfit, VITAMIN Z), ALAN SMYTH, JOE NEWMAN, TOM HOGG and STU DOUGHTY. Guitarist ALAN SMYTH was a one time engineer for PULP and The LONGPIGS but decided to start a venture of his own when he heard singer GEOFF BARRADALE practising in his studio. The two began writing and performing tracks which eventually caught the attention of 'Food' record's plugger Andy Ross (whose previous credits included BLUR and IDLEWILD). Unfortunately when ROSS had witnessed the pair performing live he was duly impressed by their lack of image and gave up all hope for the band. BARRADALE and SMYTH recruited NEWMAN, HOGG and DOUGHTY into the project and subsequently released the BACHARACH-inspired 'LOOKING FOR SPARKS' one year later. The debut single was quickly followed by another, 'HELLO WORLD', which was more uptempo, although mixed in lo-fi pop to add full effect to this minor chart placed treasure. SMYTH sensibly quit his day job making wooden wall ducks! and SEAFRUIT signed a record deal with 'Global Warming', for whom they released what was to be their one and only long-play release, the eponymous 'SEAFRUIT' (2000).

Album rating: SEAFRUIT (*6)

GEOFF BARRADALE – vocals (ex-VITAMIN Z) / **ALAN SMYTH** – guitar / **TOM HOGG** – guitar / **JOE NEWMAN** – bass, keyboards, flugelhorn / **STU DOUGHTY** – drums

		Electric Crayon	not iss.
Mar 99.	(7") (ECY 3032) **LOOKING FOR SPARKS. / TRUTH OR LIES** (cd-s+=) (ECCD 3032) – Your eyes.	☐	-
Jul 99.	(cd-s) (ECCD 3055) **HELLO WORLD / PERFECT / NOT MY SCENE** (cd-s) (ECCX 3055) – ('A'side) / Looking for sparks (acoustic) / Barefoot.	59	-
		Global Warming	not iss.
Jun 00.	(cd-ep) (WARMCD 8) **WHAT IF EVERYONE YOU EVER LOVED WASN'T THERE**	☐	-
Oct 00.	(cd) (GLOBCD 7) **SEAFRUIT** – Dirty washing / Somebody else's friend / Small town / Air / Your eyes / Rocket fuel / Looking for sparks / Assassin / Not my scene / Hello world / Truth or lies / Tenderhooks.	☐	-

SEAGULL SCREAMING KISS HER KISS HER

Formed: and discovered by CORNELIUS ... Tokyo, Japan ... 1992 by AIHA HUGURASHI and SACHIKO ITO, the girls' first release coming in the shape of 1993's 'SEAGULL TO HELL' EP; ITO was subsequently replaced by NAO KOYAMO for the follow-up, 'SWALLOW UP'. With a third member, TAKAHARU "TAKAPE" KARASHIMA, in place, this hard-working all-female trio – probably Japan's greatest ever – delivered their debut CD-album, 'GIVE THEM BACK TO ME' (1996), a stylish twee-pop dirge that paved the way for a plethora of homeland releases; by the millennium their fanbase was over 50,000. With endorsement from noneother than HOLE's COURTNEY LOVE (in way of Top 3 Newcomer of 2001), the cult underground SSKHKH subsequently toured supporting the likes of MOGWAI, MODEST MOUSE and YO LA TENGO. This promptly invited the release of a UK/US compilation, RED TALK' (2002), featuring their past several years' work. • **Covered:** FLY (Yoko Ono) / SUBTERRANEAN HOMESICK BLUES (Bob Dylan).

Album rating: RED TALK compilation (*8)

AIHA HUGURASHI – vocals, guitar / **SACHIKO ITO** – bass, vocals

		not iss.	Trumpet
May 93.	(cd-ep) <TT 502> **SEAGULL TO HELL** – Losey is my dog / A prince happy / Davy baby / Seagull's theme / Thurston & Kim & me / Mon amour (4-track demo).	-	- Japan

—— **NAO KOYAMA** – bass, vocals; repl. ITO

		not iss.	Cardinal
1994.	(cd-ep) <BDCAR-CS 001> **SWALLOW UP** – Swallow up / Stand still / Sing it for you / Dreamer goes anywhere else / N.Y. nite fever (4-track special).	-	- Japan

—— added **TAKAHARU "TAKAPE" KARASHIMA** – drums, vocals

		not iss.	Hate It, Damn It
1996.	(cd) <HDR 001CD> **GIVE THEM BACK TO ME** – Gimmie / You come to me, and give them back to me / Hawaiian bed / You and me, now / Outta head (8-track version) / No bed of roses / Naked / If I happen to fall down ... / Gimmie (brilliant shit) / Good-bye blues / Fly / Happy pills (service version) / Mid summer N.Y. / Evil / Long / Evil reprise (eat shit and die version) / Blind (yo yo session) / Darling, here I am (mono version) / Watch me dead (fly session).	-	- Japan
		not iss.	Polystar
1996.	(cd-ep) <PSCR 5431> **FLY** – It's good it's real / Fitting (Motorhead and Fuck version) / I'm a diva / Choking / If I happen to fall down (In your arms).	-	- Japan
1996.	(cd-ep) <PSCR 5533> **PINK SODA** – Foolin', but don't look back baby (Jamaicva mix) / Pink soda / Asking for it / Loopy / Pink soda (too drunk to sing version) / Subterranean homesick blues / Walk away (no end demo).	-	- Japan
1997.	(cd) <PSCR 5601> **IT'S BRAND NEW** – It's brand new / School lunch / A touch / A shotgun & me / Red talk / A shotgun & me (real body remix) / She / Cream / I feel my heart move / Criminal / Darlin' here I am / Sister of joy / Elvis.	-	- Japan
1997.	(cd-ep) <PSCR 5654> **SWEET HOME** – Angel / As long as we're together / Flower / Bare foot / Sweet home.	-	- Japan
1998.	(cd) <PSCR 5703> **17** – Coma / Double life / Down to Mexico / Rhythm voice / Slow start / Living on the same planet / Don't cry my bunny / Sister sister / Count 0 number 1 / Drive a car / Seventeen / Down to Mexico (demo).	-	- Japan
1999.	(cd-ep) <PSCR 5754> **PRETTY IN PINK** – Heaven / I'm crazy 4 U / Hello, baby it's me / Pretty in pink.	-	- Japan

—— now just **AIHA + NAO**; drums **YOSHIKI WATANABE + YASUNOBU ARAKAWA**

2000.	(cd) <PSCR 5861> **NO! NO! NO!** – No star / No telephone / No luck / Baby run / Red dress / Introduction No.9 / Krazy U / Grapefruit / Everyone's fave / A guitar for me and milk for her / Motor psycho / 8 / Do I love you enough.	-	- Japan
2001.	(cd) <PSCR 5935> **NO! NO! NO! TOUR 2000 (live)** – No star / No telephone / No luck / Introduction No.9 / Krazy 4 U / Motor psycho (chill out version) / 8 / Johnny my love / Everyone's fave / Check 1, 2 / Down to Mexico / Drive a car / Angel / 17.	-	- Japan
2001.	(cd-s) <PSCR 5952> **SENTIMENTAL JOURNEY / COUNT ZERO ZERO ZERO 1 / L'AMOUR**	-	- Japan
2001.	(cd) <PSCR 5957> **FUTURE OR NO FUTURE** – Evolution / Lullaby / Sentimental journey / Fuck it up and get hurt / Think it over / Let's dance / Chik chik A.A. / L'amour / Mo' mo' gimi' mo' / Neat neat boy / Future or no future / Six in the morning.	-	- Japan
2001.	(cd-s) <PSCR 5979> **LULLABY / PSYCHO MELODY / DOKO E IKU NO? (WHERE AM I GOING TO?)**	-	- Japan
2002.	(cd) <PSCR 6039> **DYING FOR SEAGULLS!** (compilation) – It's good it's real / If I happen to fall down / Pink soda / Asking for it / Red talk / Angel / Down to Mexico / Seventeen / I'm crazy 4 U / Pretty in pink / No star / No telephone / Evolution / Lullaby / Sentimental journey / Think it over / Doku E iku no? (Where am I going to?) / Johnny my love / The word I love you / Oui et non.	-	- Japan

– UK/US compilation/release! –

Jun 02.	(cd) *Arrivederci Baby! – Cherry Red;* <(CIAO 02CD)> **RED TALK** – Sentimental journey / Pink soda / No luck / A shotgun and me / Angel / Pretty in pink / Chik chik A.A. / Grapefruit / Asking for it / A guitar for vme and milk for her / Count 0 number 1 / Psycho melody / She / Sister sister / 8 / Mo' mo' gimi' mo' / As long as we're together / If I happen to fall down (in your arms) / Sister sister (CD-Rom).	☐	☐

SEAHORSES

Formed: based London, England ... 1996 by ex-STONES ROSES guitarist JOHN SQUIRE who allegedly 'discovered' frontman CHRIS HELME busking in his native Yorkshire. With STUART FLETCHER and ANDY WATTS completing the line-up, the band hooked up with producer Tony Visconti and quickly entered a studio in L.A. to begin work on their debut set, 'DO IT YOURSELF'. In stark contrast to the infamously drawn out sessions for the final 'ROSES album, all the tracks were laid down inside a month and the record was in the shops by Spring '97. Inevitably, the hype surrounding the whole thing tended to obscure the question of whether the record was actually any good or not; the bulk of critics (perhaps only too eager to get the bolt in to SQUIRE, a previously unassailable indie guitar god) thought not, or at least panned the set for its inoffensive blandness. Certainly, there was nothing to match the quality of any track from the STONE ROSES sublime debut, although on its own terms, the record's vaguely enjoyable, bluesy indie-rock would've counted as a decent debut by a new band. Somewhat akin to a folk-ish cross between IAN BROWN and LIAM GALLAGHER (who, incidentally, co-penned 'LOVE ME AND LEAVE ME'), HELME's singing, as with SQUIRE's guitar flash, was as competent yet ultimately forgettable as any second division Brit-rock outfit. With the album lacking any real songwriting magic (bar say 'LOVE IS THE LAW' and 'BLINDED BY THE SUN'), some fans began to wonder just who was the mysterious X factor into the STONE ROSES, although enough people thought differently to take the album to No.2 in the UK chart. With a string of successful singles and festival appearances also now under their belt, British sales of the debut are approaching the half million mark; SQUIRE may at last be achieving the success that has long seemed his due, ironically, with the most underwhelming material of his career. However, the SEAHORSES were treading water (so to speak!) during the latter half of '98, HELME expressing to mainman SQUIRE he wanted more of a say in the music/lyrics he was to sing. Inevitably, with more of a whimper than a bang, the band were no more, speculating tabloid rumours of yet another STONES ROSES reformation; HELME was meanwhile plotting his own solo career. After the end of The SEAHORSES, SQUIRE himself disappeared for a few years before delivering his solo effort in 2002, 'TIME CHANGES EVERYTHING'. A rather mediocre album from the outset, here was a songwriter with nothing to prove, unlike RICHARD ASHCROFT (who didn't do so well). Centered around jangly guitar parts, plus the wishful-thinking folk of DYLAN and NILSSON (not to mention the impending presence of the bloody ROLLING STONES), SQUIRE had managed to uphold his brilliant and taut lyricism, adding in a few hammond organs and token slide guitars. Would impress fans of PAUL WELLER, OCEAN COLOUR SCENE, et al.

Album rating: DO IT YOURSELF (*7) / John Squire: TIME CHANGES EVERYTHING (*6)

JOHN SQUIRE (b.24 Nov'62, Broadheath, Lancashire, England) – guitar / **CHRIS HELME** – vocals, acoustic guitar / **STUART FLETCHER** – bass / **ANDY WATTS** – drums, vocals

		Geffen	Geffen
May 97.	(7"/c-s/cd-s) (GFS/+C/TD 22243) **LOVE IS THE LAW. / DREAMER / SALE OF THE CENTURY**	3	–
May 97.	(cd/c/lp) (<GED/GEC/GEF 25134>) **DO IT YOURSELF**	2	–
	– I want you to know / Blinded by the sun / Suicide drive / The boy in the picture / Love is the law / Happiness is eggshaped / Love me and leave me / Round the universe / 1999 / Standing on your head / Hello.		
Jul 97.	(7"/c-s/cd-s) (GFS/+C/TD 22266) **BLINDED BY THE SUN. / KILL PUSSYCAT KILL / MOVING ON**	7	–
Sep 97.	(7"/c-s/cd-s) (GFS/+C/TD 22282) **LOVE ME AND LEAVE ME. / SHINE / FALLING IS EASY**	16	–
Dec 97.	(7"/c-s/cd-s) (GFS/+C/TD 22297) **YOU CAN TALK TO ME. / DON'T TRY / 3 WIDE**	15	–

— **MARK HEANEY** – drums; repl. WATTS

— in Feb'99, the SEAHORSES announced they had split

JOHN SQUIRE

SQUIRE – vocals, guitar + **ANDY TREACEY** – drums (of FAITHLESS) / **JONATHAN WHITE** – bass (of GROOVE ARMADA) / **JOHN ELLIS** – keyboards

		North Country	not iss.
Sep 02.	(cd/d-lp) (NCCD/NCLP 001) **TIME CHANGES EVERYTHING**	17	–
	– Joe Louis / I miss you / Shine a little light / Time changes everything / Welcome to the valley / 15 days / Transatlantic near death experience / All I really want / Strange feeling / Sophia.		
Oct 02.	(7") (NC 001) **JOE LOUIS. / HOME SWEET HOME**	43	–
	(cd-s+=) (NCCDA 001) – 15 days (home demo).		
	(cd-s) (NCCDB 001) – ('A'side) / See you on the other side / I miss you (home demo).		

SEAM

Formed: Chapel Hill, North Carolina, USA ... 1986 as BITCH MAGNET by SOOYOUNG PARK and LEXI MITCHELL. This obscure but occasionally namedropped outfit released three albums (the last featuring DAVE GRUBBS) at the turn of the decade before MAC McCAUGHAN (also of SUPERCHUNK) joined them to form SEAM. Signed to 'Homestead' ('City Slang' in Europe), the trio took a dynamic crescendo/release approach on debut album, 'HEADSPARKS' (1992), although most of the time the band crawled along at prozac pace alongside PARK's forlorn vocals. With MAC subsequently devoting all his time to the up and coming SUPERCHUNK, PARK and MITCHELL replaced him with future TORTOISE men, JOHN McENTIRE and BUNDY BROWN, before BOB RISING and second guitarist, CRAIG WHITE got involved. Now residing in Chicago and signed to local imprint, 'Touch & Go', SEAM varied their heavy-lidded music policy little on 1993's 'THE PROBLEM WITH ME', although PARK was to recruit an entire new line-up of musicians (namely REG SHRADER, WILLIAM SHIN and CHRIS MANFRIN) for future releases. These came in the shape of 'ARE YOU DRIVING ME CRAZY?' (1995) and the long-awaited but directionless 'THE PACE IS GLACIAL' (1998), SEAM yet to mine any real crossover success.
• **Covered:** WHICH WAY TO GO (Big Boys) / LOOK BACK IN ANGER (TV Personalities) / SHAME (Mark Saltzman) / DRIVING THE DYNAMITE TRUCK (Breaking Circus) / THIS AIN'T NO PICNIC (Minutemen) / HEROES (David Bowie).

Album rating: Bitch Magnet: STAR BOOTY mini (*5) / UMBER (*6) / BEN HUR (*6) / Seam: HEADSPARKS (*6) / THE PROBLEM WITH ME (*8) / ARE YOU DRIVING ME CRAZY? (*8) / THE PACE IS GLACIAL (*5)

BITCH MAGNET

SOOYOUNG PARK – vocals, guitar / **LEXI MITCHELL** – bass / **JON FINE** – drums

		What Goes On	Communion
Apr 89.	(m-lp) (GOESON 27) <COMM 7> **STAR BOOTY**		Oct88
	– Carnation / C word / Sea of pearls / Hatpins / Knucklehead / Circle K / Polio / Cantaloupe. (re-iss. Feb91 on 'Glitterhouse'; efa 08128)		

— added **DAVE GALT** – guitar

Sep 89.	(lp) (GOESON 35) <COMM 12> **UMBER**		
	– Motor / Navajo ace / Clay / Joan of Arc / Douglas leader / Goat-legged country god / Big pining / Joyless street / Punch and Judy / Americruiser. <US cd-iss. +=> – STAR BOOTY (re-iss. Feb91 on 'Glitterhouse'; efa 08129)		

DAVID GRUBBS – guitar (ex-SQUIRREL BAIT) repl. GALT

1989.	(7") <COMM 19> **VALMEAD. / PEA**	–	
	(above B-side featured CODEINE)		
1990.	(cd/c/lp) <COMM 21> **BEN HUR**	–	
	– Dragoon / Valmead / Ducks and drakes / Mesentery / Lookin' at the Devil / Gator / Spite y malice / Crescent.		

		not iss.	Waterfront
1990.	(7"red) <DAMP 148> **MESENTERY. / BIG PINING / MOTOR**		

		Caff Corp.	not iss.
1991.	(7") (CAFF 14) **SADIE. / Ducks And Drakes (by MISFITS)**		–

— split after above; PARK + MITCHELL formed SEAM, while GRUBBS formed SLINT

SEAM

SOOYOUNG PARK – vocals, guitar / **LEXI MITCHELL** – bass / **MAC McCAUGHAN** – drums (of SUPERCHUNK)

		City Slang	Homestead
Nov 91.	(7"m) <HMS 157-7> **DAYS OF THUNDER. / GRAIN / WHICH WAY TO GO**	–	
Apr 92.	(lp/cd) (EFA 04076/+CD) <HMS 177> **HEADSPARKS**		Mar92
	– Decatur / Grain / Sky city / Pins and needles / Feather / Atari / King rice / New year's / Shame / Granny 9X.		

		City Slang	Merge
Jun 92.	(7") (04074-40) <MRG 019> **GRANNY 9X. / LOOK BACK IN ANGER**		

— **BUNDY BROWN + JOHN McENTIRE** repl. MAC (back to SUPERCHUNK)

		City Slang	Trash Flow
Mar 93.	(7") (EFA 04912-45) <TF 05> **KERNEL. / SWEET PEA**		
	(12"+=/cd-s+=) (EFA 04912-02/-03) <TG 112/+CD> – Shame / Driving the dynamite truck.		

		not iss.	Summershine
Apr 93.	(7") <Shine 29> **KERNEL. / FEATHER**	–	

— **BOB RISING** – drums + **CRAIG WHITE** – guitar; repl. BROWN + McENTIRE who formed TORTOISE

		City Slang	Touch & Go
Sep 93.	(cd/c/lp) (EFA 04923-26/-06/-08) <TG 118CD> **THE PROBLEM WITH ME**		
	– Rafael / Bunch / Road to Madrid / Stage 2000 / Sweet pea / Dust and turpentine / Something's burning / The wild cat / Autopilot / Kernel.		

— **SOOYOUNG** recruited new band **REG SHRADER** – guitar / **WILLIAM SHIN** – bass / **CHRIS MANFRIN** – drums

Jun 95.	(7") (che 032) **HEY LATASHA. / MELLOW NOISE U.S.A.**		–
	(above issued on 'Che')		
Jul 95.	(cd/lp) (EFA 04960-2/-1) <TG 144CD> **ARE YOU DRIVING ME CRAZY?**		Jun95
	– Berlitz / Hey Latasha / Port of Charleston / Rainy season / Two is enough / Haole redux / Tuff luck / Broken bones / Sometimes I forget / Petty thievery.		

		Touch & Go	Touch & Go
Sep 98.	(lp/cd) <(TG 175/+CD)> **THE PACE IS GLACIAL**		
	– Little Chang, big city / Get higher / Wig / Intifada driving school / Kanawha / Nisei fight song / The prizefighters / In the sun / Inching towards Juarez / Pale marble movie / Aloha spirit.		

		Ajax	Ajax
Mar 99.	(7") <(AJAX 053)> **SUKIYAKI. / HEROES**		

— seemed to have taken a sabbatical

SEAN NA-NA

Formed: As the pseudonym of Marshall, Minnesota-born SEAN TILLMAN, along with sidekicks JON KELSON and drummer JASON RALPH. Barely out of his teens, TILLMAN formed CALVIN KRIME and issued the EP, 'PRETTY IN PINK', in 1995. After the widely ignored debut effort, 'DRESS FOR THE FUTURE' (1997), the trio released the power-punk-pop of 'YOU'RE FEELING SO ATTRACTIVE' (1998), which interpreted the same damaged lo-fi rock as PAVEMENT or early YO LA TENGO. The group split after the release of the album and TILLMAN adopted the SEAN NA-NA moniker, issuing the shaky singles collection 'AND HIS BABY BLUE' (1999), before the witty, neurotic 'DANCE 'TIL YOUR BABY IS A MAN' (2000) – TILLMAN's sly rock-infested dig at past acquaintances and foes. Outtakes from that session could be heard on 2000's 'RETURN OF THE UNICORN', before the man himself delivered what was possibly the swansong of his career, the brilliant 'MY MAJESTY' (2002). The LP, peppered with the usual TILLMAN rhetorics, this time included a varied use of instrumentation (violins, horns and a host of guitar pedals) plus a warm batch of peculiar arrangements that would've made BRIAN WILSON proud.

Album rating: Calvin Krime: DRESS FOR THE FUTURE (*5) / YOU'RE FEELING SO ATTRACTIVE (*5) / Sean Na-Na: DANCE 'TIL YOUR BABY IS A MAN (*6) / MY MAJESTY (*7)

CALVIN KRIME

SEAN TILLMANN – bass, vocals, keyboards / **JON KELSON** – vocals, guitar / **JASON RALPH** – drums

not iss. / DIY King

Nov 95. (7"ep) **PRETTY IN PINK**
– Social crash / Greens / Hybridized / My friend.

not iss. / Skernel

Oct 96. (7"ep) **KIDS INCARCERATED**
– Veryfine / Blood flows slow (fight song) / Bing Bing

Amphetam.Amphetam. Reptile / Reptile

Mar 97. (cd) <amrep 60> **DRESS FOR THE FUTURE**
– Sean Na Na / Aegis shaker / Drag dissonant / Other Jon / Personal earth station / Steve dude vs. Taurus too / Brand new Jason / My flaming arrow / Union pacific / Scram / Veryfine / Bing Bing.

Aug 98. (lp/cd) <(AMREP 71/+CD)> **YOU'RE FEELING SO ATTRACTIVE** — Apr98
– Die beautiful / Fantabuloso / 411 N. 6th St. / Inverse crickets and attractive transistors / The look, the know / Sea lions trained to hug / Mass fresh / Hunt the wumpus / Oh my goth! / Strictly business (instrumental underwater).

not iss. / Polyvinyl

Oct 98. (cd-ep) <21> **3 x 3 FOR 3 1/2**
– Mascara / This sad horse / Get off it.

— disbanded during the recording of above; JON formed The MERCURY VIRUS

SEAN NA-NA

SEAN TILLMANN – vocals, guitar

not iss. / Polyvinyl

Nov 98. (cd-ep) <23> **SEAN NA-NA**
– Two of the same name / Washington / Girls! girls! girls!

not iss. / Bread Machine

Jun 99. (7"; as SEAN NA-NA AND HIS BABY BLUE) **MEXCAL. / IN THIS HOLE**

not iss. / Heart Of A Champion

Nov 99. (7") **RISING STARS. / (other track by LUCKY JEREMY)**

not iss. / Kill Rock Stars

Jan 00. (cd-ep) <KRS 350> **SEAN NA-NA / MARY LOU LORD split**
– Princess and the pony / Stretch marks / My old France / (2 by MARY LOU LORD).

— added **NATHAN GRUMDAHL** – bass, vocals, slide guitar / **BEN WEBSTER + DAVE GATCHELL** – drums, percussion

not iss. / Troubleman

May 00. (cd) <TMR 37> **DANCE 'TIL YOUR BABY IS A MAN**
– Unicorns / The bottom / Slow to the core / Gray clouds / Cha cha cha / The ballad of coke and writhe / Mezcal (version) / Lonely moon / Rimshot Na Na / Little leaning tower.

Oct 00. (cd-ep) <TMR 61> **RETURN OF THE UNICORN EP**
– Give me a B-side / Return of the unicorn / Beh-beh-beh-beh-better / Tumor party / Big trouble / Your daddy looks dead . . .

— now with **ST. PATRICK** – bass + **BRYAN HANNA** – guitar, drums

French Kiss / French Kiss

Apr 02. (cd) <(FKS 060)> **MY MAJESTY** — Feb02
– Double date / Spread the good feeling / Give me a B side / Third life / Grew into my body / F you A-bomb / Big trouble / The human raft / Surrender foreign Lizzy / I hate saxophones / I need a girl.

SEBADOH

Formed: Boston, Massachusetts, USA . . . 1989 by LOU BARLOW, lo-fi overlord and former DINOSAUR JR member. After a less than amicable break from DINOSAUR mainman, J. MASCIS, BARLOW began writing and recording material with sticksman, ERIC GAFFNEY. Released on 'Homestead' over two albums, 'THE FREED MAN' (1989) and 'WEED FORESTIN' (1990), these acoustic sketches were (released in 1992 as a single CD package, 'FREED WEED') a taster for the fully fledged pop subversion of 'SEBADOH III' (1991). With the addition of bassist/guitarist, JASON LOWENSTEIN, the trio ventured into raucous electric territory, while keeping one foot in the acoustic camp, reconciling their love of lo-fi noise with barbed indie-folk. Though a US-only affair, the album was given a belated UK release in 1994; in the meantime, SEBADOH's output became more readily available following a deal with 'Sub Pop', the mini-set, 'ROCKIN' THE FOREST' (1992), boasting the semi-classic self-parody of 'GIMME INDIE ROCK', previously only available as an import 7". A second mini-album that year, 'SEBADOH VS HELMET', found BARLOW and Co. bravely tackling a Nick Drake cover (the timeless 'PINK MOON') with interesting results, while 'BUBBLE AND SCRAPE' (1992) was the band's most commercially successful release to date, making the UK Top 75. BARLOW continued to express his more lo-fi urges via side projects, releasing material as The FOLK IMPLOSION with (former PALACE) guitarist JOHN DAVIS and working on his own as LOU BARLOW AND HIS SENTRIDOH. Industriously (and confusingly for discographers!) prolific in the best indie tradition, BARLOW continued apace with his SEBADOH duties, releasing the acclaimed 'BAKESALE' in 1994. Though GAFFNEY had been replaced by BOB FAY, his playing still featured on an album which came as close to conventional alternative rock as anything BARLOW has yet recorded, the sound less self-consciously muted. It also marked their entry into the UK Top 40, just, while 1996's 'HARMACY' was even more accessible without compromising their indie/grunge ethos. BARLOW even had a hit single on his hands following the inclusion of FOLK IMPLOSION's 'NATURAL ONE' in Larry Clark's hotly debated 'Kids' movie, proving conclusively that lo-fi didn't necessarily entail lo-sales. Towards the end of a busy 90's for BARLOW, he delivered three excellent long-players, 'DARE TO BE SURPRISED' (1997) and 'ONE PART LULLABY' (1999) – both from the FOLK IMPLOSION – squeezed either side of SEBADOH's eponymous 'THE SEBADOH' (1999). The latter sold enough in its first week to crack the UK Top 50, while one of its highlights, 'FLAME', hit No.30(!). BARLOW's right hand man, LOEWENSTEIN, was to subsequently come up trumps with his own solo set during SEBADOH's extended lay-off (although SENTRIDOH updated their CV with 2002's 'FREE' set). 'AT SIXES AND SEVENS' (2002) mightn't have had the same immediacy as BARLOW's solo efforts but its self-produced, broodingly confrontational assault and intriguing diversions made for a promising debut.

• **Songwriters:** BARLOW and GAFFNEY (until latter repl. by FAY), some by LOWENSTEIN after 1992. Covered REJECT (Negros) / SICKLES AND HAMMERS (Minutemen) / WONDERFUL! WONDERFUL! (Edwards-Raleigh) / EVERYBODY'S BEEN BURNED (Byrds) / PINK MOON (Nick Drake) / RUN TO YOU (Bryan Adams) / BLONDE IN THE BLEACHERS (Joni Mitchell) / MARY CHRIST (Sonic Youth) / NAIMA (John Coltrane?). FOLK IMPLOSION covered SCHOOL (Nirvana) / I WON'T BACK DOWN (Tom Petty) / I SMELL A RAT (Bags) / LET A LITTLE LOVIN' (George Jones).

Album rating: THE FREED MAN (*5) / WEED FORRESTIN' (*4) / SEBADOH III (*7) / ROCKIN' THE FOREST (*4) / SEBADOH VS. HELMET (*5) / SMASH YOUR HEAD ON THE PUNK ROCK collection (*5) / BUBBLE AND SCRAPE (*7) / BAKESALE (*8) / HARMACY (*7) / THE SEBADOH (*8) / Lou Barlow & His Sentridoh: COLLECTION OF HOME RECORDINGS (*4) / ANOTHER COLLECTION OF HIS HOME RECORDINGS (*4) / LOU BARLOW & HIS SENTRIDOH (*5) / FREE SENTRIDOH: SONGS FROM LOOBIECORE (*5) / Folk Implosion: TAKE A LOOK INSIDE . . . mini (*5) / DARE TO BE SURPRISED (*6) / ONE PART LULLABY (*8) / Lou Barlow (& Rudy Trouve): SUBSONIC 6 (*5) / Jason Loewenstein: AT SIXES AND SEVENS (*6)

LOU BARLOW (b.17 Jul'66, Northampton, Massachusetts) – vocals, guitar (ex-DINOSAUR JR) / **ERIC GAFFNEY** – drums

Homestead / Homestead

Dec 89. (lp/c) <HMS 145-1/-4> **THE FREED MAN**
– Temporary dream / New worship / Subtle holy gift / My own religion / Ride the darker wave / More simple / Jealous of Jesus / Mr. Genius eyes / Perfect power / Feeding evil / Sexual confusion / Three times a day / Gate to hell / Broken / Whiley peach / I can't see / Take my hand / Pound my skinny head / I believe in fate / Waited forever / Slightest suggestion / It's so hard to fall in love / Brand new love.

Nov 90. (lp/c) <HMS 158-1/-4> **WEED FORESTIN'**
– Healthy sick / Burning out / Little man / Punch in the nose / Loose 'n' screw / Jealous evil / Moldy bread / Solid brownies / The bridge was you / Bolder / Slit your wrists / True hardcore / Stop the wheel / Made real / Close enough / Level anything / Soul mate / Nest / Narrow stories / Ladybugs / Yellow submarine / Wall of doubt / Crumbs / Growin' up with you. (UK cd-iss. Nov92 & Mar99 of above two as 'FREED WEED'; HMS 158-2)

— added **JASON LOEWENSTEIN** – bass, guitar, drums, vocals

Jul 91. (7"ep) <HMS 165-7> **GIMME INDIE ROCK**
– Gimme indie rock / Ride the darker wave / Red riding good / New king / Calling yog soggoth.
(UK-iss.Apr97 as 7"pic-d; HMS 165-7PD)

Sep 91. (cd/lp) <HMS 168-2/-1> **SEBADOH III**
– Freed pig / Sickles and hammers / Total peace / Violet execution / Scars, our eyes / Truly great thing / Kath / Perverted world / Wonderful! wonderful! / Limb by limb / Smoke a bowl / Black haired girl / Hoppin' up and down / Supernatural force / Rockstar / Downmind / Renaissance man / God told me / Holy picture / Hassle / No different / Spoiled / As the world does, the eyes of God. (UK-iss.Jul94 & Jun98 & Mar99; same)

Sonic Life / not iss.

1991. (7"m) <SL-002> **SPLIT SINGLE WITH BIG STICK**
– (untitled:-) My decision / Fire of July / Seh-bah-dough.

not iss. / Siltbreeze

Nov 91. (7"ep) <SB 009> **OVEN IS MY FRIEND**
– Oven is my friend (church police '82) / Prove it / Cheapshot / Waxbag maestro / Delicious cakes.

not iss. / Vertical

1992. (7"ep) <V-003> **ASSHOLE**
– Pig (coward) / Hung up / Slow to learn / Julienne / Violent elements / Attention / Your long journey.

SEBADOH (cont)

                                                    Domino   Sub Pop
Aug 92. (m-cd/m-lp) *(WIG CD/LP 2)* **ROCKIN' THE FOREST**
 – Gimme indie rock / Ride the darker wave / It's so hard to fall in love / Cry sis / Really insane II / Vampire / Junk bands / Mind-held.
Sep 92. (7"ep) *(DBC 001)* **SEBADOH / AZALIA SNAIL**
 – Toledo / Gondwanaland – No compass / Pete.
 (above on 'Dark Beloved Cloud'; DBC 001)
Oct 92. (m-cd/m-lp) *(WIG CD/LP 3)* **SEBADOH VS HELMET**
 – Notsur dnuora selcric / Brand new love / Mean distance / . . . Burned / New worship / Good things, proud man / P.Moon / Cecilia chime in Melee / Soulmate.
Nov 92. (cd) *<SP 176>* **SMASH YR HEAD ON PUNK ROCK**
 (compilation of above 2)
 – Crisis / Brand new love / Notsur dnuora selcric / Vampire / Good things / Cecelia chime in Melee / Everybody's been burned / Junk bonds / New worship / Pink moon / Mind meld. *(UK-iss.May98; same as US)*
Mar 93. (7") *(RUG 4)* **SOUL AND FIRE. / FANTASTIC DISASTER (amateur mix)**
 (12"+=/cd-s+=) *(RUG 4 T/CD)* – Emma get wild / Reject.
Apr 93. (cd/c/lp) *(WIG CD/MC/LP 4) <SP 192>* **BUBBLE AND SCRAPE** [63]
 – Soul and fire / Two years two days / Telecosmic alchemy / Fantastic disaster / Happily divided / Sister / Cliche / Sacred attention / Elixir is Zog / Emma get wild / Sixteen / Homemade / Forced love / No way out / Bouquet for a siren / Think (let tomorrow be) / Flood.
May 93. (7"ep) *<SP 211>* **SOUL AND FIRE / REJECT. / SISTER / BOUQUET FOR A SIREN**
Dec 93. (7") *(RUG 17)* **REBOUND. / CAREFUL**
 (12"ep+=/cd-ep+=) **FOUR SONGS EP** *(RUG 17)* – Mor backlash / Not a friend / Foreground / Naima / 40203 / Mystery man / Drumstick jumble / Lime kiln.

 ─── BARLOW, FAY + ERIC MATTHEWS were part of BELT BUCKLE who released a single on 'Sonic Bubblegum'; *GUM 013*) tracks:- Judas suicide / Pocket skylab love / Mary hair / Girl who reads.

 ─── BOB FAY – drums; repl. GAFFNEY who went solo (although still on below album)
Jul 94. (7"ep/cd-ep) *(RUG 22/+CD) <SP 267>* **SKULL. / PUNCHING MYSELF IN THE FACE REPEATEDLY, PUBLICLY / SING SOMETHING – PLATE O'HATRED**
Aug 94. (cd/c/lp) *(WIG CD/MC/LP 11) <SP 260>* **BAKESALE** [40]
 – License to confuse / Careful / Magnet's coil / Not a friend / Not too amused / Dreams / Skull / Got it / S. soup / Give up / Rebound / Mystery man / Temptation tide / Drama mine / Together or alone. *(ltd. w / free 7")*
Feb 95. (cd-ep) *<SP 284b>* **REBOUND / SOCIAL MEDICINE / ON FIRE (acoustic) / MAGNET'S COIL (acoustic) / REBOUND (acoustic)**
Jun 95. (7") *(RUG 38)* **NOT TOO AMUSED. / HANK WILLIAMS**
 (cd-s+=) *(RUG 38CD)* – ('A'-version).
Jul 96. (7") *(RUG 47)* **BEAUTY OF THE RIDE. / RIDING** [74]
 (10") *(RUG 47T)* – ('A'side) / Sixteen / Slintstrumental.
 (cd-s+=) *(RUG 47CD)* – (all 4 tracks).
Aug 96. (cd/c/d-lp) *(WIG CD/MC/LP 26) <SP 370>* **HARMACY** [38]
 – On fire / Prince – S / Ocean / Nothing like you / Crystal gypsy / Beauty of the ride / Mind reader / Sferzando! / Willing to wait / Hillbilly II / Zone doubt / Too pure / Worst thing / Love to fight / Perfect way / Can't give up / Open ended / Weed against speed / I smell a rat.
Oct 96. (7") *(RUG 50)* **OCEAN (Tim O'Heir's Ocean way remix). / WORST THING (Osterville version)**
 (cd-s+=) *(RUG 50CD)* – Third generation deadline / Portrait of the artist on the phone.

 ─── RUSS POLLARD – drums; repl. FEY
                                                    Domino   Sire
Jan 99. (7") *(RUG 80)* **FLAME (remix). / FLAME (4-track) / SWEET SURRENDER** [30]
 (cd-s) *(RUG 80CD1)* – ('A'side) / Crystal crossed / Saltwater garden.
 (cd-s) *(RUG 80CD2)* – ('A'side) / Loss of soul and shoe / Television nitelite.
Feb 99. (cd/c/lp) *(WIG CD/MC/LP 57) <31044>* **THE SEBADOH** [45]
 – It's all you / Weird / Bird in the hand / Break free / Tree / Nick of time / Flame / So long / Love is stronger / Decide / Colorblind / Thrive / Cuban / Sorry / Drag down.
Jun 99. (7") *(RUG 89)* **IT'S ALL YOU. / EMMETT PIG**
 (cd-s+=) *(RUG 89CD)* – Mind reader.

– compilations, others, etc. –

1995. (cd-ep) *Cortex; (CORX 016CD)* **MAGNET'S COIL** — Austra
 – Magnet's coil / Fancy-ass / Destitute / Perfect way / Give the drummer some / Cementville. *(UK-iss.Feb97; same)*

SENTRIDOH

LOU BARLOW
                                                    not iss.   homemade
1990. (ltd-c) *<none>* **LOSERS**
 – Smaller yard / Columbus / Love up above / Breakdown day / Sebadough / Old wife cried / Sound city / America / Wheaton / Confession / Face down / Conspiracy / Purple and green / Pet your puppy / Six days without shaving / Brotherly love / Favorite letter / Stupid asshole / Weed forestin' / Fleshy true / Mellow, cool and painfully aware / Bay city / Blind dove / Growing / Core – Nothing / Wipe it out / God won't let you die / R.A.M.O. / I will be lonely all my life / Blonde in the bleachers / You fell down the stairs / Strange love / The freed pig / Colix Juantara / Rise below slowly / Normal way / I see you running / Antheneezal.
                                                    not iss.   Shrimper
1991. (ltd-c) *<shr 12>* **LOSERS**
 – Columbus / The freed pig / Only losers / Normal way / I see you running / Anthaneezal / K-sensa-my II / Coolest hurt / Growing / Love up above / You fell down the stairs / Pink twinkie / Blonde in the bleachers / Face down / High-d / Strange love / Mellow, cool and painfully aware / Bay city baby / Blind dove / I feel good inside about me inside me / Breakdown day / Afraid of babies / Old wife cried / I will be lonely all my life / Favorite letter / Rise below slowly / Give up / Morning rain / Six days without shaving / Wipe it out / Fleshy true / Colix Juantarah / Win slow / Weed forestin' / Sebadough / Mojain plane / Try to get what you want, never get it / I'm so depressed / Wendin will / The free man.

                                                    not iss.   Smells Like Little Brother
1992. (7") *<slr 001>* **LOSERCORE. / REALLY INSANE**
Jun 93. (7"ep) *<lb-001>* **THE MYSTERIOUS SENTRIDOH EP**
 – Good in others / The spirit that kills / Weakness is the secret / Cold love / No one taught me / No matter what.
                                                    not iss.   Sub Pop
Dec 93. (7"ep) *<SP 251>* **LOU BARLOW'S 7 INCH COVER**
 – I am not mocking you / Survival / Helpless heartbreak / Dirty mind / Forever instant.
                                                    City Slang   not iss.
May 94. (cd/d-lp) *(EFA 04940-2/-1)* **LOU BARLOW AND HIS SENTRIDOH**
 – I am not mocking you / Survival / Helpless heartbreak / Dirty mind / Forever instant / Natural nature / Don't need / Endless tease / Paranoid revolution / Same old, say mold / Good in others / Spirit that kills / Weakness is the secret / Cold love / No one taught me / No matter what / Feel good / Symbiosis / Option / Alone to decide / Cranky / Machinery / Synthstrument.
                                                    Smells Like   Smells Like
Jun 94. (10"m-lp/m-cd) *<slr 08/+cd>* **WINNING LOSERS: COLLECTION OF HOME RECORDINGS**
 – Stronger / Chokechain / Only losers / Breakdown day / Rise below slowly / Dragdown memory / Not nice to be nice / Mellow, cool and painfully aware / Crackers and coffee / High school. *(UK-iss.Jul00; same as US)*
Oct 94. (d7"/m-cd; LOU BARLOW AND FRIENDS) *<(SM 12CD)>* **ANOTHER COLLECTION OF HOME RECORDINGS**
 – Run to you / Puffin' / Queen of the shore / Blonde in the bleachers / What would it be like / Feel good / Symbiosis / Cranky. *(cd+=)* – Alone to decide / Cranky / Machinery / Synthstrument. *(also cd on 'Shrimper' cd+d-lp 'LOSING YEARS') (re-iss. Jul00 on 'Mint'; MRD 004)*
                                                    Lo-Fi   not iss.
Dec 94. (7"ep) *<Low 1>* **LOUIS BARLOW'S ACOUSTIC SENTRIDOH** — French
 – Natural nature / Don't need / Endless tease / Paranoid revolution.

 ─── added guest RUSSELL POLLARD – guitar
                                                    Domino   Loobiecore
Apr 02. (cd) *(WIGCD 108) <1>* **FREE SENTRIDOH: SONGS FROM LOOBIECORE**
 – Intro / Mountain on the hill / Open door war / Blue sunshine / Choke on the rhythm / The Devil + / That kind of year / WWJD? / Over the fall / None of your goddam bizness / I love my momma / Up from the well / On the face / U can drive / Impulse / No more parties / Bad habits / Ride a hearse, build a throne / Girls come first / Don't call me writer / Songfull – Rehole / Spacescape imagination station / The cougar hood.

– compilations, etc. –

1993. (ltd-c) *Shrimper; <SHR 36>* **MOST OF THE WORST AND SOME OF THE BEST**
 – American morning '91 / Monkey rascist / Alberquerqe '89 / Ratherdie / I can't wait / Suede / Barbed wire / Nitemare / What would it be like / Run to you / Meaningless dead end / Cause for celebration / Jealous of Jesus / Mary Christ / Puffin on a pot pipe / Alone to decide.
1994. (ltd-c) *Shrimper; <SHR 48>* **WASTED PIECES**
 – Pooh piece / Stiff to the rhythm / Broken II / Be nice me / Never tried / My head really hurts (part 3) / God won't let you die / Saliva drips / Abandon / No way at all / I know before / It might be / Old man / Raise your head / Brown confessin' / Raise the bells / Conspiracy / Fun-pool / Why we swing / Nothing lasts / Heartness crane / Organ / Cello.
Oct 96. (lp/cd) *Shrimer; <(SHR 67/+CD)>* **ORIGINAL LOSING LOSERS** (tracks from early work) — May95

the FOLK IMPLOSION

LOU BARLOW + JOHN DAVIS
                                                    Chocolate Monk   not iss.
1993. (ltd-c) *<CHOC 0000005>* **WALK THRU THIS WORLD WITH THE FOLK IMPLOSION**
 – Not a man / Slam dance tonite / Kick a cutie / Stereo / Why do they hide from me / Sputnik's down / My head really hurts / School / I remember the angels / Eternal party / Third mind trouble / Walk through this world / End of the first side / Touch me all the time / A winter's day / Hey . . . / I know what I want today / . . . Hey, you don't say / I won't back down / Better than allrite / License to confuse / Let a little lovin' / So sweet I swear / End.
                                                    not iss.   Drunken Fish
1994. (7"ep) *<DF 12>* **WALK THRU THIS WORLD WITH THE FOLK IMPLOSION**
 – Eternal party / School / My head really hurts / I know what I want today / Third mind trouble / Walk through this world . . . / End of the first side / I remember the angels / Hey, you don't say / Won't back down / So sweet I swear / End.
                                                    Ubik   not iss.
1994. (7"ep) *<ubik 002>* **ELECTRIC IDIOT** — French
 – Opening day / Electric idiot / Lo-fi suicide / I reserve the right to rock / Final score.
                                                    Communion   Communion
Sep 94. (m-cd/m-lp) *<(COMM 32)>* **TAKE A LOOK INSIDE . . . .**
 – Blossom / Sputnik's down / Slap me / Chicken squawk / Spiderweb – Butterfly / Had to find out / Better than allrite / Why do they they hide / Winter's day / Boyfriend, girlfriend / Shake a little Heaven / Waltin' with yor ego / Take a look inside / Start again.
Nov 95. (cd-s) *<850430-2>* **NATURAL ONE. / CABRIDE** [29]
 (above issued on 'London')
Jan 96. (7") *<COMM 39>* **PALM OF MY HAND. / MOOD SWING**
 (cd-s+=) *<COMM 39CD>* – Opening day / Electric idiot / Lo-fi suicide / I reserve the right to rock / Final score.

— next DELUXX FOLK IMPLOSION:- LOU, JOHN, BOB + MARK PERETTA

Domino / not iss.

Mar 96. (7"ep; as D.F.I.) *(RUG 44)* **DADDY NEVER UNDERSTOOD / GREETINGS FROM SARAJEVO. / DADDY NEVER UNDERSTOOD / OVENMITT / LIQUID BREAD**

— DELUXX without LOU released 'ESKIMO LOVER' and 'SPREADABLE' 7" in 1993; BARLOW moonlighted with The SLOW BAND who backed STEVE WESTFIELD

London / not iss.

May 96. (12") *(LONX 382)* **NATURAL ONE. / ('A'-Unkle mix) / (Unkle instrumental)** — 45
(cd-s+=) *(LONCD 382)* – 'A'-Unkle No Skratch mix).
(above single taken from the movie, 'Kids')

Communion / Communion

Feb 97. (7") <*(COMM 47)*> **POLE POSITION. / OPENING DAY**
(cd-s+=) <*(COMM 47CD)*> – Summer's over.
Apr 97. (7") <*(COMM 46)*> **INSINUATION. / KEEPING SCORE**
(cd-s+=) <*(COMM 46CD)*> – Trail burn.
Jun 97. (lp/cd) <*(COMM 45/+CD)*> **DARE TO BE SURPRISED**
– Pole position / Wide web / Insinuation / Barricade / That's the trick / Checking in / Cold night / Park dub / Burning paper / (Blank paper) / Ball and chain / Fall into November / Dare to be surprised / River devotion. (w/ 12"; COMM 45M) – Insinuation / Insinuation (remix).

Domino / Interscope

Oct 99. (cd/d-lp) *(WIG CD/LP 72)* <*490336*> **ONE PART LULLABY** — Sep99
– My ritual / One part lullaby / Free to go / Serge / E.Z.L.A. / Mechanical man / Kingdom of lies / Gravity decides / Chainged to the moon / Merry-go-round / Someone you love / No need to worry / Back to the sunrise.
May 00. (7") *(RUG 104)* **FREE TO GO. / BLOSSOM / SHAKE A LITTLE HEAVEN**
(cd-s) *(RUG 104CD1)* – ('A'side) / Tomorrow may be another day / One part lullaby (instrumental).

— FOLK IMPLOSION in 2003 BARLOW + IMAAD WASIF + RUSS POLLARD

LOU BARLOW / RUDY TROUVE

LOU shared below set with dEUS man, RUDY TROUVE

Sub Rosa / Sub Rosa

Jun 00. (cd/lp) <*(SR 143 CD/V)*> **SUBSONIC 6**
– Beginning / Skipping / Nervous / Dream organ / Tough / Heavy foot / Thin-ment / Church / Jim Joe / Spoilt / End / (others by RUDY TROUVE).

JASON LOEWENSTEIN

plays everything

Domino / Sub Pop

Aug 02. (cd/lp) *(WIG CD/LP 111)* <*SP 580*> **AT SIXES AND SEVENS** — Jul02
– Codes / Casserole / Angle / Circles / I'm a shit / Crazy Santana / Upstate / Roswell to Jerusalem / H/M / NYC III / Funerals / More drugs / Mistake / Transform.
Sep 02. (7") *(RUG 143)* **CODES. / UPDATE (alt. take)**
(cd-s+=) *(RUG 143CD)* – Fall into a line / Bank / Family burden.

JOHN DAVIS

not iss. / Shrimper

1993. (ltd-c) <*SHR 042*> **STARS & SONGS**
1994. (ltd-lp) <*SHR 053*> **PURE NIGHT**

Communion / Communion

May 95. (lp/cd) <*COMM 37/+CD*> **LEAVE HOME**
– Here I am / Knocked out of the park / Goodbye for now / Always all time disco / Everyone go / That's the truth Ruth / Big billowing clouds of love / Home sweet home / So young / Start go / On fine evenings / Wipeout tonight / I hear you / Tug of war / Lullabye / Leave awe to it's devices. (UK-iss.Dec96; same)

Shrimper / Shrimper

Jan 96. (m-lp/m-cd; as JOHN DAVIS & DENNIS CALLACI) <*SHR 74/+CD*> **ROOM FOR SPACE**
– Take a walk / Room for space / Sea shore / Unclean / Saddle / Needle drag / Stand tall / Sail away. (UK-iss.Dec96; same as US)
Nov 96. (m-cd) <*SHR 85CD*> **I'LL BURN**
– I'll burn (album version) / Long range view / Topanga road / Vivid life / Automatic as apples / Circus / Endless sick hits / I'll burn (home version).
Jan 97. (lp/cd) <*SHR 90/+CD*> **BLUE MOUNTAINS**
– Jeep Cherokee / I took flight / I'll burn / Blue mountains / Narrow / Knock out / Face to the storm / Tethers / Startle / I freaked out like a big truck / Zowie pop / The way you touch me makes me laugh / Ready / Eloped – Elated.

SECRET GOLDFISH

Formed: Glasgow, Scotland ... mid-90's by PAUL TURNBULL and G LIRONEX (both ex-MACKENZIES), former FIZZBOMBS singer KATY McCULLARS and mysterious singer JOHN MOROSE. Like The POP GROUP fused with CAPTAIN BEEFHEART's 'Trout Mask Replica' period, The MACKENZIES released a couple of singles on the 'Ron Johnson' imprint, namely 'NEW BREED' and 'MEALY MOUTHS'. However, the short-lived act were better known for the funk-fuelled guitar-abuse of 'BIG JIM (THERE'S NO PUBS IN HEAVEN)', their contribution to the 'NME C86' cassette. Nearly a decade later, The SECRET GOLDFISH (not the early 80's bunch who nearly issued the 11th 'Postcard' single, 'HEY MISTER' / 'POOREST BOY IN TOWN') came to the surface with indie gems, 'SEASICK' and 'COME UNDONE', before the release of their Stephen Lironi-produced debut set 'AQUA PET ... YOU MAKE ME' (1996). Sounding much like The JESUS AND MARY CHAIN locked in a public toilet with JEFFERSON AIRPLANE and The NEW YORK DOLLS, the quartet quirkily took their name from an imaginary book credited in classic breakdown

novel 'The Catcher in the Rye'. Other singles began to follow (most notably the VIC GODARD co-penned 'SOMEWHERE IN THE WORLD' which also featured FRANCIS MACDONALD and STEVIE JACKSON), although it wasn't until summer '99 that the group returned ('JET STREAMS' was issued in 1997) with the soft and lingering third set, 'MINK RIOTS'. The album gained much attention from radio shows and music critics alike who were all baffled by the sudden change of this once indie experimental/pop collective. The MACKENZIES (i.e. GRAHAM LIRONI and IAN BEVERIDGE) were back again in the late 90's under the guise of CABS-like, MOONGOOSE. They also were part of the 'Creeping Bent' roster, releasing a shared single in '99 before recording their 'LoLeVel' set the following year. • SECRET GOLDFISH covered: THIS ARSEHOLE'S BEEN BURNED (Nectarine No.9) / SOMEWHERE IN CHINA (Shop Assistants).

Album rating: AQUA PET ... YOU MAKE ME (*5) / JET STREAMS (*6) / MINK RIOTS (*5)

MACKENZIES

G LIRONEX (b. GRAHAM LIRONI) – bass / **PAUL TURNBULL** – drums / **IAN BEVERIDGE** – keyboards

Ron Johnson / not iss.

Mar 86. (7") *(ZRON 8)* **NEW BREED. / DOG'S BREAKFAST**
Feb 87. (12"ep) *(ZRON 18)* **MEALY MOUTHS / TROUBLE. / RADIO MEALY MOUTHS / B JIM JAM**

— split after only two singles

SECRET GOLDFISH

— **TURNBULL + G LIRONEX** recruited **JOHN MOROSE** – guitar / **KATY McCULLARS** – vocals (ex-FIZZBOMBS)

Creeping Bent – Marina / not iss.

Jun 95. (7") *(bent 004)* **SEASICK. / VENUS BONDING (live)**
Apr 96. (7") *(bent 008)* **COME UNDONE. / EVERYWHERE THAT YOU GO**
Jun 96. (cd) *(bent 012cd – MA 19)* **AQUA PET ... YOU MAKE ME**
– Come undone / Tartan envy / The boy who left home to learn fear / Pet thang / Dandelion milk summer / Venus bonding: erotic Mars / I will see you through / I left one out, where did it go / Seasick / Glass mountain / The catalyst / Strawberry St. / Another short song about love and loss / Bandovian curve. (re-iss. Dec00; same)
Jul 96. (7") *(bent 016)* **DANDELION MILK SUMMER. / SNOWING IN MOUNT FLORIDA**
(cd-ep) *(bent 015cd)* **E.K.O.K. EP** – – ('A'side) / Sunless / Ambulance / Afterhours – Intuition told me.
Nov 96. (7"ep) *(bent 018)* **VENUS BONDING EP**
– Venus bonding / This arseholes been burned too many times before / Blue sky yesterday.

— **STEVEN SEVEN** – guitar; repl. LIRONEX who formed MONGOOSE

Mar 97. (7"m) *(bent 020)* **TARTAN ENVY. / RUDE AWAKENING / ALLEGRO**
Apr 97. (cd) *(MA 26 – MACD 44712)* **JET STREAMS**
– This arsehole's been burned too many times before / Casanova killer / Ambulance / Give him a great big kiss / Wasted in Carluke / Blue sky yesterday / Sunless / Tartan envy (luv'n haight version) / Allegro / Come as you are / Rude awakening / Everywhere that you go / Pink drone / Afterhours – Intuition told me. (above issued on 'Marina')
Jul 97. (7") *(bent 024)* **GIVE HIM A GREAT BIG KISS. /** (other track by Policecat)
Feb 98. (7") *(bent 032)* **PUNK DRONE. /** (other track by Scientific Support Dept.)
Jul 98. (7"pink) *(ER 193)* **SOMEWHERE IN CHINA. / X-BOYFRIEND**
(above issued on Spanish-based 'Elefant' through 'Creeping Bent')
Mar 99. (cd-ep) *(bent 038cd)* **SOMEWHERE IN THE WORLD / TOP OF THE WORLD / PINK WORLD**
Jul 99. (cd) *(bent 044cd)* **MINK RIOTS**
– Most days / All the sun / If you were me / Lashing out / World upside-down / Waterfall / 1 every 2 / Picture / Once before / Some kind of friend / Heal me. (re-iss. Dec00; same)
Aug 99. (7") *(bent 042)* **YOU'RE FUNNY 'BOUT THAT, AREN'T YOU. /** (other track by Nectarine No.9)
Nov 99. (7") *(bent 048)* **4 EXCITED PEOPLE. /** (other track by Vic Godard)

MONGOOSE

IAN BEVERIDGE + GRAHAM LIRONI – instruments, synths, etc

Oct 99. (7") *(bent 049)* **SANITISE ME. /** (other track by Element)
Sep 00. (7"; as MONGOOSE Vs SCIENTIFIC SUPPORT DEPT.) *(bent 057)* **SUBVERT NORMALITY. / GOOSE GREEN (extract)**

Realler / not iss.

Jul 01. (cd) **LO-LEVEL** — Danish
(above was scheduled by 'Creeping Bent' late '99; bent 052)

SECRET SHINE

Formed: Bristol, England ... 1990 by ex-DREAMSCAPE man JAMIE GINGELL and former PANDA POPS guitarist SCOTT PURNELL. After impressing arty-indie label 'Sarah', the duo – then monikered AMELIA'S DREAM – issued a couple of singles before changing to SECRET SHINE and recruiting PAUL VOWLES, NICK DYTE and PURNELL's brother DEAN. The sparkling dreamy guitar pop of singles 'EPHEMERAL' and

SECRET SHINE (cont)

'LOVEBIRD' helped the group crack the indie Top 20, and with the inclusion of chanteuse KATHRYN SMITH, the group began work on their debut album. 'UNTOUCHED' (1993) was to be their first and last LP, as VOWLES departed soon after its release and DYTE took over on bass, with the addition of new sticks-man TIME MORRIS. After good reviews and a healthy amount of interest, The 'GREATER THAN GOD' EP was perhaps just a boast too far and SECRET SHINE disbanded in 1994.

Album rating: UNTOUCHED mini (*5)

JAMIE GINGELL – vocals / SCOTT PURNELL – guitar (ex-PANDA POPS)

		A Turntable Friend	not iss.
Oct 91.	(7") *(TURN 07)* **UNBEARABLE. / MY ONLY FRIEND**		
		Sarah	not iss.
Oct 91.	(7"m) *(SARAH 053)* **AFTER YEARS. / SNOWFALL SORROWC / GREY SKIES**		-
——	added **DEAN PURNELL** – guitar / **PAUL VOWLES** – bass / **NICK DYTE** – drums		
Mar 92.	(7"m) *(SARAH 061)* **EPHEMERAL. / HONEY SWEET / SECRET SHINE**		-
——	added **KATHRYN SMITH** – vocals		
Mar 93.	(7") *(SARAH 071)* **LOVEBLIND. / WAY TOO HIGH** (cd-s+=) *(SARAH 071CD)* – Honey sweet.		-
Apr 93.	(lp/cd) *(SARAH 615/+CD)* **UNTOUCHED** – Suck me down / Temporal / Spellbound / So close I come / Into the ether / Toward the sky / Underworld / Sun warmed water.		-
——	**TIM MORRIS** – drums; repl. VOWLES (DYTE was now bass man)		
Apr 94.	(10"ep/cd-ep) *(SARAH 089)* **GREATER THAN GOD** – Liquid indigo / Ignite the air / Deep thinker / Elizabeth's April / Last words.		-
		Spoiler	not iss.
1995.	(7") *(SPOIL SSS01)* **WASTED AWAY**	-	- w-drawn

—— disbanded after above' the PURNELL's + GINGELL formed other bands

SECRET SQUARE (see under ⇒ APPLES IN STEREO)

SECRET STARS (see under ⇒ KARATE)

SECTOR 27 (see under ⇒ ROBINSON, Tom; 70's section)

SEE SEE RIDER

Formed: based- East Kilbride, Scotland ... late 1989 by LEWIS CHAMBERLAIN, alongside STEPHEN SANDS and female co-vocalist MAY ROCK MARSHALL. Naming themselves after a LEADBELLY song (widely covered by a variety of acts), they secured a support slot to both LLOYD COLE and The JESUS & MARY CHAIN, the latter's DOUGLAS HART augmenting the group on their inventive (shiny chrome indie-rock with darkly sexual lyrical undertones) debut recordings. SEE SEE RIDER snatched their break when BIRDLAND manager, Wayne Morris, signed them to his 'Lazy' imprint, recommending drummer PETE TWEEDIE (who had split from another band of his, The PRIMITIVES) in the process. Early in 1990, the band released their first 45/EP, 'SHE SINGS ALONE', although a series of very rock'n'roll, almost "Spinal Tap"-esque accidents put the brake on their momentum. The most serious of these occurred when MAY came a cropper after travelling pillion on a motorbike, a case of No SEE SEE RIDER, at least as far as their fans were concerned, the subsequent delay holding up the release of a follow-up single, 'STOLEN HEART' (featuring The Rolling Stones' 'HAPPY' on the flip side), until Spring 1991. By this juncture, they had taken another passenger on board, namely ex-FELT man, PHIL KING. Although the band had signed to 'Elektra', their career skidded to a halt when TWEEDIE was involved in a bust-up on stage.

Album rating: never released any

LEWIS CHAMBERLAIN – vocals, bass / MAY ROCK MARSHALL – vocals, slide guitar / STEPHEN SANDS – guitar / PETE TWEEDIE – drums (ex-PRIMITIVES)

		Lazy	not iss.
Mar 90.	(12"ep/cd-ep) *(LAZY 18 T/CD)* **SHE SINGS ALONE / SNOWFALL. / SLIP SO LOW / SEE SEE**		-
——	added **PHIL KING** – guitar (ex-SERVANTS, ex-FELT)		
May 91.	(7") *(LAZY 27)* **STOLEN HEART. / HAPPY** (12"+=/cd-s+=) *(LAZY 27 T/CD)* – Rosey singer.		-

—— Aug'91, TWEEDIE departed after a bust-up on stage
—— they disbanded when KING joined LUSH the following year

SENSURROUND (see under ⇒ MEMBRANES; in 80's section)

SENTRIDOH (see under ⇒ SEBADOH)

SERPICO (see under ⇒ MEGA CITY FOUR; in 80's section)

SET FIRE TO FLAMES (see under ⇒ GODSPEED YOU BLACK EMPEROR!)

7% SOLUTION

Formed: Austin, Texas, USA ... 1992 by guitarist, bass player and lead vocalist REESE BERMAN. SCOTT SASSER played drums on the band's full-length eponymous debut, which was a tape-only affair. Somewhat anomalous on the Austin music scene, which tends towards more traditional fare, this psychafreakadelica electrospace rock band took both fans and critics alike by storm. Named after a classic Sherlock Holmes mystery which sees the defective detective wrapped up in a cocaine addiction cocoon, the outfit laid down a tempo template for their close encounters of the sonic kind: swirling, dense, moody, esoteric cuts which explored alien internal vistas. Joined by guitarist JAMES ADKISSON on their 'SUGAR' (1993) and 'LULLABY' (1994) EP's, the band rested on their critically acclaimed laurels until they crashed back from outer space to dazzle the world with their intricate, dense, exotic LP 'ALL ABOUT SATELLITES AND SPACESHIPS' (1996). Favourably compared to their lysergic progenitors PINK FLOYD and SPACEMEN 3, these aural astronauts became (inner) spacemen 4 when they added JULIAN CAPPS to their lineup to play bass, guitar and sing back-up vocals on the 'GABRIEL'S WALTZ' (1999) set. This album was inspired by melancholic poet ANNE SEXTON and was an idiosyncratic fusion of looped dialogue, wistful wind chimes, precise drum chops, unexpectedly hard floating guitar licks and sweet bitter poetic lyrics and vocals which gracefully slowdanced the listener into sound areas most bands would never even suspect existed.

Album rating: ALL ABOUT SATELLITES AND SPACESHIPS (*6) / GABRIEL'S WALTZ (*7)

REESE BEEMAN – vocals, guitar, bass / SCOTT SASSER – drums / JAMES ADKISSON – guitar

		X-ray	X-ray
1993.	(7"ep) **SUGAR. / HALO**	-	
1996.	(cd) *<xr-001>* **ALL ABOUT SATELLITES AND SPACESHIPS** – All about satellites and spaceships / Built on sand / Revolve / Happy? / The air bends sunlight / Your kingdom, your world / The road and the common / Snuff gold and gold tilings / Blindshore / Lost / The sky suspended.	-	
——	added **JULIAN CAPPS** – bass		
Apr 98.	(7") *<(AHA 003)>* **LULLABY. / OH YEAH** (above issued on 'Hidden Agenda')		
Feb 99.	(cd) *(51233) <xr-002>* **GABRIEL'S WALTZ** – Dear Anne / The end of faith / Carousel / Bruise / Threshold / Lullaby / The innocents / Dust and ashes / Gabriel's waltz / Oh yeah.		

—— split after above

SEVEN STOREY MOUNTAIN

Formed: Arizona, USA ... 1995 by LANCE LAMMERS, JESSE EVERHART and THOMAS LANSER. SEVEN STOREY MOUNTAIN first committed their post-punk power-pop to record in 1996 via a self-titled debut EP, and followed it in 1997 with their debut album, the typically hardcore 'LEPER ETHICS' (both on the 'Art Monk' label). Their next recording was 2000's seven-track mini-album, 'BASED ON A TRUE STORY', which was recorded around late 1997 (and released on 'Deep Elm'). Their patently aggressive post-punk sound still managed to offer contagious beats and moments of melody (like on 'WASTE OF TIME'), which led to comparisons with bands like the FOO FIGHTERS and FUGAZI. By the time of the release of first full-length LP in 2002, EVERHART and LANSER had been replaced by DAVE NORWOOD (bass) and CHAD KINNEY (drums), while the band altered their moniker to SEVEN STOREY. 'DIVIDED BY ZERO' continued SS's sonic assault, although maintaining an accessibility with an indie-pop edge.

Album rating: LEPER ETHICS (*5) / BASED ON A TRUE STORY mini (*5) / DIVIDED BY ZERO (*6)

LANCE LAMMERS – vocals, guitar / JESSE EVERHART – bass, vocals / THOMAS LANSER – drums

		Art Monk	Art Monk
Mar 96.	(7"ep) *<AMC 13>* **SEVEN STOREY MOUNTAIN EP** – Your lips / Tip / Sleep. (cd-ep+=) *<AMC 13CD>* – Turned to sand.	-	
Apr 97.	(cd/lp) *<AMC 16 CD/LP>* **LEPER ETHICS** – Lasttime / Tarnish / If I . . . / Fall / Downtime / Loss of hours / Soon forget / Self-pity / Farewell gift / Enough to starve / Backslide / No promise. *(UK-iss.Apr98; same as US)*	-	
		Deep Elm	Deep Elm
Mar 00.	(m-cd) *<(DER 379CD)>* **BASED ON A TRUE STORY** – So soon / Reality time / Waste of time / Where were you / Politician / Known to lie / Unrest.		
——	**DAVE NORWOOD** – bass; repl. EVERHART		
——	**CHAD KINNEY** – drums; repl. LANSER		
Feb 02.	(cd; as SEVEN STOREY) *<(DER 404)>* **DIVIDED BY ZERO** – Instr. 1 / Unknown satellite / Flavor war / Enough already / Second Rome / Halfway / No return address / Dress rehearsal / Erase / Paper and quill.		

7 YEAR BITCH

Formed: Seattle, Washington, USA ... 1991 by SELENE VIGIL, STEFANIE SARGENT, ELIZABETH DAVIS and VALERIE AGNEW. Not short of selling points, this all-female Seattle act generated an immediate buzz with their debut single, 'LORNA', the girls' righteously browned off, distortion-drenched racket earning them fawning column inches and a PEARL JAM support slot. Even the shock death of SARGENT wasn't enough to halt the band's momentum and after a period of uncertainty they decided to carry on with new guitarist ROICI DUNNE. In the meantime the ladies released a compilation – dedicated to SARGENT – of their work to date, 'SICK 'EM', on the local 'C/Z' label; despite shying away from any real connection with the militant Riot Grrrl movement, titles like 'DEAD MEN DON'T RAPE' spelled out in black and white exactly where this band was coming from. A debut album proper, 'VIVA ZAPATA!' finally arrived in 1994, its title and subject matter no doubt influenced by sterling politico-rap tourmates RAGE AGAINST THE MACHINE. With encouraging reviews and a further round of high profile touring it was only a matter of time before the girls moved on up to a major, 'Atlantic' clinching their signatures and releasing follow-up set, 'GATO NEGRO' in 1996. • **Covered:** IT'S TOO LATE (Jim Carroll) / GO! (Tones On Tails).

Album rating: SICK 'EM (*6) / VIVA ZAPATA! (*6) / GATA NEGRO (*6)

SELENE VIGIL – guitar / **STEFANIE SARGENT** – guitar / **ELIZABETH DAVIS** – bass / **VALERIE AGNEW** – drums

		not iss.	Rathouse
1991.	(7"m) **LORNA. / NO FUCKIN' WAR / YOU SMELL LONELY** <re-iss. 1992 on 'C/Z'; >	-	

		10 Past 12	10 Past 12
Jul 92.	(10"pic-ep) <(DUMP 009)> **ANTIDISESTABLISHMENTARIANISM EP** – 8 ball / No fuckin' war / You smell / Lonely / Dead men don't rape.		

		C/Z	C/Z
Oct 92.	(pic-lp/cd) <(CZ 048/+CD)> **SICK 'EM** – Chow down / Tired of nothing / Knot / In lust you trust / Sink / Gun. (cd+=) – Lorna / You smell lonely / No fucking war / Dead men don't rape / 8-ball deluxe / Can we laugh now?		

— tragically, STEFANIE died a month before above release date
— she was repl. by **ROICI DUNNE** – guitar
— 7 YEAR BITCH split a single with THATCHER ON ACID, 'Can We Laugh Now'

| May 95. | (cd) <CZ 078> **VIVA ZAPATA!** – The scratch / Hip like junk / M.I.A. / Derailed / Cats meow / Rock a bye / It's too late / Damn good and well / Kiss my ass goodbye / Icy blue / Get lit. | - | |

		not iss.	Man's Ruin
Jan 96.	(7") <MR 026> **MISS UNDERSTOOD. / GO!**	-	

		not iss.	Atlantic
Mar 96.	(cd/c/lp) <82873-2/-4/-1> **GATA NEGRO** – The history of my future / Crying shame / Disillusion / Deep in the heart / The midst / 24,900 miles per hour / Whoopie cat / Miss understood / Sore subject / Rest my head / 2nd hand / Jack.	-	

— (mid '96) **LISA FAYE BEATTY** – guitar (ex-MUDWIMMIN) repl. DUNNE
— disbanded in 1997

SEXUAL MILKSHAKE (see under ⇒ BLAST OFF COUNTRY STYLE)

S.F. SEALS (see under ⇒ MANNING, Barbara; in 80's section)

SHADOWLAND (see under ⇒ FURTHER)

SHAMPOO

Formed: Plumstead, London, England ... 1994 by schoolgirls JACQUI BLAKE and CARRIE ASKEW. The lucky recipients of an NME Single Of The Week award for their debut, 'BLISTERS & BRUISES' (on BOB STANLEY's – ST. ETIENNE – fame 'Icerink' label), SHAMPOO emerged kicking and screaming into the music world as a kind of inverse glam-punk Barbie doll version of Riot Grrl femme-pop; a follow-up, 'BOUFFANT HEADBUTT' was delivered later in the year. All pigtails, lollipops, vacant lyrics and Smash Hits teen appeal, SHAMPOO were perhaps the most annoying girly band of the pre-SPICE GIRLS era, their self-conscious "attitude" only making the whole package even more unbearable. The truly awful 'TROUBLE' was the first result of their deal with E.M.I. subsidiary, 'Food', while 'VIVA LA MEGABABES' really was as insufferable as its title suggests. A whole album's worth of similar guff, 'WE ARE SHAMPOO', was foisted upon an unsuspecting music world in 1994 although by the time they'd got round to releasing a follow-up, 'GIRL POWER' (1996), that self same slogan was being put to far more successful use by The SPICE GIRLS.

Album rating: WE ARE SHAMPOO (*4) / GIRL POWER (*3)

CARRIE ASKEW (b. 1975) – vocals / **JACQUI BLAKE** (b. 1977) – vocals / with **CON FITZPATRICK** – producer, co-writer

		Icerink	not iss.
May 93.	(7"pink-ep) (DAVO 6) **BLISTERS AND BRUISES. / PAYDIRT / I LOVE LITTLE PUSSY**		-
Nov 93.	(12"purple/cd-s) (DAV 10 12/CD) **BOUFFANT HEADBUTT. / EXCELLENT / MONSTER**		-

		Food	Capitol
Jul 94.	(c-s/7"pink) (TC+/FOOD 51) **TROUBLE. / SCHOOL IS BORING** (cd-s+=) (CDFOOD 51) – We don't care.	11	-
Oct 94.	(c-s/7") (TC+/FOOD 54) <58444> **VIVA LA MEGABABES. / HOUSE OF LOVE** (cd-s+=) (CDFOOD 54) – Girls 'round here.	27	Sep95
Oct 94.	(cd/c/lp) (FOOD CD/TC/LP 12) <35084> **WE ARE SHAMPOO** – Trouble / Delicious / Viva la megababes / Dirty old love song / Skinny white thing / Glimmer globe / Shiny black taxi cab / Me hostage / Game boy / House of love / Shampoo you / Saddo. (re-iss. Aug95; same)	45	
Feb 95.	(7"pic-d/c-s) (FOODPD/TCFOOD 58) <58467> **DELICIOUS. / KINKY KEN** (cd-s) (CDFOOD 58) – ('A'side) / Trouble / Outta control / Trouble (mix).	21	Sep95

		Food	Atlantic
Jul 95.	(c-s) (TCFOOD 66) <87145> **TROUBLE / SHINY BLACK TAXI CAB** (cd-s+=) (CDFOOD 66) – Excellent.	36	May95
Jul 96.	(c-s/7") (TC+/FOOD 76) **GIRL POWER. / DON'T CALL ME BABE** (cd-s+=) (CDFOOD 76) – Cars.	25	
Jul 96.	(cd/c/lp) (FOOD 16 CD/TC/LP) **GIRL POWER** – Girl power / News flash / I know what boys like / Bare knuckle girl / Zap pow / War paint / You love it / Boys are us / We play dumb / I'm gonna scream / Don't call me babe.		-
Sep 96.	(7") (FOOD 83) **I KNOW WHAT BOYS LIKE. / BOUFFANT HEADBUTT** (cd-s+=) (CDFOOD 83) – Blisters and bruises / I love little pussy. (cd-s) (CDFOODS 83) – ('A'side) / ('A'mix) / Top of the pops.	42	-

— the girls split from the scene after above

SHAMS (see under ⇒ RUN ON)

SHAPIROS (see under ⇒ BLACK TAMBOURINE)

SHARKBOY

Formed: Brighton, England ... early 90's by AVY, ADRIAN OXAAL, ALAN STIRNER and JESSICA FISCHER. Bringing to mind the likes of MY BLOODY VALENTINE, MAZZY STAR, DRUGSTORE and even BLONDIE, SHARKBOY specialise in moody echo and atmosphere, AVY's breathy vocals draped like an altar cloth over the slow burning musical backdrop. Noted indie label, 'Nude' (home to SUEDE) were quick to recognise their potential, 1994 seeing the release of well received debut album, 'MATINEE'. Personnel changes ensued as JESSICA bailed out, her replacements being not one member but three, GAVIN CHEYENE, DIL DAVIES and NICK WILSON. While the critics weren't so keen to praise follow-up set, 'THE VALENTINE TAPES' (1995), AVY had nevertheless come up with another compelling musical travelogue through rootsy noir and doomed romance, knob twiddling courtesy of Phil Wright and Jem Noble (responsible for GALLON DRUNK's 'From The Heart Of Town' and 'In The Long Still Night' respectively) and violin flourishes from TINDERSTICKS man DICKON HINCHCLIFFE. • **Covers:** SOME MISUNDERSTANDING (Gene Clark) / DIAMONDS ARE FOREVER (John Barry) / WISHING ON A STAR (Candi Staton) / JE T'AIME (Serge Gainbourg).

Album rating: MATINEE (*6) / THE VALENTINE TAPES (*4)

AVY (b. Preston, England) – vocals / **ADRIAN OXAAL** (b. USA) – guitars, cello, keyboards, marimba, vocals / **ALAN STIRNER** – guitars, percussion / **JESSICA FISCHER** – bass, cello

		Nude	Tristar
Nov 93.	(12"ep/cd-ep) (NUD 7 T/CD) **CRYSTALINE. / GOLD WRAPPER / MARINVILLE 69**		-
Feb 94.	(12"ep/cd-ep) (NUD 8 T/CD) **RAZOR / BRIGHT THINGS LIE. / DEAR GILDA / SHOW ME NOW**		-
Apr 94.	(cd/c/lp) (NUDE CD/MC/LP 2) <66638> **MATINEE** – Sacramento child / My star / Forest fire / Razor / Don't walk run / Crystaline / Road / Yo yo / Sugar / Carrying some.		

— **GAVIN CHEYNE** – bass + **DIL DAVIES** – drums, percussion, marimba + **NICK WILSON** – keyboards, trumpet, percussion; repl. JESSICA

May 95.	(ltd-7") (NUD 14S) **BIG BLACK JAGUAR. / DIAMONDS ARE FOREVER**		-
Jun 95.	(ltd-7") (NUD 15S) **LITTLE LEOPARD. / WISHING ON A STAR**		-
Jun 95.	(ltd-7") (NUD 16S) **MY MAGNETIC SUSAN. / SOME MISUNDERSTANDING**		-
Jul 95.	(ltd-7") (NUD 17S) **TINY SEISMIC NIGHT. / JE T'AIME** (above releases were also under titles, 'THE VALENTINE SINGLES 1-4')		-
Sep 95.	(cd/c/lp) (NUDE CD/MC/LP 4) **THE VALENTINE TAPES** – Tiny seismic night / Big black jaguar / Take my hand / Same mother of pearl / From your eye / Blazer / Sugarmanshine / Dean / 3D angelshell / Teenage heart / Maxine.		-

— disbanded after above

SHED SEVEN

Formed: York, England ... late 1991 by RICK WITTER, PAUL BANKS, TOM GLADWIN and ALAN LEACH. Signing to 'Polydor' in 1994, the group were initially grouped in with the hopelessly contrived "new wave of new wave" scene alongside run-of-the-mill pseudo-punk revivalists like S*M*A*S*H and THESE ANIMAL MEN. Resisting the lure of the Big Smoke, the lads preferred to stay in their native York, their sound a more glam/mod retro pastiche lying somewhere between SUEDE and The

CHARLATANS. A debut single, 'MARK', had certain sections of the music press tipping them for big things and they finally assaulted the Top 30 later that summer with the 'DOLPHIN' and 'SPEAKEASY' singles. While SHED SEVEN's music was no great shakes really, the diminutive WITTER had a remarkable voice, somewhat akin to a sleazy liaison between BRETT ANDERSON and ADAM ANT (!?). They also had attitude in abundance, something which translated well in the live arena, SHED SEVEN becoming a regular attraction in the UK's sweatier venues. A debut album, 'CHANGE GIVER' (1994), wasn't exactly groundbreaking although it consolidated their limited appeal. Only a couple of unremarkable singles followed in the next year and a half, before the band returned with 'GETTING BETTER' in 1996, their biggest hit single to date. While the accompanying album, 'A MAXIMUM HIGH' (1996), drew some critical praise it ultimately failed to drag the band out of the indie second division ghetto. However, their albums were still reaching the Top 10 and singles such as 'THE HEROES' and 'DEVIL IN YOUR SHOES' weren't doing too band either; a stop-gap 'greatest hits' package, 'GOING FOR GOLD' (1999) followed the aforementioned trend. It couldn't last though and with all but the biggest guns of Britpop dead and buried by the turn of the decade, SHED SEVEN found themselves relegated to an indie label ('Artful') for 'TRUTH BE TOLD' (2001). The truth is that this was basically another average indie rock record, likely to cut some proverbial rug with diehard fans only. Recorded with new members FRASER SMITH and JOE JOHNSON (after BANKS had left to form The Rising), the album stalled at the fringes of the UK Top 40. • **Songwriters:** WITTER lyrics / group compositions. Covered JUMPING JACK FLASH (Rolling Stones) / THE JEAN GENIE (David Bowie). • **Trivia:** Said to have taken their group name, after it was revealed by ALAN the drummer that he lost his virginity in a shed aged only 7. (eh!)

Album rating: CHANGE GIVER (*6) / A MAXIMUM HIGH (*7) / LET IT RIDE (*5) / GOING FOR GOLD – THE GREATEST HITS compilation (*6) / TRUTH BE TOLD (*4)

RICK WITTER (b.1973) – vocals / **PAUL BANKS** (b.1973) – guitar / **TOM GLADWIN** (b.1973) – bass / **ALAN LEACH** (b.1970) – drums

		Polydor	Atlantic
Mar 94.	(7"green) *(YORK 1)* **MARK. / CASINO GIRL**	77	-
	(12"+/cd-s+=) *(YORK X/CD 1)* – Mobile 10.		
Jun 94.	(7"/c-s) *(YORK/YORCS 2)* **DOLPHIN. / IMMOBILITIES**	28	-
	(12"+/cd-s+=) *(YORK X/D 2)* – ('A'remix).		
Aug 94.	(7"/c-s) *(YORK/YORCS 3)* **SPEAKEASY. / AROUND YOUR HOUSE**	24	-
	(12"+/cd-s+=) *(YORKX/YORCD 3)* – Your guess is as good as mine / Dolphin.		
Sep 94.	(cd/c/lp) *(523 615-2/-4/-1) <4063>* **CHANGE GIVER**	16	-
	– Dirty soul / Speakeasy / Long time dead / Head and hands / Casino girl / Missing out / Dolphin / Stars in your eyes / Mark / Ocean pie / On an island with you.		
Nov 94.	(7"/c-s) *(YORK/YORCS 4)* **OCEAN PIE. / NEVER AGAIN**	33	-
	(12"+/cd-s+=) *(YORKX/YORCD 4)* – Sleepeasy / Sensitive.		
Apr 95.	(7"green/c-s) *(YORK/YORCS 5)* **WHERE HAVE YOU BEEN TONIGHT? / SWING MY WAVE**	23	-
	(cd-s+=) *(YORCD 5)* – This is my house.		

		Polydor	Polygram
Jan 96.	(7"/c-s) *(577 890-7/-4)* **GETTING BETTER. / ONLY DREAMING**	14	-
	(cd-s+=) *(577 890-2)* – Song seven.		
Mar 96.	(7"/c-s) *(576 215-7/-4)* **GOING FOR GOLD. / MAKING WAVES**	8	-
	(cd-s+=) *(576 215-2)* – Barracuda.		
Apr 96.	(cd/c/lp) *(<531 039-2/-4/-1>)* **A MAXIMUM HIGH**	8	
	– Getting better / Magic streets / Where have you been tonight? / Going for gold / On standby / Out by my side / Lies / This day was ours / Ladyman / Falling from the sky / Bully boy / Parallel lines. *(d-cd re-iss. Sep96; 533 416-2)* – (includes THE B-SIDES).		
May 96.	(7"ep/c-ep) *(576 596-7/-4)* **BULLY BOY / WHERE HAVE YOU BEEN TONIGHT? (live). / DOLPHIN (live) / SPEAKEASY (live)**	22	-
	(cd-ep) *(576 596-2)* – ('A'side) / Mark (live) / Ocean pie (live) / Getting better (live).		
Aug 96.	(7"/c-s) *(575 188-7/-4)* **ON STANDBY. / JUMPING JACK FLASH**	12	-
	(cd-s) *(575 273-2)* – Killing time.		
	(cd-s) *(575 188-2)* – ('A'side) / Long time dead (version) / Stepping on hearts.		
Nov 96.	(7"/c-s) *(575 929-7/-4)* **CHASING RAINBOWS. / IN COMMAND**	17	-
	(cd-s+=) *(575 928-2)* – The skin I'm in.		
Mar 98.	(7") *(569540-7)* **SHE LEFT ME ON FRIDAY. / BOTTOM UPWARDS**	11	-
	(cd-s+=) *(569541-2)* – Melpomene.		
	(cd-s) *(569543-2)* – ('A'side) / Mispent youth / You.		
May 98.	(7"/c-s) *(569916-7/-4)* **THE HEROES. / SLINKY LOVE THEME**	18	-
	(cd-s+=) *(569917-2)* – She left me on Friday (live).		
	(cd-s) *(569923-2)* – ('A'side) / She left me on Friday (live) / Forever (isn't such a long time) (live)(.		
Jun 98.	(cd/c/lp) *(557359-2/-4/-1)* **LET IT RIDE**	9	-
	– Return / Let it ride / The heroes / Halfway home / Devil in your shoes / She left me on Friday / Hole / Drink your love / Stand up and be counted / Chasing rainbows / Goodbye.		
Aug 98.	(7") *(567207-7)* **DEVIL IN YOUR SHOES. / DUMB SCENE**	37	-
	(cd-s+=) *(567207-2)* – Better late than never.		
	(cd-s) *(567205-2)* – ('A'side) / Happy now / Better late than never.		
	— now as **SHED 7**		
May 99.	(c-s) *(563874-4)* **DISCO DOWN / HANDS UP**	13	-
	(cd-s+=) *(563875-2)* – Your guess is as good as mine.		
	(cd-s) *(563877-2)* – ('A'side) / Another hole / Catapult.		
May 99.	(cd/c) *(547 442-2/553-4)* **GOING FOR GOLD – THE GREATEST HITS** (compilation)	7	-
	– Going for gold / Disco down / Getting better / Chasing rainbows / Speakeasy / She left me on Friday / On standby / Dolphin '99 / High hopes / Bully boy / Devil in your shoes / Where have you been tonight? / Ocean pie / Mark / The heroes. *(ltd d-cd; 547609-2)* – Disco down / Going for gold / The heroes / Missing out / Wired for sound / Eye in the sky / Jumping Jack Flash.		
	— **FRASER SMITH + JOE JOHNSON** – guitars, etc; repl. BANKS who formed The RISING		

		Artful	not iss.
Apr 01.	(7"/c-s) *(7/CS ARTFUL 35)* **CRY FOR HELP. / PATCHES**	30	-
	(cd-s+=) *(CDARTFUL 35)* – Working miracle.		
	(cd-s) *(CDXARTFUL 35)* – ('A'side) / Seeker / Sitting pretty.		
May 01.	(cd) *(ARTFULCD 38)* **TRUTH BE TOLD**	42	-
	– If the music don't move y'er / Eyes before / Cry for help / Thinking again / Be myself / Laughter lines / Feathers / Never felt so cold / To the wind / Love equals / Step inside your love.		
Nov 01.	(cd-s) *(CDARTFUL 37)* **STEP INSIDE YOUR LOVE / NO WAY / THE JEAN GENIE**		-

SHELLAC
(see under ⇒ BIG BLACK; see 80's section)

SHERMANS

Formed: Sweden ... late 1997 by MIKAEL MATSSON and TORBJORN THORSEN, following the disbanding of MATSSON's RED SLEEPING BEAUTY. Stateside label 'Blackbean & Placenta Tape Club' released their first recordings, 'THE SOUND OF THE SHERMANS' as a 7" single, and with the recruitment of bassist CHRISSTER NILSSON, they began performing live around Sweden. When THORSEN left to form AEROSPACE, INGELA KARLSSON was drafted in as their new vocalist. Their connections with Japanese label 'Quince' (from their RED SLEEPING BEAUTY days) proved useful when they proposed the release of a SHERMANS LP. Containing their early singles, compilation songs and new tracks, 'CASUAL' was released in Japan in 1999 (and also in the Philippines on 'Universal'). 'CASUAL' was the perfect introduction to The SHERMANS joyful, sprightly indie-pop. The same year, the band signed with 'Shelflife', who would provide distribution of their work in the US. Debut album, 'IN TECHNICOLOR', was released in America in spring 2000, and the following year the label released a re-issue of 'CASUAL' (with a few additional tracks). Also in 2001, 'Shelflife' and California's 'Sky Blue' together released the 'FALLING OUT OF LOVE' EP, which contained four new tracks. The EP title-track would soon reappear on The SHERMANS next LP, 'HAPPINESS IS TOY SHAPED', in October 2001.

Album rating: IN TECHNICOLOR (*5) / CASUAL compilation (*6) / HAPPINESS IS TOY SHAPED (*6)

TORBJORN THORSEN – vocals / **MIKAEL MATSSON** – guitar, piano, Moog + Farfisa organs, vocals (ex-RED SLEEPING BEAUTY)

		not iss.	Blackbean & Placenta
1998.	(7"ep) *<ACME 24>* **THE SOUND OF SHERMANS**	-	
	– The myth of being alone / Rush hour / Fling / Summer in your heart.		
	— **INGELA KARLSSON** – vocals; repl. THORSEN who formed AEROSPACE		

		not iss.	Shelflife
May 00.	(cd) *<LIFE 25>* **IN TECHNICOLOR**	-	
	– Practiced performance / Wrong day / Sunday morning / Dumbhead / Wasted moments / Finally April / Finding time / Crazy world / Water / Come December / Waiting for you.		
Apr 01.	(7"ep) *<FAN 013>* **HAPPY BEING LONELY**	-	
	– Happy being lonely / Best of friends / Loud and laughing / Are you near? (above issued on 'Fantastic')		
May 01.	(cd) *<LIFE 31>* **CASUAL** (compilation 1998-1999)	-	
	– The myth of being alone / Happy being lonely / My favorite cuppa / Loud and laughing / Springtime sunshine / Snowsong / Disneyland / Are you near? / Rush hour / Best of friends / Summer in your heart / My cue / Fling / Fly away / Ever after. *<cd+= not on Jap-version on 'Quince'>* – Leaving tracks / My animated world / Sun beach summer.		
	— added **CHRISTER NILSSON** – bass		
May 01.	(cd-ep) *<LIFE 34>* **FALLING OUT OF LOVE**	-	
	– Falling out of love / Shallow smile / Little Millie / Ladybug / My baby.		
Oct 01.	(cd) *<LIFE 35>* **HAPPINESS IS TOY SHAPED**	-	
	– Boy with bright eyes / Lousy judge of character / Adulthood for beginners / The umbrella song / Falling out of love / Sad kind of life / July in London / About you / Cindy Sherman / Explode / Deja vu on repeat / Catch me / What life's about / The last one.		

SHIMMER KIDS UNDERPOP ASSOCIATION

Formed: Santa Cruz, California, USA ... 1996 by ADAM DOBRER, DAVE DUNSTAN, LORELEI DAVID, JOSH BABCOCK, DAVE IBISTER and MIKE EVANS, the latter joining a year after their conception. As a psychedelic revivalist outfit, the group toured the West Coast alternative scene with their live set, which combined music and film reminiscent via the late sixties psych-out shows of bands like the GRATEFUL DEAD. Although they were more the late comers in the second generation of eccentric avant-garde acts – which centered around the Athens, Georgia-based, 'Elephant 6', label and musical collective – SKUA were not in fact part of this imprint. As well as performing with the added sonic boost of ROBIN WAGEMAN and JUSTIN WALSH, the group did a DIY cassette, in true indie fashion, on their label, 'Underpop'. Emboldened by the success of these, SKUA under their own steam, issued their debut LP proper, 'BURY MY HEART AT MAKEOUT POINT' (2000) which sold well aided by the help of indie imprint, 'Parasol'. A fine piece of intelligent and quirky songwriting, they unfortunately could not better this with their sophomore effort, 'THE NATURAL RIOT' (2002), which although it had its thoughts and heart in the right free-your-mind place, sounded all too derivative.

Album rating: BURY MY HEART AT MAKEOUT POINT (*7) / THE NATURAL RIOT (*5)

JOSH BABCOCK – vocals, guitar / **ADAM DOBRER** – bass / **DAVE ISBISTER** – piano / **DAVE DUNSTAN** – saxophone / **LORELEI DAVID** – theremin

				not iss.	own label
1996.	(ltd; cd-s)	<*none*>	**6 WAYS TIL SUNDAY**	-	
1997.	(ltd; cd-s)	<*none*>	**CARNE LEVARE**	-	

—— added **MIKE EVANS** – drums

1998.	(ltd; 7"ep)	<*none*>	**TRUE BELIEVER EP**	-	
1998.	(ltd; cd-s)	<*none*>	**CONSTANTE DOLORES DE LA CABEZA**	-	
1998.	(ltd; c-ep)	<*none*>	**THE KIDS ARE ALL FUCKED UP, VOL.1**	-	
1999.	(ltd; c-ep)	<*none*>	**THE KIDS ARE ALL FUCKED UP, VOL.2**	-	
1999.	(ltd; c-ep)	<*none*>	**THE KIDS ARE ALL FUCKED UP, VOL.3**	-	

				not iss.	Underpop
Nov 99.	(ltd; 7")	<*001*>	**STRANGE SIGNALS. / WHISTLE WHILE YOU WEEP**	-	
Aug 00.	(ltd; cd)	<*002*>	**BURY MY HEART AT MAKEOUT POINT**	-	

– Society of rockets / Ray and Carla take a vacation / Full color love affair / Bury my heart at Makeout Point / Hold him tightly, little insect / Sundowner / After the honeymoon / There's been a change in the electric age / The candidate / Last of the bright young men / Apples through the 9th key / Kiss them all goodbye / Over the wall at midnight.

| Jun 01. | (ltd; cd-ep) | <*003*> | **PRAIRIE PRAYERS** | - | |

– We're all chiefs and no Indians / The oscillator gang rides again / Left coast Neros / Country comforts / In the last days of the golden motor / The hangman's come-on / Georgia Green.

				Hidden Agenda	Hidden Agenda
Jul 02.	(cd)	<(*AHA 043CD*)>	**THE NATURAL RIOT**		

– Model kit / Like candy, like poison / Matadors in red / The getaway / Burning bridges / The soft police / Baby bankrobber / Tones in orbit / Another planet / Going in circles / The pilot and the gardener / Miss classified / The high season / October century / Se acabo, la fiesta.

SHINER

Formed: Kansas City, Missouri, USA . . . 1992 by ALLEN EPLEY, JEFF BROWN and SHAWN SHERRILL. Drummer BROWN had departed and been replaced by TIM DOW before the group secured a deal with the 'DeSoto' label. The group hit the ground running with their powerful debut, 'SPLAY', released in 1995. SHERRILL's unspectacular yet steady bass playing allowed DOW the space for his thunderous drumming which provided the perfect engine for EPLEY's raw melodic guitar playing and crisp vocals. There was no let up from the group on the 1997 follow-up, 'LULA DIVINIA'; however their SPINAL TAP-like carelessness for losing drummers meant that DOW did not feature on the 2000 release, 'STARLESS', and although replacement JASON GERRON was able enough, the record still suffered. The group that returned with the album, 'EGG' (2001), was almost unrecognisable both musically and in terms of personnel. EPLEY was the only surviving original member and was now joined by bass player PAUL MALINOWSKI, drummer JASON GERKEN and guitarist/keyboardist JOSH NEWTON. The music the group was now producing was tonally more expansive and altogether more impressive. Although the band had always produced quality, balls-out rock music, 'EGG', was a record of real substance and innovation.

Album rating: SPLAY (*5) / LULA DIVINIA (*4) / STARLESS (*5) / THE EGG (*7)

ALLEN EPLEY – vocals, guitar / **SHAWN SHERRILL** – bass / **TIM DOW** – drums; repl. JEFF BROWN

				not iss.	DeSoto
1993.	(7")	<*SH 10*>	**BROOKS. / RELEASED**	-	
1995.	(cd/lp)	<*SH 12*>	**SPLAY**	-	

– Heshe / Brooks / Complaint / Bended knee / Fetch a switch / Slipknot / Martyr / Released / Frown / Pearle.

| 1994. | (7") split w/ **MOLLY McGUIRE** | |
(above & below on 'Hit It!')
| 1995. | (7") **FLOODWATER. / COWBOY** | - | |

—— **PAUL MALINOWSKI** – bass (ex-SEASON TO RISK) repl. SHERRILL

| Mar 97. | (cd) <*SH 18*> **LULA DIVINIA** | | |

– The situationist / Chris size shoes / My life as a housewife / Lula / Third gear scratch / Sideways / Pinned / Shelflife / Jim's lament / Four feet of fence / Cake. *((UK-iss.Nov02 +=; same as US)* – Sleep it off / Two black eyes.

			not iss.	Sub Pop
1998.	(7") <*SP 403*> **SLEEP IT OFF. / HALF EMPTY**	-	

—— added **JOSH NEWTON** – guitar, keyboards

			DeSoto	DeSoto
May 00.	(7") <(*SH 33*)> **SEMPER FI. / SAILOR'S FATE**	Owned & Operated	Owned & Operated
Jun 00.	(cd) <(*OO 012CD*)> **STARLESS**		

– Spinning / Giant's chair / Kevin is gone / Unglued / The arrangement / Glass jaw test / Semper fi / Lazy eye / Rearranged / Too much of not enough / Starless.

			DeSoto	DeSoto
Oct 01.	(cd) <(*SH 41*)> **THE EGG**		

– The truth about cows / Surgery / Play dead / The top of the world / The egg / Andalusia / Bells and whistles / The simple truth / Spook the herd / Pills / Stoned.

—— disbanded in 2002

SHINING

Formed: London, England . . . 2001 by SIMON JONES and SIMON TONG, both unhappy chappies due to the breakup of THE VERVE. This outfit might've been a tad different had JONES earlier hooked up with former SEAHORSES and STONE ROSES legend JOHN SQUIRE when both were seeking co-writers. However, their brief liaison took a back seat when the latter opted for a solo career, leaving JONES to enlist the aforementioned TONG, vocalist DUNCAN BAXTER and drummer MARK HEANEY; guitarist DAN McBEAN was subsequently added. Borrowing their moniker from the Stephen King novel, The SHINING made headway via three well-received dreamy-pop singles and a Top 75 album, 'TRUE SKIES' (2002),

Album rating: TRUE SKIES (*6)

DUNCAN BAXTER – vocals / **SIMON TONG** – guitar (ex-THE VERVE) / **DAN MacBEAN** – guitar / **SIMON JONES** – bass (ex-THE VERVE) / **MARK HEANEY** – drums

				Zuma	Epic
Apr 02.	(10")	(*ZUMA 001*)	**QUICKSILVER. / DUM DUM**		
Jun 02.	(10")	(*ZUMA 002*)	**I WONDER HOW. / I GOT A FEELING**	58	
	(cd-s+=)	(*ZUMAD 002*) – Prove love.		
Sep 02.	(10")	(*ZUMA 003*)	**YOUNG AGAIN. / SOMEONE ELSE'S PLANET**	52	
	(cd-s+=)	(*ZUMAD 003B*) – Quicksilver (U.S. version) – video.		
	(cd-s)	(*ZUMAD 003A*) – ('A'side) / Waterfalls / Headspin.		
Sep 02.	(cd/lp)	(*ZUMA CD/LP 1*)	**TRUE SKIES**	73	Feb03

– Quicksilver / Young again / Find a reason / Crest of an ocean / Show you the way / I wonder how / I am the one / Danger / Find your way home / What you see / Until the end / Quicksilver (outro).

SHINS

Formed: Albuquerque, New Mexico, USA . . . 1997 by JAMES MERCER and JESSE SANDOVAL. The SHINS were originally an offshoot from MERCER and SANDOVAL's other band, FLAKE MUSIC. Originally called FLAKE when they formed in 1992, the group also featured MARTY CRANDALL and NEAL LANGFORD. FLAKE MUSIC released a number of singles, the first of which, 'MIEKE', appeared in 1993 as well as a couple of EP's. However, it would not be until 1999 before a full album was realised; 'WHEN YOU LAND HERE, IT'S TIME TO RETURN' was worth the wait and although flawed, showed great promise. It was a joyous collection of shimmering, indie-pop full of delicious melodies and a bittersweet, feel good vibe clearly inspired by the BEACH BOYS. Not content with having FLAKE MUSIC as their only musical outlet, MERCER and SANDOVAL recruited DAVE HERNANDEZ and RON SKRAESK and began performing as The SHINS. By the time the band released their debut album in 2001, HERNANDEZ and SKRAESK had already departed and MARTY CRANDALL was back in the fold. The album 'OH, INVERTED WORLD' fulfilled all that was promised by the trio's earlier incarnation. The trippy, retro sound of old was still there but the band had clearly grown in confidence and ability. The EP 'KNOW YOUR ONION' arrived the following year and featured a number of live tracks, proving the band to be every bit as competent on stage as they are in the studio.

Album rating: Flake Music: WHEN YOU LAND HERE, IT'S TIME TO RETURN mini (*8) / Shins: OH, INVERTED WORLD (*6)

FLAKE MUSIC

JAMES MERCER – vocals, guitar / **MARTY CRANDALL** – keyboards / **NEAL LANGFORD** – bass / **JESSIE SANDOVAL** – drums

				not iss.	Resin
1993.	(7"; as FLAKE)	**MIEKE. /**		-	

			not iss.	Science Project
1995.	(10"ep; as FLAKE) **SPORK**	-	
	– Nuevo / (+3).		

			not iss.	Headhunter
1997.	(7"ep; as FLAKE) **MUSIC**	-	
	– Sue defender / (+3).		

			not iss.	Omnibus
1997.	(7"; as FLAKE) <*OMNI 008*> **DELUCA. / (other by HENRY'S DRESS)**	-	
Jul 99.	(m-cd/m-lp) <*OMNI 016*> **WHEN YOU LAND HERE, IT'S TIME TO RETURN**	-	

– Spanway hits / Blast valve / Roziere / Structo / Deluca / Mieke / The shins / Vantage. *(3 untitled bonus cd tracks)*

SHINS

—— were basically the same line-up; **MERCER + SANDOVAL** brought in **CRANDALL + LANGFORD** to repl. **DAVE HERNANDEZ + RON SKRASEK**

			Omnibus	Omnibus
Aug 99.	(7"ep) <*OMNI 017*> **NATURE BEARS A VACUUM**	-	

– These bold city girls / Eating styes from elephants' eyes / We built a raft and we floated / My seventh rib.

| Jul 00. | (7") <(*OMNI 022*)> **WHEN I GOOSE STEP. / THE GLOATING SUN** | | |

SHINS (cont) — THE GREAT INDIE DISCOGRAPHY — The 1990s

	Sub Pop	Sub Pop
Mar 01. (7") <(SP 548)> **NEW SLANG. / SPHAGNUM ESPLANADE**	□	□
Jul 01. (cd) <(SPCD 550)> **OH, INVERTED WORLD**	□	□ Jun01

– Caring is creepy / One by one all day / Weird divide / Know your onion! / Girl inform me / New slang / The celibate life / Girl on the wing / Your algebra / Pressed in a book / The past and pending. (cd re-iss. Jan02; same) <(lp-iss.Apr02 on 'Omnibus'; OMNI 28)>

Apr 02. (cd-ep) <(SPCD 591)> **KNOW YOUR ONION** □ □ Jun02
– Know your onion / My seventh rib (live) / New slang (live) / Sphagnum esplanade.

SHIPPING NEWS (see under ⇒ RACHEL'S)

SHITBIRDS (see under ⇒ MARCH, April)

SHRIMP BOAT (see under ⇒ SEA AND CAKE)

SHUDDER TO THINK

Formed: Washington DC, USA ... late 1986 by STUART HILL, CHRIS MATTHEWS, MIKE RUSSELL and vocalist, CRAIG WEDREN. Hardly a typical 'Dischord' act, SHUDDER TO THINK began their career with a privately circulated demo, 'CURSE, SPELLS, VOODOO, MOOSES', in '89, before signing to IAN MacKAYE's operation and releasing 'TEN-SPOT' as their debut album proper at the turn of the decade. Eschewing a straight forward hardcore sound for a more complex, awkwardly melodic approach, the quartet attracted a cult following with albums such as 'FUNERAL AT THE MOVIES' (1991) and 'GET YOUR GOAT' (1992). Personnel ructions resulted in MATTHEWS and RUSSELL departing and being replaced by NATHAN LARSON and ADAM WADE respectively, although things took a turn for the better as 'Epic' saw potential in the band's diverse musical talents. While 'PONY EXPRESS RECORD' (1994) might've made few concessions to their new major label status, the long-awaited '50,000 B.C.' was a far more immediate affair, putting an alternative twist on everything from rootsy rock to harmony-flowing power-pop/rock. A year on, SHUDDER TO THINK made a radical move into soundtrack work, no doubt alienating part of their loyal fanbase with the atmospheric score to 'HIGH ART' and retro-pastiche of 'FIRST LOVE, LAST RITES', the latter featuring guest vocal turns by the likes of BILLY CORGAN, JEFF BUCKLEY, LIZ PHAIR, ROBIN ZANDER and JOHN DOE. With LARSON bailing out and WEDREN opting for an unfruitful solo career, STT were no more.

Album rating: TEN-SPOT (*5) / FUNERAL AT THE MOVIES mini (*5) / GET YOUR GOAT (*6) / PONY EXPRESS RECORD (*7) / 50,000 B.C. (*6) / LIVE (*5) / HIGH ART (*6) / FIRST LOVE, LAST RITES (*6)

CRAIG WEDREN – vocals, guitar / **CHRIS MATTHEWS** – guitar / **STUART HILL** – bass / **MIKE RUSSELL** – drums

	not iss.	Sammich
Mar 88. (7"ep) **IT WAS ARSON**	□	□

– Questionable / Abysmal yellow popcorn wall / Ro / It was arson.

	not iss.	Trout
May 89. (cd) **CURSE, SPELLS, VOODOO, MOOSES**	□	□

	Dischord	Dischord
Jan 90. (7") **CATCH OF THE DAY. / (split w/ UNREST)**	□	□
Jun 90. (lp/c) <(DISCHORD 46/+C)> **TEN-SPOT**	□	□

– Heaven here / Jade-dust eyes / Rags / About three dreams / Speak / Corner of my eye / Summertime train / On the rain / Vacation brain / Yes / Tony told me.

Aug 90. (7") **MEDUSA SEVEN** □ □
– Vacation brain / Boys don't mind noise.
(above issued on 'Hoss 45')

Jun 91. (m-lp/m-c) <(DISCHORD 54/+C)> **FUNERAL AT THE MOVIES** □ □
– Chocolate / Lies about the sky / Day ditty / Crosstown traffic / Red house / Funeral at the movies / I blew away / Ride that sexy horse. (cd-iss. Jul91 & Nov02 +=; DISCHORD 55) – TEN-SPOT

May 92. (lp/c/cd) <(DIS 67/+C/CD)> **GET YOUR GOAT** □ □
– Love catastrophe / Shake your halo down / White page / Goat / Pebbles / Baby drop / The hair pillow / She wears he-harem / Rain-covered cat / Funny.

— **ADAM WADE** – drums; repl. RUSSELL
— **NATHAN LARSON** – guitar; repl. MATTHEWS

	Your Choice	Your Choice
Nov 92. (7") (DIS 76V) **HIT LIQUOR. / NO ROOM 9, KENTUCKY**	□	□

Aug 94. (cd) <(YCLS 021)> **LIVE**	□	□ May94

– White page / Birthday song / Baby drop / Pebbles / Rain covered cat / I grow cold / Rag / Day ditty / Chocolate / So into you / Shake your halo down.

	Big Cat	Epic
Aug 94. (12"ep/cd-ep) (ABB 72 T/CD) <66415> **HIT LIQUOR EP**	□	□

– Hit liquor / Kissi Penny / Red house / Heaven here / Full body anchor.

Sep 94. (cd) (ABB 65CD) <57855> **PONY EXPRESS RECORD** □ □
– Hit liquor / Gang of $ / 9 fingers on you / Sweet year old / Earthquakes come home / Kissi Penny / X-French Tee shirt / No Rm. 9, Kentucky / Chakka / Own me / So into you / Trackstar / Full body anchor. (re-iss. Aug95; same)

	Big Cat	Sub Pop
Jun 95. (7") (ABB 81SCD) <SP 283> **X-FRENCH TEE SHIRT. / SHAKE YOUR HALO DOWN**	□	□

	Epic	Epic
May 97. (cd/c) (486938-2/-4) **50,000 BC**	□ Nov94	

– Call of the playground / Red house / Beauty strike / The saddest day of my life / The man who rolls / All eyes are different / Kissesmack of past action / Resident wine / She's a skull / Survival / You're gonna look fine / Love / Hop on one foot.

Jun 98. (cd) <79735> **HIGH ART** (soundtrack) □ □
– Opening / Dominoes / Cocoa butter / Mom's Mercedes / Photographic ecstasy / Gavial / Noetony / Ph balanced (for a lady) / Battle soaked / That's fat / She gives tone / Last lines / She might be waking up / Fools / End frame.

— <above issued on 'Velvel'>

Aug 98. (cd,c) <69029> **FIRST LOVE, LAST RITES** □ □
– I want someone badly / Erecting a movie star / Diamonds, sparks and all / When I was born, I was bored / Apalachian lullaby / Airfield dream / Automatic soup / Lonesome dove / Speed of love / Day ditty / The wedding is over / Jelly on the table / Just really wanna see you / I want someone badly / Final dream.

— WEDREN and LARSON were now solo artists; the former self-financed 'BLACK MARKET BABY' EP in 2002

SICBAY (see under ⇒ DAZZLING KILLMEN)

SIDI BOU SAID

Formed: Greenwich & Lewisham, South London, England ... 1990 by songwriters CLAIRE LEMMON and LOU HOWTON, alongside GAYL HARRISON and MELANIE WOODS. Named, apparently, after a town in Tunisia, this all-female outfit are definitely not your run-of-the-mill girly band. Consistently compared – much to their collective annoyance – with THROWING MUSES, there's no getting away from the similarities in terms of songwriting complexity, vocal interplay, general quirkiness and decidedly (but subtle) femininist lyrical slant. Nevertheless, SIDI BOU SAID are readily identifiable as being from this side of the pond even if the bulk of their influences – VIOLENT FEMMES, PATTI SMITH, even bluesy doomsters MASTERS OF REALITY – originate across the Atlantic. Signed to the 'Ultimate' label, the band's career got off to a shaky start with the 'BROOOCH' (1993) album which met with a lukewarm critical reception. More promising was 1995's 'BODIES' set and the attendant 'ODE TO DRINK' single, adding the influence of LED ZEPPELIN and – in the carefully arranged strings – The BEATLES to the above list. Despite their confident talk of a female revolution in rock, the group failed to make the leap to mainstream acceptance, 1996's 'OBSESSIVE' album merely underlining the fact that their introspective sound and lyrical perspective is perhaps a bit too challenging for the average (male) indie fan.

Album rating: BROOOCH (*4) / BODIES (*5) / OBSESSIVE (*5)

CLAIRE LEMMON – vocals, guitar / **LOU HOWTON** – vocals, guitar / **GAYL HARRISON** – bass / **MELANIE WOODS** – drums

	Ultimate	not iss.
Feb 93. (7") (TOPP 14) **TWILIGHT EYES. / BUZZ**	□	□

(cd-s+=) (TOPP 14CD) – Faster.

May 93. (7") (TOPP 17) **THREE SIDES. / ROMP** □ □
(12"+=/cd-s+=) (TOPP 17 T/CD) – Wild.

Oct 93. (lp) (TOPPLP 55) **BROOOCH** □ □
– Urge / My cat is my bridesmaid / Handstand / Goblin market / Thing / Glassmouth / Taste / Terrible secret / Mary Mary / Dracula / Three sides / Fallow. (re-iss. Jul94 cd/c/lp; TOPP CD/MC/LP 5)

Apr 94. (7") (TOPP 23) **THING. / LUKEWARM** □ □
(cd-s+=) (TOPP 23CD) – All these things.

— now without HOWTON

Mar 95. (10"m) (TOPP 31K) **WORMEE. / (+2)** □ □
May 95. (cd/c/lp) (TOPP CD/MC/LP 34) **BODIES** □ □
– Hyde / Practise walking / Wormee / Magnet / Bovary / Big yellow taxidermist / Ode to drink / Brittle / Lefthanded / Slitty gap / Nurse / Sicky vomit.

Jul 95. (7") (TOPP 37) **ODE TO DRINK. / FASTER (acoustic)** □ □
(cd-s+=) (TOPP 37CD) – Blood / ('A'mix).

Sep 96. (7") (TOPP 50) **FUNNYBODY. / FISHY** □ □
(cd-s+=) (TOPP 50CD) – ('A'mix).

Jan 97. (cd-s) (TOPP 57CD) **LIKE YOU / OBSESSIVE** □ □
(cd-s+=) (TOPP 57CDX) – Obsessive (new skin & long long long mixes).

Apr 97. (cd/lp) (TOPP CD/LP 53) **OBSESSIVE** □ □
– Obsessive / Like you / Funny body / Zazie / Minotaur / Harold and Maude / 20,000 horses / Seams undone / Rat king / Bella / Bridge song.

— they split after above

SIGHTS

Formed: Detroit, Michigan, USA ... early 1998 by EDDIE BARANEK and MARK LEAHEY; they later added EUGENE STROBE. Jamming since their early teens, BARANEK – who also played with fellow Detroit'ers KO AND THE KNOCKOUTS and The COME ONS – and the group were signed in 1999 to 'Spector', for whom they recorded their debut album 'ARE YOU GREEN?'. The label folded, and LA indie-darlings 'Fall Of Rome' re-issued the album in late 2001. A strange blend between British Punk and MC5 garage rock, The SIGHTS were later signed into Jim Diamond's 'Ghetto Recorders' to work on their second album proper, a move which saw them replace drummer STROBE (at this point, playing with the Witches) with DAVE SHETTLER. The group also added organist NATE CAVALIERI and delivered their sophomore set 'GOT WHAT WE WANT' (2002). A brilliantly structured garage album whose success was slightly hindered by the departure of LEAHEY two months after the album's release. Fellow Detroit veteran, MATT HATCH, later filled the position. • **Covered:** HEY GIRL (Small Faces).

Album rating: ARE YOU GREEN? (*6) / GOT WHAT WE WANT (*8)

EDDIE BARANEK – vocals, guitar / **MARK LEAHEY** – bass / **EUGENE STROBE** – drums; repl. DAVE KNEPP

	not iss.	Spectator
2000. (cd) <000> **ARE YOU GREEN?**	□	□

– All night long stay / Want is you / Sorry / I can't stand you / F# / Not one to beg / She's not the one / Finish whatcha started / Talk to you / That ain't right little girl / The hott seat / Hey girl / Are you green? <(UK+re-iss. Feb02 on 'Fall Of Rome' lp/cd; FOR 1002/+CD)>

SIGHTS (cont)

	Fall Of Rome	Fall Of Rome
Feb 02. (d7"ep; red/yellow) <(FOR 1004)> **THE SIGHTS EP**		

– If that's what you want / People / Say say / Nobody.

— added **NATE CAVALIERI** – organ

— **DAVE SHETTLER** – drums (ex-MOODS FOR MODERNS) repl. STROBE who hoined the WITCHES and the ALPHABET)

	Sweet Nothing	Fall Of Rome
Nov 02. (cd/lp) (SNCD/SNLP 022) <FOR 1007> **GOT WHAT WE WANT**		Jun02

– Don't want you back / Be like normal / Sorry revisited / It'd be nice (to have you around) / One and only / Got what I want / Last chance / Everyone's a poet / Sick and tired / Sweet little woman / Nobody.

— (August 2002) **MATT HATCH** – bass; repl. MARK

SIGUR ROS

Formed: Reykjavik, Iceland . . . early 1994 by guitarist and squeaky vocalist JON POR BIRGISSON and GEORG HOLM, later recruiting ORRI PALL DYRASON and keyboardist KJARTAN SVEINSSON. The original 3-piece line-up (consisting of BIRGISSON, HOLM and then drummer AGUST) entered a downtrodden studio and managed to record one track before their shoestring budget expired. The song was sent to 'Smekkleyse' records and was subsequently included on a compilation featuring various other artists signed to the label. The first set 'VON' (1997) was quickly delivered, pointing the road to success for these experimental debutants. At their peak, keyboard and piano player SVEINSSON was added, who arguably became a vehicle for the group's stark, uplifting and eerie sound. From 'VON BRIGOI' (the group's second set, translated: Recycle Bin), 'LEIT AF LIFI' was released as a single in summer 1998. The band had underestimated their widespread acclaim when the single rocketed to the Icelandic No.1 and stayed a further 8 weeks at the top spot! But with the good came the bad: the departure of lifelong friend and original drummer AGUST. This major setback almost put the band's future into jeopardy when they returned to the studio and came to near collapse during the recording sessions of 'AGAETIS BYRJUN' (1999). DYRASON was added to the line-up following a spectacular radio broadcasted show in the Icelandic Opera House. At the same time, SIGUR ROS had struck a deal with London based 'Fat Cat', who issued the 'SVEFN-G-ENGLAR' EP in 1999. In Iceland 'AGAETIS BYRJUN' was doing the same thing to crowds as RADIOHEAD's 'Ok Computer' did when it was released on these shores. Which, in all circumstances, is not hard to see why, since SR had (practically) the same ideals as RADIOHEAD did. Cresendos of earth quaking guitars (that didn't really sound like guitars at all), soft piano and BIRGISSON's uniquely high falsetto vocals that reminisced of the COCTEAU TWINS' 'Baby talk'. Not surprising then that multi-instrumentalists GODSPEED YOU BLACK EMPEROR! invited the 'ROS to join them on tour. The result: The greatest show on earth, quite possibly! After selling more albums in their native Iceland than a certain Ms. SPEARS (this is true!) and regretfully donating 'SVEFN-G-ENGLAR' to Tom Cruise's 'Vanilla Sky' OST, SIGUR ROS engrossed themselves in the mimbars of northern Iceland and recorded the wistful '()' in 2002. Yes, that's right – '()'. Just as The Beatles' eponymous album was christened 'The White Album' by fans, SIGUR ROS's effort became known as 'THE UNTITLED ALBUM', as no information was provided in the album sleeve and all tracks were, well, untitled. If it all sounded a bit pretentious, that's because it was, with BIRGISSON bordering on the line of childishness and pure musical poetry; '()' was an album that could not be ignored. From its grandiose opening, through to the set's middle section and coda, this was really music you could eat. Some of it sounded like GODSPEED, although slowed down to 25rpm, and BIRGISSON's promise of singing in English was missing. However, musically the LP was an elegant and mysterious journey heavily featuring the quartet's scrawled signature of falsetto vocals, eerie organ drones, sparse arrangements, plus a newly added string section to boot. Marvellous!

Album rating: VON (*6) / VON BRIGOI remixes (*5) / AGAETIS BYRJUN (*8) / () (*7)

JON POR BIRGISSON – vocals, guitar / **GEORG HOLM** – bass / **AGUST** – drums

	Smekkleysa	not iss.
1997. (cd) (SM 67CD) **VON**	-	- Iceland

– Sigur Ros / Dogun / Hun joro . . . / Leit ao lifi / Myrkur / 18 sekundur fyrir solaruppras / Hafsol / Verold ny og oo / Von / Mistur / Syndir Guos (opinberun frelsarans) / Rukrym.

— added **KJARTAN SVEINSSON** – keyboards

1998. (cd) (SM 67CDR) **VON BRIGOI / RECYCLE BIN** (remixes/recycled) – - Iceland
– Syndir Guos (by BIOGEN) / Syndir Guos (by MUM) / Leit af lifi (by PLASTMIC) / Myrkur (by ILA) / Myrkur (by DIRTY-BIX) / 180 sekundur fyrir solaruppras (by CURVER) / Hun Joro (by HASSEBRAEOUR) / Von (by GUS GUS) / Leit af lifi (by SIGUR ROS).

— **ORRI PALL DYRASON** – drums; repl. AGUST

	Fat Cat	Play It Again Sam
Oct 99. (12"ep) (12FAT 036) **SVEFN-G-ENGLAR EP**		

– Sven-g-englar / Vioar vel til lofttarasa / Verold ny og oo.
(cd-ep) (CDFAT 036) – (first two tracks) / Nyjalagio (live) / Syndir Guos (live). (re-iss. Feb00 & Apr01; same)

Mar 00. (12"ep/cd-ep) (12/CD FAT 039) **NY BATTERY** | | - |
– Rafmagnio buio / Ny battery / Bium bium bambalo / Danarfregnir og Joraofarir.

Aug 00. (cd/lp) (FAT CD/LP 11) <1> **AGAETIS BYRJUN** | 52 | |
– Into / Svefn-g-englar / Staralfur / Flugufrelsarinn / Ny batteri / Hjartao hamast (bamm bamm bamm) / Vioar vel til lofttarasa / Olsen Olsen / Agaetis byrjun / Avalon. (above issued 1999 in Iceland; SM 79CD)

— in early 2001, SIGOR ROS collaborated with HILMAR ORN HILMARSSON on the soundtrack of 'ANGELS OF THE UNIVERSE' for 'Krunk'

	Fat Cat	M.C.A.
Oct 02. (cd/lp) (FAT CD/LP 22) <AA88 113091-2> **()**	49	

– Untitled (part 1) / Untitled (part 2) / Untitled (part 3) / Untitled (part 4) / Untitled (part 5) / Untitled (part 6) / Untitled (part 7) / Untitled (part 8).

SILKWORM

Formed: Missoula, Montana, USA . . . 1987 out of EIN HEIT by co-songwriters/vocalists, JOEL PHELPS, ANDREW COHEN and TIM MIDGETT; BEN KOOSTRA was a member in the late 80's. Three years on, the trio flitted to Seattle, Washington, recruiting drummer MICHAEL DAHLQUIST in the process. A number of singles and a debut LP, 'L'AJRE' (1992), found their way to the public, although it took until early '94 for their sophomore long-player, 'IN THE WEST', to hit the more discerning indie shops. The quartet laid bare their influences (such as the MINUTEMEN and PAVEMENT) on the table, although by the time of follow-up, 'LIBERTINE' (1994), producer STEVE ALBINI (ex-BIG BLACK) had moved their hardcore ideals a little further. Following its release however, PHELPS decided to go it alone, leaving the remaining trio (who subsequently signed to 'Matador') to deliver two further sets, the ALBINI-produced 'FIREWATER' (1996) and 'DEVELOPER' (1997). In 1998, the indie-rock outfit squeezed out two albums, the double compilation, 'EVEN A BLIND CHICKEN FINDS A KERNAL OF CORN NOW AND THEN', and 'BLUEBLOOD', the latter their debut for 'Touch & Go'. Coasting into the new millennium, the SILKWORM crew gave ever more pronounced hints of the sounds and artists which had influenced them in their youth and beyond, the likes of the 'LIFESTYLE' (2000) – featuring NICKY HOPKINS on piano – and 'ITALIAN PLATINUM' (2002) albums nevertheless recycling the reference points with stringency, imagination and economy. • **Covered:** THE CHAIN (Fleetwood Mac) / IN THE BLEAK MIDWINTER + THE LITTLE DRUMMER BOY (trad) / etc.

Album rating: L'AJRE (*5) / IN THE WEST (*6) / LIBERTINE (*7) / FIREWATER (*6) / DEVELOPER (*6) / EVEN A BLIND CHICKEN FINDS A KERNAL OF CORN NOW AND THEN compilation (*6) / BLUEBLOOD (*7) / LIFESTYLE (*6) / ITALIAN PLATINUM (*5)

TIM MIDGETT – vocals, bass / **JOEL PHELPS** – vocals, guitar / **ANDREW COHEN** – vocals, guitar / **BEN KOOSTRA** – drums

	not iss.	own label
1988. (c) <none> **ADVANTAGE**	-	
1989. (c) <none> **GIRL HARBRR**	-	
1989. (c-ep) <none> **GIRL HARBRR OUT-TAKES**	-	

— (1990) **MICHAEL DAHLQUIST** – drums; repl. KOOSTRA

	not iss.	Punchdrunk
1991. (7") <PD 01> **SLIPSTREAM. / INSIDE OUTSIDE**	-	
	not iss.	Temporary Freedom
Oct 92. (ltd-lp) <TEMPO 1> **L'AJRE**	-	

– St. Patrick's day / Homoactivity / Scrawl / Three beatings / Slow burn / Little sister / Scruffy / Shithead / Pearl Harbor.

Nov 92. (ltd-7") <TEMPO 2> **THE CHAIN. / OUR SECRET**	-	
	not iss.	Blatant
1993. (7") <BLAT 007> **VIOLET. / AROUND A LIGHT**	-	
	not iss.	Stampede
1993. (7"ep) <001> **. . .HIS ABSENCE IS A BLESSING**	-	

– Motel blues / Scruffy tumor / Eye window / Pearl Harbor / No revolution.

	not iss.	Rockamundo
1993. (7") <DERBY 003> **INTO THE WOODS. / INCANDUCE CALIFORNIA**	-	
	not iss.	C/Z
Dec 93. (7") <CZ 073> **IN THE BLEAK MIDWINTER. / THE LITTLE DRUMMER BOY (ENGINE KID)**	-	
Jan 94. (cd) <CZ 071> **IN THE WEST**	-	

– Garden city blues / Dust my broom / Into the woods / Punch drunk five / Raised by tigers / Enough is enough / Parsons / Incanduce / Dremate / Pilot.

	not iss.	El Recordo
Aug 94. (cd) <ELR 01> **LIBERTINE**	-	

– There is a party in Warsaw tonight / Grotto of miracles / Cotton girl / Yen + Janet forever / Oh how we laughed / The cigarette lighters / Couldn't you wait? / A tunnel / Written on the wind / Wild in my day / Bloody eyes.

— now without PHELPS who went solo; as JOEL R.L. PHELPS

	Matador	Matador
Sep 95. (7") <(OLE 154-7)> **COULDN'T YOU WAIT? / THE GRAND TOUR**		
(cd-ep) <(OLE 154-2)> **THE MARCO COLLINS SESSIONS** – ('A'side) / Scruffy tutor / Cotton girl / Raised by tigers.		
Feb 96. (cd/d-lp) <(OLE 158-2/-1)> **FIREWATER**		

– Nerves / Drink / Wet firecracker / Slow hands / Cannibal cannibal / Tarnished angel / Quicksand / Ticket Tulane / Swings / Severance pay / The lure of beauty / Miracle mile / Drag the river / Killing my ass / Caricature of a joke / Don't make plans this Friday.

| Nov 96. (7") <(OLE 226-7)> **I NEVER MET A MAN I DIDN'T LIKE. / YOU AIN'T GOING NOWHERE / BLUE PANIC** | | |
| Dec 96. (7") <mpg 010> **QUICKSAND. / ON THE ROAD, ONE MORE TIME** | - | |

(above issued on 'My Pal God')

| Apr 97. (cd/lp) <(OLE 220-2/-1)> **DEVELOPER** | | |

– Give me some skin / Never met a man I didn't like / The city glows / Developer / The Devil is beating his wife / Ice Station Zebra / Waiting on a train / Sheep wait for wolf / Goodnight Mr. Maugham / It's too bad . . .

SILKWORM (cont)

Feb 98. (d-cd) <(OLE 259-2)> **EVEN A BLIND CHICKEN FINDS A KERNAL OF CORN NOW AND THEN** (compilation 1990-1994)
– Slipstream / Little sister / Scruffy / St. Patrick's day / Homoactivity / Scrawl / Three beatings / Slow burn / Our secret / The chain / Inside outside / Shithead / Slipstream / Scruffy tumor / No revolution / Eye window / Pearl Harbor / Motel blues / Violet / Around a light / In the bleak midwinter / Incanduce California / Insider / Hangman / The smoochy life.

                                                                              not iss. *Moneyshot*

May 98. (7"m) <8/98> **THE OTHER SIDE (S.I.T.L.). / I MUST PIANNER / I MUST PREPARE**

                                    Touch & Go *Touch & Go*

Jul 98. (cd/lp) <(TG 191 CD/LP)> **BLUEBLOOD**
– Eff / I must prepare (tablecloth tint) / Said it too late / Redeye / Empty / Elevator shaft / Beyond / Repair / Tonight we're meat / Ritz dance / Pearly gates / Clean'd me out.

─── added guest **BRETT GROSSMAN** – keyboards

Sep 00. (lp/cd) <(TG 209/+CD)> **LIFESTYLE**   *Aug00*
– Contempt / Slave wages / Treat the new guy right / Plain / Roots / Yr web / That's entertainment / Raging bull / Around the outline / Dead air / Ooh la la / The bones.

                                    12XU *Touch & Go*

Jun 02. (cd/lp) (011-2/-1) <TG 229CD> **ITALIAN PLATINUM**
– (I hope U) Don't survive / The third / The old you / Is she a sign / The brain / Bourbon beard / LR72 / White lightning / Dirty air / Young / Moving / The ram / A cockfight of feelings.

                                  not iss. *Three Lobed*

2002. (cd-ep; by TIM MIDGETT) **IT GOES LIKE THIS EP**
– As long / Portable life / Bar ice / Young / Time of the season / Something hyper.

SILVER APPLES

Formed: New York City, New York, USA ... 1967 by songwriters DANNY TAYLOR and SIMEON COXE III. A strange couple, who combined vocals with electronics and drums, they signed to 'Kapp' records for a mildly successful eponymous debut; it reached the US Top 200 lists. 'CONTACT', in 1969, was their final fling, although this is now regarded as a near-forgotten classic. The record experimented with sci-fi synths and mystical hippydom, although not sacrificing melody. Various 80's/90's outfits (i.e. SPACEMEN 3, LAIKA, WINDY & CARL) unearthed their dog-eared SILVER APPLES records, unleashing their own versions of 'A POX ON YOU', etc. Inevitably, SIMEON and a new recruit XIAN HAWKINS re-formed the duo in '96, initially only to release a one-off single, 'FRACTAL FLOW'. However, US and European tours followed soon afterwards and a string of comeback albums including 'BEACON' and 'DECATUR' (both 1998 and with drummer MICHAEL LERNER), a joint effort ('A LAKE OF TEARDROPS') with followers SPECTRUM and that long-lost third set from the SIMEON/TAYLOR days, 'THE GARDEN'. Just when things looked rosy once again, SIMEON was seriously injured in a car crash on the 1st of November, 1998. Spinal complications and a broken neck have left him badly paralysed.

Album rating: SILVER APPLES (*7) / CONTACT (*8) / BEACON (*6) / DECATUR (*6) / SILVER APPLES compilation (*7) / THE GARDEN posthumous (*5)

DANNY TAYLOR – vocals, percussion, drums / **SIMEON COXE III** (aka "The Simeon") – vocals, banjo / with poetry by **STANLEY WARREN**

                                  not iss. *Kapp*

Jul 68. (lp) <KS 3562> **SILVER APPLES**
– Oscillations / Dancing gods / Dust / Program / Velvet cave / Whirly-bird / Misty mountain / Lovefingers / Seagreen serenades. (UK-iss.Jun97; same) (cd-iss. Sep97 on 'Whirlybird'; WR 101)

Feb 69. (lp) <KS 3584> **CONTACT**
– You and I / Water / Ruby / Gypsy love / You're not foolin' me / I have known love / A pox on you / Confusion / Fantasies. (cd-iss. Sep97 on 'Whirlybird'; WR 102)

─── split and virtually disappeared from the scene for over 25 years

─── SIMEON recruited new member **XIAN HAWKINS** – keyboards

                                  Enraptured *Enraptured*

Dec 96. (7") <(RAPT45 07)> **FRACTAL FLOW. / LOVEFINGERS**

─── added **MICHAEL LERNER** – drums

                                  Whirlybird *Whirlybird*

Jan 98. (cd) <(WR 103CD)> **BEACON**
– I have known love / Together / Lovelights / You and I / Hocus pocus / Cosmic string / Ancient path / The dance / The gift / Daisy / Misty mountain. <(lp-iss.Aug98; WR 103LP)>

Mar 98. (cd) <(WR 106CD)> **DECATUR** (one track)
Sep 98. (cd) <(WR 107CD)> **BEACON REMIXED** (remixes)
– The gift / You and I / Strawberry lotus focus / String / Borrowed time / Armistice mix / Big machines / One time / Misty mountain / I have known love.

– compilations, etc. –

Jun 98. (cd) M.C.A.; <(MCD 11680)> **SILVER APPLES** (first 2 albums)
Aug 98. (cd) Whirlybird; <(WR 109CD)> **THE GARDEN**
– I don't care what people say / Tabouli noodle / Walkin' / Cannonball noodle / John Hardy / Cockroach noodle / The owl / Swamp noodle / Mustang Sally / Anasazi noodle / Again / Starlight noodle / Mad man blues / Fire ant noodle. <(lp-iss.Sep98; WR 109LP)>

SILVERFISH

Formed: London, England ... 1988 by ANDREW 'FUZZ' DUPREY, who enlisted the help of CHRIS POWFORTH and STUART WATSON to create SIVERFISH in its earliest incarnation. Subsequently installing wild Scotswoman, LESLEY RANKINE as vocalist, the band began gigging around their local Camden stomping ground. With the support of John Peel and a couple of 'Wiiija' EP's under their belt (the eponymous 'SILVERFISH' and the quaintly titled 'TOTAL FUCKING ASSHOLE'), the group released their debut album, 'FAT AXL' early in 1991, its title a reference to a journalistic comment comparing RANKINE to an overweight AXL ROSE (of GUNS N' ROSES fame). Though the group had been pigeonholed in the extremely dubious 'Camden Lurch' scene along with the likes of TH' FAITH HEALERS, SILVERFISH were clearly in a league of their own as a cursory listen to the album would testify. Over a chainsaw barrage of blues-ish guitar noise, RANKINE howled her way from originals like the self-explanatory 'SHIT OUT OF LUCK' to a sound trashing of GRANDMASTER FLASH's classic 'WHITE LINES'. Picked up by 'Creation', SILVERFISH released the brilliantly titled 'FUCKIN' DRIVIN' OR WHAT ... EP' later that summer to coincide with their triumphant Reading Festival appearance, 'BIG BAD BABY PIG SQUEAL's clarion call of 'HIPS, LIPS, TITS, POWER..' making a SILVERFISH t-shirt de rigeur. An American tour and a JIM THIRLWELL-produced Top 75 follow-up album, 'ORGAN FAN' (1992), ensued, although RANKINE (now living in New Orleans) subsequently left to form her own outfit, RUBY, alongside co-writer MARK WALK. An album, 'SALT PETER', surfaced in late '95, with RANKINE making a brooding, memorable appearance on JOOLS HOLLAND's 'Later..'. • **Songwriters:** Most by RANKINE-DUPREY or group, except ROCK ON (David Essex). • **Trivia:** Their song, 'DOLLY PARTON', contained the thigh-slapping lyrics 'Jolene, Jolene, oh f . . . off'.

Album rating: FAT AXL (*6) / ORGAN FAN (*7) / COCKEYE compilation (*6)

ANDREW 'FUZZ' DUPREY (b.14 Jun'63, Kent, England) – guitar / **LESLEY RANKINE** (b.11 Apr'65, Edinburgh, Scotland) – vocals / **CHRIS POWFORTH** (b.30 May'64, Middlesex, England) – bass / **STUART WATSON** (b.10 Nov'62, Northamptonshire, England) – drums

                                  Wiiija *Touch & Go*

Jul 89. (12"ep) (WIIIJIT 4) **SILVERFISH EP**
– Weird shit / Don't fuck / Dolly Parton / On the motorway. (re-iss. Feb93 as 'DOLLY PARTON EP'; same)

Feb 90. (7"ep/12"ep) (WIJ/12WIJ 5) **TOTAL FUCKING ASSHOLE. / DIE / DRILLER**

Jan 91. (lp/c/cd) (WIJ 6/+C/CD) <TG 67/+C/CD> **FAT AXL**
– Pink and lively / Fat painted carcass / Harry Butcher / Shit out of luck / White lines / Two marines / Spoon / Baby baby baby / Ich bin eih– / Schifttek trauser. (re-iss. Feb93 on 'Southern' cd/c/lp; 18502-2/-4/-1)

                                  Creation *Chaos-CBS*

Aug 91. (12"ep)(cd-ep) (CRE 113T)(CRESCD 113) **FUCKIN' DRIVIN' OR WHAT . . . E.P.**
– Big bad baby pig squeal / Puppy truck / Texas tea.

─── In Nov 91, LESLEY SILVERFISH was credited on 'Clawfist' collaboration with The ROCKINGBIRDS:- 'Your Good Girl's Gonna Go Bad'.

Mar 92. (12"ep)(cd-ep) (CRE 118T)(CRESCD 118) **SILVERFISH WITH SCRAMBLED EGGS**
– Crazy / Jimmy / Vitriola / Jenny.

Jun 92. (cd/lp)(c) (CRE CD/LP 118)(CCRE 118) <53316> **ORGAN FAN** *65*
– This bug / Mary Brown / Suckin' gas / Petal / Fuckin' strange way to get attention / Big bad baby pig squeal / Elvis leg / Dechainee / Scrub me mama with that boogie beat / Rock on / Joos. (lp w/free 7")

Mar 93. (7") (CRE 138) **DAMN FINE WOMAN. / SUCKING GAS**
(12"ep)(cd-ep) **DAMN FINE EP** (CRE 138T)(CRESCD 138) – ('A'side) / Scrub me mama / Petal / F.S.W.T.G.A.

Jul 93. (cd-s) <74923> **CRAZY**

─── disbanded later in '93; LESLEY formed electronica act RUBY

– compilations, others, etc. –

Aug 90. (lp/c/cd) Touch & Go; (<TGLP 56/+C/CD>) **COCKEYE**
– Dolly Parton / On the motorway / Weird shit / Don't fuck / One silver dollar / T.F.A. / Die / Driller.

SILVER JEWS

Formed: Virginia, USA ... 1990 by DAVID BERMAN, co-writer of songs by ROYAL TRUX and PAVEMENT, in fact the latter outfit provided the back-up (STEPHEN MALKMUS and BOB NASTANOVICH) on 1992's SILVER JEWS' debut release, the 'DIME MAP OF THE REEF' EP. After a long-awaited second EP/mini-set in '93, they finally came up with their first long-player, 'STARLITE WALKER' (1994). Released on the 'Drag City' ('Domino' in the UK) label, the album's off-beat alt-country stylings bore at least a spiritual comparison with the likes of PALACE and SMOG although BERMAN's cryptic lyrics and dry, LOU REED-esque vocal delivery distinguished The SILVER JEWS as backporch pioneers in their own right. With a cult fanbase already established through the PAVEMENT connection, the acclaimed follow-up set was feverishly anticipated in some quarters prior to its release in late '96. Critically acclaimed, the record featured some of BERMAN's most affecting compositions to date, not least the brilliant 'HOW TO RENT A ROOM', equal parts offhand cynicism and pained revelation. More please! was the cry and band supplied yet another masterful work with 1998's 'AMERICAN WATER'. Alongside STEVE MALKMUS (Pavement) and new recruits, MIKE FELLOWS, TIM BARNES and CHRIS STROFFOLINO, the album floated through tracks such as 'RANDOM RULES' and 'NIGHT SOCIETY'. BERMAN wasn't to return until 2001; CASSIE MARRETT having replaced MALKMUS. The brilliant and underrated 'BRIGHT FLIGHT' album contained the eerie country-tingled ballads 'TRANSYLVANIA BLUES', 'FRIDAY NIGHT FEVER' and the highlight 'TIME WILL BREAK THE WORLD'.

Album rating: ARIZONA RECORD mini (*6) / STARLITE WALKER (*7) / THE NATURAL BRIDGE (*7) / AMERICAN WATER (*7) / BRIGHT FLIGHT (*6)

DAVID BERMAN – vocals, guitar / with **STEPHEN MALKMUS** – guitar, vocals (of PAVEMENT) / **BOB NASTANOVICH** – drums (of PAVEMENT)

                                                      Domino   Drag City

May 92. (7"ep) <DC 18> **DIME MAP OF THE REEF**
– Canada / The walnut falcon / September 1999 / SVM F.T. TROOPS / THE unchained melody.

Jul 93. (m-cd) <DC 28> **ARIZONA RECORD**
– Secret knowledge of backroads / I love the rights / Jackson nightz / The war in apartment 1812 / West S / You can't trust it to remain / The wild palms / Welcome to the house of the bats / Bar scene from Star Wars.

Nov 93. (7"; as SILVER JEWS & NICO) split w/ **NEW RADIANT STORM KING**
– The sabellion rebellion / Old New York / (+ others by above).
(above issued on 'Chunk' records)

Oct 94. (cd/lp) (WIG CD/LP 15) <DC 55> **STARLITE WALKER**
– Introduction II / Trains across the sea / The moon is number 18 / Advice to the graduate / Tide to the oceans / Pan American blues / New Orleans / Country diary of a subway conductor / Living waters / Rebel Jew / Silver pageant.

— BERMAN retained MALKMUS + NASTANOVICH plus members of NEW RADIANT STORM KING:- **PEYTON PINKERTON** + **MATT HUNTER** plus **MICHAEL DEMING** – keyboards / **RIAN MURPHY** – producer, etc.

Oct 96. (cd/lp) (WIG CD/LP 28) <DC 101> **THE NATURAL BRIDGE**
– How to rent a room / Pet politics / Black and brown blues / Ballad of Reverend war character / The right to remain silent / Dallas / Inside the golden days of missing you / Albemarle station / The frontier index / Pretty eyes.

— BERMAN + MALKMUS + **MIKE FELLOWS** – bass / **CHRIS STROFFOLINO** – piano / **TIM BARNES** – drums

Sep 98. (7") (RUG 77) **SEND IN THE CLOUDS. / SELF-IGNITION**
(cd-s+=) (RUG 77CD) – Walnut falcon (live in 1990).

Oct 98. (cd/c) (WIG CD/LP 56) <DC 149CD> **AMERICAN WATER**
– Random rules / Smith & Jones forever / Night society / Federal dust / People / Blue arrangements / We are real / Send in the clouds / Like like the the the death / Bukingham rabbit / Honk if you're lonely / The wild kindness.

— **CASSIE MARRETT** – vocals; repl. MALKMUS who was already solo

Nov 01. (cd/lp) (WIG CD/LP 106) <DC 215CD> **BRIGHT FLIGHT**
– Slow education / Room games and diamond rain / Time will break the world / I remember me / Horseleg swastikas / Transylvania blues / Let's not and say we did / Tennessee / Friday night fever / Death of an heir of sorrows.

                                                      Drag City   Drag City

Nov 01. (12"ep/cd-ep) <(DC 216/+CD)> **TENNESSEE / LONG LONG GONE / I'M GONNA LOVE THE HELL OUT OF YOU / TURN YOUR GUNS AROUND**

SILVER MT. ZION
(see under ⇒ GODSPEED YOU BLACK EMPEROR!)

SILVER SUN

Formed: Camden, London, England . . . 1995 as SUN..! by songwriter JAMES BROAD and RICHARD KANE who met at a record store. The pair soon found RICHARD SAYCE and PAUL SMITH, changing their name to SILVER SUN (a German metal band was already named SUN) and signing to 'Polydor' the same year. Fusing JELLYFISH, WEEZER and the anthemic rush of SLADE with sugar-coated indie glam-pop, these post-pubescent alt-rockers scored a minor hit with 'LAVA' towards the end of '96. Early the following year, they cracked the Top 50 with 'LAST DAY', entering a purple patch as they went on to notch up three further hits and a Top 30 eponymous album. However, a summery 1998 cover of Johnny Mathis's (!!!) 'TOO MUCH, TOO LITTLE, TOO LATE' was more attuned to a teeny-pop audience, no doubt putting off many of their more discerning fans and possibly accounting for the lowly chart position (No.74) afforded sophomore effort, 'NEO WAVE' (1998). • **Covered:** XANADU (Rush) / I'M A DICK (Muffs) / YOU MAKE ME REALISE (My Bloody Valentine).

Album rating: SILVER SUN (*6) / NEO WAVE (*5)

JAMES BROAD – vocals / **PAUL SMITH** – guitar, vocals / **RICHARD KANE** – bass, vocals / **RICHARD SAYCE** – drums, vocals

                                                      Polydor   Polygram

Jul 96. (7"ep/c-ep; as SUN..!) (575112-7/-4) **E.P.**
– There will never be another me / Thickshake / Captain / Top trumps.
(cd-ep+=) (575113-2) –

Oct 96. (7"/c-s) (575686-7/-4) **LAVA. / CHANGING**   54
(cd-s+=) (575687-2) – Streets are paved with tarmac.

Feb 97. (7"/c-s) (573242-7/-4) **LAST DAY. / TRICKLE DOWN**   48
(cd-s+=) (cd-s+=) (573243-2) – Gossip.

Apr 97. (7"pink) (573826-7) **GOLDEN SKIN. / SHE'LL DO**   32
(cd-s) (573829-2) – ('A'side) / 17 times / In nature.
(cd-s) (573827-2) – ('A'side) / Hight times / It couldn't be you.

May 97. (cd/c/lp) (537208-2/-4/-1) **SILVER SUN**   30
– Test / Golden skin / Dumb / Julia / Far out / Last day / Service / Yellow light / Lava / 2 digits / This 'n' that / Wonderful / Bad haircut / Nobody / Animals feets.

Jun 97. (7"/c-s) (571174-7/-4) **JULIA. / REASONS TO LIVE**   51
(cd-s+=) (571175-2) – American metal.
(cd-s) (571177-2) – ('A'side) / Angel eyes / Made for you.

Oct 97. (7") (571422-7) **LAVA. / PART OF YOUR LIFE**   35
(cd-s) (571422-2) – ('A'side) / Tokyo E Ikitai / Fifteen / ('A'acoustic).
(cd-s) (571424-2) – ('A'side) / Built in a day / Click / Last day of your life (demo).

Jun 98. (7"/c-s) (569968-7/-4) **TOO MUCH, TOO LITTLE, TOO LATE. / XANADU**   20
(cd-s+=) (569915-2) – You made me realise / I'm a dick.

Sep 98. (c-s) (<567452-4>) **I'LL SEE YOU AROUND / FOR YOUR ART**   26   Nov98
(cd-s) (567455-2) – ('A'side) / Too much, too little, too late (acoustic) / Disguise.
(cd-s) (<567453-2>) – ('A'side) / Missed / Jessica.

Oct 98. (cd/c/lp) (559085-2/-4/-1) **NEO WAVE**   74
– Cheerleading / I'll see you around / Would've if I could've / Too much, too little, too late / Scared / There goes summer / Sharks / The prophet of the prairie / Mustard / Pixie, pixie / Hey girl friend / Only a girl / Special powers / Fire & blood / Patients / Dead end.

Nov 98. (7") (563118-7) **SHARKS. / WAYS OF LOVE**
(cd-s+=) (563118-2) – Hey girlfriend (live).
(cd-s) (563119-2) – ('A'side) / I can't wait (live) / Animals feet (live).
(cd-s) (563118-4) – ('A'side) / Too much too little too late / Lava.

— now without RICHARD SAYCE who left Feb'99; they disbanded soon after

---

SIMIAN

Formed: Manchester, England . . . late 90's by JASON SHAW, JAMES FORD, ALEX MacNAUGHTON and SIMON LORD. The latter had been summoned to Manchester by SHAW, FORD and MacNAUGHTON (who'd got together at the city's university) after they'd heard his demo tape. The quartet began writing together and quickly amassed enough material for both a debut EP, 'WATCH IT GLOW' (issued on the 'Source' label in 2000) and a debut album, 'CHEMISTRY IS WHAT WE ARE' (2001). Dropping molecular musical science that filtered classic American/British psychedelia through a post-modern, electronica-influenced lens, the group's gloopy experiments had critics doling out the kind of superlatives unwitnessed since the early days of The BETA BAND. Their touring extravaganza, The Church of Simian, preached to the unconverted while the lads immersed themselves in modern US R&B prior to the recording of their acclaimed second album, 'WE ARE YOUR FRIENDS' (2002). Much influenced by their newfound musical tastes and blessed by an unerringly upbeat pop sensibility, the record's funky, fizzing creations established a more distinctly individual path.

Album rating: WATCH IT GLOW mini (*6) / CHEMISTRY IS WHAT WE ARE (lp) (*6) / WE ARE YOUR FRIENDS (*7)

SIMON LORD – vocals / **JAMES FORD** + **ALEX MacNAUGHTON** + **JASON SHAW** – instruments/electronics

                                                      Source   Astralwerks

Nov 00. (m-cd/m-lp) (SOUR CD/LP 016) <811819> **WATCH IT GLOW**
– Drop and roll / In Siam / The wisp / Grey / Won't / (untitled). (m-cd re-iss. Apr02; SOURCDX 016)

May 01. (12"ep) (SOURV 027) **THE WISP EP**
– The wisp / The tale of Willow Hill / Turn around / What a dream.
(cd-ep+=) (SOURCDS 027) – ('A'video).

Jul 01. (cd/lp) (CDSOUR/SOURLP 021) <11005> **CHEMISTRY IS WHAT WE ARE (lp)**
– Drop and roll / The wisp / Doba / You set off my brain / How could I be right / One dimension / Tree in a corner / Orange glow / Mr. Crow / Round and around / Chamber / The tale of Willow Hill / Grey.

Oct 01. (12") (SOURT 042) **ONE DIMENSION. / OVER THE HILL / REASONS**
(cd-s) (SOURCD 042) – (first 2 tracks) / Reasons (video).
(cd-s) (SOURCDX 042) – ('A'side) / The long road / ('A'live).

Mar 02. (7") (SOUR 047) **MR. CROW. / SOCIETA**
(cd-s) (SOURCD 047) – ('A'side) / Something new / Queen May.
(cd-s) (SOURCDX 047) – ('A'side) / Into the ground / Song and dance / ('A'video).

Oct 02. (7") (SOUR 067) **NEVER BE ALONE. / NEVER BE ALONE (mobile disco mix)**
(cd-s) (SOURCD 067) – ('A'side) / Out of bed / Coins / ('A'-video).
(cd-s) (SOURCDX 067) – ('A'side) / We don't want your help / Since when.

Oct 02. (cd/lp) (CDSOUR/SOURLP 065) <42371> **WE ARE YOUR FRIENDS**
– L.A. breeze / Never be alone / Helpless / Skin / Big black gun / In between / The way I live / The swarm / When I go / She's in mind / End of the day.

SING-SING

Formed: London, England . . . 1997 by indie veterans EMMA ANDERSON (formerly of LUSH) and LISA O'NEILL (formerly of dance/electronica unit, LOCUST and guest for KID LOCO); JUSTIN WELCH (of ELASTICA) played drums on demo work. With production work from LOCUST man, MARK VAN HOEN, LISA and EMMA emerged from the studio with three songs, the first of which 'FEELS LIKE SUMMER' caught the attention of SIMON RAYMONDE and ROBIN GUTHRIE (both of COCTEAU TWINS), who released it on their 'Bella Union' imprint in autumn 1998. Now performing live with a full band, SING-SING also issued a quick follow-up 7", split with LINOLEUM. The year 2000, saw the basic duo instigate their own label,

'Aerial', to release two further single efforts, 'I'LL BE' and the re-recorded 'FEELS LIKE SUMMER'. It was inevitable that someone high up would come along. That someone was ALAN McGEE whose 'Poptones' imprint duly issued their long-awaited debut full-set, 'THE JOY OF SING-SING' (2001), a record full of dreamy pop with a cool 60's retro feel.

Album rating: THE JOY OF SING-SING (*6)

LISA O'NEILL – vocals (ex-LOCUST) / **EMMA ANDERSON** – guitar, vocals (ex-LUSH) / with various players

			Bella Union	Bella Union
Oct 98.	(cd-s) (<BELLA 8>) **FEELS LIKE SUMMER. / HIT AND RUN / COMMAND**			

—— added **POPPY GONZALEZ** – keyboards (ex-MOJAVE 3) / **SHIFTY** – bass / **MIG** – drums (ex-MOOSE, ex-MOONSHAKE)

		Fierce Panda	not iss.
Jan 99.	(7"/cd-s) (NINGNING 066/+CDS) **I CAN SEE YOU. / (other track by LINOLEUM)**		-
		Aerial	not iss.
May 00.	(7") (AEROV 001) **I'LL BE. / WESTERN**		-
	(cd-s+=) (AEROCD 001) – ('A'-dub you love mix).		
Aug 00.	(7") (AEROV 002) **FEELS LIKE SUMMER. / MAKE IT MINE**		-
	(cd-s+=) (AEROCD 002) – ('A'-scorcher mix).		
		Poptones	not iss.
Sep 01.	(7") (MC 5050S) **TEGAN. / WILLOW'S SONG**		-
Oct 01.	(cd) (MC 5050CD) **THE JOY OF SING-SING**		-

– Everything / Tegan / I'll be / Me and my friend / Far away from love / Panda eyes / Command / Feels like summer / Emigre / You don't know / Underage / I can see you. (<lp+US-iss.Sep02 on 'Manifesto'; MFO 43501LP>)

		Elefant	not iss.
Sep 02.	(7"red) (ER 241) **PANDA EYES. / OFFICE PARTY (acoustic)**		-

SINKING SHIPS (see under ⇒ HOLIDAY FLYER)

SISTERHOOD OF CONVOLUTED THINKERS (see under ⇒ EGGS)

SIX.BY SEVEN

Formed: Nottingham, England ... 1992 by five hard-working, hard-playing, hard-drinking college lads, CHRIS OLLEY, SAM HEMPTON, JAMES FOWLER, PAUL DOUGLAS and CHRIS DAVIS. Rehearsing night and day to perfect their alternative drone machine, the 12 inch 'EUROPEAN ME', finally hit the shops in the Autumn of '97. A third single for Beggars Banquet's offshoot 'Mantra', 'CANDLELIGHT' (taken from their debut set, 'THE THINGS WE MAKE'), broke into the UK Top 75, its lengthy noisy overtures classic SPACEMEN 3/SONIC YOUTH-esque affairs. If anything, the band's sound became denser on the likes of 'THE CLOSER YOU GET' (2000) and 'THE WAY I FEEL TODAY' (2002), driven by dissonant tiers of noise and neo-psychedelic nihilism, and prompting consistent comparisons with the likes of MY BLOODY VALENTINE and pseudo-grunge shoegazers SWERVEDRIVER.

Album rating: THE THINGS WE MAKE (*6) / THE CLOSER YOU GET (*7) / THE WAY I FEEL TODAY (*5)

CHRIS OLLEY – vocals, guitar / **SAM HEMPTON** – guitar / **JAMES FOWLER** – Hammond organ, tenor sax / **PAUL DOUGLAS** (b. Irvine, Scotland) – bass / **CHRIS DAVIS** – drums

		Mantra	Interscope
Sep 97.	(12") (SIX 001) **EUROPEAN ME. / BRILLIANTLY CUTE**		-
Feb 98.	(12"/cd-s) (MNT 29 T/CD) **88-92-96. / YOUR TIME / THIS**		-
Apr 98.	(7") (MNT 034) **CANDLELIGHT. / YOUNG MAN'S STRIDE**	70	-
	(12"+=/cd-s+=) (MNT 034 T/CD) – ('A'-Flaming Lips mix).		
May 98.	(cd/c/lp) (MNT CD/MC/LP 1011) <90270> **THE THINGS WE MAKE**		Oct98

– A beautiful shape / European me / Candlelight / For you / Spy song / Something wild / Brilliantly cute / Oh! dear / 88-92-96 / Comedown.

Aug 98.	(cd-s) <85001> **SIX.BY SEVEN**	-	

– European me / 88-92-96 / Your town.

Aug 98.	(7") (MNT 37) **FOR YOU. / GET A REAL TATTOO**		
	(cd-s+=) (MNT 37CD) – Oh dear (John Peel session).		
	(cd-s) (MNT 37CD2) – ('A'side) / Something wild / I'm wide open.		
May 99.	(12"ep/cd-ep) (MNT 45 T/CD) **TWO AND A HALF DAYS IN LOVE WITH YOU EP**		
	– July, August and winter / Cool TV suit / Always waiting for ...		
Oct 99.	(cd-ep) (MNT 49CD) **TEN PLACES TO DIE / ENGLAND AND A BROKEN RADIO / EUROPEAN ME (session) / HELDEN (session)**		-
	(12"ep) (MNT 49T) – (first 2 tracks) / (instrumentals).		
Mar 00.	(cd/lp) (MNT CD/LP 1017) <81017> **THE CLOSER YOU GET**		

– Eat junk become junk / Sawn off Metallica t-shirt / Ten places to die / New year / One easy ship away / My life is an accident / Don't wanna stop / Slab square / England and a broken radio / Another love song / Ovednight success / 100 & something Foxhall Road.

Jun 00.	(7") (MNT 58) **NEW YEAR. / SLEEP**		-
	(cd-s+=) (MNT 58CD) – Stoned in Hawaii.		
Nov 00.	(12"/cd-s) (MNT SIX7 T/CD) **EAT JUNK BECOME JUNK (mixes; album / Two Lone Swordsmen / Zan Lyons)**		-

—— now without HEMPTON

Oct 01.	(7") (MNT 67) **SO CLOSE. / FRAGGLE ROCK**		-
	(cd-s+=) (MNT 67CD) – Requiem for an oil spill seagull.		
Feb 02.	(7") (MNT 68) **I.O.U. LOVE. / SPEED IS IN – SPEED IS OUT (live)**	48	-
	(cd-s) (MNT 68CD) – ('A'side) / Always waiting for ... (demo) / Chanson mort-homme.		
	(cd-s) (MNT 67CD2) – ('A'-Osbourne mix) / Don't wanna stop (demo) / So close (alt. version).		
Mar 02.	(cd/lp) (MNT CD/LP 1027) <81027> **THE WAY I FEEL TODAY**	69	

– So close / I.O.U. love / All my new best friends / Flypaper for freaks / Speed is in – Speed is out / Karen O / American beer / Anyway / The way I feel today / Cafeteria rats / Bad man.

May 02.	(7") (MNT 71) **ALL MY BEST NEW FRIENDS. / SAWN OFF METALLICA T-SHIRT (live)**		
	(cd-s) (MNT 71CD) – ('A'side) / I want to destroy you / Lk 351B.		
	(cd-s) (MNT 71CD2) – ('A'demo) / Stop the world / Spiegelei und brot.		

SIX CENTS & NATALIE (see under ⇒ TULLYCRAFT)

SIX FINGER SATELLITE

Formed: Rhode Island, USA ... 1991 by J. (JEREMIAH) RYAN, JOHN MacLEAN, RICHARD PELLETIER, along with PETER PHILLIPS and CHRIS DIXON. An unorthodox signing even by 'Sub Pop' standards, SFS were a breath of fresh air to the guitar-orientated US indie scene. A kind of Stateside precursor to ADD N TO (X), if less futuristic, this combo merged elements of SUICIDE, KRAFTWERK and early 80's alt-punk using analogue synths for authenticity and smothering the sound in Dalek-style distortion and noise. Preceded by an EP, 'WEAPON', 1993's debut set, 'THE PIGEON IS THE MOST POPULAR BIRD', received surprisingly little coverage of the band in the press. Whether intentional or not, the band remained one of the most low-key acts on the 'Sub Pop' roster. They subsequently became a quartet with the addition of JAMES APT, after a further two mini-sets during the mid-90's, delivered the much-improved 'PARANORMALIZED' in 1996. Two of the album's highlights were unusual to say the least, 'SLAVE TRAITOR' was an archetypal SUICIDE dirge while 'PERICO' subjected the listener to a weird reverberating synth sound akin to a cross between a horse snoring and an elephant breaking wind! • **Covered:** GIMMIE, GIMMIE, GIMMIE (Black Flag).

Album rating: THE PIGEON IS THE MOST POPULAR BIRD (*5) / MACHINE CUISINE mini (*5) / SEVERE EXPOSURE (*6) / PARANORMALIZED (*6) / LAW OF RUINS (*6)

J. RYAN (b. JEREMIAH) – vocals, synthesizer / **JOHN MacLEAN** – synthesizers, guitar synthesizer / **RICHARD PELLETIER** – drums, drum machine / **PETER PHILLIPS** – guitar, vocals / **CHRIS DIXON** – bass

		Sub Pop	Sub Pop
Mar 92.	(cd-ep) <(SP 143)> **SIX FINGER SATELLITE EP**		
	– Weapon / Niponese national anthem / Shimkus yell / Polish the shine (satchmo).		
Oct 92.	(d7"colrd) <SP 172> **DECLARATION OF TECHNO-COLONIAL INDEPENDENCE**	-	
	– Crippled monster bearing malice / Sex transistor / (2 by GREEN MAGNET SCHOOL).		

—— **ROBERT WESTON** – bass, Moog; repl. DIXON

Aug 93.	(2x12"/cd) (SP/+CD 268) <SP 215> **THE PIGEON IS THE MOST POPULAR BIRD**		Jul93

– Home for the holy day / Laughing Larry / Funny like a clown / Deadpan / Hi-lo jerk / Love (via satellite) / Save the last dance for Larry / Solitary Hiro / Neuro-harmonic conspiracy / Takes one to know one.

—— now without PHILLIPS

Sep 94.	(10"m-lp/m-cd) (SP 133-330/-CD) <SP 261> **MACHINE CUISINE**		Jun94

– Love (via machine) / Blue melodica / The magic bus / Hans pocketwatch / The well-tempered monkey / Like to get to know you / The Greek arts / White temples.

—— **JAMES APT** – bass, clarinet; repl. WESTON

Jul 95.	(lp/cd) <(SP 299/+B)> **SEVERE EXPOSURE**		

– Bad comrade / Parlour games / White Queen to Black Knight / Pulling a train / Simian fever / Cock fight / Dark companion / Where humans go / Rabies (baby's got the) / Board the bus.

Mar 96.	(12") <SP 327> **MASSIVE COCAINE SEIZURE. / HUMAN OPERATOR**	-	
Jun 96.	(12") <LOAD 008> **CLONE THEORY**	-	

—— <above issued on 'Load'>

Jul 96.	(7"m) <SP 362> **MAN BEHIND THE GLASSES. / WAR CRIMES / DARK COMPANION**		
Sep 96.	(cd) <(SPCD 366)> **PARANORMALIZED**		

– 30 lashes / The greatest hit / Do the suicide / Coke and mirrors / Last transmission / Slave traitor / The white shadow / Paralyzed by normal life / Padded room / Perico / The great depression.

Aug 98.	(cd) <(SP 428)> **LAW OF RUINS**		

– Race against space / Surveillance house / Fall to pieces / Sea of tranquility / Law of ruins / Lonely grave / New kind of rat / White visitation / Bad aptitude.

—— might well have split as they only toured briefly in 2001

16 HORSEPOWER

Formed: Denver, Colorado, USA ... 1992 by DAVID EUGENE EDWARDS, plus JEAN YVES TOLA and PASCAL HUMBERT (the latter subsequently replaced by KEVIN SOLL after a spell in LA). Brought up under a strict religious regime, EDWARDS' preoccupation with the fire and brimstone of the Old Testament was channeled through 16 HORSEPOWER's gothic rockabilly/country stylings, the ghost of JEFFREY LEE PIERCE (ex-GUN CLUB) haunting his every phrase. EDWARDS and Co were lucky enough to secure a major label deal for their debut release, 1995's eponymous mini-CD (also known as 'HAW') being issued on A&M's offshoot 'Paradox'. A debut album, 'SACKCLOTH 'N' ASHES' (1997) was released to critical acclaim the following year, hitting the British shops (with the addition of 'HAW') in Spring '97. With HUMBERT returning and the addition of guitarist/fiddle man, JEFFREY PAUL NORLANDER (the 90's alt-country equivalent of CHARLIE DANIELS!), follow-up set, 'LOW ESTATE' (1998) benefitted from the talents of PJ HARVEY collaborator, JOHN PARRISH. Following in the spiritual footsteps of NICK CAVE can't be easy, but the gospel according to EDWARDS was further expounded upon in 'SECRET SOUTH' (2000), as ominous and haunting as any album they've yet recorded. Sounding like a reanimated ROBERT JOHNSON born again into the CARTER FAMILY, the band's head horseman continued to explore the darkest fringes of American roots music with a fervour verging on the apocalyptic. The live 'HOARSE' (2001) translated the band's dark menace with surprising intensity, a scattering of tasty covers (Creedence Clearwater Revival's 'BAD MOON RISING', Joy Division's 'DAY OF THE LORDS' and Gun Club's 'FIRE SPIRIT' among them) providing grist for EDWARDS' brimstone mill and a glimpse into the man's formative influences. 'FOLKLORE' (2002), while maintaining the band's gothic edge, simultaneously took the foot off the gas and broadened their blood red horizon, concentrating the menace into a more measured approach.

Album rating: 16 HORSEPOWER (*5) / SACKCLOTH 'N' ASHES (*8) / LOW ESTATE (*8) / SECRET SOUTH (*6) / HOARSE (*5) / FOLKLORE (*7)

DAVID EUGENE EDWARDS – vocals / **JEAN YVES TOLA** – drums (ex-PASSION FODDER) / **KEVIN SOLL** – double bass; repl. PASCAL HUMBERT

		Paradox-A&M	Paradox-A&M
Oct 95.	(cd-s) **HEEL ON THE SHOVEL / PHYLLIS RUTH / FLOWERS IN MY HEART / DEAD RUN**		-
Jun 96.	(m-cd) <(540 436-2)> **16 HORSEPOWER** – Haw / South Pennsylvania waltz / Shametown / Straight-mouth stomp / Coal black horses / I gotta gal.		Nov95
Apr 97.	(cd) <(540 591-2)> **SACKCLOTH 'N' ASHES** – I seen what I saw / Black soul choir / Scrawled in sap / Horse head / Ruthie Lingle / Harm's way / Black bush / Heel on the shovel / American wheeze / Red neck reel / Prison shoe romp / Neck on the new blade / Strong man. (UK cd+=) – 16 HORSEPOWER E.P.		Feb97

— **HUMBERT** returned to repl. KEVIN
— added **JEFFREY PAUL NORLANDER** – guitar, fiddle (ex-DENVER GENTLEMEN)

Oct 97.	(cd-ep) (582 395-2) **COAL BLACK HORSES / FOR HEAVEN'S SAKE / HAW / BRIMSTONE ROCK**		-
Jan 98.	(cd) <(540 709-2)> **LOW ESTATE** – Brimstone rock / My narrow mind / Low estate / For Heaven's sake / Sac of religion / The Denver grab / Coal black horses / Pure clob road / Phyllis Ruth / Black rung / Dead run / Golden rope / Hang my teeth on your door.		

— now without NORLANDER

		Glitterhouse	Razor & Tie
Mar 00.	(cd) (GRCD 480) <28572> **SECRET SOUTH** – Clogger / Wayfaring stranger / Cinder alley / Burning bush / Poor mouth / Silver saddle / Praying arm lane / Splinters / Just like birds / Nobody 'cept you / Straw foot.		

		Glitterhouse	Checkered Past
Mar 01.	(cd) (GRCD 497) <23> **HOARSE (live 1998)** – American wheeze / Black soul choir / Bad moon risin' / Low estate / For heaven's sake / Black lung / Horse head / South Pennsylvania waltz / Brimstone rock / Free spirit (w/ BERTRAND CANTAT) / Day of the lords.		Jun01
May 01.	(cd-s) (GRCD 525) **SPLINTERS / 'CEPT YOU**		-

		Glitterhouse	Jetset
Jul 02.	(cd) (GRCD 560) <49> **FOLKLORE** – Hutterite mile / Outlaw song / Blessed persistence / Alone and forsaken / Single girl / Beyond the pale / Horse head fiddle / Sinnerman / Flutter / La robe a parasol.		Aug02

SIXTH GREAT LAKE (see under ⇒ ESSEX GREEN)

6THS (see under ⇒ MAGNETIC FIELDS)

'68 COMEBACK (see under ⇒ GIBSON BROS.)

60 FT DOLLS

Formed: Newport, Wales ... 1993 by son of a preacher man, CARL BEVAN (oh yes he was!), MIKE COLE and RICHARD JOHN PARFITT. Spearheading the Welsh-rock revival in the seismic wake of The MANIC STREET PREACHERS, these self professed "niggers of Europe" (with regards to their place in the good old – and thankfully fast dissipating – United Kingdom) first vented their smalltown spleen with 1994's 'HAPPY SHOPPER' single. Released on their own 'Townhill' label, the single set the band up for a healthy range of major league support slots and incredibly, a Stateside deal with 'Geffen'. Unfortunately, however, the band's domestic deal with 'Rough Trade' came just as the label were on the verge of folding; this, together with the frustration felt by the whole Welsh rock community following the disappearance of The MANICS' RICHEY EDWARDS was fuel for the seething 'WHITE KNUCKLE RIDE'. Subsequently signing with R.C.A.-offshoot, 'Indolent' (home to SLEEPER), the trio began 1996 with the 'STAY' single, the long awaited debut album, 'THE BIG 3', surfacing soon after. Proving that there was more to the band than indie-punk/R&R, the record showcased a few subdued moments alongside the trademark pop-art fusing The MANICS with The JAM or MOTT THE HOOPLE. Two years passed before another single, 'ALISON'S ROOM', surfaced, its disappointing chart performance affecting sales of the "difficult" second album, 'JOYA MAGICA' (1998). Without a recording contract for some three years, RICHARD PARFITT decided to go out on his own for 2002's balladesque set 'HIGHLIGHTS IN SLOW MOTION'; much like WELLER branching out to STYLE COUNCIL some 20 years earlier! • **Songwriters:** PARFITT or COLE or both. Covered; AFTERGLOW (Small Faces) / EVERYBODY'S GOT SOMETHING TO HIDE ... (Beatles).

Album rating: THE BIG 3 (*6) / JOYA MAGICA (*4) / Richard Parfitt: HIGHLIGHTS IN SLOW MOTION (*4)

RICHARD JOHN PARFITT – vocals, guitar / **MIKE COLE** – vocals, bass / **CARL BEVAN** – drums

		Townhill	not iss.
Jul 94.	(7") (TIDY 001) **HAPPY SHOPPER. / LONDON BREEDS** (re-iss. Mar95; same)		-

		Rough Trade	not iss.
May 95.	(7") (R 379-7) **WHITEKNUCKLE RIDE. / NO.1 PURE ALCOHOL** (cd-s+=) (R 379-3) – Piss funk.		-

		Indolent	D.G.C.
Oct 95.	(7"/cd-s) (DOLLS 001/+CD) **PIG VALENTINE. / BRITISH RACING GREEN / YELLOW CANDLES**		Dec95
Jan 96.	(7"/c-s) (DOLLS 002/+MC) **STAY. / THE MAINDEE RUN** (cd-s+=) (DOLLS 002CD) – Rosalyn.	48	-
Apr 96.	(7"colrd/c-s) (DOLLS 003/+MC) **TALK TO ME. / PONY RIDE** (cd-s+=) (DOLLS 003CD) – Angel / Easy.	37	-
May 96.	(cd/c/lp) (DOLLS CD/MC/LP 004) **THE BIG 3** – New loafers / Talk to me / Stay / Hair / Happy shopper / The one / Good times / No.1 pure alcohol / Streamlined / Loser / Pig valentine / Terminal crash fear / Buzz. (lp w/ free 7") – WHITEKNUCKLE RIDE (cd re-iss. Aug99 on 'Huge & Jolly'; HNJCD 002)	36	-
Jul 96.	(7"tin/c-s) (DOLLS 005/+MC) **HAPPY SHOPPER. / AFTERGLOW** (cd-s) (DOLLS 005CD) – ('A'side) / Everybody's got something to hide (except for me and my monkey) (live) / Dr Rat.	38	-
Sep 96.	(cd-ep) <22224> **SUPERNATURAL JOY EP** – Happy shopper / White knuckle ride / British racing green / Yellow candles / Rosalyn.	-	
Nov 96.	(10"colrd-ep/cd-ep) (DOLLS 006/+CD) **HAIR / BALLERINA. / DREAMING / MESS / PRETTY HORSES**		-
Apr 98.	(7") (DOLLS 007) **ALISON'S ROOM. / TWO LANE BLACKTOP** (cd-s+=) (DOLLS 007CD2) – Time after time / Let the spirit move you. (cd-s) (DOLL 007CD1) – ('A'side) / It's over / I don't miss you / Spirit (Wubble U mix).	61	-
Jun 98.	(cd/lp) (DOLLS 008 CD/LP) **JOYA MAGICA** – Alison's room / Let it show / Baby says yeah / The biggest kick / Summer's gone / Silver screen / Back to the summer / Killer inside / Cars, bars and movie stars / I want you / Pretty little thing / Spanish. (cd re-iss. Aug99 on 'Huge & Jolly'; HNJCD 001)		

— split in 1999 after their label dropped them

RICHARD PARFITT

		Rough Trade	not iss.
Mar 02.	(cd) (RTRADECD 038) **HIGHLIGHTS IN SLOW MOTION** – Downtown / Stone honey / Summergliding / Highlights in slow motion / What we talk about / Wish I was with you / Let love in / Morning star / Freckles of gold / I took that woman home last night.		

SKYPARK (see under ⇒ FAIRWAYS)

SLANT 6

Formed: Washington D.C., USA ... mid 1992 by MYRA POWER, CHRISTINA BILLOTTE and MARGE MARSHALL. Taking their unusual moniker from a Dodge engine (c.1960's), this all-female trio began their vinyl career with a sporadic series of 7" singles and V/A compilation appearances. Having signed to local hardcore bastion, 'Discord', SLANT 6 released their debut long-player, 'SODA POP * RIP OFF', in early '94, more an overview of their progress to date rather than a cohesive body of work in itself. IAN MacKAYE (of FUGAZI) also offered his knob-twiddling skills to the follow-up, 'INZOMBIA' (1995), which developed the group's girly punk guitar assault without offering any real innovation. BILLOTTE went on to form another D.C. trio, QUIX*O*TIC, with her sister MIRA and BRENDAN MAJEWSKI. A debut single, 'HELIOTROPE', surfaced in 1998, while a debut album, 'NIGHT FOR DAY', followed in 2000. While covers of both Aaron Neville's 'TELL IT LIKE IT IS' and Black Sabbath's 'LORD OF THIS WORLD' (not to mention a clear SYD BARRETT reference on opener 'ICE CREAM SUNDAE') on follow-up 'MORTAL MIRROR', might've suggested an innovative, hybrid approach, the sub-goth posturing sounded strangely one dimensional.

Album rating: SODA POP * RIP OFF (*6) / INZOMBIA (*4) / Quix*o*tic: NIGHT FOR DAY (*4) / MORTAL MIRROR (*4)

CHRISTINA BILLOTTE – vocals, guitar (ex-AUTOCLAVE) / **MYRA POWER** – bass (ex-LUCKY 13) / **MARGE MARSHALL** – drums, organ

SLANT 6 (cont)

		Dischord	Dischord
Jul 93. (7"m) <*(DIS 85V)*> **WHAT KIND OF MONSTER ARE YOU? / SEMI-BLUE TILE / THIRTY-THIRTY VISION**
Mar 94. (cd/lp) <*(DIS 91 CD/V)*> **SODA POP * RIP OFF**
– Don't you ever? / Nights x9 / Love shock / Double edged knife / Time expired / Invisible footsteps / Poison arrows shot at heroes / Don't censor me / Blood song / Soda pop * rip off / Become your ghost / Blue angel / March 6* / What kind of monster are you? / Semi-ble tile / Thirty-thirty vision.
May 95. (cd/lp) <*(DIS 94 CD/V)*> **INZOMBIA**
– G.F.S. / Babydoll / Click-click / Instrumental / Ladybug superfly / Retro duck / Partner in crime / Victim of your own desires / Eight swimming pools / Insider spider / Mascaria / Inzombia.

| not iss. | Time Bomb |
Jul 95. (7"ep) <*128*> **split w/ The MAKE-UP**
– I love you a lot / Rebel rebel bat cat / (other 2 by the MAKE-UP).

—— disbanded after above; MYRA joined TAROT BOLERO

QUIX*O*TIC

CHRISTINA BILLOTTE – vocals, guitar, drums / **MIRA BILLOTTE** – drums, vocals, guitar / **BRENDAN MAJEWSKI** – bass, vocals, drums

| Ixor Stix | Ixor Stix |
1998. (7"m) **HELIOTROPE. / (+ 2)**
May 00. (cd) <*(IXORSTIX 3)*> **NIGHT FOR DAY**
– Make all the ghoul girls cry / Requi&es*cat / Heliotrope / Prediction of a crash / Perfume for plastic flowers / We are alone / Dead trees / Snowflakes in your eyelashes / Witch Hazel / What's so good about goodbye / My birthday party / Rhymes with crime / The seasons are the reasons / A premonition or the reason / I'm the light of the world.

—— **MICK BARR** – bass (ex-ORTHRELM) repl. BRENDAN

| Kill Rock Stars | Kill Rock Stars |
Jul 02. (lp/cd) <*KRS 381/+CD*> **MORTAL MIRROR**
– Ice cream sundae / Anonymous face / Open up the walls / The breeze / Mortal mirror / Sitting in the park / Forget to sing / On my own / To this world I must give in / Tell it like it is / Masterpeaceful / Lord of this world.

SLEATER-KINNEY

Formed: Olympia, Washington, USA ... 1994 by CARRIE BROWNSTEIN and CORIN TUCKER. The latter had cut her teeth with early 90's riot-grrrl duo HEAVENS TO BETSY (alongside drummer TRACY SAWYER), and after a handful of singles, released their one and only LP, 'CALCULATED' (1994) for 'Kill Rock Stars'). CORIN and CARRIE met at a feminist convention and became lesbian lovers for a while, CARRIE leaving her outfit, EXCUSE 17 (after the album, 'Such Friends Are Dangerous'), and forming SLEATER-KINNEY – named after a stretch of highway – with CORIN. The twin-guitar playing punk singers eventually recruited drummer, LORA McFARLANE, the all-girl trio becoming darlings of the underground feminist-rock movement, 'Riot Grrrl'. All-girl outfits including the more well-known (at the time) BIKINI KILL and HUGGY BEAR, were all the rage, having been championed by male! rock journalists, Robert Christgau and Greil Marcus. Raised on a musical diet of Scottish indie bands such as the PASTELS, the VASELINES and BEAT HAPPENING (the latter played their own Washington State in the late 80's), CARRIE and CORIN hung out with up and coming, late 80's grunge acts, most notably, NIRVANA and MUDHONEY! S-K's eponymous debut album crashed out on the radical 'Chainsaw' imprint, TONI GOGIN replacing LORA not long afterwards due to the latter's commitments with several other outfits in her homeland Australia. A second set, 'CALL THE DOCTOR' (1996), fared even better leading to major label corporates banging on their door. Shunning their advances like true punks and replacing TONI with JANET WEISS (of QUASI), SLEATER-KINNEY delivered their finest hour yet, 'DIG ME OUT' (1997). In September '98, they toured Britain heralding a long-awaited single release of 'LITTLE BABIES', while, of course, taking time out to visit their long-time musical chums north of the border. The irrepresible TUCKER subsequently teamed up with The CRABS' SARAH DOUGHTER and The LOOKERS' JUNIOR STS to form femme-punk supergroup CADALLACA, releasing their roughshod, bareback and bass-less debut, 'INTRODUCING . . .' (1998) on 'K' records. Cobbled together from farfisa, rudimentary drums and skeletal guitar, the record hovered on the verge of folksy collapse, its approach at odds with the self-consciously experimental 1999 SLEATER-KINNEY effort, 'THE HOT ROCK'. This attempt at squaring personal exploration with their trademark riot-grrrl blowout didn't always come off although it served as a catalyst for the ebullient 'ALL HANDS ON THE BAD ONE' (2000). Having recharged their creative drive, the girls returned to their trademark formula with a newfound professionalism and melodic undertow. 'ONE BEAT' (2002), meanwhile, expanded both their musical horizons and lyrical scope, influenced by a post 9/11 landscape and TUCKER's entry into motherhood.

Album rating: Heavens To Betsy: CALCULATED (*7) / Sleater-Kinney: SLEATER-KINNEY (*5) / CALL THE DOCTOR (*6) / DIG ME OUT (*7) / THE HOT ROCK (*6) / ALL HANDS ON THE BAD ONE (*6) / ONE BEAT (*6) / Cadallaca: INTRODUCING . . . (*5)

HEAVENS TO BETSY

CORIN TUCKER – vocals, bass / **TRACY SAWYER** – drums, guitar, bass, samples

| not iss. | K |
1992. (7") <*PUNK 1*> **MY SECRET. / (other by BRATMOBILE)**

| Kill Rock Stars | Kill Rock Stars |
Nov 93. (7"ep) <*KRS 209*> **THESE MONSTERS ARE REAL**
– Me and her / Monsters / Playground / Firefly.
Mar 94. (cd/c/lp) <*KRS 222 CD/C/V*> **CALCULATED**
– Nothing can stop me / Decide / Stay away / Calculated / Waitress hell / Intermission 247 / Ascemen / Donating my body to science / Terrorist / Complicated / White girl / Paralyzed.

| not iss. | Chainsaw |
Feb 95. (7"ep) **DIRECTION . . .**
– Direction / Get out of my head / The ones / Driving song.

—— after the split, TUCKER would join ...

SLEATER-KINNEY

CARRIE BROWNSTEIN (b.1975) – vocals, guitar (ex-EXCUSE 17) / **CORIN TUCKER** (b.1973) – vocals, bass / **LORA McFARLANE** – drums

| Chainsaw | Chainsaw |
Apr 95. (cd) <*CHSW 012*> **SLEATER-KINNEY**
– Don't think you wanna / The day I went away / A real man / Her again / How to play dead / Be yr mama / Sold out / Slow song / Lora's song / The last song. *(UK-iss.Jun98 on 'Matador'; OLE 267-2)*

—— **TONI GOGIN** – drums; repl. LORA who stayed in Australia

Dec 96. (lp/cd) <*(CHSW 013/+CD)*> **CALL THE DOCTOR** — Mar96
– Call the doctor / Hubcap / Little mouth / Anonymous / Stay where you are / Good things / I want to be your Joey Ramone / Taking me home / Taste test / My stuff / I'm not waiting / Heart attack. *(lp re-iss. Mar98; same) (cd re-iss. Jun98 on 'Matador'; OLE 268-2)*

| Villa Villakula | Villa Villakula |
Feb 97. (7") <*(VVK 02)*> **YOU AIN'T IT. / SURF SONG**
(re-iss. Apr98 + Mar99; same)

—— **JANET WEISS** – drums (of QUASI) repl. TONI

| Matador | Kill Rock Stars |
Oct 97. (cd/lp) *(OLE 269-2/-1)* <*KRS 279CD*> **DIG ME OUT** — Apr97
– Dig me out / One more hour / Turn it on / The drama you've been craving / Heart factory / Words and guitar / It's enough / Little babies / Not what you want / Buy her candy / Things you say / Dance song '97 / Jenny. *(re-iss. Mar98 on 'Kill Rock Stars' lp/cd; KRS 279/+CD)*
Nov 97. (10"pic-d) *(VVK 06P)* **SLEATER-KINNEY EP**
(above on 'Villa Villakula' and below released on 'Candy Ass')
Nov 97. (7") *(CAR 028)* **FREE TO FIGHT. / (other by CYPHER IN THE SNOW)**
Jun 98. (7"yellow/cd-s) *(OLE 321-7/-2)* **ONE MORE HOUR. / I WANNA BE YOUR JOEY RAMONE**
Sep 98. (7"blue/cd-s) *(OLE 326-7/-2)* **LITTLE BABIES. / I'M NOT WAITING**
Feb 99. (cd-s) *(OLE 351-2)* **A QUARTER TO THREE / BURN, DON'T FREEZE**
Feb 99. (cd/lp) *(OLE 352-2/-1)* <*KRS 321CD*> **THE HOT ROCK**
– Start together / Hot rock / End of you / Burn, don't freeze / God is a number / Banned from the end of the world / Don't talk like / Get up / One song for you / The size of your love / Living in exile / Memorize your lines / A quarter to three.
Mar 99. (7") *(OLE 354-7)* <*KRS 337*> **GET UP. / TURN IT ON**
(cd-s) *(OLE 354-2)* – ('A'side) / Words and guitar / One more hour.
May 00. (7") *(OLE 445-7)* <*KRS 364*> **YOU'RE NO ROCK'N'ROLL FUN. / MARACA**
(cd-s+=) *(OLE 445-2)* – What if I was right.
May 00. (cd/lp) *(OLE 440-2/-1)* <*KRS 360CD*> **ALL HANDS ON THE BAD ONE**
– Ballad of a ladyman / Ironclad / All hands on the bad one / Youth decay / You're no rock'n'roll fun / #1 must have / The professional / Was it a lie? / Male model / Leave you behind / Milkshake n' honey / Pompeii / The swimmer.
Aug 00. (cd-s; w-drawn) *(OLE 467-2)* **ALL HANDS ON THE BAD ONE**

| Kill Rock Stars | Kill Rock Stars |
Aug 02. (lp/cd) <*(KRS 387/+CD)*> **ONE BEAT**
– One beat / Faraway / Oh! / The remainder / Light rail coyote / Step aside / Combat rock / O2 / Prisstina / Funeral song / Hollywood ending / Sympathy.

CADALLACA

KISSY (aka CORIN TUCKER) – vocals, guitar / **DUSTY** (aka SARAH DOUGHER) – organ (of The CRABS) / **JUNIOR STS** (of The LOOKERS)

| K | K |
Sep 98. (lp/cd) <*(KLP/+CD 86)*> **INTRODUCING CADALLACA**
– Your one wish / Jun-n-July / You're my only one / Pocket games / Night vandals / Two beers late / O Chenilla / Firetrap / Winter storm '98.

SLEEPER

Formed: Ilford, Essex, England ... 1993 by LOUISE WENER and her boyfriend JON STEWART, the pair duly recruiting ANDY McCLURE and DIID OSMAN. Signing to upcoming 'R.C.A.'-offshoot, 'Indolent', SLEEPER released their debut EP in late '93, 'ALICE IN VAIN', WENER causing controversy from the off with an attack on the sacred cow of feminism. If she brought the wrath of the more radical in the female population, then she no doubt scored a few brownie points with the boys, indie lads increasingly besotted by her saucer-eyed cuteness as well as her outspoken personality. Another couple of EP's, 'SWALLOW', and 'DELICIOUS', followed in quick succession, their sexual frankness further endearing WENER to the more hormonal element of her audience. The singer had already acquired a burgeoning reputation for her lippy diatribes by the time the 'INBETWEENER' single broke the Top 20 in early '95 and the attendant interest in all things WENER ensured the debut album, 'SMART', a Top

5 placing. Getting down to the nitty gritty i.e. the music, were SLEEPER actually any good? Well, they could certainly hold their own among the Brit-pop competition although that wasn't saying much; basically they were a competent spiky guitar outfit with the odd ear-catching tune, notably the dreamy bit/noisy bit pop rush of 'VEGAS', arguably their finest moment. Later that year, the group scored a second Top 20 hit with the lightweight indie-pop of 'WHAT DO I DO NOW' followed by 'SALE OF THE CENTURY', their first Top 10 single, though by no means their best. WENER's profile was at an all-time high, her forthright views offending and delighting in equal measure; there was no middle ground with this lass, you either admired her or wished she would sod off (the aptly named SLEEPER also proved that work and pleasure were actually compatible after all). Predictably, then, a follow-up album, 'THE IT GIRL' (1996), met with decidedly mixed reviews although it sold respectably. A backlash was inevitable, however, a third set, 'PLEASED TO MEET YOU' (1997) only produced universal indifference, both critically and commercially. Being ignored is probably one thing which WENER never counted on, although it's doubtful such a feisty babe will bow out without a fight, or at least a controversial word or two. • **Songwriters:** Most by WENER or some w/ STEWART. Covered OTHER END OF THE TELESCOPE (Elvis Costello & Aimee Mann) / ATOMIC (Blondie); used on 'Trainspotting' film.

Album rating: SMART (*8) / THE IT GIRL (*6) / PLEASED TO MEET YOU (*6)

LOUISE WENER (b.30 Jul'68) – vocals, guitar / **JON STEWART** (b.12 Sep'67, Sheffield, England) – lead guitar / **DIID OSMAN** (b. KENEDIID, 10 Apr'68, Mogadishu, Somalia) – bass / **ANDY MacCLURE** (b. 4 Jul'70, Manchester, England) – drums, percussion

		Indolent	Arista
Nov 93.	(7"ep/12"ep/cd-ep) *(SLEEP 001/+T/CD)* **THE ALICE EP** – Alice in vain / Ha ha you're dead / Big nurse.	☐	–
Feb 94.	(7"ep/cd-ep) *(SLEEP 002/+CD)* **SWALLOW. / TWISTED / ONE GIRL DREAMING**	☐	–
May 94.	(7"ep/cd-ep) *(SLEEP 003/+CD)* **DELICIOUS. / LADY LOVE YOUR COUNTRYSIDE / BEDSIDE MANNERS** (12"ep+=) *(SLEEP 003T)* – Tatty.	75	–
Oct 94.	(7"mail-order) **BUCKET AND SPADE (live)** – Bedhead / Alice in vain / Swallow.	–	–
Jan 95.	(7"/c-s) *(SLEEP 006/+MC)* **INBETWEENER. / LITTLE ANNIE** (cd-s+=) *(SLEEP 006CD)* – Disco Duncan. (12"++=) *(SLEEP 006T)* – Bank.	16	–
Feb 95.	(cd/c/lp) *(SLEEP CD/MC/LP 007)* <25825> **SMART** – Inbetweener / Swallow / Delicious / Hunch / Amuse / Bedhead / Lady love your countryside / Vegas / Poor flying man / Alice in vain / Twisted / Pyrotechnician.	5	Mar95
Mar 95.	(7"blue/c-s) *(SLEEP 008/+MC)* **VEGAS. / HYMN TO HER** (12"pic-d/cd-s+=) *(SLEEP 008 T/CD)* – It's wrong to breed / Close.	33	–
Sep 95.	(7"/c-s) *(SLEEP 009/+MC)* **WHAT DO I DO NOW? / PAINT ME** (cd-s+=) *(SLEEP 009CD1)* – Room at the top. (cd-s) *(SLEEP 009CD2)* – ('A'side) / Vegas (live) / Amuse (live) / Disco Duncan (live).	14	–
Apr 96.	(7"colrd/c-s/cd-s) *(SLEEP 011/+MC/CD1)* **SALE OF THE CENTURY. / ATOMIC** (cd-s) *(SLEEP 011CD2)* – ('A'side) / Package holiday / Oh well.	10	–
May 96.	(cd/c/lp) *(SLEEP CD/MC/LP 012)* <18824> **THE IT GIRL** – Lie detector / Sale of the century / What do I do now? / Good luck Mr. Gorsky / Feeling peaky / Shrinkwrapped / Dress like your mother / Statuesque / Glue ears / Nice guy Eddie / Stop your crying / Factor 41 / Click . . . off . . . gone.	5	
Jul 96.	(7"/c-s) *(SLEEP 013/+MC)* <3064> **NICE GUY EDDIE. / INBETWEENER** (cd-s+=) *(SLEEP 013CD)* – Poker face / Blazer sleeves.	10	
Sep 96.	(7") *(SLEEP 014)* **STATUESQUE. / SHE'S A SWEETHEART** (cd-s+=) *(SLEEP 014CD1)* – Spies. (cd-s) *(SLEEP 014CD2)* – ('A'side) / ('A'-The Boxed Off mix) / Other end of the telescope / Atomic (Wubble U mix).	17	–
—	**CHRIS GIAMMALVO** – bass (of MADDER ROSE) repl. OSMAN		
Sep 97.	(7"/c-s) *(SLEEP 015/+MC)* **SHE'S A GOOD GIRL. / COME ON COME ON** (cd-s+=) *(SLEEP 015CD)* – I'm a man.	28	–
Oct 97.	(cd/c/lp) *(SLEEP CD/MC/LP 016)* **PLEASED TO MEET YOU** – Please please please / She's a good girl / Rollercoaster / Miss you / Romeo me / Breathe / You got me / Superclean / Firecracker / Because of you / Nothing is changing / Motorway man / Traffic accident.	7	–
Nov 97.	(7"clear) *(SLEEP 017)* **ROMEO ME. / C**T LONDON** (cd-s) *(SLEEP 017CD1)* – ('A'side) / This is the sound of someone else / What do I get? / Nice guy Eddie (Peel session). (cd-s) *(SLEEP 017CD2)* – ('A'side) / When will you smile? / What do I do now? (radio 1 evening session) / Motorway man (Arctic mix).	39	–
—	now with new temp bassist **DAN KAUFMANN**		
—	in early '98, they split for good		

SLINT

Formed: Louisville, Kentucky, USA . . . 1988 by former SQUIRREL BAIT partners, BRIAN McMAHAN and BRITT WALFORD, who had already teamed up with DAVID PAJO and ETHAN BUCKLER prior to the latter band's division into BASTRO and SLINT. The influential noiseniks made their debut the following year with the self-financed, STEVE ALBINI-produced album, 'TWEEZ', a willfully weird clutch of mainly instrumental guitar/bass-led creations named after their family members (including a dog!). While WALFORD (aka SHANNON DOUGHTY) moonlighted on The BREEDERS first album, 'Pod', BUCKLER would subsequently leave to form KING KONG, replacement TODD BRASHER installed as work commenced on a BRIAN PAULSON-produced follow-up set, 'SPIDERLAND'. Upon its release (on 'Touch & Go') in '91, the album generated a healthy amount of column inches praising its uncategorisable guitar-scapes, Scotland's own MOGWAI later citing the record as a pivotal reference point. While rumours circulated that the album's recording had almost sent SLINT over the edge, the individual members were obviously sane enough to work on various projects including WILL OLDHAM's PALACE BROTHERS (WALFORD, McMAHAN and BRASHER) and TORTOISE (PAJO). A final postscript to the SLINT story came in 1993 with the release of double-A side ("untitled") single, 'GLENN' / 'RHODA' (the latter a cut from '89), with McMAHAN, however, embarking on his own adventure, The FOR CARNATION with SLINT buddy PAJO; other members DOUGLAS McCOMBS, GRANT BARGER and JOHN HERNDON. This quintet released the EP, 'FLIGHT SONGS' (1995), while the mini-set 'MARSHMALLOWS' (1996) was without the much in-demand PAJO. Not released in Britian, it finally surfaced in 1997 as 'PROMISED WORKS', containing the debut EP tracks. Like in SLINT, McMAHAN enforced the dizzy guitars and whispering sung/spoken vocals that made the aforementioned group sound so interesting, GALAXIE 500 and GASTR DEL SOL were also names that were thrown in as noteworthy comparisons. Adding LEONARD COHEN-esque incoherence to the mix, a slightly surreal view of life encouraged McMAHAN's lyrics and influence to reach higher dynamic points within his sound and vision. With his brother MICHAEL on guitar, BOB BRUNO, TODD COOK and moonlighting RADAR BROS drummer STEVE GOODFRIEND, The FOR CARNATION were reborn for an album which was scheduled for release early 2000. Meanwhile, following PAJO's stint with avant-jazz combo, TORTOISE, the musical Jack-of-all trades followed a similar dusty path to the aforementioned WILL OLDHAM, on his eponymous 1997 debut solo set (released under the AERIAL-M moniker), foregoing vocals in favour of backporch strumming. Licensed from 'Drag City' to 'Domino' in the UK, the rootsy homegrown affair showed a mellower side to the normally uncompromising guitarist and paved the way for two further releases over the course of the following year, EP's 'M IS . . .' and 'OCTOBER'. PAJO's increasingly interesting full-time project AERIAL M reached a peak with the release of his remix album 'POST-GLOBAL MUSIC' (1999), a record which saw single 'WEDDING SONG NO.3' get the mixing treatment from DJ YOUR FOOD, FLACCO and BUNDY K. BROWN. A back-to-roots move, and a transformation had PAJO change what was once M, AERIAL M and M IS THE THIRTEENTH LETTER to the new post-rock infused PAPA M. He issued his best to date under this moniker, the sweeping, placid and intimately creepy 'LIVE FROM A SHARK CAGE' at the end of 1999. A slow-burning blend of echoing guitars, badly recorded keyboards and lo-fi stoned beats, the album began with the sweet chamber drone of 'ARUNDAL' moving into the xylophone driven, wintery 'ROADRUNNER'. Elsewhere on the set, PAJO advanced into the quiet eerie proportions of songwriting; the brooding atmosphere on 'CROWD OF ONE' (in which PAJO's recently deceased grandfather's answering machine messages are played over a floating ambient guitar) matches that of some of TORTOISE's more experimental works, where 'KNOCKING THE CASKET' was a banjo-laden lament, PAJO himself knocking on his acoustic guitar, to keep a beat while stomping his foot on a wooden floor. This was to ultimately lead the way for his next outing, the EP 'PAPA M SINGS', in which he put his voice to the test by singing songs in a country style, similar to friend and PALACE man WILL OLDHAM. PAJO recorded the EP on a four-track and passed it around friends. Luckily they liked it. The EP was issued on MOGWAI's 'Rock Action' in Febuary 2001 and boasted the hugely satisfying bitter-sweet/drunk love song 'JADED LOVER'. 'PISSING IN THE WIND', a donkey-paced front porch banjo track had him singing sarcastically about the 'Drag City' imprint, while the slide-guitar rambling in ode-to-a-lover 'TRUE LOVE' reminded listeners of how talented a guitarist PAJO actually was. Sure, his voice was a bit flat, but that all added to the folksy, Kentucky image honed by OLDHAM et al. Later that year, PAJO began work on his follow-up to ' . . .SHARK CAGE' and appeared as a guest on MOGWAI's 'Rock Action' album. PAJO sang again on the 2002 release 'SONGS FOR MAC' where this time PAPA M took two songs by unknowns, MAC FINLEY and AUBREY ROZIER, and covered them knowing most of his audience hadn't heard the originals. A brief and well laid-out EP, the two songs that featured were competent and displayed PAJO's trademark Louisville drawl. The set also saw a switch to the little known label 'Western Vinyl'. Meanwhile PAJO was said to be switching to the mainstream; an unlikely pairing with BILLY CORGAN and his new supergroup ZWAN.

Album rating: TWEEZ (*7) / SPIDERLAND (*8) / For Carnation: PROMISED WORKS collection of US EP's (*6) / THE FOR CARNATION (*8) / Aerial-M: AS PERFORMED BY . . . (*7) / POST-GLOBAL MUSIC (*7) / Papa M: LIVE FROM A SHARK CAGE (*8) / WHATEVER, MORTAL (*7)

BRIAN McMAHAN – vocals, guitar (ex-SQUIRREL BAIT) / **DAVID PAJO** – guitar / **ETHAN BUCKLER** – bass / **BRITT WALFORD** – drums (ex-SQUIRREL BAIT)

		Jennifer Hartman	Jennifer Hartman
Sep 89.	(lp) <*(JHR 136)*> **TWEEZ** – Ron / Nan ding / Carol / Kent / Charlotte / Darlene / Warren / Pat / Rhoda. <(re-iss. May93 on 'Touch & Go' lp/cd; TG 138/+D)>	☐	☐
—	**TODD BRASHER** – bass; BUCKLER who formed KING KONG		

		Touch & Go	Touch & Go
Mar 91.	(lp/cd) <*(TGLP 64/+cd)*> **SPIDERLAND** – Breadcrumb trail / Nosferatu man / Don, Aman / Washer / For dinner . . . / Good morning, captain. *(re-iss. Sep98; same)*	☐	☐
Sep 94.	(10"/cd-s) <*(TG 132/+cd)*> **SLINT** – Glenn / Rhoda.	☐	☐
—	had already disbanded in 1992, WALFORD + McMAHAN later joined the		

PALACE BROTHERS; the latter also formed The FOR CARNATION. PAJO (a part-timer with TFC) subsequently joined TORTOISE before forming AERIAL-M.

The FOR CARNATION

BRIAN McMAHAN with **DAVID PAJO** – guitar / **DOUGLAS McCOMBS** – bass / **JOHN HERNDON** – drums / **GRANT BARGER** – engineer, co-writer

Matador Matador

Jun 95. (cd-ep) *<(OLE 131-2)>* **FIGHT SONGS EP** Apr95
– Grace beneath the pines / How I beat the Devil / Get and stay get March.

—— **BRAD WOOD, JOHN WEISS + TIM RUTH**; repl. PAJO

Mar 96. (m-cd/m-lp) *<OLE 172-2/-1>* **MARSHMALLOWS** -
– On the swing / I wear the gold / Imyr, marshmallow / Winter lair / Salo / Preparing to receive you.

Runt not iss.

Jun 97. (cd) *(RUNT 30)* **PROMISED WORKS** (compilation of the EP and mini-set) -

—— **McMAHAN** recruited his brother **MICHAEL McMAHAN** – guitar / **BOBB BRUNO** – guitar, sampler, keyboards / **TODD COOK** – bass / **STEVE GOODFRIEND** – drums / forthcoming set in March 2000 also incl. **KIM DEAL** – vocals (ex-PIXIES) / **RACHEL HAYDEN** – vocals (of that dog.) + **JOHN McENTIRE** – (who else?, on production)

Domino Touch & Go

Mar 00. (cd/lp) *(WIG CD/LP 77) <TG 214>* **THE FOR CARNATION**
– Empowered man's blues / A tribute to / Being held / Smoother / Tales (live from the crypt) / Moonbeams.

AERIAL-M

DAVID PAJO – guitars (with **LATETIA SADIER** on first)

not iss. Palace

Dec 95. (7"; as M IS THE THIRTEENTH LETTER) *<PR 11>* **SAFELESS. / NAPOLEON** -

not iss. All City

Dec 96. (7") **VOL DE NUIT. / (other track by MONADE)** -

Domino Drag City

Sep 97. (cd/lp) *(WIG CD/LP 037) <DC 114>* **AS PERFORMED BY . . . AERIAL-M** Aug97
– Dazed and awake / Aass / Wedding song No.2 / Rachmaninoff / Skrak theme / Compassion for M / Always farewell.

Feb 98. (7"m)<cd-ep> *(RUG 062)<DC 144CD>* **M IS . . . / WEDDING THEME NO.3 / MOUNTAINS HAVE EARS** Dec97

Jun 98. (7") *(RUG 070) <DC 155>* **OCTOBER** Feb99
– Vivea / Last caress.

Feb 99. (cd/lp) *(WIG CD/LP 63) <DC 170>* **POST-GLOBAL MUSIC** Jan99
– Wedding song No.3 (FLACCO mix) / Wedding song (TIED + TICKLED TRIO remix) / Wedding song No.3 (BUNDY K. BROWN mix) / Attention span deficit disorder disruption a journey wherein (. . . seeks the gateway out of the world of red dust and learns that running between the raindrops won't save you from the chocolate thunder) (DJ YOUR FOOD mix).

PAPA M

—— aka **DAVID PAJO**

Nov 99. (cd/d-lp) *(WIG CD/LP 71) <DC 170>* **LIVE FROM A SHARK CAGE** Oct99
– Arundel / Roadrunner / Pink holler / Plastic energy man / Drunken spree / Bups / Crowd of one / I am not lonely with cricket / Knocking the casket / Up north kids / Arundel.

Jul 00. (cd-ep) *<MTOURCD 1>* **1999 TOUR EP** -
– Up north kids No.2 / She said yes.

Rock Action Sea Note

Apr 01. (cd-ep)<12"ep> *(ROCKACTCD 7) <SN 8>* **PAPA M SINGS** Jan01
– Jaded lover / Pissing in the wind / I of mine / Who am I / True love / London homesick blues.

Awkward Awkward

Nov 01. (7") *<(AWKWARD 10)>* **MAMA YOU BEEN ON MY MIND. / (other by Unhome)**

—— now augmented by **BRITT WALFORD** – drums (ex-SLINT) **WILL OLDHAM** – guitars, etc / + TARA JANE O'NEIL – guitar (ex-RODAN)

Domino Drag City

Nov 01. (cd/d-lp) *(WIG CD/LP 103) <DC 194>* **WHATEVER, MORTAL**
– Over Jordan / Beloved woman / Roses in the snow / Sorrow reigns / Krusty / The lass of Roch Royal / Many splendored thing / Glad you're here with me / Tamu / Sabotage / Purple eyelid / The unquiet grave / Northwest passage.

Western Vinyl Western Vinyl

Mar 02. (cd-ep) *<(WV 014)>* **SONGS OF MAC**
– So warped / The person and the skeleton.

—— PAJO subsequently joined ZWAN (yes, BILLY CORGAN's outfit)

SLIPSTREAM

Formed: Rugby, England . . . 1993 by MARK REFOY when he was still a member of SPIRITUALIZED. Early in 1994, SLIPSTREAM (who were completed by IAN ANDERSON, GARY LENNON and STEVE BESWICK) signed to indie label, 'Che', releasing three singles over the course of the following year, the last of which was a version of Kraftwerk's 'COMPUTER LOVE'. Their accompanying eponymous ZION TRAIN-produced album was issued in March '95, featuring some fine acoustic PINK FLOYD/CAN-ish styled songs. Later that year, two more singles preceded a compilation, although all was quiet on the SLIPSTREAM front until 1997's 'BE GROOVY OR LEAVE'.

Album rating: SLIPSTREAM (*6) / SIDE EFFECTS compilation (*6) / BE GROOVY OR LEAVE (*5)

MARK REFOY – vocals, guitar (ex-SPIRITUALIZED) / **IAN ANDERSON** – guitar / **GARY LENNON** – bass / **STEVE BESWICK** – drums

Che Carrot Top

Jul 94. (7"yellow) *(che 14)* **SUNDOWN. / SWEET MERCY / IT'S TRUE SHE SAID** -

Oct 94. (7") *(che 19)* **YOUR PRESENCE. / GIVE IT SOME TIME** -
(cd-s+=) *(che 19cd)* – Hometown / I saw your face.

Feb 95. (7"one-sided-pink) *(che 21)* **COMPUTER LOVE** -

Mar 95. (cd/c/lp) *(che 22 cd/mc/lp) <7>* **SLIPSTREAM**
– Harmony / Riverside / Pulsebeat / One step ahead / Sensurround / Computer love / Sweet mercy / Feel good again / Sundown / She passes by.

Sep 95. (7") *(che 35)* **UP IN HEAVEN. / HEARING VOICES** -

Sep 95. (7") *(che 36)* **COME BACK. / LATE TOO LATE** -

Che Elektra

Dec 95. (cd) *(che 37cd) <61875>* **SIDE EFFECTS** (singles compilation) Oct95
– Up in Heaven / Hearing voices / Come back / Late too late / Do you have an answer? / All for nothing / All the symphonies / Computer love / Your presence / Give it some time / Hometown / I saw your face / Sundown / Sweet mercy / It's true she said.

Urban Culture not iss.

Jul 96. (12") *(05)* **INTERFERENCE. / THE ABYSS** -

—— **STEVE NEW** – bass; repl. LENNON

Che Che-Warners

Jun 97. (lp/cd) *(che/+cd 69) <62083>* **BE GROOVY OR LEAVE**
– Dancing mood / You'll never catch me out again / Scars / Not there with you / There is a love / Come on and listen / Madeleine / Beneath the waves / Say it now / Leave it all behind.

Dec 97. (7") *(che 73)* **MADELEINE. / HEALING HANDS** -

Enraptured not iss.

Dec 98. (7") *(RAPT 4522)* **EVERYTHING & ANYTHING. / MIDNIGHT TRAIN** -

—— disbanded in 1999

SLOAN

Formed: Halifax, Novia Scotia, Canada . . . 1991 by CHRIS MURPHY, PATRICK PENTLAND, JAY FERGUSON and ANDREW SCOTT. Touting an unrestrained soundclash of melodic grunge and fuzz-pop, SLOAN snagged a deal with 'Geffen' after an unlikely showcase at Canada's predominantly folk orientated East Coast Music Awards. Yet by the time they'd moved on up to major label land, the band had already cut a debut EP, 'PEPPERMINT', releasing it on their own 'Murder' label in Autumn '92. Debut album, 'SMEARED', followed later that year amid positive press reaction praising the band's affecting combination of pointed lyrics and gonzoid RAMONES-style enthusiasm. Despite promising North American sales, the group parted company with 'Geffen' after follow-up set, 'TWICE REMOVED' (1994), subsequently taking time out themselves to rethink their strategy. The SLOAN crew eventually re-emerged with the self-financed 'ONE CHORD TO ANOTHER' in 1997, successfully licensing the record to 'E.M.I.' for worldwide release. The rough'n'ready pop malarky of 'NAVY BLUES' (1998) was followed by '4 NIGHTS AT THE PALAIS ROYALE' (1999), a tongue-in-cheek, double-disc tribute to their 70's rock god heroes. 1999 also saw the release of a studio set, 'BETWEEN THE BRIDGES', smoothing out the rough edges, polishing the melodies and concentrating the arrangements for a more mature pop experience. 'PRETTY TOGETHER' (2001) also made leaps and bounds in the songwriting department if never deviating too much from the tried and tested retro-friendly formula. • **Covered:** DIGNIFIED AND OLD (Jonathan Richman) / GLITTER AND GOLD (Mann-Weil) / OVER YOU (Roxy Music) / I CAN'T LET GO (Gorgoni-Taylor) / STOOD UP (. . . Grimson) / ON THE ROAD AGAIN – TRANSOMA FIVE (Canned Heat – Stereolab) / I WOULDN'T WANT TO LOSE YOUR LOVE (April Wine).

Album rating: SMEARED (*6) / TWICE REMOVED (*6) / ONE CHORD TO ANOTHER (*7) / NAVY BLUES (*7) / 4 NIGHTS AT THE PALAIS ROYALE (*5) / BETWEEN THE BRIDGES (*6) / PRETTY TOGETHER (*6)

JAY FERGUSON – vocals, guitar / **PATRICK PENTLAND** (b. N.Ireland) – guitar, vocals / **CHRIS MURPHY** – bass, vocals / **ANDREW SCOTT** – drums

Murderchords Murderchords

1992. (cd-ep) *<(MURCD 001)>* **PEPPERMINT EP**
– Marcus said / Underwhelmed / Pretty voice / Lucky for me / Sugartune / Torn. *(re-iss. May01; same)*

Geffen Geffen

Feb 93. (cd/c/lp) *<(GED/GEC/GEF 24498)>* **SMEARED**
– Underwhelmed / Raspberry / I am the cancer / Median strip / Take it in / 500 up / Marcus said / Sugartune / Left of centre / Lemonzinger / Two seater / What's there to decide. *(re-iss. May01 on 'Murderechords' lp/cd; MUR/+BD 037)*

Mar 93. (12"ep/cd-ep) *(GFST/+D 36)* **UNDERWHELMED / WHAT'S THERE TO DECIDE? / AMPED / SLEEPOVER** -

Jul 93. (12"ep/cd-ep) *(GFST/+D 45)* **I AM THE CANCER / TWO SEATER. / RAG DOLL / LAYING BLAME** -

Aug 94. (cd/c) *<(GED/GEC 24711)>* **TWICE REMOVED**
– Penpals / I hate my generation / People of the sky / Coax me / Bells on / Loosens / Worried now / Shame shame / Deeper than beauty / Snowsuit sound / Before I do / I can feel it. *(re-iss. May01 on 'Murder' lp/cd; MUR/+MD 011)*

Murderechords Capitol

Apr 97. (lp/cd) *(MUR/+MD 023) <55281>* **ONE CHORD TO ANOTHER**
– Good in everyone / Nothing left to make me wanna stay / Autobiography / Junior panthers / G turns to D / Side wins / Everything you've done wrong / Anyone who's anyone / Lines you amend / Take the bench / Can't face up / 400 metres / Let's get the party started / I can feel it. <cd+=>**PARTY** – Dignified and old / Glitter and gold / Over you / I am the cancer / I can't let go / Stood up / One the road again – Transoma five / I wouldn't want to lose your love. *(cd re-iss. May01; same)*

SLOAN (cont) — THE GREAT INDIE DISCOGRAPHY — The 1990s

1997.	(7") **THE RHODES JAM**		Murderecords / Murderecords
May 98.	(cd) <(MURCD 36)> **NAVY BLUES**		

– She says what she means / C'mon c'mon (we're gonna get it started) / Iggy & Angus / Sinking ships / Keep on thinkin' / Money city maniacs / Seems so heavy / Chester the molester / Stand by me, yeah / Suppose they close the door / On the horizon / I wanna thank you / I'm not through with you yet. (re-iss. May01; same)

Jun 99. (d-cd) <(MURCD 39)> **4 NIGHTS AT THE PALAIS (live)**
– She says what she means / The good in everyone / Coax me / The lines you amend / Marcus said / Seems so heavy / Sinking ships / Everything you've done wrong / Keep on thinkin' / Snowsuit sound / Suppose they close the door / Iggy and Angus / Bells on / Anyone who's anyone / People of the sky / 400 metres / On the horizon / I wanna thank you / G turns to D / Penpals / Money city maniacs / Deeper than beauty / I am the cancer / I can feel it / Torn / Nothing left to make me want to stay / Before I do / Underwhelmed. (re-iss. Oct00; same) (t-lp-iss.May01; MUR 038)

Nov 99. (cd) <(MRDR 40CD)> **BETWEEN THE BRIDGES**
– The N.S. / Beyond me / Don't you believe a word / Friendship / Sensory deprivation / All by ourselves / A long time coming / Waiting for slow songs / Losing California / The marquee and the moon / Take good care of the poor boy / Delivering maybes. (re-iss. Oct00; 774880040-2)

Nov 00. (cd-s) (MUR 041) **DON'T YOU BELIEVE A WORD** — B.M.G. / R.C.A.

Feb 02. (cd) (74321 88102-2) <68116> **PRETTY TOGETHER** — / Oct01
– If it feels good do it / In the movies / The other man / Dreaming of you / Pick it up and dial it / The great wall / The life of a working girl / Never seeing the ground for the sky / It's in your eyes / Who you talkin' to? / I love a long goodbye / Are you giving me back my love? / Your dreams have come true.

SLOWDIVE

Formed: Thames Valley, Reading, England ... 1990 by schoolfriends RACHEL GOSWELL and NEIL HALSTEAD. The pair duly recruited NICK CHAPLIN and belatedly accepted a final member, CHRISTIAN SAVILLE, who had been desperate to join them. After only a handful of gigs, SLOWDIVE signed to Alan McGee's 'Creation' label, where they debuted with a self-titled EP. Early the following year, the quartet scored another massive alternative chart hit with 'MORNINGRISE'. Their third EP, 'HOLDING OUR BREATH', nearly cracked the UK Top 50, the debut album, 'JUST FOR A DAY', accomplishing this feat later that year. Immersed in shimmering, distortion-happy guitars and ethereal atmospheric harmonies, their sound lay somewhere between MY BLOODY VALENTINE, The JESUS & MARY CHAIN and other "shoegazers" (RIDE and MOOSE) of that early 90's era. However, emerging grunge acts like NIRVANA were to hasten SLOWDIVE's downfall, well at least in the music press stakes where "shoegazing" bands were now looked down upon. After an 18-month hiatus, they returned with the follow-up, 'SOUVLAKI', although it was clear from their poor sales they had left it too long. An EP entitled '5EP' (their 5th) showed greater promise, using techno acts RELOAD and BANDULU to boost their now ambient direction. After their third and probably best album, 'PYGMALION' (1995), they were dropped amid a fundamental shake-up at their record label. NEIL and RACHEL were promptly snatched up by '4 a.d.', resurfacing later that year with the much underrated MOJAVE 3, actually a 5-piece completed by IAN McCUTCHEON, SIMON ROWE and POPPY (aka AUDREY RILEY). Mapping out entirely different territory from SLOWDIVE, the HALSTEAD – GOSWELL songwriting axis was now geared towards a wistful, heavy-lidded amalgam of countrified alt-folk/pop taking in the likes of LEONARD COHEN, NICK DRAKE and MAZZY STAR. This much was evident from even a cursory listen to their inaugural long-player, 'ASK ME TOMORROW'. Unfortunately it would be three long years before a follow-up, the acclaimed but generally ignored 'OUT OF TUNE' (1998). In terms of the music industry's eternal obsession with the emperor's new clothes, MOJAVE 3 resemble a threadbare favourite shirt, as comfortable and reassuring as the last time you fished it out from the bottom of the drawer. Rarely deviating from their exquisitely realised melancholia, 'EXCUSES FOR TRAVELLERS' (2000) was another gem to file alongside a growing collection with the added bonuses of a lead vocal from RACHEL GOSWELL. In fact, such was HALSTEAD's talent for writing downbeat elegies to life's emotional pitfalls that he had to release a solo album, 'SLEEPING ON ROADS' (2002) for all the ones that didn't fit onto the MOJAVE 3 albums. As such, they weren't quite up to the consummate, lugubrious quality fans have come to expect but they still stood head and shoulders above the competition. • **SLOWDIVE covered:** GOLDEN HAIR (Syd Barrett).

Album rating: JUST FOR A DAY (*6) / SOUVLAKI (*5) / PYGMALION (*7) / Mojave 5: ASK ME TOMORROW (*7) / OUT OF TUNE (*7) / EXCUSES FOR TRAVELLERS (*6) / Neil Halstead: SLEEPING ON ROADS (*6)

RACHEL GOSWELL (b.16 May'71, Hampshire, England) – vocals, guitar / **NEIL HALSTEAD** (b. 7 Oct'70, Luton, England) – vocals, guitar / **CHRISTIAN SAVILLE** (b. 6 Dec'70, Bury, England) – guitar / **NICK CHAPLIN** (b.23 Dec'70, Slough, England) – bass / **NEIL CARTER** (ex-COLOUR MARY), who had repl. original ADRIAN SELL

Creation / S.B.K.

Nov 90. (12"ep)(cd-ep) (CRE 093T)(CRESCD 093) **SLOWDIVE:- AVALYN I. / SLOWDIVE:- AVALYN II**

— **SIMON SCOTT** (b. 3 Mar'71, Cambridge, England) – drums (ex-CHARLOTTES) repl. NEIL CARTER

Feb 91. (12"ep)(cd-ep) (CRE 098T)(CRESCD 098) **MORNINGRISE. / SHE CALLS / LOSING TODAY**

Jun 91. (7") (CRE 112) **CATCH THE BREEZE. / SHINE** — 52 / —
(12"ep+=)(cd-ep+=) **HOLDING OUR BREATH** (CRE 112T)(CRESCD 112) – Albatross / Golden hair.

Aug 91. (cd/lp)(c) (CRE CD/LP 094)(CCRE 094) <98074> **JUST FOR A DAY** — 32
– Spanish air / Cedlia's dream / Catch the breeze / Ballad of Sister Sue / Erik's song / Waves / Brighter / The sadman / Primal.

1992. (cd/lp) **BLUE DAY** — —
– Slowdive:- Avalyn I / Morningrise / She calls / Losing today / Shine / Albatross.

— now without CHAPLIN

May 93. (12"ep)(cd-ep) (CRE 119T)(CRESCD 119) **OUTSIDE YOUR ROOM** — 69 / —
– Alison / So tired / Souvlaki space station / Moussaka chaos.

Jun 93. (cd/lp)(c) (CRE CD/LP 139)(CCRE 139) <88263> **SOUVLAKI** — 51 / Feb94
– Alison / Machine gun / 40 days / Sing / Here she comes / Souvlaki space station / When the Sun hits / Altogether / Melon yellow / Dagger.

Nov 93. (12"ep)(cd-ep) (CRE 157T)(CRESCD 157) **5 EP** — —
– Bandulu (in mind mix) / (open mind mix) / (in mind mix) / Reload (remix – the 147 take).
(12"ep)(cd-ep) (CRE 157TR)(CRESCD 157R) – ('A'-other mixes).

Feb 95. (cd/lp)(c) (CRE CD/LP 168)(CCRE 168) **PYGMALION** — —
– Rutty / Crazy for you / Miranda / Trellisaze / Cello / Jay's heaven / Visions of L.A. / Blue skied and clear / All of us.

— split later in the year, SIMON resurfaced in 1998 as frontman for INNER SLEEVE.

MOJAVE 3

— **RACHEL + NEIL** plus **IAN McCUTCHEON** – drums, percussion / **SIMON ROWE** – guitar / **POPPY (AUDREY RILEY)** – cello / with guest **CHRISTOPHER ANDREWS** – piano

4 a.d. / 4ad-Reprise

Oct 95. (lp/cd) (CAD 5013/+CD) <46084> **ASK ME TOMORROW** — / Feb96
– Love songs on the radio / Sarah / Tomorrow's taken / Candle song 3 / You're beautiful / Where is the love / After all / Pictures / Mercy. (cd re-iss. Jul98; GAD 5013CD)

4 a.d. / Sire

Jun 98. (cd-ep) (BAD 8011CD) **WHO DO YOU LOVE / THIS ROAD I'M TRAVELLING / BETWEEN US / WHO DO YOU LOVE (demo)**

Sep 98. (7") (AD AD 8016) **SOME KINDA ANGEL. / ALL I WANT**
(cd-s+=) (BAD 8016CD) – Go lady go.

Oct 98. (lp/cd) (CAD 8018/+CD) <31047> **OUT OF TUNE** — / Feb99
– Who do you love / Give what you take / Some kinda angel / All your tears / Yer feet / Caught behind your heel / Keep it all hid / Baby's coming home / To whom should I write.

4 a.d. / 4 a.d.

May 00. (lp/cd) (CAD2K 05/+CD) <1092> **EXCUSES FOR TRAVELLERS**
– In love with a view / Trying to reach you / My life in art / Return to sender / When you're drifting / Anyday will be fine / She broke you so softly / Prayer for the paranoid / Bringin' me home / Got my sunshine. <US+=> – Krazy koz / Always right.

NEIL HALSTEAD

with **IAN McCUTCHEON** + others

4 a.d. / 4 a.d.

Jan 02. (cd) (CAD 2202CD) <72202> **SLEEPING ON ROADS**
– Seasons / Two stones in my pocket / Driving with Bert / Hi-lo and inbetween / See you on rooftops / Martha's mantra (for the pain) / Sleeping on roads / Dreamed I saw soldiers / High hopes.

Jun 02. (cd-ep) (BAD 2212CD) **SEASONS** — —
– Seasons (surf style) / See you on rooftops (alt. version) / Sailing man / Between the bars / Seasons (Fort Lauderdale remix).

SLUDGEWORTH (see under ⇒ SCREECHING WEASEL)

SLUMBER (see under ⇒ FAT TULIPS)

SLUMBER PARTY

Formed: Detroit, Michigan, USA ... 1998 by ALICCIA BERG and GRETCHEN GONZALES, adding RACHEL KUCSULVAIN and JULIE BENJAMIN to the line-up. A slight diversion from the usual garage rock template of Detroit, SLUMBER PARTY employed a soft harmonic, psychedelic counterpart to their more abrasive peers. Beginning life on seminal indie label 'Kill Rock Stars', the group issued their self-titled debut in 2000 to rapturous acclaim from the likes of THURSTON MOORE (of SONIC YOUTH). The set, jammed with floating harmonies and spacy guitar, echoed NICO and GALAXIE 500, with BERG's chanteuse vocals stretching out beautifully over the entire set. In between projects such as The UNIVERSAL INDIANS and DR. GRETCHEN MUSICAL WEIGHTLIFTING PROGRAM (mostly involving the aforementioned MOORE) BERG and Co issued their excellent sophomore LP, 'PSYCHEDELICATE' in 2001. Just what the title suggests, SLUMBER PARTY later went on to impress former 'Creation' honcho ALAN McGEE, who signed them to his current label 'Poptones'.

Album rating: SLUMBER PARTY (*6) / PSYCHEDELICATE (*7)

GRETCHEN GONZALES – vocals, guitar (ex-UNIVERSAL INDIANS) / **ALICCIA BERG** – vocals, guitar, piano / **RACHEL KUCSULVAIN** – bass, vocals / **JULIE BENJAMIN** – drums

not iss. / Kill Rock Stars

Nov 99. (7") <KRS 334> **MAIL ORDER FREAK** — —
Aug 00. (cd) <KRS 363> **SLUMBER PARTY** — —
– Sooner or later / Certain versions / Strawberry Sunday / Trouble of my own / Any other day / Why do I care? / Fantasy / Ten little pills / All in the way / I don't mind / Retaliation / Blue sky / I'm an example. <lp-iss.2000 on 'Dulcitone'; TIBBY 5> (UK-iss.Oct01 on 'Poptones'+=; MC 5032MC) – I don't mind (video).

SLUMBER PARTY (cont)

— MARCIE BOLEN was also a member before she joined VON BONDIES

Aug 01. (cd) <KRS 377> **PSYCHEDELICATE**
 – Bag of spiders / Never again / Soldier / Everyone else I know / My little one / Heroes and zeros / You've gone too far / I'm not sad / Sometimes / I never dreamed / Depression is best.

SMALLER

Formed: Liverpool, England ... early 90's by drummer/songwriter PETER DEARY, his brother and frontman STEPHEN DEARY, plus PAUL CAVANNAGH and JASON RILEY. Boasting a chequered musical CV including a stint in early 80's popsters COOK DA BOOKS, PETER DEARY (aka DIGSY) had been slogging away at writing songs almost as long as his old mucker NOEL GALLAGHER (a guest on the debut album), the latter giving him a starring role in OASIS favourite, 'Digsy's Dinner' (from 'Definitely Maybe'). Located firmly in the hard-bitten realism school of writing, DEARY spelled out his self-admittedly cynical worldview on SMALLER's debut single, 'GOD I HATE THIS TOWN', issued in Autumn '95 on independent label, 'Better'. Over the course of the next 18 months, SMALLER delivered three singles, the latter two, 'WASTED' and 'IS', hitting the lower regions of the charts. A full length debut album, 'BADLY BADLY' (1997), carried on in the same vein, self-deprecatingly detailing the trials and tribulations of years in the pop wilderness.

Album rating: BADLY BADLY (*6)

STEPHEN DEARY – vocals, lead guitar / **PAUL CAVANNAGH** – bass / **JASON RILEY** – guitar, vocals / **PETER DEARY** – drums (ex-COOK DA BOOKS)

		Better	not iss.
Sep 95. (7") (betcd 002) **GOD I HATE THIS TOWN. / IT'S CLOSED** (cd-s+=) (betscd 002) – I hate music / (+1).			-
Apr 96. (7") (bet 005) **STRAY DOGS AND BIN BAGS. / SOMEWHERE ELSE** (cd-s+=) (betscd 005) – (+2).			-
Sep 96. (7") (bet 006) **WASTED. / AIMLESS** (cd-s+=) (betscd 006) – Garden shed / Chain of solitude.		72	-
Mar 97. (7") (bet 008) **IS. / ALL THE SAME TO ME** (cd-s+=) (betscd 008) – The pane. (cd-s) (betscd 008L) – ('A'album version) / Wasted (live) / ('A'live) / The cross (live).		55	-
Apr 97. (cd/c/lp) (bet cd/mc/lp 003) **BADLY BADLY** – Small time / The biscuit tin / Is / Whenever love lies / Wasted / On your own / God I hate this town / Ticket to Hell / Just as bad / Giz a life / In my livable hole.			-

— the group have since split

SMALL FACES

Formed: East London, England ... mid '65 by RONNIE LANE, KENNY JONES and JIMMY WINSTON, who subsequently found lead singer and ex-child actor, STEVE MARRIOTT. After a successful residency at Leicester Square's Cavern Club, the band were snapped up by 'Decca' records as potential usurpers to The WHO's mod crown. Their debut single, 'WHATCHA GONNA DO ABOUT IT' (1965) graced the Top 20 with its roughshod R&B and amid the ensuing attention the band received, WINSTON was kicked out after shamelessly trying to promote himself as the lynchpin of the group. With IAN McLAGAN drafted in as a replacement, the band hit Top 3 with the 'SHA LA LA LA LEE' (1966) single. Despite the cliched boy-meets-girl lyric, the record was a wildly exhilarating rush of amphetamine pop and suddenly The SMALL FACES were big news. After another Top 10 single and a critically acclaimed eponymous debut album, the band were being mentioned in the same breath as The BEATLES and The ROLLING STONES. Indeed, in August '66 they deposed The Fab Four's 'ELEANOR RIGBY' at the top of the charts with 'ALL OR NOTHING'. Come 1967, the band had left 'Decca' and signed with ANDREW LOOG-OLDHAM's 'Immediate' label, releasing 'HERE COMES THE NICE'. The single marked a change in direction and in keeping with the times, was vaguely psychedelic. After a similarly adventurous second album that bore a decidedly unadventurous title ('SMALL FACES' yet again), the band released their most well-known track, the slightly twee, deeply dippy 'ITCHYCOO PARK' (later reduced to dross by M-PEOPLE). Next came the abrasive 'TIN SOLDIER' (1967) single after which the band began working on their psychedelic masterpiece, 'OGDEN'S NUT GONE FLAKE' (1968). An engaging blend of trippy R&B and cockney charm, the album's influence was far reaching and it gets re-issued with the same tireless regularity as 'OCEAN WELLER SCENE' namedrop the band. Timeless as it was, the record proved to be the group's swansong and after a few singles, including the gorgeous 'AFTERGLOW (OF YOUR LOVE)' (1969), the band split with MARRIOTT flouncing off to form HUMBLE PIE.

Album rating: THE SMALL FACES (*6) / FROM THE BEGINNING out-takes (*6) / SMALL FACES (*5) / THERE ARE BUT FOUR SMALL FACES (*7) / OGDENS' NUT GONE FLAKE (*8) / THE AUTUMN STONE collection (*5)

THE ULTIMATE COLLECTION compilation (*8)

STEVE MARRIOTT (b.30 Jan'47, Bow, London) – vocals, guitar (ex-solo artist) / **JIMMY WINSTON** (b. JAMES LANGWITH, 20 Apr'45, Stratford, London) – organ / **RONNIE LANE** (b. 1 Apr'45, Plaistow, London) – bass, vocals / **KENNEY JONES** (b.16 Sep'48, Stepney, London) – drums

	Decca	Press
Aug 65. (7") (F 12208) <45-9794> **WHATCHA GONNA DO ABOUT IT?. / WHAT'S A MATTER, BABY**	14	Jan66
— IAN McLAGAN (b.12 May'45, Hounslow, England) – keyboards repl. WINSTON who went solo		
Nov 65. (7") (F 12276) **I'VE GOT MINE. / IT'S TOO LATE**		-
Jan 66. (7") (F 12317) <45-9826> **SHA-LA-LA-LA-LEE. / GROW YOUR OWN**	3	Apr66
May 66. (7") (F 12393) <45-5007> **HEY GIRL. / ALMOST GROWN**	10	Jul66
May 66. (lp) (LK 4790) **SMALL FACES** – Shake / Come on children / You better believe it / It's too late / One night stand / Whatcha gonna do about it? / Sorry she's mine / E to D / You need loving / Don't stop what you're doing / Own up / Sha-la-la-la-lee. (cd-iss. Jul88 on 'London'+= 820 572-2) – What's a matter baby / I've got mine / Grow your own / Almost grown.	3	-

	Decca	RCA Victor
Aug 66. (7") (F 12470) <45-8949> **ALL OR NOTHING. / UNDERSTANDING**	1	Sep66
Nov 66. (7") (F 12500) <47-9055> **MY MIND'S EYE. / I CAN'T DANCE WITH YOU**	4	Dec66
Feb 67. (7") (F 12565) **I CAN'T MAKE IT. / JUST PASSING**	26	-
Apr 67. (7") (F 12619) **PATTERNS. / E TO D**		-
May 67. (lp) (LK 4879) **FROM THE BEGINNING** (out-takes, demos, etc) – Runaway / My mind's eye / Yesterday, today and tomorrow / That man / My way of giving / Hey girl / Tell me have you ever seen me? / Come back and take this hurt off me / All or nothing / Baby don't do it / Plum Nellie / Sha-la-la-la-lee / You really got a hold on me / Whatcha gonna do about it?. (re-iss. Aug84; DOA 2) (cd-iss. Jan89 on 'London' w/ extra tracks; 820 766-2)	17	-

	Immediate	Immediate
Jun 67. (7") (IM 050) <1902> **HERE COMES THE NICE. / TALK TO YOU**	12	
Jun 67. (lp; mono/stereo) (IMLP/IMSP 008) **SMALL FACES** – Green circles / Become like you / Get yourself together / All our yesterdays / Talk to you / Show me the way / Up the wooden hills to Bedfordshire / Eddie's dreaming (Tell me) / Have you ever seen me / Something I want to tell you / Feeling lonely / Happy boys happy / Things are going to get better / My way of giving. (cd-iss. May91 as 'GREEN CIRCLES (FIRST IMMEDIATE ALBUM)' on 'Sequel'; NEXCD 163) (+=) – Green circles (take 2) / Donkey rides, a penny, a glass / Have you ever seen me (take 2). (cd re-iss. Apr97 on 'Essential'; ESMCD 476)	12	
Aug 67. (7") (IM 052) <501> **ITCHYCOO PARK. / I'M ONLY DREAMING**	3	16 Nov67
Nov 67. (7") (IM 062) <5003> **TIN SOLDIER. / I FEEL MUCH BETTER** (re-iss. May75; IMS 100)	9	73 Mar68
Feb 68. (lp) <Z12-52-002> **THERE ARE BUT FOUR SMALL FACES** – Here comes the nice / All or nothing / Lazy Sunday / Sha-la-la-la-lee / Collibosher / The Autumn stone / Whatcha gonna do about it? / My mind's eye / Itchycoo Park / Hey girl / The universal / Runaway / Call it something nice / I can't make it / Afterglow (of your love) / Tin soldier.	-	
Apr 68. (7") (IM 064) <5007> **LAZY SUNDAY. / ROLLIN' OVER** (re-iss. Oct82; same)	2	-
Jun 68. (lp; mono/stereo) (IMLP/IMSP 012) <Z12-52-008> **OGDENS' NUT GONE FLAKE** – Ogden's nut gone flake / Afterglow (of your love) / Long agos and worlds apart / Rene / Son of a baker / Lazy Sunday / Happiness Stan / Rollin' over / The hungry intruder / The journey / Mad John / Happy days / Toy town. <US re-iss. on 'Abkco'; 4225> (re-iss. Dec75; IML 1001) (re-iss. Jun77; IML 2001) (re-iss. export Aug78 on 'Charly'; CR 300015) (re-iss. Mar80 on 'Virgin'; V 2159) (re-iss. Oct86 on 'Castle' lp/cd+=; CLA LP/CD 116) – Tin soldier (live). (re-cd-iss. in box Feb91 on 'Castle'; CLACT 016) (cd re-iss. Feb97 on 'Original Recordings'; ORRLP 001) (cd re-iss. Apr97 on 'Essential'; ESMCD 477)	1	
Jul 68. (7") (IM 069) <5009> **THE UNIVERSAL. / DONKEY RIDES, A PENNY, A GLASS**	16	
Nov 68. (7") <5012> **THE JOURNEY. / MAD JOHN**	-	
Mar 69. (7") (IM 077) <5014> **AFTERGLOW (OF YOUR LOVE). / WHAM BAM, THANK YOU MAM**	36	
Mar 69. (d-lp) (IMAL 01/02) **THE AUTUMN STONE** (rarities, live, etc) – Here comes the nice / The Autumn stone / Collibosher / All or nothing / Red balloon / Lazy Sunday / Rollin' over / If I were a carpenter / Every little bit hurts / My mind's eye / Tin soldier / Just asking / Call it something nice / I can't make it / Afterglow (of your love) / Sha-la-la-la-lee / The universal / Itchycoo Park / Hey girl / Wide eyed girl / On the wall / Whatcha gonna do about it / Wham bam thank you mam. (re-iss. Jul84; IMLD 1) (re-iss. May86 on 'Castle' lp/c/cd; CLA LP/MC/CD 114) (re-iss. 1991) (cd re-iss. Apr97 on 'Essential'; ESMCD 477)		

— disbanded Mar'69 when STEVE MARRIOTT formed HUMBLE PIE. The remaining members became The FACES

SMALL FACTORY

Formed: Providence, Rhode Island, USA ... 1991 by ALEX KEMP, DAVE AUCHENBACH and PHOEBE SUMMERSQUASH. With their early semi-acoustic sound, SMALL FACTORY first began to acquire an East Coast indie following after impressing at the 1991 'Lotsa-Pop-Losers' festival in Washington D.C. With subsequent well-received gigs in the Northeast area, they contributed 'THE GIANT MERRY-GO-ROUND' to a fanzine flexi-disc, along with HONEYBUNCH and The BACHELOR PAD (the latter from

Glasgow). Then followed their first single release, 'SUGGESTIONS' (on the 'Collision Time' label) and a second single, 'WHAT TO WANT' (this time on 'Slumberland'). Moving into 1992, they enhanced their live reputation with a strong showing at the Providence Indie Rock Festival, a series of English dates with HEAVENLY, and then support slots touring the US with FUDGE and The DAMBUILDERS. Two further 1993 singles – 'SO WHAT ABOUT LOVE' (on 'Pop Narcotic') and 'IF YOU HURT ME' (on 'Simple Machines') – preceded the September '93 release of debut LP 'LEMON: I DO NOT LOVE YOU' (this time on 'SpinArt'). SMALL FACTORY managed to reasonably successfully translate their impressive live sound and enthusiasm onto record. With collective vocal contributions, 'LOTS TO DO' and 'KEEP ON SMILING' were typically energetic, while 'PRETENDING IT'S SUNNY' and 'JUNKY ON A GOOD DAY' express a melancholy and sobriety. Second album 'FOR IF YOU CANNOT FLY', released the following year, was driven by a constant momentum of even catchier tunes, structured around well integrated vocals and harmonies, like on 'HI HOWARD, I'M BACK'. SMALL FACTORY split-up in 1995, with KEMP and SUMMERSQUASH joining the GODRAYS – releasing a 1996 album 'SONGS FOR TV STARS' – and AUCHENBACH joining FLORA STREET. 'INDUSTRIAL EVOLUTION', released in 1996 on 'Pop Narcotic', was a compilation of SMALL FACTORY's singles from 1991-94. • Covered: Godrays – CRAZY (Versus).

Album rating: LEMON: I DO NOT LOVE YOU (*5) / FOR IF YOU CANNOT FLY (*7) / INDUSTRIAL EVOLUTION compilation (*6) / Halo Bit: GRAVITY (*4) / Godrays: SONGS FOR TV STARS (*6) / WELL COMPOSED DEATH NOTICE mini (*5)

ALEX KEMP – vocals, bass / **DAVE AUCHENBACH** – vocals, guitar / **PHOEBE SUMMERSQUASH** – vocals, drums

		not iss.	Collision Time
Sep 91.	(7"m) **SUGGESTIONS. / HAPPY TO SEE / NOT AFRAID**	-	
		not iss.	Slumberland
Apr 92.	(7"m) <SLR 13> **WHAT TO WANT. / HERE YOU COME / THE GIANT MERRY-GO-ROUND**	-	
		not iss.	Pop Narcotic
Jul 93.	(7") <NARC 005> **SO WHAT ABOUT LOVE. / WE WILL**	-	
		not iss.	Simple Machines
Aug 93.	(7") <smwh 08> **IF YOU HURT ME. / (other by TSUNAMI)**	-	
		not iss.	SpinArt
Sep 93.	(lp/cd) <SPIN 23/+CD> **LEMON: I DO NOT LOVE YOU**	-	

– I'm not giving up / Keep on smiling / What to want / What angels say / Our desert / Valentine / Lots to do / Pretending it's sunny / All your reasons / Come back down / Friends / Junky on a good day.

		Bi-Joopiter	Slumberland
Jul 94.	(7") (BIJOOP 28) <SLR 26> **LOSE YOUR WAY. / SCARED OF LOVE**		
		Quigley	Vernon Yard
Feb 95.	(7") (HREC 4) **THE LAST TIME THAT WE TALKED. / MOVIES**		-
Feb 95.	(cd/lp) (QUIG D/L 6) <YARDCD 009> **FOR IF YOU CANNOT FLY**		May94
			Nov94

– The last time that we talked / Expiration date / Hi Howard I'm back / Sensible / Everybody's happy for the first time in ages / Versus tape / The bright side / Sun goes ahh / Three months later / For when you cannot land / Sixteen years.

––– split later in 1995; AUCHENBACH joined FLORA STREET

– compilations, etc. –

Jun 96. (cd) *Pop Narcotic; <13>* **INDUSTRIAL EVOLUTION**

– Suggestions / Happy to see / Not afraid / What to want / Here you come / The giant merry-go-round / Hey Lucille / If you hurt me / So what about love / We will / Yeah / Hopefully / Lose your way / Scared of love.

HALO BIT

ALEX KEMP – vocals, guitar / **DAVE McCAFFREY** – guitar, vocals / **DICKIE WRIGHT** – bass, vocals

		not iss.	SpinArt
Aug 94.	(lp/cd) <SPIN 34/+CD> **GRAVITY**	-	

– When the sun hits me / Kiss for the one / Dreams like you / Birds not flying / Freon Wednesday / Angels and aliens / My rock & roll / Let you know / Ditched / In case she spaces / Plastic airplane / Two passing stars / W Sarah.

GODRAYS

KEMP + SUMMERSQUASH

		Vernon Yard	Vernon Yard
May 96.	(d7"ep) (YARD 021) **SONGS FOR TV STARS**		-

– Songs for TV stars / Crummy / No arms / Movie music 2.

| Oct 96. | (cd) <(YARDCD 017)> **SONGS FOR TV STARS** | | Jun96 |

– Comforting Joe / Songs for TV stars / Vampires suck / Darling / Careless / Both your names (Janus' creepy girlfriend) / Still just a night thing / 30 second song / Crummy / Boyscout thriller / Crack you up / Bother (the blushes) / Crazy / Carkeys, ponytail and gum.

Nov 96. (7"ep) (YARD 023) **THE BED SPINS EP**

––– added **COLIN RHINESMITH** – bass, keyboards

		not iss.	Sit n Spin
Apr 98.	(m-cd) <8> **WELL COMPOSED DEATH NOTICE**	-	

– Standing in a corner / Hope this makes Sheryl Crow happy / Poor Grace / Well composed death notice / Shark shaped ship / Hold tight.

––– PHOEBE subsequently guested for BRILLIANTINE

SMART WENT CRAZY

Formed: Washington D.C., USA ... 1993 by CHAD CLARK, ABRAM GOODRICH and HILARY SOLDATI; they added drummer TONY DENNISON for their self-released EP 'CUBBYHOLE'. As they began playing gigs around D.C., they recruited another guitarist, JEFF BOSWELL, and then later DEVIN OCAMPO (after DENNISON left, in mid 1997). Following their signing to D.C.'s seminal punk-rock label 'Dischord', they released their debut album, 'NOW WE'RE EVEN', in 1996. Characterized by darkly humorous and cynical lyrics, and HILARY SOLDATI's strings, the SMART WENT CRAZY sound veered towards that of JAWBOX and of course, who else?, FUGAZI. 1998's 'CON ART' was an even more raucous and pernicious slice of art-punk than their first long-player However, after their 1998 tour, they split, with OCAMPO later forming FARAQUET.

Album rating: NOW WE'RE EVEN (*6) / CON ART (*6)

CHAD CLARK – vocals, guitar, piano / **HILARY SOLDATI** – vocals, cello / **ABRAM GOODRICH** – bass / **TONY DENNISON** – drums

		not iss.	Cozy Disc
Apr 94.	(cd-ep) <#1> **CUBBYHOLE EP**	-	

– A halo and a nosebleed / Fossils in ink / Pitch black postcard / Well, you needn't.

––– added **JEFF BOSWELL** – guitar

		Dischord	Dischord
Jan 96.	(cd/lp) <(DIS 96 V/CD)> **NOW WE'RE EVEN**		

– Best and final offer / Spy vs. spy / Null set / Liked you better when you were sick / Sugar in your gas tank / That which is in the way / Gentleman caller / Garden variety hate song / Pallbearer's blues / Domestic tension / Love goes blank / Gold star / Intermission (instrumental). (cd+=) – Eat sero x-ray (by ABRAM) / Blackbird b-side (by CHAD) / M Amazon (by HILARY) / Wilt (by JEFF) / Clown (by TONY).

––– **DEVIN OCAMPO** – drums; repl. DENNISON

Nov 97. (cd/lp) <(DIS 112 CD/V)> **CON ART**

– Black kites / Exitfare / A brief conversation ending in divorce / Immutable beauty / Con art / Baker's chocolate / D.C. will do that to you / Let x = x / Funny as in funny ha-ha / Bullfighter / Hold up her hand, blocks out the sun / Song of the dodo / Tight frame loose frame / A good day / So speaks the queen bee / Tijuana 3-28-96 / Now we're even.

––– split April '98; DEVON formed FARAQUET

S*M*A*S*H

Formed: Welwyn Garden City, Hertfordshire, England ... 1992 as SMASH AT THE BLUES by ED BORRIE, SALVADOR ALESSI and ROB HAIGH. One of the most fiercely political bands since The CLASH (an obvious influence alongside the PISTOLS and the ANGELIC UPSTARTS), S*M*A*S*H made an immediate impact in summer '93 with the 'REAL SURREAL' single. Issued on their own 'Le Disques De Popcor' label, the track was followed up by early '94's 'SHAME', a double A-sided NME/Melody Maker single of the week and the subject of much controversy due to its flip side, 'LADY LOVE YOUR CUNT' (the title a reference to an essay by Germaine Greer). By this point the band were also being heralded as leaders of the much hyped "New Wave Of New Wave" scene alongside THESE ANIMAL MEN (they had previously shared an album, 1993's 'WHEELERS, DEALERS AND CHRISTINE KEELERS'), the press coverage not exactly harming them as incendiary live performances blazed a trail across the UK. The band subsequently signed to 'Hi-Rise' along with THESE ANIMAL MEN, releasing a mini-set compilation of their work to date, 'S*M*A*S*H SPRING 1994'. It broke the Top 30, as did the controversial '(I WANT TO KILL) SOMEBODY' – which infamously included a hit list of Tory MP's – the subject of censorship from Radio One. The band's political beliefs were further underlined when they played an Anti-Nazi League rally alongside BILLY BRAGG, the fact that they were more effective in a live environment than the studio confirmed with the release of a full length debut album, 'SELF ABUSED' (1994). Criticisms centred around the thin production yet amidst all the buzzsaw bluster were genuinely affecting moments such as 'REFLECTIONS OF YOU (REMEMBER ME)', 'TIME' etc. Whatever, the album failed to sell and the band concentrated on a US tour, supported by a one-off single on 'Sub Pop', 'BARRABAS'. Their return to British shores was marked with the release of mini-set, 'ANOTHER LOVE (SONG)' (1995), although it contained only a handful of genuinely new tracks. With Brit-pop now dominating the music scene, S*M*A*S*H's moment seemed to have passed and following a final single, 'REST OF MY LIFE', they officially split.

Album rating: SELF ABUSED (*6) / ANOTHER LOVE (SONG) mini (*5)

ED BORRIE – vocals, guitar / **SALVADOR ALESSI** – bass / **ROB HAIGH** – drums (ex-NIGHTMARE, ex-ASTRONAUTS)

		Les Disques	not iss.
Jul 93.	(7") (POPCOR 001) **REAL SURREAL. / DRUGS AGAIN / REVISITED NO.3**		-
Dec 93.	(c-ep) (POPCOR 002) **WHEELERS, DEALERS & CHRISTINE KEELERS**		-

– Self-abused / Kill somebody / Altruism / Bang bang bang / (5 other tracks by THESE ANIMAL MEN)

		Hi-Rise	Hut
Feb 94.	(7",7"pink/one-sided7"red) (POPCOR 003/+V) **LADY LOVE YOUR CUNT. / SHAME**	-	-
Mar 94.	(m-cd/m-c/m-lp) (FLATM CD/TC/LP 2) <3> **S*M*A*S*H SPRING 1994**	28	

– Real surreal / Drugs again / Revisited No.3 / Lady love your c*** / Shame.

S*M*A*S*H (cont)

Jul 94.	(c-ep/12"ep/cd-ep) (FLATS TC//CD 5) (I WANT TO) KILL SOMEBODY (Topper mix). / ('A'-Keith LeBlanc mix) / ('A'Gunshot headhunter mix) / ('A'-Bragg reshuffle mix)	26	
Sep 94.	(cd/c/lp) (FLAT CD/MC/LP 6) <HUSCD 6> SELF ABUSED – Revisited No.5 / Barrabas / Oh ovary / Altruism / Reflections of you (remember me) / Self abused / Scream silent / Another shark in the deep end of my swimming pool / Real surreal / Dear Lou / Bang bang bang (granta 25) / Time. (cd+=) – A.L.L.Y.C. (also other lp++=; FLATLPX 6) – Trainspotter.	59	
Nov 94.	(7") (SP 276) BARRABAS (PILOTED). / TURN ON THE WATER (above single on 'Sub Pop')		
Feb 95.	(m-cd/m-c/m-lp) (FLATM CD/TC/LP 10) ANOTHER LOVE (SONG) EP – Another love (Bobbit mix) / Petal buzz / You've got a friend who's a friend of mine / Reflections of you (remember me) (live) / Time (live) / Self abused (live) / Another love (uncut).		-
		Popcor	not iss.
Jan 96.	(7"/cd-s) (POPCOR 9/+CD) THE REST OF MY LIFE. /		-
—	broke up after above		

SMASHING PUMPKINS

Formed: Chicago, Illinois, USA ... late 80's by BILLY CORGAN, JAMES IHA, D'ARCY WRETZKY. The son of a jazz guitarist and former member of local goth band, The MARKED, CORGAN initiated The SMASHING PUMPKINS as a three piece using a drum machine, before the band recruited sticksman, JIMMY CHAMBERLAIN. After a debut single for a local label, 'I AM ONE', and the inclusion of two tracks on a local compilation album, the group came to the attention of influential Seattle label, 'Sub Pop'. After only one single, 'TRISTESSA', The SMASHING PUMPKINS moved once more, signing to Virgin subsidiary, 'Hut', in the UK, 'Caroline' in America. Produced by BUTCH VIG, a debut album, 'GISH', was released in early '92, its grunge pretensions belying a meandering 70's/psychedelic undercurrent which distanced the band from most of their contemporaries. Nevertheless, the group amassed a sizable student/grassroots following which eventually saw the debut go gold in the States, a re-released 'I AM ONE' sneaking into the UK Top 75 later that year. With the masterful 'SIAMESE DREAM' (1993), the band went from underground hopefuls to alternative rock frontrunners, the album fully realising the complex 'PUMPKINS sound in a delicious wash of noise and gentle melody. Influenced by acoustic LED ZEPPELIN fused with slices of 70's PINK FLOYD, CORGAN's croaky but effective voice was at its best on the pastel, NIRVANA-esque classics, 'TODAY' and 'DISARM', while the 'PUMPKINS went for the jugular on the likes of 'CHERUB ROCK', 'ROCKET' and 'GEEK U.S.A.'. The album made the Top 5 in Britain, Top 10 in the States, selling multi-millions and turning the band into a 'grunge' sensation almost overnight, despite the fact that their mellotron stylings and complex arrangements marked them out as closer in spirit to prog-rock than punk. Amidst frantic touring, the band released the outtakes/B-sides compilation, 'PISCES ISCARIOT' (1994), the next album proper surfacing in late '95 as the sprawling double set, 'MELLON COLLIE AND THE INFINITE SADNESS'. Dense and stylistically breathtaking, the album veered from all-out grunge/thrash to acoustic meandering and avant-rock doodlings, a less cohesive whole than its predecessor but much more to get your teeth into. Inevitably, there were criticisms of self-indulgence, though for a two-hour set, there was a surprising, compelling consistency to proceedings; among the highlights were 'BULLET WITH BUTTERFLY WINGS', 'TONIGHT, TONIGHT' and the visceral rage of '1979'. The record scaled the US charts, where The SMASHING PUMPKINS were almost reaching the commercial and critical heights of NIRVANA, the group also taking Britain by storm, headlining the 1995 Reading Festival. Never the most stable of bands, disaster struck the following year when new boy (keyboard player) JONATHAN MELVOIN died of a drugs overdose and heroin addict CHAMBERLAIN was finally kicked out. More recently (early 1998), IHA released an acclaimed solo album of acoustic strumming ('LET IT COME DOWN') while the others recorded fresh songs with a drum machine, taking things full circle. That summer, the 'PUMPKINS showed a softer side to their character when the mournful but still effective album, 'ADORE', hit the Top 5. 1999 saw two major personnel changes via the return of CHAMBERLAIN and the departure of D'ARCY (who was replaced by ex-HOLE bassist MELISSA); one last set would appear in 2000. • **Songwriters:** CORGAN, except several with IHA. Covered; A GIRL NAMED SANDOZ (Eric Burdon & The Animals) / LANDSLIDE (Fleetwood Mac) / DANCING IN THE MOONLIGHT (Thin Lizzy) / NEVER LET ME DOWN (Depeche Mode) / YOU'RE ALL I'VE GOT TONIGHT (Cars) / CLONES (WE'RE ALL) (Alice Cooper) / DREAMING (Blondie) / A NIGHT LIKE THIS (Cure) / DESTINATION UNKNOWN (Missing Persons) / SAD PETER PAN with Red Red Meat (Vic Chesnutt). • **Miscellaneous:** IHA and D'ARCY set up their own label, 'Scratchie', for whom the outfit, FULFLEJ recorded an album ('Wack-Ass Tuba Riff') in 1996 with the pair making guest appearances.

Album rating: GISH (*6) / SIAMESE DREAM (*9) / MELLON COLLIE AND THE INFINITE SADNESS (*9) / PISCES ISCARIOT compilation (*5) / THE AEROPLANE FLIES HIGH boxed set (*6) / ADORE (*5) / MACHINA – THE MACHINES OF GOD (*5) / (ROTTEN APPLES) GREATEST HITS compilation (*7) / EARPHORIA (*6) / James Iha: LET IT COME DOWN (*5)

BILLY CORGAN (b.17 Mar'67) – vocals, guitar / **JAMES IHA** (b.26 Mar'68, Elk Grove, Illinois) – guitar / **D'ARCY (WRETZKY)** (b. 1 May'68, South Haven, Michigan) – bass, vocals / **JIMMY CHAMBERLIN** (b.10 Jun'64, Joliet, Illinois) – drums

		not iss.	Limited Potential
Apr 90.	(7") <Limp 006> I AM ONE. / NOT WORTH ASKING	-	
		Glitterhouse	Sub Pop
Dec 90.	(7",7"pink) <SP 90> TRISTESSA. / LA DOLLY VITA (UK-12"+=; May93) (SP 10-137) – Honeyspider.	-	
		Hut	Caroline
Aug 91.	(12") (HUTT 6) SIVA. / WINDOW PAINE		-
Feb 92.	(12"ep/cd-ep) (HUTT/CDHUT 10) LULL EP – Rhinoceros / Blue / Slunk / Bye June (demo).		
Feb 92.	(c/c/lp) (HUT CD/MC/LP 002) <1705> GISH – I am one / Siva / Rhinoceros / Bury me / Crush / Suffer / Snail / Tristessa / Window paine / Daydream. (re-iss. May94; diff.versions cd/lp; HUT CDX/LPX 002)		Aug91
Jun 92.	(c-ep/12"ep/cd-ep) <39637> PEEL SESSIONS – Siva / A girl named Sandoz / Smiley.		-
Aug 92.	(12"ep/cd-ep) (HUTT/CDHUT 18) I AM ONE. / PLUME / STARLA (10"ep) (HUTTEN 18) – ('A'side) / Terrapin (live) / Bullet train to Osaka.	73	-
Jun 93.	(7"clear) (HUT 31) CHERUB ROCK. / PURR SNICKETY (12"/cd-s) (HUTT/CDHUT 31) – ('A'side) / Pissant / French movie theme / (Star spangled banner).	31	-
Jul 93.	(cd/c/d-lp) (HUT CD/MC/LP 011) <88267> SIAMESE DREAM – Cherub rock / Quiet / Today / Hummer / Rocket / Disarm / Soma / Geek U.S.A. / Mayonaise / Spaceboy / Silverfuck / Sweet sweet / Luna. (d-lp re-iss. Dec99 on 'Caroline'; CAROL 17401)	4	10
Sep 93.	(7"red) (HUT 37) TODAY. / APATHY'S LAST KISS (c-s/12"/cd-s) (HUTC/HUTT/CDHUT 37) – ('A'side) / Hello kitty kat / Obscured.	44	-
Feb 94.	(7"purple) (HUT 43) DISARM. / SIAMESE DREAM (12"/cd-s) (HUT T/CD 43) – ('A'side) / Soothe (demo) / Blew away. (cd-s) (HUTDX 43) – ('A'side) / Dancing in the moonlight / Landslide.	11	-
Oct 94.	(cd/c/gold-lp) <39834> PISCES ISCARIOT (compilation of B-sides & rarities) – Soothe / Frail and bedazzled / Plume / Whir / Blew away / Pissant / Hello Kitty Kat / Obscured / Landslide / Starla / Blue / A girl named Sandoz / La dolly viva / Spaced. <w/ free gold-7"; CAR 1767-7> NOT WORTH ASKING. / HONEY SPIDER II (UK-iss.Oct96 cd/c/lp; HUT CD/MC/LP 41)	-	4
		Hut	Virgin
Dec 94.	(7"peach) (HUTL 48) ROCKET. / NEVER LET ME DOWN (4x7"box-set) (SPBOX 1) SIAMESE SINGLES – (last 3 singles 1993-94 + above)		-
Oct 95.	(c-s/cd-s) (HUT C/CD 63) <38522> BULLET WITH BUTTERFLY WINGS / . . .SAID SADLY	20	25
Oct 95.	(d-cd/d-c) (CD/TC HUTD 30) <40861> MELLON COLLIE AND THE INFINITE SADNESS – DAWN TO DUSK:- Mellon Collie and the infinite sadness / Tonight, tonight / Jellybelly / Zero / Here is no why / Bullet with butterfly wings / To forgive / An ode to no one / Love / Cupid de Locke / Galapogos / Muzzle / Porcelina of the vast oceans / Take me down. // TWILIGHT TO STARLIGHT:- Where boys fear to tread / Bodies / Thirty-three / In the arms of sleep / 1979 / Tales of a scorched Earth / Thru the eyes of Ruby / Stumbleine / X.Y.U. / We only come out at night / Beautiful / Lily (my one and only) / By starlight / Farewell and goodnight. (re-iss. Apr96 on t-lp+=; HUTTLP 30) – Tonight reprise / Infinite sadness.	4	1
—	added on tour **JONATHAN MELVOIN** – keyboards (ex-DICKIES) (brother of WENDY; ex-WENDY & LISA, ex-PRINCE)		
Jan 96.	(c-ep/12"ep/cd-ep) (HUT C/T/CD 67) <38547> 1979 / UGLY. / BELIEVE / CHERRY (12"ep/cd-ep; Mar96) (HUT TX/CDX 67) – 1979 REMIXES: Vocal / Instrumental / Moby / Cement.	16	12
May 96.	(c-ep) (HUTC 69) <38547> TONIGHT, TONIGHT / MELADORI MAGPIE / ROTTEN APPLES (cd-ep+=) (HUTCD 69) – Medellia of the gray skies. (cd-ep) (HUTDX 69) – ('A'side) / Jupiter's lament / Blank / Tonite (reprise).	7	36 Jun96
—	On 12th Jul'96, MELVOIN died of a heroin overdose. CHAMBERLIN, who found him dead, was charged with drug offences and sacked by the remaining trio who were said to sick of his long-lasting drug addiction. In August, they were replaced for tour by **DENNIS FLEMION** – keyboards (ex-FROGS) + **MATT WALKER** – drums (of FILTER)		
Sep 96.	(m-cd) (HUTCD 73) <38545> ZERO EP – Zero / God / Mouths of babes / Tribute to Johnny / Marquis in spades / Pennies / Pastichio medley: (excerpts).		46 May96
Nov 96.	(cd-ep) (HUTCD 78) <38574> THIRTY THREE / THE LAST SONG / THE AEROPLANE FLIES HIGH (TURNS LEFT, LOOKS RIGHT) / TRANSFORMER (cd-ep) (HUTDX 78) – ('A'side) / The bells / My blue Heaven.	21	39
Nov 96.	(5xcd-ep;box) <SPBOX 2> THE AEROPLANE FLIES HIGH – (BULLET WITH BUTTERFLY WINGS / 1979 / TONIGHT, TONIGHT / THIRTY THREE / ZERO)	-	42
—	early in '97, CORGAN provided six songs for 'RANSOM' film soundtrack credited to conductor JAMES HORNER (Hollywood HR 62086-2)		
Jun 97.	(c-s) (W 0404C) THE END IS THE BEGINNING IS THE END / THE BEGINNING IS THE END IS THE BEGINNING (cd-s+=) (W 0404CD) – The ethers tragic / The guns of love disastrous. (12"/cd-s) (W 0410 T/CD) – ('A'mixes; 2 Fluke mixes / 2 Rabbit in The Moons mixes / Hallucination Gotham mix). (above from the film 'Batman And Robin' on 'Warners')	10	
May 98.	(7") (HUT 101) <38647> AVA ADORE. / CZARINA (c-s+=/cd-s+=) (HUT C/CD 101) – Once in a while.	11	42 Jun98
Jun 98.	(cd/c/d-lp) (CDHUT/TCHUT/HUTDLP 51) <45879> ADORE – To Sheila / Ava adore / Perfect / Daphne decends / Once upon a time / Tear / Crestfallen / Appels + oranjes / Pug / The tale of Dusty and Pistol Pete / Annie-dog / Shame / Behold! the night mare / For Martha / Blank page / 17.	5	2
Sep 98.	(c-s/cd-s) (HUT C/CD 106) <38650> PERFECT / SUMMER / PERFECT (Nellee Hooper mix) (cd-s) (HUTDX 106) – ('A'side) / Daphne descends (Oakenfold Perfecto mix) / Daphne descends (Kerry B mix).	24	54
—	**CHAMBERLAIN** was now back in the fold		
—	**MELISSA AUF DER MAUR** – bass (ex-HOLE) repl. D'ARCY		

SMASHING PUMPKINS (cont) THE GREAT INDIE DISCOGRAPHY The 1990s

Feb 00.	(c-s/cd-s) *(HUT C/CD 127)* **STAND INSIDE YOUR LOVE / SPEED KILLS**		23	-
Feb 00.	(cd/c/d-lp) *(CDHUT/HUTMC/HUTDLP 59) <48936>* **MACHINA / THE MACHINES OF GOD**		7	3

– The everlasting gaze / Rain drops & sun showers / Stand inside your love / I of the mourning / The sacred and profane / Try, try, try / Heavy metal machine / This time / The imploding voice / Glass and the ghost children / Wound / The crying tree of Mercury / With every light / Blue skies bring tears / Age of innocence.

Sep 00.	(cd-s) *(HUTCD 140)* **TRY, TRY, TRY / HERE'S TO THE ATOM BOMB**		73	-

—— the band split in November 2000; CORGAN will be back with ZWAN in '03

– compilations, etc. –

on 'Hut' UK / 'Virgin' America unless stated otherwise

Nov 01.	(cd) *(CDHUT 70) <11316>* **(ROTTEN APPLES) GREATEST HITS**		28	31

– Siva / Rhinoceros / Drown / Cherub rock / Today / Disarm / Bullet with butterfly wings / 1979 / Zero / Tonight, tonight / Eye / Ava adore / Perfect / The everlasting gaze / Stand inside your love / Try, try, try / Real love / Untitled. *(d-cd+=; CDHUTD 70)* – Lucky 13 / Aeroplane flies high (turns left looks right) / Because you are / Slow down / Believe / My mistake / Marquis in spades / Here's to the atom bomb / Sparrow / Waiting / Saturnine / Winter / One and two / No one's gonna hurt you.

Nov 02.	(cd) *(CDHUT 79) <42706>* **EARPHORIA (live)**			

– Sinfony / Quiet / Disarm / Cherub rock / Today / Bugg superstar / I am one / Pulseczar / Soma / Slunk / French movie theme / Geek U.S.A. / Mayonnaise / Silverf*** / Why am I so tired.

JAMES IHA

JAMES IHA – vocals, guitar / **NEAL CASAL** – guitar / **ADAM SCHLESINGER** – piano (of FOUNTAINS OF WAYNE) / **GREG LEISZ** – steel guitar / **JOHN GINTY** – hammond organ / **SOLOMON SNYDER** – bass / **MATT WALKER** – drums / **NINA GORDON** (of VERUCA SALT) also a part of initial basement set-up

Feb 98.	(cd/c/lp) *(CDHUT/HUTMC/HUTLP 47) <45411>* **LET IT COME DOWN**			

– Be strong now / Sound of love / Beauty / See the sun / Country girl / Jealousy / Lover, lover / Silver string / Winter / One and two / No one's gonna hurt you.

Feb 98.	(12"ep/cd-ep) *(HUT T/CD 99)* **BE STRONG NOW / MY ADVICE. / TAKE CARE / FALLING**			-

Elliott SMITH

Born: 1970, Dallas, Texas, USA, although raised from a young age by his father in Portland, Oregon, after his parents divorced. The singer/songwriter relocated to university digs in Brooklyn, New York, playing in mid-90's noisy alternative rock band, HEATMISER. They released four rare albums, 'DEAD AIR' (1993), 'YELLOW NO.5' (1994; a mini-set), 'COP AND SPEEDER' (1995) and 'MIC CITY SONS' (1996), while ELLIOTT, meantime had opted for a more sedate solo career. He delivered three very well received albums for the 'Kill Rock City' imprint, namely 'ROMAN CANDLE' (1994), 'ELLIOTT SMITH' (1995) and 'EITHER/OR' (1997) – all licensed in 1998 to the UK arm of 'Domino' – before he did a deal with 'DreamWorks'. This was due to the plaudits heaped upon him after appearing on stage alongside CELINE DION and TRISHA YEARWOOD at the "Oscars" ceremony! An unlikely story you may think, although the truth is, he provided part of the soundtrack to one of the best films of the year, 'Good Will Hunting'. His unfashionable (especially his taste in clothing and headgear – sometimes a tammy) approach was slightly reminiscent of SIMON & GARFUNKEL, BIG STAR or the lo-fi RICHARD DAVIES (of CARDINAL). His fourth album, 'XO', hit the shops later in 1998 and ELLIOTT looked certain to make his impact on the music scene. Sounding very much at home in his new big budget environment, 'FIGURE 8' (2000) found SMITH taking the opportunity to imbue his songcraft with the luxurious feel of classic BEATLES-meets-CS&N-meets-ERIC MATTHEWS while never relinquishing the skid row wisdom of his lyrical genius.

Album rating: Heatmiser: DEAD AIR (*6) / COP AND SPEEDER (*7) / MIC CITY SONS (*6) / Elliott Smith: ROMAN CANDLE (*7) / ELLIOTT SMITH (*7) / EITHER/OR (*8) / XO (*7) / FIGURE 8 (*7)

HEATMISER

ELLIOTT SMITH – vocals / **NEIL GUST** – guitar, vocals / **SAM COOMES** – bass / **TONY LASH** – drums

			not iss.	own label
1992.	(c) **THE MUSIC OF HEATMISER**		-	

– Lowlife / Bottle rocket / Buick / Just a little prick / Dirt / Mightier than you.

			not iss.	Wake
1993.	(7") **STRAY. / CAN'T BE TOUCHED**		-	

<re-iss. 1995 on 'Cavity Search'; CSR 02>

			Frontier	Frontier
Jul 93.	(cd/c) *<(31057-2/-4)>* **DEAD AIR**			Jun93

– Still / Candyland / Mock up / Dirt / Bottle rocket / Blackout / Stray / Can't be touched / Cannibal / Don't look down / Sands hotel / Low life / Buick / Dead air.

Jul 94.	(m-cd) *<(31062-2)>* **YELLOW NO.5**			

– Wake / Fortune 500 / The corner seat / Idler / Junior mint / Yellow No.5.

Apr 95.	(cd) *<(31063-2)>* **COP AND SPEEDER**			

– Disappearing ink / Bastard John / Flamel / Temper / Why did I decide to stay? / Collect to NYC / Hitting on the waiter / Busted lip / Antonio Carlos Jobim / It's not a prop / Something to lose / Sleeping pill / Trap door / Nightcap.

			Caroline	Cavity Search
Jun 95.	(7") *<CSR 7>* **SLEEPING PILL. / TEMPER**		-	
Apr 96.	(7") *<CSR 25>* **EVERYBODY HAS IT. / DIRTY DREAM**		-	
Oct 96.	(cd) *(CAR 75402) <CSR 35-2>* **MIC CITY SONS**			

– Get lucky / Plainclothes man / Low flying jets / Rest my head against the wall / Fix is in / Eagle eye / Cruel reminder / You gotta move / Pop in G / Blue highway / See you later.

—— split after SMITH was already making a name for himself as a solo act, while COOMES was in a duo with JANET WEISS called QUASI.

ELLIOTT SMITH

- vocals, drums, bass, saxophones, etc.

			not iss.	Cavity Search
Dec 94.	(cd) *<CSR 13-2>* **ROMAN CANDLE**		-	

– Roman candle / Condor avenue / No name #I / No name #II / No name #III / Drive all over town / No name #IV / The last call / Kiwi mad-dog 20-20. *(UK-iss.Mar98 on 'Cavity Search'; same as US)* *(re-iss. Aug98 on 'Domino' cd/lp; REWIG CD/LP 002)*

			Kill Rock Stars	Kill Rock Stars
Feb 95.	(7"m) *<(KRS 239)>* **NEEDLE IN THE HAY. / ALPHABET TOWN / SOME SONG**			-
Jul 95.	(lp/cd) *<KRS 246/+CD>* **ELLIOTT SMITH**		-	

– Needle in the hay / Christian brother / Clementine / Southern belle / Single file / Coming up roses / Satellite / Alphabet town / St.Ides heaven / Good to go / White lady loves you more / Biggest lie. *(UK-iss.Mar98; same)* *(re-iss. Aug98 on 'Domino' cd/lp; REWIG CD/LP 001)*

Oct 96.	(7"m) *<(KRS 266)>* **SPEED TRIALS. / ANGELES / I DON'T THINK I'M EVER GONNA FIGURE IT OUT**			
Mar 97.	(lp/cd) *<(KRS 269/+CD)>* **EITHER/OR**			

– Speed trials / Alameda / Ballad of big nothing / Between the bars / Pictures of me / No name No.5 / Rose parade / Punch and Judy / Angeles / Cupid's trick / 2:45 am / Say yes. *(UK-iss.Jun98 on 'Domino' cd/lp; WIG CD/LP 51)*

1997.	(7"; by ELLIOTT SMITH & PETE KREBS) **NO CONFIDENCE MAN. / SHIPTOWN**			-

(below issued on 'Suicide Queen')

1997.	(cd-s) *<S 005CD>* **DIVISION DAY. / NO NAME #6**			

(UK-iss.May00; same as US; re-Feb00)

Jun 98.	(7") *(RUG 74)* **BALLAD OF BIG NOTHING. / SOME SONG / DIVISION DAY**			

(cd-s+=) *(RUG 74CD)* – Angeles.

—— now with a plethora of session people + strings

			DreamWorks	DreamWorks
Aug 98.	(cd/c) *<(DRD/DRC 50048)>* **XO**			

– Sweet Adeline / Tomorrow tomorrow / Waltz #2 (XO) / Baby Britain / Pitseleh / Independence day / Bled white / Waltz #1 / Amity / Oh well, okay / Bottle up and explode! / A question mark / Everybody cares, everybody understands / I didn't understand. *<(lp-iss.on 'Bongload'/ BL 35)>*

Dec 98.	(c-s) *<(DRMS 22347)>* **WALTZ #2 (XO) / OUR THING**		52	Feb99

(cd-s+=) *(DRMCD 22347)* – How to take a fall.

Apr 99.	(7") *(DRMS7 50953)* **BABY BRITAIN. / WALTZ No.1**		55	-

(cd-s+=) *(DRMDM 50950)* – The enemy is you.
(cd-s) *(DRMDM 50951)* – ('A'side) / Some song / Bottle up and explode.

Jan 00.	(7"/cd-s) *<459037>* **HAPPINESS. / SON OF SAM**			
Apr 00.	(cd) *<(4 50225-2)>* **FIGURE 8**		37	99

– Son of Sam / Somebody that I used to know / Junk bond trader / Everything reminds me of her / Everything means nothing to me / LA / In the lost and found (honky Bach) / The roost / Stupidity tries / Easy way out / Wouldn't mama be proud? / Color bars / Happiness - The gondola man / Pretty Mary K / I better be quiet now / Can't make a sound / Bye. *<(lp-iss.Jul00 on 'Bongload'; BL 48)>*

Jun 00.	(7") *(450949-7)* **SON OF SAM. / A LIVING WILL**		55	-

(cd-s+=) *(450949-2)* – Figure 8.

Jean SMITH
(see under ⇒ MECCA NORMAL; 80's section)

Linda SMITH

Born: 1955, Baltimore, Maryland, USA. The enigma that is LINDA SMITH has been releasing music recorded on her 4-track since 1987. Early efforts such as her self-financed debut 'THE SPACE BETWEEN THE BUILDINGS' and the 1988 follow up 'DO YOU KNOW THE WAY . . .?' saw SMITH flirt between different styles as she tried to find the voice with which she was most comfortable. It was immediately evident that SMITH was most suited to the quiet introspective songs that dominated these early recordings and this was the sound she settled for as her career progressed in the 90's. It was not until 1996 that SMITH began recording digitally. The first product of this was 'NOTHING ELSE MATTERS' which still featured beautiful, poignant songs, however fans complained that the digital rendering sacrificed the trademark moody textures of SMITH's early recordings. LINDA continued to record sporadically with releases such as 1997's 'PUNCTURE' and the 2001 'EMILY'S HOUSE' reinforcing her reputation as a phenomenal songwriter. However her unwillingness to play the game meant she failed to reach a wider audience. • **Covered:** PURPLE LIPS (Nico) / IN LOVE (Raincoats) / DO YOU KNOW THE WAY TO SAN JOSE? (Burt Bacharach) / SALAD DAYS (Young Marble Giants) / etc. • **Note:** not to be confused with LINDA SMITH the rock violinist who released a few albums for 'Underground' in the early 90's.

Album rating: THE SPACE BETWEEN THE BUILDINGS + DO YOU KNOW THE WAY . . .? collection (*7) / NOTHING ELSE MATTERS (*5) / PREFERENCE (SELECTED SONGS, 1987-1991) compilation (*6) / EMILY'S HOUSE (*6) / SOMETHING NEW! (*5)

LINDA SMITH – vocals, guitar

			not iss.	Preference
1987.	(m-c) <1> **THE SPACE BETWEEN THE BUILDINGS**		-	
	– The wishing well / Girl on the train / It's your party, too / What Eleanora told Isadora / Come to my senses / But is she happy? / The space between the buildings / Put a little love in your heart.			
1988.	(m-c) <2> **DO YOU KNOW THE WAY . . .?**		-	
	– All I did / Idea / There's a / Do you know the way to San Jose? / Confidence / How funny / I could care / Take this.			

			not iss.	Harriet
May 90.	(7"m) <003> **GORGEOUS WEATHER. / THE REAL MISS CHARLOTTE / ALL THAT I CAN GIVE**		-	

			not iss.	Slumberland
Nov 93.	(7"m) <sl 016> **TIL ANOTHER TIME. / I JUST HAD TO / IN THIS**		-	

			Hoppel Di Hoy	not iss.
1994.	(7"m) **REMEMBER YOUR HEART. / WANDERING YOU KNOW / PUT IT IN WRITING**		-	- German

			not iss.	Feel Good All Over
Feb 96.	(cd) <FGAO 7005> **NOTHING ELSE MATTERS**		-	
	– The answer to your question / In no uncertain terms / I'll never see you again / For here or to go / In the hospital / Bright side / All of the blue / Only a moment / I see your face / It seems to me / Little to be won / Nothing else matters.			

			not iss.	Shrimper
1997.	(c) **I SO LIKED SPRING**		-	
	<cd-iss. 1999 on 'homemadeMusic.com'>			

			not iss.	Preference
2001.	(cd) <Pref 04> **SOMETHING NEW!**		-	
	– Something old . . . / Leaving the station / Something new! / Corporate blunders / How it was / Re enactment (with help from Abraham Lincoln) / Public life story / Purple lips / It's now / Train tune / Free and clearly / Something new! (remix by Arthur Loves Plastic).			
Feb 02.	(cd) <Pref 05> **EMILY'S HOUSE**		-	
	– Emily's house / The time of year / No 2 people / Table by the window / You changed / Night / Where were you / Club soda & lime / Emily'ss grave / Solitary pursuits / Along the quiet paths.			

– compilations, etc. –

Jun 97.	(cd) *Harriet*; <(SPY 7CD)> **PREFERENCE (SELECTED SONGS, 1987-1991)**	
	– (THE SPACE BETWEEN THE BUILDINGS / DO YOU KNOW THE WAY . . .?)	

SMOG

Formed: Silver Springs, Maryland, USA . . . 1988 by sole member, BILL CALLAHAN. The painfully introverted grandaddy of the American lo-fi scene (although he professes to loathe that particular term), CALLAHAN began releasing his bedroom creations in the late 80's as a series of mainly instrumental cassette-only affairs. All issued on his own 'Disaster' imprint, 'MACRAME GUNPLAY' (1988), 'COW' (1989), 'A TABLE SETTING' (1990) and 'TIRED MACHINE' (1990) set the tone for a debut album proper, 'SEWN TO THE SKY' (1991). This was originally released only in the States on the 'Drag City' label and carried on in the same vein as its skeletal predecessors; CALLAHAN only really began taking SMOG in a more conventionally song-structured direction with the 'FORGOTTEN FOUNDATION' (1992) album and only really started whetting critical appetites with 1993's acclaimed 'JULIUS CAESAR'. The latter set was recorded with sometime collaborator CYNTHIA 'CINDY' DALL, boasting sharper, more robust songwriting embellished with string flourishes and synth tinkling although the lyrical misery continued unabated. The mood blackened further on 1994's mini-album, 'BURNING KINGDOM', the reclusive pessimeister making WILL OLDHAM sound like a circus clown. Yet while CALLAHAN's sad-eyed music could be overbearingly claustrophobic, it was more often genuinely moving, the painstakingly recounted tales of everday heartbreak/failure featured on 'WILD LOVE' (1995) and the 'KICKING A COUPLE AROUND' EP offering up an almost voyeuristic view into the man's insular world. The bitter fruit of 'THE DOCTOR CAME AT DAWN' (1996) and 'RED APPLE FALLS' (1997) further confirmed BILL as the crown prince of sad-core, a label he'd no doubt detest even more than lo-fi. 'KNOCK KNOCK' (1999) was described as an album for teenagers and definitely one of his best, SMOG were now becoming the most popular one-man band in America. The man's ironic humour and love of wordplay were all too evident in the title of his umpteenth opus 'DONGS OF SEVOTION' (2000), wherein CALLAHAN knelt once more at the alter of his melancholy, minimalistic muse. Worshippers found much to praise in the likes of 'NINETEEN' and 'PERMANENT SMILE', the high priest of pathos wringing as much emotion from his own faltering experience as the third person character sketches. In a (undoubtedly ironic) PRINCE-like move, BILL altered the SMOG moniker to (SMOG) for 'RAIN ON LENS' (2001), a continuation of 'DONGS..' hypnotic studies of the human condition.

Album rating: SEWN TO THE SKY (*6) / FORGOTTEN FOUNDATION (*7) / JULIUS CAESAR (*8) / BURNING KINGDOM mini (*5) / WILD LOVE (*7) / THE DOCTOR CAME AT DAWN (*8) / RED APPLE FALLS (*7) / KNOCK KNOCK (*8) / DONGS OF SEVOTION (*7) / RAIN ON LENS (*7) / ACCUMULATION: NONE collection (*6)

BILL CALLAHAN (b. 1966) – vocals, guitar, etc

			not iss.	Disaster
1988.	(c) <none> **MACRAME GUNPLAY**		-	
1989.	(m-c) <none> **COW**		-	
	– Cow / Frozen at sea / Fusilage / On a scale of fish to fish / Stash / Souped up / Black olive / Hoover penny.			
1990.	(c) <none> **A TABLE SETTING**		-	
1990.	(c) <none> **TIRED TAPE MACHINE**		-	
1990.	(lp) <none> **SEWN TO THE SKY**		-	
	– Souped up II / Kings tongue / Garb / Hollow out cakes / Confederate bills and pinball slugs / Coconut cataract / Fruit bats / Peach pit / Disgust / Russian winter / Polio shimmy / Smog / Lost my key / Fried piper / Fables / Puritan work ethic / A jar of sand / I want to tell you about a man / Olive drab spectre / The weightlifter. <(re-iss.Nov95 on 'Drag City'; DC 74)>			

			not iss.	#1 hits
1991.	(7"ep) <none> **MY SHELL / ASTRONAUT.** (tracks by SUCKDOG)		-	

			Matador	Drag City
Aug 91.	(7"ep) <DC 6> **FLOATING EP**			
	– Mice / Turb / Floating / Red apples / Hole in the heart / Cursed.			
May 92.	(lp/cd) <DC 13> **FORGOTTEN FOUNDATION**			
	– Burning kingdom / Filament / High school freak / Your dress / Barometric pressure / Guitar innovator / Evil tyrant / Head of stone I / Head of stone II / Long gray hair / Kiss your lips (with LISA CARVER) / Bad ideas for country songs I / Bad ideas for country songs II / Dead river / Bad investment / Brown bag / Let me have that jar back / This insane cop / 97th street / Do the bed / I'm smiling / With a green complexion. <cd re-iss. Jan96 & Jan01; same>			

— now with **CINDY DALL** – vocals, etc

Jul 94.	(cd/lp) (OLE 097-2/-1) <DC 31> **JULIUS CAESAR**			Nov93
	– Strawberry rash / Your wedding / 37 push ups / Stalled on the tracks / One less star / Golden / When you talk / I am star wars / Connections / When the power goes out / Chosen one / What kind of angel / Stick in the mud. (cd re-iss. Jan01 on 'Domino'; REWIGCD 005)			

			City Slang	Drag City
Nov 94.	(m-cd/m-lp) (EFA 04946-2/-1) <DC 41> **BURNING KINGDOM**			Jul94
	– My shell / Renee died 1:45 / My family / Drunk on the stars / Not lonely anymore / Desert.			
Mar 95.	(7"yellow) (EFA 04951-7) <DC 38> **A HIT. / WINE STAINED LIPS**			Mar94
Apr 95.	(cd/lp) (EFA 04952-2/-1) <DC 60> **WILD LOVE**			Mar95
	– Bathysphere / Wild love / Sweet Smog children / Bathroom floor / Emperor / Limited capacity / It's rough / Sleepy Joe / Candle / Be hit / Prince alone in the studio / Goldfish bowl. (cd re-iss. Jan01 on 'Domino'; REWIGCD 007)			

			Domino	Drag City
May 96.	(12"ep/cd-ep) (RUG 45 T/CD) <DC 81> **KICKING A COUPLE AROUND EP**			Apr96
	– Your new friend / Back in school / I break horses / The orange glow of a stranger's living room.			
Sep 96.	(cd/lp) (WIG CD/LP 27) <DC 95> **THE DOCTOR CAME AT DAWN**			
	– You moved in / Somewhere in the night / Lize / Spread your bloody wings / Carmelite light / Everything you touch becomes a crutch / All your women things / Whistling teapot (rag) / Four hearts in a can / Hangman blues.			
Nov 96.	(7") (HM 19) **CAME BLUE. / SPANISH MOSS**		-	- German
	(above issued on 'Hausmusik') <below on 'Shrimper'>			
1997.	(d7") <SHR7 04> **SWING SET**		-	
May 97.	(cd/lp) (WIG CD/LP 35) <DC 116> **RED APPLE FALLS**			
	– Morning papers / Blood red bird / Red apples / I was a stranger / To be of use / Red apple falls / Ex-con / Inspirational / Finer days.			
Oct 97.	(7") (RUG 58) **EX-CON. / JUST LIKE NAPOLEON**			-
	(cd-s+=) (RUG 58CD) – Little girl shoes / Duckpond blues.			
Dec 98.	(7") <DC 161> **HELD. / COLD-BLOODED OLD TIMES**		-	
Jan 99.	(7") <DC 167> **LOOK NOW. / THE ONLY MOTHER**		-	
Feb 99.	(cd/lp) (WIG CD/LP 60) <DC 161> **KNOCK KNOCK**			Jan99
	– Let's move to the country / Held / River guard / No dancing / Teenage spaceship / Cold-blooded old times / Sweet treat / Hit the ground running / I could drive forever / Left only with love.			
May 99.	(7") (RUG 83) **HELD. / LOOK NOW / THE ONLY MOTHER**			-
	(cd-s+=) (RUG 83CD) – Held (acoustic).			
Oct 99.	(7") (RUG 98) **COLD-BLOODED OLD TIMES. / ('A'acoustic)**			-
	(cd-s+=) (RUG 98CD) – I break horses / Chosen one.			
Apr 00.	(cd/d-lp) (WIG CD/LP 76) <DC 169> **DONGS OF SEVOTION**			
	– Justice aversion / Dress sexy at my funeral / Strayed / The hard road / Easily led / Bloodflow / Nineteen / Distance / Devotion / Cold discovery / Permanent smile.			
Jul 00.	(7") (RUG 111) <DC 192> **STRAYED. / BLOODFLOW (acoustic)**			
	(cd-s) (RUG 111CD) – COW (cassette tracks).			
2000.	(cd-ep) **THE MANTA RAYS OF TIME**		-	
—	<above iss. on 'Spunk' records>			
Dec 00.	(12"ep/cd-ep) (RUG 118 T/CD) <196> **'NEATH THE PUKE TREE**			
	– I was a stranger / Your sweet entrance / A jar of sound / Orion obscured by stars / Coacheecayoo.			
Sep 01.	(cd/lp) (WIG CD/LP 99) <DC 187> **RAIN ON LENS**			
	– Rain on lens 1 / Song / Natural decline / Keep some steady friends around / Dirty pants / Lazy rain / Short drive / Live as if someone is always watching you / Rain on lens 2 / Revanchism.			

– compilations, etc. –

Nov 02.	(cd/lp) *Domino*; (WIG CD/LP 116) / *Drag City*; <DC 200CD> **ACCUMULATION: NONE** (B-sides)	
	– Astronaut / A hit / Spanish moss / Chosen one / Floating / Real live dress / Came blue / Little girl shoes / Cold blooded old times / White ribbon / I break horses / Hole in the heart.	

SMOKING POPES

Formed: Chicago, Illinois, USA . . . 1990 by punk-rock songwriter JOSH CATERER along with his brothers ELI and MATT plus MIKE FELUMLEE. Although CATERER dismissed the band's sound as punk, The SMOKING POPES generated fan base from GREEN DAY frontman BILLIE JOE and punk label 'Johann's Face', who issued their debut album 'GET FIRED' in 1993. This however, wasn't their first release as this came about in 1991 when the 'INOCULATOR' EP yielded the great 'SANDRA' track – a tribute to actress Sandra Bernhard. The major label release came in 1995 with the positively titled 'BORN TO QUIT', which had frontman CATERER singing about love while the band thrashed away relentlessly in the background. The follow up, 'DESTINATION FAILURE' (1997), saw the band taking a different approach from previous efforts. More melodies and quiet pop vocals were put into action as the band strummed delicately to CATERER's long and lonely voice. By the time of their next studio release of nostalgic covers, 'THE PARTY'S OVER' (2001), the SMOKING POPES were minus ELI. • Covered: PURE IMAGINATION (Bricusse – Newley) / SEVEN LONELY DAYS (Brown – Shuman – Shuman) / VALENTINE (. . . Nelson) / BEWITCHED (Hart – Rodgers) / THE PARTY'S OVER (Comden – Green – Styne) / FATHER ALONG (. . . Stevens) / ZING! WENT THE STRINGS OF MY HEART (. . . Hanley) / STORMY WEATHER (Arlen – Koehler) / I WAKE UP CRYING (Bacharach – David) / YOU'LL NEVER WALK ALONE (Hammersmith – Rodgers) / WHY ME (Kris Kristofferson)

Album rating: GET FIRED (*5) / BORN TO QUIT (*7) / DESTINATION FAILURE (*5) / SMOKING POPES 1991-1998 compilation (*6) / SMOKING POPES LIVE collection (*5) / THE PARTY'S OVER (*5)

JOSH CATERER – vocals, guitar / **ELI CATERER** – guitar / **MATT CATERER** – bass / **MIKE FELUMLEE** – drums

		not iss.	Carved Air
1991.	(7"ep) **INOCULATOR**	-	
	– Sandra / Brand new hairstyle / Missing out / No time for your lies / Theme from "Cheerleader".		
		not iss.	Solid Sound
1992.	(7"ep) **BREAK UP**	-	
	– Waiting around / Down the street / Never coming back / Breaking.		
1992.	(7"ep) **2**	-	
	– Writing a letter / Stars / Under the blanket / First time.		
		not iss.	Johann's Face
1993.	(7"ep) **COMIN AT YA SUCKA!**	-	
	– Heather and lace / Hang / (other 2 by GROOVY LOVE VIBES).		
1993.	(lp) <11> **GET FIRED**	-	
	– Let's hear it for love / That's where I come in / Let them die / Double fisted love / Don't be afraid / Can't find it / Off my mind / Not that kind of girlfriend / Days just wave goodbye. <cd-iss. Jun96; same>		
		Capitol	Capitol
Jan 96.	(c-s/7") (TC+/CL 764) **NEED YOU AROUND. / ADENA**		-
	(cd-s+=) (CDCL 764) – Adena (live) / Angel flying too close to the ground.		
Mar 96.	(cd/c) (CD/TC EST 2277) <33831> **BORN TO QUIT**		Nov95
	– Midnight moon / Rubella / Gotta know right now / Mrs. you and me / Just broke up / My lucky day / Need you around / Can't help the teardrops (from getting cried) / Adena / On the shoulder.		
—	<above was actually originally issued in US on 'Johann's Face' 1994>		
Jul 97.	(7") **BEFORE I'M GONE. / PASTED**		-
Sep 97.	(7") **EGG NOG**		-
	– Pure imagination / O' holy night.		
Dec 97.	(7") <58667> **I KNOW YOU LOVE ME. / NEED YOU AROUND (live)**		-
	(10"+=) – Paul.		
Mar 98.	(cd) <(8 38217-2)> **DESTINATION FAILURE**		Aug97
	– Star struck one / No more smiles / I know you love me / You spoke to me / Paul / Can't find it / Capital Cristine / Before I'm gone / Megan / Let's hear it for love / Pure imagination / I was right / They lied / End of your time / Pretty pathetic / Follow the sound.		
—	now without ELI		
		not iss.	Double Zero
Sep 01.	(cd) <8005> **THE PARTY'S OVER**	-	
	– Seven lonely days / Valentine / Bewitched / The party's over / Farther along / Zing! went the strings of my heart / Stormy weather / I wake up crying / You'll never walk alone / Why me.		

– compilations, etc. –

Dec 99.	(cd) Double Zero; <(DZO 1CD)> **SMOKING POPES 1991-1998**		Aug99
	– Brand new hairtsyle / Sandra / Wanted love / Waiting around / Down the street / Never coming back / Breaking / Run away / Writing a letter / Stars / Under the blanket / First time / Let's hear it for love / That's where I come in / Let them die / Double fisted love / Don't be afraid / Can't find it / Off my mind / Not that kind of girlfriend / Days just wave goodbye / Do something / Pasted.		
Jun 00.	(cd) Double Zero; <(DZO 3CD)> **SMOKING POPES LIVE (live)**		Jan00
	– Ramblin' rose / Off my mind / Need you around / Star struck one / No more smiles / Double fisted love / Surf (intro) / Before I'm gone / Stars / You spoke to me / Not that kind of girlfriend / Paul / Under the blanket / Gotta know right now / Days just wave goodbye / Pretty pathetic / Ramblin' rose / Writing a letter / Waiting around / Brand new hairstyle / Rubella / I know you love me.		

SMUDGE

Formed: Sydney, Australia . . . 1990 by singer/songwriter TOM MORGAN, drummer ALISON GALLOWAY and bassist PAUL DUNCAN. SMUDGE were brought together by 'Half a Cow' label-master NIC DALTON, who was compiling a compilation CD for his newly-established label, and he offered the trio the opportunity to provide a track. 'TEA, TOAST AND TURMOIL' confirmed the beginnings of SMUDGE, and they soon followed it with the 'I DON'T WANT TO BE GRANT McLENNAN' EP, which DALTON released on 'Half a Cow' (in 1991). The EP poked fun at the ex-GO-BETWEENS frontman, whose solo career had faltered somewhat.

SMUDGE continued to develop their indie-pop sound with the 1992's 'LOVE, LUST & LEMONJUICE' EP, which nearly provided them with a hit ('DIVAN') and 1993's 'SUPERHERO' EP, which contained a cover of John Waite's 'MISSING YOU'. Meanwhile, NIC DALTON had a stint on bass for the HUMMINGBIRDS (covering for friend ROBYN ST. CLARE) during their joint tour of Australia with The LEMONHEADS. DALTON and LEMONHEADS' EVAN DANDO became friends, and DALTON invited DANDO to record some tracks with him and TOM MORGAN, who by this point had formed a side-act, called SNEEZE. MORGAN and DANDO also became friends, and soon cultivated a hugely productive writing partnership, which saw MORGAN co-write the LEMONHEADS' LP title-track 'It's A Shame About Ray', and half the tracks on 'Come On Feel The Lemonheads'. Another LEMONHEADS connection was their track 'Alison's Waiting To Happen' – apparently about SMUDGE's very own Ms. GALLOWAY. Tracks from the first three SMUDGE EPs were combined with unreleased material to form the compilation 'TEA, TOAST & TURMOIL', which was released in the States in 1993 by 'Shake'. With ADAM YEE replacing DUNCAN on bass, SMUDGE recorded their full-debut, 'MANILOW', which was released later in '93. 'MANILOW' contained twenty-one punchy, playful tracks, including single 'IMPRACTICAL JOKE' (released in three countries with different b-sides) – another near-hit. Their 1994 European tour prompted the release of a UK EP, 'THE OUTDOOR TYPE', while Australia saw the release of the 'HOT SMOKE AND SASSAFRAS' EP and the 'BIG CITY POONTANG' EP – comprising the 'IMPRACTICAL JOKE' B-sides. Seeking a development of their indie-pop sound, they went to Chicago to record second LP, 'YOU, ME, CARPARK . . . NOW', hiring producer Casey Rice, using TORTOISE's JOHN McENTIRE and incorporating orchestration into their arrangements. The LP was preceded by two EPs – 'MIKE LOVE NOT WAR' and 'SLIGHT RETURN'. The 1997 release, 'MO POONTANG', was another B-side and unreleased material collection. As ALISON GALLOWAY began presenting an MTV indie show, SMUDGE became a four-piece with PETE KELLY (formerly with DISNEYFIST) joining as second guitarist. In 1998 the new-look SMUDGE recorded third LP, 'REAL McCOY, WRONG SINATRA', in a purpose built eight-track studio. It marked a return to their early, raw sound, and was recorded in only five days. The 'EIGHTEEN IN A WEEK' EP was a 1999 release, while MORGAN and DALTON still played together and occasionally released material as SNEEZE – including 2001's '70s soul influenced 'LOST THE SPIRIT TO ROCK & ROLL'. • Covered: MAKE ALL OUR DREAMS COME TRUE ('Laverne & Shirley' theme) / BERLIN CHAIR (You Am I) / SOME OF SHELLY'S BLUES (Mike Nesmith) / TRYING TO SNEEZE (Ben Lee) / etc.

Album rating: TEA, TOAST & TURMOIL compilation (*6) / MANILOW (*7) / HOT SMOKE AND SASSAFRAS mini (*5) / BIG CITY POONTANG mini collection (*4) / YOU, ME, CARPARK . . . NOW (*6) / MO POONTANG compilation (*5) / REAL McCOY, WRONG SINATRA (*6) / Sneeze: SNEEZE (*4) / LOST THE SPIRIT TO ROCK'N'ROLL (*5)

TOM MORGAN – vocals, guitar / **PAUL "DUNCS" DUNCAN** – bass / **ALISON GALLOWAY** – drums (later of GODSTAR)

		Half A Cow	not iss.
1991.	(7"ep) (moo 04) **I DON'T WANT TO BE GRANT McLENNAN**	-	- Austra
	– I don't want to be Grant McLennan / Stranglehold / Foccacia (-*). <US cd-ep-iss.1992 on 'Shock'-*/+=; SHOCKCD 004> – Dabble / Spawn.		
1992.	(cd-ep) (HAC 08) **LOVE, LUST & LEMONJUICE**	-	- Austra
	– Pulp / Plug it up / Steak and chips / Divan / Spoilt brat.		
1993.	(cd-ep) (HAC 16) **SUPERHERO**	-	- Austra
	– Superhero / Straight face down / Missing you / Outside / Make all our dreams come true / (untitled).		
		Domino	Shake
Aug 93.	(7") (RUG 7) **SUPERHERO. / MISSING YOU**		-
	(cd-s+=) (RUG 7CD) – Straight face down / Outside / untitled.		
—	**ADAM YEE** – bass (ex-HEADACHE) repl. DUNCAN		
Jan 94.	(12"ep/cd-ep) (RUG 12 T/CD) <SALD 211> **IMPRACTICAL JOKE**		
	– Impractical joke / Over / You know it / Shell hell / Hack job.		
Feb 94.	(cd/lp) (WIG CD/LP 7) <SALD 212> **MANILOW**		Sep94
	– Manilow / Ingrown / Impractical joke / Superhero / Funny you should mention that / Bodyshirt / Down about it / Little help / Desmond / Scary cassettes / Mr. Coffee man / Pulp / Dave the talking bear / Ugly, just like me / Divan / Not here for a haircut / Don't understand / Hell on hot bread / Top bunkin' Duncan / Charles in charge / Kelly.		
Jun 94.	(7"m) <BUS 40> **DESMOND. / SHELL HELL / SUCKER PUNCH**		
	(above issued on 'Bus Stop')		
Aug 94.	(12"ep/cd-ep) (RUG 24 T/CD) **THE OUTDOOR TYPE**		-
	– The outdoor type / Scary cassettes / Dave the talking bear / Not here for a haircut / Berlin chair.		
Feb 95.	(m-cd/m-lp) (WIG CD/LP 19) <SALD 219> **HOT SMOKE AND SASSAFRAS**		Apr95
	– The wrong pony / I am not the cosmos / Coal surge / My bright idea / Tenderfoot / Guess I'm a goner / All the money in the world.		
		Half A Cow	Half A Cow
1996.	(cd-ep) (HAC 54) **MIKE LOVE NOT WAR EP**	-	- Austra
	– Mike love not war / Trying to sneeze / Weep woman weep / Tenderfoot.		
1996.	(cd-ep) (HAC 56) **SLIGHT RETURN EP**	-	- Austra
	– Ingrown / Some of Shelly's blues / etc.		
1996.	(cd) (HAC 58) **YOU, ME, CARPARK . . . NOW**	-	- Austra
	– Nelson flavour / Lighten up Hank / Stash / Buddy love / Caller are you there? / It / Mike love, not war / Ingrown (slight return) / Skateboard trickery / Not nearly enough / Pedantic / A crisis of faith / Lady let's not stop the groove / Donde esta la acciones / Lonesome and then some.		

added **PETE KELLY** – guitar

Feb 99. (cd) *(HAC 73)* **REAL McCOY, WRONG SINATRA** [-] [Nov98]
– Ya we are cruel but we have our agenda / Hot potato / Nobel rot / Breadcrumb trail / Real McCoy, wrong Sinatra / The stars are coming out / Eighteen in a week / Recent Reich / Lucked out / Kokoro / Jo Jo & the guts / Lonely kid / I was born to change the world.

1999. (cd-ep) *(HAC 82)* **EIGHTEEN IN A WEEK EP** [-] [-] Austra
– Eighteen in a week / Real McCoy wrong Sinatra / Gutless wonder – a celebration of self loathing / Plenty to prove and plenty to lose / (The way outdoor type).

– compilations, etc. –

Oct 93. (lp/c/cd) *Shake; <(SALD 207/+C/D)>* **TEA, TOAST & TURMOIL**
(compilation)
– Spoilt brat / Straight face down / Outside / Make all our dreams come true / Pulp / Plug it up / Divan / Alison / I don't want to be Grant McLennan / Stranglehold / Dabble / Leroy de foix / Tea, toast & turmoil / Foccacia / Steak & chips / Babaganouj.

1995. (m-cd) *Half A Cow; (HAC 36)* **BIG CITY POONTANG** [-] [-] Austra
– The outdoor type / Touch & Go rock machine / Suckerpunch / Clodhopper / No backbone / Always a good look / Not here for a haircut / It's a guy-man-bloke thing you wouldn't understand.

Mar 98. (cd) *Half A Cow; (HAC 62)* **MO POONTANG** [-] [-]
– The outdoor type (acoustic) / Clodhopper / Suckerpunch / No backbone / Touch & Go rock machine / Not here for a haircut (haircoustic) / Good good things / Berlin chair (acoustic) / Bill / Understanding room only / Hack job / You know it / It's a guy-man-bloke thing you wouldn't understand / Clean sheets / Does your mother know? / Couldn't I just tell you / Shell hell / Over / The outdoor type (electric) / Berlin chair (electric).

SNEEZE

TOM MORGAN + NIC DALTON (ex-LEMONHEADS)

Half A Cow / not iss.

1993. (d7"ep) *(moo 06)* **SNEEZE** [-] [-] Austra
– Ying and yang telephone / Trouble in school / 2 Kates / There he is / Commencing December / Shaky ground / Doomed to visit Disneyland / Back down / Don't go (girlie) / Demand / Ripped jeans / ('Cause you're so) Sweet / Winter won out / Pedal / Accident prone / Satan / Autumnal eyes / Baby asleep / Monday at Mars with zero people / Goodbye vinyl.

1995. (cd; mail-o) *(HAC 50)* **SNEEZE** [-] [-] Austra
– Sneeze theme / (SNEEZE ep tracks) / Darth Vader helmet / Dad's trailer / Create your friends / Better days / Photo finish / I'm upset enough (pts 1 & 3) / Could run or walk / Lolly land / You put me where I am today / Climbing vulture street / Evil star / R / She's got a boyfriend / Pins and needles / Dice / Cold cold morning / (You're so) Nevermind / Explain deep December / Strawbreeze.

Apr 96. (7"ep) *(ER 177)* **SHAKY GROUND EP** [-] [-]
– Shaky ground / Trouble in school / Ripped jeans / Demand / 2 Kates / There he is / Baby asleep / Don't go (girlie)
(above issued on Spanish 'Elefant' records)

1998. (m-lp; mail-o) *(HAC 69)* **THE FOUR SEEZONS** [-] [-] Austra
– The four seezons:- Winter – Spring – Summer – Autumn / Live on Radio FBI:- Ying and yang telephone – 2 Kates – Create your friends – Photo finish – Ripped jeans – Shaky ground – Winter won out – (Don't go) Girlie – Demand – There he is – I'm upset enough (parts 1 & 3).

Aug 99. (cd-ep) *(HAC 81)* **DOCTOR OF LOVE / LOUD & TRUE** [-] [-] Austra
– Doctor of love / Rumour, conjecture, speculation, hearsay / Loud & true / When honey snaps (live) / Ninth of the ninth, ninety-nine.

Jun 01. (cd/d-lp) *(HAC 96/+V)* **LOST THE SPIRIT TO ROCK'N'ROLL** [-] [-] Austra
– Wu-Li / Too much man to be a woman / Doctor of love / Deaf girl, dumb guy, blind love / (You're not) The 'onely one / (Don't go) Distant / Dancin' dollars / Tittie bar / B.U. / I got a type / Maybe moving in together wasn't such a good idea / I want to be a woman (part 2) / Welcome back succubus / Sex gang of the year / Casual cashew daddy / I believe in Marrickville (parts 1 & 2) / Ain't no love on the road / I've lost the spirit to rock'n'roll. *(d-lp+=)* – I want to be a woman (part 1) / Too much man to be a woman (reprise) / (You've never) Had sex sober / Isle of Lesbos / Girl, it's time we had a man to man / This is the song only young girls can hear. *(UK cd-iss. Aug02 on 'Fire; FIRECD 82)*

Apr 02. (cd-ep) *(HAC 97)* **THE MAYBE MOVING IN EP** [-] [-] Austra
– Maybe moving in together wasn't such a good idea / (Love theme from) Cousin Erich / (Theme from) Smoke! / Beibi Pelu / The tittie bar suite: Tittie bar (part 2) – Girls, girls, girls, crazy girls – Nurse Jones – Tittie bar (part 3).

SMUGGLERS

Formed: Vancouver, British Columbia, Canada . . . 1988 by GRANT MARSHALL, DAVID CARSWELL, NICK THOMAS, ADAM WOODALL and PAUL PREMINGER. After a couple of singles, 'UP AND DOWN' and 'AT MARINELAND', through 1990 and 1991, these brylcreem punks made their album debut with 'ATLANTA WHISKEY FLATS' (1992). By this point, the rhythm section of WOODALL and PREMINGER had been replaced by BEEZ and BRYCE DUNN, the line-up which graced the likes of 'IN THE HALL OF FAME' (1993) and 'WET PANTS CLUB' (1994). While their goodtime, party-obsessed sound was never likely to trouble either the charts or the indie elite, the band's devoted following ensured a constant flow of frat-house rock, most recently with 'ROSIE' (2000). • **Covered:** MISS LUDELLA BLACK (Wild Billy Childish) / SMOKIN' MONKEY + SUPERCAR (Leather Uppers) / KISS LIKE A NUN (Boys) / THREE SIDES (Young Fresh Fellows) / WHAT DO YOU WANT ME TO DO? (Pointed Sticks) / PACIFICA STOMP (Frank Zappa) / LUAU! (. . . Morgan) / STAY WITH ME (. . . Shernoff).

Album rating: ATLANTA WHISKEY FLATS (*5) / IN THE HALL OF FAME (*5) / WET PANTS CLUB (*5) / SELLING THE SIZZLE (*6) / GROWING UP SMUGGLER: A TEN YEAR ANNIVERSARY LIVE compilation (*5) / ROSIE (*5)

GRANT MARSHALL – vocals / **DAVID CARSWELL** – guitar / **NICK THOMAS** – guitar / **ADAM WOODALL** – bass / **PAUL PREMINGER** – drums

not iss. / Nardwuar

1990. (7") *<Cleo 2>* **UP AND DOWN.** / [-] [-]
— **BEEZ** – bass; repl. WOODALL

not iss. / Pop Llama

1991. (10"ep) *<Cleo 3>* **AT MARINELAND** [-]
— **BRYCE DUNN** – drums; repl. PREMINGER

1992. (lp) *<PL 22>* **ATLANTA WHISKEY FLATS** [-] [-]

Apr 93. (cd) *<2121>* **IN THE HALL OF FAME** [-] [-]
– Rock'n'roll was never this fun / Your mom's the Devil / For my lover / Bourbon '92 / Sexy thing / Alan Thicke / Miss Ludella Black / My Morrissey shirt / Reid / Invitation only / Canadian ambassadors / Shake down / Flyin' buttress of love / Fun in the USA / Hey, Stephanie! / Can't be satisfied / Make you mine / Vancouver, BC / Calgarians don't dance / That is rock'n'roll.

not iss. / Screaming Apple

1993. (7") **AT GERMANY.** / [-] [-]

not iss. / Radiation

1993. (lp) *<004>* **WET PANTS CLUB** [-] [-]
– Paper doll / Luau! / La-la-la-lies / Don valley / Big house / Pacifica stomp / Time marches on / Mach 1 / Surrender / Dancin' dolly / Kiss like a nun / Amnesia. *<cd-iss. 1994; same>*

not iss. / Top Drawer

1994. (7") **TATTOO DAVE.** / (other by BUM) [-] [-]

not iss. / For Monsters

1994. (7") **GOTTA GOTTA GOTTA.** / (other by HOODS) [-] [-]

not iss. / Mint

1994. (7") **PARTY . . . PARTY . . . PARTY . . . POOPER!** / [-] [-]

not iss. / 1+2

1995. (7") **WHIPLASH!** / [-] [-]

not iss. / Rock And Roll Inc.

1995. (7"ep) **SENOR PANTSDOWN** [-] [-]

Lookout / Lookout

Jan 96. (cd-ep) *<LOOKOUT 129>* **SUMMER GAMES EP**
– She ain't no Egyptian / Elite Manila (Brent T.V.) / (other 2 tracks by The HI-FIVES).

Mar 96. (lp/cd) *<(LK 136/+CD)>* **SELLING THE SIZZLE**
– To serve, protect and entertain / Especially you / Bishy-bishy! / Big trouble / She ain't no Egyptian / Death of a romantic / Dedication / I need a vacation / B 'N' L / Pick 'em up truck / Quesy / Bad guys / Dusty's lament / Reno nickel / Barkerville.

Sep 97. (cd-ep) *<LOOKOUT 185>* **BUDDY HOLLY CONVENTION**
– Melee in Madrid / Can of love / I want, need, demand action / Buddy Holly convention / She's a machine / I love spoons.

Aug 98. (cd) *<LOOKOUT 199CD>* **GROWING UP SMUGGLER: A TEN YEAR ANNIVERSARY LIVE (live)** [-]
– Smokin' monkey / Pick 'em up truck / Paper doll / Sexy thing / To serve, protect and entertain / What do you want me to do? / Especially you / Alan Thicke / Luau! / She ain't no Egyptian / Hey, Stefanie! / Whiplash! / Stop! look! listen! / I need a vacation / Rock'n'roll was never this fun / Kiss like a nun / Supercar / Three sides / Shakedown! / Stay with me.

— **GRAHAM WATSON** – drums; repl. DUNN

Feb 00. (cd/lp) *<(LK 236 CD/LP)>* **ROSIE**
– Rock thy neighbor / Booze can / Miss Pilgrim / I'll remember / Death at Disneyland / She's another thing / Rosie / Kings of the party / Useless rocker / Coffee, tea, or me? / Teen mob! / Someone / Danko Jones' pants.

not iss. / Corduroy

2001. (7") **split w/ MACH PELICAN** [-] [-]

not iss. / Supersonicfridge

2002. (7"pic-d) **USELESS ROCKER** [-] [-]

SNAPPER

Formed: Dunedin, New Zealand . . . 1987 by songwriter and former CHILLS and CLEAN founder, PETER GUTTERIDGE, along with CHRISTINE VOICE, ALAN HAIG and DOMINIC STONES. An eponymous debut EP emerged on veteran Kiwi label, 'Flying Nun', although it was Edinburgh's 'Avalanche' imprint (an offshoot of their long established indie retail outlet) that later gave it a UK release. The label also issued their 1991 debut set, 'SHOTGUN BLOSSOM', revealing the band to be in the firmly established NZ tradition, if a little noisier and less melodic than their forebears. Employing a garage guitar/organ drone with girl/boy vocals drenched in fuzz-distortion and placed well back in the mix, the band could've been Antipodean cousins of Scotland's own JESUS & MARY CHAIN. With the subsequent establishment of a 'Flying Nun' UK base, the belated 'A.D.M.' (1996) was given a full British release. • **Note:** Not to be confused with mid-90's San Fran punks SNAP-HER ho issued sets for 'Ne Red Archives' or millennium rap artist SNAPPER.

Album rating: SHOTGUN BLOSSOM (*5) / A.D.M. (*5)

PETER GUTTERIDGE (b.19 May'61) – vocals, guitar, keyboards (ex-CHILLS, ex-CLEAN, ex-GREAT UNWASHED) / **CHRISTINE VOICE** – keyboards, vocals / **DOMINIC STONES** – guitar (ex-BIRD NEST ROYS) / **ALAN HAIG** (b. 5 Aug'61) – drums (ex-CHILLS)

Flying Nun / not iss.

May 88. (12"ep/cd-ep) *(FN/+CD 110)* **SNAPPER** [-] [-] NewZ
– Buddy / Cause of you / Death and weirdness in the surging zone / Hang on. *(UK-iss.Dec90 on 'Avalanche'; AGAP 009)*

— **DAVID KILGOUR** – guitar (ex-CLEAN) repl. STONES – he joined 3Ds

Avalanche / not iss.

Jul 91. (cd/c/lp) *(ONLY CD/MC/LP 010)* **SHOTGUN BLOSSOM**
– Pop your top / Can / Telepod fly / Eyes that shine / Dark sensation / Dead pictures / Snapper and the ocean / What are you thinking / Hot sun / I don't know / Emmanuelle / Dry spot / Rain. *(NZ-iss.1992 on 'Flying Nun'; FNCD 216)*

Dec 91. (7") *(AGAP 010)* **DARK SENSATION.** / **SNAPPER AND THE OCEAN** [-] [-]

— **MIKE DOOLEY** – drums (ex-TOY LOVE) repl. HAIG

Flying Nun / not iss.

1994. (7") *(FN 264)* **VADER.** / **GENTLE HOUR** [-] [-]

— **GUTTERIDGE + DOOLEY** now with guest backing vocalists **DEMARNIA LLOYD** (of MINK, of CLOUDBOY), **CELIA PAVLOVA** (of KING LOSER) + **CHRISTINE VOICE**

SNAPPER (cont)

Mar 96. (c/cd) *(FN/+CD 294)* **A.D.M.**
– Tomcat / Hammerhead / Small town secret / Demon / Hotchkiss / A.D.M. / Killzone 44 / Stalker / Lock and load / Used to know her name.

—— disbanded after above

– compilations, etc. –

2001. (7") *Crawlspace; (SPACE 010)* **HAMMERHEAD. / DRY SPOT** – | – NewZ

SNOW PATROL

Formed: Dundee, Scotland ... 1996 as POLARBEAR by Belfast-born Dundee University students GARY LIGHTBODY and MARK McCLELLAND; RICHARD COLBURN (with the assistance of BELLE & SEBASTIAN's STUART MURDOCH augmented early on. Unfortunately, after only one single ('STARFIGHTER PILOT') for Glasgow's Stow College label, 'Electric Honey', due to the already established US outfit POLAR BEAR (note the space!) getting the dry hump – so to speak. Subsequently inking a deal with 'Jeepster' (home to BELLE ...), SNOW PATROL gently breezed into the ears and minds of their audience via two singles, 'LITTLE HIDE' and ONE HUNDRED THINGS YOU SHOULD HAVE DONE IN BED', both highlights from the brittle guitar-pop band's debut long-player, 'SONGS FOR POLAR BEARS' (1998). Still located somewhere around Glasgow (with some sidelining with Scotland's indie conglomorate, REINDEER SECTION), the dreamy SNOW PATROL collected themselves together for a second set, 'WHEN IT'S ALL OVER WE STILL HAVE TO CLEAR UP' (2001). Bedsitter music, indeed.

Album rating: SONGS FOR POLAR BEARS (*6) / WHEN IT'S ALL OVER WE STILL HAVE TO CLEAR UP (*6)

GARY LIGHTBODY – guitar, vocals / **MARK McCLELLAND** – bass, keyboards / **RICHARD COLBURN** – drums, keyboards / with **STUART MURDOCH** – piano (of BELLE & SEBASTIAN)

                                                  Electric Honey   not iss.

Jun 97. (cd-s; as POLARBEAR) *(EHRCD 007)* **STARFIGHTER PILOT / HOLY COW / SAFETY**

—— **JOHN QUINN** – drums; repl. COLBURN

—— added live contributor: **TOM SIMPSON** – turntables

                                                  Jeepster   Imprint

Feb 98. (7") *(JPR7 004)* **LITTLE HIDE. / STICKY TEENAGE TWIN**
(cd-s+=) *(JPRCDS 004)* – Limited edition / JJ.

May 98. (7") *(JPR7 005)* **ONE HUNDRED THINGS YOU SHOULD HAVE DONE IN BED. / MY LAST GIRLFRIEND**
(cd-s+=) *(JPRCDS 005)* – T.M.T. / I could stay away forever.

Aug 98. (cd/lp) *(JPR CD/LP 004) <113141>* **SONGS FOR POLAR BEARS**
– Downhill from here / Starfighter pilot / The last shot ringing in my ears / Absolute gravity / Get balsamic vinegar ... quick you fool / Mahogany / NYC / Little hide / Make up / Velocity girl / Days without paracetamol / Fifteen minutes old / Favourite friend / One hundred things you should have done in bed. *<US cd re-iss. 1999 on 'Never'; 4039>*

Nov 98. (7") *(JPR7 007)* **VELOCITY GIRL. / ABSOLUTE GRAVITY**
(cd-s+=) *(JPRCDS 007)* – When you're right, you're right.

Jun 99. (cd-s) *(JPRCDS 013)* **STARFIGHTER PILOT (the Spynci new radio edit) / RAZE THE CITY / RIOT, PLEASE**
(cd-s) *(JPRCDS 013R)* – (remixes; Cut La Roc and Belle & Sebastian).

                                                Jeepster   Jeepster

Nov 00. (cd-s) *(JPRCDS 020)* **ASK ME HOW I AM / IN COMMAND OF CARS / TALK TO THE TREES**

Mar 01. (cd-s) *(JPRCDS 021)* **ONE NIGHT IS NOT ENOUGH / MONKEY MOBE / WORKWEAR SHOP**

Mar 01. (cd/lp) *(JPR CD/LP 012) <4052>* **WHEN IT'S ALL OVER WE STILL HAVE TO CLEAR UP**
– Never gonna fall in love again / Ask me how I am / Making enemies / Black and blue / Last ever lone gunman / If I'd found the right words to say / Batten down the hatch / One night is not enough / Chased by ... I don't know what / On/off / An olive grove facing the sea / When it's all over we still have to clear up / Make love to me forever / Firelight.

SNOWPONY

Formed: Dalston, London, England ... early 1996 by former STEREOLAB (and MOONSHAKE) keyboard player, KATHERINE GIFFORD, who hooked up with "fed-up" MY BLOODY VALENTINE bassist, DEB GOOGE. They, in turn, enlisted the aid of another indie Krautpop afficionado, MAX CORRADI (straight from QUICKSPACE SUPERSPORT and ROLLERSKATE SKINNY) and set about cutting their debut single, 'EASY WAY DOWN'. Released towards the end of the year, the platter was almost immediately followed by the EP, 'THE LITTLE GIRLS UNDERSTAND'. Sounding similar to The BREEDERS or electrophiles STEREOLAB, SNOWPONY acquired a dark but subtle range of eclectic and prolific guitar loops, popcorn synth and a labyrinth of GIFFORD's brooding, witty lyrics. Their debut set, 'THE SLOW-MOTION WORLD OF SNOWPONY' (1998), was produced (ever so crisply) by post-avant jazzateer and TORTOISE guru/drummer, JOHN McENTIRE, who twisted the quartet's style and brought it up to new and different heights. SONIC YOUTH apparently showed admiration for the troupe after the trio sampled '100%', as did lo-fi pioneers SEBADOH and sensitive types GRANDADDY, whom they supported in 1998. After taking what seemed like ages away from the music biz, SNOWPONY returned in 2001 with a new imprint, 'Dead Pan Alley' and a new album, 'SEA SHANTIES FOR SPACESHIPS'. Maintaining their foothold on electronica, trip-hop and indie, GIFFORD, GOOGE and Co searched their souls for ethereal and detached music.

Album rating: THE SLOW-MOTION WORLD OF SNOWPONY (*7) / SEA SHANTIES FOR SPACESHIPS (*6)

KATHERINE GIFFORD – vocals, keyboards, samples (ex-STEREOLAB, ex-MOONSHAKE) / **DEB GOOGE** – bass (ex-MY BLOODY VALENTINE) / **MAX CORRADI** – drums (ex-QUICKSPACE SUPERSPORT, ex-ROLLERSKATE SKINNY)

                                      See No Evil   See No Evil

Nov 96. (7") *(EVIL 001)* **EASY WAY DOWN. / GOLDEN CARRIAGE**
(cd-s+=) *(EVIL 001CD) <696209>* – Hank Williams' ass.

Dec 96. (7") *(45REV 41)* **THE LITTLE GIRLS UNDERSTAND**
– Come & sit here on your daddy's knee / Who's gonna be your daddy when I'm gone?
(above issued on 'Rough Trade Singles Club')

Jun 97. (7") *(EVIL 002)* **CHOCOLATE. / EASY WAY DOWN**
(cd-s) *(EVIL 002CD)* – ('A'side) / My brother / Kill her.

                                      Radioactive   Radioactive

Nov 98. (7") *(RAX 34)* **JOHN BROWN (TRIUMPHAL MARCH). / HAPPY ARE THE DEAD**
(cd-s+=) *(RAXTD 34)* – Golden carriage.

Feb 99. (cd) *(<RAD 11828>)* **THE SLOW-MOTION WORLD OF SNOWPONY**   Sep98
– Easy way down / A way to survive / Love letters / Bad sister / 3 Can keep a secret (if 2 are dead) / St. Lucy's gate / John Brown (triumphal march) / Titanic / Snow White / Siamese fighting fish / Pylons.

                                  Dead Pan Alley   Dead Pan Alley

Jul 01. (cd) *(<DPA 001CD>)* **SEA SHANTIES FOR SPACESHIPS**   Sep01
– Crumpled 10 / Pirate's gold / Amsterdam / A car I didn't own / Into the heart of Dalston / Starfish / Naked twister / Brown hotel (II) / My brother / Monkeys versus the universe / Pleasure gardens / Naked twister / Crumpled 10 / Chocolate (in the sun).

SOFA

Formed: Montreal, Canada ... 1993 by IAN, KEITH, BRAD and SCOTT. Like many of the militant Canadian bands on the 'Constellation' label, SOFA have endured many ups and downs in their career, spanning almost ten years. Forming in '93 as a quartet, they slowly disintegrated, but re-formed in 1995 to issue a cassette-only recording of what would end up as 'NEW ERA BUILDING' (1999), a brooding two-track EP recorded in an empty loft. They followed this eerie slice of melancholic post-punk with the full-length album 'GREY', which featured eleven tracks and a whole load of experimental, brutal, but sublime noise. Crossed between the quiet/loud of SLINT or THE FOR CARNATION, mix in a bit of SCRATCH ACID (for sheer volume) and add a twist of IAN CURTIS (if he was suddenly resurrected!) and you pretty much had the equative template for this group. Although it's easy to pigeonhole bands like these by simply slapping on a sticker that said "post-rock", SOFA went much further in terms of ambience, noise and style. On track 'MONOTONE', the ensemble exorcised some very spooky demons, likewise on the expansive droning epic 'MEDICINE HAT'. You'd be forgiven for thinking you'd walked into a good nightmare.

Album rating: GREY (*6)

IAN / KEITH / BRAD / SCOTT

                                      not iss.   own label

Jan 99. (ltd-c) **NEW ERA BUILDING**

                                      Constellation   Constellation

Mar 99. (cd) *<const 002>* **GREY**
– On – Off / Ch.2.chi / Monotone / Current / 80,000 / Red lake / Comma / The fence / Travel / Stress / Medicine hat.

SOFTIES (see under ⇒ TIGER TRAP)

SOLAR MUMUNS (see under ⇒ MOONFLOWERS)

SOLEDAD BROTHERS

Formed: Toledo, Ohio, USA ... 1998, by JOHNNY WIRICK and percussionist BEN SMITH. Peddling the blues since 1994, JOHNNY WIRICK (or WALKER, as he sometimes liked to be called), ended his stint with legendary Ohio group HENRY AND JUNE to form JOHNNY WALKER in 1997 with drummer DOUG WALKER. This was a short-lived project and came under fire when DOUG left the group leaving JOHNNY to find his replacement for a one-off gig. BEN SMITH stepped into the shoes, and fitted them nicely, causing JOHNNY to re-name themselves SOLEDAD BROTHERS, apparently after a pair of siblings whom Lomax recorded in prison back in the early 50's. They issued a 7" single on the now infamous 'Italy' records and were approached by independent distributors 'Estrus', who eventually signed the duo in early 1999. The pair began work on their debut album (2000), to be produced by JACK WHITE of The WHITE STRIPES (who also appears on the back, dressed as Uncle Sam, about to be shot by a firing squad). Self-titled and very self assertive, the group wielded the kind of two-man blues you'd expect from a Detroit band, but the Brothers Soledad fused slide-guitar, thumping tom-toms and the kind of production technique that suggested all of the songs

SOLEDAD BROTHERS (cont)

were played live, in a garage – boy, MUDDY WATERS would've been proud. 'STEAL YOUR SOUL AND DARE YOUR SPIRIT TO MOVE' was issued in 2002 to rapturous applause. Almost like a train wreck that didn't quite leave the tracks, the album was very reminiscent of The ROLLING STONES in their 'Let It Bleed' period (for further proof, check out the track 'BRAKE 'EM ON DOWN'), with JOHNNY screaming and hollering while his guitar roughly jingle-jangled in the foreground. Just as the legendary MUDDY was the STONES' muse, here it was living bluesman R.L. BURNSIDE that provided the band with inspiration, as he was congratulated on the track 'MICHIGAN LINE (HATS OFF TO R.L.)'. It was fair to say that The WHITE STRIPES were a lot more successful at their jobs than The SOLEDAD BROTHERS; with record sales and awards superseding that of the latter. But as a certain somebody once said "It's only rock'n'roll, but I like it!". • **Covered:** AIN'T NO SUNSHINE WHEN SHE'S GONE (Bill Withers).

Album rating: SOLEDAD BROTHERS (*7) / STEAL YOUR SOUL AND DARE YOUR SPIRIT TO MOVE (*6)

JOHNNY WALKER (b. JOHNNY WIRICK) – vocals, guitar, mouth organ / **BEN "SWANK" SMITH** – drums, percussion, vocals

not iss.   Italy

Nov 98. (7") <IR 007> **SUGAR & SPICE. / JOHNNY'S DEATH LETTER**

Estrus   Estrus

Nov 99. (7"red,7") <(ES 7142)> **GOSPEL ACCORDING TO JOHN. / MYSTERIOUS WAYS**

Jul 00. (lp/cd) <(ES 1271/+CD)> **SOLEDAD BROTHERS**
– Gospel according to John / What hath God wraught / The weight of the world / Front St. Front / Lovin' machine / Cadillac hips / Shining path / Rock me slow / Handle song / St. Ides of March / Sugar & spice / I-75 boogie / Do the heartstopper / Gimme back my wig / Mysterious ways.

Mar 02. (lp/cd) <(ES 1289/+CD)> **STEAL YOUR SOUL AND DARE YOUR SPIRIT TO MOVE**
– Prince among thieves / Prodigal Stones blues / This guitar says I'm sorry / Break 'em on down / Nation's bell / Hammer me down / Michigan line (hats off to R.L.) / .32 blues / Ray of love / Skidmore blues / Miracle birth / There's no sunshine when she's gone / Good Friday the 13th: part III.

SOLEX

Formed: Amsterdam, Netherlands . . . 1997 by Rotterdam-born composer and record shop owner, ELISABETH ESSELINK, who had been a member of indie-pop act, SONETIC VET. Earning its name from a small Hungarian motor scooter, protagonist ESSELINK (alongside early member GEERT DE GROOT) set up the project to broaden her musical range, and sure did accomplish it! Getting her hands on an eight track and primitive sampler, she spent most of her days rummaging around in the bargain bins and obscure jazz sections of her record shop trying to dig out any hidden gems that she could sample. The result was 1997's 'SOLEX VS. THE HITMEISTER', a Frankenstein's monster of an album, mixing old records with ESSELINK's enterprising sound, virtually creating a new breed of lo-fi techno pop. Each track featuring the name "SOLEX" (eg. 'ONE LOUDER SOLEX', 'WHEN SOLEX JUST STOOD THERE' etc.) and ESSELINK's COCTEAU TWINS-like vocals, soaring high past the ceiling and then being bounced about on a bass-ridden bungey rope. Guitars and the occasional keyboards gave 'HITMEISTER' a cultivated and delirious distinction. The follow up, 'PICK UP', was not as good as its predecessor. The samples and obscure vocals remained intact but, tragically, the album was let down by its three-part structured songs that merely existed on the famous debut. Promising, but slightly disappointing, 'Matador' still found the time to release it in 1999. Hopefully this hasn't dampened SOLEX's spirit and, hopefully, the band will return with more crazy foreign alt-pop some time in the dreamy future. ELISABETH ESSELINK's career had always been based on finding new samples from old records. 'LOW KICK AND HARD BOP' (2001) was her most accessible to date. A world away from the uncomplicated pop-sampling of FATBOY SLIM, SOLEX's fast and hard electronic noodling is more akin with the sonic breeze of The AVALANCHES, mixing bold brass with swinging lounge and a bit of warbling minced electronica for good measure. Organic sounding instrumentals also plague the set, echoing the recent boom of Folkatronica from the likes of FIUR TET and KIM HITHEROY. A decisively interesting combination, and an album worth having for alternative party music or just a plain wig-out.

Album rating: SOLEX VS. THE HITMIESTER (*8) / SOLEX ALL LIKETY(SPIT)/SOLEX WEST EP (*7) / PICK UP (*6) / LOW KICK AND HARD BOP (*7)

ELISABETH ESSELINK – vocals / with **GEERT DE GROOT** – guitar, bass, piano, cello, melodica

Matador   Matador

Mar 98. (cd/lp) (<OLE 287-2/-1>) **SOLEX VS. THE HITMEISTER**
– One louder Solex / Solex feels lucky / Solex in a slipshod style / Waking up with Solex / Solex's snag / Rolex by Solex / There's a Solex on the run / Solex all licketysplit / Solex for a while / Some Solex / When Solex just stood there / Peppy Solex.

May 98. (cd-ep) (OLE 307-2) **SOLEX ALL LICKETYSPIT. / SOLEX WEST**

—— added **MICHAEL SHAMBERG** – vocals / **ROBERT LAGERDYLE** – drums / **SHANE DELEON** – clarinet / **CORY VIELMA** – vocals

Sep 99. (cd) (<OLE 336-2>) **PICK UP**
– Pick up / Randy Costanza / Dork at 12 o'clock / That's what you get with people

like that . . . / Oh blimey! / The burglars are coming! / Superfluity / Snappy & cocky / Five star Shamberg / Chris the birthday boy / Athens – Ohio / Escargot! / Another tune like 'Not Fade Away' / That'll be $22.95.

Apr 00. (12"ep) <(OLE 362-1)> **ATHENS, OHIO**
– Athens, Ohio / Chris the birthday boy (STEWARD remix) / Randy Costanza (push up) (MOUNT FLORIDA remix) / Another tune like 'Not Fade Away' / That's what you get with people like that.
(cd-ep+=) <(OLE 362-2)> – Another tune like 'Not Fade Away' (DAMIAN O'NEILL remix).

—— now just down to ESSELINK

Sep 01. (cd) <(OLE 499-2)> **LOW KICK AND HARD BOP**
– Low kick and hard bop / Mere imposters / Have you no shame, girl? / Not a hoot! / Knee-high / Honey (Amsterdam is not L.A.!) / Shoot shoot! / Comely row / Ease up, you fundamentalist! / The dot on the I between the H and the T / Good comrades go to Heaven / Cayenne / Ololo / You say potato, I say aardappel / Look . . . no fingerprints!

SOLID GOLD HELL (see under ⇒ **S.P.U.D.**)

SOMATICS (see under ⇒ **ULTRASOUND**)

SOME VELVET SIDEWALK

Formed: Olympia, Washington, USA . . . 1987 by AL LARSEN and drummer ROBERT CHRISTIE, who opened their twee musical account via a cassette-only release, 'FROM PLAYGROUND 'TIL NOW', in '88. After a series of singles and an LP, 'APPETITE FOR EXTINCTION' (1991), CHRISTIE bailed out, leaving LARSEN to employ a new band. During rehearsals, newcomers TOBI VAIL and LOUISE OLSEN, went their own way; they had only ever played 3 gigs! However, one single surfaced from these sessions in 1992, 'EYES LIKE YOURS' for 'Seminal Twang' records. With a revolving-door line-up, LARSEN continued to release the odd SVS album until well into the 90's. His SANDY DIRT project in the mid-90's with Scots indie band, The PASTELS, released only one EP, which covered The Doors' 'SLIM SLOW RIDER'. LARSEN subsequently formed The POLAR BEARS.

Album rating: APPETITE FOR EXTINCTION (*6) / AVALANCHE (*5) / WHIRLPOOL (*7) / SHIPWRECK (*5) / GENERATE! (*5) / THE LOWDOWN (*6)

AL LARSEN – vocals, guitar / **ROBERT CHRISTIE** – drums

not iss.   A.L.

1988. (c) <none> **FROM PLAYGROUND 'TIL NOW**

not iss.   K

1988. (7"m) <IPU 008> **I KNOW. / LIFETIME / SNOW / JEAN WATTS**

1989. (7") <IPU 009> **EARTHBOUND. / LAND**

1991. (7"m) <IPU 020> **PUMPKIN PATCH. / APPLE / BURNING WORLD**

not iss.   Communion

Apr 91. (cd) <COMM 17> **APPETITE FOR EXTINCTION**
– Seasons / Old bridges / Dinosaur / Hurt / Sidewalkin' / Crayons / Snow / Alright / Moment / Sidewalk and sky / Old bridges / 20,000 leagues.

—— **TOBI VAIL** – drums; repl. CHRISTIE
—— added **LOUISE OLSEN** – bass

Seminal Twang   K

Mar 92. (7") (TWANG 12) **EYES LIKE YOURS. / EYE OF THE STORM**

—— **MARTIN BERNIER** – drums; repl. VAIL who had already joined BIKINI KILL / **DON BLAIR** – bass; repl. OLSEN

K   K

Feb 93. (lp/cd) <(KLP 010/+CD)> **AVALANCHE**
– Avalanche / Loch Ness / Curiosity / Froggy / Peaches / Little wishes / Deep sea green / No real home / Alien / Right – Wrong / Ice cream overdrive.

May 94. (lp/cd) <KLP 024/+CD> **WHIRLPOOL**
– Whirlpool / Mouse and rat / Oscar says / One bear alone / Big city plans / How will I–? / I blame you / Shame / Geological / Kicking: giant.

Oct 94. (7"ep) <(IPU 050)> **FREE FROM IT**

—— **TOBI VAIL** – drums / **DONNA DRESCH** – bassist (featured on below 1990 recording)

Jan 95. (lp/cd) <KLP 032/+CD> **SHIPWRECK** (rec.1990)
– Eyes like yours / Puppy / Empty house / Eye of the storm / Unhitched / Dumb / Boardwalkin' / Wondercat / Hopeless case / Mousetrap.

May 95. (m-cd) <KLP 019> **I SCREAM**
– Ice cream overdrive / Shame / I blame you / I cream overdrive (frozen solid mix) / Shame (misty lavender mix).

—— LARSEN recruited **NIKKI McCLURE** + **PAUL SCHUSTER**

Jun 96. (lp) <KLP 062> **GENERATE!**
– Generate! / Consequence / Circle / Altocumulus / Split the scene / Refuse / Valley of the clock / Ghost travel / Anchor / Day follows night.

Jul 96. (7") <IPU 080> **VALLEY OF THE CLOCK. / VALLEY OF THE CLOCK** (Greg Freeman remix)

Nov 97. (cd) <KLP 077CD> **THE LOWDOWN**
– The lowdown / Rewind / Valley of the clock / Drowning man / Split the scene / Hope / Valley of the thrones.

—— LARSEN subsequently formed The POLAR BEARS

SANDY DIRT

AL LARSEN with The PASTELS:- **STEPHEN, AGGI + KATRINA**

not iss.   K

Jan 96. (12"ep/cd-ep) <K 049/+CD> **SANDY DIRT**
– Klein international blue / Slim slow rider / Ship to shore / Matches / Moonlit lungs.

THE GREAT INDIE DISCOGRAPHY — The 1990s

SON, AMBULANCE

Formed: Omaha, USA ... 2000 by JOE KNAPP, who was known to the 'Saddle Creek' stable through a split collaboration, 'OH HOLY FOOLS' (2001) with BRIGHT EYES (aka CONOR OBERST). KNAPP assembled ROBERT LITTLE, JEFF KOSTER and JEFF TAFOLLA and recorded their debut album 'EUPHEMYSTIC' in 2001. With a blend of 10CC's harmonies and BEN FOLDS' rampaging piano hooks, KNAPP and Co barely had time to stop and think about the musical direction of this set, which would be more at home with American college radio, than the troubled indie connoisseur.

Album rating: OH HOLY FOOLS split w/ Bright Eyes (*5) / EUPHEMYSTIC (*4)

JOE KNAPP – vocals, multi (ex-OMAHA'S SON) / with **ROBERT LITTLE** – bass + **JEFF TAFOLLA** – keyboards + **JEFF KOSTER** – drums

	Saddle Creek	Saddle Creek
Jan 01. (cd/lp) <*LBJ 34*> **OH HOLY FOOLS**	-	

– Brown park / (BE track) / Invention of beauty / (BE track) / On the concourse / (BE track) / Katie come true / (BE track). *(UK-iss.Nov02; same as US)*

| Sep 01. (cd) <*LBJ 36*> **EUPHEMYSTIC** | - | |

– An instant death / An instant birth / Seven days / A book laid on its binding / Maria in motion / The anonymous / Like a friend / I promise you'll never grow old / A new dress for Maybell / Violet.

SONGS: OHIA

Formed: Lorain, Ohio, USA ... mid-90's as a one-man outfit by JASON MOLINA. Influenced by PALACE/WILL OLDHAM, TOM WAITS and LOU REED, he consequently began his musical dabblings playing bass in various local heavy rock outfits. Moving on from here, MOLINA began to write solo material based around his tenor-tuned guitar and falsetto singing voice. Building up confidence the singer/songwriter started making DIY home tapes of his output, which he placed under varying names like SONGS: RADIX, SONGS: UNITAS and SONGS: ALBIAN before opting for the SONGS: OHIA tag. His brilliant and unique talent was probably most closely akin to that of WILL OLDHAM's individualistic alternative country styling, although more conceptually than altogether musically. And it seemed fitting that his debut 7", 'NOR CEASE THOU NEVER NOW...' (1996), appeared on OLDHAM's 'Palace' label. MOLINA subsequently made a more stable contract signing with 'Secretly Canadian', who put out his eponymously titled full-length set, 'SONGS: OHIA' (1997). This heralded the enchanting alternative folk direction that MOLINA would take his music into; a real stand-out debut. This was followed the same year by the EP, 'HECLA AND GRIPER' (containing a Conway Twitty cover), a record which saw him team up with percussionist GEOF CUMMINGS for a more jaunty piece. The MOLINA/CUMMINGS partnership continued on into the sophomore LP 'IMPALA' (1998). As well as various singles and EPs, MOLINA and Co continued steadily on with the ensuing year's, 'AXXESS AND ACE', which saw the band at its most ambitious with the former LPs duo being joined by alternative country and folk luminaries in the shape of EDITH FROST, MICHAEL KRASSNER and DAVE PAVKOVIC (of BOXHEAD ENSEMBLE), (REX's) JULIE LIU and JOE FERGUSON (from PINETOP SEVEN). This new-found fulsome sound was only made the more incredible with the knowledge that the famous sessioners only heard most of the compositions on the days they laid down the tracks. The group's next full-length piece, the hard to get hold of album, 'THE GHOST' (1999) – only sold on his tour of that year – went back to his solo hometaping roots and displayed the dark wintry side of MOLINA's soulful playing. The post-millennium released full-length outing 'THE LIONESS' stayed with this despondent mood but witnessed the group again being enlarged, this time with the aid of AIDAN MOFFAT and DAVID GOW (of influential Scottish outfit, ARAB STRAP), (APPENDIX OUT's) ALI ROBERTS, old collaborator CUMMINGS and JONATHAN CARGILL. Also worthy of note was the MOLINA AND ROBERTS released 7", which came from the same period and which saw the two folkies covering the traditional songs 'THE GREEN MOSSY BANKS OF THE LEA' and 'TEN THOUSAND MILES' recorded in the latter's Glasgow flat. S:O's next full-length project, 'GHOST TROPIC' (2000), was probably their most far reaching, with ROBERTS staying on board and being joined by SHANE ASPEGREN (of LULLABY FOR THE WORKING CLASS), with MIKE MOGIS (of the same outfit) coming in to help engineer this eclectic set. The record showcased a wealth of world music influences from UK folk tradition to Westerns film soundtracks and a discernible dollop of Far East stylings. With 'GHOST TROPIC' still on the playlist of many a fan, SONGS: OHIA's next piece, 'DIDN'T IT RAIN' (2002), disappointed no one.

Album rating: SONGS: OHIA (*6) / HECLA & GRIPER mini (*5) / IMPALA (*5) / AXXESS & ACE (*6) / THE LIONESS (*5) / GHOST TROPIC (*7) / DIDN'T IT RAIN (*7)

JASON MOLINA – vocals, guitar, etc

	not iss.	Palace
May 96. (7"ep) **NOR CEASE THOU NEVER NOW ...**	-	

	Secretly Canadian	Secretly Canadian
Sep 96. (7"ep) <*SC 02*> **ONE PRONUNCIATION OF GLORY**	-	

– Waltham simply unite the name / Napoleon: how we have ranged.

| May 97. (cd) <*(SC 03)*> **SONGS: OHIA** | | |

– Cabwaylingo / Crab orchard / Gauley bridge / Blue jay / Tenskwatawa / White sulfur / Our republic / Big Sewell MT. / Cotton hill / Dogwood gap / Little beaver / Blue stone / U.M.W. pension. <*(lp-iss.Aug99; SC 04)*>

—— now backed by **GEOF CUMMINGS** – percussion (of PARTY GIRLS)

| Dec 97. (m-cd) <*SC 08*> **HECLA & GRIPER** | - | |

– Pass / All pass / Defenders / Declarer / Easts last heart / Reply & claim / Advice to aces / Darling ...

| Apr 98. (lp) <*SC 17*> **IMPALA** | - | |

– Ace unable to change / Easts heart divided / This time anything finite at all / Hearts newly arrived / Till morning reputations / One of those uncertain hands / Humble cause again / Rules of abscence / Just what can last. *(cd-iss. Feb00 on 'Happy Go Lucky'; HAPPY 14)*

| Aug 98. (7"ep; split w/ APPENDIX OUT) <*Bebop 3*> **NAY TIS NOT DEATH** | - | |

(above on 'Liquefaction – Bad Jazz', below on 'Acuarela')

| Dec 98. (m-cd) <*(NOIS 6)*> **OUR GOLDEN RATIO** | - | |

– There will be distance / There are no claims on you / It's your win again / When your love has gone.

—— now with **JULIE LIU** – violin (of REX) / **JOE FERGUSON** (of PINETOP SEVEN) / **MICHAEL KRASSNER** (of BOXHEAD ENSEMBLE, of LOFTY PILLARS, of EDITH FROST) / **DAVE PAVKOVIC** (of BOXHEAD ENSEMBLE) / **EDITH FROST** – vocals

| Mar 99. (cd) <*SC 24*> **AXXESS & ACE** | - | |

– Hot black silk / Love & work / Love leaves its abusers / Redhead / Captain Badass / Come back to your man / Champion / How to be perfect men / Goodnight lover.

| Mar 99. (ltd-cd) <*SC 27*> **THE GHOST** | - | - tour |
| 1999. (7"; split w/ REX) <*WEST 005*> **untitled** | | |

(above issued on 'Western Vinyl')

—— next with **ARAB STRAP** (**AIDAN MOFFAT** + **DAVID GOW**) + **APPENDIX OUT** (**ALASDAIR ROBERTS**) plus **GEOF CUMMINGS** + **JONATHAN CARGILL**

| Jan 00. (cd) <*(SC 30)*> **THE LIONESS** | | |

– Black crow / Tigress / Nervous bride / Being in love / The lioness / Coxcomb red / Back on top / Baby take a look / Just a spark.

| Oct 00. (7"; by MOLINA & ROBERTS) <*SC 16*> **MOLINA & ROBERTS** | - | |

– The green mossy banks of the Lea / Ten thousand miles.

—— next featured **MOLINA** + / **SHANE ASPEGREN** – drums (of LULLABY FOR THE WORKING CLASS)

| Nov 00. (cd) <*(SC 40)*> **GHOST TROPIC** | | |

– Lightning risked it all / Body burned away / No limits on the words / Ghost tropic / Ocean's nerves / Not just a ghost's heart / Ghost tropic / Incantation.

| 2001. (7"; split w/ ONEIDA) **untitled** | | |

(above on 'Jagjaguwar')

| Oct 01. (cd) <*(PAC 101)*> **MI SEI APPARSO COME UN FANTASMA (live in Italy 2000)** | | |

– (untitled) / (untitled) / Tigress / Being in love / (untitled) / (untitled) / Cabwaylingo. *(lp-iss.Apr02 on 'Cargo'; CAR 039)*
(above issued on 'Paper Cup')

Oct 01. (7") <*SC 61*> **THE LIONESS. / Scout Niblett: MISS MY LION**		-
Feb 02. (7") <*SC 72*> **THE GREY TOWER. / BLACK LINK TO FIRE LINK**		-
Apr 02. (lp/cd) <*(SC 65/+CD)*> **DIDN'T IT RAIN (live)**		Mar02

– Didn't it rain / Steve Albini's blues / Ring the bell / Cross the road, Molina / Blue factory flame / Two blue lights / Blue Chicago moon.

| Oct 02. (7") <*SC 75*> **KEEP IT STEADY. / UNITED OR LOST ALONE** | | - |

SONIC BOOM (see under ⇒ SPACEMEN 3)

SONORA PINE (see under ⇒ RETSIN)

SON VOLT (see under ⇒ UNCLE TUPELO)

SOUL-JUNK

Formed: San Diego, California, USA ... 1994 by former TRUMANS WATER man GLEN GALLOWAY. Continuing in the mad as a brush tradition of his erstwhile band (with which he still maintains a loose musical relationship), GALLOWAY adopted the nom de plume GLEN GALAXY and with CATHLEEN GALLOWAY proceeded to release a string of religious themed albums under the SOUL-JUNK moniker. Through the latter half of the 90's and into the new millennium, a variety of independent labels underwrote the records, each one titled after a 20th century year and seemingly picked at random. The music was as reliably unconventional as the concept with GALLOWAY cutting up the usual rag-bag of disparate influences and spontaneous inspirations; the Californian's most recent creation was 2001's mini-set, '1942'.

Album rating: 1950 (*5) / 1951 (*4) / 1952 (*6) / 1953 (*5) / 1955 (*6) / 1956 (*6) / 1942 mini (*5)

GLEN GALAXY (b. GALLOWAY) – vocals, instruments (ex/of-TRUMANS WATER) / with others which settled into **RON EASTERBROOKS** – guitar, vocals / **JON GALAXY** – bass / **BRIAN CANTRELL** – drums; (repl. early member CATHLEEN GALLOWAY)

	not iss.	Shrimper
1994. (c) <*SHR 49*> **1950**	-	

– The Lord's saxophone / Proverbs 1.20-33 / Even the archangel Michael / Father God / Shine out of darkness / I turned my back on you / Heavenly bodies will be shaken / Hosea 6.1-3 / You who are thirsty / Ephesians 2.4-10 / A holy fast / Matthew 11.28-30.

	not iss.	Holy Kiss Rex
1994. (7"ep) <*HK 01 – 142629*> **1949**	-	

– Stripes / We are healed / Isaiah 9.2-9 / 1 Peter 2.6-10.

| 1994. (cd) <*HK 02 – 142444*> **1950** | - | |

– The Lord's saxophone / Jesus light the light / I call on you Jesus / 1 John / Phillipians / Junkrock motorcade / Hebrews 10.12-17 / 1 Peter 3.15; 2.3 / So we can worship you / Phillipians 3.8-11 / Yes bless you / Hebrews 11.6 / 2 Corinthians 3.17-

SOUL-JUNK (cont)

18 / Colossians 3.1-4 acts 4.19-20 / Saved punk gospel nonet / Psalm / John 14.1-3 / Luke 21.27-33 / 2 Peter 1.16,19-21 / Rise of soul / Mark / Psalm.

			not iss.	Sub Pop
Jun 95.	(7"ep) <SP 301>	**1946**	-	

– Go away / Tombstone derby / Anointed my mouth / (Blame it on the) Mothership / Salvo!

			not iss.	Karate Brand
Jul 95.	(7"ep) <KBR 008>	**1947**	-	

– She's no peasant / Take you to a jewelers / Numchucks over / Overflows / Stay liquid.

			not iss.	Shrimper
1995.	(cd) <SHR 56>	**1951**	-	

– Spirit of God descend on us / Bread of life / Turn to joy / Forever and ever amen alright / Peace peace peace / Sovereign Lord did say / Away like a wild flower / Soul-Junk theme / Some fell along / Set you free / Jesus not religion / Struck down / No eye has seen / God does speak / Paralytic man / The life appeared / Where your treasure is / Alpha & Omega / Lifeless things / Supreamacy / I worship you.

			Homestead	Homestead
Aug 95.	(7") <(HMS 225-7)>	**1945**		

– Harbinger / Sunken reality / Crank the ruins / Gate beautiful.

Feb 96.	(cd) <(HMS 227-2)>	**1952**	-	

– In your sanctuary / Spoiler! / Pegasus on the slow tip / Like the sunrise / Sweet to my soul / Doom beat / The kingdom's fruit / Ape the rich / In their sea thru raincoats / Eyes of the spirit / Goose-eggs / Oahu strum / Cold-coct the corner / Episode / 7 horned star / Cup & dish / Seeing ear / Another dome ride / Hi-priest / Snatched from the fire / Arm in action / Throne speeda light / Nectsar sublet / Men of Memphis cracked your skull / Sideways drag / Move like kings / Soulology / Slo-jam in the end zone / Junk on lax / Kingdom of Heaven / Zion!

Nov 96.	(cd) <(HMS 236-2)>	**1953**		

– Junca de sol Andromeda / Quite right rockers / Shine out / Atonal eternal! / Young businessmen's psykick makeout / Poker of the eye / Wax presidential / Bloody men / Three thousand thirsty thoughts / The lion has roared / Some pampered gangster / Sturdy jive / Graveyard-style. *(w/ bonus CD+=)* – 1954

			not iss.	Infinite Chug
1997.	(7") <7>	**1944**		-

– Chanting her name / (+2) / Keep yr antennae up.

			Jackson Rubio	Jackson Rubio
Dec 99.	(d-cd) <(JRB 111)>	**1955**		

– Rebel syphon / Universal two-day city / Pack of goons / May my tongue be stuck up on the roof / Velodrome? / Prophecies / Old dominion / Straight from Neptune / Double-o javelin / Blunderbuss / Thrown down / Cherry stereo chariot / Moonbeam? / All men are grass / Glowing funeral / As the rain / Transubstantial peel-out // See his face / More of the illusory doorprize / Gorilla in the mix / April 42nd / Numb live & looser / Quasars? / Subwoof ape job / Yellow tooth yooth / The auriginal manglist / Down with sounds / All lids / Some true blue gum from seething teeth / Turn on the solar / Lazy rattlesnake.

			not iss.	Sarabellum
Jul 00.	(cd) <22404>	**1956**		

– Enter Venus / III-M-I / How we flow / Sarpody 1 / 3po soul / Life to false metal / K.I.N.G.D.O.M.O.G.O.D. / Eyes, externally / Monkey, flower & yarrow / Judah / Pumpfake / Lordy child (say ABBA) / Sea monsters & gargoyles / The peacemaker / Dry bones / Sweet to my soul / Red top.

			Sounds Familyre	Sounds Familyre
Oct 01.	(m-cd) <(SF 006)>	**1942**		

– Live inside the Soul-Junk cathedral / Israel and the limping hip / Soon seated / 3 fascinating shells / Weapons! / Good as dead.

SOUL SIDE (see under ⇒ GIRLS AGAINST BOYS)

SOUNDTRACK OF OUR LIVES

Formed: Gothenberg, Sweden ... 1986 as UNION CARBIDE PRODUCTIONS by EBBOT LUNDBERG, a loud talking modern Viking, er ... so to speak. UCP released a number of cranium-shredding STOOGES-esque albums – 'IN THE AIR TONIGHT' (1987), 'FINANCIALLY DISSATISFIED, PHILOSOPHICALLY TRYING' (1989), 'FROM INFLUENCE TO IGNORANCE' (1991) and 'SWING' (1992) – spread over several years before LUNDBERG started from scratch under the moniker, SOUNDTRACK OF OUR LIVES. Drinkers all, the grisly, growling LUNDBERG and his new recruits issued an album, 'EXTENDED REVELATION FOR THE PSYCHIC WEAKLINGS OF WESTERN CIVILIZATION' on 'Telegram' records in 1996 before they were scooped up by WEA subsidiary, 'Coalition'. A debut single, 'INSTANT REPEATER '99', showed them at their rawkist, psychedelic best, while their 1997 album, 'WELCOME TO THE INFANT FREEBASE', was loved by at least TIM BURGESS of The CHARLATANS. 2002 saw the SOUNDTRACK... issue their most accessible album to date, 'BEHIND THE MUSIC'. A full-on, no bull rock'n'roll album reminiscent of 'Exile On Main Street'-days, and infusing the barmiest prog-rock with gentle acoustic melodies and sweeping ballads, this LP could've only been made by Swedes. 'INFRA RIOT' opened up the album, with pounding drums and resonating guitar hooks. It was followed by a magnificent set of songs, the best of which were '21st CENTURY RIP-OFF', 'NEVERMORE' and the startling 'IN YOUR VEINS'.

Album rating: Union Carbide Productions: IN THE AIR TONIGHT (*7) / FINANCIALLY DISSATISFIED, PHILOSOPHICALLY TRYING (*6) / SWING (*5) / Soundtrack Of Our Lives: EXTENDED REVELATIONS FOR THE PSYCHIC WEAKLINGS OF WESTERN CIVILIZATION (*7) / WELCOME TO THE INFANT FREEBASE (*8) / BEHIND THE MUSIC (*7)

UNION CARBIDE PRODUCTIONS

EBBOT LUNDBERG – vocals, sax / **PATRICK CAGANIS** – guitar / **BJORN OLSSON** – guitar, sax

			Ediesta	Skyclad
Sep 88.	(lp)<cd> (CALCLP 056) <61>	**IN THE AIR TONIGHT**		Nov87

– Ring my bell / Financial declaration / Summer holiday camp / Cartoon animal / So long / In the air tonight / Three mile eyes / Teenage bankman / Pour en flirt avec toi / Down on the beach.

1989.	(cd) <71> **FINANCIALLY DISSATISFIED, PHILOSOPHICALLY TRYING**		-	-

– At dawn / Born in the 60's / San Francisco boogie / 13th trip / Down on the farm / Maximum dogbreath / Here comes God / Another rock'n'roll statement / Glad to have you back / Career opportunities / Swedish meatball revival.

			EfA	Radium
1991.	(cd) (14365) <226.05> **FROM INFLUENCE TO IGNORANCE**			

– Train song / Be myself again / Golden age / Can't hear nothing / Baritone Street / Got my eyes on you / Can't slow down / Sunset trip / Circles / Coda.

			Roadrunner	Fist Puppet
1992.	(7") <010> **HIGH SPEED ENERGY. / DOIN' MY TIME**		-	
Nov 92.	(cd) (RR 9136-2) <014> **SWING**			

– Waiting for turns / High speed energy / Mr. Untitled / Right phrase / Solution / Chameleon ride / Turn off the blues / How do you feel today? / Game boy / Beefhead / TV spiders.

SOUNDTRACK OF OUR LIVES

EBBOT LUNDBERG – vocals / **MARTIN HEDEROS** – keyboards / **IAN PERSON** – guitar / **MATTHIAS BARJED** – guitar / **KALLE GUSTAFSSON** – bass / **FREDRIK SANDSTEN** – drums

			Telegram	not iss.
1996.	(cd-ep) (15304) **THE HOMO HABILIS BLUES**			Sweden

– Galaxy gramophone / Grand Canaria / Instant repeater '99 / Greatest hit providers / Retired teenage angst.

1996.	(cd-s) (017486-2) **BLACKSTAR**	-	- Sweden
1996.	(cd) (3984 22786-2) **EXTENDED REVELATION FOR THE PSYCHIC WEAKLINGS OF WESTERN CIVILIZATION**	-	- Sweden

– Regenesis / Psychomatum X2000 / Let it come alive / Interstellar iferiority complex / Century child / Safety operation / Impacts and egos / Aqua Vera / From gravity to gold / So far / Serpentine age queen / Mega society / Black star / Love song #3105 / Jehovah sunrise / All for sale. *(all UK-iss.May98; same)*

			Coalition	not iss.
Jun 97.	(7"/c-s) (COLA 018/+C) **INSTANT REPEATER '99. / RETIRED TEENAGE ANGST / GRAND CANARIA**			-

(cd-s+=) (COLA 018CD) – ('A'side) / Blow my cool / Mantra slider / Firmament vacation / Endless song. *(re-iss. Jun98; same)*

Oct 97.	(7"/c-s) (COLA 029/+C) **MANTRA SLIDER. / WHEN LIGHTING BUGS ARRIVE**		

(cd-s+=) (COLA 029CD) – Four ages (part I) / Four ages (part II).

Nov 97.	(cd/c) (0630 18871-2/-4) **WELCOME TO THE INFANT FREEBASE**		

– Mantra slider / Firmament vacation (a soundtrack of our lives) / Underground Indian / Chromosome layer / Instant repeater '99 / Embryonic rendezvous / Four ages (pt.2) / Grand Canaria / Endless song / Confrontation camp / Blow my cool / Senior breakdown / Bendover babies / The homo habilis blues / For good / Magic Muslims / Rest in peace / Retro man / Theme from hallo / Legend in his own mind. *(re-iss. May98 on 'Telegram'; 16652-2) (d-lp-iss.Sep99 & Mar02 on 'Stickman'; PBABBLE 021)*

Apr 98.	(7"/c-s/cd-s) (COLA 045/+C/CD) **FIRMAMENT VACATION. / GREATEST HITS PROVIDERS / CLEANING SESSION RAGA**		-

		Hidden Agenda	Hidden Agenda
Jun 00.	(cd-ep) (<AHA 56>) **GIMME FIVE!**	-	Sweden

– Dow Jones syndrome / Nobrainer / It ain't free (livin' in a bubble) / James Last experience / Play station bordello.

		WEA	Universal
Feb 02.	(cd) (8573 86715-2) <156261> **BEHIND THE MUSIC**		

– Infra riot / Sister surround / In someone else's mind / Mind the gap / Broken imaginary time / 21st century rip off / Tonight / Keep the line movin' / Nevermore / Independent luxury / Ten years ahead / Still ageing / In your veins / The flood / Into the next sun. *(d-lp-iss.Mar02 on 'Stickman'; PB 031) (re-iss. Aug02 on 'Hidden Agenda'; AHA 032CD)*

May 02.	(cd-s) (WEA 345CD) **SISTER SURROUND / NEWS OF THE WORLD / SLOW DRIFT AWAY**		
Sep 02.	(cd-s) (WEA 357CD) **21ST CENTURY RIP OFF / WE'LL GET BY / LOST IN HIGHWAY**		-

SPACE

Formed: Liverpool, England ... 1993 by TOMMY SCOTT, JAMIE MURPHY, FRANNY GRIFFITHS and ANDY PARLE, all seasoned campaigners of the local music scene (TOMMY and FRANNY played in The AUSTRALIANS, whose track, 'THE GIRL WHO LOVED HER MAN ENOUGH TO KILL HIM' appeared on the 'Hit The North' various artists compilation). After a one-off single on the independent 'Home', the band were snapped up by 'Gut', a label which brought us the bare-arsed "pop thrills" of RIGHT SAID FRED. Equally camp in a more masculine kind of Scouse way, SPACE were light years removed from the shower of Brit-pop retro merchants doing the rounds in the mid-90's; the 'NEIGHBOURHOOD' single sounded like ENNIO MORRICONE waltzing round the last chance saloon to an acid-fried Mariachi soundtrack, SCOTT's robotic vocal affectations carrying lyrics cut from the same cloth as PETE SHELLEY's (Buzzcocks) creations. For all his little-boy-lost charm, SCOTT sounded pretty damn scary throughout much of the 'SPIDERS' (1996) album, his tales of losers, freaks and paranoid killers balancing black humour with unhinged Liverpudlian menace. Preceded by the voodoo-xylophone pop genius of 'FEMALE OF THE SPECIES' (a Top 20 hit and arguably one of the singles of the year) and the brassy, bouncy

SPACE (cont)

life affirming 'ME & YOU VERSUS THE WORLD' (about as commercial as SPACE get and a nod to native forebears, The Fab Four), the debut was released in late '96 to encouraging reviews and a subsequent Top 5 chart placing. Running the gamut of the band's many influences, from SINATRA and KRAFTWERK to 'South Pacific' and 'Midnight Cowboy', the album even catered for MURPHY's avowed love of techno with an acid freakout, 'GROWLER', bolted on as the closing track. Armed with a further two Top 20 hits in a re-released 'NEIGHBOURHOOD' and 'DARK CLOUDS', SPACE were ready to explore the final frontier where no (sensible) band had gone before i.e. the festival circuit. 1997 proved to be an even more hectic year, one that nearly broke them; JAMIE (at only 21, the stress of it all had played havoc with his peace of mind) pulled out on the eve of an American tour in February, TOMMY mysteriously lost his voice for a couple of months as well as being stalked and the general pressures of slogging round the world turned them into emotional wrecks. No doubt the experiences which formed the basis for follow-up Top 3 album, 'TIN PLANET' (1998), the cadets safely back on earth and ready for a new mission that resulted in two Top 10 hits, 'AVENGING ANGEL' and the tongue-in-cheek duet with CATATONIA's CERYS, 'THE BALLAD OF TOM JONES'. • **Songwriters:** Perm any SCOTT / GRIFFITHS / MURPHY and group except WE GOTTA GET OUT OF THIS PLACE (Animals).

Album rating: SPIDERS (*7) / TIN PLANET (*7) / GREATEST HITS compilation (*7)

TOMMY SCOTT – vocals, guitar / **JAMIE MURPHY** – guitar, vocals / **FRANNY GRIFFITHS** – bass / **ANDY PARLE** – drums

		Home	not iss.
Oct 95.	(c-s) *(CAHOME 1)* **MONEY / KILL ME**		-

(cd-s+=) *(CDHOME 1)* – ('A'club) / ('B'club).
(12") *(12HOME 1)* – ('A'-Lost in space remix) / ('A'-Still lost in space & safe bass mix) / ('A'-Space club mix) / ('A'-instrumental).

		Gut	Uptown – Universal
Mar 96.	(c-s) *(CAGUT 1)* **NEIGHBOURHOOD / REJECTS**	56	-

(cd-s+=) *(CDGUT 1)* – Turn me on to spiders.
(12") *(12GUT 1)* – ('A'-Live it! club) / ('A'-Live it! instrumental club) / ('A'-Pissed up stomp) / ('A'-radio).

| Jun 96. | (c-s) *(CAGUT 2)* **FEMALE OF THE SPECIES / LOONEY TUNE** | 14 | - |

(12"+=/cd-s+=) *(12/CD GUT 2)* – ('A'radio) / Give me something.

| Aug 96. | (c-s) *(CAGUT 4)* **ME & YOU VERSUS THE WORLD / SPIDERS** | 9 | - |

(cd-s+=) *(CDGUT 4)* – Life of a miser / Blow your cover.
(cd-s) *(CXGUT 4)* – ('A'mixes).

| Sep 96. | (cd/c/lp) *(GUT CD/MC/LP 1) <53028>* **SPIDERS** | 5 | Jan97 |

– Neighbourhood / Mister Psycho / Female of the species / Money / Me & you vs the world / Lovechild of the queen / No-one understands / Voodoo roller / Drop dead / Dark clouds / Major pager / Kill me / Charlie M. / Growler.

— added **DAVE PALMER** – bass

| Oct 96. | (c-s) *(CAGUT 5) <1152>* **NEIGHBOURHOOD / ONLY HALF AN ANGEL** | 11 | |

(cd-s+=) *(CDGUT 5)* – Crisis / Shut your mouth.
(cd-s) *(CXGUT 5)* – ('A'side) / Welcome to the neighbourhood / Nighthood / Neighbourhood (pissed up stomp mix).

| Feb 97. | (c-s) *(CAGUT 6)* **DARK CLOUDS / HAD ENOUGH** | 14 | - |

(cd-s+=) *(CDGUT 6)* – Children of the night / Influenza.
(cd-s) *(CXGUT 6)* – ('A'side) / Darker clouds / Storm clouds.

		Gut	Imprint
Dec 97.	(7"blue) *(7GUT 16)* **AVENGING ANGELS. / I AM UNLIKE A LIFEFORM YOU'VE NEVER MET**	6	-

(c-s) *(CAGUT 16)* – ('A'side) / Bastard me, bastard you.
(cd-s+=) *(CDGUT 16)* – Theme from "Baretta Vendetta".
(cd-s) *(CXGUT 16)* – ('A'side) / ('A'mixes:- John 'OO' Fleming Theramin mix / Ultra Vegas mix / The Jumping Soundboy mix / Franny's 'Peaceful Devil' mix / Brainbasher's 'Kick Ass Angel' mix / Jonnie Newman's 'Altered State' mix).

— **LEON CAFFREY** – drums (ex-PROPER) repl. PARLE

| Feb 98. | (7"red; with CERYS of CATATONIA) *(7GUT 18)* **THE BALLAD OF TOM JONES. / NOW SHE'S GONE** | 4 | - |

(c-s+=) *(CAGUT 18)* – Happy endings.
(cd-s++=) *(CDGUT 18)* – Stress transmissions.
(cd-s) *(CXGUT 18)* – ('A'mixes:- Cocktail Lounge mix / Dirty Beatniks mix / Sound 5 mix / Sure Is Pure dub mix / SX Dub Scratching Cuckoo mix / Tom Jones Axe To Your Head mix).

| Mar 98. | (cd/c/lp) *(GUT CD/MC/LP 5) <110683>* **TIN PLANET** | 3 | Jul98 |

– Begin again / Avenging angels / The ballad of Tom Jones / 1 o'clock / Be there / The man / A liddle buddy help from Elvis / The unluckiest man in the world / Piggies / Bad day's / There's no you / Disco dolly / Fran in Japan.

| Jun 98. | (c-s/cd-s) *(CA/CD GUT 19)* **BEGIN AGAIN / YOU ROMANTIC FOOL / NUMB THE DOUBT / INFLUENZA (flu mix)** | 21 | - |

(cd-s) *(CXGUT 19)* – ('A'side) / The ballad of Tom Jones (live) / Female of the species (live) / Avenging angels (live).

| Nov 98. | (c-s) *(CAGUT 22)* **BAD DAYS EP** | 20 | - |

– Bad days / We gotta get out of this place / The unluckiest man in the world.
(cd-s+=) *(CDGUT 22)* – Cold in the city.
(cd-s+=) *(CXGUT 22)* – Yeah right!

— late in 1999, SPACE teamed up with TOM JONES to record 'SUNNY AFTERNOON' on his comeback set, 'Reload'

| Jun 00. | (c-s/cd-s) *(CA/CD GUT 34)* **DIARY OF A WIMP / IF I EVER / RAYMOND** | 49 | - |

(cd-s+=) *(CXGUT 34)* – ('A'side) / Hell of a girl / Why can't we turn out the lights.

| Jul 02. | (cd) *(GUTCD 18)* **GREATEST HITS** (compilation) | | |

– Female of the species / Avenging angels / Neighbourhood / The ballad of Tom Jones (with CERYS MATTHEWS) / Sunny afternoon (with TOM JONES) / Money /

Begin again / We gotta get out of this place / Bad days (remix) / Dark clouds / Me & you vs. the world / Diary of a wimp / Gravity / The shit you talk is beautiful / Spiders.

SPACEHEADS
(see under ⇒ DISLOCATION DANCE; in 80's section)

SPACEHOG

Formed: Leeds, England . . . 1994 by ROYSTON LANGDON and brother ANTHONY, who hooked up with RICHARD STEEL and JOHNNY CRAGG in New York a year earlier. Signed to Elektra off-shoot, 'Hifi', in 1995, they scored a minor US hit single with 'IN THE MEANTIME' early the following year. Enjoyable if not exactly original, SPACEHOG's sound was a Glam retro-rock pastiche fusing the likes of BOWIE and SUEDE with GUNS N' ROSES, a recipe which saw them securing a Top 50 Stateside position for their debut album, 'RESIDENT ALIEN' (1995). Although they failed to make any lasting impression in the UK, the debut did scrape into the Top 40 after it was re-promoted the following year. Nevertheless, the suitably interstellar single, 'SPACE IS THE PLACE', failed to chart despite being re-released within a matter of months. After a quiet '97, the group were scheduled to release an album early '98 (a single 'CARRY ON' would precede it). In the event, 'THE CHINESE ALBUM' (1998) was hardly a departure from their tried and tested formula of tacky glam revisionism although its quasi-concept format made for a more intriguing listen. 'HOGYSSEY' (2001), meanwhile, was rather disappointing after the three year wait while the re-working of 'Also Sprach Zarathustra' (as 'THE HOGYSSEY') was downright cheesy.
• **Songwriters:** LANGDON; 'In The Meantime' phone-tone intro/outro sampled from PENGUIN CAFE ORCHESTRA tune, 'Telephone And Rubber Band'.

Album rating: RESIDENT ALIEN (*6) / THE CHINESE ALBUM (*5) / THE HOGYSSEY (*4)

ROYSTON LANGDON – vocals, bass / **RICHARD STEEL** – lead guitar / **ANTHONY LANGDON** – guitar, vocals / **JONNY CRAGG** – drums

		Elektra	Sire	
Apr 96.	(c-s/cd-s) *(EKR 218 C/CD) <64303>* **IN THE MEANTIME / TO BE A MILLIONAIRE . . . WAS IT LIKELY** (live)		32	Feb96

(cd-s+=) *(EKR 218CDX)* – Zeroes. *(re-iss. Dec96 hit UK No.27; same)*

| May 96. | (cd/c) *<7559 61834-2/-4>* **RESIDENT ALIEN** | | 49 | Oct95 |

– In the meantime / Spacehog / Starside / Candyman / Space is the place / Never coming down (part 1) / Cruel to be kind / Ship wrecked / Only a few / The last dictator / Never coming down (part 2) / Zeroes / To be a millionaire . . . was it likely? *(re-dist.Feb97 hit UK No.40)*

| Jul 96. | (c-s) *(EKR 225C)* **CRUEL TO BE KIND / THE HORROR** | | - | |

(12"+=) *(EKR 225CD)* – Crack city (live) / Starside.

| Oct 96. | (c-s) *(EKR 230C)* **SPACE IS THE PLACE (blank bar mix) / CRUEL TO BE KIND** (live) | | - | |

(cd-s+=) *(EKR 230CD)* – ('A'-lp version) / Candyman (live).

| Feb 97. | (c-s) *(EKR 234C)* **SPACE IS THE PLACE / CRUEL TO BE KIND** (live) | | - | |

(cd-s+=) *(EKR 234CD1)* – Candyman (live) / ('A'-lp version).

		Warners	Warners
Jan 98.	(7") *(W 0428)* **CARRY ON. / ONE OF THESE DAYS**	43	-

(cd-s+=) *(W 0428CD)* – Adam & Steve / Carry on (acoustic).

| Mar 98. | (cd/c) *<9362 46851-2/-4>* **THE CHINESE ALBUM** | | |

– One of these days / Goodbye violet race / Lucy's shoe / Mungo city / Skylark / Sand in your eyes / Captain Freeman / 2nd avenue / Almond kisses / Carry on / Anonymous / Beautiful girl.

| Apr 98. | (7") *(W 0439)* **MUNGO CITY. / ISLE OF MANHATTAN** | | - |

(cd-s+=) *(W 0439CD1)* – Final frontier / Skylark.
(cd-s+=) *(W 0439CD2)* – Cryogenic lover / Sand in your eyes.

		not iss.	Artemis
Apr 01.	(cd) *<751068>* **THE HOGYSSEY**	-	

– Jupiter's moon / This is America / I want to live / Earthquake / A real waste of food / Perpetual drag / Dancing on my own / And it is / The hogyssey / Strangest dream / At least I got laid / The horror. *(hidden track+=)* – I can't hear you.

SPACE NEEDLE

Formed: Long Island, New York, USA . . . 1994 by high school friends JUD EHRBAR and JEFF GATLAND. After a spell living in Rhode Island and playing drums with grunge outfit SCARCE, EHRBAR returned to Long Island, where he and GATLAND began developing the SPACE NEEDLE sound. Now signed to New York's 'Zero Hour' label, they released their debut, 'VOYAGER', in 1995. This collection of lo-fi space-rock compositions at times echoes 1970's prog-rock, and incorporates unconventional and experimental recording techniques. With the addition of guitarist ANDERS PARKER (founder of VARNALINE, a band EHRBAR has also been associated with), SPACE NEEDLE continued his sonic experimentation with 1997's 'THE MORAY EELS EAT THE SPACE NEEDLE'. Ambitious, and generally uneven, the record still contains some interesting moments ('HYAPATIA LEE', and the Mahavishnu-like 'HOT FOR KRISHNA'). EHRBAR subsequently delivered a second RESERVOIR project set, 'PINK MACHINE' (1997), having already issued an eponymous set a year earlier.

Album rating: VOYAGER (*5) / THE MORAY EELS EAT THE SPACE NEEDLE (*4) / Reservoir: RESERVOIR (*5) / PINK MACHINE (*5)

JUD EHRBAR – drums, synthesizer (ex-SCARCE) / **JEFF GATLAND** – guitar / **MAX BUCKHOLTZ** – violin

SPACE NEEDLE (cont)

1995. (cd) <ZER 1080> **VOYAGER** — Zero Hour / Zero Hour
- Eyes to the world / Dreams / Put it on the glass / Beers in Heaven / Patrick Ewing / Starry eyes / Before I lose my style / Scientific mapp / Junky's fingers / Callwood's lament.

— added **ANDERS PARKER** – guitar (of VARNALINE)

Feb 97. (cd/d-lp) <(ZER CD/LP 2080)> **THE MORAY EELS EAT THE SPACE NEEDLE** — Jan97
- Where the fuck's my wallet? / Flowers for Algernon / Never lonely alone / Love left us strangers / Hyapatia Lee / Hot for Krishna / More than goodnight / Bladewash / One kind of lullaby.

RESERVOIR

JUD EHRBAR in side-project

Jun 96. (cd) <ZER 1150> **RESERVOIR** — Zero Hour / Zero Hour
- Moonstar / Tributary / Hoover / (For LPH) Geneva / San Clementte / Gate 21 / Forum / (untitled).

Sep 97. (cd/lp) <(ZER CD/LP 2150)> **PINK MACHINE** — Jul97
- Go back / Let's fall in love again / Taking my shapes away / Weight of the world / 40 / Air Coryell / Pink machine / Right there.

SPACIOUS (see under ⇒ 3Ds)

SPAIN

Formed: Los Angeles, California, USA ... 1993 by JOSH HADEN (son of jazz legend CHARLIE HADEN, brother of PETRA and RACHEL from THAT DOG). A singer-songwriter and bass player rolled into one, JOSH cut his teeth very early (at 14!) with 'S.S.T.' hardcore jazz-rock trio, TREACHEROUS JAYWALKERS; three sets were delivered, 'SUNRISE' (1987), 'GOOD MEDICINE' (1989) and 'LA ISLA BONITA' (1990), before they folded. Bursting back onto the scene in 1995 with the cult and brooding 'THE BLUE MOODS OF...', the quartet (which included PETRA) established themselves as a good studio act that were apparently 90% shy of live audiences. The album, released on the 'Restless' label was predictably compared with early COWBOY JUNKIES and THE VELVET UNDERGROUND's self titled third album, its sparse Saturday night blues feel and moody jazz homage artwork reflected HADEN's vocals brilliantly, while the rest of the band could be heard in the background strumming quietly away as if they were trying not to wake the neighbours. As SPAIN's members lived in different cities in the States, a reformation wasn't apparent until 1999, when (and at the height of Alt Country), the group recorded the spine tingling 'SHE HAUNTS MY DREAMS'. Ten whispering tracks about lost love, high hopes and broken hearts in true country style, proved that SPAIN were the peers for such similar artists as NADINE, WHISKEYTOWN and HAZLEDINE. JOEY WARONKER, who can be heard doing the same sort of stuff on BECK's 'MUTATIONS', supplied the endless stream of rimshots and slow brushed snares while ESBJORN SVENSSON provided the occasional, but sublime, honky-tonk piano over HADEN's twenty-a-day vocals. It would be hard to imagine that in the future, SPAIN could return with an album that provoked such images of beauty and still upheld such works of passion. Expanding from their traditional trio, the group recruited permanent guitarist/keyboard player SHON SULLIVAN for 'I BELIEVE' (2001), an album which also saw the departure of WARONKER in favour of WILL HUGHES. While the changes had noticeably affected the band's sound, replacing the trademark warm minimalism with busy instrumentation (including church organ on the exquisite 'MARY'), SPAIN's dusky atmospherics were still much in evidence.
• **Note:** Not to be confused with two different acts that released 'SAETAS – CANTE DE LA SEMANA SANTA ANDALUZA' album and 'SOMETHING TO FEEL' single in the mid-90's respectively.

Album rating: Treacherous Jaywalkers: SUNRISE mini (*3) / GOOD MEDICINE (*4) / LA ISLA BONITA mini (*4) / Spain: THE BLUE MOODS OF SPAIN (*6) / SHE HAUNTS MY DREAMS (*8) / I BELIEVE (*6)

TREACHEROUS JAYWALKERS

JOSH HADEN – vocals, bass, keyboards / **QUINN HABER** – guitar / **JAMES FENTON** – drums, vocals

Sep 87. (m-lp/m-c) <(SST 126/+C)> **SUNRISE** — S.S.T. / S.S.T.
- Detonate / Can you afford the pleasure? / Sunrise / Helicopters in the sunrise. <(re-iss. May93 lp/c/cd; SST 126/+C/CD)>

Dec 89. (lp/c) <(SST 207/+C)> **GOOD MEDICINE**
- Dishes / Los tumbos / In the world / Vision pit / Pave the way / Long forgotten summer / Have you ever seen the sunrise? / Encomienda 1988 / Papa Greg / Fake / Gaze. <(re-iss. May93; same)>

— below featured **SYLVIA JUNCOSA** – vocals, keyboards (ex-LEAVING TRAINS)

May 90. (m-lp/m-cd) <(SST 217/+CD)> **LA ISLA BONITA** — Mar90
- La Isla Bonita / Ezag / Have you ever seen the sundance? / Sand / L-O-V-E / Sunride.

— hit the proverbial road after above

SPAIN

JOSH HADEN – vocals, bass / with **PETRA HADEN** – violin, vocals (of THAT DOG) / **EVAN HARTZELL** – drums

Sep 95. (cd) <(72910-2)> **THE BLUE MOODS OF SPAIN** — Restless-BMG / Restless
- It's so true / Ten nights / Dreaming of love / Untitled #1 / Her used-to-been / Ray of light / World of blue / I lied / Spiritual.

— **JOSH** now with **MERLO PODLEWSKI** – acoustic guitar / **JOEY WARONKER** – drums / plus **ESBJORN SVENSSON** – keyboards / **BJORN OLSSON** – guitar / **STEVIE KLASSON** – steel guitars / **KEN BOUDAKIAN** – guitar

Jun 99. (cd) (74321 67030-2) <72929-2> **SHE HAUNTS MY DREAMS**
- I'm leaving you / It's all over / Before it all went wrong / Hoped and prayed / Waiting for you to come / Easy lover / Bad woman blues / Nobody has to know / Every time I try / Our love is gonna live forever.

— **JOSH + MERLO** recruited **SHON SULLIVAN** – guitar, keyboards / **WILL HUGHES** – drums

Aug 01. (cd) <(73737-2)> **I BELIEVE** — Restless / Restless
- She haunts my dreams / Born to love her / You were meant for me / Do you see the light / Mary / Make your body move / I believe / Oh that feeling / If we kissed / Long time ago.

SPARE SNARE

Formed: Dundee, Scotland ... 1992 by frontman and part-time solo star (his 'A MATTER OF FACT' was played on US college radio!) JAN D. BURNETT. Along with cohorts PAUL ESPOSITO (on guitar), ALAN CORMACK (on bass) and BARRY GIBSON (on drums), they traded their early JOY DIVISION-esque meets Lo-Fi sound around the country. Forming their own 'Chute' imprint (after JAN D released a one-off under the WHITE LEATHER CLUB pseudonym), SPARE SNARE unleashed their debut single, 'SUPER SLINKY'. After a classic second and third, 'SKATEBOARD PUNK ROCKER' and 'THORNS' in '94, they surfaced the following year with a spruced up cover of Split Enz's 'I GOT YOU'. Peel sessions followed and, after a debut set, 'LIVE AT HOME' (1995) – exactly that! – they subsequently signed to the 'Deceptive' imprint (more famous for having ELASTICA on their roster). However, after only two 45's (the first being a cover of Sir Cliff's 'WIRED FOR SOUND' in the style of WIRE!), they found themselves back on the small indie imprints again. Second set, the US-only 'WESTFIELD LANE', was delivered early in '97 and was recorded on a home 4-track by multi-instrumentalist JAN, its sound a little sparse to say the least. The man in question brought back BARRY and ALAN for his next project/album, 'ANIMALS AND ME' (1998), and this was followed by even more 7" singles and a compilation the following year. Breaking free for their own musical trappings, SPARE SNARE were back in the Spring of 2001, first up being a Billy Connolly cover!, 'EVERYBODY KNOWS THAT' (backed by a rendition of the Destiny's Child number 'SAY MY NAME'!!!. • **Other covers:** STRANGE AND SILENT STAIRCASE (Number One Cup) / STOOR covered REPETITION (Edwyn Collins).

Album rating: LIVE AT HOME mini (*7) / WESTFIELD LANE (*6) / ANIMALS AND ME (*7) / LOVE YOUR EARLY STUFF compilation (*7) / CHARM (*6)

JAN D. BURNETT – vocals, guitar, synthesizer

1993. (7"one-sided; as The WHITE LEATHER CLUB) (SCOTTISH! 001) **SHANDY ON THE ROCKS** — Scottish! / not iss.

1993. (7") (CHUTE 001) <PRS 591> **SUPER SLINKY. / AS A MATTER OF FACT** — Chute / Prospective

— added **PAUL ESPOSITO** – guitar / **ALAN D. CORMACK** – bass, guitar (of MUPPET MULE) / **BARRY JAMES GIBSON** – drums (of MUPPET MULE)

Sep 94. (7") (CHUTE 003) **THORNS. / SKATEBOARD PUNK ROCKER**

Jan 95. (7"flexi) (CHUTE 004) **WHAT IS IT**

Mar 95. (7"clear/green) (che 31) **I GOT YOU. / Majesty Crush: IF JFA WERE STILL TOGETHER** (above issued for 'Che' records)

May 95. (m-cd/10"m-lp) (CHUTE CD/LP 005) <89297> **LIVE AT HOME** — Chute / Twin/Tone — Oct95
<US-title 'SPARE SNARE'>
- Thorns / Shine on now / Wired for sound / Super slinky / As a matter of fact / Skateboard punk rocker / Bugs / My better half [cd-only] / Call the birds / Thorns. (cd re-iss. Apr98 & Aug99; same)

Sep 95. (7") (PUBE 05) **BUGS. / SCRABBLE** — Love Train / not iss.

Nov 95. (7") (ASR 002) **SMILE, IT'S SUGAR. / Sone: FRENCH CAMPUS** — Anti Social / not iss.

Nov 95. (7"etched) (BLUFF 021) **WIRED FOR SOUND** — Deceptive / Prospective

Mar 96. (7") <TRG 89309> **WIRED FOR SOUND. / BUGS**

Apr 96. (7"m) (BLUFF 027) **SMILE, ITS SUGAR / INDIEKIDSUCK. / HANGING AROUND**
(c-s+=) (BLUFF 027C) – (30 minutes blank to send in for stuff).
(cd-s+=) (BLUFF 027/+CD) – Boom boom boom.

May 96. (7") (CHUTE 006) **HAIRCUT. / Lazerboy: AYE AYE CAPTAIN** — Chute / not iss.

Jun 96. (7"blue) (100GM 14) **BOOM BOOM BOOM (ONE). / (other by the SUMMER HITS)** — 100 Guitar Mania / not iss.

Jan 97. (cd) <ore 8> **WESTFIELD LANE** — not iss. / Wabana — Japan
- Action hero / James Dean poster / Let's go home and do some drugs / Before barcodes / Hit man, cha cha cha / Name with a heart / Take it, any-way / Can't you see the shit I'm in / You've got a nerve / Disturbed / Last night.

Jun 97. (7") (<BRRC 10095>) **THE MONEY PIT VOLUME ONE** — Blue Rose / Blue Rose
- Strange and silent staircase / NUMBER ONE CUP: Smile, it's sugar.

SPARE SNARE (cont)

Date	Format/Cat	Title	Label	Label2
1997.	(7"m) (RB 001)	**T.R.E.** / (other 2 by the Dakota Suite & the New Bad Things)	Rebound / Hummy And Joey	not iss. / Dutch
1997.	(7"ep) (SPAZ 03)	**LEADERS IN LIGHTCONTROL EXTENDED PLAYER EP** – Profile check / (other 2 by i.s.a.n. and David Wrench).		
Apr 98.	(7") (LISS 24)	**HARD OF HEARING.** / Coastal Cafe: **LESBIANS IN WAISTCOATS**	Lissys	not iss.

— cred on the sleeve:- **BARRY GIBSON, ALAN CORMACK & JAN BURNETT**

			Chute	not iss.
Aug 98.	(cd) (CHUTECD 010)	**ANIMALS AND ME** – I'll get by / We are the Snare / Stop complaining / If I had a hi-fi / Holding on to the shore / What's going on / The lies count / Batteries gone / My kind of crazy / Here come the storms / Hit me, Satan / They airbrushed my face / Who Lee / All I want to do is touch / We grew up / I feel the sun, and it's mine. (re-iss. Aug99; same)		

— added **ROSS MATHESON** – guitar (of STOOR)

			Third Gear	Third Gear
Mar 99.	(7") (<3G-19>)	**BRUISING YOU.** / **WHAT YOU'VE DONE**		1998

— **JAN, BARRY + ROSS** added **KEVIN DEVINE + GRAEME OGSTEN** (ALAN CORMACK was back in soon)

			Bad Jazz / Chute	not iss. / not iss.
Jan 01.	(7") (Bebop 23)	**LAUNCH.** / **CALLING IN THE . . .**		
Apr 01.	(7") (CHUTE 013)	**EVERYBODY KNOWS THAT.** / **SAY MY NAME**		
May 01.	(cd) (CHUTE 015)	**CHARM** – No soul / Taking on the sides / Surrender / Calling in the favours / Crazy sort of hum / Shakin' and rollin' / Mod girls, mod boys / Rolled over / Heady heart / Shooting off my head / Troubles.		

– compilations, etc. –

Dec 95.	(m-cd) 100 Guitar Mania: (100GM 08)	**DISCO DANCING** – As a matter of fact / Super slinky / Thorns / Skateboard punk rocker / Thorns (one) / Shine on now / Latin float / Skateboard punk rocker (one). (UK-iss.Oct97 & Aug99; same)		
Oct 99.	(cd) Che; (che 83)	**LOVE YOUR EARLY STUFF** – As a matter of fact / Super slinky / Thorns / Skateboard punk rocker / Thorns (one) / Shine on now / Latin float / Skateboard punk rocker (one) / I got you / What is it / Bugs (edit) / Scrabble / Clutch me now / Bruising you / Smile, it's sugar (one) / Wired for sound / Bugs (live) / Smile it's sugar / Indiekidsuck / Hanging around / Boom boom boom / Haircut / Aftertaste / Boom boom boom (one) / Strange and silent staircase.		

MUPPET MULE

ALAN CORMACK, BARRY GIBSON + ROY ANDERSON

			Chute	not iss.
1994.	(ltd-7"ep) (CHUTE 002)	**TESS** / **FLAYLING.** / (2 others by BROCCOLI)		

HAMFISTED

CORMACK + GIBSON (ex-members)

			Umluat	not iss.
Jun 97.	(ltd-7"ep) (UMLUAT 001)	**HAMFISTED EP** – Emma's fifteenth birthday / Bridget Riley / Get offa my bus / Class of '85.		

STOOR

ROSS MATHESON – guitar / **STEPH + SCOTT**

			Chute	not iss.
May 97.	(7") (CHUTE 007)	**REPETITION.** / **BREATHLESS**		

CONDITION BLUE

JAN BURNETT on production

Mar 98.	(7"m) (CHUTE 008)	**SINGLED OUT.** / **PRODIGAL** / **EVERYTHING ON**		

DUBREQ

JAN BURNETT + ANDY ROGERS (with stylophones)

Aug 97.	(7"one-sided) (CHUTE 011)	**DUBREQ 1**		

— added **BARRY GIBSON**

2000.	(7"one-sided) (CHUTE 012)	**DUBREQ 2**	-	- notyet

SPARKLEHORSE

Formed: Richmond, Virginia, USA . . . 1995 by former DANCING HOODS member MARK LINKOUS; this New York-based quartet issued two sets, '12 JEALOUS ROSES' (1985) and 'HALLELUJAH ANYWAY' (1988). An alternative to The REPLACEMENTS, the group enjoyed good reviews for their debut, although the long-awaited follow-up – featuring a cover of Leonard Cohen's 'DIAMONDS IN THE MINE' – fell short expectations. LINKOUS would return home to form The JOHNSON FAMILY, which duly evolved into recordless SALT CHUNK MARY. Early SPARKLEHORSE releases on 'Slow River', including 'CHORDS I'VE KNOWN' and 'HAMMERING THE CRAMPS' introduced this drawling southern singer-songwriter. Subsequently securing a deal with 'Capitol', LINKOUS supported labelmates RADIOHEAD in late '95 prior to the release of a debut single, 'SOMEDAY I WILL TREAT YOU GOOD' early the following year. A second single, a re-issue of 'HAMMERING THE CRAMPS', appeared a few months later, both tracks featuring on the tongue twistingly titled debut album, 'VIVADIXIESUBMARINETRANSMISSIONPLOT' (1996). Determinedly lo-fi, melancholic alt-country characterised by LINKOUS' catatonic vocals and influenced by the likes of TOM WAITS, NEIL YOUNG and The AFGHAN WHIGS, the album was an instant hit with the critics and even had a Top 60 showing in the UK charts. A former heroin addict, LINKOUS' health was almost the end of him when he collapsed with a heart attack and badly damaged his legs (he was also confined to a wheelchair for three months) following SPARKLEHORSE's live UK debut. When he eventually resurfaced in 1998 with the acclaimed 'GOOD MORNING SPIDER', several critics suggested that LINKOUS' near-death experience was perhaps a key factor in the vitality of the music. A record of strange beauty, 'GOOD MORNING..' segued from distorted sample-driven noise to passages of forlorn majesty with LINKOUS singing his blues against a lonely acoustic strum. Along with the likes of WILL OLDHAM and SMOG's BILL CALLAHAN, LINKOUS has become an unlikely figurehead for the lo-fi Americana scene with SPARKLEHORSE pushing the genre's boundaries while others are content to recycle. While no relf respecting SPARKLEHORSE afficionado would take the title TOO literally, 'IT'S A WONDERFUL LIFE' (2001) saw at least some sunshine straining at the wonderfully mouldering edges of LINKOUS' stained velvet curtain of sound. Reportedly recorded without the aid of stimulants, the record found a clearer headed LINKOUS getting chummy with the likes of MERCURY REV's DAVID FRIDMANN, PJ HARVEY, The CARDIGANS' NINA PERSSON and even TOM WAITS (the latter on the track 'DOG DOOR'). • **Covered:** WISH YOU WERE HERE (Pink Floyd) / WEST OF ROME (Vic Chesnutt).

Album rating: Dancing Hoods: 12 JEALOUS ROSES (*6) / HALLELUJAH ANYWAY (*4) / Sparklehorse: VIVADIXIESUBMARINETRANSMISSIONPLOT (*9) / GOOD MORNING SPIDER (*8) / IT'S A WONDERFUL LIFE (*8)

DANCING HOODS

MARK LINKOUS – guitar, vocals / **BOB BORTNICK** – vocals, guitar / **ERIC WILLIAMS** – bass / **DON SHORT** – drums

			Fun After All	Relativity
Jun 86.	(7") (FAA 104)	**BLUE LETTER.** / **ANTENNA'S UP** (12"++) (12FAA 104) – Pleasure.		-
Jul 86.	(lp) (AFTER 1) <88561-8055>	**12 JEALOUS ROSES** – Pleasure / Impossible years / Build a house / Blue letter / Girl problems / Surfing all over the world / Bye bye Jim / Watching you sleep / (Take my) Chances / She may call you up tonight / Wild and the lonely.		Nov85

— **MIKE GARACINO** – bass; repl. ERIC

1988.	(lp) <88561-8224>	**HALLELUJAH ANYWAY** – Torn away / Baby's got rockets / Better look up / Puppet dancing / Welfare shoes / Border patrol / Diamonds in the mine / Falling down / Tell you something / Crooked angel.	-	

— after the split, LINKOUS formed SALT CHUNK MARY

SPARKLEHORSE

MARK LINKOUS – vocals, guitar / **BOB RUPE** or / **ARMSTEAD WELLEFORD** – bass / **DAVID BUSH** or / **JOHNNY HOTT** – drums / **DAVID CHARLES** – electric guitar, producer

			not iss.	Slow River
Apr 95.	(7"ep) <SRR 14>	**CHORDS I'VE KNOWN EP** – Heart of darkness / Almost lost my mind / Midget in a junkyard / Dead opera star / Hatchet song.	-	
1995.	(7") <SRR 73>	**SPIRIT DITCH.** / **WAITING FOR NOTHING**	-	
1995.	(7") <SRR 74>	**HAMMERING THE CRAMPS.** / **TOO LATE** (UK-iss.Oct96; same)	-	

			Capitol	Capitol
Feb 96.	(7") <S7 19167>	**SOMEDAY I WILL TREAT YOU GOOD.** / **RAINMAKER**		-
Feb 96.	(7") (CL 766)	**SOMEDAY I WILL TREAT YOU GOOD.** / **LONDON** (cd-s+=) (CDCL 766) – In the dry.		
Apr 96.	(7") (CL 770)	**HAMMERING THE CRAMPS.** / **SPIRIT DITCH** (cd-s+=) (CDCL 770) – Dead opera star / Midget in a junkyard.		
May 96.	(cd/c/d-lp) (CD/TC+/EST 2280) <72438 32816-2/-4>	**VIVADIXIESUBMARINETRANSMISSIONPLOT** – Homecoming queen / Weird sisters / 850 double pumper Holley / Rainmaker / Spirit ditch / Tears on fresh fruit / Saturday / Cow / Little bastard choo choo / Hammering the cramps / Most beautiful widow in town / Heart of darkness / Ballad of a cold lost marble / Someday I will treat you good / Sad and beautiful world / Gasoline horseys.	58	Nov95

— LINKOUS brought in **SCOTT MINOR, PAUL WATSON + SCOTT FITZSIMMONS**

Aug 96.	(7") (CL 777)	**RAINMAKER.** / **I ALMOST LOST MY MIND** (cd-s) (CDCLS 777) – Intermission. (cd-s) (CDCL 777) – ('A'side) / Homecoming queen (live on KCRW) / Gasoline horseys (live on KCRW).	61	-
Feb 98.	(7") <SRR7-32>	**COME ON IN.** / **BLIND RABBIT CHOIR**	-	

— <above released on 'Slow River'>

— virtually **LINKOUS** with **MINOR, WATSON + SOFIA MITCHALITSIANOS** – cello / **MELISSA MOORE** – violin / **JOHNNY HOTT** – drums, piano / guests **STEPHEN McCARTHY + DAVID LOWERY + VIC CHESNUTT**

Jul 98.	(7") (CL 806)	**PAINBIRDS.** / **MARIA'S LITTLE ELBOWS** (cd-s+=) (CDCL 806) – Wish you were here / Haint / The dirt bike wreck (video).		-

SPARKLEHORSE (cont)

Jul 98. (cd/lp) *(496014-2/-1)* <36671> **GOOD MORNING SPIDER** [30] [ ] Feb99
– Pig / Painbirds / Saint Mary / Good morning spider / Sick of goodbyes / Box of stars (part one) / Sunshine / Chaos of the galaxy – Happy man / Hey, Joe / Come on in / Maria's little elbows / Cruel sun / All night home / Ghost of his smile / Hundreds of sparrows / Box of stars (part two) / Junebug.

Oct 98. (7"clear) *<(CL 808)>* **SICK OF GOODBYES. / GOOD MORNING SPIDER (session version)** [57] [ ]
(cd-s) *<CDCL 808)>* – ('A'side) / I shot a dog / Gasoline horseys.
(cd-s) *<(CDCLS 808)>* – ('A'side) / Happy place / Happy pig (session version).
Parlophone Odeon

Jun 00. (cd-ep) *(489505-2)* <69505> **DISTORTED GHOST EP** [ ] [ ] Feb00
– Happy man (Memphis version) / Waiting for nothing / Happy place / My yoke is heavy / Gasoline horsey's (live) / Happy pig (live).

—— LINKOUS now with SCOTT MINOR + DAVE FRIDMANN, ADRIAN UTLEY, JOHN PARISH, SOPHIE MICHELITSIANOS, BOB RUPE, JANE SCARPANTONI etc, + guests TOM WAITS, PJ HARVEY + NINA PERSSON
Parlophone Capitol

Jun 01. (cd) *(525616-2)* <34709> **IT'S A WONDERFUL LIFE** [49] [ ]
– It's a wonderful life / Gold day / Piano fire / Apple bed / Sea of teeth / King of nails / Eyepennies / Dog door / More yellow birds / Little fat baby / Comfort me / Babies on the sun.

Jul 01. (cd-s) *(CDCL 831)* **GOLD DAY / HELOISE / DEVIL'S NEW / MAXINE** [ ] [-]

– compilations, etc. –

Oct 02. (d-cd) *E.M.I.; (541129-2)* **VIVADIXIESUBMARINE TRANSMISSIONPLOT / GOOD MORNING SPIDER** [ ] [-]

Frankie SPARO

Born: Victoria, Canada. Although something of a mystery, FRANKIE SPARO, like label mates GODSPEED YOU BLACK EMPEROR! and DO MAKE SAY THINK, had been churning out a clattering mix of heavy noise-induced, sometimes angular and jazzy, tracks since his four-track demo tape hit 'Constellation's offices in 1998. SPARO gradually built up a live reputation in the Montreal area (which had subsequently became his new home), and with the help of other musicians in the district he recorded and issued debut album 'MY RED SCAR' (2000). A bruised and plainly simple affair, SPARO's voice transcended the sort of BILL CALLAGHAN (SMOG) kind of deftness, but still managed to sound incredibly flat and deadpan (if not croaky and strained). Mostly recorded in one-take, you can hear the tape hissing in the background, but SPARO's songs startled so much that you almost forgot this minor distraction. Particular highlights were the untangled and sweetly poisoned 'MY BASTARD HEART', the electrified lo-fi of 'HERE COMES THE FUTURE' and the full-on gushing orchestral brilliance that was 'THE LONELIEST MADEMOISELLE'. They toured with A SILVER MT. ZION in late 2000 and managed to stop off at Radio VPRO in Amsterdam, where he recorded four songs (with ZION's accompaniment). It was released the following year as 'ARENA HOSTILE', and SPARO's delicate compositions have never sounded better, especially with the addition of SOFIE's (GSYBE! and MT. ZION) weeping cello and the group's sparse electronics.

Album rating: MY RED SCARE (*6)

FRANKIE SPARO – vocals / + various Constellation musicians
Constellation Constellation

Non 00. (cd/lp) *<cst 013 cd/v>* **MY RED SCARE** [ ] [ ]
– Bastard heart / My stunning debut / Diminish me NYC / A citizen's farewell / Novak again / The loneliest mademoiselle / Send for me / This side of her / If you're fancy free / Here comes the future / The night that we stayed in.

Sep 01. (cd-ep) *<cst 017>* **ARENA HOSTILE** [ ] [ ]
– Diminish me NYC / The night that we stayed in / Here comes the future / I am waiting.

SPARTA (see under ⇒ AT THE DRIVE-IN)

SPECTRUM (see under ⇒ SPACEMEN 3)

SPEEDBALL BABY

Formed: New York City, New York, USA ... early 1994 when Bostonians RON WARD (ex-drummer of BLOOD ORANGES) and MATT VERTA-RAY (ex-MADDER ROSE) met at a friend's wedding. Completing the line-up with the rhythm section of ALI SMITH and DAVE ROY, the band signed to 'Matador' sub-label, 'P.C.P.', releasing their eponymous EP later that year. Mixing up a Molotov Cocktail of JON SPENCER-esque primal blues and raucous punk, the band served it neat on the following year's mini-set, 'GET STRAIGHT FOR THE LAST SUPPER'. The record even included a clutch of mangled covers, including the Ramones' 'BLITZKRIEG BOP' and Van Morrison's 'T.B. SHEETS'. With new drummer MARTIN OWEN, and making a foray into major label land via MCA's 'Fort Apache' subsidiary, SPEEDBALL BABY released their debut album proper, 'CINEMA!' (1996). Issued a year and a half later in Britain (on 'Konkurrent'), its release coincided with that of a mini-set on 'Sympathy For The Record Industry', 'I'M GONNA STOMP MR. HARRY LEE'. The band careered into the new millennium with 'UPTIGHT!' (2000) and 'THE BLACK-OUT' (2002), proffering more adrenalised, avant-blues and uber-cool musical righteousness; extra kudos for the guest appearance of JON SPENCER himself and even a rare cameo from legendary punk-funk agitator JAMES CHANCE. • **Covered:** CRAZY DATE (Crazy Teens) / COGNAC BLUES (Jack Kerouac).

Album rating: CINEMA! (*5) / UPTIGHT! (*6) / THE BLACK-OUT (*7)

RON WARD – vocals (ex-BLOOD ORANGES) / **MATT VERTA-RAY** – guitar (ex-MADDER ROSE) / **ALI SMITH** – bass / **DAVE ROY** – drums
P.C.P. P.C.P.

Jan 95. (7"ep) *<(PCP 018-1)>* **SPEEDBALL BABY EP** [ ] [ ]
– Speedball baby / Fucked up town / Black eyed girl / Percoset.
(cd-ep+=) *(PCP 018-2)* – Corn river.

Aug 95. (10"m-lp/m-cd) *<(PCP 023-1/-2)>* **GET STRAIGHT FOR THE LAST SUPPER** [ ] [ ]
– Phoenix hotel (pt.1) / Five dollar priest / Blitzkreig bop / Ballad of the thin / Pillbilly / Milking stool blues / T.B. sheets / The edge / Phoenix hotel (pt.2).

—— **MARTIN OWENS** – drums, percussion; repl. DAVE
not iss. Fort Apache

1996. (cd-ep) *<FA 0109>* **SPEEDBALL PETITE** [-] [ ]
– Mex blo-out / Crazy date / Toss my salad / Short term loan / Mex blo-out (reprise).
Konkurrent Fort Apache-MCA

Mar 98. (cd) *(K 182CD)* <11425> **CINEMA!** [ ] Sep96
– A stranger's skin / Rubber connection / Black cat moan / Suicide girl / Black eyed girl / Dog on fire / Skull poppin', skin tastin', love wastin' son of a bitch / Shakin' it loose / Cinema! / Toss my salad Mr. Heat / Dancin' with a fever / Drug owl.
Sympathy F Sympathy F

Apr 98. (10"m-lp/m-cd) *<(SFTRI 531/+CD)>* **I'M GONNA STOMP MR. HARRY LEE** [ ] [ ]
– Pin-up cowboy / Hate you baby / Pocket fulla fish (spoken word) / Lakeside story / Blackish man / Don't turn blue (tonight) / Speedball petite.
not iss. High Maintenance

1999. (7") *<HM 002>* **THE AL GREEN SHUFFLE. / NUMB** [-] [ ]

—— **ANDY ACTION** – drums; repl. OWENS
In The Red In The Red

Sep 00. (lp/cd) *<(ITR 072/+CD)>* **UPTIGHT!** [ ] [ ]
– I'm addictive / Dangerous top / The Al Green shuffle / December? / Mekong Sue / Hot boxin' baby / Tappin' my neighbah! / Numb / Pocket fulla fish / The crybabies (Otis) / 8 ft. cigaret / Wobbly organ.

Oct 00. (7"m) *(ITR 074)* **MEKONG SUE. / THE DIDDLER / COGNAC BLUES** [ ] [ ]

—— added **JENNY DECKER** – bass (2nd)

Jun 02. (lp/cd) *<(ITR 086/+CD)>* **THE BLACK-OUT** [ ] [ ]
– Three quarter man / Hanky-Joe digger / Do the blackout / Wanna scratch it? / Pimp hand strong / Bee in flight / Asphalt blues / The diddler / Blackjack / Baretta's my handle / Cash cow / The termite speaks / Nine eleven / The Jack Martin story / Cash cow (reprise).

SPEEDBOAT

Formed: Glasgow, Scotland ... mid-90's by former BMX BANDITS part-timer, FINLAY MACDONALD, along with like-minded SCOTT WALKER (also their producer!), ALASDAIR VANN and FRANCIS MACDONALD (also ex-BMX BANDITS, ex-PASTELS, ex-BOY HAIRDRESSERS – but no relation). Launching Glasgow's new indie-meets-country label 'Shoeshine', SPEEDBOAT's debut single, 'SATELLITE GIRL', offered up few musical surprises but pushed all the right buttons for fans of archetypal West Coast (of Scotland, that is!) melodic retro-Indie pop; well, NORMAN BLAKE (of the TEENAGE FANCLUB) did produce the record. A belated follow-up, 'LUV', was released in the summer of '97, a distinct ELVIS COSTELLO-esque edge creeping in. Sadly, SPEEDBOAT were sunk when FINLAY was given a free tranfer to, who else but TEENAGE FANCLUB; fans got a taste of what might've been with the release of posthumous retrospective, 'SATELLITE GIRL', in 1999.

Album rating: SATELLITE GIRL compilation (*6)

FINLAY MACDONALD – vocals, guitar (ex-BMX BANDITS) / **SCOTT WALKER** – vocals, guitar / **ALASDAIR VANN** – bass, vocals / **FRANCIS MACDONALD** (b.11 Sep'70, Bellshill) – drums, vocals (ex-BMX BANDITS, ex-TEENAGE FANCLUB, ex-PASTELS)
Shoeshine not iss.

May 95. (7") *(SHOE 001)* **SATELLITE GIRL. / SPEEDBOAT** [ ] [-]
(re-iss. Jul96; same)

Jul 97. (7") *(SHOE 007)* **LUV. / A-T-O-M-I-C** [ ] [-]

—— disbanded when FINLAY was talked into joining TEENAGE FANCLUB; late in 2000, FRANCIS also re-joined TFC

– compilations, etc. –

Apr 99. (cd/lp) *(SHOE CD/LP 004)* **SATELLITE GIRL** [ ] [-]
– Speedboat / Luv / The hurtin' kind / Satellite girl / Change of habit / A-T-O-M-I-C / On the run / Tidal wave / Finding a way / Outside the band.

SPEEDER

Formed: Glasgow, Scotland ... 1997 by former TEENAGE FANCLUB, PASTELS and BMX BANDITS drummer FRANK MACDONALD (aka FRANCIS), along with his own teenage fanclub! – SCOTT McCLUSKEY, JAMES CAMERON and JAMIE CAMERON. The sound of young Scotland or even arty New York perhaps, SONIC YOUTH and DINOSAUR JR being pointers in their direction, they were even featured in the Singles pages of

Kerrang! Combining dual country touches with the RADIO SWEETHEARTS and running his own label 'Shoeshine', FRANK and the boys delivered their debut single, 'EVERYTHING I DO IS WRONG', for 'Discordant' early in '98. A year and a bit later and now on 'Creeping Bent', SPEEDER released two quickfire singles, 'HEY, WHAT DO I KNOW' and 'FEELINGS', both also highlights on their much-lauded first album, 'KARMA KIDS' (2000).

Album rating: KARMA KIDS (*6)

FRANK MACDONALD (b.11 Sep'70, Bellshill, Scotland) – drums (of RADIO SWEETHEARTS, ex-PASTELS, ex-BOY HAIRDRESSERS, ex-BMX BANDITS) / **SCOTT McCLUSKEY** – vocals, guitar / **JAMIE CAMERON** – guitar / **COLIN CAMERON** – bass

		Discordant	not iss.
Jan 98.	(7") *(CORDS 011)* **EVERYTHING I DO IS WRONG. / THREE FIFTEEN**		–

		Creeping Bent	not iss.
Nov 99.	(ltd-7") *(bent 053)* **HEY, WHAT DO I KNOW. / D.O.A.**		–
Mar 00.	(cd-ep) *(bent 056cd)* **FEELINGS EP** – Feelings / Amhurst / Keychain.		–
Aug 00.	(cd) *(bent 058cd)* **KARMA KIDS** – Everything I do is wrong / Take the fun out of everything / Karma kids / Feelings / On my own / Hey, what do I know / Talk about it / Underachiever / Drag me down / To remind you / Here / No: time / Speeder skull.		–

SPEEDKING

Formed: Brooklyn, New York, USA ... 1995 out of PONY by JAMES MURPHY and MIRIAM MALTAGLIATI (on a few 'Homestead' record under the aliases, JIMMY JAMES and KITTY DuBOIS, respectively). SPEEDKING can lay claim to being one of New York's loudest, most belligerent indie-rock bands of the mid-'90s. Their relentless, pounding rhythms were accompanied by assaults of vocal sparring. They achieved some success on the live circuit, touring with SIX FINGER SATELLITE, JUNE OF 44 and SHELLAC, and released four 7"s (on different labels), like punk-funk 'MONONUCLEOSIS' and aurally injurious 'SWAY'. MURPHY had now begun experimenting with a wider and more progressive range of sounds and effects, like synths, electronics and moogs. They entered the studio in 1997 to translate this onto the tracks that would form their debut LP. Unfortunately, before the record's completion, SPEEDKING split. Their legacy was eventually recognised – and ensured – with the 2002 release of 'THE FIST AND THE LAURELS' – a two-disc compilation of their unreleased debut and earlier 7"s. The unreleased tracks were reminiscent of JOY DIVISION, with an electro punk-dance cross-over sound. '...THE LAURELS' was a collection that served to highlight SPEEDKING's impact on the '90s New York punk scene, which would lead to the emergence of acts such as The YEAH YEAH YEAHS.

Album rating: THE FIST AND THE LAURELS compilation (*7)

CHET SHERWOOD – vocals, guitar / **MIRIAM MALTAGLIATI** – bass, vocals, keyboards (ex-PONY) / **JAMES MURPHY** – drums, vocals, synths (ex-PONY)

		not iss.	Amish
1995.	(7") *<005>* **MONONUCLEOSIS. / MONOSODIUM GLUTEMATE**	–	

		not iss.	Merry Dodger
1996.	(7") **SWAY. / SPIDER VELOCE**	–	

		not iss.	Troubleman
1996.	(7") **DEVELINA. / FAKER**	–	

		not iss.	Omnibus
1996.	(7") *<OMNI 013>* **3** – SHOVE: JohnLyons8TrackMachine / SPEEDKING: Spyking.	–	

— in 1997, they recorded the 11-track CD, 'YI MA', tracks on comp

— MURPHY later formed The DFA and went into production

– compilations, etc. –

| Jul 02. | (d-cd) *Tiger Style; <(TS 027)>* **THE FIST AND THE LAURELS** – What is a mason / Yi ma / Get the dogs / Put me up against the wall / Maximum teen travel / Orphans / Hearts and flowers / Trans-resistr now / Millionth monkey / My goodbye / Mannikin / Mononucleosis / Monosodium glutemate / Sway / Spider veloce / Develina / Faker / Spyking / Tender interlude / Wabenzi / Kharis / Setting the humans on fire. | | |

Jon SPENCER BLUES EXPLOSION

Formed: New York City, New York, USA ... 1991 by former PUSSY GALORE namesake, JON SPENCER and ex-HONEYMOON KILLERS, JUDAH BAUER and RUSSELL SIMINS. Hardly blues in the conventional sense, SPENCER rather puts the emphasis on EXPLOSION, grinding out a bass-less groove-noise and howling out lip-curled soundbites. It was a formula that had its roots in the primal sludge of PUSSY GALORE and the first instalment in the JSBX saga carried on where that band left off, kind of. Released by 'Caroline' in the States and Virgin subsidiary, 'Hut', in Britain, the eponymous STEVE ALBINI-produced album surfaced in Spring '92, showcasing SPENCER's newly adopted blues drawl and revelling in defiantly dishevelled guitar abuse. Although some critics argued that SPENCER was all mouth and no trousers, so to speak, the man answered in strutting style on the likes of 'BELLBOTTOMS', one of the highlights from 1994's acclaimed 'ORANGE' album; that record, together with its 1993 predecessor, 'EXTRA WIDTH' (both released on 'Matador') really set out the band's manifesto of fractured 70's groove-funk, semi-detached melodies, hand claps, sweat dripping testimonial and sheer distorted noise. Sure, it might've been a style over substance white trash/noise interpretation of delta blues in the loosest sense but SPENCER's tongue was planted firmly in his cheek and following MTV exposure and a tour with The BEASTIE BOYS, JSBX were suddenly big news. A subsequent remix EP roped in such luminaries as BECK and if a move to 'Mute' seemed a little strange, there was no denying the blistering potential of 'NOW I GOT WORRY' (1996). From the delirious swagger of '2KINDSA LOVE' (surely a companion piece, if there ever was one, to MUDHONEY's 'Touch Me I'm Sick') to the disembodied static of Dub Narcotic's 'FUCK SHIT UP', SPENCER sounded as if he'd finally cut that deal down at the crossroads. Still, the man's recorded work only tells half the story; if you really want a baptism by BLUES EXPLOSION fire then you'll have to catch them live. 1998's STEVE ALBINI-produced set, 'ACME', was another adrenalin-fuelled taste of rock'n'roll blues although experimental sidesteps were always on show. Of late, an 'ACME +' remix LP has surfaced while his collaboration with the DUB NARCOTIC SOUND SYSTEM, 'SIDEWAYS SOUL', has also been issued. SPENCER and his crew of blues-blasting hooligans issued the frantic 'PLASTIC FANG' in April of 2002, and, although it covered no new ground whatsoever (and gave guest spots to DR. JOHN and BERNIE WORRELL), it was still a joy to hear SPENCER violently croon away – all in the name of rock'n'roll, baby! • **Songwriters:** SPENCER/ group except; LOVIN' UP A STORM (Willie Dixon).

Album rating: A REVERSE WILLIE HORTON (aka JON SPENCER BLUES EXPLOSION) (*5) / CRYPT-STYLE collection (*5) / EXTRA WIDTH (*6) / ORANGE (*7) / MO' WIDTH collection (*5) / NOW I GOT WORRY (*7) / ACME (*7) / ACME PLUS out-takes (*5) / PLASTIC FANG (*5)

JON SPENCER – vocals, guitar / **JUDAH BAUER** – guitar / **RUSSELL SIMINS** – drums

		not iss.	In The Red
Oct 91.	(7") *<ITR 007>* **SHIRT JAC. / LATCH-ON**	–	
Jan 92.	(7") *<ITR 011>* **SON OF SAM. / BENT**	–	

		not iss.	Public Popcam
Feb 92.	(lp) *<PORK 1>* **A REVERSE WILLIE HORTON** – Write a song / IEV / Exploder / Rachel / Chicken walk / White tail / '78 style / Changed / What to do / Eye to eye / Eliza Jane / History of sex / Come back / Support-a-man / Maynard Ave / Feeling of love / Vacuum of loneliness / Intro A / Biological / Water man. *(cd-iss. Apr92 as 'BLUES EXPLOSION' on 'Caroline'; CAROLCD 1719> (UK-iss.Dec93 on 'Hut' cd/lp; HUT CD/LP 3) (cd re-iss. Jun97 & Sep98 on 'Caroline'; same as US)*	–	

		not iss.	Clawfist
Jun 92.	(7"m) *clawfist 13>* **HISTORY OF SEX. / WRITE A SONG / SMOKE CIGARETTES**	–	– mail-o

		not iss.	Sub Pop
Nov 92.	(7"green) *(SP 180)* **BIG YULE LOG BOOGIE. / MY CHRISTMAS WISH**	–	

		not iss.	In The Red
Mar 93.	(7") *<ITR 019>* **TRAIN NO.3. / TRAIN NO.1**		–

		Matador	Matador
Aug 93.	(cd/c/lp; as BLUES EXPLOSION) *<(OLE 052-2/-4/-1)>* **EXTRA WIDTH** – Afro / History of lies / Black slider / Soul letter / Soul typecast / Pant leg / Hey mom / Big road / Train No.2 / Inside the world of the blues explosion / The world of sex. *(re-iss. Mar00 on 'Mute' lp/cd; JSBX 1/+CD)*		Nov93
Feb 94.	(7",7"white; as BLUES EXPLOSION) *<(OLE 077-7)>* **AFRO. / RELAX-HER**		Jul93
Oct 94.	(cd/c/lp) *<(OLE 105-2/-4/-1)>* **ORANGE** – Bellbottoms / Ditch / Dang / Very rare / Sweat / Cowboy / Orange / Brenda / Dissect / Blues x men / Full grown / Flavor / Greyhound. *(re-iss. Mar00 on 'Mute' lp/cd; JSBX 2/+CD)*		
Feb 95.	(7"white) *(OLE 111-7)* **BELLBOTTOMS. / MISS ELAINE** (12") *(OLE 111-1)* – ('A'remix) / Flavor 1 / Flavor 2. (cd-s+=) *(OLE 111-2)* – Soul typecast / Greyhound (part 1 & 2). *(the REMIXES ep of above iss.May95)*		–

		Mute	Matador – Capitol
Sep 96.	(cd/c/lp) *(cd/c+/stumm 132) <OLE 193 – 53553>* **NOW I GOT WORRY** – Skunk / Identify / Wail / Fuck shit up / 2Kindsa love / Love all of me / Chicken dog / Rocketship / Dynamite lover / Hot shot / Can't stop / Firefly child / Eyeballin / R.L. got soul / Get over here / Sticky. *(re-iss. May97; same)*	50	
Oct 96.	(7") *(MUTE 202)* **2 KINDSA LOVE. / LET'S SMERF** (cd-s) *(CDMUTE 202)* – ('A'side) / Fish sauce / Cool Vee.		
Nov 96.	(7") *<ITR 42>* **GET WITH IT. / DOWN LOW** *(above on 'In The Red')*		
Apr 97.	(7"m) *(MUTE 204)* **WAIL. / JUDAH LOVE THEME / RADIO SPOT** (7"m) *(LMUTE 204)* – ('A'-Mario C remix) / Afro (live) / Flavor (live). (cd-s) *(CDMUTE 204)* – ('A'video mix) / Yellow eyes / Buscemi / Turn up Greene.	66	
Oct 98.	(cd/lp) *(CD+/STUMM 154) <OLE 322 – 95566>* **ACME** – Calvin / Magical colours / Do you wanna get heavy? / High gear / Talk about the blues / I wanna make it all right / Lovin' machine / Bernie / Blue green Olga / Give me a chance / Desperate / Torture / Attack. *(cd re-iss. Jul00 on 'Toy's Factory'; TFCK 87163)*	72	
Nov 98.	(7"yellow) *(MUTE 222)* **MAGICAL COLOURS. / CONFUSED** (cd-s) *(CDMUTE 222)* – ('A'side) / Bacon / Get down lover.		–
Mar 99.	(7"orange) *(MUTE 226)* **TALK ABOUT THE BLUES. / WAIT A MINUTE (Moby mix)** (12") *(12MUTE 226)* – ('A'side) / Lovin' machine (Automator mix) / Calvin (zebra ranch) / ('A'-Saints and sinners remix). (cd-s+=) *(CDMUTE 226)* – ('A'-video).		–
Jun 99.	(7") *(SMALL 004)* **NEW YEAR (DESTROYER). / other track by Barry Adamson** *(above issued on 'Slut Smalls')*		–

Jon SPENCER BLUES EXPLOSION (cont)

Aug 99. (7") *(MUTE 239)* **HEAVY. / GIVE YA SOME HELL**
(12") *(12MUTE 239)* – ('A'side) / 2 kinsda love (Duck rock remix) / Attack (Detroit) / Do you wanna get heavy? (Duck rock hip'n'bass remix).
(cd-s) *(CDMUTE 239)* – ('A'side) / 2 kinsda love / Blues power / Attack (Detroit).
Sep 99. (cd/d-lp) *(CD+/STUMM 184)* <OLE 376> **ACME PLUS** (out-takes)
– Wait a minute / Get down lover / Confused / Magical colors (31 flavors) / Not yet / Get old / Bacon / Blue green / Olga (remix) / Heavy (remix) / Lap dance / Right place, wrong time / Leave me alone so I can rock again / Soul trance / Electricity / New year / Chowder / TATB (for the saints and sinners mix) / Hell / I wanna make it alright (Zebra ranch).
Mar 02. (7") *(MUTE 263)* **SHE SAID. / GHETTO MOM** [58] [-]
(cd-s) *(CDMUTE 263)* – ('A'side) / Point of view / Do you wanna get it.
(cd-s) *(LCDMUTE 263)* – ('A'side) / Then again I will / Like a bat.
Apr 02. (cd/d-lp) *(CD+/STUMM 199)* <OLE 542> **PLASTIC FANG**
– Sweet'n'sour / She said / Money rock'n'roll / Killer wolf / The midnight creep / Hold on / Down in the beast / Shakin' rock'n'roll tonight / Over and over / Mother nature / Mean heart / Point of view.
Apr 02. (7") *(ITRJBS 05)* **GHETTO MOM. / DO YOU WANNA GET IT**
(above issued on 'In The Red')
Jun 02. (7") *(MUTE 271)* **SWEET'N'SOUR. / SHAKIN' ROCK'N'ROLL TONIGHT (live at the VPRO)** [66] [-]
(cd-s) *(CDMUTE 271)* – ('A'side) / Maureen / Alex.
(cd-s) *(LCDMUTE 271)* – ('A'version) / ('A'-CD-video).

– compilations, others, etc. –

Mar 94. (cd/lp) *Crypt; (EFA 11502-2/-1)* <29> **CRYPT-STYLE** (rec.1991 NYC) [ ] [Apr92]
– Lovin' up a storm / Support a man / White tail / Maynard Ave. / '78 style / Chicken walk / Mo' chicken – Let's get funky / Watermain / Like a hawk / Big headed baby / Write a song / Eye to eye / Feeling of love / Kill a man / Rachel / History of sex / Comeback / The vacuum of loneliness.
Feb 97. (lp/cd) *Au Go Go;* <(ANDA 166/+CD)> **MO' WIDTH** [ ] [Jan95]
– Afro / Out of luck / Cherry lime / Rob K / Ole man trouble / Wet cat blues / Johnson / There stands the glass / Lion cut / Beat of the traps / Memphis soul typecast.
Oct 97. (7") *Au Go Go;* <(ANDA 231)> **ROCKETSHIP. / CHOCOLATE JOE** [-] [Austra]
(cd-s) <(ANDA 231CD)> – ('A'side) / Down low / Dynamite lover / Flavor / Full grown.
1999. (7") *Au Go Go;* <ANDA 251> **CALVIN. / CALVIN (Calvin Hill's T-Ray mix)** [-] [ ]
Mar 00. (lp/cd) *Mute; (JSBX 3/+CD)* **EXPERIMENTAL REMIXES** [ ] [-]

SPENT

Formed: Jersey City, New Jersey, USA ... early 90's by JOHN KING, ANNIE HAYDEN, JOE WESTON and ED RADICH. Unfortunately this band was another in a long line of indie rock acts who lasted only long enough to show their potential and then split. The band's origins on vinyl, the EPs 'KEEPING SECRETS' and 'SINKING IN', gained them the ear of the East Coast rock stations which stood them in a positive standing for the issue of their debut LP 'SONGS OF DRINKING AND REBELLION' (1995). Although not quite reaching the musical heights of their former singles and mini-efforts, this set nevertheless showcased the group's undoubted talent and its upfront triple guitar-led sound. Following this up with EP, 'UMBRELLA WARS', and the sophomore album 'SEAT BENEATH THE CHAIRS' a year later, it seemed the outfit definitely had staying power, while great tours with similar bands SEAM and SUPERCHUNK followed. With their songwriting prowess and muscianship, the band were an attractive option for the indie label compilation album circuit as well; appearing on the mixed bags of imprints like 'Now Sound', 'Ba-Da-Bing' and 'Motorcoat'. Summer 1997, unfortunately for fans of SPENT's work, spelled the end. KING went on that year to work with JIM WILBUR in the project HUMIDIFIER, issuing the album 'NOTHING CHANGES' (1997). HAYDEN also kept her musical leanings going working as a piano technician in New York and releasing a solo album 'THE RUB' (2001), in which she wrote the vast majority of the indie singer/songwriter material, although with added penmanship and backing from all three members of her former band. • **Covered:** A LIFE OF ILLUSION (Joe Walsh).

Album rating: SONGS OF DRINKING & REBELLION (*5) / A SEAT BENEATH THE CHAIRS (*5) / Annie Hayden: THE RUB (*5)

JOHN KING – vocals, guitar / **ANNIE HAYDEN** – guitar, keyboards, vocals / **JOE WESTON** – bass / **ED RADICH** – drums

		not iss.	Ringer Lactate
1994.	(7"ep) **KEEPING SECRETS**	-	
1994.	(7") <SPIN 29> **SINKING IN. / WEST**	not iss.	SpinArt
		not iss.	Merge
Mar 95.	(cd/c/lp) <MRG 78> **SONGS OF DRINKING & REBELLION**	-	

– Brewster station / Excuse me while I drink myself to death / West / Minty ballad / Sense of decay / Bottled mouth / Open wide / Landscaper / Santa Claus to the rescue / View from a staircase / Halfshirt / Ready ok / Brighter than day.
1996. (5") <#1> **DRESS DOWN DAY. / (other by LAMBCHOP)** [-] [ ]
(above issued on 'I-sore')
1996. (7") **REVENGING. / FOREIGN LIKE A CAR** [-] [ ]
Sep 96. (7"ep) <MRG 116> **UMBRELLA WARS EP** [ ] [ ]
– Umbrella wars / Angeleva / A life of illusion / Unwrapped, ungiven.
Oct 96. (cd/lp) <MRG 114> **A SEAT BENEATH THE CHAIRS** [-] [ ]
– Good luck line / Umbrella wars / The pilot's lament / Reupholstered / The quarter conspiracy / Until we have enough / No sign of the ponies / Under false eyelids / The blinds of her trailer / Stumble of the stairs / He's into lonely / A seat beneath the chairs.

— disbanded in July 1997

ANNIE HAYDEN

with also **JOHN KING + ED RADICH**

		Merge	Merge
Feb 01.	(cd) <(MRG 193CD)> **THE RUB**		Nov00

– Start a little late / Slip is showing / The land of nod / Alone / Wood and glue / Albatross / Red lines / Guitar lesson / Sign of your love / Pistol and glasses / Lovely to see.

SP!N (see under ⇒ GENE)

SPINANES

Formed: Portland, Oregon, USA ... 1991 by singer/songwriter REBECCA GATES and drummer SCOTT PLOUF, brought together through a mutual friend of a friend. Proving that bass players aren't essential in today's anything goes world of Lo-Fi rock'n'roll, The SPINANES drew encouraging support for their beguiling minimalism/miserabalism. After two obscure 45's on a local imprint, the duo became an unlikely signing for 'Sub Pop', releasing their debut long-player, 'MANOS', in the Autumn of '93. Critics commented on the emotional rawness of GATES' lyrics, while fans voted with their cash by placing it atop the college radio charts. Not persuaded to pack in the day jobs just yet, the fiercely independent pair (they don't even have a roadie!) knuckled down to gigs with labelmates, CODEINE. A follow-up set, the careworn 'STRAND', surfaced early in '96, another collection of harrowing tales of woe set to a picturesque musical backdrop. A subsequent split in the partnership occurred when SCOTT left for BUILT TO SPILL, leaving REBECCA to soldier on towards a third set, 'ARCHES AND AISLES', in 1998. With the latter being a solo set in all but name, GATES did the obvious thing and ditched the SPINANES moniker for her solo debut proper, 'RUBY SERIES' (2001). Partly co-written with TORTOISE's JOHN McENTIRE, the record was her most musically expansive and progressive to date, employing a raft of unlikely instrumentation such as glockenspiel, Wurlitzer organ and mellotron (played by another co-writer, NOEL KUPERSMITH).

Album rating: MANOS (*6) / STRAND (*7) / ARCHES AND AISLES (*6) / Rebecca Gates: RUBY SERIES (*5)

REBECCA GATES – vocals, guitar / **SCOTT PLOUF** – drums

		not iss.	Imp
Apr 92.	(7") **SUFFICE. / HALLOWEEN CANDY**	-	
Nov 92.	(7") **RUMMY. / HAWAIIAN BABY**	-	
		Sub Pop	Sub Pop
Sep 93.	(7") <(SP 113-291)> **SPITFIRE. / BAD KARMA**		
Nov 93.	(lp/c/cd) <(SP/+MC/CD 114-292)> **MANOS**		Oct93

– Entire / Noel, Jonah and me / Spitfire / I love that party with the monkey kitty / Uneasy / Epiphany / Manos / Dangle / Basement galaxy / Grand prize / Sunday / Shellburn.
May 94. (cd-s) <(SPCD 132-328)> **NOEL, JONAH AND ME / SUNDAY (remix) / FAME AND FORTUNE / BAD KARMA**
Jan 96. (7") <(SP 317)> **MADDING. / 10 METRE PLATFORM**
Feb 96. (lp/cd) <(SP/+CD 345)> **STRAND**
– Madding / Azure / Lines and lines / Meridian / Punchline loser / Valency / Luminous / Oceanwide / Winter on ice / Watch down / For no one else.

— now just REBECCA after PLOUF joined BUILT TO SPILL

Aug 98. (lp/cd) <(SP/+CD 417)> **ARCHES AND AISLES** [ ] [Apr98]
– Kid in candy / Greetings from the sugar lick / 72-74 / Leisure run / Love, the lazee / Sucker's trial / Slide your ass / Reach v. speed / Den trawler / Eleganza / Heisman stance.

— the SPINANES split after above

– compilations, etc. –

Apr 00. (cd-ep) *Merge;* <MRG 160> **THE IMP YEARS** [-] [-]
– Suffice / Halloween candy / Rummy / Hawaiian baby / Messy shitty / Handful of hearts.

REBECCA GATES

with **JOHN McENTIRE + SAM PREKOP + NOEL KUPERSMITH + BRIAN DECK + MIKE JORGENSEN**, etc.

		Badman	Badman
Jul 01.	(cd) <(BRCD 989)> **RUBY SERIES**		Jun01

– The seldom scene / Lure and cast / Move / In a star orbit / Doos / The colonel's circle / I received a levitation.

SPIREA X

Formed: Gourock, Scotland ... 1988 by ex-PRIMAL SCREAM member JIM BEATTIE (writer of their classic 'Velocity Girl'), who took the moniker from an old 'SCREAM b-side. Featuring a core line-up comprised of girlfriend JUDITH BOYLE and ANDY KERR, they worked on songs for well over a year before supplying a demo to a plethora of labels, eventually becoming an unlikely signing for '4 a.d.'. In spring '91, they finally unleashed their debut disc, 'CHLORINE DREAM', inspired by the life rather than death of BRIAN JONES. In fact, the single also took its musical cue from The ROLLING STONES, BEATTIE typically arrogant in his praise for the track, although for once the critics agreed. Unfortunately the public weren't so enthusiastic, neither follow-up single, 'SPEED REACTION', nor debut album, 'FIREBLADE SKIES' (named after a volume of Arthur Rimbaud's poetry), making much of an impression outside closeknit Glasgow scene. Nevertheless, the record was a pleasant enough listen, taking in the obligatory BYRDS/LOVE influences (they covered the latter's 'SIGNED D.C.') alongside SLY STONE's style funk and soul. Subsequently reduced to a duo of BEATTIE and BOYLE, SPIREA X were dropped by the label and later split in '93. Three years later, BEATTIE and the aforementioned BOYLE launched ADVENTURES IN STEREO, a project which would heavily reflect on the influence of 60's Americana (no surprise there!). Signing to up-and-coming label 'Creeping Bent', the determined duo released the 'AIRLINE' EP, which featured 'RUNWAY' and 'GOOD TIMES' as B-sides. They subsequently issued their self-titled debut album in 1997 to much critical acclaim, drawing comparisons from BRIAN WILSON to LOU REED. That said, the album definitely displayed a reoccurring '60's theme, although songs such as 'THE ATTIC WALK' and 'WE'LL MEET AGAIN' could safely be filed in a class of their own. 'ALTERNATIVE STEREO SOUNDS' (1999) was their follow-up, mainly concentrating on the same musical inventiveness, it dabbled in new-electronica et al, and came off better for it. 'EVERYTHING' and 'HANG ON' were stand-out tracks, proving the ADVENTURES had more to offer than Lo-fi musings from the BEACH BOYS era. However, 'MONOMANIA' (2000) was to be the group's finest achievement, seeing them swiftly moving into the left-field of psychedelia. Like a dimly remembered summer at the seaside, this album graced us with some summery pop/rock, not heard since the advent of love in 1967. • Covered: NOBODY'S SCARED (Subway Sect).

Album rating: FIREBLADE SKIES (*6) / Adventures In Stereo: Adventures In Stereo (*5) / ALTERNATIVE STEREO SOUNDS (*6) / MONOMANIA (*6)

JIM BEATTIE – vocals, guitar (ex-PRIMAL SCREAM) / **JUDITH BOYLE** – vocals, guitar / **ANDY KERR** – drums / with also **THOMAS McGURK** – rhythm guitar / **JAMIE O'DONNELL** – bass

	4 a.d.	4ad-Warners
Apr 91. (7") *(AD 1004)* **CHLORINE DREAM. / SPIREA RISING**		-
(12"+=/cd-s+=) *(BAD 1004/+CD)* – Risk.		
Jun 91. (7") *(AD 1006)* **SPEED REACTION. / JET PILOT**		-
(12"+=/cd-s+=) *(BAD 1006/+CD)* – What kind of love / Re action.		
Oct 91. (lp/cd)(c) *(CAD 1017/+CD)(CADC 1017)* <45001> **FIREBLADE SKIES**		
– Smile / Nothing happened yesterday / Rollercoaster / Chlorine dream / Fire and light / Spirea 9 / Speed reaction / Confusion in my soul / Signed D.C. / Sisters and brothers / Sunset dawn.		

— split in 1993 after being dropped by their label

ADVENTURES IN STEREO

JIM BEATTIE – vocals, guitar / with **JUDITH BOYLE** – vocals / **SIMON DINE**

	Creeping Bent	not iss.
Feb 96. (blue-7"ep) *(bent 010)* **E.P. 2**		-
– Airline / There was a time / Runaway / Good times.		
Jul 96. (yellow-7"ep) *(bent 013)* **E.P. 3**		-
– When we go back / Close to you / When times were young / Remain again.		
Mar 97. (cd/lp) *(bent 015/+lp)* **ADVENTURES IN STEREO**		-
– Underground sound / Cry your love away / The attic walk / Summer high / 13th floor / Airline / There was a time / Runaway / Good times / Don't you worry little one / When we go back / Flipside / When times were young / Close to you / Remain again / My buddy go / Pretty things / We'll meet again.		
Jun 97. (7") *(bent 019)* **WAVES ON. /** (track by the Leopards)		-
(cd-ep+=) *(bent 019cd)* – (tracks by the Revolutionary Corps & Spacehopper).		
Aug 97. (cd-s; promo) *(bent 022)* **WAVES ON**		-
Nov 97. (7"ep/cd-ep) *(bent 026/+cd)* **A BRAND NEW DAY**		-
– A brand new day / Nobody's scared / Pass me by / God save us. *(re-iss. Dec97 on 'Bobsled'; BOB 1)*		

— SIMON DINE formed NOONDAY UNDERGROUND

Mar 98. (7"ep/cd-ep) *(bent 028/+cd)* **DOWN IN THE TRAFFIC EP**		-
– Down in the traffic / Down in the city / Down to the sky.		
May 98. (cd) *(bent 030)* **ALTERNATIVE STEREO SOUNDS**		-
– Silence falls / Down in the traffic / Dominique K / I once knew / When you're young / Everything / Out of sight / Brand new day / Here together / Said you said / Hang out / This time / Dream surf baby / O sister / I see / Catch my soul / Long you live / Silence is. *(lp-iss.Jul98 on 'Bobsled'; BOB 2)*		

	Bobsled	not iss.
Jul 00. (7") *(BOB 10)* **INTERNATIONAL. / BABY SO RICH**		-
(cd-s+=) *(BOB 13)* – Grooves.		
Aug 00. (cd/lp) *(BOB 11/+LP)* **MONOMANIA**		-
– We will stand / International / Dust to ashes / Silence / Running / Birds / Behind the trees / Suntrips / Airkiss / Touch the rain / Ghosts / This day / When love comes in.		

— in 2000, ADVENTURES IN STEREO shared an EP, 'TRESPASSERS IN THE STEREO FIELD' with AMERICAN ANALOG SET on 'After Hours' fanzine

MOST

— were **JUDITH** and a second AIS female (they had also sidelined/guested with FUTURE PILOT AKA and MOUNT VERNON ARTS LAB

	Cooler	not iss.
May 98. (7") *(COOLER 001)* **I STOLE YOUR MAN. /**		-

SPIRES OF OXFORD
(see under ⇒ AZUSA PLANE)

SPIRITUALIZED

Formed: Rugby, England ... 1990, initially as a side project for JASON 'SPACEMAN' PIERCE, who was soon to split from SONIC BOOM and SPACEMEN 3. He retained JON MATTOCK and WILLIE B. CARRUTHERS from the latter outfit and set about getting to grips with a new 90's psychedelia. Their first release was a version of The Troggs' 'ANYWAY THAT YOU WANT ME', which squeezed into the UK Top 75. The debut album, 'LAZER GUIDED MELODIES', was awash with VELVET-tones, recycled, and heavily distorted. A three year hiatus did not deter the British buying public, who also assured the follow-up, 'PURE PHASE', of a Top 30 placing in 1995. It was blessed with a more soulful vibe, while the majestic, lo-fi rhythm lifted it from an ambient crypt. In June '97, they returned to the fold (albeit a month after schedule) with their third album, 'LADIES AND GENTLEMEN WE ARE FLOATING IN SPACE B P'. The delay was due to ELVIS PRESLEY's team of whatnots objecting to the sample of 'Can't Help Falling In Love'. Nevertheless, the album, complete with bizarre prescription pill cd packaging, duly floated into the UK Top 5. Described by one reviewer as 'album of the decade', the record met with almost universal praise while its blissful melange of retro-psych, ambient noise and gospel was a heady tonic for the Dad-rock by numbers peddled by most 'indie' bands. • **Songwriters:** PIERCE, except more covers; BORN NEVER ASKED (Laurie Anderson) / WALKING WITH JESUS (Spacemen 3) / OH HAPPY DAY (Edwin Hawkins Singers). • **Trivia:** In the early 90's, they headlined at the ICA Rock Week sponsored by Irn Bru.

Album rating: LAZER GUIDED MELODIES (*8) / PURE PHASE (*8) / LADIES AND GENTLEMEN WE ARE FLOATING IN SPACE B P (*10) / ROYAL ALBERT HALL OCTOBER 10 1997 (*8) / LET IT COME DOWN (*8)

JASON PIERCE – guitar / **WILLIE B. CARRUTHERS** – bass / **JON MATTOCK** – drums plus girlfriend **KATE RADLEY** – organ, keyboards, vocals / **MARK REFOY** – guitar, dulcimer

	Dedicated	R.C.A.
Jun 90. (7") *(ZB 43783)* **ANYWAY THAT YOU WANT ME. / STEP INTO THE BREEZE**	75	-
(12"+=/cd-s+=) *(ZT/ZD 43784)* – ('B'-part 2).		
(12") *(ZT 43780)* – ('A'remix) / ('B'-parts 2-3) / ('A'demo).		
Jun 91. (7") *(FRIGHT 053)* **FEEL SO SAD. / I WANT YOU**		-
(above is a gig freebie given away by 'Fierce' re-iss. Apr97)		
Aug 91. (7"clear) *(SPIRIT 002)* **RUN. / I WANT YOU**	59	-
(12"+=/cd-s+=) *(SPIRIT 002 T/CD)* – Luminescence (stay with me) / Effervescent (chimes).		
Nov 91. (7") *(SPIRIT 003)* **WHY DON'T YOU SMILE NOW. / SWAY**		-
(12"/cd-s) *(SPIRIT 003 T/CD)* – ('A'extended) / Sway.		
Mar 92. (7"ep/cd-ep) *(SPIRIT 004/+CD)* **I WANT YOU / YOU KNOW IT'S TRUE** (instrumental) **/ 100 BARS** (flashback)		-
Apr 92. (cd/c/2x12"lp) *(DED CD/MC/LP 004)* <66035-2/-4> **LAZER GUIDED MELODIES**	27	
– You know it's true / If I were with her now / I want you / Run / Smiles / Step into the breeze / Symphony space / Take your time / Shine a light / Angel sigh / Sway / 200 bars. *(free-7" at 'Chain With No Name' shops)* – ANY WAY THAT YOU WANT ME / WHY DON'T YOU SMILE NOW *(re-iss. Jul97; same)*		
Jul 92. (7"red) *(SPIRIT 005)* **MEDICATION. / SMILES** (Peel session)	55	-
(12") *(SPIRIT 005T)* – ('A'side) / Feel so sad (Peel session) / Angel sigh.		
(cd-s++=) *(SPIRIT 005CD)* – Space (instrumental).		
Jun 93. (7"flexi) *(SPIRIT 006)* **SMILES** (live). **/ 100 BARS** (acappella)	-	-
Jun 93. (mail-order cd) *(DEDLP 008)* **F***ED UP INSIDE**	-	-
Oct 93. (7"yellow) *(SPIRIT 007)* **GOOD TIMES / LAY BACK IN THE SUN**	49	-
(12"ep+=/cd-ep+=) *(SPIRIT 008 T/CD)* – Electric Mainline 1 + 2.		

— now without REFOY, who formed SLIPSTREAM. They issued two albums for 'Che' in 1995; 'SLIPSTREAM' & 'SIDE EFFECTS'.

SPIRITUALIZED ELECTRIC MAINLINE

SPACEMAN (JASON) + **KATE RADLEY** – keyboards, vox / **SEAN COOK** – bass, harmonica / plus **MARK REFOY** – guitar (guest only) / **JON MATTOCK** – percussion / **LEON HUNT** – banjo / **STEWART GORDON** – violin / **THE BALANESCU QUARTET** – strings / + others on wind instruments

	Dedicated	Arista
Jan 95. (cd-ep) *(SPIRIT 009CD)* **LET IT FLOW / DON'T GO / STAY WITH ME / DON'T GO / STAY WITH ME (THE INDIVIDUAL)**	30	-
(cd-ep) *(SPIRIT 009CD2)* – ('A'side) / Take good care of it / Things will never be the same / Clear rush.		
(cd-ep) *(SPIRIT 009CD3)* – ('A'side) / Medication / Take your time / Smile.		
(3xbox-cd-ep/10"ep) *(SPIRIT 009BOX/T)* – (all above).		
Feb 95. (cd/c/d-lp) *(DED CD/MC/LP 017)* <26035> **PURE PHASE**	20	Mar95
– Medication / The slide song / Electric phase / All of my tears / These blues / Let it flow / Take good care of it / Born never asked / Electric mainline / Lay back in the sun / Good times / Pure phase / Spread your wings / Feel like goin' home. *(re-iss. Jul97; same)*		
Nov 95. (cd-ep) *(74321 31178-2)* **LAY BACK IN THE SUN / THE SLIDE SONG / SPREAD YOUR WINGS** (instrumental) **/ LAY BACK IN THE SUN** (instrumental)		-
Feb 96. (12") *(SPIRT 101T)* **PURE PHASE TONES FOR DJs**		-

SPIRITUALIZED

— **DAMON REECE** – percussion + guests, repl. MATTOCK, HUNT + GORDON

Jun 97. (cd/c/lp) *(DED CD/MC/LP 034)* <18974> **LADIES AND GENTLEMEN WE ARE FLOATING IN SPACE**	4	
– Ladies and gentlemen we are floating in space / Come together / I think I'm in love / All of my thoughts / Stay with me / Electricity / Home of the brave / The individual / Broken heart / No god only religion / Cool waves / Cop shoot cop ... *(re-iss. Jan98 as 12xcd-s box; DEDCD 034A)*		

SPIRITUALIZED (cont)

Jul 97. (7") *(SPIRIT 012)* **ELECTRICITY. / COOL WAVES (instrumental)** — 32 | -
 (cd-s+=) *(SPIRIT 012CD1)* – Take your time (live) / All of my tears (live).
 (cd-s) *(SPIRIT 012CD2)* – ('A'album version) / Cop shoot cop (live) / Shine a light (live) / Electric mainline (live).
Feb 98. (7") *(SPIRIT 014)* **I THINK I'M IN LOVE. / ('A'version)** — 27 | -
 (12"+=/cd-s+=) *(SPIRIT 014 T/CD)* – ('A'-Chemical Brothers vocal & instrumental mixes).
May 98. (7") *(SPIRIT 015)* <13508> **THE ABBEY ROAD EP** — 39
 – Come together / Broken heart.
 (cd-s+=) *(SPIRIT 015CD)* – Broken heart (instrumental).
 (12"++=) *(SPIRIT 015T)* – ('A'-Richard Fearless remix) / ('A'-Two Lone Swordsmen remix).

— J(ASON) SPACEMAN, DAMON REECE, SEAN COOK, MICHAEL MOONEY, THIGHPAULSANDRA + RAYMOND (MOONSHAKE) DICKATY

Oct 98. (d-cd/d-lp) *(74321 62285-2/-1)* <19032> **ROYAL ALBERT HALL OCTOBER 10 1997 (live)** — 38 | Nov98
 – Intro / Shine a light / Electric mainline / Electricity / Home of the brave / The individual / Medication / Walking with Jesus / Take your time / No God only religion / Broken heart / Come together / I think I'm in love / Cop shoot cop / Oh happy day.

— COOK, REECE + MOONEY were sacked in June '99 and subsequently formed their own "real" band, LUPINE HOWL, who signed to 'Vinyl Hiss' for releases in early 2000

 Spaceman–Arista | Arista
Sep 01. (12") *(OPM 003)* **STOP YOUR CRYING. / ANYTHING MORE (instrumental) / ROCK'N'ROLL** — 18 | -
 (cd-s+=) *(OPM 002)* – ('A'-video).
Sep 01. (cd/d-lp) *(OPM 001 CD/LP)* <14722> **LET IT COME DOWN** — 3
 – On fire / Do it all over again / Don't just do something / Out of sight / The twelve steps / The straight and the narrow / I didn't mean to hurt you / Stop your crying / Anything more / Won't get to Heaven (the state I'm in) / Lord can you hear me.
Nov 01. (12") *(OPM 006)* **OUT OF SIGHT. / DIDN'T MEAN TO HURT YOU (instrumental) / GOING DOWN SLOW** — 65 | -
 (cd-s+=) *(OPM 005)* – ('A'-video).
Feb 02. (7") *(OPM 008)* **DO IT ALL OVER AGAIN. / ROCK AND ROLL (instrumental)** — 31 | -
 (cd-s) *(OPM 004)* – ('A'side) / On fire (evening session version) / Amazing grace (peace on earth).
 (cd-s) *(OPM 007)* – ('A'side) / Come together (Steve Lamacq session) / Going down slowly / ('A'-video).

SPITFIRE

Formed: Crawley, Sussex, England... 1990 by JEFF PRITCHER, his brother NICK, STEVE WHITE and SCOTT KENNY and MATT WISE. Signed to the 'Eve' label, this ambitious bunch of retro heads set the controls for the heart of the sun and modelled their latter day retro-indie on the likes of SPACEMEN 3, LOOP and MY BLOODY VALENTINE, with a healthy dose of strutting JIM MORRISON-style cool thrown in for good measure. After witnessing the SPITFIRE space cadets supporting his girlfriend's band, VOICE OF THE BEEHIVE, THAT PETROL EMOTION frontman, STEVE MACK, was sufficiently impressed to proffer his production skills for their debut EP, 'TRANSLUCENT'. The result saw a preponderance of such adjectives as hypnotic, compelling, dizzying etc., SPITFIRE even applying their musical weaponry to a cover of the 'Six Million Dollar Man' theme tune. By the release of follow-up EP, 'SUPERBABY', the band had relocated to Brighton and WHITE had been replaced by SIMON WALKER while JUSTIN WELCH filled the drum stool as KENNY concentrated on his other band, EVER. A bonafide full length album, 'SEX BOMB', finally emerged on 'Paperhouse' records in 1993 although the resulting sales were hardly explosive. In '96, SPITFIRE returned with the low-key 'ELECTRIC COLOUR CLIMAX' set.

Album rating: FEVERISH compilation (*6) / SEX BOMB (*6) / ELECTRIC COLOUR CLIMAX (*5)

JEFF PITCHER – vocals / **MATT WISE** – lead guitar / **STEVE WHITE** – guitar / **NICK PITCHER** – bass / **SCOTT KENNY** – drums (of EVER)

 Eve | Danceteria
Apr 91. (12"ep) *(EVER 3T)* **THE TRANSLUCENT. / DIVE / THE SIX MILLION DOLLAR MAN** — | -

— **SIMON WALKER** – guitar repl. WHITE
— **JUSTIN WELCH** – drums repl. KENNY

Aug 91. (12"ep) *(EVER 5T)* **SUPERBABY. / SUNFLOW / WOMBCHILD** — | -
Feb 92. (lp) **FEVERISH** (compilation of singles) — | -
 (UK cd-iss. Mar95 on 'Danceteria'; DANCD 097)
Mar 92. (12"red-ep) *(EVER 9T)* **FREEMACHINE** — | -
 – Freemachine / Rock and roll part 2 / (+2)..
 Paperhouse | not iss.
Aug 93. (12"ep/cd-ep) *(PAPER 025 T/CD)* **MINIMAL LOVE. / THE BALLAD OF JET HARRIS / FLUID** — | -
Oct 93. (cd/lp) *(PAP CD/LP 21)* **SEX BOMB** — | -
 – Feverish / Sex bomb / Minimal love / Kiss me / Free machine / Strawhead / Wild sunshine / Firebird / Womb child / Love lover love / Ruined.
 Lowlife | not iss.
Mar 95. (7") *(MONTY 3)* **BIG BANGER. / COME ON, GET ON** — | -
 (cd-s+=) *(MONTY 3CD)* – (+1).
 Diverse | not iss.
Aug 96. (cd) *(FULL 2CD)* **ELECTRIC COLOUR CLIMAX** — | -

— have since disbanded

SPOON

Formed: Austin, Texas, USA... early 90's by songwriter BRITT DANIEL along with JIM ENO and bassist ANDY MACGUIRE. The group, whose hybrid PIXIES, PAVEMENT and SONIC YOUTH-esque melancholic no-wave, issued their full-length LP, 'TELEPHONO' in 1996 to minor acclaim, although some critics denounced the group for "riding the coat-tails" of peers NIRVANA and WIRE. They made a mature effort to tone-down their rockier musical flurries and settled with a series of full-time bassists. The trio recorded the 'SOFT EFFECTS' EP in 1997 and signed on the dotted line for 'Elektra' records; their sophomore effort, 'SERIES OF SNAKES' was shelved and the band subsequently dropped. The album, full of wistful indie overtones and DANIEL's torn-up vocals, finally emerged in 1998. Left reeling from their major label bust-up, the group remained wary, only issuing a handful of 7" singles, 'THE AGONY OF LIFE' EP (1999) and the highly praised 'LOVE WAYS' EP in 2000. One year later, SPOON delivered 'GIRLS CAN TELL', their most accomplished work to date. It was the 'Pet Sounds' or 'Nevermind' of the band's career and ended up on many "Album Of The Year" polls in music publications and journals. From the opening song 'EVERYTHING HITS AT ONCE', SPOON seemed to be full of poison and hope, a combination at times, truly relentless. Emerging from a blend of spiky guitar riffs (akin to the likes of FUGAZI and BLACK FLAG), the often haunting and slightly erstwhile sound of 'THIS BOOK IS A MOVIE', laid out casual noir-ish experimentations, while 'CHICAGO AT NIGHT' burst with shimmering pop-rock atmospherics. It was a hard album to match and, in the tradition of RADIOHEAD, SPOON went experimental with their next release 'KILL THE MOONLIGHT' (2002). A slightly disappointing set which still saw the group's prowess intact, compared to most bland rock bands it seethed with imagination and sparks of musical genius. Just a SPOONful of sugar helps the medicine go down, as they say in Texas land.

Album rating: TELEPHONO (*6) / A SERIES OF SNEAKS (*6) / GIRLS CAN TELL (*7) / KILL THE MOONLIGHT (*5)

BRITT DANIEL – vocals, guitar / **ANDY MAGUIRE** – bass / **JIM ENO** – drums

 Matador | Matador
Mar 96. (7") <(OLE 203-7)> **ALL THE NEGATIVES HAVE BEEN DESTROYED. / IRRIGATION MAN**
 (cd-s+=) <(OLE 203-2)> – If you say so.
May 96. (cd/lp) <(OLE 201-2/-1)> **TELEPHONO** — | Apr96
 – Don't buy the realistic / Not turning off / All the negatives have been destroyed / Cvantez / Nefarious / Claws tracking / Dismember / Idiot driver / Towner / Wanted to be your friend / Theme to Wendel Stivers / Primary / The government darling / Plastic Mylar.
Jun 96. (7") *(OLE 211-7)* **NOT TURNING OFF. / PARTY UP** — | -

— **SCOTT ADAIR, BRAD SHENFELD** + (former producer) **JOHN CROSLIN** repl. MAGUIRE

Feb 97. (m-cd) <(OLE 236-2)> **SOFT EFFECTS** — | Jan97
 – Mountain to sound / Waiting for the kid to come out / I could see the dude / Get out the state / Loss leaders.

— **BRITT + JIM** added **JOSHUA ZARBO**
 not iss. | Elektra
May 98. (cd/c) <62199> **A SERIES OF SNEAKS** — |
 – Utilitarian / The minor tough / The guest list – The execution / Reservations / 30 gallon tank / Car radio / Metal detektor / June's foreign spell / Chloroform / Metal school / Staring at the board / No you're not / Quincy punk episode / Advance cassette. <lp-iss.on 'Vapor'; 46950> (UK-iss.Nov01 on '12XU'; 12XU 008-2)
 not iss. | Saddle Creek
Jun 00. (cd-s) <29> **THE AGONY OF LAFFITTE. / LAFFITTE DON'T FAIL ME NOW** — |
 12XU | Merge
Oct 00. (cd-ep) *(12XU 003-1)* <MRG 191CD> **LOVEWAYS**
 – Change my life / I didn't come here to die / Jealousy / The figures of art / Chips and dip.
Feb 01. (cd/lp) *(12XU 006-2/-1)* <MRG 495CD> **GIRLS CAN TELL**
 – Everything hits at once / Believing is art / Me and the bean / Lines in the suit / The fitted shirt / Anything you want / Take a walk / 1020 am / Take the fifth / This book is a movie / Chicago at night.
Mar 01. (7") *(12XU 004-7)* **ANYTHING YOU WANT. / SHAKE IT OFF**
 (cd-s+=) *(12XU 004-2)* – Decora.
Jul 01. (cd-s) *(12XU 007-2)* **EVERYTHING HITS AT ONCE / THE AGONY OF LAFFITTE / CHICAGO AT NIGHT (demo) / EVERYTHING HITS AT ONCE (FOR DISCOS)** — | -
Dec 01. (cd-s) *(12XU 009-2)* **CAR RADIO / ADVANCE CASSETTE** — | -
May 02. (7"ep) *(SA 05)* **SHAKE IT OFF / (+1). / (other 2 by Swearing At Motorists)** — | -
 (above issued on 'Super Asbestos')
Aug 02. (cd-s) *(12XU 016-2)* **JONATHON FISK / STAY DON'T GO / IS THIS THE LAST TIME / IN THE RIGHT PLACE AT THE RIGHT TIME** — | -
Sep 02. (cd/lp) *(12XU 014-2/-1)* <MRG 515CD> **KILL THE MOONLIGHT** — | Aug02
 – Small stakes / The way we get by / Something to look forward to / Stay don't go / Jonathon Fisk / Paper tiger / Someone something / Don't let it get you down / All the pretty girls go to the city / You gotta feel it / Back to the life / Vittorio E.
 Merge | Merge
Sep 02. (7") <(MRG 213)> **SOMEONE SOMETHING. /**

SPORTIQUE (see under ⇒ RAZORCUTS)

SPRINGHOUSE

Formed: New York City, New York, USA . . . 1988 by MITCH FRIEDLAND, LARRY HEINEMANN and JACK RABID. Early SPRINGHOUSE releases – single 'MENAGERIE KEEPER' and EP 'ESKIMO' – were followed by debut album, 'LAND FALLS' (1991), released on 'Caroline'. The track 'ESKIMO' appeared on 'LAND FALLS', and was one of several tracks to contain an Arctic or ecological theme. The songs on the aforementioned set were constructed of a layering of sounds, including FRIEDLAND's impressive nylon-stringed guitar and with vocals from FRIEDLAND and RABID. Their sound had the drive of the BUZZCOCKS, although it was probably more in common with the shoegazing sound concurrently exported from the UK. The skill and invention of their work was apparent, and saw them receive critical acclaim. 1993's 'POSTCARDS FROM THE ARCTIC' was less discordant and even better than 'LAND FALLS'. It shifted slightly away from the shoegaze sound, more towards regular indie-rock, but retained the abiding gloom of its predecessor. Following the release of 'POSTCARDS . . .', SPRINGHOUSE split, although they briefly reunited to support MARK BURGESS & THE SONS OF GOD (ex-CHAMELEONS) on their '94 US tour.

Album rating: LAND FALLS (*5) / POSTCARDS FROM THE ARCTIC (*6)

MITCH FRIEDLAND – vocals, guitars / **LARRY HEINEMANN** – bass, guitars, vocals / **JACK RAPID** – drums, vocals

		not iss.	Singles Only
1990.	(7") <SO 907> **MENAGERIE KEEPER. / SOUL ASHTRAY**	– Caroline	– Caroline
Jun 91.	(cd/c/lp) (CAR CD/C/LP 14) <CAROL 1701-2/-4/-1> **LAND FALLS** – Layers / For nothing / Eskimo / Alone / Eyesore / Again / A-ha / Open your eyes / Landslide / The sound.	–	
Oct 91.	(cd-ep) <CAROL 1466> **ESKIMO EP** – Eskimo (dark mix) / That was before / Get it going / Angels / Layers.	–	
Nov 91.	(12"ep) **SPRINGHOUSE EP** – Eyesore / Again / Open your eyes.		–
1993.	(cd/c/lp) <CAROL 1728-2/-4/-1> **POSTCARDS FROM THE ARCTIC** – Asphalt angels / All about me / Enslave me / Ghosts / Alley park / Blue snow / Worthless / Misjudgement / Time to go / Shattering cold / The light.	–	

— split in 1994

S.P.U.D.

Formed: Auckland, New Zealand . . . late 80's by GLEN LORNE CAMPBELL, MATTHEW HEINE and LANCE STRICKLAND. Taking their musical cue from the likes of The BIRTHDAY PARTY, The MELVINS or Chicago's JESUS LIZARD, S.P.U.D. delivered some rollercoaster goth-rock shows interspersed between two early 90's sets, the latter of which 'GNAW' (1991), had critics creaming themselves. Subsequently swapping members with another of NZ's finest JEAN-PAUL SARTRE EXPERIENCE (i.e. they recruited GARY SULLIVAN) and finding COLLEEN BRENNAN, a new version of the band was formed. SOLID GOLD HELL unleashed their first effort, 'SWINGIN' HOT MOTHER', in 1994, and thus a new antipodean band were on their way. However, 1996's mini-LP follow-up, 'THE BLOOD AND THE PITY', was their last, its hardcore riffery on tracks such as 'HEAVENLY BADNESS' and 'THE COUNTRY SOW' now just distant memories.

Album rating: SOUR mini (*5) / GNAW (*8) / Solid Gold Hell: SWINGIN' HOT MOTHER (*5) / THE BLOOD AND THE PITY mini (*5)

GLEN LORNE CAMPBELL – vocals, trombone / **MATTHEW HEINE** – guitar / **. . . MALONE** – / **LANCE STRICKLAND** – drums, bass, guitar (ex-HEADSHRINKERS, etc)

		Flying Nun	not iss.
1989.	(12") (FN 132) **BREAKDOWN TOWN. / SLO' GIN**	–	– NewZ
1990.	(m-lp) (FN 133) **SOUR** – Breakdown town / Jesus extreme / Jimmy Ray / Motorway / Hard hat / Drag me / Old man.	–	– NewZ
1991.	(lp/c/cd) (FN/+MC/CD 198) **GNAW** – Recliner / Creep / Fur burns / Hee ha / Mud death / Hit the road / Cleaver / I can taste / Ma friends / Go ape / D.R. muthafucka / Hard hat / Jesus extreme / Old man.	–	– NewZ
1992.	(c-s) (FN 211) **CREEP / RECLINER** (re-iss. 7"; FN 238)	–	– NewZ

— HEINE joined the JPS EXPERIENCE (JEAN-PAUL SARTRE EXPERIENCE)

SOLID GOLD HELL

CAMPBELL + HEINE plus **COLLEEN BRENNAN** – bass / **GARY SULLIVAN** – drums, trumpet (ex-GOBLIN MIX, ex-CHUG, ex-JPS EXPERIENCE)

		Flying Nun	not iss.
Aug 94.	(7") (FN 289) **SUGAR BAG. / EVIL CABARET**	–	– NewZ
Sep 94.	(lp/cd) (FN/+CD 298) **SWINGIN' HOT MOTHER** – Hot murder / Skinny kitten / Creaking heels / Daisy legs / Sugar bag / Valley of scorn / The bid tease / Bitter N Est. / The inevitable hopelessness of being.	–	
Oct 96.	(m-lp/m-cd) (FN/+CD 346) **THE BLOOD AND THE PITY** – The country sow / Gloom crasher / Heavenly badness / Motel hell / Hearse / My father before me / The blood and the pity / X-rated.	–	

— disbanded after above; SULLIVAN joined DIMMER

SPYGLASS

Formed: Seattle, Washington, USA . . . 1998 by BARBARA TRENTA/LANGE, DAVID EINMO, JOHN ROTH, CLAY MARTIN and BARRY SHAW. Making their debut in 1999 with the 'TORCH' EP, these Seattle spymasters revealed a fondness for revamped shoegazing wracked by pre-millennial tension. Their miasmic, effects-driven guitar and keyboard soundscapes were given room to breathe on the full length 'WAKE UP SLEEPYHEAD' (2000), the supper club, pseudo-goth strains of TRENTALANGE's vocals lending the music an air of unexpected sophistication. With increasingly positive noises being made by local scenesters, the group refined their darkly alchemical formula on follow-up set, 'STRATEGIES FOR THE STRANDED' (2001). • **Covered:** MOTHER (John Lennon).

Album rating: WAKE UP SLEEPYHEAD (*4) / STRATEGIES FOR THE STRANDED (*4)

BARBARA TRENTALANGE – vocals / **JOHN ROTH** – guitar, vocals / **DAVID EINMO** – guitar / **CLAY MARTIN** – bass / **BARRY SHAW** – drums

		not iss.	unknown
1999.	(cd-ep) **TORCH**	–	
2000.	(cd) <5468736> **WAKE UP SLEEPYHEAD** – Sleephead / See Jack run / Loss / Spell / Torch / Sun song / Disappearances / Marleenken / Mother.		

		Pattern 25	Orchard
Mar 02.	(cd) (P25 05) <80122-2> **STRATEGIES FOR THE STRANDED** – This heaven / Photography / Arch / Dimming stars / The longest day / China doll / Laura Tate / Untethered / The rescue.		Aug01

John SQUIRE (see under ⇒ SEAHORSES)

STARLET (see under ⇒ ACID HOUSE KINGS)

STARLINGS

Formed: London, England . . . 1989 by singer, songwriter and guitarist CHRIS SHEEHAN, with drummer BARRY BLACKER, and bassist MATT PARKIN. Initially a five-piece, SHEEHAN felt that they lacked direction, so he sacked three of them, retaining fellow Kiwi BLACKER and adding Northampton-raised PARKIN. Something of a teen-star in his native New Zealand in the '80s, he played with New Wave act the DANCE EXPONENTS, and later played guitar on CURVE's 1990 debut EP 'Blindfold'. This probably went some way to helping The STARLINGS land the support slot on CURVE's 1991 British and Irish tour. Likened to the JESUS & MARY CHAIN, they unleashed their aggressively serrated, desolate glam'n'grit sounds upon audiences throughout '91, and on their 'SAFE IN HEAVEN DEAD' and 'THE LAST ONE' EPs the same year. Their promising debut album 'VALID' (1992), was followed by 1994's 'TOO MANY DOGS', and although critically acclaimed, it wasn't a commercial success. The STARLINGS' lack of success, and reported contractual difficulties, led to their disbanding in the mid-1990s, with SHEEHAN retreating to Devon. He returned in 2000 with a solo album, 'PLANET PAINKILLER' (under the name CHRIS STARLING), and later that year joined the SISTERS OF MERCY as rhythm guitarist.

Album rating: VALID (*6) / TOO MANY DOGS (*7) / Chris Starling: PLANET PAINKILLER (*5) / SOUNDS LIKE . . . (*7)

CHRIS SHEEHAN – vocals, guitar / **MATT PARKIN** – bass / **BARRY BLACKER** – drums

		Bad Girl	not iss.
Nov 90.	(12"ep) **A LETTER FROM HEAVEN EP** – Wasn't born to follow / Letter from Heaven / Razor girl / Halloween candy / My sympathy.		–

		Anxious	Atlantic
Jun 91.	(12"ep/cd-ep) (ANX T/CD 666) **TRY. / CARE / PLEASE LEAVE**		–
Sep 91.	(12"ep/cd-ep) (ANX T/CD 700) **SAFE IN HEAVEN DEAD** – The angels share / Please stay / Thames eternal / Save in Heaven dead.		–
Nov 91.	(12"ep) (ANXT 699) **THE LAST ONE / HALLOWEEN CANDY / LAST BREATH**		–
Aug 92.	(cd) (4509 90285-2) **VALID** – Now take that / That's it you're in trouble / Unhealthy / Start again / Bad dad / Right school / Shoot up hill / Sick puppy / Jack.		–
Apr 94.	(c-ep/10"ep/cd-ep) (ANX 1018 C/TE/CD) **LOCH AANGELES MONSTER EP** – Loch AAngeles monster / As long as you feel worse / Now take that / Shoot up hill.		–
Apr 94.	(cd/c) (4509 95195-2/-4) <82621-2/-4> **TOO MANY DOGS** – Tears before bedtime / Loch AAngeles monster / Pushed and pulled / As long as you feel worse / We can save you / Mr wishy washy / Other peoples children / The party / Too many dogs / D-D-D-Dum.		
May 94.	(c-s/12"/cd-s) (ANX 1021 C/T/CD) **TEARS BEFORE BEDTIME. / OTHER PEOPLES CHILDREN**		–

— disbanded later in the year; SHEEHAN joined The SISTERS OF MERCY (twice!) and went solo

CHRIS STARLING

		EX34	not iss.
Jun 99.	(cd-s) (EX 002) **RAWHIDE BABY / GODHEADAGAIN / TENDER**		–
Oct 99.	(cd-s) (EX 003 – EX 34/11) **THE WORD / LUCKY / CHEVY**		–

STARLINGS (cont) — THE GREAT INDIE DISCOGRAPHY — The 1990s

Jan 00. (cd) (EX 001 – EX 34/31) **PLANET PAINKILLER**
– Rawhide / Mouths and brains / Saved up / The word / Bobby Slaughter saw the light / Clouds / Charles mantra overboard / Tender / Bonehead.

Mar 02. (cd) **SOUNDS LIKE . . .**
– Wendy may / Still she can't / Half life / Lost and found / Took a trip / Bar in a boat / No problemo / Let it soak in.

STARRY EYES (see under ⇒ VELOCITY GIRL)

STARS

Formed: New York, USA . . . late 90's by frontman/actor TORQUIL CAMPBELL and CHRIS SELIGMAN. Together with AMY MILLAN (who'd providing a soundtrack for the movie, 'Drowning Mona') and BIG RUDE JAKE's EVAN CRANLEY, they settled for the city of Montreal in Canada. Signed to 'Le Grand Magistery', this soulful indie-pop quartet – think SMITHS (they covered 'THIS CHARMING MAN') and early NEW ORDER – delivered their debut EP, 'A LOT OF LITTLE LIES FOR THE SAKE OF ONE BIG TRUTH', in 2000. 'NIGHTSONGS' the following year, was an album that fused romantic chamber strings with delicate electro-pop.

Album rating: NIGHTSONGS (*6)

TORQUIL CAMPBELL – vocals, guitar / **CHRIS SELIGMAN** – vocals, guitar / plus **EVAN CRANLEY** (of BIG RUDE JAKE) + **AMY MILLAN**

		Le Grand Magistery	Le Grand Magistery
Jul 00.	(cd-ep) <(HRH 014)> **A LOT OF LITTLE LIES FOR THE SAKE OF ONE BIG TRUTH** – When? / On peak hill / Going, going, gone / Theme from the Stars.		
Feb 01.	(cd) <HRH 019> **NIGHTSONGS** – Counting stars on the ceiling / My radio (AM mix) / Going, going, gone / This charming man / On peak hill / International rock star / The very thing / Write what you know / Tru / Better be heaven / Liar / Tonight / Toxic holiday / My radio.	-	
Oct 01.	(cd-ep) <(HRH 024)> **"THE COMEBACK" EP** – Krush / Violent / The aspidistra flies / Cotes de neiges / The comeback.		Jul01

STARSAILOR

Formed: Wigan, England . . . late 90's by Chorley & Warrington lads JAMES WALSH, JAMES STELFOX and BEN BYRNE with the belated arrival of keyboardist BARRY WESTHEAD. All former music students, the group lifted their name from a TIM BUCKLEY album which obviously proved to be a major influence along with VAN MORRISON and TOM WAITS. The indie quintet debuted at the 'Heavenly Social' in 2000, after having only five songs, three of which were floating around on demo tapes circulating the music industry. Giants 'E.M.I.' eventually won over the band, who were still astonished by the critical response they were receiving, it being so early on in their careers. STARSAILOR were put on tour with fellow indie guitar comrades JJ72 and ALFIE and issued their debut single 'FEVER' which would then spark a sold-out, nationwide headline tour. 'GOOD SOULS', a simple guitar-jangling lullaby followed and word seemed to be spreading as the single was another to crash into the Top 20, earning them an American tour with The DOVES and a spot on nightly comic David Letterman's show. 'LOVE IS HERE' was issued the following year to mixed reviews (one of its harshest critics being MOGWAI's STUART BRAITHWAITE who bravely said: "You can just tell JAMES WALSH would sell his granny for a Brit Award") and boasted the Top 10 single 'ALCOHOLIC', a whinging but endearing lament that would've made even THOM YORKE groan. That said, STARSAILOR obviously had a general appeal and were musically talented enough to climb as high as they did (album hit UK Top 3) in such a short period of time.

Album rating: LOVE IS HERE (*8)

JAMES WALSH – vocals, guitar / **BARRY WESTHEAD** – keyboards / **JAMES STELFOX** – bass / **BEN BYRNE** – drums

		Chrysalis	Capitol
Feb 01.	(cd-s/7"/cd-s) (CD+/CHS/+S 5123) **FEVER. / COMING DOWN / LOVE IS HERE**	18	-
Apr 01.	(c-s/7") (TC+/CHS 5125) **GOOD SOULS. / THE WAY YOUNG LOVERS DO** (c-s+=) (CDCHS 5125) – Good souls (Echoboy remix). (cd-s++=) (CDCHSS 5125) – ('A'video).	12	-
Sep 01.	(7") (CHS 5130) **ALCOHOLIC. / LET IT SHINE** (cd-s+=) (CDCHS 5130) – ('A'-original) / ('A'-video). (c-s+=) (TCCHS 5130) – Grandma's hands. (cd-s) (CDCHSS 5130) – ('A'side) / Grandma's hands / Good souls (soulsavers remix).	10	-
Oct 01.	(cd/c/lp) (535350-2/-4/-1) <7243 5 36448 2 6> **LOVE IS HERE** – Tie up my hands / Poor misguided fool / Alcoholic / Lullaby / Way to fall / Fever / She just wept / Talk her down / Love is here / Good souls / Coming down.	2	Jan02
Dec 01.	(c-s) (TCCHS 5131) **LULLABY / FROM A WHISPER TO A SCREAM / TIE UP MY HANDS (live)** (cd-s+=) (CDCHS 5131) – ('A'-video).	36	-
Mar 02.	(c-s) (TCCHS 5136) **POOR MISGUIDED FOOL / BORN AGAIN** (cd-s+=) (CDCHS 5136) – ('A'-soulsavers mix) / ('A'-video).	23	-

STARS OF THE LID

Formed: Austin, Texas, USA . . . 1994 by BRIAN McBRIDE and WINDSOR FOR THE DERBY member ADAM WILTZIE. The group first unveiled their dark ambient dirge guitar and spaced out vocal sound on the competent 1995 debut 'MUSIC FOR NITROUS OXIDE'. The 1997 follow-up, 'BALLASTED ORCHESTRA', was richly atmospheric and affecting; clearly influenced by BRIAN ENO, the group had learned how to produce music that was tonally dense whilst avoiding sounding cluttered. With the album, 'GRAVATATIONAL PULL VS. THE DESIRE FOR AN AQUATIC LIFE', released the same year, the music was a little too threadbare and consequently the album was sparse and incomplete sounding. McBRIDE kept himself busy in 1997 by also forming the group, The PILOT SHIPS, along with MONROE MUSTANG members CHRIS and MIKE LINNEN, plus CHEREE JETTON (of BEES ARE BLACK). The group released the dirgy, space rock album, 'THERE SHOULD BE AN ENTRY HERE', the same year. The following year, The STARS OF THE LID collaborated with the abstract painter JON McCAFFERTY on the album, 'PER ASPERA AD ASTRA'. McCAFFERTY had approached the band after having produced a number of works based on their debut album. The 'LID were clearly impressed and repaid the compliment by attempting to provide a soundtrack to his moody colour-wash art pieces. In 1999, the group released the brooding, 'AVEC LAUDENUM', followed by another PILOT SHIPS outing with the band, 'THE LIMITS OF PAINTING AND POETRY', in 2000. In 2001, McBRIDE and WILTZIE were reunited for their most ambitious album to date. 'TIRED SOUNDS OF STARS OF THE LID' was an epic double CD and had the sound of a band who had perfected their craft.

Album rating: MUSIC FOR NITROUS OXIDE (*6) / THE BALLASTED ORCHESTRA (*7) / GRAVATATIONAL PULL VS. THE DESIRE FOR AN AQUATIC LIFE (*5) / PER ASPERA AD ASTRA (*5) / AVEC LAUDENUM (*6) / THE TIRED SOUNDS OF STARS OF THE LID (*7) / the Pilot Ships: THERE SHOULD BE AN ENTRY HERE (*6) / THE LIMITS OF PAINTING AND POETRY (*5)

BRIAN McBRIDE – vocals, guitar / **ADAM WILTZIE** – guitar (of WINDSOR FOR THE DERBY)

		not iss.	Sedimental
Jan 95.	(c) <SEDCD 023> **MUSIC FOR NITROUS OXIDE** – Before top dead center / Adamord / Madison / Down / Lagging / (Live) Lid / Tape hiss makes me happy / The swellsong / Goodnight. (UK cd-iss. Jun99; same as US)	-	
		Kranky	Kranky
Jan 97.	(d-lp/cd) <(KRANK 015/+CD)> **THE BALLASTED ORCHESTRA** – Central Texas / Sun drugs / Down II / Taphead / Fucked up (3:57 a.m.) / Music for Twin Peaks episode #30 (pts.1 & 2) / The artificial pine / Arch song.		
Oct 97.	(cd) <(KRANK 20)> **GRAVITATIONAL PULL VS. THE DESIRE FOR AN AQUATIC LIFE** – The better angels of our nation / Cantus II: In memory of Warren Wiltzie / Jan. '69 / Lactate's moment / Be little with me.		
Feb 98.	(12") (WORM 11) **MANOUEVERING THE NOCTURNAL HUM** (above issued on 'Earworm')		-
—	added guest **JON McCAFFERTY**		
Aug 98.	(lp/cd; by STARS OF THE LID & JON McCAFFERTY) <(KRANK 028/+CD)> **PER ASPERA AD ASTRA** – Low level (listening) / Low level (listening) (continued) / Low level (listening) (continued) / Anchor states / Anchor states / Anchor states (continued) / Anchor states (continued).		
		Sub Rosa	Kranky
May 99.	(cd/lp) (SR 155 D/V) <KRANK 59> **AVEC LAUDENUM** – The atomium (pt.1) / The atomium (pt.2) / The atomium (pt.3) / Dust breeding (1,316) + / I will surround you.		Dec99
		Kranky	Kranky
Oct 01.	(t-lp/d-cd) <(KRANK 050/+CD)> **THE TIRED SOUNDS OF STARS OF THE LID** – Requiem for dying mothers (part 1) / Requiem for dying mothers (part 2) / Down 3 / Austin Texas mental hospital (part 1) / Austin Texas mental hospital (part 2) / Austin Texas mental hospital (part 3) / Broken harbours (part 1) / Broken harbours (part 2) / Broken harbours (part 3) / Mulholland / The lonely people (are getting lonelier) / Gas farming / Piano aquieu / Fac 21 / Ballad of distances (part 1) / Ballad of distances (part 2) / A lovesong (for cubs) + (part 1) / A lovesong (for cubs) + (part 2) / A lovesong (for cubs) + (part 3).		

PILOT SHIPS

BRIAN McBRIDE with **CHRIS + MIKE LINNEN** plus **CHEREE JETTON** – instruments

		At-A-Glance	At-A-Glance
Sep 97.	(cd) <(ATAG 005CD)> **THERE SHOULD BE AN ENTRY HERE** – The reverb song / Cantelope / A stop still remains / July 6th / Fun / Vessel / A song by your campfire / Pink noon / Looked over (No fun reprise).		
		BlueSanct	BlueSanct
Nov 00.	(cd) <(INR 1047CD)> **LIMITS OF PAINTING AND POETRY** – The lazy swimmer / Backyards / Find out you're nice / You've always been a dullard to me (part 2) / Deleuze / Driving off / Knotted / Sides / Pilot suicide theory.		

STEEL POLE BATH TUB

Formed: Bozeman, Montana, USA . . . late 80's by DALE FLATTUM, MIKE MORASKY and DARREN MOR-X (former MR EPP, an outfit which also featured future MUDHONEY members, MARK ARM and STEVE TURNER). Relocating to San Francisco, they signed to 'Tupelo', where they set about causing maximum aural damage with their particularly twisted brand of industrial grunge-metal, calling up the damned soul of BLACK SABBATH and The STOOGES via the latter day sonic terrorism of MINISTRY. In 1989, SPBT delivered their debut album, 'BUTTERFLY LOVE', although it would be the following year's MELVINS collaboration, 'I DREAMED I DREAMED' (borrowed from old muckers, SONIC YOUTH) that would bring them more exposure in the emerging Seattle grunge scene. Around the same time, the lads issued their follow-up set, 'LURCH', which featured an industrial strength remake of 'HEY BO DIDDLEY'. Their busiest year to date, 1991, saw STEEL POLE BATH TUB release another long-player, 'TULIP', while collaborating with fellow SF resident and former DEAD KENNEDYS frontman, JELLO BIAFRA, on the TUMOUR CIRCUS project. Two further SPBT sets, 'THE MIRACLE OF SOUND IN MOTION' (1993) and 'SOME COCKTAIL SUGGESTIONS' (1994), preceded a major label deal with 'Slash'. Although the band had cleaned up their act somewhat, 'SCARS FROM FALLING DOWN' (1995), their slightly watered down sound disappeared down the proverbial corporate plughole. In fact, the label were so enthusiastic about the follow-up that they reportedly regarded it as unlistenable, so much so in fact, that it was shelved and only released in 2002 and titled, of course, 'UNLISTENABLE'. Not that the level of sonic terrorism was any more pronounced than normal, the BATH TUB boys turning in a competent, if unremarkable set of left field experimentation. • **Covered:** PARANOID (Black Sabbath) / CHEMICAL WARFARE (Dead Kennedys) / THE GHOST (Willie Nelson) / SURRENDER + AUF WIEDERSEHEN (Cheap Trick) / WHAT I NEED (Cars).

Album rating: BUTTERFLY LOVE (*6) / LURCH mini (*6) / TULIP (*7) / THE MIRACLE OF SOUND IN MOTION (*5) / SOME COCKTAIL SUGGESTIONS mini (*5) / SCARS FROM FALLING DOWN (*5) / UNLISTENABLE (*5)

DALE FLATTUM – vocals, bass / **MIKE MORASKY** – guitar, vocals / **DARREN MOR-X** – drums

			Tupelo	B>O>N<E<R
1989.	(lp/c/cd) <BR 15> **BUTTERFLY LOVE**		-	
	– Time to die / I am Sam I am / Welcome aboard it's love / Bee sting / Hey Bo Diddley / Swerve / Thru the windshields of love / Heaven on dirt / Tear it apart.			
Jun 90.	(m-lp/cd) <BR 20> **LURCH**			
	– Christina / Lime-away / Hey you / The river / Paranoid. <cd+=> – BUTTERFLY LOVE			
Jul 90.	(7") <BR 21> **I DREAMED I DREAMED. / (other by MELVINS)**		-	
Jul 90.	(cd/lp) (TUP CD/LP 16) **LURCH / BUTTERFLY LOVE** (compilation)			-
Feb 91.	(cd/lp) (TUP CD/LP 27) <BR 26> **TULIP**			
	– Soul cannon / Sister / Quark / One thick second / Pirate 5 / Mercurochrome / Wonders of dust / The scarlet / Misty Mt. Blowtorch / Myrna Loy / Pause.			
May 92.	(7") <BR 31> **BOZEMAN. / BORSTAL** (cd-s+=) <BR 31CD> – Arizona garbage truck.		-	
Apr 93.	(cd/lp) (TUP 47-2/-1) <BR 39> **THE MIRACLE OF SOUND IN MOTION**			
	– Pseudoephedrine hydrochloride / Train to Miami / Exhale / Thumbnail / Down all the days / Cartoon / Bozeman / Borstal / 594 / Waxl.			
Jan 94.	(m-cd/m-c/m-10"lp) (TUP 051-2/-4/-1) <BR 42> **SOME COCKTAIL SUGGESTIONS..**			
	– Ray / The living end / Slip / Hit it / Speakerphone / The wasp jar.			
			not iss.	Genius
1995.	(d7"ep) <none> **TRAGEDY ECSTASY DOOM AND SO ON**		-	
	– Home is a rope / I want it now / Alice / Four barrels.			
			Slash	Slash
Jan 96.	(cd/c) <(828 685-2/-4)> **SCARS FROM FALLING DOWN**			Nov95
	– The 500 club / Population / Home is a rope / The conversation / Twist / Every thing / 3 of cups / Four barrels / Decline / Kansas City / Friday.			
			not iss.	Man's Ruin
Sep 96.	(12") <MR 11> **AUF WIEDERSEHEN. / SURRENDER**		-	

— split after above

– compilations, etc. –

Jul 94.	(cd) Your Choice; <(YCLS 019)> **LIVE (live)**		Jun94
Sep 02.	(cd) Zero To One; <(OTO 103)> **UNLISTENABLE** (rec. 1996)		
	– Spoon house – Action Man theme / Black eye fixer / What I need / Re-juvenilated / Teenage middle finger / Kinder party / Spun / Jack aloha / Hot water into steam / The good times / Cherry tomato / Glad ass / Old man bar / Park night / H2o 2 / My best friend's a girl. (3 hidden tracks)		

STEINBECKS

Formed: Melbourne, Australia ... October 1994 by former SUGARGLIDERS people, JOSH MEADOWS, his brother JOEL, ROBERT COOPER, ADAM DENNIS and BIANCA LEW. The aforementioned SUGARGLIDERS released a plethora of twee-pop 45's for 'Summershine' and 'Sarah', before accumulating their relatively large discography with a best of collection, 'WE'RE ALL TRYING TO GET THERE' (1994). Subsequently taking their cue from The BEATLES, AZTEC CAMERA and BURT BACHARACH, The STEINBECKS carried on the great antipodean tradition of utilising everything musically good about the UK and injecting it with Aussie panache. With a further series of hot singles and a lonesome album, 'AT HOME OR ABROAD WITH ...' (1996), the 5-piece found their 15 minutes worth of fame – so to speak.

Album rating: Sugargliders: WE'RE ALL TRYING TO GET THERE compilation (*6) / Steinbecks: AT HOME OR ABROAD WITH THE STEINBECKS (*6) / FROM THE WRESTLING CHAIR TO THE SEA mini (*5)

SUGARGLIDERS

JOSH MEADOWS – vocals, guitar / **JOEL MEADOWS** – guitar / **ADAM DENNIS** – guitar, trumpet / **ROBERT COOPER** – bass / **BIANCA LEW** – drums (this was actually The STEINBECKS line-up)

		Summershine	not iss.
1990.	(7"m) (SHINE 004) **SWAY. / THIS TRAVELLING SONG / PROGRESS LULLABY**		-
1991.	(7"ep) (SHINE 007) **FURLOUGH EP**		-
	– Give me some confidence / Furlough / Coffee.		
1991.	(7"ep) (SHINE 012) **BUTTERFLY SOUP EP**		-
	– Book of dreams / Fret / Police me.		
		Sarah	not iss.
Mar 92.	(7"m) (SARAH 063) **LETTER FROM A LIFEBOAT. / STRONG / WHAT WE HAD HOPED**		-
Jun 92.	(7") (MARINE 3) **ANOTHER FAUX PAS IN THE CATHEDRAL OF LOVE.**		-
	(above issued on 'Marineville')		
Oct 92.	(7"m/cd-s) (SARAH 067) **SEVENTEEN. / ALOHA STREET / FRUITLOOPIN'**		-
Mar 93.	(7"/cd-s) (SARAH 072/+CD) **AHPRAHRAN. / CORNCIRCLES / (THEME FROM) BOXVILLE**		-
May 93.	(7"/cd-s) (SARAH 077/+CD) **TRUMPET PLAY. / UNKIND / BELOVED**		-
Sep 93.	(7"/cd-s) (SARAH 083/+CD) **WILL WE EVER LEARN? / DOLLY / REINVENTING PENICILLIN**		-
Jan 94.	(7"/cd-s) (SARAH 086/+CD) **TOP 40 SCULPTURE. / 90 DAYS OF MOTHS AND RUST / YR. JACKET**		-
Feb 94.	(lp/cd) (SARAH 619/+CD) **WE'RE ALL TRYING TO GET THERE** (compilation)		-
	– Letter from a lifeboat / Strong / Seventeen / Alcha street / Ahprahran / Theme from Boxville / Unkind / Trumpet play / Will we ever learn / Reinventing penicillin / 90 days of moths and rust / Top 40 sculpture.		

STEINBECKS

— virtually the same line-up

		Summershine	Summershine
1994.	(7") <SHINE 010> **APOLLO. / MR. MUTUAL RESPECT** (UK-iss.Nov97; SHINE 54)		-
Nov 94.	(cd) <SHINEUS 013CD> **AT HOME OR ABROAD WITH THE STEINBECKS**		-
	– Apollo / Geology / 2-star hotel / Which part of no don't you understand / Same light / Fine vehicle / Smoking and driving / Change the weather / Snakes in the grass / Needless and the homely / Cosmo cosmopolitan / Listen to my heart. (UK-iss.Dec97; same)		
1997.	(7") <drive 02> **2-STAR MOTEL. / (other by BUDDHA ON THE MOON)** (above issued on 'Drive-In')	-	
Mar 98.	(m-cd/10"m-lp) (<SHINEUS 023/+LP>) **FROM THE WRESTLING CHAIR TO THE SEA**		
	– Obstreperous / Lighthouse act, 1911 / Lucky star / Boy's a dancer / Sleepyheart / Colour o' the harbour.		

STEREO BUS (see under ⇒ JEAN-PAUL SARTRE EXPERIENCE; in 80's section)

STEREOLAB

Formed: South London, England ... late 1990, by ex-indie stalwart/songwriter TIM GANE (mainman for McCARTHY), who invited lyricist girlfriend LAETITIA SADIER to join. They soon completed the initial line-up with MARTIN KEAN and JOE DILWORTH (other past indie veterans), subsequently forming their own label, 'Duophonic Super 45s'. The group released three 45's ('SUPER 45', 'SUPER ELECTRIC' & 'STUNNING DEBUT ALBUM') in 1991, the second of which was for the 'Too Pure' label (these have re-instated vinyl as worthy product, whether for limited edition collectors or just vinyl junkies who hate cd's). The following year, the eclectic ambient-boogie machine that was STEREOLAB topped the indie charts with their actual "stunning debut album", 'PENG!'. The record ran the gamut of the band's minimalist influences including VELVET UNDERGROUND, JOHN CAGE, NEU! and SPACEMEN 3. During this period, the couple introduced four new members; MARY HANSEN, SEAN O'HAGAN, DUNCAN BROWN and ANDY RAMSAY, who helped them with a busy touring schedule. In 1993, they signed to 'Elektra' in the States for a 6 figure-sum, while in the UK, they released several more 45's! and an album, 'TRANSIENT RANDOM-NOISE BURSTS WITH ANNOUNCEMENTS', which, like the classy single, 'JENNY ONDIOLINE', scraped into the UK charts (the track was premiered on Channel 4's "The Word" programme). 1994 saw them unsurprisingly hit the UK Top 20 with another double album, 'MARS AUDIAC QUINTET'. Two years later, with their best offering to date, 'EMPEROR TOMATO KETCHUP', they had established themselves as leaders of the "Metronomic Underground" scene, as the opening track suggested. Over the course of the last three years (including 1997's excellent 'DOTS AND LOOPS'), the band's sound had become increasingly characterised by the dreamy French-style vocals of LAETITIA (pronounced Le-ti-seaya), akin to a spacier SARAH CRACKNELL (of SAINT ETIENNE). Returning to the fold in August '99, STEREOLAB (complete with Gallic songstress, BRIGITTE FONTAINE) issued one of their special limited singles, 'CALIMERO', although it was not a feature on their accompanying album, 'COBRA AND PHASES GROUP PLAY VOLTAGE IN THE MILKY

NIGHT'. Officially previewed with yet another single, 'THE FREE DESIGN' (inspired by the obscure outfit of the same name!), the album was a little too twee and lightweight for some, one slightly perturbed (or disturbed?) NME critic in particular panning it enough to give zero out of ten! (a hanging offence in anyone's book). Augmented by main protagonists of the underground post-rock scene, JIM O'ROURKE and TORTOISE leader JOHN McENTIRE, STEREOLAB – after a long gap inbetween "long-playing" records – issued the near fantastic 'SOUND-DUST' (2001), a swirling trip into the uncharted territories for the group. The set matched that of the mini-album, or largely ignored 'THE FIRST OF THE MICROBE HUNTERS' (2000), which separated the band from math-rock wizards to sci-fi pop magicians. On 'SOUND-DUST' SADIER's vocals levitated through soft guitars and echoing bass guitar. Opener 'BLACK ANTS IN SOUND-DUST' was reminiscent of previous 'LAB outings, whereas 'CAPTAIN EASYCHORD' focused on being just a great space lullaby. Tragically, on the 9th of December 2002, at the age of only 36, MARY HANSEN was killed when on a bicycle trip.

Album rating: SWITCHED ON collection (*6) / PENG! (*7) / THE GROOP PLAYED "SPACE AGE BATCHELOR PAD MUSIC" (*5) / TRANSIENT RANDOM-NOISE BURSTS WITH ANNOUNCEMENTS (*8) / REFRIED ELECTOPLASM (SWITCHED ON, VOL.2) compilation (*6) / MUSIC FOR THE AMORPHOUS BODY STUDY CENTER (*8) / MARS AUDIO QUINTET (*8) / EMPEROR TOMATO KETCHUP (*9) / DOTS AND LOOPS (*8) / COBRA AND PHASES GROUP PLAY VOLTAGE IN THE MILKY NIGHT (*6) / THE FIRST OF THE MICROBE HUNTERS mini (*6) / SOUND-DUST (*7)

TIM GANE (b.12 Jul'64) – guitar, vox organ, guitar (ex-McCARTHY) / **LAETITIA SADIER** (b. 6 May'68, Paris, France) – vocals, vox organ, guitar, tambourine, moog / **GINA MORRIS** – vocals / **JOE DILWORTH** – drums (of TH' FAITH HEALERS)

Duophonic   not iss.

May 91. (10"ep-mail order) *(DS45-01)* **SUPER 45**
 – The light (that will cease to fail) / Au grand jour / Brittle / Au grand jour!.

—— added **MARTIN KEAN** (b.New Zealand) – guitar (ex-CHILLS) / **RUSSELL YATES** – live guitar (of MOOSE). **MICK CONROY** (ex-MOOSE) was also a live member early '92.

Nov 91. (7"clear,7"colrd) *(DS45-02)* **STUNNING DEBUT ALBUM: Doubt / Changer**

Too Pure   Slumberland

Sep 91. (10"ep) *(PURE 4)* **SUPERELECTRIC / HIGH EXPECTATION. / THE WAY WILL BE OPENING / CONTACT**
Apr 92. (cd/lp) *(31022) <SLR 22>* **SWITCHED ON** (compilation)   Oct92
 – Super-electric / Doubt / Au grand jour 1 / The way will be opening / Brittle / Contact / Au grand jour / High expectation / The light that will cease to fail / Changer. *(re-iss. Mar97 on 'Duophonic' cd/lp; TBC 25/24) (cd/lp re-iss. Mar99 on 'Too Pure'; PURE1 78 CD/LP)*

—— GINA departed after above

Too Pure   American

May 92. (cd,c,lp) *(PURE 11) <43018>* **PENG!**
 – Super falling star / Orgiastic / Peng! 33 / K-stars / Perversion / You little shits / The seeming and the meaning / Mellotron / Enivrez-vous / Stomach worm / Surrealchemist.

—— added **MARY HANSEN** (b. 11 Jan'66, Brisbane, Australia) – vocals, tambourine, guitar / **ANDY RAMSAY** – percussion, vox organ, bazouki; repl. DILWORTH

Sep 92. (10"ep,10"clear-ep,cd-ep) *(PURE 14)* **LOW FI**
 – Et de votre coeur endormi (Varoom!) / Laisser-faire / Elektro – He held the world in his iron grip.

—— added **SEAN O'HAGAN** – vox organ, guitar (ex-MICRODISNEY, ex-HIGH LLAMAS)

Feb 93. (7",7"pink) *<SLR 24>* **JOHN CAGE BUBBLEGUM. / ELOGE D'EROS**

—— added **DUNCAN BROWN** – bass, guitar, vocals

Mar 93. (cd,c,m-lp) *(PURE 19) <43013>* **THE GROOP PLAYED "SPACE AGE BACHELOR PAD MUSIC"**
 – Avant-garde M.O.R. / Space age bachelor pad music (mellow) / The groop play chord X / Space age bachelor pad music (foamy) / Ronco symphony / We're not adult orientated / UHF-MFP / We're not adult orientated (new wave live).

Duophonic   Elektra

Aug 93. (10"ep/cd-ep) *(DUHF D/CD 01) <8815>* **JENNY ONDIOLINE / FRUCTION / GOLDEN BALL / FRENCH DISCO**   75
Sep 93. (cd/c/2xlp) *(DUHF CD/DMC/D 02) <7559 61536-2>* **TRANSIENT RANDOM-NOISE BURSTS WITH ANNOUNCEMENTS**   62
 – Tone burst / Our trinitone blast / Pack yr romantic mind / I'm going out of my way / Golden ball / Pause / Jenny Ondioline / Analogue rock / Crest / Lock-groove lullaby.
Nov 93. (7") *(DUHF D01P)* **FRENCH DISKO (new version). / JENNY ONDIOLINE**

—— added **KATHERINE GIFFORD** – synthesizers, keyboards

Jul 94. (7"ltd) *(DUHFD 04S)* **PING PONG. / MOOGIE WONDERLAND**   45
 (10"+=/cd-s+=) *(DUHF D/CD 04)* – Pain et spectacles / Transcoma (live).
Aug 94. (cd/c/d-lp) *(DUHF CD/MC/D 05) <61669>* **MARS AUDIAC QUINTET**   16
 – Three-dee melodie / Wow and flutter / Transona five / Des etoiles electroniques / Ping pong / Anamorphose / Three longers later / Nihilist assault group / International colouring contest / The stars of our destination / Transporte sans bouger / L'enfer des formes / Outer accelerator / New orthophony / Fiery yellow. *(free clear-7" w /d-lp + cd-s on cd) (DUHF D/CD 05X)* – Klang-tang / Ulaan batter.
Oct 94. (7"ltd) *(DUHFD 07S)* **WOW AND FLUTTER. / HEAVY DENIM**   70
 (10"+=/cd-ep+=) *(DUHF D/CD 07)* – Nihilist assault group / Narco Martenot.
Apr 95. (10"ep/cd-ep) *(DUHF D/CD 08)* **AMORPHOUS BODY STUDY CENTRE**   59
 – Pop quiz / The extension trip / How to explain your internal organs overnight / The brush descends the length / Melochord seventy five / Space moment.

Sep 95. (cd/c/colrd-d-lp) *(DUHF CD/MC/D 09) / Drag City; <DC 82>* **REFRIED ECTOPLASM (SWITCHED ON – VOLUME II)** (compilation)   30
 – Harmonium / Lo boob oscillator / Mountain / Revox / French disko / Exploding head movie / Eloge d'eros / Tone burst (country) / Animal or vegetable (a wonderful wooden reason) / John Cage bubblegum / Sadistic / Farfisa / Tempter. *(d-lp re-iss. May98; same as US)*

—— **GANE / SADIER / HANSEN / RAMSAY + BROWN** added **MORGANE LHOTE** (guests; SEAN O'HAGAN / JOHN McENTIRE (of TORTOISE) + RAY DICKARTY)

—— KATHERINE GIFFORD formed indie supergroup SNOWPONY

Feb 96. (7") *(DUHFD 10S)* **CYBELE'S REVERIE. / BRIGITTE**   62
 (10"+=/cd-s+=) *(DUHF D/CD 10)* – Les yper yper sound / Young lungs.
Mar 96. (d-lp/c/cd) *(DUHF D/MC/D 11) <61640-2>* **EMPEROR TOMATO KETCHUP**   27   Apr96
 – Metronomic underground / Cybele's reverie / Percolator / Les ypersound / Spark plug / Olv 26 / The noise of carpet / Tomorrow is already here / Emperor tomato ketchup / Monstre sacre / Motoroller scalatron / Slow fast Hazel / Anonymous collective.
Apr 96. (12"ltd.) *(DS 3311)* **SIMPLE HEADPHONE MIND. / (other track by NURSE WITH WOUND)**
 (re-iss. Jun97; same)

—— now without BROWN, who was repl. by RICHARD HARRISON

Sep 96. (7") *(LISS 15)* **SHE USED TO CALL ME SADNESS. / (other by Fuxa)**
 (above on 'Lissys')
Nov 96. (7"ep)(12"ep/cd-ep) *(DUHFD 14S)(DUHF D/CD 14)* **FLUORESCENCES EP**
 – Fluorescences / Pinball / You used to call me sadness / Soop groove *2.
Dec 96. (12"; STEREOLAB & WAGON CHRIST) *(DUHFD 15)* **METROGNOMIC UNDERGROUND. /**
Sep 97. (7") *(DUHFD 16S)* **MISS MODULAR. / ALLURES**   60
 (12"+=/cd-s+=) *(DUHF D/CD 16)* – Off-on / Spinal column.
Sep 97. (cd/c/d-lp) *(DUHF CD/C/D 17) <62065>* **DOTS AND LOOPS**   19
 – Brakhage / Miss Modular / The flower called Nowhere / Prisoner of Mars / Rainbo conversation / Refractions in the plastic pulse / Parsec / Ticker-tape of the unconscious / Contronatura.

—— **SADIER, GANE, HANSEN, RAMSEY + LHOTE** were joined by **SIMON JOHNS** – bass (ex-CLEARSPOT) / **KEV HOOPER** – musical saw (ex-STUMP) / **ROB MAZUREK** – cornet / **DOMINIC MURCOTT** – marimba / plus guests **JOHN McENTIRE** (of TORTOISE) / **JIM O'ROURKE** + **SEAN O'HAGAN**

Aug 99. (7"/cd-s; STEREOLAB & BRIGITTE FONTAINE) *(DS45/+CD 25)* **CALIMERO. / (other track 'Cache Cache' by MONADE)**
Sep 99. (7") *(DUHFD 22S)* **THE FREE DESIGN. / ESCAPE POD (FROM THE WORLD OF MEDICAL OBSERVATIONS)**
 (cd-s+=) *(DUHFCD 22)* – With friends like these / Les aimes des memes.
Sep 99. (cd) *(DUHFCD 23)* **COBRA AND PHASES GROUP PLAY VOLTAGE IN THE MILKY NIGHT**
 – Fuses / People do it all the time / The free design / Blips drips and strips / Italian shoes continuum / Infinity girl / The spiracles / Op hop detonation / Puncture in the radah permutation / Velvet water / Blue milk / Caleidoscopic gaze / Strobo acceleration / The emergency kisses / Come and play in the milky night.
May 00. (m-lp/m-cd) *(DUHF D/CD 25) <62537-2>* **THE FIRST OF THE MICROBE HUNTERS**
 – Outer Bongolia / Intervals / Barock – plastik / Nomus et phusis / I feel the air (of another planet) / Household names / Retrograde mirror form.

—— O'ROURKE + McENTIRE were virtually fully-fledged 'LAB techs

Jul 01. (12"/cd-s) *(DUHF D/CD 26)* **CAPTAIN EASYCHORD / LONGLIFE LOVE. / CANNED CANDIES / MOODLES**
Sep 01. (cd/d-lp) *(DUHF CD/D 27) <62676-2>* **SOUND-DUST**
 – Black ants in sound-dust / Space moth / Captain Easychord / Baby Lulu / The black arts / Hallucinex / Double rocker / Gus the mynah bird / Naught more terrific than man / Nothing to do with me / Suggestion diabolique / Les bons bons des raisons.

—— on 9th Dec'02, MARY was killed in a bicycle accident in London

– more very limited singles, etc. –

Jun 92. (7"pink) *B.M.I.; (BMI 025)* **THE LIGHT (THAT WILL CEASE TO FAIL). / AU GRAND JOUR**
Jul 92. (7"colrd) *Duophonic; (DS45-03)* **HARMONIUM. / FARFISA**
Oct 93. (10"ep) *Clawfist; (Clawfist 20)* **CRUMB DUCK (with NURSE WITH WOUND)**
 – Animal or vegetable / Exploding head movie.
Oct 93. (7"clear) *Sub Pop; (<SP 107/283>)* **LE BOOB OSCILLATOR. / TEMPTER**
Nov 93. (7") *Teenbeat; <Teenbeat 121>* **MOUNTAIN. / ('B'by Unrest)**
Feb 98. (12"ep/cd-ep; by STEREOLAB & UI) *(DS45/+CD 19)* **FIRES**
 – St. Elmo's fire (mixes) / Less time / Impulse rah. *(re-iss/lp Aug00 on 'Bingo'; BIN 2)*
Oct 98. (d-cd/d-lp) *<DC 159>* **ALUMINIUM TUNES: SWITCHED ON VOL.3**
 – Pop quiz – The extension trip / How to play your internal organs / Brush descends the length / Melochord seventy-five / Space moment / Speedy car / Golden atoms / Olan bator / One small step / Iron man / Long hair of death / You used to call me sadness / New orthophony / One note samba – Surfboard / Cadriopo / Klang tone / Get Carter / 1000 miles an hour / Percolations / Seeperbold / Check and double check / Munich madness / Metronumero underground / Incredible He-woman.
Oct 02. (d-cd) *Strange Fruit; (SFRSCD 111)* **ABC MUSIC: THE RADIO 1 SESSIONS**

STEREOPHONICS

Formed: Cwmaman, Mid-Glamorgan, Wales . . . late 80's as The TRAGIC LOVE COMPANY by songwriter KELLY JONES, RICHARD JONES and STUART CABLE, initially treading the boards as a teenage covers band. The trio proved they were more than capable of spearheading Richard Branson's new 'V2' label with the release of debut single, 'LOOKS LIKE CHAPLIN', a melodic riffathon that had more in common with trad 70's rock and Seattle grunge than the still dominant Britpop. A Spring '97 follow-up, 'LOCAL BOY IN THE PHOTOGRAPH', came within breathing distance of the Top 50, a dizzying amalgam of the MANICS, RADIOHEAD, OASIS and BUFFALO TOM that managed to sound simultaneously contemporary and classic. JONES confirmed his newfound status as one of Britain's most promising young songwriters as The STEREOPHONICS embarked on an impressive chart run with the Top 40-breaking 'MORE LIFE IN A TRAMP'S VEST'. Late summer saw them nudge closer to the Top 20 with 'A THOUSAND TREES', the opening track on debut album, 'WORD GETS AROUND'. A massive selling UK Top 10 success, the record featured in the upper reaches of many end-of-year polls, helping to net the band a Brit Award (Best New Group) in early '98. Having seen out '97 with the moody magnificence of 'TRAFFIC', JONES and Co began the new year with a Top 20 re-issue of 'LOCAL BOY' prior to a summer of heavy touring. Towards Christmas, The STEREOPHONICS became a household name with Top 3 hit, 'THE BARTENDER & THE THIEF', proving that despite the continued predictions of its imminent demise, good old fashioned guitar-rock and solid songwriting was alive and well in Wales. The following year saw the trio peak both critically and commercially, three massive hits, 'JUST LOOKING', 'PICK A PART THAT'S NEW' and 'I WOULDN'T BELIEVE YOUR RADIO', all squeezed out of an excellent sophomore set, 'PERFORMANCE AND COCKTAILS' (1999). Welsh pop idol, TOM JONES, also called up the services of his fellow countrymen to duet with him on a Top 10 hit of 'Mama Told Me Not To Come'. Everyone's favourite trad-rockers returned in 2001 with 'JUST ENOUGH EDUCATION TO PERFORM', the record's title engendering an unlikely bout of controversy when the band – much to car manufacturer Daimler-Chrysler's disapproval – attempted to abbreviate it to 'J.E.E.P.'. Needless to say, this episode was more unpredictable than any of the meat and potatoes fare on offer within. Which isn't to say The STEREOPHONICS are worthy but dull, just that their acoustic-laced melodic rock lends itself to daytime radio play annoyingly well. Once again, JONES proved himself a master of rock classicism, taking his inspiration from the choicest, most authentic sounding 60's/70's moments and infusing them with the deftest of rootsy flourishes. Thus, try as you might to resist, singles such as 'STEP ON MY OLD SIZE NINES' and the breezy 'HAVE A NICE DAY' slowly but surely shoehorned their way into your consciousness much like that Top Gear compilation your dad used to play. While JONES is a writer who is undoubtedly maturing with age, he still lacks that strain of rugged individuality that marks out a ROD STEWART or a JOHN FOGERTY – 'HANDBAGS & GLADRAGS' indeed. • **Covered:** SUNNY AFTERNOON (Kinks) / POSITIVELY 4th STREET (Bob Dylan) / SOMETHING IN THE WAY (Nirvana) / THE OLD LAUGHING LADY + HEART OF GOLD (Neil Young) / FIRST TIME EVER I SAW YOUR FACE (Ewan MacColl) / I'M ONLY SLEEPING (Beatles) / HANDBAGS & GLADRAGS (Mike D'Abo).

Album rating: WORD GETS AROUND (*7) / PERFORMANCE AND COCKTAILS (*8) / JUST ENOUGH EDUCATION TO PERFORM (*7)

KELLY JONES (b. 3 Jun'74, Aberdare, Wales) – vocals, guitar / **RICHARD JONES** (b.23 May'74, Aberdare) – bass / **STUART CABLE** (b.19 May'70, Aberdare) – drums

		V2	V2

Nov 96. (7") (SPH 1) **LOOKS LIKE CHAPLIN. / MORE LIFE IN A TRAMP'S VEST**
(cd-s+=) (SPHD 1) – Raymond's shop.

Mar 97. (7") (SPH 2) **LOCAL BOY IN THE PHOTOGRAPH. / TWO MANY SANDWICHES** [51]
(cd-s+=) (SPHD 2) – Buy myself a small plane.

May 97. (7") (SPH 4) **MORE LIFE IN A TRAMP'S VEST. / RAYMOND'S SHOP** [33]
(cd-s+=) (SPHD 4) – Poppy day.
(cd-s) (SPHDX 4) – ('A'side) / Looks like Chaplin (live) / Too many sandwiches (live) / Last of the big time drinkers (live).

Aug 97. (7"/c-s) (VVR 500044-7/-5) **A THOUSAND TREES. / CARROT CAKE AND WINE** [22]
(cd-s+=) (VVR 500044-3) – ('A'live).
(cd-s) (VVR 500044-8) – ('A'acoustic) / Home to me (acoustic) / Looks like Chaplin (acoustic) / Summertime (acoustic).

Aug 97. (cd/c/lp) (VVR 100043-2/-4/-9) <27006> **WORD GETS AROUND** [6]
– A thousand trees / Looks like Chaplin / More life in a tramps vest / Local boy in the photograph / Traffic / Not up to you / Check my eyelids for holes / Same size feet / Last of the big time drinkers / Goldfish bowl / Too many sandwiches / Billy Daveys daughter.

Nov 97. (7"/c-s) (VVR 500094-7/-5) **TRAFFIC. / TIE ME UP TIE ME DOWN** [20]
(cd-s+=) (VVR 500094-3) – Chris Chambers / ('A'version).
(cd-s) (VVR 500094-8) – ('A'live) / More life in a tramp's vest (live) / A thousand trees (live) / Local boy in the photograph (live).

Feb 98. (7"/c-s) (VVR 500126-7/-5) **LOCAL BOY IN THE PHOTOGRAPH (remix). / WHO'LL STOP THE RAIN** [14]
(cd-s+=) (VVR 500126-3) – Check my eyelids for holes / ('A'-CD-Rom video).
(cd-s) (VVR 500126-8) – ('A'side) / Not up to you (live in session) / The last resort / Traffic (CD-rom video live).

Nov 98. (7"/c-s) (VVR 500467-7/-5) **THE BARTENDER AND THE THIEF. / SHE TAKES HER CLOTHES OFF** [3]
(cd-s+=) (VVR 500465-3) – Fiddler's green.
(cd-s) (VVR 500466-3) – ('A'live) / Traffic (live) / Raymond's shop (live).

Feb 99. (7"/c-s) (VVR 500532-7/-5) **JUST LOOKING. / POSTMEN DO NOT GREAT MOVIE HEROES MAKE (featuring Marco Migliani)** [4]
(cd-s+=) (VVR 500530-3) – Sunny afternoon.
(cd-s) (VVR 500530-0) – ('A'side) / Local boy in the photograph (live) / Same size feet (live).

Mar 99. (cd/c/lp) (VVR 100449-2/-4/-9) <27052> **PERFORMANCE AND COCKTAILS** [1] May99
– Roll up and shine / The bartender and the thief / Hurry up and wait / Pick a part that's new / Just looking / Half the lies you tell ain't true / I wouldn't believe your radio / T-shirt sun tan / Is yesterday, tomorrow, today? / A minute longer / She takes her clothes off / Plastic California / I stopped to fill my car up. (special cd+=; VVR 100449-8)

May 99. (7"/c-s) (VVR 500677-7/-5) **PICK A PART THAT'S NEW. / NICE TO BE OUT (demo)** [4]
(cd-s+=) (VVR 500677-3) – Positively 4th street / ('A'-CD-Rom video).
(cd-s) (VVR 500677-8) – ('A'acoustic) / In my day / Something in the way.

Aug 99. (7"/c-s) (VVR 500882-7/-5) **I WOULDN'T BELIEVE YOUR RADIO. / THE BARTENDER AND THE THIEF (bar version)** [11]
(cd-s+=) (VVR 500882-3) – The old laughing lady.
(cd-s) (VVR 500882-8) – ('A'live) / Pick a part that's new (live) / T-shirt suntan (live).

Nov 99. (7"/c-s) (VVR 500932-7/-5) **HURRY UP AND WAIT. / ANGIE** [11]
(cd-s+=) (VVR 500932-3) – I wouldn't believe your radio.
(cd-s) (VVR 500932-8) – ('A'live) / I stopped to fill my car up (live) / Billy Davey's daughter (live) / ('A'-video).

—— In Mar'00, the STEREOPHONICS were credited on TOM JONES' UK Top 5 smash, 'Mama Told Me Not To Come'

May 00. (cd-ep) <70041> **T-SHIRT SUNTAN EP**
– I wouldn't believe your radio / The bartender and the thief / Sunny afternoon / Positively 4th Street / Tie me up, tie me down.

—— In Sep'00, KELLY JONES collaborated with MANCHILD on their UK Top 60 hit, 'The Cliches Are True'

Mar 01. (7"/c-s) (VVR 501593-7/-5) **MR. WRITER. / MARITIM BELLE VUE IN KIEL** [5]
(cd-s+=) (VVR 501593-3) – An audience with Mr. Nice.
(cd-s) (VVR 501593-8) – ('A'-live acoustic) / Hurry up and wait (live acoustic) / Don't let me down (live acoustic).

Apr 01. (cd/c/lp) (VVR 101583-2/-4/-1) <27092> **JUST ENOUGH EDUCATION TO PERFORM** [1]
– Vegas two times / Lying in the sun / Mr. Writer / Step on my old size nines / Have a nice day / Nice to be out / Watch them fly Sundays / Everyday I think of money / Maybe / Caravan holiday / Rooftop. (cd re-iss. Nov01; VVR 101829-2)

Jun 01. (7"/c-s) (VVR 501624-7/-4) **HAVE A NICE DAY. / SURPRISE** [5]
(cd-s+=) (VVR 501624-3) – Piano for a stripper (demo).
(cd-s) (VVR 501624-8) – ('A'live acoustic) / Heart of gold (live acoustic) / I stopped to fill my car up (live acoustic).

Sep 01. (c-s) (VVR 501625-5) **STEP ON MY OLD SIZE NINES / SHOESHINE BOY** [16]
(cd-s+=) (VVR 501625-3) – I'm only sleeping / ('A'-CD-Rom).
(cd-s) (VVR 501625-8) – ('A'side) / Everyday I think of money / Just looking / ('A'live video).

Dec 01. (7"/c-s) (VVR 501775-7/-5) **HANDBAGS AND GLADRAGS. / FIRST TIME EVER I SAW YOUR FACE** [4]
(cd-s+=) (VVR 501775-3) – How.
(cd-s) (VVR 501775-8) – ('A'live) / Caravan holiday (live) / Nice to be out (live).

Apr 02. (7") (VVR 501917-7) **VEGAS TWO TIMES. / VEGAS TWO TIMES (live)** [23]
(cd-s) (VVR 501917-3) – ('A'side) / Mr Writer (live) / Watch them fly Sundays (live).

STEREO TOTAL

Formed: Adalbertsrasse, Berlin, Germany . . . 1993 by FRANCOISE CACTUS and BREZEL GORING. While the former had previously played with French femme-punks The LOLITAS, GORING had cut a number of obscure cut'n'paste albums as The SIGMUND FREUD EXPERIENCE. Scottish guitarist LESLEY CAMPBELL joined up in time for a 1995 debut EP and the cosmopolitan crew really began making waves with the release of the 'OH AH!' (1996) album. Drawing their scattershot inspiration from punk, French chanson, electro, hip-hop, classic 60's pop and literally any source that fired their Europhile imagination, the group's kitschy cut-ups were blessed/cursed with a uniquely European sense of humour. Songs about pissed-off cats and daydreaming secretaries were the order of the day, the latter getting off on a clacking typewriter hook. By the time of the record's release, Palestinian IZNOGOOD had also signed up, while ANGIE REED, came on board for 1997's 'MONOKINI' LP. The cream of the group's work to date was collected together for the listening pleasure of British and American fans on 'STEREO TOTAL' (1998), a winning blend of tacky originals and tongue-in-cheek covers including K.C. & The Sunshine Band's 'GET DOWN TONIGHT', Harpo's 'MOVIE STAR', Salt'n'Pepa's 'PUSH IT' and Serge Gainsbourg's 'JE SUIS VENU TE DIRE QUE JE M'EN VAIS'. Hot Chocolate ('HEAVEN IS IN THE BACK SEAT OF MY CADILLAC') were also given the STEREO TOTAL treatment on 1998's 'JUKEBOX ALARM' album, another riotous pile-up of pop detritus condensed into refreshingly short salvos such as 'COMICSTRIPTEASEGIRL' and 'TOUCHE-MOI'. While 1999's 'MY MELODY' (more covers, including The Beatles' 'DRIVE MY CAR' and Pizzicato 5's 'TOKYO MON AMOUR') looked like the end of the road, what with FRANCOISE going off to write another novel, the core duo of CACTUS and GORING re-emerged in 2001 with the sleeker 'MUSIQUE AUTOMATIQUE'. Eschewing the lo-fi, home recording approach of old for a more professional production, the group took their maverick, magpie sound to places it was possibly never designed to go, presumably alienating some older fans but no doubt pulling in many new ones.

Album rating: OH AH! (*5) / MONOKINI (*5) / STEREO TOTAL compilation (*5) / MY MELODY (*6) / JUKE-BOX ALARM (*5) / TOTAL POP compilation (*7) / MUSIQUE AUTOMATIQUE (*4)

FRANCOISE CACTUS (b. France) – vocals, drums (ex-LOLITAS) / **BREZEL GORING** (b. BREZEL FINSTERWALDE, Germany) – vocals, guitars, organ, synthesizer / **LESLEY CAMPBELL** (b. Scotland) – guitar / guest **IZNOGOOD** (b. Palestine) – bass-balls-bass

                                                                Desert   not iss.
1995.   (7"ep) **ALLO J'ECOUTE.** /
                                                              Bungalow   not iss.
Dec 95. (lp) *(BUNG 004LP)* **OH AH!**   – German
  – Dactylo rock / C'est la mort / Miau miau / Comme un garcon / Belami / Johnny / Morose / Je suis venu te dire que je m'en vais / Push it / Souvenir souvenir / Auf dem blauen meer / Movie star / A l'amour comme a la guerre / Get down tonight / Dans le parc / Epitaph / Moi je joue. *(UK-iss.Dec00 & Mar02 cd/lp; efa 61504-2/-1)*

───── **ANGIE REED** – guitar; repl. LESLEY
1997.   (lp) *(BUNG 011LP)* **MONOKINI**   – German
  – Ach ach liebling / Lanatique / Supergirl / Furore / Schon Von Hinten / Dlindam / Cosmonaute / Aua / Und wer wird sich mich kummern? / Tu m'as volue / Moustique / LA, Ca, USA / L'appareil a sous / Grand prix Eurovision / Ushilo sugata ga kilei. *(UK-iss.Nov00 & Mar02 cd/lp; efa 61511-2/-1)*
1997.   (cd-s) **SCHON VON HINTEN** (mixes; original / Rimini) / **THE OTHER SIDE OF YOU / SCHON VON HINTEN** (mixes; Halb / Sons of '68 & Jan Bontempi / version)
                                                              Bobsled   Bobsled – German

Sep 98. (cd) (<*BOB 003CD*> **STEREO TOTAL** (compilation)
  – Dactylo rock / C'est la mort / Furore / Schon Von Hinten / Movie star / LA, Ca, USA / Get down tonight / Comme un garcon / Ach ach leibling / Push it / Miau miau / Supergirl / Ushilo sugata ga kilei / Johnny / Morose / Dillindam / Je suis venu te dire que je m'en vais.

───── added **SAN REIMO** – organ, vocals
1999.   (7") **BEAUTYCASE.** /
1999.   (cd) <*BOB 008CD*> **MY MELODY**
  – Beautycase / I love you, Ono / Plotzlich ist alles anders / Larmes toxiques / Disc jockey / Ich liebe dich, Alexander / Tout le monde se fout des fleurs / Vilaines filles, mauvais garcons / Sous la douche / Du und dein automobil / Partir ou mourir / Ringo, I love you / Tokyo, mon amour / Milky boy bourgeois / Die krise / Joe le taxi / Tu peux conduire ma bagnole / In/out. *(UK-iss.Jul00 & Mar02 on 'Bungalow' cd/lp; efa 61565-2/-1)*
Dec 99. (cd) <*BOB 009CD*> **JUKE-BOX ALARM**
  – Holiday inn / Comicstripteasegirl / Sweet Charlotte / Touche-moi / Crazy horse / Supercool / Les minets / Oh yeah / Film d'horreur / Vertigo / Heaven is in the back seat of my Cadillac / Der schlussel / Nouvelle vague / Party anticonformiste / Holiday out. *(UK-iss.Mar02 on 'Bungalow' cd/lp; efa 61535-2/-1)*

───── now down to **CACTUS + GORING** (ANGIE REED went solo)
                                                              Bungalow Bobsled
Oct 01. (7"ep/cd-ep) **LOVE WITH THE THREE OF US**
Nov 01. (cd) <*BOB 024CD*> **MUSIQUE AUTOMATIQUE**
  – Automatic music / L'amour A3 / Ma radio / Wir tanzen in 4-eck / Les chansons d'a / Kleptomane / Adieu adieu / Forever 16 / Je suis une pouppe / Ich weiss nicht mehr genou / Le diable Nationale 7 / Exakt neutral / Ypsilon / Hep onalti'da / Love with the 3 of us. *<re-iss. Oct02 on 'Kill Rock Stars'+=; KRS 392CD>* – I think somebody should call the love police / Je reve encore de toi / The monster / Untranslatable / Wir tanzen komplixiert.
Mar 02. (12") *(efa 61599-6)* **WIR TANZEN IM VIER ECK** (remixes; Christopher Just extended / Brezel Goring / Felix Kubin / Bis / Candle Hank)   – German

            – compilations, etc. –
Feb 00. (cd) *Cherry Red;* (<*ANALOG 005CD*>) **TOTAL POP**
  – Push it / Moviestar / A l'amour comme a la guerre / Get down tonight / Comme un garcon / Moi je joue / Supergirl / Schon Von Hinten / Dilindam / Cosmonaute / Und der wird sich um mich kummen / Moustique / Holiday inn / Crazy horse / Supercool / Heaven is in the back seat of my Cadillac / Nouvelle vague / Party anticonformiste / I love you, Ono / Plotzlich ist, alles anders / Tout le monde se fout des fleurs / Partir du mourir / Ringo, I love you / Die krise. *(re-iss. Jun02; same)*

ST. ETIENNE (see under ⇒ **SAINT ETIENNE**)

STEWARD (see under ⇒ **BOYRACER**)

ST*JOHNNY

Formed: Hartford, Connecticut, USA . . . 1990 by BILL WHITTEN, TOM LEONARD, JIM ELLIOTT and WAYNE LETITIA. The group released a 7"-only single on their own label 'Asthma' records (and a second for 'Ajax') before engaging in a major label war between 'Geffen' and 'Caroline', the former getting their most wanted. Despite this, 'Caroline' issued a compilation of the two breakthrough indie EPs alongside a collection of previously unreleased songs named 'HIGH AS A KITE'. 1994 then saw the release of 'SPEED IS DREAMING', a beautiful blend of sparkling DINOSAUR JR inspired songs mixed in with lowdown filthy punk. The group subsequently recorded another album, 'LET IT COME DOWN' (1995), which received little attention despite being a sweeping melodic rock record originally intended for indie fans – although sweet sweeping spectators surprisingly gave it the proverbial thumbs up. The following year, WHITTEN reappeared with the 4-piece glam-rockin', GRAND MAL (not to be confused with 1985 'Fountain Of Youth' act or mid-90's 'Magma' dance outfit), a 1996 US-only eponymous EP being slightly upstaged by two full-sets, 'PLEASURE IS NO FUN' (1997) and 'MALEDICTIONS' (1999).

Album rating: HIGH AS A KITE (*5) / SPEED IS DREAMING (*6) / LET IT COME DOWN (*7) / Grand Mal: GRAND MAL mini (*5) / PLEASURE IS NO FUN (*6) / MALEDICTIONS (*5)

BILL WHITTEN – vocals, guitar, effects / **TOM LEONARD** – guitar, vocals, Moog synthesizer / **JIM ELLIOTT** – bass, guitar, keyboards / **WAYNE LETITIA** – drums, percussion
                                                                 not iss.   Asthma
1991.   (7"ep) <none> **4 SONGS EP (aka MY PAPER ROUTE)**
                                                                 not iss.   Ajax
1992.   (7"ep) **GO TO SLEEP.** / **HIGHWAY**
                                                              Rough Trade Caroline
Feb 93. (cd/lp) *(R 296-6/-5)* <*CAROL 1744*> **HIGH AS A KITE**   Aug93
  (compilation plus)
  – Go to sleep / God in my head / Highway / Velocity / My father's father / Matador / Black / Stupid / High as a kite / Ashes – Slashes / Unclean.
                                                                 Geffen   D.G.C.
Aug 93. (7") *(45REV 21)* **UNCLEAN.** / **GOD IN MY HEAD**
Nov 93. (7") *(GFS 59)* **A CAR OR A BOY.** / **BLACK**
Jan 94. (cd/c/lp) <(*GED/GEC/GEF 24534*)> **SPEED IS DREAMING**
  – A car or a boy / I hate rock and roll / Down the drain / I give up / What was I supposed to see / Devil's last stand / You're not my friend / You can't win / Gran Mal / Everything is beautiful / Black eye / Turbine / Stupid.

───── **WHITTEN + ELLIOTT** enlisted **JIM ROBERTS** – guitar, vocals / **JOE ROBERTS** – harmonica, slide guitar / plus **DAVE FRIDMANN** – keyboards (of MERCURY REV)
1995.   (cd/c) <*GED/GEC 24801*> **LET IT COME DOWN**
  – Scuba diving / Just when I had it under control / Bluebird / Pin the tail on the donkey / Hey teenager! / Rip off / Deliver me / Fast, cheap and out of control / After dark / Wild goose chasing / Do you wanna go out? / Million dollar bet / Salvation arm.

───── disbanded after above

GRAND MAL

BILL WHITTEN with **CARMEN LUZ QUINONES** – vocals / **JEFF MERCEL** – drums; repl. J BRYAN BOWDEN (ex-16 DELUXE) / + **DAVE FRIDMANN** – bass, piano, producer (of MERCURY REV)
                                                                 not iss. Number 6
Mar 96. (m-cd) <*37*> **GRAND MAL**
  – Hard to beat / Flyin' high / Crawling through the glass / Kill yer pain / I didn't know / Don't mean nothin'.

───── **JOHN DeVRIES** – bass, guitars, samples (ex-AGIT POP) repl. MERCEL / + guests **GRASSHOPPER** – guitars (of MERCURY REV) + **PHIL SCHUSTER** – bass
Sep 97. (cd) <*42*> **PLEASURE IS NO FUN**
  – I'm in trouble / Give yourself to the Devil / Whole lotta nuthin' / Quittin' time / Lucky stiffs / LIght as a feather / Superstars / Cold as a donor / Blow your nose / Thing to do / Don't be late.

───── **WHITTEN + DeVRIES** recruited **STEVE BORGERDING** – bass (ex-DWARVES) + **PARKER KINDERED** – drums (ex-JEFF BUCKLEY)
───── added 5th member **JONATHAN TOUBIN** – keyboards
                                                                  Slash   Slash
Nov 98. (cd-s) *(LASCD 66)* **WHOLE LOTTA NOTHING / LIFE'S A GAS / JOHNNY JACK**
Nov 99. (cd) *(8573 80843-2)* <*314 556 015*> **MALEDICTIONS**   Feb99
  – Superstars / Whole lotta nothing / Out on bail / Sixteen / Stay in bed / I'm in trouble / Picture you (as always falling) / Fun fun fun / Whizz kid / You gotta be kidding / Sucker's bet / Leave me here.

───── GRAND MAL are about to return in early 2003

J.J. STONE (see under ⇒ **GALLON DRUNK**)

STOOR (see under ⇒ **SPARE SNARE**)

Los STRAITJACKETS

Formed: Nashville, Tennesee, USA . . . mid 1988 as The STRAITJACKETS by main songwriter EDDIE ANGEL, LES JAMES "L.J." LESTER and DANNY AMIS. While this original trio never actually recorded anything, their inimitable brand of instrumental twang was blueprinted through a series of live shows and put on ice until the mid-90's. With the addition of E. SCOTT ESBECK, the group changed 'The' to 'Los', donned Mexican wrestling masks and set about perfecting their kitschy guitar instrumentals. Albums such as 'THE UTTERLY FANTASTIC AND TOTALLY UNBELIEVABLE SOUND OF LOS STRAITJACKETS' (1995), 'VIVA LOS STRAITJACKETS' (1996) and 'THE VELVET TOUCH OF LOS STRAITJACKETS' (1999) featured artfully yet affectionately crafted pieces inspired by everyone from DICK DALE and The VENTURES to ENNIO MORRICONE and classic Mexican Mariachi. LOS STRAITJACKETS are still riding the surf post-millennium, further rambunctious sets 'DAMAS Y CABALLEROS! . . .' (2001) and 'SING ALONG WITH' (2001), have stated the obvious that rock'n'roll (with a indie slant) is here to stay. • **Trivia:** BEN VAUGHN produced and appeared on most of their LPs.

Album rating: THE UTTERLY FANTASTIC AND TOTALLY UNBELIEVABLE SOUND OF LOS STRAITJACKETS (*5) / VIVA LOS STRAITJACKETS (*7) / THE VELVET TOUCH OF LOS STRAITJACKETS (*5) / DAMAS Y CABALLEROS! (*6) / SING ALONG WITH . . . (*5) / 'TIS THE SEASON FOR (*5)

EDDIE ANGEL – guitar / **DANNY AMIS** – guitar / **LES JAMES "L.J." LESTER** – drums / added **E. SCOTT ESBECK** – bass
                                                                 not iss. Sympathy F
Feb 95. (7") **GATECRASHER.** / **LONELY APACHE**

Los STRAITJACKETS (cont)

			Upstart	Upstart
Apr 95.	(cd) <(UPSTARTCD 8015)>	**THE UTTERLY FANTASTIC AND TOTALLY UNBELIEVABLE SOUND OF LOS STRAITJACKETS**	□	Mar95

– Fury! / G-man / Straightjacket / Jetty motel / Carhop / Caveman / Tailspin / University Blvd. / Gatecrusher / Itchy chicken / Della Street / Calhoun surf / Rampage / Lynxtail.

Nov 96.	(cd-s) <5>	**A MARSHMALLOW WORLD / SLEIGH RIDE / OUTTA GEAR**	–	□

When! / Upstart

Aug 96.	(cd) (WENCD 014) <UPSTARTCD 031>	**VIVA LOS STRAITJACKETS**	□	Aug96

– Cavalcade / Casbah / Wrong planet / Lonely Apache / Outta gear / Pacifica / Espionage / Swamp fire / Lawnmower / Lurking in the shadows / Brans and eggs / Venturing out / Tsunami! / Nightmare in Monte Cristo.

Yep Roc / Yep Roc

Aug 99.	(cd/lp) <(YEP 2013 CD/LP)>	**THE VELVET TOUCH OF LOS STRAITJACKETS**	□	□

– Kawanga! / Rockula / Close to Champaign / Hornet's nest / My heart will go on (love theme from . . . .) / Tempest / Tijuana boots / Sing, sing / Tabouli / Sterno / State fair / All that glitters.

Apr 01.	(cd) <YEP 2025CD>	**DAMAS Y CABALLEROS!**	□	Feb01

– Introduction of Los Straitjackets / Outta gear / State fair / Casbah / Calhoun surf / Itchy chicken / Last date / Kawanga! / I'm branded / My heart will go on (love theme from . . . .) / Squad car / Rockula / Tempest / Lynxtail / Tailspin / Pacifica / Driving guitars / Sing sing sing / Sleepwalk / Rawhide.

Evangeline / Yep Roc

Sep 01.	(cd) (GEL 4031) <YEP 2028CD>	**SING ALONG WITH . . .**	□	□

– Black is black / Chica alborotada – Tallahassee lassie / Treat her right / I ain't the one / Down the line / Rey Criollo / King Creole / California sun / I'll go down swinging / La suegra – Mother in law / Bumble bee / Shake that rat / The end of the world / A huevo.

Oct 02.	(cd) <YEP 2041>	**'TIS THE SEASON FOR . . .** (festive)	–	□

STRANGELOVE

Formed: Bristol, England . . . 1991 by PATRICK DUFF and ALEX LEE (ex-BLUE AEROPLANES), who subsequently recruited JULIAN-PRANSKY POOLE, JOE ALLEN and DAVE FRANCOLINI (of LEVITATION), the latter promptly replaced by JOHN LANGLEY. Debuting with the 'VISIONARY' EP on the independent 'Sermon' label and following it up with the acclaimed 'HYSTERIA UNKNOWN' single, the band's portentous, pseudo-goth rumblings combined with DUFF's miserabilist charisma engendered a major label signing rush. 'Food-E.M.I.' were the lucky recipients of the band's signature, releasing the morose debut album, 'TIME FOR THE REST OF YOUR LIFE' in summer '94. Hardly the success they might have hoped for, the album struggled to make the Top 75 despite some favourable reviews, STRANGELOVE's reputation among the media for being humourless and po-faced not helping them any. Previewed by the group's first Top 40 hit, 'BEAUTIFUL ALONE', 1996's follow-up set, 'LOVE AND OTHER DEMONS', continued in much the same vein with mainstream indie success continuing to elude them. Despite the sentiments of the self-loathing 'FREAK' single, a newly rehabilitated (from alcohol that is) DUFF emerged with something approaching a sense of wellbeing on 1997's eponymous 'STRANGELOVE'. Considerably more accessible and upbeat than any of the band's material to date, tracks such as 'RUNAWAY BROTHERS' and 'SOMEDAY SOON' suggested that there'd always been an indie-pop element to STRANGELOVE's goth laments, though this was hardly The BOO RADLEYS. Yet again, the record struggled to make any impact on the charts, STRANGELOVE seemingly destined to be the perpetual outsiders of 'New Grave'. • **Songwriters:** Group penned except MOTORPSYCHO NITEMARE (Bob Dylan) / IF I CAN DREAM (Skunk Anansie). • **Trivia:** Produced by ANGELO BRUSCHINI also ex-BLUE AEROPLANES.

Album rating: TIME OUT FOR THE REST OF YOUR LIFE (*7) / LOVE AND OTHER DEMONS (*6) / STRANGELOVE (*6)

PATRICK DUFF – vocals / **ALEX LEE** – guitar (ex-BLUE AEROPLANES, ex-JAZZ BUTCHER) / **JOHN LANGLEY** – drums (ex-BLUE AEROPLANES) / **JOE ALLEN** – vocals, rhythm guitar (ex-RODNEY ALLEN EXPERIENCE) / **JULIAN PRANSKY-POOLE** – bass (ex-JAZZ BUTCHER)

Sermon / not iss.

Oct 92.	(12"ep) (SERT 001)	**VISIONARY / FRONT. / CHANCES / SNAKES**	□	–
Feb 93.	(7") (SER 002)	**HYSTERIA UNKNOWN. / MY DARK**	□	–

(12"+=/cd-s+=) (SERT 002/+CD) – Walls / Sea.

Rough Trade / not iss.

Sep 93.	(7") (45REV 18)	**ZOO'D OUT. / CIRCLES**	□	–

Food-EMI / not iss.

Jun 94.	(7") (FOOD 49)	**TIME FOR THE REST OF YOUR LIFE. / IT'S SO EASY**	□	–

(12"+=/cd-s+=) (12/CD FOOD 49) – Motorpsycho nitemare.

Aug 94.	(cd/c/d-lp) (FOOD CD/TC/LP 11)	**TIME FOR THE REST OF YOUR LIFE**	69	–

– Sixer / Time for the rest of your life / Quiet day / Sand / I will burn / Low life / World outside / The return of the real me / All because of you / Fire (show me light) / Hopeful / Kite / Is there a place?. (cd re-iss. Sep97; same)

Oct 94.	(12"ep/cd-ep) (12/CD FOOD 55)	**IS THERE A PLACE? / SAND. / NOBODY'S THERE / THE KING OF SOMEWHERE ELSE**	□	–
Apr 96.	(7") (FOOD 70)	**LIVING WITH HUMAN MACHINES. / MR. HONEY CATCHER**	53	–

(cd-s+=) (CDFOODS 70) – Killing time.
(cd-s) (CDFOOD 70) – ('A'side) / Hysteria unknown / Chances / My dark.

Jun 96.	(7") (FOOD 81)	**BEAUTIFUL ALONE / VISIONARY**	35	–

(cd-s+=) (CDFOODS 81) – Zoo'd out / Sea.
(cd-s) (CDFOOD 81) – Wolf's story part I / Wolf's story part II / Wolf's story part III.

Jun 96.	(cd/c/lp) (FOOD CD/TC/LP 15)	**LOVE AND OTHER DEMONS**	44	–

– Casualties / Spiders and flies / Living with the human machines / She's everywhere / Sway / Beautiful alone / Elin's photograph / 20th century cold / 1432 / The sea of black.

Oct 96.	(7") (FOOD 82)	**SWAY / HOLD ON**	47	–

(cd-s+=) (CDFOODS 82) – Nowhere days / Ghost haddock.
(cd-s) (CDFOOD 82) – 20th century cold (live acoustic) / Moon river (live acoustic) / She's everywhere (live).

— added **NICK POWELL** – keyboards

Jul 97.	(7"white) (FOOD 97)	**THE GREATEST SHOW ON EARTH. / LIVING WITH THE HUMAN MACHINES (loop mix)**	36	–

(cd-s) (CDFOODS 97) – ('A'side) / Couples / Crofters / Ascension day.
(cd-s) (CDFOOD 97) – ('A'side) / Elin's photograph (live acoustic) / Spiders and flies (live acoustic) / If I can dream (live acoustic).

Sep 97.	(7"clear) (FOOD 105)	**FREAK. / THE FREAK**	43	–

(cd-s) (CDFOODS 105) – ('A'side) / The city song / King of the real men.
(cd-s) (CDFOOD 105) – ('A'side) / The Devil you know / Bethlehem.

Oct 97.	(cd/c/d-lp) (FOOD CD/TC/LP 24)	**STRANGELOVE**	67	–

– Superstar / Freak / Someday soon / Wellington Road / The runaway brothers / Another night in / The greatest show on Earth / Little Queenie / She's on fire / Mona Lisa / Jennifer's song.

Feb 98.	(7"red) (FOOD 110)	**ANOTHER NIGHT IN. / ANOTHER ANOTHER NIGHT IN**	46	–

(cd-s) (CDFOODS 110) – ('A'side) / The last great rock'n'roll queen / Extract from journal No.17th 1997.
(cd-s) (CDFOODS 110) – ('A'side) / The drinker / Measured in blood.

— STRANGELOVE split after above; ALEX LEE joined SUEDE

Syd STRAW

Born: Los Angeles, California, USA. The daughter of actor, Jack Straw, SYD headed for New York after leaving school and eventually landed session work for PAT BENATAR. The mid-80's saw her working with the loose alternative collective, The GOLDEN PALOMINOS, appearing on the albums, 'Visions Of Excess' and 'Blast Of Silence', although it wasn't until 1989 that the singer would record an album of her own material. Released on 'Virgin', 'SURPRISE' featured a guestlist that read like a who's who of critical faves including VAN DYKES PARKS, RY COODER, MICHAEL STIPE and RICHARD THOMPSON. Nevertheless, as any Hollywood executive knows, the big names don't always pull in the punters and as the album sank into obscurity, STRAW busied herself with other projects. Seven years went by before the release of 'WAR AND PEACE' (1996), a belated sophomore effort released on the recently reactivated 'Capricorn' label ('Mercury' in the UK) and featuring musical backing from the SKELETONS i.e. DON THOMPSON, LOU WHITNEY, KELLY BROWN and JOE TERRY. Confirming her talents as a painfully honest and insightful singer/songwriter, the record was full of rootsy odes to lost love and missed opportunities that functioned perfectly as a soundtrack for crying into your proverbial beer. When not putting her emotional life under the scalpel, STRAW was as busy as ever with other artists, working with the likes of VIC CHESNUTT and WILCO amongst others.

Album rating: SURPRISE (*7) / WAR AND PEACE (*6)

SYD STRAW – vocals (ex-GOLDEN PALOMINOS) / with a plethora of session people incl. VAN DYKE PARKS, RICHARD THOMPSON, RY COODER, MICHAEL STIPE, ANTON FIER, MARSHALL CRENSHAW, DON WAS, PETER BLEGVAD, PETER HOLSAPPLE, BENMONT TENCH, MARC RIBOT, DAVE ALVIN, MATT IRVING, BERNIE WORRELL, J.D. FOSTER, TONY LEVIN, JOHN DOE, JERRY MAROTTA, JODY HARRIS, PINO PALLADINO, CHRIS STAMEY, MICHAEL BLAIR, JIM KELTNER, ERIC AMBEL, etc

Virgin America / Virgin

Jun 89.	(lp/c/cd) (VUSLP/VUSMC/CDVUS 6) <260110>	**SURPRISE**	□	□

– Think too hard / Heart of darkness / Chasing vapor trails (this turn to cry) / Almost magic / Crazy American / Hard times / Future 40's (string of pearls) / The unanswered question / Sphinx / Racing the ruins / Golden dreams.

Sep 89.	(7") (VUS 6)	**FUTURE 40'S (STRING OF PEARLS). / TAKEN**	□	–

(12"+=/3"cd-s+=) (VUS T/CD 6) – Learning the game.

Jan 90.	(7") (VUS 16)	**THINK TOO HARD. / HARD TIMES**	□	–

(12"+=/cd-s+=) (VUS T/CD 16) – If you don't want my love / Racing to the ruins.

— during her solo recording hiatus, she helped out VIC CHESNUTT, RICKIE LEE JONES, WILCO, LEMONHEADS, DAVID SANBORN, etc.

— now with The SKELETONS as backing:- **DON THOMPSON** – guitar / **LOU WHITNEY** – bass / **KELLY BROWN** + **JOE TERRY** – keyboards / **BOBBY HICKS** – drums

Mercury / Capricorn

Jun 96.	(cd-s) <MECP 143>	**CBGB'S / (+1)**	–	□
Oct 96.	(cd) <(532457-2)>	**WAR AND PEACE**	□	May96

– Toughest girl in the world / A million miles / Time has done this / Love, and the lack of it / CBGB's / All things change / Madrid / Almost as blue / Water, please / X-ray / Howl / Static / Black squirrel / Train that takes you away.

— SYD has been a little conspicuous by her absence

STRETCHHEADS

Formed: Paisley, Scotland . . . 1987 by ANDY and P6 ('DR. TECHNOLOGY' and 'FAT BASTARD'), adding MOFUNGO DIGGS and RICHIE DEMPSEY from their Paisley school days. Serving up a platter of fun hardcore (The EX were an early inspiration), The STRETCHHEADS were an unorthodox rock concept (they wore flashy shirts and balaclavas on stage!) in that Scots bands rarely ventured into this comic book grunge-esque genre (CHOU PAHROT eat your cage out!). Poking fun at number one pop act at the time, BROS, was indeed their first musical mission, 'BROS ARE PISH', being the debut EP in question. Early the following year, a full-set of weird ideas was unveiled via their debut set, 'FIVE FINGERS, FOUR THINGERS, A THUMB, A FACELIFT AND A NEW IDENTITY' (1989). Moving from Charles Cosh's 'Moshka' (once home of The SHAMEN) to top indie imprint 'Blast First' (and with MR JASON replacing DEMPSEY on drums), the zany quartet had three releases during a prolific early 90's spell. 'EYEBALL ORIGAMI AFTERMATH WIT VEGETARIAN LEG' was a fine ooh-ah! EP, while the danceable 12" '23 SKINNER (HAVE A BANG ON THIS NUMBER)' featured a sample from the American TV sitcom theme 'Rhoda', also present on their second fool-set (sic!), 'PISH IN YOUR SLEAZEBAG' (1991). However, by the time NIRVANA's 'Nevermind' had hit the shops that Autumn, the group were facing indie oblivion. In fact, it took another couple of years and a comeback 10"EP, 'BARBED ANAL EXCITER', before the band went to ground.

Album rating: FIVE FINGERS, FOUR THINGERS, A THUMB, A FACELIFT AND A NEW IDENTITY (*4) / PISH IN YOUR SLEAZEBAG (*6)

P6 'FAT BASTARD' – vocals / **ANDY 'DR. TECHNOLOGY'** – guitar / **MOFUNGO DIGGS** – bass / **RICHIE DEMPSEY** – drums

                                            Moshka   not iss.

Nov 88. (7"ep) *(SOMA 5)* **BROS ARE PISH EP**
- Bros are pish / I should be so lucky / Confront / Headache / Everything's going to break in a minute / Worry.

— **MAC** – bass; repl. MOFUNGO

Jan 89. (lp) *(SOMALP 2)* **FIVE FINGERS, FOUR THINGERS, A THUMB, A FACELIFT AND A NEW IDENTITY**
- Fans / Long faced German / Headache / Asylum suck / Skinrip / Yiddish yoddle / Shape + cleanse / Land of Ming / Rex perplexed / Semtex / I should be so lucky / Confront / Sidatorium / Spleng / Archive footage of a fish / Everything's going to brake in a minute / Illness / Cancer / Shut up. *(cd-iss. 1991; SOMACD 2)*

— **MR. JASON** – drums; repl. DEMPSEY who later surfaced with FENN and the PH FAMILY

                                        Blast First not iss.

Nov 90. (7"ep) *(BFFP 56)* **EYEBALL ORIGAMI AFTERMATH WIT VEGETARIAN LEG EP**
- Afghanistan bananastan / Incontinent of sex / Omnipresent octopus (Russell Grant) / New thing in Egypt (Boney M).

Jan 91. (12") *(BFFP 57T)* **23 SKINNER (HAVE A BANG ON THIS NUMBER).** /

Feb 91. (lp/c/cd) *(BFFP 58/+C/CD)* **PISH IN YOUR SLEAZEBAG**
- Space ape / Trippy deadzone / A freakout / Incontinent of sex / Crazy desert man / Housewife up yer fuckin' arse music / Machine in Delhi (Gary Newman's round the world trip) / Ognob / Acid Sweeney / Mao Tse Tungs meat challenge / Space jam / HMS average nostril / Pottery owls (with innuendo) / Hairy mousaka / Fly feast. *(cd+=)* – 23 skinner (the theme from 'Rhoda') / Afghanistan bananastan / Omnipresent octopus (Russell Grant) / New thing in Egypt (Boney M).

below was a posthumous release due to their demise

Jul 93. (10"ep) *(BFFP 68)* **BARBED ANAL EXCITER EP**
- (6 tracks).

— P6 subsequently turned up on a PH FAMILY release, 'Important Information' c.1997

STRICTLY BALLROOM

Formed: Los Angeles, California, USA . . . fall of 1994 by CHRIS GUNST, IAN MACKINNON, JIMMY TAMBORELLO, JIMMY HAY and PAUL LARSON. Former radio DJs with KXLU, the band's blend of hardcore and ambient electronica – showcased on their debut LP, 'HIDE HERE FOREVER' (1997) – led many in the alternative press to label the band's sound as "enocore"; owed to the legacy of sonic explorer, BRIAN ENO, the only release the quintet would issue under the STRICTLY BALLROOM moniker. This original release was put out by 'Waxploitation', but re-issued in 2001 by 'Better Looking', by which time the group had re-formed as ARCA. Between the band's two manifestations, the individual members took time to follow other musical projects. GUNST joined The BEACHWOOD SPARKS, while TAMBORELLO formed the electronica outfit, FIGURINE, trading himself as JAMES FIGURINE, alongside two other members, DAVID and MEREDITH. After releasing the EP, 'I WAIT FOR YOU' (1998), the trio issued their debut full-length outing, 'TRANSPORTATION + COMMUNICATION = LOVE' (1999), gaining them comparisons to German master electronic magicians, KRAFTWERK. The band did much of their recordings on computer alone, and sometimes in separate locations. An idiosyncratic style which they carried through to their sophomore release, 'THE HEARTFELT' (2001), a record that was a little too robotic. TAMBORELLO continued on his mission to encompass indiecore with left-field ambience via his DNTEL project, which initially got off the ground in the mid-90's with the EP, 'SOMETHING ALWAYS GOES WRONG'. Now with a tad more time on his hands, his sophomore set, 'LIFE IS FULL OF POSSIBILITIES' (2001) – his first was a compilation – featured guest spots from CHRIS GUNST (now of BEECHWOOD SPARKS), BEN GIBBARD (DEATH CAN FOR CUTIE) and MIA DOI TOD.

Album rating: HIDE HERE FOREVER (*6) / Figurine: TRANSPORTATION + COMMUNICATION = LOVE (*5) / THE HEARTFELT (*6) / Dntel: SOMETHING ALWAYS GOES WRONG special (*5) / LIFE IS FULL OF POSSIBILITIES (*7)

CHRIS GUNST – vocals, guitar / **PAUL LARSON** – guitar / **JIMMY HAY** – keyboards, percussion / **JIMMY TAMBORELLO** – bass / **IAN MacKINNON** – drums

                                          Waxploitation Waxploitation

Aug 97. (cd) *<(WAX 0001)>* **HIDE HERE FOREVER**
- A picture / Crickets / Elevator action / Trains in the distance at night / Something that just is / This will self-destruct / Knots on a counting rope / A sudden interest in nature.

— after their split, GUNST formed BEACHWOOD SPARKS and TAMBORELLO formed FIGURINE

– others, etc. –

Apr 01. (7") *<SP 526>* **FIRE. / FIRE (remix)**

FIGURINE

JIMMY TAMBORELLO plus **DAVID + MEREDITH**

                                      not iss.   Blackbean & Placenta

Nov 98. (7") *<ACME 22>* **I WAIT FOR YOU (BY THE TELEPHONE). / YOU (live in Berlin)**

Dec 99. (cd) *<ACME 57>* **TRANSPORTATION + COMMUNICATION = LOVE**
- I wait for you (by the telephone) / F>I>G>U>R>I>N>E / New mate / An electronic address / S.O.S. / Batteries (can't help me now) / Robots / My first UFO / The European beauty / Tired eyes / Digits / Eurodiscoteque / New millennium song / International space station.

                                        Motorway not iss.

Apr 00. (7") **0 DEGREES. / OUR SONG**   – Japan

                                        not iss.   Catmobile

Apr 01. (12"ep) *<CMOB 06LP>* **JAMES VS. DAVID**
- Before I go / The life / The adventures of James Figurine / Location / M equals T3 / Our pure efficiency / David Figurine never imitates / A perfect world. *(UK-iss.Mar02; same as US)*

                                        March   March

Sep 01. (12") *<MAR 073>* **IMpossible (mixes; intro / original / fingernail / bonus beats / John Tejada / Mum / accapella)**

Dec 01. (cd) *<(MAR 070)>* **THE HEARTFELT**   Aug01
- International space station II / IMpossible / Pswd: Stdum / Rewind / Way too good / Stranger / Time (his mix) / Instrumental / Pswd: Natur / Our game (is over) / So futuristic / Pswd: Pttrn / Heartfelt / Let's make our love song.

                                        555   not iss.

Jun 02. (cd-ep) *(555CD 46)* **THE DISCARD EP**
- Miss miss / Don't stop the dancing / Connections / Not love yet / 52 original sound effects.

— TAMBORELLO (also DNTEL) subsequently joined indie supergroup POSTAL SERVICE along with BEN GIBBARD (of DEATH CAB FOR CUTIE)

– compilations, etc. –

Aug 02. (cd) *Blackbean & Placenta; <bb&ptc 345>* **RECONFIGURINE** (remixes)

DNTEL

JIMMY TAMBORELLO – electronics, bass, guitar / with guests

                                          not iss.   Phthalo

1999. (cd) *<PHTH 12>* **EARLY WORKS FOR ME IF IT WORKS FOR YOU**
- Loneliness is having no one to miss / High horses theme / Pliesex Sielking / Termites in the bathtub / Fort instructions / Curtains / Tybalt 60 / Danny loves experimental electronics / Sky pointing / Casuals / Winds let me down again / Jewel states, "the door borders".

2000. (12"ep/cd-ep) *<PHTH 19/+CD>* **SOMETHING ALWAYS GOES WRONG**
- In which our hero . . . (mixes) / The S.O.S. / A machine and a memory to keep you alive.

                                        Plug   Plug
                                      Research Research

Nov 01. (cd) *(PR 320106CD) <efa 27082>* **LIFE IS FULL OF POSSIBILITIES**   Oct01
- Umbrella / Anywhere anyone / Pillowcase / Fear of corners / Suddenly is sooner than you think / Life is full of possibilities / Why I'm so unhappy / Fireworks / (This is) The dream of Evan and Chan / Last songs.

Dec 01. (12"ep) *(PR 290103) <efa 270796>* **ANYWHERE ANYONE EP**   Jul01
- Anywhere anyone / This is how it will be all over / Anywhere anyone (nobody remix).

Sep 02. (12"/cd-s) *(PR 360204/+CD)* **(THIS IS) THE DREAM OF EVAN AND CHAN (mixes; original / safety scissors spilled my drink / Barbara Morgenstern / superpitcher kompakt / Lali puna) / YOUR HILL**

Ken STRINGFELLOW (see under ⇒ POSIES)

John P. STROHM (see under ⇒ ANTENNA)

STROKES

Formed: New York City, New York, USA . . . 1998 by JULIAN CASABLANCAS (son of Elite modeling agency CEO John Casablancas), guitarist NICK VALENSI, bass guitarist NIKOLAI FRAITURE and drummer FAB MORETTI; ALBERT HAMMOND JR would be added later. Fed up with the recent import of Nu-metal bands such as LINKIN PARK, LIMP BIZKIT and the soft post-grunge credentials of STAINED, the NME decided to promote a new form of rock music between spring and summer 2001; and The STROKES became virtually overnight the headlining act along with fellow garage rockers WHITE STRIPES. The question begged to be asked, however:

if such publicity (and some might've called it hype) wasn't used to promote this youthful garage rock band, would the public and press still deem them to be the saviours of rock? The STROKES began playing – minus HAMMOND – in 1998 where they all attended the upper-class prep school Dwight. It was there that the group discovered their love for garage rock and quickly began pulling ideas together for songs. The sound would be halfway between LOU REED's "ostrich guitar", MC5's thrash meanderings and the tunefulness of TOM PETTY. Surprisingly, the ensemble (now playing in a plush rehearsal room in the lower east side of Manhattan and with the arrival of newcomer HAMMOND) pulled off the technical trickery of the above mentioned, and, through all of the scattered influences, began to develop a sound of their own. They debuted live in spring '99, performing in such venues as NYC's 'Baby Jupiter' and 'LUNA'. Ryan Gentles was finally brought in as manager and helped them require spots at 'Mercury Lounge' and 'Bowery Ballroom'. Things were almost reaching fever pitch for The STROKES, and, alongside THE MOLDY PEACHES and ANDREW W.K., they were becoming the most talked about band in NYC. A tape, including the tracks 'SOMA', 'BARELY LEGAL' and the rip-roaring 'MODERN AGE' was sent to 'Rough Trade' in London. The label (at that time, pulling themselves out of financial difficulty) signed the band, issuing the 'MODERN AGE' EP to critical acclaim. The NME went nuts, urging the record-buying public to go out and listen to this new and exciting group. Bidding wars began in America over The STROKES distribution, with 'R.C.A.' emerging as the champions. The single 'HARD TO EXPLAIN' was issued and reached No.16 in the British charts. Now, it seemed, this group of talented young upstarts were emerging as bonafide rockstars . . . even COURTNEY LOVE wrote a song about CASABLANCAS, entitled 'But Julian, I am much older than you'. With all of the commotion, the humble and ironically titled debut album 'IS THIS IT' was premiered amid much audience anticipation in early September 2001. It reached No.2 in the UK, even with its risqué Helmut Newton-inspired cover (which was refused by Woolworth's and HMV). But as the band watched the Twin Towers collapse from their rehearsal room on September 11, they decided to pull the song 'NYC COPS' from the American release of 'IS THIS IT'. Perhaps not one of their better moves, as the above mentioned song was a blinder; perhaps the best track on the LP, and a genuine audience favourite. 'LAST NITE' appeared on single at the end of 2001, with a video accompanied by Roman Copolla, featuring a live performance from the band. Things were looking bright at the turn of the year, with the addition of a few new tracks, a sold-out tour of Britain and the re-admission of 'NYC COPS' into the live brew. Perhaps The STROKES weren't the saviours of rock, but they were sure pretty damn close.

Album rating: IS THIS IT (*9)

JULIAN CASABLANCAS – vocals / **NICK VALENSI** – guitar / **NIKOLAI FRAITURE** – bass / **FAB MORETTI** – drums / added **ALBERT HAMMOND JR** – guitar

		Rough Trade	R.C.A.
Jan 01.	(7"/cd-s) *(RTRADES/+CD 010)* **MODERN AGE. / LAST NIGHT / BARELY LEGAL** *(re-dist.Jun01)* – hit UK No.68		-
Jun 01.	(7"/cd-s) *(RTRADES/+CD 023)* **HARD TO EXPLAIN. / NEW YORK CITY COPS**	16	-
Aug 01.	(cd/lp) *(RTRADE CD/LP 030) <68101>* **IS THIS IT** – Is this it / The modern age / Soma / Barely legal / Someday / Last nite / Hard to explain / New York City cops / Trying your luck / Take it or leave it.	2	33
Nov 01.	(7"/cd-s) *(RTRADES/+CD 041)* **LAST NITE. / WHEN IT STARTED** (cd-s) *(RTRADES 041X)* – ('A'live) / Trying your luck (live) / Take it or leave it (live).	14	-
Apr 02.	(cd-ep) *(RTRADESCD 053)* **HARD TO EXPLAIN / THE MODERN AGE / LAST NITE / WHEN IT STARTED / TAKE IT OR LEAVE IT (live)**	-	- Irish
Jun 02.	(7"clear) *<7863-60554-7>* **HARD TO EXPLAIN. / NEW YORK CITY COPS** (cd-s+=) *<60533>* – Take it or leave it / Trying your luck.	-	-
Sep 02.	(7"yellow/cd-s) *(RTRADES/+CD 063)* **SOMEDAY. / ALONE, TOGETHER (home recording) / IS THIS IT (home recording)**	27	-

ST. THOMAS

Born: THOMAS HANSEN, 1976, Oslo, Norway. HANSEN is currently one of Norway's leading indie artists (and exports), and certainly its most revered alt-country act. Inspired by the music of WILL OLDHAM and NEIL YOUNG, he began writing and recording his own country-tinged compositions. After moving to Bergen in 1998, he formed the band EMILY LANG, and subsequent gigs gained them a local following. Seeking greater musical independence in 2000, he disbanded EMILY LANG and moved to Kristianland, where he reverted to writing and recording homemade four-track demos. Adopting the recording name ST. THOMAS, he self-released a 7" single and a CD-R of new music. After impressing an employee of Norwegian label 'Racing Junior' with a radio broadcast, he managed to secure distribution for his debut album. 'MYSTERIOUS WALKS' sold well in Norway, allowing him to tour using an ever-changing roster of backing musicians – billed as ST. THOMAS AND THE MAGIC CLUB. Backed by MAGIC CLUB members, THOMAS took to the studio in April 2001 to record the 'CORNERMAN' EP. Its entry into the Norwegian Top 10 prompted him to quit his job as a postman, and also led to a successful European tour. Again with MAGIC CLUB members, THOMAS soon returned to the studio to cut his second LP 'I'M COMING HOME'. Relatively huge sales in Norway led to its release in the States. The record was effectively an album of Appalachian folk songs, with the banjo and harmonica leading the way. THOMAS also adopted a falsetto vocal style, reminiscent of 'Harvest'-era NEIL YOUNG. Indeed, THOMAS' (over-)admiration of YOUNG (and WILL OLDHAM) provoked criticism from some quarters. Nevertheless, tracks like the aforementioned 'CORNERMAN' and 'THE COOL SONG' qualify him as an extremely talented contemporary songwriter/musician.

Album rating: MYSTERIOUS WALKS (*5) / I'M COMING HOME (*6)

THOMAS HANSEN – vocals, guitar / with the **MAGIC CLUB**

		Racing Junior	not iss.
Mar 01.	(cd) *(RJ 006CD)* **MYSTERIOUS WALKS** – Born again / Mysterious walks / Failure #2 / Invitation / What have I done / Walk with me / The charity ego / The proud St. Thomas / I'm coming home / Surfer's morning / Lullaby from a wannabe / Popstar – My early funeral.		-
Sep 01.	(cd-ep) *(RJCDS 009)* **THE CORNERMAN EP** – Cornerman / Goodbye Emily Lang / With the feather / Sailor.		-

now with the **BJORHAUG 49'ERS**

		City Slang	Misra
Jan 02.	(cd) *(20188-2) <13>* **I'M COMING HOME** – The cool song / Take a dance with me / Goodbye Emily Lang / Oh I have left the ground / Strangers out of blue / A nice bottle of wine / Cornerman / She married a cowboy / Failure #1 / Bookstore / Into the forest / I'm coming home #2.		May02

STUNTMAN (see under ⇒ TREEPEOPLE)

SUBAQWA

Formed: Birmingham, England . . . 1995 by art college students JUSTIN WIGGIN, NICK PELL, NICK HUMPAGE and ROB TATTERSFIELD (SIMON WEBB was invited into the fold when original drummer, POD, bailed out). After locking themselves in an (apparently) depressing cuboard for 4 years, this lap-steel laden, nonchalant quartet emerged from the deep, murky depths of NEIL FINN's psyche. However, CROWDED HOUSE meets dreamy country Lo-Fi may be a vague description of SUBAQWA, who made their name while still in art college when a friend began the enterprising 'Faith & Hope' records. Contracts were made and the group began churning out crispy, WILL OLDHAM-inspired tunes on 12" and single before debut set 'CHALK CIRCLE' was issued in 1999. The album promised much from this inspired band, who, undeniably had peers, but used them in a clever and entrancing way. A fine example of this may be tracks 'HARBOUR POINTS' and 'LITTLE GLITCHES', which both justify WIGGIN's lone and broken lyrics.

Album rating: CHALK CIRCLE (*7)

JUSTIN WIGGIN – vocals / **NICK PELL** – guitar / **NICK HUMPAGE** – guitar / **ROB TATTERSFIELD** – bass / **SIMON WEBB** – drums; repl. POD

		Faith & Hope	not iss.
Mar 99.	(7"/cd-s) *(FH 7/CD 003)* **LET IT GO. / WAVING WEST (short wave) / CHECK YOUR SPACE**		-
Jun 99.	(7"/cd-s) *(FH 7/CD 006)* **I'VE SEEN THIS BEFORE. / HOTEL SILENCE (demo) / WEDDING SOUVENIR**		-
Aug 99.	(7") *(FH7 008)* **AM-PM. / ROOM** (cd-s+=) *(FHCD 008)* – Airliner soul.		-
Aug 99.	(cd/lp) *FHCD/FHLP 009)* **CHALK CIRCLE** – Let it go / Cody's snowy memo / Little glitches / AM-PM / Backwater / Waving west / Harbour points / I've seen this before / 5 AM and falling / Hotel silence / This mountain is closed / Ricetones.		-

the group have since folded

SUBCIRCUS

Formed: London, England . . . late 1994 by North East-born frontman PETER BRADLEY JNR., Danish-born guitarist NICOLAJ BLOCH, bassist GEORGE BROWN and drummer TOMMAS ARNBY. Inspired by the success of RADIOHEAD and SUEDE, this angst-rock outfit earned a deal with 'Echo' records (home to JULIAN COPE, BABYBIRD, MOLOKO, etc), releasing their eponymous debut set in late summer '96. The relative success of minor spin off hits such as '86'd' and 'U LOVE U', seemed to bode well for the future and the group looked set to establish themselves in the States courtesy of a deal with 'Dreamworks'. Re-packaged as 'CAROUSEL', the debut album was issued once more a year later, although this strategy proved flawed as many ringside seats lay vacant. With Brit-pop taking a backseat in the ever-evolving rock mainstream, SUBCIRCUS found themselves on a highwire without a safety net when critics lambasted their long-awaited sophomore set proper, 'ARE YOU RECEIVING' (2000); RADIOHEAD they were not.

Album rating: SUBCIRCUS – CAROUSEL (*6) / ARE YOU RECEIVING (*4)

PETER BRADLEY JNR. – vocals / **NICOLAJ BLOCH** – guitar / **GEORGE BROWN** – bass / **TOMMAS ARNBY** – drums

		Echo	DreamWorks
Sep 96.	(cd/lp) *(ECH CD/LP 013)* **SUBCIRCUS** – I want you like an accident / U love U / 20th century bitch / Shelley's on the telephone / Storm fly baby / 86'd / Gravity girl & analog / Las zoot suit / Article 11 (early departure) / So strange.		-
Jan 97.	(7") *(ECS 030)* **86'D. / ARTICLE 11** (cd-s+=) *(ECSCD 030)* – Animals they'll remember you (temporary dream decay) / Gravity girl and analogue.		-

Apr 97.	(7"blue) *(ECS 034)* **U LOVE U. / CENTRAL HEATING BOILER** [61] [-] (cd-s+=) *(ECSCD 034)* – She ain't heavy. (cd-s) *(ECSXS 034)* – ('A'session) / 86'd (session) / Article 11 (session) / I want you like an accident (session).
Jun 97.	(7"bronze) *(ECS 043)* **86'D. / DISPOSABLE YOUTH** [56] [-] (gold-cd-s+=) *(ECSCD 043)* – Kill the distraction, kill your reaction / 86'd the video (CD-ROM). (cd-s) *(ECSCX 043)* – ('A'-LHB's big top mix) / ('A'-Moloko mix) / ('A'-Wide receiver sawn off dub mix).
Aug 97.	(7") *(ECS 038)* **SHELLEY'S ON THE TELEPHONE. / ('A'live demo)** (cd-s+=) *(ECSCD 038)* – Accident (live) / U love u (video). (cd-s) *(ECSCX 038)* – ('A'side) / ('A'-Fuzz Townshend mix) / ('A'-Beatniks mix) / ('A'video).
Sep 97.	(cd/c/lp) *(ECH CD/MC/LP 018)* <DRMD 50026> **CAROUSEL** – Shelley's on the telephone / 86'd / 20th century bitch / U love U / Storm fly baby / I want you like an accident / Las zoot suit / Gravity girl & analogue / Article 11 (early departure) / So strange. *(cd+=)* – Kill this distraction, kill your reaction. *(cd re-iss. Feb01; same)*
Jun 99.	(cd-s) *(ECSCD 78)* **DO YOU FEEL LOVED / DAMAGE / LONELY WILLY** [-] (cd-s) *(ECSCX 78)* – ('A'side) / Do you feel loathed? / Frequencies of a butterfly.
Nov 99.	(cd-s) *(ECSCD 80)* **FOR THOSE WHO CANNOT WEEP / SHELLEY'S ON THE TELEPHONE / DIRTY CALL** [-]
Feb 00.	(7") *(ECS 86)* **60 SECOND LOVE AFFAIR. / COME ON OUT** (cd-s+=) *(ECSCD 86)* – Mr. Sunlight.
Mar 00.	(cd/c) *(ECH CD/LP 29)* **ARE YOU RECEIVING** [-] – Man of the year / Do you feel loved / For those who cannot weep / 60 second love affair / Rented / Filthy fucker / Boys are naturally cruel / Tiredness can kill / Something to believe in / My pet poltergeist / Situation comedy.

SUB SUB (see under ⇒ DOVES)

SUCKLE

Formed: Glasgow, Scotland ... 1996 by missing VASELINES frontwoman and yoga instructor, FRANCES McKEE (also ex-PAINKILLERS), who teamed up with co-vocalist and sister MARIE McKEE; JAMES SEENAN (ex-VASELINES) was also on board at some stage. Completing the line-up with fiery redhead and SYS Electronic Music graduate ELANOR TAYLOR on flute and keyboards, art school lecturer VICKY MORTON on bass, BRIAN McEWAN on guitar and his brother KENNY (ex-LONG FIN KILLIE) on drums, SUCKLE debuted in '97 on the 'Detox' label courtesy of EP, 'HORMONAL SECRETIONS'; an obscure sophomore 12" entitled 'CYBILLA', released on FRANCES' own 'LeftHand' recordings, hit the shops the following year. Things looked increasingly brighter at the turn of the century when SUCKLE inked a deal with the much respected indie, 'Chemikal Underground' (home of The DELGADOS, etc). Their sort of comeback single, 'TO BE KING', was also the opening track on their long-awaited debut set, 'AGAINST NURTURE' (2000), a record that could be best described as a mogadon-rush retreading melodious monotone indie-pop of yesteryear.

Album rating: AGAINST NURTURE (*6)

FRANCES McKEE – vocals, guitar (ex-VASELINES, ex-PAINKILLERS) / **MARIE McKEE** – vocals / **ELANOR TAYLOR** – keyboards, flute / **BRIAN McEWAN** – guitar / **VICKY MORTON** – bass / **KENNY McEWAN** – drums (ex-LONG FIN KILLIE)

		Detox	not iss.
Apr 97.	(7"ep/cd-ep) *(7+/DTX 9703/+CD)* **HORMONAL SECRETIONS EP** – Symposium / When I was dead / Boyfriend / Circle.		
		LeftHand	not iss.
Apr 98.	(12") *(LHR 001)* **CYBILLA. / SEX WITH ANIMALS** – Syndrome / State of mind / Cybilla.		
		Chemikal Underground	Chemikal Underground
May 00.	(7") *(chem 041)* **TO BE KING. / KISS MY FEET** (cd-s+=) *(chem 041cd)* – Golden hair.		
May 00.	(lp/cd) *(chem 042/+cd)* **AGAINST NURTURE** – To be king / Earth without pleasures / Saturn / Honey suicide / How do you know / I tell you truly / Nothing / The colour song / Father's milk / So happy before / Symposium.		
Oct 00.	(12"ep/cd-ep) *(chem 045/+cd)* **THE SUN IS GOD EP** – Saturn / Wing / One made for me / Forever.		

SUEDE

Formed: London, England ... 1989 by BRETT ANDERSON, who, by 1992 had put together the final line-up of guitarist BERNARD BUTLER, bassist MATT OSMAN and drummer SIMON GILBERT (ELASTICA prime mover, JUSTINE FRISCHMANN, had also been an early member). After a single, 'BE MY GOD' / 'ART', failed to appear in 1990 on 'RML' (this lost recording was famous for featuring ex-SMITHS drummer, MIKE JOYCE), the band signed to 'Nude', precipitating a storm of media hype and adulation. Featured on the cover of NME before they had even released their debut single, the band became press darlings of a post-grunge/pre-Brit pop music scene desperate for a bit of cheap glamour. Widely touted as spiritual antecedents of The SMITHS, the group were actually closer in style to the camp affectations of mid-period BOWIE, although there was definitely a MORRISSEY-like archness to the lyrics, the glum one actually taking to covering 'MY INSATIABLE ONE' (the B-side of SUEDE's acclaimed debut effort, 'THE DROWNERS') live. Another couple of singles followed, 'METAL MICKEY' and 'ANIMAL NITRATE', these scoring successively higher chart positions. The media support, together with ANDERSON's sleazy, androgynous posturing, made him, and his band, instant heroes for a new generation of crazy, mixed up kids, the eponymous 1993 debut album quickly reaching No.1. 'Nude's takeover by 'Sony' in early that year gave the act a bit of major label muscle, ironically helping them on their way to becoming one of the biggest "indie" bands in Britain. At the beginning '94, the band scored their biggest hit single to date with the epic 'STAY TOGETHER', the track peaking at No.3. Later that Spring, gay drummer SIMON bravely went to the House Of Commons to air his views on the homosexual laws of consent, which were to be lowered from 21 to either 16 (the heterosexual age) or 18, as it finally turned out. Around the same time, more controversy dogged the group when an American jazz singer called SUEDE won her lawsuit against the band in the US, the upshot of the affair being that from that point on, the band were to be known in America as LONDON SUEDE (lucky for them they didn't come from Leatherhead!). Meantime, the group had won the Mercury Music Prize for their acclaimed debut album and were well on the way to releasing a follow-up, 'DOG MAN STAR' (1994). The last album to feature the departing BUTLER (heralded by some as the UK's most promising guitarist since JOHNNY MARR, BUTLER subsequently went on to a successful, if short lived, collaboration with DAVID McALMONT before signing to 'Creation' and embarking on a solo career), it marked something of a departure in the band's sound, a dense, ambitious set which met with a mixed critical reception. Unbowed, SUEDE swaggered on, recruiting the teenage RICHARD OAKES as BUTLER's replacement and providing a welcome diversion from the laddish excesses of Brit-pop. SUEDE's next effort, 'COMING UP' proved to be their most consistent set to date, spawning the brilliant lowlife anthem, 'TRASH' along with the similarly infectious, organic glam of 'FILMSTAR' and the dislocated melancholy of 'SATURDAY NIGHT'. A stop-gap but worthy collection of rarities and B-sides, 'SCI-FI LULLABIES' (1997) marked time before their return in the Spring of '99. 'ELECTRICITY' sparked off proceedings, the UK Top 5 single also the opening track on their No.1 Steve Osborne-produced 4th album proper, 'HEAD MUSIC' (1999). Three other retro-fied 45's ('SHE'S IN FASHION', 'EVERYTHING WILL FLOW' and 'CAN'T GET ENOUGH') were delivered to an eager kitsch fanbase who were still "into" all things glam:- BOWIE, ROXY, NUMAN, HUMAN ... A few years in the proverbial wilderness, BRETT and his beloved SUEDE team returned on the scene in summer 2002 (with ex-STRANGELOVE drummer, ALEX LEE, replacing NEIL), releasing 'A NEW MORNING', a set that didn't go straight to No.1; or even make the Top 10, or Top 20! • **Songwriters:** ANDERSON / BUTLER, except; BRASS IN POCKET (Pretenders).

Album rating: SUEDE (*8) / DOG MAN STAR (*7) / COMING UP (*7) / SCI-FI LULLABIES collection (*6) / HEAD MUSIC (*7) / A NEW MORNING (*6)

BRETT ANDERSON (b.27 Sep'67, Haywards Heath, Sussex, England) – vocals / **BERNARD BUTLER** (b. 1 May'70) – guitar, piano / **MATT OSMAN** (b. 9 Oct'67) – bass / **SIMON GILBERT** (b.23 May'65) – drums

		Nude	not iss.
Apr 92.	(7") *(nud 1s)* **THE DROWNERS. / TO THE BIRDS** [49] [-] (12"+=/cd-s+=) *(nud 1 t/cd)* – My insatiable one.		
Sep 92.	(7"/c-s) *(nud 3 s/mc)* **METAL MICKEY. / WHERE THE PIGS DON'T FLY** [17] [-] (12"+=/cd-s+=) *(NUD 3 t/cd)* – He's dead.		
		Nude-Sony	Columbia
Feb 93.	(7"/c-s) *(NUD 4 s/mc)* **ANIMAL NITRATE. / THE BIG TIME** [7] [-] (12"+=/cd-s+=) *(nud 4 t/cd)* – Painted people.		
Apr 93.	(cd/c/lp) *(NUD 1 cd/mc/lp)* <53792> **SUEDE** [1] – So young / Animal nitrate / She's not dead / Moving / Pantomime horse / The drowners / Sleeping pills / Breakdown / Metal Mickey / Animal lover / The next life. *(cd re-iss. Aug02 on 'Epic'; 473735-2)*		
May 93.	(7"/c-s) *(nud 5 s/mc)* **SO YOUNG. / HIGH RISING** [22] [-] (12"+=/cd-s+=) *(nud 5 t/cd)* – Dolly.		
Sep 93.	(cd-ep) <44K 77172> **THE DROWNERS / MY INSATIABLE ONE / TO THE BIRDS / THE BIG TIME / HE'S DEAD (live)** [-]		
Feb 94.	(7"/c-s) *(nud 9 s/mc)* **STAY TOGETHER. / THE LIVING DEAD** [3] [-] (ext;12"+=/cd-s+=) *(nud 9 t/cd)* – My dark star.		
—	An American jazz singer called SUEDE won her lawsuit against the band in the US. They are now to be called LONDON SUEDE, but thankfully only in the States.		
Mar 94.	(cd-ep) <CK 64382> **STAY TOGETHER / THE LIVING DEAD / MY DARK STAR / DOLLY HIGH RISING / STAY TOGETHER (extended)** [-]		
Sep 94.	(7"/c-s) *(nud 10 s/mc)* **WE ARE THE PIGS. / KILLING OF A FLASH BOY** [18] [-] (12"+=/cd-s+=) *(nud 10 t/cd)* – Whipsnade.		
Oct 94.	(cd/c/d-lp) *(nude 3 cd/mc/lp)* <66769> **DOG MAN STAR** [3] – Introducing the band / We are the pigs / Heroine / The wild ones / Daddy's speeding / The power / New generation / This Hollywood life / The 2 of us / Black or blue / The asphalt world / Still life. *<US-version +=>* – Modern boys. *(cd re-iss. Aug02 on 'Epic'; 477811-2)*		
—	(July'94; after rec. album) **RICHARD OAKES** – guitar; repl. BUTLER who went solo		
Nov 94.	(c-s) *(nud 11mc)* **THE WILD ONES / MODERN BOYS** [18] [-] (cd-s+=) *(nud 11cd1)* – This world needs a father. (12") *(nud 11t)* – ('A'side) / Eno's introducing the band. (cd-s) *(nud 11cd2)* – (above 2) / Asda town.		
Jan 95.	(7"/c-s) *(nud 12mc)* **NEW GENERATION. / TOGETHER** [21] [-] (12"+=/cd-s+=) *(nud 12 t/cd1)* – Bentswood boys. (cd-s) *(nud 12cd2)* – ('A'side) / Animal nitrate (live) / The wild ones (live) / Pantomime horse (live).		
—	added new member **NEIL CODLING** – keyboards, vocals		

Jul 96.	(c-s) *(nud 2mc)* **TRASH / EUROPE IS OUR PLAYGROUND**	3	-

(cd-s+=) *(nud 21cd1)* – Every Monday morning comes.
(pic-cd-s) *(nud 21cd2)* – ('A'side) / Have you ever been this low? / Another no one.

Sep 96.	(cd/c/lp) *(nude 6 cd/mc/lp)* <67911> **COMING UP**	1	

– Trash / Filmstar / Lazy / By the sea / She / Beautiful ones / Starcrazy / Picnic by the motorway / The chemistry between us / Saturday night. *(cd re-iss. Aug02 on 'Epic'; 485129-2)*

Oct 96.	(c-s) *(nud 23mc)* **BEAUTIFUL ONES / BY THE SEA (demo)**	8	-

(cd-s) *(nud 23 cd1)* – ('A'side) / Young men / The sound of the streets.
(cd-s) *(nud 23 cd2)* – ('A'side) / Money / Sam.

Jan 97.	(c-s) *(nud 24mc)* **SATURDAY NIGHT / PICNIC BY THE MOTORWAY (live)**	6	-

(cd-s) *(nud 24cd1)* – ('A'side) / W.S.D. / Jumble sale mums.
(cd-s) *(nud 24cd2)* – ('A'side) / This time / ('A'demo).
(d7") *(nud 24s)* – ('A'side) / This time / Beautiful ones / The sound of the streets.

Apr 97.	(c-s) *(nud 27mc)* **LAZY / SHE (live)**	9	-

(cd-s) *(nud 27cd1)* – ('A'side) / These are the sad songs / Feel.
(cd-s) *(nud 27cd2)* – ('A'side) / Sadie / Digging a hole.

Aug 97.	(7") *(nud 30s)* **FILMSTAR. / ('A'original demo)**	9	-

(cd-s) *(nud 30cd1)* – ('A'side) / Graffiti women / Duchess. *(w/ free video footage; Beautiful ones / Coming up.*
(cd-s) *(nud 30cd2)* – ('A'side) / Rent / Saturday night / Saturday night (cd-rom).

Oct 97.	(d-cd) *(nude 9cd)* <68857> **SCI-FI LULLABIES** (flipsides)	9	

– My insatiable one / To the birds / Where the pigs don't fly / He's dead / The big time / High rising / The living dead / My star / Killing of a flash boy / Whipsnade / Modern boys / Together / Bentswood boys / Europe is our playground // Every Monday morning comes / Have you ever been this low? / Another no one / Young men / The sound of the streets / Money / W.S.D. / This time / Jumble sale mums / These are the sad songs / Sadie / Graffiti women / Duchess. *(cd re-iss. Aug02 on 'Epic'; 488851-2)*

Apr 99.	(c-s) *(NUD 43MC)* **ELECTRICITY / IMPLIMENT, YEAH!**	5	-

(cd-s) *(NUD 43CD1)* – ('A'side) / Popstar / Killer.
(cd-s) *(NUD 43CD2)* – ('A'side) / See that girl / Waterloo.

May 99.	(cd/c/d-lp) *(NUDE 14 CD/MC/LP)* <69986> **HEAD MUSIC**	1	Jun99

– Electricity / Savoir faire / Can't get enough / Everything will flow / Down / She's in fashion / Asbestos / Head music / Elephant man / Hi-fi / Indian strings / He's gone / Crack in the Union Jack. *(cd re-iss. Aug02 on 'Epic'; 494243-2)*

Jun 99.	(c-s) *(NUD 44MC)* **SHE'S IN FASHION / DOWN (demo)**	13	-

(cd-s) *(NUD 44CD1)* – ('A'side) / Bored / Pieces of my mind.
(cd-s) *(NUD 44CD2)* – ('A'side) / Jubilee / God's gift.

Sep 99.	(c-s) *(NUD 45MC)* **EVERYTHING WILL FLOW / BEAUTIFUL ONES (live)**	24	-

(cd-s) *(NUD 45CD1)* – ('A'side) / Weight of the world / Leaving.
(cd-s) *(NUD 45CD2)* – ('A'side) / Crackhead / Seascape.

Nov 99.	(cd-s) *(NUD 47CD1)* **CAN'T GET ENOUGH / LET GO / SINCE YOU WENT AWAY**	23	-

(cd-s) *(NUD 47CD2)* – ('A'side) / Situations / Read my mind.
(cd-s) *(NUD 47CD3)* – ('A'side) / Everything will flow (Rollo's vocal mix) / She's in fashion (Lironi version) / ('A'-CD video).

— (Mar'01) **ALEX LEE** – drums (ex-BLUE AEROPLANES, ex-STRANGELOVE) repl. NEIL

Epic *Sony*

Sep 02.	(cd-s) *(672949-2)* **POSITIVITY / ONE LOVE / SIMON / POSITIVITY (video)**	16	-

(cd-s) *(672949-5)* – ('A'side) / Superstar / Cheap.

Sep 02.	(cd) *(508956-2)* <649168> **A NEW MORNING**	24	

– Positivity / Obsessions / Lonely girls / Lost in TV / Beautiful loser / Streetlife / Astrogirl / Untitled . . .morning / One hit to the body / When the rain falls. *(special cd+=; 508956-9)* – You belong to me / Oceans.

Nov 02.	(cd-s) *(673294-2)* **OBSESSIONS / COOL THING / INSTANT SUNSHINE**	29	-

(cd-s) *(673294-5)* – ('A'side) / UFO / Rainy day girl.

SUGAR

Formed: Minneapolis, USA . . . 1992 by former HUSKER DU frontman/co-writer, BOB MOULD. Upon the demise of the latter act in 1987, MOULD signed to 'Virgin America' and subsequently entered PRINCE's 'Paisley Park' studios to lay down his first solo set, 'WORKBOOK' (1989). Augmented by the former PERE UBU rhythm section of ANTON FIER and TONY MAIMONE and employing cellists JANE SCARPANTONI and STEVE HAIGLER, MOULD confounded expectations with a largely acoustic affair trading in melodic distortion for fragments of contemplative melancholy; only the closing 'WHICHEVER WAY THE WIND BLOWS' acknowledged the sonic assault of prime HUSKER DU. Despite the guaranteed critical plaudits and the more accessible nature of the material, 'WORKBOOK's sales were modest. Perhaps as a reaction, the following year's 'BLACK SHEETS OF RAIN' – again recorded with FIER and MAIMONE – was a searing return to bleaker, noisier pastures; 'HANGING TREE' remains among the most tormented work of MOULD's career, while the likes of 'HEAR ME CALLING' and 'IT'S TOO LATE' combined keening melody with blistering soloing/discordant riffing in patented MOULD fashion. When this album also failed to take off, the singer parted comapny from 'Virgin' and undertook a low-key acoustic tour. His wilderness period was brief, however, the emerging grunge vanguard citing HUSKER DU as a massive influence and inspiring MOULD to form another melodic power trio. Comprising of fellow songwriter/bassist, DAVE BARBE and drummer MALCOLM TRAVIS, SUGAR signed to 'Creation' and proceeded to cut one of the most feted albums of the era in 'COPPER BLUE' (1992). Leaner, tighter and cleaner, the record's bittersweet pop-hardcore crunch finally provided MOULD with a springboard for commercial success; a UK Top 10 hit, the album even spawned a Top 30 hit single in the sublime 'IF I CAN'T CHANGE YOUR MIND'. 'BEASTER', 1993's mini-album follow-up, took tracks from the 'COPPER BLUE' sessions and buried them in a multi-tiered blanket of howling distortion. Unsurprisingly it failed to spawn a hit, although its Top 3 success was no doubt sweet for the ever contrary MOULD, his follow-up proper, 'FILE UNDER EASY LISTENING (F.U.E.L.)' (1994), suggesting that he'd become bored with the whole concept. MOULD eventually disbanded the project in spring '96, releasing a third solo album the same year, simply titled 'BOB MOULD'. Bowing out of the music industry treadmill with 'THE LAST DOG AND PONY SHOW' (1998), MOULD eventually resurfaced in 2002 with 'MODULATE', an ambitious if ultimately flawed attempt at re-examining his muse through the lens of post-millennial electronica. • **Songwriters:** MOULD and now same with others. Covered; SHOOT OUT THE LIGHTS (Richard Thompson).

Album rating: Bob Mould: WORKBOOK (*7) / BLACK SHEETS OF RAIN (*6) / Sugar: COPPER BLUE (*9) / BEASTER mini (*7) / FILE UNDER: EASY LISTENING (*7) / BESIDES collection (*6) / Bob Mould: BOB MOULD (*8) / THE LAST DOG AND PONY SHOW (*7) / MODULATE (*4)

BOB MOULD

BOB MOULD (b.12 Oct'61, Malone, New York) – vocals, guitar, etc (ex-HUSKER DU) / with **ANTON FIER** – drums / **TONY MAIMONE** – bass, (both ex-PERE UBU) / **JANE SCARPANTONI** – cello (of TINY LIGHTS) / **STEVE HAIGLER** – cello

Virgin *Virgin*

Jun 89.	(7") *(VUS 2)* **SEE A LITTLE LIGHT. / ALL THOSE PEOPLE KNOW**		-

(12"+=/cd-s+=) *(VUS 2T/CD2)* – Shoot out the lights / Composition for the young and the old (live).

Jul 89.	(lp/cd) *(VUS LP/CD 2)* <91240> **WORKBOOK**		Apr89

– Sunspots / Wishing well / Heartbreak a stranger / See a little light / Poison years / Sinners and their repentances / Lonely afternoon / Brasilia crossed the Tranton / Compositions for the young and old / Dreaming, I amd / Whichever way the wind blows. *(re-iss. Sep90; OVED 340)*

Aug 90.	(cd/c/lp) *(VUS CD/MC/LP 21)* <91395> **BLACK SHEETS OF RAIN**		May90

– Black sheets of rain / Stand guard / It's too late / One good reason / Stop your crying / Hanging tree / The last night / Hear me calling / Out of your life / Disappointed / Sacrifice – let there be peace.

Virgin *Virgin*

May 94.	(cd) *(CDVM 9030)* <39587> **THE POISON YEARS** (compilation from first two sets)		Jul94

SUGAR

BOB MOULD – vox, guitar, keyboards, percussion / **DAVE BARBE** – bass (ex-MERCYLAND) / **MALCOLM TRAVIS** – drums, percussion (ex-ZULUS)

Creation *Rykodisc*

Jul 92.	(cd-ep) <1024> **HELPLESS / NEEDLE HITS E / IF I CAN'T CHANGE YOUR MIND / TRY AGAIN**	-	

Aug 92.	(12"ep)(cd-ep) *(CRE 126T/CRESCD 126)* **CHANGES / NEEDLE HITS E. / IF I CAN'T CHANGE YOUR MIND / TRY AGAIN**		

Sep 92.	(cd/lp)(c) *(CRE CD/LP 129)(C-CRE 129)* <RCD/RACS 10239> **COPPER BLUE**	10	

– The act we act / A good idea / Changes / Helpless / Hoover dam / The slim / If I can't change your mind / Fortune teller / Slick / Man on the Moon.

Oct 92.	(7"ep/c-ep) *(CRE+/CS 143)* <1030> **A GOOD IDEA. / WHERE DIAMONDS ARE HALOS / SLICK**	65	

(12"ep+=)(cd-ep+=) *(CRE 143T)(CRESCD 143)* – Armenia city in the sky.

Jan 93.	(7"/c-s) *(CRE+/CS 149)* **IF I CAN'T CHANGE YOUR MIND. / CLOWN MASTER**	30	

(12"+=) *(CRE 149T)* <1031> – Anyone (live) / Hoover dam (live).
(cd-s+=) *(CRESCD 149)* <1032> – ('A'side) / The slim / Where diamonds are halos.

Apr 93.	(m-cd/m-lp)(m-c) *(CRE CD/LP 153)(C-CRE 153)* <50260> **BEASTER**	3	

– Come around / Tilted / Judas cradle / JC auto / Feeling better / Walking away.

Aug 93.	(7") *(CRE 156)* **TILTED. / JC AUTO (live)**	48	-

Aug 94.	(7"/c-s) *(CRE+/CS 186)* **YOUR FAVORITE THING. / MIND IS AN ISLAND**	40	

(12"+=)(cd-s+=) *(CRE 186T)(CRESCD 186)* <1038> – Frustration / And you tell me (T.V. mix).

Sep 94.	(cd/lp)(c) *(CRE CD/LP 172)(C-CRE 172)* <10300> **FILE UNDER EASY LISTENING (F.U.E.L.)**	7	50

– Gift / Company book / Your favorite thing / What you want it to be / Gee angel / Panama city hotel / Can't help it anymore / Granny cool / Believe what you're saying / Explode and make up.

Oct 94.	(7"/c-s) *(CRE+/CS 193)* **BELIEVE WHAT YOU'RE SAYING. / GOING HOME**	73	

(cd-s+=) *(CRESCD 193)* <1039> – In the eyes of my friends / And you tell me.

Dec 94.	(cd-ep) <RCD5 1040> **GEE ANGEL / EXPLODE AND MAKE UP / SLIM / AFTER ALL THE ROADS HAVE LED TO . . .**	-	

Jul 95.	(d-cd) <10321> **BESIDES** (compilation of b-sides, live, etc)	-	-

— disbanded and BARBE formed BUZZHUNGRY / TRAVIS went to CUSTOMIZED

BOB MOULD

— solo again with various back-up

Creation *Rykodisc*

Dec 95.	(cd-s) <51050> **EGOVERRIDE**		

Apr 96.	(cd/lp) *(CRE CD/LP 188)* <10342> **BOB MOULD**	52	

– Anymore time between / I hate alternative rock / Fort Knox, King Solomon / Next time that you leave / Egoverride / Thumbtack / Hair stew / Hair stew / Deep karma canyon / Art crisis / Roll over and die.

— now with **MATT HAMMON** – drums / **ALISON CHESLEY** – cello

Aug 98.	(7") *(CRE 206)* **CLASSIFIEDS. / MOVING TRUCKS**		-

SUGAR (cont)

Aug 98. (cd/lp) (CRE CD/LP 215) <10443> **THE LAST DOG AND PONY SHOW** | 58 |
– New #1 / Moving trucks / Taking everything / First drag of the day / Classifieds / Who was around? / Skintrade / Vaporub / Sweet serene / Megamaniac / Reflecting pool / Along the way / (interview).

	Cooking Vinyl	Granary
Apr 02. (cd) (COOKCD 237) <2021> **MODULATE**		Mar02

– 180 rain / Sunset safety glass / Semper fi / Homecoming parade / Lost zoloft / Without? / Slay – Sway / The receipt / Quasar / Soundonsound / Hornery / Comeonstrong / Trade / Author's lament.

SUGARGLIDERS (see under ⇒ STEINBECKS)

Matt SUGGS (see under ⇒ BUTTERGLORY)

SUKPATCH

Formed: Minneapolis, Missouri, USA . . . early 90's by CHRIS HEIDMAN and STEPHEN CRUZE. The early SUKPATCH sound was primitive to say the least. They began recording their lo-fi indie-pop at home on a cheap four-track and distributed their cassettes amongst friends. Before long they found themselves on Seattle's 'Slabco' independent, and the cassette-only 'LITE HITS', in 1993. Enveloped in tape hiss and speed variations, 'LITE . . .' had all the technical quality of a dodgy mix-tape. Recorded TV soundbites mingled with a few promising tracks – like 'MEXICO CITY BIG VACATION', and with intermittent vocals from friend TARA, the set retained a naive charm. Following the 'SUKPATCH' (1995) and 'HOOP' EPs, they released the 'HAULIN' GRASS & SMOKIN' ASS' album in 1997. The playful, flippant indie-pop of their earlier recordings remained, although it was now fused with hip-hop and funk. Combined with their keyboards and samples, and the SUKPATCH 'home-made' feel, it was an enticing, original collection. Later in 1997, the 'HONKY TONK OPERATION' EP featured eight tracks, with Latin beats introduced on 'LANGDON ON HI', but overall it lacked the immediacy of 'HAULIN' . . .'. 1998 saw a few more single releases and SUKPATCH's signing to the BEASTIE BOYS' 'Grand Royal' imprint – making their label debut with 1999's 'TIE DOWN THAT SHINY WAVE' EP.

Album rating: LITE HITS (*5) / HAULIN' GRASS AND SMOKIN' ASS (*7)

TARA – vocals / **CHRIS HEIDMAN** – keyboards / **STEPHEN CRUZE** – keyboards

	not iss.	own label
1993. (c) <none> **LITE HITS**	–	□

– Stickerchamp / Carmine / Richland king / Little ambassador / Mexico City big vacation / Hickory tips / Lucky neighbor / Beach jeans / Chloride / Otha fish / Dixie relocation camp / The swing clip / All the juice / Juice reprise / Alligator.

— now without TARA

	Slabco	Slabco
1995. (7"ep) <SLABCO 27> **SUKPATCH EP**	–	□

– Cabo San Lucas / Empire waist / Jerry Mulligan on 45 / Miniature pee-pee.

| 1996. (7"ep) <SLABCO 33> **HOOP EP** | – | □ |

– Carving counties / Sparkin' remake / Heady crisis Eddy / Lucky neighbah floorshow.

| Mar 97. (lp/cd) <(SLABCO 36/+CD)> **HAULIN' GRASS AND SMOKIN' ASS** | □ | Feb97 |

– Flock-sultan / Florida orange / Smooth guys (American mix) / Hollow tips / C. King / Tiebreakers / Bound design / Saddle sore / Au-pair / Stained-n-strained / High-lawn / Fort Knox / Bucked hide / Straightest lines / St. Louis runs. (cd re-iss. Mar99; same)

| Sep 97. (12"ep/cd-ep) <SLABCO 38/+CD> **HONKY-TONK OPERATION E.P.** | □ | □ |

– Fleet / Lake Funt property / Langdon on hi / Sile contusion / Afternoon son / Resley / Blew spitoonias / Keys east.

	Motorway	not iss.
1997. (7") (MOTOR 013) **IDES. / BROKEN FACILITY**	□	–

	not iss.	Tonevendor
1998. (cd) <1008> **PHAZED AND RE-FUZED** (remixes)	–	□

– Flock sultan / Smooth guys / We fold at the fork / C. King / Stained-n-strained / Lakefunt property / Afternoon son ('98 mix) / Dt 100 / Fleet (in the pines mix) / Ft. Knox / Florida orange.

	not iss.	Sub Pop
1998. (7") <SP 437> **STOLEN CHROME. / BUBBLE SHAFF**	–	□

	Moshi Mishi	not iss.
Nov 98. (7") (MOSH 1001) **HEY JOLIE. / STRAY PERSUASION**	□	–

	not iss.	Grand Royal
Sep 99. (cd-ep) <GR 79CD> **TIE DOWN THAT SHINY WAVE**	–	□

– Stuck on me / One sign divine / Burnt buy / Darlin' hey / Skin tight.

— split after above

— next with **PAMELA V**

| 1990's. (c; as PATCH) **JEEP MUSIC** | – | □ |

(above was HEIDMAN himself (aka SANYO COURTS)

SULTANS OF PING F.C.

Formed: Cork, Ireland . . . 1991 by one-time near neighbours of FRANK AND WALTERS, NIALL O'FLAHERTY, PADDY O'CONNELL, ALAN McFEALY and MORTY McCARTHY. Having been caught live in their act by Martin Heath (of trendy dance label, 'Rhythm King'), The SULTANS OF PING F.C. secured an atypical UK distribution deal for their own 'Divine' imprint, kicking off with the fun-tastic 'WHERE'S ME JUMPER'. A surreal tale of a nicked jersey down the local disco, the track hit the Top 75 and briefly secured the band a role as court jesters to the music press. These Irish loonies traced a lineage back to early DAMNED through STUMP and The POGUES, newly shaken 'n' stirrred in an eccentric, hard-drinking glam pop-punk cocktail. Two further minor hits, 'STUPID KID' and 'VERONICA', also surfaced in '92, paving the way for 'Rhythm King' to team up with 'Epic' and release Top 30 breaker, 'U TALK TOO MUCH'. A debut album, the brilliantly-titled 'CASUAL SEX IN THE CINEPLEX', was given promising reviews upon its release in early '93, following the single into the Top 30. Now under the aegis of major label paymasters, The SULTANS OF PING mysteriously dropped the F.C. from their name, a ploy that backfired as subsequent singles only managed to scrape into the Top 50; a follow-up album, 'TEENAGE DRUG' (1993), fared even worse. After losing their zing they also lost their PING, abbreviating their moniker even further to simply, The SULTANS. Now back with 'Rhythm King', the lads had one final (doomed) stab at glory with the comeback album, 'GOOD YEAR FOR TROUBLE' (1996). • **Songwriters:** O'FLAHERTY, except covers; MIRACLES (Shonen Knife) / SISTERS (Yoko Ono) / RED CADILLAC AND A BLACK MOUSTACHE (Thompson-May) / BLOODSPORTS FOR ALL (Carter The Unstoppable Sex Machine).

Album rating: CASUAL SEX IN THE CINEPLEX (*6) / TEENAGE DRUG (*5) / GOOD YEAR FOR TROUBLE (*4)

NIALL O'FLAHERTY – vocals / **PADDY O'CONNELL** – guitar / **ALAN McFEALY** – bass / **MORTY McCARTHY** – drums

	Divine-Rhythm King	not iss.
Jan 92. (7"/c-s) (ATHY 01/+C) **WHERE'S ME JUMPER. / I SAID I AM I SAID**	67	–

(12"+=/cd-s+=) (ATHY 01 T/CD) – Turnip fish.

| Apr 92. (7"/c-s) (ATHY 02/+C) **STUPID KID (live). / GIVE HIM A BALL (AND A YARD OF GRASS) (live)** | 67 | – |

(12"+=/cd-s+=) (ATHY 02 T/CD) – Football hooligan (live) / No more nonsense (live).

| Oct 92. (7"/c-s) (ATHY 03/+C) **VERONICA. / TEENAGE VAMPIRE** | 69 | – |

(12"+=/cd-s+=) (ATHY 03 T/CD) – Riot at the sheepdog trials.

	Rhythm King – Epic	not iss.
Dec 92. (7") (658579-7) **U TALK TOO MUCH. / JAPANESE GIRLS**	26	–

(12"+=/10"+=/cd-s+=) (658579-6/-0/-2) – Armitage Shanks / Turnip fish.

| Feb 93. (cd/c/lp) (472495-2/-4/-1) **CASUAL SEX IN THE CINEPLEX** | 26 | – |

– Back in a tracksuit / Indeed you are / Veronica / 2 pints of rasa / Stupid kid / You talk too much / Give him a ball (and a yard of grass) / Karaoke queen / Let's go shopping / Kick me with your leather boots / Clitus Clarke.

SULTANS OF PING

| Aug 93. (12"ep) (659579-6) **TEENAGE PUNKS / HE THOUGHT I WAS YOUR BEST FRIEND. / INDEED YOU ARE / VERONICA (live)** | 49 | – |

(cd-ep) (659579-2) – (1st 3 tracks) / Crash pad chick.
(c-ep) (659579-5) – (1st 3 tracks) / Back in a tracksuit (live).

| Oct 93. (12"pic-d/c-s) (659822-6/-4) **MICHIKO / MIRACLES. / XMAS BUBBLEGUM MACHINE / STUPID KID (live)** | 43 | – |

(cd-s) (659822-2) – (1st 3 tracks) / Japanese girls (acoustic party mix).

| Nov 93. (cd/c/lp) (474716-2/-4/-1) **TEENAGE DRUG** | □ | – |

– Teenage drug / Wake up and scratch me / Teenage punks / Curse / Michiko / Love and understanding / Psychopath / Terrorist angel / Teenage rock and roll girl / Pussycat / Sisters / Pussycat (reprise) / Telephone lover / Red Cadillac and a black moustache.

| Feb 94. (c-ep/12"ep/cd-ep) (660112-4/-6/-2) **WAKE UP AND SCRATCH ME / DO RE MI. / EVERYTHING YOU DO YOU DO FOR YOU / LET'S GO SHOPPING** | 50 | – |

SULTANS

	Rhythm King	not iss.
Mar 96. (7") (ATHY 04) **MESCALINE. /**	□	–

(cd-s+=) (CDATHY 04) –

| Jul 96. (cd/lp) (ATHY 05 CD/LP) **GOOD YEAR FOR TROUBLE** | □ | – |

– Frenzy / Scar on my face / Mescaline / Good year for trouble / Young and twisted / Rubberman / Shiny boots / I've got your girl / Five years / Hero out of time / Bad boyfriend / Shake.

	Fantastic Plastic	not iss.
Aug 96. (12") (FP 001) **WHAT ABOUT THOSE SULTANS. /**	□	–

SUMMER HITS (see under ⇒ FURTHER)

SUNCATCHER

Formed: Sacramento, California, USA . . . mid 90's through a classified ad by singer/songwriter, DOUG HAMMOND, alongside BRIAN KNIGHT and ROY MURRAY; RAYMOND SANCHEZ was a 4th member. Inking a deal with 'Restless', SUNCATCHER found themselves under the glare of the media spotlight with their shiny happy debut album, 'THE GIRL THAT GOD FORGOT' (1996). Alternatively referred to as the "OWLFLOWER" album due to its cover art, the record drew obvious comparisons to STIPE/R.E.M. while recalling the poppier elements of 60's psychedelia.

Album rating: THE GIRL THAT GOD FORGOT "OWLFLOWER" (*6)

DOUG HAMMOND – vocals, guitar / **RAYMOND SANCHEZ** – guitar / **BRIAN KNIGHT** – bass / **ROY MURRAY** – drums

SUNCATCHER (cont) THE GREAT INDIE DISCOGRAPHY The 1990s

		Restless	Restless
Jul 96.	(7") **LITTLE STEVIE WONDER. / STRAWBERRY FIELDS FOREVER**	-	☐
Aug 96.	(cd) <72920> **THE GIRL THAT GOD FORGOT** (the 'OWLFLOWER' album) – The puritan song / To move you / 3 viva / Birds on the wire / Have a nice day / Trouble / The girl that good forgot / Heaven / Dandelion / Juvenelia / Trippin.	-	☐

—— disbanded in 1998

SUNDAYS

Formed: London, England ... 1988 by HARRIET WHEELER, DAVID GAVURIN and PAUL BRINDLEY, initially playing with a drum machine before recruiting sticksman PATRICK 'Patch' HANNAN. Subsequently signing to 'Rough Trade', the band's fawning music press hype was justified with the release of the semi-classic 'CAN'T BE SURE' single in early '89. A luscious slice of sugary indie, the track's reverberating guitar and fragile, bone-china vocals (courtesy of WHEELER) brought comparisons with "shoegazing" forebears The COCTEAU TWINS, some critics also mentioning THROWING MUSES. Yet The SUNDAYS were in seemingly little hurry to follow-up this indie chart topper (and minor Top 40 hit), almost a full year passing before the release of much anticipated debut album, 'READING, WRITING AND ARITHMETIC' (1990). Its glistening jangle-pop didn't disappoint and The SUNDAYS suddenly found themselves in the UK Top 5, the US Top 40 and the glare of the world's media. An ensuing continent-straddling tour together with the collapse of the band's label conspired to slow down the band's already notoriously relaxed attitude to songwriting and it was late '92 before they re-emerged via a new 'Parlophone' deal. The resulting single, 'GOODBYE', displayed a more world-weary sound (the band even covering The Rolling Stones' mournful classic, 'WILD HORSES' on the B-side) and the accompanying album, 'BLIND', sounded frayed at the edges. While the record's Top 20 placing and the success of the attendant tour suggested that The SUNDAYS' fans hadn't lost interest, their patience would be tested with a subsequent five year gap prior to a third album. When 'STATIC & SILENCE' (1997) finally arrived, critics found fault with what they saw as musical stagnation although loyal fans helped put it into the UK Top 10, proving their enduring appeal. • **Trivia:** An instrumental piece was used on the 1993 series for comedy duo, Newman & Baddiel.

Album rating: READING, WRITING AND ARITHMETIC (*8) / BLIND (*7) / STATIC & SILENCE (*6)

HARRIET WHEELER (b.26 Jun'63, Maidenhead, England) – vocals (ex-JIM JIMINEE) / **DAVID GAVURIN** (b. 4 Apr'63) – guitar / **PAUL BRINDLEY** (b. 6 Nov'63, Loughborough, England) – bass / **PATRICK 'Patch' HANNAN** (b. 4 Mar'66) – drums repl. drum machine

		Rough Trade	D.G.C.
Feb 89.	(7") (RT 218) **CAN'T BE SURE. / I KICKED A BOY** (12"+=/cd-s+=) (RT 218 T/CD) – Don't tell your mother.	45	-
Jan 90.	(lp/c/cd) (ROUGH+C/CD 148) <24277> **READING, WRITING AND ARITHMETIC** – Skin & bones / Here's where the story ends / Can't be sure / I won / Hideous towns / You're not the only one I know / A certain someone / I kicked a boy / My finest hour / Joy. (re-iss. May96 cd/c; CD/TC PCS 7378)	4	39
Jan 90.	(7") **HERE'S WHERE THE STORY ENDS. / SKIN AND BONES**	-	

		Parlophone	D.G.C.
Sep 92.	(c-s/7") (TC+/R 6319) **GOODBYE. / WILD HORSES** (cd-s+=) (CDR 6319) – Noise.	27	-
Oct 92.	(cd/c/lp) (CD/TC+/PCSD 121) <24479> **BLIND** – I feel / Goodbye / Life and soul / Marc / On Earth / God made me / Love / What do you think? / 24 hours / Blood on my hands / Medieval. (re-iss. Mar94; same)	15	
Sep 97.	(7") (R 6475) **SUMMERTIME. / NOTHING SWEET** (cd-s+=) (CDR 6475) – Gone. (cd-s) (CDRS 6475) – ('A'side) / Skin & bones (live) / Here's where the story ends (live).	15	

		Capitol	Geffen
Sep 97.	(cd/c/lp) (CD/TC+/EST 2300) <25131> **STATIC & SILENCE** – Summertime / Homeward / Folk song / She / When I'm thinking about you / I can't wait / Another flavour / Leave this city / Your eyes / Cry / Monochrome.	10	33
Nov 97.	(c-s) (TCR 6487) **CRY / THROUGH THE DARK** (cd-s+=) (CDR 6487) – Life goes on. (cd-s) (CDRS 6487) – ('A'side) / Can't be sure (demo) / You're not the only one I know (demo).	43	-

—— the band looked to have disbanded

SUNDAY'S BEST

Formed: Los Angeles, California, USA ... 1997 by PEDRO BONITO, IAN MORENO and EDWARD REYES. The trio was bolstered to a quartet when, while recording their debut 7" and a track for a compilation with producer TOM ACKERMAN (formerly of SKIPLOADER), the boys asked if he would like to come on board. ACKERMAN took them up on this invitation and moved to drum duties with MORENO taking on rhythm guitar. Their ensuing EP, 'WHERE ARE YOU NOW' (1999) and debut LP 'POISED TO BREAK' (2000), showcased their blend of pop-punk with emo-core flavourings, both competent but fairly staid early efforts. Their ensuing sophomore LP, 'THE CALIFORNIAN', was a big departure from their initial offerings, moving towards a much more lucid indie pop style, where REYES' vocal talents were allowed to shine in the extensively chilled ambience of sound. This album certainly displayed an outfit with more of a future than its more run-of-the-mill predecessor heralded.

Album rating: WHERE ARE YOU NOW mini (*5) / POISED TO BREAK (*5) / THE CALIFORNIAN (*6)

EDWARD REYES – vocals, bass / **PEDRO BONITO** – guitar / **IAN MORENO** – rhythm guitar / **TOM ACKERMAN** – drums (ex-SKIPLOADER)

		not iss.	Crank!
May 99.	(m-cd) <80218> **WHERE ARE YOU NOW** – Too soon to laugh / Red herring / You did this / Truest you / Tracing paper / Instead, he falls / Homing device.	-	

		Polyvinyl	Polyvinyl
2000.	(cd) <PRC 037CD> **POISED TO BREAK** – The hardest part / Bruise-blue / White, picket fences / Saccharine / Indian summer / When is Pearl Harbor day? / In beats like trains / Looks like a mess / Winter-owned / Congratulations.	-	

—— **JAMES TWEEDY** – bass; repl. BONITO who formed JEALOUS SOUND

| May 02. | (lp/cd) <(PRC 050/+CD)> **THE CALIFORNIAN**
– The try / The Californian / Don't let it fade / The salt mines of Santa Monica / If we had it made / Our left coast ambitions / Without meaning / Beethoven St. / Brave, but brittle ... / Los Feliz arms. | | |

SUN DIAL

Formed: South London, England ... 1985 out of MODERN ART by GARY RAMON. They/he had issued a few limited edition releases on 'Color Disc', the 1986 single, 'DREAMS TO LIVE' / 'BEAUTIFUL TRUTH', the 1987 lp, 'STEREOLAND', the 1989 one-sided 7"clear-flexi freebie, 'PENNY VALENTINE' & 'ONE-WAY TICKET', released at the same time as German-only lp, 'ALL ABOARD THE MIND TRAIN'. These recordings featured drummers DAVE MORGAN (Weather Prophets) and ED KENT alongside GERALD on guitar and occasional saxophone. SUN DIAL blasted onto the scene in the early 90's when they debuted with 'EXPLODING IN YOUR MIND'. This 12" appeared on 'Tangerine', a label formed by record dealer, Hugo Chavez-Smith. Its very limited release was rectified when Mark Heyward (of Vinyl Experience record store) set up 'UFO' records to create an outlet for future SUN DIAL recordings. The group subsequently expanded into a quartet (briefly a 5-piece) after they released their debut album, 'OTHER WAY OUT' (1991), a neo-psychedelic guitar-noise trip through the musical black hole of SPACEMEN 3 and LOOP via The STOOGES and The JESUS & MARY CHAIN. RAMON then enlisted a new-look crew of JOHN PELECH, CHRIS DALLEY and NIGEL CARPENTER for the 'OVERSPILL' EP and 'REFLECTER' (1992) LP, the former produced by Vic Keary (boss of Mushroom records), the first person to record MARC BOLAN! In 1993, after CRAIG ADRIENNE replaced PELECH, the quartet signed to 'Beggars Banquet', releasing the album, 'LIBERTINE', before RAMON reinstated the original rhythm section of CLOUGH and MORGAN. This line-up completed one further set, 'ACID YANTRA' (1995), before they were eclipsed for good. • **Songwriters:** RAMON except covers; CIRCLE SKY (Monkees) / MAGIC POTION (Open Mind) / ONLY A NORTHERN SONG (Beatles). • **Trivia:** 'OTHER WAY OUT' was voted best album in Italian magazine, 'Rockerilla'.

Album rating: OTHER WAY OUT (*8) / REFLECTER (*6) / LIBERTINE (*6) / ACID YANTRA (*6)

GARY RAMON – guitar with **DAVE MORGAN** – drums / **TONY CLOUGH** – keyboards, flute

		UFO	Continuum
Jan 91.	(12"ep/cd-ep) (45002 T/CD) **EXPLODING IN YOUR MIND (edit). / OTHER SIDE / PLAINS OF NAZCA (edit)**	☐	-

—— Note: the unreleased test pressing of above was on 'Tangerine' (TAN111)

—— Below album was also released on 'Tangerine' in 1990.

| Apr 91. | (pic-cd/c) (UFO 1 CD/MC) <19107> **OTHER WAY OUT**
– Plains of Nazca / Exploding in your mind / Magic flight / World without time / She's looking all around / Lorne blues. (cd+=) – Visitation / Other side. (re-iss. cd 1994 on 'Acme'++=; AC8003CD) – Slow motion / Fountain. | | |

—— **JOHN PELECH** – drums; repl. MORGAN

—— **CHRIS DALLEY** – bass + **NIGEL CARPENTER** – guitar (both ex-BIKINIS) repl. CLOUGH who joined SPIRAL SKY

| Sep 91. | (12"ep,12"orange-ep/cd-ep) (45002 T/CD) **OVERSPILL**
– Fireball/ Only a northern song / Never fade / Overspill. | | |

		UFO	Dutch East India
Mar 92.	(clear-lp/cd) (UFO 8/+CD) <DEI 2020> **REFLECTER** – Reflecter / Easy for you / I don't mind / Slow motion / Tremelo / Never fade / Sunstroke / Mind train. (ltd-cd+=) (UFO 8XCD) – Reflecter 2.		Apr93

		UFO	DEI
Jul 92.	(12"green-ep/cd-ep) (45008 T/CD) <2024> **FAZER** – I don't mind / Let it go / Out of place / Easy fazer. above featured **MICKY MANN** (of The SHAMEN)		

—— **CRAIG ADRIENNE** – drums; repl. PELECH

		Beggars Banquet	Beggars Banquet
Jun 93.	(lp/c/cd) (BBQ+/C/CD 138) <92326> **LIBERTINE** – Send / Going down / Watch you smile / Deep inside / Everything you see / Dual / Hold on / Around and around / Star baby / Believer.		Aug93
Oct 93.	(7"white-ep/cd-ep) (BBQ 51/+CD) **GOING DOWN / WATCH YOU SMILE. / JEWEL / STARBABY (live)**	☐	-

—— now w/out DALLEY + CARPENTER, they had become a trio (**RAMON, CLOUGH + MORGAN**) adding guest **JAKE HONEYWELL** – bass

| May 95. | (12"green/cd-s) (BBQ 54/+CD) **BAD DRUG. / FAIRGROUND** | | - |
| Jun 95. | (cd) (BBQCD 173) <92637> **ACID YANTRA**
– Red sky / Apollo / 3000 miles / Are you supernatural? / Bad drug / Fly into the sun / Rollercoaster / Nova / Yantra jam. | | Oct95 |

—— SUN DIAL disbanded after above

SUN DIAL (cont)

– compilations, etc. –

1994.	(bootleg-cd,lp) *Acme; (AC 8001)* **RETURN JOURNEY** (rec.1991 lost 2nd lp)			–	–
1996.	(red-lp,cd) *Acme; (AC 8015 LP/CD)* **LIVE DRUG**			–	–

SUNNY DAY REAL ESTATE

Formed: Seattle, Washington, USA ... early 90's by JEREMY ENIGK, WILLIAM GOLDSMITH, NATE MENDEL and DAN HOERNER. On the strength of a self-financed debut 45, 'SONG NUMBER 8 – SONG NUMBER 9', they signed to veteran US indie label, 'Sub Pop', who released their debut album, 'DIARY', the following year. As their name might suggest, SDRE offered up a brighter take on the grunge formula of their hometown, even going so far as to package their album in a day-glo pink sleeve. Despite a further promising eponymous release, the band effectively sold up with the sudden departure of ENIGK who'd converted to Christianity. MENDEL and GOLDSMITH in turn joined ex-NIRVANA drummer DAVE GROHL in his new FOO FIGHTERS project. With ENIGK having gotten at least some of his excess musical energy and neo-psychedelic questing out of his system with his one-off solo set, 'RETURN OF THE FROG QUEEN' (1996), he subsequently reformed SUNNY DAY with GOLDSMITH and new bass player J PALMER. The revamped band unveiled their bold new sound on 'HOW IT FEELS TO BE SOMETHING ON' (1998), pedalling a more complex, less strident approach shot through with the echoes of ENIGK's recent foray into the mystic. While 'LIVE' (1999) served as a competent between-album diversion, 'THE RISING TIDE' (2000) marked SUNNY DAY REAL ESTATE's creative high water mark. Richly layered, finely nuanced and characterised by an almost grand, elegant musical sweep, the record found ENIGK and Co finally coming of age.

Album rating: DIARY (*7) / SUNNY DAY REAL ESTATE (*6) / HOW IT FEELS TO BE SOMETHING ON (*7) / LIVE (*5) / THE RISING TIDE (*7) / Jeremy Enigk: RETURN OF THE FROG QUEEN (*6)

JEREMY ENIGK (b.16 Jul'74) – vocals, guitar / **DAN HOERNER** (b.13 May'69) – vocals, guitar / **NATE MENDEL** (b. 2 Dec'68) – bass / **WILLIAM GOLDSMITH** (b. 4 Jul'72) – drums

			not iss.	One Day I Stopped Breathing
1993.	(7") **SONG NUMBER 8 – SONG NUMBER 9.** /		–	
			Sub Pop	Sub Pop
Jun 94.	(lp/cd) *(SP/+CD 121-302)* <SP 246/+CD> **DIARY**			
	– Seven / In circles / Song about an angel / Round / 47 / Blankets were the stairs / Pheurton skeurto / Shadows / 48 / Grendel / Sometimes.			
Oct 95.	(lp/cd) *<(SP/+CD 316)>* **UNTITLED** ("The Pink Album")			
	– Friday / Theo B / Red elephant / 5/4 / Waffle / 8 / Iscarabaid / J'nuh / Rodeo Jones.			

— split when JEREMY found God and became a disciple of Jesus. MENDEL and GOLDSMITH were recruited by DAVE GROHL in The FOO FIGHTERS.

— **ENIGK + GOLDSMITH** reformed SDRE in 1998 with a new bassist **J PALMER**

Sep 98.	(cd) *<(SP 409)>* **HOW IT FEELS TO BE SOMETHING ON**		
	– Pillars / Roses in water / Every shining time you arrive / Two promises / 100 million / How it feels to be something on / The prophet / Guitar and video games / The shark's own private fuck / The days were golden.		
Oct 99.	(lp/cd) *<(SP/+CD 485)>* **LIVE (live)**		
	– Pillars / Guitar and video games / The blankets were the stairs / 100 million / Every shining time you arrive / Song about an angel / The prophet / J'nuh / Rodeo Jones / In circles / The days were golden.		

— **DAN HOERNER** – bass; repl. PALMER

		Time Bomb	Time Bomb
Jul 00.	(lp/cd) *(TB 3541/+CD)* **THE RISING TIDE**		Jun00
	– Killed by an angel / One / Rain song / Disappear / Snibe / The ocean / Fool in the photograph / Tearing in my heart / Television / Faces in disguise / The rising tide. (cd re-iss. Feb01 on 'R.C.A.'; 70930 43541-2)		
		Houston Party	Houston Party
Jun 01.	(7") *<(HPRV 09)>* **PILLARS. / GUITAR AND VIDEO GAMES**		

JEREMY ENIGK

with a plethora of session people

Oct 96.	(cd) *<SP 323>* **RETURN OF THE FROG QUEEN**	–	
	– Abegail Anne / Return of the frog queen / Lewis hollow / Lizard / Carnival / Call me steam / Explain / Shade and black hat / Fallen heart.		
Nov 96.	(cd-ep) *<SP 58>* **THE END SESSIONS** (U.S. tour 1997)	–	
	– Abegail Anne / Return of the frog queen / Lizard / Carnival / Explain.		

SUNSET VALLEY

Formed: Portland, Oregon, USA ... autumn 1996 by HERMAN JOLLY, JONATHAN DREWS and ERIC FURLONG. The subsequent addition of JEFF SALTZMAN and TONY LASH paved the way for the recording of debut album, 'THE NEW SPEED' (1998), an invigorating if slightly derivative instalment of harmonious, neo-psychedelic fuzz-pop. The following year's 'BOYSCOUT SUPERHERO' (1999) was as naively larger than life as its title suggested, intent on saving indie-rock's soul with a brace of bright-eyed missives. The record's more reflective moments were expanded upon with 'ICEPOND' (2001), alternatively winsome and wayward, frazzled and frustrating yet always checking in with a grace-saving melody.

Album rating: THE NEW SPEED (*5) / BOYSCOUT SUPERHERO (*6) / ICEPOND (*6)

HERMAN JOLLY – vocals / **JONATHAN DREWS** – guitar / **ERIC FURLONG** – bass / **JEFF SALTZMAN** – keyboards / **TONY LASH** – drums (ex-HEATMISER)

		Wurlitzer Jukebox	Sugar Free
Apr 98.	(cd) *<sf 007>* **THE NEW SPEED**		
	– Sky lab love scene / Blanketville / Coral man / Shanghai Shelly / Super girl / Met my mako / Red room rocket ride / Statue robot / Red Thai Sunday / Neptune pools / California now.		
1999.	(7") *(WJ 43)* **DOLL HILL. / CORAL MAN**	–	
Nov 99.	(cd) *<sf 014>* **BOYSCOUT SUPERHERO**	–	
	– I got fair / Megapills / Tornado / Happily frozen / City of bees / Heatwave one / Doll eating man / Fairy theory / Solid goldmine / Jackass crusher / Doll hill.		
		Zandzoe	not iss.
Jun 00.	(7"m) *(ZAZ 09)* **MEGA PILLS. / (+2)**		–
		not iss.	Sea Level
May 01.	(7") **PARADE ON MY RAIN. /** John Vanderslice: **MY OLD FLAME**	–	
		not iss.	Barsuk
Aug 01.	(cd) *<bark 20>* **ICEPOND**	–	
	– Say ow / Ironmen / Fall fly / Wired nights / Blackberry bushes / Help me babe / Misery jet / Nico ride / Touch you / Joseph blow / Icepond / Parade on my rain / Janey o' / Matinee idol / Nautilus sun.		

— HERMAN JOLLY was also a solo artist; 'MAD COWBOY DISEASE' album '98

SUNSHINE FIX
(see under ⇒ OLIVIA TREMOR CONTROL)

SUPERCHARGER (US)

Formed: San Francisco, California, USA ... 1990 by GREG LOWERY, DARIN RAFFELLI and KAREN SINGLETARY. This short-lived, straight-up indie punk rock group issued the ultra-rare debut, 'SUPERCHARGER' (1991), on their own 'Radio X' imprint, before signing with 'Estrus' records in 1993, and releasing the more musically accomplished 'GOES WAY OUT' (1993). After a brief tour of Europe, SUPERCHARGER split, with 'Estrus' re-issuing their debut album in 1997, which was only originally on a limited run of 500. However, the band members went on to leave a modern day punk lineage; RAFFELLI joined the lolita-esque group The DONNAS, while LOWERY formed The INFECTIONS and The ZODIAC KILLERS whilst trying to manage one of the only true DIY punk labels left – 'Rip Off' records.
• **Covered:** MYSTERY ACTION (Rezillos) / I'M A HOG FOR YOU BABY (Montesas) / BOOM BOOM (John Lee Hooker). • **Note:** Not to be confused with England's trip-hoppers SUPERCHARGER who used the name from 1997 onwards.

Album rating: SUPERCHARGER (*6) / GOES WAY OUT! (*7)

GREG LOWERY – vocals, bass / **DARIN RAEFFELLI** – guitar, vocals / **KAREN SINGLETARY** – drums, vocals

		not iss.	Radio X
1991.	(ltd-lp) *<RX 01>* **SUPERCHARGER**	–	
	– She's so cool / I broke my mind / All about Judy / Sooprize package for Mr. Mineo / The day my body vaorized / Lost cause / Phobia / Are you a boy/girl? / San Bruno / Ghost of Steve McQueen / You put the hex on me / Hey, I'm gone / Whiptofized / Hit the road / Gum flappin' baby. *<(lp/cd re-iss. Sep97 on 'Estrus'+=; ES 1240/+CD)>* – Zodiac.		
		not iss.	Pre B.S.
1992.	(7") *<P45 005>* **ICEPICK! / WANT IT BAD**	–	
		not iss.	Gearhead
1993.	(7") *<RPM 001>* **MYSTERY ACTION. /** Gas Huffer: **BAD GUY REACTION**	–	
		not iss.	Pin Up
1993.	(7"flexi-ep) *<pinup 93006>* **TOUR '93**	–	
	– Bad boy / I'm beat / (other 2 by the MUMMIES).		
		not iss.	Bag Of Hammers
1993.	(7"ep) *<BOH 009>* **REV IT UP! EP**	–	
	– Rev it up! / I got none / Take a hint / I'm a hog for you baby.		
		not iss.	Demolition Derby
1993.	(7") *<DD 001>* **LIVE AT THE PIT'S '93** (live)	–	
	– Boom boom / (other by the MUMMIES).		
		Estrus	Estrus
1993.	(7"promo) *<ESP 6>* **DON'T MESS ME UP. / LIVE FROM RADIO X**		
Jun 96.	(lp/cd) *<(ES 127/+CD)>* **GOES WAY OUT!**		May96
	– Super X / No sleep / Way out / It's alright / Buzz off / You irritate me / I took a ride (when you said I'm gone) / Bailin' out / Knockout / One way street / Sick to death / Get out of my house / Sissy jerk / Cindy Lou.		
		not iss.	Super*teem!
1996.	(7") *<45 01>* **SOOPRIZE PACKAGE FOR MR. MINEO. / SOUTH CITY PSYCHO**	–	

— disbanded + LOWERY joined The RIP-OFFS

– compilations, etc. –

1995.	(7"ep) *Pre B.S.; <P45 006>* **split w/ CAR THIEVES**	–	
	– Icepick! / Want it bad (other 2 by CAR THIEVES).		
2002.	(cd) *Rip Off; <rip off 59>* **SINGLES PARTY 1992-1993**	–	
	– Icepick! / Want it bad / Rev it up / I got none / Take a hint / I'm a hog for you baby / Bad boy / I'm beat / Don't mess me up / Live from Radio X / Mystery action / Boom boom.		

SUPERCHUNK

Formed: Chapel Hill, North Carolina, USA . . . 1989 as CHUNK by RALPH 'MAC' McCAUGHAN, STEVEN WILBUR, LAURA BALLANCE and CHUCK GARRISON. One of the original Chapel Hill bands, SUPERCHUNK (the new improved moniker implemented at the turn of the decade) kicked up a local storm with feverishly enthusiastic live performances and an eponymous debut EP (which included an unlikely but effective cover of The Shangri-las' 'TRAIN FROM KANSAS CITY') but it was 1990's 'SLACK MOTHERFUCKER' which brought them to wider attention. A brilliant pop-punk anthem for the nascent "slacker" generation, the single preceded an eponymous debut album and a growing surge of cult acclaim. The early promise was finally fulfilled with Steve Albini-produced follow-up album, 'NO POCKY FOR KITTY' (1992), a dizzying, breathless collection of noise-pop gems following a lineage from Brit pioneers like The BUZZCOCKS through FUGAZI, HUSKER DU, DINOSAUR JR., SONIC YOUTH etc. Enduring favourites like 'TOSSING SEEDS' and 'SKIP STEPS 1 & 3' favoured a straightforward, heartfelt rush of bruised melody over the more oblique approach of contemporaries like PAVEMENT; it was exactly this simplicity that earned the band such vociferous support from their fans and criticism from their detractors, as witnessed in the mixed reviews for singles compilation, 'TOSSING SEEDS' (1992). Yet despite all the predictions of imminent world domination, 1993's 'ON THE MOUTH' was met with a decidedly lukewarm reception, attempts at lengthier compositions negating the infectiousness of their best work. 'FOOLISH' (1994) and 'HERE'S WHERE THE STRINGS COME IN' (1995) redressed the balance somewhat yet save for the soaring 'HYPER ENOUGH' there was a distinct lack of the trademark, in-your-face hooks. In the meantime, frontman McCAUGHAN had been working on 'I HOPE YOUR HEART IS NOT BRITTLE' (1994), the debut album for his PORTASTATIC side-project. A further SUPERCHUNK album, 'INDOOR LIVING', surfaced on 'City Slang' in 1997, yet there's no getting away from the feeling that the band's time had come and gone. There was however, a return to form for SUPERCHUNK as legendary underground producer/musician, JIM O'ROURKE, crafted one of the band's most triumphant albums in years, the brilliant 'COME PICK ME UP' (1999). It also featured some of Chicago's finest jazz musicians JEB BISHOP, FRED LONBERG-HOLM and sax player KEN VANDERMARK. Its follow-up, 'HERE'S TO SHUTTING UP' (2001), kept much to the same standards, although it was quite evident that SUPERCHUNK and mainman McCAUGHAN had somewhat matured musically and mentally as the years had passed them. This might've had something to do with McCAUGHAN's side-project, PORTASTATIC, a slow-burning instrumental act who'd composed and released four albums since the aforementioned 1994 debut; 'SLOW NOTE FROM A SINKING SHIP' (1995), 'THE NATURE OF SAP' (1997), movie soundtrack 'LOOKING FOR LEONARD' (2001) and most recently, 'THE PERFECT LITTLE DOOR' (2001). • **Songwriters:** Group; except GIRL U WANT (Devo) / IT'S SO HARD TO FALL IN LOVE (Sebadoh) / BRAND NEW LOVE (Lou Barlow) / TRAIN FROM KANSAS CITY (Shangri-la's) / 100,000 FIREFLIES (Magnetic Fields) / LYING IN STATE (Verlaines) / I'LL BE YOUR SISTER (Motorhead) / NIGHT OF CHILL BLUE (Chills) / SCARY MONSTERS (AND SUPER CREEPS) (David Bowie) / etc. • **Trivia:** MAC guested in 1992 on SEAM's 'Headsparks' album, alongside BITCH MAGNET members.

Album rating: SUPERCHUNK (*4) / NO POCKY FOR KITTY (*8) / TOSSING SEEDS compilation (*8) / ON THE MOUTH (*6) / FOOLISH (*6) / INCIDENTAL MUSIC compilation (*8) / HERE'S WHERE THE STRINGS COME IN (*5) / INDOOR LIVING (*5) / COME PICK ME UP (*6) / HERE'S TO SHUTTING UP (*6) / Portastatic: I HOPE YOUR HEART IS NOT BRITTLE (*7) / SLOW NOTE FROM A SINKING SHIP (*5) / THE NATURE OF SAP (*5) / LOOKING FOR LEONARD (*6) / THE PERFECT LITTLE DOOR mini (*5)

MAC McCAUGHAN – vocals, guitar / **STEVEN WILBUR** – guitar / **LAURA BALLANCE** – bass / **CHUCK GARRISON** – drums

	not iss.	Merge
1989. (7"ep) <MRG 004> **THE CHUNK EP**	-	
– What do I / Train from Kansas City / My noise.		

—— **JON WURSTER** – drums; repl. CHUCK

	City Slang	Matador
May 90. (7") <MRG 007> **SLACK MOTHERFUCKER. / NIGHT CREATURES**	-	
Sep 90. (cd/c/lp) <OLE 004> **SUPERCHUNK**		
– Sick to move / My noise / Let it go / Swinging / Slow / Slack motherfucker / Binding / Down the hall / Half a life / Not tomorrow.		

—— **JIM** – guitar; repl. STEVEN

1991. (7") <MRG 014> **FISHING. / COOL**	-	
(above & below issued on 'Merge')		
1991. (7"ep) <MRG 018> **THE FREED SEED**	-	
1991. (7"ep) <ID 004> **TOWER**	-	- Austra
– Fishing / Tower / Train from Kansas City / What do I.		
(above issued on 'Messiah Complex')		
Oct 91. (7") <OLE 026> **THE BREADMAN. / CAST IRON**	-	
Jan 92. (lp/cd) (EFA 04073/+CD) <OLE 035> **NO POCKY FOR KITTY**		Oct91
– Skip steps 1 & 3 / Seed toss / Cast iron / The tower / Punch me harder / Sprung a leal / 30 xtra / Tie a rope to the back of the bus / Press / Sidewalk / Creek / Throwing things.		

	City Slang	Merge
Apr 92. (lp/c/cd) (EFA 04078/+C/CD) <MRG 20/+C/CD> **TOSSING SEEDS** (singles 1989-1991)		
– What do I / My noise / Train from Kansas City / Slack motherfucker / Night creatures / Garlic / Fishing / Cool / Breadman / Cast iron / Seed toss / It's so hard to fall in love / Brand new love.		

Oct 92. (7") (EFA 04906S) <MRG 027> **MOWER. / ON THE MOUTH**		
(12"+=/cd-s+=) (EFA 04906/+CD) <MRG 027CD> – Fishing (live).		
Jan 93. (7"ep/12"ep/cd-ep) (EFA 04910-45/-02/-03) <MRG 034CD> **THE QUESTION IS HOW FAST**		
– The question is how fast / Forged it / 100,000 fireflies.		
Feb 93. (cd/lp) (EFA 04915-2/-4) <OLE 049> **ON THE MOUTH**		
– Precision auto / From the curve / For tension / Mower package thief / Swallow that / I guess I remembered it wrong / New low / Untied / The question is how fast / Trash heap / Flawless / The only piece that you get.		

—— <above issued on 'Matador' US, below on 'Domino' UK>

Oct 93. (7") (RUG 9) <MRG 047> **RIBBON. / WHO NEEDS LIGHT**		-
Dec 93. (7") <SMWH 12> **NIGHT OF CHILL BLUE. / (other by CATERPILLAR)**	-	
(above issued on 'Simple Machines')		
Jan 94. (7") <MRG 050> **PRECISION AUTO (parts 2 & 3) (Mark R. mix)**	-	
Mar 94. (7") (EFA 04937-7) <MRG 59CD> **THE FIRST PART. / CONNECTICUT**		
(cd-s+=) (EFA 04937-2) – Foolish.		
Apr 94. (cd/lp) (EFA 04938-2/-1) <MRG 60CD> **FOOLISH**		Dec93
– Like a fool / The first part / Water wings / Driveway to driveway / Saving my ticket / Kicked in / Why do you have to put a date on everything / Without blinking / Keeping track / Revelations / Stretched out / In a stage whisper.		
Jan 95. (7"m) (EFA 04948-7) <MRG 69> **DRIVEWAY TO DRIVEWAY. / DRIVEWAY (acoustic) / SICK TO MOVE (acoustic)**		Oct94
(cd-s+=) (EFA 04948-2) – Seed toss (acoustic).		
1995. (7") **KICKED IN. / (other by TSUNAMI)**	-	
(above issued on 'Honey Bear')		
Jul 95. (cd/d-lp) (EFA 04959-2/-1) <MRG 85CD> **INCIDENTAL MUSIC 1991-95** (compilation)		
– Shallow end / Mower / On the mouth / Cadmium / Who needs light / Ribbon / Foolish / 100,000 fireflies / Invitation / Makeout bench / Baxter / Connecticut / Lying in state / Throwing things / I'll be your sister / Night of the chill blue / Forged it / Home at dawmn.		
Sep 95. (7") (EFA 04968-7) <MRG 89CD> **HYPER ENOUGH. / NEVER TOO YOUNG TO SMOKE**		Aug95
(cd-s+=) (EFA 04968-2) – Detroit has a skyline.		
Oct 95. (cd/lp) (EFA 04966-2/-1) <MRG 90CD> **HERE'S WHERE THE STRINGS COME IN**		Sep95
– Hyper enough / Silverleaf and snowy tears / Yeah, it's beautiful here too / Iron on / Sunshine state / Detroit has a skyline / Eastern terminal / Animated airplanes over Germany / Green flowers, blue fish / Here's where the strings come in / Certain stars.		
Dec 96. (cd-ep) <MRG 118CD> **THE LAUGHTER GUNS EP**	-	
– A small definition / Her royal fisticuffs / The mine has been returned to its original owner / Hero / Cool-ass mutherfuckin' bonus track – Hyper enuff part 2: The DJ's revenge.		
Aug 97. (7"ep/cd-ep) <(MRG 128/+CD)> **WATERY HANDS. / WITH BELLS ON / WATERY HANDS (Wet Wurlitzer mix)**		Jul97
Sep 97. (cd/lp) (EFA 04997-2/-1) <MRG 129CD> **INDOOR LIVING**		
– Unbelievable things / Burn last Sunday / Marquee / Watery hands / Nu bruises / Every single instinct / Song for Marion Brown / Popular music / Under our feet / European medicine / Martini's on the roof.		

	Matador	Merge
Feb 99. (7") <(MRG 148)> **THE MAJESTIC. / REG**		
Aug 99. (cd/lp) (OLE 397-2/-1) <MRG 163> **COME PICK ME UP**		
– So convinced / Hello hawk / Cursed mirror / 1000 pounds / Good dreams / Low branches / Pink clouds / Smarter hearts / Honey bee / June showers / Pulled muscle / Tiny bombs / You can always count on me (in the worst way).		
Jan 00. (cd-s) (OLE 434-2) **1000 POUNDS / WHITE NOISE / SCARY MONSTERS (AND SUPER CREEPS) / 1000 POUNDS (acoustic)**		
Sep 01. (cd) (OLE 532-2) <MRG 501> **HERE'S TO SHUTTING UP**		-
– Late century dream / Rainy streets / Phone sex / Florida's on fire / Out on the wing / The animal has left its shell / Act surprised v/ Art class (song for Yayoi Kusama) / What do you look forward to? / Drool collection.		
Oct 01. (cd-ep) (OLE 536-2) **LATE CENTURY DREAM EP**		-
– Late century dream / Length od Las Ramblas / Becoming a speck / Florida's on fire (acoustic demo).		

	Merge	Merge
Apr 02. (cd-ep) <(MRG 207CD)> **ART CLASS EP**		
– Art class / Art class (live acoustic) / Hot break / Collection of accounts.		

PORTASTATIC

MAC McCAUGHAN – vocals, multi / **JENNIFER WALKER** – bass

	Elemental	Merge
Feb 94. (lp/lp/cd) (ELM 17/+X/CD) <MRG 51CD> **I HOPE YOUR HEART IS NOT BRITTLE**		
– Mute 2 / Polaroid / Gutter / Naked pilseners / Tree killer / Creeping around / Weird time / Silver screw / Beer and chocolate bars / Had / Memphis / Receiver / Why have you come back / The main thing.		

	Matador	Matador
May 94. (7"/cd-s) <(OLE 076-7/-2)> **NAKED PILSNERS. / FEEL BETTER / JOSEPHINE**		Feb94

—— added **JON WURSTER** – guitar, keyboards, casio keyboards / **BEN BARWICK** – guitar / **CLAIRE ASHBY + ASH BOWIE** – drums

	Merge	Merge
Mar 95. (cd-ep) <MRG 80CD> **SCRAPBOOK EP**	-	
– St. Elmo's fire / Why pinch yourself / Bear that chokes / My favorite sound / Scrapbook X's.		
Jun 95. (cd) <MRG 86CD> **SLOW NOTE FROM A SINKING SHIP**	-	
– When you crashed / Skinny glasses girl / San Andreas / Taking you with me / The angels of sleep / A cunning latch / Spooky / The great escape / Running water / You can't win / Isn't that the way / On our hands / Pastime / In the manner of Anne Frank.		

SUPERCHUNK (cont) — THE GREAT INDIE DISCOGRAPHY — The 1990s

—— MAC now with JONATHAN MARX – organ, sax, trumpet, etc
Mar 97. (lp/cd) <(MRG 120/+CD)> **THE NATURE OF SAP**
– You know where to find me / A lovely Niles / Hurrican warning (ignored) / Reverse Lester / Flare / Jonathan's organ / Before you sailed around the world / Ben's revenge / Impolite cheers / Spying on the spys / BJJT / Landed / If you could sing / The nature of sap.
May 00. (cd-ep) <(MRG 180CD)> **DEL MEL DE MELAO**
– Baby / Lamento sertanejo / I fell in love one day / Nao identificado / Clareana.

—— MAC now helped by MARGARET WHITE – violin
May 01. (cd) <MRG 490CD> **LOOKING FOR LEONARD** (soundtrack)
– Looking For Leonard theme / Stmbling music / Luka's theme / "Do you speak English?" / Stealing romance / Johnny's dead / Jo's plan / Luka's theme (shake mix) / Sweethearts (organ mix) / Funeral music / Only good people wonder if they're bad / The chase / A dead end / Sweethearts of the world.
Oct 01. (m-cd; as PORTASTATIC featuring KEN VANDERMARK and TIM MULVENNA) <MRG 210CD> **THE PERFECT LITTLE DOOR**
– Had / Hey Salty / Late night wait around / Broken arm / When you crashed.

SUPER DELUXE

Formed: Seattle, Washington, USA . . . 1994 by songwriter/vocalist. guitarist, BRADEN BLAKE, along with JOHN KIRSCH, JAKE NESHEIM and CHRIS LOCKWOOD. Melodic punk-poppers swimming in the slipstream of their hometown Grunge scene, SUPER DELUXE were an adolescent hybrid of NIRVANA, the POSIES and TEENAGE FANCLUB, who initially signed to US indie, 'Tim/Kerr'. Debut album, 'FAMOUS' (1995), confirmed their precocious talent while Indolent offshoot, 'Luminous', gave it a UK release the following year. A period of high profile touring preceded a major label deal with 'Warners', through whom they issued the 1997 sophomore effort, 'VIA SATELLITE'.

Album rating: FAMOUS (*6) / VIA SATELLITE (*5)

BRADEN BLAKE – vocals, guitar / **JOHN KIRSCH** – guitar / **JAKE NESHEIM** – bass / **CHRIS LOCKWOOD** – drums

                                                                                       Luminous Tim/Kerr
Jul 96. (7") *(LUX 001)* **SHE CAME ON. / GIVE A LITTLE BIT**
(cd-s+=) *(LUX 001CD)* – Years ago / On Lisa.
Aug 96. (7") *(LUX 002)* **FAMOUS. / VIRNANA 1234**
(cd-s+=) *(LUX 002CD)* – Wilted and faded / Famous #2 (acoustic).
Sep 96. (cd/c) *(LUX CD/MC 003)* <TK95CD 106> **FAMOUS**   Oct95
– Lizadrin / Famous / She came on / Love her madly / Flustered / Disappearing / Johnny's gone fishin' / Holly's dream vacation / Smile / Suitcases / Sunshine for now. *(re-iss. Feb98 on 'Tim/Kerr' lp/cd; TK/+95CD 106)*
Dec 96. (7") *(LUX 004)* **ALL I WANTED WAS A SKATEBOARD. / GOD REST YE MERRY GENTLEMEN**
                                                                                       not iss. Warners
Jul 97. (cd/c) *<24678-2/-4>* **VIA SATELLITE**
– Your pleasure's mine / Lost in your failures / Farrah Fawcett / Love liquid wraparound / Alright / Commonplace / Divine / What's up with me / One in a million / New variations / Half asleep / I can see / Suicide doll / Years ago.
—— the band split after above

SUPERDRAG

Formed: Knoxville, Tennessee, USA . . . 1993 out of PUNCH WAGON and The USED by JOHN DAVIS, BRANDON FISHER, TOM PAPPAS and DON COFFEY JR. As DAVIS assumed the bulk of the songwriting duties and took over as frontman, the quartet coined the new moniker of SUPERDRAG and set about building up a local following. During this period the band circulated a rough demo tape, 'STEREO 360 SOUND', that eventually found its way into the hands of US indie imprint 'Darla'. In 1995, they delivered their first release, the mini-set 'THE FABULOUS 8 TRACK SOUND OF SUPERDRAG', leading to a major record deal with 'Elektra' and an impressive proper album debut, 'REGRETFULLY YOURS' (1996). In your face punk-pop with turbo-charged attitude, the record proved a favourite with the US college crowd and whetted appetites for 1998's meatier follow-up, 'HEAD TRIP IN EVERY KEY'. The band's brush with fame turned sour soon after as 'Elektra' neglected to promote the album and made it clear that SUPERDRAG weren't exactly priority. Further hassles eventually led to the label acquiescing in the band's demand to be dropped. Although PAPPAS subsequently departed and formed his own act FLESH VEHICLE (who released the 'ELASTIC PROSE' album in 2000), SUPERDRAG replaced him with SAM POWERS and set about recording 'IN THE VALLEY OF THE DYING STARS'. Cut in their own studio and released on the small 'Arena Rock Recording Company' label, the record was a cathartic musical kiss-off to their annus horribilis and paved the way for 2002's 'LAST CALL FOR VITRIOL', in which the DAVIS/POWERS writing axis came into its own. • **Covered:** SEPTEMBER GURLS (Alex Chilton) / DIANE (Husker Du).

Album rating: THE FABULOUS 8-TRACK SOUND OF SUPERDRAG mini (*6) / REGRETFULLY YOURS (*6) / HEAD TRIP IN EVERY KEY (*6) / STEREO 360 SOUND demo collection (*6) / IN THE VALLEY OF DYING STARS (*5) / LAST CALL FOR VITRIOL (*6)

PUNCH WAGON

MIKE SMITHERS – vocals, guitar / **JOHN DAVIS** – bass / **DON COFFEY JR** – drums
                                                                                       not iss. own label
1993. (c) <*none*> **PUNCH WAGON**
– My guru died / Jesus / Liquor / Parallel universe / Next time.
—— SMITHERS would subsequently form 30 AMP FUSE with DAVIS + COFFEY

USED

CHRIS HARGROVE – vocals, bass / **TOM PAPPAS** – guitar, vocals / **BRANDON FISHER** – guitar / **JOHNNY FLAME** – drums
                                                                                       not iss. own label
1993. (c) <*none*> **SHAMELESS SELF PROMOTION**
– Every stinkin' thing / Crash helmet / Be / Instrumental / Said it was me / Social plight / Hypnotized / T.A.P.S. (Terror, Angel and the Perfect Stranger) / Shallow grave.
                                                                                       not iss. Big Nothing
1993. (cd-ep) <*none*> **ROCK AND ROLL PARTY**
– Kiss me / Ultimate pop song / Tidal wave / Crash helmet / Potpourri 93.
1993. (7") <*none*> **KISS ME. / (other by The GONE DOGS)**

SUPERDRAG

JOHN DAVIS – vocals, guitar / **BRANDON FISHER** – guitar / **TOM PAPPAS** – bass / **DON COFFEY JR.** – drums
                                                                                       not iss. own label
Apr 94. (c) <*none*> **STEREO 360 SOUND**
– Whitney's theme / My prayer / Senorita / H.H.T. / Nothing good is real / Cuts and scars / Diane / Sleeping beauty / Take your spectre away. <*cd-iss. Nov98 on 'Superdrag Sound'; 001*>
                                                                                       not iss. Darla
Oct 94. (7",7"orange) <45-002> **SENORITA. / MY PRAYER / CUTS & SCARS**
Jun 95. (7",7"white) <005> **H.H.T. / NOTHING GOOD IS REAL**
Aug 95. (m-cd) <DRL 007> **THE FABULOUS 8-TRACK SOUND OF SUPERDRAG**
– Sugar / Bloody hell / Really thru / Liquor / 6/8 / Blown away / Load.
                                                                                       not iss. Arena Rock
Sep 95. (7"blue) <AR 001> **N.A. KICKER. / Husker Du: DIANE**
                                                                                       Elektra   Elektra
Oct 96. (cd) <(7559 61900-2)> **REGRETFULLY YOURS**   Apr96
– Scootin' / Cynicality / Carried / Slot machine / Garmonbozia / Phaser / Rocket / Nothing good is real / What if you don't fly / Truest love / Whitney's theme / N.A. kicker / Destination Ursa Major.
Oct 96. (cd-s) <EKR 229CD> **SUCKED OUT / SEPTEMBER GURLS (live in studio) / CYNICALITY**
Dec 96. (7") <*none*> **SLEEPING BEAUTY. / Dinky Doo: SLOW MPTION**
(above issued on 'Holbrook' records)
Mar 98. (cd/c) <62114-2/-4> **HEAD TRIP IN EVERY KEY**
– I'm expanding my mind / Hellbent / Sold you an alibi / Do the vampire / Amphetamine / Bankrupt vibration / Mr. Underground / Annetichrist / She is a holy grail / Pine away / Shuck and jive / Wrong vs. right doesn't matter / The art of dying.

—— **SAM POWERS** – bass (ex-WHO HIT JOHN) repl. PAPPAS who formed FLESH VEHICLE
                                                                                       not iss. Two Children
Jun 01. (m-cd) <*none*> **GREETINGS FROM TENNESSEE EP**
– Baby goes to 11 / Stu / I guess it's American / The emotional kind / Take your spectre away / Bloody hell / Liquor / Means so much / Bastards of young / You really got me.
                                                                                       Arena Rock Arena Rock
Oct 01. (cd) <(AR 014CD)> **IN THE VALLEY OF DYING STARS**
– Keep it close to me / Gimme animosity / Baby's waiting / Goin' out / Lighting the way / The warmth of a tomb / Bright pavilions / Ambulance driver / Unprepared / Some kind of tragedy / True believer / In the valley of dying stars.
Oct 01. (cd-ep) **ROCK SOLDIER EP**
– Lighting the way / I guess it's American / She says / My day will come / The emotional kind.
                                                                                       Vagrant Vagrant
Dec 01. (cd-ep) <(VR 358CD)> **THE ANNIVERSARY split EP**   Nov01
– (3 tracks by The ANNIVERSARY) / Take your spectre away / I guess it's American / The emotional kind.
                                                                                       Rykodisc Arena Rock
Sep 02. (cd) (RCD 16018) <AR 23CD> **LAST CALL FOR VITRIOL**   Jul02
– Baby goes to 11 / I can't wait / The staggering genius / So sincere / Extra-sensory / Feeling like I do / Way down here without you / Safe and warm / Remain yer strange / Her melancholy tune / Stu / Drag me closer to you.

– compilations, etc. –

Feb 99. (cd-ep) *Darla;* <(DRL 073)> **SENORITA EP**   Jul99
– Senorita / Cuts and scars / HHT / My prayer / Nothing good is real.

SUPER FRIENDZ

Formed: Halifax, Canada . . . 1993 by DREW YAMADA, MATT MURPHY and CHARLES AUSTIN. Not a power trio in the conventional sense, the 'FRIENDZ actually boasted two guitarists (YAMADA and MURPHY) while the drum stool was filled by a revolving cast of local movers and shakers including SLOAN's CHRIS MURPHY. A debut EP, 'BY REQUEST', appeared on the 'Murderecords' label in 1993, trailed by the 'STICKTOITIVENESS' cassette the following year. Finally, a debut album, 'MOCK UP, SCALE DOWN', was released in 1994 to widespread acclaim, their convincingly accessible brand of retro-fired, alternative power-pop going down well on the thriving Halifax scene and beyond. LONNIE JAMES was

SUPER FRIENDZ (cont)

subsequently hired as a permanent member in time to play on 1996's mini-set 'PLAY THE GAME, NOT GAMES', while an acclaimed sophomore album, 'SLIDE SHOW', followed in 1997. Sadly the 'FRIENDZ-ship came to an end later the same year as the various members determined to devote their time to other musical projects: YAMADA went on to work with INBREDS man, MIKE O'NEIL and NEUSILAND, MURPHY formed The FLASHING LIGHTS and JAMES founded his own HIGH FIVE BAND.

Album rating: MOCK UP, SCALE DOWN (*6) / SLIDE SHOW (*7) / "STICKTOITIVENESS" compilation (*6)

MATT MURPHY – guitar / **DREW YAMADA** – guitar / **CHARLES AUSTIN** – bass / **CLIFF GIBB** – drums (of THRUSH HERMIT) or **CHRIS MURPHY** – drums

			not iss.	Murderecords
1993.	(cd-ep) **BY REQUEST**		–	– Canada
1994.	(c) **STICKTOITIVENESS**		–	– Canada

— guest drummer **DAVE MARSH**

1994.	(cd) <017> **MOCK UP, SCALE DOWN**	–	– Canada

– 10 lbs / Karate man / Undertow / Down in flames / Dear old Ireland / Restricted / Come clean / Rescue us from boredom / Fireflies / Kiss the land / Stone alone / Better call / When they paid me / One day.

— now with full-time drummer **LONNIE JAMES**

1996.	(10"m-lp) <024> **PLAY THE GAME, NOT GAMES**	–	– Canada

– Green hand / Landing light / Boots / Machine green / Rescue us from boredom / Half-mast / Sorry / The Super Friendz theme.

1997.	(cd) <025> **SLIDE SHOW**	–	– Canada

– Up and running / No good reason / Stop-start / Two songs / Prattle on / Everything writes itself / Fooled at first / Forever a day / Absurd without it / Slow mothion blues / Citizens banned / Star in one / Evening sun / The world's most embarrasing moment.

— split in September, 1997; MATT MURPHY formed FLASHING LIGHTS; AUSTIN formed NEUSILAND, while others also worked on other projects

– compilations, etc. –

Jul 97.	(cd) *What Are?*; <63030> **"STICKTOITIVENESS"**	–	

– 10 lbs. / Karate man / Undertow / Rescue us from boredom / One day / Fireflies / Machine green / Kiss the land / Landing light / Green hand / Half-mast / Restricted / Better call / Down in flames / Boots / Come clean / When they paid me.

SUPER FURRY ANIMALS

Formed: Cardiff, Wales ... 1993 by GRUFF RHYS, DAFYDD IEUAN, CIAN CIARAN, GUTO PRYCE and HUW BUNFORD. Emerging from the Welsh underground scene in the mid-90's with a wholly unpronounceable EP on their native 'Ankst' label, the band whipped up a fair bit of interest from the London-based media and industry insiders alike. Alan McGee's 'Creation' subsequently took them on with the proviso that the bulk of their work be in English, the 'FURRY's famously stipulating that they never be made to work on St. David's day. Their first single for the label, 'HOMETOWN UNICORN' appeared in early '96 and dented the Top 50, while the dayglo rampage of 'GOD! SHOW ME MAGIC' made the Top 40 a couple of months later. Hailed by critics as one of the debuts of the year, the accompanying 'FUZZY LOGIC' (1996) album thrilled jaded Brit-pop fans with its dayglo showcase of deranged prog-retro pop/rock; 'MARIO MAN' was their most definitive slice of pseudo psychedelia to date while 'HANGIN' WITH HOWARD MARKS' gave them instant cool – the record's cover art depicted the various guises of "nice guy" one-time drug smuggler, MARKS. A Top 30 hit, the album spawned a further two singles in 'SOMETHING 4 THE WEEKEND' and 'IF YOU DON'T WANT ME TO DESTROY YOU', while the blase brilliance of 'THE MAN DON'T GIVE A FUCK' (repetitive line from the STEELY DAN number, 'Showbiz Kids') drew a swaggering close to a successful but inevitably controversial year, the group having been earlier banned from the Welsh BAFTA awards after a skirmish in the crowd. 1997's follow-up set, 'RADIATOR', made the Top 10, its less intense but equally compelling shenanigans threatening to take the band into the big league (they played the festival circuit that included a return to the rainy 'T In The Park' – Muddy Waters was not even invited). In May '98, after two further Top 30 hits, 'PLAY IT COOL' and 'DEMONS', the band had their biggest hit to date (#12) via non-album cut, 'ICE HOCKEY HAIR'. To end the year, 'OUT-SPACED' (a selection of rare B-sides, etc), marked time as GRUFF RHYS and his crew plotted their return. The 'NORTHERN LITES' single (which reached No.11), previewed unquestionably their finest hour to date, 'GUERILLA' (1999), a Top 10 album that featured xylophones, Caribbean brass, steel guitars, etc over some "way-out" experimental jugband psychedelia. Following the demise of 'Creation', the SUPER FURRIES were free to pursue their own cultural peccadilloes, specifically a Welsh language album on their own 'Placid Casual' imprint. Not just any old Welsh language album though, the first Welsh language record to make the UK Top 20 no less! While the significance of this may be lost on foreign readers, the fact that 'MWNG' (2000) was discussed in the UK parliament demonstrates the precedent it set. More, it was perhaps the band's most readily accessible effort to date, not so ironic when you consider the power of say, Brazilian music; often the melodies are so strong, the lyrics' meaning is besides the point. They merely function as another instrument. So with The SUPER FURRY ANIMALS and their patented brand of psyched-out leftfield pop exoctica; the melodies soar, the arrangements confound and the hooks reel you in. Although they recorded one of their best efforts on a miniscule budget, a subsequent deal with 'Columbia' presented an opportunity to go for broke on 'RINGS AROUND THE WORLD' (2001). A quasi-concept set based on the earth's ongoing disintegration, the record's technicolour melancholy represented a wild-eyed creative peak for RHYS and Co. Rarely has such digital-era indulgence reaped such endearing rewards. The single 'JUXTAPOSED WITH U' was among the highlights, a deceptive 80's AZTEC CAMERA-style croon which belied a despairing lyric railing against fat cats. From the industrial-strength ELO of the title track to the truly discomforting 'RUN! CHRISTIAN, RUN!', 'RINGS AROUND THE WORLD' truly ran kaleidoscopic rings around its indie competition.

Album rating: FUZZY LOGIC (*8) / RADIATOR (*7) / OUTSPACED collection (*6) / GUERILLA (*9) / MWNG (*7) / RINGS AROUND THE WORLD (*9)

GRUFF RHYS (b.18 Jul'70, Bethesda, Gwynedd, Wales) – vocals, guitars (ex-EMILY, ex-FFA COFFI PAWB) / **CIAN CIARAN** (b.16 Jun'76, Isle of Anglesey, Wales) – keyboards / **HUW 'Bumpf' BUNFORD** (b.15 Sep'67, Bath, England) – guitars, vocals / **GUTO PRYCE** (b. 4 Sep'72) – bass / **DAFYDD IEUAN** (b. 1 Mar'69, Isle of Anglesey) – drums, percussion, vocals (ex-ANHREFN, ex-FFA COFFI PAWB)

		Ankst	not iss.
Jun 95.	(7"ep/cd-ep) (ANKST 057/+CD) **LLANFAIRPWLLGWYNGYLLGOGERYCHWYNDROBW-LLANTYSILIOGOGOGOCHOCYNYGOFOD (IN SPACE) EP**		–

– Organ yn dy geg / Fix idris / Crys Ti / Blerwytirhwng? *(re-iss. May97; same)*

Oct 95.	(7"ep/cd-ep) (ANKST 062/+CD) **MOOG DROOG EP**		–

– Pam V / God! show me magic / Sali Mali / Focus pocus – Debiel. *(re-iss. May97; same)*

		Creation	Sony
Feb 96.	(7"/c-s) (CRE/+CS 222) **HOMETOWN UNICORN. / DON'T BE A FOOL, BILLY**	47	–

(cd-s+=) (CRESCD 222) – Lazy life (of no fixed identity).

Apr 96.	(7"/c-s) (CRE/+CS 231) **GOD! SHOW ME MAGIC. / DIM BENDITH**	33	–

(cd-s+=) (CRESCD 231) – Death by melody.

May 96.	(cd/lp)(c) (CRE CD/LP 190)(CCRE 190) <67827> **FUZZY LOGIC**	23	

– God! show me magic / Fuzzy birds / Something 4 the weekend / Frisbee / Hometown unicorn / Gathering moss / If you don't want me to destroy you / Bad behaviour / Mario man / Hangin' with Howard Marks / Long gone / For now and ever. *(cd re-iss. Feb00; same)*

Jul 96.	(7"/c-s) (CRE/+CS 235) **SOMETHING 4 THE WEEKEND. / WAITING TO HAPPEN**	18	–

(cd-s+=) (CRESCD 235) – Arnofio / Glow in the dark.

Sep 96.	(7"/c-s/cd-s) (CRE/+CS/SCD 243) **IF YOU DON'T WANT ME TO DESTROY YOU. / GUACAMOLE**	18	–

(cd-s+=) (CRESCD 243) – (Nid) Hon yw'r gan sy'n mynd I achub yr iaith (This song will save the Welsh language (not).

Dec 96.	(one-sided-7"blue) (CRE 247) **THE MAN DON'T GIVE A FUCK**	22	–

(cd-s+=) (CRESCD 247) – ('A'-Matthew 'Herbert' Herbert mix) / ('A'-Howard Marks mix).
(12"++=) (CRE 247T) – ('A'-Darren Price mix).

— In Feb'97, HUW BUNFORD was fined £700 on an earlier drug possession charge

		Creation	Flydaddy
May 97.	(7"/c-s) (CRE/+CS 252) **HERMANN LOVES PAULINE. / CALIMERO**	26	

(cd-s+=) (CRESCD 252) – Trons Mr. Urdd.

Jul 97.	(7"/c-s) (CRE/+CS 269) **THE INTERNATIONAL LANGUAGE OF SCREAMING. / WRAP IT UP**	24	

(cd-s+=) (CRESCD 269) – Foxy music / O.K.

Aug 97.	(cd/c/lp) (CRECD/CCRE/CRELP 214) <FLY 34CD> **RADIATOR**	8	

– Furryvision / The placid casual / The international language of screaming / Demons / Short painkiller / She's got spies / Play it cool / Hermann love's Pauline / Chupacabras / Torra fy ngwallt yn hir / Bass tuned to D.E.A.D. / Down a different river / Download / Mountain people.

Sep 97.	(7"/c-s) (CRE/+CS 275) **PLAY IT COOL. / PASS THE TIME**	27	–

(cd-s+=) (CRESCD 275) – Cryndod yn dy lais.

Nov 97.	(7"/c-s) (CRE/+CS 283) **DEMONS. / HIT AND RUN**	27	–

(cd-s+=) (CRESCD 283) – Carry the can.

May 98.	(7"/c-s) (CRE/+CS 288) **ICE HOCKEY HAIR. / SMOKIN'**	12	–

(12"+=)(cd-s+=) (CRE 288T)(CRESCD 288) – Mu-tron / Let's quit smokin'.

Nov 98.	(cd/lp) (CRE CD/LP 229) **OUT SPACED** (selected B-sides & rarities 1994-1998)	44	–

– The man don't give a fuck / Dim brys dim chwys / Smokin' / Dim bendith / Arnofio - Glo in the dark / Guacamole / Don't be a fool, Billy / Focus pocus – Debiel / Fix Idris / Pam V / Pass the time / Carry the can / Blerwytirhwng? *(ltd-cd; CRECD 229L) (cd re-iss. Sep99 & Feb00; same)*

May 99.	(7"/c-s) (CRE/+CS 314) **NORTHERN LITES. / RABID DOG**	11	–

(cd-s+=) (CRESCD 314) – This, that and the other.

Jun 99.	(cd/c/lp) (CRECD/CCRE/CRELP 242) <FLY 36CD> **GUERILLA**	10	

– Check it out / Do or die / The turning tide / Northern lites / Night vision / Wherever I lay my phone (that's my home) / A specific ocean / Some things come from nothing / The door to this house remains open / The teacher / Fire in my heart / The sound of life today / Chewing chewing gum / Keep the cosmic trigger happy. *(cd re-iss. Feb00; same)*

Aug 99.	(7"/c-s) (CRE/+CS 323) **FIRE IN MY HEART. / THE MATTER OF TIME**	25	–

(cd-s+=) (CRESCD 323) – Mrs Spector.

Jan 00.	(7"/c-s) (CRE/+CS 329) **DO OR DIE. / MISSUNDERSTANDING (sic)**	20	–

(cd-s+=) (CRESCD 329) – Colorblind.

		Placid Casual	Flydaddy
May 00.	(7") (PC 02) **YSBEIDIAU HEULOG. / CHARGE**		–

May 00.	(cd/c/lp)<d-cd> *(PLC 03 CD/MC/LP)* <*FLY 040*> **MWNG** – Drygioni / Ymaelodi a'r ymylon / Y gwyneb lau / Dacw hi / Nythod cacwn / Pan ddaw'r wawr / Ysbeidiau heulog / Y teimlad / Sarn Helen / Gweiddiau dwfn mawrth oer ar y blaned neifion. <*US cd+=*> – Crynodd yn dy lais / Trons mr urdd / Calimero / Sali Mali / (Nid) Hon yw'r gan sy'n mynd I achub yr iaith.		11	Jun00

Columbia Columbia

Jul 01.	(12"/c-s) *(671224-6/-4)* **JUXTAPOSED WITH U. / TRADEWINDS / HAPPINESS IS A WORN PUN** 14 -
	(cd-s+=) *(671224-2)* – ('A'-video).
Jul 01.	(cd/c/d-lp)(<*502413-2/-4/-1*>) **RINGS AROUND THE WORLD** 3 – Alternate route to Vulcan Street / Sidewalk serfer girl / (Drawing) Rings around the world / It's not the end of the world? / Receptable for the respectable / (A) Touch sensitive / Shoot Doris Day / Miniature / No sympathy / Juxtaposed with U / Presedential suite / Run! Christian, run! / Fragile happiness.
Oct 01.	(c-s/12") *(671908-4/-6)* **(DRAWING) RINGS AROUND THE WORLD / EDAM ANCHORMAN / ALL THE SHIT U DO** 28 -
	(cd-s+=) *(671908-2)* – ('A'-video).
Jan 02.	(12"/cd-s) *(672175-6/-2)* **IT'S NOT THE END OF THE WORLD? / ROMAN ROAD / GYPSY SPACE MUFFIN** 30 -

SUPERGRASS

Formed: Oxford, England ... 1991 as The JENNIFERS by schoolboy GAZ COOMBES and DANNY GOFFEY along with brother NICK and ANDY DAVIES. After a sole EP on 'Nude' (home to SUEDE), DAVIES went off to university, COOMBES and DANNY subsequently recruiting MICKEY QUINN and forming SUPERGRASS. Their raucous debut single, 'CAUGHT BY THE FUZZ', complete with a STIFF LITTLE FINGERS-like intro and a snotty, shouty vocal rampage recounting the teenage trauma of being busted for cannabis, could've conceivably come straight out of 1977. Initially released on the small 'Backbeat' label in 1994, the single was eventually re-released by 'Parlophone' after the label promptly snapped the group up in 1994. Although the track narrowly missed the Top 40, a 1995 follow-up, 'MANSIZE ROOSTER', made the Top 20, the MADNESS comparisons inevitable as SUPERGRASS wore their influences proudly on their retro sleeves. Another couple of singles followed in quick succession, 'LOSE IT' as a limited 'Sub Pop' singles club release and 'LENNY' as the group's first Top 10 hit. Few were surprised, then, when the debut album, 'I SHOULD COCO' (1995) made No.1 the following month, a proverbial grab-bag of musical styles from 60's harmony pop to sneering punk. The record's indisputable highlight was 'ALRIGHT', a perfectly formed BEACH BOYS via The YOUNG ONES' pop romp guaranteed to bring a smile to your face and proving that "Brit-pop" didn't necessarily mean second rate STRANGLERS/BLONDIE rip-offs. The song, and especially the Raleigh Chopper-riding exploits of the video, did much to crystallise The SUPERGRASS image, carefree, fun-loving lads with GAZ's wildly impressive sideburns adding to the cartoon appeal. Steven Spielberg was apparently even moved to offer the band the opportunity of starring in a 90's remake of The MONKEES! This was turned down, as was an offer for GAZ to model for Calvin Klein, the group preferring to concentrate solely on the music and downplay the novelty factor. Instead, there were two gems hidden away at the end of 'I SHOULD..' which indicated the direction SUPERGRASS were headed; the intoxicating, slow rolling 70's groove of 'TIME' and the dreamy psychedelia of 'SOFA (OF MY LETHARGY). Save a few live appearances and a solitary single, 'GOING OUT', SUPERGRASS were notably absent in 1996, tucked away once more at Sawmill Studios crafting their acclaimed follow-up, 'IN IT FOR THE MONEY'. Eventually released in Spring '97, the record was something of a departure to say the least. The impetuous buzzsaw punk-pop of old had been replaced by the dark assault of 'RICHARD III' while the bulk of the album fed off warped neo-psychedelia and stark introspection. Horn flourishes were sighted here and there, most satisfyingly on the lazy chug of the aforementioned 'GOING OUT', while parping organs and acoustic strumming were the order of the day. The enigmatic shadow of The BEATLES' 'White Album' loomed large over proceedings, especially on 'YOU CAN SEE ME' and the oom-pa-pa eccentricity of 'SOMETIMES I MAKE YOU SAD'. In fact, the only glimpse of the old SUPERGRASS came with 'SUN HITS THE SKY', a soaring, handclapping, spirit-lifting celebration of good times and faraway places. No matter though, the record's dark charm ensured the band remained a critical favourite, if not quite consolidating the commercial heights of the debut. Clearly, SUPERGRASS were looking at a long term, albums-based career, and on the strength of 'IN IT ...', the future seemed promising. In May '99, the glam BOWIE-esque 'PUMPING ON YOUR STEREO' was the first of three hit singles, the second 'MOVING' ('Dogs' by PINK FLOYD might've been "pumping on their stereo" at the time!?) previewing their self-titled third Top 3 album. However, several critics rated this as a drop in form. ALI G (Boo-y aka SACHA BARON COHEN) subsequently demolished the er, "Super-tramp" GAZ on his cult TV show; the 'SUN HITS THE SKY', indeed. The 'GRASS returned in 2002 with the brilliant 'LIFE ON OTHER PLANETS', a sweeping pop/rock album featuring COMBS' wacky strained vocals and a couple of surefire singles to boot; the infectious 'SAVE YOUR MONEY FOR THE CHILDREN' (which was just 'PUMPING ON YOUR STEREO' reprise) and the power pop punk of 'EVENING OF THE DAY'. In short, it was great to have them back. • **Covered:** STONE FREE (Jimi Hendrix) / ITCHYCOO PARK (Small Faces) / SOME GIRLS ARE BIGGER THAN OTHERS (Smiths).

Album rating: I SHOULD COCO (*9) / IN IT FOR THE MONEY (*8) / SUPERGRASS (*6) / LIFE ON OTHER PLANETS (*7)

JENNIFERS

GAZ COOMBES (b. GARETH, 8 Mar'76, Brighton, England) – vocals, guitar / **NICK GOFFEY** – guitar / **ANDY DAVIES** – bass / **DANNY GOFFEY** (b. DANIEL, 7 Feb'75, London, England) – drums

Nude-Sony not iss.

Aug 92.	(12"ep/cd-ep) *(NUD2 T/CD)* **JUST GOT BACK TODAY / ROCKS AND BOULDERS. / DANNY'S SONG / TOMORROW'S RAIN** -
—	**MICK QUINN** (b.17 Dec'69) – guitar; repl. TARA MILTON who had repl. NICK

SUPERGRASS

— now without DAVIES who went to Bristol University

Parlophone Capitol

Oct 94.	(7"/c-s) *(R/TCR 6396)* <*81769*> **CAUGHT BY THE FUZZ. / STRANGE ONES** 43 Feb95
	(cd-s+=) *(CDR 6396)* – Caught by the fuzz (acoustic).
Feb 95.	(7"/7"red/c-s) *(R/RS/TCR 6402)* <*81964*> **MANSIZE ROOSTER. / SITTING UP STRAIGHT** 20 Jun95
	(cd-s+=) *(CDR 6402)* – Odd.
Mar 95.	(7"yellow) (<*SP 281*>) **LOSE IT. / CAUGHT BY THE FUZZ (acoustic)** 75
	(above on 'Sub Pop' also feat. on Jul95 box-set 'HELTER SHELTER') *(re-iss. Sep99; same)*
Apr 95.	(7"blue/c-s) *(RS/TCR 6401)* **LENNY. / WAIT FOR THE SUN** 9 -
	(cd-s+=) *(CDR 6410)* – Sex!.
May 95.	(cd/c/lp) *(CD/TC+/PCS 7373)* <*33350*> **I SHOULD COCO** 1 Jul95 – I'd like to know / Caught by the fuzz / Mansize rooster / Alright / Lose it / Lenny / Strange ones / Sitting up straight / She's so loose / We're not supposed to / Time / Sofa (of my lethargy) / Time to go. *(7"free w/ ltd lp)* **STONE FREE. / ODD?**
Jul 95.	(c-s/7"colrd) *(TC+/R 6413)* <*82277*> **ALRIGHT. / TIME** 2 -
	(cd-s+=) *(CDR 6413)* – Condition / Je suis votre papa sucre.
	(cd-s+=) *(CDRX 6413)* – Lose it.
Feb 96.	(c-s/7"burgundy) *(TC+/R 6428)* **GOING OUT. / MELANIE DAVIS** 5 -
	(cd-s+=) *(CDR 6428)* – Strange ones (live).
Apr 97.	(cd-s/7"yellow) *(CD/+R 6461)* <*83820*> **RICHARD III. / NOTHING MORE'S GONNA GET IN MY WAY** 2 -
	(cd-s+=) *(CDRS 6461)* – 20ft halo.
	(cd-s) *(CDRS 6461)* – ('A'side) / Sometimes I make you very sad / Sometimes we're very sad.
Apr 97.	(cd/c/lp) *(CD/TC+/PCS 7388)* <*55228*> **IN IT FOR THE MONEY** 2 May97 – In it for the money / Richard III / Tonight / Late in the day / G-song / Sun hits the sky / Going out / It's not me / Cheapskate / You can see me / Hollow little reign / Sometimes I make you sad.
Jun 97.	(c-s/7") *(TC+/R 6469)* <*84187*> **SUN HITS THE SKY. / SOME GIRLS ARE BIGGER THAN OTHERS** 10
	(cd-s+=) *(CDR 6469)* – ('A'extended).
Oct 97.	(7"gold) *(R 6484)* <*84758*> **LATE IN THE DAY. / WE STILL NEED MORE (THAN ANYONE CAN GIVE)** 18
	(cd-s+=) *(CDRS 6484)* – It's not me (demo).
	(cd-s) *(CDR 6484)* – ('A'side) / Don't be cruel / The animal.
—	while SUPERGRASS took a break from the biz, DANNY moonlighted with the indie superband, LODGER, who issued a few singles in '98
—	**GAZ, DANNY + MICK** added **ROBERT COOMBES** – keyboards
May 99.	(c-s) *(TCR 6518)* **PUMPING ON YOUR STEREO / YOU'LL NEVER WALK AGAIN** 11
	(cd-s+=) *(CDRS 6518)* – Sick.
	(cd-s) *(CDR 6518)* – ('A'side) / What a shame / Lucky (no fear).
Sep 99.	(7") *(R 6524)* **MOVING. / BELIEVER** 9
	(c-s+=/cd-s+=) *(TCR/CDR 6524)* – Faraway (acoustic).
	(cd-s) *(CDRS 6524)* – ('A'side) / You too can play alright / Pumping on your stereo (CD-Rom).
Sep 99.	(cd/c) *(S 22056-2/-4)* <*542388*> **SUPERGRASS** 3 – Moving / Your love / What went wrong (in your head) / Beautiful people / Shotover hill / Eon / Mary / Jesus came from outta space / Pumping on your stereo / Born again / Faraway / Mama & papa.
Nov 99.	(7"silver) *(R 6531)* **MARY / PUMPING ON YOUR STEREO (live)** 36
	(c-s+=/cd-s+=) *(TCR/CDR 6531)* – Strange ones (live).
	(cd-s+=) *(CDRS 6531)* – Richard III (live) / Sun hits the sky (live).

Parlophone Island

Jul 02.	(ltd-7"one-sided) *(R 6583)* **NEVER DONE NOTHING LIKE THAT BEFORE** 75 -
Sep 02.	(7") *(R 6586)* **GRACE. / VELVETINE** 13 -
	(cd-s+=) *(CDRS 6586)* – Electric cowboy.
	(cd-s) *(CDR 6586)* – ('A'side) / Tishing in windows (kicking down doors) / That old song / ('A'-video).
Sep 02.	(cd/lp) *(541800-2/-1)* <*063685*> **LIFE ON OTHER PLANETS** 9 – Za / Rush hour soul / Seen the light / Brecon beacons / Can't get up / Evening of the day / Never done nothing like that before / Funniest thing / Grace / La song / Prophet 15 / Run.

– compilations, etc. –

Oct 02.	(d-cd) *EMI Catalogue; (541103-2)* **SUPERGRASS / I SHOULD COCO** -

SUPERMODEL

Formed: Egham, England ... 1995 as SUPERMODEL GT by WOLSEY WHITE and LINDSAY JAMIESON, the line-up completed by TRIANI and CHRIS. Courting controversy before they'd even got past their debut release, the band found themselves on the wrong side of parents' indignation after they'd given away free copies of the 'PENIS SIZE AND CARS' EP to kids who put in a cameo appearance in the accompanying homemade video.

SUPERMODEL (cont)

Fortunately a tabloid furore failed to materialise and SUPERMODEL were free to pursue further their campaign of combining 70's production values and American noise-pop. Dubbed ELO-fi by one imaginative critic, the group followed their idiosyncratic path via a deal with 'Fire' records, licensing out their 'NO SECOND COMING' single and 'CLUMBA MAR' debut album in 1996. A footnote to their short-lived musical history came about when THEAUDIENCE (featuring SOPHIE ELLIS BEXTOR) covered their 'PENIS SIZE ...' – ooh er. As SUPERMODEL GT once again, the band delivered their comeback sophomore set, 'POPACOPALYPSE NOW!' (2000), over 20 tracks of GUIDED BY VOICES-meets-ENNIO MORRICONE sounds.

Album rating: CLUMBA MAR (*6) / POPACOPALYPSE NOW! (*5)

WOLSEY WHITE – vocals, guitar / **LINDSAY JAMIESON** – drums / with **TRIANI** – guitar / **CHRIS** – drums

Fire   not iss.

Oct 95. (7"; as SUPERMODEL GT) *(BLAZE 96)* **PENIS SIZE AND CARS. /**
(cd-s+=) *(BLAZE 96CD)* –

Jan 96. (7") *(BLAZE 99)* **HAIRCUT. / DON'T LET THE BUGGERS GET YOU DOWN**

Mar 96. (7") *(BLAZE 104)* **NO SECOND COMING. / FLAMENCO KARAOKE**
(cd-s+=) *(BLAZE 014CD)* – Yeah.

Apr 96. (cd/lp) *(FIRE CD/LP 56)* **CLUMBA MAR**
– Houseshaker / No second coming / Where do I stand? / Moronic / Dear parent / Haircut / Edwin / You've got a gun / Satsuma / Everything you dreamt about / Clean / Penis size and cars / Housebreaker / Pluto / Chordroy messiah.

— after a long hiatus the group returned

God Bless   not iss.

Apr 00. (cd; as SUPERMODEL GT) *(NOIR 007CD)* **POPACOPALYPSE NOW!**
(re-iss. Nov01; same)

SUPERNATURALS

Formed: Glasgow, Scotland ... 1993 by JAMES McCOLL, KEN McALPINE, DEREK McMANUS, ALAN TILSTON and MARK GUTHRIE. The Scottish equivalent of HERMAN'S HERMITS, The SUPERNATURALS took the softer elements of TEENAGE FANCLUB and smiled their way WET WET WET-style into the hearts of the nation's less discerning retro-pop fans. Early in 1995, the group's first product, the disappointing mini-CD 'SITTING IN THE SUN', was available around indie shops. 'Food' records then came a-knocking and signed them on a long-term concert; the track 'SMILE' probably convinced them. Although the aforementioned 'SMILE' failed to chart first time round in '96, the frighteningly annoying follow-up, 'LAZY LOVER' gave them their first Top 40 hit. Spookily enough, the band notched up a further series of Top 30 sub-DODGY hits the following year, all included on their debut long-player, 'IT DOESN'T MATTER ANYMORE' (you could well be right, lads!). The latter opus actually made the UK Top 10 and the Glasgow boys proved they weren't quite the runt of the Brit-pop litter with 'A TUNE A DAY' (1998), a set of tongue in cheek but well crafted slacker-pop defined by the likes of Top 30 hit, 'I WASN'T BORN TO GET UP'. Having tried in vain to get 'SMILE' back into the charts via a TV ad, The SUPERNATURALS (JAMES, ALAN and newcomers PAUL MALCOLM and DAVE MITCHELL – KEN moved to St. Andrews) returned to the fold once again in September 2001, albeit a solitary single, 'FINISHING CREDITS', for the 'Koch' imprint. The next spring, an album 'WHAT WE DID LAST SUMMER' followed on from gigs on Mull, Orkneys and Shetlands.
• **Covered:** BOYS IN THE BAND (Leiber-Stoller) / BRONTOSAURUS (Move) / SKYWAY (Paul Westerberg) / YOU'RE MY BEST FRIEND (Queen).

Album rating: SITTING IN THE SUN mini (*3) / IT DOESN'T MATTER ANYMORE (*6) / A TUNE A DAY (*6) / WHAT WE DID LAST SUMMER (*5)

JAMES McCOLL – vocals, guitar / **KEN McALPINE** – keyboards, tambourine / **DEREK McMANUS** – guitar, vocals / **ALAN TILSTON** – drums / **MARK GUTHRIE** – bass

O.F.L.   not iss.

Feb 95. (m-cd) *(none)* **SITTING IN THE SUN**
– Sitting in the sun / Absence / Caroline / Slab / Godfrey / I don't think it's over (yup) / Silverback.

— around the same, three other mini demos were circulating, 'BIG EP', 'DARK STAR' and 'LET IT BLEAT'

Food   not iss.

Jul 96. (7") *(FOOD 79)* **SMILE. / CAN'T GET BACK TO NORMAL**
(cd-s+=) *(CDFOOD 79)* – Mint choc chip.

Oct 96. (c-s/7"blue) *(TC+/FOOD 85)* **LAZY LOVER. / JOSEPHINE**   34
(cd-s) *(CDFOOD 85)* – Caterpillar song.

Jan 97. (7") *(FOOD 88)* **THE DAY BEFORE YESTERDAYS MAN. / HONK WILLIAMS**   25
(cd-s+=) *(CDFOOD 88)* – Ken's song.
(cd-s) *(CDFOOD 88)* – ('A'side) / Deep in my heart I know I'm a slob / Brontosaurus.

Apr 97. (7") *(FOOD 92)* **SMILE. / STALINGRAD**   23
(cd-s+=) *(CDFOOD 92)* – Childhood sweetheart.
(cd-s) *(CDFOOD 92)* – ('A'side) / Can't get back to normal / Mint choc chip.

May 97. (cd/c) *(FOOD CD/MC/LP 21)* **IT DOESN'T MATTER ANYMORE**   9
– Please be gentle with me / Smile / Glimpse of the light / Lazy lover / Love has passed away / Dung beetle / Stammer / I don't think so / Pie in the sky / The day before yesterday's man / Prepare to land / Trees.

Jul 97. (c-s) *(TCFOOD 99)* **LOVE HAS PASSED AWAY / THE DAY BEFORE YESTERDAY'S MAN / LAZY LOVER**   38
(cd-s) *(CDFOOD 99)* – ('A'side) / Trying too hard / Rupert the bear.
(cd-s) *(CDFOODS 99)* – ('A'side) / Scandinavian girlfriend / That's not me.

Oct 97. (7") *(FOOD 106)* **PREPARE TO LAND. / STUPID LOVE SONG**   48
(cd-s+=) *(CDFOOD 106)* – Skyway.
(cd-s) *(CDFOODS 106)* – ('A'side) / High tension at Boghead / Take some time out.

Jul 98. (c-s/cd-s) *(TCFOOD/CDFOODS 112)* **I WASN'T BUILT TO GET UP / STAR WARS / BUBBLEGUM HILL**   25
(cd-s) *(CDFOOD 112)* – ('A'side) / Robot song / I just can't go on like this.

Aug 98. (cd/c) *(856893-2/-4)* **A TUNE A DAY**   21
– You take yourself too seriously / Monday mornings / Submarine song / I wasn't built to get up / Country music / Motorcycle parts / Sheffield song (I love her more than I love you) / VW song / Idiot / Magnet / Still got that feeling / Let me know / It doesn't matter anymore / Everest.

Oct 98. (7") *(FOOD 115)* **SHEFFIELD SONG (I LOVE HER MORE THAN I LOVE YOU). / I DON'T THINK IT'S OVER**   45
(cd-s+=) *(CDFOOD 115)* – X country song.
(cd-s) *(CDFOOD 115)* – ('A'side) / Boys in the band / Hang out with you.

Mar 99. (c-s) *(TCFOOD 119)* **EVEREST / YOU'RE MY BEST FRIEND**   52
(cd-s+=) *(CDFOOD 119)* – Smile (demo).
(cd-s) *(CDFOODS 119)* – ('A'side) / Let it bleat / Tomato man.

— **CRAIG** joined in Feb'99 but left Jul'00

Sep 00. (c-s) *(TCFOOD 131)* **SMILE / GLIMPSE OF THE LIGHT / SUBMARINE SONG**
(cd-s) *(CDFOOD 79)* – ('A'side) / Can't get back to normal / Mint choc chip.
above was re-iss. due to a UK TV ad

— **JAMES, KEN + ALAN** were joined by **PAUL MALCOLM** – acoustic guitar, banjo
— **DAVE MITCHELL** – keyboards; repl. KEN

Koch   not iss.

Sep 01. (cd-s) *(347956)* **FINISHING CREDITS / EASY LIFE (TV mix) / EVERYDAY THINGS CAN MAKE YOU HAPPY**

Mar 02. (cd-s) *(343970)* **WHAT WE DID LAST SUMMER / MY DOOR IS OPEN / IT'S A WONDERFUL WORLD**

May 02. (cd) *(343985)* **WHAT WE DID LAST SUMMER**
– Elle / What we did last summer / Get myself together / Wishing you were my girlfriend / Instant healing / Life is a motorway / Late for the world / Everything / Summertime / Easy life / Why / Two songbirds / Finishing credits.

SUPERSTAR

Formed: Glasgow, Scotland ... 1991 by Bellshill-born JOE McALINDEN, JIM McCULLOCH, QUENTIN McAFEE and ALAN HUTCHISON. The baby of musical maestro/trained violinist and former ex-BMX BANDITS, ex-GROOVY LITTLE NUMBERS, ex-EUGENIUS, ex-SOUP DRAGONS, JOE McALINDEN, SUPERSTAR signed to 'Creation' in '92, releasing a mini debut confusingly titled, 'GREATEST HITS VOL.1', before inking an ill-advised deal with American label, 'S.B.K.'. A period of five years subsequently elapsed before the band re-emerged on the 'Camp Fabulous' label with the mini-set, '18 CARAT', McALINDEN famously turning down an opportunity to work with BRIAN WILSON along the way. The former BEACH BOYS genius wasn't the only famous muso bod to fall under the SUPERSTAR spell, the likes of PETER BUCK (R.E.M.) and ROD STEWART (who recorded the track 'SUPERSTAR' on his recent covers album) singing the praises of their belated debut album, 'PALM TREE' (1998). Described by one critic as a cross between QUEEN and RADIOHEAD, the Glaswegian quartet tend to draw extreme reactions (usually positive) with their alternately dramatic and heart-rending sound. Beautifully crafted and seemingly wrung from McALINDEN's tortured soul, the likes of 'EVERYDAY I FALL APART' even moved three separate Radio One DJ's to name it as their single of the week. Another admirer was novelist Alan Warner, who subsequently recorded a joint single with the band in summer '98.

Album rating: GREATEST HITS VOL.1 mini (*5) / 18 CARAT mini (*6) / PALM TREE (*7)

JOE McALINDEN – vocals, guitar, piano, vocals (ex-EUGENIUS, ex-BMX BANDITS, ex-GROOVY LITTLE NUMBERS, ex-SOUP DRAGONS) / **JIM McCULLOCH** – guitar, vocals / **ALAN HUTCHISON** – bass, vocals, euphonium / **QUENTIN McAFEE** – drums, vocals

Creation   Capitol

Jun 92. (m-cd/m-lp) *(CRE CD/LP 134)* **GREATEST HITS VOL.1**
– Barfly / The reason why / She's got everything I own / Let's get lost / Taste / After taste.

1994. (cd) *<28819>* **SUPERSTAR**
– Amouricity / Feels like forever / Barfly / Don't wanna die / The reason why / I can't help it / Noise level / Let's get lost / Will I ever see you again / Thought for today / Could it be you.

— disappeared for a while after signing a new deal with 'S.B.K.'

Camp Fabulous   not iss.

Mar 97. (m-cd/m-lp) *(CFAB 001 CD/LP)* **18 CARAT**
– Superstar / The Ok corral / Why oh why / It feels so good to be with you / Bad hair day / Bumnote / Little picture.

Sep 97. (7") *(CFAB 002)* **BREATHING SPACE. / PALM TREE**
(cd-s) *(CFAB 002CD)* – ('A'side) / Blind spot / Teacher (acoustic) / Disappointed man.

Jan 98. (7") *(CFAB 003S)* **EVERY DAY I FALL APART. / EVERY SECOND HURTS**   66
(cd-s+=) *(CFAB 003CD)* – Hum / Lazy bones.

Apr 98. (7") *(CFAB 007S)* **SUPERSTAR. / HEY MONTANA SAN**   49
(cd-s+=) *(CFAB 007CD)* – Waiting room.
(cd-s) *(CFAB 007ZCD)* – ('A'side) / Monstermind / Everyday I fall apart.

SUPERSTAR (cont)

Apr 98. (cd/c/lp) *(CFAB 005X CD/MC/LP)* **PALM TREE**
 – Monstermind / Superstar / Breathing space / Sparkle / Every day I fall apart / Once again / Palm tree / And when the morning comes / Two of a kind / Life is elsewhere / Teacher.
Aug 98. (10"ep; SUPERSTAR VS. ALAN WARNER) *(CFAB 009XS)* **SUPERSTAR VS. ALAN WARNER (SOUNDCLASH)**
 – Hum (whole new meaning) / One minute story / Introduction / Life is elsewhere / Every second hurts / Little picture.
Jun 00. (7") *(CFAB 010S)* **I LOVE LOVE.** /
 (cd-s+=) *(CFAB 010CD)* –
Jul 00. (cd/lp) *(CFAB 011 XCD/LP)* **PHAT DAT**
 – Someone's watching over me / I love love / More / Had enough / Every second hurts / The gymnast / This offering / These little things / This is my world / Phat dat.
Dec 00. (2xcd-ep) *(CFAB 014XCD)* **6 MORE SONGS**
 – More / Just like me / Saint (+3).

SUPERSUCKERS

Formed: Tucson, Arizona, USA ... late 80's as BLACK SUPERSUCKERS (after a porn mag!) by EDDIE SPAGHETTI, DAN BOLTON, RON HEATHMAN and DAN SIEGAL. Following a series of singles on various US indie labels – collected together on 1992 compilation, 'THE SONGS ALL SOUND THE SAME' – the band relocated to Seattle (long before the media circus arrived) in search of work, shortened their name to SUPERSUCKERS, signed to 'Sub Pop' and embarked on a campaign of good-time grunge creation. Debut album proper, the Jack Endino-produced 'THE SMOKE OF HELL' (1992), drew comparisons with Australia's long lost COSMIC PSYCHOS while a subsequent tour with 'Sub Pop' rockabilly preacher The REVEREND HORTON HEAT brought the SUCKER musical punch to British shores for the first time. While never exactly threatening to claim NIRVANA's crown, the band continued to churn out reliably un-challenging, reinforced three-minute grunge-pop over albums such as 'LA MANO CORNUDA' (1994), 'THE SACRILICIOUS SOUNDS OF ...' (1995) and the self-explanatory 'MUST'VE BEEN HIGH' (1997). EDDIE SPAGHETTI and the dark lords of alt whatever (rock? country? folk?) returned in 1999 with the hugely impressive wrack'n'roll slider 'EVIL POWERS OF ROCK'N'ROLL'. On it, SPAGHETTI and cohorts sounded like CHEAP TRICK after a night out on the tiles, confirmed by track titles 'I WANT THE DRUGS' (pure mindblowing!), 'FISTICUFFS' and the translucent 'DIRT ROADS, DEAD ENDS AND DUST'. Following The Music Cartel's 'SPLITSVILLE' series, The SUPERSUCKERS entered the studio with weird metallers ELECTRIC FRANKENSTIEN for a disappointing split album, which included the usual collaborative covers. However, a brilliant country in-concert album, 'MUST'VE BEEN LIVE' (2002) sucked back their critics. • **Covered:** SEX & OUTRAGE (Motorhead) / BURNIN' UP (Madonna) / WHAT LOVE IS (Dead Boys) / RAZZAMANAZZ (Nazareth) / NITROGLYCERINE (Gories) / 400 BUCKS (Reverend Horton Heat) / ARE YOU READY? (Thin Lizzy) / MOTHER Mary (UFO) / THAT IS ROCK'N'ROLL (Coasters).

Album rating: THE SONGS ALL SOUND THE SAME compilation (*6) / THE SMOKE OF HELL (*6) / LA MANO CORNUDA (*6) / THE SACRILICIOUS SOUNDS OF ... (*5) / MUST'VE BEEN HIGH (*5) / HOW THE SUPERSUCKERS BECAME THE GREATEST ROCK'N'ROLL BAND IN THE WORLD compilation (*7) / THE EVIL POWERS OF ROCK'N'ROLL (*5) / SPLITSVILLE VOL.1 (*5) / MUST'VE BEEN LIVE (*4)

EDDIE SPAGHETTI – vocals, bass / **RON HEATHMAN** – guitar / **DAN BOLTON** – guitar / **DAN SEIGAL** – drums

	not iss.	Lucky
1990. (7") <LKY 002> **GRAVITY BILL. / SEX & OUTRAGE**
 <re-iss. 1993; same>

	not iss.	Sub Pop
Nov 91. (7"ep) <SP 125> **...LIKE A BIG FUCKIN' TRAIN**
 – Luck / I say fuck / Caliente / Retarded Bill / Four stroke. *(UK-iss.Sep92; SP 27/180)*

	not iss.	Sympathy F
1992. (7") <SFTRI 113> **SADDLETRAMP. / POOR AND ALRIGHT**

	Musical Tragedies	eMpTy
Apr 92. (7") <MT-135> **JUNK. / 4-STROKE / GIRL I KNOW**
Jul 92. (cd) *(EFA 11351)* <MT-162> **THE SONGS ALL SOUND THE SAME** (compilation)
 – Alright / Saddletramp / Poor / Burnin' up / Gravity Bill / Sex & outrage / What is love / Junk / 4-stroke / The girl I know / Razzamanazz. <re-iss. Sep01 on 'Hall Of'+=; 1110> – Luck / I say fuck / Second cousin. *(re-iss. Nov01 on 'Aces & Eights'+=; AE 004) (re-iss. Jan02 & Oct02 on 'Mid Fi'+=; MFRCD 001)*

	Sub Pop	Sub Pop
Oct 92. (cd)(lp) <SP 212CD)(SP 50-212> <SP 164> **THE SMOKE OF HELL** — Sep92
 – Coattail rider / Luck / I say fuck / Alone and stinking / Caliente / Tasty greens / Hell city, Hell / Hot rod rally / Drink and complain / Mighty Joe Young / Ron's got the cocaine / Sweet'n'sour Jesus / Retarded Bill / Thinkin' 'bout revenge.
May 93. (7") <SP 23-265> **DEAD HOMIEZ. / HELL CITY, HELL**
 (cd-s+=) <(SPCD 23-265)> – Poor (mexi-mix).
Nov 93. (7") <SP 225> **SHE'S MY BITCH. / DRINKIN' 'N' DRIVIN'**
Apr 94. (cd/lp) <(SP CD/LP 120-301)> **LA MANO CORNUDA**
 – Creepy jackalope eye / Seventeen poles / High ya! / On the couch / Clueless / Sugie / Mudhead / Gold top / How to maximize your kill count / I was born without a spine / Glad, damn glad / She's my bitch / The schmooze.
May 94. (7") *(SP 125-308)* <SP 249> **400 BUCKS. / (other track by REVEREND HORTON HEAT)**
 (cd-s+=) <SPCD 249> – Caliente / (other by REVEREND HORTON HEAT). *(UK-iss.Aug01; same)*
Oct 94. (7") *(SP 141-345)* **ON THE COUCH. / CAN'T RESIST**
 (cd-s+=) <(SPCD 141-345)> – Nitroglycerine / Hangliders.

— **RICK SIMS** – guitar (ex-DIDJITS) repl. HEATHMAN

Jun 95. (7") <SP 296> **BORN WITH A TAIL. / ARE YOU READY**
Jul 95. (7") <(SP 314)> **BORN WITH A TAIL. / RUN LIKE A MOTHERFUCKER**
 (cd-s+=) <(SPCD 314)> – ('A'version) / Hitting the gravel.
Sep 95. (7") <SP 315> **MARIE. / 19th MOST POWERFUL WOMAN IN ROCK**
 (cd-s+=) <SPCD 315> – Pseudopsychophramacology / Are you ready?
Sep 95. (lp/c/cd) <(SP 303/+A/CD)> **THE SACRILICIOUS SOUNDS OF THE SUPERSUCKERS**
 – Bad bad bad / Born with a tail / 19th most powerful woman in rock / Doublewide / Bad dog / Money into sin / Marie / Thing about that / Ozzy / Run like a motherfucker / Hittin' the gravel / Stoned if you want it / My victim / Don't go blue.
Nov 96. (7") <SP 384> **MOTHER MARY. / (B-side by TENDERLOIN)**
Jul 97. (cd-ep) <(SPCD 388)> **STEVE EARLE & THE SUPERSUCKERS**
 – Creepy jackalope eye / Angel is the Devil / Before they make me run / Creepy jackalope eye (without EARLE) / Angel is the Devil (EARLE vox).
Sep 97. (lp/cd) <(SP/+CD 380)> **MUST'VE BEEN HIGH** — Mar97
 – Dead in the water / Barricade / Roamin' 'round / Hungover together / Non-addictive marijuana / The captain / Blow you away / Roadworn and weary / Hangin' out with me. *(cd+=)* – Juicy pureballs / One cigarette away / Hangliders.
Aug 99. (d-lp/cd) <(SP/+CD 480)> **HOW THE SUPERSUCKERS BECAME THE GREATEST ROCK'N'ROLL BAND IN THE WORLD** (compilation)
 – Coattail rider / Creepy jackalope eye / Born with a tail / Luck / On the couch / Doublewide / Hot rod rally / She's my bitch / Bad, bad, bad / Dead in the water / How to maximize your kill count / Ron's got the cocaine / Roadworn and weary / Supersucker drive-by blues / Givin' it away / All right / Saddletramp / Can't resist / Dead Homiez / Psyched out / Hell city, Hell / Before they make me run / Blood Mary morning / Wake me when it's over / Good livin' / Monkey / Beat to shit.

	not iss.	No Lie
1999. (7") <NL 019> **WHISKEY RIVER. / (other by DON WALSER & THE PURE TEXAS BAND)**

	not iss.	Sessions
1999. (7") <sessions 16> **THAT IS ROCK'N'ROLL. / (other by HAI KARATE)**

	Koch Int.	Koch Int.
Feb 00. (cd) <(KOCCD 20801)> **THE EVIL POWERS OF ROCK'N'ROLL** — Oct99
 – The evil powers of rock'n'roll / Cool Manchu / I want the drugs / Santa Rita high / Dead meat / Stuff 'n' nonsense / Dirt roads, dead ends and dust / Fisticuffs / Gone gamblin' / My kickass life / Goin' back to Tucson / I can't hold myself in line / Hot like the sun.

	Velvel	not iss.
Oct 00. (cd-s) *(180323)* **SANTA RITA HIGH**

	Music Cartel	Music Cartel
Jan 01. (cd; split with ELECTRIC FRANKENSTEIN) <TMC 057CD> **SPLITSVILLE VOL.1**
 – Then I'm gone / Shit fire / Devil's food / Kid's got it comin' / Teenage shutdown / (others by ELECTRIC FRANKENSTEIN). *(UK-iss.Mar02; same as US)*

	Lunasound	Mid Fi
Sep 02. (cd) *(LUNA 016CD)* <1414> **MUST'VE BEEN LIVE (live)** — Nov01
 – Dead in the water / Good livin' / Roamin' 'round / Roadworn and weary / The captain / Hangin' out with me / Barricade / Drivin' nails in my coffin / Cowpoke / Don't go blue / Must've been high / One cigarette away / Alabama, Louisiana or maybe Tennessee / Hungover together / Non addictive marijuana / Ice cold beer only / The image of me / Peace in the valley / Blow you away. *(d-lp-iss.Nov02 on 'Cargo'; CARLP 050)*

SURGERY

Formed: New York City, New York, USA ... 1989 by SEAN McDONNELL, SCOTT KLEBER, JOHN LACHAPELLE and JOHN LEAMY. SURGERY unleashed their powerful KRAMER-produced debut album, 'NATIONWIDE', in 1991. The sleazy blues aspect of their otherwise visceral hardcore sound lent them an extra dimension and showed they had more to offer than many of the other groups on the circuit at this time. The 1993 EP, 'TRIM, 9TH WARD HIGH ROLLER', was another swaggering, dirty, collection of songs blending deep south blues and hard rock in the same way as WHITE STRIPES would be doing a few years down the line. After the grunge explosion of the early 90's, expectations were high that SURGERY could make a dent in the commercial market. The album 'SHIMMER' (1994) was not as successful as they had hoped and proved to be the group's last throw of the dice. Sadly, vocalist McDONNELL died of natural causes early the following year, with the remaining bandmates opting not to carry on.

Album rating: NATIONWIDE (*5) / TRIM, 9th WARD HIGH ROLLER mini (*5) / SHIMMER (*6)

SEAN McDONNELL – vocals / **SCOTT KLEBER** – guitar / **JOHN LACHAPELLE** – bass / **JOHN LEAMY** – drums

	Glitterhouse	Amphetam. Reptile
1989. (7") <Scale 17> **NOT GOING DOWN. / BLOW HER FACE**
1989. (7"; various) <Scale 18> **Dope Guns EP**
 – Action candy / (others by COWS, TAD + KING SNAKE ROOST).

	Twin/Tone	Amphetam. Reptile
Sep 90. (lp/c/cd) *(TRR 89201/+MC/CD)* <ARR 89201/+MC/CD> **NATIONWIDE**
 – Mistake / Maliblues / Breeding / Bronto / Highway 109 / Do it to it dynamo / L-7 / Drive-in fever / Caveman.
1990. (7") <Scale 27> **FEEDBACK. / FRIED**
1991. (7"; various) <Scale 34> **Ugly American Overkill EP**
 – Fun city / (others by HELMET, TAR + GOD BULLIES).

SWALLOW

Formed: Early 90's ... by Irish pair, MIKE MASON and LOUISE TREHY in London, England. The former had been a keyboard-player with INTO PARADISE, before he received his marching orders, while the latter's only previous musical background was in a directorial capacity for a SPACEMEN 3 video. After being given a tape of MASON's rough demos, singer TREHY decided to collaborate with the man and together the duo completed a more polished 3-track demo which they sent to '4 a.d.' supremo, IVO. Bluffing their way into a record deal, SWALLOW glided into pop consciousness with the very 4ad-esque 'BLOW' (1992) album, a dead ringer for MY BLOODY VALENTINE and The COCTEAU TWINS. Later in the year, the record was remixed although their highly derivative sound proved to be an albatross round their neck. Despite a couple more years of experience behind them, MASON and TREHY took flight following a final EP, 'HUSH', on 'Rough Trade'.

Album rating: BLOW (*5)

LOUISE TREHY – vocals / **MIKE MASON** – instruments (ex-INTO PARADISE)

4 a.d. / Reprise

Jul 92. (cd)(lp/c) *(CAD 2010CD)(CAD/+C 2010)* **BLOW**
– Lovesleep / Tastes like honey / Sugar your mind / Mensurral / Peekaboo / Lacuna / Oceans and blue skies / Follow me down / Halo / Cherry stars collide / Head in a cave.

Oct 92. (cd)(lp/c) *(CAD 2015CD)(CAD/+C 2015)* **BLOWBACK** (remixes)

Rough Trade / not iss.

Jun 94. (12"ep/cd-ep) *(R 322-0/-3)* **HUSH EP**
– Hush / Flooded / Watching the sun / Dear Mary.

— disbanded after above

SWEARING AT MOTORISTS

Formed: Dayton, Ohio, USA ... early 1995 by drifter and hippy-raised songwriter DAVE DOUGHMAN who gathered together a handful of songs and enlisted drummer DON THRASHER (a very appropriate second name). Cruising the Dayton scene and working as a sound engineer, DOUGHMAN recorded a 12-track album (later issued in 1998 as 'SIMPLE SOLUTIONS') which was released on cassette only to much local acclaim and was eventually picked up by Matt and John Fisher, who were laying the foundations for an independent label, 'Spare Me'. No sooner had they appeared on a modest label-sampler, SWEARING AT MOTORISTS were back in the studio compiling 'TUESDAY'S PRETZEL NIGHT' (1996), a mini album that displayed all of the duo's later traits of pop/punk/lo-fi melodies, with a bitter melancholic aftertaste. Another EP was to follow – 'FEAR OF LOW FLYING CLOUDS' (1997), this time though with a more stripped-down, acoustic flair, it signalled the end of S@M's relationship with 'Spare Me', as the band subsequently flitted to 'Secretly Canadian'. This is when their most prolific and tantalising work began to manifest; the brilliantly executed 'MORE SONGS FROM THE MELLOW STRUGGLE' (2000), the charming lo-fi DIY 'NUMBER SEVEN UPTOWN' (2000); (think early BECK in a fight with WILL OLDHAM) and the charred 'BURNT ORANGE HERSEY EP' (2000). It wasn't until two years later that SWEARING AT MOTORISTS would finally find the critical and public acclaim they deserved to have in the last century. With THRASHER leaving DOUGHMAN (to join GUIDED BY VOICES) in summer 2000, he recruited percussionist JOSEPH SIWINSKI and together they recorded the musically accessible 'ALONG THE INCLINE PLANE' (2002), a set which boasted a handful of slow-burning hushed beauties, shot straight from DOUGHMAN's heart. 2002's full-length LP 'THIS FLAG SIGNALS GOODBYE' was cut from more or less the same cloth, with DOUGHMAN demonstrating his unique and quasi-genius storytelling techniques, as well as challenging The WHITE STRIPES to a "Rock fight". Let's hope the flag really doesn't signal goodbye ... • **Covered:** VOLCANO DIVERS (Guided By Voices) / LETTER TO A FANZINE (Great Plains) / I'M STILL IN LOVE WITH YOU (Steve Earle).

Album rating: SWEARING AT MOTORISTS (*5) / FEAR OF LOW FLYING CLOUDS mini (*6) / MORE SONGS FROM THE MELLOW STRUGGLE (*8) / NUMBER SEVEN UPTOWN (*7) / THE BURNT ORANGE HERESY mini (*5) / ALONG THE INCLINED PLANE mini (*5) / THIS FLAG SIGNALS GOODBYE (*7)

DAVE DOUGHMAN – vocals, guitar / **DON THRASHER** – drums (ex-GUIDED BY VOICES)

not iss. / own label

Dec 95. (ltd-c) *(none)* **SWEARING AT MOTORISTS**
– Soundtrack for a nightmare / Resin completed the task / The king of Baltimore / New teen anthem / Reinforcing stereotypes / Similar to floral design / Derailed / Ballad of Shane and Tanya / The trouble with gravity is ... / Our adventures return / Obsessed with falling / Cabin fever. *<cd-iss. 1998 on 'Simple Solution'; ss 014>*

Spare Me / Spare Me

1996. (7"ep) *<SPARE 002>* **TUESDAY'S PRETZEL NIGHT**
– All the president's men / Feeling transparent / Painfully obvious / A drinking town / Bars close / Before the flood / Plum island / Speedracer's lament / Two blocks from the river / Smart Aleck's karma.

1996. (c-s) **THE ACADEMY AWARD FOR BEST ACTRESS / LIFE HAS NO EQUATION**
(above issued on 'Psionic')

Sep 97. (lp/cd) *<(SPARE 11/+CD)>* **FEAR OF LOW FLYING CLOUDS**
– Declaration of co-dependance / Reckless operation / Nice guy's last finish / No rest for royalty / Effects of motion / Foolish mortal / Bars close / True romance / I get lonesome / You love yourself / Reluctant pilgrim / Sometimes better than others.

not iss. / Recordhead

1997. (7"ep) *<LUNA 7>* **ENOUGH DRAMA AND THE WAY THINGS ARE**
– Barbwire sweater / Late night arithmetic (Timmy runs interference) / Duke of anxiety / Nightingale in the hanger / No more James Dean.

Secretly Canadian / Secretly Canadian

Jan 00. (cd) *<SC 29CD>* **MORE SONGS FROM THE MELLOW STRUGGLE**
– Opening theme / Creature of habits (theme from the big spill) / East of Biloxi / I'll only sleep / You're still here / Reluctant angel / Telford to North Main / A triumph for clarity / No more James Dean / The difference between listen and feel / Telford reprise / Next exit ghost town / Oxygen please / Neighborhood of sirens.

2000. (7"ep) *<none>* **STUMBLE TO THE ZERO HOUR**
– Wounding boy wonder / Pilots at the temple / The mercy of death is like flowers.
(above issued on 'Punk In My Vitamins')

Oct 00. (lp/cd) *<(SC 32/+CD)>* **NUMBER SEVEN UPTOWN**
– Flying pizza / Inadvertant Christmas song / Thin man from North Main / Prelude to a miss / Number have too many meanings to me / Dog with the lampshade head / Bullet / Calgon take me away / Maybe Zorro / Talking pictures / Flying pizza / Left on forest / Three wishes / Drunk on Monday / One more next time.

— (late 2000) **JOSEPH SIWINSKI** – drums (of the TROUBLE WITH SWEENEY) repl. THRASHER

Mar 01. (m-cd) *<(SC 47)>* **THE BURNT ORANGE HERESY** (tour cd) Dec00
– Cuando nos veramos / Lullaby ascending / Transcontinental (drunk again) / Send weed / The Calvary cross / Uneasy dreams / Borrowed sorrow / Running out of things to say.

Apr 02. (m-cd) *<(SC 74CD)>* **ALONG THE INCLINED PLANE**
– Small town, big city / 24, 40 or 65 / Can't help ourselves / Paul Williams / I'm still in love with you / Can't get you out of my head / Breathing water (relax).

May 02. (7"ep; split) *<SA 05>* **BITCH (IDLE HANDS AND THE DEVIL'S PLAYTHING) / BAD DRAWING OF THE WORST PHOTOGRAPH. / (2 others by Spoon)**
(above issued on 'Super Asbestos')

Jul 02. (lp/cd) *<(SC 68/+CD)>* **THIS FLAG SIGNALS GOODBYE** Jun02
– Over the middle bridge / This flag signals goodbye / Press the number three / Doors are closing / Fan mail for a criminal / Leaving Adams Morgan / Borrowed red bike / Drinking on the roof / Room full of you / Anything you want / Losing mine / The real thing / Collecting skylines / (It came) Out of nowhere.

SWEEP THE LEG JOHNNY

Formed: South Bend, Indiana, USA ... 1996 by former CHECK ENGINE members STEVE SOSTAK and CHRIS DALY, along with MATT ALICEA and SCOTT ANNA. Early live appearances by the group demonstrated that their fusion of progressive indie rock, jazz, industrial noise and punk could not be accommodated by any particular musical genre. The band had released a few singles and toured extensively before the appearance of their debut album, '4.9.21.30', in 1997. Against all the odds, the album managed to triumphantly blend the group's wide ranging influences without ever becoming confused. More touring followed and the release of a split single with A MINOR FOREST, came about before bass player ALICEA was replaced by JOHN BRADY. The group released their second album 'TOMORROW WE WILL RUN FASTER' in 1999. The following year DALY and SOSTAK re-formed CHECK ENGINE (alongside JOE CANNON and BRIAN WNUKOWSKI) yet continued to record with SWEEP THE LEG JOHNNY, releasing the album 'STO CAZZO!' the same year. Fans of SOSTAK and DALY were spoiled in 2002 with the release of CHECK ENGINE's debut album followed by the 4th and most consistent SWEEP THE LEG JOHNNY album, 'GOING DOWN SWINGING', a few months later.

Album rating: 4.9.21.30 (*6) / TOMORROW WE WILL RUN FASTER (*7) / STO CAZZO! (*6) / GOIN' DOWN SWINGIN' (*5) / Check Engine: CHECK ENGINE (*4)

STEVE SOSTAK – vocals, saxophone / **CHRIS DALY** – guitar / **MATT ALICEA** – bass, vocals / **SCOTT ANNA** – drums

not iss. / Estate

1996. (7") **STEGANOVA. / (other by Similarities)**

not iss. / Divot

1996. (7"ep) *<DVT 006>* **NEW BUFFALO**
– New buffalo / Insomnia pays / In the shade of the house.

Nov 97. (lp/cd) *<DVT 009/+CD>* **4.9.21.30**
– Shower scene / Insomnia pays / The face perpendicular to the shoreline / Inspection area / Sandpaper / The thought of one's own death / Building block / In the shade of the house. *(UK-iss.Dec01; same as US)*

Aug 98. (7") *<DVT 012>* **MENTAL VEHN DIAGRAM. / (other by COWPERS)**

not iss. / Tree

Sep 98. (7") **WALKING HOME ON THE EMERGENCY BED. / (other by A Minor Forest)**

— **JOHN BRADY** – bass (ex-SPANAKORZO, ex-SWING KIDS) repl. ALICEA

Southern / Southern

Apr 99. (cd/lp) *<18559-2/-1>* **TOMORROW WE WILL RUN FASTER**
– Early October / Please give me roses before I am dead / / Las cruces / Rest stop / Skin.

SWEEP THE LEG JOHNNY (cont)

Apr 00. (cd/lp) <(18569-2/-1)> **STO CAZZO!**
– The fine wrinkles; we have all of them / That than which / Walking home on the emergency bed / Bloodlines / Columbus day / The blizzard of 1999.

—— added **MITCH CHENEY** – guitar (of RUMAH SAKIT)

Jul 02. (cd/d-lp) <(18593-2/-1)> **GOING DOWN SWINGIN'**
– Sometimes my balls feel like tits / Only in a rerun / The one that goes boom / The blizzard of '99 / Rest stop / J. Daly's message to Jacob and Sylvia / Transit must suffer.

CHECK ENGINE

SOSTAK + DALY with **JOE CANNON** – guitar, vocals + **BRIAN A. WNUKOWSKI** – drums (ex-BIG'N)

	Southern	Southern
Jan 02. (cd) <(18591-2)> **CHECK ENGINE**	☐	☐

– Where's my social worker? / So, we've got some balls can balls. what else we got? / How bad (do you want it)? / I'll see you in two and two / She asked me some questions, and I answered them / Bold style / Don't make friends with salad / Nobody ever tells Jenny anything, ever / Pain don't hurt.

SWEET 75
(see under ⇒ NIRVANA; in 80's section)

SWELL

Formed: San Francisco, California, USA ... August 1987 by DAVID FREEL and SEAN KIRKPATRICK, who then added JOHN DETTMAN and TIM ADAMS, although the latter was soon replaced by MONTE VALLIER. SWELL's eponymous debut LP was self-released on their own 'Psycho Specific' label in April 1990. The early SWELL sound was acoustically driven, and steeped in hippie psychedelia, and this was fully evident on tracks like 'WOODEN HIPPIE NICE'. Other songs – like 'GET HIGH' and 'STOP' – demonstrated their knack for writing a laid-back pop-hook. Their first live date was a few months later at San Francisco's I-Beam supporting MAZZY STAR, and this was followed by a tour of California. Second LP, 'WELL?...', was released in 1992, and was a more concerted effort than their debut. Still hippie and trippy, a wider range of influences were introduced – from indie-rock like The PIXIES and The JESUS & MARY CHAIN to ENNIO MORRICONE. 'WELL?...' was given a wider release a year later, after SWELL were approached by the impressed 'Def American' label. It was around this time that DETTMAN left, although he would be replaced by TOM HAYS in time for the recording of third album '41'. The country-tinged '41', released in late-'93, was SWELL's most rounded album to date. Trouble was on the horizon though, as their self-produced fourth LP was scrapped, then the majority of their second attempt was also knocked back. Third and fourth attempts followed – involving different producers – and still no positive outcome was achieved. Finally, after shifting to New York and hooking up with producer KURT RALSKE (LOTION, The ROPERS), they had an album, only, to add insult to injury, 'American' refused to release it. Fortunately 'Beggars Banquet' did, in early 1997. The creative furore preceding the release of 'TOO MANY DAYS WITHOUT THINKING' probably explains its dark and gloomy tone, and turbulent sound. The recording and release of fifth album, 'FOR ALL THE BEAUTIFUL PEOPLE' (1998), appeared a much more agreeable process, although founder member KIRKPATRICK left, and was replaced by drummer ROB ELLIS. SWELL were now funkier, with strong basslines ('TODAY') and Stax-style horns ('EVERYTHING IS GOOD'), heightening the eclecticism of their sound. Sixth album, 'EVERYBODY WANTS TO KNOW' (2001), was effectively a solo effort by FREEL, although joined on some tracks by drummer REY WASHAM. • **Covered:** STREET FIGHTING MAN (Rolling Stones).

Album rating: SWELL (*5) / WELL? ... (*8) / 41 (*6) / TOO MANY DAYS WITHOUT THINKING (*7) / FOR ALL THE BEAUTIFUL PEOPLE (*6) / FEED mini (*5) / EVERYBODY WANTS TO KNOW (*5)

DAVID FREEL – vocals, guitar / **JOHN DETTMAN** – guitar / **MONTE VALLIER** – bass; repl. TIM ADAMS (later left 1989) / **SEAN KIRKPATRICK** – drums

	Mean	pSycho-sPecific
Apr 90. (ltd-lp) <PSY 001> **SWELL**	-	☐

– Get high / A town / Sick half of a church / Love you all / Yes and no [cd/c-only] / Stop / Dan, a son of God / Ready / Think about those days / Wooden hippie nice. <re-iss. Nov90; PSY 002> <cd/c-iss.Apr91 +=; PSY 004> (UK-iss.Feb93 on 'Mean' cd/lp; MEAN CD/LP 001) <US re-iss. Feb95 on 'Warners'; 43004>

May 91. (7") <FTD 003> **GET HIGH. / THE PRICE**

Jun 92. (cd/lp) (MEAN CD/LP 002) <PSY 005> **WELL? . . .** ☐ ☐ Feb92
– Intro / At long last / Everything / Down / Turtle song / It's okay / The price / Showbizz / Tired / Wash your brain / Soda jerk fountain / Suicide machine / Thank you, good evening. <US cd re-iss. Feb93 on 'American'; 9 45167>

—— now without DETTMAN

	Def American	Def American
Jul 93. (12"ep/cd-ep) (DAB 2 T/CD) **ROOM TO THINK E.P.**	☐	-

– At long last / Always one thing / Life's great / Give / Just get well.

	American –Beggars...	American – Warners
Mar 94. (12"ep/cd-ep) (ARB 4 T/CD) **FORGET ABOUT JESUS**	☐	-
Apr 94. (cd/lp) (ARB CD/LP 6) <45530-2/-4> **41**	☐	Nov93

– In the door, up the stairs / Is that important? / Song seven / Kinda stoned / Don't give / Smile my friend / Forget about Jesus / Here it is / You're so right / Fine day coming / (It's time to) Move on / Down the stairs, out the door. (cd+=) – Lyrics. (cd re-iss. Aug97 on 'Beggars Banquet'; BEGL 158CD)

—— FREEL + KIRKPATRICK recruited **TOM HAYS** – guitar

	Sub Pop	Sub Pop
Jul 94. (7") <(SP 264)> **SUMMER SONGS**	☐	☐

– This is how it starts / Too many days without thinking.

—— **MONTE VALLIER** – bass; returned to repl. HAYS

	Beggars Banquet	Beggars Banquet
Feb 97. (7"ep/cd-ep) (BBQ 306/+CD) **THE TRIP**	☐	-

– (I know) The Trip / So would I / Easy.

Mar 97. (cd/lp) (BBQ CD/LP 187) <80187> **TOO MANY DAYS WITHOUT THINKING** ☐ ☐
– Throw the wine / What I always wanted / Make mine you / Fuck even flow / At Lennie's / When you come over / (I know) The trip / Going up (to Portland)? / Bridgette, you love me / Sunshine everyday. (cd re-iss. Aug97; BBL 187CD)

—— **ROB ELLIS** – drums; repl. KIRKPATRICK

Aug 98. (7") (BBQ 326) **EVERYTHING IS GOOD. / 200 YEARS** ☐ -
(cd-s+=) (BBQ 326CD) – Everyday sunshine.

Aug 98. (cd) (BBQCD 203) <80203> **FOR ALL THE BEAUTIFUL PEOPLE** ☐ ☐
– Today / Oh my my / Make up your mind / I hate Christmas / Off in my head / Something to do / Pink pink rain / Blackmilk / Everything is good / Swill 9 / Tonight / Don't you know they love you?

Oct 98. (7") (BBQ 330) **MAKE UP YOUR MIND. / SAVED MY MONEY** ☐ -
(cd-s+=) (BBQ 330CD) – This is how it starts / Street fighting man.

Aug 99. (cd-ep) (RTS 26) **EP (XXVI)** ☐ -
– Fuck yew / Get higher / Come tomorrow / Two times in the sun / Golden years / Saved my money.
(above issued on 'Return To Sender')

Nov 00. (m-cd) (BBQM 349CD) **FEED** ☐ -
– Feed / Someday always comes / Like poverty / ...A velvet sun / Inside a bomb / Glad to be alone / Poverty again.

—— FREEL solo brought in **REY WASHAM** – drums

Jun 01. (cd/lp) (BBQ MCD/LP 220) 80220> **EVERYBODY WANTS TO KNOW** ☐ -
– This story / Someday always comes / ...A velvet sun / Like poverty / Inside a bomb / I don't think so / East n west / Everybody wants to know / Call me / Try me / Feed / Why not?

SWERVEDRIVER

Formed: Oxford to Camden, London, England ... late 1989 initially as SHAKE APPEAL, by ADAM FRANKLIN, JIMMY HARTRIDGE, GRAHAM BONNAR and spokesman ADRIAN VINES. This outfit issued one 7" in 1988, 'GIMME FEVER' for 'No Town'; (NO 002). SWERVEDRIVER signed to 'Creation' in the early 90's and broke through with acclaimed EP's, 'SON OF MUSTANG FORD' and 'RAVE DOWN'. Loosely associated with the 'Shoegazing' scene, SWERVEDRIVER were lent a bit of crusty credibility via FRANKLIN's dreadlocks and stoned vocals while the music was tighter and more melodic than many of their contemporaries. In 1991, they scored a minor UK hit with their third EP, 'SANDBLASTED', which preceded their classy Top 50 debut album, 'RAISE'. Although they supported the likes of The WONDER STUFF, SWERVEDRIVER were bafflingly lauded as the new UK "great white hopes" of the metal world! A 1992 Stateside tour with SOUNDGARDEN took its toll and eventually led to BONNER quitting. The band subsequently returned home and were soon another member down when VINES decided he couldn't cope. A follow-up album, 'MEZCAL HEAD' (1993), was produced by ALAN MOULDER, who had previously worked with the top-rated SMASHING PUMPKINS. Unfortunately, his midas touch didn't quite turn to gold this time around and by the release of the more solid follow-up, 'EJECTOR SEAT RESERVATION', in 1995, they were dropped by their label. Although FRANKLIN & co. were rumoured to be working out a new deal with 'Geffen', they finally reappeared on 'A&M' in early '97 with 'MAGIC BUS'. Possibly one of the unluckiest indie bands of the 90's, SWERVEDRIVER found themselves back in obscurity following the surprise collapse of the veteran label founded by Jerry Moss and Herb Alpert. A low-key EP, 'SPACE TRAVEL ROCK'N'ROLL' and album, '99th DREAM' followed in '98, although sadly it seems their moment has passed.
• **Songwriters:** HARTRIDGE / FRANKLIN penned except; JESUS (Velvet Underground).

Album rating: RAISE (*8) / MEZCAL HEAD (*6) / EJECTOR SEAT RESERVATION (*7) / 99th DREAM (*5)

ADAM FRANKLIN (b.19 Jul'68, Essex, England) – vocals, guitar / **JIMMY HARTRIDGE** (b.27 Nov'67, Oxfordshire, England) – guitar / **ADRIAN 'ADI' VINES** (b.25 Jan'68, Yorkshire, England) – bass / **GRAHAM BONNAR** (b.28 Apr'67, Glasgow, Scotland) – drums, vocals (ex-UT)

	Creation	A&M
Jul 90. (7"ep/12"ep)(cd-ep) (CRE 079/+T)(CRESCD 079) **SON OF MUSTANG FORD / VOLCANO TRASH. / KILL THE SUPERHEROES / JUGGERNAUT RIDE**	☐	-
Nov 90. (7"ep/12"ep)(cd-ep) (CRE 088/+T)(CRESCD 088) **RAVE DOWN / SHE'S BESIDE HERSELF. / AFTERGLOW / ZED HEAD**	☐	-
Jul 91. (7"ep/12"ep)(cd-ep) (CRE 102/+T)(CRESCD 102) **SANDBLASTED / OUT. / FLAWED / LAZE IT UP**	67	-
Sep 91. (cd/lp)(c) (CRE CD/LP 093)(C-CRE 093) <5376> **RAISE**	44	

– Sci-flyer / Pole-up / Son of Mustang Ford / Deep seat / Rave down / Sunset / Feel so reel / Sandblasted / Lead me where you dare. (free-12"w.a.) – SURF TWANG. / DEEP TWANG

May 92. (7") (CRE 120) **NEVER LOSE THAT FEELING. / SCRAWL AND SCREAM** 62 -
(12"+=)(cd-s+=) (CRE 120T)(CRESCD 120) – The watchman's hands / Never learn.

1018

SWERVEDRIVER (cont)

— ADI left in Sep'92. He was soon replaced by **JEZ** – drums

Aug 93. (7") *(CRE 136)* **DUEL. / PLANES OVER THE SKYLINE** (12"+=)(cd-s+=) *(CRE 136T)(CRESCD 136)* – Year of the girl. — **60** / —

Sep 93. (cd/lp)(c) *(CRE CD/LP 143)(C-CRE 143) <540129>* **MEZCAL HEAD** — **55** / Oct93
– For seeking heat / Duel / Blowin' cool / MM abduction / Last train to Satansville / Mary and Maggie / A change is gonna come / Girl on a motorbike / Duress / You find it everywhere.

Feb 94. (12"ep)(cd-ep) *(CRE 174T)(CRESCD 174)* **LAST TRAIN TO SATANSVILLE / JESUS. / SATANSVILLE REVISITED / LAND OF THE LOST**

Jul 94. (7") *(FLOWER 004)* **MY ZEPHYR (SEQUEL). / MARS**
(above 45 was a one-off for 'Flower Shop' records)

Jun 95. (12"white-ep)(c-ep/cd-ep) *(CRE 179T)(CRE CS/SCD 179)* **LAST DAY ON EARTH / MAELSTROM / I AM SUPERMAN / THE DIRECTORS CUT OF YOUR LIFE** — / —

Aug 95. (cd/lp)(c) *(CRE CD/LP 157)(C-CRE 157)* **EJECTOR SEAT RESERVATION** — / —
– Single factor salute / Bring me the head of the fortune teller / The other Jesus / Song of Jaguar E / I am Superman / Bubbling up / Ejector seat reservation / How does it feel to like Candy? / Last day on Earth / The birds. *(c+=/cd+=)* – Untitled / So downhearted. *(w/ free-7")* – FLAMING HEART / PLAN 7 SATELLITE 10.

Echostatic   not iss.

Jan 97. (d7") *(ECHO 09-10)* **WHY SAY YEAH. / IN MY TIME //** (split with SOPHIA)

A&M   not iss.
Sessions

Feb 97. (7"/cd-s) *(582130-7/-2)* **MAGIC BUS. / MAGIC BUS (edit)** — / not iss.

Cortex   Zero Hour

Jun 97. (7") *(7SMS 07)* **93 MILLION MILES FROM THE SUN (AND COUNTING). / UP FROM THE SEA** — / —

Feb 98. (cd-ep) *(CORX 050CD) <1233>* **SPACE TRAVEL ROCK'N'ROLL EP**
– 99th dream / Good ships / Hate yr kind / Stimulini.

Sonic Waves Discs   Zero Hour

Jul 98. (12"ep/cd-ep) *(SWD 098 EP/CD)* **SPACE TRAVEL, ROCK'N'ROLL EP**
– 99th dream / Good ships / Hate your kind / Stimulini.

Aug 98. (cd/lp) *(SWD 099 CD/LP) <1230>* **99th DREAM** — / Feb98
– 99th dream / Up from the sea / She weaves a tender trap / These times / Electric 77 / Stellar Caprice / Wrong treats / You've sealed my fate / In my time / Expressway / Behind the scenes of the sound and the . . .

Oct 98. (cd-ep) *(SWD 100CD)* **WRONG TREATS / HOMELESS HOMECOMING / CHATEAU IN VIRGINIA WATER** — / —

— split after above

SWIMMER (see under ⇒ TEN BENSON)

SWIRLIES

Formed: Cambridge, Massachusetts, USA ... 1990 by DAMON TUTUNJIAN, SEANA CARMODY, ANDY BERNICK and BEN DRUCKER. This appropriately monikered pseudo-psychedelic proto-"shoegazing" outfit signed to the 'Taang!' label (once home of The LEMONHEADS) and made their debut in '91 with the 'NUMBER ONE' EP. Clearly taking their cue from noise-pop experimentalists MY BLOODY VALENTINE, The SWIRLIES concocted an amorphous, effects driven sound that marked them out as spiritual cousins to UK acts like CHAPTERHOUSE, RIDE, etc. 1992's mini-set, 'WHAT TO DO ABOUT THEM', collected together the cream of the band's work to date alongside a handful of fresh tracks, none of them appearing on their debut album proper, 'BLONDER TONGUE AUDIO BATON' (1993). A solitary EP the following year marked time while the band found their feet again with newcomers CHRISTINA FILES and ANTHONY DeLUCA (replacements for SEANA and BEN), re-modelled SWIRLIES defying musical gravity once again with 1996's belated comeback set, 'THEY SPENT THEIR WILD YOUTHFUL DAYS IN THE GLITTERING WORLD OF THE SALONS'. Later that year (with ADAM PIERCE having replaced the aforementioned new members), the EP 'SNEAKY FLUTE MUSIC' hit the US indie shops, previewing 1998's full-length sequel, 'STRICTLY EAST COAST SNEAKY FLUTE MUSIC'. The SWIRLIES were about to get back on the road in early 2003 alongside The LILYS.

Album rating: WHAT TO DO ABOUT THEM mini (*5) / BLONDER TONGUE AUDIO BATON (*7) / THEY SPENT THEIR WILD YOUTHFUL DAYS IN THE GLITTERING WORLD OF THE SALONS (*6) / STRICTLY EAST COAST SNEAKY FLUTE MUSIC (*9)

DAMON TITUNJIAN – vocals, guitar / **SEANA CARMODY** – vocals, guitar / **ANDY BERNICK** – bass / **BEN DRUCKER** – drums

Slumberland   Slumberland

Jan 92. (7") *<DRYL 15>* **SARAH SITTING. / DIDN'T UNDERSTAND / CHRIS R.** — / —

1992. (7"; split w/ CUDGEL) **FISH DREAMS RED. /** — / —

Taang!   Taang!

Oct 92. (m-lp/m-cd) *<(TAANG 065/+CD)>* **WHAT TO DO ABOUT THEM**
– Tall ships / Sarah sitting / Her life of artistic freedom / Didn't understand / Upstairs / Chris R. / Cousteau.

Apr 93. (lp/cd) *<(TAANG 067/+CD)>* **BLONDER TONGUE AUDIO BATON** — / Mar93
– Bell / Vigilant always / His life of academic freedom / Pancake / Jeremy Parker / Park the car by the side of the road / Tree chopped down / Wrong tube / Wait forever.

Aug 94. (cd-ep) *<TAANG 078CD>* **BROKEDICK CAR EP** — / —
– Wrong tube / Labrea tarpit / Pancake cleaner / You're just jealous / House of pancake.

— split a 45 with PITCHBLEND

— **DAMON + ANDY** recruited newcomers **CHRISTINA FILES** – vocals / **ANTHONY DeLUCA** – drums (SEAN CARMODY formed SYRUP USA)

Apr 96. (cd) *<TAANG 101CD>* **THEY SPENT THEIR WILD YOUTHFUL DAYS IN THE GLITTERING WORLD OF THE SALONS** — / —
– French radio / In her many new found freedom / No identifier / Sounds of Sebring / San Cristobal de las Casas / You can't be told it, you must behold it / Pony / Do any of you know anything about . . . / Two girls kissing / Sterling Moss / Boys, protect yourselves from aliens / Sunn / Vehicle is invisible.

Oct 96. (cd-ep) *<TAANG 111>* **SNEAKY FLUTE MUSIC EP** — / —
– Sneaky flutes (7 pieces).

— **ADAM PIERCE** – drums; repl. DeLUCA + FILES

Apr 98. (d-lp/cd) *<(TAANG 132/+CD)>* **STRICTLY EAST COAST SNEAKY FLUTE MUSIC** — / —
– Au revoir / In harmony / Sea wolf / Adams mix / Bobs mix / River of action / Swan / No identifier / Reese's mix / Cotsey's mix / Soulsinger / #1 song / Adagio / Allegro / Finale / Torr empathy jam.

— added **ROB LAXO** – guitar (ex-WICKED FARLEYS)

— The SWIRLIES took a sabbatical for the rest of the 90's + early 00's

SYMPOSIUM

Formed: Kensington, London, England ... early '96 by fresh-faced youths and former Catholic school choirboys, ROSS CUMMINS, HAGOP TCHAPARIAN (part Armenian), WOJTEK GODZISZ (fully Polish), WILLIAM McGONAGLE and JOE BIRCH. Taking their cue from the noisy pop-punk fusion of GREEN DAY and ASH, these religiously fanatic QPR (a West London football club) fans bounded onto the indie scene in 1996 with the 'DRINK THE SUNSHINE' single. Their debut effort for 'Infectious' (home of ASH), the lads proceeded to gatecrash the Top 30 with their follow-up, 'FAREWELL TO TWILIGHT', a taster from their spunky, CLIVE LANGER/ALAN WINSTANLEY-produced Top 30 debut set, 'ONE DAY AT A TIME' (1997). The following year, SYMPOSIUM were even stronger via Top 40 album, 'ON THE OUTSIDE' (1998), a record geaturing their last hit, 'BLUE'. • **Songwriters:** GODZISZ or CUMMINGS except HARD DAY'S NIGHT (Beatles).

Album rating: ONE DAY AT A TIME mini (*7) / ON THE OUTSIDE (*8)

ROSS CUMMINS – vocals / **HAGOP TCHAPARIAN** – guitar / **WILLIAM McGONAGLE** – guitar / **WOJTEK GODZISZ** – bass / **JOE BIRCH** – drums

Infectious   Red Ant

Oct 96. (7") *(infect 30s)* **DRINK THE SUNSHINE. / DISAPPEAR** — / —
(cd-s+=) *(infect 30cd)* – Smiling.

Mar 97. (7") *(infect 34s)* **FAREWELL TO TWILIGHT. / XANTHEIN** **25** / —
(7") *(infect 34xx)* – ('A'side) / Song.
(cd-s++=) *(infect 34cd)* – Easily scared.

May 97. (cd-ep) *<RA 008-2>* **SYMPOSIUM EP** — / —
– Disappear / Xanthein / Farewell to twilight / Drink the sunshine / Easilt scared.

May 97. (7") *(infect 37s)* **ANSWER TO WHY I HATE YOU. / JIM** **32** / —
(cd-s+=) *(infect 37cd)* – Natural.
(cd-s) *(infect 37cdx)* – ('A'side) / Torquoise / Keeping the secret.

Aug 97. (7") *(infect 44s)* **FAIRWEATHER FRIEND. / ('A'live)** **25** / —
(cd-s+=) *(infect 44cd)* – Greeting song / Just so.
(cd-s+=) *(infect 44cdx)* – The answer to why I love you (live) / Disappear (live).

Oct 97. (m-cd/m-c/m-lp) *(infect 49 cd/mc/lp)* **ONE DAY AT A TIME** **29** / —
– Drink the sunshine / Farewell to twilight / Puddles / Fairweather friend / One day at a time / Fizzy / Girl with brains in her feet / Smiling.

Nov 97. (7"purple) *(infect 50s)* **DRINK THE SUNSHINE. / FIZZY** — / —

Mar 98. (7") *(infect 52s)* **AVERAGE MAN. / TWIST** **45** / —
(cd-s) *(infect 52cd)* – ('A'side) / Journey / Little things / Me.
(cd-s) *(infect 52cdx)* – ('A'side) / Hard day's night (live).

May 98. (7"pic-d) *(infect 55s)* **BURY YOU. / SCHOSTAKOWICH** **41** / —
(cd-s) *(infect 55cd)* – ('A'side) / Serenade the idiot / Standing honoured / Higher.
(cd-s) *(infect 55cdx)* – ('A'side) / Fluorescent / Mairamout / ('A'-CD-ROM video clip).

May 98. (cd/c/lp) *(infect 56 cd/mc/lp)* **ON THE OUTSIDE** **32** / —
– Impossible / The answer to why I hate you / Bury you / Blue / The end / Nothing special / Circles squares and lines / Stay on the outside / Paint the stars / Obsessive compulsive disorder / Natural / Way.

Jul 98. (7") *(infect 57s)* **BLUE. / LIFE OF RILEY** **48** / —
(cd-s+=) *(infect 57cd)* – Carnival.
(cd-s) *(infect 57cdx)* – ('A'side) / Cartwheels / Ode to the frogs.

Curveball   not iss.

May 99. (7") *(SYMP 001S)* **KILLING POSITION. / WALL OF SILENCE / THE END (live)** — / —
(cd-s+=) *(SYMP 001CD)* – Hard day's night (live at Reading).

— SYMPOSIUM split towards the end of the millennium

– compilations, etc. –

Nov 99. (cd) *Strange Fruit; (<SFRSCD 088>)* **LIVE AND IN SESSION** — / —

TAHITI 80

Formed: Paris, France ... 1993 by art students JEROME KERNER, XAVIER BOYER, PEDRO RESENDE, MEDERIC GONTIER and SYLVAIN MARCHAND. This French jangly guitar pop quintet, who seemed obsessed with bands such as The SMALL FACES or The WHO, issued their debut EP '20 MINUTES' in 1996, followed by 'I.S.A.A.C' and their first-album proper 'PUZZLE' (2000). Although having an esoteric knowledge of guitar pop, TAHITI 80 ploughed through a disappointing set of songs that really only drew from their influences without adding a single slice of individuality. A remix album was issued in 2001, with CORNELIUS stepping on board to help out with some guitar and mixing work, before the group delivered their sophomore 'WALLPAPER FOR THE SOUL' (2002). Perhaps their most accomplished album to date, the set displayed the group's musical maturity in the form of delicately crafted songs, with the odd outburst of indie pop thrown in for good measure (such as the uptempo 'FUN FAIR'). Further reason why this album was quite a marvellous release was the addition of composer and arranger RICHARD HAWSON on five tracks. Of course, HAWSON was legendary in the British music scene (NICK DRAKE, JAMES TAYLOR and a little known outfit called The BEATLES would regularly hire him), which was obviously TAHITI 80's point of reference.

Album rating: PUZZLE (*5) / WALLPAPER FOR THE SOUL (*7)

XAVIER BOYER – vocals, multi / **MEDERIC GONTIER** – guitars, vocals / **PEDRO RESENDE** – bass, synths / **SYLVAIN MARCHAND** – drums, percussion, synths

			Bobby	not iss.
1996.	(cd-ep) <001> **20 MINUTES**	–	French
– (interm? de 1) / I.S.A.A.C. / Tasteless cake / (interm? de 2) / John Steed / (interm? de 3) / Made first never forget / (interm? de 4) / Pop stars' club / 20 minutes.

			not iss.	J.V.C.
Sep 00.	(cd-s) <61106> **HEARTBEAT (mixes, etc)**	–	Japan

			Atmospherique	Minty Fresh
Sep 00.	(cd-ep) (2346-2) **I.S.A.A.C. EP**		
– I.S.A.A.C. / John Steed / So you want to be a rock'n'roll star / Montage.
Nov 00.	(7") (2381-7) **YELLOW BUTTERFLY. / DESIREE**		
	(cd-s+=) (2381-1) – Revolution 80 (millennium version).
Jun 01.	(7"/cd-s) (2393-7/-2) **A LOVE FROM OUTER SPACE. / BARBIE DRESS / WHEN THE SUN**		
Jul 01.	(cd/lp) (2349-2/-1) <70036> **PUZZLE**		Jun00
– Yellow butterfly / I.S.A.A.C. / Heartbeat / Made first never forget / Mr. Davis / Swimming suit / Hey Joe / Puzzle / Easy way out / Things are made to last forever / Revolution 80 / When the sun.
Feb 01.	(m-cd) <70039> **EXTRA PIECES**	–	
– Heartbeat (Cornelius mix) / A love from outer space / Barbie dress / Desiree / John Stead / I.S.A.A.C. / Revolution 80 (millennium version) / When the sun (sunrise version).
Oct 02.	(cd) <70046> **WALLPAPER FOR THE SOUL**	–	
– Wallpaper for the soul / 1,000 times / Separate ways / Get yourself together / The other side / Happy end / Fun fair / Soul deep / Open book / The train / Don't look below / Memories of the past.

TAGMEMICS
(see under ⇒ ART ATTACKS; 70's section)

TARNATION

Formed: San Francisco, California, USA ... 1992 by Sautee Nacoochee, Georgia-born PAULA FRAZER, a veteran of the Bay Area alt-rock acts; all-female FRIGHTWIG the most noteworthy. Prior to this and just into her teens, she had moved with her family to Arkansas, where she honed her multi-ranged soprano voice to perfection; PAULA would subsequently sing in a Bulgarian woman's choir. Having met up with former SF SEALS members, LINCOLN ALLEN and MICHELLE CERNUTO (MATT SULLIVAN would soon make it a quartet), they decided to form their own roots/alt-country group. The haunting prairie laments of TARNATION found FRAZER revisiting her presbyterian upbringing via a trademark cinematic country sound. Following a low-key self-financed debut, 'I'LL GIVE YOU SOMETHING TO CRY ABOUT' (1994), the band were signed to London label, '4 a.d.', through whom they released 1995's 'GENTLE CREATURES'. Delivered in a high, lonesome wail lying somewhere between DOLORES O'RIORDAN, GILLIAN WELCH and TAMMY WYNETTE!, FRAZER's dark narratives were set against a moody soundtrack of vibrato-shimmering guitar, subtle lap steel and shuffling percussion. Not the most immediate of approaches and one which, along with labelmates such as RED HOUSE PAINTERS and MOJAVE 3, has seen TARNATION enjoy critical acclaim without any corresponding rise in their profile. This despite one of their finest efforts to date in 1997's 'MIRADOR' album and the SMITHS-meet-The CRANBERRIES-in-Mexico brilliance of accompanying single, 'YOUR THOUGHTS AND MINE'; FRAZER was now the sole survivor, the other three being replaced by ALEX OROPEZA, BILL CUEVAS and JOE BYRNES. Her most famous moment came later that year when she duetted with TJINDER SINGH on CORNERSHOP's 'Good To Be On The Road Back Home Again'. Still, with a major label deal – courtesy of 'Reprise' – in the bag, TARNATION might yet achieve the same level of recognition as alt-country stalwarts and new labelmates WILCO. As it turned out, FRAZER was to ditch the TARNATION name and hook up with a new cast of established San Francisco-based musicians (namely PATRICK MAIN, JEFF PALMER and former SISTER DOUBLE HAPPINESS man, JIM LINDSAY) to record her debut solo set, 'INDOOR UNIVERSE' (2001). Long time fans wary of a departure from the widescreen Americana of old weren't disappointed as FRAZER once again blended her Smoky Mountain roots with smoky, noir-ish meditations on the frailties of human emotion. Viola, cello and even french horn flourishes served as a cushion for her beguiling vocals, as impressive as ever and perhaps even more vivid in their extravagant evocations of a fabled American aesthetic.

Album rating: I'LL GIVE YOU SOMETHING TO CRY ABOUT (*6) / GENTLE CREATURES (*6) / MIRADOR (*7) / Paula Frazer: INDOOR UNIVERSE (*6)

PAULA FRAZER – vocals, guitars, bass, keyboards, accordion, etc / **LINCOLN ALLEN** – guitar (ex-SF SEALS / **MATT SULLIVAN** – guitar / **MICHELLE CERNUTO** – drums (ex-SF SEALS)

			not iss.	Nuf Sed
1994.	(cd) <NONTAR 2> **I'LL GIVE YOU SOMETHING TO CRY ABOUT**	–	
– It's not easy / Yellow birds / Never an easy way / Game of broken hearts / They took you away once again / Rancho Carne humana / Big O motel / Christine / Sweat and blood / Do you fancy me / Strangers / Lonely nights / Spanking potion No.5 / The ring / Tell me it's not so.

— now with **YUMA JOE BYRNES** – drums, percussion / **JAMIE MEAGAN** – bass, guitar (+ lap steel), vocals, percussion, organ / **ALEX OROPEZA** – guitars (+ lap steel), organ, vocals / **SHEILA SCHAT** – cello, violin / **ARCH STANTON** – noise

			4 a.d.	4ad-Reprise
Sep 95.	(lp/cd) (CAD 5010/+CD) <45961> **GENTLE CREATURES**		Aug95
– Game of broken hearts / Halfway to madness / Well / Big A motel / Tell me it's not so / Two wrongs / Lonely lights / Gentle creatures / Listen to the wind / Hand / Do you fancy me / Yellow birds / Burn again / Stranger in the mirror / It's not easy. (cd re-iss. Jul98; GAD 5010CD)

— **FRAZER** now with **ALEX OROPEZA** – guitars / **BILL CUEVAS** – bass, lap steel / **JOE BYRNES** – drums

Jan 97.	(7"ltd.) (TAD 7000) **THERE'S SOMEONE. / I DIDN'T MEAN IT: PALADINA**		–
Feb 97.	(12"ep)(cd-ep) (AAD 7001)(BAD 7001CD) **YOUR THOUGHTS AND MINE / YOU'LL UNDERSTAND. / LEAVE THE SAD THINGS BEHIND / LAND THAT TIME LOST**		–
Apr 97.	(cd)(d-lp) (CAD 7004CD)(DAD 7004) <46482> **MIRADOR**		
– An awful shade of blue / Wait / A place where I know / Is she lonesome now? / Your thoughts and mine / Christine / Destiny / There's someone / Like a ghost / Idly / Little black egg / You'll understand. (cd re-iss. Jul98; GAD 7004CD)

— the band evolved into FRAZER's solo project

PAULA FRAZER

with **PATRICK MAIN** – keyboards, vocals / **JEFF PALMER** – bass (ex-SISTER DOUBLE HAPPINESS) **JIM LINDSAY** – drums (or ORANGER) / **MATT TORREY** – drums / etc.

			Evangeline	Birdman
Apr 01.	(cd) (GEL 4026) <30> **INDOOR UNIVERSE**		
– That you know / This is a song / Gone / Think of me / Not so bad, but not so good / Stay as you are / Mean things / Everywhere / Deep was the night / We met by the love lies bleeding / The only one.

TARWATER

Formed: East Berlin, Germany ... 1995 by long-time compatriots and punk rockers, BERND JESTRAM and RONALD LIPPOK (latter of TO ROCOCO ROT). After a number of homeland releases – including, '11/6 12/10', 'RABBIT MOON REMIXED' and the radio theatre play 'JOHN DONNE' – their first official album issued in the UK, 'SILUR' (means 'the Silurian Age when the Earth was underwater), came out in the Autumn of '98. An experimental masterpiece, this textured piece combined elements of CABARET VOLTAIRE and MASSIVE ATTACK, 'THE WATERSAMPLE' being the highlight. 'ANIMALS, SUNS & ATOMS' (2000) forged ahead with the band's oblique agenda, pitching assorted opaque samples into a mix of abstract rhythms, primitive instrumental elements and LIPPOK's valium-paced vocal efforts. Subsequently picked up by 'Mute', the Germans continued to explore the grey, radioactive area between mutant electro-pop and sonic tinkering on both 'NOT THE WHEEL' (2001) and 'DWELLERS ON THE THRESHOLD' (2002). • **Covered:** DOWN IN THE SEWER (Stranglers).

Album rating: 11/6 12/10 (*7) / RABBIT MOON REMIXED (*6) / SILUR (*7) / ANIMALS, SUNS & ATOMS (*6) / NOT THE WHEEL (*5) / DWELLERS ON THE THRESHOLD (*5)

BERND JESTRAM – bass, keyboards / **RONALD LIPPOK** (b. 1963) – vocals, keyboards (of TO ROCOCO ROT)

TARWATER (cont)

			Kitty-Yo	Mute	
1996.	(cd)	(KY 96004CD) **11/6 12/10**	-	-	German

– Theme / Tar / Han er der inne / Euroslut / Rome / Conquer ROM itself / New brood / Kleenex / Elbow on the quilt / Second arthyr / Inversnaid.

1996.	(m-cd) **JOHN DONNE** (radio music play)	-	-	German
1997.	(cd-s) **DOWN IN THE SEWER**	-	-	German
1997.	(cd) (KY 97005CD) **RABBIT MOON REMIXED**	-	-	German

– Rabbit moon (Las Gammas mix) / 11/6 12/10 (Elektronauten/Datec remix) / Inversnaid (atomic foam mix) / Greenwich (scabby mix) / Transfrancisco (ecchoing green mix) / Inversnaid (Ncc rado 505 finder remix) / Euroslut (spectral mix) / Rome (rabbit mix). *(UK-iss.Apr98 on 'Cap Stack'; CR 9801CD)*

Sep 98. (cd/lp) *(EFA 55213-2/-1) <6 9099>* **SILUR**
– Visit / To maouf / The watersample / Seafrance Cezanne / Silur / No more extra time / Otomo / Ford / Pomps of the subsoil / 20 miles up / To describe you / V-AT.

Jul 99. (cd-ep) *(RM 008)* **REMIX EP**
(above issued on 'Roomtone', below on 'Soul Static Sound')

Jul 99. (12"; as TARWATER featuring TIKIMAN) *(SSS 24)* **LIKE A MIRACLE**

May 00. (cd/lp) *(EFA 55229-2/-1) <6 9128>* **ANIMALS, SUNS & ATOMS**
– K.R. ? L.E.G. / All of the ants left Paris / Noon / The trees / Dauphin sun / At low frequency / Song of the moth / Early risers / Babyuniverse / Somewhere / Seven ways to fake a perfect skin.

Aug 01. (cd) *(EFA 52248-2)* **NOT THE WHEEL**
– Host – Body – Host / Expected / I want my machinery to disappear / Lost stalker / Garden / Plans / Not the wheel / Tommy tomorrow / Rejoice in the sun / Thunder's girlfriend / Spider / Warszawa on the roof / Under the green ice.

Oct 02. (cd/lp) *(EFA 55265-2/-1) <6 9188>* **DWELLERS ON THE THRESHOLD** Sep02
– 70 rupies to Paradise road / Metal flakes / Diver / 1985 / Be late / Tesla / Now / Miracle of love / Phin / Perfect shadow / Dogs and light tents / Imperator victus.

TATTLE TALE

Formed: Seattle, Washington, USA ... 1992 by singer/guitarists MADIGAN SHRIVE and JEN WOOD, schoolmates who were all of 17 and 15 years old respectively. Renowned for their raw, teenage confessional, personal-is-political-folky-feminist (somewhat overwrought, due to their tender ages) performances, TALE garnered minor fame with their series of appearances on compilations and first two singles, 'EARLY DAZE' and 'ALDER WOOD MALL'. An eponymous cassette on 'Kill Rock Stars' came next, before the duo's swansong in the form of 1995's not-particularly-well-received 'SEW TRUE' LP. However, these juvenile efforts would prove to be merely a springboard for both young women, with each of them going on to put out further releases under different guises. WOOD relocated to Santa Cruz in 1996 and recorded the solo 11-song acoustic album 'NO MORE WADING' (1997) that she put out on cassette on her own imprint 'Radar Light'. She also teamed up with THAT DOG violinist PETRA HADEN for the 'GETTING PAST THE STATIC' album (1998). This work was a catharsis hewn from the artist's own pain and confusion and was praised for the bravery of its poignant personal pop-acoustic cuts. Vocalist/cellist SHRIVE, meanwhile, would go on to create her own label, 'Moonpuss', issuing the 7" 'PLAYS WITH HERSELF', the live cassette 'FOR TUNES FROM THE F-HOLES' (1996) and studio LP 'ROCK STOP'. She then formed idiosyncratic chamber-punk trio BONFIRE MADIGAN with contrabassist SHERI OZEKI and percussionist/turntablist TOMAS PALERMO, debuting with the 'Kill Rock Stars' 7" 'BACKSEAT BUOY' (1998). The full-length '...FROM THE BURNPILE' (1998) followed soon after and, in 2000 the group, now including guitarist JENNIFER DOTY and drummer SUNSHINE HAIRE to fill out the sound – resurfaced with 'SADDLE THE BRIDGE'.

Album rating: TATTLE TALE (*4) / SEW TRUE (*5) / Jen Wood: NO MORE WADING (*6) / GETTING PAST THE STATIC (*7) / Bonfire Madigan: ...FROM THE BURNPILE with Villa VillaKula (*5) / SADDLE THE BRIDGE (*5)

MADIGAN SHRIVE – vocals, guitar, (occasional) cello, drums / **JEN WOOD** – vocals, guitar, drums

			not iss.	Pillarbox
1993.	(7") **EARLY DAZE.** /		-	
			not iss.	Chou-Chou
1993.	(7") **ALDER WOOD MALL.** /		-	
			not iss.	Kill Rock Stars
Apr 94.	(cd) <KRS 301> **TATTLE TALE**			
			not iss.	St.Francis
1995.	(cd) <2> **SEW TRUE**		-	

– Arrows / Little silver hands / Silent picture show / My nightmare / Take ten / A girl's toolbox / Blood friends / Sister blue / Fiberglass / Glass vase, cello case / Lingerie lament / Moontiwe / Holler I.

JEN WOOD

			not iss.	Radar Light
1996.	(c) <none> **NO MORE WAITING**		-	

– Aching heart / Your own words / Draining / Recharge / Bronze wound / Bullet box / Woven into Gershwin / One fist to fight / Precious light / Run with blood / Imperfect. *<cd-iss. Oct98 & re-mixed on 'Tree'; tree 07>*

— with **DANNY FRANKEL** – multi / **PETRA HADEN** – mandolin, etc

			not iss.	W.I.N.
Oct 97.	(cd) <26> **GETTING PAST THE STATIC**		-	

– Invitation to plastic / Caught halo / Three thorns torn / Bend / Candy / Sent over / Your turn / Q is for question / Bullet box / Spoken for / Stay / Ocean.

			not iss.	Tree
1999.	(ltd-7") <tree 09.6> **SHELTERING ARMS.** / Tim Kinsella: **PICTURE POSTCARD**		-	

— with **KATRINA THOMSON** – vocals + **JAYSON TOLZDOF** – guitar

May 00. (cd-ep) <tree 17> **THIS UNCONTAINABLE LIGHT**
– Ride / Lie for a lie / Let's fight / See through.

BONFIRE MADIGAN

MADIGAN SHIVE with **SHERI OZEKI** – contra bass, cello / **LAURA McFARLANE** – drums, xylophone / + a few guests

			not iss.	MoonPuss
1995.	(7"; as MADIGAN) <001> **PLAYS WITH HERSELF**		-	
1996.	(c; as MADIGAN) <none> **ForTunes FROM THE F-HOLES** (live)		-	
Nov 96.	(12"ep/cd-ep; as MADIGAN) <002> **ROCK STOP**		-	

– The girl with her foot behind her head (the contortionists song) / Pity rock / Cornerstone conspiracies / Middlenamed / Tick talk.

— **BONFIRE MADIGAN** were SHIVE + / **SHELLEY DOTY** – guitar, vocals / **TOMAS (PALERMO)** – beats, turntable / **SHERI OZEKI** – upright bass / **SUNSHINE HAIRE** – drums

			not iss.	K
1998.	(7") <IPU 87> **BACKSEAT BUOY.** /		-	
			not iss.	Kill Rock Stars
Jun 98.	(cd/c; w/ VILLA VILLAKULA) <(KRS 299 – VVK 13)> **...FROM THE BURNPILE**			

– Anthemic amendments / Smoke signals from the burnpile / Snowfell summer / For life long (scars) / Backseat buoy (revisited) / Dishes and spoons / Zamora, CA / Promised / Junebug / Tinkling on a tightrope.

— now without SHELLEY + SUNSHINE

Sep 99. (7") <KRS 330> **LESSON IN RIDE.** / **INVINCIBLE** - -
May 00. (lp/cd) <(KRS 357/+CD)> **SADDLE THE BRIDGE** - - mail-o
– Mad skywriting / Where the sky meets the sea above / Running / To find the woman in the ocean / Awake / Scraps / The debut and debauchery of Anna Magdalena / Rachel's song / (untitled) / Onion thin cello skin / Come ask her / 7 mile lane / Downtrodden up.

TEACH ME TIGER (see under ⇒ GODZUKI)

TEAM DRESCH

Formed: Portland, Oregon, USA ... 1993 by namesake DONNA DRESCH, along with KAIA KANGAROO, JODY COYOTE and MARCI MARTINEZ. One of the many queercore punk/riot grrrl outfits, TEAM DRESCH confronted all sorts of issues, religion, bigotry and themselves, via their splendid mini-set, 'PERSONAL BEST' (1994). With MELISSA JANE YORK taking MARCI's vacant drumstool, the passionate foursome issued their equally impressive sophomore long-player, 'CAPTAIN, MY CAPTAIN' (1996); again co-produced by JOHN GOODMANSON. DONNA subsequently sessioned for LOIS (MAFFEO), FIFTH COLUMN, HAZEL, PHRANC, SOME VELVET SIDEWALK and THIRD SEX, while KAIA released two albums on her ownsome (see below).

Album rating: PERSONAL BEST mini (*8) / CAPTAIN, MY CAPTAIN (*7)

DONNA DRESCH – bass, guitar / **KAIA KANGAROO** (b. KAIA LYNN WILSON) – guitar, vocals / **JODY COYOTE** (b. JODY ELIZABETH BLEYLE) – bass, guitar, vocals / **MARCI MARTINEZ** – drums

			Kill Rock Stars	Kill Rock Stars
Jun 94.	(7"m) <(KRS 227)> **3 SONG 7 INCH**			

– Hand grenade / Endtime relay / Molasses in January.

			Chainsaw	Chainsaw
Nov 94.	(m-lp/m-cd) <CHSW 11/+CD> **PERSONAL BEST**			

– Fagetarian and dyke / Hate the Christian right! / Freewheel / She's amazing / Fake fight / #1 chance pirate TV / D.A. don't care / Growing up in Springfield / Screwing yer courage. *(UK-iss.Dec96; same as US)*

— **MELISSA JANE YORK** – drums; repl. MARCI

Dec 96. (lp/cd) <(CHSW 18/+CD)> **CAPTAIN, MY CAPTAIN**
– Uncle Phranc / 107 / My dirty hands are mined / Council / Don't try suicide / To the enemies of political rock / Take on me / I'm illegal / Yes I am too, but who am I really? / Musical fanzine / Remember who you are.

			Outpunk	Outpunk
Apr 97.	(7") <(OUTPUNK 20)> **6.0 BETA**			

– Deattached / Venus Lacy.

— disbanded after above

KAIA

KAIA WILSON – vocals, guitar / with **MELISSA YORK**

			Chainsaw	Chainsaw
Dec 96.	(lp/cd) <(CHSW 14/+CD)> **KAIA**			

– 19 / Test / Salamander / Madame / 16 / Hmpphh / Statue / Delilah / No sides / Memory / Julie of the wolves / Mudball / Keep us empty.

			Mr. Lady	Mr. Lady
Feb 98.	(lp/cd) <(MRLR 01/+CD)> **LADY MAN**			

– Risk / My voice / Thread / That's my baby to you / Intermission / No drama / Little brave one 97 / Disappear without a trace / You make me cry that special way / Off / Where in the world is Greencastle....

TEENAGE FANCLUB

Formed: Glasgow, Scotland ... 1989 although earlier they had posed as The BOY HAIRDRESSERS. After a one-off single, 'GOLDEN SHOWERS' (1988), bassist GERRY LOVE was recruited and BRENDAN O'HARE replaced FRANCIS MACDONALD (who went off to join that other Glasgow institution, The PASTELS) on the drums. As TEENAGE FANCLUB, they cut the inspired chaos of the 'EVERYTHING FLOWS' (1990) single and followed

TEENAGE FANCLUB (cont)

it up with the debut album, 'A CATHOLIC EDUCATION' later the same year. The term slacker rock was surely coined with this bunch of cheeky Glaswegian wide boys in mind and if it was lazy to compare their honey-in-the-dirt melodic dischord with DINOSAUR JR., that was nothing compared to the laid back, laissez faire philosophy that fuelled (if that's not too strong a word) TEENAGE FANCLUB's ramshackle racket, both on stage and in the studio. By the release of the DON FLEMING-produced 'BANDWAGONESQUE' (1991), ('THE KING' was a sub-standard effort released to fulfil contractual obligations), the band were sounding more professional, crafting an album of langourous harmonies and chiming guitar that was a thinly veiled homage to BIG STAR as well as taking in such obvious reference points as The BYRDS, The BEACH BOYS, BUFFALO SPRINGFIELD etc. Ironically, rather than propelling TEENAGE FANCLUB into the big league, the album seemed instead to merely rekindle interest in BIG STAR's back catalogue and after a honeymoon period of being indie press darlings, the backlash was sharp and swift. The fact that the self-produced 'THIRTEEN' (1993) lacked their trademark inspired sloppiness didn't help matters any. Not that the band were overly concerned, they crafted modern retro more lovingly than most and had a loyal following to lap it up. The FANNIE's – with PAUL QUINN replacing O'HARE – further developed their niche with 'GRAND PRIX' (1995) and if it was that reliably trad, West Coast via Glasgow roots sound you were after then TEENAGE FANCLUB were your band. While they wear their influences more proudly than any other group, (O.K., so I forgot about OASIS . . .) they do it with such verve and style that it'd be churlish to write them off as mere plagiarists and they remain one of Scotland's best loved exports. Their next effort, 'SONGS FROM NORTHERN BRITAIN' (1997) was their most considered release to date, sharpening up their sound and arrangements to an unprecedented degree. But if that's what it takes to come up with something as engagingly swoonsome as 'I DON'T CARE' or 'IS THAT ENOUGH', no one's going to make much of a fuss. Now on the roster of the mighty 'Columbia' records, TEENAGE FANCLUB (complete with former BMX BANDITS man FINLAY McDONALD) returned to the fold via album No.6 proper, 'HOWDY!' (2000). Slightly back to basics and reminiscent of BIG STAR (once again!), the album only just managed to gain a UK Top 40 placing; the appropriately-titled single from it 'I NEED DIRECTION' only just dented the Top 50. Drummer and original member, FRANCIS MACDONALD, subsequently superseded QUINN for a one-off single collaboration 'DUMB DUMB DUMB' with daisy-chain hip hop stars, DE LA SOUL, although this failed miserably with the record buying public. The group were back to basics again (this time on STEPHEN PASTEL's 'Geographic' imprint) come their short but sweet set, 'WORDS OF WISDOM AND HOPE' (2002), a record that saw them collaborate with US-born songwriter JAD FAIR. Ditching their more commercial rock flair, TFC went for something a bit rougher – all thanks to FAIR – hammering out tracks 'I FEEL FINE', 'VAMPIRE'S CLAW' and 'NEAR TO YOU' (the single) to brilliant effect. • **Songwriters:** BLAKE or BLAKE-McGINLEY or group compositions except; DON'T CRY NO TEARS (Neil Young) / THE BALLAD OF JOHN AND YOKO (Beatles) / LIKE A VIRGIN (Madonna) / LIFE'S A GAS (T.Rex) / FREE AGAIN + JESUS CHRIST (Alex Chilton) / CHORDS OF FAME (Phil Ochs) / BAD SEEDS (Beat Happening) / HAVE YOU EVER SEEN THE RAIN? (Creedence Clearwater Revival) / BETWEEN US (Neil Innes) / FEMME FATALE (Velvet Underground). • **Trivia:** ALEX CHILTON (ex-BOX TOPS) guested on 1992 sessions and contributed some songs.

Album rating: A CATHOLIC EDUCATION (*6) / THE KING instrumental (*5) / BANDWAGONESQUE (*8) / THIRTEEN (*7) / DEEP FRIED FANCLUB collection (*4) / GRAND PRIX (*8) / SONGS FROM NORTHERN BRITAIN (*8) / HOWDY! (*6) / WORDS OF WISDOM AND HOPE with Jad Fair (*6)

NORMAN BLAKE (b.20 Oct'65, Bellshill, Scotland) – vocals, guitar (ex-BMX BANDITS) / **RAYMOND McGINLEY** (b. 3 Jan'64, Glasgow) – bass, vocals / **FRANCIS MACDONALD** (b.11 Sep'70, Bellshill, Scotland) – drums / **JOE McALINDEN** – violin / **JIM LAMBIE** – vibraphone

53rd & 3rd   not iss.

Jan 88. (12"; as BOY HAIRDRESSERS) *(AGARR 12T)* **GOLDEN SHOWERS. / TIDAL WAVE / THE ASSUMPTION AS AN ELEVATOR**

— **NORMAN + RAYMOND** – guitars, vocals plus **GERARD LOVE** (b.31 Aug'67, Motherwell, Scotland) – bass, vocals / **BRENDAN O'HARE** (b.16 Jan'70, Bellshill, Scotland) – drums; repl. MACDONALD who joined The PASTELS

Paperhouse   Matador

Jun 90. (7"m) *(PAPER 003)* **EVERYTHING FLOWS. / PRIMARY EDUCATION / SPEEEDER**
 (cd-ep+=) *(PAPER 003CD)* – Don't Cry No Tears. *(rel.Feb91)*

Jul 90. (cd/c/lp) *(PAP CD/MC/LP 004) <OLE 012>* **A CATHOLIC EDUCATION**   Aug90
 – Heavy metal / Everything flows / A catholic education / Too involved / Don't need a drum / Critical mass / Heavy metal II / A catholic education 2 / Eternal light / Every picture I paint / Everybody's fool. *(re-iss. cd Mar95; same) (cd re-iss. Apr02 on 'Fire'; SFIRE 001CD)*

Oct 90. (one-sided-7") *(PAPER 005)* **THE BALLAD OF JOHN AND YOKO**

Nov 90. (7"m) *<OLE 007-7>* **EVERYBODY'S FOOL. / PRIMAL EDUCATION / SPEEDER**

Nov 90. (7") *(PAPER 007) <OLE 023>* **GOD KNOWS IT'S TRUE. / SO FAR GONE**   Jan91
 (12"+=/cd-s+=) *(PAPER 007 T/CD)* – Weedbreak / Ghetto blaster.

Creation   Geffen

Aug 91. (cd/lp) *(CRE CD/LP 096)* **THE KING** (instrumental)   53   -
 – Heavy metal 6 / Mudhoney / Interstellar overdrive / Robot love / Like a virgin / The king / Opal inquest / The ballad of Bow Evil (slow and fast) / Heavy metal 9. (above originally only meant for US ears, deleted after 24 hours)

Aug 91. (7") *(CRE 105)* **STAR SIGN. / HEAVY METAL 6**   44   -
 (12"+=)(cd-s+=) *(CRE 105T)(CRESCD 105)* – Like a virgin / ('A'demo version).
 (7"ltd) *(CRE 105L)* – ('A'side) / Like a virgin.

Oct 91. (7"/c-s) *(CRE/+CS 111) <4370>* **THE CONCEPT. / LONG HAIR**   51   Jan92
 (12"+=)(cd-s+=) *(CRE 111T)(CRESCD 111)* – What you do to me (demo) / Robot love.

Nov 91. (cd)(c/lp) *(CRECD 106)(C+/CRE 106) <24461>* **BANDWAGONESQUE**   22
 – The concept / Satan / December / What you do to me / I don't know / Star sign / Metal baby / Pet rock / Sidewinder / Alcoholiday / Guiding star / Is this music?. *(cd re-iss. Jan01; same)*

Jan 92. (7"/c-s) *(CRE/+CS 115) <21708>* **WHAT YOU DO TO ME. / B-SIDE**   31
 (12"+=)(cd-s+=) *(CRE 115T)(CRESCD 115)* – Life's a gas / Filler.

Jun 93. (7"/c-s) *(CRE/+CS 130)* **RADIO. / DON'S GONE COLUMBIA**   31   -
 (12"+=)(cd-s+=) *(CRE 130T)(CRESCD 130)* – Weird horses / Chords of fame.

Sep 93. (7"/c-s) *(CRE/+CS 142)* **NORMAN 3. / OLDER GUYS**   50   -
 (12"+=)(cd-s+=) *(CRE 142T)(CRESCD 142)* – Golden glades / Genius envy.

Oct 93. (cd)(c/lp) *(CRECD 144)(C+/CRE 144) <24533>* **THIRTEEN**   14   Nov93
 – Hang on / The cabbage / Radio / Norman 3 / Song to the cynic / 120 minutes / Escher / Commercial alternative / Fear of flying / Tears are cool / Ret live dead / Get funky / Gene Clark. *(cd re-iss. Jan01; same)*

—— also in 1993, they made a joint single with BIG STAR, 'MINE EXCLUSIVELY' b/w 'PATTI GIRL', proceeds going towards Bosnia, etc

—— In Mar'94, they teamed up with DE LA SOUL on single 'FALLIN''. This was from the rock-rap album 'Judgement Day' on 'Epic' records (hit UK 59).

1994. (cd-ep) *<21887>* **AUSTRALIAN TOUR SAMPLER**   -

—— **PAUL QUINN** – drums (ex-SOUP DRAGONS) repl. O'HARE who later joined MOGWAI

Mar 95. (7"/c-s) *(CRE/+CS 175)* **MELLOW DOUBT. / SOME PEOPLE TRY TO FUCK WITH YOU**   34   -
 (cd-s+=) *(CRESCD 175)* – Getting real / About you.
 (cd-s) *(CRESCD 175X)* – ('A'side) / Have you ever seen the rain? / Between us / You're my kind.

May 95. (7"/c-s) *(CRE/+CS 201)* **SPARKY'S DREAM. / BURNED**   40   -
 (cd-s+=) *(CRESCD 201)* – For you / Headstand.
 (cd-s) *(CRESCD 201X)* – ('A'-alternative version) / Try and stop me / That's all I need to know / Who loves the sun.

May 95. (cd)(c/lp) *(CRECD 173)(C+/CRE 173) <24802>* **GRAND PRIX**   7   Jul95
 – About you / Sparky's dream / Mellow doubt / Don't look back / Verisinilitude / Neil Jung / Tears / Discolite / Say no / Going places / I'll make it clear / I gotta know / Hardcore - ballad. *(lp w/free 7")* – DISCOLITE (demo). / I GOTTA KNOW (demo) *(cd re-iss. Jan01; same)*

Aug 95. (7"/c-s) *(CRE/+CS 210)* **NEIL JUNG. / THE SHADOWS**   62   -
 (cd-s+=) *(CRESCD 210)* – My life / Every step is a way through love.
 (cd-s) *(CRESCD 210X)* – ('A'side) / Traffic jam / Hi-fi / I heard you looking.

Dec 95. (7"ep/c-ep/cd-ep) *(CRE/+CS/SCD 216)* **TEENAGE FANCLUB HAVE LOST IT EP (acoustic)**   53   -
 – Don't look back / Everything flows / Starsign / 120 mins.

—— late in '96, LOVE and McGINLEY joined forces with The VASELINES' EUGENE KELLY to form ASTROCHIMP; one single 'DRAGGIN'' for 'Shoeshine'

Creation   Sony

Jun 97. (cd-s) *(CRESCD 228)* **AIN'T THAT ENOUGH / KICKABOUT / BROKEN**   17   -
 (cd-s) *(CRESCD 228X)* – ('A'side) / Femme fatale / Jesus Christ.

Jun 97. (cd/c/lp) *(CRECD/CCRE/CRELP 196) <68202>* **SONGS FROM NORTHERN BRITAIN**   3
 – Start again / Ain't that enough / Can't feel my soul / I don't want control of you / Planets / It's a bad world / Take the long way round / Winter / I don't care / Mount Everest / Your love is the place where I come from / Speed of light. *(cd re-iss. Jan01; same)*

Aug 97. (7") *(CRE 238)* **I DON'T WANT CONTROL OF YOU. / THE COUNT**   43   -
 (cd-s+=) *(CRESCD 238)* – Middle of the road.
 (cd-s) *(CRESCD 238X)* – ('A'side) / He'd be a diamond / Live my life.

Nov 97. (7") *(CRE 280)* **START AGAIN. / AIN'T THAT ENOUGH (TOTP acoustic)**   54   -
 (cd-s+=) *(CRESCD 280)* – Take the long way round (radio).
 (cd-s) *(CRESCD 280X)* – ('A'side) / How many more years / Nothing to be done.

—— added **FINLAY McDONALD** – keyboards (ex-BMX BANDITS, ex-SPEEDBOAT); was p/t on tour

Jun 98. (7") *(CRE 298)* **LONG SHOT. / LOOPS AND STRINGS**   -

Columbia   Columbia

Oct 00. (7") *(669951-7)* **I NEED DIRECTION. / ON THIS GOOD NIGHT**   48
 (cd-s+=) *(669951-2)* – I lied / Here comes your man.

Oct 00. (cd/lp) *(<500622-2/-1>)* **HOWDY!**   33   Nov00
 – I need direction / I can't find my way home / Accidental life / Near you / Happiness / Dumb dumb dumb / Town and the city / The sun shines from you / Straight and narrow / Cul de sac / My uptight life / If I never see you again.

—— **FRANCIS MACDONALD** – drums (of Shoeshine records) repl. QUINN who quit during the middle of the last set

Jun 01. (7"; as TEENAGE FANCLUB & DE LA SOUL) *(<671213-7>)* **DUMB DUMB DUMB. / STRAIGHT AND NARROW**   Jan02
 (cd-s+=) *(671213-2)* – Thaw me / One thousand lights.

TEENAGE FANCLUB & JAD FAIR

Geographic Alternative Tentacles

Feb 02. (7") *(GEOG 013)* **NEAR TO YOU. / ALWAYS IN MY HEART**   68   -
 (cd-s+=) *(GEOG 013CD)* – Let's celebrate.

TEENAGE FANCLUB (cont)

Mar 02. (cd/lp) *(GEOG 014 CD/LP)* <*VIRUS 274*> **WORDS OF WISDOM AND HOPE** — Jan02
 – Behold the miracle / I feel fine / Near to you / Smile / Crush on you / Cupid / The power of your tenderness / Vampire's claw / Secret heart / You rock / Love's taken over / The good thing.

– compilations, others, etc. –

May 92. (7") *K;* <*IPU 26*> **FREE AGAIN. / BAD SEEDS**
Nov 92. (12"ep/cd-ep) *Strange Fruit; (SFPS/+CD 081)* **THE JOHN PEEL SESSION**
 – God knows it's true / Alcoholiday / So far gone / Long hair. *(re-iss. Dec93 & Jul95; same)*
Mar 95. (cd/c) *Fire; (FLIPCD 002)* **DEEP FRIED FANCLUB**
 – Everything flows / Primary education / Speeder / Critical mass (orig.) / The ballad of John and Yoko / God knows it's true / Weedbreak / So far gone / Ghetto blaster / Don't cry no tears / Free again / Bad seed.
Jul 95. (12"ep/cd-ep; as FRANK BLACK & TEENAGE FANCLUB) *Strange Fruit; (SFPS/+CD 091)* **PEEL SESSION**
 – Handy man / The man who was too loud / The Jacques Tati / Sister Isabel.
Apr 97. (cd) *Nectar; (NTMCD 543)* **FANDEMONIUM**
Sep 97. (7"ep) *Radiation; (RARE 033)* **TEENAGE FANCLUB EP**

TELSTAR PONIES

Formed: Glasgow, Scotland... mid-1994 by ex-18 WHEELER man, DAVID KEENAN and ex-TEENAGE FANCLUB japester, BRENDAN O'HARE; JOHN HOGARTY (ex-BMX BANDITS) was also an initial member before he joined NATIONAL PARK. With the intention of moving as far away as possible from the Scots-indie-by-numbers of KEENAN's former band, the pair eventually roped in GAVIN LAIRD and RACHEL DEVINE and set about creating a sound more in tune with cosmic sounds of CAN, FAUST etc. Signed to 'Fire' records, the band released the relatively hummable 'MAPS AND STARCHARTS' as their debut single that year, progressing to the more experimental 'NOT EVEN STARCROSSED' in summer '95. The full extent of their stellar-rock experimentation was revealed later that year on the debut album, 'IN THE SPACE OF A FEW MINUTES', while the subsequent addition of organist RICHARD YOUNGS added a further dimension to the band's sound. Follow-up set, 'VOICES FROM THE NEW MUSIC' (1996), featured some of the band's most adventurous compositions to date, not least the marathon 'DOES YOUR HEART HAVE WINGS'. Yet by the end of the year, O'HARE and LAIRD (who'd gigged around the country as CAIN) had broken ranks to form their own outfit, FIEND 1 and the short-lived MACROCOSMICA, the former later enjoying a brief tenure with fellow Glaswegian sound/noise sculptors, the mighty MOGWAI. Meanwhile, KEENAN and old chum and NATIONAL PARK member, JOHN HOGARTY, teamed up with Falkirk-born jazzman BILL WELLS to form PHANTOM ENGINEER.

Album rating: IN THE SPACE OF A FEW MINUTES (*8) / VOICES FROM THE NEW MUSIC (*7) / Fiend 1: CALEDONIAN GOTHIC (*5) / Macrocosmica: AD ASTRA (*7)

DAVID KEENAN – guitar, vocals (ex-18 WHEELER) / **RACHEL DEVINE** – guitar, piano, vocals / **GAVIN LAIRD** (b.18 Feb'70, Girvan, Ayrshire) – bass / **BRENDAN O'HARE** – drums (ex-TEENAGE FANCLUB)

Fire Instant Mayhem

Nov 94. (7") *(BLAZE 74)* **MAPS AND STARCHARTS. / THANKS BUT NO THANKS, MR. DULLI**
 (cd-s+=) (BLAZE 74CD) – Hang up.
Apr 95. (10"ep/cd-ep) *(BLAZE 85 T/CD)* **NOT EVEN STARCROSSED. / COLOR DELUXE / PATTY WATERS**
Oct 95. (7") *(BLAZE 94)* **HER NAME. / THE BALLAD OF LIBERTY VALANCE**
 (cd-s+=) (BLAZE 94CD) – Lugengeschichte (Pylon King mix) / ('A'-Pylon King mix).
Oct 95. (cd/lp) *(FIRE CD/LP 52)* **IN THE SPACE OF A FEW MINUTES**
 – The Moon is not a puzzle / Lugengeschichte / Not even starcrossed / Maya / Two's insane / Moon, don't come up tonight / Monster / Side netting / Her name / Innerhalb weniger minuten / I still believe in Christmas. *(cd re-iss. Jun02 on 'Fire'; SFIRE 015CD)*
Jan 96. (cd-ep) <*IMC 9453-2*> **MORS FACTUM MUSICA**
 – Innerhalb weniger minuten / Lugengeschichte / I still believe in Christmas trees / Does your heart have wings? / Secret outpost.
May 96. (12"/cd-s) *(BLAZE 100 T/CD)* **DOES YOUR HEART HAVE WINGS? / GHOST CHANNELS (FLEISCH-ABGEZOGEN) / GHOST CHANNELS (FLENSE)**

— added **RICHARD YOUNGS** – keyboards

Fire Velvel

Sep 96. (7") *(BLAZE 110)* **BREWERY OF EGGSHELLS. / THE FIRST KISS TAKES SO LONG**
 (cd-s+=) (BLAZE 110CD) – Wall of rock.
Oct 96. (cd/d-lp) *(FIRE CD/LP 60)* <*97100*> **VOICES FROM THE NEW MUSIC** — Mar97
 – Bells for Albert Ayler / Voices from the new music / Last outpost / Shizuka / A little cloud / Brewery of eggshells / Aegis falling / Sail her on / A feather on the breath / The fall of little summer / Does your heart have wings? / Song of Ansuz / La Vienna.
Jan 97. (cd-s) *(BLAZE 112CD)* **VOICES FROM THE NEW MUSIC** — w-drawn

— **KEENAN + DEVINE** carried on when LAIRD + O'HARE formed MACROCOSMICA (the latter subsequently joined MOGWAI in June '97)

— KEENAN, HOGARTY and jazzman BILL WELLS became PHANTOM ENGINEER

FIEND

O'HARE – guitars, vocals + **LAIRD** – guitar, vocals

God Bless God Bless

Oct 97. (cd; as FIEND 1) (<*NOIR 001CD*>) **CALEDONIAN GOTHIC**
 – Angel hair (2nd book) / Ghost kanal / Hammer into anvil empirical / Munich X / Huon pine song / Brittle horse pt.1 & 2 / Compressor / Rother / Spirit / Voyager / Origin & purpose / Rose / Traumen / Preuvial sphere (coda).
Feb 98. (cd; as FIEND 2) (<*NOIR 002CD*>) **CALEDONIAN COSMIC**
 – Testimony / Paranoic timeslip / Null / Stacy / Spacedtime / Heat and soul / Blue birthday (1st book) / The birthplace of stars.

— with also **KENNY** (from ESKA) + **RACHEL DEVINE** + **DAVE TOUGH** (of ALL TOO HUMAN, etc)

Sep 98. (cd; as FIEND 3) (<*NOIR 003CD*>) **CALEDONIAN MYSTIC**
 – Evermore / Kurz / Until these parallels are understood / Pharos light / Red pigment tattoo / Forgotten sea / Alliances / Continuum.

MACROCOSMICA

O'HARE + LAIRD plus **CERWYSS OWER** – bass, vocals + **RUSSELL McEWAN** – drums (of BLACK SUN MACHINE, of CYLINDER)

God Bless God Bless

Nov 97. (cd) (<*NOIR 004CD*>) **AD ASTRA** — Jan98
 – Rusty's arms / Orbit 48 / Ram's expo / I am the spaceship Digitalis / Lamotta / A horse can walk / Byne. *(re-iss. Nov01; same)*
May 98. (cd-ep) *(REX 002CD)* **SPACE GEEK / RA UNMOVED / WEIRD SEX DREAM #2 / LONE COP**
 (re-iss. Nov01; same)

— LAIRD departed mid-1998; meanwhile, O'HARE is part of Scot/Australian (three persons) internet link outfit, LIMINAL, who released 'aa' debut set (early '99)

LONECOP

GAVIN LAIRD + EWAN McALLAN

Static Caravan not iss.

Nov 99. (7"blue) *(VAN 10.0)* **TONE MOVIE. / HELIUM BALLOON**

Obelisk not iss.

Oct 00. (cd) *(OBOE 1)* **MY PREY BETRAYS ITSELF**
 – Tone movie / Helium balloon / Postcard / #1 / Everything burns / I try to trap this emotion for you / #2 / Jack Christ / Towards the stars / Revenge killing / #3.

TELSTAR PONIES

— re-formed in 1999 + added **RAYMOND PRIOR** – bass

— line-up now:- KEENAN, DEVINE, LAIRD plus **ALI ROBERTS** (APPENDIX OUT) + **TOM CROSSLAND** (INTERNATIONAL AIRPORT) + **BILL WELLS** (PHANTOM ENGINEER)

Geographic not iss.

Jul 01. (7") *(GEOG 008)* **FAREWELL FAREWELL. / VOICE IN THE CLOUDS**

Static Caravan – Obelisk not iss.

Nov 02. (ltd-10"m-ep) *(STATICLISK ONE)* **HARES ON THE MOUNTAIN**
 – Hares on the mountain / One hand, one heart / Terrible night / Athanasius K.

TEN BENSON

Formed: London, England-based... mid 90's out of various outfits by frontman CHRIS TECKKAM (sole survivor of SWIMMER, an act which delivered one long-player, 'PETITS POIS' in '96), the Oriental NAPOLEON CATILO (former SHIVA EFFECT drummer, a band who had one solitary 1993 single plus a 1994 album, 'YAHWEH' for 'Frog') and bassist DUNCAN LOVATT. Reclusive in nature, these overtly weird, psychedelic hillbillies mix'n'matched a variety of influences including FRANK ZAPPA, MEDICINE HEAD and GORKY'S ZYGOTIC MYNCI. Three 45's appeared between 1997 and '98, the best of which, 'EVIL CLAW', stupefied the listener into believing this might be HANK WILLIAMS and ROY ROGERS re-incarnated in some sort of manic duo. A mini-cd, '6 FINGERS OF BENSON' (1998), saw the band being pencilled in for a Reading Festival appearance. No doubt there was something far stronger than ten Benson (& Hedges) getting smoked that day. Post-millennium work has seen them release a handful of singles and two full-sets, 'HISS' (2000) and 'SATAN KIDNEY PIE' (2002).

Album rating: 6 FINGERS OF BENSON mini (*6) / HISS (*6) / SATAN KIDNEY PIE (*5)

SWIMMER

CHRIS TECKKAM – vocals, bass / **ROGER HELLIER** – guitar / **DUNCAN CAMPBELL** – guitar, organ / **HUW DAINOW** – drums

Quixotic Quixotic

Apr 94. (10") (<*QX 009-10*>) **WHIPPINGS. / BOXES**
Aug 94. (7") *(QXUK 001-7)* **SHE. / FAKING IT**
 (10"+=/cd-s+=) (QXUK 001 10/CD) – Bleach and love.

Sweet not iss.

Jun 95. (7") *(SWEE 001-7)* **SINKING MY TIN BOATS. / BREAKFAST WITH OMAR**
 (cd-s+=) (SWEE 001-CD) – Millions of me.
Jun 96. (cd) *(SWEE 004CD)* **PETITS POIS**
 above group not to be confused with another band of the same name, who issued 12" singles for the 'Spirit' imprint.

TEN BENSON

CHRIS TECKKAM – vocals, guitar / **DUNCAN LOVATT** – bass / **NAPOLEON CATILO** – drums (ex-SHIVA EFFECT)

Sweet / not iss.
- Sep 97. (7") *(SWEE 008)* **CITY HOPPERS. / TRANSPORT OVERSEAS**
- Feb 98. (7") *(SWEE 010)* **THE CLAW. / BARDOT STYLE**

Deceptive / not iss.
- Jun 98. (7") *(BLUFF 062)* **EVIL HEAT. / UNCLE BENSON**
- Jul 98. (m-cd) *(BLUFF 063CD)* **6 FINGERS OF BENSON** (compilation)
  – Evil heat / Bardot style / The claw / Transport overseas / Uncle Benson / City hoppers.
- Nov 98. (7"ep/cd-ep) *(BLUFF 066/+CD)* **UNITED COLORS OF BENSON EP**
  – Mystery man / Hell this hour / Mad ferret / Luvly guy.

Cottage / not iss.
- Feb 00. (7") *(COTTG 002)* **ROBOT TOURIST. / EVIL HEAT (Night version)**
  (cd-s+=) *(COTTG 002CD)* – (Oh I do like to be beside the) Seaside.
- Mar 00. (cd/lp) *(COTTG 003 CD/LP)* **HISS**
  – Robot tourist / I don't buy it / Raggedy man / Emporer / Dr Hemlock / Rock cottage / Magical moon / Stern / Dirty job / Under heavy riffage.
- Jun 00. (7"/cd-s) *(COTTG 004/+CD)* **I DON'T BUY IT. / SWEAT (pt.1) / SWEAT (pt.2)**
- Dec 00. (7") *(COTTG 005)* **BLACK SNOW. / SNOWMAN SNOWGIRL**
  (cd-s+=) *(COTTG 005CD)* – Listen the snow is falling.

Artrocker / not iss.
- Apr 02. (7") *(RRR45 003)* **ONE WAY TICKET. / THE LOOZIN' LINE**
- May 02. (cd) *(RRR33 002)* **SATAN KIDNEY PIE**
  – Dark forces / One way ticket / Tits / Nobody's wife / The loozin' line / Sweat (part 3) / Out of time / Come home to me / Oh general.

TENDER TRAP (see under ⇒ TALULAH GOSH)

TERMINALS

Formed: Christchurch, New Zealand ... 1988 by guitarist/vocalist STEPHEN COGLE, keyboardist MICK ELBORADO, drummer PETE STAPLETON (formerly of SCORCHED EARTH POLICY) and guitarist RUSS HUMPHRIES. Rising from the sonic ashes of obscure Christchurch experimental beatless pop combos like The VICTOR DIMISCH BAND (never to feature anyone by that name, oddly enough) and The PIN GROUP, TERMINALS quickly made their musical manifesto known. Their sound was a dark, alienated, feedback-driven bitch's brew, with a highly individualistic singer whose voice fluttered bat-like between tenor and baritone, swooping and diving from highs to lows with equal ease of register in almost operatic fervour. Releases included 'DISCONNECT' EP (1988); 'UNCOFFINED' (1990); 'DISEASE' (1992, tape-only and on 'Expressway') and 'CUL-DE-SAC' (1992). The departure of HUMPHRIES and his subsequent replacement – guitarist BRIAN CROOK – took the band back more towards its experimental roots, losing HUMPHRIES' pop sensibility and gaining a new louder, more experimental direction, as evidenced on the German-only sets 'TOUCH' (1992) and 'LITTLE THINGS' (1995). 1998 would bring the 'LIVE' album for 'Medication', a summary of the band's career with songs mostly from 'TOUCH'. Containing five obscure/unrecorded TERMINALS tracks, the album was well-received, apart from the occasionally murky sound quality.

Album rating: UNCOFFINED (*6) / TOUCH (*7) / LITTLE THINGS (*6)

VICTOR DIMISICH BAND

COGLE + STAPLETON

Flying Nun / not iss.
- 1982. (12"ep) *(VD-1)* **NATIVE WAITER EP** – NewZ
  – Native waiter / Thirteenth floor / Claude / Jonah / It's cold outside. *(re-iss. 2001 on 'Crawlspace' SPACE 005)*

—— after their split, some members joined BILL DIREEN in the BUILDERS

TERMINALS

STEPHEN COGLE – vocals / **ROSS HUMPHRIES** – guitar (ex-CLEAN, ex-PIN GROUP) / **MICK ELBORADO** – keyboards / **JOHN CHRISSTOFFELS** – bass / **PETER STAPLETON** – drums (ex-PIN GROUP + ex-SCORCHED EARTH POLICY – latter released two 'Flying Nun' EP's mid-80's)

Flying Nun / not iss.
- 1988. (12"ep) *(FN 091)* **DISCONNECT EP** – NewZ
  – Batwing / Blistering heart / Juju eyes / Turning every word around / Edie / Terminals / Cul-de-sac.
- 1990. (lp) *(FN 116)* **UNCOFFINED** – NewZ
  – No / Love, hate, revenge / Uncoffined / Before it rains / Cockroaches / All their lies / Frozen car / Gasoline / Hungry Joe / Castaway / Mothlight / Lolita.
- 1992. (cd) *(FNCD 239)* **CUL-DE-SAC** – NewZ
  – No / Love, hate, revenge / Uncoffined / Before it rains / Cockroaches / All their lies / Frozen car / Gasoline / Hungry Joe / Castaay / Mothlight / Lolita / Bating / Blistering heart / Juju eyes / Turning every word around / Edie / Terminals / Cul-de-sac.

—— **BRIAN CROOK** – guitar (of RENDERERS) repl. HUMPHRIES

Feel Good All Over / not iss.
- 1992. (7") *(8)* **WITCHDOCTORS. / PSYCHO LIVES** – NewZ

Roof Bolt / not iss.
- 1992. (7") *(RBR 005)* **MEDUSA. / SCARECROW** – NewZ

Xpressway / not iss.
- 1992. (7") *(X/WAY 17)* **DEADLY TANGO. / DO THE VOID** – NewZ

- 1992. (lp/cd) **TOUCH** – German
  – Basket case / Suicide / (What I've heard of) Wyoming / Mr. Clean / Amnesia / That thing upstairs is not my mother / Touch / Deadly tango / Janetta / Something dark / Twilight environment. *(cd+=)* – In and out of my mind.

Raffmond / not iss.
- 1995. (cd) *(014)* **LITTLE THINGS** – German
  – Coasts of the shrunken / Mekong Delta blues / Medication / Hide yourself away / Black creek / Quicksand / Little things / Ministry of lies / Messianic.

—— disbanded after above; CROOK and STAPLETON (latter also moonlighted with DADAMAH) formed FLIES INSIDE THE SUN with KIM PIETERS (also DADAMAH see – Roy MONTGOMERY)

– compilations, etc. –

- 1989. (c; as VICTOR DIMISICH BAND) *Xpressway; (X/WAY 08)* **MEKONG DELTA BLUES** – NewZ
  – It's cold outside / Crocus / Claude / Thirteenth floor / Pipeline / Walking slow / Jonah / Moonlit trance / Shade / Mekong Delta blues / Shocking pink clock / Better off dead / The cult.
- 1991. (c) *Xpressway; (X/WAY 19)* **DISEASE (LIVING OFF THE FAT OF FLYING NUN) (live)** – NewZ
  – Twilight environment / Suicide / Deadly tango / That thing up stairs is not my mother / Mr. Clean / Touch / Native waiter / Amnesia / Janetta / Do the void.
- 1998. (cd) *Medication; (001)* **LIVE** – NewZ
  – Twilight environment / Suicide / Basket case / Scatter my bones / That thing up stairs is not my mother / Cul-de-sac / Ministry of lies / Mekong Delta blues / Raining in my house / Johnny Mnemonic / Quicksand / Psycho lives / Wyoming / Do the void / Black creek.
- 1998. (cd; as VICTOR DIMISICH BAND) *Medication; (002)* **MY NAME IS K** – NewZ
  – Native waiter / Thirteenth floor / Claude / Jonah / It's cold outside / Lounge bar / Crocus / Claude / Pipeline / Such a lady / Shade / Mekong Delta blues / Shocking pink clock / Better off dead / The cult.

TERRIS

Formed: Newport, Wales ... late 90's by GAVIN GOODWIN, ALUN BOUND, NEIL DOUGMORE and OWEN MATTHEWS. The 4-piece indie lads grew up in er, terrace blocks on the outskirts of a small mining village. Influenced by the likes of BOB DYLAN, IAN CURTIS (although you wouldn't have guessed this by listening to them) and LEONARD COHEN, band members DOUGMORE, BOUND and MATTHEWS met GOODWIN in a pub after he replied to an advert they'd released in their hometown. After two years of solid practice, TERRIS began playing regularly at crowded popular venue 'Le Club' where they caught the attention of former 60ft DOLLS front man RICHARD PARFITT. He soon became their manager, inviting 'Rough Trade' talent scout Geoff Travis to view an impressive, but slightly unconvincing show. Signed to the label, they quickly issued 'THE TIME IS NOW' EP and were hailed (by the NME, at least!) as a "21st century JOY DIVISION". In a perfect world that would be fantastic, but the sad truth was TERRIS didn't quite live up to that expectation. MATTHEWS' staccato, angry vocals sounded much like the freak experiment child of TOM WAITS. The music was pretty average, with no more style and panache than Welsh neighbours SYMPOSIUM. What remained utterly ridiculous about MATTHEWS was his arrogant, know-it-all, we're-the-most-original-band-for-ages attitude that moved into hypercritical terrain once their first EP was released. Who knows, maybe in the future they will realise boasting statements achieve nothing for groups (except from spoilt rock star syndrome).

Album rating: LEARNING TO LET GO (*6)

GAVIN GOODWIN (b. 1978) – vocals / **ALUN BOUND** – guitar / **NEIL DUGMORE** – keyboards / **OWEN MATTHEWS** – drums

Rough Trade / not iss.
- Dec 99. (7"ep/cd-ep) *(RTRADES 001/+CD)* **THE TIME IS NOW EP**
  – Trial by fire / Searching for the switches / Lost October / Picture show.

Blanco Y Negro / not iss.
- Apr 00. (7"/cd-s) *(NEG 127/+CD)* **CANNIBAL KIDS. / THE TAKE DOWN: RAGGED AND SPUN OUT**
- Mar 01. (7"/c-s) *(NEG 130/+C)* **FABRICATED LUNACY. / WALKING UNDERWATER** — 62
  (cd-s+=) *(NEG 130CD)* – Where your heart hides.
- Mar 01. (cd/c/lp) *(8573 86867-2/-4/-1)* **LEARNING TO LET GO**
  – White gold way / Fabricated lunacy / Beneath the belt / Bonnie / Shapeshifter / Cannibal kids / Windvain / Petrol hours / Lost October / Vegetable days / Midnight sun / Deliverance.

TETRA SPLENDOUR

Formed: Porthcawl, Wales ... 2000 by GARETH JONES, PETER ROBERTS, KRIS MURPHY and JON MELONEY. Straight outta comprehensive, TETRA SPLENDOUR were four teens who issued three singles between 2000 and 2001; 'E.T.A.' (as ROBOTS IN THE SKY), 'MR BISHI' and the excellent 'DE-RAIL'. A sort of floating British psychedelic prog-pop rock group, they signed to 'Chrysalis' in 2002 and issued their debut LP, 'SPLENDID ANIMATION', a fusion of warped guitars, ambient beats and samples (courtesy of an Apple Mac computer) plus ROBERTS' cruising vocals. In a time when garage rock and bands that begin with 'The . . .' were being shoved down our throats, TETRA SPLENDOUR were a young and refreshing change.

Album rating: SPLENDID ANIMATION (*6)

TETRA SPLENDOUR (cont)

PETER ROBERTS – vocals / GARETH JONES – guitar / KRIS MURPHY – bass / JON MELONEY – drums

		unknown	not iss.
2000.	(7"; as ROBOTS IN THE SKY) **E.T.A.**		
		Wishakismo	not iss.
Apr 01.	(7") *(7WISH 001)* **MR. BISHI. / CENTREFOLD**		-
	(cd-s+=) *(CDWISH 001)* – Photogenius.		
Oct 01.	(7") *(7WISH 002)* **DE-RAIL. / MURIEL'S MOTORHOME (version)**		-
	(cd-s+=) *(CDWISH 002)* – Furry dice.		
		Chrysalis	not iss.
Feb 02.	(7") *(CHS 5134)* **POLLENFEVER. / FRANKENSTEIN**		-
	(cd-s+=) *(CDCHS 5134)* – De-rail (Pete's mix) / ('A'-CD-Rom).		
May 02.	(cd) *(537705-2)* **SPLENDID ANIMATION**		-
	– Landmine / Global village / E.T.A. / Pollenfever / Bless my soul / Muriel's motorhome / Mr. Bishi / De-rail / C.F.C.S. / In-flight manual / Black and grey.		

TEXAS IS THE REASON

Formed: New York City, New York, USA ... mid 1990's by Hare Krishna converts NORM ARENAS (ex-SHELTER) and CHRIS DALY (ex-108), alongside SCOT WINEGARD and GARRET KLAHN. TEXAS IS THE REASON released their, well-received, self-titled debut EP in 1995 for 'Revelation' records. The group's ability to produce melodic yet aggressive indie rock of a high standard quickly earned them a considerable fanbase. A couple of equally competent singles followed and the word on the street was that their debut album would be one to look out for. When it did arrive in 1996, 'DO YOU KNOW WHO YOU ARE?', did not disappoint and it wasn't long before the band were receiving offers from major record labels. Much to the dismay of fans this progression was never to be as the group called it quits in 1997. ARENAS and WINEGARD got together once again via indie-hardcore act, NEW END ORIGINAL, releasing the 'THRILLER' set in 2001.

Album rating: DO YOU KNOW WHO YOU ARE? (*7) / New End Original: THRILLER (*6)

GARRETT KLAHN – vocals, guitar (ex-COPPER) / **NORM ARENAS** – guitar (ex-SHELTER) / **SCOTT WINEGARD** – bass (ex-FOUNTAINHEAD) / **CHRIS DALY** – drums (ex-108)

		Revelation	Revelation
Nov 95.	(cd-ep) *<REVCD 047>* **TEXAS IS THE REASON**	-	
	– If it's here when we get back it's ours / Dressing cold / Antique.		
Mar 96.	(7") *<JT 1024>* **BLUE BOY. / (other by The PROMISE RING)**	-	
	(above issued 'Jade Tree') (below on 'Art Monk Construction')		
Apr 96.	(7") *<12.5>* **SOMETHING TO FORGET. / (other by SAMUEL).**	-	
Apr 96.	(lp/c/cd) *<(REV/+MC/CD 051)>* **DO YOU KNOW WHO YOU ARE?**		
	– Johnny on the spot / The magic bullet theory / Nickel wound / There's no way I can talk myself out of this one tonight / Something to forget / Do you know who you are? / Back and to the left / The day's refrain / A jack in one eye.		

— split in 1997; DALY joined JETS TO BRAZIL and ARENAS became a DJ and formed NEW END ORIGINAL with WINEGARD

NEW RISING SONS

KLAHN + a member of INTO PARADISE

		Grape Os	Grape Os
Jun 00.	(cd-ep) *<(GS 005)>* **THIEVES AND ANGELS**		
	– Steady sway / Put it on the wire / Falling out / Bring me around.		

NEW END ORIGINAL

ARENAS + WINEGARD with **JONAS SONZ MATRANGA** – guitar (ex-FAR) / **CHARLIE WALKER** – drums (ex-SPLIT LIP, ex-CHAMBERLAIN)

		Jade Tree	Jade Tree
Oct 01.	(lp/cd) *<(JT 1062/+CD)>* **THRILLER**		
	– Lukewarm / 14-41 / Hostage / Leper song / Titanic / Better than ever / Weary progress / #1 defender / Halo / The name / Better than this.		
		Defiance	not iss.
Oct 01.	(cd-s) *(DEFIANCE 19CD)* **LUKEWARM / ONE BIG APOLOGY / COLD SWEAT**		-

that dog.

Formed: Los Angeles, California, USA ... 1991 by ANNA WARONKER (daughter of Warner Brothers producer and top man, LENNY WARONKER), along with twin sisters RACHEL and PETRA HADEN (daughters of jazz giant, CHARLIE HADEN). Completing the line-up with 'Virgin' records employee, TONY MAXWELL, this well connected quartet issued a solitary promo single for US indie label, 'Magnatone', before securing a prestigious deal with 'D.G.C.' (4 a.d.-offshoot, 'Guernica' in the UK). Surfing on sassy girly harmonies and shot through with pussysure attitude, the band's eponymous debut album was reminiscent of The BREEDERS on uppers, drawing admiring comments from many an alternative publication. Sophomore effort, 'TOTALLY CRUSHED OUT' (1995), was even more impressive, PETRA once again adding her complementary violin touches while the likes of 'ANYMORE' and 'HOLIDAYS' tempered the grungy assault with a lilting acoustic guitar/strings tapestry. Despite never really entering the alternative premier league, the ladies (and lad!) delivered another slab of lusty, guitar-mangling frustration in the shape of 1997's 'RETREAT FROM THE SUN'. With TD taking time out, PETRA delivered her debut solo album, 'IMAGINARYLAND' (1999), which included three covers:- 'WATERMARK (Enya), 'BACH PRELUDE: No.2 IN C MINOR (Bach) and a MIRANDA SEX GARDEN SONG. Over the past half decade, she had provided backing for numerous acts including BECK, MIKE WATT, SPAIN (her brother JOSH's outfit), RENTALS, GREEN DAY and LUSCIOUS JACKSON. Although the group subsequently disbanded, WARONKER made a few forays into US TV/film work (as in composing music, not acting) and also co-produced (with her husband, veteran REDD KROSS man, STEVE McDONALD) the IMPERIAL TEEN album, 'On'. Released on her own 'Five Feet Two' label, the long awaited 'ANNA' (2002) demonstrated that her aptitude for songwriting hadn't diminished in the lengthy interim period.

Album rating: that dog. (*6) / TOTALLY CRUSHED OUT! (*8) / RETREAT FROM THE SUN (*7) / Petra Haden: IMAGINARYLAND (*5) / Anna Waronker: ANNA (*5)

ANNA WARONKER (b. 10 Jul'72) – vocals, guitar / **RACHEL HADEN** (b.11 Oct'71, New York, NY) – bass / **PETRA HADEN** (b. 11 Oct'71, NY) – violin / **TONY MAXWELL** (b. 3 Jun'68, Paris, France) – drums

		Guernica-4ad	D.G.C.
Nov 93.	(cd/lp) *(GU 6 CD/LP)* *<DGC D/C 99999>* **that dog.**		Mar94
	– Old timer / Jump / Raina / You are here / Just like me / She / Angel / Westside angst / She looks at me / Punk rock girl / Zodiac / You Family functions / She looks at me (reprise) / Paid programming / This boy. (lp w/free 7") – BUY ME FLOWERS. / (untitled) *(cd re-iss. Jul98; same)*		
Jul 95.	(cd) *<DGCD 24735>* **TOTALLY CRUSHED OUT!**	-	
	– Ms. Wrong / Silently / In the back of my mind / He's kissing Christian / Anymore / To keep you / Lip gloss / She doesn't know how / Holidays / Side part / One summer night / Michael Jordan / Rockstar.		
Apr 97.	(cd) *<DGCD 25115>* **RETREAT FROM THE SUN**	-	
	– I'm gonna see you / Never say never / Being with you / Gagged and tied / Retreat from the sun / Minneapolis / Annie / Every time I try / Long Island / Hawthorne / Did you ever / Cowboy hat / Until the day I die.		

— the quartet split in 1997

PETRA HADEN

— solo playing all instruments herself

		not iss.	Win
Mar 99.	(cd) *<19>* **IMAGINARYLAND**	-	
	– Look both ways before you cross / Cuckoo clock / Apple juice / Watermark / Bach prelude: No.2 in C minor / I'm fired / Red / Song for the whales / How are you? / Miranda Sex Garden song / Richard / Moonmilk / I.		

ANNA WARONKER

with various session people

		not iss.	Five Feet Two
Jun 02.	(cd) *<82014>* **ANNA**	-	
	– Love story / I wish you well / Beautiful / Nothing personal / John & Maria / All for you / Long time coming / Fortunes of misfortune / How do you sleep? / Perfect ten / A hollow daze / Eat me alive / The powers that be / Goodbye.		

THEE HEADCOATEES
(see under ⇒ GOLIGHTLY, Holly)

THEE HEADCOATS
(see under ⇒ CHILDISH, Wild Billy; 70's section)

THEE MICHELLE GUN ELEPHANT

Formed: Japan ... 1991 by YUSUKE CHIBA, KUJI EUNO, FUTOSHI ABE and KAZUKI KUHARA. This much heralded band of punk primitivists made their domestic debut in 1995 with the independently released 'WONDER STYLE' EP. A major label deal with 'Nippon Columbia's 'Triad' imprint led to the recording of a debut album in London with RADIOHEAD/ELASTICA engineer, Chris Brown, the resulting 'CULT GRASS STARS' (1996) followed later that year by a second domestic long player, 'HIGH TIME'. Their typically Japanese industriousness was rewarded with impressive placings on the national pop charts and rave reviews from the local press while a third album, 'CHICKEN ZOMBIES' (1997), made the Top 5. Oiling their overheated touring/recording treadmill with the greasiest rock'n'roll to ever slick its way from the East, the ELEPHANT men revved up for their 'World Psycho Blues Tour' with a fourth album, 'GEAR BLUES' (1998). This was to be the band's first Anglo/American release, hitting Western shelves in 2000 and noising up those who hadn't already heard it on import. While the most obvious blueprint for their bareback racket was The STOOGES, the lads themselves counted BILLY CHILDISH's seminal DIY troupe, THEE HEADCOATS, as their guiding influence (hence, presumably, the 'THEE' part of their name). Whatever its inspiration, the music's Elephantine, three-chord flurry and pseudo-Beat, kitsch lyrical genius (half English/half Japanese) arguably transcended its potential novelty value. The slightly darker 'RODEO TANDEM BEAT SPECTER', followed in 2002.

Album rating: CULT GRASS STARS (*6) / HIGH TIME (*6) / CHICKEN ZOMBIES (*6) / GEAR BLUES (*7) / CASANOVA SNAKE (*6) / COLLECTION compilation (*7) / RODEO TANDEM BEAT SPECTER (*5)

THEE MICHELLE GUN ELEPHANT (cont) — THE GREAT INDIE DISCOGRAPHY — The 1990s

YUSUKE CHIBA – vocals / FUTOSHI ABE – guitar / KUJI EUNO – bass / KAZUKI KUHARA – drums

		not iss.	independ..
Oct 95.	(cd-ep) WONDER STYLE	-	Japan

– Wonder style / Marshmallow monster / Why do you want to shake? / Balance / Talkin' 'bout you.

		not iss.	Triad
Feb 96.	(cd-s) WORLD'S END / KING	-	Japan
Mar 96.	(cd) CULT GRASS STARS	-	Japan

– Lizard / Strawberry garden / King / World's end (primitive version) / Toy / Black tambourine / I was walkin' & sleepin' / Dallas fried chicken / Letter to Uncle Sam / Suicide morning / Don't sulk baby / I have to sleep / Remember Amsterdam.

Aug 96.	(cd-s) CANDY HOUSE / AUTOMATIC (teansister version) / SWIMMING RADIO / STEPPIN' STONE	-	Japan
Oct 96.	(cd-s) LILY / untitled / AUTOMATIC (super karaoke)	-	Japan
Nov 96.	(cd) HIGH TIME	-	Japan

– Brand new stone / Lily / Let's get love / Sweet Monaco / Chadelier / Blue nylon shirts (from bathroom) / Bowling machine / Laugh the world! / Flash silver bus / Candy house (Texas style) / Sl(thr)ow / Baby, please go home – wave '33.

May 97.	(cd-s) CULTURE / untitled / untitled / CISCO (SHE'S GONE)	-	Japan
Aug 97.	(cd-s) GET UP LUCY / / (3 untitled)	-	Japan
Oct 97.	(cd-s) THE BIRDMEN / ROMANTIC (turkey brunch version)	-	Japan
Nov 97.	(cd) CHICKEN ZOMBIES	-	Japan

– Russian huskey / Hi! China / Mongoose / Get up Lucy / The birdmen / Boogie / I've never been you (Jesus time) / Cow / Culture / Sunny side river / Bronze master / Romantic / I've never been you (King time).

Jun 98.	(cd-s) G.W.D. / JUB	-	Japan
Aug 98.	(cd-s) OUT BLUES / SODA PRESSING	-	Japan
Oct 98.	(cd-s) SMOKIN' BILLY / untitled	-	Japan
Nov 98.	(cd) GEAR BLUES	-	

– West cabaret drive / Smokin' Billy / Satanic boom boom head / Dog way / Free devil jam / Killer beach / Brian down / Hotel bronco / Give the gallon / G.W.D. / Ash / Soul warp / Boiled oil / Danny go. <US-iss.2000 on 'Munster' d10"lp; MR 182> (UK-iss.Mar02 on 'Alive' d10"lp/cd+7"; ALIVE 040/+CD)

—— they subsequently released several Japan-only singles (not included)

		Vinyl Japan	not iss.
1998.	(7") (PAD 60) VIBE ON! / (other by the BRISTOLS)		-
		Damaged Goods	not iss.
1999.	(10"ep) (DAMGOOD 175) RUMBLE		

– Smokin' Billy / G.W.D. / Hi! China / Bowling machine (live).

May 00.	(10"ep/cd-ep) (DAMGOOD 182/+CD) PLASMA DIVE		-

– Plasma dive / Get up Lucy / Killer beach / Cisco. (re-iss. Jul02; same)

		not iss.	Estrus
2000.	(7"m) <ES 7141> WEST CABARET DRIVE. / SMOKIN' BILLY / CISCO	-	
		Munster	Munster
Dec 00.	(7"m) <(MR7 143)> GET UP LUCY. / SMOKIN' BILLY / CISCO	-	
Apr 01.	(d10"lp) <(MR 218LP)> CASANOVA SHAKE		

– Dead star end / Cobra / Young jaguar / Plasma dive / Revolver junkies / Dust bunny ride on / Naked sun / Rhapsody / Boogie's dawn / Silk / Pinhead cranberry dance / Angie motel / GT 400 / Pistol disco / Drop.

		Alive	Alive
Oct 02.	(cd) (<ALIVE 00.45CD>) RODEO BEAT TANDEM SPECTER		

– Citroen no Kodoku (the loneliness of the Citroen) / Alligator night / Abakareta sekai (the world exposed) / God jazz time / Baby stardust / Rita / Mona Lisa / Beat specter Buchanan / Turkey / Break Hazureta oreno shinzou (my heart with its brakes broken loose) / Margaret / Bird land Cindy / Beat specter Garcia / The redhead Kelly.

– compilations, etc. –

Jul 01.	(cd) Alive; (ALIVECD 043) COLLECTION		-

– Pinhead cranberry dance / Young jaguar / Hi! China / Smokin' Billy / Lily / Out blues / Why do you want to / Shake / Blue nylon shirts / Black tambourine / Boogie / Birdmen / Baby please go home / Vibe on / Revolver junkies / World's end / GT 400 / Cisco.

THEE MOTHS (see under ⇒ MAGNETIC NORTH POLE)

THEE SPEAKING CANARIES (see under ⇒ DON CABALLERO)

THESE ANIMAL MEN

Formed: Brighton, England . . . 1991 by JULIAN HOOLIGAN (HEWINGS), BOAG, PATRICK (HUSSEY) and STEVE MURRAY. Hailed as flag bearers for the hopelessly contrived 'New Wave Of New Wave' scene – as well as encouraging a glut of pointless third-rate punk throwbacks, it was also the root cause of Brit-pop – THESE ANIMAL MEN emerged in 1993 with a track on the 6-band 'Fierce Panda' punk compilation EP 'Shaggin' In The Streets'. A debut cassette EP, 'WHEELERS, DEALERS AND CHRISTINE KEELERS' (shared with S*M*A*S*H), featured five tracks, the mini-set later to resurface as 'TOO SUSSED?' in '94. Having reinvented themselves (after rather dodgy beginnings) as a would-be CLASH for the 90's – complete with retro-Adidas-chic image – the band thrived on notoriety rather than any engaging musical talent, the 'SPEEED KING' single predictably baiting the usual suspects (i.e. MP's, local councils etc.) but failing to say anything new, either musically or lyrically. After a further single, 'THIS IS THE SOUND OF YOUTH', a debut album, '(COME ON, JOIN) THE HIGH SOCIETY' surfaced later that year, critics divided over its amateur pop-punk sloganeering but generally agreeing that they'd captured something of the zeitgeist. With the mid-90's onset of the aforementioned Brit-pop, the band found themselves somewhat sidelined despite a more expansive musical outlook on mini-set, 'TAXI FOR THESE ANIMAL MEN' (1995) and follow-up album for Virgin-offshoot, 'Hut', 'ACCIDENT AND EMERGENCY' (1997).

Album rating: TOO SUSSED? mini (*5) / (COME ON, JOIN) THE HIGH SOCIETY (*6) / TAXI FOR THESE ANIMAL MEN (*5) / ACCIDENT AND EMERGENCY (*5)

BOAG – vocals / **JULIAN HOOLIGAN (HEWINGS)** – guitar / **PATRICK (HUSSEY)** – bass / **STEVE MURRAY** – drums

		Les Disques De Popcor	not iss.
Dec 93.	(c-ep) WHEELERS, DEALERS AND CHRISTINE KEELERS		-

– (5 tracks; see TOO SUSSED? m-lp) / (4 tracks by S*M*A*S*H)

		Hi-Rise	Vernon Yard
Mar 94.	(7") (FLAT 2) SPEEED KING. / JOBS FOR THE BOYS		-
Apr 94.	(7") (FLAT 3) YOU'RE NOT MY BABYLON. / WHO'S THE DADDY NOW?		-
Jun 94.	(cd/c/m-lp) (FLAT MCD/MTC/MLP 4) <VUSCD 4> TOO SUSSED?	39	

– Too sussed? (live) / Speeed king / Jobs for the boys / Who's the daddy now? / You're not my Babylon.

Sep 94.	(7"ep;pic-d/c-ep/12"ep/cd-ep) (FLAT/+C/T/CD 7) THIS IS THE SOUND OF YOUTH. / SAIL AROUND THE WORLD / HOOLIGAN'S PROGRESS	72	-
Sep 94.	(cd/c/lp) (FLAT CD/MC/LP 8) (COME ON, JOIN) THE HIGH SOCIETY	62	-

– Sharp kid / Empire building / Ambulance / This year's model / You're always right / Flawed is beautiful / This is the sound of youth / Sitting tenant / Too sussed? / (Come on, join) The high society / We are living / High society (return).

Mar 95.	(m-cd/m-c/m-lp) (FLAT CD/MC/LP 14) TAXI FOR THESE ANIMAL MEN	64	-

– You're always right / Nowhere faces / My human remains / False identification / Wait for it.

		Hut	not iss.
Jan 97.	(7"/cd-s) (HUT/+CD 76) LIFE SUPPORT MACHINE. / (MY) MAGAZINE / APRIL 7th	62	-

(cd-s) (HUTDX 76) – ('A'side) / Wichita lineman / Hammond heavy (emptyheads).

Mar 97.	(7") (HUT 81) LIGHT EMITTING ELECTRICAL WAVE. / SISTE ANNE	72	-

(cd-s+=) (HUTCD 81) – Seamen's mission lament / Louis Louis. (cd-s) (HUTDX 81) – Every bullet's (got my name on it).

Apr 97.	(cd)(c/lp) (CDHUT 40)(HUT MC/LP 40) ACCIDENT AND EMERGENCY		-

– Life support machine / So sophisticated / When your hands are tied / Monumental moneymaker / Riverboat captain / New wave girl / 24 hours to live / Going native / Ambulance man / Light emitting electrical wave / April 7th.

—— the group have since split up

THESE ARE THE SOUNDS OF KALEIDOSCOPE (see under ⇒ ROPERS)

THINGY (see under ⇒ PINBACK)

THIRD EYE FOUNDATION

Formed: Bristol, England . . . 1996 solely by drum'n'bass afficionado and ex-FLYING SAUCER ATTACK member, MATT ELLIOT, who admits to having a penchant for the wacky baccy. Having travelled the world, ELLIOT kept down a daytime job at his local Revolver records, the dreadlocked spliffhead (he has since cut his locks due to itchyness) released a few mini-cd's in 1996, namely 'SEMTEX' and 'IN VERSION', before signing for 'Domino'. The following Spring, his THIRD EYE FOUNDATION released their debut set, 'GHOST', a largely experimental journey through hip-hop and Eastern sounds. A second album, 'YOU GUYS KILL ME' (1998), was an even darker affair from the travelling man who incidentally dislikes aeroplanes. Early in 2000, TEF released their fifth full-album, 'LITTLE LOST SOUL', followed a year later by the customary remix companion set, 'I POOPOO ON YOUR JUJU' (2001). • **Note:** not to be confused with another outfit, THIRD EYE.

Album rating: SEMTEX (*6) / IN VERSION (*5) / GHOST (*6) / YOU GUYS KILL ME (*7) / LITTLE LOST SOUL (*7) / I POO POO ON YOUR JUJU remixes (*5)

MATT ELLIOT (b. 1974) – samples, etc (ex-FLYING SAUCER ATTACK)

		Planet	not iss.
Sep 96.	(7") (PUNK 015) UNIVERSAL COOLER. / I'M NOT GETTING INTO A CAR WITH YOU		-

(re-iss. Jul99; same)

		Linda's Strange Vacation	not iss.
Oct 96.	(m-cd) (LSD 02) SEMTEX		-

– Sleep / Still-life / Dreams on his fingers / Next of kin / Once when I was an Indian / Rain. (re-iss. Nov96 on 'Series 500-Domino' m-lp/m-cd; SER 502/+CD)

Oct 96.	(m-cd) (LSD 04) IN VERSION (remixes by other artists)		-

– AMP: Eternity (I and I and eye and eye and eye version) / AMP: Short wave dub / CRESCENT: Superconstellation / HOOD: Eyes / FLYING SAUCER ATTACK: Way out like David Bowman.

		Domino Series 500	not iss.
Dec 96.	(12") (SER 503) SEMTEX. / SCIENCE FICTION SEMTEX (version)		-
		Obsessive Eye	not iss.
Feb 97.	(7") (OBSESS 1) STARS ARE DOWN. / KS Kollective: (TO) A SECRET BROTHER		-

(above was a freebie given away with the group's fanzine)

	Domino	Merge
Apr 97. (cd/lp) *(WIG CD/LP 32)* <MRG 119> **GHOST**		

– What to do but cry? / Corpses as bedmates / The star's gone out / The out sound from way in / I've seen the light and it's dark / Ghosts . . . / Donald Crowhurst.

Nov 97. (12"/cd-s) *(RUG 59 T/CD)* <MRG 134CD> **SOUND OF VIOLENCE / A NAME FOR MY PAIN. / PAIN (violence mix) / CORPSES (version)**		
1998. (12"ep) *(FAT 006)* **THERE'S NO END IN SIGHT. / (other tracks by V/Vm:- Lumberjack WLTM / Female pig herder / Looks unimportant, poss, romance / Will travel, north west)**		Jan98

(above issued on 'Fat Cat')

Oct 98. (12"/cd-s) *(RUG 75 T/CD)* **FEAR OF A WACK PLANET. / A GALAXY OF SCARS (version)**		
Oct 98. (cd/lp) *(WIG CD/LP 53)* <MRG 149> **YOU GUYS KILL ME**		

– A galaxy of scars / For all the brothers and sisters / There's a fight at the end of the tunnel / An even harder shade of dark / Lions writing the bible / No dove no covenant / I'm sick and tired of being sick and tired / That would be exhibiting the same weak traits / In Bristol with a pistol.

Nov 98. (12"; shared with BUMP 'N' GRIND) *(QUANTUM 321)* **PAN ODYSSEY**

(above issued on 'Sub Rosa')

Jun 99. (7"/cd-s) *(RUG 88/+CD)* **IN BRISTOL WITH A PISTOL. / Suncoil Sect: COUNTER CULTURE (Third Eye Foundation remix)**

Jan 00. (12"/cd-s) *(RUG 102 T/CD)* **WHAT IS IT WITH YOU / ARE YOU STILL A CLICHE (WITH A TROUBLED MIND)? / WHAT IS IT WITH YOU (remote viewer version)**

Feb 00. (cd/lp) *(WIG 73 CD/LP)* <MRG 174CD> **LITTLE LOST SOUL**
– I've lost that loving feline / What is it with you / Stone cold said so / Half a tiger / Lost / Are you still a cliche? / Goddamit you've got to be kind.

Feb 01. (cd/lp) *(WIG CD/LP 91)* <MRG 499> **I POOPOO ON YOUR JUJU** (remixes by Various Artists)   May01

Fred THOMAS

Born: Ann Arbor, Michigan, USA. The schizophrenic musical career of FRED THOMAS began in 1995 when he took on the rolls of drummer, guitarist and vocalist in the group FLASHPAPR (correct spelling!) which he formed with musician/friends including JACOB DANZINGER and CARRIE SMITH. The death of drummer GEOFF STREADWICK provoked the band to release their emotional debut, 'PAIN TAPED OVER (FOREVER)', in 1998. A second and equally beautiful album, 'DO WHAT YOU MUST DO', followed the next year before THOMAS abandoned the group to form the more aggressive LOVESICK and the orchestral pop band SATURDAY LOOKS GOOD TO ME. THOMAS flirted between the two groups releasing the dreamy self-titled 'SATURDAY LOOKS GOOD TO ME' and the angsty, yet equally intricate LOVESICK album 'LOVESICK (ALL PLEASE SOUND)' both in 2000. THOMAS's prolific work rate was made all the more astonishing by both its diversity and consistency. By 2002, THOMAS had released another LOVESICK album, three more SATURDAY LOOKS GOOD TO ME albums, as well as guesting on releases by HIS NAME IS ALIVE and IDA without ever compromising the quality of the music. Amazingly THOMAS did not stop there and towards the end of the year he released his impressively titled solo debut 'EVERYTHING IS PRETTY MUCH TOTALLY FUCKED UP'.

Album rating: Flashpapr: PAIN TAPED OVER (FOREVER) (*6) / DO WHAT YOU MUST DO (*7) / NEW LEAVES (*5) / Lovesick: LOVESICK lp (*6) / LOVESICK cd (*5) / Saturday Looks Good To Me: SATURDAY LOOKS GOOD TO ME (*6) / CRUEL AUGUST MOON (*6) / I TAKE A CHANCE EVERY TIME (*6) / LOVE WILL FIND YOU (*6) / Fred Thomas: EVERYTHING IS PRETTY MUCH TOTALLY FUCKED UP (*7)

FLASHPAPR

FRED THOMAS – vocals, drums, guitar / **NIKKI MARGOSIAN** – guitar / **CARRIE SMITH** (of VON BONDIES) / **JJ HELDMAN** (of OHIO) / **JACOB DANZINGER** – violin

	not iss.	Westside Audio
Jun 96. (c) <WS 5> **SIMPLE DANCING**	-	
— THOMAS + DANZINGER plus ZACH WALLACE – stand-up bass + GEOFF STREADWICK – drums		
Jan 98. (lp) <WS 19> **PAIN TAPED OVER (FOREVER)**	-	

– Sometimes I believe in sweethearts / The frozen lake / Daylight savings / Before the war / We never mean to steal.

— tragically, GEOFF was to die during above recording

— **BEN BRACKEN** – guitar, electronics; repl. GEOFF

Aug 99. (cd) <WS 25> **DO WHAT YOU MUST DO**   -
– Were we to dance / Four rules for now / Together swarm / The air in my stomach / Untitled / Find rest / White flowers / Spanish bombs / When now began / Will the Moon be out tonight?

— added **IDA PEARLE** – violin

Sep 01. (m-cd) <web> **NEW LEAVES**   -
– After music / When flowers covered the earth / Always already there / Leave the place / Two new days / Spanish bombs.

LOVESICK

FRED THOMAS – vocals, drums, bells, etc. / plus **NIKKIE MARGOSIAN** – bass, vocals / **MICHAEL TROUTMAN** – guitar, vocals

	not iss.	demo
Jun 98. (c) <none> **LOVESICK**	-	
	not iss.	Westside Audio
Apr 99. (7") <WS 21> **ROBBY THE ROBOT. / Emergency: YOUNG BOWIE**	-	
Jul 99. (lp) <WS 24 – ALL STAR 1> **LOVESICK / THIS ROBOT KILLS**		

(above released in conjunction with 'All Star')

	not iss.	20-12
Feb 00. (7") <TWENTY TWELVE 1> **WHEN WILL WE BE AVENGED. / WHEN, IF NOT NOW? / MILLIMETERS**	-	
	not iss.	At Arms Mechanics
Mar 00. (7") <1> **QUARTERS. (other by SMALL BROWN BIKE)**	-	
	not iss.	All Please Sound
Aug 00. (lp) <1> **LOVESICK**	-	

– Reset / Sleep in cars / Falsified documents / Meet me at midnight / Invention / Faster than arrows / Tiger's ghost / New not fast.

	not iss.	Makato
May 01. (m-cd) <mkr 21> **LOVESICK**	-	

– Hateful / Where are the homes / To the dead / Stacked to the ceiling / Crown / Calm for hits / This spring's bat wings / Drum taut / Don't go out alone.

Aug 01. (7") **split w/ ALOHA**   -

SATURDAY LOOKS GOOD TO ME

FRED THOMAS with **ERIKA HOFFMAN** – vocals (of GODZUKI) / **RISA BUBERNIAK** + **BROOKE ROSSI** – vocals (of SPARKLERS) / **CHAD GILCHRIST** (of OUTRAGEOUS CHERRY)

	not iss.	Hereforeveralways
May 00. (ltd-lp) <3> **SATURDAY LOOKS GOOD TO ME**	-	

– I wish I could cry / Ladder / Obstacle / Everyday / I would find it so beautiful / No point to continue / Think about tomorrow / Don't try / I would find it so beautiful. <re-iss. Feb02 on 'Ypsilanti'+=; 7> – Ambulance / Bright green gloves / Last night I fell asleep on your floor / Car crash / I take a chance every time.

	not iss.	Little Hands
Jun 01. (cd) <lh 5> **CRUEL AUGUST MOON** (also known as 'I TAKE A CHANCE EVERY TIME')	-	

– Spring / Last night I fell asleep on your floor / Car crash / I take a chance every time / Save my life / School / Postmark / Your winter / Own.

	not iss.	Whistletap
May 02. (ltd-CD-rom) <1> **LOVE WILL FIND YOU**	-	

– Liquor store / Diary / Your small heart / When you go out tonight / We can work it out / Record store / Summer doesn't count (unless you're here) / Love will find you / Labcoat / Pet store / I get so excited.

	not iss.	Ypsilanti
Oct 02. (ltd-CD-rom) <11> **TOUR EP**	-	

– Look thru you / Light up like a lion / Sweetheart / No more plants / Summer song.

FRED THOMAS

with **JUAN GARCIA** – banjo, tambourine (ex-CORNISH IN A TURTLENECK) / **TONY CAVALLARIO** – acoustic guitar / **NATE CAVALIERI** – vibraphone (of JUDAH JOHNSON)

	not iss.	Ypsilanti
Nov 01. (CD-rom) <7> **FRED THOMAS**	-	
	not iss.	Little Hands
Feb 02. (cd) <lh 09> **EVERYTHING IS PRETTY MUCH TOTALLY FUCKED UP**	-	

– Second hand news / Rumor / Drive through / This could be the year / Don't worry / Up all night / They replace your heart / First star / Do you want to come to my party? / Last one to leave / When you fuck things up with your baby / Hearts dancing.

	not iss.	Ypsilanti
Jun 02. (CD-rom) <10> **TOUR EP**	-	
Jul 02. (3"CD-rom-s) <none> **NO ONE WILL EVER MAKE ME FEEL THIS WAY AGAIN / (split w/ ELIZABETH MITCHELL)**	-	
	not iss.	Sleep Furiously
Aug 02. (7") <1> **YOUR SIDE OF THE NIGHT. / MY SMALL HEART**	-	

Mayo THOMPSON (see under ⇒ RED CRAYOLA)

THOSE BASTARD SOULS (see under ⇒ GRIFTERS)

THOUSAND YARD STARE

Formed: Slough, Berkshire, England . . . 1988 by STEPHEN BARNES, GILES DUFFY, SEAN McDONOUGH, DOMINIC BOSTOCK and a guy called ALEX. Following a self-financed debut EP, 'WEATHERWATCHING' (on 'Stifled Aardvark'), the band accrued sufficient press interest to land a major label deal via 'Polydor'. With KEVIN MOXON having replaced ALEX, the quartet embarked upon a long journey to the Shetland Isles, undertaking an island-hopping mini tour to delighted pop-starved locals. Minor players in the shoegazing scene, THOUSAND YARD STARE might've lacked the muso intensity of RIDE or the feminine charm of LUSH but were nevertheless capable of turning out a half-decent slice of chiming guitar-pop when they felt like it. 'COMEUPPANCE' was a prime example, a UK Top 40 hit and a taster for debut album, 'HANDS ON' (1992). Given a bit of a rough ride by the press, especially when the "scene that celebrated itself" rapidly fell out of media favour, the band made little critical or commercial headway with a further two albums, 'FAIR TO MIDDLING' (1993) and 'MAPPAMUNDI' (1993). • **Songwriters:** BARNES lyrics / group penned, except STRANGE (Wire).

Album rating: HANDS ON (*7) / FAIR TO MIDDLING (*7) / MAPPAMUNDI (*4)

STEPHEN BARNES – vocals / **GILES DUFFY** – lead guitar / **ALEX** – rhythm guitar / **SEAN McDONOUGH** – bass / **DOMINIC BOSTOCK** – drums

THOUSAND YARD STARE (cont)

		Stifled Aardvark	not iss.
Nov 89.	(c-ep) *(AARD 001)* **EASTER E.P.** – Helstone / When the world was round / Sunday inverted.	□	-
May 90.	(c-ep) *(AARD 002)* **TUMBLEDOWN E.P.** – Twice times / Few and far between / Worse for wear / Wonderment.	□	-
Nov 90.	(12"ep) *(AARD 003)* **WEATHERWATCHING E.P.** – Stopgap to the world / Three doors down / Stonesthrow / Wonderment.	□	-

—— **KEVIN MOXON** – rhythm guitar; repl. ALEX

May 91.	(10"yellow-ep,12"ep,cd-ep) *(AARD 004 X/T/CD)* **KEEPSAKE E.P.** – Buttermouth / Twicetimes / Weatherwatching one / Another on and on.	□	-
Oct 91.	(12"ep/10"blue-ep/c-ep/cd-ep) *(AARD 005 T/X/C/CD)* **SEASONSTREAM E.P.** – 0-0 a.e.t. / Village end / Keepsake / Worse for wear.	65	-
Nov 91.	(12";one-sided gig freebie) *(AARD 006)* **STRANGE. / TWICE TIMES**	-	-

—— Note; 'Stifled Aardvark' were now licensed to 'Polydor'.

Jan 92.	(7"/10"red) *(AARD 007/+X)* **COMEUPPANCE. / WISH A PERFECT** (12"+=/cd-s+=) *(AARD 007 T/CD)* – Standoffish.	37	-
Feb 92.	(cd/c/10"lp) *(AARD 008 – 513001-2/-4/-1)* **HANDS ON** – 0-0 A.E.T. / Thisness / Comeuppance / Cottager / Seasonstream / Junketing / Nonplussed / Absentee / Last up first to go / Buttermouth / Wideshire.*(lp w/ free 10"ep)*	38	-
Apr 92.	(10"ep) *(AARD 009)* **LIVE BOOTLEG E.P. (live)** – 3 doors down / Buttermouth / Twicetimes / Village end.	□	-
Jun 92.	(12"ep/cd-ep/10"green or clear-ep) *(AAR DT/CD/X 010)* **SPINDRIFT E.P.** – Wideshire two / Hand, son (live) / Happenstance? (live) / Moccapune e.p.	58	-
Mar 93.	(cd)(blue-lp) *(AAR 11CD)(AARLP 11)* **FAIR TO MIDDLING** (compilation) – No score after extra time / Village end / Weatherwatching – Another on and on / Three doors down / Stonesthrow / Buttermouth / Twice times / Keepsake / Worse for wear / Wonderment.	□	-
May 93.	(7") *(AARD 012)* **VERSION OF ME. / STRANGE** (cd-s+=/12"clear+=) *(AAR CD/DT 012)* – Darkness of her eyes / ('A'demo version). (cd-s) *(AARDD 012)* – ('A'side) / Spacehopper / Happenstance (live) / Comeuppance (live).	57	-
May 93.	(cd/c/lp) *(519359-2/-4/-1)* **MAPPAMUNDI** – Version of me / God's P45 / Tragedy No.6 / Debutante / One and all / Snoozer / Half size / Small change / Monsieur Bour and his coat / Naturesway (Earth watching) / What's your level? / Downtown mystic.	□	-

—— disbanded after above

3Ds

Formed: Dunedin, New Zealand . . . 1988 by DAVID SAUNDERS, DENISE ROUGHAN and DOMINIC STONES. Another product of Dunedin's esteemed indie scene, The 3Ds debuted with the 'FISH TALES' EP in 1990, by which time DAVID MITCHELL had expanded the band into a quartet. A second EP, 'SWARTHY SONGS FOR SWABS', appeared in 1991 while debut album, 'HELLZAPOPPIN', more than made the grade the following year. Although their demented, melodic noise-pop wasn't entirely out of keeping with Dunedin forebears such as The CHILLS and The CLEAN, the most obvious and oft quoted musical referent was The PIXIES. With SAUNDERS' occasionally manic yelp tempered by ROUGHAN's gentler touch, not to mention the occasional lavishing of instrumental exotica, the record steered firmly clear of the pack and signalled that things were still looking up down under. 'THE VENUS TRAIL' (1993) confirmed this impression, sharpening their skewed musical wits still further while simultaneously divesting themselves of their derivative tag. With SAUNDERS and MITCHELL having already moonlighted in the band MAGICK HEADS, MITCHELL (this time with ROUGHAN, his wife) announced another side project, The GHOST CLUB, with 1996's haunting 'Flying Nun' single, 'BELOVED'. The lacklustre 3Ds album 'STRANGE NEWS FROM THE ANGELS' (1997) seemed to confirm that MITCHELL's mind was elsewhere and his new project reached creative fruition in 2001 with the 'GHOSTCLUBBING' album. • **Covered:** BABY'S ON FIRE (Eno).

Album rating: FISH TALES mini (*5) / SWARTHY SONGS FOR SWABS mini (*6) / HELLZAPOPPIN' (*7) / THE VENUS TRAIL (*6) / STRANGE NEWS FROM THE ANGELS (*5) / Ghost Club: GHOSTCLUBBING (*6) / Goblin Mix + Exploding Budgies: THE COMPLETE . . . compilation (*6)

DAVID SAUNDERS – vocals, guitar / **DENISE ROUGHAN** – vocals, bass (ex-LOOK BLUE GO PURPLE) / **DOMINIC STONES** – drums (ex-SNAPPER guitarist) / **DAVID MITCHELL** – guitar (ex-PLAGAL GRIND, ex-EXPLODING BUDGIES, ex-GOBLIN MIX)

		Flying Nun	First Warning
1990.	(m-lp) *(FN 150)* **FISH TALES** – First church / Dreams of Herge / Evil kid / Fish tails / Evocation of W.C. Fields / Mud sacrifice / The ball of purple cotton.	-	- NewZ
1991.	(m-lp) *(FN 167)* **SWARTHY SONGS FOR SWABS** – Sing-song / Bunny / Ritual tragick / Meluzina man / Nimmo's dream / Grimace.	-	- NewZ

—— added guest **RACHEL KING** – bass

| 1991. | (cd)(c) *(FNCD 188)(FNMC 187)* <72705-75706-4/-4> **FISH TALES / SWARTHY SONGS FOR SWABS** (compilation)
 – (added+=) – Hairs / One eye opened. | □ | - |

—— guest now **ALAN STARRETT**

| Jul 92. | (cd/c) *(FNCD/FNMC 225)* <72705-75709-2/-4> **HELLZAPOPPIN'**
 – Outer space / Ugly day / Sunken head / Swallows / Sunken treasure / Hellzapoppin' / Leave the dogs to play / Hairs / Something in the water / Homo necans / One eye opened / Teacher is dead / Jewel. | □ | Sep91 |
| 1992. | (7"/c-s) *(FN/+TC 241)* **OUTER SPACE. / BABY'S ON FIRE** | - | - NewZ |

		Flying Nun	Merge
1993.	(7") <MRG 043> **BEAUTIFUL THINGS. / SUMMER STONE**	-	-
Mar 94.	(7") <MRG 064> **HEY SUESS. / RIVER BURIAL**	-	-
Mar 94.	(cd-ep) *(FNCD 297)* **HEY SUESS / MAN ON THE VERGE OF A NERVOUS BREAKDOWN / RIVER BURIAL** (w/ free cd-ep) *(FNCD 261)* – BEAUTIFUL THINGS / SUMMER STONE / SONG FOR THE WHOLE WORLD	□	-
Apr 94.	(cd/lp) *(FNCD/FNLP 281)* <MRG 065 CD/C> **THE VENUS TRAIL** – Hey Suess / Philadelphia rising / Cash none / The golden grove / The Venus trail / Beautiful things / Man on the verge of a nervous breakdown / Jane air / The young and the restless / Summer stone / Ice / Spooky. *(cd re-iss. Sep98; same)*	□	1993

		Flying Nun	NewZ
1995.	(cd-ep) *(FNCD 319)* **CATERWAULING** – Big heart / Free agent / Lightening tree / Cold harbour.	-	- NewZ
Jan 96.	(cd/c) *(FNCD/FNMC 351)* **STRANGE NEWS FROM THE ANGELS** – Dust / Seven days of kindness / Fangworld / Animal / Vector 27 / Riding the whale / The fiery angel / Ben / Devil red / Big red heart / I believe in you / Castaway / Carrion days / The wish.	□	-
Mar 96.	(7") *(FN 361)* **DUST. / FALLEN ANGEL** (cd-ep+=) *(FNCD 361)* **DUST EP** – Animal / Strange news from the angels.	-	- NewZ

SPACIOUS

—— aka **DAVID SAUNDERS**

		Flying Nun	not iss.
Feb 96.	(7"m) *(FN 355)* **VECTOR 27. / RIDING THE WHALE / I BELIEVE IN YOU**	-	- NewZ

GHOST CLUB

DAVID MITCHELL + DENISE ROUGHAN

		Xpressway	not iss.
1991.	(7"m; as DAVID MITCHELL & DENISE ROUGHAN) *(X/WAY 21)* **DEAD DOG IN PORT CHALMERS / DOGS. / GREY FUNNEL LINE**	-	- NewZ

—— next with **JIM ABBOTT** – drums

		Flying Nun	not iss.
Jan 96.	(7") *(FN 356)* **BELOVED. / THE CRYING ROOM**	-	- NewZ
Jul 01.	(cd) *(FNCD 416)* **GHOSTCLUBBING** – Punch (your brother) / Precious blood / Cool air / Unterwasser fotos / Diver X / Break the law / Howl of the duck / Late lamentable fire / Tote oma / Ghost Club theme song / Tiny cuts.	-	- NewZ

– DAVID MITCHELL's earlier projects –

on 'Flying Nun'

1984.	(12"ep; EXPLODING BUDGIES) *(FN 033)* **GROTESQUE SINGERS EP** – Thorn: field / Kenneth Anger / Hank Marvin / See you around the stones / Sunflower.	-	- NewZ
1985.	(12"ep; GOBLIN MIX) *(FN 046)* **GOBLIN MIX EP** – Lament / The water / Time away / The unusual wish.	-	- NewZ
1987.	(m-lp/m-c; GOBLIN MIX) *(FN/+MC 074)* **SON OF GOBLIN MIX** – Venus fleye trap / The winter song / The drinking man's curse / Coleridge / Up from the sink / Fruit of the womb.	-	- NewZ
1990.	(cd/c; GOBLIN MIX / EXPLODING BUDGIES) *(FNCD/FNMC 193)* **THE COMPLETE . . .** – GROTESQUE SINGERS EP / GOBLIN MIX EP / Travelling grave / SON OF GOBLIN MIX EP / Ely's on smack.	-	- NewZ

THRUM

Formed: Bellshill, Lanarkshire, Scotland . . . 1992 by JOHNNY SMILLIE, DAVE McGOWAN, GARY JOHNSTON and singer MONICA QUEEN. Following the established pedigree of homegrown indie bands (TEENAGE FANCLUB, BMX BANDITS etc.), THRUM specialised in updating the classic sounds of West Coast Americana with one ear cocked to the 90's US alternative scene. Released as the first fruits of a deal with 'Fire' records, an eponymous debut EP surfaced in 1993 (containing a tortured version of Roy Orbison's 'CRYING') and confirmed early live evidence of potential Laurel Canyon via Bellshill greatness. Further acclaim was heaped upon singles, 'SO GLAD' and 'HERE I AM', prior to a long awaited debut album, 'RIFFERAMA' (1994). NEIL YOUNG was an obvious and oft-quoted influence with SMILLIE's rootsy guitar workouts complemented by MONICA's powerful MARIA McKEE meets DOLLY PARTON vocal. Perhaps the timing wasn't right as despite constantly being tipped for big things, THRUM seemed to be forever struggling around the toilet circuit, playing their emotive country-rock to a core of fans but failing to interest the wider music buying public. In 1997, MONICA returned to the limelight via a special guest vocalist spot on BELLE AND SEBASTIAN's classic 'Lazy Line Painter Jane'; her terrific countrified larynx arguably the best singing indie-pop performance ever; also listen to her duets with the JAYHAWKS, GRANT LEE BUFFALO and SHANE MacGOWAN. Memories of the aforementioned John Peel favourite were still ripe in the minds of non-STEPS fans all over the country, when the girl from Bellshill released her debut solo single for 'Creeping Bent', '77X'. With SMILLIE still contributing to production, writing and guitar work on this September 2000 platter, MONICA Q was back to her old best, especially on third track 'CAMP FIRE CRACKLING'. She subsequently followed this with her debut album 'TEN SORROWFUL MYSTERIES' in Febuary 2002. Co-written and produced by THRUM's JOHN SMILLIE, the set featured ten tracks full of blissful country melodies a la EMMYLOU HARRIS. If QUEEN was the Scottish equivalent of ALISON KRAUSS, then SMILLIE was the DAVID RAWLINGS of Scottish country/folk, with his gentle compositions fitting QUEEN's gliding field-hollers. 'TEAR BEHIND MY SMILE' was an accented folk ballad, while the hypnotic 'WHERE DO YOU SLEEP' was just one reason why this LP should've been in the record collections of many.

Album rating: RIFFERAMA (*6) / Monica Queen: TEN SORROWFUL MYSTERIES (*7)

MONICA QUEEN – vocals, guitar / **JOHNNY SMILLIE** – guitar, vocals / **DAVE McGOWAN** – bass, vocals / **GARY JOHNSTON** – drums

		Fire	not iss.
Apr 93.	(12"ep/cd-ep) (BLAZE 64 T/CD) **THRUM EP**		-
	– Lullaby / Illegitimate clown (mix) / Does anybody know? / Crying (live).		
Jan 94.	(7") (BLAZE 67) **SO GLAD / GIVE A LITTLE**		-
	(12"+=/cd-s+=) (BLAZE 67 T/CD) –		
Jun 94.	(7") (BLAZE 70) **HERE I AM. / WAITING FOR THE SUN**		-
	(7") (7SM 3) – ('A'side) / Get a life.		
	(cd-s) (BLAZE 70CD) – (all 3 tracks).		
Sep 94.	(cd/c/lp) (FIRE CD/MC/LP 38) **RIFFERAMA**		-
	– Rifferama / Purify / So glad / You wish / Lullaby II / Here I am / Hey Joe / Won't be long / Nowhere to run / Almost done.		
Dec 94.	(7") (BLAZE 81) **PURIFY. / IF EVERY DAY WAS LIKE CHRISTMAS DAY**		-

— disbanded the following year, MONICA subsequently provided vocals for BELLE & SEBASTIAN on their classic track, 'Lazy Line Painter Jane' . . .

MONICA QUEEN

— MONICA was still augmented by co-songwriter **JOHN SMILLIE**

		Creeping Bent	not iss.
Sep 00.	(cd-ep) (bent 060cd) **77X e.p.**		-
	– 77X / Stay up all night / Camp fire crackling.		
Feb 02.	(cd) (bent 063cd) **TEN SORROWFUL MYSTERIES**		-
	– I'm sorry darling / State of grace / Do something pretty / Only love / Tear behind my smile / Broken wing / 260 / 77x / Promise for Thomas / Where do you sleep.		

THRUSH PUPPIES

Formed: Manchester, England . . . early 1994 by JULIE "JOOLS" McLARNON (of Irish parentage) along with LAUREN. Enthused by a mutual hatred of the male race, both women thought they'd tell the world how much they despised and didn't need the male sex . . . by fixating on and writing songs about them. Recruiting oestrogen-challenged bass player ANTONY, they released the subtly-titled 'STAND OR SQUAT' 7" (on 'Abstract Sounds') in 1994, which they shared with FLATBACK 4. Sharing their brand of riot grrrl-like oestrogenocide primal scream punk ranting with the world, they released a slew of limited 7"s and CD singles over the next few years. These included a spot on the 'Abstract Sounds' 'Amplified' (1994) compilation album with the tracks 'PIG / SO SWALLOW' (their demo), the 'MAYQUEEN' EP, 'I CAME' 7", 'LET IT LIE' 7" and 'LULLABYS FROM LEVENSHULME' EP. THRUSH PUPPIES caused chaos on tours with The MUFFS and MUDHONEY, horrifying record label '4 a.d.' when they convinced a retarded dwarf to dance on stage during their gigs. However, tiring of her exhausting, juvenile anti-male screeching polemics, McLARNON formed the acoustic solo project BRIDGET STORM (with LAUREN on occasional backing vocals) in 1999. Having cut her musical chops at the George Martin instituted School of Recording Technology at Salford University and Manchester's legendary Strawberry Studios, recording sessions for the likes of NEW ORDER, HAPPY MONDAYS, The CHARLATANS and others, McLARNON was always going to be about more than one-note PMT-bawling-and-brawling. A debut 600-only 7" 'BRIDGET STORM' EP was championed by John Peel and XFM, selling out on word of mouth alone in a couple of weeks and getting McLARNON signed to 'Rough Trade'. It also managed to secure her a series of support slots on UK tours with the likes of LOW, SMOG and ARAB STRAP. STORM was compared favourably to the likes of DUSTY SPRINGFIELD, MARY TIMONY and The WALKABOUTS, and the 7" 'TERRESTRIAL LIVING', showcasing a tougher side of the project, followed in November 2000. The subsequent 'SLEEP' EP was released on the prestigious 'Bad Jazz' label, crossing vast stretches of sonic terrain from quiet acoustic introspection to Moog-smeared grind. McLARNON then retired into a basement full of drums and wires to complete her universally-praised 'HERE'S WHAT'S LEFT' (2002) debut album.

Album rating: Bridget Storm: HERE'S WHAT'S LEFT (*7)

JOOLS (b. JULIE McLARNON) – vocals, bass / **ANTONY** – guitar / **LAUREN** – drums

		Abstract	not iss.
1994.	(7"ep) (ABS 107) **STAND OR SQUAT ep** (split w/ Flatback)		-
	– Pig / Back.		

— **RICKY CUMMINGS** – guitar, 2nd bass; vocals; repl. ANTONY

		Too Damn Loud	not iss.
Mar 95.	(ltd-cd-ep) (2DMCD 06) **MAYQUEEN EP**		-
	– Mayqueen / Shallow / Ladybird / Mine.		
Aug 95.	(ltd-7"purple) (2DM 08) **I CAME. / TART BINT**		-

		Detox Artifacts – 4 a.d.	not iss.
1997.	(7") (7dxt 9701) **LET IT LIE. / LOOK AT ME WHEN I'M TALKING TO YOU**		-
	(cd-ep+=) **LULLABYS FROM LEVENSHULME** – Pathological liar / Dressed like a girl.		

— split later in 1997; RICKY formed indie quintet MONOMANIA; released the CD-singles, 'WHAT NEXT' and 'IN YOUR ELEMENT' for 'Uglyman'.

BRIDGET STORM

JULIE – vocals, multi / with **LAUREN** + 1 other female

		Analogue	not iss.
Sep 99.	(ltd-cd-ep) (acat 002) **2 tracks by BRIDGET STORM + 1 each by Transicord + Robot Donut**		-
Oct 00.	(7") (acat 005) **TERRESTRIAL LIVING. / BOY FROM TO**		-
	(cd-s+=) (acat 005) – (+1).		

		Bad Jazz	not iss.
Mar 01.	(7"ep) (BEBOP 30) **THE SLEEP EP**		-
	– Polar baby part III / Elvis injection / Sleep.		

		Analogue	not iss.
Jun 02.	(cd) (acat 006) **HERE'S WHAT'S LEFT**		-
	– Wake / Oraine / Losing it / Stitches / Quaalude interlude / Conditioning / Terrestrial living / Hush hush pills / Boy from Towerhill / Here's what's left / Felt something go (vocal version).		

TIGER

Formed: London, England . . . early '96 by DAN LAIDLER, JULIE SIMS, and three others. On the strength of a one-off single, 'SHINING IN THE WOODS', for the 'Fierce Panda' imprint, TIGER signed to Island offshoot, 'Trade 2', the FALL comparisons abound due to their Moog attacking indie rock. Two further singles, 'RACE' and 'MY PUPPET PAL', were also unleashed that year, although they were minor hits, it was their debut set, 'WE ARE PUPPETS' (1996), that critics took note of. In 1998, they roared back into gear with the 'FRIENDS' single (from the sophomore 'ROSARIA' set), the much maligned and misunderstood bunch of one-time NME darlings were back. • **Note:** Not to be confused with the late 80's outfit.

Album rating: WE ARE PUPPETS (*7) / ROSARIA (*6)

DAN LAIDLER – vocals / **JULIE SIMS** – guitar, vocals / **DIDO** – bass, Moog / **TINA** – keyboards / – drums

		Fierce Panda	not iss.
Jun 96.	(7") (NING 22) **SHINING IN THE WOOD. / WHERE'S THE LOVE**		-
	(cd-s+=) (NING 22CD) – Bicycle.		

		Trade 2	Bar None
Aug 96.	(7") (TRDS 004) **RACE. / HONEY FRIENDS**	37	-
	(c-s+=) (TRDMC 004) – I'm in love with an RAF nurse.		
	(cd-s++=) (TRDCD 004) – Time tunnel cellar.		
Nov 96.	(7"/c-s) (TRD S/MC 005) **MY PUPPET PAL. / ICICLE**	62	-
	(cd-s+=) (TRDCD 005) – Flea's song.		
Nov 96.	(cd/c/lp) (TRD CD/MC/LP 1002) **WE ARE PUPPETS**		-
	– My puppet pal / Shamed all over / Race / Bollinger farm / Storm injector / Depot / On the rose / Sorry monkeys / Cateader reddle / She's o.k. / Ray Travey / Keep in touch.		
Feb 97.	(7") (TRDS 008) **ON THE ROSE. / ON SPANISH FARMLAND**	57	-
	(cd-s+=) (TRSCD 008) – Babe.		
	(cd-s) (TRDCX 008) – ('A'side) / Ray Travez (live) / Depot (session) / I am in love with an RAF nurse (session).		
Apr 97.	(m-cd) <72> **SHINING IN THE WOOD**	-	
	– Shining in the wood / Where's the love? / Honey friends / Time tunnel cellar / Bicycle / I'm in love with an RAF nurse.		

— now a quartet

Aug 98.	(7") (TRDS 013) **FRIENDS. / WENSLEYDALE**	72	-
	(cd-s+=) (TRDCD 013) – Bottle of juice.		
	(cd-s) (TRDCX 013) – ('A'side) / White Saab, dark night / Rouge Robyn.		
Sep 98.	(7") (TRDS 014) **GIRL FROM THE PETROL STATION. / PAUL YOUNG**		-
	(cd-s+=) (TRDCD 014) – Sea shandy.		
	(cd-s) (TRDCX 014) – ('A'side) / God it's good / Rolling Rose.		
Oct 98.	(cd/lp) (TRD CD/LP 1006) **ROSARIA**		-
	– Friends / I was a rollin' stone / Speak to me / Girl from petrol station / Candy Andy / Birmingham / Root cage / Soho soul / Bee song / Our simple life / River / Rox baroque. (re-iss. May99 on 'Tugboat'; TUGCD 010)		

— split after above

TIGER TRAP

Formed: Sacramento, California, USA . . . 1992 by schoolfriends ROSE MELBERG and ANGELA LOY, who enlisted JEN BRAUN and HEATHER DUNN. Taking their moniker from an episode in the 'Calvin and Hobbes' comic series, the group – although only issuing one album – made a huge impact on the US indie pop scene. Debuting via a split 7" with BRATMOBILE – TT's contribution being the track 'WORDS AND SMILES' – they followed it up with their second single, 'SUPERCRUSH', on the influential indie imprint 'K'. Their ensuing eponymously-titled first LP, 'TIGER TRAP', reached the shops in 1993 and caused quite a stir on the alternative pop scene with its jangly light guitar work and well-penned lyrical content. The equally fine EP 'SOUR GRASS' followed. Unfortunately by the end of 1993 the band suddenly split following a gig. DUNN moved on to play with the outfit LOIS. The talented MELBERG meanwhile cruised through the rest of the 90s in various musical projects. Within the next year MELBERG had formed the GO SAILOR unit with the aid of PAUL CURRAN (of CRIMPSHRINE) and AMY GEDDES (from HENRY'S DRESS). GO

SAILOR was on the whole a moonlighting project for its three members, and over the next two years they recorded and issued three EPs, which were later collected on the self-titled compilation, 'GO SAILOR' (1996). The sound on this set continuing in the same vein as MELBERG's former band. During those two years, MELBERG also moved north up the West Coast to Portland, Oregon, where she met PRETTY FACE's JEN SBRAGIA and put togther the more substantial SOFTIES. The twosome debuted with the 7", 'LOVESEAT', following it up with their first full-length outing, 'IT'S LOVE', that same year. This set heralded a quieter, more bare-bones pop sound than MELBERG's erstwhile projects. The SOFTIES were back again three years later courtesy of their second LP, 'WINTER PAGEANT', a record which drew from the same subdued musical bag as its predecessors. By this time MELBERG and SBRAGIA were also dabbling with another side-project, THREE PEEPS, which included PETER GREEN (of CLASS fame). 1997 also witnessed MELBERG tripping further up the western coast of North America to Vancouver, Canada, where she went for the backseat approach playing drums for the newly formed GAZE which consisted of herself, MIKO HOFFMAN and MEGAN MALLETT. The Canadian-based indie popsters debuted with the 7", 'SEEDLESS' (1997), which was succeeded a year later by their debut LP, 'MITSUMERU', a set which showcased their skill for the catchy pop hook. Their aptitude was proven again on their sophomore album, 'SHAKE THE POUNCE', which arrived the next year. While still pounding the skins for HOFFMAN and MALLETT, MELBERG found time to put out the solo full-length offering, 'PORTOLA' (1998). This set displayed what a talent she was in her own right with its beautiful collection of mainly acoustic backed numbers and served as one of her career highlights. The SOFTIES (ROSE and JEN) returned to the fold via their third set, 'HOLIDAY IN RHODE ISLAND' (2000), a delicate and lovelorn bunch of jangle-pop.

Album rating: TIGER TRAP (*7) / Softies: IT'S LOVE (*7) / WINTER PAGEANT (*5) / HOLIDAY IN RHODE ISLAND (*7) / Gaze: MITSUMERU (*5) / SHAKE THE POUNCE (*5) / Go Sailor: GO SAILOR mini (*4) / Rose Melberg: PORTOLA (*7)

ROSE MELBERG – vocals, guitar / **ANGELA LOY** – vocals, guitar / **JEN BRAUN** – bass / **HEATHER DUNN** – drums

		not iss.	4 Letter Words
Dec 92.	(7") **WORDS AND SMILES. / (split w/ BRATMOBILE)**	- / K	K
Jun 93.	(7"ep) <IPU 36> **SUPERCRUSH EP**		
Jul 93.	(lp/c/cd) <(KLP 17/+MC/CD)> **TIGER TRAP**		

– Puzzle pieces / You're sleeping / Eight wheels / Super crush / Tore a hole / Words and smiles / For sure / You and me / Supreme nothing / CHRSTN / My broken heart / Prettiest boy.

Feb 94.	(7") <SLR 33> **ALIEN SPACE SONG. / HENRY'S DRESS: Feathers**	-	
	(above issued on 'Slumberland')		
Jul 95.	(cd-ep) <K 23CD> **SOUR GRASS EP**	-	

– Sour grass / Carrie's song / Don't ask / Treasure / Sweet heart.

SOFTIES

ROSE MELBERG – vocals, guitar, keyboards / **JEN SBRAGIA** – vocals, guitar (ex-PRETTY FACE)

		not iss.	Slumberland
Jul 94.	(7"ep) <SLR 41> **LOVE SEAT EP**	-	

– Love seat / That and everything / Goodbye / You don't like me anymore.

		K	K
Apr 95.	(7") <IPU 056> **HE'LL HAVE TO KNOW. /**		
Oct 95.	(lp/cd) <(KLP 43/+CD)> **IT'S LOVE**		

– Hello rain / I love you more / Charms around your wrist / Could I / Until you tell / Awful mess / This house / It's love / Alaska / Fragile don't crush / Heart condition / Follow me / I can't get no satisfaction thank God / Perfect afternoon.

Mar 96.	(10"ep/cd-ep) <SLR 47> **THE SOFTIES**	-	

– Snow like this / Selfish / All in good time / Half as much / Sixteen months / Count to ten / Postal blue / Pedestal.
(above issued on 'Slumberland', below on 'Double Agent')

1997.	(7"ep; as THREE PEEPS) <DA 2> **THE THREE PEEPS**	-	

– My heaven, my sky / My one true love / Mr. Spaceman.
(above group:- MELBERG, SBRAGIA + vocalist PETER GREEN)

Jan 97.	(lp/cd) <(KLP 61/+CD)> **WINTER PAGEANT**		

– Pack your things and go / So sad / Over / No one at all / Tracks and tunnels / Excellent / My foolish way / The best days / Fortune / Splintered hands / About you / Anywhere but here / Winter pageant / Make up your mind.

May 97.	(7") <IPU 079> **THE BEST DAYS. / AS SKITTISH AS ME**		
Oct 00.	(cd/lp) <(KLP 119 CD/V)> **HOLIDAY IN RHODE ISLAND**		Sep00

– Sleep away your troubles / The places we go / These sad times / The beginning of the end / Just a day / Me and the bees / Holiday in Rhode Island / Favorite shade of blue / You and only / Sturdies bay / Saint Agnes / If you stayed / Write it down / My empty arms.

GAZE

ROSE MELBERG – drums! / **MIKO HOFFMAN** – vocals, guitar / **MEGAN MALLETT** – vocals, bass

Sep 97.	(7"ep) <IPU 084> **SEEDLESS EP**	-	
Feb 98.	(cd) <(KLP 80CD)> **MITSUMERU**		

– Shady / Jelly-bean / Bob again / 400 ad / Anyway / Portrait / Preppy villain / Peeking shows his ignorance / Listen / Eric idol / Seedless / Turquoise / X-real / You glow.

Jan 99.	(cd) <(KLP 87CD)> **SHAKE THE POUNCE**		

– So early to tell / The snake song / From the inside / Detail queen / Tea or coffee / Mr. Oh so suave and debonaire / Nine lives to Rigel Five / He makes all the girls smile (with his smile) / Sunday night waterworks / Noticed me / A new home / Static / I wonder / In the midst.

GO SAILOR

ROSE MELBERG – vocals / **PAUL CURRAN** – bass (of CRIMPSHRINE) / **AMY** – drums (of HENRY'S DRESS)

		not iss.	Yo Yo
1995.	(7"ep) <YOYO 7-1> **FINE DAY FOR SAILING**	-	

– Last year / A fine day for sailing / I'm still crying / I just do / Bigger than the ocean / Silly.

		not iss.	Slumberland
Jul 95.	(7"ep) <SLR 36> **LONG DISTANCE EP**	-	

– Long distance / Windy / Blue sky / The boy who sailed around the world.

		Lookout!	Lookout!
Mar 96.	(7"blue-ep) <LK 137> **DON'T GO EP**		

– Don't go / Ray of sunshine / Together forever in love / Every day.

Aug 96.	(m-cd) <(LK 153)> **GO SAILOR**		

– Last year / A fine day for sailing / I'm still crying / I just do / Bigger than an ocean / Silly / Long distance / Windy / Blue sky / The boy who sailed around the world / Don't go / Ray of sunshine / Together forever in love / Every day.

ROSE MELBERG

		not iss.	Slumberland
1994.	(7"flexi) <WISH 3> **CUPID**	-	
		not iss.	Double Agent
Nov 98.	(cd) <DA 009> **PORTOLA**	-	

– Deep purple / Golden Gate Bridge / Happy birthday to me / Devoted to you / Loose talk / Another cup of coffee / Stitch / I will / My heaven, my sky / Mr. Spaceman / The love we could have had.

Kevin TIHISTA's RED TERROR
(see under ⇒ TRIPLE FAST ACTION)

Mary TIMONY (see under ⇒ HELIUM)

TINDERSTICKS

Formed: Nottingham, England … 1988 as ASPHALT RIBBONS, by STUART STAPLES, DAVE BOULTER and DICKON HINCHCLIFFE, the line-up completed by NEIL FRASER, MARK COLWILL and AL McCAULEY. Abandoning their previous TRIFFIDS/GO-BETWEENS-esque indie attempts, the group adopted a darkly brooding hybrid of faded-glamour easy listening and semi-acoustic strumming, incorporating swooning strings, mournful violin, frantic flamenco and hints of country. Surely the heartbroken, doomed romantic to top all doomed romantics, STAPLES' low-key mumblings were somehow utterly compelling, his often barely audible melange of NICK CAVE, LEE HAZLEWOOD and TOM WAITS capable of expressing every nuance in the music regardless of what he was actually saying. The TINDERSTICKS came to critical notice with only their second single, 'MARBLES', a lo-fi STAPLES monologue cosetted by an aching melody. Released on their own 'Tippy Toe' label, the track was unanimously awarded Single Of The Week by both NME and Melody Maker, creating a buzz which would eventually see the group sign to the newly formed 'This Way Up' label. Previewed by the string-drenched melancholy of the 'CITY SICKNESS' single, the eponymous 'TINDERSTICKS' was released in late '93. A dense, bleakly beautiful, seedily glamorous near 80-minute epic, the record was so strikingly different from anything else around (save for maybe GALLON DRUNK or NICK CAVE) it sounded timeless. From the edgy resignation of 'WHISKEY & WATER' to the lovelorn lament of 'RAINDROPS', this was one of the most luxuriantly dark albums of the 90's, reeking of failed relationships and nicotine-stained despair. With gushing praise from the music press, both for the album and their hypnotic live shows, The TINDERSTICKS even managed to scrape a Top 60 chart placing. Released simultaneously with the album was a cover of John Barry's 'WE HAVE ALL THE TIME IN THE WORLD' alongside GALLON DRUNK on a 'Clawfist' 7", the latter group's TERRY EDWARDS having guested on the album and subsequently adding string arrangements on their next long player. Preceded by a cover of the late Townes Van Zandt's 'KATHLEEN', 'TINDERSTICKS' (same title, different album) was finally released in Spring '95, its grainy noir narratives and downtrodden country enhanced with exquisite orchestration. There were no great stylistic leaps, just a further exploration and refinement of the blurred shadows and twilit corners that graced the debut. An undisputed highlight was the goose-bump country duet with The WALKABOUTS' CARLA TORGERSON, 'TRAVELLING LIGHT', released as a single that summer. The TINDERSTICKS were also in the process of refining their live sound, or rather expanding it, with the help of a full orchestra; the gorgeous results can be heard on concert set, 'THE BLOOMSBURY THEATRE 12.3.95'. Unable to sustain such a money draining enterprise for too long, The TINDERSTICKS-plus-orchestra phase reached its zenith during a hugely successful week long residency at London's ICA theatre in late '96. The same year also saw the group's first foray into soundtrack work, scoring the music for French art film, 'Nenette et Boni'. Largely instrumental, the piano and bass-led main theme was fleshed out with the moving 'TINY TEARS' (or 'PETITES GOUTTES D'EAU' in French) from the second album; hardly essential but a pleasant listen all the same. Following the group's own fears that the fragile balance of The TINDERSTICKS' muse was becoming unworkable, the difficult third album, 'CURTAINS' was finally completed in a fevered rush of creativity and released in Summer '97. Less sprawling and more cohesive than previous efforts, it was also bolder and more accessible, STAPLES actually singing comprehensibly on the bulk of the tracks. Predictably, there were also more strings than ever, HINCHCLIFFE's orchestral flourishes crescendoing majestically on 'DON'T LOOK DOWN' and achieving a pathos only previously glimpsed before on 'LET'S PRETEND', JESUS ALEMANY's mariachi-style trumpet a bittersweet counterpart. There was even another country duet, 'BURIED BONES', a brilliantly executed NANCY/LEE-style sparring match featuring the velvet tones of BONGWATER's ANNE MAGNUSON. Lyrically, the themes remained reliably unchanged, tales of everyday lust and disillusionment dripping from STAPLES' lips like the honey from his claws as described in the gripping, unsettling 'BEARSUIT'. And, with 'BALLAD OF TINDERSTICKS', STAPLES indicated that they don't take this music business lark TOO seriously. After a stop-gap 'best of' album, 'DONKEYS' was released in '98, TINDERSTICKS were back to their mournful best courtesy of 1999's 'SIMPLE PLEASURE'. Opening with the minor hit, 'CAN WE START AGAIN?' and then a cover of Odyssey's dancefloor hit(!), 'IF YOU'RE LOOKING FOR A WAY OUT', it was clear to see the familiar 'STICKS territory had been given a modern day injection. Switching to another label was perhaps the best possible thing to happen to TINDERSTICKS who issued their dark melancholic set 'CAN OUR LOVE . . .' in 2001. A jazzy, but yet still tortoise speed release, STAPLES' crooning, brooding, COHEN-esque vocals reached new heights of intimacy on songs such as 'DYING SLOWLY' and 'SWEET RELEASE'. The group returned one year later to issue the soundtrack for Claire Denis' post-feminist, cannibal movie 'TROUBLE EVERY DAY', which marked the group's second collaboration with the director after her debut film 'Nenette et Boni'. As usual, the tone set was a dark one, STAPLES providing only one vocal track, to much eerie and frightening effect. If there was any justice, TINDERSTICKS would be bigger than OASIS; as it is they remain a treasured secret for anyone who's ever glimpsed the universe through the bottom of a wine glass. • **Other covers:** KOOKS (David Bowie) / I'VE BEEN LOVING YOU TOO LONG (Otis Redding & Jerry Butler) / HERE (Pavement). • **Trivia:** JON LANGFORD of The THREE JOHNS, produced early ASPHALT RIBBONS material.

Album rating: Asphalt Ribbons: OLD HORSE & OTHER SONGS (*4) / Tindersticks: TINDERSTICKS (*8) / THE SECOND TINDERSTICKS ALBUM (*7) / THE BLOOMSBURY THEATRE 12.3.95 (*6) / NANETTE ET BONI soundtrack (*6) / CURTAINS (*8) / DONKEYS 92-97 compilation (*7) / SIMPLE PLEASURE (*8) / CAN OUR LOVE (*7) / TROUBLE EVERY DAY (*6)

ASPHALT RIBBONS

STUART STAPLES – vocals / **DICKON HINCHCLIFFE** – violin / **DAVE BOULTER** – keyboards / **BLACKHOUSE** – guitar / **FRASER** – bass / **WATT** – drums

	In-Tape	not iss.
Oct 89. (7"ep) (IT 063) **THE ORCHARD**		-
– Over again / Red sauce / Greyhound / I used to live T.		
May 90. (7"m) (IT 068) **GOOD LOVE. / LONG LOST UNCLE / THE DAY I TURNED BAD**		-

— (Alongside new stablemates MY LIFE WITH PATRICK, their new label below issued a free flexi sampler with 'Zip Code' fanzine; cat no. LILY 001)

	Tiger Lily	not iss.
Apr 91. (12"ep) (LILY 002) **PASSION, COOLNESS, INDIFFERENCE, BOREDOM, MOCKERY, CONTEMPT, DISGUST**		-

	E.T.T.	not iss.
Aug 91. (m-lp) (E 101) **OLD HORSE & OTHER SONGS**		-
– Rosemarie / Old horse / State inside / The distance between us / Strong hands / Downside. (cd-iss. Apr92; E 101-2)		

TINDERSTICKS

— were formed by **STUART, DICKON and DAVE**, plus Londoners **NEIL FRASER** – guitar / **MARK COLWILL** – bass / **AL McCAULEY** – drums

	Tippy Toe	No.6
Nov 92. (7") (TIPPY TOE 1) **PATCHWORK. / MILKY TEETH**		
Mar 93. (10"ep) (TIPPY TOE – che 2) **MARBLES / JOE STUMBLE. / FOR THOSE . . . / BENN**		

— Below featured dual vox of **NIKI SIN** of HUGGY BEAR.

	Rough Trade Sing. Club	not iss.
Mar 93. (7") (45REV 16) **A MARRIAGE MADE IN HEAVEN. / (instrumental)**		

	Domino	No.6
Jul 93. (7"ep) (RUG 6) **UNWIRED E.P.**		-
– Feeling relatively good / Rottweilers and mace / She / Kooks.		
Sep 93. (7") <KAR 028> **MARBLES. / FOR THOSE NOT BEAUTIFUL**	-	

	This Way Up	Bar None
Sep 93. (7"/cd-s) (WAY 1811/1833) **CITY SICKNESS. / UNTITLED / THE BULLRING**		-
Oct 93. (cd/c/lp) (518306-2/-4/-1) <46> **TINDERSTICKS**	56	
– Nectar tyed / Sweet, sweet man (pt.1) / Whiskey & water / Blood / City sickness / Patchwork / Marbles / The Walt blues / Milky teeth (pt.2) / Sweet, sweet man (pt.2) / Jism / Piano song / Tie dye / Raindrops / Sweet, sweet man (pt.3) / Her / Tea stain / Drunk tank / Paco de Renaldo's dream / The not knowing. (lp+=) – Fruitless. (re-iss. Jun97; same)		
Oct 93. (7") (XPIG 21) **WE HAVE ALL THE TIME IN THE WORLD – JAMES BOND THEME. / (other by Gallon DRunk)**		
(above issued on 'Clawfist')		

— 'Tippy Toe' also gave away 7" 'LIVE IN BERLIN' at gigs.

Jan 94. (7"ep/10"ep/cd-ep) (WAY 2811/2888/2833) **KATHLEEN EP**	61	-
– Kathleen / Summat Moon / A sweet sweet man / E-type Joe.		

— In Aug'94, they appeared on Various Artists EP on 'Blue Eyed Dog'; track 'LOVE BITES', and others by STRANGELOVE / GOD MACHINE + BREED.

	This Way Up	London
Mar 95. (7") (WAY 38-11) **NO MORE AFFAIRS. / (instrumental)**	58	-
(cd-s+=) (WAY 38-33) – Fruitless.		
Apr 95. (cd/c/d-lp) (526303-2/-4/-1) <6303> **THE SECOND TINDERSTICKS ALBUM**	13	Oct95
– El diablo en el ojo / My sister / Tiny tears / Snowy in F minor / Seaweed / Vertraven 2 / Talk to me / No more affairs / Singing / Travelling light / Cherry blossoms / She's gone / Mistakes / Vertraven 3 / Sleepy song. (ltd.lp w/ free one-sided-7") – PLUS DE LIAISONS		
Jun 95. (7") <SP 297> **THE SMOOTH SOUNDS OF TINDERSTICKS**	-	
– Here / Harry's dilemma.		

— <above issued for 'Sub Pop'>

Jul 95. (7"/cd-s) (WAY 45-11) **TRAVELLING LIGHT. / WAITING 'ROUND YOU / I'VE BEEN LOVING YOU TOO LONG**	51	-
Oct 95. (cd/d-10"lp) (528597-2/-1) **THE BLOOMSBURY THEATRE 12.3.95 (live)**	32	-
– El diablo en el ojo / A night in / Talk to me / She's gone / My sister / No more affairs / City sickness / Vertrauen II / Sleepy song / Jism / Drunk tank / Mistakes / Tiny tears / Raindrops / For those . . . (d-lp+= *)		

	This Way Up	Bar None
Oct 96. (cd/lp) (524300-2/-1) <99> **NENETTE ET BONI (Original Soundtrack)**		
– Ma souer / La passerelle / Les gateaux / Camions / Nenette est la / Petites chiennes / Nosterfrau / Petites gouttes d'eau / Les Cannes a peche / La mort de Felix / Nenette s'en va / Les bebes / Les fleurs / Rumba.		

	This Way Up	Polygram
May 97. (12"ep/cd-ep) (WAY 61-22/-33) **BATHTIME. / MANALOW / SHADOWS / PACO'S THEME**	38	-
(cd-ep) (WAY 61-66) – ('A'side) / Kathleen / Here / Tyed.		
Jun 97. (cd/c/lp) (<524344-2/-4/-1>) **CURTAINS**	37	
– Another night in / Rented rooms / Don't look down / Dick's slow song / Fast one / Ballad of Tindersticks / Dancing / Let's pretend / Desperate man / Buried bones / Bearsuit / (Tonight) Are you trying to fall in love again / I was your man / Bathtime / Walking.		
Oct 97. (7") (WAY 65-22) **RENTED ROOMS. / ('A'-Swing version)**	56	
(cd-s+=) (WAY 65-33) – Make believe.		
(cd-s) (WAY 65-66) – ('A'side) / Cherry blossoms (live) / She's gone (live) / Rhumba (live).		

	Island	Island
Sep 98. (cd/lp) (CID/ILPS 8074) <524588> **DONKEYS 92-97 (A COLLECTION OF SINGLES ° RARITIES ° UNRELEASED RECORDINGS)** (compilation)		
– Patchwork / Marbles / Her / City sickness / Travelling light / I've been loving you too long / Plus de liaisons / Here / Tiny tears / Bathtime / A marriage made in Heaven / For those . . .		
Aug 99. (7") (IS 756) **CAN WE START AGAIN? / ONE WAY STREET**	54	-
(cd-s+=) (CID 756) – A little time.		
(cd-s) (CIDX 756) – ('A'demo) / Puppy fat / Desperate man (alternate version).		
Aug 99. (cd) (CID 8085) <546372> **SIMPLE PLEASURE**	36	
– Can we start again? / If you're looking for a way out / Pretty words / From the inside / If she's torn / Before you close your eyes / (You take) This heart of mine / I know that loving / CF GF. (lp-iss.Sep99 on 'Simply Vinyl'; SVLP 112)		

	Beggars Banquet	Beggars Banquet
Dec 00. (7"/cd-s) (SINS 001/1CD) **WHAT IS A MAN. / (instrumental)**		-
May 01. (cd/lp) (BBQ CD/LP 222) <80222> **CAN OUR LOVE . . .**	47	
– Dying slowly / People keep comin' around / Tricklin' / Can our love . . . / Sweet release / Don't ever get tired / No man in the world / Chilitetime.		
Oct 01. (cd/lp) (BBQ CD/LP 225) <80225> **TROUBLE EVERY DAY**		
– Opening titles / Dream / Houses / Maid theme 1 / Room 321 / Computer / Notre Dame / Killing theme / Taxi to Core / Core on stairs – Love theme (Shane and June) / Maid theme (end) / Closing titles / Killing theme (alternate version) / Trouble every day.		

TINY MONROE

Formed: Camden, North London, England . . . early 90's by Indian Glaswegian, NJ, alongside RICHARD DAVIES, STEVEN WALKER, GARRY BECKER and DAN NEUMANN. Following a number of respectable tour supports, the band were picked up by LUSH manager, Howard Gough's 'Laurel' label and proceeded to release a debut single, 'VHF 855V' (the name of NJ's car number plate!) in early '94. Dominated by the sensual vocals of frontwoman/songwriter, NJ, the band's sound had a definite late 70's/early 80's pop feel, confirmed by 1996's debut album, 'VOLCANOES' (1996). The lush synth flourishes of single, 'OPEN INVITATION', for example, were strangely reminiscent of prime 'Gazza' NUMAN. Still, the rootsy Southern-fried slide on 'MIRROR' indicated that they weren't about to become ambassadors for the threatened 80's revival just yet.

Album rating: VOLCANOES (*6)

NJ (b. Gorbals, Glasgow, Scotland) – vocals / **RICHARD DAVIES** – guitar / **STEVEN WALKER** – guitar / **GARRY BECKER** – bass / **DAN NEUMANN** – drums (ex-BRIGANDAGE)

	Laurel	not iss.
Mar 94. (7") (LAUREL 1) **VHF 855V. / UNDER THE SKIN**		-
Jun 94. (7"ep/10"ep/cd-ep) (LAUREL 2/+T/CD) **THE CREAM EP**		-
– Cream bun / Jealousy / Brittle bones / Sonic blue.		
Apr 96. (7") (LAU 9) **SHE. / THE PARTY'S OVER**		-
(cd-s+=) (LAUCD 9) – Really happy.		
Jun 96. (12") (LAU 10) **OPEN INVITATION. / ANOTHER STATION**		-
(cd-s+=) (LAUCD 10) – Mirror.		
Jul 96. (cd/c/lp) (828804-2/-4/-1) **VOLCANOES**		-
– She / Cream bun / Love of the bottle / Open invitation / Snake in the grass / VHF 855V / Brittle bones / Secret place / Skin beach / Women in love / Bubble.		

— split after **ALEX CULPIN** (bass) + **JON SOLOMON** (drums) were added

TOASTED HERETIC

Formed: Galway, Ireland ... by singer JULIAN GOUGH, DECLAN COLLINS, NEIL FARRELL, BREFFNI O'ROURKE and ANGUS MCMAHON; bassist BARRY WALLACE would later complete the line-up post-1992. COLLINS and FARRELL began writing "mostly bad" unrecorded songs in primary school. TOASTED HERETIC (who obviously know how Joan of Arc felt) played their first gig in 1986 on the back of a lorry in Salthill, Galway. By 1989 the band had recorded two lo-fi cassette-only albums ('SONGS FOR SWINGING CELIBATES' in 1988 'CHARM AND ARROGANCE' in 1989) at FARRELL's living room on a Tascam 244, which was a second-hand 4-track portastudio. They released these efforts on their own 'Bananafish' label, selling them by mail order, a 4-star review from English music magazine Q helping ensure decent enough sales. After playing the Reading Festival, a new music seminar in New York and some gigs in London, the band recorded the 'GALWAYS AND LOS ANGELES' single in 1991 for record label 'Liquid', well received for its milk bottle percussion, Harrier jump jet samples, etc, as well as wiggly guitar playing and GOUGH's arch, wry, witty MORRISSEY-like lyrics. HERETIC also recorded 'ANOTHER DAY, ANOTHER RIOT' single in 1992 and a full-length album under the same title before the 'Liquid' label evaporated after a distribution deal with Warner Brothers fell apart. After a brief tour of France the band recorded the 'MINDLESS OPTIMISM' (1994) album and put it out on 'Bananafish', reckoning that it was the first album of theirs to have a coherent feel to it. Little or nothing much has been heard of them since.

Album rating: ANOTHER DAY, ANOTHER RIOT (*6) / MINDLESS OPTIMISM (*5)

JULIAN GOUGH – vocals / **DECLAN COLLINS** – guitars, sequencing / **BREFFNI O'ROURKE** – rhythm guitar / **AENGUS McMAHON** – bass / **NEIL FARRELL** – drums, sequencing

Bananafish / not iss.

1988. (c) *(BAN 1)* **SONGS FOR SWINGING CELIBATES** – Irish
– Sodom tonight / Very naughty party / Galway Bay / Black contact lenses / Goodbye to Berlin / Love theme from "Yeats: The Movie" / Still life with guitar / Bouncing off the boulders / The best things in life are mine.

1989. (c) *(BAN 2)* **CHARM & ARROGANCE** – Irish
– You make girls unhappy / Abandon the galleries / Stay tonight / Some drugs / Here comes the new year / Lost & found / L.S.D. (isn't what it used to be) / Drown the browns / Charm & arrogance / Go to sleep / You can always go home.

1990. (12"ep/c-ep) *(BAN/+C 3)* **THE SMUG E.P.** – Irish
– Don't you wish you were good? / They didn't teach music in my school / Sun says hi / Let's get drunk.

—— (1991) now without O'ROURKE

Liquid-WEA / not iss.

Nov 91. (7"/12"/c-s) *(LQ/+EP/MC 1)* **GALWAY AND LOS ANGELES. / LIVING AT THE WRONG SPEED / GALWAY AND LOS ANGELES (Dragons are extra version)**

—— added **BARRY WALLACE** – bass (AENGUS now on rhythm guitar)

Oct 92. (7"ep/c-ep/12"ep/cd-ep) *(LQ/+MC/EP/CD 3)* **ANOTHER DAY, ANOTHER RIOT / FOOD FOR BREAKFAST. / HA HA HA / MEET MR MORRISON**

Nov 92. (cd/c) *(LQCD/LQMC 2)* **ANOTHER DAY, ANOTHER RIOT**
– Unrealistic / Another day, another riot / Going public / Don't scuff my tan / Money loves you / Song of the beggar king / Tarty girls / Forgotten / Big happy ending / Galway and Los Angeles / An enormous request / Thanks for the clothes / Heretic boulevard / Galway Bay.

Bananafish / not iss.

1994. (cd/c) *(BAN CD/C 4)* **MINDLESS OPTIMISM** – Irish
– Maybe we should talk / Passenger jets / Anglepoise lamp / Lightning / It's all over / Here comes the new year / Heart attack / Mummy are we there yet / Living in my time / Don't tell me we don't live.

—— split in 1995; re-formed briefly in '96

TOMORROWLAND

Formed: Ann Arbor, Michigan, USA ... spring 1996 by NICK BROCKNEY and STEVE BAKER. Specialising in fractured, freeform electronica, the duo secured the release of their first single, 'I WISH I WAS AN ANGEL SO I COULD SLEEP ON THE MOON', on the Japanese 'Motorway' imprint. After following up with 'FUTURIST' for the 'Burnt Hair' label, they were contracted by 'Darla' with a view to recording the sixth volume in their 'Bliss Out' series. The resulting 'STEREOSCOPIC SOUNDWAVES' (1997) allowed their painstakingly crafted, semi-structured ambient textures room to breathe over the course of a whole album. Chicago label, 'Kranky' stepped into the breach for follow-up, 'SEQUENCE OF THE NEGATIVE SPACE CHANGES' (1998). Although BROCKNEY was heavily involved in his job with video installations and BAKER with printmaking, the pair managed to unfetter another set, 'MICROBE' (2001).

Album rating: STEREOSCOPIC SOUNDWAVES (*4) / SEQUENCE OF THE NEGATIVE SPACE CHANGES (*4) / MICROBE (*4)

NICK BROCKNEY – vocals, multi (ex-CHILDREN'S ICE CREAM) / **STEVE BAKER** – bass, guitar, drums

Motorway / not iss.

1996. (7") *(MOTOR 015)* **I WISH I WAS AN ANGEL SO I COULD SLEEP ON THE MOON. /** – Japan

not iss. / Burnt Hair

May 97. (7") *<015>* **FUTURIST. / SEA OF TRANQUILITY**

Darla / Darla

Jul 97. (lp/cd) *<(DRL 042/+CD)>* **STEREOSCOPIC SOUNDWAVES**
– Arrival / Spiraea / 100101111 / A drop of golden sun / Sea of serenity / Kepler planet harmonies.

Kranky / Kranky

Aug 98. (lp/cd) *<(KRANK 029/+CD)>* **SEQUENCE OF NEGATIVE SPACE CHANGES**
– Butterflies / Sunspot / Venus / Synapse / Dustbot / Saturn / Oxygen / Sequence / Sunbeam / Mantric.

Darla / not iss.

Feb 99. (12"blue) *(DRL 072)* **PEOPLE MOVER. / SUBTRACTIVE SYNTHESIS**

not iss. / Red Antenna

Mar 01. (cd) *<RA 002>* **MICROBE**
– DNA / Diode / People mover (Hudson Bldng version) / Skyway / Minutiae / Nautical / Geometrid / Antigravity / Velcro / Module / Neutron / Vapor / Microbe / Polymer / Molecule / Galactica.

TOMPAULIN

Formed: Sheffield, England ... 1999 by STACEY, KATIE, AMOS, JAMIE HOLMAN and SIMON TROUGHT. Named after the Irish critic / lecturer of the same name, TOMPAULIN issued an abundance of singles between 2000 and 2002. All collected in the 'EVERYTHING WAS BEAUTIFUL AND NOTHING HURT' (2002) compilation, the group were still busy recording their debut album, 'THE TOWN AND THE CITY', for uber indie label 'Track & Field'. A wistful and delicate group reminscent of BELLE & SEBASTIAN, when the real Tom Paulin was asked to review them himself by the NME he quipped, "I think it's quite beautiful". Not only have the band been recording their eagerly awaited debut release but TROUGHT and HOLMAN have moonlighted in SISTER VANILLA and lead vocalist STACEY has recorded with CIARON SOUNDSYSTEM. Watch this space like a hawk!

Album rating: THE TOWN AND THE CITY (*7)

STACEY – vocals / **TAP** (b. SIMON TROUGHT) – guitar / **JAMIE HOLMAN** – bass / **CIARON** – drums

Action / not iss.

Nov 99. (7") *(TAKE 013)* **BALLAD OF THE BOOTBOYS. / WEDDING SONG**

Mar 00. (7"ep) *(WORM 58)* **CARCRASH E.P.**
– Slender / My life as a carcrash.
(above issued on 'Earworm')

Jun 00. (7") *(TAKE 014)* **SLENDER. / MY LIFE AS A CARCRASH**
(cd-s+=) *(TAKE 014CD)* – Them vs. us.

Track & Field / not iss.

Jan 01. (7") *(LANE 03)* **IT'S A GIRLS WORLD. / SECOND RATE REPUBLIC (4 track demo) / MY PERFECT GIRLFRIEND (4 track demo)**

Ugly Man / not iss.

Oct 01. (7") *(UGLY 27V)* **MY LIFE AT THE MOVIES. / THE LOVE DOCTOR**
(cd-s) *(UGLY 27)* – ('A'side) / All your favourite records / North.

Nov 01. (cd/lp) *(MAN 3/+V)* **THE TOWN AND THE CITY**
– My life at the movies / Richard Brautigan / Daydreaming / Short affairs / My life on buses / Westholme girls / Kicking and punching / The boy hairdresser / The good doctor / All the great writers and me / Je suis un partisan / Second rate republic. *(cd re-iss. Aug02; same)*

Track & Field / not iss.

Aug 02. (7"/cd-s) *(LANE 15/+CD)* **GIVE ME A RIOT IN THE SUMMERTIME. / SWING LOW STUART / THE SADNESS OF THINGS**

TOMPOT BLENNY

Formed: Nottingham, England ... 1992 initially as SPAM by singer/bassist CARL and guitarist CRAIG (yes, not only did they come up with one of the worst band names ever, they didn't use their surnames). They released only one song under this name, a track called 'KRYSTALS' on the Loughborough University label 'Quarantine'. After changing their meaty moniker to the no-less-obscure TOMPOT BLENNY (named after a British freshwater fish) they were one of the first bands signed to MATT HAYNES' label 'Shinkansen', which he started after the distressing demise of his legendary indie imprint 'Sarah'. They released the vinyl-only three-song 7" EP 'THINKING OF WAYS TO KEEP YOU WARM' (1996) and the 'GREEN IS THE BEST COLOUR' EP (1996), which were two of the first five singles on 'Shinakansen', the latter CD of which included all three tracks from 'THINKING ...' as well as the wonderfully-named 'THE SHORT-HAIRED GIRL IN THE LEFT-LEGGED PINEAPPLE', a tribute to a female worker in a strangely-named Loughborough record shop. The angular, sparse, mostly-acoustic, from-lullaby-to-janglebrain sound of these EPs was complemented by the addition of drummer ALAN on the 'FOUND UNDER BLANKETS' (2000) LP. This twee, tender, acoustic, breathy album placed a greater emphasis on a further-to-the-front-of-the-song rhythm section than previous efforts and showcased a much fuller sound.

Album rating: FOUND UNDER BLANKETS mini (*6)

CARL – vocals, guitar, bass / **CRAIG** – lead guitar

May 96. (7"m) *(SHINKANSEN 2)* **THINKING OF WAYS OF KEEPING YOU WARM. / SLEEPWAITING FOR TRAINS / SMILE AGAIN**
Nov 96. (7"ep) *(SHINKANSEN 5)* **GREEN IS THE BEST COLOUR**
– Dr. Fitzpiers / Green is the best colour / The short-haired girl in the left-legged pineapple.
(cd-ep+=) *(SHINKANSEN 5CD)* – THINKING OF WAYS OF KEEPING YOU WARM EP.

—— added **ALAN** – drums

Nov 00. (m-cd) *(SHINKANSEN 28)* **FOUND UNDER BLANKETS**
– Red light Ryan / Don't let her know / Ingleberry / Artless aliens / Real-life Scooby-Doo / Falling / Roses jar / Found under blankets.

Jenny TOOMEY (see under ⇒ TSUNAMI)

TO ROCOCO ROT

Formed: Berlin, Germany … 1994 by KREIDLER bassist, STEFAN SCHNEIDER, along with the LIPPOK brothers, ROBERT and RONALD. Latter day carriers of the experimental electronic flame originally lit by Germanic forebears such as KRAFTWERK and TANGERINE DREAM, the palindromically monikered TO ROCOCO ROT were originally conceived as a multi-media art project. Attempting to align these ideas within the context of post-rock minimalism, the trio made their musical debut in 1996 with an eponymous German-only album, drawing praise from both the alternative-rock and electronic scenes alike. The reception was positive enough for 'Kitty-Yo' to give the album a full UK release as '.CD' (1997), critics comparing the record's undulating grooves to Stateside practioners like TORTOISE, TRANS AM and ROME. By this point, the group had already begun to make waves in Britain and America with the more trance-Europe-expressive 'VEICULO', released some five months previously. Meanwhile, SCHNEIDER was developing his own project, KREIDLER, along with THOMAS KLEIN and ANDREAS REIHSE; they subsequently recruited DJ, DETLEF WEINRICH. Taking their moniker from an old clapped-out motorbike, KREIDLER conceived their own blend of Krautrock, fusing TORTOISE-esque musings with organic pop. A debut album, 'WEEKENDER' (1996), found its own groovy niche among the avant-garde indie anorak brigade. Now similar to MOUSE ON MARS, although a tad more conformist, the 'COLDNESS' single (remixed by Mute boss, DANIEL MILLER), was taken from their second set, 'APPEARANCE AND THE PARK' (1998). The post-electro combo issued the down-beat angular set 'THE AMATEUR VIEW' in 1999 and 'MUSIC IS A HUNGRY SOUND' in 2001, the latter was a collaboration with I-SOUND and boasted a broader musical range in terms of harmonics, hooks and general electro sounds. A few months after its release came another KREIDLER album, 'KREIDLER' (2001), an electro-dance effort that saw appearances from MOMUS and LEO GARCIA.

Album rating: TO ROCOCO ROT / .CD (*5) / VEICULO (*6) / THE AMATEUR VIEW (*7) / MUSIC IS A HUNGRY GHOST (*6) / Kreidler: WEEKENDER (*7) / APPEARANCE AND THE PARK (*7) / KREIDLER (*6)

ROBERT LIPPOK – guitar, electronics / **RONALD LIPPOK** – drums, effects / **STEFAN SCHNEIDER** – bass, organ, turntables (of KREIDLER)

EFA not iss.

1996. (cd) *(707120)* **TO ROCOCO ROT** — German
– Im lilienthal / Kritische masse I / Veramun / Dekothek / Polo star / Susse kuche / National velvet / Tour de repechage / Testfield / Parabola. *(UK-iss.Jul97 as '.CD' on 'Kitty Yo'+=; KITTY 010)* – Weiter / Schon sehr viel telefoniert / Kabine / Autonachmittag.

City Slang Emperor Jones

Feb 97. (cd/lp) *(efa 04990-2/-1) <15>* **VEICULO**
– Micromanaged / He loves me / Modern homes / Moto / Mit dir in der gegend / Leggiero / Geheimnis eines mantels / Extra / Fach / Lips / Merano / Allover dezent / Lift.
Oct 97. (12"ep)<cd-ep> *(efa 049941) <19>* **PARIS 25** Feb98
– Lift (denso) / Mit dir in der gegend (sehr) / Dual use / History on discs / Days between stations.
Apr 98. (12"ep) *(12FAT 007)* **SHE UNDERSTANDS THE DYNAMICS. / THINGS HAVE A WAY OF HAPPENING BY THEMSELVES / RUPTURE IN A FINE AND STEADY DAY**
(above issued on 'Fat Cat' below on 'Soul Static Sound')
Nov 98. (m-cd; as TO ROCOCO + D) *(SSS 23)* **TRRD**
– Set this / Sandy piece / As compasses / Go copabei / Allem was du machst / A day long.

City Slang Mute

Mar 99. (10") *(efa 087181)* **TELEMA. / TELEMA (LANGS) / EVEN**
Apr 99. (cd) *(847349-2) <9095>* **THE AMATEUR VIEW**
– I am in the world with you / Telema / Prado / A little asphalt here and there / This sandy piece / Tomorrow / Greenwich / Cars / She loves animals / Die dinge des lebens / Das blau und der Morgen.
Sep 99. (cd-s) *(efa 08724-2)* **CARS**
– Cars / Cars (variant) / Rocket fuel / Casper.
Apr 01. (cd/lp; as TO ROCOCO ROT and I-SOUND) *(20177-2/-1) <9153>* **MUSIC IS A HUNGRY GHOST** May01
– A number of things / For a moment / How we never went to bed / First / From dream to daylight / Your secrets, a few words / Along the route / Overhead / Koko / Pantone / Mazda in the mist / She tended to forget / The trance of travel.
Oct 01. (12"ep/cd-ep) *(20186-6/-2) <9163>* **PANTONE EP** Sep01
– Pantone (red) / The trance of travel (gets) / Brett zwei (plus) / I wanted to meet him / Fishermen dressed like Joseph Beuys.

KREIDLER

STEFAN SCHNEIDER – bass / **ANDREAS REIHSE** – keyboards / **THOMAS KLEIN** – drums / **DETLEF WEINRICH** – turntables, etc

Kiff/SM Mute

Nov 96. (lp/cd) *(KIFF 004/+CD)* **WEEKENDER**
– Traffic way / Shaun / Spat / La capital / Sand colour classic / Lio / Polaroid / Desto / Reflections / Hillwood / Telefon / La fille en beige / If / Schodringers katze. *(re-iss. Jun97 on 'Play It Again Sam' cd/lp; PIAS 556500-20/-10)*
Jun 97. (12"ep/cd-ep) *(EFA 07323-1/-2)* **RESPORT EP**
– Anti – Car (remixed by ERIK) / Boccia (remixed by ERIK) / Boccia (remixed by PYROLATOR) / Kookai (remixed by ROBERT LIPPOK) / Anti – Car (remixed by LAN) / Boccia (remixed by LAN). *(re-iss. & remixed Nov97; STU 04)*
(above on 'Stewardess' and could have been issued earlier in Germany)
Jul 97. (12"ep) *(KIFF 006)* **FECHTERIN. / SHIVER / OBJEKT METAL**
Apr 98. (12"ep) *(KIFF 010)* **AU PAIR (mixes). / GAIN / AUTOMATIC TUNNEL**
(cd-ep) *(KIFF 010CD)* – (first 2 tracks) / Now the necessity.
May 98. (cd/lp) *(KIFF 011 CD/LP) <9088>* **APPEARANCE AND THE PARK** Mar99
– Tuesday / Il songo di una cosa / Plus / She woke up and the world had changed / Necessity now / Good morning city / Sneak preview / Au pair / After the preview / Coldness / Venetian blind / Cube. *(cd+=)* – Coldness (Sunroof mix).
Sep 98. (12") *(KIFF 013)* **COLDNESS (mixes:- Sunroof mix / Shantel mix / April & Clyne velocity mix / In cold dub)**
(cd-s+=) *(KIFF 013CD)* – ('A'-Sunroof instrumental).

2000 Wonder Mute

Nov 00. (cd/lp) *(efa 64153-2/-1) <9144>* **KREIDLER**
– Circles / Mnemorex (with MOMUS) / Do it / The main / Bewitched / Sans soleil / Beauties / Ashes / The boy who wonders / Estatico (with LEO GARCIA) / Lanzelot.

TORTOISE

Formed: Chicago, Illinois, USA … 1990 by DOUG McCOMBS and JOHN HERNDON, who started jamming together with JOHN McENTIRE, BUNDY K BROWN and DAN BITNEY. This cult outfit initially crawled out of their collective shell with a series of early 90's EP's before finally unleashing their eponymous debut in '94. Remixed by STEVE ALBINI on the following year's blistering EP, 'RHYTHMS, RESOLUTIONS & CLUSTERS', the record proved TORTOISE to be the foremost purveyors of cut'n'mix avant-jazz. In 1996, their second album, 'MILLIONS NOW LIVING WILL NEVER DIE' (featuring the STEREOLAB trio of TIM, LAETITIA and MARY) was even better, opening with the psychedelic/Krautrock marathon of 'DJED'. This 20-minute track was subsequently given the 'Mo Wax' treatment, the extent of the band's appeal illustrated by their impressive run of collaborations over the course of the next year. The hard-working McENTIRE, who was also a part-time member of RED CRAYOLA and The SEA AND CAKE, returned to the studio at the end of the year, beavering away on what was yet another classic TORTOISE set, 'TNT' (1998). A segued journey from cool avant-jazz rock that unsuspectingly flowed into complex rhythmical landscapes, the record proved a hard listen for alt-rock buffs. JOHN McENTIRE (who also sidelined with the SEA AND CAKE), subsequently found his niche in soundtrack work, although 'REACH THE ROCK' (1999) was too pretentious and complex for some. After a one-off collaboration ('IN THE FISHTANK') with Dutch indie-meisters, The EX, TORTOISE resumed their position as electronica's top groovesters via their fourth album proper, 'STANDARDS' (2001) – their first for the seminal UK imprint, 'Warp'. McENTIRE and the group "prog"-ressed with every mixed-up, well-rehearsed bass and vibraphone beat, although it didn't quite match the experimentation of their previous work. The trio of PARKER, HERNDON and BITNEY were also behind ISOTOPE 17, an inevitable TORTOISE offshoot which catered to the guys' jazzier urges. Also featuring MATT LUX, ROB MAZUREK and SARA P. SMITH, the ensemble debuted in 1997 with 'THE UNSTABLE MOLECULE', a supple, low-key excursion into the kind of fusion territory where even most Chicago outfits, never mind conventional lo-fi experimentalists, wouldn't dare to venture. 'UTONIAN AUTOMATIC' (1999) extended their intrepid musical brief while the 'COMMANDER MINDFUCK/DESIGNER' remix EP, released the same year, offered up dynamic reworkings of selected live performances. 'WHO STOLE THE I WALKMAN?' followed in 2000.

Album rating: TORTOISE (*8) / RHYTHMS, RESOLUTIONS & CLUSTERS remixes (*6) / MILLIONS NOW LIVING WILL NEVER DIE (*9) / DIGEST COMPENDIUM OF … compilation (*7) / TNT (*8) / IN THE FISHTANK mini; with The Ex (*5) / STANDARDS (*7) / Isotope 217: THE UNSTABLE MOLECULE mini (*7) / COMMANDER MINDFUCK mini (*6) / UTONIAN AUTOMATIC (*6) / WHO STOLE THE I WALKMAN? (*4) / John McEntire: REACH THE ROCK soundtrack (*5)

JOHN McENTIRE – synthesizers, drums, vibraphone (ex-BASTRO, ex-SHRIMP BOAT) / **BUNDY K BROWN** – guitar, bass (ex-GASTR DE SOL) / **DOUG McCOMBS** – bass (ex-ELEVENTH DREAM DAY) / **JOHNNY HERNDON** – drums, synthesizers, vibraphone (ex-POSTER CHILDREN) / **DAN BITNEY** – synthesizers, percussion, multi (ex-TAR BABIES) / 6th member **CASEY RICE** – soundman

not iss. Torsion

1993. (7") *<003>* **MOSQUITO. / ONIONS WRAPPED IN RUBBER / GOOSENECK**

not iss. Soul Static

1994. (7") *<SOUL 7>* **WHY WE FIGHT. / WHITEWATER**
(UK-iss.Jan95; same)

City Slang Thrill Jockey

1994. (12") *<THRILL 006>* **LONESOME SOUND. / RESERVOIR / SHEETS**

TORTOISE (cont)

Jan 95. (cd/lp) *(EFA 04950-2/-1)* <THRILL 013> **TORTOISE**
– Magnet pulls through / Night air / Ry Cooder / Onions wrapped in rubber / Tin cans and twine / Spiderwebbed / His second story island / On noble / Flyrod / Cornpole brunch. *(cd-iss. remixed May97; TKCB 71016) (lp re-iss. Jun97 on 'Thrill Jockey'; THRILL 013)*

Apr 95. (12") *(Dodgey Beast; DS 3309)* **GAMERA. / CLIFF DWELLER SOCIETY**
(12") *(DS 3309S)* – ('A'mixes).

Jun 95. (m-cd/m-lp) *(EFA 04957-2/-1)* <THRILL 019> **RHYTHMS, RESOLUTIONS & CLUSTERS: REMIXED AND RARE**
– Alcohall / Your new rod / Cobwebbed / Match incident / Not quite east of the Ryan / Initial gesture protraction.

── **DAVE PAJO** – guitar (ex-SLINT) repl. BUNDY who formed DIRECTIONS IN MUSIC for one eponymous set; he and McCOMBS were also part of alt-supergroup, PULLMAN.

Jan 96. (cd/lp) *(EFA 04972-2/-1)* <THRILL 025> **MILLIONS NOW LIVING WILL NEVER DIE**
– Djed / Glass museum / A survey / The taut and the tame / Dear grandma and grandpa / Along the banks of rivers. *(cd-iss. Japanese version May97; TKCB 70931)*

Apr 96. (12"; by TORTOISE Vs U.N.K.L.E./JOHN McENTIRE) *(SHELL 001)* <TJ 12.1> **DJED (bruise blood mix). / TJED**

Jul 96. (12"; by TORTOISE Vs BUNDY BROWN) <TJ 12.2> **ROME**

Jul 96. (12"; by TORTOISE Vs OVAL) *(SHELL 002)* <TJ 12.3> **MUSIC FOR WORK GROUPS EP**
– The bubble economy (mix by Marcus Popp) / Learning curve (mix by Marcus Popp).

Sep 96. (12"; by TORTOISE VS SPRING HEEL JACK) *(SHELL 003)* <TJ 12.4> **GALAPAGOS 1 (Spring Heel Jack remix). / REFERENCE RESISTANCE GATE (Jim O'Rourke remix)**
(re-iss. Jun97 on 'Thrill Jockey'; TJ 124)

Oct 96. (12"; by TORTOISE Vs LUKE VIBERT/BUNDY K BROWN) *(SHELL 004)* <TJ 12.5> **THE TAUT AND THE TAME. / FIND THE ONE (WAIT, ABSTRACTION NO . . .)**

── In 1996, they also shared a single with STEREOLAB, 'VAUS' / 'SPEEDY CAR', released on 'Duophonic'; *D-UHF-D12*)

── **JEFF PARKER** – guitar; repl. PAJO who formed AERIAL M

Mar 98. (cd/d-lp) *(EFA 08705-2/-1)* <THRILL 050> **TNT**
– Swung from the gutters / Ten-day interval / I set my face to the hillside / The equator / A simple way to go faster than light that does not work / The suspension bridge at Iguazu Falls / Four-day interval / In Sarah, Mencken, Christ, and Beethoven there were women and men / Almost always is nearly enough / Jetty / Everglade.

Jul 98. (ltd-12"; TORTOISE VS. DERRICK CARTER) *(087096)* **IN SARAH, MENCKEN, CHRIST, AND BEETHOVEN THERE WERE WOMEN AND MEN**
– (D's winter crazy mix) / (D's winter outtake).
(above was issued on 'Rephlex' (below on 'Fishtank/Konkurrent')

May 99. (m-cd/m-lp; by TORTOISE & THE EX) *(FISH 5 CD/LP)* **IN THE FISHTANK**
– Lawn of the limb / Pooh song / Central heating / Pleasure as usual / Did you comb / Huge hidden spaces.

Feb 01. (cd/lp) *(WARP CD/LP 081)* <THRILL 089> **STANDARDS** [Warp / Thrill Jockey]
– Seneca / Eros / Benway / Firefly / Six pack / Eden 2 / Monica / Blackjack / Eden 1 / Speakeasy.

– compilations, others, etc. –

May 97. (cd) *Thrill Jockey; <(TKCB 70932)>* **A DIGEST COMPENDIUM OF TORTOISE'S WORLD**   1996
– Tin cans & twine / Alcohall / Night air / Gooseneck / Onions wrapped in rubber / Spiderwebbed / Cobnebbed / Your new rod / Ry Cooder (the beer incident) / Not quite east of the Ryan / Reservoir / Cornpone brunch / Whitewater / Initial gesture protraction.

Apr 98. (cd) *Thrill Jockey; <(TKCB 71016)>* **TORTOISE REMIXED** (all the 4 collaboration/Vs singles)   1996

Oct 01. (m-cd) *Thrill Jockey; <(THRILL 122-2)>* **GENTLY CUPPING THE CHIN OF THE APE**
– Waihopai / Peering / Seneca (video) / Tortoise 98 (video) / Rehearsal 2001 (video).

ISOTOPE 217

JEFF PARKER – guitar / **JOHN HERNDON** – percussion / **DAN BITNEY** – percussion / **MATT LUX** – bass (of HEROIC DOSES) / **ROB MAZUREK** – trumpet (of CHICAGO UNDERGROUND DUO) / **SARA P. SMITH** – trombone

Jan 98. (lp/cd) <(THRILL 049/+CD)> **THE UNSTABLE MOLECULE** [Thrill Jockey / Thrill Jockey Nov97]
– Kryptonite smokes the red line / Beneath the undertow / La jetee / Phonometrics / Prince Namor / Audio boxing.

Mar 99. (m-cd) <(ASTO 6 CD/LP)> **COMMANDER MINDFUCK**
– Hodah / User password: Lebar.
(above credited DESIGNER – CASEY RICE – and issued on 'Aesthetics')

Aug 99. (lp/cd) <(THRILL 063/+2)> **UTONIAN AUTOMATIC**
– Luh / Audio champion / New beyond / Rest for the wicked / Looking after life on Mars / Solaris / Real MC's.

Aug 00. (lp/cd) <(THRILL 080/+CD)> **WHO STOLE THE I WALKMAN?**
– Ham-o-lodge / Space krikts / Meta bass / Moonlex / Kidtronix / (untitled) / Moot ang / Sint_D / Input / (untitled) / (untitled).

JOHN McENTIRE

── his debut solo album (although shared with others)

Feb 99. (7"pic-d) <(HEF 13)> **split w/ SEA AND CAKE** [Hefty / Hefty]

Mar 99. (cd) <(HEFT 14CD)> **REACH THE ROCK** (Original Soundtrack)
– In a thimble (TORTOISE) / Criminal record / Overview / Stolen car / Drift (BUNDY K. BROWN) / Quinn goes to town / Window lights (SEA AND CAKE) / Reverse migraine (POLVO) / Lise arrives / The kiss / Main title / Dreams of being king (DIANOGAH). *(lp-iss.Nov99; HEFT 014LP)*

TOWN & COUNTRY

Formed: Chicago, Illinois, USA . . . late 90's by JOSH ABRAMS, BEN VIDA, LIZ PAYNE and JIM DORLING. Utilising relatively exotic instrumentation such as contrabass and harmonium, and manipulating it into highly complex, note-perfect anti-structures of sound, the quartet followed in the established Chicago mould, at least in terms of their uncompromising bent for experimentation. Where they differed was in their wholly acoustic approach to their minimalistic art, always keeping the volume to an initially disconcerting minimum and drawing obvious inspiration from the likes of JOHN FAHEY. Signed to where else but 'Thrill Jockey' after the release of an eponymous 1998 debut set, the group evolved their subtle aesthetic over the albums 'IT ALL HAS TO DO WITH IT' (2000) and 'C'MON' (2002).

Album rating: TOWN & COUNTRY (*6) / DECLARATION DAY mini (*5) / IT ALL HAS TO DO WITH IT (*5) / C'MON (*7)

BEN VIDA – guitar, trumpet / **JOSH ABRAMS** – piano, contrabass / **LIZ PAYNE** – contrabass / **JIM DORLING** – harmonium

Jan 99. (cd) <(BOXCD 006)> **TOWN & COUNTRY** [Box Media / Box Media Nov98]
– The Loam hazard / Crossings / And see / But the lids / So that I may come back.

May 00. (m-cd) <(THRILL 083CD)> **DECLARATION DAY** [Thrill Jockey / Thrill Jockey]
– Give your baby a standing ovation / Spicer / Off season. *(re-iss. Mar02; same)*

Oct 00. (lp/cd) <(THRILL 088/+CD)> **IT ALL HAS TO DO WITH IT**
– Hindeburg / Hat versus food / Fine Italian hand / That old feeling. *(cd re-iss. Mar02; same)*

Feb 02. (cd) <(THRILL 114CD)> **C'MON**
– Going to Kamakura / I'm appealing / Garden / The bells / I am so very cold / Palms / Bookmobile.

── note that avant-garde, PILLOW (LIZ PAYNE, BEN VIDA, FRED LONBERG-HOLM + MIKE COLLIGAN), released a few post-millennium releases, 'PILLOW', 'FIELD ON WATER' and 'THREE HENRIES'.

TRACK STAR

Formed: San Francisco, California, USA . . . early 1990's by WYATT CUSICK and MATTHEW TROY. Having already featured on a couple of split singles, TRACK STAR released their debut EP, 'SOMETIME, WHAT'S THE DIFFERENCE', in 1995. The music was sensitive, jangling indie-pop in the same vein as bands such as SEBADOH, and displayed no ambition to stretch the genre. The band's unwillingness to experiment was again evident on their first full-length album 'COMMUNICATION BREAKS'. The album was competent enough and may have made more of an impact had it been released 10 years earlier however, by 1997 this limited sub genre had been wrung dry. The band continued to coast on their next release, 'LION DESTROYED THE WHOLE WORLD', and once again the album was nice but not spectacular enough to transcend its lack of originality.

Album rating: COMMUNICATION BREAKS (*6) / LION DESTROYED THE WHOLE WORLD (*7)

WYATT CUSICK – vocals, guitar, bass / **MATTHEW TROY** – vocals, guitar, bass / + drum machine

1994. (7") <KD 002> **NO BIG DEAL. / PUSH IT** [not iss. / Kick Down]

1994. (c; split w/ RAISLER) **RAISLER SEXACUTE TRACK STAR**
(above was also issued on 'Bad Deal Hypenosis' records)

Oct 95. (10"m-lp) <SG 024> **SOMETIMES, WHAT'S THE DIFFERENCE?** [not iss. / Silver Girl]

1996. (7"ep) <CRD 02> **CRASHED OUT / AUGUST. / (other by Kid Dynamo)** [not iss. / Chocolate River]

Nov 97. (lp/cd) <DIE 002/+CD> **COMMUNICATION BREAKS** [Die Young Stay / Die Young Stay Oct97]
– Alien idea / Lifestyles . . . / These horses carry blood / One hundred degrees / Payback / All hands / Low rent – High life / Revenge fantasy / Owen's ghetto punch / Sooner it dies / Big fuck you / The something very winning / Dead today / Bleeding guns / This ios number forty two / West Coast weather.

1999. (7") **REMOVABLE PARTS. / THE VIEW FROM SPACE** [not iss. / Suicide Squeeze]

1999. (7") <OMNI 032> **THE CHORD. / GREEN TO GOLD** [not iss. / Omnibus]

── CUSICK joined The AISLERS SET for a time in the late 90's

── **BRIAN GIRGUS** – drums (ex-LOWERCASE) repl. drummer/drum machine

May 02. (cd) <(BLR 011)> **LION DESTROYED THE WHOLE WORLD** [Better Looking / Better Looking]
– Feet first / The one we play / Green to gold / Pretty close to nothing / October! / November / Goodbye to the dream / Something to do / Amy, tell me why / Cross country / The end / Cities on cities.

TRAM

Formed: London, England... 1997 by singer/songwriter PAUL ANDERSON and drummer NICK AVERY. After playing together in a '90s power-pop band, ANDERSON and AVERY decided to broaden their horizons and create music more pertinent to their own vision. They signed to independent label 'Jetset', then in 1999 released debut LP 'HEAVY BLACK FRAME'. Recorded with the assistance of friends CLIVE and MARTINE from BROKEN DOG, TRAM's debut was an emotional, intimate collection of gentle, mellow instrumental arrangements, plaintive lyrics, and hushed vocals (from ANDERSON). There was a New Romantic quality to ANDERSON's yearning, and they drew comparisons with SMOG and LOW, although if anything the TRAM sound was even more muted and sedate. Within 'HEAVY...' was a diverse, yet subtle, range of influences, like the country-tinged 'WHEN IT'S ALL OVER' and the jazzy 'EXPECTATIONS'. Second album 'FREQUENTLY ASKED QUESTIONS' followed in 2001, and expanded on the orchestral range and the solemnity of their debut. Although using some additional musicians, ANDERSON and AVERY worked largely alone, recording the vocals and instrumental parts separately, then mixing them on computer. AVERY's sparse rhythms and beats were accompanied by pianos and synthesizers, and occasionally violins ('YES BUT FOR HOW LONG'), saxophone ('FOLK'), and a JOHN PARISH slide guitar on their cover of Tim Buckley's 'ONCE I WAS'. Now with a budget at their disposal, TRAM entered the studio to record their third album 'A KIND OF CLOSURE', employing horns and strings and looking to achieve a 'live' feel. '...CLOSURE' maintains the resonance of their previous two albums, although it didn't represent any significant progression.

Album rating: HEAVY BLACK FRAME (*6) / FREQUENTLY ASKED QUESTIONS (*7) / A KIND OF CLOSURE (*5)

PAUL ANDERSON – vocals, guitar, etc. / **NICK AVERY** – drums / with **IDA AKESSON** – keyboards / **IAN PAINTER** – bass

		Piao!	Jetset
Jul 97.	(7") *(PIAO 11)* **NOTHING LEFT TO SAY. / I'VE BEEN HERE ONCE BEFORE**		–
Jun 98.	(7") *(PIAO 14)* **HIGH GROUND. / INSTRUMENTAL**		–
Mar 99.	(cd/lp) *(PIAO 16 CD/LP)* *<JETSET 23>* **HEAVY BLACK FRAME**		Sep99

– Nothing left to say / Expectations / Too scared to sleep / Like clockwork / Home / I've been here once before / High ground / When it's all over / Reason why / You can go now (if you want).

		Liquefaction	not iss.
Mar 99.	(7"ep) *(Duske 10)* **SONGS FROM THE STURDY CHARIOT**		–

– Too scared to sleep / I can't lie to you / Underneath the ceiling / Prom.

—— added **FIONA BRICE** – piano, violin / + others

		Setanta	Jetset
Feb 01.	(cd) *(SETCD 083)* *<JETSET 35>* **FREQUENTLY ASKED QUESTIONS**		

– Now we can get on with our lives / Giving up / Once I was / Yes but for how long / He walk alone / This sacred day / Folk / Social disease / Are you satisfied / Underneath the ceiling / Light a candle on my birthday.

| May 02. | (cd) *(SETCD 095)* *<JETSET 45>* **A KIND OF CLOSURE** | | |

– Three years / Forlorn labour / A kind of closure / A painful education / Theme / Forgive me dear / Fools / Only then / The hope has been taken away / You let me down / Understand.

TRANS AM

Formed: Maryland & Washington DC, USA... 1990 by college graduates, PHIL MANLEY, NATHAN MEANS and SEBASTIAN THOMPSON. More tongue-in-cheek than many of their supposed post-rock contemporaries, TRANS AM set out to prove that Americans do actually have a sense of irony, using experimental dexterity to exaggerate the cliches of prime 70's prog-rock (i.e. YES, KING CRIMSON, etc) on their eponymous debut mini-set. After a lengthy gestation period, the JOHN McENTIRE (TORTOISE)-produced record eventually emerged on 'Thrill Jockey' early in 1996. Exactly a year later, the band returned with sophomore effort, 'SURRENDER TO THE NIGHT' (1997), its cheesy title(s) belying a more straightforwardly retro outing that paid homage to the likes of KRAFTWERK. The following year, TRANS AM continued their back-to-the-future road trip with 'THE SURVEILLANCE' album, a more sophisticated hybrid of digitally enhanced instrumental rock ambience. TRANS AM returned in 1999 to issue their folly into the world of psychedelic instrumentations, 'FUTUREWORLD', a sparse, robotic, shimmering set full of acoustic warmth and minimal charm. One year later, they delivered the Japanese-only set of rarities, B-sides and singles, entitled 'YOU CAN ALWAYS GET WHAT YOU WANT' and the brilliant 'RED LINE' album, which packed a personal post-rock punch and silenced most of their critics who claimed they were average "TORTOISE imitators". However, follow-up 'T.A.' (2002) was cited as their weakest set to date, proving that the musos might have a point.

Album rating: TRANS AM (*7) / SURRENDER TO THE NIGHT (*5) / THE SURVEILLANCE (*6) / FUTUREWORLD (*6) / YOU CAN ALWAYS GET WHAT YOU WANT (*5) / RED LINE (*7) / T.A. (*4)

PHIL MANLEY – guitar, keyboards / **NATHAN MEANS** – bass, keyboards / **SEBASTIAN THOMPSON** – drums, drum programming

		not iss.	S.K.A.M.
1993.	(7"ep) **S.K.A.M. split** (live in Chapel Hill)	–	

– American kooter / Simulacrum / Man-machine.

		not iss.	Strength
1995.	(7") **NOW YOU DIE, THRIDDLE FOOL. / (other by other artist)**	–	

		City Slang	Thrill Jockey
Apr 96.	(m-cd/m-lp) *(efa 04977-2/-1)* *<THRILL 024>* **TRANS AM**		Jan96

– Ballbados / Enforcer / Technology corridor / Trans am / Firepoker / A single ray of light on an otherwise cloudy day / Prowler / Orlando / Love affair / American kooter. *(cd re-iss. Dec00; same as US)*

| Nov 96. | (12"ep) *<HAPPY 06>* **ILLEGAL ASS** | – | |

– Illegal ass / Koln / Randy groove.

—— <issued on 'Happy Go Lucky'> *(UK-iss.Apr98; same as US)*

| Feb 97. | (cd/lp) *(efa 04988-2/-0)* *<THRILL 038>* **SURRENDER TO THE NIGHT** | | |

– Motr / Cologne / Illegalize it / Love commander / Rough justice / Zero tolerance / Tough love / Night dreaming / Night dancing / Carboforce / Surrender to the night.

| Mar 98. | (cd/lp) *<THRILL 054/+LP>* **THE SURVEILLANCE** | – | |

– Armed response / Prowler '97 / The campaign / Access control / Endgame / E.S.I. / Home security / Extreme measures / Shadow boogie / Stereo situation. *(UK cd-iss. Jun00 on 'City Slang'; 845642-2)*

| Aug 98. | (12") *(PM 003)* **INSTICTIVE CODES** | | – |

(above issued on 'Phont Music')

		Thrill Jockey	Thrill Jockey
Apr 99.	(cd/lp) *<(THRILL 062/+LP)>* **FUTUREWORLD**		

– 1999 / Television eyes / Futureworld / City in flames / Am rhein / Cocaine computer / Runners standing still / Futureworld II / Positron / Sad and young. *(re-iss. Oct01; same)*

| 1999. | (cd-ep) *<URA-006>* **WHO DO WE THINK YOU ARE?** (Australian Tour EP) | | – |

– Funky guy / Slow response / Surface of the sun / When the method is right (pressure mix) / Crystal lite (positive mix) / Wildwood flower.
(above issued on 'Spunk!')

| May 00. | (cd) *<(THRILL 082)>* **YOU CAN ALWAYS GET WHAT YOU WANT (compilation)** | | |

– American kooter (live) / Simulacrum (live) / Man-machine (live) / Illegal ass / Koln / Randy groove / Now you die, thriddle fool / Strong sensations / Security breach / Asian taste / Nazi/hippie empire / Am rhein (party mix) / Monica's story / Love commander (live) / Surrender (live) / Rough justice (live) / Night dancing (live). *(re-iss. Oct01; same)*

| Sep 00. | (cd/d-lp) *<(THRILL 087)>* **RED LINE** | | |

– Let's take the fresh step together / I want it all / Casual Friday / Polizei (zu spat) / Village in bubbles / For now and forever / Play in the summer / Where do you want to fuck today? / Don't bundle up / Mr. Simmons / Diabolical cracker / I'm coming down / The dark gift / Air and space / Talk you all tight / Lunar landing / Bad cat / Slow response / Getting very nervous / Ragged agenda / Shady grove. *(re-iss. Oct01; same)*

| Oct 01. | (m-cd/m-lp; as TRANS CHAMPS) *<(THRILL 107/+LP)>* **DOUBLE EXPOSURE** | | |

– Give it to you / The big machine / First comes Sunday morning / Then comes Saturday night / Somebody like you.

| May 02. | (cd/lp) *<(THRILL 109 CD/LP)>* **T.A.** | | |

– Cold war / Molecules / Run with me / Bonn / Basta / Different kind of love / You will be there / Derek Fisher / Party station / Positive people / Afternight / C sick / Feed on me / Infinite wavelength.

| Sep 02. | (cd-ep) *<(THRILL 1226)>* **EXTREMIXXX** (remixes) | | |

– Cold war (a grape dope bombs and more mix) / Infinite wavelength (Dabrye mix) / Cold war (Jonathan Kwar is stupid mix) / Different kind of love (Dan the automator mix) / Different kind of love (Prefuse 73 mix) / Different kind of love (Prefuse 73 instrumental).

TRASH CAN SINATRAS

Formed: Irvine, Ayrshire, Scotland... late 80's by FRANCIS READ, PAUL LIVINGSTON, GEORGE McDAID, and brothers JOHN and STEPHEN DOUGLAS. Possibly a band out of their time, TRASH CAN SINATRAS early 90's material echoed the sounds of the early 80's 'Postcard' era, particularly AZTEC CAMERA. Signed to 'Go! Discs', the quintet released their debut EP, 'OBSCURITY KNOCKS' (chancing their arm a bit with a title that would later become a self-fulfilling prophecy!), a follow-up track, 'ONLY TONGUE CAN TELL', preceding the band's debut album, 'CAKE' (1990). As well as breaking into the UK Top 75, the record was a surprise success Stateside, eventually spending three months in the US Top 200 after gaining exposure through the influential college radio circuit. With the pressure on to "crack America", transatlantic touring kept the 'SINATRAS' off the domestic scene for almost three years. When they did return, McDAID had been replaced by DAVID HUGHES on UK Top 50 comeback set, 'I'VE SEEN EVERYTHING' (1993), the album's relative success promoted by the preceding single, 'HAYFEVER'. Marginalised in Britain and overtaken by the grunge scene in the States, TCS went to ground for a further three years, re-emerging with a series of singles in mid '96. An accompanying third album, 'A HAPPY POCKET', failed to win any new support while the old fans appeared to have unceremoniously dumped them, obviously preffering a bit of GARBAGE instead. Around the same time, the TCS worked on stage with the production of Irvine Welsh's 'Marabou Stork Nightmares'. STEPHEN DOUGLAS soon resurfaced in a new outfit, JOHNSON, a gothic NICK CAVE/SCOTT WALKER-esque 5-piece featuring one-time members of The JOHNSTONE BRASS BAND, WONDER BOY BUCKLEY and SLINKY. A handful of singles (with FRANCIS as co-producer) appeared on their own 'Play' imprint around the turn of the decade. JOHNSON's talented frontman PETER ROSS continued to write songs and was the mainman behind OSTLE BAY, a collaboration with TRASH CAN SINATRAS. Their recent album, 'LOVE FROM OSTLE BAY' (2002), displayed a delicate blend of early arty 'Postcard' moods although just a tad out of time. • **Covered:** SENSES WORKING OVERTIME (Xtc) / LITTLE THINGS (THAT KEEP US TOGETHER) (Scott Walker) / BORN FREE (hit; Matt Monro) / YOU ONLY LIVE TWICE (John Barry).

Album rating: CAKE (*6) / I'VE SEEN EVERYTHING (*5) / A HAPPY POCKET (*4) / Ostle Bay: LOVE FROM OSTLE BAY (*6)

FRANCIS READ (b. 1966) – vocals / **PAUL LIVINGSTON** (b. 1970) – guitar / **JOHN DOUGLAS** (b. 1963) – guitar / **GEORGE McDAID** (b. 1966) – bass / **STEPHEN DOUGLAS** – drums

                                                                            Go! Discs   Polygram

Feb 90. (7"ep/c-ep) *(GOD/+MC 34)* **OBSCURITY KNOCKS EP**
 – Obscurity knocks / Who's he? / The best man's fall.
 (12"ep+=/cd-ep+=) *(GOD X/CD 34)* – Drunken chorus.

May 90. (7"/c-s) *(GOD/+MC 41)* **ONLY TONGUE CAN TELL. / USELESS**
 (12"+=/cd-s+=) *(GOD X/CD 41)* – Tonight you belong to me.

Jun 90. (cd/c/lp) *(<828 201-2/-4/-1>)* **CAKE**   74   Jan91
 – Obscurity knocks / Maybe I should drive / Thrupenny tears / Even the odd / The best man's fall / Circling the circumference / Funny / Only tongue can tell / You made me feel / January's little joke.

Oct 90. (7"/c-s) *(GOD/+MC 46)* **CIRCLING THE CIRCUMFERENCE. / MY MISTAKE**
 (12"+=/cd-s+=) *(GOD X/CD 46)* – White horses.

Jan 91. (c-s) *<869 314-4>* **OBSCURITY KNOCKS / WHO'S HE**   –

—— **DAVID HUGHES** – bass; repl. McDAID

Apr 93. (7"/c-s) *(GOD/+MC 98)* **HAYFEVER. / SAY**   61
 (12"+=/cd-s+=) *(GOD X/CD 98)* – Kangaroo court / Skin diving.

May 93. (cd/c/lp) *(<828 408-2/-4/-1>)* **I'VE SEEN EVERYTHING**   50
 – Easy read / Hayfever / Bloodrush / Worked a miracle / The perfect reminder / Killing the cabinet / Orange fell / I'm immortal / Send for Henny / Iceberg / One at a time / I've seen everything / The hairy years / Earlies.

Jun 93. (7"/c-s) *(GOD/+MC 100)* **I'VE SEEN EVERYTHING. / HOUSEPROUD / I'M THE ONE WHO FAINTED**
 (12"+=/cd-s+=) *(GOD X/CD 100)* – Ask Davy.

Nov 95. (cd-ep) *(TCMCD 1)* **FIVE HUNGRY JOES E.P.**   –
 – No gasoline / Mr. Grisly / Aberration / A boy and a girl / I must fly. *(note:- this EP was a mail-order promo)*

Mar 96. (7"ep/cd-ep) *(GOD/+CD 141)* **THE MAIN ATTRACTION EP**   –
 – The main attraction / Stainless Stephen / Charlie's atlas / Jane's estranged.

May 96. (7"/c-s) *(GOD/+MC 147)* **TWISTED AND BENT. / MR. GRISLY**
 (cd-s+=) *(GODCD 147)* – No gasoline / Aberration.

May 96. (cd/c/lp) *(<828 696-2/-4/-1>)* **A HAPPY POCKET**   Sep96
 – Outside / Twisted and bent / Unfortunate age / To sir with love / Make yourself at home / The main attraction / How can I apply . . . ? / The pop place / The genius I was / The sleeping policeman / I must fly / I'll get them in / The safecracker / The therapist.

Jul 96. (7"/c-s) *(GOD/+MC 151)* **HOW CAN I APPLY. / SAVE ME**   –
 (cd-s+=) *(GODCD 151)* – A worm with a head / Little things (that keep us together).

Dec 96. (7"/c-s) *(GOD/+MC 157)* **TO SIR WITH LOVE. / CLAW**
 (12"+=/cd-s+=) *(GOD X/CD 157)* – A boy and a girl / You only live twice.

—— disbanded the following year; STEPHEN turned up in JOHNSON

JOHNSON

PETER ROSE – vocals, guitar / **STEPHEN DOUGLAS** – drums, percussion, acoustic guitar, vocals / **RAFE FITZPATRICK** – violin / **CLARE HANLEY** – cornet, organ, vocals / **JOHNNY MITCHELL** – bass

Feb 99. (7") *(PLAY 001)* **TRIPPING WITH THE MOONLIGHT. / FLIPSIDE HEAD**

May 99. (7") *(PLAY 002)* **SAVOURY BODY SHOW. / SWEAR I WAS THERE**   –

Oct 99. (7") *(PLAY 003)* **SKIN AND GOLD. / PARADISE (live)**   –

Apr 00. (7") *(PLAY 004)* **BLONDE ON BLUE. / BARE AND BLUE**   –

—— there is a JOHNSON CD-album in the pipeline

OSTLE BAY

PETER ROSE – vocals, guitar / **STEPHEN DOUGLAS** – drums, percussion / **JOHN DOUGLAS** – guitar, keyboards / **PAUL LIVINGSTON** – guitar / **GRANT WILSON** – bass / **JODY STODDART** – guitar, harmonica (of HEIRLOOM) / with also **CLARE HANLEY** – cornet

Sep 02. (cd) *(PLAY 008)* **LOVE FROM OSTLE BAY**
 – Ostle Bay / Dusting the sun / The one / Music box / Did I ever say / Wish I was with you / Won't you / Windows on the pavement / Tuesday / Farming for diamonds / Out of those eyes.

TRASHMONK
(see under ⇒ DREAM ACADEMY; 80's section)

TRAVIS

Formed: Glasgow, Scotland . . . 1991 as GLASS ONION by ANDY DUNLOP and NEIL PRIMROSE, who'd both been members of RUNNING RED. Songwriting singer FRAN HEALY was invited to join the fresh-faced guitar-pop quintet (with the MARTYN brothers), replacing the original female vocalist soon after. In 1993, FRAN's mother advanced the lads some cash to cut a demo and this led to a publishing contract with 'Sony'. Winning a trip to the New Music Seminar in New York via first place in a talent contest might've given them an early break had they attended, although they did manage to squeeze out an eponymous EP the same year. With the band going nowhere fast, changes had to be made and by March '96, the MARTYN brothers had made way for FRAN's Glasgow School Of Art chum, DOUGIE PAYNE (ANDY had also been a student); TRAVIS were now in circulation. Following a self-financed debut single, 'ALL I WANT TO DO IS ROCK', the quartet were taken under the wing of (ex-Go! Discs man) Andy McDonald's 'Independiente' (still through 'Sony') early in '97. Subsequently relocating to London, TRAVIS released their controversial follow-up single, 'U16 GIRLS', apparently a paeon to the charms of underage females. A re-vamp of their hard-to-find debut single followed it into the Top 40 and suddenly TRAVIS were one of the hippest new names on the block. Though HEALY was a charismatic frontman, the Top 10 debut album, 'GOOD FEELING', illustrated at the time the one-dimensional nature of much of their material. Nevertheless, the record did spawn two further Top 40 hits, 'TIED TO THE 90'S' and 'HAPPY', indicating that there was at least some potential for the future. After a relatively quiet '98 – although 'MORE THAN US' became their biggest hit to date at No.16 – TRAVIS were back the following March. Taking a softer, laid back approach (70's BREAD come to mind!), the quartet achieved a deserved second Top 20 spot with the beautiful ballad 'WRITING TO REACH YOU'. Further successes came in the shape of 'DRIFTWOOD', 'WHY DOES IT ALWAYS RAIN ON ME?' and 'TURN', all songwriting masterpieces from the critically acclaimed No.1 follow-up set, 'THE MAN WHO' (1999). TRAVIS were fast becoming the United Kingdom's No.1 band and by the start of the year 2000 they were given that accolade by winning the now prestigious Brit award. OASIS (who had been tops until recently!) invited nice guy HEALY and Co to support them on a US tour, the American audiences eventually being won over by their sheer honest enthusiasm and talent. While many critics predictably put the boot in, you could bet your bottom dollar they had a secret copy of UK chart-topper 'THE INVISIBLE BAND' (2001) hidden away for furtive listening pleasure. TRAVIS simply write great songs, occasionally something more but rarely anything less. On first listen, the deceptively simple single, 'SING' may sound trite, but its subtle, banjo inflected power deepens with every spin, enveloping you in a dizzying aura of elemental truth. Similarly the lyrics of 'SIDE' were the butt of cheap jibes yet their sentiment leaks into the consciousness like a zen koan. The band's lack of image and endearing avoidance of any flirtations with the vagaries of musical fashion merely accentuates the strength of the material. While there was nothing on the album that matched the searing melancholy of say, 'WRITING TO REACH YOU', chances are you'll still be playing this album next year, and the next, and the next . . . However, disaster struck the band on the 9th of July 2002, when drummer PRIMROSE accidently hit his upper torso on the bottom of a swimming pool in France. He underwent extensive surgery to his neck, accumulating in the cancellation of the group's entire European tour (as well as V2002). All was said to be well, though, with PRIMROSE making a slow but steady recovery, the group being set to enter the studio. • **Covered:** BE MY BABY (Ronettes) / BABY ONE MORE TIME (Britney Spears) / ALL THE YOUNG DUDES (Mott The Hoople) / HERE COMES THE SUN (Beatles).

Album rating: GOOD FEELING (*7) / THE MAN WHO (*8) / THE INVISIBLE BAND (*7)

GLASS ONION

FRAN HEALY (b. Stafford, England) – vocals, guitar; repl. female / **ANDY DUNLOP** – guitar / **NEIL PRIMROSE** – drums / . . . **MARTYN** – bass / . . . **MARTYN** – keyboards

                                                                own label   not iss.

Nov 93. (cd-ep) *(GLASSCD 001)* **GLASS ONION**
 – Dream on / The day before / Free soul / Whenever she comes around.

TRAVIS

—— **DOUGIE PAYNE** – bass; repl. the MARTYN brothers

                                                                Red
                                                                Telephone   not iss.

Oct 96. (10"ep) *(PHONE 001)* **ALL I WANT TO DO IS ROCK. / THE LINE IS FINE / FUNNY THING**
                                                                Independiente Independiente

Mar 97. (7"pic-d/c-s) *(ISOM 1 S/CS)* **U16 GIRLS. / HAZY SHADES OF GOLD / GOOD TIME GIRLS**   40   –
 (c-s+=/cd-s+=) *(ISOM 1MS)* – Good feeling.

Jun 97. (7") *(SOM 3S) <6080>* **ALL I WANT TO DO IS ROCK. / BLUE ON A BLACK WEEKEND**   39   Apr98
 (cd-s+=) *(ISOM 3MS)* – Combing my hair.
 (cd-s) *(ISOM 3SMS)* – ('A'side) / "20" / 1922.

Aug 97. (7"/cd-s) *(ISOM 5S/+MS) <6084>* **TIED TO THE 90's. / ME BESIDE YOU**   30   Apr98
 (cd-s) *(ISOM 5MS)* – ('A'side) / City in the rain / Whenever she comes around / Standing on my own.

Sep 97. (cd/c/lp) *(ISOM 1 CD/MC/LP) <68239>* **GOOD FEELING**   9   Oct97
 – All I want to do is rock / U16 girls / Line is fine / Good day to die / Good feeling / Midsummer nights dreamin' / Tied to the 90's / I love you anyways / Happy / More than us / Falling down / Funny thing. *(re-iss. Nov99; same) (re-dist.Jun01)* – hit No.19

Oct 97. (c-s) *(ISOM 6CS) <6081>* **HAPPY / UNBELIEVERS**   38   Apr98
 (cd-s+=) *(ISOM 6MS)* – Everyday faces.
 (cd-s) *(ISOM 6SMS)* – ('A'side) / When I'm feeling blue (days of the week) / Mother.

Mar 98. (7"ep/c-ep/cd-ep) *(ISOM 11 S/CS/MS)* **MORE THAN US E.P.**   16   –
 – More than us (with Anne Dudley) / Give me some truth / All I want to do is rock (with Noel Gallagher) / Funny thing (mixed by Tim Simenon).
 (cd-s) *(ISOM 11SMS)* – (lead track) / Beautiful bird (demo version) / Reason (with Susie Hug) / More than us (acoustic version).

Mar 99. (7"/c-s) *(ISOM 22 S/CS)* **WRITING TO REACH YOU. / ONLY MOLLY KNOWS**   14   –
 (cd-s+=) *(ISOM 22MS)* – Green behind the ears.
 (cd-s) *(ISOM 22SM)* – ('A'side) / Yeah yeah yeah yeah / High as a kite.

May 99. (c-s) *(ISOM 27CS)* **DRIFTWOOD / WRITING TO REACH YOU (Deadly Avenger remix)**   13   –
 (cd-s+=) *(ISOM 27SMS)* – Wtiting to reach you (Deadly Avenger instrumental remix).
 (cd-s) *(ISOM 27MS)* – ('A'side) / Be my baby / Where is the love.

May 99. (cd/c/lp) *(ISOM 9 CD/MC/LP) <62151>* **THE MAN WHO**   1   Apr00
 – Writing to reach you / The fear / As you are / Driftwood / The last laugh of the

TRAVIS (cont)

laughter / Turn / Why does it always rain on me? / Luv / She's so strange / Slide show. *(lp w/free 12"; ISOM 27T)* – WRITING TO REACH YOU (Deadly Avenger mixes). *(special ltd-cd+=; ISOM 9CDX)* – Blue flashing light / Writing to reach you / Driftwood. *(cd re-iss. Aug02; same)*

Aug 99. (c-s) *(ISOM 33CS)* **WHY DOES IT ALWAYS RAIN ON ME? / VILLAGE MAN** — 10 / -
(cd-s+=) *(ISOM 33MS)* – Driftwood (live).
(cd-s) *(ISOM 33SMS)* – ('A'side) / The urge for going / Slide show (live).

Nov 99. (c-s) *(ISOM 39CS)* **TURN / DAYS OF OUR LIVES** — 8 / -
(cd-s+=) *(ISOM 39MS)* – River.
(cd-s) *(ISOM 39SMS)* – ('A'side) / We are monkeys / Baby one more time.

Jun 00. (7"/c-s) *(ISOM 45 S/CS)* **COMING AROUND. / CONNECTION** — 5 / -
(cd-s+=) *(ISOM 45MC)* – Just the faces change.
(cd-s) *(ISOM 45SMS)* – ('A'side) / Rock'n'(salad) roll / The weight.

May 01. (7"/c-s) *(ISOM 49 S/CS)* **SING. / KILLER QUEEN** — 3 / -
(cd-s+=) *(ISOM 49MS)* – Ring out the bell.
(cd-s) *(ISOM 49SMAS)* – ('A'side) / You don't know what I'm like / Beautiful.

Jun 01. (cd/c/lp) *(ISOM 25 CD/MC/LP) <85788>* **THE INVISIBLE BAND** — 1 / 39
– Sing / Dear diary / Side / Pipe dreams / Flowers in the window / The cage / Safe / Follow the light / Last train / Afterglow / Indefinitely / The Humpty Dumpty love song.

Sep 01. (7"/c-s) *(ISOM 54 S/CS)* **SIDE. / ALL THE YOUNG DUDES (live)** — 14 / -
(cd-s+=) *(ISOM 54MS)* – ('A'side) / Driftwood (live).
(cd-s) *(ISOM 54SMS)* – ('A'side) / You're a big girl now / Ancient train.

Mar 02. (c-s) *(ISOM 56CS)* **FLOWERS IN THE WINDOW / A LITTLE BIT OF SOUL** — 18 / -
(cd-s+=) *(ISOM 56MS)* – Here comes the sun.
(cd-s) *(ISOM 56SMS)* – ('A'side) / Central station / No cigar.
(7") *(ISOM 56S)* – ('A'side) / Here comes the sun.

TREEPEOPLE

Formed: Boise, Idaho, USA . . . late 80's out of STATE OF CONFUSION by DOUG MARTSCH, SCOTT SCHMALJOHN, PAT BROWN and WAYNE RHINO. Debuting on the 'Toxic Shock' label with 1989's 'GUILT, REGRET, EMBARRASSMENT', this pre-grunge alternative outfit were spiritual cousins to the likes of GREEN RIVER and HUSKER DU, employing a twin-guitar attack that never veered too far from punk primitivism while putting an emphasis on melody. Sticksman, RHINO was replaced by TONY DALLAS REED for 1992's 'C/Z'-released follow-up, 'SOMETHING VICIOUS FOR TOMORROW', a record that mauled The Smiths' 'BIGMOUTH STRIKES AGAIN'. In true Spinal Tap style, yet another drummer, ERIC AKRE, was in place for 'JUST KIDDING' (1993), the band summing up the slacker ethos with 'ANYTHING'S IMPOSSIBLE'. MARTSCH was the next one to climb down, leaving the TREEPEOPLE and later joining BUILT TO SPILL; the gap was subsequently filled with JOHN POLLE and ERIC CARNELL; the line-up on the band's fourth and final album, 'ACTUAL RE-ENACTMENT' (1994). ERIC, SCOTT and JOHN reunited in the short-lived STUNTMAN.
• **Covered:** ANDY WARHOL (David Bowie) / CLOUDS IN MY COFFEE (Carly Simon) / DAMNATION DAWN (Aqua The Clown) / MORE THAN A FEELING (Boston) / WEB IN FRONT (Archers Of Loaf) / WILD WORLD (Cat Stevens).
Album rating: GUILT, REGRET, EMBARRASSMENT (*6) / SOMETHING VICIOUS FOR TOMORROW mini (*4) / JUST KIDDING (*7) / ACTUAL RE-ENACTMENT (*5) / Stuntman: STUNTMAN (*4)

DOUG MARTSCH – vocals, guitar / **SCOTT SCHMALJOHN** – guitar, vocals / **PAT BROWN** – bass / **WAYNE RHINO** – drums

not iss. *Silence*

1989. (c-ep) *<SILENCE 01>* **NO MOUTH PEPETTING**
1989. (7"ep) *<SEP 02>* **IMPORTANT THINGS. / IN MY HEAD / HANDCUFFS**
1989. (12"ep) *<SILENCE 03>* **TIME WHORE EP**
– Party / Tongues on thrones / Lives / Radio man / Size of a quarter / Time whore.

not iss. *Toxic Shock*

1989. (cd) *<23>* **GUILT, REGRET, EMBARRASSMENT**
– No doubt / Andy Warhol / Gre / Lost / Transitional devices / Pity / (I'm gonna) Miss you (when you're dead) / Wasted on you / Stay / Chunks of milk / Everytime when I fall down and my head hits the floor hard / Trailer park.

1991. (7"ep) *<TOX 18>* **split w/ HOUSE OF LARGE SIZES**
– Neil's down / Bankrupt in Hoven / (+2 by other artist).

not iss. *Sonic Bubblegum*

1991. (7") *<GUM 002>* **MISTAKE. / BALLARD BITTER**

TONY DALLAS REED – drums; repl. the departing RHINO (on some)

C/Z *C/Z*

Mar 92. (m-lp/m-cd) *<(CZ 040/+CD)>* **SOMETHING VICIOUS FOR TOMORROW**
– Liquid boy / It's alright now ma / Something vicious for tomorrow / Big mouth strikes again / Filter / Ad campaigns / Funnelhead. *<US cd-iss. w/+=>* – TIME WHORE EP

ERIC AKRE – drums (ex-CHRIST ON A CRUTCH) repl. BROWN (REED took over bass!)

SCHMALJOHN + AKRE recruited newcomers (**JOHN POLLE** – guitar + **ERIC CARNELL** – bass) when MARTSCH left to form BUILT TO SPILL

Soil *C/Z*

1993. (7") **HIDE AND FIND OUT. / DAMNATION DAWN**
1993. (7") *<CZ 050>* **OUTSIDE IN. / HIDE AND FIND OUT**
1993. (cd) *<CZ 054>* **JUST KIDDING**
– Today / In C / Cartoon brew / Ballard bitter / Clouds and faces / Fishbasket / Nod and blink / Anything's impossible / Neil's down / Outside in.

1994. (cd) *<CZ 080>* **ACTUAL RE-ENACTMENT**
– Wha'd I mean to think you said / Feed me / Slept through mine / Heinz von Foerster / Boot straps / Liver vs. heart / Better days / Bag of wood / Low / Will we ever / Too long.

not iss. *Sonic Bubblegum*

Feb 94. (d7"ep) *<GUM 016>* **MEET AT THE END. / WEB IN FRONT // (split w/ ARCHERS OF LOAF)**

— split after above . . .

STUNTMAN

SCOTT, ERIC + JOHN

not iss. *Link*

Feb 96. (cd) *<100>* **STUNTMAN**
– Bleed / 8 women & 2 to 3 men / Nighttime theater / Slaves / Nose dive / The feminist / Take it wrong / Wax pattern / Before going under / The Devil / Good enough.

TREE FORT ANGST

Formed: Washington D.C. & Baltimore, Maryland, USA . . . 1991 when singer/songwriter and former ST. CHRISTOPHER stalwart, TERRY BANKS, released a cassette-only LP under the moniker, TREE FORT ANGST. The following year, BANKS enlisted friends JOHN GOTSCHALK and HUNTER DUKE to provide a vehicle for songs he was developing that were more suited to a complete band sound. TFA's output was far from prolific and over the next six years they only managed to produce four EP's and a handful of appearances on compilation albums. The best of their recordings along with several new songs appeared on the 1997 compilation, 'KNEE DEEP IN THE ROCOCO EXCESS OF TREE FORT ANGST'. The jangling guitar sound of their music was reminiscent of The WEDDING PRESENT and was suitably accompanied by bittersweet-knowing lyrics.
Album rating: KNEE-DEEP IN THE ROCOCO EXCESS OF . . . compilation (*5) / LAST PAGE IN THE BOOK OF LOVE (*6)

TERRY BANKS – vocals, guitar (ex-ST. CHRISTOPHER)

not iss. *A Turntable Friend*

Apr 92. (7"ep) *<TURN 09>* **SIX SONGS EP**
– You should have seen the one that got away / I'm not giving up on you / Four years, six months, two days / Shining example / Eternal pledge / Ascension.

— added **JOHN GOTSCHALK** – bass / **HUNTER DUKE** – drums

not iss. *Velodrome*

Nov 92. (7"ep) **BUZZING WITH BEAUTY & WONDER**

not iss. *Ad Lithium Pop*

Oct 93. (7"flexi) *<ADLIB 3>* **PARTING KISS**

not iss. *Bus Stop*

Jul 94. (7"ep) *<BUS 39>* **TILTING AT WINDMILLS EP**

— split in the summer of '94 (below single posthumous); TERRY was to join GLO-WORM and later The SATURDAY PEOPLE

not iss. *Stickboy*

1995. (7") *<STICK 003>* **HOPE. /**

– compilations, etc. –

Mar 97. (cd) *Bus Stop; <(BUS 1007-2)>* **KNEE-DEEP IN THE ROCOCO EXCESS OF . . .** — / Dec96
– Tuesday / Found out / Bell weather / 20 hours / In-between / Hope / Tilting at windmills / Save me / This is the day / Why couldn't you see this coming? / The one that got away / Fin de siecle / Hope (practice room jamboree) / Trampoline / Drunk on your senses / Miss you essay / Parting kiss / Four years, six months, two days / Under the sun / Bad Ronald.

Sep 02. (cd) *Foxboy; <003>* **LAST PAGE IN THE BOOK OF LOVE**
(above set + 10 tracks).

TREMBLING BLUE STARS
(see under ⇒ FIELD MICE)

TRENCHMOUTH

Formed: Chicago, Illinois, USA . . . 1990 by FRED ARMISEN, CHRIS DEZUTTER, WAYNE MONTANA and DAMON LOCKS. A band that quite simply perched itself on the edges of the alternative fusing punk sensibility and attitude via combinations ranging from hardcore to dub ska. Touchstones include the post-punk of GANG OF FOUR, the recording techniques of LEE PERRY and their left-field native peers TORTOISE. Their debut full-length outing, 'CONSTRUCTION OF NEW ACTION' (1992), centered more around raw guitar power, although suffice to say every album they put out was distinctly different from its predecessor with the linear similarity being their quest for breaking up the boundaries. This was evident on their aptly-titled second LP, 'INSIDE THE FUTURE' (1993). Following on from this came their brilliant third album, 'VS. THE LIGHT OF THE SUN' (1994), a record heralding their foray into dubby basslines and art-rock lyrical rantings courtesy of LOCKS. Although not quite hitting the heights of its former, their fourth offering 'THE BROADCASTING SYSTEM' (1996), was still an admirable effort and delved further into Jamaican/CLASH soundsystem noodlings.

TRENCHMOUTH (cont)

Unfortunately this record also marked the end for the band. ARMISEN took a left-turn and continued to nurse his creative urges as a performance artist. Meanwhile, LOCKS and MONTANA teamed up with DAN FLIEGEL to form The ETERNALS which carried on the dub project although with a more avant-jazz inflected flavour. They debuted in 1999 with the EP 'WHERE WILL WE LIVE NOW' and 7" 'CHAPTER AND VERSE', before moving on the following year to issue the self-titled premier LP, 'THE ETERNALS' which garnered the knob-twiddling assistance of none other than JOHN McENTIRE (of TORTOISE fame and CASEY RICE).

Album rating: CONSTRUCTION OF NEW ACTION – VOLUME ONE: FIRST THERE WAS MOVEMENT (*5) / INSIDE THE FUTURE (*5) / VS. THE LIGHT OF THE SUN (*7) / THE BROADCASTING SYSTEM (*6) / the Eternals: THE ETERNALS (*5)

DAMON LOCKS – vocals, percussion / **CHRIS DeZUTTER** – guitar / **WAYNE FONTANA** – bass / **FRED ARMISEN** – drums

Skene! Skene!

Nov 92. (cd) *(SR 89222CD)* <20> **CONSTRUCTION OF NEW ACTION – VOLUME ONE: FIRST THERE WAS MOVEMENT**
– The volcanic action of my soul / Ultraman / Friction! / Sordo Ciego / Bear in mind / Siberia / Oxygen gum / History history / Gold / Chalk / Detonation speech: A last ditch effort.

Sep 93. (cd) <30> **INSIDE THE FUTURE**
– Telescopic / Power to the amplifier / The dawning of a new sound system / Yes, this is the place / Timing is everything (struck by lightning) / Capsule / Confectionery / In the event of a struggle / The future vs. centrifugal force / Sea of serenity (swing version) / Hit men will suffocate the city / Now I have tasted life.

Sep 94. (cd) <38> **VS. THE LIGHT OF THE SUN**
– Washington! Washington! / A prescription written in a different language / Here come the automata / How I became invincible / Set the oven at 400° / Saw a ghost / The effects of radiation / Doing the flammability / A man without lungs / Bricks should have wings. *<re-iss. 1995 on 'East West'; 61738>*

Runt Skene!

1995. (cd) **VOLUMES, AMPLIFIERS, EQUALIZERS** (compilation)
– Power to the amplifier / The dawning of a new sound system / The volcanic action of my soul / Timing is everything (struck by lightning) / Friction! / Making money for freak machines / The future vs. centrifugal force / Ultraman / I believe in me / Sea of serenity / Hit men will suffocate the city / Gold / Confectionery / Detonation speech: a last ditch effort / Telescopic.

Mar 97. (cd) *(RUNT 21)* <40> **THE BROADCASTING SYSTEM** May96
– Picking up interference / Broadcasting from the heart / The fire and the wire colossus / In high contrast / Moving with momentum / Overthrower / Contrast beneath the surface / Onus / Interference.

— ARMISEN became a comedic entertainer after they split

ETERNALS

DAMON LOCKS – vocals, keyboards, samples / **WAYNE MONTANA** – bass, guitar, keyboards / **DAN FLIEGEL** – percussion, guitar

not iss. Thrill Jockey

1999. (12") *<THRILL 12.16>* **CHAPTER AND VERSE**
(UK-iss.Apr02; same as US)

1999. (12") *<THRILL 12.18>* **WHERE WILL WE LIVE NOW?**

Aesthetics De Soto

Nov 00. (d-lp)<cd> *(AST 014)* <SE SOTO 37> **THE ETERNALS** Oct00
– Billions of people / Stirring up weather / Feverous times / Phase 3 (or never ending transformation) / Eternally yours / Forever people / Eternals 2000 / Bewilderness / The beginning and the end.

TRIBE 8

Formed: San Francisco, California, USA ... 1991 by LYNN BREEDLOVE, LYNN FLIPPER, SLADE BELLUM, TANTRUM and LESLIE NEWMAN. Having met while working for a lesbian escort service, the girls decided to form a band with the promise of not only riches and loads of female groupies but a platform for their zealous feminism and radical politics. As heard on their 1993 debut set, 'BY THE TIME WE GET TO COLORADO', TRIBE 8's queercore punk caught the attention of JELLO BIAFRA who quickly procured them for his 'Alternative Tentacles' label. While not prancing around on stage with a dildo sticking out of her tartan trousers, BREEDLOVE was hard at work in the studio with her bosom buddies, banging out the likes of 'ALLEN'S MOM' (1994), 'FIST CITY' (1995) and 'SNARKISM' (1996). The dyke warriors reached their artistic zenith with 'ROLE MODELS FOR AMERIKA' (1998), choosing none other than The SPICE GIRLS as support for the subsequent tour.
• Covered: THINK (Aretha Franklin) / RADAR LOVE (Golden Earring) / RISE ABOVE (Black Flag).

Album rating: BY THE TIME WE GET TO COLORADO mini (*5) / FIST CITY (*5) / SNARKISM (*6) / ROLE MODELS FOR AMERIKA (*5)

LYNN BREEDLOVE – vocals / **LESLIE MAH** (b. NEWMAN) – lead guitar, vocals / **LYNN FLIPPER** – rhythm guitar, vocals / **LYNN PAYNE** – bass, vocals / **SLADE BELLUM** – drums, vocals

not iss. own label

1992. (7"ep/c-ep/cd-ep) **THERE'S A DYKE IN THE PIT EP**

not iss. Lickout

1993. (7") **BITCHES IN BREW. /**

Outpunk Outpunk

Jun 93. (cd/c) *<OUT 7 CD/MC>* **BY THE TIME WE GET TO COLORADO**
– Lezbophobia / 1 party 2 many / Masochist's medley / Easy virtue / Censor this / Crash crush.

Nov 94. (7"ep/cd-ep) *<OUT 13/+CD>* **ALLEN'S MOM**

Alternative Alternative Tentacles Tentacles

Jan 95. (cd) *<VIRUS 156CD>* **FIST CITY**
– Manipulate / Seraphim / Butch in the streets / Romeo and Julio / What? / Kick / Neanderthal dyke / Freedom / Allen's mom / Femme bitch top / Think / Flippersnapper / Barnyard poontang / All I can do / Frat pig. *(UK-iss.Apr00; same as US)*

Nov 95. (cd-ep) *<VIRUS 173>* **ROADKILL CAFE EP**
– Wrong bathroom / Radar love / Ice cream man (live) / Manipulate (live).

May 96. (cd/lp) *<(VIRUS 181 CD/LP)>* **SNARKISM** Apr96
– Republican lullaby / Tranny chaser / She said / A sad poem / Ez virtue / Checking out your babe / Jim, darby & Sid / Wrong bathroom / People hate me / Mendo hoo-ha / Oversize ego / Dead clothed boys / Speed fortress.

Mar 98. (cd/lp) *<(VIRUS 212 CD/LP)>* **ROLE MODELS FOR AMERIKA**
– Sunbears / Old skool, new skool / Sleep deprivation / Junkyard dog / Ta ta ta's / What the papers didn't say / Queen of the scene / Castration song #22 / Rise above / Daredevil delivery / Het punx (Opie 'n' Alli's song) / Takin' out the trash / Estrofemme / Haldol shuffle / Prison blues / Hapa girl / Sunbears (extended dance mix).

— split soon after above

TRIPLE FAST ACTION

Formed: Chicago, Illinois, USA ... January 1993 by WES KIDD, BRIAN ST. CLAIR and KEVIN TIHISTA. Picking up where KIDD and ST. CLAIR's previous band, RIGHTS OF THE ACCUSED, left off, this Chicago trio released a clutch of singles before making their debut in 1996 with the DON FLEMING-produced 'BROADCASTER' (1996). Despite having been signed up by 'Capitol' in the post-Nirvana grunge goldrush, TRIPLE FAST ACTION's competent if unremarkable grunge-oriented melodic punk was never likely to shift enough units to satisfy major label demand. No surprise then, that their sophomore effort was the independently released 'CATTLEMEN DON'T' (1997). It also proved to be their parting shot although TIHISTA went on to a solo career following the band's official split in 1998. With KIDD as his manager, TIHISTA secured a single deal with British indie label, 'Easy Tiger', releasing 'LOSE THE DRESS' in late 2000. An eponymous EP followed on 'Rough Trade' and TIHISTA was subsequently signed to 'Atlantic' Stateside subsidiary 'Division One'. Released as KEVIN TIHISTA'S RED TERROR, 'DON'T BREATHE A WORD' (2001) possessed a BEATLES-ish, retro-pop feel in stark contrast to its death metal-esque moniker. With strings and horns courtesy of the CLARK brothers TOM and ELLIS (whose home studio the tracks were recorded in), and violinist MERRITT LEAR, the record's humble tales of romantic doom marked TIHISTA out as a promising if not particularly original songsmith. 'JUDO' (2002), a collection of songs recorded at the same time as those on the debut (and originally intended for inclusion on a double set), was unsurprisingly very similar in atmosphere and approach to that record if not quite as consistent.

Album rating: BROADCASTER (*6) / CATTLEMEN DON'T (*5) / Kevin Tihista's Red Terror: KEVIN TIHISTA'S RED TERROR mini (*5) / DON'T BREATHE A WORD (*5) / JUDO (*4)

WES KIDD – vocals, guitar / **KEVIN TIHISTA** (b. Walnut Creek, Calif.) – bass, vocals / **BRIAN ST. CLAIR** – drums / **RONNIE SCHNEIDER** – guitar / on tour:- **SCOTT LUCAS** – guitar (of LOCAL H)

not iss. Limited Potential

1994. (7") *<LP 006>* **REVVED UP. / SALLY TREE**
(UK-iss.1997 on 'Regal';)

not iss. Hit It!

May 95. (7") **RONNIE'S PANTS. / AEROSMITH**

not iss. Capitol

Apr 96. (10"lp/cd) *<32142-1/-2>* **BROADCASTER**
– Areosmith / Anna (get your gun) / Revved up / Bird again / (untitled) / Don't tell / American city world / Cheery / Rest my head / Never ever care / Sally tree / Paris / Superstar. *(cd+=)* – Bedhead.

Deep Elm Deep Elm

Jul 98. (cd) *<(DER 364CD)>* **CATTLEMEN DON'T** Oct97
– Ronnie's theme / Pure / Heroes / If / Cattlemen don't / Eurogirl / The rescue / I'm ready / Duck and run / Sent them straight / Yeah / Operator / No doubt / Bearer of bad news.

— WES KIDD went into production; BRIAN joined LOCAL H

KEVIN TIHISTA'S RED TERROR

KEVIN TIHISTA – vocals, bass, guitar / **ELLIS CLARK** – multi

Easy! Tiger not iss.

Oct 00. (7"m) *(MUSE 008)* **LOSE THE DRESS. / OH NO NOT AGAIN / YOU'LL BE BACK SOMEDAY**

RoughTrade not iss.

Jun 01. (cd/lp) *(RTRADE CD/LP 015)* **KEVIN TIHISTA'S RED TERROR**
– Sucker / Beautiful / Doctor (emergency mix) / 2nd look / Stoopid boy / Back to Budapest.

Blanco Y Negro Atlantic

Oct 01. (cd) *(0927 41555-2)* <83456> **DON'T BREATHE A WORD** Sep01
– Just not enough / Lose the dress / Sucker / Pretty please / Don't breathe a word / Doctor / Outta site, ouuta mind / I love her / Stoopid boy / Don't you know / Beautiful / You're going to kill me.

Parasol Parasol

Jul 02. (cd) *<(PARCD 080)>* **JUDO**
– Back to Budapest / One more day / I'm in love with girls / Second look / You're making other plans / You don't have to be sorry / Love plays a dirty game / You will be back someday / Come on now / Oh no, not again / Hymn / That's for sure.

TRIPPING DAISY (see under ⇒ POLYPHONIC SPREE)

TRISTEZA

Formed: San Diego, California, USA ... 1997 by CHRISTOPHER SPRAGUE, JIMMY LAVALLE, LUIS HERMOSILLO, STEPHEN SWESEY and JIMMY LEHNER. A debut single, 'FORESHADOW', previewed the quartet's instrumental post-rock sound fully embraced on 1999's 'SPINE AND SENSORY'. Subtle, cerebral and not wholly immediate, the comparisons with the likes of TORTOISE were unavoidable and like the latter's most involving work, rewarded repeated listening. The subsequent release of their own EP instalment in the 'INSOUND TOUR SUPPORT' series confirmed their commitment to live work as a key tool in developing their sound. This much was evident with the well received 'DREAMS SIGNALS IN FULL CIRCLES' (2000), an even more richly textured outing produced by The PULSARS' DAVE TRUMFIO.

Album rating: SPINE AND SENSORY (*7) / DREAM SIGNALS IN FULL CIRCLES (*6) / MIXED STYLES remixes (*5)

JIMMY LAVALLE – guitar / **CHRISTOPHER SPRAGUE** – guitar / **STEPHEN SWESEY** – keyboards / **LUIS HERMOSILLO** – bass / **JIMMY LEHNER** – drums

		not iss.	Caffeine vs. Nicotine
1998.	(7") **FORESHADOW. / SMOKE THROUGH GLASS**	–	

		Jonathan Whisky	not iss.
1999.	(7") **ZACHARIAH. / (other by The REMOTE VIEWER)**		–

		not iss.	Makato
1999.	(cd) <16> **SPINE AND SENSORY**	–	

– Golden hill / Beige finger / RMS 2000 / When we glow / Memphis emphasis / Muerte en tu sueno / Electrolytes / The marionette / Cinematography / A little distance.

		Tiger Style	Tiger Style
Aug 00.	(7") <TS 008> **ARE WE PEOPLE. / WHEN MORNING STEALS THE SKY**	–	
Sep 00.	(cd) <(TS 010CD)> **DREAM SIGNALS IN FULL CIRCLES**		

– Building peaks / Respira / City of the future / Shifty drifty / Aurora Borealis / I am a cheetah / Chiaroscuro / Are we people / Opiate slopes.

Feb 01.	(7") <RR 007> **MACRAME. / RMS 2000 (remix)**	–	

(above issued on 'Rocket Racer', below on 'Gravity')

Apr 01.	(cd-ep) <41> **TRISTEZA EP**	–	

– These walls / Stop grass / Japan mountain / Panic power / The magic hour / Auxilio mate.

Feb 02.	(cd) <(TS 014CD – RR 015)> **MIXED SIGNALS** (remixes by V/A)		

– Shifty / Peaks / Cheetah / Drifty / Building / Casio / Futuro / Chiaroscuro / Opiate / Respira / We are people.

TRUE LOVE ALWAYS

Formed: Charlottesville, Virginia, USA ... October 1995 out of OPERATION LOVE by JOHN LINDAMAN and MATT DATESMAN. With TOBIN RODRIGUEZ completing the line-up, these hopeless musical romantics earned their first break via the auspices of MARK ROBINSON and his celebrated 'Teenbeat' label. After releasing a debut single, 'MEDITERRANEAN', in 1996, the band followed up with 'WHEN WILL YOU BE MINE' later the same year. Drawing comparisons with UNREST and similar tweemeisters, the trio's loose-limbed, bittersweet bossa-pop nevertheless had more of a swing to it than most practitioners. The trio further refined their BELLE & SEBASTIAN-esque sound over the albums 'HOPEFULLY' (1998), 'TORCH' (2000) and 'CLOUDS' (2002), the latter with TONY ZANELLA replacing RODRIGUEZ. • **Covered:** TONGUE (R.E.M.).

Album rating: WHEN WILL YOU BE MINE (*7) / HOPEFULLY (*6) / TORCH (*6) / SPRING COLLECTION compilation (*7) / CLOUDS (*5)

JOHN LINDAMAN – vocals, guitar / **MATT DATESMAN** (b. Atlanta, Georgia) – drums (of FLIN FLON) / **TOBIN RODRIGUEZ** – bass

		TeenBeat	TeenBeat
1996.	(7") <TEENBEAT 219> **MEDITERRANEAN. / SWEET TIME**	–	
Mar 97.	(cd) <TEENBEAT 239> **WHEN WILL YOU BE MINE**		

– Don't take it easy / Yearbook / I've got a crush on you / Party time / All along the basement / Cigarette star / Shame on you / Summertime time / Bicycle rider / Everyone knows / Dionne. *(UK-iss.Jan 01; same as US)*

1997.	(7") <MOTOR 021> **SECRET SCENES. / MY SHIT**		

(above issued on 'Motorway')

1998.	(7") <TEENBEAT 259> **TAKE ME OVER. / R U COPING W/ ME**	–	
Jul 98.	(cd) <TEENBEAT 269> **HOPEFULLY**	–	

– More / Show & prove / Cashmere / The winter months / 127 m.p.h. / Spring collection / IWW / Spelling B / Ill systems / Things to do today – 1). Try / Teenage Stonehenge.

1999.	(7") <TEENBEAT 279> **BURIED TREASURE. / HOPELESSLY DEVOTED**		
Apr 00.	(cd) <(TEENBEAT 299)> **TORCH**		

– Stream up / Underneath / Sunshine / 100 years of you / In it to win it / Torch / The losing part / Rockets + jets / Furs / Windows fade / Sheets.

— (late 1999) **TONY ZANELLA** – bass; repl. RODRIGUEZ

Dec 02.	(cd) <TEENBEAT 329> **CLOUDS**	–	

– Give me the colors / Let the rain blow in / For you alone / Sidewalks and spaces / The garden's inside / Bachelor bare / Summer books / I can only see you smile / Modesto / Peel away / Tracing the rays.

– compilations, etc. –

Aug 01.	(cd) TeenBeat; <(TEENBEAT 309)> **SPRING COLLECTION**		

– Mediterranean / Sweet time / Secret static / Top / Hopelessly devoted / Take me over / R U coping w/ me / Secret scenes / Tongue / Faust / Buried treasure / Je suis souviens / Silence of the mind / Windows fade / Shy song / September / Making love.

TRUMANS WATER

Formed: San Diego, California, USA ... 1991 by ELY MOYAL, GLENN GALLOWAY and brothers KEVIN and KIRK BRANSTETTER. Debuting in 1992 with 'OUR SCARS LIKE BADGES', the band were quick off the mark with a follow-up set, 'OF THICK TUM', initial copies of the latter coming complete with a hand-painted sleeve. Aired in its entirety by DJ, John Peel, the album captured their chaotic disharmony (like BEEFHEART on punk pills fused with lo-fi no wave retro) in full flow. Live on his Radio One show, Peel subsequently offered them a session, which led to a contract with 'Elemental'. First up was a double-album, 'SPASM SMASH XXXOXOX OX & ASS' (1993), a schizoid sprawl of nigh on unintelligible avant-pop/indie-rock. Defying all recognised music business convention, the wacky Californians proceeded to release four LP's in '94, 'GODSPEED THE PUNCHLINE', being the first in the 'GODSPEED' series and perhaps unsurprisingly, their last for 'Elemental'. The band certainly weren't taking the 'MILKTRAIN TO PAYDIRT' (1995), the latter set sending them on a one-way ticket to obscurity after receiving short shrift in the press. Unfortunately the band weren't able to simply 'COUGH FORTH SUCH DILEMMAS' (the name of a US-only cassette in '96), still searching for the 'FRAGMENTS OF A LUCKY BREAK' in '98. TRUMANS WATER surfaced again in 2001, courtesy of an eponymous set. • **Covered:** CARS (Gary Numan) / RADAR 1941 (Sun City Girls). • **Trvia:** GLEN was left facing a hefty 5-figure bill after failing to graduate from Naval College in the early 90's.

Album rating: OF THICK TUM (*8) / GODSPEED THE PUNCHLINE (*5) / MILKTRAIN TO PAYDIRT (*5) / FRAGMENTS OF A LUCKY BREAK (*5) / TRUMANS WATER (*5)

KEVIN BRANSTETTER – vocals, bass / **KIRK BRANSTETTER** – guitar, vocals / **GLENN GALLOWAY** – guitar, vocals / **ELY MOYAL** – drums

		not iss.	Justice My Eye
1992	(lp) **OF THICK TUM**	–	

– Deep grub yonder / 665 / Yakboy = nurturer / Nick Long ding barn / Tooth ferry / Disindependence / Well nigh dusk / Wings spred wide I thot "ignition" / Jamellopy / Spurning of Angel Peg / Sorry about the blood / Fong / Girler too. *(UK-iss.Jan93 on 'Homestead' cd+=/lp; HMS 192-2/-1)* – Secret blood thirst / Large organs / Johnny Pissoff & the red angel meets / Yakboy = enabler (alt. take).

		not iss.	Way Out
1992.	(7"ep) <004> **JUBILEEEEE** (instrumental)	–	

– Enter slumlord / Rash of hotbed / Static clobber blass / 4 spux spux / Infinite xplosion antennae / Schism now / Groundwave / Transistor seizure / Blare scara blaze / Self-righteous underage billions obliviate you.

		not iss.	Homestead
Nov 92.	(7"ep) <HMS 190-7> **OUR SCARS LIKE BADGES**	–	

– Apolitix / Mind yer altar / Another movement / Sad sailor story.

		not iss.	Drunken Fish
Dec 92.	(7"ep,7"clear-ep) <DF 03> **LAUGH LIGHTS LIT**	–	

– Habits are spirits / Silver tongue please / X-ray eyes or.

		–	
Apr 93.	(7"m) <DF 06> **HEY FISH. / MR. E / EMPTY QUEEN**	–	

		Elemental	Homestead
Apr 93.	(d-lp/cd) <ELM 9/+CD> <HMS 199-1/-2> **SPASM SMASH XXXOXOX OX & ASS**		Mar93

– Aroma of Gina Arnold / Speeds exceeding / Good blood after bad / Rations / Death to dead things / Sun go out / Bludgeon elites and stagger / Limbs / Athlete who is suck / Top of morning / Lo priest / Soar ossinaxx at long last / Our doctor thinks we're blind / Fingers / Steps ahead of our minds / La jolly my armpit / K-song / Mindstab, forklift to milktruck / Bladder stomp: Krautrack / The sad skinhead. *(cd re-iss. Jan99; same)*

Sep 93.	(10"ep/cd-ep) (ELM 14/+CD) **10 X MY AGE**		–

– Empty queen II / Second bass drum / Enflamed (sic) / Paid squat / Parabolic / Action sound deadman.

Jan 94.	(lp/s/lp/cd) (ELM 15/+X/CD) <HMS 209-2> **GODSPEED THE PUNCHLINE**		

– Destroy 1998 / Long end of a firearm / All wet west of Washington / Hair junk fibre / Ungalaxy / Antsmashes yer star (dead airwaves) / Enflamed / Outpatient lightspeed / Infinity times zero / Sucker mystique / Playboy stabtone bloodbath go / Slander in new slang / No big (wave) star / Theme of blast / Fuller piston vinegar / .22 / Horsesense / Spaceship next door. *(cd re-iss. Jan99; same)*

		not iss.	Drunken Fish
1994.	(m-lp) <DF 10> **GODSPEED THE STATIC**	–	

– Kick penmanship / Sweet sister Gay / Shower stopper shower stopper shower stopper shower stopper yeah / California lies.

		not iss.	Way Out Sound
1994.	(lp/cd) <#8> **GODSPEED THE VORTEX**	–	

– Total x-stasis / Odor is free / Syrup is tangled / Swordfish in the trees / Ominous blips fore / True-star down / New rupture / Soup of volts / New rapture / Ominous blips aft / Freon. *(cd+=)* – Way out No.7 / The 20 minute song.

		not iss.	Homestead
1994.	(m-lp; some blue) <HMS 193-1> **GODSPEED THE HEMORRHAGE**	–	

– Small-jut master / Jagged bottlecap jangle / Knuckle suggestion / Amplify idea / Storm / Ordinance / Ordinance (ctd).

		not iss.	Sympathy F
1994.	(7") <SFTRI 255> **SKYJACKER. / FLOORJACKER / FINEST DONUT THEME SONG**	–	

		not iss.	Clawfist
1994.	(7"ep) <*CF 25*> **SPAZZ ROCKDANCE INFERNO**	-	

– New kinda radio / Do the spazz / Bat cave / Ride the no-wave.

—— now without GLENN who formed SOUL-JUNK

		not iss.	Howardian
1995.	(7"ep) <*002*> **THE FIRST DEAD MAN OF DILUVIA**		

– Standing on his back / 4th & early 5th / Consort of the crane / Emphasis off.

		Homestead	Homestead
Aug 95.	(cd/lp) <(*HMS 221-2/-1*)> **MILKTRAIN TO PAYDIRT**		

– Mechanical days safety system / Unitraction bath / Lick observatory spectroheliscope / Stares from new enemies / Vexation fruits / Sour synapse – St. Job int'l Gore / Concussed / American fat / Irly traitor consent / Mnemonic elfnlock / Siski you armiger / Asleep sneeze / Off peak arson / Wind and rain over wings.

		Footprinr	not iss.
1996.	(7"ep) (*Foot 04*) **THE GREAT FLOOD**	-	- Belg

– Underwater / I drive a UFO / Icestorm / Windstorm.

—— <'Union Pole' issued US cassette, 'COUGH FORTH SUCH DILEMMAS' in '96>

		Runt	Runt
Jun 97.	(cd) <(*RUNT 28*)> **ACTION ORNAMENTS**		

– 3 straps nose to rear / 4 story friend / A hurting helping / Mood strain / Angels spit stars / Skeeter dope / Gold plated pissin troff / Mutual blood tied force / Curl up to yer empty years / Restore restore and destroy / Flying in a coin operated universe / Shoe lace or else / Car sliced lies.

		Justice My Eye	Justice My Eye
Apr 98.	(cd) <(*JME 006*)> **APISTOGRAMMA**		

– I've been here before though I don't remember it / Skrimshaw skalps / Family style / Blistered and soft / Cy30 – Cy30B / The end is a cinch to see even behind me / Rocket #9 / Minus time space plus soul time / Prune the laggards / Ballad of Finn McCool / Slum summer.

		Emperor Jones	Emperor Jones
Aug 98.	(cd) <(*EJ 23CD*)> **FRAGMENTS OF A LUCKY BREAK**		

– Obstacle / Lyrical nozzle / Strat-as-fear / Wealth in a flask / Sky landslide / Your courage / Woed world whirlers / Tiny world with the jitters / Mall removal machine / 60 seconds over medium / Worth of wait / Matter smasher / Water for a thirsty city / Someday you'll be king / All eye and movement. *(lp-iss. on 'Infinite Chug'; CHUG 10LP)*

		Infinite Chug	not iss.
Oct 98.	(7") (*CHUG 11*) **ABSTRACTER JET NINE. / (split with I'M BEING GOOD + GRAVEL SAMWIDGE + PENTHOUSE)**		

		not iss.	Sub Pop
2000.	(7") <*SP 519*> **MISS SPACESHIP. / RADAR 1941**	-	-

		Delboy	Emperor Jones
Mar 02.	(lp)<cd> **TRUMAN'S WATER**		Jun01

– Miss Spaceship / Who owns the sun / Wilt banana / Radar 1941 *[UK-only]* / Self-censored *[US-only]* / Limping towards oblivion / Ondele clouds / Rinsed in ashes *[US-only]* / Cars *[UK-only]* / Failure to quit *[US-only]* / Equatorial Antarctica / Second wind *[US-only]* / Limits of the new deal *[US-only]* / La bonita cancion / Messed possession *[US-only]* / Another day in the dream museum / Sun tastes like fire.

– compilations, others, etc –

Apr 95.	(cd) *Strange Fruit; (SFRCD 133)* **PEEL SESSIONS**		-

– All wet est of Washington / Long end of a firearm / Large organs / Seven holes / Hair junk fiver (sic?) / Death to dead things / Girler too / Esoterica of Abyssynia / Kingdom of Heaven / No naked lights / True tilt pinball / Lick observatory / Go-go dancer solidified / Electro muerta / Talking hockey with strangers / St. Job (international gore).

TSE TSE FLY

Formed: Leeds, England ... early 90's by JAYNE LOCKEY, SIMON CLEAVE and PAUL DORRINGTON (the latter joining The WEDDING PRESENT before any releases). All three of these members would go on to join indie legends The WEDDING PRESENT at various times, the FLY's primary claim to fame, and this Leeds-guitar-squall-sound is reflected in TSE TSE FLY recordings. FLY kicked off their alternative sonic rock career with the release of their debut 10" 'DUCKWEED SMUGGLED HOME' (1992) on 'Ablution' records. This somewhat undistinguished release was sonically categorized alongside the likes of SONIC YOUTH and THAT DOG, but established the band's signature boy-on-girl-on-boy tag-team vocal style, alternating between male and female often in the same song, alongside meaty, beaty, big and bouncy US-alternative-style ripping guitar riffs. The record see-sawed between quiet, stellar female backing vocals ('ENDORPHIN') and upbeat and punky ('TADPOLE PART ONE'). But it was with the 7", 'FOX UNDER DIESEL', that the FLY came into their own. Using left-of-field samples (including dogs and telephones), melancholic tunes, distorted boom bass and swirling, vertiginous guitar effects, the band finally broke free of their US and UK mentors to forge their own verging-on-the-psychedelic-in-places sound. 'Cherry Red' released 'MUDFLAT JOEY', which was a combination of two EPs recorded for the label. This 12-song CD contained a couple of the songs ('M1' and 'ROO MOLE SUIT') from 'DIESEL' and was produced by Richard Formby, producer of The TELESCOPES and SPECTRUM. 'Pehr' records released a compilation CD with 'DUCKWEED SMUGGLED HOME', 'FOX UNDER DIESEL' and four previously unreleased tracks. This would be the sum total of the band's legacy, aside from the obvious WEDDING PRESENT-style sound apparent in some of the songs.

Album rating: MUDFLAT JOEY (*7) / TSE TSE FLY collection (*7)

JAYNE LOCKEY – vocals, bass / **SIMON CLEAVE** – vocals, guitar / (PAUL DORRINGTON

		Ablution	not iss.
1992.	(10"ep) **DUCKWEED SMUGGLED HOME EP**		-

– Quasi / Replicas / Endorphin / Splee / Tadpole part one.

		Morphene	not iss.
1993.	(7"ep) **FOX UNDER DIESEL EP**		-

– M1 / Happy punk / Itch four four / Mew.

		Cherry Red	not iss.
Jun 94.	(7") (*CHERRY 134*) **SCAFFOLDING. / CUBBY HOLE**		-

(cd-s+=) (*CDCHERRY 134*) – Us / Semi-flattened squirrel.

Oct 94.	(cd/lp) (*CD+/BRED 117*) **MUDFLAT JOEY**		-

– M1 / Jonah / Talk to me / Dog-eared / On purpose / Lido / Roo mole suit / Itchy / Some day soon / Non-ferrous / Kitchen / Hogwash.

—— split after above; both LOCKEY and CLEAVE joined The WEDDING PRESENT; the latter is now part of DAVID GEDGE's most recent project CINERAMA

– compilations, etc. –

Jul 01.	(ltd-cd) *Pehr; <004>* **TSE TSE FLY**	-	

– DUCKWEED SMUGGLED HOME ep / FOX UNDER DIESEL ep / Roo mole suit / Prayer wheel / Samaritan / Engineer.

TSUNAMI

Formed: Arlington, Virginia, USA ... 1990 by KRISTIN THOMSON, JENNY TOOMEY, ANDREW WEBSTER and JOHN PAMER. Enthusiastic exponents of the original DIY punk ethic, TSUNAMI (a tidal wave!) were that rare example of a band walking it like they talk it. As well as being an outlet for their own product, the THOMSON/TOOMEY-run 'Simple Machines' (Washington DC-based) label has released material by such semi-legendary alternative/hardcore acts as SUPERCHUNK and NATION OF ULYSSES. Following a debut 1991 EP, 'HEADRINGER' and a series of imaginatively packaged singles ('MATCHBOOK', for instance, was under the guise of a book of matches), a fully formed debut album, 'DEEP END', surfaced in 1993. Bursting with fizzing guitar-pop tunes written largely from a feminine angle, the record was well received in indie circles where Riot Grrrl was the flavour of the month. A slot on the 1993 Lollapalooza tour – where they also set up a 'Simple Machines' stall – was followed in early '94 by the release of a follow-up set, 'THE HEART'S TREMOLO'. TOOMEY's other bands included CHOKE, GEEK and her offshoot super-"indie"-group, LIQUORICE (along with DAN LITTLETON and TREY MANY). 1994 was also the year TOOMEY set about consummating her long standing musical partnership with DAN LITTLETON. At the behest of '4 a.d.' head bod, Ivo Watts-Russell, the pair got together as LIQUORICE to record the 'LISTENING CAP' (1995) album. An acoustic-based affair, the record's stripped down feel was in marked contrast to TSUNAMI's aural assault. With PALMER subsequently resuming his college education, the group were eventually obliged to hire a new drummer in the shape of LUTHER 'TRIP' GRAY (who'd previously played with the likes of SEA SAW and DELTA 72). Long awaited as it was, 'A BRILLIANT MISTAKE' (1997) was to be the final chapter in the long running TSUNAMI saga. With JENNY TOOMEY now the executive producer of The Future Music Coalition, and casualty from bands such as GEEK and the aforementioned LIQUORICE, she issued the subtle 'ANTIDOTE' (2001) set, featuring the brilliant backing rhythm section courtesy of the LAMBCHOP players and spread over two discs. The album even featured a floating rendition of Curtis Mayfield's 'FOOL FOR YOU', produced by LAMBCHOP's MARK NEVERS. TOOMEY resurfaced one year later with a bizarre covers album of songs by FRANKLIN BRUNO, entitled 'TEMPTING: JENNY TOOMEY SINGS THE SONGS OF FRANKLIN', which, interestingly enough, featured JOEY BURNS and JOHN CONVERTINO of CALEXICO and GIANT SAND fame.

Album rating: DEEP END (*7) / THE HEART'S TREMOLO (*8) / WORLD TOUR AND OTHER DESTINATIONS compilation (*6) / A BRILLIANT MISTAKE (*7) / Liquorice: LISTENING CAP (*5) / Geek: GRADE SCHOOL BONER (*4) / Jenny Toomey: ANTIDOTE (*7) / TEMPTING (*5)

JENNY TOOMEY – guitar, vocals / **KRISTIN THOMSON** – guitar, vocals / **ANDREW WEBSTER** – bass, vocals / **JOHN PAMER** – drums

		Simple Machines	Simple Machines
Feb 91.	(demo-c-s) <*none*> **COW ARCADE**	-	
Jul 91.	(7") <(*HMS 179*)> **GENIUS OF CRACK. / ANSWERMAN**		
	(above issued on 'Homestead')		
Aug 91.	(7"ep) <*SMR 4.5*> **HEADRINGER EP**	-	
	– Flameproof suit / World tour / Ski trip / Kickball babe / Candyman.		
Jan 92.	(7") <*SP 137*> **LEFT BEHIND. / (other by VELOCITY GIRL)**	-	
	(above on 'Sub Pop')		
Dec 92.	(7") <*SMR 14*> **COULD HAVE BEEN CHRISTMAS. / (other by Velocity Girl)**		-
Jan 93.	(7") <*SMR 16*> **DINER**		
	– Load hog / Gold digger.		
	(below on 'I.T.Q.')		
Mar 93.	(7") <(*IVR 1*)> **BEAUTIFUL ARLINGTON. / (other artists)**		Dec92
Apr 93.	(7"ep) <(*SMR 18*)> **MATCHBOOK / IN A NAME. / NOT LIVING / BOSSANOVA**		
May 93.	(cd/c/lp) <(*SMR 13 CD/C/V*)> **DEEP END**		

– In a name / The spook / Slugger / Lucky / Water's edge / Genius of crack / 460 / Sniffy / Valentine / Skinny / Waxed / Writing letters / Stupid like a fox.

Aug 93.	(7") <*smwh 08 / SMR 26*> **KIDDING ON THE SQUARE. / (other by Small Factory)**		
	(above shared on 'Working Holiday' label)		
Apr 94.	(7") <(*SMR 24*)> **BE LIKE THAT. / NEWSPAPER**		
May 94.	(cd/c/lp) <(*SMR 25 CD/C/V*)> **THE HEART'S TREMOLO**		

– Loud is as loud does / Quietnova / Be like that / Fast food medicine / Kidding on the square / Slaw / Cowed by the bla bla / The heart's tremolo / Bride d-elegance / Fits and starts.

TSUNAMI (cont)

May 94. (cd-ep) <SMR 29> **COWED BY THE BLAH BLAH (split w/ RODAN and EGGS)**
Feb 95. (7") **SHE CRACKED. / (other by SUPERCHUNK)**
(above issued on 'Huggy Bear' records)
Apr 95. (cd) <(SMR 33CD)> **WORLD TOUR & OTHER DESTINATIONS** (compilation)
– Flameproof suit / World tour / Ski trip / Kickball babe / Candyman / Genius of crack / Answerman / Left behind / Punk means cuddle / Could have been Christmas / Load hog / Goldigger / Beauty (pt.2) / Brick book building / Sometimes a notion / Walking tour / Crackers / Not living / Bossa nova / Kidding on the square / Newspaper / Courage.

—— **TRIP GREY** – drums; repl. PAMER
—— added **AMY DOMINGUES** – bass, cello + **BOB MASSEY** – guitar, keyboards

Aug 97. (7") <SMR 52> **POODLE. / OLD CITY**
Sep 97. (cd) <(SMR 53CD)> **A BRILLIANT MISTAKE**
– Old grey mare / Great mimes / Double shift / Enter misguided / The workers are punished / Liar's dice (flight of the chickens) / The match / Poodle / Unbridled / DMFH / David Foster Wallace / Hocky / PBS.

LIQUORICE

JENNY TOOMEY – vocals, guitar (of GRENADINE) / **DAN LITTLETON** – guitar, vocals (of IDA) / **ROB CHRISTIANSEN** – bass / **TREY MANY** – drums (of HIS NAME IS ALIVE)

4 a.d.   4ad-Warners

Jul 95. (lp/cd) (CAD 5008/+CD) <45902> **LISTENING CAP**
– Trump suit / Team player / Keeping the weekend free / Drive around / Cheap cuts / Trump suit (edit) / Jill of all trades / No excuses / Breaking the ice / Blew it.

not iss.   Simple Machines

Nov 95. (7"m) <SMR 38> **STALLS. / ARTIFACTS / SQUAWK OF THE TOWN**

—— (1997) **LUTHER GREY** – drums; repl. TREY
—— LIQUORICE were inactive since 1999

GEEK

with **JENNY TOOMEY** etc

not iss.   Thrilladonna

Sep 00. (cd-ep) <5000> **SMELLS LIKE TUNA**
– Brain peel / Give it back / Your eyes / Away / Rise.
May 01. (cd) <5002> **GRADE SCHOOL BONER**
– I don't care / Away / Out of control / Brain peel / Your eyes / I don't give a fuck / Give it back / Whore / Kandy / Stop / My own / Unsure.

JENNY TOOMEY

with a plethora of session people + ex-TSUNAMI members

Misra   Misra

Oct 01. (cd) <MRS 010CD> **ANTIDOTE**
– Patsy Cline / Baby would it matter / Word traffic / Fall on me / Clear cut / Breezewood, PA / Needmore, PA / Useless excuses / Unclaimed / Charm city / The smell of him / When you get cold / Know from me / Artful dodger / Fool for you / Further unclaimed.

—— next with composer **FRANKLIN BRUNO**

Oct 02. (cd) <(MRS 016CD)> **TEMPTING: SINGS THE SONGS OF FRANKLIN BRUNO**
– Your inarticulate boyfriend / Decoy / Cheat / Empty sentiment / Just because it's dying / Masonic eye / Tempting / Pointless triangle / Unionbusting / Let's stay in / Only a monster / Every little bit hurts.

TUFNELS
(see under ⇒ BIRD NEST ROYS; see 80's section)

TUGBOAT 3001 A.D. (see under ⇒ FURTHER)

TULLYCRAFT

Formed: Seattle, Washington, USA . . . 1994 by ex-CRAYON members SEAN TOLLEFSON and JEFF FELL, along with former WIMP FACTOR 14 guitarist, GARY MIKLUSEK. CRAYON had chalked up only one album, 'BRICK FACTORY' before they bit the dust. TULLYCRAFT more or less picked up where CRAYON left off with their 1996 debut, 'OLD TRADITIONS, NEW STANDARDS'. Both groups were too easily defined by critics as twee pop when in fact their music featured a neurotic edginess not characteristic of that sub genre. Having set such high standards for themselves, the group's second album was going to have to be spectacular, and unfortunately it wasn't. 'CITY OF SUBARUS' had all the same ingredients as their debut, however, it was slightly under cooked. A singles collection in 1999 and an anthology of material from TOLLEFSON'S sporadic side-project, SIX CENTS & NATALIE, filled the gap between this and their 2002 album, 'BEAT, SURF, FUN', which was a welcome return to form by the band. • **Covered:** HEROES & VILLAINS (Pooh Sticks) / FALLING OUT OF LOVE (WITH YOU) (6ths / Stephin Merritt) / PUMPKIN PATCH (Some Velvet Sidewalk) / Six Cents covered TRUE COLORS (Cyndi Lauper) / YOUR CLASS (BMX Bandits) / THE WATER SONG (Mountain Goats) / etc.

Album rating: Crayon: BRICK FACTORY (*7) / Tullycraft: OLD TRADITIONS, NEW STANDARDS (*6) / CITY OF SUBARUS (*5) / THE SINGLES collection (*6) / BEAT SURF FUN (*6) / Six Cents & Natalie: SHOW ME THE HONEY collection (*4) / WHEN PUNK FELL TO EARTH compilation (*7)

CRAYON

SEAN TOLLEFSON – vocals, bass / **BRAD** – vocals, guitar / **JEFF FELL** – drums

not iss.   own label

1991. (ltd-c) <none> **A CARTWHEEL FOR A KISS**

not iss.   Harriet

Sep 91. (7"m) <9> **MATCHBOX. / ANOTHER KING OF THE WORLD / GREEN STAMP**
Jun 92. (7"ep) <12> **MOOMINLAND EP**
– Secret goldfish / St. Michael and the killer whale / Cupid said / Sit by me / All the stars / Barney, garney.
1993. (7") **FOREVER NEARLY TRUE. / Grover: 3-D Girl**
(above issued on 'Gritty Kitty' / below on 'Cher Doll')
1993. (7") <CHER 01> **THIS DREAM IS GONE. / Veronica Lake: SLEEPYHOUSE**
Aug 93. (7") <19> **THE SNAPTIGHT WARS. / PUMPKIN PATCH**
Mar 94. (cd) <SPY 2> **BRICK FACTORY**
– Live it with baby / Small / Chutes and ladders / The snap-tight wars / Crown / Western flyer / Pedal / Honey bunny / Hope in evert train / Reason 2600 Snow globe / Schirm loop / Jenny don't be sad / Knee-high Susan.

TULLYCRAFT

SEAN + JEFF / + GARY MIKLUSEK – guitar (ex-WIMP FACTOR 14)

Wurlitzer Jukebox   Harriet

May 95. (7"m) <30> **TRUE BLUE. / SKYWAY / SUPERBOY & SUPERGIRL**
—— (note that the title track was not included on 'THE SINGLES' comp)

not iss.   Little Teddy

1995. (7"ep) <Lite 738> **1ST STRING TEENAGE HIGH**
– 1st string teenage high / Not quite burning bridges / Piano mlessons for beauty queens / Stay cool I'll see you next summer.

—— in 1995, the TULLYCRAFT track, 'Pink Lemonade' featured on a split 'PaperCut' records EP alongside tracks by CUB, RAGGEDY ANN + WEAKLING
—— in 1995, another 7"ep on 'Sweet Bamboo' (issued w/ White Bread fanzine) – featuring the track 'PITNEY BOSE' alongside PUMPERNICKEL, CUPPA JOE and AL LARSEN & KATRINA MITCHELL
—— in 1996, 'Glove Puppet' fanzine issued 7" EP (featuring TULLYCRAFT's 'She's Got The Beat') alongside PUSH KINGS, PEST 500 & TIZZY

1996. (cd)<lp> <SPY 5><BITE 31> **OLD TRADITIONS, NEW STANDARDS**
– Willie goes to the seashore / Josie / Mental obsession / Wish I'd kept a scrap book / Superboy & Supergirl / Sweet / Dollywood / Pop songs your new boyfriend's too stupid to know about / Then again, maybe I don't / Meet me in Las Vegas / Cammy & the count / Miracles are hard to find. (UK lp-iss.Aug98 +=; same as US) – (2 extra tracks). <(re+UK cd-iss. Jan00 on 'Darla'; DRL 102)>
1996. (7") (WJ 13) **JOSIE. / LOOK HOW WE KILLED THE RIOT GRRRLS**
1996. (7"m) <CHER 7> **BAILEY PARK. / SWEET / PEDAL**
(above issued on 'Cher Doll')

1997. (7") <40> **HEROES AND VILLAINS. / (other by RIZZO)**

KittyBoo

1997. (7"ep) <BOO!-002> **TEAM BUNNYGRUNT vs. TEAM TULLYCRAFT**
– Break seaside (and over) / Maybe baby / (two by BUNNYGRUNT).

not iss.   100 Guitar Mania

1997. (7") **SHE'S GOT THE BEAT. / (other by AVACADO BABY)**

—— added **CHRIS MUNFORD** – keyboards, guitar (ex-INCREDIBLE FORCE OF JUNIOR)

Cher Doll – Cher Doll – Darla   Darla

Mar 98. (lp/cd) <(DRL 055/+CD)> **CITY OF SUBARUS**
– 8 great ways / Belinda / Ticket tonight / Crush this town / Godspeed / Miss Douglas county / Actives and pledges / The lives of Cleopatra / Bee sting stings / Vacation in Christine, ND.

—— (1999) now without GARY
—— (2000) added **HAROLD** (ex-guest) guitar

Little Teddy   Little Teddy

Jan 02. (7") <(LITE7 49)> **TWEE. / FALLING OUT OF LOVE (WITH YOU)**

not iss.   Magic Marker

Apr 02. (cd/lp) <MMR 20 CD/LP> **BEAT SURF FUN**
– Twee / Glitter & twang / Christine, ND / Wild bikini / DIY queen / Cowgirls on parade / I kept the Beach Boys / Orange cake mix / Knockout / Radio theme / Sent to the Moon / Who needs what.

– compilations, etc. –

Jan 00. (cd) *Darla;* <(DRL 101)> **THE SINGLES**   Oct99
– Skyway / Superboy & Supergirl / Pop songs your new boyfriend's too stupid to know about / Pink lemonade / Bailey park / Pedal / Josie / 1st string teenage high / Not quite burning bridges / Piano lessons for beauty queens / Stay cool I'll see you in the summer / Falling out of love (with you) / Guyana punch / She's got the beat / Break seaside (and over) / Maybe baby / Heoes and villains / They're not tyring on the dance floor / 8 great ways / Crush the scene / Look how we killed the riot grrrls / Loveless.

SIX CENTS & NATALIE

SEAN TOLLEFSON with at first **MELISSA JETER** – vocals

not iss.   own label

1991. (c) <none> **WATER MACHINE**
1992. (c) <none> **TRESSEL**
1993. (c) <none> **LET'S PRETEND WE'RE MARRIED**

TULLYCRAFT (cont)

			not iss.	Harriet
Aug 92.	(7") <HARR 14> BOYFRIENDS. /		-	
1994.	(7") SUMMER'S GONE BUT A LOT GOES. /		-	
1995.	(7") WHEN PUNK FELL TO EARTH. /		-	

—— he added **JEFF FELL** – guitar (on tour)

– compilations, etc. –

on 'Blackbean & Placenta Tape Club' unless mentioned otherwise
1999. (cd) <BBPTC 83> **SHOW ME THE HONEY**
– Quilting bee / One for me / Spoiler / Needed to / Fly with me / Qubic / Sing-a-long / Nutra-sweet / Sea scout / Reason 2600 / Beach girl / Red and green / Just one / XYZ / A little cranky / No tag backs / Boyfriends / My love is a flower / Dumb stupid song / Cowboys and spaceships / When I was your boyfriend / New term / Stephanie / All the best things / Wait for me / Secret goldfish / (untitled).
2002. (cd) <BBPTC 195> **WHEN PUNK FELL TO EARTH**

TURIN BRAKES

Formed: Balham, London, England ... 1998 by OLLIE KNIGHTS and GALE PARADJANIAN (a guy). Acting as Britain's own KINGS OF CONVENIENCE, TURIN BRAKES have been fighting the NAM (New Acoustic Movement) war since the release of their 1999 EP 'THE DOOR'. Comprising of hushed acoustic tracks with multi-talented OLLIE KNIGHTS on vocals and PARADJANIAN playing whatever took his fancy, the set helped them grab the attention of independent label 'Source', who issued two EP's 'FIGHT OR FLIGHT' and 'THE STATE OF THINGS' in 2000, whilst re-issuing 'THE DOOR'. After much attention from the music press and MTV's own 'alternative' music channel MTV2, the duo had a Top 40 chart position with their debut album 'THE OPTIMIST LP' (2001). The set, with added percussion, piano and emotive strings, spawned three further Top 40 singles, the best being the sublime 'MIND OVER MONEY', with KNIGHTS' vocal gymnastics being a particular highlight.

Album rating: THE OPTIMIST LP (*8)

OLLIE KNIGHTS – vocals, guitar / **GALE PARADJANIAN** – multi

		Anvil	not iss.
Jun 99.	(ltd;7"ep/cd-ep) (ANV 027/+CDS) **'THE DOOR' EP**		-
	– The door / By TV light / Nowhere / The road.		

		Source	Astralwerks
Aug 00.	(d7"ep/cd-ep) (SOUR V/CDS 008) **THE STATE OF THINGS EP**		-
	– The boss / Balham to Brooklyn / All away / The state of things.		
Oct 00.	(7"ep/cd-ep) (SOUR V/CDS 012) **FIGHT OR FLIGHT EP**		-
	– Mind over money / Nine to five / Emergency 72 / Christine.		
Feb 01.	(7"ep/cd-ep) (SOUR V/CDS 024) **THE DOOR EP**	67	-
	– The door / Reach out / Boss.		
Mar 01.	(cd/lp) (SOUR CD/LP 023) <30696> **THE OPTIMIST LP**	27	May01
	– Feeling oblivion / Underdog (save me) / Emergency 72 / Future boy / The door / The state of things / By TV light / Slack / Starship / The road / Mind over money / The optimist.		
Apr 01.	(7") (SOURV 015) **UNDERDOG (SAVE ME). / BALHAM TO BROOKLYN**	39	-
	(cd-s+=) (SOURCDS1 015) – The door (live).		
	(cd-s) (SOURCDS2 015) – ('A'side) / Nowhere / Feeling oblivion (live) / ('A'-video).		
Jul 01.	(7") (SOUR 038) **MIND OVER MONEY. / STONE**	31	-
	(cd-s+=) (SOURCDX 038) – Tunnel.		
	(cd-s) (SOURCD 038) – ('A'extended) / Road (session) / Sunjets – Heavy 2 (instrumental) / ('A'-video).		
Oct 01.	(7") (SOUR 041) **EMERGENCY 72. / EVERYBODY KNOWS**	41	-
	(cd-s+=) (SOURCDX 041) – The first time / ('A'video).		
	(cd-s) (SOURCD 041) – ('A'extended) / The last time / Lasso.		
Oct 02.	(7") (SOUR 064) **LONG DISTANCE. / LOST AND FOUND**	22	-
	(cd-s+=) (SOURCD 064) – ('A'-The Bees remix).		
	(cd-s) (SOURCDX 064) – ('A'side) / ('A'-Max Tundra remix) / Soul less (home recording).		

TUSCADERO

Formed: Washington D.C., USA ... 1993 by MELISSA FARRIS (vocals, guitar) and MARGARET MCCARTNEY (vocals, guitar). TUSCADERO (who named themselves after SUZI QUATRO's 'Happy Days' character 'Leather Tuscadero') were one of a slew of bands who hit their mid-20s in the early-to-mid-90s ... decided they didn't want to grow up ... and then set about recapturing their lost childhoods on record. They also set about reeling in the bygone years by baiting their bubblegum pop-punk hooks with sweet, choice memories of teenage years, television, problems with boyfriends and parents ... and a general sonic smorgasbord of the immature-but-happy popular culture references that characterize much of that musical subgenre in general. Blowing breathy bubblegum pop ballad bubbles they first hit the retro popcult scene with the 'MT. PLEASANT / NANCY DREW' EP in 1994 (for 'Teenbeat' records) and then 'THE PINK ALBUM' (1994), which would be remixed by MARK ROBINSON of UNREST and re-released by 'Elektra' when they signed the band two years later. Until then, 'Teenbeat' would release a series of EPs in 1995: 'STEP INTO MY WIGGLE ROOM'; 'ANGEL IN A HALF SHIRT'; and the 'ROBINSON' EP. After the redone 'PINK' album, TUSCADERO recorded 'MY WAY OR THE HIGHWAY', their first LP specifically for 'Elektra'. This would once again fall back on the tried-and-tested-to-destruction fuzzpunk pop-cult formula of teen melodrama, joyful alienation and comic book worship. McCARTNEY would subsequently play for HOT PURSUIT, while FARRIS would reprise her fuzzy power chords in stripped-down form for Washington outfit, DAME FATE, when they formed in the summer of 1999 along with YALAN PAPILLION (vocals/bass) and SPECK (drummer). Their debut album 'TIME AND TIDE, WAIT FOR NO MAN' (2002) was released on the 'Lovitt' label, and its melancholy, moody, gothic, musically eclectic running time appeared to quiet approval and hope for good things on their next album.

Album rating: THE PINK ALBUM (*6) / STEP INTO MY WIGGLE ROOM mini (*5) / MY WAY OR THE HIGHWAY (*6) / Hot Pursuit: THE THRILL DEPARTMENT (*6) / Dame Fate: TIME AND TIDE, WAIT FOR NO MAN (*5)

MELISSA FARRIS – vocals, guitar, organ / **MARGARET McCARTNEY** – vocals, guitar, flute / **PHIL SATLOF** – bass, piano, timpani, vocals / **JACK HORNADY** – drums, vocals

		Teenbeat	Teenbeat
May 94.	(ltd-7") <(TEENBEAT 139)> **MT. PLEASANT. / NANCY DREW**		
Aug 94.	(ltd-7") <(TEENBEAT 149)> **ANGEL IN A HALF-SHIRT. / POSTER BOY**		Nov93
Aug 95.	(lp/cd) <(TEENBEAT 159-1/-2)> **THE PINK ALBUM**		Nov94
	– Heat lightnin' / Candy song / Game song / Latex dominatrix / Just my size / Dime a dozen / Lovesick / Mt. Pleasant / Nancy Drew / Hollywood handsome / Leather idol / Crayola. <re-iss. & re-mixed 1996 on 'Elektra'; 61918>		
Sep 95.	(7"ep) <TEENBEAT 169> **THE MARK ROBINSON REMIXES EP**	-	
	– Paper crown / The sky is cold blue / Pleasure idle / Sweet sweet sugar pops / So sick of you / I am king oil / Your chocolate bells.		
Oct 95.	(m-lp/m-cd) <(TB 179-1/-2)> **STEP INTO MY WIGGLE ROOM**		
	– Holidays R hell / Angel in a half-shirt / Poster boy / Dreams of the tanker / Sways / Given up / Sonic yogurt / Palmer: all-star jam.		

		not iss.	Elektra
Apr 98.	(cd,c) <62170> **MY WAY OR THE HIGHWAY**	-	
	– Queen for a day / Paper dolls / Freak magnet / Not my Johnny / Hot head / Tiny shiny boyfriend / Dr. Doom / Tickled pink / Evil eye / You got your pride / Cathy Ray / Liquid center / Temper temper / Mutiny. <also on 'Teenbeat'; TB 259>		

—— split in '99; FARRIS + SATLOF were also behind The PROJECT (with MARK ROBINSON; ex-UNREST) while McCARTNEY moonlighted with HOT PURSUIT

HOT PURSUIT

MARGARET McCARTNEY – vocals, bass / **EVELYN HURLEY** – vocals, guitar (ex-BLAST OFF COUNTRY STYLE) / **GINGER CROCKETT** – drums

		Teenbeat	Teenbeat
Jan 99.	(7") <TEENBEAT 264> **BASKETBALL. / HAWAII**	-	-
Jul 00.	(cd) <(TEENBEAT 289)> **THE THRILL DEPARTMENT**		
	– Summer song / Timonium two-step / Mail call / Goldenhead / Tobingets a bonus / Mousetime USA / Spring cleaning / Why married? / Revolutionary war song / Lucky seven.		

DAME FATE

MELISSA FARRIS – vocals, guitar / **YALAN PAPILLION** – bass, vocals (ex-MISS MAY '66, ex-SHANGHAI LILY, ex-AVEC DES PAPILLIONS) / **SPECK** – drums

		not iss.	Lovitt
May 02.	(cd) <LOV 029> **TIME AND TIDE, WAIT FOR NO MAN**	-	
	– Crisp winter / Forget him / River letters / Lovely drug / Stealing hearts / Poison wings of a butterfly / Ceilings / Lights out.		

TWELVE THOUSAND DAYS
(see under ⇒ EYELESS IN GAZA; in 80's section)

27 VARIOUS
(see under ⇒ POLARA; in 80's section)

22 PISTEPIRKKO

Formed: North Finland ... late 70's by P-K KERANEN, his brother ASKO KERANEN and ESPE HAVERINEN. Naming themselves after a type of beetle, they won Helsinki's Battle Of The Bands in '82, quickly spreading their unique RAMONES-meets-CAPTAIN BEEFHEART style. The trio released their first single in '85, finally getting around to a full set of tracks on their 1987 debut, 'THE KINGS OF HONG KONG'. A second album, 'BARE BONE NEST', fused a varied mix'n'match batch of genres, while three years on, their dark and moody major label debut, 'BIG LUPU', now fused A-HA vocals with SMASHING PUMPKINS or VELVET UNDERGROUND. Another lengthy break ensued, until 1996's trip-hop and dub attempt, 'RUMBLE CITY LA LA LAND', failed to achieve its goal. Continuing their trend of selected ambience, drones and general experimental electronica, 22-PISTEPIRKKO issued what could've been considered their first 'summer', or, shudder 'pop' record. Simmering with day-glo warmth and a tentative ear for melodies, 'RALLY OF LOVE' (2001) still maintained the group's instantly recognisible mix of beats, loops and samples et al, but this time with a melodic spin. Pretty much like BOARD OF CANADA's trippy wavering psychedelic electro sound, but without being too sinister.

Album rating: THE KINGS OF HONG KONG (*6) / BARE BONE NEST (*6) / BIG LUPU (*6) / RUMBLE CITY, LA LA LAND (*5) / ELEVEN (*7) / DOWNHILL CITY (*5) / RALLY OF LOVE (*6)

P-K KERANEN – vocals, guitar / **ASKO KERANEN** – bass, keyboards / **SEPE HAVERINEN** – drums, vocals

22 PISTEPIRKKO (cont)

				Pygmi	not iss.
1988.	(cd) **THE KINGS OF HONG KONG**			-	- Finland

– I'm back / Geronimo / Last night / Big bed / Hong Kong king / Hank's TV set / Don't try to tease me / I'm staying now / Lost lost love / B-instrumental / Motorcycle man / Searching & looking / Horseman's son.

		Sonet	not iss.
Oct 90.	(cd) *(SNTCD 1007)* **BARE BONE NEST**		-

– Frankenstein / Don't go home Joe / Don't play cello / You're mine blues / Shoe bayou / Night train miss / Fly on / Bone bone baby / Round table blues / Till I day I die / She's so alone / Save my soul / Bare bone nest. *(re-iss. Jul00 on 'Clear Spot'; 05420-2)*

Sep 91. (m-lp) *(SONL 22)* **22 PISTEPIRKKO**

		Spirit – Polygram	not iss.
1992.	(cd) **BIG LUPU**	-	- Finland

– Bubblegum couple / Don't say I'm so evil / Household affairs / Tired of being drunk / Birdy / I'm right / Crippled and blind blues / Texacoson / Papa / Swamp blues / All night cafe / She's so shy / Hawk walk.

		Bare Bone Business	not iss.
Mar 96.	(cd) *(BBBCD 002)* **RUMBLE CITY, LA LA LAND**		-

– Wild Billy / Oo my head / (Just a) Little bit more / Tokyo tiger / Snowy Dave / At the everybody's / I never said / I do do I / Gimme some water / Blue balloon / Nappy king blues / Coffee girl.

		Clearspot	Clearspot
Oct 98.	(cd/lp) *(efa 05409-2/-1)* <019> **ELEVEN**		

– Taxi 74 / Onion soup / Coma moon / Sad lake city / Boardroom walk / Hey man / Let the Romeo weep / Morning / Frustration / Shadows.

Nov 98. (cd-s) *(efacd 05449)* <021> **ONION SOUP / MILES & NEMO / ROMEO INSTRUMENTAL**

Jul 00. (cd) *(efa 05418-2)* **DOWNHILL CITY** (original soundtrack)
– Fabian's theme / Downhill city / Fujisan / Say wrong / Let the Romeo weep / Snowy Dave-99 / Doris drives away / Sascha's theme / Where's the moon, Joey? / Coffee girl 2 / Truth / Fujisan (beatbox jam) / Roundabout 2 / Tokyo (Aleksei Borisov remix).

Sep 01. (cd-s) *(060299)* **THIS TIME / THIS TIME (basement take)**

Oct 01. (cd/lp) *(060201-2/-1)* **RALLY OF LOVE**
– Quicksand / This time / Car wash / Freeman / Bloodstopper / I'm a moon around you / Moving a lawn / Waiting for the train / D-day / Metro blues / Rally of love.

– compilations, etc. –

1996.	(cd) *Bare Bone Business; (531 588-2)* **ZIPCODE** (remixes)	-	- Finland

– Tired of being drunk / Swamp blues / Wild Billy / Roundabout / I never said / Little bit more / Snowy Dave / Oo my head / Oo my head / Don't play cello / Don't say I'm so evil / Horror o'horrible / Bubblegum couple / Gimme some water / Birdy.

2 FOOT FLAME
(see under ⇒ MECCA NORMAL; 80's section)

TYDE (see under ⇒ FURTHER)

UGLY CASANOVA (see under ⇒ MODEST MOUSE)

Ui

Formed: New York City, New York, USA ... 1991 by SASHA FRERE-JONES (a music journo and ex-DOLORES bassist), CLEM WALDMANN, ALEX WRIGHT and DAVID WEEKS – however, WRIGHT and WEEKS had departed from the band before their debut EP, 'TWO-SIDED' (1994), and were replaced by jazz bassist WILBO WRIGHT. A free-range, post experimental/instrumental combo, it was no surprise that Ui hung about with the JOHN McENTIRE (TORTOISE) set in the early 90's. Delivering their 'UNLIKE' EP in 1995, they toured with the aforementioned TORTOISE and LABRADFORD before signing with Chicago's ultra-cool 'Southern' records. 'SIDELONG', the group's debut LP, appeared in 1996 and displayed the same robust, instrumental clamour once honed by the maverick SLINT. Funky duelling bass riffs, odd time signatures and mumbled sung/spoken lyrics were Ui's bag and the entire album reeked of deliberate "math rock", akin to the likes of TRANS AM, POLVO and The SEA & CAKE. After a brief flirtation with TECHNO ANIMAL and STEREOLAB (producing the rather interesting electronia of 'FIRES' (1997), under the nom de plume, UILAB), the ensemble issued their sophomore set, 'LIFELIKE' (1998), which mixed and matched their post-rock antics with some beautiful electronic ambience. Like looking at good, complex, modern architecture, Ui displayed the hallmarks of their neatly constructed, neo-conservative facade.

Album rating: SIDELONG (*7) / LIFELIKE (*6)

SASHA FRERE-JONES – vocals, bass, guitar, banjo (ex-DOLORES) / **CLEM WALDMANN** – drums, percussion / **ALEX WRIGHT** – bass (ex-DOLORES) / **DAVID WEEKS** – DJ, samples

		Hemiola	not iss.
Dec 93.	(12"ep) **THE 2-SIDED EP**		-

– At nako / Pinata / I will not make inconsiderate requests / Horn crown label / Lull / Ring / Scrape.

— now without WRIGHT + WEEKS; added **WILBO WRIGHT** – bass, cello

		not iss.	Lunamoth
Oct 95.	(m-cd) <*LUNAMOTH 05*> **UNLIKE REMIXES VOL.I**	-	

– Horn crown label / Ring (descriptive mix 1) / Sexy photograph / Ring / The piano / Ring (descriptive mix 2).

		Soul Static	Soul Static
Feb 96.	(12"ep) *(SOUL 10)* **THE SHARPIE EP**		

– The sharpie / Have a good time / Skeletons.

Feb 96. (7") *(SOUL 11)* **MATCH MY FOOT. / MATCH MY FOOT (Darryl Moore remix)**

Feb 96. (one-sided-7") *(SOUL 12)* **MATCH MY FOOT (D-mix 2)**

		Southern	Southern
Apr 96.	(cd/lp) <*(18535-2/-1)*> **SIDELONG**		

– August song / The long egg / Sexy photograph / Top requests / Golden child / The piano / Painted hill / Drive towards the smoke / Butterfly who / Johnny.

Jul 96. (12"ep) <*(18540-1)*> **DROPPLIKE EP**   Sep96
– Dropplike (Darryl Moore remix) / Liquid leg (Daryll Moore remix) / Slow burner (Ganger remix).

Feb 98. (12"ep/cd-ep; as UiLAB) *(2)* **FIRES**
– St. Elmo's fire (radio) / Less time / St. Elmo's fire (red corona) / St. Elmo's fire (spatio-dynamic) / Impulse rah! / St. Elmo's fire (snow).
(above was a collaboration with STEREOLAB and issued on 'Bingo')

Apr 98. (cd/lp) <*(18547-2/-1)*> **LIFELIKE**
– Drive until he sleeps / Blood in the air / Undersided / Digame / Laceria / Molloy's march / Green of the melon / Spilling / The fortune one knows no anxiety / News to go farther / Acer rubrum / Exeunt.

Nov 99. (12"ep/cd-ep) <*(18571-1/-2)*> **THE IRON APPLE**
– Mrs. Lady Lady / Blue pietro / Ms. Lady / Golden pietro / Run pietro.

— (Jan'01) added **ERIK SANKO**; expect an album mid-2003

– compilations, etc. –

Oct 97. (cd) *Southern; <(18549)>* **THE 2-SIDED EP / THE SHARPIE EP**   Feb98

UKRAINIANS

Formed: Leeds, England ... initially as a sideline for The WEDDING PRESENT (PETER SOLOWKA's father handed down the tradition of playing the mandolin and balalaika) on a series of John Peel sessions (released as 'UKRAINSKI VISTUPI V JOHNA PEELA' in the Spring of '89). A few years later, after he parted company with DAVID GEDGE & co., PETER formed The

UKRAINIANS with other like-minded traditionalists, lyricist LEN LIGGINS and ROMAN REMEYNES. Signed to top roots label, 'Cooking Vinyl', the group unveiled their eponymous debut album in Autumn '91, turning their impressively authentic Eastern European folk style to The SMITHS. Yes, The SMITHS (!), LIGGINS sounding too close to MORRISSEY for comfort on the likes of 'BATYAR' (i.e. 'Bigmouth Strikes Again') and 'KOROLEVA NE POLERMA' ('The Queen Is Dead'), the 'PISNI IZ THE SMITHS' EP possibly proving that there's always been an er . . . Balkans element to The SMITHS' sound. Following the replacement of REMEYNES with STEPAN PASICZNYK, The UKRAINIANS released a follow-up set, 'VORONY' (1993), this time turning their dolorous charm to a reading of the Velvet Underground's 'VENUS IN FURS' (under the guise of 'CHEKAAANYA'). 1994's 'KULTURA', meanwhile, was a rockier affair (courtesy of new members DAVE LEE, PAUL DINO and MICHAEL L.B. WEST) combining breakneck stompalongs like 'EUROPA' with more easy going fare in the vein of the countrified 'HORILKA'. Nigh on four years passed before the band inflicted the self explanatory 'PRINCE' EP on an unsuspecting public, SOLOWKA and his minstrels lending a measure of threadbare austerity to the lavish creations of the artist formerly known as. With the long-awaited 'REPUBLIKA' (2002), the folk revisionists set their sights on the SEX PISTOLS, cranking out rather ridiculous versions of 'ANARCHY IN THE UK' and 'PRETTY VACANT'. Nevertheless, these detracted only slightly from what was otherwise the most accomplished album of their career by dint of its more reverent treatment of Eastern European tradition.

Album rating: THE UKRAINIANS (*5) / VORONY (*5) / KULTURA (*5) / DRINK TO MY HORSE! collection (*5) / RESPUBLIKA (*7)

THE 'Legendary' LEN LIGGINS (b. London, England) – vocals, violin (ex-SINISTER CLEANERS) / **PETER SOLOWKA** – guitars, mandolin, vocals (ex-WEDDING PRESENT) / **ROMAN REMEYNES** – accordion, vocals

		Cooking Vinyl	Omnium
Sep 91.	(cd/c) *(COOK CD/C 044)* <2002> **THE UKRAINIANS**		

– Oi divchino / Hopak / Ti moyi radoshchi / Zavtra / Slava kobzarya / Dity plachut / Cherez richku, cherez hal / Pereyidu / Tebe zhdu / Son. *(cd re-iss. JUl02 on 'Gumbo'; GUMBOCD 028)*

— **STEPAN PASICZNYK** – accordion, vocals; repl. ROMAN

Jan 93.	(cd-ep) *(FRYCD 023)* **PISNI IZ THE SMITHS**		-

– Batyar (Bigmouth strikes again) / Koroleva ne Polerma (The Queen is dead) / M'yaso – Ubivstvo (Meat is murder) / Spivaye solovey (What difference does it make?).

		Cooking Vinyl	Xenophile
Feb 93.	(cd/c) *(COOK CD/C 054)* <4015> **VORONY**		

– Vorony / Koroleva ne Polerma (The Queen is dead) / Chi skriptsi hrayu / Sche raz / Nadia pishla / Doroha / Rospryahaite / Durak / Sertsem i dusheyu / Dvi lebidky / De ye moya mila? / Teper mi hovorymo / Chekannya (Venus in furs).

— now with also **DAVE LEE** – drums / **PAUL DINO** – Briggs bass guitar / **MICHAEL L.B. WEST** – mandolin, duda, piano

		Cooking Vinyl	Cooking Vinyl
Sep 94.	(cd) *(<COOKCD 070>)* **KULTURA**		

– Polityka / UkrainAmerica / Kievskiy express / Smert / Horilka / Slava / Europa / Kinets / Tycha voda / Zillya zelenenke / Ya / Tsyhanochka / Dyakuyu i dobranich.

— little was heard from them for just under 4 years

Aug 98.	(cd-ep) *(FRYCD 071)* **PRINCE E.P.**		-

– Nothing compares 2 U / Sign 'o' the times / Purple rain.

		Zirka	not iss.
Feb 01.	(cd) *(ZRKCD 1)* **DRINK TO MY HORSE!** (collection 1989-1994)		-

– Oi divchino / Cherez richku cherez hai / Davni chasy / Teper my hovorymo / Yikhav kozak za zanai / Ti moyi radoshchi / Zavtra / Sertsem I dusheyu / Hopak / Na skriptsi hrayu / Koroleva ne pomerla (The Queen is dead) / Chekannya (Venus in furs) / Kievskiy express / Tykha voda / Batyar (Bigmouth strikes again) / Europa / Rospryahaite / Tsyhanochka / Davni chasy / Verkhovyno.

Jun 02.	(cd-s) *(ZRKCDS 2)* **ANARCHY IN THE UK**		-

		not iss.	Omnium
Oct 02.	(cd) <2028> **RESPUBLIKA**	-	

– Ty zh mene pidmanula (You deceived me) / Anarchy in the UK / Chervona rozha troyaka (Three red roses) / Horila sosna (The pine tree was burning) / Arkan (The lasso) / Oi vydno selo (You can see a village) / Srebrncia / Stoyit yavir nad vodoyu (The maple tree stood at the water's edge) / Oi na hori (On the hill) / Pretty vacant / Reve ta stohne dnipr shyrokyy (The broad river Dnieper roars and moans) / Nalyvaimo brattya (Let's fill out drinking cups, brothers) / O Ukraino (Oh Ukraine).

ULTRABABYFAT

Formed: Santa Cruz, California, USA . . . 1992 by Nashville-born, Atlanta, Georgia students SHONALI BHOWMIK and MICHELLE DUBOIS. These two musicians met at age eight when they were both taking violin lessons in their native city of Nashville, and would stay in contact with each other as they state-hopped to California before arriving in Georgia for their formation. Recruiting bassist LAURIE GARNIER and drummer MAURICIO CAREY, they called themselves BABYFAT and released their debut album, 'DRAGONS GO AWAY' (1995) on 'Sister Ruby' records. In 1998, the group became ULTRABABYFAT and, with new bassist BRITTA PHILLIPS (ex-BELLTOWER) and SHANE SANDERS on sticks, they released the uneven indie harmonic pop rock 'SILVER TONES SMILE' album (1998). Three years on, the garage-cum-surf-(s)punk 'EIGHT BALLS IN REVERSE' LP (2001) would cement the band's reputation as entertaining-but-stuck-in-the-lower-leagues songsmiths.

Album rating: DRAGONS GO AWAY as Babyfat (*4) / SILVER TONES SMILE (*4) / EIGHT BALLS IN REVERSE (*5)

SHONALI BHOWMIK – vocals, guitar / **MICHELLE DUBOIS** – vocals, guitar / **LAURIE GARNIER** – bass / **MAURICIO CAREY** – drums

		not iss.	Sister Ruby
Apr 95.	(cd; as BABYFAT) <16> **DRAGONS GO AWAY**	-	

– Mandible man / Green / In a kelp bed / Sour mash / Bent on / Dust pet / Sloth / Mean thing / Crazy / Wrapped up / Mud / October / Shattered pins / What he said.

— **BRITTA PHILLIPS** – bass (ex-BELLTOWER) repl. GARNIER

— **JEFF SULLIVAN** – drums; repl. SHANE SANDERS who repl. CAREY

		not iss.	Velvel
Jul 98.	(cd) <79700> **SILVER TONES SMILE**	-	

– Twist / Bent on / T.C.B.A. / Plenty / Salem / 100 watts / Water / What he said / Jonesin' / Peacock throne / St. Augustine / Stupid / Ringside.

— although BRITTA spent time with LUNA, she returned to the fold for . . .

		Orange	Orange
Jun 01.	(cd) <(OR 010)> **EIGHT BALLS IN REVERSE**		May01

– Gunshy / Bored in Paris / Water tower / Diamondback / Already there / Apple tree / Star's lament / Underground / Chapel of yesterdays / Shake n' bake / The fool / Bury me / Crash bang highway / Sawdust and coffee.

ULTRASOUND

Formed: Newcastle, England . . . early 90's by the bulky (ex-POSSESSION) singer, TINY and guitarist RICHARD GREEN, whom he had met at a music course at Wakefield College. The pair decided to form wacky CARDIACS-induced outfit, SLEEPY PEOPLE, adding drummer ANDY PEACE in the process. Relocating to London (Acton, actually), they added VANESSA BEST on bass and MATT JONES on keyboards, although times were tough playing gigs for next to nothing and trying to explain that to the dole office the next day. TINY, with a look between EDDIE IZZARD on a very bad night and a chubby MORRISSEY, began to attract the right people to ULTRASOUND gigs. Among the A&R pack was 'Virgin' supremo himself, Richard Branson, who was enticed to go and see them perform by staff at his offshoot imprint, 'V2'. Fortunately, they played at NME's Unsigned Bands Gig early the following year, releasing a debut 45, 'SAME BAND', for 'Fierce Panda' soon after. This in turn, led to 'Nude' records subsequently giving them a deal, their second single, 'BEST WISHES', breaking the hard working quintet into the UK Top 75. In the summer of '98, they cracked the Top 30 with the excellent 'STAY YOUNG', although 'I'LL SHOW YOU MINE IF YOU SHOW ME YOURS', failed to register. Released the following March, 'FLOOTLIT WORLD' (a non-album cut) continued ULTRASOUND's chart campaign and previewed the double-CD debut album, 'EVERYTHING PICTURE'. A tad ambitious, overblown and retro 70's (especially in format!), the 100-minute plus set was just too much for the average punter although it did break into the Top 30. ULTRASOUND split soon after in October 1999. GREEN had already instigated The SOMATICS, a psychedelic guitar outfit with STEPHANIE GREEN and BRUCE RENSHAW. They issued the single 'LAST DAYS OF AN OLD TOWN' on Oxford's 'Shifty Disco' label in 2000, subsequently followed by the Chris Blair-produced, debut self-titled album in 2001. • **Covered:** Neil Young's 'HEY, HEY, MY, MY (INTO THE BLACK)', Pere Ubu's 'FINAL SOLUTION' and the Beatles' 'GETTING BETTER'.

Album rating: EVERYTHING PICTURE (*6) / Somatics: THE SOMATICS (*6)

TINY (b. ANDREW VICTOR WOOD, 1962, Birkenhead, Liverpool) – vocals / **RICHARD GREEN** – guitar / **MATT JONES** – keyboards / **VANESSA BEST** – bass / **ANDY PEACE** – drums

		Fierce Panda	not iss.
Jul 97.	(ltd-7"/cd-s) *(NING 35/+CD)* **SAME BAND. / OVER THERE / FLOODLIT WORLD**		-

		Nude	not iss.
Feb 98.	(ltd;10"/cd-s) *(NUD 33 T/CD)* **BEST WISHES / KURT RUSSELL / BLACK HOLE**	68	-
Jun 98.	(7") *(NUD 35S)* **STAY YOUNG. / UNDERWATER LOVE STORY**	30	-
	(cd-s+=) *(NUD 35CD1)* – Can't say no.		
	(cd-s) *(NUD 35CD2)* – ('A'side) / Football meat / Hey, hey, my, my (into the black).		
Oct 98.	(12"/cd-s) *(NUD 39 T/CD)* **I'LL SHOW YOU MINE IF YOU SHOW ME YOURS. / LOVESICK / ONE PLUS ONE / FINAL SOLUTION**		-
Mar 99.	(7") *(NUD 41S)* **FLOODLIT WORLD. / DEATH OF A DRAG RACER**	39	-
	(cd-s+=) *(NUD 41CD1)* – We will find love / Getting better.		
	(cd-s+=) *(NUD 41CD2)* – I'll show you mine (CD-Rom).		
Apr 99.	(d-cd/c/d-lp) *(NUDE 12 CDX/MC/LP)* **EVERYTHING PICTURE**	23	-

– Cross my heart / Same band / Stay young / Suckle / Fame thing / Happy times (are coming) // Aire & Calder / Sentimental song / Floodlit world / My impossible dream / Everything picture.

— ULTRASOUND disbanded in October 1999; MATT JONES would subsequently become MINUTEMAN who released an technoid album, 'RESIGNED TO LIFE' (2002). VANESSA BEST tried to embark on a solo career, while WOOD and PEACE reunited for a few ULTRASOUND outings; most got back together as SLEEPY PEOPLE to make one set, 'BURST NAILS IN A SHARP WALL' (1999).

SOMATICS

RICHARD GREEN – vocals, guitar / **STEPHANIE GREEN** – vocals, bass / **BRUCE RENSHAW** – drums, percussion

		Shifty Disco	not iss.
Jun 01.	(cd-s) *(DISCO 0106)* **LAST DAYS IN AN OLD TOWN / ASHES TO COAL**		-

ULTRA VIVID SCENE

Formed: New York City, New York, USA ... 1988 as a vehicle for singer/songwriter KURT RALSKE, who flitted between the local jazz and hardcore scenes. He then moved to London, England in '86, forming the bands NOTHING BUT HAPPINESS and CRASH. Having gained a contract with the UK label, '4 a.d.', KURT subsequently returned to New York where he formed UVS and it wasn't long before his eponymous HUGH JONES-produced debut set scaled the UK indie charts. Trading in a bubblegum ambient sound influenced by The VELVET UNDERGROUND and latter day noise merchants The JESUS & MARY CHAIN, RALSKE's insinuating vocals and uncompromising subject matter (perversion, suicide, mental illness, etc.) made him a kind of transatlantic spiritual cousin of MOMUS. Previous to this, he'd released the 'SHE SCREAMED' EP, which included his tribute to HANK WILLIAMS and the MARQUIS DE SADE; 'NOT IN LOVE (HIT BY A TRUCK)'. The man's 1990 follow-up album fared even better, attracting considerable interest from the US college circuit. He finally gave up solo/group work, moving into production for singer LIDA HUSIK after 1992's slightly disappointing 'REV' album.

Album rating: ULTRA VIVID SCENE (*8) / JOY 1967-1990 (*7) / REV (*6)

NOTHING BUT HAPPINESS

KURT RALSKE (b. 1967) – guitar / **DAVID MAREADY BOWAN** / **BILL GERSTALL** / **LYNN CUTHBERTSON**

		Remorse	Justine
Jun 86.	(7") *(LOST 1)* <*JUS 002*> **COULDN'T MAKE YOU MINE. / NARCOTICS DAY**		Feb89
Mar 87.	(lp) *(REMLP 1)* **DETOUR** – For waitress friends / Striped songs / Battle hymn / Buried in the flowers / Facsimile / Don't laugh / Couldn't make you mine / My summer dress / Blue kiss / Narcotics day.		–

CRASH

had already been formed by **KURT** plus **MARK DUMAIS** – vocals, guitar, main songwriter / **BILL CAREY** – guitar (ex-EXCENTRICKS) / **ADAM WRIGHT** – bass / **BYRON GUTHRIE** – drums

		Remorse	Justine
Nov 86.	(12"ep) *(LOST 2)* <*JUS 001*> **DON'T LOOK NOW (NOW!). / INTERNATIONAL VELVET / DON'T LOOK NOW (acoustic)**		Jun88
Nov 86.	(12"ep) *(LOST 4)* **ALMOST. / MY MACHINE / ON AND ON (version)**		–
Feb 87.	(lp) *(REMLP 2)* **I FEEL FINE** – Almost / Craig egg / International velvet / I go round / Superfly / Everything under the sun / I feel fine / My machine / On and on / Rings, chains and groups / Get set / John stood by / What I found. *(cd+=)* – (1 track).		–
Aug 87.	(7") *(LOSS 6)* **BRIGHT COLOURED LIGHTS. / IN MY HEAD**		–

— Disbanded soon after above. BYRON joined JOHN MOORE'S EXPRESSWAY and CAREY joined SOMETHING PRETTY BEAUTIFUL. It was an entirely different CRASH that issued for 'Creation', a single 'SUNBURST' early '89.

ULTRA VIVID SCENE

KURT RALSKE – vocals, everything (solo)

		4 a.d.	Columbia
Aug 88.	(12"ep/cd-ep) *(BAD 806/+CD)* **SHE SCREAMED / WALKIN' AFTER MIDNIGHT / NOT IN LOVE (HIT BY A TRUCK)**		–
Oct 88.	(lp/c)(cd) *(CAD/+C 809)(CAD 809CD)* <47485> **ULTRA VIVID SCENE** – She screamed / Crash / You didn't say please / Lynne-Marie 2 / Nausea / Mercy seat / Dream of love / Lynne-Marie / This isn't real / The whore of God / Bloodline / How did it feel / Hail Mary.		
1989.	(7") <*JUS 003*> **SLOW YOU DOWN. / TOTALLY FREE**	–	

— added **KRISTAN KRAMER** – bass / **MAZORA CREAGER** – cello, vocals / + the re turning **BYRON GUTHRIE** – drums

Mar 89.	(7") *(AD 906)* **MERCY SEAT. / CODINE**		–
	(12"+=/cd-s+=) – H like in Heaven / ('A'-lp version).		
Jul 89.	(7"ltd.shop-freebie) *(AD 908)* **SOMETHING TO EAT. / H LIKE IN HEAVEN**	–	–

— **KURT** retained **BYRON** + recruited **COLLIN RAE** – rhythm guitar / **ANN HOLLIS** – bass

Apr 90.	(7"ep/c-ep/12"ep/cd-ep) *(BAD/+C/T/CD 0004)* <73371> **STARING AT THE SUN / THREE STARS (*** version). / CRASH / SOMETHING BETTER**		
Apr 90.	(cd)(lp/c) *(CAD 0005CD)(CAD/+C 0005)* **JOY 1967-1990** – It happens every time / Staring at the sun / Three stars / Special one / Grey turns white / Poison / Guilty pleasure / Extra ordinary / Beauty No.2 / The kindest cut / Praise the law / Lightning.		–
Nov 90.	(7")<cd-ep> *(AD 0016)* <73534> **SPECIAL ONE. / KIND OF A DRAG**		–

— **RALSKE** recruited entire new line-up; **JACK DALEY** – bass / **JULIAN KLEPACZ** – drums

		Beggars Banquet	not iss.
Apr 02.	(7") *(BBQ 359)* **LEMONADE. / KILL TIME (OR IT KILLS YOU)**		–
	(cd-s+=) *(BBQ 359CD)* – Almost an introduction.		
May 02.	(cd/lp) *(BBQ CD/LP 227)* **THE SOMATICS** – For Claudette / Lemonade / Last days in an old town / LS2 9LZ / There is a happy land / Quietly / Come on heal me / Urban 45 / Guilt trip / Goodbye 25.		–

Oct 92.	(cd)(lp/c) *(CAD 2017CD)(CAD/+C 2017)* <53133> **REV** – Candida / Cut-throat / Mirror to mirror / The portion of delight / Thief's love song / How sweet / Medicating angels / Blood and thunder / This is the way.		
Feb 93.	(12"ep/cd-ep) *(BAD 3003/+CD)* **BLOOD AND THUNDER EP** – Blood and thunder (remix) / Don't look now (now!) / Candida (theme from 'Red Pressure Mounting') / Winter song.		–

— as said, KURT concentrated on production demands until he released an ambient set under the moniker, CATHARS, in 1999

UNBELIEVABLE TRUTH

Formed: Abingdon, Oxford, England ... 1993 by school friends JASON MOULSTER, NIGEL POWELL and ANDY YORKE (yes, that YORKE!). Having paid their musical dues in various bands in and around their home town, MOULSTER and POWELL hooked up with YORKE upon his return from Moscow (where he'd completed a degree in Russian literature) and set about forming a band of their own. Of course, any hopes that the group might be able to avoid the inevitable comparisons with elder brother THOM's mighty RADIOHEAD were doomed from the beginning. Especially as their music dealt in a similar vein of melancholic atmospherics (vaguely akin to a cross between latter day TALK TALK and AMERICAN MUSIC CLUB) and soul searching of the long dark night variety. Nevertheless, ANDY's voice was singled out for particular praise by critics, his tonsils possessed of enough individual character to deflect any predictable murmurs of family influence. Similarly, UNBELIEVABLE TRUTH's rise to cult acclaim has apparently been achieved with a dignified determination not to ride on the coat-tails of sibling success, the band attracting the attentions of 'Virgin' records after an early 1997 effort, 'BUILDING' for 'Shifty Disco'. After three further singles over the course of the next year and a bit (most notably Top 40 breakers, 'HIGHER THAN REASON' and 'SOLVED'), their debut album, 'ALMOST HERE', appeared in May '98. Fittingly navel gazing listening for one of the most overcast summers anyone can remember, the record almost made the UK Top 20 despite mixed reviews. Whether they can build upon this and truly emerge from the shadow of big brother remains to be seen; success on the scale of RADIOHEAD really would be unbelievable. ANDY YORKE and Co issued the soft-rock album, 'SORRYTHANKYOU', in July 2000, just as his brother's band were set to deliver the long-awaited 'Kid A'. It translated on the record itself just how much of a catch-22 situation poor ANDY had found himself in; to stay as far away from sounding like RADIOHEAD as he possibly could, which, in turn, only made matters worse as The UNBELIEVABLE TRUTH had ceased to progress musically. Regrettably, they split for good in September 2000. • **Trivia:** In 1997, they made an appearance on the quaintly-titled 'Fierce Panda' compilation, 'Cry Me A Liver'.

Album rating: ALMOST HERE (*7) / SORRYTHANKYOU (*5) / MISC. MUSIC double compilation (*5)

ANDY YORKE – vocals, guitar / **JASON MOULSTER** – bass / **NIGEL POWELL** – drums, keyboards, acoustic guitar

		Shifty Disco	not iss.
Feb 97.	(7") *(DISCO 9702)* **BUILDING. / TOO MANY THINGS TO LEARN**		–

		Virgin	Virgin
Oct 97.	(7"/c-s) *(VS/+C 1657)* **STONE. / FINEST LITTLE SPACE** (cd-s+=) *(VSCDT 1657)* – Roadside No.1 / Tyretracks.		–
Feb 98.	(7"/c-s) *(VS/+C 1676)* **HIGHER THAN REASON. / WHO'S TO KNOW** (cd-s+=) *(VSCDT 1676)* – Coming round / Revolution.	38	–
Apr 98.	(7"/c-s) *(VS/+C 1684)* **SOLVED. / NEVERMIND** (cd-s+=) *(VSCDT 1684)* – Yesterday never leaves / There if you want it.	39	–
May 98.	(cd/c/lp) *(<CDVX/TCV/V 2849>)* **ALMOST HERE** – Solved / Angel / Stone / Same mistakes / Forget about me / Settle down / Finest little space / Building / Almost here / Higher than reason / Be ready.	21	
Jul 98.	(7"/c-s) *(VS/+C 1697)* **SETTLE DOWN. / DUNE SEA** (cd-s+=) *(VSCDT 1697)* – Circle.	46	–

		Shifty Disco	not iss.
May 00.	(cd-s) *(DISCOQUICK 5)* **AGONY / ROADSIDE NO.2 / NIGHTLIGHT**		–
Jul 00.	(cd-s) *(DISCOQUICK 6)* **LANDSLIDE / EVERYBODY HAS TO EAT / HEAVEN SENT ME**		–
Sep 00.	(cd) *(SHIFTY 0002)* **SORRYTHANKYOU** – Landslide / A name / Disarm / Pedestrian / Home again / Daylight / Shed your skin / Advice to a lover / Agony / Covers / Hypnotist / I can't wait / Let it flow. *(d-lp-iss.Oct00; SHIFTY 0002V)*		–

— the band split after farewell show on 16 Sep'00

– compilations, etc. –

May 01.	(d-cd) *Shifty Disco; (UBTDIY 001)* **MISC. MUSIC** (b-sides, outtakes // live farewell show) – Life without this / Building / Roadside No.2 / Landslide / In the beginning / Believe in anger / Some of these people / Nightlight / Over / History / Fiction / Unwanted gift / Ciao! my shining star / All this time / Heaven sent me / Mea culpa / Everyone has to eat / Disaster / Whose side are you on? / Roadside No.1 (live) // Almost here / Pedestrian / Landslide / Who's to know / Stone / Home again / Daylight / Hypnotist / Higher than reason / Forget about me / Coveres / From this height / Building / Agony / Finest little space / Solved / I can't wait.		–

UNCLE TUPELO

Formed: Belleville, Illinois, USA ... 1987 by schoolmates JEFF TWEEDY and JAY FARRAR (who had played in punk outfit, The PRIMITIVES – US), MIKE HEIDORN completing the line-up. A band that have achieved almost legendary status among alternative country afficionados, UNCLE TUPELO christened a whole movement with the release of their seminal debut album, 'NO DEPRESSION' (1990). Issued on the small 'Rockville' label, the record translated the raw expression and sonic assault of punk into a contemporary country context; the spirit of what TWEEDY and FARRAR were trying to do was best illustrated on the title track, an impressive excavation of an ancient CARTER FAMILY song yearning for the sanctuary of Heaven, performed with as much conviction as any bonafide gospel act. Follow-up set, 'STILL FEEL GONE' (1991) continued in the same vein, developing and updating country in a fashion a damn sight closer to GRAM PARSONS' cosmic vision than the polished dross coming out of Nashville. Yet it was the stark testimony of the PETER BUCK-produced 'MARCH 16-20' (1992) that really cut to the heart of American roots tradition, a breathtaking album of grainy originals and hard-bitten folk covers. While the quality of the songwriting arguably outstripped almost anything released under the banner of country/alt-country in the past twenty years, it was the bruised beauty of the vocals (especially FARRAR) that really brought on the goose-bumps and belied UNCLE TUPELO's relative youthfulness. The likes of 'GRINDSTONE', 'BLACK EYE' and the traditional 'MOONSHINER' resonated with what sounded like the careworn resignation of a lifetime's toil and trouble, the whole album religious in its rawness. Released to rave reviews, it didn't take long for word to spread and with major labels eager for a piece of the action, FARRAR and TWEEDY opted to sign for 'Reprise' (home to spiritual forefathers PARSONS and NEIL YOUNG amongst others). With FARRAR and TWEEDY maintaining a hard-drinking, volatile relationship at the best of times, 'ANODYNE' (1993) proved to be the final product of their mercurial partnership. A return to more upbeat material, the album featured a rousing cover of Doug Sahm's 'GIVE BACK THE KEY TO MY HEART' (featuring the cult Texan roots man on guitar) alongside more reflective fare like the gorgeously plaintive 'SLATE', one of the most perfectly formed compositions in the FARRAR/TWEEDY canon with fiddle arrangements to break the hardest heart. While many mourned the band's passing, fans could look forward to the prospect of two solo projects, FARRAR's SON VOLT and TWEEDY's WILCO. The latter outfit (comprising TWEEDY, JAY BENNETT, JOHN STIRRATT and UNCLE TUPELO veterans MAX JOHNSTON and KEN COOMER) were first off the starting block with 1994's 'A.M.'. An enjoyable enough set of uptempo country-rock, it was nevertheless eclipsed by the 1996 follow-up, 'BEING THERE', a sprawling double set drawing comparisons with The STONES' 'Exile On Main Street' and hailed as one of the albums of the year. Reaching far beyond TWEEDY's patented musical boundaries to encompass everything from bar-room belters to Spector-esque rock/pop, the record proved conclusively that FARRAR's other half was blessed with his own distinct musical vision. Fans yearning for the down-at-heel spirit of UNCLE TUPELO's moodier moments were comforted by the fact that FARRAR himself was still treading the dirt-road backstreets of country's dark underbelly with SON VOLT, releasing 'TRACE' in 1994 and 'STRAIGHTAWAYS' in late '96; 'WIDE SWING TREMELO' (1998) was their most recent set. While some critics railed against what they perceived as the unrelenting miserabilism of FARRAR's approach (especially with regards to the SON VOLT live experience), there was no disputing the quality or honesty of the writing. While both camps continue to come up with the goods, the prospect of an UNCLE TUPELO reunion is still tantalisingly within reach. However, WILCO returned in the summer of '98, an unlikely collaboration with English bard BILLY BRAGG on a memorable WOODY GUTHRIE tribute album, 'MERMAID AVENUE', kept the duo ticking over fine style. The following March, the leaders of the alt-country/folk scene released their long-awaited third set, 'SUMMERTEETH' (1999), a UK Top 40 record (Top 100 in the US) that boasted some breezy old tales opening with minor UK hit, 'CAN'T STAND IT'. A second volume of GUTHRIE re-writes, 'MERMAID AVENUE VOL.2' (2000) couldn't come up with anything quite as affecting as say, 'CALIFORNIA STARS' but it had its moments. WILCO's penchant for uptempo roots-rock wasn't always the best vehicle for presenting the legendary socialist's humourous protest-folk, BRAGG often stealing the limelight. After 'STRAIGHTAWAYS', FARRAR took time out from SON VOLT (they split 1999) to record 'SEBASTAPOL' (2001) an album of self-conscious beauty, but of beauty all the same. Acoustic numbers such as the whispering 'CLEAR DAY THUNDER' and 'OUTSIDE THE DOOR' evoked that folksy UNCLE TUPELO formula, where as 'BARSTOW' and 'DAMN SHAME' had FARRAR's own personalised stamp. Elsewhere on the set, he had trouble dealing with the process alone (after all he was always best with a collaborator), although the man proved he was still a great contender in the American alt country scene. TWEEDY moved even further from both his old sparring partner and his musical roots with 'YANKEE HOTEL FOXTROT' (2002), a record the band believed in so much they spent a hefty sum buying it back from 'Reprise'. While JIM O'ROURKE's off-kilter production opened up angles seemingly irreconcilable with the limited roots-rock sound of yore, the results were never less than intriguing and often brilliantly conceived. • **Songwriters**: All compositions FARRAR – TWEEDY except arrangements of traditional tunes, plus covers: I WANNA DESTROY YOU (Soft Boys) / NO DEPRESSION (A.P.Carter) / JOHN HARDY (Leadbelly) / ATOMIC POWER (Louvin Brothers/B.Bain) / BLUE EYES (Gram Parsons) / SIN CITY (Flying Burrito Brothers) / I WANNA BE YOUR DOG (Stooges) / EFFIGY (Creedence Clearwater Revival). • **Other info**: TWEEDY was also an integral part of y'alternative supergroup, GOLDEN SMOG, alongside members of the JAYHAWKS, SOUL ASYLUM, RUN WESTY RUN and BIG STAR.

Album rating: NO DEPRESSION (*8) / STILL FEEL GONE (*9) / MARCH 16-20 (*7) / ANODYNE (*8) / 1989-1993: AN ANTHOLOGY (*8) / Wilco: A.M. (*8) / BEING THERE (*8) / SUMMERTEETH (*8) / YANKEE HOTEL FOXTROT (*6) / Son Volt: TRACE (*7) / STRAIGHTAWAYS (*6) / WIDE SWING TREMELO (*7) / Jay Farrar: SEBASTAPOL (*6)

JEFF TWEEDY (b.25 Aug'67) – vocals, guitar, bass / **JAY FARRAR** (b.26 Dec'66) – vocals, guitar / **MICHAEL HEIDORN** – drums

		Rockville	Rockville
Aug 90.	(lp) <ROCK 6050-1> **NO DEPRESSION**	-	
	– Graveyard shift / That year / Before I break / No depression / Factory belt / Whiskey bottle / Outdone / Train / Life worth livin' / Flatness / So called friend / Screen door / John Hardy. (UK cd-iss. Sep97; ROCK 6050-2)		
Sep 90.	(7") <ROCK 6055-7> **I GOT DRUNK. / SIN CITY**	-	
Sep 91.	(7") <ROCK 6069-7> **GUN. / I WANNA DESTROY YOU**	-	
Sep 91.	(lp) <ROCK 6070-1> **STILL FEEL GONE**	-	
	– Gun / Looking for a way out / Fall down easy / Nothing / Still be around / Watch me fall / Punch drunk / Postcard / D. Boon / True to life / Cold shoulder / Discarded / If that's alright. (UK-iss.cd Nov92 on 'Yellow Moon'; BUFF 001CD)		
Nov 92.	(7") <(ROCK 6089-7)> **SAUGET WIND. / LOOKING FOR A WAY OUT (acoustic) / TAKE MY WORD**		
Mar 93.	(cd/c/lp) <(ROCK 6110-2/-4/-1)> **MARCH 16-20, 1992**		Aug92
	– Grindstone / Coalminers / Wait up / Criminals / Shaky ground / Satan, your kingdom must come down / Black eye / Moonshiner / I wish my baby was born / Atomic power / Lilli Schull / Warfare / Fatal wound / Sandusky / Wipe the clock.		

— **KEN COOMER** – drums + **JOHN STIRRATT** – bass; repl. HEIDORN

		Warners	Sire
Oct 93.	(cd/c) (9362 45330-2/-4) <45424> **ANODYNE**		
	– Slate / Acuff-Rose / The long cut / Give back the key to my heart / Chickamauga / New Madrid / Anodyne / We've been had / Fifteen keys / High water / No sense in lovin' / Steal the crumbs.		

— arguments arose, FARRAR subsequently forming SON VOLT with MICHAEL HEIDORN

– compilations, etc. –

May 95.	(c) *Dutch East*; <6110> **STILL FEEL GONE / MARCH 16-20, 1992**		
May 02.	(cd) *Sony*; (507612-2) <62223> **1989-1993: AN ANTHOLOGY**		Mar02
	– No depression / Screen door / Graveyard shift / Whiskey bottle / Outdone / I got drunk / I wanna be your dog / Gun / Still be around / Looking for a way out (acoustic) / Watch me fall / Sauget wind / Black eye / Moonshiner / Fatal wound / Grindstone / Effigy / The long cut / Chickamuuga / New Madrid / We've been had (live). <(d-lp-iss.Jun02 on 'Sundazed'; SCLP 5153)>		

WILCO

JEFF TWEEDY with remaining UNCLE TUPELO members **STIRRATT + COOMER**

		Warners	Reprise
Apr 95.	(cd) <(9362 45857-2)> **A.M.**		
	– I must be high / Casino queen / Box full of letters / Shouldn't be ashamed / Pick up the change / I thought IU held you / That's not the issue / It's just that simple / Should've been in love / Passenger side / Dash 7 / Blue eyed soul / Too far apart.		
Jul 95.	(c-s) (W 0306MC) **BOX FULL OF LETTERS / I AM NOT WILLING**		
	(cd-s+=) (W 0306) – Who were you thinking of (live).		

— added **JAY BENNETT** – guitar

Feb 97.	(d-cd) <(9362 46236-2)> **BEING THERE**		73 Nov96
	– Misunderstood / Forget the flowers / I got you (at the end of the century) / Red eyed and blue / (Was I) In your dreams / Dreamer in my dreams / Lonely one / Why would you wanna live / Kingpin / Someone else's song / Outta mind (outta sight) / Someday soon / Sunken treasure / Say you miss me / Hotel Arizona / What's the world got in store / Far far away / Monday.		
Apr 97.	(cd-ep) (W 0397CD) **OUTTA SIGHT (OUTTA MIND) / OUTTA MIND (OUTTA SIGHT) / THIRTEEN / A LASTING FONDER**		-

— In the middle of '98, WILCO collaborated with BILLY BRAGG on a tribute album ('MERMAID AVENUE') to WOODY GUTHRIE

Mar 99.	(cd/c/lp) <(9362 47282-2/-4/-1)> **SUMMERTEETH**	38	78
	– Can't stand it / She's a jar / A shot in the arm / We're just friends / I'm always in love / Nothing'severgonnastandinmyway (again) / Pieholden suite / How to fight loneliness / Via Chicago / ELT / My darling / When you wake up feeling old / Summer teeth / In a future age.		
Apr 99.	(cd-s) (W 475CD1) **CAN'T STAND IT / STUDENT LOAN ZERO / TRIED AND TRUE**	67	
	(cd-s) (W 475CD2) – ('A'side) / Sunken treasure (solo acoustic) / I'm always in love (solo acoustic).		
Jun 99.	(c-s/cd-s) (W 496 C/CD2) **A SHOT IN THE ARM / VIA CHICAGO (demo) / SHE'S A JAR**		
	(cd-s) (W 496CD1) – ('A'side) / ELT (demo) / True love will find you in the end.		

— a 2nd 'MERMAID AVENUE' (VOL.2) was issued with BILLY BRAGG in mid'00

— **GLENN KOTSCHE** – drums; repl. COOMER

— **LEROY BACH** – guitar; repl. BENNETT

		Nonesuch	Nonesuch
Apr 02.	(cd) <(7559 79669-2)> **YANKEE HOTEL FOXTROT**	40	13
	– I am trying to break your heart / Kamera / Radio cure / War on war / Jesus, etc. / Ashes of American flags / Heavy metal drummer / I'm the man who loves you / Pot kettle black / Poor places / Reservations. (d-lp-iss.Nov02 on 'Sundazed'; SCLP 5161)>		
May 02.	(cd-s) (NONE 001CD) **WAR ON WAR / THE GOOD PART / I'M THE MAN WHO LOVES YOU (live)**		-

SON VOLT

JAY FARRAR – vocals, guitar, organ, harmonica, songwriter / **DAVE BOQUIST** – guitars, fiddle, banjo, lap steel / **JIM BOQUIST** – bass, backing vocals / **MIKE HEIDORN** – drums

Warners   Warners

Oct 95. (cd/c) <(9362-46010-2/-4)> **TRACE**   Sep95
– Windfall / Live free / Tear stained eye / Route / Ten second news / Drown / Loose string / Out of the picture / Catching on / Too early / Mystifies me.

— with guests **ERIC HEYWOOD** – pedal steel, mandolin / **PAULI RYAN** – tambourine

Aug 97. (cd) <(9362-46518-2/-4)> **STRAIGHTAWAYS**   44   May97
– Caryatid easy / Back into the world / Picking up the signal / Left a slide / Creosote / Cemetery savior / Last minute shakedown / Been set free / No more parades / Way down Watson.

Oct 98. (cd/c) <(9362 47059-2/-4)> **WIDE SWING TREMELO**   93
– Straightface / Driving the view / Jodel / Medicine hat / Strands / Flow / Dead man's clothes / Right on through / Chanty / Carry you down / Question / Streets that time walks / Hanging blue side / Blind hope.

JAY FARRAR

with **DAVID RAWLINGS, TOM RAY, MATT PENCE, JON WURSTER, DADE FARRAR, JOHN AGNELLO, KELLY JOE PHELPS + GILLIAN WELCH**

Epic   Artemis

Oct 01. (cd) (504570-2) <751093> **SEBASTAPOL**   Sep01
– Feel free / Clear day thunder / Voodoo candle / Barstow / Damn shame / Damaged son / Prelude (make it alright) / Dead promises / Feedkill chain / Make it alright / Fortissimo wah / Drain / Different eyes / Outside the door / Equilibrium / Direction / Vitamins.

Nov 02. (cd-ep) <751138> **THIRDSHIFTGROTTOSLACK**   -
– Greenwich time / Damn shame / Station to station / Kind of madness / Dues.

UNION CARBIDE PRODUCTIONS
(see under ⇒ SOUNDTRACK OF OUR LIVES)

UNISEX (see under ⇒ TELESCOPES; 80's section)

UNWED SAILOR (see under ⇒ ROADSIDE MONUMENT)

UNWOUND

Formed: Tumwater, Olympia, Washington, USA ... 1990/91 by JUSTIN TROSPER, VERN RUMSEY and BRANDT SANDENO. The earliest release from this post-punk indie noise-rock group was in 1992 when UNWOUND issued two singles for 'Kill Rock Stars' before recording an album. The self-titled album was delayed as drummer SANDENO left the band (subsequently replaced by SARAH LUND), resurfacing in 1995 for the 'Honey Bear' label. By that time, the band had three albums under their belt, the exhilarating 'FAKE TRAIN' (1993), 'NEW PLASTIC IDEAS' (1994) and 'THE FUTURE OF WHAT' (1995). The band's sound came close to something between FUGAZI, SONIC YOUTH and the BUZZCOCKS, while their melodies and structures were put to great effect and the distortion added a raw element to the post-Washington grunge/punk scene. In 1996, the group added 'REPETITION' to their list of albums, releasing their best long-player to date, 'CHALLENGE FOR A CIVILIZED SOCIETY'. The stand out track on the album was 'UNTITLED', a startling wig-out that went from hardcore rock to calm sax-laden jazz to violent punk, and all in eight minutes.

Album rating: UNWOUND (*5) / FAKE TRAIN (*5) / NEW PLASTIC IDEAS (*6) / THE FUTURE OF WHAT (*7) / REPETITION (*5) / CHALLENGE FOR A CIVILIZED SOCIETY (*6) / FURTHER LISTENING compilation (*7) / A SINGLE HISTORY 1991-1997 compilation (*6) / LEAVES TURN INSIDE YOU (*7)

JUSTIN TROSPER – vocals, guitar / **VERN RUMSEY** – bass / **BRANDT SANDENO** – drums

Kill Rock   Kill Rock
Stars   Stars

1991. (7"m) <KRS 203> **CATERPILLAR. / MISERFERIC CONDITION / LOVE AND FEAR**   -

1992. (7"m) <KRS 205> **KANDY KORN RITUALS. / AGAINST / HATING IN D**   -

not iss.   Punk In My Vitamins

1992. (lp) <PNMV 06> **UNWOUND**   -
– Antifreeze / Rising blood / Understand & forget / Fingertips / You bite my tongue / Stuck in the middle of nowhere again / Warmth prospect / Kid is gone / Kandy korn rituals. <cd-iss. Aug95 on 'Honey Bear'; hb 07>

not iss.   Gravity

Jan 93. (7"m) <gravity 6> **YOU BITE MY TONGUE. / KID IS GONE CHANT OF VENGEANCE / UNDERSTAND AND FORGET**   -
<re-iss. 1996; same>

— (1993) **SARAH LUND** – drums (ex-WITCHYPOO, ex-BELGIAN WAFFLES) repl. SANDENO

Kill Rock   Kill Rock
Stars   Stars

Mar 94. (lp/cd) <(KRS 210/+CD)> **FAKE TRAIN**   Jul93
– Dragnalus / Lucky acid / Nervous energy / Valentine card / Kantina / Were, and was or is / Honourosis / Pure pan sugar / Gravity slips / Star spangled hell / Ratbite / Feeling real.

Apr 94. (cd/lp) <(KRS 223 CD/V)> **NEW PLASTIC IDEAS**
– Entirely different matters / What was wound / Envelope / Hexenzscene / Abstraktions / All soul's day / Usual dosage / Arboretum / Fiction friction.

Jun 94. (7") <KRS 225> **MKULTRA. / TOTALITY**   -

Nov 94. (7"m) <TMU 1> **NEGATED / SAID SERIAL. / CENSUS**   -
(above issued on 'Troubleman Unlimited')

Jul 95. (cd) <(KRS 245CD)> **THE FUTURE OF WHAT**   Apr95
– New energy / Demolished / Natural disasters / Re-enact stupid / Equally stupid / Pardon my French / Descension / Accidents on purpose / Petals like bricks / Vern's answer to the masses / Here come the dogs / Disappoint / Swan / Full explanation of answer / Excuse me but pardon my French.

Apr 96. (cd) <KRS 261CD> **REPETITION**   -
– Message received / Corpse pose / Unauthorized autobiography / Lowest common denominator / Sensible / Lady elect / Fingernails on a chalkboard / Murder movies / Next exit / Devoid / Go to Dallas an take a left / For your entertainment.

May 96. (7") <KRS 262> **CORPSE POSSE. / EVERYTHING IS WEIRD**   -

1996. (7") <hb 012> **untitled. / (other by STEEL POLE BATH TUB)**   -
(above issued on 'Honey Bear')

Dec 97. (12"ep) <(KRS 288)> **THE LIGHT AT THE END OF THE TUNNEL IS A TRAIN**
– Mile me deaf / No tech / Solo sonata / The light at the end of the tunnel is a train.

Jan 98. (lp/cd) <(KRS 289/+CD)> **CHALLENGE FOR A CIVILIZED SOCIETY**
– Data / Laugh track / Meets the plastics / The world is flat / Sonata for loudspeakers / Mile me deaf / No tech / Side effects of being tired / Lifetime achievement award / What went wrong. <(re-iss. Jan99 on 'Matador' cd=/lp+=; OLE 335-2/-1)> – XLNT / The light at the end of the tunnel is a train.

not iss.   Troubleman

1999. (7") <TMU 015> **TORCH SONG. / (split w/ VERSUS)**   -

Matador   Matador

Apr 01. (d-cd/d-lp) <(OLE 469-2/-1)> **LEAVES TURN INSIDE YOU**
– We invent you / Look a ghost / December / Treachery / Terminus / Demons sing love songs / Off this century / One lick less / Scarlette / October all over / Summer freeze / Radio Gra / Below the salt / Who cares.

– compilations, etc. –

May 99. (cd) *Matador; (OLE 341-2)* **FURTHER LISTENING**   -
– All souls day / Valentine card / Corpse pose / Kantina / You bite my tongue / Were, are and was or is / Here comes the dogs / Petals like bricks / Envelope / Murder movies / Rising blood / Miserific condition / Dragnalus / Kid is gone / Equally stupid / Message received / Unauthorised autobiography / Swan / Arboretum / Hating in D.

Jul 99. (lp) *Lovitt; (LVT 004LP)* **UNWOUND LIVE IN EUROPE (live)**

Sep 99. (lp/cd) *Kill Rock Stars; <(KRS 345/+CD)>* **A SINGLE HISTORY 1991-1997**
– Mile me deaf / Broken E strings / Totally / MK ultra / Seen not heard / Caterpillar / Miserific condition / Everything is weird / Negated / Said serial / Census / Plight / Stumbling block / Eternalux / New radio hit / The light at the end of the tunnel is a train / Crab nebula.

Mar 01. (12"ep) *Speakerphone; (SIS 2)* **IN LONDON**   -
– Hexenzsene / Side effects of being tired / Kantina / Were are and was or is.

URUSEI YATSURA

Formed: Glasgow, Scotland ... 1994 by FERGUS LAWRIE, GRAHAM KEMP, plus brother and sister IAN and ELAINE GRAHAM. Part of the US-influenced Glasgow indie scene, their low-key debut release was a very rare mini-lp, 'ALL HAIL URUSEI YATSURA' (1995), a follow-up single, 'PAMPERED ADOLESCENT', receiving airplay from Radio One stalwarts John Peel and Mark Radcliffe. This exposure resulted in an indie Top 30 hit, with London's 'Che' records picking them up for a long-term deal. A handful of singles, including 'SIAMESE', 'PLASTIC ASHTRAY' and 'KEWPIES LIKE WATERMELON', preceded a debut album proper, the self-explanatory 'WE ARE URUSEI YATSURA', in the Spring of '96. Arty bubblegum noise merchants trading in a PAVEMENT meets SONIC YOUTH meets T.REX style, these colourful kitschy characters amassed further critical acclaim with another clutch of three minute gems over the course of the next two years. From 'PHASERS ON STUN' to their first Top 75 entry 'STRATEGIC HAMLETS' to summer '97's 'FAKE FUR', the band were building up to their first Top 40 hit, 'HELLO TIGER', in early '98. URUSEI YATSURA's (YATSURA only in the States!) ultra hip factor was enough to persuade 'Warners' to enter into a part deal with 'Che', the result being a collection of the aforementioned singles, 'SLAIN BY URUSEI YATSURA' (1998). The latter's title track was inspired by their finest moment to date, minor hit single 'SLAIN BY ELF'.

• **Trivia:** Their moniker roughly translates as a troublemaking female android in Japanese.

Album rating: ALL HAIL URUSEI YATSURA mini (*5) / WE ARE URUSEI YATSURA (*8) / SLAIN BY URUSEI YATSURA (*8) / EVERYBODY LOVES URUSEI YATSURA (*6)

FERGUS LAWRIE (b.23 Jan'68, Marlborough, England) – vocals, guitar / **GRAHAM KEMP** (b. 3 Dec'68, Inverness, Scotland) – vocals, guitar / **ELAINE GRAHAM** (b.16 Jun'70) – bass / **IAN GRAHAM** (b.19 Oct'72) – drums, percussion, programming

Hipster   not iss.

Jan 95. (m-lp) *(hip 001)* **ALL HAIL URUSEI YATSURA**   -
– It is / Death 2 everyone / Yeah / Saturn / On your mind / Teenage dream. *(m-cd iss.Mar98 on 'Tiny Superhero'; SuperCD 005)*

Modern Independent   not iss.

Apr 95. (7"burgundy) *(mir 001)* **PAMPERED ADOLESCENT. / (other track by the Blisters)**   -

Che   Primary

Sep 95. (7",7"orange) *(che 38)* **SIAMESE. / LO-FI SCARY BALLOONS**   -

Nov 95. (7") *(PUBE 08)* **KERNAL. / TEENDREAM**   -
(above issued on 'Love Train')

Feb 96. (7",7"pink) *(che 46-7) <64338>* **PLASTIC ASHTRAY. / GOT THE SUN**
(cd-s+=) *(che 46-2)* – Miramar / Yatsura kill taster.

Apr 96. (7") *(che 53)* **KEWPIES LIKE WATERMELON. / MAJESTY**   83
(cd-ep) **STUNRAY EP** *(che 53) <66011>* – Sucker / Burriko girl.

URUSEI YATSURA (cont)

May 96. (cd/lp,orange-lp) *(che 54 cd/lp)* <*61957*> **WE ARE URUSEI YATSURA**
– Siamese / First day on a new planet / Pow R. Ball / Kewpies like watermelon / Phasers on stun – Sola kola / Black hole love / Velvy blood / Plastic ashtray / Death 2 everyone / Pachinko / Kernel / Road song. *(re-iss. Sep97; same)*

—— shared a tour freebie 7" – che 59- (via the track 'PHASERS (live)' with MOGWAI and BACKWATER

Aug 96. (d7",cd-ep) *(che 62)* <*66011*> **PHASERS ON STUN. / THE LOVE THAT BRINGS YOU DOWN // THE POWER OF NEGATIVE THINKING. / SID AND NANCY**

Oct 96. (7") *(100gm 18)* **SILVER KREST. / (other track by the DELGADOS)**
(above iss. on '100 Guitar Mania' as part of 'Stolen Ecstasy' series)

Feb 97. (7") *(che 67)* **STRATEGIC HAMLETS. / KOZEE HEART** 64
(7") *(che 67s)* – ('A'side) / Revir.
(cd-s+=) *(che 67cd)* – Down home Kitty.

Jun 97. (7"white) *(che 70)* **FAKE FUR. / SILVER KREST** 58
(cd-s+=) *(che 73cd)* – Nova static / Secret crush.
(cd-s) *(che 73cd2)* – ('A'side) / Pampered adolescent / Bewitched / Saki & cremola.

Jun 97. (cd-s) <*62084*> **FAKE FUR / STRATEGIC HAMLETS**

Aug 97. (cd; as YATSURA) <*62084*> **PULPO!** (compilation)
– Strategic hamlets / Down home Kitty / Pampered adolescent / Kozee heart / Miramar / Saki & Cremola / Fake fur / Silver krest / Got the sun / Nova static / Revir / The power of negative thinking / The love that brings you down.

Feb 98. (7") *(che 75)* **HELLO TIGER. / VANILLA STARLET** 40
(cd-s+=) *(che 75cd1)* – Vent axia.
(cd-s) *(che 75cd2)* – ('A'-Peel session version) / Nae dice nae dice (Peel session version) / Everybody hang out.

Che-Warners   Sire

Mar 98. (cd) *(che 76cd – <3984-22221-2>)* **SLAIN BY URUSEI YATSURA** 64
– Glo starz / Hello tiger / Strategic hamlets / No 1 cheesecake / Superfi / No no girl / Flaming skull / Slain by elf / King of lazy / Exidor / Fake fur / Skull in action / Amber.

May 98. (7") *(che 80)* **SLAIN BY ELF. / HAIL TO THE NEW POOR** 63
(cd-s+=) *(che 80cd2)* – What's wrong with me.
(cd-s) *(che 80cd1)* – ('A'side) / Nu style / Subatomic.

Beggars Banquet   not iss.

Nov 99. (d7"white-ep/cd-ep) *(BBQ 342/+CD)* **YON KYOKU IRI EP**
– Kaytronika / Still exploding / Nobody knows we're stars / Mother of the MBK.

Oni   not iss.

Aug 00. (7") *(ONIV7 1)* **LOUCHE 33. / PLANET OF THE SKULLS**
(cd-s+=) *(ONICDS 1)* – I'm vexed.

Sep 00. (cd/lp) *(ONI CD/LP 2)* **EVERYBODY LOVES URUSEI YATSURA**
– Louche 33 / Eastern youth / Superdeformer / Silver dragon / Uji bomb / Our shining path / Kubrick in town / Random cruise / Faking it / Thank you / Sores / Osaka white.

Mar 01. (7") *(ONIV7 2)* **EASTERN YOUTH. / THE HEARTS YOU BREAK**

—— URUSEI YATSURA have now disbanded

USED (see under ⇒ SUPERDRAG)

Drag City   Drag City

Jun 99. (cd/d-lp) <*(DC 164 CD/LP)*> **TALKER**
– Bumps and guys / Running from Kabob / Go to bruises / More horror / Apollo, don't you crust? / Breeze, it's your high school / Stupid deep indoors / (untitled) / So long bonus.

Apr 01. (cd/lp) <*(DC 208 CD/LP)*> **ACRE THRILLS**
– (11 untitled tracks).

—— **ADAM VIDA** – drums (ex-EDITH FROST) repl. SAMSON

U.S. MAPLE

Formed: Chicago, Illinois, USA ... early 1995 out of SHORTY and The MERCURY PLAYERS by AL JOHNSON, MARK SHIPPY, TODD RITTMAN and PAT SAMSON. After an initial 7", 'STUCK', the group released the brilliantly titled, JIM O'ROURKE-produced album, 'LONG HAIR IN THREE STAGES' (1995). While their post-modern, deconstructivist approach made for a cerebral, challenging listen, their love of bluesy, proudly unreconstructed rock was a clearly a driving factor underpinning all the experimentation. Hardly surprising then, their respective choice of Dion & The Belmonts' 'THE WANDERER' and AC/DC's 'SIN CITY' for two separate tribute albums both released in 1996 and featuring the cream of the Chicago scene. O'ROURKE was again at the helm for 1997's 'SANG PHAT EDITOR', an even more thrillingly incoherent, engagingly angular rock dissection which further endeared the band to critics. A move to 'Drag City' (they'd previously been signed to 'Skin Graft') and a change of producer (former SWANS man, MICHAEL GIRA) did nothing to harm U.S. MAPLE's sonic mission; on the contrary, the leaden, dirge-like genius of GIRA's old band had obviously rubbed off on them judging by the sludgy, caustic burn of 'TALKER' (1999).

Album rating: LONG HAIR IN THREE STAGES (*7) / SANG PHAT EDITOR (*6) / TALKER (*6) / ACRE THRILLS (*5)

AL JOHNSON – vocals (ex-SHORTY) / **MARK SHIPPY** – guitar (ex-SHORTY) / **TODD RITTMAN** – guitar (ex-MERCURY PLAYERS) / **PAT SAMSON** – drums (ex-MERCURY PLAYERS)

Skin Graft   Skin Graft

Sep 95. (7") <*GR 19*> **STUCK. / WHEN A MAN SAYS "OW"**

Nov 95. (lp/cd) <*(GR 33/+CD)*> **LONG HAIR IN THREE STAGES**   Oct95
– Hey king / Letter to ZZ Top / Home-made stuff / Magic job / The state was bad / Aplomado / You know what will get you you know where / When a man say "ow" / Northward / Lady to Biug.

1996. (7") <*SB 29*> **THE WANDERER. / WHOA COMPLAINS**
(above issued on 'Sonic Bubblegum')

Jun 97. (lp/cd) <*(GR 44/+CD)*> **SANG PHAT EDITOR**
– Coming back to damnit / Songs that have no making out / La click / Mountain top / Missouri twist / Through with six six six / Home it's O.K.

VAN PELT (see under ⇒ LAPSE)

VARNALINE

Formed: New York, USA ... mid 90's as a one-man vehicle for singer-songwriter ANDERS PARKER. 1996's eponymous debut album consisted of songs PARKER had previously recorded on a four-track, initially only as a private project. Picked up by indie label, 'Zero Hour', the tracks introduced PARKER as a man of rootsy introspection even if he was loathe to have his work labelled as 'Lo-fi'. Recruiting his brother JOHN and ex-SCARCE sticksman, JUD EHRBAR, for live work, VARNALINE secured a slot on the 1996 Lollapalooza shindig amid favourable critical comparisons with the likes of BIG STAR. As well as sidelining in experimental sister projects such as SPACE NEEDLE and RESERVOIR, PARKER found time to cut a one-off single, 'PARTY NOW', and work on the second album, 'MAN OF SIN' (1997). The eponymous 'VARNALINE' (1997) was followed by a mini-set, 'A SHOT AND A BEER' (1998) and third full length album, 'SWEET LIFE' (1998). The latter's winning blend of earthy Americana and subtle experimentation was to be his last for a few years as the label went bankrupt and PARKER was temporarily left without a creative home. Roots renaissance man STEVE EARLE came to the rescue, setting the stage for the acclaimed 'SONGS IN A NORTHERN KEY' (2001) wherein VARNALINE expanded their musical palette with flourishes of trombone and vibes.

Album rating: VARNALINE (*7) / MAN OF SIN (*4) / A SHOT AND A BEER mini (*4) / SWEET LIFE (*6) / SONGS IN A NORTHERN KEY (*6)

ANDERS PARKER – vocals, guitar (also of SPACE NEEDLE) / with **BOB MacKAY** – bass

		Rykodisc	Zero Hour
Aug 96.	(cd) (RCD 10368) <ZERCD 1130> **MAN OF SIN**		Feb96

– The hammer goes down / Gary's paranoia / Lbs / Thorns and such / Little pills / Dust / No decision, no discipline / Want you / Green again / In the year of dope.

—— **JOHN PARKER** – bass, pump organ; repl. MacKAY

—— added **JUD EHRBAR** – drums (of SPACE NEEDLE)

		Zero Hour	Zero Hour
May 97.	(cd) <ZERCD 2130> **VARNALINE**	-	

– Lights / Meet me on the ledge / Sky'd out / Why are you unkind / Empire blues / Really can't say / Velocity / My time / Understanding H / God in your eyes. (UK-iss.Nov97; same)

Jan 98.	(m-cd) <(ZERC 3130)> **A SHOT AND A BEER**		Oct97

– Hear the birds cry / The only one / In your orbit / Bardust / Judges seventeen / Don't come home.

Aug 98.	(cd) <(ZERC 0413D)> **SWEET LIFE**		

– Gulf of Mexico / Northern lights / Now you're dirt / All about love / While you were sleeping / Saviours / This is the river / Underneath the mountain / Fuck and fight / Mare imbrium / Tonight / Sweet life.

—— added **DEAN JONES** – trombone, piano

		not iss.	Artemis
Jul 01.	(cd) <751077> **SONGS IN A NORTHERN KEY**	-	

– Still dream / Song / Indian summer breakdown / Blackbird fields / Blue flowers on the highway / The drunkard's wish / Difference / Anything from now / Down the street / Green eyed stars / Sister and the chrome waves / I don't want / Let it all come down / Broken song / Murder crow.

VEES (see under ⇒ JALE)

VEHICLE FLIPS

Formed: Pittsburgh, Pennsylvania, USA ... 1994 by FRANK BOSCOE, TIM PARKER, ERIK LIPSKY and TIM HOFFMAN. Soon after the group's formation, guitarist LIPSKY and drummer HOFFMAN departed making way for JEFF SCHRECKENGOST and CRAIG WHITMAN respectively. The group debuted in 1995 with the album 'IN ACTION'. The sound was similar to that of BOSCOE's previous band WIMP FACTOR 14, who had released the good natured album, 'ANKLE DEEP', in 1993. With the VEHICLE FLIPS debut, BOSCOE had once again ticked all the boxes required for producing a standard indie pop album. The jangly guitars, wistful lyrics and bittersweet melodies were all in place, though this formulaic approach meant the album was limited and struggled to shine. Personnel changes and BOSCOE's improving skills as a songwriter meant that the 1998 follow-up, 'THE PREMISE UNRAVELED', was altogether more individual and impressive. However standards dropped for the group's final album, 'FOR YOU I PINE' (2000). BOSCOE returned in 2002 with his new band The GAZETTEERS courtesy of a new album 'TERRITORY SONGS'. Once again BOSCOE trusted the same familiar sound, although this time his multi-instrumentalist band mates, ROB CHRISTIANSEN (ex-EGGS) and STEVE SILVERSTEIN, afforded him a greater tonal range.

Album rating: Wimp Factor 14: ANKLE DEEP (*5) / Vehicle Flips: IN ACTION (*4) / THE PREMISE UNRAVELED (*6) / FOR YOU I PINE (*5) / Gazetteers: TERRITORY SONGS mini (*6)

WIMP FACTOR 14

FRANK BOSCOE – vocals, guitar / **GARY MIKLUSEK** – guitar

		not iss.	Harriet
Mar 91.	(7") <5> **TRAIN SONG. / I'LL SEND YOU A POSTCARD**	-	
1991.	(one-sided;7") <FLW 006> **ONE FOR THE RECORD BOOKS** (above issued on 'Four Letter Words')	-	
Sep 92.	(7") <15> **BOTCH. /**	-	
Aug 93.	(cd) <SPY 1> **ANKLE DEEP**	-	

– Jittery and wobbling / The heart of my stupefaction / I is for incomplete / Steam rolling, but it wasn't steam rolling / How to avoid losing small objects / Stationary from work / (It's ok to work for) Rockwell international / Role model glue / Ankle of repose / Tale of the loophole guy / Stratego / Holiday park flyer / 1993 comeback player of the year / Adjustment. <lp-iss.on 'Little Teddy'; 003>

Oct 93.	(7") <23> **MIRACLE MILE. /**	-	

—— after they split, GARY joined TULLYCRAFT and FRANK formed ...

VEHICLE FLIPS

FRANK BOSCOE with **JEFF SCHRECKENGOST** – guitar; repl. ERIK LIPSKY / **TIM PARKER** – bass / **CRAIG WHITMAN** – drums; repl. TIM HOFFMAN

		Hemiola	Harriet
Nov 94.	(7"m) <29> **OUR RETURNING CHAMPION. /**	-	
Sep 95.	(cd) <SPY 4> **IN ACTION**	-	

– Insincerity showcase / The eye opener / Steelers' fight song / Marashino / Potomac / City of fireworks / Hot apple pushover (to be an optimist) / Platitude man / The clean slate / Going to New Mexico / Could've, should've / An evening with Mr. Clyde.

Mar 96.	(7"m) (HEM 012) **IMPRESSED BEYOND BELIEF. / FORMULA REJECTION SONG / CITRONELLA**		-

—— added **PAUL BOSCOE** – vocals + **JESSE TRBOVICH** – guitar

1996.	(7"m) <005> **A HOUSEHOLD EXPATRIATE. /** (above issued on 'Rover') (below on 'Numeric')	-	- Japan
1996.	(7") **OMPOMPANOOSUC. / STERLING**	-	

—— (1996) **ERIC TOPOLSKY** – multi; repl. PAUL + JESSE

—— (1996) **TIM WILLIAMS** – drums; repl. CRAIG

Feb 97.	(7") <38> **TERMINUS. / SALAD BAR**	-	

—— (1998) **JOHN LANCIA** – drums; repl. TIM + ERIC

		not iss.	Magic Marker
Dec 98.	(cd) <MMR 3> **THE PREMISE UNRAVELED**	-	

– Requiem for a canceled program / Security / Welcome to the big ten conference / Song of the slag pile / Florence scene report / Swope street theme / Self-pity / Bitter coffee song / Expendable you / Regarding telephones / Octoraro / Honeywell round thermostat.

Mar 00.	(cd) <MMR 9> **FOR YOU I PINE**	-	

– Where the capital flows / City beautiful / Parcel post / Trouble on the western survey / Bus pass / Song for Pahaquarry, NJ (1824-1997) / Graduation party / Icejam / Anti-hymn / Parcel post (return to sender).

GAZETTEERS

FRANK BOSCOE recruited **ROB CHRISTIANSEN** – multi (ex-EGGS, ex-SISTERHOOD OF CONVOLUTED THINKERS) / **STEVE SILVERSTEIN** – (ex-CHRISTMAS DECORATIONS) / guests **JEANNINE DUFREE** + **PAUL BOSCOE**

		not iss.	Magic Marker
Aug 02.	(m-cd) <MMR 22> **TERRITORY SONGS**	-	

– Now let us flee / Vacationland / Rainbow warriors / Our Danish heritage / Shoichi yokoi / Unbridgeable / Bedroom community / Palm meadows / Come play in Aberdeen! / Poor little Rhode Island.

VELDT

Formed: Raleigh, North Carolina, USA ... 1986 by identical twins DONNY and DANNY CHAVIS, the line-up being completed by MARTIN LEVI and DAVID BURRIS. This multi-racial alt-rock band were heavily influenced by the dark post-punk guitar sound of British acts such as the CURE, PSYCHEDELIC FURS and JAMC, eventually signing to 'Stardog' (home to MOTHER LOVE BONE) for a LINCOLN FONG-produced mini set in '92; officially an eponymous affair, the record was sometimes referred to as 'MARIGOLDS' due to its sleeve art. The VELDT furthered developed their loose-limbed rhythmic indie sound over a succession of albums beginning with 1994's 'AFRODISIAC'.

Album rating: THE VELDT (*5) / AFRODISIAC (*6) / UNIVERSE BOAT (*5)

DONNY CHAVIS – vocals, guitar / **DANNY CHAVIS** – guitar, vocals / **DAVID BURRIS** – bass / **MARTIN LEVI** – drums

		Mercury	Stardog
Oct 92.	(m-cd/m-c) (864 409-2/-4) <771150-2/-4> **THE VELDT (MARIGOLDS)**		

– CCCP / She stoops to conquer / (untitled) / Pleasure toy / Tinsel town / (untitled) / Chartreuse / Willow tree / Reprise.

VELDT (cont)

Feb 94. (cd/c) <518349-2/-4> **AFRODISIAC**
– Intro (I'll say anything) / It's over / Soul in a jar / You take the world / Revolutionary sister / Interlude (station id) / Juicy sandwich / Heather / Until you're forever / Interlude (V.E.L.D.T.) / Wanna be where you are / Daisy chain / Dusty blood / Last call / I couldn't care less / Outro (shaved) / Soul in a jar (drug store mix) / Soul in a jar (guitar mix).

                                                                   not iss.   Yesha

1996. (cd) **UNIVERSE BOAT**

                                        not iss.   End Of The World

May 98. (cd) </1> **LOVE AT FIRST HATE**
– (untitled tracks).

—— split after above

VELOCETTE

Formed: North London, England ... May 1997 by former COMET GAIN members SARAH BLEACH, SAM PLUCK and JAX COOMBES. Nearly a year on, VELOCETTE were darlings of the NME and Melody Maker when their debut, 'GET YOURSELF TOGETHER', was made 'Single Of The Week'. Mixing a unique blend of laid-back jazz, folk and frantic beats, VELOCETTE certainly grabbed the listener with their newfound sound. Further 45's for 'Wiiija', 'SPOILED CHILDREN' and 'REBORN', preceded their enterprising first album, 'FOURFOLD REMEDY' (1998). But were they good enough to break through into the mainstream? The answer was no as they took time out from the spotlight. • **Covered:** PERFUME (Paris Angels).

Album rating: FOURFOLD REMEDY (*6)

SARAH BLEACH – vocals / **JAX COOMBES** – bass, keyboards, synthesizer / **SAM PLUCK** – guitars, vocals / + session people

                                               Wiiija   Wiiija

Mar 98. (d7"ep/cd-ep) (WIJ 68) **GET YOURSELF TOGETHER**
– Get yourself together / Upstream / Don't care / Get yourself together (French version).

Jun 98. (7") (WIJ 073) **SPOILED CHILDREN. / PERFUME**
(cd-s+=) (WIJ 073CD) – Strip polka.

Nov 98. (7") (WIJ 089) **REBORN. / SISTER**
(cd-s+=) (WIJ 089CD) – Slow dancing angels.

Nov 98. (cd/lp) <(WIJ CD/LP 1077)> **FOURFOLD REMEDY**
– Reborn / Bitterscene / Sirena / Unkind / Where are we? / Get yourself together / Spoiled children / Submarines / Somebody's waiting / That ain't mine.

Mar 99. (7") (WIJ 094) **BITTERSCENE. / BOSSANOVA**
(cd-s+=) (WIJ 094CD) – Catch the sun.

—— the group disappeared after above; another VELOCETTE (a dance group) were around during the 90's

VELOCITY GIRL

Formed: Washington D.C., USA ... 1989 by ARCHIE MOORE (part-time with BLACK TAMBOURINE) and KELLY RILES, who had met at university and only initially intended performing together for a one-off party. Taking their moniker from a PRIMAL SCREAM B-side, they recruited BRIAN NELSON (also of BLACK TAMBOURINE), JIM SPELLMAN and the classically-trained SARAH SHANNON, releasing a handful of singles on obscure labels and making a few appearances via some V/A compilations. These were collected together on the US-only 'THE HORRIBLE TRUTH' mini-set (issued eponymously in the UK in '93. Now signed to grunge bastion, 'Sub Pop', they released 'CRAZY TOWN', although critics noted that their 80's influenced WEATHER PROPHETS/JUNE BRIDES-style jangling was miles apart from NIRVANA et al. VELOCITY GIRL's follow-up, '!SIMPATICO!' (1994), was produced by John Porter (a man more famous for having worked with ROXY MUSIC and The SMITHS), his influence lending the record even more of an Anglicised sheen. Save for a solitary single on 'Heaven' records in '95, all was quiet in the VELOCITY GIRL camp until '96's 'GILDED STARS AND ZEALOUS HEARTS'. ARCHIE MOORE had already moonlighted with another project, HEARTWORMS, and after a couple of indie-pop sets, 'SPACE ESCAPADE' (1995) and 'DURING' (1998), he settled for new post-millennium venture, The SATURDAY PEOPLE. • **Covered:** YOUR SILENT FACE (New Order) / YOU'RE SO GOOD TO ME (Beach Boys) / SEVEN SEAS (Echo & The Bunnymen) / BREAKING LINES (Pastels).

Album rating: 6 SONGS mini compilation (*5) / COPACETIC (*7) / !SIMPATICO! (*6) / GILDED STARS AND ZEALOUS HEARTS (*6) / Heartworms: SPACE ESCAPADE (*5) / DURING (*6) / Saturday People: THE SATURDAY PEOPLE (*5)

SARAH SHANNON (b. 7 Oct'69) – vocals / **ARCHIE MOORE** (b. 3 Jun'68) – guitar, bass, vocals (also of BLACK TAMBOURINE) / **KELLY RILES** (b.22 Mar'67, Encino, Calif.) – guitar, bass / **BRIAN NELSON** (b. 2 Nov'67) – guitar (also of BLACK TAMBOURINE) / **JIM SPELLMAN** (b. 5 Nov'67) – drums

                                         not iss.   Slumberland

Nov 90. (7") <DRYL 004> **I DON'T CARE IF YOU GO. / ALWAYS**

Feb 91. (7") <Shine 006> **I DON'T CARE IF YOU GO. / NOT AT ALL / I DON'T CARE IF YOU GO (acoustic)**
(above on 'Slumberland' records)

Nov 91. (7") <DRYL 010> **MY FORGOTTEN FAVORITE. / WHY SHOULD I BE NICE TO YOU?**

                                         Sub Pop   Sub Pop

Jan 92. (7") <SP 137> **WARM – CRAWL. / (other track by Tsunami)**

Nov 92. (7"green) (60/227) <SP 179> **CRAZY TOWN. / CREEPY**
(12"+=/cd-s+=) (61/228) – My forgotten favourite.

Dec 92. (7") <SMR 014> **MERRY CHRISTMAS, I LOVE YOU. / (other track by Tsunami)**
(above issued on 'Simple Machines')

Apr 93. (lp/c/cd) (SP/+MC/CD 75-242) <SP 196/+A/B> **COPACETIC**   Mar93
– Pretty sister / Crazy town / Copacetic / Here comes / Pop loser / Living well / Chang / Audrey's eyes / Lisa librarian / 57 waltz / Cany apples / Catching squirrels.

Jul 93. (7") (SP 112-228) **AUDREY'S EYES. / STUPID THING**

May 94. (7") <SP 257> **SORRY AGAIN. / MARZIPAN**
(cd-s+=) <SP 257b> – Diamond jubilee / Labrador (original).

Jun 94. (7") (SP 130/322) **I CAN'T STOP SMILING. / MARZIPAN**

Jun 94. (7") <MRG 061> **YOUR SILENT FACE. / YOU'RE SO GOOD TO ME**

Jul 94. (cd/lp) (SP/+CD 122-303) <SP 247/+A/B> **!SIMPATICO!**
– Sorry again / There's only one thing left to say / Tripping wires / I can't stop smiling / All-consumer / Drug girls / Rubble / Labrador / Hey you, get off my moon / Medio core / What you left behind / Wake up, I'm leaving. (

Nov 95. (7") (HV 13) **SEVEN SEAS. / BREAKING LINES**
(above issued on 'Heaven' records)

Feb 96. (7"glitter) <(SP 341)> **NOTHING. / ANATOMY OF A GUTLESS WONDER**

Mar 96. (lp/cd) <(SP/+CD 340)> **GILDED STARS & ZEALOUS HEARTS**
– Gilded stars / Nothing / Just like that / Same old city / Go coastal / Lose something / It's not for you / Zealous heart / Only ones / Finest hour / Blue in spite / Formula 1 throwaway / For the record / One word.

—— disbanded later in 1996

                                         Shute   not iss.

Nov 97. (7") (Shute No.8) **BREAKING LINES. / (split with CHISEL)**

– compilations, etc. –

Jun 93. (m-cd) Slumberland; <(SLR 023CD)> **THE HORRIBLE TRUTH EP**   Mar93
– I don't care if you go / Always / My forgotten favorite / Why should I be nice to you? / Not at all / I don't care if you go (acoustic).

STARRY EYES

SHANNON + SPELLMAN + RILES

                                        not iss.   Radiopaque

Feb 98. (7") <015> **DISAPPEAR. / RADIO!**
(cd-ep+=) <014> **STARRY EYES EP** – Getting over my surprise / N-N-N-Nervous.

HEARTWORMS

ARCHIE MOORE with **TRISHA ROY** – vocals, bass (of BELMONDO) / **CHRIS NORBORG** – drums (of CHISEL) / **CHRISTOPER "CHIP" PORTER** (of SABINE)

                                        not iss.   Darla

1994. (7") **THANKS FOR THE HEADACHE. / LITTLE HANDS OF CONCRETE**

May 95. (cd) <drl 4> **SPACE ESCAPADE**
– Thanks for the headache / Sunday girl / Girl don't tell me / Blues for a heartworm / I won't lose my patience / Creep / Two suns / Sleep is kind / Really, really, reaaly sorry (parts 1-2) / Space escapade / Blues for a heartworm (acoustic).

1995. (7"flexi) <none> **BLUES FOR A HEARTWORM. / (other by the APPLES)**
(above issued on 'Wurlitzer Jukebox')

—— **ARCHIE + TRISH** with **KEVIN MOORE + SCOTT**

Jun 96. (cd-ep) <drl 16> **ENEMIES EP**
– I don't need to know / Two suns / Enemies / Sometimes I never / Wisdom teeth.

                                         Pop Factory   Pop Factory

1997. (7"m) <PROOF 004> **IF EVERYTHING GOES AS PLANNED. / (+2)**

May 98. (cd) <(POOF 13CD)> **DURING**   Mar98
– Holland / Prescription sunglasses / The candle, the radio and the television show / There you go / Wish / Then I saw you praying / Visiting hours / If everything goes as planned / During / Amnesia / Pop factory on strike.

                                         not iss.   Ace Fu

1998. (7") <4> **split w/ CALIFORNIA STADIUM**

                                         not iss.   Brittle Stars

Nov 99. (7") <bsr 004> **FIRE ENGINE RED. / GLARE**

SATURDAY PEOPLE

ARCHIE MOORE – bass, keyboards, vocals / **TERRY BANKS** – guitar (ex-TREE FORT ANGST) / **GREG PAVLOVCAK** – guitar, vocals (of CASTAWAY STONES) / **DAN SEARING** – drums (of ROPERS)

                                         not iss.   Brittle Stars

Dec 99. (7") <bsr 005> **TWILIGHT STORY. / THE CASTLE**

                                         Slumberland   Slumberland

Nov 00. (7") <SLR 60> **CALIFORNIA GIRLS. / SLIPPING THROUGH YOUR FINGERTIPS**

Jul 01. (7") <SLR 63> **GRACE. / (other by the CLIENTELE)**

Nov 01. (lp/cd) <(SLR 67/+CD)> **THE SATURDAY PEOPLE**
– No matter where you are / Find out / Upside-down girl / Grace / Working for the weekend / That settles that / Slipping through your fingertips / The man without qualities (part 2) / California girls / Sound of yesterday / Lullabye in the rain / Twilight story / The man without qualities (part 1) / The castle / Ghost of a chance.

VELO-DELUXE (see under ⇒ ANTENNA)

VELVET CRUSH

Formed: Rhode Island, Providence, New York, then settling in Boston, USA ... 1988 by PAUL CHASTAIN (a former solo artist), RIC MENCK and Milwaukee-raised JEFFREY BORCHARDT, all having had previous experience in the indie scene. As The CHOO CHOO TRAIN, CHASTAIN and MENCK cut a handful of singles, 'THIS PERFECT DAY', 'THE BRIAR ROSE' and 'HIGH', the latter two for UK label, 'Subway'. The VELVET

CRUSH began as a beat/psychedelic fusion of The FLAMIN' GROOVIES, BIG STAR and The REPLACEMENTS. First up was a TEENAGE FANCLUB (they also supported the band in late '91) number, 'EVERYTHING FLOWS', a track that led them to sign for Alan McGee's 'Creation' label. That year, they also unleashed their much loved debut album, 'IN THE PRESENCE OF GREATNESS' (apparently recorded on an 8-track at their friend's pad), a companion piece to the 'FANCLUB's 'Bandwagonesque'; BRENDON O'HARE admitted that the towering MENCK was to him, a pillar of inspiration. A few years in the making, the MITCH EASTER-produced 'TEENAGE SYMPHONIES TO GOD' was, appropriately enough, released on American Independence Day, 4th Of July 1994. The lads subsequently worked with STEPHEN DUFFY through the mid to late 90's, eventually surfacing minus 'Creation' with a third VELVET CRUSH set, 'HEAVY CHANGES', in 1998. 'CRUSH man MENCK issued a solo compilation of early, hard-to-find singles and titled it 'THE BALLAD OF RIC MENCK' (1996). Featuring some recordings made under the moniker of The SPRINGFIELDS, MENCK also included his sundrenched covers of The Hollies' 'CLOWN' and Matthew Sweet's 'WE ARE GONNA BE ALRIGHT'. Meanwhile, CHASTAIN and SWEET were recording material in L.A., intended for a CHASTAIN solo project. After MENCK heard some of the songs, he proposed the idea of developing a "soft rock" album to his fellow band mate. CHASTAIN obliged and, with the material already recorded, coupled with some of MENCK's own songs, the group issued 'SOFT SOUNDS' in 2002. Not a soft rock album in as much as say, BRYAN ADAMS, VELVET CRUSH had taken delicate melodies and applied them to acoustic rock songs. A startling album from its opening track – and a first for the usually melodic feedback-induced duo. • **Covered:** MR. SPACEMAN (Byrds) / ONE HUNDRED YEARS (Gram Parsons) / WHY NOT YOUR BABY + ELEVATOR OPERATOR (Gene Clark).

Album rating: IN THE PRESENCE OF GREATNESS (*7) / TEENAGE SYMPHONIES TO GOD (*6) / HEAVY CHANGES (*6) / FREE EXPRESSION (*6) / ROCK CONCERT live (*4) / A SINGLE ODESSEY compilation (*7) / TIMELESS MELODIES compilation (*7) / MELODY FREAKS compilation (*7) / SOFT SOUNDS (*7) / Paul Chastain & Ric Menck: HEY WIMPUS collection (*6) / Ric Menck: THE BALLAD OF RIC MENCK (*7)

PAUL CHASTAIN

1985. (12"ep) <psma-001965> **HALO EP**
– Halo / Am I right / Focused / Every other time / Outside circle / Comes round.
— The STUPID CUPIDS were PAULIE, RICKY + DARREN COOPER
1987. (7"flexi; as PAULIE CHASTAIN) <none> **RAINING ALL DAY. / Stupid Cupids: BIG BLUE FUZZ**
— COOPER later formed THREE HOUR TOUR, who issued '1969' in 1996

CHOO CHOO TRAIN

PAUL CHASTAIN – vocals, bass / **RIC MENCK** – drums (ex-DRATS, ex-PAINT SET)

1987. (7") **THIS PERFECT DAY. / HAPPY BICYCLE**
Jul 88. (12"ep) (SUBWAY 20T) **THE BRIAR ROSE**
– Briar rose / Big blue buzz / Nothing else! / Flower field / Every little knight / Catch another breath.
Nov 88. (7") (SUBWAY 23) **HIGH. / WISHING ON A STAR**
(12"+=) (SUBWAY 23T) – My best friend / When Sunday comes / Parasol!

SPRINGFIELDS

PAUL CHASTAIN + RIC MENCK

Aug 88. (7"m) (SARAH 010) <BUS 001> **SUNFLOWER. / CLOWN / ARE WE GONNA BE ALRIGHT?**
Nov 88. (7"; as BAG-O-SHELLS) <BUS 002> **MARKERS. / ALMOST HOME**
1990. (7"; as BAG-O-SHELLS) <BUS 009> **POCKETBOOK. / BACK IN YOUR TOWN / WHATEVER HAPPENED TO MY LIFE?**
Jan 91. (7") <PB 005> **TOMORROW ENDS TODAY. / SHE SWIRLS AROUND ME**
Feb 91. (7") (SARAH 040) **WONDER. / TOMORROW ENDS TODAY**
1991. (7"ep/cd-ep) (TWANG 8/+CD) <SHINE 005> **TRANQUIL. / REACH FOR THE STARS / MILLION TEARS**

VELVET CRUSH

— **CHASTAIN + MENCK** added **JEFFREY BORCHARDT** – guitar, vocals (ex-WHITE SISTERS)

1990. (7") <BUS 007> **IF NOT TRUE. / ONE THING TWO BELIEVE**
1990. (7"flexi) <RAVE 16FX> **WALKING OUT ON LOVE. / (other track by The Golden Dawn)**
(above issued on 'Raving Pop Blast')
1991. (7"ep) <BUS 011> **ASH & EARTH / CIRCLING THE SUN. / EVERYTHING FLOWS / SHE CRACKED**
Jun 91. (7") (TWANG 3) **EVERYTHING FLOWS. / ASH & EARTH / CIRCLING THE SUN**

Oct 91. (cd/c) (CRECD/C-CRE 109) <RL 05-2/-4> **IN THE PRESENCE OF GREATNESS**
– Window to the world / Drive me down / Ash & earth / White soul / Superstar / Blind faith / Speedway baby / Stop / Asshole / Die a little every day. <(cd re-iss. Oct01 on 'Action Musik'+=; AMCD 104)> – Circling the sun / Everything flows / She cracked.
Apr 92. (7") (CRE 122) **WINDOW TO THE WORLD. / ATMOSPHERE**
(12"ep)(cd-ep) **THE POST GREATNESS E.P.** (CRE 122T)(CRESCD 122) – The gentle breeze / Butterfly position.
— added guest **DAVE GIBBS** – guitar (of GIGOLO AUNTS)
Oct 92. (12"ep)(cd-ep) (CRE 139T)(CRESCD 139) **DRIVE ME DOWN (SOFTLY). / ATMOSPHERE / SLIP AWAY**
Jun 94. (7") <PAR 001> **HOLD ME UP. / MR. SPACEMAN**
Jun 94. (7") (CRE 146) **HOLD ME UP. / DON'T YOU SLIP AWAY FROM ME**
(12"+=)(cd-s+=) (CRE 146T)(CRESCD 146) – One hundred year from now.
Jul 94. (cd/lp)(c) (CRECD/CRELP/C-CRE 130) <6444-2> **TEENAGE SYMPHONIES TO GOD**
– Hold me up / My blank pages / Why not your baby / Time wraps around you / Atmosphere / #10 / Faster days / Somethings goota give / This life is killing me / Weird summer / Star trip / Keep on lingerin'.
— now worked with (STEPHEN) DUFFY on two sets, 'Duffy' (1995) and 'I Love My Friends' (1998)
— **CHASTAIN + MENCK** added **JEFF UNDERHILL** – guitar (of HONEYBUNCH) + **PETER PHILLIPS**
Jun 98. (cd/lp) <(AMCD/AMLP 102)> **HEAVY CHANGES**
– Play for keeps / Standing still / Fear of flying / Think it over / Ever after / Used to believe / Wake up / God speed / White satin bed / Live for now / Seen better days. (cd re-iss. Oct98 on 'Cooking Vinyl'; COOKCD 163)
1999. (cd/lp) <Bob-6> **FREE EXPRESSION**
– Kill me now / Worst enemy / Between the lines / Goin' to my head / Heaven knows / Roman candle / Melody No.1 / Things get better / Gentle breeze / All together / Shine on me / Unlucky one. (UK-iss.Feb01; same)
Dec 00. (7"green) <(Bob 14)> **GENTLE BREEZE. / ON MY SIDE**
(cd-s+=) <(Bob 15)> – Party line.
— now down to **CHASTAIN + MENCK**

Oct 02. (cd) <(AMCD 106)> **SOFT SOUNDS**
– Don't take me down / Rollin' in my sleep / Some kind of light / Save me a place / In your time / Forever, for now / She goes on / Vanishing point / Duchess / Party line (samba) / Late in the day.

– compilations, etc. –

on 'Action Musik' unless stated otherwise)
Mar 92. (lp/cd; as CHOO CHOO TRAIN) Suborg; (SUBORG 015/+CD) **BRIAR HIGH** (THE 1988 SINGLES)
Mar 98. (cd; as PAUL CHASTAIN & RIC MENCK) <(AMCD 100)> **HEY WIMPUS: THE EARLY RECORDINGS OF PAUL CHASTAIN & RIC MENCK**
– Briar rose / Big blue buzz / There before the dawn / Nothing else / Flower field / Every little knight / Catch another breath / High / Wishing on a star / My best friend / When Sunday comes / Parasol / Walking out on love.
Feb 01. (cd) Action Musik; <(AMCD 101)> **ROCK CONCERT (live at Cabaret Metro, Chicago)**
– Window to the world / My blank pages / Ash and earth / Time wraps around you / Atmosphere / This life is killing me / Hold me up / Remember the lightning.
Oct 01. (cd) Action Musik; <(AMCD 103)> **A SINGLE ODESSEY**
– If not true / One thing two believe / Circling the sun / Everything flows / She cracked / Atmosphere / Gentle breeze / Butterfly position / Drive me down (acoustic) / Remember the lightning / Elevator operator / One hundred years from now / Don't you slip away from me / It's been too long and it's too late now / Be someone tonight / Leisure 40 / The thing that you do / Party line / On my side.
Nov 01. (cd) Epic; <80960> **TIMELESS MELODIES**
– If not true / Ash and earth / Window to the world / Blind faith / Superstar / Gentle breeze / Butterfly position / Drive me down (acoustic) / Star trip (original) / Time wraps around you (original) / Hold me up / Weird summer / Why not your baby / Atmosphere / Fear of flying / Think it over / Be someone tonight / Goin' to my head / Worst enemy / Things get better / Please don't take me down / Staying found.
Jul 02. (cd) Action Musik; <(AMCD 105)> **MELODY FREAKS** (demos & outtakes 1990-1996)
– Star trip / Time wraps around you / Hold me up / Standing down / Further over you / Beside yourself / Seen better days / Turn down / My blank pages / This life is killing me / Weird summer / One thing two believe / Reunion day / The real one / If not true / Goin' to my head / Heaven knows / Keep on lingerin'.

RIC MENCK

Nov 97. (cd) <(SHINEUS 16)> **THE BALLAD OF RIC MENCK**
– Perfect day / The bicycle song / Clown / Sunflower / Are we gonna be alright? / Tomorrow ends today / Wonder / She swirls around me / Million tears / Reachin' for the stars / Tranquil.

VENT 414 (see under ⇒ WONDER STUFF)

VERBENA

Formed: Birmingham, Alabama, USA . . . 1994 by vocalist SCOTT BONDY, drummer LES NUBY and bassist DANIEL JOHNSTON (not to be confused with the Austin troubadour of the same name). The bluesey rock trio began life as SHALLOW, but drummer NUBY was replaced with REMY ZERO's LOUIS SCHEFANO and singer/guitarist ANNE MARIE GRIFFIN was added to the line-up. They were now VERBENA, and after a live performance, BONDY and Co were approached by 'Merge' to issue an EP, which would become 'PILOT PARK' released in 1996. Pressured back into the band after this brief success, drummer NUBY re-joined and the group headed into the studio with DAVE FRIDMANN (of MERCURY REV and FLAMING LIPS fame). The result was the rocking KEEF'n'MICK-esque (there's even a track called 'ME & KEITH') mix of rocky R&B soul, paired with floating LYNYRD SKYNYRD-style melodies and ANNE MARIE GRIFFIN's contrasting harmonies. 'Capitol' records pricked-up their ears, as did DAVE GROHL (of FOO FIGHTERS), who offered to produce the band's major-label debut; the stinging, abrasive 'INTO THE PINK' (1999). However, the band took a dive and strayed away from music . . . until 2003.

Album Rating: SOULS FOR SALE (*6) / INTO THE PINK (*5)

SCOTT BONDY – vocals, guitar / **DANIEL JOHNSTON** – bass / **LOUIS SCHEFANO** – drums (ex-REMY ZERO) repl. LES NUBY / **ANNE MARIE GRIFFIN** – vocals, guitar, bass

		Setanta	Merge
Oct 95.	(7"m) *(SET 020)* **I SAY SO. / SILVER QUEEN / EVER RENT A HEART?**	□	-
1996.	(cd-ep) *<MRG 102>* **PILOT PARK**	-	□
	– I say so / ***** **** / Silver queen / Everyday shoes / Pony express / Ever rent a heart?		
Mar 97.	(cd-s) *(SETCD 031)* **HEY, COME ON**	□	-
May 97.	(cd/lp) *(SET CD/LP 035)* *<MRG 115>* **SOULS FOR SALE**	□	Apr97
	– Hot blood / Shaped like a gun / Junk for fashion / Song that ended your career / Desert / Hey, come on / Me & Keith / So what / Postcard blues / Kiss yourself.		
Aug 97.	(7") *(SET 037)* **SHAPED LIKE A GUN. / POSTCARD BLUES**	□	-

— **LES NUBY** – drums; repl. LOUIS

		not iss.	Capitol
Jun 99.	(cd) *<59280>* **INTO THE PINK**	-	□
	– Lovely isn't love / Into the pink / Baby got shot / John Beverly / Pretty please / Monkey, I'm your man / Prick the sun / Oh my / Submissionary / Bang bang / Depression is a fashion / Sympathy was dead / Big skies, black rainbows.		

— **NICK DAVISTON** – bass, vocals; repl. GRIFFIN

— they will release an album in 2003

VERMONT (see under ⇒ PROMISE RING)

VERONICA LAKE

Formed: Ann Arbor, Michigan, USA . . . 1990 by singer/songwriter TIM SENDRA, a man very obviously influenced by that iconic pre-war Hollywood actress of the same name. Along with CHIP PORTER and R. SCOTT KELLY, the trio debuted in 1992 on the seminal "indie" imprint courtesy of vinyl single billed as 'THE MAN WHO WAS NOT WITH IT'. The twee-pop act delivered a quickfire series of limited edition 7"ers over the ensuing year or so, culminating with 1993's, 'THRENODY'. After they split, SENDRA was subsequently discovered in an equally low-key outfit, MADISON ELECTRIC.

Album rating: never released any

TIM SENDRA – vocals, guitar / **CHRISTOPER "CHIP" PORTER + R. SCOTT KELLY**

		not iss.	Bus Stop
1992.	(7") *<BUS 018>* **THE MAN WHO WAS NOT WITH IT**	-	□
	– This is my world (you can have it) / See me when you are 16.		
		not iss.	Cher Doll
1992.	(7") *<CHER 001>* **SLEEPYHOUSE. / (other by CRAYON)**	-	□
		not iss.	SpinArt
1993.	(7") *<SPART 3E>* **WHEN YOU SMILE. / INSECURE BABY**	-	□
		not iss.	Simple Machines
May 93.	(7") *<smwh 006>* **SAINTS ABOVE. / (split w/ BRATMOBILE)**	-	□
		not iss.	Silver Girl
1993.	(7"ep; as VERONICA LAKE ORCHESTRA) **Winter's Mist**	-	□
	– Emma maybe / (other artists).		
		not iss.	Audrey's Diary
1993.	(7") *<004.93>* **THRENODY. / IN THE CLOUDS**	-	□

— disbanded in 1993

MADISON ELECTRIC

— aka **TIM SENDRA**

		not iss.	Drive-in
Apr 96.	(7"ep) *<DRIVE 1>* **Tonights Features EP**	-	□
	– V-neck.		
		not iss.	Quiddity
1996.	(7") *<QUID 003>* **HEAVY PETAL. /**	-	□

VERSUS

Formed: New York City, New York, USA . . . 1992 out of FLOWER (a band who released an album, 'HOLOGRAM SKY' 1991 and several 45's subsequently appearing on collections, 'CONCRETE SKY' 1994 and 'THE BEST OF FLOWER' 1995) and SATURNINE, by its leader, RICHARD BALUYUT and cohort, FONTAINE TOUPS. Debuting soon after with the 7", 'INSOMNIA', the band followed this up with their opening mini-effort EP, 'LET'S ELECTRIFY!' (1993). They moved on with the release of their debut full-length offering, 'THE STARS ARE INSANE' (1994) – the band wished to title it 'MEAT, SPORTS AND ROCK' but were persuaded against it by their label not wishing to alienate members of the record-buying public. A set which was both competent and mature in its approach, although lacking some of the balls of their earlier deliveries. Their ensuing compilation, 'DEAD LEAVES' (1995), featured a swathe of previously released singles and other material including the standout track, 'TIN FOIL STAR'. Their rather disappointing 'DEEP RED' EP of the following year, did however contain a new guitarist in the shape of another BALUYUT brother, JAMES. Fortunately the band came back strongly with the long-player, 'SECRET SWINGERS', which contained some of their best work since 'LET'S ELECTRIFY'. This move into a more airey dream rock style continued on to the next LP, 'TWO CENTS PLUS TAX' (1998), helped by the assistance of new drummer PATRICK RAMOS who had replaced the departing ED. This progression towards a lighter poppier feel seemed to be purposeful when their fifth album proper 'AFTERGLOW' hit the shops in 1999. Running alongside the band's work was TOUPS' side-project CONTAINE, which had been accidentally formed in 1993 when the full line-up of VERSUS were unable to play a live show causing TOUPS to seek the assistance of CONNIE LOVATT (of ALKALINE and PACIFIC OCEAN fame) for the stage appearnace. The pair continued in the studio with debut, airy-pop EP, 'I WANT IT ALL', helped by the stickwork of DAVE FRANK. Three years later saw the issue of their first full-length album proper, 'ONLY COWARDS WALK LIKE COWARDS'. With some great comedy song titles and the drumming of ED BALUYUT, this set moved into a more raucous indie rock arena from its laid-back pop predecessor. • **Covered:** SHANGRI-LA (Kinks) / OUT IN THE STREETS (Shangri-La's) / SHANGRI-LA (Jeff Lynne). • **Note:** Another VERSUS released an EP on 'Gold & Liebe' in '98.

Album rating: LET'S ELECTRIFY! mini (*6) / THE STARS ARE INSANE (*5) / DEAD LEAVES (*5) / SECRET SWINGERS (*7) / TWO CENTS PLUS TAX (*5) / HURRAH (*4) / Containe: I WANT IT ALL mini (*6) / ONLY COWARDS WALK LIKE COWARDS (*8)

RICHARD BALUYUT – vocals, guitar / **FONTAINE TOUPS** – vocals, bass / **ED BALUYUT** – drums

		not iss.	Land Speed
1992.	(7") **INSOMNIA. / ASTRONAUT**	-	□
		not iss.	Pop Narcotic
1992.	(7") **BRIGHT LIGHT. / FOREST FIRE**	-	□
		not iss.	Remora
1993.	(m-lp) *<001>* **LET'S ELECTRIFY!**	-	□
	– (4 tracks) / Noogie / Sea girl.		
		Simple Machines	Simple Machines
Mar 93.	(7") *<(WHJAN)>* **TIN FOIL STAR. / (other by SCRAWL)**	□	□
		not iss.	K
1994.	(7") *<IPU 44>* **FROG. / (GO TELL IT TO THE) MOUNTAIN**	-	□
		Teenbeat	Teenbeat
May 94.	(lp/c/cd) *<(TEENBEAT 142/+C/CD)>* **THE STARS ARE INSANE**	□	□
	– Thera / Circle / Fallow / River / Mirror mirror / Be-9 / Deserte / Blade of grass / Janet / Solar democrat / Wind me up / I'll be you. *(cd re-iss. Feb95 on 'Cloudland'; RAIN 011CD)*		
Nov 94.	(7") *<TEENBEAT 152>* **BIG HEAD ON. / N.I.T.A.**	-	□
Apr 95.	(lp/c/cd) *<(TEENBEAT 162/+C/CD)>* **DEAD LEAVES** (compilation)	□	□
	– Astronaut / Forest fire / Insomnia / Venus Victoria / Another face / Bright light / Merry-go-round / Tin foil star / Cross the street / Crazy / Sunburned / Flax. *(cd re-iss. May95 on 'Cloudland'; RAIN 015CD)*		

— added **JAMES BALUYUT** – guitar, drums, synthesizer; repl. ED

		Teenbeat	Teenbeat – Caroline
Mar 96.	(12"ep/cd-ep) *<(TB 192-1/-2)>* **DEEP RED EP**	□	□
	– Shooting star / Linus / Lost time / Dead city / Deep red.		
Sep 96.	(lp – cd) *<(TB 222 – CAROL 004CD)<7533>* **SECRET SWINGERS**	□	Jul96
	– Lose that dress / Yeah you / Glitter of love / Ghost story / Use as directed / Double suicide (mercy killing) / Jealous / Shower song / Angels rush in / One million / Heart is a diamond.		
		Caroline	Caroline
Aug 96.	(7") *<(7CAR 007)>* **YEAH YOU. / KNOW NOTHING**	□	□
Oct 96.	(7") *<(7CAR 010)>* **GLITTER OF LOVE. / FOREST FIRE**	□	□
	(cd-s+=) *<(CDCAR 010)>* – Reveille.		

— **PATRICK RAMOS** – drums; repl. ED

May 98.	(cd) *<7557>* **TWO CENTS PLUS TAX**	□	□
	– Atomic kid / Dumb fun / Never be o.k. / Morning glory / Radar follows you / Underground / Spastic reaction / Crazy-maker (I'm still in love with you) / Jack & Jill / Mouth of Heaven.		
		Merge	Merge
Feb 99.	(cd-ep) *<MRG 156>* **AFTERGLOW**	□	□
	– Crashing the afterglow / Raining / True believer / Off the hook / Santa Maria.		
Apr 00.	(cd-ep) *<MRG 176>* **SHANGRI-LA**	□	□
	– Shangri-la / Shangri-la / Out in the streets / Shangri-la.		
Oct 00.	(lp/cd) *<(MRG 186/+CD)>* **HURRAH**	□	□
	– My Adidas / Eskimo / Play dead / Said too much / You'll be sorry / Frederick's		

CONTAINE

FONTAINE TOUPS – vocals, bass / **CONNIE LOVATT** – vocals / with **DAVE FRANK** – drums

	not iss.	Enchante
1994. (m-lp) <*001*> **I WANT IT ALL**	–	

– Shooting me down / Hem / Mean song / Lemon cake / You don't owe me / Big blue car / You / Tired eyes.

— added guest **ED BALUYUT** – drums

Feb 97. (cd) <*002*> **ONLY COWARDS WALK LIKE COWARDS** | – | |

– I notice everything / Why why why / Why waste your time? / Shy song (or, I want to fuck you) / It's not easy being wrong / Mean song pt.II / Instrumental / Say please / Sad sad luck / Your brother's a star / Change the world / Summer / Only cowards walk like cowards / Reprise (the money song) (or the I hate my boyfriend song or the I hate your band song).

— disbanded when CONNIE formed PACIFIC OCEAN, who issued one album for the same label, 'BIRDS DON'T THINK THEY'RE FLYING' <*003*>

VERUCA SALT

Formed: Chicago, Illinois, USA ... early '93 by NINA GORDON and LOUISE POST, who were soon joined by STEVE LACK and NINA's brother JIM SHAPIRO. In mid-94 they enjoyed a minor indie hit with debut single, 'SEETHER' and amid the major label chequebook scramble that followed, opted to remain independent for the 'AMERICAN THIGHS' album later that year. Named after a line in AC/DC's classic track, 'You Shook Me All Night Long', the album was a promising blast of punk-pop directed from a distinctly femme-rock perspective, at times akin to a surreal fusion of a mellow BREEDERS or a heavy PIXIES. Following a further succession of minor US hits including a re-released 'SEETHER' and 'NUMBER ONE BLIND', the band signed to the 'Outpost-MCA' imprint for follow-up set, 'EIGHT ARMS TO HOLD YOU' (1997). Once again taking its title from rock'n'roll history (the original moniker intended for The BEATLES' 'Help' film), the record found the girls utilising a more satisfying sonic palate while retaining the edge that had made their earlier work so compelling. With the subsequent departure of both SHAPIRO and GORDON amid much bitterness and infighting, POST completely reconfigured the group with new members STEPHEN FITZPATRICK, SUZANNE SOKOL and JIMMY MADLA. The issue of her bust-up with both POST and FOO FIGHTERS man, DAVE GROHL informed much of the album's lyrical sting, while musically the ferocious guitar attack harked back to the halcyon era of grunge. • **Songwriters:** GORDON or POST except; BODIES (Sex Pistols) / STACEY PLEASE (Morris-Felsenthal) / MY SHARONA (Knack). • **Trivia:** Named after a character in Roald Dahl's 'Charlie And The Chocolate Factory'.

Album rating: AMERICAN THIGHS (*7) / EIGHT ARMS TO HOLD YOU (*7) / RESOLVER (*4)

NINA GORDON – vocals / **LOUISE POST** – vocals, guitar / **STEVE LACK** – bass / **JIM SHAPIRO** – drums

	Scared Hitless	Minty Fresh
Jun 94. (7") (*FRET 003S*) **SEETHER. / ALL HAIL ME**	61	–
(cd-s+=) (*FRET 003CD*) – Stacey please.		

	Hi-Rise	Minty Fresh
Oct 94. (cd/c/lp) (*FLAT CD/MC/LP 9*) <*24732*> **AMERICAN THIGHS**		69

– Get back / All hail me / Seether / Spiderman '79 / Forsythia / Wolf / Celebrate you / Fly / Number one blind / Victrola / Twinstar / 25. (*lp w /free one-sided 12"+=*) (*FLATLPX 9*) – SLEEPING WHERE I WANT

Nov 94. (7"/c-s) (*FLAT/+C 12*) **SEETHER. / STRAIGHT**	73	–
(12"+=/cd-s+=) (*FLAT T/SDG 12*) – She's a brain.		
Jan 95. (7"green) (*FLAT 16*) <*9*> **NUMBER ONE BLIND. / BODIES**	68	
(12"+=/cd-s+=) (*FLAT T/SCD 16*) – Aurora.		
Jun 95. (7") (*FLAT 19*) **VICTROLA. / MY SHARONA**		
(10"+=/cd-s+=) (*FLAT EN/SCD 19*) <*65051*> – Sundown (live).		
Apr 96. (cd-ep) <*22212*> **BLOW IT OUT YOUR ASS IT'S VERUCA SALT**	–	

– Shimmer like a girl / I'm taking Europe with me / New York mining disaster 1996 / Disinherit.

— **STACY JONES** – drums (ex-LETTERS TO CLEO) repl. SHAPIRO

	Outpost	Outpost
Feb 97. (7") (*OPRS 22197*) **VOLCANO GIRLS. / GOOD DISASTER**	56	–
(cd-s+=) (*OPRCD 22197*) – Sleeper car.		
(cd-s) (*OPRXD 22197*) – ('A'side) / Pale green / One more page of insincerity please.		
Mar 97. (cd/c) <(*OP CD/C 30001*)> **EIGHT ARMS TO HOLD YOU**		55 Feb97

– Straight / Volcano girls / Don't make me prove it / Awesome / One last time / With David Bowie / Benjamin / Shutterbug / The morning said / Sound of the bell / Loneliness is worse / Stoneface / Venus man trap / Earthcrosser.

Aug 97. (7") (*OPRS 22261*) **BENJAMIN. / THE SPEED OF CANDY (demo)**	75	
(7") (*OPRSX 22261*) – ('A'side) / Never met her (demo).		
(cd-s+=) (*OPRCD 22261*) – Swedish fish (demo).		

— when GORDON went solo (for 'Warners' set, 'Tonight And The Rest Of My Life' – 2001) POST recruited **STEPHEN FITZPATRICK** – guitar / **SUZANNE SOKOL** – bass / **JIMMY MADLA** – drums

	Beyond	Beyond
May 00. (cd) <(*63985 78103-2*)> **RESOLVER**		

– The same person / Born entertainer / Best you can get / Wet suit / Yeah man / Imperfectly / Officially dead / Only you know / Disconnected / All dressed up / Used to know her / Pretty boys / Hellraiser. (*re-iss. Sep01 on 'Artful'; ARTFULCD 41*)

	Artful	not iss.
Nov 01. (cd-s) (*CDARTFUL 38*) **BORN ENTERTAINER / YEAH MAN / IMPERFECTLY**		–

VERVE

Formed: Wigan, England ... 1990 by local college lads RICHARD ASHCROFT (the main writer), NICK McCABE, SIMON JONES and PETER SALISBURY. They were soon supporting the likes of RIDE and SPIRITUALIZED, signing to 'Hut' in 1991. The following year, they released three singles, the spiralling psychedelia of 'ALL IN THE MIND', 'SHE'S A SUPERSTAR' & 'GRAVITY GRAVE'. In early summer of '93, they had a minor hit with 'BLUE', a taster for the debut album, 'A STORM IN HEAVEN', which made the UK Top 30. The album delivered on the promise of the early singles; an amorphous melange of trippy rock and liquid space-jazz ambience. Ambitious and cocksure, they toured the States, subsequently coming unstuck with US label VERVE, who forced them to slightly change their name to THE VERVE. In 1995, they unleashed a second album, 'A NORTHERN SOUL', a much darker, more intense affair featuring more conventional song structures. Although the album went Top 20, they announced they were splitting several months later, the 'HISTORY' single apparently their swan song. Just when the band were poised to enter the big league, it looked as if they'd missed the boat, McCABE and ASHCROFT's quarrelling, together with well documented drug problems, seemingly to blame for the band's demise. By February '97, however, they got it together sufficiently to reform and their first single of the year was to many, their best song yet, the grandiose, string-laden 'BITTER SWEET SYMPHONY' (written by MICK JAGGER and KEITH RICHARDS for The ANDREW LOOG OLDHAM ORCHESTRA). The song crashed into the UK chart at No.2 thanks to a glorious video featuring a tense, jaywalking ASHCROFT barging into everyone in sight! A follow-up, 'THE DRUGS DON'T WORK', went straight in at No.1, as did parent album, 'URBAN HYMNS' (1997). It seemed THE VERVE could do no wrong, although tensions between ASHCROFT and the others were coming to a head; McCABE would subsequently announce his retirement from stage work in July '98 (veteran pedal steel man BJ COLE was enlisted). The Americans had already taken the band into their hearts by this time, the aforementioned third set hitting the Top 30 and going platinum in the process. However by May 1999, THE VERVE were history, "astral man" ASHCROFT opting for a solo career with his SPIRITUALIZED wife KATE RADLEY in tow. And what a picture of domestic bliss he painted on 'ALONE WITH EVERYBODY' (2000), his first solo set and a marked transition from the anguished soul-searching of his best work with THE VERVE. Eloquent string arrangements, folky strumming and contented musings on life's basic essentials made for one of the best solo debuts in years. A lucky man? It certainly seemed so. ASHCROFT returned in 2002 to deliver 'HUMAN CONDITIONS', a slighty bitter sophomore record, that seemed to isolate VERVE fans even more. Reverting into a world of deliberate melancholy, ASHCROFT even dabbled with the world's smallest violin. Themes of God, lost love and difficult relationships have all been explored before by ASHCROFT et al, nevertheless it reached UK No.3. Yet its only saving grace remained in the brilliant closing track 'NATURE IS THE LAW' (excuse the cheesy title), which featured BRIAN WILSON on backing harmonies.

Album rating: A STORM IN HEAVEN (*7) / NO COME DOWN collection (*6) / A NORTHERN SOUL (*8) / URBAN HYMNS (*9) / Richard Ashcroft: ALONE WITH EVERYBODY (*7) / HUMAN CONDITIONS (*6)

RICHARD ASHCROFT (b.11 Sep'71) – vocals, guitar / **NICK McCABE** (b.14 Jul'71) – lead guitar / **SIMON JONES** (b.29 Jul'72) – bass / **PETER SALISBURY** (b.24 Sep'71) – drums

	Hut	Vernon Yard
Mar 92. (7") (*HUT 12*) **ALL IN THE MIND. / ONE WAY TO GO**		–
(12"+=/cd-s+=) (*HUT T/CD 12*) – A man called Sun.		
Jun 92. (7"/ext-12"/ext-cd-s) (*HUT/+H/CD 16*) **SHE'S A SUPERSTAR. / FEEL**	66	–
Oct 92. (10"ep) (*HUTEN 21*) **GRAVITY GRAVE EP**		–
– Gravity grave / Endless life / She's a superstar (live).		
(12"+=/cd-s++) (*HUT T/CD 21*) – ('A'extended) / Endless life / A man called Sun (live).		
Jan 93. (m-cd) (<*HUTUS 1*>) **THE VERVE E.P.** (compilation)	–	
– Gravity grave / A man called Sun / She's a superstar / Endless life / Feel. (*UK-iss.Sep97 on 'Vernon Yard'; YARDCD 001*)		
May 93. (12"ep) (*HUTT 29*) **BLUE. / TWILIGHT / WHERE THE GEESE GO**	69	–
(10"ep+=/cd-ep+=) (*HUT EN/CD 29*) – No come down.		
Jun 93. (cd/c/lp) (*CDHUT/HUTMC/HUTLP 10*) <*87950*> **A STORM IN HEAVEN**	27	
– Star sail / Slide away / Already there / Beautiful mind / The sun, the sea / Virtual world / Make it 'til Monday / Blue / Butterfly / See you in the next one (have a good time).		
Sep 93. (7"pink) (*HUT 35*) **SLIDE AWAY. / 6 O'CLOCK**		–
(12"/cd-s) (*HUT T/CD 35*) – ('A'side) / Make it 'til Monday (acoustic) / Virtual world (acoustic).		
May 94. (cd) (*CDHUT 18*) **NO COMEDOWN** (rare / b-sides)		–
– No come down / Blue (USA mix) / Make it 'til Monday (acoustic) / Butterfly (acoustic) / Where the grease go / 6 o'clock / One way to go / Gravity grave (live) / Twilight. (*re-iss. Sep97 on 'Vernon Yard'; YARDCD 007*)		

THE VERVE

Apr 95. (7"burgundy) (*HUT 54*) **THIS IS MUSIC. / LET THE DAMAGE BEGIN**	35	–
(12"+=/cd-s+=) (*HUT T/CD 54*) – You and me.		
Jun 95. (7"green/c-s) (*HUT/+C 55*) **ON YOUR OWN. / I SEE THE DOOR**	28	–
(cd-s+=) (*HUTCD 55*) – Little gem / Dance on your bones.		

VERVE (cont)

Jul 95. (cd/c/d-lp) *(CDHUT/HUTMC/HUTLP 27)* <40437> **A NORTHERN SOUL** — 13
— A new decade / This is music / On your own / So it goes / A northern soul / Brainstorm interlude / Drive you home / History / No knock on my door / Life's an ocean / Stormy clouds / Stormy clouds (reprise).
Sep 95. (c-s) *(HUTC 59)* **HISTORY / BACK ON MY FEET AGAIN** 24 —
(cd-s+=) *(HUTCD 59)* — On your own (acoustic) / Monkey magic (Brainstorm mix).
(cd-s) *(HUTDX 59)* — ('A'extended) / Grey skies / Life's not a rehearsal.

— originals re-formed adding **SIMON TONG** — guitar, keyboards

| | | Hut | Virgin |

Jun 97. (7") *(HUTLH 82)* <38634> **BITTER SWEET SYMPHONY. / SO SISTER** 2 12 Mar98
('A'extended; cd-s+=) *(HUTDX 82)* — Echo bass.
(c-s/cd-s) *(HUT C/DG 82)* — ('A'side) / Lord I guess I'll never know / Country song / ('A'radio version).
Sep 97. (c-s/cd-s) *(HUT C/DG 88)* **THE DRUGS DON'T WORK / THREE STEPS / THE DRUGS DON'T WORK (original demo)** 1 —
(cd-s) *(HUTDX 88)* — ('A'extended) / Bitter sweet symphony (James Lavelle remix) / The crab / Stamped.
Sep 97. (cd/c/lp) *(<44913-2/-4/-1>)* **URBAN HYMNS** 1 23
— Bitter sweet symphony / Sonnet / The rolling people / The drugs don't work / Catching the butterfly / Neon wilderness / Space and time / Weeping willow / Lucky man / One day / This time / Velvet morning / Come on.
Nov 97. (c-s/cd-s) *(HUT C/DG 92)* **LUCKY MAN / NEVER WANNA SEE YOU CRY / HISTORY** 7 —
(cd-s) *(HUT DX 92)* — ('A'side) / MSG / The longest day / Lucky man (happiness more or less).
Feb 98. (cd-ep) *<13112-2>* **FIVE BY FIVE** — —
— Come on / The rolling people / Lucky man (radio edit) / Catching the butterfly / Space and time.

— THE VERVE announced their demise in '99; JONES (and later TONG) formed The SHINING

– compilations, etc. –

Mar 98. (ltd-12"ep) **BITTER SWEET SYMPHONY (original) / LORD I GUESS I'LL NEVER KNOW. / BITTER SWEET SYMPHONY (James Lavelle mix) / COUNTRY SONG** — —
Mar 98. (ltd-12"ep) **THE DRUGS DON'T WORK / THREE STEPS. / THE DRUGS DON'T WORK (demo) / THE CRAB** — —
Mar 98. (ltd-12"ep) **LUCKY MAN / NEVER WANNA SEE YOU CRY. / MSG / THE LONGEST DAY** — —
Mar 98. (ltd-12"ep) **SONNET / STAMPED. / SO SISTER / ECHO BASS** — —
(the import cd-single version of the above single <895075-2> actually hit UK No.74 in May '98)

RICHARD ASHCROFT

— with various session people incl. **PETER SALISBURY**

| | | Hut | Virgin |

Apr 00. (c-s) *(HUTC 128)* **A SONG FOR THE LOVERS / PRECIOUS STONE** 3 —
(12"+=/cd-s+=) *(HUT T/CD 128)* — Could be a country thing city thing blues thing.
Jun 00. (c-s) *(HUTC 136)* **MONEY TO BURN / XXYY** 17 —
(12"+=/cd-s+=) *(HUT T/CD 136)* — Leave me high.
Jun 00. (cd/c/lp) *(CDHUTX/HUTMCX/HUTLP 63)* <49494> **ALONE WITH EVERYBODY** 1 Jul00
— A song for the lovers / I get my beat / Brave new world / New York / You on my mind in my sleep / Crazy world / On a beach / Money to burn / Slow was my heart / C'mon people (we're making it now) / Everybody.
Sep 00. (c-s) *(HUTC 138)* **C'MON PEOPLE (WE'RE MAKING IT NOW) / A SONG FOR THE LOVERS (remix)** 21 —
(12"+=/cd-s+=) *(HUT T/CD 138)* — Make a wish.
Oct 02. (7") *(HUT 161)* **CHECK THE MEANING. / MIRACLE** 11 —
(cd-s+=) *(HUTCD 161)* — ('A'-Chris Potter remix) / ('A'-video).
Oct 02. (cd/d-lp) *(CDHUT/HUTDLP 77)* <13383> **HUMAN CONDITIONS** 3 —
— Check the meaning / Buy it in bottles / Bright lights / Paradise / God in the numbers / Science of silence / Man on a mission / Running away / Lord I've been trying / Nature is the law.

VERY SECRETARY

Formed: Champaign-Urbana, Illinois, USA ... March 1997 by brothers DAVID and ALLEN JOHNSON, TIM ADAMSON and ROY EWING. Driven (if that's not too strong a word) by the fragile muse of DAVID JOHNSON, the quartet issued their debut album, 'BEST POSSIBLE SOUVENIR', in 1998. As an exercise in indie-pop melancholia, the record verged on the miserabilist without resorting to self-indulgence, JOHNSON's subtle phrasing leaving a lasting impression. With ADAMSON subsequently being replaced by violinist RACHEL DIETKUS, the band unveiled a richer, more eloquent sound on sophomore set, 'STANDING IN THE SHADE' (1999), already hinted at with their contribution, 'NAGARKOT', to the 'Tree' record's 'Postmarked Stamps' compilation. Their own volume of the 'IN SOUND TOUR SUPPORT' series was to be their final release, the group disbanding around the time of the EP's release.

Album rating: BEST POSSIBLE SOUVENIR mini (*6) / STANDING IN THE SHADE (*7)

DAVID JOHNSON – vocals, guitar / **TIM ADAMSON** – guitar / **ALLEN JOHNSON** – bass / **ROY EWING** – drums (ex-BRAID)

| | | Mud | Mud |

Feb 98. (m-cd) <*(MUDCD 031)*> **BEST POSSIBLE SOUVENIR** — —
— Under a rug / Best possible souvenir / Piped in from a hometown / Trade-off / Charity / Brace period / Composure.

— **RACHAEL DIETKUS** – violin; repl. ADAMSON

Sep 99. (cd) <*(MUDCD 037)*> **STANDING IN THE SHADE** — —
— Feeling cheated / This lovesick / Sister psyche / Politic / Paper bag / Countryless / Sharp dressers / Paid to forget / Permanence / Giannini eyes.

VINES

Formed: Sydney, Australia ... late 1999 by frontman CRAIG NICHOLLS, a NIRVANA-obsessed McDonalds worker who pulled together PATRICK MATTHEWS, RYAN GRIFFITHS and DAVID OLLIFFE. Named after NICHOLLS' dad's band from the 60's (although they were called The VYNES), the group began performing at house parties where they would amuse the guests with NIRVANA and MUDHONEY covers. It wasn't until 2001 that they issued their debut single, a roaring number entitled 'FACTORY', which sounded like a lost song from COBAIN and crew, with screeching vocals aplenty and a chorus to die for. This led to their signing with 'Heavenly' in the UK, and The VINES were shipped off to L.A. to record their debut album, all the while being compared to Jesus by the ever reliable NME. It wasn't until summer 2002 that the ensemble would return, clutching a handful of admittedly great rock songs with the unfettering of the album 'HIGHLY EVOLVED'. 'GET FREE', the debut single was grunge from the very first note, with NICHOLLS even singing in unison with his guitar – just like COBAIN. The hollowed out sound of 'OUTTATHAWAY' was much more intense, and the 90-minute pop/punk blast of 'HIGHLY EVOLVED' was just a smack in the face. However it was not all grind-core grunge; the group also showed their 'sensitive' side (with NICHOLLS basically saying "look how tortured I am") with such trite stuff as 'AUTUMN SHADE' and the cringeworthy 'HOMESICK', all pianos and welling tears. During interviews with the group NICHOLLS also admitted that his two favourite things were "a McDonalds meal and a SUEDE album". McDonalds was bad enough, but SUEDE!

Album rating: HIGHLY EVOLVED (*7)

CRAIG NICHOLLS – vocals, guitar / **PATRICK MATTHEWS** – bass, vocals / **DAVID OLLIFFE** – drums

| | | Rex | not iss. |

Oct 01. (ltd-7") *(REKD 195)* **FACTORY. / AIN'T NO ROOM / DROWN THE BAPTISTS** — —

| | | Heavenly | Capitol |

Apr 02. (7"/cd-s) *(HVN 112/+CD)* **HIGHLY EVOLVED. / SUN CHILD** 32 —

— **HAMISH ROSSER** – drums; repl. OLLIFFE
— added **RYAN GRIFFITHS** – guitar

Jun 02. (7") *(HVN 113)* **GET FREE. / BLUES RIFF** 24 Jul02
(cd-s) *(HVN 113CD)* <550942> – ('A'side) / Down at the club / Hot leather.
Jul 02. (lp/cd) *(HVNLP 36/+CD)* <537527> **HIGHLY EVOLVED** 3 —
— Highly evolved / Autumn shade / Outtathaway / Sunshinin' / Homesick / Get free / Country yard / Factory / In the jungle / Mary Jane / Ain't no room / 1969.
Oct 02. (7") *(HVN 120)* **OUTTATHAWAY. / MS. JACKSON** 20 —
(cd-s+=) *(HVN 120CDS)* <551223> – Country yard (live) / ('A'-David LaChapelle video).
(cd-s) *(HVN 120CD)* <551215> – ('A'side) / Don't go (demo) / Get free (live) / ('A'-Alastair McKevitt US film video).

VIOLET INDIANA
(see under ⇒ COCTEAU TWINS; in 80's section)

VIVA SATELLITE! (see under ⇒ EGGS)

VIVA SATURN
(see under ⇒ RAIN PARADE; in 80's section)

VON BONDIES

Formed: Detroit, Michigan, USA ... 2000 out of The BABY KILLERS by JASON STOLLSTEIMER (ex-COBRA YOUTH), MARCIE BOLEN, CARRIE SMITH and DON BLUM. Garage rock didn't come any dirtier and rawer than The VON BONDIES style of thrash'n'tickle. Influenced by peers The DIRTBOMBS, SOLEDAD BROTHERS and, of course, JACK WHITE of The WHITE STRIPES, the ensemble recorded cuts 'IT CAME FROM JAPAN' (a deafening experience) and 'NITE TRAIN', before being snapped up by 'Sympathy For The Record Industry' in 2001 and sent on a whirlwind tour across the US. Word had already hit the streets in Britain, and along with The WHITE STRIPES came promise of The VON BONDIES and their sonic attack. JACK WHITE produced the album 'LACK OF COMMUNICATION' (2001), a messy, fractured, skeletal record that possessed infinite passion and harked back to the good ol' days of MC5. Lying somewhere between GUITAR WOLF's searing, screeching guitars and BLONDIE's proto-punk New Wave days, the set switched from one style to the next; EDDIE COCHRAN's in there somewhere, and so was the grinding rhythm'n'blues of JIMMY REED. Yet, it was a very Detroit kind of record – dirty, polluted and very impassioned. Things just came together for a lot of bands from the State of Detroit at the turn

VON BONDIES (cont)

of the new millennium, proving that their New Yorker cousins weren't getting away with having all the fun. • **Covered:** BRING IT ON HOME TO ME (Sam Cooke).

Album rating: LACK OF COMMUNICATION (*7)

JASON STOLLSTEIMER – vocals, guitar / **MARCIE BOLEN** – guitar, vocals (ex-SLUMBER PARTY) / **LAUREN WILCOX** – bass / **DON BLUM** – drums

			not iss.	D-wreckEd-hiT
2000.	(7") <DET 001>	**NITE TRAIN. / GOIN' DOWN**	-	

— **CARRIE SMITH** – bass; repl. WILCOX

			Sympathy F	Sympathy F
2001.	(7") <SFTRI 667>	**IT CAME FROM JAPAN. / RED HEAD DEVIL** (UK-iss.Sep02 on 'Sweet Nothing' c-s; CSSN 012)	-	
Jul 01.	(lp/cd) <(SFTRI 658/+CD)>	**LACK OF COMMUNICATION** – Lack of communication / It came from Japan / Shallow grave / Going down / Cass and Henry / Nite train / No sugar mama / Cryin' / In the act / Please please man / Sound of terror. (hidden cd track+=) – Bring it on home to me. (re-iss. Apr02 on 'Sweet Nothing'; SNCD/SNLP 015)		-
Dec 01.	(7"clear-ep) (FLB 118)	**X-MAS SURPRISE PACKAGE VOLUME 4** – Ain't no chimney in the big house / SOLEDAD BROTHERS: Hang my star / MISTREATERS: Santa stole my baby. (above on 'Flying Bomb', below on 'Must Destroy')		
Nov 02.	(ltd-7"one-sided) (DESTROYER 2)	**TELL ME WHAT YOU SEE**		-

VON HEMMLING (see under ⇒ APPLES IN STEREO)

VOODOO QUEENS

Formed: London, England ... late '93 by former MAMBO TAXI drummer turned songwriter/singer/guitarist ANJALI BHATIA, her sister RAJNI and cousin ANJULA. Bolstering their amateurish sound (they had only previously mastered their unstruments) with two other Asian-descent females, bassist ELLA (also of MAMBO TAXI) and new drummer SUNNY. Bassist MARY DEIGAN was a member before joining The HANGOVERS in '97.

Album rating: CHOCOLATE REVENGE (*6)

ANJALI BHATIA – vocals, guitar (ex-MAMBO TAXI) / **RAJNI** – keyboards / **ANJULA** – guitar / **ELLA** – bass (of MAMBO TAXI) SUNNY – drums

			Too Pure	not iss.
May 93.	(7") (PURE 021)	**SUPERMODEL-SUPERFICIAL. / CHOCOLATE (MELT IN YOUR MOUTH)**		-
Jul 93.	(7"/7"pink) (PURE S/L 024)	**KENUWEE HEAD. / KENUWEE HEAD (backwards) / GIRL SOLO** (10") (PURE 024) – ('A'side / Lucky bag / ('A'edit). (cd-s) (PURECD 024) – ('A'edit) / Guitar baby / Supermodel-superficial / Chocolate (melt in your mouth).		-
Dec 93.	(lp/cd) (PURE L/CD 030)	**CHOCOLATE REVENGE** – You're dumped / Princess of the voodoo beat / Neptune / Summer sun / I'm not bitter – I just want to kill you / Faceache / Indian filmstar / Cactus trees / Shopping girl maniac / Chocolate eyes / My favourite handbag.		-

— **MARY DEIGAN** – bass; repl. ELLA

May 94.	(cd-s) (PURE 037CD)	**F IS FOR FAME / I'M NOT BITTER – I JUST WANT TO KILL YOU / YOU'LL LOSE A GOOD THING**		-

			Strange Fruit	not iss.
Jun 94.	(cd) (SFRCD 125)	**PEEL SESSIONS** – Kenuwee head / Summer sun / Princess of the voodoo beat / Supermodel – superficial / Chocolate eyes / Shopping girl maniac / Indian filmstar / My favourite handbag.		-

			Voodoo Dirt	not iss. Dirt
Jul 95.	(7") (VOODOO 001)	**EAT THE GERMS. / HAIRY 2ch**		-
Jul 97.	(7") (<DRT 010>)	**NEPTUNE. / I'M NOT BITTER (I JUST WANT TO KILL YOU)**		

— split after above; DEIGAN joined The HANGOVERS

V-TWIN

Formed: Glasgow, Scotland ... 1996 by JASON MacPHAIL and MIKE McGAUGHRIN after meeting at Art school. Lifting their name from an advanced motorcycle engine, V-TWIN became the darlings of the experimental scene in Glasgow during 1998 along with MOGWAI and BELLE AND SEBASTIAN. However, the only thing that this warped ambient pop outfit have in common with the latter is that fleeting members of B&S have graced V-TWIN's skewed, unbalanced musical landscape. Describing themselves as "the New York Dolls playing techno", cult label 'Domino' relesed their debut single 'GIFTED' in 1998 to much critical acclaim. These two as yet unknown soldiers battled it to the death, using breakbeats, dislocated guitar sounds and warm keyboards as unthreatening weapons in a sliding vista of strangulated pop. 'IN THE LAND OF THE PHAROAHS (DARK TOURISM)' – a part of Domino's electronic offshoot 'Series 500' – followed in 1999, as did the sublime single 'THANKYOU BABY' and it's B-side 'DERAILED' (with B&S man STUART DAVID riding the faders and making the odd contribution). After a long break, MacPHAIL and McGAUGHRIN returned in September 2000 with a further single 'DELINQUENCY', another piece of fragmented brilliance that was and is V-TWIN. It would two full years before they came up with their sophomore set, 'THE BLUES IS A MINEFIELD' (2002). • **Covered:** LUNAN (Simon Shaw) / AN AMONITE FOR BILL (Lindsay Cooper).

Album rating: FREE THE TWIN mini (*6) / THE BLUES IS A MINEFIELD (*6)

JASON MacPHAIL – vocals / **MIKE McGAUGHRIN** – guitar / with a plethora of guests incl. **KATRINA** – vocals (of PASTELS)

			Domino	Drag City
Jun 98.	(7") (RUG 68)	**GIFTED. / SOUND AS EVER**		-
Aug 98.	(12") (SER 509)	**IN THE LAND OF THE PHAROAHS (DARK TOURISM). / IN THE LAND OF THE PHAROAHS (the Cinema mix)** (above issued on 'Series 500'; part of 'Domino')		-

— next with guests **CHRIS GEDDES** (of BELLE AND SEBASTIAN) plus **STUART DAVID** – producer (of BELLE AND SEBASTIAN)

Aug 99.	(7") (RUG 95)	**THANKYOU BABY. / DERAILED** (cd-s+=) (RUG 95CD) – Lunan.		-
Sep 00.	(12"/cd-s) (RUG 106 T/CD)	**DELINQUENCY (Gareth Jones mix) / DELINQUENCY (Jagz Kooner mix). / DELINQUENCY (Adam & Eve mix) / AN AMONITE FOR BILL (Adam & Eve mix)**		-
Oct 00.	(cd) (WIGCD 86)	**FREE THE TWIN** (compilation) – Delinquency / Derailed / In the land of the pharoahs (dark tourism) / Thankyou baby / Sound as ever / Lunan / Delinquency / Delinquency / An amonite for Bill / In the land of the pharoahs.		-
Sep 02.	(7") (RUG 147)	**CALL A MEETING. / YOU CAN'T PUT YOUR ARMS AROUND A MEMORY**		-
Oct 02.	(cd) (WIGCD 114)	**THE BLUES IS A MINEFIELD** – Call a meeting / Despot blues / Needle in the red / Muddy fox / Swissair / V-Twin city rockers / Delinquency / Get your wings / The emperor is dead / Across the lanes.		-

THE GREAT INDIE DISCOGRAPHY — The 1990s

Tom WAITS

Born: 7 Dec'49, Pomona, California, USA. Signed to 'Asylum' in 1973, after being spotted at the Troubadour club. His debut album 'CLOSING TIME' produced by Jerry Yester (ex-LOVIN' SPOONFUL), didn't sell greatly, but it did contain 'OL '55' which was soon covered by The EAGLES on their album 'On The Border'. 'THE HEART OF SATURDAY NIGHT' (1974) was more proficient, his downtrodden JACK KEROUAC meets CHARLES BUKOWSKI persona beginning to develop. With his distinctive Billy Goat Gruff vocals he sounded frighteningly like he'd been drinking industrial strength paint stripper since childhood. A born raconteur, his sharply observed tales of American lowlife were set against a musical backdrop of smokey blues and jazz stylings. The live album 'NIGHTHAWKS AT THE DINER' (1975) was WAITS in his element, reeling off wry vignettes with casual ease. 'SMALL CHANGE' (1976) was a confident step forward, his booze-sodden recollections more focused and his songwriting more complex on tracks like 'TOM TRAUBERT'S BLUES'. He even attempted to cultivate his parched vocals on 'FOREIGN AFFAIR' (1977), duetting with BETTE MIDLER for 'I NEVER TALK TO STRANGERS'. With 'BLUE VALENTINE' (1978) and 'HEARTATTACK AND VINE' (1980), WAITS opted for a combination of supple R&B tracks and heartbroken love ballads, the latter set spawning the haunting 'JERSEY GIRL' which was later covered by BRUCE SPRINGSTEEN. This was the end of an era for the maverick singer/songwriter as he signed to 'Island' and employed a more experimental strategy. The gloriously titled 'SWORDFISHTROMBONES' (1983) introduced the new WAITS sound, a surrealistic cut up of mutant jazz, skewed rhythms, jarring guitar and wildly inspired lyrics. 'RAIN DOGS' (1985) advanced this formula, again employing an array of session musicians to realise his eccentric musical vision. Adapted from a song on 'SWORDFISHTROMBONES', 'FRANK'S WILD YEARS' (1987) was the soundtrack to a musical stage show that included the brilliant horn-driven weirdness of 'HANG ON ST. CHRISTOPHER'. 'BIG TIME' (1988) was similar in tone, taking material from all his 'Island' recordings to date. With a string of acting credits already behind him as well as 1983's 'ONE FROM THE HEART' soundtrack, he scored JIM JARMUSCH's 'NIGHT ON EARTH' in 1992. His next album proper was 'BONE MACHINE', released later the same year. The title was apt, a stark collection of minimalistic clankings and dark, muted musings. 'BLACK RIDER' (1993) held the musical fruits of a collaboration between director ROBERT WILSON and uber-Beat poet WILLIAM BURROUGHS. It was six long years before WAITS returned to the fold, the 'Epitaph' label (more identified with today's hardcore/punk scene) astonishingly taking up the reins for his marvellous comeback set, 'MULE VARIATIONS' (1999); if his gruff vox could be singled out as one type of music, it would indeed be "hard core". Now nearly fifty years of age (and looking every part of it!), WAITS had his first UK Top 10 success with 'MULE . . .', and even more importantly, his debut into the American Top 30. WAITS is an artist with defiantly singular vision and is a rare commodity in a marketplace where so often the blind lead the blind in a musical wild goose chase for the next trend. Why bother with a double set when two simultaneously-released single albums will do, May 2002's 'BLOOD MONEY' and 'ALICE', gave WAITS another cross-Atlantic success. • **Songwriters:** Pens own songs except; WHAT KEEPS MAN ALIVE (Kurt Weill) / HEIGH-HO (from 'Snow White') / IT'S ALL RIGHT WITH ME (Cole Porter). From 1987, his material was co-written with wife and Irish playwright Kathleen Brennan, whom he married on the 31st December '81. • **Filmography:** PARADISE ALLEY (bit-part 1978) / WOLFEN (cameo 1979) / STONE BOY (cameo 1980) / ONE FROM THE HEART (1981 cameo + soundtrack) / THE OUTSIDERS (1983) / RUMBLEFISH (1983) / THE COTTON CLUB (1984 cameo) / DOWN BY LAW (1986) / IRONWEED (1988) / COLD FEET (1989) / SHORT CUTS (1993) / THE FISHER KING (1990). • **Trivia:** In the late 70's, he parted company with girlfriend/singer RICKIE LEE JONES. In 1991, he sued a radio ad company for using a soundalike in a chips commercial and won nearly $2.5 million.

Album rating: CLOSING TIME (*7) / THE HEART OF SATURDAY NIGHT (*6) / NIGHTHAWKS AT THE DINER (*6) / SMALL CHANGE (*8) / FOREIGN AFFAIRS (*6) / BLUE VALENTINE (*6) / HEARTATTACK AND VINE (*7) / BOUNCED CHECKS compilation (*6) / ONE FROM THE HEART soundtrack with Crystal Gayle (*6) / SWORDFISHTROMBONES (*9) / THE ASYLUM YEARS compilation (*8) / RAIN DOGS (*9) / FRANKS WILD YEARS soundtrack (*7) / BIG TIME (*7) / NIGHT ON EARTH soundtrack (*5) / BONE MACHINE (*8) / THE BLACK RIDER (*5) / BEAUTIFUL MALADIES – THE ISLAND YEARS compilation (*8) / MULE VARIATIONS (*7) / BLOOD MONEY (*7) / ALICE (*7)

TOM WAITS – vocals, piano, accordion

			Asylum	Elektra
May 73.	(lp) *(SYL 9007)* <*SD 5061*>	**CLOSING TIME**		

– Ol' 55 / I hope that I don't fall in love with you / Virginia Ave/ Old shoes (and picture postcards) / Midnight lullaby / Martha / Rosie / Lonely / Ice cream man / Little trip to Heaven (on the wings of your love) / Grapefruit moon / Closing time. *(re-iss. Jun76; K 53030) (cd-iss. Feb93 on 'WEA'; 960836-2)*

| May 73. | (7") **OL '55. / MIDNIGHT LULLABY** | – | |
| Jan 74. | (lp) *(K 53035)* <*7E 1015*> **THE HEART OF SATURDAY NIGHT** | | |

– New coat of paint / San Diego serenade / Semi suite / Shiver me timbers / Diamonds on my windshield / (Looking for) The heart of Saturday night / Fumblin' with the blues / Please call me baby / Depot, depot / Drunk on the Moon / The ghosts of Saturday night (after hours at Napoleon's pizza house). *(re-iss. Jun76; same) (cd-iss. 1989 on 'WEA'; 960 597-2)*

Mar 74.	(7") <*45213*> **DIAMONDS ON MY WINDSHIELD. / SAN DIEGO SERENADE**	–	
Jun 75.	(7") <*45233*> **NEW COAT OF PAINT. / BLUE SKIES**	–	
Oct 75.	(7") <*45262*> **(LOOKING FOR) THE HEART OF SATURDAY NIGHT. / DIAMONDS ON MY WINDSHIELD**	–	

—— with **MIKE MELVOIN** – piano / **JIM HUGHART** – bass / **BILL GOODWIN** – drums

| Dec 75. | (d-lp) *(SYSP 903)* <*7E 2008*> **NIGHTHAWKS AT THE DINER** (live) | | Oct75 |

– (opening intro) / Emotional weather report / (intro) / On a foggy night / (intro) / Eggs and sausage / (intro) / Better off without a wife / Nighthawk postcards (from Easy street) / (intro) / Warm beer and cold women / (intro) / Puttnam County / Spare parts 1 (a nocturnal emission) / Nobody / (intro) / Big Joe and Phantom 309 / Spare parts 2 and closing. *(re-iss. Jun76; K 63002) (cd-iss. 1989 on 'WEA'; 960 620-2)*

—— retained **HUGHART** + new **SHELLY MANNE** – drums / **LEW TABACKIN** – tenor sax

| Nov 76. | (7") <*45371*> **STEP RIGHT UP. / THE PIANO HAS BEEN DRINKING (NOT ME)** | – | |
| May 77. | (lp) *(K 52050)* <*7E 1078*> **SMALL CHANGE** | | **89** Nov 76 |

– Tom Traubert's blues / Step right up / Jitterbug boy / I wish I was in New Orleans / The piano has been drinking (not me) / Invitation to the blues / Pasties and a g-string / Bad liver and a broken heart / The one that got away / Small change / I can't wait to get off work. *(cd-iss. 1989 on 'WEA'; 960 612-2)*

—— **FRANK VICARI** – tenor sax / **JACK SHELDON** – trumpet repl. TABACKIN

| Oct 77. | (lp) *(K 53068)* <*7E 1117*> **FOREIGN AFFAIRS** | | |

– Cinny's waltz / Muriel / I never talk to strangers / Jack and Neal – California here I come / A sight for sore eyes / Potter's field / Burma shave / Barber shop / Foreign affair. *(cd-iss. Mar95 on 'WEA'; 7559 60618-2)*

—— **RICK LAWSON** – drums repl. MANNE / added **ROLAND BAUTISTA + RAY CRAWFORD** – guitar / **BYRON MILLER** – bass / **DA WILLIE CONGA** – piano / **HAROLD BATTISTE** – piano

| Apr 79. | (7") <*45539*> **SOMEWHERE. / RED SHOES BY THE DRUGSTORE** | – | |
| Aug 79. | (lp) *(K 53088)* <*6E 162*> **BLUE VALENTINE** | | |

– Somewhere / Red shoes by the drugstore / Christmas card from a hooker in Minneapolis / Romeo is bleeding / Wrong side of the road / Whistlin' past the graveyard / Kentucky Avenue / A sweet little bullet from a pretty blue gun / Blue valentines. *(cd-iss. Feb93; 7559 60533-2)*

—— retained **HUGHART + BAUTISTA** + new **LARRY TAYLOR** – upright bass / **RONNIE BARRON** – organ / **GREG COHEN** – bass / **PLAS JOHNSON** – sax / **BIG JOHN THOMASSIE** – drums

| Oct 80. | (lp/c) *(K/K4 52252)* <*6E 295*> **HEARTATTACK AND VINE** | | **96** |

– Saving all my love for you / On the nickel / In shades / Downtown / Jersey girl / Til the money runs out / Mr. Segal / Ruby's arms. *(cd-iss. 1989 on 'WEA') (re-iss. cd May93; 7559 60547-2)*

| Dec 80. | (7") <*47077*> **JERSEY GIRL. / HEARTATTACK AND VINE** | – | |
| Nov 81. | (lp/c) *(K/K4 52316)* **BOUNCED CHECKS** (compilation, some live) | | – |

– Heartattack and vine / Jersey girl / Eggs and sausage / I never talk to strangers / The piano has been drinking (not me) / Whistlin' past the graveyard / Mr. Henry / Diamonds on my windshield / Burma shave / Tom Traubert's blues.

—— now with many session people from above incl. **VICTOR FELDMAN** – percussion

			C.B.S.	Columbia
Feb 83.	(lp; TOM WAITS & CRYSTAL GAYLE) *(70215)* <*37703*> **ONE FROM THE HEART** (Film Soundtrack)		

– (opening montage): Tom's piano intro – Once upon a town – The wages of love / Is there any way out of this dream / Picking up after you / Old boyfriends / Broken bicycles / I beg your pardon / Little boy blue / (instrumental montage): The tango – Circus girl / You can't unring a bell / This one's from the heart / Take me home / Presents / (others by CRYSTAL GAYLE only). *(cd-iss. Jan91)*

—— **FRED TACKETT** – guitar + **STEPHEN TAYLOR HODGES** – drums repl. BAUTISTA + LAWSON / added **FRANCIS THUMM** – pump organ / **RANDY ALDCROFT** – horns

			Island	Island
Sep 83.	(lp/c) *(ILPS/ICM 9762)* <*90095*> **SWORDFISHTROMBONES**	**62**	

– Underground / Shore leave / Dave the butcher / Johnsburg, Illinois / 16 shells from a thirty-ought-six / Town with no cheer / In the neighbourhood / Just another sucker on the vine / Frank's wild years / Swordfishtrombones / Down, down, down / Soldier's things / Gin soaked boy / Trouble's braids / Rainbirds. *(re-iss. Sep86 lp/c; same) (cd-iss. Nov87; CID 9762) (re-iss. cd Jun89; IMCD 48) (re-iss. lp Jan94 + May94; ILPM 9762)*

| Oct 83. | (7") *(IS 141)* **IN THE NEIGHBOURHOOD. / FRANK'S WILD YEARS** | | |

—— **MARC RIBOT** – guitar + **MICHAEL BLAIR** – drums, percussion repl. TACKETT, THUMM + HODGES / **WILLIAM SCHIMMEL** – piano / **RALPH CARNEY** – sax, clarinet + **BOB FUNK** – trombone repl. FELDMAN + ALDCROFT

| Oct 85. | (lp/c)(cd) *(ILPS/ICT 9803)(CID 131)* <*90299*> **RAIN DOGS** | **29** | |

– Singapore / Clap hands / Cemetery polka / Jockey full of bourbon / Tango till they're sore / Big black Mariah / Diamonds and gold / Hang down your head / Time / Rain dogs / Midtown / Ninth and headpin / Gun Street girl / Union square / Blind love / Walking Spanish / Downtown train / Bride of Rain dog / Anywhere I lay my head. *(re-iss. cd.Aug89 & Apr91; IMCD 49)*

| Nov 85. | (7"/12") *(IS/12IS 253)* **DOWNTOWN TRAIN. / TANGO 'TILL THEY'RE SORE** | | |

Feb 86.	(7") *(IS 260)* **IN THE NEIGHBOURHOOD. / SINGAPORE**				
	(d7"+=) *(ISD 260)* – Tango till they're sore (live) / Rain dogs (live).				
	(12") *(12IS 260)* – ('A'side) Jockey full of bourbon / Tango till they're sore (live) / 16 shells from a thirty-ought-six (live).				

—— Past live group **FRED TACKETT** – guitar / **RICHIE HAYWARD** – drums / **LARRY TAYLOR** – upright bass. Retained only **TAYLOR, CARNEY, SCHIMMEL** / new: **MORRIS TEPPER** – guitar / **FRANCIS THUMM** – pump organ (on some) / guest **DAVID HIDALGO** – accordion

Aug 87. (lp/c/cd) *(ITW/+C/CD 3) <90572>* **FRANKS WILD YEARS (soundtrack)** [20]
– Hang on St. Christopher / Straight to the top (rhumba) / Blow wind blow / Temptation / Innocent when you dream (barroom) / I'll be gone / I'll take New York / Telephone call from Istanbul / Cold cold ground / Train song / Yesterday is here / Please wake me up / Frank's theme / More than rain / Way down in the hole / Straight to the top (Vegas). *(re-iss. cd.Jun89 & Apr91; IMCD 50)*

—— 1988 live band **WILLIE SCHWARZ** – keyboards, accordion repl. SCHIMMEL + TEPPER

Sep 88. (lp/c/cd) *(ITW/+CD 4) <90987>* **BIG TIME (live)** [84]
– 16 shells from a thirty-ought-six / Red shoes / Cold cold ground / Way down in the hole / Falling down / Strange weather / Big black Mariah / Rain dogs / Train song / Telephone call from Istanbul / Gun street girl / Time. *(cd+=)* – Underground / Straight to the top / Yesterday is here / Johnsburg, Illinois / Ruby's arms / Clap hands. *(cd-iss. Mar97; IMCD 249)*

Sep 88. (7") *(IS 370)* **16 SHELLS FROM A THIRTY-OUGHT-SIX (live). / BIG BLACK MARIAH (live)**
(12"+=) *(12IS 370)* – Ruby's arms (live).

May 92. (cd/c) *<510929-2/-4/>* **NIGHT ON EARTH (soundtrack)**
– Back in the good old world / Los Angeles mood (chromium descentions) / Los Angeles theme (another private dick) / New York theme (hey, you can have that heart attack outside, buddy) / New York mood (a new haircut and a busted lip) / Baby, I'm not a baby anymore (Beatrice theme) / Good old world (waltz) / Carnival (Brunello del Montalcino) / On the old side of the world (vocal) / Good old world (gypsy instrumental) / Paris mood (un de fromage) / Dragging a dead priest / Helsinki mood / Carnival Bob's confession / Good old world (waltz vocal) / On the other side of the world (instrumental).

Aug 92. (7") *(IS 537)* **GOIN' OUT WEST. / A LITTLE RAIN**
(10"+=/cd-s+=) *(10IS/CID 537)* – The ocean doesn't want me / Back in the good old world (gypsy).

Sep 92. (cd/c/lp) *(CID/ICT/ILPS 9993) <512580>* **BONE MACHINE** [26]
– Earth died screaming / Dirt in the ground / Such a scream / All stripped down / Who are you / The ocean doesn't want me / Jesus gonna behave / A little rain / In the Colosseum / Goin' out west / Murder in the red barn / Black wings / Whistle down the wind / I don't wanna grow up / Let me get up on it / That feel.

Nov 93. (cd/c/lp) *(CID/ICT/ILPS 8021) <518559>* **THE BLACK RIDER** [47]
– Lucky day overture / The black rider / November / Just the right bullets / Black box theme / 'T ain't no sin / Flash pan hunter intro / That's the way / The briar and the rose / Russian dance / Gospel train-orchestra / I'll shoot the Moon / Flash pan hunter / Crossroads / Gospel train / Interlude / Oily night / Lucky day / The last rose of summer / Carnival.

—— 3 of above tracks were co-written with author WILLIAM S. BURROUGHS

Epitaph Epitaph

Apr 99. (cd/c/lp) *<(8 6547-2/-4/-1)>* **MULE VARIATIONS** [9] [30]
– Big in Japan / Lowside of the road / Hold on / Get behind the mule / House where nobody lives / Cold water / Pony / What's he building? / Black market baby / Eyeball kid / Picture in a frame / Chocolate Jesus / Georgia Lee / Filipino box spring hog / Take it with me / Come on up to the house.

Jun 99. (cd-s) *(1020-2)* **HOLD ON / BIG IN JAPAN / FLEDDERJON**

Anti- Anti-

May 02. (cd/lp) *<(8 6629-2/-1)>* **BLOOD MONEY** [21] [32]
– Misery is the river of the world / Everything goes to hell / Coney Island baby / All the world is green / God's away on business / Another man's vine / Knife chase / Lullaby / Starving in the belly of a whale / The part you throw away / Woe / Calliope / A good man is hard to find.

May 02. (cd/lp) *<(8 6632-2/-1)>* **ALICE** [20] [33]
– Alice / Everything you can think / Flower's grave / No one knows I'm gone / Kommienezuspadt / Poor Edward / Table top Joe / Lost in the harbour / We're all mad here / Watch her disappear / Reeperbahn / I'm still here / Fish & bird / Barcarolle / Fawn.

– compilations, etc. –

Apr 84. (d-lp/c) *Asylum; (960 321-1/-4)* **THE ASYLUM YEARS**
– Diamonds on my windshield / (Looking for) The heart of Saturday night / Martha / The ghosts of Saturday night / Grapefruit Moon / Small change / Burma slave / I never talk to strangers / Tom Traubert's blues / Blue valentine / Potter's field / Kentucky avenue / Somewhere / Ruby's arms. *(cd-iss. Oct86; 960 494-2)* – (omitted 9 tracks but added 3 others).

Jul 91. (cd/c/lp) *Edsel; (ED/C+/ED 332)* **THE EARLY YEARS** (rare & demos)
– Goin' down slow / Poncho's lament / I'm your late night evening prostitute / Had me a girl / Ice cream man / Rockin' chair / Virginia Ave. / Midnight lullabye / When you ain't got nobody / Little trip to Heaven / Frank's song / Looks like I'm up shit creek again / So long I'll see you. *(re-iss. Feb97 & Mar98 on 'Manifesto'; PT 340601)*

Nov 92. (d-cd) *Island; (ITSCD 5)* **SWORDFISHTROMBONES / RAIN DOGS**

Feb 93. (cd/c) *Edsel; (ED CD/MC 371)* **THE EARLY YEARS VOL.2**
– Hope I don't fall in love with you / Ol' 55 / Mockin bird / In between love / Blue skies / Nobody / I want you / Shiver me timbers / Grapefruit moon / Diamonds on my windshield / Please call me, baby / So it goes / Old shoes. *(re-iss. Feb97 & Mar98 on 'Manifesto'; PT 340602)*

Mar 93. (7"/c-s) *Elektra; (EKR 162/+C)* **HEARTATTACK AND VINE. / BLUE VALENTINES**
(cd-s+=) *(EKR 162CD)* – On a foggy night (live) / Intro to a foggy night (live).

Jun 98. (d-cd) *Island; (524 519-2)* **BEAUTIFUL MALADIES – THE ISLAND YEARS** [63]
– Hang on St. Christopher / Temptation / Clap hands / The back rider / Underground / Jockey full of bourbon / Earth died screaming / Innocent when you dream (78) / The heart of the top / Frank's wild years / Singapore / Shore leave / Johnsburg, Illinois / Way down in the hole / Strange weather (live) / Cold, cold ground (live) / November / Downtown train / 16 shells from a thirty-ought six / Jesus gonna be here / Good old world (waltz) / I don't wanna grow up / Time.

Nov 01. (cd) *Burning Airlines; (PILOT 082)* **DIME STORE NOVELS VOL.1**

Mar 02. (cd) *Rhino; <(8122 78351-2)>* **USED SONGS 1973-1980**

WALKMEN (see under ⇒ JONATHAN FIRE*EATER)

WANNADIES

Formed: Skelleftea, Sweden … 1989 by PAR WIKSTEN, CHRISTINA BERGMARK, STEFAN SCHONFELT, FREDERIK SCHONFELT and GUNNAR KARLSSON. Moving to Stockholm, the group secured a deal with independent label, 'Snap', releasing an eponymous debut set the same year. Four years in the making, 'AQUANAUTIC' found the group working with ROXETTE songwriter, PER GESSLE; as might be expected, the results were less than rocking, although 'R.C.A.'-offshoot, 'Indolent', had enough faith in their indie-pop potential to sign them up in 1995. While it missed the chart first time round, the giddy, starry-eyed rush of 'YOU & ME SONG' introduced The WANNADIES as jangling indie fops in the finest tradition of the genre. On the right side of twee, just, the single was a taster for debut album, 'BE A GIRL', released the same month; with the same stilted-English charm as forebears, ABBA, the Swedish popsters traced a time-honoured lineage through the likes of The BYRDS, The DREAM ACADEMY, The GO-BETWEENS etc., right up to modern day practitioners like TEENAGE FANCLUB and served with an extra helping of BLUR-style attitude. After a further couple of minor hits with 'MIGHT BE STARS' and 'HOW DOES IT FEEL', the group finally made the Top 20 in Spring '96 with a re-released 'YOU & ME SONG'. The following year, they continued their steady rise to major league status with the single, 'HIT', a hit! no less from the follow-up set, BAGSY ME. Protracted record company disputes helped ensure The WANNADIES' lengthy absence from the rock world and conceivably added to the more downbeat mood of the belated 'YEAH' (2000). Produced by The CARS' RIC OCASEK, the album was a musically mature effort that achieved a more cohesive sound and greater depth without necessarily sacrificing their saccharine pop, candy-coated appeal. • **Songwriters:** Group, except; LEE REMICK (Go-Betweens) / NEW LIFE (Depeche Mode) / BLISTER IN THE SUN (Violent Femmes) / I'M A MAN (Spencer Davis Group) / CHILDREN OF THE REVOLUTION (T.Rex) / I GOT A RIGHT (Iggy Pop).

Album rating: WANNADIES (*6) / AQUANAUTIC (*6) / BE A GIRL (*8) / BAGSY ME (*7) / THE WANNADIES compilation (*7) / YEAH (*5)

PAR WIKSTEN – vocals / **CHRISTINA BERGMARK** – keyboards, vocals / **STEFAN SCHONFELDT** – guitar / **FREDRIK SCHONFELDT** – bass / **GUNNAR KARLSSON** – drums / **MALMQUIST**

		West Side	not iss.
1989.	(cd-s) *(we 009)* **THE BEAST CURES THE LOVER / THIS TIME I WANT MORE**	-	- Sweden
		M.N.W.	not iss.
1989.	(cd-s) *(mnws 140)* **MY HOME TOWN / BLACK WATERS**	-	- Sweden
1989.	(cd-s) *(mnws 150)* **HEAVEN / CHILDREN OF THE REVOLUTION**	-	- Sweden
		Snap	not iss.
1989.	(lp) *(snap 002)* **WANNADIES**	-	-

– Together / Heaven / My home town / Things that you love / How beautiful is the Moon / Innocent me / So many lies / Smile / Anything / Black waters / The beast cures the lover / Children of the revolution / Lee Remick. *(re-iss. cd Jan94; RESNAP 002)*

1992.	(cd-s) *(snapc 5)* **THINGS THAT I WOULD LOVE TO HAVE UNDONE / LUCKY YOU / A PLACE TO GO**	-	- Sweden
1992.	(cd-s) *(snapc 10)* **SO HAPPY NOW / IN THE ALTOGETHER / BIRDS**	-	-
Jan 93.	(cd) *(snap 005)* **AQUANAUTIC**		

– Everything's true / Cherry man / Things that I would love to have undone / Love is dead / So happy now / Lucky you / 1.07 / December days / Something to tell / Suddenly I missed her / God knows / Never killed anyone / I love you love me.

Jul 93. (cd-ep) *(snapc 15)* **CHERRY MAN EP**
– Cherry man / Love is dead (from Hell to Skellefte version) / Lee Remick / I'm a man / Blister in the sun.

Jun 94. (cd-s) *(snapc 26)* **LOVE IN JUNE / I GOT A RIGHT**

—— now without MALMQUIST

		Indolent	R.C.A.
Aug 95.	(7"colrd/c-s) *(DIE 002/+MC)* **YOU & ME SONG. / BLISTER IN THE SUN**		-

(cd-s+=) *(DIE 002CD)* – Lift me up (don't let me down).

Aug 95. (cd/c/lp) *(DIE CD/MC/LP 002)* **BE A GIRL**
– You and me song / Might be stars / Love in June / How does it feel? / Sweet nymphet / New world record / Dying for more / Soon you're dead / Do it all the time / Dreamy Wednesdays / Kid. *(re-dist.Apr96)* (cd re-iss. Sep99 on 'R.C.A.'; 74321 32546-2)

Oct 95. (c-s) *(DIE 003MC)* **MIGHT BE STARS / CHERRY MAN** [51]
(cd-s+=) *(DIE 003CD1)* – Lee Remick / Love is dead.
(cd-s) *(DIE 003CD2)* – ('A'side) / New life / So happy now / Things that I would love to have undone.

Feb 96. (c-s/cd-s) *(DIE 004 MC/CD1)* **HOW DOES IT FEEL? / DYING FOR MORE (live) / LOVE IN JUNE (live) / MIGHT BE STARS (live)** [53]
(cd-s) *(DIE 004CD2)* – ('A'side) / Let go oh oh / I'm a man / Never killed anyone.

Apr 96. (7"colrd/c-s) *(DIE 005/MC)* **YOU & ME SONG. / BLISTER IN THE SUN** [18]
(cd-s) *(DIE 005CD)* – ('A'side) / Everybody loves me / I like you a lalalala lot / You & me song (lounge version).

Aug 96. (7"/c-s) (DIE 006/+MC) **SOMEONE SOMEWHERE. / DISAPPOINTED** | 38 | - |
 (cd-s) (DIE 006CD) – ('A'side) / Why / Goodbye.
Oct 96. (7"/c-s) (DIE 007/+MC) **FRIENDS. / WE WERE SITTING IN A CAR ON OUR WAY FROM MOLD TO BATH AS A !** | | - |
 (cd-s) (DIE 007CD) – ('A'side) / Trick me / Can't get enough of that.
Apr 97. (7"colrd) (DIE 009) **HIT. / CRUCIFY ME** | 20 | - |
 (cd-s+=) (DIE 009CD1) – Pathetico.
 (cd-s) (DIE 009CD2) – ('A'side) / As if you care / (Yeah yeah yeah) In your face.
May 97. (cd/c)(lp-box) (DIE CD/MC 008)(DIELP 008S) **BAGSY ME** | 37 | - |
 – Because / Friends / Someone somewhere / Oh yes (it's a mess) / Shorty / Damn it I said / Silent people / What you want / Hit / Bumble bee boy / Combat honey / That's all. (lp+=) – What's the fuss. (cd re-iss. Sep99 on 'R.C.A.'; 74321 42982-2)
Jun 97. (7") (DIE 010) **SHORTY. / ARE YOU EXCLUSIVE** | 41 | - |
 (cd-s+=) (DIE 010CD1) – Short people.
 (cd-s) (DIE 010CD2) – ('A'side) / Taking the easy way out / That's all.
Sep 97. (7"/c-s) (DIE 011/+MC) **YOU AND ME SONG. / JUST CAN'T GET ENOUGH** | | |
 (cd-s) (DIE 011CD) – ('A'side) / Love in June / How does it feel / Love is dead.
Oct 97. (cd,c) <67433> **THE WANNADIES** (compilation) | - | |
 – Might be stars / Because / Friends / You and me song / Someone somewhere / Damn it I said / How does it feel / Oh yes (it's a mess) / Shorty / Silent people / What you want / Hit / That's all.

---- **ERIK DAHLGREN** – drums; repl. GUNNAR

| | R.C.A. | not iss. |

Feb 00. (cd-s) (74321 74555-2) **YEAH / PRINCESS SPOON / AFTER ALL** | 56 | - |
 (cd-s) (74321 73455-2) – ('A'side) / Trick me.
Mar 00. (cd/c) (74321 68702-2/-4) **YEAH** | 73 | - |
 – I love myself / Yeah / No holiday / Big fan / Don't like you (what the hell are we supposed to do) / String song / Can't see me now / Kill you / (You) / Low enough / Idiot boy / Friend or foe / Ball / ...Have another one.
Jun 00. (c-s) (74321 76502-4) **BIG FAN / LOVE AND HATE** | | |
 (cd-s+=) (74321 76502-) – Yeah (video).

---- The WANNADIES released another Swedish-only CD, 'BEFORE AND AFTER' for 'Indolent' in May 2002

– compilations, etc. –

Mar 98. (cd) Snap; (XRESNAP 3) **SKELLEFTEA** | | - |

Dean WAREHAM (see under ⇒ GALAXIE 500)

WARLOCKS

Formed: Los Angeles, California, USA ... on the 4th of July 1998, by none other than indie stoner BOBBY HECKSHER, who was a tad cynical after being shunted by the music industry after two failed bands, CHARLES BROWN SUPERSTAR and MAGIC PACER. HECKSHER, who had also collaborated with BECK on his shambolic – but worthy – 'Stereopathic Soul Manure', had left CHARLES BROWN SUPERSTAR and MAGIC PACER after two full-length albums and decided to bring together an eight-piece (the line-up changes with the weather) rock collective who musically fused the brains of HAWKWIND and the balls of KYUSS. After recording a loose demo, The WARLOCKS signed a double album deal with the USA's oldest existing indie label, 'Bomp!' and issued the VELVET UNDERGROUND-esque, self-titled EP in 2000. This featured 'COCAINE BLUES', a slack-jawed cover version of Luke Jordan's 1927 blues 78, 'Song For Nico' and the ball-busting 'JAM OF THE WARLOCKS' (in its 12-minute entirety). By 2001, the group had expanded to nine members and issued the brilliant 'RISE AND FALL' set, which included redux versions of 'SONG FOR NICO' (cleaned up and more psychedelic) and 'JAM OF THE WITCHES', which was the opening track and a blinding fifteen minutes long. Elsewhere the ensemble displayed their QOTSA qualities; 'SKULL DEATH DRUM JAM', did what it said on the tin, whereas 'HOUSE OF GLASS' played like a rather melodically disturbed MELVINS track (their avant-garde period, of course). HECKSHER did a pretty decent impression of LOU REED, but then again, many have done for years. Musically, the instrumentation and sludgey arrangements fitted perfectly with The WARLOCKS' bummed-out, drugged-up image. The band quickly unfettered the 'PHOENIX' EP, and subsequently 'THE PHOENIX ALBUM' in 2002, being conveniently placed in the "stoner-rock" brackets. But The WARLOCKS' sound, no matter how similar it was to KYUSS or QOTSA, had a more open-top, sinister feel and the walls of sound swept the listener away with a pulsating sonic backdraft.

Album rating: THE WARLOCKS mini (*6) / RISE AND FALL (*7) / THE PHOENIX ALBUM (*8)

BOBBY HECKSHER – vocals, bass, guitar / **JEFF LEVITZ** – guitar / **COREY GRANET** – guitar / **HUNTER CROWLEY** – guitar / **CALEB SWEAZY** – bass, acoustic guitar / **LAURA GRISBY** – organ, tambourine, vocals / **JASON ANCHONDO** – drums / **DANNY HOLE** – drums

| | Bomp! | Bomp! |

Nov 00. (m-cd) <(BCD 4080)> **WARLOCKS** | | |
 – Cocaine blues / Song for Nico / Jam of the zombies / Caveman rock / Angry demons / Jam of the warlocks.
Nov 01. (cd) <(BCD 4082)> **RISE AND FALL** | | Oct01 |
 – Jam of the witches / House of glass / Skull death drum jam / Whips of mercy / Song for Nico / Left and right of the Moon / Motorcycles / Heavy bomber / Laser beam. (also iss.Oct01 on 'Evangeline'; GEL 4035) – (different order tracks).

| | Tree | Tree |

Jul 02. (7") <(TREE 018)> **BABY BLUE. / DILUADED** | | |

---- added **LARRY HARDY** – voices

| | Birdman | Birdman |

Aug 02. (m-lp/m-cd) <(BMR 40/+CD)> **PHOENIX EP** | | Jul02 |
 – Baby blue / Oh Sandy / Stone hearts / Minneapolis mad man. (cd+=) – (hidden extended jam).
Nov 02. (lp/cd) <(BMR 41/+CD)> **THE PHOENIX ALBUM** | | |
 – Shake the dope out / Hurricane heart attack / Baby blue / Stickman blues / Cosmic letdown / The dope feels good / Moving and shaking / Inside outside / Stone hearts / Oh Shadie.

WARM JETS

Formed: Bromley, England ... 1995 by LOUIS JONES, ED GRIMSHAW, PAUL NOBLE (ex-EAT) and former PALE SAINTS bassist, COLLEEN BROWNE. Driven by JONES' sound-vision of a new-wave futurism taking in such diverse influences as WIRE, TALKING HEADS, KRAFTWERK and BRIAN ENO (whose 'Here Come The Warm Jets' album inspired their name), the band found themselves signed to hip 'Island'-backed indie label, 'This Way Up', after only a few gigs. A debut EP, 'AUTOPIA', appeared in Autumn '96, critics namechecking the likes of The FLAMING LIPS and TIGER (formed by JONES' erstwhile girlfriend, JULIE) in an attempt to come halfway towards describing the JETS' complex sound. Recorded with the help of veteran studio man, Glyn Johns, follow-up EP, 'NEVER NEVER' confirmed the band's mission to explore music's deepest, darkest frontiers, while a much anticipated debut Top 40 album, 'FUTURE SIGNS', saw The WARM JETS hailed as one of the UK's most promising post-Brit-pop bands. Pity they didn't see the future signs. • **Covered:** THE MODEL (Kraftwerk).

Album rating: FUTURE SIGNS (*6)

LOUIS JONES – vocals / **PAUL NOBLE** – guitar (ex-EAT) / **COLLEEN BROWNE** – bass (ex-PALE SAINTS, ex-PARACHUTE MEN. ex-HEART THROBS) / **ED GRIMSHAW** – drums

| | This Way Up | This Way Up |

Sep 96. (d7"ep/cd-ep) (WAY 53-11/-33) **AUTOPIA. / SUNFREEZE // WIRES. / LIVERPOOL STREET** | | - |
Apr 97. (7"m) (WAY 58-11) **NEVER NEVER. / SIGNS 2 / THE MODEL (acoustic)** | | - |
 (cd-s+=) (WAY 58-33) – In another picture.
Jun 97. (7"m) (WAY 63-11) **MOVE AWAY. / METEORITES / DEAD STAR BOYS** | | - |
 (cd-s+=) (WAY 63-33) – Undertow.
 (cd-s) (WAY 63-66) – ('A'side) / Down down down / 2 shots / Beauty number 3 (demo).
Sep 97. (7"m) (WAY 66-11) **HURRICANE. / DESERT CATS / DAKOTA** | | - |
 (cd-s+=) (WAY 66-33) – Forever.
 (cd-s) (WAY 66-66) – ('A'side) / Just like you / Never never (live) / Hurricane (demo).

---- **AKI SHIBAHARA** – bass; repl. COLLEEN

Feb 98. (7"gold) (WAY 67-11) **NEVER NEVER. / TOKYO LIMBO** | 37 | - |
 (cd-s) (WAY 67-33) – ('A'side) / On the floor / There is still a mystery.
 (cd-s) (WAY 67-66) – ('A'side) / Underground / RTZ.
Feb 98. (cd/c/lp) (<524534-2/-4/-1>) **FUTURE SIGNS** | 40 | |
 – Move away / Never never / Hurricane / Vapour trails / Future signs / Romero / Autopia / Maestro / Red drag / Meteorites / Silver surfer / Liverpool Street.

| | Island | not iss. |

Apr 98. (7") (IS 697) **HURRICANE. / SOFT SONG** | 34 | - |
 (cd-s+=) (CID 697) – Dakota.
 (cd-s) (CISX 697) – ('A'side) / Faster faster / Just like you.

---- the group split after above

Anna WARONKER (see under ⇒ that dog.)

Laura WATLING

Born: New York, USA. LAURA WATLING began recording music with the West Coast-based AUTOCOLLANTS, alongside guitarists ED MAZZUCCO and TIM MORRIS, plus drummer DWAYNE PALASEK. The AUTOCOLLANTS, although claiming a small fanbase, enjoyed little success. Their first EP in '96, 'CASA', showcased everything they had to offer. It was pleasant yet standard twee-pop with WATLING's breezy vocals the only notable feature. Another EP, 'TENNIS RACKET', followed in 1997. However, the band split soon afterwards, although by this point WATLING and PALASEK had formed CARTWHEEL. Their first recording appeared on the 1997 V/A compilation 'This Is Sterephonic Sunshine'. Again it was minimal pop, with the duelling boy/girl vocals making them sound like a bubblegum BEAUTIFUL SOUTH. WATLING was also keeping herself busy with CASINO ASHTRAYS who released their debut 'BUS TO VEGAS' in 1998; it seemed also as though WATLING had found a partner in RAOL DE LA CRUZ who could construct music befitting her vocals. 1999 saw the release of an AUTOCOLLANTS retrospective, 'WHY COULDN'T THINGS JUST STAY THE SAME', as well as CARTWHEEL's first EP 'TUMBLE'. After relocating to North Carolina, WATLING began recording as a solo artist releasing two albums, 'EARLY MORNING WALK' and 'TWENTY-FIVE', in 2001.

Album rating: WHY COULDN'T THINGS JUST STAY THE SAME? compilation (*7) / Laura Watling: EARLY MORNING WALK (*7) / TWENTY-FIVE mini (*6)

LAURA WATLING – vocals, bass / **TIM MORRIS** – guitar / **ED MAZZUCCO** – guitar / **DWAYNE PALASEK** – trumpet

1996. (7") <LIFE 3> **GAS MONEY** — not iss. / Shelflife
 – We can't have it all / Nothing at all.

1996. (7"ep) <TINT 002> **CASA EP** — not iss. / Tinseltones
 – Casa / Polyensemble / Another Thursday / Beyond the reef.

1997. (7"ep) <drive 04> **TENNIS RACKET** — not iss. / Drive-In
 – Tennis racket / Candy coated kisses / Four and a half / The simple things.

—— split when LAURA moved to California to form The CASINO ASHTRAYS

– compilations, etc. –

Aug 99. (cd) *Shelflife*; <LIFE 9> **WHY COULDN'T THINGS JUST STAY THE SAME?**
 – We can't have it all / Nothing at all / Casa / Polyensemble / Another Thursday / Beyond the reef / Tennis racket / Candy coated kisses / Four and a half / The simple things / Apple vines / High school summer / Trio.

CASINO ASHTRAYS

LAURA WATLING – vocals, multi / **RAOUL DE LA CRUZ** – vocals, guitar (ex-CHA CHA CHA, ex-TEST PILOT)

1998. (c-ep) <none> **JUST LIKE ME** — not iss. / Popgun

1998. (cd-ep) <TK 007> **BUS TO VEGAS** — not iss. / Twee Kitten
 – Bus to Vegas / Been here since November / Invincible.

—— added **BETH** – vocals (ex-ABERDEEN)

—— disbanded when LAURA formed . . .

CARTWHEEL

LAURA + DWAYNE

1999. (7"ep) **TUMBLE** — not iss. / Sandcastle

LAURA WATLING

—— with also guest **DWAYNE** – trumpet

Sep 00. (7"ep) <LIFE 14> **WHAT'S YOUR FAVORITE COLOR?** — not iss. / Shelflife
 – One more way to amuse myself / Passing time / My fondest wish / Christmas trees in July.

Jun 01. (cd) <LIFE 33> **EARLY MORNING WALK**
 – Same / Perfect penmanship / We're still fun / It's all I can do / My fondest wish / Back and forth / Recover / World falls into place / The one for you / Grey day / Atlantis / You're gonna have to change your ways / October / Early morning walk / Another place / Time is never on our side.

Aug 01. (m-cd) <SRS 2> **TWENTY-FIVE** — not iss. / Sofa – HongK
 – Good times never last / The wonderful disappointment / You've got everything / Cleaning / What you say and what you really mean / This river will never run dry / Under the ice.

WATTS (see under ⇒ MONO MEN)

WAVE ROOM

Formed: by Forfar-born Scotsman HAMISH MACKINTOSH (ex-FUEL), an atmospheric songwriter and singer in the mould of MATT JOHNSON (THE THE), PETER GABRIEL or even LLOYD COLE. HAMISH MACKINTOSH who was friends with LOWLIFE and even featured with local band FUEL who signed to 'Midnight Music' and sounded like COCTEAU TWINS, The SMITHS and LOWLIFE. Subsequently teaming up with former COCTEAU TWINS guitarist ROBIN GUTHRIE and his new label/project, 'Bella Union', The WAVE ROOM scored a hit with the ENO-esque, ambient-indie fanclub via an impressive debut, 'LOVE MEDICINE' (2000). Also present alongside the pairing was dub bass giant JAH WOBBLE (ex-PiL), vocalist MANNEY POKU and a host of other "World"ly instrumentalists.
Album rating: LOVE MEDICINE (*6) / Fuel: THE BACK OF THIS BEYOND (*4)

FUEL

HAMISH MacKINTOSH – vocals, instruments

Jan 88. (lp) (NISHI 2013) **THE BACK OF THIS BEYOND** Nightshift / not iss.
 – Age and present past / Heaven's 7th palace / A copper Davidfield / In the land of Prestor John / Philomel / Wind rose / Charon / White water shroud / Myrida streams / Sacred blue / Winter fair.

—— HAMISH subsequently moved to 'Midnight Music' and joined LOWLIFE

WAVE ROOM

MACKINTOSH with **ROBIN GUTHRIE** – guitar, bass / **JAH WOBBLE** – bass / **MITSUO TATE** – guitar / etc.

Jul 00. (cd) (<BELLACD 20>) **LOVE MEDICINE** Bella Union / Bella Union – Jul01
 – Atlas of hands / Dreaming in tongues / Anywhere here is now / One for the river / Memory one / Second box / Houdini / Manna / Oneday someday soon / Love medicine.

Ben WEASEL (see under ⇒ SCREECHING WEASEL)

WEBB BROTHERS

Formed: Chicago, Illinois, USA . . . 1998 by the sons of singer/composer JIMMY WEBB, CHRISTIAAN and JUSTIN. The "partnership" between the two gifted musicians apparently started when CHRISTIAAN began writing brilliant pop songs at the age of 11! Time passed quickly, and a demo of 11 tracks that the pair had recorded (titled 'EXCERPTS FROM THE BIOSPHERE') reached A&R hands in January '98. Some twelve months later the majestic, space ridden, 'EXCERPTS . . .' was released through the 'Easy! Tiger' imprint, although available only on a limited 1000 copies basis. This was subsequently followed up by the similarly titled debut album, 'BEYOND THE BIOSPHERE' (on 'East West'), which seemed to be heavily inspired by HARRY NILSSON's conceptual album, 'The Point', its strange cocktail of pop harmonies and lo-fi acoustics (a fusion of CROSBY, STILLS & NASH and NIRVANA quite possibly!) thrown in for good measure.
Album rating: BEYOND THE BIOSPHERE (*8) / MAROON (*7)

CHRISTIAAN WEBB – vocals, keyboards / **JUSTIN WEBB** – vocals, guitar / with BEITR FUHRMAN – bass / MICHAEL DUGGAN – cello / NEAL OSTROVSKY – drums, guitar / KENNY ANDERSON – trumpet / BILL McFARLAND – trombone

Jan 99. (ltd-7"ep) (MUSE 005) **EXCERPTS FROM BEYOND THE BIOSPHERE** Easy! Tiger / not iss.
 – Cold fingers / The filth of it all / I'm over & I know it.

Jul 99. (cd/lp) <(3984 28323-2/-1)> **BEYOND THE BIOSPHERE** eastwest / eastwest
 – Beyond the biosphere / She drifts into my room / Sour grapes / Cold fingers / What have we become / The filth of it all / Biosphere (reprise) / You took it wrong / Drink and drown / Got no worries / I'm over and I know it.

Nov 99. (7") (WEA 243) **COLD FINGERS. / HEALTY AND HANDSOME**
 (cd-s+=) (WEA 243CD) – I'm over and I know it (+ CD-Rom video).

Sep 00. (cd/c/lp) (8573 83217-2/-4) **MAROON**
 – The liar's club / I can't believe you're gone / All the cocaine in the world / Summer people / Low grade fever / Marooned / Intermission / Fluorescent lights / In a fashion / Suddenly awake / Powder pale / Are you happy now? / Sleep if you can.

Feb 01. (12"/cd-s) (WEA 320 E/CD1) **I CAN'T BELIEVE YOU'RE GONE. / IRIS / NOBODY HAS TO KNOW** 69 / –
 (cd-s) (WEA 320CD2) – ('A'side) / Blame it on yourself / ('A'version).

WEEN

Formed: New Jersey, USA . . . early 1985 by 14-year-old MICKEY MELCHIONDO and AARON FREEMAN (alias DEAN and GENE WEEN). They worked together in a farm commune on a 4-track cassette machine for the last half of the 80's, the first fruits of this released as a double album in 1990, 'GOD WEEN SATAN – THE ONENESS'. Its underground cult success led KRAMER of BONGWATER to put out 'THE POD' (1992), named after the home they had just been evicted from. After a brief stint on 'Sub Pop', they were signed to 'Elektra' in 1993, Creation off-shoot 'August' subsequently taking up an option on their album, 'PURE GUAVA'. They were later dropped by the label although the UK division of 'Flying Nun' released their next effort, 'CHOCOLATE AND CHEESE'. DEAN and p/t WEEN'er CALVIN CALSIUS had a few hip-hop attempts as The MOIST BOYZ for The BEASTIE BOYS' 'Grand Royal' label. 1996's '12 GOLDEN COUNTRY GREATS' was psychedelic country of the weirdo variety, shot through with WEEN's inimitable warped humour. Following on from this, the lads completed another set of inspired rock'n'roll piss-taking in 'THE MOLLUSK' (1997). The late 90's was time well spent as the WEEN boys plotted their comeback via 2000's 'WHITE PEPPER' set; the pastiches were still there, at the expense this time of STEELY DAN, JIMMY BUFFETT and er, Burt Reynolds. A concert set, 'PAINTIN' THE TOWN BROWN: WEEN LIVE 1990-1998' was released prior to this. • **Covered:** SHOCKADELICA (Prince).
Album rating: GOD WEEN SATAN – THE ONENESS (*8) / THE POD (*7) / PURE GUAVA (*6) / CHOCOLATE AND CHEESE (*6) / 12 GOLDEN COUNTRY GREATS (*4) / THE MOLLUSK (*6) / PAINTIN' THE TOWN BROWN: WEEN LIVE 1990-1998 collection (*5) / WHITE PEPPER (*6)

DEAN WEEN (b. MICHAEL MELCHIONDO) – vocals, guitar, etc / **GENE WEEN** (b. AARON FREEMAN) – vocals, guitar, etc

1987. (c) <TEENBEAT 15> **SYNTHETIC SOCKS** not iss. / Teenbeat
 – Baked potatoe / Cops / Hence it came (instrumental) / Living together / Once I lived / Anything quickly (instrumental) / Get back here son (take the .45) / Go. go. stop. no / Ho ho ho / Some weird shit / Eurshishyshen / Tree (instrumental) / Love / Justcruisin' / Acoustic lawn jam / I hate snuggles / Style of carpet (instrumental) / Collectives / Cheese fries / I had a party / What do you think about women? / Sea of Mellchis / Investigating tornadoes / Today it is my birthday / Sonata in A#G overture (instrumental) / Happy family / School days / Prank calls (literally).

1987. (c-ep) <none> **THE CRUCIAL SQUEEGIE LIP** not iss. / Bird O'Prey
 – (interview with Jeff Rusnak) / Talk to me about Erica Glabb / Intro – Nippy wiffle / Jelly II / Boobtalk / Boobs (nice version) / Go! / Stresstabs / Drinktalk / I drink a lot / Jessica / Red as Satan / Murphy flattens his frustrations / Cowbell / Ingrown Mayo / Duke of denim / Blow it out your ass / You fucked up / Talkthing / I drink a

WEEN (cont)

lot (nice version) / Hey bullfrog / Smash my head / (You) Piss me off / Justalking / Blue hair / Sweetness (parts 1 & 2) / Refrigerator that wouldn't close (live) / Mind fuck / Livetalk / Boognish / Boobs II / Yolk / Schnagenhausen / We seen Ween Bean / Yeah sure / Oik / Jelly I / Outroview.

1988. (c-ep) <*none*> **AXIS: BOLD AS BOOGNISH**
– Kill everything / Tweet tweet / Going to the beach / I like you / Bumblebee / Emily / David the negro / The iron whore / Wanton nougat / Smoke my brain / Ann (live) / Aqua-man / She said, she said / The journey into Dinh / Gene's lament (tree love theme) / Opus 51 fugue trilogy in A (take me to the tree): a) Yurtle swimming, b) The tree, c) Bertha gets the mooshy mooshy, d) The kitty & the squirrel, e) The departure / On.

1988. (12"ep) <*none*> **THE LIVE BRAIN WEDGIE! // WAD EXCERPTS**
– You fucked up / Jelly / The refrigerator that wouldn't close / I like you / I drink a lot / Nippy wiffle // In the node of Golgotha / I got a weasel / Hippy smell / Stacey / Gladiola heartbreaker.

Twin/Tone Twin/Tone

Nov 90. (cd/d-lp) <*(TTR 89186-2/-1)*> **GOD WEEN SATAN – THE ONENESS**
– You fucked up / Tick / I'm in the mood / I gots a weasel / Fat Lenny / Cold + wet / Bumblebee / Don't laugh (I love you) / Never squeal / Up on th' hill / Wayne's pet youngin' / Nicole / Common bitch / El camino / Old Queen Cole / Nan / Licking the palm for Guava / Mushroom festival in Hell / L.M.L.Y.P. / Papa zit / Old man thunder / Birthday boy / Blackjack / Squelch the weasel / Marble tulip juicy tree / Puffy cloud (puffi claude). *(re-iss. cd Jul95; same)*

not iss. Sub Pop

Jan 92. (7") <*SP 214*> **SKYCRUISER. / CRUISE CONTROL**

Shimmy Shimmy
Disc   Disc

Feb 92. (cd/d-lp) <*(SDE 9238 DD/DLP)*> **THE POD**
– Strap on the jammy pac / Dr. Rock / Frank / Sorry Charlie / Pollo Asado / Right to the ways and the rules of the world / Captain Fantasy / Demon sweat / Molly / Can U taste the waste? / Don't sweat it / Laura / Boing / Mononucleosis / Oh my dear (falling in love) / Sketches of winkle / Alone / Moving away / She fucks me / Pork roll egg and cheese / The stallion (pt.2). *(re-iss. Apr95 & Jan01 on 'Flying Nun' d-lp/cd; FN/+CD 322)*

Creation –
August   Elektra

Jan 93. (cd/lp) *(RUST 002 CD/LP)* <*61428*> **PURE GUAVA**   Nov92
– Little Birdy / Tender situation / The stallion (part 3) / Big Jim / Push th' little daisies / The going gets tough from the getgo / Reggaejunkiejew / I play it off legit / Pumpin' 4 the man / Sarah / Springtheme / Flies on my dick / I saw Gener cryin' in his sleep / Touch my tooter / Mourning glory / Loving U thru it all / Hey fat boy (asshole) / Don't get 2 close (2 my fantasy) / Poop ship destroyer.

Aug 93. (12"ep/cd-ep) *(CAUG 004 T/CD)* **PUSH TH' LITTLE DAISIES (shitless edit) / PUSH TH' LITTLE DAISIES (happier than shit version) / ODE TO RENE. / I SMOKE SOME GRASS (REALLY REALLY HIGH) / MANGO WOMAN / PUSH TH' LITTLE DAISIES (funky drummer mix)**

not iss. White Label

Jul 93. (7"ep) <*#57*> **SKY CRUISER**
– Skycruiser / Big Jilm / Don't get 2 close (2 my fantasy) / Cover it with gas and set it on fire.

not iss. Vital

1993. (7"clear) <*VMS 20*> **I'M FAT A. / I'M FAT B**
above featured **CALVIN CELSIUS** – vocals
—— added **ANDREW WEISS** – multi + **CLAUDE COLEMAN JR.** – drums

Flying Nun Elektra

Jan 95. (7"pic-d) *(FN 321)* **VOODOO LADY. / BUENAS TARDES AMIGO**
(cd-s+=) *(FNCD 321)* – There's a pig / Valleso.
(7") *(FNSP 321)* – ('A'side) / Cover it with gas and set it on fire.

Jan 95. (d-lp/cd) *(FN/+CD 314)* <*61639*> **CHOCOLATE AND CHEESE**   Sep94
– Take me away / Spinal menegitis / Freedom of '76 / I can't put my finger on it / A tear for eddie / Roses are free / Baby back / Mister, would you please help my pony? / Drifter in the dark / Voodoo lady / Joppa road / Candi / Buenas tardes, amigo / The HIV song / What Deaner was talkin' about / Don't spit when you eat. *(cd re-iss. Jan01; same)*

Apr 95. (7") *(FN 327)* **FREEDOM OF '76. / POLLO ASADO**
(cd-s+=) *(FNCD 327)* – ('A'-shaved dog mix) / Now I'm freaking out.
(7"pic-d) *(FNSP 327)* – ('A'-Shaved dog mix) / Bakersfield.

Jul 96. (7") *(FN 387)* **PISS UP A ROPE. / YOU WERE THE FOOL**
(cd-s+=) *(FNCD 387)* – So long Jerry.

Aug 96. (lp/s-lp/c/cd) *(FN/+SP/MC/CD 386)* <*61909*> **12 COUNTRY GREATS**   Jul96
– I'm holding you / Japanese cowboy / Piss up a rope / I don't want to leave you on the farm / Pretty girl / Powder blue / Mister Richard smoker / Help me scrape the mucus of my brain / You were the fool / Fluffy. *(cd re-iss. Jan01; same)*

not iss. Diesel Only

Feb 97. (7"yellow) **PISS UP A ROPE. / SWEET TEXAS FIRE**

—— in 1997, DEAN, GENE, ANDREW + CLAUDE COLEMAN teamed up with BOREDOMS members to release a record as Z-ROCK HAWAII

Mushroom Elektra

Sep 97. (cd/lp) *(MUSH 3 CD/LP)* <*62013*> **THE MOLLUSK**   Jun97
– I'll be dancing in the show tonight / The mollusk / Polka dot tail / I'll be you're Jonny on the spot / Mutilated lips / The Blarney stone / It's gonna be (alright) / The golden eel / Cold blows the wind / Pink eye (on my leg) / Waving my dick in the wind / Buckingham green / Ocean man / She wanted to leave.

—— In Aug'98, WEEN appeared with 'BEACON LIGHT' on the UK Top 20 b-side of a FOO FIGHTERS single

Jul 99. (d-cd/t-lp) *(MUSH 55 CD/LP)* <*62264*> **PAINTIN' THE TOWN BROWN: WEEN LIVE 1990-1998 (live)**   Jun99
– Mushroom festival in Hell / Japanese cowboy / Mountain dew / Bumblebee / Voodoo lady / Ode to Rene / Mister Richard Smoker / Doctor Rock / I can't put my finger on it / Cover it with gas and set it on fire / Awesome sound / Tender situation / Mister would you please help my pony? / I saw Gener cryin' in his sleep / Marble tulip juicy tree / She fucks me / Poor ship destroyer / Vallejo / Puffycloud.

May 00. (cd/lp) *(MUSH 69 CD/LP)* <*62449*> **WHITE PEPPER**
– Exactly where I'm at / Flutes of Chi / Even if you don't / Bananas and blow / Stroker ace / Ice castles / Back to Basom / The grobe / Pandy Fackler / Stay forever / Falling out / She's your baby.

Jul 00. (7"red-ep/cd-ep) *(MUSH 78 S/CDS)* **STAT FOREVER. / WHO DAT? / THE GROBE**

Sep 00. (7"green) *(MUSH 73S)* **EVEN IF YOU DON'T. / CORNBREAD RED**
(cd-s+=) – *(MUSH 73CDS)* – Cornbread red (dub mix).

MOIST BOYZ

DEAN WEEN + CALVIN CELSIUS (MICKEY MOIST + DICKIE MOIST) alter-ego outfit remixed by The BEASTIE BOYS on their label

not iss. X-ploit

1994. (7"red) **O.G. SIMPSON. / O.G. SIMPSON (afraid of the facts that we kick radio edit)**

Grand Grand
Royal Royal

Jan 96. (m-lp/m-cd) <*GR 004/+CD*> **MOISTBOYZ**
– Carjack / I.O. (fuck no) / U blow / Supersoaker Md50 / I am the jury / Adios amigo. *(UK-iss.Apr97; same as US)*

1995. (7"m) **SECOND-HAND SMOKER. / POWERVICE / CRANK**
(above issued on 'Arson' records)

Nov 96. (lp/cd) <*GR 037/+CD*> **MOISTBOYZ VOL.2**
– It ain't rude / Second hand smoker / Larry and cool / Rock, stock, barrel / Man of the year / American made and duty-free / Crank / Powervice / Keep the fire alive / Good morning America. *(UK-iss.Mar98; same as US)*

WEEZER

Formed: Los Angeles, California, USA ... 1993 by RIVERS CUOMO, MATT SHARP and PATRICK WILSON. Signing to 'Geffen' and recruiting final member, BRIAN BELL, the group released their eponymous RIC OCASEK-produced debut album in September '94. Helped by the transatlantic success of singles such as 'UNDONE – THE SWEATER SONG' and the pogo-pop of 'BUDDY HOLLY', the album became one of the year's biggest sellers. Often described as The PIXIES meeting The BEACH BOYS, their blaring college 'nerd'-rock saw WEEZER riding the crest of an American 'new wave' triggered by the likes of GREEN DAY and OFFSPRING. Meanwhile, MATT SHARP was also busy with a side project, The RENTALS (comprising CHERIELYNN WESTRICH, ROD CERVERA, PETRA HADEN, PAT WILSON and JIM RICHARDS), releasing an album of New Wave-esque songs in 'RETURN OF THE RENTALS' (1995/96). A second WEEZER album, 'PINKERTON' (1996), was much of the same, although it brought the band a bit of grief when the American security firm of the same name brought legal action. WEEZER released their third long-awaited set, 'THE GREEN ALBUM', in May 2001, bringing back geek-rock to the masses. After a year of touring, self-produced 'MALADROIT' (2002), a sort of companion piece to 'THE GREEN ALBUM' was released into the US Top 5. Short, sweet and very melodic (as always), CUOMO and crew had created another half-an-hour blast of guitar pop that was impossible not to like. Reasons why? Well, the faux-thrash metal piss-take 'DEATH AND DESTRUCTION', or jangling opener 'AMERICAN GIGOLO' or the catchy head-bopping single 'KEEP FISHING', which featured the entire cast of The Muppets in its video. Reasons to be cheerful, 1, 2, 3! • **Songwriters:** CUOMO, a few w/ WILSON.

Album rating: WEEZER (*7) / PINKERTON (*7) / THE GREEN ALBUM (*8) / MALADROIT (*6) / Rentals: RETURN OF THE RENTALS (*5) / SEVEN MORE MINUTES (*6)

RIVERS CUOMO – vocals / **BRIAN BELL** – guitar, vocals / **MATT SHARP** – bass, vocals / **PATRICK WILSON** – drums

Geffen D.G.C.

Jan 95. (7"blue) *(GFS 85)* <*19378*> **UNDONE – THE SWEATER SONG. / HOLIDAY**   35   57 Sep94
(c-s+=/cd-s+=) *(GFS C/TD 85)* – Mykel & Carli / Susanne.

Feb 95. (cd/c/lp) <*(GED/GEC/GEF 24629)*> **WEEZER**   23   16 Aug94
– My name is Jonas / No one else / The world has turned and left me here / Buddy Holly / Undone – the sweater song / In the garage / Holiday / Only in dreams. *(lp re-iss. Mar02 on 'Universal'; AA694 93045-1)*

Apr 95. (7"/c-s) *(GFS/+C 88)* **BUDDY HOLLY. / JAMIE**   12   –
(cd-s+=) *(GFSTD 88)* – My name is Jonas / Surf wax America.

Jul 95. (10"ep/c-ep/cd-ep) *(GFS V/CTD 95)* **SAY IT AIN'T SO (remix). / NO ONE ELSE (live acoustic) / JAMIE (live acoustic)**   37

Sep 96. (7"/c-s) *(GFS/+C 22167)* **EL SCORCHO. / YOU GAVE YOUR LOVE TO ME SOFTLY**   50   –
(cd-s+=) *(GFSTD 22167)* – Devotion.

Oct 96. (cd/c) <*(GED/GEC 25007)*> **PINKERTON**   43   19
– Tired of sex / Getchoo / No other one / Why bother / Across the sea / Good life / El Scorcho / Pink triangle / Falling for you / Butterfly.

RENTALS

MATT SHARP – vocals, bass, Moog synthesizer / plus **CHERIELYNN WESTRICH** – vocals / **ROD CERVERA** – guitar / **PETRA HADEN** – violin, vocals / **JIM RICHARDS** – keyboards / **PAT WILSON** – drums

Warners Maverick

Jan 96. (cd/c) <*(9362 46093-2/-4)*> **RETURN OF THE RENTALS**   Nov95
– Love I'm searching for / Waiting / Friends of P. / Move on / Please let that be you / My summer girl / Brilliant boy / Naive / These days / Sweetness and tenderness.

Mar 96. (c-s) *(W 0340C)* **FRIENDS OF P. / SO SOON**
(cd-s+=) *(W 0340CD)* – Love I'm searching for.

Sire Sire

Apr 99. (cd/c) <*(9362 46680-2/-4)*> **SEVEN MORE MINUTES**
– Getting by / Hello hello / She says it's alright / Cruise / Barcelona / Say goodbye forever / Overlee / Big daddy C / Keep sleeping / The man with two brains / Must be wrong / Insomnia / She says it's alright (reprise) / My head is in the sun / Jumping around.

WEEZER

— re-formed for 2001

		Geggen	Interscope
May 01.	(cd) *(493061-2)* <*493045*> **THE GREEN ALBUM**	31	4

– Don't let go / Photograph / Hash pipe / Island in the sun / Crab / Knock-down drag-out / Smile / Simple pages / Glorious days / O girlfriend / I do *[UK-only]*.

| Jul 01. | (7") *(497567-7)* **HASH PIPE. / TEENAGE VICTORY SONG** | 21 | - |

(c-s) *(497567-4)* – ('A'side) / Starlight.
(cd-s+=) *(497564-2)* – ('A'-Jimmy Pop remix) / ('A'-video).

| Oct 01. | (7") *(497616-7)* **ISLAND IN THE SUN. / ALWAYS** | 31 | - |

(cd-s+=) *(497610-2)* – Oh Lisa / ('A'-video).
(cd-s) *(297616-2)* – ('A'side) / Sugar booger / My best friends are gone.

| May 02. | (cd) *(493325-2)* <*493241*> **MALADROIT** | 16 | 3 |

– American gigolo / Dope noise / Keep fishin' / Take control / Death and destruction / Slob / Burndt jamb / Space rock / Slave / Fall together / Possibilities / Love explosion / December *(UK+=)* – Living without you (version) / Island in the sun (version). *(lp-iss.May02; same as US)*

| Sep 02. | (7") *(497771-7)* **KEEP FISHIN'. / PHOTOGRAPH (live)** | 29 | - |

(cd-s+=) *(497771-2)* – Death and destruction (live) / ('A'-video).
(cd-s) *(497792-2)* – ('A'side) / Slob (live) / Knockdown drag out (live).

WEIRD WAR (see under ⇒ MAKE-UP)

WE KNOW WHERE YOU LIVE (see under ⇒ WONDER STUFF)

Bill WELLS

Born: c.1963, Falkirk, Scotland. Completely self-taught, BILL WELLS began forging his idiosyncratic path through the jazz idiom in the late 80's. Learning his trade by playing in clubs, he eventually started writing his own arrangements and initially offered them to BOBBY WISHART. With the latter declining WELLS' offer, he was given the impetus to found his own band, The BILL WELLS OCTET. Comprising some of the most talented musicians on the Scottish jazz scene (PHIL and TOM BANCROFT), the group has become a regular fixture in Edinburgh and Glasgow's smokier clubs although WELLS' singular musical vision has not always enjoyed the favour of critics. Although influenced by the melodic innovation of BRIAN WILSON and BURT BACHARACH as well as GIL EVANS and CHARLES MINGUS, WELLS has carved his own unique niche of experimental jazz – described by one critic as "structured chaos" – that doesn't lend itself to pigeonholing. Although he's yet to release his own album, the man has regularly recorded the OCTET in live performance and has subsequently sold the tapes at gigs. This has seen the message spread to cult indie artists such as STEREOLAB and BELLE & SEBASTIAN. In fact, the latter outfit's STEVIE JACKSON and ISOBEL CAMPBELL guested at a BILL WELLS gig in Stirling which also featured respected jazz improviser LOL COXHILL. WELLS recently recorded a collaborative set with COXHILL, following on from his pairing with FUTURE PILOT AKA on 1999's 'Domino' album, 'BILL WELLS vs . . .'. Prior to this, BILL teamed up with DAVID KEENAN (ex-TELSTAR PONIES) and JOHN HOGARTY (ex-BMX BANDITS) to deliver a one-off eponymous set as PHANTOM ENGINEER, while more recently (late 2000), the jazz outcast released the solo 'INCORRECT PRACTICE' set. A brooding, but jazzy collection of songs, the album saw WELLS moving into more organic territory, with his sampled keyboard loops and staccato jazz rhythms playing over STEVIE JACKSON's (BELLE & SEBASTIAN) harmonica-driven arrangements and LINDSAY COOPER's sliding tuba. A scathing Scottish alternative to Chicago's TORTOISE (or the very similar SALLERYMAN), proving that post-rock jazz isn't just played by clever Americans in suits and ties. In spring 2002, The Falkirk "bairn" came up with two sets, 'ALSO IN WHITE' with his TRIO and 'GHOST OF YESTERDAY' a collaborative BILLIE HOLIDAY-type album with ISOBEL CAMPBELL.

Album rating: THE BILLS OCTET vs FUTURE PILOT A.K.A. (*6) / INCORRECT PRACTICE (*7) / ALSO IN WHITE (*6) / GHOST OF YESTERDAY with Isobel Campbell (*6)

BILL WELLS – instruments

		Domino	not iss.
Apr 99.	(cd/lp) *(Wig 58 cd/lp)* **THE BILL WELLS OCTET vs FUTURE PILOT A.K.A.**		-

– Introduction / In your short life / Chimps / No funerals this morning / Advert / Requiem pour un con / Pink Kitty / Olympic material / Advert – Prepare for shutdown / Om namah shivaya.

BILL WELLS TRIO

		Geographic	not iss.
Dec 00.	(cd/lp) *(GEOG 005 CD/LP)* **INCORRECT PRACTICE**		-

– Incorrect practice / Strangers by the shore / Burmac / Four cows / Bad plumbing / Presentation piece #2.

| May 02. | (cd/lp) *(GEOG 015 CD/LP)* **ALSO IN WHITE** | | - |

– Presentation piece 1 / Record collectors / Singleton / Jab the chemistry teacher / The last guitar lesson / New ascending staircase / Also in white / Inappropriate behaviour / Euphonia / DADE.

BILL WELLS and ISOBEL CAMPBELL

		Creeping Bent	not iss.
Jun 02.	(cd) *(bent 067cd)* **GHOST OF YESTERDAY**		-

– All alone / Who needs you / Please don't do it in here / Preacher boy / Tell me more and more (and then some) / Somebody's on my mind.

WENDYS

Formed: Edinburgh, Scotland . . . early 1990 by brothers JONATHAN and ARTHUR RENTON, alongside IAN WHITE and JOHNNY MacARTHUR. This all-male outfit were lucky enough to gain an early support slot with The HAPPY MONDAYS, encouraged by SHAUN RYDER's dad Derek to send in a demo to their label, 'Factory'. Subsequently signed to Anthony Wilson's imprint through A&R man Phil Sachs, who also became their manager, The WENDYS' short career consisted of a couple of singles and an IAN BROUDIE-produced album, 'GOBBLEDYGOOK' (1991). Manchester in approach, despite their Caledonian roots, the band were virtually clones of other 'Factory' outfits; the aforementioned HAPPY MONDAYS, JAMES or even an optimistic JOY DIVISION.

Album rating: GOBBLEDYGOOK (*5) / SIXFOOT WINGSPAN lost set (*6)

JONATHAN RENTON – vocals / **IAN WHITE** – guitars / **ARTHUR RENTON** – bass / **JOHNNY MacARTHUR** – drums

		own label	not iss.
1990.	(c) *(none)* **WENDY'S**		-

– Ceiling / Sickbag / Spinster / You stopped me dead.

		Factory	East West
Feb 91.	(7"/12"/cd-s) *(FAC 289/T/CD)* **THE SUN'S GOING TO SHINE FOR ME SOON. / EVERYBODY**		-
Apr 91.	(7"/c-s) *(FAC 297)* **PULLING MY FINGERS OFF. / I FEEL SLOWLY**		-

(12"+=/cd-s+=) *(FAC 297 T/CD)* – More than enough (instrumental).

| May 91. | (lp/c/cd) *(FAC 285/+C/CD)* <*91754*> **GOBBLEDYGOOK** | | |

– Something's wrong somewhere / Pulling my fingers off / Half blind / Suckling / Removal / Gobbledygook / I want you and I want your friend / Soon is fine / Half pie / I feel lovely / The sun's going to shine for me soon.

| Sep 91. | (12"ep/cd-ep) *(FAC 337 T/CD)* **I INSTRUCT** | | - |

– Enjoy the things you fear / Newspaper cows / The pop song (live) / The sun's going to shine for me soon (live).

— disappeared from the scene when Factory went bust

– compilations, etc. –

| Apr 00. | (cd) *Starshaped; (STARS 001)* **SIXFOOT WINGSPAN** (their shelved set from 1992) | | - |

WESTERN ELECTRIC (see under ⇒ LONG RYDERS; in 80's section)

WESTON

Formed: Pennsylvania, USA . . . 1990 by DAVE WESTON. Archetypal American "losers" and presumably the sworn enemy of their "jock" classmates, WESTON emerged in 1995 with their first instalment of determinedly breezy teenage neurosis, 'A REAL LIFE STORY OF A TEENAGE REBELLION'. Two-bit, harmony heavy pop-punk in the mould of The PIXIES but all the more effective for its heartfelt simplicity, the record won WESTON many admirers among both critics and newly converted grunge fans. With its success came the release of 'SPLITSVILLE' (1995), a collection of early singles and covers including The Buggles' 'VIDEO KILLED THE RADIO STAR'. Their self-explanatory sophomore effort, meanwhile, 'GOT BEAT UP' (1996), kept flying the flag for the geek brigade, recounting tales of hopeless infatuation and bullying against upbeat, unerringly infectious hooks. 'MATINEE' (1997) kept up the momentum although the lads weren't sounding quite so fresh-faced, while the live split with DOC HOPPER, 'STEPCHILDREN OF ROCK' (1998) featured a cover of Suicidal Tendencies' definitive 'INSTITUTIONALIZED'. It had to happen sometime; 'THE MASSED ALBERT SOUNDS' (2000) was the sound of a decidedly more mature band, both lyrically and musically. A slick WESTON may be something of a contradiction in terms and while many older fans might have been appalled, there was at least some merit to be found in their new sound.

Album rating: A REAL-LIFE STORY OF TEENAGE REBELLION (*7) / SPLITSVILLE compilation (*5) / GOT BEAT UP (*6) / MATINEE (*6) / THE MASSED ALBERT SOUNDS (*5)

DAVE WESTON – vocals, guitar / (+ 3 others)

		not iss.	Gern Blandsten
Aug 95.	(lp/cd) <*GERN 13/+CD*> **A REAL-LIFE STORY OF TEENAGE REBELLION**	-	

– Just like Kurt / Little mile '94 / Fafi / Feet / Mr. Lazo / Two 2 / The truth about Rodney / Galaxy, galaxy / Feelings stipit feelings / David Soul / Lovely, fragile February / Flower / Always on my mind.

| Nov 95. | (cd) <*GERN 23CD*> **SPLITSVILLE** (compilation) | - | |

– Redhead girl / Hard to say goodbye / Dinosaur / Tattoo monkey / She don't know me / I feel like dying / Young pa / Elephant / Naked and alone / Video killed the radio star.

WESTON (cont)

		Go Kart	Go Kart
Oct 96.	(cd/lp) <(GKCD/GKLP 019)> **GOT BEAT UP**		Apr96

– Retarded / Me and Rene / No kind of superstar / New shirt / Heather Lewis / Your summer dresses bore me / Just like you / Teenage love affair / Superbus 23 / Clumsy shy / Varsity sweater / Got beat up / Running stupid / Heartbreak sandwich.

Oct 97.	(cd/lp) <(GKCD/GKLP 033)> **MATINEE**		Aug97

– Opening chord / Record shop / My favourite mistake / Indie rock star / Uninspired / Mrs. Perfect girl / Next to you at night / Lonely when I'm with you / Matinee / In April sometime / Radio.

| Sep 98. | (cd/lp) <GKCD/GKLP 029> **THE STEPCHILDREN OF ROCK** (split w/ DOC HOPPER) | - | |

– Teenage love affair / Retarded / Me and Rene / No kind of superstar / Just like Kurt / Mrs. Perfect girl / Just like you / Superbus 23 / Little mile / My favourite mistake / Varsity sweater / Feet / New shirt / Heather Lewis / Feelings stupit feelings / Mr. Lazo / (other tracks by DOC HOPPER).

		not iss.	Universal
Sep 00.	(cd) <159345> **THE MASSED ALBERT SOUNDS**	-	

– I just quit rock & roll / To some I'm genius / Kiss like an angel / Wonderdrug / Radio / Summer's over / Liz Phair / My favourite high / You haunt me / El differente / Volume hater / I just quit rock & roll (reprise).

WHEAT

Formed: Taughton, Massachusetts, USA . . . 1996 by one-time mysterious trio led by SCOTT LEVESQUE and BRENDAN HARNEY; the pair soon enlisted RICKY BRENNAN. Their debut 45, 'DEATHCAR', was given the prestigious mantle of NME's Single Of The Week, the lo-fi, SPARKLEHORSE-esque outfit reaping even more plaudits with their accompanying 'MEDEIROS' album in spring 1998. Lo-fi slo-core with ambient hazes, it paved the way for another elegant and melancholic album. 'HOPE AND ADAMS' (1999) – co-produced by MERCURY REV'S DAVE FRIDMANN – swept them into the new millennium with comfort and ease; sadly, WHEAT have been of late, a little conspicuous by the absence.

Album rating: MEDEIROS (*7) / HOPE AND ADAMS (*6)

SCOTT LEVESQUE – vocals, guitar / **RICKY BRENNAN** – guitar / **BRENDAN HARNEY** – drums

		Easy Tiger	Easy Tiger
Jul 98.	(7") <(MUSE 003)> **DEATH CAR. / HOPE & ADAMS**		
		Sugar Free	Sugar Free
Aug 98.	(cd) <(SF 004-2)> **MEDEIROS**		Apr98

– Prepise / Death car / Karmic episodes / Tubesoft / Soft polluted blacks / Summer / Leslie West / Girl singer / Working man's manifesto / Reprise. (UK-iss.Jul00 as 'WHEAT'; 0414)

		City Slang	Sugar Free
Aug 99.	(7") (08727-7) **OFF THE PEDESTAL. / FLAT BACK**		-
Oct 99.	(cd/lp) (08726-2/-1) <SF 013-2> **HOPE AND ADAMS**		

– This wheat / Slow fade / Don't I hold you / San Diego / Raised ranch revolution / San Diego / No one ever told me / Be brave / Who's the one / Off the pedestal / And someone with strengths / Body talk (part 1) / Body talk (part 2) / More than you'll ever know / Roll the road.

| Nov 99. | (7"m/cd-s) (08728-7/-2) **DON'T I HOLD YOU. / NEW BOYFRIEND / MORE THAN YOU'LL EVER KNOW** | | - |
| May 00. | (7") (20157-7) **RAISED RANCH REVOLUTION. / AND FIRST YOU SEE A SUPERSTAR, THEN YOU DON'T** | | - |

(cd-s+=) (20157-2) – Headphone recorder.

WHIPPED CREAM

Formed: Gothenburg, Sweden . . . 1989 by ELISABETH PUNZIS, JC (aka JORGEN CREMONESE), LARS ERIK GRIMELUND and JONAS SONESSON. Successfully proving that Scandinavia has more to offer than ABBA clones and Eurocheese, WHIPPED CREAM signed to 'M.N.W.' (in Sweden) and set about reinventing psychedelia Nordic style on their debut album, 'WHIPPED CREAM AND OTHER DELIGHTS' (1990). Although the band disputed the MY BLOODY VALENTINE comparisons, their swirling guitar atmospherics bore at least superficial similarities with the shoegazers while the bizarre dual vocals of ELISABETH and JC lent an exotic slant to proceedings. Critics fell over themselves to praise follow-up, 'TUNE IN THIS CENTURY' (1992), its eddying, churning inventiveness receiving almost universal plaudits, while the choice of Captain Beefheart's 'OBSERVATORY CREST' as a single release suggested the Swedes weren't exactly pandering to any notions of indie convention.

Album rating: WHIPPED CREAM & OTHER DELIGHTS (*6) / TUNE IN THE CENTURY (*7) / HORSE MOUNTAIN (*5)

JORGEN CREMONESE – vocals, guitars / **ELIZABETH PUNZIS** – vocals / **JONAS ONESSON** – bass / **LARS ERIK GRIMELUND** – drums

		Snap	Chameleon
1990.	(cd) (SNAP 1) <61355> **WHIPPED CREAM & OTHER DELIGHTS**		1993

– Explosion / Remember / Silver 1 / Let us try it out / Wishing / This time, next time / Theodora wine / I know you're mine / Whatever / Together. (cd-iss. Jan94 +=; RESNAP 001) – Come together / Explosion '93.

| Sep 92. | (cd) (SNAP 3) **TUNE IN THE CENTURY** | | - |

– Yes / Tune in the century / Wait for a minute / Lay down beside / Give away / Sensational / Virtuosity / Observatory crest / Up the country / Come and find / Beyond the sun.

Mar 93.	(cd-s) (SNAPC 8) **OBSERVATORY CREST / SOMETHING NEW / SILVER PART 2**	-	- Sweden
May 93.	(cd-s) **COME TOGETHER / SILVER PART III / WISHING**	-	- Sweden
Jun 94.	(cd-s) (SNAPC 013) **YOU AND I / . . . AND I HAVE THIS DREAM**		-

| Jul 94. | (cd) (SNAP 014) **HORSE MOUNTAIN** | | - |

– L.O.V.E. / Fire / You and I / I just waited / Spare me . . . / You know the time is right / Fresh / Still got the blues / Starshine / Horse mountain / UCP / Ways.

— disbanded after above

WHIPPING BOY

Formed: Dublin, Ireland . . . 1988 by FERGHAL McKEE, PAUL PAGE, MYLES McDONNELL and COLM HASSETT. Beginning life as a covers band, WHIPPING BOY signed to 'Cheree' at the turn of the decade and proceeded to release a couple of EP's, 'THE WHIPPING BOY' and 'I THINK I MISS YOU', the band's growing infamy and cult acclaim (with album, 'SUBMARINE' in 1992 – leading to a major label deal with 'Columbia'; comparisons with compatriots CATHAL COUGHLAN/FATIMA MANSIONS were inevitable, not least insofar as McKEE had earned himself a well documented reputation for onstage erm, spontaneity. Musically, WHIPPING BOYS' brooding guitar sound encompassed echoes of MY BLOODY VALENTINE and JOY DIVISION, driven by a Celtic boldness, occasional squalls of Seattle-style grunge and a lyrical grit. All these ingredients helped make 'HEARTWORM' (1995) a worthy second album, its cause helped by lavish praise for singles 'TWINKLE', cracked love narrative, 'WE DON'T NEED NOBODY ELSE' and McKEE's vivid portrayal of a rough'n'ready upbringing, 'WHEN WE WERE YOUNG'. The latter was backed by a cover of Lou Reed's 'CAROLINE SAYS II', hardly a sterling choice to deflect accusations of lyrical misogyny from the Irish press. The group disbanded in 1998 leaving behind a posthumous album release a few years later. • **More covers:** SUSPICIOUS MINDS (Elvis Presley). • **Note:** Not the same band from the US who released an lp in 1983, 'The Sound Of No Hands Clapping', and another band on 'Grand Theft Auto'.

Album rating: SUBMARINE (*6) / HEARTWORM (*6) / WHIPPING BOY (*5)

FERGHAL McKEE – vocals / **PAUL PAGE** – guitar / **MYLES McDONNELL** – bass, vocals / **COLM HASSETT** – drums

		own label	not iss.
Apr 89.	(c-ep) (none) **SWEET MANGLED THING EP**	-	- Ire

– Velvet crush / Alligator smile / Highwayman / I think I miss you / Happy.

		Cheree	not iss.
Aug 90.	(12"ep) (CHEREE 8T) **WHIPPING BOY E.P.**		-

– Switchblade smile / Valentine '69 / Sugar I swear.

| Feb 91. | (12"ep) (CHEREE 11T) **I THINK I MISS YOU E.P.** | | - |

– Daze / Highwayman / I think i miss you / She makes me ill.

		Liquid	not iss.
Sep 92.	(lp/cd) (LQ/+CD 1) **SUBMARINE**		- Ire

– Safari / Beatle / Sushi / Favourite sister / Astronaut blues / Bettyclean / Buffalo / Snow / Valentine '69 / Submarine.

| Dec 92. | (7") (LQ 4) **FAVOURITE SISTER. / SAFARI** | | - Ire |

		Columbia	Sony
Jul 95.	(7"/c-s) (661371-7/-4) **TWINKLE. / A NATURAL**		

(cd-s+=) (661371-2) – Plaything / Favourite sister (live).

| Oct 95. | (7"clear/c-s) (662220-7/-4) **WE DON'T NEED NOBODY ELSE. / HERE I AM** | 51 | - |

(cd-s+=) (662220-2) – Disappointed.
(cd-s) (662220-5) – ('A'side) / Twinkle (acoustic) / ('A'-acoustic).

| Oct 95. | (cd/c/blue-lp) (480281-2/-4/0) <67486> **HEARTWORM** | | |

– Twinkle / When we were young / Tripped / The honeymoon is over / We don't need nobody else / Blinded / Personality / Users / Fiction / Morning rise. (cd hidden track+=) – A natural.

| Jan 96. | (7"red/c-s) (662806-7/-4) **WHEN WE WERE YOUNG. / AS THE DAY GOES** | 46 | - |

(cd-s+=) (662806-2) – ('A'-Philo version) / Caroline says II.
(above Philo version, sampled PHIL LYNOTT; Thin Lizzy)

| May 96. | (7"white) (663227-7) **TWINKLE. / THE HONEYMOON IS OVER (live)** | 55 | - |

(cd-s+=) (663227-2) – Fiction (live) / Tripped (live).
(cd-s) (663227-5) – ('A'side) / Blinded (live) / Personality (live) / Users (live).

— WHIPPING BOY split in 1998 shelving an album until . . .

		Low Rent	not iss.
Nov 00.	(cd) (LOWRENT 2001) **WHIPPING BOY**		

– So much for love / Bad books / Pat the almighty / Mutton / Fly / That was then, this is now / One to call my own / Puppets / Who am I? / Ghost of Elvis / No place to go.

WHISTLER (see under ⇒ EMF)

WHITE LEATHER CLUB (see under ⇒ SPARE SNARE)

WHITE OCTAVE

Formed: Chapel Hill, North Carolina, USA . . . 1998 by former CURSIVE main man STEPHEN PEDERSON together with LINCOLN HANCOCK and ROBERT BIGGERS. An additional guitarist, FINN COHEN, joined up for the recording of a debut album, 'STYLE NO.6312' (2000). Nerd-rock presidents WEEZER (minus the camp humour) were an obvious influence on the album's driving, impassioned emo-rock although PEDERSON's unflinching confessionals were never likely to hit the pop charts. The band subsequently contributed 'LOOKING PAST THE SKY' to the 'Deep Elm' compilation, 'I Guess This Is Goodbye: The Emo Diaries, Chapter Five', while a sophomore album, 'MENERGY', appeared in 2001.

Album rating: STYLE NO.6312 (*6) / MENERGY (*5)

STEPHEN PEDERSON – vocals, guitar (ex-CURSIVE) / **FINN COHEN** – guitar / **LINCOLN HANCOCK** – bass, vocals / **ROBERT P. BIGGERS JR.** – drums

			Deep Elm	Deep Elm
Nov 00.	(cd) <(DER 394CD)> **STYLE NO.6312**			Apr00

– Appeals for insertion / Crashing the clarion / Devise executes / Etc. / Call the kiss / Piss and vinegar / Adult entertainment / Crossing the rubicon / No resolution theory / This is not a subsistence existence / South / Guts and black stuff / Style No.6312.

			Initial	Initial
Jul 01.	(cd) <(INITIAL 044CD)> **MENERGY**			Jan01

– The constant is zero / Splashed into serpents / Animal chin / La vista / Wait / The house is flatlined / Powerlines / Move in time / Weight / Menstrumental.

WHITEOUT

Formed: Greenock, Scotland ... early 90's by teenagers ANDREW CALDWELL and ERIC LINDSAY, along with PAUL CARROLL and STUART SMITH. Hailing squarely from the Bellshill/TEENAGE FANCLUB school of sugary harmonies and retro songwriting, WHITEOUT were nothing if not instantly recognisable as Scottish. Signed to 'Silvertone', the band released 'NOT TIME' as their debut single and, incredibly in retrospect, embarked on a co-headlining tour with OASIS. Further prestigious support slots and festival dates followed along with a further series of singles, 'STARRCLUB', 'DETROIT' and 'JACKIE'S RACING'. The latter was their most successful release, displaying a healthy affection for 60's West Coast pop a la LOVIN' SPOONFUL and The MAMAS & THE PAPAS. B-side, 'SO CONFUSED', meanwhile, brought to mind the harmonies of 'American Beauty'-era GRATEFUL DEAD. Yet trawling the cobwebbed corridors of America's rock'n'roll hall of fame proved insufficient to elevate WHITEOUT beyond second division status, their debut album, 'BITE IT', released at the tail end of '95 to less than overwhelming reviews. When they were dropped by 'Silvertone', ERIC and PAUL (who had now taken over vocal duties from the departing ANDREW) found drummer MARK FAIRHURST, releasing an EP, 'KICKOUT', and album, 'BIG WOW' (1998) on their own 'Yoyo' label.
• **Note:** not to be confused with the WHITE OUT who issued an eponymous set or the US group on 'Ecstatic Peace' records.

Album rating: BITE IT (*4) / BIG WOW (*4)

ANDREW CALDWELL – vocals / **ERIC LINDSAY** – guitar / **PAUL CARROLL** – bass / **STUART SMITH** – drums

		Silvertone	not iss.
Apr 94.	(7"/c-s) (ORE/+C 64) **STARRCLUB. / AND I BELIEVE**		-
	(12"+=/cd-s+=) (ORE T/CD 64) – Higher.		
Sep 94.	(7"/c-s) (ORE/+C 66) **DETROIT. / JUST PASSIN' THROUGH, KID**	73	-
	(12"+=/cd-s+=) (ORE T/CD 66) – Dee Troyt.		
Feb 95.	(7"/c-s) (ORE/+C 68) **JACKIE'S RACING. / COUSIN JANE**	72	-
	(12"+=/cd-s+=) (ORE T/CD 68) – So confused.		
May 95.	(7"/c-s) (ORE/+C 76) **NO TIME. / GET ME THROUGH**		-
	(cd-s+=) (ORECD 76) – U drag me.		
Jun 95.	(cd/c/lp) (ORE CD/C/LP 536) **BITE IT**	71	-

– Thirty eight / No time / We should stick together / Jackie's racing / Shine on you / No more tears / Altogether / U drag me / Baby don't give up on me yet / You left me seeing stars / Everyday / Untitled / Detroit.

— **ERIC + PAUL** took over vocal duties from the departing ANDREW

— **MARK FAIRHURST** – drums (a past member) repl. STUART

		Yoyo	not iss.
Nov 97.	(cd-ep) (YOCD 02) **KICKOUT EP**		-

– Kickout / I don't wanna hear about it / Heaven sent / To carry us through.

| Jun 98. | (cd) (YOLP 01) **BIG WOW** | | - |

– Kickout / Heaven sent / Selling up / Through all the rain / 435 / I don't wanna hear about it / Running for cover / Out on the town / Take it with ease / Get back what you give / Back where I used to be.

— **EGGY + FUDGE** repl. MARK, although WHITEOUT split soon after

WHITE STRIPES

Formed: Detroit, Michigan, USA ... 1997 by brother and sister JACK and MEG WHITE. The former began his musical career in Michigan's local outfit GO, before recruiting his sister MEG to play percussion in what would ultimately become The WHITE STRIPES. Clad in matching red and white clothes (apparently they even smoke Embassy Royals because of their clever color scheme), the duo debuted with the single 'LET'S SHAKE HANDS' (1997), issued on the 'Italy' imprint, after whipping up a storm on the local garage/underground rock circut. Two more singles followed and the group flitted to champions of the independent scene 'Sympathy For The Record Industry', where their self-titled album was released. It was good enough to generate column inches and critics seemed most impressed with covers of blues classics 'STOP BREAKING DOWN BLUES' and 'ST. JAMES INFIRMARY BLUES'. Whilst still borrowing a variation of sounds from the likes of The WHO and MC5, JACK's love for the blues was apparent: he continuously cited giant of the genre CHARLEY PATTON as his immediate influence, and frequently covered some of his songs in The STRIPES' live sets. This love of country blues was even more obvious come the sophomore LP 'DE STIJL' (1998), named after the abstract art movement led by Dutch artist Gerrit Rietveld. Stand-out tracks included the rock-steady 'LITTLE BIRD', 'TRUTH DON'T MAKE A NOISE' and a worthy Son House cover 'DEATH LETTER'. A break was imminent and JACK took to producing some of the scene's most promising acts during the period between 1999-2000. The VON BONDIES and The SOLEDAD BROTHERS were just two of the groups that had impressed him, and judging by the cover of the latter's debut album, he was happy to dress up as Uncle Sam, get propped up against a wall and shot by a firing squad (but don't worry, ladies and gents, he didn't really suffer for his art). That aside, it was time for him and MEG to venture back into the studio to record what was to become their breakthrough album, 'WHITE BLOOD CELLS' (2001). On the eve of its premiere, the NME claimed that the WHITE STRIPES, along with fellow garage rockers The STROKES, were destined to become the future of rock music. Even the tabloids caught on, with the Sun hailing them as "Stripe-tastic". Meanwhile, normally MOR radio station Radio 4 caught the STRIPE's buzz, as did John Peel, who casually compared them to The SEX PISTOLS. Rolling Stone magazine reckoned that Detroit was the new Seattle, but JACK STRIPE was unfazed, claiming he'd rather hang-out with fellow musicians The VON BONDIES than pay attention to the hype. A sold-out tour followed, plus a reputed $1m move to 'X.L.' records, once home to The PRODIGY. Singles 'HOTEL YOBA'- named after a "doss-house" – and 'FELL IN LOVE WITH A GIRL' followed, both charting in the Top 20. • **Covers:** LOOK ME OVER CLOSELY (T. Gilkyson) / JOLENE (Dolly Parton) / ONE MORE CUP OF COFFEE (Bob Dylan) / STOP BREAKING DOWN (Robert Johnson) / ST. JAMES INFIRMARY BLUES (J. Primrose) / LORD, SEND ME AN ANGEL + YOUR SOUTHERN CAN IS MINE (Blind Willie McTell) / DEATH LETTER (Son House) / PARTY OF SPECIAL THINGS TO DO + CHINA PIG + ASHTRAY HEART (Captain Beefheart) / RATED X (Loretta Lynn).

Album ratings: THE WHITE STRIPES (*7) / DE STIJL (*7) / WHITE BLOOD CELLS (*8)

JACK WHITE (b. JOHN) – vocals, guitar, piano / **MEG WHITE** – drums, tambourine

		not iss.	Italy
1997.	(7"red,7") <IR 003> **LET'S SHAKE HANDS. / LOOK ME OVER CLOSELY**	-	
1998.	(7"white,7") <IR 006> **LAFAYETTE BLUES. / SUGAR NEVER TASTED SO GOOD**	-	

		Sympathy F	Sympathy F
Jun 99.	(lp/cd) <(SFTRI 577/+CD)> **THE WHITE STRIPES**		

– Jimmy the exploder / Stop breaking down / The big three killed my baby [cd-only] / Suzy Lee / Sugar never tasted so good [cd-only] / Wasting my time / Cannon / Astro / Broken bricks / When I hear my name / Do / Screwdriver / One more cup of coffee [cd-only] / Little people / Slicker drips / St. James infirmary blues / I fought piranhas. (UK re-iss. Apr01; same) <(re-iss. Sep01 on 'X.L.' lp/cd; XLLP/XLCD 149)>

| Jun 99. | (7"red) <SFTRI 578> **THE BIG THREE KILLED MY BABY. / RED BOWLING BALL RUTH** | - | |

(UK-iss.Jan02; same as US)

| Jun 00. | (lp/cd) <(SFTRI 609/+CD)> **DE STIJL** | | |

– You're pretty good looking / Hello operator / Little bird / Apple blossom / I'm bound to pack it up / Death letter / Sister, do you know my name? / Truth doesn't make a noise / A boy's best friend / Let's build a home / Jumble, jumble / Why can't you be nicer to me? / Your southern can is mine. (UK re-iss. Apr01; same) <(re-iss. Sep01 on 'X.L.' lp/cd; XLLP/XLCD 150)>

| Aug 00. | (7"pic-d,7") <SFTRI 619> **HELLO OPERATOR. / JOLENE** | - | |

(UK-iss.Jan02; same as US)

| Nov 00. | (7"red,7"; tour) <SFTRI 645> **LORD, SEND ME AN ANGEL. / YOU'RE PRETTY GOOD LOOKING (trendy American remix)** | - | - Austra |

(UK-iss.Jan02; same)

| Jan 01. | (7") <SP 527> **PARTY OF SPECIAL THINGS TO DO. / CHINA PIG / ASHTRAY HEART** | - | |

— <above issued for 'Sub Pop' singles club>

| Jul 01. | (lp/cd) <(SFTRI 660/+CD)> **WHITE BLOOD CELLS** | 55 | |

– Dead leaves and the dirty ground / Hotel Yorba / I'm finding it harder to be a gentleman / Fell in love with a girl / Expecting / Little room / The union forever / The same boy you've always known / We're going to be friends / Offend in every way / I think I smell a rat / Aluminium / I can't wait / Now Mary / I can learn / This protector. <re-iss. Sep01 on 'X.L.' lp/cd; XLLP/XLCD 151)>

		X.L.	X.L.
Nov 01.	(7") <(XLS 139)> **HOTEL YORBA (live at the Hotel Yorba). / RATED X (live at the Hotel Yorba)**	26	
	(cd-s+=) <(XLS 139CD)> – ('A'-video).		
Feb 02.	(7") (XLS 142) **FELL IN LOVE WITH A GIRL. / I JUST DON'T KNOW WHAT TO DO WITH MYSELF**	21	-
	(cd-s+=) (XLS 142CD2) – Lovesick (live) / ('A'-video).		
	(cd-s) (XLS 142CD) – ('A'side) / Let's shake hands / Lafayette blues.		
Sep 02.	(7") (XLS 148) **DEAD LEAVES AND THE DIRTY GROUND. / STOP BREAKING DOWN**	25	-
	(cd-s+=) (XLS 148CD) – Suzy Lee.		

WHITE TOWN

Formed: As a vehicle for DIY singer/songwriter, JYOTI MISHRA, born 30 July, 1966 (Rourkela, India), but raised in Derby, England. At the age of twelve, MISHRA began playing piano and by his late teens (around the explosion of early electronica and Chicago House music) he became increasingly interested in keyboards and synthesizers. However, by 1987 the air was rife with guitar bands such as R.E.M., The HOUSEMARTINS and PRIMAL SCREAM. MISHRA set up WHITE TOWN, coined after the local Indian slang for the small suburbs in which he lived. Initially, the group began playing jangle-indie pop and were even confident enough to support PRIMAL SCREAM and The SEA URCHINS. WHITE TOWN issued their eponymous EP on 'Satya' in 1990, but it did very poorly – even for an indie – and the rest of MISHRA's

WHITE TOWN (cont)

backing band left, leaving him to finish off their second EP 'ALAIN DELON' and the debut album 'SOCIALISM, SEXISM AND SEXUALITY' (1994). As far as MISHRA was concerned, the affair with WHITE TOWN was over. He consistently made home recordings of little synthy dance tracks in his bedroom as a reaction to playing in a guitar band for five years. Finally in 1996, MISHRA reluctantly issued 'ABORT, RETRY, FAIL?', an EP of four-track recorded keyboard music, with scratching parts and samples galore. A track featured on that EP – 'YOUR WOMAN' – would go on to become WHITE TOWN's best-known song, but E.M.I. were just interested in MISHRA's simple keyboard hooks and kooky samples, signing him to 'Chrysalis' in late 1996. The single of 'YOUR WOMAN', which fused his deadpan vocals with a clarinet sample from Lew Stone's 'My Woman' (from the 30's!), became an instant hit and even reached the No.1 spot in Britain. MISHRA's second WHITE TOWN outing, 'WOMEN IN TECHNOLOGY' (1997), was also a commercial and critical success, and although it spawned several more singles, 'YOUR WOMAN' was its only hit. Scorned by the one-hit-wonder syndrome, MISHRA retreated back to his home town and issued the considerably more indie 'PEEK & POKE' (1999), an album which was largely ignored and rebuked by the music press.

Album rating: SOCIALISM, SEXISM & SEXUALITY (*4) / WOMEN IN TECHNOLOGY (*5) / PEEK & POKE (*3)

JYOTI MISHRA – vocals, keyboards, samples / with three other members

		Satya	not iss.
1990.	(7"ep) *(01)* **WHITE TOWN EP**		-
		Lovely	not iss.
Dec 90.	(7"flexi) *(LOFA 006)* **DARLY ABBEY: COLD AS HELL**		-
	(re-iss. Nov96; same)		
		Parasol	not iss.
1991.	(7") *(PAR 004)* **ALL SHE SAID. /**		-

— now only **MISHRA** on his own

Jan 92.	(7"ep) *(PAR 008)* **ALAIN DELON EP**		-
1992.	(7"ep) *(ER 106)* **FAIRWEATHER FRIEND EP**		-
	(above issued on 'Elefant')		
1992.	(7") *(PAR 016)* **BEWITCHED EP**		-
	(re-iss. Nov96; same)		
Jul 94.	(cd) *(PARCD 021)* **SOCIALISM, SEXISM, SEXUALITY**		-

– Heather's party / All summer in a day / An idiot sings / Why I hate Christmas / Turn away / My baby will love me / Insincere / That's just so / Fairweather friend / Waiting / Ian / The girl that I see / If I had a gun / Back on the shelf / Lie, lie, lie / Bewitched / Fucked again / Save the earth (but save me) / Deep within / Then I'll be sane. *(re-iss. Nov96; same)*

Nov 96.	(cd-ep) *(PARCD 004)* **ABORT, RETRY, FAIL EP**		-

– Your woman / Give me some pain / Theme tune for a mid-afternoon game show / Theme for a late-night documentary about the dangers of drugs.

		Chrysalis	Capitol
Jan 97.	(12"/c-s) *(12/TC CHS 5052)* <58638> **YOUR WOMAN / GIVE ME SOME PAIN /** ('A'-Fights 2000 mix)	**1**	**23** Mar97

(cd-s+=) *(CDCHS 5052)* – Theme for a mid-afternoon game show / Theme for late night documentary about drug abuse.

Feb 97.	(cd/c) *(CD/TC CHR 6120)* <56129> **WOMEN IN TECHNOLOGY**		**84** Apr97

– Undressed / Thursday night at the Blue Note / Week next June / Your woman / White town / Shape of love / Wanted / Function of the orgasm / Going nowhere somehow / Theme for an early evening sitcom / Death of my desire / Once I flew.

May 97.	(c-s) *(TCCHS 5058)* **UNDRESSED / FAMOUS**	**57**	-

(cd-s+=) *(CDCHSS 5058)* – One more day / Your woman.
(cd-s) *(CDCHS 5058)* – ('A'mix) / Theme for an early morning romantic mini series / Theme for an early evening American sitcom.

		Parasol	Parasol
Aug 98.	(cd-ep) *(<PAR 030>)* **ANOTHER LOVER EP**		May99

– Another lover / Theme for leaving Derby / Theme for a violent videogame / I ain't commercial.

Feb 00.	(cd) *(PARCD 044)* **PEEK & POKE**		-

– Another lover / Why I hate drugs / Duplicate / Every second counts / Anyway / In my head / Bunny boiler / She left for Paris / Theme for Alan Mathison Turing / I'm alone / The story of my life / Excerpts from an essay. *(re-iss. May00 & Apr02 on 'Bzangy Groink'; GROINK 1CD)*

WHO

Formed: Chiswick & Hammersmith, London, England ... 1964 as The HIGH NUMBERS, by ROGER DALTREY, PETE TOWNSHEND, JOHN ENTWISTLE and DOUG SANDOM. After making his impromptu mid-set debut at an early gig, manic sticksman, KEITH MOON, was immediately recruited in favour of the struggling SANDERS. At his first show proper, MOON reportedly mystified colleagues by roping his drums to some pillars before the show. All became clear when the drummer proceeded to knock seven shades of proverbial shit out of them during a solo, the kit actually bouncing off the floor! And thus was completed the line-up that would make their mark as one of the most pivotal, not to mention aggressive bands in rock history. Manager PETE MEADON introduced the band to the burgeoning "Mod" scene and shaped their image accordingly as a musical voice for the sharply dressed, scooter-riding young rebels, a movement that TOWNSHEND in particular felt a strong affinity with, and whose frustrations he'd document in his early, indignant blasts of raw rock'n'roll. A strutting, gloriously arrogant piece of R&B, the band's debut one-off 45 for 'Fontana', 'I'M THE FACE', was released the same month as the experienced managerial team of KIT LAMBERT and CHRIS STAMP took the reins from MEADON and began a concerted campaign for chart domination. Later that year, the band were re-christened The WHO and by this time had begun to perfect their powerful stageshow, TOWNSHEND developing his ferocious "windmilling" power-chord guitar style while the band courted controversy and delighted crowds by smashing their instruments in a cathartic rage. Rejected by major labels, they eventually secured a deal with 'Decca' US, through producer SHEL TALMY. Released in Britain via 'Decca's UK subsidiary, 'Brunswick', 'I CAN'T EXPLAIN' (1965) introduced a more melodic sound and gave the band their first chart hit. The single climbed into the top 10 after TV appearances on 'Ready Steady Go' (which later adopted the track as its theme tune) and Top Of The Pops, 'ANYWAY, ANYHOW, ANYWHERE' following it later that summer. For most people however, The WHO really arrived with the seminal rebel anthem, 'MY GENERATION'. A stuttering, incredibly focused piece of amphetamine aggression, it galvanised legions of disaffected youths and only The SEX PISTOLS ever equalled it for sheer snide factor. It reached No.2 and was closely followed by the similarly titled debut album which included 'THE KIDS ARE ALRIGHT', probably TOWNSHEND's most explicit alignment with his "Mod" following. But if the kids were alright, The WHO's deal with SHEL TALMY certainly wasn't, or at least that's what the band thought, and after releasing their next single, 'SUBSTITUTE' (1966), on a new label, they became embroiled in a court battle over TALMY's right to produce the group. Despite TALMY winning a royalty on all the band's recordings for another five years, The WHO came out fighting, releasing a string of hits including 'I'M A BOY' (1966), 'HAPPY JACK' (1966) and the wistful ode to masturbation, 'PICTURES OF LILY' (1967). The title track from 'A QUICK ONE' (1966) was a patchy, prototype of the rock opera concept TOWNSHEND would later refine towards the end of the decade. Elsewhere on the album, tracks like ENTWISTLE's 'BORIS THE SPIDER' and TOWNSHEND's 'HAPPY JACK' possessed the same quirky Englishness that was the essence of The KINKS, and The WHO only really began to make some headway in America after their incendiary performance at The Monterey Pop Festival in the summer of '67. 'THE WHO SELL OUT' (1967), a mock concept album, contained the sublime 'I CAN SEE FOR MILES', a spiralling piece of neo-psychedelia that had a spiritual partner in the equally trippy 'ARMENIA CITY IN THE SKY'. With 'TOMMY' (1969), TOWNSHEND ushered in the dreaded concept of the 'Rock Opera'. Yet with his compelling story of a "deaf, dumb and blind kid" who finds release through pinball, he managed to carry the whole thing off. 'PINBALL WIZARD' and 'SEE ME, FEEL ME' were classic TOWNSHEND. The album was even made into a film by maverick director Ken Russell and later into a successful West End show. After this artful tour de force, the band released the legendary 'LIVE AT LEEDS' (1970) album while they worked on TOWNSHEND's latest idea, the 'LIFEHOUSE' project. An ambitious attempt at following up 'TOMMY', the venture was later aborted, although some of the material was used as the basis for the landmark 'WHO'S NEXT' album. Released in 1971, the record heralded a harder rocking sound with the anthemic 'WON'T GET FOOLED AGAIN' and 'BABA O'REILLY'. Immaculately produced, it still stands as The WHO's most confident and cohesive work and only No.1 album. TOWNSHEND finally created a follow-up to TOMMY with 'QUADROPHENIA' in 1973. A complex, lavishly embellished piece that saw him retrospectively examining the Mod sub-culture he'd so closely identified with. The project was later made into a film, inspiring a whole new wave of neo-Mod bands at the turn of the decade.

Album rating: MY GENERATION (*7) / A QUICK ONE (*6) / THE WHO SELL OUT (*7) / MAGIC BUS – THE WHO ON TOUR (*5) / TOMMY (*8) / THE WHO LIVE AT LEEDS (*8) / WHO'S NEXT (*10) / MEATY, BEATY, BIG AND BOUNCY compilation (*9) / QUADROPHENIA (*9) / ODDS AND SODS collection (*5)

ROGER DALTREY (b. 1 Mar'45) – vocals / **PETE TOWNSHEND** (b.19 May'45) – guitar, vocals / **JOHN ENTWISTLE** (b. 9 Oct'44) – bass, vocals / **KEITH MOON** (b.23 Aug'47) – drums, vocals repl. DOUG SANDOM

		Fontana	not iss.
Jul 64.	(7"; as The HIGH NUMBERS) *(TF 480)* **I'M THE FACE. / ZOOT SUIT**		-

(re-iss. Feb65) (re-iss. Mar80 on 'Back Door', hit UK No.49) (US re-iss. Mar80 as The WHO on 'Mercury')

		Brunswick	Decca
Jan 65.	(7") *(05926)* <31725> **I CAN'T EXPLAIN. / BALD HEADED WOMAN**	**8**	**93** Feb65
	(US re-iss. 1973 on 'MCA')		
May 65.	(7") *(05935)* **ANYWAY ANYHOW ANYWHERE. / DADDY ROLLING STONE**	**10**	-
Jun 65.	(7") *<31801>* **ANYWAY ANYHOW ANYWHERE. / ANYTIME YOU WANT ME**	-	-
Oct 65.	(7") *(05944)* <32058> **MY GENERATION. / SHOUT & SHIMMY**	**2**	-
Nov 65.	(7") *<31877>* **MY GENERATION. / OUT IN THE STREET**	-	**74**
Dec 65.	(lp) *(LAT 8616)* <74664> **MY GENERATION**	**5**	

– Out in the street / I don't mind / The good's gone / La-la-la-lies / Much too much / My generation / The kid's are alright / Please please please / It's not true / I'm a man / A legal matter / The ox. *(US title 'THE WHO SING MY GENERATION') (UK re-iss. Oct80 on 'Virgin' lp/c; V/TCV 2179)* – (hit UK No.20) (cd-iss. 1990;)

		Reaction	Decca
Mar 66.	(7") *(591 001)* <6409> **SUBSTITUTE. / WALTZ FOR A PIG** ("The WHO ORCHESTRA")	**5**	

—— (some copies 'INSTANT PARTY' or 'CIRCLES' on b-side)
<above on US 'Atco'; re-iss. Aug67; 6509>

Aug 66.	(7") *(591 004)* <32058> **I'M A BOY. / IN THE CITY**	**2**	Dec66
Dec 66.	(7") *(591 010)* **HAPPY JACK. / I'VE BEEN AWAY**	**3**	-
Dec 66.	(lp) *(593 002)* <74892> **A QUICK ONE** <US-title 'HAPPY JACK'>	**4**	**67** May67

– Run run run / Boris the spider / Whiskey man / I need you / Heatwave / Cobwebs and strange / Don't look away / See my way / So sad about us / A quick one, while he's away. *(re-iss. Aug88 on 'Polydor' lp/c)(cd); (SPE LP/MC 114)(835 782-2) (cd re-iss. Jun95 & Apr97; 527758-2)*

WHO (cont)

Mar 67.	(7") <32114>	HAPPY JACK. / WHISKEY MAN		- Track	24 Decca
Apr 67.	(7") (604 002) <32156>	PICTURES OF LILY. / DOCTOR DOCTOR		4	51 Jun67
Jul 67.	(7") (604 006)	THE LAST TIME. / UNDER MY THUMB		44	-
Oct 67.	(7") (604 011)	I CAN SEE FOR MILES. / SOMEONE'S COMING		10	-
Oct 67.	(7") <32206>	I CAN SEE FOR MILES. / MARY ANN WITH THE SHAKY HANDS		-	9
Jan 68.	(lp; mono/stereo) (612/613 002) <74950>	THE WHO SELL OUT		13	48

– Armenia, city in the sky / Heinz baked beans / Mary Anne with the shaky hands / Odorono / Tattoo / Our love was, is / I can see for miles / I can't reach you / Medac / Silas Stingy / Sunrise / Tattoo / Rael (1 and 2). (re-iss. Aug88 on 'Polydor' lp/c)(cd; (SPE LP/MC 115) (cd re-iss. Jun95 & Apr97 on 'Polydor'; 527 759-2)

Mar 68.	(7") <32288>	CALL ME LIGHTNING. / DR. JEKYLL & MR. HIDE		-	40
Jun 68.	(7") (604 023)	DOGS. / CALL ME LIGHTNING		25	-
Jul 68.	(7") <32362>	MAGIC BUS. / SOMEONE'S COMING		-	25
Oct 68.	(7") (604 024)	MAGIC BUS. / DR. JEKYLL & MR. HIDE		26	-
Oct 68.	(lp) <75064>	MAGIC BUS – (THE WHO ON TOUR) (live)		-	39

– Disguises / Run run run / Dr. Jekyll & Mr. Hide / I can't reach you / Our love was, is / Call me Lightning / Magic bus / Someone's coming / Doctor doctor / Bucket T. / Pictures of ily.

Nov 68.	(lp; mono/stereo) (612/613 006)	DIRECT HITS (compilation)		-	-

– Bucket T. / I'm a boy / Pictures of Lily / Doctor doctor / I can see for miles / Substitute / Happy Jack / The last time / In the city / Call me Lightning / Mary-Anne with the shaky hand / Dogs.

Mar 69.	(7") (604 027) <32465>	PINBALL WIZARD. / DOGS (part 2)		4	19
	<US re-iss. 1973 on 'MCA'>				
May 69.	(d-lp) (613 013-014) <7205>	TOMMY		2	4

– Overture / It's a boy / 1921 / Amazing journey / Sparks / Eyesight for the blind / Miracle cure / Sally Simpson / I'm free / Welcome / Tommy's holiday camp / We're not gonna take it / Christmas / Cousin Kevin / The acid queen / Underture / Do you think it's alright / Fiddle about / Pinball wizard / There's a doctor / Go to the mirror / Tommy can you hear me / Smash the mirror / Sensation. (re-iss. Jul84 on 'Polydor'; 2486 161/2) (d-cd-iss. Apr89; 800 077-2)

Jul 69.	(7") <32519>	I'M FREE. / WE'RE NOT GONNA TAKE IT		-	37
Mar 70.	(7") (604 036) <32670>	THE SEEKER. / HERE FOR MORE		19	44
May 70.	(lp) (2406 001) <79175>	LIVE AT LEEDS (live)		3	4

– Young man / Substitute / Summertime blues / Shakin' all over / My generation / Magic bus. (re-iss. Nov83 on 'Polydor' lp/c; SPE LP/MC 50) (cd-iss. May88 on 'Polydor'; 825 339-2) (cd re-iss. Feb95 on 'Polydor', hit No.59 & Apr97; 527 169-2)

Jul 70.	(7") (2094 002)	SUMMERTIME BLUES (live). / HEAVEN AND HELL		38	-
Jul 70.	(7") <32708>	SUMMERTIME BLUES (live). / HERE FOR MORE		-	27
Sep 70.	(7") <32729>	SEE ME, FEEL ME. / WE'RE NOT GONNA TAKE IT / OVERTURE FROM TOMMY		-	12
	<US re-iss. 1973 on 'MCA'>				
Sep 70.	(7"w-drawn) (2094 004)	SEE ME, FEEL ME. / OVERTURE FROM TOMMY			
Jul 71.	(7") (2094 009) <32846>	WON'T GET FOOLED AGAIN. / I DON'T EVEN KNOW MYSELF		9	15
Sep 71.	(lp) (2408 102) <79182>	WHO'S NEXT		1	4 Aug71

– Baba O'Riley / Bargain / Love ain't for keeping / My wife / Song is over / Getting in tune / Going mobile / Behind blue eyes / Won't get fooled again. (re-iss. Nov83 on 'Polydor' lp/c; SPE LP/MC 49)(813 651-2) (cd re-iss. Aug96; 527760-2)

Oct 71.	(7") (2094 012)	LET'S SEE ACTION. / WHEN I WAS A BOY		16	-
Nov 71.	(7") <32888>	BEHIND BLUE EYES. / MY WIFE		-	34
Dec 71.	(lp/c) (2406/3191 006) <79184>	MEATY, BEATY, BIG AND BOUNCY (compilation)		9	11 Nov71

– I can't explain / The kids are alright / Happy Jack / I can see for miles / Pictures of Lily / My generation / The seeker / Anyway, anyhow, anywhere / Pinball wizard / A legal matter / Boris the spider / Magic bus / Substitute / I'm a boy. (re-iss. 1974)

Jun 72.	(7") (2094 102) <32983>	JOIN TOGETHER. / BABY DON'T YOU DO IT		9	17

– In Oct72, PETE TOWNSHEND was another like ENTWISTLE to issue debut solo album 'WHO CAME FIRST'. It scraped into UK Top30. He issued more throughout 70's-80's (see . . .) In Apr'73, ROGER DALTREY hit the singles chart with GIVING IT ALL AWAY. It was a cut from debut album DALTREY.

Jan 73.	(7") (2094 106) <33041>	RELAY. / WASPMAN		21 Track	39 Dec72 M.C.A.
Oct 73.	(7") (2094 115)	5:15. / WATER		20	-
Oct 73.	(7") <40152>	5:15. / LOVE REIGN O'ER ME		-	-
Nov 73.	(d-lp) (2657 002) <10004>	QUADROPHENIA		2	2

– I am the sea / The real me / Quadrophenia / Cut my hair / The punk and the godfather / I'm one / Dirty jobs / Helpless dancer / Is it in my head? / I've had enough / 5:15 / Sea and sand / Drowned / Bell boy / Doctor Jimmy / The rock / Love, reign o'er me. (re-iss. Sep79 on 'Polydor' d-lp)(d-c; 2657013)(3526001) (d-cd-iss. Jan87 on 'Polydor'; 831074-2)

Nov 73.	(7") <40152>	LOVE, REIGN O'ER ME. / WATER		-	76
Jan 74.	(7") <40182>	THE REAL ME. / I'M ONE		-	92

WILCO (see under ⇒ UNCLE TUPELO)

WILLARD GRANT CONSPIRACY

Formed: Boston, Massachusetts, USA ... 1996 out of The FLOWER TAMERS and The LAUGHING ACADEMY, initially as an informal weekly get together for various local musicians/songwriters. The group (California-rasised ROBERT FISHER, PAUL AUSTIN and Co.) eventually took on a more permanent nature for the recording of a self-financed debut album, '3 A.M. SUNDAY @ FORTUNE OTTO'S'. Following in the brooding shadow of such mood masters as NICK CAVE, TINDERSTICKS and The WALKABOUTS, WILLARD GRANT CONSPIRACY revel in detailing life's seedier side to a rootsy, downbeat musical backdrop incorporating such traditional instrumentation as mandolin, bouzouki, etc. Their self-styled "swamp noir" sound was finally brought to a UK audience via 1998's 'FLYING LOW' on the influential 'Slow River' label. One of last year's finest alt-country releases, highlights included loser's anthem, 'EVENING MASS', a grim meditation on life's hardships also featured on the brilliant 'Uncut' magazine compilation, 'Sounds Of The New West'. The desert doomsters were back with more neo-Gothic roots manoeuvres on 1999's 'MOJAVE', alternating their bleak alt-country with a snatch of heart of darkness punk and – on, marathon coda, 'THE VISITOR' – striking out into more exploratory, quasi-psychedelic territory. WGC love their dark irony and 'EVERYTHING'S FINE' (2001) proffered more monochrome snapshots of lives in desperate need of salvation, the revelatory, sonorous timbre of FISHER's vocal reverberating through the dense instrumentation like a distant thunderclap. On paper a seemingly irreconcilable partnership, the pairing of WGC and Dutch electronicists TELE:FUNK was fascinating in practice. Released as part of Amsterdam label 'Konkurrent's series of intriguing collaborations, the 'IN THE FISHTANK' (2001) EP proved that the grainy stamp of tradition resonated perhaps even more deeply when availed of technology's organic pulse.

Album rating: 3 A.M. SUNDAY @ FORTUNE OTTO'S (*6) / FLYING LOW (*6) / MOJAVE (*5) / EVERYTHING'S FINE (*6) / IN THE FISHTANK with Telefunk (*6)

ROBERT FISHER – vocals, guitar / **PAUL AUSTIN** – guitars / **JAMES APT** – guitars / **DAVE CURRY** – viola / + other guests

				not iss.	Dahlia
1996.	(cd)	3 A.M. SUNDAY @ FORTUNE OTTO'S		-	

– Morning is the end of the day / Clockwork timing device / The ostrich song / Siren on the rocks / The only story I tell / Child's prayer / Unrequited / If bojangles couldn't dance / Oh Mary / Bring it down.

1997.	(7") <DHL 0020>	WAKE ME WHEN I'M UNDER		-	

– (track by CHRIS & CARLA) / Arch's lullabye.

				Slow River	Slow River
Mar 98.	(cd) <(SRRCD 35)>	FLYING LOW			Aug98

– The smile at the bottom of the ladder / Evening mass / August list / St. John Street / House is not a home (Palmdale, CA) / Bring the monster inside / No such thing as clean / It doesn't matter / Eephus pitch / Water / Split tender.

– added guests **CHRIS BROKAW** (of COME), **MALCOLM TRAVIS** (ex-SUGAR) + **EDITH FROST** (solo artist)

May 99.	(cd) <(SRRCD 46)>	MOJAVE			

– Another lonely night / Color of the sun / The work song / How to get to Heaven / Archy's lullaby / Go, Jimmy, go / I miss you best / Cat nap in the boom boom room / Front porch / Love has no meaning / Sticky / Right on time / The visitor.

1999.	(cd-ep)	COLOR OF THE SUN		-	

– Color of the sun / The work song / Love doesn't / Sticky (alt. version) / Massachusetts.

Oct 00.	(cd) <(SRRCD 58)>	EVERYTHING'S FINE			Feb01

– Notes from the waiting room / Christmas in Nevada / Kite flying / Wicked / Hesitation / Ballad of John Parker / Southend of a northbound train / The beautiful song / Drunkard's prayer / Closing time / Massachusetts.

				Fishtank	Fishtank
Jan 02.	(m-cd; by WILLARD GRANT CONSPIRACY & TELEFUNK) <(FISH 8CD)>	IN THE FISHTANK			

– Twistification / Cuckoo / Grun grun / Near the cross / Just a little rain / Dig a hole in the meadow.

– AUSTIN would subsequently team up with TERRI MOELLER (of WALKABOUTS) to form TRANSMISSIONARY 6; they released an eponymouse set in 2002

WILLIAM (see under ⇒ JESUS & MARY CHAIN)

Astrid WILLIAMSON

Born: c.1971, Shetlands. After attending music college in Glasgow, she took the long trip south to London where she found work playing piano in a cocktail bar. More exciting horizons beckoned as she became frontwoman for GOYA DRESS, an indie act signed to the 'Nude' label. She subsequently struck out on a solo career following the band's demise in late '96. A subtle, sophisticated singer-songwriter as well as a classically trained pianist and multi-instrumentalist, ASTRID was compared to veteran femme confessionalists such as CAROLE KING and JONI MITCHELL although commentators found her highly original, evocative style hard to pin down. Indie lable 'Nude' were convinced of both her genius as a songwriter and her potential as an albums artist, putting up the budget for ASTRID to work on a debut album with producer Malcolm Burn (BOB DYLAN, PATTI SMITH, IGGY POP) in New Orleans. The resulting 'BOY FOR YOU' (1998) album had critics reaching for the superlatives, praising her crystalline melodies, prophetic introspection and lucid way with a pithy lyric. Neither 'I AM THE BOY FOR YOU' or the narrative 'HOZANNA' made much headway as single releases although 'Nude' MD, Saul Galpern seems to be committed to her longer term development. ASTRID's talent also came to the attention of JOHNNY MARR who recruited her earthy vocal chords for ELECTRONIC's 1999 album, 'Twisted Tenderness'. Dropped by 'Nude' records, she found it a little difficult to get back into the mainstream. Finally, in August 2002, ASTRID WILLIAMSON (now using her full moniker) delivered an internet-only release, 'CARNATION' – available at www.astridwilliamson.net – a top set that was made for Radio 2 and possibly a proper CD release.

Astrid WILLIAMSON (cont)

Album rating: BOY FOR YOU (*5) / CARNATION (*6)

ASTRID

ASTRID WILLIAMSON – vocals, guitar / with session people

                                                                     Nude   Imprint

Jul 98. (cd-s) *(NUD 36CD1)* **I AM THE BOY FOR YOU / WORLD AT YOUR FEET** (original) **/ SOMEONE I SHOULD LOVE** (demo)
(cd-s2) *(NUD 36CD2)* – ('A'side) / ('A'demo) / Sing for me (acoustic).
Aug 98. (cd/c) *(NUDE 10 CD/MC)* <112719> **BOY FOR YOU**
– I am the boy for you / Everyone's waiting / What do you... / World at your feet / Sing for me / Someone / Hozanna / If I loved you / Outside / Say what you mean.
Sep 98. (c-s) *(NUD 40C)* **HOZANNA / FAN**
(cd-s+=) *(NUD 40CD)* – Hozanna (acoustic mix).

ASTRID WILLIAMSON

                                                    internet not iss.

Aug 02. (web) **CARNATION**
– Never enough / Love / To love you / Bye and bye / Blood horizon / Calling / Girlfriend / Tumbling into blue / Lucky / Call for beauty.

WIMP FACTOR 14 (see under ⇒ VEHICLE FLIPS)

WINDMILLS

Formed: Southend-on-Sea, England... 1987 by ROY THIRLWALL, brother TONY and DAN PANKHURST plus drummer ROB CLARKE. Might well have been all forgotten as The WINDMILLS only breezed in one solitary single in 1988, 'THE DAY DAWNED ON ME', before breaking up in 1990. However, they made a surprise return in 1999 (with a new drummer, PETE SPICER) with the release of a comeback single, 'THREE SIXTY DEGREES', which was followed by a debut album 'EDGE OF AUGUST' (2000) and an EP, 'DRUG AUTUMN'. It was not until the delivery of the 'SUNLIGHT' album in 2001 that the group displayed their full capabilities. Their jangly guitar pop, which had always sounded like a pale imitation of the HOUSEMARTINS, now carried its own stamp. The group had grown in confidence and were now playing the kind of fresh charming indie-styled pop they had always wished they could. The band again displayed what might've been with the release of the 'WALKING AROUND THE WORLD' EP. This collection of songs was their most complete and heart-felt to date and, if released a decade or so earlier, could have sat comfortably alongside the work of The SMITHS. Not content with leading The WINDMILLS, THIRLWALL moonlighted with side-project, the MELODIE GROUP. Luscious, jangly and dreamy best described his 6-track mini-set, confusingly-titled 'SEVEN SONGS' (2000) – hail to The ORCHIDS, EAST VILLAGE and FELT.

Album rating: EDGE OF AUGUST (*5) / SUNLIGHT (*6) / Melodie Group: SEVEN SONGS mini (*5)

ROY THIRLWALL – vocals, guitar / **TONY PANKHURST** – guitar / **DAN PANKHURST** – bass / **ROB CLARKE** – drums

                                                    S.T.S.   not iss.

1988. (7") *(STS 2)* **THE DAY DAWNED ON ME. / DOLPHINS**

— split in 1990; re-formed in 1998

— **PETE SPICER** – drums; repl. CLARKE

                                                  Matinee Matinee

May 99. (7") *(matinee 011)* **THREE SIXTY DEGREES. / BAD LUCK CHARM**
Jan 00. (cd) *(matcd 002)* **EDGE OF AUGUST**
– Last night / GoodNewsBadNews / Tired and emotional / Three sixty degrees / Bad luck charm / Bad days will end / Want / Edge of August / Not my fault / Git / As if / Turn you out of doors.
Oct 00. (cd-ep) *(matinee 021)* **DRUG AUTUMN EP**
– Everything is new each day / Drug autumn / Are we still where we were? / Want.
Apr 01. (cd-ep) *(matinee 024)* **WHEN IT WAS WINTER EP**
– When it was winter / Pounds, shillings and pence / Snow white / Good riddance to bad rubbish.

— **ROB CLARKE** – drums; repl. SPICER

Oct 01. (cd) *(<matcd 014>)* **SUNLIGHT**
– Unkiss / Pounds, shillings and pance / Taxi fare / When it was winter / She's so hard / Boxing glove / Cloud five / Be groovy or leave / Untouch / Drug autumn.
Jul 02. (cd-ep) *(<matinee 038>)* **WALKING AROUND THE WORLD EP**   May02
– What was it for? / Amelia / Walking around the world / What was it for? (video).

MELODIE GROUP

ROY THIRLWALL – vocals, guitars, etc.

                                                    Matinee Matinee

Jul 00. (m-cd) *(matcd 007)* **SEVEN SONGS**
– Wildest dream / Skin dive / Granny dress / Callow fellow / Jean Genet / Swimming pool.
Dec 00. (cd-ep) *(matinee 020)* **RAINCOAT**
– You've got the whole world in your mouth / Raincoat / Magic robot / Goodbye.
Dec 01. (7"ep) *(matinee 033)* **SUMMERNESS**
– Summerness / Nineteen eighty nine / Small grinning thing.

WINDSOR FOR THE DERBY

Formed: Tampa, Florida, USA... 1994 by DAN MATZ, JASON McNEELEY and GREG ANDERSON. Having relocated to Austin, Texas, the band debuted in 1996 with the album, 'CALM HADES FLOAT'. Like so many bands in America at this time, the group's sound was created by burying the vocals and drums under waves of effect-laden guitars and although, especially for a first effort, it wasn't bad, there was nothing to separate them from the pack. A self-titled EP, released the same year, was of similar quality, as was the 1997 album, 'MINNIE GREUNZFELDT'. It was in 1999 and with the release of the album, 'DIFFERENCE AND REPETITION', that the band started to forge an identity of their own. Ironically this can be attributed to guest members such as ADAM WILTZIE of STARS OF THE LID. Following the release of the album, the band scaled down to a duo with only MATZ and McNEELEY remaining. Having shed the other band members, the group returned with fittingly aero-dynamic music. The band had not completely abandoned their previous sound, they had simply made it lighter and less claustrophobic, which allowed the melodies (think DURUTTI COLUMN and SLINT) room to breath and build, proving that sometimes less is more.

Album rating: CALM HADES FLOAT (*6) / MINNIE GREUNZFELDT (*6) / DIFFERENCE AND REPETITION (*6) / EARNEST POWERS compilation (*5) / THE EMOTIONAL RESCUE LP (*7)

DAN MATZ – guitar / **JASON McNEELEY** – guitar / **GREG ANDERSON** – drums / **ADAM WILTZIE** – mixer (of STARS OF THE LID)

                                       Trance   Trance
                                       Syndicate Syndicate

Jan 96. (7") *<TR 45>* **split w/ DESAFINADO**
May 96. (cd/lp) *<(TR 46 CD/LP)>* **CALM HADES FLOAT**
– (7 untitled tracks).
Jan 97. (cd-ep) *<TR 54CD>* **METROPOLITAN THEN POLAND**
– Exposito / Moving Florida / Slow death / Slow death + / The Electric Co.
Jul 97. (12"; split w/ DRAIN) *<TR 57>* **KAHANEK INCIDENT, VOL.1**
Oct 97. (cd/lp) *<(TR 63 CD/LP)>* **MINNIE GREUNZFELDT**
– Fat angel / Skinny ghost / Stasis bass trap / No techno w/drums / When I see scissors / Useless arm / Skimming.

                                    not iss. Young God

Jun 99. (cd) *<YG 9>* **DIFFERENCE AND REPETITION**
– (untitled) / Shoes McCoat / (untitled) / Shaker / The egg / Nico / Lost in cycles.

                                    Speakerphone not iss.

Nov 00. (7") *(DIAL 008)* **MELT CLOSE. / DONKEY**

                                    Holophonor not iss.

Jul 01. (12"ep) *(HOLO 002)* **THE EMOTIONAL RESCUE EP**
– Piranha / Horse in cork / Horse in glass / Emotional rescue.

— **MATZ + McNEELEY** trimmed down

                                     Aesthetics Aesthetics

Oct 01. (cd-ep) *<(AST 21CD)>* **THE AWKWARDNESS EP**
– The emotional rescue / I change. C? / Ice age blues / Awkwardness / Now I know the sea.

— **MATZ** recruited **CHRISTIAN GOYER + KARL BAUER + LESLIE SISSON**

Oct 02. (cd) *<AST 24CD>* **THE EMOTIONAL RESCUE LP**
– The same / Now I know the sea / Emotional rescue / Fall of '68 / Indonesian guitars / Mythologies / Awkwardness / Another rescue / Donkey ride.

– compilations, etc. –

Mar 02. (cd) *Emperor Jones; <EJ 36>* **EARNEST POWERS**
– (11 untitled tracks).

WINDY & CARL

Formed: Dearborn, Michigan, USA... 1991 by bassist WINDY WEBER and guitarist CARL HULTGREN. By the time the pair met, HULTGREN had already self-financed a space-fixated, instrumental demo, 'PORTAL', subsequently released in revamped form circa late 1995. In the meantime, WINDY & CARL made their official debut with the 'WATERSONG' single, again released on a self-financed label, 'Blue Flea'. Fleshing out their feedback-droning, cosmic ambient sound, the duo recruited guitarist/keysman RANDALL NIEMAN and percussionist BRENDA MARKOVICH, releasing the 'DRIFTING' EP in early '95 as ONCE DREAMT. Due to the departure of BRENDA and RANDALL (the latter forming FUXA), it would be a few years before the arrival of any fresh material, although fans were treated to a series of singles culminating with early '98's 'Kranky' album, 'DEPTHS'. These singles further refined the somehow indefinable WINDY & CARL aesthetic, absorbing WINDY's amorphous, filmic utterings into swathes of soporific electronica. 'WINDY & CARL & THE LOTHARS' (2000) compiled assorted excerpts from the respective artists' live work at the various 'Terrastock' nu-psychedelia festivals, including a collaboration between HULTGREN and The LOTHARS on opener '3rd STAGE'. The WINDY & CARL section of the album, meanwhile, was represented by 'THROUGH THE PORTAL' and 'BALLAST'. The well received 'CONSCIOUSNESS' (2001), meanwhile, took the duo further out into the realms of pure sound and its brain-chemistry altering possibilities, transcending the conceit of much ambient music by unhinging its very structure.

Album rating: PORTAL (*5) / DRAWING OF SOUND (*6) / A DREAM OF BLUE (*6) / ANTARTICA (*5) / DEPTHS (*5) / CONSCIOUSNESS (*6)

CARL HULTGREN – guitar / **WINDY WEBER** – bass, vocals

not iss. / Blue Flea

Dec 93. (7") **WATERSONG. / DRAGONFLY** [-] [ ]

— added **RANDALL NIEMAN** – guitar, keyboards / **BRENDA MARKOVICH** – percussion

Feb 95. (cd-ep; as ONCE DREAMT) *<BLUEFLEA 05>* **DRIFTING EP** [-] [ ]
(c-ep iss.Apr96)

— now without MARKOVICH + NIEMAN (the latter formed FUXA)

not iss. / Ba Da Bing

Nov 94. (cd) *<BING 004>* **PORTAL** (early + new) [-] [ ]
– Preparation / Awhile / Ode to spaceman / Firebursts / Sound ignition / Approach – Descend / Exploration / Departure / Glowing – Colorful / Gravital loft / Through the portal. *(UK-iss.Nov97; same as US)*

not iss. / Burnt Hair

1995. (7") *<singe 8>* **split w/ HOPEWELL** [-] [ ]

Blue Flea / Blue Flea

Mar 97. (lp) *<(BLUEFLEA 07R)>* **DRAWING OF SOUND** [ ] [ ] Mar96
– You / Lighthouse / Venice / Awhile / Whisper.

Ochre / Ochre

Oct 97. (10"lp/cd) *<(OCH 17/+CD)>* **A DREAM OF BLUE** [ ] [ ]
– A dream of blue / Kate / Hypnos. *(re-iss. Feb99; same)*

Darla / Darla

Jan 98. (lp/cd) *<(DRL 027/+CD)>* **ANTARTICA** [ ] [ ] Feb97
– Antartica / Traveling / Sunrise.

Kranky / Kranky

Feb 98. (cd/d-lp) *<(KRANK 024 CD/LP)>* **DEPTHS** [ ] [ ] Mar98
– Sirens / Undercurrent / Set adrift / Depths / The silent ocean / Aquatica / Surfacing.

Apr 00. (lp) *(WORMSS 7)* **split w/ SADDAR BAZAAR** [ ] [-]
(above on 'Earworm', below issued on 'Blue Flea')

Nov 00. (cd) *<BLFL 11>* **WINDY & CARL & THE LOTHARS** [-] [ ]
– 3rd stage / Through the portal / Ballast / Dust mah space broom.
(above with various artists, the LOTHARS, MAIN, ALASTAIR GALBRAITH)

Mar 01. (lp/cd) *<(KRANK 045/+CD)>* **CONSCIOUSNESS** [ ] [ ]
– The sun / Balance (trembling) / Elevation / The llama's dream / Consciousness / Resolution.

— in 2001, a tour cd-ep was split w/ LANDING for 'Wobbly' records

WISDOM OF HARRY
(see under ⇒ WEATHER PROPHETS; 80's section)

WITCH HAZEL

Formed: Kent, Ohio, USA . . . 1992 by KEVIN CORAL, MIKE SPLIT, JASON RICHARDSON and MARK F. The group released their debut single to widespread critical acclaim the following year. It was not until 1995 that the group displayed their full potential with both the EP 'BEESWAX' and the full-length 'LANDLOCKED'. The sound of the album was derivative of BRIAN WILSON packed with lush harmonies and infectious melodies. Occasionally the band sounded as though they had bitten off more than they could chew although all the signs of a promising future were in place. A six track EP, 'IT'S ALL TRUE', recorded in 1998 but not released until 2000, was a more controlled effort with the group not allowing their multi-layered sound to become muddled. This new found confidence was carried over to their next full-length album 'THIS WORLD, THEN THE FIREWORKS . . .' (2001), which sounded more groovy and less formulaic than anything they had produced before.

Album rating: LANDLOCKED (*5) / IT'S ALL TRUE mini (*8) / THIS WORLD, THEN THE FIREWORKS . . . (*6)

KEVIN CORAL (b. 3 Jan'68) – guitar, keyboards, multi / **MARK F.** (b.12 Apr'71) – vocals / **MIKE SPLIT** (b.26 Aug'71) – bass

not iss. / Bubblegum Smile

1993. (7") *<1>* **JUST DON'T TRY. / PLAIN** [-] [ ]

Elefant / Brilliant

1993. (d7"ep; split w/ The TECHNICAL JED) *(ER 124 <ANT 04>* **KRAMER'S BEACH DOUBLE** [ ] [ ]
– (2 by The TECHNICAL JED) / Believe mention.

not iss. / Sonic Swirl

1994. (7"ep) *<SWIRL 002>* **COUGH SYRUP. / (other by MOMMYHEADS)** [-] [ ]

not iss. / Get Go

1995. (7"ep) *<5>* **BEESWAX EP** [-] [ ]

Flydaddy / Flydaddy

Dec 95. (cd/lp) *<(FLY 014 CD/LP)>* **LANDLOCKED** [ ] [ ] Sep95
– Gone tomorrow / Chinese apples / Secrets of the spider world / Honey stick / Blonde on blonde / Lemon grove kids / Rosewater crescent / Autumnal void / Pink grapefruit cocktail / Peking opera blues / Hideous sun demon / Do you dig worms? *(re-iss. Feb99; same)*

Camera Obscura / Camera Obscura

Jun 98. (m-cd; as WITCH HAZEL SOUND) *<CAM 012CD>* **IT'S ALL TRUE** [-] [ ]
– The libertine revisited / Fontaine / Pacific – Atlantic / The secret grave girl / Hawthorne / Frank's dream. *(UK-iss.Apr00; same as US)*

not iss. / Hidden Agenda

Nov 01. (cd) *<AHA! 028>* **THIS WORLD, THEN THE FIREWORKS . . .** [-] [ ]
– Music becomes vibration / 2 or 3 things I know about her / Fireworks / Providence / Blue city / Sun horse Moon horse / The guild of splinters / Kiss of tomorrow / Halo of brass / Kiss me monster / Ballad of Constance Money / The boy with green hair.

WITNESS

Formed: Wigan, England . . . 1994 by GERARD STARKE and RAY CHAN, who toured around the city while working as record company talent scouts in the height of Brit pop. STARKE was allegedly drunk every night while CHAN closely observed a million chord strumming minimalists. The two had decided to form a group of their own on the basis that they sounded nothing like OASIS or CAST etc. DYLAN KEETON was recruited as bassist and the three made up a startling demo that reached THE VERVE's PR and virtually signed on the spot. Keyboard-player JULIAN PRANSKY-POOLE and drummer JON LANGLEY (ex-STRANGELOVE and BLUE AEROPLANES) were the final instalments into the group, the band subsequently releasing the zen-like titled 'BEFORE THE CALM', an album that reflected on certain moods expressed throughout. Although sounding rather similar to THE VERVE, WITNESS had created their own tortured sound whith blistering laments such as 'SECOND LIFE' and the single 'SCARS'. The post-NICK DRAKE like 'FREEZING OVER MORNING' contained one of the best lines of the year:- "Sometimes I stride like royalty, while other times I crawl", proving, in WITNESS' case, that heartache is a delicate subject. In 2001, "Wigan's answer to R.E.M." provided their adoring fanbase with a second LP instalment, courtesy of 'UNDER A SUN', STARKE's unique vocal range helping pad out their Americana-meets-60's type rock. • **Note:** They are WITNESS U.K. in the States.

Album rating: BEFORE THE CALM (*8) / UNDER A SUN (*7)

GERALD STARKE – vocals / **RAY CHAN** – guitar / **DYLAN KEETON** – bass / **JULIAN PRANSKY-POOLE** – keyboards, guitar / **JON LANGLEY** – drums (ex-STRANGELOVE, ex-BLUE AEROPLANES)

Valient / not iss.

Nov 98. (7") *(VAL 001)* **QUARANTINE. / INTO THE WAVES** [ ] [-]

Island / M.C.A.

Mar 99. (7") *(IS/CID 740)* **SCARS. / MORE MILES AWAY / LONG FIRST CHAPTER** [71] [-]

Jun 99. (7") *(IS 749)* **AUDITION. / BLIND SOUL MIME** [71] [-]
(cd-s+=) *(CID 749)* – Drinking song.

Jul 99. (cd) *(CID 8084) <25061>* **BEFORE THE CALM** [59] [ ]
– Second life / Scars / Freezing over morning / Hijacker / My own old song / So far gone / Cause and effect / Heirloom / Audtion / My friend will see me through / Still.

Sep 99. (7") *(IS 758)* **HIJACKER. / LOWJACKER** [ ] [-]
(cd-s) *(CID 758)* – ('A'side) / Quarantine (acoustic) / Before the calm.

Jul 01. (7") *(IS 778)* **YOU ARE ALL MY OWN INVENTION. / LIGHTEN UP** [ ] [-]
(cd-s) *(CID 778)* – ('A'side) / Don't suffer fools / This sober.

Jul 01. (cd) *(CID 8107) <586034>* **UNDER A SUN** [62] [ ] Sep01
– Here's one for you / You are all my own invention / Dividing line / Under a sun / Till the morning / Closing up / My time alone / Warning song / Mines / So here be well again / Avalanche / My boat. *(bonus+=)* – Pushchair.

Nov 01. (7") *(IS 784)* **HERE'S ONE FOR YOU. / IN MINIATURE** [ ] [-]
(cd-s+=) *(CID 784)* – Pendulum.

WOLF COLONEL

Formed: Portland, Oregon, USA . . . late 1996 as the solo acoustic project of guitarist/singer JASON ANDERSON. Receiving a bolt of inspirational lightning from a recent ELLIOTT SMITH gig, ANDERSON began playing around the Lewis & Clark College campus, including cramped performances in his dorm room. The singer/songwriter met CALVIN JOHNSON from 'K' records at a HALO BENDERS show and started sending him self-released cassettes such as 'THIS IS COMPTON' and 'SEX RIOT'. JOHNSON eventually recorded a WOLF COLONEL session at his Dub Narcotic studio when ANDERSON added drums and bass to the aural proceedings, resulting in the release of the 'WOLF COLONEL' EP in 1999. Frontman ANDERSON recruited bassist RYAN WISE (also of DEAR NORA), ADAM FORKNER (of YUME BITSU, with whom ANDERSON also moonlighted as drummer) and rhythm guitarist JAKE LONGSTRETH for a subsequent tour. The LPs 'VIKINGS OF MINT' (2000) and 'THE CASTLE' (2000) would follow in short order. Both releases were well-received and praised for their playful indie and pop-punk eccentricity, with ANDERSON (penning all the material and playing nearly all the instruments) showing a knack for constructing surreal, idiosyncratic song titles like 'THESE AQUATIC DROIDS', 'MISTER EASTER AEROPLANE' and 'THE ALMOND GORILLA', even if influences like GUIDED BY VOICES and SUPERCHUNK were still a bit too obvious in the mix. With the release of the 'SOMETHING / EVERYTHING' LP (2002) however, ANDERSON had found his own true voice. The album's title was a nod to TODD RUNDGREN's 'Something / Anything' and, working with producers PHIL ELVRUM, CALVIN JOHNSON and ADAM FORKNER, 24-year-old ANDERSON came up with a confident, cheery work that ranged in sound from hip-hop to pop-punk to piano without missing a beat.

Album rating: VIKINGS OF MINT mint (*6) / THE CASTLE (*5) / SOMETHING – EVERYTHING! (*5)

JASON ANDERSON (b. 1978, South Sutton, New Hampshire, USA) – vocals, guitar, organ

K / K

Feb 99. (7"ep) *<IPU 090>* **WOLF COLONEL** [-] [ ]
– What it is / Didn't know what was in store / The penguin entropy retractor / Motorcycle cop / Be with you tonight / Down where the others play / Don't freeze the mayonnaise / True.

— added **JAKE LONGSTRETH** – guitar / **RYAN WISE** – bass (of DEAR NORA) / **ADAM FORKNER** – drums (of YUME BITSU)

Feb 00. (m-cd) <KCD 107> **VIKINGS OF MINT**
– A medium rootbeer / Mister Easter aeroplane / The emperor in the sky / These aquatic droids / The clam, the owl / Moral of the story / Agave's lament / Uncle of France / Dear Elliott / Know what the story is / T-resistible / You ignore me / The Idean ocean / The top seven singles club / Scared of a snail.

---- **KEVIN JOHNSON** – drums; repl. FORKNER

Sep 00. (cd) <(KCD 114)> **THE CASTLE**
– The perspective / Is this what we asked for? / Pet you over / The almond gorilla / I swear I am / We'll always have Phoenix / Sabotage the alley / Fantasy soccer / He goes places no one goes / Here we go my friends / Nectarine island / Jerusalem / Russian sandwiches / Cookie saucer / Dirty dream.

---- now with **FORKNER** again

Sep 02. (cd) <(KCD 132)> **SOMETHING / EVERYTHING!** Aug02
– Astronaut, astronaut / Moon song / From Wisconsin / Break the news / One thousand ways / Citizen's arrest / Jet ski accidents / Sophomore / The most delicious part / Now we choose / That's my life / Thinking about you / The goodbye / Bless us now.

WOLFIE

Formed: Champaign-Urbana, Illinois, USA . . . 1991 as SLACKJAWED by JOE ZIEMBA, MIKE DOWNEY and R.J. PORTER. After releasing a couple of DIY tapes, the arrival of ZIEMBA's girlfriend AMANDA LYONS cemented the band and they changed their name to WOLFIE. A single, 'DON'T TURN IT OFF', was issued on the 'Grand Theft Auto' label in 1997 while a debut album, 'AWFUL MESS MYSTERY' (1998), more fully revealed the delights of their fresh-faced, synth-plonking indie-pop. Sophomore set, 'WHERE'S WOLFIE' (1999), favoured a slightly more retro feel although the infectious harmonies were as naively endearing as ever. ZIEMBA and LYONS also released material as BUSYTOBY, an outfit which initially included SARGE lady RACHEL SWITZKY before she was replaced by JENNY MANGUN. After a homespun cassette, the project was taken on board by 'Parasol', who released a single, 'ME, MY DRUMS AND YOU', in 1998 and an album, 'IT'S GOOD TO BE ALIVE', the following year.

Album rating: AWFUL MESS MYSTERY (*6) / WHERE'S WOLFIE (*6) / TALL DARK HILL (*7) / BusyToby: IT'S GOOD TO BE ALIVE (*7)

JOE ZIEMBA – vocals, bass / **MIKE DOWNEY** – vocals, guitar / **R.J. PORTER** – drums / added **AMANDA LYONS** – vocals, keyboards

not iss. GrandTheft Autumn

Sep 97. (7"m) <006> **DON'T TURN IT OFF. / VFM / PUTTING IT TOGETHER**

Parasol Parasol

Feb 98. (7"m) <(MUD 025)> **MOCKHOUSE. / MULTIMATIC MONTHS / IT'S TOUGH**
May 98. (10"lp) <(MUD 033)> **AWFUL MESS MYSTERY**
– I know I know I know / Mockhouse / Hey it's finally yay / Yeah yeah you / Subroutine the reward / Ikat me / Lazy weekend, dtormy season / Gettin' the reach that I need / Life saver socks / Everybody ought to know / I gotta, U gotta / Iron orange, iron blue / Want to practice (you do). <(cd-iss. Oct00; MUD 033CD)>
Nov 98. (7") <(PAR 037)> **YOU'RE LUCKY I'M SKINNY. / GINGER ALE YAWN**
Apr 99. (cd) <(PARCD 048)> **WHERE'S WOLFIE**
– Little bee is dancin' / Steely Dan / Mr. and Mrs. Season / Busy, busy, busy / I'm an engineer / Forget about Friday / Ain't no good news / On loan to satellite / Knew it knew it / Buying an empire / It's Thursday, not Sunday (thankl goodness) / Ambulances east / So brother / You're lucky I'm skinny / You're gonna fall into it, but I'll always.

Kindercore Kindercore

Jun 00. (cd-ep) <(KC 041CD)> **WOLFIE, THE COAT AND THE HAT**
– THey call me leaves / It's hard luck being me / The all good people / Rachel Carson / Calvin grove / Two birds.

Kittridge Kittridge

Jul 00. (7"m) <(KITT 005)> **HEAVY LADY. / ALL DAY I'M THINKING OF YOU / WHEN YOU FALL ASLEEP AT NIGHT**

March March Jun00

Jun 01. (cd) <(MAR 069)> **TALL DARK HILL**
– What I want from the world / A checkered begonia / Waiting for the night to end / Everybody knows how to cry / Gwendolyn / Crab and the sandy beach / Living island is real / Slip of a shingle / You are a woman / Happy state of Mr. Bubbins.

BUSYTOBY

ZIEMBA + LYONS – vocals, keyboards

not iss. unknown

1997. (c; as STEREOTOMY) **THE HUMAN IS THE KEYBOARD'S MOTOR**
1998. (c; as STEREOTOMY) **YOU LOVE THE CRICKETS**

Parasol Parasol

Jul 98. (7") <PAR 035> **ME, MY DRUMS, AND YOU. /**
Dec 99. (cd) <(PAR 050CD)> **"IT'S GOOD TO BE ALIVE"** Oct99
– Sparrow, somehow you know / The band / Ms. Thripp / Hey Hali / Big big brother / Dear momma and poppa / I been waiting / Greenwood Ave., Jonathan Lane / Just you and me know who / The very strange rabbit / The fateful day / House on a hill / Maia and leaves / A quiet night at home / The day we'll meet a cloud / Why it's good to be alive. <(lp-iss.Jun00; PARLP 050)>

Jen WOOD (see under ⇒ TATTLE TALE)

WORKDOGS (see under ⇒ GIBSON BROS.)

WORLD OF TWIST

Formed: Manchester, England . . . 1989 by GORDON KING, TONY OGDEN, JULIA McSHELLS, ADGE and ANDY HOBSON. One of the many bands skulking in the floppy fringes of the baggy movement, WORLD OF TWIST signed to 'Virgin'-offshoot, 'Circa', scoring a near-Top 40 hit with their debut single, 'THE STORM'. A follow-up track, 'SONS OF THE STAGE', achieved a similar feat in spring '91, by which point the group had been reduced to a trio of KING, OGDEN and new recruit NICHOLAS SANDERSON. Although a John Peel session helped boost their credibility, the 'SWEETS' single barely nudged into the Top 60 later the same year. Many critics intrigued by the band's colourful, adventurous indie-pop weren't so impressed by the debut album, 'QUALITY STREET' (1991), while a re-released version of their Rolling Stones cover, 'SHE'S A RAINBOW', smacked of last-gasp desperation. SANDERSON and KING changed direction and subsequently formed EARL BRUTUS. • **Songwriters:** Group except: THIS TOO SHALL PASS AWAY (Honeycombs).

Album rating: QUALITY STREET (*5)

GORDON KING – guitar / **TONY OGDEN** – vocals / **JULIA McSHELLS** (MC SHELLS) – synthesizers / **ANDY HOBSON** – keyboards / **ADGE** – visuals

Circa not iss.

Nov 90. (7") (YR 55) **THE STORM. / SHE'S A RAINBOW** 42
(12"+=/cd-s+=) (YR/+T/CD 55) – (2 other 'A'&'B' versions).
(12"+=) (YRT 55) – Blackpool Tower suite.

---- now reduced to **KING, OGDEN** + new recruit **NICHOLAS SANDERSON** – percussion

Mar 91. (7") (YR 62) **SONS OF THE STAGE. / LIFE AND DEATH (remix)** 47
(12"+=/cd-s+=) (YR T/CD 62) – ('A'version).
Sep 91. (7") (YR 72) **SWEETS. / THIS TOO SHALL PASS AWAY** 58
(cd-s+=) (YRCD 72) – The storm / Sons of the stage.
Oct 91. (c/cd/lp) (CIRC/+D/A 17) **QUALITY STREET** 50
– Lose my way / Sons of the stage / This too shall pass away / Jelly baby / Speed wine / The lights / On the scene / Sweets / The spring / The storm. (cd+=)R – She's a rainbow / Life and death.
Feb 92. (7") (YR 82) **SHE'S A RAINBOW. / LOSE MY WAY** 62
(12"+=/cd-s+=) (YR T/CD 82) – ('A'mixes).

---- disbanded June '92; SANDERSON + KING formed EARL BRUTUS

WOULD BE'S

Formed: Kingcourt, Dublin, Ireland . . . 1989 by the shy youthful sextet of MATTIE FINNEGAN (main songwriter), his brothers EAMONN and PAUL, plus JULIE O'DONNELL, PASCAL SMITH and AIDIN O'REILLY. Filling in a Celtic gap between The SMITHS and The SUNDAYS, The WOULD BE'S' short-lived career consisted of a handful of early 90's singles for the 'Decoy' label. Debut effort, 'I'M HARDLY EVER WRONG', displayed the group's trademark dry wit, while a further couple of early 90's releases, the EP's 'SILLY SONGS FOR CYNICAL PEOPLE' and 'MY RADIO SOUNDS DIFFERENT IN THE DARK', saw EILEEN GOGAN coming in for JULIE. However, the band disappeared when they finally got decent jobs (sorry, ed!); EILEEN subsequently became part of The REVENANTS alongside former STARS OF HEAVEN mainman, STEPHEN RYAN.

Album rating: never released any

MATTIE FINNEGAN – vocals / **JULIE O'DONNELL** – vocals / **PASCAL SMITH, AIDIN O'REILLY, EAMONN FINNEGAN + PAUL FINNEGAN**

Decoy not iss.

Mar 90. (7") (DYS 13) **I'M HARDLY EVER WRONG. / GREAT EXPECTATIONS**
(12"+=) (DYS 13T) – I want to say what goes without saying / There is there are that's all.

---- JULIE left to go back to school; repl. by **EILEEN GOGAN**

May 91. (12"ep/cd-ep) (DECOY 18 T/CD) **SILLY SONGS FOR CYNICAL PEOPLE**
– Funny ha ha / Cynical song / All this rubbish is true / Logic makes no sense to me.
Nov 91. (12"ep) (DYT 26) **THE WONDERFUL EP**
– My radio sounds different in the dark / Would be song / Damn mistake.

---- split after above; but re-formed for comeback single

C.M.R. not iss.

2001. (cd-ep) (CMCD 001) **SOME OTHER PLANET / ALL THIS RUBBISH IS TRUE (acoustic gubbins) / SOME OTHER PLANET (karaoke mix)**

Shannon WRIGHT (see under ⇒ CROWSDELL)

THE GREAT INDIE DISCOGRAPHY — The 1990s

XINLISUPREME

Formed: Oita, Japan . . . 2000 by YASUMI OKANO and TAKA YUKI SHOUJI. Brandishing an idiosyncratic take on the Japanese experimental rock aesthetic, XINLISUPREME secured a deal with London's 'Fat Cat' label, for whom they released a debut single in early 2002, 'ALL YOU NEED IS LOVE WAS NOT TRUE'. Again twisting a Beatles song for its title, the full-length 'TOMORROW NEVER COMES' followed a few months later. While an obvious reference point would be The BOREDOMS, experimental New York punk was also a clear influence on their schizophrenic, genre-hopping dynamic. Lurching from all-out sonic attack to hushed meditation and constructed from contradictory yet complementary layers and textures, the record's compelling complexity had the critics frothing. A mini-set, 'MURDER LICENSE', followed later the same year.

Album rating: TOMORROW NEVER COMES (*7) / MURDER LICENSE mini (*6)

YASUMI OKANO – multi-instruments / **TAKAYUKI SHOUJI** – multi-instruments

		Fat Cat	Fat Cat
Dec 01.	(7"m) *(7FAT 002)* **ALL YOU NEED IS LOVE WAS NOT TRUE. / KYORO / CLOSE**		-
Mar 02.	(cd) *(<FATSP 03>)* **TOMORROW NEVER COMES**		
	– Kyoro / Goodbye for all / Symmetry / All you need is love was not true / Suzu / I drew a picture of myself / Under a clown / Amaryllis / You died in the sea / Untitled / Fatal sisters opened umbrella / Nameless song.		
Oct 02.	(m-cd) *(<FATSP 06>)* **MURDER LICENSE**		Dec02
	– Murder license / I drew a picture of my eyes / Front of you / Sakae / I.T.D.O.O.M. / Count down / Nameless song.		

YEAH YEAH YEAHS

Formed: New York City. New York, USA . . . 2000 by KAREN O, a student from Ohio who flitted to NY and subsequently met guitarist NICK ZINNER and drummer BRAIN CHASE. Dubbed the "Strokes' favourite new band" (Christ, isn't everyone!), because one of them wore a YEAH YEAH YEAHS' badge while playing on an American chatshow, this 3-piece outfit didn't deserve being introduced like that in the wake of NYC's other trendy garage rockers. However, if one could describe the sound of O and her cohorts, it would most likely include a ROYAL TRUX's rock-out sludginess and POLLY JEAN HARVEY's precise eroticism mixed with garage guts and slut-chic. After a handful of support gigs with the likes of The WHITE STRIPES and BOSS HOG, they recorded and issued their self-titled EP in 2001, which was produced by JERRY TEEL, himself a member of BOSS HOG. After touring even more, another EP arrived on 'Touch and Go' records, entitled 'MACHINE' (in 2002), and displayed KAREN O's raw, sexually driven grind-house stompers (barely backed by only guitar and drums), which were harshly reminiscent of early BIKINI KILL, especially on screamers such as 'ART STAR' and 'BANG'. The next big thing in 2003.

KAREN O – vocals / **NICK ZINNER** – guitar / **BRIAN CHASE** – drums

		Wichita	Shifty
Apr 02.	(12"ep/cd-ep) *(WEBB 029 T/CD) <05>* **YEAH YEAH YEAHS EP**		Nov01
	– Bang / Mystery girl / Art star / Miles away / Our time. *<US re-iss. Mar02 on 'Touch & Go'; T&G 238>*		
		Wichita	Touch & Go
Nov 02.	(7"ep/cd-ep) *(WEBB 036 S/CD) <T&G 244>* **MACHINE EP**	37	
	– Machine / Graveyard / Pin (remix).		

James YORKSTON (& THE ATHLETES)

Born: Kingsbarns, Fife, Scotland. YORKSTON began his musical explorations at the tender age of eight when he made his own musical entertainment with a pal named MIKE. Influenced by the songwriting talents of such eclectic artists as ANNE BRIGGS and The BHUNDU BOYS, YORKSTON flitted to Edinburgh with his girlfriend (when they were seventeen). He remained a vital part of the city's music scene supporting such acts as BERT JANSCH and JOHN MARTYN (the latter eventually invited him on a 30-date support tour) as well as joining noisekins HUCKLEBERRY. He eventually left the group ("I was going deaf . . .", he commented) to pursue his own adventures in Hi-Fi, finally accumulating in a demo tape which was passed through industry hands until it landed on the desk of seminal radio DJ John Peel. The man played selected tracks from the tape live on air, which resulted in 'Bad Jazz' issuing the single 'MOVING UP COUNTRY / ROARING THE GOSPEL' (split with Scottish cult hero LONE PIGEON) to critical acclaim. Folky and very hushed, YORKSTON had a lot in common with fellow Scots APPENDIX OUT, with band members FAISAL, REUBEN, DOUGIE, SUN-LI and HOLLY exemplifying the WILL OLDHAM/PALACE factor. A proper signing with 'Domino' was on the cards, with himself and The ATHLETES issuing seminal 'THE LANG TOUN' single in 2002, complete with a complementary remix by none other than KEIRAN HEBDEN (of FOUR TET). 'ST. PATRICK' was issued months later as a warm-up to his debut set 'MOVING UP COUNTRY' (2002), a placid and very emotive introduction. Contained within were the aforementioned singles as well as a few surprises that thwarted the notion that YORKSTON was just another "Scottish folk singer".

Album rating: MOVING UP COUNTRY (*8)

JAMES YORKSTON – vocals, acoustic guitar (ex-HUCKLEBERRY) / **DOUGIE** – bass / **FAISAL** – drums / **RUEBEN** – harmonium, piano / **SUN LI** – violin / **HOLLY** – mandolin, pipes, whistles

		Bad Jazz	not iss.
Jan 01.	(7"m) *(BEBOP 21)* **MOVING UP COUNTRY. / ROARING THE GOSPEL / ARE YOU COMING HOME TONIGHT?**		-
Jan 02.	(7") *(BEBOP 33)* **ST. PATRICK. / (other by LONE PIGEON)**		-
		Domino	Domino
Mar 02.	(10") *(RUG 136T)* **THE LANG TOUN. / THE LANG TOUN (Four Tet remix)**		-

James YORKSTON (& THE ATHLETES) (cont)

May 02. (10") (RUG 141T) **ST. PATRICK. / ST. PATRICK (Vitus mix)**
(cd-s+=) (RUG 141CD) – Catching eyes / Blue Madonna's.
Jun 02. (cd/lp) (<WIG CD/LP 107>) **MOVING UP COUNTRY**
– In your hands / St. Patrick / Sweet Jesus / Tender to the blues / Moving up country / Cheating the game / I spy dogs / 6:30 is way too early / Patient song / I know my love.
Sep 02. (10"/cd-s) (RUG 145 T/CD) **TENDER TO THE BLUES. / 6:30 (Reuben's string mix) / A MAN WITH MY SKILLS / HARES ON THE MOUNTAIN; OLD MAID**

YOU AM I

Formed: Sydney, Australia . . . 1989 by TIM ROGERS, his brother JAIMMIE, along with NICK TISCHLER. A few years year, JAIMMIE was substituted by MARK TUNALEY, ROGERS being the only original remaining when ANDY KENT replaced TISCHLER; two EP's ('SNAKETIDE' and 'GODAMN') having already hit the independent shops. 'SOUND AS EVER' proceeded the excellent 1994 single 'BERLIN CHAIR' when it was released on a small independent Australian label. After SONIC YOUTH's LEE RANALDO produced the ensemble's fourth EP, 'COPROLALIA', success in America began to surface and 'Warner Bros' (home to the FLAMING LIPS) re-issued their debut album before releasing 'HI-FI WAY' in 1996. The sophomore set delivered some of the best SONIC YOUTH/VELVET UNDERGROUND-esque tracks in recent years, with YOU AM I mixing in their own blend of aggressive rock and ballads only the PIXIES could achieve before them. A large US tour got the group busy until the following year when they retreated back into the studio, this time attempting to repeat the formula by recording the mellow, mod-influenced 'HOURLY DAILY' (1997). Their most uncompromising album to date, ' . . . #4 RECORD', subsequently followed it in 1998, clashing with the sound of another popular group The LILYS, who seemed to have incorporated their style somewhat. YOU AM I have since released two further studio sets, the impressive 'DRESS ME SLOWLY' (2001) and 'DELIVERANCE' (2002), the latter replacing HITCHCOCK with BRUCE HAYMES.

Album rating: SNAKE TIDE mini (*5) / SOUND AS EVER (*6) / HI FI WAY (*7) / HOURLY DAILY (*6) / YOU AM I'S #4 RECORD (*5) / SATURDAY NIGHT AROUND TEN (*5) / DRESS ME SLOWLY (*6) / DELIVERANCE (*5)

TIM ROGERS – vocals, guitar, organ / **NICK TISCHLER** – bass, vocals / **MARK TUNALEY** – drums; repl. JAIMME ROGERS

Survival / not iss.

Jul 92. (m-cd) (SUR 522CD) **SNAKE TIDE**
– High chair / Burn to stay / Shame / Crazy you is / White and skinny / Drink it dry / New face / Conscience / Snake tide.
Dec 92. (cd-ep) **GODAMN EP** — / — Austra

—— **ANDY KENT** – bass; repl. TISCHLER

not iss. / RooArt

Sep 93. (cd-ep) <2550> **COPROLALIA EP**
– Cool hand Luke / Last thing you can depend on / Can't get started / In case you're wandering / Embarrassed.

not iss. / Restless

Oct 94. (cd-s) <72791> **BERLIN CHAIR / CAN'T EXPLAIN / JAIMME (makers mark version) / ALL I WANT TO DO IS ROCK**
Oct 94. (cd) <72795> **SOUND AS EVER**
– Coprolalia / Berlin chair / Trainspottin' / Adam's ribs / Rosedale / Forever and easy / Everyone's to blame / Jaimmie's got a gal / Who's leaving you now? / Ordinary / You scare me / Sound as ever. <re-iss. Jul95 on 'Warners'; 45936>

—— **RUSSELL HOPKINSON** – drums, percussion; repl. TUNALEY

Warners / Warners

Apr 96. (cd) <46078> **HI FI WAY**
– Ain't gone and open / Minor Byrd / She digs her / Cathy's clown / Jewels and bullets / Purple sneakers / Pizza guy / Applecross wing commander / Stray / Handwasher / Punkarella / Ken (the mother nature's son) / Gray / How much is enough?

—— added **GREG HITCHCOCK** – brass

Feb 97. (cd) <(9362 46520)> **HOURLY DAILY**
– Hourly, daily / Good mournin' / Mr. Milk / Soldiers / Trike / Tuesday / Opportunities / If we can't get it together / Flag fall $1.80 / Wally raffles / Heavy comfort / Dead letter chours / Baby clothes / Please don't ask me to smile / Who takes who home.
Mar 97. (c-s) (W 0395C) **GOOD MOURNIN' / I'LL MAKE YOU HAPPY**
(cd-s+=) (W 0395CD) – (You must fight to live) On the planet of the apes.
Jun 97. (c-s/cd-s) (W 0400 C/CD) **MR. MILK / SIX**
Feb 98. (cd-s) (55994-2) **WHAT I DON'T KNOW 'BOUT YOU / YOU WANT IT SO BAD / CATHY'S CLOWN (live) / THE APPLE CROSS WING COMMANDER (live)**
Apr 98. (cd/c) (9362 46875-2/-4) **YOU AM I'S #4 RECORD**
– Junk / Cream & the crock / What I don't know 'bout you / Fifteen / Top of the morn' & slip of the day / Billy / Come home wit' me / Heavy heart / Rumble / Guys, girls, guitars / Plans / . . . And vandalism. (UK cd re-iss. Jul00 on 'Roo Art'; 74321 57699-2)

Roo Art / Roo Art

Jun 98. (cd-s) (74321 57892-2) **RUMBLE / ARSE-KICKIN' LADY FROM THE NORTH-WEST / I LIVE UNDER THE FLIGHT PATH**
Aug 98. (cd-ep) (74321 60550-2) **HEAVY HEART / WHAT I DON'T KNOW ABOUT YOU / MIDNIGHT TO SIX MAN / SHE'S SO FINE**
Jan 00. (cd) (74321 70136-2) **SATURDAY NIGHT AROUND TEN (live)**
– Arse kickin' lady from the northwest / Mr Milk / Jamie's got a gal / Stray / Gasoline

for two / Fifteen / Berlin chair / Junk / Minor Byrd / Heavy heart / Round ten / Purple sneakers / Cathy's clown / Rumble / TRike / How much is enough / Ramblin' rose.
Jul 01. (cd) <(74321 84768-2)> **DRESS ME SLOWLY**
– Judge Roy / Get up / Beautiful girl / Damage / Doug Sahm / Watcha doin' to me / Satisfied mind / Bring some sun back / Weeds / Gone, gone, gone / Sugar / Kick a hole in the sky / End o' the line.

—— **BRUCE HAYMES** – organ, piano; repl. HITCHCOCK

Sep 02. (cd) <74321 95761-2> **DELIVERANCE**
– Words of sadness / Who put the devil in you / 'Til the clouds roll away / Ribbons and bows / Deliverance / One trick pony / The wrong side now / Nifty lil' number like you / City lights / Crash / Nuthin's ever gone be the same again / When you know what you want.

YOU FANTASTIC! (see under ⇒ DAZZLING KILLMEN)

YOUNG & SEXY

Formed: Vancouver, British Columbia, Canada . . . 1993 by former lovers PAUL HIXON PITTMAN and LUCY BRAIN together with RON 'FRANKIE' TEARDROP, TEDDY BOIS and ANDRE LAGACE. Signed to the hip'n'happening 'Mint Records', the group's lovingly crafted, alluringly melodic music bracketed them perfectly with the label's roster of winsome pop dreamers. The widely acclaimed 'STAND UP FOR YOUR MOTHER' (2002) revealed PITTMAN's incurable BEATLES fixation and wry way with a lyric, not to mention BRAIN's luxuriant harmonies, all vital ingredients in YOUNG & SEXY's musical make-up bag.

Album rating: STAND UP FOR YOUR MOTHER (*7)

PAUL HIXON PITTMAN – vocals, acoustic guitar / **LUCY BRAIN** – vocals / **ANDRE LAGACE** – bass, guitar; repl. COLIN McLAINE / **TEDDY BOIS** – keyboards / **RON "FRANKIE" TEARDROP** (b. Austria) – drums

Mint / Mint

Jun 02. (cd) <(MRD 058)> **STAND UP FOR YOUR MOTHER** / Mar02
– Stand up for your mother / Chikubi / The city you live in is ugly / Silent film star / Lies, ties and battlefields / Better / Scott / Car bought for a son / Last year's hopes / Television / Take what you got / Bobby baby.

YOUNGER YOUNGER 28'S

Formed: London, England . . . 1998 by ex-cabaret player JOE NORTHERN, wedding keyboardist G.I. JIMMY D and vocalists LIZ THOMAS and ANDIE PAGE. Winning that year's Battle Of The Bands competition at 'In the City', 'V2' records had the 4-piece snapped up in an instant, releasing their first single, 'WE'RE GOING OUT', in 1999. Heavily relying on a vast ad campaign, the platter saw the band gain credit from fellow bands, radio stations and music journalists, who heralded the cheesey electronica/indie pop act as a unique PULP alternative. Quite frankly, the quartet could sound at times like a bad karaoke nightmare that not even your gran would hire to play at her retirement party, although many could see the tongue-in-cheek appeal. Phoney synths, out of key SHAMPOO-esque singing, awful keyboards and playful lyrics were all apparent on their next 45 which, BILLIE, if she was given the chance, could probably do much better. CURE fans were not enthralled when the group chose to cover their 'INBETWEENDAYS' early in 2000; it certainly didn't help sales of their inaugural album, 'SOAP'.

Album rating: SOAP (*4)

JOE NORTHERN – guitar / **G.I. JIMMY D** – keyboards / **LIZ THOMAS** – vocals / **ANDIE PAGE** – vocals

internet / not iss.

Feb 99. (ltd-7") (none) **LIPSTICK, CIGARETTES, PACKET OF THREE. / (untitled)**

V2 / not iss.

May 99. (7"pink) (VVR 500694-7) **WE'RE GOING OUT. / VALERIE** 61
(cd-s+=) (VVR 500694-3) – Married man.
(cd-s) (VVR 500764-3) – ('A'side) / (2-'A'-Mint Royale mixes).
Oct 99. (7"yellow) (VVR 500847-7) **NEXT BIG THING. / GINGER DETERMINATION**
(cd-s+=) (VVR 500847-3) – Karaoke queen.
(cd-s) (VVR 500847-8) – ('A'side) / (2-'A'-D-Bop mixes).
Feb 00. (7") (VVR 500931-7) **INBETWEENDAYS. / SUGAR SWEET DREAMS**
(cd-s+=) (VVR 500931-3) – Two timer (crap in bed).
(cd-s) (VVR 501207-3) – ('A'side) / Psychoworld / We want a man.
Mar 00. (cd) (VVR 100836-2) **SOAP**
– Sugar sweet dreams / Next big thing / We nearly made it / First love / Julie / We're going out / Dirty Harry / Teenage mum / Gary / Valerie / No more yesterdays / In between days.

—— the group disappeared after above

Richard YOUNGS

Born: early 1970's, England. RICHARD YOUNGS is easily one of the most experimental and prolific artists to have emerged in Scotland during the 90's. His jazzy avant-garde variations of well-crafted and lengthy musical landscapes were first unearthed in 1990 on a self-distributed LP, 'ADVENT'. From this humble beginning, the singer/songwriter, pianist, multi-instrumentalist went on to collaborate with SIMON WICKHAM-SMITH on over a dozen sets culminating with 1999's WYATT/OLDHAM meets

Richard YOUNGS (cont)

HAMMILL/VAN DER GRAAF offering, 'METALLIC SONATAS'. Prior to this (and not including more collabs with BRIAN LAVELLE), solo RICHARD was at his most creative courtesy of the gorgeous and weepy 'SAPPHIE' (1998). Originally issued for 'Oblique' records, the 37-minute/3-song set saw light of day again in 2000 as his first release for Bloomington, Indiana label, 'Jagjaguwar'. YOUNGS returned to his Edinburgh stamping ground for New Year 2001 and performed several gigs (on a stool) to promote his umpteenth set, 'MAKING PAPER'. Kicking off with the 19-minute 'WARRIORS' track, it was clear RICHARD's avant-meets-Prog affiliations were heralding the start of something new. This was even clearer come the songsmith's next set, 'MAY' (2002). A desolate, sparse collection of sweet folk songs, YOUNGS knew his practices well, with his NICK DRAKE/NIC JONES-esque beauty mixed in with his avant-guitar doodlings. Very much in the same vein as JIM O'ROURKE and others currently honing their skills in the obscure folk community, YOUNGS managed to add simple poetics into tracks such as 'NEON WINTER' and the, um, gliding 'GLIDING'. Hard to categorise, and hard to get into at first, the listener's lack of patience was quickly polarised by his eclectic arrangements and modest production skills.

Album rating (selective): ADVENT (*4) / RADIOS (*3) / FESTIVAL (*7) / SITE – REALM (*5) / RADIOS VOL.2 (*4) / RED & BLUE BEAR: OPERA (*4) / HOUSE MUSIC (*5) / SAPPHIE (*6) / MAKING PAPER (*6) / MAY (*7)

RICHARD YOUNGS – piano, vocals, guitar, multi

No Fans / not iss.

1990. (lp) <none> **ADVENT**
 – Part I / Part II / Part III. <cd-iss. Nov97 on 'Table Of The Elements'; NIOBIUM 41>
1990. (d-lp; as RICHARD YOUNGS & SIMON WICKHAM-SMITH) <none> **LAKE**
 – Pt.1:- Lake – Anti-social behaviour – Anti-social behaviour in Iceland / Pt.2:- Let them eat records – Dance: help the ages (give them a heart) / Pt.3:- Chord / Pt.4:- Bells – Redenhall – Goat. <cd-iss. Oct00 on 'V.H.F.'; VHF 52>

— in 1991, RICHARD featured on A BAND's 'Any Old Records' 7" (later – 1997 – they also released an untitled CD-album). SIMON, RICHARD, A BAND and SALIVATING REGINA issued a 7"EP for 'Baby Huey'.

not iss. / Forced Exposure

1992. (lp; as RICHARD YOUNGS & SIMON WICKHAM-SMITH) **CEAUCESCU**
1993. (lp; as NEIL / RICHARD / SIMON / STEWART) **DURIAN DURIAN**

— in 1993, YOUNGS featured on the ARTEX – A LOT set on 'Siltbreeze'
1993. (lp) <FE 035> **NEW ANGLOID SOUND**

not iss. / Insample

1994. (7") <001> **ST. HELENA. / JUNIPER**

not iss. / Fourth Dimension

1994. (7"; as RICHARD YOUNGS & SIMON WICKHAM-SMITH) **WORRIED ABOUT HEAVEN. / MUSCLES IN YOUR HEAD**
1995. (10"ep; as RICHARD YOUNGS & SIMON WICKHAM-SMITH) **444D**

not iss. / Majora

1994. (lp; as RICHARD YOUNGS & SIMON WICKHAM-SMITH) **ASTHMA & DIABETES**
1996. (lp; as RICHARD YOUNGS & SIMON WICKHAM-SMITH) **ENEDKEG**

not iss. / Slask

1994. (cd; as SIMON WICKHAM-SMITH & RICHARD YOUNGS) <SLACD 008> **KRETINMUSAK**
 (UK-iss.Jul00; same as US)

not iss. / Crank Automotive

1995. (7"; as RICHARD YOUNGS Vs. LEATHER MOLE) **DENNY. / TWECHAR**

not iss. / Ignivomous

1996. (lp; as RICHARD YOUNGS & SIMON WICKHAM-SMITH) **KNISH**

— next with **NEIL** – synthesizers

not iss. / TableOfThe Elements

Jun 96. (cd) <21> **FESTIVAL**
 – Alban stands here / Nil a.m. / Angel Petrina Bell / Nathan Rice / The sea is madness.

V.H.F. / V.H.F.

Dec 95. (lp; as RICHARD YOUNGS & MATTHEW BOWER) <VHF 20> **SITE – REALM**
Apr 96. (cd; as STEPHEN TODD & RICHARD YOUNGS) <VHF 22> **GEORGIANS**
 – Bananas 'n' muffins / Granite eye / Sixteen OO / Higher grit / Lady of Staines / Techno won ton / Hannibal / Perranuthroe / Berry.
Mar 97. (cd; as RICHARD YOUNGS & SIMON WICKHAM-SMITH) <(VHF 27)> **RED AND BLUE BEAR: OPERA**
 – 3 parts.

— in 1997/8, YOUNGS and WICKHAM-SMITH also issued 'VEIL (FOR GREG)' on 'Insignificant' imprint, plus a 7" 'THE ENIGMA OF ROTONS' for 'Hell's Half Halo'.
Apr 98. (cd; as RICHARD YOUNGS & SIMON WICKHAM-SMITH) <(VHF 35)> **PULSE OF THE ROOSTERS**
 – On a bus / Shanti deva / Up a tree / My 4-sleeve hairshirt / By the sea / Learners.

— in 1998, YOUNGS featured on ILK's CD-set 'ZENITH' for 'No Fans'
1998. (cd) <007> **HOUSE MUSIC**

— <above iss. on 'Meme'>

Feb 99. (cd; as RICHARD YOUNGS & SIMON WICKHAM-SMITH) <(VHF 40)> **METALLIC SONATAS**
 – Metallic sonatas (nos.1-15).

Jagjaguwar / Jagjaguwar

Jul 00. (cd) <(JAG 19)> **SAPPHIE** <rec.1998 for 'Oblique'>
 – Soon it will be fire / A fullness of light in your soul / The graze of days.
Feb 01. (m-cd) <(JAG 26)> **MAKING PAPER**
 – Warriors / The world is silence in your head / Only haligonian.

— note: too, that RICHARD appeared on a plethora of V/A sets/EP's
Mar 02. (cd) <(JAG 43CD)> **MAY**
 – Neon winter / Bloom of all / Trees that fall / Wynding hills of Maine / Gilding / Wynd time wynd.

BRIAN LAVELLE & RICHARD YOUNGS

— **BRIAN** – guitars, keyboards + **RICHARD**

Freek / Freek

Mar 96. (cd) <FRR 018> **RADIOS**
 – It and distribution . . . / Monstrously, in process . . . / Molecular field physicist . . . / Our thin processes . . . / Description level of forces that meagre alphabet B / That meagre alphabet B / Alphabet B / B.
Aug 96. (cd) <FRR 023> **RADIOS 2**
 – Beach / Coded Easter Cork completes visiting arrival / Rhymie has / Attractions: Place: Oval: Hock / Halls (0141) buildings / Meadow and price underground trails / Wedged prior every date / Monument / Protection courses / Estuary in 3190.
Jun 98. (3xcd-set) <(FRR 028)> **RADIOS 345**

YUME BITSU

Formed: Portland, Oregon, USA ... 1998 by guitarist/vocalist ADAM FORKNER, guitarist FRANZ PRICHARD, keyboardist ALEX BUNDY and drummer JASON ANDERSON, who also anchors indie rock band WOLF COLONEL. YUME BITSU derive their name from the Japanese for 'dream beats', their aural aesthetic from space rock and, judging by song titles like 'MOTHMEN MEET THE COUNCIL OF FROGS' and 'THE FRIGID, FRIGID, FRIGID BODY OF DR. T.J' ... from possibly smoking way too much crack. The band's sojourn into trippified cosmic grooves commenced on the 'YUME BITSU' LP (1998), a mostly instrumental release which presented the unsuspecting listener with an experimental musical mix which ran the gauntlet from arhythmic wall-of-soundcheck to sculpted, delicate, freefloating distortion. The 'GIANT SURFACE MUSIC FALLING TO EARTH LIKE JEWELS FROM THE SKY' (1999) LP blended fathomless, droning sonic Rorschach blot compositions with punchy, visceral psyche-pop tunes. Both of these first two albums were released on the 'Ba Da Bing!' label. The year 2000 then saw YUME BITSU move to 'K' records and cut their next two albums 'AUSPICIOUS WINDS' (2000 – the title refers to the Japanese High Tea ceremony, continuing their Oriental theme) and 'GOLDEN VESSYL OF SOUND' (2002). Black holes of space rock sensurround sound swirled through both albums, drawing listeners into explorations of inner and outer universes with inescapable gravity, guitars whipping and twirling lazily in their depths. '... VESSYL...' contained nine tracks, none of which bore a title. The songs in question were created out of improvisations and fragments and unstructured pieces, as opposed to being more linear, logical, straightforward pieces of work, and the band felt it wouldn't suit the album's ambience to impose titles on the compositions. Crack was obviously, once again, cheap and readily available that week. Continuing the space (cadet) theme, keyboardist BUNDY released the 'PLANETARIUM MUSIC' LP on 'K', with guitarist FORKNER also teaming up with members of LANDING to form SURFACE OF ECEON on the 'THE KING BENEATH THE MOUNTAIN' LP, which was straight-up escape velocity space rock once again.

Album rating: GIANT SURFACE MUSIC FALLING TO EARTH LIKE JEWELS FROM THE SKY (*5) / YUME BITSU (*5) / AUSPICIOUS WINDS (*6) / THE GOLDEN VESSYL OF SOUND (*5)

ADAM FORKNER – vocals, guitar (of WOLF COLONEL) / **FRANZ PRICHARD** – guitar / **ALEX BUNDY** – keyboards / **JASON ANDERSON** – drums (of WOLF COLONEL)

Bad Da Bing! / Ba Da Bing!

Oct 98. (cd) <(BING 015)> **GIANT SURFACE MUSIC FALLING TO EARTH LIKE JEWELS FROM THE SKY**
 – Of freedom and flight / The end of pain is near / Travels over seascapes / Flight of the navigator / Where fog blurs and covers, emptiness prevails.
Dec 99. (cd) <(BING 020)> **YUME BITSU**
 – Team Yume / I wait for you / Surface I / Truth / Surface II / The frigid, frigid, frigid body of Dr. T.J. Eckleberg.

K / K

Nov 00. (cd/lp) <(KLP 121 CD/V)> **AUSPICIOUS WINDS**
 – The wedding procession / Doctor trips / Sharp, twisted / Mothmen meet the council of frogs / Into the hole.
May 02. (cd) <KLP 137> **THE GOLDEN VESSYL OF SOUND**
 – Song one / Song two / Song three / Song four / Song five / Song six / Song seven / Song eight / Song nine.

Planaria / not iss.

Aug 02. (lp) (PR 015LP) **DRYYSTONIAN DREAMSCAPES / Andrew Rieger: TENTACLES**

— (ANDREW RIEGER was of ELF POWER)

YUMMY FUR

Formed: Glasgow, Scotland ... 1994 by JOHN McKEOWN, MARK GIBBONS, BRIAN McDOUGALL, MARK LEIGHTON and PAUL THOMPSON; the sound of young Scotland a decade or so on from the 'Postcard' era. The YUMMY FUR took off in their frantic world of Sci-Fi pop (KRAFTWERK meeting ENO/ROXY MUSIC comes to mind) via the excellent Peel/Lamacq fave, '...THUS, A POLITICAL RECORD' single/EP. Moving from Newcastle-based 'Slampt Underground' to London's 'Guided Missile', the quirky quartet issued the excellent follow-up 45, 'KODAK NANCY EUROPE' in 1995, while a third label, the Glasgow-run 'Vesuvius' also had the YUMMY's on their books. Choosing to write 1-minute bites instead of the more conventional 2-3 minute tracks, the prolific group delivered a succession of singles and a handful of albums including three for 'Guided...', 'NIGHT CLUB' (1996), the 60-track(!) 'KINKY CINEMA' (1997) and 'SEXY WORLD' (1998). Meanwhile, 'Vesuvius' also got into the game by releasing the mini-set, 'MALE SHADOW AT 3 O'CLOCK', arguably their best work to date under one fur-lined roof. Towards the end of '98, they had become a bit more electronic and even shared a single with THE KARELIA, EL HOMBRE TRAJEADO and MOGWAI; one of the band is now in ska-Punks the AMPHETAMEANIES.

Album rating: NIGHT CLUB (*6) / KINKY CINEMA (*4) / MALE SHADOW AT 3 O'CLOCK mini (*6) / SEXY WORLD (*5)

JOHN McKEOWN – vocals, guitar / **BRIAN McDOUGALL** – guitar / **MARK GIBBONS** – keyboards / **MARK LEIGHTON** – bass / **PAUL THOMPSON** – drums, machine

                                                  Slampt Underground / not iss.

Feb 95. (7"ep) *(SLAMPT 27)* **MUSIC BY WALT DISNEY BUT PLAYED BY YURI GAGARIN – THUS A POLITICAL RECORD**
– Goosebump / + 9

                                           Guided Missile / not iss.

Jul 95. (7"ep) *(GUIDE 6)* **KODAK NANCY EUROPE**
– Documentary of a kid / Amelia Scoptophilia / The creplica / Xplosion / Tracy Katz / Car park / Male slut / Everything's turning to plastic / British sounds / The Candy Darling show.

Sep 96. (cd) *(GUIDE 10CD)* **NIGHT CLUB**
– Plastic cowboy / Prole birthday / Kirsty Cooper / Theme from Ultrabra / Films / Chelovek / Republic of Salo / Rollerderby / Theoretically pink / Kodak Nancy Europe / Carry on nurse / I am a 'cosmetic man' / Roxy girls / Klaxxon education film / Exact copy of H. Friendly / Sergeant jumper / Chines bookie. *(lp-iss.on 'Slampt Underground'; SLAMPT 43)*

Dec 96. (7"m) *(GUIDE 12)* **PLASTIC COWBOY. / FLAPPY CLOWN DISCO / CHINESE BOOKIE**

Jan 97. (7") *(POMP 008)* **SUPERMARKET. / THE CAREER SAVER**
(above on 'Vesuvius')

Mar 97. (7") *(GUIDE 13)* **POLICEMAN. / 70'S CAR CRASH**

Sep 97. (7") *(ROX 001)* **STEREO GIRLS. / ALWAYS CRASHING IN THE SAME CAR**
(above issued on 'Roxy' label)

Sep 97. (cd) *(GUIDE 22CD)* **KINKY CINEMA**
– Documentary of a kid / Amelia Scoptophilia / The replica / Xplosion / Tracy Katz / Car park / Male slut / Everything's turning to plastic / British sounds / The Candy Darling show / Goosebump / Frankenstein a go-go / Mondo coyote / Ice cream van / British children on smack / Hong Kong in stereo / Independent pop song / Popcorn / The Walt Disney murder club / 90's / Shrinky-dinc / Cosmonauts and carbonauts / Gimme cigarettes / Policemanoid / The optical meat dress / Gimmick / Pop art documentary / Found a girlfriend / Plastic cowboy (new wave) / Father Ubu repents / Vanilla Minelli / Fiery Jack / Car smash / Kodak Nancy Euro '96 / I am consumer man / The dummy / Liliput / Monophonic yum yum / Flappy clown Garry / Prostitutes / Cabaret punks / Escape from Oz / Mao Tse-Tung / Eyeball popping madness / Yummy Fur vs The Stooges / The monotony song / The yummy tummy / Bugs Bunny / Pink pop girls / Discord / Shaggy / Amphetamine education movie / Our peppermint scene / Candy Clark / Super 8 recording / Actress / Theoretically blue / Saturday night Mo-Mo / Phoning the Fundus / Brian at the gates of dawn.

Feb 98. (m-lp/m-cd) *(POMP 012/+CD)* **MALE SHADOW AT 3 O'CLOCK**
– St. John of the cross / Catholic / Department / Colonel Blimp / The Canadian flag / Vacuum cleaner.
(above issued on 'Vesuvius')

Jun 98. (7") *(SHaG 13.08)* **Club Beatroot Part Eight**
– This is Andrew Sinclair / (other track by OLYMPIA)
(above in conjunction with 'Flotsam & Jetsam' & 'The 13th Note')

Jun 98. (ltd-7") *(GUIDE 29)* **SHOOT THE RIDICULANT. / SHOOT THE RIDICULANT (part 2)**

Nov 98. (cd/lp) *(GUIDE 32 CD/LP)* **SEXY WORLD**
– Sexy world / Playboy Japan (1971) / In the company of women / British eyeballs Ltd. / Cryptdang / Analogue people / 50 million bees / Deathclub / Fantastic legs / 801 / The ballad of Piggy Wings / Young pop things / Shoot the ridiculant.

— also in Nov'98, the track 'SHIVERS' featured on the 'GLASGOW' V/A EP along with EL HOMBRE TRAJEADO, MOGWAI and the KARELIA

YUM-YUM (see under ⇒ HOLMES, Chris)

Yukio YUNG

Born: TERRY BURROWS, 14 Jan'63, Ipswich, England. A self-taught multi-instrumentalist with a fondness for classic 60's psychedelia, this computer incredibly prolific computer whizz began releasing records in the mid-80's via his own 'Hamster' imprint. The JUNG ANALYSTS – who released 'THE WISHING BALLOONS' in '84 – was to be the first of many pseudonyms BURROWS would use throughout his chequered career. Through the late 80's, he also worked with ALAN JENKINS and MARTIN HOWELLS as The CHRYSANTHEMUMS, as part of which he began assuming the stage name YUKIO YUNG. When the band split in 1991, BURROWS retained the name for his first full-length solo release (he'd previously issued the mini-set, 'EXCREMENT', in 1989), 'TREE-CLIMBING GOATS' (1992). Follow-up effort, 'ART POP STUPIDITY' (1993) was a cut'n'paste effort constructed solely out of samples yet artistically miles from the kind of electronica which would come to the fore in the mid to late 90's. YUNG was more concerned with crafting clever homages to his musical heroes than exploring the limits of sound yet his sampledelic creations were exquisitely executed nonetheless. Even the covers were expertly crafted: 'LOOK AT ME I'M YOU' by underrated 60's psych act, Blossom Toes and a fond reading of E.L.O.'s 'MR. BLUE SKY'. The latter appeared in slightly different form on the following year's 5-track tribute, 'JEFF LYNNE'. Also featuring 'XANADU', '10538 OVERTURE', 'LIVIN' THING' and 'END OF THE ROAD', the EP revealed the extent of the man's LYNNE fetish yet reinvented the songs rather than blindly parroting them. More cover strangeness followed with the B-side of the 'KEEP THE BLACK FLAG FLYING' single; the bizarre 'RESERVOIR GIRLS (YUKIO'S DREAM)' was an operatically themed tribute to the film of the same name spliced with the Ray, Goodman and Brown chestnut, 'GIRLS'. The German-issued EP's, 'GOODBYE PORK-PIE BRAIN' and 'HELLO PULSING VEIN' followed in '95 while the Suffolk maverick also worked with R. STEVIE MOORE on 1995's 'OBJECTIVITY' EP. Alongside YUNG's versions of his favourite MOORE songs, he put in a fine reading of Robert Wyatt's 'GOD SONG'. The following year, along with HOWELLS, he re-activated his old band under the slightly altered moniker of CHRYS&THEMUMS.

Album rating: EXCREMENT (*4) / TREE-CLIMBING GOATS (*4) / ART POP STUPIDITY (*5) / A BRAINLESS DECONSTRUCTION OF THE POPULAR SONG (*4)

YUKIO YUNG – vocals, instruments

                                    Logical Fish / not iss.

Mar 89. (m-lp) *(LOGICAL 3)* **EXCREMENT**

                                    not iss. / Little Teddy

1992. (lp) **TREE-CLIMBING GOATS**

1993. (lp) *<LITE 002>* **ART POP STUPIDITY**
– Jimmy Pursey / See you Tuesday / Intercourse with Barbara Steele / His problem's boring me / Look at me, I'm you / Perfectly human, thank you / A big dead man / Not, in fact, the time / Old dickhead is back / Deconstruction 1-2-3 / Big binoculars / No one went to Heaven / Mr. Blue Sky / It's so mysterious.

1993. (cd) **A BRAINLESS DECONSTRUCTION OF THE POPULAR SONG**
(above issued on 'Mermaid')

1994. (7"ep) *<LITE 715>* **JEFF LYNNE**
– Mr. Blue Sky / Xanadu / 10538 overture / Livin' thing / End of the road.

1994. (7") **KEEP THE BLACK FLAG FLYING. / RESERVOIR GIRLS (YUKIO'S DREAM #6)**

                                    Pink / not iss.

1995. (10"ep) **GOODBYE PORK-PIE BRAIN** — German
1995. (10"ep) **HELLO PULSING VEIN** — German
1995. (cd-ep) **(MOSTLY) WATER** — German

— next with **R. STEVIE MOORE**

1995. (cd-ep) **OBJECTIVITY** — German

— after a couple of collaborations, BURROWS teamed up once again to re-form CHRYS&THEMUMS

ZABRINSKI

Formed: Carmarthen, Wales ... late 90's by school friends MATTHEW DURBRIDGE (vocals/guitar), IWAN MORGAN (electronica/keyboards) and GARETH RICHARDSON (guitar); they relocated to Cardiff where they were joined by RHUN LENNY (bass) and OWAIN JONES (drums). Their 2000 self-released debut album 'SCREEN MEMORIES' led to a record deal with 'Ankst', and radio sessions for John Peel. ZABRINSKI's electro-psychedelic pop was now reaching a consistently wider audience – assisted further by supporting GORKY'S ZYGOTIC MYNCI on their UK tour of 2001. Indeed, ZABRINSKI have naturally been compared to fellow Welsh acts like GORKY'S and the SUPER FURRY ANIMALS, although their youthfully nonchalant attitude is very much their own. Their widely-acclaimed second LP 'YETI' soon followed, and marked a positive progression in their sound, courtesy of a winning blend of rock guitars and electronics. Considered their finest yet, 2002's 'KOALA KO-ORDINATION', with tracks like the epic 'RELEASE THE HOUNDS' and the brooding 'BLEN', affirmed ZABRINSKI as one of the UK's most promising and gifted bands.

Album rating: SCREEN MEMORIES (*7) / YETI (*8) / KOALA KO-ORDINATION (*8)

MATTHEW DURBRIDGE – vocals, guitar / **GARETH RICHARDSON** – guitar / **IWAN MORGAN** – electronics, keyboards / **RHUN LENNY** – bass / **OWAIN JONES** – drums

			Microgram	not iss.
Dec 00.	(cd)	*(MICRO 001)* **SCREEN MEMORIES**		-

– You'll find out / Apoplexy now / Absence makes the mind wander / Melody made / Commandos / Mangled on my brain / Drums kill your mind / Calm the chaos (interlude) / Echoes and wells / Dusk / Breakbeat lullaby / Me Gustan let Tutankamhun / Wise babies / You'll find outro.

			Booby Trap	not iss.
Mar 01.	(cd-s)	*(BOOB 005CD)* **FREEDOM OF THE HIWAY / RATTLESNAKE ON ICE**		-
			Ankst	not iss.
Dec 01.	(cd)	*(ANKSTCD 99)* **YETI**		-

– The 100th Yeti / Freedom of the hiway / Mishi Brei / Pan pan, vino vino / 3968 / Celwyddwallt / Bullied into boxing / Download my files / Rattlesnake on ice / Where's my boat.

Nov 02. (cd) *(ANKSTCD 106)* **KOALA KO-ORDINATION**
– Blen / Koala ko-ordination / Switzerland / Pan Central / Black Forest science friction / Splenetical / Floodback / Raid the farm / I ask the questions / Plus 3 / Release the hounds.

Thalia ZEDEK (see under ⇒ COME)

ZE MALIBU KIDS (see under ⇒ REDD KROSS)

ZEN GUERRILLA

Formed: Newark, Delaware, USA ... 1990 by MARCUS DURANT, RICH MILLMAN, CARL HOME and ANDY DUVALL. Old-skooled, roughnecked rock'n'roll revivalists with an appetite for soulful, MC5-style musical invective, ZEN GUERRILLA released a couple of early EP's before an admiring JELLO BIAFRA furnished them with an 'Alternative Tentacles' album deal. 'POSITRONIC RAYGUN' (1998), together with a further couple of albums on 'Sub Pop', 'TRANCE STATES IN TONGUES' (1999) and 'SHADOWS ON THE SUN' (2001), announced the arrival of that rare commodity these days, an alternative rock band whose influences stretched back further than the early 90's. More importantly perhaps, their musical reach encompassed both black and white musical heritage without differentiating between the two, dredging up dirty blues, earthen funk, primitive metal and even gospel. • **Covered:** IF 6 WAS 9 (Jimi Hendrix) / NILE SONG (Pink Floyd) / EMPTY HEART (Rolling Stones) / MOONAGE DAYDREAM (David Bowie) / CHANGE IS GONNA COME (Sam Cooke) / MAMA'S LITTLE ROCKET (Little Richard) / HUNGRY WOLF (X) / THE SEEKER (Who) / THE TROOPER (Iron Maiden) / MOB RULES (Black Sabbath).

Album rating: ZEN GUERRILLA (*4) / POSITRONIC RAYGUN (*4) / TRANCE STATES IN TONGUES (*5) / SHADOWS ON THE SUN (*5)

MARCUS DURANT – vocals / **RICH MILLMAN** – guitar / **CARL HORNE** – bass / **ANDY DUVALL** – drums

			not iss.	Insect
1991.	(7")	*<INS 01>* **GET IT. / DADDY LONGLEGS**	-	
1992.	(7")	*<INS 02>* **VAMP. / DEAD GIVEAWAY**	-	
			Compulsive	Compulsive
Mar 93.	(cd)	*<(OPS 8)>* **ZEN GUERRILLA**		

– Vamp / Friction / Icy water / Platinum cat / Crawl / Solar station / If 6 was 9 / Daddy long legs.

			not iss.	Union Hall
1993.	(7")	*<none>* **PULL. / NILE SONG**	-	
1994.	(7")	*<none>* **CROW. / UNUSUAL**	-	
			not iss.	Insect
1996.	(cd-ep)	*<INS 07>* **INVISIBLE "LIFTEE" PAD**	-	

– Chicken scratch / Slip knot / Wee wee hours / Dirty jewel / Tin can / Jig-a-boo [not on re-issue]. <m-cd-iss. 1997 on 'Alternative Tentacles'+=; VIRUS 195> – GAP-TOOTH CLOWN

1997. (cd-ep) *<INS 08>* **GAP-TOOTH CLOWN** -
– Auto pilot / Crow / Lipstick / Gospel tent / Unusual.

			Alternative Tentacles	Alternative Tentacles
Sep 97.	(7")	*<VIRUS 198>* **TROUBLE SHAKE. / CHANGE IS GONNA COME**	-	
Feb 98.	(lp/cd)	*<(VIRUS 211/+CD)>* **POSITRONIC RAYGUN**		Jan98

– Saucerships to ragtime / Trouble shake / Roachman / She's radar / Tomato cup / Fingers / Empty heart / Swamp / 54 stars and stripes / Healing in the water / 2000 watts over the south side / Frequency out. *(cd re-iss. May98 on 'Lockjaw'; LJCD 009)*

			not iss.	Allied
1999.	(one-sided-7"pic-d)	*<Allied 99>* **MAMA'S LITTLE ROCKET**	-	
			Epitaph	not iss.
1999.	(7")	*(EP 1041)* **GHETTO CITY VERSION. / HUNGRY WOLF**		-
			Epitaph	Sub Pop
Sep 99.	(cd/c)	*(6571-2/-1)* *<SP 475>* **TRANCE STATES IN TONGUES**		

– Pins and needles / Slow motion rewind / Mod riot / Black-eyed boogie / Peppermint / What I got / Cold duck / Heart attack / Ghetto city version / Preacher's promise / Magpie / Moonage daydream.

Nov 00. (7") *<(SP 511)>* **THE SEEKER. / HALF STEP**
Nov 00. (7") *<(ES 7155)>* **DIRTY MILE. / HAM AND EGGS**
(above issued on 'Estrus', below on 'Safety Pin')
Dec 00. (7") *<SP 025>* **THE TROOPER. / MOB RULES**
Aug 01. (lp/cd) *<(SP 530/+CD)>* **SHADOWS ON THE SUN**
– Barbed wire / Inferno / Staring into midnight / Smoke rings / Graffiti hustle / Captain infinity / Subway transmission / Dirty mile / Evening sun / Fifth and Cecil B. / Where's my halo? / Shadows / Zombies and hobos / Fingers.

			not iss.	Flapping Jet
Dec 01.	(12"pic-d)	*<FJ 025>* **HEAVY MELLOW**	-	

– Ghetto city version / Trouble shake / Heart attack / Old floor shiver / Radio ghost.

ZEPHYRS

Formed: Edinburgh, Scotland ... late 1999 by the NICOL brothers STUART and DAVID, one-time partners in the LARRY MARSHALL FANCLUB, DOLLFUSS and INDIAN INK; DAVID was also a member of 'Narodnik' outfit, the VULTURES. With moonlighters SHALEPH O'NEILL (the PIGPEN guitarist) and drummer ROBIN JONES (from THE BETA BAND), The ZEPHYRS (taking their name from the revolutionary skateboarding team from the '70's) blew in from the East to play some local live sets. Early the following year, the brothers were joined by former POLICECAT, GORDON KILGOUR, the drummer duly augmenting the trio's studio sound for their debut set, 'IT'S OKAY NOT TO SAY ANYTHING' (2000). A celebratory live outing at the Tron – featuring MOGWAI's STUART BRAITHWAITE as guest DJ – saw The ZEPHYRS merge with JONATHAN KILGOUR (DAVID's twin), who had also set himself free from POLICECAT. A much sought-after cassette including their best-known track, 'STARGAZER', was given away to fans at the door, while subsequent tours with 'Evol' stablemates, I AM SCIENTIST, followed on that April. The aforementioned album was mostly recorded at a substation in Cowdenbeath(!), that 4-track sound working wonders on numbers such as opener 'I CAME FOR THAT'. Further session work for BBC Scotland that same April, saw the band premiere three new songs, 'MOUNT MISERY', 'SETTING SUN' and a version of the Mongers' 'LONG'. With new members STUART CAMPBELL and Bristol-born Edinburgh Uni student CAROLINE BARBER, the 6-piece ZEPHYRS re-surfaced on vinyl once again, this time with a new version of 'STARGAZER', recorded for MOGWAI's 'Rock Action' imprint. Largely overlooked by the British music press (if not the King-Tut's crowd), The ZEPHYRS bounded back with the astonishing 'WHEN THE SKY COMES DOWN IT COMES DOWN ON YOUR HEAD' (2001), a lush country-tinged ode to GRAM PARSONS and LOW, which featured guests ranging from MOJAVE 3, STEREOLAB and some time ARAB STRAP collaborator ADEL BETHEL (whose sweetened larynx made the track 'MODERN BEATS' even more poignant). Other standout tracks 'SETTING SUN' and 'PAINT YOUR HOUSE' redefined Scottish country, with its immaculate blend of wispy folk-electronica and laid-back, front-porch beats. Move over LAMBCHOP, GIANT SAND et al, there's a new kind of country in town.

Album rating: IT'S OKAY NOT TO SAY ANYTHING (*7) / WHEN THE SKY COMES DOWN IT COMES DOWN ON YOUR HEAD (*8)

STUART NICOL (b.1972, Currie, Edinburgh) – guitar, vocals / **DAVID NICOL** (b.1968, Currie) – bass, keyboards (ex-VULTURES) / **JONATHAN KILGOUR** (b.21 Oct'68, Glasgow) – vocals, guitar, squeezebox (ex-POLICECAT, ex-ROYAL BRONCO, ex-PASTELS) / **GORDON KILGOUR** (b.21 Oct'68, Glasgow) – drums, guitar, vocals (ex-POLICECAT, ex-ROYAL BRONCO, ex-MONGERS) / **STEWART CAMPBELL** (b.1974, Glasgow) – harmonica, keyboards / **CAROLINE BARBER** (b.1979, Bristol, England) – cello, keyboards

ZEPHYRS (cont)

					Evol	Evol
Mar 00.	(cd)	(<evol 10>)	**IT'S OKAY NOT TO SAY ANYTHING**			

– I came for that / The most revealing hymn / In your arms / Go-go bar / Tork – Dolphin Avenue / The first guitar / Jewish hotel / ABC / Obeyesssekere / Sunglasses – Cathedral. *(re-iss. Dec00; same)*

Mar 00. (c; ltd-freebie) (<evol 11>) **001 TO 100** – -
– Urges / Stargazer / Carpentry.

				Rock Action	not iss.
Nov 00.	(7"/cd-s)	(ROCKACT/+CD 6)	**STARGAZER. / URGES**		

				Southpaw	not iss.
Sep 01.	(lp/cd)	(PAW/+CD 002)	**WHEN THE SKY COMES DOWN IT COMES DOWN ON YOUR HEAD**		–

– The buildings aren't going anywhere / Modern beats / Mount misery / Setting sun / The green tree / Paint your house / Murder of a small man / Stargazer / Ballad of the green tree.

				Acuarela	not iss.
Jul 02.	(cd-ep)	(NOIS 24)	**THE LOVE THAT WILL GUIDE YOU BACK HOME**		–

– The love that will guide you back home / Carpentry / Obeyessekere / I came for that (Stuart Braithwaite remix).

ZOMBIES

Formed: St. Albans, England ... 1963 by ROD ARGENT, COLIN BLUNSTONE, HUGH GRUNDY and PAUL ATKINSON. In early 1964, after winning a local band competition, they signed to 'Decca' and soon had a massive worldwide hit with the classic 'SHE'S NOT THERE'. With its distinctive churning organ and portentous overtones, the single instantly marked the band out from the rest of the Brit-Beat pack, especially in America where the song climbed to No.2. The equally classy 'TELL HER NO', again reaped success across the Atlantic but strangely stiffed in the UK. Despite a fine debut album, 'BEGIN HERE' (1965) and a string of well-crafted singles, the band met with zero success in the UK and even their early success in America wasn't repeated. 'Decca' duly declined to renew their contract and they signed to 'C.B.S.' in 1967. Although The ZOMBIES split in frustration before its release, 'ODESSEY AND ORACLE' (deliberate spelling mistake!) was their masterstroke. A concept album of sorts, the record boasted an exquisitely arranged combination of sublime harmonies and jazz-inflected instrumentation, BLUNSTONE's unmistakable high vocals floating overhead. Though the album barely scraped into the top 100, it was an ironic twist of fate when the compelling 'TIME OF THE SEASON' single became an American million seller. The band reformed briefly (minus BLUNSTONE and WHITE) and released a couple of singles without success, ARGENT going on to form, funnily enough, ARGENT, while BLUNSTONE carved out a fairly successful solo career. • **Songwriters:** ARGENT-WHITE penned, except for the ubiquitous covers; GOT MY MOJO WORKING (Muddy Waters) / YOU'VE REALLY GOT A HOLD ON ME (Smokey Robinson) / ROADRUNNER (Bo Diddley) / SUMMERTIME (Gershwin) / GOIN' OUT OF MY HEAD (Little Anthony & The Imperials) / etc. • **Trivia:** Early in 1966, they made a cameo appearance in the film, 'Bunny Lake Is Missing'. They were known as the most intelligent pop group of the mid-60's, after leaving school with over fifty 'O' and 'A' levels between them.

Album rating: BEGIN HERE (*6) / ODESSEY & ORACLE (*8) / NEW WORLD (*3) / THE BEST OF THE ZOMBIES compilation (*8)

COLIN BLUNSTONE (b.24 Jun'45, Hatfield, England) – vocals / **ROD ARGENT** (b.14 Jun'45, St.Albans) – piano, keyboards, vocals / **PAUL ATKINSON** (b.19 Mar'46, Cuffley, England) – guitar / **CHRIS WHITE** (b. 7 Mar'43, Barnet, England) – bass repl. PAUL ARNOLD / **HUGH GRUNDY** (b. 6 Mar'45, Winchester, England) – drums

				Decca	Parrot
Jul 64.	(7") (F 11940) <9695>	**SHE'S NOT THERE. / YOU MAKE ME FEEL GOOD**		12	2 Oct64
Oct 64.	(7") (F 12004)	**LEAVE ME BE. / WOMAN**			–
Jan 65.	(7") (F 12072) <9723>	**TELL HER NO. / WHAT MORE CAN I DO**		42	6
Mar 65.	(7") (F 12125) <9747>	**SHE'S COMING HOME. / I MUST MOVE**			58
Apr 65.	(lp) (LK 4679) <7001>	**BEGIN HERE** <US-title 'THE ZOMBIES'>			39 Feb65

– Roadrunner / Summertime / I can't make up my mind / The way I feel inside / Work 'n' play / You've really got a hold on me / She's not there / Sticks and stones / Can't nobody love you / Woman / I don't want to know / I remember when I loved her / What more can I do / I got my mojo working. *(re-iss. Nov84; DOA 4) (re-iss. Jul86 on 'See For Miles' US version) (cd-iss. Aug92 on 'Repertoire'+=;)* – You make me feel good / Leave me be / Tell her no / She's coming home / I must move / Kind of girl / It's alright with me / Sometimes / Whenever you're ready / I love you / Is this the dream / Don't go away / Remember you / Just out of reach / Indication / How we were before / I'm going home.

Jun 65.	(7") <9769>	**I WANT YOU BACK AGAIN. / ONCE UPON A TIME**	–	95
Sep 65.	(7") (F 12225) <9786>	**WHENEVER YOU'RE READY. / I LOVE HER**		
Nov 65.	(7") (F 12296) <9821>	**IS THIS A DREAM. / DON'T GO AWAY**		Apr66
Jan 66.	(7") (F 12322) <9797>	**REMEMBER YOU. / JUST OUT OF REACH**		
Jun 66.	(7") (F 12426) <3004>	**INDICATION. / HOW WE WERE BEFORE**		
Nov 66.	(7") (F 12495)	**GOTTA GET A HOLD ON MYSELF. / THE WAY I FEEL INSIDE**		–
Mar 67.	(7") (F 12584)	**GOIN' OUT OF MY HEAD. / SHE DOES EVERYTHING FOR ME**		–

				C.B.S.	Columbia
May 67.	(7") (F 12798)	**I LOVE YOU. / THE WAY I FEEL INSIDE**			
Sep 67.	(7") (2960)	**FRIENDS OF MINE. / BEECHWOOD PARK**			
Nov 67.	(7") (3087) <44363>	**CARE OF CELL 44. / MAYBE AFTER HE'S GONE**			

(re-iss. Mar74 on 'Epic';)

– disbanded late '67; posthumous release below resurrected group in '69

				C.B.S.	Date
Apr 68.	(lp; stereo/mono) (S+/BPG 63280) <4013>	**ODYSSEY AND ORACLE**			95 Mar69

– Care of Cell 44 / A rose for Emily / Maybe after he's gone / Beechwood park / Brief candles / Hung up on a dream / Changes / I want her she wants me / This will be our year / Butcher's tale (Western Front 1914) / Friends of mine / Time of the season. *(re-iss. Dec86 on 'Razor';) (cd-iss. Aug92 on 'Repertoire'+=)* – I call you mine / She loves the way they love her / Imagine the swan / Smokey day / If it don't work out / I know she will / Don't cry for me / Walking in the sun / Conversation off Floral Street / I want you back again / Gotta get hold of myself / Goin' out of my head / She does everything for me / Nothing's changed / I could spend the day / Girl help me.

Apr 68.	(7") (3380) <1604>	**TIME OF THE SEASON. / I'LL CALL YOU MINE**		
Jul 68.	(7") <1612>	**THIS WILL BE OUR YEAR. / BUTCHERS TALE (WESTERN FRONT 1914)**		
Feb 69.	(7") <1628>	**TIME OF THE SEASON. / FRIENDS OF MINE**	–	3

ZUMPANO

Formed: Vancouver, British Columbia, Canada ... mid 90's by namesake drummer JASON ZUMPANO and his musical colleagues MICHAEL LEDWIDGE, CARL NEWMAN and STEFAN NIEMANN. Signing to NIRVANA and SPACEMEN 3 imprint 'Sub Pop', the band released the cheekily titled 'LOOK WHAT THE ROOKIE DID' in 1995, giving host to a celebrated and catchy debut. 60's influence infected this amusing, post-pop creation which included such gems as 'I DIG YOU' and the WEBB cover 'ROSECRANS BOULEVARD'. The ZOMBIES veil was, however, torn when the guitar-pop combo delivered a soft and melodic second set, 'GOIN' THROUGH CHANGES' (1996), which resembled something like The RADAR BROS or SPAIN more than their key inspirators CHEAP TRICK and BRIAN WILSON. The album paced through like a tortoise with nowhere special to go, releasing hope for a band that may find themselves dodging in and out of the lo-fi circle in the foreseeable future. With ZUMPANO out of the way, CARL opted for a fresh approach via indie rock supergroup, The NEW PORNOGRAPHERS. Together with DAN BEJAR (of DESTROYER), JOHN COLLINS (of THEE EVAPORATORS), TODD FANCEY, KURT DAHLEARE (of LIMBLIFTER) and vocalist NEKO CASE, they delivered the glam/power-pop set, 'MASS ROMANTIC' (2000).

Album rating: LOOK WHAT THE ROOKIE DID (*7) / GOIN' THROUGH CHANGES (*5) / New Pornographers: MASS ROMANTIC (*6)

CARL NEWMAN – vocals, guitar / **MICHAEL LEDWIDGE** – keyboards, guitar / **STEFAN NIEMANN** – bass, guitar / **JASON ZUMPANO** – drums

				Sub Pop	Sup Pop
Jan 95.	(lp/c/cd) (SP/+MC/CD 140-344) <SP 277>	**LOOK WHAT THE ROOKIE DID**			

– Party rages on / Oh that Atkinson girl / Rosecrans boulevard / Platinum is best served cold / Evil black magic / Temptation / I dig you / Wraparound shades / Snowflakes & heartaches / Jeez Louise / (She's a) Full-bloodied Sicilian.

Sep 96.	(cd) <(SPCD 372)>	**GOIN' THROUGH CHANGES**		

– Behind the beehive / Broca's ways / Throwing stars / Here's the plan / Only reason under the sun / Millionaire poets / Let's fight / It doesn't take a genius / Sylvia hotel / Momentum / Angel with the good news / Some sun.

– split after above; LEDWIDGE joined NEAR CASTLEGAR who released one mini-CD, 'IN JANUARY'.

NEW PORNOGRAPHERS

CARL NEWMAN – vocals, guitar / **JOHN COLLINS** – bass (of THEE EVAPORATORS) / **DAN BEJAR** – vocals (of DESTROYER) / **KURT DAHLEARE** – drums (ex-LIMBLIFTER) repl. FISHER ROSE / **TODD FANCEY** – guitar / + **NEKO CASE** – vocals

				Mint	Mint
Nov 00.	(cd) <(MRD 043)>	**MASS ROMANTIC**			

– Mass romantic / The fake headlines / The slow descent into alcoholism / Mystery hours / Jackie / Letter from an occupant / To wild homes / The body says no / Execution day / Centre for holy wars / The Mary Martin show / Breakin' the law.

ZUZU'S PETALS

Formed: Minneapolis, Minnesota, USA ... 1990 by songwriters COLEEN ELWOOD and LAURIE LINDEEN, the all-girl trio being completed by drummer VICKIE BARNES who was substituted by LINDA PITMON after one single. A further 45, 'HOW LONG' (for Shimmy Disc offshoot, 'Kokopop') saw ZUZU'S PETALS – who at one point were competing for the ZUZU's moniker with around half a dozen other outfits – signed to 'TwinTone'. Strangely enough, licensed to 'Roadrunner' in Europe, the band's debut set, 'WHEN NO ONE'S LOOKING' (1993), revealed them to be distant cousins

ZUZU'S PETALS (cont)

of BELLY or The BREEDERS, although critics found their combination of shouty vocals and basic indie-pop difficult to pigeonhole. • **Covered:** BRAND NEW KEY (Melanie) / HUMAN BEING (New York Dolls). • **Trivia:** ZUZU'S PETALS stems from Frank Capra's great B&W movie, 'It's A Wonderful Life', as well as being the name of a poem by William Blake.

Album rating: WHEN NO ONE'S LOOKING (*5) / THE MUSIC OF YOUR LIFE (*4)

LAURIE LINDEEN – vocals, guitar / **COLEEN ELWOOD** – bass, vocals / **VICKIE BARNES** – drums

			not iss.	Susstones
Jul 90.	(7") <IMS 547> **BABBLIN' MULES. / SHIPWRECKED**	-	

─── **LINDA PITMON** – drums, percussion; repl. BARNES

		not iss.	Comm 3
Jun 91.	(7"m) <C3 3091> **JACKALS. / CATAGORIES / JOHANNE**	-	
		not iss.	Kokopop
Jun 92.	(7") <KOKO 003> **HOW LONG. / PSYCHO TAVERN**	-	
	(cd-s+=) <KOKO 003CD> – Brand new key.		

		Roadrunner	TwinTone
Feb 93.	(cd/lp) (RR 9099-2/-1) <89229> **WHEN NO ONE'S LOOKING**		Jan93

– Cinderella's daydream / God cries / Madrid / Gypsies cove / Johanne / Psycho tavern / Dork magnet / White trash love / Happy birthday / How long / Rum'n coke / Sisters / Sweat pea / Jackhals.

May 93. (12"ep/cd-ep) (RR 2384-6/-3) **CINDERELLA'S DAYDREAM / STANDING BY THE SEA. / GOD CRIES / HUMAN BEING**

Jan 95. (cd/lp) (RR 8975-2/-1) <89260> **THE MUSIC OF YOUR LIFE** Aug94
– Do not / Come true / Chatty chatty / Girl he first met / Remembering why / Don't bother / Feel like going home / Johnny / Slacks / Love bullet / Happy.

		not iss.	Delmore
Jan 95.	(7") <DE7 10> **COME TRUE. / STAR BABY**	-	

─── split after above

Index

Bold type indicates entries which were not included in the 1st edition of the book.

ITEMS WITH SHADING are The "Icons of Indie".

1

1-SPEED BIKE (see under GODSPEED YOU BLACK EMPEROR!)
13th FLOOR ELEVATORS 541
14 ICED BEARS 338
16 HORSEPOWER 973
18th DYE 724
18 WHEELER 724
100 FLOWERS (see under URINALS)
101'ERS 109
10,000 MANIACS 534

2

2 FOOT FLAME (see under MECCA NORMAL)
22 PISTEPIRKKO 1043
23 SKIDOO 549
27 VARIOUS (see under POLARA)
28th DAY (see under MANNING, Barbara)

3

3Ds 1029

5

5 STYLE 741
54•40 331

6

6THS (see under MAGNETIC FIELDS)
60 FT DOLLS 974
'68 COMEBACK (see under GIBSON BROS.)

7

7% SOLUTION 965
7 YEAR BITCH 966

8

8 EYED SPY (see under LUNCH, Lydia)
8 STOREY WINDOW 725

9

90 DAY MEN 891
999 105

A

ABBC (see under CALEXICO)
ABERDEEN 586
aBLe 586
ABLE TASMANS 191
ABSOLUTE GREY 191
ABUNAI! 586
A.C. ACOUSTICS 587
A CAMP (see under CARDIGANS)
ACCELERATORS 191
A CERTAIN RATIO 192
ACETONE 587
ACID HOUSE KINGS 587
A.C. MARIAS 193
ACT (see under LEER, Thomas)
A.C. TEMPLE 193
ACTION FIGURES 588
ACTION SWINGERS 589
ADAM & THE ANTS 3
ADAMSON, Barry 193
ADD N TO (X) 589
ADEN 589
ADORABLE 590
ADULT NET 194
ADVENTURES IN STEREO (see under SPIREA X)
ADVERTS 4
AEREOGRAMME (see under FUKUYAMA)
AERIAL-M (see under SLINT)
AFGHAN WHIGS 590
AFRAID OF MICE 194
AGE OF CHANCE 195
A HANDFUL OF DUST (see under DEAD C.)
A HOUSE 195
AINTS! (see under LAUGHINGCLOWNS)
AIRHEAD 591
AIR MIAMI (see under UNREST)
AIRPORT 5 (see under GUIDED BY VOICES)
AISLERS SET (see under HENRY'S DRESS)
ALBERTO Y LOST TRIOS PARANOIAS 5
ALCOHOL FUNNYCAR 591
ALFIE 591
ALICE DONUT 196
ALIEN CRIME SYNDICATE (see under MEICES)
ALIEN SEX FIEND 196
ALISON'S HALO 592
ALL ABOUT EVE 197
ALL NATURAL LEMON & LIME FLAVORS 592
ALMOND, Marc 198
ALPHA STONE (see under DARKSIDE)
ALTAMONT (see under PORCUPINETREE)
ALTERED IMAGES 200
ALTERNATE LEARNING (see under GAME THEORY)
ALTERNATIVE TV 5
ALUMINUM GROUP 592
ALWAYS 201
AM/FM 593
AMBITIOUS LOVERS (see under DNA)
AMELIA (see under TALULAH GOSH)
AMERICAN ANALOG SET 593
AMERICAN FOOTBALL (see under JOAN OF ARC)
AMERICAN MUSIC CLUB 201
A MINOR FOREST 593
AMNESIA (see under MEDICINE)
AMP 594
AMPHETAMEANIES 594
AMPS (see under BREEDERS)
ANASTASIA SCREAMED 595
AND ALSO THE TREES 203
ANDERSON, Laurie 6
...AND YOU WILL KNOW US BY THE TRAIL OF DEAD 595
AN EMOTIONAL FISH 595
ANGEL CORPUS CHRISTI 203
ANGELFISH (see under GOODBYE MR MACKENZIE)
ANGELICA 596
ANGELIC UPSTARTS 7
ANGELS OF LIGHT (see under SWANS)
ANGORA (see under HEART THROBS)
ANIMALS THAT SWIM 596
ANNIE CHRISTIAN 597
ANNIVERSARY 597
ANOTHER SUNNY DAY 204
ANT (see under HEFNER)
ANT, Adam (see under ADAM & THE ANTS)
ANTENNA 597
ANTIETAM 204
ANTI-GROUP (see under CLOCKDVA)
ANXIETY, Annie 204
APARTMENTS 205
APPENDIX OUT 598

APPLES (IN STEREO) 598
APPLESEED CAST 598
APPLIANCE 599
A PRIMARY INDUSTRY (see under ULTRAMARINE)
ARABESQUE / BEAUMONT (see under BLUEBOY)
ARAB STRAP 600
ARCHERS OF LOAF 600
ARCWELDER 601
A.R.E. WEAPONS 602
A.R. KANE 205
ARMOURY SHOW (see under SKIDS)
ARNOLD 602
ART & LANGUAGE (see under RED CRAYOLA)
ART ATTACKS 8
ARTERY 206
ART OBJECTS (see under BLUE AEROPLANES)
ASH 602
ASH, Daniel (see under BAUHAUS)
ASHA VIDA 603
ASHBY 603
ASHCROFT, Richard (see under VERVE)
ASHLEY PARK 603
ASHTRAY BOY 604
ASIAN DUB FOUNDATION 604
ASPERA AD ASTRA 605
ASPHALT RIBBONS (see under TINDERSTICKS)
ASSOCIATES 206
ASS PONYS 605
ASTLEY, Virginia 207
ASTRID 605
ASTRID (see under WILLIAMSON, Astrid)
ASTRO CHIMP (see under VASELINES)
ATHLETICO SPIZZ '80 (see under SPIZZ)
AT THE DRIVE-IN 606
ATTILA THE STOCKBROKER 208
AUBURN LULL 606
AUDIO LEARNING CENTER (see under POND)
AU PAIRS 208
AUTEURS 607
AUTOCLAVE (see under HELIUM)
AUTOCOLLANTS (see under WATLING, Laura)
AVANT GARDENERS 8
AVENGERS 9
AVOCADO BABY (see under MILKY WIMPSHAKE)
A WITNESS 209
AZTEC CAMERA 209
AZURE RAY 608
AZUSA PLANE 608

B

B-52's 11
BAADER-MEINHOF (see under AUTEURS)
BABES IN TOYLAND 609
BABYBIRD 610
BABYLON DANCE BAND (see under ANTIETAM)
BACHARACH, Burt 611
BACHMANN, Eric / BARRY BLACK (see under ARCHERS OF LOAF)
BACK TO THE PLANET 611
BACKWATER 611
BAD BRAINS 210
BAD DREAM FANCY DRESS (see under KING OF LUXEMBOURG)
BADLY DRAWN BOY 612
BADOWSKI, Henry 9
BAILEY, Chris (see under SAINTS)
BAILTER SPACE 211
BALANCING ACT 211
B.A.L.L. 212
BALL, Edward 9
BALLBOY 612
BAMBULE (see under CINdYTALK)
BANDIT QUEEN 613
BAND OF HOLY JOY 212
BAND OF SUSANS 213

BAND OF ... BLACKY RANCHETTE (see under GIANT SAND)
BANE, Honey (see under FATAL MICROBES)
BANGER, Ed (see under NOSEBLEEDS)
BANNED 11
BARCELONA 613
BARDO POND 613
BARDOTS 614
BAREFOOT CONTESSA 614
BARE JR. 614
BARK PSYCHOSIS 614
BARLOW, Lou (see under DINOSAUR JR.)
BARONE, Richard (see under BONGOS)
BARRACUDAS 213
BARRETT, Syd 214
BASH & POP (see under REPLACEMENTS)
BASINGER (see under CHESTERFIELDS)
BASTRO (see under SQUIRREL BAIT)
BATES, Martyn (see under EYELESS IN GAZA)
BATHERS 215
BATHGATE, Alec (see under TALL DWARFS)
BATORS, Stiv (see under DEAD BOYS)
BATS 215
BATTERSHELL 615
BAUHAUS 216
BAWL 615
BAY (see under ARAB STRAP)
BEACH BOYS 615
BEACHBUGGY 616
BEACHWOOD SPARKS 616
BEAR 617
BEASTS OF BOURBON (see under SCIENTISTS)
BEAT (see under NERVES)
BEAT HAPPENING 218
BEATLES 617
BEATNIK FILMSTARS 618
BEAT RODEO 219
BEAUMONT (see under BLUEBOY)
BECAUSE (see under FURNITURE)
BECK 619
BECKER, Pete (see under EYELESS IN GAZA)
BEDHEAD 620
BEEFEATER 220
BEEZUS 620
BEIRUT SLUMP (see under LUNCH, Lydia)
BELL, Chris 220
BELLATRIX 621
BELLE AND SEBASTIAN 621
BELLINI (see under DON CABALLERO)
BELLRAYS 622
BELLTOWER 622
BELLY 622
BELOVED 220
BENNY PROFANE (see under ROOM)
BENSON, Brendan 623
BERRY, Heidi 221
BERRYHILL, Cindy Lee 222
BETA BAND 623
BETTIE SERVEERT 624
BEULAH 624
BEVIS FROND 222
BIAFRA, Jello (see under DEAD KENNEDYS)
BIBLE 223
BICYCLE THIEF (see under THELONIOUS MONSTER)
BID (see under MONOCHROME SET)
BIFF BANG POW! (see under McGEE, Alan)
BIFFY CLYRO 624
BIF NAKED 625
BIG BLACK 224
BIG DIPPER (see under EMBARRASSMENT)
BIG FLAME 225
BIG IN JAPAN 12
BIG LEAVES 625
BIG RAY (see under STUPIDS)
BIG STAR 225
BIG'N 625
BIKERIDE 626

INDEX

BIKESHED (see under MAGNETIC NORTH POLE)
BIKINI KILL 626
BILLY MAHONIE 627
BIRDDOG 627
BIRDIE (see under EAST VILLAGE)
BIRDLAND 627
BIRD NEST ROYS 226
BIRDSONGS OF THE MESOZOIC 226
BIRTHDAY PARTY (see under CAVE, Nick)
BIS 628
BISHOPS (see under COUNT BISHOPS)
BITCH MAGNET (see under SEAM)
BITING TONGUES 227
BIVOUAC 628
BJORK 227
BLACK 229
BLACK, Frank (see under PIXIES)
BLACK BOX RECORDER (see under AUTEURS)
BLACK DICE 629
BLACK FLAG 12
BLACK GRAPE (see under HAPPY MONDAYS)
BLACK HEART PROCESSION 629
BLACK RANDY & THE METRO SQUAD 13
BLACK REBEL MOTORCYCLE CLUB 629
BLACK SWAN NETWORK (see under OLIVIA TREMOR CONTROL)
BLACK TAMBOURINE 630
BLACKTOP (see under DIRTBOMBS)
BLADE, Andy (see under EATER)
BLAGGERS I.T.A. 630
BLAKE, Karl 230
BLAKE BABIES (see under HATFIELD, Juliana)
BLAMELESS 631
BLAST OFF COUNTRY STYLE 631
BLEACH 632
BLEED 632
BLESSED ETHEL 632
BLIND MR. JONES 632
BLINK 633
BLINK-182 633
BLISTERS (see under KARELIA)
BLONDE REDHEAD 633
BLONDIE 14
BLOOD ON THE SADDLE 231
BLOOMSDAY (see under BATHERS)
BLOW UP 231
BLUE AEROPLANES 232
BLUEBEAR (see under BEATNIK FILMSTARS)
BLUEBOY 634
BLUE NILE 233
BLUE ORCHIDS 233
BLUETIP 635
BLUETONES 635
BLUMFELD 635
BLUR 636
BLURT 234
BLYTH POWER 234
B-MOVIE 235
BMX BANDITS 236
BOARDS OF CANADA 637
BOB 236
BODINES 237
BOGSHED 237
BOLAN, Marc 237
BOMB PARTY 238
BONE-BOX 638
BONE ORCHARD 239
BONFIRE MADIGAN (see under TATTLE TALE)
BONGOS 239
BONGWATER 240
BONHAM, Tracy 638
BONNEY, Simon (see under CRIME & THE CITY SOLUTION)
BONNIE 'PRINCE' BILLY (see under OLDHAM, Will)
BOOMTOWN RATS 15
BOON EXPERIENCE!, Clint (see under INSPIRAL CARPETS)
BOO RADLEYS 638
BOOTH AND THE BAD ANGEL (see under JAMES)

BOOTS FOR DANCING 240
BORED GAMES (see under STRAITJACKET FITS)
BORLAND, Adrian (see under SOUND)
BOSS HOG (see under PUSSY GALORE)
BOUQUET 639
BOURGIE BOURGIE (see under QUINN, Paul)
BOWERY ELECTRIC 639
BOWIE, David 241, 639
BOWLFISH 640
BOWS 640
BOW WOW WOW 241
BOX 242
BOXCAR RACER (see under BLINK-182)
BOXHEAD ENSEMBLE 640
BOYFRIEND 641
BOYRACER 641
BOYS 16
BOY SETS FIRE 642
BOYS NEXT DOOR (see under CAVE, Nick)
B-PEOPLE 243
BRADFORD 243
BRAGG, Billy 243
BRAID 643
BRAIN DONOR (see under COPE, Julian)
BRAINIAC 643
BRANCA, Glenn 245
BRANDON'S 10:51, Kirk (see under SPEAR OF DESTINY)
BRANDTSON 643
BRASSY 644
BRATMOBILE 644
BRAVE CAPTAIN 644
BREAKING CIRCUS (see under RIFLE SPORT)
BREATHLESS 245
BREEDERS 645
BREL, Jacques 246
BRIAN JONESTOWN MASSACRE 645
BRICK LAYER CAKE 646
BRIDESHEAD 646
BRIDEWELL TAXIS 646
BRIDGET STORM (see under THRUSH PUPPIES)
BRIGHT 647
BRIGHTER 647
BRIGHT EYES 647
BRILLIANT CORNERS 246
BRILLIANTINE (see under DAMBUILDERS)
BRINSLEY SCHWARZ 17
BRITISH SEA POWER 648
BROADCAST 648
BROCCOLI 648
BROKEN SPINDLES (see under FAINT)
BROTHER JT 649
BROWN, Ian 650
BROWN, Steven (see under TUXEDOMOON)
BRUNO, Franklin (see under NOTHING PAINTED BLUE)
BRUNTNELL, Peter 650
BUBONIQUE (see under COUGHLAN, Cathal)
BUCKLEY, Jeff 650
BUDDHA ON THE MOON 651
BUFFALO DAUGHTER 651
BUFFALO SPRINGFIELD 651
BUFFALO TOM 652
BUFF MEDWAYS (see under CHILDISH, Wild Billy)
BUILDERS/BILDERS (see under DIREEN, Bill)
BUILT TO SPILL 653
BUNNYGRUNT 653
BURGESS, Mark (see under CHAMELEONS)
BURNEL, JJ (see under STRANGLERS)
BURNING AIRLINES (see under JAWBOX)
BURNING BRIDES 654
BUSH TETRAS 247
BUSY SIGNALS 654
BUSYTOBY (see under WOLFIE)
BUTLER, Bernard 654
BUTTER 08 (see under CIBO MATTO)

BUTTERFLY CHILD 655
BUTTERGLORY 655
BUTTHOLE SURFERS 247
BUZZCOCKS 18
BYRDS 248

C

CABARET VOLTAIRE 20
CABLE 656
CADALLACA (see under SLEATER-KINNEY)
CAGNEY & LACEE (see under GALAXIE 500)
CAKE 656
CAKEKITCHEN (see under THIS KIND OF PUNISHMENT)
CAKE LIKE 656
CALE, John 22
CALEXICO 657
CALIFONE (see under RED RED MEAT)
CALL AND RESPONSE 657
CALVIN KRIME (see under SEAN NA-NA)
CAMBER 657
CAMBERWELL NOW (see under THIS HEAT)
CAMERA OBSCURA 658
CAMPAG VELOCET 658
CAMPER VAN BEETHOVEN 250
CAN 658
CANDIDATE 659
CANDYLAND 660
CANDYSKINS 660
CANE 141 661
CANNANES 251
CAPITOL CITY DUSTERS 661
CAPTAIN AMERICA (see under VASELINES)
CAPTAIN BEEFHEART 252
CAPTAIN SENSIBLE 23
CAPTAINS OF INDUSTRY (see under WRECKLESS ERIC)
CAPTAIN SOUL 661
CAP'N JAZZ (see under JOAN OF ARC)
CARDIACS 254
CARDIGANS 661
CARDINAL (see under Davies, Richard)
CARE (see under WILD SWANS)
CARETAKER RACE 255
CAROUSEL (see under RAZORCUTS)
CARPETTES 24
CARROLL, Cath 255
CARTER, Chris (see under CHRIS AND COSEY)
CARTER THE UNSTOPPABLE SEX MACHINE 662
CARTWHEEL (see under WATLING, Laura)
CASH AUDIO 663
CASINO ASHTRAYS (see under WATLING, Laura)
CASSANDRA COMPLEX 256
CAST 664
CASTAWAY STONES (see under BLACK TAMBOURINE)
CASTOR 664
CATATONIA 664
CATERAN 256
CAT HEADS 257
CATHERINE WHEEL 665
CATHETERS 666
CAT POWER 666
CAT'S MIAOW! 666
CAVE, Nick 24
C-CAT TRANCE 257
CECIL 667
CELIBATE RIFLES 257
CELL 668
CENTRO-MATIC 668
CERBERUS SHOAL 668
CERVENKA, Exene (see under X)
C. GIBBS GROUP (see under MORNING GLORIES)
CHA CHA 2000 (see under PROLAPSE)
CHA CHA COHEN 669
CHADBOURNE, Eugene 26
CHADWICK, Guy (see under HOUSE OF LOVE)

CHAINSAW KITTENS 669
CHAMBERS, Ken (see under MOVING TARGETS)
CHAMELEONS 258
CHANCE, James 27
CHAPPAQUIDDICK SKYLINE (see under PERNICE BROTHERS)
CHAPTERHOUSE 670
CHARLATANS (UK) 670
CHARLOTTES 260
CHARMING 671
CHASTAIN, Paul (see under VELVET CRUSH)
CHAVEZ 671
CHE (see under MODERN EON)
CHEAP (see under ADVERTS)
CHECK ENGINE (see under SWEEP THE LEG JOHNNY)
CHEEKY MONKEY 672
CHELSEA 28
CHEMICAL PEOPLE 260
CHEMICAL PILOT (see under McGEE, Alan)
CHESNUTT, Vic 672
CHESTERFIELDS 260
CHESTNUT STATION 672
CHEVRON, Phil (see under RADIATORS FROM SPACE)
CHICKS ON SPEED 672
CHILDISH, Wild Billy 29
CHILDREN'S HOUR (see under HEADLESS CHICKENS)
CHILLS 261
CHILTON, Alex (see under BIG STAR)
CHIMERA 673
CHINA DRUM 673
CHISEL 673
CHIXDIGGIT! 674
CHOCOLATE (see under STUPIDS)
CHOCOLATE USA 674
CHOIR INVISIBLE 262
CHOO CHOO TRAIN (see under VELVET CRUSH)
CHOU PAHROT 32
CHRIS & CARLA (see under WALKABOUTS)
CHRIS AND COSEY 262
CHROME 32
CHROME CRANKS 675
CHRYSANTHEMUMS (see under DEEP FREEZE MICE)
CHUBBIES 675
CHUG (see under LOOK BLUE GO PURPLE)
CHUMBAWAMBA 263
CHUNK (see under SUPERCHUNK)
CHURCH 264
CIAO BELLA 676
CIBO MATTO 676
CINdYTALK 267
CINEMA 676
CINERAMA (see under WEDDING PRESENT)
CINNAMON 676
CINNAMON (see under ASHLEY PARK)
CIRCULATORY SYSTEM (see under OLIVIA TREMOR CONTROL)
CIRCUS LUPUS 677
CITIZEN FISH (see under SUBHUMANS)
CLAN OF XYMOX (see under XYMOX)
CLAPP, Allen (see under ORANGE PEELS)
CLARK, Anne 267
CLARKSON, Jay 268
CLASH 34
CLASS 677
CLAW HAMMER 677
CLEAN 268
CLEANERS FROM VENUS 269
CLEARLAKE 677
CLIENTELE 678
CLINIC 678
CLINTON (see under CORNERSHOP)
CLOCKDVA 271
CLOSE LOBSTERS 272
CLOUDBERRY JAM 679
CLUB 8 (see under ACID HOUSE KINGS)
COAL PORTERS (see under LONG RYDERS)

INDEX

COAST 679
COAX (see under DENTISTS)
COBRA VERDE 679
COCKEYED GHOST 680
COCTAILS 680
COCTEAU TWINS 272
CODEINE 680
CODY 681
COHEN, Leonard 273
COIL 274
COLD COLD HEARTS (see under BRATMOBILE)
COLDPLAY 681
COLD WATER FLAT 681
COLE, Lloyd 274
COLENSO PARADE 275
COLLINS, Edwyn 276
COLORBLIND JAMES EXPERIENCE 277
COLOSSAMITE (see under DAZZLING KILLMEN)
COMBUSTIBLE EDISON 681
COME 682
COME ONS 682
COMET 683
COMET GAIN 683
COMING UP ROSES (see under DOLLY MIXTURE)
COMMANDER VENUS (see under BRIGHT EYES)
COMPOUND RED 683
COMPULSION 684
COMSAT ANGELS 278
CONDITION BLUE (see under SPARE SNARE)
CONFETTI (see under FAT TULIPS)
CONN, Bobby 684
CONTAINE (see under VERSUS)
CONTORTIONS (see under CHANCE, James)
Cooper CLARKE, John 33
COOPER TEMPLE CLAUSE 685
COPE, Julian 279
COP SHOOT COP 685
CORAL 685
CORN DOLLIES 280
CORNDOLLY 686
CORNELIUS 686
CORNERSHOP 686
CORNWALL, Hugh (see under STRANGLERS)
CORPORATION OF NOISE (see under BALL, Edward)
CORTINAS 36
COSEY FANNI TUTTI (see under CHRIS AND COSEY)
COSMIC ROUGH RIDERS 687
COSTELLO, Elvis 36
COTTON MATHER 688
COUGHLAN, Cathal 281
COUNT BISHOPS 39
COUNTRY TEASERS 688
COUNTY, Wayne/Jayne 40
COURTNEY LOVE (see under LOIS)
COUSTEAU 689
COWBOY JUNKIES 282
COWS 689
COXON, Graham (see under BLUR)
CRABS 689
CRACKER 690
CRACKNELL, Sarah (see under SAINT ETIENNE)
CRAMPS 40
CRANBERRIES 690
CRANES 691
CRASH (see under ULTRA VIVID SCENE)
CRASS 42
CRAUSE, Ian (see under DISCO INFERNO)
CRAVATS 42
CRAWLING CHAOS 283
CRAYON (see under TULLYCRAFT)
CRAZYHEAD 283
CREAMS (see under DEEP FREEZE MICE)
CREATION 692
CREATURES (see under SIOUXSIE & THE BANSHEES)
CREEPER LAGOON 692
CREEPERS (see under RILEY, Marc)
CRESCENT 693

CRIME 43
CRIME & THE CITY SOLUTION 284
CRINGER (see under J CHURCH)
CRISIS (see under DEATH IN JUNE)
CRISPY AMBULANCE 284
CROCKETTS 693
CROOK, Brian (see under RENDERERS)
CROOKED FINGERS (see under ARCHERS OF LOAF)
CROWD 285
CROWNHATE RUIN (see under HOOVER)
CROWSDELL 693
CRUCIFUCKS (see under LOUDSPEAKER)
CRUNT (see under BABES IN TOYLAND)
CUB 694
CUBAN HEELS 43
CUB COUNTRY (see under JETS TO BRAZIL)
CUCKOO (see under JETPLANE LANDING)
CUD 285
CUDDLY TOYS 43
CUL DE SAC 694
CULTURE SHOCK (see under SUBHUMANS)
CUNNINGHAM, David (see under FLYING LIZARDS)
CUNNINGHAM, John 695
CUPOL (see under WIRE)
CURE 44
CURRENT 93 286
CURSIVE 695
CURVE 696
CYNICS 286
CYRFF, y 287
CZUKAY, Holger (see under CAN)

D

D4 706
DADAMAH (see under MONTGOMERY, Roy)
D.A.F. 288
DAHLIA, Blag (see under DWARVES)
DAINTEES (see under STEPHENSON, Martin)
DAISIES (see under MEDAL)
DAISY CHAINSAW 697
DALEK I LOVE YOU 289
DALI'S CAR (see under BAUHAUS)
DALL, Cynthia 697
DAMBUILDERS 697
DAME FATE (see under TUSCADERO)
DAMNED 46
DAMON & NAOMI (see under GALAXIE 500)
DANCING DID 289
DANCING HOOD (see under SPARKLEHORSE)
DANDO, Evan (see under LEMONHEADS)
DANDY WARHOLS 698
DANGEROUS GIRLS 47
DANIELSON FAMILE 698
DANNY & DUSTY (see under GREEN ON RED)
DANSE SOCIETY 289
DARKSIDE 699
DARK STAR (see under LEVITATION)
DARLING BUDS 290
DARYLL-ANN 699
DAS DAMEN 290
DASHBOARD CONFESSIONAL 700
DATBLYGU 291
DATSUNS 700
DAVID DEVANT & HIS SPIRIT WIFE 700
DAVIES, Richard 700
DAVIS, John (see under SEBADOH; the FOLK IMPLOSION)
DAWN OF THE REPLICANTS 701
DAX, Danielle 291
DAZZLING KILLMEN 702
dB's 47
DEAD BOYS 48
DEAD C. 292
DEAD CAN DANCE 293
DEAD FAMOUS PEOPLE 294

DEAD KENNEDYS 49
DEAD MILKMEN 294
DEAF SCHOOL 50
DEAL 6000, Kelley 702
DEAR NORA 702
DEATH CAB FOR CUTIE 703
DEATHFOLK (see under GERMS)
DEATH IN JUNE 295
DEATH OF SAMANTHA (see under COBRA VERDE)
DECORATORS 296
DEEBANK, Maurice (see under FELT)
DEEP FREEZE MICE 296
DELAKOTA 703
DELGADO, Gabi (see under D.A.F.)
DELGADOS 703
DELICATESSEN 704
DELICIOUS MONSTER 704
DELMONAS (see under CHILDISH, Wild Billy)
DELTA 5 298
DELTA 72 705
DEMOLITION DOLL RODS 705
DEMON PREACHERS (see under ALIEN SEX FIEND)
DENIM (see under FELT)
DENISON / KIMBALL TRIO (see under JESUS LIZARD)
DENTISTS 298
DEPARTMENT S 299
DEPARTURE LOUNGE 705
DEPECHE MODE 299
DESAPARECIDOS (see under BRIGHT EYES)
DESC (see under KHAYA)
DESPERATE BICYCLES 51
DESTROY ALL MONSTERS 51
dEUS 705
DEUTSCHE AMERIKANISCHE FREUNDSCHAFT (see under D.A.F.)
DEUX FILLES (see under KING OF LUXEMBOURG)
DEVIANTS (see under PINK FAIRIES)
DeVILLE, Willy (see under MINK DeVILLE)
DEVILS (see under DUFFY, Stephen)
DEVINE & STATTON (see under LUDUS)
DEVO 51
DEVOTO, Howard (see under MAGAZINE)
DHARMA BUMS 706
DIAGRAM BROS (see under DISLOCATION DANCE)
DIANOGAH 706
DICKIES 52
DICKS (see under SISTER DOUBLE HAPPINESS)
DICTATORS 53
DIESELHED 707
DIFFORD & TILBROOK (see under SQUEEZE)
DIF JUZ 301
DiFRANCO, Ani 707
DIGGERS 708
DIGGLE, Steve (see under BUZZCOCKS)
DILS 54
DIMMER (see under STRAITJACKET FITS)
DIM STARS (see under HELL, Richard)
DiNIZIO, Pat (see under SMITHEREENS)
DINOSAUR JR. 302
DIODES 54
DIREEN, Bill 303
DIRTBOMBS 708
DIRTY THREE 709
DISCO INFERNO 710
DISCOUNT 710
DISKOTHI Q 710
DISLOCATION DANCE 303
DISMEMBERMENT PLAN 711
DISSOLVE (see under MONTGOMERY, Roy)
DISTRACTIONS 54
DIVINE COMEDY 711
DIVINE HORSEMEN (see under FLESH EATERS)
DIVISION OF LAURA LEE 712
DMZ 55
DNA 55
DNTEL (see under STRICTLY BALLROOM)

D.O.A. 56
DOCTORS OF MADNESS 57
DODGY 712
DOE, John (see under X)
DOG FACED HERMANS 304
DOIRON, Julie (see under ERIC'S TRIP)
DOLEFUL LIONS 713
DOLL 57
DOLL BY DOLL 57
DOLLY MIXTURE 304
DOLPHIN BROTHERS (see under JAPAN)
DO MAKE SAY THINK 713
DOME (see under WIRE)
DON CABALLERO 714
DONELLY, Tanya (see under BELLY)
DONNAS 714
DONNER PARTY 305
DONOVAN 715
DOOR AND THE WINDOW (see under ALTERNATIVE TV)
DOORS 305
DOROTHY (see under RAINCOATS)
DOS (see under MINUTEMEN)
DOUBLE HAPPYS (see under STRAITJACKET FITS)
DOVES 715
DOWNES, Graeme (see under VERLAINES)
DOWNY MILDEW 306
DRAGS 716
DRAIN (see under BUTTHOLE SURFERS)
DRAKE, Nick 716
DR CALCULUS (see under DUFFY, Stephen)
DREAM ACADEMY 307
DREAM SYNDICATE 307
DRESSY BESSY 717
DR. FRANK (see under MR. T EXPERIENCE)
DRIBBLING DARTS OF LOVE (see under SNEAKY FEELINGS)
DRIFT (see under EYELESS IN GAZA)
DRINKING ELECTRICITY 308
DRIVE LIKE JEHU (see under ROCKET FROM THE CRYPT)
DR. MIX & THE REMIX (see under METAL URBAIN)
DRONES 58
DROOGS 58
DROP NINETEENS 717
DRUGSTORE 717
DRUMS & TUBA (see under PAUL NEWMAN)
DRUNK 718
DUB NARCOTIC SOUND SYSTEM (see under BEAT HAPPENING)
DUBREQ (see under SPARE SNARE)
DUBSTAR 718
DUET EMMO (see under WIRE)
DUFFY, Stephen 308
DUKES OF STRATOSPHEAR (see under XTC)
DUMP (see under YO LA TENGO)
DURUTTI COLUMN 310
DURY, Baxter 719
DURY, Ian 59
DUSTDEVILS 311
DWARVES 311
DYLAN, Bob 312
DYLANS 719

E

E.A.R. (see under EXPERIMENTAL AUDIO RESEARCH)
EARL BRUTUS 720
EARLY DAY MINERS 720
EARWIG 720
EASTERHOUSE 313
EAST RIVER PIPE 721
EAST VILLAGE 313
EASY 721
EASYWORLD 721
EAT 314
EATER 61
ECHO & THE BUNNYMEN 314
ECHOBELLY 315
ECHOBOY 722
ECKMAN, Chris (see under WALKABOUTS)

INDEX

EDDIE & THE HOT RODS 61
EDGE, Damon (see under CHROME)
ED GEIN'S CAR 316
EGGMAN (see under BOO RADLEYS)
EGGS 723
EGGSTONE 723
**EIGHTIES MATCHBOX
B-LINE DISASTER 724**
EINSTURZENDE NEUBAUTEN 316
EITZEL, Mark (see under AMERICAN MUSIC CLUB)
ELASTICA 725
ELBOW 725
ELECTRAFIXION (see under ECHO & THE BUNNYMEN)
ELECTRASY 726
ELECTRELANE 726
ELECTRIC CHAIRS (see under COUNTY, Wayne/Jayne)
ELECTRIC COMPANY (see under MEDICINE)
ELECTRIC EELS 62
ELECTRIC SOFT PARADE 726
ELECTRIC SOUND OF JOY 727
ELECTRO GROUP 727
ELECTRONIC (see under NEW ORDER)
ELECTROSCOPE 727
ELEVENTH DREAM DAY 317
ELF POWER 727
EL HOMBRE TRAJEADO 728
ELLIS ISLAND SOUND (see under WEATHER PROPHETS)
EMBARRASSMENT 318
EMBRACE [US] 318
EMBRACE [Eng] 728
EMF 729
ENO, Brian 730
ENON 731
EPILEPTICS (see under FLUX OF PINK INDIANS)
ERASE ERRATA 731
ERICKSON, Roky (see under 13th FLOOR ELEVATORS)
ERIC'S TRIP 732
ESKA 732
ESP SUMMER (see under HIS NAME IS ALIVE)
ESSENCE 319
ESSENTIAL LOGIC (see under LOGIC, Lora)
ESSEX GREEN 733
ETERNALS (see under TRENCHMOUTH)
ETHER 733
ETHYLINE (see under SCREECHING WEASEL)
ETHYL MEATPLOW (see under GERALDINE FIBBERS)
ETON CROP 319
EUGENIUS (see under VASELINES)
EUPHONE 733
EVEN AS WE SPEAK 734
EVERCLEAR 734
EVEREST THE HARD WAY (see under FIRE ENGINES)
EVERLASTING THE WAY (see under JUNE OF 44)
EVERYTHING BUT THE GIRL 320
EX, the 321
EXHAUST (see under GODSPEED YOU BLACK EMPEROR!)
EXILE INSIDE (see under MY LIFE STORY)
EXPENDABLES (see under CLARKSON, Jay)
EXPERIMENTAL AUDIO RESEARCH (see under SPACEMEN 3)
EXPERIMENTAL POP BAND (see under BRILLIANT CORNERS)
EXPLODING WHITE MICE 322
EXTRA GLENNS (see under MOUNTAIN GOATS)
EYELESS IN GAZA 322

F

FABULOUS 735
FAD GADGET 324
FAINT 735

FAIR, Jad (see under HALF JAPANESE)
FAIRWAYS 736
FAITH (see under EMBRACE)
FAITH HEALERS, Th' 736
FAITH OVER REASON 737
FALCO, Tav 325
FALL 63
FALSE PROPHETS 326
FAMILY CAT 737
FAMILY FODDER 326
FANATICS (see under OCEAN COLOUR SCENE)
FARINA, Geoff (see under KARATE)
FARM 326
FARMER'S BOYS 327
FARRAR, Jay (see under UNCLE TUPELO)
FARREN, Mick (see under PINK FAIRIES)
FASHION 66
FASTBACKS 328
FATAL MICROBES 66
FATIMA MANSIONS (see under COUGHLAN, Cathal)
FAT TULIPS 738
FAUST 738
FEELIES 328
FELICE, John, & THE LOWDOWNS (see under REAL KIDS)
FELT 329
FIAT LUX 330
FIELD MICE 739
FIEND (see under TELSTAR PONIES)
FIER, Anton (see under GOLDEN PALOMINOS)
FIGURINE (see under STRICTLY BALLROOM)
FINGERPRINTZ 67
FINITRIBE 331
FIRE ENGINES 332
fIREHOSE (see under MINUTEMEN)
FIRE PARTY 333
FIREWATER 740
FISCHER-Z 67
FISH & ROSES (see under RUN ON)
FISHER-TURNER, Simon, (SFT) (see under KING OF LUXEMBOURG)
FISK, Steve (see under PELL MELL)
FITZGERALD, Patrik 68
FITZ OF DEPRESSION 740
FIVE GO DOWN TO THE SEA 333
FIVE OR SIX 333
FIVER 740
FIVE THIRTY 334
FIZZBOMBS (see under JESSE GARON & THE DESPERADOES)
FLAG OF CONVENIENCE (see under BUZZCOCKS)
FLAKE MUSIC (see under SHINS)
FLAMING LIPS 334
FLAMINGOES 741
FLAMING STARS 741
FLAMIN' GROOVIES 68
FLASHPAPR (see under THOMAS, Fred)
FLATMATES 335
FLESH EATERS 69
FLESH FOR LULU 335
FLESHTONES 70
FLIES INSIDE THE SUN 742
FLIN FLON (see under UNREST)
FLIPPER 336
FLOAT UP CP (see under RIP, RIG + PANIC)
FLOUR (see under RIFLE SPORT)
FLOWCHART 742
FLOWERED UP 743
FLOWERS 336
FLOYD, Gary (see under SISTER DOUBLE HAPPINESS)
FLUF 743
FLUFFY 744
FLUID 337
FLUX OF PINK INDIANS 337
FLYING COLOR 337
FLYING LIZARDS 71
FLYING MEDALLIONS 744
FLYING SAUCER ATTACK 744
FLY PAN AM (see under GODSPEED YOU BLACK EMPEROR!)
FLYS 71

FOEHN 745
FOIL 745
FOLK DEVILS (see under LOWERY, Ian)
FOLK IMPLOSION (see under SEBADOH)
FONTANELLE (see under JESSAMINE)
FOO FIGHTERS 745
FOR AGAINST 338
FOR CARNATION (see under SLINT)
FOREVER PEOPLE (see under RAZORCUTS)
FOR SQUIRRELS 746
FOR STARS 746
FORSTER, Robert (see under GO-BETWEENS)
FORTUNATE SONS (see under BARRACUDAS)
FOSCA (see under ORLANDO)
FOUNTAINS OF WAYNE 746
FOUR TET (see under FRIDGE)
FOWLEY, Kim 339
FOXX, John 339
FRAME, Roddy (see under AZTEC CAMERA)
FRANK & WALTERS 747
FRANK CHICKENS 340
FRAZER, Paula (see under TARNATION)
FRAZIER CHORUS 340
FREAKWATER (see under ELEVENTH DREAM DAY)
FREAKY REALISTIC 747
FREE DESIGN 748
FREEHEAT (see under JESUS & MARY CHAIN)
FREE KITTEN (see under SONIC YOUTH)
FREEZE (see under CINdYTALK)
FREIWILLIGE SELBSTKONTROLLE 341
FRENCH KICKS 749
FRENTE! 749
FRESHIES 72
FRETBLANKET 749
FRIDAY, Gavin (see under VIRGIN PRUNES)
FRIDGE 749
FRIENDS OF BETTY (see under RED RED MEAT)
FRIENDS OF DEAN MARTINEZ 750
FROM BUBBLEGUM TO SKY (see under CIAO BELLA)
FROST, Edith 751
FROSTED AMBASSADOR (see under OLIVIA TREMOR CONTROL)
FRUIT (see under KITCHENS OF DISTINCTION)
F.S.K. (see under FREIWILLIGE SELBSTKONTROLLE)
FUCK 751
FUDGE 751
FUGAZI 341
FUKUYAMA 752
FURNITURE 342
FURTHER 752
FUTURE BIBLE HEROES (see under MAGNETIC FIELDS)
FUTURE PILOT AKA 753
FUXA 753
FUZZBOX (see under WE'VE GOT A FUZZBOX…)
FUZZTONES 343
FUZZY 754

G

GADGETS (see under THE THE)
GAINSBOURG, Serge 754
GALAS, Diamanda 344
GALAXIE 500 755
GALBRAITH, Alastair 344
GALLON DRUNK 756
GAME THEORY 345
GANGER 757
GANG OF FOUR 73
GARAGELAND 758
GARBAGE 758
GARNER, Sue (see under RUN ON)
GAS HUFFER 759
GASTR DEL SOL (see under SQUIRREL BAIT)
GATE (see under DEAD C.)

GATES, Rebecca (see under SPINANES)
GAUNT 759
GAY DAD 760
GAYE BYKERS ON ACID 346
GAZE (see under TIGER TRAP)
GAZETTEERS (see under VEHICLE FLIPS)
GEAR (see under CHESTERFIELDS)
GEEK (see under TSUNAMI)
GEE MR. TRACY 346
GELB, Howe (see under GIANT SAND)
GENE 760
GENE LOVES JEZEBEL 346
GENERATION X 74
GENEVA 761
GENTLE WAVES (see under BELLE AND SEBASTIAN)
GERALDINE FIBBERS 762
GERBILS 762
GERMANO, Lisa 762
GERMS 74
GERRARD, Lisa (see under DEAD CAN DANCE)
GET UP KIDS 763
GHOST CLUB (see under 3Ds)
GHOST DANCE 348
GIANT SAND 348
GIBSON BROS. 763
GIGOLO AUNTS 764
GILBERT & LEWIS (see under WIRE)
GILBERTO, Astrud 765
GILL, Andy (see under GANG OF FOUR)
GINN / GONE, Greg (see under BLACK FLAG)
GIRA, Michael (see under SWANS)
GIRL OF THE WORLD (see under CAT'S MIAOW!)
GIRLS AGAINST BOYS 765
GIRLS AT OUR BEST 350
GIST (see under YOUNG MARBLE GIANTS)
GITS 766
GLAND SHROUDS (see under BLAKE, Karl)
GLASS ONION (see under TRAVIS)
GLAXO BABIES 350
GLITTERBOX 766
GLOVE (see under SIOUXSIE AND THE BANSHEES)
GLO-WORM (see under BLACK TAMBOURINE)
GLUCK, Jeremy (see under BARRACUDAS)
GNAC 767
GO, the 767
GO-BETWEENS 350
GOBLIN MIX / EXPLODING BUDGIES (see under 3Ds)
GOD, MOTHER & COUNTRY (see under RIP, RIG + PANIC)
GODARD (& SUBWAY SECT), Vic 75
GOD BULLIES 767
GODFATHERS 352
GOD IS MY CO-PILOT 768
GODRAYS (see under SMALL FACTORY)
**GODSPEED YOU
BLACK EMPEROR! 769**
GODSTAR 770
GODZUKI 771
GO HOLE (see under GENE)
GO KART MOZART (see under FELT)
GOLDBLADE (see under MEMBRANES)
GOLDEN PALOMINOS 353
GOLDEN SMOG 771
GOLDTHORPE, Mark (see under ARTERY)
GOLIGHTLY, Holly 771
GOMEZ 772
GOODBYE MR MACKENZIE 354
GOOD LIFE (see under CURSIVE)
GOOD MISSIONARIES (see under ALTERNATIVE TV)
GORDONS (see under BAILTER SPACE)
GORE, Martin L. (see under DEPECHE MODE)
GORIES (see under DIRTBOMBS)
GORILLAS 76
GORILLAZ (see under BLUR)
GORKY'S ZYGOTIC MYNCI 773

INDEX

GORL, Robert (see under D.A.F.)
GO SAILOR (see under TIGER TRAP)
GO TEAM (see under BEAT HAPPENING)
GOTHIC ARCHIES (see under MAGNETIC FIELDS)
GOYA DRESS 774
GRAB GRAB THE HADDOCK (see under MARINE GIRLS)
GRANDADDY 774
GRAND MAL (see under ST*JOHNNY)
GRANDPABOY (see under REPLACEMENTS)
GRANEY, Dave (see under MOODISTS)
GRANING, Chick (see under ANASTASIA SCREAMED)
GRANT LEE BUFFALO 775
GRAPE (see under CHESTERFIELDS)
GRASSHOPPER & THE GOLDEN CRICKETS (see under MERCURY REV)
GRAY, David 775
GREAT DIVIDE (see under BIBLE)
GREAT LEAP FORWARD (see under BIG FLAME)
GREAT OUTDOORS (see under FARMER'S BOYS)
GREAT UNWASHED (see under CLEAN)
GREEN, Adam (see under MOLDY PEACHES)
GREEN DAY 776
GREENFIELD, Dave (see under STRANGLERS)
GREENHORNES 777
GREEN ON RED 355
GREEN TELESCOPE (see under THANES)
GRENADINE (see under UNREST)
GRIFFIN, Sid (see under LONG RYDERS)
GRIFTERS 777
GRIMBLE GRUMBLE 778
GROOVE FARM (see under BEATNIK FILMSTARS)
GROOVY LITTLE NUMBERS 356
GRUBBS, David (see under SQUIRREL BAIT)
GUADALCANAL DIARY 356
GUANA BATZ 356
GUIDED BY VOICES 357
GUITAR WOLF 778
GUMBALL (see under B.A.L.L.)
GUN CLUB 359
GUPPYBOY (see under ESSEX GREEN)
GUSTER 778
GUTTERBALL (see under DREAM SYNDICATE)
GUV'NER 778
G.W. McLENNAN (see under GO-BETWEENS)
GYMSLIPS 360
GYRES 779

H

HADEN, Petra (see under that dog.)
HAGAR THE WOMB 361
HAGEN, Nina 76
HAGERTY, Neil Michael (see under ROYAL TRUX)
HAIG, Paul (see under JOSEF K)
HAINES, Luke (see under AUTEURS)
HAIR & SKIN TRADING CO. 779
HALF-HANDED CLOUD 779
HALF JAPANESE 77
HALF MAN HALF BISCUIT 361
HALF STRING 780
HALL, John S. (see under KING MISSILE)
HALLIDAY, Toni (see under CURVE)
HALO BENDERS (see under BEAT HAPPENING)
HALO BIT (see under SMALL FACTORY)
HALO OF FLIES 362
HALSTEAD, Neil (see under SLOWDIVE)
HAMFISTED (see under SPARE SNARE)
HANDSOME FAMILY 780
HANGED UP (see under SACKVILLE)
HANGOVERS 780
HAPPY FAMILY (see under MOMUS)
HAPPY FLOWERS 362
HAPPY MONDAYS 363
HARBOR, Pearl, & THE EXPLOSIONS 364
HARCOURT, Ed 781
HARD-ONS 365
HARDY, Francoise 781
HARMONY ROCKETS (see under MERCURY REV)
HARPER, Charlie (see under UK SUBS)
HARRY CREWS (see under LUNCH, Lydia)
HARRY, Debbie/Deborah (see under BLONDIE)
HART, Grant (see under HUSKER DU)
HARVEST MINISTERS 781
HARVEY DANGER 782
HARVEY, PJ 781
HASH JAR TEMPO (see under MONTGOMERY, Roy)
HATFIELD, Juliana 783
HAVEN 784
HAWKS (see under DUFFY, Stephen)
HAWLEY, Richard (see under LONGPIGS)
HAYDEN 784
HAYDEN, Annie (see under SPENT)
HAYWARD, Charles (see under THIS HEAT)
HEAD, Jowe (see under SWELL MAPS)
HEAD, Michael (see under SHACK)
HEADLESS CHICKENS 365
HEARTBREAKERS (see under THUNDERS, Johnny)
HEART THROBS 366
HEARTWORMS (see under VELOCITY GIRL)
HEAT, Reverend Horton 784
HEATMISER (see under SMITH, Elliott)
HEATON, Angie (see under CORNDOLLY)
HEAVENLY (see under TALULAH GOSH)
HEAVENS TO BETSY (see under SLEATER-KINNEY)
HEAVY STEREO 785
HEAVY VEGETABLE (see under PINBACK)
HEAZLEWOOD, Chris (see under KING LOSER)
HEFNER 785
HELEN LOVE 786
HELIUM 786
HELL, Richard 79
HELLACOPTERS 787
HENDRICKS TRIO, Karl 788
HENDRIX, Jimi 366
HENRY'S DRESS 788
HENTCHMEN 789
HERO, Stephen (see under KITCHENS OF DISTINCTION)
HEROIC DOSES (see under 5 STYLE)
HERON 789
HERSH, Kristin (see under THROWING MUSES)
HER SPACE HOLIDAY 789
HERZFELD (see under McCARTHY)
HE SAID (see under WIRE)
HEWERDINE, Boo (see under BIBLE)
HEX (see under CHURCH)
HIGH 790
HIGH BACK CHAIRS 790
HIGH FIDELITY 790
HIGH FIVE 367
HIGH LLAMAS 790
HIGSONS 367
HINDU LOVE GODS (see under R.E.M.)
HINKLER, Simon (see under ARTERY)
HIS NAME IS ALIVE 791
HITCHCOCK, Robyn 80
HIT PARADE 368
HIVES 792
HOFFMAN, Kristian (see under MUMPS)
HOGGBOY 792
HOLE 792
HOLIDAY FLYER 793
HOLLY & THE ITALIANS 368
HOLLYWOOD BRATS 82
HOLMES, Chris 794
HOLY CHILDHOOD 794
HOLY JOY (see under BAND OF HOLY JOY)
HONEYBUNCH 794
HONEYMOON KILLERS 368
HONEYRIDER 794
HOOD 795
HOODOO GURUS 369
HOOVER 795
HOPE, Peter (see under BOX)
HOPE BLISTER (see under THIS MORTAL COIL)
HOPEWELL 796
HOPPER 796
HORMONES 796
HOTALACIO (see under FLUX OF PINK INDIANS)
HOT HOT HEAT 796
HOT MONKEY (see under GRIFTERS)
HOT PURSUIT (see under TUSCADERO)
HOT ROD (see under REVOLVER)
HOT ROD CIRCUIT 797
HOT SNAKES (see under ROCKET FROM THE CRYPT)
HOUSEHUNTERS (see under SWELL MAPS)
HOUSEMARTINS 370
HOUSE OF LOVE 370
HOVERCRAFT 797
H.P. ZINKER 797
HUCKLEBERRY 798
HUGGY BEAR 798
HUGO LARGO 371
HULA 371
HULA BOY (see under BOYRACER)
HUM 799
HUMAN LEAGUE 82
HUMPERS 799
HUNGRY GHOSTS 800
HUNGRY I (see under EYELESS IN GAZA)
HUNT (CLUB), Miles (see under WONDER STUFF)
HUNTERS AND COLLECTORS 372
HURRAH! 373
HURRICANE #1 800
HUSKER DU 373
HYBRIDS (see under ECHOBOY)
HYDROPLANE (see under CAT'S MIAOW)

I

I AM KLOOT 801
I AM THE WORLD TRADE CENTER (see under KINCAID.)
ICARUS LINE 801
ICICLE WORKS (see under McNABB, Ian)
IDA 801
IDAHO 802
IDHA 802
IDLEWILD 802
IDYLL SWORDS (see under POLVO)
IHA, James (see under SMASHING PUMPKINS)
IKARA COLT 803
I, LUDICROUS 375
IMAGINARY FRIEND (see under BUDDHA ON THE MOON)
IMPERIAL DRAG (see under JELLYFISH)
I'M SO HOLLOW 375
INBREDS 803
INCA BABIES 375
INDIANS IN MOSCOW 375
IN EMBRACE 376
INNER SLEEVE 804
INSIDES (see under EARWIG)
INSPIRAL CARPETS 804
INTERNATIONAL AIRPORT 805
(INTERNATIONAL) NOISE CONSPIRACY (see under REFUSED)
INTERPOL 805
IN THE NURSERY 376
INTO A CIRCLE 377
IRVING 805
ISOTOPE 217 (see under TORTOISE)
IT'S IMMATERIAL 377
IVY (N.Y.C.) 806

J

J, David (see under BAUHAUS)
JACK 807
JACK DRAG 807
JACK FROST (see under CHURCH)
JACKIE-O MOTHERFUCKER 808
JACKNIFE LEE (see under COMPULSION)
JACKOFFICERS (see under BUTTHOLE SURFERS)
JACOBITES (see under SWELL MAPS)
JACOB'S MOUSE 808
JACQUES (see under JACK)
JAKE BURNS & THE WHEEL (see under STIFF LITTLE FINGERS)
JALE 808
JAM 83
JAMES 378
JAMES, Denise 809
JAMES ORR COMPLEX (see under ESKA)
JAMIE WEDNESDAY (see under CARTER THE UNSTOPPABLE SEX MACHINE)
JANE (& BARTON) (see under MARINE GIRLS)
JANE POW 809
JANITORS 379
JANOVITZ, Bill (see under BUFFALO TOM)
JANSEN / BARBIERI (see under JAPAN)
JANUARY 809
JAPAN 85
JAPANCAKES 809
JARBOE (see under SWANS)
JASMINE MINKS 379
JAWBOX 810
JAWBREAKER 810
JAYHAWKS 380
JAZZATEERS 380
JAZZ BUTCHER 381
JAZZ CANNON (see under MADDER ROSE)
J CHURCH 811
JEAN-PAUL SARTRE EXPERIENCE 382
JEEVAS (see under KULA SHAKER)
JEFFERIES, Peter (see under THIS KIND OF PUNISHMENT)
JELLYFISH 812
JELLYFISH KISS 813
JENNIFERS (see under SUPERGRASS)
JESSAMINE 813
JESSE GARON & THE DESPERADOES 382
JESUS & MARY CHAIN 383
JESUS LIZARD 384
JETPLANE LANDING 813
JETS TO BRAZIL 814
JETT BRANDO (see under ALL NATURAL LEMON & LIME FLAVORS)
JILTED JOHN 87
JIMMY EAT WORLD 814
JIM'S SUPER STEREOWORLD (see under CARTER THE UNSTOPPABLE SEX MACHINE)
JJ72 815
J.J. STONE (see under GALLON DRUNK)
JOAN OF ARC 815
JOBSON, Richard (see under SKIDS)
JOCASTA 816
JOHN AND MARY (see under 10,000 MANIACS)
JOHNBOY 816
JOHNNY & THE SELF-ABUSERS (see under SIMPLE MINDS)
JOHNSON, Mike (see under DINOSAUR JR.)
JOHNSON, Will (see under CENTRO-MATIC)
JOHNSTON, Daniel 385
JOHNSTON, Freedy 816
JOLT (see under SENSELESS THINGS)
JONATHAN FIRE*EATER 817
JONES, Stephen (see under BABYBIRD)
JOOLZ 386
JOSEF K 386
JOY DIVISION 87
JOYRIDERS (see under CATERAN)

INDEX

JPS EXPERIENCE (see under JEAN-PAUL SARTRE EXPERIENCE)
JULIE RUIN (see under BIKINI KILL)
JUMBO 817
JUNE BRIDES 387
JUNE OF 44 817
JUNIOR VARSITY 818
JUNIOR VARSITY KM 818
JUNIPER (see under MONDO CRESCENDO)
JUPITER AFFECT (see under THREE O'CLOCK)
JURADO, Damien 818

K

KAIA (see under TEAM DRESCH)
KALIMA (see under A CERTAIN RATIO)
KARATE 819
KARELIA, the 820
KARN, Mick (see under JAPAN)
KATASTROPHY WIFE (see under BABES IN TOYLAND)
KATO, Nash (see under URGE OVERKILL)
KEAREY, Ian (see under BLUE AEROPLANES)
KEATING, Matt 820
KENICKIE 820
KENNY PROCESS TEAM 821
KENT, Klark (see under POLICE)
KEPONE 821
KEY, Tara (see under ANTIETAM)
KHAYA 821
KID SILVER (see under ROLLERSKATE SKINNY)
KILBEY, Steve (see under CHURCH)
KILBURN & THE HIGH ROADS (see under DURY, Ian)
KILGOUR, David (see under CLEAN)
KILLDOZER 388
KILLER TWEEKER BEES (see under BLACK FLAG)
KILLING JOKE 388
KILLJOYS 88
KILLS (see under DISCOUNT)
KINCAID. 822
KING ADORA 822
KING BISCUIT TIME (see under BETA BAND)
KING BLANK (see under LOWERY, Ian)
KING KONG 822
KING LOSER 823
KINGMAKER 823
KING MISSILE 389
KING OF LUXEMBOURG 390
KING OF THE SLUMS 391
KINGSBURY MANX 824
KINGS OF CONVENIENCE 824
KING SOUND QUARTET (see under DIRTBOMBS)
KINKS 824
KINKY MACHINE (see under RIALTO)
KIPPINGTON LODGE (see under BRINSLEY SCHWARZ)
KIRK, Richard H. (see under CABARET VOLTAIRE)
KITCHEN (see under BIS)
KITCHENS OF DISTINCTION 392
KITEMONSTER (see under ASTRID)
KLEENEX 88
K-LINE (see under STUPIDS)
KNIFE IN THE WATER 825
KNOX, Chris (see under TALL DWARFS)
KO AND THE KNOCKOUTS 826
KOMEDA 826
KOPPES, Peter (see under CHURCH)
KOSTARS (see under LUSCIOUS JACKSON)
KOUFAX 826
KOZELEK, Mark (see under RED HOUSE PAINTERS)
KRAFTWERK 826
KRAMER (see under BONGWATER)
KRAMER, Wayne (see under MC5)
KRAY CHERUBS (see under ART ATTACKS)
KREIDLER (see under TO ROCOCO ROT)
KRUMMENACHER, Victor (see under CAMPER VAN BEETHOVEN)
KUEPPER, Ed (see under LAUGHING CLOWNS)
KUKL (see under BJORK)
KULA SHAKER 827
KUSTOMIZED (see under VOLCANO SONS)
KWELLER, Ben (see under RADISH)
KYOKO (see under BEATNIK FILMSTARS)

L

L7 846
LABRADFORD 828
LADYBUG TRANSISTOR 828
LADYTRON 829
LAETO 829
LAGWAGON 829
LAIKA 830
LAKE, Kirk 830
L/A/L (see under LOVE AS LAUGHTER)
LAMBCHOP 830
LAND OF NOD 831
LANEGAN, Mark (see under SCREAMING TREES)
LANGFORD, Jon (see under MEKONS)
LANGLEY, Gerard (see under BLUE AEROPLANES)
LAPSE 831
LARD (see under DEAD KENNEDYS)
LARMOUSSE 832
LASSIE FOUNDATION 832
LAST 89
LAUGHING APPLE (see under McGEE, Alan)
LAUGHING CLOWNS 393
LAUGHING HYENAS 395
LAZER BOY 832
LAZYCAME (see under JESUS & MARY CHAIN)
LAZY COWGIRLS 395
LA'S 393
LEARY, Paul (see under BUTTHOLE SURFERS)
LEATHER NUN 396
LEAVES 833
LEAVING TRAINS 397
LE COUPE 833
LEE, Arthur (see under LOVE)
LEER, Thomas 90
LEGENDARY PINK DOTS 398
LE MANS 833
LEMONHEADS 398
LEMON KITTENS (see under BLAKE, Karl)
LEN BRIGHT COMBO (see under WRECKLESS ERIC)
LENNON, Don 833
LENOLA 834
LEO / PHARMACISTS, Ted (see under CHISEL)
LEOPARDS 834
LES SAVY FAV 834
LE TIGRE (see under BIKINI KILL)
LETTER E (see under JUNE OF 44)
LETTERS TO CLEO 835
LET'S ACTIVE 400
LEVELLERS 835
LEVEN, Jackie (see under DOLL BY DOLL)
LEVITATION 836
LEYTON BUZZARDS 90
LIARS 836
LIBERTINES 837
LIBERTY CAGE (see under MEN THEY COULDN'T HANG)
LIBIDO 837
LIBRANESS (see under POLVO)
LICKS (see under FLUX OF PINK INDIANS)
LIFE WITHOUT BUILDINGS 837
LIFT TO EXPERIENCE 837
LIGHTNING SEEDS 400
LILAC TIME (see under DUFFY, Stephen)
LILIPUT (see under KLEENEX)
LILYS 837
LINDSAY, Arto (see under DNA)
LINOLEUM 838
LIQUORETTE (see under CORNDOLLY)

LIQUORICE (see under TSUNAMI)
LITTLE ANNIE (see under ANXIETY, Annie)
LITTLE RED ROCKET (see under AZURE RAY)
LITTLE VILLAGE (see under LOWE, Nick)
LLAMA FARMERS 838
LLOYD, Richard (see under TELEVISION)
LLOYD, Robert (see under NIGHTINGALES)
LODGER 839
LOEWENSTEIN, Jason (see under SEBADOH)
LOFT (see under WEATHER PROPHETS)
LOFTUS (see under RED RED MEAT)
LOFTY PILLARS (see under BOXHEAD ENSEMBLE)
LOGIC, Lora 90
LOIS 839
LONE PIGEON 839
LONESOME ORGANIST (see under 5 STYLE)
LONG FIN KILLIE (see under BOWS)
LONGPIGS 840
LONG RYDERS 401
LOOK BLUE GO PURPLE 402
LOOP 402
LOOPER 840
LORDS OF THE NEW CHURCH (see under DEAD BOYS)
LORELEI 841
LORI & THE CHAMELEONS 403
LOTHARS (see under ABUNAI!)
LOTION 841
LOTUS EATERS (see under WILD SWANS)
LOUD FAMILY (see under GAME THEORY)
LOUDSPEAKER 403
Lou LORD, Mary 841
LOVE 842
LOVE AND ROCKETS (see under BAUHAUS)
LOVE AS LAUGHTER 843
LOVE BATTERY 844
LOVE CORPORATION (see under BALL, Edward)
LOVEJOY (see under BLUEBOY)
LOVELETTER (see under KING OF LUXEMBOURG)
LOVESICK (see under THOMAS, Fred)
LOVE SPIT LOVE (see under PSYCHEDELIC FURS)
LOVES UGLY CHILDREN 844
LOVE TRACTOR 403
LOVICH, Lene 91
LOW 844
LOWCRAFT 845
LOWE, Alex 845
LOWE, Nick 91
LOWERY, Ian 404
LOWGOLD 846
LOWLIFE 404
LUCKSMITHS 846
LUCKY PIERRE (see under ARAB STRAP)
LUCKY SPERMS (see under HALF JAPANESE)
LUDUS 405
LUGWORM 847
LULLABY FOR THE WORKING CLASS 847
LUNA (see under GALAXIE 500)
LUNACHICKS 847
LUNCH, Lydia 92
LUNCHBOX 848
LUNE 848
LUNGFISH 848
LUNG LEG 849
LUPINE HOWL 849
LURKERS 94
LUSCIOUS JACKSON 849
LUSH 850
LUXURIA (see under MAGAZINE)
LYDON, John (see under PUBLIC IMAGE LTD.)
LYNC (see under LOVE AS LAUGHTER)

LYNNFIELD PIONEERS 850
LYRES 405

Mac / Mc

McCARTHY 408
McCAUGHEY, Scott (see under YOUNG FRESH FELLOWS)
McCOMB, Dave (see under TRIFFIDS)
McCULLOCH, Ian (see under ECHO & THE BUNNYMEN)
McDOWALL, Rose (see under STRAWBERRY SWITCHBLADE)
McENTIRE, John (see under TORTOISE)
McGEE, Alan 409
MACKENZIE, Billy (see under ASSOCIATES)
MacKENZIES (see under SECRET GOLDFISH)
MacLEAN, Bryan (see under LOVE)
McLUSKY 863
McNABB, Ian 410

M

MACHISMO (see under JACOB'S MOUSE)
MACROCOSMICA (see under TELSTAR PONIES)
MADDER ROSE 851
MADISON ELECTRIC (see under VERONICA LAKE)
MAD SCENE (see under CLEAN)
MAGAZINE 95
MAGIC DIRT 851
MAGICDRIVE 852
MAGIC HOUR (see under GALAXIE 500)
MAGICK HEADS (see under BATS)
MAGNAPOP 852
MAGNETIC FIELDS 852
MAGNETIC NORTH POLE 853
MAGNOLIAS 406
MAGOO 854
MAIDS OF GRAVITY 854
MAIN (see under LOOP)
MAJESTIC 855
MAKE-UP 855
MALARIA! 406
MALE NURSE 856
MALKMUS, Stephen (see under PAVEMENT)
MALLINDER, Stephen (see under CABARET VOLTAIRE)
MAMBO TAXI 856
MAN FROM DELMONTE 406
MANIC STREET PREACHERS 856
MANIFESTO (see under EMBRACE)
MANNING, Barbara 407
MANNING, Roger (see under JELLYFISH)
MAN OR ASTRO-MAN? 858
MANSUN 859
MANTARAY 859
MAPS OF JUPITER (see under MAGNETIC NORTH POLE)
MARBLES (see under APPLES IN STEREO)
MARC & THE MAMBAS (see under ALMOND, Marc)
MARCH, April 860
MARCH VIOLETS 407
MARINE GIRLS 408
MARINE RESEARCH (see under TALULAH GOSH)
MARION 860
MARK FOUR (see under CREATION)
MARS 96
MARS, Chris (see under REPLACEMENTS)
MARS VOLTA (see under AT THE DRIVE-IN)
MARTHA & THE MUFFINS 96
MASCIS, J. (see under DINOSAUR JR.)
MASS (see under WOLFGANG PRESS)
MASTERS OF THE HEMISPHERE 861
MATCHING MOLE (see under WYATT, Robert)
MATTHEWS, Eric 861
matt pond PA 861

INDEX

MAXIMUM JOY (see under GLAXO BABIES)
MAYDAY (see under LULLABY FOR THE WORKING CLASS)
MAZARIN 862
MAZINGA PHASER 862
MAZZY STAR 862
MC5 96
MEAT PUPPETS 411
MEAT WHIPLASH (see under MOTORCYCLE BOY)
MECCA NORMAL 412
MEDAL 863
MEDALARK 11 (see under BODINES)
MEDICINE 863
MEDIUM MEDIUM (see under C-CAT TRANCE)
ME FIRST AND THE GIMME GIMMES 864
MEGA CITY FOUR 413
MEICES 865
MEKONS 97
MELBERG, Rose (see under TIGER TRAP)
MELODIE GROUP (see under WINDMILLS)
MELODY UNIT 865
MELONS (see under FAT TULIPS)
MEL-O-TONES (see under WALKING SEEDS)
MELT (see under HAGAR THE WOMB)
MELT-BANANA 865
MELVINS 413
MELYS 866
MEMBERS 99
MEMBRANES 414
ME ME ME (see under ELASTICA)
MENCK, Ric (see under VELVET CRUSH)
MENSWE@R 866
MEN THEY COULDN'T HANG 415
MEN WITHOUT HATS 416
MERCURY PROGRAM 867
MERCURY REV 867
MERRITT, Stephin (see under MAGNETIC FIELDS)
METAL URBAIN 99
METEORS 417
MEXICO 70 868
MIAOW (see under CARROLL, Cath)
MICE (see under ALL ABOUT EVE)
MICRODISNEY (see under COUGHLAN, Cathal)
MIDGET 868
MIDWAY STILL 869
MIGHTY LEMON DROPS 418
MIGHTY MIGHTY 419
MIGHTY WAH! (see under WAH!)
MIGHTY FLASHLIGHT (see under RITES OF SPRING)
MILKY WIMPSHAKE 869
MILLER, Roger (see under MISSION OF BURMA)
MILLTOWN BROTHERS 870
MILTON, Ted (see under BLURT)
MIMI (see under HUGO LARGO)
MINDERS 870
MINEKAWA, Takako 871
MINK DeVILLE 100
MINK LUNGS 871
MINNY POPS 419
MINOR THREAT (see under FUGAZI)
MINTY 871
MINUS 5 (see under YOUNG FRESH FELLOWS)
MINUTEMEN 419
MIRACLE LEGION 420
MIRANDA SEX GARDEN 871
MIRRORS (see under STYRENES)
MISFITS 100
MISSION 421
MISSION OF BURMA 422
MOB (see under BLYTH POWER)
MOCK TURTLES 423
MODELS 101
MODERN ENGLISH 423
MODERN EON 424
MODERN LOVERS (see under RICHMAN, Jonathan)
MODEST MOUSE 872

MO-DETTES 424
MOFUNGO 424
MOGWAI 873
MO-HO-BISH-O-PI 873
MOISTBOYZ (see under WEEN)
MOJAVE 3 (see under SLOWDIVE)
MOLDY PEACHES 874
MOLES (see under DAVIES, Richard)
MOLLY HALF HEAD 874
MOMUS 425
MONACO (see under NEW ORDER)
MONDO CRESCENDO 874
MONGERS (see under POLICECAT)
MONGOOSE (see under SECRET GOLDFISH)
MONKEYWRENCH (see under MUDHONEY)
MONKS OF DOOM (see under CAMPER VAN BEETHOVEN)
MONOCHROME SET 101
MONOGRAPH 875
MONO MEN 875
MONROE MUSTANG 876
MONSTERLAND 876
MONTGOMERY, Roy 426
MOODISTS 427
MOOD SIX 427
MOOG COOKBOOK (see under JELLYFISH)
MOONEY SUZUKI 876
MOONFLOWERS 877
MOONSHAKE (see under WOLFHOUNDS)
MOORE, Thurston (see under SONIC YOUTH)
MOOSE 877
MOPED, Johnny 102
MORELLA'S FOREST 878
MORNING GLORIES 878
MORNING STAR (see under MOONFLOWERS)
MORPHINE 878
MORRICONE, Ennio 879
MORRISSEY 428
MOST (see under SPIREA X)
MOTELLO, Elton 103
MOTHMEN 429
MOTOR BOYS MOTOR (see under SCREAMING BLUE MESSIAHS)
MOTORCYCLE BOY 429
MOTOR LIFE CO. 879
MOULD, Bob (see under HUSKER DU)
MOUNTAIN GOATS 880
MOUNT VERNON ARTS LAB 881
MOVIETONE 881
MOVING TARGETS 430
MOXHAM, Stuart, & THE ORIGINAL ARTISTS (see under YOUNG MARBLE GIANTS)
MR. T EXPERIENCE 430
MUDHONEY 431
MUFFS (see under PANDORAS)
MULCAHY, Mark (see under MIRACLE LEGION)
MULE 881
MULL HISTORICAL SOCIETY 882
MUMMIES 882
MUMPS 103
MUPPET MULE (see under SPARE SNARE)
MURDER CITY DEVILS 882
MURPHY, Peter (see under BAUHAUS)
MURRAY, Pauline, (& THE INVISIBLE GIRLS) (see under PENETRATION)
MURRY THE HUMP 883
MUSE 883
MUSIC 884
MUSIC FOR PLEASURE 432
MUSIC TAPES (see under CHOCOLATE USA)
MUTTON BIRDS 884
MX-80 SOUND 103
MY BLOODY VALENTINE 884
MY DAD IS DEAD 433
MY FAVORITE 885
MY LIFE STORY 885
MY VITRIOL 886

N

NADA SURF 887
NAKED PREY 434
NAKED RAYGUN 434
NAKED SEE (see under FOIL)
NAMES 434
NANCY BOY 887
NATIONAL PARK 887
NATIONAL SKYLINE (see under HUM)
NATION OF ULYSSES (see under MAKE-UP)
NATIVE HIPSTERS 435
NATIVE NOD (see under LAPSE)
NAVIGATOR 887
NAYSAYER (see under RETSIN)
NECTARINE No.9 (see under FIRE ENGINES)
NED'S ATOMIC DUSTBIN 888
NEGATIVE TREND (see under FLIPPER)
NEGATIVLAND 435
NERVES 104
NERVOUS EATERS 104
NEU! 888
NEUROTICS (see under NEWTOWN NEUROTICS)
NEUTRAL MILK HOTEL 889
NEW AMSTERDAMS (see under GET UP KIDS)
NEW BOMB TURKS 889
NEWELL, Martin (see under CLEANERS FROM VENUS)
NEW END ORIGINAL (see under TEXAS IS THE REASON)
NEW FAST AUTOMATIC DAFFODILS 890
NEWMAN, Colin (see under WIRE)
NEW MODEL ARMY 436
NEW ORDER 437
NEW PORNOGRAPHERS (see under ZUMPANO)
NEW RACE (see under RADIO BIRDMAN)
NEW RADIANT STORM KING 890
NEW RISING SONS (see under TEXAS IS THE REASON)
NEWTOWN NEUROTICS 439
NEW YORK DOLLS 104
NICE (see under ASHTRAY BOY)
NICO 440
NIGHTBLOOMS 891
NIGHTINGALES 441
NIPS / NIPPLE ERECTORS (see under POGUES)
NIRVANA 441
NOBACON, Danbert (see under CHUMBAWAMBA)
NOCTURNAL PROJECTIONS (see under THIS KIND OF PUNISHMENT)
NOMADS 443
NO-MAN (see under PORCUPINE TREE)
NO MAN IS ROGER MILLER (see under MISSION OF BURMA)
NOMEANSNO 443
NON 444
NOONDAY UNDERGROUND 891
NORDENSTAM, Stina 892
NORMAL 106
NORTHERN PICTURE LIBRARY (see under FIELD MICE)
NORTHERN UPROAR 892
NORTHSIDE 892
NOSEBLEEDS 106
NOTHING BUT HAPPINESS (see under ULTRA VIVID SCENE)
NOTHING PAINTED BLUE 893
NOTSENSIBLES 106
NOTWIST 893
NOVA, Heather 894
NOVAK STATE CONSPIRACY (see under VENUS FLY TRAP)
NOVA MOB (see under HUSKER DU)
NOVOCAINE 894
NOW IT'S OVERHEAD (see under AZURE RAY)
NUBILES 894
NUMAN, Gary 106
NUMBER ONE CUP 895

NUNS 109
NURSE WITH WOUND 445
NYLON, Judy (see under SNATCH)
N.Y. LOOSE 895

O

OASIS 896
OBABEN 897
OBLIVIANS 897
OCEAN BLUE 898
OCEAN COLOUR SCENE 898
OCTOBER, Gene (see under CHELSEA)
OCTOPUS 899
OEDIPUSSY (see under PERFECT DISASTER)
OFFHOOKS (see under THANES)
OF MONTREAL 900
OH OK (see under MAGNAPOP)
OINGO BOINGO 446
OLDHAM, Will 900
O-LEVEL (see under BALL, Edward)
OLIVELAWN (see under FLUF)
OLIVIA TREMOR CONTROL 902
OLYMPIC DEATH SQUAD (see under UNREST)
OMD (see under ORCHESTRAL MANOEUVRES IN THE DARK)
ONEIDA 902
ONE LADY OWNER 903
ONLY ONES 109
OOBERMAN 903
OP8 (see under GIANT SAND)
OPAL (see under MAZZY STAR)
ORANGE (see under STRAITJACKET FITS)
ORANGE CAKE MIX 903
ORANGE CAN 904
ORANGE DELUXE (see under FIVE THIRTY)
ORANGE JUICE (see under COLLINS, Edwyn)
ORANGE PEELS 905
ORANGER 905
ORCHESTRAL MANOEUVRES IN THE DARK 446
ORCHIDS 448
ORGANISATION (see under KRAFTWERK)
ORIGINAL MIRRORS 448
ORIGINAL SINS (see under BROTHER J.T.)
ORLANDO 905
O'ROURKE, Jim 906
ORTON, Beth 907
OSTLE BAY (see under TRASH CAN SINATRAS)
OTHER TWO (see under NEW ORDER)
OUTCASTS 110
OUTRAGEOUS CHERRY 907
OUTSIDERS (see under SOUND)
OVA (see under FAITH OVER REASON)
OWEN (see under JOAN OF ARC)
OWLS (see under JOAN OF ARC)
OXES 907

P

P (see under BUTTHOLE SURFERS)
PACIFIC RADIO (see under MONOGRAPH)
PACK (see under SPEAR OF DESTINY)
PAGANS 111
PAIN TEENS 449
PALACE (see under OLDHAM, Will)
PALE 908
PALE FOUNTAINS (see under SHACK)
PALE SAINTS 908
PALOOKAS (see under SWELL MAPS)
PANDORAS 449
PANOPLY ACADEMY... 909
PANSY DIVISION 909
PANTHER BURNS (see under FALCO, Tav)
PAPA M (see under SLINT)
PAPAS FRITAS 910
PARACHUTE MEN 450
PARADISE MOTEL 910
PARFITT, Richard (see under 60 FT DOLLS)

INDEX

PARIS ANGELS 910
PARISH, John, & POLLY JEAN HARVEY (see under HARVEY, PJ)
PARKINSONS 911
PARSONS, Gram 911
PARTRIDGE, Andy (see under XTC)
PASSAGE 111
PASSIONS 450
PASSMORE SISTERS 450
PASTELS 450
PATTERN 912
PAUL NEWMAN 912
PAVEMENT 913
PEACH COBBLER (see under RUN ON)
PEDRO THE LION 914
PEECHEES 914
PEEPS INTO FAIRYLAND 914
PELL MELL 451
PENETRATION 112
PENTHOUSE 915
PERE UBU 112
PERFECT DISASTER 452
PERFUME 915
PERMANENT GREEN LIGHT (see under THREE O'CLOCK)
PERNICE BROTHERS 915
PERRETT, Peter (see under ONLY ONES)
PERRY, Brendan (see under DEAD CAN DANCE)
PERRY, Mark (see under ALTERNATIVE TV)
PHAIR, Liz 916
PHANTOM ENGINEER 916
PHANTOM SURFERS 916
PHELPS, Joel R.L. 917
PHILLIPPS, Martin (see under CHILLS)
PHILLIPS, Grant Lee (see under GRANT LEE BUFFALO)
PHOTON BAND 917
PHOTOS 452
PHRANC 453
PIANO MAGIC 917
PIE FINGER (see under FIRE ENGINES)
PIERCE, Jeffrey Lee (see under GUN CLUB)
PIGBAG 453
PiL (see under PUBLIC IMAGE LTD.)
PILOT (see under DHARMA BUMS)
PILOTCAN 918
PILOT SHIPS (see under STARS OF THE LID)
PINBACK 918
PINEHURST KIDS 919
PIN GROUP (see under MONTGOMERY, Roy)
PINK FAIRIES 114
PINK FLOYD 919
PINK INDUSTRY (see under PINK MILITARY)
PINK KROSS 920
PINK MILITARY 454
PIPE 920
PIXIES 454
PIZZICATO FIVE 456
PLACEBO 920
PLAIN, John (see under LURKERS)
PLANES MISTAKEN FOR STARS 921
PLANET WILSON (see under RED GUITARS)
PLASMATICS 115
PLASTIC BERTRAND 116
PLASTICLAND 456
PLAY DEAD 457
PLIMSOULS 457
PLUSH 921
PLUTO MONKEY (see under DAWN OF THE REPLICANTS)
P'O (see under WIRE)
POGUES 457
POISON GIRLS 116
POLAK (see under ADORABLE)
POLARA 921
POLICE 117
POLICECAT 922
POLLARD, Robert (see under GUIDED BY VOICES)
POLVO 922
POLYPHONIC SPREE 923
POND 923
PONY CLUB 924

POOH STICKS 459
POP, Iggy 118
POP GROUP 120
POPGUNS 924
POPINJAYS 924
POP RIVETS (see under CHILDISH, Wild Billy)
POPSICLE 925
POP WILL EAT ITSELF 460
PORCUPINE TREE 925
PORK DUKES 121
PORTASTATIC (see under SUPERCHUNK)
POSIES 926
POSITIVE NOISE 461
POSSIBILITIES 927
POSSUM DIXON 927
POSTER CHILDREN 927
#POUNDSIGN# 928
PRAG VEC 121
PRAM 928
PREKOP, Sam (see under SEA AND CAKE)
PRESTON SCHOOL OF INDUSTRY 929
PREWITT, Archer (see under COCTAILS)
PRIMAL SCREAM 461
PRIMEVALS 462
PRIMITIVES 463
PRINCIPLE, Peter (see under TUXEDOMOON)
PRISONERS 463
PRISONSHAKE 929
PRITCHARD, Bill 464
PROFESSIONALS (see under SEX PISTOLS)
PROJECT (see under UNREST)
PROLAPSE 929
PROMISE RING 930
PSYCHEDELIC FURS 464
PSYCHED UP JANIS 930
PSYCHIC TV 465
PSYCLONE RANGERS 930
PUBLIC IMAGE LTD. 121
PUDDLE 466
PULLMAN 931
PULP 467
PULSARS 931
PUNCH WAGON (see under SUPERDRAG)
PUNISHMENT OF LUXURY 122
PUPPY LOVE BOMB (see under HORMONES)
PURE MORNING (see under CLINIC)
PURESSENCE 931
PURSEY, Jimmy (see under SHAM 69)
PUSHERMAN 931
PUSH KINGS 932
PUSSYCAT TRASH (see under MILKY WIMPSHAKE)
PUSSY GALORE 468
PUSSYWILLOWS (see under MARCH, April)
P.W. LONG'S REELFOOT (see under MULE)
PYLON 469

Q

Q AND NOT U 932
QUASI 932
QUEEN, Monica (see under THRUM)
QUEERS 470
? & THE MYSTERIANS 470
QUICKSPACE (SUPERSPORT) (see under FAITH HEALERS, Th')
QUINN, Paul 471
QUIX*O*TIC (see under SLANT 6)

R

RACEBANNON 933
RACHEL'S 933
RADAR BROS. 934
RADIAL SPANGLE 934
RADIATORS FROM SPACE 123
RADIO 4 934
RADIO BIRDMAN 124
RADIOHEAD 935

RADIO STARS 124
RADISH 936
RAILROAD JERK 936
RAILWAY CHILDREN 472
RAIN 936
RAINCOATS 125
RAINER MARIA 937
RAIN PARADE 472
RAIN TREE CROW (see under JAPAN)
RAINY DAY (see under MAZZY STAR)
RAJ QUARTET (see under MONOCHROME SET)
RAMONES 125
RAM RAM KINO (see under CRISPY AMBULANCE)
RANALDO, Lee (see under SONIC YOUTH)
RANDOM, Eric 473
RANK & FILE (see under DILS)
RANKINE, Alan 473
RAPED (see under CUDDLY TOYS)
RAPEMAN (see under BIG BLACK)
RAPTURE 937
RAZORCUTS 473
REAL KIDS 127
REAL PEOPLE 937
RECORDS 128
RED AUNTS 937
RED CRAYOLA 938
REDD KROSS 474
RED GUITARS 475
RED HOUSE PAINTERS 939
RED KRAYOLA (see under RED CRAYOLA)
RED LETTER DAY 476
RED LORRY YELLOW LORRY 476
RED MONKEY (see under MILKY WIMPSHAKE)
RED RED MEAT 939
REDSKINS 477
RED SLEEPING BEAUTY (see under ACID HOUSE KINGS)
REED, Dougal (see under FAITH HEALERS, Th')
REED, Lou 477
REEGS (see under CHAMELEONS)
REFLECTIONS (see under ALTERNATIVE TV)
REFUSED 940
REGULAR FRIES 941
REINDEER SECTION 941
REININGER, Blaine L. (see under TUXEDOMOON)
RELICT (see under CLIENTELE)
R.E.M. 479
REMA REMA (see under WOLFGANG PRESS)
RENALDO & THE LOAF 481
RENDERERS 942
RENTALS (see under WEEZER)
REPLACEMENTS 481
RESERVOIR (see under SPACE NEEDLE)
RESIDENTS 128
RETSIN 942
REV, Martin (see under SUICIDE)
REVELL, Graeme (see under S.P.K.)
REVENANTS (see under STARS OF HEAVEN)
REVENGE (see under NEW ORDER)
REVILLOS (see under REZILLOS)
REVOLUTIONARY CORPS OF TEENAGE JESUS 943
REVOLVER 943
REVOLVING PAINT DREAM 483
REZILLOS 130
RHATIGAN, Suzanne 943
RHYTHM SISTERS 483
RIALTO 944
RICE, Boyd (see under NON)
RICH KIDS 131
RICHMAN, Jonathan 131
RIDE 944
RIFF RAFF (see under BRAGG, Billy)
RIFLE SPORT 483
RIG 945
RILEY, Marc, & The CREEPERS 483
RIMBAUD, Penny (see under CRASS)
RIP (see under GALBRAITH, Alastair)
RIP, RIG + PANIC 484

RITCHIE, Brian (see under VIOLENT FEMMES)
RITES OF SPRING 485
RIVERDALES (see under SCREECHING WEASEL)
RIZZO 945
ROADSIDE MONUMENT 945
ROBERTS, Alasdair (see under APPENDIX OUT)
ROBINSON, Mark (see under UNREST)
ROBINSON, Tom 132
ROCKET FROM THE CRYPT 946
ROCKET FROM THE TOMBS (see under PERE UBU)
ROCKETSHIP 947
ROCKINGBIRDS 947
RODAN (see under RACHEL'S)
ROLAND, Paul 485
ROLLERSKATE SKINNY 947
ROLLING STONES 486
ROMEO VOID 487
ROOM 487
ROPERS 948
ROSA MOTA 948
ROSE OF AVALANCHE 487
ROSITA (see under KENICKIE)
ROSS, Malcolm 948
ROTE KAPELLE (see under JESSE GARON & THE DESPERADOES)
ROXY MUSIC 948
ROYAL BRONCO (see under POLICECAT)
ROYAL FAMILY AND THE POOR 488
ROYAL TRUX 949
RUBELLA BALLET 488
RUDE CLUB 950
RUDI 134
RUIZ, The Legendary Jim (Group) 950
RUMAH SAKIT 950
RUMBLEFISH 489
RUNAWAYS 134
RUN ON 950
RUSSELL, Bruce (see under DEAD C)
RUTH'S REFRIGERATOR (see under DEEP FREEZE MICE)
RUTS 134
RYE COALITION 951

S

SABALON GLITZ (see under HOLMES, Chris)
SACKVILLE 952
SAD LOVERS AND GIANTS 489
SAFE HOME (see under NIGHTBLOOMS)
SAGE, Greg (see under WIPERS)
SAINT ETIENNE 952
SAINT LOW (see under MADDER ROSE)
SAINTS 136
SAINT SOPHIA 953
SALAD 953
SALAKO 954
SALARYMAN (see under POSTER CHILDREN)
SALAS-HUMARA, Walter (see under SILOS)
SALMON, Kim, & THE SURREALISTICS (see under SCIENTISTS)
SALOON 954
SALVATION 490
SAMMY 954
SANDOVAL, Hope, & THE WARM INVENTIONS (see under MAZZY STAR)
SANDY DIRT (see under SOME VELVET SIDEWALK)
SARGE 955
SATAN'S RATS (see under PHOTOS)
SATURDAY LOOKS GOOD TO ME (see under THOMAS, Fred)
SATURDAY PEOPLE (see under VELOCITY GIRL)
SATURNINE 955
SATURN V (see under RAZORCUTS)
SAVAGE PENCIL (see under ART ATTACKS)
SAVAGE REPUBLIC 490
SAVES THE DAY 955

INDEX

SAXON, Sky (see under SEEDS)
SCARCE (see under ANASTASIA SCREAMED)
SCARFO 956
SCARS 491
SCENIC (see under SAVAGE REPUBLIC)
SCHEER 956
SCHNEIDER, Fred (see under B-52's)
SCHOPPLER, Fran (see under JESSE GARON & THE DESPERADOES)
SCIENTISTS 491
SCISSOR GIRLS 956
SCORPIO RISING 957
SCOTT, Robert (see under BATS)
SCOTT 4 957
SCRATCH ACID (see under JESUS LIZARD)
SCRAWL 492
SCREAMING BLUE MESSIAHS 493
SCREAMING TREES 493
SCREECHING WEASEL 957
SCRITTI POLITTI 137
SCUD MOUNTAIN BOYS 959
SEA AND CAKE 959
SEAFOOD 959
SEAFRUIT 960
SEAGULL SCREAMING KISS HER KISS HER 960
SEAHORSES 961
SEAM 961
SEAN NA-NA 962
SEA URCHINS 494
SEBADOH 962
SECOND LAYER (see under SOUND)
SECRET GOLDFISH 964
SECRET SHINE 964
SECRET SQUARE (see under APPLES IN STEREO)
SECRET STARS (see under KARATE)
SECTION 25 495
SECTOR 27 (see under ROBINSON, Tom)
SEEDS 495
SEE SEE RIDER 965
SENATE (see under SPEAR OF DESTINY)
SENSELESS THINGS 496
SENSURROUND (see under MEMBRANES)
SENTRIDOH (see under SEBADOH)
SERGEANT, Will (see under ECHO & THE BUNNYMEN)
SERIOUS DRINKING 497
SERPICO (see under MEGA CITY FOUR)
SERVANTS 497
SET FIRE TO FLAMES (see under GODSPEED YOU BLACK EMPEROR!)
SEVEN STOREY MOUNTAIN 965
SEX CLARK FIVE 497
SEX GANG CHILDREN 498
SEX PISTOLS 138
SEXUAL MILKSHAKE (see under BLAST OFF COUNTRY STYLE)
SFERIC EXPERIMENT (see under KING LOSER)
S.F. SEALS (see under MANNING, Barbara)
SHACK 498
SHADOWLAND (see under FURTHER)
SHAKE (see under REZILLOS)
SHAM 69 140
SHAMPOO 966
SHAMS (see under RUN ON)
SHANGRI-LA'S 499
SHAPES 141
SHAPIROS (see under BLACK TAMBOURINE)
SHARKBOY 966
SHAW, Sandie 500
SHED SEVEN 966
SHELLAC (see under BIG BLACK)
SHELLEY, Pete (see under BUZZCOCKS)
SHELLEYAN ORPHAN 500
SHERMANS 967
SHIMMER KIDS UNDERPOP ASSOCIATION 967
SHINER 968
SHINING 968
SHINS 968
SHIPPING NEWS (see under RACHEL'S)
SHIRTS 141
SHITBIRDS (see under MARCH, April)
SHOCKABILLY (see under CHADBOURNE, Eugene)
SHOCKED, Michelle 501
SHOCK HEADED PETERS (see under BLAKE, Karl)
SHOES 141
SHONEN KNIFE 501
SHOP ASSISTANTS 502
SHRIEKBACK 502
SHRIMP BOAT (see under SEA AND CAKE)
SHRUBS 503
SHUDDER TO THINK 969
SICBAY (see under DAZZLING KILLMEN)
SIDDLEYS 503
SIDI BOU SAID 969
SID PRESLEY EXPERIENCE (see under GODFATHERS)
SIDEBOTTOM, Frank (see under FRESHIES)
SIEVEY, Chris (see under FRESHIES)
SIGHTS 969
SIGUR ROS 970
SILKWORM 970
SILOS 504
SILVER APPLES 971
SILVERFISH 971
SILVER JEWS 971
SILVER MT. ZION (see under GODSPEED YOU BLACK EMPEROR!)
SILVER SUN 972
SIMIAN 972
SIMPLE MINDS 142
SING-SING 972
SINK (see under STUPIDS)
SINKING SHIPS (see under HOLIDAY FLYER)
SIOUXSIE & THE BANSHEES 144
SIR HORATIO (see under A CERTAIN RATIO)
SISTER DOUBLE HAPPINESS 504
SISTERHOOD OF CONVOLUTED THINKERS (see under EGGS)
SISTERS OF MERCY 505
SIX.BY SEVEN 973
SIX CENTS & NATALIE (see under TULLYCRAFT)
SIX FINGER SATELLITE 973
SIXTH GREAT LAKE (see under ESSEX GREEN)
SKELETAL FAMILY 506
SKEPTICS 506
SKIDS 145
SKI PATROL (see under LOWERY, Ian)
SKYPARK (see under FAIRWAYS)
SLANT 6 974
SLAUGHTER & THE DOGS 146
SLAUGHTER JOE 507
SLEATER-KINNEY 975
SLEEPER 975
SLINT 976
SLIPSTREAM 977
SLITS 147
SLOAN 977
SLOWDIVE 978
SLUDGEWORTH (see under SCREECHING WEASEL)
SLUMBER (see under FAT TULIPS)
SLUMBER PARTY 978
SMALLER 979
SMALL FACES 979
SMALL FACTORY 979
SMART WENT CRAZY 980
S*M*A*S*H 980
SMASHING PUMPKINS 981
SMEAR/RUTHENSMEAR, Pat (see under GERMS)
SMITH, Elliott 982
SMITH, Jean (see under MECCA NORMAL)
SMITH, Linda 982
SMITH, Patti 148
SMITH, t.v. (see under ADVERTS)
SMITHEREENS 507
SMITHS 508
SMOG 983
SMOKING POPES 983
SMUDGE 984
SMUGGLERS 985
SNAKES OF SHAKE 509
SNAPPER 985
SNATCH 149
SNEAKY FEELINGS 510
SNEETCHES 510
SNIVELLING SHITS 149
SNOW PATROL 986
SNOWPONY 986
SNUFF 511
SOFA 986
SOFT BOYS (see under HITCHCOCK, Robyn)
SOFT CELL (see under ALMOND, Marc)
SOFTIES (see under TIGER TRAP)
SOLAR MUMUNS (see under MOONFLOWERS)
SOLEDAD BROTHERS 986
SOLEX 987
SOLID GOLD HELL (see under S.P.U.D.)
SOMATICS (see under ULTRASOUND)
SOME VELVET SIDEWALK 987
SON, AMBULANCE 988
SONGS: OHIA 988
SONIC BOOM (see under SPACEMEN 3)
SONICS 149
SONIC YOUTH 511
SONORA PINE (see under RETSIN)
SON VOLT (see under UNCLE TUPELO)
SOUL ASYLUM 513
SOULED AMERICAN 514
SOUL-JUNK 988
SOUL SIDE (see under GIRLS AGAINST BOYS)
SOUND 514
SOUNDTRACK OF OUR LIVES 989
SOUP DRAGONS 515
SOUTHERN CULTURE ON THE SKIDS 516
SPACE 989
SPACEHEADS (see under DISLOCATION DANCE)
SPACEHOG 990
SPACEMEN 3 517
SPACE NEEDLE 990
SPACE NEGROS 519
SPACIOUS (see under 3Ds)
SPAIN 991
SPARE SNARE 991
SPARKLEHORSE 992
SPARO, Frankie 993
SPARTA (see under AT THE DRIVE-IN)
SPEAR OF DESTINY 519
SPECTRUM (see under SPACEMEN 3)
SPEEDBALL BABY 993
SPEEDBOAT 993
SPEEDER 993
SPEEDKING 994
SPEED THE PLOUGH 521
SPENCER BLUES EXPLOSION, Jon 994
SPENT 995
SP!N (see under GENE)
SPINANES 995
SPIREA X 995
SPIRES OF OXFORD (see under AZUSA PLANE)
SPIRITUALIZED 996
SPITFIRE 997
SPIZZ 150
S.P.K. 521
SPOON 997
SPORTIQUE (see under RAZORCUTS)
SPRINGFIELDS (see under VELVET CRUSH)
SPRINGHOUSE 998
SPROUT, Tobin (see under GUIDED BY VOICES)
S.P.U.D. 998
SPYGLASS 998
SQUEEZE 150
SQUIRE, John (see under SEAHORSES)
SQUIRREL BAIT 522
ST*JOHNNY 1003
STAMEY, Chris 152
STARLET (see under ACID HOUSE KINGS)
STARLINGS 998
STARRY EYES (see under VELOCITY GIRL)
STARS 999
STARSAILOR 999
STARS OF HEAVEN 523
STARS OF THE LID 999
STATE OF PLAY (see under CURVE)
STATIC (see under BRANCA, Glenn)
STAYRCASE (see under THANES)
ST. CHRISTOPHER 523
STEEL POLE BATH TUB 999
STEINBECKS 1000
STEPHEN (see under CLEAN)
STEPHENSON, Martin 523
STEREO BUS (see under JEAN-PAUL SARTRE EXPERIENCE)
STEREOLAB 1000
STEREOPHONICS 1002
STEREO TOTAL 1002
ST. ETIENNE (see under SAINT ETIENNE)
STEWARD (see under BOYRACER)
STEWART, Douglas T. (see under BMX BANDITS)
STEWART, Mark (see under POP GROUP)
STIFF LITTLE FINGERS 153
STINKY TOYS 154
STOCKHOLM MONSTERS 524
STONE ROSES 525
STOOGES (see under POP, Iggy)
STOOR (see under SPARE SNARE)
STRAITJACKET FITS 526
STRAITJACKETS, Los 1003
STRANGE, Richard (see under DOCTORS OF MADNESS)
STRANGELOVE 1004
STRANGLERS 154
STRAW, Syd 1004
STRAWBERRY SWITCHBLADE 526
STRETCHHEADS 1004
STRICTLY BALLROOM 1005
STRIDE, Pete (see under LURKERS)
STRINGFELLOW, Ken (see under POSIES)
STROHM, John P. (see under ANTENNA)
STROKES 1005
STRUMMER, Joe (see under CLASH)
ST. THOMAS 1006
STUART, Dan (see under GREEN ON RED)
STUMP 527
STUNTMAN (see under TREEPEOPLE)
STUPIDS 527
STYLE COUNCIL (see under WELLER, Paul)
STYRENE, Poly (see under X-RAY SPEX)
STYRENES 156
SUBAQWA 1006
SUBCIRCUS 1006
SUBHUMANS [Canada] 157
SUBHUMANS [Eng] 528
SUB SUB (see under DOVES)
SUBURBAN NIGHTMARE (see under DWARVES)
SUBWAY SECT (see under GODARD, Vic)
SUCKLE 1007
SUDDEN, Nikki (see under SWELL MAPS)
SUDDEN SWAY 529
SUEDE 1007
SUGAR 1008
SUGARCUBES (see under BJORK)
SUGARGLIDERS (see under STEINBECKS)
SUGGS, Matt (see under BUTTERGLORY)
SUICIDE 157
SUICIDE COMMANDOS (see under BEAT RODEO)
SUKPATCH 1009
SULTANS OF PING F.C. 1009
SUMMERHILL (see under SNAKES OF SHAKE)
SUMMER HITS (see under FURTHER)
SUN AND THE MOON (see under CHAMELEONS)
SUNCATCHER 1009
SUNDAYS 1010
SUNDAY'S BEST 1010
SUN DIAL 1010
SUNNY DAY REAL ESTATE 1011
SUNSET VALLEY 1011
SUNSHINE FIX (see under OLIVIA TREMOR CONTROL)

INDEX

SUPERCHARGER (US) 1011
SUPERCHUNK 1012
SUPER DELUXE 1013
SUPERDRAG 1013
SUPER FRIENDZ 1013
SUPER FURRY ANIMALS 1014
SUPERGRASS 1015
SUPERMODEL 1015
SUPERNATURALS 1016
SUPERSTAR 1016
SUPERSUCKERS 1017
SURGERY 1017
SURGICAL PENIS KLINIK (see under S.P.K.)
SWALLOW [USA] 529
SWALLOW [London] 1018
SWAMP CHILDREN (see under A CERTAIN RATIO)
SWANS 529
SWEARING AT MOTORISTS 1018
SWEEP THE LEG JOHNNY 1018
SWEET 75 (see under NIRVANA)
SWELL 1019
SWELL MAPS 158
SWERVEDRIVER 1019
SWIMMER (see under TEN BENSON)
SWIMMING POOL Q'S 531
SWIRLIES 1020
SYLVIAN, David (see under JAPAN)
SYMPOSIUM 1020

T

TABLE 161
TAGMEMICS (see under ART ATTACKS)
TAHITI 80 1021
TALKING HEADS 161
TALL DWARFS 532
TALULAH GOSH 533
TAPPI TiKARRASS (see under BJORK)
TARNATION 1021
TARWATER 1021
TATE, Troy 534
TATER TOTZ (see under REDD KROSS)
TATTLE TALE 1022
TEACH ME TIGER (see under GODZUKI)
TEAM DRESCH 1022
TEARDROP EXPLODES (see under COPE, Julian)
TEENAGE FANCLUB 1022
TEENAGE FILMSTARS (see under BALL, Edward)
TEENAGE JESUS & THE JERKS (see under LUNCH, Lydia)
TELESCOPES 534
TELEVISION 162
TELEVISION PERSONALITIES 163
TELSTAR PONIES 1024
TEN BENSON 1024
TENDER TRAP (see under TALULAH GOSH)
TERMINALS 1025
TERRIS 1025
TESTCARD-F (see under GEE MR. TRACY)
TETRA SPLENDOUR 1025
TEXAS IS THE REASON 1026
THANES 535
that dog. 1026
THAT PETROL EMOTION 536
THEATRE OF HATE (see under SPEAR OF DESTINY)
THEE HEADCOATEES (see under GOLIGHTLY, Holly)
THEE HEADCOATS (see under CHILDISH, Wild Billy)
THEE MICHELLE GUN ELEPHANT 1026
THEE MIGHTY CAESARS (see under CHILDISH, Wild Billy)
THEE MILKSHAKES (see under CHILDISH, Wild Billy)
THEE MOTHS (see under MAGNETIC NORTH POLE)
THEE SPEAKING CANARIES (see under DON CABALLERO)
THELONIOUS MONSTER 537
THEORETICAL GIRLS (see under BRANCA, Glenn)

THESE ANIMAL MEN 1027
THESE ARE THE SOUNDS OF KALEIDOSCOPE (see under ROPERS)
THESE IMMORTAL SOULS 537
THE THE 537
THEY MIGHT BE GIANTS 539
THINGY (see under PINBACK)
THINKING FELLERS UNION LOCAL 282 540
THIN WHITE ROPE 540
THIRD EYE FOUNDATION 1027
THIRST (see under BLUE ORCHIDS)
THIS HEAT 164
THIS KIND OF PUNISHMENT 542
THIS MORTAL COIL 544
THOMAS, David (see under PERE UBU)
THOMAS, Fred 1028
THOMPSON, Mayo (see under RED CRAYOLA)
THORN, Tracey (see under EVERYTHING BUT THE GIRL)
THOSE BASTARD SOULS (see under GRIFTERS)
THOSE NAUGHTY LUMPS 165
THOUSAND YARD STARE 1028
THREE JOHNS 544
THREE O'CLOCK 545
THROBBING GRISTLE 165
THROWING MUSES 545
THROWN UPS (see under MUDHONEY)
THRUM 1029
THRUSH PUPPIES 1030
THUNDERS, Johnny 166
TIGER 1030
TIGER LILY (see under ULTRAVOX)
TIGER TRAP 1030
TIHISTA's RED TERROR, Kevin (see under TRIPLE FAST ACTION)
TIMES (see under BALL, Edward)
TIMONY, Mary (see under HELIUM)
TINDERSTICKS 1031
TIN HUEY 167
TIN TIN (see under DUFFY, Stephen)
TINY MONROE 1032
TOASTED HERETIC 1033
TOILING MIDGETS (see under AMERICAN MUSIC CLUB)
TOLMAN, Russ (see under TRUE WEST)
TOMORROWLAND 1033
TOMPAULIN 1033
TOMPOT BLENNY 1033
TONES ON TAIL (see under BAUHAUS)
TONG, Winston (see under TUXEDOMOON)
TOOMEY, Jenny (see under TSUNAMI)
TO ROCOCO ROT 1034
TORTOISE 1034
TOVEY, Frank (see under FAD GADGET)
TOWN & COUNTRY 1035
TOYAH 167
TOY LOVE (see under TALL DWARFS)
TRACK STAR 1035
TRAM 1036
TRANS AM 1036
TRANSLATOR 547
TRASH CAN SINATRAS 1036
TRASHMONK (see under DREAM ACADEMY)
TRAVIS 1037
TREACHEROUS JAYWALKERS (see under SPAIN)
TREE FORT ANGST 1038
TREEPEOPLE 1038
TREMBLING BLUE STARS (see under FIELD MICE)
TRENCHMOUTH 1038
T. REX (see under BOLAN, Marc)
TRIBE 8 1039
TRIFFIDS 547
TRIPLE FAST ACTION 1039
TRIPPING DAISY (see under POLYPHONIC SPREE)
TRISTEZA 1040
TROTSKY ICEPICK (see under URINALS)
TRUE BELIEVERS 548
TRUE LOVE ALWAYS 1040
TRUE WEST 548
TRUMANS WATER 1040

TRYPES (see under FEELIES + SPEED THE PLOUGH)
TSE TSE FLY 1041
TSUNAMI 1041
TUBES 168
TUBEWAY ARMY (see under NUMAN, Gary)
TUFNELS (see under BIRD NEST ROYS)
TUGBOAT 3001 A.D. (see under FURTHER)
TULLYCRAFT 1042
TUMOUR CIRCUS (see under DEAD KENNEDYS)
TURBINES 549
TURIN BRAKES 1043
TUSCADERO 1043
TUXEDOMOON 169
TV PERSONALITIES (see under TELEVISION PERSONALITIES)
TWANG 549
TWELVE THOUSAND DAYS (see under EYELESS IN GAZA)
TWINK (see under PINK FAIRIES)
TWINKEYZ 171
TWO NICE GIRLS 550
TYDE (see under FURTHER)
TYRANNOSAURUS REX (see under BOLAN, Marc)

U

UGLY CASANOVA (see under MODEST MOUSE)
Ui 1044
UK DECAY 550
UKRAINIANS 1044
UK SUBS 172
ULTRABABYFAT 1045
ULTRAMARINE 551
ULTRASOUND 1045
ULTRA VIVID SCENE 1046
ULTRAVOX 173
UNBELIEVABLE TRUTH 1046
UNCLE TUPELO 1047
UNDERNEATH (see under BLAKE, Karl)
UNDERTONES 174
UNION CARBIDE PRODUCTIONS (see under SOUNDTRACK OF OUR LIVES)
UNISEX (see under TELESCOPES)
UNREST 551
UNWANTED 175
UNWED SAILOR (see under ROADSIDE MONUMENT)
UNWOUND 1048
URGE OVERKILL 552
URINALS 175
URUSEI YATSURA 1048
USED (see under SUPERDRAG)
USERS 176
U.S. MAPLE 1049
UT 553

V

VALVES 177
VANIAN, Dave, & THE PHANTOM CHORDS (see under DAMNED)
VANILLA, Cherry 177
VAN PELT (see under LAPSE)
VARNALINE 1050
VASELINES 554
VEES (see under JALE)
VEGA, Alan (see under SUICIDE)
VEHICLE FLIPS 1050
VELDT 1050
VELOCETTE 1051
VELOCITY GIRL 1051
VELO-DELUXE (see under ANTENNA)
VELVET CRUSH 1051
VELVET MONKEYS (see under B.A.L.L.)
VELVET UNDERGROUND 554
VENT 414 (see under WONDER STUFF)
VENUS FLY TRAP 556
VERBENA 1053
VERLAINE, Tom (see under TELEVISION)
VERLAINES 556
VERMONT (see under PROMISE RING)
VERONICA LAKE 1053

VERSUS 1053
VERUCA SALT 1054
VERVE 1054
VERY SECRETARY 1055
VERY THINGS (see under CRAVATS)
VIBRATORS 177
VICTIMS OF PLEASURE (see under ASTLEY, Virginia)
VINCENT, Holly Beth (see under HOLLY & THE ITALIANS)
VINES 1055
VIOLENT FEMMES 557
VIOLET INDIANA (see under COCTEAU TWINS)
VIRGIN PRUNES 557
VIVA SATELLITE! (see under EGGS)
VIVA SATURN (see under RAIN PARADE)
VOLCANO SUNS 559
VON BONDIES 1055
VON HEMMLING (see under APPLES IN STEREO)
VOODOO QUEENS 1056
V-TWIN 1056

W

WAH! 560
WAITRESSES 179
WAITS, Tom 1057
WAKE 561
WAKE OOLOO (see under FEELIES)
WALKABOUTS 561
WALKER, Scott 563
WALKINGSEEDS 563
WALKMEN (see under JONATHAN FIRE*EATER)
WALL 564
WALL OF VOODOO 564
WALTONES 565
WANDERERS (see under SHAM 69)
WANNADIES 1058
WAREHAM, Dean (see under GALAXIE 500)
WARLOCKS 1059
WARM JETS 1059
WARONKER, Anna (see under that dog.)
WATLING, Laura 1059
WATT, Ben (see under EVERYTHING BUT THE GIRL)
WATT, Mike (see under MINUTEMEN)
WATTS (see under MONO MEN)
WATTS, John (see under FISCHER-Z)
WAVE ROOM 1060
WAYBILL, Fee (see under TUBES)
WE ARE GOING TO EAT YOU (see under HAGAR THE WOMB)
WEASEL, Ben (see under SCREECHING WEASEL)
WEATHER PROPHETS 565
WEBB BROTHERS 1060
WEBSTER, Gregory (see under RAZORCUTS)
WEDDING PRESENT 566
WEEDS (see under STRAITJACKET FITS)
WEEKEND (see under YOUNG MARBLE GIANTS)
WEEN 1060
WEEZER 1061
WEIRDOS 179
WEIRD WAR (see under MAKE-UP)
WE KNOW WHERE YOU LIVE (see under WONDER STUFF)
WELLER, Paul 568
WELLS, Bill 1062
WENDYS 1062
WESTERBERG, Paul (see under REPLACEMENTS)
WESTERN ELECTRIC (see under LONG RYDERS)
WESTLAKE, David (see under SERVANTS)
WESTON 1062
WE'VE GOT A FUZZBOX AND WE'RE GONNA USE IT 570
WHEAT 1063
WHIPPED CREAM 1063
WHIPPING BOY 1063
WHISTLER (see under EMF)
WHITE, James (& THE BLACKS) (see under CHANCE, James)

INDEX

WHITE LEATHER CLUB (see under SPARE SNARE)
WHITE OCTAVE 1063
WHITEOUT 1064
WHITE STRIPES 1064
WHITE TOWN 1064
WHO 1065
WILCO (see under UNCLE TUPELO)
WILD ANGELS (see under JAZZATEERS)
WILD FLOWERS 570
WILD SWANS 571
WILLARD GRANT CONSPIRACY 1066
WILLIAM (see under JESUS & MARY CHAIN)
WILLIAMS, Harvey (see under ANOTHER SUNNY DAY)
WILLIAMSON, Astrid 1066
WILLSON-PIPER, Marty (see under CHURCH)
WILSON, Phil (see under JUNE BRIDES)
WIMP FACTOR 14 (see under VEHICLE FLIPS)
WIN (see under FIRE ENGINES)
WINDBREAKERS 572
WINDMILLS 1067
WINDSOR FOR THE DERBY 1067
WINDY & CARL 1067
WIPERS 179
WIRE 180
WISDOM OF HARRY (see under WEATHER PROPHETS)
WISHING STONES 572
WITCH HAZEL 1068
WITNESS 1068
WOLF COLONEL 1068
WOLFGANG PRESS 572
WOLFHOUNDS 573
WOLFIE 1069
WONDER STUFF 574
WOOD, Jen (see under TATTLE TALE)
WOODENTOPS 575
WORKDOGS (see under GIBSON BROS.)
(WORLD OF) SKIN (see under SWANS)
WORLD OF TWIST 1069
WOULD-BE-GOODS 575
WOULD BE'S 1069
WRECKLESS ERIC 182
WRECK SMALL SPEAKERS ON EXPENSIVE STEREOS (see under DEAD C)
WRIGHT, Mr. (Kevin) (see under ALWAYS)
WRIGHT, Shannon (see under CROWSDELL)
WYATT, Robert 576
WYLIE, Pete (see under WAH!)
WYNN, Steve (see under DREAM SYNDICATE)

X

X 183
XINLISUPREME 1070
X-MAL DEUTSCHLAND 577
X-RAY SPEX 184
XTC 185
XYMOX 577

Y

YACHTS 187
YEAH JAZZ 578
YEAH YEAH NOH 578
YEAH YEAH YEAHS 1070
YO LA TENGO 579
YORKSTON, James (& THE ATHLETES) 1070
YOU AM I 1071
YOU FANTASTIC! (see under DAZZLING KILLMEN)
YOUNG & SEXY 1071
YOUNG, Neil 580
YOUNGER YOUNGER 28'S 1071
YOUNG FRESH FELLOWS 581
YOUNG MARBLE GIANTS 582
YOUNGS, Richard 1071
YUME BITSU 1072
YUMMY FUR 1073
YUM-YUM (see under HOLMES, Chris)
YUNG, Yukio 1073
YUNG WU (see under FEELIES)

Z

ZABRINSKI 1074
ZEDEK, Thalia (see under COME)
ZE MALIBU KIDS (see under REDD KROSS)
ZEN GUERRILLA 1074
ZEPHYRS 1074
ZODIAC MOTEL (see under BIRDLAND)
ZOMBIES 1075
ZUMPANO 1075
ZUZU'S PETALS 1075

Out-takes

Due to the evolvement of Indie music over the last decade or so (see the Introduction for more details), there have been a plethora of out-takes (mostly Metal or Dance) which have resulted in their omission from this (indie-only) 2nd Edition.

You can find these following artists in:–
The Great Metal Discography II, The Great Rock Discography VI or V, and of course the 1st edition of *The Great Alternative & Indie Discography.*

3 COLOURS RED
3 MUSTAPHAS 3
4-SKINS
7 SECONDS
12 RODS

'A'
ABRASIVE WHEELS
ACACIA
ACTIFED
ACTION PACT
ADICTS
ADOLESCENTS
ADRENALIN O.D.
ADVENTURES
AGENT ORANGE
AGNOSTIC FRONT
ALABAMA 3
ALARM
G.G. ALLIN
ANGRY SAMOANS
ANTI
ANTI-NOWHERE LEAGUE
ANTI-PASTI
A POPULAR HISTORY OF SIGNS
ASSERT
ASTROPUPPEES
ATARI TEENAGE RIOT

BABY CHAOS
BAD RELIGION
BALAAM AND THE ANGEL
BAMBI SLAM
BANGLES
BATFISH BOYS
BEAT FARMERS
BEDLAM AGO GO
BETTER THAN EZRA
BIG BOYS
BIG CHIEF
BLASTERS
BLITZ
BOLLOCK BROTHERS
BOREDOMS
BOTTLE ROCKETS
BRACKET
BRAD
Brian BRAIN
BRIGANDAGE
Caspar BROTZMANN
BUSINESS

CAIFANES
CALL
CAUSE FOR ALARM
CHANNEL 3
CHINA CRISIS
Ted CHIPPINGTON
CHRISTIAN DEATH
CHRON GEN
CIRCLE JERKS
CITIZENS' UTILITIES
CIV
COCKNEY REJECTS
COCK SPARRER
COLLAPSED LUNG
CONCRETE BLONDE
CONFLICT
CONNELLS

Chris CONNELLY
CRASH TEST DUMMIES
Marshall CRENSHAW
CYCLEFLY

DANCE HALL CRASHERS
DEL FUEGOS
DEL-LORDS
DEMENTED ARE GO
DESCENDENTS
DESTRUCTORS
DIE CHEERLEADER
DIG
DISORDER
DIVINYLS
Don DIXON
DOCTOR & THE MEDICS
DOGSTAR
DOWN BY LAW
DROPKICK MURPHYS
DUST JUNKYS

EELS
EJECTED
EXPLOITED

FASTBALL
FEAR
FISHBONE
FLINCH
FLOWERPOT MEN
FOETUS
FRONTLINE ASSEMBLY
FRONT 242
FU MANCHU
FUTURE SOUND OF LONDON

GANG GREEN
GBH
GIN BLOSSOMS
GOOBER PATROL
GRAPES OF WRATH
GROOP DOGDRILL
GROTUS

H2O
HAZELDINE
HELMET
HONEYCRACK
Dave HOWARD

ICE
INFA-RIOT
I START COUNTING

JAGS
JANUS STARK
J.F.A.
JOYRIDER

KANTE
James KING
KING PRAWN
KMFDM
Die KREUZEN
Die KRUPPS
K'S CHOICE

LAIBACH
LAUGH
LIGHT A BIG FIRE
LIGOTAGE
LINUS
LONDON

Shane MacGOWAN & THE POPES
David McALMONT
MEAT BEAT MANIFESTO
MODELS
MOTORS
MUNDY

NECROS
NITZER EBB
Mojo NIXON
NOFX
NUT

Hazel O'CONNOR
OI POLLOI
OMEGA TRIBE
OUR DAUGHTER'S WEDDING
OUR LADY PEACE
OUT OF MY HAIR

PAW
PENNYWISE
PETER & THE TEST-TUBE BABIES
POISON IDEA
PRESIDENTS OF THE UNITED STATES
  OF AMERICA
PRIMUS
PROPAGANDA

RADICAL DANCE FACTION
RANCID
RED SNAPPER
REFRESHMENTS
RENEGADE SOUNDWAVE
RIOT SQUAD
R.O.C.
Henry ROLLINS
ROME

SCREAM
SEEFEEL
SENSER
SHAMEN
SHEEP ON DRUGS
Jane SIBERRY
SICK OF IT ALL
SIGUE SIGUE SPUTNIK
SKINNY PUPPY
SKREWDRIVER
SKUNK ANANSIE
SKY CRIES MARY
SMASHING ORANGE
SNFU
SOCIAL DISTORTION
SOFA SURFERS
SOUL COUGHING
SPELL
SPLODGENESSABOUNDS
SPONGE
STABBING WESTWARD
STANFORD PRISON
SUICIDAL TENDENCIES

TAD
TANSADS
TENPOLE TUDOR
TEST DEPT
THEE HYPNOTICS
THERAPY?
THERMADORE
TOADIES
TONIC
TOWERING INFERNO
TOY DOLLS
TRIBUTE TO NOTHING
TRULY
T.S.O.L.

VAPORS
VERVE PIPE
VICE SQUAD
VOICE OF THE BEEHIVE
VULGAR BOATMEN

WATERBOYS
WHALE
Victoria WILLIAMS
WISHPLANTS
Jah WOBBLE
WORLD DOMINATION

YARGO
YELLO
YOSSARIAN
YOUNG GODS
YOUTH BRIGADE (Wash'n DC)
YOUTH BRIGADE (Hollywood)

ZEKE
ZOUNDS